MW01249030

BUC
USED BOAT
PRICE GUIDE

1905-1983 MODELS

Statistically Authenticated
Current Market Prices for ...
OUTBOARDS • INBOARDS • SAILBOATS
OUTDRIVES • POWERBOATS
HOUSEBOATS • CUSTOM BOATS
with Area, Condition and Equipment Scales
and a Complete Cross Referenced Index

96th Edition 2009

BUC RESEARCH
INFORMATION YOU CAN TRUST® SINCE 1961

PUBLISHED BY

BUC RESEARCH

1314 Northeast 17th Court, Ft Lauderdale, FL 33305
800-327-6929, 954-565-6715, Fax: 954-561-3095

Library of Congress Catalog No. 63-35604

ISBN 978-0-9816019-7-7

Purchase two or more BUC Used Boat Price Guides at discounted prices and receive BUCValuPro.com Memberships FREE[*].
See Page iii for login and activation details.

Subscription prices, U.S. and Foreign

BUC Used Boat Price Guide (Vol. I 1997-2008 models) List Price	$95
BUC Used Boat Price Guide (Vol. II 1984-1996 models) List Price	$85
BUC Used Boat Price Guide (Vol. III 1905-1983 models) List Price	$69
Buy Volumes I & II, receive $14 book discount & ONE FREE BUCValuPro.com Membership, a $27.95 per month value.*	**$166**
Buy Volumes I, II & III, receive $34 book discount & TWO FREE BUCValuPro.com Memberships, a $32.95 per month value.*	**$215**

- Plus Postage -
$8 for single Volume I, II or III
$10 for the Two Volume Set (Vol. I & II)
$12 for the Three Volume Set (Vol. I, II & III)
- FLORIDA residents add sales tax -

OVERSEAS AIR SHIPMENT RATES FOR PREPAID ORDERS:
Add $35 for single Volume I, II or III
Add $40 for Two Volume Set (Vol. I & II)
Add $50 for Three Volume Set (Vol. I, II & III)

TO ORDER:
email orders@BUC.com, or call 800-327-6929 or 954-565-6715
If you require 10 or more BUCValuPro.com Login's, please call or email for a customized quotation.

QUANTITY DISCOUNTS for **BUC Used Boat Price Guides** and **BUCValuPro.com** Memberships are also available at
http://wwwBUC.com

CONTENTS

> Purchase two or more BUC Used Boat Price Guides at discounted prices and receive BUCValuPro.com Memberships FREE*.

If you have previously registered your BUC Personal Login, go to: http://www.BUCValuPro.com

To activate a new membership and create your own BUC Personal Login, go to http://www.BUCValuPro.com/freetrial. Enter your BUC Customer Number & Free Trial Code: UB94

If you have any questions call:
800-327-6929 or (954) 565-6715

If you have purchased a single copy of the BUC Used Boat Price Guide Volume I or Volume II, you can receive a FREE BUCValuPro Membership by purchasing an additional copy or volume. Or, you can supplement your Book purchase with a BUCValuPro Membership at a special price. (Sign in according to the instructions above).

Prices, promotions & free trials are subject to change or withdrawal without notice.
*Free BUCValuPro.com Memberships, unless renewed, expire according to the terms on www.BUC.com or upon publication of the next edition whichever comes first.

PREFACE

This 96th edition of the BUC Used Boat Price Guide contains the current retail price of more than 440,000 used pleasure boats. Over 75,000 additions and other changes have been made since the last edition. The unique formulas used in depreciating or appreciating the various boats utilize the prices of actual used boat sales reported by dealers, brokers and surveyors from all geographical areas of the United States and Canada.

This edition contains a method for adjusting for variation due to area location and condition. Be sure to read the instructions. The cross-referenced trade name index indicates the boat type and length for each trade name. This should facilitate finding listings where two or more manufacturers have used one trade name.

Many other changes have also been made. To gain maximum benefit from this book and a deeper understanding of the subtleties of boat and engine evaluation, we suggest rereading the Introduction and How To Use This Book sections from time to time, especially first time or casual users. Referencing a price without regard to Area, Equipment and Condition Scales is a misusage and likely to be detrimental to your requirements.

Sometimes we are asked why we do not show the original list price of the various boats along with the current retail high for each boat. Since the list price of any boat has little bearing on its ultimate used market value, it only tends to confuse both the user of the price guide and the consumer.

For prices of used boats 1997-2008, see BUC's Used Boat Price Guide Volume I; and for used boats 1984-1996, see BUC's Used Boat Price Guide Volume II, the 96th Editions.

Walter J. Sullivan, III
Fort Lauderdale, Florida
January 2009

INTRODUCTION

DEPRECIATION OF BOATS

There are all kinds of depreciation techniques. A straight-line method is often used by accountants and bookkeepers. It's a tidy way to devalue capital equipment over its expected useful life, but the values obtained with this method have no relationship to the market values of recreational boats.

The straight-line depreciation technique generally tends to separate the buyer and seller rather than invite them to negotiate. The only way to accurately determine and project the depreciation curve of a used recreational vessel is to study the market place to see what buyers are actually paying for boats in light of all the current economic factors.

Determining depreciation or appreciation by market demand is not an easy task because it requires analysis of actual used boat sales. BUC analyzes the market through Used Boat Sales Reports received from corresponding dealers, brokers and surveyors, and through analysis of current listing prices. Our expert staff, using the very latest computers and sophisticated software, studies the information statistically for different geographical regions. The various plotted value curves are usually unique to a manufacturer. In some cases, patterns vary across major model lines of the same manufacturer.

Some vessels hold their price after the first year and over a period of years before they show noticeable depreciation. Others drop rapidly in value right from the beginning. Still others may show an initial drop and then a plateau, or drop in a series of steps. Many consumers and some brokers are not aware that boats can actually appreciate in value at times.

The market value of boats depends heavily on current economic conditions, both general and those specifically influencing luxury industries. Rates can fluctuate monthly which is why you should check each evaluation with www.BUCValuPro.com. Alternatively, you may wish to take advantage of BUC's Personalized Boat Evaluation Service by calling our office. There is a small charge for this service but you will have the very latest pricing information customized to your vessel.

Analysis of the recreational boat market is a science as well as a business. Forty-seven years of studying almost 63 billion dollars in used boat transactions has taught us that many common opinions have no basis in fact. For instance, there is no standard relationship between the manufacturer's suggested list price in the year of manufacture and the current retail market value. Another big lesson is that the patterns of depreciation for boats are substantially different from airplanes or automobiles.

Please take note that the prices shown in this guide are current retail prices, also commonly known as actual cash value, fair market value, or just market value. Trade-in value is discussed on page ixx.

DATA RECORDING AND COMPILATION

A network of cooperating dealers, brokers, and surveyors located throughout the United States and Canada complete Used Boat Sales Reports, shown below, and mail them to BUC every six months.

All aspects of each transaction shown on the Used Boat Sales Report are stored in a database where they can be accessed for analysis by our statisticians.

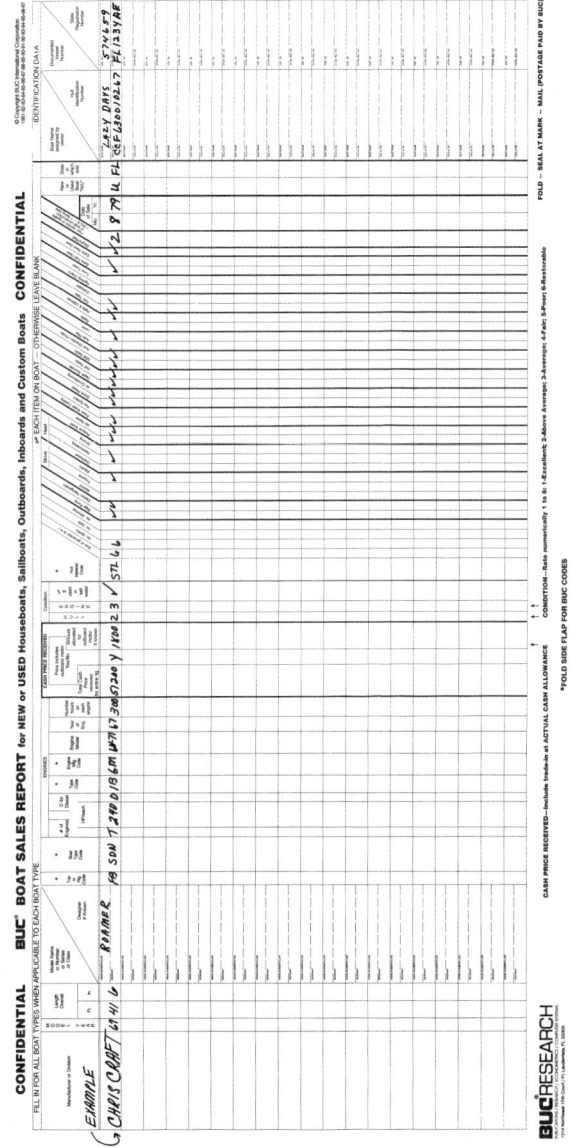

For the purpose of price analysis, sales reports are separated into different geographical areas, typically:

1) North Atlantic Coast
2) South Atlantic and Florida
3) Gulf of Mexico exclusive of Florida Coast
4) Great Lakes and Midwest
5) Northern Pacific Coast (Eureka, CA to Canadian border)
6) Southern Pacific Coast (Eureka, CA to Mexican border)
7) Canada, Great Lakes Area only

Obviously, reported prices of boats reflect myriad variations due to location, condition and the kind and quantity of optional equipment and accessories found on the boat. Special computer programs adjust each reported sale price to reflect a boat in BUC CONDITION with average equipment located in the North Atlantic Area.

The database of reported prices are then passed through various other programs to plot curves by manufacturer, model and year (a typical positively skewed curve is shown below). These prices are then curve fit with historical data on the same company to smooth out the rate before publishing the adjusted Retail Prices in this book. The sophistication and accuracy of this system is unequaled.

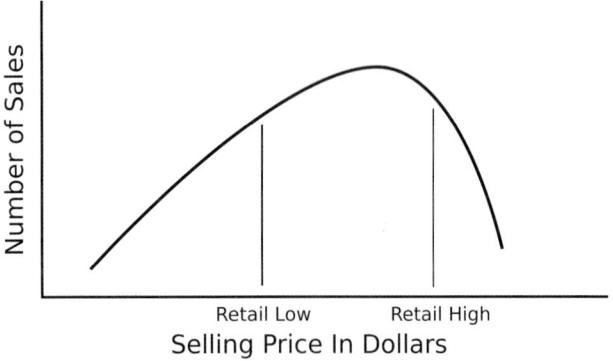

Selling Price In Dollars

RETAIL HIGH AND LOW

Technically speaking, the price range published by BUC under the columns Retail Low and Retail High is a statistical confidence interval, which means that the average of all sales of that particular model boat will most likely fall within the given range. Despite the precision of proven techniques however, compared to BUC's published current market prices, the actual selling prices of boats can show a huge variance even for two boats exactly alike in design, condition and amount of equipment. This is because unique circumstances influence the buyer and seller in every transaction. The following are just a few causes of price variance:

- Minor optional equipment included in the boat but difficult to separate from the price.
- Buying intensity of the customer.
- Highly competitive conditions in a particular geographic area.
- Sales made by firms with different overhead requirements.
- Weather conditions affecting the opportunity of using the boat.
- Terms of payment offered or asked by the buyer and/or his source of credit.
- Distress sales.
- Condition of hull, engine and equipment not properly described.

As you can see the potential causes for price variances are numerous. As a matter of fact, it is not unusual to have a range in reported sales from 30 to 60% of the median price. BUC could, of course, have published the highest and lowest prices reported, but the range in dollars would be so great as to have no practical value to any of our users. The statistically determined Retail Lows and Highs published by BUC are between generally between 8 and 16%. This is a meaningful range on which your business can profitably function.

Knowing the retail price range that has been statistically determined by market data will help you in your decision making. The wider the range, the less firm the price. Conversely, firmer prices exist when the range is small. Very popular well-known boats tend to have prices that are established in a tighter range. In any case, you know that the average of all sales, when adjusted for area and condition, will likely fall between the Retail Low and the Retail High.

Some boats will not have published prices. This is done occasionally when the number or quality of the sales reports is insufficient to be accurate, or if the received reports indicate a sudden price swing. After all, not every used boat is sold and reported every year. Although our statisticians are confident in their comparative techniques, it occasionally happens that we are not able to sufficiently pinpoint the fair market value of some models of boats. When this happens, asterisks (**) will be published in the price columns.

BUC is sometimes asked about the effect of prices reported by those wishing to influence our studies for nefarious purposes, including supporting their own profit or pride. Be assured that false reports are very easy to detect statistically. When a reported price is found to be fictitious, the entire Used Boat Sales Report for that correspondent is deemed useless and their reported prices are removed from the file. This is regrettable. The efforts of the person filing the Sales Reports could have been valid and useful to everyone, but most of all to himself. Ironically, he has excluded the mathematical influence of his local business conditions in the calculation of the very models that he sells.

With all the subtleties to consider, use your new BUC Used Boat Price Guide as a guide, tempered by your own understanding of the market. Most importantly, use the Area and Conditic Adjustment Scales found on the inside of the front cover.
page xvi for instructions.

BUC ᴦ

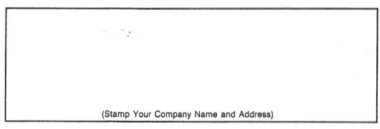
BOAT and YACHT APPRAISAL FORM

BUC's Boat and Yacht Appraisal Form has been designed to assist banks, credit unions, dealers, brokers, surveyors, and others interested in performing a thorough inspection and evaluation of boats, engines, and trailers. It has evolved over many years and includes virtually all the descriptive and equipment items that significantly affect Current Market Value. Because it secures and records a detailed description in a structured way it is a valuable aid to decision making.

The form is designed to be used in conjunction with the latest BUC Used Boat Price Guides. For appraisals of stock, semi-custom, custom and one-of-a-kind boats and yachts on an individual basis, call BUC at 800-327-6929 after completing this form and request BUC's Personalized Boat Evaluation Service℠. The fee for this service can be charged to your credit card or to your account if such has been previously established.

(PLEASE PRINT LEGIBLY)

BOAT DESCRIPTION

| • BOAT NAME | RESERVED ☐ YES ☐ NO | EX-NAME | • MANUFACTURER | DESIGNER |

| • MODEL YEAR | MFG. YEAR | • MODEL NAME/NUMBER | • BOAT TYPE • | • TOP/RIG • | • BOAT IS ☐ USED ☐ NEW |

| • LENGTH OVERALL | LENGTH WATERLINE | BEAM | DRAFT (MAX) | DRAFT (MIN) | WEIGHT (DISPL) | BALLAST (LBS / TYPE) |

| ft. in. | ft. in. | ft. in. | ft. in. | ft. in. | | |
| • HULL MATERIAL • | HULL CONFIGURATION • | DECK MATERIAL | SLEEPS | STATE ROOMS | SAIL AREA |

| SPEED(mph)CRUISE@RPM | SPEED(mph)MAX@RPM | GALS/HR CRUISE | GALS/HR MAX | RANGE(miles) | FUEL TANK(gal)(matrl) | WATER TANK(gal)(matrl) |

| COLOR HULL | COLOR DECK | • HULL ID #(HIN) | • DOC VESSEL NUMBER | • STATE NUMBER |

ENGINE DESCRIPTION

| • TYPE: • ☐ OB ☐ IB ☐ JET | • # OF ENGINES | • HORSEPOWER EACH | • FUEL TYPE ☐ GAS ☐ DSL | MANUFACTURER • | MODEL | • MODEL YEAR |

| HOURS SINCE NEW | HOURS SINCE MAJOR OVERHAUL | OVERHAUL DATE | SERIAL# PORT | SERIAL# STARBOARD |

TRAILER DESCRIPTION

| • MANUFACTURER | • MFG YEAR | MODEL | • CAPACITY | • # WHEELS | • TANDEM ☐ YES ☐ NO | TRAILER SERIAL#(VIN) | REGISTRATION # |

LOCATION OF BOAT

| • MARINA / YARD / STREET ADDRESS / SLIP | • CITY | • STATE | • ZIP | • COUNTRY (if not U.S.) |

| DOCKMASTER/CONTACT | CAPTAIN ABOARD ☐ YES ☐ NO | CAPTAIN'S NAME | CAPTAIN'S PHONE(A/C & #) | BOAT PHONE(A/C & #) |

OWNER DATA

| • OWNER NAME | COMPANY | • HOME PHONE(A/C & #) | • BUS PHONE(A/C & #) |

| • ADDRESS | • CITY | • STATE | • ZIP | • COUNTRY (if not U.S.) |

| HOMEPORT CITY(if different) | STATE | COUNTRY (if not U.S.) | MARINA |

OWNER IS:
☐ FORMER CLIENT
☐ NEW CLIENT, IF NEW SOURCE OF REFERRAL _____

APPRAISER USE ONLY

DATE INSPECTED	INSPECTED BY	STORED:	REASON FOR APPRAISAL:
		☐ INSIDE ☐ COVERED ☐ DOCKSIDE	☐ INSURANCE ☐ BUY ☐ TRADE-IN ☐ ESTATE ☐ OTHER
		☐ OUTSIDE ☐ UNCOVERED SLIP #____	☐ SURVEY ☐ SELL ☐ DONATE ☐ BROKER LISTING

CALCULATION SECTION

CURRENT BUC PRICE (Adjusted for Area only) . . . . $ _____ (A)

Cost to Repair/Replace (column 1 on back page) . . . . $ _____ (B)

Cost to Repair/Replace (column 2 on back page) . . . . $ _____ (C)

Total Cost to Recondition Boat for Resale (Add B to C) . . . . $ _____ (D)

CURRENT RESALE VALUE (Subtract D from A) . . . . $ _____ (E)

ALLOWANCE FOR PROFIT ON RESALE (estimated storage, advertising, insurance, profit and other overhead) $ _____ (F)

ACTUAL CASH ALLOWANCE/TRADE-IN VALUE (Subtract F from E or multiply E × .75) . . . . $ _____ (G)

> NOTE: The current BUC price is a price for a GOOD BOAT, ready for sale *WITHOUT ANY ADDITIONAL WORK*. See complete definition of BUC Condition in the latest edition of BUC's Used Boat Price Guide.

ITEMS INDICATED WITH A BULLET (•) ARE MANDATORY. • SEE YOUR BUC USED BOAT PRICE GUIDE, PAGE 1, FOR SUGGESTED ABBREVIATIONS

© 1984 BUC International Corporation   BUC AF 8406-5

These forms come 50 to a pad and can be ordered directly from BUC.
Call our toll free number: 800-327-6929 or write:
BUC Research
1314 NE 17th Ct.
Ft Lauderdale, FL 33305

X

ACCESSORIES & EQUIPMENT ON BOARD

Check the box to the left of each item to indicate that the vessel you are appraising has this item. Check a box to the right to indicate whether the item should be repaired or replaced, and insert the cost to repair or replace. Checking the box to the left and not checking either repair or replace will indicate that the item exists on the vessel and is in functional condition. The blank spaces for manufacturer, model, size, number, etc. for some items can be completed at your option. If you select to use BUC's Personalized Boat Evaluation Service℠, it may be desirable to provide this information since the precision of BUC's Evaluation may depend on such detailed information.

	Repair	Replace $

ACCOMMODATIONS & FURNISHINGS
Overall Condition: ☐ Mint ☐ Above Average ☐ Good ☐ Fair ☐ Poor
- ☐ Carpeting ☐ Drapes
- ☐ Cushions ☐ Linens
- ☐ Dinette
- ☐ Furniture: Chairs (#)_____ Table(s) (#)_____ Sofa(s) (#)_____
- ☐ Head(s)(#)_____ ☐ Overboard ☐ Recir ☐ Hold; ☐ Elec ☐ Man
- ☐ Helmseat
- ☐ Insulation: ☐ Thermal ☐ Acoustical
- ☐ Owner & Guest Berths: (#)_____ Staterooms: (#)_____
- ☐ Master Stateroom is: ☐ Fwd. ☐ Aft ☐ Amidship; has ☐ Head ☐ Shower
  ☐ Tub; with: ☐ King ☐ Queen ☐ Double ☐ Twin ☐ Vee Berths
- ☐ Guest Berths(#)_____ Guest Heads (#)_____ Guest Showers(#)_____
- ☐ Crew Berths(#)_____ Crew Heads(#)_____ Crew Showers(#)_____
  Separate Captain's Quarters: ☐ Yes ☐ No
- ☐ Conv Dinette Sleeps (#)_____ ☐ Conv Settee Sleeps (#)_____
- ☐ Stereo ☐ Television(s)(#)_____
- ☐ Video Recorder ☐ Wet Bar

GALLEY & LAUNDRY
Overall Condition: ☐ Mint ☐ Above Average ☐ Good ☐ Fair ☐ Poor
- ☐ Dishwasher
- ☐ Clothes Washer ☐ Clothes Dryer
- ☐ Galley: ☐ Up ☐ Down
- ☐ Garbage Disposal
- ☐ Ice Maker: Mfg/Mdl
- ☐ Refrigeration: ☐ Refrigerator ☐ Ice Box ☐ Deep Freeze
- ☐ Stove: ☐ Alcohol ☐ Propane/Butane ☐ Elec w/o Oven
  ☐ Electric w/Oven ☐ Microwave Oven
- ☐ Water Heater
- ☐ Water Maker: Mfg_____ Capacity (gals) _____
- ☐ Water System: ☐ Pressure ☐ Manual ☐ Dockside
- ☐ Trash Compactor

•ELECTRONICS & NAVIGATION
Overall Condition: ☐ Mint ☐ Above Average ☐ Good ☐ Fair ☐ Poor
- ☐ Auto Pilot: Mfg/Mdl
- ☐ Compass(es) (#)_____ Size (1)_____ Size (2)_____
- ☐ Depth Sounder: ☐ Flasher/Digital ☐ Recording: Mfg
- ☐ Direction Finder: Mfg/Mdl_____ ☐ Auto (ADF) ☐ Man (RDF)
- ☐ Hailer ☐ Intercom
- ☐ Lorar: Mfg/Mdl_____ ☐ Auto Track ☐ Interface
- ☐ Navigation Lights
- ☐ Radar: Mfg/Mdl_____ Range (miles)_____
- ☐ Radios: ☐ CB; ☐ VHF: Mfg/Mdl_____ Channels_____
- ☐ SSB: Mfg/Mdl_____ Channels_____ Watts_____
- ☐ Rudder Indicator ☐ Wind Speed Indicator
- ☐ Satellite Navigation: Mfg/Mdl
- ☐ Synchronizers
- ☐ Speed & Distance Logs: Mfg/Mdl

•ELECTRICAL EQUIPMENT
Overall Condition: ☐ Mint ☐ Above Average ☐ Good ☐ Fair ☐ Poor
- ☐ Air Cond:_____ BTUs_____ ☐ Reverse Cycle
- ☐ Batteries: (#)_____; Amp hours: _____; ☐ Battery Parallel
- ☐ Battery Charger: ☐ Auto ☐ Man;_____ AMPs
- ☐ Electrical System: Shippower ☐ 12V ☐ 24V ☐ 32V; Shorepower ☐ 110 ☐ 220
- ☐ Dockside Electrical Cable(s) ☐ Constavolt (Converter)
- ☐ Generator: Mfg_____ K.W._____ Hours_____
- ☐ Heater only (Separate from A/C)
- ☐ Lights
- ☐ Switches, fuses, circuit breakers
- ☐ Wiring overall

DECK & SAFETY
Overall Condition: ☐ Mint ☐ Above Average ☐ Good ☐ Fair ☐ Poor
- ☐ Anchor(s) w/Lines: (#)_____; ☐ Anchor Davit(s)
- ☐ Bilge Blower(s): (#)_____
- ☐ Bilge Pump(s): (#)_____ ☐ Auto ☐ Man
- ☐ Bow Rails ☐ Side Stanchions w/Lifelines
- ☐ Canvas Covers: ☐ Winter ☐ Mooring ☐ Drop Curtains
  ☐ Enclosed Curtains ☐ Bimini Top ☐ Dodger ☐ Cockpit Awning
  ☐ Flybridge Curtains ☐ Camper Top
- ☐ CG Package: (Anchor, Bell, Compass, Cushions, Fenders,
  Flares, Horn, Jackets, and Lights)
- ☐ Deck Wash Down System: ☐ Fresh Water ☐ Salt Water
- ☐ Dinghy Davits: ☐ Elec ☐ Man
- ☐ Dinghy ☐ Raft: Mfg_____ LOA_____
  Eng_____ HP_____
- ☐ Docking Lights: ☐ Transom ☐ Bow
- ☐ Fenders and Lines
- ☐ Fire System: ☐ CO² ☐ Halon; ☐ Auto ☐ Man
- ☐ Life Jackets & Life Rings: (#)_____
- ☐ Rails & Lifelines
- ☐ Search Lights: ☐ Single ☐ Dual; ☐ Remote Control: ☐ Manual ☐ Electric
- ☐ Swim Platform ☐ Swim (Boarding) Ladder
- ☐ Windlass ☐ Windshield Wipers

COST TO REPAIR/REPLACE COLUMN 1 (line B front page) $ _____

•FISHING EQUIPMENT
Overall Condition: ☐ Mint ☐ Above Average ☐ Good ☐ Fair ☐ Poor
- ☐ Bait Freezer ☐ Cockpit Sink
- ☐ Downriggers ☐ Fish Gear & Tackle
- ☐ Fish Box ☐ Live Well
- ☐ Fishing Chairs (#)_____ Mfg_____
- ☐ Outriggers: Mfg_____ Length (ft)_____
- ☐ Rods (#)_____ ☐ Reels (#)_____; ☐ Rod Holders (#)_____
- ☐ Tuna Tower or Half Tower: Mfg_____ Height (ft)_____
- ☐ Transom Door

SAILS & RIGGING
Overall Condition: ☐ Mint ☐ Above Average ☐ Good ☐ Fair ☐ Poor
- ☐ Cruising Equipped ☐ Racing Equipped
- ☐ Rigging: Material
- ☐ Roller Furling, Make/Type: (Main, Jib, etc.)
- ☐ Sails: ☐ Dacron ☐ Nylon;(#)_____ Types: ☐ Main ☐ Jib ☐ Spinnaker
  ☐ (#)1 Genoa ☐ (#)2 Genoa ☐ Mizzen ☐ Staysail;
  Mfg. of most: _____
- ☐ Winches: (#)_____ Mfg of most: _____

ENGINE/ENGINE ROOM/CONTROLS/DRIVE
Overall Condition: ☐ Mint ☐ Above Average ☐ Good ☐ Fair ☐ Poor
- ☐ Bow Thrusters: Mfg/Mdl:
- ☐ Clutch: ☐ Mechanical ☐ Hydraulic
- ☐ Controls: ☐ Cabin ☐ Cockpit ☐ Bridge ☐ Tower
  ☐ Side Console ☐ Center Console
- ☐ Ejectors
- ☐ Engine Alarm(s) ☐ Emergency Engine Stop
- ☐ Engine Block(s)
- ☐ Fresh Water Cooling System ☐ Fuel Filters
- ☐ Fuel Shut Off Valve: ☐ Stove ☐ Engines
- ☐ Fume Detector
- ☐ Lube Oil Storage & Transfer System
- ☐ Manifolds
- ☐ Muffler(s)
- ☐ Points & Plugs
- ☐ Extra Propeller(s) (#)_____
- ☐ Raw Water Sea Strainer(s)
- ☐ Reduction Drive: Ratios _____
- ☐ Rudder(s)
- ☐ Extra Shaft(s) (#)_____
- ☐ Stabilizers: Mfg/Mdl:
- ☐ Steering: ☐ Man ☐ Hydrt; ☐ Wheel ☐ Tiller
- ☐ Strut(s)
- ☐ Trim Tabs: Mfg/Mdl:
- ☐ Wiring Harnesses

PAINT/VARNISH/STAINS
Overall Condition: ☐ Mint ☐ Above Average ☐ Good ☐ Fair ☐ Poor
Boat has: ☐ Awlgrip ☐ Imron
- ☐ Bottom
- ☐ Cockpit
- ☐ Deck
- ☐ Interior
- ☐ Super Structure
- ☐ Topsides
- ☐ Transom

OTHER MISCELLANEOUS
- ☐ Cradle
Deck (describe) _____

Hull (describe) _____

Super Structure (describe) _____

Other (describe) _____

COST TO REPAIR/REPLACE COLUMN 2 (line C front page) $ _____

TO ORDER BUC'S PERSONALIZED BOAT EVALUATION SERVICE℠

• YOUR NAME   • COMPANY NAME   • AREA CODE & PHONE NUMBER

• ADDRESS   • CITY   • STATE   • ZIP   • COUNTRY

ARE YOU THE BOAT'S OWNER   ARE YOU CURRENTLY, OR HAVE YOU PREVIOUSLY BEEN, A BUC CUSTOMER?
☐ YES   ☐ YES   ☐ NO
☐ NO   IF YES, CUSTOMER NUMBER

BUC'S PERSONALIZED BOAT EVALUATION SERVICE HELPS TO ESTABLISH CURRENT MARKET AND OTHER VALUE AS OF A GIVEN DATE. THE FEE IS $45 PER VESSEL. TO DETERMINE VALUES FOR MORE THAN ONE DATE REQUIRES A FEE OF $30 FOR EACH ADDITIONAL DATE. THERE IS A $15.00 SERVICE CHARGE FOR ONE DAY PHONE SERVICE AND $25.00 SERVICE CHARGE FOR PHONE SERVICE WITH TWO HOUR TURNAROUND. FOREIGN CLIENTS MUST ADD COST OF RETURN PHONE CALL.

TO ORDER BY MAIL: COMPLETE THIS FORM AND MAIL TO BUC INFORMATION SERVICES, 1314 NE 17 CT., FT. LAUDERDALE, FL 33306
PLEASE ENCLOSE YOUR CHECK FOR THE FULL AMOUNT DUE (ADD 5% SALES TAX IF FLORIDA RESIDENT) OR USE YOUR CREDIT CARD. PLEASE COMPLETE APPROPRIATE BOXES BELOW.

PAYMENT IS: ☐ BY CHECK   ☐ BY CREDIT CARD: CARD NO.   EXPIRATION DATE
                                 ☐ AMERICAN EXPRESS
AMOUNT ENCLOSED $_____   ☐ MASTER CARD ☐ VISA

TO ORDER BY PHONE: COMPLETE THIS FORM BEFORE CALLING AND HAVE YOUR CREDIT CARD INFORMATION READILY AVAILABLE (SEE LINE ABOVE) AND CALL 1-800-327-6929 IN U.S. (FLORIDA AND FOREIGN DIAL DIRECT (305) 565-6715.)

These forms come 50 to a pad and can be ordered
directly from BUC.
Call our toll free number: 800-327-6929 or write:
BUC Research
1314 NE 17th Ct.
Ft Lauderdale, FL 33305

HOW TO USE THIS BOOK

For proper usage of this publication, it is essential that the user understand the Preface (page v) and the Introduction (page vi). Please read those sections before proceeding with this one.

MINIMUM IDENTIFYING INFORMATION

To arrive at the current retail price of a used boat, the following minimum information is usually required:
1) Manufacturer's name;
2) Model year;
3) The Length Overall;
4) Name and/or Model;
5) Engine Horsepower and Type and whether single, twin, gas or diesel;
6) The Location of the Vessel;
7) A BUC Rating as to its Engine and Hull Condition;
8) Details regarding Extra or Optional Equipment and Accessories.

USING THE INDEX

The index of this book represents thousands of hours of compilation. It is a combination of a manufacturers index and a cross-referenced model name index. This index warrants your attention and understanding because it can save you many hours of fruitless searching.

Unless you are very familiar with a particular listing, it is advisable to look up the manufacturer's name for all boats because it often reveals the unexpected. You will discover that many boat manufacturers have had name changes or have been acquired by other companies. You may also discover more than one manufacturer with the same or similar manufacturing name.

If the name is not listed as a manufacturer, check for a cross-reference, since the common trade names are often mistaken for corporate names. More information on how to use the index can be found on the first page of the index section.

IF YOU DON'T FIND THE BOAT

If you have the necessary information to identify a boat, have properly used the index and are still unable to find the listing, then recheck your source of information. In ninety percent of the cases, the reason for failing to find a listing is improper model year or length data. We gather model data not only directly from the manufacturers themselves, but also from other public sources. Additional models may exist, but BUC has found through various surveys that thirty-four percent of all boats owners cannot or will not properly describe their boat. Even in the trade, twenty-two percent of the inquiries to BUC have incorrect names or specifications.

One of the most common causes of not finding the model is

the confusion between the year of manufacture and the model year. Our listings are categorized by model year, which is not necessarily the same as the calendar year in which the boat was manufactured. Another very common identification problem is confusing the Length Overall (LOA) with the Length On Deck (LOD). Some manufacturers have reported the model to us with the Length On Deck in the LOA field, but list the LOA in their marketing literature. For a boat that has a large swim platform, bowsprit or sloped transom, this can make it difficult to find the model in our book. Sometimes, the numbers in the model name are a clue to solving this riddle.

Yet another area of confusion occurs when people round off inch measurements to the next highest or lowest foot. For example, some boat owner may be so used to bragging about his 31 footer that he has completely forgotten that the actual LOA is 30'1".

It is important to keep these points in mind since most states have titling and registration laws that allow the registrant to offer verbal testimony regarding a boat's specifications. In cases, however, where the boat may not be listed, please bring it to the attention of the research staff.

NOTES ABOUT OUR LISTINGS

Certain listing parameters have been utilized throughout the book with which you should familiarize yourself.

Boats with Engines

When a number appears in the column labeled "HP" under the "ENGINE" description, it can mean several things. If the engine type "TP" is outboard (OB) then the number indicated is the maximum horsepower outboard engine recommended by the manufacturer. The engine is not included in price. If the "TP" is any other inboard installation — HD, IB, IO, JT, SD, TD, VD (see Page 1 for Engine Type abbreviation) — then the number under "HP" is the horsepower of each engine. Single engines have no entry under the column headed "#" but twins will show a "T"; triple, an "R"; quadruple, a "Q". Engines are included in the price of non-outboard power boats. A "D" after the "HP" number indicates a diesel engine.

Older boats offered for sale after the engine has been replaced or rebuilt should receive more favorable treatment when using the BUC CONDITION/EQUIPMENT SCALE. When using the BUC Appraisal Form to determine boat evaluation, the cost of the new engine and installation is not to be added to the BUC price. Allow instead for better condition.

Sailboats

Retail prices for sailboats include standing and running rigging and one set of working sails unless otherwise indicated. The prices do not reflect any racing sails or extra racing equipment although most reported sales for sailboats list extra sails and associated gear. Use the BUC CONDITION/EQUIPMENT SCALE or the BUC APPRAISAL FORM for including the retail value of extra winches, pedestal steerers, etc. Regardless of size, a sailboat is considered an auxiliary when a horsepower appears in the column indicated "HP".

Outboard Boats

Outboard boats are priced without engines or trailer and minimal equipment. Although sales reports often include the value of the engine, these reports have been adjusted accordingly. The price of the motor or the price of a trailer must be added to the boat price.

Custom Built Boats

Custom built boats have no published or suggested list prices. They are usually built to the specifications of the original purchaser and vary considerably in the quality of construction and the manner in which they are equipped, powered and finished. We only assign values to custom built boats using BUC's Personalized Evaluation Service.

Our studies of this unique market have proven that comparison of features and characteristics help to determine each boat's position in the "For Sale" universe. Using powerful statistical computing techniques, our experienced staff will research each boat individually to determine the current market value of the boat, taking into account the vessel's location, condition and its complete inventory of features and equipment. The modest fee for this service can barely compare to the potential cost of a misevaluation. Call BUC (+1-954-565-6715) for complete details about the Personalized Evaluation Service, and to receive the evaluation forms.

Outboard Motors and Trailers

Outboard motors and trailers are only listed in Volume I since older models of these components tend to depreciate based only on condition rather than age. For information on how to use those listings, please see page xx of Volume I of the BUC Used Boat Price Guice.

USING THE LISTINGS

Near the top of every page are column headings. See the example figure on the next page. The numbered columns correspond to these descriptions:

1 LOA	Length Overall expressed in feet and inches.
2 NAME AND/OR MODEL	Descriptive Name or Model Information.
3 TOP/RIG	Indicates kind of Top for outboards and powerboats or the Rig style for sailboats (for example, SLP = Sloop or FB = Flybridge. See Key to BUC Codes on page 1 or inside back cover.)
4 BOAT TYPE	Describes Boat Type (See Key to BUC Codes on page 1 or inside back cover.)
5 HULL MTL	Describes the Hull Material (See Key to BUC Codes on page 1 or inside back cover.)

6 HULL TP	Describes the Hull Configuration (See Key To BUC Codes on page 1 or inside back cover.)
7 ENGINE TP	Describes the type of power plant that is or could be installed (for example IB = Inboard, see Key To BUC Codes on page 1 or inside back cover). If horsepower is shown, the engine is included in price.
8 ENGINE #	The prefix "T" indicates Twin installation; "R", Triple; "Q", Quad. Blank means Single engine.
9 ENGINE HP	The horsepower of each engine included in the price. The suffix "D" indicates Diesel and blank after the number means Gas engine(s). A number followed by a C in the HP column means that the number should be multiplied by 100. For example, T10CD indicates Twin 1000 Horsepower Diesel engines.
10 ENGINE MFG	The manufacturer of the engine(s) listed in the previous column.
11 BEAM FT IN	The boat's Beam in feet and inches.
12 WGT LBS	Approximate Weight in pounds. A number with a "T" suffix (like 35T) indicates the weight in Tons.
13 DRAFT FT IN	The draft of the boat in feet and inches.
14 RETAIL LOW	The current market Retail Low price for the North Atlantic area.
15 RETAIL HIGH	The current market Retail High price for the North Atlantic area.

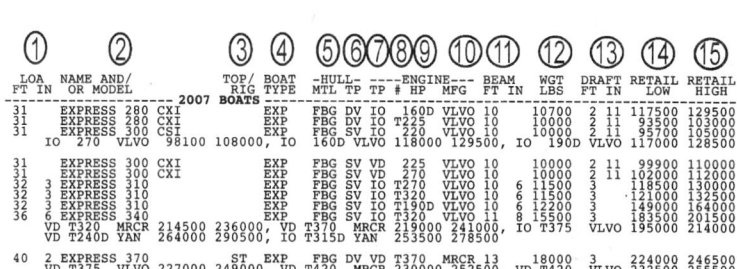

```
  ①       ②          ③  ④  ⑤⑥⑦⑧⑨      ⑩⑪  ⑫  ⑬  ⑭    ⑮
 LOA   NAME AND/      TOP/ BOAT -HULL- ----ENGINE--- BEAM   WGT  DRAFT RETAIL RETAIL
FT IN  OR MODEL       RIG  TYPE MTL TP TP # HP  MFG  FT IN  LBS  FT IN  LOW    HIGH
---------------------- 2007 BOATS -----------------------------------------------
 31   EXPRESS 280 CXI       EXP  FBG DV IO  160D VLVO 10         10700 2 11 117500 129500
 31   EXPRESS 280 CXI       EXP  FBG DV T225 VLVO 10             10000 2 11  93500 103000
 31   EXPRESS 300 CSI       EXP  FBG SV IO  220  VLVO 10         10000 2 11  95700 105000
      IO 270 VLVO 98100 108000, IO 160D VLVO 118000 129500, IO 190D VLVO 117000 128500

 31   EXPRESS 300 CXI       EXP  FBG SV VD  225  VLVO 10         10000 2 11  99900 110000
 31   EXPRESS 300 CXI       EXP  FBG SV VD  270  VLVO 10         10000 2 11 102000 112000
 32  3 EXPRESS 310          EXP  FBG SV IO T270  VLVO 10  6      11500 3    118500 130000
 32  3 EXPRESS 310          EXP  FBG SV IO T320  VLVO 10  6      11500 3    121000 132500
 32  3 EXPRESS 310          EXP  FBG SV IO T190D VLVO 10  6      12200 3    149000 164000
 36  6 EXPRESS 340          EXP  FBG SV IO T320  VLVO 11  8      15500 3    183500 201500
      VD T320 MRCR 214500 236000, VD T370 MRCR 219000 241000, IO T375 VLVO 195000 214000
      VD T240D YAN 264000 290500, IO T315D YAN 253500 278500

 40  2 EXPRESS 370      ST  EXP  FBG DV VD T370  MRCR 13         18000 3    224000 246500
      VD T375 VLVO 227000 249000, VD T420 MRCR 230000 252500, VD T420 VLVO 232500 255500
      VD T315D YAN 283000 311000
```

The BUC Used Boat Price Guide is organized first by Manufacturer Name. Within the manufacturer's listing, the boats are separated into groups by Model Year. Within each year, the models are listed in order of increasing Length Overall (LOA) and then by increasing horsepower and number of engines.

When a particular model has more than four different engine options they are stacked in three columns under the basic model description. In other words, the LOA, Name and/or Model, Top/Rig, Boat Type, Hull Material, Hull Type, Beam, Weight and Draft are not repeated but the Engine Type, Number of engines, Horsepower, Fuel, Engine Manufacturer and Retail Price range are listed three to a line under the basic listing. The three columns are separated by commas. Read from left to right on each line and ignore the column headings for these stacked engine options.

If the price difference between two or more engine options is relatively small, then the engine manufacturer is omitted and a range of horsepowers is printed in the horsepower column (shown as a low value and a high value with a dash between them). In this case, apply the retail price range to any engine whose horsepower falls within the horsepower range. See below, for an example of a horsepower range listing.

LOA FT IN	NAME AND/ OR MODEL	TOP/ RIG	BOAT TYPE	-HULL- MTL TP	----ENGINE--- TP # HP MFG	BEAM FT IN	WGT LBS	DRAFT FT IN	RETAIL LOW	RETAIL HIGH
			--- 1998 BOATS ---							
23 7	2300 SC	OP	CUD	FBG SV	IO 220-310	8 4	4700	3 1	16900	20600
23 7	2300 SR	OP	RNBT	FBG SV	IO 220-310	8 4	4100	3 1	14500	17900
25 3	2400 SCR	OP	CR	FBG SV	IO 190-250	8 6	5000	2 11	19400	22300
27 8	2700 SR	OP	CR	FBG SV	IO 250-310	8 3	5850	3 1	23100	27000

Finding A Listing

After properly identifying the boat in question and utilizing the boat manufacturer, trade name and model name Index, refer to the page where the manufacturer's listing starts.

Select the Model Year (for example, ---2003 BOATS---). Read down the list until you find the appropriate Length Overall (LOA). Check the model name of the listing, then the top or rig and the boat type. Next select the correct engine type, the number of engines, the horsepower, fuel type and the engine manufacturer. In some cases, you may have to check the hull material if a particular hull was built with different materials. Models with optional construction variances might follow a group of models with numerous engine options. For example, a 40-foot Express Cruiser with a Flybridge would follow a 40-foot Express Cruiser with a Hard Top.

Under the columns "Retail Low" and "Retail High" is the fair market value price range of the boat in U.S. Dollars for a boat in BUC Condition and located in the North Atlantic area. Obviously, if the boat you are evaluating meets this definition, use the published prices. If not, the range is easily and precisely adjusted by using the BUC AREA ADJUSTMENT SCALE and the BUC CONDITION/EQUIPMENT SCALE (both found on the inside front cover). You may, if you wish, use the BUC APPRAISAL FORM.

RETAIL PRICE ADJUSTMENTS

The prices for used boats listed in BUC's Used Boat Price Guides are for boats that have about average equipment appropriate for the boat's size, are in BUC Condition and are located in the North Atlantic Area. To determine the current retail price of a boat that varies in location, equipment or condition from these assumptions, you must know how to adjust for AREA, CONDITION and EQUIPMENT.

Use of the Area Adjustment Scale

Inside the front cover of each BUC Used Boat Price Guide is an Area Adjustment Scale. This chart shows the percentage that is to be added or subtracted to the Retail Price range in order to obtain the correct price range for a geographical area other than the North Atlantic. To use this scale, find the percentage adjustment where the area and boat type/boat length intersect. The entry in the intersected box will be a plus or minus percent. If the boat does not require a CONDI- TION/EQUIPMENT adjustment, merely add or subtract the indicated percentage to the published BUC Retail Low and Retail High. If, as is usually the case, the boat requires a CONDITION/EQUIPMENT adjustment, then add the adjustment percentages together (see example below).

Example: A 30' sailboat located on the east coast of Florida	Low	High
Published BUC retail	$70,800	$77,800
South Atlantic Area Adjustment, subtract 5%	−3,540	−3,890
Current Retail market value	$67,260	$73,910

Use of the Condition/Equipment Scale

For a quick determination of the market value of a used boat in other than BUC Condition, use the CONDITION/EQUIPMENT SCALE found inside the front cover. This unique scale has been compiled by studying the selling price of boats reported to us by dealers and brokers to the condition rating they indicate on these reports. Clearly, use of this scale will not be as accurate as a detailed analysis, using, for examle, the BUC APPRAISAL FORM (see below). However, it is quite sufficient for every day use, and especially convenient when interacting with a customer who wants a general idea of the value of his boat.

Banks, finance companies, credit unions, insurance companies, assessors and other government agencies will find themselves using the SCALES almost exclusively. Dealers, brokers and surveyors will use this technique most of the time especially as experience with the BUC Book increases. However, professionals in the industry will also frequently use check lists like the BUC APPRAISAL FORM for an accurate, detailed evaluation, carefully listing and evaluating the price effect of extra equipment and various condition deficiencies.

Example: A 40' sundeck trawler in high Above BUC Condition	Low	High
Published BUC retail	$336,500	$369,500
High end of Above BUC, add 15%	50,475	55,425
Current Retail market value	$386,975	$424,925

Using Both AREA and CONDITION Adjustments

When both the AREA ADJUSTMENT SCALE and the CONDITION/EQUIPMENT SCALE are necessary for the same boat, add the percentages together before adjusting the published Retail Prices.

Example: A 26' sport fisherman in Seattle in Fair Condition	Low	High
Published BUC retail	$70,100	$77,100
Combine Northern Pacific, +15%, and Fair Condition, -10%.		
+5% net adjustment	3,505	3,855
Current Retail market value	$73,605	$80,955

Use of Appraisal Forms

The BUC APPRAISAL FORM was created to help you record and analyze a boat's condition and equipment inventory. It provides a convenient documentation of the cost to repair, equip or recondition a vessel to bring it up to the level of BUC Condition. These forms can be used everyday in your business to assist with the cost control of trade-in, storage and repair. A reproduction of the form appears on pages x and xi.

To use the BUC APPRAISAL FORM,

1. Find the correct listing in the BUC Used Boat Price Guide.
2. Adjust the Retail High only for Area, not condition.
3. Record the area-adjusted Retail High on line (A) of the Form.
4. Add together the Cost To Repair/Replace from columns 1 and 2 of the back of the page, and put that cost on line (D).
5. Subtract (D) from (A). That is the current High Retail of the boat, on line (E) of the Form.
6. Divide the original Retail Low by the original Retail High to obtain the range percentage. Then multiply this percentage by the adjusted Retail High from step 5, line (E), in order to obtain the adjusted Retail Low.

Example: A 33' Open Express in Texas on the Gulf Coast needing minor repairs. The BUC published Retail range is $173,000-190,000.

BUC published Retail High	$190,000
Adjust for AREA, Gulf Coast, 33', minus 10%	−19,000
Adjusted Retail High	171,000
Dealer estimates the total amount to recondition the boat for resale (to BUC Condition)	−8,500
Current Retail High value for this boat	$162,500
The original Retail Low divided by the original Retail High, 173000÷190000	91%
Current Retail Low value for this boat	$147,875

For the example boat above, the current Retail range, adjusted for area and reconditioning, is $147,875-162,500.

If the completion of the BUC APPRAISAL FORM reveals that the boat has no significant deficiencies, but rather there are extras, or recent major reconditioning, then the situation is somewhat more complicated. One cannot just add the value of the extras to the Retail range. Our studies have shown that money added to a vessel beyond BUC Condition does not necessarily increase the value dollar-for-dollar.

For example, take an older model boat that has had a recent $60,000 re-powering and $40,000 of interior upgrades, and is now in good condition with no deficiencies. It is not correct to just add $100,000 to the BUC Retail Low and High, because some large part of that expense may have just returned the boat to BUC Condition. More likely, professionals in the industry will use their knowledge to evaluate whether this boat is in "Above BUC Condition" or perhaps "Bristol". Then, the appropriate adjustment percentage will be added to the BUC Retail range.

Determination of Trade-In Price (or actual cash allowance)

We do not calculate or publish a trade-in value because every firm has its own overhead or profit margin. Generally, the trade-in allowance used by most dealers is 70 to 80 percent of the current market retail. The reasons for a variation in the margin are numerous but might typically be: size of the organization, whether salespeople are commissioned or employed, building location, yard costs, showroom expense and financial costs.

There are two common techniques for handling trade-ins. The first is a little round-about. The dealer allows the buyer of a new boat full market value on his trade-in (exactly what he expects to sell it for) but the new boat is not discounted or is discounted very little. This technique has been used successfully by a number of dealers throughout the years. However, the mathematics become tangled and the cost of the used boat to your business and the possible potential profit that could be derived on resale is confused with the new boat sale.

Alternatively, separate the new and used boat sales even if they are involved in the same transaction. For the trade-in, adjust the published BUC price with the Area, Condition and Equipment Scales, and perhaps make-ready repairs such as waxing or bottom painting, along with any factors you might use for local conditions. Then subtract the amount of profit you expect to realize on resale, and subtract your cost of sales overhead, including the cost to store the boat, advertising and salesman's commission. The net result is the trade-in value.

You can divide the net figure resulting after subtracting all those profit and cost items by the adjusted retail price for your area. This coefficient, as a percentage, is your trade-in margin. The trade-in margin can be used to quickly and roughly calculate any other trade-in. Merely multiply your margin by the Retail price after adjusting for area and condition.

BOAT PRICING SECTION
Key to BUC Codes

BOAT TYPE

AIR	Airboat
BASS	Bass
BUOY	Buoy Tender
B/R	Bowrider
CBNCR	Cabin Cruiser
CAMPR	Camper
CANOE	Canoe
CTRCN	Center Console Fisherman
COMM	Commercial
CNV	Convertible
CR	Cruiser
CRCPT	Cruiser with Cockpit
CUD	Cuddy
DECK	Deck Style Boat
DGY	Dinghy
DCCPT	Double Cabin Cockpit
DCFD	Double Cabin Flush Deck
DCMY	Double Cabin Motor Yacht
DNEST	Downeast
EXP	Express
EXPSF	Express Fisherman
FSH	Fisherman
FLATS	Flats Fisherman
FH	Floating Home
FD	Flush Deck
FDCR	Flush Deck Cruiser
FDPH	Flush Deck with Pilothouse
HB	Houseboat
ICE	Ice Boat
JTSKI	Jet Ski
JON	Jon (or John)
KAYAK	Kayak
LNCH	Launch
LRMY	LRC Motor Yacht
LRMYC	LRC Motor Yacht with Cockpit
LRPH	LRC with Raised Pilothouse
LRPHC	LRC with Raised Pilothouse and Cockpit
LRRD	LRC with Raised Aft Deck
LRRDC	LRC with Raised Aft Deck and Cockpit
LRSDN	LRC Sedan
LRTC	LRC with Trunk Cabin
LRTCC	LRC with Trunk Cabin and Cockpit
MS	Motor Sailor
MY	Motor Yacht
MYCPT	Motor Yacht with Cockpit
MYDKH	Motor Yacht with Deckhouse
MYXDH	Motor Yacht with Ext. Deckhouse
MYFD	Motor Yacht with Flush Deck
MYPH	Motor Yacht with Pilothouse
MYSD	Sun Deck Motor Yacht
MYSDC	Sun Deck Motor Yacht with Cockpit
OFF	Offshore
OPFSH	Open Fish
OVNTR	Overnighter
PEDAL	Pedal Boat
PW	Personal Watercraft
PH	Pilothouse
PRAM	Pram
RACE	Racing Runabout
ROW	Row Boat
RNBT	Runabout
SBD	Sailboard
SAIL	Sailboat
SA/CR	Sailboat-Cruising
SA/OD	Sailboat-One Design
SA/RC	Sailboat-Racer/Cruiser
SCDAC	Sail, Cursing-Deckhouse-Aft Cockpit
SCDCA	Sail, Cruising-Deckhouse-Center and Aft Cockpits
SCDCC	Sail, Cruising-Deckhouse-Center Cockpit
SCFAC	Sail, Cruising-Aft Cockpit
SCFCC	Sail, Cruising-Center Cockpit
SCFCA	Sail, Cruising-Center and Aft Cockpits
SCPHO	Sail, Cruising-Pilothouse (Only)
SCPAC	Sail, Cruising-Pilothouse-Aft Cockpit
SCPBR	Sail, Cruising-Pilothouse-Bridge
SCPCC	Sail, Cruising-Pilothouse-Center Cockpit
SCPCA	Sail, Cruising-Pilothouse-Center and Aft Cockpits
SMPHO	Motorsailer-Pilothouse (Only)
SMPAC	Motorsailer-Pilothouse-Aft Cockpit
SMPBR	Motorsailer-Pilothouse—Bridge
SMPCC	Motorsailer-Pilothouse-Center Cockpit
SMPCA	Motorsailer-Pilothouse-Center and Aft Cockpits
SRCAC	Sail, Racer/Cruiser-Aft Cockpit
SRCCC	Sail, Racer/Cruiser-Center Cockpit
SRCCA	Sail, Racer/Cruiser-Center and Aft Cockpits
SROAC	Sail, Racer/Cruiser-One Design
SRRAC	Sail, Racer Only-Aft Cockpit
SRRAD	Sail, Racer Only-Aft Cockpit-Deckpit
SDN	Sedan Cruiser
SDNSF	Sedan Sport Fisherman
SKI	Ski
SPTCR	Sport Cruiser
SF	Sport Fisherman
TRWL	Trawler
TRMY	Trawler Motor Yacht
TRMYC	Trawler Motor Yacht with Cockpit
TRRD	Trawler with Raised Aft Deck
TRRDC	Trawler with Raised Aft Deck and Cockpits
TRSDN	Trawler Sedan
TRTC	Trawler with Trunk Cabin
TRTCC	Trawler with Trunk Cabin and Cockpit
TRPH	Trawler with Raised Pilothouse
TRPHC	Trawler with Raised Pilothouse and Cockpit
TCMY	Triple Cabin Motor Yacht
TUG	Tug Boat
UTL	Utility (or Open)
W/T	Walkthru Windshield
WKNDR	Weekender
YTFS	Yacht Fisherman

HULL CONFIGURATION

BB	Bilge Boards
BK	Bulb Keel
CT	Catamaran
CB	Centerboard
DB	Daggerboard
DV	Deep Vee
DS	Displacement
FL	Flatbottom
KL	Keel
KC	Keel-Centerboard
LB	Leeboards
OR	Outrigger
PN	Pontoon (or Platform)
RB	Round Bottom
SD	Semi Displacement
SV	Semi Vee (or Modified Vee)
SK	Swing Keel (or Drop Keel)

HULL CONFIGURATION (Continued)

TR	Tri Hull (or Cathedral)
TM	Trimaran
TH	Tunnel Hull
TK	Twin Keels (Fin Keels)
WK	Wing Keel

ENGINE TYPE

EL	Electric
HD	Hydraulic Drive
IB	Inboard
IO	Inboard-Outdrive (stern drive)
OB	Outboard
SD	Sail Drive
SE	Seadrive
TD	Tunnel Drive
VD	Vee-Drive
JT	Water Jet Propulsion

HULL MATERIAL

ABS	Acetyl Butyl Styrene
ARX	Airex
AL	Aluminum
A/S	Aluminum over Steel
C/S	Carbon Fiber Sandwich
CDR	Cedar
WCM	Cold Molded Wood
FC	Ferro Cement
FBG	Fiberglass
FBC	Fiberglass Composite
F/S	Fiberglass Sandwich
F/W	Fiberglass over Wood
FOM	Foam
INF	Inflatable
RIB	Inflatable with Rigid Bottom
IRON	Iron
KEV	Kevlar
L/P	Lapstrake Plywood
LEAD	Lead
MHG	Mahogany
M/P	Mahogany over Plywood
MONL	Monel
P/C	Planked Cedar
P/M	Planked Mahogany
P/P	Planked Plywood
PL	Plastic
PLY	Plywood
PVC	Polyvinylchloride
RR	Reinforced Rubber
RIB	Rigid Inflatable
RLX	Royalex
R/N	Rubber over Nylon
STL	Steel
S/S	Stainless Steel
SAN	Styrene Acetyl Nitride
TEK	Teak
V/N	Vinyl over Nylon
VEF	Virtual Engineered Composites
WD	Wood
CVS	Wood/Canvas

TOP or RIG

CAT	Cat Rig
CUT	Cutter Rig
EPH	Enclosed Pilothouse
EPF	Enclosed Pilothouse with Flybridge
EPS	Enclosed Pilothouse with Sun Deck
FB	Flybridge
F+H	Fly Bridge with Half Tower
F+M	Fly Bridge with Marlin Tower
F+T	Fly Bridge with Tuna Tower
GAF	Gaff Rig
HT	Hard Top
H+H	Hard Top with Half Tower
H+M	Hard Top with Marlin Tower
H+T	Hard Top with Tuna Tower
KTH	Ketch Rig
LAT	Lateen (or Lug Rig)
OP	Open
TH	Open with Half Tower
MT	Open with Marlin Tower
RA	Open with Radar Arch
ST	Open with Soft Top (Bimini Top)
TT	Open with T-Top
TT	Open with Tuna Tower
SCH	Schooner
SLP	Sloop Rig
SQ	Square Sail Rig
TT	Tuna Tower
YWL	Yawl Rig

MISCELLANEOUS OTHER ABBREVIATIONS

CUS	Custom
DKHS	Deckhouse
DLX	Deluxe
DIN	Dinette
DISPL	Displacement
EXT	Extended
F	Fire Engines
FM	Fixed Motor
FWC	Fresh Water Cooled
HP	Horsepower
LOA	Length Overall
LWL	Length at Waterline
MAX	Maximum
MIN	Minimum
MLD	Molded
MTR	Motor
NA	Not Announced (or not available at time of compilation)
OPT	Optional
PRMDK	Promenade Deck
Q	(before HP) Quad Engines
RIV	Riveted
SLPR	Sleeper
SPIN	Spinnaker
STD	Standard
TL	Tilt
TR	Trim
R	(before HP) Triple Engines
T	(after HP) Turbine Engines
TB	Turbocharged
T	(before HP) Twin Engines
WGT	Weight
WELD	Welded

ENGINE MANUFACTURER

ALAS	Alaska Diesel Electric/Lugger
ALBN	Albin
ALLI	Allison Engine Co.
AMER	American Diesel
AMDL	American Diesel Corp.
AMML	American Marine Ltd.
BENZ	Mercedes-Benz
BMW	BMW Marine Products
BPM	BPM Volcano
BMC	British Marine Cmpnts.
SEAG	British Seagull Co.
BUIC	Buick
BUKH	Bukh (USA) Inc.

ENGINE MANUFACTURER (Continued)

CPWR	C-Power (Marine) Ltd.
CADI	Cadillac
CARN	Carniti/Pennsylvania Development
CARY	Cary Marine Engines
CAT	Caterpillar, Inc.
CHAL	Challenger
CHEV	Chevrolet
CC	Chris Craft
CHRY	Chrysler Marine
CBRA	Cobra Power Inc.
COMM	Commander Marine Co.
CNTL	Continental
CORR	Correct Craft
CRUS	Crusader Marine Engines
CUM	Cummins Engine Co. Inc.
CUYA	Cuyuna
DATS	Datsun
DAY	Daytona Marine Engine Corp.
DEER	John Deere
DD	Detroit Diesel
DUTZ	Deutz MWM
DRAK	Drake
EAST	Easthope Industries Ltd.
EICK	Eickert
ESCO	Escort
ESKA	Eska Company
EVIN	Evinrude Motors
FARY	Faryman Diesel Engines
FIAT	Fiat Marine
FIBF	Fiberform
FLAG	Flagship Marine Engine Co. Inc.
FRCE	Force Outboards
FORD	Ford Motor Co.
FUJI	Fuji
GARD	Gardner
GE	General Electric
GM	General Motors
GLAS	Glastron Engines
GRAY	Graymarine Engines
GREN	Greenwich
HAM	CNF Hamelton & Co. Ltd.
HARD	Hardin Marine
HAWK	Hawk Marine Power Inc.
HERC	Hercules Motors Corp.
HINO	Hino Motors Inc.
HOLM	Holman and Moody Inc.
HOME	Homelite
HOND	Honda Marine
HUST	Hustler Hi-Tec Marine
HYDR	Hydro Marine
INDM	Indmar Products Co. Inc.
INT	Interceptor (Crusader) (Eaton)
IF	Isotta Fraschini SPA
ISUZ	Isuzu Diesel of North America
IVCO	Iveco Aifo
JOHN	Johnson Outboard
J&T	Johnson & Towers
KAAM	Kaama
KAWA	Kawasaki
KELV	Kelvin
KERM	Kermath Engine Works
KOHL	Kohler
KRUP	Krupp Mak
KUBT	Kubota
LANC	Lancing Marine
LATH	Lathrop
LEHM	Lehman Power Corp./Ford
LEYL	Leyland Thornycroft
LINC	Lincoln
LIST	Lister Petter Ltd.
LOMB	Lombardini Marine Spa
LYC	Lycoming
MACK	Mack Diesel Power
MAN	MAN Marine Engines
MDS	Marine Drive Systems
MPC	Marine Power Corp.
MRNR	Mariner Outboards
MCCU	McCulloch/Firestone
MRCR	Mercury Marine/Mercruiser
MERC	Mercury Outboards
MERL	Merlin Marine Engines
MAID	Mermaid Marine Engines Ltd.
MITS	Mitsubishi
MITY	Mity Mite
MTU	MTU of North America
MGW	Muncie Gear Works
MWM	M.W.M. Murphy
NANI	Nanni Diesel BV
NAPR	Napier Deltic Paxmans
NISS	Nissan Marine
OMC	OMC Stern Drive
OSCO	Osco Motors Corp.
OWEN	Owens
PACE	Pacemaker
PACK	Packard
PALM	Palmer
PANT	Panther Marine Engines
PARS	Parsons Engineering Ltd.
PATH	Pathfinder Marine
PAX	Paxman Diesels
PEN	Peninsular Marine Inc.
PERK	Perkins North America
PETT	Petter Diesels
PEUG	Peugot Motors of America
PISC	Pisces
PCM	Pleasurecraft Marine Engines Co.
RCA	RCA Marine Division
REN	Renault
RIVA	Riva Marine Engines
RR	Rolls Royce
SAAB	Saab Scania
SABB	Sabb Motor A/S
SABR	Sabre Engines Inc.
SEAK	Sea King/Montgomery Ward
SEA	Seamaster Marine Division
SEAR	Sears Roebuck & Co.
SETK	Seatek Marine Power
SOLE	Sole Diesel
SOLM	Soloman Technology
STER	Sterling
STRN	Stern Power
S&S	Stewart & Stevenson
SUZU	Suzuki
TAN	Tanaka (USA) Co. Ltd.
THOR	Thornycroft/Leyland
TOHU	Tohatsu
UNIF	Uniflite
UNIV	Universal/Medalist/Atomic
USMA	US Marine Power Corp.
DAF	Van Dorns
DENO	Vetus – Den Ouden, Inc.
VW	Volkswagon Marine Div, N.A. Inc.
VMMD	V-M Marine Diesel
VLVO	Volvo Penta of America
WANK	Wankle
WATE	Watermota Ltd.
WAUK	Waukesha
WEST	Westerbeke Corp.
WICK	Wickstrom
WOLF	Wolfpack Marine
YAMA	Yamaha Motor Corp.
YAN	YanmarDiesel Engine Co. Ltd.

1

A & T MARINE SERVICES INC
COAST GUARD MFG ID- AJK

Call 1-800-327-6929 for BUC Personalized Evaluation Service
Or, for 1980 to 1981 boats, sign onto www.BUCValuPro.com

A B C CUSTOM CATAMARANS

Call 1-800-327-6929 for BUC Personalized Evaluation Service
Or, for 1980 to 1983 boats, sign onto www.BUCValuPro.com

A C MANUFACTURING CO INC
DIV OF ANACAPRI YACHT SALES   See inside cover to adjust price for area
HIALEAH GARDENS FL 3301 COAST GUARD MFG ID- ACW
FOR MORE RECENT MODELS SEE ANACAPRI MARINE INC

LOA FT IN	NAME AND/ OR MODEL	TOP/ RIG	BOAT TYPE	-HULL- MTL TP	----ENGINE--- TP # HP MFG	BEAM FT IN	WGT LBS	DRAFT FT IN	RETAIL LOW	RETAIL HIGH
				1978 BOATS						
19 3	ANGLER	OP	OPFSH	FBG SV	OB	8	1800		3600	4200
22 3	ANGLER	OP	OPFSH	FBG SV	OB	8	2300		5050	5800
22 3	ANGLER	OP	OPFSH	FBG SV	IB 175	8	2300		3600	4150
22 3	NEWPORT		RNBT	FBG SV	OB	8	2500		5350	6150
22 3	NEWPORT		RNBT	FBG SV	IB 175	8	2500		3750	4400
22 3	TORINO		CUD	FBG SV	OB	8	2700		5650	6500
22 3	TORINO		CUD	FBG SV	IB 175	8	2700		3900	4500
23 7	ERIKA	SLP	SAIL	FBG CB		7 8	2400	1 4	5350	6150
24 10	ANGLER	OP	OPFSH	FBG SV	IB 225-235	8	3800		5650	6500
24 10	HOLIDAY		CR	FBG SV	IB 235	8	3840		5750	6650
24 10	VAGABOND		CR	FBG SV	IB 235	8	3950		5900	6750
				1977 BOATS						
19 3	ANGLER	OP	OPFSH	FBG SV	OB	8	1800		3600	4150
22 3	ANGLER	OP	OPFSH	FBG SV	OB	8	2300		5000	5700
22 3	ANGLER	OP	OPFSH	FBG SV	IO 175	8	2300		3750	4350
22 3	ANGLER	OP	OPFSH	FBG SV	IB 225	8	2300		3500	4050
22 3	NEWPORT		RNBT	FBG SV	OB	8	2500		5300	6100
22 3	NEWPORT	OP	RNBT	FBG SV	IO 175	8	2500		3500	4050
22 3	TORINO	HT	CUD	FBG SV	OB	8	2700		5600	6450
22 3	TORINO	HT	CUD	FBG SV	IO 175	8	2700		3850	4450
23 7	ERIKA	SLP	SAIL	FBG CB		7 8	2400	1 4	5150	5900
24 10	ANGLER	OP	OPFSH	FBG SV	IB 225	8	3800		5400	6250
24 10	ANGLER	OP	OPFSH	FBG SV	IO 235	8	3840		5950	6850
24 10	HOLIDAY	HT	CR	FBG SV	IO 235	8	3840		5700	6550
24 10	VAGABOND	OP	OPFSH	FBG SV	IO 235	8	3950		6100	7000
				1976 BOATS						
19 3	ANGLER	OP	OPFSH	FBG SV	OB	8	1580	7	3250	3800
22 3	ANGLER	OP	OPFSH	FBG SV	OB	8	3040	2 4	6000	6900
22 3	ANGLER	OP	OPFSH	FBG SV	IO 165 OMC	8	3040	2 4	4450	5100
22 3	ANGLER	OP	OPFSH	FBG SV	IB 165 OMC	8	3040	2 4	3950	4600
22 3	DIPLOMAT V230	HT	CR	FBG SV	OB	8	3040	2 4	6000	6900
22 3	DIPLOMAT V230	HT	CR	FBG SV	IB 165-235	8	3240	2 4	4000	4850
22 3	DIPLOMAT V230	FB	CR	FBG SV	IB 165-235	8	3240	2 4	4000	4850
22 3	NEWPORT V230	OP	RNBT	FBG SV	OB	8	3040	2 4	6000	6900
22 3	NEWPORT V230	OP	RNBT	FBG SV	IB 165-235	8	3240	2 4	4000	4900
22 3	NEWPORT V230	OP	RNBT	FBG SV	IB T120	8	3240	2 4	4300	5200
22 3	NEWPORT V230	OP	RNBT	FBG SV	IB T140	8	3240	2 4	4450	5400
22 3	TORINO V230	OP	CUD	FBG SV	OB	8	3040	2 4	6000	6900
22 3	TORINO V230	OP	CUD	FBG SV	IB 165-235	8	3440	2 4	4150	5050
22 3	TORINO V230	OP	CUD	FBG SV	IB T120-T140	8	3440	2 4	4450	5550
22 3	TORINO V230	HT	CUD	FBG SV	IB 165-235	8	3440	2 4	4150	5050
22 3	TORINO V230	HT	CUD	FBG SV	IB T120-T140	8	3440	2 4	4450	5550
23 7	ERIKA	SLP	SAIL	FBG KC		7 6	2000	1 4	5850	6750
24 10	ANGLER	OP	OPFSH	FBG SV	IO 165 OMC	8	3800	2 4	5800	6700
24 10	ANGLER	OP	OPFSH	FBG SV	IB 165 OMC	8	3800	2 4	5150	5950
24 10	HOLIDAY V250	OP	CR	FBG SV	IB 225-235	8	3840	2 4	5400	6250
24 10	HOLIDAY V250	OP	CR	FBG SV	IB T140-T165	8	3840	2 4	5400	7000
24 10	HOLIDAY V250	HT	CR	FBG SV	IB 225-235	8	3840	2 4	5400	6250
24 10	HOLIDAY V250	HT	CR	FBG SV	IB T140-T165	8	3840	2 4	5700	7000
24 10	HOLIDAY V250	FB	CR	FBG SV	IB 225-235	8	3840	2 4	5400	6250
24 10	HOLIDAY V250	FB	CR	FBG SV	IB T140-T165	8	3840	2 4	5700	7000
24 10	VAGABOND	OP	OPFSH	FBG SV	IO 225 OMC	8	3950	2 4	6150	7100
24 10	VAGABOND	OP	OPFSH	FBG SV	IB 225 OMC	8	3950	2 4	5450	6250
24 10	VAGABOND	HT	OPFSH	FBG SV	IO 225 OMC	8	3950	2 4	6150	7100
24 10	VAGABOND	HT	OPFSH	FBG SV	IB 225 OMC	8	3950	2 4	5450	6250
24 10	VAGABOND	FB	OPFSH	FBG SV	IO 225 OMC	8	3950	2 4	6150	7100
24 10	VAGABOND	FB	OPFSH	FBG SV	IB 225 OMC	8	3950	2 4	5450	6250
				1973 BOATS						
19	ANGLER	OP	OPFSH	FBG	OB	8	1725	7	3350	3900
22	ANGLER	OP	OPFSH	FBG	OB	8	3040	1	5750	6650
22	ANGLER	OP	OPFSH	FBG	IO 165 OMC	8	3040	1	4800	5550
22	DIPLOMAT	HT	CR	FBG	IO 120 OMC	8	3440	1	4950	5650
22	DIPLOMAT	FB	CR	FBG	IO 120 OMC	8	3550	1	5050	5800
22	NEWPORT	OP	RNBT	FBG	IO 165-255	8	3240	1	4550	5450
22	NEWPORT	OP	RNBT	FBG	IO T120-T225	8	3240	1	5150	6250
22	TORINO	OP	CUD	FBG	IO 165-255	8	3440	1	5000	6000
22	TORINO	OP	CUD	FBG	IO T120-T225	8	3440	1	5650	6850
25	ANGLER	OP	OPFSH	FBG	IO 165-255	8	3500	1	6150	7550
25	ANGLER	OP	OPFSH	FBG	IO T120-T225	8	3500	1	6950	8650
25	HOLIDAY	OP	CR	FBG	IO 165-255	8	3840	1	6250	7650
25	HOLIDAY	OP	CR	FBG	IO T120-T225	8	3840	1	7000	8700
				1971 BOATS						
19	LIGHTNING	SLP	SA/OD	FBG CB		6 6	700	5	1950	2350
22		EXP		FBG SV	IO 155 OMC	8	3400	2 4	5250	6000
22	ANGLER	OP	OPFSH	FBG SV	IO 155 OMC	8	3100	2 4	5000	6000
22	DIPLOMAT	HT		FBG SV	IO 155 OMC	8	3400	2 4	5000	5750
22	NEWPORT		RNBT	FBG SV	IO 155 OMC	8	3200	2 4	4750	5500
22	TORINO		CUD	FBG SV	IO 155 OMC	8	3400	2 4	5250	6000
25	ANGLER	OP	OPFSH	FBG SV	IO 155 OMC	8	3500	2 4	6500	7500
25	HOLIDAY		CR	FBG SV	IO 155 OMC	8	3700	2 4	6450	7450
25	HOLIDAY	OP	CR	FBG SV	IO 225	8			6950	8000
				1970 BOATS						
22	ANGLER		OPFSH	FBG DV	IO 155 OMC	8	3100	3	5400	6200
22	ANGLER		OPFSH	FBG SV	OB	8	2400	1	4900	5650
22	DIPLOMAT	HT	CR	FBG DV	IO 155 OMC	8	3400	3	5400	6200
22	NEWPORT		RNBT	FBG DV	IO 155 OMC	8	3200	3	4950	5650
25	ANGLER		OPFSH	FBG DV	IO 155 OMC	8	3500	3	6750	7750
25	ESQUIRE		CR	FBG DV	IO 155 OMC	8	3800	3	6700	7700
25	HOLIDAY		CR	FBG DV	IO 155 OMC	8	3700	3	6700	7700
				1968 BOATS						
22			OVNTR	FBG	IO 155		3040		5400	6200
22	ANGLER	OP	OPFSH	FBG	IO 155		3040		5700	6550

A J S SANDWICH YT CONS LTD

Call 1-800-327-6929 for BUC Personalized Evaluation Service
Or, for 1974 to 1980 boats, sign onto www.BUCValuPro.com

A M & T COMPANY
SHIELDS INC   COAST GUARD MFG ID- AHH

Call 1-800-327-6929 for BUC Personalized Evaluation Service
Or, for 1982 to 1986 boats, sign onto www.BUCValuPro.com

ABBATE

INTERNATIONAL CUSTOM YACHTS

Call 1-800-327-6929 for BUC Personalized Evaluation Service
Or, for 1979 to 1985 boats, sign onto www.BUCValuPro.com

ABBOTT BOATS LTD
SARNIA ONTARIO CANADA   COAST GUARD MFG ID- ZBL See inside cover to adjust price for area

For more recent years, see the BUC Used Boat Price Guide, Volume 1 or Volume 2

LOA FT IN	NAME AND/ OR MODEL	TOP/ RIG	BOAT TYPE	-HULL- MTL TP	----ENGINE--- TP # HP MFG	BEAM FT IN	WGT LBS	DRAFT FT IN	RETAIL LOW	RETAIL HIGH
				1983 BOATS						
22	ABBOTT 22	SLP	SAIL	FBG KL OB		7 6	3100	3 10	5350	6150
26 9	SOLING	SLP	SA/OD	FBG KL		6 3	2300	4 6	5200	6000
33 4	ABBOTT 33	SLP	SA/OD	FBG KL SD	VLVO	8 3	6057	5 5	17100	19500
				1982 BOATS						
22	ABBOTT 22	SLP	SAIL	FBG KL OB		7 6	3100	3 10	5050	5800
26 9	SOLING	SLP	SA/OD	FBG KL		6 3	2300	4 6	4900	5650
33 4	ABBOTT 33	SLP	SA/OD	FBG KL SD	9D VLVO	8 3	6057	5 5	16200	18400
				1981 BOATS						
22	ABBOTT 22	SLP	SAIL	FBG KL OB		7 6	3100	3 10	4750	5450
26 9	SOLING	SLP	SA/OD	FBG KL		6 3	2300	4 6	4650	5350
33 4	ABBOTT 33	SLP	SA/OD	FBG KL SD	9D VLVO	8 3	6057	5 5	15200	17300

ABBOTT BOATS LTD

-CONTINUED   See inside cover to adjust price for area

LOA FT IN	NAME AND/ OR MODEL	TOP/ RIG	BOAT TYPE	HULL MTL TP	TP	ENGINE # HP	MFG	BEAM FT IN	WGT LBS	DRAFT FT IN	RETAIL LOW	RETAIL HIGH
			1980 BOATS									
22	ABBOTT 22	SLP	SA/RC FBG	KL	IB	D		7 6	3100	3 10	5500	6350
26 9	SOLING	SLP	SA/OD FBG	KL				6 3		4 3	7100	8200
33 3	ABBOTT 33	SLP	SA/RC FBG	KL	IB	9D	VLVO	8 2	6057	5 5	14600	16500
			1979 BOATS									
22	ABBOTT 22	SLP	SA/CR FBG	KL	OB			7 6	3100	3 10	4350	5050
26 9	SOLING	SLP	SA/OD FBG	KL				6 3	2200	4 3	4100	4750
33 4	ABBOTT 33	SLP	SA/OD FBG	KL	IB	9D	VLVO	8 3	6057	5 5	14000	15900
			1978 BOATS									
22	ABBOTT 22	SLP	SA/CR FBG	KL				7 6	3000	3 10	4050	4750
25 2	FOLKBOAT	SLP	SA/CR FBG	KL				7 2	4700		6650	7650
			1977 BOATS									
26 9	SOLING	SLP	SA/OD FBG	KL				6 3	2233	4 3	3850	4500
			1976 BOATS									
26 9	SOLING	SLP	SA/OD FBG	KL				6 3	2200	4 3	3700	4300
			1975 BOATS									
22	ABBOTT 22	SLP	SA/CR FBG	KL				7 6	3300	3 8	4000	4650
26 9	SOLING	SLP	SA/OD FBG	KL				6 3	2200	4 3	3600	4200
			1974 BOATS									
26 9	SOLING	SLP	SA/OD FBG	KL				6 3	2200	4 3	3500	4050
			1973 BOATS									
26 9	SOLING	SLP	SA/OD FBG	KL				6 3	2200	4 3	3400	3950
			1972 BOATS									
26 9	SOLING	SLP	SA/OD FBG	KL				6 3	2200	4 3	3350	3900
			1971 BOATS									
26 9	SOLING	SLP	SA/OD FBG	KL				6 3	2200	4 3	3300	3800
			1970 BOATS									
26 9	SOLING	SLP	SA/OD FBG	KL				6 3	2200	4 3	3200	3750
			1969 BOATS									
26 9	SOLING	SLP	SA/OD FBG	KL				6 3	2200	4 3	3150	3700
			1967 BOATS									
25	FOLKBOAT	SLP	SA/OD FBG	KL				7 3	4700	3 11	5150	5950
25	FOLKBOAT	SLP	SA/OD WD	KL				7 3	4700	3 11	5150	5950
			1966 BOATS									
29 2	DRAGON	SLP	SA/OD WD	KL				6 4	3747	3 10	4750	5500
			1965 BOATS									
29 2	DRAGON	SLP	SA/OD WD	KL				6 4	3747	3 10	4750	5450
			1941 BOATS									
29	VISITOR	SLP	SAIL WD	KL	IB	D		8		4 6	16600	18800
31 4	OVER-NITER	SLP	SAIL WD	KL	IB	D		8 6		4 7	24500	27300
38 10	WEEK-ENDER	SLP	SAIL WD	KL	IB	D		9 9		5 10	49100	54000

ABEKING & RASMUSSEN YACHT YD

LEMWERDER GERMANY D-27805   See inside cover to adjust price for area

For more recent years, see the BUC Used Boat Price Guide, Volume 1 or Volume 2

LOA FT IN	NAME AND/ OR MODEL	TOP/ RIG	BOAT TYPE	HULL MTL TP	TP	ENGINE # HP	MFG	BEAM FT IN	WGT LBS	DRAFT FT IN	RETAIL LOW	RETAIL HIGH
			1973 BOATS									
29 2	DRAGON	CUT	SA/OD FBG	KL				6 4	3747	3 11	8250	9500
29 2	DRAGON	CUT	SA/OD WD	KL				6 4	3747	3 11	8250	9500
			1972 BOATS									
29 2	DRAGON	CUT	SA/OD WD	KL				6 4	3747	3 11	8050	9250
			1971 BOATS									
29 2	DRAGON	CUT	SA/OD WD	KL				6 4	3747	3 11	7900	9100
			1970 BOATS									
29 2	DRAGON	CUT	SA/OD WD	KL				6 4	3747	3 11	7750	8900
			1969 BOATS									
29 2	DRAGON	CUT	SA/OD WD	KL				6 4	3747	3 11	7650	8800
			1968 BOATS									
29 2	DRAGON	CUT	SA/OD WD	KL				6 4	3747	3 11	7550	8650
			1967 BOATS									
29 2	DRAGON	CUT	SA/OD WD	KL				6 4	3747	3 11	7450	8550
			1966 BOATS									
29 2	DRAGON	CUT	SA/OD WD	KL				6 4	3747	3 10	7400	8500
			1965 BOATS									
29 2	DRAGON	CUT	SA/OD WD	KL				6 4	3747	3 10	7350	8450

ABLE CUSTOM YACHTS

DIV OF TRENTON MARINE INC
ELLSWORTH ME 04605-9705 COAST GUARD MFG ID- XRA   See inside cover to adjust price for area

For more recent years, see the BUC Used Boat Price Guide, Volume 1 or Volume 2

LOA FT IN	NAME AND/ OR MODEL	TOP/ RIG	BOAT TYPE	HULL MTL TP	TP	ENGINE # HP	MFG	BEAM FT IN	WGT LBS	DRAFT FT IN	RETAIL LOW	RETAIL HIGH
			1983 BOATS									
32 1	WHISTLER 32	CAT	SAIL FBG	KC	IB	16D	UNIV	10 6	11986	3 8	55500	61000
33 5	INTERNATL-ONE-DESIGN	SLP	SAIL FBG	KC	IB	D		6 9	7120	5 4	32800	36400
			1982 BOATS									
32 1	WHISTLER 32	CAT	SAIL FBG	KC	IB	16D	UNIV	10 6	11986	3 8	52600	57800
33 5	INTERNATL-ONE-DESIGN	SLP	SAIL FBG	KC	IB	D		6 9	7120	5 4	31000	34500

ABLE SHIPWRIGHTS INC

E HAMPTON CT 06424   COAST GUARD MFG ID- TFA   See inside cover to adjust price for area

LOA FT IN	NAME AND/ OR MODEL	TOP/ RIG	BOAT TYPE	HULL MTL TP	TP	ENGINE # HP	MFG	BEAM FT IN	WGT LBS	DRAFT FT IN	RETAIL LOW	RETAIL HIGH
			1977 BOATS									
20	ABLE 20	SLP	SAIL FBG	KL	OB			7 4	2500	2 6	5350	6150
			1976 BOATS									
20	ABLE 20	SLP	SAIL FBG	KL	OB			7 4	2500	2 6	5200	5950
23 10	ABLE-POITIN	SLP	SAIL F/S	KL	OB			10	3750	4	8250	9450
23 10	ABLE-POITIN	SLP	SAIL F/S	KL	IB	5D- 7D		10	3900	4	9500	10900

ACAPULCO YACHTS

COAST GUARD MFG ID- APX

Call 1-800-327-6929 for BUC Personalized Evaluation Service
Or, for 1969 to 1977 boats, sign onto www.BUCValuPro.com

ACE SPEEDBOAT CO

COAST GUARD MFG ID- ACI

Call 1-800-327-6929 for BUC Personalized Evaluation Service
Or, for 1983 to 1985 boats, sign onto www.BUCValuPro.com

ACHILLES YACHTS LTD

COAST GUARD MFG ID- BMC
FORMERLY BUTLER MOULDINGS

Call 1-800-327-6929 for BUC Personalized Evaluation Service
Or, for 1968 to 1987 boats, sign onto www.BUCValuPro.com

ACTION CRAFT INC

CAPE CORAL FL 33909-290 COAST GUARD MFG ID- AFQ See inside cover to adjust price for area

For more recent years, see the BUC Used Boat Price Guide, Volume 1 or Volume 2

LOA FT IN	NAME AND/ OR MODEL	TOP/ RIG	BOAT TYPE	HULL MTL TP	TP	ENGINE # HP	MFG	BEAM FT IN	WGT LBS	DRAFT FT IN	RETAIL LOW	RETAIL HIGH
			1983 BOATS									
17 3	BACK-BAY 17-3	OP	FSH FBG	SV	OB			6 7	750	9	2800	3300
17 3	BONEFISHER 17-3	OP	FSH FBG	SV	OB			6 7		9	3200	3700
17 3	PACEMAKER	OP	RNBT FBG	SV	OB			6 7	750	9	2900	3350

ACTION MARINE INC

COAST GUARD MFG ID- ACM

Call 1-800-327-6929 for BUC Personalized Evaluation Service
Or, for 1977 to 1979 boats, sign onto www.BUCValuPro.com

ACTION MARINE INC

Call 1-800-327-6929 for BUC Personalized Evaluation Service
Or, for 1971 boats, sign onto www.BUCValuPro.com

QUINCY ADAMS BOAT YARD

QUINCY MA   See inside cover to adjust price for area

LOA FT IN	NAME AND/ OR MODEL	TOP/ RIG	BOAT TYPE	HULL MTL TP	TP	ENGINE # HP	MFG	BEAM FT IN	WGT LBS	DRAFT FT IN	RETAIL LOW	RETAIL HIGH
			1966 BOATS									
37 8	U-S-ONE-DESIGN	SLP	SA/OD MHG	KL				7		5 6	21600	24000

LOA FT IN	NAME AND/ OR MODEL	TOP/ RIG	BOAT TYPE	MTL	-HULL- TP	TP	----ENGINE--- # HP	MFG	BEAM FT IN	WGT LBS	DRAFT FT IN	RETAIL LOW	RETAIL HIGH
			1965 BOATS										
38	U-S-ONE-DESIGN	SLP	SA/OD	MHG	KL				7		5 4	21800	24300

LAIRD ADAMS ENGINEERING LTD

Call 1-800-327-6929 for BUC Personalized Evaluation Service
Or, for 1980 boats, sign onto www.BUCValuPro.com

ADLER & BARBOUR YACHT SERVICE

PELHAM NY 10803   See inside cover to adjust price for area

For more recent years, see the BUC Used Boat Price Guide, Volume 1 or Volume 2

LOA FT IN	NAME AND/ OR MODEL	TOP/ RIG	BOAT TYPE	MTL	-HULL- TP	TP	----ENGINE--- # HP	MFG	BEAM FT IN	WGT LBS	DRAFT FT IN	RETAIL LOW	RETAIL HIGH
			1983 BOATS										
43 10	PETERSON 44	CUT	SA/RC	FBG	KL	IB		D	12 11	29000	6 4	100000	110000
			1982 BOATS										
43 10	PETERSON 44	CUT	SA/RC	FBG	KL	IB		D	12 11	29000	6 4	94900	104500
			1981 BOATS										
43 10	PETERSON 44	CUT	SA/RC	FBG	KL	IB		D	12 11	29000	6 4	89900	98700
			1980 BOATS										
43 10	PETERSON 44	CUT	SA/RC	FBG	KL	IB		D	12 11	29000	6 4	85600	94000
46 7	VAGABOND 47	KTH	SA/RC	FBG	KL	IB		D	13 5	40000	5 6	113000	124000
			1979 BOATS										
43 10	PETERSON 44	CUT	SA/CR	FBG	KL	IB		D	12 11	29000	6 4	81700	89800
46 7	VAGABOND 47	KTH	SA/CR	FBG	KL	IB		D	13 5	40000	5 6	107500	118500
			1978 BOATS										
43 10	PETERSON 44	CUT	SA/CR	FBG	KL	IB		D	12 11	29000	6 4	78200	85900
46 7	VAGABOND 47	KTH	SA/CR	FBG	KL	IB		D	13 5	40000	5 7	103000	113000
			1977 BOATS										
43 10	PETERSON 44	CUT	SA/CR	FBG	KL	IB	60D		12 11	30000	6 4	76200	83700
46 7	VAGABOND 47	KTH	SA/RC	FBG	KL	IB		D	13 5	40000	5 6	98800	108500
			1976 BOATS										
46 7	VAGABOND 47	KTH	SA/RC	FBG	KL	IB		D	13 5	40000	5 6	95000	104500
			1975 BOATS										
45 5	BLUEWATER 46	KTH	SA/CR	FBG	KL	IB		D	13 8	29000	5 4	77200	84900
46	U-S 46	YWL	SA/CR	FBG	KC	IB		D	12	25000	5 2	70300	77300
46 7	VAGABOND 47	KTH	SA/RC	FBG	KL	IB		D	13 5	40000	5 6	91500	100500
			1974 BOATS										
46	U-S 46 CTR CPT	YWL	SA/CR	FBG	KC	IB		D	12	25000	5 2	67900	74600
46 7	VAGABOND 47 CTR CPT	KTH	SA/RC	FBG	KL	IB		D	13 5	40000	5 6	88400	97100
			1973 BOATS										
46	U-S 46	YWL	SA/CR	FBG	KC	IB		D	12	25000	5 2	65700	72200
46 7	VAGABOND 47	KTH	SA/RC	FBG	KL	IB		D	13 5	40000	5 6	85600	94000

ADMIRALTY LTD

Call 1-800-327-6929 for BUC Personalized Evaluation Service
Or, for 1983 to 1984 boats, sign onto www.BUCValuPro.com

ADPRE BOAT CORP

COAST GUARD MFG ID- ADP

Call 1-800-327-6929 for BUC Personalized Evaluation Service
Or, for 1974 boats, sign onto www.BUCValuPro.com

ADRIATIC YACHTS INC

COAST GUARD MFG ID- AYD

Call 1-800-327-6929 for BUC Personalized Evaluation Service
Or, for 1980 to 1983 boats, sign onto www.BUCValuPro.com

ADVANCE SAILBOAT CORP

COAST GUARD MFG ID- ADS

Call 1-800-327-6929 for BUC Personalized Evaluation Service
Or, for 1961 to 1982 boats, sign onto www.BUCValuPro.com

ADVENTURE YACHT CO INC

MARINA DEL REY CA 90292 COAST GUARD MFG ID- AYA See inside cover to adjust price for area

LOA FT IN	NAME AND/ OR MODEL	TOP/ RIG	BOAT TYPE	MTL	-HULL- TP	TP	----ENGINE--- # HP	MFG	BEAM FT IN	WGT LBS	DRAFT FT IN	RETAIL LOW	RETAIL HIGH
			1983 BOATS										
34 6	FANTASIA 35	SLP	SA/CR	FBG	KL	IB		D	11	21000	4 8	47800	52500
			1982 BOATS										
34 6	FANTASIA 35	SLP	SA/CR	FBG	KL	IB		D	11	21000	4 8	44700	49700
			1981 BOATS										
34 6	FANTASIA 35	SLP	SA/CR	FBG	KL	IB		D	11	21000	4 8	42100	46700
			1980 BOATS										
34 6	FANTASIA	SLP	SA/CR	FBG	KL	IB	33D	YAN	11	21000	4 8	40200	44600
34 6	FANTASIA	CUT	SA/CR	FBG	KL	IB	33D	YAN	11	21000	4 8	40200	44600
35	HARRIS 35	SLP	SA/CR	FBG	KL	IB		D	11 4	18000	5	35000	38900
			1979 BOATS										
34 6	FANTASIA	SLP	SA/CR	FBG	KL	IB		D	11	22000	4 8	40300	44800
35 10	MAGELLAN	KTH	SA/CR	FBG	KL	IB		D	11 10	19000		35600	39600
			1978 BOATS										
34 6	FANTASIA	SLP	SA/CR	FBG	KL	IB	40D	PISC	11	22000	4 8	38800	43100
34 6	FANTASIA	CUT	SA/CR	FBG	KL	IB	40D	PISC	11	22000	4 8	38800	43100
			1977 BOATS										
34 6	FANTASIA 35	SLP	SA/CR	FBG	KL	IB	40D		11	23200	5	39300	43700

ADVENTURER YACHT CO

Call 1-800-327-6929 for BUC Personalized Evaluation Service
Or, for 1961 to 1966 boats, sign onto www.BUCValuPro.com

AEOLUS BOATS

Call 1-800-327-6929 for BUC Personalized Evaluation Service
Or, for 1966 to 1967 boats, sign onto www.BUCValuPro.com

AERO MARINE INDUSTRIES LTD

Call 1-800-327-6929 for BUC Personalized Evaluation Service
Or, for 1978 to 1979 boats, sign onto www.BUCValuPro.com

AERO-NAUTICAL INC

SKIMMAR BOATS   COAST GUARD MFG ID- SKM

Call 1-800-327-6929 for BUC Personalized Evaluation Service
Or, for 1959 to 1977 boats, sign onto www.BUCValuPro.com

AEROCRAFT INC

TECUMSEH MI 49286   See inside cover to adjust price for area

For more recent years, see the BUC Used Boat Price Guide, Volume 1 or Volume 2

LOA FT IN	NAME AND/ OR MODEL	TOP/ RIG	BOAT TYPE	MTL	-HULL- TP	TP	----ENGINE--- # HP	MFG	BEAM FT IN	WGT LBS	DRAFT FT IN	RETAIL LOW	RETAIL HIGH
			1982 BOATS										
16 6	MALIBU		RNBT	FBG	DV	OB			6 11	1388		2200	2600
16 6	MALIBU		RNBT	FBG	IO		120		7 4	1980		2950	3450
16 6	MUSTANG I		RNBT	FBG	TR	OB			7	1388		2200	2600
17 6	MONTE-CARLO		RNBT	FBG	DV	OB			7 4	1478		2350	2700
17 6	MONTE-CARLO		RNBT	FBG	DV	IO	140		7 4	2140		3300	3800
17 6	MUSTANG II		RNBT	FBG	TR	IO	140		7 4	2230		3350	3900
20 7	MACH II-C		CUD	FBG	DV	IO	170		8	2965		5150	5900
			1981 BOATS										
16 6	MALIBU		RNBT	FBG	DV	OB			6 11	1338		2050	2450
16 6	MALIBU		RNBT	FBG	DV	IO	120-170		6 11	1980		2850	3300
16 6	MUSTANG I		RNBT	FBG	TR	OB			7	1290		2000	2400
17 6	MONTE-CARLO		RNBT	FBG	DV	OB			7 4	1478		2300	2700
17 6	MONTE-CARLO		RNBT	FBG	DV	IO	140-230		7 4	2103		3200	3900
17 6	MUSTANG II		RNBT	FBG	TR	IO	140-230		7 4	2153		3250	3950
20 7	MACH II-C		RNBT	FBG	DV	IO	170-260		8	2965		5050	6150
			1980 BOATS										
16 6	MALIBU		RNBT	FBG	DV	OB			6 11	1388		2150	2500
16 6	MALIBU	OP	RNBT	FBG	DV	IO	140-170		6 11			2800	3300
16 6	MUSTANG I		RNBT	FBG	TR	OB			7	1438		2200	2600
16 6	MUSTANG I	OP	RNBT	FBG	TR	IO	140-170		7			2850	3300
17 6	MONTE-CARLO		RNBT	FBG	DV	OB			7 4	1528		2300	2700
17 6	MONTE-CARLO I	OP	RNBT	FBG	DV	IO	140-230		7			3150	3900
17 6	MONTE-CARLO II	OP	RNBT	FBG	DV	IO	230		7			3250	3800

AEROCRAFT INC — CONTINUED

See inside cover to adjust price for area

LOA FT IN	NAME AND/OR MODEL	TOP/RIG	BOAT TYPE	HULL MTL TP	ENGINE TP # HP MFG	BEAM FT IN	WGT LBS	DRAFT FT IN	RETAIL LOW	RETAIL HIGH
1980 BOATS										
17 6	MUSTANG II		RNBT	FBG TR	OB	7 4	1578		2350	2750
17 6	MUSTANG II	OP	RNBT	FBG TR	IO 140-230	7 4			3250	3900
20	MUSTANG III	OP	RNBT	FBG TR	IO 165-260	7 10			4600	5600
20 7	MACH II-C		CUD	FBG DV	IO 260	8			5250	6050
20 7	MACH IIC		CUD	FBG DV	OB	8	2163		3450	4050
20 7	MACH IIR		RNBT	FBG DV	OB	8	2063		3350	3900
20 7	MACH IIR	OP	RNBT	FBG DV	IO 165-260	8			3750	5800
22	MACH III		RNBT	FBG DV	IO 165-260	7 11			5300	6450
1979 BOATS										
16 6	MALIBU	OP	RNBT	FBG DV	OB	6 11	1388		2050	2450
16 6	MUSTANG I	OP	RNBT	FBG TR	OB	7	1438		2200	2550
17 6	MONTE-CARLO	OP	RNBT	FBG DV	OB	7 4	1528		2300	2700
17 6	MONTE-CARLO I	OP	RNBT	FBG DV	IO 230	7 4	2453		3550	4150
17 6	MONTE-CARLO II	OP	RNBT	FBG DV	IO 230	7 4	2453		3550	4150
17 6	MUSTANG II	OP	RNBT	FBG TR	OB	7 4	1578		2350	2700
17 6	MUSTANG II	OP	RNBT	FBG TR	IO 170-230	7 4	2503		3500	4200
20	MUSTANG III	OP	RNBT	FBG TR	IO 260	7 10	3100		5000	5700
20 7	MACH II	OP	RNBT	FBG DV	IO 260	8	3000		5050	5800
21 7	MACH IIC	OP	CUD	FBG DV	OB	8	2063		3500	4050
21 7	MACH IIR	OP	RNBT	FBG DV	OB	8	2063		3500	4050
22	MACH III	OP	CUD	FBG DV	IO 260	7 11	3400		6100	7000
1978 BOATS										
16 6	MALIBU	ST	RNBT	FBG DV	OB	6 11			2050	2450
16 6	MALIBU	ST	RNBT	FBG DV	IO 120-165	6 11	2300		3050	3550
16 6	MARLIN	ST	RNBT	FBG DV	OB	6 11	1388		2050	2450
16 6	MUSTANG I	ST	RNBT	FBG TR	OB	7	1438		2150	2500
16 6	MUSTANG I	ST	RNBT	FBG TR	IO 120-165	7	2350		3100	3650
17 6	MONTE-CARLO I	ST	RNBT	FBG DV	OB	7 4	1528		2300	2650
17 6	MONTE-CARLO I	ST	RNBT	FBG DV	IO 140-228	7 4	2453		3450	4150
17 6	MONTE-CARLO II	ST	RNBT	FBG DV	IO 140-228	7 4	2403		3400	4100
17 6	MUSTANG II	ST	RNBT	FBG TR	OB	7 4	1578		2300	2700
17 6	MUSTANG II	ST	RNBT	FBG TR	IO 140-228	7 4	2503		3500	4150
20	MUSTANG III	ST	RNBT	FBG TR	IO 165-260	7 10	3100		4750	5750
20 7	MACH II C	ST	CUD	FBG DV	OB	8	2163		3350	3900
20 7	MACH II C	ST	CUD	FBG DV	IO 165-260	8	3100		5150	6250
20 7	MACH II R	ST	RNBT	FBG DV	OB	8	2163		3350	3900
20 7	MACH II R	ST	RNBT	FBG DV	IO 165-260	8	3000		4800	5850
22	MACH III	ST	RNBT	FBG DV	IO 165-260	7 11	3400		5550	6700
1977 BOATS										
16 6	MALIBU	ST	RNBT	FBG DV	OB	6 11	1380		2000	2400
16 6	MALIBU	ST	RNBT	FBG DV	IO 120-175	6 11	2146		2950	3500
16 6	MUSTANG I	ST	RNBT	FBG TR	OB	7	1431		2050	2450
16 6	MUSTANG I	ST	RNBT	FBG TR	IO 120-175	7	2196		3050	3550
17 6	MONTE-CARLO I	ST	RNBT	FBG DV	OB	7 4	1498		2200	2600
17 6	MONTE-CARLO I	ST	RNBT	FBG DV	IO 140-235	7 4	2453		3500	4250
17 6	MONTE-CARLO II	ST	RNBT	FBG DV	IO 140-235	7 4	2403		3450	4200
17 6	MUSTANG II	ST	RNBT	FBG TR	OB	7 4	1548		2300	2650
17 6	MUSTANG II	ST	RNBT	FBG TR	IO 140-235	7 4	2503		3500	4300
17 6	MUSTANG III	ST	RNBT	FBG TR	IO 165 MRCR	7 10	3253		4300	5000
20	MUSTANG III	ST	RNBT	FBG DV	IO 170-235	7 10	3253		4950	5850
22	MACH III	ST	CUD	FBG DV	IO 165-235	7 11	3533		6100	7150
1976 BOATS										
16 6	MALIBU	OP	RNBT	FBG DV	OB	7	1200		1750	2100
16 6	MALIBU	OP	RNBT	FBG DV	IO 140-165	7	1200		2400	2800
16 6	MUSTANG I	OP	RNBT	FBG TR	OB	7	1350		1950	2300
16 6	MUSTANG I	OP	RNBT	FBG TR	IO 140-165	7	1350		2500	2900
17 5	MUSTANG I	OP	RNBT	FBG TR	OB	7 4	1575		2300	2650
17 5	MUSTANG I	OP	RNBT	FBG TR	IO	7 4	1575		**	**
17 5	MUSTANG I	OP	RNBT	FBG TR	IO 188	7 4	1575		2950	3450
17 8	MONTE-CARLO I	OP	RNBT	FBG DV	OB	7 4	1500		2200	2550
17 8	MONTE-CARLO I	OP	RNBT	FBG DV	IO 165-233	7 4	1500		2950	3600
17 8	MONTE-CARLO II	OP	RNBT	FBG DV	IO 165	7 4			3350	3900
20	MUSTANG III	OP	RNBT	FBG DV	IO 188-280	7 10			4800	5950
22	MACH III	OP	CUD	FBG DV	IO 188	7 11			5850	6750
1975 BOATS										
16 6	MALIBU	ST	RNBT	FBG DV	IO 120-140	7	2100		3100	3650
17 5	MUSTANG I	ST	RNBT	FBG DV	IO 140 MRCR	7	2100		3150	3650
17 5	MUSTANG II	ST	RNBT	FBG SV	OB	7 4	1450		2050	2450
17 5	MUSTANG II	ST	RNBT	FBG SV	IO 140-188	7 4	2450		3650	4300
17 5	MUSTANG II	ST	RNBT	FBG SV	IO 390 BERK	7 4	2450		5900	6800
17 6	MUSTANG II	ST	RNBT	FBG DV	IO 120-140	7	2100		3300	3850
17 8	MONTE-CARLO	ST	RNBT	FBG DV	OB	7 4	1400		2050	2400
17 8	MONTE-CARLO	ST	RNBT	FBG DV	IO 140-188	7 4	2400		3650	4300
17 8	MONTE-CARLO	ST	RNBT	FBG DV	IO 390 BERK	7 4	2400		5900	6800
20	MARLIN	ST	RNBT	FBG SV	IO 140-188	7 10	2900		4850	5600
20	MUSTANG III	ST	RNBT	FBG SV	IO 165-188	7 10	2800		4750	5450
1974 BOATS										
16 6	MALIBU		RNBT	FBG DV	IO 120	7	2100	2 6	3200	3750
16 6	MALIBU		RNBT	FBG DV	JT 140 OMC	7	2100	2 6	3100	3600
16 6	MALIBU		RNBT	FBG DV	IO 140	7	2100	2 6	3250	3750
16 6	MUSTANG		RNBT	FBG SV	IO 120	7	2100	2 6	3200	3750
16 6	MUSTANG		RNBT	FBG SV	JT 140 OMC	7	2100	2 6	3100	3600
16 6	MUSTANG		RNBT	FBG SV	IO 140	7	2100	2 6	3250	3750
17 5	MONTEREY		RNBT	FBG SV	OB	7 4	1450	10	2050	2450
17 5	MONTEREY		RNBT	FBG SV	IO 120	7 4	2450	2 5	3750	4400
	JT 140 OMC 3550 4150, IO 140-188 3800 4450, JT 245-390 3750 4350									
17 8	MONTE-CARLO		RNBT	FBG DV	OB	7 4	1400	10		2400
17 8	MONTE-CARLO		RNBT	FBG DV	IO 120	7 4	2400	2 5	3650	4400
	JT 140 OMC 3550 4150, IO 140-188 3800 4450, JT 245-390 3750 4350									
20	MARLIN		FSH	FBG SV	IO 120-188	7 10	2900	2 6	5500	6350
20	MARQUIS		RNBT	FBG SV	IO 120-188	7 10	2800	2 6	4900	5700
20	MARQUIS		RNBT	FBG SV	JT 245-390	7 10	2800	2 6	4700	5400
20	MONTCLAIR		CR	FBG	IO 140-188	7 10	3400	2 6	5750	6700
23 8	MARINER		CUD	FBG	IO 165-188	7 10	3500	2 8	7150	8250
23 8	MARINER		CUD	FBG	IO T140	7 10	3500	2 8	8100	9300
1973 BOATS										
16 6	MALIBU		RNBT	FBG DV	IO 120	7	1100		2550	2950
16 6	MALIBU		RNBT	FBG DV	JT 140 OMC	7	1100		2350	2700
16 6	MALIBU		RNBT	FBG DV	IO 140	7	1100		2550	2950
16 6	MUSTANG		RNBT	FBG SV	IO 120	7	1100		2350	2700
16 6	MUSTANG		RNBT	FBG SV	JT 140 OMC	7	1100		2550	2950
16 6	MUSTANG		RNBT	FBG SV	IO 140	7	1100		2550	2950
17 5	MONTEREY		RNBT	FBG SV	OB	7 4	1450		2050	2450
17 5	MONTEREY		RNBT	FBG SV	IO 120	7 4	1450		3100	3600
	JT 140 OMC 2800 3250, IO 140-188 3100 3700, JT 245-330 2950 3450									
17 8	MONTE-CARLO		RNBT	FBG DV	OB	7 4	1400		2000	2400
17 8	MONTE-CARLO		RNBT	FBG DV	IO 120	7 4	1400		3150	3650
	JT 140 MRCR 2800 3250, IO 140-188 3150 3700, JT 245-330 3000 3450									
20	MARQUIS		RNBT	FBG SV	IO 120-188	7 10	2800		5050	5850
	JT 245 OMC 4550 5250, IO 245 5250 6050, JT 330 BERK 4550 5250									
20	MONTCLAIR		CR	FBG	IO 140-245	7 10	3400		5950	7050
1972 BOATS										
16 6	MALIBU		RNBT	FBG DV	IO 120-188	7	2100		3450	4050
16 6	MUSTANG		RNBT	FBG DV	IO 120	7	2100		3450	4000
17 5	MONTEREY		RNBT	FBG SV	IO 188	7	2100		3500	4050
17 5	MONTEREY		RNBT	FBG SV	OB	7 4	1200		1750	2100
17 5	MONTEREY		RNBT	FBG SV	IO 120-245	7 4	2100		3700	4600
17 8	MONTE-CARLO		RNBT	FBG DV	IO 120-245	7 4	2100		3750	4900
20	MARQUIS		RNBT	FBG SV	IO 120-245	7 10	2800		5200	6300
21	MEDITERRANEAN		RNBT	FBG DV	IO 120-245	7			5700	6850
1971 BOATS										
16 5	NASSAU		RNBT	FBG SV	IO 120-140	6 6			3300	3850
17 2	CARIBBEAN		RNBT	FBG SV	IO 120-140	6 10			3550	4100
17 5	DT-175	OP	RNBT	FBG TR	OB	7 4	1200		1750	2100
17 5	MONTEREY	OP	RNBT	FBG TR	IO	7 4	1200		2100	2100
18 7	ATLANTIC		RNBT	FBG DV	OB	7			4000	4800
18 8	BAHAMA		RNBT	FBG SV	OB	7 2	1275		1900	2250
18 8	BAHAMA		RNBT	FBG DV	IO 120-200	7 2			4100	4850
21	GALAXY		CR	FBG DV	IO 160-210	8			6200	7250
21	GALAXY		CUD	FBG DV	IO 160-210	8			6200	7250
1970 BOATS										
16 5	NASSAU		RNBT	FBG TR	IO 120	6 6	1630	8	3100	3600
17	COHO	ST	RNBT	AL RB	IO 120	6 10	1120		2900	3400
17 2	CARIBBEAN		RNBT	FBG SV	IO 120	6 10	1632	9	3350	3900
18 7	ATLANTIC		RNBT	FBG DV	IO 120	7	2000	10	4050	4900
18 8	BAHAMA		RNBT	FBG TR	IO 160	7 2	2180	9	4300	5000
21	GALAXY		CR	FBG DV	IO 160	7 11	2195	1 2	5500	6300
21	GALAXY CD		CUD	FBG DV	IO 160	7 11	3070	1 1	6500	7450
1969 BOATS										
16 5	NASSAU		RNBT	FBG TR	IO 120	6 10			3500	4100
17	COHO		RNBT	AL	IO 80	6 10			3750	4350
17	COHO SR CO-18		RNBT	AL RB	IO 80	6 10	1120		3000	3500
17 2	CARIBBEAN		RNBT	FBG SV	OB	6 10	1580		2200	2600
17 3	YORK		RNBT	FBG	IO 120	6 10			3750	4400
18 7	ATLANTIC		RNBT	FBG	IO 120	7			3800	4400
18 7	ATLANTIC		RNBT	FBG	IO 120	7			4300	5000
18 8	BAHAMA		RNBT	FBG DV	IO 120-175	7	2000		4150	4900
18 8	BAHAMA		RNBT	FBG	IO 155	7 2			4450	5100

LOA FT IN	NAME AND/ OR MODEL	TOP/ RIG	BOAT TYPE	-HULL- MTL TP	----ENGINE--- TP # HP MFG	BEAM FT IN	WGT LBS	DRAFT FT IN	RETAIL LOW	RETAIL HIGH
					1969 BOATS					
18 8	BAHAMA		RNBT	FBG TR	IO 120-175	7 2	2000		4250	5000
21	GALAXY	CR	FBG		IO 155	8			6650	7600
21	GALAXY	CR	FBG	DV	IO 155-175	8	2700		6250	7250
21	GALAXY	CUD	FBG	DV	IO 155-175	8	3000		6600	7650
					1968 BOATS					
16 5	MAVERICK MA-16		RNBT	FBG	IO 80-120	6 6	1225		2950	3400
17 3	YORK		RNBT	FBG	IO 120	6 10	1750		3700	4300
18 7	ATLANTIC		RNBT	FBG	IO 155-160	7	2000		4350	5050
21	GALAXY	CR	FBG		IO 155-160	8	2700		6500	7450
					1967 BOATS					
16 5	MAVERICK MA-16		RNBT	FBG	IO 80		1100		3050	3500
16 5	ROGUE		RNBT	FBG	IO 80	6 6			3750	4350
17 3	YORK		RNBT	FBG	IO 120		1750		3850	4450
21	GALAXY	CR	FDC		IO 150		2700		6700	7700
21	GALAXY	CR	FBG		IO 225		3000		7300	8400
					1966 BOATS					
17	CHALLENGER CH-18		RNBT	AL	OB				2150	2500
17	CHALLENGER SPORT		RNBT	AL	OB				1900	2250
17 3	YORK YO-18		RNBT	FBG	OB				2100	2450
17 3	YORK YO-18		RNBT	FBG	OB 110				4200	4900
17 3	YORK YOS-18 SPORT		RNBT	FBG	OB				1900	2250
21	GALAXY	CR	FBG		IO 150-225				7300	8600
					1965 BOATS					
17	CHALLENGER CH-18		RNBT	AL	OB				2000	2400
17 4	YORK YO-18		RNBT	FBG	OB				2000	2400
17 4	YORK YO-18		RNBT	FBG	IO				**	**
17 4	YORK YO-18		RNBT	FBG	IO 110				4400	5050
					1964 BOATS					
17 4	YORK YO-18		RNBT	FBG	OB				2000	2400
17 4	YORK YO-18		RNBT	FBG	IO				**	**
					1963 BOATS					
17	TRIUMPH TR-17		RNBT	AL	OB				2050	2450
18	YORK YO-18		RNBT	FBG	OB				2250	2600
					1962 BOATS					
16 9	IMPERIAL IM-18		RNBT	FBG	IO 85-100				4700	5400
17 2	ADVENTURER AD-18		RNBT	FBG	OB				2050	2450

AEROMARINE CORP

Call 1-800-327-6929 for BUC Personalized Evaluation Service
Or, for 1983 to 1984 boats, sign onto www.BUCValuPro.com

AEROMARINE PLASTICS CORP

Call 1-800-327-6929 for BUC Personalized Evaluation Service
Or, for 1959 to 1961 boats, sign onto www.BUCValuPro.com

AIRBOATS INC

Call 1-800-327-6929 for BUC Personalized Evaluation Service
Or, for 1959 to 1961 boats, sign onto www.BUCValuPro.com

AKAMAI FIBERGLASSING CORP
COAST GUARD MFG ID- AKI

Call 1-800-327-6929 for BUC Personalized Evaluation Service
Or, for 1983 boats, sign onto www.BUCValuPro.com

AKSJESELSKAPET ANCAS

Call 1-800-327-6929 for BUC Personalized Evaluation Service
Or, for 1967 boats, sign onto www.BUCValuPro.com

ALAJUELA YACHT CORP
HUNTINGTON BEACH CA 926 COAST GUARD MFG ID- AYC See inside cover to adjust price for area
FOR MORE RECENT YEARS SEE CHAPMAN YACHT CORP

LOA FT IN	NAME AND/ OR MODEL	TOP/ RIG	BOAT TYPE	-HULL- MTL TP	----ENGINE--- TP # HP MFG	BEAM FT IN	WGT LBS	DRAFT FT IN	RETAIL LOW	RETAIL HIGH
					1982 BOATS					
33 1	CHAPMAN 33	CUT	SA/CR	FBG KL	IB 27D WEST	10 8	13500	4 9	46400	51000
38	CHAPMAN 38	CUT	SA/CR	FBG KL	IB 40D PERK	11 6	27000	5 7	84700	93000
48 4	CHAPMAN 48		SA/CR	FBG KL	IB 85D PERK	13 10	29500	6 9	125000	137500
48 4	CHAPMAN 48	CUT	SA/CR	FBG KL	IB 85D PERK	13 10	29500	6 9	122000	134000
48 4	CHAPMAN 48	KTH	SA/CR	FBG KL	IB 85D PERK	13 10	29500	6 9	130500	143000
					1981 BOATS					
33	ALAJUELA 33	CUT	SA/CR	FBG KL	IB D	10 8	13500	4 9	43600	48400
33 1	ALAJUELA 33	SCH	SA/CR	FBG KL	IB D	10 8	13500	4 9	43700	48500
33 1	ALAJUELA 33	KTH	SA/CR	FBG KL	IB D	10 8	13500	4 9	44000	48800
38	ALAJUELA 38 MK-11	SCH	SA/CR	FBG KL	IB D	11 6	27000	5 7	81800	89900
38	ALAJUELA 38 MK-11	CUT	SA/CR	FBG KL	IB D	11 6	27000	5 7	80900	88900
38	ALAJUELA 38 MK-11	KTH	SA/CR	FBG KL	IB D	11 6	27000	5 7	84400	92700
48 4	ALAJUELA 48	SCH	SA/CR	FBG KL	IB D	13 10	29500	6 9	116000	127500
48 4	ALAJUELA 48	CUT	SA/CR	FBG KL	IB D	13 10	29500	6 9	116000	127500
48 4	ALAJUELA 48	KTH	SA/CR	FBG KL	IB D	13 10	29500	6 9	124000	136000
					1980 BOATS					
33 1	ALAJUELA 33	CUT	SA/CR	FBG KL	IB D	10 8	13500	4 9	41500	46200
38	ALAJUELA 38 MK-II	CUT	SA/CR	FBG KL	IB D	11 6	27000	5 7	77000	84600
					1979 BOATS					
33 1	ALAJUELA 33	CUT	SA/CR	FBG KL	IB D	10 8	13500		39700	44100
38	ALAJUELA 38	CUT	SA/CR	FBG KL	IB D	11 6	27000	5 7	73600	80900
					1978 BOATS					
33	ALAJUELA 33	CUT	SA/CR	FBG KL	IB 27D PISC	11	13500	4 11	38000	42300
38	ALAJUELA 38	CUT	SA/CR	FBG KL	IB 40D PISC	11 6	27000	5 7	70300	77200
					1977 BOATS					
38	ALAJUELA 38	CUT	SA/CR	FBG KL	IB 35D VLVO	11 6	27000	5 7	67400	74100
38	ALAJUELA 38	CUT	SA/CR	FBG KL	IB 40D PISC	11 6	27000	5 7	67500	74100
38	ALAJUELA 38	CUT	SA/CR	FBG KL	IB 50D PERK	11 6	27000	5 7	67300	74000
					1976 BOATS					
38	ALAJUELA 38	CUT	SA/CR	FBG KL	IB D	11 6	27000	5 7	65100	71500
					1975 BOATS					
38	ALAJUELA 38	CUT	SA/CR	FBG KL	IB D	11 6	27000	5 7	62800	69000

ALAMEDA BOAT WORKS

Call 1-800-327-6929 for BUC Personalized Evaluation Service
Or, for 1973 boats, sign onto www.BUCValuPro.com

ALBEMARLE BOATS INC
BRUNSWICK@DIV OF
EDENTON NC 27932   COAST GUARD MFG ID- XWR   See inside cover to adjust price for area

For more recent years, see the BUC Used Boat Price Guide, Volume 1 or Volume 2

LOA FT IN	NAME AND/ OR MODEL	TOP/ RIG	BOAT TYPE	-HULL- MTL TP	----ENGINE--- TP # HP MFG	BEAM FT IN	WGT LBS	DRAFT FT IN	RETAIL LOW	RETAIL HIGH
					1983 BOATS					
20 7	ALBEMARLE 21	OP	CUD	FBG DV	OB	8	2500	2 6	7050	8100
20 7	ALBEMARLE 21	OP	CUD	FBG DV	IO 170-200	8	3450	2 6	6250	7500
20 7	ALBEMARLE 21	OP	CUD	FBG DV	IO 130D-165D	8	3600	2 6	8050	9350
23 7	ALBEMARLE 24	OP	SF	FBG DV	OB	8	3200	2 6	10200	11600
23 7	ALBEMARLE 24	OP	SF	FBG DV	IO 260	8	4100	2 6	9900	11600
23 7	ALBEMARLE 24	OP	SF	FBG DV	IO 130D-165D	8	4100	2 6	12600	15000
23 7	ALBEMARLE 24	OP	SF	FBG DV	IO T138-T185	8	4100	2 6	11000	12500
					1982 BOATS					
20 7	ALBEMARLE 21	OP	CUD	FBG DV	IO 200 VLVO	8	3450	2 6	6400	7350
20 7	ALBEMARLE 21	OP	CUD	FBG DV	IO 130D VLVO	8	3600	2 6	7850	9050
23 7	ALBEMARLE 24	OP	SF	FBG DV	OB	8	3200	2 6	10000	11300
23 7	ALBEMARLE 24	OP	SF	FBG DV	IO 260 VLVO	8	4100	2 6	10000	11400
23 7	ALBEMARLE 24	OP	SF	FBG DV	IO 155D VLVO	8	4200	2 6	12800	14500
23 7	ALBEMARLE 24	OP	SF	FBG DV	IO T185 MRCR	8	4200	2 6	10600	12100

ALBIN BOATS
BLADEN COMPOSITES LLC   See inside cover to adjust price for area
BLADENBORO NC 28320   COAST GUARD MFG ID- AUL

For more recent years, see the BUC Used Boat Price Guide, Volume 1 or Volume 2

LOA FT IN	NAME AND/ OR MODEL	TOP/ RIG	BOAT TYPE	-HULL- MTL TP	----ENGINE--- TP # HP MFG	BEAM FT IN	WGT LBS	DRAFT FT IN	RETAIL LOW	RETAIL HIGH
					1983 BOATS					
26 9	ALBIN 27	HT	DC	FBG	IB 61D LEHM	9 8	4500	2 6	15200	17300
28 7	CUMULUS 28	SLP	SA/CR	FBG KL	IB 12D YAN	9 3	7056	5 3	18100	20100
35 6	STRATUS 36	SLP	SA/CR	FBG KL	IB 20D YAN	10 10	11466	5 11	29800	33100
35 9	ALBIN 36	FB	TRWL	FBG DS	IB 120D LEHM	13 2	18500	3 6	77000	84700
36	PALM-BEACH ALBIN 36	FB	DCMY	FBG SV	IB 158D VLVO	12 6	16000	4	68600	75400
40 3	ALBIN 40	FB	TRWL	FBG DS	IB 120D LEHM	13 8	26000	3 6	89000	97800

LOA FT	LOA IN	NAME AND/ OR MODEL	TOP/ RIG	BOAT TYPE	-HULL- MTL	-HULL- TP	ENGINE TP	ENGINE # HP	ENGINE MFG	BEAM FT	BEAM IN	WGT LBS	DRAFT FT	DRAFT IN	RETAIL LOW	RETAIL HIGH
		1983 BOATS														
41	6	NIMBUS 42	SLP	SA/CR	FBG	KL	IB	42D	PATH	12	6	21500	5	10	60200	66100
42	6	ALBIN 43	FB	TRWL	FBG	DS	IB	T120D	LEHM	14	6	30000	4	1	104500	115000
47	9	PALM-BEACH ALBIN 48	FB	TCMY	FBG	SV	IB	T158D	VLVO	14		25000	3	6	96300	106000
48	4	ALBIN 49 TRI-CABIN	FB	TRWL	FBG	DS	IB	T120D	LEHM	15		39050	3	8	113500	125000
48	4	ALBIN 49 TRI-CABIN	FB	TRWL	FBG	DS	IB	T158D	VLVO	15		39050	3	8	115000	126500
48	4	ALBIN 49 TRI-CABIN	FB	TRWL	FBG	DS	IB	T210D	CAT	15		40050	3	8	119500	131500
48	6	ALBIN 49 SEDAN	FB	TRWL	FBG	DS	IB	T124D	VLVO	14	7	34000	4	5	104500	115000
		1982 BOATS														
28	7	CUMULUS 28	SLP	SA/CR	FBG	KL	IB	12D	YAN	9	6	7056	5	3	16600	18900
35	6	STRATUS 36	SLP	SA/CR	FBG	KL	IB	22D	YAN	10	10	11466	5	11	28000	31200
35	9	ALBIN 36	FB	TRWL	FBG	DS	IB	120D	LEHM	13	2	18500	3	6	74000	81400
41	2	NIMBUS 42	SLP	SA/CR	FBG	KL	VD	50D	PATH	12	6	21500	5	10	56000	61600
42	6	ALBIN 43	FB	TRWL	FBG	DS	IB	T120D	LEHM	14	6	30000	4	1	99900	110000
48	4	ALBIN 49 TRI-CABIN	FB	TRWL	FBG	DS	IB	T120D	LEHM	15		39050	3	8	108500	119500
48	4	ALBIN 49 TRI-CABIN	FB	TRWL	FBG	DS	IB	T210D	CAT	15		39050	3	8	113000	124500
		1981 BOATS														
28	1	ALBIN 85 CUMULUS	SLP	SA/CR	FBG	KL	IB	12D	YAN	9	3	7055	5	3	15500	17600
28	7	CUMULUS 28	SLP	SA/CR	FBG	KL	IB	12D	YAN	9	6	7056	5	3	15600	17800
35	6	STRATUS 36	SLP	SA/CR	FBG	KL	IB	22D	YAN	10	10	11466	5	11	26400	29300
35	9	ALBIN 36	FB	TRWL	FBG	DS	IB	120D	LEHM	13	2	18500	3	6	71200	78200
40	3	ALBIN 40	FB	TRWL	FBG	DV	IB	120D		13	8				85500	93900
41	2	NIMBUS 42	SLP	SA/CR	FBG	KL	VD	50D	PATH	12	6	21500	5	10	52700	57900
42	6	ALBIN 43	FB	TRWL	FBG	DS	IB	T120D	FORD	14	6	30000	4	1	95100	104500
48	4	ALBIN 49 TRI-CABIN	FB	TRWL	FBG	DS	IB	T120D	FORD	15		39050	3	8	103500	113500
48	6	ALBIN 49 SUNDECK	FB	TRWL	FBG	DS	IB	T120D	FORD	14	7	34000	4	5	95800	105500
		1980 BOATS														
28	7	CUMULUS 28	SLP	SA/CR	FBG	KL	IB	12D	YAN	9	6	7056	5	3	14900	17000
32	6	ALBIN 33	FB	TRWL	FBG	DS	IB	120D		11	6	16000			56400	62000
35	6	STRATUS 36	SLP	SA/CR	FBG	KL	IB	22D	YAN	10	10	11466	5	11	25200	28000
35	9	ALBIN 36	FB	TRWL	FBG	DS	IB	120D	LEHM	13	2	18500	3	6	68500	75300
35	9	ALBIN 36	FB	TRWL	FBG	DS	IB	160D		13	2	18500			68600	75400
40		ALBIN 40	FB	TRWL	FBG	DS	IB	120D		13	6				81900	90000
40		ALBIN 40	FB	TRWL	FBG	DS	IB	T120D		13	6				85800	94300
41	2	NIMBUS 42	SLP	SA/CR	FBG	KL	IB	50D	PATH	12	6	21500	5	10	50300	55300
42	6	ALBIN 43	FB	TRWL	FBG	DS	IB	120D		14	6	30000			87200	95800
42	6	ALBIN 43	FB	TRWL	FBG	DS	IB	T120D	LEHM	14	6	30000	4	1	89300	98100
42	6	ALBIN 43 SUNDECK	FB	TRWL	FBG	DS	IB	T120D	LEHM	14	6	30000	4	1	94900	104000
48	4	ALBIN 49 TRI-CABIN	FB	TRWL	FBG	DS	IB	T120D	LEHM	15	1	39050	3	8	98700	108500
48	6	ALBIN 49 SEDAN	FB	TRWL	FBG	DS	IB	T120D	LEHM	14	7	34000	4	5	87200	95900
48	6	ALBIN 49 SUNDECK	FB	TRWL	FBG	DS	IB	T120D	LEHM	14	7	34000	4	5	95600	105000
49	4	ALBIN 49	FB	TRWL	FBG	DS	IB	T120D		15		34000			91300	100500
		1979 BOATS														
27	11	CUMULUS 28	SLP	SA/CR	FBG	KL	IB	12D	YAN	9	3	7056	5	3	14200	16100
29	9	SCAMPI 30	SLP	SA/RC	FBG	KL	IB	12D	FARY	9	9	7000	5	3	14400	16400
32	6	ALBIN 33	FB	TRWL	FBG	DS	IB	120D	LEHM	11	5	16800	3	7	56100	61600
35	9	ALBIN 36	FB	TRWL	FBG	DS	IB	120D	LEHM	13	2	18500	3	6	65900	72400
35	9	ALBIN 36	FB	TRWL	FBG	DS	IB	T120D	LEHM	13	2	18500	3	6	68900	75700
42	6	ALBIN 43	FB	TRWL	FBG	DS	IB	120D	LEHM	14	6	30000	3	9	83200	91500
42	6	ALBIN 43	FB	TRWL	FBG	DS	IB	T120D	LEHM	15		30000	3	9	85800	94300
48	4	ALBIN 49	FB	TRWL	FBG	DS	IB	T120D	LEHM	15		34000	3	9	87400	96100
		1978 BOATS														
19		ALBIN 5.7	SLP	SAIL	FBG	SK	OB			7	11	1763	1	11	2800	3250
25		ALBIN 25 DELUXE	ST	DC	FBG	DS	IB	35D	VLVO	8	6	3860	2	4	10900	12400
25		ALBIN 25 FISHERMAN	ST	FSH	FBG	DS	IB	35D	VLVO	8	6	3860	2	4	10900	12400
25	11	ALBIN 7.9	SLP	SA/CR	FBG	KL	IB	8D	VLVO	8	9	4200	4	7	7750	8900
26	11	ALBIN 8.2 MS	SLP	MS	FBG	KL	IB	35D	VLVO	9	9	7496	3	11	14500	16500
27	1	VEGA	SLP	SA/CR	FBG	KL	IB	13D	VLVO	8	1	5070	3	10	9650	11000
29	11	BALLAD	SLP	SA/CR	FBG	KL	IB	13D	VLVO	9	8	7276	5	1	14500	16500
30	2	ALBIN 30	HT	DC	FBG	DS	IB	130D	PERK	10	5	8380	2	8	26200	29200
35	9	ALBIN 36	FB	TRWL	FBG	DS	IB	120D	LEHM	13	2	18500	3	6	63500	69700
		1977 BOATS														
19		ALBIN 5.7	SLP	SAIL	FBG	SK	OB			7	11	1763	1	11	2700	3150
25		ALBIN 25 DELUXE	ST	DC	FBG	DS	IB	36D	VLVO	8	6	3860	2	4	10500	11900
25		ALBIN 25 FISHERMAN	ST	FSH	FBG	DS	IB	36D	VLVO	8	6	3640	2	4	10000	11300
25	11	ALBIN 7.9	SLP	SA/CR	FBG	KL	IB	8D	VLVO	8	9	4200	4	7	7500	8600
26	11	ALBIN 8.2 MS	SLP	MS	FBG	KL	IB	35D	VLVO	9	9	7496	3	11	14000	15900
27	1	VEGA	SLP	SA/CR	FBG	KL	IB	10D	VLVO	8	1	5070	3	10	9350	10600
29	11	BALLAD	SLP	SA/CR	FBG	KL	IB	10D	VLVO	9	8	7276	5	1	14000	15900
30	2	ALBIN 30	HT	DC	FBG	DS	IB	115D-130D		10	5	8380	2	8	25500	28300
		1976 BOATS														
23	4	VIGGEN	SLP	SAIL	FBG	KL				7	4	3090	3	8	4550	5250
25		ALBIN 25 DELUXE	ST	DC	FBG	DS	IB	36D	VLVO	8	6	3860	2	4	10100	11500
25		ALBIN 25 FISHERMAN	ST	FSH	FBG	DS	IB	36D	VLVO	8	6	3640	2	4	9600	10900
25	11	ALBIN 7.9	SLP	SA/CR	FBG	KL	IB	8D	VLVO	8	9	4200	4	7	7250	8350
27	1	VEGA	SLP	SA/CR	FBG	KL	IB	10D	VLVO	8		5070	3	10	9050	10300
29	11	BALLAD	SLP	SA/CR	FBG	KL	IB	10D	VLVO	9	8	7276	5	1	13600	15400
30	2	ALBIN 30	HT	DC	FBG	DS	IB	85D-100D		10	5	8380	2	8	23000	25600
		1975 BOATS														
25		ALBIN 25	ST	DC	FBG	DS	IB	36D	VLVO	8	6	3860	2	4	9850	11200
25		ALBIN 25 FISHERMAN	ST	FSH	FBG	DS	IB	36D	VLVO	8	6	3640	2	4	9350	10600
25	11	ALBIN 7.9	SLP	SA/CR	FBG	KL	IB	8D	VLVO	8	9	4200	4	7	7050	8100
27	1	VEGA	SLP	SA/CR	FBG	KL	IB	10D	VLVO	8		5070	3	10	8800	10000
29	11	BALLAD	SLP	SA/CR	FBG	KL	IB	10D	VLVO	9	8	7276	5	1	13200	15000
		1974 BOATS														
25		ALBIN 25	ST	DC	FBG	DS	IB	36D	VLVO	8	6	3860	2	4	9600	10900
27	1	VEGA	SLP	SA/CR	FBG	KL	IB	10D	VLVO	8		5070	3	10	8450	9750
29	11	BALLAD 30	SLP	SA/CR	FBG	KL	IB	10D	VLVO	9	8	7276	5	1	12800	14600
		1973 BOATS														
25		ALBIN 25	ST	DC	FBG	DS	IB	36D	VLVO	8	6	3860	2	4	9300	10600
25		ALBIN 25 FISHERMAN	ST	FSH	FBG	DS	IB	36D	VLVO	8	6	3860	2	4	9350	10600
27	1	VEGA	SLP	SA/CR	FBG	KL	IB	10D	VLVO	8		5070	3	10	8250	9500
29	11	BALLAD	SLP	SA/CR	FBG	KL	IB	10D	VLVO	9	8	7276	5	1	12500	14200
33	8	SINGOALLA	SLP	SA/RC	FBG	KL	IB	20D	ALBN	10	10	10030	5	2	17300	19600
		1972 BOATS														
27	1	VEGA	SLP	SA/CR	FBG	KL	IB	12D	ALBN	8		5070	3	8	8100	9300
		1971 BOATS														
25		ALBIN 25	ST	DC	FBG	DS	IB	22D	ALBN	8	6	3860	2	4	8850	10100
27	1	VEGA	SLP	SA/CR	FBG	KL	IB	12D	ALBN	8		5070	3	10	7950	9100
		1970 BOATS														
25		ALBIN 25		DC	FBG	SV	IB	20D		8	2	3500	2	1	7700	8850
27	1	VEGA	SLP	SA/CR	FBG	KL	IB	12D	ALBN	8		5020	3	10	7700	8850
33	8	SINGOALLA	SLP	SA/RC	FBG	KL	IB	20D	ALBN	10	10	8820	5	1	14300	16300
		1969 BOATS														
25		ALBIN 25	ST	DC	FBG	DS	IB	20D		8	6	3860	2	4	8350	9600
27	1	VEGA	SLP	SA/CR	FBG	KL	IB	12D	ALBN	8		5020	3	10	7600	8750
		1968 BOATS														
27	1	VEGA	SLP	SA/CR	FBG	KL	IB	12D	ALBN	8		5070	3	10	7550	8700
		1967 BOATS														
27	1	VEGA OCEAN CRUISER	SLP	SA/CR	FBG	KL	IB	12D	ALBN	8		5070	3	10	7500	8600

ALBRIGHT BOAT & MARINE CO

Call 1-800-327-6929 for BUC Personalized Evaluation Service
Or, for 1959 to 1961 boats, sign onto www.BUCValuPro.com

ALCAN MARINE PRODUCTS

DIV OF ALCAN CANADA PROD LTD
PRINCEVILLE PQ CANADA COAST GUARD MFG ID- ZCB

See inside cover to adjust price for area

For more recent years, see the BUC Used Boat Price Guide, Volume 1 or Volume 2

LOA FT	LOA IN	NAME AND/ OR MODEL	TOP/ RIG	BOAT TYPE	-HULL- MTL	-HULL- TP	ENGINE TP	ENGINE # HP	ENGINE MFG	BEAM FT	BEAM IN	WGT LBS	DRAFT FT	DRAFT IN	RETAIL LOW	RETAIL HIGH
		1983 BOATS														
16	4	MONZA	ST	RNBT	FBG	SV	IO	120		6	9	1280			3700	4300
16	8	LE-MANS	ST	SKI	FBG	SV	IO	120-185		7		1200			3550	4250
17	9	APOLLO X18	ST	RNBT	FBG	SV	OB			7	3	1410			1850	2200
17	9	COSMOS X18	ST	RNBT	FBG	SV	IO	140-225		7	3	1355			4550	5450
17	9	GEMINI X18	ST	RNBT	FBG	SV	IO	140-225		7	3	1415			4600	5550
18	2	OLYMPIAN		RNBT	FBG	DV	IO	185-225		7	8	1450			5000	5900
18	4	CENTURION	ST	RNBT	AL	SV	IO	120-140		6	8	1070			4350	5050
18	4	LAURENTIDE 1088	ST	RNBT	AL	SV	IO	120-140		6	8	1065			4350	5050
18	4	MARLIN	ST	RNBT	AL	SV	IO	120-140		6	8	1095			4400	5050
18	4	MONTEREY 1087	ST	RNBT	AL	SV	IO	120-140		6	8	1090			4350	5050
19	10	CAPRI	ST	RNBT	FBG	DV	IO	185-225		8		2000			6200	7300
19	10	GRAND-PRIX SUPER		RNBT	FBG	SV	IO	185-225		7	4	1580			5550	6550
19	10	RIVIERA	ST	CUD	FBG	DV	IO	140-260		6	8	2000			5700	7050
		1982 BOATS														
16	4	MONZA	ST	RNBT	FBG	SV	IO	120-185		6	9	1280			3600	4250
16	8	LE-MANS	ST	SKI	FBG	SV	IO	120-185		7		1200			3500	4100
17	9	APOLLO X18	ST	RNBT	FBG	SV	OB			7	3	1410			1750	2100
17	9	COSMOS X18	ST	RNBT	FBG	SV	IO	140-230		7	3	1355			4400	5350
17	9	GEMINI X18	ST	RNBT	FBG	SV	IO	140-230		7	3	1415			4450	5400
18	4	CENTURION	ST	RNBT	AL	SV	IO	120-140		6	8	1070			4200	4900
18	4	LAURENTIDE 1088	ST	RNBT	AL	SV	IO	120-140		6	8	1065			4200	4900
18	4	MARLIN	ST	RNBT	AL	SV	IO	120-140		6	8	1095			4200	4900
18	4	MONTEREY 1087	ST	RNBT	AL	SV	IO	120		6	8	1090			4200	4850
18	4	MONTEREY 1087	ST	RNBT	AL	SV	IO	140		8		1090			4850	5600
19	10	RIVIERA	ST	CUD	FBG	DV	IO	140-260		8		2000			6100	7500
		1981 BOATS														
16	4	MONZA	ST	RNBT	FBG	SV	IO	120-140		6	9	1280			3550	4150
16	4	SEVILLE	ST	RNBT	FBG	SV	IO	120-140		6	9	1185			3450	4000

LOA FT IN	NAME AND/ OR MODEL	TOP/ RIG	BOAT TYPE	HULL MTL	HULL TP	HULL TP	ENGINE #	ENGINE HP	ENGINE MFG	BEAM FT IN	WGT LBS	DRAFT FT IN	RETAIL LOW	RETAIL HIGH
1981 BOATS														
16 8	LE-MANS	ST	SKI	FBG	SV	IO		120–140		7	1200		3400	4000
17 9	APOLLO X18	ST	RNBT	FBG	SV	OB				7 3	1410		1700	2000
17 9	APOLLO X18	ST	RNBT	FBG	SV	IO		155		7 3	1410		4350	5000
17 9	COSMOS X18	ST	RNBT	FBG	SV	IO		140–200		7 3	1355		4250	5050
17 9	GEMINI X18	ST	RNBT	FBG	SV	OB				7 3	1415		1700	2000
17 9	GEMINI X18	ST	RNBT	FBG	SV	IO		140–200		7 3	1415		4300	5100
17 9	SATELLITE X18	ST	RNBT	FBG	SV	IO		155		7 3	1300		4200	4900
18 2	OLYMPIAN	ST	RNBT	FBG	DV	IO		185–225		7 8	1450		4750	5650
18 4	CENTURION	ST	RNBT	AL	SV	IO		120–140		6 8	1070		4100	4750
18 4	LAURENTIDE 1088	ST	RNBT	AL	SV	IO		120–140		6 8	1065		4100	4750
18 4	MARLIN	ST	RNBT	AL	SV	IO		120–140		6 8	1095		4100	4750
18 4	MONTEREY 1087	ST	RNBT	AL	SV	IO		120–140		6 8	1090		4100	4750
19 10	RIVIERA	ST	CUD	FBG	DV	IO		185–260		8	2000		6050	7050
19 11	GRAND-PRIX SUPER	ST	RNDT	FBC	DV	IO		185–225		7 4	1580		5250	6200
23 7	GYPSY		EXP		SV			165		8			11400	12900
1978 BOATS														
16 5	SUPER-SPORT 2008	ST	RNBT	FBG	TR	IO		140		6 7	1379		3500	4100
16 10	LE-MANS 2009	ST	RNBT	FBG	SV	IO		140		7	1292		3650	4250
18 4	CENTURION 1886	ST	RNBT	AL	SV	IO		120–140		6 8	1670		4400	5050
18 4	MARLIN 1888	ST	RNBT	AL	SV	IO		120–140		6 8	1710		4400	5100
18 6	JUMBO 1061	OP	FSH	AL	SV	OB				6 9	2070		2000	2350
18 9	OSPREY 2006	ST	RNBT	FBG	SV	IO		170–175		7	1550		4550	5250
19 11	GRAND-PRIX SUPR 2007	ST	RNBT	FBG	DV	IO		188–190		7 4	2137		5600	6450
22 9	CAPRI DELUXE 2011	ST	CUD	FBG	DV	IO		188–190		7 8	3155		9450	10700
22 9	CAPRI STANDARD 2012	ST	CUD	FBG	DV	IO		188–190		7 8	3155		8500	9750
1977 BOATS														
16 4	MONZA 2004	ST	RNBT	FBG	SV	IO		140		6 9	1200		3350	3900
16 5	SUPER-SPORT 2008	ST	RNBT	FBG	TR	IO		140		6 7	1379		3550	4100
16 10	LE-MANS 2009	ST	RNBT	FBG	SV	IO		140		7	1292		3650	4250
18 2	OLYMPIAN 2010	ST	RNBT	FBG	DV	IO		188–190		7 8	1875		4950	5700
18 9	MISTRESS 2006	ST	RNBT	FBG	SV	IO		170	MRCR	7			4400	5050
19 11	GRAND-PRIX SUPR 2007	ST	RNBT	FBG	SV	IO		188–190		7 4	2137		5650	6450
22 9	CAPRI 2011	ST	CUD	FBG	DV	IO		188–190		7 8	3155		9050	10300
23 9	GYPSY 2001	ST	CBNCR	FBG	SV	IO		188–190		8	3279		10900	12400
23 9	GYPSY 2001	HT	CBNCR	FBG	SV	IO		188–190		8	3279		10900	12400
1976 BOATS														
16 4	MONZA 2004	ST	RNBT	FBG	SV	IO				6 9	1821		**	**
16 5	SUPER-SPORT 2008	ST	RNBT	FBG	TR	IO				6 7	2000		**	**
16 10	LE-MANS 2009	ST	RNBT	FBG	SV	IO				7	1800		**	**
17	LE-MARQUIS 2003	ST	RNBT	FBG	SV	IO				7	2230		**	**
18 2	OLYMPIAN 2010	ST	RNBT	FBG	DV	IO				7 8	2720		**	**
19 11	GRAND-PRIX SUPR 2007	ST	RNBT	FBG	DV	IO				7 4	2938		**	**
22 9	CAPRI 2011	ST	CUD	FBG	DV	IO				7 8	4000		**	**
23 9	GYPSY 2001	ST	CR	FBG	SV	IO				8	4080		**	**
23 9	GYPSY 2001	HT	CR	FBG	SV	IO				8	4080		**	**
1975 BOATS														
16 2	MONZA V 162	ST	RNBT	FBG	SV	IO		140–165		6 10	1120	3 6	3350	3950
17 2	C172	OP	RNBT	FBG	SV	IO		140–165		6 10	1125	2 7	3700	4350
17 7	LE-MARQUIS V 177	ST	RNBT	FBG	SV	IO		165–188		6 10	1450	3 10	4150	4900
19	GRAND-PRIX V190	ST	RNBT	FBG	SV	IO		165–225			3630		8500	9950
20	GRAND-PRIX SUP V200	ST	RNBT	FBG	SV	IO		188–225			3630		7200	8450
24	GYPSY V 240	ST	RNBT	FBG	SV	IO		188–245		8	3630	6 9	10600	12400
1974 BOATS														
16 2	MONZA			FBG		IO		140–160		6 10	1100	2	3250	3800
16 4	FLEETWOOD		RNBT	FBG	SV	IB				6 8	765		**	**
17	LE-MANS		RNBT	FBG	SV	IB				6 10	860		**	**
17	RIVIERA			FBG		IO		140–160		6 10	1000	2	3500	4050
17 7	LE-MARQUIS			FBG		IO		140–200		6 10	1400	2	3900	4650
19	GRAND-PRIX			FBG		IO		165–240		7 2	2000	2	5250	6350
24	GYPSY			FBG		IO		188–275		7 11	4000	2	11700	13900
1973 BOATS														
16 4	MONZA	ST	RNBT	FBG	SV	IO		140		6 9	1821		4450	5150
16 5	SUPER-SPORT	ST	RNBT	FBG	TR	IO		120		6 7	2000		4650	5350
17	RIVIERA		RNBT	FBG	TR	IO		140		6 10			3950	4600
17 8	LE-MARQUIS	ST	RNBT	FBG	SV	IO		140		7	2230		5400	6200
19 11	GRAND-PRIX	ST	RNBT	FBG	SV	IO		188		7 4	2938		7150	8200
23 9	GYPSY		CR	FBG	SV	IO		188		8	4080		12800	14600
1972 BOATS														
16 2	MONZA		RNBT	FBG	SV	IO		120–155		6 10		2	3850	4500
17	RIVIERA W/T		RNBT	FBG	SV	IO		140–165		6 10		2	4100	4800
17 7	LE-MARQUIS W/T		RNBT	FBG	SV	IO		140–165		6 10		2	4400	5100
19	GRAND-PRIX		RNBT	FBG	DV	IO		188–225		7 2		2	5200	6150
24	GYPSY		CR	FBG	DV	IO		188–250		8		2	13400	15600

ALCAR BOAT COMPANY
COAST GUARD MFG ID- ATJ

C B BOATWORKS

Call 1-800-327-6929 for BUC Personalized Evaluation Service
Or, for 1980 to 2004 boats, sign onto www.BUCValuPro.com

ALCOM MARINE INC
DIXIE DORY   COAST GUARD MFG ID- AWP

Call 1-800-327-6929 for BUC Personalized Evaluation Service
Or, for 1977 to 1981 boats, sign onto www.BUCValuPro.com

ALCORT SAILBOATS INC
WATERBURY CT 06708   COAST GUARD MFG ID- AMF See inside cover to adjust price for area
FORMERLY ALCORT SAILBOATS INC

For more recent years, see the BUC Used Boat Price Guide, Volume 1 or Volume 2

LOA FT IN	NAME AND/ OR MODEL	TOP/ RIG	BOAT TYPE	HULL MTL	HULL TP	HULL TP	ENGINE #	ENGINE HP	ENGINE MFG	BEAM FT IN	WGT LBS	DRAFT FT IN	RETAIL LOW	RETAIL HIGH
1983 BOATS														
21 1	A-M-F 2100	SLP	SA/RC	FBG	CB					8	2200	1	3650	4250
21 1	AMF 2100	SLP	SA/OD	FBG	CB					8	2200	4	3650	4250
1982 BOATS														
21 1	AMF 2100	SLP	SAIL	FBG	CB					8	2200	1	3450	4000
1981 BOATS														
21 1	AMF 2100	SLP	SAIL	FBG	CB					8	2200	4	3250	3800
22 7	PY-23	SLP	SA/RC	FBG	KL					8	2950		4300	5000
22 7	PY-23	SLP	SA/OD	FBG	KL					8	2950	4 9	4300	5000
26 4	PY-26	SLP	SA/RC	FBG	KL					9 6	6900		11500	13100
26 4	PY-26	SLP	SA/OD	FBG	KL					9 6	6900	6 7	11500	13100
1980 BOATS														
21 1	AMF 2100	SLP	SAIL	FBG	CB					8	2200	4	3100	3600

ALDEN DESIGNED YACHTS
BOSTON MA   See inside cover to adjust price for area

CATHIE HALL
RI 02840

LOA FT IN	NAME AND/ OR MODEL	TOP/ RIG	BOAT TYPE	HULL MTL	HULL TP	HULL TP	ENGINE #	ENGINE HP	ENGINE MFG	BEAM FT IN	WGT LBS	DRAFT FT IN	RETAIL LOW	RETAIL HIGH
1966 BOATS														
39 9		KTH	SAIL	FBG		IB		D	WEST				54400	59800
1953 BOATS														
38 10	GRAVES BUILT	YWL	SAIL		KL	IB		D	GRAY	9 9	19075	5 9	50500	55500
1948 BOATS														
39 9		SLP	SAIL	WD		IB		25	UNIV				49200	54000
1947 BOATS														
35		SLP	SAIL	WD		OB							35700	39700
1939 BOATS														
31 4	MALABAR		SAIL	WD		IB		22D	GRAY				35500	39500
32	RAINBOW		SAIL	WD		IB		30D	GRAY				43100	47900
1936 BOATS														
34 6		YWL	SAIL	WD		IB		25D	VLVO				55200	60600
1935 BOATS														
35		YWL	SAIL	WD		IB		D	LATH				57500	63200
1931 BOATS														
45		SCH	SAIL	KC		IB		40D		12 6		4 3	155500	171000
1929 BOATS														
38		SLP	SAIL	WD		IB		25D	GRAY				98800	108500

ALDEN OCEAN SHELLS INC
ALDEN OCEAN SHELL
FORMERLY MARTIN MARINE CO INC

Call 1-800-327-6929 for BUC Personalized Evaluation Service
Or, for 1971 to 1999 boats, sign onto www.BUCValuPro.com

ALDEN YACHTS
PORTSMOUTH RI 02871

FORMERLY JOHN G ALDEN

See inside cover to adjust price for area

For more recent years, see the BUC Used Boat Price Guide, Volume 1 or Volume 2

LOA FT IN	NAME AND/ OR MODEL	TOP/ RIG	BOAT TYPE	-HULL- MTL TP TP #	----ENGINE--- HP MFG	BEAM FT IN	WGT LBS	DRAFT FT IN	RETAIL LOW	RETAIL HIGH
--- 1983 BOATS ---										
44 2	ALDEN 44	SLP	SA/RC FBG KC IB	50D PERK	12 6	25000	8 9	119500	131000	
75	ADLEN 75	KTH	SA/RC FBG KC IB	100D	18	98400	6 6	**	**	
--- 1982 BOATS ---										
44 2	ALDEN 44	SLP	SA/RC FBG KC IB	50D PERK	12 6	25000	4 11	112500	123500	
75	ALDEN 75	KTH	SA/RC FBG KC IB	100D	18	98400	6 6	**	**	
--- 1981 BOATS ---										
44 2	ALDEN 44	SLP	SA/RC FBG KC IB	50D PERK	12 6	25000	8 9	105500	116000	
75	ALDEN 75	KTH	SA/RC FBG KC IB	100D	18	98400	6 6	**	**	
--- 1980 BOATS ---										
44 2	ALDEN 44	SLP	SA/RC FBG KC IB	50D PERK	12 6	25000	8 9	101000	111000	
75	ALDEN 75	KTH	SA/RC FBG KC IB	100D	18	98400	6 6	**	**	
--- 1979 BOATS ---										
44 2	ALDEN 44	CUT	SA/CR FBG KC IB	40D WEST	12 6	24500	4 11	96400	106000	
--- 1978 BOATS ---										
44 2	ALDEN 44	CUT	SA/CR FBG KC IB	40D WEST	12 6	24500	4 11	92900	102000	
44 2	ALDEN 44	SLP	SA/RC FBG KC IB	40D WEST	12 6	24500	4 11	92900	102000	
47	ALDEN 47	KTH	SA/CR FBG KL IB	70D PERK	12 9	32680	5 8	133000	146000	
58 7	ALDEN 58	KTH	SA/CR FBG KC IB	130D PERK	15 2	54000	5 4	339500	373000	
58 7	ALDEN 58	KTH	SA/CR FBG KC IB	130D PERK	15 2	54000	5 4	339500	373000	
61 6	ALDEN 61	KTH	MS FBG KL IB	250D CAT	16	65000	5	404500	444500	
--- 1977 BOATS ---										
43 11	ALDEN 44	SLP	SA/RC FBG KC IB	D	12 6	24500		88000	96700	
47	ALDEN 47	KTH	SA/CR FBG KC IB	D PERK	12 9	32680	5 8	128500	141000	
58 7	ALDEN 58	KTH	SA/CR FBG KC IB	130D PERK	15 2	54000	5 4	328000	360500	
61 6	ALDEN 61	KTH	MS FBG KL IB	250D CAT	16	65000	5	391000	429500	
--- 1976 BOATS ---										
43 9	ALDEN 44	KTH	SA/CR FBG KC IB	D	12 6	27000	4 9	88300	97100	
47	ALDEN 47	KTH	SA/CR FBG KL IB	70D PERK	12 9	32680	5 8	124500	137000	
47	ALDEN 47	KTH	SA/CR FBG KL IB	85D PERK	12 9	32680	5 8	124500	137000	
58 7	ALDEN 58	KTH	SA/CR FBG KC IB	130D PERK	15 2	54000	5 4	318000	349500	
61 6	ALDEN 61	KTH	MS FBG KL IB	250D CAT	16	65000	5	378500	416000	
--- 1975 BOATS ---										
47	DOLPHIN 47	KTH	SA/CR FBG KC IB	70D PERK	12 9	32680	5 8	121000	133000	
58 7	BOOTHBAY-CHALLENGER	KTH	SA/CR FBG KC IB	130D PERK	15 2	54000	5 4	309000	339500	
58 7	BOOTHBAY-CHALLENGER	KTH	SA/CR FBG KC IB	130D PERK	15 2	54000	5 4	309000	339500	
58 7	BOOTHBAY-EXPLORER	KTH	SA/CR FBG KL IB	130D PERK	15 2	54000	5 4	309000	339500	
--- 1974 BOATS ---										
44 9	DOLPHIN 45	KTH	SA/CR FBG KC IB	70D PERK	12 9	32600	5 8	98900	108500	
47	WELLINGTON 47	KTH	SA/CR FBG KL IB	130D PERK	12 9	45000	5	135000	148000	
58 7	BOOTHBAY CHALLENGER	KTH	SA/CR FBG KL IB	130D PERK	15 2	54000	5 4	300500	330500	
58 7	BOOTHBAY EXPLORER	KTH	SA/CR FBG KL IB	130D PERK	15 2	54000	5 4	300500	330500	
60	VOYAGER	TRWL	FBG DS IB	250	16	65000	5 3	288000	316500	
63		MY	AL IB T	17 4		4 6	**	**		
63		MY	AL IB T870	17 4		4 6	776500	853500		
--- 1973 BOATS ---										
41 7	CARAVELLE	SLP	SA/CR FBG KL IB	37D WEST	11	20000	5 10	57400	63000	
44 9	DOLPHIN 45	KTH	SA/CR FBG KL IB	85D PERK	12 9	33000	5 8	97200	107000	
58 7	BOOTHBAY CHALLENGER	KTH	SA/CR FBG KL IB	130D PERK	15 2	54000	5 4	296500	326000	
58 7	BOOTHBAY EXPLORER	KTH	SA/CR FBG KL IB	130D PERK	15 2	54000	5 4	290000	318500	
60	VOYAGER	TRWL	FBG DS IB	250	16	65000	5 3	276000	303500	
--- 1972 BOATS ---										
41 7	CARAVELLE	SLP	SA/CR FBG KL IB	37D WEST	11	20000	5 10	56100	61700	
44 9	DOLPHIN 45	KTH	SA/CR FBG KL IB	70D PERK	12 9	33000	5 8	94900	104500	
58 7	BOOTHBAY-CHALLENGER	KTH	SA/CR FBG KL IB	130D PERK	15 2	54000	5 4	287000	315000	
58 7	BOOTHBAY-EXPLORER	KTH	SA/CR FBG KL IB	130D PERK	15 2	54000	5 4	287000	315000	
--- 1971 BOATS ---										
41 7	CARAVELLE	SLP	SA/CR FBG KL IB	37D WEST	11	20000	5 11	55000	60400	
41 7	CARAVELLE	YWL	SA/CR FBG KL IB	37D WEST	11	20000	5 11	55000	60400	
41 7	DOLPHIN 42	KTH	SA/CR FBG KL IB	D	12 9	29600	5 3	69800	76700	
44 3	ALDEN 44	TRWL	SA/CR FBG KC OB	T130D PERK	13 4	31000		130000	151500	
46 11	ALDEN 47	KTH	SA/CR FBG KC OB	D	13 4	45000		123000	135000	
58		SF	FBG DS IB	250	15	63000	5	240000	264000	
58 7	BOOTHBAY-CHALLENGER	KTH	SA/CR FBG KL IB	130D PERK	15 2	54000	5 4	281000	309500	
59 5		CR	FBG DS IB	250	16	63000	5	243500	267500	
60		TRWL	FBG RB IB	250	16	65000	5 3	254000	279500	
--- 1970 BOATS ---										
46 11	ALDEN 47	KTH	SA/CR FBG KL IB	130D	15 2	54000	5 4	123500	135000	
58		SF	FBG DS IB	250	15	63000	5	230500	253000	
58 7	BOOTHBAY CHALLENGER	KTH	SA/CR FBG KL IB	140D	15 2	53300	3 4	275500	302500	
59 5	OFFSHORE POWER CR	SDN	FBG DS IB	250	16	63000	5	254500	280000	
60		TRWL	FBG RB IB	250	16	65000	5 3	244000	268000	
--- 1969 BOATS ---										
41 7	CARAVELLE	SLP	SA/CR FBG KL IB	30D	11	18000	5 10	49700	54600	
41 7	CARAVELLE	YWL	SA/CR FBG KL IB	30D	11	18000	5 10	49700	54600	
46 11	ISLANDER 47	KTH	SA/CR FBG KL IB	130	13 4	45000	5	120000	132000	
58	VOYAGER	SF	FBG RB IB	250D	15	63000	5	211000	232000	
58 7	BOOTHBAY	KTH	SA/CR FBG KC IB	140	15 2	11500	5 4	199000	218500	
58 7	BOOTHBAY	KTH	SA/CR FBG KC IB	140	15 2	11500	7 9	199000	218500	
59 5	VOYAGER	CR	FBG RB IB	250D	16	63000	5	218000	239500	
59 6	VOYAGER	CR	FBG RB IB	250D	16	63000	5	219500	241000	
60	VOYAGER	TRWL	FBG RB IB	250D	16	65000	5 3	228500	251500	
--- 1968 BOATS ---										
41 7	CARAVELLE	SLP	SA/CR FBG KL IB	30D	11	18000	5 10	49000	53900	
41 7	CARAVELLE	YWL	SA/CR FBG KL IB	30D	11	18000	5 10	49000	53900	
44 6	COUNTESS CUSTOM	KTH	SA/CR FBG KL IB	80D	12	28000	5 4	80900	88900	
49	SEA-SAILER	KTH	SA/CR FBG CB IB	60	13 3	44200	5	132000	145000	
58 7	BOOTHBAY-CHALLENGER	KTH	SA/CR FBG KL IB	140	12	53300	5 4	265500	291500	
--- 1967 BOATS ---										
36 4	MISTRAL	SLP	SA/CR FBG KL IB	D	10 6		5	34600	38400	
38 6	CHALLENGER	YWL	SA/CR FBG KL IB	D	11		5	43400	48200	
41 7	CARVELLE	SLP	SA/CR FBG KL IB	D	11	18000	5 10	48600	53400	
41 7	CARVELLE	YWL	SA/CR FBG KL IB	D	11	18000	5 10	48600	53400	
44 6	COUNTESS CUSTOM	KTH	SA/CR FBG KL IB	D	12		5 4	73100	80400	
50 4	ALDEN 50	SLP	SA/CR FBG KL IB	D	13 2		6 6	132000	145000	
--- 1966 BOATS ---										
36 4	MISTRAL 36	SLP	SA/CR FBG KL IB	D	10 6		5	34300	38100	
38 6	CHALLENGER	YWL	SA/CR FBG KL IB	D	11		5	43000	47800	
41 7	CARAVELLE	SLP	SA/CR FBG KL IB	D	11	18000	5 8	48100	52900	
41 7	CARAVELLE	YWL	SA/CR FBG KL IB	D	11	18000	5 8	48100	52900	
--- 1965 BOATS ---										
36 4	MISTRAL	YWL	SAIL FBG KL IB	D	10 6		4 9	34000	37800	
38 6	CHALLENGER	YWL	SAIL FBG KL IB	D	11		4 7	42700	47400	
41 7	CARAVELLE	YWL	SAIL FBG KL IB	D	11	18000	5 8	47800	52500	
47	LADY-HELENE	KTH	SAIL FBG KL IB	D	12		5	105000	115500	
57	MONTAUK 57	CR	WD IB	200	15 9		5	188500	207000	
--- 1959 BOATS ---										
30	PRISCILLA	SLP	SAIL WD KL IB	D	8 6		4 3	20000	22200	
36	MALABAR 36	YWL	SAIL WD IB	D				33900	37700	
38 5		YWL	SAIL FBG IB	D				41700	46300	
41	WES'COASTER	SLP	SAIL WD IB	D				53700	59000	
42	NORDFARER	YWL	SAIL WD IB	D				57200	62900	
43	WHITE-CAP	MS	WD IB	D				75100	82600	
46	CRUISING-SP	FSH	IB	D				**	**	
50	STEEL-SHRIMPER	CR	IB	D				**	**	
60	BROADVIEW	CR	IB	D				**	**	
--- 1941 BOATS ---										
31	MALIBAR-JUNIOR					9163		29400	32700	
34	BARNACLE	SLP	SA/CR WD IB	D GRAY	8 5	11262	5 4	35400	39400	
36 5	COASTWISE-CRUISER	CUT	SA/CR WD IB	D	9	12864	5 3	40100	44600	
42 2	OFF-SOUNDINGS	CUT	SA/CR WD IB	D	10	20000	5 10	74500	81900	
42 2	OFF-SOUNDINGS	YWL	SA/CR WD IB	D	10	20000	5 10	74500	81900	
--- 1939 BOATS ---										
36 5	COASTWISE-CRUISER	CUT	SA/CR WD IB	D GRAY	9	12864	5 3	42700	47400	
42 2	OFF-SOUNDINGS	CUT	SA/CR WD IB	D GRAY	10	20000	5 10	79300	87100	
42 2	OFF-SOUNDINGS	YWL	SA/CR WD IB	D GRAY	10	20000	5 10	79300	87100	
--- 1937 BOATS ---										
38		YWL	SA/CR WD KL IB	D GRAY	10 5	14650	5 3	52800	58000	
39 4		CUT	SA/CR WD KL IB	D GRAY	10 5	15617	5 3	58000	63800	
--- 1936 BOATS ---										
30 9		SLP	SA/CR WD IB	D	9 8	9163	5	34500	38300	
35 10		CUT	SA/CR WD IB	D	10 5	12864	5 3	47500	52200	
35 10		YWL	SA/CR WD IB	D	10 5	12864	5 3	47500	52200	

ALEUTIAN MARINE INTL INC
COAST GUARD MFG ID- AEM

Call 1-800-327-6929 for BUC Personalized Evaluation Service
Or, for 1976 to 1978 boats, sign onto www.BUCValuPro.com

ALGLAS CORP
EGG HARBOR CITY NJ

See inside cover to adjust price for area

SEE ALSO PACEMAKER YACHT COMPANY

LOA FT IN	NAME AND/ OR MODEL	TOP/ RIG	BOAT TYPE	-HULL- MTL TP TP #	----ENGINE--- HP MFG	BEAM FT IN	WGT LBS	DRAFT FT IN	RETAIL LOW	RETAIL HIGH
--- 1970 BOATS ---										
26		FB	CR FBG IB	210 CRUS	9 6	5500	2	8600	9850	
26		SF	FBG IB	210-260	9 6	5500	2	8550	10100	
26		SF	FBG IB	T155 CHRY	9 6	5500	2	9300	10600	

LOA FT	LOA IN	NAME AND/ OR MODEL	TOP/ RIG	BOAT TYPE	-HULL- MTL	-HULL- TP	----ENGINE--- TP # HP MFG	BEAM FT	BEAM IN	WGT LBS	DRAFT FT	DRAFT IN	RETAIL LOW	RETAIL HIGH
		1970 BOATS												
26		4 SLEEPER		EXP	FBG		IB 210-260	9	6	5500	2		8600	10100
28	4			EXP	FBG		IB 210-260	10	11	6079	2	5	11100	13000
28	4			EXP	FBG		IB T210-T260	10	11	6079	2	5	12700	15000
28	4			EXP	FBG		IB T 85D PERK	10	11	6079	2	5	15300	17400
28	4			SF	FBG		IB 210-260	10	11	7604	2	5	12200	14300
28	4			SF	FBG		IB T210-T260	10	11	7604	2	5	13700	16100
28	4			SF	FBG		IB T 85D PERK	10	11	7604	2	5	18400	20500
31		4 SLEEPER		SF	FBG		IB 160D-170D	11	10	12500	2	4	26700	29700
31		4 SLEEPER		SF	FBG		IB T210-T260	11	10	12500	2	4	20300	23100
31		4 SLEEPER		SF	FBG		IB T160D PERK	11	10	12500	2	4	29100	32300
31		6 SLEEPER		EXP	FBG		IB 160D-170D	11	10	12500	2	4	27800	30800
31		6 SLEEPER		EXP	FBG		IB T210-T260	11	10	12500	2	4	20800	23800
31		6 SLEEPER		EXP	FBG		IB T160D PERK	11	10	12500	2	4	29900	33200
31		6 SLEEPER		SDN	FBG		IB 160D-170D	11	10	12500	2	4	29900	33300
31		6 SLEEPER		SDN	FBG		IB T210-T260	11	10	12500	2	4	22400	25900
31		6 SLEEPER		SDN	FBG		IB T160D PERK	11	10	12500	2	4	33100	36800
31		6 SLEEPER		SF	FBG		IB 160D-170D	11	10	12500	2	4	27700	30700
31		6 SLEEPER		SF	FBG		IB T210-T260	11	10	12500	2	4	21400	24400
31		6 SLEEPER		SF	FBG		IB T160D PERK	11	10	12500	2	4	30300	33600
33				DC	FBG		IB T210-T260	13	2	13500	2	6	24900	28300
33			FB	SDNSF	FBG		IB T210-T260	13	2	13500	2	6	24800	28200
33			FB	SDNSF	FBG		IBT140D-T170D	13	2	13500	2	6	33400	37900
33			FB	SF	FBG		IB T210-T260	13	2	13500	2	6	24800	28100
33			FB	SF	FBG		IBT140D-T170D	13	2	13500	2	6	33400	38000
33		4 SLEEPER		EXP	FBG		IB T210-T260	13	2	13500	2	6	25000	28300
33		4 SLEEPER		EXP	FBG		IBT140D-T170D	13	2	13500	2	6	33500	38100
33		6 SLEEPER		SDN	FBG		IB T210-T260	13	2	13500	2	6	26600	30500
33		6 SLEEPER		SDN	FBG		IBT140D-T170D	13	2	13500	2	6	36300	41600
37	10			DC	FBG		IB T260 CRUS	13	10	18000	2	9	38700	43000
		IB T320 CRUS 39300 43600, IB T170D CUM 43000 47700, IB T216D GM											44200	49100
		IB T283D GM 46600 51200, IB T290D GM 46900 51500												
37	10			SDNSF	FBG		IB T260 CRUS	13	10	18000	2	9	38100	42400
		IB T320 CRUS 38700 43000, IB T170D CUM 42800 47600, IB T216D GM											44100	49000
		IB T283D GM 46500 51100, IB T290D GM 46700 51300												
43		6 SLEEPER		MY	FBG		IB T320 CRUS	14	6	30000	3	1	67700	74400
		IB T216D GM 70700 77700, IB T283D GM 75100 82500, IB T290D GM											75600	83000
		IB T300D GM 76200 83800												
48		COCKPIT 6 SLPR	HT	MYCPT	FBG		IB T320 CRUS	14	6		3		**	**
		IB T283D GM 72600 79800, IB T290D GM 73600 80900, IB T300D CUM											75100	82500
		IB T370D CUM 84500 92900												
		1969 BOATS												
24	6		FB	EXP	FBG		IB 210-250	9	6	5450	2		7700	9000
24	6	4 SLEEPER		EXP	FBG		IB 210-250	9	6	5450	2		7250	9000
24	6	4 SLEEPER		SF	FBG	RB	IB 210-250	9	6	5200	2		7000	8650
24	6	EXPRESS CRUISER		EXP	FBG		IO T120 VLVO	9	6	5450	2		15200	17300
24	6	EXPRESS CRUISER		EXP	FBG	RB	IB 210 CRUS	9	6	5450	2		8300	9550
24	6	SPORT FISHERMAN		SF	FBG		IO T120 VLVO	9	6	5200	2		16700	18900
24	6	SPORT FISHERMAN		SF	FBG	RB	IB 210 CRUS	9	6	5200	2		8000	9200
24	6	WAHOO			FBG	RB	IB 150-210	9	6	4500	1	10	6550	7800
28	3	EXPRESS CRUISER		EXP	FBG	RB	IB T210 CRUS	10	10				12300	14000
28	4			EXP	FBG		IB 210-250	10	11	6079	2	5	10600	12400
28	4			EXP	FBG		IB T210-T250	10	11	7379	2	5	13000	15200
28	4			SF	FBG		IB 210-250	10	11	6314	2	5	10800	12500
28	4			SF	FBG		IB T210-T250	10	11	7604	2	5	13100	15300
31		4 SLEEPER		EXP	FBG		IB 210-250	11	10	12500	2	4	18100	21000
31		4 SLEEPER		EXP	FBG		IB 170D CRUS	11	10	12500	2	4	26700	29700
31		4 SLEEPER		EXP	FBG		IB T210-T250	11	10	12500	2	4	20000	22600
31		4 SLEEPER		SF	FBG		IB 210-250	11	10	12500	2	4	18800	21100
31		4 SLEEPER		SF	FBG		IB 170D CRUS	11	10	12500	2	4	26500	29400
31		4 SLEEPER		SF	FBG		IB T210-T250	11	10	12500	2	4	20500	22800
31		6 SLEEPER		EXP	FBG		IB 210-250	11	10	12500	2	4	18300	21200
31		6 SLEEPER		EXP	FBG		IB 170D CRUS	11	10	12500	2	4	27000	30000
31		6 SLEEPER		EXP	FBG		IB T210-T250	11	10	12500	2	4	20200	22900
31		6 SLEEPER		SDN	FBG		IB 210-250	11	10	12500	2	4	18800	22300
31		6 SLEEPER		SDN	FBG		IB 170D CRUS	11	10	12500	2	4	29400	32600
31		6 SLEEPER		SDN	FBG		IB T210-T250	11	10	12500	2	4	21600	24700
31		6 SLEEPER	FB	SF	FBG		IB 210-250	11	10	12500	2	4	18900	21100
31		6 SLEEPER	FB	SF	FBG		IB 170D CRUS	11	10	12500	2	4	28100	31300
31		6 SLEEPER	FB	SF	FBG		IB T210-T250	11	10	12500	2	4	20200	22900
31		EXPRESS CRUISER		EXP	FBG	RB	IB 210 CRUS	11	10	12500	2	4	19900	22200
31		EXPRESS CRUISER		EXP	FBG	SV	IB T210 CRUS	11	10	12500	2	4	20100	22400
31		SEDAN		SDN	FBG	SV	IB 210 CRUS	11	10	12500	2	4	20600	22900
31		SEDAN		SDN	FBG	SV	IB T210 CRUS	11	10	12500	2	4	21600	24000
31		SPORT FISHERMAN		SF	FBG	SV	IB T210 CRUS	11	10	12500	2	4	20100	22300
33			FB	SDNSF	FBG		IB T210-T250	13	2	13500	2	6	23800	27000
33			FB	SDNSF	FBG		IB T170D CRUS	13	2	13500	2	6	33400	37100
33			FB	SF	FBG		IB T210-T250	13	2	13500	2	6	23700	26800
33			FB	SF	FBG		IB T170D CRUS	13	2	13500	2	6	33400	37200
33		4 SLEEPER		EXP	FBG		IB T210-T250	13	2	13500	2	6	22600	27200
33		4 SLEEPER		EXP	FBG		IB T170D CRUS	13	2	13500	2	6	33500	37300
33		6 SLEEPER		SDN	FBG		IB T210-T290	13	2	13500	2	6	24100	29800
33		6 SLEEPER		SDN	FBG		IB T320 PACE	13	2	13500	2	6	27400	30400
33		6 SLEEPER		SDN	FBG		IB T170D CRUS	13	2	13500	2	6	36600	40700
33		EXPRESS CRUISER		EXP	FBG	SV	IB T210 CRUS	13	2	13500	2	6	25300	28100
33		SEDAN		SDN	FBG	SV	IB T210 CRUS	13	2	13500	2	6	27000	30000
33		SPORT FISHERMAN		SF	FBG	SV	IB T210 CRUS	13	2	13500	2	6	23800	26400
42		MOTOR YACHT		MY	FBG	SV	IB T320 CRUS	14	6	30000	3	1	64500	70800
43				MY	FBG		IB T320 PACE	14	6	30000	3	1	64800	71300
		1968 BOATS												
24	6		FB	EXP	FBG		IB 210-250	9	6	5450	2		7450	8650
24	6		FB	EXP	FBG		IB 96D	9	6	5450	2		10800	12300
24	6		FB	EXP	FBG		IB T120 VLVO	9	6	5450	2		7850	9000
24	6	4 SLEEPER		EXP	FBG		IB 210-250	9	6	5450	2		7450	8650
24	6	4 SLEEPER		EXP	FBG		IB 96D	9	6	5450	2		10800	12300
24	6	4 SLEEPER		EXP	FBG		IB T120 VLVO	9	6	5450	2		7850	9000
24	6	4 SLEEPER		SF	FBG		IB 210-250	9	6	5200	2		7200	8350
24	6	4 SLEEPER		SF	FBG		IB 96D	9	6	5200	2		10400	11800
24	6	4 SLEEPER		SF	FBG		IO T120 VLVO	9	6	5200	2		17200	19600
24	6	WAHOO		CTRCN	FBG	SV	IB 50 CHRY	9	6	4500	1	10	5900	6750
24	6	WAHOO		CTRCN	FBG	SV	IB 210 CHRY	9	6	4500	1	10	6450	7400
31		4 SLEEPER		EXP	FBG		IB 170D	11	10	12500	2	4	26400	29300
31		4 SLEEPER		EXP	FBG		IB T210 CHRY	11	10	12500	2	4	19300	21400
31		4 SLEEPER		EXP	FBG	DV	IB 210-250	11	10	12500	2	4	18000	20300
31		4 SLEEPER		EXP	FBG	SV	IB T250	11	10	12500	2	4	19700	21900
31		4 SLEEPER		SF	FBG	DV	IB 210-250	11	10	12500	2	4	17100	20400
31		4 SLEEPER		SF	FBG	DV	IB 170D CHRY	11	10	12500	2	4	25700	28600
31		4 SLEEPER		SF	FBG	DV	IB T210-T250	11	10	12500	2	4	19300	22000
31		6 SLEEPER		EXP	FBG	DV	IB 210-250	11	10	12500	2	4	18200	20600
31		6 SLEEPER		EXP	FBG	DV	IB 170D CHRY	11	10	12500	2	4	26600	29500
31		6 SLEEPER		EXP	FBG	DV	IB T210-T250	11	10	12500	2	4	19500	22100
31		6 SLEEPER		SDN	FBG	DV	IB 210-250	11	10	12500	2	4	19000	21500
31		6 SLEEPER		SDN	FBG	DV	IB 170D CHRY	11	10	12500	2	4	28700	31900
31		6 SLEEPER		SDN	FBG	DV	IB T210-T250	11	10	12500	2	4	20800	23800
31		6 SLEEPER		SF	FBG	DV	IB 210 CHRY	11	10	12500	2	4	18800	20900
31		6 SLEEPER	FB	SF	FBG	DV	IB 250	11	10	12500	2	4	18500	20500
31		6 SLEEPER	FB	SF	FBG	DV	IB 170D	11	10	12500	2	4	27600	30600
31		6 SLEEPER	FB	SF	FBG	DV	IB T210-T250	11	10	12500	2	4	19400	22100
33			FB	SDNSF	FBG	DV	IB T210-T320	13	2	13500	2	6	23000	26900
33			FB	SDNSF	FBG	DV	IBT130D-T185D	13	2	13500	2	6	31800	36800
33			FB	SF	FBG		IB T250-T320	13	2	13500	2	6	23300	26600
33			FB	SF	FBG		IBT130D-T185D	13	2	13500	2	6	31800	36800
33			FB	SF	FBG	DV	IB T210 CHRY	13	2	13500	2	6	22900	25500
33		4 SLEEPER		EXP	FBG	DV	IB T210-T320	13	2	13500	2	6	23100	27100
33		4 SLEEPER		EXP	FBG	DV	IBT130D-T185D	13	2	13500	2	6	31900	37000
33		6 SLEEPER		SDN	FBG	DV	IB T210-T320	13	2	13500	2	6	24600	29300
33		6 SLEEPER		SDN	FBG	DV	IBT130D-T185D	13	2	13500	2	6	34500	40500
43	2			MY	FBG	DV	IB T320	14	6	27000	3	2	58900	64700
		IB T216D 68200 74900, IB T283D 72500 79600, IB T300D											73600	80900
		1967 BOATS												
24	5			EXP	FBG		IB 250			5450			7250	8300
24	5	CUSTOM		SF	FBG		IB 250			5200			6950	8000
33		4 SLEEPER DLX		EXP	FBG		IB T190-T250			13500			21800	25000
33		4 SLEEPER DLX		EXP	FBG		IB T170D			13500			31900	35500
33		4 SLEEPER DLX	FB	EXP	FBG		IB T190-T250			13500			21800	25000
33		4 SLEEPER DLX	FB	EXP	FBG		IB T170D			13500			31900	35500
33		6 SLEEPER		SDN	FBG		IB T190-T250			13500			23100	26700
33		6 SLEEPER	FB	SDN	FBG		IB T190-T250			13500			23100	26700
33		6 SLEEPER	FB	SDN	FBG		IB T170D			13500			34900	38700
		1966 BOATS												
24	5			EXP	FBG		IB 185-220						6900	7950
24	5	CUSTOM		SF	FBG		IB 185-220						6650	7650
24	5	CUSTOM	FB	SF	FBG		IB 185-220						6700	7750
33		6 SLEEPER DELUXE		EXP	FBG		IB T185-T320						21000	25000

CONTINUED ON NEXT PAGE

LOA FT IN	NAME AND/ OR MODEL	TOP/ RIG	BOAT TYPE	-HULL- MTL TP	ENGINE TP # HP MFG	BEAM FT IN	WGT LBS	DRAFT FT IN	RETAIL LOW	RETAIL HIGH
				1966 BOATS						
33 6	SLEEPER DELUXE		EXP	FBG	IB T170D				33100	36800
33 6	SLEEPER DELUXE	FB	EXP	FBG	IB T185-T320				21000	25000
33 6	SLEEPER DELUXE	FB	EXP	FBG	IB T170D				33100	36800

ALIM-MARINE
DIV OF ALIM ASSOCIATION

Call 1-800-327-6929 for BUC Personalized Evaluation Service
Or, for 1962 to 1965 boats, sign onto www.BUCValuPro.com

ALINDALE MFG CO INC
COAST GUARD MFG ID- ADL

Call 1-800-327-6929 for BUC Personalized Evaluation Service
Or, for 1979 to 1984 boats, sign onto www.BUCValuPro.com

ALL FAMILY CRAFT INC
DIV OF PLAYCRAFT BOATS   COAST GUARD MFG ID- CDG

Call 1-800-327-6929 for BUC Personalized Evaluation Service
Or, for 1979 to 2008 boats, sign onto www.BUCValuPro.com

ALL SEASON INDUSTRIES INC
MARKLE IN 46770   COAST GUARD MFG ID- ALS See inside cover to adjust price for area

For more recent years, see the BUC Used Boat Price Guide, Volume 1 or Volume 2

LOA FT IN	NAME AND/ OR MODEL	TOP/ RIG	BOAT TYPE	-HULL- MTL TP	ENGINE TP # HP MFG	BEAM FT IN	WGT LBS	DRAFT FT IN	RETAIL LOW	RETAIL HIGH
				1983 BOATS						
16 4	IMPERIAL T164		RNBT	FBG TR	OB	7 4	890		1700	2050
16 11	IMPERIAL V171		RNBT	FBG DV	OB	6 9	1060		2050	2450
17	IMPERIAL V173	OP	RNBT	FBG DV	OB	6 10	900		1750	2100
17	IMPERIAL V176	ST	RNBT	FBG DV	OB	6 10	1300		2450	2850
17	REGENCY VR175	ST	RNBT	FBG DV	IO 120-170	6 10	1850		1700	2050
17	REGENCY VR176	ST	RNBT	FBG DV	OB	6 10	900		1750	2100
17 2	IMPERIAL V170		RNBT	FBG DV	IO 185	6 10	1770		1700	2000
17 8	IMPERIAL V180	OP	RNBT	FBG DV	IO 120-198	7 3	1980		1900	2300
17 8	IMPERIAL V181	OP	RNBT	FBG DV	OB	7 3	1140		2300	2650
17 8	IMPERIAL V182	OP	RNBT	FBG DV	IO 120-198	7 3	1990		1900	2300
17 8	IMPERIAL V183	OP	RNBT	FBG DV	OB	7 3	1150		2300	2650
17 8	REGENCY VR180	ST	RNBT	FBG DV	IO 120-198	7 3	1980		1900	2300
17 8	REGENCY VR181	ST	RNBT	FBG DV	OB	7 3	1140		2300	2650
17 8	REGENCY VR182	ST	RNBT	FBG DV	IO 120-198	7 3	1980		1900	2300
17 8	REGENCY VR183	ST	RNBT	FBG DV	OB	7 3	1140		2300	2650
19 6	CITATION VC200	OP	RNBT	FBG DV	IO 120-260	7 11	2478		2450	3100
19 6	CITATION VC201	OP	RNBT	FBG DV	OB	7 11	1978		3550	4150
19 6	IMPERIAL V190	OP	RNBT	FBG DV	IO 120-260	7 11	2978		2750	3400
19 6	IMPERIAL V191	OP	RNBT	FBG DV	OB	7 11	1978		3300	3800
19 6	IMPERIAL V192	OP	RNBT	FBG DV	IO 120-260	7 11	2978		2750	3400
19 6	IMPERIAL V193	OP	RNBT	FBG DV	OB	7 11	1978		3300	3800
19 6	REGENCY VR190	OP	RNBT	FBG DV	IO	7 11	2978		**	**
19 6	REGENCY VR191	OP	RNBT	FBG DV	OB	7 11	1978		4100	4800
19 6	REGENCY VR192	ST	RNBT	FBG DV	IO 120-260	7 11	2978		2750	3400
19 6	REGENCY VR193	ST	RNBT	FBG DV	OB	7 11	1380		2800	3250
19 6	REGENCY VRC200		CUD	FBG DV	IO 120-260	7 9	2988		2800	3500
20 10	CITATION VC210	OP	RNBT	FBG DV	IO 170-260	7 11	3000		3250	4000
22 10	CITATION VC230	OP	RNBT	FBG DV	IO 170-260	7 11	3867		4300	5200
24 5	CITATION VC240		CR	FBG DV	IO 188-255	8 5			5200	6200
				1982 BOATS						
16 11	IMPERIAL V171	OP	RNBT	FBG DV	OB	6 9	1060		2000	2400
17	IMPERIAL V173	OP	RNBT	FBG DV	OB	6 10	900		1750	2050
17	IMPERIAL V176	ST	RNBT	FBG DV	OB	6 10	1300		2400	2800
17	REGENCY VR176	ST	RNBT	FBG DV	OB	6 10	900		1750	2050
17 8	IMPERIAL V180	OP	RNBT	FBG DV	IO 120-228	7 3	1980		1850	2300
17 8	IMPERIAL V181	OP	RNBT	FBG DV	OB	7 3	1140		2250	2600
17 8	IMPERIAL V182	OP	RNBT	FBG DV	IO 120-228	7 3	1990		1850	2300
17 8	IMPERIAL V183	OP	RNBT	FBG DV	OB	7 3	1150		2250	2600
17 8	REGENCY VR180	ST	RNBT	FBG DV	IO 120-228	7 3	1980		1800	2300
17 8	REGENCY VR181	ST	RNBT	FBG DV	OB	7 3	1140		2250	2600
17 8	REGENCY VR182	ST	RNBT	FBG DV	IO 120-228	7 3	1980		1850	2300
17 8	REGENCY VR183	ST	RNBT	FBG DV	OB	7 3	1140		2250	2600
19 6	CITATION VC200	OP	RNBT	FBG DV	IO 120-260	7 11	2478		2400	3000
19 6	CITATION VC201	OP	RNBT	FBG DV	OB	7 11	1978		3500	4100
19 6	CITATION VC211	OP	RNBT	FBG DV	OB	7 11			2750	3200
19 6	IMPERIAL V190	OP	RNBT	FBG DV	IO 120-228	7 11	2978		2650	3200
19 6	IMPERIAL V190	OP	RNBT	FBG DV	IO 260	7 11	2978		2850	3300
19 6	IMPERIAL V191	OP	RNBT	FBG DV	OB	7 11	1978		3050	3550
19 6	IMPERIAL V192	OP	RNBT	FBG DV	IO 120-228	7 11	2978		2650	3200
19 6	IMPERIAL V192	OP	RNBT	FBG DV	IO 260	7 11	2978		2850	3300
19 6	IMPERIAL V193	OP	RNBT	FBG DV	OB	7 11	1978		3250	3800
19 6	IMPERIAL VC200	OP	RNBT	FBG DV	IO 120	7 9	1920		2150	2500
19 6	IMPERIAL VC201	OP	RNBT	FBG DV	OB	7 10	1978		3500	4050
19 6	REGENCY VCR200	ST	CUD	FBG DV	IO 120-260	7 11	1978		2300	2850
19 6	REGENCY VCR201	ST	CUD	FBG DV	IO	7 11	1390		2750	3200
19 6	REGENCY VR190	OP	RNBT	FBG DV	IO 120	7 11	2978		2700	3150
19 6	REGENCY VR191	OP	RNBT	FBG DV	OB	7 11	1978		4100	4800
19 6	REGENCY VR192	ST	RNBT	FBG DV	IO 120-260	7 11	2978		2700	3300
19 6	REGENCY VR193	OP	RNBT	FBG DV	OB	7 11	1380		2700	3150
20 10	CITATION VC210	OP	RNBT	FBG DV	IO 170-260	7 11	3000		3200	3900
22 10	CITATION VC230	OP	RNBT	FBG DV	IO 170-260	7 11	3867		4200	5050
24 5	CITATION VC240		CR	FBG DV	IO 188	8 5			5050	5800
				1981 BOATS						
17	IMPERIAL V173	OP	RNBT	FBG DV	OB	6 10	900		1700	2050
17	IMPERIAL V176	ST	RNBT	FBG DV	OB	6 10	1300		2350	2750
17	REGENCY VR176	ST	RNBT	FBG DV	OB	6 10	900		1700	2050
17 8	IMPERIAL V180	OP	RNBT	FBG DV	IO 120-230	7 3	1980		1800	2250
17 8	IMPERIAL V181	OP	RNBT	FBG DV	OB	7 3	1140		2200	2550
17 8	IMPERIAL V182	OP	RNBT	FBG DV	IO 120-230	7 3	1990		1800	2250
17 8	IMPERIAL V183	OP	RNBT	FBG DV	OB	7 3	1150		2200	2550
17 8	REGENCY VR180	ST	RNBT	FBG DV	IO 120-200	7 3	1980		1800	2200
17 8	REGENCY VR180	ST	RNBT	FBG DV	IO 228 MRCR	7 3	1980		1900	2250
17 8	REGENCY VR181	ST	RNBT	FBG DV	OB	7 3	1140		2200	2550
17 8	REGENCY VR182	ST	RNBT	FBG DV	IO 120-228	7 3	1980		1800	2250
17 8	REGENCY VR183	ST	RNBT	FBG DV	OB	7 3	1140		2200	2550
18 6	BARON T-186	ST	RNBT	FBG TR	OB	7 2	1500		2750	3150
18 6	BARON T-187	ST	RNBT	FBG TR	IO 120-228	7 2	1500		1950	2450
19 6	IMPERIAL V190	OP	RNBT	FBG DV	IO 120-260	7 11	2978		2600	3250
19 6	IMPERIAL V191	OP	RNBT	FBG DV	OB	7 11	1978		3600	4200
19 6	IMPERIAL V192	OP	RNBT	FBG DV	IO 120-260	7 11	2978		2650	3250
19 6	IMPERIAL V193	OP	RNBT	FBG DV	OB	7 11	1978		3750	4350
19 6	IMPERIAL VC200	OP	RNBT	FBG DV	IO 120-260	7 11	2478		2400	2950
19 6	IMPERIAL VC201	OP	RNBT	FBG DV	OB	7 11	1978		2950	3400
19 6	REGENCY VCR200	ST	CUD	FBG DV	IO 120-260	7 11	1978		2250	2800
19 6	REGENCY VCR201	ST	CUD	FBG DV	IO	7 11	1390		2700	3100
19 6	REGENCY VR192	ST	RNBT	FBG DV	IO 120-260	7 11	2978		2650	3250
19 6	REGENCY VR193	ST	RNBT	FBG DV	OB	7 11	1380		2650	3100
20 10	IMPERIAL VC120	OP	RNBT	FBG DV	OB 170 MRCR	7 11	3000		3150	3650
20 10	IMPERIAL VC211	OP	RNBT	FBG DV	OB	7 11	1650		3400	3950
20 11	CITATION VC210		CR	FBG DV	IO 165	8			3300	3800
22 10	IMPERIAL VC230	OP	RNBT	FBG DV	IO 170 MRCR	7 11	3867		4100	4800
23 1	CITATION VC230		CR	FBG DV	IO 170	8			4400	5100
24 5	CITATION VC240		CR	FBG DV	IO 188	8 5			5000	5750
				1980 BOATS						
16 11	IMPERIAL T171	OP	RNBT	FBG TR	OB	6 11	1240		2250	2650
17 2	IMPERIAL V171	OP	RNBT	FBG DV	OB	7	980		1800	2150
17 8	IMPERIAL V180	OP	RNBT	FBG DV	IO 120-230	7 3	1980		1800	2250
17 8	IMPERIAL V181	OP	RNBT	FBG DV	OB	7 3	1140		2150	2500
17 8	IMPERIAL V182	OP	RNBT	FBG DV	IO 120-230	7 3	1990		2150	2650
17 8	IMPERIAL V183	OP	RNBT	FBG DV	OB	7 3	1150		2150	2650
17 8	REGENCY VR180	ST	RNBT	FBG DV	IO 120-200	7 3	1980		1800	2200
17 8	REGENCY VR180	ST	RNBT	FBG DV	IO 228 MRCR	7 3	1980		1900	2250
17 8	REGENCY VR181	ST	RNBT	FBG DV	OB	7 3	1140		2150	2500
17 8	REGENCY VR182	ST	RNBT	FBG DV	IO 120-228	7 3	1980		1800	2250
17 8	REGENCY VR183	ST	RNBT	FBG DV	OB	7 3	1140		2150	2500
18 6	BARON T-186	ST	RNBT	FBG TR	OB	7 2	1500		2700	3100
18 6	BARON T-187	ST	RNBT	FBG TR	IO 120-228	7 2	2200		1950	2450
19 6	IMPERIAL V190	OP	RNBT	FBG DV	IO 120-230	7 11	2978		2600	3150
19 6	IMPERIAL V190	OP	RNBT	FBG DV	IO 260	7 11	2978		2800	3250
19 6	IMPERIAL V191	OP	RNBT	FBG DV	OB	7 11	1978		3200	3700
19 6	IMPERIAL V192	OP	RNBT	FBG DV	IO 120-260	7 11	2978		2650	3250
19 6	IMPERIAL V193	OP	RNBT	FBG DV	OB	7 11	1978		3250	3750
19 6	IMPERIAL VC200	OP	RNBT	FBG DV	IO 120-260	7 11	2478		2350	2950
19 6	IMPERIAL VC201	OP	RNBT	FBG DV	OB	7 11	1978		3650	4250
19 6	REGENCY VCR200	ST	CUD	FBG DV	IO 120-260	7 11	1978		2250	2800

LOA FT IN	NAME AND/ OR MODEL	TOP/ RIG	BOAT TYPE	-HULL- MTL TP	TP	----ENGINE--- # HP MFG	BEAM FT IN	WGT LBS	DRAFT FT IN	RETAIL LOW	RETAIL HIGH
			1980 BOATS								
19 6	REGENCY VCR201	ST	CUD	FBG DV	OB		7 11	1390		2650	3050
19 6	REGENCY VR192	ST	RNBT	FBG DV	IO	120-260	7 11	2978		2600	3250
19 6	REGENCY VR193	ST	RNBT	FBG DV	OB		7 11	1380		2600	3050
21	VC210		CR	FBG DV	IO	228	7 11			3350	3900
24	V240C		CR	FBG DV	IO	228	8 6			4950	5650
			1979 BOATS								
17	IMPERIAL T-171	OP	RNBT	FBG TR	OB		6 11	1120		2000	2400
17	IMPERIAL V-171	OP	RNBT	FBG DV	OB		7	1520		2600	3000
17	IMPERIAL V-173	OP	RNBT	FBG DV	OB		6 10	1100		1950	2350
19	IMPERIAL T-186	OP	RNBT	FBG TR	OB		7 2			2500	2950
19	IMPERIAL T-187	OP	RNBT	FBG TR	IO	170	7 2			1900	2250
19	V-190	OP	RNBT	FBG DV	IO	200	7 11	3000		2550	3000
19	V-191	OP	RNBT	FBG DV	OB		7 11	1978		3150	3650
19	V-192	OP	RNBT	FBG DV	IO	200	7 11	3000		2600	3050
19	V-193	OP	RNBT	FBG DV	OB		7 11	1978		3250	3800
21	VOYAGER VC-210		CR	FBG DV	IO	228	7 11			3350	3900
24	EXPLORER V-240C		CR	FBG DV	IO	228	8 6			4950	5650
			1978 BOATS								
16 11	IMPERIAL T171	ST	RNBT	FBG TR	OB		6 11	1120		1950	2350
17	IMPERIAL V173	ST	RNBT	FBG DV	OB		6 10	1100		1950	2300
17 2	IMPERIAL V170	ST	RNBT	FBG DV	IO	120-170	7	2250		1850	2200
17 2	IMPERIAL V171	ST	RNBT	FBG DV	OB		7	1520		2550	3000
17 8	IMPERIAL V180	ST	RNBT	FBG DV	IO	120-198	7 3	1915		1800	2150
18 6	IMPERIAL T186	ST	RNBT	FBG TR	OB		7 2	1500		2600	3050
18 6	IMPERIAL T187	ST	RNBT	FBG TR	IO	120-235	7 2	2400		2050	2550
20 11	VOYAGER VC210	ST	CUD	FBG DV	IO	165-255	8	3280		3500	4300
20 11	VOYAGER VC210	ST	CUD	FBG DV	IO	T120-T170	8			3800	4450
20 11	VOYAGER VC210HT	HT	CUD	FBG DV	IO	165-255	8	3450		3650	4400
20 11	VOYAGER VC210HT	HT	CUD	FBG DV	IO	T120-T170	8			3800	4450
24 5	EXPLORER V240C	OP	CBNCR	FBG DV	IO	188-255	8 5	4800		6600	7850
24 5	EXPLORER V240C	OP	CBNCR	FBG DV	IO	T120-T255	8 5			6350	7750
			1977 BOATS								
16 11	RANGER V-170	ST	RNBT	FBG TR	IO	170-200	6 11	1705		1700	2150
16 11	RANGER T-171	ST	RNBT	FBG TR	OB		6 11	1120		1950	2300
17 1	AVENGER V-173	ST	RNBT	FBG SV	OB		6 10	1100		1950	2300
17 1	AVENGER V-174	ST	RNBT	FBG SV	IO	130-170	6 10	1725		1700	2100
17 8	CHARGER V-180	ST	RNBT	FBG DV	IO	120-165	7 3	1815		1750	2200
17 8	CHARGER V-180	ST	RNBT	FBG DV	IO	170-188	7 3	1930		1850	2300
18 6	BARON T-186	ST	RNBT	FBG TR	OB		7 2	1500		2600	3000
18 6	BARON T-187	ST	RNBT	FBG TR	IO	120-165	7 2	2200		2000	2500
18 6	BARON T-187	ST	RNBT	FBG TR	IO	170-188	7 2	2315		2050	2550
20 10	VOYAGER VC-210	ST	CUD	FBG DV	IO	165-233	8	3280		3550	4250
20 10	VOYAGER VC-210HT	HT	CUD	FBG DV	IO	165-233	8	3450		3700	4400
24 5	EXPLORER V-240C	ST	CR	FBG DV	IO	188-255	8 6	4800		5800	6900
			1976 BOATS								
16 11	RANGER T170	OP	RNBT	FBG TR	IO	130-165	6 11	1840		1800	2150
17 1	AVENGER V173	OP	RNBT	FBG DV	OB		6 10	1100		1900	2250
17 1	AVENGER V174	OP	RNBT	FBG DV	IO	130 VLVO	6 6	1800		1750	2050
17 8	CHARGER V180	OP	RNBT	FBG DV	IO	140-165	7 3	1915		1850	2200
17 8	CHARGER V180	OP	RNBT	FBG DV	IO	170 VLVO	7 3	1915		1950	2350
18 6	BARON T186	OP	RNBT	FBG DV	OB		7 2	1500		2550	2950
18 6	BARON T187	OP	RNBT	FBG DV	IO	165	7 2	2200		2050	2450
18 6	BARON T187	OP	RNBT	FBG DV	IO	170 VLVO	7 2	2200		2250	2600
18 6	EXPLORER TC188	OP	CUD	FBG TR	OB		7 2	1500		2550	2950
18 6	EXPLORER TC189	OP	CUD	FBG TR	IO	140-170	7 2	2200		2150	2650
20 10	VOYAGER VC210	OP	CUD	FBG DV	IO	188-233	8	3280		3650	4500
			1975 BOATS								
17 3	AVENGER V173	OP	RNBT	FBG DV	OB		6 6	1265		2200	2550
17 3	AVENGER V174	OP	RNBT	FBG DV	IO	120-165	6 6	1915		1750	2100
17 10	CHARGER V180	OP	RNBT	FBG DV	IO	140-165	7 1	2000		1950	2350
18 6	BARON T186	ST	RNBT	FBG TR	OB		7 5	1500		2550	2950
18 6	BARON T187	ST	RNBT	FBG TR	IO	140-188	7 5	2200		2250	2600
20 10	VOYAGER VC210	OP	CUD	FBG DV	IO	165-233	7 11	3280		3750	4500
			1974 BOATS								
17 3	SCAT 1750			FBG	OB		6 2	1500		2400	2800
18 6	BARON 1900			FBG	OB		7 4	1500		2500	2900
18 6	BARON 1950			FBG	IO	120-188	7 4	2300		2250	2750

ALLEMAN ENTERPRISES
COAST GUARD MFG ID- ALE

Call 1-800-327-6929 for BUC Personalized Evaluation Service
Or, for 1965 to 1978 boats, sign onto www.BUCValuPro.com

ALLEN BOAT CO
COAST GUARD MFG ID- TGA

Call 1-800-327-6929 for BUC Personalized Evaluation Service
Or, for 1965 to 2009 boats, sign onto www.BUCValuPro.com

ALLIED BOAT CO INC
ALLIED YACHTS   See inside cover to adjust price for area
CATSKILL NY 12414   COAST GUARD MFG ID- ABC

LOA FT IN	NAME AND/ OR MODEL	TOP/ RIG	BOAT TYPE	-HULL- MTL TP	TP	----ENGINE--- # HP MFG	BEAM FT IN	WGT LBS	DRAFT FT IN	RETAIL LOW	RETAIL HIGH
			1982 BOATS								
30 6	SEAWIND	KTH	SA/RC	FBG KL	IB	D WEST	9 3	12080	4 2	32100	35700
30 6	SEAWIND I	CUT	SA/RC	FBG KL	IB	D	9 3	12080	4 2	32100	35700
30 6	SEAWIND I	KTH	SA/RC	FBG KL	IB	D	9 3	12080	4 2	32100	35700
31 7	SEAWIND II	CUT	SA/CR	FBG KL	IB	D WEST	10 5	14900	4 6	39800	44200
31 7	SEAWIND II	KTH	SA/RC	FBG KL	IB	D WEST	10 5	14900	4 6	39800	44200
31 7	SEAWIND II	CUT	SA/CR	FBG KL	IB	D	10 5	14900	4 6	39800	44200
31 7	SEAWIND II	KTH	SA/RC	FBG KL	IB	D	10 5	14900	4 6	39800	44200
36	PRINCESS 36	CUT	SA/CR	FBG KL	IB	D	11	15400	4 5	43000	47700
36	PRINCESS 36	CUT	SA/CR	FBG KL	IB	40D WEST	11	15400	4 5	43100	47900
36	PRINCESS 36	KTH	SA/CR	FBG KL	IB	D	11	15400	4 5	43000	47700
36	PRINCESS 36	KTH	SA/CR	FBG KL	IB	40D WEST	11	15400	4 5	43100	47900
38 10	MISTRESS 39	KTH	SA/RC	FBG KL	IB	D	12	20800	4 6	63800	70100
38 10	MISTRESS 39MK III	KTH	SA/RC	FBG KL	IB	D	12	20800	4 6	58300	64100
41 9	XL-2-42	SLP	SA/RC	FBG KL	IB	D	11 6	19770	4 6	66600	73200
41 9	XL-2-42	YWL	SA/RC	FBG KL	IB	D	11 6	19770	4 6	66600	73200
			1981 BOATS								
30 6	SEAWIND II	CUT	SA/RC	FBG KL	IB	D	9 3	12080	4 2	30400	33800
30 6	SEAWIND II	KTH	SA/RC	FBG KL	IB	D	9 3	12080	4 2	30400	33800
31 7	SEAWIND II	CUT	SA/RC	FBG KL	IB	D	10 5	14900	4 6	37700	41900
31 7	SEAWIND II	KTH	SA/RC	FBG KL	IB	D	10 5	14900	4 6	37700	41900
36	PRINCESS 36	CUT	SA/CR	FBG KL	IB	D	11	15400	4 6	40700	45200
36	PRINCESS 36	KTH	SA/CR	FBG KL	IB	D	11	15400	4 6	40700	45200
38 10	MISTRESS 39	KTH	SA/RC	FBG KL	IB	D	12	20800	4 6	60800	66800
38 10	MISTRESS 39 MK III	KTH	SA/RC	FBG KL	IB	D	12	20800	4 6	55000	60400
			1980 BOATS								
31 7	SEAWIND II	CUT	SA/CR	FBG KL	IB	D	10 5	16000	4 6	38900	43200
31 7	SEAWIND II	KTH	SA/CR	FBG KL	IB	D	10 5	16000	4 6	38900	43200
36	ALLIED 36	CUT	SA/CR	FBG KL	IB	D	11	15400	4 6	39200	43500
36	ALLIED 36	KTH	SA/CR	FBG KL	IB	D	11	15400	4 6	39200	43500
39	ALLIED 39	CUT	SA/CR	FBG KL	IB	D	12	20800	4 6	56000	61600
39	ALLIED 39	KTH	SA/CR	FBG KL	IB	D	12	20800	4 6	56000	61600
39	ALLIED 39	CUT	SA/CR	FBG KL	IB	D	12	20800	4 6	56100	61600
52 11	ALLIED 52	CUT	SA/CR	FBG KL	IB	D	14 7	46000	5 7	151000	166000
52 11	ALLIED 52	KTH	SA/CR	FBG KL	IB	D	14 7	46000	5 7	151000	166000
			1979 BOATS								
31 7	SEA-WIND II	CUT	SA/CR	FBG KL	IB	D	10 5	14900	4 6	35100	39000
31 7	SEA-WIND II	KTH	SA/CR	FBG KL	IB	D	10 5	14900	4 6	35100	39000
36	PRINCESS 36	CUT	SA/CR	FBG KL	IB	D	11	16400	4 6	40100	44600
36	PRINCESS 36	KTH	SA/CR	FBG KL	IB	D	11	16400	4 6	40100	44600
39 9	SEA-VENTURE 40	KTH	SA/CR	FBG KL	IB	D	12 1	21800	4 7	58200	64000
			1978 BOATS								
31 7	SEAWIND II	KTH	SAIL	FBG KL	IB	25D WEST	10 5	14900	4 6	34100	37900
36	CONTESSA 36	KTH	SA/RC	FBG KL	IB	37D WEST	11	16400	4 6	39000	43300
36	PRINCESS 36	SLP	SAIL	FBG KL	IB	37D WEST	11	15400	4 6	37000	41100
36	PRINCESS 36	KTH	SAIL	FBG KL	IB	37D WEST	11	15400	4 6	37000	41100
38 8	MISTRESS MARK III	KTH	SAIL	FBG KL	IB	37D WEST	12	20800	4 6	52000	57100
38 9	MISTRESS 39 GT CABIN	KTH	SAIL	FBG KL	IB	37D WEST	12	20800	4 6	52700	57900
38 9	MISTRESS 39 TRUNK	KTH	SAIL	FBG KL	IB	37D WEST	12	20800	4 6	51600	56700
40	WRIGHT 40	SLP	SAIL	FBG KC	IB	37D	12	19000	4 2	52000	57200
40	WRIGHT 40	KTH	SAIL	FBG KC	IB	37D	12	19000	4 2	52000	57300
41 9	XL-2-42	SLP	SAIL	FBG KC	IB	37D WEST	11 6	19770	4 2	57200	62800
41 9	XL-2-42	YWL	SAIL	FBG KC	IB	37D WEST	11 6	19770	4 2	57200	62800
			1977 BOATS								
31 7	SEAWIND II	KTH	SAIL	FBG KL	IB	27 PALM	10 5	14900	4 6	33200	36900
31 7	SEAWIND II	KTH	SAIL	FBG KL	IB	30D WEST	10 5	14900	4 6	33200	36900
36	PRINCESS 36	SLP	SAIL	FBG KL	IB	37D WEST	11	15400	4 6	36000	40000
36	PRINCESS 36	KTH	SAIL	FBG KL	IB	37D WEST	11	15400	4 6	36000	40000
38 9	MISTRESS 39 GT CABIN	KTH	SAIL	FBG KL	IB	37D WEST	12	20800	4 6	51900	57100
38 9	MISTRESS 39 TRUNK	KTH	SAIL	FBG KL	IB	37D WEST	12	20800	4 6	50800	55800
38 9	MISTRESS MK III	KTH	SAIL	FBG KL	IB	37D WEST	12	20800	4 6	49600	54500
41 9	XL-2-42	SLP	SAIL	FBG KC	IB	37D WEST	11 6	19000	4 2	54300	59700
41 9	XL-2-42	YWL	SAIL	FBG KC	IB	37D WEST	11 6	19000	4 2	54300	59700

LOA FT	LOA IN	NAME AND/ OR MODEL	TOP/ RIG	BOAT TYPE	-HULL- MTL	-HULL- TP	ENGINE TP	ENGINE # HP	ENGINE MFG	BEAM FT	BEAM IN	WGT LBS	DRAFT FT	DRAFT IN	RETAIL LOW	RETAIL HIGH
		1976 BOATS														
31	7	SEAWIND II	KTH	SAIL	FBG	KL	IB	25D	WEST	10	5	14900	4	6	32400	36000
36		CONTESSA 36	KTH	SAIL	FBG	KL	IB	25D	WEST	11		14400	4	6	35100	39000
36		PRINCESS 36	KTH	SAIL	FBG	KL	IB	25D	WEST	11		14400	4	6	30800	34300
38	7	MISTRESS MARK III	KTH	SAIL	FBG	KL	IB	37D	WEST	12		20800	4	6	49200	54000
38	9	MISTRESS 39	KTH	SAIL	FBG	KL	IB	37D	WEST	12		20800	4	6	49500	54400
41	9	XL-2-42	SLP	SAIL	FBG	KC	IB	37D	WEST	11	6	19000	4	2	53000	58300
41	9	XL-2-42	YWL	SAIL	FBG	KC	IB	37D	WEST	11	6	19000	4	2	53000	58300
		1975 BOATS														
36		PRINCESS	SLP	SAIL	FBG	KL	IB	25D	WEST	11		14400	4	6	32200	35800
36		PRINCESS	KTH	SAIL	FBG	KL	IB	25D	WEST	11		14400	4	6	32200	35800
38	7	MISTRESS GREAT CBN	KTH	SAIL	FBG	KL	IB	40D	WEST	12		20800	4	6	49200	54000
38	7	MISTRESS MARK III	KTH	SAIL	FBG	KL	IB	40D	WEST	12		20800	4	6	47300	52000
38	7	MISTRESS TRUNK CBN	KTH	SAIL	FBG	KL	IB	40D	WEST	12		20800	4	6	48200	53000
41	9	XL-2 42 MARK III	SLP	SAIL	FBG	SK	IB	40D	WEST	11	6	19770	8	5	53100	58400
41	9	XL-2 42 MARK III	YWL	SAIL	FBG	SK	IB	40D	WEST	11	6	19770	8	5	53100	58400
		1974 BOATS														
29	11	CHANCE 30.30 MORC		SAIL	FBG		IB	27	PALM	10		11200	5	3	22900	25500
30	6	SEAWIND	SLP	SAIL	FBG		IB	27	PALM	9	3	12080	4	2	25000	27800
30	6	SEAWIND	KTH	SAIL	FBG		IB	27	PALM	9	3	12080	4	2	25000	27800
30	7	CHANCE 30.30 IOR		SAIL	FBG		IB	27	PALM	10		11200	5	3	23100	25700
33		LUDERS	SLP	SAIL	FBG		IB	27	PALM	10		12800	5		26800	29800
34	6	SEABREEZE	SLP	SAIL	FBG		IB	27	PALM	10	3	13000	3	10	27600	30700
34	6	SEABREEZE	YWL	SAIL	FBG		IB	27	PALM	10	3	13000	3	10	27600	30700
36		CONTESSA 36	KTH	SAIL	FBG		IB	27D	WEST	11		15000	4	6	32800	36400
36		PRINCESS 36	SLP	SAIL	FBG		IB	27D	WEST	11		14400	4	6	31600	35100
36		PRINCESS 36	KTH	SAIL	FBG		IB	27D	WEST	11		14400	4	6	31600	35100
38	8	MISTRESS 39	KTH	SA/CR	FBG	KL	IB	D		12		20800	4	6	47500	52300
41		X-L-2	SLP	SAIL	FBG		IB	37D	PERK	11	6	19000	4	2	48800	53600
41		X-L-2	YWL	SAIL	FBG		IB	37D	PERK	11	6	19000	4	2	48800	53600
		1973 BOATS														
29	11	CHANCE 30.30 MORC		SAIL	FBG		IB	27	PALM	10		11200	5	3	22500	25000
30	6	SEAWIND	SLP	SAIL	FBG		IB	27	PALM	9	3	12080	4	2	24500	27200
30	6	SEAWIND	KTH	SAIL	FBG		IB	27	PALM	9	3	12080	4	2	24500	27200
30	7	CHANCE 30.30 IOR		SAIL	FBG		IB	27	PALM	10		11200	5	3	22700	25200
33		LUDERS	SLP	SAIL	FBG		IB	27	PALM	10		12800	5		26300	29300
34	6	SEABREEZE	SLP	SAIL	FBG	KC	IB	27		10	3	13000	3	10	27100	30100
34	6	SEABREEZE	KTH	SAIL	FBG	KC	IB	27		10	3	13000	3	10	27100	30100
36		CONTESSA 36		SAIL	FBG		IB	27D	WEST	11		14400	4	6	33500	37200
36		PRINCESS 36		SAIL	FBG		IB	27D	WEST	11		14400	4	6	28600	31700
38	8	MISTRESS	KTH	SAIL	FBG		IB	40D	WEST	12		20800	4	6	46700	51300
39	10	ALLIED	SLP	SAIL	FBG	KC	IB	27		10	3	17000	5	10	41600	46200
39	10	ALLIED	KTH	SAIL	FBG	KC	IB	27		10	3	17000	5	10	41600	46200
41	1	X-L-2	SLP	SAIL	FBG	KC	IB	37D		11	6	19000	4	2	48300	53100
41	1	X-L-2	YWL	SAIL	FBG	KC	IB	37D		11	6	19000	4	2	48300	53100
		1972 BOATS														
29	11	CHANCE 30.30 MORC		SAIL	FBG		IB	27D	PALM	10		11200	5	3	22200	24600
30	6	SEAWIND	SLP	SAIL	FBG		IB	27D	PALM	9	3	12080	4	2	24100	26800
30	6	SEAWIND	KTH	SAIL	FBG		IB	27D	PALM	9	3	12080	4	2	24100	26800
30	7	CHANCE 30.30 IOR		SAIL	FBG		IB	27D	PALM	10		11200	5	3	22300	24800
33		LUDERS	SLP	SAIL	FBG		IB	27D	PALM	10		12800	5		25900	28700
34	6	SEABREEZE	SLP	SAIL	FBG		IB	27D	PALM	10	3	13000	3	10	26700	29700
34	6	SEABREEZE	YWL	SAIL	FBG		IB	27D	PALM	10	3	13000	3	10	26700	29700
36		PRINCESS 36		SAIL	FBG		IB	27D	WEST	11		14400	4	6	30400	33700
38	8	MISTRESS	KTH	SAIL	FBG		IB	40D	WEST	12		20800	4	6	45700	50200
41		X-L-2	YWL	SAIL	FBG		IB	37D	PERK	11	6	19000	4	2	47100	51800
		1971 BOATS														
24	3	GREENWICH 24	SLP	SAIL	FBG		OB			7	3	3825	3		5350	6150
29	11	CHANCE 30.30 MORC		SAIL	FBG		IB	27D	PALM	10		11200	5	3	21600	24000
30	6	SEAWIND	KTH	SAIL	FBG		IB	27D	PALM	9	3	12080	4	2	23500	26100
30	7	CHANCE 30.30 CCA		SAIL	FBG		IB	27D	PALM	10		11200	5	3	21800	24200
33		LUDERS	SLP	SAIL	FBG		IB	27D	PALM	10		12800	5		25200	28000
34	6	SEABREEZE 35	SLP	SAIL	FBG		IB	27D	PALM	10	3	13000	3	10	26000	28900
34	6	SEABREEZE 35	YWL	SAIL	FBG		IB	27D	PALM	10	3	13000	3	10	26000	28900
39	10	ALLIED 39		SAIL	FBG		IB	27D	PALM	10	3	17000	5	10	40300	44700
41	1	X-L-2	SLP	SAIL	FBG		IB	37D	PERK	11	6	19000	4	2	46100	50700
41	1	X-L-2	YWL	SAIL	FBG		IB	37D	PERK	11	6	19000	4	2	46100	50700
		1970 BOATS														
24	3	GREENWICH 24	SLP	SAIL	FBG	KL	OB			7	3	3825	3		5250	6000
30	6	SEAWIND 30	SLP	SAIL	FBG	KL	IB	18D	ALBN	9	3	12080	4	4	22900	25400
30	6	SEAWIND 30	KTH	SAIL	FBG	KL	IB	18D	ALBN	9	3	12080	4	4	22900	25400
33		LUDERS	SLP	SAIL	FBG	KL	IB	22D	PALM	10		12800	5	4	24600	27300
34	6	SEABREEZE 35	SLP	SAIL	FBG	KC	IB	22D	PALM	10	3	13600	3	10	26500	29400
34	6	SEABREEZE 35	YWL	SAIL	FBG	KC	IB	22D	PALM	10	3	13600	3	10	26500	29400
39	6	ALLIED 39	SLP	SAIL	FBG	KL	IB	22D	PALM	10		18200	5	10	40300	44800
39	6	ALLIED 39	YWL	SAIL	FBG	KL	IB	22D	PALM	10		18200	5	10	40300	44800
41	6	X-L-2	SLP	SAIL	FBG	KC	IB	37D	PERK	11	6	20400	4	2	47900	52600
41	6	X-L-2	YWL	SAIL	FBG	KC	IB	37D	PERK	11	6	20400	4	2	47900	52600
		1969 BOATS														
24	3	GREENWICH 24	SLP	SAIL	FBG	KL	OB			7	3	3825	3		5100	5900
30	6	SEAWIND 30	SLP	SAIL	FBG	KL	IB	18D	ALBN	9	3	12080	4	4	22400	24900
30	6	SEAWIND 30	KTH	SAIL	FBG	KL	IB	18D	ALBN	9	3	12080	4	4	22400	24900
33		LUDERS	SLP	SAIL	FBG	KL	IB	22D	PALM	10		12800	5		24000	26700
34	6	SEABREEZE 35	SLP	SAIL	FBG	KC	IB	22D	PALM	10	3	13600	7		25900	28800
34	6	SEABREEZE 35	YWL	SAIL	FBG	KC	IB	22D	PALM	10	3	13600	7		25900	28800
41	6	X-L-2	SLP	SAIL	FBG	KC	IB	37D	WEST	11	3	17500	4	2	42400	47100
41	6	X-L-2	YWL	SAIL	FBG	KC	IB	37D	WEST	11	3	17500	4	2	42400	47100
		1968 BOATS														
24	3	GREENWICH 24	SLP	SAIL	FBG	KL	OB			7	3	3825	3		5000	5750
30	6	SEAWIND	SLP	SAIL	FBG	KL	IB	18D		9	3	12080	4	4	21900	24400
30	6	SEAWIND	KTH	SAIL	FBG	KL	IB	18D		9	3	12080	4	4	21900	24400
33		LUDERS	SLP	SAIL	FBG	KL	IB	22D		10		12800	5		23500	26200
34	6	SEABREEZE	SLP	SAIL	FBG	KC	IB	22D		10	3	13600	3	10	25400	28200
34	6	SEABREEZE	YWL	SAIL	FBG	KC	IB	22D		10	3	13600	3	10	25400	28200
		1967 BOATS														
30	6	SEAWIND	SLP	SAIL	FBG		IB	30D							21500	23900
30	6	SEAWIND	KTH	SAIL	FBG		IB	30D							21500	23900
30	6	SEAWIND 30	SLP	SAIL	FBG		IB	25D				12080			21500	23900
30	6	SEAWIND 30	KTH	SAIL	FBG		IB	25D				12080			21500	23900
33		LUDERS	SLP	SAIL	FBG		IB	30D							27100	30100
33		LUDERS 33	SLP	SAIL	FBG		IB	25D				12800			23100	25700
34	6	SEABREEZE	SLP	SAIL	FBG		IB	30D							28400	31600
34	6	SEABREEZE	YWL	SAIL	FBG		IB	30D							28400	31600
34	6	SEABREEZE 34	SLP	SAIL	FBG		IB	25D				13600			24900	27700
34	6	SEABREEZE 34	YWL	SAIL	FBG		IB	25D				13600			24900	27700
		1966 BOATS														
30	6	SEAWIND	SLP	SAIL	FBG	KL	IB	25D- 30D		9	3				21200	23500
30	6	SEAWIND	KTH	SAIL	FBG	KL	IB	25D- 30D		9	3		4	4	21200	23500
33		LUDERS	SLP	SAIL	FBG	KL	IB	25D- 40D		9	11		5		26700	29600
34	6	SEABREEZE	SLP	SAIL	FBG	KC	IB	40D		10	3		3	10	28000	31100
34	6	SEABREEZE	SLP	SAIL	FBG	KL	IB	25D		10	3		3	10	27900	31000
34	6	SEABREEZE	YWL	SAIL	FBG	KC	IB	25D- 40D		10	3		3	10	27900	31100
		1965 BOATS														
30	6	SEAWIND	SLP	SAIL	FBG		IB	25D- 30D		9	3		4	4	20900	23200
30	6	SEAWIND	KTH	SAIL	FBG		IB	25D- 30D							20900	23200
34	6	SEABREEZE 35	SLP	SAIL	FBG		IB	25D- 30D							27500	30600
34	6	SEABREEZE 35	YWL	SAIL	FBG		IB	25D- 30D		10	3		3	10	27500	30600
		1964 BOATS														
30	6	SEAWIND	KTH	SAIL	FBG		IB	25D		9	3		4	4	20600	22900
34	6	SEABREEZE	SLP	SAIL	FBG		IB	25D		10	3		3	10	27200	30200
34	6	SEABREEZE	YWL	SAIL	FBG		IB	25D		10	3		3	10	27200	30200
		1963 BOATS														
30	6	SEAWIND	SLP	SAIL	FBG		IB	30D							20400	22700
		1962 BOATS														
30	6	SEAWIND	SLP	SAIL	FBG		IB	30D							20200	22500

ALLIED MARINE

MIAMI FL 33125

See inside cover to adjust price for area

LOA FT	LOA IN	NAME AND/ OR MODEL	TOP/ RIG	BOAT TYPE	-HULL- MTL	-HULL- TP	ENGINE TP	ENGINE # HP	ENGINE MFG	BEAM FT	BEAM IN	WGT LBS	DRAFT FT	DRAFT IN	RETAIL LOW	RETAIL HIGH
		1969 BOATS														
46		CUSTOM		SF	WD	SV	IB	T255D	GM	15			3	8	149500	164000
52	6	CUSTOM		SF	WD	SV	IB	T370D	CUM	16	4		3	3	216500	238000
60		CUSTOM		SF	WD	SV	IB	T461D	GM	16	6		3	6	294000	323000

ALLISON BOATS INC

COAST GUARD MFG ID- ALT

Call 1-800-327-6929 for BUC Personalized Evaluation Service
Or, for 1982 to 2009 boats, sign onto www.BUCValuPro.com

ALLMAND BOATS

JOHN ALLMAND
MIAMI FL 33157   COAST GUARD MFG ID- JAB   See inside cover to adjust price for area

For more recent years, see the BUC Used Boat Price Guide, Volume 1 or Volume 2

```
 LOA   NAME AND/           TOP/ BOAT  -HULL- ----ENGINE---   BEAM   WGT  DRAFT  RETAIL RETAIL
FT IN  OR MODEL            RIG  TYPE  MTL TP TP # HP  MFG    FT IN  LBS  FT IN   LOW   HIGH
------------------------- 1983 BOATS ------------------------------------------------------
30  9 ALLMAND 312          SLP SA/CR FBG KL IB   D    11 4 12850  4        23700 26300
30  9 ALLMAND SAIL 31      SLP SA/CR FBG KL IB   D    11 4 11100  3 10     20400 22700
30  9 ALLMAND TRI-CAB 31   SLP SA/CR FBG KL IB   D    11 4 13000  4        24000 26600
34  9 ALLMAND 35 PH        SLP SA/CR FBG KL IB               12000  4 11   22300 24800
34  9 ALLMAND RAISED CAB   SLP SA/CR FBG KL IB   D    11 8 15500  5  2     28300 31500
34  9 ALLMAND TRI-CAB 35   SLP SA/CR FBG KL IB   D    11 8 15100  5  2     27700 30700
------------------------- 1982 BOATS ------------------------------------------------------
30  9 ALLMAND SAIL 31      SLP SA/CR FBG KL IB  16D UNIV 11 4 11100 3 10   19200 21300
34  9 ALLMAND 35 PH        SLP SA/CR FBG KL IB  24D   11 8 12000  4 11     21000 23300
------------------------- 1981 BOATS ------------------------------------------------------
25  9 FREEDOM 26           OP  EXP  FBG SV OB           9 9  4900  2  3    12000 13600
25  9 FREEDOM 26           OP  EXP  FBG SV IO  225 VLVO 9 9  4900  2  3     6150  7100
      IB  225  COMM  7150  8200, IO  228  MRCR  6100  7000, IB 228-255      7150  8300
      IO  260        6250  7300, IO 130D-155D   6550  7800, IO T145  VLVO   6700  7700
      IO T170  MRCR  6700  7700, IB T170-T228   7850  9450

25  9 FREEDOM 26           HT  EXP  FBG SV OB           9 9  4900  2  3    12000 13600
25  9 FREEDOM 26           HT  EXP  FBG SV IO  225 VLVO 9 9  4900  2  3     6150  7100
      IB  225  COMM  7150  8200, IO  228  MRCR  6100  7000, IB 228-255      7150  8300
      IO  260        6250  7300, IO 130D-155D   6550  7800, IO T145  VLVO   6700  7700
      IO T170  MRCR  6700  7700, IB T170-T228   7850  9450

25  9 FREEDOM 26           FB  EXP  FBG SV OB           9 9  4900  2  3    12000 13600
25  9 FREEDOM 26           FB  EXP  FBG SV IO  225 VLVO 9 9  4900  2  3     6150  7100
      IB  225  COMM  7150  8200, IO  228  MRCR  6100  7000, IB 228-255      7150  8300
      IO  260        6250  7300, IO 130D-155D   6550  7800, IO T145  VLVO   6700  7700
      IO T170  MRCR  6700  7700, IB T170-T228   7850  9450

25  9 FREEDOM 26 OSF       OP  SF   FBG SV OB           9 9  4900  2  3    12000 13600
25  9 FREEDOM 26 OSF       OP  SF   FBG SV IO  225 VLVO 9 9  4900  2  3     7000  8050
      IB  225  COMM  7100  8200, IO  228  MRCR  6900  7950, IB 228-255      7150  8300
      IO  260        7100  8300, IO 124D  VLVO  8400  9650, IO 130D-155D    8150  9700
      IB 200D  PERK  9950 11300, IO T145  VLVO  7650  8750, IO T170  MRCR   7600  8750
      IB T170-T228   7850  9400, IB T124D VLVO 10700 12200

25  9 FREEDOM 26 OSF       HT  SF   FBG SV OB           9 9  4900  2  3    12000 13600
25  9 FREEDOM 26 OSF       HT  SF   FBG SV IO  225 VLVO 9 9  4900  2  3     7000  8050
      IB  225  COMM  7100  8150, IO  228  MRCR  6900  7950, IB 228-255      7100  8300
      IO  260        7100  8300, IO 124D  VLVO  8400  9650, IO 130D-155D    8150  9700
      IB 200D  PERK  9900 11300, IO T145  VLVO  7600  8750, IO T170  MRCR   7600  8750
      IB T170-T228   7800  9400, IB T124D VLVO 10700 12200

28    RANGER 28                EXP  FBG SV OB              11              14900 16900
28    RANGER 28            ST  EXP  FBG SV IB  T225 COMM 11   8000  2  6   16100 18300
28    RANGER 28            HT  EXP  FBG SV IB  T225 COMM 11   8000  2  6   16100 18300
28    RANGER 28            FB  EXP  FBG SV IB  T225 COMM 11   8000  2  6   16100 18300
28    RANGER 28            FB  SF   FBG SV IB  T225 COMM 11   8000  2  6   16100 18300
30  9 ALLMAND SAIL 31      SLP SA/CR FBG KL IB 16D- 24D 11 4 11100  3 10   19000 21100
30  9 ALLMAND SAIL 31      SLP SA/RC FBG KL IB 16D- 24D 11 4 11100  3 10   19200 21300
30  9 ALLMAND SAIL 31/II   SLP SA/CR FBG KL IB 15D- 24D 11 4 11100  3 10   18300 20300
30  9 ALLMAND SAIL 31/II   SLP SA/RC FBG KL IB 15D- 24D 11 4 11100  3 10   18300 20300
34    CLASSIC 34           HT  SDN  FBG SV IB  T225 COMM 11  12000  2  8   30300 33600
34    CLASSIC 34           FB  SDN  FBG SV IB  T225 COMM 11  12000  2  8   30300 33600
34    CLASSIC 34           FB  SF   FBG SV IB  T225 COMM 11  12000  2  8   28700 31900

34    CLASSIC 34 DELUXE    HT  SDN  FBG SV IB  T225 COMM 11  12000  2  8   30300 33600
34    CLASSIC 34 DELUXE    FB  SDN  FBG SV IB  T225 COMM 11  12000  2  8   30300 33600
34  9 ALLMAND 35 PH        SLP SA/CR FBG KL IB 24D- 27D 11 4 12000  4 11   19300 22000
34  9 ALLMAND 35 PH        CUT SA/CR FBG KL IB 24D- 27D 11 4 12000  3 11   19300 21500
34  9 ALLMAND 35 PH SHOAL  SLP SA/CR FBG KL IB 24D UNIV 11 4 12000  3 11   20200 22400
34  9 ALLMAND 35 PH SHOAL  CUT SA/CR FBG KL IB 24D- 27D 11 4 12000  3 11   20200 22400
------------------------- 1980 BOATS ------------------------------------------------------
25  9 FREEDOM 26           OP  CUD  FBG SV IO  130D      9 9        2  3    6650  7600
25  9 FREEDOM 26           OP  EXP  FBG SV IO  130D      9 9        2  3    6650  6900
25  9 FREEDOM 26           OP  EXP  FBG SV IO  225 COMM  9 9  4900  2  3    6850  7850
25  9 FREEDOM 26           HT  EXP  FBG SV IO  225       9 9        2  3    6000  6900
25  9 FREEDOM 26           HT  EXP  FBG SV IO  225 COMM  9 9  4900  2  3    6850  7850
25  9 FREEDOM 26           HT  EXP  FBG SV IO  130D      9 9        2  3    6650  7650
25  9 FREEDOM 26           FB  EXP  FBG SV IO  225       9 9        2  3    6000  6900
25  9 FREEDOM 26           FB  EXP  FBG SV IO  225 COMM  9 9  4900  2  3    6850  7850
25  9 FREEDOM 26           FB  EXP  FBG SV IO  130D      9 9        2  3    6650  7650
25  9 OFF-SHORE FSH        OP  CUD  FBG SV OB            9 9  4300             11300 12900
25  9 OFF-SHORE FSH        OP  CUD  FBG SV IB  225       9 9  4600  2  3    5800  6650
25  9 OFF-SHORE FSH        OP  CUD  FBG SV IB  225 COMM  9 9  4600  2  3    6600  7600

25  9 OFF-SHORE FSH        OP  CUD  FBG SV IO  130D      9 9        2  3    6650  7600
28    RANGER 28            ST  EXP  FBG SV IB  225 COMM 11   8000  2  6   13800 15700
28    RANGER 28            HT  EXP  FBG SV IB  225 COMM 11   8000  2  6   13800 15700
28    RANGER 28            FB  EXP  FBG SV IB  225 COMM 11   8000  2  6   13800 15700
28    RANGER 28                SF   FBG SV OB             11             14600 16600
28    RANGER 28            FB       FBG SV IB  225 COMM 11   8000  2  6   13800 15700
28    RANGER 28            FB  SF   FBG SV IB  T225      11             15400 17500
30  9 ALLMAND SAIL 31      SLP SA/CR FBG KL IB   D    11 4 11100  3 10   17100 19400
30  9 ALLMAND SAIL 31      SLP SA/RC FBG KL IB   D    11 4 11100  3 10   17100 19400
34    CLASSIC 34           HT  SDN  FBG SV IB  T225 COMM 11  12000  2  8   29000 32200
34    CLASSIC 34           FB  SDN  FBG SV IB  T225 COMM 11  12000  2  8   29000 32200
34    CLASSIC 34           FB  SF   FBG SV IB  T225 COMM 11  12000  2  8   27500 30500

34    CLASSIC 34 DELUXE    HT  SDN  FBG SV IB  T225 COMM 11  12000  2  8   29000 32200
34    CLASSIC 34 DELUXE    FB  SDN  FBG SV IB  T225 COMM 11  12000  2  8   29000 32200
------------------------- 1979 BOATS ------------------------------------------------------
22  6 ALLMAND 22.5         SLP SAIL FBG CB                8     2700  1  3   3000  3500
22 10 CITATION CONVERTIBLE ST  CUD  FBG SV IO  225        8     3400  2  2   3800  4450
22 10 CITATION CONVERTIBLE ST  CUD  FBG SV IO  225        8     3400  2  2   4100  4800
22 10 CITATION HARDTOP     HT  CUD  FBG SV IO  225        8     3400  2  2   3800  4450
22 10 CITATION HARDTOP     HT  CUD  FBG SV IO  225        8     3400  2  2   4100  4800
22 10 FISHERMAN CUD        OP  CTRCN FBG SV IO 225        8     3400  2  2   4100  4800
22 10 TICONDEROGA          FB  CUD  FBG SV IO  225        8     3400  2  2   3800  4450
22 10 TICONDEROGA          FB  CUD  FBG SV IO  225        8     3400  2  2   4100  4800
22 10 WEEKENDER CUD        ST  WKNDR FBG SV IO 225        8     3400  2  2   3800  4450
23  9 ALLMAND 23           SLP SAIL FBG SK                8     3090  1  4   3550  4100
23  9 ALLMAND AMS 23       CUT MS   FBG CB IB             8     3600  1  4   4000  4650
23  9 ALLMAND AMS 23       CUT MS   FBG CB IB   D         8     3600  1  4   4550  5250

25  9 FREEDOM 26 EXP       OP  EXP  FBG SV IO  225 VLVO 9 9  4900  2  3    6100  7000
      IB  225  COMM  6550  7500, IO T140-T170 6600 7600, IB T225  COMM     7500  8650
25  9 FREEDOM 26 EXP       HT  EXP  FBG SV IO  225 VLVO 9 9  4900  2  3    6100  7000
      IB  225  COMM  6550  7550, IO T140-T170 6600 7600, IB T225  COMM     7500  8650
25  9 FREEDOM 26 EXP       FB  EXP  FBG SV IO  225 VLVO 9 9  4900  2  3    6100  7000
      IB  225  COMM  6550  7550, IO T140-T170 6600 7600, IB T225  COMM     7500  8650
25  9 OFF-SHORE FSH        OP  CUD  FBG SV IB  200 CHRY 9 9  4600  2  3    6200  7150
      IO  225  VLVO  5850  6750, IB 225  COMM  6300  7250, IO T140-T170     6400  7350
      IB T225  COMM  7350  8450

28    RANGER 28 EXP        ST  EXP  FBG SV IB  T225-T255 11  8000  2  6   14800 17100
28    RANGER 28 EXP        ST  EXP  FBG SV IB  T200D CHRY 11 8000  2  6   21700 24100
28    RANGER 28 EXP        HT  EXP  FBG SV IB  T225-T255 11  8000  2  6   14800 17100
28    RANGER 28 EXP        HT  EXP  FBG SV IB  T200D CHRY 11 8000  2  6   21700 24100
28    RANGER 28 EXP        FB  EXP  FBG SV IB  T225-T255 11  8000  2  6   14800 17100
28    RANGER 28 EXP        FB  EXP  FBG SV IB  T200D CHRY 11 8000  2  6   21700 24100
28    RANGER 28 EXP        FB  SF   FBG SV IB  T225-T255 11  8000  2  6   14800 17100
28    RANGER 28 EXP        FB  SF   FBG SV IB  T200D CHRY 11 8000  2  6   21800 24200
30  9 ALLMAND SAIL 31      SLP SA/CR FBG KL IB 16D REN 11 4 11100  3 10   16400 18600
30  9 ALLMAND SAIL 31      SLP SA/RC FBG KL IB 16D REN 11 4 11100  3 10   16400 18600
34    CLASSIC 34           HT  SDN  FBG SV IB  T225-T330 11 12000  2  8   27100 30100
34    CLASSIC 34           HT  SDN  FBG SV IBT200D-T210D 11 12000  2  8   36100 40500

34    CLASSIC 34           FB  SDN  FBG SV IB  T225-T330 11 12000  2  8   27200 32100
34    CLASSIC 34           FB  SDN  FBG SV IBT200D-T210D 11 12000  2  8   36100 40500
34    CLASSIC 34           HT  SDN  FBG SV IB  T225-T330 11 12000  2  8   26400 30700
34    CLASSIC 34           HT  SDN  FBG SV IBT200D-T210D 11 12000  2  8   33600 37600
34    CLASSIC 34           FB  SDN  FBG SV IB  T225-T330 11 12000  2  8   26400 30700
34    CLASSIC 34           FB  SDN  FBG SV IBT200D-T210D 11 12000  2  8   33600 37600
34    CLASSIC 34 DLX       HT  SDN  FBG SV IB  T225-T330 11 12000  2  8   33500 37200
34    CLASSIC 34 DLX       HT  SDN  FBG SV IBT200D-T210D 11 12000  2  8   37200 41700
34    CLASSIC 34 DLX       FB  SDN  FBG SV IB  T225-T330 11 12000  2  8   28400 33400
34    CLASSIC 34 DLX       FB  SDN  FBG SV IBT200D-T210D 11 12000  2  8   37200 41700
------------------------- 1978 BOATS ------------------------------------------------------
22 10 CITATION CONVERTIBLE ST  CUD  FBG SV IO  170 MRCR  8  3400  2  2    3800  4400
      IO  225  COMM  3800  4400, IB 225  COMM  3950  4600, IO 228  MRCR    3850  4500
      IO T120-T140   4250  5200
22 10 CITATION HARDTOP     HT  CUD  FBG SV IO  170 MRCR  8  3400  2  2    3800  4400
      IO  225  COMM  3800  4400, IB 225  COMM  3950  4600, IO 228  MRCR    3850  4500
      IO T120-T140   4250  5200
22 10 FISHERMAN            OP  CTRCN FBG SV IO 225        8  3400  2  2    4050  4750
```

```
ALLMAND BOATS            -CONTINUED    See inside cover to adjust price for area
  LOA  NAME AND/            TOP/ BOAT -HULL- ----ENGINE--- BEAM  WGT  DRAFT RETAIL RETAIL
  FT IN  OR MODEL           RIG  TYPE MTL TP TP # HP MFG   FT IN  LBS  FT IN  LOW   HIGH
-------------------- 1978 BOATS ----------------------------------------------------------
 22 10 FISHERMAN           OP  CTRCN FBG SV IB  225        8      3400  2  2  3950  4600
 22 10 TICONDEROGA         FB  CUD   FBG SV IO  170  MRCR  8      3400  2  2  3800  4400
       IO  225  COMM  3800 4400, IB  225  COMM  3950  4600, IO 228  MRCR  3850  4500
       IO T120-T140  4250 5200'

 22 10 WEEKENDER           ST  WKNDR FBG SV IO 170-228     8      3400  2  2  3800  4500
 23    ALLMAND 22.5        SLP SAIL  FBG CB IB   12        8      2700  1  2  3200  3700
 24    ALLMAND 24          SLP SAIL  FBG CB IB   12        8      3090  1  2  3650  4250
 24    ALLMAND HMS         CUT SAIL  FBG CB IB   12        8      3360  1  4  3900  4550
 25  9 FREEDOM EXPRESS     OP  EXP   FBG SV IO  225  COMM  9   9  4900  2  3  6000  6900
       IB  225  COMM  6300 7200, IO T140-T170  6650  7650, IB T225  COMM  7200  8300

 25  9 FREEDOM EXPRESS     HT  EXP   FBG SV IO  225  COMM  9   9  4900  2  3  6000  6900
       IB  225  COMM  6300 7200, IO T140-T170  6650  7650, IB T225  COMM  7200  8300

 25  9 FREEDOM FLYBRIDGE   FB  EXP   FBG SV IO  225  COMM  9   9  4900  2  3  6000  6900
       IB  225  COMM  6300 7200, IO T140-T170  6650  7650, IB T225  COMM  7200  8300

 28    RANGER 28           ST  EXP   FBG SV IB T225-T255  11      8000  2  6 13800 16400
 28    RANGER 28           HT  EXP   FBG SV IB T225-T255  11      8000  2  6 13800 16400
 28    RANGER 28           FB  EXP   FBG SV IB T225-T255  11      8000  2  6 13800 16400
 28    RANGER 28           FB  SF    FBG SV IB T225-T255  11      8000  2  6 14200 16400
 28    RANGER 28 DELUXE    ST  EXP   FBG SV IB T225-T255  11      8000  2  6 14500 17200
 28    RANGER 28 DELUXE    HT  EXP   FBG SV IB T225-T255  11      8000  2  6 14500 17200
 28    RANGER 28 DELUXE    FB  EXP   FBG SV IB T225-T255  11      8000  2  6 14500 17100
 30    ALLMAND 30          SLP SAIL  FBG KL IB   30        11  4  9800  4  1 13800 15700
 34    CLASSIC 34          HT  SDN   FBG SV IB T225-T330  11     12000  2  8 26000 30700
 34    CLASSIC 34          HT  SDN   FBG SV IBT200D-T210D 11     12000  2  8 34700 39000
 34    CLASSIC 34          FB  SDN   FBG SV IB T225-T330  11     12000  2  8 26100 30800
 34    CLASSIC 34          FB  SDN   FBG SV IBT200D-T210D 11     12000  2  8 34800 39000

 34    CLASSIC 34          HT  SF    FBG SV IB T225-T330  11     12000  2  8 25300 29500
 34    CLASSIC 34          HT  SF    FBG SV IBT200D-T210D 11     12000  2  8 32300 36200
 34    CLASSIC 34          FB  SF    FBG SV IB T225-T330  11     12000  2  8 25300 29500
 34    CLASSIC 34          FB  SF    FBG SV IBT200D-T210D 11     12000  2  8 32300 36200
 34    CLASSIC 34 DELUXE   HT  SDN   FBG SV IB T225-T330  11     12000  2  8 27300 32100
 34    CLASSIC 34 DELUXE   HT  SDN   FBG SV IBT200D-T210D 11     12000  2  8 35800 40100
 34    CLASSIC 34 DELUXE   FB  SDN   FBG SV IB T225-T330  11     12000  2  8 27300 32100
 34    CLASSIC 34 DELUXE   FB  SDN   FBG SV IBT200D-T210D 11     12000  2  8 35800 40100
-------------------- 1977 BOATS ----------------------------------------------------------
 22 10 CENTER CONSOLE      OP  FSH   FBG SV IB  225  COMM  8      3400  2  2  3800  4450
 22 10 CITATION CONVERTIBLE ST CUD   FBG SV IO 165-190     8      3400  2  2  3850  4600
       IO  225  COMM  3850 4500, IB  225  COMM  3800  4400, IO  255  COMM  3950  4550
       IO T130-T140  4600 5300'

 22 10 CITATION HARDTOP    HT  CUD   FBG SV IO 165-190     8      3400  2  2  3850  4600
       IO  225  COMM  3850 4500, IB  225  COMM  3800  4400, IO  255  COMM  3950  4550
       IO T130-T140  4600 5300'

 22 10 STINGER-WASP        OP  RNBT  FBG SV OB        8           3400  2  2  8100  9300
 22 10 STINGER-WASP        OP  RNBT  FBG SV IO 130-165     8      3400  2  2  3700  4300
 22 10 TICONDEROGA         FB  CUD   FBG SV IO 165-190     8      3400  2  2  3850  4600
       IO  225  COMM  3850 4500, IB  225  COMM  3800  4400, IO  255  COMM  3950  4550
       IO T130-T140  4600 5300'

 22 10 WEEKENDER           ST  WKNDR FBG SV IO 188-190     8      3400  2  2  3850  4500
 25  9 FREEDOM EXPRESS     OP  EXP   FBG SV IO  225  COMM  9   9  4900  2  3  6100  7000
       IB  225  COMM  6000 6900, IO T225  COMM  7000  8050, IB T225  COMM  6900  7950

 25  9 FREEDOM FLYBRIDGE   FB  EXP   FBG SV IO  225  COMM  9   9  4900  2  3  6100  7000
       IB  225  COMM  6050 6950, IO T225  COMM  7000  8050, IB T225  COMM  6900  7950

 28    RANGER 28           ST  EXP   FBG SV IB T225-T255  11      8000  2  6 13200 15300
 28    RANGER 28           HT  EXP   FBG SV IB T225-T255  11      8000  2  6 13200 15300
 28    RANGER 28           FB  EXP   FBG SV IB T225-T255  11      8000  2  6 13200 15300
 28    RANGER 28           FB  SF    FBG SV IB T225-T255  11      8000  2  6 13200 15300
 28    RANGER 28 DELUXE    ST  EXP   FBG SV IB T225-T255  11      8000  2  6 14000 16200
 28    RANGER 28 DELUXE    HT  EXP   FBG SV IB T225-T255  11      8000  2  6 14000 16200
 28    RANGER 28 DELUXE    FB  EXP   FBG SV IB T225-T255  11      8000  2  6 14000 16200
 28    RANGER 28 DELUXE    FB  SF    FBG SV IB T225-T255  11      8000  2  6 14000 16200
 34    CLASSIC 34          HT  SDN   FBG SV IB T225-T255  11      8000  2  6 23000 26100
 34    CLASSIC 34          HT  SF    FBG SV IB T225-T255  11      8000  2  6 20700 23400
 34    CLASSIC 34          FB  SF    FBG SV IB T225-T255  11      8000  2  6 20700 23400
 34    CLASSIC 34 DELUXE   HT  SDN   FBG SV IB T225-T255  11      8000  2  6 24200 27400

 34    CLASSIC 34A         FB  SDN   FBG SV IB T225-T255  11      8000  2  6 23200 26300
 34    CLASSIC 34A DELUXE  FB  SDN   FBG SV IB T225-T255  11      8000  2  6 24300 27600
 34    CLASSIC 34B         FB  SDN   FBG SV IB T225-T255  11      8000  2  6 22900 26000
 34    CLASSIC 34B DELUXE  FB  SDN   FBG SV IB T225-T255  11      8000  2  6 24000 27200
-------------------- 1976 BOATS ----------------------------------------------------------
 22 10 CITATION CONVERTIBLE OP CUD   FBG SV IO 165-190     8      3900  2  2  4400  5200
       IB  225  FORD  4000 4650, IO 233-235     4500  5150, IO T120-T140  4900  5850

 22 10 CITATION HARDTOP    HT  CUD   FBG SV IO 165-235     8      3900  2  2  4400  5200
 22 10 CITATION HARDTOP    HT  CUD   FBG SV IO T120-T140   8      3600  2  6  4900  5850
 22 10 FISHERMAN-CTR CONSOL OP CUD   FBG SV IB  225  FORD  8      3900  2  2  4050  4700
 22 10 STINGER HORNET      FB  FSH   FBG SV IO 188-235     8      3600  2  6  4400  5150
 22 10 STINGER HORNET      FB  FSH   FBG SV IO T120-T140   8      3600  2  6  4900  5900
 22 10 STINGER WASP        OP  RNBT  FBG SV IO 130-165     8      3200  2  6  3650  4250
 22 10 STINGER-HORNET      FB  FSH   FBG SV OB        8           3600  2  6  7200  8300
 22 10 STINGER-WASP        OP  RNBT  FBG SV OB        8           3200  2  6  6700  8300
 22 10 TICONDEROGA         FB  CUD   FBG SV IO 165-235     8      3900  2  2  4400  5200
 22 10 TICONDEROGA         FB  CUD   FBG SV IO T120-T140   8      3900  2  2  4900  5850
 22 10 WEEKENDER           HT  WKNDR FBG SV IO 165-235     8      3900  2  2  4400  5200
 22 10 WEEKENDER           HT  WKNDR FBG SV IO T120-T140   8      3900  2  2  4900  5850

 25  9 FREEDOM 26          OP  EXP   FBG SV IO 188-190     9   9  4900  2  8  6150  7050
       IB  225  FORD  5800 6650, IO T130  VLVO  6850  7900, IB T130  VLVO  6150  7050
       IO T140        6750 7750'

 28    RANGER 28           ST  EXP   FBG SV IB T225-T350  11      8000  2  6 12700 15800
 28    RANGER 28           HT  EXP   FBG SV IB T225-T350  11      8000  2  6 12700 15800
 28    RANGER 28           FB  EXP   FBG SV IB T225-T350  11      8000  2  6 12700 15900
 28    RANGER 28           FB  SF    FBG SV IB T225-T350  11      8000  2  6 12700 15900
 28    RANGER 28 DELUXE    ST  EXP   FBG SV IB T225-T350  11      8000  2  6 13400 16600
 28    RANGER 28 DELUXE    HT  EXP   FBG SV IB T225-T350  11      8000  2  6 13400 16600
 28    RANGER 28 DELUXE    FB  EXP   FBG SV IB T225-T350  11      8000  2  6 13400 16600
 34    CLASSIC 34          HT  SDN   FBG SV IB T225-T350  11     12000  2  8 24300 29000
 34    CLASSIC 34          HT  SF    FBG SV IB T225-T350  11     12000  2  8 23300 27400
 34    CLASSIC 34 A        FB  SDN   FBG SV IB T225-T350  11     12000  2  8 24500 29200
 34    CLASSIC 34 B        FB  SDN   FBG SV IB T225-T350  11     12000  2  8 24200 28900

 34    CLASSIC 34 B        FB  SF    FBG SV IB T225-T350  11     12000  2  8 23300 27400
 34    CLASSIC 34 DELUXE   HT  SDN   FBG SV IB T225-T350  11     12000  2  8 24800 29600
 34    CLASSIC 34 DELUXE A FB  SDN   FBG SV IB T225-T350  11     12000  2  8 25000 29800
-------------------- 1975 BOATS ----------------------------------------------------------
 22 10 CENTER CONSOLE FSH  OP  CUD   FBG SV IB  233  MRCR  8      3500  2  2  3550  4150
 22 10 CITATION CONV       OP  CUD   FBG SV IO 120-225     8      3400  2  2  4050  4800
       IO  233  MRCR  4150 4850, IO 233-235     3500  4200, IO  255  MRCR  4250  4950
       IO T120-T165  4600 5600'

 22 10 CITATION HARDTOP    HT  CUD   FBG SV IO 120-225     8      3400  2  2  4050  4800
       IO  233  MRCR  4150 4850, IB 233-235     3500  4200, IO  255  MRCR  4250  4950
       IO T120-T165  4600 5600'

 22 10 TICONDEROGA         FB  CUD   FBG SV IO 120-225     8      3400  2  2  4050  4800
       IO  233  MRCR  4150 4850, IB 233-235     3500  4200, IO  255  MRCR  4250  4950
       IO T120-T165  4600 5600'

 28    RANGER 300 A        FB  SF    FBG SV IB T233-T350  11      8000  2  6 12300 15300
 28    RANGER 300 A TWIN ST FB SF    FBG SV IB T233-T350  11      8000  2  6 12900 15900
 28    RANGER 300 EXPRESS  HT  EXP   FBG SV IB T233-T350  11      8000  2  6 12600 15600
 28    RANGER 300 FLYBRIDGE FB SF    FBG SV IB T233-T350  11      8000  2  6 12600 15600
 28    RANGER 300 HARDTOP  HT  SDN   FBG SV IB T233-T350  11      8000  2  6 13800 16400
 34    FB LESS PILOT HOUSE FB  SF    FBG SV IB T233-T350  11      8000  2  8 19200 22800
 34    FB SEDAN A          FB  EXP   FBG SV IB T233-T350  11      8000  2  8 22900 27300
 34    FB SEDAN B          FB  EXP   FBG SV IB T233-T350  11      8000  2  8 22600 26800
 34    HARDTOP SEDAN A     HT  SDN   FBG SV IB T233-T350  11      8000  2  8 21900 25200
-------------------- 1974 BOATS ----------------------------------------------------------
 22 10 CITATION            HT  CUD   FBG   IO 120-188      8      4000  2  2  4700  5500
       IO  225  MRCR  4850 5550, IO 225  OMC   4800  5550, IB  225  MRCR  3350  3900
       IO T120-T165  5250 6350'

 22 10 CITATION CONV       OP  CUD   FBG   IO 120-188      8      3800  2  2  4550  5300
       IO  225  MRCR  4700 5400, IO 225  OMC   4650  5350, IB  225  MRCR  3350  3900
       IO T120-T165  5100 6150'

 22 10 SARATOGA 23         CR  RNBT  FBG SV IO 120         8      3000  2    4200  4850
 22 10 STINGER 23          OP  RNBT  FBG SV IO 120         8      3000  2    3600  4300
       IO  225  OMC   3700 4300, IB  225  MRCR  3100  3600, IO T120-T140  4150  5100

 22 10 TICONDEROGA         FB.       FBG   IO 120-188      8      4000  2  2  4500  5250
       IO  225  MRCR  4600 5300, IO 225  OMC   4600  5300, IB  225  MRCR  3350  3900
       IO T120-T165  5000 6050'


 96th ed. - Vol. III              CONTINUED ON NEXT PAGE                            15
```

LOA FT	IN	NAME AND/ OR MODEL	TOP/ RIG	BOAT TYPE	-HULL- MTL	TP	TP	ENGINE # HP	MFG	BEAM FT	IN	WGT LBS	DRAFT FT	IN	RETAIL LOW	RETAIL HIGH
		1974 BOATS														
28		RANGER 300	OP	EXP	FBG		IB	350		11		8000	2	6	11500	13000
28		RANGER 300	OP	EXP	FBG		IB	T225-T325		11		8000	2	6	12000	14700
28		RANGER 300	HT	EXP	FBG		IB	350		11		8000	2	6	11500	13000
28		RANGER 300	HT	EXP	FBG		IB	T225-T325		11		8000	2	6	12000	14700
28		RANGER 300	FB	EXP	FBG		IB	350		11		8000	2	6	11500	13000
28		RANGER 300	FB	EXP	FBG		IB	T225-T325		11		8000	2	6	12000	14700
28		RANGER 300 A	FB	SF	FBG		IB	350		11		8000	2	6	11500	13100
28		RANGER 300 A	FB	SF	FBG		IB	T225-T325		11		8000	2	6	12200	14700
28		RANGER 300 B	FB	SF	FBG		IB	350		11		8000	2	6	11500	13100
28		RANGER 300 B	FB	SF	FBG		IB	T225-T325		11		8000	2	6	12200	14700
28		RANGER 300 B TWIN		SF	FBG		IB	350		11		8000	2	6	11500	13000
28		RANGER 300 B TWIN		SF	FBG		IB	T225-T330		11		8000	2	6	12000	14700
34		ALLMAND	FB	SF	FBG		IB	350		11		8000	2	0	17500	19900
34		ALLMAND	FB	SF	FBG		IB	T225-T330		11		8000	2	8	18500	21600
34		ALLMAND 34	HT	SDN	FBG		IB	350		11		8000	2	8	20100	22300
34		ALLMAND 34	HT	SDN	FBG		IB	T225-T330		11		8000	2	8	20900	24100
34		ALLMAND A	FB	SDN	FBG		IB	350		11		8000	2	8	20100	22300
34		ALLMAND A	FB	SDN	FBG		IB	T225-T330		11		8000	2	8	21300	24200
34		ALLMAND B	FB	SDN	FBG		IB	350		11		8000	2	8	20100	22300
34		ALLMAND B	FB	SDN	FBG		IB	T225-T330		11		8000	2	8	21000	23900
		1973 BOATS														
19		NOVA	OP	SKI	FBG	SV	IO	245		8		3000	3		2950	3400
19	3	FISHERMAN 19		RNBT	FBG	SV	OB			8		2000			4200	4850
22	10	CITATION	HT	CUD	FBG		IO	120-188		8		4000	2	2	4850	5650
		IO 225 OMC 4950 5700, IB 225 MRCR 3600 4200, IO T130 VLVO													5750	6600
22	10	CITATION CONV	OP	CUD	FBG		IO	140-188		8		3800	2	2	4700	5450
		IO 225 MRCR 4800 5550, IO 225 OMC 4800 5500, IB 225 MRCR													3500	4050
		IO T120-T130 5250 6350														
22	10	SARATOGA			FBG		IO	165-225		8		4000	2	2	4650	5450
22	10	STINGER 23	OP	RNBT	FBG		IO	120-188		8		3000	2		3750	4400
		IO 225 MRCR 3850 4500, IO 225 OMC 3850 4450, IB 225 MRCR													3000	3500
22	10	TICONDEROGA	FB		FBG		IO	120-188		8		4000	2	2	4650	5400
		IO 225 OMC 4700 5450, IB 225 MRCR 3650 4200, IO T120-T140													5150	6250
25		ALLMAND 25	OP	CNV	FBG	SV	IO	T165		8		4000	2	8	7400	8550
25		ALLMAND 25	HT	CR	FBG	SV	IO	T165		8		4000	2	8	6250	7200
28		RANGER 300		EXP	FBG		IB	T225-T255		11		8000	2	6	11500	13400
28		RANGER 300	HT	EXP	FBG		IB	T225-T255		11		8000	2	6	11500	13400
28		RANGER 300	FB	EXP	FBG		IB	T225-T255		11		8000	2	6	11500	13400
28		RANGER 300 A	FB	SF	FBG		IB	T225-T255		11		8000	2	6	11700	13400
28		RANGER 300 B	FB	SF	FBG		IB	T225-T330		11		8000	2	6	11600	14100
28		RANGER 300 B TWIN	FB	SF	FBG		IB	T225-T325		11		8000	2	6	11800	14100
34		ALLMAND	FB	SF	FBG		IB	T225-T280		11		8000	2	8	17400	20400
34		ALLMAND 34	HT	SDN	FBG		IB	T225-T255		11		8000	2	8	20100	22800
34		ALLMAND A	FB	SDN	FBG		IB	T225-T330		11		8000	2	8	20400	23100
34		ALLMAND B	FB	SDN	FBG		IB	T225-T280		11		8000	2	8	20100	22700
		1972 BOATS														
19		SUPER-NOVA			FBG		IO	245	OMC	8		3000	3		3050	3550
22	10	CITATION CONV CUSTOM	OP	CUD	FBG		IO	130-225		8		3400	2	2	4650	5350
22	10	CITATION CONV CUSTOM	OP	CUD	FBG		IO	T130-T140		8		3800	2	2	5750	6600
22	10	CITATION CUSTOM	HT	CUD	FBG		IO	130-225		8		3400	2	2	4650	5350
22	10	CITATION CUSTOM	HT	CUD	FBG		IO	T130-T165		8		3800	2	2	5750	6600
22	10	STINGER	OP	RNBT	FBG		OB			8		3000	2		7250	8300
22	10	STINGER	OP	RNBT	FBG		IO	120-225		8			2		4200	5050
22	10	STINGER	OP	RNBT	FBG		IO	T130	VLVO	8			2		5050	5800
22	10	TICONDEROGA CUSTOM	FB		FBG		IO	165-225		8			2	2	4250	5050
22	10	TICONDEROGA CUSTOM	FB		FBG		IO	T120-T165		8			2	2	4800	5850
25		ALLMAND 25	HT		FBG		IO	188-225		8		4000	2	8	5600	6600
25		ALLMAND 25	HT		FBG		IO	T120-T165		8		4000	2	8	6150	7350
25		ALLMAND 25	OP	CNV	FBG		IO	188-225		8		4000	2	8	6850	8050
25		ALLMAND 25	OP	CNV	FBG		IO	T165	MRCR	8		4000	2	8	7650	8800
28		RANGER 300	HT	EXP	FBG		IB	T215-T270		11		8000	2	6	11000	13000
28		RANGER 300	FB	EXP	FBG		IB	T215-T330		11		8000	2	6	11000	13600
28		RANGER 300 A	FB	SF	FBG		IB	T215-T330		11		8000	2	6	11100	13600
28		RANGER 300 B	FB	SF	FBG		IB	T215-T270		11		8000	2	6	11000	13100
34		ALLMAND 34	FB	EXP	FBG		IO	T225-T325		11		12000	2	8	28800	34000
34		ALLMAND 34	FB	EXP	FBG		IO	T210D	CUM	11		12000	2	8	33400	37100
34		ALLMAND 34	HT	SDN	FBG		IO	T325	MRCR	11		12000	2	8	32500	36200
		1971 BOATS														
19		JUMPER	OP	RACE	FBG		IO	140	MRCR	6	9	2100			2250	2600
19		SUPER-JUMPER	OP	RACE	FBG		IO	235	FORD	6	9	2100			2350	2750
19		SUPER-NOVA	OP	SKI	FBG		IO	235	OMC	8		2000	3		2500	2950
19		SUPER-NOVA	OP	SKI	FBG		IO	290	HOLM	8		2000	3		2800	3250
22	10	CITATION CUSTOM	OP	CUD	FBG		IO	140-235		8		3500	2	2	4750	5600
22	10	CITATION CUSTOM	OP	CUD	FBG		IO	T 90-T165		8		3500	2	2	5300	6200
22	10	CITATION CUSTOM	HT	CUD	FBG		IO	130-235		8		3700	2	2	5050	5850
22	10	CITATION CUSTOM	HT	CUD	FBG		IO	T 90-T165		8		3700	2	2	5500	6400
22	10	STINGER			FBG		IO	90-235		8		3200	2		4200	5050
22	10	STINGER			FBG		IO	T 90	OMC	8		3200	2		4800	5500
22	10	TICONDEROGA		SDN	FBG		IO	130-235		8		4000	2	2	5350	6150
22	10	TICONDEROGA		SDN	FBG		IO	T 90-T165		8		4000	2	2	5800	6750
22	10	TICONDEROGA CUSTOM	FB		FBG		IO	130-235		8		4000	2	2	5100	5850
22	10	TICONDEROGA CUSTOM	FB		FBG		IO	T 90-T165		8		4000	2	2	5500	6450
25		ALLMAND 25	HT		FBG		IO	155-235		8		4000	2	8	5650	6900
		IO 270-325 6200 7650, IO T 90-T165 6200 7600, IO T215 MRCR													6900	7950
25		ALLMAND 25	FB		FBG		IO	155-235		8		4000	2	8	5650	6900
		IO 270-325 6200 7650, IO T 90-T165 6200 7600, IO T215 MRCR													6900	7950
25		ALLMAND 25	OP	CNV	FBG		IO	155-235		8		4000	2	8	6850	8400
25		ALLMAND 25	OP	CNV	FBG		IO	270-325		8		4000	2	8	7600	9200
25		ALLMAND 25	OP	CNV	FBG		IO	T 90-T215		8		4000	2	8	7500	9250
28		RANGER 300		EXP	FBG		IB	T215-T270		11		8000	2	6	10600	12600
28		RANGER 300	HT	EXP	FBG		IB	T215-T270		11		8000	2	6	10600	12600
28		RANGER 300	FB	EXP	FBG		IB	T215-T270		11		8000	2	6	10600	12600
28		RANGER 300 A	FB	SF	FBG		IB	T215-T270		11		8000	2	6	10600	12700
28		RANGER 300 B	FB	SF	FBG		IB	T215-T270		11		8000	2	6	10500	12600
34		ALLMAND 34	HT	CR	FBG		IB	T225-T325		11			2	8	19200	22000
34		ALLMAND 34		EXP	FBG		IB	T225-T325		11			2	8	20900	24300
34		ALLMAND 34	FB	EXP	FBG		IB	T225-T325		11			2	8	20900	24300
34		ALLMAND 34		SF	FBG		IB	T225-T325		11			2	8	18100	21100
		1970 BOATS														
22	10	CITATION CUSTOM	OP	CUD	FBG	SV	IO	130-215		8			2	2	4950	5700
22	10	CITATION CUSTOM	OP	CUD	FBG	SV	IO	T120		8			2	2	5450	6250
22	10	CITATION CUSTOM	HT	CUD	FBG	SV	IO	130-215		8			2	2	4950	5700
22	10	CITATION CUSTOM	HT	CUD	FBG	SV	IO	T120		8			2	2	5450	6250
22	10	TICONDEROGA CUSTOM	FB	SF	FBG	SV	IO	130-215		8			2	2	5700	6550
22	10	TICONDEROGA CUSTOM	FB	SF	FBG	SV	IO	T120		8			2	2	6250	7200
24	6	SENECA		RNBT	FBG	SV	IO	130		8			2	4	6300	7250
24	6	TICONDEROGA		SDNSF	FBG		IO	130		8			2	4	7700	8850
24	6	TICONDEROGA SALON		SF	FBG		IO	130		8			2	4	7700	8850
25	4	ALLMAND 25	OP	CNV	FBG	SV	IO	155-215		8			2	2	8250	9950
25	4	ALLMAND 25	OP	CNV	FBG	SV	IO	270	MRCR	8			2	2	9150	10400
25	4	ALLMAND 25	OP	CNV	FBG	SV	IO	T120-T215		8			2	2	9350	11100
25	4	ALLMAND 25	HT	RNBT	FBG	SV	IO	155-270		8			2	2	6400	7950
25	4	ALLMAND 25	HT	RNBT	FBG	SV	IO	T120-T215		8			2	2	7100	8700
28		RANGER 300	OP	EXP	FBG	SV	IB	250	MRCR	11			2	2	9400	10700
		IO 270 MRCR 15900 18000, IO 325 MRCR 16500 18700, IB 325 MRCR													9700	11000
		IO T155-T165 16300 18700, IO T210 OMC 17100 19400, IB T210 OMC													10300	11700
		IO T215 MRCR 17200 19500, IB T215-T325 10200 12600														
28		RANGER 300	HT	EXP	FBG	SV	IB	250	MRCR	11			2	2	9400	10700
		IO 270 MRCR 15900 18000, IO 325 MRCR 16500 18700, IB 325 MRCR													9700	11000
		IO T155-T165 16300 18700, IO T210 OMC 17100 19400, IB T210 OMC													10300	11700
		IO T215 MRCR 17200 19500, IB T215-T325 10200 12600														
28		RANGER 300	FB	EXP	FBG	SV	IB	250	MRCR	11			2	2	9400	10700
		IO 270 MRCR 15900 18000, IO 325 MRCR 16500 18700, IB 325 MRCR													9700	11000
		IO T155-T165 16300 18700, IO T210 OMC 17100 19400, IB T210 OMC													10300	11700
		IO T215 MRCR 17200 19500, IB T215-T325 10200 12600														
28		RANGER 300	FB	SF	FBG	SV	IB	250	MRCR	11			2	2	9400	10700
		IO 270 MRCR 18500 20600, IO 325 MRCR 19000 21100, IB 325 MRCR													9700	11000
		IO T155-T165 19000 21100, IO T210 OMC 19700 21800, IB T210 OMC													10300	11700
		IO T215 MRCR 19800 22000, IB T215-T325 10200 12600														
		1969 BOATS														
23		CHAMPLAIN	FB	SF	FBG	SV	IO	120-225		8		3800	2	2	6000	7150
23		CHAMPLAIN	FB	SF	FBG	SV	IO	T120		8		4200	2	2	7100	8600
23		CHAMPLAIN	FB	SF	FBG	SV	IO	T 60D-T70D		8		5300	2	2	11700	13300
23		CITATION	HT	CUD	FBG	SV	IO	120-225		8		3600	2	2	5350	6250
23		CITATION	HT	CUD	FBG	SV	IO	T120		8		4000	2	2	6250	7550
23		CITATION	HT	CUD	FBG	SV	IO	T 60D-T70D		8		5100	2	2	9550	10800
23		CITATION CONV	OP	CUD	FBG	SV	IO	120-225		8		3400	2	2	5150	6100
23		CITATION CONV	OP	CUD	FBG	SV	IO	T120		8		3800	2	2	6050	7300
23		CITATION CONV	OP	CUD	FBG	SV	IO	T 60D-T70D		8		4900	2	2	9350	10600
23		SARATOGA	FB	CR	FBG	SV	IO	165-225		8		4100	2	2	5750	6850
23		SARATOGA	FB	CR	FBG	SV	IO	T120		8		4400	2	2	6650	8050

CONTINUED ON NEXT PAGE

ALLMAND BOATS   -CONTINUED   See inside cover to adjust price for area

LOA FT IN	NAME AND/ OR MODEL	TOP/ RIG	BOAT TYPE	-HULL- MTL TP TP	----ENGINE--- # HP MFG	BEAM FT IN	WGT LBS	DRAFT FT IN	RETAIL LOW	RETAIL HIGH
					1969 BOATS					
23	SARATOGA	FB	CR	FBG SV IO	T 60D-T70D 8		5500	2 2	10000	11300
23	SARATOGA		EXP	FBG SV IO	120 VLVO 8			2 2	5150	5900
23	SENECA	ST	UTL	FBG SV IO	120-225 8		3400	2 2	5450	6450
23	SENECA	ST	UTL	FBG SV IO	T120 8		3800	2 2	6350	7700
23	SENECA	ST	UTL	FBG SV IO	T 60D-T70D 8		4900	2 2	11600	13200
23	TICONDEROGA		SDNSF	FBG SV IO	120 VLVO 8			2 2	5850	6750
23	TICONDEROGA	FB	SF	FBG SV IO	120-225 8		3800	2 2	6800	8050
23	TICONDEROGA	FB	SF	FBG SV IO	T120 8		4200	2 2	7850	9500
23	TICONDEROGA	FB	SF	FBG SV IO	T 60D-T70D 8		5300	2 2	12700	14500
25	ALLMAND 25		CBNCR	FBG SV IO	155-210 11		4000	2 2	8000	9450
25	ALLMAND 25		CBNCR	FBG SV IO	T120-T210 11		4000	2 4	8850	10200
28	RANGER 300	HT	EXP	FBG SV IO	250-325 11		8500	2 2	16700	20000
	IO T155-T165 17400 19900, IB T175 CHRY 11200, IO T200 MRCR 18400 20500									
	IO T210 INT 18600 20600, IO T210 OMC 18500 20600, IB T210-T225 10100 11600									
	IO T 92D VLVO 20900 23300									
28	RANGER 300	FB	EXP	FBG SV IO	T155-T165 11		9000	2 2	18300	20500
	IB T175 CHRY 10100 11500, IO T200 MRCR 19000 21100, IO T210 INT 19100 21200									
	IO T210 OMC 19100 21200, IB T210-T225 10400 11900									
28	RANGER 300	FB	SF	FBG SV IO	250-325 11		9500	2 2	20600	23900
	IO T155-T165 21300 23800, IB T175 CHRY 10400 11900, IO T200 MRCR 22000 24400									
	IO T210 INT 22100 24600, IO T210 OMC 22100 24500, IB T210-T225 10700 12300									
28	RANGER 300 CONV	OP	EXP	FBG SV IO	250-325 11		8000	2 2	16200	19400
	IO T155-T165 16900 19400, IB T175 CHRY 9550 10800, IO T200 MRCR 17500 19900									
	IO T210 INT 18100 20100, IO T210 OMC 18000 20000, IB T210-T225 9800 11300									
	IO T 92D VLVO 19900 22100									
					1968 BOATS					
23	CHAMPLAIN	FB		FBG	IO 120-225		3800		5300	6500
23	CHAMPLAIN	FB		FBG	IO T110-T120 8		4100	2 2	6300	7350
23	CHAMPLAIN	FB		FBG	IO T 60D-T70D 8		5300	2 2	9600	10900
23	CITATION	HT	CUD	FBG	IO T120 8		4000	2 2	6500	7450
23	SARATOGA	FB	CR	FBG	IO 120-225 8		4000	2 2	5800	7100
23	SARATOGA	FB	CR	FBG	IO T110-T120 8		4300	2 2	6850	8000
23	SARATOGA	FB	CR	FBG	IO T 60D-T70D 8		5500	2 2	10300	11700
23	SENECA	ST	UTL	FBG	IO 70D 8		4900	2 2	12200	13900
23	TICONDEROGA	FB		FBG	IO T 60D 8		5300		9600	10900
23	TICONDEROGA	FB	SF	FBG	IO 120-225 8		3800	2 2	6450	7850
23	TICONDEROGA	FB	SF	FBG	IO T110-T120 8		4100	2 2	7650	8950
23	TICONDEROGA	FB	SF	FBG	IO T 70D 8		4200	2 2	11300	12900
24 6	CITATION	HT	CUD	FBG	IO 120-225 8		3600	2 2	5750	7150
24 6	CITATION	HT	CUD	FBG	IO T110-T120 8		3900	2 2	6850	7950
24 6	CITATION	HT	CUD	FBG	IO T 60D-T70D 8		5100	2 2	10200	11600
24 6	CITATION CONV	OP	CUD	FBG	IO 120-225 8		3400	2 2	5500	6900
24 6	CITATION CONV	OP	CUD	FBG	IO T110-T120 8		3700	2 2	6600	7750
24 6	CITATION CONV	OP	CUD	FBG	IO T 60D-T70D 8		4900	2 2	9950	11300
24 6	SENECA	ST	UTL	FBG	IO 120-225 8		3400	2 2	5850	7300
24 6	SENECA	ST	UTL	FBG	IO T110-T120 8		3700	2 2	7000	8200
24 6	SENECA	ST	UTL	FBG	IO T 60D 8		4900	2 2	12400	14100
25	ALLMAND 25			FBG	IO 155 11		4000	2 2	6750	7750
25	ALLMAND 25			FBG	IO 160-210 11			2 2	7700	9100
25	ALLMAND 25			FBG	IO T120-T210 11			2 2	8450	10300
28	RANGER 300	HT	EXP	FBG	IO T155-T210 11		8000	2 2	17400	21200
28	RANGER 300	FB	EXP	FBG	IO T155-T210 11		8500	2 2	18400	21700
28	RANGER 300 CONV	OP	EXP	FBG	IO T155-T210 11		7500	2 2	16900	20700
					1967 BOATS					
23	CHAMPLAIN	FB		FBG	IO 140-165		3800		5150	6050
	IO 185-225 5650 6500, IO T110-T120 6150 7200, IO T 60D-T70D 9500 10800									
23	CITATION	HT	CUD	FBG	IO 140-225		3600		5550	6800
23	CITATION	HT	CUD	FBG	IO T110-T120		3900		6600	7700
23	CITATION	HT	CUD	FBG	IO T 60D-T70D		5100		10200	11600
23	CITATION CONV	OP	CUD	FBG	IO 140-225		3400		5350	6550
23	CITATION CONV	OP	CUD	FBG	IO T110-T120		3700		6400	7450
23	CITATION CONV	OP	CUD	FBG	IO T 60D-T70D		4900		9950	11300
23	SARATOGA	FB	CR	FBG	IO 140-225		4000		6000	7300
23	SARATOGA	FB	CR	FBG	IO T110-T120		4300		7050	8250
23	SARATOGA	FB	CR	FBG	IO T 60D-T70D		5500		10700	12100
23	SENECA	ST	UTL	FBG	IO 140-225		3400		5650	6900
23	SENECA	ST	UTL	FBG	IO T110-T120		3700		6750	7850
23	SENECA	ST	UTL	FBG	IO T 60D-T70D		4900		12300	14000
23	TICONDEROGA	FB		FBG	IO 140-225		3800		5850	7100
23	TICONDEROGA	FB		FBG	IO T110-T120		4100		6800	7950
23	TICONDEROGA	FB		FBG	IO T 60D-T70D		5300		10300	11700
28	RANGER 300		CR	FBG	IB T150 11			2 4	8650	9900
					1966 BOATS					
23	CHAMPLAIN 23 SKIFF	FB		FBG	IO 140-225 8		3800	2	4700	5600
	IO 310 5400 6250, IO 170D 7450 8550, IO T110-T150 5450 6350									
	IO T 60D 8200 9400									
23	CITATION	HT	CUD	FBG	IO 140-225 8		3600	2	5550	6500
	IO 310 6200 7150, IO 170D 7800 8950, IO T110-T150 6250 7200									
	IO T 60D 8800 10000									
23	CITATION CONV	OP	CUD	FBG	IO 140-225 8		3400	2	5550	6500
	IO 310 6200 7150, IO 170D 7800 8950, IO T110-T150 6250 7200									
	IO T 60D 8800 10000									
23	SARATOGA 23	FB	EXP	FBG	IO 140-225 8		4000	2	5550	6500
	IO 310 6200 7150, IO 170D 7950 9150, IO T110-T150 6250 7200									
	IO T 60D 9000 10200									
23	SENECA 23	ST	UTL	FBG	IO 140-225 8		3400	2	5850	6850
	IO 310 6550 7550, IO 170D 9050 10300, IO T110-T150 6600 7600									
	IO T 60D 10000 11300									
23	TICONDEROGA 23	FB		FBG	IO 140-225 8		4000	2	6450	6750
	IO 310 6400 7350, IO 170D 8350 9600, IO T110-T150 6450 7400									
	IO T 60D 9450 10700									
28	RANGER 300	OP	EXP	FBG	IO T150 8			2 2	18100	20100
28	RANGER 300	HT	EXP	FBG	IO T150 8			2 2	18100	20100
28	RANGER 300	FB	EXP	FBG	IO T150 8			2 2	18100	20100
					1965 BOATS					
23	CITATION	HT	CUD	FBG	IO 140-225				5700	6700
	IO 310 6400 7350, IO T110-T160 6450 7450, IO T 60D 9100 10400									
23	CITATION CONVERTIBLE	OP	CUD	FBG	IO 140-225				5700	6700
	IO 310 6400 7350, IO T110-T165 6450 7500, IO T 60D 9100 10400									
23	SARATOGA	FB	CBNCR	FBG	IO 140-225				6400	7550
	IO 310 7200 8250, IO T110-T165 7250 8400, IO T 60D 10300 11700									
23	TICONDEROGA	FB		FBG	IO 140-225				5450	6400
	IO 310 6100 7000, IO T110-T165 6150 7100, IO T 60D 9200 10400									

ALLOY MANUFACTURING LTD
COAST GUARD MFG ID- AYM

Call 1-800-327-6929 for BUC Personalized Evaluation Service
Or, for 1973 to 1977 boats, sign onto www.BUCValuPro.com

ALLWEATHER BOATS INC
COAST GUARD MFG ID- AWT

Call 1-800-327-6929 for BUC Personalized Evaluation Service
Or, for 1981 to 2008 boats, sign onto www.BUCValuPro.com

ALMAR BOATS
COAST GUARD MFG ID- AUC

Call 1-800-327-6929 for BUC Personalized Evaluation Service
Or, for 1973 to 1996 boats, sign onto www.BUCValuPro.com

ALOA MARINE S A
CONSTRUCTION NAVALES
CANNES LABOCCA FRANCE   COAST GUARD MFG ID- SEB   See inside cover to adjust price for area

LOA FT IN	NAME AND/ OR MODEL	TOP/ RIG	BOAT TYPE	-HULL- MTL TP TP	----ENGINE--- # HP MFG	BEAM FT IN	WGT LBS	DRAFT FT IN	RETAIL LOW	RETAIL HIGH
					1978 BOATS					
23 10	ALOA 23R STD	SLP	SA/CR	F/S KL IB	8 2		2207	3 9	4900	5600
25 7	ALOA 25 M	SLP	SA/CR	F/S KL IB	6D REN 8 10		4000	4 5	9450	10700
25 7	ALOA 25 STD	SLP	SA/RC	F/S KL IB	8 10		3750	4 5	8300	9500
27 3	ALOA 27 DLX	SLP	SA/CR	F/S KL IB	8D YAN 9 3		5960	4 10	15000	17000
29 10	ALOA 29 STD	SLP	SA/CR	F/S KL IB	10D VLVO 10 2		6840	5 1	19300	21400

96th ed. - Vol. III   CONTINUED ON NEXT PAGE   17

LOA FT	LOA IN	NAME AND/ OR MODEL	TOP/ RIG	BOAT TYPE	HULL MTL	HULL TP	ENGINE TP	ENGINE # HP	ENGINE MFG	BEAM FT	BEAM IN	WGT LBS	DRAFT FT	DRAFT IN	RETAIL LOW	RETAIL HIGH
		1978 BOATS														
34	10	ALOA MS 35	SLP	MS	F/S	KL	IB	25D- 35D		11	10	10800	4	7	30100	34100
37	3	ALOA MY 36/4	FB	TRWL	F/S	DS	IB	T 80D	PERK	12	10	18700	3	4	75000	82400
37	3	ALOA MY 36/6	FB	TRWL	F/S	DS	IB	T120D	PERK	12	10	18760	3	4	76800	84300
45	3	ALOA MS 45	KTH	MS	F/S	KL	IB	80D	PERK	13	9	24280	5	3	67300	73900
		1977 BOATS														
25	7	ALOA 25	SLP	SA/CR	FBG	KL	IB	6D	REN	8	10	3750	4	5	8550	9800
27	3	ALOA 27	SLP	SA/CR	FBG	KL	IB	8D	YAN	9	2	5950	4	10	14500	16400
29	10	ALOA 29	SLP	SA/CR	FBG	KL	IB	12D	REN	10	2	6800	4		18800	20800
37	4	ALOA M 36	FB	TRWL	FBG	DS	IB	T 80D	PERK	12	10	18750	3	4	72300	79400
37	4	ALOA M 36	FB	TRWL	FBG	DS	IB	T120D	PERK	12	10	18750	3	4	73800	81100
45	3	ALOA MS 45	KTH	MS	F/S	KL	IB	80D	PERK	13	10	24250	5	3	64900	71300
		1975 BOATS														
29		ALOA 29	SLP	SA/CR	FBG	KL	IB	10D	REN	10	2	6944	5	4	17100	19400
34		ALOA 34	SLP	SA/CR	FBG	KL	IB	24D	FARY	10	10	10080	5	6	25800	28700
		1974 BOATS														
28	6	ALOA 29	SLP	SA/CR	FBG	KL	IB	10D	REN	10	10	6820	5	4	16000	18100
34	1	ALOA 34	SLP	SA/CR	FBG	KL	IB	22D	FARY	10	10	9900	5	6	24700	27500

ALOHA YACHTS INTERNATIONAL

WHITBY ONTARIO CANADA COAST GUARD MFG ID- ZUY See inside cover to adjust price for area
FORMERLY OUYANG BOAT WORKS LTD

For more recent years, see the BUC Used Boat Price Guide, Volume 1 or Volume 2

LOA FT	LOA IN	NAME AND/ OR MODEL	TOP/ RIG	BOAT TYPE	HULL MTL	HULL TP	ENGINE TP	ENGINE # HP	ENGINE MFG	BEAM FT	BEAM IN	WGT LBS	DRAFT FT	DRAFT IN	RETAIL LOW	RETAIL HIGH
		1983 BOATS														
26	9	ALOHA 8.2	SLP	SA/CR	FBG	KL	IB	8D	BMW	9	6	5200	4	4	12200	13800
28		ALOHA 8.5	SLP	SA/CR	FBG	KL	SD	13D	WEST	9	5	6750	4	4	16600	18900
32	5	ALOHA 32	SLP	SA/CR	FBG	KL	VD	21D	WEST	10	10	9800	4	6	26400	29300
34		ALOHA 10.4	SLP	SA/CR	FBG	KL	IB	21D	WEST	11	2	13600	5	6	36400	40400
34		ALOHA 10.4 SHOAL	SLP	SA/CR	FBG	KL	IB	21D	WEST	11	2	13600	4	7	36400	40400
		1982 BOATS														
26	9	ALOHA 8.2	SLP	SA/CR	FBG	KL	OB			9	6	5200	4	4	11000	12500
26	9	ALOHA 8.2	SLP	SA/CR	FBG	KL	IB	7D	BMW	9	6	5200	4	4	11400	13000
28		ALOHA 8.5	SLP	SA/CR	FBG	KL	SD	13D	WEST	9	5	6750	4	4	15600	17800
28		ALOHA 8.5	SLP	SA/CR	FBG	KL	VD	13D	WEST	9	5	6750	4	4	15600	17800
32	5	ALOHA 32	SLP	SA/CR	FBG	KL	IB	21D	UNIV	10	10	9800	4	9	24800	27600
34		ALOHA 10.4	SLP	SA/CR	FBG	KL	IB	21D	WEST	11	2	13600	5	6	34200	38000
34		ALOHA 10.4 SHOAL	SLP	SA/CR	FBG	KL	IB	21D	WEST	11	2	13800	4	6	34700	38600
		1981 BOATS														
26	9	ALOHA 8.2	SLP	SA/CR	FBG	KL	OB			9	6	5200	4	4	10300	11700
26	9	ALOHA 8.2	SLP	SA/CR	FBG	KL	IB	7D	BMW	9	6	5200	4	4	10800	12200
28		ALOHA 8.5	SLP	SA/CR	FBG	KL	SD	13D- 16D		9	5	6750	4	4	14700	16700
34		ALOHA 10.4	SLP	SA/CR	FBG	KL	IB	23D- 24D		11	2	13600	5	6	32200	35800
		1980 BOATS														
19	6	MATILDA 20	SLP	SA/CR	FBG	KL				7	10	1550	4	2	2750	3200
23		MATILDA 23	SLP	SA/CR	FBG	CB				8	3	4600			7150	8200
26	9	ALOHA 26	SLP	SA/CR	FBG	KL	OB			9	6	5200	4	4	9850	11200
26	9	ALOHA 26	SLP	SA/CR	FBG	KL	SD	8D	VLVO	9	6	5200	4	4	10300	11700
28		ALOHA 28	SLP	SA/CR	FBG	KL	SD	12D- 13D		9	5	6750	4	4	14000	15900
34		ALOHA 34	SLP	SA/CR	FBG	KL	IB	24D- 30D		11	2	13600	5	6	30700	34200
34		ALOHA 34 SHOAL	SLP	SA/CR	FBG	KL	IB	24D- 30D		11	2	13600	4	7	30700	34200
		1979 BOATS														
26	9	ALOHA 26	SLP	SA/CR	FBG	KL	SD	12	OMC	9	6	5200	4	4	9700	11000
26	9	ALOHA 26	SLP	SA/CR	FBG	KL	SD	8D	VLVO	9	6	5200	4	4	9900	11300
28		ALOHA 28	SLP	SA/CR	FBG	KL	SD	13D- 30D		9	5	6750	4	4	13500	15500
34		ALOHA 34	SLP	SA/CR	FBG	KL	SD	23D- 30D		11	2	13680	5	6	29700	33100
		1978 BOATS														
19	6	MATILDA 20	SLP	SA/CR	FBG	CB	OB			7	10	1550		9	2550	2950
22	6	MATILDA 23	SLP	SA/CR	FBG	KC	OB			8	3	4600	2		6550	7500
28		ALOHA 28	SLP	SA/CR	FBG	KL	IB	13D	VLVO	9	5	6750	4	4	13000	14800
34		ALOHA 34	SLP	SA/CR	FBG	KL	IB	30	UNIV	11	2	11700	4	6	24600	27300
		1977 BOATS														
19	6	MATILDA 20	SLP	SA/CR	FBG	SK	OB			7	10	1550		9	2450	2850
23	6	MATILDA 23 ECONOMY	SLP	SA/CR	FBG	KC	OB			8	2	4650	2		6050	6950
23	6	MATILDA 23 STANDARD	SLP	SA/CR	FBG	KC	OB			8	2	4650	2		7100	8150
28		ALOHA 28	SLP	SA/CR	FBG	KL	IB	10D		9	5	6750	4	4	12500	14200
34		ALOHA 34	SLP	SA/CR	FBG	KL	IB	24D		11	2	12000	5	6	23700	26300
34		ALOHA 34 DELUXE	SLP	SA/CR	FBG	KL	IB	24D		11	2	12000	5	6	25200	28000
		1976 BOATS														
16	2	MATILDA 16	SLP	SAIL	FBG	CB	OB			5	1	870		9	1700	2000
19	6	MATILDA 20	SLP	SAIL	FBG	CB	OB			7	10	1550		9	2400	2800
23		MATILDA 23	SLP	SAIL	FBG	KC	OB			8	2	3500	2		4700	5400
28		ALOHA 28	SLP	SAIL	FBG	KL	IB	30	UNIV	9	5	6750	4	4	12000	13700
28		ALOHA 28	SLP	SAIL	FBG	KL	IB	10D- 12D		9	5	6750	4	4	12100	13800
28		ALOHA 28	CUT	SAIL	FBG	KL	IB	30	UNIV	9	5	6750	4	4	12000	13700
28		ALOHA 28	CUT	SAIL	FBG	KL	IB	10D- 12D		9	5	6750	4	4	12100	13800
34		ALOHA 34	SLP	SAIL	FBG	KL	IB	30	UNIV	11	2	12900	5	5	25200	28000
34		ALOHA 34	SLP	SAIL	FBG	KL	IB	22D- 24D		11	2	12900	5	5	25400	28200
		1975 BOATS														
19	6	MATILDA	SLP	SAIL	FBG	CB	OB			7	10	1550	4	2	2350	2700
28		ALOHA 28	SLP	SAIL	FBG	KL	OB			9	5	6750	4	4	11500	13100
28		ALOHA 28	SLP	SAIL	FBG	KL	IB	30	UNIV	9	5	6750	4	4	11700	13300
28		ALOHA 28	CUT	SAIL	FBG	KL	OB			9	5	6750	4	4	11500	13100
28		ALOHA 28	CUT	SAIL	FBG	KL	IB	10D	FARY	9	5	6750	4	4	11800	13400
34		ALOHA 34	SLP	SAIL	F/S	KL	IB	30	UNIV	11	2	11700	5	6	22300	24800
34		ALOHA 34	SLP	SAIL	F/S	KL	IB	10D	FARY	11	2	11700	5	6	22400	24900
		1974 BOATS														
19	6	MATILDA		SAIL	FBG	CB	OB			7	10	1550		9	2300	2650
28		ALOHA 28		SAIL	FBG	KL	IB	10D	FARY	9	5	6750	4	4	11500	13000
34		ALOHA 34	SLP	SA/CR	FBG	KL	IB	10D	FARY	11	2	11700	5	5	21800	24200
		1973 BOATS														
19	6	MATILDA		SAIL	FBG	CB	OB			7	10	1550			2250	2600
28		ALOHA 28		SAIL	FBG	KL	IB	10D	FARY	9	5	6750			11200	12700
		1972 BOATS														
19	6	MATILDA	SLP	SAIL	FBG	CB	OB			7	10	1550		9	2200	2550

ALPA

COAST GUARD MFG ID- ALG

INTERNATIONAL YACHT AGENGY LTD

Call 1-800-327-6929 for BUC Personalized Evaluation Service
Or, for 1976 to 1977 boats, sign onto www.BUCValuPro.com

ALPHA CATAMARANS INC

COAST GUARD MFG ID- APA

Call 1-800-327-6929 for BUC Personalized Evaluation Service
Or, for 1974 to 1975 boats, sign onto www.BUCValuPro.com

ALTAY DISTRIBUTORS

Call 1-800-327-6929 for BUC Personalized Evaluation Service
Or, for 1977 to 1978 boats, sign onto www.BUCValuPro.com

ALUMACRAFT BOAT COMPANY

ST PETER MN 56082 COAST GUARD MFG ID- ACB See inside cover to adjust price for area

For more recent years, see the BUC Used Boat Price Guide, Volume 1 or Volume 2

LOA FT	LOA IN	NAME AND/ OR MODEL	TOP/ RIG	BOAT TYPE	HULL MTL	HULL TP	ENGINE TP	ENGINE # HP	ENGINE MFG	BEAM FT	BEAM IN	WGT LBS	DRAFT FT	DRAFT IN	RETAIL LOW	RETAIL HIGH
		1971 BOATS														
16		SEA-AIRA 1700	OP	RNBT	FBG	SV	IO	130		6	4		2		3150	3700
16		X-PRESS 160	OP	RNBT	FBG	SV	IO	120-165		7			2		3300	3900
16	7	M-PRESS 165	OP	RNBT	FBG	TR	IO	120-155		7	2		2		3700	4350
17	4	X-PRESS 180	OP	RNBT	FBG	DV	IO	120-235		7					3800	4700
18	2	CATALINA 1901	OP		AL	TR	IO	140-215		7	3	1245	2		3450	4150
18	4	X-PRESS 200	OP	RNBT	FBG	DV	IO	155-215		7	7				4400	5200
		1970 BOATS														
16		KINGSTON 1600		RNBT	FBG	DV	IO	120-160		7		1565	2		3250	4000
16		KINGSTON 1600		RNBT	FBG	DV	IO	165	VLVO	7		1565	2		3500	4050
16		SEA-AIRA DLX	OP	RNBT	FBG	SV	IO	130	CHRY	6	4	1395			2900	3350
16		X-PRESS 100		RNBT	FBG	SV	IO	200		7		2000	2		3750	4350
16	8	JAMAICA 1700	OP	RNBT	FBG	TR	IO	120-165		7	3	1600	2		3500	4350
17	4	KINGSTON 1800		RNBT	FBG	DV	IO	120-210		7		1700	2		3700	4550
18	3	CATALINA-QUEEN		RNBT	AL	TR	IO	120-165		7	3	1930	2		4200	5150
18	4	AMBASSADOR 2000		RNBT	FBG		IO	155-210		7	7	2000	2		4450	5400
		1969 BOATS														
16		SEA-AIRA 1700		RNBT	FBG		IO	80		6	4				3350	3900
16		SEA-AIRA 1700		RNBT	FBG	SV	IO	120	VLVO	6	4	1395	1	9	3200	3750
16	8	JAMAICA 1700		RNBT	FBG	TR	IO	120-160		7	3				4000	4650
17	4	KINGSTON 1800		RNBT	FBG		IO	120		7					4050	4750
17	4	KINGSTON 1800		RNBT	FBG	DV	IO	120-210		7		1700	2		3800	4700
18	1	CATALINA-QUEEN		RNBT	AL	TR	IO	120		7	3				4500	5150
18	1	CATALINA-QUEEN		UTL	AL		IO	120		7	3				4800	5500
18	1	CATALINA-QUEEN 1900		RNBT	FBG	TR	IO	120-160		7	3	1930	2		4200	5150
18	1	CATALINA-QUEEN 1901		RNBT	FBG	TR	IO	120-160		7	3	1930	2		4400	5300
18	4	AMBASSADOR 2000		RNBT	FBG		IO	155		7	7				4650	5350

```
ALUMACRAFT BOAT COMPANY        -CONTINUED      See inside cover to adjust price for area
LOA   NAME AND/       TOP/ BOAT  -HULL- ----ENGINE---  BEAM  WGT   DRAFT RETAIL RETAIL
FT IN OR MODEL        RIG  TYPE   MTL TP TP # HP  MFG   FT IN LBS   FT IN LOW    HIGH
-------------------- 1969 BOATS ----------------------------------------------------------
18  4 AMBASSADOR 2000       RNBT FBG SV IO 155-210   7 7 2000  2    4600   5400
-------------------- 1968 BOATS ----------------------------------------------------------
16    SEA-AIRA          OP  RNBT FBG    IO 110-120   6 4  805       2500   2900
17  4 SWEET V-17        OP  RNBT FBG    IO 120-160   7    1800 2 1  4000   4700
18  1 QUEEN-MERRIE      OP  RNBT AL     IO 120       6 4 1480  1 9  3700   4300
18  4 AMBASSADOR        OP       FBG    IO 155-160   7 7 2000  2    4650   5350
-------------------- 1967 BOATS ----------------------------------------------------------
16    CORDELLA              AL     IO      OMC       1524        **     **
16    SEA-AIRA              FBG    IO      OMC        915        **     **
16    SEA-AIRA              FBG    IO 80-110          805       2400   2800
18  1 QUEEN-MERRIE     RNBT AL     OB                1783       1750   2050
18  1 QUEEN-MERRIE     RNBT AL     IO 120            1005       4050   4700
18  4 AMBASSADOR       RNBT FBG    IO 155-160        2000       4800   5600
-------------------- 1966 BOATS ----------------------------------------------------------
16    CORDELLA         RNBT AL     IO 60- 90   6 4              3700   4300
16    SEA-AIRA         RNBT FBG    IO 60- 90   6 4              3700   4300
18  1 KING-FISHERMAN   FSH  AL     IO 60-120                    5400   6250
18  1 QUEEN-MERRIE     RNBT AL     IO 110-120                   5000   5750
18  4 AMBASSADOR       RNBT FBG    IO 120-150   7 7             5150   5900
18  4 WAVERLY          CR   FBG    IO 120-150   7 7             5250   6050
-------------------- 1965 BOATS ----------------------------------------------------------
18  1 KING-FISHERMAN   FSH  AL     IO 110-120                   5600   6450
18  1 QUEEN-MERRIE     RNBT AL     IO 110-120                   5200   5950
18  4 AMBASSADOR       RNBT FBG    IO 120                       5250   6050
18  4 WAVERLY          CR   FBG    IO 150                       5400   6200
-------------------- 1964 BOATS ----------------------------------------------------------
18  1 QUEEN-MERRIE     RNBT AL     IO 110                       5350   6150
-------------------- 1963 BOATS ----------------------------------------------------------
18    QUEEN-MERRIE     RNBT AL     IO 10                        5500   6350
-------------------- 1962 BOATS ----------------------------------------------------------
18    QUEEN-MERRIE DELUXE RNBT AL  IB 80                        1800   2150
```

ALUMINUM BOATS & CANOES INC
PRINCECRAFT

Call 1-800-327-6929 for BUC Personalized Evaluation Service
Or, for 1967 boats, sign onto www.BUCValuPro.com

ALUMINUM CO OF CANADA LTD

Call 1-800-327-6929 for BUC Personalized Evaluation Service
Or, for 1970 boats, sign onto www.BUCValuPro.com

ALUMINUM CRUISERS INC
LOUISVILLE KY 40213   COAST GUARD MFG ID- ALC See inside cover to adjust price for area

For more recent years, see the BUC Used Boat Price Guide, Volume 1 or Volume 2

```
LOA   NAME AND/        TOP/ BOAT  -HULL- ----ENGINE---  BEAM  WGT   DRAFT RETAIL RETAIL
FT IN OR MODEL         RIG  TYPE  MTL TP TP # HP  MFG    FT IN LBS   FT IN LOW    HIGH
-------------------- 1983 BOATS ----------------------------------------------------------
28    MARINETTE             HT EXP AL SV IB 225    CHRY 11  5800 2     12100 13800
28    MARINETTE             FB EXP AL SV IB 225-250     11  5800 2     12100 14000
28    MARINETTE             HT SDN AL SV IB 225-250     11  7000 2     14900 17200
28    MARINETTE             FB SDN AL SV IB 225-250     11  6000 2     13500 15600
28    MARINETTE             HT SDN AL SV IB T225-T250   11  6000 2     15400 17600
28    MARINETTE             FB SDN AL SV IB 225-250     11  6000 2     13500 15600
28    MARINETTE             FB SDN AL SV IB T225-T250   11  6000 2     15400 17600
28    MARINETTE FISHERMAN   FB EXP AL SV IB 225-250     11  5600 2     11900 13800
28    MARINETTE FISHERMAN   FB EXP AL SV IB T225-T250   11  6800 2     14700 17100
28    MARINETTE SPORTSMAN   HT SF  AL SV IB 225-250     11  5000 2     11500 13300
28    MARINETTE SPORTSMAN   HT SF  AL SV IB T225-T250   11  5000 2     13400 15600

28    MARINETTE SPORTSMAN   FB SF  AL SV IB 225-250     11  5000 2     11500 13300
28    MARINETTE SPORTSMAN   FB SF  AL SV IB T225-T250   11  5000 2     13400 15600
32  6 MARINETTE             HT EXP AL SV IB T225-T250   12  9000 2     25600 29000
32  6 MARINETTE             FB EXP AL SV IB T225-T250   12  9000 2     25600 29000
32  6 MARINETTE             HT SDN AL SV IB T225-T250   12  9500 2     25000 28400
32  6 MARINETTE             FB SDN AL SV IB T225-T250   12  9500 2     25000 28400
32  6 MARINETTE FISHERMAN   FB EXP AL SV IB T225-T250   12  8800 2     25600 28900
38  7 MARINETTE             HT DCMY AL SV IB T330 CHRY 13 6 13000 2 6  41200 45800
38  7 MARINETTE             FB DCMY AL SV IB T330 CHRY 13 6 13000 2 6  41200 45800
38  7 MARINETTE             HT MY  AL SV IB T330  CHRY 13 6 12000 2 6  38700 43000
38  7 MARINETTE             FB MY  AL SV IB T330  CHRY 13 6 12000 2 6  38700 43000
-------------------- 1982 BOATS ----------------------------------------------------------
28    MARINETTE             HT EXP AL SV IB 225-250     11  5800 2     11600 13400
28    MARINETTE             HT EXP AL SV IB T225-T250   11  7000 2     14200 16500
28    MARINETTE             FB EXP AL SV IB 225-250     11  5800 2     11600 13400
28    MARINETTE             FB EXP AL SV IB T225-T250   11  7000 2     14200 16500
28    MARINETTE             HT SDN AL SV IB 225-250     11  6000 2     12900 15000
28    MARINETTE             HT SDN AL SV IB T225-T250   11  6000 2     14800 16800
28    MARINETTE             FB SDN AL SV IB 225-250     11  6000 2     12900 15000
28    MARINETTE             FB SDN AL SV IB T225-T250   11  6000 2     14800 16800
28    MARINETTE FISHERMAN   FB EXP AL SV IB 225-250     11  5600 2     11400 13200
28    MARINETTE FISHERMAN   FB EXP AL SV IB T225-T250   11  6800 2     14100 16300
28    MARINETTE SPORTSMAN   HT SF  AL SV IB 225-250     11  5000 2     11000 12700
28    MARINETTE SPORTSMAN   HT SF  AL SV IB T225-T250   11  5000 2     12800 14900

28    MARINETTE SPORTSMAN   FB SF  AL SV IB 225-250     11  5000 2     11000 12700
28    MARINETTE SPORTSMAN   FB SF  AL SV IB T225-T250   11  5000 2     12800 14900
32  6 MARINETTE             HT EXP AL SV IB T225-T250   12  9000 2     24500 27700
32  6 MARINETTE             FB EXP AL SV IB T225-T250   12  9000 2     24500 27700
32  6 MARINETTE             HT SDN AL SV IB T225-T250   12  9500 2     23900 27100
32  6 MARINETTE             FB SDN AL SV IB T225-T250   12  9500 2     23900 27100
32  6 MARINETTE FISHERMAN   FB EXP AL SV IB T225-T250   12  8800 2     24500 27600
37    MARINETTE             HT DC  AL SV IB T250 CHRY 13 6 12500 2 6   35800 39700
37    MARINETTE             HT DC  AL SV IB T330 CHRY 13 6 12800 2 6   37300 41400
37    MARINETTE             FB DC  AL SV IB T250 CHRY 13 6 12500 2 6   35800 39700
37    MARINETTE             FB DC  AL SV IB T330 CHRY 13 6 12800 2 6   37300 41400

37    MARINETTE             HT SDN AL SV IB T250 CHRY 13 6 11000 2 6   32300 35900
37    MARINETTE             HT SDN AL SV IB T330 CHRY 13 6 11300 2 6   33800 37600
37    MARINETTE             FB SDN AL SV IB T250 CHRY 13 6 11000 2 6   32300 35900
37    MARINETTE             FB SDN AL SV IB T330 CHRY 13 6 11300 2 6   33800 37600
-------------------- 1981 BOATS ----------------------------------------------------------
28    MARINETTE             HT EXP AL SV IB 225-250     11  5800 2     11100 12800
28    MARINETTE             HT EXP AL SV IB T225-T250   11  7000 2     13600 15800
28    MARINETTE             FB EXP AL SV IB 225-250     11  5800 2     11100 12800
28    MARINETTE             FB EXP AL SV IB T225-T250   11  7000 2     13600 15800
28    MARINETTE             HT SDN AL SV IB 225-250     11  6000 2     12400 14300
28    MARINETTE             HT SDN AL SV IB T155-T250   11  7100 2     14200 16300
28    MARINETTE             FB SDN AL SV IB 225-250     11  6000 2     12400 14300
28    MARINETTE             FB SDN AL SV IB T155-T250   11  7100 2     14200 16300
28    MARINETTE FISHERMAN   FB EXP AL SV IB 225-250     11  5600 2     10900 12700
28    MARINETTE FISHERMAN   FB EXP AL SV IB T225-T250   11  6800 2     13500 15600
32  6 MARINETTE             HT EXP AL SV IB T225-T250   12  9000 2     23500 26500
32  6 MARINETTE             FB EXP AL SV IB T225-T250   12  9000 2     23500 26500

32  6 MARINETTE             HT SDN AL SV IB T225-T250   12  9500 2     22900 26000
32  6 MARINETTE             FB SDN AL SV IB T225-T250   12  9500 2     22900 26000
32  6 MARINETTE FISHERMAN   FB EXP AL SV IB T225-T250   12  8800 2     23400 26400
37    MARINETTE             HT DC  AL SV IB T250 CHRY 13 6 12500 2 6   34100 37900
37    MARINETTE             HT DC  AL SV IB T330 CHRY 13 6 12800 2 6   35500 39500
37    MARINETTE             FB DC  AL SV IB T250 CHRY 13 6 12500 2 6   34100 37900
37    MARINETTE             FB DC  AL SV IB T330 CHRY 13 6 12800 2 6   35500 39500
37    MARINETTE             HT SDN AL SV IB T250 CHRY 13 6 11000 2 6   30800 34200
37    MARINETTE             HT SDN AL SV IB T330 CHRY 13 6 11300 2 6   32200 35800
37    MARINETTE             FB SDN AL SV IB T250 CHRY 13 6 11000 2 6   30800 34200
37    MARINETTE             FB SDN AL SV IB T330 CHRY 13 6 11300 2 6   32200 35800
-------------------- 1980 BOATS ----------------------------------------------------------
28    MARINETTE             HT EXP AL SV IB 225  CHRY 11  5800 2       10600 12100
28    MARINETTE             HT EXP AL SV IB 225  CHRY 11  7000 2       13100 14900
28    MARINETTE             FB EXP AL SV IB 225  CHRY 11  5800 2       10600 12100
28    MARINETTE             FB EXP AL SV IB 225  CHRY 11  7000 2       13100 14900
28    MARINETTE             HT FSH AL SV IB 225  CHRY 11  5600 2       10500 11900
28    MARINETTE             FB FSH AL SV IB 225  CHRY 11  6800 2       12900 14700
28    MARINETTE             HT FSH AL SV IB 225  CHRY 11  5600 2       10500 11900
28    MARINETTE             FB FSH AL SV IB 225  CHRY 11  6800 2       12900 14700
28    MARINETTE             HT SDN AL SV IB 225  CHRY 11  7000 2       11800 13500
28    MARINETTE             FB SDN AL SV IB 225  CHRY 11  7000 2       11800 13500
28    MARINETTE             HT SDN AL SV IB T155 CRUS 11  7000 2       13600 15400
28    MARINETTE             FB SDN AL SV IB T155 CRUS 11  7000 2       13600 15400

32  6 MARINETTE             HT EXP AL SV IB T225-T250   12  9000 2     22500 25800
32  6 MARINETTE             FB EXP AL SV IB T225-T250   12  9000 2     22500 25800
32  6 MARINETTE             HT FSH AL SV IB T225 CHRY 12  8800 2       18800 21300
32  6 MARINETTE             FB FSH AL SV IB T225 CHRY 12  8800 2       18800 20800
32  6 MARINETTE             HT SDN AL SV IB T225 CHRY 12  9500 2       22000 25000
32  6 MARINETTE             FB SDN AL SV IB T225 CHRY 12  9500 2       22000 24400
37    MARINETTE             HT DC  AL SV IB T250 CHRY 13 6 12500 2 6   32500 36100
37    MARINETTE             HT DC  AL SV IB T330 CHRY 13 6 12800 2 6   33900 37600
```

ALUMINUM CRUISERS INC -CONTINUED See inside cover to adjust price for area

LOA FT	LOA IN	NAME AND/ OR MODEL	TOP/ RIG	BOAT TYPE	-HULL- MTL	-HULL- TP	ENGINE TP	ENGINE # HP	ENGINE MFG	BEAM FT	BEAM IN	WGT LBS	DRAFT FT	DRAFT IN	RETAIL LOW	RETAIL HIGH
		1980 BOATS														
37		MARINETTE	FB	DC	AL	SV	IB	T250	CHRY	13	6	12500	2	6	32500	36100
37		MARINETTE	FB	DC	AL	SV	IB	T330	CHRY	13	6	12800	2	6	33900	37600
37		MARINETTE	HT	SDN	AL	SV	IB	T250	CHRY	13	6	11000	2	6	29300	32600
37		MARINETTE	HT	SDN	AL	SV	IB	T330	CHRY	13	6	11300	2	6	30800	34200
37		MARINETTE	FB	SDN	AL	SV	IB	T250	CHRY	13	6	11000	2	6	29300	32600
37		MARINETTE	FB	SDN	AL	SV	IB	T330	CHRY	13	6	11300	2	6	30800	34200
		1979 BOATS														
28		MARINETTE	HT	EXP	AL	SV	IB	225-250		11		5800	2		10200	11800
28		MARINETTE	HT	EXP	AL	SV	IB	T225-T250		11		7000	2		12500	14500
28		MARINETTE	FB	EXP	AL	SV	IB	225-250		11		5800	2		10200	11800
28		MARINETTE	FB	EXP	AL	SV	IB	T225-T250		11		7000	2		12500	14500
28		MARINETTE	HT	FSH	AL	SV	IB	225-250		11		5800	2		10200	11800
28		MARINETTE	HT	FSH	AL	SV	IB	T225-T250		11		7000	2		12500	14500
28		MARINETTE	FB	FSH	AL	SV	IB	225-250		11		5800	2		10200	11800
28		MARINETTE	FB	FSH	AL	SV	IB	T225-T250		11		7000	2		12500	14500
32		MARINETTE	HT	EXP	AL	SV	IB	T225-T250		12		9000	2		20800	23600
32		MARINETTE	FB	EXP	AL	SV	IB	T225-T250		12		9000	2		20800	23600
32		MARINETTE	HT	FSH	AL	SV	IB	T225-T250		12		9000	2		16900	19500
32		MARINETTE	FB	FSH	AL	SV	IB	T225-T250		12		9000	2		16900	19500
32		MARINETTE	HT	SDN	AL	SV	IB	T225-T250		12		9500	2		20400	23200
32		MARINETTE	FB	SDN	AL	SV	IB	T225-T250		12		9500	2		20400	23200
37		MARINETTE	HT	DC	AL	SV	IB	T250	CHRY	13	6	12500	2	6	31100	34500
37		MARINETTE	HT	DC	AL	SV	IB	T350	CHRY	13	6	12500	2	6	32200	35800
37		MARINETTE	FB	DC	AL	SV	IB	T250	CHRY	13	6	12500	2	6	31100	34500
37		MARINETTE	FB	DC	AL	SV	IB	T350	CHRY	13	6	12500	2	6	32200	35800
37		MARINETTE	HT	SDN	AL	SV	IB	T250	CHRY	13	6	11000	2	6	28000	31100
37		MARINETTE	HT	SDN	AL	SV	IB	T350	CHRY	13	6	11000	2	6	29300	32500
37		MARINETTE	FB	SDN	AL	SV	IB	T250	CHRY	13	6	11000	2	6	28000	31100
37		MARINETTE	FB	SDN	AL	SV	IB	T350	CHRY	13	6	11000	2	6	29300	32500
		1978 BOATS														
28		MARINETTE	HT	EXP	AL	SV	IB	225-330		10	5	5800	2		9700	11800
28		MARINETTE	HT	EXP	AL	SV	IB	T225	CHRY	10	5	7000	2		11900	13500
28		MARINETTE	FB	EXP	AL	SV	IB	225-330		10	5	5800	2		9700	11800
28		MARINETTE	FB	EXP	AL	SV	IB	T225	CHRY	10	5	7000	2		11900	13500
28		MARINETTE	HT	FSH	AL	SV	IB	225	CHRY	10	5	5800	2		9700	11000
28		MARINETTE	HT	FSH	AL	SV	IB	T225-T250		10	5	7000	2		11900	13600
28		MARINETTE	FB	FSH	AL	SV	IB	225	CHRY	10	5	5800	2		9700	11000
28		MARINETTE	FB	FSH	AL	SV	IB	T225-T250		10	5	7000	2		11900	13600
32	6	MARINETTE	HT	EXP	AL	SV	IB	T225-T250		12		9000	2		20700	23400
32	6	MARINETTE	FB	EXP	AL	SV	IB	T225-T250		12		9000	2		20700	23400
32	6	MARINETTE	HT	FSH	AL	SV	IB	T225-T250		12		9000	2		16900	19600
32	6	MARINETTE	FB	FSH	AL	SV	IB	T225-T250		12		9000	2		16900	19600
32	6	MARINETTE	HT	SDN	AL	SV	IB	T225-T250		12		9500	2		20200	22900
32	6	MARINETTE	FB	SDN	AL	SV	IB	T225-T250		12		9500	2		20200	22900
37		MARINETTE	HT	DC	AL	SV	IB	T250	CHRY	13	6	12200	2	6	29300	32500
37		MARINETTE	HT	DC	AL	SV	IB	T330	CHRY	13	6		2	6	35100	39000
37		MARINETTE	FB	DC	AL	SV	IB	T250	CHRY	13	6	12200	2	6	29300	32500
37		MARINETTE	FB	DC	AL	SV	IB	T330	CHRY	13	6		2	6	35100	39000
37		MARINETTE	HT	SDN	AL	SV	IB	T250	CHRY	13	6	11000	2	6	26800	29800
37		MARINETTE	HT	SDN	AL	SV	IB	T330	CHRY	13	6	11000	2	6	27700	30800
37		MARINETTE	FB	SDN	AL	SV	IB	T250	CHRY	13	6	11000	2	6	26800	29800
37		MARINETTE	FB	SDN	AL	SV	IB	T330	CHRY	13	6	11000	2	6	27700	30800
		1977 BOATS														
28		MARINETTE	HT	EXP	AL	SV	IB	225	CHRY	10	5	5800	2		9350	10600
28		MARINETTE	HT	EXP	AL	SV	IB	T225	CHRY	10	5	7000	2		11400	13000
28		MARINETTE	FB	EXP	AL	SV	IB	225	CHRY	10	5	5800	2		9350	10600
28		MARINETTE	FB	EXP	AL	SV	IB	T225	CHRY	10	5	7000	2		11400	13000
28		MARINETTE	HT	FSH	AL	SV	IB	225	CHRY	10	5	5800	2		9350	10600
28		MARINETTE	HT	FSH	AL	SV	IB	T225	CHRY	10	5	7000	2		11400	13000
32	6	MARINETTE	HT	EXP	AL	SV	IB	T225	CHRY	12		9000	2		19900	22100
32	6	MARINETTE	FB	EXP	AL	SV	IB	T225	CHRY	12		9000	2		19900	22100
32	6	MARINETTE	HT	FSH	AL	SV	IB	T225	CHRY	12		9000	2		16200	18500
32	6	MARINETTE	HT	SDN	AL	SV	IB	T225	CHRY	12		9500	2		19400	21500
32	6	MARINETTE	FB	SDN	AL	SV	IB	T225	CHRY	12		9500	2		19400	21500
37		MARINETTE	HT	DC	AL	SV	IB	T250	CHRY	13	6	13000	2	6	29200	32400
37		MARINETTE	HT	DC	AL	SV	IB	T330	CHRY	13	6	13250	2	6	30300	33600
37		MARINETTE	FB	DC	AL	SV	IB	T250	CHRY	13	6	13500	2	6	29900	33200
37		MARINETTE	FB	DC	AL	SV	IB	T330	CHRY	13	6	13750	2	6	31000	34400
37		MARINETTE	HT	SDN	AL	SV	IB	T250	CHRY	13	6	11000	2	6	25700	28500
37		MARINETTE	HT	SDN	AL	SV	IB	T330	CHRY	13	6	11250	2	6	26900	29800
37		MARINETTE	FB	SDN	AL	SV	IB	T250	CHRY	13	6	11000	2	6	25700	28500
37		MARINETTE	FB	SDN	AL	SV	IB	T330	CHRY	13	6	11250	2	6	26900	29800
		1976 BOATS														
28		MARINETTE	HT	EXP	AL	SV	IB	225	CHRY	10	5	5800	2		9000	10200
28		MARINETTE	HT	EXP	AL	SV	IB	T225	CHRY	10	5	7000	2		11000	12500
28		MARINETTE	FB	EXP	AL	SV	IB	225	CHRY	10	5	5800	2		9000	10200
28		MARINETTE	FB	EXP	AL	SV	IB	T225	CHRY	10	5	7000	2		11000	12500
28		MARINETTE	HT	FSH	AL	SV	IB	225	CHRY	10	5	5800	2		9000	10200
28		MARINETTE	HT	FSH	AL	SV	IB	T225	CHRY	10	5	7000	2		11000	12500
28		MARINETTE	FB	FSH	AL	SV	IB	225	CHRY	10	5	5800	2		9000	10200
28		MARINETTE	FB	FSH	AL	SV	IB	T225	CHRY	10	5	7000	2		11000	12500
32	6	MARINETTE	HT	EXP	AL	SV	IB	T225	CHRY	12		9000	2		19100	21200
32	6	MARINETTE	FB	EXP	AL	SV	IB	T225	CHRY	12		9000	2		19100	21200
32	6	MARINETTE	HT	FSH	AL	SV	IB	T225	CHRY	12		9000	2		15600	17700
32	6	MARINETTE	FB	FSH	AL	SV	IB	T225	CHRY	12		9000	2		15600	17700
32	6	MARINETTE	HT	SDN	AL	SV	IB	T225	CHRY	12		9500	2		18800	20900
32	6	MARINETTE	FB	SDN	AL	SV	IB	T225	CHRY	12		9500	2		18800	20900
37		MARINETTE	HT	SDN	AL	SV	IB	T250	CHRY	13	6	11000	2	6	24600	27400
37		MARINETTE	HT	SDN	AL	SV	IB	T330	CHRY	13	6	11250	2	6	25800	28600
37		MARINETTE	HT	SDN	AL	SV	IB	T225D	CAT	13	6	13500	2	6	35000	38900
37		MARINETTE	FB	SDN	AL	SV	IB	T250	CHRY	13	6	11000	2	6	24600	27400
37		MARINETTE	FB	SDN	AL	SV	IB	T330	CHRY	13	6	11250	2	6	25800	28600
37		MARINETTE	FB	SDN	AL	SV	IB	T225D	CAT	13	6	13500	2	6	35000	38900
		1975 BOATS														
28		MARINETTE	HT	EXP	AL	SV	IB	225-250		10	5	5800	2		8550	9950
28		MARINETTE	HT	EXP	AL	SV	IB	T225-T250		10	5	7000	2		10500	12200
28		MARINETTE	HT	FSH	AL	SV	IB	225-250		10	5	5800	2		8550	9950
28		MARINETTE	HT	FSH	AL	SV	IB	T225-T250		10	5	7000	2		10600	12200
32	4	MARINETTE	HT	EXP	AL	DV	IB	225-250		11	6		2		16500	19000
32	4	MARINETTE	HT	EXP	AL	DV	IB	T225-T250		11	6	9000	2		18200	20600
32	4	MARINETTE	FB	EXP	AL	DV	IB	225-250		11	6		2		16500	19000
32	4	MARINETTE	FB	EXP	AL	DV	IB	T225-T250		11	6	9000	2		18200	20600
32	4	MARINETTE	HT	FSH	AL	DV	IB	T225-T250		11	6	9000	2		14700	17000
32	4	MARINETTE	FB	FSH	AL	DV	IB	T225-T250		11	6	9000	2		14700	17000
32	4	MARINETTE	HT	SDN	AL	DV	IB	T225-T250		11	6	9500	2		17400	20200
32	4	MARINETTE	FB	SDN	AL	DV	IB	T225-T250		11	6	9500	2		17400	20200
37		MARINETTE	HT	SDN	AL	DV	IB	T250	CHRY	13	6	11000	2	6	23700	26300
37		MARINETTE	HT	SDN	AL	DV	IB	T330	CHRY	13	6	11000	2	6	24400	27100
37		MARINETTE	HT	SDN	AL	DV	IB	T225D	CAT	13	6	15000	2	6	35700	39700
37		MARINETTE	FB	SDN	AL	DV	IB	T250	CHRY	13	6	11000	2	6	23700	26300
37		MARINETTE	FB	SDN	AL	DV	IB	T330	CHRY	13	6	11000	2	6	24400	27100
37		MARINETTE	FB	SDN	AL	DV	IB	T225D	CAT	13	6	15000	2	6	35700	39700
		1974 BOATS														
28		MARINETTE		EXP	AL		IB	225-250		10	5	5410	2		7950	9300
28		MARINETTE		EXP	AL		IB	T225-T250		10	5	6520	2		9850	11400
28		MARINETTE	FB	EXP	AL		IB	225-250		10	5	5410	2		7950	9300
28		MARINETTE	FB	EXP	AL		IB	T225-T250		10	5	6520	2		9850	11400
28		MARINETTE		FSH	AL		IB	225-250		10	5	5410	2		7950	9350
28		MARINETTE		FSH	AL		IB	T225-T250		10	5	6520	2		9850	11200
28		MARINETTE	FB	SF	AL		IB	225-250		10	5	5410	2		7950	9300
28		MARINETTE	FB	SF	AL		IB	T225-T250		10	5	6520	2		9850	11400
32	4	MARINETTE		EXP	AL		IB	225-250		11	6	8380	2		15400	17700
32	4	MARINETTE		EXP	AL		IB	T225-T250		11	6	9490	2		17300	19700
32	4	MARINETTE	FB	EXP	AL		IB	225-250		11	6	8380	2		15400	17700
32	4	MARINETTE	FB	EXP	AL		IB	T225-T250		11	6	8380	2		17000	19700
32	4	MARINETTE		FSH	AL		IB	225-250		11	6	8510	2		12800	14700
32	4	MARINETTE		FSH	AL		IB	T225-T250		11	6	9620	2		14300	16300
32	4	MARINETTE		SDN	AL		IB	225-250		11	6	8700	2		14800	17000
32	4	MARINETTE		SDN	AL		IB	T225-T250		11	6	9800	2		16800	19300
32	4	MARINETTE	FB	SDN	AL		IB	225-250		11	6	8700	2		14800	17000
32	4	MARINETTE	FB	SDN	AL		IB	T225-T250		11	6	8700	2		16600	19300
32	4	MARINETTE	FB	SF	AL		IB	225-250		11	6	8510	2		12700	14700
32	4	MARINETTE	FB	SF	AL		IB	T225-T250		11	6	8510	2		14000	16200
37		MARINETTE		SDN	AL		IB	T250	CHRY	13	6	12000	3		25100	27800
37		MARINETTE	FB	SDN	AL		IB	T250	CHRY	13	6	12000	3		25100	27800
41		SEA-CREST	HT	HB	AL	SV	IB	T225		13	6	13170	2	4	21600	24000
41		SEA-CREST	FB	HB	AL	SV	IB	T225		13	6	13170	2	4	21600	24000
		1973 BOATS														
28		MARINETTE		EXP	AL		IB	225-250		10	5	5410	2		7650	8950
28		MARINETTE		EXP	AL		IB	T225-T250		10	5	6520	2		9500	11000
28		MARINETTE	FB	EXP	AL		IB	225-250		10	5	6060	2		8000	9350
28		MARINETTE	FB	EXP	AL		IB	T225-T250		10	5	7170	2		9850	11400
28		MARINETTE		FSH	AL		IB	225-250		10	5	5410	2		7650	8950
28		MARINETTE		FSH	AL		IB	T225-T250		10	5	6520	2		9500	11000
32	4	MARINETTE		EXP	AL		IB	225-250		11	6	8380	2		14800	17100
32	4	MARINETTE		EXP	AL		IB	T225-T250		11	6	9490	2		16600	19200
32	4	MARINETTE	FB	EXP	AL		IB	225-250		11	6	9030	2		15000	17300
32	4	MARINETTE	FB	EXP	AL		IB	T225-T250		11	6	10140	2		16800	19400
32	4	MARINETTE		FSH	AL		IB	T225-T250		11	6		2		13800	15900

CONTINUED ON NEXT PAGE

LOA FT	LOA IN	NAME AND/ OR MODEL	TOP/ RIG	BOAT TYPE	HULL MTL	HULL TP	ENGINE TP	ENGINE # HP	ENGINE MFG	BEAM FT	BEAM IN	WGT LBS	DRAFT FT	DRAFT IN	RETAIL LOW	RETAIL HIGH
1973 BOATS																
32	4	MARINETTE		SDN	AL		IB	T225-T250		11	6		2		16200	18800
32	4	MARINETTE	FB	SDN	AL		IB	T225-T250		11	6		2		16200	18800
41		SEA-CREST	HT	HB	AL		IB	T225	CHRY	13	6	12470	2	4	20800	23100
41		SEA-CREST	HT	HB	AL		IB	T250	CHRY	13	6	12470	2	4	20900	23200
41		SEA-CREST	FB	HB	AL		IB	T225	CHRY	13	6	13170	2	4	21500	23900
41		SEA-CREST	FB	HB	AL		IB	T250	CHRY	13	6	13170	2	4	21600	24000
1972 BOATS																
28		MARINETTE		EXP	AL		IB	225-250		10	5	5410	2		7350	8600
28		MARINETTE		EXP	AL		IB	T225-T250		10	5	6520	2		9150	10600
28		MARINETTE	FB	EXP	AL		IB	225-250		10	5	6060	2		7700	9000
28		MARINETTE	FB	EXP	AL		IB	T225-T250		10	5	7170	2		9450	11000
28		MARINETTE		FSH	AL		IB	225-250		10	5	5410	2		7350	8650
28		MARINETTE		FSH	AL		IB	T225-T250		10	5	6520	2		9200	10600
32	4	MARINETTE		EXP	AL		IB	225-250		11	6	8380	2		14300	16400
32	4	MARINETTE		EXP	AL		IB	T225-T250		11	6	9490	2		16000	18400
32	4	MARINETTE	FB	EXP	AL		IB	225-250		11	6	9030	2		14400	16600
32	4	MARINETTE	FB	EXP	AL		IB	T225-T250		11	6	10140	2		16100	18600
32	4	MARINETTE		FSH	AL		IB	T225-T250		11	6		2		13200	15300
32	4	MARINETTE		SDN	AL		IB	T225-T250		11	6		2		15600	18100
41		SEA-CREST	HT	HB	AL		IB	T225	CHRY	13	6	12470	2	4	20600	22900
41		SEA-CREST	HT	HB	AL		IB	T250	CHRY	13	6	12470	2	4	20700	23000
41		SEA-CREST	FB	HB	AL		IB	T225	CHRY	13	6	13170	2	4	21400	23700
41		SEA-CREST	FB	HB	AL		IB	T250	CHRY	13	6	13170	2	4	21500	23800
1971 BOATS																
28		MARINETTE		EXP	AL		IB	225-250		10	5	5410	2		7100	8300
28		MARINETTE		EXP	AL		IB	T225-T250		10	5	6520	2		8800	10200
28		MARINETTE	FB	EXP	AL		IB	225-250		10	5		2		7650	8900
28		MARINETTE	FB	EXP	AL		IB	T225-T250		10	5		2		8700	10200
28		MARINETTE		FSH	AL		IB	225-250		10	5	5410	2		7100	8300
28		MARINETTE		FSH	AL		IB	T225-T250		10	5	6520	2		8850	10200
28		MARINETTE		SF	AL		IB	225-250		10	5	5410	2		7100	8300
28		MARINETTE		SF	AL		IB	T225-T250		10	5	6520	2		8800	10200
32	4	MARINETTE		EXP	AL		IB	225-250		11	6	8380	2		13700	15800
32	4	MARINETTE		EXP	AL		IB	T225-T250		11	6	8380	2		15100	17500
32	4	MARINETTE	FB	EXP	AL		IB	225-250		11	6		2		14100	16300
32	4	MARINETTE	FB	EXP	AL		IB	T225-T250		11	6		2		15500	17900
32	4	MARINETTE		FSH	AL		IB	T225-T250		11	6		2		12700	14700
39	11	SEA-CREST	HT	HB	AL		IB	T225	CHRY	12		11000	2	4	19300	21500
39	11	SEA-CREST	HT	HB	AL		IB	T250	CHRY	12		11000	2	4	19400	21600
39	11	SEA-CREST	FB	HB	AL		IB	T225	CHRY	12		11000	2	4	19300	21500
39	11	SEA-CREST	FB	HB	AL		IB	T250	CHRY	12		11000	2	4	19400	21600
1970 BOATS																
28		MARINETTE		EXP	AL	SV	IB	225	CHRY	10	6	4900	2		6600	7550
28		MARINETTE		EXP	AL	SV	IB	T225	CHRY	10	6	5700	2		8050	9250
28		MARINETTE		FSH	AL	SV	IB	T225	CHRY	10	6	6200	2		8250	9500
32	3	MARINETTE		EXP	AL	SV	IB	225	CHRY	11	6	6300	2	2	12700	14400
32	3	MARINETTE		EXP	AL	SV	IB	T225	CHRY	11	6	7300	2	2	14300	16300
32	3	MARINETTE		FSH	AL	SV	IB	T225	CHRY	11	6	7600	2	2	11800	13400
39	10	SEA-CREST		HB	AL	SV	IB	T225	CHRY	12		11000	2	7	19100	21200
1969 BOATS																
28		MARINETTE		EXP	AL	SV	IB	210	CHRY	10	6	4875	2		6250	7200
28		MARINETTE		EXP	AL	SV	IB	T210	CHRY	10	6	5705	2		7650	8750
28		MARINETTE		FSH	AL	SV	IB	T210	CHRY	10	6	6135	2		7850	9000
32	3	MARINETTE		EXP	AL	SV	IB	210	CHRY	11	6	6100	2	2	12100	13700
32	3	MARINETTE		EXP	AL	SV	IB	T210	CHRY	11	6	7110	2	2	13600	15400
32	3	MARINETTE		FSH	AL	SV	IB	210	CHRY	11	6	6350	2	2	9950	11300
32	3	MARINETTE		FSH	AL	SV	IB	T210	CHRY	11	6	7360	2	2	11200	12700
34		RIVER-CRUISER		HB	AL	SV	VD	210	CHRY	12		7250	2	4	13200	15000
34		RIVER-CRUISER		HB	AL	SV	VD	T210	CHRY	12		8750	2	4	16700	18900
1968 BOATS																
28		MARINETTE		EXP	AL	DV	IB	210	CHRY	10	6	4875	2		6050	6950
28		MARINETTE		EXP	AL	DV	IB	T210	CHRY	10	6	5705	2		7350	8450
28		MARINETTE		FSH	AL	DV	IB	210	CHRY	10	6	5125	2		6150	7050
28		MARINETTE		FSH	AL	DV	IB	T210	CHRY	10	6	6135	2		7550	8650
32	3	MARINETTE		EXP	AL	DV	IB	210	CHRY	11	6	6100	2	2	11600	13200
32	3	MARINETTE		EXP	AL	DV	IB	T210	CHRY	11	6	7110	2	2	13100	14900
32	3	MARINETTE		FSH	AL	DV	IB	210	CHRY	11	6	6350	2	2	9600	10900
32	3	MARINETTE		FSH	AL	DV	IB	T210	CHRY	11	6	7360	2	2	10800	12300
34		RIVER-CRUISER		HB	AL	SV	VD	210	CHRY	12		7250	2	4	13100	14900
34		RIVER-CRUISER		HB	AL	SV	VD	T210	CHRY	12		8400	2	4	16100	18300
1967 BOATS																
26		MARINETTE		EXP	AL		IB	210				4175			4300	5000
26		MARINETTE	HT	EXP	AL		IB	210							4950	5700
26		MARINETTE		FSH	AL		IB	210				4325			4400	5050
26		MARINETTE		OVNTR	AL		IB	210				3950			4150	4800
26		MARINETTE	HT	SF	AL		IB	210							5200	6000
32	3	MARINETTE		EXP	AL		IB	210							12000	13700
32	3	MARINETTE		EXP	AL		IB	T210				6975			12600	14400
32	3	MARINETTE	HT	EXP	AL		IB	210							12000	13700
32	3	MARINETTE	HT	EXP	AL		IB	T210							13100	14900
32	3	MARINETTE		FSH	AL		IB	T210				7225			10400	11800
32	3	MARINETTE	HT	SF	AL		IB	T210							10600	12000
34		RIVER-CRUISER		HB	AL	SV	IB	210							18200	20200
34		RIVER-CRUISER		HB	AL	SV	IB	T210				7200			14400	16400
1966 BOATS																
26		MARINETTE		EXP	AL		IB	195		10	2		1	9	4800	5550
31	3	MARINETTE 4 SLEEPER		EXP	AL		IB	195		10	4		1	10	9200	10500
31	3	MARINETTE 4 SLEEPER		EXP	AL		IB	T190		10	4		1	10	10200	11600
31	3	MARINETTE 4 SLEEPER		SF	AL		IB	T190		10	4		1	10	8450	9700
31	3	MARINETTE 6 SLEEPER		EXP	AL		IB	195		10	4		1	10	9400	10700
31	3	MARINETTE 6 SLEEPER		EXP	AL		IB	T190		10	4		1	10	10500	11900
31	3	MARINETTE 6 SLEEPER		SF	AL		IB	T190		10	4		1	10	8650	9900
37	6	SEA-CREST	FB	HB	AL	SV	IB	T238		13			2	6	22400	24800
1965 BOATS																
26		MARINETTE		EXP	AL		IB	195							4600	5250
31	3	MARINETTE 4 SLEEPER		EXP	AL		IB	195							9150	10400
31	3	MARINETTE 4 SLEEPER		EXP	AL		IB	T190							10100	11500
31	3	MARINETTE 4 SLEEPER		SF	AL		IB	T190							8350	9600
36	2	MARINETTE		SF	AL		IB	T195		13			2	6	19900	22100
1964 BOATS																
26		MARINETTE		EXP	AL		IB	195							4400	5100
31		MARINETTE		EXP	AL		IB	195							8400	9650
31		MARINETTE		EXP	AL		IB	T160							9200	10500
57		MARINETTE 57		SF	AL		IB	T310		22			3		75600	83000
1963 BOATS																
31		MARINETTE		EXP	AL		IB	188							8100	9300
31		MARINETTE		EXP	AL		IB	T160							8900	10100
1962 BOATS																
30	6	MARINETTE		EXP	AL		IB	188	GRAY	9	2	5000	2		6850	7850
30	6	MARINETTE		EXP	AL		IB	T160	GRAY	9	2	5000	2		7550	8700
1961 BOATS																
30	6	MARINETTE		EXP	AL		IB	188	GRAY	9	2	5000	2		6700	7700
1960 BOATS																
30	6	MARINETTE		EXP	AL		OB			9	2	5000	1	10	22800	25300
30	6	MARINETTE		EXP	AL		IB	70-109		9	2	5000	1	10	5900	6950
30	6	MARINETTE		EXP	AL		IB	T 70	GRAY	9	2	5000	1	10	6250	7200

ALURA

MARLSBORO NJ 07746

See inside cover to adjust price for area

LOA FT	LOA IN	NAME AND/ OR MODEL	TOP/ RIG	BOAT TYPE	HULL MTL	HULL TP	ENGINE TP	ENGINE # HP	ENGINE MFG	BEAM FT	BEAM IN	WGT LBS	DRAFT FT	DRAFT IN	RETAIL LOW	RETAIL HIGH
1967 BOATS																
32	6	ALURA 32		CR	FBG		IB	238		12	4		2	10	13200	15000

ALWEST MARINE

COAST GUARD MFG ID- ALM

Call 1-800-327-6929 for BUC Personalized Evaluation Service
Or, for 1971 to 1974 boats, sign onto www.BUCValuPro.com

AMAPALA YACHTS

AMAPALA MARINE SA
SAN DIEGO CA 92124 COAST GUARD MFG ID- AXJ

See inside cover to adjust price for area

LOA FT	LOA IN	NAME AND/ OR MODEL	TOP/ RIG	BOAT TYPE	HULL MTL	HULL TP	ENGINE TP	ENGINE # HP	ENGINE MFG	BEAM FT	BEAM IN	WGT LBS	DRAFT FT	DRAFT IN	RETAIL LOW	RETAIL HIGH
1981 BOATS																
34	11	AMAPALA 35	FB	SPTCR	FBG	SV	IO	T330	CHRY	13	10	17671	2	3	35500	39400
39	9	AMAPALA 40	FB	SPTCR	FBG	SV	IO	T330	CHRY	15	4	24490	2	7	43600	48400
39	9	AMAPALA 40	FB	SPTCR	FBG	SV	IO	T251D	CAT	15	4	24490	2	7	53800	59200
39	9	AMAPALA 40	FB	SPTCR	FBG	SV	IO	T410D	GM	15	4	24490	2	7	58400	64100

CHANTIERS AMEL
17812 PERIGNY CEDEX FRANCE   See inside cover to adjust price for area

For more recent years, see the BUC Used Boat Price Guide, Volume 1 or Volume 2

LOA FT IN	NAME AND/ OR MODEL	TOP/ RIG	BOAT TYPE	HULL MTL TP	TP	ENGINE # HP	MFG	BEAM FT IN	WGT LBS	DRAFT FT IN	RETAIL LOW	RETAIL HIGH
					1978 BOATS							
35	KIRK	SLP	SAIL	FBG KL	IB	25D	VLVO	10	10000	5 5	29700	33000
41	EUROS	KTH	SAIL	FBG KL	IB	75D	VLVO	11	14000	5 5	57700	63400
45	MARAMU	KTH	SAIL	FBG KL	IB	62D	PERK	13 4	20000	6 4	85500	93900
53	MELTEM	KTH	SAIL	FBG KL	IB	106D	VLVO	14 1	30000	6 6	150500	165500
					1977 BOATS							
36 2	KIRK	SLP	SAIL	FBG KL	IB	30D		9 10	10200	5 4	31100	34500
40 6	EUROS	KTH	SAIL	FBG KL	IB	50D		10 10	14000	5 5	54400	59800
52 6	MELTEM	KTH	SAIL	FBG KL	IB	100D		14	30000	6 4	142000	156000
					1976 BOATS							
36 2	KIRK	KTH	SAIL	FBG KL	IB	20D	VLVO	9 11	11648	5 5	34100	37900
40 6	EUROS	KTH	SAIL	FBG KL	IB	75D	REN	10 10	15680	5 5	57700	63400
52 6	MELTEM	KTH	SAIL	FBG KL	IB	100D	REN	14 11	33600	6 5	141500	155500

AMERGLASS N V

Call 1-800-327-6929 for BUC Personalized Evaluation Service
Or, for 1972 to 1973 boats, sign onto www.BUCValuPro.com

AMERICAN BOAT DIST
AM-JET BOATS   COAST GUARD MFG ID- AEN

Call 1-800-327-6929 for BUC Personalized Evaluation Service
Or, for 1980 boats, sign onto www.BUCValuPro.com

AMERICAN BOATBUILDING COMPANY
WARWICK RI   See inside cover to adjust price for area

LOA FT IN	NAME AND/ OR MODEL	TOP/ RIG	BOAT TYPE	HULL MTL TP	TP	ENGINE # HP	MFG	BEAM FT IN	WGT LBS	DRAFT FT IN	RETAIL LOW	RETAIL HIGH
					1963 BOATS							
31 7	GALAXY	SLP	SAIL	FBG	OB						10700	12200
40 7	BLOCK-ISLANDER	SLP	SAIL	FBG	OB						24700	27400
					1962 BOATS							
31 7	GALAXY	SLP	SAIL	FBG	OB						10700	12100
40 9	BLOCK-ISLANDER	SLP	SAIL	FBG	OB						24800	27500
					1961 BOATS							
21	PRIVATEER		BASS	FBG	IB	60		8		1 8	1850	2200
22 6	SEA-SPRITE	SLP	SA/CR	FBG KL				7		3 1	3300	3850
32	GALAXY	SLP	SAIL	FBG KL	OB			10 2		5	10700	12100
32 10	SAYONARA		CR	FBG	IB	T270		11		2 4	14400	16400
40	BLOCK-ISLANDER	SLP	SAIL	FBG	OB			11 9		3 11	24600	27300
40	BLOCK-ISLANDER	YWL	SAIL	FBG	OB			11 9		3 11	24500	27300
					1960 BOATS							
21	PRIVATEER		BASS	FBG	IB	95		8		2	1900	2250
21	PRIVATEER		CBNCR	FBG	IB	120		8 6		2	2650	3050
21	PRIVATEER		CUD	FBG	IB	95		8		2	2550	3000
22 6	SEA-SPRITE	SLP	SA/CR	FBG KL				7		3	3300	3850
24	CORSAIR		BASS	FBG	IB	120		8 6		2	4100	4750
24	CORSAIR		CBNCR	FBG	IB	120		8 6		2	3600	4200
24	CORSAIR		SF	FBG	IB	120		8 6		2	3900	4550
31 7	GALAXY	SLP	SA/CR	FBG CB	OB			10 2			11300	12800
31 7	GALAXY	SLP	SA/CR	FBG KL	OB			10 2		5	11300	12800
32 10	SAYONARA			FBG	IB	270-370		11		2 4	13000	15300
40 8	BLOCK-ISLAND	SLP	SA/CR	FBG KL	OB			11 9			25400	28200
40 8	BLOCK-ISLAND	SLP	SA/CR	FBG KL	OB			11 9		3 4	25400	28200
40 8	BLOCK-ISLAND	YWL	SA/CR	FBG CB	OB			11 9		3 4	25400	28200
					1959 BOATS							
21	PRIVATEER	OP	BASS	FBG	IB	95		8			1850	2200
21	PRIVATEER		CBNCR	FBG	IB	95		8			2450	2800
21	PRIVATEER		CUD	FBG	IB	95		8			2500	2950
22 6	SEA-SPRITE	SLP	SAIL	KL				7		3	3300	3850
24	CORSAIR	OP	BASS	FBG	IB	120		8 6			4050	4700
24	CORSAIR		CBNCR	FBG	IB	120		8 6			3550	4150
24	CORSAIR		SF	FBG	IB	120		8			3850	4450
31 7	GALAXY	SLP	SAIL	KL				10 11		5	10800	12300
40	BLOCK-ISLANDER	YWL	SAIL	FBG KC	IB	32D				4 3	31200	34700
40 8	BLOCK-ISLAND 40	SLP	SAIL	CB				11 9		5	24300	27000

AMERICAN CAR & FOUNDRY CO
A C F
NEW YORK NY   See inside cover to adjust price for area

LOA FT IN	NAME AND/ OR MODEL	TOP/ RIG	BOAT TYPE	HULL MTL TP	TP	ENGINE # HP	MFG	BEAM FT IN	WGT LBS	DRAFT FT IN	RETAIL LOW	RETAIL HIGH
					1939 BOATS							
26	ROAMER	OP	EXP	WD	IB						**	**
32	WANDERER	OP	EXP	WD	IB						**	**
34		HT	CBNCR	WD	IB						**	**
38		OP	EXP	WD	IB	T160					31900	35400
42	VOYAGER	HT	CBNCR	WD	IB	T 73					**	**
42	VOYAGER	HT	DC	WD	IB	T 73					54900	60300
43					IB	T250	CHRY				**	**
46		HT	DC	WD	IB	T					**	**
					1938 BOATS							
72					IB	500D	GM				**	**
					1937 BOATS							
26	ROAMER	OP	EXP		IB		CHRY				**	**
32					IB	190	GRAY				**	**
32	WANDERER	OP	EXP	MHG	IB		CHRY				**	**
32	WANDERER DELUXE	HT	EXP	MHG	IB		CHRY				**	**
34		HT	CR	MHG	IB		CHRY				**	**
38		OP	EXP	MHG	IB	T110	GRAY				32600	36300
40		HT	CBNCR	MHG	IB	T100					**	**
40		HT	DC	MHG	IB	175					54700	60100
42	VOYAGER	HT	CBNCR	MHG	IB	T 73	CHRY	11 3			**	**
42	VOYAGER	HT	DC	MHG	IB	T 73	CHRY	11 3			56400	62000
46		HT	DC	MHG	IB		CHRY				**	**
47		HT	MY	MHG	IB	175					78000	85700
54		HT	MY	MHG	IB	T175					79400	87300
68		HT	MY	MHG	IB	T175					154000	169500
					1936 BOATS							
26		OP	CR	WD	IB		8				**	**
38			EXP	WD	IB	T	SCRI				**	**
					1935 BOATS							
40				WD	IB	400	CHEV				**	**
					1934 BOATS							
39		HT	CR	WD	IB	T105					44300	49200
					1932 BOATS							
30		HT	CBNCR	WD	IB						**	**
30		HT	DC	WD	IB						**	**
30			RNBT	WD	IB						**	**
38		HT	CR	WD	IB	T					**	**
39		HT	CR	WD	IB						**	**
40		HT	CR	WD	IB						**	**
40		HT	DC	WD	IB						**	**
46		HT	DC	WD	IB						**	**
47		HT	MY	WD	IB						**	**
54		HT	MY	WD	IB						**	**
68		HT	MY	WD	IB						**	**
					1931 BOATS							
30		HT	CBNCR	WD	IB	75					15600	17700
39		HT	CR	WD	IB	T					**	**
46		HT	DC	WD	IB	T110					77100	84700
					1928 BOATS							
54					IB	T165D	GM				**	**

AMERICAN CATAMARANS LTD

Call 1-800-327-6929 for BUC Personalized Evaluation Service
Or, for 1971 to 1972 boats, sign onto www.BUCValuPro.com

AMERICAN FIBERGLASS CORP
STAMFORD CT 06902   COAST GUARD MFG ID- AFC   See inside cover to adjust price for area

LOA FT IN	NAME AND/ OR MODEL	TOP/ RIG	BOAT TYPE	HULL MTL TP	TP	ENGINE # HP	MFG	BEAM FT IN	WGT LBS	DRAFT FT IN	RETAIL LOW	RETAIL HIGH
					1979 BOATS							
17 7	AMERICAN 2+2	SLP	SA/CR	FBG KC	OB			7	1500		2850	3300
17 7	DISCOVERER	SLP	SA/OD	FBG CB	OB			6	650		1850	2200
21	AMERICAN 21	SLP	SA/CR	FBG DB	OB			8	2200		3750	4400
					1978 BOATS							
17 7	AMERICAN 2+2	SLP	SAIL	FBG KC	OB			7	950	1 4	2150	2500
17 7	DISCOVERER	SLP	SA/OD	FBG CB	OB			6 4	650	9	1800	2100
21	AMERICAN 21	SLP	SAIL	FBG SK	OB			8	2200	1 6	3650	4200

AMERICAN FIBERGLASS CORP   -CONTINUED   See inside cover to adjust price for area

LOA FT IN	NAME AND/ OR MODEL	TOP/ RIG	BOAT TYPE	-HULL- MTL TP	TP	----ENGINE--- # HP MFG	BEAM FT IN	WGT LBS	DRAFT FT IN	RETAIL LOW	RETAIL HIGH
------------------- 1977 BOATS ---
17	MINI-TONNER	SLP	SAIL	FBG	CB OB	7		950	4	2050	2450
------------------- 1976 BOATS ---
17	MINI-TONNER 2+2	SLP	SAIL	FBG	KC OB	7 1		900	1 5	1950	2300
------------------- 1966 BOATS ---
30	TEX-TRI 30 6 SLEEPER	SAIL	FBG	CT						14300	16200

AMERICAN INT'L YACHT CORP
COAST GUARD MFG ID- AYE

Call 1-800-327-6929 for BUC Personalized Evaluation Service
Or, for 1971 to 1973 boats, sign onto www.BUCValuPro.com

AMERICAN LEISURE PRODUCTS INC

Call 1-800-327-6929 for BUC Personalized Evaluation Service
Or, for 1972 boats, sign onto www.BUCValuPro.com

AMERICAN MARC INC

Call 1-800-327-6929 for BUC Personalized Evaluation Service
Or, for 1960 to 1961 boats, sign onto www.BUCValuPro.com

AMERICAN MARINE LTD
NEWPORT BEACH CA   See inside cover to adjust price for area

LOA FT IN	NAME AND/ OR MODEL	TOP/ RIG	BOAT TYPE	-HULL- MTL TP	TP	----ENGINE--- # HP MFG	BEAM FT IN	WGT LBS	DRAFT FT IN	RETAIL LOW	RETAIL HIGH
------------------- 1969 BOATS ---
34 9	MAGELLAN 36	SLP	SA/CR	WD	KL IB	35D	10 7	15000	4 5	31100	34500
38 6	MAGELLAN 39	SLP	SA/CR	WD	KL IB	60D	11 6	17521	4 9	38100	42300
46	MAGELLAN 46	KTH	SA/CR	WD	KL IB	90D	12 8	32594	5 3	70700	77700
------------------- 1968 BOATS ---
34 9	MAGELLAN 35	SLP	SA/CR	WD	KL IB	35D	10 7	15000	4 5	30800	34200
38 6	MAGELLAN 39		SA/CR	WD	KL IB	60D	11 6	17521	4 9	37700	41900
46	MAGELLAN 46	KTH	SA/CR	WD	KL IB	90D	12 8	32594	5 3	69900	76800
------------------- 1967 BOATS ---
34 6	MAGELLAN 35	SLP	SA/CR	WD	KL IB	D	10 7		4 8	30400	33800
38 6	MAGELLAN 39	SLP	SA/CR	WD	KL IB	D	11 5		4 9	37000	41100
38 6	MAGELLAN 39	KTH	SA/CR	WD	KL IB	D	11 5		4 9	37000	41200
45 8	MAGELLAN 46	SLP	SA/CR	WD	KL IB	D	12 8		5 3	68100	74800
45 8	MAGELLAN 46	KTH	SA/CR	WD	KL IB	D	12 8		5 3	68200	74900

AMERICAN MARINER IND
ORANGE CA 92665   COAST GUARD MFG ID- AMX See inside cover to adjust price for area

LOA FT IN	NAME AND/ OR MODEL	TOP/ RIG	BOAT TYPE	-HULL- MTL TP	TP	----ENGINE--- # HP MFG	BEAM FT IN	WGT LBS	DRAFT FT IN	RETAIL LOW	RETAIL HIGH
------------------- 1983 BOATS ---
20 9	AMERICAN 6.5	SLP	SA/CR	FBG	KL		7 10	2500	2 2	2550	3000
23	AMERICAN 7.0	SLP	SA/CR	FBG	KL		7 10	3500	2 2	3600	4200
24 9	AMERICAN 7.5	SLP	SA/CR	FBG	KL		8	4600	2 4	5050	5800
26 9	AMERICAN 8.0	SLP	SA/CR	FBG	KL		8	5600	2 4	6500	7450
27 6	AMERICAN 8.5	MS		FBG	KL IB	D	8	6500	2 4	8500	9750
29 11	AMERICAN 9.0	SLP	SA/CR	FBG	KL IB		10 8	10000	3 8	13700	15600
------------------- 1982 BOATS ---
20 9	AMERICAN 6.5	SLP	SA/CR	FBG	KL OB		7 10	2500	2 2	2400	2800
23	AMERICAN 7.0	SLP	SA/CR	FBG	KL OB		7 10	3500	2 2	3400	3950
24	AMERICAN 7.5	SLP	SA/CR	FBG	KL OB		8	4600	2 4	4700	5400
24	AMERICAN 7.5II	SLP	SA/CR	FBG	KL OB	D YAN	8	4800	2 4	5350	6200
26 9	AMERICAN 8.0	SLP	SA/CR	FBG	KL IB	D YAN	8	5600	2 4	6450	7400
26 9	AMERICAN 8.0II	SLP	SA/CR	FBG	KL IB		8	5800	2 4	7050	8100
27 6	AMERICAN 8.5MS	SLP	SA/CR	FBG	KL IB	D YAN	8	6200	2 4	7350	8450
27 6	AMERICAN 8.5MS	SLP	SA/CR	FBG	KL IB	D YAN	8	6500	2 4	8000	9200
29 11	AMERICAN 9.0	SLP	SA/CR	FBG	KL IB	23D YAN	10 8	10000	3 6	12900	14700
------------------- 1981 BOATS ---
20 9	AMERICAN 6.5	SLP	SA/CR	FBG	KL OB		7 10	2500	2 2	2300	2650
23	AMERICAN 7.0	SLP	SA/CR	FBG	KL OB		7 10	3500	2 2	3200	3750
24	AMERICAN 7.5	SLP	SA/CR	FBG	KL OB		8	4600	2 4	4400	5050
24	AMERICAN 7.5II	SLP	SA/CR	FBG	KL OB	15D	8	4800	2 4	5050	5850
26 9	AMERICAN 8.0	SLP	SA/CR	FBG	KL IB	15D	8	5600	2 4	6050	7000
26 9	AMERICAN 8.0II	SLP	SA/CR	FBG	KL IB	15D	8	5800	2 4	6600	7600
27 6	AMERICAN 8.5MS	SLP	SA/CR	FBG	KL IB	15D	8	6500	2 4	7500	8650
29 11	AMERICAN 9.0	SLP	SA/CR	FBG	KL IB		10 8	10000	3 6	12200	13800
------------------- 1980 BOATS ---
20 9	AMERICAN 6.5	SLP	SA/CR	FBG	KL OB		7 10	2500	2 2	2200	2550
23	AMERICAN 7.0	SLP	SA/CR	FBG	KL OB		7 10	3500	2 2	3050	3550
24	AMERICAN 7.5	SLP	SA/CR	FBG	KL OB		8	4600	2 4	4150	4850
24	AMERICAN 7.5II	SLP	SA/CR	FBG	KL OB	15D YAN	8	4800	2 4	4850	5550
26 9	AMERICAN 8.0	SLP	SA/CR	FBG	KL IB		8	5600	2 4	5800	6650
26 9	AMERICAN 8.0II	SLP	SA/CR	FBG	KL IB	15D YAN	8	5800	2 4	6350	7250
27 6	AMERICAN 8.5MS	SLP	SA/CR	FBG	KL IB	15D YAN	8	6500	2 4	7200	8300
29 11	AMERICAN 9.0	SLP	SA/CR	FBG	KL IB	15D YAN	10 8	10000	3 6	11600	13200
------------------- 1979 BOATS ---
20 9	AMERICAN 6.5	SLP	SA/CR	FBG	KL OB		7 10	2500	2 2	2050	2450
23	AMERICAN 7.0	SLP	SA/CR	FBG	KL OB		7 10	3500	2 2	2950	3450
24	AMERICAN 7.5	SLP	SA/CR	FBG	KL OB		8	4600	2 4	4650	4650
24	AMERICAN 7.5II	SLP	SA/CR	FBG	KL OB	15D YAN	8	4800	2 4	4700	5400
26 9	AMERICAN 8.0	SLP	SA/CR	FBG	KL IB		8	5600	2 4	5600	6400
26 9	AMERICAN 8.0II	SLP	SA/CR	FBG	KL IB	15D YAN	8	5800	2 4	6100	7000
27 6	AMERICAN 8.5MS	SLP	SA/CR	FBG	KL IB	15D YAN	8	6500	2 4	6950	7950
------------------- 1978 BOATS ---
22 9	AMERICAN 7.0	SLP	SA/CR	FBG	KL OB		7 10	3300	2 2	2650	3100
24	AMERICAN 7.5	SLP	SA/CR	FBG	KL OB		7 11	4300	2 4	3600	4200
24	AMERICAN 7.5D	SLP	SA/CR	FBG	KL OB	16D BALD	7 11	4300	2 4	4300	4950
26 6	AMERICAN 8.0	SLP	SA/CR	FBG	KL IB		7 11	5300	2 4	5050	5800
26 6	AMERICAN 8.0D	SLP	SA/CR	FBG	KL IB	16D BALD	7 11	5600	2 4	5600	6450
27 6	AMERICAN 8.5MS	SLP	SA/CR	FBG	KL IB	16D BALD	7 11	6300	2 4	6450	7400
29 9	AMERICAN	SLP	SA/CR	FBG	KL IB	D	10	7000	3 9	7400	8550
------------------- 1977 BOATS ---
22	AMERICAN 22	SLP	SA/CR	FBG	KL OB	15 OMC	7 10	2800	2 2	2200	2600
22	AMERICAN 22	SLP	SA/CR	FBG	KL OB	8D YAN	7 10	2800	2 2	2350	2750
22	AMERICAN 22	SLP	SA/CR	FBG	KL OB		7 10	2800	2 2	2700	3150
23 8	AMERICAN 24	SLP	SA/CR	FBG	KL OB	15 OMC	8	3500	2 4	2850	3300
23 8	AMERICAN 24	SLP	SA/CR	FBG	KL OB	8D YAN	8	3500	2 4	3000	3500
23 8	AMERICAN 24	SLP	SA/CR	FBG	KL OB		8	3500	2 4	3200	3750
26 6	AMERICAN 26	SLP	SA/CR	FBG	KL IB	15 OMC	8	4500	2 4	4100	4800
26 6	AMERICAN 26	SLP	SA/CR	FBG	KL IB	8D YAN	8	4500	2 4	4200	4900
26 6	AMERICAN 26	SLP	SA/CR	FBG	KL IB		8	4500	2 4	4500	5050
27 6	AMERICAN 28 MS	SLP	MS	FBG	KL IB	8D YAN	8	5500	2 4	5400	6250
------------------- 1976 BOATS ---
23	AMERICAN 23	SLP	SAIL	FBG	KL OB		7 11	3000	2 4	2350	2750
26	AMERICAN 26	SLP	MS	FBG	KL OB	8D YAN	7 11	5500	2 4	5050	5800
26	AMERICAN 26	SLP	SAIL	FBG	KL OB		7 11	4000	2 4	3500	4050
------------------- 1975 BOATS ---
23	AMERICAN 23	SLP	SAIL	FBG	KL OB		8	3000	2 4	2300	2700
26	AMERICAN 26	SLP	SAIL	FBG	KL OB		8	4000	2 4	3400	3950
28	AMERICAN 28	SLP	MS	FBG	KL IB	15D- 25D	8	6000	2 4	5650	6550

AMERICAN RIVER MFG COMPANY
COAST GUARD MFG ID- ARU

Call 1-800-327-6929 for BUC Personalized Evaluation Service
Or, for 1982 to 2002 boats, sign onto www.BUCValuPro.com

AMERICAN SKIER
AMERICAN SKIER BOAT COR COAST GUARD MFG ID- SKI

Call 1-800-327-6929 for BUC Personalized Evaluation Service
Or, for 1977 to 1995 boats, sign onto www.BUCValuPro.com

AMERICAN SLEEK CRAFT INC
SLEEK CRAFT
SANTA FE SPRINGS CA 906 COAST GUARD MFG ID- SLE   See inside cover to adjust price for area
FORMERLY SLEEK CRAFT BOATS

For more recent years, see the BUC Used Boat Price Guide, Volume 1 or Volume 2

LOA FT IN	NAME AND/ OR MODEL	TOP/ RIG	BOAT TYPE	-HULL- MTL TP	TP	----ENGINE--- # HP MFG	BEAM FT IN	WGT LBS	DRAFT FT IN	RETAIL LOW	RETAIL HIGH
------------------- 1983 BOATS ---
18	REBEL	OP	SKI	FBG SV	JT	320 BERK	7 2	925		3500	4100
18	SPORTSTER	OP	SKI	FBG SV	JT	320-325	7 2	925		3500	4250
19	KAUAI	OP	SKI	FBG SV	JT	320-325	7 2	925		3950	4550
20 2	ARISTOCRAT	OP	SKI	FBG SV	OB		7 2	950		2350	2750
20 2	ARISTOCRAT	OP	SKI	FBG SV	JT	320-325	7 2	950		4550	5200
20 2	ARISTOCRAT	OP	SKI	FBG TH	OB		7 2	950		2450	2850
20 2	ARISTOCRAT			FBG TH	IO	228 MRCR	7 2	950		2950	3450
	JT 320 BERK	4800	5500,	JT	325	BERK 4700	5400, JT	325	HARD	4700	5400

LOA FT IN	NAME AND/ OR MODEL	TOP/ RIG	BOAT TYPE	-HULL- MTL TP	----ENGINE--- TP # HP MFG	BEAM FT IN	WGT LBS	DRAFT FT IN	RETAIL LOW	RETAIL HIGH
				1983 BOATS						
20	2 ARISTOCRAT	OP	SKI	FBG TH	JT 325 PANT	7 2	950		5000	5750
20	2 ARISTOCRAT	OP	SKI	FBG TH	VD 325 HARD	7 2	950		4400	5050
20	2 ARISTOCRAT	OP	SKI	FBG TH	VD 325 PANT	7 2	950		6750	7750
20	2 SST	OP	SKI	FBG TH	OB	7 2	950		2550	2950
20	2 SST	OP	SKI	FBG TH	IO 228 MRCR	7 2	950		3650	4250
	JT 320 BERK 5100	5850, JT	325	BERK	5000 5750, JT	325	HARD		5000	5750
	JT 325 PANT 5300	6100, VD	325	HARD	4700 5400, VD	325	PANT		7200	8300
20	2 SSU	OP	SKI	FBG SV	JT 320-325	7 2	950		4950	5950
21	JR-EXECUTIVE	OP	SPTCR	FBG TH	OB				5550	6350
21	3 DIPLOMAT	OP	SPTCR	FBG SV	OB				5650	6500
21	3 DIPLOMAT	OP	SPTCR	FBG SV	IO 228 MRCR	7 2	1550		3800	4450
21	3 DIPLOMAT	OP	SPTCR	FBG SV	IO 260	7 2	1550		3950	4850
21	3 DIPLOMAT	OP	SPTCR	FBG SV	IO 320-325	7 2	1550		5200	5950
21	3 DIPLOMAT	OP	SPTCR	FBG TH	OB				3600	6500
21	3 DIPLOMAT	OP	SPTCR	FBG TH	IO 228-260	7 2	1550		4000	4900
21	3 DIPLOMAT	OP	SPTCR	FBG TH	JT 320-325	7 2	1550		5450	6250
21	3 JR-EXECUTIVE	OP	SPTCR	FBG SV	OB	7 2	1550		3800	4450
21	3 JR-EXECUTIVE	OP	SPTCR	FBG SV	IO 228 MRCR	7 2	1550		3750	4350
	IO 260 MRCR 3800	4450, IO	260	VLVO	4150 4850, JT	320	BERK		5150	5900
	JT 325 BERK 5100	5850, JT	325	HARD	5100 5850, JT	325	PANT		5400	6200
	VD 325 HARD 4800	5550, VD	325	PANT	7200 8250					
21	3 JR-EXECUTIVE	OP	SPTCR	FBG TH	IO 228 MRCR	7 2	1550		3800	4400
	IO 260 4100	5050, JT	320	BERK	5400 6200, JT	325	BERK		5350	6150
	JT 325 HARD 5350	6150, JT	325	PANT	5650 6500, VD	325	HARD		5050	5800
	VD 325 PANT 7550	8650								
23	EXECUTIVE	OP	CUD	FBG DV	OB	8	1800		4600	5300
23	EXECUTIVE	OP	CUD	FBG DV	IO 228-260	8	1800		4550	5650
	JT 320 BERK 6100	7000, JT	325	BERK	6100 7000, JT	325	HARD		6100	7000
	JT 325 PANT 6100	7000, VD	325	HARD	5750 6600					
26	AMBASSADOR	OP	CUD	FBG DV	IO 260	8	2000		7050	8300
26	AMBASSADOR	OP	CUD	FBG DV	JT 320-325	8	2000		9150	10400
30	MONTEREY	OP	OFF	FBG DV	IO T290-T330	8	6500		19700	22600
36	COMMODORE	OP	OFF	FBG DV	IO T330 MRCR	8	8000		27300	30300
36	CONDOR	OP	OFF	FBG DV	IO T290 VLVO	8	8000		27400	30400
36	CONDOR	OP	OFF	FBG DV	IO T330 MRCR	8	8000		28400	31600
				1982 BOATS						
18	REBEL	OP	SKI	FBG SV	JT 320-325	7 2	925		3350	3900
18	SPORTSTER	OP	SKI	FBG SV	JT 320-325	7 2	925		3350	3900
19	KAUAI	OP	SKI	FBG SV	JT 320-325	7 2	925		3750	4350
20	2 ARISTOCRAT	OP	SKI	FBG SV	IO 225 MRCR	7 2	950		3150	3650
20	2 ARISTOCRAT	OP	SKI	FBG SV	JT 320-325	7 2	950		4550	5250
20	2 ARISTOCRAT	OP	SKI	FBG TH	IO 225 MRCR	7 2	950		3200	3750
	JT 320 BERK 4750	5450, JT	325	HARD	4750 5450, JT	325	PANT		4750	5450
	VD 325 BERK 4350	5000, VD	325	HARD	4350 5000, VD	325	PANT		6650	7650
20	2 SST	OP	SKI	FBG TH	IO 225 MRCR	7 2	950		3200	3750
	JT 320 BERK 4750	5450, JT	325	HARD	4750 5450, JT	325	PANT		4750	5450
	VD 325 BERK 4350	5000, VD	325	HARD	4350 5000, VD	325	PANT		6650	7650
20	2 SSV	OP	SKI	FBG SV	JT 320-325	7 2	950		4550	5250
21	3 DIPLOMAT	OP	SPTCR	FBG SV	IO 225 MRCR	7 2	1550		3650	4250
21	3 DIPLOMAT	OP	SPTCR	FBG SV	IO 260	7 2	1550		3800	4700
21	3 DIPLOMAT	OP	SPTCR	FBG SV	JT 320-325	7 2	1550		4950	5700
21	3 DIPLOMAT	OP	SPTCR	FBG TH	IO 225 MRCR	7 2	1550		3850	4500
21	3 DIPLOMAT	OP	SPTCR	FBG TH	IO 260	7 2	1550		4000	4950
21	3 DIPLOMAT	OP	SPTCR	FBG TH	JT 320-325	7 2	1550		5250	6050
21	3 JR-EXECUTIVE	OP	SPTCR	FBG SV	IO 225 MRCR	7 2	1550		3600	4200
	IO 260 3800	4650, JT	320	BERK	4900 5650, JT	325	HARD		4900	5650
	JT 325 PANT 4900	5650, VD	325	BERK	4600 5300, VD	325	HARD		4900	5300
	VD 325 PANT 6850	7900								
21	3 JR-EXECUTIVE	OP	SPTCR	FBG TH	IO 225 MRCR	7 2	1550		3800	4400
	IO 260 4000	4900, JT	320	BERK	5200 5950, JT	325	HARD		5200	5950
	JT 325 PANT 5200	5950, VD	325	BERK	4850 5550, VD	325	HARD		4850	5550
	VD 325 PANT 7250	8300								
23	AMBASSADOR	OP	CUD	FBG DV	IO 260	8	2000		4700	5650
23	AMBASSADOR	OP	CUD	FBG DV	JT 320-325	8	2000		5950	6850
23	EXECUTIVE	OP	CUD	FBG DV	IO 225-260	8	1800		4450	5500
	JT 320 BERK 5850	6700, JT	325	HARD	5850 6700, JT	325	PANT		5850	6700
	VD 325 BERK 5500	6300								
26	AMBASSADOR		CUD	FBG DV	IO 260	8	2000		6900	8100
26	AMBASSADOR		CUD	FBG DV	JT 325	8	2000		8650	9950
30	COMMODORE	OP	OFF	FBG DV	IO T330 MRCR	8	8000		20700	23000
30	MONTEREY	OP	OFF	FBG DV	IO T290-T330	8	6500		19200	22000
				1979 BOATS						
18	REBEL	OP	RNBT	FBG DV	JT	7 2	925		**	**
18	SPORTSTER	OP	RNBT	FBG DV	JT	6 8	800		**	**
19	KAUAI	OP	SKI	FBG DV	JT	7 2	925		**	**
20	2 ARISTOCRAT	OP	RNBT	FBG DV	OB	7 3	950		2300	2650
20	2 ARISTOCRAT	OP	RNBT	FBG TH	OB	7 3	950		**	**
20	2 ARISTOCRAT	OP	RNBT	FBG DV	JT	7 3	950		2300	2650
20	2 ARISTOCRAT	OP	RNBT	FBG TH	JT	7 3	950		**	**
20	2 SST	OP	RNBT	FBG DV	JT	7 3	950		**	**
20	2 SST	OP	RNBT	FBG TH	JT	7 3	950		**	**
21	3 DIPLOMAT	OP	SKI	FBG DV	JT	7 3	1550		**	**
21	3 DIPLOMAT	OP	SKI	FBG DV	VD	7 3	1550		**	**
21	3 DIPLOMAT	OP	SKI	FBG TH	JT	7 3	1550		**	**
21	3 DIPLOMAT	OP	SKI	FBG TH	IO	7 3	1550		**	**
21	3 DIPLOMAT	OP	SKI	FBG TH	VD	7 3	1550		**	**
21	3 JR-EXECUTIVE	OP	SKI	FBG DV	JT	7 3	1550		**	**
21	3 JR-EXECUTIVE	OP	SKI	FBG DV	IO	7 3	1550		**	**
21	3 JR-EXECUTIVE	OP	SKI	FBG DV	VD	7 3	1550		**	**
21	3 JR-EXECUTIVE	OP	SKI	FBG TH	JT	7 3	1550		**	**
21	3 JR-EXECUTIVE	OP	SKI	FBG TH	IO	7 3	1550		**	**
21	3 JR-EXECUTIVE	OP	SKI	FBG TH	VD	7 3	1550		**	**
23	EXECUTIVE	OP	CUD	FBG DV	IO	8	1800		**	**
23	EXECUTIVE	OP	CUD	FBG DV	VD	8	1800		**	**
23	EXECUTIVE	OP	CUD	FBG DV	JT T	8	1800		**	**
26	AMBASSADOR	OP	CUD	FBG DV	IO T	8	2000		**	**
26	AMBASSADOR	OP	CUD	FBG DV	VD T	8	2000		**	**
36	COMMANDER	OP	CR	FBG DV	IO T	8	8000		**	**
				1978 BOATS						
18	REBEL	OP	RNBT	FBG DV	JT	7 2	925		**	**
18	SPORTSTER	OP	RNBT	FBG DV	JT	6 8	800		**	**
18	1 MAKAI	OP	RNBT	FBG DV	JT	7 2	900		**	**
18	6 KAWAI	OP	SKI	FBG DV	OB	7 2	925		1850	2150
18	6 KAWAI	OP	SKI	FBG DV	JT	7 2	925		**	**
20	2 ARISTOCRAT	OP	RNBT	FBG DV	OB	7 3	950		2300	2650
20	2 ARISTOCRAT	OP	RNBT	FBG DV	IO 255-260	7 3	950		3500	4050
20	2 STREAKER	OP	RNBT	FBG TH	JT	7 3	950		**	**
21	3 DIPLOMAT	OP	FSH	FBG DV	JT	7 3	1550		**	**
21	3 DIPLOMAT	OP	SKI	FBG DV	JT	7 3	1550		**	**
21	3 JR-EXECUTIVE	OP	SKI	FBG DV	JT	7 3	1550		**	**
23	EXECUTIVE		CUD	FBG DV	JT	8	1800		**	**
25	6 AMBASSADOR		CUD	FBG DV	JT	8	2000		**	**
				1975 BOATS						
17	MONTEREY	OP	RNBT	FBG DV	OB	7 2			2000	2350
17	MONTEREY	OP	RNBT	FBG DV	JT 325 OLDS	7 5			2500	2900
18	REBEL	OP	RNBT	FBG SV	JT 325 OLDS	7 5			2750	3200
18	SPORTSTER	OP	RNBT	FBG DV	JT 325 OLDS	6 8			3000	3500
20	2 STREAKER	OP	RNBT	FBG DV	JT 325 OLDS	7 5			3450	4050
21	JR-EXECUTIVE	HT	CR	FBG DV	JT 325 OLDS	7 7			4200	4900
22	6 EXECUTIVE	HT	CR	FBG DV	JT 325 OLDS	7 8			5150	5900
24	6 AMBASSADOR	HT	CR	FBG DV	JT 325 OLDS	7 8			6000	6900

AMERICAN YACHT COMPANY

Call 1-800-327-6929 for BUC Personalized Evaluation Service
Or, for 1963 to 1966 boats, sign onto www.BUCValuPro.com

AMPRO INDUSTRIES
DORION VAUDREUIL QUE CA COAST GUARD MFG ID- MYL See inside cover to adjust price for area
FORMERLY MIRAGE YACHTS LTD

For more recent years, see the BUC Used Boat Price Guide, Volume 1 or Volume 2

LOA FT IN	NAME AND/ OR MODEL	TOP/ RIG	BOAT TYPE	-HULL- MTL TP	----ENGINE--- TP # HP MFG	BEAM FT IN	WGT LBS	DRAFT FT IN	RETAIL LOW	RETAIL HIGH
				1983 BOATS						
25	KIRBY 25	SLP	SA/RC	FBG KL	OB	8 9	3100	4 2	5350	6150
25	MIRAGE 25	SLP	SA/RC	FBG KL	OB	9 6	4300	4 4	7200	8250
25	MIRAGE 25	SLP	SA/RC	FBG KL	SD 8 VLVO	9 6	4300	4 4	7450	8550

AMPRO INDUSTRIES — CONTINUED

See inside cover to adjust price for area

```
LOA   NAME AND/      TOP/ BOAT  -HULL- ----ENGINE---  BEAM  WGT  DRAFT RETAIL RETAIL
FT IN OR MODEL       RIG  TYPE  MTL TP TP #  HP  MFG  FT IN LBS  FT IN  LOW   HIGH
------------------- 1983 BOATS ----------------------------------------------------
27    MIRAGE 27      SLP SA/RC FBG KL SD      8  VLVO  9  3 5500  4  4 10800 12300
27    MIRAGE 27      SLP SA/RC FBG KL IB 8D  YAN   9  3 5500  4  4 11100 12600
30    KIRBY 30       SLP SA/RC FBG KL IB 8D  YAN  10  3 5500  5   12600 14300
30    MIRAGE 30      SLP SA/RC FBG KL IB 15D YAN  10  6 7000  4  3 16100 18300
33  6 MIRAGE 33      SLP SA/RC FBG KL IB 15D- 20D YAN 11  8 9300  5   22800 25300
------------------- 1982 BOATS ----------------------------------------------------
25    KIRBY 25       SLP SA/RC FBG KL OB          8  9 3100  4  2  5050  5800
27    MIRAGE 27      SLP SA/RC FBG KL IB    D     9  3 5500  4  4 10500 11900
30    KIRBY 30       SLP SA/RC FBG KL IB    D    10  3 5500  5   11900 13500
33    MIRAGE 33      SLP SA/RC FBG KL IB    D    11  6 9000  5   20700 23000
------------------- 1981 BOATS ----------------------------------------------------
25    KIRBY 25       SLP SA/RC FBG KL OB          8  9 3100  4  2  4750  5450
27    MIRAGE 27      SLP SA/RC FBG KL IB    D     9  3 5500  4  4  9850 11200
30    KIRBY 30       SLP SA/RC FBG KL IB    D    10  3 5500  5   11200 12700
------------------- 1979 BOATS ----------------------------------------------------
23 10 MIRAGE 24      SLP SA/CR FBG KL OB          8  5 3600  4    4500  5200
25    KIRBY 25       SLP SA/CR FBG KL OB          8  9 3100  4  2  4500  5050
26  2 MIRAGE 26      SLP SA/CR FBG KL OB          9  3 5200  4  3  7700  8850
26  2 MIRAGE 26      SLP SA/CR FBG KL SD 15  OMC  9  3 5200  4  3  7900  9100
------------------- 1978 BOATS ----------------------------------------------------
23 10 MIRAGE 24      SLP SA/CR FBG KL OB          8  5 3600  4    4350  5000
26  2 MIRAGE 26      SLP SA/CR FBG KL OB          9  3 5200  4  4  7450  8550
26  2 MIRAGE 26      SLP SA/CR FBG KL SD 15  OMC  9  3 5200  4  4  7600  8750
27 11 MIRAGE 27      SLP SA/CR FBG KL IB 12D YAN  9  3 6830  4  3 11300 12900
------------------- 1977 BOATS ----------------------------------------------------
27    MIRAGE 27      SLP SA/CR FBG KL IB 12D YAN  9  2 6850  4  2 10500 12000
------------------- 1976 BOATS ----------------------------------------------------
23 10 MIRAGE 24      SLP SAIL  FBG KL OB          8  5 3700  4    4150  4800
27    MIRAGE 27      SLP SAIL  FBG KL IB 12D YAN  9  3 6500  4  3  9650 11000
------------------- 1975 BOATS ----------------------------------------------------
23 10 MIRAGE 24      SLP SA/CR FBG KL IB    D     8  5 3700  4    4550  5250
27    MIRAGE 27      SLP SA/CR FBG KL IB    D     9  3 6800  4  2  9850 11200
```

AMSTERDAM SHIPYARD INC
AMSTERDAM HOLLAND

See inside cover to adjust price for area

```
LOA   NAME AND/        TOP/ BOAT  -HULL- ----ENGINE---  BEAM  WGT  DRAFT RETAIL RETAIL
FT IN OR MODEL         RIG  TYPE  MTL TP TP #  HP  MFG  FT IN LBS  FT IN  LOW   HIGH
------------------- 1965 BOATS --------------------------------------------------------
21  6 CINDERELLA       SLP SAIL  FBG TK           7           2  2 2800  3250
24  9 MERIDIAN         SLP SAIL  FBG KL           7           3  3 4350  5000
29    TRIPP-LENTCH     SLP SAIL  FBG KL           9           4  6 6050  6950
------------------- 1961 BOATS --------------------------------------------------------
26  3 STANDARD CABIN CR    CBNCR FBG     IB T 65  8  9        2  8 22500 25000
33  6 SWIFTSURE        SLP SA/CR FBG CB OB       10             15900 18000
------------------- 1960 BOATS --------------------------------------------------------
26  3 STANDARD CABIN CR    CBNCR FBG     IB T 65  8  9        2  8 22100 24500
33  6 SWIFTSURE        SLP SA/CR FBG CB OB       10             15900 18100
```

ANACAPA BOAT CO
LOS ANGELES HARBOR MARINE CO

Call 1-800-327-6929 for BUC Personalized Evaluation Service
Or, for 1965 to 1968 boats, sign onto www.BUCValuPro.com

ANACAPRI MARINE INC
MIAMI FL 33142   COAST GUARD MFG ID- AKR   See inside cover to adjust price for area
FOR OLDER MODELS SEE A C MANUFACTURING CO INC

For more recent years, see the BUC Used Boat Price Guide, Volume 1 or Volume 2

```
LOA   NAME AND/         TOP/ BOAT  -HULL- ----ENGINE---  BEAM  WGT  DRAFT RETAIL RETAIL
FT IN OR MODEL          RIG  TYPE  MTL TP TP #  HP   MFG FT IN LBS  FT IN  LOW   HIGH
------------------- 1983 BOATS ------------------------------------------------------------
19    PROFESSIONAL V190   OP CTRCN FBG DV OB                              4900  5600
19    PROFESSIONAL V190   OP CTRCN FBG DV IO 120-175                      2750  3400
22    ANGLER V220 CTRCN   HT CUD  FBG DV IO 120-228  8         3040 2 4  4800  5700
        IO 290 VLVO 5350  6150, IO 130D VLVO 5950  6850, IO T120-T140 5350 6450

22    NEWPORT V220        OP RNBT FBG SV OB          8         3240 2 4  9750 11100
22    NEWPORT V220        OP RNBT FBG SV IO 120-230  8              2 4  4750  5800
        IO 260-290 5000  6250, IO 130D VLVO 5850  6700, IO T120-T170 5400 6500

22    NEWPORT V220        HT RNBT FBG SV OB          8         3240 2 4  9750 11100
22    NEWPORT V220        HT RNBT FBG SV IO 120-230  8              2 4  4750  5800
        IO 260-290 5000  6250, IO 130D VLVO 5850  6700, IO T120-T170 5400 6500

22    TORINO V220         OP CUD  FBG SV IO 200-290   8        3440 2 4  5300  6600
22    TORINO V230         OP CUD  FBG SV OB           8        2720 2 4  8700 10000
22    TORINO V230         OP CUD  FBG SV IO 120-200   8        3440 2 4  5050  6000
22    TORINO V230         OP CUD  FBG SV IO 130D VLVO 8        3440 2 4  6350  7300
22    TORINO V230         HT CUD  FBG SV OB           8        2720 2 4  8700 10000
22    TORINO V230         HT CUD  FBG SV IO 120-230   8        3440 2 4  5050  6150
        IO 260-290 5300  6600, IO 130D VLVO 6350  7300, IO T120-T170 5700 6900

22  3 ANGLER V220 CTRCN   HT CUD  FBG SV OB          8         2400 2 4  8050  9250
22  3 ANGLER V220 CTRCN   HT CUD  FBG SV IO 120  MRCR 8        2400 2 4  4150  4800
        IO 120-230 4700  5700, IO 260 5000  5950, IO T120-T170 5350 6200

22  3 ANGLER V220 CTRCN   FB CUD  FBG SV OB          8         2400 2 4  8050  9250
22  3 ANGLER V220 CTRCN   FB CUD  FBG SV IO 120-230  8         3040 2 4  4700  5750
        IO 260 5950, IO 290 VLVO 5450  6250, IO 130D VLVO 6000 6900
        IO T120-T170 5400 6550

22  3 ANGLER V220 CTRCN   OP OPFSH FBG SV OB         8         2400 2 4  8050  9250
22  3 ANGLER V220 CTRCN   OP OPFSH FBG SV IO 120-230 8         3040 2 4  5000  6150
        IO 260 6350, IO 290 VLVO 5800  6650, IO 130D VLVO 7550 8700
        IO T120-T170 5750 7000

22  3 ANGLER V220 CTRCN   TT OPFSH FBG SV OB         8         2400 2 4  8050  9250
22  3 ANGLER V220 CTRCN   TT OPFSH FBG SV IO 120-230 8         3040 2 4  5000  6150
        IO 260 6350, IO 290 VLVO 5800  6650, IO 130D VLVO 7550 8700
        IO T120-T170 5750 7000

24 10 ANBLER V250 CTRCN   HT CUD  FBG SV OB          8         3400 2 4 11800 13500
24 10 ANGLER V250 CTRCN   HT CUD  FBG SV IO 170-230  8         3800 2 4  6250  7600
        IO 260-290 6650  8150, IO 130D VLVO 7250  8300, IO T120-T185 7050 8450

24 10 ANGLER V250 CTRCN   FB CUD  FBG SV OB          8         3400 2 4 11800 13400
24 10 ANGLER V250 CTRCN   OP CUD  FBG SV OB          8         3400 2 4 11800 13400
24 10 ANGLER V250 CTRCN   OP OPFSH FBG SV IO 170-230 8         3800 2 4  6600  8000
        IO 260-290 7000  8600, IO 130D VLVO 9050 10300, IO T120-T185 7400 8900

24 10 ANGLER V250 CTRCN   TT OPFSH FBG SV OB          8        3400 2 4 11800 13400
24 10 ANGLER V250 CTRCN   TT OPFSH FBG SV IO 170-230  8        3800 2 4  6600  8000
        IO 260-290 7000  8600, IO 130D VLVO 9050 10300, IO T120-T170 7400 8900

24 10 HOLIDAY V250        OP CUD  FBG SV OB          8         3700 2 4 12400 14100
24 10 HOLIDAY V250        OP CUD  FBG SV IO 185-260  8         4000 2 4  6550  8100
        IO 290 VLVO 7300 8400, IO 130D VLVO 7500  8650, IO T120-T170 7250 8700

24 10 HOLIDAY V250        HT CUD  FBG SV OB          8         4000 2 4  6550  8100
24 10 HOLIDAY V250        HT CUD  FBG SV IO 185-260  8         4000 2 4  6550  8100
        IO 290 VLVO 7300 8400, IO 130D VLVO 7500  8650, IO T120-T170 7250 8700

24 10 HOLIDAY V250        FB CUD  FBG SV OB          8         3700 2 4 12400 14100
24 10 HOLIDAY V250        FB CUD  FBG SV IO 185-260  8         4000 2 4  6550  8100
        IO 290 VLVO 7300 8400, IO 130D VLVO 7500  8650, IO T120-T170 7250 8700

31    CUSTOM              RNBT FBG SV IO 200        10         8000   10700 12200
41    CUSTOM              EXP  FBG SV IO T330        9         8000   31800 35300
------------------- 1982 BOATS ------------------------------------------------------------
22    NEWPORT V220        OP RNBT FBG SV OB          8         3240 2 4  9550 10900
22    NEWPORT V220        OP RNBT FBG SV IO 140-230  8              2 4  4650  5650
        IO 260-290 4900  6100, IO 130D VLVO 5700  6550, IO T120-T170 5250 6350

22    NEWPORT V220        HT RNBT FBG SV OB          8         3240 2 4  9550 10900
22    NEWPORT V220        HT RNBT FBG SV IO 140-230  8              2 4  4650  5650
        IO 260-290 4900  6100, IO 130D VLVO 5700  6550, IO T120-T170 5250 6350

22    TORINO              FB CUD  FBG SV OB          8         2720 2 4  8550  9800
22    TORINO V220         OP CUD  FBG SV OB          8         2720 2 4  8550  9800
22    TORINO V220         OP CUD  FBG SV IO 140-230  8         3440 2 4  4950  6000
        IO 260-290 5200  6450, IO 130D VLVO 6200  7100, IO T120-T170 5550 6750

22    TORINO V220         HT CUD  FBG SV OB          8         2720 2 4  8550  9800
22    TORINO V220         HT CUD  FBG SV IO 140-230  8         3440 2 4  4950  6000
        IO 260-290 5200  6450, IO 130D VLVO 6200  7100, IO T120-T170 5550 6750

22  3 ANGLER V220 CTRCN   HT CUD  FBG SV OB          8         2400 2 4  7900  9100
22  3 ANGLER V220 CTRCN   HT CUD  FBG SV IO 140-230  8         3040 2 4  4600  5550
22  3 ANGLER V220 CTRCN   HT CUD  FBG SV IO 260      8         3040 2 4  4850  5800
22  3 ANGLER V220 CTRCN   HT CUD  FBG SV IO T140 OMC 8         3040 2 4  5200  6000
```

```
 LOA  NAME AND/                TOP/ BOAT  -HULL- ----ENGINE--- BEAM   WGT  DRAFT RETAIL RETAIL
 FT IN OR MODEL                RIG TYPE   MTL TP TP # HP  MFG   FT IN  LBS  FT IN  LOW   HIGH
--------------------- 1982 BOATS --------------------------------------------------------------
22  3 ANGLER V220 CTRCN        FB  CUD    FBG SV OB          8    2400  2  4  7900   9100
22  3 ANGLER V220 CTRCN        FB  CUD    FBG SV IO 140-260  8    3040  2  4  4600   5550
22  3 ANGLER V220 CTRCN        FB  CUD    FBG SV IO T120-T170 8   3040  2  4  5200   6050
22  3 ANGLER V220 CTRCN        OP  OPFSH  FBG SV OB          8    2400  2  4  7900   9100
22  3 ANGLER V220 CTRCN        OP  OPFSH  FBG SV IO 140-230  8    3040  2  4  4900   6000
       IO 260     5200         6200, IO 290  VLVO  5650  6500, IO 130D VLVO  7350   8500
       IO T120-T170 5600       6850

22  3 ANGLER V220 CTRCN        TT  OPFSH  FBG SV OB          8    2400  2  4  7900   9100
22  3 ANGLER V220 CTRCN        TT  OPFSH  FBG SV IO 140-230  8    3040  2  4  4900   6000
       IO 260     5200         6200, IO 290  VLVO  5650  6500, IO 130D VLVO  7350   8500
       IO T120-T170 5600       6850

24 10 ANGLER V250 CTRCN        HT  CUD    FBG SV OB          8    3400  2  4  11600  13200
24 10 ANGLER V250 CTRCN        HT  CUD    FDG CV IO  260 MRCR 8   3800  2  4  6500   7450
24 10 ANGLER V250 CTRCN        HT  CUD    FBG SV IO T120 MRCR 8   3800  2  4  6850   7900
24 10 ANGLER V250 CTRCN        FB  CUD    FBG SV OB          8    3400  2  4  11600  13200
24 10 ANGLER V250 CTRCN        OP  OPFSH  FBG SV OB          8    3400  2  4  11600  13200
24 10 ANGLER V250 CTRCN        OP  OPFSH  FBG SV IO 165-230  8    3800  2  4  6400   7800
       IO 260-290  6850        8400, IO 130D VLVO  8850 10100, IO T120-T185  7200   8700

24 10 ANGLER V250 CTRCN        TT  OPFSH  FBG SV OB          8    3400  2  4  11600  13200
24 10 ANGLER V250 CTRCN        TT  OPFSH  FBG SV IO 165-230  8    3800  2  4  6400   7800
       IO 260-290  6850        8400, IO 130D VLVO  8850 10100, IO T120-T185  7200   8700

24 10 HOLIDAY V250             OP  CUD    FBG SV OB          8    3700  2  4  12200  13900
24 10 HOLIDAY V250             OP  CUD    FBG SV IO 185-260  8    4000  2  4  6350   7900
       IO 290  VLVO  7150      8200, IO 130D VLVO  7300  8400, IO T120-T185  7050   8550

24 10 HOLIDAY V250             HT  CUD    FBG SV OB          8    3700  2  4  12200  13900
24 10 HOLIDAY V250             HT  CUD    FBG SV IO 185-260  8    4000  2  4  6350   7900
       IO 290  VLVO  7150      8200, IO 130D VLVO  7300  8400, IO T120-T185  7050   8550

24 10 HOLIDAY V250             FB  CUD    FBG SV OB          8    3700  2  4  12200  13900
24 10 HOLIDAY V250             FB  CUD    FBG SV IO 185-260  8    4000  2  4  6350   7900
       IO 290  VLVO  7150      8200, IO 130D VLVO  7300  8400, IO T120-T185  7050   8550
--------------------- 1981 BOATS --------------------------------------------------------------
22    NEWPORT V220             OP  RNBT   FBG SV OB          8    3240        9400  10700
22    NEWPORT V220             OP  RNBT   FBG SV IO 140-260  8               4600   5700
       IO 290  VLVO  5200      6000, IO 130D VLVO  5600  6400, IO T120-T170  5150   6250

22    NEWPORT V220             HT  RNBT   FBG SV OB          8    3240        9400  10700
22    NEWPORT V220             HT  RNBT   FBG SV IO 140-260  8               4600   5700
       IO 290  VLVO  5200      6000, IO 130D VLVO  5600  6400, IO T120-T170  5150   6250

22    NEWPORT V220             FB  RNBT   FBG SV OB          8    3240        9400  10700
22    NEWPORT V220             FB  RNBT   FBG SV IO 140-260  8               4600   5700
       IO 290  VLVO  5200      6000, IO 130D VLVO  5600  6400, IO T120-T170  5150   6250

22    NEWPORT V220             TT  RNBT   FBG SV OB          8    3240        9400  10700
22    NEWPORT V220             TT  RNBT   FBG SV IO 140-260  8               4600   5700
       IO 290  VLVO  5200      6000, IO 130D VLVO  5600  6400, IO T120-T170  5150   6250

22    TORINO V220              OP  CUD    FBG SV OB          8    2720  2  4  8400   9650
22    TORINO V220              OP  CUD    FBG SV IO 140-230  8    3440  2  4  4850   5900
       IO 260-290  5100        6350, IO 130D VLVO  6050  6950, IO T120-T170  5450   6650

22    TORINO V220              HT  CUD    FBG SV OB          8    2720  2  4  8400   9650
22    TORINO V220              HT  CUD    FBG SV IO 140-230  8    3440  2  4  4850   5900
       IO 260-290  5100        6350, IO 130D VLVO  6050  6950, IO T120-T170  5450   6650

22    TORINO V220              FB  CUD    FBG SV OB          8    2720  2  4  8400   9650
22    TORINO V220              FB  CUD    FBG SV IO 140-230  8    3440  2  4  4850   5900
       IO 260-290  5100        6350, IO 130D VLVO  6050  6950, IO T120-T170  5450   6650

22    TORINO V220              TT  CUD    FBG SV OB          8    3440        9700  11000
22    TORINO V220              TT  CUD    FBG SV IO 140-230  8    3440  2  4  4850   5900
       IO 260-290  5100        6350, IO 130D VLVO  6050  6950, IO T120-T170  5450   6650

22  3 ANGLER V-230             SF         FBG DV OB          8    2400        7750   8950
22  3 ANGLER V220 CTCRN        HT  CUD    FBG SV IO 130D VLVO 8   3040        5750   6600
22  3 ANGLER V220 CTRCN        HT  CUD    FBG SV OB          8    2400  2  4  7800   8950
22  3 ANGLER V220 CTRCN        HT  CUD    FBG SV IO 140-230  8    3040  2  4  4550   5500
       IO 260      4750        5700, IO 290  VLVO  5200  6000, IO T120 MRCR  5150   5950
       IO T120-T170 5850       6700

22  3 ANGLER V220 CTRCN        FB  CUD    FBG SV OB          8    2400  2  4  7800   8950
22  3 ANGLER V220 CTRCN        FB  CUD    FBG SV IO 140-230  8    3040  2  4  4550   5500
       IO 260      4750        5700, IO 290  VLVO  5200  6000, IO 130D VLVO  5750   6600
       IO T120-T170 5900       6800

22  3 ANGLER V220 CTRCN        OP  OPFSH  FBG SV OB          8    2400        7750   8950
22  3 ANGLER V220 CTRCN        OP  OPFSH  FBG SV IO 140-230  8    3040        4800   5900
       IO 260      5100        6100, IO 290  VLVO  5550  6350, IO 130D VLVO  7250   8350
       IO T120-T170 5500       6700

22  3 ANGLER V220 CTRCN        TT  OPFSH  FBG SV OB          8    2400        7750   8950
22  3 ANGLER V220 CTRCN        TT  OPFSH  FBG SV IO 140-230  8    3040        4800   5900
       IO 260      5100        6100, IO 290  VLVO  5550  6350, IO 130D VLVO  7250   8350
       IO T120-T170 5500       6700

24 10 ANGLER V250              HT  CUD    FBG SV OB          8    3400  2  4  11400  13000
24 10 ANGLER V250 CTRCN        HT  CUD    FBG SV IO 165-230  8    3800        6000   7300
       IO 260-290  6400        7800, IO 130D VLVO  6900  7950, IO T120-T185  6750   8100

24 10 ANGLER V250              FB  CUD    FBG SV OB          8    3400  2  4  11400  13000
24 10 ANGLER V250 CTRCN        FB  CUD    FBG SV IO 165-230  8    3800        6000   7300
       IO 260-290  6400        7800, IO 130D VLVO  6900  7950, IO T120-T185  6750   8150

24 10 ANGLER V250              OP  OPFSH  FBG SV OB          8    3400        11400  13000
24 10 ANGLER V250 CTRCN        OP  OPFSH  FBG SV IO 165-230  8    3800        6300   7650
       IO 260-290  6700        8250, IO 130D VLVO  8600  9850, IO T120-T185  7100   8500

24 10 ANGLER V250              TT  OPFSH  FBG SV OB          8    3400        11400  13000
24 10 ANGLER V250 CTRCN        TT  OPFSH  FBG SV IO 165-230  8    3800        6300   7650
       IO 260-290  6700        8250, IO 130D VLVO  8600  9850, IO T120-T185  7100   8550

24 10 HOLIDAY V250             OP  CUD    FBG SV OB          8    3700  2  4  12000  13600
24 10 HOLIDAY V250             OP  CUD    FBG SV IO 185-260  8    4000  2  4  6250   7750
       IO 290  VLVO  7000      8050, IO 130D VLVO  7200  8250, IO T120-T185  6950   8400

24 10 HOLIDAY V250             HT  CUD    FBG SV OB          8    3700  2  4  12000  13600
24 10 HOLIDAY V250             HT  CUD    FBG SV IO 185-260  8    4000  2  4  6250   7750
       IO 290  VLVO  7000      8050, IO 130D VLVO  7200  8250, IO T120-T185  6950   8400

24 10 HOLIDAY V250             FB  CUD    FBG SV OB          8    3700  2  4  12000  13600
24 10 HOLIDAY V250             FB  CUD    FBG SV IO 185-260  8    4000  2  4  6250   7750
       IO 290  VLVO  7000      8050, IO 130D VLVO  7200  8250, IO T120-T185  6950   8400

24 10 HOLIDAY V250             TT  CUD    FBG SV OB          8    3700  2  4  12000  13600
24 10 HOLIDAY V250             TT  CUD    FBG SV IO 185-260  8    4000  2  4  6250   7750
       IO 290  VLVO  7000      8050, IO 130D VLVO  7200  8250, IO T120-T185  6950   8400

25    ANGLER V-250             SF         FBG DV OB          8    3400        11600  13200
--------------------- 1980 BOATS --------------------------------------------------------------
22    NEWPORT V220             OP  RNBT   FBG SV OB          8    3240        9300  10600
22    NEWPORT V220             OP  RNBT   FBG SV IO 140-260  8               4550   5650
       IO 290  VLVO  5150      5900, IO 130D-145D  5500  6750, IO T120-T140  5100   6150

22    NEWPORT V220             HT  RNBT   FBG SV OB          8    3240        9300  10600
22    NEWPORT V220             HT  RNBT   FBG SV IO 140-260  8               4550   5650
       IO 290  VLVO  5150      5900, IO 130D-145D  5500  6750, IO T120-T140  5100   6150

22    NEWPORT V220             FB  RNBT   FBG SV OB          8    3240        9300  10600
22    NEWPORT V220             FB  RNBT   FBG SV IO 140-260  8               4550   5650
       IO 290  VLVO  5150      5900, IO 130D-145D  5500  6750, IO T120-T140  5100   6150

22    TORINO V220              OP  CUD    FBG SV OB          8    2720  2  4  8250   9500
22    TORINO V220              OP  CUD    FBG SV IO 140-230  8    3440  2  4  4800   5800
       IO 260-290  5050        6250, IO 130D-145D  6000  7350, IO T120-T140  5400   6550

22    TORINO V220              HT  CUD    FBG SV OB          8    2720  2  4  8250   9500
22    TORINO V220              HT  CUD    FBG SV IO 140-230  8    3440  2  4  4800   5800
       IO 260-290  5050        6250, IO 130D-145D  6000  7350, IO T120-T140  5400   6550

22    TORINO V220              FB  CUD    FBG SV OB          8    2720  2  4  8250   9500
22    TORINO V220              FB  CUD    FBG SV IO 130-260  8    3440  2  4  4900   6000
22    TORINO V220              FB  CUD    FBG SV IO 290  VLVO 8    3440  2  4  5450   6250
22    TORINO V220              FB  CUD    FBG SV IO T120-T140 8   3440  2  4  5400   6550
22  3 ANGLER V220 CTRCN        OP  OPFSH  FBG SV OB          8    2400        7650   8800
22  3 ANGLER V220 CTRCN        OP  OPFSH  FBG SV IO 140-230  8    3040        4750   5800
       IO 260      5050        6000, IO 290  VLVO  5500  6300, IO 130D-145D  7150   8800

22  3 ANGLER V220 CTRCN        TT  OPFSH  FBG SV OB          8    2400        7650   8800
22  3 ANGLER V220 CTRCN        TT  OPFSH  FBG SV IO 140-230  8    3040        4750   5800
       IO T120-T140 5450       6600
```

```
 LOA   NAME AND/        TOP/ BOAT  -HULL-  ----ENGINE---  BEAM  WGT  DRAFT RETAIL RETAIL
FT IN  OR MODEL         RIG  TYPE  MTL TP TP # HP  MFG    FT IN LBS  FT IN  LOW   HIGH
-------------------- 1980 BOATS --------------------------------------------------------
22  3 ANGLER V220 CTRCN  TT OPFSH FBG DV OB  250         8       3040        5050  6000
   IO 290  VLVO  5500  6300, IO 130D-145D  7150  8800, IO T120-T140      5450  6600

22  3 ANGLER V230           OPFSH FBG DV OB          8           7650  8800
22  3 TORINO V230           CR    FBG DV OB          8           9250 10500
24 10 ANGLER V250 CTRCN  OP OPFSH FBG SV OB          8       3400      11200 12800
24 10 ANGLER V250 CTRCN  OP OPFSH FBG SV IO 165-230  8       3800       6250  7600
   IO 260-290  6650  8150, IO 130D-145D  8450 10300, IO T120-T170       7000  8450

24 10 ANGLER V250 CTRCN  TT OPFSH FBG SV OB          8       3400      11200 12800
24 10 ANGLER V250 CTRCN  TT OPFSH FBG SV IO 165-230  8       3800       6250  7600
   IO 260-290  6650  8150, IO 130D-145D  8500 10300, IO T120-T170       7000  8450

24 10 HOLIDAY V250       OP CUD   FBG SV OB          8       3700 2 4  11800 13400
24 10 HOLIDAY V250       OP CUD   FBG SV IO 198-260  8       4000 2 4   6200  7650
   IO 290  VLVO  6900  7950, IO 130D-145D  7100  8600, IO T120-T228    6850  8550
   IO T260 MRCR  7700  8850

24 10 HOLIDAY V250       HT CUD   FBG SV OB          8       3700 2 4  11800 13400
24 10 HOLIDAY V250       HT CUD   FBG SV IO 185-260  8       4000 2 4   6200  7650
   IO 290  VLVO  6900  7950, IO 130D-145D  7100  8600, IO T120-T170    6850  8250

24 10 HOLIDAY V250       FB CUD   FBG SV OB          8       3700 2 4  11800 13400
24 10 HOLIDAY V250       FB CUD   FBG SV IO 185-260  8       4000 2 4   6200  7650
   IO 290  VLVO  6900  7950, IO 130D-145D  7100  8600, IO T120-T170    6850  8250
-------------------- 1979 BOATS --------------------------------------------------------
22    NEWPORT V230       OP RNBT  FBG SV IO           8      3240       9150 10400
22    NEWPORT V230       OP RNBT  FBG SV IO 140-228   8      3240       4350  5150
22    NEWPORT V230       OP RNBT  FBG SV IO T120-T140 8      3240       4950  5700
22    TORINO V230        OP CUD   FBG SV OB           8           2 4   8900 10100
22    TORINO V230        OP CUD   FBG SV IO 140-230   8      3440 2 4   4750  5600
22    TORINO V230        OP CUD   FBG SV IO T120-T140 8      3440 2 4   5400  6200
22    TORINO V230        HT CUD   FBG SV OB           8           2 4   8900 10100
22    TORINO V230        HT CUD   FBG SV IO 140-230   8      3440 2 4   4750  5600
22    TORINO V230        HT CUD   FBG SV IO T120-T140 8      3440 2 4   5400  6200
22    TORINO V230        FB CUD   FBG SV OB           8           2 4   8900 10100
22    TORINO V230        FB CUD   FBG SV IO 140-230   8      3440 2 4   4750  5600
22    TORINO V230        FB CUD   FBG SV IO T120-T140 8      3440 2 4   5400  6200

22  3 ANGLER V230 CTRCN  OP OPFSH FBG SV OB           8                 7550  8650
22  3 ANGLER V230 CTRCN  OP OPFSH FBG SV IO 140-250   8      3040       4700  5650
22  3 ANGLER V230 CTRCN  OP OPFSH FBG SV IO T120-T140 8      3040       5450  6250
24    MARLIN V240        OP RNBT  FBG SV IO 140-250                     5500  6550
24    MARLIN V240        OP RNBT  FBG SV IO T120-T140                   6200  7150
24    SUPERSPORT V240    OP RNBT  FBG SV IO 140-250                     5500  6550
24    SUPERSPORT V240    OP RNBT  FBG SV IO T120-T170                   6200  7200
24 10 ANGLER V250 CTRCN  OP OPFSH FBG SV OB           8                11500 13100
24 10 ANGLER V250 CTRCN  OP OPFSH FBG SV IO 165-250   8      3800       6200  7500
24 10 ANGLER V250 CTRCN  OP OPFSH FBG SV IO T120-T170 8      3800       7000  8300
24 10 HOLIDAY V250       OP CR    FBG SV OB           8           2 4  12100 13700

24 10 HOLIDAY V250       OP CR    FBG SV IO 198-200   8      4000 2 4   6250  7150
24 10 HOLIDAY V250       OP CR    FBG SV IO T140-T170 8      4000 2 4   6950  8150
24 10 HOLIDAY V250       HT CR    FBG SV OB           8           2 4  12100 13700
24 10 HOLIDAY V250       HT CR    FBG SV IO 198-200   8      4000 2 4   6250  7150
24 10 HOLIDAY V250       HT CR    FBG SV IO T140-T170 8      4000 2 4   6950  8150
24 10 HOLIDAY V250       FB CR    FBG SV OB           8           2 4  12100 13700
24 10 HOLIDAY V250       FB CR    FBG SV IO 198-200   8      4000 2 4   6250  7150
24 10 HOLIDAY V250       FB CR    FBG SV IO T140-T170 8      4000 2 4   6950  8150
```

ANCHOR INDUSTRIES
MARR'S LEISURE PRODUCTS COAST GUARD MFG ID- ZAI

Call 1-800-327-6929 for BUC Personalized Evaluation Service
Or, for 1980 to 1984 boats, sign onto www.BUCValuPro.com

ANCHOR LINE MARINE

Call 1-800-327-6929 for BUC Personalized Evaluation Service
Or, for 1961 boats, sign onto www.BUCValuPro.com

ANCHOR MARINE INC
IMPORTERS LM GLASFIBER COAST GUARD MFG ID- LMJ

Call 1-800-327-6929 for BUC Personalized Evaluation Service
Or, for 1983 to 1994 boats, sign onto www.BUCValuPro.com

ANCHOR PLASTICS INC
DECK BOATS   COAST GUARD MFG ID- ANP

Call 1-800-327-6929 for BUC Personalized Evaluation Service
Or, for 1963 to 1994 boats, sign onto www.BUCValuPro.com

THE ANCHORAGE INC
DYER BOATS
WARREN RI 02885   COAST GUARD MFG ID- DYE   See inside cover to adjust price for area

For more recent years, see the BUC Used Boat Price Guide, Volume 1 or Volume 2

```
 LOA   NAME AND/        TOP/ BOAT  -HULL-  ----ENGINE---  BEAM  WGT  DRAFT RETAIL RETAIL
FT IN  OR MODEL         RIG  TYPE  MTL TP TP # HP  MFG    FT IN LBS  FT IN  LOW   HIGH
-------------------- 1983 BOATS --------------------------------------------------------
28  6 DYERCRAFT 29         CR    FBG RB IB 225       9 5 7000   40000  44400
28  6 DYERCRAFT 29      OP LNCH  FBG RB IB 170       9 5        32500  36100
28  6 DYERCRAFT 29         OFF   FBG RB IB 225       9 5 7000   40300  44800
39  8 DYERCRAFT 40         CR    FBG RB IB 110      12 6       134000 147500
39  8 DYERCRAFT 40         DC    FBG RB IB 240D     12 6       154000 169000
39  8 DYERCRAFT 40         SF    FBG RB IB T250     12 6       154500 169500
-------------------- 1982 BOATS --------------------------------------------------------
28  6 DYERCRAFT 29         CR    FBG RB IB 225       9 5        43200  48000
28  6 DYERCRAFT 29      OP LNCH  FBG RB IB 170       9 5        35700  39700
28  6 DYERCRAFT 29         OFF   FBG RB IB 225       9 5        35800  39800
39  8 DYERCRAFT 40         CR    FBG RB IB 110      12 6       128500 141000
39  8 DYERCRAFT 40         DC    FBG RB IB T250     12 6       199500 219000
39  8 DYERCRAFT 40         SF    FBG RB IB T250     12 6       148000 162500
-------------------- 1981 BOATS --------------------------------------------------------
28  6 DYERCRAFT 29         CR    FBG RB IB 225       9 5        41300  45900
28  6 DYERCRAFT 29         LNCH  FBG RB IB 170       9 5        34500  38300
28  6 DYERCRAFT 29         OFF   FBG RB IB 225       9 5        34400  38200
39  8 DYERCRAFT 40         CR    FBG RB IB 110      12 6       122500 134500
39  8 DYERCRAFT 40         DC    FBG RB IB T250     12 6       190000 209000
39  8 DYERCRAFT 40         SF    FBG RB IB T250     12 6       141000 155000
-------------------- 1980 BOATS --------------------------------------------------------
16        GLAMOUR GIRL   OP UTL  FBG SV OB           6 1 1000    6650  7650
16        GLAMOUR GIRL   OP UTL  FBG SV IB 130       5 9         6350  7300
16        GLAMOUR GIRL   OP UTL  FBG RB IB 225     D 5 9          **    **
28  6 DYERCRAFT 29         BASS  FBG RB IB 225       9 5 7000   34800  38700
28  6 DYERCRAFT 29         BASS  FBG RB IB       D   9 5 7000    **    **
28  6 DYERCRAFT 29         CR    FBG RB IB 225       9 5 7000   35100  39000
28  6 DYERCRAFT 29         CR    FBG RB IB       D   9 5 7000    **    **
28  6 DYERCRAFT 29         LNCH  FBG RB IB       D   9 5 7000    **    **
28  6 DYERCRAFT 29      OP LNCH  FBG RB IB 170       9 5 7000   28500  31700
39  8 DYERCRAFT 40         CR    FBG RB IB 110      12 6       116500 128000
39  8 DYERCRAFT 40         DC    FBG RB IB 110      12 6       181500 199500
39  8 DYERCRAFT 40         SF    FBG RB IB T250     12 6       134500 148000
-------------------- 1979 BOATS --------------------------------------------------------
16  2 GLAMOUR-GIRL       OP UTL  FBG SV IB           6 5 1000    6500  7500
16  2 GLAMOUR-GIRL       OP UTL  FBG SV IB 130       5 9         6150  7050
16  2 GLAMOUR-GIRL       OP UTL  FBG RB IB           5 9          **    **
28  6 DYER HARDTOP       HT SF   FBG RB IB 225-330   9 5 6700   32300  38100
28  6 DYER HARDTOP       HT SF   FBG RB IB 120D-185D 9 5 6700 2 6 34700  44800
28  6 DYER OFFSHORE BASS OP SF   FBG RB IB 225-330   9 5 6700   32500  38400
28  6 DYER OFFSHORE BASS OP SF   FBG RB IB 120D-185D 9 5 6700 2 6 37000  45200
28  6 DYER TRUNK CABIN   OP SPTCR FBG RB IB 225-330  9 5 6700   33000  39100
28  6 DYER TRUNK CABIN   OP SPTCR FBG RB IB 120D-185D 9 5 6700 2 6 37500  45900
39  8 DYERCRAFT             CR   FBG RB IB 110      12 6       111500 122500
39  8 DYERCRAFT             CR   FBG RB IB 250      12 6       112500 123500

39  8 DYERCRAFT             DC   FBG RB IB T250     12 6       173500 192500
39  8 DYERCRAFT             DC   FBG RB IB T330     12 6       175000 192500
39  8 DYERCRAFT             SF   FBG RB IB T250     12 6       128500 141000
39  8 DYERCRAFT             SF   FBG RB IB T330     12 6       130000 143000
-------------------- 1978 BOATS --------------------------------------------------------
16        GLAMOUR-GIRL   OP UTL  FBG SV IB           6 1         6400  7350
16  2 GLAMOUR-GIRL          UTL  FBG SV IB 30        5 9         5350  6250
16  2 GLAMOUR-GIRL          UTL  FBG RB IB 37D       5 9         5000  5900
28  6 DYER HARDTOP       HT SF   FBG RB IB 225       9 5 8000 2 7 33700  37500
28  6 DYER HARDTOP       HT SF   FBG RB IB 160D-225D 9 5 8000 2 7 34700  50500
28  6 DYER OFFSHORE BASS ST SF   FBG RB IB 225  CHRY 9 5 6700 2 6 31200  34700
28  6 DYER OFFSHORE BASS ST SF   FBG RB IB 225D      9 5 6700 2 6 40500  45000
28  6 DYER TRUNK CABIN   ST SPTCR FBG RB IB 225      9 5 7800 2 7 34000  37800
```

THE ANCHORAGE INC -CONTINUED See inside cover to adjust price for area

LOA FT	LOA IN	NAME AND/ OR MODEL	TOP/ RIG	BOAT TYPE	HULL MTL	HULL TP	ENGINE TP	ENGINE # HP	ENGINE MFG	BEAM FT	BEAM IN	WGT LBS	DRAFT FT	DRAFT IN	RETAIL LOW	RETAIL HIGH
		1978 BOATS														
28	6	DYER TRUNK CABIN	ST	SPTCR	FBG	RB	IB	120D-225D		9	5	7800	2	7	42300	51000
39	8	DYERCRAFT		CR	FBG		IB	110		12	6				106500	117000
39	8	DYERCRAFT		CR	FBG		IB	250D		12	6				124500	136500
39	8	DYERCRAFT		DC	FBG		IB	T250		12	6				166000	182000
39	8	DYERCRAFT		DC	FBG		IB	T330D		12	6				142000	156000
39	8	DYERCRAFT		SF	FBG		IB	T250		12	6				122500	134500
39	8	DYERCRAFT		SF	FBG		IB	T330D		12	6				139000	152500
		1977 BOATS														
16		DYERCRAFT	OP	UTL	FBG		OB			5	9	1000	1	5	6300	7250
16	4	GLAMOUR-GIRL	OP	UTL	FBG		IB	30		5	9		1	5	4450	5100
16	4	GLAMOUR-GIRL	OP	UTL	FBG		IB	30D		5	9		1	5	8050	9250
20		GLAMOUR-GIRL	OP	UTL	FBG		OB			5	9	1200			7500	8600
28	6	DYERCRAFT 29		CR	FBG	RB	IB	225		9	5		2	6	34900	38800
28	6	DYERCRAFT 29		CR	FBG	RB	IB	225D		9	5		2	6	42000	46700
39	8	DYERCRAFT 40		SF	FBG		IB			12	6		2	9	**	**
		1976 BOATS														
16		GLAMOUR-GIRL	OP		FBG	SV	IB	130		5	9				4600	5250
16	4	GLAMOUR-GIRL	OP	UTL	FBG	SV	OB			6	1	900			5600	6450
20		GLAMOUR-GIRL	OP	UTL	FBG	SV	OB			6	1	1080			6650	7650
28	6	DYERCRAFT		CR	FBG	SV	IB	225		9	5				33500	37300
28	6	DYERCRAFT		CR	FBG	SV	IB	D		9	5				**	**
39	8	DYERCRAFT		SF	FBG	SV	IB			12	6				**	**
39	8	DYERCRAFT		SF	FBG	SV	IB	D		12	6				**	**
		1975 BOATS														
16	2	GLAMOUR-GIRL	OP	UTL	FBG	SV	IB	30		5	9		1	5	4000	4650
16	2	GLAMOUR-GIRL	OP	UTL	FBG	SV	IB	37D		5	9		1	5	7700	8900
16	2	YACHT TENDER		UTL	FBG		IB	30		5	9		1	5	4000	4650
16	2	YACHT TENDER		UTL	FBG		IB	37D		5	9		1	5	7700	8900
16	4	GLAMOUR-GIRL	OP	UTL	FBG	SV	OB			6	1	900	1	5	5550	6400
20		GLAMOUR-GIRL	OP	UTL	FBG	SV	OB			6	1	1080			6600	7600
28	6	DYERCRAFT 29		CR	FBG		IB	225-330		9	5		2	6	32200	37600
28	6	DYERCRAFT 29		OFF	FBG		IB	225-330		9	5		2	6	26700	31500
28	6	DYERCRAFT 29	OP	UTL	FBG		IB	170-250		9	5		2	6	34300	39300
39	8	DYERCRAFT 40		CR	FBG		IB	110		12	6		2	9	93600	103000
39	8	DYERCRAFT 40		CR	FBG		IB	250		12	6		2	9	94600	104000
39	8	DYERCRAFT 40		DC	FBG		IB	T250		12	6		2	9	146000	160500
39	8	DYERCRAFT 40		DC	FBG		IB	T330		12	6		2	9	147500	162000
39	8	DYERCRAFT 40		LNCH	FBG		IB			12	6				**	**
39	8	DYERCRAFT 40		SF	FBG		IB	T250		12	6		2	9	108000	118500
39	8	DYERCRAFT 40		SF	FBG		IB	T330		12	6		2	9	109000	120000
		1974 BOATS														
16	2	FISH		UTL	FBG		IB	30	UNIV	5	9	1050	1	5	2600	3050
16	2	FISH		UTL	FBG		IB	37D		5	9	1050	1	5	6950	8000
16	2	YACHT TENDER		UTL	FBG		IB	30	UNIV	5	9	1050	1	5	2850	3300
16	2	YACHT TENDER		UTL	FBG		IB	37D		5	9	1050	1	5	6950	8000
16	4	GLAMOUR-GIRL	OP	UTL	FBG	SV	OB			6	1	810			5000	5750
20		GLAMOUR-GIRL	OP	UTL	FBG	SV	OB			6	1	1080			6550	7500
28	6	OFFSHORE		BASS	FBG		IB	225-365		9	5	6700	2	6	26700	32200
28	6	OFFSHORE		BASS	FBG		IB	131D-210D		9	5	6700	2	6	31600	38600
28	6	OFFSHORE	HT	BASS	FBG		IB	225-365		9	5	6700	2	6	26700	32200
28	6	OFFSHORE	HT	BASS	FBG		IB	131D-210D		9	5	6700	2	6	31600	38600
39	8	DYER 40 CUSTOM			FBG		IB			12	5		2	9	**	**
39	8	DYERCRAFT 40		DC	FBG		IB	T250		12	5		2	9	141000	155000
39	8	DYERCRAFT 40		DC	FBG		IB	T330		12	5		2	9	142500	156500
39	8	DYERCRAFT 40		SF	FBG		IB	T250		12	5		2	9	104000	114500
39	8	DYERCRAFT 40		SF	FBG		IB	T330		12	5		2	9	105500	116000
39	8	DYERCRAFT SIGHTSEER		CR	FBG		IB	110		12	5		2	9	90400	99400
39	8	DYERCRAFT SIGHTSEER		DC	FBG		IB	250		12	5		2	9	137500	151000
		1973 BOATS														
16	2	FISH		UTL	FBG		IB	30	UNIV	5	9	950	1	5	2500	2900
16	2	YACHT TENDER		UTL	FBG		IB	30	UNIV	5	9	995	1	5	2550	2950
16	4	GLAMOUR-GIRL		FSH	FBG		IO	120	MRCR	6	1	1560	2	4	6100	7000
16	4	GLAMOUR-GIRL		RNBT	FBG		IO	120	MRCR	6	1	1530	2	4	5950	6850
16	4	GLAMOUR-GIRL	OP	UTL	FBG	SV	OB			6	1	900			5450	6300
18	9	DELTA		SAIL	FBG		OB			6	1	550		6	3000	3500
20		GLAMOUR-GIRL		FSH	FBG		IO	120-140		6	1	1990	1	11	8300	9600
20		GLAMOUR-GIRL		RNBT	FBG		IO	120-140		6	1	1950	1	11	7500	8700
20		GLAMOUR-GIRL	OP	UTL	FBG	SV	OB			6	1	1080			6500	7450
28	6	DYERCRAFT 29 STYLE A			FBG		IB	200-250		9	5		2	6	28600	32500
28	6	DYERCRAFT 29 STYLE A			FBG		IB	140D-155D		9	5		2	6	33500	37800
28	6	DYERCRAFT 29 STYLE B			FBG		IB	200-250		9	5		2	6	28800	32900
28	6	DYERCRAFT 29 STYLE B			FBG		IB	140D-155D		9	5		2	6	33700	38100
28	6	OFFSHORE		BASS	FBG		IB	200-250		9	5		2	6	27200	31100
28	6	OFFSHORE		BASS	FBG		IB	140D-155D		9	5		2	6	33400	37800
39	8	DYERCRAFT 40		CR	FBG	RB	IB	T300		12	6		2	9	91200	100000
39	8	DYERCRAFT 40		DC	FBG	RB	IB	T300		12	6		2	9	136000	149000
39	8	DYERCRAFT 40		SF	FBG	RB	IB	T300		12	6		2	9	100500	110000
		1972 BOATS														
16	4	GLAMOUR-GIRL	OP	UTL	FBG	DS	IB	30		6	1	900			2550	2950
16	4	GLAMOUR-GIRL	OP	UTL	FBG	SV	OB			6	1	900			5450	6250
16	4	GLAMOUR-GIRL	OP	UTL	FBG	SV	IB	30		6	1	900			2550	2950
16	4	GLAMOUR-GIRL	OP	UTL	FBG	SV	IO	90-120		6	1	900			5550	6400
16	4	GLAMOUR-GIRL	OP	UTL	FBG	SV	IO	90D		6	1	900			11200	12800
18	9	DYER-DELTA	SLP	SA/OD	FBG	CB				6	1			6	3350	3900
20		GLAMOUR-GIRL	OP	UTL	FBG	SV	OB			6	1	1080			6450	7400
20		GLAMOUR-GIRL	OP	UTL	FBG	SV	IB	65		6	1	1080			4650	5350
		IO 90-140 7850 9050, IB 150 5400 6200, IO 90D													13800	15600
28	6	DYERCRAFT		CR	FBG	SV	IB	130-265		9	5	6700	2	6	23200	28300
28	6	DYERCRAFT		OFF	FBG	SV	IB	170		9	5	6700	2	6	24400	27100
28	6	DYERCRAFT		OFF	FBG	SV	IB	T265		9	5	6700	2	6	28900	32200
39	8	DYERCRAFT		CR	FBG	DS	IB	110		12	6	18000	2	9	85300	93800
39	8	DYERCRAFT		CR	FBG	DS	IB	T300		12	6	18000	2	9	89900	98800
39	8	DYERCRAFT		SF	FBG	DS	IB	250		12	6	18000	2	9	82900	91100
39	8	DYERCRAFT		SF	FBG	DS	IB	T300		12	6	18000	2	9	86500	95000
		1971 BOATS														
16	2	GLAMOUR-GIRL		UTL	FBG		IB	30D	UNIV	5	9	1050	1	5	6700	7700
16	2	GLAMOUR-GIRL TENDER		UTL	FBG		IB	30D	UNIV	5	9	1095	1	5	6800	7800
16	4	GLAMOUR-GIRL		FSH	FBG		IO	65D	MRCR	6	1	1240	2	4	10700	12200
16	4	GLAMOUR-GIRL		FSH	FBG		IB	70D	UNIV	6	1	1350	2	4	8200	9400
16	4	GLAMOUR-GIRL		RNBT	FBG		IO	65D	MRCR	6	1	1230	2	4	8850	10100
18	9	DYER DELTA		SAIL	FBG		OB			6	1	550		6	2850	3350
20		GLAMOUR-GIRL		FSH	FBG		IO	90-140		6	1	1720	1	11	8400	9800
20		GLAMOUR-GIRL		RNBT	FBG		IO	90-140		6	1	1700	1	11	7650	8900
28	6	DYERCRAFT OFFSHORE		OFF	FBG		IB	170-277		9	5		2	6	22200	26200
28	6	DYERCRAFT OFFSHORE		OFF	FBG		IB	115D-155D		9	5		2	6	33400	37200
28	6	DYERCRAFT STYLE A			FBG		IB	170-250		9	5		2	6	26000	30100
28	6	DYERCRAFT STYLE A			FBG		IB	145D	GM	9	5		2	6	32000	35500
28	6	DYERCRAFT STYLE B			FBG		IB	170-250		9	5		2	6	26300	30400
28	6	DYERCRAFT STYLE B			FBG		IB	145D	GM	9	5		2	6	32200	35800
39	8	DYERCRAFT 40		CR	FBG	DS	IB	110		12	6	14500	2	9	70000	76900
		IB 160 70500 77500, IB 110D 78000 85800, IB 160D													78900	86700
39	8	DYERCRAFT 40		DC	FBG	DS	IB	110		12	6	18000	2	9	80900	88900
		IB T300 85200 93600, IB T110D 95800 105500, IB T300D													105000	115500
39	8	DYERCRAFT 40		SF	FBG	DS	IB	130		12	6	16600	2	9	74600	82000
		IB 130D 83100 91400, IB T300 78600 86400, IB T300D													97900	107500
		1970 BOATS														
16	2	GLAMOUR-GIRL		UTL	FBG		IB	30	UNIV	5	9	950	1	5	2200	2550
16	2	YACHT TENDER		UTL	FBG	SV	IB	30	UNIV	5	9	995	1	5	2250	2650
16	4	GLAMOUR-GIRL		FSH	FBG	SV	IO	90-120		6	1	1390	2		6300	7700
16	4	GLAMOUR-GIRL		RNBT	FBG	SV	IO	90-120		6	1	1360	2		6200	7550
16	4	GLAMOUR-GIRL 16	OP		FBG	SV	OB			6	1	900	2		5500	6300
18	9	DELTA	SLP	SA/OD	FBG	CB	OB			6	1	550		6	2800	3250
20		GLAMOUR-GIRL		FSH	FBG	SV	IO	80-120		6	1	1820	2		8900	10500
20		GLAMOUR-GIRL		RNBT	FBG	SV	IO	90-120		6	1	1780	2		8000	9500
20		GLAMOUR-GIRL 20			FBG	SV	OB			6	1	1080	2		7600	8750
20		YACHT-CLUB		LNCH	FBG	SV	IB	30	UNIV	6	1	1700	1	10	7850	9000
28	6	DYERCRAFT CRUISER 29		CR	FBG	RB	IB	130		9	5	6680	2	6	21600	24000
28	6	DYERCRAFT LAUNCH 29		LNCH	FBG	RB	IB	150D	PALM	9	5	6200	2	6	25300	28100
28	6	OFFSHORE		BASS	FBG		IB	195	PALM	9	5		2	6	24300	27000
28	6	OFFSHORE		BASS	FBG		IB	155D	PALM	9	5		2	6	31500	35000
28	6	STYLE A			FBG		IB	110D-140D							31200	35000
28	6	STYLE A		LNCH	FBG	RB	IB	200-225		9	5		2	5	22100	24900
39	8	DYERCRAFT 40			FBG	RB	IB	110		6	1	18000	1	10	131000	143500
39	8	DYERCRAFT 40			FBG	RB	IB	110		12	6	14500	2	9	70500	77500
39	8	DYERCRAFT 40		DC	FBG	RB	IB			12	6	18000	2	9	**	**
39	8	DYERCRAFT 40		SF	FBG	RB	IB	130		12	6	16600	2	9	72100	79200
39	8	DYERCRAFT 40		SF	FBG	RB	IB	D		12	6	16600	2	9	**	**
		1969 BOATS														
16	2	GLAMOUR-GIRL		UTL	FBG	SV	IB	30	UNIV	5	9	950	1	5	2050	2450
16	2	YACHT TENDER		UTL	FBG	SV	IB	30	UNIV	5	9	995	1	5	2200	2550
16	4	GLAMOUR-GIRL		FSH	FBG	SV	IO	80-120		6	1	1390	2		6550	7950
16	4	GLAMOUR-GIRL		RNBT	FBG	SV	IO	80-120		6	1	1360	2		6400	7800
16	4	GLAMOUR-GIRL		UTL	FBG		OB			6	1	900			5450	6250
18	8	DYER-DELTA	SLP	SA/OD	FBG					6	1			6	3150	3700
18	9	DELTA	SLP	SAIL	FBG	CB	OB			6	1	550		6	2750	3200
20		GLAMOUR-GIRL		FSH	FBG		IB	150	UNIV	6	1		1	10	6700	7700
20		GLAMOUR-GIRL		FSH	FBG		IB	70D	UNIV	6	1	1750	1	10	9400	10700
20		GLAMOUR-GIRL		FSH	FBG	SV	IO	80-140		6	1	1820	1	11	9200	10900

 CONTINUED ON NEXT PAGE

LOA FT	LOA IN	NAME AND/ OR MODEL	TOP/ RIG	BOAT TYPE	-HULL- MTL	-HULL- TP	ENGINE TP	ENGINE # HP	ENGINE MFG	BEAM FT	BEAM IN	WGT LBS	DRAFT FT	DRAFT IN	RETAIL LOW	RETAIL HIGH
		1969 BOATS														
20		GLAMOUR-GIRL		LNCH	FBG		IO	120		6	1		2	1	14300	16200
20		GLAMOUR-GIRL		LNCH	FBG		IB	30D	UNIV	6	1	1700	1	10	12900	14600
20		GLAMOUR-GIRL		UTL	FBG		OB			6	1	1080			6450	7400
20		GLAMOUR-GIRL YHT CLB		LNCH	FBG		IB	100		6	1		1	10	8450	9700
20		YACHT CLUB LAUNCH		RNBT	FBG		IO	80-140		6	1	1780			8250	9900
28	6	DYERCRAFT		LNCH	FBG	RB	IB	150	PALM	9	5	6200	2	6	18200	20200
28	6	DYERCRAFT		LNCH	FBG	RB	IB	150D	PALM	9	5	6200	2	6	24800	27600
28	6	DYERCRAFT 29		BASS	FBG		IB	225		9	5	6680	2	6	22200	24700
28	6	DYERCRAFT OFFSHORE		BASS	FBG		IB	195	PALM	9	5	6300	2	6	21200	23600
28	6	DYERCRAFT STYLE A		CR	FBG		IB	165-225		9	5		2	6	24700	28300
28	6	DYERCRAFT STYLE A		CR	FBG		IB	110D-140D		9	5		2	6	30300	34000
28	6	DYERCRAFT STYLE B			FBG		IB	165-225		9	5		2	6	24200	27700
28	6	DYERCRAFT STYLE B			FBG		IB	110D-140D		9	5		2	6	30200	33900
39	8	DYERCRAFT 40		DC	FBG		IB	T300		12	6		2	9	118000	129500
39	8	DYERCRAFT 40		SF	FBG		IB	T300		12	6		2	9	87000	95700
39	8	DYERCRAFT SIGHTSEER		CR	FBG		IB	250		12	6		2	9	75900	83400
		1968 BOATS														
16	2	GLAMOUR-GIRL		UTL	FBG		IB	30	UNIV			950			2200	2600
16	2	GLAMOUR-GIRL TENDER	OP	UTL	FBG		IB	30	UNIV	5	9	995	1	5	2050	2450
16	4	GLAMOUR-GIRL	OP	FSH	FBG		IO	60-120		5	9	1350	1	5	6450	8000
16	4	GLAMOUR-GIRL	OP	RNBT	FBG		IO	60-120		5	9	1320	2		6400	7850
18	9	DYER DELTA	SLP	SAIL	FBG	CB	OB			6	1	550		6	2450	2850
20		GLAMOUR-GIRL	OP	FSH	FBG		IO	60-140		6	1	1780	1	10	9450	11300
20		GLAMOUR-GIRL	OP	FSH	FBG		IO	60D		6	1	2400	1	10	16600	18900
20		GLAMOUR-GIRL	OP	RNBT	FBG		IO	60-140		6	1	1740	1	10	8500	10200
20		GLAMOUR-GIRL	OP	RNBT	FBG		IO	60D		6	1	2375	1	10	12700	14400
20		YACHT CLUB	OP	LNCH	FBG		IO	100		6	1		1	10	14800	16800
28	6	DYERCRAFT		OFF	FBG		IB		PALM	9	5	6300	2	5	**	**
28	6	DYERCRAFT		OFF	FBG		IB	D		9	5		2	5	**	**
28	6	DYERCRAFT 29	OP	LNCH	FBG		IO	195		9	5		2	6	25800	28700
28	6	DYERCRAFT 29	OP	SF	FBG		IO	225		9	5		2	6	45700	50300
28	6	DYERCRAFT 29 STYLE A		CR	FBG		IB	165		9	5	6680	2	6	20700	23000
28	6	DYERCRAFT 29 STYLE A		CR	FBG		IB	190-225		9	5		2	6	24000	27200
28	6	DYERCRAFT 29 STYLE A		CR	FBG		IB	130D-140D		9	5		2	6	29600	33300
28	6	DYERCRAFT 29 STYLE B		CR	FBG		IB	165-225		9	5		2	6	23900	27400
28	6	DYERCRAFT 29 STYLE B		CR	FBG		IB	130D-140D		9	5		2	6	29600	33300
39	8	DYERCRAFT		DC	FBG		IB		PALM	12	6	18000	2	9	**	**
39	8	DYERCRAFT		DC	FBG		IB	D		12	6		2	9	**	**
39	8	DYERCRAFT	OP	EXP	FBG		IB		PALM	12	6	14500	2	9	**	**
39	8	DYERCRAFT	OP	EXP	FBG		IB	D		12	6		2	9	**	**
39	8	DYERCRAFT		SF	FBG		IB		PALM	12	6	16600	2	9	**	**
39	8	DYERCRAFT		SF	FBG		IB	D		12	6		2	9	**	**
39	8	DYERCRAFT 40		DC	FBG		IO	T300		12	6		2	9	185500	204000
39	8	DYERCRAFT 40		SF	FBG		IO	T300		12	6		2	9	152500	167500
		1967 BOATS														
16	2	GLAMOUR-GIRL		UTL	FBG		IB	30				950			2100	2500
16	2	GLAMOUR-GIRL TENDER		UTL	FBG		IB	30				995			2200	2550
16	4	GLAMOUR-GIRL		FSH	FBG		IO	60				1350			7300	8350
16	4	GLAMOUR-GIRL		FSH	FBG		IB	60		6	1		2		2750	3200
16	4	GLAMOUR-GIRL		FSH	FBG		IO	80-120				1390			7400	8950
16	4	GLAMOUR-GIRL		RNBT	FBG		IO	60-120				1320			7150	8750
16	4	GLAMOUR-GIRL		UTL	FBG		OB			6	1	900			5450	6250
18	9	DYER DELTA		SAIL	FBG		OB					550			2400	2800
20		FISHERMAN 20		FSH	FBG		IB	60		6	1		1	10	5600	6450
20		GLAMOUR-GIRL		FSH	FBG		IO	60-140				1780			11500	13600
20		GLAMOUR-GIRL		FSH	FBG		IO	60D				2400			20100	22400
20		GLAMOUR-GIRL		RNBT	FBG		IO	60-140				1740			10300	12200
20		GLAMOUR-GIRL		RNBT	FBG		IO	60D				2375			14700	16700
20		GLAMOUR-GIRL		UTL	FBG		OB			6	1	1080			6450	7400
20		YACHT-CLUB		LNCH	FBG		IO	60		6	1		2	1	15200	17300
20		YACHT-CLUB	OP	LNCH	FBG		IB	45		6	1		1	10	7150	8250
28	6	DYERCRAFT 29		CR	FBG		IB	130		9	5		2	6	22900	25500
28	6	DYERCRAFT 29	OP	LNCH	FBG		IB	110		9	5		2	6	19500	21700
28	6	DYERCRAFT 29		SF	FBG		IB	110		9	5		2	6	20900	23200
28	6	DYERCRAFT 29 STYLE A			FBG		IB	165-225							22900	26200
28	6	DYERCRAFT 29 STYLE A			FBG		IB	130D-140D							29200	32800
28	6	DYERCRAFT 29 STYLE B			FBG		IB	165-225							23300	26500
28	6	DYERCRAFT 29 STYLE B			FBG		IB	130D-140D							29200	32800
39	8	DYERCRAFT 40		DC	FBG		IB	110		12	6		2	9	106500	117000
39	8	DYERCRAFT 40		SF	FBG		IB	130		12	6		2	9	78200	85900
39	8	DYERCRAFT 40		UTL	FBG		IB	110		12	6		2	9	36500	40600
		1966 BOATS														
16	2	GLAMOUR-GIRL		UTL	FBG		IB	30		5	9		1	5	2700	3150
16	2	GLAMOUR-GIRL TENDER		UTL	FBG		IB	30		5	9		1	5	2950	3450
16	4	GLAMOUR-GIRL		FSH	FBG		IO	60-120		6	1		2		7000	8050
16	4	GLAMOUR-GIRL		RNBT	FBG		IO	60-120		6	1		2		8000	9250
16	4	GLAMOUR-GIRL		UTL	FBG	SV	OB			6	1	900			5450	6250
18	9	DYER DELTA	SLP	SAIL	FBG	CB	OB			6	1	550		6	2400	2750
20		GLAMOUR-GIRL		FSH	FBG		IO	60-140		6	1		2	3	13200	15000
20		GLAMOUR-GIRL		FSH	FBG		IO	60D		6	1		2	3	21600	24000
20		GLAMOUR-GIRL		RNBT	FBG		IO	60-140		6	1		2	2	11200	12700
20		GLAMOUR-GIRL		RNBT	FBG		IO	60D		6	1		2	2	15700	17900
20		GLAMOUR-GIRL		UTL	FBG	SV	OB			6	1	1080			6450	7400
28	6	DYERCRAFT 29	OP	LNCH	FBG	RB	IB	110		9	5		2	6	18800	20900
28	6	DYERCRAFT 29 STYLE A		SF	FBG		IB	165-225		9	5		2	6	20500	23600
28	6	DYERCRAFT 29 STYLE A		SF	FBG		IB	130D-140D		9	5		2	6	27900	31400
28	6	DYERCRAFT 29 STYLE B		SF	FBG		IB	165-225		9	5		2	6	20800	23700
28	6	DYERCRAFT 29 STYLE B		SF	FBG		IB	130D-140D		9	5		2	6	27900	31400
39	8	DYERCRAFT 40		DC	FBG	RB	IB	110		12	6		2	9	103500	114000
39	8	DYERCRAFT 40		SF	FBG	RB	IB	110		12	6		2	9	75700	83200
		1965 BOATS														
16	2	GLAMOUR-GIRL		UTL	FBG		IB								**	**
16	2	GLAMOUR-GIRL TENDER		UTL	FBG		IB								**	**
16	4	GLAMOUR-GIRL		FSH	FBG		IO	100-140							7650	8850
16	4	GLAMOUR-GIRL		FSH	FBG		IO	60D							12600	14300
16	4	GLAMOUR-GIRL		RNBT	FBG		IO	100-140							8700	10000
16	4	GLAMOUR-GIRL		RNBT	FBG		IO	60D							10600	12000
20		GLAMOUR-GIRL		FSH	FBG		IO	100-140							15600	17800
20		GLAMOUR-GIRL		FSH	FBG		IO	60D							24400	27100
20		GLAMOUR-GIRL		RNBT	FBG		IO	100-140							12900	14700
20		GLAMOUR-GIRL		RNBT	FBG		IO	60D							18400	20400
28	6	DYERCRAFT		CR	FBG		IB	225		9	5		2	6	22200	24600
28	6	DYERCRAFT		FSH	FBG		IB	225		9	5		2	6	21600	24100
39	8	DYERCRAFT		CR	FBG		IB			12	5		2	9	**	**
		1964 BOATS														
16	2	GLAMOUR-GIRL		FSH	FBG		OB								3800	4400
16	2	GLAMOUR-GIRL TENDER		UTL	FBG		OB								2900	3350
16	4	GLAMOUR-GIRL		FSH	FBG		IO	110							7900	9100
16	4	GLAMOUR-GIRL		RNBT	FBG		IO	110							9100	10300
20		GLAMOUR-GIRL		FSH	FBG		IO								**	**
20		GLAMOUR-GIRL		FSH	FBG		IO	100-140							16100	18300
20		GLAMOUR-GIRL		FSH	FBG		IO	50D							24700	27500
20		GLAMOUR-GIRL		RNBT	FBG		IO								**	**
		1963 BOATS														
16	2	GLAMOUR-GIRL		FSH	FBG		IB	30							2250	2600
16	2	GLAMOUR-GIRL TENDER		UTL	FBG		IB	30							2700	3150
16	4	GLORIFIED		RNBT	FBG		IB	60							3300	3850
16	4	GLORIFIED GLAMOUR		FSH	FBG		IB	60							2500	2900
28	6	DYERCRAFT		CNV	FBG		IB	135-200							21900	25500
28	6	DYERCRAFT		CR	FBG		IB	135-200							20200	23000
28	6	DYERCRAFT COMMUTER			FBG		IB	135-200							19800	22700
39	8	DYERCRAFT 40			FBG		IB	T240							62700	68900
		1962 BOATS														
16	2	GLAMOUR-GIRL		FSH	FBG		IB	30							2150	2500
16	2	GLAMOUR-GIRL		FSH	FBG		IB	60- 70							2400	2900
16	2	GLAMOUR-GIRL		FSH	FBG		IB	80							2600	3000
16	2	GLAMOUR-GIRL TENDER		UTL	FBG		IB	30- 60							2650	3300
16	2	GLAMOUR-GIRL TENDER		UTL	FBG		IB	70							2900	3350
28	6	DYERCRAFT 29		CNV	FBG		IB	135-200							21300	24800
28	6	DYERCRAFT 29		CR	FBG		IB	135-200							19700	22400
28	6	DYERCRAFT 29	FB	EXP	FBG		IB	135-200							19000	21900
39	8	DYERCRAFT 40			FBG		IB	T240							61200	67300
		1961 BOATS														
28	6	DYERCRAFT 29		SF	FBG	RB	IB	220		9	5		2	6	18500	20600
39	6	DYERCRAFT 40		CR	FBG		IB	T220		12	6		2	8	62500	68700
		1960 BOATS														
16		GLAMOUR-GIRL		UTL	FBG		IB	70							2900	3350
16		GLAMOUR-GIRL TENDER		UTL	FBG		IB	70							2900	3350
29		DYERCRAFT 29		SF	FBG		IB	220							18900	21000
40		DYERCRAFT 40		CR	FBG		IB	T220							63400	69700
		1959 BOATS														
19	11	GLAMOUR-GIRL		UTL	FBG		OB			7	3				5500	6300
19	11	GLAMOUR-GIRL		UTL	FBG		IB	65		7	3				5850	6700
28	6	DYERCRAFT 29		SF	FBG		IB			7					**	**
		1949 BOATS														
26		DYER-DHOW-SENIOR	SLP	SAIL	WD		IB								13500	15400
		1941 BOATS														
18		MARLIN	SLP	SA/OD	WD	KL									3100	3600
21		DYERCRAFT	OP	CR	WD		IB								**	**

 CONTINUED ON NEXT PAGE

LOA FT IN	NAME AND/ OR MODEL	TOP/ RIG	BOAT TYPE	-HULL- MTL TP TP	----ENGINE--- # HP MFG	BEAM FT IN	WGT LBS	DRAFT FT IN	RETAIL LOW	RETAIL HIGH
--------------------	1939 BOATS									
18	MARLIN	SLP	SA/OD	WD KL				3	3300	3800
--------------------	1928 BOATS									
21		RNBT	WD	IB	GRAY 5 9				**	**

ANDERSON'S BOAT YARD

Call 1-800-327-6929 for BUC Personalized Evaluation Service
Or, for 1975 to 1976 boats, sign onto www.BUCValuPro.com

ANDROMACHE YACHTS
COAST GUARD MFG ID- ANH

Call 1-800-327-6929 for BUC Personalized Evaluation Service
Or, for 1977 boats, sign onto www.BUCValuPro.com

ANGLER BOAT CO

Call 1-800-327-6929 for BUC Personalized Evaluation Service
Or, for 1960 boats, sign onto www.BUCValuPro.com

ANGLER BOAT CORP
MIAMI FL 33147   COAST GUARD MFG ID- ANG See inside cover to adjust price for area

For more recent years, see the BUC Used Boat Price Guide, Volume 1 or Volume 2

LOA FT IN	NAME AND/ OR MODEL	TOP/ RIG	BOAT TYPE	-HULL- MTL TP TP	----ENGINE--- # HP MFG	BEAM FT IN	WGT LBS	DRAFT FT IN	RETAIL LOW	RETAIL HIGH
--------------------	1983 BOATS									
18	3 V-19BR	ST	RNBT	FBG SV IO	120 VLVO	7 5	1230		1750	2050
18	3 V-19H	ST	RNBT	FBG SV IO	138 VLVO	7 5	1230		1700	2000
18	3 V-19H	ST	RNBT	FBG SV IO	175 VLVO	7 5	1230		1750	2050
18	3 V-19H	ST	RNBT	FBG SV IO	T175 VLVO	7 5	1230		2150	2500
18	8 V-19F	OP	FSH	FBG SV OB		8	1570		1700	2050
20	1 V-21BR	ST	RNBT	FBG SV OB		8	1715		2850	3350
20	1 V-21BR	ST	RNBT	FBG SV IO	120-140	8	1715		2350	2850
	IO 170 MRCR	2350	2750, IB 170	OMC	3250	3750, IO 175-230			2450	2950
	IO T120 MRCR	2650	3100, IO T120	OMC	2600	3050, IO T120-T175			2850	3400
20	1 V-21CC	ST	CUD	FBG SV OB		8	1775		2950	3400
20	1 V-21CC	ST	CUD	FBG SV IO	120-200	8	1775		2450	3050
	IO 225-230	2650	3100, IO 290-330		3000	3600, IO 130D VLVO			3450	4000
	IO T120 MRCR	2750	3200, IO T120	OMC	2750	3200, IO T120-T175			3000	3550
22	V-22F	OP	CTRCN	FBG SV OB		8	1940	10	3450	4000
22	V-22F	OP	CTRCN	FBG SV IO	120-230	8		10	3300	4150
	IO 260	3550	4300, IO 290-330		3950	4750, IO 130D VLVO			5850	6750
	IB 150D S&S	6600	7600, IO T165D VLVO		8000	9150				
22	V-22PF	OP	CTRCN	FBG SV IO	185 OMC	8			3350	3850
22	V-22PF	OP	CTRCN	FBG SV IO	130D VLVO	8			5850	6750
22	V-22WA	OP	FSH	FBG DV OB		8	3000		4750	5450
22	V-22WA	OP	FSH	FBG DV IO	120-230	8	3000		3800	4700
	IO 260	4000	4850, IO 290-330		4450	5250, IO 130D VLVO			5850	6750
	IB 150D S&S	6600	7600, IO 155D VLVO		6050	7000				
23	6 V-24CC	ST	CUD	FBG DV OB		8	3000		5200	6000
23	6 V-24CC	ST	CUD	FBG DV IO	200-230	8	3400		4050	4950
	IO 260	4250	5100, IO 290-330		4650	5450, IO 130D VLVO			5100	5850
	IB 150D S&S	7200	8250, IO 165D VLVO		5300	6050, IO T120-T200			4700	5800
	IO T225-T260	5150	6200							
23	6 V-24HS	HT	SDN	FBG DV OB		8	2400		4350	5000
23	6 V-24HS	HT	SDN	FBG DV IO	185-260	8			4850	5950
	IO 290-330	5350	6300, IO 130D VLVO		6250	7150, IB 150D S&S			8700	10000
	IO 165D VLVO	6350	7300, IO T120-T230		5450	6750, IO T260			5850	7150
	IO T165D VLVO	8300	9550							
25	9 FREEDOM 26	OP	EXP	FBG DV OB		9 9	4900	2 3	7700	8850
25	9 FREEDOM 26	OP	EXP	FBG DV IO	225 VLVO	9 9	4900	2 3	6450	7400
	IB 225 COMM	7950	9150, IO 228 MRCR		6400	7350, IB 255			8100	9300
	IO 260	6550	7650, IO 130D-165D		6950	8350, IO T138 VLVO			7200	8250
	IO T170 MRCR	7200	8300, IB T170-T225		9000	10700, IO T228 MRCR			7600	8700
25	9 FREEDOM 26	HT	EXP	FBG DV OB		9 9	4900	2 3	7850	9050
25	9 FREEDOM 26	HT	EXP	FBG DV IO	225 VLVO	9 9	4900	2 3	6450	7400
	IB 225 COMM	7950	9150, IO 228 MRCR		6400	7350, IB 255			8100	9300
	IO 260	6550	7650, IO 130D-165D		6950	8350, IO T138 VLVO			7200	8250
	IO T170 MRCR	7200	8300, IB T170-T225		9000	10700, IO T228 MRCR			7600	8700
25	9 FREEDOM 26	FB	EXP	FBG DV OB		9 9	4900	2 3	7750	8900
25	9 FREEDOM 26	FB	EXP	FBG DV IO	225 VLVO	9 9	4900	2 3	6450	7400
	IB 225 COMM	7950	9150, IO 228 MRCR		6400	7350, IB 255			8100	9300
	IO 260	6550	7650, IO 130D-165D		6950	8350, IO T138 VLVO			7200	8250
	IO T170 MRCR	7200	8300, IB T170-T225		9000	10700, IO T228 MRCR			7600	8700
25	9 FREEDOM 26	OP	SF	FBG DV OB		9 9	4900	2 3	7600	8750
25	9 FREEDOM 26	OP	SF	FBG DV IO	225 VLVO	9 9	4900	2 3	7250	8350
	IB 225 COMM	7800	8950, IO 228 MRCR		7200	8250, IB 255			7900	9100
	IO 260	7350	8600, IB 124D VLVO		9150	10400, IO 130D-165D			8550	10300
	IB 200D PERK	10800	12200, IO T138 VLVO		8100	9300, IO T170 MRCR			8100	9300
	IB T170-T225	8850	10400, IO T228 MRCR		8500	9800, IB T124D VLVO			11800	13500
25	9 FREEDOM 26	HT	SF	FBG DV OB		9 9	4900	2 3	7600	8750
25	9 FREEDOM 26	HT	SF	FBG DV IO	225 VLVO	9 9	4900	2 3	7100	8150
	IB 225 COMM	7550	8700, IO 228 MRCR		7500	8100, IB 255			7750	8900
	IO 260	7200	8400, IB 124D VLVO		8950	10200, IO 130D-165D			8300	10100
	IB 200D PERK	10500	11900, IO T138 VLVO		7900	9100, IO T170 MRCR			7950	9100
	IB T170-T225	8550	10200, IO T228 MRCR		8300	9550, IB T124D VLVO			11600	13200
27	V-27CC	ST	CUD	FBG DV OB		8 9	3500		9000	10200
27	V-27CC	ST	CUD	FBG DV IO	200-260	8 9			6700	8300
	IO 290-330	7450	8900, IO 130D VLVO		6700	7700, IB 150D S&S			9700	11000
	IO 165D VLVO	7200	8300, IO T138-T200		7600	9450, IO T225-T260			8450	9900
	IO T290-T330	9350	10900, IO T165D VLVO		9850	11200				
27	V-27FB	FB	SDN	FBG DV OB		8 9	6200		8900	10100
27	V-27FB	FB	SDN	FBG DV IO	198-290	8 9			6900	11700
	IO 330 MRCR	10600	12000, IO 130D VLVO		13200	15000, IB 150D S&S			19400	21500
	IO 165D VLVO	13600	15500, IO T138-T260		10500	13200, IO T290-T330			12000	13900
	IO T165D VLVO	16700	19000							
27	V-27HS	HT	CUD	FBG DV OB		8 9			9150	10400
27	V-27HS	HT	CUD	FBG DV IO	198-260	8 9			6700	8300
	IO 290-330	7450	8900, IO 130D VLVO		6700	7700, IB 150D S&S			9700	11000
	IO 165D VLVO	7200	8300, IO T140-T198		7500	9250, IO T200-T225			8050	9700
	IO T260	8650	10100, IO T165D VLVO		9850	11200				
27	V-27HS	HT	SDN	FBG DV IO	198-290	8 9			9600	11700
	IO 330 MRCR	10600	12000, IO 130D VLVO		13200	15000, IB 150D S&S			19400	21500
	IO 165D VLVO	13600	15500, IO T138-T230		13000	15000, IO T260-T330			11600	13900
	IO T165D VLVO	16700	19000							
--------------------	1982 BOATS									
18	3 V-19BR	ST	RNBT	FBG SV IO	175 VLVO	7 5	1230		1700	2000
18	3 V-19BR	ST	RNBT	FBG SV IO	125-175 OMC	7 5	1230		1800	2150
18	3 V-19CC	ST	CUD	FBG SV IO	125-175	7 5	1300		1700	2000
18	3 V-19FB	FB	RNBT	FBG SV IO	120	7 5			1900	2250
18	3 V-19H	ST	RNBT	FBG SV IO	T175 VLVO	7 5	1230		2050	2450
18	8 V-19F	OP	FSH	FBG SV OB		8	1570	8	1800	2150
20	1 V-21BR	ST	RNBT	FBG SV OB		8	1715		2800	3200
20	1 V-21BR	ST	RNBT	FBG SV IO	120-200	8	1715		2250	2800
	IO 225-260	2450	3000, IO 290-330		2750	3350, IO 130D VLVO			3150	3650
	IO T120-T140	2550	3200, IO T145-T200		2750	3250				
20	1 V-21CC	ST	CUD	FBG SV OB		8	1775		2900	3350
20	1 V-21CC	ST	CUD	FBG SV IO	120-200	8	1775		2350	2950
	IO 225-260	2600	3150, IO 290-330		3000	3550, IO 130D VLVO			3350	3900
	IO T120	2700	3100, IO T125-T200		2900	3450				
22	V-22F	OP	CTRCN	FBG SV OB		8		10	4450	5150
22	V-22F	OP	CTRCN	FBG SV IO	120-200	8		10	3200	3950
	IO 225-260	3450	4150, IO 290-330		3800	4600, IO 130D VLVO			5700	6500
	IB 150D S&S	6400	7350, IO T155D VLVO		7550	8650				
22	V-22PF	OP	CTRCN	FBG SV OB		8			3650	4250
22	V-22PF	OP	CTRCN	FBG SV IO	185-200	8			3200	3950
	IO 225-260	3450	4150, IO 290-330		3800	4600, IO 130D VLVO			5700	6500
23	6 V-24CC	ST	CUD	FBG DV OB		8	3000		5100	5850
23	6 V-24CC	ST	CUD	FBG DV IO	185-260	8			4600	5650
	IO 290-330	5100	6000, IO 130D VLVO		6050	6950, IB 150D S&S			8400	9650
	IO 155D VLVO	6200	7100, IO T120-T230		5200	6450, IO T250-T260			5800	6650

```
ANGLER BOAT CORP          -CONTINUED    See inside cover to adjust price for area
LOA  NAME AND/          TOP/ BOAT   -HULL-  ----ENGINE---  BEAM    WGT  DRAFT RETAIL RETAIL
FT IN OR MODEL          RIG  TYPE   MTL TP TP # HP MFG   FT IN   LBS  FT IN  LOW   HIGH
-------------------- 1982 BOATS --------------------------------------------------------
23  6 V-24CC            ST  CUD  FBG DV IO T155D VLVO  8                    7950   9150
23  6 V-24HS            HT  SDN  FBG DV OB            8                     5100   5850
23  6 V-24HS            HT  SDN  FBG DV IO 185-260    8                     4700   5750
    IO 290-330   5200   6100, IO 130D VLVO   6050   6950, IB 150D S&S      8350   9600
    IO 155D VLVO 6150   7050, IO T120-T230   5250   6550, IO T250-T260     5900   6750
    IO T155D VLVO 7950  9150

27    V-27CC            ST  CUD  FBG DV OB            8  9                  8950  10200
27    V-27CC            ST  CUD  FBG DV IO 198-260    8  9                  6500   8050
    IO 290-330   7200   8550, IO 130D VLVO   6450   7450, IB 150D S&S      9350  10600
    IO 155D VLVO 6850   7900, IO T140-T198   7250   9000, IO T200-T260     7800   9600
    IO T290-T330 9050  10600, IO T155D VLVO  9350  10600

27    V-27FB            FB  SDN  FBG DV OB            8  9                  8500   9800
27    V-27FB            FB  SDN  FBG DV IO 198-290    8  9                  9300  11400
    IO 330 MRCR 10300  11600, IO 130D VLVO  12900  14700, IB 150D S&S     18600  20700
    IO 155D VLVO 13200 15000, IO T140-T230  10100  12600, IO T260-T330    11200  13400
    IO T155D VLVO 16000 18200

27    V-27HS            HT  CUD  FBG DV OB            8  9                  8950  10100
27    V-27HS            HT  CUD  FBG DV IO 198-260    8  9                  6500   8050
    IO 290-330   7200   8550, IO 130D VLVO   6450   7450, IB 150D S&S      9350  10600
    IO 155D VLVO 6850   7900, IO T140-T198   7250   9000, IO T200-T260     7800   9700
    IO T155D VLVO 9350  10600

27    V-27HS            HT  SDN  FBG DV IO 198-290    8                     9150  11200
    IO 330 MRCR 10100  11500, IO 130D VLVO  12800  14500, IB 150D S&S     18400  20400
    IO 155D VLVO 13100 14900, IO T140-T230  10000  12400, IO T250-T330    11200  13300
    IO T155D VLVO 15500 17600
-------------------- 1981 BOATS --------------------------------------------------------
18  8 V-19F             OP  FSH  FBG SV OB            8       1570         1850   2200
20  1 V-21BR            ST  RNBT FBG DV OB            8       1715         2750   3200
20  1 V-21BR            ST  RNBT FBG SV IO 120-198    8       1715         2200   2700
    IO 200       2250   2750, IO 225-260    2400   2950, IO 290-330       2700   3250
    IO 130D VLVO 3100   3600, IO T140 OMC   2500   2900, IO T140-T200     2700   3150

20  1 V-21CC            ST  CUD  FBG DV OB            8       1775         2850   3300
20  1 V-21CC            ST  CUD  FBG SV IO 185-200    8       1775         2350   2850
    IO 225-260   2500   3050, IO 290-330    2800   3450, IO 130D VLVO     3200   3750
    IO T140 OMC  2600   3000, IO T140-T200  2850   3300

22    V-22F             OP  CTRCN FBG SV OB           8                    5100   5850
22    V-22F             OP  CTRCN FBG SV IO 228-260   8                    3400   4250
22    V-22F             OP  CTRCN FBG SV IO 290-330   8                    3900   4650
22    V-22PF            OP  CTRCN FBG SV IO 130D VLVO 8                    5700   6600
22    V-22PF            OP  CTRCN FBG SV OB           8                    2850   3300
22    V-22PF            OP  CTRCN FBG SV IO 185-200   8                    3100   3850
    IO 225-290   3350   4050, IO 330 MRCR   3650   4250, IO 130D VLVO     5350   6150

23  6 V-24CC            ST  CUD  FBG DV OB            8                    5150   5900
23  6 V-24CC            ST  CUD  FBG DV IO 185-260    8                    4500   5550
    IO 290-330   5000   5850, IO 130D-150D  5850   7050, IO T140-T200     5000   6200

23  6 V-24HS            HT  SDN  FBG DV OB            8                    5000   5750
23  6 V-24HS            HT  SDN  FBG DV IO 185-260    8                    4550   5600
    IO 290-330   5050   5950, IO 130D-150D  5850   7000, IO T140-T200     5100   6300

27    V-27CC            ST  CUD  FBG DV IO            8                    **     **
27    V-27FB            FB  SDN  FBG DV IO            8                    **     **
27    V-27HS            HT  SDN  FBG DV IO            8                    **     **
-------------------- 1980 BOATS --------------------------------------------------------
18  3 V-19BR            ST  RNBT FBG SV IO 120       7  5                  1850   2300
    IO 140 MRCR 1800   2150, IO 140 OMC    1800   2100, IO 140-185        1950   2300

18  3 V-19CC            ST  CUD  FBG SV IO 120 MRCR  7  5                  1850   2200
18  3 V-19CC            ST  CUD  FBG SV IO 120 OMC   7  5                  1850   2200
18  3 V-19CC            ST  CUD  FBG SV IO 120-185   7  5                  1950   2350
18  3 V-19H             ST  RNBT FBG SV IO 120 MRCR  7  5                  1750   2100
18  3 V-19H             ST  RNBT FBG SV IO 120 OMC   7  5                  1750   2100
18  3 V-19H             ST  RNBT FBG SV IO 120-185   7  5                  1850   2250
20  1 V-21BR            ST  RNBT FBG SV OB           8       1715         2750   3150
20  1 V-21BR            ST  RNBT FBG SV IO 120-200   8                    2600   3200
    IO 225-260   2800   3400, IO 290-330    3100   3700, IO 130D VLVO     3800   4450
    IO T140-T200 2900   3600

20  1 V-21CC            ST  CUD  FBG SV OB           8       1775         2800   3250
20  1 V-21CC            ST  CUD  FBG SV IO 120-200   8                    2700   3350
    IO 225-260   2950   3550, IO 290-330    3200   3900, IO 130D VLVO     4200   4850
    IO T140-T200 3050   3750

21  8 V-22F             OP  CTRCN FBG SV IO 120-250  8                    3000   3750
21  8 V-22F             OP  CTRCN FBG SV IO 260      8                    3200   3900
21  8 V-22F             OP  CTRCN FBG SV IO 290-330  8                    3550   4300
22    V-22PF            OP  CTRCN FBG SV OB          8                    3900   4550
23  6 V-24CC            ST  CUD  FBG DV OB           8       3000         4950   5700
23  6 V-24CC            ST  CUD  FBG DV IO 185-250   8       3400         3750   4600
    IO 260       3950   4750, IO 290-330    4250   5100, IO 130D-150D     4750   5700
    IO T140-T200 4350   5350

23  6 V-24HS            HT  SDN  FBG DV OB           8       3000         4950   5700
23  6 V-24HS            HT  SDN  FBG DV IO 185-250   8       3400         3750   4600
    IO 260       3950   4750, IO 290-330    4250   5100, IO 130D-150D     4750   5700
    IO T140-T200 4350   5400
-------------------- 1979 BOATS --------------------------------------------------------
18  3 V-19BR            ST  RNBT FBG SV IO 120 MRCR  7  5                  1800   2150
18  3 V-19BR            ST  RNBT FBG SV IO 120 OMC   7  5                  1800   2100
18  3 V-19BR            HT  RNBT FBG SV IO 120-170   7  5                  1900   2300
18  3 V-19CC            ST  CUD  FBG SV IO 120 MRCR  7  5                  1800   2150
18  3 V-19CC            ST  CUD  FBG SV IO 120 OMC   7  5                  1800   2150
18  3 V-19CC            ST  CUD  FBG SV IO 120-170   7  5                  1950   2300
18  3 V-19H             ST  RNBT FBG SV IO 120 MRCR  7  5                  1750   2100
18  3 V-19H             ST  RNBT FBG SV IO 120 OMC   7  5                  1750   2050
18  3 V-19H             ST  RNBT FBG SV IO 120-170   7  5                  1850   2250
20  2 V-21BR            ST  RNBT FBG SV OB           8       1715         2700   3150

20  2 V-21BR            ST  RNBT FBG SV IO 120-200   8                    2600   3150
    IO 225-260   2750   3400, IO 290-330    3050   3700, IO 130D VLVO     3800   4400
    IO T140-T200 2900   3550

20  2 V-21CC            ST  CUD  FBG SV OB           8       1775         2800   3250
20  2 V-21CC            ST  CUD  FBG SV IO 120-200   8                    2700   3350
    IO 225-260   2900   3550, IO 290-330    3200   3900, IO 130D VLVO     4150   4800
    IO T140-T200 3000   3700

21  8 V-22F             OP  CTRCN FBG SV OB          8                    3800   4400
21  8 V-22F             OP  CTRCN FBG SV IO 120-250  8                    3000   3700
21  8 V-22F             OP  CTRCN FBG SV IO 260      8                    3150   3900
21  8 V-22F             OP  CTRCN FBG SV IO 290-330  8                    3500   4250
23  6 V-24CC            ST  CUD  FBG DV OB           8       3000         5000   5750
23  6 V-24CC            ST  CUD  FBG DV IO 185-250   8       3400         3400   4200
    IO 260       3550   4300, IO 290-330    3900   4700, IO 130D-150D     4400   5300
    IO T140-T198 3950   4850, IO T200        4000   4950

23  6 V-24HS            HT  SDN  FBG DV OB           8       3000         4900   5600
23  6 V-24HS            HT  SDN  FBG DV IO 185-250   8       3400         3700   4550
    IO 260       3900   4700, IO 290-330    4200   5050, IO 130D-150D     4700   5650
    IO T140-T200 4350   5350
-------------------- 1978 BOATS --------------------------------------------------------
19  8 V-19BR            ST  RNBT FBG SV IO 120-170   7  5                  2250   2700
19  8 V-19CC            ST  RNBT FBG SV IO 120-170   7  5                  2300   2800
19  8 V-19H             ST  RNBT FBG SV IO 120-170   7  5                  2200   2650
20  1 V-21BR            ST  RNBT FBG SV OB           8       1725         2700   3100
20  1 V-21BR            ST  RNBT FBG SV IO 120-240   8                    2550   3200
20  1 V-21BR            ST  RNBT FBG SV IO 255-260   8                    2850   3350
20  1 V-21BR            ST  RNBT FBG SV IO 130D VLVO 8                    3750   4350
20  1 V-21CC            ST  CUD  FBG SV OB           8       1775         2750   3200
20  1 V-21CC            ST  CUD  FBG SV IO 120-200   8                    2650   3300
    IO 225-240   2750   3350, IO 255-260    3000   3500, IO 130D VLVO     4100   4800

21  8 V-22F             OP  OPFSH FBG SV IO          8  2100  8 3350      4100   4700
23  6 V-24CC            ST  CUD  FBG DV IO          8  2400              4000   4700
23  6 V-24CC            ST  CUD  FBG DV IO 185-260   8                    4300   5350
23  6 V-24CC            ST  CUD  FBG DV IO 130D-150D 8                    4900   6000
23  6 V-24CC            ST  CUD  FBG DV IO T140-T200 8                    4900   6000
23  6 V-24HS            HT  SDN  FBG DV IO          8  2400              4000   4650
23  6 V-24HS            HT  SDN  FBG DV IO 185-260   8                    4400   5400
23  6 V-24HS            HT  SDN  FBG DV IO 130D-150D 8                    5650   6700
23  6 V-24HS            HT  SDN  FBG DV IO T140-T200 8                    5000   6100
-------------------- 1977 BOATS --------------------------------------------------------
18  2 V19 BOW RIDER     ST  RNBT FBG SV IO 75D VLVO  7  5  1230          2000   2400
18  2 V19 BOW RIDER     ST  RNBT FBG SV IO 106D VLVO 7  5  1230          2200   2550
18  2 V19 CUDDY CABIN   ST  CUD  FBG SV IO 75D VLVO  7  5  1300          2100   2500
18  2 V19 CUDDY CABIN   ST  CUD  FBG SV IO 106D VLVO 7  5  1300          2250   2650
18  2 V19 HARD DECK     ST  RNBT FBG SV IO 75D VLVO  7  5  1140          2000   2400
```

96th ed. - Vol. III   CONTINUED ON NEXT PAGE   31

ANGLER BOAT CORP   -CONTINUED   See inside cover to adjust price for area

LOA FT IN	NAME AND/ OR MODEL	TOP/ RIG	BOAT TYPE	-HULL- MTL TP	----ENGINE--- TP # HP MFG	BEAM FT IN	WGT LBS	DRAFT FT IN	RETAIL LOW	RETAIL HIGH
					------ 1977 BOATS ------					
18 2	V19 HARD DECK	ST	RNBT	FBG SV IO	106D VLVO	7 5	1140		2150	2550
20 1	V21 BOW RIDER	ST	RNBT	FBG SV OB		8	1715		2650	3100
20 1	V21 BOW RIDER	ST	RNBT	FBG SV IO	120-190	8	1715		2150	2650
20 1	V21 BOW RIDER	ST	RNBT	FBG SV IO	75D-106D	8	1715		2750	3400
20 1	V21 CUDDY CABIN	ST	CUD	FBG SV OB		8	1775		2700	3150
20 1	V21 CUDDY CABIN	ST	CUD	FBG SV IO	120-190	8	1775		2250	2750
20 1	V21 CUDDY CABIN	ST	CUD	FBG SV IO	75D-106D	8	1775		2900	3550
21 8	V22 FISHERMAN	OP	FSH	FBG SV OB		8			3800	4400
23 8	V24 CUDDY CABIN	ST	CUD	FBG DV OB		8			4950	5700
23 8	V24 CUDDY CABIN	ST	CUD	FBG DV IO	188-255	8			4400	5400
23 8	V24 CUDDY CABIN	ST	CUD	FBG DV IO	T165-T175	8			5000	6000
23 8	V24 CUDDY CABIN	ST	CUD	FBG DV IO	T75D-T106D	8			6800	8200
23 8	V24 FISHERMAN		FSH	FBG DV OB		8			4850	5550
23 8	V24 FISHERMAN		FSH	FBG DV IO	188-255	8			5200	6350
23 8	V24 FISHERMAN		FSH	FBG DV IO	T165-T175	8			5900	7100
23 8	V24 FISHERMAN		FSH	FBG DV IO	T75D-T106D	8			9300	11000
23 8	V24 HARDTOP SEDAN	HT	SDN	FBG DV OB		8			4850	5550
23 8	V24 HARDTOP SEDAN	HT	SDN	FBG DV IO	188-255	8			4500	5500
23 8	V24 HARDTOP SEDAN	HT	SDN	FBG DV IO	T165-T175	8			5100	6100
23 8	V24 HARDTOP SEDAN	HT	SDN	FBG DV IO	T75D-T106D	8			6800	8200
					------ 1976 BOATS ------					
18 2	V19 BOW RIDER	ST	RNBT	FBG SV IO	106D VLVO	7 5	1230	9	2200	2600
18 2	V19 CUDDY CABIN	ST	CUD	FBG SV IO	106D VLVO	7 5	1230	9	2300	2650
18 2	V19 HARD DECK	ST	RNBT	FBG SV IO	106D VLVO	7 5	1230	9	2200	2600
20 1	V21 BOW RIDER	ST	RNBT	FBG SV OB		8	1715	9	2650	3050
20 1	V21 BOW RIDER	ST	RNBT	FBG SV IO	120-170	8	1715	9	2200	2700
20 1	V21 BOW RIDER	ST	RNBT	FBG SV IO	106D VLVO	8	1715	9	2950	3450
20 1	V21 CUDDY CABIN	ST	CUD	FBG SV OB		8	1775	9	2700	3150
20 1	V21 CUDDY CABIN	ST	CUD	FBG SV IO	120-170	8	1775	9	2250	2800
20 1	V21 CUDDY CABIN	ST	CUD	FBG SV IO	106D VLVO	8	1775	9	3100	3600
21 8	V22 FISHERMAN	OP	FSH	FBG SV OB		8	1775	9	2900	3350
21 8	V22 FISHERMAN	OP	FSH	FBG SV IO	120-170	8	1775	9	2700	3350
21 8	V22 FISHERMAN	OP	FSH	FBG SV IO	106D VLVO	8	1775	9	4400	5050

ANKER MARINE PRODUCTS

Call 1-800-327-6929 for BUC Personalized Evaluation Service
Or, for 1969 boats, sign onto www.BUCValuPro.com

ANKOR CRAFT

Call 1-800-327-6929 for BUC Personalized Evaluation Service
Or, for 1978 to 1979 boats, sign onto www.BUCValuPro.com

ANNAPOLIS SAILBOAT BLD INC
ANNAPOLIS MD 21401   COAST GUARD MFG ID- ASB See inside cover to adjust price for area

LOA FT IN	NAME AND/ OR MODEL	TOP/ RIG	BOAT TYPE	-HULL- MTL TP	----ENGINE--- TP # HP MFG	BEAM FT IN	WGT LBS	DRAFT FT IN	RETAIL LOW	RETAIL HIGH
					------ 1973 BOATS ------					
17 7	DISCOVERER	SLP	SA/OD	FBG CB OB		6 4	650	9	1850	2250
					------ 1972 BOATS ------					
17 7	DISCOVERER	SLP	SA/OD	FBG CB OB		6 4	650	9	1850	2200
20 4	SEVERN	SLP	SA/CR	FBG KC OB		7	1700	1 8	3150	3650
					------ 1971 BOATS ------					
17 7	DISCOVERER	SLP	SA/OD	FBG CB OB		6 4	650	9	1800	2150
20 4	SEVERN 20	SLP	SA/RC	FBG KC OB		7	1400	1 8	2800	3250
					------ 1970 BOATS ------					
17 7	DISCOVERER	SLP	SA/OD	FBG CB OB		6 4	650	9	1750	2100
20 4	SEVERN 20	SLP	SA/RC	FBG KC OB		7	1400	1 8	2750	3150
					------ 1969 BOATS ------					
17 7	DISCOVERER	SLP	SA/OD	FBG CB OB		6 4	650	9	1750	2050
20 5	SEVERN	SLP	SAIL	FBG KC OB		7		1 8	3000	3450
					------ 1967 BOATS ------					
21 4	RELIANCE	SLP	SA/OD	FBG KC OB		6 11		1 9	2800	3250
					------ 1966 BOATS ------					
21 4	RELIANCE	SLP	SA/OD	FBG KC OB		6 11		1 9	2750	3250
					------ 1965 BOATS ------					
21 4	RELIANCE	SLP	SA/OD	FBG KC OB		6 11		3 8	2750	3200

ANNAPOLIS YACHT SHOP
ANNAPOLIS MD 21403   COAST GUARD MFG ID- AYH See inside cover to adjust price for area
SEE ALSO TA CHIAO BROS YACHT BLDG CO

LOA FT IN	NAME AND/ OR MODEL	TOP/ RIG	BOAT TYPE	-HULL- MTL TP	----ENGINE--- TP # HP MFG	BEAM FT IN	WGT LBS	DRAFT FT IN	RETAIL LOW	RETAIL HIGH
					------ 1980 BOATS ------					
35 1	ANNAPOLIS 35	CUT	SA/CR	FBG KL IB	D	11	19000	5 4	52600	57800
40 10	PERRY 41	SLP	SA/CR	FBG KL IB	D	12	22300	6	69200	76000
42 6	OFFSHORE 43	CUT	SA/CR	FBG KL IB	D	12 2	29500	6	86300	94800
46 7	PERRY 47	KTH	SA/CR	FBG KL IB	D	13 6	34400	6 4	108500	119000
46 9	EASTPORT 47	KTH	SA/CR	FBG KL IB	75D	13 2	30000	6	103000	113000
					------ 1979 BOATS ------					
40 10	PERRY 41	SLP	SA/CR	FBG KL IB	D	12	22300		66500	73100
46 7	PERRY 47	KTH	SA/CR	FBG KL IB	D	13 6	30400		98700	108500
					------ 1946 BOATS ------					
46 8		HT	MY	WD	IB T	12 4		3 6	**	**
53 9		HT	MY	WD	IB T	15		3 9	**	**
59 11		HT	MY	WD	IB T	15		4 6	**	**
					------ 1939 BOATS ------					
34	ANNAPOLIS	HT	CR	WD	IB T	10		3	**	**

ANSTEY YACHTS LTD
TRAPPER YACHTS LTD

Call 1-800-327-6929 for BUC Personalized Evaluation Service
Or, for 1970 to 1979 boats, sign onto www.BUCValuPro.com

ANSWER MARINE CORP
MIAMI FL 33147   COAST GUARD MFG ID- AKM See inside cover to adjust price for area

For more recent years, see the BUC Used Boat Price Guide, Volume 1 or Volume 2

LOA FT IN	NAME AND/ OR MODEL	TOP/ RIG	BOAT TYPE	-HULL- MTL TP	----ENGINE--- TP # HP MFG	BEAM FT IN	WGT LBS	DRAFT FT IN	RETAIL LOW	RETAIL HIGH
					------ 1983 BOATS ------					
18 5	RUNABOUT 18	OP	RNBT	FBG DV IO	140 MRCR	7 3		9	3000	3500
18 6	FISHING MACHINE 18	OP	OPFSH	FBG DV IO	140	7 3		9	3550	4150
20 10	DIVEMASTER	ST	UTL	FBG SV IO	138-200	8	2850	10	5250	6100
20 10	FAMILY-SPORTSMAN 21	ST	CUD	FBG SV OB		8	2100	10	2000	2350
20 10	FAMILY-SPORTSMAN 21	ST	CUD	FBG SV IO	138-200	8	3100	10	5150	5950
20 10	FISH-MASTER 21	ST	FSH	FBG DV OB		8	1850	10	1850	2200
20 10	FISH-MASTER 21	ST	FSH	FBG DV IO	138-200	8	2550	10	4900	5700
20 10	FISHING-MACHINE 21	OP	CTRCN	FBG DV OB		8	1850	10	1850	2200
20 10	FISHING-MACHINE 21	OP	CTRCN	FBG DV IO	138-200	8	2850	10	5100	5950
23 6	FAMILY-SPORTSMAN 24	ST	CUD	FBG DV OB		8	2800	1 3	2900	3350
23 6	FAMILY-SPORTSMAN 24	ST	CUD	FBG DV IO	170-200	8	3800	1 3	6450	7700
23 6	FAMILY-SPORTSMAN 24	ST	CUD	FBG DV SE	205 OMC	8	3800	1 3	3600	4150
23 6	FAMILY-SPORTSMAN 24	ST	CUD	FBG DV IO	225-290	8	3800	1 3	6750	8350
23 6	FAMILY-SPORTSMAN 24	ST	CUD	FBG DV IO	T138-T188	8	3800	1 3	7700	8850
23 6	FAMILY-SPORTSMAN 24	ST	CUD	FBG DV SE	T205 OMC	8	3800	1 3	3600	4150
23 6	FISHING-MACHINE 24	OP	CTRCN	FBG DV OB		8	2800	1 3	2900	3350
23 6	FISHING-MACHINE 24	OP	CTRCN	FBG DV IO	170-200	8	3900	1 3	7100	8450
23 6	FISHING-MACHINE 24	OP	CTRCN	FBG DV SE	205 OMC	8	3900	1 3	3650	4250
23 6	FISHING-MACHINE 24	OP	CTRCN	FBG DV IO	225-290	8	3900	1 3	7400	9100
23 6	FISHING-MACHINE 24	OP	CTRCN	FBG DV IO	T138-T188	8	3900	1 3	8350	9600
23 6	FISHING-MACHINE 24	OP	CTRCN	FBG DV SE	T205 OMC	8	3900	1 3	3650	4250
23 6	HARDTOP 24	HT	SDN	FBG DV OB		8		1 3	3050	3550
23 6	HARDTOP 24	HT	SDN	FBG DV IO	170-200	8		1 3	7100	8400
23 6	HARDTOP 24	HT	SDN	FBG DV SE	205 OMC	8		1 3	**	**
23 6	HARDTOP 24	HT	SDN	FBG DV IO	225-290	8		1 3	7400	9000
23 6	HARDTOP 24	HT	SDN	FBG DV IO	T138-T188	8		1 3	8300	9500
23 6	HARDTOP 24	HT	SDN	FBG DV SE	T205 OMC	8		1 3	**	**
23 6	SPORT FISHERMAN	FB	SF	FBG DV OB		8	3500	1 3	3400	3950
23 6	SPORT FISHERMAN	FB	SF	FBG DV IO	170-200	8	4700	1 3	10000	11700
23 6	SPORT FISHERMAN	FB	SF	FBG DV SE	205 OMC	8	4700	1 3	4050	4700
23 6	SPORT FISHERMAN	FB	SF	FBG DV IO	225-290	8	4700	1 3	10400	12500
23 6	SPORT FISHERMAN	FB	SF	FBG DV IO	T138-T188	8	4700	1 3	11700	13200
23 6	SPORT FISHERMAN	FB	SF	FBG DV SE	T205 OMC	8	4700	1 3	4050	4700
23 6	SUPERSPORT 24	ST	CUD	FBG DV OB		8	3300	1 3	3250	3800
23 6	SUPERSPORT 24	ST	CUD	FBG DV IO	170-198	8	4000	1 3	6700	8250
23 6	SUPERSPORT 24	ST	CUD	FBG DV IO	200	8	4300	1 3	7150	8500
23 6	SUPERSPORT 24	ST	CUD	FBG DV SE	205 OMC	8	4000	1 3	3700	4300
23 6	SUPERSPORT 24	ST	CUD	FBG DV IO	225-230	8	4300	1 3	7450	8550
	IO 260 MRCR 7400	8550,	IO	260 OMC	7400	8500,	IO 260	VLVO	7650	8800
	IB 260 OMC 8600	9850,	IO	290 VLVO	7900	9100,	IO T140-T188		8000	9600

32   CONTINUED ON NEXT PAGE   96th ed. - Vol. III

LOA FT	LOA IN	NAME AND/ OR MODEL	TOP/ RIG	BOAT TYPE	HULL MTL	HULL TP	ENGINE TP	ENGINE # HP	ENGINE MFG	BEAM FT	BEAM IN	WGT LBS	DRAFT FT	DRAFT IN	RETAIL LOW	RETAIL HIGH
		1983 BOATS														
23	6	SUPERSPORT 24	ST	CUD	FBG	DV	SE	T205	OMC	8		4000	1	3	3700	4300
		1982 BOATS														
20	10	DIVEMASTER	ST	UTL	FBG	SV	IO	140-200		8		2850		10	4900	5950
20	10	FAMILY-SPORTSMAN 21	ST	CUD	FBG	SV	OB			8		2100		10	1950	2350
20	10	FAMILY-SPORTSMAN 21	ST	CUD	FBG	SV	IB			8		3100		10	**	**
20	10	FAMILY-SPORTSMAN 21	ST	CUD	FBG	SV	IO	140-200		8		3100		10	4800	5800
20	10	FISH-MASTER 21	ST	FSH	FBG	DV	OB			8		1850		10	1750	2100
20	10	FISH-MASTER 21	ST	FSH	FBG	DV	IB			8		2550		10	**	**
20	10	FISH-MASTER 21	ST	FSH	FBG	DV	IO	140-200		8		2550		10	4550	5550
20	10	FISHING-MACHINE 21	OP	CTRCN	FBG	SV	OB			8		1850		10	1750	2100
20	10	FISHING-MACHINE 21	OP	CTRCN	FBG	SV	IO	140-200		8		2850		10	4800	5750
23	6	FAMILY-SPORTSMAN 24	ST	CUD	FBG	DV	OB			8		2800	1	3	2800	3250
23	6	FAMILY-SPORTSMAN 24	ST	CUD	FBG	DV	IO	170-260		8		3800	1	3	6300	7750
23	6	FAMILY-SPORTSMAN 24	ST	CUD	FBG	DV	IO	290	VLVO	8		3800	1	3	7050	8100
23	6	FAMILY-SPORTSMAN 24	ST	CUD	FBG	DV	IO	T140-T185		8		3800	1	3	7150	8600
23	6	FISHING-MACHINE 24	OP	CTRCN	FBG	DV	OB			8		2800	1	3	2800	3250
23	6	FISHING-MACHINE 24	OP	CTRCN	FBG	DV	IO	170-260		8		3900	1	3	6900	8500
23	6	FISHING-MACHINE 24	OP	CTRCN	FBG	DV	IO	290	VLVO	8		3900	1	3	7700	8850
23	6	FISHING-MACHINE 24	OP	CTRCN	FBG	DV	IO	T140-T185		8		3900	1	3	7850	9350
23	6	HARDTOP 24	HT	SDN	FBG	DV	OB			8		3100	1	3	3050	3500
23	6	HARDTOP 24	HT	SDN	FBG	DV	IO	170-260		8			1	3	6850	8450
23	6	HARDTOP 24	HT	SDN	FBG	DV	IO	290	VLVO	8			1	3	7650	8750
23	6	HARDTOP 24	HT	SDN	FBG	DV	IO	T140-T185		8			1	3	7700	9250
23	6	SPORT FISHERMAN	FB	SF	FBG	DV	OB			8		3500	1	3	3300	3850
23	6	SPORT FISHERMAN	FB	SF	FBG	DV	IO	170-290		8		4700	1	3	9700	12100
23	6	SPORT FISHERMAN	FB	SF	FBG	DV	IO	T140-T185		8		4700	1	3	10900	12800
23	6	SUPERSPORT 24	ST	CUD	FBG	DV	OB			8		3300	1	3	3150	3700
23	6	SUPERSPORT 24	ST	CUD	FBG	DV	IO	170-198		8		4000	1	3	6550	8050
		IO 200-230 6950 8300, IB 255 8000 9450, IO 260													7200	8550
		IB 270 CRUS 8150 9350, IO 290 VLVO 7700 8850, IB 330-350													8250	9750
		IB 124D VLVO 10500 12000, IB 185D PERK 12200 13800, IO T140-T185													7850	9300
		1981 BOATS														
20	10	DIVEMASTER	ST	UTL	FBG	SV	IO	140-200		8		2850		10	5700	6900
20	10	FAMILY SPORTSMAN 21	ST	CUD	FBG	SV	OB			8		2100		10	1900	2300
20	10	FAMILY SPORTSMAN 21	ST	CUD	FBG	SV	IB			8		2800		10	**	**
20	10	FAMILY SPORTSMAN 21	ST	CUD	FBG	SV	IO	140-200		8		3100		10	5550	6700
20	10	FISH MASTER	ST	RNBT	FBG	SV	OB			8		1850		10	1700	2050
20	10	FISH MASTER	ST	RNBT	FBG	SV	IB			8		2550		10	**	**
20	10	FISH MASTER	ST	RNBT	FBG	SV	IO	140-200		8		2850		10	5100	6150
20	10	FISHING MACHINE 21	OP	CTRCN	FBG	SV	OB			8		1850		10	1700	2050
20	10	FISHING MACHINE 21	OP	CTRCN	FBG	SV	IO	140	MRCR	8		2850		10	5500	6350
20	10	FISHING MASTER 21	OP	CTRCN	FBG	SV	IO	140-200		8		2850		10	5500	6700
23	6	FAMILY SPORTS	ST	FSH	FBG	DV	OB			8		2800	1	3	2750	3200
23	6	FAMILY SPORTS	ST	FSH	FBG	DV	IO	170	MRCR	8		3900	1	3	8400	9650
23	6	FAMILY SPORTS	ST	FSH	FBG	DV	IO	170-230		8			1	3	9350	10600
23	6	FAMILY SPORTS	ST	FSH	FBG	DV	IB	470	MRCR	8			1	3	12200	13800
23	6	FAMILY SPORTSMAN 24	OP	CTRCN	FBG	DV	OB			8		2800	1	3	2750	3200
23	6	FAMILY SPORTSMAN 24	OP	CTRCN	FBG	DV	IO	170-260		8		3900	1	3	8050	9950
23	6	FAMILY SPORTSMAN 24	OP	CTRCN	FBG	DV	IO	290	VLVO	8		3900	1	3	9100	10300
23	6	FAMILY SPORTSMAN 24	OP	CTRCN	FBG	DV	IO	T140	MRCR	8		3900	1	3	9250	10500
23	6	FAMILY SPORTSMAN 24	ST	FSH	FBG	DV	IO	260-290		8		3900	1	3	8850	10800
23	6	FAMILY SPORTSMAN 24	ST	FSH	FBG	DV	IB	350	CRUS	8			1	3	11100	12700
23	6	FAMILY SPORTSMAN 24	ST	FSH	FBG	DV	IO	T140-T185		8		3900	1	3	9650	12100
23	6	FISHING-MACHINE	OP	CTRCN	FBG	DV	IO	T140-T185		8		3900	1	3	9100	11000
23	6	FLYBRIDGE 24	FB	SF	FBG	DV	IO	170-260		8		4700	1	3	11600	14300
23	6	FLYBRIDGE 24	FB	SF	FBG	DV	IO	290	VLVO	8		4800	1	3	12900	14700
23	6	FLYBRIDGE 24	FB	SF	FBG	DV	IO	T140-T185		8		4800	1	3	13200	15600
23	6	HARDTOP 24	HT	SDN	FBG	DV	OB			8			1	3	2900	3350
23	6	HARDTOP 24	HT	SDN	FBG	DV	IO	170-260		8			1	3	8000	9850
23	6	HARDTOP 24	HT	SDN	FBG	DV	IO	290	VLVO	8			1	3	9000	10200
23	6	HARDTOP 24	HT	SDN	FBG	DV	IO	T140-T185		8			1	3	9150	10800
23	6	SPORT FISHERMAN	FB	SF	FBG	DV	OB			8		3500	1	3	3200	3750
23	6	SPORT FISHERMAN	FB	SF	FBG	DV	IO	170	MRCR	8		4800	1	3	11800	13400
23	6	SUPERSPORT	ST	CUD	FBG	DV	OB			8		3300	1	3	3100	3600
23	6	SUPERSPORT	ST	CUD	FBG	DV	IO	170-230		8		4300	1	3	8100	9700
		IB 255 9100 10700, IO 260 8400 9950, IB 270 CRUS													9300	10600
		IO 290 VLVO 9050 10300, IB 330-350 9400 11100, IB 124D VLVO													12000	13700
		IB 185D PERK 14200 16100, IO T140-T185 9200 10900														
		1980 BOATS														
20	10	BOWRIDER	ST	RNBT	FBG	SV	OB			8		1850		10	1700	2000
20	10	BOWRIDER	ST	RNBT	FBG	SV	IO	140		8		2850		10	5000	6050
		IO 170 MRCR 5050 5800, IB 170 MRCR 5800 6650, IO 185-200													5050	6200
		IB 220 CRUS 6000 6900, IO 230 OMC 5150 5950, IB 230-350													6400	7450
20	10	CUDDY	ST	CUD	FBG	SV	OB			8		2100		10	1750	2100
20	10	CUDDY	ST	CUD	FBG	SV	IO	140		8		3100		10	5300	6400
		IO 170 MRCR 5350 6150, IB 170 MRCR 5750 6600, IO 185-200													5350	6550
		IB 220-228 5950 6850, IO 230 OMC 5450 6300, IB 230-270													5800	7050
		IB 330-350 6200 7500, IB 130D 10200 11600														
20	10	CUDDY SUPREME	ST	CUD	FBG	SV	OB			8		2100		10	1950	2300
20	10	CUDDY SUPREME	ST	CUD	FBG	SV	IO	140		8		3100		10	5600	6700
		IO 170 MRCR 5600 6450, IB 170 MRCR 6000 6900, IO 185-200													5600	6850
		IB 220-228 6200 7150, IO 230 OMC 5700 6600, IB 230-350													6600	7700
20	10	DIVEMASTER	OP	UTL	FBG	SV	IO	140		8		2850		10	5650	6700
		IO 170 MRCR 5650 6500, IB 170 MRCR 5750 6600, IO 185-200													5650	6800
		IB 220-228 5950 6850, IO 230 OMC 5750 6650, IB 230-350													6100	7450
		IB 130D 8600 9900														
20	10	OPEN FISHERMAN	OP	CTRCN	FBG	SV	IO	140		8		2850		10	5450	6500
		IO 170 MRCR 5450 6300, IB 170 MRCR 5550 6350, IO 185-200													5450	6600
		IB 220-228 5750 6600, IO 230 OMC 5550 6400, IB 230-350													5850	7150
		IB 130D 9100 10300														
20	10	RUNABOUT	ST	RNBT	FBG	SV	IO	140		8		2850		10	4950	5950
		IO 170 MRCR 5000 5750, IB 170 MRCR 5700 6550, IO 185-200													5000	6100
		IB 220-228 5900 6800, IO 230 OMC 5100 5850, IB 230-270													5750	7000
		IB 330-350 6100 7400														
23	6	FISHING-MACHINE	OP	CTRCN	FBG	DV	OB			8		2800	1	3	2700	3100
23	6	FISHING-MACHINE	OP	CTRCN	FBG	DV	IO	140	VLVO	8		3900	1	3	8100	9300
		IO 170 MRCR 7950 9100, IB 170 MRCR 8350 9600, IO 185-200													7900	9450
		IB 220 CRUS 8550 9850, IO 225 VLVO 8300 9550, IO 228 MRCR													8100	9300
		IB 228 MRCR 8400 9700, IO 230 OMC 8050 9250, IB 230 OMC													8650	9950
		IO 250 OMC 8150 9350, IB 255 8450 10000, IO 260													8250	9800
		IB 270 CRUS 8650 9950, IO 290 VLVO 8950 10200, IB 330-350													8800	10400
		IB 124D VLVO 11400 13000, IB 185D PERK 13200 15000, IO T140-T185													9100	10800
23	6	SEA FAL			FBG	DV	OB			8			1	3	2850	3300
23	6	SEA FAL			FBG	DV	IO	140	VLVO	8			1	3	7400	8500
		IO 170 MRCR 7250 8350, IB 170 MRCR 8850 10000, IO 185-200													7250	8600
		IB 220 CRUS 9050 10300, IO 225 VLVO 7600 8700, IO 228 MRCR													7400	8500
		IB 228 MRCR 8900 10100, IO 230 OMC 7350 8450, IB 230 OMC													9150	10400
		IO 250 OMC 7450 8550, IB 255 8950 10500, IO 260													7550	9050
		IB 270 CRUS 9100 10400, IO 290 VLVO 8150 9350, IB 330-350													9200	10800
		IB 124D VLVO 12800 14500, IB 185D PERK 14900 16900, IO T140-T185													8300	9900
23	6	SEDAN CRUISER	HT	SDN	FBG	DV	OB			8			1	3	2850	3300
23	6	SEDAN CRUISER	HT	SDN	FBG	DV	IO	140	VLVO	8			1	3	8050	9250
		IO 170 MRCR 7900 9100, IB 170 MRCR 9050 10300, IO 185-200													7900	9350
		IB 220 CRUS 9250 10500, IO 225 VLVO 8250 9450, IO 228 MRCR													8050	9250
		IB 228 MRCR 9100 10400, IO 230 OMC 8000 9200, IB 230 OMC													9350	10600
		IO 250 OMC 8100 9300, IB 255 9150 10700, IO 260													8200	9700
		IB 270 CRUS 9350 10600, IO 290 VLVO 8850 10100, IB 330-350													9400	11100
		IB 124D VLVO 12700 14400, IB 185D PERK 14800 16800, IO T140-T185													9000	10600
23	6	SPORT FISHERMAN	FB	SF	FBG	DV	OB			8		3500	1	3	3150	3650
23	6	SPORT FISHERMAN	FB	SF	FBG	DV	IO	140	VLVO	8		4800	1	3	11800	13500
		IO 170 MRCR 11600 13200, IB 170 MRCR 11400 12900, IO 185-200													11600	13600
		IB 220 CRUS 11600 13200, IO 225 VLVO 12100 13700, IO 228 MRCR													11800	13400
		IB 228 MRCR 11400 13000, IO 230 OMC 11800 13400, IB 230 OMC													11700	13300
		IO 250 OMC 11900 13500, IB 255 11500 13400, IO 260													12000	14000
		IB 270 CRUS 11700 13300, IO 290 VLVO 12800 14500, IB 330-350													11800	13800
		IB 124D VLVO 15000 17100, IB 185D PERK 17500 19900, IO T140-T185													13000	15300
23	6	SUPERSPORT	ST	CUD	FBG	DV	OB			8		3300	1	3	3050	3500
23	6	SUPERSPORT	ST	CUD	FBG	DV	IO	140	VLVO	8		4300	1	3	8150	9350
		IO 170 MRCR 7950 9150, IB 170 MRCR 8550 9800, IO 185-200													7950	9450
		IB 220 CRUS 8850 10000, IO 225 VLVO 8300 9550, IO 228 MRCR													8100	9300
		IB 228 MRCR 8600 9900, IO 230 OMC 8050 9250, IB 230 OMC													8950	10200
		IO 250 OMC 8150 9400, IB 255 8650 10200, IO 260													8250	9800
		IB 270 CRUS 8900 10100, IO 290 VLVO 8900 10100, IB 330-350													9000	10600
		IB 124D VLVO 11600 13100, IB 185D PERK 13400 15200, IO T140-T185													9050	10700

ANTIGUA SAILING YACHTS LTD

Call 1-800-327-6929 for BUC Personalized Evaluation Service
Or, for 1981 boats, sign onto www.BUCValuPro.com

ANTRIM MARINE

Call 1-800-327-6929 for BUC Personalized Evaluation Service
Or, for 1983 boats, sign onto www.BUCValuPro.com

APHRODITE NORTH AMERICAN

SEATTLE WA 98103   See inside cover to adjust price for area

LOA FT IN	NAME AND/ OR MODEL	TOP/ RIG	BOAT TYPE	-HULL- MTL TP	TP	----ENGINE--- # HP MFG	BEAM FT IN	WGT LBS	DRAFT FT IN	RETAIL LOW	RETAIL HIGH
---	--- --- 1983	BOATS	---								
32 8	INTERNATIONAL 101	SLP	SA/CR	FBG KL	IB	D	7 10	6160	5 4	21600	24000
41 4	BIANCA 414	SLP	SA/RC	FBG KL	IB	D	9 6	14990	7 5	62400	68600
---	--- --- 1982	BOATS	---								
32 8	INTERNATIONAL 101	SLP	SA/CR	FBG KL	IB	D	7 10	6160	5 4	20500	22800
41 4	BIANCA 414	SLP	SA/RC	FBG KL	IB	D	9 6	14990	7 5	58900	64700
---	--- --- 1981	BOATS	---								
32 8	INTERNATIONAL 101	SLP	SA/CR	FBG KL	IB	D	7 10	6160	5 4	19500	21700
41 4	BIANCA 414	SLP	SA/RC	FBG KL	IB	D	9 6	14990	7 5	56000	61600
---	--- --- 1980	BOATS	---								
32 8	INTERNATIONAL 101	SLP	SA/CR	FBG KL	IB	D	7 10	6160	5 4	18700	20800
41 4	BIANCA 414	SLP	SA/RC	FBG KL	IB	D	9 6	14990	7 5	53500	58800
---	--- --- 1979	BOATS	---								
33 8	INTERNATIONAL 101	SLP	SA/OD	FBG KL	IB	D	7 10	6160		17300	19700

APOLLO BOATS INC

ST PETERSBURG FL   COAST GUARD MFG ID- APL See inside cover to adjust price for area

LOA FT IN	NAME AND/ OR MODEL	TOP/ RIG	BOAT TYPE	-HULL- MTL TP	TP	----ENGINE--- # HP MFG	BEAM FT IN	WGT LBS	DRAFT FT IN	RETAIL LOW	RETAIL HIGH
---	--- --- 1978	BOATS	---								
19	APOLLO 19		OP	OPFSH FBG	SV OB		8	1200		1700	2000
19	SALTY			FSH FBG	OB		7 6	1500		2000	2400
21 11	APOLLO 22		OP	OPFSH FBG	SV OB		8	1500		2450	2850
21 11	APOLLO 22		OP	OPFSH FBG	SV IO	120-175	8	2600		3300	4000
	IO 190 OMC 3450		4000,	IB 190		3700	4300, IO	198 MRCR		3450	4050
	IB 198 MRCR 3400		3950,	IO 228		3500	4100, IB	105D CHRY		5100	5850
	IB 130D PERK 5850		6700								
21 11	APOLLO 22 LINER		OP	OPFSH FBG	SV OB		8	1900		3000	3500
22	SALTY			FSH FBG	OB		8	1700		2750	3200
23 7	APOLLO 24		OP	CUD FBG	DV OB		8	3150		4850	5600
23 7	APOLLO 24		OP	CUD FBG	DV IO	165-250	8	4000		4550	5550
23 7	APOLLO 24		OP	CUD FBG	DV IO	330 MRCR	8	4000		5150	5950
23 7	APOLLO 24		OP	CUD FBG	DV IO	T120-T228	8	4000		5050	6000
23 8	MAXIM 24		OP	CUD FBG	DV IO	235	8	4750		5300	6100
23 8	MAXIM 24		OP	CUD FBG	DV IO	330 MRCR	8	4750		5850	6700
23 8	MAXIM 24		OP	CUD FBG	DV IO	T228	8	4750		5900	6800
26 2	APOLLO 26		OP	EXP FBG	SV IB	190-225	9 6	5800		7200	8300
	IO 235 7000		8050,	IB 260-270		7400	8600, IO	T228		7950	9150
	IB T230 8350		9550								
26 2	APOLLO 26		OP	OPFSH FBG	SV IB	198 MRCR	9 6	5000		6450	7450
31	MAXIM V		OP	EXP FBG	DV IB	T225	9 4	8700		14600	16600
	IO T250 13900		15800,	IB T250		14900	16900, IO	T260 MRCR		14000	15900
	IO T330 MRCR 14800		16800,	IB T330-T350		15700	18100				
31	MAXIM V		OP	SPTCR FBG	DV IB	T233	9 4	8300		13200	14900
	IO T250 12400		14100,	IB T250		13300	15100, IO	T260 MRCR		12500	14200
	IO T330 MRCR 13200		15000,	IB T330-T350		14000	16200				
---	--- --- 1977	BOATS	---								
22	APOLLO 22V		OP	OPFSH FBG	SV OB		8	1400		2250	2650
22	APOLLO 22V		OP	OPFSH FBG	SV IO	120-140	8	2200		3100	3600
22	APOLLO 22V		OP	OPFSH FBG	SV IO	155 CHRY	8	2300		2900	3400
24	APOLLO 24		OP	CUD FBG	DV OB		8	2900		4550	5250
24	APOLLO 24		OP	CUD FBG	DV IO	165-235	8	3800		4550	5500
24	APOLLO 24		OP	CUD FBG	DV IO	280 MRCR	8	4050		5000	5750
26	APOLLO			EXP FBG	SV IB	225 CHRY	9 8	5400		6600	7600
31	MAXIM-V			EXP FBG	DV IO	T233-T330	9 5	8200	2 10	13800	17100
31	MAXIM-V			SPTCR FBG	DV IO	T233-T280	9 5	8000	2 10	12300	14700
31	MAXIM-V			SPTCR FBG	DV IB	T330	9 5	8400	2 10	13600	15400
---	--- --- 1976	BOATS	---								
22	APOLLO 22-V		OP	OPFSH FBG	SV OB		8	1400		2250	2600
22	APOLLO 22-V		OP	OPFSH FBG	SV IO	120-140	8	2200		3200	3700
23 7	APOLLO 24 LONG DECK		OP	CUD FBG	DV IO	165-280	8	3700		4500	5450
23 7	APOLLO 24 LONG DECK		OP	CUD FBG	DV IO	T120-T165	8	3700		4950	5750
23 7	APOLLO 24 SHORT DECK		OP	CUD FBG	DV IO	165-280	8	3700		4500	5450
23 7	APOLLO 24 SHORT DECK		OP	CUD FBG	DV IO	T120-T165	8	3700		4950	5750
31	MAXIM-V		OP	EXP FBG	DV IO	T188-T280	9 4	8000		13600	16600
31	MAXIM-V		OP	EXP FBG	DV IB	T330-T350	9 4	8000		14200	16400
31	MAXIM-V SPORT BOAT		OP	SPTCR FBG	DV IO	T188-T280	9 4	8000		12100	14900
31	MAXIM-V SPORT BOAT		OP	SPTCR FBG	DV IB	T330-T350	9 4	8000		12900	14900
---	--- --- 1975	BOATS	---								
20	20		SLP	SAIL FBG	SK OB		7 4	1800	4 6	3600	4150
20 6	21		SLP	SAIL FBG	KL OB		7 8	1800	2	3650	4250
22	22V		OP	OPFSH FBG	SV OB		8	1400	2	2200	2550
23 7	24 CENTER CONSOLE		OP	OPFSH FBG	DV IO	165-233	8	3800	2 6	4950	5800
23 7	24 CENTER CONSOLE		OP	OPFSH FBG	DV IO	T120-T165	8	3800	2 6	5550	6400
23 7	24 LONG DECK		ST	CUD FBG	DV IO	165-233	8	3800	2 6	4700	5500
23 7	24 LONG DECK		ST	CUD FBG	DV IO	T120-T165	8	3800	2 6	5200	6000
23 7	24 SHORT DECK		ST	CUD FBG	DV IO	165-233	8	3800	2 6	4700	5500
23 7	24 SHORT DECK		ST	CUD FBG	DV IO	T120-T165	8	3800	2 6	5200	6000
31	MAXIM V		ST	SPTCR FBG	DV IO	T280 MRCR	9 3	8000	3	13500	15400
31	MAXIM V		ST	SPTCR FBG	DV IB	T330 CHRY	9 3	8000	3	12300	14000
---	--- --- 1974	BOATS	---								
23 7	APOLLO 24			FBG	IO	165-188	8	3700		4550	5250
23 7	APOLLO 24			FBG	IO	T120-T165	8	3700		5050	5850
31	MAXIM V			FBG	IO	250 CHRY	9 4	8000		9300	10600
31	MAXIM V			FBG	IO	300 CRUS	9 4	8000		13100	14800
31	MAXIM V			FBG	IB	300-350	9 4	8000		9550	11100
---	--- --- 1973	BOATS	---								
24	MAXIM V			FBG	IO	188 MRCR	8	4000	2 6	5050	5850
24	MAXIM V			FBG	IO	T120-T165	8	4200	2 6	5800	6900
31 3	MAXIM V			FBG	IO	T188 MRCR	9 4	7500	2 6	14300	16200
	IB T225-T250 9900		11400,	IO T255		15100	17200, IB	T330 CHRY		10600	12100

APPLEBY MFG CO

COAST GUARD MFG ID- APB

Call 1-800-327-6929 for BUC Personalized Evaluation Service
Or, for 1961 to 1976 boats, sign onto www.BUCValuPro.com

AQUA CRAFT BOAT CO

Call 1-800-327-6929 for BUC Personalized Evaluation Service
Or, for 1965 to 1972 boats, sign onto www.BUCValuPro.com

AQUA KING

Call 1-800-327-6929 for BUC Personalized Evaluation Service
Or, for 1968 to 1971 boats, sign onto www.BUCValuPro.com

AQUA SPORT CANADA LTD

LAVAL BOATS   See inside cover to adjust price for area
SPORT CRAFT
FABREVLL PQ CANADA   COAST GUARD MFG ID- ZAS

For more recent years, see the BUC Used Boat Price Guide, Volume 1 or Volume 2

LOA FT IN	NAME AND/ OR MODEL	TOP/ RIG	BOAT TYPE	-HULL- MTL TP	TP	----ENGINE--- # HP MFG	BEAM FT IN	WGT LBS	DRAFT FT IN	RETAIL LOW	RETAIL HIGH
---	--- --- 1983	BOATS	---								
17	CONCORDE V-170	ST	RNBT	FBG DV	IO	120 MRCR	6 7	1400		4200	4900
---	--- --- 1982	BOATS	---								
17	CONCORDE V-170	ST	RNBT	FBG SV	IO	120-170	6 7			4250	5000
---	--- --- 1981	BOATS	---								
17	CONCORDE V-170	ST	RNBT	FBG SV	IO	140 MRCR	6 7			4150	4850
---	--- --- 1980	BOATS	---								
17	CONCORDE V-170	ST	RNBT	FBG SV	IO	120-170	6 7			4100	4800

AQUA-STAR LTD

Call 1-800-327-6929 for BUC Personalized Evaluation Service
Or, for 1979 to 2000 boats, sign onto www.BUCValuPro.com

AQUADYNE BOAT COMPANY INC

COAST GUARD MFG ID- AXD

Call 1-800-327-6929 for BUC Personalized Evaluation Service
Or, for 1977 boats, sign onto www.BUCValuPro.com

AQUARIUS YACHTS INC

SARASOTA FL 33580 COAST GUARD MFG ID- AYW See inside cover to adjust price for area
SEE ALSO TOP SAIL YACHTS INC

For more recent years, see the BUC Used Boat Price Guide, Volume 1 or Volume 2

LOA FT	LOA IN	NAME AND/ OR MODEL	TOP/ RIG	BOAT TYPE	-HULL- MTL	-HULL- TP	ENGINE TP	ENGINE # HP	ENGINE MFG	BEAM FT	BEAM IN	WGT LBS	DRAFT FT	DRAFT IN	RETAIL LOW	RETAIL HIGH
		1983 BOATS														
24		PILOT	CUT	SA/CR	FBG	KL	IB	D		9		8900	4		22800	25400
32		PILOT	CUT	SA/CR	FBG	KL	IB	18D	VLVO	9		8900	4		26200	29100
		1982 BOATS														
32		PILOT MARCONI	CUT	SA/CR	FBG	KL	IB	13D	VLVO	9		8900	4		24700	27400
32		PILOT TOPS'L	GAF	SA/CR	FBG	KL	IB	13D	VLVO	9		8900	4		24700	27400
		1981 BOATS														
32		PILOT MARCONI	CUT	SA/CR	FBG	KL	IB	13D	VLVO	9		8900	4		23200	25800
32		PILOT TOPS'L	GAF	SA/CR	FBG	KL	IB	13D	VLVO	9		8900	4		23200	25800
		1980 BOATS														
32		PILOT MARCONI	CUT	SA/CR	FBG	KL	IB	13D	VLVO	9		8900	4		22000	24400
32		PILOT TOPS'L	GAF	SA/CR	FBG	KL	IB	13D	VLVO	9		8900	4		22000	24400
35		PACKET	CUT	SA/CR	FBG	KL	IB	23D	VLVO	9	1	16000	4		39100	43400
		1979 BOATS														
32		PILOT TOPS'L	CUT	SA/CR	FBG	KL	IB	12D	FARY	9		9000	4		21300	23700

AQUASPORT

DIV OF GENMAR INDUSTRIES See inside cover to adjust price for area
SARASOTA FL 34243 COAST GUARD MFG ID- ASP

For more recent years, see the BUC Used Boat Price Guide, Volume 1 or Volume 2

LOA FT	LOA IN	NAME AND/ OR MODEL	TOP/ RIG	BOAT TYPE	-HULL- MTL	-HULL- TP	ENGINE TP	ENGINE # HP	ENGINE MFG	BEAM FT	BEAM IN	WGT LBS	DRAFT FT	DRAFT IN	RETAIL LOW	RETAIL HIGH
		1983 BOATS														
17		OSPREY 170 CC	OP	CTRCN	FBG	SV	OB			6	10	1150		8	2200	2600
19	6	OSPREY 19-6 CC	OP	CTRCN	FBG	SV	OB			7	8	1550		9	2950	3450
20	2	AQUASPORT 200 CCP	OP	CTRCN	FBG	DV	OB			7	10	1900	1		4000	4650
20	2	AQUASPORT 200 EF	ST	CUD	FBG	DV	OB			7	10	2000	1		4200	4900
22	2	AQUASPORT 22-2 CCP	OP	CTRCN	FBG	DV	OB			8		2200		10	5000	5750
22	2	AQUASPORT 22-2 FF	ST	CUD	FBG	DV	OB			8		2200	1		5050	5800
22	2	AQUASPORT 22-2 FF	ST	CUD	FBG	DV	IO	170-200		8			1		5900	6800
24	6	AQUASPORT 246 CCP	OP	CTRCN	FBG	DV	OB			8		2600	1		6300	7200
24	6	AQUASPORT 246 CCP	TT	CTRCN	FBG	DV	OB			8		2550	1		6200	7150
24	6	AQUASPORT 246 EF	ST	CUD	FBG	DV	OB			8		2900	1		6950	7950
24	6	AQUASPORT 246 EF	ST	CUD	FBG	DV	SE		OMC	8		2900	1		**	**
24	6	AQUASPORT 246 EF	ST	CUD	FBG	DV	IO	228-260		8			1		7600	8900
24	6	AQUASPORT 246XF		CR	FBG	DV	IO	360		8					9550	10900
26	6	AQUASPORT 266EF		FSH	FBG	DV	IB	T230		10		7000			16200	18400
28	6	AQUASPORT 286EF		FSH	FBG	SV	IB	T230		11					22700	25200
28	6	AQUASPORT 286XF	TT	SF	FBG	DV	IB	230	MRCR	11		9500	2	6	21600	24000
31		286 EXPRESS FISH	ST	CBNCR	FBG	DV	IO	220-270		11			2	6	23500	27100
		1982 BOATS														
17		OSPREY 170 CC	OP	CTRCN	FBG	SV	OB			6	10	1150		8	2150	2500
17	6	AQUASPORT 176 FF		RNBT	FBG	DV	OB			7	1	1500			2700	3100
18	8	AQUASPORT 188 FF	ST	RNBT	FBG	DV	OB			7	9	1500		10	2750	3200
19	6	AQUASPORT 19-6 DLX	ST	CUD	FBG	DV	IO	170		7	8	1750		9	2550	2950
19	6	AQUASPORT 19-6 FF	ST	CUD	FBG	DV	IO	170		7	8	1750		9	2550	2950
19	6	OSPREY 19-6 CC	OP	CTRCN	FBG	SV	OB			7	8	1500		9	2800	3250
20	2	AQUASPORT 200 CCP	OP	CTRCN	FBG	DV	OB			7	10	1800	1		3750	4400
20	2	AQUASPORT 200 EF	ST	CUD	FBG	DV	OB			7	10	2000	1		4100	4750
22	2	AQUASPORT 22-2 CCP	OP	CTRCN	FBG	DV	OB			8		2100	1		4700	5400
22	2	AQUASPORT 22-2 FF	ST	CUD	FBG	DV	OB			8		2200	1		4950	5650
22	2	AQUASPORT 22-2 FF	ST	CUD	FBG	DV	IO	170-200		8		2200	1		4200	4900
22	2	AQUASPORT 22-2 FFDLX	ST	CUD	FBG	DV	IO		BMW	8		2200	1		**	**
22	2	OSPREY 22-2 CC	OP	CTRCN	FBG	DV	IB	190-228		7	11	1800		9	4750	5500
22	2	OSPREY 22-2 CC	OP	CTRCN	FBG	DV	IB	50D	BMW	7	11	1800		9	6450	7450
22	2	OSPREY 22-2 CC	OP	CTRCN	FBG	SV	OB			7	11	1800		9	4100	4750
22	2	OSPREY 22-2 CCDLX	OP	CTRCN	FBG	DV	IB	190-228		7	11	1800		9	4750	5500
22	2	OSPREY 22-2 CCDLX	OP	CTRCN	FBG	DV	IB	50D	BMW	7	11	1800		9	6450	7450
24	6	AQUASPORT 246 CCP	OP	CTRCN	FBG	DV	OB			8		2550	1		6050	6950
24	6	AQUASPORT 246 CCP	TT	CTRCN	FBG	DV	OB			8		2550	1		6050	7000
24	6	AQUASPORT 246 EF	ST	CUD	FBG	DV	OB			8		2900	1		6800	7800
24	6	AQUASPORT 246 EF	ST	CUD	FBG	DV	IO	228-260		8		3400	1		6200	7350
24	6	AQUASPORT 246 EF DLX	ST	CUD	FBG	DV	OB			8		2900	1		6800	7800
24	6	AQUASPORT 246 FF DLX	ST	CUD	FBG	DV	IO	228-260		8		2750	1		5550	6600
24	6	AQUASPORT 286 XF	TT	SF	FBG	DV	IB	230-260		8		9500	2	6	16800	19200
28	6	AQUASPORT 286 XF	TT	SF	FBG	DV	IB			11		9500	2	6	**	**
28	6	AQUASPORT 286 XF	TT	SF	FBG	DV	IB	155D	VLVO	11		9500	2	6	27600	30700
		1981 BOATS														
17		OSPREY 170 CC	OP	CTRCN	FBG	DV	OB			6	10	1150		7	2050	2450
17	6	AQUASPORT 176 FF		RNBT	FBG	DV	OB			7	1	1500			2600	3050
18	8	AQUASPORT 188 FF	ST	RNBT	FBG	DV	OB			7	9	1500		10	2600	3050
18	8	AQUASPORT 188 FF DLX	ST	RNBT	FBG	DV	OB			7	9	1500		10	2800	3250
18	8	SPORT-RIDER 188	ST	RNBT	FBG	DV	OB			7	9	1500		10	2600	3050
18	8	SPORT-RIDER 188 DLX	ST	RNBT	FBG	DV	OB			7	9	1500		10	2800	3250
19	6	AQUASPORT 19-6 DLX	ST	CUD	FBG	DV	OB			7	8	1750		9	3300	3800
19	6	AQUASPORT 19-6 DLX	ST	CUD	FBG	DV	IO	130-170		7	8	1750		9	2750	3200
19	6	AQUASPORT 19-6 FF	ST	CUD	FBG	DV	OB			7	8	1750		9	2900	3400
19	6	AQUASPORT 19-6 FF	ST	CUD	FBG	DV	IO	130-170		7	8	1750		9	2550	3000
19	6	OSPREY 19-6 CC	OP	CTRCN	FBG	DV	OB			7	8	1500		9	2650	3100
19	6	OSPREY 19-6 CC DLX	OP	CTRCN	FBG	DV	OB			7	8	1500		9	2850	3300
20	2	AQUASPORT 200 CCP	OP	CTRCN	FBG	DV	OB			7	10	1800			3550	4150
20	2	AQUASPORT 200 CCPDLX	OP	CTRCN	FBG	DV	OB			7	10	1800			3800	4450
20	2	AQUASPORT 200 EF	ST	CUD	FBG	DV	OB			7	10	2000	1		4000	4650
22	2	AQUASPORT 22-2 CCP	OP	CTRCN	FBG	DV	OB			8		2100			4450	5150
22	2	AQUASPORT 22-2 CCPDL	OP	CTRCN	FBG	DV	OB			8		2100			4750	5450
22	2	AQUASPORT 22-2 FF	ST	CUD	FBG	DV	OB			8		2200	1		4550	5250
22	2	AQUASPORT 22-2 FF	ST	CUD	FBG	DV	IO		BMW	8		2200	1		**	**
22	2	AQUASPORT 22-2 FF	ST	CUD	FBG	DV	IO	170-200		8		2200	1		3950	4900
22	2	AQUASPORT 22-2 FFDLX	ST	CUD	FBG	DV	OB			8		2200	1		5100	5850
22	2	AQUASPORT 22-2 FFDLX	ST	CUD	FBG	DV	IO		BMW	8		2200	1		**	**
22	2	AQUASPORT 22-2 FFDLX	ST	CUD	FBG	DV	IO	170-200		8		2200	1		4250	5250
22	2	OSPREY 22-2 CC	OP	CTRCN	FBG	DV	OB			7	11	1800		9	3900	4550
22	2	OSPREY 22-2 CC	OP	CTRCN	FBG	DV	IB	170-228		7	11	1800		9	4450	5200
22	2	OSPREY 22-2 CC	OP	CTRCN	FBG	DV	IB	50D	BMW	7	11	1800		9	6150	7050
22	2	OSPREY 22-2 CCDLX	OP	CTRCN	FBG	DV	OB			7	11	1800		9	4100	4800
22	2	OSPREY 22-2 CCDLX	OP	CTRCN	FBG	DV	IB	170-228		7	11	1800		9	4600	5350
22	2	OSPREY 22-2 CCDLX	OP	CTRCN	FBG	DV	IB	50D	BMW	7	11	1800		9	6300	7250
24	6	AQUASPORT 246 CCC	OP	CTRCN	FBG	DV	OB			8		2550	1		5950	6850
24	6	AQUASPORT 246 CCC	OP	CTRCN	FBG	DV	IO	190-260		8			1		7200	8400
24	6	AQUASPORT 246 CCC	TT	CTRCN	FBG	DV	OB			8		2550	1		5950	6800
24	6	AQUASPORT 246 CCC	TT	CTRCN	FBG	DV	IO	190-260		8			1		7200	8400
24	6	AQUASPORT 246 CCCDLX	OP	CTRCN	FBG	DV	OB			8		2550	1		7000	8000
24	6	AQUASPORT 246 CCCDLX	OP	CTRCN	FBG	DV	IO	190-260					1		7300	8500
24	6	AQUASPORT 246 CCCDLX	TT	CTRCN	FBG	DV	OB			8		2550	1		5950	6800
24	6	AQUASPORT 246 CCCDLX	TT	CTRCN	FBG	DV	IO	190-260		8			1		7200	8400
24	6	AQUASPORT 246 CCP	OP	CTRCN	FBG	DV	OB			8		2550	2		5250	6050
24	6	AQUASPORT 246 CCP	TT	CTRCN	FBG	DV	OB			8		2550	1		5950	6800
24	6	AQUASPORT 246 CCPDLX	OP	CTRCN	FBG	DV	OB			8		2550			5500	6300
24	6	AQUASPORT 246 EF	ST	CUD	FBG	DV	OB			8		2900	1		6450	7400
24	6	AQUASPORT 246 EF	ST	CUD	FBG	DV	IO	228-260		8		2900	1		5500	6600
24	6	AQUASPORT 246 EF DLX	ST	CUD	FBG	DV	OB			8		2900	1		6850	7850
24	6	AQUASPORT 246 EF DLX	ST	CUD	FBG	DV	IO	228-260		8		2900	1		5700	6750
24	6	AQUASPORT 246 FF	ST	CUD	FBG	DV	OB			8		2750	1		5900	6800
24	6	AQUASPORT 246 FF	ST	CUD	FBG	DV	IO	190-260		8		2750	1		5350	6250
24	6	AQUASPORT 246 FF DLX	ST	CUD	FBG	DV	OB			8		2750	1		6850	7900
24	6	AQUASPORT 246 FF DLX	ST	CUD	FBG	DV	IO	190-260		8		2750	1		5750	6700
24	6	AQUASPORT 240 CCPDLX	TT	CTRCN	FBG	DV	OB			8		2550	1		5950	6800
		1980 BOATS														
17		AQUASPORT 170	OP	CTRCN	FBG	SV	OB			6	10	1175			2050	2450
17		AQUASPORT 170 CC	OP	OPFSH	FBG	SV	OB			6	10	1175		8	2000	2350
17	6	AQUASPORT 176 FF	ST	CUD	FBG	SV	OB			7	1	1500		8	2550	3000
17	6	AQUASPORT 176FF		CUD	FBG	SV	OB			7	1	1500			2550	3000
18	8	AQUASPORT 188 FF	ST	RNBT	FBG	DV	OB			7	9	1650		10	2800	3300
18	8	AQUASPORT 188FF		RNBT	FBG	SV	OB			7	9	1650			2800	3300
18	8	SPORT-RIDER 188	ST	RNBT	FBG	DV	OB			7	9	1650		10	2800	3300
18	8	SPORTRIDER 188		RNBT	FBG	SV	OB			7	9	1650			2800	3300
19	6	AQUASPORT 19-6 CC	OP	OPFSH	FBG	SV	OB			7	8	1500		9	2700	3150
19	6	AQUASPORT 19-6 FF	ST	CUD	FBG	SV	OB			7	8	1650		9	2900	3400
19	6	AQUASPORT 19-6 FF	ST	CUD	FBG	SV	IO	140-185		7	8	2100	1		2650	3100
19	6	AQUASPORT 196FF		CTRCN	FBG	SV	OB			7	8	1500			2700	3150
19	6	AQUASPORT 196FF		CUD	FBG	SV	OB			7	8	1650			2900	3400
20	2	AQUASPORT 200 CCP	OP	CTRCN	FBG	DV	OB			7	10	1800	1		3600	4200
20	2	AQUASPORT 200 EF	ST	CUD	FBG	DV	OB			7	10	2000	1		3950	4600
20	2	CABIN-WALK-A-ROUND			FBG	DV	OB			7	10	1850			3700	4300

CONTINUED ON NEXT PAGE

LOA FT	LOA IN	NAME AND/ OR MODEL	TOP/ RIG	BOAT TYPE	-HULL- MTL	-HULL- TP	ENGINE TP	# HP	MFG	BEAM FT	BEAM IN	WGT LBS	DRAFT FT	DRAFT IN	RETAIL LOW	RETAIL HIGH
		1980 BOATS														
20	2	PROFESSIONAL 200		CTRCN	FBG	DV	OB			7	10	1800			3600	4200
22	2	AQUASPORT 22-2 CCP	OP	OPFSH	FBG	DV	OB			8		2100	1		4550	5250
22	2	AQUASPORT 22-2 FF	ST	CUD	FBG	SV	OB			7	11	1850		9	4100	4750
22	2	AQUASPORT 22-2 FF	ST	CUD	FBG	SV	IO	170-228		7	11	2400	1		4200	5000
22	2	AQUASPORT 22-2 FFV	ST	CUD	FBG	DV	OB			8		2200	1		4750	5450
22	2	AQUASPORT 22-2 FFV	ST	CUD	FBG	DV	IO	170-228		8		2200	1		4100	4850
22	2	AQUASPORT 22-2FF		CUD	FBG	SV	OB			7	11	1900			4200	4850
22	2	AQUASPORT 22-2FFV		CUD	FBG	DV	OB			8		2200			4750	5450
22	2	PROFESSIONAL 222		CTRCN	FBG	DV	OB			8		2100			4500	5200
24	6	AQUASPORT 246		CTRCN	FBG	DV	OB			8		2550			6200	7150
24	6	AQUASPORT 246 CCC	ST	CUD	FBG	DV	IO	226-260		8			1		7200	8850
24	6	AQUASPORT 246 CCC	OP	OPFSH	FBG	DV	OB			8		2550	1		5850	6700
24	6	AQUASPORT 246 CCC	TT	OPFSH	FBG	DV	OB			8			1		7850	9050
24	6	AQUASPORT 246 CCC	TT	OPFSH	FBG	DV	IO	228-260		8			1		7200	8450
24	6	AQUASPORT 246 CCP	OP	OPFSH	FBG	DV	OB			8		2550	1		5850	6700
24	6	AQUASPORT 246 CCP	ST	OPFSH	FBG	DV	OB			8		2550	1		5850	6700
24	6	AQUASPORT 246 EF	ST	CUD	FBG	DV	OB			8		2900	1	1	6500	7450
24	6	AQUASPORT 246 FFV	ST	CUD	FBG	DV	OB			8		2550	1		5900	6800
24	6	AQUASPORT 246 FFV	ST	CUD	FBG	DV	IO	228-260		8			1		7250	8300
24	6	AQUASPORT 246FF		CUD	FBG	DV	OB			8		2550			5900	6800
24	6	PROFESSIONAL 246		CTRCN	FBG	DV	OB			8		2550			5400	6200
		1979 BOATS														
17		AQUASPORT 170	OP	OPFSH	FBG	SV	OB			6	10	1150		8	1900	2250
17	4	XSCAPE 180 BR	OP	RNBT	FBG	TR	OB			7	4	1350		7	2350	2750
17	6	AQUASPORT 176 FF	OP	CUD	FBG	SV	OB			7	1	1500		8	2550	2950
18	8	XSCAPE 190 BR	OP	RNBT	FBG	DV	OB			7	9	1500		10	2600	3050
18	8	XSCAPE 190 FD	OP	RNBT	FBG	DV	OB			7	9	1500		10	2600	3050
19	6	AQUASPORT 19-6	OP	CUD	FBG	SV	OB			7	8	1450		9	2650	3050
19	6	AQUASPORT 19-6	OP	CUD	FBG	SV	IO	140-185		7	8	2100		9	2650	3100
19	6	AQUASPORT 19-6	OP	OPFSH	FBG	SV	OB			7	8	1450		9	2600	3000
20	2	AQUASPORT 200 CCP	OP	CTRCN	FBG	DV	OB			7	10	1900		9	3700	4300
22	2	AQUASPORT 22-2	OP	CUD	FBG	SV	OB			7	11	1800		9	3950	4550
22	2	AQUASPORT 22-2	OP	CUD	FBG	SV	IO	170-228		7	11	2400		9	4200	5000
22	2	AQUASPORT 22-2	OP	OPFSH	FBG	SV	OB			7	11	1800		9	3900	4550
22	2	AQUASPORT 22-2 CCP	OP	CTRCN	FBG	DV	OB			8			1		5800	6700
22	2	AQUASPORT 22-2 FF	OP	CUD	FBG	SV	IO	240	OMC	7	11	2400		9	4350	5000
22	2	AQUASPORT 22-2 FFV	OP	CUD	FBG	DV	OB			8			1		5950	6850
22	2	AQUASPORT 22-2 FFV	OP	CUD	FBG	DV	IO	170-228		8		2200	1		4050	4850
22	2	AQUASPORT 22-2 FFV	OP	CUD	FBG	DV	IO	240	MRCR	8		2800	1		4750	5450
24	6	AQUASPORT 246 CCC		CUD	FBG	DV	OB			8			1		8000	9200
24	6	AQUASPORT 246 CCC		CUD	FBG	DV	IO	260-288		8			1		7400	8700
24	6	AQUASPORT 246 CCP	OP	CTRCN	FBG	DV	OB			8		2650	1		5850	6700
24	6	AQUASPORT 246 CCP	TT	CTRCN	FBG	DV	OB			8		2200	1		5150	5900
24	6	AQUASPORT 246 FF	OP	CUD	FBG	DV	OB			8			1		8000	9200
24	6	AQUASPORT 246 FF	OP	CUD	FBG	DV	IO	228-260		8			1		7200	8500
		1978 BOATS														
17		AQUASPORT 170	OP	OPFSH	FBG	SV	OB			6	10	1175		8	1900	2250
17	4	XSCAPE 180	OP	RNBT	FBG	TR	OB			7	4	1550		7	2550	2950
18	8	XSCAPE 190 BR	OP	RNBT	FBG	DV	OB			7	9	1650		10	2750	3150
18	8	XSCAPE 190 FD	OP	RNBT	FBG	DV	OB			7	9	1650		10	2750	3150
19	6	AQUASPORT 19-6	OP	OPFSH	FBG	SV	OB			7	8	1450		9	2550	2950
19	6	AQUASPORT 19-6 FF	OP	CUD	FBG	SV	OB			7	8	1650		9	2850	3300
19	6	AQUASPORT 19-6 FF	OP	CUD	FBG	SV	IO	140-175		7	8	2100			2650	3100
20	2	AQUASPORT 200 CCP	OP	CTRCN	FBG	DV	OB			7	10	1900		9	3600	4200
22	2	AQUASPORT 22-2	OP	OPFSH	FBG	SV	OB			7	11	1900		9	4000	4650
22	2	AQUASPORT 22-2 CCP	OP	CTRCN	FBG	DV	OB			8		2200			4500	5200
22	2	AQUASPORT 22-2 FF	OP	CUD	FBG	SV	OB			7	11	1900		9	4050	4700
22	2	AQUASPORT 22-2 FF	OP	CUD	FBG	SV	IO	170-190		7	11	2800			4650	5350
22	2	AQUASPORT 22-2 FFV	OP	CUD	FBG	DV	OB			8		2200	1		4600	5300
22	2	AQUASPORT 22-2 FFV	OP	CUD	FBG	DV	IO	170-240		8					5650	6600
24	6	AQUASPORT 246 CCP	OP	CTRCN	FBG	DV	OB			8		2650	1		5750	6600
24	6	AQUASPORT 246 FF	OP	CUD	FBG	DV	OB			8		2650	1		5850	6750
24	6	AQUASPORT 246 FF	OP	CUD	FBG	DV	IO	228-260		8					7300	8550
		1977 BOATS														
17		AQUASPORT 170	OP	OPFSH	FBG	SV	OB			6	10	1150		8	1850	2200
17	4	XSCAPE 180	OP	RNBT	FBG	TR	OB			7	4	1550		7	2500	2950
19	6	AQUASPORT 19-6	OP	OPFSH	FBG	SV	OB			7	8	1450		9	2500	2950
19	6	AQUASPORT 19-6FF	OP	CUD	FBG	SV	OB			7	8	1450		9	2550	3000
19	6	AQUASPORT 19-6FF	OP	CUD	FBG	SV	IO	140		7	8	2100		9	2700	3150
22	2	AQUASPORT 22-2	OP	OPFSH	FBG	SV	OB			7	11	1800		9	3800	4400
22	2	AQUASPORT 22-2	OP	OPFSH	FBG	SV	IB	230-233		7	11	2600	2		4650	5300
22	2	AQUASPORT 22-2FF	OP	CUD	FBG	SV	OB			7	11	1800		9	3800	4450
22	2	AQUASPORT 22-2FF	OP	CUD	FBG	SV	IO	165-190		7	11	2400		9	4300	5000
24		AQUASPORT 240	OP	OPFSH	FBG	SV	OB			8		2500		10	5300	6100
24		AQUASPORT 240	OP	OPFSH	FBG	SV	IO	165-235		8		2500			5150	6100
24		AQUASPORT 240	OP	OPFSH	FBG	SV	IB	255-260		8		2500		10	4850	5800
24		AQUASPORT 240	OP	OPFSH	FBG	SV	IB	160D	PERK	8		2500		10	7950	9150
24	6	AQUASPORT 246FF	OP	CUD	FBG	DV	OB			8		2650	1	2	5800	6650
24	6	AQUASPORT 246FF	OP	CUD	FBG	DV	IO	233-235		8		2650	1	2	5450	6300
		1976 BOATS														
17		AQUASPORT 170	OP	FSH	FBG	SV	OB			6	10	1100		7	1800	2150
19	6	AQUASPORT 19-6 CTR	OP	FSH	FBG	SV	OB			7	8	1450		8	2500	2900
19	6	AQUASPORT 19-6 CTR	ST	SPTCR	FBG	SV	IO	140	MRCR	7	8	2100	1	10	2750	3200
19	6	AQUASPORT 19-6 FF	ST	SPTCR	FBG	SV	OB			7	8	1450		8	2500	2900
19	6	AQUASPORT 19-6 FF	ST	SPTCR	FBG	SV	IO	140	OMC	7	8	2100	1	10	2750	3200
22	2	AQUASPORT 22-2 CTR	OP	OPFSH	FBG	SV	OB			7	10	1800		9	3750	4350
22	2	AQUASPORT 22-2 CTR	OP	OPFSH	FBG	SV	IB	233-235		7	10	2600	2		4200	5100
22	2	AQUASPORT 22-2 FF	ST	SPTCR	FBG	SV	OB			7	10	1800		9	3750	4350
22	2	AQUASPORT 22-2 FF	ST	SPTCR	FBG	SV	IO	165		7	10	2400	2		4450	5100
24		AQUASPORT 240 CTR	OP	OPFSH	FBG	SV	OB			8		2150		11	4600	5300
24		AQUASPORT 240 CTR	OP	OPFSH	FBG	SV	IO	165-235		8		2800	2		5600	6600
		IB 255 5500 6550, IB 165D PERK 9800 11100, IO T140													7300	8400
24		AQUASPORT 240 CUDDY	ST	CUD	FBG	SV	OB			8		2450		11	5200	5950
24		AQUASPORT 240 CUDDY	ST	CUD	FBG	SV	IO	165-235		8		3600	2		6250	7300
24		AQUASPORT 240 CUDDY	ST	CUD	FBG	SV	IO	T140		8		4250	2	2	7800	8950
24		AQUASPORT 240 SIDE	OP	OPFSH	FBG	SV	OB			8		2100		11	4550	5200
24		AQUASPORT 240 SIDE	OP	OPFSH	FBG	SV	IO	165-235		8		3250	2		6150	7250
		1975 BOATS														
17		AQUASPORT 170	OP	FSH	FBG	SV	OB			6	10	1100		8	1800	2150
19	6	AQUASPORT 19-6	OP	FSH	FBG	SV	OB			7	8	1450		9	2450	2850
19	6	AQUASPORT 19-6	OP	FSH	FBG	SV	IO	140		7	8	2100		10	3000	3500
19	6	AQUASPORT 19-6 FF	OP	W/T	FBG	SV	OB			7	8	1650		10	2700	3150
22	2	AQUASPORT 22-2	OP	FSH	FBG	SV	OB			7	11	1800		9	3650	4250
22	2	AQUASPORT 22-2	OP	FSH	FBG	SV	IO	165		7	11	2400	2		4850	5550
22	2	AQUASPORT 22-2	OP	FSH	FBG	SV	IB	215-233		7	11	3200	2		4600	5500
24		AQUASPORT 240 CENTER	OP	FSH	FBG	SV	OB			8		2200		10	4650	5350
24		AQUASPORT 240 CENTER	OP	FSH	FBG	SV	IO	165-235		8		3000	2		6050	7100
		IB 250-260 5750 6850, IB 160D PERK 9700 11000, IO T140													7300	8350
24		AQUASPORT 240 CUDDY	OP	CUD	FBG	SV	OB			8		2600		10	5400	6200
24		AQUASPORT 240 CUDDY	OP	CUD	FBG	SV	IO	165-235		8		3200	2		5950	7400
24		AQUASPORT 240 CUDDY	OP	CUD	FBG	SV	IO	T140		8		3800	2		7450	8600
24		AQUASPORT 240 SIDE	OP	FSH	FBG	SV	OB			8		2400		10	4950	5700
24		AQUASPORT 240 SIDE	OP	FSH	FBG	SV	IO	165-235		8		3100	2		6150	7550
		1974 BOATS														
17		AQUASPORT	OP	FSH	FBG	SV	OB			6	10	1150		7	1850	2200
19	6	AQUASPORT	OP	FSH	FBG	SV	OB			7	8	1550		9	2550	2950
19	6	AQUASPORT	OP	FSH	FBG	SV	IO	140		7	8	2200		9	3200	3700
22	2	AQUASPORT	OP	FSH	FBG	SV	IO	165		7	11	2450		9	5050	5800
22	2	AQUASPORT	OP	RNBT	FBG	SV	OB			7	11	1750		9	3600	4200
24		AQUASPORT	OP	CUD	FBG	SV	OB			8		2700		10	5500	6350
24		AQUASPORT	OP	CUD	FBG	SV	IO	165-225		8		3650		10	6700	7800
24		AQUASPORT	OP	CUD	FBG	SV	IO	T140		8		5400		10	10000	11400
24		AQUASPORT	OP	FSH	FBG	SV	OB			8		2600		10	5250	6050
24		AQUASPORT	OP	FSH	FBG	SV	IO	165-188		8		3550		10	6950	8050
24		AQUASPORT	OP	FSH	FBG	SV	IO	T140	MRCR	8		5300		10	10400	11800
24		AQUASPORT	OP	RNBT	FBG	SV	IO	225	OMC	8		3550		10	6250	7200
24		AQUASPORT	OP	RNBT	FBG	SV	IO	T140	OMC	8		5300		10	9250	10500
		1973 BOATS														
17		AQUASPORT 170	OP	FSH	FBG	SV	OB			6	10	1150	7	1	1850	2200
19	6	AQUASPORT 19-6	OP	FSH	FBG	SV	OB			7	8	1500	9		2500	2900
19	6	AQUASPORT 19-6	OP	FSH	FBG	SV	IO	140	MRCR	7	8	2100	9		3200	3750
19	6	AQUASPORT 19-6	OP	RNBT	FBG	SV	IO	140	OMC	7	8	2100	9		2950	3400
22	2	AQUASPORT 22-2	OP	FSH	FBG	SV	OB			7	11	1750	10		3550	4100
22	2	AQUASPORT 22-2	OP	FSH	FBG	SV	IO	165		7	11	2450	10		5200	6000
24		AQUASPORT 240	OP	FSH	FBG	SV	OB			8		2600	10		5250	6000
24		AQUASPORT 240	OP	FSH	FBG	SV	IO	165-225		8		3550	10		7200	8350
24		AQUASPORT 240 CC	OP	CUD	FBG	SV	OB			8		2700		10	5450	6300
24		AQUASPORT 240 CC	OP	CUD	FBG	SV	IO	165-225		8		3660		10	6950	8100
24		AQUASPORT 240 CC	OP	CUD	FBG	SV	IO	T140		8		4150		10	8450	9750
		1972 BOATS														
17		AQUASPORT CUSTOM	OP	FSH	FBG		OB			6	10	1050	7	1	1700	2000
19	6	AQUASPORT			FBG		IO	120		7	10	2450	8	1	3250	3800
19	6	AQUASPORT	OP	FSH	FBG		OB			7	10	1350	8	1	2300	2700
22	2	AQUASPORT			FBG		IO	120		7	11	2450	9		4850	5550
22	2	AQUASPORT	OP	FSH	FBG		OB			7	11	1750	9		3500	4100
24		AQUASPORT			FBG		IO	155-225		8		3550	10	1	6650	7800
24		AQUASPORT	OP	FSH	FBG		OB			8		2500	10	1	5050	5800

 CONTINUED ON NEXT PAGE

LOA FT IN	NAME AND/ OR MODEL	TOP/ RIG	BOAT TYPE	MTL	-HULL- TP	TP	----ENGINE--- # HP MFG	BEAM FT IN	WGT LBS	DRAFT FT IN	RETAIL LOW	RETAIL HIGH
							1971 BOATS					
17 2	170 CUS	OP	FSH	FBG		OB	6 10	1250		7	1950	2350
19 1	AQUASPORT 19-1	GULL	FSH	FBG		OB	7 6	1675		8	2600	3000
19 1	OSPREY	OP	FSH	FBG		OB	7 6	1675		8	2600	3000
22 2	AQUASPORT 22-2	OP	FSH	FBG		OB	7 10	2000		8	3900	4550
23 6	AQUASPORT 236		FSH	FBG	SV	IO 155	8			1 6	8950	10100
23 6	AQUASPORT 236		FSH	FBG	SV	IO T220	8			1 6	10100	11500
23 6	AQUASPORT 236	SF	FBG	SV	IO 155	8			1 6	9200	10500
23 6	AQUASPORT 236	SF	FBG	SV	IO T220	8			1 6	10500	11900
24	SEA-HUNTER		FBG		IO 155-215	8		3400			6650	7750
24	SEA-HUNTER	OP	FSH	FBG		OB	8		2500	10	5050	5800
							1970 BOATS					
19 1	AQUASPORT 19-1	OP	FSH	FBG		OB	7 6	1100		8	1900	2250
19 1	OSPREY 19-1	OP	FSH	FBG	SV	OB	7 6	1100		8	1900	2250
22 2	AQUASPORT 22-2	OP	FSH	FBG		OB	7 8	1400		8	2900	3350
							1969 BOATS					
19 1	AQUASPORT 19-1	OP	FSH	FBG		OB	7 6	1100		8	1900	2250
22 2	AQUASPORT 22-2	OP	FSH	FBG		OB	7 8	1400		8	2900	3350
							1968 BOATS					
22	AQUASPORT 22-2	OP	FSH	FBG		OB	7 10	1500		8	3050	3550
							1967 BOATS					
22	AQUASPORT 22-2	OP	FSH	FBG		OB				.	5400	6200
							1966 BOATS					
22 2	AQUASPORT 22-2	OP	FSH	FBG		OB					5450	6250

ARCO

Call 1-800-327-6929 for BUC Personalized Evaluation Service
Or, for 1959 boats, sign onto www.BUCValuPro.com

ARENA CRAFT PRODUCTS INC

Call 1-800-327-6929 for BUC Personalized Evaluation Service
Or, for 1961 to 1971 boats, sign onto www.BUCValuPro.com

ARGO BOAT MFG CO INC
ARGO CRAFT

Call 1-800-327-6929 for BUC Personalized Evaluation Service
Or, for 1961 to 1967 boats, sign onto www.BUCValuPro.com

ARGOSY MARINE CORP
FORT LAUDERDALE FL   See inside cover to adjust price for area

LOA FT IN	NAME AND/ OR MODEL	TOP/ RIG	BOAT TYPE	MTL	-HULL- TP	TP	----ENGINE--- # HP MFG	BEAM FT IN	WGT LBS	DRAFT FT IN	RETAIL LOW	RETAIL HIGH
							1971 BOATS					
32		SF	AL	SV	IB T150D GM	12		12000	2 6	58400	64200	
60 3		MY	AL	SV	IB T390D GM	17 4		57000	4 6	264500	290500	

ARGOSY YACHT SALES

Call 1-800-327-6929 for BUC Personalized Evaluation Service
Or, for 1970 to 1971 boats, sign onto www.BUCValuPro.com

ARKADY MARINE INC

Call 1-800-327-6929 for BUC Personalized Evaluation Service
Or, for 1982 to 1986 boats, sign onto www.BUCValuPro.com

ARROW GLASS BOAT & MFG CORP
DIV OF GENERAL MARINE IND   See inside cover to adjust price for area
PANAMA CITY FL 32404   COAST GUARD MFG ID- CGM

For more recent years, see the BUC Used Boat Price Guide, Volume 1 or Volume 2

LOA FT IN	NAME AND/ OR MODEL	TOP/ RIG	BOAT TYPE	MTL	-HULL- TP	TP	----ENGINE--- # HP MFG	BEAM FT IN	WGT LBS	DRAFT FT IN	RETAIL LOW	RETAIL HIGH
							1979 BOATS					
16 7	STINGER		RNBT	FBG	DV	OB	6 11	1285			1950	2350
17 4	CHEETAH B/R		RNBT	FBG	TR	OB	7	1100			1750	2100
17 4	MARLIN B/R		RNBT	FBG		OB	7	1073			1700	2050
18 3	CAPRI B/R		RNBT	FBG	DV	OB	7 4	1400			2250	2600
18 3	CAPRI B/R		RNBT	FBG	DV	IO 228	7 4				1750	2100
18 3	MATADOR		RNBT	FBG	TR	IO 228	7 2				1700	2050
18 3	RIVIERA		RNBT	FBG	DV	IO 228	7 4				1700	2050
20 1	SIESTA		CR	FBG	DV	IO 228	8				2400	2800
							1978 BOATS					
16 7	STINGER	ST	RNBT	FBG	DV	OB	6 11	1285			1950	2300
17 4	CHEETAH B/R	ST	RNBT	FBG	TR	OB	7	1100			1750	2050
18 3	CAPRI B/R	ST	RNBT	FBG	DV	OB	7 4	1423			2250	2600
18 3	CAPRI B/R	ST	RNBT	FBG	DV	IO 120-228	7 4	2593			1850	2250
18 3	CAPRI B/R	ST	RNBT	FBG	DV	IO 240-260	7 4	2650			1950	2400
18 3	MATADOR B/R	ST	RNBT	FBG	TR	IO 120-170	7 2	2437			1750	2200
18 3	MATADOR B/R	ST	RNBT	FBG	TR	IO 185-228	7 2	2723			1900	2350
18 3	MATADOR B/R	ST	RNBT	FBG	TR	IO 240-260	7 2	2780			2000	2400
18 3	RIVIERA	ST	RNBT	FBG	DV	IO 120-240	7 4	2593			1850	2300
18 3	RIVIERA	ST	RNBT	FBG	DV	IO 260 MRCR	7 4	2650			2000	2400
20 1	SIESTA	ST	CUD	FBG	DV	IO 140-228	8	3200			2500	3100
20 1	SIESTA	ST	CUD	FBG	DV	IO 240-260	8	3420			2700	3200
							1977 BOATS					
16 7	STINGER	ST	RNBT	FBG	DV	OB	6 11	1285			1950	2300
17 4	CHEETAH	ST	RNBT	FBG	TR	OB	7	1100			1700	2050
17 4	MARLIN	ST	RNBT	FBG		OB	7	1073			1700	2000
18 3	BONITA	OP	FSH	FBG	DV	OB	7 4	1340			2050	2450
18 3	CAPRI	ST	RNBT	FBG	DV	OB	7 4	1425			2200	2600
18 3	CAPRI	ST	RNBT	FBG	DV	IO 140-175	7 4	2146			1700	2100
18 3	CAPRI	ST	RNBT	FBG	DV	IO 188-235	7 4	2352			1800	2250
18 3	MATADOR	ST	RNBT	FBG	TR	IO 140-175	7 2	2619			1850	2300
18 3	MATADOR	ST	RNBT	FBG	TR	IO 188-235	7 2	2825			1950	2400
18 3	RIVIERA	ST	RNBT	FBG	DV	IO 140-175	7 4	2169			1700	2100
18 3	RIVIERA	ST	RNBT	FBG	DV	IO 188-235	7 4	2375			1800	2250
20 1	SIESTA	ST	CUD	FBG	DV	IO 140-235	7 4	3370			2500	3000
							1976 BOATS					
16 3	JAGUAR	ST	RNBT	FBG	TR	OB	6 6	1145			1700	2050
17 4	CHEETAH	ST	RNBT	FBG	TR	OB	7	1092			1700	2000
17 4	MARLIN	OP	RNBT	FBG	TR	OB	7	1096			1700	2000
18 1	TIGRE	ST	RNBT	FBG	TR	OB	7 1	1392			1700	2150
18 1	TIGRE	ST	RNBT	FBG	DV	IO 233-235	7 1	2331			1800	2150
18 3	CAPRI	ST	RNBT	FBG	DV	IO 140-235	7 4	2800			2000	2450
18 3	CAPRI	ST	RNBT	FBG	DV	IO 255 MRCR	7 4	2800			2200	2550
18 3	RIVIERA	ST	RNBT	FBG	DV	IO 100-255	7 4	2800			2000	2450
20 1	ASTRA	ST	RNBT	FBG	DV	IO 140-255	8				2350	2850
							1975 BOATS					
16 3	JAGUAR	ST	RNBT	FBG	TR	OB	6 6	1145			1700	2050
16 3	JAGUAR J-200	ST	RNBT	FBG	TR	OB	6 6	1145			1700	2050
17 4	CHEETAH	OP	RNBT	FBG	TR	OB	7	1092			1700	2000
17 4	CHEETAH C-300	OP	RNBT	FBG	TR	OB	7	1092			1700	2000
17 4	MARLIN	OP	RNBT	FBG	TR	OB	7	1096			1700	2000
18 1	FIESTA	OP	RNBT	FBG	TR	OB	7 1	1132			1750	2100
18 1	TIGRE	ST	RNBT	FBG	TR	OB	7 1	1392			2100	2500
18 1	TIGRE	ST	RNBT	FBG	DV	IO 165-190	7 1	2089			1700	2050
18 1	TIGRE	ST	RNBT	FBG	DV	IO 233-235	7 1	2331			1850	2250
18 1	TIGRE T-400	OP	RNBT	FBG	TR	OB	7 1	1392			2100	2500
18 10	FALCON	ST	RNBT	FBG	DV	JT	7 3	2561			**	2400
18 10	FALCON	ST	RNBT	FBG	DV	IO 165-245	7 3	2511			1950	2400
18 10	FALCON	ST	RNBT	FBG	DV	IO 255 MRCR	7 3	2843			2300	2650
18 10	OSPREY	ST	RNBT	FBG	DV	OB	7 3	1822			2300	2700
20 4	BLUEFIN	ST	RNBT	FBG	DV	OB	8	2028			3100	3600
20 4	NOCTURNE	ST	RNBT	FBG	DV	OB	8	1823			2900	3350
20 4	NOCTURNE	ST	RNBT	FBG	DV	JT	8	3062			**	**
20 4	NOCTURNE	ST	RNBT	FBG	DV	IO 165-245	8	3012			2500	3000
20 4	NOCTURNE	ST	RNBT	FBG	DV	IO 255 MRCR	8	3344			2800	3250
							1974 BOATS					
18 1	TIGRE	ST	RNBT	FBG	TR	OB	7	1280			1950	2300
18 1	TIGRE	ST	RNBT	FBG	DV	IO 140-225	7	2220			1800	2150
18 10	FALCON	ST	RNBT	FBG	DV	JT	7 3				**	**
18 10	FALCON	ST	RNBT	FBG	DV	IO 165	7 3	2390			2000	2450
18 10	FALCON	ST	RNBT	FBG	DV	IO 188-255	7 3				2150	2650
18 10	OSPREY	ST	RNBT	FBG	DV	OB	7	1405			2200	2550
20 4	BLUEFIN	OP	RNBT	FBG	DV	OB	8				2800	3250
20 4	NOCTURNE	ST	RNBT	FBG	DV	OB	8	1780			2800	3300
20 4	NOCTURNE	ST	RNBT	FBG	DV	JT	8	2365			**	**
20 4	NOCTURNE	ST	RNBT	FBG	DV	IO 165-225	8	2365			2300	2750
							1973 BOATS					
18 10	FALCON	ST	RNBT	FBG	DV	IO 140-225	7 3	2390			2000	2500
18 10	FALCON	ST	RNBT	FBG	DV	JT 455 OLDS	7 3	2390			1950	2350
18 10	OSPREY	ST	RNBT	FBG	DV	OB	7 3	1405			2200	2550
20 4	ASTRA	HT	RNBT	FBG	DV	IO	8	2525			**	**

ARROW GLASS BOAT & MFG CORP   -CONTINUED

See inside cover to adjust price for area

LOA FT IN	NAME AND/ OR MODEL	TOP/ RIG	BOAT TYPE	MTL	-HULL- TP	TP	# HP	ENGINE MFG	BEAM FT IN	WGT LBS	DRAFT FT IN	RETAIL LOW	RETAIL HIGH
_____ 1973 BOATS													
20 4	BLUEFIN	OP	FSH	FBG	DV	OB			8	1980		3000	3500
20 4	NOCTURNE	OP	RNBT	FBG	DV	OB			8	1780		2800	3250
20 4	NOCTURNE	OP	RNBT	FBG	DV	IO	165-255		8	2365		2350	2900
_____ 1972 BOATS													
18 6	FALCON	ST	RNBT			IO			7 2			**	**
20 4	BLUEFIN	OP	RNBT	FBG	DV	OB			8	1980		3000	3500
20 4	NOCTURNE	OP	RNBT	FBG	DV	OB			8	1780		2800	3250
20 4	NOCTURNE	OP	RNBT	FBG	DV	IO	155-225		8	2365		2400	2900
20 4	POLARIS	OP	RNBT	FBG	DV	OB			8	1860		2900	3350
20 4	POLARIS	OP	RNBT	FBG	DV	IO	155-225		8	2525		2500	2950
_____ 1971 BOATS													
17 4	CHEETAH	ST	RNBT	FBG	TR	IO			7	1830		**	**
18	RIVIERA	ST	RNBT	FBG	DV	IO			6 10	2200		**	**
20 4	NOCTURNE	OP	RNBT	FBG	DV	OB			8	1780		2800	3250
20 4	NOCTURNE	OP	RNBT	FBG	DV	IO			8	2365		**	**
20 4	POLARIS	OP	CUD	FBG	DV	OB			8	1860		2900	3350
20 4	POLARIS	OP	CUD	FBG	DV	IO			8	2525		**	**
_____ 1970 BOATS													
17 4	CHEETAH	ST	RNBT	FBG	TR	IO	165		7	1830		1800	2150
18	RIVIERA	ST	RNBT	FBG	DV	IO	165		6 10	2200		2000	2400
20 4	NOCTURNE	OP	RNBT	FBG	DV	IO	270		8	2365		2800	3250
20 4	POLARIS	OP	RNBT	FBG	DV	IO	270		8	2525		2900	3350
_____ 1969 BOATS													
17 4	CHEETAH		RNBT	FBG	TR	IO	160	OMC	7	2000		1900	2250
17 4	CHEETAH	OP	RNBT	FBG	TR	IO	125		7	1830		1850	2200
17 4	CHEETAH CUSTOM		RNBT	FBG	TR	IO	120		7	1970		1900	2250
18	RIVIERA		RNBT	FBG	DV	IO	120-210		6 10			2000	2450
18	RIVIERA	OP	RNBT	FBG	DV	IO	120	MRCR	6 10	2200		2050	2400
20 4	MAKO			FBG	DV	IO	120	MRCR	8	2315		2600	3050
20 4	MAKO		RNBT	FBG	SV	IO	120-210		8	3300		3200	3800
20 4	NOCTURNE		RNBT	FBG	SV	IO	120-210		8	3500		3350	3950
20 4	NOCTURNE	OP	RNBT	FBG	DV	IO	120	MRCR	8	2365		2650	3100
_____ 1968 BOATS													
17 2	STINGRAY	OP	RNBT	FBG	SV	IO	200	OMC	6 10	2000		1950	2350
17 2	STINGRAY CUSTOM	OP	RNBT	FBG	SV	IO	200	OMC	6 10	1970		1950	2300
17 4	CHEETAH	OP	RNBT	FBG	TR	IO	160	OMC	7	2000		1950	2350
17 4	CHEETAH CUSTOM	OP	RNBT	FBG	TR	IO	120	OMC	7	1970		1950	2300
20 4	MAKO	SF	FBG	SV	IO	225	OMC			8	3300		4050	4700
20 4	NOCTURNE	OP	RNBT	FBG	SV	IO	225	OMC	8	3500		3550	4100
_____ 1967 BOATS													
17 2	STINGRAY			FBG		IO	120-160			1760		1800	2200
17 2	STINGRAY			FBG		IO	185-200					1850	2300
20 4	MAKO			FBG		IO	120-155			2500		2850	3400
	IO 160-200	3100	3650, IO	225			3400	3950, IO	T 80-T120			3700	4450
20 4	NOCTURNE			FBG		IO	120-155			2800		3050	3800
	IO 185	3300	3800, IO	200			3550	4150, IO	T 80-T120			3900	4700
_____ 1966 BOATS													
17 2	COBRA	RNBT		FBG		OB			6 10	1100		1700	2000
17 2	STINGRAY			FBG		IO	110-200		6 10			1900	2300
19 2	EMPRESS	RNBT		FBG		OB			7 8	1650		2450	2850
19 2	EMPRESS	RNBT		FBG		IO	110		7 8			2900	3350
19 2	OLYMPIA	OFF		FBG		OB			7 8	1600		2400	2800
19 2	OLYMPIA	OFF		FBG		IO	110		7 8			3200	3700
_____ 1965 BOATS													
17 2	BARRACUDA	FSH		FBG		IO						**	**
17 2	BARRACUDA	FSH		FBG		IO	110-160					2150	2550
17 2	COBRA	RNBT		FBG		OB						2300	2650
17 2	STINGRAY			FBG		IO						**	**
17 2	STINGRAY			FBG		IO	110-160					1950	2350
19 2	EMPRESS	RNBT		FBG		OB						2550	2950
19 2	EMPRESS	RNBT		FBG		IO						**	**
19 2	EMPRESS	RNBT		FBG		IO	110-225					3050	3700
19 2	OLYMPIA			FBG		OB						2500	2900
19 2	OLYMPIA			FBG		IO						**	**
19 2	OLYMPIA			FBG		IO	110-225					3050	3700

ARTHUR MARINE

Call 1-800-327-6929 for BUC Personalized Evaluation Service
Or, for 1971 to 1972 boats, sign onto www.BUCValuPro.com

ASH CRAFT
FORMERLY WAGEMAKER

Call 1-800-327-6929 for BUC Personalized Evaluation Service
Or, for 1959 to 1962 boats, sign onto www.BUCValuPro.com

ASTRAL YACHTS
HALMATIC LTD
P091JR ENGLAND

POOLE PORSET ENG

See inside cover to adjust price for area

LOA FT IN	NAME AND/ OR MODEL	TOP/ RIG	BOAT TYPE	MTL	-HULL- TP	TP	# HP	ENGINE MFG	BEAM FT IN	WGT LBS	DRAFT FT IN	RETAIL LOW	RETAIL HIGH
_____ 1983 BOATS													
57	ASTRAL-ADVENTURER	FB	MY	FBG	SV	IB	T550D	GM	17 9	54000	4 3	250000	274500
68	ASTRAL-ARIES	FB	MY	FBG	DV	IB	T675D	GM	17 6	68000	4 9	408500	449000
68	ASTRAL-ARIES	FB	MY	FBG	DV	IB	T925D	GM	17 6	68000	4 9	440500	484000
68	ASTRAL-ARIES	FB	MY	FBG	DV	IB	T10CD	MTU	17 6	68000	4 9	468000	514500
_____ 1982 BOATS													
57	ASTRAL-ADVENTURER	FB	MY	FBG	SV	IB	T550D	GM	17 9	54000	4 3	238500	262000
68	ASTRAL-ARIES	FB	MY	FBG	DV	IB	T675D	GM	17 6	68000	4 9	390500	429500
68	ASTRAL-ARIES	FB	MY	FBG	DV	IB	T925D	GM	17 6	68000	4 9	420500	462500
68	ASTRAL-ARIES	FB	MY	FBG	DV	IB	T10CD	MTU	17 6	68000	4 9	447500	492000
_____ 1981 BOATS													
57	ASTRAL ADVENTURER	FB	MY	FBG	SV	IB	T550D	GM	17 9	54000	4 3	227500	250000
68	ASTRAL ALGARVE	FB	MY	FBG	DV	IB	T675D	GM	17 6	68000	4 9	372000	409000
68	ASTRAL ALGARVE	FB	MY	FBG	DV	IB	T925D	GM	17 6	68000	4 9	400500	440500
68	ASTRAL ALGARVE	FB	MY	FBG	DV	IB	T11CD	MTU	17 6	68000	4 9	443000	487000
_____ 1980 BOATS													
57	ASTRAL 55	FB	MY	FBG	DV	IB	T510D	GM	17 9	54000	4 3	212000	233000
68	ASTRAL 65	FB	MY	FBG	DV	IB	T D	GM	17 6	68000	4 9	**	**
68	ASTRAL 65	FB	MY	FBG	DV	IB	T675D	GM	17 6	68000	4 9	355000	390000
68	ASTRAL 65	FB	MY	FBG	DV	IB	T925D	GM	17 6	68000	4 9	382000	420000
75 5	ASTRAL 75	FB	MY	FBG	DV	IB	T675D	GM				**	**

ATLANTA BOAT WORKS
ARISTO-CRAFT BOAT CORP
ATLANTA GA 30306

COAST GUARD MFG ID- ATL

See inside cover to adjust price for area

LOA FT IN	NAME AND/ OR MODEL	TOP/ RIG	BOAT TYPE	MTL	-HULL- TP	TP	# HP	ENGINE MFG	BEAM FT IN	WGT LBS	DRAFT FT IN	RETAIL LOW	RETAIL HIGH
_____ 1980 BOATS													
20 4	ARISTO-CRAFT		RNBT	FBG	DV	IO	120		7 7			3300	3850
_____ 1979 BOATS													
19	ARISTO-CRAFT	OP	RNBT	FBG	DV	IO	120-170		7 7	1850		2850	3350
19	ARISTO-CRAFT	HT	RNBT	FBG	DV	IO	120-170		7 7	1850		2850	3350
_____ 1978 BOATS													
19	ARISTO-CRAFT	OP	RNBT	FBG	DV	IO	120-170		7 7	1900	3	2900	3400
19	ARISTO-CRAFT	HT	RNBT	FBG	DV	IO	120-170		7 7	1900	3	2900	3400
_____ 1977 BOATS													
19	ARISTO-CRAFT	OP	RNBT	FBG	DV	IO	120-165		7 7	1580		2800	3250
19	ARISTO-CRAFT	HT	RNBT	FBG	DV	IO	120-165		7 7	1580		2800	3250
_____ 1976 BOATS													
19	ARISTO-CRAFT 19	OP	RNBT	FBG	DV	IO	120-165		7 9	1865	2	3050	3600
19	ARISTO-CRAFT 19	HT	RNBT	FBG	DV	IO	120-165		7 9	1865	2	3050	3600
_____ 1975 BOATS													
19	ARISTO-CRAFT 19	OP	RNBT	FBG	DV	IO	120-165		7 9	1650	3	3000	3500
_____ 1974 BOATS													
19 1	ARISTO-CRAFT 19	HT	RNBT	FBG	DV	IO	120-165		7 7	1665	1 10	3100	3750
_____ 1973 BOATS													
19 1	ARISTO-CRAFT 19	HT	RNBT	FBG	DV	IO	120-165		7 7	1665	1 10	3200	3850
_____ 1972 BOATS													
19 1	ARISTO-CRAFT 19	HT	RNBT	FBG	DV	IO	120-165		7 7	1665	1 10	3250	3900
_____ 1971 BOATS													
19 1	ARISTO-CRAFT 19	HT		FBG	DV	IO	120-165		7 7	1625	1 10	3350	3900
19 1	ARISTO-CRAFT 19	HT		FBG	DV	IO	120-165		7 7	1625	1 10	3350	3900
_____ 1970 BOATS													
19 1	NINETEEN			FBG	DV	IO	120-165		7 7	1625	1 10	3450	4100
_____ 1969 BOATS													
19	NINETEEN		RNBT	FBG	DV	IO	120-160		7 7	1560		3550	4350
19 1	NINETEEN		RNBT	FBG	DV	IO	120	MRCR	7 7	1625	1 10	3650	4250
_____ 1968 BOATS													
19	NINETEEN	OP		FBG		IO	120-160		7 7	1560		3600	4250
19	NINETEEN			FBG		IO	120-160		7 7	1645		3650	4400
_____ 1967 BOATS													
18 3	EIGHTEEN			FBG		IO	120			1400		3450	4000
18 3	EIGHTEEN	HT		FBG		IO	120			1400		3450	4000

```
ATLANTA BOAT WORKS            -CONTINUED      See inside cover to adjust price for area
  LOA  NAME AND/          TOP/ BOAT -HULL- ----ENGINE--- BEAM   WGT  DRAFT RETAIL RETAIL
  FT IN  OR MODEL         RIG  TYPE MTL TP TP # HP  MFG  FT IN  LBS  FT IN  LOW   HIGH
  ------------------- 1966 BOATS ------------------------------------------------------
  16  5 FUNLINER                    FBG  IO 110    MRCR  7  2              2850   3350
  18  3 EIGHTEEN                    FBG  IO 110          7  9              3850   4500
  ------------------- 1965 BOATS ------------------------------------------------------
  17  5 ARISTO-CRAFT FUNLINR        FBG  IO 110-120                        3400   3950
  ------------------- 1964 BOATS ------------------------------------------------------
  16  4 ARISTO-CRAFT FUNLINR        FBG  IO 80-110                         2850   3350
```

ATLANTA MARINE LTD

Call 1-800-327-6929 for BUC Personalized Evaluation Service
Or, for 1980 boats, sign onto www.BUCValuPro.com

ATLANTIC CITY CATBOATS
NAVESINK YACHT SALES INC   See inside cover to adjust price for area
SEA BRIGHT NJ 07760

For more recent years, see the BUC Used Boat Price Guide, Volume 1 or Volume 2

```
  LOA  NAME AND/          TOP/ BOAT -HULL- ----ENGINE--- BEAM   WGT  DRAFT RETAIL RETAIL
  FT IN  OR MODEL         RIG  TYPE MTL TP TP # HP  MFG  FT IN  LBS  FT IN  LOW   HIGH
  ------------------- 1983 BOATS ------------------------------------------------------
  21  3 ATLANTIC-CITY KITTY GAF SA/CR FBG CB IB    D     9  6   5300  2    12200  13900
  24    ATLANTIC-CITY CAT   GAF SA/CR FBG CB IB    D    11      8000  2    20400  22700
  ------------------- 1982 BOATS ------------------------------------------------------
  24    ATLANTIC-CITY CAT BT GAF SA/CR FBG CB IB 12D BMW 11     8000  2    19200  21300
```

ATLANTIC YACHT CO

Call 1-800-327-6929 for BUC Personalized Evaluation Service
Or, for 1960 to 1970 boats, sign onto www.BUCValuPro.com

ATLANTIC YACHT CORPORATION
ST AUGUSTINE BOAT WORKS INC   See inside cover to adjust price for area
PALATKA FL 32178   COAST GUARD MFG ID- AYU
                          FORMERLY ATLANTIC YACHT & SHIPBUILDING CORP

For more recent years, see the BUC Used Boat Price Guide, Volume 1 or Volume 2

```
  LOA  NAME AND/          TOP/ BOAT -HULL- ----ENGINE--- BEAM   WGT  DRAFT RETAIL RETAIL
  FT IN  OR MODEL         RIG  TYPE MTL TP TP # HP  MFG  FT IN  LBS  FT IN  LOW   HIGH
  ------------------- 1983 BOATS ------------------------------------------------------
  29  7 ATLANTIC LONG RANGE  FB  CR  FBG DS IB   165  CRUS 12   12000  3    28900  32200
  36  7 ATLANTIC LONG RANGE  FB  CR  FBG DS IB  120D LEHM 13  9 17000  3  6 63400  69600
      IB T270  CRUS  60400  66300, IB T120D LEHM 65300  71800, IB T124D VLVO 64500  70900
      IB T158D VLVO 65100  71500, IB T205D GM   67700  74400
  43  8 ATLANTIC LONG RANGE  FB DCMY FBG DS IB  T350  CRUS 14   30000  3 .5 126500 139000
      IB T120D LEHM 127000 139500, IB T210D CAT 127500 140500, IB T300D CAT 140000 154000
      IB T300D GM  139000 152500
  46  9 ATLANTIC LONG RANGE  FB DCMY FBG DS IB  T350  CRUS 16   34000  3  9 116000 127500
      IB T120D LEHM 133500 146500, IB T300D CAT 127000 139500, IB T300D GM 126000 138500
  46  9 ATLANTIC LONG RANGE  FB YTFS FBG DS IB  T350  CRUS 16   34000  3  9 122500 134500
      IB T375  GM   127000 140000, IB T300D CAT 133000 146000, IB T300D GM 132500 145500
      IB T355D CAT  144500 158500
  ------------------- 1982 BOATS ------------------------------------------------------
  36  7 PRAIRIE 37 LRC       FB  CR  FBG DS IB  T205D GM  13  9 17000  3  3 64500  71100
  36  7 PRAIRIE 37 LRC       FB TRWL FBG DS IB  T120D LEHM 13  9 17000  3  3 64500  70900
  43  9 ATLANTIC LONG RANGE  HT DCMY FBG DS IB  T210D CAT  14   30000  3  6 122500 134500
  43  9 ATLANTIC LONG RANGE  HT DCMY FBG DS IB  T300D CAT  14   30000  3  6 135000 148000
  43  9 ATLANTIC LONG RANGE  FB DCMY FBG DS IB  T300D GM   14   30000  3  6 133500 146500
  43  9 ATLANTIC LONG RANGE  FB DCMY FBG DS IB  T210D CAT  14   30000  3  6 124500 137000
  43  9 ATLANTIC LONG RANGE  FB DCMY FBG DS IB  T300D CAT  14   30000  3  6 134000 147500
  43  9 ATLANTIC LONG RANGE  FB DCMY FBG DS IB  T300D GM   14   30000  3  6 133000 146000
  43  9 ATLANTIC LONG RANGE  HT TRWL FBG DS IB  T120D LEHM 14   30000  3  6 123000 135000
  43  9 ATLANTIC LONG RANGE  FB TRWL FBG DS IB  T120D LEHM 14   30000  3  6 122500 134500
  46  9 PRAIRIE 47 LRC       HT DCMY FBG DS IB  T300D CAT  16   34000  3  9 128500 141500
  46  9 PRAIRIE 47 LRC       HT DCMY FBG DS IB  T300D GM   16   34000  3  9 128000 141000
  46  9 PRAIRIE 47 LRC       FB DCMY FBG DS IB  T300D CAT  16   34000  3  9 127500 140500
  46  9 PRAIRIE 47 LRC       FB DCMY FBG DS IB  T300D GM   16   34000  3  9 127500 140000
  46  9 PRAIRIE 47 LRC       HT TRWL FBG DS IB  T120D LEHM 16   34000  3  9 139500 153500
  46  9 PRAIRIE 47 LRC       FB TRWL FBG DS IB  T120D LEHM 16   34000  3  9 138500 152000
  46  9 PRAIRIE 47 YF        FB YTFS FBG DS IB  T300D CAT  16   34000  3  9 134500 147500
  46  9 PRAIRIE 47 YF        FB YTFS FBG DS IB  T300D GM   16   34000  3  9 134000 147000
  48  8 ATLANTIC 49          FB YTFS FBG DS IB  T310       14              120500 132500
  ------------------- 1981 BOATS ------------------------------------------------------
  43  9 ATLANTIC LONG RANGE  HT DCMY FBG DS IB  T130D PERK 14   32000  3  6 122500 134500
      IB T160D PERK 116000 127500, IB T200D PERK 121000 133000, IB T210D CAT 122500 134500
      IB T300D CAT  134000 147000
  43  9 ATLANTIC LONG RANGE  FB TRWL FBG DS IB  T130D PERK 14   32000  3  6 122500 134500
      IB T160D PERK 124000 136000, IB T200D PERK 126000 138000, IB T210D CAT 126000 138500
      IB T260D CAT  128500 141500
  48  8 ATLANTIC 49          YTFS FBG DS IB  T210D        14              102000 112000
  ------------------- 1980 BOATS ------------------------------------------------------
  43  8 ATLANTIC 44          FB TRWL FBG DS IB  T260D      14   30000  3  5 114000 125500
  43  9 ATLANTIC 44          FB TRWL FBG DS IB  T120D LEHM 14   32000  3  6 113000 124500
      IB T128D GM  113500 125000, IB T210D CAT 117500 129500, IB T310D CAT 122500 135000
  ------------------- 1979 BOATS ------------------------------------------------------
  43  9 ATLANTIC 44          FB TRWL FBG DS IB  T120D LEHM 14   30000  3  6 103500 114000
  43  9 ATLANTIC 44          FB TRWL FBG DS IB  T150D GM   14   30000  3  6 105000 115000
  43  9 ATLANTIC 44          FB TRWL FBG DS IB  T210D CAT  14   30000  3  6 108000 118500
  ------------------- 1978 BOATS ------------------------------------------------------
  43  9 ATLANTIC 44 AMERICAN FB TRWL FBG DS IB  T120D LEHM 14   32000  3  6 95400 105000
      IB T150D LEHM  96500 106000, IB T210D CAT  99700 109500, IB T250D CAT 101500 111500
  43  9 ATLANTIC 44 EUROPEAN FB TRWL FBG DS IB  T120D LEHM 14   32000  3  6 98900 108500
      IB T150D LEHM  99900 110000, IB T210D CAT 103000 113000, IB T250D CAT 104500 115000
  43  9 MEDITERRANEAN A44    FB TRWL FBG DS IB  T120D LEHM 14   32000  3  6 101500 111500
      IB T150D LEHM 102500 112500, IB T210D CAT 105500 115500, IB T250D CAT 106500 117500
  ------------------- 1977 BOATS ------------------------------------------------------
  43  9 ATLANTIC 44          FB TRWL FBG DS IB  T120D      14   28000  3  6 90900  99900
```

ATLANTIC YACHT SERVICES
COAST GUARD MFG ID- AYS

Call 1-800-327-6929 for BUC Personalized Evaluation Service
Or, for 1981 boats, sign onto www.BUCValuPro.com

ATLANTIC YACHTS & MARINE LTD

Call 1-800-327-6929 for BUC Personalized Evaluation Service
Or, for 1981 to 1983 boats, sign onto www.BUCValuPro.com

ATLANTIC YACHTS LTD

Call 1-800-327-6929 for BUC Personalized Evaluation Service
Or, for 1981 boats, sign onto www.BUCValuPro.com

AURORA YACHTS LTD
COAST GUARD MFG ID- ZAX

Call 1-800-327-6929 for BUC Personalized Evaluation Service
Or, for 1977 to 1978 boats, sign onto www.BUCValuPro.com

AURORAGLAS INC
COAST GUARD MFG ID- AJC

Call 1-800-327-6929 for BUC Personalized Evaluation Service
Or, for 1979 to 1981 boats, sign onto www.BUCValuPro.com

AVENGER-PEMBROKE YACHTS
CORAL GABLES FL 33146   See inside cover to adjust price for area

```
  LOA  NAME AND/          TOP/ BOAT -HULL- ----ENGINE--- BEAM   WGT  DRAFT RETAIL RETAIL
  FT IN  OR MODEL         RIG  TYPE MTL TP TP # HP  MFG  FT IN  LBS  FT IN  LOW   HIGH
  ------------------- 1970 BOATS ------------------------------------------------------
  39            DC          FBG    T225D CAT  13 10 22000  3  6 65600  72100
  39            DC          FBG SV T216D GM   13 10 22000  3  7 64000  70300
  39  AVENGER   DC          FBG SV IB T300 CHRY 13 10      3  6 49500  54400
  39  AVENGER   SDNSF       FBG SV IB T300 CHRY 13 10 23500  3  6 60400  66400
```

LOA FT IN	NAME AND/ OR MODEL	TOP/ RIG	BOAT TYPE	-HULL- MTL TP	----ENGINE--- TP # HP MFG	BEAM FT IN	WGT LBS	DRAFT FT IN	RETAIL LOW	RETAIL HIGH
	--------------- 1970 **BOATS**									
39	AVENGER		SDNSF	FBG SV	IB T216D GM	13 10	23500	3 7	67300	73900
39	AVENGER		SDNSF	FBG SV	IB T225D CAT	13 10	23500	3 7	68900	75700
	--------------- 1969 **BOATS**									
39		DC	FBG	IB	IB T216 GM	13 10	19500	3 8	49800	54700
	IB T300 CHRY 48000	52700,	IB T216D GM		56500 62100, IB T225D CAT				59600	65500
39		HT DC	FBG	IB	IB T300 CHRY	13 10		3 6	47600	52300
39		HT DC	FBG	IB	IB T216D GM	13 10		3 7	58000	63800
39		HT DC	FBG	IB	IB T225D CAT	13 10		3 7	59600	65500
39		SDNSF	FBG	IB	IB T300 CHRY	13 10		3 6	52500	57700
39		FB	SDNSF FBG	IB	IB T300 CHRY	13 10	18000	3 6	47100	51700
	IB T160D PERK 54000	59400,	IB T216D GM		56500 62100, IB T225D CAT				61900	68000
	--------------- 1968 **BOATS**									
39		DC	FBG	IB	IB T295 CHRY	13 10	18000	3 6	45700	50200
39		DC	FBG	IB	IB T216D GM	13 10	19750	3 7	55300	60800
39		SDN	FBG	IB	IB T295 CHRY	13 8	17500	3 6	44700	49600
39		SDN	FBG	IB	IB T216D GM	13 8	19250	3 7	54900	60300
39	COCKPIT	DCCPT	FBG	IB	IB T295 CHRY	13 10	18000	3 6	45700	50200
39	COCKPIT	DCCPT	FBG	IB	IB T216D GM	13 10	19750	3 7	55400	60900
	--------------- 1967 **BOATS**									
38	8 AVENGER 39			FBG	IB T295		17500		42700	47500
38	8 AVENGER 39			FBG	IB T216D		17500		48500	53300
38	8 AVENGER 39	HT		FBG	IB T295		17500		42700	47500
38	8 AVENGER 39	HT		FBG	IB T216D		17500		48500	53300
38	9 AVENGER 39		CR	FBG	IB T295	13 6		3 2	45700	50200
38	9 AVENGER 39		FSH	FBG	IB T295	13 6		3 2	44800	49800
38	9 AVENGER 39	HT	HB	FBG	IO T210	13 6		3 2	29200	32400
38	9 AVENGER 39	HT	HB	FBG	IB T295	13 6		3 2	29400	32600
	--------------- 1966 **BOATS**									
38	9 AVENGER 39		CR	FBG SV	IB T200	13 4		3	42800	47500
38	9 AVENGER 39		SF	FBG SV	IB T200	13 4		3	43700	48500
38	9 AVENGER 39 AFT CPT		CR	FBG SV	IB T200	13 4		3	45500	50000

AVON INFLATABLES LTD
AVON RUBBER PLC
STEVENSVILLE MD 21666   COAST GUARD MFG ID- AVB   See inside cover to adjust price for area

IMTRA CORPORATION
CLEARWATER FL 34622

For more recent years, see the BUC Used Boat Price Guide, Volume 1 or Volume 2

LOA FT IN	NAME AND/ OR MODEL	TOP/ RIG	BOAT TYPE	-HULL- MTL TP	----ENGINE--- TP # HP MFG	BEAM FT IN	WGT LBS	DRAFT FT IN	RETAIL LOW	RETAIL HIGH
	--------------- 1983 **BOATS**									
17 10	SEARIDER 5M DLX	OP	CTRCN	FBG DV	OB	6 6	630		3400	3950
17 10	SEARIDER 5M RESCUE	OP	CTRCN	FBG DV	OB	6 6	660		3550	4150

CHARLES AXTMANN
Call 1-800-327-6929 for BUC Personalized Evaluation Service
Or, for 1970 to 1972 boats, sign onto www.BUCValuPro.com

AZTEC BOATS
Call 1-800-327-6929 for BUC Personalized Evaluation Service
Or, for 1965 to 1979 boats, sign onto www.BUCValuPro.com

B & R MAST RIGGING
FORMERLY B&R DESIGNS
Call 1-800-327-6929 for BUC Personalized Evaluation Service
Or, for 1977 to 1994 boats, sign onto www.BUCValuPro.com

B & W CORONET BOATS
Call 1-800-327-6929 for BUC Personalized Evaluation Service
Or, for 1976 to 1988 boats, sign onto www.BUCValuPro.com

B Y PLASTICS LTD
C STRIKE   COAST GUARD MFG ID- ZBZ
Call 1-800-327-6929 for BUC Personalized Evaluation Service
Or, for 1975 to 1979 boats, sign onto www.BUCValuPro.com

BAHA CRUISER BOATS INC
MAYO FL 32066   COAST GUARD MFG ID- VBH See inside cover to adjust price for area

For more recent years, see the BUC Used Boat Price Guide, Volume 1 or Volume 2

LOA FT IN	NAME AND/ OR MODEL	TOP/ RIG	BOAT TYPE	-HULL- MTL TP	----ENGINE--- TP # HP MFG	BEAM FT IN	WGT LBS	DRAFT FT IN	RETAIL LOW	RETAIL HIGH
	--------------- 1983 **BOATS**									
24	BAHA DAY CRUISER		CR	FBG DV	IO 228	8	6000		8150	9400
24	BAHA EXPRESS CRUISER		EXP	FBG DV	IO 228	8	6000		8150	9400
24	BAHA EXPRESS CRUISER		EXP	FBG DV	IB 228	8	6000		10100	11400
24	BAHA SPORT FISHERMAN		SF	FBG DV	IO 228	8	5000		8000	9200
24	BAHA SPORT FISHERMAN		SF	FBG DV	IB 228	8	5000		8550	9850
26	1 BAHA EXPRESS CRUISER		EXP	FBG DV	IO 260	10 6	8000		11200	12800
26	1 BAHA EXPRESS CRUISER		EXP	FBG DV	IB 260	10 6	8000		13800	15700
26	1 BAHA FAMILY	FB	CR	FBG DV	IO 260	10 6	8000		11200	12800
26	1 BAHA FAMILY	FB	CR	FBG DV	IB 260	10 6	8000		13800	15700
26	1 BAHA SPORT FISHERMAN		SF	FBG DV	IO 260	10 6	7000		11700	13300
26	1 BAHA SPORT FISHERMAN		SF	FBG DV	IB 260	10 6	7000		12600	14300
26	1 BAHA-TOURNAMENT		SF	FBG DV	IO 260	10 6	7500		12200	13900
26	1 BAHA-TOURNAMENT		SF	FBG DV	IB 260	10 6	7500		13200	15000
31	1 BAHA FAMILY	FB	CR	FBG DV	IB T260	11 2	12000		24500	27200
31	1 BAHA SPORT FISHERMAN		SF	FBG DV	IB T260	11 2	11000		21200	23600
31	1 BAHA-TOURNAMENT		SF	FBG SV	IB T260	11 2	11000		26700	29700
	--------------- 1982 **BOATS**									
24	BAHA DAY CRUISER	OP	SPTCR	FBG SV	IO 198-260	8	6000		7900	9300
24	BAHA EXPRESS CRUISER	OP	EXP	FBG SV	IO 198-260	8	6000		7900	9300
26	2 BAHA EXPRESS CRUISER	OP	EXP	FBG SV	IO 260-330	10 6	8000		11000	13100
26	2 BAHA EXPRESS CRUISER	OP	EXP	FBG SV	IO T120-T170	10 6	8000		11200	13100
26	2 BAHA EXPRESS CRUISER	OP	EXP	FBG SV	IO T D	10 6	8000		**	**
26	2 BAHA FAMILY FB	FB	SDN	FBG SV	VD 255	10 6	8000		13900	15700
	IO 260 11500	13100,	IO 330		12200 13900, IB 330				14400	16300
	VD 330 14400	16300,	VD D	**	**, IO T140				11900	13500
	IO T170 12100	13800,	VD T170		14700 16700, IO T D				**	**
	VD T D **	**								
26	2 BAHA SPORT FISHERMAN	OP	SF	FBG SV	IO 228	10 6	7000		11200	12700
	IO 228 11900	13500,	IO 260		11400 13000, IB 260				12000	13700
	IO 330 12100	13700,	IO 330		12400 14100, IO T140-T170				11800	13700
26	2 BAHA-TOURNAMENT		SF	FBG SV	IO 260	10 6	7500		12000	13600
26	2 BAHA-TOURNAMENT		SF	FBG SV	IB 260	10 6	7500		12600	14300
31	1 BAHA FAMILY FB	FB	SDN	FBG SV	IB 330	11 2	12000		23600	26300
	IB D VLVO **	**	, IB		330D				25000	29900
	IB T D VLVO	**	**							
31	1 BAHA SPORT FISHERMAN	OP	SF	FBG SV	IB 330	11 2	11000		21500	23800
	IB D VLVO	**	**, IB	T228-T330	22500 26600, IB T D VLVO				**	**
31	1 BAHA-TOURNAMENT		TT	SF	FBG SV	IB 255-330	11 2	11000		20800	23800
	IB D CAT	**	**, IB	D CUM	** **, IB D VLVO				**	**
	IB T228-T330 22500	26600,	IB T D VLVO		**, IB T200D CHRY				28700	31900
	--------------- 1981 **BOATS**									
24	BAHA DAY CRUISER	OP	SPTCR	FBG SV	IO 198-260	7 11	6000		7750	9150
24	BAHA DAY CRUISER	OP	SPTCR	FBG SV	IO T D	7 11	6000		**	**
24	BAHA EXPRESS CRUISER	OP	EXP	FBG SV	IO 198-260	7 11	6000		7750	9150
24	BAHA EXPRESS CRUISER	OP	EXP	FBG SV	IO T D	7 11	6000		**	**
26	BAHA EXPRESS CRUISER	OP	EXP	FBG SV	IO 228-330	10 6	8000		8700	10800
	IO D	**	**, IO	T120-T170	9150 10800, IO T D				**	**
26	2 BAHA FAMILY FB		FB	SDN	FBG SV	IO 228	10 6	8000		11100	12700
	VD 228-255	13100	15100, IO	D	11400 12900, IO T120-T170				12000	13600
	VD 330 13800	15600, IO	D		** **, IO T120-T170				11500	13600
26	2 BAHA SPORT FISHERMAN	OP	SF	FBG SV	IO 228	10 6	7000		11000	12500
	IB 228-255	11400	13100, IO	260	11200 12800, IO D				**	**
	IB D	**	**							
31	1 BAHA FAMILY FB		FB	SDN	FBG SV	IB 330	11 2	12000		22600	25200
	IB 330D CAT	31400	34900, IB	T228-T330	23900 28600, IB T D VLVO				**	**

```
LOA  NAME AND/              TOP/ BOAT  -HULL- ----ENGINE--- BEAM   WGT  DRAFT RETAIL RETAIL
FT IN  OR MODEL             RIG  TYPE  MTL TP TP # HP  MFG  FT IN  LBS  FT IN  LOW   HIGH
-------------------- 1981 BOATS ----------------------------------------------------------
31  1 BAHA SPORT FISHERMAN OP   SF   FBG SV IB  330          11  2 11000        20500 22800
    IB    D VLVO    **    ** , IB T228-T330  21500  25500, IB T   D VLVO   **        **    **
31  1 BAHA-TOURNAMENT       TT   SF   FBG SV IB  255-330     11  2 11000        19900 22800
    IB    D CAT    **    ** , IB   D CUM      **    ** , IB   D VLVO   **        **    **
    IB T228-T330  21500  25500, IB T   D VLVO   **    ** , IB T200D CHRY        27600 30700
-------------------- 1980 BOATS ----------------------------------------------------------
26  2 FAMILY               FB   CR   FBG SV IO             11  2                  **    **
26  2 FAMILY EXPRESS CR    OP   EXP  FBG SV IO             10  6                  **    **
31  1 BAHA FAMILY FSHERMAN FB   SF   FBG SV IO             11  2                  **    **
31  1 BAHA SPORTFISHERMAN  OP   SF   FBG SV IO             11  2                  **    **
```

BAHAMAS SEACRAFT INC

Call 1-800-327-6929 for BUC Personalized Evaluation Service
Or, for 1960 to 1961 boats, sign onto www.BUCValuPro.com

BAHNER CUSTOM BOATS

Call 1-800-327-6929 for BUC Personalized Evaluation Service
Or, for 1979 boats, sign onto www.BUCValuPro.com

BAILEYS BOAT WORKS
COAST GUARD MFG ID- BYU

Call 1-800-327-6929 for BUC Personalized Evaluation Service
Or, for 1912 to 1983 boats, sign onto www.BUCValuPro.com

BAJA MARINE CORP
BUCYRUS OH 44820-0151   COAST GUARD MFG ID- AGC See inside cover to adjust price for area
                           FORMERLY AEROGLASTICS CORP

For more recent years, see the BUC Used Boat Price Guide, Volume 1 or Volume 2

```
LOA  NAME AND/              TOP/ BOAT  -HULL- ----ENGINE--- BEAM   WGT  DRAFT RETAIL RETAIL
FT IN  OR MODEL             RIG  TYPE  MTL TP TP # HP  MFG  FT IN  LBS  FT IN  LOW   HIGH
-------------------- 1983 BOATS ----------------------------------------------------------
16  1 160BR                OP   RNBT FBG SV OB             6  8   845        1750  2100
16  1 TRI-16               OP   RNBT FBG TR OB             6 10   845        1750  2100
16  1 TRI16                OP   RNBT FBG TR OB             6  8   845        1750  2100
16  2 164B                 OP   RNBT FBG SV OB             6 10   850        1750  2100
16  2 164FS                OP   RNBT FBG SV OB             6 10   925        1900  2300
16  2 164HLS               OP   BASS FBG SV OB             6 10   900        1850  2200
16  2 164SS                OP   SKI  FBG SV OB             6 10   830        1700  2000
16  8 170BR                OP   RNBT FBG SV OB             7  1  1000        2100  2500
16  8 170BR                OP   RNBT FBG SV IO 140-188     7  1  1500        1850  2250
16  8 170SS                OP   SKI  FBG SV OB             7  1  1000        2050  2450
18  4 184BR                OP   RNBT FBG SV OB             7  1  1050        2350  2750
18  4 184BR                OP   RNBT FBG SV IO 140-188     7  1  1885        2300  2750
18  4 184BR                OP   RNBT FBG SV JT 260-360     7  1  1885        3500  4100
18  4 184FS                OP   RNBT FBG SV OB             7  1  1200        2550  3000
18  4 184HLS               OP   BASS FBG SV OB             7  1  1100        2400  2800
18  4 184SS                OP   SKI  FBG SV OB             7  1  1050        2300  2700
18  4 184SS                OP   SKI  FBG SV IO 140-188     7  1  1885        2200  2600
18  4 184SS                OP   SKI  FBG SV JT 260-360     7  1  1885        3400  3950
19  3 190BR                OP   RNBT FBG SV OB             7  3  1200        2650  3050
19  3 190BR                OP   RNBT FBG SV IO 140-230     7  3  2175        2600  3150
      JT  260    CHEV 3950  4550, IO 260        2800   3250, JT 300-360        3950  4550
19  3 TWILIGHT-CRUISER 190 ST   CUD  FBG DV OB             7  3  1335        2850  3300
19  3 TWILIGHT-CRUISER 190 ST   CUD  FBG DV IO  170   MRCR 7  3  2350        2800  3250
      IO  170  OMC   2750  3250, IB  170        3400   4150, IO  185  OMC      2800  3250
      IB  185  OMC   3600  4200, IO  188  MRCR  2800   3300, IB  188  MRCR     3400  4000
      IO  198  MRCR  2850  3300, IB  198  MRCR  3450   4000, JT  200  CHEV     3900  4550
      IO  200  OMC   2800  3250, IB  200  OMC   3600   4200, IO  228  MRCR     3900  3350
      IB  228  MRCR  3450  4000, IO  230  OMC   2850   3350, IB  230  OMC      3650  4250
      IO  260  MRCR  3000  3500, IO  260  OMC   3000   3450, IB  260           3500  4300
      JT 300-360     3950  4600
20  3 200BR                OP   RNBT FBG SV OB             7  4  1300        3000  3500
20  3 200SS                OP   SKI  FBG SV OB             7  4  1200        2800  3250
20  3 200SS                OP   SKI  FBG SV IO 198-230     7  4  2245        3650  4350
      JT  260    CHEV 5450  6250, IO 260        3900   4500, JT 300-360        5450  6250
20  3 20BR                 OP   RNBT FBG SV OB             7  4  1300        3000  3500
21  7 210                  OP   CUD  FBG SV IO 198-230     8        3400        5650  6550
      IO  260  MRCR  5850  6750, IO 260-330     6700   7700, IO T170-T188      6350  7450
22  6 TWILIGHT-CRUISER 220 OP   CUD  FBG DV IO 198-260     8                      6300  7500
23  9 240BR                OP   CR   FBG DV OB             7  9         2450     5700  6550
23  9 240BR                OP   CR   FBG DV IO 198-260     7  9                   7000  8250
23  9 CARRERA 240               SPTCR FBG DV IB  198       7  9         3000     7050  8100
23  9 CARRERA 240          ST   SPTCR FBG DV IO 188-260    7  9                   6950  8300
23  9 CARRERA DLX               SPTCR FBG DV IB  198       7  9         2220     6100  7000
32  1 OFFHORE 3200         OP   SPTCR KEV DV IO T370  MRCR 8  4         5980    22300 24800
32  1 OFFSHORE 3200        OP   SPTCR SV IO T370          8  4                   21700 24100
32  1 OFFSHORE 3200        OP   SPTCR KEV DV IO T330 MRCR 8  4         5980     21700 24100
32  1 OFFSHORE 3200        OP   SPTCR SV IO T370          8  4                   22400 24800
32  1 OFFSHORE 3200        OP   SPTCR DV IO T330 MRCR     8  4         5980     22300 24800
32  1 OFFSHORE 3200        OP   SPTCR DV IO T330          8  4                   21700 24100
32  1 OFFSHORE 3200        OP   SPTCR KEV DV IO T330-T370 8  4                   21700 24800
-------------------- 1982 BOATS ----------------------------------------------------------
16  1 160BR                     RNBT FBG TR OB             6  8   845        1700  2050
16  8 TRI-16                    RNBT FBG TR OB             6 10   845        1700  2050
16  8 171BR                     RNBT FBG SV OB             7  1   960        1950  2350
16  8 171SS                     RNBT FBG SV OB             7  1   940        1900  2300
17  7 180BR                     RNBT FBG SV OB             7  5  1050        2250  2600
17  7 180BR                     RNBT FBG SV IB 140         7  5  1050        2300  2700
17  7 180BR                     RNBT FBG SV JT 295         7  5  1825        3300  3800
17  7 180SS                     RNBT FBG SV OB             7  5  1010        2150  2500
17  7 180SS                     RNBT FBG SV JT 295         7  5  1785        3250  3800
18  4 184BR                     RNBT FBG SV OB             7  1  1100        2350  2750
18  4 184SS                     RNBT FBG SV OB             7  1  1050        2300  2650
18  4 BASS BOAT                 BASS FBG SV OB             7  1  1100        2350  2750
19  3 190BR                     RNBT FBG SV IB 140         7  5  1117        2450  2900
19  3 190BR                     RNBT FBG SV JT 295         7  5  1217        2750  3200
19  3 190BR                     RNBT FBG SV IB 140         7  5  2175        3800  4400
19  3 190TC                     RNBT FBG SV OB             7  5  1335        2800  3250
19  3 190TC                     RNBT FBG SV IB 140         7  5  2350        2750  3200
20  4 20SS                      RNBT FBG SV JT 295         7  5  2350        3950  4550
20  4 20SS                      RNBT FBG SV IB 198         7  5  1340        3000  3500
20  4 20SS                      RNBT FBG SV JT 295         7  4  1340        4100  4800
22  6 220PC                     RNBT FBG DV IB 228         8        1950     5300  6200
23  9 CARRERA 240 DLX      CR   FBG DV IB 198              7  9  3000        5300  6150
23  9 CARRERA SS           CR   FBG DV IB 198              7  9  2200        6750  7750
-------------------- 1981 BOATS ----------------------------------------------------------
17  7 180BR                     RNBT FBG SV OB             7  5  1050        2200  2550
17  7 180BR                     RNBT FBG SV IB 140         7  5                   2950  3400
17  7 180BR                     RNBT FBG SV JT 295         7  5                   3500  4100
17  7 180SS                     RNBT FBG SV OB             7  5  1010        2050  2450
17  7 180SS                     RNBT FBG SV JT 295         7  5                   3500  4100
19  3 190BR                     RNBT FBG SV OB             7  5  1117        2400  2800
19  3 190BR                     RNBT FBG SV IB 140         7  5                   3650  4250
19  3 190BR                     RNBT FBG SV JT 295         7  5                   4200  4900
19  3 190TC                     RNBT FBG SV OB             7  5  1335        2700  3150
19  3 190TC                     RNBT FBG SV IB 140         7  5                   3650  4250
20  4 200SS                     RNBT FBG SV IB 198         7  5                   4650  5350
20  4 20SS                      RNBT FBG SV JT 295         7  5                   5300  6050
20  4 20SS                      RNBT FBG SV IB 198         7  4  1340        2950  3400
22  6 220PC                     RNBT FBG DV IB 228         8                      7050  8100
23  9 CARRERA 240          CR   FBG DV IB 198              7  9                   7850  9150
23  9 CARRERA SS           CR   FBG DV IB 198              7  9                   7850  9000
-------------------- 1980 BOATS ----------------------------------------------------------
17  7 180BR                     RNBT FBG SV OB             7  5   980        2050  2450
17  7 180BR                     RNBT FBG SV IB 140         7  5                   2450  2850
17  7 180BR                     RNBT FBG SV IB 140         7  5                   2800  3250
17  7 180BR                     RNBT FBG SV JT 295         7  5                   3350  3900
17  7 180SS                     RNBT FBG SV OB             7  5   940        1800  2150
17  7 180SS                     RNBT FBG SV IB 140         7  5                   2350  2750
17  7 180SS                     RNBT FBG SV JT 295         7  5                   3350  3900
19  3 19BR                      RNBT FBG SV IB 140         7  5                   2750  3200
19  3 19BC                      RNBT FBG SV OB             7  5  1060        1950  2300
19  3 19BR                      RNBT FBG SV IB 140         7  5                   2750  3200
19  3 19BR                      RNBT FBG SV IB 260         7  5                   3650  4250
```

LOA FT	IN	NAME AND/OR MODEL	TOP/RIG	BOAT TYPE	MTL	TP	TP	#	HP	MFG	BEAM FT	IN	WGT LBS	DRAFT FT	IN	RETAIL LOW	RETAIL HIGH
		1980 BOATS															
19	3	19BR		RNBT	FBG	SV	JT		295-360		7	5				3800	4700
19	3	19TC		RNBT	FBG	SV	OB				7	5	1120			2600	3000
19	3	19TC		RNBT	FBG	SV	IO		140		7	5				3150	3700
19	3	19TC		RNBT	FBG	SV	IB		140-260		7	5				3700	4300
19	3	19TC		RNBT	FBG	SV	JT		295-360		7	5				4300	5000
20	4	20SS		RNBT	FBG	SV	OB				7	4	1140			2550	2950
20	4	20SS		RNBT	FBG	SV	IO		198		7	4				3700	4350
20	4	20SS		RNBT	FBG	SV	IB		198-260		7	4				4500	5250
20	4	20SS		RNBT	FBG	SV	JT		295-360		7	4				5050	5800
23	9	CARRERA 240 DLX		CR	FBG	DV	IB		198-330		7	9				8200	9450
23	9	CARRERA SS		CR	FBG	DV	IB		198		7	9				6850	7850
23	9	CARRERA SS		CR	FBG	DV	IB		330		7	9				7800	8950
		1979 BOATS															
18		180BR	OP	RNBT	FBG	SV	OB				7	5	980			1950	2350
18		180BR	OP	RNBT	FBG	SV	IO		140		7	5				2550	3000
18		180SS	OP	RNBT	FBG	SV	OB				7	5	940			1900	2250
18		180SS	OP	RNBT	FBG	SV	IO		140		7	5				2350	2750
19		19BR	OP	RNBT	FBG	SV	OB				7	5	1060			2200	2550
19		19BR	OP	RNBT	FBG	SV	IO		140		7	5				2900	3400
19		19TC		RNBT	FBG	SV	OB				7	5	1120			2300	2700
19		19TC		RNBT	FBG	SV	IO		140		7	5				2900	3400
20		20SS	OP	RNBT	FBG	SV	OB				7	4	1140			2450	2850
20		20SS	OP	RNBT	FBG	SV	IO		198		7	4				3650	4250
		1977 BOATS															
18		18 JET	OP	RNBT	FBG	SV	IB		290		7	2	1780			2350	2700
19		19BR	OP	RNBT	FBG	SV	OB				7	5	1105			2200	2550
19		19BR	OP	RNBT	FBG	SV	IO		140		7	5	1780			2350	2700
19		19BR	OP	RNBT	FBG	SV	IB		290		7	5	1780			2550	2950
19		19TC		RNBT	FBG	SV	IO		140		7	5	1285			2500	2900
19		19TC		RNBT	FBG	SV	IO		140		7	5				3000	3450
19		19TC		RNBT	FBG	SV	IB		290		7	5				3200	3750
		1976 BOATS															
18	1	18V	OP	RNBT	FBG		IB		295-360		8	8				2900	3650
19	2	18VB-V	OP	RNBT	FBG		OB				7	6	1680			2850	3300
19	2	19-TC	OP	RNBT	FBG	DV	IB		140-295		8	10				3300	4050
19	2	19-TC		RNBT	FBG	DV	IB		360		8	10				3650	4250
		1974 BOATS															
18	1	V-1800J		RNBT	FBG		JT		500	BERK	7	8	1789			2450	2850

JOHN BAKER LTD
COAST GUARD MFG ID- JBK

Call 1-800-327-6929 for BUC Personalized Evaluation Service
Or, for 1976 to 1978 boats, sign onto www.BUCValuPro.com

BALBOA MARINA

Call 1-800-327-6929 for BUC Personalized Evaluation Service
Or, for 1961 boats, sign onto www.BUCValuPro.com

BALBOA YACHTS
SEE COASTAL RECREATION INC

Call 1-800-327-6929 for BUC Personalized Evaluation Service
Or, for 1979 boats, sign onto www.BUCValuPro.com

BALD MOUNTAIN BOAT WORKS

Call 1-800-327-6929 for BUC Personalized Evaluation Service
Or, for 1966 to 1967 boats, sign onto www.BUCValuPro.com

BALDWINSVILLE SHIPBLD CORP
COAST GUARD MFG ID- BWN

Call 1-800-327-6929 for BUC Personalized Evaluation Service
Or, for 1973 to 1981 boats, sign onto www.BUCValuPro.com

BALLENGER BOATBUILDING
COAST GUARD MFG ID- BUZ

Call 1-800-327-6929 for BUC Personalized Evaluation Service
Or, for 1971 to 1983 boats, sign onto www.BUCValuPro.com

BALTIC EXPORT-IMPORT CORP

Call 1-800-327-6929 for BUC Personalized Evaluation Service
Or, for 1960 boats, sign onto www.BUCValuPro.com

BALTIC YACHTS LTD
SF68555 BOSUND FINLAND   See inside cover to adjust price for area

BALTIC YACHTS USA INC
MARBLEHEAD MA 01945

For more recent years, see the BUC Used Boat Price Guide, Volume 1 or Volume 2

LOA FT	IN	NAME AND/OR MODEL	TOP/RIG	BOAT TYPE	MTL	TP	TP	#	HP	MFG	BEAM FT	IN	WGT LBS	DRAFT FT	IN	RETAIL LOW	RETAIL HIGH
		1983 BOATS															
37		BALTIC 37	SLP	SA/CR	FBG	KL	SD		23D	VLVO	12		13600	5	9	78600	86400
38		BALTIC 38DP	SLP	SA/CR	FBG	KL	SD		30D	YAN	12	4	14300	7	3	86000	94500
38	1	BALTIC 39	SLP	SA/CR	FBG	KL	SD		23D	VLVO	12		18000	6	11	103000	113500
41	11	BALTIC 42DP	SLP	SA/CR	FBG	KL	SD		50D	PERK	13	4	18400	7	11	124000	136500
50	11	BALTIC 51	SLP	SA/CR	FBG	KL	SD		61D	VLVO	15	3	34390	8	11	259000	284500
62	11	BALTIC 63	SLP	SA/CR	FBG	KL	IB		D		17	5	52500	10	6	510000	561500
79	8	BALTIC 80	SLP	SA/CR	FBG	KL	IB		D		18	5	83600	12	7	**	**
		1982 BOATS															
37		BALTIC 37	SLP	SA/CR	FBG	KL	IB		D		12		13600	6	9	74200	81600
38	1	BALTIC 39	SLP	SA/CR	FBG	KL	IB		D		12	7	18000	6	9	97700	107500
41	11	BALTIC 42	SLP	SA/CR	FBG	KL	IB		D		13	4	18400	7	10	117500	129000
50	11	BALTIC 51	SLP	SA/CR	FBG	KL	IB		D		15	4	34300	9		244000	268500
64		BALTIC 64	SLP	SA/CR	FBG	KL	IB		D		17	5	64000	11		549000	603000
64		BALTIC 64	SLP	SA/CR	FBG	KL	IB		D		17	5	64000	11		549000	603000
64		BALTIC 64	SLP	SA/CR	FBG	KC	IB		D		17	5	64000	11		549000	603000
64		BALTIC 64	KTH	SA/CR	FBG	KL	IB		D		17	5	64000	11		549000	603000
		1981 BOATS															
37		BALTIC 37	SLP	SA/CR	FBG	KL	IB		D		12			6	7	84700	93000
38	1	BALTIC 39	SLP	SA/CR	FBG	KL	IB		D		12	5		6	9	79500	87300
41	11	BALTIC 42	SLP	SA/CR	FBG	KL	IB		D		12	6		7	1	115000	126500
50	11	BALTIC 51	SLP	SA/CR	FBG	KL	IB		D		15			9		208000	228500
		1980 BOATS															
32	8	BALTIC 33	SLP	SA/CR	FBG	KL	IB		D		10	5		5	5	55700	61300
37		BALTIC 37	SLP	SA/CR	FBG	KL	IB		D		12			6	7	80600	88500
38	1	BALTIC 39	SLP	SA/CR	FBG	KL	IB		D		12	5		6	9	75600	83100
41	11	BALTIC 42	SLP	SA/CR	FBG	KL	IB		D		12	6		7	1	110000	120500
46	2	BALTIC 46	SLP	SA/CR	FBG	KL	IB		D		13	7		7	5	151000	166000
50	11	BALTIC 51	SLP	SA/CR	FBG	KL	IB		D		15			8		198000	218500
		1979 BOATS															
32	8	BALTIC 33	SLP	SA/CR	FBG	KL	IB		D		10	5		5	9	53600	58900
38	1	BALTIC 39	SLP	SA/CR	FBG	KL	IB		D		12	5		6	9	72700	79900
41	11	BALTIC 42	SLP	SA/CR	FBG	KL	IB		D		12	6		7	1	105500	116000
46	2	BALTIC 46	SLP	SA/CR	FBG	KL	IB		D		13	7		7	5	145000	159500

BALTZER SHIPYARDS
NEWBURYPORT MA   See inside cover to adjust price for area

LOA FT	IN	NAME AND/OR MODEL	TOP/RIG	BOAT TYPE	MTL	TP	TP	#	HP	MFG	BEAM FT	IN	WGT LBS	DRAFT FT	IN	RETAIL LOW	RETAIL HIGH
		1954 BOATS															
26		CAMP-CRUISER	HT	CBNCR	WD	SV	VD		100	GRAY	8	6				6200	7100
38	8		HT	SDN	WD	RB	IB		T145	NORD	12	4		3	6	39200	43600
38	8		HT	SDN	WD	RB	IB		T200	CHRY	12	4				39500	43800
		1953 BOATS															
31	4		HT	EXP	WD	RB	IB		160	CHRY	9	9				14300	16300
33		CAPE-ISLAND	HT	SDN	WD	RB	IB				11					**	**
36	10		HT	DC	WD	RB	IB				11	10				**	**
36	10	VOYAGEUR	HT	SDN	WD	RB	IB				11	10				**	**
		1952 BOATS															
32	10	CAPE-ISLANDER	OP	EXP	WD	RB	IB		100		10	2		3		17500	19900
32	10	CAPE-ISLANDER	HT	SDN	WD	RB	IB		100		10	2		3		15700	17800
36		VOYAGEUR	HT	SDN	WD	RB	IB				11					**	**
40		SEAMASTER	HT	MY	WD	RB	IB				11					**	**
		1950 BOATS															
32			HT	SPTCR	WD	RB	IB									**	**
33		VOYAGEUR	HT	CR	WD	RB	IB									**	**
36	6	VOYAGEUR	HT	SDN	WD	RB	IB		100	PACK	11			3	4	31300	34800
40		SEAMASTER	HT	MY	WD	RB	IB		T	PACK						**	**

LOA FT IN	NAME AND/ OR MODEL	TOP/ RIG	BOAT TYPE	-HULL- MTL TP	ENGINE TP # HP	MFG	BEAM FT IN	WGT LBS	DRAFT FT IN	RETAIL LOW	RETAIL HIGH
					1949 BOATS						
28	VOYAGEUR JUNIOR	HT	CBNCR	WD	RB IB					**	**
33 4	VOYAGEUR	HT	CBNCR	WD	RB IB					**	**
40 6	SEAMASTER	HT	CR	WD	RB IB		12 4			**	**
40 6	SEAMASTER	FB	SF	WD	RB IB		12 4			**	**
					1941 BOATS						
32 6	DREADNAUGHT	HT	SDN	WD	RB IB 100	KERM	10 10		3	13800	15700
					1939 BOATS						
34 6		HT	CR	WD	RB IB		10 5		3 6	**	**
					1937 BOATS						
32			SDN	WD	RB IB 85	KERM				13200	15000

BANANA BOAT COMPANY
DIV OF MULTI TRANS   COAST GUARD MFG ID- BCV

Call 1-800-327-6929 for BUC Personalized Evaluation Service
Or, for 1977 to 1980 boats, sign onto www.BUCValuPro.com

BANSHEE INTERNATIONAL INC
COAST GUARD MFG ID- BSD

Call 1-800-327-6929 for BUC Personalized Evaluation Service
Or, for 1974 to 1986 boats, sign onto www.BUCValuPro.com

BARBERIS YACHTS/SMI
LARCHMONT NY 10538   See inside cover to adjust price for area

For more recent years, see the BUC Used Boat Price Guide, Volume 1 or Volume 2

LOA FT IN	NAME AND/ OR MODEL	TOP/ RIG	BOAT TYPE	-HULL- MTL TP	ENGINE TP # HP	MFG	BEAM FT IN	WGT LBS	DRAFT FT IN	RETAIL LOW	RETAIL HIGH
					1983 BOATS						
23 4	SHOW 24	SLP	SA/CR	FBG KL	OB		8 2	2100	4 5	5250	6050
27 6	SHOW 27	SLP	SA/CR	FBG KL	IB 8D	YAN	9 8	4840	5 6	13000	14800
27 6	SHOW 27 SHOAL	SLP	SA/CR	FBG KL	IB 8D	YAN	9 8	4840	4 11	13000	14800
29 6	SHOW 29	SLP	SA/CR	FBG KL	SD 15D	YAN	10 2	6380		18100	20100
29 6	SHOW 29 SHOAL	SLP	SA/CR	FBG KL	IB 15D	YAN	10 2	6380	5 7	18100	20100
29 6	SHOW 30	SLP	SA/CR	FBG KC	IB 15D	YAN	10 2	6380		18100	20100
33 8	SHOW 34	SLP	SA/CR	FBG KC	IB 23D	YAN	11 2	10780	6	30700	34100
33 8	SHOW 34 SHOAL	SLP	SA/CR	FBG KC	IB 23D	YAN	11 2	10780		30700	34100
37 8	SHOW 38	SLP	SA/CR	FBG KL	IB 23D	YAN	12 7	11220		35800	39800
37 8	SHOW 38	SLP	SA/CR	FBG KL	IB 23D	YAN	12 7	11220		35800	39800
37 8	SHOW 38 SHOAL	SLP	SA/CR	FBG KL	IB 23D	YAN	12 7	11220	6 3	35800	39800
41 5	SHOW 42	SLP	SA/CR	FBG KC	IB 50D	PERK	13	18480	5 6	63800	70100
41 5	SHOW 42	SLP	SA/CR	FBG KL	IB 50D	PERK	13	18480	6 10	63800	70100
41 5	SHOW 42 SHOAL	SLP	SA/CR	FBG KL	IB 50D	PERK	13	18480	5 8	63800	70100

BARBOUR BOATS INC
COAST GUARD MFG ID- BAB

Call 1-800-327-6929 for BUC Personalized Evaluation Service
Or, for 1953 to 1971 boats, sign onto www.BUCValuPro.com

BARCONE MARINE CORP
COAST GUARD MFG ID- BMC

Call 1-800-327-6929 for BUC Personalized Evaluation Service
Or, for 1971 to 1972 boats, sign onto www.BUCValuPro.com

BARNES

Call 1-800-327-6929 for BUC Personalized Evaluation Service
Or, for 1948 to 1967 boats, sign onto www.BUCValuPro.com

BARRACUDA

Call 1-800-327-6929 for BUC Personalized Evaluation Service
Or, for 1959 to 1961 boats, sign onto www.BUCValuPro.com

BARTEL BOATS
COAST GUARD MFG ID- RTC

Call 1-800-327-6929 for BUC Personalized Evaluation Service
Or, for 1982 to 1996 boats, sign onto www.BUCValuPro.com

BARTON ENTERPRISES

Call 1-800-327-6929 for BUC Personalized Evaluation Service
Or, for 1965 boats, sign onto www.BUCValuPro.com

BASS BOATS INC
COAST GUARD MFG ID- BBT

Call 1-800-327-6929 for BUC Personalized Evaluation Service
Or, for 1965 to 1968 boats, sign onto www.BUCValuPro.com

BAY CITY BOATS INC

Call 1-800-327-6929 for BUC Personalized Evaluation Service
Or, for 1952 to 1968 boats, sign onto www.BUCValuPro.com

BAY ISLAND YACHTS

Call 1-800-327-6929 for BUC Personalized Evaluation Service
Or, for 1983 boats, sign onto www.BUCValuPro.com

BAY YACHTS
COAST GUARD MFG ID- BYT

Call 1-800-327-6929 for BUC Personalized Evaluation Service
Or, for 1974 to 1977 boats, sign onto www.BUCValuPro.com

BAYCRAFT BOAT SHOP
COAST GUARD MFG ID- BB7
FORMERLY LUNENBURG DORY

Call 1-800-327-6929 for BUC Personalized Evaluation Service
Or, for 1983 boats, sign onto www.BUCValuPro.com

BAYCRAFT MARINE

Call 1-800-327-6929 for BUC Personalized Evaluation Service
Or, for 1983 to 1985 boats, sign onto www.BUCValuPro.com

BAYFIELD BOAT YARD LTD
CLINTON ONTARIO CANADA   COAST GUARD MFG ID- ZBY See inside cover to adjust price for area

For more recent years, see the BUC Used Boat Price Guide, Volume 1 or Volume 2

LOA FT IN	NAME AND/ OR MODEL	TOP/ RIG	BOAT TYPE	-HULL- MTL TP	ENGINE TP # HP	MFG	BEAM FT IN	WGT LBS	DRAFT FT IN	RETAIL LOW	RETAIL HIGH
					1983 BOATS						
25	BAYFIELD 25	SLP	SA/CR	FBG KL	IB 9D	YAN	8	3500	2 11	9550	10900
29	BAYFIELD 29	CUT	SA/CR	FBG KL	IB 18D	YAN	10 2	7100	3 6	21900	24300
32	BAYFIELD 32	CUT	SA/CR	FBG KL	IB 18D	YAN	10 6	9600	3 9	31200	34700
32	BAYFIELD 32	KTH	SA/CR	FBG KL	IB 18D	YAN	10 6	9600	3 9	31200	34700
32 2	BAYFIELD 32C	CUT	SA/CR	FBG KL	IB 18D	YAN	10 6	9600	3 9	31200	34600
					1982 BOATS						
25	BAYFIELD 25	SLP	SA/CR	FBG KL	IB 8D	YAN	8	3500	2 11	9000	10200
29	BAYFIELD 29	CUT	SA/CR	FBG KL	IB 12D	YAN	10 2	7100	3 6	20500	22800
32	BAYFIELD 32	CUT	SA/CR	FBG KL	IB 15D	YAN	10 6	9600	3 9	29400	32700
32	BAYFIELD 32-C	CUT	SA/CR	FBG KL	IB 15D	YAN	10 6	10000	3 9	30600	34000
					1981 BOATS						
25	BAYFIELD 25	SLP	SA/CR	FBG KL	IB 8D	YAN	8	3500	2 11	8400	9650
29	BAYFIELD 29	CUT	SA/CR	FBG KL	IB 12D	YAN	10 2	7100	3 6	19300	21500
32	BAYFIELD 32	CUT	SA/CR	FBG KL	IB 15D	YAN	10 6	9600	3 9	27600	30700
32	BAYFIELD 32	KTH	SA/CR	FBG KL	IB 15D	YAN	10 6	9600	3 9	27600	30700
32	BAYFIELD 32-C	CUT	SA/CR	FBG KL	IB 15D	YAN	10 6	10000	3 9	28800	32000

LOA FT	LOA IN	NAME AND/ OR MODEL	TOP/ RIG	BOAT TYPE	HULL MTL	HULL TP	ENGINE TP	ENGINE # HP	ENGINE MFG	BEAM FT	BEAM IN	WGT LBS	DRAFT FT	DRAFT IN	RETAIL LOW	RETAIL HIGH
		1980 BOATS														
25		BAYFIELD 25	SLP	SA/CR	FBG	KL	IB	8D	YAN	8		3500	2	11	8000	9200
29		BAYFIELD 29	CUT	SA/CR	FBG	KL	IB	12D	YAN	10	2	7100	3	6	18700	20700
32		BAYFIELD 32	CUT	SA/CR	FBG	KL	IB	15D	YAN	10	6	9600	3	9	26400	29300
		1979 BOATS														
25		BAYFIELD 25	SLP	SA/CR	FBG	KL	IB	8D	YAN	8		3500	2	11	7700	8850
29		BAYFIELD 29	CUT	SA/CR	FBG	KL	IB	12D	YAN	10	2	7100	3	6	17500	19900
32		BAYFIELD 32	CUT	SA/CR	FBG	KL	IB	15D	YAN	10	6	9600	3	9	25400	28200
32		BAYFIELD 32	KTH	SA/CR	FBG	KL	IB	15D	YAN	10	6	9600	3	9	25400	28200
		1978 BOATS														
25		BAYFIELD 25	SLP	SA/CR	FBG	KL	IB	8D	YAN	8		3500	2	11	7400	8550
29		BAYFIELD 29	CUT	SA/CR	FBG	KL	IB	12D	YAN	10	2	7100	3	5	16900	19200
32		BAYFIELD 32	CUT	SA/CR	FBG	KL	IB	15D	YAN	10	6	9500	3	9	24200	26900
32		BAYFIELD 32	CUT	SA/CR	FBG	KL	VD	20D	YAN	10	6	9500	3	9	24200	26900
32		BAYFIELD 32	KTH	SA/CR	FBG	KL	IB	15D	YAN	10	6	9500	3	9	24200	26900
32		BAYFIELD 32	KTH	SA/CR	FBG	KL	VD	20D	YAN	10	6	9500	3	9	24200	26900
		1977 BOATS														
25		BAYFIELD 23/25	SLP	SA/CR	FBG	KL	IB	8D	YAN	8		3500	2	11	7200	8250
29		BAYFIELD 27/29	CUT	SA/CR	FBG	KL	IB	12D	YAN	10		7100	3	5	16300	18600
32		BAYFIELD 30/32	CUT	SA/CR	FBG	KL	IB	12D	YAN	10	6	9500	3	9	23400	26000
32		BAYFIELD 30/32	CUT	SA/CR	FBG	KL	VD	20D	YAN	10	6	9500	3	9	23400	26000
32		BAYFIELD 30/32	KTH	SA/CR	FBG	KL	IB	12D	YAN	10	6	9500	3	9	23400	26000
32		BAYFIELD 30/32	KTH	SA/CR	FBG	KL	VD	20D	YAN	10	6	9500	3	9	23400	26000
		1976 BOATS														
25		BAYFIELD 23/25	SLP	SAIL	FBG	KL	IB	8D	YAN	8		3500	2	11	6950	8000
32		BAYFIELD 30/32	CUT	SAIL	FBG	KL	IB	24D	FARY	10	6	9500	3	9	22700	25200
		1975 BOATS														
25		BAYFIELD 23/25	SLP	SAIL	FBG	KL	IB	7D	WEST	8		3000	2	6	6000	6900
27		BAYFIELD 26/27	CUT	SAIL	FBG	KL	IB	8D	YAN	8	6	4000	2	9	8200	9400
32		BAYFIELD 30/32	CUT	SAIL	FBG	KL	IB	24D	FARY	10	6	8500	3	9	19700	21900
		1974 BOATS														
25		BAYFIELD 23	SLP	SA/CR	FBG	KL	IB	7D	WEST	8			2	6	7600	8750
32		BAYFIELD 30	SLP	SA/CR	FBG	KL	VD	30	UNIV	10		8500	3	9	19200	21300

BAYHEAD YACHT CORP

PT PLEASANT BEACH NJ COAST GUARD MFG ID- BYC See inside cover to adjust price for area

LOA FT	LOA IN	NAME AND/ OR MODEL	TOP/ RIG	BOAT TYPE	HULL MTL	HULL TP	ENGINE TP	ENGINE # HP	ENGINE MFG	BEAM FT	BEAM IN	WGT LBS	DRAFT FT	DRAFT IN	RETAIL LOW	RETAIL HIGH
		1974 BOATS														
30	7	TOURNAMENT FISHERMAN		SF	FBG		IB	T330-T350		11	6	12500	2	6	31900	36000
30	7	TOURNAMENT FISHERMAN		SF	FBG		IB	T210D-T225D		11	6	13500	2	6	44600	50900
		1973 BOATS														
30	9	TOURNAMENT FISHERMAN		SF	FBG		IB	T330	CHRY	11		13500	2	4	31700	35200
30	9	TOURNAMENT FISHERMAN		SF	FBG		IB	T210D	CUM	11			2	4	38900	43200
		1972 BOATS														
30				SF	WD		IB	T330	CHRY	11	2	11000	2	6	27000	30000
33		PURSUIT		SF	WD		IB	T330	CHRY	11	6	13500	2	9	36700	40800
36		SUPER-PURSUIT		FSH	WD		IB	T330	CHRY	13		17000	2	10	47300	51900
36		SUPERSPORT		EXP	WD		IB	T330	CHRY	13		17000	2	10	49100	54000
38		MARAUDER		SF	WD		IB	T425	DAY	13	6	19500	3		57900	63600
40		COMMUTER		SF	WD		IB	T425	DAY	14		22500	3	3	68100	74800
42			FB	SDN	WD		IB	T425	DAY	14	6	25000	3	4	79800	87700
43		CANYON-COMMUTER		SF	WD		IB	T325D	GM	14	8	27500	3	6	101000	111000
44		SEASPACE		MY	WD		IB	T325D	GM	15		33000	4		111000	121500
		1971 BOATS														
30				SF	WD		IB	T300	CHRY	11	2	11000	2	6	25600	28500
33		PURSUIT		SF	WD		IB	T300	CHRY	11	6	13500	2	9	34800	38700
36		SUPER-PURSUIT		FSH	WD		IB	T325	CHRY	13		17000	2	10	45000	50000
36		SUPERSPORT		EXP	WD		IB	T325	CHRY	13		17000	2	10	47300	52000
38		MARAUDER		SF	WD		IB	T425	DAY	13	6	19500	3		55800	61400
40		COMMUTER		SF	WD		IB	T425	DAY	14		22500	3	3	65700	72200
42			FB	SDN	WD		IB	T425	DAY	14	6	25000	3	4	77000	84600
43		CANYON-COMMUTER		SF	WD		IB	T300D	GM	14	8	27500	3	6	95700	105000
44		SEASPACE		MY	WD		IB	T325D	GM	15		33000	4		107000	117500
		1970 BOATS														
30		BIMINI		SF	WD	RB	IB	T210	CHRY	11		10000	2	6	23000	25500
33		PURSUIT		SF	WD		IB	T300	CHRY	11	6	13000	2	8	33100	36800
36		SUPER-PURSUIT		SF	WD	RB	IB	T325	CHRY	13		16000	2	9	42800	47500
36		SUPERSPORT		EXP	WD	RB	IB	T300	CHRY	13		16000	2	9	43400	48300
38		MARAUDER		SF	WD	RB	IB	T425	DAY	13	6	18000	3		51200	56300
40		COMMUTER		SF	WD	RB	IB	T425	DAY	14		20000	3		58700	64500
40		DECKHOUSE	FB	CR	WD	RB	IB	T425	DAY	14		21500	3	3	63900	70200
43		CANYON-COMMUTER		SF	WD	RB	IB	T425	DAY	14	6	25000	3	6	80600	88600
44		SEASPACE		MY	WD	RB	IB	T283D	GM	15		30000	4		94000	103500
		1969 BOATS														
30		BIMINI		SF	WD	RB	IB	T210	CHRY	11		10000	2	6	22100	24600
33		PURSUIT		SF	WD	RB	IB	T300	CHRY	11	6	13000	2	8	31900	35400
36		SUPER-PURSUIT		SF	WD	RB	IB	T325	CHRY	13		16000	2	9	41300	45900
36		SUPERSPORT		EXP	WD	RB	IB	T300	CHRY	13		16000	2	9	42000	46700
38		MARAUDER		SF	WD	RB	IB	T425	DAY	13	6	18000	3		50000	54900
40		COMMUTER		SF	WD	RB	IB	T425	DAY	14		20000	3		56700	62300
40		DECKHOUSE	FB	CR	WD	RB	IB	T425	DAY	14		21500	3	3	62100	68200
43		CANYON-COMMUTER		SF	WD	RB	IB	T425	DAY	14	6	25000	3	6	77900	85600
44		SEASPACE		DCMY	WD	RB	IB	T283D	GM	15		30000	4		92000	101000
		1968 BOATS														
30				SF	WD		IB	T225	CHRY	11		10000	2	6	21700	24100
33		PURSUIT		SF	WD		IB	T320	CHRY	11	6	13000	2	8	31000	34400
36		SUPER-PURSUIT		SF	WD		IB	T320	CHRY	13		16000	2	9	39900	44400
36		SUPERSPORT		EXP	WD		IB	T320	CHRY	13		16000	2	9	40900	45500
38		MARAUDER		SF	WD		IB	T425	DAY	13	6	18000	3		48400	53200
40			FB	MYDKH	WD		IB	T425	DAY	14		21500	3	3	59700	65600
40		COMMUTER		SF	WD		IB	T425	DAY	14		20000	3		54900	60300
43		CANYON-COMMUTER		SF	WD		IB	T425	DAY	14	6	25000	3	6	75400	82800
44		SEASPACE		MY	WD		IB	T283D	DAY	15		30000	4		87500	96200
		1967 BOATS														
30		BIMINI		SF	L/P		IB	T238		11			2	4	18600	20700
30		BIMINI	OP	SF	P/C		IB	T220							18600	20700
33				SF	P/C		IB	T220							25600	28500
33		PURSUIT		SF	L/P		IB	T280		11	6		2	6	26200	29100
33		PURSUIT		SF	P/C		IB	T290							26400	29400
36		PURSUIT		SF	L/P		IB	T280		12	6		2	8	35900	39900
36		PURSUIT		SF	P/C		IB	T290							35100	39000
36		SUPERSPORT		EXP	P/C		IB	T290							37600	41800
38		MARAUDER		SF	L/P		IB	T277		13			2	10	45900	50400
38		MARAUDER		SF	P/C		IB	T380							45900	50500
40			FB	SDN	L/P		IB	T277		13	6		3		54500	59900
40			FB	SDN	P/C		IB	T380							54600	60000
40		COMMUTER		SF	L/P		IB	T277		13	6		3		54400	59800
40		COMMUTER		SF	P/C		IB	T435							55300	60800
43		CANYON-COMMUTER		SF	P/C		IB	T435							73400	80700
44		SEASPACE	FB	DCMY	P/C		IB	T283D							81700	89800
		1966 BOATS														
30				SF	WD		IB	T225							17600	20000
30		CARIBBEAN		CR	WD		IB	T300							19700	21900
33	6			SF	WD		IB	T225							26000	28900
33	6	PURSUIT		SF	WD		IB	T280		11	6		2	4	26400	29400
36	6	PURSUIT		SF	WD		IB	T280		12	6		2	5	36400	40400
36	6	SUPERSPORT		EXP	WD		IB	T250		12	6		2	5	38700	43000
38		MARAUDER		SF	WD		IB	T300		13			2	6	44200	49100
40		COMMUTER		SF	WD		IB	T300		13			3		54500	59900
42		COMMUTER		SF	WD		IB	T380D		13	6		3	6	85100	93600
43		SEASPACE		DC	WD		IB	T280D		14			3	6	83000	91200
		1965 BOATS														
30				SF	WD		IB	T225							16900	19300
33	6	PURSUIT		SF	WD		IB	T290							25700	28600
36	6	PURSUIT		SF	WD		IB	T290							34500	38300
36	6	SUPERSPORT		EXP	WD		IB	T290							36900	41000
38		MARAUDER		SF	WD		IB	T380							42800	47600
40		COMMUTER		SF	WD		IB	T425							52400	57600
42		COMMUTER		SF	WD		IB	T380D							80500	88500
44		SEASPACE		MY	WD		IB	T283D							78700	86500
		1964 BOATS														
30				SF	WD		IB	T225							16300	18600
33		PURSUIT		SF	WD		IB	T280							23600	26200
36		PURSUIT		SF	WD		IB	T280							32100	35600
38		MARAUDER		SF	WD		IB	T300							40500	45000
40		COMMUTER		SF	WD		IB	T300							49200	54100
42		COMMUTER		SF	WD		IB	T380D							78400	86100
		1963 BOATS														
30	2			SF	WD		IB	T225							16500	18800
30	2	BIMINI		CR	WD		IB	T225							16900	19200
30	2	CARIBBEAN		CR	WD		IB	T300							18100	20100
30	2	CARIBBEAN		SF	WD		IB	T225							15300	17300
33	6			SF	WD		IB	T225							27800	30900
33	6	BIMINI		SF	WD		IB	T225							19000	21100
33	6	PURSUIT	FB	SF	WD		IB	T225							23400	26000
36	3	PURSUIT	FB	SF	WD		IB	T300							32200	35800
36	3	SUPERSPORT		EXP	WD		IB	T225							33800	37500
36	3	SUPERSPORT		EXP	WD		IB	T120D							41200	45700
38		MARAUDER	FB	SF	WD		IB	T300							39700	44100
40		COMMUTER	FB	SF	WD		IB	T300							48200	52900
		1961 BOATS														
30		CARIBBEAN		CR	L/P		IB	450		10			2	6	15600	17700
30		DAY SPORTFISHERMAN		SF	L/P		IB	376		10			2	6	14200	16100

CONTINUED ON NEXT PAGE

BAYHEAD YACHT CORP -CONTINUED See inside cover to adjust price for area

LOA FT	LOA IN	NAME AND/ OR MODEL	TOP/ RIG	BOAT TYPE	HULL MTL	HULL TP	ENGINE TP	ENGINE # HP	ENGINE MFG	BEAM FT	BEAM IN	WGT LBS	DRAFT FT	DRAFT IN	RETAIL LOW	RETAIL HIGH
		1961 BOATS														
33		EXPRESS CR		CR	L/P		IB	450		11			2	6	22600	25100
33		PURSUIT		SF	L/P		IB	450		11			2	6	21200	23600
36		SUPERSPORT		EXP	L/P		IB	550		12			2	9	34300	38100
		1960 BOATS														
30				SF	WD		IB	T280	GRAY						15100	17100
30	3	CARIBBEAN		EXP	CDR		IB	T177-T300		10	7		2	4	16700	20300
30	3	DAY SPORTFISHERMAN		SF	CDR		IB	T177-T240		10	7		2	3	14300	16800
33	6	EXPRESS SPORTFISHRMN		SF	CDR		IB	T225-T300		11			2	4	22000	25200
36	6	SUPERSPORT		EXP	CDR		IB	T225		12			2	6	34100	37800
36	6	SUPERSPORT		EXP	CDR		IB	T300		12			2	6	34600	38400
		1959 BOATS														
30		BLUEWATER DAY SPORT		FSH	L/P		IB	300		10	6				13500	15300
36		SUPERSPORT		EXP	L/P		IB	300		12					30700	34100

BAYLINER MARINE CORP

DIV OF BRUNSWICK
ARLINGTON WA 98223

COAST GUARD MFG ID- BLB
ALSO SEE TROPHY

See inside cover to adjust price for area

For more recent years, see the BUC Used Boat Price Guide, Volume 1 or Volume 2

LOA FT	LOA IN	NAME AND/ OR MODEL	TOP/ RIG	BOAT TYPE	HULL MTL	HULL TP	ENGINE TP	ENGINE # HP	ENGINE MFG	BEAM FT	BEAM IN	WGT LBS	DRAFT FT	DRAFT IN	RETAIL LOW	RETAIL HIGH
		1983 BOATS														
18	8	CAPRI 1950 B/R	ST	RNBT	FBG	DV	IO	120-175		7	6	1995	2	8	2500	3100
18	8	CAPRI 1950 C/B	ST	RNBT	FBG	DV	IO	120-175		7	6	1950	2	8	2500	3100
18	8	CAPRI CUD 1950	ST	CUD	FBG	DV	IO	120-175		7	6	2045	2	9	2750	3200
18	8	COBRA 1950	ST	RNBT	FBG	DV	IO	170	MRCR	8		2316	2	11	2850	3300
18	8	COBRA 1950	ST	RNBT	FBG	DV	IO	225-260		8		2316	2	11	3050	3700
20	1	EXPLORER 2070	ST	CR	FBG	SV	IO	120	VLVO	8		2870	2	9	4100	4750
20	1	TROPHY FSH 2060	ST	FSH	FBG	SV	IO	120	VLVO	8		2725			4200	4850
20	8	CIERA 2150	ST	CR	FBG	DV	IO	120-225		8		3150	3		4500	5350
22	3	EXPLORER 2270	HT	CR	FBG	SV	IO	120	VLVO	8		4200	3	2	5950	6800
22	3	TROPHY FSH 2260	ST	FSH	FBG	SV	IO	120	VLVO	8		3600			5600	6450
22	9	COBRA OFF 2350	ST	SPTCR	FBG	DV	IO	260		8		3650	3	4	5600	6700
23	8	CIERA COMM BR 2450	FB	CBNCR	FBG	DV	IO	170-260		8		4350	3		7300	8950
23	8	CIERA COMM BR 2450	FB	CBNCR	FBG	DV	IO	T120-T170		8		4350	3		8400	9650
23	8	CIERA SB 2450	ST	CR	FBG	DV	IO	170-260		8		3950	3		6000	7400
23	8	CIERA SB 2450	ST	CR	FBG	DV	IO	T120-T170		8		3950	3		6950	7950
26	1	EXPLORER 2670	HT	CR	FBG	SV	IO	120	VLVO	8		5500	2	2	8150	9350
27		VICTORIA SB 2750	ST	CR	FBG	DV	IO	T120-T175		8		5440			9600	11600
27		VICTORIA SUNBR 2750	ST	CR	FBG	DV	IO	260		8		5440	3	3	9400	10700
27		VICTORIA SUNBR 2750	ST	CR	FBG	DV	IO	T170	MRCR	8		5440	3	3	9950	11300
27	5	CONTESSA SB 2850	ST	CR	FBG	DV	IO	260		10		6440			10800	12400
27	5	CONTESSA SB 2850	ST	CR	FBG	DV	IO	T120-T175		10		6440			11100	13200
27	5	CONTESSA SB 2850	ST	CR	FBG	DV	IO	T225	VLVO	10		6440			12200	13900
27	5	CONTESSA SDN BR 2850	FB	CBNCR	FBG	DV	IO	260		10		6770			13700	15700
27	5	CONTESSA SDN BR 2850	FB	CBNCR	FBG	DV	IO	T120-T225		10		6770			13900	16500
31	7	CONQUEST SUNBR 3250	ST	CBNCR	FBG	DV	IO	T225	VLVO	11	11	10150			24000	26700
31	7	CONQUEST SUNBR 3250	FB	OFF	FBG	DV	IO	T260		11	11	10150	3		19700	21900
31	7	CONQUEST SUNBR 3250	FB	OFF	FBG	DV	VD	T350		11	11	10150	3		25800	28600
31	7	CONQUEST SUNBR 3250	FB	OFF	FBG	DV	VD	T155D	VLVO	11	11	10950	3		28300	31400
32	1	EXPLORER 3270	FB	MY	FBG	DV	IB	T140		11	6	12950			27900	31000
32	1	EXPLORER 3270	FB	MY	FBG	DV	IB	T 90D	BMC	11	6	12950			35300	39200
32	1	EXPLORER COMD BR3270	FB	DCMY	FBG	SV	IB	T165		11	6	13400			28700	31900
38	2	EXPLORER CB 3870	FB	DCMY	FBG	SV	IB	T130D	BMC	13	5	19608			57800	63500
40		BODEGA 4050	FB	MY	FBG	SV	IB	T454		14		23000	3	6	68000	74800
40		BODEGA 4050	FB	MY	FBG	SV	IB	T286D	VLVO	14		23000	3	6	72200	79300
		1982 BOATS														
16	6	FORCE 1650	ST	RNBT	FBG	DV	IO	140	MRCR	7	2	1545			1850	2200
16	8	MUTINY 1750	ST	RNBT	FBG	DV	IO	120	MRCR	6	10	1700			1900	2250
16	8	MUTINY 1750	ST	RNBT	FBG	DV	IO	125	VLVO	6	10	1700			2000	2400
16	8	MUTINY 1750 B/R	ST	RNBT	FBG	DV	IO	120	MRCR	6	10	1745			1900	2300
16	8	MUTINY 1750 B/R	ST	RNBT	FBG	DV	IO	125	VLVO	6	10	1745			2050	2400
16	8	MUTINY 1750 OFFSHORE	ST	RNBT	FBG	DV	IO	140	MRCR	6	10	1700			1900	2250
18	6	LIBERTY 2050	ST	CUD	FBG	DV	IO	120-175		7	4	2225			2600	3200
18	8	CAPRI 1950 B/R	ST	RNBT	FBG	DV	IO	120-175		7	6	1995			2450	3050
18	8	CAPRI 1950 C/B	ST	RNBT	FBG	DV	IO	120-175		7	6	1950			2450	3000
18	8	EAGLE 1950	ST	RNBT	FBG	DV	IO	170-175		8		1950			2550	3150
18	8	EAGLE 1950	ST	RNBT	FBG	DV	IO	225-260		8		1950			2800	3400
18	8	EAGLE 1950 OFFSHORE	ST	RNBT	FBG	DV	IO	170-175		8		2316			2750	3350
18	8	EAGLE 1950 OFFSHORE	ST	RNBT	FBG	DV	IO	225-260		8		2316			3000	3650
20	1	EXPLORER 2070	ST	CR	FBG	SV	IO	125	VLVO	8		2870			4000	4650
20	1	TROPHY 2010		FSH	FBG		OB			8		2700			3500	4100
20	8	SANTIAGO OFF 2250	ST	SPTCR	FBG	DV	IO	120-175		8		2500			3700	4500
20	8	SANTIAGO OFF 2250	ST	SPTCR	FBG	DV	IO	225-260		8		2500			3950	4800
22	3	EXPLORER 2270	HT	CR	FBG	DV	IO	60D		8		4200			6650	7650
22	3	EXPLORER 2270	HT	CR	FBG	SV	IO	125	VLVO	8		4200			5800	6650
22	3	TROPHY 2260		FSH	FBG		IO	125	VLVO	8		3600			5500	6300
22	8	MONTEREY 2350	FB	CR	FBG	DV	IO	225-260		8		4525			6400	7400
22	8	MONTEREY SUNBR 2350	ST	CR	FBG	DV	IO	170-260		8		4095			5700	6900
22	8	MONTEREY SUNBR 2350	ST	CR	FBG	DV	IO	T145	VLVO	8		3975			6500	7500
22	9	COBRA OFF 2350	ST	SPTCR	FBG	DV	IO	260		8		3650			5500	6550
22	9	COBRA OFF 2350	ST	SPTCR	FBG	DV	IO	330	MRCR	8		3650			6100	7000
22	9	COBRA OFF 2350	ST	SPTCR	FBG	DV	IO	T170	MRCR	8		3650			5950	6850
24	9	SARATOGA 2550	FB	CR	FBG	DV	IO	260	MRCR	8		5010			7650	8800
24	9	SARATOGA 2550	FB	CR	FBG	DV	IO	T145	VLVO	8		5010			8300	9550
24	9	SARATOGA 2550	FB	CR	FBG	SV	IO	260	VLVO	8		5010			7800	9000
24	9	SARATOGA SUNBR 2550	ST	CR	FBG	DV	IO	228-260		8		4740			7200	8650
24	9	SARATOGA SUNBR 2550	ST	CR	FBG	DV	IO	T125-T145		8		4740			7950	9200
24	9	SARATOGA SUNBR 2550	ST	CR	FBG	SV	IO	225	VLVO	8		4740			7300	8400
26	1	EXPLORER 2670		CR	FBG	SV	IB	125-140		8		5500			9550	11000
26	1	EXPLORER 2670		CR	FBG	SV	IB	90D	BMC	8		5500			11500	13100
26	1	TROPHY 2660		FSH	FBG		IO	125	VLVO	8		5250			8150	9400
26	1	TROPHY 2660		FSH	FBG	SV	IO	140	VLVO	8		5250			8250	9500
26	1	TROPHY 2660		FSH	FBG	SV	IO	90D	BMC	8		5250			10300	11700
27		VICTORIA 2750	FB	CR	FBG	DV	IO	260	MRCR	8		5770			9400	10700
27		VICTORIA 2750	FB	CR	FBG	DV	IO	T125-T170		8		5840			9800	11400
27		VICTORIA 2750	FB	CR	FBG	SV	IO	260	VLVO	8		5770			9500	10800
27		VICTORIA SUNBR 2750	ST	CR	FBG	DV	IO	260	MRCR	8		5440			9200	10400
27		VICTORIA SUNBR 2750	ST	CR	FBG	DV	IO	T145-T170		8		5440			9650	11100
27		VICTORIA SUNBR 2750	ST	CR	FBG	SV	IO	260	VLVO	8		5440			9300	10500
27	11	ENCOUNTER 2950	FB	SDN	FBG	DV	VD	T155	VLVO	11	5	11300			20300	22500
		IO T170 MRCR 16700 18900, IB T170 19200 21300, IO T200-T260													17200	20400
		VD T350 VLVO 23200 25800, IB T130D VLVO 30400 33800														
27	11	ENCOUNTER SUNBR 2950	ST	CR	FBG	DV	IO	260		11	5	9645			13800	15800
		IO T170 MRCR 14400 16300, IB T170 16500 18700, IO T200-T260													14800	17600
		IO T130D VLVO 18900 21000, VD T155D VLVO 25400 28300														
31	7	CONQUEST SUNBR 3150	ST	OFF	FBG	DV	IO	T260		11	11	10150	3		19200	21400
31	7	CONQUEST SUNBR 3150	ST	OFF	FBG	DV	VD	T350		11	11	10150	3		24600	27400
31	7	CONQUEST SUNBR 3150	ST	OFF	FBG	DV	IO	T130D	VLVO	11	11	10150	3		19100	21200
31	7	CONQUEST SUNBR 3250	ST	OFF	FBG	DV	VD	T135D	VLVO	11	11	10150	3		25400	28300
31	7	CONQUEST SUNBR 3250	FB	OFF	FBG	DV	IO	T260		11	11	10800	3		19500	21700
31	7	CONQUEST SUNBR 3250	FB	OFF	FBG	DV	IO	T130D	VLVO	11	11	10800	3		20100	22300
31	7	CONQUEST SUNBR 3250	FB	OFF	FBG	DV	VD	T155D	VLVO	11	11	10950	3		27200	30200
32	1	EXPLORER 3270	FB	MY	FBG	DV	IB	T145		11	6	12950			26800	29800
32	1	EXPLORER 3270	FB	MY	FBG	DV	IB	T90D-T165D		11	6	12950			33900	41000
32	1	EXPLORER 3270	FB	MY	FBG	SV	IB	T140		11	6	12950			26700	29700
40		BODEGA 4050	FB	MY	FBG	SV	IB	T330		14		23000	3	6	61900	68000
		IB T130D VLVO 64800 71200, IB T270D 69800 76700, IB T310D GM													71400	78400
		1981 BOATS														
16	6	FORCE 1650	ST	RNBT	FBG	DV	IO	140	MRCR	7	2	1545			1800	2150
16	8	MUTINY 1750	ST	RNBT	FBG	DV	IO	120	MRCR	6	10	1700			1850	2200
16	8	MUTINY 1750	ST	RNBT	FBG	DV	IO	120	VLVO	6	10	1700			2000	2350
16	8	MUTINY 1750 B/R	ST	RNBT	FBG	DV	IO	120	MRCR	6	10	1745			1900	2250
16	8	MUTINY 1750 B/R	ST	RNBT	FBG	DV	IO	120	VLVO	6	10	1745			2000	2400
16	8	MUTINY 1750 OFFSHORE	ST	RNBT	FBG	DV	IO	140	MRCR	6	10	1700			1850	2200
18	6	LIBERTY 2050	ST	CUD	FBG	DV	IO	120-170		7	4	2225			2550	3100
18	8	EAGLE 1900	ST	RNBT	FBG	DV	OB			8		1388			2000	2400
18	8	EAGLE 1900 B/R	ST	RNBT	FBG	DV	OB			8		1433			2050	2450
18	8	EAGLE 1950	ST	RNBT	FBG	DV	IO	170	MRCR	8		1950			2550	2950
18	8	EAGLE 1950	ST	RNBT	FBG	DV	IO	225-260		8		1950			2750	3350
18	8	EAGLE 1950 B/R	ST	RNBT	FBG	DV	IO	170	MRCR	8		1995			2550	2950
18	8	EAGLE 1950 B/R	ST	RNBT	FBG	DV	IO	225-260		8		1995			2750	3400
18	8	EAGLE 1950 OFFSHORE	ST	RNBT	FBG	DV	IO	170	MRCR	8		2316			2700	3150
18	8	EAGLE 1950 OFFSHORE	ST	RNBT	FBG	DV	IO	225-260		8		2316			2950	3600
19	7	EXPLORER 2170	ST	CR	FBG	DV	IO	120	VLVO	7	9	2450			3100	3600
20	8	SANTIAGO 2200		OPFSH	FBG	DV	OB			8		2195			3300	3800
20	8	SANTIAGO OFF 2250	ST	FSH	FBG	DV	IO	120-225		8		2938			4200	5200
20	8	SANTIAGO OFF 2250	ST	FSH	FBG	DV	IO	260		8		2938			4500	5400
20	8	SANTIAGO OFF 2250	ST	SPTCR	FBG	DV	IO	120-170		8		2500			3650	4400
20	8	SANTIAGO OFF 2250	ST	SPTCR	FBG	DV	IO	225-260		8		2500			3900	4750
22	3	EXPLORER 2270	HT	CR	FBG	DV	IO	120	VLVO	8		4200			5700	6550
22	3	EXPLORER 2270	HT	CR	FBG	DV	IO	60D		8		4200			6550	7500
22	8	MONTEREY 2350	FB	CR	FBG	DV	IO	225-260		8		4325			6100	7200
22	8	MONTEREY 2350	ST	CUD	FBG	DV	IO	198-260		8		3650			5200	6400

CONTINUED ON NEXT PAGE

LOA		NAME AND/	TOP/	BOAT	-HULL-		----ENGINE---			BEAM		WGT	DRAFT		RETAIL	RETAIL
FT	IN	OR MODEL	RIG	TYPE	MTL	TP	TP	# HP	MFG	FT	IN	LBS	FT	IN	LOW	HIGH
		1981 BOATS														
22	8	MONTEREY 2350	ST	CUD	FBG	DV	IO	130D	VLVO	8		3650			6350	7300
22	8	MONTEREY 2350	ST	EXP	FBG	DV	IO	198-260		8		3975			5500	6800
22	8	MONTEREY SUNBR 2350	ST	CR	FBG	DV	IO	198-260		8		3975			5500	6800
22	8	MONTEREY SUNBR 2350	ST	CR	FBG	DV	IO	T145	VLVO	8		3975			6400	7400
22	9	COBRA OFF 2350	ST	SPTCR	FBG	DV	IO	260		8		3650			5400	6450
22	9	COBRA OFF 2350	ST	SPTCR	FBG	DV	IO	330	MRCR	8		3650			6000	6900
22	9	COBRA OFF 2350	ST	SPTCR	FBG	DV	IO	T170	MRCR	8		3650			5850	6750
24	9	SARATOGA 2550	FB	CR	FBG	DV	IO	260		8		5010			7550	8850
24	9	SARATOGA 2550	FB	CR	FBG	DV	IO	T145	VLVO	8		5010			8200	9400
24	9	SARATOGA 2550	HT	SDN	FBG	DV	IO	225-260		8		4860			7600	9000
24	9	SARATOGA 2550	HT	SDN	FBG	DV	IO	T145	VLVO	8		4860			8300	9550
24	9	SARATOGA SUNBR 2550	ST	CR	FBG	DV	IO	225-260		8		4740			7200	8500
24	9	SARATOGA SUNBR 2550	ST	CR	FBG	DV	IO	T145D	VLVO	8		4740			10500	11900
26	1	EXPLORER 2670	HT	CR	FBG	DV	IO	120-140		8		5500			7050	9150
26	1	EXPLORER 2670	HT	CR	FBG	DV	IO	60D		8		5500			8350	9600
27		VICTORIA 2750	FB	CR	FBG	DV	IO	260		8		5770			9300	10700
27		VICTORIA 2750	FB	CR	FBG	DV	IO	130D	VLVO	8		5840			9600	10900
27		VICTORIA 2750	FB	CR	FBG	DV	IO	T145-T170		8		5770			9750	11200
27		VICTORIA SUNBR 2750	ST	CR	FBG	DV	IO	260		8		5440			9050	10400
27		VICTORIA SUNBR 2750	ST	CR	FBG	DV	IO	T145-T170		8		5440			9500	10900
27	11	ENCOUNTER 2950	FB	SDN	FBG	DV	IO	T200-T260		11	5	11300			16900	20100
27	11	ENCOUNTER 2950	FB	SDN	FBG	DV	IB	T130D	VLVO	11	5	11300			29200	32500
27	11	ENCOUNTER 2950	FB	SDN	FBG	DV	VD	T130D	VLVO	11	5	11300			29200	32500
27	11	ENCOUNTER SUNBR 2950	ST	CR	FBG	DV	IO	T170-T260		11	5	8645			13300	16400
27	11	ENCOUNTER SUNBR 2950	ST	CR	FBG	DV	IO	T130D	VLVO	11	5	8645			16700	18900
31	7	CONQUEST 3150	ST	OFF	FBG	DV	IO	T130D	VLVO	11	11	10150	3		17500	19900
31	7	CONQUEST 3250	FB	SDN	FBG	DV	IO	T		11	11	11300	3		**	**
31	7	CONQUEST 3250	FB	SDN	FBG	DV	IO	T260		11	11	11300	3		22400	24900
31	7	CONQUEST 3250	FB	SDN	FBG	DV	IO	T130D		11	11	11300	3		24100	26800
31	7	CONQUEST EXP 3150	ST	OFF	FBG	DV	IO	T		11	11	10150	3		**	**
31	7	CONQUEST SPORTB 3250	FB	SPTCR	FBG	DV	IO	T		11	11	10800	3		**	**
31	7	CONQUEST SUNBR 3150	ST	OFF	FBG	DV	VD	T		11	11	10150	3		**	**
31	7	CONQUEST SUNBR 3150	ST	OFF	FBG	DV	IO	T260		11	11	10150	3		19200	21300
31	7	CONQUEST SUNBR 3150	ST	OFF	FBG	DV	IO	T130D	VLVO	11	11	10150	3		20000	22200
31	7	CONQUEST SUNBR 3250	FB	OFF	FBG	DV	VD	T		11	11	10800	3		**	**
31	7	CONQUEST SUNBR 3250	FB	OFF	FBG	DV	IO	T260		11	11	10800	3		19200	21400
31	7	CONQUEST SUNBR 3250	FB	OFF	FBG	DV	IO	T130D	VLVO	11	11	10800	3		19800	22000
32	1	EXPLORER 3270	FB	MY	FBG	DV	IB	T140		11	6	12950			25600	28400
32	1	EXPLORER 3270	FB	MY	FBG	DV	IB	T 60D-T90D		11	6	12950			32100	36300
32	1	EXPLORER COM BR	FB	MY	FBG	DV	IB	T140		11	6	13400			25800	28600
32	1	EXPLORER COM BR	FB	MY	FBG	DV	IB	T 60D-T90D		11	6	13400			33000	37000
35		BRISTOL 3550	FB	MY	FBG	DV	IB	224D	VLVO	13	1	16000	3	2	41500	46100
35		BRISTOL 3550	FB	MY	FBG	DV	IB	T330		13	1	16000	3	2	37000	41100
35		BRISTOL 3550	FB	MY	FBG	DV	IB	T210D	CUM	13	1	16000	3	2	45700	50300
40		BODEGA 4050	FB	MY	FBG	SV	IB	T330		14		23000	3	6	59000	64800
		IB T130D 62600 68800, IB T270D 66500 73000, IB T310D GM													68000	74700
		1980 BOATS														
16	6	FORCE 505	ST	RNBT	FBG	DV	IO	120-140		7	2	1545			1800	2150
16	8	MUTINY 1750	ST	RNBT	FBG	DV	IO	120	MRCR	6	10	1700			1850	2200
16	8	MUTINY 1750	ST	RNBT	FBG	DV	IO	120-140		6	10	1700			1950	2350
16	8	MUTINY 1750 B/R	ST	RNBT	FBG	DV	IO	120	MRCR	6	10	1745			1850	2250
16	8	MUTINY 1750 B/R	ST	RNBT	FBG	DV	IO	120-140		6	10	1745			2000	2350
17	3	QUARTERMASTER 1950	ST	RNBT	FBG	DV	IO	120	MRCR	7	4	1875			2100	2500
17	3	QUARTERMASTER 1950	ST	RNBT	FBG	DV	IO	120-170		7	4	1875			2250	2650
17	3	QUARTERMASTER B/R	ST	RNBT	FBG	DV	IO	120-170		7	4	1910			2150	2650
18	6	ADMIRALTY 2050	ST	RNBT	FBG	DV	IO	120-200		7	4	2150			2400	3000
18	6	ADMIRALTY 2050	ST	RNBT	FBG	DV	IO	225	VLVO	7	4	2150			2650	3100
18	6	LIBERTY 2050	ST	CUD	FBG	DV	IO	120-198		7	4	2225			2500	3100
18	6	LIBERTY 2050	ST	CUD	FBG	DV	IO	200-225		7	4	2225			2700	3250
18	8	EAGLE 1900	ST	RNBT	FBG	DV	OB			8		1388			1950	2350
18	8	EAGLE 1900 B/R	ST	RNBT	FBG	DV	OB			8		1433			2000	2400
18	8	EAGLE 1950	ST	RNBT	FBG	DV	IO	120-200		8		1950			2500	3100
18	8	EAGLE 1950	ST	RNBT	FBG	DV	IO	225-260		8		1950			2700	3350
18	8	EAGLE 1950 B/R	ST	RNBT	FBG	DV	IO	120-200		8		1995			2500	3150
18	8	EAGLE 1950 B/R	ST	RNBT	FBG	DV	IO	225-260		8		1995			2750	3350
20	8	SANTIAGO 2200	OP	OPFSH	FBG	DV	OB			8		2195			3200	3750
20	8	SANTIAGO CUDDY 2250	OP	CTRCN	FBG	DV	IO	120-228		8		2838			4050	5050
20	8	SANTIAGO CUDDY 2250	OP	CTRCN	FBG	DV	IO	260		8		2838			4400	5250
20	8	SANTIAGO CUDDY 2250	ST	OVNTR	FBG	DV	IO	120-200		8		2225			3400	4200
20	8	SANTIAGO CUDDY 2250	ST	OVNTR	FBG	DV	IO	225-260		8		2225			3700	4450
20	8	SANTIAGO OFF 2250	ST	FSH	FBG	DV	IO	120-228		8		2938			4150	5150
20	8	SANTIAGO OFF 2250	ST	FSH	FBG	DV	IO	260		8		2938			4450	5350
20	8	SANTIAGO OFF 2250	ST	SPTCR	FBG	DV	IO	120-200		8		2500			3600	4450
20	8	SANTIAGO OFF 2250	ST	SPTCR	FBG	DV	IO	225-260		8		2500			3850	4700
22	8	MONTEREY 2350	FB	CR	FBG	DV	IO	198-260		8		4675			6200	7550
22	8	MONTEREY 2350	FB	CR	FBG	DV	IO	130D	VLVO	8		4675			7350	8450
22	8	MONTEREY 2350	ST	CUD	FBG	DV	IO	170-260		8		3650			5100	6350
22	8	MONTEREY 2350	ST	CUD	FBG	DV	IO	130D	VLVO	8		3650			6300	7250
22	8	MONTEREY 2350	ST	EXP	FBG	DV	IO	170-260		8		3975			5450	6750
22	8	MONTEREY 2350	ST	EXP	FBG	DV	IO	130D	VLVO	8		3975			6650	7600
24	9	SARATOGA 2550	FB	CR	FBG	DV	IO	198-260		8		5010			7200	8750
24	9	SARATOGA 2550	FB	CR	FBG	DV	IO	130D	VLVO	8		5010			8350	9600
24	9	SARATOGA 2550	FB	CR	FBG	DV	IO	T140	MRCR	8		5010			7850	9000
24	9	SARATOGA 2550	ST	OFF	FBG	DV	IO	198-260		8		4400			6500	7950
24	9	SARATOGA 2550	ST	OFF	FBG	DV	IO	130D	VLVO	8		4400			7350	8450
24	9	SARATOGA 2550	ST	OFF	FBG	DV	IO	T140	VLVO	8		4400			7350	8450
24	9	SARATOGA 2550	HT	SDN	FBG	DV	IO	198-260		8					7050	8650
24	9	SARATOGA 2550	HT	SDN	FBG	DV	IO	130D	VLVO	8					8250	9450
24	9	SARATOGA 2550	HT	SDN	FBG	DV	IO	T140	VLVO	8					8000	9200
24	9	SARATOGA SUNBR 2550	ST	CR	FBG	DV	IO	198-260		8		4740			6900	8450
24	9	SARATOGA SUNBR 2550	ST	CR	FBG	DV	IO	130D	VLVO	8		4740			8000	9200
26	1	EXPLORER 2650	ST	CR	FBG	SV	IO	120-140		8		5500			7750	9050
26	1	EXPLORER 2650	ST	CR	FBG	SV	IO	23D- 36D		8		5500			7850	9150
26	1	EXPLORER 2650	ST	CR	FBG	SV	IB	70D	CHRY	8		5500			10500	12000
27		VICTORIA 2750	FB	CR	FBG	DV	IO	225-260		8		5840			9150	10700
27		VICTORIA 2750	FB	CR	FBG	DV	IO	130D	VLVO	8		5840			9500	10800
27		VICTORIA 2750	FB	CR	FBG	DV	IO	T140-T170		8		5840			9700	11200
27		VICTORIA SUNBR 2750	ST	CR	FBG	DV	IO	225-260		8		5770			9050	10600
27		VICTORIA SUNBR 2750	ST	CR	FBG	DV	IO	T140-T200		8		5770			9650	11600
27	11	ENCOUNTER 2950	FB	SDN	FBG	DV	IO	T170-T228		11	5	11300			16200	19400
		IB T255 19800 22100, IO T260 MRCR 17400 19700, IO T260 VLVO													17500	19900
		IB T260 CRUS 20000 22200, IB T130D VLVO 28100 31200, VD T130D VLVO													28100	31200
27	11	ENCOUNTER OFF 2950	ST	OFF	FBG	DV	IO	260-330		11	5	8500			12700	15000
		IO T170-T228 13200 15700, IO T260 MRCR 14100 16000, IO T260 VLVO													14200	16200
		IB T260 CRUS 16000 18200, IO T130D VLVO 16100 18300, IB T130D VLVO													20500	22800
27	11	ENCOUNTER OFF2950	ST	OFF	FBG	DV	IB	T255		11	5	8500			15800	18000
27	11	ENCOUNTER SUNBR 2950	ST	CR	FBG	DV	IO	260-330		11	5	8645			12600	15000
27	11	ENCOUNTER SUNBR 2950	ST	CR	FBG	DV	IO	T170-T260		11	5	8645			13200	16300
27	11	ENCOUNTER SUNBR 2950	ST	CR	FBG	DV	IO	T130D	VLVO	11	5	8645			16500	18800
31	7	CONQUEST 3150	ST	OFF	FBG	DV	IO	T200-T228		11	11	10000	3		18300	20600
		IO T260 MRCR 18900 21000, IO T260 VLVO 18900 21100, IB T260-T330													21400	24800
		IO T130D VLVO 18700 20700														
31	7	CONQUEST 3150	FB	SDN	FBG	DV	IO	T225-T228		11	11	11300	3		21600	24100
		IO T260 MRCR 22200 24700, IO T260 VLVO 22200 24700, IB T260 CRUS													25400	28300
		IO T130D VLVO 23900 26600, IB T130D VLVO 30000 33400														
31	7	CONQUEST 3250	ST	OFF	FBG	DV	IO	T170-T198		11	11	10000			17500	20200
31	7	CONQUEST 3250	ST	OFF	FBG	DV	IB	T255		11	11	10000			21400	23700
31	7	CONQUEST 3250	ST	OFF	FBG	DV	IB	T130D	VLVO	11	11	10000			23200	25800
31	7	CONQUEST EXP3250		EXP	FBG	DV	IB	T255		11	11	10000			22600	25100
31	7	CONQUEST EXP3250		EXP	FBG	DV	IB	T130D		11	11	10000			25100	27800
31	7	CONQUEST SPORTB 3150	FB	OFF	FBG	DV	IO	T200-T228		11	11	10850	3		18600	21000
		IO T260 MRCR 19100 21200, IO T260 VLVO 19100 21200, IB T260-T330													21800	25200
		IO T130D VLVO 19700 21900														
31	7	CONQUEST SPORTB 3250	FB	OFF	FBG	DV	IO	T170-T198		11	11	10850			18300	20700
31	7	CONQUEST SPORTB 3250	FB	OFF	FBG	DV	IB	T130D	VLVO	11	11	10850			24700	27500
31	7	CONQUEST SUNBR3250		CR	FBG	DV	IB	T255		11	11	11300			23100	25700
31	7	CONQUEST SUNBR3250		CR	FBG	DV	IB	T130D		11	11	11300			26900	29900
35		BRISTOL 3550	FB	MY	FBG	DV	IB	T330	CRUS	13	1	16000	3	2	35600	39600
35		BRISTOL 3550	FB	MY	FBG	DV	IB	T210D	CUM	13	1	16000	3	2	43500	48400
35		BRISTOL 3550	FB	MY	FBG	DV	IB	T224D	VLVO	13	1	16000	3	2	43700	48500
40		BODEGA 4050	FB	MY	FBG	SV	IB	T330	CRUS	14		23000	3	6	56700	62300
		IB T130D VLVO 58900 64700, IB T270D VLVO 62100 68200, IB T310D GM													64900	71300
		1979 BOATS														
16	8	MUTINY 1750	ST	RNBT	FBG	DV	IO	120	MRCR	6	10	1825			1900	2250
16	8	MUTINY 1750	ST	RNBT	FBG	DV	IO	120-140		6	10	1825			2000	2400
17	1	CUTLASS 1850	ST	RNBT	FBG	TR	IO	120	MRCR	6	6	1795			1900	2250
17	1	CUTLASS 1850	ST	RNBT	FBG	TR	IO	120-170		6	6	1795			2000	2400
17	3	QUARTERMASTER 1950	ST	RNBT	FBG	DV	IO	120-170		7	4	1990			2200	2650
17	3	QUARTERMASTER B/R	ST	RNBT	FBG	DV	IO	120-170		7	4	1990			2250	2700
18	6	ADMIRALTY 2050	ST	CUD	FBG	DV	IO	120-200		7	4	2593			2750	3400
18	6	ADMIRALTY 2050	ST	CUD	FBG	DV	IO	225-228		7	4	2593			3000	3500
18	6	ADMIRALTY 2050	ST	RNBT	FBG	DV	IO	120-200		7	4	2413			2550	3200

CONTINUED ON NEXT PAGE

LOA FT	IN	NAME AND/ OR MODEL	TOP/ RIG	BOAT TYPE	-HULL- MTL	TP	TP	----ENGINE--- # HP	MFG	BEAM FT	IN	WGT LBS	DRAFT FT	IN	RETAIL LOW	RETAIL HIGH
		1979 BOATS														
18	6	ADMIRALTY 2050	ST	RNBT	FBG	DV	IO	225-228		7	4	2413			2800	3250
18	6	ADMIRALTY 2050 B/R	ST	RNBT	FBG	DV	IO	120-200		7	4	2463			2600	3200
18	6	ADMIRALTY 2050 B/R	ST	RNBT	FBG	DV	IO	225-228		7	4	2463			2850	3300
19	7	LIBERTY 2150	HT	CAMPR	FBG	DV	IO	120-200		7	9	2763			3150	3850
19	7	LIBERTY 2150	HT	CAMPR	FBG	DV	IO	225-228		7	9	2763			3400	3950
19	7	LIBERTY 2150	ST	CUD	FBG	DV	IO	120-200		7	9	2763			3150	3850
19	7	LIBERTY 2150	ST	CUD	FBG	DV	IO	225-228		7	9	2763			3400	3950
20	8	SANTIAGO CUDDY 2250	OP	CTRCN	FBG	DV	IO	120-228		8		2838			4050	5050
20	8	SANTIAGO CUDDY 2250	OP	CTRCN	FBG	DV	IO	255-260		8		2838			4550	5250
20	8	SANTIAGO CUDDY 2250	ST	OVNTR	FBG	DV	IO	120-200		8		2563			3650	4500
20	8	SANTIAGO CUDDY 2250	ST	OVNTR	FBG	DV	IO	225-260		8		2563			3900	4700
20	8	SANTIAGO OFF 2250	ST	FSH	FBG	DV	IO	120-228		8		2938			4150	5150
20	8	SANTIAGO OFF 2250	ST	FSH	FBG	DV	IO	255-260		8		2938			4650	5350
20	8	SANTIAGO OFF 2250	ST	SPTCR	FBG	DV	IO	120-228		8		2838			3850	4800
20	8	SANTIAGO OFF 2250	ST	SPTCR	FBG	DV	IO	255-260		8		2838			4250	4950
21	2	SKAGIT SUNBR 2275	ST	OFF	FBG	DV	IO	198-260		8		3975			5050	6200
22	3	NISQUALLY 2350	FB	CR	FBG	DV	IO	198-255		8		4825			6200	7550
22	3	NISQUALLY 2350	FB	CR	FBG	DV	IO	130D	VLVO	8		4825			7350	8450
24	6	SARATOGA 2550	HT	EXP	FBG	DV	IO	198-260		8		5171			7300	8850
24	6	SARATOGA 2550	HT	EXP	FBG	DV	IO	T120-T140		8		5171			7900	9450
24	6	SARATOGA SUNBR 2550	ST	CR	FBG	DV	IO	198-260		8		5725			7950	9550
24	6	SARATOGA SUNBR 2550	ST	CR	FBG	DV	IO	130D	VLVO	8		5725			9400	10700
24	6	SARATOGA SUNBR 2550	ST	CR	FBG	DV	IO	T120-T200		8		5725			8550	10400
24	9	SARATOGA 2550	FB	CR	FBG	DV	IO	198-260		8		5429			7650	9250
24	9	SARATOGA 2550	FB	CR	FBG	DV	IO	130D	VLVO	8		5429			9000	10200
24	9	SARATOGA 2550	FB	CR	FBG	DV	IO	T120-T170		8		5429			8250	9800
24	9	SARATOGA 2550	OP	OFF	FBG	DV	IO	198-260		8		4829			6950	8450
24	9	SARATOGA 2550	OP	OFF	FBG	DV	IO	130D	VLVO	8		4829			7950	9150
24	9	SARATOGA 2550	OP	OFF	FBG	DV	IO	T120-T170		8		4829			7500	9000
24	9	SARATOGA 2550	HT	SDN	FBG	DV	IO	198-260		8					7050	8600
24	9	SARATOGA 2550	HT	SDN	FBG	DV	IO	130D	VLVO	8					8200	9450
24	9	SARATOGA 2550	HT	SDN	FBG	DV	IO	T120-T170		8					7650	9200
27		VICTORIA 2750	FB	CR	FBG	DV	IO	225-260		8		5951			9200	10700
27		VICTORIA 2750	FB	CR	FBG	DV	IO	130D	VLVO	8		5951			9650	11000
27		VICTORIA 2750	FB	CR	FBG	DV	IO	T120-T170		8		5951			9450	11300
27		VICTORIA SUNBR 2750	ST	OFF	FBG	DV	IO	225-260		8		6025			9250	10700
27		VICTORIA SUNBR 2750	ST	OFF	FBG	DV	IO	T120-T200		8		6025			9450	11700
27		VICTORIA SUNBR 2750	ST	OFF	FBG	DV	IO	T225-T260		8		6025			10500	12300
27	4	BOUNTY 2850	FB	CR	FBG	DV	IO	255-260		10	4	7200	2	10	11000	12500
27	4	BOUNTY 2850	FB	CR	FBG	DV	IO	130D	VLVO	10	4	7200	2	10	12000	13600
27	4	BOUNTY 2850	FB	CR	FBG	DV	IO	T170-T255		10	4	7200	2	10	11500	14300
29	4	ENCOUNTER 3050	FB	SPTCR	FBG	DV	VD	T		10	4	9410	2	10	**	**
29	4	ENCOUNTER 3050	FB	SPTCR	FBG	DV	IO	T198-T260		10	4	9410	2	10	14400	17200
29	4	ENCOUNTER 3050	FB	SPTCR	FBG	DV	IO	T130D	VLVO	10	4	9410	2	10	17100	19400
31	7	CONQUEST 3150	ST	OFF	FBG	DV	IB	T		11	11	10000	3		**	**
		IO T200-T260 18200 21000, IB T330 CC 21400 23700, IO T130D VLVO													18600	20700
31	7	CONQUEST 3150	HT	OFF	FBG	DV	IB	T		11	11	10000	3		**	**
		IO T200-T260 18200 21000, IB T330 CC 21400 23700, IO T130D VLVO													18600	20700
31	7	CONQUEST 3150	FB	OFF	FBG	DV	IB	T		11	11	10000	3		**	**
		IO T200-T260 18200 21000, IB T330 CC 21400 23700, IO T130D VLVO													18600	20700
31	7	CONQUEST SUNBR 3150	ST	SPTCR	FBG	DV	IO	T200-T260		11	11	10150	3		19100	22100
31	7	CONQUEST SUNBR 3150	ST	SPTCR	FBG	DV	IO	T130D	VLVO	11	11	10150	3		20100	22300
35		BRISTOL 3550	FB	MY	FBG	DV	IB	T330	CC	13	1	16000	3	2	34000	37800
35		BRISTOL 3550	FB	MY	FBG	DV	IB	T215D	CUMM	13	1	16000	3	2	42100	46800
40		BODEGA 4050	FB	MY	FBG	DV	IB	T330	CC	14		23000	3	6	53700	59100
40		BODEGA 4050	FB	MY	FBG	DV	IB	T265D	GM	14		23000	3	6	60400	66400
		1978 BOATS														
16	5	CASCADE 1750	OP	RNBT	FBG	TR	IO	120	MRCR	6	6	1650			1750	2100
16	5	CASCADE 1750	OP	RNBT	FBG	TR	IO	130-140		6	6	1650			1900	2250
16	9	MUTINY 1750	OP	RNBT	FBG	DV	IO	120	MRCR	7	1	1875			2000	2400
16	9	MUTINY 1750	OP	RNBT	FBG	DV	IO	130-140		7	1	1875			2150	2550
16	9	MYSTIC 1850	OP	RNBT	FBG	TR	IO	120	MRCR	7	5	1850			2050	2450
16	9	MYSTIC 1850	OP	RNBT	FBG	TR	IO	130-170		7	5	1850			2200	2600
17	3	QUARTERMASTER 1950	OP	B/R	FBG	DV	IO	120	MRCR	7	3	1775			1950	2300
17	3	QUARTERMASTER 1950	OP	B/R	FBG	DV	IO	130-170		7	3	1775			2050	2450
17	3	QUARTERMASTER 1950	OP	RNBT	FBG	DV	IO	120	MRCR	7	3	1750			2050	2400
17	3	QUARTERMASTER 1950	OP	RNBT	FBG	DV	IO	130-170		7	3	1750			2200	2550
18	6	ADMIRALTY 2000 B/R	OP	RNBT	FBG	DV	OB			7	3	1225			1700	2050
18	6	ADMIRALTY 2050	OP	OVNTR	FBG	DV	IO	120-198		7	3	2100			2450	3000
18	6	ADMIRALTY 2050	OP	OVNTR	FBG	DV	IO	200-260		7	3	2100			2650	3300
18	6	ADMIRALTY 2050	OP	OVNTR	FBG	DV	IO	300	PHS	7	3	2100			2950	3400
18	6	ADMIRALTY 2050 B/R	OP	RNBT	FBG	DV	IO	120-200		7	3	2150			2400	3000
18	6	ADMIRALTY 2050 B/R	OP	RNBT	FBG	DV	IO	225-260		7	3	2150			2650	3200
18	6	ADMIRALTY 2050 B/R	OP	RNBT	FBG	DV	IO	300	PHS	7	3	2150			2850	3350
18	7	JAMAICA 1950	OP	RNBT	FBG	TR	IO	120-198		7	5	2000			2400	2900
18	7	JAMAICA 1950	OP	RNBT	FBG	TR	IO	200-228		7	5	2000			2550	3050
19	3	CALYPSO 2000	OP	RNBT	FBG	DV	OB			7	8	1300			1850	2200
19	3	CALYPSO 2050	OP	RNBT	FBG	DV	IO	198-225		7	8	2625			2950	3650
19	3	CALYPSO 2050	OP	RNBT	FBG	DV	IO	255-300		7	8	2625			3250	3850
19	7	LIBERTY 2150	ST	CUD	FBG	DV	IO	120-200		7	9	2450			2950	3650
19	7	LIBERTY 2150	ST	CUD	FBG	DV	IO	225-228		7	9	2450			3200	3750
19	7	LIBERTY 2150	HT	CUD	FBG	DV	IO	120-200		7	9	2450			2950	3650
19	7	LIBERTY 2150	HT	CUD	FBG	DV	IO	225-228		7	9	2450			3200	3750
19	7	LIBERTY 2150	ST	FSH	FBG	DV	IO	120-200		7	9	2500			3150	3900
19	7	LIBERTY 2150	ST	FSH	FBG	DV	IO	225-228		7	9	2500			3400	3950
19	7	LIBERTY 2150	HT	FSH	FBG	DV	IO	120-200		7	9	2500			3150	3900
19	7	LIBERTY 2150	HT	FSH	FBG	DV	IO	225-228		7	9	2500			3400	3950
20	8	SANTIAGO CUDDY 2200	ST	FSH	FBG	DV	IO	120-200		8		2275			3650	4500
20	8	SANTIAGO CUDDY 2200	ST	FSH	FBG	DV	IO	225-300		8		2275			3950	4900
20	8	SANTIAGO CUDDY 2200	ST	OVNTR	FBG	DV	IO	120-200		8		2225			3450	4250
20	8	SANTIAGO CUDDY 2200	ST	OVNTR	FBG	DV	IO	225-300		8		2225			3700	4600
20	8	SANTIAGO OFF 2200	ST	CUD	FBG	DV	IO	120-200		8		2500			3600	4450
20	8	SANTIAGO OFF 2200	ST	CUD	FBG	DV	IO	225-300		8		2500			3900	4800
20	8	SANTIAGO OFF 2200	ST	FSH	FBG	DV	IO	120-200		8		2550			3850	4750
20	8	SANTIAGO OFF 2200	ST	FSH	FBG	DV	IO	225-300		8		2550			4150	5150
21	2	SKAGIT SUNBR 2250	ST	OFF	FBG	DV	IO	198-260		8		3950			5050	6250
21	2	SKAGIT SUNBR 2250	ST	OFF	FBG	DV	IO	300	PHS	8		3950			5550	6350
22	5	NISQUALLY 2350	FB	CR	FBG	DV	IO	198-300		8		4790			6300	7750
22	5	NISQUALLY 2350	FB	CR	FBG	DV	IO	T130	VLVO	8		4790			7150	8250
22	5	NISQUALLY 2350	HT	EXP	FBG	DV	IO	198-300		8		4440			5900	7350
22	5	NISQUALLY 2350	HT	SDN	FBG	DV	IO	198-300		8		4120			5600	6950
22	5	NISQUALLY 2350	HT	SDN	FBG	DV	IO	T130	VLVO	8		4120			6450	7450
24	6	SARATOGA 2550	HT	EXP	FBG	DV	IO	198-300		8		4900			7050	8750
24	6	SARATOGA 2550	HT	EXP	FBG	DV	IO	T120-T140		8		4900			7650	9150
24	6	SARATOGA 2550	ST	FSH	FBG	DV	IO	198-300		8		4200			6650	8300
24	6	SARATOGA 2550	ST	FSH	FBG	DV	IO	130D	VLVO	8		4200			9300	10600
24	6	SARATOGA 2550	ST	FSH	FBG	DV	IO	T130	VLVO	8		4200			7550	8700
24	6	SARATOGA 2550	ST	OFF	FBG	DV	IO	198-300		8		4800			6900	8550
		IO 130D VLVO 8050 9250, IO T120-T200 7500 9200, IO T225 VLVO													8200	9400
24	6	SARATOGA 2550	HT	OFF	FBG	DV	IO	198-300		8		4300			6350	7900
24	6	SARATOGA 2550	HT	OFF	FBG	DV	IO	130D	VLVO	8		4300			7350	8450
24	6	SARATOGA 2550	HT	OFF	FBG	DV	IO	T120-T140		8		4300			6950	8350
27		VICTORIA 2750	FB	CR	FBG	DV	IO	198-300		8		5700			8800	10800
27		VICTORIA 2750	FB	CR	FBG	DV	IO	130D	VLVO	8		5700			9400	10700
27		VICTORIA 2750	FB	CR	FBG	DV	IO	T120-T200		8		5700			9350	11600
27		VICTORIA 2750	ST	OFF	FBG	DV	IO	198-300		8		6000			9050	11000
		IO 130D VLVO 9850 11200, IO T120-T200 9500 11700, IO T225-T255													10600	12400
27	4	BOUNTY 2850	FB	CR	FBG	DV	IO	255	VLVO	10	4	7846	3		11700	13200
27	4	BOUNTY 2850	FB	CR	FBG	DV	IO	130D	VLVO	10	4	7846	3		13200	15000
27	4	BOUNTY 2850	FB	CR	FBG	DV	IO	T198-T225		10	4	7846	3		12400	14600
29	4	ENCOUNTER 3050	FB	SPTCR	FBG	DV	IO	225	VLVO	10	4	9410	3		13400	15200
		IB 250 CHRY 14100 16000, IO 255 VLVO 13600 15500, IO T198 MRCR													14500	16400
		IO T130D VLVO 17200 19600														
32	3	MONTEGO 3350	FB	MY	FBG	DV	IB	T250	CHRY	11	5	12500	3		24800	27500
32	3	MONTEGO 3350	FB	MY	FBG	DV	IO	T255-T260		11	5	12500	3		27100	30200
32	3	MONTEGO 3350	FB	MY	FBG	DV	IO	T130D	VLVO	11	5	12500	3		32400	36000
40		BODEGA 4050	FB	TCMY	FBG	DV	IB	T330		14		23000	3	6	51400	56500
40		BODEGA 4050	FB	TCMY	FBG	DV	IB	T310D	GM	14		23000	3	6	59200	65100
		1977 BOATS														
16	5	CASCADE 1750	ST	RNBT	FBG	TR	IO	120	MRCR	7	5	1650			1950	2300
16	5	CASCADE 1750	ST	RNBT	FBG	TR	IO	130-170		7	5	1650			2050	2450
16	9	MUTINY 1750	ST	RNBT	FBG	DV	IO	120	MRCR	7	1	1875			2050	2400
16	9	MUTINY 1750	ST	RNBT	FBG	DV	IO	130-170		7	1	1875			2200	2550
16	9	MYSTIC 1850	ST	RNBT	FBG	TR	IO	120	MRCR	7	5	1850			2100	2450
16	9	MYSTIC 1850	ST	RNBT	FBG	TR	IO	130-170		7	5	1850			2250	2600
17	7	QUARTERMASTER 1950	ST	B/R	FBG	DV	IO	120-200		7	2	2075			2200	2750
17	7	QUARTERMASTER 1950	ST	B/R	FBG	DV	IO	225	VLVO	7	2	2075			2400	2800
17	7	QUARTERMASTER 1950	ST	RNBT	FBG	DV	IO	120-200		7	2	1975			2250	2800
17	7	QUARTERMASTER 1950	ST	RNBT	FBG	DV	IO	225	VLVO	7	2	1975			2450	2850
18	7	JAMAICA 1950	HT	EXP	FBG	TR	IO	120-170		7	5	2275			2650	3250
18	7	JAMAICA 1950	ST	RNBT	FBG	TR	IO	120-190		7	5	2000			2450	3000
18	7	JAMAICA 1950	ST	RNBT	FBG	TR	IO	200-225		7	5	2000			2600	3100

 CONTINUED ON NEXT PAGE

BAYLINER MARINE CORP -CONTINUED See inside cover to adjust price for area

LOA FT	LOA IN	NAME AND/ OR MODEL	TOP/ RIG	BOAT TYPE	-HULL- MTL	-HULL- TP	ENGINE TP	# HP	MFG	BEAM FT	BEAM IN	WGT LBS	DRAFT FT IN	RETAIL LOW	RETAIL HIGH
		1977 BOATS													
19	3	CALYPSO 2000	ST	RNBT	FBG	DV	OB			7	8	1300		1800	2150
19	3	CALYPSO 2050	ST	RNBT	FBG	DV	IO	225-300		7	8	2625		3150	3950
19	7	ADMIRALTY 2050	ST	FSH	FBG	DV	IO	120-170		7	8	2325		3050	3750
19	7	ADMIRALTY 2050	ST	RNBT	FBG	DV	IO	120-200		7	9	2250		2800	3450
19	7	ADMIRALTY 2050	ST	RNBT	FBG	DV	IO	225	VLVO	7	9	2250		3000	3500
19	7	ADMIRALTY 2050	HT	RNBT	FBG	DV	IO	120-200		7	9	2250		2800	3450
19	7	ADMIRALTY 2050	HT	RNBT	FBG	DV	IO	225	VLVO	7	9	2250		3000	3500
19	7	LIBERTY 2150	ST	CUD	FBG	DV	IO	120-200		7	9	2450		3000	3700
19	7	LIBERTY 2150	ST	CUD	FBG	DV	IO	225	VLVO	7	9	2450		3250	3800
19	7	LIBERTY 2150	HT	CUD	FBG	DV	IO	120-200		7	9	2450		3000	3700
19	7	LIBERTY 2150	HT	CUD	FBG	DV	IO	225	VLVO	7	9	2450		3250	3800
19	7	LIBERTY 2150	ST	FSH	FBG	DV	IO	120-170		7	9	2500		3200	3900
21	2	SKAGIT 2250	ST	CUD	FBG	DV	IO	170-255		8		3275		4650	5600
21	2	SKAGIT 2250	HT	CUD	FBG	DV	IO	170-255		8		3275		4650	5600
21	2	SKAGIT 2250	ST	OFF	FBG	DV	IO	170-255		8		3720		5050	6100
21	2	SKAGIT 2250	HT	OFF	FBG	DV	IO	170-255		8		3720		5050	6100
21	2	SKAGIT 2250	HT	SDN	FBG	DV	IO	170-255		8		3720		5050	6100
22	5	NISQUALLY 2350	FB	CR	FBG	DV	IO	188-255		8		4790		6350	7750
22	5	NISQUALLY 2350	FB	CR	FBG	DV	IO	T130	VLVO	8		4790		7300	8350
22	5	NISQUALLY 2350	HT	EXP	FBG	DV	IO	188-255		8		4440		6000	7350
22	5	NISQUALLY 2350	HT	SDN	FBG	DV	IO	188-255		8		4120		5650	6950
22	5	NISQUALLY 2350	HT	SDN	FBG	DV	IO	T130	VLVO	8		4120		6550	7550
24	6	SARATOGA 2550	ST	CR	FBG	DV	IO	188-255		8		4800		7050	8600
24	6	SARATOGA 2550	ST	CR	FBG	DV	IO	T120-T140		8		4800		7650	9150
24	6	SARATOGA 2550	HT	EXP	FBG	DV	IO	188-255		8		4900		7150	8700
24	6	SARATOGA 2550	HT	EXP	FBG	DV	IO	T130	VLVO	8		4900		8050	9250
24	6	SARATOGA 2550	ST	FSH	FBG	DV	IO	188-255		8		4200		6750	8250
24	6	SARATOGA 2550	ST	FSH	FBG	DV	IO	T130	VLVO	8		4200		7700	8850
24	6	SARATOGA 2550	ST	OFF	FBG	DV	IO	188-255		8		4300		6450	7900
24	6	SARATOGA 2550	ST	OFF	FBG	DV	IO	T120-T140		8		4300		7050	8450
24	6	SARATOGA 2550	HT	OFF	FBG	DV	IO	188-255		8		4300		6450	7900
24	6	SARATOGA 2550	HT	OFF	FBG	DV	IO	T120-T140		8		4300		7050	8450
27		VICTORIA 2750	FB	CR	FBG	DV	IO	188-255		8		6040		9200	11000
27		VICTORIA 2750	FB	CR	FBG	DV	IO	T120-T200		8		6040		9750	12100
27	4	BOUNTY 2850	FB	MY	FBG	DV	IO	250-255		10	4	7200		13700	15700
27	4	BOUNTY 2850	FB	MY	FBG	DV	IO	T188-T200		10	4	7200		14900	17300
29	4	ENCOUNTER 3050	FB	MY	FBG	DV	IO	T225	VLVO	10	4	9410		19000	21100
		IO T250 PHS 19300 21500, IB T250 CHRY 16500 18700, IO T255												19400	21700
32	3	MONTEGO 3350	FB	MY	FBG	DV	IO	T250	PHS	11	5	12500		27500	30500
32	3	MONTEGO 3350	FB	MY	FBG	DV	IB	T250	CHRY	11	5	12500		23800	26400
32	3	MONTEGO 3350	FB	MY	FBG	DV	IO	T255		11	5	12500		27600	30700
		1976 BOATS													
16	1	MUTINY 1750	ST	RNBT	FBG	DV	IO	120		6	10	1650		1850	2200
16	1	MUTINY 1750	ST	RNBT	FBG	DV	IO	130-140		6	10	1650		1950	2350
16	5	CASCADE 1750	ST	RNBT	FBG	TR	IO	120		6	6	1700		1850	2200
16	5	CASCADE 1750	ST	RNBT	FBG	TR	IO	130-140		6	6	1700		2000	2350
17	7	QUARTERMASTER 1950	ST	RNBT	FBG	DV	IO	120-200		7	2	1900		2250	2850
17	7	QUARTERMASTER 1950	ST	RNBT	FBG	DV	IO	225	VLVO	7	2	1900		2500	2900
18	7	JAMAICA 1900	ST	RNBT	FBG	TR	OB			7	5	1250		1700	2000
18	7	JAMAICA 1950	ST	RNBT	FBG	TR	IO	120-200		7	5	2250		2650	3250
18	7	JAMAICA 1950	ST	RNBT	FBG	TR	IO	225	VLVO	7	5	2250		2850	3350
19	3	CALYPSO 2050	ST	RNBT	FBG	DV	IO	188-250		7	8			2850	3550
19	3	CALYPSO 2050	ST	RNBT	FBG	DV	IO	300	CC	7	8			3250	3800
19	7	ADMIRALTY 2050	ST	FSH	FBG	DV	IO	120-170		7	9	2450		3250	3950
19	7	ADMIRALTY 2050	ST	RNBT	FBG	DV	IO	120-200		7	9	2450		2950	3650
19	7	ADMIRALTY 2050	ST	RNBT	FBG	DV	IO	225	VLVO	7	9	2450		3200	3750
19	7	ADMIRALTY 2050	HT	RNBT	FBG	DV	IO	120-200		7	9	2450		2950	3650
19	7	ADMIRALTY 2050	HT	RNBT	FBG	DV	IO	225	VLVO	7	9	2450		3200	3750
19	7	LIBERTY 2150	ST	CUD	FBG	DV	IO	120-200		7	9	2600		3200	3950
19	7	LIBERTY 2150	ST	CUD	FBG	DV	IO	225	VLVO	7	9	2600		3450	4000
19	7	LIBERTY 2150	HT	CUD	FBG	DV	IO	120-200		7	9	2600		3200	3950
19	7	LIBERTY 2150	HT	CUD	FBG	DV	IO	225	VLVO	7	9	2600		3450	4000
21	2	SKAGIT 2250	FB	CR	FBG	DV	IO	165-255		8		4000		5300	6400
21	2	SKAGIT 2250	ST	CUD	FBG	DV	IO	130-255		8		4000		5400	6400
21	2	SKAGIT 2250	HT	CUD	FBG	DV	IO	130-255		8		4000		5400	6400
21	2	SKAGIT 2250	ST	OFF	FBG	DV	IO	165-255		8		3500		4800	5850
21	2	SKAGIT 2250	HT	OFF	FBG	DV	IO	165-255		8		3500		4800	5850
21	2	SKAGIT 2250		SDN	FBG	DV	IO	165-255		8				4400	5350
22	5	NISQUALLY 2350	FB	CR	FBG	DV	IO	165-255		8		4600		6300	7550
22	5	NISQUALLY 2350	FB	CR	FBG	DV	IO	T130	VLVO	8		4600		7250	8350
22	5	NISQUALLY 2350	HT	SDN	FBG	DV	IO	165-255		8		3800		5450	6550
22	5	NISQUALLY 2350	HT	SDN	FBG	DV	IO	T130	VLVO	8		3800		6400	7350
24	6	SARATOGA 2550	HT	EXP	FBG	DV	IO	165-255		8		4800		7150	8600
24	6	SARATOGA 2550	HT	EXP	FBG	DV	IO	T120-T200		8		4800		7850	9700
24	6	SARATOGA 2550	HT	FSH	FBG	DV	IO	165-255		8				7400	8900
24	6	SARATOGA 2550	HT	FSH	FBG	DV	IO	T130	VLVO	8				8450	9700
24	6	SARATOGA 2550	ST	OFF	FBG	DV	IO	165-255		8		4100		6350	7650
24	6	SARATOGA 2550	ST	OFF	FBG	DV	IO	T120-T200		8		4100		7000	8700
24	6	SARATOGA 2550	HT	OFF	FBG	DV	IO	165-255		8		4100		6350	7650
24	6	SARATOGA 2550	HT	OFF	FBG	DV	IO	T120-T200		8		4100		7000	8700
26	3	VICTORIA 2750	FB	CR	FBG	DV	IO	188-255		8		5600		8600	10300
26	3	VICTORIA 2750	FB	CR	FBG	DV	IO	T120-T200		8		5600		9300	11500
26	3	VICTORIA 2750	FB	DC	FBG	DV	IO	188-255		8		5600		9850	11700
26	3	VICTORIA DC 2750	HT	EXP	FBG	DV	IO	188-255		8		5600		8600	10300
27	4	BOUNTY 2850		CR	FBG	DV	IO	250		10	4			10700	12200
29	4	ENCOUNTER 3050		CR	FBG	DV	IO	T230		10	4			14200	16100
29	4	ENCOUNTER 3050		CR	FBG	DV	IB	T230		10	4			13000	14800
32	3	MONTEGO		MY	FBG	DV	IO	T260		11	5			26600	29500
32	3	MONTEGO		MY	FBG	DV	IB	T260		11	5			21500	23900
		1975 BOATS													
16	1	MUTINY 1750	ST	RNBT	FBG	DV	IO	120		6	10	1650		1900	2250
16	1	MUTINY 1750	ST	RNBT	FBG	DV	IO	130-140		6	10	1650		2050	2400
16	5	CASCADE 1750	ST	RNBT	FBG	TR	IO	120		6	6	1700		1900	2300
16	5	CASCADE 1750	ST	RNBT	FBG	TR	IO	130-140		6	6	1700		2050	2450
16	9	DISCOVERY 1850	OP	RNBT	FBG	DV	IO	130	VLVO	7	1	1800		2300	2650
17	7	QUARTERMASTER 1950	ST	RNBT	FBG	DV	IO	120-188		7	2	1900		2300	2900
17	7	QUARTERMASTER 1950	ST	RNBT	FBG	DV	IO	200-225		7	2	1900		2500	3000
18	7	JAMAICA 1950	ST	RNBT	FBG	TR	IO	120-140		7	5	1250		2300	2800
18	7	JAMAICA 1950	ST	RNBT	FBG	TR	IO	165-200		7	5	2250		2750	3400
18	7	JAMAICA 1950	ST	RNBT	FBG	TR	IO	225	VLVO	7	5	2250		2950	3450
20	11	ADMIRALTY 2050	ST	RNBT	FBG	DV	IO	120-165		7	9	2300		3550	4300
20	11	ADMIRALTY 2050	ST	RNBT	FBG	DV	IO	170-225		7	9	2450		3850	4600
20	11	LIBERTY 2150	ST	CUD	FBG	DV	IO	120-165		7	9	2450		3850	4650
20	11	LIBERTY 2150	ST	CUD	FBG	DV	IO	170-225		7	9	2600		4150	4950
21	2	SKAGIT 2250	FB	CR	FBG	DV	IO	165-255		8		4000		5450	6600
21	2	SKAGIT CAMPER 2250	ST	CR	FBG	DV	IO	165-255		8		2900		4400	5400
21	2	SKAGIT OFFSHORE 2250	ST	CUD	FBG	DV	IO	165-255		8		3500		4950	6050
22	5	NISQUALLY 2350	FB	CR	FBG	DV	IO	165-255		8		4450		6350	7800
22	5	NISQUALLY 2350	HT	SDN	FBG	DV	IO	165-255		8		3800		5600	6800
24	6	SARATOGA 2550	HT	EXP	FBG	DV	IO	165-255		8		4800		7400	8900
24	6	SARATOGA 2550	HT	EXP	FBG	DV	IO	T120-T200		8		5000		8350	10300
24	6	SARATOGA OFF 2550	ST	CUD	FBG	DV	IO	165-255				4100		6650	8050
24	6	SARATOGA OFF 2550	ST	CUD	FBG	DV	IO	T120-T200				4100		7400	9200
26	3	VICTORIA 2750	FB	CR	FBG	DV	IO	188-255		8		5400		8650	10400
26	3	VICTORIA 2750	FB	CR	FBG	DV	IO	T120-T200		8		5600		9550	11900
26	3	VICTORIA 2750	FB	CR	FBG	DV	IO	T225	VLVO	8		5600		10700	12200
29	4	ENCOUNTER 3050	FB	CR	FBG	DV	IO	255	MRCR	10	4	8700		14100	16000
		IO T225 VLVO 15500 17700, IB T250 CHRY 13400 15300, IO T255 MRCR												15800	18000
29	4	ENCOUNTER 3050	HT	SDN	FBG	DV	IO	255	MRCR	10	4	8100		14900	16900
		IO T225 VLVO 16800 19100, IB T250 CHRY 14600 16600, IO T255 MRCR												17200	19600
29	4	ENCOUNTER OFF 3050	ST	CR	FBG	DV	IO	255	MRCR	10	4	7600		13400	15200
		IO T225 VLVO 15000 17000, IB T250 CHRY 13000 14700, IO T255 MRCR												15300	17400
32	3	MONTEGO 3350	FB	CR	FBG	DV	IO	T225-T255		11	5	12500		23300	26300
		1974 BOATS													
16	1	MUTINY 1750			FBG		IO	120	MRCR	6	10	1665		1850	2200
16	1	MUTINY 1750			FBG		IO	130-140		6	10	1665		2000	2400
16	7	MYSTIC 1850			FBG		IO	120-140		7	5	2200		2400	2950
16	9	DISCOVERY 1850			FBG		IO	120-140		7	1			2200	2650
17	7	QUARTERMASTER 1950			FBG		IO	120-165		7	2	1900		2350	2900
17	7	QUARTERMASTER 1950			FBG		IO	170-225		7	2			2650	3100
17	7	QUARTERMASTER 1950			FBG		IO	455	BERK	7	2			5550	6400
18	7	JAMAICA 1950			FBG		IO	120-225		7	5			2750	3400
18	7	JAMAICA 1950			FBG		IO	455	BERK	7	5			5800	6700
19	7	ADMIRALTY 2050			FBG		IO	120-215		7	9			3100	3750
19	7	ADMIRALTY 2050			FBG		IO	225-255		7	9			3200	3850
19	7	ADMIRALTY 2050			FBG		IO	455	BERK	7	9			6350	7300
19	7	ADMIRALTY 2050	HT		FBG		IO	120-215		7	9			3100	3750
19	7	ADMIRALTY 2050	HT		FBG		IO	225-255		7	9			3250	3900
19	7	ADMIRALTY 2050	HT		FBG		IO	455	BERK	7	9			6350	7300
19	7	LIBERTY 2150			FBG		IO	120-255		7	9			3650	4450
19	7	LIBERTY 2150	HT		FBG		IO	120-255		7	9			3600	4450
21	2	SKAGIT	HT	CAMPR	FBG		IO	120-255		8				4650	5700

 CONTINUED ON NEXT PAGE

```
LOA  NAME AND/        TOP/ BOAT -HULL- ----ENGINE--- BEAM  WGT  DRAFT RETAIL RETAIL
FT IN  OR MODEL        RIG  TYPE MTL TP TP # HP  MFG  FT IN LBS  FT IN  LOW   HIGH
-------------------------- 1974 BOATS ---------------------------------------
21  2 SKAGIT 2250            CAMPR FBG    IO 120   MRCR 8     2500           4150  4800
21  2 SKAGIT 2250            CAMPR FBG    IO 120-255  8                      4650  5700
21  2 SKAGIT 2250            EXP   FBG    IO 120-255  8                      4650  5700
21  2 SKAGIT 2250 OFFSHORE   OFF   FBG    IO 120-255  8                      4650  5700
21  2 SKAGIT OFFSHORE     HT OFF   FBG    IO 120-255  8                      4650  5700
22  5 NISQUALLY 2350      FB       FBG    IO 130-255  8                      5850  6900
22  5 NISQUALLY 2350      FB       FBG    IO T120-T140 8                     6400  7750
22  5 NISQUALLY 2350         EXP   FBG    IO 130   VLVO 8    2950           5050  5800
22  5 NISQUALLY 2350         EXP   FBG    IO 140-255  8                      6000  7300
22  5 NISQUALLY 2350         EXP   FBG    IO T120-T130 8                     6750  8100
24  6 SARATOGA 2550       FB       FBG    IO 165      8                      7250  8300
24  6 SARATOGA 2550       FB       FBG    IO 170-255  8      5860           8950 10200

24  6 SARATOGA 2550       FB       FBG    IO T120-T200 8                     7950  9850
24  6 SARATOGA 2550          EXP   FBG    IO 130-255  8                      7550  9000
24  6 SARATOGA 2550          EXP   FBG    IO T120-T170 8                     8250  9950
24  6 SARATOGA OFFSHORE      OFF   FBG    IO 130-255  8                      7550  8950
24  6 SARATOGA OFFSHORE      OFF   FBG    IO T120-T200 8                     8200 10100
24  6 SARATOGA OFFSHORE   HT OFF   FBG    IO 130-255  8                      7550  8950
24  6 SARATOGA OFFSHORE   HT OFF   FBG    IO T120-T200 8                     8200 10100
26  3 VICTORIA 2750       FB       FBG    IO 170   VLVO 8                    8600  9850
      IO 188-255  9650  11000, IO T120-T188  9400 11400, IO T200 VLVO 10400 11800

32  3 MONTEGO 3350        FB       FBG    VD T165-T255 11  5 10500          17600 20000
-------------------------- 1973 BOATS ---------------------------------------
16    TAHITI 1650                  FBG    IO 140   MRCR 6  8 1620           1850  2200
16  1 MUTINY 1750                  FBG    IO 120       6 10                 1750  2100
16  1 MUTINY 1750                  FBG    IO 130-140   6 10 1665            2050  2450
16  9 DISCOVERY 1850               FBG    IO 120-165   7  1                 2250  2700
17  7 QUARTERMASTER                FBG    IO 120-188   7  2                 2550  3200
17  7 QUARTERMASTER                FBG    JT 270   BERK 7 2                 2350  2700
18  7 JAMAICA 1900                 FBG    IO 120-165   7  5                 2850  3350
18  7 JAMAICA 1900                 FBG    JT 270   BERK 7 5                 2550  3000
19  2 ADMIRALTY             HT     FBG    IO 120-225   7  6                 3000  3650
19  2 ADMIRALTY             HT     FBG    IO 255   MRCR 7 6                 3200  3750
19  2 ADMIRALTY             HT     FBG    JT 270   BERK 7 6                 2650  3100

19  2 ADMIRALTY 2050               FBG    IO 120-225   7  6                 3000  3650
19  2 ADMIRALTY 2050               FBG    IO 255   MRCR 7 6                 3200  3750
19  2 ADMIRALTY 2050               FBG    JT 270   BERK 7 6                 2650  3100
20  4 LIBERTY CC                   FBG    IO 120-255   7  6                 3900  4850
20  4 LIBERTY CC            HT     FBG    IO 120-255   7  6                 3900  4850
21  2 SKAGIT 2250             SPTCR FBG   IO 120-255   8                    4800  5800
21  2 SKAGIT OFFSHORE         OFF   FBG   IO 120-255   8                    4800  5800
21  2 SKAGIT OFFSHORE      HT OFF   FBG   IO 120-255   8                    4800  5800
22  5 NISQUALLY            FB       FBG   IO 140-255   8                    5900  7100
22  5 NISQUALLY            FB       FBG   IO 105D  CHRY 8                   7450  8600
22  5 NISQUALLY            FB       FBG   IO T120-T140 8                    6650  8000

22  5 NISQUALLY               EXP   FBG   IO 140-255   8                    6200  7450
22  5 NISQUALLY               EXP   FBG   IO 105D  CHRY 8                   7500  8650
22  5 NISQUALLY               EXP   FBG   IO T120-T130 8                    7000  8400
22  5 NISQUALLY               SDN   FBG   IO 140-255   8                    6200  7450
22  5 NISQUALLY               SDN   FBG   IO T120-T130 8                    7000  8400
24  6 SARATOGA                EXP   FBG   IO 165-170   8                    7750  8900
      IB 188-255  5750  6800, IB 105D CHRY  9350 10600, IB T120-T170 6000 7400

24  6 SARATOGA OFFSHORE       OFF   FBG   IO 165-255   8                    7700  9200
24  6 SARATOGA OFFSHORE       OFF   FBG   IO T120-T188 8                    8450 10200
24  6 SARATOGA OFFSHORE       OFF FBG DV  IO 165-225   17                   9400 10900
24  6 SARATOGA OFFSHORE    HT OFF   FBG   IO 165-255   8                    7700  9200
24  6 SARATOGA OFFSHORE    HT OFF   FBG   IO 105D  CHRY 8                  10900 12400
24  6 SARATOGA OFFSHORE    HT OFF   FBG   IO T120-T188 8                    8450 10200
26  3 VICTORIA 2750        FB       FBG   IO 188-255   8      5285          9400 10700
      IO 105D CHRY 11700 13300, IO T120-T188  9650 11800, IO T105D CHRY 14300 16300
-------------------------- 1972 BOATS ---------------------------------------
16    SUPER TAHITI                 FBG   IO 120-140   6  7 1620            1900  2300
16  2 MUTINY                       FBG   IO 120-130   6  6 1610            1900  2300
16 10 DISCOVERY II                 FBG   IO 120-140   7  1 1800            2300  2850
17  4 WILLAPA                      FBG   IO 120       6  9 1740            2250  2650
17  4 WILLAPA                      FBG   IO 130-140   6  9                 2450  2850
17  8 QUARTERMASTER                FBG   IO 120       7  1 1970            2500  2900
17  8 QUARTERMASTER                FBG   IO 130-255   7  1                 2800  3350
17  8 QUARTERMASTER                FBG   JT 270   BERK 7 1                 2250  2650
19  2 ADMIRALTY                    FBG   IO 120-225   7  8 2270            3100  3850
19  2 ADMIRALTY                    FBG   IO 255   WAUK 7 8                 3350  3900
19  2 ADMIRALTY                    FBG   JT 270   BERK 7 8                 2600  3000

20  1 LIBERTY                CR     FBG   IO 120-165   7  8 2575           4100  5100
20  1 LIBERTY                CR     FBG   IO 170-255   7  8                4500  5250
22  2 NISQUALLY              EXP    FBG   IO 120       8      3400          5650  6500
22  2 NISQUALLY              EXP    FBG   IO 130-255   8                    6500  7600
22  2 NISQUALLY              EXP    FBG   IO T120-T170 8                    7100  8650
22  2 NISQUALLY              SDN    FBG   IO 120       8      2950          5150  5900
22  2 NISQUALLY              SDN    FBG   IO 130-255   8                    6500  7600
22  2 NISQUALLY              SDN    FBG   IO T120-T170 8                    7100  8650
23  9 SARATOGA            FB        FBG   IO 215   MRCR 8                   7550  8650
23  9 SARATOGA            FB        FBG   IO T130  VLVO 8                   8500  9750
23  9 SARATOGA               EXP    FBG   IO 165       8      3850          6700  7750
23  9 SARATOGA               EXP    FBG   IO 170-255   8                    9950 11400

23  9 SARATOGA               EXP    FBG   IO T120-T170 8                   10500 12400
23  9 SARATOGA OFFSHORE      OFF    FBG   IO 165-255   8                    7850  9300
23  9 SARATOGA OFFSHORE      OFF    FBG   IO T120-T170 8                    8600 10300
26  2 VICTORIA               SDN    FBG   IO 165-225   8                    9500 11400
26  2 VICTORIA               SDN    FBG   IO T120-T170 8                   10600 12900
26  2 VICTORIAN           FB        FBG   IO 215   MRCR 8                   9450 11700
26  2 VICTORIAN           FB        FBG   IO T130-T170 8                   10200 12100
-------------------------- 1971 BOATS ---------------------------------------
16 10 DISCOVERY                    FBG   IO 120   MRCR 6  7 1700           2200  2550
17  4 WILLAPA                      FBG   IO 120-140   6  9 1740            2300  2700
17  7 QUARTERMASTER                FBG   IO 120-215   7  1                 2700  3300
17  7 QUARTERMASTER                FBG   IO 455   PALM 7  1                6100  7000
19  2 ADMIRALTY                    FBG   IO 120-215   7  8 2250            3200  3950
19  2 ADMIRALTY                    FBG   IO 455   PALM 7  8 2250           6650  7550
20  1 LIBERTY                      FBG   IO 120-215   7  8 2475            3950  4750
23  9 SARATOGA               EXP    FBG   IO 155-215   8      3800          6850  8000
23  9 SARATOGA               EXP    FBG   IO 155-215   8      3800          7650  8800
23  9 SARATOGA OFFSHORE      OFF    FBG   IO T120-T140 8      3450          6400  7500
23  9 SARATOGA OFFSHORE      OFF    FBG   IO T120-T140 8      3450          7200  8300
-------------------------- 1970 BOATS ---------------------------------------
16 10 DISCOVERY           RNBT  FBG DV IO 120-165   6  8        1 4        2500  2900
16  3 WILLAPA             RNBT  FBG TR IO 120-140   6  8        1 4        2550  2950
18 11 CORONET             RNBT  FBG DV OB    120    7  5        1 5        1850  2200
18 11 CORONET             RNBT  FBG DV OB    120    7  5 2000   1 3        3100  3600
19  3 ADMIRALTY           CBNCR FBG DV IO 120-215   7  9 1450  1 5        4200  5000
19  3 ADMIRALTY           RNBT  FBG DV IO 120-215   7  9 2500  1 5        3600  4300
20    LIBERTY                   FBG DV IO 120-215   7  9 2500  1 5        4100  4900
20    LIBERTY             CBNCR FBG DV IO 120-215   7  9 2800  1 5        4950  5700
23  9 SARATOGA            CBNCR FBG DV IO 165-215   8    4200  1 7        8800 10100
23  9 SARATOGA OFFSHORE   OFF   FBG DV IO 165-215   8    3700  1 7        6950  8100
-------------------------- 1969 BOATS ---------------------------------------
16    TAHITI              SKI   FBG DV IO 120-140   6  8      1450         1950  2300
16 10 DISCOVERY           RNBT  FBG DV IO 120-160   6  8      1700         2450  2950
18 11 CORONET             RNBT  FBG DV OB    120    7  5      1400         1800  2150
18 11 CORONET             RNBT  FBG DV IO 120-160   7  8      2000         3200  3800
19  5 ADMIRALTY           RNBT  FBG DV IO 140-200   7  7      2200         3400  4150
19  5 ADMIRALTY           CBNCR FBG DV IO 120-200   7  7      2300         3900  4700
19  5 ADMIRALTY           RNBT  FBG DV IO 120   MRCR 7  7     2300         3450  4050
-------------------------- 1968 BOATS ---------------------------------------
16 10 CORONET             OP    RNBT FBG   IO 120   MRCR 7  6 2000         2950  3400
16 10 DISCOVERY           OP    RNBT FBG   IO 120   MRCR 7  6 1550         2450  2900
16 10 DISCOVERY           OP    RNBT FBG   IO 160       7  6              2700  3100
18 10 CORNET              OP    RNBT FBG   OB         7  7 1350           1750  2100
18 10 CORNET              OP    RNBT FBG   IO 160     7  8               3550  4100
-------------------------- 1967 BOATS ---------------------------------------
16 10 BAYLINER            RNBT  FBG DV IO 80        6  8                  2750  3200
```

BAYON CUSTOM BOATS
COAST GUARD MFG ID- CBB
FORMERLY CUSTOM BOATS BY BAYON

Call 1-800-327-6929 for BUC Personalized Evaluation Service
Or, for 1977 to 1983 boats, sign onto www.BUCValuPro.com

BAYRUNNER BOATS INC
COAST GUARD MFG ID- BYN

Call 1-800-327-6929 for BUC Personalized Evaluation Service
Or, for 1974 boats, sign onto www.BUCValuPro.com

BAYSTAR MARINE DIVISION

Call 1-800-327-6929 for BUC Personalized Evaluation Service
Or, for 1970 to 1971 boats, sign onto www.BUCValuPro.com

BB10 MANUFACTURING INC
COAST GUARD MFG ID- BB9

Call 1-800-327-6929 for BUC Personalized Evaluation Service
Or, for 1982 to 1988 boats, sign onto www.BUCValuPro.com

BEACH-CRAFT
LOUISIANA MO   See inside cover to adjust price for area

LOA FT IN	NAME AND/ OR MODEL	TOP/ RIG	BOAT TYPE	-HULL- MTL TP	TP	ENGINE # HP	MFG	BEAM FT IN	WGT LBS	DRAFT FT IN	RETAIL LOW	RETAIL HIGH
1966 BOATS												
16 7	SPORT SKIER		CKI	FBG	OB			6 5	720		1700	2050
16 8			RNBT	FBG DV	OB			6 6	875		2050	2450
16 8			RNBT	FBG DV	IO	90		6 6			3650	4250
1965 BOATS												
16 7	17 SPORTS		SKI	FBG	OB						1700	2050
16 7	STINGER 17			FBG	OB						2300	2650

BEACHCAT BOATS INC
OLDSMAR FL 34677   COAST GUARD MFG ID- MXB See inside cover to adjust price for area

For more recent years, see the BUC Used Boat Price Guide, Volume 1 or Volume 2

LOA FT IN	NAME AND/ OR MODEL	TOP/ RIG	BOAT TYPE	-HULL- MTL TP	TP	ENGINE # HP	MFG	BEAM FT IN	WGT LBS	DRAFT FT IN	RETAIL LOW	RETAIL HIGH
1982 BOATS												
25 4	BEACHCOMBER 25	CAT	SA/CR	FBG CB	OB			8	4000	11	11200	12800
25 4	BEACHCOMBER 25	CAT	SA/CR	FBG CB	IB	8D- 15D		8	5300	1 3	15500	17800
1981 BOATS												
25 4	BEACHCOMBER 25	CAT	SA/CR	FBG CB				8	4500		11200	12800
25 4	BEACHCOMBER 25	KTH	SA/CR	FBG CB				8	4500		11200	12800
32	SANDPIPER 32	CAT	SA/CR	FBG BB	IB	12D	YAN	8	7500		25300	28100
32	SANDPIPER 32	SCH	SA/CR	FBG BB	IB	12D	YAN	8	7500		25300	28100
1980 BOATS												
25 4	BEACHCOMBER 25	CAT	SA/CR	FBG CB				8	4000		9800	11100
25 4	BEACHCOMBER 25	KTH	SA/CR	FBG CB				8	4000		9800	11100
32	SANDPIPER 32	CAT	SA/CR	FBG BB	IB	12D	YAN	8	7500		24700	27500
32	SANDPIPER 32	SCH	SA/CR	FBG BB	IB	12D	YAN	8	7500		24700	27500
1979 BOATS												
25	BEACHCOMBER 25	CAT	SA/CR	FBG CB	OB			8	4000	11	9750	11100
32	SANDPIPER 32 SPARPIE	SCH	SA/CR	FBG BB	IB	12D	YAN	8	7400	1 7	23300	25900
1978 BOATS												
32	SANDPIPER 32 SHARPIE	SCH	SA/CR	FBG SK	OB			8	6500	1 7	20100	22300
32	SANDPIPER 32 SHARPIE	SCH	SA/CR	FBG SK	IB	12D	YAN	8	6500	1 7	20100	22300

BEACHCOMBER FIBERGLASS TECH
COAST GUARD MFG ID- BXG
FORMERLY BEACHCOMBER BOAT BUILDING

Call 1-800-327-6929 for BUC Personalized Evaluation Service
Or, for 1965 to 1988 boats, sign onto www.BUCValuPro.com

BEACHCRAFT MARINE CORP
COAST GUARD MFG ID- BCC

Call 1-800-327-6929 for BUC Personalized Evaluation Service
Or, for 1976 to 1983 boats, sign onto www.BUCValuPro.com

BEAUVAIS MARINE INC
COAST GUARD MFG ID- TUV

Call 1-800-327-6929 for BUC Personalized Evaluation Service
Or, for 1980 to 1982 boats, sign onto www.BUCValuPro.com

BEAVER GLASS HULLS LTD
COAST GUARD MFG ID- ZBG

Call 1-800-327-6929 for BUC Personalized Evaluation Service
Or, for 1968 to 1983 boats, sign onto www.BUCValuPro.com

BEE CRAFT INC
COAST GUARD MFG ID- BEE

Call 1-800-327-6929 for BUC Personalized Evaluation Service
Or, for 1961 to 1983 boats, sign onto www.BUCValuPro.com

THE BEEBE CO

Call 1-800-327-6929 for BUC Personalized Evaluation Service
Or, for 1960 boats, sign onto www.BUCValuPro.com

BEL-CRAFT INC
LINKWOOD MD 21835   See inside cover to adjust price for area

LOA FT IN	NAME AND/ OR MODEL	TOP/ RIG	BOAT TYPE	-HULL- MTL TP	TP	ENGINE # HP	MFG	BEAM FT IN	WGT LBS	DRAFT FT IN	RETAIL LOW	RETAIL HIGH
1966 BOATS												
25 8			EXP	WD	IB	220					6000	6900
30	SEMI-ENCLOSED		EXP	WD	IB	220					11200	12700
30	SEMI-ENCLOSED		EXP	WD	IB	T195-T220					12200	14200
30	TANGIER		EXP	WD	IB	220		10 10		2 2	11200	12700
30	TANGIER		EXP	WD	IB	T195-T220		10 10		2 2	12200	14100
30	TANGIER	FB	EXP	WD	IB	220		10 10		2 2	11200	12700
30	TANGIER	FB	EXP	WD	IB	T195-T220		10 10		2 2	12200	14100
30	TANGIER SPORTS		SPTCR	WD	IB	220		10 10		2 2	10600	12000
30	TANGIER SPORTS		SPTCR	WD	IB	T195-T220		10 10		2 2	11500	13300
1965 BOATS												
25 8			EXP	WD	IB	190-220					5450	6350
25 8		HT	EXP	WD	IB	190-220					5700	6650
25 8	SEMI-ENCLOSED		EXP	WD	IB	190-220					6000	7000
25 8	SPORTSMAN			WD	IB	190-220					5200	6050
25 8	SPORTSMAN	HT		WD	IB	190-220					5550	6450
25 8	SPORTSMAN			WD	IB	190-220					5550	6450
25 8	SPORTSMAN SEMI-ENCL			WD	IB	190-220					5850	6850
28 8		HT	EXP	WD	IB	210-220					9400	10700
28 8		HT	EXP	WD	IB	T190-T220					10200	11900
28 8		FB	EXP	WD	IB	210-220					9400	10700
28 8		FB	EXP	WD	IB	T190-T220					10200	11900
28 8	4 SLEEPER		EXP	WD	IB	210-220					9000	10300
28 8	4 SLEEPER		EXP	WD	IB	T190-T220					9800	11500
28 8	SEMI-ENCLOSED		EXP	WD	IB	210-220					9650	11100
28 8	SEMI-ENCLOSED		EXP	WD	IB	T190-T220					10500	12200
28 8	SPORTSMAN			WD	IB	210-220					7600	8750
28 8	SPORTSMAN			WD	IB	T190-T220					8550	10100
28 8	SPORTSMAN	HT		WD	IB	210-220					9400	10800
28 8	SPORTSMAN	HT		WD	IB	T190-T220					10300	11900
28 8	SPORTSMAN	FB		WD	IB	210-220					7700	8900
28 8	SPORTSMAN	FB		WD	IB	T190-T220					8600	10300
28 8	SPORTSMAN SEMI-ENCL			WD	IB	210-220					8400	9700
28 8	SPORTSMAN SEMI-ENCL			WD	IB	T190-T220					9400	10900
28 8	TANGIER	FB		WD	IB	210-220					11100	12700
28 8	TANGIER	FB		WD	IB	T190-T220					11900	13600
28 8	TANGIER		EXP	WD	IB	210-220					9400	10700
28 8	TANGIER		EXP	WD	IB	T190-T220					10300	11900
28 8	TANGIER SEMI-ENCL			WD	IB	210-220					12200	13900
28 8	TANGIER SEMI-ENCL			WD	IB	T190-T220					12900	14900
31 8		FB	EXP	WD	IB	T190-T220					14500	16800
31 8	SEMI-ENCLOSED		EXP	WD	IB	T190-T220					14500	16800
31 8	SEMI-ENCLOSED	FB	SF	WD	IB	T190-T220					11900	13800
1964 BOATS												
26		EXP		WD	IB	178-225					5550	6550
26		SF		WD	IB	178-225					5850	6900
26	DELUXE			WD	IB	178-225					5400	6350
26	SPORTSMAN DLX			WD	IB	225-280					9350	10800
29		EXP		WD	IB	225					9300	11400
29		EXP		WD	IB	T105-T188					10300	11700
29	DELUXE	SF		WD	IB	225-280					8950	10500
29	DELUXE	SF		WD	IB	T105-T188					8950	11000
29	DELUXE	SF		WD	IB	225-280					10000	11400
29	SPORTSMAN DLX			WD	IB	225-280					9400	10900
29	SPORTSMAN DLX			WD	IB	T105-T188					9350	11500
29	SPORTSMAN DLX			WD	IB	T225					10400	11800

BEL-CRAFT INC -CONTINUED See inside cover to adjust price for area

LOA FT	LOA IN	NAME AND/ OR MODEL	TOP/ RIG	BOAT TYPE	-HULL- MTL	-HULL- TP	ENGINE TP	ENGINE # HP	ENGINE MFG	BEAM FT	BEAM IN	WGT LBS	DRAFT FT	DRAFT IN	RETAIL LOW	RETAIL HIGH
1964 BOATS																
32				EXP	WD		IB	T188-T225							14500	16900
32			FB	EXP	WD		IB	T188-T225							14500	16900
32		DELUXE		SF	WD		IB	T188-T225							11800	13800
1963 BOATS																
24	7			EXP	WD		IB	150-225							4750	5600
24	7			SF	WD		IB	150-190							4150	4900
24	7	BEL-AIR SKIFF	OP		WD		IB	100-190							4400	5350
24	7	SPORTSMAN DLX			WD		IB	150-190							4550	5350
28	2			EXP	WD		IB	T100-T150							7600	9350
28	2			EXP	WD		IB	T178-T188							8350	9700
28	2			SF	WD		IB	T100-T150							7500	9200
28	2			SF	WD		IB	T178-T188							8250	9550
28	2	SPORTSMAN DLX			WD		IB	T100-T150							7300	9000
28	2	SPORTSMAN DLX			WD		IB	T178-T188							8100	9350
31				EXP	WD		IB	T100-T188							11600	14300
31				SF	WD		IB	T100-T188							9700	12000
31		SPORTSMAN DLX			WD		IB	T100-T188							9150	11300
1962 BOATS																
24	6	R-10		UTL	WD		IB	100-150							2800	3500
24	6	R-10		UTL	WD		IB	185-188							3100	3600
24	6	R-10-D	HT	CR	WD		IB	100-188							4500	5400
24	6	R-7 DLX		EXP	WD		IB	135-188							4600	5400
24	6	SHELTER CABIN R-8		CR	WD		IB	100-188							4500	5400
24	6	SPORTSMAN CUS R-9-C			WD		IB	135-188							4400	5200
24	6	SPORTSMAN R-9 DELUXE			WD		IB	135-188							4400	5200
24	6	SPORTSMAN R-9-S			WD		IB	100-188							4250	5200
31		DELUXE		SF	WD		IB	T100-T185							9500	11600
31		SEMI-ENCLOSED		EXP	WD		IB	T100-T185							11400	14000
31		SPORTSMAN			WD		IB	T100-T185							8950	11000
31		SPORTSMAN CUS			WD		IB	T100-T185							8950	11000
31		SPORTSMAN DLX			WD		IB	T100-T185							8950	11000

BELL BOY

AMERICAN MARINE IND INC
TACOMA WA 98421 COAST GUARD MFG ID- AMM

See inside cover to adjust price for area

LOA FT	LOA IN	NAME AND/ OR MODEL	TOP/ RIG	BOAT TYPE	-HULL- MTL	-HULL- TP	ENGINE TP	ENGINE # HP	ENGINE MFG	BEAM FT	BEAM IN	WGT LBS	DRAFT FT	DRAFT IN	RETAIL LOW	RETAIL HIGH
1983 BOATS																
17	10	BALLERINA 1875		RNBT	FBG	DV	IO	120-228		7					2900	3550
17	10	BARRACUDA 1820		RNBT	FBG	DV	IO	120-228		7					2900	3550
17	10	BEACHCOMBER 1830		RNBT	FBG	DV	IO	120-228		7					2900	3550
18		BANDIT 1810		RNBT	FBG	DV	OB			7		1400			2500	2900
18	11	CUTLASS 1950		RNBT	FBG	DV	IO	120-228		7	1				3100	3750
19	6	BONITA 2010		RNBT	FBG	DV	IO	120-228		8					3700	4500
19	6	MARLIN 2030		RNBT	FBG	DV	IO	120-228		8					3700	4500
19	6	RIVIERA 2070		RNBT	FBG	DV	IO	120-228		8					3700	4500
19	6	VIKING 2050		RNBT	FBG	DV	IO	120-228		8					3700	4500
21	6	ALASKA 2210		RNBT	FBG	DV	IO	120-228		8					5650	6650
21	6	BLUEWATER 2215		RNBT	FBG	DV	IO	120-228		8					5650	6650
21	6	OVERNIGHTER 2220		OVNTR	FBG	DV	IO	120-228		8					5950	7000
1982 BOATS																
17	10	BALLERINA 1875		RNBT	FBG	DV	IO	120-228		7					2850	3450
17	10	BARRACUDA 1820		RNBT	FBG	DV	IO	120-228		7					2850	3450
17	10	BEACHCOMBER 1830		RNBT	FBG	DV	IO	120-228		7					2850	3450
18		BANDIT 1810		RNBT	FBG	DV	OB			7		1400			2450	2850
18	11	CUTLASS 1950		RNBT	FBG	DV	IO	120-228		7	1				3000	3650
19	6	BONITA 2010		RNBT	FBG	DV	IO	120-228		8					3600	4350
19	6	MARLIN 2030		RNBT	FBG	DV	IO	120-228		8					3600	4350
19	6	RIVIERA 2070		RNBT	FBG	DV	IO	120-228		8					3600	4350
19	6	VIKING 2050		RNBT	FBG	DV	IO	120-228		8					3600	4350
21	6	ALASKA 2210		RNBT	FBG	DV	IO	120-228		8					5500	6500
21	6	BLUEWATER 2215		RNBT	FBG	DV	IO	120-228		8					5500	6500
21	6	OVERNIGHTER 2220		OVNTR	FBG	DV	IO	120-228		8					5800	6800
1981 BOATS																
17	10	BALLERINA 1875		RNBT	FBG	DV	IO	120-228		7					2750	3350
17	10	BARRACUDA 1820		RNBT	FBG	DV	IO	120-228		7					2750	3350
17	10	BEACHCOMBER 1830		RNBT	FBG	DV	IO	120-228		7					2750	3350
18		BANDIT 1810		RNBT	FBG	DV	OB			7		1400			2450	2800
18	11	CUTLASS 1950		RNBT	FBG	DV	IO	120-228		7	1				2950	3550
19	6	BONITA 2010		RNBT	FBG	DV	IO	120-228		8					3550	4250
19	6	MARLIN 2030		RNBT	FBG	DV	IO	120-228		8					3550	4250
19	6	VIKING 2050		RNBT	FBG	DV	IO	120-228		8					3550	4250
21	6	OVERNIGHTER 2220		OVNTR	FBG	DV	IO	120-228		8					5650	6700
1980 BOATS																
16	9	BALLERINA	OP	RNBT	FBG	DV	IO	120		7		2200			2400	2750
16	9	BANDIT		RNBT	FBG	DV	OB			7		1400			2350	2750
16	9	BEACHCOMBER	OP	RNBT	FBG	DV	IO	120		7		2400			2500	2900
16	9	BOLERO	OP	RNBT	FBG	DV	IO	120		7					2400	2800
16	9	BONITA		RNBT	FBG	DV	OB			7		1400			2350	2700
17		BARRACUDA	OP	RNBT	FBG	DV	IO	120		7		2200			2400	2800
18		CUTLASS	OP	SKI	FBG	DV	IO	120		7		2500			2650	3050
18	5	ALASKA	HT	RNBT	FBG	DV	IO	120		8					3050	3550
18	5	BONITA	OP	RNBT	FBG	DV	IO	120		8		2600			3050	3550
18	5	MARLIN	OP	RNBT	FBG	DV	IO	120		8		2600			2800	3250
18	5	RIVIERA	OP	RNBT	FBG	DV	IO	120		8		2600			3450	4000
18	5	VIKING	HT	RNBT	FBG	DV	IO	120		8		2600			3100	3600
20	5	ALASKA	HT	RNBT	FBG	DV	IO	120		8		2900			4100	4750
20	5	BLUE-WATER	HT	RNBT	FBG	DV	IO	120		8		2900			3700	4300
20	5	BONNEVILLE		EXP	FBG	DV	IO	120		8					4450	5100
20	5	OVERNIGHTER	HT	OVNTR	FBG	DV	IO	120		8		3300			4500	5150
20	5	SARATOGA		RNBT	FBG	DV	IO	120		8					3900	4550
22	3	SPORT SEDAN		SDN	FBG	DV	IO	185		8					5800	6650
24	3	VAGABOND		EXP	FBG	DV	IO	185		8					6950	8000
1979 BOATS																
16	9	BALLERINA 175	ST	RNBT	FBG	DV	IO	120	OMC	7		2400			2400	2800
16	9	BALLERINA 175	ST	RNBT	FBG	DV	IO	120-200		7		2400			2600	3100
16	9	BANDIT 170	OP	RNBT	FBG	DV	OB			7		1400			2350	2700
16	9	BEACHCOMBER 173	ST	RNBT	FBG	DV	IO	120	OMC	7		2400			2500	2900
16	9	BEACHCOMBER 173	ST	RNBT	FBG	DV	IO	120-200		7		2400			2650	3200
16	9	BOLERO 172	OP	RNBT	FBG	DV	IO	120-170		7		2400			2450	3050
16	9	BOLERO 172	OP	RNBT	FBG	DV	IO	200		7		2400			2500	3100
18		CUTLASS 185	ST	SKI	FBG	DV	IO	120-170		7	1	2500			2600	3200
18		CUTLASS 185	ST	SKI	FBG	DV	IO	200-228		7	1	2500			2650	3300
18		CUTLASS 185	ST	SKI	FBG	DV	IO	255-260		7	1	2500			3000	3500
18	5	ALASKA 191	HT	RNBT	FBG	DV	IO	120-170		8		2600			3050	3850
18	5	ALASKA 191	HT	RNBT	FBG	DV	IO	200	OMC	8		2600			3100	3600
18	5	ALASKA 191	HT	RNBT	FBG	DV	IO	200-260		8		2600			3350	4100
18	5	BONITA 190	ST	RNBT	FBG	DV	IO	120-170		8		2600			2950	3650
18	5	BONITA 190	ST	RNBT	FBG	DV	IO	200	OMC	8		2600			3000	3500
18	5	BONITA 190	ST	RNBT	FBG	DV	IO	200-260		8		2600			3300	4000
18	5	MARLIN 195	ST	RNBT	FBG	DV	IO	120-170		8		2600			3050	3850
18	5	MARLIN 195	ST	RNBT	FBG	DV	IO	200	OMC	8		2600			3100	3600
18	5	MARLIN 195	ST	RNBT	FBG	DV	IO	200-260		8		2600			3350	4100
18	5	RIVIERA 197	HT	RNBT	FBG	DV	IO	120-170		8		2600			2950	3650
18	5	RIVIERA 197	HT	RNBT	FBG	DV	IO	200	OMC	8		2600			3000	3500
18	5	RIVIERA 197	HT	RNBT	FBG	DV	IO	200-260		8		2600			3250	4000
18	5	VIKING 194	HT	RNBT	FBG	DV	IO	120-170		8		2600			3000	3750
18	5	VIKING 194	HT	RNBT	FBG	DV	IO	200	OMC	8		2600			3050	3550
18	5	VIKING 194	HT	RNBT	FBG	DV	IO	200-260		8		2600			3350	4050
20	5	ALASKA 210	HT	RNBT	FBG	DV	IO	120-228		8		2900			3850	4750
20	5	ALASKA 210	HT	RNBT	FBG	DV	IO	255-260		8		2900			4300	5000
20	5	BONNEVILLE 217	ST	EXP	FBG	DV	IO	120-228		8		3500			4400	5350
20	5	BONNEVILLE 217	ST	EXP	FBG	DV	IO	255-260		8		3500			4850	5550
20	5	OVERNIGHTER 220	ST	OVNTR	FBG	DV	IO	120-228		8		3300			4400	5350
20	5	OVERNIGHTER 220	ST	OVNTR	FBG	DV	IO	255-260		8		3300			4900	5600
20	5	SARATOGA 215	ST	RNBT	FBG	DV	IO	120-228		8		2900			3850	4750
20	5	SARATOGA 215	ST	RNBT	FBG	DV	IO	255-260		8		2900			4300	5000
22	3	SPORT SEDAN 230	HT	SDN	FBG	DV	IO	200-260		8		4200			5800	7100
24	3	COMMANDER 255	FB	CBNCR	FBG	DV	IO	255	VLVO	8		5000			8900	10100
24	3	VAGABOND 250	HT	EXP	FBG	DV	IO	200-260		8		4600			6950	8400
1978 BOATS																
16	9	SV1700	OP	RNBT	FBG	DV	OB			7		1400			2300	2700
16	9	SV1700	OP	RNBT	FBG	DV	IO	120-198		7		2000			2250	2700
16	9	SV1705	ST	RNBT	FBG	DV	OB			7		1400			2300	2700
16	9	SV1705	ST	RNBT	FBG	DV	IO	120-198		7		2000			2250	2700
18	5	LV1900	OP	RNBT	FBG	DV	IO	120-198		8		2400			3000	3500
18	5	LV1905	ST	RNBT	FBG	DV	IO	120-198		8		2400			3000	3500
18	5	LV1910	HT	RNBT	FBG	DV	IO	120-198		8		2500			2950	3500
18	5	LV1915	HT	RNBT	FBG	DV	IO	120-198		8		2500			3200	3750
18	5	SV1900	OP	RNBT	FBG	DV	IO	120-198		8		2400			2950	3450
18	5	SV1905	ST	RNBT	FBG	DV	IO	120-198		8		2400			2950	3450
18	5	SV1910	HT	RNBT	FBG	DV	IO	120-198		8		2500			2900	3450
18	5	SV1915	HT	RNBT	FBG	DV	IO	120-198		8		2500			3150	3650
20	5	ALASKA LV2110-A	HT	CUD	FBG	DV	IO	120-240		8		3000			4200	5000
20	5	ALASKA SV2110-A	HT	CUD	FBG	DV	IO	120-240		8		3000			4150	4900
20	5	LV2100	OP	RNBT	FBG	DV	IO	120-240		8		2800			3900	4600

 CONTINUED ON NEXT PAGE

LOA FT IN	NAME AND/OR MODEL	TOP/RIG	BOAT TYPE	HULL MTL TP	ENGINE TP # HP MFG	BEAM FT IN	WGT LBS	DRAFT FT IN	RETAIL LOW	RETAIL HIGH
					--- 1978 BOATS ---					
20 5	LV2105	ST	RNBT	FBG DV	IO 120-240	8	2800		3900	4600
20 5	LV2110	HT	RNBT	FBG DV	IO 120-240	8	3000		3900	4650
20 5	LV2115	HT	RNBT	FBG DV	IO 120-240	8	3000		4200	4950
20 5	LV2120	OP	OVNTR	FBG DV	IO 120-240	8	3400		4600	5400
20 5	LV2120	HT	OVNTR	FBG DV	IO 120-240	8	3400		4600	5400
20 5	LV2145	HT	CUD	FBG DV	IO 120-240	8	3200		4400	5200
20 5	SV2100	OP	RNBT	FBG DV	IO 120-240	8	2800		3800	4550
20 5	SV2105	ST	RNBT	FBG DV	IO 120-240	8	2800		3800	4550
20 5	SV2110	HT	RNBT	FBG DV	IO 120-240	8	3000		3800	4600
20 5	SV2115	HT	RNBT	FBG DV	IO 120-240	8	3000		4100	4900
20 5	SV2120	OP	OVNTR	FBG DV	IO 120-240	8	3400		4550	5350
20 5	SV2120	HT	OVNTR	FBG DV	IO 120-240	8	3400		4550	5350
20 5	SV2145	HT	CUD	FBG DV	IO 120-240	8	3200		4300	5100
22 3	LV2300	HT	SDN	FBG DV	IO 170-240	8	4000		5600	6550
24 3	LV2520	HT	EXP	FBG DV	IO 170-240	8	4500		6850	8050
24 3	LV2530	FB	SDN	FBG DV	IO 170-240	8	4800		7250	8550
24 3	SV2520	HT	EXP	FBG DV	IO 170-240	8	4500		6700	7950
24 3	SV2530	FB	SDN	FBG DV	IO 170-240	8	4800		7200	8400
					--- 1977 BOATS ---					
18 5	LV1900	OP	RNBT	FBG DV	IO 120-198	7 10	2500		2950	3450
18 5	LV1905	OP	RNBT	FBG DV	IO 120-198	7 10	2500		3150	3700
18 5	LV1915	HT	RNBT	FBG DV	IO 120-198	7 10	2600		3100	3650
18 5	SV1900	OP	RNBT	FBG DV	IO 120-198	7 10	2500		2900	3400
18 5	SV1905	OP	RNBT	FBG DV	IO 120-198	7 10	2500		3100	3650
18 5	SV1915	HT	RNBT	FBG DV	IO 120-198	7 10	2600		3050	3600
20 5	LV2100	OP	RNBT	FBG DV	IO 120-235	8	2900		4000	4750
20 5	LV2105	ST	RNBT	FBG DV	IO 120-235	8	2900		4000	4750
20 5	LV2115	HT	RNBT	FBG DV	IO 120-235	8	2900		4000	4750
20 5	LV2120	ST	OVNTR	FBG DV	IO 120-235	8	3300		4750	5450
20 5	LV2140	HT	OVNTR	FBG DV	IO 120-235	8			4600	5400
20 5	LV2145		OVNTR	FBG DV	IO 120-235	8			4650	5400
20 5	SV2100	OP	RNBT	FBG DV	IO 120-235	8	2900		3950	4650
20 5	SV2105	ST	RNBT	FBG DV	IO 120-235	8	2900		3950	4650
20 5	SV2115	HT	RNBT	FBG DV	IO 120-235	8	2900		3950	4650
20 5	SV2120	ST	OVNTR	FBG DV	IO 120-235	8	3300		4450	5250
20 5	SV2140	HT	OVNTR	FBG DV	IO 120-235	8			4550	5300
20 5	SV2145		RNBT	FBG DV	IO 120-235	8			3950	4700
22 3	LV2300	HT	SDN	FBG DV	IO 170-288	8	4200		5850	6850
24 3	LV2520	HT	EXP	FBG DV	IO 170-288	8	4600		7050	8350
24 3	LV2530	FB	SDN	FBG DV	IO 170-288	8	5000		7550	8950
24 3	SV2520	HT	EXP	FBG DV	IO 170-235	8	4600		6950	8200
24 3	SV2530	FB	SDN	FBG DV	IO 170-235	8	5000		7450	8750
					--- 1976 BOATS ---					
18	XL195 HI-PERF	OP	RNBT	FBG DV	IO 140-235	7 1	2400		2750	3350
18	XL195 HI-PERF	OP	RNBT	FBG DV	JT 290 BERK	7 1	2400		3300	3850
18	XL196 HI-PERF	OP	RNBT	FBG DV	IO 140-235	7 1	2400		2700	3300
18	XL196 HI-PERF	OP	RNBT	FBG DV	JT 290 BERK	7 1	2400		3250	3750
18 6	LV1900	OP	RNBT	FBG DV	OB	7 4	1400		2100	2500
18 6	LV1900	OP	RNBT	FBG DV	IO 120-200	7 4	2500		2950	3650
18 6	LV1905	OP	RNBT	FBG DV	OB	7 4	1400		2550	2950
18 6	LV1905	ST	RNBT	FBG DV	IO 120-200	7 4	2500		2950	3650
18 6	LV1910	HT	RNBT	FBG DV	OB	7 4	1500		2450	2850
18 6	LV1910	HT	RNBT	FBG DV	IO 120-200	7 4	2600		2950	3650
18 6	LV1915	HT	RNBT	FBG DV	OB	7 4	1600		2550	2950
18 6	LV1915	HT	RNBT	FBG DV	IO 120-200	7 4	2600		3100	3850
20 6	LV2100	OP	RNBT	FBG DV	IO 120-235	8	2800		3950	4800
20 6	LV2100	OP	RNBT	FBG DV	IO 240 VLVO	8	2800		4250	4950
20 6	LV2105	ST	RNBT	FBG DV	IO 120-235	8	2800		3950	4800
20 6	LV2105	ST	RNBT	FBG DV	IO 240 VLVO	8	2800		4250	4950
20 6	LV2115	HT	RNBT	FBG DV	IO 120-235	8	2900		4000	4900
20 6	LV2115	HT	RNBT	FBG DV	IO 240 VLVO	8	2900		4400	5050
20 6	LV2120	OP	CUD	FBG DV	IO 120-235	8	3000		4250	5200
20 6	LV2120	OP	CUD	FBG DV	IO 240 VLVO	8	3000		4650	5350
20 6	LV2120	HT	CUD	FBG DV	IO 120-235	8	3000		4250	5350
20 6	LV2120	HT	CUD	FBG DV	IO 240 VLVO	8	3000		4650	5350
20 6	LV2140	HT	CUD	FBG DV	IO 120-235	8	2900		4150	5100
20 6	LV2140	HT	CUD	FBG DV	IO 240 VLVO	8	2900		4600	5250
22 3	LV2300	HT	SDN	FBG DV	IO 175-240	8	4400		6150	7500
22 3	LV2300	HT	SDN	FBG DV	IO T120-T140	8	4400		6850	8200
22 3	LV2350	HT	OFF	FBG DV	IO 175-240	8	4500		6400	7850
22 3	LV2350	HT	OFF	FBG DV	IO T120-T140	8	4500		7100	8450
24 3	LV2520	HT	EXP	FBG DV	IO 170-240	8	5000		7800	9200
24 3	LV2520	HT	EXP	FBG DV	IO T120-T140	8	5000		8550	10200
24 3	LV2530	FB	SDN	FBG DV	IO 170-240	8	5000		7850	9300
24 3	LV2530	FB	SDN	FBG DV	IO T120-T140	8	5000		8650	10300
					--- 1975 BOATS ---					
17 1	LV1800	ST	RNBT	FBG DV	OB	7 1	1300		2100	2500
17 1	LV1800	ST	RNBT	FBG DV	IO 120-190	7 1	2050		2450	2900
17 1	LV1805	ST	RNBT	FBG DV	OB	7 1	1350		2200	2550
17 1	LV1805	ST	RNBT	FBG DV	IO 120-190	7 1	2100		2500	2950
17 1	LV1810	HT	RNBT	FBG DV	OB	7 1	1450		2150	2500
17 1	LV1810	HT	RNBT	FBG DV	IO 120-190	7 1	2200		2500	2950
17 1	LV1815	HT	RNBT	FBG DV	OB	7 1	1450		2450	2850
17 1	LV1815	HT	RNBT	FBG DV	IO 120-190	7 1	2200		2700	3150
18	EX190	ST	RNBT	FBG DV	IO 140-235	7 1	2400		2750	3350
18	EX190	OP	RNBT	FBG DV	JT 295-330	7 1	2400		3100	3600
18	EX191	HT	RNBT	FBG DV	IO 140-235	7 1	2400		2650	3300
18	EX191	OP	RNBT	FBG DV	JT 295-330	7 1	2400		3000	3500
18	XL195	OP	RNBT	FBG DV	IO 140-235	7 1	2400		2900	3550
18	XL195	OP	RNBT	FBG DV	JT 295-330	7 1	2400		3350	3850
18	XL196	OP	RNBT	FBG DV	IO 140-235	7 1	2400		2850	3500
18	XL196	OP	RNBT	FBG DV	JT 295-330	7 1	2400		3200	3700
18	XL197	OP	RNBT	FBG DV	IO 140-235	7 1	2400		2800	3450
18	XL197	OP	RNBT	FBG DV	JT 295-330	7 1	2400		3150	3650
19 1	LV2000	ST	RNBT	FBG DV	IO 120-235	7 7	2400		3100	3750
19 1	LV2005	ST	RNBT	FBG DV	IO 120-235	7 7	2450		3150	3850
19 1	LV2010	HT	RNBT	FBG DV	IO 120-235	7 7	2550		3150	3850
19 1	LV2015	HT	RNBT	FBG DV	IO 120-235	7 7	2550		3400	4000
19 1	LV2040	HT	RNBT	FBG DV	IO 120-235	7 7	2650		3300	3950
19 1	LV2050	HT	RNBT	FBG DV	IO 120-235	7 7	2650		3400	4050
21 3	LV2220	HT	CUD	FBG DV	IO 120-235	8	2850		4450	5300
22 3	LV2300	HT	SDN	FBG DV	IO 175-235	8	4000		5850	6900
22 3	LV2300	HT	SDN	FBG DV	IO T120-T140	8	4000		6500	7500
22 3	LV2330	FB	SPTCR	FBG DV	IO 175-235	8	4300		6550	7800
22 3	LV2330	FB	SPTCR	FBG DV	IO T120-T140	8	4300		7250	8350
22 3	LV2340	ST	OFF	FBG DV	IO 175-235	8	4000		6000	7100
22 3	LV2340	HT	OFF	FBG DV	IO T120-T140	8	4000		6650	7650
22 3	LV2350	HT	OFF	FBG DV	IO 175-235	8	4000		6000	7100
22 3	LV2350	HT	OFF	FBG DV	IO T120-T140	8	4000		6650	7650
24 3	LV2500	OP	SDN	FBG DV	IO 175-235	8	4500		7250	8550
24 3	LV2500	OP	SDN	FBG DV	IO T120-T140	8	4500		8250	9550
24 3	LV2520	HT	EXP	FBG DV	IO 175-235	8	4500		7150	8400
24 3	LV2520	HT	EXP	FBG DV	IO T120-T140	8	4500		8150	9400
24 3	LV2530	FB	SPTCR	FBG DV	IO 175-235	8	4650		7600	9050
24 3	LV2530	FB	SPTCR	FBG DV	IO T120-T140	8	4650		8650	10000
					--- 1974 BOATS ---					
17 1	LV1800	ST		FBG	OB	7 1	1300		2050	2450
17 1	LV1800	ST		FBG	IO 120-190	7 1	2100		2450	3050
17 1	LV1800	ST		FBG	IO 200 VLVO	7 1	2100		2700	3100
17 1	LV1800	ST		FBG	JT 270 BERK	7 1	2100		2600	3000
17 1	LV1805	ST		FBG	OB	7 1	1325		2100	2500
17 1	LV1805	ST		FBG	IO 120-190	7 1	2125		2500	3100
17 1	LV1805	ST		FBG	IO 200 VLVO	7 1	2125		2750	3150
17 1	LV1805	ST		FBG	JT 270 BERK	7 1	2125		2600	3100
17 1	LV1810	HT		FBG	OB	7 1	1375		2200	2550
17 1	LV1810	HT		FBG	IO 120-190	7 1	2175		2600	3100
17 1	LV1810	HT		FBG	IO 200 VLVO	7 1	2175		2750	3200
17 1	LV1810	HT		FBG	JT 270 BERK	7 1	2175		2600	3050
17 1	LV1815	HT		FBG	OB	7 1	1395		2250	2600
17 1	LV1815	HT		FBG	IO 120-190	7 1	2200		2550	3150
17 1	LV1815	HT		FBG	IO 200 VLVO	7 1	2200		2750	3200
17 1	LV1815	HT		FBG	JT 270 BERK	7 1	2200		3050	3550
19 1	LV2000	ST		FBG	IO 120-190	7 9	2435		3200	3950
19 1	LV2000	ST		FBG	IO 200-225	7 9	2435		3450	4100
19 1	LV2000	ST		FBG	JT 270 BERK	7 9	2435		3200	3750
19 1	LV2005	ST		FBG	IO 120-190	7 9	2460		3300	3950
19 1	LV2005	ST		FBG	IO 200-225	7 9	2460		3450	4100
19 1	LV2005	ST		FBG	JT 270 BERK	7 9	2460		3250	3750
19 1	LV2010	HT		FBG	IO 120-200	7 9	2535		3300	4100
19 1	LV2010	HT		FBG	IO 225	7 9	2535		3400	4150
19 1	LV2010	HT		FBG	JT 270 BERK	7 9	2535		3300	3850
19 1	LV2010	HT		FBG	IO 120-200	7 9	2560		3300	4100
19 1	LV2015	HT		FBG	IO 225	7 9	2560		3400	4150
19 1	LV2015	HT		FBG	JT 270 BERK	7 9	2560		3350	3850
19 1	LV2040	HT		FBG	IO 120-225	7 9	2600		3350	4150
19 1	LV2040	HT		FBG	JT 270 BERK	7 9	2600		3300	3850

BELL BOY -CONTINUED

See inside cover to adjust price for area

LOA FT	IN	NAME AND/OR MODEL	TOP/RIG	BOAT TYPE	HULL MTL	HULL TP	ENG TP	HP	MFG	BEAM FT	IN	WGT LBS	DRAFT FT	IN	RETAIL LOW	RETAIL HIGH
		1974 BOATS														
19	1	LV2050	HT		FBG		IO	120-225		7	9	2600			3400	4250
19	1	LV2050	HT		FBG		JT	270	BERK	7	9	2600			3400	3950
22	3	LV2300		SDN	FBG		IO	140-255		8		4200			6350	7650
22	3	LV2300		SDN	FBG		IO	T120-T140		8		4200			7100	8450
22	3	LV2310		SF	FBG		IO	140-255		8		4000			6850	8300
22	3	LV2310		SF	FBG		IO	T120-T140		8		4000			7550	9200
22	3	LV2320		EXP	FBG		IO	140-255		8		4400			6450	7850
22	3	LV2320		EXP	FBG		IO	T120-T140		8		4400			7200	8600
22	3	LV2330	FB		FBG		IO	140-255		8		4500			6400	7700
22	3	LV2330	FB		FBG		IO	T120-T140		8		4500			7100	8450
24	3	LV2500		SDN	FBG		IO	165-255		8		4400			7400	9000
24	3	LV2500		SDN	FBG		IO	T120-T140		8		4400			8450	10100
24	3	LV2510		SF	FBG		IO	165-255		8		4500			8300	9950
24	3	LV2510		SF	FBG		IO	T120-T140		8		4500			9500	11200
24	3	LV2520		EXP	FBG		IO	165-255		8		4600			7550	9150
24	3	LV2520		EXP	FBG		IO	T120-T140		8		4600			8600	10300
24	3	LV2530	FB		FBG		IO	165-255		8		4700			7400	9000
24	3	LV2530	FB		FBG		IO	T120-T140		8		4700			8450	10100
24	3	LV2540		OFF	FBG		IO	165-255		8		4200			7050	8450
24	3	LV2540		OFF	FBG		IO	T120-T140		8		4200			8050	9650
		1973 BOATS														
17	1	LV1800	ST		FBG		OB			7	1	1275			2000	2400
17	1	LV1800	ST		FBG		IO	120-165		7	1	2075			2550	2950
17	1	LV1800	HT		FBG		OB			7	1	1350			2150	2500
17	1	LV1800	HT		FBG		IO	120-165		7	1	2150			2600	3050
17	6	LT1800			FBG	TR	OB			7	2	1300			2100	2450
17	6	LT1800			FBG	TR	IO	120-140		7	2	2100			2650	3050
19	1	LV2000	ST		FBG		OB			7	7				2350	2750
19	1	LV2000	ST		FBG		IO	120-225		7	7	2400			3200	3900
19	1	LV2000	HT		FBG		OB			7	7				2350	2750
19	1	LV2000	HT		FBG		IO	120-225		7	7				3350	4000
21	3	LV2200	ST		FBG		IO	120-225		8		2500			4300	5050
21	3	LV2210	HT		FBG		IO	120-225		8		2650			4450	5200
21	3	LV2220		OVNTR	FBG		IO	120-225		8		2850			4800	5650
21	3	LV2230		EXP	FBG		IO	120-225		8		2650			4550	5300
21	3	LV2240		EXP	FBG		IO	120-225		8		2650			4400	5150
24	3	LV2500	HT	SDN	FBG		IO	165-255		8		4400			7750	9250
24	3	LV2500		SDN	FBG		IO	100D	CHRY	8		4400			9350	10600
24	3	LV2510		SF	FBG		IO	165-255		8		4450			8500	10200
24	3	LV2510		SF	FBG		IO	100D	CHRY	8		4450			11200	12700
24	3	LV2510		SF	FBG		IO	T120-T140		8		4450			9750	11100
24	3	LV2520		EXP	FBG		IO	165-255		8		4500			7750	9250
24	3	LV2520		EXP	FBG		IO	100D	CHRY	8		4500			9350	10600
24	3	LV2520		EXP	FBG		IO	T120-T140		8		4500			8850	10100
24	3	LV2530	FB		FBG		IO	165-255		8		4800			7850	9400
24	3	LV2530	FB		FBG		IO	100D	CHRY	8		4800			9450	10700
24	3	LV2530	FB		FBG		IO	T120-T140		8		4800			8950	10200
		1972 BOATS														
17	1	LV1800	ST		FBG		OB			7	1	1275			2000	2400
17	1	LV1800	ST		FBG		IO	120-165		7	1	2075			2600	3150
17	1	LV1800	HT		FBG		OB			7	1	1350			2150	2500
17	1	LV1800	HT		FBG		IO	120-165		7	1	2150			2650	3150
17	6	LT1800			FBG	TR	OB			7	2	1100			1800	2150
17	6	LT1800			FBG	TR	IO	120-140		7	2	1900			2600	3000
19	1	LV2000	ST		FBG		OB			7	9	1500			2450	2850
19	1	LV2000	ST		FBG		IO	120-225		7	9	2400			3400	4250
19	1	LV2000	ST		FBG		IO	255	WAUK	7	9	2600			3850	4450
19	1	LV2000	HT		FBG		IO	120-225		7	9	2500			3500	4350
19	1	LV2000	HT		FBG		IO	255	WAUK	7	9	2700			3900	4550
21	3	LV2200	ST		FBG		IO	120-225		8		2550			4400	5400
21	3	LV2200	ST		FBG		IO	255	WAUK	8		2750			4850	5600
21	3	LV2200	HT		FBG		IO	120-225		8		2650			4500	5500
21	3	LV2200	HT		FBG		IO	255	WAUK	8		2825			4950	5650
21	3	LV2200		EXP	FBG		IO	120-255		8		3000			4950	6150
21	3	LV2200		OVNTR	FBG		IO	120-255		8					5450	6600
21	3	LV2200		OVNTR	FBG		IO	120-225		8		2850			4950	6000
21	3	LV2200	HT	OVNTR	FBG		IO	255	WAUK	8		3000			5500	6650
24	3	LV2500		EXP	FBG		IO	165-255		8		4425			7900	9550
24	3	LV2500		EXP	FBG		IO	T120-T140		8		5150			10100	11500
24	3	LV2500	HT	EXP	FBG		IO	165-255		8					8100	9650
24	3	LV2500	HT	EXP	FBG		IO	T120-T140		8					9250	10600
		1971 BOATS														
16	1	LV1700			FBG		IO	140	MRCR	6	6	1750			2200	2550
17	1	LV1800	ST		FBG		OB			7	1	1275			2000	2400
17	1	LV1800	ST		FBG		IO	155-165		7	1	2075			2700	3150
17	1	LV1800	HT		FBG		OB			7	1	1350			2150	2500
17	1	LV1800	HT		FBG		IO	155-165		7	1	2150			2750	3250
17	6	LT1800			FBG	TR	IO	140-155		7	2	1900			2700	3150
19	1	LV2000	ST		FBG		OB			7	9	1500			2450	2850
19	1	LV2000	ST		FBG		IO	215		7	9	2400			3600	4200
19	1	LV2000	HT		FBG		OB			7	9	1600			2550	3000
19	1	LV2000	HT		FBG		IO	215		7	9	2500			3700	4300
21	3	LV2200	ST		FBG		IO	215		8		2550			4650	5350
21	3	LV2200	HT		FBG		IO	215		8		2650			4750	5500
21	3	LV2200		EXP	FBG		IO	215		8		3000			5200	6000
21	3	LV2200		OVNTR	FBG		IO	215		8		2850			5250	6050
24	3	LV2500		EXP	FBG		IO	215		8		4500			8400	9650
25	10	V2600		EXP	F/W		IB	225	CHRY	9	2	5000	2	6	6850	7900
25	10	V2600		EXP	F/W		IB	T140		9	2	5000	2	6	7400	8500
		1970 BOATS														
17	1	BONITA		RNBT	FBG	SV	OB			7	1	1200			1950	2300
17	1	BONITA	ST	RNBT	FBG	SV	IO	120		7	1				3050	3550
18	8	BOLERO		RNBT	FBG	TR	IO	120		7	11				3850	4450
19	1	BONNEVILLE		RNBT	FBG	SV	OB			7	10	1500			2450	2850
19	1	BONNEVILLE	ST	RNBT	FBG	SV	IO	120		7	10				3900	4550
21	3	BEACHCOMBER		RNBT	FBG	DV	IO	120		8					5800	6650
21	3	BEACHCOMBER		OVNTR	FBG	DV	IO	120		8					5850	6700
21	3	BEACHCOMBER	ST	RNBT	FBG	DV	IO	120		8					5100	5850
		1969 BOATS														
17	1	BONITA		RNBT	FBG	DV	IO	160	OMC	7	1			11	3150	3650
17	1	BONITA	ST	RNBT	FBG		OB			7	1	1050			1750	2050
17	1	BONITA	ST	RNBT	FBG	DV	IO	160	MRCR	7	1			11	3150	3700
17	1	BONITA	HT	RNBT	FBG		OB			7	1	1125			1850	2200
19	1	BONNEVILLE		RNBT	FBG	DV	IO	210	OMC	7	9		1		4050	4700
19	1	BONNEVILLE	ST	RNBT	FBG		OB			7	9	1250			2200	2550
19	1	BONNEVILLE	ST	RNBT	FBG	DV	IO	210	MRCR	7	9		1		4100	4750
19	1	BONNEVILLE	HT	RNBT	FBG		OB			7	9	1350			2300	2700
21	3	BEACHCOMBER		RNBT	FBG	DV	IO	210		8			1	3	6100	7000
21	3	BEACHCOMBER		OVNTR	FBG	DV	IO	210		8			1	3	6150	7050
21	3	BEACHCOMBER		RNBT	FBG	DV	IO	210	OMC	8			1	1	5300	6100
21	3	BEACHCOMBER	ST	RNBT	FBG	DV	IO	210	MRCR	8			1	1	5350	6150
		1968 BOATS														
17	1	BONITA	ST		FBG		OB			7	1	1200			1950	2300
17	1	BONITA	ST		FBG		OB	80-160		7	1				3100	3500
17	1	BONITA	HT		FBG		OB			7	1				2250	2600
17	1	BONITA	HT		FBG		IO	80-160		7	1				3100	3650
19	1	BONNEVILLE	ST		FBG		OB			7	10	1500			2450	2850
19	1	BONNEVILLE	ST		FBG		IO	120-210		7	10				4050	4850
19	1	BONNEVILLE	HT		FBG		OB			7	10				2350	2750
19	1	BONNEVILLE	HT		FBG		IO	120-210		7	10				4050	4850
21	3	BEACHCOMBER	ST		FBG		IO	120-210		7	11				5550	6500
21	3	BEACHCOMBER	HT		FBG		IO	120-210		7	11				5550	6500
21	3	BEACHCOMBER		EXP	FBG		IO	120-210		7	11				6200	7250
21	3	BEACHCOMBER		OVNTR	FBG		IO	120-210		7	11				6250	7300
		1967 BOATS														
16	4	BONITA 17 CUSTOM			FBG		OB								2350	2750
16	4	BONITA 17 CUSTOM	HT		FBG		OB								3100	3650
16	4	BONITA CUSTOM			FBG		IO	80-160							3250	3600
16	4	BONITA CUSTOM	HT		FBG		IO	80-160							3050	3550
16	4	BONITA SPORT 17			FBG		OB								2050	2450
16	4	BONITA SPORT 17			FBG		IO	80-160							2950	3500
18	4	BONNEVILLE CUSTOM			FBG		OB								2400	2750
18	4	BONNEVILLE CUSTOM			FBG		IO	120-200							4050	4800
18	4	BONNEVILLE CUSTOM	HT		FBG		OB								2550	2750
18	4	BONNEVILLE CUSTOM	HT		FBG		IO	120-200							4000	4750
18	4	BONNEVILLE SPORT 19			FBG		OB								2250	2600
18	4	BONNEVILLE SPORT 19			FBG		IO	120-200							3900	4650
19	9	BEACHCOMBER		EXP	FBG		IO	120-200							5500	6400
19	9	BEACHCOMBER 20	HT		FBG		IO	120-200							5000	5800
19	9	BEACHCOMBER CUSTOM			FBG		IO	120-200							5000	5900
19	9	BEACHCOMBER SPORT 20			FBG		IO	120-200							4850	5750
		1966 BOATS														
16	4	BONITA 17 CUSTOM			FBG		OB								2350	2750
16	4	BONITA 17 CUSTOM			FBG		IO	60							3250	3750
16	4	BONITA 17 CUSTOM			FBG		IO	110							3200	3700
16	4	BONITA 17 CUSTOM			FBG		IO	110-120							3450	3600
16	4	BONITA CUSTOM	HT		FBG		OB								2250	2600
16	4	BONITA CUSTOM	HT		FBG		IO	60-120							3150	3900
16	4	BONITA SPORT 17			FBG		OB								2050	2450
16	4	BONITA SPORT 17			FBG		IO	60							3050	3550

 CONTINUED ON NEXT PAGE

BELL BOY — CONTINUED

LOA FT IN	NAME AND/OR MODEL	TOP/RIG	BOAT TYPE	HULL MTL	HULL TP	ENG TP	#	HP	MFG	BEAM FT IN	WGT LBS	DRAFT FT IN	RETAIL LOW	RETAIL HIGH
1966 BOATS														
16 4	BONITA SPORT 17			FBG		IO		110					3050	3550
16 4	BONITA SPORT 17			FBG		IO		110-120					3350	3850
18 4	BARRACUDA CUSTOM			FBG		OB							2450	2850
18 4	BARRACUDA CUSTOM			FBG		IO		110-200					4250	5200
18 4	BARRACUDA CUSTOM	HT		FBG		OB							2350	2750
18 4	BARRACUDA CUSTOM	HT		FBG		IO		110-200					4150	5100
18 4	BARRACUDA SPORT 19			FBG		OB							2300	2650
18 4	BARRACUDA SPORT 19			FBG		IO		110-200					4050	5000
18 4	BONNEVILLE	EXP		FBG		OB							2300	2700
18 4	BONNEVILLE	EXP		FBG		IO		110-150					4100	5000
18 4	BONNEVILLE CUSTOM			FBG		OB							2350	2750
18 4	BONNEVILLE CUSTOM			FBG		IO		110-150					4100	5100
18 4	BONNEVILLE CUSTOM	HT		FDG		OB							2250	2650
18 4	BONNEVILLE CUSTOM	HT		FBG		IO		110-150					4050	5000
18 4	BONNEVILLE SPORT 19			FBG		OB							2150	2500
18 4	BONNEVILLE SPORT 19			FBG		IO		110-150					3950	4900
19 9	BEACHCOMBER 20	HT		FBG		IO		110-200					5150	6150
19 9	BEACHCOMBER CUSTOM			FBG		IO		110-200					5200	6300
19 9	BEACHCOMBER SPORT 20			FBG		IO		110-200					5050	6100
1965 BOATS														
16 4	BONITA 17 CUSTOM			FBG		OB							2350	2750
16 4	BONITA 17 CUSTOM			FBG		IO		110-120					3450	4050
16 4	BONITA CUSTOM			FBG		OB							2250	2600
16 4	BONITA CUSTOM	HT		FBG		IO		110-120					3300	3850
16 4	BONITA SPORT 17			FBG		OB							2100	2450
16 4	BONITA SPORT 17			FBG		IO		110-120					3300	3900
18 4	BONNEVILLE CUSTOM			FBG		OB							2400	2800
18 4	BONNEVILLE CUSTOM			FBG		IO		110-150					4500	5200
18 4	BONNEVILLE CUSTOM	HT		FBG		OB							2300	2700
18 4	BONNEVILLE CUSTOM	HT		FBG		IO		110-150					4250	5000
18 4	BONNEVILLE SPORT 19			FBG		OB							2250	2600
18 4	BONNEVILLE SPORT 19			FBG		IO		110-150					4300	5000
18 6	BARRACUDA CUSTOM			FBG		OB							2400	2800
18 6	BARRACUDA CUSTOM			FBG		IO		110-150					4250	4950
18 6	BARRACUDA CUSTOM	HT		FBG		OB							2350	2700
18 6	BARRACUDA CUSTOM	HT		FBG		IO		110-150					4050	4750
18 6	BARRACUDA SPORT 19			FBG		OB							2250	2600
18 6	BARRACUDA SPORT 19			FBG		IO		110-150					4100	4800
23 6	BAHAMA 23			FBG		IO		110-150					9750	11100
1963 BOATS														
16	BAYONET 16	RNBT		FBG		OB							2300	2650
16	BONANZA 16			FBG		OB							2250	2650
16	BONANZA 16			FBG		IO		80-100					3450	4000
18	BONNEVILLE 18			FBG		OB							2300	2700
18	BONNEVILLE 18			FBG		IO		80-140					4500	5200
1962 BOATS														
16	BONNIE 16	CR		FBG		OB							2300	2650
16	BONNIE 16	CR		FBG		IO		80					3700	4300
16	BONNIE 16	RNBT		FBG		OB							2300	2700
16	BONNIE 16	RNBT		FBG		IO		80					3750	4350
17	BETA 17	CR		FBG		OB							2250	2650
17	BETA 17	CR		FBG		IO		80					4000	4650
17	BETA 17	EXP		FBG		OB							2250	2650
17	BETA 17	EXP		FBG		IO		80					3700	4300
17	BETA 17	RNBT		FBG		OB							2300	2650
17	BETA 17	RNBT		FBG		IO		80					3950	4600
20	BLAZER 20	EXP		FBG		OB							3350	3850
20	BLAZER 20	EXP		FBG		IO		80					7050	8100
1961 BOATS														
17	BETA 17	EXP		FBG		OB				7	1250		2050	2450
17	BETA 17	EXP		FBG		IO		80		7			3850	4450
17	BETA 17	RNBT		FBG		OB				7			4100	4750
17	BETA 17	HT	RNBT	FBG		OB				7	1025		1750	2100
17	BETA 17	HT	RNBT	FBG		IO		80		7			4100	4750
18 5			EXP	FBG		OB				7 3	1370		2350	2700
18 5			EXP	FBG		IO		80		7 3			4700	5400
18 5		HT	RNBT	FBG		OB				7 3	1290		2250	2650
18 5		HT	RNBT	FBG		IO		80		7 3			4900	5600
20	BLAZER 20	EXP		FBG		OB				7 3	1800		3150	3650
20	BLAZER 20	EXP		FBG		IO		80		7 11			7250	8350
20	BLAZER 20	SDN		FBG		IO		80		7 11	1750		3050	3550
20	BLAZER 20	SDN		FBG		IO		80		7 11			6900	7950
1960 BOATS														
18 5			EXP	FBG		OB							2400	2750
18 5			EXP	FBG		IO		160					5100	5850
18 5			RNBT	FBG		OB							2400	2800
18 5			RNBT	FBG		IO		160					5300	6100
18 5		ST	RNBT	FBG		OB							2400	2800
18 5		ST	RNBT	FBG		IO		160					5300	6100
18 5		HT	RNBT	FBG		OB							2400	2800
18 5		HT	RNBT	FBG		IO		160					5300	6100
18 5			SDN	FBG		OB							2400	2750
18 5			SDN	FBG		IO		160					5400	6200
1959 BOATS														
18 5	404	HT	EXP	FBG		OB				7 4	1190		2050	2450
21 2	EXPRESS	CR		FBG		OB				7 10	1750		3300	3800

BELL INDUSTRIES

DIV OF TAHITI BOAT   COAST GUARD MFG ID- TAH

Call 1-800-327-6929 for BUC Personalized Evaluation Service
Or, for 1970 to 1981 boats, sign onto www.BUCValuPro.com

BELLE CRAFT INC

NAPLES FL 33942   See inside cover to adjust price for area

LOA FT IN	NAME AND/OR MODEL	TOP/RIG	BOAT TYPE	HULL MTL	HULL TP	ENG TP	#	HP	MFG	BEAM FT IN	WGT LBS	DRAFT FT IN	RETAIL LOW	RETAIL HIGH
1979 BOATS														
24	BELLE-CRAFT	CUD		AL	SV	OB				8	1900		8550	9850
28	BELLE-CRAFT	CR		AL	SV	OB				8	4200		21700	24100
28	BELLE-CRAFT	CR		AL	SV	IB		200D		8	6100		17200	19500
32	BELLE-CRAFT	CR		AL	SV	IB		T200D		11 9	14000		41400	46000
37	BELLE-CRAFT	CR		AL	SV	IB		T200D		13	16000		53800	59100
55	BELLE-CRAFT	SF		AL	SV	IB		T450D		14	42000		145500	160000
1978 BOATS														
24	BELLE-CRAFT	CUD		AL	SV	OB				8	1900		8450	9700
28	BELLE-CRAFT	CR		AL	SV	OB				8	4200		21300	23700
28	BELLE-CRAFT	CR		AL	SV	IB		200D		8	6100		16500	18800
32	BELLE-CRAFT	CR		AL	SV	IB		T200D		11 9	14000		39800	44300
37	BELLE-CRAFT	CR		AL	SV	IB		T200D		13	16000		51500	56500
55	BELLE-CRAFT	SF		AL	SV	IB		T450D		14	42000		139500	153000

BELLEVILLE MARINE YARDS LTD

BELLEVILLE CANADA   See inside cover to adjust price for area

LOA FT IN	NAME AND/OR MODEL	TOP/RIG	BOAT TYPE	HULL MTL	HULL TP	ENG TP	#	HP	MFG	BEAM FT IN	WGT LBS	DRAFT FT IN	RETAIL LOW	RETAIL HIGH
1970 BOATS														
31 2	CORVETTE	SLP	SA/CR	FBG	KC			30		9 1	4000	3 3	6800	7800
35 8	FRIGATE	SLP	SA/CR	FBG	KC			30		10 2	5300	3 7	9400	10700
39 8	CRUSADER	SLP	SA/CR	FBG	KC			30		11 2	8405	4	20700	23000
1969 BOATS														
31 2	CORVETTE	SLP	SA/CR	FBG	KC	IB		30		9 1	8545	3 3	14700	16700
35 8	FRIGATE	SLP	SA/CR	FBG	KC	IB		30		10 2	11575	3 7	21200	23500
35 8	INVADER	SLP	SA/CR	FBG	KL	IB		30		10 2	16000	4 9	18600	20700
39 8	CRUSADER	SLP	SA/CR	FBG	KC	IB		30		11 2	18225	4 6	36900	41000
1968 BOATS														
31 3	CORVETTE	SLP	SA/CR	PLY	KC	IB		30		9 3	8545	3 3	14500	16500
35 8	INVADER	SLP	SA/CR	PLY	KL	IB		30		10 3	10000	4 9	18400	20400

BENDER SHIPBUILDING CORP

Call 1-800-327-6929 for BUC Personalized Evaluation Service
Or, for 1968 to 1969 boats, sign onto www.BUCValuPro.com

BENETEAU USA

CHANTIERS BENETEAU S/A-FRANCE   See inside cover to adjust price for area
MARION SC 29571   COAST GUARD MFG ID- BEY

For more recent years, see the BUC Used Boat Price Guide, Volume 1 or Volume 2

LOA FT IN	NAME AND/OR MODEL	TOP/RIG	BOAT TYPE	HULL MTL	HULL TP	ENG TP	#	HP	MFG	BEAM FT IN	WGT LBS	DRAFT FT IN	RETAIL LOW	RETAIL HIGH
1983 BOATS														
29 6	BENETEAU R/C 28	SLP	SA/RC	FBG	KL	IB			D	9	5300	4 3	14300	16300
31 6	BENETEAU R/C 30	SLP	SA/RC	FBG	KL	IB			D	10 6	7100	4 3	19800	22000
32 9	BENETEAU R/C 32	SLP	SA/RC	FBG	KL	IB			D	11 1	8000	5 10	22200	24600

LOA FT	LOA IN	NAME AND/ OR MODEL	TOP/ RIG	BOAT TYPE	-HULL- MTL	-HULL- TP	ENGINE TP	ENGINE # HP	ENGINE MFG	BEAM FT	BEAM IN	WGT LBS	DRAFT FT	DRAFT IN	RETAIL LOW	RETAIL HIGH
		1983 BOATS														
35	2	BENETEAU R/C 35	SLP	SA/RC	FBG	KL	IB	D		12	2	10500	6	3	29100	32300
40	2	BENETEAU R/C 38	SLP	SA/RC	FBG	KL	IB	D		12	9	15655	4	11	48900	53800
43	8	BENETEAU R/C 42	SLP	SA/RC	FBG	KL	IB	D		13	2	18600	7	3	62900	69100
		1982 BOATS														
27	11	BENETEAU R/C 27	SLP	SA/RC	FBG	KL	IB	D		9	11	5300	5	2	13100	14900
29	6	BENETEAU R/C 30	SLP	SA/RC	FBG	KL	IB	D		9	6	7650	5	6	19700	21900
31	9	BENETEAU R/C30E	SLP	SA/CR	FBG	KL	IB	17D	VLVO	10	7	7070	5	6	18800	20900
31	9	BENETEAU R/C30ESHOAL	SLP	SA/RC	FBG	KL	IB	17D	VLVO	10	7	7070	4	3	18800	20900
32		BENETEAU M/S 32	KTH	MS	FBG	KL	IB	40D	PERK	9	10	12600	4	6	32900	36600
32	9	BENETEAU R/C32	SLP	SA/RC	FBG	KL	IB	15D	YAN	11	1	7390	5	10	19200	21400
32	9	BENETEAU R/C32 SHOAL	SLP	SA/RC	FBG	KL	IB	15D	YAN	11	1	7390	4	4	19200	21400
35	2	BENETEAU R/C 35	SLP	SA/RC	FBG	KL	IB	15D	YAN	12	2	10485	6	3	27300	30300
35	2	BENETEAU R/C 35	SLP	SA/RC	FBG	KL	IB	25D	REN	12	2	10485	6	3	27300	30300
35	2	BENETEAU R/C35 SHOAL	SLP	SA/RC	FBG	KL	IB	15D	YAN	12	2	10485	4	5	27300	30300
35	2	BENETEAU R/C35 SHOAL	SLP	SA/RC	FBG	KL	IB	25D	REN	12	2	10485	4	5	27300	30300
37	2	BENETEAU M/S 37	KTH	MS	FBG	KC	IB	50D	PERK	11	9	17660	4	4	44900	49900
37	2	BENETEAU M/S 37	KTH	MS	FBG	KL	IB	50D	PERK	11	9	17660	5	9	44900	49900
43	8	BENETEAU R/C42	SLP	SA/CR	FBG	KL	IB	50D	PERK	13	2	18600	7	3	59000	64900
43	8	BENETEAU R/C42 SHOAL	SLP	SA/RC	FBG	KL	IB	50D	PERK	13	2	18600	5	5	59000	64900
		1981 BOATS														
24	5	EVASION 25	SLP	SA/CR	FBG	KL	IB	D		8	10	6100	3	10	12700	14500
27	4	BENETEAU M/S 25	SLP	MS	FBG	KL	IB	12D- 15D		8	10	6100	3	10	14000	15900
27	11	BENETEAU R/C 27	SLP	SA/RC	FBG	KL	IB	8D	YAN	9	11	5300	5	2	12300	13900
27	11	BENETEAU R/C27 SHOAL	SLP	SA/RC	FBG	KL	IB	8D	YAN	9	11	5300	4	5	12300	13900
29	6	BENETEAU R/C 30	SLP	SA/RC	FBG	KL	IB	8D- 15D		9	6	7650	5	6	18700	20800
32		BENETEAU M/S 32	KTH	MS	FBG	KL	IB	40D	PERK	9	10	12600	4	6	31000	34400
35	2	BENETEAU R/C 35	SLP	SA/RC	FBG	KL	IB	15D	YAN	12	2	10485	6	3	25600	28500
35	2	BENETEAU R/C 35	SLP	SA/RC	FBG	KL	IB	25D	REN	12	2	10485	6	3	25700	28500
35	2	BENETEAU R/C35 SHOAL	SLP	SA/RC	FBG	KL	IB	15D	YAN	12	2	10485	4	5	25600	28500
35	2	BENETEAU R/C35 SHOAL	SLP	SA/RC	FBG	KL	IB	25D	REN	12	2	10485	4	5	25700	28500
37	2	BENETEAU M/S 37	KTH	MS	FBG	KC	IB	50D	PERK	11	9	17660	4	4	42200	46900
37	2	BENETEAU M/S 37	KTH	MS	FBG	KL	IB	50D	PERK	11	9	17660	4	4	42200	46900
		1980 BOATS														
26	11	EVASION 25	SLP	MS	F/S	KL	IB	12D- 15D		8	9	6050	3	10	13100	14900
27	4	BENETEAU M/S 25	SLP	MS	FBG	KL	IB	12D- 15D		8	10	6100	3	10	13300	15200
27	7	FIRST 27	SLP	SA/RC	FBG	KL	IB	8D- 16D		9	10	5280	5	1	11600	13200
27	7	FIRST 27 SHOAL	SLP	SA/RC	FBG	KL	IB	8D- 16D		9	10	5280	4	5	11600	13200
27	11	BENETEAU R/C 27	SLP	SA/RC	FBG	KL	IB	8D	YAN	9	11	5300	5	2	11700	13300
27	11	BENETEAU R/C27 SHOAL	SLP	SA/RC	FBG	KL	IB	8D	YAN	9	11	5300	4	5	11700	13300
28		EVASION 28	SLP	MS	F/S	KL	IB	25D	VLVO	9	6	9600	3	10	22100	24500
29	6	BENETEAU R/C 30	SLP	SA/RC	FBG	KL	IB	8D- 15D		9	6	7650	5	6	18600	20700
29	6	FIRST 30	SLP	SA/RC	FBG	KL	IB	8D- 16D		9	6	7650	5	6	16800	19900
32		BENETEAU M/S 32	KTH	MS	FBG	KL	IB	25D- 40D		9	10	12600	4	6	29600	32900
32		EVASION 32	KTH	MS	F/S	KL	IB	25D- 40D		9	10	12600	4	6	29600	32900
35	2	BENETEAU R/C 35	SLP	SA/RC	FBG	KL	IB	15D	YAN	12	2	10485	6	3	24500	27200
35	2	BENETEAU R/C 35	SLP	SA/RC	FBG	KL	IB	25D	REN	12	2	10485	6	3	24500	27300
35	2	BENETEAU R/C35 SHOAL	SLP	SA/RC	FBG	KL	IB	15D	YAN	12	2	10485	4	5	24500	27200
35	2	BENETEAU R/C35 SHOAL	SLP	SA/RC	FBG	KL	IB	25D	REN	12	2	10485	4	5	24500	27300
37	2	BENETEAU M/S 37	KTH	MS	FBG	KC	IB	40D	PERK	11	9	17660	4	4	40200	44700
37	2	BENETEAU M/S 37	KTH	MS	FBG	KC	IB	60D	FORD	11	9	17660	4	4	40600	45100
		1979 BOATS														
28		EVASION 28	SLP	MS	F/S	KL	IB	25D	VLVO	9	6	9600	3	10	21200	23600
29	6	LE-FIRST 30	SLP	SA/RC	FBG	KL	IB	8D- 16D		9	6	7650	5	6	16800	19100
32		EVASION 32	KTH	MS	F/S	KL	IB	25D- 40D		9	10	12600	4	6	28400	31600
		1978 BOATS														
28		ESCAPADE 28	SLP	SA/CR	F/S	KL	IB	12D	YAN	9	6	9600	3	10	20400	22600
28		EVASION 28	SLP	MS	F/S	KL	IB	23D	VLVO	9	6	9600	3	10	20400	22700
29	6	LE-FIRST 30	SLP	SA/RC	FBG	KL	IB	8D- 16D		9	6	7040	5	6	14900	16900
32		EVASION 32	KTH	MS	F/S	KL	IB	25D- 40D		9	10	12600	4	6	27400	30500

JAY R BENFORD & ASSOC INC

Call 1-800-327-6929 for BUC Personalized Evaluation Service
Or, for 1972 to 1986 boats, sign onto www.BUCValuPro.com

BENNETT BROTHERS YACHTS INC

MAMARONECK NY 10543 See inside cover to adjust price for area
FORMERLY STEVENS YACHTS OF ANNAPOLIS

For more recent years, see the BUC Used Boat Price Guide, Volume 1 or Volume 2

LOA FT	LOA IN	NAME AND/ OR MODEL	TOP/ RIG	BOAT TYPE	-HULL- MTL	-HULL- TP	ENGINE TP	ENGINE # HP	ENGINE MFG	BEAM FT	BEAM IN	WGT LBS	DRAFT FT	DRAFT IN	RETAIL LOW	RETAIL HIGH
		1982 BOATS														
46	10	STEVENS 47	CUT	SA/CR	FBG	KL	IB	65D	LEHM	14	3	32000	6		139000	152500
		1981 BOATS														
46	10	STEVENS 47	SLP	SA/CR	FBG	KL	IB	D		14	4	31220	6		129500	142500

BERTRAM INTERNATIONAL

MIAMI FL 33152 COAST GUARD MFG ID- BRY See inside cover to adjust price for area

LOA FT	LOA IN	NAME AND/ OR MODEL	TOP/ RIG	BOAT TYPE	-HULL- MTL	-HULL- TP	ENGINE TP	ENGINE # HP	ENGINE MFG	BEAM FT	BEAM IN	WGT LBS	DRAFT FT	DRAFT IN	RETAIL LOW	RETAIL HIGH
		1974 BOATS														
63		BERTRAM-INTERNATL		MY	FBG	DV	IB	T480D		16	4				241500	265500
		1973 BOATS														
63		BERTRAM-INTERNATL		MY	FBG	DV	IB	T480D		16	4				232500	255500
		1971 BOATS														
55				SF	FBG	DV	IB	T360D	CAT	16	3	40000	4		115500	127000
55	9			CR	FBG	DV	IB	T360D	CAT	16	3	42000	4		110500	121500
55	9			MY	FBG	DV	IB	T360D	CAT	16	3	44000	4	6	120500	132500
63				CR	FBG	DV	IB	T460D	CAT	16	3	60000	4	6	204500	225000
63				MY	FBG	DV	IB	T460D	CAT	16	3	63000	4	6	216000	237000
63				SF	FBG	DV	IB	T460D	CAT	16	3	60000	4	6	189000	208000
63		BERTRAM-INTERNATL	FB	MY	FBG	DV	IB	T460D	CAT	16	4				214000	235500
		1970 BOATS														
56		BERTRAM-INTERNATL		MY	FBG		IB	T D							**	**
		1969 BOATS														
62	3	BERTRAM-INTERNATL	KTH	SA/CR	STL	KC	IB	160		16		77000	6		258000	283500
63		BERTRAM-INTERNATL	FB	MY	FBG		IB	T460D	CAT	16	4				200000	220000
76			FB	MY	FBG		IB	T480D	GM						**	**

BERTRAM YACHT INC

MIAMI FL 33142 COAST GUARD MFG ID- BER See inside cover to adjust price for area

For more recent years, see the BUC Used Boat Price Guide, Volume 1 or Volume 2

LOA FT	LOA IN	NAME AND/ OR MODEL	TOP/ RIG	BOAT TYPE	-HULL- MTL	-HULL- TP	ENGINE TP	ENGINE # HP	ENGINE MFG	BEAM FT	BEAM IN	WGT LBS	DRAFT FT	DRAFT IN	RETAIL LOW	RETAIL HIGH
		1983 BOATS														
26	2	26 II SPORT CONV	OP	SPTCR	FBG	DV	OB			10		5100			14900	16900
26	2	26 II SPORT CONV	OP	SPTCR	FBG	DV	IB	T165	CRUS	10		6700	3		23600	26300
28	6	FLYBRIDGE CRUISER	FB	SDN	FBG	DV	IB	T230	MRCR	11		11820	2	8	37600	41700
28	6	FLYBRIDGE CRUISER	FB	SDN	FBG	DV	IB	T124D	VLVO	11		11930	2	8	53600	58900
28	6	HARDTOP	HT	SPTCR	FBG	DV	IB	T230	MRCR	11		11020	2	7	33900	37600
28	6	HARDTOP	HT	SPTCR	FBG	DV	IB	T124D	VLVO	11		11130	2	7	47200	51900
28	6	SPORT CONVERTIBLE	OP	SPTCR	FBG	DV	IB	T230	MRCR	11		10400	2	7	32900	36500
28	6	SPORT FISHERMAN	FB	SF	FBG	DV	IB	T230	MRCR	11		11320	2	8	34700	38500
28	6	SPORT FISHERMAN	FB	SF	FBG	DV	IB	T124D	VLVO	11		11430	2	8	48100	52800
30	7	FLYBRIDGE CRUISER	FB	SDN	FBG	DV	IB	T350	CRUS	11	2	13910	3		50100	55100
30	7	FLYBRIDGE CRUISER	FB	SDN	FBG	DV	IB	T140D-T210D		11	2	15350	3		66700	78300
30	7	HARDTOP	HT	SPTCR	FBG	DV	IB	T350		11	2				36000	40000
30	7	SPORT-FISHERMAN		SF	FBG	DV	IB	T350		11	2				35100	39000
32	11	FLYBRIDGE CRUISER	FB	SDN	FBG	DV	IB	T320	CRUS	12	6	20730	3		65100	71600
32	11	FLYBRIDGE CRUISER	FB	SDN	FBG	DV	IB	T270D		12	6	22730	3		99100	109000
33		FLYBRIDGE CRUISER	FB	CR	FBG	DV	IB	T350		12	8				47700	52400
33		SPORT FISHERMAN	FB	SDNSF	FBG	DV	IB	T320	CRUS	12	6	20930	3		62700	68900
33		SPORT FISHERMAN	FB	SDNSF	FBG	DV	IB	T270D		12	6	21565	3		90200	99100
33		SPORT FISHERMAN		SF	FBG	DV	IB	T350		12	8				43300	48100
35	2	CONVERTIBLE 35 II	FB	CNV	FBG	DV	IB	T215D	CUM	13	3	24500	3		106000	116500
35	2	CONVERTIBLE 35 II	FB	CNV	FBG	DV	IB	T300D	CAT	13	3	24500	3		113000	124000
35	4	CONVERTIBLE 35 II	FB	CNV	FBG	DV	IB	T350	CRUS	13	3	22500	3	1	81400	89500
38	5	CONVERTIBLE 38 III	FB	CNV	FBG	DV	IB	T300D	CAT	13	3	30400	4		131500	144500
38	5	CONVERTIBLE 38 III	FB	CNV	FBG	DV	IB	T305D	GM	13	3	30400	4		129500	142500
38	5	CONVERTIBLE 38 III	FB	CNV	FBG	DV	IB	T380D	CUM	13	3	30400	4		134000	147500
42	6	CONVERTIBLE	FB	CNV	FBG	DV	IB	T435D	GM	14	10	39400	4		167500	184000
42	6	CONVERTIBLE	FB	CNV	FBG	DV	IB	T450D	CUM	14	10	39400	4		168500	185000
42	6	YACHT	FB	MY	FBG	DV	IB	T330D	GM	14	10	39000	4		158500	174500
46	6	CONVERTIBLE	FB	CNV	FBG	DV	IB	T462D	GM	16		44900	4	6	163500	179500
46	6	CONVERTIBLE	FB	CNV	FBG	DV	IB	T570D	GM	16		44900	4	6	174500	192000
46	6	CONVERTIBLE MDL II	FB	CNV	FBG	DV	IB	T462D	GM	16		44900	4	6	177500	195000
46	6	CONVERTIBLE MDL II	FB	CNV	FBG	DV	IB	T570D	GM	16		44900	4	6	190000	208500
46	6	YACHT	FB	MY	FBG	DV	IB	T462D	GM	16		45600	4	8	172000	189000
46	6	YACHT	FB	MY	FBG	DV	IB	T570D	GM	16		45600	4	8	182500	200500
54		CONVERTIBLE	FB	CNV	FBG	DV	IB	T675D	GM	16	11	65000	4	10	306500	337000
54		CONVERTIBLE	FB	CNV	FBG	DV	IB	T800D		16	11	65000	4	10	326000	358000

 CONTINUED ON NEXT PAGE

LOA FT	LOA IN	NAME AND/ OR MODEL	TOP/ RIG	BOAT TYPE	-HULL- MTL	-HULL- TP	ENGINE TP	ENGINE # HP	ENGINE MFG	BEAM FT	BEAM IN	WGT LBS	DRAFT FT	DRAFT IN	RETAIL LOW	RETAIL HIGH
		1983 BOATS														
58	3	CONVERTIBLE	FB	CNV	FBG	DV	IB	T675D	GM	17	11	90000	5	6	400000	439500
58	3	YACHT	FB	MY	FBG	DV	IB	T675D	GM	17	11	87500	5	4	403000	442500
		1982 BOATS														
28	6	FLYBRIDGE CRUISER	FB	SDN	FBG	DV	SE	T205	OMC	11		11130	3		23300	25900
28	6	FLYBRIDGE CRUISER	FB	SDN	FBG	DV	IB	T230	MRCR	11		11820	2	8	34600	38500
28	6	FLYBRIDGE CRUISER	FB	SDN	FBG	DV	IB	T130D	VLVO	11		12320	2	8	53100	58300
28	6	FLYBRIDGE CRUISER II	FB	SDN	FBG	DV	IB	T230	MRCR	11		11820	2	8	37300	41400
28	6	FLYBRIDGE CRUISER II	FB	SDN	FBG	DV	IB	T130D	VLVO	11		12420	2	8	53400	58700
28	6	HARDTOP	HT	SPTCR	FBG	DV	IB	T230	MRCR	11		11020	2	7	32400	36000
28	6	HARDTOP	HT	SPTCR	FBG	DV	IB	T130D	VLVO	11		11620	2	7	47300	52000
28	6	SPORT CONVERTIBLE	OP	SPTCR	FBG	DV	SE	T205	OMC	11		9400	3		24500	27200
28	6	SPORT CONVERTIBLE	OP	SPTCR	FBG	DV	IB	T230	MRCR	11		10400	2	7	31500	35000
28	6	SPORT FISHERMAN	FB	SF	FBG	DV	IB	T230	MRCR	11		11320	2	8	33300	37000
28	6	SPORT FISHERMAN	FB	SF	FBG	DV	IB	T130D	VLVO	11		11920	2	8	48100	52800
30	7	FLYBRIDGE CRUISER	FB	SDN	FBG	DV	IB	T350	CRUS	11	2	13300	3	1	47600	52300
30	7	FLYBRIDGE CRUISER	FB	SDN	FBG	DV	IB	T140D-T210D		11	2	14100	3	1	60500	73300
30	7	HARDTOP	HT	SPTCR	FBG	DV	IB	T350	CRUS	11	2	12500	3		42400	47100
30	7	HARDTOP	HT	SPTCR	FBG	DV	IB	T140D-T210D		11	2	13600	3		54400	67000
30	7	SPORT FISHERMAN	FB	SF	FBG	DV	IB	T350	CRUS	11	2	13300	3	1	43200	48000
30	7	SPORT FISHERMAN	FB	SF	FBG	DV	IB	T140D-T210D		11	2	14100	3	1	55800	66900
32	11	FLYBRIDGE CRUISER	FB	SDN	FBG	DV	IB	T350	CRUS	12	6	20000	3		62500	68700
32	11	FLYBRIDGE CRUISER	FB	SDN	FBG	DV	IB	T260D-T270D		12	6	22000	3		92700	102000
33		SPORT FISHERMAN	FB	SDNSF	FBG	DV	IB	T350	CRUS	12	6	19400	3	1	58900	64800
33		SPORT FISHERMAN	FB	SDNSF	FBG	DV	IB	T260D-T270D		12	6	21565	3	1	86200	94800
35	2	CONVERTIBLE 35 II	FB	CNV	FBG	DV	IB	T350	CRUS	13	3	20500	3		73600	80900
35	2	CONVERTIBLE 35 II	FB	CNV	FBG	DV	IB	T215D	CUM	13	3	23000	3		98100	107500
35	2	CONVERTIBLE 35 II	FB	CNV	FBG	DV	IB	T300D	CAT	13	3	23000	3		104500	114500
38	5	CONVERTIBLE 38 III	FB	CNV	FBG	DV	IB	T275D	GM	13	3	28857	4	2	117000	128500
38	5	CONVERTIBLE 38 III	FB	CNV	FBG	DV	IB	T300D	CAT	13	3	28500	4	2	119500	131500
38	5	CONVERTIBLE 38 III	FB	CNV	FBG	DV	IB	T380D	CUM	13	3	30400	4	2	128000	140500
42	6	CONVERTIBLE	FB	CNV	FBG	DV	IB	T435D	GM	14	10	39400	4		160000	175500
42	6	CONVERTIBLE	FB	CNV	FBG	DV	IB	T450D	CUM	14	10	38566	4		158500	174000
42	6	YACHT	FB	MY	FBG	DV	IB	T335D	GM	14	10	39000	4		152000	167000
46	6	CONVERTIBLE	FB	CNV	FBG	DV	IB	T462D	GM	16		43000	4	6	159000	174500
46	6	CONVERTIBLE	FB	CNV	FBG	DV	IB	T570D	GM	16		43600	4	6	170500	187500
46	6	YACHT	FB	MY	FBG	DV	IB	T462D	GM	16		45600	4	8	164500	181000
46	6	YACHT	FB	MY	FBG	DV	IB	T570D	GM	16		45600	4	8	175000	192000
54		CONVERTIBLE	FB	CNV	FBG	DV	IB	T675D	GM	16	11	63000	4	10	285500	314000
54		CONVERTIBLE	FB	CNV	FBG	DV	IB	T800D	GM	16	11	63000	4	10	304000	334500
58	3	CONVERTIBLE	FB	CNV	FBG	DV	IB	T675D	GM	17	11	90000	5	6	383500	421500
58	3	YACHT	FB	MY	FBG	DV	IB	T675D	GM	17	11	87000	5	4	385500	423500
		1981 BOATS														
28	6	FLYBRIDGE CRUISER	FB	SDN	FBG	DV	IB	T228	MRCR	11		11820	2	8	34400	38200
28	6	FLYBRIDGE CRUISER	FB	SDN	FBG	DV	IB	T124D-T130D		11		11920			49500	56100
28	6	HARDTOP	HT	SPTCR	FBG	DV	IB	T228	MRCR	11		11020	2	7	31000	34500
28	6	HARDTOP	HT	SPTCR	FBG	DV	IB	T130D	VLVO	11		11620	2	7	45000	50000
28	6	SPORT CONVERTIBLE	OP	SPTCR	FBG	DV	IB	T228	MRCR	11		10400	2	7	30100	33500
28	6	SPORT FISHERMAN	FB	SF	FBG	DV	IB	T228	MRCR	11		11320	2	8	31900	35500
28	6	SPORT FISHERMAN	FB	SF	FBG	DV	IB	T130D	VLVO	11		11920	2	8	46500	51100
30	7	BAHIA-MAR		SPTCR	FBG	DV	IB	T330		11	2				32500	36200
30	7	FLYBRIDGE CRUISER	FB	SDN	FBG	DV	IB	T330	MRCR	11	2	13300	3	1	44400	49400
30	7	FLYBRIDGE CRUISER	FB	SDN	FBG	DV	IB	T140D-T210D		11	2	14100	3	1	58200	70400
30	7	HARDTOP	HT	SPTCR	FBG	DV	IB	T330	MRCR	11	2	12500	3		40000	44500
30	7	HARDTOP	HT	SPTCR	FBG	DV	IB	T140D-T210D		11	2	13600	3		52300	64400
30	7	SPORT FISHERMAN	FB	SF	FBG	DV	IB	T330	MRCR			13300	3	1	40900	45400
30	7	SPORT FISHERMAN	FB	SF	FBG	DV	IB	T140D-T210D		11	2	14100	3	1	53700	64300
32	11	FLYBRIDGE CRUISER	FB	SDN	FBG	DV	IB	T330	MRCR	12	6	20000	3		59200	65000
32	11	FLYBRIDGE CRUISER	FB	SDN	FBG	DV	IB	T270D	CAT	12	6	22000	3		89700	98600
33		SPORT FISHERMAN	FB	SDNSF	FBG	DV	IB	T330	MRCR	12	6	19400	3	1	55900	61400
33		SPORT FISHERMAN	FB	SDNSF	FBG	DV	IB	T270D	CAT	12	6	21565	3	1	83300	91600
35	2	CONVERTIBLE 35 II	FB	CNV	FBG	DV	IB	T350	CRUS	13	3	20500	3		70500	77500
35	2	CONVERTIBLE 35 II	FB	CNV	FBG	DV	IB	T215D	CUMM	13	3	22500	3		93200	102500
35	2	CONVERTIBLE 35 II	FB	CNV	FBG	DV	IB	T300D	CAT	13	3	22500	3		99100	109000
38	5	CONVERTIBLE 38 III	FB	CNV	FBG	DV	IB	T330	MRCR	13	3	26000	4	2	91500	100500
		IB T275D GM 111500 122500, IB T300D CAT 114000 125500, IB T380D CUM													122000	134000
42	6	CONVERTIBLE	FB	CNV	FBG	DV	IB	T420D	CUM	14	10				133500	146500
42	6	CONVERTIBLE	FB	CNV	FBG	DV	IB	T435D	GM	14	10	39400	4		152500	167500
42	6	CONVERTIBLE	FB	CNV	FBG	DV	IB	T450D	CUMM	14	10	38566	4		151500	166500
42	6	YACHT	FB	MY	FBG	DV	IB	T335D	GM	14	10	39000	4		145000	159000
46	6	CONVERTIBLE	FB	CNV	FBG	DV	IB	T462D	GM	16		43000	4	6	152500	167500
46	6	CONVERTIBLE	FB	CNV	FBG	DV	IB	T570D	GM	16		43600	4	6	163500	179500
46	6	YACHT	FB	MY	FBG	DV	IB	T462D	GM	16		45600	4	8	157500	173500
46	6	YACHT	FB	MY	FBG	DV	IB	T570D	GM	16		45600	4	8	167500	184000
54		CONVERTIBLE	FB	CNV	FBG	DV	IB	T675D	GM	16	11	63000	4	10	272000	299000
54		CONVERTIBLE	FB	CNV	FBG	DV	IB	T800D	GM	16	11	63000	4	10	290000	318500
58	3	CONVERTIBLE	FB	CNV	FBG	DV	IB	T675D	GM	17	11	90000	5	6	366000	402500
58	3	YACHT	FB	MY	FBG	DV	IB	T675D	GM	17	11	87000	5	4	367500	404000
		1980 BOATS														
28		FLYBRIDGE CRUISER	FB	SDN	FBG	DV	IB	T228	MRCR	11		7500	2	7	26800	29800
28		HARDTOP	HT	SPTCR	FBG	DV	IB	T228	MRCR	11		7500	2	7	24300	27000
28		SPORT CONVERTIBLE	OP	SPTCR	FBG	DV	IB	T228	MRCR	11		7500	2	7	24300	27000
28		SPORT FISHERMAN	FB	SF	FBG	DV	IB	T228	MRCR	11		7500	2	7	24400	27100
30	7	BAHIA-MAR	OP	SPTCR	FBG	DV	IB	T330	MRCR	11	2	9400	2	9	32100	35700
30	7	BAHIA-MAR	OP	SPTCR	FBG	DV	IB	T140D-T195D		11	2	9400	2	9	37100	44100
30	7	BAHIA-MAR	HT	SPTCR	FBG	DV	IB	T330	MRCR	11	2	9400	2	9	32000	35600
30	7	BAHIA-MAR	HT	SPTCR	FBG	DV	IB	T140D-T195D		11	2	9400	2	9	36900	44300
30	7	FLYBRIDGE CRUISER	FB	SDN	FBG	DV	IB	T330	MRCR	11	2	10600	2	9	40600	45200
30	7	FLYBRIDGE CRUISER	FB	SDN	FBG	DV	IB	T140D-T210D		11	2	10600	2	9	47700	57600
30	7	HARDTOP	HT	SPTCR	FBG	DV	IB	T330	MRCR	11	2	9400	2	8	32200	35800
30	7	HARDTOP	HT	SPTCR	FBG	DV	IB	T140D-T210D		11	2	9400	2	8	37200	45200
30	7	SPORT FISHERMAN	FB	SF	FBG	DV	IB	T330	MRCR	11	2	10300	2	8	36400	40500
30	7	SPORT FISHERMAN	FB	SF	FBG	DV	IB	T140D-T210D		11	2	10300	2	8	41300	50000
32	11	FLYBRIDGE CRUISER	FB	SDN	FBG	DV	IB	T330	MRCR	12	8				44100	49000
32	11	FLYBRIDGE CRUISER	FB	SDN	FBG	DV	IB	T270D	CAT	12	8				64000	70400
33		SPORT FISHERMAN	FB	SDNSF	FBG	DV	IB	T330	MRCR	12	8				45900	50400
33		SPORT FISHERMAN	FB	SDNSF	FBG	DV	IB	T270D	CAT	12	8				61200	67300
35		CONVERTIBLE	FB	CNV	FBG	DV	IB	T330	MRCR	13					55200	60700
35		CONVERTIBLE	FB	CNV	FBG	DV	IB	T215D	CUM	13					77000	84600
38	6	CONVERTIBLE 38 III	FB	CNV	FBG	DV	IB	T330	MRCR	13	3	26000	3	7	88000	96700
38	6	CONVERTIBLE 38 III	FB	CNV	FBG	DV	IB	T270D	CAT	13	3	28500	3	7	108000	118500
38	6	CONVERTIBLE 38 III	FB	CNV	FBG	DV	IB	T275D	GM	13	3	28500	3	7	106000	116500
42	6	CONVERTIBLE	FB	CNV	FBG	DV	IB	T420D	CUM	14	10	35000	4		132500	146000
42	6	CONVERTIBLE	FB	CNV	FBG	DV	IB	T435D	GM	14	10	35000	4		134500	148000
42	6	YACHT	HT	MY	FBG	DV	IB	T335D	GM	14	10	34000	3	9	125500	137500
42	6	YACHT	FB	MY	FBG	DV	IB	T335D	GM	14	10	34000	3	9	125000	137500
46	6	CONVERTIBLE	FB	CNV	FBG	DV	IB	T420D	CUM	16			4	6	139500	153500
46	6	CONVERTIBLE	FB	CNV	FBG	DV	IB	T435D	GM	16			4	6	141000	155000
46	6	YACHT	HT	MY	FBG	DV	IB	T435D	GM	16		43000	4	6	146000	160500
46	6	YACHT	FB	MY	FBG	DV	IB	T435D	GM	16		43000	4	6	145500	159500
58	3	CONVERTIBLE	FB	CNV	FBG	DV	IB	T675D	GM	17	11	80000	5		335500	368500
58	5	YACHT	FB	MY	FBG	DV	IB	T675D	GM	17	11	75000	5		327500	360000
		1979 BOATS														
28		FLYBRIDGE CRUISER	FB	SDN	FBG	DV	IB	T228	MRCR	11		7500	2	7	26300	29300
28		HARDTOP	HT	SPTCR	FBG	DV	IB	T228	MRCR	11		7500	2	7	23900	26500
28		SPORT CONVERTIBLE	OP	SPTCR	FBG	DV	IB	T228	MRCR	11		7500	2	7	23900	26500
28		SPORT FISHERMAN	FB	SF	FBG	DV	IB	T228	MRCR	11		7500	2	7	23900	26600
30	7	BAHIA-MAR	HT	SPTCR	FBG	DV	IB	T330	MRCR	11	2	9400	2	9	31500	35000
30	7	BAHIA-MAR	HT	SPTCR	FBG	DV	IB	T140D-T195D		11	2	9400	2	9	36500	43400
30	7	FLYBRIDGE CRUISER	FB	SDN	FBG	DV	IB	T330	MRCR	11	2	10600	2	9	39900	44300
30	7	FLYBRIDGE CRUISER	FB	SDN	FBG	DV	IB	T140D-T210D		11	2	10600	2	9	47000	56700
30	7	HARDTOP	HT	SPTCR	FBG	DV	IB	T330	MRCR	11	2		2	8	30700	34100
30	7	HARDTOP	HT	SPTCR	FBG	DV	IB	T140D-T210D		11	2		2	8	35300	43300
30	7	SPORT FISHERMAN	FB	SF	FBG	DV	IB	T330	MRCR	11	2	10300	2	8	35700	39700
30	7	SPORT FISHERMAN	FB	SF	FBG	DV	IB	T140D-T210D		11	2	10300	2	8	40700	49200
33		CONVERTIBLE	FB	CNV	FBG	DV	IB	T330	MRCR	12	8				45600	50100
33		CONVERTIBLE	FB	CNV	FBG	DV	IB	T215D	CUM	12	8				60000	66000
33		SPORT FISHERMAN	FB	SDNSF	FBG	DV	IB	T330	MRCR	12	8				44500	49500
33		SPORT FISHERMAN	FB	SDNSF	FBG	DV	IB	T270D	CAT	12	8				60300	66300
35		CONVERTIBLE	FB	CNV	FBG	DV	IB	T330	MRCR	13					54200	59600
35		CONVERTIBLE	FB	CNV	FBG	DV	IB	T215D	CUM	13					75900	83400
38	6	CONVERTIBLE 38 III	FB	CNV	FBG	DV	IB	T330	MRCR	13	3	28500	3	7	93000	102000
38	6	CONVERTIBLE 38 III	FB	CNV	FBG	DV	IB	T270D	CAT	13	3	28500	3	7	105500	116000
38	6	CONVERTIBLE 38 III	FB	CNV	FBG	DV	IB	T270D	CUM	13	3	28500	3	7	103000	113000
42	6	CONVERTIBLE	FB	CNV	FBG	DV	IB	T335D	GM	14	10		4		117500	129000
42	6	CONVERTIBLE	FB	CNV	FBG	DV	IB	T420D	CUM	14	10		4		125000	137000
42	6	CONVERTIBLE	FB	CNV	FBG	DV	IB	T435D	GM	14	10		4		127000	139500
42	6	YACHT	FB	MY	FBG	DV	IB	T335D	GM	14	10	34000	3	9	122000	134500
46	6	CONVERTIBLE	FB	CNV	FBG	DV	IB	T420D	CUM	16			4	6	135500	148500
46	6	CONVERTIBLE	FB	CNV	FBG	DV	IB	T435D	GM	16			4	6	137000	150500
46	6	YACHT	FB	MY	FBG	DV	IB	T435D	GM	16		43000	4	6	141000	155000
58	3	CONVERTIBLE	FB	CNV	FBG	DV	IB	T675D	GM	17	11	80000	5		327000	359500
58	5	YACHT	FB	MY	FBG	DV	IB	T675D	GM	17	11	75000	5		320000	352000
		1978 BOATS														
28		FLYBRIDGE CRUISER	FB	SDN	FBG	DV	IB	T228	MRCR	11		7500	2	7	25900	28700
28		HARDTOP	HT	SPTCR	FBG	DV	IB	T228	MRCR	11		7500	2	7	23500	26100
28		SPORT CONVERTIBLE	OP	SPTCR	FBG	DV	IB	T228	MRCR	11		7500	2	7	23500	26100
28		SPORT FISHERMAN	FB	SF	FBG	DV	IB	T228	MRCR	11		7500	2	7	23500	26100

56 CONTINUED ON NEXT PAGE 96th ed. - Vol. III

BERTRAM YACHT INC -CONTINUED See inside cover to adjust price for area

LOA FT	IN	NAME AND/ OR MODEL	TOP/ RIG	BOAT TYPE	-HULL- MTL	TP	----ENGINE--- TP	# HP	MFG	BEAM FT	IN	WGT LBS	DRAFT FT	IN	RETAIL LOW	RETAIL HIGH
		1978 BOATS														
30	7	BAHIA-MAR	OP	SPTCR	FBG	DV	IB	T228-T330		11	2	9400	2	9	28900	34400
30	7	BAHIA-MAR	OP	SPTCR	FBG	DV	IB	T140D-T210D		11	2	9400	2	9	36000	43600
30	7	BAHIA-MAR	HT	SPTCR	FBG	DV	IB	T228-T330		11	2	9400	2	9	28800	34200
30	7	BAHIA-MAR	HT	SPTCR	FBG	DV	IB	T140D-T210D		11	2	9400	2	9	35800	43700
30	7	FLYBRIDGE CRUISER	FB	SDN	FBG	DV	IB	T228-T330		11	2	10600	2	9	36100	43500
30	7	FLYBRIDGE CRUISER	FB	SDN	FBG	DV	IB	T140D-T225D		11	2	10600	2	9	46400	57000
30	7	HARDTOP	HT	SPTCR	FBG	DV	IB	T228-T330		11	2	9400	2	8	28900	34600
30	7	HARDTOP	HT	SPTCR	FBG	DV	IB	T140D-T225D		11	2	9400	2	8	36200	44700
30	7	SPORT FISHERMAN	FB	SF	FBG	DV	IB	T228-T330		11	2	10300	2	8	32800	39000
30	7	SPORT FISHERMAN	FB	SF	FBG	DV	IB	T140D-T225D		11	2	10300	2	8	40100	49300
33		CONVERTIBLE	FB	CNV	FBG	DV	IB	T228-T330		12	8				41600	49200
33		CONVERTIBLE	FB	CNV	FBG	DV	IB	T240D	CUM	12	8				60600	66600
35		CONVERTIBLE	FB	CNV	FBG	DV	IB	T330	MRCR	13					53200	58500
35		CONVERTIBLE	FB	CNV	FBG	DV	IB	T225D	CAT	13					76100	83600
35		CONVERTIBLE	FB	CNV	FBG	DV	IB	T240D	CUM	13					76000	83600
38	6	CONVERTIBLE 38 III	FB	CNV	FBG	DV	IB	T330	MRCR	13	3	25000	3	7	81600	89600
38	6	CONVERTIBLE 38 III	FB	CNV	FBG	DV	IB	T270D	CUM	13	3	25000	3	7	91300	100500
42	6	CONVERTIBLE	FB	CNV	FBG	DV	IB	T330	MRCR	14	10	35000	4		105000	115500
42	6	CONVERTIBLE	FB	CNV	FBG	DV	IB	T335D	GM	14	10	35000	4		119500	131500
42	6	CONVERTIBLE	FB	CNV	FBG	DV	IB	T420D	CUM	14	10	35000	4		127000	139500
42	6	YACHT	HT	MY	FBG	DV	IB	T330	MRCR	14	10	34000	3	9	105000	115500
42	6	YACHT	HT	MY	FBG	DV	IB	T335D	GM	14	10	34000	3	9	120000	131500
42	6	YACHT	FB	MY	FBG	DV	IB	T330	MRCR	14	10	34000	3	9	105000	115500
42	6	YACHT	FB	MY	FBG	DV	IB	T335D	GM	14	10	34000	3	9	119500	131500
46	6	CONVERTIBLE	FB	CNV	FBG	DV	IB	T435D	GM	16			4	6	133000	146500
46	6	YACHT	FB	MY	FBG	DV	IB	T435D	GM	16		43000	4	6	137000	150500
58	3	CONVERTIBLE	FB	CNV	FBG	DV	IB	T650D	GM	17	11	80000	5		315500	346500
58	5	YACHT	FB	MY	FBG	DV	IB	T650D	GM	17	11	75000	5		309000	340000
		1977 BOATS														
26		HARDTOP	HT	SPTCR	FBG	DV	IO	T165	MRCR	10		5500	2	6	17400	19700
26		SPORT CONVERTIBLE	OP	CR	FBG	DV	IO	T165	MRCR	10		5500	2	6	17400	19700
26		SPORT FISHERMAN	FB	SF	FBG	DV	IO	T165	MRCR	10		5500	2	6	20100	22300
28		FLYBRIDGE CRUISER	FB	SDNSF	FBG	DV	IB	T225-T233		11		7500	2	7	23000	25700
28		HARDTOP	HT	SPTCR	FBG	DV	IB	T225-T233		11		7500	2	7	23000	25700
28		SPORT CONVERTIBLE	OP	SPTCR	FBG	DV	IB	T225-T233		11		7500	2	7	23000	25700
28		SPORT FISHERMAN	FB	SF	FBG	DV	IB	T225-T233		11		7500	2	7	23100	25800
30	7	BAHIA-MAR	OP	SPTCR	FBG	DV	IB	T233-T330		11	2	9400	2	7	28400	33800
30	7	BAHIA-MAR	OP	SPTCR	FBG	DV	IB	T140D-T210D		11	2	9400	2	7	35500	43000
30	7	FLYBRIDGE CRUISER	FB	SDNSF	FBG	DV	IB	T233-T330		11	2	10600	2	9	32600	38600
30	7	FLYBRIDGE CRUISER	FB	SDNSF	FBG	DV	IB	T140D-T225D		11	2	10600	2	9	40300	49400
30	7	HARDTOP	HT	SPTCR	FBG	DV	IB	T233-T330		11	2	9400	2	8	28400	33800
30	7	HARDTOP	HT	SPTCR	FBG	DV	IB	T140D-T225D		11	2	9400	2	8	35500	44100
30	7	SPORT FISHERMAN	FB	SF	FBG	DV	IB	T233-T330		11	2	10300	2	8	32400	38300
30	7	SPORT FISHERMAN	FB	SF	FBG	DV	IB	T140D-T225D		11	2	10300	2	8	39600	48600
33		CONVERTIBLE	FB	SDNSF	FBG	DV	IB	T233-T330		12	8				40900	47700
33		CONVERTIBLE	FB	SDNSF	FBG	DV	IB	T240D	CUM	12	8				56900	62500
35		CONVERTIBLE	FB	SDNSF	FBG	DV	IB	T330	MRCR	13		14850	3		53000	58300
35		CONVERTIBLE	FB	SDNSF	FBG	DV	IB	T225D	CAT	13		18700	3		74500	81900
35		CONVERTIBLE	FB	SDNSF	FBG	DV	IB	T240D	CUM	13		18700	3		74300	81600
42	6	CONVERTIBLE	FB	SDNSF	FBG	DV	IB	T330	MRCR	14	10	35000	4		104000	114000
42	6	CONVERTIBLE	FB	SDNSF	FBG	DV	IB	T335D	GM	14	10	35000	4		118000	130000
42	6	CONVERTIBLE	FB	SDNSF	FBG	DV	IB	T420D	CUM	14	10	35000	4		125500	138000
42	6	YACHT	FB	MY	FBG	DV	IB	T330	MRCR	14	10	34000	3	9	103000	113000
42	6	YACHT	FB	MY	FBG	DV	IB	T335D	GM	14	10	34000	3	9	117000	129000
46	6	CONVERTIBLE	FB	SDNSF	FBG	DV	IB	T350D	GM	16			4	6	126000	138000
46	6	CONVERTIBLE	FB	SDNSF	FBG	DV	IB	T435D	GM	16			4	6	133500	146500
46	6	YACHT	FB	MY	FBG	DV	IB	T435D	GM	16		43000	4	6	133500	147000
58	5	CONVERTIBLE	FB	SDNSF	FBG	DV	IB	T		17	11		5		**	**
58	5	YACHT	FB	MY	FBG	DV	IB	T480D	GM	17	11	65000	5		241500	265500
58	5	YACHT	FB	MY	FBG	DV	IB	T650D	GM	17	11	65000	5		271000	298000
		1976 BOATS														
26		HARDTOP	HT	SPTCR	FBG	DV	IO	T165	MRCR	10		5500	2	6	18600	20700
26		SPORT CONVERTIBLE	OP	CR	FBG	DV	IO	T165	MRCR	10		5500	2	6	18600	20700
26		SPORT FISHERMAN	FB	SF	FBG	DV	IO	T165	MRCR	10		5500	2	6	21100	23500
28		FLYBRIDGE CRUISER	FB	SDNSF	FBG	DV	IB	T225-T233		7	6	7500	2	6	21300	23800
28		HARDTOP	HT	SPTCR	FBG	DV	IB	T225-T233		7	4	7500	2	4	21200	23800
28		SPORT FISHERMAN	FB	SF	FBG	DV	IB	T225-T233		7	6	7500	2	5	21300	23900
31		BAHIA-MAR	OP	SPTCR	FBG	DV	IB	T233-T350		8	6	9400	1	10	27700	33400
31		BAHIA-MAR	OP	SPTCR	FBG	DV	IB	T140D-T225D		8	6	9400	1	10	34200	42400
31		FLYBRIDGE CRUISER	FB	SDNSF	FBG	DV	IB	T233-T350		11	2	10600	2	11	33200	39700
31		FLYBRIDGE CRUISER	FB	SDNSF	FBG	DV	IB	T140D-T225D		11	2	11662	2	11	42800	53000
31		HARDTOP	HT	SPTCR	FBG	DV	IB	T233-T350		8	10	9400	2		27900	33600
31		HARDTOP	HT	SPTCR	FBG	DV	IB	T140D-T225D		8	10	9400	2		34400	42600
31		SPORT FISHERMAN	FB	SF	FBG	DV	IB	T233-T350		9	2	10300	3		29000	34700
31		SPORT FISHERMAN	FB	SF	FBG	DV	IB	T140D-T210D		9		11462	2	10	39200	47700
31		SPORT FISHERMAN	FB	SF	FBG	DV	IB	T225D	CAT	9	2	12205	3		44500	49500
35		CONVERTIBLE	FB	SDNSF	FBG	DV	IB	T350	MRCR	10	8	14850	3	8	51700	56800
35		CONVERTIBLE	FB	SDNSF	FBG	DV	IB	T225D	CAT	11	4	18700	3	2	73200	80500
35		CONVERTIBLE	FB	SDNSF	FBG	DV	IB	T240D	CUM	11	4	18700	3	2	73000	80200
38		CONVERTIBLE	FB	SDNSF	FBG	DV	IB	T320D	CUM	11	10	24836	2	7	92500	101500
42		CONVERTIBLE	FB	SDNSF	FBG	DV	IB	T350	MRCR	14	10	35000	4		104000	114500
42		CONVERTIBLE	FB	SDNSF	FBG	DV	IB	T335D	GM	14	10	35000	4		116500	128000
42		CONVERTIBLE	FB	SDNSF	FBG	DV	IB	T420D	CUM	14	10	35000	4		123500	135500
42		YACHT	FB	MY	FBG	DV	IB	T350	MRCR	14	10	34000	3	9	102500	112500
42		YACHT	FB	MY	FBG	DV	IB	T320D	CUM	14	10	34000	3	9	113500	125000
42		YACHT	FB	MY	FBG	DV	IB	T335D	GM	14	10	34000	3	9	115000	126500
46		CONVERTIBLE	FB	SDNSF	FBG	DV	IB	T350D	GM	13			3	6	112000	123000
46		CONVERTIBLE	FB	SDNSF	FBG	DV	IB	T435D	GM	13			3	6	119500	131500
46		YACHT	FB	MY	FBG	DV	IB	T435D	GM	13	1	43000	3	8	149500	164500
58		YACHT	FB	MY	FBG	DV	IB	T525D	GM	17	11	65000	5		244000	268000
58		YACHT	FB	MY	FBG	DV	IB	T675D	GM	17	11	65000	5		268000	294500
		1975 BOATS														
26		HARDTOP	HT	SPTCR	FBG	DV	IO	165-233		10		5500	2	6	17000	20200
26		SPORT CONVERTIBLE	ST	SPTCR	FBG	DV	IO	165-233		10		5500	2	6	17000	20200
26		SPORT FISHERMAN	FB	SF	FBG	DV	IO	165-233		10		5500	2	6	19800	22900
28		FLYBRIDGE CRUISER	FB	SDNSF	FBG	DV	IB	T225		11		10000	2	7	25400	28300
28		HARDTOP	HT	SPTCR	FBG	DV	IB	T225		11		10000	2	7	25500	28400
28		SPORT FISHERMAN	FB	SF	FBG	DV	IB	T225		11		10000	2	7	26100	29100
30	7	BAHIA-MAR	ST	SPTCR	FBG	DV	IB	T225-T350		11	2	9400	2	7	27300	33100
30	7	BAHIA-MAR	ST	SPTCR	FBG	DV	IB	T140D-T225D		11	2	9400	2	7	34800	43200
30	7	FLYBRIDGE CRUISER	FB	SDNSF	FBG	DV	IB	T225-T350		11	2	10600	2	9	31400	37800
30	7	FLYBRIDGE CRUISER	FB	SDNSF	FBG	DV	IB	T140D-T225D		11	2	10600	2	9	39500	48400
30	7	HARDTOP	HT	SPTCR	FBG	DV	IB	T225-T350		11	2	9400	2	8	27300	33100
30	7	HARDTOP	HT	SPTCR	FBG	DV	IB	T140D-T225D		11	2	9400	2	8	34800	43200
30	7	SPORT FISHERMAN	FB	SF	FBG	DV	IB	T225-T350		11	2	10300	2	8	31100	37500
30	7	SPORT FISHERMAN	FB	SF	FBG	DV	IB	T140D-T225D		11	2	10300	2	8	38800	47600
35		CONVERTIBLE	FB	SDNSF	FBG	DV	IB	T350	MRCR	13		21000			59900	65800
35		CONVERTIBLE	FB	SDNSF	FBG	DV	IB	T240D	CUM	13		21000			78100	85900
37	8	CONVERTIBLE	FB	SDNSF	FBG	DV	IB	T320D	CUM	14	5	28830	3	6	90700	99600
38	6	YACHT	HT	MY	FBG	DV	IB	T350	MRCR	13		22000	3	6	70900	77900
38	6	YACHT	HT	MY	FBG	DV	IB	T320D	CUM	13		22000	3	6	81900	90000
42	6	SPORT FISHERMAN	FB	SF	FBG	DV	IB	T335D	GM	14	10	35000	4		116500	128000
42	6	YACHT	HT	MY	FBG	DV	IB	T320D	CUM	14	10	34000	3	9	112000	123000
42	6	YACHT	HT	MY	FBG	DV	IB	T335D	GM	14	10	34000	3	9	113500	124500
42	6	YACHT	FB	MY	FBG	DV	IB	T320D	CUM	14	10	34000	3	9	111500	122500
42	6	YACHT	FB	MY	FBG	DV	IB	T335D	GM	14	10	34000	3	9	113000	124500
46	6	CONVERTIBLE	FB	SDNSF	FBG	DV	IB	T350D	GM	16		42300	4	6	118500	130000
46	6	CONVERTIBLE	FB	SDNSF	FBG	DV	IB	T435D	GM	16		42300	4	6	126000	138500
46	6	YACHT	HT	MY	FBG	DV	IB	T350D	GM	16		43000	4	6	122500	134500
46	6	YACHT	HT	MY	FBG	DV	IB	T435D	GM	16		43000	4	6	128500	141000
46	6	YACHT	FB	MY	FBG	DV	IB	T350D	GM	16		43000	4	6	122000	134000
46	6	YACHT	FB	MY	FBG	DV	IB	T435D	GM	16		43000	4	6	127500	140500
58	5	YACHT	HT	MY	FBG	DV	IB	T650D	GM	17	11	70000	5		281500	309500
58	5	YACHT	FB	MY	FBG	DV	IB	T650D	GM	17	11	70000	5		278000	305500
		1974 BOATS														
24	8		FB	SF	FBG	DV	IB	225		9	11	4750	2	4	12800	14500
24	8		FB	SF	FBG	DV	IO	T165	MRCR	9	11	4750	2	4	20300	22500
24	8		HT	SPTCR	FBG	DV	IB	225		9	11	4700	2	3	12600	14400
24	8		HT	SPTCR	FBG	DV	IO	T165	MRCR	9	11	4700	2	3	17400	19700
24	8	SPORT CONVERTIBLE	OP	CR	FBG	DV	IB	225		9	11	4500	2	3	12200	13900
24	8	SPORT CONVERTIBLE	OP	CR	FBG	DV	IO	T165	MRCR	9	11	4500	2	3	16900	19200
28			FB	SDNSF	FBG	DV	IB	T225	MRCR	11	2	7000	2	7	21300	23600
28			FB	SF	FBG	DV	IB	T225	MRCR	11	2	7000	2	7	21300	23700
28			HT	SPTCR	FBG	DV	IB	T225	MRCR	11	2	7000	2	7	21300	23700
30	7		FB	SDNSF	FBG	DV	IB	T225-T325		11	2	9600	2	9	28500	33900
30	7		FB	SDNSF	FBG	DV	IB	T140D-T210D		11	2	9600	2	9	36900	44600
30	7		FB	SF	FBG	DV	IB	T225-T325		11	2	9300	2	8	25200	30000
30	7		FB	SF	FBG	DV	IB	T140D-T210D		11	2	9300	2	8	32300	39100
30	7		HT	SPTCR	FBG	DV	IB	T225-T325		11	2	8800	2	8	26500	31600
30	7		HT	SPTCR	FBG	DV	IB	T140D-T210D		11	2	8800	2	8	33300	40600
30	7	BAHIA-MAR	OP	SPTCR	FBG	DV	IB	T225-T325		11	2	8120	2	7	26000	31100
30	7	BAHIA-MAR	OP	SPTCR	FBG	DV	IB	T140D-T210D		11	2	8120	2	7	31900	39200
35			FB	SDNSF	FBG	DV	IB	T325	MRCR	13		21000	3		58400	64100
35			FB	SDNSF	FBG	DV	IB	T225D	CAT	13		21000	3		78000	85700
35			FB	SDNSF	FBG	DV	IB	T240D	CUM	13		21000	3		77800	85500
37	8		FB	SDNSF	FBG	DV	IB	T320D	CUM	14	5	26163	3	6	82700	90900
38	6		HT	MY	FBG	DV	IB	T325	MRCR	13		22000	3	6	69300	76200

 CONTINUED ON NEXT PAGE

LOA FT	IN	NAME AND/ OR MODEL	TOP/ RIG	BOAT TYPE	-HULL- MTL	TP	ENGINE TP	# HP	MFG	BEAM FT	IN	WGT LBS	DRAFT FT	IN	RETAIL LOW	RETAIL HIGH
1974 BOATS																
38	6		HT	MY	FBG	DV	IB	T283D	GM	13		22000	3	6	79200	87100
42	6		HT	MY	FBG	DV	IB	T320D	CUM	14	10	29000	3	9	102000	112000
42	6		HT	MY	FBG	DV	IB	T335D	GM	14	10	34000	3	9	116000	127500
46	6		FB	MY	FBG	DV	IB	T350D	GM	16		43000	4	6	127500	140000
46	6		FB	MY	FBG	DV	IB	T395D	GM	16		43000	4	6	132500	145500
46	6		FB	SDNSF	FBG	DV	IB	T350D	GM	16			4	6	138000	152000
46	6		FB	SDNSF	FBG	DV	IB	T395D	GM	16			4	6	144500	158500
1973 BOATS																
25	10		FB	SF	FBG	DV	IO	T165	MRCR	9	11	4750	2	4	22800	25400
25	10		HT	SPTCR	FBG	DV	IO	T165	MRCR	9	11	4700	2	4	19800	22000
25	10	SPORT CONVERTIBLE	OP	CR	FBG	DV	IO	T165	MRCR	9	11	4500	2	4	19400	21500
28			FB	SDNSF	FBG	DV	IB	T225	MRCR	11		7000	2	5	20900	23200
28			FB	SF	FBG	DV	IB	T225	MRCR	11		7000	2	5	20900	23300
28			HT	SPTCR	FBG	DV	IB	T225	MRCR	11		7000	2	4	20900	23200
30	7		FB	SDNSF	FBG	DV	IB	T225-T325		11	2	10562	2	9	30300	35900
30	7		FB	SDNSF	FBG	DV	IB	T140D-T210D		11	2	11662	2	10	41800	50700
30	7		FB	SF	FBG	DV	IB	T225-T325		11	2	10362	2	9	30200	35800
30	7		FB	SF	FBG	DV	IB	T140D-T210D		11	2	11462	2	10	41300	50100
30	7		HT	SPTCR	FBG	DV	IB	T225-T325		11	2	9562	2	8	26600	31600
30	7		HT	SPTCR	FBG	DV	IB	T140D-T210D		11	2	11062	2	10	40300	48100
30	7	BAHIA-MAR	OP	SPTCR	FBG	DV	IB	T225-T325		11	2	9362	2	8	26400	31500
30	7	BAHIA-MAR	OP	SPTCR	FBG	DV	IB	T140D-T210D		11	2	10462	2	8	38900	47600
35			FB	SDNSF	FBG	DV	IB	T325	MRCR	13		16200	2	8	51200	56300
35			FB	SDNSF	FBG	DV	IB	T225D	CAT	13		19100	3	2	73300	80600
35			FB	SDNSF	FBG	DV	IB	T240D	CUM	13		19400	3	2	73800	81100
37	8		FB	SDNSF	FBG	DV	IB	T283D	GM	14	5	24836	3	6	77000	84600
37	8		FB	SDNSF	FBG	DV	IB	T320D	CUM	14	5	24836	3	6	78300	86100
38	6	SALON	HT	CR	FBG	DV	IB	T325	MRCR	13	5	22000	3	6	66600	73200
38	6	SALON	HT	CR	FBG	DV	IB	T283D	GM	13	5	22000	3	6	76300	83800
42	6		HT	MY	FBG	DV	IB	T320D	CUM	14	10	34000	3	9	113000	124000
42	6		HT	MY	FBG	DV	IB	T335D	GM	14	10	34000	3	9	114500	126000
46	6		FB	MY	FBG	DV	IB	T435D	GM	16		43000	4	6	134500	148000
46	6		FB	SDNSF	FBG	DV	IB	T350D	GM	16		37400	4	6	122500	135000
46	6		FB	SDNSF	FBG	DV	IB	T435D	GM	16		38600	4	6	137000	151000
1972 BOATS																
25	10		FB	SF	FBG	DV	IO	T165	MRCR	9	11	4750	2	4	24100	26800
25	10		HT	SPTCR	FBG	DV	IO	T165	MRCR	9	11	4700	2	3	20900	23200
25	10	SPORT CONVERTIBLE	OP	CR	FBG	DV	IO	T165	MRCR	9	11	4500	2	3	20400	22700
28			FB	SDNSF	FBG	DV	IO	T215	MRCR	11		7000	2	7	33800	37600
28			FB	SF	FBG	DV	IO	T215	MRCR	11		7000	2	7	33800	37600
28			HT	SPTCR	FBG	DV	IO	T215	MRCR	11		7000	2	7	29700	33000
30	7		FB	SDNSF	FBG	DV	IO	T215-T325		11	2	9600	2	9	45700	54400
30	7		FB	SDNSF	FBG	DV	IB	T140D-T170D		11	2	9600	2	9	36800	42300
30	7		FB	SF	FBG	DV	IO	T215-T325		11	2	9300	2	8	40000	48400
30	7		FB	SF	FBG	DV	IB	T140D-T170D		11	2	9300	2	8	32200	37100
30	7		HT	SPTCR	FBG	DV	IO	T215-T325		11	2	8800	2	8	36800	44700
30	7		HT	SPTCR	FBG	DV	IB	T140D-T170D		11	2	8800	2	8	33200	38300
30	7	BAHIA-MAR	OP	SPTCR	FBG	DV	IO	T215-T325		11	2	8120	2	7	36200	44100
30	7	BAHIA-MAR	OP	SPTCR	FBG	DV	IB	T140D-T170D		11	2	8120	2	7	31800	36900
35			FB	SDNSF	FBG	DV	IO	T325	MRCR	13		19281			91100	100000
35			FB	SDNSF	FBG	DV	IB	T210D	CUM	13		19281			72200	79400
35			FB	SDNSF	FBG	DV	IB	T225D	CAT	13		19281			73600	80900
35			FB	SF	FBG	DV	IO	T325	MRCR	13		19281			91100	100000
35			FB	SF	FBG	DV	IB	T210D	CUM	13		19281			72200	79400
35			FB	SF	FBG	DV	IB	T225D	CAT	13		19281			73600	80900
37	8		FB	SDNSF	FBG	DV	IO	T325	MRCR	14	5		3	6	75900	83400
37	8		FB	SDNSF	FBG	DV	IB	T283D	GM	14	5		3	6	60700	66700
37	8		FB	SF	FBG	DV	IO	T325	MRCR	14	5		3	6	81300	89300
37	8		FB	SF	FBG	DV	IB	T283D	GM	14	5		3	6	75100	82500
38	6	SALON	HT	CR	FBG	DV	IO	T325	MRCR	13		22000	3	6	77100	84700
38	6	SALON	HT	CR	FBG	DV	IB	T283D	GM	13		22000	3	6	76800	84400
46	6		FB	SDNSF	FBG	DV	IB	T350D	GM	16		37400	4	6	121000	133000
46	6		FB	SDNSF	FBG	DV	IB	T395D	GM	16		38600	4	6	130000	143000
1971 BOATS																
24		MOPPIE		CAMPR	FBG	DV	IO	T165	MRCR	8		3800	3	1	16400	18600
24		MOPPIE II		RNBT	FBG	DV	IO	165	MRCR	8		3500	2	4	12900	14700
24	8		FB	SF	FBG	DV	IO	T165	MRCR	9	11	4750	2	4	24000	26700
24	8		FB	SF	FBG	DV	IB	T200	CHRY	9	11	6300	2	3	16400	18600
24	8		HT	SPTCR	FBG	DV	IO	T165	MRCR	9	11	4700	2	3	20700	23000
24	8		HT	SPTCR	FBG	DV	IB	T200	CHRY	9	11	5700	2	3	15100	17200
24	8	BAHIA-MAR	OP	SPTCR	FBG	DV	IO	T165	MRCR	9	11	4450	2	3	20100	22300
24	8	SPORT CONVERTIBLE	OP	CR	FBG	DV	IO	T165	MRCR	9	11	4500	2	3	20200	22400
24	8	SPORT CONVERTIBLE	OP	CR	FBG	DV	IB	T200	CHRY	9	11	5500	2	3	14700	16700
28			FB	SDNSF	FBG	DV	IO	T215	MRCR	11		6500	2	7	34800	38600
28			FB	SF	FBG	DV	IO	T215	MRCR	11		6500	2	7	34800	38600
28			HT	SPTCR	FBG	DV	IO	T215	MRCR	11		6500	2	7	30500	33900
30	7		FB	SDNSF	FBG	DV	IO	T215-T325		11	2	9600	2	9	48100	57500
30	7		FB	SDNSF	FBG	DV	IB	T140D-T170D		11	2	9600	2	9	36700	42300
30	7		FB	SF	FBG	DV	IO	T215-T325		11	2	9300	2	8	42300	51100
30	7		FB	SF	FBG	DV	IB	T140D-T170D		11	2	9300	2	8	32200	37100
30	7		HT	SPTCR	FBG	DV	IO	T215-T325		11	2	8800	2	7	39000	47300
30	7		HT	SPTCR	FBG	DV	IB	T140D-T170D		11	2	8800	2	7	33200	38300
30	7	BAHIA-MAR	OP	SPTCR	FBG	DV	IO	T215-T325		11	2	8120	2	7	38300	46600
30	7	BAHIA-MAR	OP	SPTCR	FBG	DV	IB	T140D-T170D		11	2	8120	2	7	31800	36900
35			FB	SDNSF	FBG	DV	IO	T325	MRCR	13		19281			96400	106000
35			FB	SDNSF	FBG	DV	IB	T210D	CUM	13		19281			72200	79300
35			FB	SF	FBG	DV	IO	T325	MRCR	13		19281			96400	106000
35			FB	SF	FBG	DV	IB	T210D	CUM	13		19281			72200	79300
37	8		FB	SDNSF	FBG	DV	IO	T325	MRCR	14	5		3	6	80200	88200
37	8		FB	SDNSF	FBG	DV	IB	T283D	GM	14	5		3	6	60000	66000
37	8		FB	SF	FBG	DV	IO	T325	MRCR	14	5		3	6	86000	94500
37	8		FB	SF	FBG	DV	IB	T283D	GM	14	5		3	6	74200	81500
38	6	SALON	HT	CR	FBG	DV	IO	T325	MRCR	13		22000	3	6	81600	89600
38	6	SALON	HT	CR	FBG	DV	IB	T283D	GM	13		22000	3	6	75900	83500
46			FB	SF	FBG	DV	IO	T350D	GM	15	6		4	6	166000	182500
46			FB	SF	FBG	DV	IB	T390D	GM	15	6		4	6	114000	125000
1970 BOATS																
20	3	BAHIA-MAR	OP	RNBT	FBG	DV	IO	160	MRCR	8		2500	1	4	9300	10600
20	3	BARON	OP	RNBT	FBG	DV	IO	160-235		8		2500	1	4	9650	11100
20	3	MOPPIE	OP	RNBT	FBG	DV	IO	160	MRCR	8		2300	1	4	9150	10400
20	3	MOPPIE	HT	RNBT	FBG	DV	IO	160	MRCR	8		2300	1	4	9150	10400
20	3	SPORTSMAN	OP	CTRCN	FBG	DV	IO	160	MRCR	8		2400	1	4	10200	11600
25	11		HT	CR	FBG	DV	IO	T120-T160		9	11	4450	1	6	21900	25300
25	11		HT	CR	FBG	DV	IB	T200	CHRY	9	11	4450	1	6	13900	15800
25	11		FB	SF	FBG	DV	IO	T120-T160		9	11	4250	1	6	24600	28500
25	11		FB	SF	FBG	DV	IB	T200	CHRY	9	11	4250	1	6	13700	15500
25	11	BAHIA-MAR	OP	SPTCR	FBG	DV	IO	T120-T160		9	11	4200	1	6	21300	24600
25	11	SPORT CONVERTIBLE	OP	CR	FBG	DV	IO	T120-T160		9	11	4250	1	6	21400	24700
25	11	SPORT CONVERTIBLE	OP	CR	FBG	DV	IB	T200	CHRY	9	11	4250	1	6	13600	15500
28		BARON	OP	RNBT	FBG	DV	IO	T200-T235		7	10	4400	1	11	21100	24500
30	7		HT	EXP	FBG	DV	IB	T225-T325		11	2	9400	2	8	28100	33500
30	7		HT	EXP	FBG	DV	IB	T140D-T170D		11	2	9400	2	8	38300	44200
30	7		FB	SDNSF	FBG	DV	IB	T225-T325		11	2	9600	2	9	26800	31900
30	7		FB	SDNSF	FBG	DV	IB	T140D-T170D		11	2	9600	2	9	36800	42400
30	7		FB	SF	FBG	DV	IB	T225-T325		11	2	9300	2	8	23700	28200
30	7		FB	SF	FBG	DV	IB	T140D-T170D		11	2	9300	2	8	32200	37100
30	7		HT	SPTCR	FBG	DV	IB	T210-T325		11	2	8800	2	7	24600	29700
30	7		HT	SPTCR	FBG	DV	IB	T140D-T170D		11	2	8800	2	7	33200	38400
30	7	BAHIA-MAR	OP	SPTCR	FBG	DV	IB	T225-T325		11	2	8800	2	7	24900	29700
30	7	BAHIA-MAR	OP	SPTCR	FBG	DV	IB	T140D-T170D		11	2	9650	2	7	35000	40300
35			FB	SDNSF	FBG	DV	IB	T300	CHRY	13		19281	2	9	52200	57300
35			FB	SDNSF	FBG	DV	IB	T325	MRCR	13		19281	2	9	52700	57900
35			FB	SDNSF	FBG	DV	IB	T216D	GM	13		19281	2	9	72700	79900
37	8		FB	SF	FBG	DV	IB	T325	MRCR	14	5	24373	3	6	63800	70200
37	8		FB	SF	FBG	DV	IB	T390	MRCR	14	5		3	6	54200	59600
37	8		FB	SF	FBG	DV	IB	T283D	GM	14	5		3	6	73400	80700
38	6	SALON	FB	CR	FBG	DV	IB	T325	MRCR	13		22000	3	6	65800	72300
38	6	SALON	FB	CR	FBG	DV	IB	T283D	GM	13		22000	3	6	75200	82600
1969 BOATS																
20	3		HT	RNBT	FBG	DV	IO	160-210		8		2400	1	4	9800	11500
20	3	BAHIA-MAR	OP	RNBT	FBG	DV	IO	160-210		8		2500	1	4	9650	11500
20	3	BARON	OP	RNBT	FBG	DV	IO	160-225		8		2500	1	4	10300	11700
20	3	MOPPIE	OP	RNBT	FBG	DV	IO	160-210		8		2300	1	4	9600	11000
20	3	SPORTSMAN	OP	CTRCN	FBG	DV	IO	160	MRCR	8		2400	1	4	10800	12200
25	11		HT	EXP	FBG	DV	IO	T120-T160		9	11	4880	1	6	24300	28000
25	11	BAHIA-MAR	OP	SPTCR	FBG	DV	IO	T120-T160		9	11	4200	1	6	22500	26100
25	11	MARK II	HT	CR	FBG	DV	IO	T120-T160		9	11	4450	1	6	23100	26700
25	11	MARK II	HT	CR	FBG	DV	IB	T195	CHRY	9	11	4450	1	6	13700	15500
25	11	MARK II	FB	SF	FBG	DV	IO	T120-T160		9	11	4250	1	6	26000	30100
25	11	MARK II	FB	SF	FBG	DV	IB	T195	CHRY	9	11	4250	1	6	13400	15200
25	11	MARK II SPORT CONV	OP	CR	FBG	DV	IO	T120-T160		9	11	4250	1	6	22600	26200
25	11	MARK II SPORT CONV	OP	CR	FBG	DV	IB	T195	CHRY	9	11	4250	1	6	13400	15200
28		BARON	OP	RNBT	FBG	DV	IO	T225	HOLM	7	10		1	11	24500	27200
30	7		FB	CR	FBG	DV	IB	T210-T325		11	2	9600	2	9	24800	29800
30	7		FB	CR	FBG	DV	IB	T140D-T170D		11	2	9600	2	9	35000	40300
30	7		HT	EXP	FBG	DV	IB	T210-T325		11	2	9400	2	8	27400	33000
30	7		HT	EXP	FBG	DV	IB	T140D-T170D		11	2	9400	2	8	38400	44300

58 CONTINUED ON NEXT PAGE 96th ed. - Vol. III

BERTRAM YACHT INC -CONTINUED See inside cover to adjust price for area

LOA FT	IN	NAME AND/ OR MODEL	TOP/ RIG	BOAT TYPE	-HULL- MTL	TP	----ENGINE--- TP	# HP	MFG	BEAM FT	IN	WGT LBS	DRAFT FT	IN	RETAIL LOW	RETAIL HIGH
1969 BOATS																
30	7		FB	SF	FBG	DV	IB	T210-T325		11	2	9300	2	8	23100	27800
30	7		FB	SF	FBG	DV	IB	T140D-T216D		11	2	9300	2	8	32300	39400
30	7	BAHIA-MAR	OP	SPTCR	FBG	DV	IB	T210-T325		11	2	8800	2	7	24200	29300
30	7	BAHIA-MAR	OP	SPTCR	FBG	DV	IB	T140D-T216D		11	2	9650	2	7	35100	42800
30	7	MARK II	HT	CR	FBG	DV	IB	T210-T325		11	2	8800	2	7	24200	29200
30	7	MARK II	HT	CR	FBG	DV	IB	T140D-T216D		11	2	8800	2	7	33200	40800
35		CARIBE	HT	SDN	FBG	DV	IB	T300	CHRY	13		14300	2	9	47900	52600
35		CARIBE	HT	SDN	FBG	DV	IB	T180D	GM	13			2	9	70400	77300
35		CARIBE	FB	SF	FBG	DV	IB	T300	CHRY	13		19281	2	9	51400	56500
35		CARIBE	FB	SF	FBG	DV	IB	T180D	GM	13		19281	2	9	71600	78600
37	9	SALON	HT	CR	FBG	DV	IB	T277	SEA	13		19000	2	8	55300	60800
		IB T290 CHRY 55300 60800, IB T300 CHRY 55400 60900, IB T216D GM													62400	68500
		IB T220D CRUS 61500 67600														
38	1	SALON	HT	CR	FBG	DV	IB	T325		13		22000			63800	70200
38	3	SPORT FISHERMAN		SF		DV	IB	300	CHRY			20000	3	9	58700	64500
55	9	DIPLOMAT		MY	FBG	DV	IB	360D	CAT	16	3	44000	4		103000	113000
55	9	ENVOY		MY	FBG	DV	IB	360D	CAT	16	3	42000	4		101000	111000
1968 BOATS																
20	3		HT	RNBT	FBG	DV	IO	160-200		8		2400	1	4	10400	12100
20	3	BAHIA-MAR	OP	RNBT	FBG	DV	IO	160-200		8		2800	1	4	11200	13100
20	3	MOPPIE	OP	RNBT	FBG	DV	IO	160-200		8		2300	1	4	10200	11900
25	11		HT	EXP	FBG	DV	IO	T120-T160		9	11	4880	1	9	25700	30300
25	11	BAHIA-MAR	OP	SPTCR	FBG	DV	IO	T120-T160		9	11	4200	1	6	23800	28300
25	11	MARK II	HT	CR	FBG	DV	IO	T120-T160		9	11	4450	1	6	24500	29000
25	11	MARK II	HT	CR	FBG	DV	VD	T195	CHRY	9	11	5700	1	6	15300	17400
25	11	MARK II	FB	SF	FBG	DV	IO	T120-T160		9	11	4550	1	7	28500	33800
25	11	MARK II	FB	SF	FBG	DV	VD	T195	CHRY	9	11	5850	1	7	15600	17700
25	11	MARK II SPORT CONV	OP	CR	FBG	DV	IO	T120-T160		9	11	4250	1	6	23900	28400
25	11	MARK II SPORT CONV	OP	CR	FBG	DV	VD	T195	CHRY	9	11	5500	1	6	15000	17000
30	7		HT	CR	FBG	DV	IB	T210-T290		11	2	8800	1	11	23900	28100
30	7		HT	CR	FBG	DV	IB	T140D	GM	11	2	9650	1	11	35200	39100
30	7		HT	CR	FBG	DV	IB	T170D-T216D		11	2	10560	1	11	40600	45100
30	7		FB	CR	FBG	DV	IB	T210-T290		11	2	9500	1	11	24300	28600
30	7		FB	CR	FBG	DV	IB	T140D-T170D		11	2	10500	1	11	39200	47300
30	7		HT	EXP	FBG	DV	IB	T210-T290		11	2	9400	1	11	27000	31800
30	7		HT	EXP	FBG	DV	IB	T140D-T170D		11	2	10250	1	11	38600	46700
30	7		FB	SF	FBG	DV	IB	T210-T290		11	2	9500	1	11	22900	26900
30	7		FB	SF	FBG	DV	IB	T140D-T216D		11	2	10500	1	11	39200	47300
30	7	BAHIA-MAR	OP	SPTCR	FBG	DV	IB	T210-T290		11	2	8800	1	10	23900	28200
30	7	BAHIA-MAR	OP	SPTCR	FBG	DV	IB	T140D	GM	11	2	9650	1	10	35300	39200
30	7	BAHIA-MAR	OP	SPTCR	FBG	DV	IB	T170D-T216D		11	2	10460	1	10	40400	44900
35		CARIBE		SDN			IB	T300		12	11		2	6	46300	50900
37	9	SALON	HT	CR	FBG	DV	IB	T277	SEA	13		20850	3		59000	64800
		IB T290 CHRY 54900 60300, IB T216D GM 68000 74700, IB T220D CRUS													66600	73200
1967 BOATS																
20	3		HT	RNBT	FBG	DV	IO	150-200		8		2400	1	4	10900	12500
20	3		HT	RNBT	FBG	DV	IO	60D	ROVR	8		2400	1	4	13700	15500
20	3	BAHIA-MAR	OP	RNBT	FBG	DV	IO	150-200		8		2500	1	4	11200	12700
20	3	BAHIA-MAR	OP	RNBT	FBG	DV	IO	60D	ROVR	8		2500	1	4	13900	15800
20	3	MOPPIE	OP	RNBT	FBG	DV	IO	150-200		8		2300	1	4	10700	12300
20	3	MOPPIE	OP	RNBT	FBG	DV	IO	60D	ROVR	8		2300	1	4	13500	15300
25	11		HT	EXP	FBG	DV	IO	T120-T160		9	11	4880	1	9	27200	32000
25	11		HT	EXP	FBG	DV	IO	T 60D	ROVR	9	11	5575	1	9	33600	37400
25	11	BAHIA-MAR	OP	SPTCR	FBG	DV	IO	T120-T160		9	11	4200	1	6	25200	30000
25	11	BAHIA-MAR	OP	SPTCR	FBG	DV	IO	T 60D	ROVR	9	11	4925	1	6	30500	33900
25	11	MARK II	HT	CR	FBG	DV	IO	T120-T160		9	11	4450	1	6	25900	30700
25	11	MARK II	HT	CR	FBG	DV	IO	T 60D	ROVR	9	11	5175	1	6	31700	35200
25	11	MARK II	FB	SF	FBG	DV	IO	T120-T160		9	11	4500	1	7	30000	35500
25	11	MARK II	FB	SF	FBG	DV	IO	T 60D	ROVR	9	11	5225	1	7	40200	44700
25	11	MARK II SPORT CONV	OP	CR	FBG	DV	IO	T120-T160		9	11	4250	1	6	25300	30100
25	11	MARK II SPORT CONV	OP	CR	FBG	DV	IO	T 60D	ROVR	9	11	4975	1	6	30700	34100
30	7		HT	CR	FBG	DV	IB	T210-T290		11	3	8800	2	7	23600	27700
30	7		HT	CR	FBG	DV	IB	T140D-T216D		11	3	9650	2	7	35500	43200
30	7		FB	CR	FBG	DV	IB	T210-T290		11	3	9500	2	7	24000	28200
30	7		FB	CR	FBG	DV	IB	T140D	GM	11	3	10500	2	7	39400	43800
30	7		HT	EXP	FBG	DV	IB	T210-T290		11	3	9400	2	7	26700	31400
30	7		HT	EXP	FBG	DV	IB	T140D	GM	11	3	10250	2	7	38800	43200
30	7		FB	SF	FBG	DV	IB	T210-T290		11	3	9500	2	7	22600	26500
30	7		FB	SF	FBG	DV	IB	T140D-T216D		11	3	10500	2	7	39400	47600
30	7	BAHIA-MAR	OP	SPTCR	FBG	DV	IB	T210-T290		11	3	8800	2	7	23600	27800
30	7	BAHIA-MAR	OP	SPTCR	FBG	DV	IB	T140D-T216D		11	3	9650	2	7	35500	43200
37	9		FB	CR	FBG	DV	IB	T290	CHRY			19000			57300	63000
		IB T216D GM 62200 68400, IB T283D GM 64700 71100, IB T300D CUM													65000	71400
		IB T370D CUM 67300 74000														
37	9	SALON	HT	CR	FBG	DV	IB	T290	CHRY	13		19000	3		54500	59900
37	9	SALON	HT	CR	FBG	DV	IB	T216D	GM	13			3		60500	66500
1966 BOATS																
20	3	BAHIA-MAR	OP	RNBT	FBG	DV	IO	150-200		8		2500	1	4	11800	13500
20	3	BAHIA-MAR	OP	RNBT	FBG	DV	IO	60D	MRCR	8		2500	1	4	14700	16700
20	3	MOPPIE	OP	RNBT	FBG	DV	IO	150-200		8		2300	1	4	11300	13100
20	3	MOPPIE	OP	RNBT	FBG	DV	IO	60D		8		2300	1	4	14200	16200
25	11		HT	EXP	FBG	DV	IO	T110-T150		9	11	4200	1	9	26300	30500
25	11		HT	EXP	FBG	DV	IO	T 60D		9	11	4500	1	9	30000	33400
25	11	BAHIA-MAR	OP	SPTCR	FBG	DV	IO	T110-T150		9	11	4500	1	6	27300	32200
25	11	MARK II	HT	CR	FBG	DV	IO	T110-T150		9	11	4450	1	6	27100	31300
25	11	MARK II	HT	CR	FBG	DV	IO	T 60D		9	11	4700	1	6	31100	34500
25	11	MARK II	FB	SF	FBG	DV	IO	T110-T150		9	11	4500	1	7	31400	37100
25	11	MARK II	FB	SF	FBG	DV	IO	T 60D		9	11	4700	1	7	39200	43500
25	11	MARK II SPORT CONV	OP	CR	FBG	DV	IO	T110-T150		9	11	4250	1	6	26500	30700
25	11	MARK II SPORT CONV	OP	CR	FBG	DV	IO	T 60D		9	11	4500	1	6	30100	33400
30	7		HT	CR	FBG	DV	IB	T290	CHRY	11	3	8800	2	7	24600	27400
30	7		HT	CR	FBG	DV	IB	T140D-T216D		11	3	9650	2	7	35700	43500
30	7		FB	CR	FBG	DV	IB	T290	CHRY	11	3	9500	2	7	25100	27800
30	7		FB	CR	FBG	DV	IB	T140D	GM	11	3	10500	2	7	39700	44100
30	7		HT	EXP	FBG	DV	IB	T290	CHRY	11	3	9500	2	7	27900	31000
30	7		HT	EXP	FBG	DV	IB	T140D	GM	11	3	10500	2	7	39700	44100
30	7		FB	SF	FBG	DV	IB	T290	CHRY	11	3	9500	2	7	23500	26200
30	7		FB	SF	FBG	DV	IB	T140D	GM	11	3	10500	2	7	39700	44100
30	7	BAHIA-MAR	OP	SPTCR	FBG	DV	IB	T210-T290		11	3	8800	2	7	23300	27400
30	7	BAHIA-MAR	OP	SPTCR	FBG	DV	IB	T140D	GM	11	3	9650	2	7	35800	39700
37	9		FB	CR	FBG	DV	IB	T290	CHRY	14	5	19000			50000	55000
		IB T181D GM 55900 61400, IB T280D GM 59300 65100, IB T300D CUM													58700	64500
		IB T370D CUM 62000 68200														
1965 BOATS																
20	3	MOPPIE	OP	RNBT	FBG	DV	IO	150	MRCR	8		2300	1	2	12000	13600
24	7		HT	EXP	FBG	DV	IO	T110-T150		9	11		1	5	29200	33400
24	7	BAHIA-MAR	OP	SPTCR	FBG	DV	IO	T110-T150		9	11		1	5	28800	33000
24	7	MARK II	FB	SF	FBG	DV	IO	T110-T150		9	11		1	5	30100	34100
24	7	MARK II SPORT CONV	OP	CR	FBG	DV	IO	T110-T150		9	11	4750	1	5	28300	32700
24	7	SPORT CONVERTIBLE	OP	CR	FBG	DV	IO	T110-T150		9	11	4750	1	5	28300	32700
24	7	SPORT CONVERTIBLE	HT	CR	FBG	DV	IO	T110-T150		9	11		1	5	29100	32800
30	6		HT	CR	FBG	DV	IB	T280-T310		11	3		2	4	24500	27800
30	6		HT	CR	FBG	DV	IB	T130D-T180D		11	3		2	4	36900	43400
30	6		FB	CR	FBG	DV	IB	T280-T310		11	3		2	4	24500	27800
30	6		FB	CR	FBG	DV	IB	T130D	GM	11	3		2	4	36900	41000
30	6		HT	EXP	FBG	DV	IB	T280-T310		11	3		2	4	27500	31200
30	6		HT	EXP	FBG	DV	IB	T130D	GM	11	3		2	4	46400	51000
30	6		FB	SF	FBG	DV	IB	T280-T310		11	3		2	4	23200	26300
30	6		FB	SF	FBG	DV	IB	T130D	GM	11	3		2	4	33800	37500
37	9		FB	CR	FBG	DV	IB	T310	CHRY	14	6		3	5	40900	45400
		IB T181D GM 54500 59900, IB T280D GM 57800 63500, IB T300D GM													58700	64500
		IB T370D GM 62100 68200														
37	9		HT	EXP	FBG	DV	IB	T280	CHRY	14	6		3	5	41400	46000
		IB T310 CHRY 41700 46300, IB T181D GM 65100 71500, IB T280D													68300	75100
1964 BOATS																
25			HT	EXP	FBG	DV	IO	T110-T140							30200	34500
25		SPORT CONVERTIBLE	OP	SPTCR	FBG	DV	IO	T110-T140							29800	34000
31			HT	CR	FBG	DV	IB	T280-T315		11	3		2	4	25200	28600
31			HT	CR	FBG	DV	IB	T130D	GM	11	3		2	4	37800	42000
31			FB	CR	FBG	DV	IB	T280-T315		11	3		2	4	25200	28600
31			FB	CR	FBG	DV	IB	T130D	GM	11	3		2	4	37800	42000
31			HT	EXP	FBG	DV	IB	T280-T315		11	3		2	4	28400	32300
31			HT	EXP	FBG	DV	IB	T130D	GM	11	3		2	4	47600	52300
31			FB	SF	FBG	DV	IB	T280-T315		11	3		2	4	23700	27000
31			FB	SF	FBG	DV	IB	T130D	GM	11	3		2	4	34500	38400
31		SPORT CONVERTIBLE	OP	SPTCR	FBG	DV	IB	T280-T315		11	3		2	4	24500	27900
31		SPORT CONVERTIBLE	OP	SPTCR	FBG	DV	IB	T130D	GM	11	3		2	4	34800	38600
37	9		FB	CR	FBG	DV	IB	T315	CHRY	14	1		1	11	42000	46700
37	9		FB	CR	FBG	DV	IB	T181D	GM	14	1		1	11	55600	61000
37	9		FB	CR	FBG	DV	IB	T300D	CUM	14	1		1	11	59300	65200

CONTINUED ON NEXT PAGE

```
LOA   NAME AND/        TOP/ BOAT  -HULL- ----ENGINE---  BEAM  WGT  DRAFT RETAIL RETAIL
FT IN OR MODEL         RIG  TYPE  MTL TP TP # HP  MFG   FT IN LBS  FT IN  LOW   HIGH
--------------------- 1963 BOATS -----------------------------------------------------
25                     HT   EXP   FBG DV IO T100-T110                       31800 35500
25   SPORT CONVERTIBLE OP   SPTCR FBG DV IO T 80-T110                       30900 35000
31                     FB   CR    FBG DV IB T280   CHRY 11 3        2 4     24800 27600
31                     FB   CR    FBG DV IB T130D  GM   11 3        2 4     38200 42500
31                     HT   EXP   FBG DV IB T280   CHRY 11 3        2 4     28100 31200
31                     HT   EXP   FBG DV IB T130D  GM   11 3        2 4     47900 52600
31                     FB   SF    FBG DV IB T280   CHRY 11 3        2 4     23400 26000
31                     FB   SF    FBG DV IB T130D  GM   11 3        2 4     34900 38800
31                     HT   SPTCR FBG DV IB T280   CHRY 11 3        2 4     24200 26900
31                     HT   SPTCR FBG DV IB T130D  GM   11 3        2 4     35200 39100
31   SPORT CONVERTIBLE OP   SPTCR FBG DV IB T280   CHRY 11 3        2 4     24200 26900
31   SPORT CONVERTIBLE OP   SPTCR FBG DV IB T130D  GM   11 3        2 4     35200 39100

37 8                   FB   CR    FBG DV IB T288        14 1        1 11    41700 46300
     IB T325   42200 46900, IB T181D GM 55300 60700, IB T300D CUM 59000 64900
--------------------- 1962 BOATS -----------------------------------------------------
24 6                   HT   EXP   FBG DV IO T110                            33400 37100
24 6 SPORT CONVERTIBLE OP   SPTCR FBG DV IO T 80-T110                       32500 36500
30 4                   HT   EXP   FBG DV IB T280   CHRY                     25200 28000
30 4                   FB   SF    FBG DV IB T280   CHRY                     21600 24000
30 4                   HT   SPTCR FBG DV IB T280   CHRY                     23400 26000
30 4                   FB   SPTCR FBG DV IB T280   CHRY                     23400 26000
30 4 SPORT CONVERTIBLE OP   SPTCR FBG DV IB T280   CHRY      9262           23300 25900
--------------------- 1961 BOATS -----------------------------------------------------
31                     FB   SF    FBG DV IB T280   CHRY                     23500 26100
31   BERTRAM V-31      FB   SF    FBG    IB 170         11          2 4     20000 22200
31   BERTRAM V-31           SPTCR FBG    IB  70         11          2 4     19700 21900
31   BERTRAM V-31      HT   SPTCR FBG    IB 170         11          2 4     20200 22400
31   MOPPIE            FB   EXP   FBG DV IB T345                            29400 32700
```

BERWICK YACHTS

Call 1-800-327-6929 for BUC Personalized Evaluation Service
Or, for 1980 to 1983 boats, sign onto www.BUCValuPro.com

BIANCHI & CECCHI

Call 1-800-327-6929 for BUC Personalized Evaluation Service
Or, for 1970 to 1979 boats, sign onto www.BUCValuPro.com

BIMINI RUNNER MARINE PROD INC
COAST GUARD MFG ID- BPN

Call 1-800-327-6929 for BUC Personalized Evaluation Service
Or, for 1978 to 1982 boats, sign onto www.BUCValuPro.com

BLACKBIRD RACING TEAM
B R T   COAST GUARD MFG ID- BBM
FORMERLY BLACKBIRD MARINE

Call 1-800-327-6929 for BUC Personalized Evaluation Service
Or, for 1976 to 1984 boats, sign onto www.BUCValuPro.com

BLACKFIN YACHT CORP
FT LAUDERDALE FL 33335   COAST GUARD MFG ID- KMA See inside cover to adjust price for area
FORMERLY KARANDA MARINE INC

For more recent years, see the BUC Used Boat Price Guide, Volume 1 or Volume 2

```
LOA   NAME AND/          TOP/ BOAT  -HULL- ----ENGINE---   BEAM  WGT   DRAFT RETAIL RETAIL
FT IN OR MODEL           RIG  TYPE  MTL TP TP # HP   MFG   FT IN LBS   FT IN  LOW   HIGH
--------------------- 1983 BOATS --------------------------------------------------------
25 2 BLACK-FIN COMBI     OP   SF    FBG DV OB              8     4500  2 9    19200 21300
25 2 BLACK-FIN COMBI     OP   SF    FBG DV IB 350    CRUS  8     5160  2 9    15200 17300
     IB 158D-250D  21900 27100, IB T165-T260 17600 20900, IB T124D VLVO 25700 28600

25 2 BLACK-FIN COMBI     TT   SF    FBG DV OB              8     4500  2 9    19100 21200
25 2 BLACK-FIN COMBI     TT   SF    FBG DV SE 205    OMC   8     5160  2 9    20200 22400
25 2 BLACK-FIN COMBI     TT   SF    FBG DV IB 350    CRUS  8     5160  2 9    15000 17100
     IB 158D-250D  21900 27100, IB T165-T260 17500 20900, IB T124D VLVO 26000 28900

25 2 BLACK-FIN FISHERMAN OP   SF    FBG DV OB              8     4500  2 9    18800 20900
25 2 BLACK-FIN FISHERMAN OP   SF    FBG DV SE 205    OMC   8     5160  2 9    19800 22000
25 2 BLACK-FIN FISHERMAN OP   SF    FBG DV IB 350    CRUS  8     5160  2 9    15300 17300
     IB 158D-250D  22000 27300, IB T165-T260 18000 21000, IB T350 CRUS 20300 22500
     IB T124D VLVO 26000 28900

25 2 BLACK-FIN FISHERMAN TT   SF    FBG DV OB              8     4500  2 9    18900 20900
25 2 BLACK-FIN FISHERMAN TT   SF    FBG DV SE 205    OMC   8     5160  2 9    19800 22000
25 2 BLACK-FIN FISHERMAN TT   SF    FBG DV IB 350    CRUS  8     5160  2 9    15500 17600
     IB 158D-250D  22100 27300, IB T165-T350 18000 22500, IB T124D VLVO 25700 28600

29 4 BLACK-FIN           OP   FSH   FBG DV SE T205   OMC   10 6  8400  2 7    27500 30500
29 4 BLACK-FIN           OP   FSH   FBG DV IB T270-T350    10 6  8400  2 7    29800 35200
29 4 BLACK-FIN           OP   FSH   FBG DV IBT158D-T235D   10 6  8400  2 10   40000 48600
29 4 BLACK-FIN           TT   FSH   FBG DV SE T205   OMC   10 6  8400  2 7    27800 30900
29 4 BLACK-FIN           TT   FSH   FBG DV IB T270-T350    10 6  8400  2 10   29800 35200
29 4 BLACK-FIN           TT   FSH   FBG DV IBT158D-T235D   10 6  9650  2 10   40000 48600
31 9 BLACK-FIN           FB   SF    FBG DV IB T350   CRUS  11 11 11640 2 8    44300 49200
31 9 BLACK-FIN           FB   SF    FBG DV IBT235D-T355D   11 11 11640 2 8    58300 71000
31 9 BLACK-FIN           F+T  SF    FBG DV IB T350   CRUS  11 11 11640 2 8    44300 49200
31 9 BLACK-FIN           F+T  SF    FBG DV IBT235D-T355D   11 11 13680 2 8    58300 70900
32 6 BLACK-FIN COMBI     OP   SF    FBG DV OB              9 9   6500  2 8    37000 41100
32 6 BLACK-FIN COMBI     OP   SF    FBG DV SE T205   OMC   9 9   8450  2 8    36500 40500

32 6 BLACK-FIN COMBI     OP   SF    FBG DV IB T350-T400    9 9   8450  2 8    33500 38700
32 6 BLACK-FIN COMBI     OP   SF    FBG DV IBT235D-T250D   9 9   10470 2 8    45600 51900
32 6 BLACK-FIN COMBI     TT   SF    FBG DV OB              9 9   6500  2 8    37100 41200
32 6 BLACK-FIN COMBI     TT   SF    FBG DV SE T205   OMC   9 9   8450  2 8    36600 40700
32 6 BLACK-FI. COMBI     TT   SF    FBG DV IB T350-T400    9 9   8450  2 8    33800 38800
32 6 BLACK-FIN COMBI     TT   SF    FBG DV IBT235D-T250D   9 9   10470 2 8    46300 53200
32 6 BLACK-FIN FISHERMAN OP   SF    FBG DV OB              9 9   6500  2 8    36200 40200
32 6 BLACK-FIN FISHERMAN OP   SF    FBG DV SE T205   OMC   9 9   8450  2 8    37100 41200
32 6 BLACK-FIN FISHERMAN OP   SF    FBG DV IB T350   CRUS  9 9   8450  2 8    37500 41700
32 6 BLACK-FIN FISHERMAN OP   SF    FBG DV IB T400   MRCR  9 9   10470 2 8    42500 47200
32 6 BLACK-FIN FISHERMAN OP   SF    FBG DV IBT235D-T250D   9 9   10470 2 8    50300 55700

32 6 BLACK-FIN FISHERMAN TT   SF    FBG DV OB              9 9   6500  2 8    36400 40500
32 6 BLACK-FIN FISHERMAN TT   SF    FBG DV SE T205   OMC   9 9   8450  2 8    37100 41200
32 6 BLACK-FIN FISHERMAN TT   SF    FBG DV IB T350   CRUS  9 9   8450  2 8    37500 41700
32 6 BLACK-FIN FISHERMAN TT   SF    FBG DV IB T400   MRCR  9 9   10470 2 8    42500 47300
32 6 BLACK-FIN FISHERMAN TT   SF    FBG DV IBT235D-T250D   9 9   10470 2 8    50300 55900
39   BLACK-FIN           FB   SF    FBG DV IB T350   PERK  14 4  32000 3      127000 140000
39   BLACK-FIN           FB   SF    FBG SV IB T350   CRUS  14 4  32000 3      109500 120500
     IB T300D CAT 123500 136000, IB T350D CAT 127000 139500, IB T350D PERK 127000 140000
     IB T355D CAT 127500 140000, IB T450D GM 132000 145000

39   BLACK-FIN           F+T  SF    FBG SV IB T350   CRUS  14 4  32000 3      109500 120500
     IB T300D CAT 123500 136000, IB T350D CAT 127000 139500, IB T350D PERK 127000 140000
     IB T450D GM 132000 145000
--------------------- 1982 BOATS --------------------------------------------------------
25 2 BLACK-FIN COMBI     OP   SF    FBG DV OB              8     4500         19100 21200
25 2 BLACK-FIN COMBI     OP   SF    FBG DV IB 205-350      8     5160         13700 16600
     IB 205D GM 22500 25000, IB 300D CAT 25400 28300, IB T165 CRUS 16800 19100
     IB T124D VLVO 24700 27500

25 2 BLACK-FIN COMBI     TT   SF    FBG DV OB              8     4500         19000 21100
25 2 BLACK-FIN COMBI     TT   SF    FBG DV IB 205-350      8     5160         13700 16500
     IB 205D GM 22500 24900, IB 300D CAT 25400 28300, IB T165 CRUS 16800 19100
     IB T124D VLVO 24700 27500

25 2 BLACK-FIN FISHERMAN OP   SF    FBG DV OB              8     4500         18400 20600
25 2 BLACK-FIN FISHERMAN OP   SF    FBG DV IB 205-350      8     5160         13600 16600
     IB 205D GM 22600 25100, IB 300D CAT 25700 28500, IB T165 CRUS 16800 19100
     IB T124D VLVO 25000 27700

25 2 BLACK-FIN FISHERMAN TT   SF    FBG DV OB              8     4500         18500 20600
25 2 BLACK-FIN FISHERMAN TT   SF    FBG DV IB 205-350      8     5160         13700 16600
     IB 205D GM 22600 25100, IB 300D CAT 25700 28500, IB T165 CRUS 16900 19200
     IB T124D VLVO 25000 27800

27 11 BLACK-FIN COMBI     OP   SF   FBG DV IB T205-T350    9 10  7590         25700 28600
27 11 BLACK-FIN COMBI     OP   SF   FBG DV IBT148D-T235D   9 10  9620         34100 41500
27 11 BLACK-FIN COMBI     TT   SF   FBG DV IB T205-T350    9 10  7590         25700 28500
27 11 BLACK-FIN COMBI     TT   SF   FBG DV IBT148D-T235D   9 10  9620         19400 23100
27 11 BLACK-FIN FISHERMAN OP   SF   FBG DV IB T205-T350    9 10  7590         34000 41500
27 11 BLACK-FIN FISHERMAN OP   SF   FBG DV IBT148D-T235D   9 10  9620         24900 27700
27 11 BLACK-FIN FISHERMAN TT   SF   FBG DV IB T205-T350    9 10  7590         35700 43700
27 11 BLACK-FIN FISHERMAN TT   SF   FBG DV IBT148D-T235D   9 10  9620         25100 27800
```

```
BLACKFIN YACHT CORP          -CONTINUED       See inside cover to adjust price for area

  LOA  NAME AND/           TOP/ BOAT  -HULL- ----ENGINE---  BEAM   WGT  DRAFT RETAIL RETAIL
  FT IN  OR MODEL           RIG TYPE  MTL TP TP # HP  MFG   FT IN  LBS  FT IN  LOW   HIGH
-------------------- 1982 BOATS -----------------------------------------------------------
27 11 BLACK-FIN FISHERMAN  TT  SF    FBG DV IB T205-T350   9 10   7590        23100  28500
27 11 BLACK-FIN FISHERMAN  FB  SF    FBG DV IBT148D-T235D  9 10   9620        35800  43800
31  9 BLACK-FIN            FB  SF    FBG DV IB T350  CRUS 11 11  11640        42400  47100
31  9 BLACK-FIN            FB  SF    FBG DV IBT205D-T300D 11 11  13680        54700  65100
32  6 BLACK-FIN COMBI      OP  SF    FBG DV OB            9  9   6500        36300  40300
32  6 BLACK-FIN COMBI      OP  SF    FBG DV IB T205  OMC  9  9   8450        29800  33200
32  6 BLACK-FIN COMBI      OP  SF    FBG DV IB T235-T350  9  9  10470        33700  37400
32  6 BLACK-FIN COMBI      OP  SF    FBG DV IB T300D CAT  9  9  10470        48600  53400
32  6 BLACK-FIN COMBI      TT  SF    FBG DV OB            9  9   6500        36400  40400
32  6 BLACK-FIN COMBI      TT  SF    FBG DV IB T205-T350  9  9   8450        30400  36500
32  6 BLACK-FIN COMBI      TT  SF    FBG DV IBT235D-T300D 9  9  10470        44400  55200
32  6 BLACK-FIN FISHERMAN  OP  SF    FBG DV OB            9  9   6500        35300  39200

32  6 BLACK-FIN FISHERMAN  OP  SF    FBG DV IB T205-T350  9  9   8450        32100  39200
32  6 BLACK-FIN FISHERMAN  OP  SF    FBG DV IBT235D-T300D 9  9  10470        48100  56500
32  6 BLACK-FIN FISHERMAN  TT  SF    FBG DV OB            9  9   6500        35600  39500
32  6 BLACK-FIN FISHERMAN  TT  SF    FBG DV IB T205-T350  9  9   8450        32100  39300
32  6 BLACK-FIN FISHERMAN  TT  SF    FBG DV IBT235D-T300D 9  9  10470        47900  57000
-------------------- 1981 BOATS -----------------------------------------------------------
25  2 BLACK-FIN COMBI      OP  SF    FBG DV OB            8      4500  2  9  18800  20900
25  2 BLACK-FIN COMBI      OP  SF    FBG DV IB  350  CRUS 8      5160  2  9  14000  15900
      IB 205D-225D  21600 24500, IB 300D CAT  24500  27200, IB T165  CRUS 16100  18300
      IB T124D VLVO 23800 26500

25  2 BLACK-FIN COMBI      TT  SF    FBG DV OB            8      4500  2  9  18700  20800
25  2 BLACK-FIN COMBI      TT  SF    FBG DV IB  350  CRUS 8      5160  2  9  14000  15900
      IB 205D-225D  21500 24400, IB 300D CAT  24500  27200, IB T165  CRUS 16100  18300
      IB T124D VLVO 23800 26400

25  2 BLACK-FIN FISHERMAN  OP  SF    FBG DV OB            8      4500  2  9  18100  20100
25  2 BLACK-FIN FISHERMAN  OP  SF    FBG DV IB  350  CRUS 8      5160  2  9  13900  15800
      IB 205D-225D  21700 24600, IB 300D CAT  24700  27400, IB T165  CRUS 16100  18300
      IB T124D VLVO 24000 26700

25  2 BLACK-FIN FISHERMAN  TT  SF    FBG DV OB            8      4500  2  9  18200  20200
25  2 BLACK-FIN FISHERMAN  TT  SF    FBG DV IB  350  CRUS 8      5160  2  9  14000  15900
      IB 205D-225D  21800 24600, IB 300D CAT  24700  27400, IB T165  CRUS 16100  18300
      IB T124D VLVO 24000 26700

27 11 BLACK-FIN COMBI      OP  SF    FBG DV OB            9 10   5820  2 11  25300  28100
27 11 BLACK-FIN COMBI      OP  SF    FBG DV IB  300D CAT  9 10   7810  3      28300  31500
27 11 BLACK-FIN COMBI      OP  SF    FBG DV IB T270-T350  9 10   7590  2  6  21900  25900
27 11 BLACK-FIN COMBI      OP  SF    FBG DV IBT205D-T235D 9 10   9620  2  9  35400  39900
27 11 BLACK-FIN COMBI      TT  SF    FBG DV OB            9 10   5820  2 11  25300  28100
27 11 BLACK-FIN COMBI      TT  SF    FBG DV IB  300D CAT  9 10   7810  3      28300  31400
27 11 BLACK-FIN COMBI      TT  SF    FBG DV IB T270-T350  9 10   7590  2  6  21900  25800
27 11 BLACK-FIN COMBI      TT  SF    FBG DV IBT205D-T235D 9 10   9620  2  9  35400  39900
27 11 BLACK-FIN FISHERMAN  OP  SF    FBG DV OB            9 10   5820  2 11  24500  27200
27 11 BLACK-FIN FISHERMAN  OP  SF    FBG DV IB  300D CAT  9 10   7810  3      29600  32900
27 11 BLACK-FIN FISHERMAN  OP  SF    FBG DV IB T270-T350  9 10   7590  2  6  22800  27000
27 11 BLACK-FIN FISHERMAN  OP  SF    FBG DV IBT205D-T235D 9 10   9620  2  9  37200  42000

27 11 BLACK-FIN FISHERMAN  TT  SF    FBG DV OB            9 10   5820  2 11  24600  27400
27 11 BLACK-FIN FISHERMAN  TT  SF    FBG DV IB  300D CAT  9 10   7810  3      29600  32900
27 11 BLACK-FIN FISHERMAN  TT  SF    FBG DV IB T270-T350  9 10   7590  2  6  22800  27000
27 11 BLACK-FIN FISHERMAN  TT  SF    FBG DV IBT205D-T235D 9 10   9620  2  9  37200  42000
31  9 BLACK-FIN 32         FB  SF    FBG DV IB T350  CRUS 11 11  11640  2  5  40600  45100
31  9 BLACK-FIN 32         FB  SF    FBG DV IBT205D-T300D 11 11  13680  2  8  52600  62600
32  6 BLACK-FIN COMBI 33   OP  SF    FBG DV OB            9  9   6500  2  8  35500  39500
32  6 BLACK-FIN COMBI 33   OP  SF    FBG DV IB T350  CRUS 9  9   8450  2  8  34400  38300
32  6 BLACK-FIN COMBI 33   OP  SF    FBG DV IBT205D-T300D 9  9  10470  2 11  45500  54900
32  6 BLACK-FIN COMBI 33   TT  SF    FBG DV OB            9  9   6500  2  8  35500  39500
32  6 BLACK-FIN COMBI 33   TT  SF    FBG DV IB T350  CRUS 9  9   8450  2  8  34300  38100
32  6 BLACK-FIN COMBI 33   TT  SF    FBG DV IBT205D-T300D 9  9  10470  2 11  44700  53800

32  6 BLACK-FIN FISH 33    OP  SF    FBG DV OB            9  9   6500  2  8  34600  38400
32  6 BLACK-FIN FISH 33    OP  SF    FBG DV IB T350  CRUS 9  9   8450  2  8  33800  37500
32  6 BLACK-FIN FISH 33    OP  SF    FBG DV IBT205D-T300D 9  9  10470  2 11  44500  54300
32  6 BLACK-FIN FISH 33    TT  SF    FBG DV OB            9  9   6500  2  8  35000  38900
32  6 BLACK-FIN FISH 33    TT  SF    FBG DV IB T350  CRUS 9  9   8450  2  8  33900  37700
32  6 BLACK-FIN FISH 33    TT  SF    FBG DV IBT205D-T300D 9  9  10470  2 11  45500  56200
-------------------- 1980 BOATS -----------------------------------------------------------
25  2 BLACK-FIN COMBI      OP  SF    FBG DV IB 250-350    8              12500  15300
      IB 210D-270D  21300 25400, IB T170-T255  15400  18200, IB T124D VLVO 23000  25600

25  2 BLACK-FIN COMBI      TT  SF    FBG DV IB  350  CRUS 8      5160  2  9  13500  15300
      IB 270D CAT   22900 25400, IB T170-T255  15300  18100, IB T124D VLVO 23000  25500

25  2 BLACK-FIN FISHERMAN  OP  SF    FBG DV IB  350  CRUS 8      5160  2  9  13300  15100
      IB 270D CAT   22900 25400, IB T170-T255  15200  18000, IB T124D VLVO 23000  25500

25  2 BLACK-FIN FISHERMAN  TT  SF    FBG DV IB  350  CRUS 8      5160  2  9  13300  15100
      IB 270D CAT   22900 25400, IB T170-T255  15200  18100, IB T124D VLVO 23000  25600

27 11 BLACK-FIN COMBI      OP  SF    FBG DV IB  350  CRUS 9 10   6560  2 11  18400  20500
      IB 270D-300D  26600 29700, IB T220-T350  21800  25300, IB T124D VLVO 30900  34300
      IBT235D-T250D 35700 40500

27 11 BLACK-FIN FISHERMAN  OP  SF    FBG DV IB  350  CRUS 9 10   6560  2 11  18400  20400
      IB 270D CAT   26300 29200, IB T124D VLVO 30800  34200, IB T235D VLVO 34700  38500

27 11 BLACK-FIN FISHERMAN  TT  SF    FBG DV IB  350  CRUS 9 10   6560  2 11  18800  20900
      IB 270D CAT   27600 30600, IB T225       21200  23600, IB T124D VLVO 32000  35500
      IB T235D VLVO 36300 40300

27 11 BLACK-FIN FISHERMAN  TT  SF    FBG DV IB  350  CRUS 9 10   6560  2 11  18800  21000
27 11 BLACK-FIN FISHERMAN  TT  SF    FBG DV IBT124D VLVO  9 10   9620  2  9  32000  35600
27 11 BLACK-FIN FISHERMAN  TT  SF    FBG DV IB T235D VLVO 9 10   9620  2  9  36300  40300
31  9 BLACK-FIN 32         FB  SF    FBG DV IB T350  CRUS 11 11  11640  2  5  38000  42200
31  9 BLACK-FIN 32         FB  SF    FBG DV IBT205D-T270D 11 11  13680  2  8  51400  50400
32  6 BLACK-FIN COMBI      OP  SF    FBG DV IB T210-T270  9  9   8450  2  8  43000  46200
32  6 BLACK-FIN COMBI 33   OP  SF    FBG DV IB T300D      9      10875        44000  48900
32  6 BLACK-FIN COMBI 33   OP  SF    FBG DV IBT300-T350   9  9   6500  2  8  32000  36900
32  6 BLACK-FIN COMBI 33   OP  SF    FBG DV IBT235D-T270D 9  9  10470  2 11  44600  51700
32  6 BLACK-FIN COMBI 33   TT  SF    FBG DV IBT235D-T270D 9  9  10470  2 11  43200  36800
32  6 BLACK-FIN COMBI 33   TT  SF    FBG DV IBT235D-T270D 9  9  10470  2 11  44700  51900

32  6 BLACK-FIN FISH 33    OP  SF    FBG DV IBT210-T270D  9  9   8450  2 11  31100  35800
32  6 BLACK-FIN FISH 33    OP  SF    FBG DV IBT235D-T270D 9  9  10470  2 11  43400  50800
32  6 BLACK-FIN FISH 33    TT  SF    FBG DV IBT210-T270D  9  9   8450  2 11  31500  36200
32  6 BLACK-FIN FISH 33    TT  SF    FBG DV IBT235D-T270D 9  9  10470  2 11  43900  51100
-------------------- 1979 BOATS -----------------------------------------------------------
23  2 BLACK-FIN COMBI      OP  FSH   FBG SV IB 220-270    8      3900  2  4   9300  10700
23  2 BLACK-FIN COMBI      OP  FSH   FBG SV IB 125D VLVO  8      4900  2  4  14100  16000
23  2 BLACK-FIN COMBI      TT  FSH   FBG SV IB 220-270    8      3900  2  4  10600  12000
23  2 BLACK-FIN COMBI      TT  FSH   FBG SV IB 125D VLVO  8      4900  2  4  14000  16000
23  2 BLACK-FIN FISHERMAN  OP  FSH   FBG SV IB 220-270    8      3900  2  4   8650  10000
23  2 BLACK-FIN FISHERMAN  OP  FSH   FBG SV IB 125D VLVO  8      4900  2  4  13500  15300
23  2 BLACK-FIN FISHERMAN  TT  FSH   FBG SV IB 220-270    8      3900  2  4  10100  10100
23  2 BLACK-FIN FISHERMAN  TT  FSH   FBG SV IB 125D VLVO  8      4900  2  4  13500  15400
25  2 BLACK-FIN COMBI      OP  SF    FBG DV IB 250-350    8      5100  2 10  12100  14600
      IB 210D-270D  20300 24000, IB T215-T225  15000  17600, IB T125D VLVO 21300  23700

25  2 BLACK-FIN COMBI      TT  SF    FBG DV IB 250-350    8      5100  2 10  12000  14600
      IB 210D-270D  20200 23900, IB T215-T225  15000  17600, IB T125D VLVO 21300  23700

25  2 BLACK-FIN FISHERMAN  OP  SF    FBG DV IB 250-350    8      5100  2  7  11700  14300
      IB 210D-270D  20100 23800, IB T215-T225  14800  17300, IB T125D VLVO 21300  23600

25  2 BLACK-FIN FISHERMAN  TT  SF    FBG DV IB 250-350    8      5100  2  7  11800  14300
      IB 210D-270D  20200 23900, IB T215-T225  14800  17400, IB T125D VLVO 21300  23600

27 11 BLACK-FIN COMBI      OP  SF    FBG DV IB  350  CRUS 9 10   6400  2 10  16800  19000
      IB 210D-270D  22500 26500, IB T220-T350  19500  23800, IBT125D-T192D 24900  30800
      IBT210D-T270D 29500 35600

27 11 BLACK-FIN COMBI      TT  SF    FBG DV IB  350  CRUS 9 10   6400  2 10  16800  19000
      IB 210D-270D  22500 26500, IB T220-T350  19400  23800, IBT125D-T192D 24900  30800
      IBT210D-T270D 29500 35600

27 11 BLACK-FIN FISHERMAN  OP  SF    FBG DV IB  350  CRUS 9 10   6400  2 10  18200  20300
      IB 210D-270D  23800 28200, IB T220-T350  19900  24500, IBT125D-T192D 26500  32000
      IBT210D-T270D 30700 37200

27 11 BLACK-FIN FISHERMAN  TT  SF    FBG DV IB  350  CRUS 9 10   6400  2 10  18200  20300
      IB 210D-270D  23800 28200, IB T220-T350  19900  24500, IBT125D-T192D 26500  32000
      IBT210D-T270D 30700 37200

32  6 BLACK-FIN COMBI 33   OP  SF    FBG DV IB  350  CRUS 9  9   7500  3  2  27300  30400
      IB 210D CAT   31200 34700, IB 270D CAT   32500  36100, IB T270-T350  30300  35400
      IBT192D-T270D 40800 49800

32  6 BLACK-FIN COMBI 33   TT  SF    FBG DV IB  350  CRUS 9  9   7500  3  2  27300  30400
      IB 210D CAT   31400 34900, IB 270D CAT   32700  36400, IB T270-T350  30200  35300
      IBT192D-T270D 40800 50000
```

```
       LOA   NAME AND/        TOP/  BOAT  -HULL-  ----ENGINE---   BEAM    WGT   DRAFT  RETAIL RETAIL
       FT IN OR MODEL         RIG   TYPE  MTL TP  TP #  HP  MFG   FT IN   LBS   FT IN  LOW    HIGH
-------------------- 1979 BOATS -----------------------------------------------------------------------
32  6 BLACK-FIN FISH 33       OP    SF    FBG DV  IB   350  CRUS  9  9    7500  3  2   27300  30400
      IB  210D CAT   31200  34700,  IB  270D CAT   32500  36100,  IB  T270-T350  29100  34200
      IBT190D-T270D  40700  48800

32  6 BLACK-FIN FISH 33       TT    SF    FBG DV  IB   350  CRUS  9  9    7500  3  2   27300  30400
      IB  210D CAT   31400  34900,  IB  270D CAT   32700  36400,  IB  T270-T350  29200  34300
      IBT190D-T270D  40700  49100

-------------------- 1978 BOATS -----------------------------------------------------------------------
23  2 BLACK-FIN LAUNCH        OP    FSH   FBG SV  IB   215-270     8     3900  2  4    8400   9950
23  2 BLACK-FIN LAUNCH        OP    FSH   FBG SV  IB        D GM   8     3900  2  4     **     **
23  2 BLACK-FIN LAUNCH        OP    FSH   FBG SV  IB   125D-140D   8     3900  2  4   11400  13700
23  2 BLACK-FIN LAUNCH        TT    FSH   FBG SV  IB   215-270     8     3900  2  4    8400   9950
23  2 BLACK-FIN LAUNCH        TT    FSH   FBG SV  IB        D GM   8     3900  2  4     **     **
23  2 BLACK-FIN LAUNCH        TT    FSH   FBG SV  IB   125D-140D   8     3900  2  4   11400  13700
24  4 BLACK-FIN COMBI         OP    CUD   FBG DV  IB   250-350     8     4300  2  7    9700  11800
      IB 197D-215D   15900  19000,  IB  270D CAT   18300  20400,  IB  T185-T225  12500  14900
      IB T125D VLVO  18600  20700

24  4 BLACK-FIN COMBI         TT    CUD   FBG DV  IB   250-350     8     4300  2  7    9700  11800
      IB 197D-215D   15900  19000,  IB  270D CAT   18300  20400,  IB  T185-T225  12500  14900
      IB T125D VLVO  18600  20700

24  4 BLACK-FIN FISHERMAN     OP    OPFSH FBG DV  IB   250-350     8     4300  2  7    9700  11800
      IB 197D-215D   16000  19100,  IB  270D CAT   18400  20400,  IB  T185-T225  12600  15000
      IB T125D VLVO  18700  20700

24  4 BLACK-FIN FISHERMAN     TT    OPFSH FBG DV  IB   250-350     8     4300  2  7    9700  11800
      IB 197D-215D   16000  19100,  IB  270D CAT   18400  20400,  IB  T185-T225  12600  15000
      IB T125D VLVO  18700  20700

-------------------- 1977 BOATS -----------------------------------------------------------------------
23    BLACK-FIN 23            OP    FSH   FBG DV  IB   220-255     8     3800  2  4    8000   9300
23    BLACK-FIN 23            OP    FSH   FBG DV  IB   130D-200D   8     3800  2  4   11800  13800
24  4 BLACK-FIN FISHERMAN     OP    FSH   FBG DV  IB   233-350     8     4300  2  7    9400  11200
24  4 BLACK-FIN FISHERMAN     OP    FSH   FBG DV  IB   200D-210D   8     5200  2  8   15500  18500
24  4 BLACK-FIN FISHERMAN     OP    FSH   FBG DV  IB   T185-T215   8     5400  1 11   12100  13900
24  4 BLACK-FIN FISHERMAN     TT    FSH   FBG DV  IB   233-350     8     4300  2  7    9400  11400
24  4 BLACK-FIN FISHERMAN     TT    FSH   FBG DV  IB   200D-210D   8     5200  2  8   15500  18500
24  4 BLACK-FIN FISHERMAN     TT    FSH   FBG DV  IB   T185-T215   8     5400  1 11   12100  13900
24  4 BLACK-FIN-COMBI         OP    CUD   FBG DV  IB   233-350     8     4300  2  7    9400  11400
24  4 BLACK-FIN-COMBI         OP    CUD   FBG DV  IB   200D-210D   8     5200  2  8   15500  18500
24  4 BLACK-FIN-COMBI         OP    CUD   FBG DV  IB   T185-T225   8     5400  1 11   12100  13900
24  4 BLACK-FIN-COMBI         TT    CUD   FBG DV  IB   233-350     8     4300  2  7    9400  11400
24  4 BLACK-FIN-COMBI         TT    CUD   FBG DV  IB   200D-210D   8     5200  2  8   15500  18500
24  4 BLACK-FIN-COMBI         TT    CUD   FBG DV  IB   T185-T215   8     5400  1 11   12100  13900
-------------------- 1976 BOATS -----------------------------------------------------------------------
24  4 BLACK-FIN 24 COMBI      OP    CUD   FBG DV  IB   233-350     8     4300  2  7    9000  10900
24  4 BLACK-FIN 24 COMBI      OP    CUD   FBG DV  IB   225D CAT    8     6000  2  8   17500  19900
24  4 BLACK-FIN 24 COMBI      OP    CUD   FBG DV  IB   T185-T215   8     5400  1 11   11600  13300
24  4 BLACK-FIN 24 FISHER     OP    FSH   FBG DV  IB   233-350     8     4300  2  7    9000  10900
24  4 BLACK-FIN 24 FISHER     OP    FSH   FBG DV  IB   225D CAT    8     6000  2  8   17500  19900
24  4 BLACK-FIN 24 FISHER     OP    FSH   FBG DV  IB   T185-T215   8     5400  1 11   11700  13400
-------------------- 1975 BOATS -----------------------------------------------------------------------
24    ESPRIT 24                     FBG DV  IO   225         8                       11100  12600
24  4 BLACK-FIN 24            OP    FSH   FBG DV  IB   233  MRCR         4300  2  3    8550   9850
24  4 BLACK-FIN 24            OP    FSH   FBG DV  IB   T165-T225   8     5300  2  3   10900  12700
24  4 BLACK-FIN 24 COMBI      OP    W/T   FBG DV  IB   233-350     8     4300  2  3    8550  10400
-------------------- 1974 BOATS -----------------------------------------------------------------------
24  3 BLACK-FIN 24                  SF    FBG     IB   225-255     8     4130  2  3    7900   9150
24  3 BLACK-FIN 24                  SF    FBG     IB   T130-T185   8     4130  2  3    8350  10200
```

THE BLAGG BOAT CO LTD
COAST GUARD MFG ID- BGG

Call 1-800-327-6929 for BUC Personalized Evaluation Service
Or, for 1979 to 1983 boats, sign onto www.BUCValuPro.com

BLAKE BOAT WORKS

Call 1-800-327-6929 for BUC Personalized Evaluation Service
Or, for 1983 to 1985 boats, sign onto www.BUCValuPro.com

BLUE BAY MARINE
DIV OF THERMAL MFG CO

Call 1-800-327-6929 for BUC Personalized Evaluation Service
Or, for 1965 to 1969 boats, sign onto www.BUCValuPro.com

BLUE BUOY YACHT COMPANY
TORRANCE CA 90501   COAST GUARD MFG ID- BBU See inside cover to adjust price for area

```
       LOA   NAME AND/        TOP/  BOAT  -HULL-  ----ENGINE---   BEAM    WGT   DRAFT  RETAIL RETAIL
       FT IN OR MODEL         RIG   TYPE  MTL TP  TP #  HP  MFG   FT IN   LBS   FT IN  LOW    HIGH
-------------------- 1978 BOATS -----------------------------------------------------------------------
16  3 BLUE-BUOY 16            SLP   SAIL  FBG CB               7  6   450        4     1900   2250
21    DEL-REY 21              SLP   SA/CR FBG SK  OB           7      1200  1          2900   3350
24    DEL-REY 24              SLP   SA/CR FBG KL  OB           8      4500  3 10       6900   7950
26    SEAQUEST 26             SLP   SA/CR FBG KL  IB           8      5800  4        10500  11900
31    DEL-REY 31              SLP   SA/CR FBG KL  IB    D PISC 10 2  10000  5       22800  25400
45    DEL-REY 45              SLP   SA/CR FBG KL  IB    D      12 4  32000  6  6    75000  82400
47    DEL-REY 47              KTH   SA/CR FBG KL  IB    D LEHM 12 10 34000  6  8    85900  94400
-------------------- 1975 BOATS -----------------------------------------------------------------------
26    SEAQUEST 26             SLP   SAIL  FBG KL  OB           8      5800  4         9400  10700
31    DEL-REY 31              SLP   SAIL  FBG KL  IB    8D     10 2  10000  5       20500  22800
45    DEL-REY 50              SCH   SAIL  FBG KL  IB    65D    12    33000  6       66800  73400
45    DEL-REY 50              CUT   SAIL  FBG KL  IB    65D    12    33000  6       66300  72700
45    DEL-REY 50              KTH   SAIL  FBG KL  IB    65D    12    33000  6       71200  78200
-------------------- 1972 BOATS -----------------------------------------------------------------------
24    DEL-REY 24                    SAIL  FBG     OB           7 10         3  8     5700   6550
24    DEL-REY 24                    SAIL  FBG     OB    7D     7 10         3  8     7150   8250
26    SEAQUEST 26                   SAIL  FBG     OB           8      5800  4         8600   9800
31    DEL-REY 31                    SAIL  FBG     IB    10D    10 2  10000  5       18800  20900
45    DEL-REY 50                    SAIL  FBG     IB    50D    12    33000  6       62000  68200
-------------------- 1969 BOATS -----------------------------------------------------------------------
21    DEL-RAY 21              SLP   SAIL  FBG KL               7 10         3  2     2300   2700
23    DEL-RAY 23              SLP   SAIL  FBG KL               7 10         3  5     5150   5950
24    DEL-RAY 24              SLP   SA/OD FBG KL               7 10         3  8     6600   7550
31    DEL-RAY 31              SLP   SA/CR FBG KL  IB    D      10 4         5       17200  19600
50    DEL-RAY 50              CUT   SA/CR FBG KL  IB    D      12 4         6       71400  78400
50    DEL-RAY 50              KTH   SA/CR FBG KL  IB    D      12 4         6       75900  83400
-------------------- 1968 BOATS -----------------------------------------------------------------------
24    DEL-REY 24              SLP   SAIL  FBG KL               7 10         3  8     5550   6400
31    DEL-REY 31              SLP   SAIL  FBG KL  IB           10 2         5       18300  20300
50    DEL-REY 50              SLP   SAIL  FBG KL  IB           12 4               74400  81800
-------------------- 1967 BOATS -----------------------------------------------------------------------
24    DEL-REY 24              SLP   SA/CR FBG KL               7 10         3  8     5450   6250
31    DEL-REY 31              SLP   SA/CR FBG KL  IB    30D    10 4         9       17600  20000
50    DEL-REY 50              SCH   SA/CR FBG KL  IB    D      12 4         6       21900  79100
50    DEL-REY 50              CUT   SA/CR FBG KL  IB    D      12 4         6       71400  78500
50    DEL-REY 50              YWL   SA/CR FBG KL  IB    D      12 4         6       73300  80600
50    DEL-REY 50              KTH   SA/CR FBG KL  IB    D      12 4         6       76000  83500
```

BLUE FIN INDUSTRIES INC
DIV OF BRUNSWICK MARINE COAST GUARD MFG ID- BFF

Call 1-800-327-6929 for BUC Personalized Evaluation Service
Or, for 1980 to 1988 boats, sign onto www.BUCValuPro.com

BLUE MFG CO
BLUE STAR

Call 1-800-327-6929 for BUC Personalized Evaluation Service
Or, for 1959 to 1961 boats, sign onto www.BUCValuPro.com

BLUE SEA INDUSTRIAL CO LT
TAIPEI TAIWAN ROC   See inside cover to adjust price for area

For more recent years, see the BUC Used Boat Price Guide, Volume 1 or Volume 2

```
       LOA   NAME AND/        TOP/  BOAT  -HULL-  ----ENGINE---   BEAM    WGT   DRAFT  RETAIL RETAIL
       FT IN OR MODEL         RIG   TYPE  MTL TP  TP #  HP  MFG   FT IN   LBS   FT IN  LOW    HIGH
-------------------- 1983 BOATS -----------------------------------------------------------------------
27  2 BLUE-SEA 27             CUT   SA/CR FBG KL  IB   8D  YAN    9 10  9750       4  30100  33500
34  2 BLUE-SEA 34             SLP   SA/CR FBG KL  IB   30D YAN    11   22800  5     71400  78400
34  2 BLUE-SEA 34             CUT   SA/CR FBG KL  IB   30D YAN    11   22800  5  6  71300  78400
36    BLUE-SEA 36SDN          FB    TRWL  FBG DS  IB                                  **     **
41    BLUE-SEA 41             CUT   SA/CR FBG KL  IB   30D YAN    14   26000  6     87700  96300
```

BLUE SEA INDUSTRIAL CO LT   -CONTINUED   See inside cover to adjust price for area

LOA FT IN	NAME AND/ OR MODEL	TOP/ RIG	BOAT TYPE	-HULL- MTL TP TP	----ENGINE--- # HP MFG	BEAM FT IN	WGT LBS	DRAFT FT IN	RETAIL LOW	RETAIL HIGH
					1983 BOATS					
41	BLUE-SEA 41	CUT	SA/CR	FBG KL IB	50D	14	26000	6	88000	96700
45 5	BLUE-SEA 46	CUT	MS	FBG KL IB	80D FORD	13 9	34800	6	120500	132000
45 5	BLUE-SEA 46	KTH	MS	FBG KL IB	80D FORD	13 9	34800	6	121000	133000

BLUE STREAK INDUSTRIES
COAST GUARD MFG ID- BLU

Call 1-800-327-6929 for BUC Personalized Evaluation Service
Or, for 1973 to 1975 boats, sign onto www.BUCValuPro.com

BLUE WATER BOAT WORKS
AMARILLO TX 79105   COAST GUARD MFG ID- BWH See inside cover to adjust price for area

LOA FT IN	NAME AND/ OR MODEL	TOP/ RIG	BOAT TYPE	-HULL- MTL TP TP	----ENGINE--- # HP MFG	BEAM FT IN	WGT LBS	DRAFT FT IN	RETAIL LOW	RETAIL HIGH
					1983 BOATS					
22 7	BLACKWATCH	CUT	SA/CR	FBG KL		7 11	2300	2	7850	9000
					1982 BOATS					
20 7	BLACKWATCH	CUT	SA/CR	FBG KL		7 11	2300	2	6900	7900
					1981 BOATS					
22 7	BLACKWATCH	CUT	SA/CR	FBG KL OB		7 11	2300	2	6950	7950
					1980 BOATS					
24	BLACKWATCH	CUT	SA/CR	FBG KL OB		7 11	2200	2	6900	7900

BLUE WATER BOATS
NORDIC TUGS INC
WOODINVILLE WA   COAST GUARD MFG ID- BLW   See inside cover to adjust price for area

LOA FT IN	NAME AND/ OR MODEL	TOP/ RIG	BOAT TYPE	-HULL- MTL TP TP	----ENGINE--- # HP MFG	BEAM FT IN	WGT LBS	DRAFT FT IN	RETAIL LOW	RETAIL HIGH
					1983 BOATS					
46 3	INGRID 38	KTH	SA/CR	FBG KL IB	D	11 4	26000	5 5	119500	131000

BLUEFIN MARINE INC
FT LAUDERDALE FL   See inside cover to adjust price for area

LOA FT IN	NAME AND/ OR MODEL	TOP/ RIG	BOAT TYPE	-HULL- MTL TP TP	----ENGINE--- # HP MFG	BEAM FT IN	WGT LBS	DRAFT FT IN	RETAIL LOW	RETAIL HIGH
					1975 BOATS					
25 10	BLUEFIN 26	OP	SF	FBG SV IB	D	11 2	5000	2 7	**	**
25 10	BLUEFIN 26	OP	SF	FBG SV IB	T233-T350	11 2	5000	2 7	8200	10200
					1974 BOATS					
25 10	BLUEFIN 26	OP	SF	FBG	IB	350 MRCR	11 2	5000	2 7	7650	8800
	IB 210D-240D	10500	12500, IB T200-T255		7950 9500, IBT140D-T180D	12100	14600			
					1973 BOATS					
25 10	BLUEFIN 26	OP	SF	FBG	IB	325 MRCR	11 2	5000	2 7	6950	8000
	IB 210D SABR	9450	10700, IB T225-T255		8000 9450, IB T180D SABR	13000	14800			

BLUENOSE BOATYARD

Call 1-800-327-6929 for BUC Personalized Evaluation Service
Or, for 1970 boats, sign onto www.BUCValuPro.com

BLUEWATER
MORA MN 55051   COAST GUARD MFG ID- BTL See inside cover to adjust price for area
FORMERLY BOATEL YACHTS

For more recent years, see the BUC Used Boat Price Guide, Volume 1 or Volume 2

LOA FT IN	NAME AND/ OR MODEL	TOP/ RIG	BOAT TYPE	-HULL- MTL TP TP	----ENGINE--- # HP MFG	BEAM FT IN	WGT LBS	DRAFT FT IN	RETAIL LOW	RETAIL HIGH
					1983 BOATS					
43	BLUEWATER 43	SPTCR	FBG DV IB	T350	14 4	31000	3 6	87400	96100	
47	BLUEWATER	FB	SDN	FBG SV IB	T 85D PERK	15	29000	3 4	63500	69800
	IB T135D PERK	66400	73000, IB T210D CAT		70400 77400, IB T300D CAT		74800	82100		
	IB T305D GM	74700	82100							
47 10	BLUEWATER	FB	SDN	FBG SV IB	T350 CRUS 15		30000	3 8	70900	77900
52	BLUEWATER	FB	SDN	FBG SV IB	T 85D PERK	15	32000	3 2	88100	96800
	IB T135D PERK	89500	98400, IB T210D CAT		93800 103000, IB T300D CAT		100000	110000		
	IB T305D GM	98800	108500							
52 10	BLUEWATER	FB	MY	FBG SV IB	T350 CRUS 15		35000	3 8	99600	109500
	IB T 85D PERK	91400	100500, IB T135D PERK		92600 101500, IB T210D CAT		96900	106500		
	IB T300D CAT	103500	113500, IB T305D GM		101500 112000, IB T410D J&T		114500	124500		
52 10	BLUEWATER	FB	SDN	FBG SV IB	T350 CRUS 15		33000	3 8	100500	110000
52 10	BLUEWATER	FB	SDN	FBG SV IB	T410D J&T 15		33000	3 8	114500	124000
54	BLUEWATER 54	SDN	FBG DV IB	T350	14 8	37000	3 6	113500	124500	
54	BLUEWATER 54	SDN	FBG DV IB	T210D	14 8	37000	3 6	100500	110500	
					1982 BOATS					
40	BLUEWATER	HT	SDN	FBG SV IB	T350	13			61300	67400
40	BLUEWATER	HT	SDN	FBG SV IB	T210D	13			78100	85800
43	BLUEWATER	FB	SPTCR	FBG SV IB	T350 CRUS 14	4 31000	3 6	76700	84300	
	IB T210D CAT	78300	86100, IB T275D GM		82100 90200, IB T300D CAT		85100	93500		
	IB T410D GM	92000	101000							
45	BLUEWATER	HT	SDN	FBG SV IB	T350	13			55500	61000
45	BLUEWATER	HT	SDN	FBG SV IB	T210D	13			59700	65600
47	BLUEWATER	FB	SDN	FBG SV IB	T350 CRUS 13	4	29000	3 4	66400	73000
	IB T 85D PERK	60600	66600, IB T135D PERK		63400 69700, IB T210D CAT		67200	73800		
	IB T275D GM	70000	76900, IB T300D CAT		71300 78400					
52	BLUEWATER	FB	SDN	FBG SV IB	T350 CRUS 15		32000	3 2	93600	103000
	IB T 85D PERK	84600	92900, IB T135D PERK		85900 94400, IB T210D CAT		90000	98900		
	IB T275D GM	92500	101500, IB T300D CAT		96100 105500					
54	BLUEWATER	FB	SDN	FBG SV IB	T350 CRUS 14	8 37000	3 6	102000	112500	
	IB T210D CAT	94500	104000, IB T275D GM		97500 107200, IB T300D CAT		102000	112500		
	IB T410D GM	113500	125000							
					1981 BOATS					
35	BLUEWATER	FB	TCMY	FBG SV IB	T270 CRUS 13		19000	2 10	38600	42900
35	BLUEWATER	FB	TCMY	FBG SV IB	T350 CRUS 13		19000	2 10	39800	44200
35	BLUEWATER	FB	TCMY	FBG SV IB	T210D CAT 13		19000	2 10	49500	54400
40	BLUEWATER	FB	SDN	FBG SV IB	T270 CRUS 13		22000	2 10	59500	65400
40	BLUEWATER	FB	SDN	FBG SV IB	T350 CRUS 13		22000	2 10	60600	66600
40	BLUEWATER	FB	SDN	FBG SV IB	T210D CAT 13		22000	2 10	67400	74600
40	BLUEWATER	FB	TCMY	FBG SV IB	T270 CRUS 13		22000	2 10	62600	68800
40	BLUEWATER	FB	TCMY	FBG SV IB	T350 CRUS 13		23000	2 10	63700	70000
40	BLUEWATER	FB	TCMY	FBG SV IB	T210D CAT 13		23000	2 10	70100	77100
43	BLUEWATER	FB	SPTCR	FBG SV IB	T350 CRUS 14	4 31000	3 6	73100	80300	
	IB T210D CAT	74600	82000, IB T260D CAT		78100 85900, IB T275D GM		78200	85900		
	IB T410D GM	87600	96300							
45	BLUEWATER	FB	SDN	FBG SV IB	T270 CRUS 13		25000	3 1	57800	63500
45	BLUEWATER	FB	SDN	FBG SV IB	T350 CRUS 13		25000	3 1	60300	65900
45	BLUEWATER	FB	SDN	FBG SV IB	T210D CAT 13		25000	3 1	62500	68700
53 7	BLUEWATER	FB	SDN	FBG SV IB	T350 CRUS 14	8 37000	3 6	97000	106500	
	IB T210D CAT	90600	99000, IB T260D CAT		94200 103500, IB T275D GM		93400	102500		
	IB T410D GM	108000	118500							
					1980 BOATS					
35	BLUEWATER	HT	TCMY	FBG SV IB	T220 CRUS 13		19000	2 10	36500	40500
	IB T270 CRUS	37000	41100, IB T350 CRUS		38200 42400, IB T210D		47400	52100		
	IB T225D CAT	48000	52800							
35	BLUEWATER	FB	TCMY	FBG SV IB	T220 CRUS 13		19000	2 10	36500	40500
	IB T270 CRUS	37000	41100, IB T350 CRUS		38200 42400, IB T225D CAT		48000	52800		
40	BLUEWATER	HT	SDN	FBG SV IB	T270 CRUS 13		22000	2 10	56700	62300
	IB T350 CRUS	57700	63400, IB T210D		63400 69700, IB T225D CAT		65100	71600		
40	BLUEWATER	FB	SDN	FBG SV IB	T270 CRUS 13		22000	2 10	58600	62400
40	BLUEWATER	FB	SDN	FBG SV IB	T350 CRUS 13		22000	2 10	57800	63500
40	BLUEWATER	FB	SDN	FBG SV IB	T225D CAT 13		23000	2 10	65200	71600
40	BLUEWATER	HT	TCMY	FBG SV IB	T270 CRUS 13		23000	2 10	59600	65500
40	BLUEWATER	HT	TCMY	FBG SV IB	T350 CRUS 13		23000	2 10	60700	66700
40	BLUEWATER	HT	TCMY	FBG SV IB	T225D CAT 13		23000	2 10	67300	74000
40	BLUEWATER	FB	TCMY	FBG SV IB	T270 CRUS 13		23000	2 10	59700	65600
40	BLUEWATER	FB	TCMY	FBG SV IB	T350 CRUS 13		23000	2 10	60700	66700
40	BLUEWATER	FB	TCMY	FBG SV IB	T225D CAT 13		23000	2 10	67300	74000
43	BLUEWATER	FB	SDNSF	FBG SV IB	T350 CRUS 14	4 31000	3 6	67500	74200	
	IB T210D CAT	69700	76600, IB T260D CAT		73100 80300, IB T270D CUM		72500	79600		
45	BLUEWATER	HT	SDN	FBG SV IB	T270 CRUS 13		25000	3 1	55800	60800
	IB T350 CRUS	57400	63100, IB T210D		59300 65100, IB T225D CAT		60400	66400		
45	BLUEWATER	FB	SDN	FBG SV IB	T270 CRUS 13		25000	3 1	55100	60500

```
 LOA  NAME AND/          TOP/ BOAT -HULL- ----ENGINE--- BEAM  WGT  DRAFT RETAIL RETAIL
 FT IN OR MODEL          RIG  TYPE MTL TP TP # HP  MFG  FT IN  LBS  FT IN  LOW    HIGH
------------------- 1980 BOATS -------------------------------------------------------
 45   BLUEWATER          FB   SDN  FBG SV IB T350  CRUS 12    25000 3 1  57200  62800
 45   BLUEWATER          FB   SDN  FBG SV IB T225D CAT  13    25000 3 1  60200  66100
 53  7 BLUEWATER AFT STATRM FB SDN FBG SV IB T350  CRUS 14  8 36000 3 6  91400 100500
      IB T210D CAT  87900  96600, IB T260D CAT  91200 100500, IB T270D CUM  92000 101000

 53  7 BLUEWATER CRUISER FB  SDN  FBG SV IB T350  CRUS 14  8 36000 3 6  86200  94800
      IB T210D CAT  83700  92000, IB T260D CAT  87100  95700, IB T270D CUM  85900  94400
------------------- 1979 BOATS -------------------------------------------------------
 35   BLUEWATER          HT   TCMY FBG SV IB T220  CRUS 13    19000 2 10 35000  38900
 35   BLUEWATER          HT   TCMY FBG SV IB T270  CRUS 13    19000 2 10 35500  39400
 35   BLUEWATER          HT   TCMY FBG SV IB T225D CAT  13    19000 2 10 46500  51100
 35   BLUEWATER          FB   TCMY FBG SV IB T220  CRUS 13    19000 2 10 35000  38900
 35   BLUEWATER          FB   TCMY FBG SV IB T270  CRUS 13    19000 2 10 35500  39400
 35   BLUEWATER          FB   TCMY FBG SV IB T225D CAT  13    19000 2 10 46500  51100
 40   BLUEWATER          HT   SDN  FBG SV IB T270  CRUS 13    22000 2 10 54200  59600
 40   BLUEWATER          HT   SDN  FBG SV IB T350  CRUS 13    22000 2 10 55200  60700
 40   BLUEWATER          HT   SDN  FBG SV IB T225D CAT  13    22000 2 10 62200  68300
 40   BLUEWATER          FB   SDN  FBG SV IB T270  CRUS 13    22000 2 10 54300  59700
 40   BLUEWATER          FB   SDN  FBG SV IB T350  CRUS 13    22000 2 10 55300  60800
 40   BLUEWATER          FB   SDN  FBG SV IB T225D CAT  13    22000 2 10 62200  68400

 40   BLUEWATER          HT   TCMY FBG SV IB T270  CRUS 13    23000 2 10 56900  62600
 40   BLUEWATER          HT   TCMY FBG SV IB T350  CRUS 13    23000 2 10 57900  63700
 40   BLUEWATER          HT   TCMY FBG SV IB T225D CAT  13    23000 2 10 64300  70700
 40   BLUEWATER          FB   TCMY FBG SV IB T270  CRUS 13    23000 2 10 57000  62600
 40   BLUEWATER          FB   TCMY FBG SV IB T350  CRUS 13    23000 2 10 58000  63700
 40   BLUEWATER          FB   TCMY FBG SV IB T225D CAT  13    23000 2 10 64300  70700
 45   BLUEWATER          HT   SDN  FBG SV IB T270  CRUS 13    25000 3 1  52800  58000
 45   BLUEWATER          HT   SDN  FBG SV IB T350  CRUS 13    25000 3 1  54800  60200
 45   BLUEWATER          HT   SDN  FBG SV IB T225D CAT  13    25000 3 1  57900  63400
 45   BLUEWATER          FB   SDN  FBG SV IB T270  CRUS 13    25000 3 1  52600  57800
 45   BLUEWATER          FB   SDN  FBG SV IB T350  CRUS 13    25000 3 1  54800  60000
 45   BLUEWATER          FB   SDN  FBG SV IB T225D CAT  13    25000 3 1  57500  63200
------------------- 1978 BOATS -------------------------------------------------------
 35   BLUEWATER          HT   TCMY FBG SV IB T220  CRUS 13    19000 2 10 33500  37300
 35   BLUEWATER          HT   TCMY FBG SV IB T270  CRUS 13    19000 2 10 34100  37800
 35   BLUEWATER          FB   TCMY FBG SV IB T220  CRUS 13    19000 2 10 33500  37300
 35   BLUEWATER          FB   TCMY FBG SV IB T270  CRUS 13    19000 2 10 34100  37800
 38   ECONOMY CATAMARAN  HT   HB   STL CT OB        14          23700  26300
 40   BLUEWATER          HT   TCMY FBG SV IB T270  CRUS 13    22000 2 10 52000  57100
      IB T350  CRUS  52900  58200, IB T225D CAT  59500  65300, IB T350D      62500  68700

 40   BLUEWATER          FB   SDN  FBG SV IB T270  CRUS 13    22000 2 10 52100  57200
      IB T350  CRUS  52900  58100, IB T225D CAT  59500  65400, IB T350D      62500  68700

 40   BLUEWATER          HT   TCMY FBG SV IB T270  CRUS 13    23000 2 10 54400  59800
      IB T350  CRUS  55400  60900, IB T225D CAT  61500  67600, IB T350D      64500  70900

 40   BLUEWATER          FB   TCMY FBG SV IB T270  CRUS 13    23000 2 10 54500  59900
      IB T350  CRUS  55400  60900, IB T225D CAT  61500  67600, IB T350D      64500  70900

 44   STANDARD CATAMARAN HT   HB   STL CT OB        14    14000 1 4  31700  35300
 45   BLUEWATER          HT   SDN  FBG SV IB T270  CRUS 13    25000 2 10 50500  55500
      IB T350  CRUS  52400  57600, IB T225D CAT  55200  60600, IB T350D      59000  64800

 45   BLUEWATER          FB   SDN  FBG SV IB T270  CRUS 13    25000 2 10 50300  55300
      IB T350  CRUS  52200  57400, IB T225D CAT  55000  60400, IB T350D      58700  64600

 50   DELUXE             HT   HB   STL CT OB        14    20000 1 10 43300  48100
------------------- 1977 BOATS -------------------------------------------------------
 34   CATAMARAN          HT   HB   STL CT OB        12    10000 1 4  34200  38000
 35   GULFSTREAM 410     HT   MY   FBG SV VD T220  CRUS 13    19000 3   33200  36900
 35   GULFSTREAM 410     HT   MY   FBG SV VD T270  CRUS 13    19000 3   33800  37500
 35   GULFSTREAM 410     HT   MY   FBG SV VD T175D CRUS 13    19000 3   43000  47800
 35   GULFSTREAM 410     FB   MY   FBG SV VD T220  CRUS 13    19000 3   33200  36900
 35   GULFSTREAM 410     FB   MY   FBG SV VD T270  CRUS 13    19000 3   33800  37500
 35   GULFSTREAM 410     FB   MY   FBG SV VD T175D CRUS 13    19000 3   43000  47800
 40   BLUEWATER 450      HT   MY   FBG SV VD T220  CRUS 13    23000 2 10 51700  56900
 40   BLUEWATER 450      HT   MY   FBG SV VD T270  CRUS 13    23000 2 10 51900  57100
 40   BLUEWATER 450      FB   MY   FBG SV VD T175D CRUS 13    23000 2 10 56600  62200
 40   BLUEWATER 450      FB   MY   FBG SV VD T270  CRUS 13    23000 2 10 51800  56900
 40   BLUEWATER 450      FB   MY   FBG SV IB T270  CRUS 13    23000 2 10 52000  57100

 40   BLUEWATER 450      FB   MY   FBG SV IB T175D CRUS 14    23000 2 10 56600  62200
 42   CATAMARAN          HT   HB   STL CT OB        14    13000 1 4  29400  31500
 43   ADVENTURER 43      HT   HB   STL CT OB        12    12000     26300  29200
 44   DELUXE CATAMARAN   HT   HB   STL CT OB        14    14000 1 4  31400  34800
 47   ISLANDER 470       HT   MY   FBG SV VD T220  CRUS 13    25000 2 10 47400  52100
 47   ISLANDER 470       HT   MY   FBG SV VD T270  CRUS 13    25000 2 10 48000  52700
 47   ISLANDER 470       HT   MY   FBG SV VD T175D CRUS 13    25000 2 10 49600  54500
 47   ISLANDER 470       FB   MY   FBG SV VD T220  CRUS 13    25000 2 10 47200  51800
 47   ISLANDER 470       FB   MY   FBG SV VD T270  CRUS 13    25000 2 10 47700  52500
 47   ISLANDER 470       FB   MY   FBG SV IB T175D CRUS 13    25000 2 10 49400  54300
 50   ADVENTURER CUSTOM 50 HT  HB  STL CT OB        14    20000     42800  47600
 52   DELUXE CATAMARAN   HT   HB   STL CT OB        14    20000 1 6  44700  49600
------------------- 1976 BOATS -------------------------------------------------------
 35   GULFSTREAM         HT   MY   FBG SV IO 255   MRCR 13    19000 3 2  37500  41700
      VD T220  CRUS  31900  35400, IB T225  CHRY  31800  35300, IB T250  CHRY      32100  35600

 35   GULFSTREAM         FB   MY   FBG SV IO 255   MRCR 13    19000 3 2  30400  33800
      VD T220  CRUS  31900  35400, IB T225  CHRY  31800  35300, IB T250  CHRY      32100  35600

 40   BLUEWATER          HT   MY   FBG SV IO T220  CRUS 13    22000 2 10 48200  53000
      VD T225  CHRY  47800  52500, VD T250  CHRY  47900  52700, IO T255  MRCR  50600  55600
      VD T330  CHRY  48500  53300, VD T175D CRUS  52600  57800

 40   BLUEWATER          FB   MY   FBG SV VD T220  CRUS 13    22000 2 10 48300  53000
      VD T225  CHRY  47900  52600, VD T250  CHRY  47900  52700, IO T255  MRCR  50700  55700
      VD T330  CHRY  48500  53300, VD T175D CRUS  52600  57800

 42  5 ADVENTURER        HT   HB   STL CT          12    12000 1 4  26200  29100
 47   ISLANDER           HT   MY   FBG SV VD T250  CHRY 13    25000 2 10 45000  50000
      IO T255  MRCR  46000  50600, VD T270  CRUS  46000  50500, VD T330  CHRY  46500  51100
      VD T175D CRUS  47600  52300

 47   ISLANDER           FB   MY   FBG SV VD T250  CHRY 13    25000 2 10 44800  49700
      IO T255  MRCR  45800  50300, VD T270  CRUS  45800  50300, VD T330  CHRY  46200  50800
      VD T175D CRUS  47300  52000

 50   ADVENTURER         HT   HB   STL CT          14    20000 1 10 42400  47100
------------------- 1975 BOATS -------------------------------------------------------
 40   BLUEWATER          HT   MY   FBG DV VD 250   CHRY 13    22000 2 10 44400  49300
      VD  330  CHRY  44700  49600, VD T225  CHRY  46000  50500, IO T255  MRCR  52000  57100
      VD T175D CRUS  50600  55700

 40   BLUEWATER          FB   MY   FBG DV VD 250   CHRY 13    22000 2 10 44500  49400
      VD  330  CHRY  44700  49600, VD T225  CHRY  46000  50600, IO T255  MRCR  52100  57200
      VD T175D CRUS  50700  55700

 42  5 ADVENTURER        HT   HB   STL CT OB        12    12000 1 4  25900  28800
 47   ISLANDER           HT   MY   FBG DV VD 330   CHRY 13    25000 2 8  41500  46100
      VD T250  CHRY  43200  48000, IO T255  MRCR  47000  51700, VD T175D CRUS  46500  50200

 47   ISLANDER           FB   MY   FBG DV VD 330   CHRY 13    25000 2 8  41300  45900
      VD T250  CHRY  43000  47800, IO T255  MRCR  46800  51400, VD T175D CRUS  44900  49900
------------------- 1974 BOATS -------------------------------------------------------
 40   BLUEWATER               SDN  FBG    IB 330   CHRY 13    22000 2 10 42500  47200
      IB T225  CHRY  43300  48200, IB T255  WAUK  43500  48400, IB T140D GM   48200  52900

 40   BLUEWATER          FB   SDN  FBG    IB 330   CHRY 13    22000 2 10 42600  47400
      IB T225  CHRY  43400  48300, IB T255  WAUK  43600  48500, IB T140D GM   48200  53000

 42  5 ADVENTURER        HT   HB   STL CT OB        12    12000 1 4  25700  28500
 47   ISLANDER           HT   HB   FBG    IB 250   CHRY 13    25000 2 8  46700  51300
      IB  330  CHRY  47300  51900, IB T255  WAUK  48900  53800, IB T140D GM   55000  60400

 47   ISLANDER           FB   HB   FBG    IB 250   CHRY 13    25000 2 8  46700  51300
      IB  330  CHRY  47300  51900, IB T255  WAUK  48900  53800, IB T140D GM   55000  60400
------------------- 1973 BOATS -------------------------------------------------------
 37   TRADEWIND          IO   MY   FBG    IO 225   MRCR 12    12000 2 2  32800  36400
      IO  255  MRCR  33200  36900, IO T155  CHRY  36500  40600, IO T165  MRCR  36600  40600
      VD T225  CHRY  37500  41700

 42  5 ADVENTURER        HT   HB   STL CT OB        12    12000 1 4  25500  28300
 47   ISLANDER               HB   FBG    IO T225   CHRY 13    22000 2 4  47000  51700
      IB T250  CHRY  45900  50500, IO T255  MRCR  47800  52500, VD T220D PALM  56600  62200
------------------- 1972 BOATS -------------------------------------------------------
 37   TRADEWIND               HB   FBG    IO 165   MRCR 12    13000 2 2  33700  37500
      IO  225  CHRY  34100  37900, IO  270   MRCR  34800  38700, IO  280  CHRY  35000  38900
      IO  325  MRCR  36600  40600, IO T165  MRCR  36300  40300
```

```
 LOA   NAME AND/       TOP/ BOAT  -HULL-  ----ENGINE---  BEAM   WGT   DRAFT RETAIL RETAIL
FT IN   OR MODEL       RIG  TYPE  MTL TP TP # HP  MFG    FT IN  LBS   FT IN  LOW    HIGH
------------------ 1972 BOATS -----------------------------------------------------------
37   TRADEWIND              FB HB  FBG  IO   165 MRCR 12         2 2  36400 40400
     IO  225 CHRY 36700  40800, IO 270  MRCR 37400 41600, IO  280 CHRY 37700 41900
     IO  325 MRCR 39400  43800, IO 106D VLVO 37100 41300, IO T165 MRCR 39100 43500

47   ISLANDER                  HB  FBG  IO T225 CHRY 13  21000  2 4  45700 50200
     VD T250 CHRY 44100 49000, IO T270 MRCR 47000 51600, VD T300 CHRY 44700 49600

47   ISLANDER               FB HB  FBG  IO T225 CHRY 13         2 4  44100 49000
     VD T250 CHRY 43100 47900, IO T270 MRCR 45900 50500, IO T280 CHRY 46400 50900
------------------ 1971 BOATS -----------------------------------------------------------
37   TRADEWIND                 HB  FBG  IO   215 MRCR 12  12240 2 2  32500 36200
     IO  250 CHRY 33000 36600, IO 270 MRCR 33300 37000, IO T165 MRCR 34800 38600

37   TRADEWIND              FB HB  FBG  IO   215 MRCR 12         2 2  36400 40400
     IO  250 CHRY 36800 40900, IO 270 MRCR 37100 41300, IO T165 MRCR 36400 43100

47   ISLANDER                  HB  FBG  IO T215 MRCR 13  21480  2 4  45600 50100
47   ISLANDER                  HB  FBG  IO T250 CHRY 13  21480  2 4  46400 51000
47   ISLANDER                  HB  FBG  IO T270 MRCR 13  21480  2 4  47100 51700
47   ISLANDER               FB HB  FBG  IO T215 MRCR 13         2 4  43600 48500
47   ISLANDER               FB HB  FBG  IO T250 CHRY 13         2 4  44400 49300
47   ISLANDER               FB HB  FBG  IO T270 MRCR 13         2 4  45600 50100
------------------ 1970 BOATS -----------------------------------------------------------
34   BARRACUDA                 HB  STL CT          12       8000 1 10 26700 29700
37   COUGAR                    HB  FBG IO   270 MRCR 12    11000 1 6  33000 34400
37   COUGAR                    HB  FBG IO T160     MRCR 12 11600 1 6  33400 37100
37   COUGAR                 FB HB  FBG IO   270 MRCR 12    11150 1 6  31300 34700
47   ADVENTURER                HB  AL  CT          12       9000 1 10 19800 22000
47   COUGAR SUPER           FB HB  FBG IO T270 MRCR 13     16250 2    40400 44900
47   COUGAR SUPER SS           HB  FBG IO T160 MRCR 13     15000 2    36700 40700
47   COUGAR SUPER SS           HB  FBG IO T270 MRCR 13     16000 2    40000 44500
------------------ 1969 BOATS -----------------------------------------------------------
33   BARRACUDA 33              HB  STL CT          10            1 6  20700 23000
35   COUGAR 35                 HB  FBG IB   250 MRCR 12          1 6  38300 42600
35   COUGAR 35              FB HB  FBG IB   250 MRCR 12          1 6  38300 42600
37   DEL-RIO 37                HB  STL IB   225 MRCR 11          1 6  34100 37900
37   DEL-RIO 37                HB  STL IB T150 MRCR 11           1 6  35800 39800
38   EXPLORER 38               HB  STL CT          12            1 6  21900 24300
50   EL-DORADO 50              HB  STL IB   225 MRCR 12          1 6  46000 50500
50   EL-DORADO 50              HB  STL IB T150 MRCR 12           1 6  47600 52300
50   EL-DORADO 50              HB  STL IB T225 MRCR 12           1 6  47900 52700
------------------ 1968 BOATS -----------------------------------------------------------
33   BARRACUDA 33              HB  STL CT             10    7500 1 6  24800 27600
37   DEL-RIO 37                HB  STL DV IO   225    11   11000 1 6  28800 31900
37   DEL-RIO 37                HB  STL DV IO T150     11   11000 1 6  30700 34100
38   EXPLORER 38               HB  STL CT OB          12    9000 1 6  22400 24900
50   EL-DORADO 50              HB  STL IO   225       12   17000 1 6  38900 43200
50   EL-DORADO 50              HB  STL IO T150        12   17000 1 6  40800 45300
50   EL-DORADO 50              HB  STL IO T225        12   17000 1 6  41500 46100
------------------ 1967 BOATS -----------------------------------------------------------
33   BARRACUDA 33              HB  AL  OB            10          1 6  22800 25300
33   BARRACUDA 33              HB  STL OB            10          1 6  20900 23200
37   DEL-RIO 37                HB  AL  IO   225      11          1 6  35200 39200
37   DEL-RIO 37                HB  STL IO   225      11          1 6  34100 37900
37   DEL-RIO 37                HB  AL  IO T150       11          1 6  37200 41400
37   DEL-RIO 37                HB  STL IO T150       11          1 6  36100 40100
38   EXPLORER 38               HB  AL  OB            10    7983  1 6  20400 22600
38   EXPLORER 38               HB  STL OB            10    7983  1 6  20100 22400
50   EL-DORADO 50              HB  AL  IO   225      12          1 6  46000 50600
50   EL-DORADO 50              HB  STL IO   225      12          1 6  45800 50300
50   EL-DORADO 50              HB  AL  IO T150       12          1 6  47900 52600
50   EL-DORADO 50              HB  STL IO T150       12          1 6  47700 52400

50   EL-DORADO 50              HB  AL  IO T225       12          1 6  48400 53200
50   EL-DORADO 50              HB  STL IO T225       12          1 6  48100 52900
------------------ 1966 BOATS -----------------------------------------------------------
33   BARRACUDA 33              HB  AL  OB            10          1 6  22700 25200
33   BARRACUDA 33              HB  STL OB            10          1 6  20800 23100
37   DEL-RIO 37                HB  AL  IO   210      11          1 6  34900 38800
37   DEL-RIO 37                HB  STL IO   210      11          1 6  33800 37600
37   DEL-RIO 37                HB  AL  IO   225      11          1 6  35000 38900
37   DEL-RIO 37                HB  STL IO   225      11          1 6  33900 37700
37   DEL-RIO 37                HB  AL  IO T150       11          1 6  37000 41100
37   DEL-RIO 37                HB  STL IO T150       11          1 6  35900 39800
37   DEL-RIO 37                HB  AL  IO T160       11          1 6  37100 41200
37   DEL-RIO 37                HB  STL IO T160       11          1 6  35900 39900
38   EXPLORER 38               HB  AL  OB            12          1 6  21700 24100
38   EXPLORER 38               HB  STL OB            12          1 6  21500 23900

42   F-420                         AL  IO   210      12          1 6  64800 71200
42   F-420                         STL IO   210      12          1 6  64800 71000
42   F-420                         AL  IO   225      12          1 6  65000 71400
42   F-420                         STL IO   225      12          1 6  65000 71400
42   F-420                         AL  IO T150       12          1 6  66700 73300
42   F-420                         STL IO T150       12          1 6  66700 73300
42   F-420                         AL  IO T160       12          1 6  67000 73600
42   F-420                         STL IO T160       12          1 6  67000 73600
44   C-440                     HB  AL  OB            12          1 6  31100 34600
44   C-440                     HB  STL OB            12          1 6  31100 34600
44   C-440                     HB  AL  IO T150       12          1 6  37500 41600
44   C-440                     HB  STL IO T150       12          1 6  37400 41500

44   C-440                     HB  AL  IO T160       12          1 6  37500 41700
44   C-440                     HB  STL IO T160       12          1 6  37400 41500
50   EL-DORADO 50              HB  AL  IO   210      12          1 6  45700 50200
50   EL-DORADO 50              HB  STL IO   210      12          1 6  45800 49900
50   EL-DORADO 50              HB  AL  IO   225      12          1 6  45800 50300
50   EL-DORADO 50              HB  STL IO   225      12          1 6  45600 50100
50   EL-DORADO 50              HB  AL  IO T150       12          1 6  47600 52300
50   EL-DORADO 50              HB  STL IO T150       12          1 6  47700 52400
50   EL-DORADO 50              HB  AL  IO T160       12          1 6  47600 52100
50   EL-DORADO 50              HB  STL IO T210       12          1 6  48100 52900
50   EL-DORADO 50              HB  AL  IO T210       12          1 6  47900 52600

50   EL-DORADO 50              HB  AL  IO T225       12          1 6  48100 52900
50   EL-DORADO 50              HB  STL IO T225       12          1 6  47800 52600
52   SEA-RAY 52                HB  AL               12          1 6  43800 48700
52   SEA-RAY 52                HB  STL              12          1 6  40400 44900
52   SEA-RAY 52                HB  AL  IO T150       12          1 6  57000 62600
52   SEA-RAY 52                HB  STL IO T150       12          1 6  52300 57600
52   SEA-RAY 52                HB  AL  IO T160       12          1 6  57000 62600
52   SEA-RAY 52                HB  STL IO T160       12          1 6  52300 57500
------------------ 1965 BOATS -----------------------------------------------------------
33   BARRACUDA 33              HB  AL  OB            10          1 2  22500 25000
33   BARRACUDA 33              HB  STL OB            10          1 2  20500 22900
36   DEL-RIO 36                HB  AL  IO   160      12          1 2  30100 33400
36   DEL-RIO 36                HB  STL IO   160      12          1 2  29200 32400
36   DEL-RIO 36                HB  AL  IO   210      12          1 2  30300 33700
36   DEL-RIO 36                HB  STL IO   210      12          1 2  29400 32600
36   DEL-RIO 36                HB  AL  IO T160       12          1 2  32500 36100
36   DEL-RIO 36                HB  STL IO T160       12          1 2  31500 35000
37   EXPLORER 37               HB  AL  OB            12          1 10 19500 21700
37   EXPLORER 37               HB  STL OB            12            10 19300 21400
50   EL-DORADO 50              HB  AL  IO   210      13          1 3  44900 49900
50   EL-DORADO 50              HB  STL IO   210      13          1 3  44700 49700

50   EL-DORADO 50              HB  AL  IO T160       13          1 3  47400 52100
50   EL-DORADO 50              HB  STL IO T160       13          1 3  47200 51900
50   EL-DORADO 50              HB  AL  IO T210       13          1 3  47800 52600
50   EL-DORADO 50              HB  STL IO T210       13          1 3  47600 52300
------------------ 1964 BOATS -----------------------------------------------------------
32   EXPLORER 32               HB  AL  IO            12          1 2  40200 44700
32   EXPLORER 32               HB  STL IO            12          1 2  37000 41100
42   DEL-RIO 42                HB  AL  IO            12            10 33400 37100
42   DEL-RIO 42                HB  STL IO            12            10 32200 35800
------------------ 1963 BOATS -----------------------------------------------------------
31   EXPLORER 31               HB  STL IO            12          1 2  36200 40200
37   DEL-RIO 37                HB  STL IO            11          1 10 33300 37000
42   ADVENTURER 42             HB  STL IO            14          1 2  32100 35600
```

BLUEWATER YACHT BLD LTD
TAIPEI TAIWAN   COAST GUARD MFG ID- BYY See inside cover to adjust price for area

For more recent years, see the BUC Used Boat Price Guide, Volume 1 or Volume 2

```
 LOA   NAME AND/       TOP/ BOAT  -HULL-  ----ENGINE---  BEAM   WGT   DRAFT RETAIL RETAIL
FT IN   OR MODEL       RIG  TYPE  MTL TP TP # HP  MFG    FT IN  LBS   FT IN  LOW    HIGH
------------------ 1983 BOATS -----------------------------------------------------------
46  7  VAGABOND-VOYAGER KTH SA/RC FBG KL IB  85D LEHM 13  5 40000 5 6 126500 139000
------------------ 1982 BOATS -----------------------------------------------------------
41  8  VAGABOND 42     CUT SA/CR FBG KL IB  65D LEHM 12 10 28500 5 6  88900  97700
41  8  VAGABOND 42     KTH SA/CR FBG KL IB  65D LEHM 12 10 28500 5 6  89000  97800
46  7  VAGABOND 47     KTH SA/CR FBG KL IB  85D LEHM 13  5 40000 5 3 119500 131500
```

BLUEWATER YACHT BLD LTD   -CONTINUED   See inside cover to adjust price for area

LOA FT IN	NAME AND/ OR MODEL	TOP/ RIG	BOAT TYPE	-HULL- MTL TP	----ENGINE--- TP # HP MFG	BEAM FT IN	WGT LBS	DRAFT FT IN	RETAIL LOW	RETAIL HIGH
			1981 BOATS							
41 8	VAGABOND 42	KTH	SA/CR FBG KL	IB	65D LEHM	12 10	29000	5 6	85200	93600
46 7	VAGABOND 47	KTH	SA/CR FBG KL	IB	80D LEHM	13 8	40000	5 3	113500	124500
			1980 BOATS							
41 8	VAGABOND 42	CUT	SA/CR FBG KL	IB	65D LEHM	12 10	29000	5 6	81900	90100
41 8	VAGABOND 42	KTH	SA/CR FBG KL	IB	65D LEHM	12 10	29000	5 6	82000	90100
46 7	VAGABOND 47	KTH	SA/CR FBG KL	IB	80D LEHM	13 8	40000	5 3	109000	120000
			1978 BOATS							
47	VAGABOND-VOYAGER	KTH	SA/CR FBG KL	IB	85D	13 5	40000	5 3	104000	114000
			1973 BOATS							
42	BLUEWATER 42	TRWL	FBG	IB 256		14		4	46000	50600
			1971 BOATS							
39 4	BLUEWATER 40	TRWL	FBG	IB	120D GM		32000	4 3	54100	59500
40 10	BLUEWATER 41	KTH	SA/CR FBG KL	IB	50D PERK	12 2	28000	6	62800	69100
44	BLUEWATER 44	TRWL	WD	IB	T120D GM	14	37000	4 3	63600	69900
44 9	SEAWANDERER	KTH	SA/CR WD KL	IB	50D PERK	13	39000	5 6	82100	90200
46	BLUEWATER	KTH	SA/CR WD KL	IB	70	13	42000	6	87000	95600
46	CLIPPER 46	KTH	SAIL WD	IB	50D VLVO	13 3	41900	5 8	87700	96300
47	VAGABOND 47	KTH	SA/CR FBG	IB	70D PERK	13 4	40000	5 6	87900	96600

BOAT COMPANY OF MYSTIC
COAST GUARD MFG ID- BTK

Call 1-800-327-6929 for BUC Personalized Evaluation Service
Or, for 1979 boats, sign onto www.BUCValuPro.com

THE BOAT YARD INC
COAST GUARD MFG ID- TBY

Call 1-800-327-6929 for BUC Personalized Evaluation Service
Or, for 1971 to 1975 boats, sign onto www.BUCValuPro.com

BOATEL MARINE INC
PAGE AZ 86040   See inside cover to adjust price for area

For more recent years, see the BUC Used Boat Price Guide, Volume 1 or Volume 2

LOA FT IN	NAME AND/ OR MODEL	TOP/ RIG	BOAT TYPE	-HULL- MTL TP	----ENGINE--- TP # HP MFG	BEAM FT IN	WGT LBS	DRAFT FT IN	RETAIL LOW	RETAIL HIGH
			1983 BOATS							
36	BOATEL 36	HT	HB	STL PN	OB	14	10000		13200	15000
44	BOATEL 44	HT	HB	STL PN	OB	14			14700	16700
50	BOATEL 50	HT	HB	STL PN	OB	14	15000		17200	19500
52	BOATEL 52	HT	HB	STL PN	OB	14			23700	26400
			1982 BOATS							
36	BOATEL 36	HT	HB	STL PN	OB	14	10000		13000	14800
44	BOATEL 44	HT	HB	STL PN	OB	14			14400	16400
50	BOATEL 50	HT	HB	STL PN	OB	14	15000		16800	19100
52	BOATEL 52	HT	HB	STL PN	OB	14			23300	25900
			1981 BOATS							
36	BOATEL 36	HT	HB	STL CT	OB	14	10000		12000	13600
44	BOATEL 44	HT	HB	STL CT	OB	14			14000	15900
50	BOATEL 50	HT	HB	STL CT	OB	14	15000		16700	19000
			1980 BOATS							
36	CATAMARAN	HT	HB	STL PN	OB	14			13800	15600
44	CATAMARAN	HT	HB	STL PN	OB	14			14000	15900
50	CATAMARAN	HT	HB	STL PN	OB	14			18600	20700
			1979 BOATS							
36	ECONOMY	HT	HB	STL PN	OB	14			13600	15400
44	STANDARD	HT	HB	STL PN	OB	14			13800	15600
50	DELUXE	HT	HB	STL PN	OB	14			18300	20400
			1971 BOATS							
34	BARRACUDA	HT	HB	STL PN	OB	10	7500	3	10100	11400
37	TRADEWIND	HT	HB	FBG SV	IO	10	13000	2 2	16200	18500
41	ADVENTURER	HT	HB	STL PN	OB	12	11000	1 4	11100	12700
			1969 BOATS							
33	BARRACUDA	HT	HB	STL		10		6	7650	8800
33	BARRACUDA	HT	HB	STL PN	OB	10	7500	3	9900	11300
35	COUGAR	HT	HB	FBG	IO 250	9		1 6	15000	17000
35	COUGAR	HT	HB	FBG SV	IO 250	10	10000	3	15100	17100
38	DEL-RIO	HT	HB	STL	IO 225	9		1 6	14900	16900
38	DEL-RIO	HT	HB	STL SV	IO 225	12	11000	3	12300	14000
38	EXPLORER	HT	HB	STL	OB	9		1 6	13700	15600
38	EXPLORER	HT	HB	STL PN	OB	12	9000	3	10500	11900
38	SEA-RAY	HT	HB	AL	IO 225	9		1 6	17300	19600
50	EL-DORADO	HT	HB	STL SV	IO T450	12	17000	3	25700	28600
50	ELDORADO	HT	HB	STL	IO T150	10		1 6	21600	24000
			1966 BOATS							
33	C-33	HT	HB	STL CT	OB	10		1 4	7350	8450
37	F-37	HT	HB	STL CT	IO 225	11		10	15200	17200
42	C-42	HT	HB	STL CT	IO T150	12		1 4	16300	18500
50	F-50	HT	HB	STL CT	IO 225	12		10	20500	22800
			1961 BOATS							
30	EXPLORER	HT	HB	AL CT	OB	14	5000	1	6450	7400
30	VAGABOND	HT	HB	STL CT	OB	8	3000		1800	2100
37	ADVENTURER	HT	HB	AL CT	OB	14	7000		8850	10000
			1960 BOATS							
27	ADVENTURER	HT	HB	AL CT	OB	14	7000	1	**	**
27	ADVENTURER	HT	HB	FBG CT	OB	14	7000	1	**	**
29	VAGABOND	HT	HB	STL CT	OB	8	3000	8	1800	2100
30	EXPLORER	HT	HB	AL CT	OB	14	5000	1	6400	7350
30	EXPLORER	HT	HB	FBG CT	OB	14	5000	1	6450	7400

DER BOATHAUS
THE SHARPIE SHOPPE

Call 1-800-327-6929 for BUC Personalized Evaluation Service
Or, for 1982 boats, sign onto www.BUCValuPro.com

BOATS UNLIMITED CORP
BEACHCOMBER BOATS   COAST GUARD MFG ID- GPD

Call 1-800-327-6929 for BUC Personalized Evaluation Service
Or, for 1981 boats, sign onto www.BUCValuPro.com

BOCA GRANDE BOATS
SARASOTA FL 34243   COAST GUARD MFG ID- BQA See inside cover to adjust price for area

For more recent years, see the BUC Used Boat Price Guide, Volume 1 or Volume 2

LOA FT IN	NAME AND/ OR MODEL	TOP/ RIG	BOAT TYPE	-HULL- MTL TP	----ENGINE--- TP # HP MFG	BEAM FT IN	WGT LBS	DRAFT FT IN	RETAIL LOW	RETAIL HIGH
			1974 BOATS							
26	DIVE-MASTER 26		UTL	FBG SV	OB	8	3200	1	6800	7850
26	DIVE-MASTER 26		UTL	FBG SV	IO 165	8	3200	1	13000	14700
	JT 185	10400	11900, IO T170		15700 17900, JT T185				12900	14700
26	PASS-MASTER 26		OPFSH	FBG SV	JT 185	8	3200	1	10200	11600
26	PASS-MASTER 26		OPFSH	FBG SV	JT T185	8	3200	1	12600	14300
26	PASS-MASTER 26	OP	OPFSH	FBG SV	OB	8	3200	1	7050	8100
26	PASS-MASTER 26	OP	OPFSH	FBG SV	IO 165	8	3200	1	12700	14400
26	PASS-MASTER 26	OP	OPFSH	FBG SV	IO T170	8	3200	1	15300	17400
26	PASS-MASTER 26	FB	SF	FBG SV	OB	8	3440	1	7200	8250
26	PASS-MASTER 26	FB	SF	FBG SV	IO 165	8	3440	1	14500	16400
	JT 185	10700	12200, IO T170		17400 19800, JT T185				13200	15000
28 2	GULF-MASTER	FB	SF	FBG SV	IB T225	11 2		1 10	21900	24300
32	GULF-MASTER	FB	SF	FBG SV	IB T225-T300	11 6		2	29100	34100
			1973 BOATS							
26	PASS-MASTER 26		FBG		OB	8	3200	1	7050	8100
26	PASS-MASTER 26		FBG		IO 188 MRCR	8	4495	1	15600	17700
26	PASS-MASTER 26		FBG		IO T165-T170	8	4950	1	19000	21500
40 3	SILVER-KING	FB	SF	FBG	IB 600D	13 6		2 3	105500	116000

JAMES A BOCK & CO INC
UNITED YACHT BROKERS INC

Call 1-800-327-6929 for BUC Personalized Evaluation Service
Or, for 1959 to 1982 boats, sign onto www.BUCValuPro.com

BOE CRAFT

Call 1-800-327-6929 for BUC Personalized Evaluation Service
Or, for 1968 to 1970 boats, sign onto www.BUCValuPro.com

BONANZA MOLDING CORP
COAST GUARD MFG ID- BNM

Call 1-800-327-6929 for BUC Personalized Evaluation Service
Or, for 1973 to 1980 boats, sign onto www.BUCValuPro.com

BONITO BOAT CORP
NARRAGANSETT RI 02882   COAST GUARD MFG ID- BNA See inside cover to adjust price for area

LOA FT IN	NAME AND/ OR MODEL	TOP/ RIG	BOAT TYPE	-HULL- MTL TP	----ENGINE--- TP # HP MFG	BEAM FT IN	WGT LBS	DRAFT FT IN	RETAIL LOW	RETAIL HIGH
			---- 1977 BOATS							
19 8	LEMA 20	OP	OPFSH	FBG SV	IO 140 MRCR	8 4	3000	1 4	4300	5000
25 8	BONITO 26	OP	CUD	FBG SV	IO 255 MRCR	11 1	6000	1 5	10600	12100
25 8	BONITO 26	OP	OPFSH	FBG SV	IO 255 MRCR	11 1	6000	1 5	11100	12600
			---- 1976 BOATS							
25 8	BONITO		CUD	FBG SV	IO 255	11 1	6000	2 2	10900	12400
25 8	BONITO	OP	RNBT	FBG SV	IO 255	11 1	6000	2 2	10100	11400
			---- 1975 BOATS							
25 8	BONITO		CUD	FBG SV	IB 250	11 1	6000	2 2	9500	10800
25 8	BONITO		CUD	FBG SV	IB 325	11 1	6000	2 2	12000	13600
25 8	BONITO		CUD	FBG SV	IB 325	11 1	6000	2 2	9850	11200
25 8	BONITO	OP	OPFSH	FBG SV	IB 250	11 1	6000	2 2	9450	10700
25 8	BONITO	OP	OPFSH	FBG SV	IB 325	11 1	6000	2 2	12500	14200
25 8	BONITO	OP	OPFSH	FBG SV	IB 325	11 1	6000	2 2	9700	11000
			---- 1974 BOATS							
25 8	BONITO		CUD	FBG SV	IB 225	11 1	6000	2 4	11400	13000
25 8	BONITO		CUD	FBG SV	IB 325	11 1	6000	2 4	9450	10700
25 8	BONITO		CUD	FBG SV	IO T165	11 1	6000	2 4	12300	14000
25 8	BONITO		OPFSH	FBG SV	IO 225	11 1	6000	2 4	11900	13500
25 8	BONITO		OPFSH	FBG SV	IB 255	11 1	6000	2 4	9100	10300
25 8	BONITO		OPFSH	FBG SV	IO T165	11 1	6000	2 4	12800	14600

BONITO BOATS INC
COAST GUARD MFG ID- BNT

Call 1-800-327-6929 for BUC Personalized Evaluation Service
Or, for 1975 to 1986 boats, sign onto www.BUCValuPro.com

BONUM MARIN AB
FORMERLY LARSSON TRADE AB

Call 1-800-327-6929 for BUC Personalized Evaluation Service
Or, for 1965 to 1986 boats, sign onto www.BUCValuPro.com

ROBERT BOOMER AGENCY

Call 1-800-327-6929 for BUC Personalized Evaluation Service
Or, for 1960 to 1968 boats, sign onto www.BUCValuPro.com

BOOTH ENTERPRISES
COAST GUARD MFG ID- ZQT

Call 1-800-327-6929 for BUC Personalized Evaluation Service
Or, for 1976 to 1999 boats, sign onto www.BUCValuPro.com

BOOTHBAY BOATS INC

Call 1-800-327-6929 for BUC Personalized Evaluation Service
Or, for 1959 to 1967 boats, sign onto www.BUCValuPro.com

BORGE BRINGSVAERD'S VERFT

Call 1-800-327-6929 for BUC Personalized Evaluation Service
Or, for 1973 to 1978 boats, sign onto www.BUCValuPro.com

BORHAMEN

Call 1-800-327-6929 for BUC Personalized Evaluation Service
Or, for 1919 boats, sign onto www.BUCValuPro.com

BORRESENS BAADEBYGGERI A/S
COAST GUARD MFG ID- BBG

Call 1-800-327-6929 for BUC Personalized Evaluation Service
Or, for 1965 to 2001 boats, sign onto www.BUCValuPro.com

BORUM BOATS INC
COAST GUARD MFG ID- BRM
FORMERLY WATER WAYS ENTERPRISES INC

Call 1-800-327-6929 for BUC Personalized Evaluation Service
Or, for 1959 to 1980 boats, sign onto www.BUCValuPro.com

BOSSOMS BOATYARD LTD

Call 1-800-327-6929 for BUC Personalized Evaluation Service
Or, for 1978 to 1994 boats, sign onto www.BUCValuPro.com

BOSTON WHALER INC
EDGEWATER FL 32141   COAST GUARD MFG ID- BWC See inside cover to adjust price for area
FORMERLY FISHER PIERCE CO INC

For more recent years, see the BUC Used Boat Price Guide, Volume 1 or Volume 2

LOA FT IN	NAME AND/ OR MODEL	TOP/ RIG	BOAT TYPE	-HULL- MTL TP	----ENGINE--- TP # HP MFG	BEAM FT IN	WGT LBS	DRAFT FT IN	RETAIL LOW	RETAIL HIGH
			---- 1983 BOATS							
16 7	MONTAUK	OP	CTRCN	F/S SV	OB	6 2	900	9	3100	3600
16 7	NEWPORT	OP	RNBT	F/S SV	OB	6 2	950	9	3250	3800
16 7	SPORT	OP	UTL	F/S SV	OB	6 2	850	9	2750	3200
16 7	STRIPER	OP	BASS	F/S SV	OB	6 2	850	9	2900	3350
17	HARPOON 5.2	SLP	SA/OD	F/S CB	OB	7 6	565	5	3050	3550
18 6	GTX18	OP	RNBT	F/S	OB	7 2	1250	10	5650	6500
18 6	GTX18	OP	RNBT	F/S	OB 188-260	7 2	2950	1	4250	5250
18 6	NEWPORT 18	OP	RNBT	F/S DV	OB	7 2	1150	10	4950	5700
18 6	OUTRAGE 18	OP	CTRCN	F/S DV	OB	7 2	1250	10	5100	5900
19 10	OUTRAGE V-20	OP	OPFSH	F/S DV	OB	7 5	1650	11	6050	6950
19 10	REVENGE 20	OP	CR	F/S DV	OB	7 5	1950	11	6550	7550
20 4	HARPOON 6.2	SLP	SA/CR	F/S CB	OB	8	1700	3 6	6100	7000
22 3	OUTRAGE 22	OP	FSH	F/S DV	IO 188 MRCR	7 5	3050	1 2	7350	8450
22 3	OUTRAGE 22	OP	OPFSH	F/S DV	OB	7 5	2050	1 2	6750	7750
22 3	OUTRAGE 22	OP	OPFSH	F/S DV	IO	7 5	3050	1 2	**	**
22 3	OUTRAGE 22	OP	OPFSH	F/S DV	IO 170 OMC	7 5	3050	1 2	7250	8350
22 3	OUTRAGE 22 CUDDY	OP	CUD	F/S DV	OB	7 5	2250	1 2	7500	8600
22 3	OUTRAGE 22 CUDDY	OP	CUD	F/S DV	IO	7 5	3050	1 2	**	**
22 3	OUTRAGE 22 CUDDY	OP	CUD	F/S DV	IO 170-188	7 5	3050	1 2	6850	8000
22 3	REVENGE 22	OP	CR	F/S DV	OB	7 5	2350	1 2	8850	10000
22 3	REVENGE 22	OP	CR	F/S DV	IO	7 5	3350	1 2	**	**
22 3	REVENGE 22	OP	CR	F/S DV	IO 170-188	7 5	3350	1 2	7300	8500
22 3	REVENGE 22 CUDDY	OP	CUD	F/S DV	OB	7 5	2350	1 2	8350	9600
22 3	REVENGE 22 CUDDY	OP	CUD	F/S DV	IO	7 5	3350	1 2	**	**
22 3	REVENGE 22 CUDDY	OP	CUD	F/S DV	IO 170-188	7 5	3350	1 2	7300	8500
24 7	FRONTIER 25XC	OP	UTL	F/S DV	OB	8	3500	1 4	12600	14400
24 7	FRONTIER 25XC	OP	UTL	F/S DV	IO	8	4670	1 4	**	**
24 7	FRONTIER 25XC	OP	UTL	F/S DV	IO 188 MRCR	8	4670	1 4	11500	13100
24 7	FRONTIER 25XC	OP	UTL	F/S DV	SE 205 OMC	8	4670	1 4	15200	17200
24 7	FRONTIER 25XC	OP	UTL	F/S DV	IO 260	8	4670	1 4	12000	13700
24 7	OUTRAGE 25	OP	FSH	F/S DV	OB	8	3000	1 4	8500	9750
24 7	OUTRAGE 25	OP	FSH	F/S DV	IO	8	4670	1 4	**	**
24 7	OUTRAGE 25	OP	FSH	F/S DV	IO 188 MRCR	8	4670	1 4	11600	13200
24 7	OUTRAGE 25	OP	FSH	F/S DV	SE 205 OMC	8	4670	1 4	11200	12700
24 7	OUTRAGE 25	OP	FSH	F/S DV	IO 260	8	4670	1 4	12100	13700
24 7	OUTRAGE 25 CUDDY	OP	CUD	F/S DV	OB	8	3000	1 4	9400	10700
24 7	OUTRAGE 25 CUDDY	OP	CUD	F/S DV	IO	8	4670	1 4	**	**
24 7	OUTRAGE 25 CUDDY	OP	CUD	F/S DV	IO 188 MRCR	8	4670	1 4	10800	12300
24 7	OUTRAGE 25 CUDDY	OP	CUD	F/S DV	SE 205 OMC	8	4670	1 4	12200	13800
24 7	OUTRAGE 25 CUDDY	OP	CUD	F/S DV	IO 260	8	4670	1 4	14600	16500
24 7	REVENGE 25	OP	CR	F/S DV	OB	8	4000	1 4	**	**
24 7	REVENGE 25	OP	CR	F/S DV	IO	8	5000	1 4	**	**
24 7	REVENGE 25	OP	CR	F/S DV	IO 188 MRCR	8	5000	1 4	11500	13100
24 7	REVENGE 25	OP	CR	F/S DV	SE 205 OMC	8	5000	1 4	16400	18600
24 7	REVENGE 25	OP	CR	F/S DV	IO 260	8	5000	1 4	12000	13600
24 7	REVENGE 25 CUDDY	OP	CUD	F/S DV	OB	8	4000	1 4	11200	12700
24 7	REVENGE 25 CUDDY	OP	CUD	F/S DV	IO	8	4670	1 4	**	**

LOA FT	IN	NAME AND/ OR MODEL	TOP/ RIG	BOAT TYPE	-HULL- MTL	HULL TP	ENGINE TP	# HP	MFG	BEAM FT	BEAM IN	WGT LBS	DRAFT FT	DRAFT IN	RETAIL LOW	RETAIL HIGH
		1983 BOATS														
24	7	REVENGE 25 CUDDY	OP	CUD	F/S	DV	IO	188	MRCR	8		4670	1	4	11100	12600
24	7	REVENGE 25 CUDDY	OP	CUD	F/S	DV	SE	205	OMC	8		4670	1	4	12300	14000
24	7	REVENGE 25 CUDDY	OP	CUD	F/S	DV	IO	260		8		4670	1	4	11500	13100
		1982 BOATS														
16	7	MONTAUK	OP	CTRCN	F/S	SV	OB			6	2	900		9	3050	3500
16	7	NEWPORT	OP	RNBT	F/S	SV	OB			6	2	950		9	3200	3700
16	7	SPORT	OP	UTL	F/S	SV	OB			6	2	850		9	2700	3150
16	7	STRIPER 17	OP	FSH	F/S	SV	OB			6	2	850		9	2750	3200
17		HARPOON 5.2	SLP	SA/OD	F/S	CB	OB			7	6	565		5	2850	3300
18	6	GTX 18V	OP	RNBT	F/S	DV	IO	185	MRCR	7	2	1745	1		3200	3750
18	6	NEWPORT 18	OP	RNBT	F/S	DV	OB			7	2	1150		10	4850	5600
18	6	OUTRAGE 18	OP	CTRCN	F/S	DV	OB			7	2	1250		10	5050	5800
19	10	OUTRAGE V-20	OP	OPFSH	F/S	DV	OB			7	5	1500		11	5550	6400
19	10	REVENGE 20	OP	CR	F/S	DV	OB			7	5	1950		11	6450	7400
20	4	HARPOON 6.2	SLP	SA/CR	F/S	CB	OB			8		1700	3	6	5700	6550
22	3	OUTRAGE 22	OP	FSH	F/S	DV	IO		OMC	7	5	3050	1	2	**	**
22	3	OUTRAGE 22	OP	FSH	F/S	DV	IO	185	MRCR	7	5	3050	1	2	7150	8250
22	3	OUTRAGE 22	OP	OPFSH	F/S	DV	OB			7	5	2050	1	2	6650	7650
22	3	REVENGE 22 CUDDY	OP	CUD	F/S	DV	OB			7	5	2350	1	2	8000	9200
22	3	REVENGE 22 CUDDY	OP	CUD	F/S	DV	IO		OMC	7	5	3350	1	2	**	**
22	3	REVENGE 22 CUDDY	OP	CUD	F/S	DV	IO	185	MRCR	7	5	3350	1	2	7200	8300
24	7	FRONTIER 25XC	OP	UTL	F/S	DV	OB			8		3500	1	4	12400	14000
24	7	OUTRAGE 25	OP	CTRCN	F/S	DV	OB			8		3000	1	4	8250	9500
24	7	OUTRAGE 25	OP	CUD	F/S	DV	OB			8		3500	1	4	9400	10700
24	7	OUTRAGE 25	OP	CUD	F/S	DV	IO			8		4670	1	4	**	**
24	7	REVENGE 25 CUDDY	OP	CUD	F/S	DV	OB			8		4000	1	4	11000	12500
24	7	REVENGE 25 CUDDY	OP	CUD	F/S	DV	IO	260	MRCR	8		5000	1	4	11700	13300
		1981 BOATS														
16	7	MONTAUK	OP	CTRCN	F/S	SV	OB			6	2	900		9	3000	3450
16	7	NEWPORT	OP	RNBT	F/S	SV	OB			6	2	950		9	3150	3650
16	7	SPORT	OP	UTL	F/S	SV	OB			6	2	850		9	2650	3050
16	7	STRIPER 17		FSH	F/S	SV	OB			6	2	850			2700	3150
17		HARPOON 5.2	SLP	SA/OD	F/S	CB	OB			7	6	565		5	2700	3100
19	10	OUTRAGE V-20	OP	OPFSH	F/S	SV	OB			7	5	1500		11	5450	6300
19	10	REVENGE 20		CR	F/S	DV	OB			7	5	1950			6350	7300
20	4	HARPOON 6.2	SLP	SA/CR	F/S		OB			8		1700	3	6	5350	6150
21	4	OUTRAGE SPECIAL	OP	OPFSH	F/S	SV	OB			7	4	1600		10	5650	6500
22	3	OUTRAGE 22	OP	FSH	F/S	DV	IO	185	MRCR	7	5	3050			7050	8100
22	3	OUTRAGE V-22	OP	OPFSH	F/S	SV	OB			7	5	2050	1	2	6350	7300
22	3	REVENGE 22		CR	F/S	DV	IO	185	MRCR	7	5	3350			7100	8150
22	3	REVENGE V-22	OP	CR	F/S	SV	OB			7	5	2350	1	2	7300	8400
24	7	OUTRAGE 25	OP	FSH	F/S	DV	OB			8		3000			8150	9350
		1980 BOATS														
16	7	MONTAUK	OP	CTRCN	F/S	SV	OB			6	2	900		9	2950	3400
16	7	NEWPORT	OP	RNBT	F/S	SV	OB			6	2	950		9	3100	3600
16	7	SPORT	OP	UTL	F/S	SV	OB			6	2	850		9	2600	3000
17		HARPOON 5.2	SLP	SA/OD	F/S	CB				7	6	565		5	2550	2950
19	10	OUTRAGE V-20	OP	OPFSH	F/S	SV	OB			7	5	1500		11	5400	6200
21	4	OUTRAGE	OP	FSH	F/S	SV	OB			7	4	1600		10	5400	6200
21	4	REVENGE	OP	RNBT	F/S	SV	OB			7	4	1800		10	5650	6500
22	3	OUTRAGE V-22	OP	OPFSH	F/S	SV	OB			7	5	2050	1	2	6250	7150
22	3	REVENGE V-22	OP	CR	F/S	SV	OB			7	5	2350	1	2	7200	8250
		1979 BOATS														
16	7	MONTAUK	OP	CTRCN	F/S	SV	OB			6	2	900		9	3000	3500
16	7	NEWPORT	OP	RNBT	F/S	SV	OB			6	2	950		9	3200	3700
16	7	SPORT	OP	UTL	F/S	SV	OB			6	2	850		9	2750	3200
17		HARPOON 5.2	SLP	SA/OD	F/S	CB				7	6	565		5	2450	2850
19	4	REVENGE	OP	RNBT	F/S	SV	OB			7	4	1500		10	5050	5850
19	10	OUTRAGE V-20	OP	OPFSH	F/S	SV	OB			7	5	1500		11	5200	5950
21	4	OUTRAGE	OP	FSH	F/S	SV	OB			7	4	1600		10	5900	6800
21	4	REVENGE	OP	RNBT	F/S	SV	OB			7	4	1800		10	6600	7600
22	3	OUTRAGE V-22	OP	OPFSH	F/S	SV	OB			7	5	2050	1	2	7550	8650
22	3	REVENGE V-22	OP	CR	F/S	SV	OB			7	5	2350	1	2	8500	9750
		1978 BOATS														
16	7	LOW PROFILE	OP	UTL	F/S	SV	OB			6	2	950		9	3000	3500
16	7	MONTAUK	OP	CTRCN	F/S	SV	OB			6	2	900		9	3000	3500
16	7	NEWPORT	OP	RNBT	F/S	SV	OB			6	2	950		9	3150	3650
16	7	SPORT	OP	UTL	F/S	SV	OB			6	2	850		9	2700	3150
17		HARPOON 5.2	SLP	SA/OD	F/S	CB				7	6	565		5	2350	2700
19	4	OUTRAGE	OP	OPFSH	F/S	SV	IO	165		7	4	2600			4400	5050
19	4	REVENGE	OP	RNBT	F/S	SV	OB			7	4	1500		10	5000	5750
19	4	REVENGE	OP	RNBT	F/S	SV	IO	165		7	4	1500			3250	3750
19	10	OUTRAGE	OP	OPFSH	F/S	SV	OB			7	5	1500		11	5150	5900
21	4	OUTRAGE	OP	FSH	F/S	SV	OB			7	4	1600		10	5850	6700
21	4	REVENGE	OP	RNBT	F/S	SV	OB			7	4	1800		10	6550	7500
		1977 BOATS														
16	7	MONTAUK	OP	FSH	F/S	SV	OB			6	2	850		9	2800	3250
16	7	NEWPORT	OP	RNBT	F/S	SV	OB			6	2	950		9	3100	3650
16	7	SPORT	OP	UTL	F/S	SV	OB			6	2	900		9	2850	3300
17		HARPOON 5.2	SLP	SA/OD	F/S	CB				7	6	565		5	2300	2650
19	4	OUTRAGE	OP	FSH	F/S	SV	OB			7	4	1500		10	4950	5700
19	4	OUTRAGE	OP	FSH	F/S	SV	IO	165-175		7	4	2600		10	4450	5150
19	4	REVENGE	OP	RNBT	F/S	SV	OB			7	4	1600		10	5200	6000
19	4	REVENGE	OP	RNBT	F/S	SV	IO	165-175		7	4	2700		10	4150	4800
21	4	OUTRAGE	OP	FSH	F/S	SV	OB			7	4	1600		10	5750	6600
21	4	REVENGE	OP	RNBT	F/S	SV	OB			7	4	1800		10	6450	7400
		1976 BOATS														
16	7	BASS BOAT	OP	BASS	FBG	SV	OB			6	2	950			3100	3600
16	7	MONTAUK 17	OP	UTL	FBG	SV	OB			6	2	900			2950	3400
16	7	NEWPORT 17	OP	UTL	FBG	SV	OB			6	2	950			2950	3450
16	7	SAKONNET 17	OP	UTL	FBG	SV	OB			6	2	900			2700	3150
16	7	SPORT 17	OP	UTL	FBG	SV	OB			6	2	850			2700	3100
19	4	OUTRAGE	OP	UTL	FBG	SV	OB			7	4	1500			4450	5100
19	4	OUTRAGE	OP	UTL	FBG	SV	IO	165		7	4	2600			4600	5250
19	4	REVENGE	OP	UTL	FBG	SV	OB			7	4	1600			4650	5350
19	4	REVENGE	OP	UTL	FBG	SV	IO	165		7	4	1600			3700	4300
21		YANKEE-VOYAGER		CR	FBG		IO	188-233		8			2		5650	6700
21	4	OUTRAGE	OP	FSH	FBG	SV	OB			7	4	1600		10	5700	6500
21	4	REVENGE	OP	RNBT	FBG	SV	OB			7	4	1800			6400	7350
		1975 BOATS														
16	7	BARE HULL	OP	UTL	FBG	TR	OB			6	2	550		8	1700	2050
16	7	BASS BOAT	OP	BASS	FBG	TR	OB			6	2	950		8	3100	3600
16	7	CURRITUCK	OP	UTL	FBG	TR	OB			6	2	650		8	2000	2400
16	7	KATAMA	OP	UTL	FBG	TR	OB			6	2	850		8	2650	3100
16	7	MONTAUK	OP	UTL	FBG	TR	OB			6	2	900		8	2800	3250
16	7	NEWPORT	OP	RNBT	FBG	TR	OB			6	2	950		8	3100	3600
16	7	SAKONNET	OP	UTL	FBG	TR	OB			6	2	770		8	2400	2800
19	4	OUTRAGE	OP	UTL	FBG	TR	OB			7	4	1500		10	4400	5050
19	4	OUTRAGE	OP	UTL	FBG	TR	IO	165		7	4	2400	1		4550	5200
19	4	REVENGE	OP	RNBT	FBG	TR	IO	165		7	4	2600	1		4300	5000
19	4	REVENGE	OP	UTL	FBG	TR	OB			7	4	1600		10	4600	5300
21	4	OUTRAGE	OP	FSH	FBG	TR	OB			7	4	1600		10	5600	6450
21	4	REVENGE	OP	RNBT	FBG	TR	OB			7	4	1800		10	6350	7250
		1974 BOATS														
16	7		OP	BASS	FBG	TR	OB			6	7	950			3050	3550
16	7	CURRITUCK	OP	UTL	FBG	TR	OB			6	2	650			2000	2400
16	7	KATAMA	OP	UTL	FBG	TR	OB			6	7	700			2250	2600
16	7	MONTAUK	OP	UTL	FBG	TR	OB			6	2	850			2650	3050
16	7	SAKONNET	OP	UTL	FBG	TR	OB			6	7	900			2800	3250
19	4	OUTRAGE	OP	UTL	FBG	TR	OB			7	4	1500			4200	4900
19	4	REVENGE	OP	UTL	FBG	TR	OB			7	4	1500			4500	5150
21	4	OUTRAGE	OP	FSH	FBG	TR	OB			7	4	1600			5550	6400
21	4	REVENGE	OP	RNBT	FBG	TR	OB			7	4	1800			6300	7200
		1973 BOATS														
16	7			BASS	FBG		OB			6	2	800			2600	3050
16	7	COHASSET			FBG	TR	OB			6	2	800			2650	3050
16	7	CURRITUCK	OP	UTL	FBG	TR	OB			6	2	650			2000	2400
16	7	KATAMA	OP	UTL	FBG	TR	OB			6	2	800			2350	2700
16	7	NAUSET			FBG	TR	OB			6	2	800			2300	2700
16	7	SAKONNET	OP	UTL	FBG	TR	OB			6	2	800			2650	3050
16	7	TASHMOO			FBG	TR	OB			6	2	800			2850	3300
19	4	BOSTON-WHALER 19			FBG	TR	OB			7	4	1350			4550	5200
21	4	OUTRAGE	OP	FSH	FBG	TR	OB			7	4	1600			5550	6350
		1972 BOATS														
16	7			BASS	FBG		OB			6	2	800			2600	3050
16	7	EASTPORT			FBG		OB			6	2	800			2600	3000
16	7	KATAMA			FBG		OB			6	2	800			2450	2850
16	7	MINOT			FBG		OB			6	2	750			2450	2850
16	7	NAUSET			FBG		OB			6	2	800			2400	2800
16	7	SAKONNET			FBG		OB			6	2	800			2800	3250
16	7	TASHMOO			FBG		OB			6	2	800			2750	3200
21	4	OUTRAGE BARE HULL	OP	FSH	FBG		OB			7	4	1550			5350	6150
21	4	OUTRAGE I	OP	FSH	FBG		OB			7	4	1750			5950	6850
21	4	OUTRAGE II	OP	FSH	FBG		OB			7	4	1800			6050	7000
21	4	OUTRAGE III	OP	FSH	FBG		OB			7	4	1650			5650	6500
		1971 BOATS														
16	7	CURRITUCK	OP	RNBT	FBG		OB			6	2	700			2350	2700
16	7	EASTPORT	OP	RNBT	FBG		OB			6	2	800			2650	3100
16	7	KATAMA	OP	RNBT	FBG		OB			6	2	800			2500	2900
16	7	MENEMSHA	OP	CR	FBG		OB			6	2	1200			3750	4350
16	7	MINOT	OP	RNBT	FBG		OB			6	2	750			2450	2850
16	7	NAUSET	OP	RNBT	FBG		OB			6	2	800			2450	2850
16	7	SAKONNET	OP	RNBT	FBG		OB			6	2	800			2900	3350

 CONTINUED ON NEXT PAGE

```
BOSTON WHALER INC          -CONTINUED      See inside cover to adjust price for area
   LOA   NAME AND/              TOP/ BOAT  -HULL- ----ENGINE---  BEAM   WGT  DRAFT RETAIL RETAIL
  FT IN  OR MODEL               RIG  TYPE  MTL TP TP # HP MFG   FT IN   LBS  FT IN  LOW    HIGH
------------------------- 1971 BOATS ----------------------------------------------------------
  21  4  OUTRAGE               OP  FSH   FBG     OB              7   4  1600         5500   6300
------------------------- 1970 BOATS ----------------------------------------------------------
  16  7  CURRITUCK             OP  RNBT  FBG     OB              6   2   700         2350   2700
  16  7  EASTPORT              OP  RNBT  FBG     OB              6   2   800         2700   3100
  16  7  KATAMA                OP  RNBT  FBG     OB              6   2   800         2450   2850
  16  7  MENEMSHA              OP  CR    FBG     OB              6   2  1200         3750   4350
  16  7  MINOT                 OP  RNBT  FBG     OB              6   2   750         2450   2850
  16  7  NAUSET                OP  RNBT  FBG     OB              6   2   800         2450   2850
  16  7  SAKONNET              OP  RNBT  FBG     OB              6   2   800         2900   3400
------------------------- 1969 BOATS ----------------------------------------------------------
  16  7  CURRITUCK             OP  RNBT  FBG     OB              6   2   700         2300   2700
  16  7  EASTPORT              OP  RNBT  FBG     OB              6   2   900         2900   3400
  16  7  KATAMA                OP  RNBT  FBG     OB              6   2   800         2550   2950
  16  7  MENEMSHA              OP  CR    FBG     OB              6   2  1200         3750   4350
  16  7  MINOT                 OP  RNBT  FBG     OB              6   2   750         2500   2900
  16  7  NAUSET                OP  RNBT  FBG     OB              6   2   800         2700   3150
  16  7  SAKONNET              OP  RNBT  FBG     OB              6   2   900         2950   3400
------------------------- 1968 BOATS ----------------------------------------------------------
  16  7  CURRITUCK             OP  RNBT  FBG     OB              6   2   700         2350   2700
  16  7  EASTPORT              OP  RNBT  FBG     OB              6   2   900         2950   3400
  16  7  MENEMSHA              OP  CR    FBG     OB              6   2  1200         3750   4350
  16  7  NAUSET                OP  RNBT  FBG     OB              6   2   800         2650   3050
  16  7  SAKONNET              OP  RNBT  FBG     OB              6   2   900         2950   3450
------------------------- 1967 BOATS ----------------------------------------------------------
  16  7  EASTPORT              OP  RNBT  FBG     OB              6   2   500         2050   2450
  16  7  NAUSET                OP  RNBT  FBG     OB              6   2   500         1750   2050
  16  7  SAKONNET              OP  RNBT  FBG     OB              6   2   500         2050   2450
------------------------- 1966 BOATS ----------------------------------------------------------
  16  7  EASTPORT              OP  RNBT  FBG     OB              6   2   500         2050   2450
  16  7  NAUSET                OP  RNBT  FBG     OB              6   2   500         1750   2100
  16  7  SAKONNET              OP  RNBT  FBG     OB              6   2   500         2050   2450
------------------------- 1965 BOATS ----------------------------------------------------------
  16  7  EASTPORT              OP  RNBT  FBG     OB              6   2   500         2050   2400
  16  7  NAUSET                OP  RNBT  FBG     OB              6   2   500         1750   2100
  16  7  SAKONNET              OP  RNBT  FBG     OB              6   2   500         2100   2450
------------------------- 1964 BOATS ----------------------------------------------------------
  16  7  EASTPORT              OP  RNBT  FBG     OB              6   2   500         2050   2450
  16  7  NAUSET                OP  RNBT  FBG     OB              6   2   500         1750   2100
  16  7  SAKONNET              OP  RNBT  FBG     OB              6   2   500         2100   2500
------------------------- 1963 BOATS ----------------------------------------------------------
  16  7  EASTPORT              OP  RNBT  FBG     OB              6   2   500         2000   2350
  16  7  NAUSET                OP  RNBT  FBG     OB              6   2   500         1700   2050
  16  7  SAKONNET              OP  RNBT  FBG     OB              6   2   500         2050   2400
------------------------- 1962 BOATS ----------------------------------------------------------
  16  7  BARE HULL             OP  RNBT  FBG     OB              6   2   500         1750   2050
  16  7  EASTPORT              OP  RNBT  FBG     OB              6   2   500         1750   2050
  16  7  NAUSET                OP  RNBT  FBG     OB              6   2   500         1750   2050
------------------------- 1961 BOATS ----------------------------------------------------------
  16  7  EASTPORT              OP  RNBT  FBG     OB              6   2   500         1750   2100
  17     NAUSET                OP  RNBT  FBG     OB              6   2   500         1800   2150
```

BOSWORTH MARINE

Call 1-800-327-6929 for BUC Personalized Evaluation Service
Or, for 1965 boats, sign onto www.BUCValuPro.com

BOTNIA-MARIN OY AB

Call 1-800-327-6929 for BUC Personalized Evaluation Service
Or, for 1980 to 1996 boats, sign onto www.BUCValuPro.com

BOUNTY ENTERPRISES INC
COAST GUARD MFG ID- BFK

Call 1-800-327-6929 for BUC Personalized Evaluation Service
Or, for 1979 to 1983 boats, sign onto www.BUCValuPro.com

BOW MARINE
COAST GUARD MFG ID- BWM

Call 1-800-327-6929 for BUC Personalized Evaluation Service
Or, for 1965 to 1980 boats, sign onto www.BUCValuPro.com

BOWLAND MARINE
COAST GUARD MFG ID- BWZ

Call 1-800-327-6929 for BUC Personalized Evaluation Service
Or, for 1983 boats, sign onto www.BUCValuPro.com

BOWMAN MANUFACTURERS INC

Call 1-800-327-6929 for BUC Personalized Evaluation Service
Or, for 1959 to 1969 boats, sign onto www.BUCValuPro.com

BOWMAN YACHTS
DIV OF EMSWORTH MARINE SALES   See inside cover to adjust price for area
EMSWORTH ENGLAND

```
   LOA   NAME AND/              TOP/ BOAT  -HULL- ----ENGINE---  BEAM    WGT  DRAFT RETAIL RETAIL
  FT IN  OR MODEL               RIG  TYPE  MTL TP TP # HP MFG   FT IN    LBS  FT IN  LOW    HIGH
------------------------- 1982 BOATS -----------------------------------------------------------
  49  3  BOWMAN 49            CUT  SA/CR FBG KL IB   70D PERK  14      28800  7   6 184500 202500
  49  3  BOWMAN 49            KTH  SA/CR FBG KL IB   70D PERK  14      28800  5  10 184500 202500
  57     BOWMAN 57            KTH  SA/CR FBG CB IB   70D PERK  14   8  41300  5  10 286000 314000
  57     BOWMAN 57            KTH  SA/CR FBG KL IB   70D PERK  14   8  41300  8   4 286000 314000
  70     BOWMAN 70            KTH  SA/CR FBG KL IB T120D PERK  17   1    50T  8   6 609000 669500
------------------------- 1978 BOATS -----------------------------------------------------------
  36  8  BOWMAN 36            SLP  SAIL  FBG KC IB   47D PERK  11   4  17100  3   9  65600  72100
  36  8  BOWMAN 36            SLP  SAIL  FBG KL IB   47D PERK  11   4  18600  5   6  70400  77300
  36  8  BOWMAN 36            KTH  SAIL  FBG KC IB   47D PERK  11   4  17100  3   9  65600  72100
  36  8  BOWMAN 36            KTH  SAIL  FBG KL IB   47D PERK  11   4  18600  5   6  70400  77300
  40     BOWMAN 40            SLP  SAIL  FBG KL IB   47D PERK  11   1  18570  5   4  81400  89400
  44  4  BOWMAN CORSAIR       SLP  SAIL  FBG KC IB   47D PERK  12  11  23500  3   1 115600 126000
  44  4  BOWMAN CORSAIR       SLP  SAIL  FBG KL IB   47D PERK  12  11  23500  7   3 115600 126000
  44  4  BOWMAN CORSAIR       YWL  SAIL  FBG KC IB   47D PERK  12  11  23500  3   1 115600 126000
  44  4  BOWMAN CORSAIR       YWL  SAIL  FBG KL IB   47D PERK  12  11  23500  7   3 115600 126000
  44 11  BOWMAN 45            SLP  SAIL  FBG KC IB   47D PERK  13      21370  7     113500 124500
  44 11  BOWMAN 45            SLP  SAIL  FBG KL IB   47D PERK  13      21370  5   8 113500 124500
  44 11  BOWMAN 45 SHOAL      SLP  SAIL  FBG KL IB   47D PERK  13      21370  5   8 113500 124500

  44 11  BOWMAN 45 SHOAL      KTH  SAIL  FBG KL IB   47D PERK  13      21370  5   8 113500 124500
  45  8  BOWMAN 46            SLP  SAIL  FBG KC IB   47D PERK  12  11  23500  5   3 123500 135500
  45  8  BOWMAN 46            SLP  SAIL  FBG KL IB   47D PERK  12  11  23500  5   3 123500 135500
  45  8  BOWMAN 46            YWL  SAIL  FBG KC IB   47D PERK  12  11  23500  5   3 123500 135500
  45  8  BOWMAN 46            YWL  SAIL  FBG KL IB   47D PERK  12  11  23500  7   3 123500 135500
  48 11  BOWMAN 49            FB   CR    FBG SV IB T200D CAT   15   3  36000  4   6  96800 106500
  54     BOWMAN 54            KTH  MS    STL KL IB T 70D FORD  14      51520  8   6 216500 238000
  57     BOWMAN 57            SLP  SAIL  FBG KC IB   72D PERK  14   8  41276  9     245000 269500
  57     BOWMAN 57            SLP  SAIL  FBG KL IB   72D PERK  14   8  41276  8   4 245000 269500
  57     BOWMAN 57            CUT  SAIL  FBG KC IB   72D PERK  14   8  41276  5   9 245000 269500
  57     BOWMAN 57            CUT  SAIL  FBG KL IB   72D PERK  14   8  41276  7     245000 269500

  57     BOWMAN 57            KTH  SAIL  FBG KL IB   72D PERK  14   8  41276  8   4 245000 269500
  57     BOWMAN 57 DEEP DRAFT SLP  SAIL  FBG KL IB   72D PERK  14   8  41276  8   4 245000 269500
  57     BOWMAN 57 DEEP DRAFT CUT  SAIL  FBG KL IB   72D PERK  14   8  41276  8   4 245000 269500
  57     BOWMAN 57 DEEP DRAFT KTH  SAIL  FBG KL IB   72D PERK  14   8  41276  8   4 245000 269500
  61     ENDURANCE 61         SLP  SAIL  FBG KC IB  100D SABB  15   3  57640  4   6 306500 336500
  61     ENDURANCE 61         SLP  SAIL  FBG KL IB  100D SABB  15   3  57640 10   0 306500 336500
  61     ENDURANCE 61         KTH  SAIL  FBG KC IB  100D SABB  15   3  57640  4   6 306500 336500
  61     ENDURANCE 61         KTH  SAIL  FBG KL IB  100D SABB  15   3  57640 10   0 306500 336500
  66     BOWMAN 66            KTH  SAIL  FBG KC IB  140D PERK  16   5  79520  8     412000 452500
  66     BOWMAN 66            KTH  SAIL  FBG KL IB  140D PERK  16   5  79520  8     412000 452500
------------------------- 1977 BOATS -----------------------------------------------------------
  36     BOWMAN 36            SLP  SA/CR FBG KC IB   47D PERK  11   4  18000  3   9  65600  72000
  36     BOWMAN 36            SLP  SA/CR FBG KL IB   47D PERK  11   4  18000  3   9  65600  72000
  36     BOWMAN 36            KTH  SA/CR FBG KC IB   47D PERK  11   4  18000  3   9  65600  72000
  36     BOWMAN 36            KTH  SA/CR FBG KL IB   47D PERK  11   4  18000  3   9  65600  72000
  40     BOWMAN 40            SLP  SA/CR FBG KL IB   47D PERK  11   4  23520  5   4  92900 102000
  44  4  BOWMAN-CORSAIR       SLP  SA/CR FBG KC IB   47D PERK  12  11  23500  3   1 111500 123000
  44  4  BOWMAN-CORSAIR       SLP  SA/CR FBG KL IB   47D PERK  12  11  23500  7   3 111500 123000
  44  4  BOWMAN-CORSAIR       YWL  SA/CR FBG KC IB   47D PERK  12  11  23500  3   1 111500 123000
  44  4  BOWMAN-CORSAIR       YWL  SA/CR FBG KL IB   47D PERK  12  11  23500  7   3 111500 123000
  44  9  BOWMAN 45            YWL  SAIL  FBG KL IB   47D PERK  13      21370  7     109500 120000
  44  9  BOWMAN 45            YWL  SAIL  FBG KL IB   47D PERK  13      21370  5   8 109500 120000
  45  7  BOWMAN 46            SLP  SA/CR FBG KL IB   47D PERK  12  11  23500  7     119500 131500

  45  7  BOWMAN 46            SLP  SA/CR FBG KC IB   47D PERK  12  11  23500  7     119500 131500
  45  7  BOWMAN 46            YWL  SA/CR FBG KC IB   47D PERK  12  11  23500  5   3 119500 131500
```

LOA FT IN	NAME AND/ OR MODEL	TOP/ RIG	BOAT TYPE	-HULL- MTL TP TP	----ENGINE--- # HP MFG	BEAM FT IN	WGT LBS	DRAFT FT IN	RETAIL LOW	RETAIL HIGH
--- 1977 BOATS ---										
45 7	BOWMAN 46	YWL	SA/CR	FBG KL IB	47D PERK	12 11	23500	7	119500	131500
54	BOWMAN 54	KTH	SA/CR	STL KL IB T	70D FORD	14	50000	6 6	210000	230500
57	BOWMAN 57	KTH	SA/CR	FBG KL IB	72D PERK	14 6	42000	8 3	240000	263500
74	BOWMAN 74	KTH	SA/CR	FBG KL IB	D PERK	18	74000	9	**	**
--- 1976 BOATS ---										
36	BOWMAN 36	SLP	SA/CR	FBG KC IB	47D PERK	11 4	18600	3 9	65800	72300
36	BOWMAN 36	SLP	SA/CR	FBG KC IB	47D PERK	11 4	18600	5 6	65800	72300
36	BOWMAN 36	KTH	SA/CR	FBG KC IB	47D PERK	11 4	18600	3 9	65800	72300
36	BOWMAN 36	KTH	SA/CR	FBG KL IB	47D PERK	11 4	18600	5 6	65800	72300
40	BOWMAN 40	SLP	SA/CR	FBG KL IB	47D PERK	11 1	23520	5 4	90600	99600
44 4	BOWMAN-CORSAIR	SLP	SA/CR	FBG KC IB	47D PERK	12 11	23500	5 3	109000	120000
44 4	BOWMAN-CORSAIR	SLP	SA/CR	FBG KL IB	47D PERK	12 11	23500	5 3	109000	120000
45 8	BOWMAN 46	YWL	SA/CR	FBG KC IB	47D PERK	12 11	23500	5 3	117500	129000
45 8	BOWMAN 46	YWL	SA/CR	FBG KL IB	47D PERK	12 11	23500	7	117500	129000
57	BOWMAN 57	KTH	MS	FBC KL IB	68D BENZ	14 6	42000	8 4	234500	257500

BRABOURNE MARINE LTD

Call 1-800-327-6929 for BUC Personalized Evaluation Service
Or, for 1966 to 1970 boats, sign onto www.BUCValuPro.com

BRADFORD YACHT SALES

FT LAUDERDALE FL 33312   COAST GUARD MFG ID- BYL See inside cover to adjust price for area

LOA FT IN	NAME AND/ OR MODEL	TOP/ RIG	BOAT TYPE	-HULL- MTL TP TP	----ENGINE--- # HP MFG	BEAM FT IN	WGT LBS	DRAFT FT IN	RETAIL LOW	RETAIL HIGH
--- 1979 BOATS ---										
25	RUM-RUNNER	CUD		AL SV IB	T185D PERK	11	7800	2 2	21500	23900
--- 1978 BOATS ---										
25	CENTER CONSOLE		CTRCN	AL SV IB	T185D	11	7800		20000	22200
72		HT	MY	AL SV IB	T650D	19 2	60000		**	**
--- 1968 BOATS ---										
39	SALAR 39	KTH	MS	FBG	D	11 3		5 3	52500	57700
63	DELFINO		MY	STL	IB T350	17		4 9	279000	306500
63	DELFINO		MY	STL	IB T530	17		4 9	282000	310000
72	GABBIANO		MY	STL	IB T700	17		3 8	**	**

BRANSON BOAT CO

COAST GUARD MFG ID- BBY

Call 1-800-327-6929 for BUC Personalized Evaluation Service
Or, for 1965 to 1975 boats, sign onto www.BUCValuPro.com

BRERONS INC

COAST GUARD MFG ID- TVS

Call 1-800-327-6929 for BUC Personalized Evaluation Service
Or, for 1976 to 1977 boats, sign onto www.BUCValuPro.com

BREUIL BOAT COMPANY

ENTERPRISE YACHTS   See inside cover to adjust price for area
MIAMI FL   COAST GUARD MFG ID- XBV

LOA FT IN	NAME AND/ OR MODEL	TOP/ RIG	BOAT TYPE	-HULL- MTL TP TP	----ENGINE--- # HP MFG	BEAM FT IN	WGT LBS	DRAFT FT IN	RETAIL LOW	RETAIL HIGH
--- 1971 BOATS ---										
36 6		FB	SF	FBG	IB T210D	12 6		2 6	49500	54400
--- 1967 BOATS ---										
26		OP		FBG	IO 210				16400	18700
27			UTL	FBG	IB T170 SEA				9150	10400
31		FB	EXP	FBG	IB T210				19600	21800
36		FB	SDN	FBG	IB T300 CHRY				33400	37200
--- 1966 BOATS ---										
27		FB	EXP	FBG	IB T225				10400	11800
28 1	ENTERPRISE		EXP	WD	IB 225 CHRY	9 4		2 5	10800	12300
28 1	ENTERPRISE	FB	SF	FBG	IB T210 CHRY	9 4		2 5	11900	13500
28 1	ENTERPRISE		UTL	FBG	IB T210	9 4		2 5	10200	11600
31 6	ENTERPRISE DLX		SDN	FBG	IB T210	11 2		2 5	19700	21800
31 6	ENTERPRISE DLX	FB	SF	FBG	IB T210	11 2		2 5	16000	18200
35 9	ENTERPRISE DLX		EXP	FBG	IB T210	13 3		2 6	26800	29700
35 9	ENTERPRISE DLX		SDN	FBG	IB T210	13 3		2 6	29400	32600
35 9	ENTERPRISE DLX	FB	SF	FBG	IB T300 CHRY	13 3		2 6	29000	32200
--- 1965 BOATS ---										
18	ENTERPRISE		RNBT	FBG	OB				3550	4150
18	ENTERPRISE		RNBT	FBG	IO 110				5200	5950
27 4		OP	UTL	FBG	IB 210				7800	8950
27 4		OP	UTL	FBG	IB T210				9200	10500
27 4	SPORT		CR	FBG	IB 225-325				9400	11300

IB 250D DAY 15600 17700, IB T225-T325 10700 13100, IB T380 DAY 12100 13800
IB T140D 17000 19300

31 6			EXP	FBG	IO T190-T310				43000	51900
31 6			EXP	FBG	IO D				**	**
31 6		FB	SF	FBG	IO T190-T310				40300	49100
31 6		FB	SF	FBG	IO D				**	**
31 6	DELUXE		SDN	FBG	IO T190-T310				43000	52500
31 6	DELUXE		SDN	FBG	IO D				**	**
31 6	SPORT		UTL	FBG	IO T190-T310				36000	43700
31 6	SPORT		UTL	FBG	IO T D				**	**
36			FB CR	FBG	IB T224				27800	30900

IB T225 27800 30900, IB T280 28200 31400, IB T325 28700 31900
IB T380 29600 32800, IB T195D 36300 40400

36			SDN	FBG	IB T224				30900	34300

IB T225 30900 34300, IB T280 31400 34900, IB T325 32000 35500
IB T380 32900 36500, IB T195D 43600 48500

36	DELUXE		SF	FBG	IB T224				30000	33300

IB T225 30000 33300, IB T280 30400 33800, IB T325 30900 34300
IB T380 31600 35100, IB T195D 37900 42100

37			SF	FBG	IB				**	**
37	VOYAGER		DC	FBG	IB T225 GRAY				40300	44700
42			DCMY	FBG	IB T275				56500	62100
42			SF	FBG	IB T275				36800	40900
42	INFERNO		SAIL	FBG	IB				47400	52100
--- 1964 BOATS ---										
28		OP	UTL	FBG	IB T190				10600	12100
36			SDN	FBG	IB T290 CHRY				30700	34100
36		FB	SDN	FBG	IB T300 HOLM				30900	34300
--- 1963 BOATS ---										
31 6	CUSTOM		SF	FBG	IB T280				14900	16900
31 6	SC CUSTOM		SF	FBG	IO T310				47500	52200
36 9	CUSTOM		SF	WD	IB T280				32100	35600
41 11	CUSTOM		SPTCR	WD	IB T280				46500	51100
--- 1962 BOATS ---										
35	ENTERPRISE		EXP	WD	IB T230				23400	26000
35	ENTERPRISE		SF	WD	IB T230				20900	23200
--- 1961 BOATS ---										
35 4	ENTERPRISE 35			WD	IB T225	13 3		2 6	23700	26300
42 4	ENTERPRISE 42			WD	IB T275	14 6		2 9	57600	63300
--- 1960 BOATS ---										
35			SF	WD	IB 225				18900	21000
35			SF	WD	IB 225				20000	22200
40			SF	WD	IB 225				41900	46600
40			SF	WD	IB T225				42900	47700
42			SDN	WD	IB 275				51300	56400
42			SDN	WD	IB 275				53800	59100
42			SF	WD	IB 275				25100	27900
42			SF	WD	IB 275				31600	35100
--- 1959 BOATS ---										
35			SF	L/P	IB T225	13 8			19500	21600
40			SF	L/P	IB T225	13 8			41300	45900

BREVARD BOAT WORKS INC

FLEETWING   COAST GUARD MFG ID- BVD

Call 1-800-327-6929 for BUC Personalized Evaluation Service
Or, for 1970 to 1973 boats, sign onto www.BUCValuPro.com

BRIGHTON YACHTS INC

DELTA CLIPPER   See inside cover to adjust price for area
LA VERGNE TN 37167   COAST GUARD MFG ID- BYA

LOA FT IN	NAME AND/ OR MODEL	TOP/ RIG	BOAT TYPE	-HULL- MTL TP TP	----ENGINE--- # HP MFG	BEAM FT IN	WGT LBS	DRAFT FT IN	RETAIL LOW	RETAIL HIGH
--- 1977 BOATS ---										
37	DELTA-CLIPPER 37A	HT	HB	FBG DV IO	255 MRCR	12	15000	2 10	21000	23400
37	DELTA-CLIPPER 37A	FB	HB	FBG DV IO	255 MRCR	12	15000	2 10	21000	23300

```
BRIGHTON YACHTS INC          -CONTINUED        See inside cover to adjust price for area
 LOA   NAME AND/       TOP/ BOAT  -HULL-  ----ENGINE---  BEAM    WGT   DRAFT  RETAIL  RETAIL
FT IN  OR MODEL        RIG TYPE  MTL TP TP # HP  MFG     FT IN   LBS   FT IN  LOW     HIGH
-------------------- 1977 BOATS --------------------------------------------------------------
37    DELTA-CLIPPER 37A    FB  HB    FBG DV VD T165  PCM  12     15000  2 10  21800   24200
      IO T233  MRCR  22300  24800, VD T233  MRCR  22000  24500, IO T255  MRCR  22900   25500
      VD T255  MRCR  21800  24200, VD T255  PCM   22100  24600
37    DELTA-CLIPPER 37B    HT  HB    FBG DV IO  233   MRCR 12    15000  2 10  20600   22900
      IO  255  MRCR  20600  22900, VD T165  PCM   21100  23400, IO T233  MRCR  22200   24700
      VD T233  MRCR  21300  23700, IO T255  MRCR  22300  24800, VD T255  MRCR  21400   23800
37    DELTA-CLIPPER 37B    FB  HB    FBG DV IO  233   MRCR 12    15000  2 10  20600   22900
      IO  255  MRCR  20600  22900, VD T165  PCM   21100  23500, IO T233  MRCR  22200   24700
      VD T233  MRCR  21400  23800, IO T255  MRCR  22400  24900, VD T255  MRCR  21500   23900
43    DELTA-CLIPPER 43     HT  HB    FBG DV VD T233  MRCR 12     19000  2 10  22600   25100
      IO T255  MRCR  23500  26100, VD T255  MRCR  22700  25200, VD T255  PCM   22700   25200
43    DELTA-CLIPPER 43     FB  HB    FBG DV VD T233  MRCR 12     19000  2 10  22600   25100
      IO T255  MRCR  23500  26100, VD T255  MRCR  22700  25200, VD T255  PCM   22700   25200
-------------------- 1976 BOATS --------------------------------------------------------------
30    DELTA-CLIPPER 30     HT  HB    FBG SV IO  165-255  9   6  12000  1  3  17200   20000
      VD T165  PCM   18600  20700, IO T225  MRCR  19100  21300, VD T225  PCM   18900   21000
      IO T255  MRCR  19600  21700, VD T255  PCM   19000  21100
37    DELTA-CLIPPER 37A    HT  HB    FBG SV IO  255   MRCR 12    15000   3    20500   22800
      VD T165  PCM   21200  23600, IO T225  MRCR  21900  24300, IO T233  MRCR  22000   24400
      VD T233  MRCR  21500  23900, IO T255  MRCR  22300  24800, VD T255  MRCR  21600   24000
      VD T255  PCM   21600  24000
37    DELTA-CLIPPER 37A    FB  HB    FBG SV IO  255   MRCR 12    15000   3    20500   22800
      VD T165  PCM   21200  23600, IO T225  MRCR  21900  24300, IO T233  MRCR  22000   24400
      VD T233  MRCR  21500  23900, IO T255  MRCR  22300  24800, VD T255  MRCR  21600   24000
      VD T255  PCM   21600  24000
37    DELTA-CLIPPER 37B    HT  HB    FBG SV IO  225   MRCR 12    16500   3    21400   23800
      IO  233  MRCR  21400  23800, IO  255  MRCR  21600  24000, VD T165  PCM   22300   24800
      IO T225  MRCR  22900  25500, VD T225  PCM   22500  25000, IO T233  MRCR  23000   25600
      VD T233  MRCR  22600  25100, IO T255  MRCR  23400  26000, VD T255  MRCR  22600   25200
37    DELTA-CLIPPER 37B    FB  HB    FBG SV IO  225   MRCR 12    16500   3    21400   23800
      IO  233  MRCR  21400  23800, IO  255  MRCR  21600  24000, VD T165  PCM   22300   24800
      IO T225  MRCR  22900  25500, VD T225  PCM   22500  25000, IO T233  MRCR  23000   25600
      VD T233  MRCR  22600  25100, IO T255  MRCR  23400  26000, VD T255  MRCR  22600   25200
43    DELTA-CLIPPER 43     HT  HB    FBG SV VD T233  MRCR 12    21000   3    23400   26000
      IO T255  MRCR  24300  27000, VD T255  MRCR  23500  26100, VD T255  PCM   23500   26100
43    DELTA-CLIPPER 43     FB  HB    FBG SV VD T233  MRCR 12    21000   3    23400   26000
      IO T255  MRCR  24300  27000, VD T255  MRCR  23500  26100, VD T255  PCM   23500   26100
-------------------- 1975 BOATS --------------------------------------------------------------
37    DELTA-CLIPPER 37A    HT  HB    FBG SV IO  255   MRCR 12    15000  2 10  20700   23000
      VD T165  PCM   21400  23700, IO T225  MRCR  22000  24500, VD T225  MRCR  21000   23300
      IO T255  MRCR  22400  24900, VD T255  PCM   21300  23700
37    DELTA-CLIPPER 37A    FB  HB    FBG SV IO  255   MRCR 12    15000  2 10  20700   23000
      VD T165  PCM   21300  23700, IO T225  MRCR  22000  24400, VD T225  MRCR  21000   23400
      IO T255  MRCR  22300  24800, VD T255  PCM   21300  23700
37    DELTA-CLIPPER 37B    HT  HB    FBG SV IO  225   MRCR 12    15000  2 10  20100   22300
      IO  255  MRCR  20000  22200, VD T165  PCM   20700  23000, IO T225  MRCR  21300   23600
      VD T225  PCM   21500  23900, IO T255  MRCR  21800  24200
37    DELTA-CLIPPER 37B    FB  HB    FBG SV IO  225   MRCR 12    15000  2 10  20100   22300
      IO  255  MRCR  20000  22300, VD T165  PCM   20700  23000, IO T225  MRCR  21300   23700
      VD T225  PCM   21400  23800, IO T255  MRCR  21800  24200
43    DELTA-CLIPPER 43     HT  HB    FBG SV VD T233       12    21000  2 10  23200   25700
43    DELTA-CLIPPER 43     HT  HB    FBG SV IO  T255  MRCR 12    21000  2 10  24000   26700
43    DELTA-CLIPPER 43     HT  HB    FBG SV VD T255  PCM  12     21000  2 10  23200   25700
43    DELTA-CLIPPER 43     FB  HB    FBG SV VD T233  MRCR 12     21000  2 10  23200   25700
43    DELTA-CLIPPER 43     FB  HB    FBG SV IO  T255  MRCR 12    21000  2 10  24000   26700
43    DELTA-CLIPPER 43     FB  HB    FBG SV VD T255  PCM  12     21000  2 10  23200   25800
-------------------- 1973 BOATS --------------------------------------------------------------
37    DELTA-CLIPPER 37     HT  HB    FBG SV VD  255       12    15000  2 10  20000   22200
43    DELTA-CLIPPER 43     HT  HB    FBG SV VD T233       12    19000  2 10  21600   24000
-------------------- 1972 BOATS --------------------------------------------------------------
37    DELTA-CLIPPER       HT  HB    FBG SV IO  225       12            1  8  19800   22000
43    DELTA-CLIPPER       HT  HB    FBG SV IB T225       12            2     22100   24500
```

BRIGHTON YACHTS LTD
COAST GUARD MFG ID- ZBR

Call 1-800-327-6929 for BUC Personalized Evaluation Service
Or, for 1981 to 1983 boats, sign onto www.BUCValuPro.com

BRISTOL BLUEWATER BOATS INC
COAST GUARD MFG ID- BXD

Call 1-800-327-6929 for BUC Personalized Evaluation Service
Or, for 1977 to 1983 boats, sign onto www.BUCValuPro.com

BRISTOL BOAT COMPANY
BRISTOL RI 02809   COAST GUARD MFG ID- BTY See inside cover to adjust price for area
                        FOR OLDER MODELS SEE SAILSTAR BOATS INC

For more recent years, see the BUC Used Boat Price Guide, Volume 1 or Volume 2

```
 LOA   NAME AND/       TOP/ BOAT  -HULL-  ----ENGINE---  BEAM    WGT   DRAFT  RETAIL  RETAIL
FT IN  OR MODEL        RIG TYPE  MTL TP TP # HP  MFG     FT IN   LBS   FT IN  LOW     HIGH
-------------------- 1983 BOATS --------------------------------------------------------------
19  7  BRISTOL 19      SLP SAIL   FBG KL                  6   6  2724   2  9   5950    6850
24  7  BRISTOL 24      SLP SA/CR  FBG KL  IB      D      10      5920   3  5  16200   18400
27  3  BRISTOL 27.7    SLP SA/CR  FBG KL  IB      D      10      7000   3  5  21700   24100
29 11  BRISTOL 29.9    SLP SA/RC  FBG KC  IB  16D UNIV   10  2  8650   3  9  28900   32300
29 11  BRISTOL 29.9    SLP SA/RC  FBG KC  IB  16D UNIV   10  2  8650   4  4  28900   32100
32  1  BRISTOL 32      SLP SA/RC  FBG KC  IB  16D UNIV    9  5 11300   3  6  39600   44000
32  1  BRISTOL 32      SLP SA/RC  FBG KL  IB  16D UNIV    9  5 11300   3  8  39600   44000
32  1  BRISTOL 32      KTH SA/RC  FBG KC  IB  16D UNIV    9  5 11300   3  6  39600   44000
32  1  BRISTOL 32      KTH SA/RC  FBG KL  IB  16D UNIV    9  5 11300   3  8  39600   44000
35  6  BRISTOL 35.5    SLP SA/RC  FBG KC  IB  24D UNIV   10 10 15000   3  9  56400   62000
35  6  BRISTOL 35.5    SLP SA/RC  FBG KL  IB  24D UNIV   10 10 15000   5  6  56400   62000
38  4  BRISTOL 38.8    SLP SA/RC  FBG KC  IB  44D UNIV   12  1 19150   4   78500   86200
40  2  BRISTOL 40      SLP SA/RC  FBG KC  IB  40D WEST   10  9 17580   4   82400   90500
40  2  BRISTOL 40      SLP SA/RC  FBG KL  IB  40D WEST   10  9 17580   5  5  82400   90500
40  2  BRISTOL 40      YWL SA/RC  FBG KC  IB  40D WEST   10  9 17580   4   82400   90500
40  2  BRISTOL 40      YWL SA/RC  FBG KL  IB  40D WEST   10  9 17580   5  5  82400   90500
41  2  BRISTOL 41.1    SLP SA/RC  FBG KC  IB  50D WEST   12 11 26530   4  6 110500  121500
45  3  BRISTOL 45.5    SLP SA/RC  FBG KC  IB  58D WEST   13  3 34660   4 11 145500  159500
45  3  BRISTOL 45.5    SLP SA/RC  FBG KL  IB  58D WEST   13  3 34660   4 11 145500  160000
-------------------- 1982 BOATS --------------------------------------------------------------
19  7  BRISTOL 19      SLP SAIL   FBG KL  OB              6   6  2724   2  9   5500    6400
24  7  BRISTOL 24      SLP SA/CR  FBG KL  IB      D      10      5920   3  5  15100   17200
27  3  BRISTOL 27.7    SLP SA/CR  FBG KL  IB      D      10      7000   3  5  20400   22700
29 11  BRISTOL 29.9    SLP SA/RC  FBG KC  IB  15D YAN    10  2  8650   3  9  27300   30300
29 11  BRISTOL 29.9    SLP SA/RC  FBG KC  IB  15D YAN    10  2  8650   4  4  27200   30200
32  1  BRISTOL 32      SLP SA/RC  FBG KC  IB  15D YAN     9  5 11300   3  6  37000   41200
32  1  BRISTOL 32      SLP SA/RC  FBG KL  IB  15D YAN     9  5 11300   3  8  37000   41200
32  1  BRISTOL 32      YWL SA/RC  FBG KC  IB  15D YAN     9  5 11300   3  6  37100   41200
32  1  BRISTOL 32      YWL SA/RC  FBG KL  IB  15D YAN     9  5 11300   3  8  37100   41200
32  1  BRISTOL 32      KTH SA/RC  FBG KC  IB  15D YAN     9  5 11300   3  6  37000   41200
32  1  BRISTOL 32      KTH SA/RC  FBG KL  IB  15D YAN     9  5 11300   3  8  37000   41200
35  6  BRISTOL 35.5    SLP SA/RC  FBG KC  IB  22D YAN    10 10 15000   3  9  52800   58000
35  6  BRISTOL 35.5    SLP SA/RC  FBG KC  IB  22D YAN    10 10 15000   5  6  52800   58000
38  4  BRISTOL 38.8    SLP SA/RC  FBG KC  IB  44D UNIV   12  1 19150   4   73400   80700
40  2  BRISTOL 40      SLP SA/RC  FBG KC  IB  40D WEST   10  9 17580   4   77100   84700
40  2  BRISTOL 40      SLP SA/RC  FBG KL  IB  40D WEST   10  9 17580   5  5  77100   84700
40  2  BRISTOL 40      YWL SA/RC  FBG KC  IB  40D WEST   10  9 17580   4   77100   84700
40  2  BRISTOL 40      YWL SA/RC  FBG KL  IB  40D WEST   10  9 17580   5  5  77100   84700
40  2  BRISTOL 40      KTH SA/RC  FBG KC  IB      D      10  9 17580   4   76800   84400
40  2  BRISTOL 40      KTH SA/RC  FBG KL  IB      D      10  9 17580   5  5  76800   84400
41  2  BRISTOL 41.1    SLP SA/RC  FBG KC  IB  50D WEST   12 11 26530   4  6 103500  114000
45  3  BRISTOL 45.5    SLP SA/RC  FBG KC  IB  60D WEST   13  3 34660   4 11 136000  149500
45  3  BRISTOL 45.5    SLP SA/RC  FBG KL  IB  60D WEST   13  3 34660   4 11 136000  149500
-------------------- 1981 BOATS --------------------------------------------------------------
19  7  BRISTOL 19      SLP SA/CR  FBG KL  OB              6   6  2724   2  9   5200    6000
24  7  BRISTOL 24      SLP SA/CR  FBG KL  IB      D      10      5920   3  5  13500   15000
27  3  BRISTOL 27.7    SLP SA/CR  FBG KL  IB  12D YAN    10      7000   4  5  19100   21200
29 11  BRISTOL 29.9    SLP SA/RC  FBG KC  IB  15D YAN    10  2  8650   3  8  25500   28400
29 11  BRISTOL 29.9    SLP SA/RC  FBG KC  IB  15D YAN    10  2  8650   4  4  25500   28400
32  1  BRISTOL 32      SLP SA/RC  FBG KC  IB  15D YAN     9  5 11300   3  6  34700   38500
32  1  BRISTOL 32      SLP SA/CR  FBG KL  IB  15D YAN     9  5 11300   3  8  34700   38500
```

BRIGHTON YACHTS LTD

BRISTOL BOAT COMPANY -CONTINUED See inside cover to adjust price for area

LOA FT	LOA IN	NAME AND/ OR MODEL	TOP/ RIG	BOAT TYPE	-HULL- MTL	-HULL- TP	ENGINE TP	ENGINE # HP	ENGINE MFG	BEAM FT	BEAM IN	WGT LBS	DRAFT FT	DRAFT IN	RETAIL LOW	RETAIL HIGH
		1981 BOATS														
32	1	BRISTOL 32	YWL	SA/CR	FBG	KC	IB	D		9	5	11300	4	8	34700	38500
32	1	BRISTOL 32	YWL	SA/CR	FBG	KL	IB	D		9	5	11300	4	8	34700	38500
32	1	BRISTOL 32	KTH	SA/CR	FBG	KC	IB	15D	YAN	9	5	11300	3	6	34700	38500
32	1	BRISTOL 32	KTH	SA/CR	FBG	KL	IB	15D	YAN	9	5	11300	4	8	34700	38500
35	6	BRISTOL 35.5	SLP	SA/CR	FBG	KC	IB	22D	YAN	10	10	15000	3	9	49400	54300
35	6	BRISTOL 35.5	SLP	SA/CR	FBG	KL	IB	22D	YAN	10	10	15000	5	9	49400	54300
40	2	BRISTOL 40	SLP	SA/CR	FBG	KC	IB	40D	WEST	10	9	17580	4		72200	79300
40	2	BRISTOL 40	SLP	SA/CR	FBG	KL	IB	40D	WEST	10	9	17580	5	5	72200	79300
40	2	BRISTOL 40	YWL	SA/CR	FBG	KC	IB	40D	WEST	10	9	17580	4		72200	79300
40	2	BRISTOL 40	YWL	SA/CR	FBG	KL	IB	40D	WEST	10	9	17580	5	5	72200	79300
40	2	BRISTOL 40	KTH	SA/RC	FBG	KC	IB	D		10	9	17580	5	5	71900	79000
40	2	BRISTOL 40	KTH	SA/RC	FBG	KL	IB	D		10	9	17580	5	5	71900	79000
41	2	BRISTOL 41.1	SLP	SA/CR	FBG	KC	IB	50D	WEST	12	11	26530	4	6	97000	106500
41	2	BRISTOL 41.1	KTH	SA/RC	FBG	KC	IB	D		12	11	26530	4	6	97000	106500
45	3	BRISTOL 45.5	SLP	SA/CR	FBG	KC	IB	60D	WEST	13	3	34660	4	11	127500	140000
45	3	BRISTOL 45.5	KTH	SA/CR	FBG	KC	IB	60D	WEST	13	3	34660	4	11	127500	140000
		1980 BOATS														
19	7	BRISTOL 19	SLP	SA/CR	FBG	KL	OB			6	6	2724	2	9	4950	5700
24	7	BRISTOL 24	SLP	SA/CR	FBG	KL	OB			8		5920	3	5	12600	14300
27	3	BRISTOL 27.7	SLP	SA/CR	FBG	KL	IB	12D	YAN	10		7000	4	5	18300	20300
29	11	BRISTOL 29.9	SLP	SA/CR	FBG	KL	IB	15D	YAN	10	2	8650	4	4	24300	27000
32		BRISTOL 32	SLP	SA/CR	FBG	KL	IB	15D	YAN	9	5	11300	4	8	32900	36600
32	1	BRISTOL 32	SLP	SA/CR	FBG	CB	IB	15D	YAN	9	5	11300			33000	36600
32	1	BRISTOL 32	YWL	SA/CR	FBG	CB	IB	15D	YAN	9	5	11300			33000	36600
32	1	BRISTOL 32	YWL	SA/CR	FBG	KL	IB	15D	YAN	9	5	11300	4	8	33000	36600
35	6	BRISTOL 35.5	SLP	SA/RC	FBG	CB	IB	22D	YAN	10	10	15000			47300	52000
35	6	BRISTOL 35.5	SLP	SA/RC	FBG	KL	IB	22D	YAN	10	10	15000	5	9	47300	52000
40	2	BRISTOL 40	SLP	SA/RC	FBG	CB	IB	40D	WEST	10	9	17580			68600	75400
40	2	BRISTOL 40	SLP	SA/RC	FBG	KL	IB	40D	WEST	10	9	17580	5	5	68600	75400
40	2	BRISTOL 40	KTH	SA/RC	FBG	CB	IB	40D	WEST	10	9	17580			68600	75400
40	2	BRISTOL 40	KTH	SA/RC	FBG	KL	IB	40D	WEST	10	9	17580	5	5	68600	75400
45	3	BRISTOL 45.5	SLP	SA/RC	FBG	CB	IB	60D	WEST	13	3	34664			121000	133000
		1979 BOATS														
19	7	BRISTOL 19	SLP	SA/CR	FBG	KL	OB			6	6	2724	2	9	4750	5450
24	7	BRISTOL 24	SLP	SA/CR	FBG	KL	OB			8		5920	3	5	12000	13700
24	7	BRISTOL 24	SLP	SA/CR	FBG	KL	IB	12D	YAN	8		5920	3	5	12900	14600
27	3	BRISTOL 27.7	SLP	SA/CR	FBG	KC	IB	8D-	15D	10		7000			17000	19500
27	3	BRISTOL 27.7	SLP	SA/CR	FBG	KL	IB	8D-	15D	10		7000	4	5	17000	19500
29	11	BRISTOL 29.9	SLP	SA/CR	FBG	KC	IB	15D-	24D	10	2	8650	3	6	23300	25900
29	11	BRISTOL 29.9	SLP	SA/CR	FBG	KL	IB	15D-	24D	10	2	8650	4	4	23200	25800
32	1	BRISTOL 32	SLP	SA/CR	FBG	KC	IB	15D-	24D	9	5	11300	3	6	31600	35100
32	1	BRISTOL 32	SLP	SA/CR	FBG	KL	IB	15D-	24D	9	5	11300	4	8	31600	35100
32	1	BRISTOL 32	YWL	SA/CR	FBG	KC	IB	15D-	24D	9	5	11300	3	6	31600	35100
32	1	BRISTOL 32	YWL	SA/CR	FBG	KL	IB	15D-	24D	9	5	11300	4	8	31600	35100
35	6	BRISTOL 35.5	SLP	SA/CR	FBG	KC	IB	22D	WEST	10	10	15000	3	9	44800	49800
		IB 22D YAN 44800 49700, IB 30D WEST 44900 49900, IB 40D WEST													45000	50000
35	6	BRISTOL 35.5	SLP	SA/CR	FBG	KL	IB	22D	WEST	10	10	15000	5	9	44800	49800
		IB 22D YAN 44800 49700, IB 30D WEST 44900 49900, IB 40D WEST													45000	50000
40	2	BRISTOL 40	SLP	SA/CR	FBG	KC	IB	40D	WEST	10	9	17580	4		65700	72200
40	2	BRISTOL 40	SLP	SA/CR	FBG	KL	IB	40D	WEST	10	9	17580	5	5	65700	72200
40	2	BRISTOL 40	YWL	SA/CR	FBG	KC	IB	40D	WEST	10	9	17580	4		65700	72200
40	2	BRISTOL 40	YWL	SA/CR	FBG	KL	IB	40D	WEST	10	9	17580	5	5	65700	72200
45	3	BRISTOL 45.5	SLP	SA/CR	FBG	KC				13	3	34660	4	11	113500	125000
45	3	BRISTOL 45.5	YWL	SA/CR	FBG	KC				13	3	34660	4	11	113500	125000
		1978 BOATS														
22		BRISTOL 22	SLP	SA/CR	FBG	KC	OB			7	9	2850	3	6	5050	5800
22		BRISTOL 22	SLP	SA/CR	FBG	KL	OB			7	9	2850	3	6	5050	5800
24	7	BRISTOL 24	SLP	SA/CR	FBG	KL	OB			8		5920	3	5	11500	13100
26		BRISTOL 26	SLP	SA/CR	FBG	KC	OB			8		5500	2	10	11600	13700
27	2	BRISTOL 27	SLP	SA/CR	FBG	KL	IB			8		6600	4		15100	17200
29	11	BRISTOL 29.9	SLP	SA/CR	FBG	KC	IB	30		10	2	8650	4	4	22200	24700
30		BRISTOL 30	SLP	SA/CR	FBG	KC	IB	30		9	2	8400	3	4	21600	24000
32	1	BRISTOL 32	SLP	SA/CR	FBG	KC	IB	30		9	5	10800	4	8	29000	32200
34	3	BRISTOL 34	SLP	SA/CR	FBG	KC	IB	30		10	5	11500	5	6	32100	35700
34	8	BRISTOL 35	SLP	SA/CR	FBG	KC	IB	30		10		12500	3	9	35100	39000
35	5	BRISTOL 35.5	SLP	SA/CR	FBG	KC	IB	30D		10	10	15000	5	9	42900	47700
39	9	BRISTOL 40	SLP	SA/CR	FBG	KC	IB	30		10	9	17580	4		60400	66300
42	2	BRISTOL 42.2	KTH	SA/CR	FBG		IB			12	6	27500	5		87800	96500
		1977 BOATS														
19	7	BRISTOL 19	SLP	SA/CR	FBG	KL	OB			6	6	2850	2	9	4550	5250
22		CARAVEL 22	SLP	SA/CR	FBG	KC	OB			7	9	2850			4900	5600
22		CARAVEL 22	SLP	SA/CR	FBG	KL	OB			7	9	2850	3	6	4900	5600
24	7	BRISTOL 24	SLP	SA/CR	FBG	KL	OB			8		5920	3	5	11100	12600
24	7	BRISTOL 24	SLP	SA/CR	FBG	KL	IB	8D	YAN	8		5920	3	5	11800	13400
26		BRISTOL 26	SLP	SA/CR	FBG	KC	OB			8		5500	2	10	11200	12700
26		BRISTOL 26	SLP	SA/CR	FBG	KL	OB			8		5700	3	10	11600	13200
27	2	BRISTOL 27	SLP	SA/CR	FBG	KL	IB	30	UNIV	8		6600	4		14600	16500
27	2	BRISTOL 27	SLP	SA/CR	FBG	KL	IB	10D	WEST	8		6600	4		14800	16800
30		BRISTOL 30	SLP	SA/CR	FBG	KC	IB	30	UNIV	9	2	8400	3	4	20800	23200
30		BRISTOL 30	SLP	SA/CR	FBG	KC	IB	10D-	20D	9	2	8400	3	4	20900	23200
30		BRISTOL 30	SLP	SA/CR	FBG	KL	IB	30	UNIV	9	2	8400	4	6	20800	23100
30		BRISTOL 30	SLP	SA/CR	FBG	KL	IB	10D-	20D	9	2	8400	4	6	20900	23300
32	1	BRISTOL 32	SLP	SA/CR	FBG	KC	IB	30	UNIV	9	5	10800			27900	31000
32	1	BRISTOL 32	SLP	SA/CR	FBG	KC	IB	20D-	25D	9	5	10800			27900	31100
32	1	BRISTOL 32	SLP	SA/CR	FBG	KL	IB	30	UNIV	9	5	10800	4	8	27900	31000
32	1	BRISTOL 32	SLP	SA/CR	FBG	KL	IB	20D-	25D	9	5	10800	4	8	27900	31100
32	1	BRISTOL 32	YWL	SA/CR	FBG	KC	IB	30	UNIV	9	5	10800			27900	31000
32	1	BRISTOL 32	YWL	SA/CR	FBG	KC	IB	20D-	25D	9	5	10800			27900	31100
32	1	BRISTOL 32	YWL	SA/CR	FBG	KL	IB	30	UNIV	9	5	10800	4	8	27900	31000
32	1	BRISTOL 32	YWL	SA/CR	FBG	KL	IB	20D-	25D	9	5	10800	4	8	27900	31100
34	3	CARIB 34	SLP	SA/CR	FBG	KC	IB	30	UNIV	10	5	11500	4		30900	34300
34	3	CARIB 34	SLP	SA/CR	FBG	KC	IB	20D-	25D	10	5	11500	4		31100	34600
34	3	CARIB 34	SLP	SA/CR	FBG	KL	IB	30	UNIV	10	5	11500	5	6	30900	34300
34	3	CARIB 34	SLP	SA/CR	FBG	KL	IB	20D-	25D	10	5	11500	5	6	31100	34600
34	8	BRISTOL 35	SLP	SA/CR	FBG	KC	IB	30	UNIV	10		12500	3	9	33800	37600
34	8	BRISTOL 35	SLP	SA/CR	FBG	KC	IB	20D-	25D	10		12500	3	9	34100	37900
34	8	BRISTOL 35	SLP	SA/CR	FBG	KL	IB	30	UNIV	10		12500	5		33800	37600
34	8	BRISTOL 35	SLP	SA/CR	FBG	KL	IB	20D-	25D	10		12500	3	9	34100	37900
34	8	BRISTOL 35	YWL	SA/CR	FBG	KC	IB	30	UNIV	10		12500	3	9	33800	37600
34	8	BRISTOL 35	YWL	SA/CR	FBG	KC	IB	20D-	25D	10		12500	3	9	34100	37900
34	8	BRISTOL 35	YWL	SA/CR	FBG	KL	IB	30	UNIV	10		12500	3	9	33800	37600
34	8	BRISTOL 35	YWL	SA/CR	FBG	KL	IB	20D-	25D	10		12500	3	9	34100	37900
39	9	BRISTOL 40	SLP	SA/CR	FBG	KC	IB	30	UNIV	10	9	17580	4		58100	63900
39	9	BRISTOL 40	SLP	SA/CR	FBG	KC	IB	25D	WEST	10	9	17580	4		59000	64900
39	9	BRISTOL 40	SLP	SA/CR	FBG	KL	IB	30	UNIV	10	9	17580	5	5	58100	63900
39	9	BRISTOL 40	SLP	SA/CR	FBG	KL	IB	25D	WEST	10	9	17580	5	5	59000	64900
39	9	BRISTOL 40	YWL	SA/CR	FBG	KC	IB	30	UNIV	10	9	17580	4		58100	63900
39	9	BRISTOL 40	YWL	SA/CR	FBG	KC	IB	25D	WEST	10	9	17580	4		59000	64900
39	9	BRISTOL 40	YWL	SA/CR	FBG	KL	IB	30	UNIV	10	9	17580	5	5	58100	63900
39	9	BRISTOL 40	YWL	SA/CR	FBG	KL	IB	25D	WEST	10	9	17580	5	5	59000	64900
		1976 BOATS														
19	7	BRISTOL 19	SLP	SAIL	FBG	KL	OB			6	6	2724	2	9	4200	4900
22		BRISTOL 22	SLP	SAIL	FBG	KC	OB			7	9	2850	3	6	4700	5400
22		BRISTOL 22	SLP	SAIL	FBG	KL	OB			7	9	2850	3	6	4700	5400
24	7	BRISTOL 24	SLP	SAIL	FBG	KL	OB			8		5920	3	5	10700	12200
26		BRISTOL 26	SLP	SAIL	FBG	KC	OB			8		5700	3	10	11200	12800
26		BRISTOL 26	SLP	SAIL	FBG	KL	OB			8		5700	3	10	11200	12800
27	2	BRISTOL 27	SLP	SAIL	FBG	KL	IB	30	UNIV	8		6600	4		14100	16000
27	2	BRISTOL 27	SLP	SAIL	FBG	KL	IB	10D	WEST	8		6600	4		14300	16200
28		BRISTOL 28	SLP	SAIL	FBG	KL	IB	30	UNIV	9	6	8400	5		18900	21000
28		BRISTOL 28	SLP	SAIL	FBG	KL	IB	10D	WEST	9	6	8400	5		19000	21200
30		BRISTOL 30	SLP	SAIL	FBG	KC	IB	30	UNIV	9	2	8400	3	4	20100	22400
30		BRISTOL 30	SLP	SAIL	FBG	KC	IB	10D-	20D	9	2	8400	3	4	20200	22500
30		BRISTOL 30	SLP	SAIL	FBG	KL	IB	30	UNIV	9	2	8400	4	6	20100	22300
30		BRISTOL 30	SLP	SAIL	FBG	KL	IB	10D-	20D	9	2	8400	4	6	20200	22500
32	1	BRISTOL 32	SLP	SAIL	FBG	KC	IB	30	UNIV	9	5	10800			27000	30000
32	1	BRISTOL 32	SLP	SAIL	FBG	KC	IB	20D	WEST	9	5	10800			27000	30000
32	1	BRISTOL 32	SLP	SAIL	FBG	KL	IB	30	UNIV	9	5	10800	4	8	27000	30000
32	1	BRISTOL 32	SLP	SAIL	FBG	KL	IB	20D	WEST	9	5	10800	4	8	27000	30000
32	1	BRISTOL 32	YWL	SAIL	FBG	KC	IB	30	UNIV	9	5	10800			27000	30000
32	1	BRISTOL 32	YWL	SAIL	FBG	KC	IB	20D	WEST	9	5	10800			27000	30000
32	1	BRISTOL 32	YWL	SAIL	FBG	KL	IB	30	UNIV	9	5	10800	4	8	27000	30000
32	1	BRISTOL 32	YWL	SAIL	FBG	KL	IB	20D	WEST	9	5	10800	4	8	27000	30000
34	3	BRISTOL 34	SLP	SAIL	FBG	KC	IB	30	UNIV	10	5	11500	5	6	29900	33200
34	3	BRISTOL 34	SLP	SAIL	FBG	KC	IB	20D-	25D	10	5	11500	5	6	30100	33500
34	3	BRISTOL 34	SLP	SAIL	FBG	KL	IB	30	UNIV	10	5	11500	5	6	29900	33200
34	3	BRISTOL 34	SLP	SAIL	FBG	KL	IB	20D-	25D	10	5	11500	5	6	30100	33500
34	8	BRISTOL 35	SLP	SAIL	FBG	KC	IB	30	UNIV	10		12500	5		32700	36300
34	8	BRISTOL 35	SLP	SAIL	FBG	KC	IB	20D-	25D	10		12500	5		32900	36700
34	8	BRISTOL 35	SLP	SAIL	FBG	KL	IB	30	UNIV	10		12500	5		32700	36300
34	8	BRISTOL 35	SLP	SAIL	FBG	KL	IB	20D-	25D	10		12500	5		32900	36700
34	8	BRISTOL 35	YWL	SAIL	FBG	KC	IB	30	UNIV	10		12500	5		32700	36300
34	8	BRISTOL 35	YWL	SAIL	FBG	KC	IB	20D-	25D	10		12500	5		32900	36700
34	8	BRISTOL 35	YWL	SAIL	FBG	KL	IB	30	UNIV	10		12500	5		32700	36300
34	8	BRISTOL 35	YWL	SAIL	FBG	KL	IB	20D-	25D	10		12500	5		32900	36700

 CONTINUED ON NEXT PAGE

BRISTOL BOAT COMPANY -CONTINUED See inside cover to adjust price for area

LOA FT	IN	NAME AND/ OR MODEL	TOP/ RIG	BOAT TYPE	-HULL- MTL	TP	ENGINE TP	# HP	MFG	BEAM FT	IN	WGT LBS	DRAFT FT	IN	RETAIL LOW	RETAIL HIGH
1976 BOATS																
39	9	BRISTOL 40	SLP	SAIL	FBG	KC	IB	30	UNIV	10	9	17580	5	5	56100	61700
39	9	BRISTOL 40	SLP	SAIL	FBG	KC	IB	25D	WEST	10	9	17580	5	5	57000	62600
39	9	BRISTOL 40	SLP	SAIL	FBG	KL	IB	30	UNIV	10	9	17580	5	5	56100	61700
39	9	BRISTOL 40	SLP	SAIL	FBG	KL	IB	25D	WEST	10	9	17580	5	5	57000	62600
39	9	BRISTOL 40	YWL	SAIL	FBG	KC	IB	30	UNIV	10	9	17580	5	5	56100	61700
39	9	BRISTOL 40	YWL	SAIL	FBG	KC	IB	25D	WEST	10	9	17580	5	5	57000	62600
39	9	BRISTOL 40	YWL	SAIL	FBG	KL	IB	30	UNIV	10	9	17580	5	5	56100	61700
39	9	BRISTOL 40	YWL	SAIL	FBG	KL	IB	25D	WEST	10	9	17580	5	5	57000	62600
39	11	BRISTOL TC-440	SLP	MS	FBG	KL	IB	50D	PERK	12	6	27500	5		78000	85700
39	11	BRISTOL TC-440	SLP	MS	FBG	KL	IB	85D	PERK	12	6	27500	5		78000	85700
39	11	BRISTOL TC-440	KTH	MS	FBG	KL	IB	50D	PERK	12	6	27500	5		78000	85700
39	11	BRISTOL TC-440	KTH	MS	FBG	KL	IB	85D	PERK	12	6	27500	5		78400	86200
1975 BOATS																
19	7	CORINTHIAN 19	SLP	SAIL	FBG	KL	OB			6	6	2724	2	9	4100	4750
22		CARAVEL 22	SLP	SAIL	FBG	CB	OB			7	9	2850	3	6	4600	5300
22		CARAVEL 22	SLP	SAIL	FBG	KL	OB			7	9	2850	3	6	4600	5300
24	7	CORSAIR 24	SLP	SAIL	FBG	KL	OB			8		5920	3	5	10400	11800
26		BRISTOL 26	SLP	SAIL	FBG	CB	OB			8		5500	2	10	10500	11900
26		BRISTOL 26	SLP	SAIL	FBG	KL	OB			8		5700	3	10	10900	12400
27	2	BRISTOL 27	SLP	SAIL	FBG	KL	IB	30	UNIV	8		6600	4		13600	15500
27	2	BRISTOL 27	SLP	SAIL	FBG	KL	IB	10D	WEST	8		6600	4		13800	15700
30		BRISTOL 30	SLP	SAIL	FBG	CB	IB	30	UNIV	9	2	8400	3	4	19500	21600
30		BRISTOL 30	SLP	SAIL	FBG	CB	IB	10D-	20D	9	2	8400	3	4	19500	21800
30		BRISTOL 30	SLP	SAIL	FBG	KL	IB	30	UNIV	9	2	8400	4	6	19500	21600
30		BRISTOL 30	SLP	SAIL	FBG	KL	IB	10D-	20D	9	2	8400	4	6	19500	21800
32	1	BRISTOL 32	SLP	SAIL	FBG	CB	IB	30	UNIV	9	5	10800	4	8	26100	29000
32	1	BRISTOL 32	SLP	SAIL	FBG	CB	IB	20D	WEST	9	5		4	8	27100	30100
32	1	BRISTOL 32	SLP	SAIL	FBG	KL	IB	30	UNIV	9	5	10800	4	8	26100	29000
32	1	BRISTOL 32	SLP	SAIL	FBG	KL	IB	20D	WEST	9	5		4	8	27100	30100
32	1	BRISTOL 32	YWL	SAIL	FBG	CB	IB	30	UNIV	9	5	10800	4	8	26100	29000
32	1	BRISTOL 32	YWL	SAIL	FBG	CB	IB	20D	WEST	9	5	10800	4	8	26200	29100
32	1	BRISTOL 32	YWL	SAIL	FBG	KL	IB	30	UNIV	9	5	10800	4	8	26100	29000
32	1	BRISTOL 32	YWL	SAIL	FBG	KL	IB	20D	WEST	9	5	10800	4	8	26200	29100
34	3	BRISTOL 34	SLP	SAIL	FBG	CB	IB	30	UNIV	10	5	11500	4	6	28900	32100
34	3	BRISTOL 34	SLP	SAIL	FBG	CB	IB	20D-	50D	10	5	11500	4	6	29100	32500
34	3	BRISTOL 34	SLP	SAIL	FBG	KL	IB	30	UNIV	10	5	11500	5	6	28900	32100
34	3	BRISTOL 34	SLP	SAIL	FBG	KL	IB	20D-	50D	10	5	11500	5	6	29100	32500
34	8	BRISTOL 35	SLP	SAIL	FBG	CB	IB	30	UNIV	10		12500	3	9	31700	35200
34	8	BRISTOL 35	SLP	SAIL	FBG	CB	IB	20D-	50D	10		12500	3	9	31900	35600
34	8	BRISTOL 35	SLP	SAIL	FBG	KL	IB	30	UNIV	10		12500	5		31700	35200
34	8	BRISTOL 35	SLP	SAIL	FBG	KL	IB	20D-	50D	10		12500	5		31900	35600
34	8	BRISTOL 35	YWL	SAIL	FBG	CB	IB	30	UNIV	10		12500	3	9	31700	35200
34	8	BRISTOL 35	YWL	SAIL	FBG	CB	IB	20D-	50D	10		12500	3	9	31900	35600
34	8	BRISTOL 35	YWL	SAIL	FBG	KL	IB	30	UNIV	10		12500	5		31700	35200
34	8	BRISTOL 35	YWL	SAIL	FBG	KL	IB	20D-	50D	10		12500	5		31900	35600
39	9	BRISTOL 40	SLP	SAIL	FBG	CB	IB	30	UNIV	10	9	17580	4		54400	59800
39	9	BRISTOL 40	SLP	SAIL	FBG	CB	VD	40D	WEST	10	9	17580	4		55500	61000
39	9	BRISTOL 40	SLP	SAIL	FBG	CB	VD	50D	PERK	10	9	17580	4		55200	60700
39	9	BRISTOL 40	SLP	SAIL	FBG	KL	IB	30	UNIV	10	9	17580	5	5	54400	59800
39	9	BRISTOL 40	SLP	SAIL	FBG	KL	VD	40D	WEST	10	9	17580	5	5	55500	61000
39	9	BRISTOL 40	SLP	SAIL	FBG	KL	VD	50D	PERK	10	9	17580	5	5	55200	60700
39	9	BRISTOL 40	YWL	SAIL	FBG	CB	IB	30	UNIV	10	9	17580	4		54400	59800
39	9	BRISTOL 40	YWL	SAIL	FBG	CB	VD	40D	WEST	10	9	17580	4		55500	61000
39	9	BRISTOL 40	YWL	SAIL	FBG	CB	VD	50D	PERK	10	9	17580	4		55200	60700
39	9	BRISTOL 40	YWL	SAIL	FBG	KL	IB	30	UNIV	10	9	17580	5	5	54400	59800
39	9	BRISTOL 40	YWL	SAIL	FBG	KL	VD	40D	WEST	10	9	17580	5	5	55500	61000
39	9	BRISTOL 40	YWL	SAIL	FBG	KL	VD	50D	PERK	10	9	17580	5	5	55200	60700
39	11	BRISTOL 440 TC	SLP	SAIL	FBG	KL	IB	40D	WEST	12	6	27500	5		75800	83300
39	11	BRISTOL 440 TC	SLP	SAIL	FBG	KL	IB	50D	PERK	12	6	27500	5		75500	83000
39	11	BRISTOL 440 TC	KTH	SAIL	FBG	KL	IB	40D	WEST	12	6	27500	5		75900	83400
39	11	BRISTOL 440 TC	KTH	SAIL	FBG	KL	IB	50D	PERK	12	6	27500	5		75500	83000
1974 BOATS																
19	7	CORINTHIAN 19	SLP	SAIL	FBG	KL	OB			6	6	2724	2	9	3950	4600
22		CARAVEL 22	SLP	SAIL	FBG	CB	OB			7	9	2850	3	6	4450	5150
22		CARAVEL 22	SLP	SAIL	FBG	KL	OB			7	9	2850	3	6	4450	5150
26		SAILSTAR 26	SLP	SAIL	FBG	CB	OB			8		5700	3	10	10600	12000
26		SAILSTAR 26	SLP	SAIL	FBG	KL	OB			8		5700	3	10	10600	12000
27	2	BRISTOL 27	SLP	SAIL	FBG	KL	IB	30	UNIV	8		6600	4		13200	15000
30		BRISTOL 30	SLP	SAIL	FBG	CB	IB	30	UNIV	9	2	8400	4	6	18900	21000
30		BRISTOL 30	SLP	SAIL	FBG	KL	IB	30	UNIV	9	2	8400	4	6	18800	20900
32	1	BRISTOL 32	SLP	SAIL	FBG	CB	IB	30	UNIV	9	5	10800	4	8	25400	28200
32	1	BRISTOL 32	SLP	SAIL	FBG	KL	IB	30	UNIV	9	5	10800	4	8	25400	28200
32	1	BRISTOL 32	YWL	SAIL	FBG	KL	IB	30	UNIV	9	5	10800	4	8	25400	28200
32	1	BRISTOL 32	YWL	SAIL	FBG	KL	IB	37D	WEST	9	5	10800	4	8	25400	28200
34	3	BRISTOL 34	SLP	SAIL	FBG	KL	IB	30	UNIV	10	5	11500	5	6	28100	31200
34	3	BRISTOL 34	SLP	SAIL	FBG	KL	IB	37D	WEST	10	5	11500	5	6	28400	31600
34	8	BRISTOL 35	SLP	SAIL	FBG	CB	IB	30	UNIV	10		12500	3	9	30800	34200
34	8	BRISTOL 35	SLP	SAIL	FBG	KL	IB	30	UNIV	10		12500	5		30800	34200
34	8	BRISTOL 35	YWL	SAIL	FBG	KL	IB	30	UNIV	10		12500	5		30800	34200
34	8	BRISTOL 35	YWL	SAIL	FBG	KL	IB	37D	WEST	10		12500	5		31100	34600
39	9	BRISTOL 40	SLP	SAIL	FBG	CB	IB	30	UNIV	10	9	17580	4		52800	58100
39	9	BRISTOL 40	SLP	SAIL	FBG	KL	IB	30	UNIV	10	9	17580	5	5	52800	58100
39	9	BRISTOL 40	YWL	SAIL	FBG	KL	IB	30	UNIV	10	9	17580	5	5	52800	58100
39	9	BRISTOL 40	YWL	SAIL	FBG	KL	IB	37D	WEST	10	9	17580	5	5	53900	59200
1973 BOATS																
19	7	CORINTHIAN 19	SLP	SAIL	FBG	KL	OB			6	6	2724	2	9	3900	4500
22		CARAVEL 22	SLP	SAIL	FBG	CB	OB			7	9	2850	3	6	4350	5000
22		CARAVEL 22	SLP	SAIL	FBG	KL	OB			7	9	2850	3	6	4350	5000
26		SAILSTAR 26	SLP	SAIL	FBG	CB	OB			8		5500	3	10	9950	11300
26		SAILSTAR 26	SLP	SAIL	FBG	KL	OB			8		5700	3	10	10300	11700
27	2	BRISTOL 27	SLP	SAIL	FBG	KL	IB	30	UNIV	8		6600	4		12900	14600
30		BRISTOL 30	SLP	SAIL	FBG	CB	IB	30	UNIV	9	2	8400	4	6	18500	20600
30		BRISTOL 30	SLP	SAIL	FBG	KL	IB	30	UNIV	9	2	8400	4	6	18500	20500
32	1	BRISTOL 32	SLP	SAIL	FBG	CB	IB	30	UNIV	9	5	10800	4	8	24800	27600
32	1	BRISTOL 32	SLP	SAIL	FBG	KL	IB	30	UNIV	9	5	10800	4	8	24800	27600
32	1	BRISTOL 32	YWL	SAIL	FBG	CB	IB	37D	WEST	9	5	10800	4	8	24800	27600
32	1	BRISTOL 32	YWL	SAIL	FBG	KL	IB	30	UNIV	9	5	10800	4	8	24800	27600
34	3	BRISTOL 34	SLP	SAIL	FBG	CB	IB	37D	WEST	10	5	11500	5	6	27700	30800
34	3	BRISTOL 34	SLP	SAIL	FBG	KL	IB	30	UNIV	10	5	11500	5	6	27400	30500
34	8	BRISTOL 35	SLP	SAIL	FBG	CB	IB	30	UNIV	10		12500	3	9	30000	33400
34	8	BRISTOL 35	SLP	SAIL	FBG	KL	IB	30	UNIV	10		12500	5		30000	33400
34	8	BRISTOL 35	YWL	SAIL	FBG	CB	IB	37D	WEST	10		12500	5		30400	33800
34	8	BRISTOL 35	YWL	SAIL	FBG	KL	IB	30	UNIV	10		12500	5		30000	33400
39	9	BRISTOL 40	SLP	SAIL	FBG	CB	IB	30	UNIV	10	9	17580	4		51600	56700
39	9	BRISTOL 40	SLP	SAIL	FBG	KL	IB	30	UNIV	10	9	17580	5	5	51600	56700
39	9	BRISTOL 40	YWL	SAIL	FBG	CB	IB	37D	WEST	10	9	17580	5	5	52600	57800
39	9	BRISTOL 40	YWL	SAIL	FBG	KL	IB	30	UNIV	10	9	17580	5	5	51600	56700
1972 BOATS																
19	7	CORINTHIAN 19	SLP	SAIL	FBG	KL	OB			6	6	2724	2	9	3800	4400
22		CARAVEL 22	SLP	SAIL	FBG	CB	OB			7	9	2850	3	6	4200	4900
22		CARAVEL 22	SLP	SAIL	FBG	KL	OB			7	9	2850	3	6	4200	4900
26		SAILSTAR 26	SLP	SAIL	FBG	CB	OB			7	9	5500	3	10	9750	11100
27	2	BRISTOL 27	SLP	SAIL	FBG	KL	IB	30	UNIV	7	9	6600	4		12600	14300
30		BRISTOL 30	SLP	SAIL	FBG	CB	IB	30	UNIV	7	9	6600	4		13800	15700
30		BRISTOL 30	SLP	SAIL	FBG	KL	IB	30	UNIV	7	9	6600	4		13800	15700
32	1	BRISTOL 32	SLP	SAIL	FBG	CB	IB	30	UNIV	9	5	10800	4	8	24300	27000
32	1	BRISTOL 32	SLP	SAIL	FBG	KL	IB	30	UNIV	9	5	10800	4	8	24300	27000
32	1	BRISTOL 32	YWL	SAIL	FBG	CB	IB	37D	WEST	9	5	10800	4	8	24300	27000
32	1	BRISTOL 32	YWL	SAIL	FBG	KL	IB	30	UNIV	9	5	10800	4	8	24300	27000
34	3	BRISTOL 34	SLP	SAIL	FBG	CB	IB	37D	WEST	10	5	11500	5	6	27200	30200
34	3	BRISTOL 34	SLP	SAIL	FBG	KL	IB	30	UNIV	10	5	11500	5	6	26900	29900
34	8	BRISTOL 35	SLP	SAIL	FBG	CB	IB	30	UNIV	10		12500	3	9	29400	32700
34	8	BRISTOL 35	SLP	SAIL	FBG	KL	IB	30	UNIV	10		12500	5		29400	32700
34	8	BRISTOL 35	YWL	SAIL	FBG	CB	IB	37D	WEST	10		12500	5		29800	33100
34	8	BRISTOL 35	YWL	SAIL	FBG	KL	IB	30	UNIV	10		12500	5		29400	32700
39	9	BRISTOL 40	SLP	SAIL	FBG	CB	IB	30	UNIV	10	9	17580	4		50500	55500
39	9	BRISTOL 40	SLP	SAIL	FBG	CB	IB	37D	WEST	10	9	17580	5	5	51500	56600
39	9	BRISTOL 40	SLP	SAIL	FBG	KL	IB	30	UNIV	10	9	17580	5	5	50500	55500
1971 BOATS																
19	7	BRISTOL 19	SLP	SAIL	FBG	KL	OB			6	6	2724	2	9	3750	4350
22		BRISTOL 22	SLP	SAIL	FBG	KL	OB			7	9	2850	3	6	4150	4800
24	7	BRISTOL 24	SLP	SAIL	FBG	KL	OB			8		5920	3	5	9500	10800
26		HERRESHOFF 26	SLP	SAIL	FBG	CB	OB			8		5500	3	10	9550	10900
26		HERRESHOFF 26	SLP	SAIL	FBG	KL	OB			8		5700	3	10	9900	11300
27	2	BRISTOL 27	SLP	SAIL	FBG	KL	OB			8			4		8850	10000
27	2	BRISTOL 27	SLP	SAIL	FBG	KL	IB	30	UNIV	8		6600	4		12400	14000
29	2	BRISTOL 29	SLP	SAIL	FBG	CB	IB	30	UNIV	9	2	8400	4	6	16700	19000
29	2	BRISTOL 29	SLP	SAIL	FBG	KL	IB	30	UNIV	9	2	8400	4	6	16700	19000
30		BRISTOL 30	SLP	SAIL	FBG	CB	IB	30	UNIV	9	2	8400	4	6	17300	19700
30		BRISTOL 30	SLP	SAIL	FBG	KL	IB	30	UNIV	9	2	8400	4	6	17300	19700
32	1	BRISTOL 32	SLP	SAIL	FBG	CB	IB	30	UNIV	9	5	10800	4	8	23900	26500
32	1	BRISTOL 32	SLP	SAIL	FBG	CB	IB	37D	WEST	9	5	10800	4	8	23900	26500
32	1	BRISTOL 32	SLP	SAIL	FBG	KL	IB	30	UNIV	9	5	10800	4	8	23900	26500
32	1	BRISTOL 32	SLP	SAIL	FBG	KL	IB	37D	WEST	9	5	10800	4	8	23900	26500
34	4	BRISTOL 34	SLP	SAIL	FBG	KL	IB	30	UNIV	10	6	11500	5	6	26500	29400
34	4	BRISTOL 34	SLP	SAIL	FBG	KL	IB	37D	WEST	10	6	11500	5	6	26800	29700
34	8	BRISTOL 35	SLP	SAIL	FBG	CB	IB	30	UNIV	10		12500	5		28900	32100
34	8	BRISTOL 35	SLP	SAIL	FBG	CB	IB	37D	WEST	10		12500	5		29200	32500

96th ed. - Vol. III
CONTINUED ON NEXT PAGE
73

BRISTOL BOAT COMPANY -CONTINUED See inside cover to adjust price for area

LOA FT	LOA IN	NAME AND/ OR MODEL	TOP/ RIG	BOAT TYPE	-HULL- MTL	-HULL- TP	ENGINE TP	ENGINE # HP	ENGINE MFG	BEAM FT	BEAM IN	WGT LBS	DRAFT FT	DRAFT IN	RETAIL LOW	RETAIL HIGH
		1971 BOATS														
34	8	BRISTOL 35	SLP	SAIL	FBG	KL	IB	30	UNIV	10		12500	5		28900	32100
34	8	BRISTOL 35	SLP	SAIL	FBG	KL	IB	37D	WEST	10		12500	5		29200	32500
39	3	BRISTOL 39	SLP	SAIL	FBG	CB	IB	30	UNIV	10	9	17580	5	5	48000	52700
39	3	BRISTOL 39	SLP	SAIL	FBG	CB	IB	37D	WEST	10	9	17580	5	5	48900	53800
39	3	BRISTOL 39	SLP	SAIL	FBG	KL	IB	30	UNIV	10	9	17500	5	5	47800	52600
39	3	BRISTOL 39	SLP	SAIL	FBG	KL	IB	37D	WEST	10	9	17500	5	5	48800	53600
39	11	SEA-LION	SLP	SA/CR	FBG	KL	IB	110		12	6	26000	5		65300	71700
40	9	BRISTOL 41	SLP	SA/CR	FBG	KL	IB	D		11	2		6	10	68900	75700
		1970 BOATS														
27	2		SLP	SAIL	FBG	KL	OB			8		6600	4		10600	12100
27	2	BRISTOL 27	SLP	SA/CR	FBG	KL	OB			8		6600	4		11900	13600
27	2	BRISTOL 27 CRUISER	SLP	SA/CR	FBG	KL				8		6600	4		11300	12800
27	2	BRISTOL 27 DINETTE	SLP	SA/CR	FBG	KL				8		6600	4		11700	13300
27	2	BRISTOL 27 DINETTE	SLP	SAIL	FBG	KL	OB			8		6600	4		13300	15100
27	2	WEEKENDINC CRUISER	SLP	SA/CR	FBG	KL				8		6600	4		9400	10700
29	6	BRISTOL 29	SLP	SA/CR	FBG	KC	IB	30D		8	11	9600	3	4	19600	21800
29	6	BRISTOL 29	SLP	SAIL	FBG	CB	IB	30D		8	11	9600	3	4	19600	21800
32	2	BRISTOL 32	SLP	SA/CR	FBG	KC	IB	30D		9	6	10300	4	7	22500	25000
32	2	BRISTOL 32	YWL	SA/CR	FBG	KC	IB	30D		9	6	10300	4	7	22500	25000
32	2	BRISTOL 32	SLP	SAIL	FBG	CB	IB	30D		9	6	10300	4	7	22500	25000
33	4	BRISTOL 33	SLP	SA/CR	FBG	KC	IB	30D		10	3	11900	5	7	26500	29400
33	4	BRISTOL 33	YWL	SA/CR	FBG	KC	IB	30D		10	3	11900	5	7	26500	29400
33	4	BRISTOL 33		SAIL	FBG	CB	IB	30D		10	3	11900	5	7	26500	29400
34	8	BRISTOL 35	SLP	SA/CR	FBG	KC	IB	30D		10		12450	3	9	28600	31800
34	8	BRISTOL 35	YWL	SA/CR	FBG	KC	IB	30D		10		12450	3	9	28600	31800
34	8	BRISTOL 35	SLP	SAIL	FBG	CB	IB	30D		10		12450	3	9	28600	31800
38		ALERION	SLP	SA/CR	FBG	KL	IB	30D		10	9	17300	6	3	43700	48600
38		ALERION		SAIL	FBG	KL	IB	30D		10	9	17300	6	3	43700	48600
39	1	BRISTOL 39	SLP	SA/CR	FBG	KC	IB	30D		10	9	17600	3	11	47700	52400
39	1	BRISTOL 39	YWL	SA/CR	FBG	KC	IB	30D		10	9	17600	3	11	47700	52400
39	1	BRISTOL 39	SLP	SAIL	FBG	CB	IB	30D		10	9	17600	3	11	47700	52400
39	11	SEA-LION	SLP	SA/CR	FBG	KL	IB	110		12	6	26000	5		64200	70600
39	11	SEA-LION		SAIL	FBG	KL	IB	110		12	6	26000	5		64200	70600
41	6	OFFSHORE 42		DC	FBG	SV	IB	128D	FORD	13	6	27600	4		55900	61400
41	6	OFFSHORE 42		OFF	FBG	SV	IB	T110D	PALM	13	6	26700	4		60000	65900
		1969 BOATS														
27	2	BRISTOL 27 DINETTE	SLP	SAIL	FBG	KL	OB			8		6600	4		12700	14400
27	2	BRISTOL 27 STD	SLP	SAIL	FBG	KL	OB			8		6600	4		12300	14000
27	2	BRISTOL 27 WEEKENDER	SLP	SAIL	FBG	KL	OB			8		6600	4		10400	11800
29	2	BRISTOL 29 DINETTE	SLP	SAIL	FBG	CB	IB	30	UNIV	8	11	8400	4	6	16700	19000
29	2	BRISTOL 29 DINETTE	SLP	SAIL	FBG	CB	IB	25D	GRAY	8	11	8400	4	6	16900	19200
29	2	BRISTOL 29 DINETTE	SLP	SAIL	FBG	KL	IB	30	UNIV	8	11	8400	4	6	16100	18200
29	2	BRISTOL 29 DINETTE	SLP	SAIL	FBG	KL	IB	25D	GRAY	8	11	8400	4	6	16200	18400
29	2	BRISTOL 29 STD	SLP	SAIL	FBG	CB	IB	30	UNIV	8	11	8400	4	6	16500	18700
29	2	BRISTOL 29 STD	SLP	SAIL	FBG	CB	IB	25D	GRAY	8	11	8400	4	6	16600	18900
29	2	BRISTOL 29 STD	SLP	SAIL	FBG	KL	IB	30	UNIV	8	11	8400	4	6	15500	17600
29	2	BRISTOL 29 STD	SLP	SAIL	FBG	KL	IB	25D	GRAY	8	11	8400	4	6	15700	17800
31	10	BRISTOL 31 XL	SLP	SAIL	FBG	KL	IB	30	UNIV	9	5	10600	5		22700	25200
31	10	BRISTOL 31 XL	SLP	SAIL	FBG	KL	IB	25D	GRAY	9	5	10600	5		22700	25300
32	1	BRISTOL 32	SLP	SAIL	FBG	CB	IB	30	UNIV	9	5	10800	4	7	23200	25800
32	1	BRISTOL 32	SLP	SAIL	FBG	CB	IB	25D	GRAY	9	5	10800	4	7	23200	25800
32	1	BRISTOL 32	SLP	SAIL	FBG	KL	IB	30	UNIV	9	5	10800	4	8	23200	25800
32	1	BRISTOL 32	SLP	SAIL	FBG	KL	IB	25D	GRAY	9	5	10800	4	8	23200	25800
32	1	BRISTOL 32	YWL	SAIL	FBG	CB	IB	30	UNIV	9	5	10800	4	7	23200	25800
32	1	BRISTOL 32	YWL	SAIL	FBG	CB	IB	25D	GRAY	9	5	10800	4	7	23200	25800
32	1	BRISTOL 32	YWL	SAIL	FBG	KL	IB	30	UNIV	9	5	10800	4	8	23200	25800
32	1	BRISTOL 32	YWL	SAIL	FBG	KL	IB	25D	GRAY	9	5	10800	4	8	23200	25800
33	7	BRISTOL 33	SLP	SAIL	FBG	KL	IB	30	UNIV	10	3	12800	5	8	28100	31200
33	7	BRISTOL 33	SLP	SAIL	FBG	KL	IB	25D	GRAY	10	3	12800	5	8	28200	31300
34	8	BRISTOL 35 DINETTE	SLP	SAIL	FBG	KL	IB	30	UNIV	10		12500	5		27700	30800
34	8	BRISTOL 35 DINETTE	SLP	SAIL	FBG	KL	IB	25D	GRAY	10		12500	5		27900	31000
34	8	BRISTOL 35 STD	SLP	SAIL	FBG	CB	IB	30	UNIV	10		12500	3	9	29000	32300
34	8	BRISTOL 35 STD	SLP	SAIL	FBG	CB	IB	25D	GRAY	10		12500	3	9	29300	32500
34	8	BRISTOL 35 STD	SLP	SAIL	FBG	KL	IB	30	UNIV	10		12500	5		27600	30600
34	8	BRISTOL 35 STD	SLP	SAIL	FBG	KL	IB	25D	GRAY	10		12500	5		27800	30900
38		ALERION	SLP	SA/CR	FBG	KL	IB	30D		10	9	17300	6	3	43100	47900
39	3	BRISTOL 39 DINETTE	SLP	SAIL	FBG	CB	IB	30	UNIV	10	9	17500	4		47700	52400
39	3	BRISTOL 39 DINETTE	SLP	SAIL	FBG	CB	IB	25D	GRAY	10	9	17500	4		48000	52800
39	3	BRISTOL 39 DINETTE	SLP	SAIL	FBG	KL	IB	30	UNIV	10	9	17500	5	4	46200	50700
39	3	BRISTOL 39 DINETTE	SLP	SAIL	FBG	KL	IB	25D	GRAY	10	9	17500	5	4	46700	51400
39	3	BRISTOL 39 STD	SLP	SAIL	FBG	CB	IB	30	UNIV	10	9	17500	4		47400	52100
39	3	BRISTOL 39 STD	SLP	SAIL	FBG	CB	IB	25D	GRAY	10	9	17500	4		47700	52500
39	3	BRISTOL 39 STD	SLP	SAIL	FBG	KL	IB	30	UNIV	10	9	17500	5	4	45800	50400
39	3	BRISTOL 39 STD	SLP	SAIL	FBG	KL	IB	25D	GRAY	10	9	17500	5	4	46400	51000
		1968 BOATS														
19	7	BRISTOL 19	SLP	SAIL	FBG		OB			6	6	2724	2	9	3600	4200
22		BRISTOL 22	SLP	SAIL	FBG	CB	OB			7	9	2850	3	6	4000	4650
22		BRISTOL 22	SLP	SAIL	FBG	KL	OB			7	9	2850	3	6	4000	4650
24	7	BRISTOL 24	SLP	SAIL	FBG		OB			8		5920	3	5	9200	10400
26		BRISTOL 26	SLP	SAIL	FBG	CB	OB			8		5500	2	10	9250	10500
26		BRISTOL 26	SLP	SAIL	FBG	KL	OB			8		5700	3	10	9550	10800
27	2	BRISTOL 27 DINETTE	SLP	SAIL	FBG	KL	OB			8		6600	4		12700	14400
27	2	BRISTOL 27 STD	SLP	SAIL	FBG	KL	OB			8		6600	4		12200	13900
27	2	BRISTOL 27 WEEKENDER	SLP	SAIL	FBG	KL	OB			8		6600	4		10100	11500
29	2	BRISTOL 29 DINETTE	SLP	SAIL	FBG	KC	IB	30	UNIV	8	11	8400	4	6	15500	17600
29	2	BRISTOL 29 STD	SLP	SAIL	FBG	KC	IB	30	UNIV	8	11	8400	4	6	15500	17600
29	2	BRISTOL 30 DINETTE	SLP	SAIL	FBG	CB	IB	30	UNIV	8	11	8400	4	6	16600	18900
29	2	BRISTOL 30 STD	SLP	SAIL	FBG	CB	IB	30	UNIV	8	11	8400	4	6	16600	18900
32	1	BRISTOL 32	SLP	SAIL	FBG	CB	IB	30	UNIV	9	5	10800	4	7	23000	25500
32	1	BRISTOL 32	SLP	SAIL	FBG	KL	IB	30	UNIV	9	5	10800	4	8	23000	25500
32	1	BRISTOL 32	YWL	SAIL	FBG	CB	IB	30	UNIV	9	5	10800	4	7	23000	25500
32	1	BRISTOL 32	YWL	SAIL	FBG	KL	IB	30	UNIV	9	5	10800	4	8	23000	25500
34	3	BRISTOL 34	SLP	SAIL	FBG		IB	30	UNIV	10	3	12800	5	6	28100	31300
34	8	BRISTOL 35 DINETTE	SLP	SAIL	FBG	CB	IB	30	UNIV	10		12500	3	9	28400	31600
34	8	BRISTOL 35 DINETTE	SLP	SAIL	FBG	KL	IB	30	UNIV	10		12500	5		27100	30200
34	8	BRISTOL 35 STD	SLP	SAIL	FBG	CB	IB	30	UNIV	10		12500	3	9	28400	31600
34	8	BRISTOL 35 STD	SLP	SAIL	FBG	KL	IB	30	UNIV	10		12500	5		27100	30200
39	3	BRISTOL 39 DINETTE	SLP	SAIL	FBG	CB	IB	30	UNIV	10	9	17500	5	4	47000	51600
39	3	BRISTOL 39 DINETTE	SLP	SAIL	FBG	KL	IB	30	UNIV	10	9	17500	5	4	45000	50000
39	3	BRISTOL 39 STD	SLP	SAIL	FBG	CB	IB	30	UNIV	10	9	17500	5	4	47000	51600
39	3	BRISTOL 39 STD	SLP	SAIL	FBG	KL	IB	30	UNIV	10	9	17500	5	4	45000	50000
		1967 BOATS														
27	2	BRISTOL 27	SLP	SA/CR	FBG	KL	IB	25D				6600			12100	13700
27	2	BRISTOL 27 WKNDR	SLP	SAIL	FBG	KL	OB					6600			11500	13100
29	2	BRISTOL 29	SLP	SAIL	FBG	KL	IB	25D							14300	16200
29	2	BRISTOL 29 DINETTE	SLP	SAIL	FBG	KL	IB	25D							14500	16500
32	1	BRISTOL 32	SLP	SAIL	FBG	CB	IB	25D				10800			22800	25400
32	1	BRISTOL 32	SLP	SAIL	FBG	KL	IB	25D				10800			22800	25400
32	1	BRISTOL 32	YWL	SAIL	FBG	CB	IB	25D				10800			22800	25400
32	1	BRISTOL 32	YWL	SAIL	FBG	KL	IB	25D				10800			22800	25400
34	8	BRISTOL 35	SLP	SAIL	FBG	CB	IB	31D- 40D				12500			27800	31000
34	8	BRISTOL 35	SLP	SAIL	FBG	KL	IB	31D- 40D				12500			27800	30900
34	8	BRISTOL 35	YWL	SAIL	FBG	CB	IB	31D- 40D				12500			27800	31000
34	8	BRISTOL 35	YWL	SAIL	FBG	KL	IB	31D- 40D				12500			27800	30900
39	3	BRISTOL 39	SLP	SAIL	FBG	CB	IB	31D				17580			46700	51300
39	3	BRISTOL 39	SLP	SAIL	FBG	CB	IB	40D				17580			46900	51500
39	3	BRISTOL 39	SLP	SAIL	FBG	KL	IB	31D				17580			46700	51300
39	3	BRISTOL 39	SLP	SAIL	FBG	KL	IB	40D				17580			46900	51500
39	3	BRISTOL 39	YWL	SAIL	FBG	CB	IB	31D				17580			46700	51300
39	3	BRISTOL 39	YWL	SAIL	FBG	CB	IB	40D				17580			46900	51500
39	3	BRISTOL 39	YWL	SAIL	FBG	KL	IB	31D				17580			46700	51300
39	3	BRISTOL 39	YWL	SAIL	FBG	KL	IB	40D				17580			46900	51500
		1966 BOATS														
27	2	BRISTOL 27	SLP	SA/CR	FBG	KL	OB			8		6600	4		11500	13000
27	2	BRISTOL 27	SLP	SA/CR	FBG	KL	IB	25D		8		6600	4		12000	13700
27	2	BRISTOL 27 WEEKENDER	SLP	SAIL	FBG	KL	OB			8		6600	4		11500	13000
29	2	BRISTOL 29	SLP	SA/CR	FBG	KL	IB	25D		8	11	8400	4	6	15900	18000
32	1	BRISTOL 32	SLP	SAIL	FBG	CB	IB	25D		9	6	10800			22700	25200
32	1	BRISTOL 32	SLP	SAIL	FBG	KL	IB	25D		9	6	10800	4	8	22700	25200
32	1	BRISTOL 32	YWL	SAIL	FBG	CB	IB	25D		9	6	10800			22700	25200
32	1	BRISTOL 32	YWL	SAIL	FBG	KL	IB	25D		9	6	10800	4	8	22700	25200
34	8	BRISTOL 35	SLP	SA/CR	FBG	CB	IB	25D		10		12500			27600	30700
34	8	BRISTOL 35	SLP	SA/CR	FBG	KL	IB	25D		10		12500	5		27600	30700
39	3	BRISTOL 39	SLP	SA/CR	FBG	CB	IB	30D		10	9	17580			46500	51100
39	3	BRISTOL 39	SLP	SA/CR	FBG	KL	IB	30D		10	9	17580	5	5	46500	51100
39	3	BRISTOL 39	YWL	SA/CR	FBG	CB	IB	30D		10	9	17580			46400	51000
39	3	BRISTOL 39	YWL	SA/CR	FBG	KL	IB	30D		10	9	17580	5	5	46400	51000

BRISTOL BOAT CORP

Call 1-800-327-6929 for BUC Personalized Evaluation Service
Or, for 1961 boats, sign onto www.BUCValuPro.com

BRISTOL BOATS

Call 1-800-327-6929 for BUC Personalized Evaluation Service
Or, for 1960 boats, sign onto www.BUCValuPro.com

BRISTOL BOATS LTD
OAKLAND CA 94611   See inside cover to adjust price for area

LOA FT IN	NAME AND/ OR MODEL	TOP/ RIG	BOAT TYPE	-HULL- MTL TP	----ENGINE--- TP # HP MFG	BEAM FT IN	WGT LBS	DRAFT FT IN	RETAIL LOW	RETAIL HIGH
					1980 BOATS					
42	BRISTOL		TRWL	FBG DS	IB T120D	13 6	29000		76500	84100

BRISTOL YACHTS
DIV ALLEN QUIMBY VENEER CO

Call 1-800-327-6929 for BUC Personalized Evaluation Service
Or, for 1953 to 1962 boats, sign onto www.BUCValuPro.com

BRISTOL YACHTS INT'L
B Y I LTD N V   See inside cover to adjust price for area
NETHERLANDS ANT   COAST GUARD MFG ID- BNV

LOA FT IN	NAME AND/ OR MODEL	TOP/ RIG	BOAT TYPE	-HULL- MTL TP	----ENGINE--- TP # HP MFG	BEAM FT IN	WGT LBS	DRAFT FT IN	RETAIL LOW	RETAIL HIGH
					1978 BOATS					
37 10	BRISTOL OFFSHORE 38	FB	TRWL	FBG DS	IB 130D PERK	12 6	22000	3 11	55000	60400
41 6	BRISTOL OFFSHORE 42	FB	TRWL	FBG DS	IB 130D PERK	13 6	26700	4 6	69300	76100
41 6	BRISTOL OFFSHORE 42	FB	TRWL	FBG DS	IB T130D LEHM	13 6	26700	4 6	72200	79400
					1977 BOATS					
37 10	BRISTOL OFFSHORE 38	FB	TRWL	FBG DS	IB 130D PERK	12 6	22000	3 11	52700	57900
37 10	BRISTOL OFFSHORE 38	FB	TRWL	FBG DS	IB T130D PERK	12 6	22000	3 11	56000	61600
41 6	BRISTOL OFFSHORE 42	FB	TRWL	FBG DS	IB 130D PERK	13 6	26700	4	66300	72900
41 6	BRISTOL OFFSHORE 42	FB	TRWL	FBG DS	IB T130D PERK	13 6	26700	4	70000	76900
					1976 BOATS					
37 10	BRISTOL OFFSHORE 38	FB	TRWL	FBG DS	IB T160D	12 6	22000	3 11	53600	58800
37 10	BRISTOL OFFSHORE 38	FB	TRWL	FBG DS	IB T220D	12 6	22000	3 11	55000	60400
41 6	BRISTOL OFFSHORE 42	FB	TRWL	FBG DS	IB T160D	13 6	26700	4	67000	73700
41 6	BRISTOL OFFSHORE 42	FB	TRWL	FBG DS	IB T220D	13 6	26700	4	68500	75300
					1975 BOATS					
37 10	BRISTOL OFFSHORE 38	FB	TRWL	FBG DS	IB T160D	12 6	22000	3 11	51400	56500
37 10	BRISTOL OFFSHORE 38	FB	TRWL	FBG DS	IB T220D	12 6	22000	3 11	52800	58000
41 6	BRISTOL OFFSHORE 42	FB	TRWL	FBG DS	IB T160D	13 6	26700	4	64400	70700
41 6	BRISTOL OFFSHORE 42	FB	TRWL	FBG DS	IB T220D	13 6	26700	4	65800	72300
					1974 BOATS					
37 10	BRISTOL OFFSHORE 38	FB	TRWL	FBG DS	IB 130D	12 6	22000	3 11	46600	51200
41 6	BRISTOL OFFSHORE 42	FB	TRWL	FBG DS	IB 130D	13 6	26700	4	58400	64200
					1971 BOATS					
37 9	BRISTOL OFFSHORE 37	FB	TRWL	FBG DS	IB 128D FORD	12 6	22000	3 11	41100	45700
37 9	BRISTOL OFFSHORE 37	FB	TRWL	FBG DS	IB T128D FORD	12 6	22000	3 11	43400	48200
37 9	BRISTOL OFFSHORE 37	FB	TRWL	FBG DS	IB T200D	12 6	22000	3 11	44700	49600
41 6	BRISTOL OFFSHORE 42	FB	TRWL	FBG DS	IB 128D FORD	13 6	26700	4	52400	57500
41 6	BRISTOL OFFSHORE 42	FB	TRWL	FBG DS	IB T200D	13 6	26700	4	56300	61900

BRITISH YACHTS

Call 1-800-327-6929 for BUC Personalized Evaluation Service
Or, for 1966 boats, sign onto www.BUCValuPro.com

BRITISH YACHTS LIMITED
COAST GUARD MFG ID- BYZ
FORMERLY NORTHSHORE YACHT YARDS LTD

Call 1-800-327-6929 for BUC Personalized Evaluation Service
Or, for 1980 to 1985 boats, sign onto www.BUCValuPro.com

BRITT BROTHERS

Call 1-800-327-6929 for BUC Personalized Evaluation Service
Or, for 1929 boats, sign onto www.BUCValuPro.com

BROADWATER BOAT COMPANY
MAYO MD 21106   COAST GUARD MFG ID- BWB See inside cover to adjust price for area

LOA FT IN	NAME AND/ OR MODEL	TOP/ RIG	BOAT TYPE	-HULL- MTL TP	----ENGINE--- TP # HP MFG	BEAM FT IN	WGT LBS	DRAFT FT IN	RETAIL LOW	RETAIL HIGH
					1977 BOATS					
21	LITTLE-MARINER	CR	FBG DV	IB	165 PCM	8		3 6	4900	5650
24	EXPRESS	EXP	FBG DV	IB	215 PCM	8		3 6	6150	7050
24	SPORT CRUISER	SPTCR	FBG DV	IB	185 PCM	8		3 6	6050	7000
27	EXPRESS	EXP	FBG DV	IB	215 PCM	10		3 6	8450	9700
33	EXPLORER	FB	CR	FBG DV	IB T185 PCM	11		3 6	17500	19900
33	EXPRESS		EXP	FBG DV	IB T185 PCM	11		3 6	19700	21900
					1976 BOATS					
21 8	LITTLE-MARINER	CR	FBG DV	IB	165 PCM	8	4500	2 6	4900	5600
33	MARK III	CR	FBG DV	IB	T165 PCM	11	9200	2 6	16900	19200
					1975 BOATS					
21 8	LITTLE-MARINER	FB	CR	FBG SV	VD 165 WAUK	8	4500	2 6	4700	5400
21 8	LITTLE-MARINER	FB	CR	FBG SV	VD 185 WAUK	8	4500	2 6	4700	5400
31	BAY-BREEZE	FB	CR	FBG SV	225-350	11	8200	2 6	15100	18100
33	BAY-BREEZE	FB	CR	FBG SV	T165 WAUK	11	8200	2 6	15800	18000
33	MARK-III-EXPLORER	FB	SDN	FBG SV	225-350	11	9200	2 6	16300	19800
33	MARK-III-EXPLORER	FB	SDN	FBG SV	T165 WAUK	11	9200	2 6	17300	19700
					1974 BOATS					
21 8	LITTLE-MARINER	EXP	FBG DV	IO	165 WAUK	8	4500	2 6	5400	6250
21 8	LITTLE-MARINER	EXP	FBG DV	IO	185 WAUK	8	4500	2 6	5400	5150
30	EXPRESS	EXP	F/W	DV	IB 225 CHRY	10	7000	2	11100	12600
33	EXPLORER	SPTCR	FBG DV	IB	225 CHRY	11	9200	2 6	14900	16900
33	EXPRESS	EXP	FBG DV	IB	225 CHRY	11	8200	2 6	16200	18400
					1973 BOATS					
21 8	LITTLE-MARINER		FBG	IB	165 WAUK	8		2	4300	5000
25		EXP	F/W	IB	165 WAUK	10	4900	2	5650	6500
25	EXPLORER		F/W	IB	165 WAUK	10	4900	2	5650	6500
25	TILGHMAN		F/W	IB	165 WAUK	10	4500	2	5350	6150
30		EXP	F/W	IB	225 CHRY	10	7000	2	10700	12100
30		SDN	F/W	IB	225 CHRY	10	7400	2	10700	12200
30	EXPLORER		F/W	IB	225 CHRY	10	7200	2	9300	10500
31 9		EXP	F/W	IB	225 CHRY	10	8000	2	13500	15400
31 9	EXPLORER MARK III		F/W	IB	225 CHRY	10	9000	2	11500	13100
33		DC	F/W	IB	T165 WAUK	10 10		3	16000	18200
33		SDN	F/W	IB	225 CHRY	10 10	9000	2	15100	17100
					1972 BOATS					
25		EXP	PLY	IB	165 WAUK	10	4900	2	5400	6200
25	EXPLORER	FB	PLY	IB	165 WAUK	10	4900	2	5400	6200
25	TILGHMAN		FSH	F/W	DV IB 165-225	10		2	5350	6300
25	TILGHMAN		SF	PLY	IB 165 WAUK	10	4500	2	5050	5800
30		EXP	PLY	IB	225 CHRY	10	7000	2	10300	11700
30		SDN	PLY	IB	225 CHRY	10	7400	2	10300	11700
30	EXPLORER	FB	PLY	IB	225 CHRY	10	7200	2	8900	10100
32		EXP	PLY	IB	225 CHRY	10	8000	2	13600	15400
32	EXPLORER	FB	PLY	IB	225 CHRY	10	8000	2	11200	12700
33		DC	PLY	IB	T165 WAUK	10 10	11000	2 6	15300	17400
33		SDN	PLY	IB	225 CHRY	10 10	10000	2 6	14800	16800
					1971 BOATS					
25		EXP	WD	IB	150 GRAY	10	4900	2	5150	5950
25	EXPLORER		WD	IB	150 GRAY	10	4950	2	5200	6000
25	TILGHMAN		WD	IB	150 GRAY	10	4500	2	4850	5600
30		EXP	WD	IB	225 CHRY	10	6900	2 2	9800	11100
30		SDN	WD	IB	225 CHRY	10 2	6900	2 4	9750	11100
30	EXPLORER		WD	IB	225 CHRY	10	6900	2 4	8350	9600
31 9	BAY-BREEZE		WD	IB	225 CHRY	10 10	8000	2 4	10500	11900
31 9	EXPLORER		WD	IB	225 CHRY	10 10	8200	2 4	10500	11900
33		DC	WD	IB	100D	10 10	10000	2 4	18200	20200
33		DC	WD	IB	T150 GRAY	10 10	10000	2 4	14800	16800
33		SDN	WD	IB	225 CHRY	10 10	9000	2 4	13800	15800
33		SDN	WD	IB	100D	10 10	9000	2 4	15800	17900
					1970 BOATS					
25		EXP	MHG	SV	150 GRAY	10	5000	2	5050	5800
25	ANCHORLINE	HT	HB		150	10 6		2	**	**
27	FISHAWK 27			PLY	SV 225 CHRY	10 10	6000	2	6500	7450
29 7	BAY-BREEZE	EXP	PLY	SV	225 CHRY	10 10	7000	2	9250	10500
29 7	EXPLORER 29	FB	CR	PLY	SV 225 CHRY	10 10	7000	2	8350	9550
31	BAY-BREEZE 31		EXP	PLY	SV 225 CHRY	10 10	8000	2	11100	12600
33			SDN	PLY	IB 225 CHRY	10 10	10000	2	13700	15500
					1969 BOATS					
25	ANCHOR-LINE 25	HT	HB	F/W	130	8		2	**	**
25	ANCHORLINE 25	HT	HB	FBG	SV IO 120	10 6		2	**	**
27	FISHAWK		CR	PLY	IB 210 CHRY	10 10		2	6550	7550
27	FISHAWK 27		CR	MHG	IB 210 CHRY	10 10	6000	2	6200	7150
29 7	BAY-BREEZE		EXP	MHG	IB 210 CHRY	10 10	7000	2	8700	10000
29 7	BAY-BREEZE		EXP	PLY	IB 210 CHRY	10		2	**	**
29 7	BUCCANEER	FB	CR	FBG	IB 210 CHRY	10		2	7850	9050
29 7	BUCCANEER		EXP	FBG	IB 210 CHRY	10		2	8600	9850

LOA FT IN	NAME AND/ OR MODEL	TOP/ RIG	BOAT TYPE	-HULL- MTL TP	TP	ENGINE # HP	MFG	BEAM FT IN	WGT LBS	DRAFT FT IN	RETAIL LOW	RETAIL HIGH
1969 BOATS
29 7	BUCCANEER 30			MHG	IB	210	CHRY	10	8000	2	7800	8950
29 7	EXPLORER	FB	CR	PLY	IB	210	CHRY 10 10			2	**	**
29 7	EXPLORER 29	FB	CR	MHG	IB	210	CHRY 10 10		7000	2	7950	9150
31	BAY-BREEZE		EXP	PLY	IB	210	CHRY 10 10			2	10300	11700
31	BAY-BREEZE 31		CR	MHG	IB	210	CHRY 10 10		8000	2	9500	10800
33	SALON		EXP	MHG	IB	300	INT 11 11		11000	3	14500	16500
33	SALON-EXPRESS		EXP	PLY	IB	210	CHRY 11 11			3	13100	14900
34	ANCHOR-LINE 34	HT	HB	F/W	IO	325	9			2	11200	12700
34	ANCHORLINE 34	HT	HB	FBG	SV IO	325	11 11			2	11200	12700
1968 BOATS
27	FISHAWK			PLY	IB	210	CHRY 10 10		6000	2	6000	6900
29 7		HT	EXP	PLY	IB	210	CHRY 10 10		7000	2	8400	9650
29 7	BUCCANEER		EXP	FBG	IB	210	CHRY 10		8000	2	8700	10000
29 7	BUCCANEER EXPLORER		FBC	FBC	IB	210	CHRY 10		8000	2	7500	8650
29 7	EXPLORER	FB		PLY	IB	210	CHRY 10 10		7000	2	7250	8300
31	BAY-BREEZE			PLY	IB	210	CHRY 10 10		8000	2	8500	9800
33	SALON		EXP	PLY	IB	300	11 11		11000	3	14000	15900
1967 BOATS
23	BROADWATER			MHG	IB	195			3200		2900	3350
23	LITTLE-MARINER	CR	PLY	IB		8			2	**	**
26 7	FISHAWK		EXP	PLY	IB	10				2	**	**
28	LITTLE-MARINER	CR	PLY	IB		10			2	**	**
29 7	BAY-BREEZE		EXP	PLY	IB	10				2	**	**
29 7	BROADWATER			MHG	IB	210			7000		6950	8000
29 7	BUCCANEER 30			FBG	IB	210			8000		7300	8400
29 7	BUCCANEER 30	HT		FBG	IB	210			8000		7300	8400
33	EXPRESS		EXP	PLY	IB		11 11			3	**	**
36	BROADWATER			MHG	IB	T150			12500		18900	21000
36	EXPRESS		EXP	PLY	IB		11 11			3	**	**
36	SEDAN		SDN	PLY	IB		11 11			3	**	**
1966 BOATS
23	LITTLE-MARINER		CNV	WD	IB	165	8			1 7	3500	4050
23	LITTLE-MARINER		EXP	WD	IB	165	8			1 7	3550	4100
26 6	FISHAWK		SF	WD	IB	190-195	10			2	5050	5850
26 6	SEA-FLYER		EXP	WD	IB	210	10			2	5400	6200
26 6	SEA-FLYER	HT	EXP	WD	IB	210-235	10			2	5400	6300
29 7	BAY-BREEZE		EXP	WD	IB	210-235	10			2	7700	8950
29 7	BAY-BREEZE	HT	EXP	WD	IB	210-235	10			2	7700	8950
29 7	BAY-BREEZE	FB	EXP	WD	IB	210-235	10			2	7700	9000
36			EXP	WD	IB	T150	11 11			3	17500	19900
36		FB	EXP	WD	IB	T150	11 11			3	17600	20000
1965 BOATS
23	FISHAWK			WD	IB	120-190					3350	4000
23 8	LITTLE-MARINER			WD	IB	210					3700	4350
23 8	LITTLE-MARINER		CNV	WD	IB	210					3700	4350
26 6			EXP	WD	IB	210					5200	6000
26 6		HT	EXP	WD	IB	210					5200	6000
29 7			EXP	WD	IB	210					7450	8600
29 7		HT	EXP	WD	IB	210					7450	8600
1964 BOATS
23 8			EXP	WD	IB	210					3600	4150
23 8	CONV		EXP	WD	IB	210					3750	4350
26			EXP	WD	IB	210					4250	4950
26		HT	EXP	WD	IB	210					4250	4950
29 7			EXP	WD	IB	210					7200	8300
29 7		HT	EXP	WD	IB	210					7200	8300
29 7			SF	WD	IB	210					6250	7200
1961 BOATS
16	UTILITY		UTL	PLY	OB		6 10	700			1950	2350
19 3		HT		PLY	OB		7 4	1000			3100	3600
19 3	CRUISER		CR	PLY	OB		7 4	1450			4150	4850
21	CRUISER		CR	PLY	OB		7 8	1650			5250	6050
21	CRUISER		CR	PLY	IB	100	7 8			1 2	2600	3000

BROOKE MARINE LTD

Call 1-800-327-6929 for BUC Personalized Evaluation Service
Or, for 1971 boats, sign onto www.BUCValuPro.com

C J BROOM & SONS LTD

Call 1-800-327-6929 for BUC Personalized Evaluation Service
Or, for 1976 boats, sign onto www.BUCValuPro.com

BROWARD MARINE INC

DANIA BEACH FL 33004   COAST GUARD MFG ID- BWD See inside cover to adjust price for area

LOA FT IN	NAME AND/ OR MODEL	TOP/ RIG	BOAT TYPE	-HULL- MTL TP	TP	ENGINE # HP	MFG	BEAM FT IN	WGT LBS	DRAFT FT IN	RETAIL LOW	RETAIL HIGH
1983 BOATS
38 3	CATAMARAN RACER			AL	CT IB			11			**	**
77	MOTOR YACHT		MY	AL	SV IB			19			**	**
1982 BOATS
38 3	CATAMARAN RACER			AL	CT IB			11			**	**
67 1	BROWARD	FB	MY	AL	DV IB	T	D GM	17 10		4 6	**	**
70	BROWARD	FB	MY	AL	DV IB	T	D GM	17 10		4 6	**	**
72 5	RAISED BRIDGE	FB	MY	AL	SV IB	T550D GM		18			**	**
75	BROWARD	FB	MY	AL	DV IB	T	D GM	18 5		4 7	**	**
77	MOTOR YACHT		MY	AL	SV IB			19			**	**
1979 BOATS
67 1	BROWARD		MY	AL	DV IB	T	D GM	17 10		4 6	**	**
70	BROWARD		MY	AL	DV IB	T	D GM	17 10		4 6	**	**
75	BROWARD		MY	AL	DV IB	T	D GM	18 5		4 7	**	**
1974 BOATS
73			MY	WD	IB	T255D GM		18 2		4 7	**	**
74 4			MY	AL	IB	T255D GM		18 2		4 7	**	**
1972 BOATS
46			FB	SF	FBG	IB	T370D CUM				116000	127500
1971 BOATS
46 2	ANGLER		SF	FBG	IB	T280D GM		14 8	28000	3	101000	111000
1970 BOATS
46 2	ANGLER		SF	FBG SV	IB	280D GM		14 8	28000	3	89200	98100
1969 BOATS
46 2	ANGLER		SF	FBG SV	IB	T280D GM		14 8	28000	3	94400	104000
1968 BOATS
46 2	ANGLER		SF	FBG	IB	T280D GM		14 8	28000		91400	100500
1957 BOATS
39		FB	SF	WD	IB	T218D GM					45800	50400

BROWN-HUTCHINSON INC

TWIN-ALUME PONTOON BOAT COAST GUARD MFG ID- BHN

Call 1-800-327-6929 for BUC Personalized Evaluation Service
Or, for 1967 to 1979 boats, sign onto www.BUCValuPro.com

BROWNELL BOAT YARD INC.

MATTAPOISETT MA 02739-0 COAST GUARD MFG ID- BBW See inside cover to adjust price for area

For more recent years, see the BUC Used Boat Price Guide, Volume 1 or Volume 2

LOA FT IN	NAME AND/ OR MODEL	TOP/ RIG	BOAT TYPE	-HULL- MTL TP	TP	ENGINE # HP	MFG	BEAM FT IN	WGT LBS	DRAFT FT IN	RETAIL LOW	RETAIL HIGH
1967 BOATS
24 1	BASS BOAT		BASS	P/M	IB	135	8 5			2 2	10300	11700
26 6	BASS BOAT		BASS	P/M	IB	150	9 8			2 5	16300	18500
32 2	SPORT FISH		SF	P/M	IB	170	11			2 6	27400	30400
36 2	SPORT FISH		SF	P/M	IB	215	12 6			2 10	48100	52800
39 11	SPORT FISH		SF	P/M	IB	T225	13 2			2 9	71600	78700
46	SPORT FISH		SF	P/M	IB	T225	14 2			3 2	114200	125500
1965 BOATS
24 1	BASS BOAT		BASS	WD	IB	120	8 5			2 2	9600	10900
32 2	BORWNELL		CR	WD	IB	150	11			2 6	26300	29300
32 2	BROWNELL		SF	WD	IB	150	11			2 6	25300	28100
36	BROWNELL		CR	WD	IB	175					45600	50100
46	BROWNELL		CR	WD	IB	225					74100	81400

JOHN BROWNING & ASSOC

COAST GUARD MFG ID- JBA

Call 1-800-327-6929 for BUC Personalized Evaluation Service
Or, for 1969 to 1977 boats, sign onto www.BUCValuPro.com

BRUNO & STILLMAN

NEWINGTON NH 03801 COAST GUARD MFG ID- BSY See inside cover to adjust price for area

LOA FT	LOA IN	NAME AND/ OR MODEL	TOP/ RIG	BOAT TYPE	HULL MTL	HULL TP	ENGINE TP	# HP	ENGINE MFG	BEAM FT	BEAM IN	WGT LBS	DRAFT FT	DRAFT IN	RETAIL LOW	RETAIL HIGH
		1983 BOATS														
29	6	SPORT CRUISER		SPTCR	FBG	DS	IB	85D		10	2				38800	43100
35		SPORT CRUISER		SPTCR	FBG	DS	IB	130D		11	6		2	10	62500	68700
		1982 BOATS														
29	6			SPTCR	FBG	DS	IB	85D		10	2				37300	41500
35				SPTCR	FBG	DS	IB	130D		11	6	11000			60100	66000
		1981 BOATS														
35				SPTCR	FBG	DS	IB	130D		11	6	11000	2	10	57700	63500
35		SPORTFISHERMAN		SF	FBG	DS	IB	130D	PERK	11	6	11000			55200	60700
		1980 BOATS														
35		B&S		CR	FBG	DS	IB	130D		11	6	11000			55600	61000
35		B&S		SF	FBG	DS	IB	130D		11	6	11000			52800	58100
35		B-&-S WORKBOAT		PH	FBG	DS	IB	120		11	6	10000			45700	50200
42		B-&-S WORKBOAT		PH	FBG	DS	IB	120		13	8	19000			66800	73400
55		B-&-S WORKBOAT		PH	FBG	DS	IB	250D		16		40000			132500	145500
		1979 BOATS														
35		B-&-S		CR	FBG	DS	IB	130D		11	6	11000			53500	58800
35		B-&-S		SF	FBG	DS	IB	130D		11	6	11000			50800	55900
35		B-&-S WORKBOAT		PH	FBG	DS	IB	220		11	6	10000			44100	49000
42		B-&-S WORKBOAT		PH	FBG	DS	IB	220		13	8	19000			65200	71600
55		B-&-S WORKBOAT		PH	FBG	DS	IB	250D		16		40000			126500	139500
		1978 BOATS														
35		B-&-S		CR	FBG	DS	IB	130D		11	6	11000			51500	56600
35		B-&-S		CR	FBG	DS	IB	210D		11	6	11000			51100	56100
35		B-&-S		SF	FBG	DS	IB	130D		11	6	11000			49000	53800
35		B-&-S WORKBOAT		PH	FBG	DS	IB	220		13	8	10000			39500	43900
42		B-&-S WORKBOAT		PH	FBG	DS	IB	220		13	8	19000			62300	68500
55		B-&-S WORKBOAT		PH	FBG	DS	IB	250D		16		40000			121500	133500
		1977 BOATS														
35		B-&-S WORKBOAT		PH	FBG	DS	IB	220		11	6	10000	2	10	40600	45100
		IB 101D GM 49900 54800, IB 128D FORD 49200 54100, IB 130D PERK 49400 54300														
		IB 140D GM 49000 53800, IB 160D PERK 49000 53800, IB 180D PERK 49000 53800														
		IB 210D CAT 49600 54500, IB 216D GM 49400 54200														
42	3	B-&-S WORKBOAT		PH	FBG	DS	IB	220		13	8	19340	4		60600	66600
		IB 140D GM 73800 81100, IB 145D GM 73900 81200, IB 165D CAT 74800 82100														
		IB 180D PERK 75100 82500, IB 210D CAT 68100 74800, IB 216D GM 67700 74400														
		IB 225D GM 68200 74900, IB 250D CAT 70200 77100, IB 290D GM 71700 78700														
		IB 310D J&T 73000 80200														
55		B-&-S WORKBOAT		PH	FBG	DS	IB	240D	GM	16		40000	5	3	110000	120500
		IB 270D CAT 113500 124500, IB 325D CAT 115000 126500, IB 325D GM 112000 123000														
		IB 490D GM 120000 131500														
		1976 BOATS														
35		B-&-S WORKBOAT		PH	FBG	DS	IB	220		11	6	10000	2	10	39000	43300
42	3	B-&-S WORKBOAT		PH	FBG	DS	IB	220		13	8	20880	4		61600	67700
55		B-&-S WORKBOAT		PH	FBG	DS	IB	250D	CAT	16		44800	5	3	113000	124500
		1975 BOATS														
35		B-&-S WORKBOAT		PH	FBG	RB	IB	190	PALM	11	6	10000	2	10	37100	41200
42	3	B-&-S WORKBOAT		PH	FBG	RB	IB	190	PALM	13	8	20000	4		56600	62200
55		B-&-S WORKBOAT		PH	FBG	RB	IB	375D	CAT	16		40000	5	3	107500	118000
		1972 BOATS														
30	6	FRIENDSHIP	GAF	SA/CR	FBG	KL	IB	30D		10			4	6	19600	21800
30	6	FRIENDSHIP	SLP	SA/CR	FBG	KL	IB	30D		10			4	6	19600	21800
		1971 BOATS														
30	6	FRIENDSHIP 30	SLP	SAIL	FBG	KL	IB	25D	GRAY	10		12500	4	6	23600	26200
		1970 BOATS														
30	6	FRIENDSHIP	SLP	SAIL	FBG	KL	IB	15D	VLVO	10		12540	4	6	23300	25800
		1969 BOATS														
30	6	FRIENDSHIP	SLP	SAIL	FBG	KL	IB	15D	VLVO						18800	20900

BRYANT BOATS

COAST GUARD MFG ID- BMA

Call 1-800-327-6929 for BUC Personalized Evaluation Service
Or, for 1959 to 1962 boats, sign onto www.BUCValuPro.com

BUCCANEER YACHTS

DIV OF BAYLINER MARINE CORP
EVERETT WA 98206 COAST GUARD MFG ID- BLB See inside cover to adjust price for area

LOA FT	LOA IN	NAME AND/ OR MODEL	TOP/ RIG	BOAT TYPE	HULL MTL	HULL TP	ENGINE TP	# HP	ENGINE MFG	BEAM FT	BEAM IN	WGT LBS	DRAFT FT	DRAFT IN	RETAIL LOW	RETAIL HIGH
		1980 BOATS														
22		BUCCANEER 220	SLP	SA/CR	FBG	KL	OB			7	11	2450	4	1	2800	3250
25		BUCCANEER 250	SLP	SA/CR	FBG	KL	OB			8		3750	4	7	4450	5100
25		BUCCANEER 255	SLP	SA/CR	FBG	KL	IB	8D	VLVO	8		4070	4	7	5150	5900
27		CORINTHIAN 27	SLP	SA/CR	FBG	KL	OB			9	6	6050	5		7450	8550
27		CORINTHIAN 27	SLP	SA/CR	FBG	KL	IB	8D- 13D		9	6	6250	5		8000	9350
29	3	BUCCANEER 295	SLP	SA/CR	FBG	KL	IB	13D	VLVO	10	3	6800	5	1	8900	10100
29	11	CORINTHIAN 30	SLP	SA/CR	FBG	KL	IB	13D	VLVO	10	3	7000	5	7	9150	10400
30		BUCCANEER 305	SLP	SA/CR	FBG	KL	IB	23D- 36D		10	2	10000	4		13100	15000
32	10	BUCCANEER 335	SLP	SA/CR	FBG	KL	IB	13D	VLVO	10	6	9300	5	6	11900	13500
		1979 BOATS														
22		BUCCANEER 220	SLP	SA/CR	FBG	KL	OB			7	11	2450	3		2750	3200
22		BUCCANEER 220 SHOAL	SLP	SA/CR	FBG	KL	OB			7	11	2450			2650	3100
25		BUCCANEER 250	SLP	SA/CR	FBG	KL	OB			8		3750	3	6	4250	4950
25		BUCCANEER 250 SHOAL	SLP	SA/CR	FBG	KL	OB			8		3750			4150	4850
27	6	BUCCANEER 272	SLP	SA/CR	FBG	KL	OB			8		5200	4		6200	7100
27	6	BUCCANEER 277	SLP	SA/CR	FBG	KL	IB	8D- 13D		8		6050	4		7450	8600
29	3	BUCCANEER 295	SLP	SA/CR	FBG	KL	IB	13D	VLVO	12	3	6800	5	7	8450	9750
29	3	BUCCANEER 305	SLP	SA/CR	FBG	KL	IB	23D- 36D		12	2	10000	4		12700	14500
32	10	BUCCANEER 335	SLP	SA/CR	FBG	KL	IB	13D	VLVO	12	6	9300	6	1	11400	13000
		1978 BOATS														
20	5	BUCCANEER 200	SLP	SAIL	FBG	KL	OB			8		2100	1	9	2300	2700
20	10	BUCCANEER 210	SLP	SA/CR	FBG	KL	OB			8		3000	2		2900	3400
23	8	BUCCANEER 240	SLP	SA/CR	FBG	KL	OB			8		4000	2	6	4100	4750
26	8	BUCCANEER 270	SLP	SA/CR	FBG	KL	OB			8		5000	2	3	5650	6450
26	8	BUCCANEER 275	SLP	SA/CR	FBG	KL	IB	8D- 13D		8		5850	2	3	6900	8000
26	8	BUCCANEER 285	SLP	SA/CR	FBG	KL	IB	13D	VLVO	8		6050	2	3	7200	8250
27	6	BUCCANEER 272	SLP	SA/CR	FBG	KL	OB			8		5200	4		5950	6850
27	6	BUCCANEER 277	SLP	SA/CR	FBG	KL	IB	8D- 13D		8		6050	4		7200	8300
29	3	BUCCANEER 295	SLP	SA/CR	FBG	KL	IB	13D	VLVO	10	3	6800	5	7	8150	9400
30		BUCCANEER 305	SLP	SA/CR	FBG	KL	IB	23D- 35D		10	2	10000	4		12200	13900
32		BUCCANEER 325	SLP	SA/CR	FBG	KL	IB	35D	VLVO	10	2	12500	4		14800	16900
32	10	BUCCANEER 335	SLP	SA/CR	FBG	KL	IB	13D	VLVO	10	6	9300	6	1	11000	12500
		1977 BOATS														
20	5	BUCCANEER 200	SLP	SAIL	FBG	KL	OB			8		2100	1	9	2250	2600
20	10	BUCCANEER 210	SLP	SA/CR	FBG	KL	OB			8		3000	2		2800	3250
23	8	BUCCANEER 240	SLP	SA/CR	FBG	KL	OB			8		4000	2	6	3950	4600
23	8	BUCCANEER 245	SLP	SA/CR	FBG	KL	IB	8D	VLVO	8		4250	2	3	4650	5350
26	8	BUCCANEER 270	SLP	SA/CR	FBG	KL	OB			8		5000	2	3	5450	6250
26	8	BUCCANEER 275	SLP	SA/CR	FBG	KL	IB	10D	VLVO	8		5850	2	3	6700	7700
26	8	BUCCANEER 285	SLP	SA/CR	FBG	KL	IB	10D	VLVO	8		6050	2	3	6900	7950
30		BUCCANEER 305	SLP	SA/CR	FBG	KL	IB	25D	VLVO	10	2	10000	4		11800	13400
32		BUCCANEER 325	SLP	MS	FBG	KL	IB	36D	VLVO	10	2	12500	4		14200	16100
		1976 BOATS														
20	10	BUCCANEER 210	SLP	SAIL	FBG	KL	OB			8		3000	2		2750	3150
23	8	BUCCANEER 240	SLP	SAIL	FBG	KL	OB			8		4000	2	3	3850	4450
26	8	BUCCANEER 270	SLP	SAIL	FBG	KL	OB			8		5000	2	3	5250	6050
26	8	BUCCANEER 270	SLP	SAIL	FBG	KL	IB	10D	VLVO	8		5000	2	3	5550	6400
32		BUCCANEER 320	SLP	SAIL	FBG	KL	IB	36D	VLVO	10	2	12500	3	6	13800	15600
		1975 BOATS														
20	10	BUCCANEER 210	SLP	SAIL	FBG	KL	OB			8		3000	2		2650	3100
23	8	BUCCANEER 240	SLP	SAIL	FBG	KL	OB			8		4000	2	3	3750	4350
23	8	BUCCANEER 240	SLP	SAIL	FBG	KL	IB	10D	VLVO	8		4000	2	3	4150	4800
26	8	BUCCANEER 270	SLP	SAIL	FBG	KL	OB			8		5000	2	3	5100	5900
26	8	BUCCANEER 270	SLP	SAIL	FBG	KL	IB	10D	VLVO	8		5000	2	3	5400	6200
32		BUCCANEER 320	SLP	SAIL	FBG	KL	IB	36D	VLVO	10	2	12500	3	6	13400	15200

WM BUCHAN BOAT COMPANY

Call 1-800-327-6929 for BUC Personalized Evaluation Service
Or, for 1972 to 1977 boats, sign onto www.BUCValuPro.com

BUCHAN YACHTS LTD

Call 1-800-327-6929 for BUC Personalized Evaluation Service
Or, for 1979 to 1985 boats, sign onto www.BUCValuPro.com

BUCKLER BOAT COMPANY LTD

Call 1-800-327-6929 for BUC Personalized Evaluation Service
Or, for 1977 to 1978 boats, sign onto www.BUCValuPro.com

THE BUEHLER CORP
TURBOCRAFT   COAST GUARD MFG ID- BLR

Call 1-800-327-6929 for BUC Personalized Evaluation Service
Or, for 1959 to 1979 boats, sign onto www.BUCValuPro.com

BUHLERS YACHTS LTD

Call 1-800-327-6929 for BUC Personalized Evaluation Service
Or, for 1977 to 1984 boats, sign onto www.BUCValuPro.com

BURGER BOAT COMPANY
MANITOWOC WI 54220   COAST GUARD MFG ID- BRG See inside cover to adjust price for area

For more recent years, see the BUC Used Boat Price Guide, Volume 1 or Volume 2

LOA NAME AND/ FT IN OR MODEL		TOP/ RIG	BOAT TYPE	-HULL- MTL TP	----ENGINE--- TP # HP MFG	BEAM FT IN	WGT LBS	DRAFT FT IN	RETAIL LOW	RETAIL HIGH
----------------- 1976	**BOATS**									
72 2		FB	MY	AL	IB T650D GM				**	**
----------------- 1974	**BOATS**									
75 COCKPIT		FB	MYCPT	AL	IB T550D GM				**	**
----------------- 1973	**BOATS**									
72 2		FB	MY	AL	IB T650D GM				**	**
----------------- 1972	**BOATS**									
71 4		FB	MY	FBG	IB T525D GM				568000	624500
----------------- 1971	**BOATS**									
64		FD	AL		IB T350D GM				295000	324000
----------------- 1970	**BOATS**									
66		FD	AL		IB T400D CAT				318500	350000
----------------- 1969	**BOATS**									
64 2		HT FD	AL		IB T350D GM				277500	305000
67		MY			IB T350D				372000	409000
----------------- 1968	**BOATS**									
62		MY	AL		IB T350D GM				314500	345500
64		HT FD	AL		IB T350D GM				266500	293000
----------------- 1967	**BOATS**									
64		FD	AL		IB T350D GM				258500	284000
----------------- 1965	**BOATS**									
65		FB FD	AL		IB T350D GM				255500	281000
----------------- 1963	**BOATS**									
63		FD	AL		IB T336D GM				231000	253500
----------------- 1954	**BOATS**									
54		FB	MY	STL	IB T235D GM				125000	137500
----------------- 1951	**BOATS**									
53		FB	MY	WD	IB T D GM	14			**	**
----------------- 1950	**BOATS**									
59		FD	STL		IB T235D GM				140500	154500
----------------- 1949	**BOATS**									
53		HT	MY	STL	IB				**	**
----------------- 1948	**BOATS**									
57		FD			IB T D GM	14 6		4 6	**	**
----------------- 1946	**BOATS**									
45		SAIL	STL		IB				74900	82300
54		HT MY	STL		IB				**	**
----------------- 1937	**BOATS**									
16 SNIPE		SAIL	WD						2150	2500
23 SAILETTE		SAIL	WD						6350	7300
23 STAR		SAIL	WD						6350	7300
28 SEAFLOW		SAIL	WD						13800	15700
33 SAILBOY		SAIL	WD						28000	31100
34		HT	SDN	WD	IB				**	**
46		FB	MY	WD	IB				**	**
----------------- 1936	**BOATS**									
22 9		SLP	SAIL	WD KL	7		3450	2 6	6900	7900
----------------- 1935	**BOATS**									
22 9		SLP	SAIL	WD KL	7		3450	2 6	7150	8200
----------------- 1907	**BOATS**									
42				WD	IB 90D UNIV				**	**

JOHN BURN & ASSOC LTD
MARK ELLIS DESIGN LTD

Call 1-800-327-6929 for BUC Personalized Evaluation Service
Or, for 1978 to 1980 boats, sign onto www.BUCValuPro.com

BURNS CRAFT INC
BURNS MANUFACTURING INC   See inside cover to adjust price for area
LEXINGTON AL 35648   COAST GUARD MFG ID- BCI
                        FOR OLDER MODELS SEE NAUTA-CRAFT INC

For more recent years, see the BUC Used Boat Price Guide, Volume 1 or Volume 2

LOA NAME AND/ FT IN OR MODEL	TOP/ RIG	BOAT TYPE	-HULL- MTL TP	----ENGINE--- TP # HP MFG	BEAM FT IN	WGT LBS	DRAFT FT IN	RETAIL LOW	RETAIL HIGH
--------------- 1982 BOATS									
40 6 ELDORADO	HT	SDN	FBG SV	IB T	12 6	23000	2 11	**	**
40 6 ELDORADO	FB	SDN	FBG SV	IB T	12 6	23000	2 11	**	**
40 6 ELDORADO	FB	SDN	FBG SV	IB T235D VLVO	12 6	23000	2 11	51000	56000
48 3 BURNS-CRAFT 48	FB	TCMY	FBG SV	IB T	15 2	34000	3 6	**	**
48 3 BURNS-CRAFT 48	FB	TCMY	FBG SV	IB T235D VLVO	15 2	34000	3 6	70600	77600
--------------- 1981 BOATS									
40 6 ELDORADO	HT	SDN	FBG SV	IB T	12 6	23000	2 11	**	**
40 6 ELDORADO	HT	SDN	FBG SV	IB T235D VLVO	12 6	23000	2 11	48600	53400
40 6 ELDORADO	FB	SDN	FBG SV	IB T	12 6	23000	2 11	**	**
40 6 ELDORADO	FB	SDN	FBG SV	IB T330	12 6	23000	2 11	44800	49800
40 6 ELDORADO	FB	SDN	FBG SV	IB T235D VLVO	12 6	23000	2 11	48600	53400
43 NAUTA-LINE 43	FB	HB	FBG SV	VD T270 CRUS	13 5	24000	2 5	35900	39900
43 NAUTA-LINE 43	FB	HB	FBG SV	VD T350 CRUS	13 5	24000	2 5	37400	41500
--------------- 1980 BOATS									
37 SEVILLE	HT	SDN	FBG DV	IB T198	12 6	18000		30000	33300
40 6 ELDORADO	FB	SDN	FBG DV	IB T330	12 6	23000	2 11	42800	47500
--------------- 1979 BOATS									
37 SEVILLE	HT	SDN	FBG SV	IB 198	12 6	20000	2 4	29800	33100
37 SEVILLE	HT	SDN	FBG SV	IB T330	12 6	20000	2 4	31600	35100
37 SEVILLE	FB	SDN	FBG SV	IB 198	12 6	20000	2 4	29800	33100
37 SEVILLE	FB	SDN	FBG SV	IB T330	12 6	20000	2 4	31600	35100
38 BURNS-CRAFT	HT	HB	FBG TR	IO 228	12			27800	30900
41 SEVILLE-ELDORADO	HT	SF	FBG SV	IB 198	12 6	23000	2 11	41200	45800
41 SEVILLE-ELDORADO	HT	SF	FBG SV	IB T330	12 6	23000	2 11	39600	44000
41 SEVILLE-ELDORADO	FB	SF	FBG SV	IB 198	12 6	23000	2 11	41200	45800
41 SEVILLE-ELDORADO	FB	SF	FBG SV	IB T330	12 6	23000	2 11	39600	44000
43 BURNS-CRAFT	HT	HB	FBG TR	IB T228	14			29900	33200
--------------- 1978 BOATS									
37 SEVILLE	HT	SDN	FBG DV	IB 228 MRCR	12 6	20900	2 4	29500	32700
IB 233 MRCR 29500	32800,	IB	250	CC 29500	32800,	IB 330	CC	29800	33100
IB 330 MRCR 29800	33100,	IB		D **	**,	IB T228	MRCR	30500	33800
37 SEVILLE	FB	SDN	FBG DV	IB 228 MRCR	12 6	20900	2 4	29500	32800
IB 233 MRCR 29500	32800,	IB	250	CC 29500	32800,	IB 330	CC	29800	33100
IB 330 MRCR 29800	33100,	IB		D **	**,	IB T228	MRCR	30500	33800
37 1 BURNS-CRAFT	HT	HB	FBG TR	IO 228 MRCR	12	16000		30300	33600
IO 330 MRCR 32300	35900,	VD	T225	CC 33000	36700,	IO T228	MRCR	32600	36200
VD T228 MRCR 33100	36700,	VD	T250	CC 33200	36900,	VD T255	MRCR	33200	36900
IO T330 MRCR 36700	40800,	VD	T330	CC 34300	38100,	VD T330	MRCR	34300	38100
37 1 BURNS-CRAFT	FB	HB	FBG TR	IO 228 MRCR	12	16000		30300	33600
IO 330 MRCR 32300	35900,	VD	T225	CC 33000	36700,	IO T228	MRCR	32600	36200
VD T228 MRCR 33100	36700,	VD	T250	CC 33200	36900,	VD T255	MRCR	33200	36900
IO T330 MRCR 36700	40800,	VD	T330	CC 34300	38100,	VD T330	MRCR	34300	38100
43 BURNS-CRAFT	HT	HB	FBG TR	IO 228 MRCR	14	19000		30500	33900
IO 330 MRCR 32400	36000,	VD	T225	CC 31700	35200,	IO T228	MRCR	32600	36300
VD T228 MRCR 31700	35300,	VD	T250	CC 31800	35400,	VD T255	MRCR	31900	35400
IO T330 MRCR 36500	40600,	VD	T330	CC 32800	36500,	VD T330	MRCR	32800	36500
43 BURNS-CRAFT	FB	HB	FBG TR	IO 228 MRCR	14	19000		30500	33900
IO 330 MRCR 32400	36000,	VD	T225	CC 31700	35200,	IO T228	MRCR	32600	36300
VD T228 MRCR 31700	35300,	VD	T250	CC 31800	35400,	VD T255	MRCR	31900	35400
IO T330 MRCR 36500	40600,	VD	T330	CC 32800	36500,	VD T330	MRCR	32800	36500
--------------- 1977 BOATS									
32 BURNS-CRAFT	HT	HB	FBG TR	IO 255 MRCR	12	11000	1 4	22100	24500
32 BURNS-CRAFT	HT	HB	FBG TR	IO T255 MRCR	12	11000	1 4	22100	24500
32 BURNS-CRAFT	FB	HB	FBG TR	IO 255 MRCR	12	11000	1 4	22400	27100
32 BURNS-CRAFT	FB	HB	FBG TR	IO T255 MRCR	12	11000	1 4	24400	27100
36 6 SEVILLE	HT	SDN	F/S DV	IB T233 MRCR	12 6	13000	2 4	21400	23700
VD T233 MRCR 21400	23700,	IB	T250	CC 21500	23900,	VD T250	CC	21500	23900
IB T330 CC 22100	24600,	VD	T330	CC 22100	24600,	IB T130D LEHM		23100	25700
VD T130D LEHM 23100	25700								
36 6 SEVILLE	FB	SDN	F/S DV	IB T233 MRCR	12 6	13000	2 4	21400	23700
VD T233 MRCR 21400	23700,	IB	T250	CC 21500	23900,	VD T250	CC	21500	23900

```
 LOA  NAME AND/        TOP/ BOAT  -HULL- ----ENGINE--- BEAM  WGT  DRAFT RETAIL RETAIL
FT IN OR MODEL         RIG TYPE   MTL TP TP # HP MFG  FT IN  LBS  FT IN  LOW    HIGH
-------------------- 1977 BOATS -------------------------------------------------
36  6 SEVILLE           FB  SDN  F/S DV IB T330  CC   12  6 13000  2  4 22100  24600
      VD T330  CC 22100 24600, IB T130D LEHM 23100 25700, VD T130D LEHM 23100 25700
43    BURNS-CRAFT       HT  HB   FBG TR IO 255  MRCR 14    16000  1  8 27600  30600
      VD T215  CC 28500 31700, VD T233 MRCR 28600 31700, VD T250 CC 28700 31800
      IO T255  MRCR 30000 33300, VD T255 MRCR 28700 31900, VD T330 CC 29600 32900
      VD T350  MRCR 30000 33400
43    BURNS-CRAFT       FB  HB   FBG TR IO 255  MRCR 14    16000  1  8 27600  30600
      VD T215  CC 28500 31700, VD T233 MRCR 28600 31700, VD T250 CC 28700 31800
      IO T255  MRCR 30000 33300, VD T255 MRCR 28700 31900, VD T330 CC 29600 32900
      VD T350  MRCR 30000 33400
50    BURNS-CRAFT       HT  HB   FBG SV VD T215  CC   15    23000  2  9 39600  44000
      VD T233  MRCR 39700 44100, VD T250 CC 39800 44200, IO T255 MRCR 42700 47500
      VD T255  MRCR 39800 44200, VD T330 CC 40800 45300, VD T350 MRCR 41200 45800
50    BURNS-CRAFT       FB  HB   FBG SV VD T215  CC   15    23000  2  9 39600  44000
      VD T233  MRCR 39700 44100, VD T250 CC 39800 44200, IO T255 MRCR 42700 47500
      VD T255  MRCR 39800 44200, VD T330 CC 40800 45300, VD T350 MRCR 41200 45800
-------------------- 1976 BOATS -------------------------------------------------
32    BURNS-CRAFT       HT  HB   FBG TR IO 233-255  12    11000  1  4 21600  24200
32    BURNS-CRAFT       HT  HB   FBG TR IO T233-T255 12    11000  1  4 23700  26800
32    BURNS-CRAFT       FB  HB   FBG TR IO 233-255  12    11000  1  4 21600  24200
32    BURNS-CRAFT       FB  HB   FBG TR IO T233-T255 12    11000  1  4 23700  26800
43    BURNS-CRAFT       HT  HB   FBG TR IO 255  MRCR 14    11000  1  8 28000  31100
      VD T215  CC 28900 32100, VD T233 MRCR 29000 32200, VD T250 CC 29100 32300
      IO T255  MRCR 30400 33800, VD T255 MRCR 29100 32300, VD T330 CC 30000 33400
      VD T350  MRCR 30500 33800
43    BURNS-CRAFT       FB  HB   FBG TR IO 255  MRCR 14          1  8 28000  31100
      VD T215  CC 28900 32100, VD T233 MRCR 29000 32200, VD T250 CC 29100 32300
      IO T255  MRCR 30400 33800, VD T255 MRCR 29100 32300, VD T330 CC 30000 33400
      VD T350  MRCR 30500 33800
50    BURNS-CRAFT       HT  HB   FBG TR VD T215  CC   15    23000  2  9 40800  45300
      VD T233  MRCR 45400 45400, VD T250 CC 40900 45500, IO T255 MRCR 43800 48600
      VD T255  MRCR 41000 45500, VD T330 CC 42000 46600, VD T350 MRCR 42400 47200
50    BURNS-CRAFT       FB  HB   FBG TR VD T215  CC   15    23000  2  9 40800  45300
      VD T233  MRCR 40900 45400, VD T250 CC 40900 45500, IO T255 MRCR 43800 48600
      VD T255  MRCR 41000 45500, VD T330 CC 42000 46600, VD T350 MRCR 42400 47200
-------------------- 1975 BOATS -------------------------------------------------
32    BURNS-CRAFT       HT  HB   FBG TR IB T225     12    11000  1  4 21100  23500
38    BURNS-CRAFT       HT  HB   FBG SV IB T225     15          27000  30000
38    BURNS-CRAFT       HT  HB   FBG TR IB T225     14          26800  29800
50    BURNS-CRAFT       HT  HB   FBG SV IB T225     15          39300  43600
-------------------- 1974 BOATS -------------------------------------------------
32    BURNS-CRAFT       HT  HB   FBG TR IB  225     12    11000  1  4 20900  23300
43    BURNS-CRAFT       HT  HB   FBG TR IB T225     12          1  8 28200  31300
45    BURNS-CRAFT       HT  HB   FBG SV IB  225     15          29200  32500
50    BURNS-CRAFT       HT  HB   FBG SV IB T225     15    23000  2  9 38400  42700
-------------------- 1973 BOATS -------------------------------------------------
32    BURNS-CRAFT       HT  HB   FBG TR IO  225     12    11000  1  4 21000  23300
35    BURNS-CRAFT       HT  HB   FBG    IO  225     12          19000  21200
43    BURNS-CRAFT       HT  HB   FBG TR VD T215     14    16000  1  8 27300  30400
45    BURNS-CRAFT       HT  HB   FBG    VD T215     15          30300  33600
50    BURNS-CRAFT       HT  HB   FBG SV VD T215     15    23000  2  9 38000  42200
-------------------- 1971 BOATS -------------------------------------------------
31  8 BURNS-CRAFT       HT  HB   FBG    IO  225     12    10000  1  6 19400  21600
35    BURNS-CRAFT       HT  HB   FBG        225     12    12000  1  8 21700  24200
      IB  225 21600 24000, IO T225 23700 26300, IB T225 23200 25800
42 10 BURNS-CRAFT       HT  HB   FBG    IO T225     15    16000  2    27700  30800
44    BURNS-CRAFT       HT  HB   FBG    IO T225     15    18000  2    34400  38200
44    BURNS-CRAFT       HT  HB   FBG    IO T225     15    18000  2    33000  36700
49    BURNS-CRAFT       HT  HB   FBG    IB T300     15    20000  2    40500  45000
49    BURNS-CRAFT       HT  HB   FBG    IB T300     15    20000  2    36700  40800
52    BURNS-CRAFT       HT  HB   STL    IO T300     15    22000  2    43800  48700
-------------------- 1970 BOATS -------------------------------------------------
31  8 31              HT  HB   FBG SV IO  225     12    10000         18900  21100
42 10 42              HT  HB   FBG SV IO  225     15    16000         24300  27000
49    49              HT  HB   FBG SV IO  300     15    22000         37100  41300
52    52              HT  HB   STL SV IO  300     15    22000         40000  44500
```

BURR BROS BOATS INC
COAST GUARD MFG ID- BRR

Call 1-800-327-6929 for BUC Personalized Evaluation Service
Or, for 1959 to 1974 boats, sign onto www.BUCValuPro.com

BUZZARD'S BAY BOATS INC
COAST GUARD MFG ID- BBV

Call 1-800-327-6929 for BUC Personalized Evaluation Service
Or, for 1974 to 1975 boats, sign onto www.BUCValuPro.com

C & B MARINE
COAST GUARD MFG ID- CNJ

Call 1-800-327-6929 for BUC Personalized Evaluation Service
Or, for 1981 to 1985 boats, sign onto www.BUCValuPro.com

C & C YACHTS
FAIRPORT HARBOR OH 4400 COAST GUARD MFG ID- ZCC See inside cover to adjust price for area

C & C YACHTS
FAIRPORT HARBOR OH 44077
FORMERLY C & C INTERNATIONAL YACHTS

For more recent years, see the BUC Used Boat Price Guide, Volume 1 or Volume 2

```
 LOA  NAME AND/        TOP/ BOAT  -HULL- ----ENGINE--- BEAM  WGT  DRAFT RETAIL RETAIL
FT IN OR MODEL         RIG TYPE   MTL TP TP # HP MFG  FT IN  LBS  FT IN  LOW    HIGH
-------------------- 1983 BOATS -------------------------------------------------
25  2 C-&-C 25         SLP SAIL FBG KL OB          8  8  4600  4  3 11400  12900
27 11 C-&-C 27         SLP SA/CR FBG KL IB  15D    9  1  5800  4  6 16800  19000
28  7 C-&-C 29         SLP SA/CR FBG KL IB  15D    9  6  6700  5  4 19900  22100
30    C-&-C 30         SLP SA/CR FBG KL IB  15D   10    8000  5    23800  26400
31  6 C-&-C 32         SLP SA/CR FBG KC IB  15D   10  3 10485  4    30400  33700
31  6 C-&-C 32         SLP SA/CR FBG KL IB  15D   10  3  9680  5  8 29800  33100
33  6 C-&-C 34         SLP SA/CR FBG KC IB  23D   11    11090  4    34300  38200
33  6 C-&-C 34         SLP SA/CR FBG KL IB  23D   11    10100  5 11 31300  34800
34  8 C-&-C 35         SLP SA/CR FBG KC IB  23D   10  2 10800  6  5 33900  37700
34 11 LANDFALL 35      SLP SA/CR FBG KL IB  30D   10  8 13000  4 10 40700  45200
37  7 C-&-C 37         SLP SA/CR FBG KC IB  30D   10    14300    48100  52800
37  7 C-&-C 37         SLP SA/CR FBG KL IB  30D   11  8 14300  6  8 48100  52800
37  7 LANDFALL 38      SLP SA/CR FBG KL IB  30D   10    16700  5    54600  60100
39  7 C-&-C 40         SLP SA/CR FBG KL IB  30D   10  8 16300  4 10 50100  55100
42  1 LANDFALL 43      SLP SA/CR FBG KL IB  60D   12  8 24600  5  6 85800  94200
42  1 LANDFALL 43      SLP SA/CR FBG KL IB  60D   12  8 24600  5  6 85800  94300
47  6 LANDFALL 48      CUT SA/CR FBG KL IB  85D   14    35600  6  2 128000 140500
62  5 C-&-C 62         KTH SA/CR FBG KC IB  100D  15  2 62000  8  2 336500 369500
62  5 C-&-C 62         KTH SA/CR FBG KL IB  100D  15  2 62000  8  2 336500 369500
-------------------- 1982 BOATS -------------------------------------------------
24    C-&-C 24         SLP SA/RC FBG KL OB          8  9  3200  4    7150   8200
25  2 C-&-C 25         SLP SAIL FBG KL OB          8  8  4100  4  3  9600  10900
25  2 C-&-C 25         SLP SAIL FBG KL SD  15  OMC 8  8  4100  4  3 10300  11700
27 11 C-&-C 27         SLP SAIL FBG KL IB  15D YAN 9  1  5500  4  6 15000  17000
      C-&-C 30         SLP SA/RC FBG KL OB  15D YAN 10    8000  5    24400  24900
30    MEGA 30          SLP SA/RC FBG KL OB          7 11 6589  5  2 18100  20100
30    MEGA 30          SLP SA/RC FBG SK OB          7 11 6589    18100  20100
31  6 C-&-C 32         SLP SAIL FBG KC IB  15D YAN 10  3 10485  4    30400  33800
31  6 C-&-C 32         SLP SAIL FBG KL IB  15D YAN 10  3  9680  5  8 28100  31200
33  6 C-&-C 34         SLP SAIL FBG KC IB  20D YAN 11    11090  4    32300  35900
33  6 C-&-C 34         SLP SAIL FBG KL IB  20D YAN 11    10100  5 11 29500  32800
34 11 LANDFALL 35      SLP SAIL FBG KL IB  30D YAN 10  8 13000  4 10 38300  42600
35  8 C-&-C 36         SLP SAIL FBG KC IB  30D YAN 11  6 12000  4    37300  41400
35  8 C-&-C 36         SLP SAIL FBG KL IB  30D YAN 11  8 12000  5 11 35100  39000
37  7 C-&-C 37         SLP SA/RC FBG KL IB  30D YAN 11  8 14300  6  7 45600  50100
37  7 C-&-C 38         SLP SA/RC FBG KL IB  30D YAN 11  8 14700  6  8 45900  50500
37  7 LANDFALL 38      SLP SAIL FBG KL IB  30D YAN 12    15000  5    47400  52100
39  7 C-&-C 40         SLP SAIL FBG KC IB  30D YAN 12  8 17985  4  9 59600  65500
39  7 C-&-C 40         SLP SAIL FBG KL IB  30D YAN 12  8 17985  6  8 52100  57200
47  6 LANDFALL 48      SLP SAIL FBG KL IB  80D PERK 14    31600  6  7 114500 125500
-------------------- 1981 BOATS -------------------------------------------------
24    C-&-C 24         SLP SAIL FBG KL OB          8 10  3200  4    6700   7700
25  2 C-&-C 25         SLP SAIL FBG KL OB          8  8  4100  4  3  9050  10300
25  2 C-&-C 25         SLP SAIL FBG KL SD      OMC 8  8  4100  4  3  9750  11100
```

LOA FT	LOA IN	NAME AND/ OR MODEL	TOP/ RIG	BOAT TYPE	-HULL- MTL	-HULL- TP	ENGINE TP	ENGINE # HP	ENGINE MFG	BEAM FT	BEAM IN	WGT LBS	DRAFT FT	DRAFT IN	RETAIL LOW	RETAIL HIGH
		1981 BOATS														
27	11	C-&-C 27	SLP	SAIL	FBG	KL	IB	12D	YAN	9		5500	4	6	14100	16000
30		C-&-C 30	SLP	SAIL	FBG	KL	IB	15D	YAN	10		8000	5		21100	23400
31	6	C-&-C 32	SLP	SAIL	FBG	KC	IB	15D	YAN	10	3	10485	4		28600	31800
31	6	C-&-C 32	SLP	SAIL	FBG	KL	IB	15D	YAN	10	3	9680	5	8	26400	29300
33	6	C-&-C 34	SLP	SAIL	FBG	KC	IB	20D	YAN	11		11090	4		30400	33800
33	6	C-&-C 34	SLP	SAIL	FBG	KL	IB	20D	YAN	11		10100	5	11	27700	30800
34	11	LANDFALL 35	SLP	SAIL	FBG	KL	IB	30D	YAN	10	8	13000	4	10	36000	40000
35	8	C-&-C 36	SLP	SAIL	FBG	KC	IB	30D	YAN	11	6	12800	4		35100	39000
35	8	C-&-C 36	SLP	SAIL	FBG	KL	IB	30D	YAN	11	6	12000	5	11	33000	36700
37	7	C&C 38	SLP	SA/RC	FBG	KL	OB			12			6	1	38100	42300
37	7	LANDFALL 38	SLP	SAIL	FBG	KL	IB	30D	YAN	12		15000	5		44100	49000
39	7	C-&-C 40	SLP	SAIL	FBG	KC	IB	30D	YAN	12	8	17985	4	9	56100	61600
39	7	C-&-C 40	SLP	SAIL	FBG	KL	IB	30D	YAN	12	8	17100	7		54100	59500
47	6	LANDFALL 48	SLP	SAIL	FBG	KL	IB	80D	PERK	14		31600	6	7	107500	118000
		1980 BOATS														
24		C-&-C 24	SLP	SA/RC	FBG	KL				8	9	3200	4		6400	7350
24		C-&-C 24	SLP	SAIL	FBG	KL	OB			8	10	3200	4		6400	7350
25	1	C-&-C 25	SLP	SAIL	FBG	KL	OB			8	7	4000	4	3	8300	9550
26	4	ENCOUNTER 26	SLP	SA/CR	FBG	KL	IB	D		10		6170	3	11	14500	16400
27	11	C-&-C 27	SLP	SA/RC	FBG	KL	IB	D		9	1	5500	4	5	13400	15200
27	11	C-&-C 27	SLP	SAIL	FBG	KL	IB	D	YAN	9		5500	4	6	13400	15300
29	7	C-&-C 29	SLP	SA/RC	FBG	KL	IB	D		10	4	7500	5	3	19200	21300
29	11	MEGA 30	SLP	SA/OD	FBG	CB	OB			7	11	4500	2		11100	12700
29	11	MEGA 30	SLP	SA/OD	FBG	CB	OB			7	11	6589	5		16400	18700
29	11	MEGA 30	SLP	SA/RC	FBG	KL				7	11	4500	3	6	10400	11800
30		C-&-C 30	SLP	SA/RC	FBG	KL	IB	D		10		7703	5		19400	21500
30		C-&-C 30	SLP	SAIL	FBG	KL	IB	D	YAN	10		8000	5		20200	22400
31	6	C-&-C 32	SLP	SAIL	FBG	KC	IB	D	YAN	10	3	10485			27300	30300
31	6	C-&-C 32	SLP	SAIL	FBG	KL	IB	D	YAN	10	3	9680	5	8	25200	28000
33	6	C-&-C 34	SLP	SAIL	FBG	KC	IB	D	YAN	11		11090			29000	32300
33	6	C-&-C 34	SLP	SAIL	FBG	KL	IB	D	YAN	11		10100	5	11	26500	29400
33	7	C-&-C 34	SLP	SA/RC	FBG	KL	IB	D		11		10000	5	11	26200	29200
35	7	C-&-C 36	SLP	SA/RC	FBG	KL	IB	D		11	6	12000	5	11	31500	35000
35	8	C-&-C 36	SLP	SAIL	FBG	KC	IB	D	YAN	11	6	12800	4		33500	37200
35	8	C-&-C 36	SLP	SAIL	FBG	KL	IB	D	YAN	11	6	12000	5	11	31500	35000
37	7	C-&-C 38	SLP	SA/RC	FBG	KL	IB	D		12		14700	6	1	41400	46000
37	7	LANDFALL 38	SLP	SA/CR	FBG	KL	IB	D		12		15000	5		42100	46800
37	7	LANDFALL 38	SLP	SAIL	FBG	KL	IB	D	YAN	12		15000	5		42200	46900
39	5	C-&-C 40	SLP	SA/RC	FBG	KL	IB	D		12	8	17710	7		52600	57800
39	7	C-&-C 40	SLP	SAIL	FBG	KC	IB	D	YAN	12	8	17985	4	9	53800	59200
39	7	C-&-C 40	SLP	SAIL	FBG	KL	IB	D	YAN	12	8	17100	7		51900	57100
39	7	CUSTOM 40	SLP	SA/RC	FBG	KC	IB	D		12	8	17000	8	6	51600	56700
41	8	LANDFALL 42	SLP	SA/CR	FBG	KL	IB	D		12	6	18000	5		58900	64800
47	6	LANDFALL 48	SLP	SAIL	FBG	KL	IB	D	PERK	14		31600	6	7	102500	113000
		1979 BOATS														
24		C-&-C 24	SLP	SAIL	FBG	KL	OB			8	10	3200	4		6150	7100
26	4	ENCOUNTER 26	SLP	SAIL	FBG	KL	IB	8D	YAN	10		6170	3	7	13800	15700
27	11	C-&-C 27	SLP	SAIL	FBG	KL	IB	D		9		5500	4	6	12900	14600
29	7	C-&-C 29	SLP	SAIL	FBG	KL	IB	D		10	5	7500	5	3	18600	20700
29	11	MEGA 30	SLP	SA/OD	FBG	CB	OB			7	11	4500	2		10700	12200
30		C-&-C 30	SLP	SAIL	FBG	KL	IB	D		10		8000	5		19400	21500
33	6	C-&-C 34	SLP	SAIL	FBG	KL	IB	D		11		10100	5	11	25500	28300
35	8	C-&-C 36	SLP	SAIL	FBG	KC	IB	D		11	6	12800	4		32200	35800
35	8	C-&-C 36	SLP	SAIL	FBG	KL	IB	D		11	6	12000	5	11	30300	33600
37	9	LANDFALL 38	SLP	SAIL	FBG	KL	IB	D		12	2	15000	5		40800	45300
39	7	C-&-C 40	SLP	SAIL	FBG	KC	IB	D		12	8	17985	4	9	51700	56800
39	7	C-&-C 40	SLP	SAIL	FBG	KL	IB	D		12	8	17100	7		49800	54800
		1978 BOATS														
24		C-&-C 24	SLP	SAIL	FBG	KL	OB			8	10	3200	4		5600	6450
24		COMPETITION 24	SLP	SA/RC	FBG	KL	OB			8	10	3200	4		5950	6800
24		NIAGARA 24	SLP	SAIL	FBG	KL	OB			8	10	3200	4		6250	7200
26	4	C-&-C 26	SLP	SAIL	FBG	KL	IB	7D		10		5200	4	7	11300	12800
27	11	C-&-C 27	SLP	SAIL	FBG	KL	IB	D		10		5800	4	6	13100	14900
29	7	C-&-C 29	SLP	SAIL	FBG	KL	IB	30	UNIV	10	5	7500	5	3	17400	19800
29	7	C-&-C 29	SLP	SAIL	FBG	KL	IB	D		10	5	7500	5	3	17600	20000
29	7	C-&-C 29 SHOAL DRAFT	SLP	SAIL	FBG	KL	IB	30	UNIV	10	5	7500			17500	19800
29	7	C-&-C 29 SHOAL DRAFT	SLP	SAIL	FBG	KL	IB	D		10	5	7500			17600	20000
30		C-&-C 30	SLP	SAIL	FBG	KL	IB	30	UNIV	10		8000	5		18700	20700
30		C-&-C 30	SLP	SAIL	FBG	KL	IB	D		10		8000	5		18900	21000
33	6	C-&-C 34	SLP	SAIL	FBG	KL	IB	30	UNIV	11		10100	5	11	24400	27100
33	6	C-&-C 34	SLP	SAIL	FBG	KL	IB	D		11		10100	5	11	24500	27300
35	8	C-&-C 36	SLP	SAIL	FBG	KL	IB	30	UNIV	11	6	12000	5	11	29000	32200
35	8	C-&-C 36	SLP	SAIL	FBG	KL	IB	D		11	6	12000	5	11	29200	32400
37		C-&-C CUSTOM ONE TON	SLP	SA/CR	FBG	KL	IB	D		11	6	14600	5	10	37300	41400
37	7	C-&-C 38	SLP	SAIL	FBG	KL	IB	30	UNIV	12		14700	6	1	37800	42000
37	7	C-&-C 38	SLP	SAIL	FBG	KL	IB	D		12		14700	6	1	38400	42700
39	7	C-&-C 40	SLP	SA/RC	FBG	KL	IB	22D	WEST	12	8	17700	7		49000	53800
41	8	LANDFALL 42	SLP	SA/CR	FBG	KL	IB	50D	PERK	12	6	18000	5		54400	59800
42		C-&-C 42	SLP	SA/CR	FBG	KL	IB	40D		12	11	20200	7	2	59400	65200
61		C-&-C CUSTOM 61	SLP	SA/CR	FBG	KL	IB	D		15	1	48155	8	3	226000	248500
		1977 BOATS														
24		C-&-C 24	SLP	SAIL	FBG	KL	OB			8	9	3200	4		5350	6150
24		NIAGARA 24	SLP	SAIL	FBG	KL	OB			8	9	3200	4		6100	7000
25	2	C-&-C 25	SLP	SAIL	FBG	KL	IB	7D	WEST	8	9	4800	3	10	9600	10900
26	4	C-&-C 26	SLP	SAIL	FBG	KL	IB	7D	WEST	10		5200	4	7	10800	12300
27	11	C-&-C 27	SLP	SAIL	FBG	KL	IB	30	UNIV	10		5800	4	6	12500	14200
29	7	C-&-C 29	SLP	SAIL	FBG	KL	IB	30	UNIV	10	1	7500	5	3	16800	19100
30		C-&-C 30	SLP	SAIL	FBG	KL	IB	30	UNIV	10		8000	5		18000	20000
30		C-&-C 30	SLP	SAIL	FBG	KL	IB	D		10		8000	5		18300	20300
32	11	C-&-C 33	SLP	SAIL	FBG	KL	VD	30	UNIV	10	7	9800	5	6	22900	25400
36	7	C-&-C CUSTOM ONE TON	SLP	SAIL	FBG	KL	IB	D		11	6	14600	5	10	35600	39500
37	7	C-&-C 38	SLP	SAIL	FBG	KL	IB	30	UNIV	12		14700	6	1	36500	40600
37	7	C-&-C 38	SLP	SAIL	FBG	KL	IB	D		12		14700	6	1	37100	41200
41	8	LANDFALL 42	SLP	SAIL	FBG	KL	IB	D		12	6	18000	5		52800	58000
41	8	LANDFALL 42	SLP	SAIL	FBG	KL	IB	40D		12	6	18000	5		52700	57900
42	7	C-&-C 42	SLP	SAIL	FBG	KL	IB	D		12	11	20200	7	2	59100	65000
42	7	C-&-C 42	SLP	SAIL	FBG	KL	IB	40D		12	11	20200	7	2	59000	64800
44	5	C-&-C CUSTOM 44	SLP	SAIL	FBG	KL	IB	D		13		23400	7	4	70100	77000
46	4	C-&-C 46	SLP	SAIL	FBG	KL	IB	D		12	2	26700	7	6	81700	89800
46	4	C-&-C 46	SLP	SAIL	FBG	KL	IB	45D		12	2	26700	7	6	81500	89500
61	3	C-&-C CUSTOM 61	SLP	SAIL	FBG	KL	IB	D		15	1	48155	8	3	219000	240500
		1976 BOATS														
24		C-&-C 24	SLP	SAIL	FBG	KL	OB			8	9	3200	4		5050	5800
24		COMPETITION 24	SLP	SAIL	FBG	KL	OB			8	9	3200	4		6150	7050
24		NIAGARA 24	SLP	SAIL	FBG	KL	OB			8	9	3200	4		5500	6300
24		SHARK	SLP	SA/OD	FBG	KL	OB			6	10	2200	3		4250	4950
25	2	C-&-C 25	SLP	SAIL	FBG	KL	IB	7D	WEST	8	9	4138	3	10	8100	9300
27	11	C-&-C 27	SLP	SAIL	FBG	KL	IB	30	UNIV	9	2	5500	4	6	11500	13000
30		C-&-C 30	SLP	SAIL	FBG	KL	IB	30	UNIV	10		7900	5		16900	19200
30		C-&-C 30	SLP	SAIL	FBG	KL	IB	D		10		7900	5		17100	19400
32	10	C-&-C CUSTOM 3/4	SLP	SAIL	FBG	KL	IB	D		10	7	9800	5	6	22200	24700
32	11	C-&-C 33	SLP	SAIL	FBG	KL	IB	30	UNIV	10	7	9800	5	6	22200	24600
32	11	C-&-C 33	SLP	SAIL	FBG	KL	IB	D		10	7	9800	5	6	22200	24700
36	7	C-&-C CUSTOM 1-TON	SLP	SAIL	FBG	KL	IB	D		11	6	14600	5	10	34400	38300
37	7	C-&-C 38	SLP	SAIL	FBG	KL	IB	30	UNIV	12		14700	6	1	35400	39300
37	7	C-&-C 38	SLP	SAIL	FBG	KL	IB	D		12		14700	6	1	35900	39900
44	5	C-&-C CUSTOM 44	SLP	SAIL	FBG	KL	IB	D		13		23400	7	4	67900	74600
46		C-&-C 46	SLP	SAIL	FBG	KL	IB	D		13	8	26700	7	6	78000	85700
48	1	C-&-C CUSTOM 48	SLP	SAIL	FBG	KL	IB	D		13	8	28100	7	3	87900	96600
61	3	C-&-C CUSTOM 61	SLP	SAIL	FBG	KL	IB	D		15	1	57300	8	3	231500	254500
		1975 BOATS														
24		SHARK	SLP	SAIL	FBG	KL	OB			6	10	2200	3		4100	4800
25	2	C-&-C 25	SLP	SAIL	FBG	KL	OB			8	9	4138	3	10	7250	8350
25	2	C-&-C 25	SLP	SAIL	FBG	KL	IB	D		8	9		3	10	8550	9850
27	11	C-&-C 27	SLP	SAIL	FBG	KL	IB	30	UNIV	9	2	5500	4	6	11100	12700
30		C-&-C 30	SLP	SAIL	FBG	KL	IB	30	UNIV	10		7700	5		15900	18100
32	10	C-&-C 3/4 TON	SLP	SAIL	FBG	KL	IB	D		10	6	9800	5	6	21600	24000
32	11	C-&-C 33	SLP	SAIL	FBG	KL	VD	30	UNIV	10	7	9800	5	6	21500	23900
35	6	C-&-C 35	SLP	SAIL	FBG	KL	IB	30	UNIV	10	7	13800	5	6	30100	33500
36	7	C-&-C CUSTOM ONE TON	SLP	SAIL	FBG	KL	IB	D		11	6	14600	5	10	33500	37200
44	5	C-&-C CUSTOM 44	SLP	SAIL	FBG	KL	IB	D		13		23400	7	4	65900	72400
48	1	C-&-C CUSTOM 48	SLP	SAIL	FBG	KL	IB	D		13	8	28100	7	3	85400	93800
59	10	C-&-C CUSTOM 50	SLP	SAIL	FBG	KL	IB	D		14	6	31500	8		177000	194500
61	3	C-&-C CUSTOM 61	SLP	SAIL	FBG	KL	IB	D		15	1	57300	8	3	225000	247000
		1974 BOATS														
24		SHARK		SAIL	FBG		OB			6	10	2200	3		4000	4650
25	2	C-&-C 25		SAIL	FBG		OB			8	9	4200	3	10	7150	8250
27	4	C-&-C 27		SAIL	FBG		IB	30	UNIV	9	2	5200	4	3	10100	11500
30		C-&-C 30		SAIL	FBG	KL	IB	30	UNIV	10		7900	5		15900	18100
35	6	C-&-C 35		SAIL	FBG	KL	IB	30	UNIV	10	6	13800			29300	32600
39	3	C-&-C 39		SAIL	FBG		IB	30	UNIV	11	6	17000	6	3	40500	45000
43	4	C-&-C CUSTOM 43	SLP	SAIL	FBG	KL	IB	D		12	10		7		67800	74500
48	1	C-&-C CUSTOM 48	SLP	SAIL	FBG	KL	IB	D		13	8	28100	7	3	83100	91300
49	10	C-&-C CUSTOM 50	SLP	SAIL	FBG	KL	IB	D		14	6	31500	8		96200	105500
61	3	C-&-C CUSTOM 61	SLP	SAIL	FBG	KL	IB	D		15	1	57300	8	3	219000	240500
		1973 BOATS														
24		SHARK		SAIL	FBG		OB			6	10	2200	3		3900	4550
25	2	C-&-C 25		SAIL	FBG		OB			8	9	4200	3	10	7000	8050
27	4	C-&-C 27		SAIL	FBG		IB	30	UNIV	9	2	5950	4	3	11300	12800

```
C & C YACHTS              -CONTINUED      See inside cover to adjust price for area
  LOA  NAME AND/          TOP/ BOAT  -HULL-  ----ENGINE---  BEAM   WGT  DRAFT RETAIL RETAIL
 FT IN  OR MODEL          RIG  TYPE  MTL TP  TP # HP  MFG   FT IN  LBS  FT IN  LOW    HIGH
------------------- 1973 BOATS -----------------------------------------------------------
 30    C-&-C 30                SAIL  FBG KL IB     30  UNIV 10     7900   5     15600  17700
 34  7 C-&-C 35                SAIL  FBG    IB     30  UNIV 10   7 10500   5  3 22100  24600
 39  3 C-&-C 39                SAIL  FBG    IB     30  UNIV 11   6 17000   6  3 39500  43900
 43  4 C-&-C 43           SLP  SAIL  FBG KL IB    40D       12  10       7     65800  72400
 49  9 C-&-C 50           SLP  SAIL  FBG KL IB    40D       14   6 31500   8     92800 102000
 61  3 C-&-C 61           SLP  SAIL  FBG KL IB    40D       15   1 57300   8  3 212500 233500
------------------- 1972 BOATS -----------------------------------------------------------
 24    SHARK             SLP  SA/CR FBG KL IB      D         6  10  2200   3      4400   5100
 24    SHARK                  SAIL  FBG    OB      D         6  10  2200   3      3800   4450
 25  1 HR 25             SLP  SA/RC FBG KL         8              3600   3  6   5700   6550
 27    C-&-C 27          SLP  SA/CR FBG KL IB      D         9   2  6000   4  3 11200  12700
 27  4 C-&-C 27               SAIL  FBG    IB     30  UNIV  9   2  5950   4  3 11000  12500
 30    C-&-C 30          SLP  SA/CR FBG KL IB      D        10       7800   5     15200  17300
 30    C-&-C 30               SAIL  FBG    IB     30  UNIV 10       7900   5     15200  17300
 34  7 C-&-C 35               SAIL  FBG    IB     30  UNIV 10   7 10500   5  3 21600  24100
 35    C-&-C 35          SLP  SA/CR FBG KL IB      D        10   7 10500   5  3 21600  24000
 35  1 C-&-C 36R         SLP  SA/RC FBG KL IB      D        11   1 12700   6     26000  28900
 39    C-&-C 39          SLP  SA/CR FBG KL IB      D        11   6 16800   6  3 38500  42800
 39  3 C-&-C 39               SAIL  FBG    IB     30  UNIV 11   6       6  3 49900  54900

 40  8 C-&-C 40C         SLP  SA/CR FBG KL IB      D        13     18500   4 11 44700  49700
 40  8 C-&-C 40C         YWL  SA/CR FBG KL IB      D        13     18500   4 11 44700  49700
 40  8 C-&-C 40C         KTH  SA/CR FBG KL IB      D        13     18500   4 11 44700  49700
 43  4 C-&-C 43          SLP  SA/RC FBG KL IB      D        12  10 21500   7     55500  61000
 49  9 C-&-C 50          SLP  SA/CR FBG KL IB      D        14   6 31100   8     70400  99900
 61  6 C-&-C 61          SLP  SA/RC FBG KL IB      D        15   1 48155   8  3 192000 210500
------------------- 1971 BOATS -----------------------------------------------------------
 24    SHARK                  SAIL  FBG    OB                6  10  2200   3      3750   4350
 24  7 REDLINE 25             SAIL  FBG    OB                8      4115   5      6350   7300
 25  1 HR 25                  SAIL  FBG    OB                8      3600   3  6   5800   6650
 27  4 C-&-C 27               SAIL  FBG    IB     30  UNIV  9   2  5950   4  3 10800  12300
 30    C-&-C 30               SAIL  FBG    IB     30  UNIV 10       7900   5     14900  16900
 31  3 CORVETTE 31            SAIL  FBG    IB     30  UNIV  9   2  8545   7     16800  19100
 34  7 C-&-C 35               SAIL  FBG    IB     30  UNIV 10   7 10500   5  3 21200  23600
 35  1 C-&-C 36R              SAIL  FBG    IB     30  UNIV 11   2 13000   6     25900  28800
 39  8 C-&-C 40               SAIL  FBG    IB    35D  WEST 11   2 18985   8     42700  47500
 40  8 C-&-C 40C              MS    FBG    IB    35D  WEST 11   1 18500   4 11 43800  48600
 41  5 REDLINE 41 MK 2        SAIL  FBG    IB     30  UNIV 11   2 19700   6  9 46700  51300
 61  6 C-&-C 61          SLP  SAIL  FBG KL IB    50D       15   1 48155   8  3 187000 205500
------------------- 1968 BOATS -----------------------------------------------------------
 35  3 CORVETTE          SLP  SAIL  FBG KC IB      D         9   2       3  3 18100  20100
 35  8 INVADER           SLP  SAIL  FBG KL IB      D        10   3       4 10 18100  20100
 41  5 REDLINE 41        SLP  SAIL  FBG KL IB      D        11   2       6  4 36300  40300

C & L BOATWORKS
DIV OF WATERHOUSE & MAY LTD                        See inside cover to adjust price for area
PICKERING ONTARIO CANAD COAST GUARD MFG ID- CLW
                        FOR OLDER MODELS SEE CROCE & LOFTHOUSE SAILCRAFT

         For more recent years, see the BUC Used Boat Price Guide, Volume 1 or Volume 2
  LOA  NAME AND/          TOP/ BOAT  -HULL-  ----ENGINE---  BEAM   WGT  DRAFT RETAIL RETAIL
 FT IN  OR MODEL          RIG  TYPE  MTL TP  TP # HP  MFG   FT IN  LBS  FT IN  LOW    HIGH
------------------- 1983 BOATS -----------------------------------------------------------
 18  6 SANDPIPER 565      SLP  SAIL  FBG SK OB       7   1       1200  10     3150   3650
------------------- 1982 BOATS -----------------------------------------------------------
 18  6 SANDPIPER 565      SLP  SAIL  FBG SK OB       7   1       1200  10     2950   3400
------------------- 1981 BOATS -----------------------------------------------------------
 18  6 SANDPIPER 565      SLP  SAIL  FBG SK OB       7   1       1200  10     2750   3200
------------------- 1980 BOATS -----------------------------------------------------------
 18  6 SANDPIPER 565      SLP  SAIL  FBG SK OB       7   1       1200  10     2600   3050
------------------- 1979 BOATS -----------------------------------------------------------
 18  6 SANDPIPER 565      SLP  SAIL  FBG SK OB       7   1       1200  10     2500   2900
------------------- 1978 BOATS -----------------------------------------------------------
 18  6 SANDPIPER 565      SLP  SA/CR FBG SK OB       7         1300  10     2500   2900
------------------- 1977 BOATS -----------------------------------------------------------
 18  6 SANDPIPER 565      SLP  SAIL  FBG SK OB       7   1       1300  10     2400   2800
------------------- 1976 BOATS -----------------------------------------------------------
 18  6 SANDPIPER 565      SLP  SAIL  FBG SK OB       7   1       1300  10     2300   2700

C C C ENTERPRISES
COAST GUARD MFG ID- NCC

Call 1-800-327-6929 for BUC Personalized Evaluation Service
Or, for 1980 to 1983 boats, sign onto www.BUCValuPro.com

C I M A

Call 1-800-327-6929 for BUC Personalized Evaluation Service
Or, for 1970 to 1978 boats, sign onto www.BUCValuPro.com

C M MARINE INC
COAST GUARD MFG ID- CEG

Call 1-800-327-6929 for BUC Personalized Evaluation Service
Or, for 1978 to 1980 boats, sign onto www.BUCValuPro.com

C M S YACHTS INC
COAST GUARD MFG ID- VMY

Call 1-800-327-6929 for BUC Personalized Evaluation Service
Or, for 1978 to 1980 boats, sign onto www.BUCValuPro.com

C S K CATAMARANS

Call 1-800-327-6929 for BUC Personalized Evaluation Service
Or, for 1971 boats, sign onto www.BUCValuPro.com

C S Y
TENAFLY NJ 07670                                   See inside cover to adjust price for area

         For more recent years, see the BUC Used Boat Price Guide, Volume 1 or Volume 2
  LOA  NAME AND/          TOP/ BOAT  -HULL-  ----ENGINE---  BEAM   WGT  DRAFT RETAIL RETAIL
 FT IN  OR MODEL          RIG  TYPE  MTL TP  TP # HP  MFG   FT IN  LBS  FT IN  LOW    HIGH
------------------- 1982 BOATS -----------------------------------------------------------
 33  4 CIGNET 33          SLP  SA/CR FBG KL IB    40D  WEST 11     14000   4  6 34700  38600
 37  4 CIGNET 37          SLP  SA/CR FBG KL IB    50D  PERK 12     18000   4  6 45600  50100
 37  3 CIGNET 37          CUT  SA/CR FBG KL IB    50D  PERK 12     18000   4  6 45600  50100
 44  3 CIGNET 44          SLP  SA/CR FBG KL IB    62D  PERK 13   4 37000   6  6 88700  97400
 44  3 CIGNET 44          CUT  SA/CR FBG KL IB    62D  PERK 13   4 37000   6  6 88700  97400
 44  3 CIGNET 44 PH       SLP  SA/CR FBG KL IB    85D  PERK 13   4 38000   6  6 90100  99000
 44  3 CIGNET 44 PH       CUT  SA/CR FBG KL IB    85D  PERK 13   4 38000   6  6 90100  99000
 44  3 CIGNET 44 PH       KTH  SA/CR FBG KL IB    85D  PERK 13   4 38000   6  6 90100  99000
 44  3 CIGNET 44 W/T      SLP  SA/CR FBG KL IB    62D  PERK 13   4 37000   6  6 88700  97400
 44  3 CIGNET 44 W/T      CUT  SA/CR FBG KL IB    62D  PERK 13   4 37000   6  6 88700  97400
 44  3 CIGNET 44 W/T      KTH  SA/CR FBG KL IB    62D  PERK 13   4 37000   6  6 88700  97400
------------------- 1981 BOATS -----------------------------------------------------------
 33  4 CSY 33 AFT CPT          CUT  SA/CR FBG KL IB    40D  WEST 11     15200   5     35800  39800
 33  4 CSY 33 AFT CPT    SHOAL CUT  SA/CR FBG KL IB    40D  WEST 11     15200   3 11 35400  39300
 37  3 CSY 37 AFT CPT          CUT  SA/CR FBG KL IB    50D  PERK 12     19689   4  8 46500  51100
 37  3 CSY 37 AFT CPT    SHOAL CUT  SA/CR FBG KL IB    50D  PERK 12     19689   4  8 46500  51100
 44    BOTTOM-LINE 44 PH       CUT  SA/CR FBG KL IB    85D  PERK 13   4       4 11 84000  92300
 44    BOTTOM-LINE 44 PH       CUT  MS    FBG KL IB    85D  PERK 13   4 37000   6  6 83600  91900
 44    CSY 44 MID CPT          CUT  SA/CR FBG KL IB    62D  PERK 13   4 37000   4 11 84000  92300
 44    CSY 44 MID CPT    SHOAL CUT  SA/CR FBG KL IB    62D  PERK 13   4 37000   4 11 84000  92300
 44    CSY 44 PH               KTH  SA/CR FBG KL IB    85D  PERK 13   4 38000   6  6 84800  93200
 44    CSY 44 PH SHOAL         KTH  SA/CR FBG KL IB    85D  PERK 13   4 38000   4 11 84800  93200
 44    CSY 44 WALK THRU        CUT  SA/CR FBG KL IB    62D  PERK 13   4 37000   6  6 83400  91700
 44    CSY 44 WALK THRU        KTH  SA/CR FBG KL IB    62D  PERK 13   4 37000   6  6 83400  91700
 44    CSY 44 WALK THRU SHL CUT  SA/CR FBG KL IB    62D  PERK 13   4 37000   4 11 83400  91700
 44    CSY 44 WALK THRU SHL KTH  SA/CR FBG KL IB    62D  PERK 13   4 37000   4 11 83400  91700
------------------- 1980 BOATS -----------------------------------------------------------
 33  4 CSY 33 AFT CPT          CUT  SA/CR FBG KL IB    40D  WEST 11     15200   5     34300  38100
 33  4 CSY 33 AFT CPT          CUT  SA/CR FBG KL IB    40D  WEST 11     15200   5     34500  38300
 33  4 CSY 33 AFT CPT    SHOAL CUT  SA/CR FBG KL IB    40D  WEST 11     15200   3 11 34000  37800
 37  3 CSY 37 AFT CPT          CUT  SA/CR FBG KL IB    50D  PERK 12     19689   4  8 44300  49200
 37  3 CSY 37 AFT CPT    SHOAL CUT  SA/CR FBG KL IB    50D  PERK 12     19689   4  8 44300  49200
 44    CSY 44 MID CPT          CUT  SA/CR FBG KL IB    62D  PERK 13   4 37000   6  6 74100  81400
 44    CSY 44 MID CPT    SHOAL CUT  SA/CR FBG KL IB    62D  PERK 13   4 37000   4 11 74100  81400
 44    CSY 44 PH               KTH  SA/CR FBG KL IB    85D  PERK 13   4 38000   6  6 82000  90100
 44    CSY 44 PH SHOAL         KTH  SA/CR FBG KL IB    85D  PERK 13   4 38000   4 11 81200  89200
 44    CSY 44 WALK THRU        CUT  SA/CR FBG KL IB    62D  PERK 13   4 37000   6  6 86400  94900
 44    CSY 44 WALK THRU        KTH  SA/CR FBG KL IB    62D  PERK 13   4 37000   6  6 80800  88800
 44    CSY 44 WALK THRU SHL CUT  SA/CR FBG KL IB    62D  PERK 13   4 37000   4 11 85300  93800
 44    CSY 44 WALK THRU SHL KTH  SA/CR FBG KL IB    62D  PERK 13   4 37000   4 11 79800  87700
```

LOA FT IN	NAME AND/ OR MODEL	TOP/ RIG	BOAT TYPE	-HULL- MTL TP	ENGINE TP # HP	MFG	BEAM FT IN	WGT LBS	DRAFT FT IN	RETAIL LOW	RETAIL HIGH
				1979 BOATS							
33 4	CSY 33	CUT	SA/CR FBG	KL IB	30D	WEST	11	15200	5	33400	37100
33 4	CSY 33 SHOAL	CUT	SA/CR FBG	KL IB	30D	WEST	11	15200	3 11	32900	36600
37 3	CSY 37 PLAN A	CUT	SA/CR FBG	KL IB	50D	PERK	12	19689	6	43700	48600
37 3	CSY 37 PLAN A SHOAL	CUT	SA/CR FBG	KL IB	50D	PERK	12	19689	4 8	43200	48000
37 3	CSY 37 PLAN B	CUT	SA/CR FBG	KL IB	50D	PERK	12	19689	6	42500	47300
37 3	CSY 37 PLAN B SHOAL	CUT	SA/CR FBG	KL IB	50D	PERK	12	19689	4 8	42100	46800
44	CSY 44 MID CPT	CUT	SA/CR FBG	KL IB	64D	PERK	13 4	37000	6 6	78200	85900
44	CSY 44 MID CPT SHOAL	CUT	SA/CR FBG	KL IB	64D	PERK	13 4	37000	4 11	77400	85100
44	CSY 44 PILOT HOUSE	KTH	SA/CR FBG	KL IB	85D	PERK	13 4	38000	4 11	79100	86900
44	CSY 44 PILOT HOUSE	KTH	SA/CR FBG	KL IB	85D	PERK	13 4	38000	6 6	79100	86900
				1978 BOATS							
37 3	CSY 37	CUT	SAIL FBG	KL IB	40D	WEST	12	19689	6	41800	46500
37 3	CSY 37 SHOAL	CUT	SAIL FBG	KL IB	40D	WEST	12	19689	4 8	41800	46500
44	CSY 44 MID CPT	CUT	SAIL FBG	KL IB	60D	WEST	13 4	37000	4 11	75900	83400
44	CSY 44 MID CPT	CUT	SAIL FBG	KL IB	60D	WEST	13 4	37000	6 6	75900	83400
44	CSY 44 PILOT HOUSE	KTH	SAIL FBG	KL IB	60D	WEST	13 4	38000	4 11	77000	84600
44	CSY 44 PILOT HOUSE	KTH	SAIL FBG	KL IB	60D	WEST	13 4	38000	6 6	77000	84600
				1977 BOATS							
37 3	CSY 37	CUT	SA/CR FBG	KL IB	40D	WEST	12	18500	6	38700	43000
44	CSY 44	CUT	SA/CR FBG	KL IB	60D	WEST	13 4	35475	6 6	72300	79500

C-KIP YACHTS

Call 1-800-327-6929 for BUC Personalized Evaluation Service
Or, for 1980 boats, sign onto www.BUCValuPro.com

CABO RICO YACHTS

FT LAUDERDALE FL 33316   COAST GUARD MFG ID- CQB See inside cover to adjust price for area

For more recent years, see the BUC Used Boat Price Guide, Volume 1 or Volume 2

LOA FT IN	NAME AND/ OR MODEL	TOP/ RIG	BOAT TYPE	-HULL- MTL TP	ENGINE TP # HP	MFG	BEAM FT IN	WGT LBS	DRAFT FT IN	RETAIL LOW	RETAIL HIGH
				1983 BOATS							
41	CABO-RICO 38	CUT	SA/CR FBG	KL IB	50D	PERK	11 4	20000	5	101000	111000
				1982 BOATS							
41	CABO-RICO 38	CUT	SA/CR FBG	KL IB	50D	PERK	11 4	20000	5	95800	105500
				1981 BOATS							
41	CABO-RICO 38	CUT	SA/CR FBG	KL IB	50D	PERK	11 4	20000	5	90900	99900
				1980 BOATS							
41	CABO-RICO 38	CUT	SA/CR FBG	KL IB	50D	PERK	11 4	20000	5	87500	96100

CABOTCRAFT INDUSTRIES LTD

SYDNEY NS CANADA   COAST GUARD MFG ID- ZBD See inside cover to adjust price for area

LOA FT IN	NAME AND/ OR MODEL	TOP/ RIG	BOAT TYPE	-HULL- MTL TP	ENGINE TP # HP	MFG	BEAM FT IN	WGT LBS	DRAFT FT IN	RETAIL LOW	RETAIL HIGH
				1979 BOATS							
19 5	CAPE-ISLAND		CR FBG	OB	7		9			3450	4000
19 5	CAPE-ISLAND		CR FBG	IB	130	7	9			2100	2500
35 7	CABOT 36	SLP	SA/CR FBG	KL IB	D	11 8	17000	4 9		40400	44800
35 7	CABOT 36	CUT	SA/CR FBG	KL IB	D	11 8	17000	4 9		40100	44600
41 3	CAPE-ISLAND		CR FBG	IB	120D	14 8				31900	35400
41 3	CAPE-ISLAND		CR FBG	IB	225D	14 8				33000	36700
				1978 BOATS							
35 7	CABOT 36	SLP	SAIL F/S	KL IB	50D	PERK	11 8	16000	4 9	36800	40900
35 7	CABOT 36	CUT	SAIL F/S	KL IB	50D	PERK	11 8	16000	4 9	36600	40700
				1977 BOATS							
35 7	CABOT 36	SLP	SAIL FBG	KL IB	25D	VLVO	11 8	15000	4 9	33800	37600
35 7	CABOT 36	CUT	SAIL FBG	KL IB	25D	VLVO	11 8	15000	4 9	33700	37400
				1976 BOATS							
35 7	CABOT 36	SLP	SAIL FBG	KL IB	25D	VLVO	11 8	15000	4 9	33000	36600
35 7	CABOT 36	CUT	SAIL FBG	KL IB	25D	VLVO	11 8	15000	4 9	32800	36500
				1975 BOATS							
35 7	CABOT 36	SLP	SAIL F/S	KL IB	25D	VLVO	11 8	15000	4 9	32100	35700
35 7	CABOT 36	CUT	SAIL F/S	KL IB	25D	VLVO	11 8	15000	4 9	32000	35500
				1974 BOATS							
35 7	CABOT 36	SLP	SA/CR FBG	KL IB	25D	VLVO	11 8	14500	4 9	30600	34000
35 7	CABOT 36	CUT	SA/CR FBG	KL IB	25D	VLVO	11 8	14500	4 9	30400	33800

CADDILAC

Call 1-800-327-6929 for BUC Personalized Evaluation Service
Or, for 1956 boats, sign onto www.BUCValuPro.com

CADDO BOAT MFG CO

NELSON-DYKES CO INC   COAST GUARD MFG ID- LMA

Call 1-800-327-6929 for BUC Personalized Evaluation Service
Or, for 1977 to 1985 boats, sign onto www.BUCValuPro.com

CADILLAC SAIL CRAFT

Call 1-800-327-6929 for BUC Personalized Evaluation Service
Or, for 1965 to 1972 boats, sign onto www.BUCValuPro.com

CAL-PACIFIC MARINE LTD

COAST GUARD MFG ID- CNI

Call 1-800-327-6929 for BUC Personalized Evaluation Service
Or, for 1983 boats, sign onto www.BUCValuPro.com

CAL-PEARSON

BETHESDA MD 20814-3601   COAST GUARD MFG ID- CAB See inside cover to adjust price for area
                          formerly LEAR SIEGLER MARINE

For more recent years, see the BUC Used Boat Price Guide, Volume 1 or Volume 2

LOA FT IN	NAME AND/ OR MODEL	TOP/ RIG	BOAT TYPE	-HULL- MTL TP	ENGINE TP # HP	MFG	BEAM FT IN	WGT LBS	DRAFT FT IN	RETAIL LOW	RETAIL HIGH
				1983 BOATS							
25 3	CAL 25	SLP	SA/CR FBG	KL OB	9			4500	4 6	9400	10700
25 3	CAL 25 SHOAL	SLP	SA/CR FBG	KL OB	9			4500	3 6	9400	10700
26 8	CAL 25 SHOAL	SLP	SA/CR FBG	KL IB	11D UNIV	9		4500	3 6	10200	11500
26 8	CAL 27 II	SLP	SA/CR FBG	KL IB	9			5200	4	11800	13500
26 8	CAL 27 II	SLP	SA/CR FBG	KL IB	8D YAN	9		5200	4	12400	14100
26 8	CAL 27 II SHOAL	SLP	SA/CR FBG	KL IB	9			5200	4	11800	13500
26 8	CAL 27 II SHOAL	SLP	SA/CR FBG	KL IB	8D YAN	9		5200	4	12400	14100
30	CAL 9.2	SLP	SA/RC FBG	KL IB	11D UNIV	10 4	7000	5 7	18400	20500
30	CAL 9.2 SHOAL	SLP	SA/RC FBG	KL IB	11D UNIV	10 4	7000	4 7	18400	20500
30	CAL 9.2R	SLP	SA/RC FBG	KL IB	11D UNIV	10 4	7000	5 10	20000	22300
31 6	CAL 31	SLP	SA/CR FBG	KL IB	16D UNIV	10		9170	5	25400	28200
31 6	CAL 31 SHOAL	SLP	SA/CR FBG	KL IB	16D UNIV	10		9170	4 3	25400	28200
35	CAL 35	SLP	SA/CR FBG	KL IB	32D UNIV	10 11	13000	6	36600	40700
35	CAL 35 SHOAL	SLP	SA/CR FBG	KL IB	32D UNIV	10 11	13000	4 11	36600	40700
39	CAL 39	SLP	SA/CR FBG	KL IB	44D UNIV	12	19000	6 8	57200	62800
39	CAL 39 SHOAL	SLP	SA/CR FBG	KL IB	44D UNIV	12	19000	6 8	57200	62800
39	CAL 39 TALL RIG	SLP	SA/CR FBG	KL IB	44D UNIV	12	19000	6 8	57400	63000
				1982 BOATS							
25 3	CAL 25	SLP	SA/CR FBG	KL OB	9			4500	4 6	9000	10200
25 3	CAL 25	SLP	SA/CR FBG	KL OB	11D UNIV	9		4500	4 6	9650	10900
25 3	CAL 25 SHOAL	SLP	SA/CR FBG	KL OB	9			4500	3 6	9000	10200
25 3	CAL 25 SHOAL	SLP	SA/CR FBG	KL OB	11D UNIV	9		4500	3 6	9650	10900
30	CAL 9.2	SLP	SA/RC FBG	KL IB	11D UNIV	10 4	7000	5 7	18000	20000
30	CAL 9.2 SHOAL	SLP	SA/RC FBG	KL IB	11D UNIV	10 4	7000	4 7	18000	20000
31 6	CAL 31	SLP	SA/CR FBG	KL IB	16D UNIV	10		9170	5	24100	26800
35	CAL 35	SLP	SA/CR FBG	KL IB	32D UNIV	11 3	13000	6	34700	38600
35	CAL 35 SHOAL	SLP	SA/CR FBG	KL IB	32D UNIV	11 3	13000	4 11	34700	38600
39	CAL 39	SLP	SA/CR FBG	KL IB	40D PATH	12	17000	6 8	49900	54800
39	CAL 39 SHOAL	SLP	SA/CR FBG	KL IB	40D PATH	12	17000	6 8	49900	54800
				1981 BOATS							
25 3	CAL 25	SLP	SA/CR FBG	KL OB SD	15 OMC	9		4500	4 6	8400	9650
25 3	CAL 25	SLP	SA/CR FBG	KL OB	11D UNIV	9		4500	4 6	8800	10000
25 3	CAL 25	SLP	SA/CR FBG	KL OB	9			4500	4 6	8400	9650
25 3	CAL 25 SHOAL	SLP	SA/CR FBG	KL OB SD	15 OMC	9		4500	3 6	8400	9650
25 3	CAL 25 SHOAL	SLP	SA/CR FBG	KL OB	11D UNIV	9		4500	3 6	8800	10000
25 3	CAL 25 SHOAL	SLP	SA/CR FBG	KL OB	9			4500	3 6	8400	9650
26 7	CAL 27	SLP	SA/RC FBG	KL IB	9			6700	4 3	15400	16400
30	CAL 9.2	SLP	SA/RC FBG	KL IB	11D UNIV	10 4	7000	5 7	16700	19000
30	CAL 9.2 SHOAL	SLP	SA/RC FBG	KL IB	11D UNIV	10 4	7000	4 7	16700	19000
31 6	CAL 31	SLP	SA/CR FBG	KL IB	16D UNIV	10		9170	5	22800	25400
35	CAL 35	SLP	SA/CR FBG	KL IB	32D UNIV	11 3	13000	6	32900	36500
35	CAL 35 SHOAL	SLP	SA/CR FBG	KL IB	32D UNIV	11 3	13000	4 11	32900	36500
39	CAL 39	SLP	SA/CR FBG	KL IB	40D PATH	12	17000	6 8	47500	52200
39	CAL 39 SHOAL	SLP	SA/CR FBG	KL IB	40D PATH	12	17000	5 6	47500	52200

LOA FT	LOA IN	NAME AND/ OR MODEL	TOP/ RIG	BOAT TYPE	-HULL- MTL	-HULL- TP	ENGINE TP	#	HP	MFG	BEAM FT	BEAM IN	WGT LBS	DRAFT FT	DRAFT IN	RETAIL LOW	RETAIL HIGH
		1980 BOATS															
25	3	CAL 25	SLP	SA/CR	FBG	KL	OB				9		4500	4	6	8100	9300
25	3	CAL 25	SLP	SA/CR	FBG	KL	SD		15	OMC	9		4500	4	6	8400	9650
25	3	CAL 25	SLP	SA/CR	FBG	KL	IB		11D	UNIV	9		4500	4	6	8850	10000
25	3	CAL 25 SHOAL	SLP	SA/CR	FBG	KL	OB				9		4500	3	6	8100	9300
25	3	CAL 25 SHOAL	SLP	SA/CR	FBG	KL	SD		15	OMC	9		4500	3	6	8400	9650
25	3	CAL 25 SHOAL	SLP	SA/CR	FBG	KL	IB		11D	UNIV	9		4500	3	6	8850	10000
26	7	CAL 27	SLP	SA/CR	FBG	KL	IB		11D	UNIV	9	4	6700	4	3	13800	15700
31	6	CAL 31	SLP	SA/CR	FBG	KL	IB		16D	UNIV	10		9170	5		22000	24400
35		CAL 35	SLP	SA/CR	FBG	KL	IB		32D	UNIV	11	3	13000	6		31700	35200
35		CAL 35 SHOAL	SLP	SA/CR	FBG	KL	IB		32D	UNIV	11	3	13000	4	11	31700	35200
39		CAL 39	SLP	SA/CR	FBG	KL	IB		39D	PERK	12		17000	6	8	45000	50000
39		CAL 39 SHOAL	SLP	SA/CR	FBG	KL	IB		39D	PERK	12		17000	5	6	45000	50000
		1979 BOATS															
25	3	CAL 25	SLP	SA/CR	FBG	KC	OB				9		4500	3		7850	9000
25	3	CAL 25	SLP	SA/CR	FBG	KC	IB		8D	YAN	9		4500	3		8400	9700
25	3	CAL 25	SLP	SA/CR	FBG	KL	OB				9		4500	4	6	7850	9000
25	3	CAL 25	SLP	SA/CR	FBG	KL	IB		8D	YAN	9		4500	4	6	8400	9700
26	7	CAL 27	SLP	SA/CR	FBG	KL	IB		D	UNIV	9	4	6700	4	3	13400	15300
31	6	CAL 31	SLP	SA/CR	FBG	KC	IB		13D	VLVO	10		9170			21300	23600
31	6	CAL 31	SLP	SA/CR	FBG	KL	IB		13D	VLVO	10		9170	5		21300	23600
33	6	CAL 34	SLP	SA/CR	FBG	KL	IB		24D	WEST	9	3	10200	4	9	23900	26600
39		CAL 39	SLP	SA/CR	FBG	KL	IB		50D	PERK	12		17000	6	8	42800	47500
39		CAL 39 SHOAL	SLP	SA/CR	FBG	KL	IB		50D	PERK	12		17000	5	6	42800	47500
39		CAL 39 TC	SLP	SA/CR	FBG	KL	IB		50D	PERK	12		17000	6	8	44600	49600
39		CAL 39 TC SHOAL	SLP	SA/CR	FBG	KL	IB		50D	PERK	12		17000	5	6	44600	49600
		1978 BOATS															
25	3	CAL 25	SLP	SA/CR	FBG	KL	OB				9		4500	4	6	7600	8750
25	3	CAL 25	SLP	SA/CR	FBG	KL	IB		8D	YAN	9		4500	4	6	8200	9400
26	7	CAL 27	SLP	SA/CR	FBG	KL	OB				9	4	6700	4	3	12500	14200
26	7	CAL 27	SLP	SA/CR	FBG	KL	IB		30	UNIV	9	4	6700	4	3	12800	14500
26	7	CAL 27	SLP	SA/CR	FBG	KL	IB		12D	FARY	9	4	6700	4	3	13000	14700
29	3	CAL 29	SLP	SA/CR	FBG	KL	IB		30	UNIV	9	3	8000	4	9	16900	19200
29	3	CAL 29	SLP	SA/CR	FBG	KL	IB		12D	WEST	9	3	8000	4	9	17000	19400
33	6	CAL 34	SLP	SA/CR	FBG	KL	IB		30	UNIV	10		10200	5		23100	25600
33	6	CAL 34	SLP	SA/CR	FBG	KL	IB		24D	WEST	10		10200	5		23200	25800
39		CAL 39	SLP	SA/CR	FBG	KL	IB		45D	PERK	12		17000	6	8	39800	44200
39		CAL 39 TRI CBN	SLP	SA/CR	FBG	KL	IB		45D	PERK	12		17000	6	8	45000	50000
45	6	CAL 46	SLP	SA/CR	FBG	KL	IB		85D	PERK	12	6	30000	5		78900	86700
45	6	CAL 46	KTH	SA/CR	FBG	KL	IB		85D	PERK	12	6	30000	5		78900	86700
		1977 BOATS															
20		CAL 20	SLP	SA/CR	FBG	KL	OB				7		1950	3	4	3150	3650
25		CAL 25	SLP	SA/CR	FBG	KL	OB				8		4000	4		6500	7500
26	7	CAL 2-27	SLP	SAIL	FBG	KL	OB				9	3	6700	4	3	12200	13800
26	7	CAL 2-27	SLP	SAIL	FBG	KL	IB		30	UNIV	9	3	6700	4	3	12400	14100
26	7	CAL 2-27	SLP	SAIL	FBG	KL	IB		12D	FARY	9	3	6700	4	3	12600	14400
29		CAL 2-29	SLP	SAIL	FBG	KL	IB		30	UNIV	9	3	8000	4	6	16300	18600
29		CAL 2-29	SLP	SAIL	FBG	KL	IB		12D	FARY	9	3	8000	4	6	16400	18700
33	3	CAL 34 III	SLP	SAIL	FBG	KL	IB		30	UNIV	10		10200	5		22500	25000
33	3	CAL 34 III	SLP	SAIL	FBG	KL	IB		25D	WEST	10		10200	5		22600	25100
45	6	CAL 46 III	SLP	SAIL	FBG	KL	IB		85D	PERK	12	6	30000	5		76800	84400
45	6	CAL 46 III	KTH	SAIL	FBG	KL	IB		85D	PERK	12	6	30000	5		76800	84400
		1976 BOATS															
20		CAL 20	SLP	SA/CR	FBG	KL	OB				7		1950	3	4	3050	3550
25		CAL 25	SLP	SAIL	FBG	KL	OB				8		4000	4		6350	7300
26	7	CAL 2-27	SLP	SAIL	FBG	KL	OB				9	3	6700	4	3	11900	13500
26	7	CAL 2-27	SLP	SAIL	FBG	KL	IB		30	UNIV	9	3	6700	4	3	12100	13800
26	7	CAL 2-27	SLP	SAIL	FBG	KL	IB		12D	FARY	9	3	6700	4	3	12300	14000
29		CAL 2-29	SLP	SAIL	FBG	KL	IB		12D	FARY	9	3	8000	4	6	16500	18800
29		CAL 29	SLP	SAIL	FBG	KL	OB				9	3	8000	4	6	15800	18000
29		CAL 29	SLP	SAIL	FBG	KL	IB		30	UNIV	9	3	8000	4	6	15900	18100
29		CAL 29	SLP	SAIL	FBG	KL	IB		12D	FARY	9	3	8000	4	6	15600	17700
30		CAL 3-30	SLP	SA/RC	FBG	KL	IB		30	UNIV	10	2	10500	5	6	21900	24300
30		CAL 3-30	SLP	SA/RC	FBG	KL	IB		12D	FARY	10	2	10500	5	6	22000	24400
30		CAL 3-30	SLP	SAIL	FBG	KL	IB		30	UNIV	10	2	10500	5	6	21900	24300
30		CAL 3-30	SLP	SAIL	FBG	KL	IB		12D	FARY	10	2	10500	5	6	22000	24400
33	3	CAL 2-34	SLP	SAIL	FBG	KL	IB		25D		10		9500	5		20500	22800
33	3	CAL 34	SLP	SAIL	FBG	KL	VD		30	UNIV	10		10200	5		21900	24300
45	6	CAL 2-46	SLP	SAIL	FBG	KL	IB		85D	PERK	12	6	33000	5		78300	86000
45	6	CAL 2-46	KTH	SAIL	FBG	KL	IB		85D	PERK	12	6	33000	5		78300	86000
		1975 BOATS															
20		CAL 20	SLP	SAIL	FBG	KL	OB				7		1950	3	4	3000	3450
20	6	CAL 21	SLP	SAIL	FBG	SK	OB				6	8	1100	4	3	2300	2650
25		CAL 25	SLP	SAIL	FBG	KL	OB				8		4000	4		6200	7150
26	7	CAL 2-27	SLP	SAIL	FBG	KL	IB		12D	VLVO	9	3	6700	4	3	12100	13700
29		CAL 2-29	SLP	SAIL	FBG	KL	IB		12D	FARY	9	3	8000	4	6	15700	17800
29		CAL 29	SLP	SAIL	FBG	KL	IB		25	UNIV	9	3	8000	4	6	15600	17700
30		CAL 3-30 SHORT BOAT	SLP	SAIL	FBG	KL	IB		25D	GRAY	10	2	10500	5	6	21500	23900
30	2	CAL 3-30 LONG BOAT	SLP	SAIL	FBG	KL	IB		25D	GRAY	10	2	10500	5	6	21600	24000
33	3	CAL 2-34	SLP	SAIL	FBG	KL	IB		24D	FARY	10		9500	5		20100	22300
35	1	CAL 35	SLP	SAIL	FBG	KL	IB		50D	PERK	11		15000	4	8	31600	35100
45	6	CAL 2-46	KTH	SAIL	FBG	KL	IB		85D	PERK	12	6	30000	5		73300	80500
		1974 BOATS															
20		CAL 20	SLP	SAIL	FBG	KL	OB				7		1950	3	4	2900	3400
20	6	CAL 21	SLP	SAIL	FBG	SK	OB				6	8	1100	4	3	2250	2600
24	2	CAL T/4	SLP	SA/CR	FBG	KL	OB				8		4000	4		5750	6600
25		CAL 25	SLP	SA/CR	FBG	KL	OB				8		4000	4		6100	7000
27	5	CAL 27	SLP	SAIL	FBG	KL	OB				9		5400	4	6	9400	10700
27	5	CAL T/2	SLP	SAIL	FBG	KL	OB				9		5400	4	6	9550	10800
29		CAL 2-29	SLP	SA/CR	FBG	KL	IB		12D		9	3	8000	4	6	15400	17500
29		CAL 29	SLP	SAIL	FBG	KL	OB				9	3	8000	4	6	15100	17200
30	2	CAL 3-30	SLP	SAIL	FBG	KL	IB		D		10	2	10500	5	6	21100	23500
32	8	CAL 33	SLP	SA/CR	FBG	KL	IB		D		10	4	10800	6		22300	24700
35	1	CAL 35	SLP	SAIL	FBG	KL	IB		D	PERK	11		15000	4	8	30800	34300
35	1	CAL 35	KTH	SAIL	FBG	KL	IB		D	PERK	11		15000	4	8	30800	34300
45	6	CAL 2-46	SLP	SAIL	FBG	KL	IB		85D	PERK	12	6	30000	5		71800	78900
45	6	CAL 2-46	KTH	SAIL	FBG	KL	IB		85D	PERK	12	6	30000	5		71800	78900
		1973 BOATS															
20		CAL 20	SLP	SAIL	FBG	KL	OB				7		1950	3	4	2850	3350
20	6	CAL 21	SLP	SAIL	FBG	SK	OB				6	8	1100	4	3	2200	2550
24	2	CAL T/4	SLP	SAIL	FBG	KL	OB				8		4000	4		5600	6450
25		CAL 25	SLP	SAIL	FBG	KL	OB				8		4000	4		5950	6850
27	5	CAL 27	SLP	SAIL	FBG	KL	OB				9		5400	4	6	8950	10200
27	5	CAL 27	SLP	SAIL	FBG	KL	IB		6D	WEST	9		5400	4	6	9600	10900
27	5	CAL T/2	SLP	SA/CR	FBG	KL	IB		6D	WEST	9		5400			9600	10900
27	5	CAL T/2	SLP	SAIL	FBG	KL	OB				9		5400			9650	11000
29		CAL 29	SLP	SAIL	FBG	KL	OB				9	3	8000	4	6	14900	16900
29		CAL 29	SLP	SAIL	FBG	KL	IB		30	UNIV	9	3	8000	4	6	15000	17000
30	2	CAL 3-30	SLP	SAIL	FBG	KL	IB		D		10	2	10500	5	6	20700	23000
32	8	CAL 33	SLP	SAIL	FBG	KL	IB		25	UNIV	10	4	10800	6		21800	24200
38	8	CAL 39	SLP	SAIL	FBG	KL	IB		30	UNIV	11	8	14600	6		31300	34800
38	8	CAL 39	SLP	SAIL	FBG	KL	IB		40D	PERK	11	8	14600	6		31800	35400
38	8	CAL 39 DLX	SLP	SAIL	FBG	KL	IB		30	UNIV	11	8	14600	6		34000	37800
38	8	CAL 39 DLX	SLP	SAIL	FBG	KL	IB		40D	PERK	11	8	14600	6		34400	38200
45	6	CAL 2-46	SLP	SA/CR	FBG	KL	IB		85D	PERK	12	6	30000	5		70500	77400
45	6	CAL 2-46	KTH	SAIL	FBG	KL	IB		85D	PERK	12	6	30000	5		70500	77400
		1972 BOATS															
20		CAL 20	SLP	SAIL	FBG	KL	OB				7		1950	3	4	2800	3250
20	6	CAL 21	SLP	SAIL	FBG	SK	OB				6	8	1100	4	3	2100	2500
24	1	CAL T/4	SLP	SAIL	FBG	KL	OB				8		4000	4		5450	6300
25		CAL 25	SLP	SAIL	FBG	KL	OB				8		4000	4		5850	6700
27	5	CAL 27	SLP	SAIL	FBG	KL	OB				9		5400	4	6	9150	10400
27	5	CAL 27	SLP	SAIL	FBG	KL	IB		6D	WEST	9			4	6	10100	11500
29		CAL 29	SLP	SAIL	FBG	KL	OB				9	3	8000	4	6	14500	16500
29		CAL 29	SLP	SAIL	FBG	KL	IB		30	UNIV	9	3	8000	4	6	14700	16700
30	2	CAL 2-30	SLP	SAIL	FBG	KL	IB		30	UNIV	9		10300	5		19800	22000
32	8	CAL 33	SLP	SAIL	FBG	KL	IB		30	UNIV	10	4	10000	5	6	19800	22000
35	6	CAL 36	SLP	SA/CR	FBG	KL	IB		135D		10	4	12000	5	8	24900	27600
38	8	CAL 39	SLP	SAIL	FBG	KL	IB		40	UNIV	11	8	14600	6		30700	34100
38	8	CAL 39	SLP	SAIL	FBG	KL	IB		50D	PERK	11	8	14600	6		31200	34700
38	8	CAL 39 DLX	SLP	SAIL	FBG	KL	IB		40	UNIV	11	8	14600	6		33400	37100
38	8	CAL 39 DLX	SLP	SAIL	FBG	KL	IB		50D	PERK	11	8	14600	6		33800	37500
39	4	CAL 40	SLP	SAIL	FBG	KL	IB		D		11		15000	5	7	34500	38300
42	8	CAL 43	SLP	SAIL	FBG	KL	IB		40	UNIV	11	6	20000	6	6	48500	53200
42	8	CAL 43	SLP	SAIL	FBG	KL	IB		50D	PERK	11	6	20000	6	6	49000	53900
45	6	CAL 46	SLP	SA/CR	FBG	KL	IB		75D		12	6	30000	5		69200	76000
		1971 BOATS															
20		CAL 20	SLP	SAIL	FBG	KL	OB				7		1950	3	4	2750	3200
20	6	CAL 21	SLP	SAIL	FBG	SK	OB				6	8	1100	4	3	2050	2450
24		CAL 2-24	SLP	SAIL	FBG	KL	OB				7	9	3700	4		4950	5650
25		CAL 25	SLP	SAIL	FBG	KL	OB				8		4000	4		5700	6550
27	5	CAL 27	SLP	SAIL	FBG	KL	OB				9		5400	4	6	8900	10100
29		CAL 29	SLP	SAIL	FBG	KL	OB				9	3	8000	4	6	14200	16100
29		CAL 29	SLP	SAIL	FBG	KL	IB		30	UNIV	9	3	8000	4	6	14300	16200
30	2	CAL 2-30	SLP	SAIL	FBG	KL	IB		30	UNIV	9		10300	5		19300	21500
33	3	CAL 34	SLP	SAIL	FBG	KL	IB		30	UNIV	10		9500	5		18500	20600
35	6	CAL	SLP	SA/CR	FBG	KL	IB		50D	PERK	10	4	12000	5	8	23800	26400
38	8	CAL 39	SLP	SAIL	FBG	KL	IB		40	UNIV	11	8	14600	6		29900	33200
38	8	CAL 39	SLP	SAIL	FBG	KL	IB		50D	PERK	11	8	14600	6		30500	33900

 CONTINUED ON NEXT PAGE

LOA FT IN	NAME AND/ OR MODEL	TOP/ RIG	BOAT TYPE	HULL MTL TP	ENGINE TP # HP MFG	BEAM FT IN	WGT LBS	DRAFT FT IN	RETAIL LOW	RETAIL HIGH
				1971 BOATS						
38 8	CAL 39 DLX	SLP	SAIL	FBG KL	IB 40 UNIV	11 8	14600	6	32500	36100
38 8	CAL 39 DLX	SLP	SAIL	FBG KL	IB 50D PERK	11 8	14600	6	32900	36500
39 4	CAL 40	SLP	SAIL	FBG KL	IB 25D GRAY	11	15000	5 7	33500	37200
39 4	CAL 40	SLP	SAIL	FBG KL	IB 50D PERK	11	15000	5 7	33600	37300
42 8	CAL 43	SLP	SAIL	FBG KL	IB 40 UNIV	11 6	20000	6 6	47500	52200
42 8	CAL 43	SLP	SAIL	FBG KL	IB 50D PERK	11 6	20000	6 6	47800	52500
45 6	CAL	SLP	SA/CR	FBG KL	IB 85D PERK	12 6	30000	5	67200	73900
				1970 BOATS						
20	CAL 20	SLP	SA/OD	FBG KL	OB	7	1950	3 4	2650	3100
20 6	CAL 21	SLP	SAIL	FBG SK	OB	6 8	1100	4 9	2000	2400
24	CAL 2-24	SLP	SAIL	FBG KL	OB	7 9	3700	4	4800	5550
25	CAL 25	SLP	SAIL	FBG KL	OB	8	4000	4	5550	6400
29	CAL 29	SLP	SAIL	FBG KL	OB	9 3	8000	4 6	13800	15700
29	CAL 29	SLP	SAIL	FBG KL	IB 30 UNIV	9 3	8000	4 6	14000	15900
30 2	CAL 2-30	SLP	SAIL	FBG KL	IB 30 UNIV	9	10300	5	19100	21200
33 3	CAL 34	SLP	SAIL	FBG KL	IB 30 UNIV	10	9500	5	18100	20100
35 6	CAL 36	SLP	SAIL	FBG KL	IB 30 UNIV	10 4	11200	5 8	21500	23900
35 6	CAL CRUISING 36	SLP	SA/CR	FBG KL	IB 50D PERK	10 4	12000	5 8	23200	25800
39 4	CAL 40	SLP	SAIL	FBG KL	IB 25D GRAY	11	15000	5 7	32700	36300
42 8	CAL 43	SLP	SA/CR	FBG KL	IB D GRAY		20000	6 6	47100	51800
42 8	CAL 43	SLP	SA/CR	FBG KL	IB D PERK		20000	6 6	46900	51500
45 6	CAL CRUISING 46	SLP	SA/CR	FBG KL	IB 85D PERK	12 6	30000	5	65600	72100
47 9	CAL 48	SLP	SAIL	FBG	IB 50D PERK	12	25000	6 6	67300	74000
				1969 BOATS						
20	CAL 20	SLP	SAIL	FBG KL	OB	7	1950	3 4	2600	3050
24	CAL 2-24	SLP	SAIL	FBG KL	OB	7 9	3700	4	4700	5400
25	CAL 25	SLP	SAIL	FBG KL	OB	8	4000	4	5450	6250
28	CAL 28	SLP	SAIL	FBG KL	OB	9	6000	4 6	9650	11000
30 2	CAL 2-30	SLP	SAIL	FBG KL	IB 30 UNIV	9	10300	5	18600	20700
33 3	CAL 34	SLP	SAIL	FBG KL	IB 30 UNIV	10	9500	5	17300	19600
35 6	CAL 36	SLP	SAIL	FBG KL	IB 30 UNIV	10 4	11200	5 8	21000	23300
35 6	CAL CRUISING 36	SLP	SA/CR	FBG KL	IB 50D PERK	10 4	12000	5 8	22700	25200
37	CAL 37	SLP	SAIL	FBG KL	IB D				30500	33800
39 4	CAL 40	SLP	SAIL	FBG KL	IB	11	15000	5 7	32100	35600
45 6	CAL CRUISING 46	SLP	SA/CR	FBG KL	IB 85D PERK	12 6	30000	5	64100	70500
47 9	CAL 48	SLP	SAIL	FBG KL	IB 50D PERK	12	25000	6 6	65800	72300
				1968 BOATS						
20	CAL 20	SLP	SAIL	FBG KL	OB	7	1950	3 4	2550	2950
24	CAL 2-24	SLP	SAIL	FBG KL	OB	7 9	3700	4	4650	5300
25	CAL 25	SLP	SAIL	FBG KL	OB	8	4000	4	5350	6100
28	CAL 28	SLP	SAIL	FBG KL	OB	9	6000	4 6	9450	10700
33 3	CAL 34	SLP	SAIL	FBG KL	IB 30D	10	9500	5	17000	19300
35 6	CAL 36	SLP	SAIL	FBG KL	IB 30D	10 4	11200	5 8	20800	23100
39 4	CAL 40	SLP	SAIL	FBG KL	IB 36D	11	15000	5 7	31400	34900
45 6	CAL 46	SLP	SA/CR	FBG KL	IB 85D	12 6	30000	5	63100	69400
47 9	CAL 48	SLP	SAIL	FBG KL	IB 50D	12	25000	6 6	64700	71100
				1967 BOATS						
20	CAL 20	SLP	SA/OD	FBG KL		7	1950	3 4	2550	2900
24	CAL 2-24	SLP	SA/OD	FBG KL		7 9	3700	4 6	4550	5200
25	CAL 25	SLP	SA/OD	FBG KL		8	4000	4	5000	5750
28	CAL 28	SLP	SA/OD	FBG KL		9	6000	4 6	8050	9250
30	CAL 2-30	SLP	SA/OD	FBG KL		10	10300	4 6	15400	17500
35 6	CAL 36	SLP	SA/CR	FBG KL	IB D	10 4		5 8	20900	23200
39 4	CAL 40	SLP	SAIL	FBG KL	IB D	11	15000	5 7	30800	34300
45 6	CAL 46	SLP	SAIL	FBG KL	IB D	12 6		5	55300	65100
47 9	CAL 48	SLP	SA/CR	FBG KL	IB D	12		6 6	52300	79400
				1966 BOATS						
20	CAL 20	SLP	SAIL	FBG KL	OB				2500	2950
24	CAL 24	SLP	SA/OD	FBG KC		8		2 6	3600	4150
25	CAL 25	SLP	SAIL	FBG KL	OB				4800	5500
28	CAL 28	SLP	SAIL	FBG KL	OB				9400	10700
30	CAL 30	SLP	SAIL	FBG KL	IB 30D				11700	13300
35 6	CAL 36	SLP	SAIL	FBG KL	IB 30D				20600	22900
39 4	CAL 40	SLP	SAIL	FBG KL	IB 31D	11	15000		30300	33700
				1965 BOATS						
20	CAL 20	SLP	SAIL	FBG KL	OB	7		3 4	2500	2900
24	CAL 24	SLP	SAIL	FBG KC	OB	8		4 6	4200	4900
25	CAL 25	SLP	SAIL	FBG KL	OB	8		4	4750	5450
28	CAL 28	SLP	SAIL	FBG KL	OB	9		4	9250	10500
30	CAL 30	SLP	SAIL	FBG KL	OB	10		4 6	10200	11600
39 4	CAL 40	SLP	SAIL	FBG KL	IB D	11	15000	5 7	29900	33200
				1963 BOATS						
20	CAL 20	SLP	SAIL	FBG KL	OB				2400	2800
24	CAL 24	SLP	SAIL	FBG KC	OB				4100	4750
30	CAL 30	SLP	SAIL	FBG KL	OB				9950	11300
				1959 BOATS						
24	CAL 24	SLP	SAIL	FBG KL		8			4000	4650

CALIBER BOATS INC

CALIBER BOATS   COAST GUARD MFG ID- AER

Call 1-800-327-6929 for BUC Personalized Evaluation Service
Or, for 1977 boats, sign onto www.BUCValuPro.com

CALIBER YACHTS INC

CLEARWATER FL 33762   COAST GUARD MFG ID- CYQ See inside cover to adjust price for area
FORMERLY CALIBER YACHT CORP

For more recent years, see the BUC Used Boat Price Guide, Volume 1 or Volume 2

LOA FT IN	NAME AND/ OR MODEL	TOP/ RIG	BOAT TYPE	HULL MTL TP	ENGINE TP # HP MFG	BEAM FT IN	WGT LBS	DRAFT FT IN	RETAIL LOW	RETAIL HIGH
				1983 BOATS						
27 6	CALIBER 28	SLP	SA/RC	FBG KL	IB 15D YAN	10 10	6300	3 11	18200	20200

CALIFORNIA BOAT MFG INC

COAST GUARD MFG ID- CAL

Call 1-800-327-6929 for BUC Personalized Evaluation Service
Or, for 1974 boats, sign onto www.BUCValuPro.com

CALIFORNIA STEAMBOATS INC

COAST GUARD MFG ID- CSI

Call 1-800-327-6929 for BUC Personalized Evaluation Service
Or, for 1983 boats, sign onto www.BUCValuPro.com

CALKINS CRAFT BOAT CO

Call 1-800-327-6929 for BUC Personalized Evaluation Service
Or, for 1960 to 1961 boats, sign onto www.BUCValuPro.com

WENDELL H CALKINS NA

Call 1-800-327-6929 for BUC Personalized Evaluation Service
Or, for 1965 to 1969 boats, sign onto www.BUCValuPro.com

CAMELOT YACHTS

COAST GUARD MFG ID- KMT

Call 1-800-327-6929 for BUC Personalized Evaluation Service
Or, for 1982 to 1988 boats, sign onto www.BUCValuPro.com

CAMMENGAS JACHT-EN SCHEEPWERF

WORMERVEER HOLLAND   See inside cover to adjust price for area

LOA FT IN	NAME AND/ OR MODEL	TOP/ RIG	BOAT TYPE	HULL MTL TP	ENGINE TP # HP MFG	BEAM FT IN	WGT LBS	DRAFT FT IN	RETAIL LOW	RETAIL HIGH
				1967 BOATS						
30 4	COMMODORE	SLP	SAIL	STL KL	IB	8 10		4 3	11400	12900
32	COMMANDER	SLP	SAIL	STL KL	IB	9 4		4 8	12500	14200
34	GOODWIN	SLP	SA/RC	STL KL	IB	10 2		9 2	18800	20800
34 2	CAPTAIN	SLP	SAIL	STL KL	IB	9 7		4 8	27000	30000
42 10	TREWES	MS		STL KL	IB 60D	12 2		5 1	60900	67000
48	VANGUARD	KTH	SA/CR	STL KL	IB	12 8		5 9	71300	78400
49 5	WEST-INDIES	KTH	SA/CR	STL KL	IB	13 3		6	80100	88100
55	VALIANT	MS		STL KL	IB 126D	14 6		6	132500	146000
58 9	VENTURA	KTH	SA/CR	STL KL	IB	15		6 8	127500	140500

CAMPBELL BOAT CO

COAST GUARD MFG ID- CBL

Call 1-800-327-6929 for BUC Personalized Evaluation Service
Or, for 1974 boats, sign onto www.BUCValuPro.com

CAMPBELL YACHTS INC

SANTA ANA CA 92704   COAST GUARD MFG ID- PDG See inside cover to adjust price for area

LOA FT IN	NAME AND/ OR MODEL	TOP/ RIG	BOAT TYPE	-HULL- MTL TP	----ENGINE--- TP # HP MFG	BEAM FT IN	WGT LBS	DRAFT FT IN	RETAIL LOW	RETAIL HIGH
1976 BOATS										
37 1	OHLSON 38	SLP	SA/CR FBG	KL IB	25D	10 3	14900	5 7	38700	42900
37 1	OHLSON 38	YWL	SA/CR FBG	KL IB	25D	10 3	14900	5 7	38700	42900
38	OFFSHORE	OFF	FBG	IB	160	14 6		3 10	32700	36400
47	MOTOR YACHT	MY	FBG	IB	T185	15 4		4	138500	152000
52	MOTOR YACHT	MY	FBG	IB	T225	17 10		5	150500	165500
56	MOTOR YACHT	MY	FBG	IB	T225	17 10		5	173000	190000
60	MOTOR YACHT	MY	FBG	IB	T225	17 10		5	196500	216000
65	MOTOR YACHT	MY	FBG	IB	T225	17 10		5	402000	442000
75	MOTOR YACHT	MY	FBG	IB	T600	23		5 6	**	**
1975 BOATS										
28 11	OHLSON 8.8	SLP	SA/CR FBG	KL IB	12D	9 5	6600	5 2	17100	19500
34 6	OHLSON 35	SLP	SA/CR FBG	KL IB	19D	10 6	10400	5 11	26800	29800
37 1	OHLSON 38	SLP	SA/CR FBG	KL IB	25D	10 3	14900	5 7	37500	41700
37 1	OHLSON 38	YWL	SA/CR FBG	KL IB	25D	10 3	14900	5 7	37500	41700
38	OHLSON ONE-TON	SLP	SA/CR FBG	KL IB	30D	11 10	16000	6 7	40400	44900
1974 BOATS										
28 11	OHLSON 8.8	SLP	SA/CR FBG	KL IB	12D	9 5	6600	5 2	16700	18900
34 6	OHLSON 35	SLP	SA/CR FBG	KL IB	19D	10 6	10400	5 11	26100	29000
37 1	OHLSON 38	SLP	SA/CR FBG	KL IB	25D	10 3	14900	5 7	36500	40600
37 1	OHLSON 38	YWL	SA/CR FBG	KL IB	25D	10 3	14900	5 7	36500	40600
38	OHLSON ONE TON	SLP	SA/CR FBG	KL IB	30D	11 10	16000	6 7	39400	43700
1973 BOATS										
28 11	OHLSON 8.8	SLP	SA/CR FBG	KL IB	12D	9 5	6600	5 2	16300	18500
34 6	OHLSON 35	SLP	SA/CR FBG	KL IB	19D	10 6	10400	5 11	25500	28300
37 1	OHLSON 38	SLP	SA/CR FBG	KL IB	25D	10 3	14900	5 7	35600	39600
37 1	OHLSON 38	YWL	SA/CR FBG	KL IB	25D	10 3	14900	5 7	35600	39600
1971 BOATS										
31	HARMONY	SLP	SAIL FBG	KL IB	19	9 2	10750	4 8	26200	29100
33	NANTUCKET 33	SLP	SAIL FBG	KL IB	12	10 2		5 4	23900	26500
34 6	OHLSON 35	SLP	SAIL FBG	KL IB	19D	10 6	10400	5 11	24400	27100
37 3	OHLSON 38	SLP	SAIL FBG	KL IB	19	10 3	14900	5 7	33800	37600
37 3	OHLSON 38	YWL	SAIL FBG	KL IB	19	10 3	14900	5 7	33800	37600
40 9	OHLSON 41	SLP	SAIL FBG	KL IB		11	20000	6 1	46800	51400
40 9	OHLSON 41	YWL	SAIL FBG	KL IB		11	20000	6 1	46800	51400
43 6	OHLSON 44	SLP	SAIL FBG	KL IB		11 6	24500	6 3	59000	64800
43 6	OHLSON 44	YWL	SAIL FBG	KL IB		11 6	24500	6 3	59000	64800
44 6	OHLSON 45	SLP	SAIL FBG	KL IB		12 10	25000	6 8	62500	68700
44 6	OHLSON 45	YWL	SAIL FBG	KL IB		12 10	25000	6 8	62500	68700

CAMPBELL-SHEEHAN INC

LARCHMONT NY 10538   COAST GUARD MFG ID- CNS See inside cover to adjust price for area

LOA FT IN	NAME AND/ OR MODEL	TOP/ RIG	BOAT TYPE	-HULL- MTL TP	----ENGINE--- TP # HP MFG	BEAM FT IN	WGT LBS	DRAFT FT IN	RETAIL LOW	RETAIL HIGH
1975 BOATS										
17	STREAKER	RNBT	FBG	DV IO	130	5 10			6550	7500
38	CAMPBELL	OFF	FBG	IB	T225	14 6		3 10	59200	65000
47	CAMPBELL	MY	FBG	IB	T225	15		4	214000	235000
56	CAMPBELL	MY	FBG	IB	T350	18		5	308500	339000
60	CAMPBELL	MY	FBG	IB	T350	18		5	308500	339000
65	CAMPBELL	MY	FBG	IB	T350	18		5	725500	797000
1974 BOATS										
16	CAMPBELL	RNBT	FBG	DV OB		6 9	900		2400	2750
47	CAMPBELL	MY	FBG	IB	T225	15		3 10	205500	226000
52	CAMPBELL	MY	FBG	IB	T350	17		4 8	228500	251000
56	CAMPBELL	MY	FBG	IB	T550	18		4 10	318500	350000
60	CAMPBELL	MY	FBG	IB	T600	18		5	359000	394500
65	CAMPBELL	MY	FBG	IB	T	18		5 2	**	**
76	CAMPBELL	MY	FBG	IB	T	24		6 8	**	**
1972 BOATS										
28 11	OHLSON 8.8	SLP	SA/RC FBG	KL IB	12D	9 5	6600	5 2	18200	20300
34 6	OHLSON 35	SLP	SA/RC FBG	KL IB	19D	10 6	10400	5 11	28300	31400
37 1	OHLSON 38	SLP	SA/RC FBG	KL IB	25D	10 3	14900	5 7	40600	45100
1970 BOATS										
20	SHARK	SLP	SA/OD FBG	CT IB	D	10		6	2750	3200
20	TORNADO	SLP	SA/OD WD	CT IB	D	10		5	2750	3200
31	HARMONY	SLP	SA/CR FBG	KL IB	19D	9 2	10750	4 8	28800	32000
33	NANTUCKET 33	SLP	SA/CR FBG	KL IB	12D	10 2	10000	5 4	26300	29300
37 3	OHLSON 38	SLP	SA/CR FBG	KL IB	19D	10 3	14900	5 7	39100	43500
37 3	OHLSON 38	YWL	SA/CR FBG	KL IB	19D	10 3	14900	5 7	39100	43500
40 9	OHLSON 41	SLP	SA/CR AL	KL IB	D	11	20000	6 1	55600	61200
40 9	OHLSON 41	SLP	SA/CR AL	KL IB	D	11	20000	6 1	55600	61200
40 9	OHLSON 41	SLP	SA/CR AL	KL IB	D	11	20000	6 1	55600	61200
40 9	OHLSON 41	YWL	SA/CR AL	KL IB	D	11	20000	6 1	55600	61200
40 9	OHLSON 41	YWL	SA/CR AL	KL IB	D	11	20000	6 1	55600	61200
43 6	OHLSON 44	SLP	SA/CR AL	KL IB	D	11 6	24500	6 3	70300	77300
43 6	OHLSON 44	SLP	SA/CR WD	KL IB	D	11 6	24500	6 3	70300	77300
43 6	OHLSON 44	SLP	SA/CR WD	KL IB	D	11 6	24500	6 3	70300	77300
43 6	OHLSON 44	YWL	SA/CR AL	KL IB	D	11 6	24500	6 3	70300	77300
43 6	OHLSON 44	YWL	SA/CR WD	KL IB	D	11 6	24500	6 3	70300	77300
44 6	OHLSON 45	SLP	SA/CR FBG	KL IB	D	12 10	25000	6 8	74500	81900
44 6	OHLSON 45	SLP	SA/CR WD	KL IB	D	12 10	25000	6 8	74500	81900
44 6	OHLSON 45	SLP	SA/CR AL	KL IB	D	12 10	25000	6 8	74500	81900
44 6	OHLSON 45	YWL	SA/CR WD	KL IB	D	12 10	25000	6 8	74500	81900
1969 BOATS										
20	SHARK	SLP	SAIL FBG	CT IB	D	10	550	6	2700	3150
31	HARMONY	SLP	SA/CR AL	KL IB	19D	9 2	10750	4 8	28300	31500
33	NANTUCKET 33	SLP	SA/CR AL	KL IB	D	10 2		5 4	25900	28800
33	NANTUCKET 33	SLP	SA/CR FBG	KL IB	12D	10 2	10000	5 4	25900	28800
37 3	OHLSON 38	SLP	SA/CR FBG	KL IB	19D	10 3	14900	5 7	38500	42800
37 3	OHLSON 38	YWL	SA/CR FBG	KL IB	19D	10 3	14900	5 7	38500	42800
40 9	OHLSON 41	SLP	SA/CR AL	KL IB	D	11	20000	6 1	54800	60200
44 6	OHLSON 45	SLP	SA/CR AL	KL IB	D	12 10		6 8	73300	80600
44 6	OHLSON 45	SLP	SA/CR AL	KL IB	D	12 10	25000	6 8	73300	80600
44 6	OHLSON 45	YWL	SA/CR AL	KL IB	D	12 10		6 8	73300	80600
44 6	OHLSON 45	YWL	SA/CR WD	KL IB	D	12 10	25000	6 8	73300	80600
1968 BOATS										
31	HARMONY	SLP	SA/CR FBG	KL IB	D	9 2		4 8	28000	31100
33	NANTUCKET 33	SLP	SA/CR AL	KL IB	D	10 2		5 4	25600	28400
37 3	OHLSON 38	SLP	SA/CR FBG	KL IB	D	10 3		5 7	38200	42400
40 9	OHLSON 41	SLP	SA/CR AL	KL IB	D	11		6 1	54000	59400
40 9	OHLSON 41	SLP	SA/CR FBG	KL IB	D	11		6 1	54000	59400
40 9	OHLSON 41	SLP	SA/CR STL	KL IB	D	11		6 1	54000	59400
43 6	OHLSON 44	SLP	SA/CR AL	KL IB	D	11 6		6 6	68300	75100
43 6	OHLSON 44	SLP	SA/CR FBG	KL IB	D	11 6		6 6	68300	75100
43 6	OHLSON 44	SLP	SA/CR STL	KL IB	D	11 6		6 6	68300	75100
1966 BOATS										
26	OHLSON 26	SLP	SA/CR P/M	KL IB	D VLVO	8		4 1	12600	14300
36 3	OHLSON 36	SLP	SA/CR P/M	KL IB	25D GRAY	9 8		5	36700	40700
36 3	OHLSON 36	SLP	SA/CR P/M	KL IB	25D GRAY	9 8		5	36700	40700
40 9	OHLSON 41	SLP	SA/CR STL	KL IB	30 UNIV	11		6	38100	42300
1965 BOATS										
26	OHLSON	SLP	SAIL FBG	KL IB	D	8		4 1	12500	14200
26 6	OHLSON	SLP	SAIL FBG	KL IB	D	8 9		5	15200	17300
30	OHLSON A	SLP	SAIL FBG	KL IB	D	8 2		4 6	25300	28400
36 7	OHLSON 37	SLP	SAIL FBG	KL IB	D	9 8		5	36600	40700
40 9	OHLSON 41	SLP	SAIL FBG	KL IB	D	11		6 1	52500	57700

CAMPER & NICHOLSONS INC

GOSPORT HAMPSHIRE ENGLA COAST GUARD MFG ID- CNL See inside cover to adjust price for area

For more recent years, see the BUC Used Boat Price Guide, Volume 1 or Volume 2

LOA FT IN	NAME AND/ OR MODEL	TOP/ RIG	BOAT TYPE	-HULL- MTL TP	----ENGINE--- TP # HP MFG	BEAM FT IN	WGT LBS	DRAFT FT IN	RETAIL LOW	RETAIL HIGH
1983 BOATS										
30 6	NICHOLSON 31	SLP	SA/CR FBG	KL IB	D	10 3	14000	5	57000	62600
35 3	NICHOLSON 35	SLP	SA/CR FBG	KL IB	D	10 5	17000	5 6	67900	74600
39	NICHOLSON 39	SLP	SA/CR FBG	KL IB	D	11 6	23000	5 6	89900	98800
40	NICHOLSON 40 AFT	KTH	SA/CR FBG	KL IB	D	11 6	24400	5 9	96000	105500
40	NICHOLSON 40PH	SLP	SA/CR FBG	KL IB	D	11 6	23300	5 6	93100	102500
43 2	NICHOLSON 44	KTH	SA/CR FBG	KL IB	D	12 2	28000	6 3	117000	128500
47 8	NICHOLSON 48	KTH	SA/CR FBG	KL IB	D	12 11	31240	6 3	152000	167000
54 5	NICHOLSON 55	KTH	SA/CR FBG	KL IB	D	14 4	35000	8 3	241500	265500
57 7	NICHOLSON 58	SLP	SA/CR CB	KL IB	D	15 7	52500	8 6	342500	376000
57 7	NICHOLSON 58	KTH	SA/CR FBG	KL IB	D	15 7	52500	8 6	342500	376000
57 7	NICHOLSON 58	SLP	SA/CR CB	KL IB	D	15 7	52500	8 6	342500	376000
57 7	NICHOLSON 58	KTH	SA/CR FBG	KL IB	D	15 7	52500	8 6	342500	376500
70	NICHOLSON 70	KTH	SA/CR FBG	KL IB	D	17 1	51T	8 6	691500	760000
1982 BOATS										
30 6	NICHOLSON 31	SLP	SA/CR FBG	KL IB	D	10 3	14000	5	53800	58900
35 3	NICHOLSON 35	SLP	SA/CR FBG	KL IB	D	10 5	17000	5 6	63900	70200
39	NICHOLSON 39	SLP	SA/CR FBG	KL IB	D	11 6	23000	5 6	84600	93000
40	NICHOLSON 40 AFT	KTH	SA/CR FBG	KL IB	D	11 6	24400	5 9	90300	99300
40	NICHOLSON 40PH	SLP	SA/CR FBG	KL IB	D	11 6	23300	5 6	87500	96200
43 2	NICHOLSON 44	KTH	SA/CR FBG	KL IB	D	12 2	28000	6 3	110000	121000
47 8	NICHOLSON 48	KTH	SA/CR FBG	KL IB	D	12 11	31240	6 3	143000	157000
54 5	NICHOLSON 55	KTH	SA/CR FBG	KL IB	D	14 4	35000	8 3	227500	250000
70	NICHOLSON 70	KTH	SA/CR FBG	KL IB	D	17 1	51T	8 6	652000	716500

LOA FT	IN	NAME AND/ OR MODEL	TOP/ RIG	BOAT TYPE	-HULL- MTL	TP	----ENGINE--- TP	#	HP	MFG	BEAM FT	IN	WGT LBS	DRAFT FT	IN	RETAIL LOW	RETAIL HIGH
		1981 BOATS															
27	2	NICHOLSON 27	SLP	SA/CR	FBG	KL	IB		D		9	7	6448	4	7	19800	22000
27	2	NICHOLSON 27	SLP	SA/CR	FBG	TK	IB		D		9	7	6448	4	7	19800	22000
30	1	NICHOLSON 303	SLP	SA/RC	FBG	KL	IB		D		10	3	6000	5	9	21000	23300
30	6	NICHOLSON 31	SLP	SA/CR	FBG	KL	IB		D		10	4	14000	5		50400	55400
34	5	NICHOLSON 345	SLP	SA/RC	FBG	KL	IB		D		11		11500	6	1	41600	46200
35	3	NICHOLSON 35	SLP	SA/CR	FBG	KL	IB		D		10	5	17000	5	6	60100	66000
39		NICHOLSON 39	KTH	SA/CR	FBG	KL	IB		D		11	6	23000	5	6	79500	87400
40		NICHOLSON 40 AFT	KTH	SA/CR	FBG	KL	IB		D		11	6	24400	5	9	85000	93400
40		NICHOLSON 40 PH	SLP	SA/CR	FBG	KL	IB		D		11	6	23300	5	6	82300	90500
43	2	NICHOLSON 44	KTH	SA/CR	FBG	KL	IB		D		12	3	28000	5	6	103500	114000
47	8	NICHOLSON 48	KTH	SA/CR	FBG	KL	IB		D		12	11	31240	5	6	134500	148000
54	5	NICHOLSON 55	KTH	SA/CR	FBG	KL	IB		D		14	4	35000	8	3	214000	235000
70		NICHOLSON 70	KTH	SA/CR	FBG	KL	IB		D		17	1	51T	8	6	615000	676000
		1979 BOATS															
30		NICHOLSON HALF TON	SLP	SA/RC	FBG	KL	IB		D		10	3	6000	5	9	19200	21300
30	3	NICHOLSON 303	SLP	SA/CR	FBG	KL	IB		D		10	3	5733	5	7	18700	20800
30	6	NICHOLSON 31	SLP	SA/CR	FBG	KL	IB		D		10	4	13000	5		42700	47400
32	1	NICHOLSON 33	SLP	SA/RC	FBG	KL	IB		D		10	5	10000	6	1	34000	37800
34		NICHOLSON 345	SLP	SA/CR	FBG	KL	IB		D							38300	42500
35	3	NICHOLSON 35	SLP	SA/CR	FBG	KL	IB		D		10	5	15620	5	6	51100	56200
39		NICHOLSON 39	KTH	SA/CR	FBG	KL	IB		D		11	6	20000	5	6	65900	72400
40		NICHOLSON 40	SLP	SA/CR	FBG	KL	IB		D		11	6	20000	5	6	68200	74900
43	2	NICHOLSON 44	KTH	SA/CR	FBG	KL	IB		D		12	3	22200	5	6	83800	92000
47	8	NICHOLSON 48	KTH	SA/CR	FBG	KL	IB		D		12	11	31240	5	6	123500	135500
54	5	NICHOLSON 55	KTH	SA/CR	FBG	KL	IB		D		14	4	35000	8	3	196500	216000
70		NICHOLSON 70	KTH	SA/CR	FBG	KL	IB		D		17	1	51T	8	6	561000	616500
		1978 BOATS															
30		NICHOLSON HALF TON	SLP	SA/CR	FBG	CB	IB		8D		10	3	6000	5	9	18600	20700
31		NICHOLSON	SLP	SA/CR	FBG	KL	IB		12D		10	4	13000	5		41600	46200
33		NICHOLSON	SLP	SA/CR	FBG	CB	IB		12D		10	5	10000	5	11	32400	36000
35		NICHOLSON	SLP	SA/CR	FBG	KL	IB		48D		10	5	15620	5	6	49400	54300
39		NICHOLSON	KTH	SA/CR	FBG	KL	IB		50D		11	6	20000	5	6	63600	69900
44		NICHOLSON	KTH	SA/CR	FBG	KL	IB		72D		12	3	22220	5	6	84900	93200
48		NICHOLSON	KTH	SA/CR	FBG	KL	IB		72D		12	11	31200	5	6	121000	133000
55		NICHOLSON	KTH	SA/CR	FBG	KL	IB		72D		14	4	38000	8	3	199000	219000
70		NICHOLSON	KTH	SA/CR	FBG	KL	IB	T	95D		17	1	52T	8	6	511500	562000
		1977 BOATS															
30		NICHOLSON	SLP	SA/CR	FBG	KL	IB		10D		9	6	7700	5	7	23000	25500
30	6	NICHOLSON	SLP	SA/CR	FBG	KL	IB		12D		10	4	13000	5		39700	44100
32	1	NICHOLSON	SLP	SA/CR	FBG	KL	IB		12D		10	5	10000	5	11	31700	35200
35	3	NICHOLSON	SLP	SA/CR	FBG	KL	IB		48D		10	5	15620	5	6	47700	52400
39		NICHOLSON	KTH	SA/CR	FBG	KL	IB		50D		11	6	20000	5	6	61500	67600
43	2	NICHOLSON	KTH	SA/CR	FBG	KL	IB		72D		12	3	22220	5	6	78400	86100
47	8	NICHOLSON	KTH	SA/CR	FBG	KL	IB		72D		12	11	31200	5	6	115000	126500
54	5	NICHOLSON	KTH	SA/CR	FBG	KL	IB		72D		14	4	38000	8	3	184500	202500
70		NICHOLSON	KTH	SA/CR	FBG	KL	IB	T	95D		17	1	52T	8	6	492500	541000
		1976 BOATS															
29		NICHOLSON 30	SLP	SA/CR	FBG	KL	IB		10D		9	9	7055	5	7	19600	21700
32	1	NICHOLSON 33	SLP	SA/CR	FBG	KL	IB				10	5	10046	5	11	30800	34200
33		NICHOLSON 32	SLP	SA/CR	FBG	KL	IB		20D		9	3	13670	5	6	41100	45700
35	3	NICHOLSON 35	SLP	SA/CR	FBG	KL	IB		37D		10	5	15655	5	6	46500	51100
37	10	NICHOLSON 38	KTH	SA/CR	FBG	KL	IB		37D		10	6	15905	5	2	48300	53000
42		NICHOLSON 42	SLP	SA/CR	FBG	KL	IB		62D		12	2	22265	5	6	71600	78700
42		NICHOLSON 42	KTH	SA/CR	FBG	KL	IB		62D		12	2	22265	5	6	71600	78700
47	8	NICHOLSON 48	KTH	SA/CR	FBG	KL	IB		62D		12	11	31200	5	6	111000	122000
54	5	NICHOLSON 55	SLP	SA/CR	FBG	KL	IB		62D		14	4	38140	8	3	178000	195500
54	5	NICHOLSON 55	KTH	SA/CR	FBG	KL	IB		62D		14	4	38140	8	3	178500	196000
70		NICHOLSON 70	KTH	SA/CR	FBG	KL	IB	T	95D		17	1	52T	8	6	475000	522000
		1975 BOATS															
29		NICHOLSON HALF TON	SLP	SA/CR	FBG	KL	IB		10D		9	9	7055	5	7	19000	21100
33		NICHOLSON 32	SLP	SA/CR	FBG	KL	IB		20D		9	3	13670	5	6	39900	44400
35	3	NICHOLSON 35	SLP	SA/CR	FBG	KL	IB		37D		10	5	15655	5	6	44700	49600
37	10	NICHOLSON 38	KTH	SA/CR	FBG	KL	IB		37D		10	6	15905	5	2	47100	51800
41		NICHOLSON 42	SLP	SA/CR	FBG	KL	IB		62D		12	2	22265	5	6	66700	73300
41		NICHOLSON 42	KTH	SA/CR	FBG	KL	IB		62D		12	2	22265	5	6	66700	73300
47	8	NICHOLSON 48	KTH	SA/CR	FBG	KL	IB		62D		12	11	31200	5	6	108000	118500
54	5	NICHOLSON 55	SLP	SA/CR	FBG	KL	IB		62D		14	4	38140	8	3	172500	189500
54	5	NICHOLSON 55	KTH	SA/CR	FBG	KL	IB		62D		14	4	38140	8	3	173000	190500
70		NICHOLSON 70	KTH	SA/CR	FBG	KL	IB	T	95D		17	1	52T	8	6	459500	505000
		1974 BOATS															
28	11	NICHOLSON 30	SLP	SA/CR	FBG	KL	IB		D		9	9	7055	5	8	18700	20800
33		NICHOLSON 32	SLP	SA/CR	FBG	KL	IB		20D		9	2	13670	5	6	38900	43200
35	3	NICHOLSON 35	SLP	SA/CR	FBG	KL	IB		D		10	5	15655	5	6	43500	48300
37	10	NICHOLSON 38 CTR CPT	KTH	SA/CR	FBG	KL	IB		D		10	6	15905	5	2	45800	50300
41		NICHOLSON 42 CTR CPT	SLP	SA/CR	FBG	KL	IB		D		12	2	22265	5	6	64700	71200
41		NICHOLSON 42 CTR CPT	KTH	SA/CR	FBG	KL	IB		D		12	2	22265	5	6	64700	71200
47	8	NICHOLSON 48 CTR CPT	KTH	SA/CR	FBG	KL	IB		D		12	11	31200	5	6	105000	115500
54	10	NICHOLSON 55 CTR CPT	SLP	SA/CR	FBG	KL	IB		D		14	4	38140	8	6	173000	190000
54	10	NICHOLSON 55 CTR CPT	KTH	SA/CR	FBG	KL	IB		D		14	4	38140	8	6	174000	191500
		1973 BOATS															
28	11	NICHOLSON 30	SLP	SA/CR	FBG	KL	IB		D		9	9	7055	5	8	18300	20300
33		NICHOLSON 32	SLP	SA/CR	FBG	KL	IB		D		9	2	13670	5	6	37900	42200
35	3	NICHOLSON 35	SLP	SA/CR	FBG	KL	IB		D		10	5	15620	5	6	42300	47000
37	10	NICHOLSON 38	KTH	SA/CR	FBG	KL	IB		D		10	6	15905	5	2	44200	49100
43	3	NICHOLSON 43	SLP	SAIL	FBG	KL	IB		D		11	6	20000	6	9	66100	72600
43	8	NICHOLSON 45	SLP	SA/CR	FBG	KL	IB		D		12	3		7	1	79300	87200
47	8	NICHOLSON 48	KTH	SA/CR	FBG	KL	IB		D		12	11	31200	5	6	102500	113000
53	10	NICHOLSON 55	SLP	SA/CR	FBG	KL	IB		D		14	4	38140	8	3	157500	173500
53	10	NICHOLSON 55	KTH	SA/CR	FBG	KL	IB		D		14	4	38140	8	3	158500	174000
		1972 BOATS															
32		NICHOLSON 32	SLP	SA/RC	FBG	KL	IB		D		9	3		5	6	27700	30800
35	3	NICHOLSON 35	SLP	SA/RC	FBG	KL	IB		D		10	5		5	6	44100	49000
37	10	NICHOLSON 38	KTH	SA/CR	FBG	KL	IB		D		10	6		5	2	57400	63100
43	3	NICHOLSON 43	SLP	SA/RC	FBG	KL	IB		D		11	6		6	9	76100	83600
54	5	NICHOLSON 55	SLP	SA/CR	FBG	KL	IB		D		14	4		8	3	158000	173500
		1971 BOATS															
32		NICHOLSON 32	SLP	SA/CR	FBG	KL	IB		D		9	3		5	6	27200	30200
37	10	NICHOLSON 38	KTH	SA/CR	FBG	KL	IB		D		10	6		5	2	56300	61800
43	3	NICHOLSON 43	SLP	SA/CR	FBG	KL	IB		D		11	6		6	9	74600	82000
54	5	NICHOLSON 56	SLP	SA/CR	FBG	KL	IB		D		14	4		8	3	154500	170000
54	5	NICHOLSON 56	KTH	SA/CR	FBG	KL	IB		D		14	4		8	3	156000	171000

CAMPER-CRAFT INC

COAST GUARD MFG ID- CGE

Call 1-800-327-6929 for BUC Personalized Evaluation Service
Or, for 1978 boats, sign onto www.BUCValuPro.com

CAMPION MARINE INC

KELOWNA BC CANADA V1X 7 COAST GUARD MFG ID- ZBI See inside cover to adjust price for area

For more recent years, see the BUC Used Boat Price Guide, Volume 1 or Volume 2

LOA FT	IN	NAME AND/ OR MODEL	TOP/ RIG	BOAT TYPE	-HULL- MTL	TP	----ENGINE--- TP	#	HP	MFG	BEAM FT	IN	WGT LBS	DRAFT FT	IN	RETAIL LOW	RETAIL HIGH
		1982 BOATS															
16	2	SEVERN 160		RNBT	FBG	DV	IO		120		6	5	1350			1800	2100
16	3	ARROW 160		SKI	FBG	DV	OB				6	7	800			1850	2200
16	8	KOOTENAY 170		SKI	FBG	SV	OB				6	8	800			1850	2200
17	6	ALERT 180		RNBT	FBG	DV	OB				7	2	1200			2850	3300
17	6	ALERT 180		RNBT	FBG	DV	IO		120		7	2	1500			2250	2600
17	6	BOWRIDER 180		RNBT	FBG	DV	OB				7	2	1200			2850	3300
17	6	BOWRIDER 180		RNBT	FBG	DV	IO		120		7	2	1500			2250	2600
17	6	CRUISETTE 180		CR	FBG	DV	OB				7	2	1200			2800	3250
18	6	CRUISETTE 190		CR	FBG	DV	OB				7	2	1700			3700	4300
18	6	SQUALLY 190		RNBT	FBG	DV	OB				7	2	1300			3100	3600
18	6	SQUALLY 190		RNBT	FBG	DV	IO		120		7	2	1600			2450	2850
18	6	SQUALLY 190	HT	RNBT	FBG	DV	IO		120		7	2	1600			2450	2850
20	6	DISCOVERY 210		RNBT	FBG	DV	OB				7	2	1900			4950	5700
20	6	DISCOVERY 210		RNBT	FBG	DV	IO		140		8		1850			3150	3650
21		MONASHEE 220		CBNCR	FBG	DV	IO		184		8					4750	5450
21		SKEENA 220-CB		CR	FBG	DV	IO		140		8					4350	5000
23	10	ADVENTURE 250		SPTCR	FBG	DV	IO		120		8	10				6300	7250
23	10	HAIDA OFFSHORE 250		CR	FBG	DV	IO		225		8	10				6450	7400
25	10	TOBA 270		SDN	FBG	DV	IO		225		9	4				9150	10400
29	11	TRAWLER 300		TRWL	FBG	DV	IO		75		11	11				13000	14700
		1981 BOATS															
16	2	SEVERN 16		RNBT	FBG	DV	IO		120		6	5				2150	2500
16	3	ARROW 16		SKI	FBG	DV	OB				6	7	1350			2900	3400
16	3	SEVERN 16		RNBT	FBG	DV	OB				6	5	1000			2300	2650
17	6	ALERT 17		RNBT	FBG	DV	OB				7	2	1200			2750	3200
17	6	ALERT 17		RNBT	FBG	DV	IO		120		7	2				2700	3150
17	6	BOWRIDER 17		RNBT	FBG	DV	OB				7	2	1200			2750	3200
17	6	BOWRIDER 17		RNBT	FBG	DV	IO		120		7	2				2700	3150
17	6	CRUISETTE 17		CR	FBG	DV	OB				7	2	1200			2700	3150
18	6	CRUISETTE 18		CR	FBG	DV	OB				7	2	1700			3600	4200
18	6	SQUALLY 18		RNBT	FBG	DV	OB				7	2	1300			3000	3500
18	6	SQUALLY 18		RNBT	FBG	DV	IO		120		7	2				2900	3400
20	6	DISCOVERY 20		RNBT	FBG	DV	IO		140-240		8					3950	4600
21		MONASHEE 21		CBNCR	FBG	DV	IO		184		8					4650	5350
21		SKEENA 21		CR	FBG	DV	IO		140		8					4250	4950

 CONTINUED ON NEXT PAGE

LOA FT	LOA IN	NAME AND/ OR MODEL	TOP/ RIG	BOAT TYPE	-HULL- MTL	-HULL- TP	TP	ENGINE # HP	ENGINE MFG	BEAM FT	BEAM IN	WGT LBS	DRAFT FT	DRAFT IN	RETAIL LOW	RETAIL HIGH
		1981 BOATS														
23	10	ADVENTURE 24		SPTCR	FBG	DV	IO	120		8	10				6200	7150
23	10	HAIDA OFFSHORE 24		CR	FBG	DV	IO	225		8	10				6300	7250
25	10	TOBA 26		SDN	FBG	DV	IO	225		9	4				9000	10200
29	11	TRAWLER 29		TRWL	FBG	DV	IO	75		11	11				12800	14500
		1980 BOATS														
16	2	SEVERN		RNBT	FBG	DV	IO	120		6	5				2100	2500
16	3	ARROW	OP	SKI	FBG	DV	OB			6	7	800			1700	2050
16	3	SEVERN	OP	RNBT	FBG	DV	OB			6	5	1000			2250	2600
17	6	ALERT		RNBT	FBG	DV	IO	120		7	2				2650	3100
17	6	ALERT	OP	RNBT	FBG	DV	OB			7	2	1200			2650	3050
17	6	ALERT	HT	RNBT	FBG	DV	OB			7	2	1200			2700	3150
17	6	BOWRIDER		RNBT	FBG	DV	IO	120		7	2				2700	3150
17	6	BOWRIDER	OP	RNBT	FBG	DV	OB			7	2	1200			2750	3200
17	6	CRUISETTE	OP	CR	FBG	DV	OB			7	2	1200			2650	3100
18	6	CRUISETTE	OP	CR	FBG	DV	OB			7	2	1700			3500	4100
18	6	SQUALLY		RNBT	FBG	DV	IO	120		7	2				2900	3350
18	6	SQUALLY	OP	RNBT	FBG	DV	OB			7	2	1300			2950	3400
18	6	SQUALLY	HT	RNBT	FBG	DV	OB			7	2	1400			3100	3600
18	6	SQUALLY	HT	RNBT	FBG	DV	IO	120		7	2				2900	3350
20	6	CORTES		RNBT	FBG	DV	IO	140		8					3900	4550
20	6	CORTES	OP	RNBT	FBG	DV	OB			7	2	1900			4750	5450
20	6	CORTES	HT	RNBT	FBG	DV	OB			7	2	2100			5100	5850
21		GULF-ISLANDER		CR	FBG	DV	IO	140		8					3850	4450
21		SKEENA		CR	FBG	DV	IO	140		8					4650	5300
23	10	HAIDA		CR	FBG	DV	IO	225		8	10				6250	7200
25	10	TOBA		CR	FBG	DV	IO	225		9	4				8250	9500
		1979 BOATS														
16	2	SEVERN		RNBT	FBG	DV	OB			6	5	1000			2150	2550
16	2	SEVERN		RNBT	FBG	DV	IO	120-140		6	5	1600			1850	2250
16	3	ARROW	OP	SKI	FBG	DV	OB			6	7	900			1900	2300
17	6	ALERT	OP	RNBT	FBG	DV	OB			7	2	1200			2600	3050
17	6	ALERT	OP	RNBT	FBG	DV	IO	140-190		7	2	2000			2400	2900
17	6	ALERT	HT	RNBT	FBG	DV	OB			7	2	1200			2650	3050
17	6	ALERT	HT	RNBT	FBG	DV	IO	140-190		7	2	2000			2450	2900
17	6	ALERT W/T	OP	RNBT	FBG	DV	OB			7	2	1200			2650	3100
17	6	ALERT W/T	OP	RNBT	FBG	DV	IO	140-190		7	2	2000			2450	2900
17	6	CRUISETTE		CR	FBG	DV	OB			7	2	1700			3350	3900
18	6	CRUISETTE		CR	FBG	DV	OB			7	2	1900			3700	4300
18	6	CRUISETTE		CR	FBG	DV	IO	140-200		7	2				2950	3500
18	6	SQUALLY	OP	CR	FBG	DV	OB			7	2	1400			3000	3500
18	6	SQUALLY	OP	CR	FBG	DV	IO	140-200		7	2				2950	3500
18	6	SQUALLY	HT	CR	FBG	DV	OB			7	2	1400			3000	3500
18	6	SQUALLY	HT	CR	FBG	DV	IO	140-200		7	2				2950	3500
19		GULF-ISLANDER		CR	FBG	DV	IO	140-200		8					3250	3850
19		SOUNDER		CR	FBG	DV	OB			8	2	2100			4000	4650
19		SOUNDER		CR	FBG	DV	IO	140-200		8	2	2700			3450	4100
21		SOUNDER		CR	FBG	DV	OB			8	2	2350			5500	6350
21		SOUNDER		CR	FBG	DV	IO	185-230		8	2	3000			4200	5000
23	10	HAIDA		CR	FBG	DV	IO	225-260		8	10				6250	7350
25	10	TOBA		CR	FBG	DV	IO	225-260		9	6				8300	9750
		1978 BOATS														
16	2	SEVERN 16	ST	RNBT	FBG	SV	OB			6	5	1000			2100	2500
16	2	SEVERN 16	ST	RNBT	FBG	SV	IO	120		6	5	1600			1900	2250
		IO 140 MRCR 1900 2250, IO 140 OMC 1850 2200, IO 140 VLVO													2000	2400
16	3	ARROW 16	OP	RNBT	FBG	SV	OB			6	7	900			1900	2250
17	6	ALERT 17-1/2	ST	RNBT	FBG	SV	OB			7	2	1200			2600	3000
17	6	ALERT 17-1/2	ST	RNBT	FBG	SV	IO	120-198		7	2	2000			2450	3050
17	6	ALERT 17-1/2	ST	RNBT	FBG	SV	IO	200	VLVO	7	2	2000			2650	3100
17	6	ALERT 17-1/2	HT	RNBT	FBG	SV	OB			7	2				3400	4000
17	6	ALERT 17-1/2	HT	RNBT	FBG	SV	IO	120-198		7	2	2000			2450	3050
17	6	ALERT 17-1/2	HT	RNBT	FBG	SV	IO	200	VLVO	7	2	2000			2650	3100
17	6	ALERT 17-1/2 B/R	ST	RNBT	FBG	SV	OB			7	2	1250			2650	3100
17	6	ALERT 17-1/2 B/R	ST	RNBT	FBG	SV	IO	120-198		7	2	2000			2450	3050
17	6	ALERT 17-1/2 B/R	ST	RNBT	FBG	SV	IO	200	VLVO	7	2	2000			2650	3100
17	6	ALERT CRUISETTE	OP	RNBT	FBG	SV	OB			7	2				3400	4000
17	6	ALERT CRUISETTE	OP	RNBT	FBG	SV	IO	120-198		7	2	2000			2450	3050
17	6	ALERT CRUISETTE	OP	RNBT	FBG	SV	IO	200	VLVO	7	2	2000			2650	3100
17	6	CHRISTINA 17-1/2	ST	RNBT	FBG	SV	IO	120-198		7	2	2400			2700	3300
17	6	CHRISTINA 17-1/2	ST	RNBT	FBG	SV	IO	200	VLVO	7	2	2400			2900	3350
18	6	SQUALLY 18-1/2	ST	RNBT	FBG	SV	OB								3750	4350
18	6	SQUALLY 18-1/2	ST	RNBT	FBG	SV	IO	120-228							3000	3700
18	6	SQUALLY 18-1/2	HT	RNBT	FBG	SV	OB								3750	4350
18	6	SQUALLY 18-1/2	HT	RNBT	FBG	SV	IO	120-228							3000	3700
18	6	SQUALLY CRUISETTE	OP	RNBT	FBG	SV	OB								3750	4350
18	6	SQUALLY CRUISETTE	OP	RNBT	FBG	SV	IO	120-200							3000	3700
18	6	SQUALLY CRUISETTE	OP	RNBT	FBG	SV	IO	225-228							3050	3750
19		GULF-ISLANDER 19	HT	WKNDR	FBG	SV	IO	120-200		7	10	3100			3700	4550
19		GULF-ISLANDER 19	HT	WKNDR	FBG	SV	IO	225-228		7	10	3100			3750	4600
19		SOUNDER 19	ST	RNBT	FBG	SV	OB			7	10	2100			3950	4600
19		SOUNDER 19	ST	RNBT	FBG	SV	IO	120-200		7	10	2700			3250	4050
19		SOUNDER 19	ST	RNBT	FBG	SV	IO	225-228		7	10	2700			3350	4100
19		SOUNDER 19	HT	RNBT	FBG	SV	IO	120-200		7	10	2700			3250	4050
19		SOUNDER 19	HT	RNBT	FBG	SV	IO	225		7	10	2700			3350	4100
19		SOUNDER 19	HT	WKNDR	FBG	SV	IO	120-228		7	10	2700			3400	4100
19		TYEE 19	ST	RNBT	FBG	SV	IO	120-200		7	10				3150	3900
19		TYEE 19	ST	RNBT	FBG	SV	IO	225-228		7	10				3200	3950
21		CHRISTINA 21	ST	RNBT	FBG	SV	IO	165-240		7	10	3250			4100	5150
21		CHRISTINA 21	ST	RNBT	FBG	SV	IO	255-260		7	10	3250			4550	5250
21		GULF-ISLANDER 21	HT	WKNDR	FBG	SV	IO	165-260		7	10	3400			4500	5600
21		MONASHEE 21	ST	WKNDR	FBG	SV	IO	165-260		7	10	3500			4600	5700
21		MONASHEE 21	HT	WKNDR	FBG	SV	IO	165-260		7	10	3500			4600	5700
21		SKEENA 21	HT	SDN	FBG	SV	IO	165-260		7	10	3650			4700	5900
21		SKEENA 21	FB	WKNDR	FBG	SV	IO	165-260		7	10	3650			4700	5900
21		SOUNDER 21	ST	RNBT	FBG	SV	OB			7	10	2350			5400	6200
21		SOUNDER 21	ST	RNBT	FBG	SV	IO	165-228		7	10	3000			3900	4850
21		SOUNDER 21	ST	RNBT	FBG	SV	IO	240-260		7	10	3000			4050	5000
21		SOUNDER 21	HT	WKNDR	FBG	SV	IO	165-228		7	10	3000			4100	5100
21		SOUNDER 21	HT	WKNDR	FBG	SV	IO	240-260		7	10	3000			4200	5250
23	10	HAIDA 24	FB	CR	FBG	SV	IO	165-260		8	9	5500			7800	9400
		IO 330 MRCR 8600 9900, IO 130D VLVO 9150 10400, IO T120-T200													8450	10200
23	10	HAIDA 24	HT	SDN	FBG	SV	IO	165-260		8	9	5500			7800	9400
		IO 330 MRCR 8600 9900, IO 130D VLVO 9150 10400, IO T120-T200													8450	10200
25	10	TOBA 26	FB	CR	FBG	SV	IO	165-260		9	4	6000			8850	10700
		IO 330 MRCR 9900 11300, IO 130D VLVO 10200 11600, IO T120-T200													9500	11700
25	10	TOBA 26	HT	SDN	FBG	SV	IO	165-260		9	4	6000			9300	11300
		IO 330 MRCR 10600 12000, IO 130D VLVO 11100 12600, IO T120-T200													10100	12500

CANADIAN SAILCRAFT

BRAMPTON ONTARIO CANADA COAST GUARD MFG ID- ZCU See inside cover to adjust price for area

For more recent years, see the BUC Used Boat Price Guide, Volume 1 or Volume 2

LOA FT	LOA IN	NAME AND/ OR MODEL	TOP/ RIG	BOAT TYPE	-HULL- MTL	-HULL- TP	TP	ENGINE # HP	ENGINE MFG	BEAM FT	BEAM IN	WGT LBS	DRAFT FT	DRAFT IN	RETAIL LOW	RETAIL HIGH
		1983 BOATS														
27		CS 27	SLP	SA/RC	FBG	KL	IB	8D	YAN	9	4	6100	5	2	17100	19400
27		CS 27 SHOAL	SLP	SA/RC	FBG	KL	IB	8D	YAN	9	4	6500	3	11	18600	20700
32	8	CS 33	SLP	SA/RC	FBG	KL	IB	20D	BUKH	10	8	10000	5	9	32600	36300
32	8	CS 33 SHOAL	SLP	SA/RC	FBG	KL	IB	20D	BUKH	10	8	10000	4	5	32600	36300
36	6	CS 36	SLP	SA/RC	FBG	KL	IB	30D	WEST	11	6	15500	6	3	51000	56000
36	6	CS 36 SHOAL	SLP	SA/RC	FBG	KL	IB	30D	WEST	11	6	15500	4	11	51000	56000
		1981 BOATS														
27		CS 27	SLP	SA/RC	FBG	KL	IB	8D	YAN	9	4	6100	5	2	15300	17400
27		CS 27 SHOAL	SLP	SA/RC	FBG	KL	IB	8D	YAN	9	4	6500	3	11	16400	18600
32	8	CS 33	SLP	SA/RC	FBG	KL	IB	21D	WEST	10	8	10000	5	9	29300	32600
32	8	CS 33 SHOAL	SLP	SA/RC	FBG	KL	IB	21D	WEST	10	8	10000	4	5	29300	32600
36	6	CS 36	SLP	SA/RC	FBG	KL	IB	30D	WEST	11	6	15500	6	3	46100	50600
36	6	CS 36 SHOAL	SLP	SA/RC	FBG	KL	IB	30D	WEST	11	6	15500	4	11	46100	50600
		1979 BOATS														
21	6	CS 22	SLP	SA/RC	FBG	KC	OB			8		2200	2		4100	4750
27		CS 27	SLP	SA/RC	FBG	KL	IB	8D		9	4	6500	5	2	15200	17300
36	6	CS 36	SLP	SA/RC	FBG	KL	IB	30D		11	6	15500	6	3	42400	47100
		1978 BOATS														
21	6	CS 22	SLP	SA/RC	FBG	KC	OB			8		2200	2		4000	4650
27		CS 27	SLP	SA/RC	FBG	KL	IB	8D	YAN	9	4	6100	5	2	13900	15800
27		CS 27 SHOAL DRAFT	SLP	SA/RC	FBG	KL	IB	8D	YAN	9	4	6500	3	11	14800	16800
		1977 BOATS														
21	6	CS 22	SLP	SA/RC	FBG	KC	OB			8		2200	2		3900	4500
27		CS 27	SLP	SA/RC	FBG	KL	IB	8D	YAN	9	4	6100	5	2	13500	15400
27		CS 27 SHOAL	SLP	SA/RC	FBG	KL	IB	8D	YAN	9	4	6500	3	11	14400	16400
		1975 BOATS														
21	7	CS 22	SLP	SAIL	FBG	KC	OB			8		2200	5		3700	4300
27		CS 27	SLP	SAIL	FBG	KC	OB			9	4	5150	4	8	10400	11900
27		CS 27	SLP	SAIL	FBG	KC	IB	8D	YAN	9	4	5150	4	8	10900	12400

 CONTINUED ON NEXT PAGE

```
LOA  NAME AND/          TOP/ BOAT  -HULL- ----ENGINE--- BEAM  WGT  DRAFT RETAIL RETAIL
FT IN  OR MODEL         RIG TYPE   MTL TP TP # HP  MFG  FT IN LBS  FT IN  LOW    HIGH
------------------- 1974 BOATS -----------------------------------------------------
21  7 CS-22            SLP SAIL  FBG KC OB        8     2200   5      3650   4250
29  7 CSN-30           SLP SAIL  FBG    OB        9 10  7600   5  7  16700  19000
------------------- 1973 BOATS -----------------------------------------------------
21  8 CS-22                SAIL  FBG KC OB        8     2200          3600   4150
```

THE CANADIAN TRIMARAN CO LTD

Call 1-800-327-6929 for BUC Personalized Evaluation Service
Or, for 1967 boats, sign onto www.BUCValuPro.com

CANAVERAL CUSTOM BOATS INC

CAPE CANAVERAL FL 32920 COAST GUARD MFG ID- DBJ See inside cover to adjust price for area
FORMERLY DELTA BOATS INC

For more recent years, see the BUC Used Boat Price Guide, Volume 1 or Volume 2

```
LOA  NAME AND/          TOP/ BOAT  -HULL- ----ENGINE--- BEAM  WGT  DRAFT RETAIL RETAIL
FT IN  OR MODEL         RIG TYPE   MTL TP TP #  HP   MFG FT IN LBS FT IN  LOW    HIGH
------------------- 1983 BOATS -----------------------------------------------------
25    PUMA            ST  CUD  FBG SV SE  155  OMC   9  6            12200  13900
25    PUMA            ST  CUD  FBG SV IB  255  PCM   9  6   5800  2  11700  13300
25    PUMA            ST  CUD  FBG SV IO  155D VLVO 9  6   5800  2  11100  12600
25    PUMA            ST  CUD  FBG SV IB 158D-210D  9  6   5800  2  15000  18400
25    PUMA            ST  CUD  FBG SV SE T115 OMC   9  6   5800  2  15400  17500
25    PUMA            HT  CUD  FBG SV SE  155  OMC   9  6            12200  13800
25    PUMA            HT  CUD  FBG SV IB  255  PCM   9  6   5800  2  11700  13300
25    PUMA            HT  CUD  FBG SV IO  155D VLVO 9  6   5800  2  11100  12600
25    PUMA            HT  CUD  FBG SV IB 158D-210D  9  6   5800  2  15000  18400
25    PUMA            HT  CUD  FBG SV SE T115 OMC   9  6   5800  2  15400  17500
25    PUMA            FB  CUD  FBG SV OB            9  6   5800  2  15400  17500
25    PUMA            FB  CUD  FBG SV SE  155  OMC   9  6            12100  13700

25    PUMA            FB  CUD  FBG SV IB  255  PCM   9  6             9700  11000
25    PUMA            FB  CUD  FBG SV IO  155D VLVO 9  6   5800  2  11100  12600
25    PUMA            FB  CUD  FBG SV IB 158D-210D  9  6   5800  2  15000  18400
34  6 OFFSHORE 34     FB  OFF  FBG  D  CUM  12  8 18000 3  6    **     **
      IB 300D-410D  53200  58900, IB T  D CUM  **   ** , IBT200D-T300D  54000  62300

36  2 CLIMAX 36           FB       FBG  IB T235D VLVO 12  2            71100  78200
      IB T250D J&T  73000  80200, IO T286D VLVO  51900  57100, IB T310D GM   75300  82700

38    COMMERCIAL          HT  OFF  FBG SV IB  D CUM  12  5 19000 3       **     **
      IB  250D J&T  70400  77300, IB  260D GM  70300  77300, IB  300D CAT  72200  79300
      IB  310D GM   71400  78500, IB  410D J&T  74600  82000, IB T  D CUM    **     **
      IB T195D PCM  74300  81700, IB T200D PERK 76000  83500, IB T235D VLVO 74200  81500
      IB T286D VLVO 76100  83700, IB T300D CAT  80700  88700, IB T310D GM   79200  87000
      IB T410D J&T  86100  94600

38    FLYBRIDGE SEDAN    FB  SDN  FBG SV IB  300D CAT  12  5          3  72400  79500
38    FLYBRIDGE SEDAN    FB  SDN  FBG SV IB T250D J&T  12  5          3  77300  84900
38    SPORT FISHERMAN    FB  SF   FBG SV IB  D CUM  12  5 19000 3       **     **
      IB  250D J&T  70300  77300, IB  260D GM  70300  77300, IB  286D VLVO 69900  76800
      IB  300D CAT  72200  79300, IB  310D GM  71400  78400, IB  410D J&T  74700  82100
      IB T  D CUM    **     ** , IB T200D PERK 76100  83600, IB T210D CAT  76400  84000
      IB T250D J&T  76900  84500, IB T260D GM  76900  84500, IB T286D VLVO 76400  83900
      IB T300D CAT  80900  88900, IB T310D GM  79400  87300, IB T410D J&T  86400  95000

38  4 PASSENGER 38CGA   FB  OFF  FBG SV IB  300D CAT  12  5 19000 3  6  73600  80800
38  4 PASSENGER 38CGA   FB  OFF  FBG SV IB T250D J&T  12  5 19000 3  6  78200  86000
------------------- 1982 BOATS -----------------------------------------------------
25    PUMA 25           ST  CUD  FBG SV IB        10     5800  2      **     **
25    PUMA 25           ST  CUD  FBG SV IB  90D-172D 10   5800  2  13700  17100
25    PUMA 25           ST  CUD  FBG SV IB 200D-210D 10   5800  2  15500  18100
25    PUMA 25           HT  CUD  FBG SV IB        10     5800  2      **     **
25    PUMA 25           HT  CUD  FBG SV IB  90D-172D 10   5800  2  13700  17100
25    PUMA 25           HT  CUD  FBG SV IB 200D-210D 10   5800  2  15500  18100
25    PUMA 25           FB  CUD  FBG SV IB        10     5800  2      **     **
25    PUMA 25           FB  CUD  FBG SV IB  90D-172D 10   5800  2  13700  17100
25    PUMA 25           FB  CUD  FBG SV IB 200D-210D 10   5800  2  15500  18100
34  6 COMMERCIAL        HT  OFF  FBG SV VD T200D CAT 12  8 17000 3  6  49800  54800
34  6 OFFSHORE 34       FB  OFF  FBG SV IB 240D-410D 12  8 18000 3  6  50900  56500
34  6 OFFSHORE 34       FB  OFF  FBG IBT200D-T300D   12  8 18000 3  6  51800  59900

38    COMMERCIAL          HT  OFF  FBG SV IB  210D CAT  12  5 19000 3  67100  73700
      IB  260D GM   67100  73800, IB  270D CUM  67100  73800, IB  270D GM   67300  73900
      IB  300D CAT  68900  75700, IB  410D J&T  71200  78300, IB T200D PERK 72600  79700
      IB T260D GM   73200  80500, IB T270D CUM  73300  80500, IB T270D GM   73700  81000
      IB T285D VLVO 72600  79800, IB T300D CAT  77000  84600, IB T410D J&T  82200  90300

38    FLYBRIDGE SEDAN    FB  SDN  FBG SV IB  300D CAT  12  5          3  69000  75900
38    SPORT FISHERMAN    FB  SF   FBG SV IB  210D CAT  12  5 19000 3  67000  73700
      IB  260D GM   67100  73700, IB  270D CUM  67100  73700, IB  270D GM   67300  73900
      IB  285D VLVO 66700  73300, IB  300D CAT  68900  75700, IB  410D J&T  71300  78400
      IB T200D PERK 72600  79800, IB T210D CAT  72900  80200, IB T260D GM   73400  80700
      IB T270D CUM  73500  80700, IB T270D J&T  79800  81200, IB T285D VLVO 72800  80000
      IB T300D CAT  77200  84900, IB T410D J&T  82500  90600

38  4 PASSENGER 38C6A   FB  OFF  FBG SV IB T400D PERK 12  5 19000 3  6  85300  93700
------------------- 1981 BOATS -----------------------------------------------------
25    PUMA 25           ST  CUD  FBG SV IB  255  PCM   9  6   5800  2  10700  12200
25    PUMA 25           ST  CUD  FBG SV IB 200D-210D   9  6   5800  2  14800  17000
25    PUMA 25           HT  CUD  FBG SV IB  255  PCM   9  6   5800  2  10700  12200
25    PUMA 25           HT  CUD  FBG SV IB 200D-210D   9  6   5800  2  14800  17000
25    PUMA 25           FB  CUD  FBG SV IB  255  PCM   9  6   5800  2  10700  12200
25    PUMA 25           FB  CUD  FBG SV IB 200D-210D   9  6   5800  2  14800  17000
34  6 OFFSHORE 34       FB  OFF  FBG SV IB 210D-410D  12  8          3  6  59800  65700
34  6 OFFSHORE 34       FB  OFF  FBG IBT185D-T245D    12  8          3  6  59300  66100
38    COMMERCIAL        HT  OFF  FBG SV IB 195D VLVO  12  5          2 10  62300  68400
      IB  197D GM  62900  69100, IB  245D VLVO 62900  69100, IB  270D CUM  63800  70100
      IB  270D GM  64000  70400, IB  275D CAT  65000  71400, IB  300D CAT  65500  72000
      IB  410D J&T 67800  74500

38    COMMERCIAL          FB  OFF  FBG SV IB  216D GM  12  5          2 10  63200  69400
      IB  235D VLVO 62800  69000, IB  245D VLVO 62900  69100, IB  270D CUM  63800  70200
      IB  270D GM  64000  70400, IB  275D CAT  65000  71400, IB  300D CAT  65500  72000
      IB  410D J&T 67800  74500
------------------- 1980 BOATS -----------------------------------------------------
25    PUMA 25           ST  CUD  FBG SV IB  255  CHRY  9  6   5800  2  10200  11600
25    PUMA 25           ST  CUD  FBG SV IB 200D-210D   9  6   5800  2  14200  16300
25    PUMA 25           HT  CUD  FBG SV IB  255  CHRY  9  6   5800  2  10200  11600
25    PUMA 25           HT  CUD  FBG SV IB 200D-210D   9  6   5800  2  14200  16300
25    PUMA 25           FB  CUD  FBG SV IB  255  CHRY  9  6   5800  2  10200  11600
25    PUMA 25           FB  CUD  FBG SV IB 200D-210D   9  6   5800  2  14200  16300
34  6 OFFSHORE 34       FB  OFF  FBG SV IB 210D-410D  12  8          3  6  57500  63200
34  6 OFFSHORE 34       FB  OFF  FBG SV IB  T  D CUM  12  8          3  6    **     **
34  6 OFFSHORE 34       FB  OFF  FBG IBT200D-T286D    12  8          3  6  57800  63900
38    COMMERCIAL        HT  OFF  FBG SV IB  197  VLVO 12  5          3  6  49800  54700
      IB  235 VLVO 49900  54800, IB  16 D GM  45000  50000, IB  260D CAT  47500  52200
      IB  270D CUM 46700  51400, IB  270D GM  46900  51500, IB  410D J&T  50400  55300
------------------- 1979 BOATS -----------------------------------------------------
25    PUMA 25           ST  CUD  FBG SV IB  255  PCM  10     5800  2   9950  11300
25    PUMA 25           ST  CUD  FBG SV IB  200D CHRY 10     5800  2  13800  15700
25    PUMA 25           HT  CUD  FBG SV IB  255  PCM  10     5800  2   9950  11300
25    PUMA 25           HT  CUD  FBG SV IB  200D CHRY 10     5800  2  13800  15700
25    PUMA 25           FB  CUD  FBG SV IB  255  PCM  10     5800  2   9950  11300
25    PUMA 25           FB  CUD  FBG SV IB  200D CHRY 10     5800  2  13800  15700
34  6 OFFSHORE 34       FB  OFF  FBG SV IB           12  8          3  6    **     **
------------------- 1978 BOATS -----------------------------------------------------
25    PUMA 25           ST  EXP  FBG SV IB           9  6   5800  2    **     **
25    PUMA 25           ST  EXP  FBG SV IB  200D CHRY 9  6   5800  2  13200  15000
25    PUMA 25           FB  EXP  FBG SV IB           9  6   5800  2    **     **
25    PUMA 25           FB  EXP  FBG SV IB  200D CHRY 9  6   5800  2  13200  15000
25    PUMA 25           HT  EXP  FBG SV IB  255  PCM  9  6   5800  2   9500  10800
25    PUMA 25           HT  EXP  FBG SV IB  200D CHRY 9  6   5800  2  13200  15000
25    PUMA 25           FB  EXP  FBG SV IB           9  6   5800  2    **     **
25    PUMA 25           FB  EXP  FBG SV IB  255  PCM  9  6   5800  2   9500  10800
25    PUMA 25           FB  EXP  FBG SV IB  200D CHRY 9  6   5800  2  13200  15000
```

CANOE COVE MFG LTD

SIDNEY BC CANADA   COAST GUARD MFG ID- CVE See inside cover to adjust price for area

For more recent years, see the BUC Used Boat Price Guide, Volume 1 or Volume 2

```
LOA  NAME AND/          TOP/ BOAT  -HULL- ----ENGINE--- BEAM  WGT  DRAFT RETAIL RETAIL
FT IN  OR MODEL         RIG TYPE   MTL TP TP #  HP   MFG FT IN LBS FT IN  LOW    HIGH
------------------- 1983 BOATS -----------------------------------------------------
37    CRUSADER          FB  SF   FBG SV VD T340      13    22000 3  4  70100  77000
      VD T165D GM  76800  84400, VD T200D PERK 79000  86800, VD T205D GM   77900  85600
      VD T216D GM  78300  86000, VD T225D CAT  80000  87900, VD T230D CUM  78500  86200
      VD T260D GM  80000  88000, VD T270D CUM  80100  88000, VD T300D CAT  83600  91900
```

```
LOA  NAME AND/          TOP/ BOAT  -HULL-  ----ENGINE---  BEAM    WGT   DRAFT RETAIL RETAIL
FT IN OR MODEL          RIG  TYPE  MTL TP TP # HP  MFG   FT IN   LBS   FT IN  LOW    HIGH
----------------- 1983 BOATS -----------------------------------------------------------------
37    SPORTS SEDAN       FB   DC    FBG SV VD T340      13  2 23000  3   4  72200  79300
      VD T165D GM   79000 86800, VD T200D PERK  81100  89100, VD T205D GM    80000  87900
      VD T216D GM   80400 88300, VD T225D CAT   82100  90200, VD T230D CUM   80600  88600
      VD T260D GM   82100 90300, VD T270D CUM   82200  90400, VD T300D CAT   85800  94200

37    TRUANT 370 PILOT HSE SLP SA/CR F/S KL IB  42D PATH 12  2 18000  5  9  71600  78700
37    TRUANT 370 PILOT HSE CUT SA/CR F/S KL IB  42D PATH 12  2 18000  5  9  71600  78700
37    TRUANT 370 TRIAD     SLP SA/CR F/S KL IB  42D PATH 12  2 18000  5  9  73500  80700
37    TRUANT 370 TRIAD     CUT SA/CR F/S KL IB  42D PATH 12  2 18000  5  9  71600  78700
41    COHO TRI-CABIN       FB   TCMY  FBG SV VD T340     13  2 25000  3  4  96100 105500
      VD T165D GM   99100 109000, VD T200D PERK 103000 113000, VD T205D GM   102000 112000
      VD T216D GM  102500 112500, VD T225D CAT  105000 115000, VD T230D CUM  103000 113500
      VD T260D GM  105500 116000, VD T270D CUM  106000 116500, VD T300D CAT  110500 121500

41    SPORTS SEDAN       FB   DC    FBG SV VD T340     13  2 25000  3  4  93500 103000
      VD T165D GM   96900 106500, VD T200D PERK 100500 110500, VD T205D GM    99300 109000
      VD T216D GM  100000 110000, VD T225D CAT  102000 112500, VD T230D CUM  100500 110500
      VD T260D GM  103000 113000, VD T270D CUM  103000 113500, VD T300D CAT  107500 118500

45  8 COHO TRI-CABIN     FB   TCMY  FBG SV VD T216D GM   14  9 40000  4  4  146000 160500
      VD T225D CAT  148000 163000, VD T230D CUM  148500 163000, VD T260D GM   153000 168500
      VD T270D CUM  154500 169500, VD T295D CUM  158000 173500, VD T300D CAT  159500 175500
      VD T310D J&T  160500 176000, VD T410D J&T  172500 189500

48    COHO TRI-CABIN     FB   TCMY  FBG SV VD T216D GM   14  9 45000  4  4  171000 188000
      VD T225D CAT  168500 185000, VD T230D CUM  169000 186000, VD T260D GM   174000 191000
      VD T270D CUM  175000 192500, VD T295D CUM  178500 196000, VD T300D CAT  180500 198000
      VD T310D J&T  181000 198500, VD T410D J&T  192000 210500

48    SPORTS SEDAN       FB   SDN   FBG SV VD T260D GM   14  9 45000  4  4  166000 182500
      VD T270D CUM  166500 183000, VD T295D CUM  168000 184500, VD T300D CAT  169500 186000
      VD T310D J&T  169500 186000, VD T410D J&T  176000 193000

53    COHO FOUR-CABIN    FB   MY    FBG SV VD T216D GM   14  9 50000  4  4  128500 141000
      VD T225D CAT  130500 143500, VD T230D CUM  131000 144000, VD T260D GM   135500 149000
      VD T295D CUM  142000 156500, VD T300D CAT  143500 157500, VD T310D J&T  145500 160000
      VD T410D J&T  162500 179000

53    MOTOR YACHT        FB   MY    FBG SV VD T260D GM   14  9 55000  4  4  154500 170000
      VD T270D CUM  156500 171500, VD T295D CUM  164000 180000, VD T300D CAT  165000 181500
      VD T310D J&T  167000 183500, VD T398D GM  182000 200000, VD T410D J&T  184000 202500
      VD T425D CUM  186500 204500

53    SPORTS SEDAN       FB   SDN   FBG SV VD T260D GM   14  9 50000  4  4  169000 186000
      VD T270D CUM  171000 188000, VD T295D CUM  175500 193000, VD T300D CAT  176500 194000
      VD T310D J&T  178500 196000, VD T410D J&T  194500 213500
------------------ 1982 BOATS ---------------------------------------------------------------
37    CRUSADER           FB   SF    FBG SV VD T350      13   22000  3  4  67100  73700
      VD T165D GM   73300 80500, VD T200D PERK  75400  82800, VD T216D GM    74700  82100
      VD T225D CAT  76300 83800, VD T230D CUM   74900  82300, VD T260D CAT   77800  85500
      VD T260D GM   76400 83900, VD T270D CUM   76500  84000

41    COHO TRI-CABIN     FB   TCMY  FBG SV VD T350      13  2 25000  3  4  92100 101500
      VD T165D GM   94600 104000, VD T200D PERK  98300 108000, VD T216D GM    97900 107500
      VD T225D CAT  100000 110000, VD T230D CUM  98400 108000, VD T260D CAT  102500 112500
      VD T260D GM  101000 111000, VD T270D CUM 101000 111000, VD T310D CAT  106500 117000

41    SPORTS SEDAN       FB   DC    FBG SV VD T330      13  2 25000  3  4  88900  97700
      VD T165D GM   92500 101500, VD T200D PERK  96000 105500, VD T216D GM    95400 105000
      VD T225D CAT  97500 107000, VD T230D CUM  95900 105500, VD T260D CAT   99800 109500
      VD T260D GM   98100 108000, VD T270D CUM  98300 108000

45  8 COHO TRI-CABIN     FB   TCMY  FBG SV VD T216D GM   14  9 40000  4  4  139500 153500
      VD T225D CAT  141500 155500, VD T230D CUM  142000 156000, VD T260D CAT  147000 161500
      VD T260D GM  146500 161000, VD T270D CUM  147500 162000, VD T295D CUM  151000 166000
      VD T310D GM  153000 168000, VD T410D GM  164500 181000

48    COHO TRI-CABIN     FB   TCMY  FBG SV VD T216D GM   14  9 45000  4  4  163500 180000
      VD T225D CAT  161000 177000, VD T230D CUM  161500 177500, VD T260D GM   166500 183000
      VD T260D GM  166500 182500, VD T270D CUM  167500 184000, VD T295D CUM  170500 187500
      VD T310D GM  172500 189500, VD T410D GM  183000 201000

48    SPORTS SEDAN       FB   SDN   FBG SV VD T260D CAT  14  9 45000  4  4  159500 175000
      VD T260D GM  158500 174500, VD T270D CUM  159000 174500, VD T295D CUM  160500 176500
      VD T310D GM  161500 177500, VD T410D GM  168000 184500

53    COHO FOUR CABIN    FB   MY    FBG SV VD T216D GM   14  9 50000  4  4  125000 137500
      VD T225D CAT  127000 140000, VD T230D CUM  127500 140500, VD T260D GM   133000 146000
      VD T260D GM  132500 145500, VD T270D CUM  134500 148000, VD T295D CUM  139000 153000
      VD T310D GM  142000 156000, VD T410D GM  159000 175000

53    MOTOR YACHT        FB   MY    FBG SV VD T260D CAT  14  9 55000  4  4  147500 162000
      VD T260D GM  147500 162000, VD T270D CUM  149000 164000, VD T295D CUM  156500 172000
      VD T310D GM  159000 175000, VD T398D GM  173500 190500, VD T410D GM  175500 193000
      VD T425D CUM  178000 195500

53    SPORTS SEDAN       FB   SDN   FBG SV VD T260D CAT  14  9 50000  4  4  161500 177500
      VD T260D GM  161500 177500, VD T270D CUM  163000 179500, VD T295D CUM  167500 184000
      VD T310D GM  170000 186500, VD T410D GM  185000 203000
------------------ 1981 BOATS ---------------------------------------------------------------
37    CRUSADER           FB   SF    FBG SV VD T350      13   22000  3  4  64000  70300
      VD T155D CHRY  69600 76500, VD T200D PERK  71800  78900, VD T216D GM    71200  78200
      VD T225D CAT  72700 79900, VD T230D CUM   71400  78400, VD T260D CAT   74100  81500
      VD T260D GM   72800 80000, VD T270D CUM   72800  80100

41    COHO TRI-CABIN     FB   TCMY  FBG SV VD T350      13  2 25000  3  4  87800  96500
      VD T155D CHRY  89500 98300, VD T200D PERK  93700 103000, VD T216D GM    93200 102500
      VD T225D CAT  95300 104500, VD T230D CUM  93800 103000, VD T260D CAT   96100 105500
      VD T270D CUM  96300 106000, VD T310D CAT 101500 111500

41    SPORTS SEDAN       FB   DC    FBG SV VD T330      13  2 25000  3  4  84700  93100
      VD T155D CHRY  87600 96200, VD T200D PERK  91400 100500, VD T216D GM    90900  99900
      VD T225D CAT  92900 102000, VD T230D CUM  92700 102000, VD T260D CAT   95100 104500
      VD T260D GM   93500 102500, VD T270D CUM  93700 103000

45  8 COHO TRI-CABIN     FB   TCMY  FBG SV VD T216D GM   14  9 40000  4  4  133000 146000
      VD T225D CAT  135000 148500, VD T230D CUM  135000 148500, VD T260D CAT  140000 154000
      VD T260D GM  139500 153000, VD T270D CUM  140500 154500, VD T295D CUM  144000 158000
      VD T310D GM  146000 160000, VD T410D GM  157000 172500

48    COHO TRI-CABIN     FB   TCMY  FBG SV VD T216D GM   14  9 45000  4  4  156000 171500
      VD T225D CAT  153500 168500, VD T230D CUM  154000 169000, VD T260D CAT  159000 174500
      VD T260D GM  158500 174000, VD T270D CUM  159500 175500, VD T295D CUM  162500 178500
      VD T310D GM  164500 181000, VD T410D GM  174500 191500

48    SPORTS SEDAN       FB   SDN   FBG SV VD T260D CAT  14  9 45000  4  4  152000 167000
      VD T260D GM  151000 166000, VD T270D CUM  151500 166500, VD T295D CUM  153000 168000
      VD T310D GM  154000 169500, VD T410D GM  160000 175500

53    COHO FOUR CABIN    FB   MY    FBG SV VD T216D GM   14  9 50000  4  4  119500 131000
      VD T225D CAT  121500 133500, VD T230D CUM  122000 133500, VD T260D CAT  126500 139000
      VD T260D GM  126000 138500, VD T270D CUM  128000 141000, VD T295D CUM  132500 145500
      VD T310D GM  135000 148500, VD T410D GM  151500 166500

53    MOTOR YACHT        FB   MY    FBG SV VD T260D CAT  14  9 55000  4  4  140500 154500
      VD T260D GM  140500 154500, VD T270D CUM  142000 156000, VD T295D CUM  149000 164000
      VD T310D GM  151500 166500, VD T398D GM  165500 181500, VD T410D GM  167000 183500
      VD T425D CUM  169500 186000

53    SPORTS SEDAN       FB   SDN   FBG SV VD T260D CAT  14  9 50000  4  4  154000 169000
      VD T260D GM  154000 169000, VD T270D CUM  155500 171000, VD T295D CUM  159500 175500
      VD T310D GM  162000 178000, VD T410D GM  176000 193500
------------------ 1980 BOATS ---------------------------------------------------------------
37    CHALLENGER         FB   SDN   FBG SV VD T350      13   22000  3  4  61700  67800
      VD T155D CHRY  67000 73600, VD T200D PERK  69400  76300, VD T216D GM    68800  75600
      VD T225D CAT  70300 77300, VD T230D CUM   69100  75900, VD T260D CAT   71800  78900
      VD T260D GM   70500 77400, VD T270D CUM   70600  77600

41    COHO TRI-CABIN     FB   TCMY  FBG SV VD T350      13  2 25000  3  4  83800  92100
      VD T155D CHRY  85300 93800, VD T200D PERK  89500 100500, VD T216D GM    89000  97700
      VD T225D CAT  90900 99900, VD T230D CUM   89300  98300, VD T260D CAT   91600 100500
      VD T270D CUM  91900 101000

41    SPORTS SEDAN       FB   DC    FBG SV VD T330      13  2 25000  3  4  80800  88800
      VD T155D CHRY  83500 91800, VD T200D PERK  87200  95800, VD T216D GM    86700  95300
      VD T225D CAT  88600 97400, VD T230D CUM   87200  95800, VD T260D CAT   90700  99700
      VD T260D GM   89200 98000, VD T270D CUM   89400  98200

45  8 COHO TRI-CABIN     FB   TCMY  FBG SV VD T216D GM   14  9 40000  4  4  127000 139500
      VD T225D CAT  128500 141500, VD T230D CUM  129000 141500, VD T260D CAT  133500 146500
      VD T260D GM  133000 146000, VD T270D CUM  134000 147500, VD T295D CUM  137000 150500
      VD T310D GM  139000 153000, VD T410D GM  149500 164500
```

```
 LOA  NAME AND/           TOP/ BOAT -HULL- ----ENGINE--- BEAM  WGT DRAFT RETAIL RETAIL
 FT IN OR MODEL           RIG  TYPE MTL TP TP # HP MFG  FT IN  LBS FT IN  LOW    HIGH
------------------- 1980 BOATS --------------------------------------------------------
 48    COHO TRI-CABIN       FB  TCMY  FBG SV VD T216D GM  14   9 45000  4  4 149000 163500
       VD T225D CAT 146000 160500, VD T230D CUM 147000 161500, VD T260D CAT 151500 166500
       VD T260D GM  151000 166000, VD T270D CUM 152500 167500, VD T295D CUM 155000 170500
       VD T310D GM  157000 172500, VD T410D GM  166500 183000

 48    SPORTS SEDAN         FB  SDN   FBG SV VD T260D CAT  14   9 45000  4  4 145000 159000
       VD T260D GM  144000 158500, VD T270D CUM 144500 159000, VD T295D CUM 146000 160500
       VD T310D GM  147000 161500, VD T410D GM  152500 167500

 53    COHO FOUR CABIN      FB  MY    FBG SV VD T260D GM   14   9 50000  4  4 114000 125000
       VD T225D CAT 115500 127000, VD T230D CUM 116000 127500, VD T260D CAT 120500 132500
       VD T260D GM  120500 132500, VD T270D CUM 122500 134500, VD T295D CUM 126500 139000
       VD T310D GM  129000 142000, VD T410D GM  144500 159000

 53    MOTOR YACHT          FB  MY    FBG SV VD T260D CAT  14   9 55000  4  4 134000 147500
       VD T260D GM  134000 147500, VD T270D CUM 135500 149000, VD T295D CUM 142500 156500
       VD T310D GM  144500 159000, VD T398D GM  158000 173500, VD T410D GM  159500 175000
       VD T425D CUM 161500 177500
-------------------- 1979 BOATS --------------------------------------------------------
 37    CHALLENGER           FB  SDN   FBG SV VD T350      13     22000  3  4  59000  64900
       VD T160D PERK 65100  71500, VD T216D GM  65800  72300, VD T225D CAT  67200  73800
       VD T230D CUM 66000  72500, VD T270D CUM  67400  74100

 41    COHO TRI-CABIN       FB  TCMY  FBG SV VD T350      13   2 25000  3  4  80100  88000
       VD T160D PERK 82900  91100, VD T216D GM  85000  93400, VD T225D CAT  86800  95400
       VD T230D CUM 85500  93900, VD T270D CUM  87800  96500

 41    SPORTS SEDAN         FB  DC    FBG SV VD T350      13   2 25000  3  4  77900  85600
       VD T160D PERK 81200  89200, VD T216D GM  82800  91000, VD T225D CAT  84600  93000
       VD T230D CUM 83300  91500, VD T270D CUM  85400  93800

 45    8 COHO TRI-CABIN     FB  TCMY  FBG SV VD T216D GM  14   9 40000  4  4 121000 133000
       VD T225D CAT 123000 135000, VD T230D CUM 123000 135000, VD T250D CAT 126000 138500
       VD T270D CUM 128000 140500, VD T295D CUM 131000 144000, VD T310D GM  133000 146000
       VD T410D GM  143000 157000

 48    COHO TRI-CABIN       FB  TCMY  FBG SV VD T216D GM  14   9 45000  4  4 142000 156000
       VD T225D CAT 139500 153500, VD T230D CUM 140000 154000, VD T250D CAT 143500 157500
       VD T270D CUM 145500 160000, VD T295D CUM 148000 163000, VD T310D GM  150000 164500
       VD T410D GM  159000 174500

 48    SPORTS SEDAN         FB  SDN   FBG SV VD T310D GM  14   9 45000  4  4 140000 153500
 48    SPORTS SEDAN         FB  SDN   FBG SV VD T410D GM  14   9 45000  4  4 145500 160000
 53    COHO FOUR CABIN      FB  MY    FBG SV VD T216D GM  14   9 50000  4  4 108500 119500
       VD T225D CAT 110500 121500, VD T230D CUM 111000 122000, VD T250D CAT 114000 125000
       VD T270D CUM 117000 128500, VD T307D CUM 123000 135500, VD T310D GM  123000 135500
       VD T410D GM  138000 152000

 53    MOTOR YACHT          FB  MY    FBG SV VD T250D CAT  14   9 55000  4  4 126500 139000
       VD T270D CUM 129500 142500, VD T307D CUM 137500 151500, VD T310D GM  138000 152000
       VD T380D GM  148000 163000, VD T410D CUM 152500 167500, VD T425D CUM 154500 169500
-------------------- 1978 BOATS --------------------------------------------------------
 37    CHALLENGER           FB  SDN   FBG SV VD T350      13         3  4  44600  49600
       VD T160D PERK 52800  58000, VD T185D PERK 53600  58900, VD T216D GM   53500  58800
       VD T225D CAT 54900  60300, VD T240D CUM  54100  59400

 41    CHALLENGER           FB  SDN   FBG SV VD T350      13   2     3  4  67600  74300
       VD T160D PERK 72200  79300, VD T185D PERK 73200  80400, VD T216D GM   73300  80500
       VD T225D CAT 75000  82400, VD T240D CUM  74000  81300, VD T270D CUM  75400  82900

 41    COHO TRI-CABIN       FB  TCMY  FBG SV VD T350      13   2     3  4  69500  76400
       VD T160D PERK 71000  78000, VD T185D PERK 72500  79700, VD T216D GM   73100  80300
       VD T225D CAT 74900  82300, VD T240D CUM  74100  81500

 41    SPORTS SEDAN         FB  SPTCR FBG SV VD T350      13   2     3  4  40900  45500
       VD T160D PERK 60300  66300, VD T185D PERK 61900  68000, VD T216D GM   62500  68700
       VD T225D CAT 64300  70700, VD T240D CUM  63600  69900, VD T270D CUM  65500  71900

 45    COHO TRI-CABIN       FB  TCMY  FBG SV VD T216D GM  14   9     4  4  97400 107000
       VD T225D CAT 99100 109000, VD T240D CUM 100000 110000, VD T240D GM  100000 110000
       VD T250D CAT 102000 112000, VD T270D CUM 103500 113500, VD T295D CUM 106500 117000

 48    COHO                 FB  TCMY  FBG SV VD T216D GM  14   9     4  4 116000 127500
       VD T225D CAT 118500 130000, VD T240D CUM 121000 133000, VD T240D GM  121000 133000
       VD T250D CAT 123000 135500, VD T270D CUM 125000 137500, VD T295D CUM 128000 140500

 53    COHO FOUR CABIN      FB  MY    FBG SV VD T216D GM  14   9     4  4  98800 108500
       VD T225D CAT 99300 109000, VD T240D CUM  96800 106500, VD T240D GM  101500 111500
       VD T250D CUM 99900 110000, VD T270D CUM 101500 111500, VD T295D CUM 103500 114000

 53    MOTOR YACHT          FB  MY    FBG SV VD T216D GM  14   9     4  4 121500 133500
       VD T225D CAT 122000 134000, VD T240D CUM 118500 130500, VD T240D GM  123500 136000
       VD T250D CAT 122000 134000, VD T270D CUM 124000 136000, VD T295D CUM 125500 138000
       VD T425D CUM 124500 137000, VD T425D GM  124500 137000
-------------------- 1977 BOATS --------------------------------------------------------
 37    CHALLENGER           FB  SDN   FBG DV IB T350 MRCR 13         3  4  42700  47500
       IB T160D PERK 50600  55600, IB T185D PERK 51300  56400, IB T216D GM   51300  56300
       IB T225D CAT 52600  57800, IB T240D CUM  51800  56900

 41    CHALLENGER           FB  SDN   FBG DV IB T350 MRCR 13   2     3  4  64900  71300
       IB T160D PERK 69200  76000, IB T185D PERK 70200  77100, IB T216D GM   70300  77200
       IB T225D CAT 71900  79000, IB T240D CUM  71000  78000

 41    COHO                 FB  TCMY  FBG DV IB T350 MRCR 13   2     3  4  68300  75000
       IB T160D PERK 69800  76700, IB T185D PERK 71500  78500, IB T216D GM   72200  79400
       IB T225D CAT 74000  81300, IB T240D CUM  73400  80600

 45    8 COHO               FB  TCMY  FBG DV IB T216D GM  14   9     4  4 107500 118000
       IB T225D CAT 109500 120000, IB T240D CUM 110000 121000, IB T240D GM  110500 121500
       IB T340D CUM 118000 129500

 48    COHO                 FB  TCMY  FBG DV IB T216D GM  14   9     4  4 114000 125500
       IB T225D CAT 116000 127500, IB T240D CUM 118000 129500, IB T240D GM  118000 130000
       IB T340D CUM 126500 139000

 53    COHO FOUR CABIN      FB  MY    FBG DV IB T216D GM  14   9     4  4 106500 117500
       IB T225D CAT 107000 118000, IB T240D CUM 106500 117500, IB T240D GM  106500 117500
       IB T320D CUM 113000 124000, IB T425D CUM 119500 131500, IB T425D GM  119500 131500

 53    MOTOR YACHT          FB  TCMY  FBG DV IB T216D GM  14   9     4  4 114000 125500
       IB T225D CAT 115500 126500, IB T240D CUM 117000 128500, IB T240D GM  116500 128500
       IB T320D CUM 124500 137000, IB T425D CUM 133000 146000, IB T425D GM  133000 146000
-------------------- 1976 BOATS --------------------------------------------------------
 37    CHALLENGER           FB  SDN   FBG SV IB T350 MRCR 13         3    41000  45500
       VD T160D PERK 48500  53300, VD T216D GM  49200  54000, VD T225D CAT  50400  55400
       VD T240D CUM 49700  54600

 37    CRUSADER             FB  SDNSF FBG SV IB T350 MRCR 13         3    40800  45400
       VD T160D PERK 49900  54800, VD T216D GM  50400  55400, VD T225D CAT  51600  56700
       VD T240D CUM 50800  55900

 41    CHALLENGER           FB  SDN   FBG SV VD T350 MRCR 13   2     3  4  62100  68300
       VD T160D PERK 66300  72900, VD T216D GM  67300  74000, VD T225D CAT  68900  75700
       VD T240D CUM 68000  74700

 41    COHO                 FB  DC    FBG SV VD T350 MRCR 13   2     3  4  69700  76600
       VD T160D PERK 74400  81800, VD T216D GM  76100  83700, VD T225D CAT  77800  85500
       VD T240D CUM 77100  84700

 41    CRUSADER             FB  SDNSF FBG SV VD T350 MRCR 13   2     3  4  77500  85100
       VD T160D PERK 51800  56900, VD T216D GM  54200  59500, VD T225D CAT  55900  61400
       VD T240D CUM 55400  60800

 45    COHO                 FB  DC    FBG SV VD T216D GM  14   9     4  2  93300 102500
       VD T225D CAT 95000 104500, VD T240D CUM  95900 105500, VD T265D GM   98600 108500
       VD T340D CUM 106500 117000

 48    COHO                 FB  DC    FBG SV VD T216D GM  14   9     4  2    **     **
       VD T225D CAT   **     **  , VD T240D CUM   **     **  , VD T265D GM    **     **
       VD T340D CUM  **     **

 53    COHO                 FB  DC    FBG SV VD T216D GM  15         4  2 102000 112000
       VD T240D CUM 104500 115000, VD T270D CUM 107000 117500, VD T340D CUM 114000 125000
       VD T400D CUM 119000 130500, VD T425D CUM 121000 133000

 53    MOTOR YACHT          FB  TCMY  FBG SV VD T216D GM  15         4  2 106500 117000
       VD T240D CUM 109000 119500, VD T265D GM  111000 122000, VD T340D CUM 117500 129000
       VD T400D CUM 122000 134000, VD T425D CUM 124000 136500
-------------------- 1975 BOATS --------------------------------------------------------
 37    CHALLENGER           HT  SDN   FBG SV IB T350 MRCR 13   2 20500  3  4  47500  52200
       IB T160D PERK 51900  57000, IB T185D PERK 52600  57800, IB T216D GM   52500  57700
```

```
CANOE COVE MFG LTD        -CONTINUED   See inside cover to adjust price for area
  LOA  NAME AND/          TOP/ BOAT  -HULL- ----ENGINE---  BEAM    WGT  DRAFT RETAIL RETAIL
FT IN  OR MODEL           RIG  TYPE  MTL TP TP # HP  MFG   FT IN   LBS  FT IN  LOW   HIGH
--------------------- 1975 BOATS ----------------------------------------------------------
37   CHALLENGER           HT  SDN   FBG SV IB T225D CAT  13 2 20500 3  4 53700 59000
37   CHALLENGER           HT  SDN   FBG SV IB T240D CUM  13 2 20500 3  4 53000 58200
37   CHALLENGER           FB  SDN   FBG SV IB T350  MRCR 13 2 20500 3  4 47500 52200
     IB T160D PERK 51900 57000, IB T185D PERK  52600  57800, IB T216D GM      52500 57700
     IB T225D CAT  53700 59000, IB T240D CUM   53000  58200

37   CRUSADER             HT  SF    FBG SV IB T350  MRCR 13 2 20000 3  4 46100 50700
     IB T160D PERK 50400 55400, IB T185D PERK  50900  56000, IB T216D GM      50800 55900
     IB T225D CAT  52000 57200, IB T240D CUM   51300  56300

37   CRUSADER             FB  SF    FBG SV IB T350  MRCR 13 2 20000 3  4 46100 50700
     IB T160D PERK 50400 55400, IB T185D PERK  50900  56000, IB T216D GM      50800 55900
     IB T225D CAT  52000 57200, IB T240D CUM   51300  56300

41   CHALLENGER           FB  SDN   FBG SV IB T350  MRCR        22000      57200 62900
     IB T160D PERK 61400 67500, IB T185D PERK  62300  68400, IB T216D GM      62300 68400
     IB T225D CAT  63700 70000, IB T240D CUM   62800  69000

41   COHO                 FB  TCMY  FBG SV IB T350  MRCR 13 2 24000 3  4 67100 73700
     IB T160D PERK 69500 76400, IB T185D PERK  70900  77900, IB T216D GM      71500 78600
     IB T225D CAT  73200 80400, IB T240D CUM   72600  79700

48   COHO                     TCMY  FBG SV IB T160D PERK        36000      115000 126500
     IB T216D GM   85900 94400, IB T225D CAT   87600  96200, IB T240D CUM     90400  99300
     IB T255D GM   93100 102500, IB T320D CUM 102500 112500, IB T425D CUM    117500 129000

53   COHO                 FB  TCMY  FBG SV IB T160D PERK        40000      86100  94600
     IB T216D GM   83100 91300, IB T225D CAT   85300  93800, IB T240D CUM     85500  93900
     IB T255D GM   85800 94300, IB T320D CUM   93300 102500, IB T425D CUM    109000 119500
--------------------- 1973 BOATS ----------------------------------------------------------
37   CHALLENGER           SDN  FBG SV IB T240D      13 2       3  4 43800 48600
41   COHO                 TCMY FBG SV IB T350       13 2       3  4 58000 63800
48   COHO                 TCMY FBG SV IB T160D      14 9       4  2 83300 91600
53   COHO                 TCMY FBG SV IB T160D      15         4  2 105000 115500
--------------------- 1972 BOATS ----------------------------------------------------------
37   CHALLENGER           FB  CR  FBG SV IB T160    13 2           34500 38300
37   CHALLENGER           FB  CR  FBG SV IB T225    13 2           34800 38700
37   CRUSADER             FB  SF  FBG SV IB T160    13 2           33700 37400
37   CRUSADER             FB  SF  FBG SV IB T225    13 2           34000 37800
41                        FB  SF  FBG SV IB T160    13 2           49300 54100
41                        FB  SF  FBG SV IB T225    13 2           51200 56200
41   CHALLENGER           FB  CR  FBG SV IB T160    13 2           39000 43400
41   CHALLENGER           FB  CR  FBG SV IB T225    13 2           39900 44300
41   COHO                 FB  SF  FBG SV IB T160    13 2           49500 54400
41   COHO                 FB  SF  FBG SV IB T225    13 2           51800 56900
48                        FB  SF  FBG SV IB T210    14 9           62800 69000
48                        FB  SF  FBG SV IB T370    14 9           67500 74200

48   COMMODORE            FB  MY  FBG SV IB T210    14 9           66800 73400
48   COMMODORE            FB  MY  FBG SV IB T370    14 9           73200 80400
53   COMMODORE            FB  MY  FBG SV IB T210    14 9           89400 98300
53   COMMODORE            FB  MY  FBG SV IB T370    14 9           102500 112500
--------------------- 1971 BOATS ----------------------------------------------------------
37   CHALLENGER           SDN  FBG DV IB T270    13           3   33000 36700
37   CHALLENGER           SDN  FBG DV IB T390    13           3   34600 38400
37   CRUSADER             SF   FBG DV IB T270    13           3   33400 37100
37   CRUSADER             SF   FBG DV IB T390    13           3   34900 38700
41 1 WESTPORTER           CR   FBG DV IB T325    13 2       3  4 40000 44400
41 1 WESTPORTER           CR   FBG DV IB T390    13 2       3  4 41500 46100
41 6                      SDN  FBG DV IB T325    13 2       3  4 58600 64400
41 6                      SDN  FBG DV IB T370    13 2       3  4 62300 68500
41 6                      SF   FBG DV IB T325    13 2       3  4 34600 38500
41 6                      SF   FBG DV IB T390    13 2       3  4 35900 39900
41 6 CHALLENGER           SDN  FBG DV IB T325    13 2       3  4 63400 69700
41 6 CHALLENGER           SDN  FBG DV IB T390    13 2       3  4 63600 69800

48                        MY   FBG DV IB T215D   14 9       3 10 75900 83400
48                        MY   FBG DV IB T370D   14 9       3 10 90700 99600
```

CANTIERI NAVALE BENETTI
VIA REGGIO ITALY   See inside cover to adjust price for area
For more recent years, see the BUC Used Boat Price Guide, Volume 1 or Volume 2

```
  LOA  NAME AND/          TOP/ BOAT  -HULL- ----ENGINE---  BEAM    WGT  DRAFT RETAIL RETAIL
FT IN  OR MODEL           RIG  TYPE  MTL TP TP # HP  MFG   FT IN   LBS  FT IN  LOW   HIGH
--------------------- 1983 BOATS ----------------------------------------------------------
75 6 BENETTI 21D          EPH MY   STL    IB T270D VLVO 17      10 3   **    **
--------------------- 1981 BOATS ----------------------------------------------------------
75 6                      FB  MY   STL    IB T180D VLVO 17       8 6   **    **
--------------------- 1978 BOATS ----------------------------------------------------------
75 6 23 S                     MY   STL    IB T650D              **    **
--------------------- 1977 BOATS ----------------------------------------------------------
77   23S                  EPH MY   STL    IB T650D GM   21      6     **    **
--------------------- 1972 BOATS ----------------------------------------------------------
65 6                      FB  MYFD STL    IB T800D MTU  17 6    6     494000 542500
70                        FB  MYFD STL SD IB T800D MTU  17 6    6     432500 475500
--------------------- 1971 BOATS ----------------------------------------------------------
65 7                      FB  MY   STL    IB T600D GM   18      6     446000 490000
--------------------- 1969 BOATS ----------------------------------------------------------
75                        MY   STL    IB T650D DD   18 10     7 3   **    **
--------------------- 1967 BOATS ----------------------------------------------------------
78 9                      OP  MY   STL    IB T650D GM   19 8    4 11  **    **
--------------------- 1966 BOATS ----------------------------------------------------------
65   MOTOR YACHT          FB  MYFD STL    IB T480D GM   17      4     266500 293000
78 9 24M                  MY   STL    IB T680D      18 1    6 3   **    **
--------------------- 1963 BOATS ----------------------------------------------------------
66   DELFINO              MY   STL    IB T330D      16 5         299500 329000
```

CANYON CORPORATION
COAST GUARD MFG ID- HAJ

Call 1-800-327-6929 for BUC Personalized Evaluation Service
Or, for 1979 to 1984 boats, sign onto www.BUCValuPro.com

CAPE COD SHIPBUILDING CO
WAREHAM MA 02571   COAST GUARD MFG ID- CAC See inside cover to adjust price for area
For more recent years, see the BUC Used Boat Price Guide, Volume 1 or Volume 2

```
  LOA  NAME AND/          TOP/ BOAT  -HULL- ----ENGINE---  BEAM    WGT  DRAFT RETAIL RETAIL
FT IN  OR MODEL           RIG  TYPE  MTL TP TP # HP  MFG   FT IN   LBS  FT IN  LOW   HIGH
--------------------- 1983 BOATS ----------------------------------------------------------
16 1 GEMINI               SLP SAIL  FBG CB OB        5  7  440     7   3350  3900
17   CAPE-COD-CAT         GAF SAIL  FBG CB OB        7 11 2200  1  8   8050  9250
18   RHODES 18            SLP SAIL  FBG CB OB        6  3  800     7   4700  5400
18   RHODES 18            SLP SAIL  FBG CB OB        6  3  920     8   5050  5800
18 3 GOLDENEYE            SLP SAIL  FBG KL OB        6  4 2500  3   8850 10100
20 1 GAUNTLET             SLP SAIL  FBG KL OB        6  6  950  3  9 5450  6250
24 3 RAVEN                SLP SA/OD FBG CB OB        7     1170     7   7300  8400
30   BLUE-CHIP 30         SLP SA/CR FBG KL IB     D  9  6 9500  4  3 40100 44600
30 3 SHIELDS              SLP SAIL  FBG KC OB        6  5 4600  4  9 18600 20700
30 6 ATLANTIC             SLP SAIL  FBG KC OB        6  6 4559  4  9 18800 20900
44   MERCER 44            SLP SA/RC FBG KC IB     D  11 9 27000 4  3 122500 135000
44   MERCER 44            YWL SA/RC FBG KC IB     D  11 9 27000 4  3 122500 134500
--------------------- 1982 BOATS ----------------------------------------------------------
16 1 GEMINI               SLP SAIL  FBG CB OB        5  7  440     7   3200  3700
16 5 CAPE-COD-CAT         GAF SAIL  FBG CB OB        7 11 2200  1  8   7600  8750
18   RHODES 18            SLP SAIL  FBG CB OB        6  3  800     7   4500  5150
18   RHODES 18            SLP SAIL  FBG CB OB        6  3  920  2  8 4750  5500
18 3 GOLDENEYE            SLP SAIL  FBG KL OB        6  4 2500  3   8300  9550
20 1 GAUNTLET             SLP SAIL  FBG KL OB        6  6  950  3  9 5150  5900
24 3 RAVEN                SLP SA/OD FBG CB OB        7     1170     7   6900  7950
30   BLUE-CHIP 30         SLP SA/CR FBG KL IB     D  9  6 9500  4  3 37000 42500
30 3 SHIELDS              SLP SA/OD FBG KL OB        6  5 4600  4  9 17400 19800
30 6 ATLANTIC             SLP SAIL  FBG KC OB        6  6 4559  4  9 17500 19900
44   MERCER 44            SLP SA/RC FBG KC IB     D  11 9 27000 4  3 117000 128500
44   MERCER 44            YWL SA/RC FBG KC IB     D  11 9 27000 4  3 117000 128000
--------------------- 1981 BOATS ----------------------------------------------------------
16 1 GEMINI TWIN BOARDS   SLP SAIL  FBG CB OB        5 11  440     7   3000  3500
17   CAPE-COD-CAT         GAF SAIL  FBG CB OB        7 11 2200  1  8   7200  8300
18   RHODES               SLP SAIL  FBG CB OB        6  3  800     7   4300  4900
18   RHODES               SLP SAIL  FBG CB OB        6  3  920  2  8 4550  5250
18 3 GOLDENEYE            SLP SAIL  FBG KL OB        6  4 2500     7   7850  9050
20 1 GAUNTLET             SLP SAIL  FBG KL OB        6  6  950  3  9 4900  5600
24 3 RAVEN                SLP SA/OD FBG CB OB        7     1170     7   6550  7550
30   BLUE-CHIP 30         SLP SA/CR FBG KL IB     D  9  6 9500  4  3 36000 40000
30 3 SHIELDS              SLP SA/OD FBG KL OB        6  5 4600  4  9 16600 18900
30 6 ATLANTIC             SLP SAIL  FBG KC OB        6  6 4559  4  9 16800 19100
44   MERCER 44            SLP SA/RC FBG KC IB     D  11 9 27000 4  3 112000 123000
44   MERCER 44            YWL SA/RC FBG KC IB     D  11 9 27000 4  3 112000 123000
```

LOA FT	IN	NAME AND/ OR MODEL	TOP/ RIG	BOAT TYPE	-HULL- MTL	TP	ENGINE TP	# HP	MFG	BEAM FT	IN	WGT LBS	DRAFT FT	IN	RETAIL LOW	RETAIL HIGH
1980 BOATS																
16	1	GEMINI	SLP	SAIL	FBG	CB	OB			5	7	440		7	2900	3400
17		CAPE-COD-CAT	GAF	SAIL	FBG	KL	OB			7	11	2200	1	8	6950	8000
17		CAPE-COD-CAT	GAF	SAIL	FBG	KL	IB	7D	WEST	7	11	2200	1	8	10500	11900
18		RHODES	SLP	SAIL	FBG	CB	OB			6	3	800		7	4050	4700
18		RHODES	SLP	SAIL	FBG	KL	OB			6	3	920	2	8	4400	5050
18	3	GOLDENEYE	SLP	SAIL	FBG	KL	OB			6	4	2500	3		7550	8700
20	1	GAUNTLET	SLP	SAIL	FBG	KL	OB			6	6	950	3	9	4700	5400
24	3	RAVEN	SLP	SA/OD	FBG	CB	OB			7		1170		7	6300	7250
30	3	SHIELDS	SLP	SA/OD	FBG	KL	OB			6	5	4600	4	9	15700	17800
30	6	ATLANTIC	SLP	SAIL	FBG	KC	OB			6	6	4559	4	9	16100	18200
1979 BOATS																
16	1	GEMINI	SLP	SAIL	FBG	LB	OB			5	7	440		7	2800	3250
17		CAPE-COD-CAT	GAF	SAIL	FBG	KL	OB			7	11	2200	1	8	6750	7750
17		CAPE-COD-CAT	GAF	SAIL	FBG	KL	IB	D		7	11	2200	1	8	10600	12000
18		RHODES	SLP	SAIL	FBG	CB	OB			6	3	800		7	3950	4550
18		RHODES	SLP	SAIL	FBG	KL	OB			6	3	920	2	8	4200	4900
18	3	GOLDEN-EYE	SLP	SAIL	FBG	KL	OB			6	4	2500			7350	8400
20	1	GAUNTLET	SLP	SAIL	FBG	KL	OB			6	6	950	3	9	4550	5250
24	3	RAVEN	SLP	SA/OD	FBG	CB	OB			7		1170		7	6100	7000
1978 BOATS																
16	1	GEMINI	SLP	SAIL	FBG	LB	OB			5	7	440		7	2750	3200
17		CAPE-COD-CAT	CAT	SAIL	FBG	KL				7	11	2200	1	8	6550	7500
18		GOLDEN-EYE	SLP	SAIL	FBG	KL				6	4		3		5000	5750
18		RHODES	SLP	SAIL	FBG	CB	OB			6	3	800		7	3800	4450
20	1	GAUNTLET	SLP	SAIL	FBG	KL	OB			6	6	950	3	9	4450	5100
24	3	RAVEN	SLP	SA/OD	FBG	CB	OB			7		1100		7	5800	6700
29	10	BLUE-CHIP 30	SLP	SA/CR	FBG	KL	IB	20D		9	6	9000	4	3	30300	33600
30	3	SHIELDS	SLP	SA/OD	FBG	KL	OB			6	4	4600	4	9	14700	16700
44		MERCER	YWL	SA/CR	F/S	KL	IB	37D		11	9	28000	4		101500	111500
1977 BOATS																
16	1	GEMINI	SLP	SAIL	FBG	LB	OB			5	7	440		7	2650	3100
17		CAPE-COD-CAT	CAT	SAIL	FBG	CB	OB			7	11	2200	1	8	6350	7300
17		CAPE-COD-CAT	CAT	SAIL	FBG	CB	IB	5D-	6D	7	11	2200	1	8	9500	10800
17		CAPE-COD-CAT	CAT	SAIL	FBG	KL	OB			7	11	2200	1	11	6350	7300
17		CAPE-COD-CAT	CAT	SAIL	FBG	KL	IB	5D-	6D	7	11	2200	1	11	9500	10800
18		RHODES	SLP	SAIL	FBG	CB	OB			6	3	800		7	3700	4300
18		RHODES	SLP	SAIL	FBG	KL	OB			6	3	920	2	8	3950	4600
18	3	GOLDEN-EYE	SLP	SAIL	FBG	KL	OB			6	4	2500	3		6950	7950
20	1	GAUNTLET	SLP	SAIL	FBG	KL	OB			6	6	950	3	9	4250	4950
24	3	RAVEN	SLP	SA/OD	FBG	CB	OB			7		1170		7	5750	6650
29	10	BLUE-CHIP 30	SLP	SA/CR	FBG	KL	IB	15D		9	6	9500	4	3	30900	34400
30	3	SHIELDS	SLP	SA/OD	FBG	KL	OB			6	6	4600	4	9	14000	15900
44		MERCER	YWL	SA/CR	FBG	KC	IB	37D		11	9	27000	4	3	96100	105500
1976 BOATS																
16	1	GEMINI	SLP	SAIL	FBG	CB	OB			5	7	440		7	2600	3000
17		CAPE-COD-CAT	CAT	SAIL	FBG	KC	OB			7	11	2200	1	8	6200	7150
18		RHODES	SLP	SAIL	FBG	CB	OB			6	3	800		7	3600	4200
18		RHODES	SLP	SAIL	FBG	KL	OB			6	3	920	2	8	3850	4500
18	3	GOLDEN-EYE	SLP	SAIL	FBG	KL	OB			6	4	2500	3		6750	7750
20		GAUNTLET	SLP	SAIL	FBG	KL	OB			6	6	950	3	9	4150	4850
24	3	RAVEN	SLP	SA/OD	FBG	CB	OB					1170		7	5650	6450
29	10	BLUE-CHIP 30	SLP	SAIL	FBG	KL	IB	15D	WEST	9	6	9000	4	6	28400	31500
30	3	SHIELDS	SLP	SA/OD	FBG	KL	OB			6	6	4600	4	9	13600	15400
44		MERCER	SLP	SAIL	F/S	KC	IB	36D	WEST	11	9	28000	4	3	95100	104500
44		MERCER	YWL	SAIL	F/S	KC	IB	36D	WEST	11	9	28000	4	3	95100	104500
1975 BOATS																
16	1	GEMINI	SLP	SAIL	FBG	LB	OB			5	7	440		7	2550	2950
17		CAPE-COD-CAT	CAT	SAIL	FBG	CB	OB					2200			6050	6950
18		RHODES	SLP	SAIL	FBG	CB	OB			6	3	800	4		3550	4100
18		RHODES	SLP	SAIL	FBG	KL	OB			6	3	920	2	8	3800	4400
18	3	GOLDEN-EYE	SLP	SAIL	FBG	KL	OB			6	4	2500	3		6600	7600
20	1	GAUNTLET	SLP	SAIL	FBG	KL	OB			6	6	950	3	9	4100	4750
24	3	RAVEN	SLP	SA/OD	FBG	CB	OB			7		1170	5	4	5500	6350
29	10	BLUE-CHIP 30	SLP	SA/CR	FBG	KL	IB	15D		9	6	9500	4	3	29200	32500
30	3	SHIELDS	SLP	SA/OD	FBG	KL	OB			6	6	4600	4	9	13300	15100
44		MERCER	SLP	SAIL	F/S	KC	IB	D	WEST	11	9	27000	9		91100	100000
44		MERCER	YWL	SAIL	F/S	KC	IB	D	WEST	11	9	27000	9		91100	100000
1974 BOATS																
16	1	GEMINI	SLP	SAIL	FBG		OB			5	7	440			2500	2900
17		CAPE-COD CAT		SAIL	FBG		OB			7	11	2200	1	8	5950	6850
18		RHODES	SLP	SAIL	FBG	CB	OB			6	3	800			3450	4050
18		RHODES	SLP	SAIL	FBG	KL	OB			6	3	920	2	8	3700	4300
18	3	GOLDEN-EYE	SLP	SAIL	FBG		OB			6	4	2500	3		6500	7450
20	1	GAUNTLET		SAIL	FBG		OB			6	6	950			4000	4650
24	3	RAVEN	SLP	SA/OD	FBG	CB	OB			7		1170			5400	6200
29	10	BLUE-CHIP		SAIL	FBG		IB	16D	WEST	9	6	9500	4	3	28500	31700
30	3	SHIELDS	SLP	SA/OD	FBG	KL	OB			6	6	4600	4	9	12900	14700
44		MERCER		SAIL	FBG		IB	38D	WEST	11	9	27000			88300	97100
1973 BOATS																
16	1	GEMINI	SLP	SAIL	FBG		OB			5	7	440			2450	2850
17		CAPE-COD CAT		SAIL	FBG		OB			7	11	2200	1	8	5850	6700
18		RHODES	SLP	SAIL	FBG	CB	OB			6	3	800	4		3400	3950
18		RHODES	SLP	SAIL	FBG	KL	OB			6	3	920	4		3650	4250
18	3	GOLDEN-EYE	SLP	SAIL	FBG		OB			6	4	2500	3		6350	7300
20	1	GAUNTLET	SLP	SAIL	FBG		OB			6	6	950	3	9	3900	4550
24	3	RAVEN	SLP	SA/OD	FBG	CB	OB			7		1170			5300	6100
29	10	CAPE-COD 30		SAIL	FBG		IB	16D		9	6		4	3	25300	28100
44		MERCER	SLP	SA/CR	FBG	KC	IB	D		11	9	27000	4	3	86400	94900
44		MERCER	YWL	SA/CR	FBG	KC	IB	D		11	9	27000	4	3	86300	94900
1972 BOATS																
16	1	GEMINI	SLP	SAIL	FBG		OB			5	7	440	3	4	2400	2800
18		RHODES		SAIL	FBG	CB	OB			6	3	800	4		3350	3900
18		RHODES		SAIL	FBG	KL	OB			6	3	920	2	8	3550	4150
18	3	GOLDEN-EYE	SLP	SAIL	FBG		OB			6	4	2500	3		6200	7150
20	1	GAUNTLET	SLP	SAIL	FBG		OB			6	6	950	3	9	3850	4450
23		MARLIN		SA/CR	FBG		OB			7	2	3200	3	3	8550	9850
23		MARLIN	SLP	SA/CR	FBG	KL	IB	D		7	2	3200	3	3	10000	11400
23		MARLIN		SAIL	FBG		OB			7	2	2800	3	3	7700	8900
23		MARLIN DAY SAILER		SAIL	FBG		OB			7	2	3000	3	3	8150	9350
24	3	RAVEN	SLP	SA/OD	FBG	CB	OB			7		1175	5	4	5200	5950
29		CAPE-COD THIRTY		SAIL	FBG		IB	16D		9	6	3250	4	3	9350	10600
29	10	BLUE-CHIP	SLP	SA/CR	FBG	KL	IB	22D		9	6		5		25300	28100
44		MERCER	SLP	SAIL	FBG		OB			11	9		4	3	82700	90900
44		MERCER	YWL	SAIL	FBG		OB			11	9		4	3	82700	90900
1971 BOATS																
16	1	GEMINI	SLP	SAIL	FBG		OB			5	7	440	3	4	2350	2700
16	8	RANGER	OP	RNBT	FBG	SV	OB			5	11	650		7	2050	2450
18		RHODES	SLP	SAIL	FBG	CB	OB			6	3	800	4		3250	3800
18		RHODES	SLP	SAIL	FBG	KL	OB			6	3	920	2	8	3450	4050
18	3	GOLDEN-EYE	SLP	SAIL	FBG		OB			6	4	2500	3		6050	6950
20		GEMINI II		SAIL	FBG		OB			5	7	950	3	4	3750	4350
20	1	GAUNTLET	SLP	SAIL	FBG		OB			6	6	950	3	9	3750	4350
23		MARLIN		SA/CR	FBG		OB			7	2	3200	3	3	8350	9600
23		MARLIN	SLP	SA/CR	FBG	KL	IB	D		7	2	3200	3	3	9750	11100
23		MARLIN		SAIL	FBG		OB			7	2	2800	3	3	7550	8650
23		MARLIN DAY SAILER		SAIL	FBG		OB			7	2	3000	3	3	7950	9100
24	3	RAVEN	SLP	SA/OD	FBG	CB	OB			7		1175	5	4	5050	5800
29	10	CAPE-COD 30	SLP	SA/CR	FBG	KL	IB	22D		9	6	7100	5		19900	22100
44		MERCER	SLP	SAIL	FBG		OB			11	9		4	3	81000	89000
44		MERCER	YWL	SAIL	FBG		OB			11	9		4	3	81000	89000
1970 BOATS																
16	1	GEMINI	SLP	SA/OD	FBG	BB	OB			5	7	440		7	2300	2650
16	8	RANGER		RNBT	FBG	SV	OB			5	11	650		7	2100	2450
18		RHODES	SLP	SA/OD	FBG	CB	OB			6	3	800		7	3150	3700
18		RHODES	SLP	SA/OD	FBG	KL	OB			6	3	920	2	8	3400	3950
18	3	GOLDEN-EYE	SLP	SAIL	FBG	KL	OB			6	4	2500	3		5900	6800
20		GAUNTLET	SLP	SAIL	FBG	KL	OB			6	6	950	3	9	3650	4250
20		GEMINI II	SLP	SAIL	FBG	CB	OB			5	7	950		9	3650	4250
23		MARLIN	SLP	SA/CR	FBG	KL	OB			7	2	3200	3	3	8150	9350
23		MARLIN	SLP	SA/CR	FBG	KL	IB	D		7	2	3200	3	3	9550	10800
23		MARLIN	SLP	SAIL	FBG	KL	OB			7	2	2800	3	3	7350	8450
23		MARLIN DAY SAILER	SLP	SAIL	FBG		OB			7	2	3000	3	3	7750	8900
24	3	RAVEN	SLP	SA/OD	FBG	CB	OB			7		1175	5	4	4950	5650
29	10	BLUE-CHIP	SLP	SA/CR	FBG	KL				9	6		4	3	14100	16000
29	10	CAPE-COD 30	SLP	SA/CR	FBG	KL	IB	22D		9	6	7100	4	3	19400	21600
44		MERCER	SLP	SAIL	FBG	KC	OB			11	9	27000	4	3	80800	88800
44		MERCER	YWL	SAIL	FBG	KC	OB			11	9	27000	4	3	80800	88800
1969 BOATS																
16	1	GEMINI	SLP	SA/OD	FBG	CB				5	7			7	3800	4450
16	1	GEMINI	SLP	SAIL	FBG	BB	OB			5	7	440	3	4	2250	2600
16	8	RANGER		RNBT	FBG	SV	OB			5	11	650		7	2100	2500
18		RHODES	SLP	SA/OD	FBG	CB	OB			6	3	800		7	3100	3600
18		RHODES	SLP	SA/OD	FBG	KL	OB			6	3	920	2	8	3300	3850
18	3	GOLDENEYE	SLP	SAIL	FBG	KL				6	4	2500	3		5800	6650
20		GAUNTLET	SLP	SAIL	FBG	KL	OB			6	6	950	3	9	3550	4150
20		GEMINI II	SLP	SAIL	FBG	CB	OB			5	7	950		9	3550	4150
23		MARLIN	SLP	SA/CR	FBG	KL	OB			7	2	3200	3	3	7950	9150
23		MARLIN	SLP	SA/CR	FBG	KL	IB	D		7	2	3200	3	3	9350	10700
23		MARLIN	SLP	SAIL	FBG	KL	OB			7	2	2800	3	3	7200	8250
23		MARLIN DAY SAILER	SLP	SAIL	FBG	KL	OB			7	2	3000	3	3	7550	8700
24	3	RAVEN	SLP	SA/OD	FBG	CB	OB			7		1175		7	4850	5550

 CONTINUED ON NEXT PAGE

CAPE COD SHIPBUILDING CO — CONTINUED

See inside cover to adjust price for area

LOA FT	IN	NAME AND/OR MODEL	TOP/RIG	BOAT TYPE	HULL MTL	HULL TP	TP	# HP	MFG	BEAM FT	IN	WGT LBS	DRAFT FT	IN	RETAIL LOW	RETAIL HIGH
———— 1969 BOATS																
29	10	CAPE-COD 30	SLP	SAIL	FBG	KL	OB	22D		9	6	7100	4	3	18900	21000
30	6	ATLANTIC	SLP	SAIL	FBG	KL	OB			6	6	4559	4	9	11400	12900
44		MERCER	SLP	SAIL	FBG	KC	OB			11	9	27000	4	3	78700	86500
44		MERCER	YWL	SAIL	FBG	KC	OB			11	9	27000	4	3	78600	86400
———— 1968 BOATS																
16	1	GEMINI	SLP	SAIL	FBG	BB	OB			5	7	440		7	2200	2550
16	8	RANGER	OP		FBG	SV	OB			5	11	650		7	2100	2500
18		RHODES	SLP	SAIL	FBG	CB	OB			6	3	800		7	3050	3550
18		RHODES	SLP	SAIL	FBG	KL	OB			6	3	920	2	8	3250	3750
18	3	GOLDEN-EYE	SLP	SA/CR	FBG	KL				6	4	2500	3		5650	6500
20		GAUNTLET	SLP	SAIL	FBG	KL	OB			6	6	950	3	9	3500	4050
20		GEMINI II	SLP	SAIL	FBG	CB	OB			6	6	950		9	3500	4050
23		MARLIN	SLP	SA/CR	FBG	KL	OB			7	2	3200	3	3	7800	8950
23		MARLIN	SLP	SA/CR	FBG	KL	OB	16D		7	2	3200	3	3	9350	10600
23		MARLIN	SLP	SAIL	FBG	KL	OB			7	2	2800	3	3	7050	8100
23		MARLIN DAY SAILER	SLP	SAIL	FBG	KL	OB			7	2	3000	3	3	7400	8500
24	3	RAVEN	SLP	SA/OD	FBG	CB	OB			7		1175		7	4750	5450
30	6	ATLANTIC	SLP	SAIL	FBG	KL	OB			6	6	4559	4	9	11600	13100
44		CAPE-COD-MERCER	SLP	SA/CR	FBG	KC	OB			11	9	27000	4	3	81800	89900
———— 1967 BOATS																
16	1	GEMINI	SLP	SAIL	FBG		OB					440			2150	2500
16	8	RANGER		RNBT	FBG		OB			6		650			2100	2500
18		RHODES	SLP	SAIL	FBG	CB	OB					800			3000	3450
18		RHODES	SLP	SAIL	FBG	KL	OB					920			3200	3700
18	3	GOLDEN-EYE	SLP	SA/CR	FBG	KL				6	4		3		3900	4500
23		MARLIN		SA/CR	FBG		OB					3200			7650	8800
23		MARLIN	SLP	SA/CR	FBG	KL	OB	16D		7	2	3200	3	3	9200	10400
23		MARLIN		SAIL	FBG		OB					2800			6900	7950
23		MARLIN DAY SAILER		SAIL	FBG		OB					3000			7300	8350
24	3	RAVEN	SLP	SA/OD	FBG	CB	OB					1175			4650	5350
29	10	BLUE-CHIP	SLP	SA/CR	FBG	KL	OB			9	6		4	3	11300	12800
30	6	ATLANTIC		SAIL	FBG		OB					4559			11300	12900
44		MERCER	SLP	SA/CR	FBG	KL	OB			11	9		4	3	86700	95300
44		MERCER	YWL	SA/CR	FBG	KL	OB			11	9		4	3	86600	95200
———— 1966 BOATS																
16	1	GEMINI	SLP	SA/OD	FBG	BB	OB			5	7	440		7	2100	2450
16	8	RANGER	OP	RNBT	FBG	SV	OB			5	11	650		7	2150	2500
18		RHODES	SLP	SA/OD	FBG	CB	OB			6	3	800		7	2950	3400
18		RHODES	SLP	SA/OD	FBG	KL	OB			6	3	920	2	8	3150	3650
18	3	GOLDEN-EYE	SLP	SAIL	FBG	KL				6	4	2500	3		5450	6300
23		MARLIN	SLP	SA/CR	FBG	KL	OB			7	2	3200	2	2	7550	8650
23		MARLIN	SLP	SA/CR	FBG	KL	IB	16D		7	2	3200	3	3	9050	10300
23		MARLIN	SLP	SAIL	FBG	KL	OB			7	2	2800	3	2	6800	7800
23		MARLIN DAY SAILER	SLP	SAIL	FBG	KL	OB			7	2	3000	3	2	7150	8200
24	3	RAVEN	SLP	SA/OD	FBG	CB	OB			7		850		7	4150	4850
29	10	CAPE-COD 30	SLP	SA/CR	FBG	KL	IB	22		9	6	7100	4	3	18100	20200
30	6	ATLANTIC	SLP	SA/OD	FBG	KL	OB			6	6	4559	4	9	11100	12600
44		MERCER	SLP	SA/CR	FBG	KC	IB	50D		11	9	27000	4	3	78000	85700
———— 1965 BOATS																
16	1	GEMINI	SLP	SAIL	FBG		OB								3550	4150
16	8	RANGER	OP	RNBT	FBG		OB								3450	4050
16	8	RANGER	OP	RNBT	FBG		IO	40							3800	4400
18		RHODES	SLP	SAIL	FBG	CB	OB								3750	4350
18		RHODES	SLP	SAIL	FBG	KL	OB								3750	4350
18	3	GOLDEN-EYE	SLP	SAIL	FBG										3750	4400
23		MARLIN		SA/CR	FBG										7400	8550
23		MARLIN		SAIL	FBG										7000	8050
23		MARLIN DAY SAILER		SAIL	FBG										7850	9000
24	3	RAVEN	SLP	SA/OD	FBG	CB	OB								5050	5800
29	10	CAPE-COD THIRTY		SAIL	FBG		IB	16D							22300	24800
30	3	SHIELDS	SLP	SA/OD	FBG	KL	OB								10900	12400
———— 1964 BOATS																
16	1	GEMINI	SLP	SAIL	FBG		OB								3500	4100
16	8	RANGER	SLP	SAIL	FBG		OB								2950	3450
18		RHODES	SLP	SAIL	FBG		OB								3700	4300
23		MARLIN		SA/CR	FBG		OB								7350	8400
23		MARLIN		SAIL	FBG		OB								6900	7950
23		MARLIN DAY SAILER		SAIL	FBG		OB								7750	8900
24	3	RAVEN	SLP	SA/OD	FBG	CB	OB								5000	5750
29	10	CAPE-COD THIRTY		SAIL	FBG		IB	16D							22000	24400
30	3	SHIELDS	SLP	SA/OD	FBG	KL	OB								10700	12200
———— 1963 BOATS																
16	1	GEMINI	SLP	SAIL	FBG		OB								3450	4050
18		RHODES	SLP	SAIL	FBG		OB								3650	4250
23		MARLIN		SA/CR	FBG		OB								7250	8350
23		MARLIN		SAIL	FBG		OB								6850	7850
23		MARLIN DAY SAILER		SAIL	FBG		OB								7650	8800
24	3	RAVEN	SLP	SA/OD	FBG	CB	OB								4950	5650
———— 1962 BOATS																
16		GEMINI	SLP	SAIL	FBG		OB								3450	4000
18		RHODES	SLP	SAIL	FBG		OB								3650	4250
23		MARLIN		SAIL	FBG		OB								7200	8250
24	3	RAVEN	SLP	SA/OD	FBG	CB	OB								4900	5600
———— 1961 BOATS																
16	11	MARLIN	SLP	SA/OD	FBG	KL							3	3	2900	3350
17		RANGER		RNBT			OB			5	11	650			2250	2650
18		RHODES 18	SLP	SA/CR	FBG	KC				6	3			4	3600	4200
23		MARLIN	SLP	SA/OD	FBG	KL	OB			7	2		3	3	7150	8200
24	3	RAVEN	SLP	SA/OD	FBG	CB				7					7100	8200
30	6	ATLANTIC	SLP	SA/OD	FBG	KL				6	6		4	9	12500	14200
———— 1960 BOATS																
18		MERCURY	SLP	SA/OD	FBG	KL				5	4		3	1	3600	4200
18		RHODES	SLP	SA/OD	FBG	KL				6	3		2	8	3600	4200
19				CR			OB								4000	4650
23		MARLIN		SA/OD	FBG	KL				7	2		3	3	6500	7450
24	2	RAVEN	SLP	SA/OD	FBG	CB				7				7	7050	8100
———— 1959 BOATS																
18		RHODES	SLP	SAIL	FBG	KC									3600	4150
19				CBNCR			OB					1100			3800	4450
23		MARLIN	SLP	SAIL	FBG	KL	OB						3	5	7050	8150
24		RAVEN	SLP	SAIL	FBG	CB									8100	9300
———— 1946 BOATS																
18		BABY-KNOCKABOUT		SA/OD	PLY	CB									4150	4800
18		RHODES		SA/OD	PLY										4150	4800
31		ADVANCED-TRAINER	SLP	SA/OD	PLY	KL									14500	16500
32			OP	FSH	PLY		IB	D							**	**
———— 1941 BOATS																
18		RHODES	SLP	SA/OD	WD	KC									4800	5500
18		RHODES	SLP	SA/OD	WD										4800	5500
23		KNOCKABOUT	SLP	SA/OD	WD	KC									8850	10100
23		KNOCKABOUT	SLP	SA/OD	WD	KL									8850	10100
———— 1939 BOATS																
23		SENIOR-KNOCKABOUT	SLP	SA/OD	WD	KC				6	4		1	8	9350	10600
———— 1937 BOATS																
16		VEE 16	SLP	SAIL	WD	CB								10	5150	5900
18		BABY-KNOCKABOUT	SLP	SAIL	WD	CB				5	10			10	5450	6250
22	10	SENIOR-KNOCKABOUT	SLP	SAIL	WD	KC				6	6		1	8	10600	12100
26			SLP	SAIL	WD										15900	18100
———— 1936 BOATS																
16		VEE 16	SLP	SAIL	CDR	CB				6	3			1	5300	6100
18		BABY-KNOCKABOUT	SLP	SAIL	CDR	CB									5600	6450
23		CRUISING	SLP	SAIL	CDR										11100	12800
———— 1931 BOATS																
16		SPEEDCOM		RNBT	WD		IB	35D							3300	3850
18		BABY-KNOCKABOUT		SAIL	WD	CB									6750	7750
20				RNBT	WD		IB	D							**	**
26			SLP	SAIL		KC	IB	D	PALM	8	6		2	6	29900	33200

CAPE CODDER CO
COAST GUARD MFG ID- AGU

Call 1-800-327-6929 for BUC Personalized Evaluation Service
Or, for 1980 to 1983 boats, sign onto www.BUCValuPro.com

CAPE DORY YACHTS INC
AMITYVILLE NY 11701   COAST GUARD MFG ID- CDN   See inside cover to adjust price for area

For more recent years, see the BUC Used Boat Price Guide, Volume 1 or Volume 2

LOA FT	IN	NAME AND/OR MODEL	TOP/RIG	BOAT TYPE	HULL MTL	HULL TP	TP	# HP	MFG	BEAM FT	IN	WGT LBS	DRAFT FT	IN	RETAIL LOW	RETAIL HIGH
———— 1983 BOATS																
18	6	TYPHOON DAYSAILER	SLP	SAIL	FBG	KL	OB			6	4	1900	2	7	6000	6850
18	6	TYPHOON WEEKENDER	SLP	SAIL	FBG	KL	OB			6	4	1900	2	7	6150	7050
22	4	CAPE-DORY 22	SLP	SAIL	FBG	KL	OB			7	4	3200	3		7900	9100
25	3	CAPE-DORY 25D	SLP	SAIL	FBG	KL	IB	8D	YAN	8	3	5120	3	6	14200	16100
27	1	CAPE-DORY 27	SLP	SA/CR	FBG	KL	IB	13D	WEST	8	6	7500	4		22600	25100
28	2	CAPE-DORY 28	SLP	SA/CR	FBG	KL	IB	15D	VLVO	8	11	8000	4		28000	31100
30	3	CAPE-DORY 30	CUT	SA/CR	FBG	KL	IB	15D	VLVO	9		10000	4	2	31900	35500
33	1	CAPE-DORY 33	SLP	SA/CR	FBG	KL	IB	30D	UNIV	10	3	13300	4	10	42900	47600
36	2	CAPE-DORY 36	CUT	SA/CR	FBG	KL	IB	50D	PERK	10	8	16100	5		62500	68700

LOA FT	IN	NAME AND/ OR MODEL	TOP/ RIG	BOAT TYPE	-HULL- MTL	TP	ENGINE TP	# HP	MFG	BEAM FT	IN	WGT LBS	DRAFT FT	IN	RETAIL LOW	RETAIL HIGH
		1983 BOATS														
45	2	CAPE-DORY 45	CUT	SA/CR	FBG	KL	IB	52D	WEST	13		24000	6	3	106500	117000
45	2	CAPE-DORY 45	KTH	SA/CR	FBG	KL	IB	52D	WEST	13		24000	6	3	106500	117000
		1982 BOATS														
18	6	TYPHOON DAYSAILER	SLP	SAIL	FBG	KL	OB			6	4	1900	2	7	5700	6550
18	6	TYPHOON WEEKENDER	SLP	SAIL	FBG	KL	OB			6	4	2000	2	7	5850	6700
22	4	CAPE-DORY 22	SLP	SAIL	FBG	KL	OB			7	4	3200	3		7500	8650
24	10	CAPE-DORY 25	SLP	SAIL	FBG	KL	OB			7	3	4000	3		9700	11000
25	3	CAPE-DORY 25D	SLP	SAIL	FBG	KL	IB	8D	YAN	8		5120	3	6	13500	15300
27	1	CAPE-DORY 27	SLP	SA/CR	FBG	KL	IB	8D	YAN	8	6	7500	4		21300	23700
28	1	CAPE-DORY 28	SLP	SA/CR	FBG	KL	IB	13D	VLVO	8	11	9000	4		26400	29400
30	3	CAPE-DORY 30	CUT	SA/CR	FBG	KL	IB	13D	VLVO	9		10000	4	2	30200	33600
33	1	CAPE-DORY 33	SLP	SA/CR	FBG	KL	IB	23D	VLVO	10	3	13300	4	10	40600	45100
36	2	CAPE-DORY 36	CUT	SA/CR	FBG	KL	IB	50D	PERK	10	8	16100	5		59200	65100
		1981 BOATS														
18	6	TYPHOON DAYSAILER	SLP	SAIL	FBG	KL	OB			6	4	2000	2	7	5350	6150
18	6	TYPHOON WEEKENDER	SLP	SAIL	FBG	KL	OB			6	4	2000	2	7	5750	6600
22	4	CAPE-DORY 22	SLP	SAIL	FBG	KL	OB			7	4	3200	3		7100	8200
24	10	CAPE-DORY 25	SLP	SAIL	FBG	KL	OB			7	3	4000	3		9250	10500
27	1	CAPE-DORY 27	SLP	SA/CR	FBG	KL	IB	8D	YAN	8	6	7500	4		20200	22400
28	1	CAPE-DORY 28	SLP	SA/CR	FBG	KL	IB	13D	VLVO	8	11	9000	4		25100	27800
30	3	CAPE-DORY 30	CUT	SA/CR	FBG	KL	IB	13D	VLVO	9		10000	4	2	28700	31900
33	1	CAPE-DORY 33	SLP	SA/CR	FBG	KL	IB	23D	UNIV	10	3	13300	4	10	38500	42700
36	2	CAPE-DORY 36	CUT	SA/CR	FBG	KL	IB	50D	PERK	10	8	16100	5		56100	61700
		1980 BOATS														
18	6	TYPHOON DAYSAILER	SLP	SAIL	FBG	KL	OB			6	4	1900	2	7	5200	5950
18	6	TYPHOON WEEKENDER	SLP	SAIL	FBG	KL	OB			6	3	2000	2	7	5350	6150
24	10	CAPE-DORY 25	SLP	SAIL	FBG	KL	OB			7	3	4000	3		8900	10100
27	1	CAPE-DORY 27	SLP	SA/CR	FBG	KL	IB	8D		8	6	7500	4		19400	21500
28	1	CAPE-DORY 28	SLP	SA/CR	FBG	KL	IB	15D		8	11	9000	4		24100	26800
30	3	CAPE-DORY 30	CUT	SA/CR	FBG	KL	IB	15D		9		10000	4	2	27600	30700
30	3	CAPE-DORY 30	KTH	SA/CR	FBG	KL	IB	15D		9		10000	4	2	27600	30700
33	1	CAPE-DORY 33	SLP	SA/CR	FBG	KL	IB	23D	VLVO	10	3	13300	4	10	37000	41100
36	2	CAPE-DORY 36	CUT	SA/CR	FBG	KL	IB	50D	PERK	10	8		5		54000	59400
		1979 BOATS														
18	6	TYPHOON DAYSAILER	SLP	SAIL	FBG	KL	OB			6	4	1900	2	7	5050	5800
18	6	TYPHOON WEEKENDER	SLP	SAIL	FBG	KL	OB			6	4	2000	2	7	5200	5950
24	10	CAPE-DORY 25	SLP	SAIL	FBG	KL	OB			7	3	4000	3		8500	9750
27	1	CAPE-DORY 27	SLP	SA/CR	FBG	KL	IB	8D	YAN	8	6	7350	4		18600	20700
28	2	CAPE-DORY 28	SLP	SA/CR	FBG	KL	IB	15D	VLVO	8	11	9000	4		23400	26000
30	3	CAPE-DORY 30	CUT	SA/CR	FBG	KL	IB	15D	VLVO	9		10000	4	2	26700	29700
30	3	CAPE-DORY 30	KTH	SA/CR	FBG	KL	IB	15D	VLVO	9		10000	4	2	26700	29700
36	2	CAPE-DORY 36	CUT	SA/CR	FBG	KL	IB	50D	PERK	10	8	16100	5		45800	50300
		1978 BOATS														
18	6	TYPHOON WEEKENDER	SLP	SAIL	FBG	KL	OB			6	3	2000	2	7	5000	5750
24	10	CAPE-DORY 25	SLP	SAIL	FBG	KL	OB			7	3	4000	3		8250	9500
27	1	CAPE-DORY 27	SLP	SAIL	FBG	KL	IB	8D	YAN	8	6	7350	4		18100	20100
28	1	CAPE-DORY 28	SLP	SAIL	FBG	KL	IB	13D	VLVO	8	10	9000	4		22700	25200
30	2	CAPE-DORY 30	CUT	SAIL	FBG	KL	IB	13D	VLVO	9		10000	4	2	25900	28800
30	2	CAPE-DORY 30	KTH	SAIL	FBG	KL	IB	13D	VLVO	9		10000	4	2	25900	28800
		1977 BOATS														
18	6	TYPHOON DAYSAILER	SLP	SAIL	FBG	KL	OB			6	3	1800	2	7	4600	5300
18	6	TYPHOON WEEKENDER	SLP	SA/CR	FBG	KL	OB			6	3	2000	2	7	4900	5600
24	10	CAPE-DORY 25	SLP	SA/CR	FBG	KL	OB			7	3	4000	3		8050	9250
27	1	CAPE-DORY 27	SLP	SA/CR	FBG	KL	IB	8D	YAN	8	6	7500	4		17600	20000
28	1	CAPE-DORY 28	SLP	SA/CR	FBG	KL	IB	12D	FARY	8	10	9000	4		22100	24500
30	2	CAPE-DORY 30	SLP	SA/CR	FBG	KL	IB	12D	YAN	9		10000	4	2	25300	28100
30	2	CAPE-DORY 30-K	KTH	SA/CR	FBG	KL	IB	12D	YAN	9		10000	4	2	25300	28100
		1976 BOATS														
18	6	TYPHOON	SLP	SAIL	FBG	KL	OB			6	3	2000	2	7	4750	5450
18	6	TYPHOON DAYSAILER	SLP	SAIL	FBG	KL	OB			6	3	1800	2	7	4500	5200
24	10	CAPE-DORY 25	SLP	SAIL	FBG	KL	OB			7	3	4000	3		7850	9000
27	2	CAPE-DORY 27	SLP	SAIL	FBG	KL	IB	8D		8	6	7350	4		16800	19100
28	1	CAPE-DORY 28	SLP	SAIL	FBG	KL	IB	25D	VLVO	8	11	9000	4		21700	24100
30	3	CAPE-DORY 30	KTH	SAIL	FBG	KL	IB	18D	YAN	9		10000	4	2	24700	27400
		1975 BOATS														
18	6	TYPHOON	SLP	SAIL	FBG	KL				6	3	1900	2	7	4550	5200
18	6	TYPHOON DAYSAILER	SLP	SAIL	FBG	KL				6	3	1800	2	7	4400	5050
24	10	CAPE-DORY 25	SLP	SAIL	FBG	KL				7	3	3900	3		7300	8400
28	1	CAPE-DORY 28	SLP	SAIL	FBG	KL	IB	25D	VLVO	8	11	9000	4		21200	23500
		1974 BOATS														
18	6	ALBERG-TYPHOON		SAIL	FBG		OB			6	3	1900	2	7	4450	5100
24	10	CAPE-DORY 25		SAIL	FBG		OB			7	3	3850	3		7250	8350
30		CAPE 30	SLP	SAIL	FBG	KL	IB	18D	YAN	9	3	9350	4	5	22000	24500
		1973 BOATS														
18	6	ALBERG-TYPHOON		SAIL	FBG		OB			6	3	1900	2	7	4300	5000
24	10	CAPE 25		SAIL	FBG		OB			7	3	3850	3		7100	8200
30		CAPE 30	SLP	SAIL	FBG	KL	IB	18D	YAN	9	3	9350	4	5	21600	24000
		1972 BOATS														
18	6	ALBERG-TYPHOON		SAIL	FBG		OB			6	3	1900	2	7	4200	4900
30		CAPE 30		SAIL	FBG		IB	18	UNIV	9	3	9350	4	5	21000	23400
		1971 BOATS														
18	6	ALBERG-TYPHOON		SAIL	FBG		OB			6	3	1900	2	7	4100	4800
		1970 BOATS														
18	4	ALBERG-TYPHOON	SLP	SA/OD	FBG	KL	OB			6	4	1750	2	7	3850	4450
		1969 BOATS														
18	6	CAPE-DORY TYPHOON	SLP	SAIL	FBG	KL	OB			6	3	2000	2	7	4050	4700
		1968 BOATS														
18	6	CAPE-DORY TYPHOON	SLP	SAIL	FBG	KL	OB			6	3	2000	2	7	3900	4500
		1967 BOATS														
18	6	CAPE-DORY TYPHOON	SLP	SAIL	FBG	KL	OB			6	3	2000	2	7	3800	4450

CAPE FOULWEATHER BOATS

COAST GUARD MFG ID- CFH

Call 1-800-327-6929 for BUC Personalized Evaluation Service
Or, for 1979 to 1983 boats, sign onto www.BUCValuPro.com

CAPE YACHTS LTD

COAST GUARD MFG ID- CYA

Call 1-800-327-6929 for BUC Personalized Evaluation Service
Or, for 1974 to 1977 boats, sign onto www.BUCValuPro.com

CAPITAL YACHTS INC

NEWPORT
HARBOR CITY CA 90710-08 COAST GUARD MFG ID- CPY

See inside cover to adjust price for area

For more recent years, see the BUC Used Boat Price Guide, Volume 1 or Volume 2

LOA FT	IN	NAME AND/ OR MODEL	TOP/ RIG	BOAT TYPE	-HULL- MTL	TP	ENGINE TP	# HP	MFG	BEAM FT	IN	WGT LBS	DRAFT FT	IN	RETAIL LOW	RETAIL HIGH
		1983 BOATS														
24		NEPTUNE 24	SLP	SAIL	FBG	KL	OB			8		3200	5		5250	6050
24		NEPTUNE 24	SLP	SAIL	FBG	SK	OB			8		3200	2		5250	6050
27		NEWPORT 27SII	SLP	SA/RC	FBG	KL	IB	15D	UNIV	9	2	6500	5	2	12700	14400
27	2	GULF 27	SLP	SA/CR	FBG	KL	IB	15D	UNIV	9	4	6900	5	2	13600	15400
28		NEWPORT 28II	SLP	SA/RC	FBG	KL	IB	15D	UNIV	9	6	7000	5	2	14000	15900
28	8	GULF 29	SLP	SA/CR	FBG	KL	IB	15D	UNIV	9	4	7500	4	6	15200	17300
30		NEWPORT 30 III	SLP	SA/RC	FBG	KL	IB	20D	UNIV	10	8	9000	5	3	19100	21200
32		GULF 32	SLP	SA/CR	FBG	KL	IB	D		10		14000	5	2	29400	32700
33		NEWPORT 33	SLP	SA/RC	FBG	KL	IB	20D	UNIV	10	10	9500	6		20100	22400
41		NEWPORT 41SII	SLP	SA/RC	FBG	KL	IB	40D	UNIV	11	3	18000	6	3	45500	50000
		1982 BOATS														
24		NEPTUNE 24	SLP	SAIL	FBG	KL	OB			8		3200	4	8	5000	5700
24		NEPTUNE 24	SLP	SAIL	FBG	SK	OB			8		3200	2	6	5000	5700
27		NEWPORT 27	SLP	SA/RC	FBG	KL	IB	D		9	2	6500	4	3	12000	13700
27	2	GULF 27	SLP	SA/CR	FBG	KL	IB	D		9	4	6900	4	2	12800	14600
28		NEWPORT 28	SLP	SA/RC	FBG	KL	IB	D		9	6	7000	4	6	13300	15100
28	8	GULF 29	SLP	SA/CR	FBG	KL	IB	D		9	4	7500	4	6	14500	16400
30		NEWPORT 30 II	SLP	SA/RC	FBG	KL	IB	D		10	6	8000	4	9	15700	17900
32		GULF 32	SLP	SA/CR	FBG	KL	IB	D		10		14000	5	2	27900	31000
33		NEWPORT 33	SLP	SA/CR	FBG	KL	IB	D		10	10	10000			20100	22300
41		NEWPORT 41 MKII	SLP	SA/RC	FBG	KL	IB	40D	UNIV	11	3	17500	6	3	41900	46600
41		NEWPORT 41S	SLP	SA/RC	FBG	KL	IB	D		11	3	18000	6	3	42600	47400
		1981 BOATS														
24		NEPTUNE 24	SLP	SAIL	FBG	KL	OB			8		3200	5		4700	5450
24		NEPTUNE 24	SLP	SAIL	FBG	SK	OB			8		3200	2		4700	5450
27		NEWPORT 27	SLP	SA/RC	FBG	KL	OB			9	2	6500	4	3	10900	12400
27	2	GULF 27	SLP	SA/CR	FBG	KL	OB			9	4	6900	4	2	11700	13300
28		NEWPORT 28	SLP	SA/RC	FBG	KL	OB			9	6	7000	4	6	12200	13900
28	8	GULF 29	SLP	SA/CR	FBG	KL				9	4	7500	4	6	12300	14000
30		NEWPORT 30 II	SLP	SA/RC	FBG	KL	OB			10	6	8000	4	9	14700	16700
32		GULF 32	SLP	SA/CR	FBG	KL	IB	D		10		14000	5		26400	29400
41		NEWPORT 41S	SLP	SA/RC	FBG	KL	OB			11	3	18000	6	3	39300	43700
		1980 BOATS														
24		NEPTUNE 24	SLP	SA/CR	FBG	BB				8		3000	3	6	4300	5000
27		NEWPORT 27S	SLP	SA/CR	FBG	KL	IB	D		9	2	6500	4	3	11000	12500
28		NEWPORT 28	SLP	SA/RC	FBG	KL	IB	D		9	6	7000	4	6	12100	13800
30		NEWPORT 30 II	SLP	SA/RC	FBG	KL	IB	D		10	6	8000	4	9	14300	16300
32		GULF 32	SLP	SA/CR	FBG	KL	IB	D		10		15000	5	2	27200	30200
41		NEWPORT 41S	SLP	SA/RC	FBG	KL	IB	D		11	3	18000	6	3	38900	43200

CONTINUED ON NEXT PAGE

LOA FT	LOA IN	NAME AND/ OR MODEL	TOP/ RIG	BOAT TYPE	-HULL- MTL	-HULL- TP	ENGINE TP	ENGINE # HP	ENGINE MFG	BEAM FT	BEAM IN	WGT LBS	DRAFT FT	DRAFT IN	RETAIL LOW	RETAIL HIGH
		1979 BOATS														
24		NEPTUNE 24	SLP	SA/CR	FBG	KL	OB			8		3200	3	6	4400	5100
27		NEWPORT 27S	SLP	SA/CR	FBG	KL	OB			9	2	6000	4	3	9450	10700
28		NEWPORT 28	SLP	SA/CR	FBG	KL	IB	D		9	6	7000	4	6	11800	13400
30		NEWPORT 30 II	SLP	SA/CR	FBG	KL	IB	D		10	6	8000	4	9	13900	15800
32		GULF 32	SLP	SA/CR	FBG	KL	IB	D		10		15000	5	2	26300	29300
41		NEWPORT 41S	SLP	SA/CR	FBG	KL	IB	D		11	3	18000	6	3	37600	41800
		1978 BOATS														
24		NEPTUNE 24	SLP	SAIL	FBG	KC	OB			8		3200	2		4250	4950
27		NEWPORT 27S	SLP	SAIL	FBG	KL	OB			9	2	6000	4	3	9150	10400
27		NEWPORT 27S	SLP	SAIL	FBG	KL	IB	30	UNIV	9	2	6000	4	3	9400	10700
27		NEWPORT 27S	SLP	SAIL	FBG	KL	IB	D	YAN	9	2	6000	4	3	9500	10800
28		NEWPORT 28	SLP	SAIL	FBG	KL	IB	30	UNIV	9	6	7000	4	6	11200	12800
28		NEWPORT 28	SLP	SAIL	FBG	KL	IB	D		9	6	7000	4	6	11400	13000
30		NEWPORT 30II	SLP	SAIL	FBG	KL	IB	30	UNIV	10	6	8500	4	9	14100	16100
30		NEWPORT 30II	SLP	SAIL	FBG	KL	IB	12D		10	6	8500	4	9	14200	16400
30		NEWPORT 30II SHOAL	SLP	SAIL	FBG	KL	IB	30	UNIV	10	6	8500	4	9	14300	16300
30		NEWPORT 30II SHOAL	SLP	SAIL	FBG	KL	IB	12D		10	6	8500	4	9	14400	16400
32		GULF 32	CUT	SA/CR	FBG	KL	IB	22D	WEST	10		13000	5	2	22300	24700
41		NEWPORT 41	SLP	SAIL	FBG	KL	IB	30D	PERK	11	3	18000	6	3	36300	40300
		1977 BOATS														
24		NEPTUNE 24	SLP	SAIL	FBG	KC	OB			8		3200	2		4150	4800
27		NEWPORT 27S	SLP	SAIL	FBG	KL	OB			9	2	6000	4	3	8900	10100
27		NEWPORT 27S	SLP	SAIL	FBG	KL	IB	30	UNIV	9	2	6000	4	3	9100	10400
27		NEWPORT 27S	SLP	SAIL	FBG	KL	IB	D	YAN	9	2	6000	4	3	9300	10600
28		NEWPORT 28 SHOAL	SLP	SAIL	FBG	KL	OB			9	6	7000	4		10800	12200
28		NEWPORT 28 SHOAL	SLP	SAIL	FBG	KL	IB	30D		9	6	7000	4		11100	12700
30		NEWPORT 30II	SLP	SAIL	FBG	KL	IB	30	UNIV	10	6	8500	4	9	13800	15600
30		NEWPORT 30II	SLP	SAIL	FBG	KL	IB	D		10	6	8500	4	9	14100	16000
30		NEWPORT 30II SHOAL	SLP	SAIL	FBG	KL	IB	30	UNIV	10	6	8500	4		14000	15900
30		NEWPORT 30II SHOAL	SLP	SAIL	FBG	KL	IB	D		10	6	8500	4		14300	16200
32		GULF 32	CUT	SA/CR	FBG	KL	IB	25D		10		13000	5	2	21700	24100
41		NEWPORT 41S	SLP	SAIL	FBG	KL	IB	50D	PERK	11	3	18000	6	3	35500	39400
		1976 BOATS														
20	6	NEWPORT	SLP	SA/OD	FBG	KL	OB			7	6	2500	3	3	2900	3350
24		NEPTUNE 24	SLP	SAIL	FBG	KC	OB					3200	2		4050	4700
27		NEWPORT 27S	SLP	SAIL	FBG	KL	IB	30	UNIV			6000	4	3	8900	10100
28		NEWPORT 28	SLP	SAIL	FBG	KL	IB	30	UNIV			7000	4		10700	12100
30		NEWPORT 30II	SLP	SAIL	FBG	KL	IB	30	UNIV			8500	4		13500	15400
32		GULF 32	SLP	SAIL	FBG	KL	IB	D				13000	5	2	21100	23500
41		NEWPORT 41S	SLP	SAIL	FBG	KL	IB	D	PERK			18000	6	3	34500	38400
		1975 BOATS														
20	6	NEWPORT	SLP	SA/OD	FBG	KL	OB			7	6	2500	3	3	2800	3300
27		NEWPORT 27S	SLP	SA/CR	FBG	KL	IB	D		9	2	6000	4	3	8850	10100
28		NEWPORT 28	SLP	SA/CR	FBG	KL	IB	D		9	6	7000	4	6	10600	12000
30		NEWPORT 30II	SLP	SA/CR	FBG	KL	IB	D		10	6	8000	4	9	12500	14200
41		NEWPORT 41S	SLP	SA/CR	FBG	KL	IB	D		11	3	18000	6	3	34000	37700
		1974 BOATS														
27		NEWPORT 27S	SLP	SA/CR	FBG	KL	IB	D		9	2	6000	4	3	8600	9850
28		NEWPORT 28	SLP	SA/CR	FBG	KL	IB	D		9	6	7000	4	6	10400	11800
30		NEWPORT 30II	SLP	SA/CR	FBG	KL	IB	D		10	6	8000	4	9	12300	13900
41		NEWPORT 41S	SLP	SA/CR	FBG	KL	IB	D		11	3	18000	6	3	33300	37000
		1973 BOATS														
20	6	NEWPORT	SLP	SA/OD	FBG	KL	OB			7	6	2500	3	4	2700	3150
27		NEWPORT 27	SLP	SAIL	FBG	KL	IB	30D		9	2	6000	4	3	8550	9800
30		NEWPORT 30	SLP	SAIL	FBG	KL	IB	30D		10	6	8000	4	9	12100	13700
41		NEWPORT 41	SLP	SAIL	FBG	KL	IB	D		11		18000	6	3	32600	36300

CAPRI HOUSEBOATS

Call 1-800-327-6929 for BUC Personalized Evaluation Service
Or, for 1969 to 1970 boats, sign onto www.BUCValuPro.com

CAPRI SAILBOATS

DIV OF CATALINA YACHTS
WOODLAND HILLS CA 91367 COAST GUARD MFG ID- CPS

See inside cover to adjust price for area

For more recent years, see the BUC Used Boat Price Guide, Volume 1 or Volume 2

LOA FT	LOA IN	NAME AND/ OR MODEL	TOP/ RIG	BOAT TYPE	-HULL- MTL	-HULL- TP	ENGINE TP	ENGINE # HP	ENGINE MFG	BEAM FT	BEAM IN	WGT LBS	DRAFT FT	DRAFT IN	RETAIL LOW	RETAIL HIGH
		1983 BOATS														
21		VICTORY 21	SLP	SA/OD	FBG	KL	OB			6	3	1350	3		2600	3050
24	7	CAPRI 25	SLP	SA/OD	FBG	KL	OB			9	2	2785	4	2	4700	5450
29	6	CAPRI 30	SLP	SA/OD	FBG	KL	OB			11	2	4985	5	2	9650	11000
29	6	CAPRI 30	SLP	SA/OD	FBG	KL	IB	7D	BMW	11	2	4985	5	2	9850	11200
		1982 BOATS														
21		VICTORY 21	SLP	SA/OD	FBG	KL	OB			6	3	1350	3		2450	2850
24	7	CAPRI 25	SLP	SA/OD	FBG	KL	OB			9	2	2785	4	2	4450	5150
29	6	CAPRI 30	SLP	SA/OD	FBG	KL	OB			11	2	4985	5	2	9150	10400
29	11	CAPRI 30	SLP	SA/OD	FBG	KL	OB			11	2	3800	5	5	6900	7950
		1981 BOATS														
21		VICTORY 21	SLP	SA/OD	FBG	KL	OB			6	3	1350	3		2350	2700
24	7	CAPRI 25	SLP	SA/OD	FBG	KL	OB			9	2	2785	4	2	4150	4850
		1980 BOATS														
21		VICTORY 21	SLP	SA/OD	FBG	KL	OB			6	3	1350	3		2250	2600
24	7	CAPRI 25	SLP	SA/OD	FBG	KL	OB			9	2	2785	4	2	3950	4600
		1979 BOATS														
21		VICTORY 21	SLP	SA/OD	FBG	KL	OB			6	3	1350	3		2100	2500
24	7	CAPRI 25	SLP	SA/OD	FBG	KL	OB			9	2	2875	4	2	3900	4550
		1978 BOATS														
21		VICTORY 21	SLP	SA/OD	FBG	KL	OB			6	3	1350	3		2000	2400
		1977 BOATS														
21		VICTORY 21	SLP	SA/OD	FBG	KL	OB			6	3	1350	3		1950	2300
		1976 BOATS														
21	6	CATALINA 22	SLP	SAIL	FBG	KL	OB			7	8	2150	3	6	2500	2900
21	6	CATALINA 22	SLP	SAIL	FBG	SK	OB			7	8	1850	1	8	2300	2700
		1975 BOATS														
21		VICTORY 21	SLP	SA/OD	FBG	KL	OB			6	3	1350	3		1850	2200
		1974 BOATS														
21		VICTORY 21	SLP	SA/OD	FBG	KL	OB			6	3	1350	3		1800	2150
		1973 BOATS														
21		VICTORY 21	SLP	SA/OD	FBG	KL	OB			6	3	1350	3		1750	2050
		1970 BOATS														
21		VICTORY 21	SLP	SA/OD	FBG	KL	OB			6	3	1500	3	6	1750	2050

CAPTAINS CRAFT HOUSEBOAT

COAST GUARD MFG ID- CPT

Call 1-800-327-6929 for BUC Personalized Evaluation Service
Or, for 1975 to 1979 boats, sign onto www.BUCValuPro.com

CARAVELA YACHTS LTD

Call 1-800-327-6929 for BUC Personalized Evaluation Service
Or, for 1979 boats, sign onto www.BUCValuPro.com

CARAVELLE POWERBOATS INC

AMERICUS GA 31709 COAST GUARD MFG ID- VCN See inside cover to adjust price for area
FORMERLY CARAVELLE BOATS INC

For more recent years, see the BUC Used Boat Price Guide, Volume 1 or Volume 2

LOA FT	LOA IN	NAME AND/ OR MODEL	TOP/ RIG	BOAT TYPE	-HULL- MTL	-HULL- TP	ENGINE TP	ENGINE # HP	ENGINE MFG	BEAM FT	BEAM IN	WGT LBS	DRAFT FT	DRAFT IN	RETAIL LOW	RETAIL HIGH
		1975 BOATS														
16	8	STING-RAY CIV-17	ST	RNBT	FBG	DV	IO	140	MRCR	6	11	2000	2	8	2450	2850
16	8	STING-RAY COV-17	ST	RNBT	FBG	DV	OB			6	11	1200			1700	2050
16	9	SHARK CIT-17	ST	RNBT	FBG	TR	IO	120-165		6	8	2050	2	8	2450	2900
17	6	BARRACUDA CIT-18	ST	RNBT	FBG	TR	IO	140-190		7		2300	2	8	2800	3300
17	6	BARRACUDA COT-18	ST	RNBT	FBG	TR	OB			7		1450			2050	2450
18	4	CHIMERA CIV-19	ST	RNBT	FBG	DV	IO	165-233		7	6	2600	2	8	3250	3950
18	4	CHIMERA CIV-19	ST	RNBT	FBG	DV	IO	390	HARD	7	6	2600	2	8	5100	5850
18	4	CHIMERA COV-19	ST	RNBT	FBG	DV	OB			7	6	1800			2450	2850
19		POMPANO CIT-20	ST	RNBT	FBG	TR	IO	188-190		7	6	2700	2	8	3500	4050
19		STRIPER COV-20	ST	OPFSH	FBG	DV	IO			8		1600	2	8	**	**
20	9	OFFSHORE CIV-22	ST	CUD	FBG	DV	IO	188-233		7	11	3500	2	8	4900	5800
20	9	WAHOO CIV-22	ST	CUD	FBG	DV	IO	188-233		7	11	3500	2	8	5500	6450
24		BONITO CIV-24	ST	CUD	FBG	DV	IO	188-233				4000	3		6950	8100
24		BONITO CIV-24	ST	CUD	FBG	DV	IO	T140-T188				4000	3		7650	8900
		1974 BOATS														
16	8	STING-RAY IV			FBG		OB			6	11	1200			1700	2050
16	8	STING-RAY IV			FBG		IO	140-165		6	11	2000	2	8	2450	2850
16	8	STING-RAY IV			FBG		JT	390	HARD	6	11	2000			2450	2850
16	9	SHARK IV			FBG		OB			6	8	1250			1750	2100
16	9	SHARK IV			FBG		IO	140		6	8	2050	2	8	2450	2850
17	6	BARRACUDA IV			FBG		OB			7		1450			2000	2400
17	6	BARRACUDA IV			FBG		IO	165-188		7		2300	2	8	2800	3300
17	6	BARRACUDA IV			FBG		JT	390	HARD	7		2300			2750	3150
18	4	CHIMERA IV			FBG		OB			7	6	1800			2400	2800
18	4	CHIMERA IV			FBG		IO	165-225		7	6	2600	2	8	3300	3900

 CONTINUED ON NEXT PAGE

LOA FT	LOA IN	NAME AND/ OR MODEL	TOP/ RIG	BOAT TYPE	-HULL- MTL	-HULL- TP	ENGINE TP	ENGINE # HP	ENGINE MFG	BEAM FT	BEAM IN	WGT LBS	DRAFT FT	DRAFT IN	RETAIL LOW	RETAIL HIGH
		1974 BOATS														
18	4	CHIMERA IV			FBG		JT	390	HARD	7	6	2600			3150	3650
19		POMPANO IV			FBG		OB			7	6	1800			2450	2900
19		POMPANO IV			FBG		IO	165-225		7	6	2700	2	8	3500	4150
20	9	WAHOO		OVNTR	FBG		IO	165-225		7	11	3500	2	8	5350	6250
20	9	WAHOO	HT	OVNTR	FBG		IO	165-225		7	11	3500	2	8	5350	6250
20	9	WAHOO IV			FBG		IO	165-225		7	11	3500	2	8	5100	5950
24	10	MARLIN IV			FBG		IO	225		8		6200	2	8	10200	11600
24	10	MARLIN IV			FBG		IO	T165-T188		8		6200	2	8	11000	12600
		1973 BOATS														
16	8	STING-RAY II			FBG		OB			6	11	1200			1700	2000
16	8	STING-RAY II			FBG		IO	130-165		6	11	2050			2700	3150
17	6	BARRACUDA II			FBG		OB			7		1450			2000	2400
17	6	BARRACUDA II			FBG		IO	130-165		7		2300			3050	3550
18	2	CHIMERA			FBG		OB			7	6	1800			2400	2800
18	2	CHIMERA			FBG		IO	165-225		7	6	2400			3250	3850
19		POMPANO			FBG		OB			7	6	1800			2450	2850
19		POMPANO			FBG		IO	165-225		7	6	2400			3400	4050
20	9	WAHOO			FBG		IO	165-246		7	11	3200			4950	5900
20	9	WAHOO		CAMPR	FBG		IO	165-246		7	11	3500			5550	6600
		1972 BOATS														
16		STING-RAY CX-162-A			FBG		IO	120	MRCR	6	4	1550			2050	2450
16		STING-RAY CX-162-K			FBG		IO	140	MRCR	6	4	1550			2050	2450
16	11	WHIP-RAY CX-174-A			FBG		IO	120	MRCR	7		1600			2350	2750
16	11	WHIP-RAY CX-174-K			FBG		IO	140	MRCR	7		1600			2400	2800
16	11	WHIP-RAY CX-174-R			FBG		IO	120	OMC	7		1600			2400	2800
17	5	BARRACUDA CX-176-A			FBG		IO	120	MRCR	7		1775			2600	3000
17	5	BARRACUDA CX-176-B			FBG		IO	165	MRCR	7		1775			2600	3050
17	5	BARRACUDA CX-176-K			FBG		IO	140	MRCR	7		1775			2600	3050
17	5	BARRACUDA CX-176-R			FBG		IO	120	OMC	7		1775			2600	3000
17	5	BARRACUDA CX-176-S			FBG		IO	165	OMC	7		1775			2600	3050
18	2	CHIMERA CX-183			FBG		OB			7	6	1600			2250	2600
18	2	CHIMERA CX-184-B			FBG		IO	165	MRCR	7	6	2400			3300	3850
18	2	CHIMERA CX-184-K			FBG		IO	140	MRCR	7	6	2400			3300	3850
18	2	CHIMERA CX-184-P			FBG		IO	188	MRCR	7	6	2400			3350	3900
18	2	CHIMERA CX-184-S			FBG		IO	165	OMC	7	6	2400			3300	3850
18	2	CHIMERA CX-184-T			FBG		IO	225	OMC	7	6	2400			3400	3950
19		POMPANO CX-191			FBG		OB			7	6	1600			2300	2650
19		POMPANO CX-192-B			FBG		IO	165	MRCR	7	6	2400			3500	4050
19		POMPANO CX-192-K			FBG		IO	140	MRCR	7	6	2400			3500	4050
19		POMPANO CX-192-P			FBG		IO	188	MRCR	7	6	2400			3550	4100
19		POMPANO CX-192-S			FBG		IO	165	OMC	7	6	2400			3500	4050
19		POMPANO CX-192-T			FBG		IO	225	OMC	7	6	2400			3600	4150
20	9	WAHOO CX-212-B			FBG		IO	165	MRCR	7	11	3200			5100	5850
20	9	WAHOO CX-212-P			FBG		IO	188	MRCR	7	11	3200			5150	5900
20	9	WAHOO CX-212-S			FBG		IO	165	OMC	7	11	3200			5100	5850
20	9	WAHOO CX-212-T			FBG		IO	225	OMC	7	11	3200			5200	5950
20	9	WAHOO CX-212-U			FBG		IO	245	OMC	7	11	3200			5250	6050
		1971 BOATS														
16		STING-RAY CX-162-A			FBG		IO	120	MRCR	6	4	1550			2150	2500
16	11	WHIP-RAY CX-174-A			FBG		IO	120	MRCR	7		1600			2450	2900
16	11	WHIP-RAY CX-174-C			FBG		IO	120	OMC	7					2750	3200
16	11	WHIP-RAY CX-174-D			FBG		IO	155	OMC	7					2800	3250
16	11	WHIP-RAY CX-174-K			FBG		IO	140	MRCR	7					2800	3250
17	5	BARRACUDA CX-176-A			FBG		IO	120	MRCR	7		1775			2700	3150
17	5	BARRACUDA CX-176-B			FBG		IO	165	MRCR	7					2900	3400
17	5	BARRACUDA CX-176-C			FBG		IO	120	OMC	7					2850	3300
17	5	BARRACUDA CX-176-D			FBG		IO	155	OMC	7					2850	3350
17	5	BARRACUDA CX-176-K			FBG		IO	140	MRCR	7					2900	3350
17	10	MARLIN CX-181			FBG		OB			6	10	1330			1900	2250
20	9	CX-212-B			FBG		IO	165	MRCR	7	11				5100	5850
20	9	WAHOO CX-212-L			FBG		IO	215	MRCR	7	11	2800			4950	5700
20	9	WAHOO CX-212-M			FBG		IO	215	OMC	7	11				5150	5950
20	9	WAHOO CX-212-O			FBG		IO	235	OMC	7	11				5200	6000
		1969 BOATS														
16		STING-RAY CX162		RNBT	FBG	DV	IO	120		6	4	1600			2450	2850
17	5	BARRACUDA CX172		RNBT	FBG	TR	IO	160		7		1900			3100	3600
17	10	MARLIN CX182		RNBT	FBG	DV	IO	160-175		6	10	1900			3100	3650

CARD CRAFT INC

Call 1-800-327-6929 for BUC Personalized Evaluation Service
Or, for 1959 boats, sign onto www.BUCValuPro.com

CARGILE INC

CUTTER BOATS
NASHVILLE TN 37211 COAST GUARD MFG ID- CAR

See inside cover to adjust price for area

LOA FT	LOA IN	NAME AND/ OR MODEL	TOP/ RIG	BOAT TYPE	-HULL- MTL	-HULL- TP	ENGINE TP	ENGINE # HP	ENGINE MFG	BEAM FT	BEAM IN	WGT LBS	DRAFT FT	DRAFT IN	RETAIL LOW	RETAIL HIGH
		1982 BOATS														
30		CUTTER		CR	FBG	DV	IO	260		8		6000			18000	20000
		1981 BOATS														
30		CUTTER	FB	CBNCR	FBG	DV	IO	260	VLVO	8		6000	1	4	23000	25500
		1980 BOATS														
30		CUTTER		CR	FBG	DV	IO	260		8	6	5600			17100	19400
30		CUTTER		CR	FBG	DV	IB	260		8	6	5600			19700	21900
		1979 BOATS														
30		CUTTER	FB	CBNCR	FBG	SV	IO	260	VLVO	8		5400	2	8	22000	24500
		IO 130D VLVO 22600 25100, IO T260 VLVO 22600 25100, IO T130D VLVO													27900	31000
		1978 BOATS														
28		CUTTER		CR	FBG	SV	IO	250		8		5000			13800	15700
28		CUTTER		CR	FBG	SV	IO	T250		8		5000			16400	18600
30		CUTTER	FB	CR	FBG	SV	IO	250-255		8		6700	1	6	18000	20200
30		CUTTER	FB	CR	FBG	SV	IO	T250		8		6700	1	6	20400	22600
		1977 BOATS														
28		CUTTER	FB	CR	FBG	SV	IO	165-225		8		5000	2	10	12900	15600
		IO 300 CC 14600 16500, IO T130-T170 14500 17300, IO T300 CC													17600	20000
28		CUTTER SPORTSMAN	FB	SF	FBG	SV	IO	165-225		8		5000	2	10	14900	17900
		IO 300 CC 16800 19000, IO T130-T170 16600 19900, IO T300 CC													20500	22700
28		SPORTSMAN SPECIAL	FB	CR	FBG	SV	IO	165-225		8		5000	2	10	13200	15900
		IO 300 CC 14900 16900, IO T130-T170 14700 17600, IO T300 CC													18300	20400
30		CUTTER	FB	CR	FBG	SV	IO	250	CC	8		5700	2	10	17300	19600
30		CUTTER	FB	CR	FBG	SV	IO	T250	CC	8		5700	2	10	20200	22500
		1976 BOATS														
28		CUTTER	FB	CR	FBG	SV	IO	165-225		8		5000	2	10	13200	16000
		IO 300 CC 14900 17000, IO T130-T170 14800 17700, IO T300 CC													18500	20500
28		CUTTER SPORTSMAN	FB	SF	FBG	SV	IO	165-225		8		5000	2	10	15200	18400
		IO 300 CC 17200 19500, IO T130-T170 17100 20400, IO T300 CC													21000	23300
28		SPORTSMAN SPECIAL	FB	CR	FBG	SV	IO	165-225		8		5000	2	10	13500	16300
		IO 300 CC 15200 17300, IO T130-T170 15100 18000, IO T300 CC													18800	20900
		1975 BOATS														
28		CUTTER	FB	EXP	FBG	SV	IO	165-255		8		4800	2	10	13400	16600
28		CUTTER	FB	EXP	FBG	SV	IO	300	CC	8		4800	2	10	15200	17300
28		CUTTER	FB	EXP	FBG	SV	IO	T130-T165		8		4800	2	10	14900	17800
28		CUTTER SPORTSMAN	FB	EXP	FBG	SV	IO	165-255		8		4800	2	10	13800	17000
28		CUTTER SPORTSMAN	FB	EXP	FBG	SV	IO	300	CC	8		4800	2	10	15600	17700
28		CUTTER SPORTSMAN	FB	EXP	FBG	SV	IO	T130-T165		8		4800	2	10	15300	18100
		1974 BOATS														
28		CUTTER CRUISER		HB	FBG		IO	165-255		8		4800	2	10	**	**
28		CUTTER CRUISER		HB	FBG		IO	300	CRUS	8		4800	2	10	**	**
28		CUTTER CRUISER		HB	FBG		IO	T130-T165		8		4800	2	10	**	**
		1973 BOATS														
28		CUTTER CRUISER		HB	FBG		IO	165-225		8	10	4800	2	10	**	**
28		CUTTER CRUISER		HB	FBG		IO	300	CRUS	8	10	4800	2	10	**	**
28		CUTTER CRUISER		HB	FBG		IO	T130-T165		8	10	4800	2	10	**	**
		1972 BOATS														
28		CUTTER CRUISER		HB	FBG		IO	165-225		8		4800	2	10	**	**
28		CUTTER CRUISER		HB	FBG		IO	T130-T165		8					**	**
40		SPORTLINER	HT	HB	FBG	FL	IO			13			1	2	27700	30800
46		QUEENLINER	HT	HB	FBG	FL	IO			13			1	2	31500	35000
49		LEISURELINER	HT	HB	FBG	FL	IO			13			1	2	34000	37800
54		FUNLINER	HT	HB	FBG	FL	IO			13			1	2	48600	53400
59		HOMELINER	HT	HB	FBG	FL	IO			15			1	4	50700	55700
		1971 BOATS														
28		CUTTER CRUISER		HB	FBG		IO	225-250		8		4800	2	10	**	**
28		CUTTER CRUISER		HB	FBG		IO	325	MRCR	8			2	2	**	**
28		CUTTER CRUISER		HB	FBG		IO	T120-T225		8			2	2	**	**
40		SPORTLINER		HB	FBG		IO			13			1	2	27500	30500
		IO 120 MRCR 27300 30300, IO 165 MRCR 27300 30400, IO 225 CC													27600	30700
		IO 270 MRCR 28200 31300, IO 325 MRCR 29600 32800, IO T120 MRCR													29200	32500
		IO T165 MRCR 29300 32600, IO T225 CC 29900 33200, IO T270 MRCR													31000	34500
		IO T325 MRCR 33800 37500														
46		QUEENLINER		HB	FBG		IO			13			1	2	31200	34700

CONTINUED ON NEXT PAGE

```
 LOA  NAME AND/      TOP/ BOAT  -HULL- ----ENGINE---  BEAM   WGT  DRAFT RETAIL RETAIL
 FT IN  OR MODEL     RIG  TYPE  MTL TP TP # HP  MFG    FT IN  LBS  FT IN  LOW    HIGH
--------------------- 1971 BOATS ----------------------------------------------------
 46   QUEENLINER         HB    FBG  IO  120   MRCR 13         1 2  31000  34500
      IO 165 MRCR 31100 34600, IO 225  CC  31300 34800, IO 270  MRCR     31800  35400
      IO 325 MRCR 33000 36700, IO T120 MRCR 32700 36400, IO T165 MRCR    32800  36500
      IO T210 MRCR 33200 36800, IO T225 CC  33300 37100, IO T325 MRCR    36700  40800

 49   LEISURELINER       HB    FBG  IO        13             1 2  33700  37500
      IO 120 MRCR 33600 37300, IO 165  MRCR 33600 37300, IO 225  CC      33900  37600
      IO 270 MRCR 34300 38200, IO 325  MRCR 35600 39500, IO T120 MRCR    35300  39200
      IO T165 MRCR 35300 39300, IO T225 CC  35900 39800, IO T270 MRCR    36800  40900
      IO T325 MRCR 39300 43600

 54   FUNLINER           HB    FBG  IO        13             1 2  48200  52900
      IO 120 MRCR 47900 52700, IO 165  MRCR 48000 52800, IO 225  CC      48300  53100
      IO 270 MRCR 48900 53700, IO 325  MRCR 50000 54900, IO T120 MRCR    49600  54500
      IO T165 MRCR 49700 54700, IO T225 CC  50300 55300, IO T270 MRCR    51500  56600
      IO T325 MRCR 53900 59200

 59   HOMELINER          HB    FBG  IO        15             1 4  50300  55200
      IO 120 MRCR 50100 55000, IO 165  MRCR 50100 55100, IO 225  CC      50400  55400
      IO 270 MRCR 51000 56000, IO 325  MRCR 52400 57600, IO T120 MRCR    52000  57200
      IO T165 MRCR 52100 57300, IO T225 CC  52700 57900, IO T270 MRCR    53500  58700
      IO T325 MRCR 56200 61800
--------------------- 1970 BOATS ----------------------------------------------------
 28   CUTTER CRUISER  HT HB  FBG SV IO 120-250     8    6500  2 2   **     **
      IO 325 MRCR ** ** , IO T120-T250 ** ** , IO T325 MRCR  **      **     **

 40   SPORTLINER      HT HB  FBG FL OB        10    8000  1   15200  17300
      IO 120 MRCR 18200 20200, IO 160  MRCR 18200 20200, IO 225  CC      18500  20600
      IO 250 MRCR 18800 20900, IO 325  MRCR 20200 22500, IO T120 MRCR    19900  22100
      IO T160 MRCR 20000 22200, IO T225 CC  20600 22900, IO T250 MRCR    21100  23500
      IO T325 MRCR 23900 26600

 46   QUEENLINER      HT HB  FBG FL OB        10    12000 1   20000  22200
      IO 120 MRCR 22000 24500, IO 160  MRCR 22100 24500, IO 225  CC      22300  24800
      IO 250 MRCR 22600 25100, IO 325  MRCR 23800 26400, IO T120 MRCR    23500  26100
      IO T160 MRCR 23600 26200, IO T225 CC  24100 26800, IO T250 MRCR    24500  27300
      IO T325 MRCR 27500 30500

 47   LEASURELINER    HT HB  FBG FL OB        10    13000 1   21600  24000
      IO 120 MRCR 22600 25100, IO 160  MRCR 22600 25100, IO 225  CC      24100  26700
      IO 250 MRCR 24300 27000, IO 325  MRCR 25800 28600, IO T120 MRCR    25500  28300
      IO T160 MRCR 25500 28400, IO T225 CC  26000 28900, IO T250 MRCR    26500  29400
      IO T325 MRCR 29400 32700

 54   FUNLINER        HT HB  FBG FL OB        10    16000 1   33100  36800
      IO 120 MRCR 36200 40200, IO 160  MRCR 36200 40200, IO 225  CC      36500  40600
      IO 250 MRCR 36800 40900, IO 325  MRCR 38100 42400, IO T120 MRCR    38100  42400
      IO T160 MRCR 38200 42500, IO T225 CC  38500 42800, IO T235 MRCR    38700  43000
      IO T250 MRCR 39000 43400

 59   HOMELINER       HT HB  FBG FL OB        12    26000 1   43000  47800
      IO 120 MRCR 47300 52000, IO 160  MRCR 47400 52000, IO 225  CC      47700  52400
      IO 250 MRCR 47900 52700, IO 325  MRCR 49600 54500, IO T120 MRCR    49300  54200
      IO T160 MRCR 49400 54300, IO T225 CC  49700 54600, IO T250 MRCR    50200  55200
      IO T325 MRCR 53300 58500
--------------------- 1969 BOATS ----------------------------------------------------
 36   PORTLINER       HT HB  FBG    OB        10             1    20900  23200
 36   SPORTLINER      HT HB  FBG    IO 120    10             1    25500  28300
 40   SPORTLINER         HB  FBG FL OB        10    8000     1    15100  17200
      IO 120 18000 20100, IO 160  18100 20100, IO 225  CC          18400  20400
      IO 250 18700 20700, IO 325  20100 22300, IO T120            20000  22300
      IO T160 19800 22000, IO T225 20400 22700, IO T250           21000  23300
      IO T325 23800 26400

 43   QUEENLINER      HT HB  FBG    OB        10             1 1  24000  26700
 43   QUEENLINER      HT HB  FBG    IO 160    10             1 1  28700  31800
 46   QUEENLINER         HB  FBG FL OB        10    12000    1 1  19900  22100
      IO 120 21900 24300, IO 160  21900 24400, IO 225  CC          22200  24600
      IO 250 22400 24900, IO 325  23600 26200, IO T120            23300  25900
      IO T160 23400 26000, IO T225 23900 26600, IO T250           24400  27100
      IO T325 27300 30300

 50   FUNLINER        HT HB  FBG    OB        10             1 2  25300  28100
 50   FUNLINER        HT HB  FBG    IO 210    10             1 2  35000  38900
 53   FUNLINER           HB  FBG FL OB        10    16000    1 2  32300  35900
      IO 120 35300 39300, IO 160  35400 39300, IO 225  CC          35700  39700
      IO 250 36000 40000, IO 325  37700 41800, IO T120            37300  41500
      IO T160 37400 41600, IO T225 38000 42200, IO T250           38200  42400
      IO T325 41300 45900

 57   HOMELINER          HB  FBG FL OB        12    26000    1 2  41700  46300
      IO 120 46000 50500, IO 160  46000 50500, IO 225  CC          46300  50900
      IO 250 46600 51200, IO 325  48300 53000, IO T120            47900  52600
      IO T160 48000 52700, IO T225 48600 53400, IO T250           49100  54000
      IO T325 52200 57300

 57   HOMELINER       HT HB  FBG    IO 210    12             1 6  49400  54300
 57   HOMELINER       HT HB  FBG    IO 250    12             1 6  49800  54700
--------------------- 1968 BOATS ----------------------------------------------------
 34 10 SPORTLINER 190    HB  FBG FL OB        11    8000     1    21200  23500
 34 10 SPORTLINER 190    HB  FBG FL IO 120-250   11  8000    1    23800  26800
 34 10 SPORTLINER 190    HB  FBG FL IO T120-T250 11  8000    1    25800  29700
 42 10 QUEENLINER 260    HB  FBG FL OB        11    12000    1 1  20500  22800
      IO 120 22700 25200, IO T120 22700 25300, IO 210          22900  25500
      IO 250 23300 25800, IO T160 24500 27200, IO T210         24600  27300
      IO T210 25000 27700, IO T250 25700 28500

 49 10 FUNLINER 330      HB  FBG FL OB        13    16000    1 2  25400  28200
      IO 120 28400 31600, IO 160  28500 31600, IO 210          28600  31800
      IO 250 28900 32100, IO T120 30100 33400, IO T160         30200  33500
      IO T210 30500 33900, IO T250 31100 34600

 59 10 HOMELINER CUSTOM  HB  FBG FL IO 120    13    23000    1 6  44500  49500
      IO 160 44400 49500, IO 210  44800 49800, IO 250          45600  50100
      IO T120 46900 51600, IO T160 47000 51700, IO T210        47400  52100
      IO T250 48100 52900
--------------------- 1966 BOATS ----------------------------------------------------
 45   FUNLINER 45     HT HB  FBG FL IO 120    10              10  25100  27900
 56   HOMELINER 56    HT HB  FBG FL IO 120    10             1 9  43700  48600
 70   HOMELINER 70    HT HB  FBG FL IO 120    10             1 9  50500  55400
```

CARGO FISHING BOAT CO

Call 1-800-327-6929 for BUC Personalized Evaluation Service
Or, for 1981 boats, sign onto www.BUCValuPro.com

CARIBBEAN YACHTS
COAST GUARD MFG ID- ZFK

Call 1-800-327-6929 for BUC Personalized Evaluation Service
Or, for 1983 boats, sign onto www.BUCValuPro.com

CARIBE INDUSTRIES INC

Call 1-800-327-6929 for BUC Personalized Evaluation Service
Or, for 1977 to 1993 boats, sign onto www.BUCValuPro.com

CARLSON BOATS

Call 1-800-327-6929 for BUC Personalized Evaluation Service
Or, for 1965 to 1969 boats, sign onto www.BUCValuPro.com

RICHARD D CARLSON

Call 1-800-327-6929 for BUC Personalized Evaluation Service
Or, for 1959 to 1977 boats, sign onto www.BUCValuPro.com

SUNE CARLSSON

Call 1-800-327-6929 for BUC Personalized Evaluation Service
Or, for 1977 to 1978 boats, sign onto www.BUCValuPro.com

CAROLINA YACHTS
STRANDBERG ENGR LABS IN COAST GUARD MFG ID- CYS

Call 1-800-327-6929 for BUC Personalized Evaluation Service
Or, for 1981 boats, sign onto www.BUCValuPro.com

CAROLINE BOAT WORKS INC

Call 1-800-327-6929 for BUC Personalized Evaluation Service
Or, for 1959 to 1960 boats, sign onto www.BUCValuPro.com

CARRERA POWERBOAT CORP
MIAMI FL 33166   COAST GUARD MFG ID- CBC See inside cover to adjust price for area

For more recent years, see the BUC Used Boat Price Guide, Volume 1 or Volume 2

LOA FT IN	NAME AND/ OR MODEL	TOP/ RIG	BOAT TYPE	-HULL- MTL TP	ENGINE TP # HP	MFG	BEAM FT IN	WGT LBS	DRAFT FT IN	RETAIL LOW	RETAIL HIGH
---	--- 1982 BOATS										
23 8	CARRERA SS7M	OP	OFF	FBG DV	OB		7		1 6	5750	6600
29 7	CARRERA SS9M	OP	OFF	FBG DV	IB T350	CRUS	8	7000		23900	26500
29 10	CARRERA SS9M	OP	OFF	FBG DV	IO T260-T370		8	7500		19200	23600
29 10	CARRERA SS9M	OP	OFF	FBG DV	IO T400	MRCR	8	7500		22000	24400
29 10	CARRERA SS9M	OP	OFF	FBG DV	IB T240D REN		8	7500		29900	33200
35 8	COREICA 36	OP	OFF	FBG DV	IO T330	MRCR	8 6	8500		38600	42900
	IB T350 CRUS 46800		51400, IO	T370	MRCR	40100 44500,	IO T400	MRCR	41400	46000	
	IB T240D REN 53900		59200								
39	CARRERA SS12M	OP	OFF	FBG DV	IO T330	MRCR	9 8	10000		40600	45100
39	CARRERA SS12M	OP	OFF	FBG DV	IO T370	MRCR	9 8	10000		42500	47300
39	CARRERA SS12M	OP	OFF	FBG DV	IO T400	MRCR	9 8	10000		44400	49300
39 2	CARRERA SS12M	OP	OFF	FBG DV	IB T240D REN		9 8	10000		72100	79200
---	--- 1981 BOATS										
23 8	CARRERA SS7M	OP	OFF	FBG DV	OB		7		1 6	5600	6450
23 8	CARRERA SS7M	OP	OFF	FBG DV	IO 260	MRCR	7	4500	1 6	8150	9350
	IO 330-370 8950		11000, IO	400	MRCR	10400 11800,	IO T170-T260		8800	10700	
29 7	CARRERA SS9M	OP	OFF	FBG DV	IO T350	CRUS	8	7000		19700	21900
29 10	CARRERA SS9M	OP	OFF	FBG DV	IO T260-T370		8	7500		19100	23200
29 10	CARRERA SS9M	OP	OFF	FBG DV	IO T400	MRCR	8	7500		21600	24000
29 10	CARRERA SS9M	OP	OFF	FBG DV	IO T240D REN		8	7500		22200	24700
35 8	CORSICA 36	OP	OFF	FBG DV	IO T330	MRCR	8 6	8500		38000	42200
	IO T350 CRUS 38700		43000, IO	T370	MRCR	39400 43800,	IO T400	MRCR	40800	45300	
	IO T240D REN 39800		44200								
39	CARRERA SS12M	OP	OFF	FBG DV	IO T330	MRCR	9 8	10000		39900	44400
39	CARRERA SS12M	OP	OFF	FBG DV	IO T370	MRCR	9 8	10000		41900	46500
39	CARRERA SS12M	OP	OFF	FBG DV	IO T400	MRCR	9 8	10000		43700	48500
39 2	CARRERA SS12M	OP	OFF	FBG DV	IO T240D REN		9 8	10000		49200	54000
---	--- 1980 BOATS										
23 8	CARRERA SS7M	OP	OFF	FBG DV	IO 260	MRCR	7	4500	1 6	8050	9250
23 8	CARRERA SS7M	OP	OFF	FBG DV	IO 330-370		7	4500	1 6	8900	10900
23 8	CARRERA SS7M	OP	OFF	FBG DV	IO T170-T260		7	4500	1 6	8650	10600
29 10	CARRERA SS9M	OP	OFF	FBG DV	IO T260-T370		8	7500		18900	23000
29 10	CARRERA SS9M	OP	OFF	FBG DV	IO T400	MRCR	8	7500		21400	23900
29 10	CARRERA SS9M	OP	OFF	FBG DV	IO T D REN		8	7500		**	**
39 2	CARRERA SS12M	OP	OFF	FBG DV	IO T D REN		9 8	10000		**	**
---	--- 1979 BOATS										
23 8	CARRERA SS7M	OP	OFF	FBG DV	IO 330	MRCR	7 1	4500	1 6	8900	10100
---	--- 1978 BOATS										
23 8	CARRERA SS7M	OP	SPTCR	FBG DV	IO 260	MRCR	7 1	4200	1 6	7700	8850
23 8	CARRERA SS7M	OP	SPTCR	FBG DV	IO 330	MRCR	7 1	4200	1 6	8450	9700
23 8	CARRERA SS7M	OP	SPTCR	FBG DV	IO T165	MRCR	7 1	4200	1 6	8250	9500

CARRI-CRAFT CATAMARANS INC
WAUWATOSA WI 53226-3439 COAST GUARD MFG ID- CRR See inside cover to adjust price for area
FORMERLY CARRI-CRAFT INC

For more recent years, see the BUC Used Boat Price Guide, Volume 1 or Volume 2

LOA FT IN	NAME AND/ OR MODEL	TOP/ RIG	BOAT TYPE	-HULL- MTL TP	ENGINE TP # HP	MFG	BEAM FT IN	WGT LBS	DRAFT FT IN	RETAIL LOW	RETAIL HIGH
---	--- 1975 BOATS										
45	CRUIS-ADER	HB	FBG	CT IB T215	14 2				3 6	37300	41500
45	CRUIS-ADER	HB	FBG	CT IB T225	14 2				3 6	38700	41500
45	CRUIS-ADER	HB	FBG	CT IB T350	14 2				3 6	39300	43700
45	SPORT FISHER	SF	FBG	CT IB T215	14 2					49400	54300
57	CRUIS-ADER	HB	FBG	CT IB T225	14 2				3 6	60500	66500
57	CRUIS-ADER	HB	FBG	CT IB T270	14 2				3 6	60900	66900
57	CRUIS-ADER	HB	FBG	CT IB T350	14 2				3 6	62500	68700
57	SPORT FISHER	SF	FBG	CT IB T270	14 2					79300	87100
---	--- 1974 BOATS										
45	CARRI-CRAFT FISHDECK	HB	FBG	CT IB T215	14			25000	3 8	47800	52600
45	CARRI-CRAFT FISHDECK	HB	FBG	CT IB T185D PERK	14			25000	3 8	57100	62700
45	CARRI-CRAFT FULL CBN	HB	FBG	CT IB T215	14			28000	3 8	50000	55000
45	CARRI-CRAFT FULL CBN	HB	FBG	CT IB T185D PERK	14			28000	3 8	59300	65100
57	CARRI-CRAFT FISHDECK	HB	FBG	CT IB T270	14			35000	3 8	**	**
57	CARRI-CRAFT FISHDECK	HB	FBG	CT IB T185D PERK	14			35000	3 8	**	**
57	CARRI-CRAFT FULL CBN	HB	FBG	CT IB T270	14			38000	3 8	**	**
57	CARRI-CRAFT FULL CBN	HB	FBG	CT IB T185D PERK	14			38000	3 8	**	**
---	--- 1973 BOATS										
45	CRUIS-ADER	HB	FBG	CT IB T185D	14			25000	3 8	54900	60300
45	SPORT FISHER	SF	FBG	CT IB T215	14 2					45600	50200
57	CRUIS-ADER	HB	FBG	CT IB T185D	14			35000	3 8	**	**
57	SPORT FISHER	SF	FBG	CT IB T270	14 2					73400	80600
---	--- 1972 BOATS										
45	CRUIS-ADER	HB	FBG	CT IB T185D	14			25000	3 8	54400	59800
45	CRUIS-ADER	MY	FBG	CT IB T215	12					43700	48600
45	CRUIS-ADER	MY	FBG	CT IB T325	12					44800	49800
45	CRUIS-ADER	MY	FBG	CT IB T D	12					**	**
45	CRUIS-ADER	SF	FBG	CT IB T215	12					44600	49600
45	CRUIS-ADER	SF	FBG	CT IB T325	12					46100	50700
45	CRUIS-ADER	SF	FBG	CT IB T D	12					**	**
57	SPORT FISHER	SF	FBG	CT IB T185D PERK	14			35000	3 8	43500	48300
57	CRUIS-ADER	MY	FBG	CT IB T215	12					66000	72600
	IB T270 66200		72800, IB	T325		66700 73200,	IB T D		**	**	
57	CRUIS-ADER	SF	FBG	CT IB T215	12					68200	75000
	IB T270 70000		77000, IB	T325		71400 78500,	IB T D		**	**	
57	SPORT FISHER	SF	FBG	CT IB T270	14 2					70700	77700
---	--- 1971 BOATS										
45	CRUIS-ADER	HB	FBG	CT IB T185D	14			25000	3 8	54000	59300
45	SPORT FISHER	SF	FBG	CT IB T215	14 2					41900	46600
57	CRUIS-ADER	HB	FBG	CT IB T185D	14			35000	3 8	**	**
57	SPORT FISHER	SF	FBG	CT IB T270	14 2					68200	75000
---	--- 1970 BOATS										
45	2 CASA-RIO-Y-MAR	HB	FBG	IB T215	MRCR 12		9 18000		3 6	39500	43900
	IB T250 MRCR 39700		44100, IB	T300	CHRY	40000 45400,	IB T325	MRCR	40800	45300	
57	CASA-GRANDE	HB	FBG	IB T250	MRCR 12		9 22000		3 6	51200	56200
	IB T270 MRCR 51500		56600, IB	T300	CHRY	51200 56300,	IB T325	MRCR	52000	57100	
	IB T160D PERK 58700		64500								
---	--- 1969 BOATS										
44	CASA-EL-HOMBRE	HB	FBG	PN IB T210	CHRY 12			17000	2	31900	35500
44	CASA-RIO-Y-MAR	HB	FBG	PN IB T210	CHRY 12			17000	2	44100	49000
44	CASA-SEGUNDA	HB	FBG	PN IB T210	CHRY 12			17000	2	37100	41200
56	CASA-GRANDE	HB	FBG	PN IB T210	CHRY 12			21000	2	49400	54300
---	--- 1968 BOATS										
42		CR		CR	FBG CT IO T160	12		16000	2 10	56800	62400
42		FB	CR	FBG CT IO T160	12			16000	2 10	56800	62400
42		HB		STL CT OB			10	6500	1 10	11400	13000
42	OCEANAIRE	HB	FBG	CT IO T120	10			8400	1 10	20900	23200
42	OCEANAIRE	HB	FBG	CT IO T120	10			8400	1 10	20900	23200
52	CONTINENTAL	HB	STL	CT IO T120	10			13500	1 10	36200	40300
54	CONTINENTAL	CR	FBG	CT IO T210	12			22000	2 10	46100	50700
54	CONTINENTAL	HB	STL	CT IO T160	10			14000	1 10	38300	42600
---	--- 1967 BOATS										
42		CR		CR	FBG CT IO T160				16000		52900	58200
42		FB	CR	FBG CT IO T160				16000		53100	58300
54		CR		CR	FBG CT IO T210				22000		43900	48800
54	CUSTOM CRUISER	CR	FBG	IB T225	14				2	47300	52000
---	--- 1966 BOATS										
42	OCEANAIRE	HT	HB	STL CT IO T110	10			8400	1 3	20700	23000
52	CONTINENTAL	HT	STL	CT IO T110	10			13500	1 3	35800	39700
54	CONTINENTAL	HT	STL	CT IO T150	10			14000	1 3	37800	42000
---	--- 1960 BOATS										
30	CATAMARAN HOUSEBOAT	HT	HB	STL	OB		8	3200	1 8	5050	5800

CARTER CRAFT CORP

Call 1-800-327-6929 for BUC Personalized Evaluation Service
Or, for 1960 to 1961 boats, sign onto www.BUCValuPro.com

CARTER MARINE INC
COSTA MESA CA 92627   COAST GUARD MFG ID- CMX See inside cover to adjust price for area

FT	IN	NAME AND/OR MODEL	TOP/RIG	BOAT TYPE	HULL MTL	TP	ENG TP	#	HP	MFG	BEAM FT IN	WGT LBS	DRAFT FT IN	RETAIL LOW	RETAIL HIGH
		1974 BOATS													
28	3	SAFARI 28			FBG		IO		T		8	6700	1 7	**	**
		1973 BOATS													
28	3	SAFARI 28			FBG		IO		T		8		1 7	**	**
		1972 BOATS													
28	3	SAFARI 28			FBG		IO		T		8		1 7	**	**

CARTER OFFSHORE INC
NAHANT MA 01908   COAST GUARD MFG ID- CTR See inside cover to adjust price for area

FT	IN	NAME AND/OR MODEL	TOP/RIG	BOAT TYPE	HULL MTL	TP	ENG TP	#	HP	MFG	BEAM FT IN	WGT LBS	DRAFT FT IN	RETAIL LOW	RETAIL HIGH
		1976 BOATS													
29	9	CARTER 30	SLP	SAIL	FBG	KL	IB		10D		10 1	7300	5	17500	19900
32	7	CARTER 33	SLP	SAIL	FBG	KL	IB		D		11	8000	5 6	19800	22000
32	9	CARTER 3/4 TON	SLP	SAIL	FBG	KL	IB		D		11 2	10910	6	26900	29900
37		CARTER 37	SLP	SAIL	FBG	KL	IB		35D		11 11	15300	6 4	38100	42300
37		CARTER ONE TON	SLP	SAIL	FBG	KL	IB		D		11 9	15300	6 3	38100	42300
39		CARTER 39	SLP	SAIL	FBG	KL	IB		35D		12 9	18500	6 9	47600	52400
40	11	CARTER TWO TON	SLP	SAIL	FBG	KL	IB		D		12 3	18800	6 11	51900	57000
		1975 BOATS													
29	9	CARTER 30	SLP	SAIL	FBG	KL	IB		10D	YAN	10 1	7300	5	17000	19400
32	7	CARTER 33	SLP	SAIL	FBG	KL	IB		10D	VLVO	11	8000	5 6	19200	21300
32	9	CARTER 3/4 TON	SLP	SAIL	FBG	KL	IB		20D	VLVO	11 2	10910	6	26100	29000
35	8	TEXAS 1 TON	SLP	SAIL	FBG	KL	IB		27D	PISC	11 8	14200	6 3	33700	37500
37		CARTER 37	SLP	SAIL	FBG	KL	HD		37D	WEST	11 11	15300	6 4	37100	41200
39		CARTER 39	SLP	SAIL	FBG	KL	HD		37D	WEST	12 9	18500	6 9	46400	51000
		1974 BOATS													
32	7	CARTER 33	SLP	SAIL	FBG	KL	IB		25D	VLVO	11	8000	5 6	18900	21000
37		CARTER ONE TON	SLP	SAIL	FBG	KL	IB		50D	PERK	11 9	15300	6 4	33900	39900
39		CARTER 39	SLP	SAIL	FBG	KL	IB		37D	WEST	12 9	18500	6 9	44700	49600
		1973 BOATS													
32	7	CARTER 33	SLP	SAIL	FBG	KL	IB		10D	VLVO	11	8000	5 6	18400	20500
37		CARTER ONE TON	SLP	SAIL	FBG	KL	IB		35D	PERK	11 9	15300	6 4	35000	38900
39		CARTER 39	SLP	SAIL	FBG	KL	IB		35D	PERK	12 9	18500	6 9	43300	48100
42		CARTER 42	SLP	SAIL	FBG	KL	IB		D		12 5		6 10	50100	55100
		1972 BOATS													
32	7	CARTER 33	SLP	SAIL	FBG		IB		25D	VLVO	11	8000	5 6	18000	20000

CARTER OFFSHORE LTD
Call 1-800-327-6929 for BUC Personalized Evaluation Service
Or, for 1981 to 1986 boats, sign onto www.BUCValuPro.com

R S CARTER YACHT CO INC
Call 1-800-327-6929 for BUC Personalized Evaluation Service
Or, for 1970 boats, sign onto www.BUCValuPro.com

J B CARTWRIGHT CUSTOM YTS
Call 1-800-327-6929 for BUC Personalized Evaluation Service
Or, for 1976 to 1981 boats, sign onto www.BUCValuPro.com

CARVER BOAT CORPORATION
PULASKI WI 54162   COAST GUARD MFG ID- CDR See inside cover to adjust price for area

For more recent years, see the BUC Used Boat Price Guide, Volume 1 or Volume 2

FT	IN	NAME AND/OR MODEL	TOP/RIG	BOAT TYPE	HULL MTL	TP	ENG TP	#	HP	MFG	BEAM FT IN	WGT LBS	DRAFT FT IN	RETAIL LOW	RETAIL HIGH
		1983 BOATS													
23		MONTEREY 2357	OP	EXP	FBG	SV	IO		225	VLVO	8	4000	2 10	7550	8650
25	8	MONTEREY 2687	OP	EXP	FBG	SV	IO		225-260		8	5300	2 10	9800	11500
25	8	MONTEREY 2687	OP	EXP	FBG	SV	VD		270	CRUS	8	5300	2 10	12300	14000
25	8	MONTEREY 2687	OP	EXP	FBG	SV	IO		130D	VLVO	8	5300	2 10	10700	12200
25	8	SANTA-CRUZ 2667	FB	CBNCR	FBG	SV	IO		225-260		8	5400	2 10	11100	12800
25	8	SANTA-CRUZ 2667	FB	CBNCR	FBG	SV	VD		270	CRUS	8	5400	2 10	12600	14300
25	8	SANTA-CRUZ 2667	FB	CBNCR	FBG	SV	IO		130D	VLVO	8	5400	2 10	13500	15300
28		AFT-CABIN 2807	ST	CR	FBG	SV	IB		350	CRUS	11 1		2 10	22400	24900
		IB 158D VLVO 27800 30900, IB T220-T250 23400 26300, IB T158D VLVO 31800 35300													
28		MARINER 2897	FB	SDN	FBG	SV	IB		350	CRUS	11 1	10300	2 10	22500	25000
		IB 158D VLVO 29700 33000, IB T220-T250 23500 26500, IB T158D VLVO 33800 37600													
32		AFT-CABIN 3207	FB	MY	FBG	SV	IB		225D	PCM	11 7	12000	2 10	36400	40400
32		AFT-CABIN 3207	FB	MY	FBG	SV	IB		T250-T270		11 7	12000	2 10	34500	35500
32		AFT-CABIN 3207	FB	MY	FBG	SV	IB		T158D	VLVO	11 7	12000	2 10	38500	42700
32	9	MARINER 3396	FB	SDN	FBG	SV	VD		T250-T270		12	11620	3 2	32800	
32	9	MARINER 3396	FB	SDN	FBG	SV	IB		T155D	VLVO	12	11620	3 3	34300	38100
35	7	AFT CABIN 3607	FB	MY	FBG	SV	IB		225D	CRUS	12 6	18500	3 2	50400	55400
		IB 235D VLVO 50200 55200, IB T350 CRUS 44700 49700, IB T225D CRUS 44500 49400													
		1982 BOATS													
23		MONTEGO 2357	OP	CR	FBG	SV	IO		185-260		8	4000	2 10	6650	8200
25	8	MONTEREY 2687	OP	EXP	FBG	SV	IO		225-260		8	5300	2 10	9600	11200
25	8	MONTEREY 2687	OP	EXP	FBG	SV	VD		270	CRUS	8	5300	2 10	11800	13400
25	8	MONTEREY 2687	OP	EXP	FBG	SV	IO		130D	VLVO	8	5300	2 10	10500	11900
25	8	MONTEREY 2687	HT	EXP	FBG	SV	IO		225-260		8	5300	2 10	9600	11200
25	8	MONTEREY 2687	HT	EXP	FBG	SV	VD		270	CRUS	8	5300	2 10	11800	13400
25	8	MONTEREY 2687	HT	EXP	FBG	SV	IO		130D	VLVO	8	5300	2 10	10500	11900
25	8	SANTA-CRUZ 2667	FB	CBNCR	FBG	SV	IO		225-260		8	5400	2 10	10800	12500
25	8	SANTA-CRUZ 2667	FB	CBNCR	FBG	SV	VD		270	CRUS	8	5400	2 10	12000	13700
25	8	SANTA-CRUZ 2667	FB	CBNCR	FBG	SV	IO		130D	VLVO	8	5400	2 10	13200	15000
28	4	MARINER 2896	FB	SDN	FBG	SV	IO		225	VLVO	10 4	8320	2 11	13600	15400
		IO 250 PCM 13700 15600, VD 250 PCM 16700 18900, IO T220 CRUS 21100													
		VD T220 CRUS 19100 21200, IO T225 VLVO 15500 17700, VD T330 MRCR 19800 22100													
28	4	SANTA-CRUZ 2866	FB	CBNCR	FBG	SV	VD		250	PCM	10 4	7630	3 4	17000	19400
		IB T220 18800 20800, IO T225 VLVO 15900 18100, IB T124D VLVO 25700 28600													
29	10	AFT-CABIN 3007	FB	SDN	FBG	SV	IB		124D	VLVO	11 4	10500	2 10	28300	31400
29	10	AFT-CABIN 3007	FB	SDN	FBG	SV	IB		T165-T220		11 4	10500	2 10	23900	27800
29	10	SEDAN 3027	HT	SDN	FBG	SV	IB		T	PCM	11 4	10100	2 10	**	**
		IB T170-T220 24900 29000, IB T124D VLVO 32400 36000, VD T124D VLVO 36300 36300													
29	10	SEDAN 3027	FB	SDN	FBG	SV	IB		220	CRUS	11 4	10100	2 10	23200	25800
		IB T170-T250 24900 29700, IB T124D VLVO 32400 36000, VD T124D VLVO 36300 36300													
32	9	MARINER 3396	FB	SDN	FBG	SV	VD		T250-T270		12	11620	3 3	27800	31400
32	9	MARINER 3396	FB	SDN	FBG	SV	IB		T124D	VLVO	12	11620	3 3	31800	35300
35	7	AFT CABIN 3607	FB	MY	FBG	SV	IB		225	CRUS	12 6	18500	3 3	47800	43100
		IB T350 CRUS 42800 47500, IB T225D CRUS 52500 57700, IB T225D PCM 52500 57700													
		IB T250D CRUS 53400 58700													
		1981 BOATS													
23		MONTEGO 2357	OP	CR	FBG	SV	IO		185-260		8	4000	2 10	6550	8050
23		MONTEGO 2357	OP	CR	FBG	SV	IO		130D	VLVO	8	4000	2 10	7950	9150
25		OFFSHORE 2347	OP	OFF	FBG	SV	IO		225-260		8	4000	2 10	7900	8050
25	8	MONTEREY 2687	OP	EXP	FBG	SV	IO		225-260		8	5300	2 10	9450	11000
25	8	MONTEREY 2687	OP	EXP	FBG	SV	VD		270	CRUS	8	5300	2 10	11300	12800
25	8	MONTEREY 2687	OP	EXP	FBG	SV	IO		130D	VLVO	8	5300	2 10	10300	11700
25	8	MONTEREY 2687	HT	EXP	FBG	SV	IO		225-260		8	5300	2 10	9600	11100
25	8	MONTEREY 2687	HT	EXP	FBG	SV	VD		270	CRUS	8	5300	2 10	11300	12800
25	8	SANTA-CRUZ 2667	FB	CBNCR	FBG	SV	IO		225-260		8	5400	2 10	10600	12300
25	8	SANTA-CRUZ 2667	FB	CBNCR	FBG	SV	VD		270	CRUS	8	5400	2 10	13100	13100
28	4	MARINER 2896	FB	SDN	FBG	SV	IO		255-270		10 4	8320		16000	18400
28	4	MARINER 2896	FB	SDN	FBG	SV	IB		T220-T330		10 4	8320	2 11	18300	21300
28	4	SANTA-CRUZ 2866	FB	CBNCR	FBG	SV	VD		255-270		10 4	7630	3 4	16400	18900
		IB T220 CRUS 17600 20000, IO T225 VLVO 15700 17800, IB T228-T302 17500 20100													
29	10	AFT-CABIN 3007	FB	SDN	FBG	SV	IB		124D	VLVO	11 4	10500	2 10	27200	30200
		IB T PCM ** **, IB T165-T270 22900 27800, IB T350-T470 26400 30400													
		IB T124D VLVO 30300 33700													
32	9	MARINER 3396	FB	SDN	FBG	SV	IB		T250	PCM	12	11620	3 3	26600	29600
32	9	MARINER 3396	FB	SDN	FBG	SV	VD		T250-T270		12	11620	3 3	26700	30000
32	9	MARINER 3396	FB	SDN	FBG	SV	IB		T124D	VLVO	12	11620	3 3	30600	34000
32	9	VOYAGER 3326	FB	SDN	FBG	SV	VD		T250-T270		12	12600	3 3	26500	29900
32	9	VOYAGER 3326	FB	SDN	FBG	SV	IB		T124D	VLVO	12	12600	3 3	31200	34600
		1980 BOATS													
23		MONTEGO 2357	OP	CR	FBG	SV	IO		225-260		8	4000	2 10	6750	8000
23		MONTEGO 2357	OP	CR	FBG	SV	IO		130D		8	4000	2 10	8200	9400
25		OFFSHORE 2347	OP	OFF	FBG	SV	IO		225-260		8	4000	2 10	6950	8200
25		OFFSHORE 2347	OP	OFF	FBG	SV	IO		130D	VLVO	8	4000	2 10	8100	9300
25	8	MONTEREY 2687	OP	EXP	FBG	SV	IO		225-260		8	5300	2 10	9400	10900
25	8	MONTEREY 2687	OP	EXP	FBG	SV	IB		85D	PERK	8	5300		12700	14400

```
LOA   NAME AND/        TOP/ BOAT -HULL- ----ENGINE--- BEAM  WGT  DRAFT RETAIL RETAIL
FT IN OR MODEL         RIG  TYPE MTL TP TP # HP MFG   FT IN LBS  FT IN LOW    HIGH
------------------ 1980 BOATS ----------------------------------------------------
25 8 MONTEREY 2687        OP  EXP   FBG SV IO 130D VLVO      5300         10400 11900
25 8 SANTA-CRUZ 2667      FB  CBNCR FBG SV IO 225-260  8     5400  2 10  10500 12200
     IB 270    11000 12500, IB  85D PERK 12900 14600, IO 130D        13100 14900

26   EXPRESS              EXP FBG SV IO 225       8  5175          7800  8950
26   EXPRESS              EXP FBG SV IB 270       8  5175          9150 10400
26   EXPRESS              EXP FBG SV IO 130D      8  5175          8600  9850
28 4 MARINER 2896    FB SDN   FBG SV IB T220-T225  10 4 8320 2 11 17100 19600
28 4 MARINER 2896    FB SDN   FBG SV IB T130D PERK 10 4 8320 2 11 23500 26100
28 4 SANTA-CRUZ 2866 FB CBNCR FBG SV IB T220-T225  10 4 7630 3  4 16800 19200
28 4 SANTA-CRUZ 2866 FB CBNCR FBG SV IBT124D-T130D 10 4 7630 3  4 23800 27400
28 4 VOYAGER 2826    FB SDN   FBG SV IB T220-T225  10 4 9000 2 11 18800 21000
28 4 VOYAGER 2826    FB SDN   FBG SV IB T130D PERK 10 4 9000 3  5 25700 28500
32 9 MARINER 3396    FB SDN   FBG SV IB T250-T270  12   11620 3 3 25600 20000
32 9 MARINER 3396    FB SDN   FBG SV IBT124D-T130D 12   11620 3 3 29400 33100

32 9 VOYAGER 3326    FB SDN   FBG SV IB T250-T270  12   12600 3 3 25500 28600
32 9 VOYAGER 3326    FB SDN   FBG SV IBT124D-T130D 12   12600 3 3 30000 33700
------------------ 1979 BOATS ----------------------------------------------------
23   MONTEGO 2357     FB CR    FBG SV IO 225-260      8 4000 2 10  6750  7950
23   MONTEGO 2357     OP CR    FBG SV IO 130D VLVO    8 4000 1  3  7850  9050
25 2 MONTEREY 2586    ST EXP   FBG SV IO 225-260      8 5175 1  3  8850 10300
25 2 MONTEREY 2586    ST EXP   FBG SV IO 130D VLVO    8 5175 1  3  9750 11100
25 2 MONTEREY 2586    HT EXP   FBG SV IO 225-260      8 5175 1  3  8850 10300
25 2 MONTEREY 2586    HT EXP   FBG SV IO 130D VLVO    8 5175 1  3  9750 11100
25 2 SANTA-CRUZ 2566  FB CBNCR FBG SV IO 225-260      8 5250 1  3 10900 12600
25 2 SANTA-CRUZ 2566  FB CBNCR FBG SV IO 130D VLVO    8 5250 1  3 13500 15300
28 4 MARINER 2896     FB SDN   FBG SV VD 270  CRUS 10 4 8320 3  4 14900 16900
28 4 MARINER 2896     FB SDN   FBG SV IO 330  MRCR 10 4 8320 3  5 14200 16100
28 4 MARINER 2896     FB SDN   FBG SV    T220      10 4 8800 2 11 16800 19000

28 4 SANTA-CRUZ 2866  FB CBNCR FBG SV VD 270  CRUS 10 4 8000 3  4 15500 17600
     IO 330 MRCR 15600 17700, VD T220 17100 19500, VD T130D VLVO 24500

28 4 VOYAGER 2826     FB SDN   FBG SV IO 330  MRCR 10 4 9000 3  5 15300 17400
28 4 VOYAGER 2826     FB SDN   FBG SV VD T220      10 4 9000 2 11 18000 20100
32 9 MARINER 3396     FB SDN   FBG SV VD T255-T270 12   11620 3  3 24500 27600
32 9 VOYAGER 3326     FB SDN   FBG SV VD T255-T270 12   12600 3  3 24400 27500
------------------ 1978 BOATS ----------------------------------------------------
22 2 CAMPER 2276      ST CAMPR FBG SV IO 185-240     8 3420         5900  6950
22 2 CAMPER 2276      HT CAMPR FBG SV IO 185-240     8 3420         5900  6950
25 2 RANGER 2546      ST CBNCR FBG SV IO 228-260     8 4500         8300  9750
25 2 RANGER 2546      ST CBNCR FBG SV IO 130D VLVO   8 4500        10500 11900
25 2 RANGER 2546      ST CBNCR FBG SV IO T140        8 4500         8900 10100
25 2 RANGER 2546      HT CBNCR FBG SV IO 228-260     8 4500         8300  9750
25 2 RANGER 2546      HT CBNCR FBG SV IO 130D VLVO   8 4500        10500 11900
25 2 RANGER 2546      HT CBNCR FBG SV IO T140        8 4500         8900 11300
25 2 SANTA-CRUZ 2566  FB CBNCR FBG SV IO 228-260     8 4860        12900 14600
28 4 MARINER 2896     FB SDN   FBG SV IO 228  MRCR 10 4 8320       14800 16800
     VD 270 CRUS 15200 17300, IO 330 MRCR 16100 18300, VD T215-T220 16200 18500

28 4 SANTA-CRUZ 2866  FB CBNCR FBG SV IO 228  MRCR 10 4 7630       14200 16100
     VD 270 CRUS 14600 16600, IO 330 MRCR 15400 17500, VD 192D VLVO 20100 22400
     IB T215-T225 15400 17700, VD T125D VLVO 22100 24500

28 4 VOYAGER 2826     FB CBNCR FBG SV VD T215-T220 10 4 9000       18000 20100
32 9 MARINER 3396     FB CBNCR FBG SV VD T250-T270 12   11620      25000 27800
32 9 VOYAGER 3326     FB CBNCR FBG SV VD T250-T270 12   12600      24900 28000
------------------ 1977 BOATS ----------------------------------------------------
22 2 CAMPER 2276      ST CAMPR FBG SV IO 175-235      8 3420 1 3  6000  7100
22 2 CAMPER 2276      HT CAMPR FBG SV IO 175-235      8 3420 1 3  6000  7100
25 4 CAMPER 2576      ST CAMPR FBG SV IO 188-240      8 4600 1 3  7200  8750
25 4 CAMPER 2576      HT CAMPR FBG SV IO 188-240      8 4600 1 3  7200  8750
25 4 RANGER 2546      ST CR    FBG SV IO 188-240      8 4500 1 3  6900  8350
25 4 RANGER 2546      HT CR    FBG SV IO 188-240      8 4500 1 3  6900  8350
25 4 SANTA-CRUZ 2566  FB CR    FBG SV IO 233-240      8 4860 1 3  8850 10300
28 4 MARINER 2896     FB SDN   FBG SV IO 255  MRCR 10 4 8020 1 7 12500 14300
28 4 MARINER 2896     FB SDN   FBG SV IB T215-T233 10 4 8320 2 6 13700 15700
28 4 SANTA-CRUZ 2866  FB SDN   FBG SV IO 255  MRCR 10 4 7300 2 6 11900 13500
28 4 SANTA-CRUZ 2866  FB CR    FBG SV IB 255  PCM  10 4 7200 2 6 11600 13200
28 4 SANTA-CRUZ 2866  FB CR    FBG SV IB T215-T233 10 4 7630 2 6 13100 15000

32 9 MARINER 3396     FB CR    FBG SV IB T233-T255 12   11620 2 3 20600 23200
33   VOYAGER          FB SPTCR FBG SV IB T233      12         19700 21900
------------------ 1976 BOATS ----------------------------------------------------
22 2 CAMPER 2276      OP    FBG SV IO 175-235        8 3420 1 3  6150  7300
22 2 CAMPER 2276      HT    FBG SV IO 175-235        8 3420 1 3  6150  7300
25   MONTEREY 2585    HT CR FBG SV IO 188-235        8 4590 1 3  8850 10300
25   SANTA-CRUZ 2565  FB CR FBG SV IO 188-235        8 4610 1 3  8550 10100
28 4 MARINER 2896     FB CR FBG SV IO 255  MRCR   10 4 8320 1 7 13100 14900
28 4 MARINER 2896     FB CR FBG SV IB T215-T233   10 4 8320 2 6 13100 15100
28 4 SANTA-CRUZ 2866  FB CR FBG SV IO 255  MRCR   10 4 7630 1 7 12400 14100
28 4 SANTA-CRUZ 2866  FB CR FBG SV IB T215-T230   10 4 7630 2 6 12500 14500
32 6 MARINER 3395     FB CR FBG SV VD T233-T255   12   11220 2 3 18700 21000
32 6 MONTEREY 3385    HT CR FBG SV IB T233-T255   12   10340 2 3 18100 20400
------------------ 1975 BOATS ----------------------------------------------------
25   MONTEREY 2585    HT EXP FBG SV IO 188-233      8 4590 1 2  9150 10700
25   SANTA-CRUZ 2565  FB SF  FBG SV IO 188-233      8 4610 1 2 10100 11500
28 2 MARINER 2895     FB SDN FBG SV IO 255  MRCR 10 4 6800 2 9 14500 16500
28 2 MARINER 2895     FB SDN FBG SV VD T215-T233 10 4 6800 2 9 13900 16000
28 2 MONTEREY 2885    HT EXP FBG SV IO 255  MRCR 10 4 6405 2 9 11900 13500
28 2 MONTEREY 2885    HT EXP FBG SV IB T215-T230 10 4 6405 2 9 13200 15400
28 2 MONTEREY 2885    FB EXP FBG SV IO 255  MRCR 10 4 6405 2 9 11900 13500
28 2 MONTEREY 2885    FB EXP FBG SV IB T215-T230 10 4 6405 2 9 13200 15400
28 2 SANTA-CRUZ 2865  FB SF  FBG SV IO 255  MRCR 10 4 6412 2 9 11300 12900
28 2 SANTA-CRUZ 2865  FB SF  FBG SV IB T215-T230 10 4 6412 2 6 12600 14600
32 6 MARINER 3395     FB SDN FBG SV VD T233-T255 12   11220 2 3 19200 21400
32 6 MONTEREY 3385    HT EXP FBG SV IB T233-T255 12   10340 2 6 16800 19000

32 6 MONTEREY 3385    FB EXP FBG SV IB T233-T255 12   10340      16800 19400
------------------ 1974 BOATS ----------------------------------------------------
22   2275             CAMPR FBG IO 165-225       8 3470 1 3  6800  8100
25   MONTEREY 2585          FBG IO 188-225       8 4115 1 3  8550 10000
25   SANTA-CRUZ 2565        FBG IO 188-225       8 4380 1 3  8700 10200
28 2 MARINER 2895           FBG IO 255  MRCR  10 4 7350 1 7 15100 17200
28 2 MARINER 2895           FBG IB T185 WAUK  10 4 7350 2 6 16200 18400
28 2 MONTEREY 2885          FBG IB T185-T215  10 4 7630 2 3 13300 15500
28 2 MONTEREY 2885    FB    FBG IB T185-T215  10 4 7630 2 6 13300 15500
28 2 SANTA-CRUZ 2865        FBG IB T225 MRCR  12 4 7430 2 6 12500 14500
32 6 MONTEREY 3385    FB    FBG IB T225 MRCR  12   11200 2 3 16500 18800
33   VOYAGER          SPTCR FBG SV IB T225    12         17000 19300
------------------ 1973 BOATS ----------------------------------------------------
22   2275             CAMPR FBG IO 165-188    8 3470 1 3  7000  8300
25   MONTEREY 2585          FBG IO 188-255    8 4115 1 3  8950 10700
25   SANTA-CRUZ 2565  FB    FBG IO 188-255    8 4380 1 3  9050 10800
28   COMMODORE 2845   FB    FBG IB T185-T215 10 4 7280 1 2 12500 14600
28   MARINER 2890     FB    FBG L/P IO 255 WAUK 10 4 7280 2 6 13100 15300
28   MARINER 2890     FB    FBG L/P VD 255 WAUK 10 4 7280 2 9 13400 15700
28   MARINER 2890     FB    FBG L/P VD T140 MRCR 10 4 7680 1 9 14100 16100
31 2 MONTEREY 3180    FB    FBG L/P IB T185-T215 8 9730 1 3 18500 20600
31 2 MONTEREY 3180    FB    FBG L/P IB 130D VLVO 8 9730 2 6 18500 20600
31 2 MONTEREY 3180    FB    FBG L/P IB T185-T215 8 9730 2 6 12000 14000

31 2 VOYAGER 3120     FB    FBG L/P IB T185-T215 8 9575 1 9 20100 22300
31 2 VOYAGER 3120     FB    FBG L/P IB T185-T215 8 9575 2 6 13200 15300
31 2 VOYAGER 3120     FB    FBG L/P IB T185-T215 8 9575 1 9 20100 22300
31 2 VOYAGER 3120     FB    FBG L/P IB T188-T215 8 9575 2 6 13200 15300
------------------ 1972 BOATS ----------------------------------------------------
22   2275             CAMPR    FBG IO 155-225  8 3470 1 2  7200  8650
22   MONTEGO 2285     OP CR    FBG IO 155-225  8 3590 1 2  8100  9750
25   MONTEREY                  FBG IO 188-225  8 4115 1 3  6900  8350
25   MONTEREY                  FBG IO 188-225  8 4425 1 2  8050  9250
25   SANTA-CRUZ 2565           FBG IO T140 MRCR 8 4380 1 3  9350 11100
25   SANTA-CRUZ 2565           FBG IO T140 MRCR 8 4700 1 3 10800 12300
28   HOLIDAY 2870    L/P       FBG IO 225      2 6010 1 7 12500 14400
     IB 215 8050 9300, IO 225 OMC 12600 14300, IO T140-T155 13700 15800

28   MARINER 2890    L/P       FBG IO 215 MRCR 10 4 7280 1 7 13500 15300
     IB 215 MRCR 8850 10100, IO 225 OMC 13600 15400, IO T140 MRCR 14600 16600

28   MONTEREY        L/P       FBG IB 215 MRCR 10 4 7620 1 7 15400 17400
     IB 215 MRCR 10000 11400, IO 225 OMC 14700 17500, IO T140-T155 15400 16600

31 2 MONTEREY        L/P       FBG IB T155-T225 11 8 9430 1 9 21400 25300
31 2 VOYAGER 3120    L/P       FBG IB T155-T165 11 8 9575 1 9 12500 14500
31 2 VOYAGER 3120    L/P       FBG IB T185 WAUK 11 8 9575 1 9 12700 14400
31 2 VOYAGER 3120    L/P       FBG IB T188-T215 11 8 9575 1 9 20800 23800
------------------ 1971 BOATS ----------------------------------------------------
21   HOLIDAY         L/P       IO 120-155  8 2350 1 10 4150 5200
21   MONTEREY        L/P       IO 120-155  8 2630    10 4350 4850
22   HOLIDAY         L/P FBG   IO 140-215  8 2730 1    5050 6100
22   HOLIDAY         CAMPR FBG IO 140-215  8 2830 1    5400 6550
22   MONTEGO         OP CR FBG IO 140-215  8 3550 1    8000 9650
```

```
 LOA  NAME AND/           TOP/ BOAT -HULL- ----ENGINE--- BEAM   WGT  DRAFT RETAIL RETAIL
FT IN OR MODEL            RIG  TYPE MTL TP  TP # HP  MFG  FT IN  LBS  FT IN  LOW    HIGH
-------------------- 1971 BOATS --------------------------------------------------------
24  7 MONTEREY                L/P        IO 155-215       8     3950 1 2  6550  8000
24  7 MONTEREY                L/P        IO T120-T140     8     4550 1 2  8100  9550
24  7 SANTA-CRUZ              L/P        IO 155-215       8     4215 1 2  7350  8900
24  7 SANTA-CRUZ              L/P        IO T120-T140     8     4865 1 2  9150 10700
28    HOLIDAY                 L/P        IB 210  OMC  10 2 5195 1 7  9200 10500
      IO  215  MRCR 15400 17500, IO 215 OMC 15200 17200, IB 215-250       9200 10900
      IO T120-T165 16300 20100

28    MARINER                 L/P        IB 210  OMC  10 2 6525 1 7  7700  8850
      IO  215  MRCR 12900 14700, IO 215 OMC 12700 14400, IB 215-250       7750  9300
      IO T120-T165 13500 16400

28    MONTEREY                L/P        IB 210  OMC  10 2 6150 1 7  8650  9950
      IO  215  MRCR 14500 16500, IO 215 OMC 14300 16300, IB 215-250       8600 10300
      IO T120-T165 15400 18800

31  2 MONTEREY                L/P        IO T155-T165 11 8 8320 1 9 21500 24200
      IB T210  OMC  13000 14700, IO T215 MRCR 23000 25500, IO T215 OMC   22800 25400
      IB T215  MRCR 13000 14700
-------------------- 1970 BOATS --------------------------------------------------------
16    STINGRAY CX-162         RNBT FBG DV IO 120        6  4 1590      2100  2500
16 11 WHIP-RAY CX-174         RNBT FBG DV IO 120        7    1600      2400  2800
17  5 BARRACUDA CX-171   OP         FBG TR OB           7    1125      1750  2100
17  5 BARRACUDA CX-176         RNBT FBG TR IO 120       7    1775      2600  3000
17  5 BARRACUDA CX-L73 PRM OP       FBG TR OB           7    1150      1800  2150
17 10 MARLIN CX-182           RNBT FBG DV IO 120        6 10 1930      2700  3150
21    HOLIDAY                 CR       MHG IO 120       8    2350   1 6 4800  5550
21    HOLIDAY                 CR       MHG IO 140-155   8       1 6 5400  6250
21    MONTEREY                CR       MHG IO 120       8    2640   1 6 4550  5200
21    MONTEREY                CR       MHG IO 140-155   8       1 6 5100  5850
24  7                         HT   CAMPR MHG IO 155-160 8    3825   1 11 7250  8400
24  7                         HT   CAMPR MHG IO 165-215 8       1 11 10600 12200

24  7                         HT   CAMPR MHG IO T120-T155 8     1 11 11400 13000
24  7 HOLIDAY                 HT   CR   MHG IO 155-160  8    3700   1 11 7550  8750
24  7 HOLIDAY                 HT   CR   MHG IO 165-215  8       1 11 10700 12300
24  7 HOLIDAY                 HT   CR   MHG IO T120-T155 8      1 11 11600 13300
24  7 MONTEREY                HT   CR   MHG IO 155-160  8    3950   1 11 7000  8100
24  7 MONTEREY                HT   CR   MHG IO 165-215  8       1 11 10500 12000
24  7 MONTEREY                HT   CR   MHG IO T120-T155 8      1 11 11200 12700
24  7 SANTA-CRUZ              HT   CR   MHG IO 155  OMC 8    4590   1 11 8350  9600
24  7 SANTA-CRUZ              HT   SF   MHG IO 160  MRCR 8   4590   1 11 9600 10900
24  7 SANTA-CRUZ              HT   SF   MHG IO 165-215  8       1 11 12100 13900
24  7 SANTA-CRUZ              HT   SF   MHG IO T120-T155 8      1 11 13000 14900

26  8                         HT   CAMPR MHG IO 210-215 10 6 5200 2 10 10800 13500
26  8                         HT   CAMPR MHG IB 225 CHRY 10 6    2 10 7100  8150
26  8                         HT   CAMPR MHG IO T120-T165 10 6  2 10 12500 14700
26  8 MONTEREY                HT   CR   MHG IO 210-215 10 6 5530 2 10 10500 12700
26  8 MONTEREY                HT   CR   MHG IB 225 CHRY 10 6    2 10 6700  7700
26  8 MONTEREY                HT   CR   MHG IO T120-T165 10 6   2 10 11800 13900
26  8 SANTA-CRUZ              HT   SF   MHG IO T120 OMC 10 6 6100 2 10 12300 14000
26  8 SANTA-CRUZ              HT   SF   MHG IO 210-215 10 6    2 10 13600 15500
26  8 SANTA-CRUZ              HT   SF   MHG IB 225 CHRY 10 6   2 10 7100  8200
26  8 SANTA-CRUZ              HT   SF   MHG IO T120-T165 10 6  2 10 14300 16900
31  2 MONTEREY                HT   CR   MHG IO 325 MRCR 11 8 8730 3 2 21600 24000
31  2 MONTEREY                HT   CR   MHG IO T155-T215 11 8   3 2 22900 26600

31  2 MONTEREY                HT   CR   MHG IB T225 CHRY 11 8   3 2 14300 16200
-------------------- 1969 BOATS --------------------------------------------------------
19  4 HOLIDAY                 CBNCR MHG SV IO 120-210 7 10 2170    7 4050  4700
21  4 HOLIDAY                 CUD  MHG SV IO 120      8    2350    10 5050  5800
21  4 HOLIDAY                 CUD  MHG SV IO 155-210  8       10 5900  6900
21  4 MONTEREY                CBNCR MHG SV IO 120-210 8    2640    10 5200  6450
24  7                         HT   CAMPR MHG SV IO 155-225 8 4250 1 2 8100  9650
24  7                         HT   CAMPR MHG SV IO T120    8    1 2 11800 13100
24  7 HOLIDAY                 HT        MHG SV IO 155-225 8    1 2 11200 13100
24  7 HOLIDAY                 HT        MHG SV IO T120    8    1 2 12200 13800
24  7 HOLIDAY                 CR        MHG SV IO 155-225 8 4250 1 2 8600 10300
24  7 HOLIDAY                 CR        MHG SV IO T120    8    1 2 12500 14200
24  7 MONTEREY                EXP       MHG SV IO 155-225 8 4500 1 2 7950  9450
24  7 MONTEREY                EXP       MHG SV IO T120    8    1 2 11100 12600

24  7 SANTA-CRUZ              SF        MHG SV IO 155-225 8 4429 2  9600 11300
24  7 SANTA-CRUZ              SF        MHG SV IO T120    8    2  13500 15300
24  7 SANTA-CRUZ 2560         SF        MHG    IB 300     8    2  5400  6250
26  8                         HT   CAMPR MHG IO 155-210 10 6 5050 2 6 10600 12500
      IO  225  MRCR 11200 12700, IB 225-300  6850  8200, IO T120-T160  12900 15200
26  8 MONTEREY                CR   MHG IO 155-210 10 6 5400 2 4 10300 12200
      IO  225  MRCR 10900 12400, IB 225-300  6000  7250, IO T120-T160  11400 13400
26  8 SANTA-CRUZ              SF   MHG IO 155-210 10 6 5200 2 4 12300 14500
      IO  225  MRCR 13000 14700, IB 225-300  6850  8200, IO T120-T160  14700 17300
-------------------- 1968 BOATS --------------------------------------------------------
19  4 1950                    OP   CAMPR WD OB        7 10 1260    10 2850  3350
19  4 1950                    OP   CAMPR WD OB 120-210 7 10       1 5150  6150
19  4 HOLIDAY 1970            CR        WD OB 120-210 7 10 1270   1 2950  3450
19  4 HOLIDAY 1970            CR        WD OB 120-185 7 10 1970   1 5050  6300
19  4 HOLIDAY 1970            CR        WD OB 210     7 10        1 5550  6300
19  4 RANGER 1940             OP   RNBT WD OB 120 MRCR 7 10 1220  1 2450  2850
19  4 RANGER 1940             OP   RNBT WD OB 120     7 10 1920   1 4150  4800
19  4 RANGER 1940             OP   RNBT WD IO 120-210 7 10        1 4600  5450
21    2150                    OP   CAMPR WD OB 120 MRCR 8   1560  1 6 3300  3850
21    2150                    OP   CAMPR WD OB       8    2260   1 6 5750  6650
21    2150                    OP   CAMPR WD IO 120 MRCR 8     1 6 6350  7450
21    HOLIDAY 2170            OP   CAMPR WD OB       8    1650   1 6 3250  3750

21    HOLIDAY 2170            CR        WD IO 120 MRCR 8  2350  1 6 5450  6300
21    HOLIDAY 2170            CR        WD IO 155-210 8     1 6 6350  7450
21    MONTEREY 2180           EXP       WD OB       8    1840   1 6 3950  4600
21    MONTEREY 2180           EXP       WD IO 120 MRCR 8  2540  1 6 6400  7350
21    MONTEREY 2180           EXP       WD IO 155-210 8     1 6 7050  8250
21    RANGER 2140             OP   RNBT WD OB       8    1560   1  3000  3500
21    RANGER 2140             OP   RNBT WD IO 120 MRCR 8  2220  1  4950  5700
21    RANGER 2140             OP   RNBT WD IO 155-210 8     1  5700  6700
24  7 2550                    HT   CAMPR WD IO 155-160 8 4250 1 11 6700  7700
24  7 2550                    HT   CAMPR WD IO 185-225 8    1 11 9050 10500
24  7 2550                    HT   CAMPR WD IO T120    8    1 11 9700 11000

24  7 HOLIDAY 2570            CBNCR WD IO 155-225 8 4250 1 11 7650  8800
24  7 HOLIDAY 2570            CBNCR WD IO 185-225 8    1 11 10200 11800
24  7 HOLIDAY 2570            CBNCR WD IO T120    8    1 11 11000 12500
24  7 MONTEREY 2580           EXP   WD IO 155-160 8 4500 1 11 7300  8400
24  7 MONTEREY 2580           EXP   WD IO 185-225 8    1 11 9450 10900
24  7 MONTEREY 2580           EXP   WD IO T120    8    1 11 10100 11500
24  7 SANTA-CRUZ 2560         SF    WD IO 155-160 8 4429 1 11 8550  9850
24  7 SANTA-CRUZ 2560         SF    WD IO 185-225 8    1 11 11200 12900
26  8 2750                    HT   CAMPR WD IO 155-160 10 6 5050 1 11 9000 10300
26  8 2750                    HT   CAMPR WD IO 185-225 10 6   1 11 10200 11900
26  8 2750                    HT   CAMPR WD IO T120-T160 10 6 1 11 10900 12800

26  8 MONTEREY 2780           EXP   WD IO 155-210 10 6 5400 2 6 10200 12100
26  8 MONTEREY 2780           EXP   WD IO 225     10 6    2 6 11500 13100
26  8 MONTEREY 2780           EXP   WD IO T120-T160 10 6   2 6 12000 14100
26  8 SANTA-CRUZ 2760         SF    WD IO 155-160 10 6 5200 2 6 11200 12700
26  8 SANTA-CRUZ 2760         SF    WD IO 185-225 10 6    2 6 12500 14600
-------------------- 1967 BOATS --------------------------------------------------------
16  3 CITATION                RNBT L/P IO 60        6 4      2800  3300
16  3 COMMANDER CUSTOM             WD OB 60- 80       735     1800  2100
16  3 COMMANDER CUSTOM             WD OB 60- 80               3550  4100
17  5 CAPTAIN                      WD OB 120-200     1050     2600  3050
17  5 CAPTAIN                      WD OB 120-200               4500  5400
17  5 COMMANDER CUSTOM             WD OB 120         1010     2500  2900
17  5 COMMANDER CUSTOM             WD OB 120         1010     3750  4350
17  5 COMMANDER CUSTOM             WD OB 120-200               4250  5050
19  4                         CAMPR WD OB 120-200    1350     2250  2600
19  4                         CAMPR WD OB 120-200               4350  5050
19  4 HOLIDAY                      WD OB 120-200     1450     2500  2900
19  4 HOLIDAY                      WD OB 120-200               3750  4600

19  4 RANGER                       WD OB 120-200     1320     1900  2250
19  4 RANGER                       WD OB 120-200               3050  3650
21                            CAMPR WD OB 120-200    1600     3250  3750
21                            CAMPR WD OB 120-200               5400  6400
21                            CAMPR WD OB T 80                  6300  7250
21    MONTEREY                     WD OB 120-200               2500  2900
21    MONTEREY                     WD OB T 80        3800     5950  6850
21    MONTEREY                     WD OB 120-200               6000  6900
21    RANGER                       WD OB T 80        1520     2750  3250
21    RANGER                       WD OB 120-200               4250  5150
21    RANGER                       WD OB T 80                  5700  6700

24  7                         CAMPR WD IO 120-225              11700 13600
24  7                         CAMPR WD IO T 80-T120            12500 14400
24  7 MONTEREY                     WD IO 120         4500     8300  9500
```

CARVER BOAT CORPORATION   -CONTINUED   See inside cover to adjust price for area

LOA FT IN	NAME AND/ OR MODEL	TOP/ RIG	BOAT TYPE	HULL MTL	HULL TP	ENG TP	#	HP	MFG	BEAM FT IN	WGT LBS	DRAFT FT IN	RETAIL LOW	RETAIL HIGH
1967 BOATS														
24 7	MONTEREY			WD		IO		120-225					12100	13700
24 7	MONTEREY			WD		IO		T 80-T120					12300	14300
24 7	RANGER			WD		IO		120-225					9150	10800
24 7	RANGER			WD		IO		T 80-T120					9950	11900
26 8	MONTEREY			WD		IO		150			5150		10700	12200
26 8	MONTEREY			WD		IO		155-225					11900	14200
26 8	MONTEREY			WD		IO		T120-T160					13000	15300
26 8	RANGER	HT		WD		IO		150			4800		9650	11000
26 8	RANGER	HT		WD		IO		155-225					11100	13300
26 8	RANGER	HT		WD		IO		T120-T160					12200	14400
26 8	RANGER	FB		WD		IO		150-225					11100	13300
26 8	RANGER	FB		WD		IO		T120-T160					12200	14400
1966 BOATS														
16 3	CITATION		RNBT	WD		TO		60		6 4			2900	3400
16 3	COMMANDER CUSTOM		RNBT	WD		OB				6 4	735		1850	2250
17 4	CAPTAIN		SKI	WD		OB				7 1	1170		2750	3200
17 4	CAPTAIN		SKI	WD		IO		110-200		7 1			4500	5350
17 4	COMMANDER CUSTOM		RNBT	WD		OB				7 1	1110		2800	3250
17 4	COMMANDER CUSTOM		RNBT	WD		IO		110-200		7 1			5100	6000
18 10			CAMPR	WD		OB				7 6	1230		2000	2400
18 10			CAMPR	WD		IO		110-200		7 6			3750	4450
18 10	HOLIDAY		CBNCR	WD		OB				7 6	1225		2200	2550
18 10	HOLIDAY		CBNCR	WD		IO		110-200		7 6			4100	4900
18 10	RANGER		RNBT	WD		OB				7 6	1200		1750	2050
18 10	RANGER		RNBT	WD		IO		110-200		7 6			3400	4050
20 4			CAMPR	WD		OB				8	1525		2600	3050
20 4			CAMPR	WD		IO		110-200		8			4800	5650
20 4			CAMPR	WD		IO		T 60		8			5750	6600
20 4	MONTEREY		CBNCR	WD		OB				8			2500	2900
20 4	MONTEREY		CBNCR	WD		IO		110-200		8			5700	6650
20 4	MONTEREY		CBNCR	WD		IO		T 60		8			6650	7650
20 4	RANGER		RNBT	WD		OB				8	1525		2350	2700
20 4	RANGER		RNBT	WD		IO		110-200		8			4500	5300
20 4	RANGER		RNBT	WD		IO		T 60		8			5250	6050
24 4			CAMPR	WD		IO		110-225		8			8650	10300
24 4			CAMPR	WD		IO		T 60-T120		8			9600	11100
24 4	MONTEREY		CBNCR	WD		IO		110-225		8			8950	10600
24 4	MONTEREY		CBNCR	WD		IO		T 60-T120		8			9900	11400
24 4	MONTEREY			WD		IO		110-225		8			7250	8650
24 4	RANGER			WD		IO		T 60-T120		8			8000	9400
26 6			CR	WD		IO		150-225		10			12800	15300
26 6			CR	WD		IO		T110-T120		10			13900	15900
26 6	MONTEREY		CBNCR	WD		IO		150-225		10			14500	17600
26 6	MONTEREY		CBNCR	WD		IO		T110-T120		10			15900	18400
1965 BOATS														
16 1	COMMANDER CUSTOM			WD		OB							1750	2050
17 3	CAPTAIN			WD		OB							2750	3200
17 3	CAPTAIN			WD		IO		110-120					5100	5850
17 3	COMMANDER CUSTOM			WD		OB							2350	2700
17 3	COMMANDER CUSTOM			WD		IO		110-120					4650	5350
17 3	SPORTSMAN			WD		IO		110-120					2650	3050
18 8	CAPTAIN			WD		OB							3450	4000
18 8	CAPTAIN			WD		IO		110-150					6400	7350
18 8	COMMANDER CUSTOM			WD		OB							2950	3450
18 8	COMMANDER CUSTOM			WD		IO		110-150					5850	6750
18 8	HOLIDAY		CBNCR	WD		OB							2000	2400
18 8	HOLIDAY		CBNCR	WD		IO		110-120					4200	4900
20 3			CAMPR	WD		OB							2550	3000
20 3			CAMPR	WD		IO		110-150					4700	5400
20 3	CATALINA	HT		WD		OB							2100	2500
20 3	CATALINA	HT		WD		IO		110-150					4800	5500
20 3	MONTEREY		CBNCR	WD		OB							2500	2900
20 3	MONTEREY		CBNCR	WD		IO		110-150					5750	6600
20 3	RANGER			WD		OB							1850	2200
20 3	RANGER			WD		IO		110-150					4200	4900
22 7			CAMPR	WD		OB							3850	4450
22 7			CAMPR	WD		IO		110-150					6950	8000
22 7	CATALINA	HT		WD		OB							3200	3700
22 7	CATALINA	HT		WD		IO		110-150					6750	7750
22 7	MONTEREY		CBNCR	WD		OB							3400	4000
22 7	MONTEREY		CBNCR	WD		IO		110-150					6050	6950
22 7	RANGER			WD		OB							2850	3300
22 7	RANGER			WD		IO		110-150					5950	6850
1964 BOATS														
16	COMMANDER			WD		IO		80					2250	2600
16	COMMANDER CUSTOM			WD		IO		80					4000	4650
17			CAMPR	WD		IO		80-120					3600	4200
17	CAPTAIN			WD		OB							2700	3150
17	CAPTAIN			WD		IO		80-120					5150	6000
17	COMMANDER			WD		IO		80-120					2650	3150
17	COMMUTER			WD		IO		80-120					2850	3300
19			CAMPR	WD		OB							2400	2750
19			CAMPR	WD		IO		80-150					4000	4650
19	COMMUTER			WD		OB							2200	2550
19	COMMUTER			WD		IO		80-150					3850	4500
22			CAMPR	WD		OB							3750	4350
22			CAMPR	WD		IO		110-150					6950	8000
22	CARIBBEAN CUSTOM			WD		OB							2550	2950
22	CARIBBEAN CUSTOM			WD		IO		120-150					6900	7950
27	COMMODORE			WD		IO		150	MRCR				14200	16200
1963 BOATS														
17 2	CAPTAIN			WD		OB							2800	3250
17 2	CAPTAIN			WD		IO		80-110					5100	5850
19			CAMPR	WD		OB							2400	2800
19	CAPTAIN			WD		OB							3250	3800
19	CAPTAIN			WD		IO		110-120					6750	7850
19	CARIBBEAN			WD		OB							2150	2500
19	CARIBBEAN CUSTOM			WD		OB							2550	2950
19	CARIBBEAN CUSTOM			WD		IO		110-120					4250	5000
19	COMMUTER			WD		OB							1800	2150
19	COMMUTER			WD		IO		110-120					3700	4300
27			CR	WD		IO		120-140					13900	16000
27			CR	WD		IB		195					5350	6150
27			CR	WD		IO		T110-T140					15300	18000
1962 BOATS														
17 2	CAPTAIN			WD		OB							2400	2800
17 2	CAPTAIN			WD		IO		80					5250	6050
17 11	CAPTAIN			WD		OB							2500	2950
19	CAPTAIN			WD		OB							3300	3850
19	CAPTAIN			WD		IO		120					7000	8050
19	CARIBBEAN			WD		OB							2200	2550
19	CARIBBEAN CUSTOM			WD		OB							2200	2550
19	CARIBBEAN CUSTOM			WD		IO		120					4100	4750
19	COMMUTER			WD		OB							2200	2550
19	COMMUTER			WD		IO		120					4100	4750
24 8	CUSTOM			CR	WD	IO		120					13700	15600
1961 BOATS														
17 10	CAPTAIN		RNBT	PLY		OB				6 9	750		2100	2500
18 4			CR	PLY		OB				7 2	1025		1750	2050
19 8			CR	PLY		OB				7	1088		1900	2250
19 8	CARIBBEAN		CR	PLY		OB				7	1100		1950	2300
1960 BOATS														
16	COMMANDER CUSTOM		RNBT	WD		OB							2000	2400
17	CAPTAIN		RNBT	WD		OB							2850	3350
20			CR	WD		OB							2650	3050
20	CARIBBEAN		CR	WD		OB							2650	3050
20	CARIBBEAN CUSTOM		CR	WD		OB							2650	3050
20	COMMUTER		CR	WD		OB							2650	3050
20	CUSTOM		CR	WD		OB							2650	3050
1959 BOATS														
17	CAPTAIN		RNBT	MHG		OB				6 6	660		1800	2150

CARVER MARINE INC

Call 1-800-327-6929 for BUC Personalized Evaluation Service
Or, for 1980 boats, sign onto www.BUCValuPro.com

CARY MARINE

GRAND HAVEN MI 49417   COAST GUARD MFG ID- CRM   See inside cover to adjust price for area

For more recent years, see the BUC Used Boat Price Guide, Volume 1 or Volume 2

LOA FT IN	NAME AND/ OR MODEL	TOP/ RIG	BOAT TYPE	HULL MTL	HULL TP	ENG TP	#	HP	MFG	BEAM FT IN	WGT LBS	DRAFT FT IN	RETAIL LOW	RETAIL HIGH
1983 BOATS														
43	CARY 43	OP	OFF	FBG	DV		R	370	MRCR	10 2	16000	2 6	89000	97800
49 10	CARY 50	OP	OFF	FBG	DV		T	370	MRCR	14 6	28000	3	115500	127000
	IB T570D GM	219000	241000,	IO Q370	MRCR	135000	148500,	IO Q500					152500	167500

102   CONTINUED ON NEXT PAGE   96th ed. - Vol. III

LOA FT	LOA IN	NAME AND/ OR MODEL	TOP/ RIG	BOAT TYPE	HULL MTL	HULL TP	ENGINE TP	# HP	MFG	BEAM FT	BEAM IN	WGT LBS	DRAFT FT	DRAFT IN	RETAIL LOW	RETAIL HIGH
		1983 BOATS														
49	10	CARY 50	OP	OFF	FBG	DV	IB	Q240D	REN	14	6	28000	3		234500	257500
49	10	CARY 50	FB	OFF	FBG	DV	IB	T570D	GM	14	6	28000	3		222000	244000
		IO Q370 MRCR 137000 150500, IB Q240D REN 238000 261500, IB Q500D REN 301500 331500														
49	10	FLYBRIDGE	FB	SDN	FBG	DV	IB	T550D	GM	14	9	36000	4	1	259000	285000
49	10	SPORT 2+2	OP	OFF	KEV	DV	IO	Q400	MRCR	14	9	20000	3		138000	151500
		1982 BOATS														
43		CARY 43	OP	OFF	FBG	DV	IO	R370	MRCR	10	2	16000	2	6	86800	95400
48	10	FLYBRIDGE	FB	SDN	FBG	DV	IB	T550D	GM	14	6	36000	4	1	239500	263000
48	10	SPORT 2+2	OP	OFF	KEV	DV	IO	Q400	MRCR	14	6	20000	3		125000	137500
48	10	SPORT YACHT	OP	OFF	FBG	DV	IO	T400	MRCR	14	6	30000	3	10	129000	141500
49	10	CARY 50	OP	OFF	FBG	DV	IO	T370	MRCR	14	6	28000	3		113000	124000
		IB T570D GM 212000 233000, IO Q370 MRCR 132000 145000, IO Q500 CARY 149000 163500														
		IB Q240D REN 223500 246000														
49	10	CARY 50	FB	SDN	FBG	DV	IO	T370	MRCR	14	6	30000	3		115500	127000
49	10	CARY 50	FB	SDN	FBG	DV	IO	Q370	MRCR	14	6	32000	3		135500	149000
49	10	CARY 50	FB	SDN	FBG	DV	IB	Q240D	REN	14	6	32000	3		230000	253000
		1981 BOATS														
48	10	FLYBRIDGE	FB	SDN	FBG	DV	IB	T550D	GM	14	9	30000	3	10	212500	233500
48	10	SPORT 2+2	OP	OFF	KEV	DV	IO	Q400	MRCR	14	9	20000	3		123000	135000
48	10	SPORT YACHT	OP	OFF	FBG	DV	IO	T400	MRCR	14	9	25000	3	10	120500	132500
49	10	CARY 50	OP	OFF	FBG	DV	IO	Q370	MRCR	14	6	25000	3		129000	141500
49	10	CARY 50	OP	OFF	FBG	DV	IO	Q500		14	6	25000	3		146500	161000
		1980 BOATS														
48	10	FLYBRIDGE	FB	SDN	FBG	DV	IB	T550D	GM	14	9	30000	3	10	202500	222500
48	10	SPORT 2+2	OP	OFF	KEV	DV	IO	Q400	MRCR	14	9	20000	3	6	122000	134000
48	10	SPORT YACHT	OP	OFF	FBG	DV	IO	T400	MRCR	14	9	25000	3	10	119000	131000
		1978 BOATS														
27	10	CARY 28	OP	SF	FBG	SV	IB	T225-T250		9	10	7500	2	6	25800	28800
27	10	CARY 28	TT	SF	FBG	SV	IB	T225-T250		9	10	7500	2	6	26100	29100
29	1	CARY 29 ET	OP	CR	FBG	DV	IO	T330	MRCR	8		5700	1	8	24800	27500
32	6	CARY 32 SE	OP	CR	FBG	DV	IO	T330	MRCR	9	9	8000	2	10	40100	44500
32	6	CARY 32 SF	OP	SF	FBG	DV	IB	T330		9	9	8000	3		38900	43300
32	6	CARY 32 SF	OP	SF	FBG	DV	IB	T D	GM	9	9	8000	3		**	**
32	6	CARY 32 SF	TT	SF	FBG	DV	IB	T330		9	9	8000	3		39000	43400
32	6	CARY 32 SF	TT	SF	FBG	DV	IB	T D	GM	9	9	8000	3		**	**
32	6	CARY 32 SS	OP	RNBT	FBG	DV	IB	T330		9	9	8000	3		40700	45300
32	6	CARY 32 SS	OP	RNBT	FBG	DV	IB	T D	GM	9	9	8000	3		**	**
48	10	CARY 49 C	OP	EXP	FBG	DV	IB	T580D	GM	14	9	31200	14	9	161000	177000
48	10	CARY 49 S	OP	EXP	FBG	DV	IB	T580D	GM	14	9	30000	14	9	149000	163500
48	10	CARY 50	FB	SDN	FBG	DV	IB	T580D	GM	14	9	35000	14	9	176500	194000
		1977 BOATS														
29	1	E/ET		RNBT	FBG	DV	IO	T280		8					21900	24300
32		CARY 32 SF		SF	FBG	DV	IB	T330D		9	9				54500	59900
32		CARY 32 SS		RNBT	FBG	DV	IB	T330D		9	9				48600	53400
32	6	CARY 32 SF		SF	FBG	DV	IB	T330		9	9	8500	3		37500	41700
32	6	CARY 32 SS		RNBT	FBG	DV	IB	T330		9	9	8500	3		39300	43700
32	6	SE		SPTCR	FBG	DV	IO	T280		9	9		2	10	37600	41800
49		CARY 49		CR	FBG	DV	IB	T550D		14		30000	3	10	135500	148500
		1976 BOATS														
29	1	CARY 29 ET	OP	CR	FBG	DV	IO	T280	MRCR	8		5700	1	8	23400	26000
32	6	CARY 32 SE	OP	CR	FBG	DV	IO	T280	MRCR	9	9	8500	2	10	40300	44800
32	6	CARY 32 SF	OP	SF	FBG	DV	IB	T330	CC	9	9	8500	3		36000	40000
32	6	CARY 32 SF	OP	SF	FBG	DV	IB	T160D-T200D		9	9	8500	3		39700	46300
32	6	CARY 32 SF	TT	SF	FBG	DV	IB	T330	CC	9	9	8500	3		36100	40100
32	6	CARY 32 SF	TT	SF	FBG	DV	IB	T160D-T200D		9	9	8500	3		39700	46300
32	6	CARY 32 SS	OP	RNBT	FBG	DV	IB	T330	CC	9	9	8500	2	10	37500	41700
32	6	CARY 32 SS	OP	RNBT	FBG	DV	IB	T160D-T210D		9	9	8500	2	10	40900	48300
48	10	CARY 49 S	OP	CR	FBG	DV	IB	T430D	BENZ	14	9	23500	3	10	111000	122000
48	10	CARY 49 S	OP	CR	FBG	DV	IB	T465D	GM	14	9	23500	3	10	113500	124500
48	10	CARY 49 S	OP	CR	FBG	DV	IB	T555D	GM	14	9	23500	3	10	120000	132000
		1975 BOATS														
26		CARY ET-26		RNBT	FBG	DV	IO	T170		8			3		15700	17900
26		CARY ET-26		RNBT	FBG	DV	IO	T300		8			3		18900	21000
29		CARY ET-29		RNBT	FBG	DV	IO	T188-T300		8			3		21100	25600
29		CARY S-29	OP	OPFSH	FBG	DV	IO	T170		8			3		24200	26900
29		CARY S-29	OP	OPFSH	FBG	DV	IB	T225		8			3		21900	24400
32	6	32SE SPORT RUNABOUT	OP	RNBT	FBG	DV	IO	T280-T395		9	9	8500	2	6	33000	39900
32	6	32SF SPORT FISHER	OP	SF	FBG	DV	IB	T350	CRUS	9	9	8300	2	6	35000	38900
32	6	32SF SPORT FISHER	TT	SF	FBG	DV	IB	T350	CRUS	9	9	8300	2	6	35100	39000
32	6	32SS SPORT RUNABOUT	OP	RNBT	FBG	DV	IB	T330	CC	9	9	8300	2	6	35900	39900
32	6	32SS SPORT RUNABOUT	TT	RNBT	FBG	DV	IB	T330	CC	9	9	8300	2	6	36000	40000
48	10	49S SPORTSMAN	OP	SPTCR	FBG	DV	IB	T465D	GM	14	9	23500	3	4	109000	120000
		1974 BOATS														
28	10	SPORTSMAN 29			FBG		IB	T250	CHRY	8	2		2	5	24700	27500
32	6			SF	FBG		IB	T330	CHRY	9	9		2	6	34200	38000
32	6	SUPER SPORT 32			FBG		IB	T330	CHRY	9	9		2	6	35000	38900
48	10			SF	FBG		IB	T370D		14	9		3	10	115500	126500
48	10	SPORT 49			FBG		IB	T370D		14	9	23500	3	10	106000	116500
48	10	SPORT 49			FBG		IB	T465D	GM	14	9	23500	3	10	112000	123000
		1973 BOATS														
27	10			SF	FBG		IB	T330	CHRY	9	10	7200	2	6	22100	24500
27	10			SPTCR	FBG		IB	T330	CHRY	9	10	7200	2	6	24500	27200
29	8			SF	FBG		IB	T250	CHRY	8		5500	2	10	19700	21900
32	6			SF	FBG		IB	T330	CHRY	9	9	7800	2	8	29600	32900
32	6			SPTCR	FBG		IB	T330	CHRY	9	9	7800	2	8	33800	37600
32	6	CUSTOM		SF	FBG		IB	T330	CHRY	9	9	7800	2	8	33800	37600
49	10			SF	FBG		IB	T525	FORD	14	8		3	6	115500	127000
49	10			SF	FBG		IB	T370D	CUM	14	8	23000	3	6	106000	116500
49	10		FB	SPTCR	FBG		IB	T525	FORD	14	8		3	6	115500	127000
49	10		FB	SPTCR	FBG		IB	T370D	CUM	14	8	25000	3	6	101000	111000
		1972 BOATS														
18	6	CARY 19		RNBT	FBG	SV	OB			6	8	1270			2500	2900
26	3	SPEEDSTER			FBG	DV	IB	375		8	2		2	9	14300	16200
27	10	SPORTSMAN			FBG		IB	T330	CHRY	9	10	7200	2	6	21800	24200
31	9	SPORTSMAN			FBG		IO	T330	CHRY	9	6		2	8	36200	40200
49	10			SF	FBG		IB	T450	FORD	14	8		3	6	102000	112500
49	10			SF	FBG		IB	T370D	CUM	14	8	25000	3	6	99900	110000
49	10	SPORTSMAN			FBG		IB	T450	FORD	14	8		3	6	97400	107000
49	10	SPORTSMAN			FBG		IB	T370D	CUM	14	8	23000	3	6	98600	108500
		1971 BOATS														
18	6	CARY 19		RNBT	FBG	SV	OB			6	8	1270		8	2500	2900
26	3	SPEEDSTER			FBG		IB	375	CHRY	8	2	4600	2	9	12900	14700
26	3	SPEEDSTER			FBG		IB	500	DAY	8	2	4600	2	9	14400	16300
27	10	SPORTSMAN			FBG		IB	T330	CHRY	9	10	7200	2	6	20900	23200
31	9	SPORTSMAN			FBG		IO			9	6		2	8	**	**
49	10			SF	FBG		IB	T370D	CUM	14	6	25000	3	6	96400	106000
49	10	SPORTSMAN			FBG		IB	T370D	CUM	14	3	23000	3	6	95100	104500
		1970 BOATS														
18	6	CARY 19	OP	RNBT	FBG	SV	OB			6	8	1200		8	2400	2800
27	10	CARY 28 SPORTSMAN		CR	FBG	DV	IB	T140D	GM	9	10	8100	2	6	29500	32800
27	10	CARY 28 SPORTSMAN		RNBT	FBG	DV	IB	T325	CHRY	9	10	7200	2	6	21200	23600
		1969 BOATS														
27	10	OCEAN RUNABOUT		RNBT	FBG	DV	IB	400		9	10	7200	2	6	18700	20800
27	10	OCEAN RUNABOUT		RNBT	FBG	DV	IB	T210		9	10	7200	2	6	19100	21200

CARY RACING TEAM INC

COAST GUARD MFG ID- CYR

Call 1-800-327-6929 for BUC Personalized Evaluation Service
Or, for 1977 boats, sign onto www.BUCValuPro.com

CASCADE YACHTS INC

PORTLAND OR 97218 COAST GUARD MFG ID- YCS See inside cover to adjust price for area

For more recent years, see the BUC Used Boat Price Guide, Volume 1 or Volume 2

LOA FT	LOA IN	NAME AND/ OR MODEL	TOP/ RIG	BOAT TYPE	HULL MTL	HULL TP	ENGINE TP	# HP	MFG	BEAM FT	BEAM IN	WGT LBS	DRAFT FT	DRAFT IN	RETAIL LOW	RETAIL HIGH
		1983 BOATS														
22	11	CASCADE 23	SLP	SA/RC	FBG	DB	OB			7	8	2500	1	8	4750	5500
27	1	CASCADE 27	SLP	SA/RC	FBG	KL	IB	8D	FARY	8	10	6500	4	6	15300	17400
29		CASCADE 29	SLP	SA/RC	FBG	KL	IB	12D	FARY	8	2	8000	4	9	20600	22900
36		CASCADE 36	SLP	SA/RC	FBG	KL	IB	24D	FARY	10		13000	5	6	34900	38800
41	9	CASCADE 42	SLP	SA/CR	FBG	KL	IB	32D	FARY	11	8	18450	6		54400	59800
41	9	CASCADE 42	SLP	SA/CR	FBG	KL	IB	40D	PERK	11	8	18450	6		54300	59600
41	9	CASCADE 42	KTH	SA/CR	FBG	KL	IB	32D	FARY	11	8	18450	6		54400	59800
41	9	CASCADE 42	KTH	SA/CR	FBG	KL	IB	40D	PERK	11	8	18450	6		54300	59600
42	6	CASCADE 42 CS	SLP	SA/CR	FBG	KL	IB	32D	FARY	12		19000	6		56800	62400
42	6	CASCADE 42 CS	SLP	SA/CR	FBG	KL	IB	40D	PERK	12		19000	6		56600	62200
42	6	CASCADE 42 CS	KTH	SA/CR	FBG	KL	IB	32D	FARY	12		19000	6		56800	62400
42	6	CASCADE 42 CS	KTH	SA/CR	FBG	KL	IB	40D	PERK	12		19000	6		56600	62200
		1982 BOATS														
22	11	CASCADE 23	SLP	SA/RC	FBG	DB	OB			7	8	2500	1	8	4550	5200
27	1	CASCADE 27	SLP	SA/RC	FBG	KL	IB	8D	FARY	8	10	6500	4	6	14500	16500
29		CASCADE 29	SLP	SA/RC	FBG	KL	IB	12D	FARY	8	2	8500	4	9	20800	23100
36		CASCADE 36	SLP	SA/RC	FBG	KL	IB	24D	FARY	10		13000	5	6	33100	36700
41	9	CASCADE 42	SLP	SA/CR	FBG	KL	IB	32D	FARY	11	8	18450	6		51600	56600
41	9	CASCADE 42	SLP	SA/CR	FBG	KL	IB	40D	PERK	11	8	18450	6		51400	56500
41	9	CASCADE 42	KTH	SA/CR	FBG	KL	IB	32D	FARY	11	8	18450	6		51600	56600
41	9	CASCADE 42	KTH	SA/CR	FBG	KL	IB	40D	PERK	11	8	18450	6		51400	56500

 CONTINUED ON NEXT PAGE

CASCADE YACHTS INC -CONTINUED
See inside cover to adjust price for area

LOA FT IN	NAME AND/ OR MODEL	TOP/ RIG	BOAT TYPE	HULL MTL TP	TP	ENGINE # HP	MFG	BEAM FT IN	WGT LBS	DRAFT FT IN	RETAIL LOW	RETAIL HIGH
				1982 BOATS								
42 6	CASCADE 42 CS	SLP	SA/CR	FBG KL	IB	32D	FARY	12	19000	6	53800	59100
42 6	CASCADE 42 CS	SLP	SA/CR	FBG KL	IB	40D	PERK	12	19000	6	53700	59000
42 6	CASCADE 42 CS	KTH	SA/CR	FBG KL	IB	32D	FARY	12	19000	6	53800	59100
42 6	CASCADE 42 CS	KTH	SA/CR	FBG KL	IB	40D	PERK	12	19000	6	53700	59000
				1981 BOATS								
22 11	CASCADE 23	SLP	SA/RC	FBG DB	OB			7 8	2500	1 8	4250	4950
27 1	CASCADE 27	SLP	SA/RC	FBG KL	IB	7D	FARY	8 10	6500	4 6	13700	15600
36	CASCADE 36	SLP	SA/RC	FBG KL	IB	24D	FARY	10	13000	5 6	31300	34800
41 9	CASCADE 42	SLP	SA/CR	FBG KL	IB	40D	PERK	11 8	18450	6	48700	53600
41 9	CASCADE 42	KTH	SA/CR	FBG KL	IB	40D	PERK	11 8	18450	6	48700	53600
42 6	CASCADE 42 CS	SLP	SA/CR	FBG KL	IB	40D	PERK	12	19000	6	50900	55900
42 6	CASCADE 42 CS	KTH	SA/CR	FBG KL	IB	40D	PERK	12	19000	6	50900	55900
				1980 BOATS								
27 1	CASCADE 27	SLP	SA/RC	FBG KL	IB	7D	FARY	8 10	6500	4 6	13200	15000
29	CASCADE 29	SLP	SA/RC	FBG KL	IB	12D	FARY	8 2	8500	4 9	19200	21300
36	CASCADE 36	SLP	SA/CR	FBG KL	IB	40D	PERK	10	13000	5 6	30200	33500
42	CASCADE 42	SLP	SA/CR	FBG KL	IB	40D	PERK	11 2	18450	6	47500	52300
42	CASCADE 42	KTH	SA/CR	FBG KL	IB	40D	PERK	11 2	18450	6	47500	52300
43	CASCADE 42 CS	SLP	SA/CR	FBG KL	IB	40D	PERK	12	19000	6	49900	54800
43	CASCADE 42 CS	KTH	SA/CR	FBG KL	IB	40D	PERK	12	19000	6	49900	54800
				1979 BOATS								
27 1	CASCADE 27	SLP	SA/CR	FBG KL	IB	8D		8 10	6500	4 6	12900	14700
				1978 BOATS								
29	CASCADE 29	SLP	SA/CR	FBG KL	IB	12D	VLVO	8 2	8000	4 9	16600	18800
36 2	CASCADE 36	SLP	SA/CR	FBG KL	IB	25D	VLVO	10	13000	5 6	28400	31600
42	CASCADE 42	SLP	SA/CR	FBG KL	IB	40D	PERK	11 2	18000	6	43600	48400
				1977 BOATS								
29	CASCADE 29	SLP	SAIL	FBG KL	IB	15D		8 2	7500	4 9	15100	17200
36 2	CASCADE 36	SLP	SAIL	FBG KL	IB	35D		10	13000	5 6	27800	30800
36 2	CASCADE 36	KTH	SAIL	FBG KL	IB	35D		10	13000	5 6	27800	30800
42	CASCADE 42	SLP	SAIL	FBG KL	IB	45D		11 2	18000	6	42700	47500
42	CASCADE 42	KTH	SAIL	FBG KL	IB	45D		11 2	18000	6	42700	47500
				1976 BOATS								
29	CASCADE 29	SLP	SAIL	FBG KL	IB	15D- 23D		8 2	9000	4 9	18200	20300
29	CASCADE 29	KTH	SAIL	FBG KL	IB	15D- 23D		8 2	9000	4 9	18200	20300
36 2	CASCADE 36	SLP	SAIL	FBG KL	IB	23D	VLVO	10	14000	5 6	28900	32100
36 2	CASCADE 36	SLP	SAIL	FBG KL	IB	25D	WEST	10	14000	5 6	28900	32100
36 2	CASCADE 36	KTH	SAIL	FBG KL	IB	23D	VLVO	10	14000	5 6	28900	32100
36 2	CASCADE 36	KTH	SAIL	FBG KL	IB	25D	WEST	10	14000	5 6	28900	32100
42	CASCADE 42	SLP	SAIL	FBG KL	IB	35D	VLVO	11 2	18000	6	41600	46200
42	CASCADE 42	SLP	SAIL	FBG KL	IB	37D	WEST	11 2	18000	6	41700	46300
42	CASCADE 42	KTH	SAIL	FBG KL	IB	35D	VLVO	11 2	18000	6	41600	46200
42	CASCADE 42	KTH	SAIL	FBG KL	IB	37D	WEST	11 2	18000	6	41700	46300
42 3	CASCADE	SLP	SA/CR	FBG KL	IB	35D	VLVO	12 1	18000	6 2	41900	46600
42 3	CASCADE	SLP	SA/CR	FBG KL	IB	37D	WEST	12 1	18000	6 2	42000	46700
42 3	CASCADE	KTH	SA/CR	FBG KL	IB	35D	VLVO	12 1	18000	6 2	41900	46600
42 3	CASCADE	KTH	SA/CR	FBG KL	IB	37D	WEST	12 1	18000	6 2	42000	46700
				1974 BOATS								
29	CASCADE 29		SAIL	FBG	IB	25D	VLVO	8 2	7500	4 9	14200	16100
36	CASCADE 36		SAIL	FBG	IB	25D	WEST	10	13500	5 6	26800	29700
42	CASCADE 42		SAIL	FBG	IB	38D	WEST	11 2	20000	6	42500	47200
				1973 BOATS								
29	CASCADE 29	SLP	SAIL	FBG KL	IB	15D		8 2	9000	4 9	16700	19000
36 2	CASCADE 36	SLP	SAIL	FBG KL	IB	25D		10	14000	5 6	27100	30200
36 2	CASCADE 36	KTH	SAIL	FBG KL	IB	25D		10	14000	5 6	27100	30200
42	CASCADE 42	SLP	SAIL	FBG KL	IB	37D		11 2	18000	6	39100	43400
42	CASCADE 42	KTH	SAIL	FBG KL	IB	37D		11 2	18000	6	39100	43400
				1972 BOATS								
29	CASCADE 29	SLP	SA/OD	FBG KL	IB	D		8 2	7500	4 9	13600	15400
36 2	CASCADE 36	KTH	SA/CR	FBG KL	IB	D		10	13500	5 6	25700	28600
41 9	CASCADE 42	KTH	SA/CR	FBG KL	IB	D		11 2	18500	6	38600	42900
				1971 BOATS								
29	CASCADE 29	SLP	SA/OD	FBG KL	IB	D		8 2		5 2	15000	17100
36 2	CASCADE 36	KTH	SA/CR	FBG KL	IB	25D		10	12000	5 6	22500	25000
				1970 BOATS								
29	CASCADE 29	SLP	SA/OD	FBG KL	IB	UNIV		8 2	7500	4 9	12800	14500
29	CASCADE 29	SLP	SA/OD	FBG KL	IB	D	VLVO	8 2	7500	4 9	12900	14700
36	CASCADE 36	SLP	SA/CR	FBG KL	IB	D		10		5 6	23600	26200
42	CASCADE 42	SLP	SA/CR	FBG KL	IB	D		11 2		6	42600	47300
				1969 BOATS								
29	CASCADE 29	SLP	SA/OD	FBG KL	IB	D		8 2	7500	4 9	12600	14300
34	CHINOOK 34	SLP	SA/CR	FBG CB	IB	D		9		3 10	19600	21700
36	CASCADE 36	SLP	SA/CR	FBG KL	IB	D		10	13500	5 6	23700	26300
42	CASCADE 42	SLP	SA/CR	FBG KL	IB	D		11 2	18500	6	36200	40200
				1968 BOATS								
29	CASCADE 29	SLP	SAIL	FBG KL	IB			8 2		5 2	12800	14500
34	CHINOOK 34	SLP	SAIL	FBG CB	OB			9		3 10	18900	21000
36	CASCADE 36	SLP	SAIL	FBG KL	IB			10		5 6	18800	20900
42	CASCADE 42	SLP	SAIL	FBG KL	IB			11 2		6	36800	40900
				1967 BOATS								
29	CASCADE 29	SLP	SA/OD	FBG KL	IB	25		8 2	7500	5 2	12000	13600
34	CHINOOK 34	SLP	SA/CR	FBG CB	IB	25		9		3 10	26400	29300
34	CHINOOK 34	KTH	SA/CR	FBG CB	IB	25		9		3 10	26400	29300
42	CASCADE 42	SLP	SA/CR	FBG KL	IB	40		11 2		6	36400	40400
42	CASCADE 42	KTH	SA/CR	FBG KL	IB	40		11 2		6	36400	40400
				1966 BOATS								
29	CASCADE 29	SLP	SA/OD	FBG KL	IB	25		8 2	7500	5 2	11800	13400
34	CHINOOK 34	SLP	SA/CR	FBG CB	IB	25		9		3 10	25900	28800
34	CHINOOK 34	KTH	SA/CR	FBG CB	IB	25		9		3 10	26000	28800
42	CASCADE 42	SLP	SA/CR	FBG KL	IB	40		11 2		6	35800	39700
42	CASCADE 42	KTH	SA/CR	FBG KL	IB	40		11 2		6	35800	39700
				1965 BOATS								
29	CASCADE 29	SLP	SAIL	FBG KL	IB			8 2		4 9	12100	13800

CAT KETCH CORP
MIAMI FL 33146   COAST GUARD MFG ID- CKI See inside cover to adjust price for area

For more recent years, see the BUC Used Boat Price Guide, Volume 1 or Volume 2

LOA FT IN	NAME AND/ OR MODEL	TOP/ RIG	BOAT TYPE	HULL MTL TP	TP	ENGINE # HP	MFG	BEAM FT IN	WGT LBS	DRAFT FT IN	RETAIL LOW	RETAIL HIGH
				1983 BOATS								
30 10	HERRESHOFF 31	KTH	SRCAC	FBG KL	IB	11D	BMW	10 4	8640	4	27700	30700
38	HERRESHOFF 38	KTH	SA/RC	FBG KL	IB	35D	BMW	11 6	13080	4 5	46000	50500
				1982 BOATS								
30 10	HERRESHOFF 31	KTH	SRCAC	FBG KL	IB	11D		10 4	8640	4	26000	28900
37	HERRESHOFF 37	KTH	SA/CR	FBG KL	IB	24D		11 3	12000	4 9	38000	42200

CAT LIMBO MARINE
COAST GUARD MFG ID- XKH

Call 1-800-327-6929 for BUC Personalized Evaluation Service
Or, for 1983 to 1984 boats, sign onto www.BUCValuPro.com

CATALINA BOAT MFG CO
HIALEAH FL 33013   See inside cover to adjust price for area

LOA FT IN	NAME AND/ OR MODEL	TOP/ RIG	BOAT TYPE	HULL MTL TP	TP	ENGINE # HP	MFG	BEAM FT IN	WGT LBS	DRAFT FT IN	RETAIL LOW	RETAIL HIGH
				1968 BOATS								
20 2	V-20			FBG	IO	120					5200	5950
23 4	V-24			FBG	IO	155-225					7700	9000
23 4	V-24			FBG	IO	T120					8650	9950

CATALINA YACHTS INC
WOODLAND HILLS CA 91367 COAST GUARD MFG ID- CTY See inside cover to adjust price for area

For more recent years, see the BUC Used Boat Price Guide, Volume 1 or Volume 2

LOA FT IN	NAME AND/ OR MODEL	TOP/ RIG	BOAT TYPE	HULL MTL TP	TP	ENGINE # HP	MFG	BEAM FT IN	WGT LBS	DRAFT FT IN	RETAIL LOW	RETAIL HIGH
				1983 BOATS								
21 6	CATALINA 22 POP TOP	SLP	SA/CR	FBG SK	OB			7 8	2250	2	3800	4400
21 6	CATALINA 22 STD DECK	SLP	SA/CR	FBG SK	OB			7 8	2490	3 6	4000	4700
21 6	CATALINA 22 STD DECK	SLP	SA/CR	FBG SK	OB			7 8	2250	2	3750	4350
25	CATALINA 25	SLP	SA/CR	FBG KL	OB			8	4550	4	8000	9150
25	CATALINA 25	SLP	SA/CR	FBG SK	OB			8	4150	2 8	7300	8400
26 10	CATALINA 27	SLP	SA/CR	FBG KL	OB			8 10	6850	4	13200	15000
26 10	CATALINA 27	SLP	SA/CR	FBG KL	IB	11D- 21D		8 10	6850	4	13700	15700
26 10	CATALINA 27 SHOAL	SLP	SA/CR	FBG KL	OB			8 10	7300	3 5	14200	16100
26 10	CATALINA 27 SHOAL	SLP	SA/CR	FBG KL	IB	11D		8 10	7250	3 5	14600	16700
29 11	CATALINA 30	SLP	SA/CR	FBG KL	IB	11D- 21D		10 10	10200	5	21800	24300
29 11	CATALINA 30 SHOAL	SLP	SA/CR	FBG KL	IB	11D- 21D		10 10	10650	4 4	22800	25400
35 7	CATALINA 36	SLP	SA/CR	FBG KL	IB	21D	UNIV	11 11	15000	5	31800	35400
38 3	CATALINA 38	SLP	SA/CR	FBG KL	IB	24D	UNIV	11 11	15900	6 9	35900	39900
38 3	CATALINA 38 SHOAL	SLP	SA/CR	FBG KL	IB	24D	UNIV	11 11	16700	4 11	37300	41500
				1982 BOATS								
21 6	CATALINA 22 POP TOP	SLP	SA/CR	FBG SK	OB			7 8	2490	3 6	3800	4450
21 6	CATALINA 22 POP TOP	SLP	SA/CR	FBG SK	OB			7 8	2250	2	3600	4150
21 6	CATALINA 22 STD DECK	SLP	SA/CR	FBG SK	OB			7 8	2490	3 6	3750	4350

LOA FT	LOA IN	NAME AND/ OR MODEL	TOP/ RIG	BOAT TYPE	-HULL- MTL	-HULL- TP	ENGINE TP	# HP	MFG	BEAM FT	BEAM IN	WGT LBS	DRAFT FT	DRAFT IN	RETAIL LOW	RETAIL HIGH
		1982 BOATS														
21	6	CATALINA 22 STD DECK	SLP	SA/CR	FBG	SK	OB			7	8	2250	2		3500	4100
25		CATALINA 25	SLP	SA/CR	FBG	KL	OB			8		4550	4		7500	8650
25		CATALINA 25	SLP	SA/CR	FBG	SK	OB			8		4150	2	8	6850	7900
26	10	CATALINA 27	SLP	SA/CR	FBG	KL	OB			8	10	6850	4		12400	14100
26	10	CATALINA 27	SLP	SA/CR	FBG	KL	IB	11D- 30D		8	10	6850	4		12900	14900
26	10	CATALINA 27 SHOAL	SLP	SA/CR	FBG	KL	OB			8	10	7300	3	5	13300	15100
26	10	CATALINA 27 SHOAL	SLP	SA/CR	FBG	KL	IB	11D- 30D		8	10	7300	3	5	13800	15900
29	11	CATALINA 30	SLP	SA/CR	FBG	KL	OB			10	10	10200	5	3	20300	22600
29	11	CATALINA 30	SLP	SA/CR	FBG	KL	IB	11D- 30D		10	10	10200	5	3	20500	22900
29	11	CATALINA 30 SHOAL	SLP	SA/CR	FBG	KL	OB			10	10	10650	4	4	21300	23600
29	11	CATALINA 30 SHOAL	SLP	SA/CR	FBG	KL	IB	11D- 30D		10	10	10650	4	4	21500	23900
35	7	CATALINA 36	SLP	SA/CR	FBG	KL	IB	21D	UNIV	11	11	15000	5	5	29900	33300
35	7	CATALINA 36	SLP	SA/RC	FBG	KL	IB	25D	UNIV	11	11	13000	5	4	26300	29200
38	3	CATALINA 38	SLP	SA/CR	FBG	KL	IB	24D	UNIV	11	10	15900	6	9	33800	37600
38	3	CATALINA 38 SHOAL	SLP	SA/CR	FBG	KL	IB	24D	UNIV	11	10	16700	4	11	35100	39000
		1981 BOATS														
21	6	CATALINA 22	SLP	SA/CR	FBG	KL	OB			7	8	2490	3	6	3550	4150
21	6	CATALINA 22	SLP	SA/CR	FBG	SK	OB			7	8	2250	2		3350	3900
25		CATALINA 25	SLP	SA/CR	FBG	KL	OB			8		4550	4		7050	8100
25		CATALINA 25	SLP	SA/CR	FBG	SK	OB			8		4150	2	8	6450	7450
26	10	CATALINA 27	SLP	SA/CR	FBG	KL	OB			8	10	6850	4		11700	13300
26	10	CATALINA 27	SLP	SA/CR	FBG	KL	IB	30D		8	10	6850	4		12200	14000
26	10	CATALINA 27 SHOAL	SLP	SA/CR	FBG	KL	OB			8	10	7300	3	5	12500	14200
26	10	CATALINA 27 SHOAL	SLP	SA/CR	FBG	KL	IB	30D		8	10	7300	3	5	13000	14900
29	11	CATALINA 30	SLP	SA/CR	FBG	KL	IB	11D- 30D		10	10	10200	5	3	19300	21500
29	11	CATALINA 30 SHOAL	SLP	SA/CR	FBG	KL	IB	11D- 30D		10	10	10650	4	4	20200	22500
38	3	CATALINA 38	SLP	SA/CR	FBG	KL	IB	24D	UNIV	11	10	15900	6	9	31800	35300
38	3	CATALINA 38 SHOAL	SLP	SA/CR	FBG	KL	IB	24D	UNIV	11	10	16700	4	11	33000	36700
		1980 BOATS														
21	6	CATALINA 22	SLP	SA/CR	FBG	KL	OB			7	8	2490	3	6	3400	3950
21	6	CATALINA 22	SLP	SA/CR	FBG	SK	OB			7	8	2250	1	8	3200	3700
25		CATALINA 25	SLP	SA/CR	FBG	KL	OB			8		4550	4		6750	7750
25		CATALINA 25	SLP	SA/CR	FBG	SK	OB			8		4150	2	8	6150	7100
26	10	CATALINA 27	SLP	SA/CR	FBG	KL	OB			8	10	6550	4		10400	11800
26	10	CATALINA 27	SLP	SA/CR	FBG	KL	IB	30D		8	10	6550	4		10900	12600
26	10	CATALINA 27 SHOAL	SLP	SA/CR	FBG	KL	OB			8	10	6550	3	5	10900	12400
26	10	CATALINA 27 SHOAL	SLP	SA/CR	FBG	KL	IB	30D		8	10	6550	3	5	11300	13000
29	11	CATALINA 30	SLP	SA/CR	FBG	KL	IB	11D- 30D		10	10	10200	5	3	18400	20500
29	11	CATALINA 30 SHOAL	SLP	SA/CR	FBG	KL	IB	11D- 30D		10	10	10200	4	4	18900	21100
38	3	CATALINA 38	SLP	SA/CR	FBG	KL	IB	24D	UNIV	11	10	15900	6	9	30400	33700
		1979 BOATS														
21	6	CATALINA 22	SLP	SA/CR	FBG	KL	OB			7	8	2350	3	6	3150	3650
21	6	CATALINA 22	SLP	SA/CR	FBG	SK	OB			7	8	2350	1	8	3150	3650
25		CATALINA 25	SLP	SA/CR	FBG	KL	OB			8		4550	4		6500	7450
25		CATALINA 25	SLP	SA/CR	FBG	SK	OB			8		4550	2	8	6500	7450
26	10	CATALINA 27	SLP	SA/CR	FBG	KL	OB			8	10	6850	4		10500	11900
26	10	CATALINA 27	SLP	SA/CR	FBG	KL	IB	30D		8	10	6850	4		11000	12600
26	10	CATALINA 27 SHOAL	SLP	SA/CR	FBG	KL	OB			8	10	6850	3	5	11000	12500
26	10	CATALINA 27 SHOAL	SLP	SA/CR	FBG	KL	IB	30D		8	10	6850	3	5	11400	13100
29	11	CATALINA 30	SLP	SA/CR	FBG	KL	IB	30D		10	10	10200	5	3	17300	19800
29	11	CATALINA 30 SHOAL	SLP	SA/CR	FBG	KL	IB	30D		10	10	10200	4	4	18200	20200
38	3	CATALINA 38	SLP	SA/CR	FBG	KL	IB	22D	YAN	11	10	15900	6	9	29200	32400
38	3	CATALINA 38	SLP	SA/CR	FBG	KL	IB	30D	UNIV	11	10	15900	6	9	29300	32500
		1978 BOATS														
21	6	CATALINA 22	SLP	SA/CR	FBG	KL	OB			7	8	2150	3	6	2850	3350
21	6	CATALINA 22	SLP	SA/CR	FBG	SK	OB			7	8	1850	1	8	2650	3050
25		CATALINA 25	SLP	SA/CR	FBG	KL	OB			8		4550	4		6250	7200
25		CATALINA 25	SLP	SA/CR	FBG	SK	OB			8		4150	2		5700	6550
26	10	CATALINA 27	SLP	SA/CR	FBG	KL	OB			8	10	6550	4		9850	11200
26	10	CATALINA 27	SLP	SA/CR	FBG	KL	IB	30	UNIV	8	10	6550	4		10100	11500
26	10	CATALINA 27	SLP	SA/CR	FBG	KL	IB	7D	PETT	8	10	6550	4		10200	11600
29	11	CATALINA 30	SLP	SA/CR	FBG	KL	OB			10	10	10200	5	3	16400	18700
29	11	CATALINA 30	SLP	SA/CR	FBG	KL	IB	30	UNIV	10	10	10200	5	3	16600	18800
29	11	CATALINA 30	SLP	SA/CR	FBG	KL	IB	12D	YAN	10	10	10200	5	3	16600	18900
29	11	CATALINA 30 SHOAL	SLP	SA/CR	FBG	KL	OB			10	10	10200	4	4	17100	19400
29	11	CATALINA 30 SHOAL	SLP	SA/CR	FBG	KL	IB	30	UNIV	10	10	10200	4	4	17100	19400
29	11	CATALINA 30 SHOAL	SLP	SA/CR	FBG	KL	IB	12D	YAN	10	10	10200	4	4	17200	19500
38	3	CATALINA 38	SLP	SA/CR	FBG	KL	IB	30	UNIV	11	9	14750	6	7	26200	29100
38	3	CATALINA 38	SLP	SA/CR	FBG	KL	IB	22D	YAN	11	9	14750	6	7	26500	29500
		1977 BOATS														
21	6	CATALINA 22	SLP	SA/CR	FBG	KL	OB			7	8	2150	3	6	2750	3200
21	6	CATALINA 22	SLP	SA/CR	FBG	SK	OB			7	8	1850	1	8	2550	2950
25	1	CATALINA 25	SLP	SA/CR	FBG	KL	OB			7	11	4150	4		5550	6400
25	1	CATALINA 25	SLP	SA/CR	FBG	SK	OB			7	11	4150	2		5550	6400
26	10	CATALINA 27	SLP	SA/CR	FBG	KL	OB			8	10	6550	4		9550	10800
26	10	CATALINA 27	SLP	SA/CR	FBG	KL	IB	30	UNIV	8	10	6550	4		9750	11100
26	10	CATALINA 27	SLP	SA/CR	FBG	KL	IB	6D	PETT	8	10	6550	4		9850	11200
29	11	CATALINA 30	SLP	SA/CR	FBG	KL	IB	30	UNIV	10	10	10200	5	3	16000	18200
29	11	CATALINA 30	SLP	SA/CR	FBG	KL	IB	12D	YAN	10	10	10200	5	3	16100	18300
29	11	CATALINA 30 SHOAL	SLP	SA/CR	FBG	KL	IB	30	UNIV	10	10	10200	4	4	16500	18800
29	11	CATALINA 30 SHOAL	SLP	SA/CR	FBG	KL	IB	12D	YAN	10	10	10200	4	4	16500	18800
38	2	CATALINA 38	SLP	SA/CR	FBG	KL	IB	30	UNIV	11	9	16000	6	6	26900	29900
38	2	CATALINA 38	SLP	SA/CR	FBG	KL	IB	22D	YAN	11	9	16000	6	6	27200	30300
		1976 BOATS														
21	6	CATALINA 22	SLP	SAIL	FBG	KL	OB			7	8	2150	3	6	2700	3100
21	6	CATALINA 22	SLP	SAIL	FBG	SK	OB			7	8	1850	1	8	2450	2850
25		CATALINA 25	SLP	SAIL	FBG	KL	OB			7	11	4200	4		5400	6200
25		CATALINA 25	SLP	SAIL	FBG	SK	OB			7	11	4000	2	6	5150	5950
26	10	CATALINA 27	SLP	SAIL	FBG	KL	OB			8	10	6500	4		9200	10500
26	10	CATALINA 27	SLP	SAIL	FBG	KL	IB	30	UNIV	8	10	6700	4		9650	11000
26	10	CATALINA 27	SLP	SAIL	FBG	KL	IB	7D	PETT	8	10	6700	4		9750	11100
29	11	CATALINA 30	SLP	SAIL	FBG	KL	IB	30	UNIV	10	10	10000	5		15400	17500
29	11	CATALINA 30	SLP	SAIL	FBG	KL	IB	12D	YAN	10	10	10000	5		15500	17600
38	2	CATALINA	SLP	SAIL	FBG	KL	IB			11	9	16000	6	3	26100	29000
		1975 BOATS														
21	6	CATALINA 22	SLP	SAIL	FBG	KL	OB			7	8	2150	3	6	2600	3050
21	6	CATALINA 22	SLP	SAIL	FBG	SK	OB			7	8	1850	1	8	2400	2800
26	10	CATALINA 27	SLP	SAIL	FBG	KL	OB			8	10	6800	4		9400	10700
26	10	CATALINA 27	SLP	SAIL	FBG	KL	IB	30	UNIV	8	10	6800	4		9550	10800
26	10	CATALINA 27	SLP	SAIL	FBG	KL	IB	8D	PETT	8	10	6800	4		9650	11000
29	11	CATALINA 30	SLP	SAIL	FBG	KL	IB	30	UNIV	10	10	10000	5		15000	17000
29	11	CATALINA 30	SLP	SAIL	FBG	KL	IB	12D	YAN	10	10	10000	5		15100	17100
		1974 BOATS														
21	6	CATALINA 22	SLP	SAIL	FBG	KL	OB			7	8	2150	3	6	2550	2950
21	6	CATALINA 22	SLP	SAIL	FBG	SK	OB			7	8	1850	1	8	2300	2700
26	10	CATALINA 27	SLP	SAIL	FBG	KL	OB			8	10	6550	4		8700	10000
26	10	CATALINA 27	SLP	SAIL	FBG	KL	IB	30	UNIV	8	10	6550	4		9000	10200
29	11	CATALINA 30	SLP	SAIL	FBG	KL	IB			10	10	9800	5		14300	16200
		1973 BOATS														
21	6	CATALINA 22	SLP	SAIL	FBG	KL	OB			7	8	1850	3	6	2300	2650
21	6	CATALINA 22	SLP	SAIL	FBG	SK	OB			7	8	2150	1	8	2500	2900
26	10	CATALINA 27	SLP	SAIL	FBG	KL	OB			8	10	6550	4		8450	9750
26	10	CATALINA 27	SLP	SAIL	FBG	KL	IB	30	UNIV	8	10	6550	4		8650	9950
		1972 BOATS														
21	6	CATALINA 22	SLP	SAIL	FBG	KL	OB			7	8	2150	3	6	2400	2800
21	6	CATALINA 22	SLP	SAIL	FBG	SK	OB			7	8	1850	1	8	2250	2600
26	10	CATALINA 27	SLP	SAIL	FBG	KL	OB			8	10	5650	4		7100	8150
		1971 BOATS														
21	6	CATALINA 22	SLP	SAIL	FBG	KL	OB			7	8	2150	3	6	2350	2750
21	6	CATALINA 22	SLP	SAIL	FBG	SK	OB			7	8	1850	1	8	2200	2550
26	10	CATALINA 27	SLP	SAIL	FBG	KL	OB			8	10	5650	4		6950	8000
		1970 BOATS														
21	6	CATALINA 22	SLP	SA/AC	FBG	KL	OB			7	8	2150	3	6	2350	2700
21	6	CATALINA 22	SLP	SAIL	FBG	SK	OB			7	8	1850	1	8	2150	2500
26	10	CATALINA 27	SLP	SAIL	FBG	KL	OB			8	10	5650	4		6800	7850

CATAMARAN CO INC

Call 1-800-327-6929 for BUC Personalized Evaluation Service
Or, for 1959 to 1960 boats, sign onto www.BUCValuPro.com

CATAMARAN DESIGN & SALES

Call 1-800-327-6929 for BUC Personalized Evaluation Service
Or, for 1970 boats, sign onto www.BUCValuPro.com

CATAMARAN MOTOR YACHTS

Call 1-800-327-6929 for BUC Personalized Evaluation Service
Or, for 1970 boats, sign onto www.BUCValuPro.com

KENNETH CAVANAUGH

Call 1-800-327-6929 for BUC Personalized Evaluation Service
Or, for 1976 to 1984 boats, sign onto www.BUCValuPro.com

CBC LYMAN

FT MYERS FL 33916 COAST GUARD MFG ID- LYM See inside cover to adjust price for area
ALSO LYMAN INDUSTRIES INC

For more recent years, see the BUC Used Boat Price Guide, Volume 1 or Volume 2

LOA FT	IN	NAME AND/ OR MODEL	TOP/ RIG	BOAT TYPE	-HULL- MTL	TP	----ENGINE--- TP	# HP	MFG	BEAM FT	IN	WGT LBS	DRAFT FT	IN	RETAIL LOW	RETAIL HIGH
		1982 BOATS														
24	4	BISCAYNE 24	OP	RNBT	FBG	RB	IB	220	CRUS	8	11	4600	2	1	13600	15500
24	4	SPORTSMAN 24	OP	RNBT	FBG	RB	IB	220-228		8	11	4400	2	1	13200	15000
24	4	SPORTSMAN 24	OP	RNBT	FBG	RB	IB	124D-145D		8	11	4400	2	1	16500	19800
26	7	CRUISETTE 26	OP	FSH	FBG	RB	IB	220-270		9	1	5200	2	4	17100	20000
26	7	CRUISETTE 26	OP	FSH	FBG	RB	IB	124D-145D		9	1	5200	2	4	19600	22700
26	7	CRUISETTE 26	HT	FSH	FBG	RB	IB	220-270		9	1	5500	2	4	18000	20600
26	7	CRUISETTE 26	HT	FSH	FBG	RB	IB	124D-145D		9	1	5500	2	4	20300	23800
26	7	FISHERMAN/SLEEPER 26	OP	FSH	FBG	RB	IB	220-270		9	1	4900	2	4	16600	19500
26	7	FISHERMAN/SLEEPER 26	OP	FSH	FBG	RB	IB	124D-160D		9	1	4900	2	4	18600	22700
26	7	FISHERMAN/SLEEPER 26	HT	FSH	FBG	RB	IB	220-270		9	1	5200	2	4	17100	20000
26	7	FISHERMAN/SLEEPER 26	HT	FSH	FBG	RB	IB	124D-160D		9	1	5200	2	4	19600	23700
		1981 BOATS														
24	4	BISCAYNE 24	OP	RNBT	FBG	RB	IB	220-228		8	11	4600	2	1	13100	14900
24	4	BISCAYNE 24	OP	RNBT	FBG	RB	IB	124D-145D		8	11	4600	2	1	16400	19600
24	4	SPORTSMAN 24	OP	RNBT	FBG	RB	IB	220-228		8	11	4400	2	1	12700	14400
24	4	SPORTSMAN 24	OP	RNBT	FBG	RB	IB	124D-145D		8	11	4400	2	1	15800	19100
26	7	CRUISETTE 26	OP	FSH	FBG	RB	IB	220-270		9	1	5200	2	4	16400	19200
26	7	CRUISETTE 26	OP	FSH	FBG	RB	IB	124D-145D		9	1	5200	2	4	18800	22100
26	7	CRUISETTE 26	HT	FSH	FBG	RB	IB	220-270		9	1	5500	2	4	16900	19800
26	7	CRUISETTE 26	HT	FSH	FBG	RB	IB	124D-145D		9	1	5500	2	4	19800	22900
26	7	FISHERMAN/SLEEPER	OP	FSH	FBG	RB	IB	124D-130D		9	1	4900	2	4	17500	20500
26	7	FISHERMAN/SLEEPER	OP	FSH	FBG	RB	IB	160D	PERK	9	1	4900	2	4	19900	22100
26	7	FISHERMAN/SLEEPER	HT	FSH	FBG	RB	IB	130D-160D		9	1	5200	2	4	19400	22800
26	7	FISHERMAN/SLEEPER 26	OP	FSH	FBG	RB	IB	220-270		9	1	4900	2	4	15900	18600
26	7	FISHERMAN/SLEEPER 26	OP	FSH	FBG	RB	IB	145D	ISUZ	9	1	4900	2	4	19000	21100
26	7	FISHERMAN/SLEEPER 26	HT	FSH	FBG	RB	IB	220-270		9	1	5200	2	4	16400	19200
26	7	FISHERMAN/SLEEPER 26	HT	FSH	FBG	RB	IB	124D-145D		9	1	5200	2	4	18800	22100
		1980 BOATS														
24	4	BISCAYNE 24	OP	RNBT	FBG	RB	IB	220-228		8	11	4600	2	1	12500	14200
24	4	BISCAYNE 24	OP	RNBT	FBG	RB	IB	130D-145D		8	11	4600	2	1	16400	18900
24	4	SPORTSMAN 24	OP	RNBT	FBG	RB	IB	220-228		8	11	4400	2	1	12200	13900
24	4	SPORTSMAN 24	OP	RNBT	FBG	RB	IB	130D-145D		8	11	4400	2	1	15900	18300
26	7	CRUISETTE 26	OP	FSH	FBG	RB	IB	220-270		9	1	5200	2	4	15700	18400
26	7	CRUISETTE 26	OP	FSH	FBG	RB	IB	145D	ISUZ	9	1	5200	2	4	19100	21200
26	7	CRUISETTE 26	HT	FSH	FBG	RB	IB	220-270		9	1	5500	2	4	16200	18900
26	7	CRUISETTE 26	HT	FSH	FBG	RB	IB	145D	ISUZ	9	1	5500	2	4	19800	22000
26	7	FISHERMAN/SLEEPER 26	OP	FSH	FBG	RB	IB	220-270		9	1	4900	2	4	15200	17800
26	7	FISHERMAN/SLEEPER 26	OP	FSH	FBG	RB	IB	145D	ISUZ	9	1	4900	2	4	18200	20300
26	7	FISHERMAN/SLEEPER 26	HT	FSH	FBG	RB	IB	220-270		9	1	5200	2	4	15700	18400
26	7	FISHERMAN/SLEEPER 26	HT	FSH	FBG	RB	IB	124D-145D		9	1	5200	2	4	18100	21200
		1979 BOATS														
19	4	SEBRING 19	OP	RNBT	FBG	SV	IO	120-170		7	4		2	1	4600	5300
24	4	BISCAYNE 24	OP	RNBT	FBG	RB	IB	220-228		8	11	4600	2	1	12100	13700
24	4	BISCAYNE 24	OP	RNBT	FBG	RB	IB	124D-145D		8	11	4600	2	1	15100	18200
24	4	SPORTSMAN 24	OP	RNBT	FBG	RB	IB	220-228		8	11	4400	2	1	11700	13300
24	4	SPORTSMAN 24	OP	RNBT	FBG	RB	IB	124D-145D		8	11	4400	2	1	14700	17700
26	7	CRUISETTE 26	OP	WKNDR	FBG	RB	IB	220-270		9	1	5200	2	4	15400	18100
26	7	CRUISETTE 26	OP	WKNDR	FBG	RB	IB	124D-145D		9	1	5200	2	4	17400	20900
26	7	CRUISETTE 26	HT	WKNDR	FBG	RB	IB	220-270		9	1	5500	2	4	15900	18700
26	7	CRUISETTE 26	HT	WKNDR	FBG	RB	IB	124D-145D		9	1	5500	2	4	18700	21900
26	7	FISHERMAN/SLEEPER 26	OP	FSH	FBG	RB	IB	200-270		9	1	4900	2	4	14400	17100
26	7	FISHERMAN/SLEEPER 26	OP	FSH	FBG	RB	IB	124D-145D		9	1	4900	2	4	16200	19500
26	7	FISHERMAN/SLEEPER 26	OP	FSH	FBG	RB	IB	160D-200D		9	1	4900	2	4	18400	21300
26	7	FISHERMAN/SLEEPER 26	HT	FSH	FBG	RB	IB	200-270		9	1	5200	2	4	14800	17600
26	7	FISHERMAN/SLEEPER 26	HT	FSH	FBG	RB	IB	124D-145D		9	1	5200	2	4	17100	20400
26	7	FISHERMAN/SLEEPER 26	HT	FSH	FBG	RB	IB	160D-200D		9	1	5200	2	4	19200	22200
		1978 BOATS														
19	4	SEBRING 19	OP	RNBT	FBG	SV	IO	120-185		7	4	2000	2	1	4100	5050
24	4	BISCAYNE 24	OP	RNBT	FBG	RB	IB	220-225		8	11	4600	2	1	11600	13200
24	4	SPORTSMAN 24	OP	RNBT	FBG	RB	IB	220-225		8	11	4400	2	1	11200	12700
26	2	CRUISETTE 26	OP	WKNDR	FBG	RB	IB	220-270		9	1	5400	2	4	14700	17200
26	2	CRUISETTE 26	HT	WKNDR	FBG	RB	IB	220-270		9	1	5800	2	4	15400	17900
26	2	FISHERMAN/SLEEPER 26	OP	FSH	FBG	RB	IB	220-270		9	1	5000	2	4	13700	16100
26	2	FISHERMAN/SLEEPER 26	HT	FSH	FBG	RB	IB	220-270		9	1	5400	2	4	14400	16800
28		GULFSTREAM 28	FB	EXP	FBG	SV	VD	250-350		11	3	9500	2	9	21400	24800
28		GULFSTREAM 28	FB	EXP	FBG	SV	VD	T220-T225		11	3	10500	2	9	24200	26900
		1977 BOATS														
19	4	SEBRING 19	OP	RNBT	FBG	SV	IO	120		7	4	2000	2	1	4150	4800
24	4	BISCAYNE 24	OP	RNBT	FBG	RB	IB	225		8	11	4000	2	1	10300	11700
24	4	SPORTSMAN 24	OP	RNBT	FBG	RB	IB	225		8	11	4000	2	1	9700	11000
26	2	CRUISETTE 26	OP	WKNDR	FBG	RB	IB	225		9	1	4500	2	4	12700	14400
26	2	FISHERMAN/SLEEPER 26	OP	FSH	FBG	RB	IB	225		9	1	4500	2	4	12400	14100
28		GULFSTREAM 28	FB	SDN	FBG	RB	IB	T225		11	3	10000	2	9	24100	26800
		1976 BOATS														
19	4	SEBRING 19	OP	RNBT	FBG	RB	IO	140-170		7	4	2000	2	1	4200	4950
24	4	BISCAYNE 24	OP	RNBT	FBG	RB	IO	225		8	11	4000	2	1	9800	11100
24	4	SPORTSMAN 24	OP	RNBT	FBG	RB	IO	225		8	11	4000	2	1	9200	10500
26	2	CRUISETTE 26	OP	WKNDR	FBG	RB	IO	250		9	1	4500	2	4	12800	14600
28		GULFSTREAM 28	FB	SDN	FBG	RB	IO	280		11	3	10000	2	9	22200	24600
28		GULFSTREAM 28	FB	SDN	FBG	RB	IO	T225		11	3	10000	2	9	24000	26700
		1975 BOATS														
19	4	SEBRING 19	OP	RNBT	FBG	SV	IO	120-170		7	4	2000	2	1	4350	5050
24	4	BISCAYNE 24	OP	RNBT	FBG	RB	IB	220-225		8	11	4000	2	1	9650	11000
24	4	SPORTSMAN 24	OP	RNBT	FBG	RB	IB	220-225		8	11	4000	2	1	9100	10300
26	2	CRUISETTE 26	OP	WKNDR	FBG	RB	IB	220-270		9	1	4500	2	4	11800	13900
28		GULFSTREAM 28	FB	SDN	FBG	RB	VD	280-350		11	3	10000	2	9	20900	24100
28		GULFSTREAM 28	FB	SDN	FBG	RB	VD	T220-T225		11	3	10000	2	9	22600	25100
		1974 BOATS														
19	4	SEBRING 19 DELUXE	ST	RNBT	FBG	SV	IO	120-155		7	4	2000	2	1	4500	5200
24	4	BISCAYNE 24	ST	RNBT	FBG	RB	IB	190-225		8	11	4000	2	1	9050	10500
24	4	SPORTSMAN 24	ST	RNBT	FBG	RB	IB	190-225		8	11	4000	2	1	8500	10000
26	2	SLEEPER 26	OP	CUD	L/P	RB	IB	225-270		9	1	3700	2	4	9850	11500
28		GULFSTREAM 28	FB	SDN	FBG	RB	IB	280-350		11	3	10000	2	9	20000	23000
28		GULFSTREAM 28	FB	SDN	FBG	RB	IB	T220-T225		11	3	10000	2	9	22000	24400
		1973 BOATS														
19	4	SEBRING 19	OP	RNBT	FBG		IO	120-200		7	4	2000	2	1	4650	5450
24	4	BISCAYNE 24	OP	RNBT	FBG		IB	200-220		8	11	3000	2	1	7250	8500
24	4	SPORTSMAN 24	OP	RNBT	FBG		IB	200-220		8	11	3000	2	1	6900	8100
26	2	CRUISETTE 26	OP	WKNDR	L/P	RB	IB	225-270		9	1	3700	2	4	9950	11800
28		GULFSTREAM	FB		FBG		IB	300-350		11	3	9500	2	9	18000	20600
28		GULFSTREAM	FB		FBG		IB	T200-T225		11	3	10000	2	9	19600	22200
28		GULFSTREAM	FB	SDN	FBG		IB	280	CHRY	11	3	9500	2	9	19000	21100
28		GULFSTREAM	FB	SDN	FBG		IB	T190	PALM	11	3	10000	2	9	20600	22800
		1972 BOATS														
19	4	SEBRING 19	OP	RNBT	FBG		IO	120-155		7	4	2000	2	1	4800	5550
23				RNBT	L/P		IB	200-220		8	9	3000	2	1	6300	7400
23		GULFSTREAM	OP	CUD	L/P		IB	200-220		8	9	3000	2	1	6250	7300
24	4	BISCAYNE 24	OP	RNBT	FBG		IB	200-220		8	11	3000	2	1	6750	7950
26	2			CR	L/P		IB	220-270		9	1	3600	2	4	9150	10800
26	2		HT	CR	L/P		IB	220-270		9	1	3700	2	4	9250	10900
26	2	CRUISETTE 26	OP	WKNDR	L/P		IB	220-270		9	1	3700	2	4	9650	11300
26	2	CRUISETTE 26	HT	WKNDR	L/P		IB	220-270		9	1	3800	2	4	9800	11500
26	2	GULFSTREAM	OP	SF	L/P		IB	220-270		9	1	3600	2	4	8850	10400
29	10	GULFSTREAM	OP	SF	L/P		IB	T220-T270		10	9	7400	2	7	16500	19500
29	10	GULFSTREAM	HT	SF	L/P		IB	T220-T270		10	9	7700	2	7	16600	19600
29	10	GULFSTREAM	FB	SF	L/P		IB	T220-T270		10	9	7800	2	7	17400	20500
29	10	ISLANDER	HT	SDN	L/P		IB	T220-T270		10	9	7700	2	7	19900	22800
29	10	ISLANDER	FB	SDN	L/P		IB	T220-T270		10	9	7800	2	7	19900	22900
29	10	ISLANDER	HT	SPTCR	L/P		IB	T220-T270		10	9	7700	2	7	18400	21200
29	10	ISLANDER	FB	SPTCR	L/P		IB	T220-T270		10	9	7800	2	7	18400	21300
29	10	MARINER		EXP	L/P		IB	T220-T270		10	9	7700	2	7	20000	22800
29	10	MARINER	HT	EXP	L/P		IB	T220-T270		10	9	7800	2	7	20100	22900
29	10	SPORTSMAN	HT	SDN	L/P		IB	270	CRUS	10	9	7700	2	7	18100	20100
29	10	SPORTSMAN	HT	SDN	L/P		IB	T220-T250		10	9	7700	2	7	19900	22600
29	10	SPORTSMAN	FB	SDN	L/P		IB	T220-T270		10	9	7800	2	7	19900	22900
29	10	SPORTSMAN	OP	SPTCR	L/P		IB	T220-T270		10	9	7400	2	7	18100	21000
29	10	SPORTSMAN	HT	SPTCR	L/P		IB	225-270		10	9	7700	2	7	15900	18600
29	10	SPORTSMAN	HT	SPTCR	L/P		IB	T220	CRUS	10	9	7700	2	7	18300	20300
29	10	SPORTSMAN	FB	SPTCR	L/P		IB	T220-T270		10	9	7800	2	7	18300	21200
35	2	SEA-HAWK	HT	EXP	L/P		IB	T220	CRUS	12	3	13600	2	8	35200	39100
		IB T225 CHRY 35100 39000, IB T235 CC 35200 39200, IB T250 CHRY 35400 39300														
		IB T270 CRUS 35800 39800, IB T280 CHRY 35800 39700														
35	2	SEA-HAWK	FB	EXP	L/P		IB	T220	CRUS	12	3	13600	2	8	35200	39100
		IB T225 CHRY 35100 39000, IB T235 CC 35300 39200, IB T250 CHRY 35400 39300														
		IB T270 CRUS 35900 39800, IB T280 CHRY 35800 39800														
		1971 BOATS														
23				RNBT	PLY		IB	200-210		8	9	3000	2	1	6100	7200
23		OFFSHORE		OFF	PLY		IB	200-210		8	9	3000	2	1	6100	7200
26	2			CR	PLY		IB	210-260		9	1	3600	2	4	8700	10300
26	2		HT	CR	PLY		IB	210-260		9	1	3600	2	4	8700	10400
26	2	CRUISETTE	OP	WKNDR	PLY		IB	210-260		9	1	3700	2	4	9250	10900
26	2	CRUISETTE	HT	WKNDR	PLY		IB	210-260		9	1	3700	2	4	9250	10900
26	2	OFFSHORE		OFF	PLY		IB	210-260		9	1	3600	2	4	8350	9950

CONTINUED ON NEXT PAGE

LOA		NAME AND/	TOP/	BOAT	-HULL-		----ENGINE---			BEAM		WGT	DRAFT		RETAIL	RETAIL
FT	IN	OR MODEL	RIG	TYPE	MTL	TP	TP	# HP	MFG	FT	IN	LBS	FT	IN	LOW	HIGH
1971 BOATS																
29	8	MARINER		EXP	PLY	DS	IB	T220		10	9		2	7	19500	21600
29	8	OFFSHORE		CUD	PLY	DS	IB	T220		10	9		2	7	15600	17700
29	9			EXP	PLY		IB	T210-T260		10	9	7700	2	7	19000	22000
29	9		HT	EXP	PLY		IB	T210-T260		10	9	7700	2	7	19000	22000
29	9	ISLANDER	HT	SPTCR	PLY		IB	T210-T260		10	9	7700	2	7	17000	20100
29	9	ISLANDER	FB	SPTCR	PLY		IB	T210-T260		10	9	7700	2	7	17000	20100
29	9	SPORTSMAN	OP	SPTCR	PLY		IB	T210-T260		10	9	7400	2	7	16900	19900
29	9	SPORTSMAN	HT	SPTCR	PLY		IB	T210-T260		10	9	7400	2	7	16900	19900
29	9	SPORTSMAN	FB	SPTCR	PLY		IB	T210-T260		10	9	7400	2	7	16900	19900
35	2	SEA-HAWK	HT	EXP	PLY		IB	T210	CRUS	12	3	13600	2	6	33700	37500
		IB T225 CHRY 33700 37500, IB T250 CHRY 34000 37800, IB T260 CRUS 34300 38100														
		IB T280 CHRY 34400 38200														
35	2	SEA-HAWK	FB	EXP	PLY		IB	T210	CRUS	12	3	13600	2	6	33800	37500
		IB T225 CHRY 33800 37500, IB T250 CHRY 34100 37800, IB T260 CRUS 34400 38200														
		IB T280 CHRY 34400 38300														
1970 BOATS																
22	2			CR	PLY	RB	IB	200-220		7	11	2750	2	2	5150	6100
22	2		HT	CR	PLY	RB	IB	200-220		7	11	2750	2	2	5150	6100
23		OFFSHORE		OFF	PLY	RB	IB	200-220		8	9	3000	2	1	5850	6900
26	2			CR	PLY	RB	IB	210-260		9	1	3600	2	4	8350	9950
26	2		HT	CR	PLY	RB	IB	210-260		9	1	3600	2	4	8350	9950
26	2	CRUISETTE	OP	WKNDR	PLY	RB	IB	210-260		9	1	3700	2	4	8900	10500
26	2	CRUISETTE	HT	WKNDR	PLY	RB	IB	210-260		9	1	3700	2	4	8900	10500
26	2	OFFSHORE		OFF	PLY	RB	IB	210-260		9	1	3600	2	4	8050	9600
29	9	ISLANDER	HT	SPTCR	PLY	RB	IB	T210-T260		10	9	7700	2	7	16400	19400
29	9	ISLANDER	FB	SPTCR	PLY	RB	IB	T210-T260		10	9	7700	2	7	16400	19400
29	9	MARINER		EXP	PLY	RB	IB	T210-T260		10	9	7700	2	7	18300	21100
29	9	MARINER	HT	EXP	PLY	RB	IB	T210-T260		10	9	7700	2	7	18300	21100
29	9	SPORTSMAN	OP	SPTCR	PLY	RB	IB	T210-T260		10	9	7400	2	7	16200	19200
29	9	SPORTSMAN	HT	SPTCR	PLY	RB	IB	T210-T260		10	9	7400	2	7	16200	19200
29	9	SPORTSMAN	FB	SPTCR	PLY	RB	IB	T210-T260		10	9	7400	2	7	16200	19200
1969 BOATS																
16	3	STANDARD		RNBT	PLY		IO	150		6	3	905	2		2950	3450
16	3	STANDARD	OP	RNBT	L/P	RB	OB			6	3	655		10	1850	2250
18	2	STANDARD	OP	RNBT	L/P	RB	OB			7	1	855	1	1	2600	3050
18	2	STANDARD	OP	RNBT	PLY	RB	IO	120	MRCR	7	1	1105	1	8	4100	4750
19	6		OP	RNBT	PLY	RB	IB	165	INT	7	4	2300	2		3500	4100
19	6	STANDARD	OP	RNBT	PLY	RB	IO	120	MRCR	7	4	2200	1	10	5550	6350
22	2	SLEEPER		CR	PLY	RB	IO	160	MRCR	7	11	2450	2		7900	9050
22	2	SLEEPER		CR	PLY	RB	IB	200	CHRY	7	11	2650	2		4900	5600
26	2			EXP	PLY	RB	IB	225	CHRY	9	1	4000	2	4	8300	9550
26	2	CRUISETTE	OP	WKNDR	PLY	RB	IB	225	CHRY	9	1	3600	2	4	8400	9650
26	2	OFFSHORE		OFF	PLY	RB	IB	225	CHRY	9	1	3600	2	4	7750	8900
26	2	SLEEPER		CR	PLY	RB	IB	225	CHRY	9	1	3500	2	4	7950	9100
29	6	ISLANDER	HT	SPTCR	PLY	RB	IB	T225	CHRY	10	9	7600	2	7	15500	17700
29	6	MARINER		EXP	PLY	RB	IB	T225	CHRY	10	9	7600	2	7	16900	19200
29	6	SPORTSMAN	OP	SPTCR	PLY	RB	IB	T225	CHRY	10	9	7600	2	7	15500	17700
1968 BOATS																
16	3	STANDARD	OP	RNBT	L/P		OB			6	3	655	1	8	1900	2250
16	3	STANDARD	OP	RNBT	WD		IO	60		6	3	905	1	8	3000	3500
18	2	STANDARD	OP	RNBT	L/P		OB			7	1	855	1	8	2650	3050
18	2	STANDARD	OP	RNBT	WD		IO	80		7	1	1105	1	8	4200	4900
19	6		OP	RNBT	WD		IO	120		7	4	2200	1	10	5700	6550
19	6		OP	RNBT	WD		IB	165		7	4	2300	2		3400	3950
22	2	SLEEPER	OP	CUD	WD		IO	120-160		7	11	2450	2		8000	9250
22	2	SLEEPER	OP	CUD	WD		IB	195		7	11	2650	2	2	4700	5400
26			OP	CUD	WD		IB	250	CHRY						9150	10400
26	2			EXP	WD		IB	210		9	1	4000	2	4	7950	9150
26	2	CRUISETTE	OP	WKNDR	WD		IB	210		9	1	3600	2	4	8000	9200
26	2	SLEEPER	OP	CUD	WD		IB	210		9	1	3500	2	4	7500	8650
29	6	ISLANDER	HT	SPTCR	WD		IB	T210		10	9	7600	2	7	14800	16800
29	6	MARINER		EXP	WD		IB	T210		10	9	7600	2	7	16100	18300
29	6	SPORTSMAN	OP	SPTCR	WD		IB	T210		10	9	7600	2	7	14800	16800
1967 BOATS																
16	3	DELUXE	OP	RNBT	L/P		OB			6	3	655			2050	2450
16	3	RUNABOUT		RNBT	L/P		IO	60		6	3		1	8	4000	4650
16	3	STANDARD	OP	RNBT	L/P		OB			6	3	655			1700	2050
18					WD		IB	60	GRAY						**	
18	2				L/P		IO	120	MRCR	7	1	1205	1	8	4150	4850
18	2	DELUXE	OP	RNBT	L/P		OB			7	1	855			2850	3350
18	2	STANDARD	OP	RNBT	L/P		OB			7	1	855			2400	2800
19	6			RNBT	L/P		IO	120		9	4	2300	1	10	6950	8000
19	6			RNBT	L/P		IB	150-160		7	3	2500	2		3350	3900
22	2			CR	L/P		IO	120-160		7	11	2550	2		8500	9800
22	2			CR	L/P		IB	165-195		7	11	2750	2	2	4600	5350
22	2		HT	CR	L/P		IB	165-195		7	11	2750	2	2	4600	5350
26	2			CR	L/P		IB	190-210		9	1	3600	2	4	7250	8450
26	2		HT	CR	L/P		IB	190-210		9	1	3600	2	4	7250	8450
26	2	CRUISETTE	OP	WKNDR	L/P		IB	190-210		9	1	3700	2	4	7650	8950
26	2	CRUISETTE	HT	WKNDR	L/P		IB	190-210		9	1	3700	2	4	7650	8950
29	6			CR	L/P		IB	210		10	9	7700	2	7	12700	14400
29	6	ISLANDER	HT	SPTCR	L/P		IB	210		10	9	7700	2	7	12700	14400
29	6	ISLANDER	FB	SPTCR	L/P		IB	210		10	9	7700	2	7	12700	14400
29	6	MARINER		RNBT	L/P		IB	210		10	9		2	7	11400	13000
29	6	SPORTSMAN	OP	SPTCR	L/P		IB	210				7400			12500	14200
29	6	SPORTSMAN	HT	SPTCR	L/P		IB	210				7400			12500	14200
1966 BOATS																
16	3			RNBT	L/P		IO	60		6	3	1005			3250	3800
16	3	DELUXE	OP	RNBT	L/P		OB			6	3	655			2100	2500
16	3	STANDARD	OP	RNBT	L/P		OB			6	3	655			1700	2000
18	2			RNBT	PLY		IO	60		7	1	1205			4600	5300
18	2	DELUXE	OP	RNBT	PLY		OB			7	1	855			2650	3100
18	2	STANDARD	OP	RNBT	L/P		OB								3750	4400
19	6			RNBT	WD		IO	110		7	3		1	10	6650	7600
19	6			RNBT	WD		IB	150-165		7	3		2		3350	3950
21	1			RNBT	WD		IO	110		7	8		2		8400	9650
21	1			RNBT	WD		IO	150		7	8		2		8400	9700
21	1			RNBT	WD		IB	150-190		7	8		2	2	4250	5050
21	1		HT	RNBT	WD		IB	150-190		7	8		2	2	4250	5050
25	1			CR	WD		IB	190-220		8	10		2	4	7300	8500
25	1		HT	CR	WD		IB	190-220		8	10		2	4	7300	8500
25	1	CRUISETTE	OP	WKNDR	WD		IB	190-220		8	10		2	4	7500	8750
25	1	CRUISETTE	HT	WKNDR	WD		IB	190-220		8	10		2	4	7500	8750
28	3	ISLANDER	HT	SPTCR	WD		IB	T190-T195		10	6		2	7	11400	13000
28	3	ISLANDER	FB	SPTCR	WD		IB	T190-T195		10	6		2	7	11400	13000
28	3	MARINER		CR	WD		IB	T190-T195		10	6		2	7	11300	13000
28	3	SPORTSMAN	OP	SPTCR	WD		IB	T190-T195		10	6		2	7	11400	13000
1965 BOATS																
16		DELUXE	OP	RNBT	L/P		OB								2500	2950
16		STANDARD	OP	RNBT	L/P		OB								2000	2400
18		DELUXE	OP	RNBT	L/P		OB								4200	4850
18		STANDARD	OP	RNBT	L/P		OB								3400	3900
19					WD		IO	110							5950	7200
19				RNBT	WD		IB	80-120							2900	3500
19				RNBT	WD		IB	140							3100	3600
21					WD		IO	110-150							8550	10200
21			HT		WD		IO	110-150							8550	10200
21				RNBT	WD		IB	140-195							4150	4950
21			HT	RNBT	WD		IB	140-195							4150	4950
25				CR	WD		IB	190-220							7050	8250
25			HT	CR	WD		IB	190-220							7050	8250
28				CR	WD		IB	T190-T195							10600	12100
28		ISLANDER	HT	SPTCR	WD		IB	T190-T195							10700	12200
28		SPORTSMAN	OP	SPTCR	WD		IB	T190-T195							10700	12200
1964 BOATS																
16	2	DELUXE	OP	RNBT	L/P		OB								2550	3000
16	2	STANDARD	OP	RNBT	L/P		OB								2000	2400
18	2				WD		IO	80- 85							5100	5850
18	2	DELUXE	OP	RNBT	L/P		OB								4200	4900
18	2	STANDARD	OP	RNBT	L/P		OB								3400	3950
21	2				WD		IO	105-140							9000	10300
21	2			RNBT	WD		IB	138-178							4050	4800
25	1			RNBT	WD		IB	138-220							6500	7800
26					WD		IB	188	BUIC						**	**
28	3			CR	WD		IB	T188-T190							10500	11900
28	3	ISLANDER	HT	SPTCR	WD		IB	T188-T190							10500	12000
1963 BOATS																
16	2		OP	RNBT	L/P		OB								2300	2700
18	2				WD		IO	80- 85							5300	6050
18	2		OP	RNBT	L/P		OB								3850	4450
20	6				WD		IO	100							9000	10200
20	6			RNBT	WD		IB	109-178							3650	4500
24	6			CR	WD		IB	109-188							6150	7400
1962 BOATS																
16	2		OP	RNBT	L/P		OB								2350	2700
18	2				WD		IO	80							5450	6250
18	2		OP	RNBT	L/P		OB								3850	4500
20	6				WD		IO	100-178							9300	10600

 CONTINUED ON NEXT PAGE

LOA FT IN	NAME AND/ OR MODEL	TOP/ RIG	BOAT TYPE	-HULL- MTL TP	----ENGINE--- TP # HP	MFG	BEAM FT IN	WGT LBS	DRAFT FT IN	RETAIL LOW	RETAIL HIGH
---	--- --- 1962 BOATS										
20 6			RNBT	WD	IB 109-178					3550	4350
24 6			CR	WD	IB 109-188					5950	7200
---	--- --- 1961 BOATS										
16 2		OP	RNBT	L/P	OB		6 1	600		1800	2150
18 2		OP	RNBT	L/P	OB		7	1000		3150	3650
20 6			RNBT	L/P	IB 109		7 7		2 4	3350	3900
24 2			CUD	L/P	IB 109-135		8 9		2 4	5650	6550
24 6			CUD	WD	IB 188					5950	6850
---	--- --- 1960 BOATS										
16		OP	RNBT	L/P	OB					2350	2750
17		OP	RNBT	L/P	OB					3300	3850
18			RNBT	WD	OB					3900	4550
18	ISLANDER		RNBT	WD	60					2050	2400
19			RNBT	L/P	IB 60		6 10		2 6	2250	2650
19			RNBT	L/P	IB 125		6 10		2 6	2450	2850
19	ISLANDER		UTL	WD	IB 135					2400	2800
23			RNBT	L/P	IB 109-188		8		2 10	5000	6050
23	2 BERTH		CR	WD	IB 170					5600	6450
23	ISLANDER		UTL	WD	IB 170					5600	6450
23	SLEEPER		RNBT	L/P	IB 109-188		8		2 10	5500	6500
---	--- --- 1959 BOATS										
16	WO/FWD DK	OP	RNBT	L/P	OB					2400	2750
16 7		OP	RNBT	L/P	OB			540		1700	2000
17 2		OP	RNBT	L/P	OB			730		2350	2700
18 4		OP	RNBT	L/P	OB			900		2900	3400
18 4	ISLANDER		RNBT	L/P	IB 60		6 10			1950	2300
19 2	ISLANDER		RNBT	L/P	IB 109-135		6 10			2400	2900
23	ISLANDER		RNBT	L/P	IB 135-170		8			5300	6200
23	ISLANDER SLEEPER			L/P	IB 170		8			5350	6150
---	--- --- 1958 BOATS										
17		OP	RNBT	L/P	OB					3350	3900
18		OP	RNBT	L/P	OB					3950	4600
18	ISLANDER		RNBT	WD	IB 109					2200	2550
19			RNBT	WD	IB 109					2550	2950
23			UTL	WD	IB 125-135					5300	6150
---	--- --- 1957 BOATS										
16		OP	RNBT	L/P	OB					2400	2800
18			RNBT	WD	IB 100					2100	2500
18		OP	RNBT	L/P	OB					3950	4600
18	ISLANDER		RNBT	WD	IB 100					2100	2500
18 4				WD	IB 100	GRAY				**	**
23			UTL	WD	IB 125					5300	6050
---	--- --- 1956 BOATS										
18				WD	IB 90	GRAY				**	**
18			RNBT	WD	IB 100					2050	2450
18		OP	RNBT	L/P	OB					4000	4650
18	ISLANDER		RNBT	WD	IB 100					2050	2450
22	ISLANDER		RNBT	WD	IB 125					3900	4500
---	--- --- 1955 BOATS										
18			RNBT	WD	IB 60					1900	2300
18	ISLANDER		RNBT	WD	IB 60					1900	2300
20			RNBT	WD	IB 100					2950	3400
---	--- --- 1954 BOATS										
18	ISLANDER		RNBT	WD	IB 60					1900	2250
---	--- --- 1953 BOATS										
18	ISLANDER		RNBT	WD	IB 60					1850	2200
---	--- --- 1952 BOATS										
18	ISLANDER		RNBT	WD	IB 60					1850	2200
---	--- --- 1951 BOATS										
18	ISLANDER		RNBT	WD	IB 60					1800	2150
---	--- --- 1950 BOATS										
18	ISLANDER		RNBT	WD	IB 60					1800	2150
---	--- --- 1949 BOATS										
18	ISLANDER		RNBT	WD	IB 60					1800	2150
---	--- --- 1948 BOATS										
18	ISLANDER		RNBT	WD	IB 60					1750	2100
---	--- --- 1947 BOATS										
18	ISLANDER		RNBT	WD	IB 60					1750	2100
---	--- --- 1946 BOATS										
18	ISLANDER		RNBT	WD	IB 60					1750	2100
20		OP	RNBT	WD	IB					**	**
22		OP	RNBT	WD	IB					**	**
---	--- --- 1941 BOATS										
17	ISLANDER	OP	RNBT	WD	IB	GRAY				**	**
18		OP	RNBT	WD	IB	GRAY				**	**
19 6		OP	RNBT	WD	IB					**	**
21		OP	RNBT	WD	IB					**	**
24		OP	RNBT	WD	IB					**	**

CEE BEE MANUFACTURING INC
COAST GUARD MFG ID- CBM
FORMERLY CEE BEE MANUFACTURING CO

Call 1-800-327-6929 for BUC Personalized Evaluation Service
Or, for 1968 to 2004 boats, sign onto www.BUCValuPro.com

CELEBRITY BOATS
DIV SEA DOO / SKI DOO   See inside cover to adjust price for area
GRAND-MERE QUEBEC G9T 5 COAST GUARD MFG ID- QDO

For more recent years, see the BUC Used Boat Price Guide, Volume 1 or Volume 2

LOA FT IN	NAME AND/ OR MODEL	TOP/ RIG	BOAT TYPE	-HULL- MTL TP	----ENGINE--- TP # HP	MFG	BEAM FT IN	WGT LBS	DRAFT FT IN	RETAIL LOW	RETAIL HIGH
---	--- --- 1982 BOATS										
16 11	170VBR	ST	RNBT	FBG SV	IO 120-185		7 1	1250	6	2200	2550
16 11	170VBR	ST	RNBT	FBG SV	IO 120-185		7 1	2380	6	2250	2800
16 11	170VCD	ST	RNBT	FBG SV	OB		7 1	2380	6	2250	2600
18 8	188V	ST	RNBT	FBG SV	OB		7 8	1550	6	2650	3050
18 8	188VBR	ST	RNBT	FBG SV	IO 120-200		7 8	2420	6	2650	3200
18 8	188VBR	ST	RNBT	FBG SV	IO 228-260		7 8	2650	6	2800	3350
20 5	210V CUDDY	ST	FSH	FBG SV	IO 120-260		8	3250	7	3950	4900
20 5	210V RNBT	ST	CUD	FBG SV	IO 120-260		8	3250	7	3750	4650
20 5	210VBR	ST	RNBT	FBG SV	IO 120-260		8	3250	7	3600	4400
---	--- --- 1981 BOATS										
16 11	170V	ST	RNBT	FBG SV	IO 120-185		7 1	2160		2050	2450
16 11	170VBR	ST	RNBT	FBG SV	IO		7 1	1350	6	2300	2650
16 11	170VBR	ST	RNBT	FBG SV	IO 120-170		7 1	2160	6	2050	2450
16 11	170VBR	ST	RNBT	FBG SV	IO 185		7 1	2650		2350	2750
18 8	188V	ST	RNBT	FBG SV	OB		7 8			3250	3750
18 8	188VBR	ST	RNBT	FBG SV	IO 170-260		7 8	2650	6	2650	3300
20 5	210V CUDDY	ST	FSH	FBG SV	IO 198-260		8	3250	7	3950	4800
20 5	210V RNBT	ST	CUD	FBG SV	IO 198-260		8	3250	7	3750	4550
20 5	210VBR	ST	RNBT	FBG SV	IO 198-260		8	3250	7	3600	4350
---	--- --- 1980 BOATS										
16 11	170VBR	ST	RNBT	FBG SV	IO 120-170		7 1	1350	6	2200	2600
16 11	170VBR	ST	RNBT	FBG SV	IO 120-170		7 1	2160	6	2050	2450
18 2	182VBR	ST	RNBT	FBG SV	IO 165-260		7 8	2650	6	2600	3200
18 8	190VBR	ST	RNBT	FBG SV	IO 165-260		8			2900	3550
20 5	210V CUDDY		FSH	FBG SV	IO 198-260		8	3250	7	3900	4750
20 5	210V RNBT		CUD	FBG SV	IO 198-260		8	3250	7	3700	4500
20 5	210VBR	ST	RNBT	FBG SV	IO 198-260		8	3250	7	3550	4300
---	--- --- 1979 BOATS										
16 4	165VBR	ST	RNBT	FBG TR	IO 120-170		6 5	2150		1850	2250
16 9	170VBR	ST	RNBT	FBG SV	IO 120-170		7 1	1950		1900	2250
18 2	182VBR	ST	RNBT	FBG SV	IO 140-230		7 6	2600		2500	3050
20 5	210V FISHERMAN	ST	FSH	FBG SV	IO 198-260		8	3100		3800	4650
20 5	210VBR	ST	RNBT	FBG SV	IO 198-260		8	3100		3450	4200
20 5	SUNCRUISER 200	ST	CR	FBG SV	IO 140-260		8	3100		3550	4400

CELESTIAL YACHT LTD
GEMCRAFT LTD   See inside cover to adjust price for area
KOWLOON HONG KONG   COAST GUARD MFG ID- CYH

For more recent years, see the BUC Used Boat Price Guide, Volume 1 or Volume 2

LOA FT IN	NAME AND/ OR MODEL	TOP/ RIG	BOAT TYPE	-HULL- MTL TP	----ENGINE--- TP # HP	MFG	BEAM FT IN	WGT LBS	DRAFT FT IN	RETAIL LOW	RETAIL HIGH
---	--- --- 1983 BOATS										
44	CELESTIAL	KTH	SA/CR	FBG KL	HD 61D	LEHM	13 2	26300	5 6	81300	89300
44 4	CONSTELLATION 44	KTH	SA/CR	FBG KL	HD	D	13 9	27000	5 8	83700	92000
48	CELESTIAL	KTH	SA/CR	FBG KL	HD 65D	LEHM	13 6	28000	6	101500	112000
56	CELESTIAL 56	KTH	SA/RC	FBG KL	HD	D	15 4	42000	8 6	197500	217000
---	--- --- 1982 BOATS										
43	CELESTIAL	KTH	SA/CR	FBG KL	HD 65D	LEHM	13 1	24000	5 6	69600	76500
46	CELESTIAL	KTH	SA/CR	FBG KL	HD 65D	LEHM	13 6	29000	6	88000	96800
47	CELESTIAL	KTH	SA/CR	FBG KL	HD 65D	LEHM	13 6	29500	6	93000	102000
56	CELESTIAL 56	KTH	SA/RC	FBG KL	HD	D	15 4	42000	8 6	186500	205000
---	--- --- 1981 BOATS										
43	CELESTIAL	KTH	SA/CR	FBG KL	HD 65D	LEHM	13 1	24000	5 6	65500	71900
46	CELESTIAL	KTH	SA/CR	FBG KL	HD 65D	LEHM	13 6	29000	6	82800	91000
56	CELESTIAL 56	KTH	SA/RC	FBG KL	HD	D	13 9	42000	8 6	175500	193000

LOA FT IN	NAME AND/ OR MODEL	TOP/ RIG	BOAT TYPE	-HULL- MTL TP	----ENGINE--- TP # HP MFG	BEAM FT IN	WGT LBS	DRAFT FT IN	RETAIL LOW	RETAIL HIGH
					1980 BOATS					
46	CELESTIAL	KTH	SA/CR	FBG KL	HD 65D LEHM 13	6	31000	6	81400	89500

CENTARK IND INC
COAST GUARD MFG ID- CNH

Call 1-800-327-6929 for BUC Personalized Evaluation Service
Or, for 1977 to 1980 boats, sign onto www.BUCValuPro.com

CENTRAL BOAT WORKS

Call 1-800-327-6929 for BUC Personalized Evaluation Service
Or, for 1960 boats, sign onto www.BUCValuPro.com

CENTRAL ENGINEERING

Call 1-800-327-6929 for BUC Personalized Evaluation Service
Or, for 1968 to 1969 boats, sign onto www.BUCValuPro.com

CENTURIAN CORPORATION
COAST GUARD MFG ID- CTX

Call 1-800-327-6929 for BUC Personalized Evaluation Service
Or, for 1957 to 1978 boats, sign onto www.BUCValuPro.com

CENTURION BOATS INC
MERCED CA 95340   COAST GUARD MFG ID- CEE See inside cover to adjust price for area
FOR MORE RECENT MODELS SEE FINELINE

LOA FT IN	NAME AND/ OR MODEL	TOP/ RIG	BOAT TYPE	-HULL- MTL TP	----ENGINE--- TP # HP MFG	BEAM FT IN	WGT LBS	DRAFT FT IN	RETAIL LOW	RETAIL HIGH
					1983 BOATS					
16	6 16SK	OP	RNBT	FBG SV	OB	7	750		2250	2650
17	8 18SK	OP	RNBT	FBG SV	OB	7	850		2650	3050
19	TRUTRAC	OP	SKI	FBG SV	IB 250 PCM	6 10	2250	2	5200	6000
20	4 BAREFOOT	OP	SKI	FBG SV	OB	6 10	1350		4500	5150
20	8 SPORT 20	OP	RNBT	FBG SV	IO	7 10	2450		**	**
24	9 CLASSIC 25	OP	CUD	FBG SV	IO	8	4000		**	**
					1982 BOATS					
19	TRUTRAC	OP	SKI	FBG SV	IB 250 PCM	6 10	2250	2	5000	5700
20	4 BAREFOOT	OP	SKI	FBG SV	OB	6 10	1350		4400	5100

CENTURY BOAT COMPANY
C & C MANUFACTURING INC
PANAMA CITY FL 32404   COAST GUARD MFG ID- CGM   See inside cover to adjust price for area

For more recent years, see the BUC Used Boat Price Guide, Volume 1 or Volume 2

LOA FT IN	NAME AND/ OR MODEL	TOP/ RIG	BOAT TYPE	-HULL- MTL TP	----ENGINE--- TP # HP MFG	BEAM FT IN	WGT LBS	DRAFT FT IN	RETAIL LOW	RETAIL HIGH
					1983 BOATS					
16	5 CENTURY 1000	OP	RNBT	FBG SV	OB	7	1065	2 7	1800	2150
16	5 CENTURY 1000 B/R	OP	RNBT	FBG SV	OB	7	1065	2 7	1800	2150
16	5 CENTURY 1000 B/R	OP	RNBT	FBG SV	IO 120-188	7	1065	2 7	1700	2050
16	5 RIVIERA 5-METER	OP	RNBT	FBG SV	IO 120-188	7	1760	2 3	2050	2500
17	7 RESORTER 18	OP	RNBT	FBG SV	IB 225-250	7	1510	2 1	2750	3450
17	7 RESORTER 18	OP	RNBT	FBG SV	IB 270 CRUS	7	1510	2 1	3000	3500
17	7 THOROUGHBRED SKIER18	OP	RNBT	FBG SV	IB 225-250	7	1510	2 1	2750	3450
17	7 THOROUGHBRED SKIER18	OP	RNBT	FBG SV	IB 270 CRUS	7	1510	2 1	3000	3500
17	10 CENTURY 2000	ST	RNBT	FBG SV	IO 120-230	7 7	1900	2 1	2350	2900
17	10 CENTURY 2000	ST	RNBT	FBG SV	IO 260	7 7	1900	2 1	2600	3050
17	10 CENTURY 2000 B/R	ST	RNBT	FBG SV	IO 120-230	7 7	1900	2 1	2450	3000
17	10 CENTURY 2000 B/R	ST	RNBT	FBG SV	IO 260	7 7	1900	2 1	2700	3100
17	10 CENTURY 2000 SPT	ST	RNBT	FBG SV	IO 120-230	7 7	1900	2 1	2500	3050
17	10 CENTURY 2000 SPT	ST	RNBT	FBG SV	IO 260	7 7	1900	2 1	2750	3200
17	10 CENTURY 2000 SPT B/R	ST	RNBT	FBG SV	IO 120-230	7 7	1900	2 1	2600	3150
17	10 CENTURY 2000 SPT B/R	ST	RNBT	FBG SV	IO 260	7 7	1900	2 1	2800	3250
18	11 CENTURY 3000 B/R	ST	RNBT	FBG SV	IO 170-230	8	2150	2 1	2800	3400
18	11 CENTURY 3000 B/R	ST	RNBT	FBG SV	IO 260	8	2150	2 1	3050	3500
18	11 CENTURY 3000 SPT B/R	ST	RNBT	FBG SV	IO 170-230	8	2150	2 1	2950	3600
18	11 CENTURY 3000 SPT B/R	ST	RNBT	FBG SV	IO 260	8	2150	2 1	3200	3750
18	11 CENTURY 3000CC	ST	CUD	FBG SV	IO 170-230	8	2000	2 3	2900	3500
18	11 CENTURY 3000CC	ST	CUD	FBG SV	IO 260	8	2000	2 3	3150	3650
19	1 ARABIAN 200	OP	SKI	FBG SV	IO 198-260	7 3	1900	2 3	2550	3200
19	1 ARABIAN 200	OP	SKI	FBG SV	IO 330 CHRY	7 3	1900	2 3	3500	4100
19	1 ARABIAN 200	OP	SKI	FBG SV	VD 350 CRUS	7 3	1900	2 3	3850	4450
19	7 MUSTANG 195	OP	RNBT	FBG SV	IO 120-188	7 5	1300	2 3	2500	2950
19	8 RIVIERA 6-METER	OP	SKI	FBG SV	IO 170-260	7 4	1775	2 3	2600	3100
20	10 CENTURY 4000 SPT	ST	CUD	FBG SV	IO 170-260	8	2675	2 8	3500	4300
20	10 CENTURY 4000CC	ST	CUD	FBG SV	IO 170-260	8	3250	2 8	3900	4800
20	11 CTS	OP	SKI	FBG SV	IB 250-350	7 6	1500	2 2	3400	4200
20	11 CTS	OP	SKI	FBG SV	IB 350 CRUS	7 6	1500	2 2	3900	4550
20	11 CTS-CENTURY TOUR SKI	OP	SKI	FBG SV	IB 225 CHRY	7 6	1500	2 2	3400	3950
21	10 CORONADO 21	ST	RNBT	FBG SV	IB 330-350	7 11	2140	2 2	4400	5400
21	10 CORONADO CARDEL	ST	RNBT	FBG SV	VD 330 CHRY	7 11	2200	2 2	4450	5100
21	10 CORONADO-CARDEL	ST	RNBT	FBG SV	IO 260	7 11	2200	2 2	3400	3950
21	10 CORONADO-CARDEL	ST	RNBT	FBG SV	VD 350 CRUS	7 11	2200	2 2	4700	5400
22	7 RANGEMASTER 5000	ST	CUD	FBG SV	IO 170-260	8	3050	2 8	4150	5050
22	8 CENTURY 5000 SUN EXP	OP	CUD	FBG SV	IO 170-260	8	3720	2 8	4800	5750
22	8 CENTURY 5000CC	ST	CUD	FBG SV	IO 170-260	8	3000	2 8	4150	5050
26	4 CENTURY 7000	ST	CUD	FBG SV	IO 198-260	8	3900	2 10	6250	7650
26	4 CENTURY 7000	ST	CUD	FBG SV	IO T120-T188	8	3900	2 10	6800	8300
26	4 CENTURY 7000 EXP	ST	EXP	FBG SV	IO 198-260	8	4100	2 10	6400	7800
26	4 CENTURY 7000 EXP	ST	EXP	FBG SV	IO T120-T188	8	4100	2 10	6950	8450
26	4 CENTURY 7000 SUN EXP	ST	CUD	FBG SV	IO 198-260	8	4100	2 10	6400	7800
26	4 CENTURY 7000 SUN EXP	ST	CUD	FBG SV	IO T120-T188	8	4100	2 10	6950	8450
26	4 CORTEZ 270	OP	CUD	FBG SV	IO 198-260	8	4200	2 10	6500	7900
26	4 CORTEZ 270	OP	CUD	FBG SV	IO T120-T188	8	4200	2 10	7000	8750
26	4 CORTEZ 270	OP	CUD	FBG SV	IO T260 MRCR	8	4200	2 10	8300	9500
29	CORTEZ-ELEGANTE	FB	DCCPT	FBG SV	IO 330 MRCR	10 7	8400	2	12500	14200
29	CORTEZ-ELEGANTE	FB	DCCPT	FBG SV	IB T225-T270	10 7	8400	2	16400	19500
29	1 CORTEZ-GRANDE	ST	DC	FBG SV	IO 330 MRCR	10 6	8000	2 10	12900	14700
29	1 CORTEZ-GRANDE	ST	DC	FBG SV	IB T188-T270	10 6	8000	2 10	14300	17400
					1982 BOATS					
16	5 CENTURY 1000	OP	RNBT	FBG SV	OB	7	1065	2 8	1700	2050
16	5 CENTURY 1000	OP	RNBT	FBG SV	IO 120-185	7		2 9	1800	2400
16	5 CENTURY 1000 B/R	OP	RNBT	FBG SV	OB	7	1065	2 9	1900	2150
16	5 CENTURY 1000 B/R	OP	RNBT	FBG SV	IO 120-185	7		2 9	2050	2450
16	5 RIVIERA	OP	RNBT	FBG SV	IO 120-185	7	1760	2	2000	2450
17	7 RESORTER 18	OP	RNBT	FBG SV	IB 270 CRUS	7	2550	2 1	3600	4200
17	10 CENTURY 2000	ST	RNBT	FBG SV	IO 120-230	7 7	2300	2 1	2500	3100
17	10 CENTURY 2000	ST	RNBT	FBG SV	IO 260	7 7	2300	2 1	2750	3200
17	10 CENTURY 2000 B/R	ST	RNBT	FBG SV	IO 120-230	7 7	2300	2 1	2600	3150
17	10 CENTURY 2000 B/R	ST	RNBT	FBG SV	IO 260	7 7	2300	2 1	2800	3250
17	10 CENTURY 2000 SPT	ST	RNBT	FBG SV	IO 120-230	7 7	2300	2 1	2700	3300
17	10 CENTURY 2000 SPT	ST	RNBT	FBG SV	IO 260	7 7	2300	2 1	2900	3400
17	10 CENTURY 2000 SPT B/R	ST	RNBT	FBG SV	IO 120-260	7 7	2300	2 1	2750	3450
18	11 CENTURY 3000	ST	RNBT	FBG SV	IO 170-260	8	2500	2 1	3050	3600
18	11 CENTURY 3000 B/R	ST	RNBT	FBG SV	IO 170-260	8	2500	2 1	2950	3600
18	11 CENTURY 3000 B/R	ST	RNBT	FBG SV	IO 260	8	2500	2 1	3100	3700
18	11 CENTURY 3000 SPT	ST	RNBT	FBG SV	IO 170-260	8	2500	2 1	3300	3850
18	11 CENTURY 3000 SPT	ST	RNBT	FBG SV	IO 260	8	2500	2 1	3150	3800
18	11 CENTURY 3000 SPT B/R	ST	RNBT	FBG SV	IO 170-260	8	2500	2 1	3400	3950
18	11 CENTURY 3000CC	ST	CUD	FBG SV	IO 170-260	8	2300	2 3	3300	4100
19	1 ARABIAN 200	OP	SKI	FBG SV	IO 198-260	7 3	2850	2 3	3050	3750
19	1 ARABIAN 200	OP	SKI	FBG SV	VD 330 CRUS	7 3	2850	2 3	4450	5100
19	6 RIVIERA 6-METER	OP	SKI	FBG SV	IO 120-230	7	2500	2 9	2850	3450
19	6 RIVIERA 6-METER	OP	SKI	FBG SV	IO 170-230	7	2500	2 9	3100	3600
20	10 CENTURY 4000 SPT	ST	CUD	FBG SV	IO 170-260	8		2 8	3750	4600
20	10 CENTURY 4000CC	ST	CUD	FBG SV	IO 170-260	8		2 8	3850	4700
21	10 CORONADO 21	ST	RNBT	FBG SV	IB 350 CRUS	7 11	3300	2 2	5500	6300
21	10 CORONADO 21	HT	RNBT	FBG SV	IB 350 CRUS	7 11	3300	2 2	5600	6300
21	10 CORONADO-CARDEL	ST	RNBT	FBG SV	IO 260	7 11	3300	2 2	4050	4700
21	10 CORONADO-CARDEL	ST	RNBT	FBG SV	IO 350 CRUS	7 11	3300	2 2	5500	6300
22	7 RANGEMASTER 5000	ST	CUD	FBG SV	IO 170-260	8	4050	2 9	4950	5950
22	9 CENTURY 5000CC	ST	CUD	FBG SV	IO 170-260	8	4050	2 9	4950	5950
22	9 CORTEZ 230	OP	CUD	FBG SV	IO 170-260	8		2 9	4950	5950
24	7 CENTURY 5000 SUN EXP	OP	CUD	FBG SV	IO 170-260	8	4300		5700	6900
26	4 CENTURY 7000 EXP	ST	EXP	FBG SV	IO 170-260	8	5270	2 10	7050	8650
26	4 CENTURY 7000 EXP	ST	EXP	FBG SV	IO T120-T185	8	5270	2 10	7700	9400
26	4 CENTURY 7000 SUN EXP	ST	CUD	FBG SV	IO 198-260	8	5520	2 10	7250	8900
26	4 CENTURY 7000 SUN EXP	ST	CUD	FBG SV	IO T120-T185	8	5520	2 10	7900	9600
26	4 CENTURY 7000	ST	CUD	FBG SV	IO 198-260	8	4800	2 10	6850	8300

CENTURY BOAT COMPANY -CONTINUED See inside cover to adjust price for area

LOA FT	LOA IN	NAME AND/ OR MODEL	TOP/ RIG	BOAT TYPE	-HULL- MTL	-HULL- TP	ENGINE TP	ENGINE # HP	ENGINE MFG	BEAM FT	BEAM IN	WGT LBS	DRAFT FT	DRAFT IN	RETAIL LOW	RETAIL HIGH
		1982 BOATS														
26	5	CENTURY 7000	ST	CUD	FBG	SV	IO	T120-T185		8		4800	2	10	7350	9050
26	5	CORTEZ 270	OP	CUD	FBG	SV	IO	198-260		8		4800	2	10	6850	8300
26	5	CORTEZ 270	OP	CUD	FBG	SV	IO	T120-T185		8		4800	2	10	7350	9050
28	6	CORTEZ 300	OP	CUD	FBG	SV	VD	T270	CRUS	10	7		2	10	13700	15500
		1981 BOATS														
16	4	RIVIERA	OP	RNBT	FBG	SV	IO	120-185		7		1760			1950	2400
17	7	RESORTER 18	OP	RNBT	FBG	SV	IB	270	CRUS	7		2550	2	1	3450	4000
17	10	CENTURY 2000	ST	RNBT	FBG	SV	IO	120-230		7	7	2300	2	1	2450	3000
17	10	CENTURY 2000	ST	RNBT	FBG	SV	IO	260		7	7	2300	2	1	2800	3250
17	10	CENTURY 2000 B/R	ST	RNBT	FBG	SV	IO	120-260		7	7	2300	2	1	2650	3300
18	11	CENTURY 3000	ST	RNBT	FBG	SV	IO	170-230		8			2	1	2950	3550
18	11	CENTURY 3000	ST	RNBT	FBG	SV	IO	260		8		2500	2	1	3150	3700
18	11	CENTURY 3000 B/R	ST	RNBT	FBG	SV	IO	170-230		8			2	1	3000	3600
18	11	CENTURY 3000 B/R	ST	RNBT	FBG	SV	IO	260		8		2500	2	1	3250	3750
18	11	CENTURY 3000CC	ST	CUD	FBG	SV	IO	170-230		8			2	3	3150	3800
18	11	CENTURY 3000CC	ST	CUD	FBG	SV	IO	260		8		2750	2	3	3500	4050
19		ARABIAN 200	OP	SKI	FBG	SV	IO	200	OMC	7	3		2	3	2450	2850
19	1	ARABIAN 200	OP	SKI	FBG	SV	IO	198-230		7	3		2	3	2450	2950
19	1	ARABIAN 200	OP	SKI	FBG	SV	IO	260		7	3	2850	2	3	3200	3700
19	1	ARABIAN 200	OP	SKI	FBG	SV	VD	350	CRUS	7	3		2	3	3550	4100
20	10	CENTURY 4000CC	ST	CUD	FBG	SV	IO	170-260		8		3250	2	8	3800	4650
21	10	CORONADO 21	OP	RNBT	FBG	SV	IB	330	MRCR	7	11	3300	2	2	5000	5800
21	10	CORONADO 21	HT	RNBT	FBG	SV	IB	330	MRCR	7	11		2	2	5100	5850
22	9	CENTURY 5000CC	ST	CUD	FBG	SV	IO	198-260		8			2	8	4700	5850
22	9	CORTEZ 230	OP	CUD	FBG	SV	IO	198-260		8			2	8	4700	5850
24	7	SUN BRIDGE 5000	OP	CUD	FBG	SV	IO	198-260		8		4300			5700	6800
26	4	CENTURY 7000 EXP	ST	EXP	FBG	SV	IO	198-260		8		5270	2	10	7050	8500
26	4	CENTURY 7000 EXP	ST	EXP	FBG	SV	IO	T120-T185		8		5270	2	10	7550	9250
26	5	CENTURY 7000	ST	CUD	FBG	SV	IO	198-260		8			2	10	6700	8150
26	5	CENTURY 7000	ST	CUD	FBG	SV	IO	T120-T185		8		4800	2	10	7250	8850
26	5	CENTURY 7000CC	ST	CUD	FBG	SV	IO	230-260		8			2	10	6850	8100
26	5	CORTEZ 270	OP	CUD	FBG	SV	IO	198-260		8			2	10	6700	8100
26	5	CORTEZ 270	OP	CUD	FBG	SV	IO	T120-T185		8		4800	2	10	7250	8850
28	6	CORTEZ 300	OP	CUD	FBG	SV	VD	T270	CRUS	10	7		2	10	13100	14900
		1980 BOATS														
16	8	ARABIAN 180		RNBT	FBG	SV	IO	140-170		6	11	2500			2400	2800
16	8	ARABIAN 180	OP	SKI	FBG	SV	IO	120-198		6	11	2500	2	1	2300	2700
16	8	CENTURY 180	ST	RNBT	FBG	SV	IO	120-170		6	11	2250	2	1	2300	2700
17	7	RESORTER 18	OP	RNBT	FBG	SV	IB	255		7		2550	2	1	3150	3900
17	10		ST	RNBT	FBG	SV	IO	228	MRCR	7	7		2	1	2650	3100
17	10	CENTURY 2000	ST	RNBT	FBG	SV	IO	120-228		7	7	2300	2	1	2500	3000
17	10	CENTURY 2000	ST	RNBT	FBG	SV	IO	260		7	7	2300	2	1	2750	3200
17	10	CENTURY 2000 B/R	ST	RNBT	FBG	SV	IO	120-198		7	7	2300	2	1	2650	3150
17	10	CENTURY 2000 B/R	ST	RNBT	FBG	SV	IO	260		7	7	2300	2	1	2850	3300
17	10	CENTURY 2500 B/R	ST	RNBT	FBG	SV	IO	120-228		7	5	2350	2		2550	3000
17	10	CENTURY 2500 B/R	ST	RNBT	FBG	SV	IO	260		7	5	2350	2		2800	3250
18	1	CENTURY 190	ST	RNBT	FBG	SV	IO	120-228		7	3	2400	2	3	2550	3000
18	1	CENTURY 190	ST	RNBT	FBG	SV	IO	260		7	3	2400	2	3	2800	3250
18	1	CENTURY 190 B/R	ST	RNBT	FBG	SV	IO	120-260		7	3	2400	2	3	2650	3300
18	11	CENTURY 3000	ST	RNBT	FBG	SV	IO	120-140		8		2500	2	1	2750	3400
18	11	CENTURY 3000	ST	RNBT	FBG	SV	IO	170-260		8		2500			2950	3650
18	11	CENTURY 3000 B/R	ST	RNBT	FBG	SV	IO	120-260		8		2500	2	1	3150	3750
18	11	CENTURY 3000CC	ST	CUD	FBG	SV	IO	120-260		8		2750	2	3	3200	4000
19	1	ARABIAN 200	ST	RNBT	FBG	SV	IO	170		7	3	2850			3050	3550
19	1	ARABIAN 200	OP	SKI	FBG	SV	IO	120-228		7	3	2850	2	3	2950	3400
		VD 255 MRCR 2950 3450, IO 260 3150 3650, VD 330 MRCR 3150 3650														
19	1	CENTURY 200	ST	RNBT	FBG	SV	IO	120-228		7	3	2500	2	3	2800	3350
19	1	CENTURY 200	ST	RNBT	FBG	SV	IO	260		7	3	2500	2	3	3000	3500
19	1	CENTURY 200CC	ST	CUD	FBG	SV	IO	120-198		7	3	2700	2	5	3000	3600
19	1	CENTURY 200CC	ST	CUD	FBG	SV	IO	260		7	3	2700	2	5	3250	3800
19	6	CENTURY 3500	ST	RNBT	FBG	SV	IO	170-228		7	6	2600			3000	3650
19	6	CENTURY 3500 B/R	ST	RNBT	FBG	SV	IO	120-260		7	6	2600	2	1	3000	3700
20	10	CENTURY 4000CC	ST	CUD	FBG	SV	IO	170-260		8		3250	2	8	3750	4600
22	9	CENTURY 200CC	ST	RNBT	FBG	SV	IO	40-228		7	3		2	5	4050	4850
22	9	CENTURY 5000CC	ST	CUD	FBG	SV	IO	170-260		8		4000	2	8	4850	5800
22	9	CENTURY 5000CC	ST	CUD	FBG	SV	IO	T120		8		4000			5400	6200
22	9	CORTEZ 230	OP	CUD	FBG	SV	IO	198-228		8			2	8	4700	5450
22	9	CORTEZ 230	OP	CUD	FBG	SV	IO	T120-T260		8		4000			5400	6700
22	9	SPORTSMAN 230	OP	RNBT	FBG	SV	IO	170-260		8		4000	2	8	4600	5450
22	9	SPORTSMAN 230	ST	RNBT	FBG	SV	IO	198-228		8			2	8	4250	5000
24	7	CENTURY 6000	ST	CUD	FBG	SV	IO	198-260		8			2	10	5750	7050
24	7	CENTURY 6000	ST	CUD	FBG	SV	IO	T120-T170		8		4600	2	10	6450	7400
24	7	CENTURY 6000	ST	CUD	FBG	SV	IO	T260		8		4600	2	10	7100	8150
26	5	CENTURY 7000	ST	CUD	FBG	SV	IO	198-260		8			2	10	6650	8100
26	5	CENTURY 7000	ST	CUD	FBG	SV	IO	T120-T198		8		4800	2	10	7150	8900
26	5	CENTURY 7000	ST	CUD	FBG	SV	IO	T260		8		4800	2	10	8350	9600
26	5	CORTEZ 270	OP	CUD	FBG	SV	IO	198-260		8			2	10	6650	8050
26	5	CORTEZ 270	OP	CUD	FBG	SV	IO	T120-T198		8		4800	2	10	7150	8900
26	5	CORTEZ 270	OP	CUD	FBG	SV	IO	T228-T260		8			2	10	8000	9600
28	1	CENTURY 8000	ST	CUD	FBG	SV	IO	260	MRCR	8			2	10	8400	9650
28	1	CENTURY 8000	ST	CUD	FBG	SV	IO	T170-T198		8		5580	2	10	8400	10500
28	1	CENTURY 8000	ST	CUD	FBG	SV	IO	T228-T260		8			2	10	9450	10700
28	6	CORTEZ 300	OP	CUD	FBG	SV	VD	255	MRCR	10	7		2	10	10900	12400
28	6	CORTEZ 300	OP	CUD	FBG	SV	VD	T170		10	7				11500	13100
28	6	CORTEZ 300	OP	CUD	FBG	SV	VD	T228-T330		10	7	9260	2	10	13300	16200
		1979 BOATS														
16	8	ARABIAN 180	ST	SKI	FBG	SV	IO	120-200		6	11	2500	2	1	2300	2700
16	8	CENTURY 180	ST	RNBT	FBG	SV	IO	120-170		6	11	2250	2	1	2300	2700
17	10	CENTURY 2000	ST	RNBT	FBG	SV	IO	140-200		7	7	2300	2	1	2600	3050
17	10	CENTURY 2000 B/R	ST	RNBT	FBG	SV	IO	165-230		7	7	2350	2	1	2600	3150
17	10	CENTURY 2500	ST	RNBT	FBG	SV	IO	165-200		7	5	2350	2		2600	3050
18	1	CENTURY 190	ST	RNBT	FBG	SV	IO	120-230		7	3	2400	2	3	2600	3150
18	1	CENTURY 190 B/R	ST	RNBT	FBG	SV	IO	165-200		7	5	2450	2	3	2700	3150
18	11	CENTURY 3000	ST	RNBT	FBG	SV	IO	165-230		8		2500	2	1	2900	3500
18	11	CENTURY 3000	ST	RNBT	FBG	SV	IO	260		8		2500	2	1	3150	3650
18	11	CENTURY 3000 B/R	ST	RNBT	FBG	SV	IO	165-260		8		2500	2	1	3000	3750
19	1	ARABIAN 200	ST	SKI	FBG	SV	IO	228-260		7	3	2850	2	3	3050	3650
19	1	CENTURY 200	ST	RNBT	FBG	SV	IO	120-230		7	3	2500	2	3	2800	3400
19	1	CENTURY 200CC	ST	CUD	FBG	SV	IO	140-260		7	3	2700	2	5	3000	3750
19	6	CENTURY 3500	ST	RNBT	FBG	SV	IO	165-260		7	6	2600	2	1	3000	3700
20	10	CENTURY 4000	ST	CUD	FBG	SV	IO	198-260		8		3250	2	8	3800	4600
22	9	CENTURY 230	ST	CUD	FBG	SV	IO	198-260		8		4000	2	8	4850	5600
22	9	CENTURY 230	ST	CUD	FBG	SV	IO	T120	MRCR	8		4000	2	8	5400	6200
22	9	CENTURY 5000	ST	CUD	FBG	SV	IO	228-260		8		4000	2	8	4650	5600
22	9	CENTURY 5500	ST	CUD	FBG	SV	IO	228-260		8		4000	2	8	5100	6100
22	9	CENTURY 5500	ST	CUD	FBG	SV	IO	T140	MRCR	8		4000	2	8	5400	6200
22	9	CORTEZ 230	ST	CUD	FBG	SV	IO	228-260		8		4000	2	8	5550	6400
22	9	CORTEZ 230	ST	CUD	FBG	SV	IO	T170	MRCR	8		4000	2	8	5450	6250
24	8	CENTURY 250	ST	CUD	FBG	SV	IO	228	MRCR	8		4500	2	10	5950	6800
24	8	CENTURY 250	ST	CUD	FBG	SV	IO	T120	MRCR	8		4500	2	10	6350	7300
24	8	CENTURY 6000	ST	CUD	FBG	SV	IO	198-260		8		4600	2	10	5950	7100
24	8	CENTURY 6000	ST	CUD	FBG	SV	IO	T140-T170		8		4600	2	10	6500	7600
26	5	CENTURY 270	ST	CUD	FBG	SV	IO	228-260		8		4700	2	10	6750	8000
26	5	CENTURY 7000	ST	CUD	FBG	SV	IO	198-260		8		4800	2	10	6650	7650
26	5	CENTURY 7000	ST	CUD	FBG	SV	IO	T120-T170		8		4800	2	10	7150	8250
26	5	CENTURY 7500	ST	CUD	FBG	SV	IO	228-260		8		4800	2	10	6950	8200
26	5	CENTURY 7500	ST	CUD	FBG	SV	IO	T140-T170		8		4800	2	10	7700	8850
26	5	CORTEZ 270	ST	CUD	FBG	SV	IO	228-260		8		4800	2	10	7450	8800
26	5	CORTEZ 270	ST	CUD	FBG	SV	IO	T170-T260		8		4800	2	10	8100	9600
		1978 BOATS														
16	8	ARABIAN 180	OP	RNBT	FBG	SV	IO	120-198		6	11	2500	2		2400	2900
16	8	CENTURY 180	ST	RNBT	FBG	SV	IO	120-170		6	11	2250	2	1	2300	2700
17	6	CENTURY 2000	ST	RNBT	FBG	SV	IO	120-198		7	5	2300	2	1	2500	3000
17	10	TRV 190	ST	RNBT	FBG	SV	IO	120-198		7	5	2350	2		2600	3050
18	1	CENTURY 190	ST	RNBT	FBG	SV	IO	120-235		7	4	2400	2	3	2650	3200
18	6	CENTURY 3000	ST	RNBT	FBG	SV	IO	120-235		8		2500	2	3	2900	3500
19		ARABIAN 200	OP	RNBT	FBG	SV	IO	170-260		7	4	2850	2	1	3050	3800
19		ARABIAN 200	OP	RNBT	FBG	SV	VD	330		7	4	2850	2	1	3600	4450
19	1	CENTURY 200	ST	RNBT	FBG	SV	IO	120-235		7	4	2500	2	3	2850	3450
19	1	CENTURY 200CC	ST	CUD	FBG	SV	IO	140-235		7	4	2700	2	3	3050	3700
19	5	TRV 200	ST	RNBT	FBG	SV	IO	165-235		7	6	2600	2	1	3000	3600
20	6	CENTURY 4000	ST	CUD	FBG	SV	IO	185-260		8		3250	2	10	3700	4550
22	6	CENTURY 230	ST	CUD	FBG	SV	IO	185-260		8		4000	2	6	4200	5150
22	6	CENTURY 230	ST	CUD	FBG	SV	IO	T120-T170		8		4000	2	6	4850	5700
22	6	CENTURY 5000	ST	CUD	FBG	SV	IO	185-260		8		4000	2	10	4800	5750
22	6	CENTURY 5000	ST	CUD	FBG	SV	IO	T120-T170		8		4000	2	10	5350	6200
22	6	CORTEZ 230	ST	CUD	FBG	SV	IO	185-260		8		4000	2	8	5350	6400
22	6	CORTEZ 230	ST	CUD	FBG	SV	IO	T120-T170		8		4000	2	8	5900	6750
24	7	CENTURY 250	ST	CUD	FBG	SV	IO	185-260		8		4600	2	10	5700	6900
24	7	CENTURY 250	ST	CUD	FBG	SV	IO	T120-T170		8		4600	2	10	6300	7400
24	7	CENTURY 6000	ST	CUD	FBG	SV	IO	185-260		8		4600	2	10	6100	7350
24	7	CENTURY 6000	ST	CUD	FBG	SV	IO	T120-T170		8		4600	2	10	6650	7800
26	3	CENTURY 270	ST	CUD	FBG	SV	IO	185-260		8		4800	2	10	6000	7350
26	3	CENTURY 270	ST	CUD	FBG	SV	IO	T120-T170		8		4800	2	10	6600	8050
26	3	CENTURY 7000	ST	CUD	FBG	SV	IO	185-260		8		4800	2	10	6350	7800
26	3	CENTURY 7000	ST	CUD	FBG	SV	IO	T120-T170		8		4800	2	10	6950	8450

110
CONTINUED ON NEXT PAGE
96th ed. - Vol. III

LOA FT	LOA IN	NAME AND/ OR MODEL	TOP/ RIG	BOAT TYPE	-HULL- MTL	-HULL- TP	ENGINE TP	ENGINE # HP	ENGINE MFG	BEAM FT	BEAM IN	WGT LBS	DRAFT FT	DRAFT IN	RETAIL LOW	RETAIL HIGH
		1978 BOATS														
26	3	CORTEZ 270	ST	CUD	FBG	SV	IO	185-260		8		4800	2	10	7350	8950
26	3	CORTEZ 270	ST	CUD	FBG	SV	IO	T120-T170		8		4800	2	10	7900	9450
		1977 BOATS														
16	8	ARABIAN 180	OP	RNBT	FBG	SV	IO	120-188		6	11	2500	2		2450	2900
16	8	ARABIAN 180	OP	RNBT	FBG	SV	IB	233	MRCR	6	11	2500	2		2600	3050
16	8	RAVEN 180	ST	RNBT	FBG	SV	OB			6	11	1200	1	6	1800	2100
16	8	RAVEN 180	ST	RNBT	FBG	SV	IO	120-170		6	11	2200	1	10	2300	2700
18	1	RAVEN 190	ST	RNBT	FBG	SV	IO	120-235		7	4	2400	2	1	2650	3250
19		ARABIAN 200	OP	RNBT	FBG	SV	IO	188-233		7	4	2850			3150	3750
19		ARABIAN 200	OP	RNBT	FBG	SV	IB	330		7	4	2850			3400	4000
19	1	RAVEN 200	ST	RNBT	FBG	SV	IO	120-235		7	4	2500	2	3	2900	3500
19	1	RAVEN 210CC	ST	CUD	FBG	SV	IO	120-235		7	4	2700	2	3	3100	3750
19	5	TRV 200	ST	RNBT	FBG	SV	IO	120-235		7	6	2600	2	1	3050	3700
22	6	CORTEZ 230	OP	CUD	FBG	SV	IO	188-280		8		4100	2	5	5000	6100
22	6	CORTEZ 230	OP	CUD	FBG	SV	IO	T170	MRCR	8		4100	2	5	5600	6400
22	6	RAVEN 230	ST	UTL	FBG	SV	IO	233-235		8		3700	2	5	5000	5700
24	7	RAVEN 250	ST	CR	FBG	SV	IO	188-280		8		4000	2	5	5450	6700
24	7	RAVEN 250	ST	CR	FBG	SV	IO	T120-T140		8		4000	2	5	6000	6950
24	7	RAVEN 250	HT	CR	FBG	SV	IO	188-280		8		4000	2	5	5450	6700
24	7	RAVEN 250	HT	CR	FBG	SV	IO	T120-T140		8		4000	2	5	6000	6950
26	3	RAVEN 270	ST	CR	FBG	SV	IO	188-280		8		4800	2	5	6700	8350
26	3	RAVEN 270	ST	CR	FBG	SV	IO	T120-T140		8		4800	2	5	7250	8500
26	3	RAVEN 270	HT	CR	FBG	SV	IO	188-280		8		4800	2	5	6700	8350
26	3	RAVEN 270	HT	CR	FBG	SV	IO	T120-T140		8		4800	2	5	7250	8500
28	3	VENTURER 300	ST	CR	FBG	SV	IB	T233-T250		10	7	7200	2	10	10400	12000
28	3	VENTURER 300	HT	CR	FBG	SV	IB	T233-T250		10	7	7200	2	10	10400	12000
28	3	VENTURER 300	FB	CR	FBG	SV	IB	T233-T250		10	7	7200	2	10	10400	12000
		1976 BOATS														
16	1	TRIDENT 16	OP	RNBT	FBG	TR	IO	120-140		6	5	2000	2		2050	2450
16	1	TRIDENT 16	ST	RNBT	FBG	TR	OB			6	5	1275	1		1850	2200
16	8	ARABIAN 180	OP	RNBT	FBG	SV	IO	120-188		6	11	2550	2		2550	3000
16	8	ARABIAN 180	OP	RNBT	FBG	SV	IB	233	MRCR	6	11	2550	2		2550	2950
16	8	RAVEN 180	ST	RNBT	FBG	SV	OB			6	11	1520	1	3	2200	2550
16	8	RAVEN 180	ST	RNBT	FBG	SV	IO	120-165		6	11	2250	2	1	2400	2800
16	8	SABRE 180	OP	RNBT	FBG	SV	IB	225-233		6	11	2500	2		2450	2900
17	6	TRIDENT 18	OP	RNBT	FBG	TR	IO	120-235		7	2	2530	2	3	2700	3300
17	6	TRIDENT 18	ST	RNBT	FBG	TR	OB			7	2	1700	1	3	2400	2750
18	1	RAVEN 190	ST	RNBT	FBG	SV	IO	120-235		7	4	2400	2	3	2750	3350
19		ARABIAN 200	OP	RNBT	FBG	SV	IO	188-233		7	4	2850	2		3200	3850
19		ARABIAN 200	OP	RNBT	FBG	SV	IB	330-350		7	4	2850	2		3300	3950
19		SABRE 200	OP	RNBT	FBG	SV	IB	330-350		7	4	2800	2		3250	3900
19		SABRE 200 GULL WING	HT	RNBT	FBG	SV	IB	330-350		7	4	2800	2		3250	3900
19	1	RAVEN 200	ST	RNBT	FBG	SV	IO	120-235		7	4	2500	2	3	2950	3600
19	1	RAVEN 210CC	ST	CUD	FBG	SV	IO	120-235		7	4	2700	2	3	3200	3850
19	1	RAVEN 210CC	HT	CUD	FBG	SV	IO	120-235		7	4	2700	2	3	3200	3850
21	10	CORONADO 21	HT	RNBT	FBG	SV	IB	330-350		8		3400	2		4100	4900
21	10	RAVEN 224	ST	RNBT	FBG	SV	IO	165-235		8		2970	2	2	3700	4450
21	10	RAVEN 225	HT	RNBT	FBG	SV	IO	165-235		8		3000	2	2	3750	4450
24	7	RAVEN 250	ST	CR	FBG	SV	IO	188-255		8		4600	2	10	6200	7400
24	7	RAVEN 250	ST	CR	FBG	SV	IO	T120-T165		8		4600	2	10	6750	7900
24	7	RAVEN 250	HT	CR	FBG	SV	IO	188-255		8		4600	2	10	6200	7400
24	7	RAVEN 250	HT	CR	FBG	SV	IO	T120-T165		8		4600	2	10	6750	7900
26	3	RAVEN 270	ST	CR	FBG	SV	IO	188-255		8		4850	2	10	6900	8400
26	3	RAVEN 270	ST	CR	FBG	SV	IO	T120-T165		8		4850	2	10	7500	9000
26	3	RAVEN 270	HT	CR	FBG	SV	IO	188-255		8		4850	2	10	6900	8400
26	3	RAVEN 270	HT	CR	FBG	SV	IO	T120-T165		8		4850	2	10	7500	9000
28	3	VENTURER 300	ST	CR	FBG	SV	IB	T233-T250		10	7	7000	2	10	9900	11400
28	3	VENTURER 300	HT	CR	FBG	SV	IB	T233-T250		10	7	7000	2	10	9900	11400
28	3	VENTURER 300	FB	CR	FBG	SV	IB	T233-T250		10	7	7000	2	10	9900	11400
		1975 BOATS														
16	1	TRIDENT 16	ST	RNBT	FBG	TR	OB			6	5	1275	1		1800	2150
16	1	TRIDENT 16	ST	RNBT	FBG	TR	IO	120-140		6	5	2000	1	2	2200	2550
16	4	RESORTER 16	ST	RNBT	FBG	FL	IB	225-233		6	8	2190	1	9	2100	2550
16	4	SKI-FURY 16	OP	RNBT	FBG	SV	IB	225-255		6	8	2380	2		2250	2650
16	7	RAVEN 180	ST	RNBT	FBG	SV	OB			6	11	1520	1	3	2150	2500
16	7	RAVEN 180	ST	RNBT	FBG	SV	IO	140-165		6	11	2250	2	1	2450	2850
16	8	MARK II	OP	RNBT	FBG	SV	IO	188	MRCR	6	11	2500	2		2650	3100
16	8	MARK II	OP	RNBT	FBG	SV	VD	250	CHRY	6	11	2500	2		2400	2750
16	8	MARK II	OP	RNBT	FBG	SV	JT	390	HARD	6	11	2500	2		2750	3250
17	6	TRIDENT 18	ST	RNBT	FBG	TR	OB			7	2	1700	1	2	2350	2750
17	6	TRIDENT 18	ST	RNBT	FBG	TR	IO	165-190		7	2	2530	2	3	2800	3300
17	7	RESORTER 18	ST	RNBT	FBG	SV	IB	233-330		7		2550	2	1	2550	3150
17	7	RESORTER 18	ST	RNBT	FBG	SV	IB	350	MRCR	7		2550	2	1	2800	3250
18	1	RAVEN 190	ST	UTL	FBG	SV	IO	188-225		7	4	2500	2	1	3150	3750
19		SABRE 19	HT	RNBT	FBG	SV	IB	233-330		7	4	2810	2	1	3000	3650
19		SABRE 19	HT	RNBT	FBG	SV	IB	350	MRCR	7	4	2810	2	1	3250	3750
19	1	RAVEN 200	ST	UTL	FBG	SV	IO	188-235		7	4	2610	2	1	3450	4150
19	2	ARABIAN 19	ST	RNBT	FBG	SV	VD	330-350		7	4	2850	2	1	3200	3800
19	2	SKI-FURY 19	OP	RNBT	FBG	SV	IB	233-330		7	3	2700	2	1	2950	3550
19	2	SKI-FURY 19	OP	RNBT	FBG	SV	IB	350	MRCR	7	3	2700	2	1	3150	3700
21	10	CORONADO 21	HT	RNBT	FBG	SV	IB	330-350		7	11	3400	2	2	3950	4700
21	10	RAVEN 220	ST	UTL	FBG	SV	IO	188-235		7	10	3100	2	2	4400	5200
21	10	RAVEN 225	ST	UTL	FBG	SV	IO	188-235		7	10	3510	2	2	4800	5600
23	6	BUCCANEER 24			FBG	SV	IO	225		9		3250	2	3	4750	5450
26	3	RAVEN 270	ST	UTL	FBG	SV	IO	188-233		8		4800	2	3	7500	8950
26	3	RAVEN 270	ST	UTL	FBG	SV	IO	T120-T165		8		4800	2	3	8150	9800
28	3	VENTURER 28	ST	UTL	FBG	SV	IB	T225		10	7	7000	3		9450	10800
		1974 BOATS														
16	1	TRIDENT 16			FBG		IO	120-140		6	5	2000	1	2	2100	2500
16	1	TRIDENT 16	ST	RNBT	FBG	TR	OB			6	5		1		1800	2100
16	4	RESORTER 16			FBG		IB	225		6	8	2190	1	9	1900	2300
16	4	SKI-FURY 16		SKI	FBG		IB	225-255		6	9	2380	2		2000	2450
16	8	MARK II			FBG		IO	188	MRCR	6	11	2500	2		2650	3050
		VD 225 CHRY 2200 2550, IB 250 CHRY 2200 2550, JT 330-390													2550	2950
16	8	RAVEN 17			FBG		IO	120-165		6	11	2250	2	3	2450	2850
16	8	RAVEN 17	ST	RNBT	FBG	SV	OB			6	11	1520	2	3	2100	2500
17	6	TRIDENT 18			FBG		IO	165-188		7	2	2530	2	3	2800	3300
17	6	TRIDENT 18	ST	RNBT	FBG	TR	OB			7	2	1700	1	3	2350	2700
17	7	RESORTER 18			FBG		IB	225-330		7		2500	2	1	2300	2850
19	1	ARABIAN 19			FBG		VD	330-350		7	4	2850	2	1	2950	3700
19	1	RAVEN 19			FBG		IO	165-250		7	4	2500	2	3	3100	3850
19	1	RAVEN 19			FBG		JT	330-390		7	4	2500	2	3	2950	3450
19	2	SKI-FURY 19		SKI	FBG		IB	225-330		7	3	2700	2	1	2700	3300
21	10	CORONADO 21			FBG		IB	330-350		7	11	3350	2	1	3700	4550
21	10	RAVEN 22			FBG		IO	165-188		7	10	3100	2	2	4050	4750
21	10	RAVEN 22			FBG		IO	225	OMC	7	10	3100	2	2	4100	4800
21	10	RAVEN 22			FBG		VD	225-330		7	10	3100	2	2	3350	4100
21	10	RAVEN 22 DELUXE			FBG		IO	165-188		7	10	3150	2	2	4100	4800
21	10	RAVEN 22 DELUXE			FBG		IO	225	OMC	7	10	3150	2	2	4150	4850
21	10	RAVEN 22 DELUXE			FBG		VD	225-330		7	10	3150	2	2	3400	4100
23	6	BUCCANEER 24			FBG		IO	188	MRCR	9		3550	2	3	5100	5900
		IO 225 OMC 5150 5950, IB 225-330 4200 5050, IB T115 VLVO													4550	5250
		1973 BOATS														
16	1	TRIDENT 16			FBG		IO	120-140		6	5		1	2	1800	2150
16	1	TRIDENT 16	ST	RNBT	FBG	TR	OB			6	5	1950	1	2	2600	3050
16	4	SKI-FURY 16		SKI	FBG		IB	190-250		6	9	2150	2		1800	2150
16	8	MARK II			FBG		JT		OLDS	6	9	2150	1	11	**	**
		IO 165-188 2450 2850, VD 225 CHRY 1850 2200, IB 250 CHRY													1850	2200
		JT 330 BERK 2250 2650														
16	8	RAVEN 17			FBG		IO	120-165		6	11	2100	2	3	2400	2850
17	6	TRIDENT 18			FBG		IO	165-188		7	2	2160	2	3	2650	3150
17	7	RESORTER 18			FBG		IB	225-330		7	7	2380	1	9	2250	2800
19	1	ARABIAN 19			FBG		VD	330	CHRY	7	4				2500	2900
19	1	ARABIAN 19			FBG		VD	350	CRUS	7	4	2650			2950	3400
19	1	RAVEN 19			FBG		IO	165-250		7	4		2	3	3050	3750
21	10	CORONADO 21			FBG		IB	330	CHRY	7	11	3300	2	3	3500	4100
21	10	CORONADO 21			FBG		IB	350	CRUS	7	11	3450	2	3	3800	4450
21	10	RAVEN 21			FBG		IO	165-188		7	10	2900	2	2	4000	4700
		IO 225 OMC 4100 4750, IB 225 CHRY 3100 3600, VD 225 CHRY													3100	3600
		IO 250 CHRY 4200 4900, IB 250 CHRY 3100 3600, VD 250 CHRY													3100	3600
		IB 330 CHRY 3250 3750, VD 330 CHRY 3250 3750														
22	1	BUCCANEER 22			FBG		IO	188	MRCR	7	10	3100	2	3	4250	4950
		IO 225 OMC 4350 5000, IB 225 CHRY 3250 3800, VD 225 CHRY													3250	3800
		IO 250 CHRY 4450 5150, IB 250 CHRY 3300 3800, VD 250 CHRY													3300	3800
		IB 330 CHRY 3400 3950, VD 330 CHRY 3400 3950														
23	6	BUCCANEER 24			FBG		IO	225	OMC	9		3250			5050	5800
		IB 225 CHRY 3800 4450, VD 225 CHRY 3800 4450, IO 250 CHRY													5150	5900
		IB 250 CHRY 3850 4450, VD 250 CHRY 3850 4450, IB 330 CHRY													3950	4600
		IB T115 VLVO 4800 5500														
		1972 BOATS														
16	8	MARK II			FBG		IO	155-188		6	9	2150	1	11	2500	2950
16	8	MARK II			FBG		IB	225-250		6	9	2150	1	11	1750	2150
16	8	MARK II			FBG		JT	330	BERK	6	9	2150	1	11	2200	2550

 CONTINUED ON NEXT PAGE

```
LOA   NAME AND/       TOP/ BOAT -HULL- ---ENGINE---  BEAM  WGT  DRAFT RETAIL RETAIL
FT IN OR MODEL        RIG  TYPE MTL TP TP # HP  MFG  FT IN LBS  FT IN  LOW    HIGH
----------------------------- 1972 BOATS -----------------------------------------
16  8 RAVEN 17             FBG      IO 120-165  6 11 2100  2  3  2500   2950
17  6 TRIDENT 18           FBG      IO 155-188  7  2 2160  2  3  2700   3250
17  7 RESORTER 18          FBG      IO 225-330  7  7 2380  1  9  2200   2700
19  1 ARABIAN 19           FBG      IO 250  CHRY 7 4             3700   4300
19  1 ARABIAN 19           FBG      IB 330  CHRY 7 4             2400   2750
19  1 RAVEN 19             FBG      IO 155-250  7  4        2  3 3100   3700
21 10 CORONADO 21          FBG      IB 330  CHRY 7 11 3300  2  3 3400   3950
21 10 RAVEN 21             FBG      IO 165-188  7 10 2900  2  2 4150   4850
      IO  225  OMC  4200 4900, IB 225 CHRY 3000 3450, VD 225 CHRY 3000 3450
      IO  250  CHRY 4400 5050, IB 250 CHRY 3000 3500, VD 250 CHRY 3000 3500
      IB  330  CHRY 3100 3600, VD 330 CHRY 3100 3600

22  1 BUCCANEER 22         FBG      IO 188 MRCR 7 10 3100  2  3 4450   5100
      IO  225  OMC  1500 5150, IB 225 CHRY 3150 3650, VD 225 CHRY 3150 3650
      IO  250  CHRY 4600 5300, IB 250 CHRY 3150 3700, VD 250 CHRY 3150 3700
      IB  330  CHRY 3300 3800, VD 330 CHRY 3300 3800

23  6 BUCCANEER 24         FBG      IO 188 MRCR 9      3250      5150   5950
      IO  225  OMC  5200 6000, IB 225 CHRY 3700 4250, VD 225 CHRY 3700 4300
      IO  250  CHRY 5300 6100, IB 250 CHRY 3700 4300, VD 250 CHRY 3700 4300
      IB  330  CHRY 3800 4450, IB T115 VLVO 4600 5300, IO T170 VLVO 6950 8000
----------------------------- 1971 BOATS -----------------------------------------
16  1 BUCCANEER 16         FBG      IO 120-165  6  8 1855  2  2 2300   2700
16  8 MARK II              FBG      IO 155-215  6  9 2150  1 11 2550   3100
16  8 MARK II              FBG      IB 225-250  6  9 2150  1 11 1700   2050
16  8 MARK II              FBG      JT 330  BERK 6  9 2150  1 11 2050   2450
16  8 RAVEN 17             FBG      IO 155-165  6 11 2100  2  3 2550   3050
16  8 RAVEN 17             FBG      IO 170-215  6 11 2100  2  3 2750   3200
17  6 BUCCANEER 18         FBG      IO 155-165  6 11 2070  2  1 2700   3150
17  6 BUCCANEER 18         FBG      IO 225  CHRY 6 11 2070  2  1 1800   2150
17  6 TRIDENT 18           FBG      IO 155-215  7  2 2160  2  3 2800   3500
17  7 RESORTER 18          FBG      IB 225  CHRY 7  7 2380  1  9 2050   2450
17  7 RESORTER 18          FBG      IB 250      7  7 2380  1  9 2050   2600
17  7 RESORTER 18          FBG      IB 330  CHRY 7  7 2380  1  9 2250   2600

19  1 ARABIAN 19           FBG      IB 320-330  7  4      2  1 2400   2800
21 10 CORONADO 21          FBG      IB 320-375  7 11 3300 2  3 3350   3950
21 10 RAVEN 21             FBG      IO 165-215  7 10 2900 2  2 4300   5150
      IB  225  CHRY 2850 3350, VD 225 CHRY 2850 3350, IB 330 CHRY 3000 3500
      VD  330  CHRY 3000 3500

22  1 BUCCANEER 22         FBG      IO 165-215  7 10 3100 2  3 4600   5300
22  1 BUCCANEER 22         FBG      IB 225  CHRY 7 10 3100 2  3 3050   3500
22  1 BUCCANEER 22         FBG      VD 225  CHRY 7 10 3100 2  3 3050   3500
23  6 BUCCANEER 24         FBG      IB 225-330  9      3250 2  3 3550   4250
23  6 BUCCANEER 24         FBG      IB T115 VLVO 9     3550 2  3 4000   4650
----------------------------- 1970 BOATS -----------------------------------------
16  4 BUCCANEER 16         FBG      IO 120-165  6  2 1920  1  7 2350   2750
16  4 CHEETAH 16      RNBT FBG      IB 220-250  6  8 2060  1  9 1700   2000
16  8 CHEETAH 17 MARK II RNBT FBG   IO 155-215  6  9 2150  1 11 2750   3350
16  8 CHEETAH 17 MARK II RNBT FBG   IB 225  CHRY 6  9 2150  1 11 1750   2050
17  6 BUCCANEER 18         FBG      IO 155-165  6 11 2070  2   2800   3300
17  6 BUCCANEER 18         FBG      IB 220-225  7    2150  2   1800   2150
17  7 RESORTER 18          FBG      IB 225  CHRY 7    2150  1  9 1900   2250
      IB  250  INT  1900 2300, IB 250 MRCR 1900 2300, IB 250 OMC 2050 2450

17  7 RESORTER 18     RNBT FBG      IB 210      7    1865  1  3 1900   2250
17  8 TRIDENT 18      RNBT FBG      IO 155-215  7  2 1865  1  3 2250   3350
19  5 ARABIAN 19           FBG      IB 300      7  3      2400   2800
21 10 CORONADO 21          FBG      IB 300  INT 7 11 3300 2  3 3100   3600
21 10 CORONADO 21     HT RNBT FBG   IB 300-335  7 11 3300 2  3 3400   3700
22    BUCCANEER 22         FBG      IO 210-215  7  8 3180  1  5 4750   5500
22    BUCCANEER 22         FBG      IB 225-250  7  8 3140  1  5 2900   3400
23  8 BUCCANEER 24      CR  FBG DV  IB 225-300  9    3740  2  4 3750   4550
23  8 BUCCANEER 24      CR  FBG DV  IB T110 VLVO 9   4120  2  4 4250   4950
----------------------------- 1969 BOATS -----------------------------------------
16  4 CHEETAH 16      RNBT FBG      IO 210      6  8 2060  1  9 2850   3300
17  6 BUCCANEER      RNBT FBG SV IO 165         7    2  5 3100   3600
17  6 BUCCANEER 18   RNBT FBG SV IO 165  INT    7    2070  2  1 1750   2050
17  7 RESORTER FGL 17 RNBT FBG SV IB 235-250    7    2380  1 10 1900   2300
17  7 RESORTER FGL 17 HT RNBT FBG SV IB 235-250 7    2580  1 10 2000   2400
19                        WD      IB 250              2     **    **
19  3 BUCCANEER 18    RNBT FBG DV IO 160-165    7    2370  2  5 3550   4150
19  5 ARABIAN FGL 19  RNBT FBG SV IB 300        7  3 2750  1 11 2400   2850
19  5 RESORTER FGL 19 RNBT FBG SV IB 300        7  3 2600  1 10 2350   2750
19  5 RESORTER FGL 19 HT RNBT FBG SV IB 300     7  3 2910  1 10 2500   2950
20  6 TRIDENT 20      UTL  FBG TR IO T130 CHRY  8    3000  1 11 5700   6550
21 10 CORONADO FGL 21 RNBT FBG SV IB 300-325    7 11 3000 2  3 2850   3350

21 10 CORONADO FGL 21 HT RNBT FBG SV IB 300-325 7 11 3300 2  3 3000   3550
23  3 BUCCANEER 23    RNBT FBG SV IO 160-210    9    3550  2  6 5850   6850
23  3 BUCCANEER 23    RNBT FBG SV IB 225-300    9    3250  2  3 3250   3850
----------------------------- 1968 BOATS -----------------------------------------
17  6 BUCCANEER 18    OP   FBG      IO 120-200  7    2350  1  1 3200   3850
17  6 RESORTER 17     HT RNBT MHG   IB 210-250  6 11      1  6 1750   2100
17  6 RESORTER FGL-17 HT RNBT MHG   IB 210-250  7  4      1  8 1850   2150
19  4 RESORTER 19          MHG      IB 250-290  7  3 1760  1  8 1850   2250
19  4 RESORTER 19     HT   MHG      IB 250-290  7  3      1  8 2200   2600
19  4 RESORTER FGL-19      MHG      IB 250-290  7  6 1850  1  8 1900   2350
19  4 RESORTER FGL-19 HT   MHG      IB 250-290  7  6      1  8 2250   2650
19  5 ARABIAN 19           FBG      IB 285-290  7  3 1950  1  9 1950   2350
19  5 ARABIAN FGL-19       FBG      IB 285-290  7  6 2020  1  8 2000   2400
20  6 TRIDENT 20      OP   FBG TH OB              8  1820  10   3600   4200
20  6 TRIDENT 20      OP   FBG      IO T 80      8  2450  10   4800   5550
21    CORONADO 21     RNBT MHG      IB 250-335   8  2140  1 10 2250   2700

21    CORONADO 21     HT   MHG      IB 250-335   8         1 10 2550   3100
23    BUCCANEER 23    OP   FBG DV   IO 155-200   9              5850   6750
----------------------------- 1967 BOATS -----------------------------------------
17  6 RESORTER 17          FBG DV   IO 120       7              2850   3250
19  4 RESORTER 19          MHG      IB 238-290   7    1760  1  1750   2100
19  4 RESORTER 19     HT   MHG      IB 238-290   7              1900   2300
19  4 RESORTER FGL-19      FBG      IB 238-290   7    1850       1750   2150
19  4 RESORTER FGL-19 HT   MHG      IB 238-290   7              1900   2300
19  5 ARABIAN 19           FBG      IB 285-290   7    1950       1850   2200
19  5 ARABIAN FGL-19       FBG      IB 285-290   7    2020       1850   2250
20  6 TRIDENT 20           FBG      IO T 60            5300   6100
20  6 TRIDENT 20      OP RNBT FBG TH OB                4500   5150
21    CORONADO 21          MHG      IB 238-300   8    2140       2050   2500
21    CORONADO 21          MHG      IB 325       8    2140       2200   2550
21    CORONADO 21     HT   MHG      IB 238-325   8              2350   2900

22    RAVEN 22             MHG      IB 210-220   8    2160       2200   2600
22    RAVEN 22        HT   MHG      IB 210-220   8              2850   3300
23    BUCCANEER            FBG      IO 155-225   9              5750   6750
23    BUCCANEER 23         FBG DV   IO 150       9              6050   6950
26  1 RAVEN 26             MHG      IB 220-290   9    3100       3750   4650
26  1 RAVEN 26             MHG      IB T150      9    3100       4150   4850
26  1 RAVEN 26        HT   MHG      IB 220-290   9              4750   5700
26  1 RAVEN 26        HT   MHG      IB T150      9              5150   5900
26  1 RAVEN 26        HT   MHG      IB 220-290   9              4750   5700
26  1 RAVEN 26        FB   MHG      IB T150      9              5150   5700
27  1 VENTURER 27    FB   MHG      IB T220      9              6000   6900
----------------------------- 1966 BOATS -----------------------------------------
18    SABRE 18        RNBT WD SV IB 210-250     7  5      1  8 1700   2050
18    SABRE 18        HT   WD SV IB 210-250     7  5      1  8 1700   2050
19  2 RAVEN 19             UTL  WD SV IB 185     7  4      1  7 1800   2100
19  3 RESORTER 19          RNBT WD SV IB 238-290 7  3      1  7 1950   2400
19  3 RESORTER 19     HT   RNBT WD SV IB 238-290 7  3      1  7 1950   2400
19  5 ARABIAN 19           RNBT WD SV IB 285     7  3      1  7 1900   2400
21    CORONADO 21          RNBT WD SV IB 238-330 8         1 10 2350   2900
21    CORONADO 21     HT   RNBT WD SV IB 238-330 8         1 10 2500   2900
21    RESORTER 21          RNBT WD SV IB 238-290 7  8      1 10 2200   2750
21    RESORTER 21     HT   RNBT WD SV IB 238-290 7  8      1 10 2300   2750
22    RAVEN 22             UTL  WD SV IB 210     7  8      1  9 4900   5650
      IB  210       2050 2400, IO 220       4950 5700, IB 220       2050 2400

22    RAVEN 22        HT UTL WD SV IO 210       7  8      1  9 4900   5650
      IB  210       2050 2400, IO 220       4950 5700, IB 220       2050 2400

26  1 RAVEN 26             UTL  WD SV IB 220-290 9  8      2    4400   5250
26  1 RAVEN 26             UTL  WD SV IB T150    9  8      2    4750   5450
26  1 RAVEN 26        HT   UTL  WD SV IB 220-290 9  8      2    4400   5450
26  1 RAVEN 26        HT   UTL  WD SV IB T150    9  8      2    4750   5450
27  1 VENTURER 27    SA/CR WD    IB 220-280     10  2      2  1 9700  11200
27  2 VENTURER 27    SA/CR WD    IB T220        10  2      2  1 10300 11800
33                        EXP  P/M  IB 220      12  6      2  6 11200 12700
----------------------------- 1965 BOATS -----------------------------------------
19    RESORTER 19          WD      IB 175             1700   2000
19    RESORTER 19     HT   WD      IB 220-280         1700   2100
19    RESORTER 19          WD      IB 220-280         1700   2100
21    CORONADO 21          WD      IB 220-330         2350   2800
21    CORONADO 21     HT   WD      IB 220-330         2450   2850
21    RESORTER 21          WD      IB 220-280         2000   2400
21    RESORTER 21          WD      IB 238-280         2250   2600
```

LOA FT	IN	NAME AND/ OR MODEL	TOP/ RIG	BOAT TYPE	-HULL- MTL	TP	----ENGINE--- TP	# HP	MFG	BEAM FT	IN	WGT LBS	DRAFT FT	IN	RETAIL LOW	RETAIL HIGH
		1965 BOATS														
21		RESORTER 21	HT		WD		IB	220							1950	2300
21		RESORTER 21	HT		WD		IB	238-280							2250	2600
22		RAVEN 22			WD		IB	210-220							2650	3050
22		RAVEN 22	HT		WD		IB	210-220							2650	3050
26		RAVEN 26			WD		IB	220-280							4450	5250
26		RAVEN 26			WD		IB	T150-T160							4750	5550
26		RAVEN 26	HT		WD		IB	220-280							4450	5250
26		RAVEN 26	HT		WD		IB	T150-T160							4750	5550
26		RAVEN 26	FB		WD		IB	220-280							4450	5250
26		RAVEN 26	FB		WD		IB	T150-T160							4750	5550
27	6			EXP	WD		IB	220-280							5950	7050
27	6			EXP	WD		IB	170D							11100	12600
27	6			EXP	WD		IB	T220							6650	7650
27	6		HT	EXP	WD		IB	220-280							5950	7050
27	6		HT	EXP	WD		IB	170D							11100	12600
27	6		HT	EXP	WD		IB	T220							6650	7650
33				EXP	WD		IB	220-280							10900	12600
33				EXP	WD		IB	T155D-T170D							20300	22800
33			FB	EXP	WD		IB	220-280							10900	12600
33			FB	EXP	WD		IB	T155D-T170D							20300	22800
33				SDN	WD		IB	220-280							10200	11900
33				SDN	WD		IB	T155D-T170D							19100	21300
33			FB	SDN	WD		IB	220-280							10200	11900
33			FB	SDN	WD		IB	T155D-T170D							19100	21300
45	5	CUSTOM	MY		WD		IB	T280							36500	40500
		IB T195D 40600 45200, IB T215D 41400 46000, IB T270D													42400	47100
		IB T300D 43000 47800, IB T308D 43200 47900, IB T370D													44600	49600
		1964 BOATS														
19	3	RESORTER 19			WD		IB	220-280							1700	2050
19	3	RESORTER 19	HT		WD		IB	220-280							1700	2050
20	8	CORONADO 21			WD		IB	220-325							2050	2550
20	8	CORONADO 21			WD		IB	330							2200	2600
20	8	CORONADO 21	HT		WD		IB	220-325							2050	2550
20	8	CORONADO 21	HT		WD		IB	330							2200	2600
21		RESORTER 21			WD		IB	210-280							2100	2550
21		RESORTER 21	HT		WD		IB	210-280							2100	2550
21	11	RAVEN 22			WD		IB	210-215							2550	2950
21	11	RAVEN 22	HT		WD		IB	210-215							2550	2950
22					WD		IB	215	GRAY						**	**
25	10	RAVEN 26			WD		IB	215-280							4150	5050
25	10	RAVEN 26			WD		IB	T150-T160							4550	5300
25	10	RAVEN 26	HT		WD		IB	215-280							4150	5050
25	10	RAVEN 26	HT		WD		IB	T150							4550	5250
25	10	RAVEN 26	HT		WD		IB	T650							7150	8200
25	10	RAVEN 26	FB		WD		IB	215-280							4150	5050
25	10	RAVEN 26	FB		WD		IB	T150-T160							4550	5300
27		CLIPPER 27			WD		IB	195-280							4450	5400
27		CLIPPER 27			WD		IB	T195							5150	5900
27		CLIPPER 27	HT		WD		IB	195-280							4450	5400
27		CLIPPER 27	HT		WD		IB	T195							5150	5900
29		CLIPPER 29			WD		IB	T215							6950	8000
29		CLIPPER 29	HT		WD		IB	T215							7050	8100
29		CLIPPER 29	HT	PH	WD		IB	T215							7450	8550
29		GULFSTREAM 29			WD		IB	T215							7550	8700
29		VENTURER 29			WD		IB	T215							6550	7550
29		VENTURER 29	FB		WD		IB	T215							7050	8100
33		EL-DORADO CUSTOM			WD		IB	T215-T280							10500	12100
33		EL-DORADO CUSTOM			WD		IB	T135D							14900	16900
33		EL-DORADO CUSTOM	FB		WD		IB	T215-T280							10400	12000
33		EL-DORADO CUSTOM	FB		WD		IB	T135D							14800	16900
33		VENTURER			WD		IB	T215-T280							9900	11500
33		VENTURER			WD		IB	T135D							14400	16400
33		VENTURER	FB		WD		IB	T215-T280							10000	11600
33		VENTURER	FB		WD		IB	T135D							14500	16500
45			MY		WD		IB	T280							34800	38600
		IB T215D 39100 43500, IB T270D 40100 44600, IB T300D													40700	45200
		IB T308D 41300 45900, IB T370D 42600 47400														
		1963 BOATS														
16	11	SUN-SLED 17			WD		IO	100-136							3050	3550
17	10	TRINIDAD 18			WD		IO	80-100							3350	3900
21		CORONADO 21			WD		IB	225-300							2000	2450
21	11	RAVEN 22			WD		IB	190-215							2450	2850
25	10	RAVEN 26			WD		IB	215-280							4050	4850
25	10	RAVEN 26			WD		IB	T145							4350	5050
26	1	CLIPPER 26			WD		IB	215-225							4100	4800
29		CLIPPER 29			WD		IB	T215-T225							6800	7850
29		GULFSTREAM 29			WD		IB	T215-T225							7400	8550
29		VENTURER 29			WD		IB	T215-T225							6150	7150
33		EL-DORADO CUSTOM			WD		IB	T215-T225							10100	11500
33		VENTURER 33			WD		IB	T215-T225							9550	10900
		1962 BOATS														
17		SUN-SLED 17			WD		IO	100							3200	3700
18		TRINIDAD 18			WD		IO	100							3500	4050
21		CORONADO 21			WD		IB	225-325							1950	2450
22		RAVEN 22			WD		IB	170-190							2400	2800
26		RAVEN 26			WD		IB	215							3950	4600
		1961 BOATS														
21		CORONADO		RNBT	WD		IB	225-325		7	7		1	9	1950	2450
21	11	RAVEN		UTL	WD		IB	170-188		7	10		1	9	1750	2050
		1960 BOATS														
21					WD		IB	300	CHRY						**	**
21		CORONADO			WD		IB	170-275							1850	2300
21		CORONADO			WD		IB	325							2000	2350
22		RAVEN			WD		IB	170-177							2300	2700
		1959 BOATS														
21					P/M		IB	225	GRAY	7	8				**	**
21		CORONADO			P/M		IB	135-215		7	8				1750	2200
21		CORONADO			P/M		IB	275		7	8				1850	2200
21		CORONADO		RNBT	P/M		IB	300		7	8				1950	2300
22		RAVEN			L/P		IB	109-135		7	10				2150	2550
22		RAVEN	HT		L/P		IB	170		7	10				2250	2600
		1958 BOATS														
16		NOMAD	OP	RNBT	WD		OB								1800	2100
21					WD		IB	238	GRAY						**	**
21		CORONADO		RNBT	WD		IB	135-215							1850	2250
21		CORONADO		RNBT	WD		IB	275							1950	2300
22		RAVEN	HT		WD		IB	109-170							2100	2600
55					WD		IB	300D	GM						**	**
		1957 BOATS														
16		SEAFLYTE			WD		OB								1750	2100
21					WD		IB	200	CHRY						**	**
21		CORONADO			WD		IB	135-225							1750	2150
21		CORONADO			WD		IB	275-300							1800	2200
22		RAVEN			WD		IB	75-112							2000	2450
22		RAVEN			WD		IB	135							2100	2500
		1956 BOATS														
16		SEAFLYTE			WD		OB								1750	2100
16		SPORTSMAN IMPERIAL			WD		OB								1750	2100
21					WD		IB	175	GRAY						**	**
		1955 BOATS														
16		IMPERIAL SPORTSMAN			WD		OB								1750	2100
16		SEAFLYTE 16 DLX LAP			WD		OB								1750	2100
		1954 BOATS														
16		SEAFLYTE			WD		OB								1750	2100
		1953 BOATS														
16		SPORTSMAN IMPERIAL			WD		OB								1750	2100
		1952 BOATS														
16		SPORTSMAN IMPERIAL			WD		OB								1750	2100
16		SPORTSMAN ROYAL			WD		OB								1750	2100
16		SPORTSMAN STANDARD			WD		OB								1750	2100
		1951 BOATS														
16		SPORTSMAN IMPERIAL			WD		OB								1750	2100
16		SPORTSMAN ROYAL			WD		OB								1750	2100
16		SPORTSMAN STANDARD			WD		OB								1750	2100
		1950 BOATS														
16		SPORTSMAN IMPERIAL			WD		OB								1800	2100
16		SPORTSMAN ROYAL			WD		OB								1800	2100
16		SPORTSMAN STANDARD			WD		OB								1800	2100
		1946 BOATS														
19			OP	RNBT	MHG		IB								**	**
		1932 BOATS														
16		PIONEER		RNBT	MHG		IB		GRAY	5	6				**	**
16		SEA-MAID 46		RNBT	MHG		IB		GRAY						**	**
16		TRAVELER			MHG		OB								2000	2400
17		SEA-MAID 47		RNBT	MHG		IB		GRAY						**	**
18		SEA-MAID 49		RNBT	MHG		IO	32	GRAY						11000	12500
18		SEA-MAID 65		RNBT	MHG		IO	65	GRAY						11000	12500
22		SEA-KING		RNBT	MHG		VD	66	GRAY						3300	3850

CONTINUED ON NEXT PAGE

LOA FT IN	NAME AND/ OR MODEL	TOP/ RIG	BOAT TYPE	-HULL- MTL TP		----ENGINE--- TP # HP MFG	BEAM FT IN	WGT LBS	DRAFT FT IN	RETAIL LOW	RETAIL HIGH
			1929 **BOATS**							
28				WD	IB	200 KERM				**	**

CHALLENGER BOATS INC
COAST GUARD MFG ID- CHE

Call 1-800-327-6929 for BUC Personalized Evaluation Service
Or, for 1978 boats, sign onto www.BUCValuPro.com

CHALLENGER MARINE CORP
COAST GUARD MFG ID- CGC

Call 1 800 327 6929 for BUC Personalized Evaluation Service
Or, for 1959 to 1977 boats, sign onto www.BUCValuPro.com

CHALLENGER YACHT CORP
WILMINGTON CA 90744   COAST GUARD MFG ID- CYC See inside cover to adjust price for area

LOA FT IN	NAME AND/ OR MODEL	TOP/ RIG	BOAT TYPE	-HULL- MTL TP		----ENGINE--- TP # HP MFG	BEAM FT IN	WGT LBS	DRAFT FT IN	RETAIL LOW	RETAIL HIGH
			1980 **BOATS**								
32 2	CHALLENGER 32	SLP	SA/CR FBG KL	IB	55D PERK	11 2	12800	4 10	30200	33500
34 8	CHALLENGER 35	SLP	SA/CR FBG KL	IB	55D PERK	11 6	14800	4 6	37600	41800
34 8	CHALLENGER 35	KTH	SA/CR FBG KL	IB	55D PERK	11 6	14800	4 6	37800	42000
40 8	CHALLENGER 41	KTH	SA/CR FBG KL	IB	55D PERK	13 6	26700	5 6	74400	81800
44 8	CHALLENGER 45	KTH	SA/CR FBG KL	IB	65D PERK	15	44000	6	102000	112000
50 4	CHALLENGER 50	KTH	SA/CR FBG KL	IB	85D PERK	16 6	68000	6 6	130500	143500
			1979 **BOATS**								
32 2	CHALLENGER 32	SLP	SA/CR FBG KL	IB	55D PERK	11 2	12800	4 10	29000	32200
34 8	CHALLENGER 35	SLP	SA/CR FBG KL	IB	55D PERK	11 6	13600	4 6	33400	37100
34 8	CHALLENGER 35	KTH	SA/CR FBG KL	IB	55D PERK	11 6	13900	4 6	34300	38100
40 8	CHALLENGER 41	SLP	SA/CR FBG KL	IB	55D PERK	13 6	25650	5 6	65700	72200
40 8	CHALLENGER 41	KTH	SA/CR FBG KL	IB	55D PERK	13 6	25925	5 6	69700	76600
50 4	CHALLENGER 50	KTH	SA/CR FBG KL	IB	85D PERK	16	68700	6	125000	137500
			1978 **BOATS**								
32	CHALLENGER 32	SLP	SA/CR FBG KL	IB	55D PERK	11 2	12800	4 10	27800	30900
35	CHALLENGER 35	SLP	SA/CR FBG KL	IB	55D PERK	11 6	13400	4 6	32400	36000
35	CHALLENGER 35	KTH	SA/CR FBG KL	IB	55D PERK	11 6	13900	4 6	33400	37100
41	CHALLENGER 41	SLP	SA/CR FBG KL	IB	55D PERK	13 4	25650	5 6	63100	69300
41	CHALLENGER 41	KTH	SA/CR FBG KL	IB	55D PERK	13 4	25925	5 6	67000	73600
50	CHALLENGER 50	KTH	SA/CR FBG KL	IB	85D PERK	16	68700	6	119000	130500
			1977 **BOATS**								
32 2	CHALLENGER 32	SLP	SA/CR FBG KL	IB	70D	11 2	12800	4 10	27000	30000
34 8	CHALLENGER 35	SLP	SA/CR FBG KL	IB	70D	11 6	13600	4 8	30700	34100
34 8	CHALLENGER 35	KTH	SA/CR FBG KL	IB	70D	11 6	13900	4 8	31600	35100
40 4	CHALLENGER 41	SLP	SA/CR FBG KL	IB	70D	13	25650	5 6	60600	66600
40 4	CHALLENGER 41	KTH	SA/CR FBG KL	IB	70D	13	25925	5 6	64500	70800
50 4	CHALLENGER 50	KTH	SA/CR FBG KL	IB	100D	16	68700	6	115500	127000
			1976 **BOATS**								
29 6	CHALLENGER 29	SLP	SA/CR FBG KL	IB	D	11	9200	3 10	18700	20800
32 2	CHALLENGER 32	SLP	SA/CR FBG KL	IB	70D	11 2	12800	4 10	26200	29100
34 8	CHALLENGER 35	SLP	SA/CR FBG KL	IB	70D	11 6	13800	4 6	30000	33300
34 8	CHALLENGER 35	KTH	SA/CR FBG KL	IB	70D	11 6	13800	4 6	30300	33700
40 4	CHALLENGER 41	SLP	SA/CR FBG KL	IB	70D	13	25600	5 6	58800	64600
40 4	CHALLENGER 41	KTH	SA/CR FBG KL	IB	70D	13	25600	5 6	61500	67600
50 4	CHALLENGER 50	SLP	SA/CR FBG KL	IB	100D	16	56000	6 6	100500	110000
50 4	CHALLENGER 50	KTH	SA/CR FBG KL	IB	100D	16	56000	6 6	104000	114000
			1975 **BOATS**								
32 2	CHALLENGER 32	SLP	SA/CR FBG KL	IB	55D	11 2	12800	4 10	25400	28200
34 8	CHALLENGER 35	SLP	SA/CR FBG KL	IB	55D	11 6	13600	4 5	29000	32200
34 8	CHALLENGER 35	SLP	SA/CR FBG KL	IB	55D	11 6	13800	4 5	29600	32900
39 11	CHALLENGER 40	SLP	SA/CR FBG KL	IB	D	12 10	24800	5 6	53100	60600
39 11	CHALLENGER 40	KTH	SA/CR FBG KL	IB	D	12 10	24800	5 6	58200	63900
40 4	CHALLENGER 41	SLP	SA/CR FBG KL	IB	55D	13	25650	5 6	56600	62200
40 4	CHALLENGER 41	KTH	SA/CR FBG KL	IB	55D	13	25925	5 6	59600	65500
42 11	CHALLENGER 43	SLP	MS FBG KL	IB	D	13	25700	5 6	56500	62100
42 11	CHALLENGER 43	KTH	MS FBG KL	IB	D	13	25700	5 6	59500	65400
44 11	CHALLENGER 45	KTH	SA/CR FBG KL	IB	D	14 4	44000	5	83700	92000
46	CHALLENGER 46	KTH	SA/CR FBG KL	IB	100D	14 6	36450	5	77600	85300
50 4	CHALLENGER 50	KTH	SA/CR FBG KL	IB	100D	16	68700	6 6	1070000	1175000
			1974 **BOATS**								
32 2	CHALLENGER 32	SLP	SA/CR FBG KL	IB	30D	11 2	12800	4 10	24700	27500
34 8	CHALLENGER 35	SLP	SA/CR FBG KL	IB	30D	11 6	13600	4 4	28000	31100
34 8	CHALLENGER 35	KTH	SA/CR FBG KL	IB	55D	11 6	13800	4 4	28400	31500
39 11	CHALLENGER 40	SLP	SA/CR FBG KL	IB	30D	PERK	12 10	24800	5 6	52900	58100
39 11	CHALLENGER 40	KTH	MS FBG KL	IB	55D	PERK	12 10	24800	5 6	55900	61400
42 11	CHALLENGER 42	CTRCPT	KTH	MS FBG KL	IB	85D	13	5 6	103500	113500
50 4	CHALLENGER 50	KTH	SA/CR FBG KL	IB	85D	15 6	68700	6 6	103500	113500
			1973 **BOATS**								
32 2	CHALLENGER 32	SLP	SA/CR FBG KL	IB	30 UNIV	11 2	12800	4 10	24100	26800
32 2	CHALLENGER 32	SLP	SA/CR FBG KL	IB	55D PERK	11 2	12800	4 10	24100	26800
35 4	CHALLENGER 35	SLP	SA/CR FBG KL	IB	55D PERK	11 6	14600	4 4	29400	32700
39 11	CHALLENGER 40	SLP	SA/CR FBG KL	IB	30 UNIV	12 10	28800	6	56000	61500
39 11	CHALLENGER 40	SLP	SA/CR FBG KL	IB	55D PERK	12 10	28800	6	59100	64900
39 11	CHALLENGER 40	KTH	SA/CR FBG KL	IB	55D PERK	12 10	28800	6	59800	65700
40	CHALLENGER 40	SLP	SA/CR FBG KL	IB	55D PERK	12	28800	6	56800	62400
42 6	CHALLENGER 42	KTH	SA/CR FBG KL	IB	55D PERK	13	28000	6	60200	66100
48 11	CHALLENGER 48	KTH	SA/CR FBG KL	IB	85D	15 4	46000	6	83900	92200
50 4	CHALLENGER 50	KTH	SA/CR FBG KL	IB	85D PERK	15	48000	6 6	89000	97800
			1972 **BOATS**								
32 2	CHALLENGER 32	SLP	SA/CR FBG KL	IB	30 UNIV	11 2	12600	4 10	23200	25800
39 11	CHALLENGER 40	SLP	SA/CR FBG KL	IB	50D PERK	12 10	26800	5	52700	57900
50 4	CHALLENGER 50	KTH	SA/CR FBG KL	IB	85D PERK	15 6	48000	6 6	86500	95000
			1971 **BOATS**								
32 2	CHALLENGER 32	SLP	SA/CR FBG KL	IB	30 UNIV	11 2	12800	4 10	23100	25600
37	CHALLENGER 37	SLP	SA/CR FBG KL	IB	D	12 8		5 4	33200	36900
50 10	CHALLENGER 50	SLP	SA/CR FBG KL	IB	D	14 6		6 10	91600	100500
50 10	CHALLENGER 50	KTH	SA/CR FBG KL	IB	D	14 6		6 10	94800	104000
			1970 **BOATS**								
26 6	CHALLENGER 26	SLP	SA/RC FBG KL	IB	D	9		3 11	9100	10400
26 8	CHALLENGER 26	SLP	SA/RC FBG KL	IB	D	9	5900	3 10	9250	10500
32 2	CHALLENGER 32	SLP	SA/CR FBG KL	IB	30 UNIV	11 2	12800	4 10	22700	25200
37 2	CHALLENGER 37	SLP	SA/RC FBG KL	IB	D	11 6		6	29500	32800
37 6	CHALLENGER 37	SLP	SA/RC FBG KL	IB	D	12 1	14300	6	28400	31600
41 3	CHALLENGER 41	SLP	SA/RC FBG KL	IB	D	12		6	50000	54900
41 9	CHALLENGER 41	SLP	SA/RC FBG KL	IB	D	14 3	19000	6	41200	45800

CHALLENGER YACHTS LTD
COAST GUARD MFG ID- ZCY

Call 1-800-327-6929 for BUC Personalized Evaluation Service
Or, for 1970 to 1978 boats, sign onto www.BUCValuPro.com

CHAMPION BOATS

Call 1-800-327-6929 for BUC Personalized Evaluation Service
Or, for 1959 to 1969 boats, sign onto www.BUCValuPro.com

CHAMPION BOATS
AQUA DYNAMICS INC

Call 1-800-327-6929 for BUC Personalized Evaluation Service
Or, for 1966 to 1973 boats, sign onto www.BUCValuPro.com

CHAMPIONSHIP TUNNEL HULL
GRASS EQUIP & SUPPLIES INC

Call 1-800-327-6929 for BUC Personalized Evaluation Service
Or, for 1983 boats, sign onto www.BUCValuPro.com

CHAN SIEW TIN COMPANY
COAST GUARD MFG ID- TXN

ASSOCIATED YACHT BROKERS INC

Call 1-800-327-6929 for BUC Personalized Evaluation Service
Or, for 1980 to 1986 boats, sign onto www.BUCValuPro.com

CHANCE AND ASSOCIATES INC

Call 1-800-327-6929 for BUC Personalized Evaluation Service
Or, for 1960 to 1964 boats, sign onto www.BUCValuPro.com

CHANCE AND COMPANY

OYSTER BAY NY 11771 COAST GUARD MFG ID- CHF See inside cover to adjust price for area

LOA FT	LOA IN	NAME AND/ OR MODEL	TOP/ RIG	BOAT TYPE	HULL MTL	HULL TP	ENGINE TP	# HP	ENGINE MFG	BEAM FT	BEAM IN	WGT LBS	DRAFT FT	DRAFT IN	RETAIL LOW	RETAIL HIGH
		1977 BOATS														
28	7	QUARTER-TON	SLP	SA/RC	FBG	KL	IB	D		9	4	6830	5	1	6900	7900
28	10	MOTOR SAILER	SLP	MS	FBG	KL	IB	D		9	4	9791	5	2	10200	11600
32	11	OFFSHORE-ONE	SLP	SA/CR	FBG	KL	IB	D		9	3	13590	6		16400	18600
55	3	DWL 48	SLP	MS	FBG	KC	IB	D		13	6	42000	4		99100	109000
		1976 BOATS														
28	7	HALF-TON-CUP	SLP	SAIL	FBG	KL	IB	15D	VLVO	9	4	6830	5		6600	7550
28	10	MOTOR SAILER	SLP	MS	FBG	KL	IB	50D	PERK	9	4	9480	5	2	9550	10800
33		OFFSHORE ONE	SLP	SAIL	FBG	KL	IB	200D	BUKH	9	4	13590	6		15400	17500
55	3	DWL 48	SLP	MS	FBG	KC	IB	D		13	6	42000	4		95500	105000
		1975 BOATS														
28	7	CJ29	SLP	SA/RC	FBG	KL	IB	D		9	4	7400	5	4	6950	8000
33		OFFSHORE ONE	SLP	SAIL	FBG	KL	IB	12D	VLVO	9	4	12000	6		13200	15000
39		CHANCE 39/33	SLP	SAIL	FBG	KL	IB	20D	WEST	11	3	18500	6	9	28000	31100
42		CHANCE 42/36	SLP	SAIL	FBG	KL	IB	35D	VLVO	11	7	22000	7	8	35000	38900
52		CHANCE 52/45	KTH	SAIL	FBG	CB	IB	35D	VLVO	14	1	34000	10		71700	78800
55	3	CHANCE 55-C	SLP	MS	FBG	KC	IB	D		13	6	44000	4	6	92800	102000
55	3	CHANCE 55-C	KTH	MS	FBG	KC	IB	D		13	6	44000	4	6	94900	104000
		1974 BOATS														
33		CHANCE 29	SLP	SAIL	FBG		OB			9	4	15500	6	9	16800	19100
36	5	CHANCE ONE TONNER		SAIL	FBG	CB	OB			10	6	12000			16000	18100
39	3	CHANCE 39 CUTTER		SAIL	FBG		OB			11	3	15800	7	1	24700	27400
42	2	CHANCE 42		SAIL	FBG		OB			11	7	17800	7	9	29900	33200
52		CHANCE YACHT		SAIL	FBG		OB			14	5	37000	9	9	68100	74800

CHANNEL MARINE

COAST GUARD MFG ID- CNM

Call 1-800-327-6929 for BUC Personalized Evaluation Service
Or, for 1972 to 1974 boats, sign onto www.BUCValuPro.com

LLOYD CHANNING ASSOC

Call 1-800-327-6929 for BUC Personalized Evaluation Service
Or, for 1977 to 1978 boats, sign onto www.BUCValuPro.com

CHAPARRAL BOATS INC

NASHVILLE GA 31639 COAST GUARD MFG ID- FGB See inside cover to adjust price for area
FORMERLY FIBERGLASS FABRICATORS INC

For more recent years, see the BUC Used Boat Price Guide, Volume 1 or Volume 2

LOA FT	LOA IN	NAME AND/ OR MODEL	TOP/ RIG	BOAT TYPE	HULL MTL	HULL TP	ENGINE TP	# HP	ENGINE MFG	BEAM FT	BEAM IN	WGT LBS	DRAFT FT	DRAFT IN	RETAIL LOW	RETAIL HIGH
		1983 BOATS														
16	6	CHAPARRAL 167 VB	ST	RNBT	FBG	DV	IO	120		7	2				2550	3000
16	6	CHAPARRAL 177VB DLX	ST	RNBT	FBG	DV	OB			7	2	1300			1950	2300
16	6	CHAPARRAL 177VB DLX	ST	RNBT	FBG	DV	IO	120-140		7	2	1900			2450	2850
16	6	LUXURY SPT 177VBR	ST	RNBT	FBG	DV	OB			7	2	1400			2050	2450
16	6	LUXURY SPT 177VBR	ST	RNBT	FBG	DV	IO	120-140		7	2	2000			2500	2900
17	4	CHAPARRAL 185 BR	ST	RNBT	FBG	DV	IO	120		7	2				2700	3150
17	8	CHAPARRAL 187 BR	ST	RNBT	FBG	DV	IO	140		7	2				2750	3200
17	8	CHAPARRAL 187 CD	ST	RNBT	FBG	DV	OB			7	2	1250			1900	2250
17	8	CHAPARRAL 187 CD	ST	RNBT	FBG	DV	IO	140		7	2				2750	3200
17	8	CHAPARRAL 187V	ST	RNBT	FBG	DV	OB			7	2	1500			2250	2600
17	8	CHAPARRAL 187V	ST	RNBT	FBG	DV	IO	140		7	2	2200			2800	3250
17	8	CHAPARRAL 187V	ST	RNBT	FBG	DV	IO	260		7	2	2200			3050	3550
18	3	CHAPARRAL 194VBR	ST	RNBT	FBG	DV	OB			7	2	1400			2100	2500
18	3	CHAPARRAL 194VBR	ST	RNBT	FBG	DV	IO	120-185		7	2	2100			2850	3350
19	3	CHAPARRAL 198CV	ST	CUD	FBG	DV	IO	170-260		8		2900			3950	4900
19	3	CHAPARRAL 198VBR	ST	RNBT	FBG	DV	OB			8		1900			2700	3150
19	3	CHAPARRAL 198VBR	ST	RNBT	FBG	DV	IO	170-260		8		2700			3650	4500
19	3	CHAPARRAL 204V	ST	FSH	FBG	DV	OB			8		2000			2700	3150
21		CHAPARRAL 21	ST	CTRCN	FBG	DV	OB			8		2700			4500	5200
21		CHAPARRAL 214V	ST	CUD	FBG	DV	OB			8		2500			4400	5050
21		CHAPARRAL 214V	ST	CUD	FBG	DV	IO	170-260		8		3400			5250	6350
23		CHAPARRAL 235V	ST	CUD	FBG	DV	IO	198-260		8		4125			6750	8050
23		CHAPARRAL 238	ST	FSH	FBG	DV	OB			8		3000			5550	6350
23		CHAPARRAL 238V	ST	CR	FBG	DV	IO	198-260		8		4500			7250	8600
24	4	CHAPARRAL 244V	ST	CUD	FBG	DV	IO	185-260		8		3900			6950	8300
24	4	CHAPARRAL 244V	ST	CUD	FBG	DV	IO	T120-T170		8		3900			7650	8950
31		BOMBAY-CLIPPER	SLP	SAIL	FBG	KL	IB	D		11		11000	3	5	21900	24300
		1982 BOATS														
16	6	CHAPARRAL 167 STD	ST	RNBT	FBG	DV	OB			7	2	1450			1950	2350
16	6	CHAPARRAL 167 VB DLX	ST	RNBT	FBG	DV	OB			7	2	1450			2200	2550
16	6	CHAPARRAL 167 VB DLX	ST	RNBT	FBG	DV	IO	140	MRCR	7	2	2050			2450	2800
16	6	CHAPARRAL 167 VBR	ST	RNBT	FBG	DV	IO	120	MRCR	7	2	2050			2400	2800
16	6	LUXURY SPORT 167 VBR	ST	RNBT	FBG	DV	IO	120-140		7	2	2050			2500	2900
17	6	CHAPARRAL 185	ST	RNBT	FBG	TR	IO	120-185		7	6	2250			2800	3450
17	8	CHAPARRAL 187 V	ST	RNBT	FBG	DV	OB			7	2	1550			2250	2600
17	8	CHAPARRAL 187 V	ST	RNBT	FBG	DV	IO	140-200		7	2	2250			2800	3450
17	8	CHAPARRAL 187 V	ST	RNBT	FBG	DV	IO	225-260		7	2	2250			3050	3750
17	8	CHAPARRAL 187 VBR	ST	RNBT	FBG	DV	OB			7	2	1550			2250	2600
17	8	CHAPARRAL 187 VBR	ST	RNBT	FBG	DV	IO	140-200		7	2	2250			2800	3450
17	8	CHAPARRAL 187 VBR	ST	RNBT	FBG	DV	IO	225-260		7	2	2250			3050	3750
18	3	CHAPARRAL 194 V DLX	ST	RNBT	FBG	DV	OB			7	2	1550			2300	2650
18	3	CHAPARRAL 194 V DLX	ST	RNBT	FBG	DV	IO	120-185		7	2	2150			2800	3450
18	3	CHAPARRAL 194 V STD	ST	RNBT	FBG	DV	OB			7	2	1550			2200	2600
18	3	CHAPARRAL 194 V STD	ST	RNBT	FBG	DV	IO	120-185		7	2	2150			2800	3400
19	3	CHAPARRAL 198 V DLX	ST	CUD	FBG	DV	IO	170-230		8		2750			3750	4650
19	3	CHAPARRAL 198 V DLX	ST	CUD	FBG	DV	IO	260		8		2750			4000	4850
19	3	CHAPARRAL 198 VB DLX	ST	RNBT	FBG	DV	IO	170-230		8		2750			3600	4500
19	3	CHAPARRAL 198 VB DLX	ST	RNBT	FBG	DV	IO	260		8		2750			3850	4700
19	3	CHAPARRAL 198 VBRDLX	ST	RNBT	FBG	DV	OB			8		1950			2650	3100
19	3	CHAPARRAL 204 DLX	ST	OPFSH	FBG	DV	OB			8		2000			2650	3050
21		CHAPARRAL 214 V DLX	ST	CUD	FBG	DV	OB			8		2550			4350	5000
21		CHAPARRAL 214 V DLX	ST	CUD	FBG	DV	IO	170-230		8		3350			5100	6200
21		CHAPARRAL 214 V DLX	ST	CUD	FBG	DV	IO	260		8		3350			5350	6400
23		CHAPARRAL 238		OVNTR	FBG	DV	OB			8		3000			5450	6250
23		CHAPARRAL 238	ST	OVNTR	FBG	DV	IO	198-260		8		4400			6950	8650
24	4	CHAPARRAL 244 V DLX	ST	CUD	FBG	DV	IO	198-260		8		3950			6850	8450
24	4	CHAPARRAL 244 V DLX	ST	CUD	FBG	DV	IO	T120-T170		8		3950			7550	8850
31		BOMBAY-CLIPPER	SLP	SAIL	FBG	KL	IB	20D	YAN	11		11000	3	5	20800	23100
		1981 BOATS														
16	6	CHAPARRAL 167 STD	ST	RNBT	FBG	DV	OB			7	2	1450			1900	2250
16	6	CHAPARRAL 167 VB DLX	ST	RNBT	FBG	DV	OB			7	2	1450			2150	2500
16	6	CHAPARRAL 167 VB DLX	ST	RNBT	FBG	DV	IO	140	MRCR	7	2	2050			2500	2900
16	6	CHAPARRAL 167 VBR	ST	RNBT	FBG	DV	IO	120	MRCR	7	2	2050			2500	2900
16	6	LUXURY SPORT 167 VBR	ST	RNBT	FBG	DV	IO	120-140		7	2	2050			2350	2750
17	6	CHAPARRAL 185	ST	RNBT	FBG	TR	IO	120-185		7	6	2250			2800	3400
17	8	CHAPARRAL 187 V	ST	RNBT	FBG	DV	OB			7	2	1550			2150	2550
17	8	CHAPARRAL 187 V	ST	RNBT	FBG	DV	IO	140-198		7	2	2250			2750	3350
		IO 200 OMC 2750 3200, IO 200-230 2950 3500, IO 260 MRCR 2950 3450														
		IO 260 OMC 2950 3400, IO 260 VLVO 3200 3700														
17	8	CHAPARRAL 187 VBR	ST	RNBT	FBG	DV	OB			7	2	1550			2150	2550
17	8	CHAPARRAL 187 VBR	ST	RNBT	FBG	DV	IO	140-198		7	2	2250			2750	3350
		IO 200 OMC 2750 3200, IO 200-230 2950 3500, IO 260 MRCR 2950 3450														
		IO 260 OMC 2950 3400, IO 260 VLVO 3200 3700														
18	3	CHAPARRAL 194 V DLX	ST	RNBT	FBG	DV	OB			7	2	1550			2250	2600
18	3	CHAPARRAL 194 V DLX	ST	RNBT	FBG	DV	IO	120-185		7	2	2150			2750	3450
18	3	CHAPARRAL 194 V STD	ST	RNBT	FBG	DV	OB			7	2	1550			2150	2500
18	3	CHAPARRAL 194 V STD	ST	RNBT	FBG	DV	IO	120-185		7	2	2150			2700	3350
19	3	CHAPARRAL 198 V	ST	CUD	FBG	DV	IO	228	MRCR	8		2750			3800	4400
19	3	CHAPARRAL 198 V DLX	ST	CUD	FBG	DV	IO	170-230		8		2750			3700	4600
19	3	CHAPARRAL 198 V DLX	ST	CUD	FBG	DV	IO	260		8		2750			3900	4800
19	3	CHAPARRAL 198 VB DLX	ST	RNBT	FBG	DV	IO	170-230		8		2750			3550	4400
19	3	CHAPARRAL 198 VB DLX	ST	RNBT	FBG	DV	IO	260		8		2750			3800	4600
19	3	CHAPARRAL 198 VBR	ST	RNBT	FBG	DV	OB			8		1950			2600	3050
21		CHAPARRAL 214 V DLX	ST	CUD	FBG	DV	OB			8		2550			4250	4950
21		CHAPARRAL 214 V DLX	ST	CUD	FBG	DV	IO	165-230		8		3350			5000	6100
21		CHAPARRAL 214 V DLX	ST	CUD	FBG	DV	IO	260		8		3350			5250	6300
24	4	CHAPARRAL 244 V DLX	ST	CUD	FBG	DV	IO	198-260		8		3950			6750	8300
24	4	CHAPARRAL 244 V DLX	ST	CUD	FBG	DV	IO	T120-T185		8		3950			7450	8950
31		BOMBAY CLIPPER	SLP	SAIL	FBG	KL	IB	20D	YAN	11		11000	3	5	19700	21900
		1980 BOATS														
16	6	CHAPARRAL 167 VBR	ST	RNBT	FBG	DV	OB			7	2	1450			1950	2350
16	6	CHAPARRAL 167 VBR	ST	RNBT	FBG	DV	IO	120-140		7	2	2050			2400	2800
17	4	CHAPARRAL 177 BR		RNBT	FBG	SV	OB			7	2	1400			1950	2300
17	4	CHAPARRAL 177 BR		RNBT	FBG	SV	IO	120		7	2				2550	3000
17	6	CHAPARRAL 185	ST	RNBT	FBG	TR	IO	120-185		7	6	2250			2750	3350
17	8	CHAPARRAL 187 V	ST	RNBT	FBG	DV	OB			7	2	1550			2100	2500
17	8	CHAPARRAL 187 V	ST	RNBT	FBG	DV	IO	140-198		7	2	2250			2700	3300
17	8	CHAPARRAL 187 V	ST	RNBT	FBG	DV	IO	200		7	2	2250			2750	3400
17	8	CHAPARRAL 187 V	ST	RNBT	FBG	DV	IO	225-260		7	2	2250			3000	3650
17	8	CHAPARRAL 187 VBR	ST	RNBT	FBG	DV	OB			7	2	1550			2100	2500

CONTINUED ON NEXT PAGE

LOA FT	LOA IN	NAME AND/ OR MODEL	TOP/ RIG	BOAT TYPE	-HULL- MTL	-HULL- TP	TP	ENGINE # HP	MFG	BEAM FT	BEAM IN	WGT LBS	DRAFT FT	DRAFT IN	RETAIL LOW	RETAIL HIGH
		1980 BOATS														
17	8	CHAPARRAL 187 VBR	ST	RNBT	FBG	DV	IO	140-198		7	2	2250			2700	3300
17	8	CHAPARRAL 187 VBR	ST	RNBT	FBG	DV	IO	200		7	2	2250			2750	3400
17	8	CHAPARRAL 187 VBR	ST	RNBT	FBG	DV	IO	225-260		7	2	2250			3000	3650
18	3	CHAPARRAL 194 V DLX	ST	RNBT	FBG	DV	OB			7	2	1550			2200	2550
18	3	CHAPARRAL 194 V DLX	ST	RNBT	FBG	DV	IO	120-185		7	2	2150			2750	3350
18	3	CHAPARRAL 194 V STD	ST	RNBT	FBG	DV	OB			7	2	1550			2050	2450
18	3	CHAPARRAL 194 V STD	ST	RNBT	FBG	DV	IO	120-185		7	2	2150			2700	3300
19	3	CHAPARRAL 198 V	ST	CUD	FBG	DV	IO	170-230		8		2750			3650	4550
19	3	CHAPARRAL 198 V	ST	CUD	FBG	DV	IO	260		8		2750			3900	4750
19	3	CHAPARRAL 198 VBR	ST	RNBT	FBG	DV	OB			8		1950			2550	2950
19	3	CHAPARRAL 198 VBR	ST	RNBT	FBG	DV	IO	170-230		8		2750			3500	4400
19	3	CHAPARRAL 198 VBR	ST	RNBT	FBG	DV	IO	260		8		2750			3750	4550
21		CHAPARRAL 214 V	ST	CUD	FBG	DV	OB			8		2550			4150	4800
21		CHAPARRAL 214 V	ST	CUD	FBG	DV	IO	165-230		8		3350			4950	6050
21		CHAPARRAL 214 V	ST	CUD	FBG	DV	IO	260		0		3350			5250	6250
24	4	CHAPARRAL 244 V		CUD	FBG	DV	IO	190		8					7100	8150
24	4	CHAPARRAL 244 V	ST	CUD	FBG	DV	IO	185-260		8		3950			6650	8250
24	4	CHAPARRAL 244 V	ST	CUD	FBG	DV	IO	T120-T185		8		3950			7350	8850
		1979 BOATS														
16	6	CHAPARRAL 167 VBR	ST	RNBT	FBG	DV	IO	140		7	2	1700		8	2250	2600
17	4	CHAPARRAL 177 TV	ST	RNBT	FBG	TR	IO	188	MRCR	7	2	2000		8	2550	2950
17	8	CHAPARRAL 187 V	ST	RNBT	FBG	DV	OB			7	2	1350		8	1700	2050
17	8	CHAPARRAL 187 V	ST	RNBT	FBG	DV	IO	120		7	2	2200		8	2650	3100
17	8	CHAPARRAL 187 V	ST	RNBT	FBG	DV	IO	260		7	2	2200		8	2900	3400
17	8	CHAPARRAL 187 VBR	ST	RNBT	FBG	DV	OB			7	2	1350		8	2000	2350
17	8	CHAPARRAL 187 VBR	ST	RNBT	FBG	DV	IO	120		7	2	2200		8	2650	3100
17	8	CHAPARRAL 187 VBR	ST	RNBT	FBG	DV	IO	260		7	2	2200		8	2900	3400
18	3	CHAPARRAL 19 VBR	ST	RNBT	FBG	DV	OB			7	2	1450		6	2000	2350
18	3	CHAPARRAL 19 VBR	ST	RNBT	FBG	DV	IO	120-170		7	2	2200		6	2750	3250
19	3	CHAPARRAL 198 V	ST	CUD	FBG	DV	IO	170-260		8		3000		10	3850	4750
19	3	CHAPARRAL 198 VBR	ST	RNBT	FBG	DV	OB			8		1800		10	2400	2800
19	3	CHAPARRAL 198 VBR	ST	RNBT	FBG	DV	IO	165-260		8		2600		10	3400	4250
21		CHAPARRAL 21 V	ST	CUD	FBG	DV	OB			8		2550	1		4050	4750
21		CHAPARRAL 21 V	ST	CUD	FBG	DV	IO	165-260		8		3300	1		4900	5950
24	4	CHAPARRAL 244 V	ST	CUD	FBG	DV	IO	165-260		8		4000	1	2	6700	8050
24	4	CHAPARRAL 244 V	ST	CUD	FBG	DV	IO	T170		8		4000	1	2	7550	8700
		1978 BOATS														
16	5	CHAPARRAL 165 DELUXE	OP	RNBT	FBG	TR	IO	120-140		6	6	1700	1	8	2050	2450
17	8	CHAPARRAL 18	OP	RNBT	FBG	TR	IO	120-170		6	11	2000	2		2500	2950
17	8	CHAPARRAL 187 DELUXE	OP	RNBT	FBG	DV	IO	120-240		7	2	2000	2		2550	3150
17	8	CHAPARRAL 187 DELUXE	OP	RNBT	FBG	DV	IO	260	MRCR	7	2	2000	2		2800	3300
18	3	CHAPARRAL 19	OP	OPFSH	FBG	DV	OB			7	2	1300	1	6	1750	2050
18	3	CHAPARRAL 19	OP	RNBT	FBG	DV	OB			7	2	1300	1	6	1800	2150
18	3	CHAPARRAL 19	OP	RNBT	FBG	DV	IO	120-170		7	2	2100	2		2700	3200
19	1	CHAPARRAL 198 DELUXE	OP	RNBT	FBG	DV	IO	165-260		8		2800	2		3550	4400
21		CHAPARRAL 21	OP	CUD	FBG	DV	OB			8		2000	2		3400	3950
21		CHAPARRAL 21	OP	CUD	FBG	DV	IO	165-260		8		3000	2	6	4700	5650
21		CHAPARRAL 21	OP	OPFSH	FBG	DV	OB			8		2000	2		3400	3950
24	4	CHAPARRAL 244	OP	CUD	FBG	DV	IO	185-260		8		4000	2	6	6750	8100
24	4	CHAPARRAL 244	OP	CUD	FBG	DV	IO	280D	VLVO	8		4000	2	6	9550	10900
24	4	CHAPARRAL 244	OP	CUD	FBG	DV	IO	T120-T165		8		4000	2	6	7500	8750
		1977 BOATS														
16	5	CHAPARRAL 165 DELUXE	ST	RNBT	FBG	TR	IO	120-140		6	6	1700			2200	2550
16	5	CHAPARRAL 165 STD	ST	RNBT	FBG	TR	IO	120-140		6	6	1700			2050	2450
17	8	CHAPARRAL 18T DELUXE	ST	RNBT	FBG	TR	OB			7	2	1200			1750	2050
17	8	CHAPARRAL 18T DELUXE	ST	RNBT	FBG	TR	IO	120-165		7	2	2000			2650	3100
17	8	CHAPARRAL 18T STD	ST	RNBT	FBG	TR	IO	120-165		7	2	2000			2550	3000
17	8	CHAPARRAL 18V DELUXE	ST	RNBT	FBG	DV	IO	120-170		7	2	2000			2650	3100
18	3	CHAPARRAL 19V	ST	FSH	FBG	DV	OB			7	2	1300			1750	2050
18	3	CHAPARRAL 19V DELUXE	ST	RNBT	FBG	DV	OB			7	2	1300			1800	2150
18	3	CHAPARRAL 19V DELUXE	ST	RNBT	FBG	DV	IO	120-165		7	2				2800	3300
18	3	CHAPARRAL 19V STD	ST	RNBT	FBG	DV	OB			7	2	1300			1700	2050
18	3	CHAPARRAL 19V STD	ST	RNBT	FBG	DV	IO	120-165		7	2				2700	3200
21		CHAPARRAL 21V	ST	CUD	FBG	DV	OB			8		2000			3350	3900
21		CHAPARRAL 21V DELUXE	ST	CUD	FBG	DV	IO	140-235		8		3000			4750	5650
21		CHAPARRAL 21V STD	ST	CUD	FBG	DV	IO	140-235		8		3000			4700	5550
24	4	CHAPARRAL 244 DELUXE	ST	CUD	FBG	DV	IO	165-255		8		4000			7050	8450
24	4	CHAPARRAL 244 DELUXE	ST	CUD	FBG	DV	IO	T120-T170		8		4000			7800	9100
24	4	CHAPARRAL 244 STD	ST	CUD	FBG	DV	IO	165-255		8		4000			6600	7950
24	4	CHAPARRAL 244 STD	ST	CUD	FBG	DV	IO	T120-T170		8		4000			7400	8700
		1976 BOATS														
16	5	CHAPARRAL 165 DELUXE	ST	RNBT	FBG	TR	IO	120-140		6	6	1700			2250	2750
16	5	CHAPARRAL 165 STD	ST	RNBT	FBG	TR	IO	120-140		6	6	1700			2150	2700
17	8	CHAPARRAL 18 DELUXE	ST	RNBT	FBG	TR	OB					1200			1700	2050
17	8	CHAPARRAL 18 DELUXE	ST	RNBT	FBG	TR	IO	120-170				2000			2750	3350
17	8	CHAPARRAL 18 STD	ST	RNBT	FBG	TR	IO	120-170				2000			2600	3250
18	3	CHAPARRAL 19V DELUXE	ST		FBG	DV	OB			7	2	1300			1700	2050
18	3	CHAPARRAL 19V DELUXE	ST		FBG	DV	IO	120-170		7	2				2900	3550
18	3	CHAPARRAL 19V FISH	ST	FSH	FBG	DV	OB			7	2	1300			1700	2050
18	3	CHAPARRAL 19V STD	ST	RNBT	FBG	DV	OB			7	2	1300			1750	2100
18	3	CHAPARRAL 19V STD	ST	RNBT	FBG	DV	IO	120-170		7	2				2850	3500
21		CHAPARRAL 21	ST	CUD	FBG	DV	OB			8		2000			3350	3850
21		CHAPARRAL 21 DELUXE	ST	CUD	FBG	DV	IO	140-235		8		3000			4900	5850
21		CHAPARRAL 21 STD	ST	CUD	FBG	DV	IO	140-235		8		3000			4800	5700
24	4	CHAPARRAL 224 DELUXE	ST	CUD	FBG	DV	IO	165-255		8		4000			7000	8450
24	4	CHAPARRAL 224 DELUXE	ST	CUD	FBG	DV	IO	T120-T170		8		4000			7800	9500
24	4	CHAPARRAL 224 STD	ST	CUD	FBG	DV	IO	165-255				4000			7100	8550
24	4	CHAPARRAL 224 STD	ST	CUD	FBG	DV	IO	T120-T170				4000			7900	9600
		1975 BOATS														
16	5	CHAPARRAL 165 DLX	OP	RNBT	FBG	TR	IO	120-140		6	6	1700	1	8	2300	2850
16	5	CHAPARRAL 165 STD	OP	RNBT	FBG	TR	IO	120-140		6	6	1700	1	8	2200	2700
17	8	CHAPARRAL 18T DLX	OP	RNBT	FBG	TR	OB			6	11	1200	1	2	1700	2000
17	8	CHAPARRAL 18T DLX	OP	RNBT	FBG	TR	IO	120-170		6	11	2000	2		2750	3400
17	8	CHAPARRAL 18T DLX	OP	RNBT	FBG	TR	IO	465		6	11	2000	2		6300	7250
17	8	CHAPARRAL 18T STD	OP	RNBT	FBG	TR	IO	120-170		6	11	2000	2		2650	3300
18	3	CHAPARRAL 19V DLX	OP	RNBT	FBG	DV	OB			7	2	1300	1	6	1800	2100
18	3	CHAPARRAL 19V DLX	OP	RNBT	FBG	DV	IO	120-170		7	2	2100	2	6	2950	3650
18	3	CHAPARRAL 19V STD	OP	FSH	FBG	DV	OB			7	2	1300	1	6	1700	2050
18	3	CHAPARRAL 19V STD	OP	RNBT	FBG	DV	OB			7	2	1300	1	6	1700	2000
18	3	CHAPARRAL 19V STD	OP	RNBT	FBG	DV	IO	120-170		7	2	2100	2	6	2900	3550
20	3	CHAPARRAL 21	OP	RNBT	FBG	DV	OB			8		1800	2	6	2950	3400
20	3	CHAPARRAL 21	OP	RNBT	FBG	DV	IO	120-165		8		2200	2	6	3900	4550
21		CHAPARRAL	OP	RNBT	FBG	DV	OB			8		1800	2	6	3050	3550
21		CHAPARRAL	OP	RNBT	FBG	DV	IO	120-165		8		2200	2	6	4050	4750
21		CHAPARRAL 21V CUDDY	OP	CUD	FBG	DV	OB			8		2000	2	6	3300	3850
21		CHAPARRAL 21V CUDDY	OP	CUD	FBG	DV	IO	140-165		8		3000	2	6	5000	5750
21		CHAPARRAL 21V STD	OP	CUD	FBG	DV	IO	165-235		8		3000	2	6	5000	5950
24	4	CHAPARRAL 244V CUDDY	OP	CUD	FBG	DV	IO	165-255		8		4000	2	6	7250	8700
24	4	CHAPARRAL 244V CUDDY	OP	CUD	FBG	DV	IO	T120-T170		8		4000	2	6	8050	9800
		1973 BOATS														
17	8	CHAPARRAL 18		RNBT	FBG	TR	IO	120		6	11	2000	2		2900	3350
18	3	CHAPARRAL 19		RNBT	FBG	DV	OB			7	2	1300	1	6	1700	2050
24	4	CHAPARRAL 244		CUD	FBG	DV	IO	165		8		4000	2	6	7750	8900

CHAPMAN & KALAYJIAN

COSTA MESA CA COAST GUARD MFG ID- CAK See inside cover to adjust price for area

LOA FT	LOA IN	NAME AND/ OR MODEL	TOP/ RIG	BOAT TYPE	-HULL- MTL	-HULL- TP	TP	ENGINE # HP	MFG	BEAM FT	BEAM IN	WGT LBS	DRAFT FT	DRAFT IN	RETAIL LOW	RETAIL HIGH
		1963 BOATS														
36	2	LAPWORTH 36		SAIL	WD		IB	25D							33100	36800
39	11	LAPWORTH 40		SAIL	WD		IB	31D							48500	53300
		1960 BOATS														
39	11	LAPWORTH 40	SLP	SAIL	WD	KL	IB	D		10	6		5	6	48700	53500

CHAPMAN YACHT CORP

COAST GUARD MFG ID- AYC
FORMERLY ALAJUELA YACHT CORP

Call 1-800-327-6929 for BUC Personalized Evaluation Service
Or, for 1983 boats, sign onto www.BUCValuPro.com

CHARGER BOATS INC

CONCORD LK ONTARIO CANADA See inside cover to adjust price for area
ALSO AMF

For more recent years, see the BUC Used Boat Price Guide, Volume 1 or Volume 2

LOA FT	LOA IN	NAME AND/ OR MODEL	TOP/ RIG	BOAT TYPE	-HULL- MTL	-HULL- TP	TP	ENGINE # HP	MFG	BEAM FT	BEAM IN	WGT LBS	DRAFT FT	DRAFT IN	RETAIL LOW	RETAIL HIGH
		1983 BOATS														
18		CHARGER 18DL	OP	RNBT	F/S	DV	OB			6	9	900			3350	3900
18		CHARGER 18DL	OP	RNBT	F/S	DV	IO	170-185		6	9	900			2950	3450
18		CHARGER 18DL	OP	RNBT	F/S	DV	IO	260		6	9	900			3250	3750
18		CHARGER 18SK	OP	RNBT	F/S	DV	OB			6	9	800			3050	3550
20	2	CHARGER 20	OP	RNBT	F/S	DV	OB			8		1400			5300	6100
20	2	CHARGER 20	OP	RNBT	F/S	DV	IO	260		8		1400			4800	5500

 CONTINUED ON NEXT PAGE

LOA FT	LOA IN	NAME AND/ OR MODEL	TOP/ RIG	BOAT TYPE	-HULL- MTL	-HULL- TP	ENGINE TP	ENGINE # HP	ENGINE MFG	BEAM FT	BEAM IN	WGT LBS	DRAFT FT	DRAFT IN	RETAIL LOW	RETAIL HIGH
		1983 BOATS														
20	2	CHARGER 20	OP	RNBT	F/S	DV	IO	330		8		1400			5650	6500
30		CHARGER 30	OP	RNBT	F/S	DV	OB			8		3500			25600	28400
30		CHARGER 30	OP	RNBT	F/S	DV	IO	T330	MRCR	8		3500			17000	19300

CHARGER/AFC INC

DIV RICHLAND DIVERSIFIED IND
RICHLAND MO 65556 COAST GUARD MFG ID- RDA
FOR LATER YEARS SEE PLAY-CRAFT PONTOONS
See inside cover to adjust price for area

For more recent years, see the BUC Used Boat Price Guide, Volume 1 or Volume 2

LOA FT	LOA IN	NAME AND/ OR MODEL	TOP/ RIG	BOAT TYPE	-HULL- MTL	-HULL- TP	ENGINE TP	ENGINE # HP	ENGINE MFG	BEAM FT	BEAM IN	WGT LBS	DRAFT FT	DRAFT IN	RETAIL LOW	RETAIL HIGH
		1983 BOATS														
16		160V SE	OP	BASS	FBG	DV	OB			6	10	850			2750	3200
16	4	165V	OP	RNBT	FBG	DV	OB			7	2	1100			3550	4100
16	4	165V	OP	RNBT	FBG	DV	IO			7	2	1850			**	**
17	1	CHARGER 747XLT	OP	BASS	FBG	SV	OB			6	2	950			3200	3700
17	1	CHARGER 747XLT	OP	BASS	FBG	SV	IO	140		6	2	1650			2400	2800
17	1	CHARGER 747XLV	OP	BASS	FBG	SV	OB			6	2	900			3050	3500
17	1	CHARGER 747XLV	OP	BASS	FBG	SV	IO	140		6	2	1550			2350	2700
17	3	FOXFIRE 170T SE	OP	BASS	FBG	DV	OB			7	2				3200	3700
17	3	FOXFIRE 170V SE	OP	BASS	FBG	DV	OB			7	2	1000			3350	3900
17	6	CHARGER 175V SE	OP	BASS	FBG	SV	OB			7		1050			3500	4100
17	8	CHARGER 180VBR	OP	RNBT	FBG	DV	OB			7	3	1350			4400	5050
17	8	CHARGER 180VBR	OP	RNBT	FBG	DV	IO	140		7	3	2350			3050	3550
17	11	CHARGER 270V	OP	BASS	FBG	SV	OB			7		1800			5350	6150
18	11	CHARGER 290	OP	BASS	FBG	TR	IO	140		7		1800			3100	3600
19	2	CHARGER 200VBR	OP	RNBT	FBG	DV	IO	260		7	8	2650			3900	4550
19	2	M-F-G 19	SLP	SAIL	FBG	KL				7		1600	2	2	4850	5550
21	2	2150V	OP	RNBT	FBG	DV	IO			7	9	2950			**	**
22	7	C-23		SAIL	FBG		OB			7	11	2900			7750	8900
		1982 BOATS														
16		160V SE	OP	BASS	FBG	DV	OB			6	10	850			2700	3150
16		260V SE	OP	BASS	FBG	DV	OB			6	9	875			2800	3250
16	4	165V	OP	RNBT	FBG	DV	OB			7	2	850			2750	3200
16	4	165V	OP	RNBT	FBG	DV	IO			7	2	1250			**	**
17	1	CHARGER 747XLT	OP	BASS	FBG	SV	OB			6	2	950			3100	3600
17	1	CHARGER 747XLT	OP	BASS	FBG	SV	IO	140		6	2				2350	2700
17	1	CHARGER 747XLV	OP	BASS	FBG	SV	OB			6	2	900			2950	3450
17	1	CHARGER 747XLV	OP	BASS	FBG	SV	IO	140		6	2	1550			2300	2700
17	3	170T	OP	RNBT	FBG	TR	IO	140		6	10	2100			2650	3100
17	6	CHARGER 175V SE	OP	BASS	FBG	SV	OB			7		950			3150	3700
17	8	CHARGER 180VBR	OP	RNBT	FBG	DV	OB			7	3	1350			4250	4950
17	8	CHARGER 180VBR	OP	RNBT	FBG	DV	IO	140		7	3	2350			3000	3450
17	11	170V	OP	BASS	FBG	SV	IO	170		7					2800	3300
17	11	CHARGER 270V	OP	BASS	FBG	SV	OB			7		1050			3500	4050
18	11	CHARGER 290	OP	BASS	FBG	TR	IO	140		7		1800			3000	3500
19	2	BANDIT 19	SLP	SAIL	FBG	KL	OB			7		1600	2	2	4600	5250
19	2	CHARGER 200VBR	OP	RNBT	FBG	DV	IO	260		7	8	2800			3950	4550
21	2	2150V	OP	RNBT	FBG	DV	IO			7	9	2950			**	**
22	7	C-23	OP	SAIL	FBG		OB			7	11	2900			7300	8400
		1981 BOATS														
17	1	CHARGER 747XLT		BASS	FBG	SV	OB			6	2	950			3050	3550
17	1	CHARGER 747XLT		BASS	FBG	SV	IO	140		6	2	1650			2350	2750
17	1	CHARGER 747XLV		BASS	FBG	SV	OB			6	2	900			2900	3400
17	1	CHARGER 747XLV		BASS	FBG	SV	IO	140		6	2	1550			2300	2650
17	3	CHARGER 170T		RNBT	FBG	TR	OB			6	10	1250			3900	4500
17	3	CHARGER 170T		RNBT	FBG	TR	IO	140		6	10	2100			2600	3050
17	6	CHARGER 175V SE		BASS	FBG	SV	OB			7		950			3100	3600
17	8	CHARGER 180VBR		RNBT	FBG	DV	OB			7	3	1350			4200	4850
17	8	CHARGER 180VBR		RNBT	FBG	DV	IO	140		7	3	2350			2950	3400
17	11	CHARGER 170V	OP	BASS	FBG	SV	OB			7		950			3150	3650
17	11	CHARGER 170VBR		RNBT	FBG	DV	IO	170	MRCR	7		1800			2600	3000
17	11	CHARGER 270V		BASS	FBG	SV	OB			7		1050			3450	4000
18	11	CHARGER 290		BASS	FBG	TR	IO	140		7		1800			2950	3450
19	2	CHARGER 200VBR		RNBT	FBG	DV	IO	260		7	8	2800			3850	4500
19	2	M-F-G 19	SLP	SAIL	FBG	KL	OB			7		1600	2	2	4250	4950
		1980 BOATS														
17	1	CHARGER 747XLT		BASS	FBG	SV	OB			6	2	950			3000	3500
17	1	CHARGER 747XLT		BASS	FBG	SV	IO	140		6	2	1650			2350	2700
17	1	CHARGER 747XLV		BASS	FBG	SV	OB			6	2	900			2850	3350
17	1	CHARGER 747XLV		BASS	FBG	SV	IO	140		6	2	1550			2250	2650
17	3	CHARGER 170T		RNBT	FBG	TR	OB			6	10	1250			3850	4450
17	3	CHARGER 170T		RNBT	FBG	TR	IO	140		6	10	2100			2600	3000
17	6	CHARGER 175V SE		BASS	FBG	SV	OB			7		950			3050	3550
17	8	CHARGER 180VBR		RNBT	FBG	DV	OB			7	3	1350			4100	4800
17	8	CHARGER 180VBR		RNBT	FBG	DV	IO	140		7	3	2350			2900	3400
17	11	CHARGER 170V		BASS	FBG	SV	OB			7		950			3100	3600
17	11	CHARGER 170V		BASS	FBG	SV	IO	140-170		7					2750	3200
17	11	CHARGER 270V		BASS	FBG	SV	OB			7		1050			3350	3900
18	11	CHARGER 290		BASS	FBG	TR	IO	140		7		1800			2950	3400
19	2	CHARGER 200VBR		RNBT	FBG	DV	IO	260		7	8	2800			3800	4450
19	2	CHARGER 200VBR		RNBT	FBG	SV	IO	170		7	7	2650			3450	4050
19	2	CHARGER 200VBR SS		RNBT	FBG	DV	IO	260		7	8	2800			3850	4500
		1979 BOATS														
17	1	CHARGER 747XLT	OP	BASS	FBG	TR	OB			6	2	950			2950	3450
17	1	CHARGER 747XLV	OP	BASS	FBG	DV	OB			6	2	850			2700	3100
17	11	CHARGER 170V	OP	BASS	FBG	DV	OB			7		950			3050	3550
17	11	CHARGER 170Z	OP	BASS	FBG	TR	OB			7		1000			3200	3700
17	11	CHARGER 270V	OP	BASS	FBG	DV	OB			7		1050			3350	3900
17	11	CHARGER 270Z	OP	BASS	FBG	TR	OB			7		1050			3300	3800
18	11	CHARGER 290Z	OP	BASS	FBG	TR	OB			7		1200			3800	4450
18	11	CHARGER 290Z	OP	BASS	FBG	TR	IO	140		7		1800			2950	3400
19	2	CHARGER 19VBR	OP	RNBT	FBG	DV	IO	200	OMC	7	8	2800			3600	4200
19	2	CHARGER 19VBR S/S	OP	RNBT	FBG	DV	IO	198	MRCR	7	8	2800			3650	4200
		1978 BOATS														
16	3	CII	OP	FSH	FBG		OB			5	5	775			2350	2750
17	1	CHARGER 747XL	OP	BASS	FBG	TR	OB			6	3	900			2800	3250
17	1	CHARGER 747XL-V	OP	BASS	FBG	DV	OB			6	2	850			2650	3100
18		CHARGER 170Z	OP	BASS	FBG	TR	OB			7		1000			3150	3650
18		CHARGER 170Z-V	OP	BASS	FBG	DV	OB			7		950			3000	3500
18		CHARGER 270Z	OP	BASS	FBG	TR	OB			7		1050			3250	3750
18		CHARGER 270Z-V	OP	BASS	FBG	DV	OB			7		1050			3300	3850
19		CHARGER 290Z	OP	BASS	FBG	TR	OB			7		1200			3800	4400
19		CHARGER 290Z	OP	BASS	FBG	TR	IO	140		7		1200			2700	3150
		1977 BOATS														
16	3	CHARGER II	OP	BASS	FBG	TR	OB			5	3	700			2100	2500
17	1	CHARGER 747XL	OP	BASS	FBG	TR	OB			6	2	925			2800	3300
		1976 BOATS														
16	3	CHARGER II	OP	BASS	FBG	TR	OB			5	5	775			2300	2700
16	3	CHARGER III	OP	BASS	FBG	TR	OB			5	5	775			2300	2700
16	3	CHARGER V	OP	BASS	FBG	TR	OB			5	5	875			2600	3000
17	1	747XL	OP	FSH	FBG	TR	OB			6	2	900			2700	3150
		1975 BOATS														
16	3	CHARGER III	OP	BASS	FBG	TR	OB			5	5	775			2300	2700
16	3	CHARGER IV	OP	BASS	FBG	TR	OB			5	5	775			2300	2700
16	3	CHARGER V	OP	BASS	FBG	TR	OB			5	5	875			2550	3000

CHARLESTON FIBER GLASS

DIV OF REINELL INDUSTRIES

Call 1-800-327-6929 for BUC Personalized Evaluation Service
Or, for 1976 boats, sign onto www.BUCValuPro.com

CHARTER MARINE CORP

COAST GUARD MFG ID- CVV

Call 1-800-327-6929 for BUC Personalized Evaluation Service
Or, for 1978 boats, sign onto www.BUCValuPro.com

CHASER YACHT SALES INC

ERIN ONTARIO CANADA COAST GUARD MFG ID- ZCD See inside cover to adjust price for area

LOA FT	LOA IN	NAME AND/ OR MODEL	TOP/ RIG	BOAT TYPE	-HULL- MTL	-HULL- TP	ENGINE TP	ENGINE # HP	ENGINE MFG	BEAM FT	BEAM IN	WGT LBS	DRAFT FT	DRAFT IN	RETAIL LOW	RETAIL HIGH
		1980 BOATS														
39	11	CHASER 39	CUT	SAIL	FBG	KL	IB	35D	PERK	12		17500	5	6	34600	38400
		1977 BOATS														
29	3	CHASER HALF-TON	SLP	SAIL	FBG	KL	IB	19	UNIV	10	2	7200	5	7	13900	15900
32	10	CHASER 33 3/4 TON	SLP	SA/CR	F/S	KL	IB	19	UNIV	10	6	9300	6	1	18600	20700
		1976 BOATS														
29		CHASER HALF-TON	SLP	SAIL	F/S	KL	IB	19	UNIV	10	2	5280	5	7	9800	11200
32	10	CHASER 33	SLP	SAIL	F/S	KL	IB	19	UNIV	10	6	7800	6		14800	16800
35	10	PETERSON ONE-TON	SLP	SAIL	FBG	KL	IB	D		11	8	13000	6	6	23100	25700
39	11	PETERSON TWO-TON	SLP	SAIL	FBG	KL	IB	D		12	7	20000	7	3	33200	36800

CHECKMATE BOATS INC

BUCYRUS OH 44820 COAST GUARD MFG ID- CHK See inside cover to adjust price for area

For more recent years, see the BUC Used Boat Price Guide, Volume 1 or Volume 2

LOA FT	LOA IN	NAME AND/ OR MODEL	TOP/ RIG	BOAT TYPE	-HULL- MTL	-HULL- TP	ENGINE TP	ENGINE # HP	ENGINE MFG	BEAM FT	BEAM IN	WGT LBS	DRAFT FT	DRAFT IN	RETAIL LOW	RETAIL HIGH
		1983 BOATS														
17	8	DIPLOMAT	OP	RNBT	FBG	DV	OB			7	4	1875			2200	2550
17	8	DIPLOMAT	OP	RNBT	FBG	DV	IO	140-185		7	6	1875			2750	3250
17	8	SPORTFIRE	OP	RNBT	FBG	DV	IO	140-185		7	6	1875			2750	3250
18	10	ELUDER	OP	RNBT	FBG	DV	IO	140-198		7	6	2000			3000	3550
18	10	ELUDER	OP	RNBT	FBG	DV	IO	260	MRCR	7	6	2000			3250	3800
18	11	EXCITER	OP	RNBT	FBG	DV	IO	140-198		7	5	1975			3000	3550
18	11	EXCITER	OP	RNBT	FBG	DV	IO	260	MRCR	7	5	1975			3250	3800
20	1	ENCHANTER	OP	RNBT	FBG	DV	OB			7	6	1275			1950	2350
20	1	ENTERTAINER	OP	RNBT	FBG	DV	OB			7	6	1150			1800	2150
20	8	ENCHANTER	OP	RNBT	FBG	DV	IO	140-260		7	6	2350			3850	4800
20	8	ENCHANTER	OP	RNBT	FBG	DV	JT	364	CHEV	7	6	2350			5800	6650
20	8	ENTERTAINER	OP	RNBT	FBG	DV	IO	140-260		7	6	2175			3750	4650
20	8	ENTERTAINER	OP	RNBT	FBG	DV	JT	364	CHEV	7	6	2175			5600	6450
23	1	ENFORCER	OP	RNBT	FBG	DV	OB			7	7	2000			3150	3650
23	3	ENFORCER	OP	RNBT	FBG	DV	IO	260		7	7				5500	6350
24	7	CONVINCOR	OP	RNBT	FBG	DV	OB			7	8	2400			4000	4650
25	3	CONVINCOR	OP	RNBT	FBG	DV	IO	260		7	6				7250	8350
		1982 BOATS														
17	8	DIPLOMAT	OP	RNBT	FBG	DV	IO	140-185		7	6	2175			2850	3400
17	8	SPORTFIRE	OP	RNBT	FBG	DV	IO	140-185		7	6	2175			2850	3350
18	10	ELUDER	OP	RNBT	FBG	DV	IO	140-198		7	6	2000			2950	3500
18	10	ELUDER	OP	RNBT	FBG	DV	IO	260	MRCR	7	6	2000			3200	3700
18	11	EXCITER	OP	RNBT	FBG	DV	IO	140-198		7	5	1975			2900	3450
18	11	EXCITER	OP	RNBT	FBG	DV	IO	260	MRCR	7	5	1975			3150	3700
20	1	ENCHANTER	OP	RNBT	FBG	DV	OB			7	6	1275			1900	2300
20	1	ENTERTAINER	OP	RNBT	FBG	DV	OB			7	6	1150			1750	2100
20	8	ENCHANTER	OP	RNBT	FBG	DV	IO	140-260		7	6	2350			3800	4700
20	8	ENTERTAINER	OP	RNBT	FBG	DV	IO	140-260		7	6	2175			3650	4550
23	4	ENFORCER	OP	RNBT	FBG	DV	OB			7	8	2100			3200	3750
24	7	CONVINCOR	OP	RNBT	FBG	DV	OB			7	8	2400			3900	4550
		1981 BOATS														
18	1	PERSUADER	OP	RNBT	FBG	DV	JT	324	FORD	7	1	2000			3900	4550
18	10	ELUDER	OP	RNBT	FBG	DV	IO	140-198		7	6	2000			2900	3450
18	10	ELUDER	OP	RNBT	FBG	DV	IO	260	MRCR	7	6	2000			3150	3650
18	11	EXCITER	OP	RNBT	FBG	DV	IO	140-198		7	5	1975			2900	3400
18	11	EXCITER	OP	RNBT	FBG	DV	IO	260	MRCR	7	5	1975			3100	3650
20	1	ENCHANTER	OP	RNBT	FBG	DV	OB			7	6	1275			1850	2250
20	1	ENTERTAINER	OP	RNBT	FBG	DV	OB			7	6	1150			1700	2050
20	8	ENCHANTER	OP	RNBT	FBG	DV	IO	140-260		7	6	2350			3750	4650
20	8	ENCHANTER	OP	RNBT	FBG	DV	JT	324-364		7	6	2350			5300	6100
20	8	ENTERTAINER	OP	RNBT	FBG	DV	IO	140-260		7	6	2175			3600	4500
20	8	ENTERTAINER	OP	RNBT	FBG	DV	JT	324-364		7	6	2175			5150	5900
		1980 BOATS														
16	8	TRIMATE IV		RNBT	FBG	TR	IO	140		7	4				2500	2900
18	1	PERSUADER	OP	RNBT	FBG	DV	JT	309-324		7	1				3850	4500
18	3	ELUDER	OP	RNBT	FBG	DV	IO	140-198		7	6	2100			2850	3350
18	3	ELUDER	OP	RNBT	FBG	DV	IO	260	MRCR	7	6	2100			3100	3600
20	1	ENCHANTER	OP	RNBT	FBG	DV	OB			7	6	1500			2100	2500
20	8	ENCHANTER	OP	RNBT	FBG	DV	IO	140-260		7	6	2600			3900	4800
20	8	ENCHANTER	OP	RNBT	FBG	DV	JT	309-364		7	6				5450	6300
20	8	ENTERTAINER	OP	RNBT	FBG	DV	IO	140-260		7	6	2585			3850	4800
20	8	ENTERTAINER	OP	RNBT	FBG	DV	JT	324-364		7	6	2585			5300	6100
		1979 BOATS														
16	8	TRI-MATE IV	OP	RNBT	FBG	TR	IO	140-170		7	4	1420			2200	2550
18	1	PERSUADER	OP	RNBT	FBG	DV	JT		FORD	7	2	2135			**	**
18	1	PERSUADER	OP	RNBT	FBG	DV	JT		OLDS	7	2	2135			**	**
18	1	PERSUADER	OP	RNBT	FBG	DV	JT	330-360		7	2	2135			3700	4300
18	3	ELUDER	OP	RNBT	FBG	DV	IO	140-228		7	6	2100			2850	3450
18	3	ELUDER	OP	RNBT	FBG	DV	IO	260		7	6	2100			3100	3600
20	1	ENCHANTER	OP	CUD	FBG	DV	OB			7	6	1500			2050	2450
20	1	ENTERTAINER	OP	RNBT	FBG	DV	OB			7	6	1550			2100	2500
20	8	ENCHANTER	OP	CUD	FBG	DV	JT		FORD	7	6	2600			**	**
20	8	ENCHANTER	OP	CUD	FBG	DV	IO	140-260		7	6	2600			4050	5050
20	8	ENTERTAINER	OP	RNBT	FBG	DV	IO	140-260		7	6	2585			3850	4800
		1978 BOATS														
16	9	TRI-MATE IV	OP	RNBT	FBG	TR	IO	140-170		7	3	1420			2200	2550
18	1	JET-MATE II	OP	RNBT	FBG	DV	JT	324	FORD	6	8	2020			3350	3900
19	9	CONVINSOR	OP	RNBT	FBG	DV	IO	140-228		7	7	1650			2900	3500
19	9	CONVINSOR	OP	RNBT	FBG	DV	IO	260	MRCR	7	7	1650			3150	3650
19	9	CONVINSOR	OP	RNBT	FBG	DV	JT	320	FORD	7	7	1650			3700	4300
20	2	ENCHANTER	OP	RNBT	FBG	DV	OB			7	6	1200			1700	2000
20	2	ENCHANTER	OP	RNBT	FBG	DV	IO	170-260		7	6				3950	4850
20	2	ENCHANTER	OP	RNBT	FBG	DV	JT	460	FORD	7	6				4900	5650
		1976 BOATS														
16	8	TRI-MATE IV	OP	RNBT	FBG	TR	IO	120-140		7	4	1600			2350	2750
17	4	INMATE I	OP	RNBT	FBG	DV	IO	120-140		7	5	1353			2350	2750
17	4	INMATE II	OP	RNBT	FBG	DV	IO	233	MRCR	7	5	1353			2500	2900
18	1	JETMATE	OP	RNBT	FBG	DV	JT		FORD	7	5	1875			**	**
18	1	JETMATE	OP	RNBT	FBG	DV	JT	324-440		7	5	1875			3200	3700
		1975 BOATS														
17		INMATE	OP	RNBT	FBG		IO	140-233		7	3		1		2750	3350
17		JETMATE	OP	RNBT	FBG		IB	325		7	3		1		2700	3100
17		JETMATE	OP	RNBT	FBG		IB	450		7	3		1		3400	3950
		1974 BOATS														
17		CHECKMATE MX-17			FDG		IO	140-200		7	2	1500			2350	2850
18	3	CHECKMATE JETMATE		SKI	FBG		JT	325-450		6	11	1800			2700	3150
		1973 BOATS														
18	3	JETMATE			FBG		JT	390		6	11	1675			2550	2950

CHEOY LEE SHIPYARDS LTD

FT LAUDERDALE FL 33316 COAST GUARD MFG ID- CHL See inside cover to adjust price for area

CHEOY LEE SHIPYARD
LAI CHI KOK KOWLOON HONG KONG

For more recent years, see the BUC Used Boat Price Guide, Volume 1 or Volume 2

LOA FT	LOA IN	NAME AND/ OR MODEL	TOP/ RIG	BOAT TYPE	-HULL- MTL	-HULL- TP	ENGINE TP	ENGINE # HP	ENGINE MFG	BEAM FT	BEAM IN	WGT LBS	DRAFT FT	DRAFT IN	RETAIL LOW	RETAIL HIGH
		1983 BOATS														
27	11	CHEOY-LEE 28	FB	TRWL	FBG	DS	IB	80D	LEHM	10	9	14500	2	10	38000	42200
31	11	CHEOY-LEE 32	SLP	SA/CR	FBG	KL	IB	80D		10	6	11300	4	6	34700	38600
31	11	CHEOY-LEE 32	KTH	SA/CR	FBG	KL	IB	80D		10	6	11300	4	6	34700	38600
31	11	CHEOY-LEE 32	FB	TRWL	FBG	DS	IB	80D	LEHM	12		19000	4	5	51200	56300
31	11	CHEOY-LEE 32 AFT CBN	FB	TRWL	FBG	DS	IB	80D	LEHM	12		19000	4	5	58100	63900
32		CHEOY-LEE 32	FB	TRWL	FBG	DS	IB	120D		12		19000	4	5	55300	60800
32		CHEOY-LEE 32 AFT CBN	FB	TRWL	FBG	DS	IB	120D		12		19000	4	5	62400	68500
32	11	CLIPPER 33	CUT	SA/CR	FBG	KL	IB	25D		10		12000	4		36900	41000
32	11	CLIPPER 33	KTH	SA/CR	FBG	KL	IB	25D		10		12000	4		36900	41000
34	10	CHEOY-LEE 35	SLP	SA/CR	FBG	KL	IB	25D		11	2	14300	5	4	44500	49400
34	10	CHEOY-LEE 35	KTH	SA/CR	FBG	KL	IB	25D		11	2	14300	5	4	44500	49400
34	11	CHEOY-LEE 35	FB	TRWL	FBG	DS	IB	120D	LEHM	12		21000	3	7	68100	74900
35	7	CLIPPER 36	CUT	SA/CR	FBG	KL	IB	25D		10	9	16250	5	3	50800	55900
35	7	CLIPPER 36	KTH	SA/CR	FBG	KL	IB	25D		10	9	16250	5	3	50800	55900
35	9	MIDSHIPMAN 36	SLP	SA/CR	FBG	KL	IB	D		11	6	15000	4		47900	52600
35	9	MIDSHIPMAN 36	KTH	SA/CR	FBG	KL	IB	D		11	6	15000	4		47900	52600
37	11	CHEOY-LEE 38	SLP	SA/CR	FBG	KL	IB	35D		12		17500	5	8	58100	63800
37	11	CHEOY-LEE 38	KTH	SA/CR	FBG	KL	IB	35D		12		17500	5	8	58100	63800
38		CHEOY-LEE	FB	SF	FBG		IB	T210D	J&T			24000			86800	95300
40		CHEOY-LEE 40	FB	TRWL	FBG	DS	IB	T120D	LEHM	14		38000	4	8	130500	143000
40	9	CHEOY-LEE 41	SLP	SA/CR	FBG	KL	IB	35D		12	6	22000	6		77800	85500
40	9	CHEOY-LEE 41	YWL	SA/CR	FBG	KL	IB	35D		12	6	22000	6		77800	85500
40	9	CHEOY-LEE 41	KTH	SA/CR	FBG	KL	IB	35D		12	6	22000	6		77800	85500
40	11	PEDRICK 41	SLP	SA/CR	FBG	KL	IB	37D		12	9	21130			76400	84000
40	11	PEDRICK 41	YWL	SA/CR	FBG	KL	IB	37D		12	9	21130			76400	84000
42		CHEOY-LEE	FB	SF	FBG		IB	T210D	J&T			25374			100500	110500
42	5	CLIPPER 42	SCH	SA/CR	FBG	KL	IB	37D		12	1	23500	5	9	87900	96600
42	5	CLIPPER 42	KTH	SA/CR	FBG	KL	IB	37D		12	1	23500	5	9	87900	96600
42	9	CHEOY-LEE 43	CUT	MS	FBG	KL	IB	120D	LEHM	13	2	34000	5		111500	122500
42	9	CHEOY-LEE 43	KTH	MS	FBG	KL	IB	120D	LEHM	13	2	34000	5		111500	122500
43	10	CHEOY-LEE 44 AFT	CUT	SA/CR	FBG	KL	IB	37D		13	3	27200	6		102500	113000
43	10	CHEOY-LEE 44 AFT	KTH	SA/CR	FBG	KL	IB	37D		13	3	27200	6		102500	113000
43	10	CHEOY-LEE 44 MID	CUT	SA/CR	FBG	KL	IB	37D		13	3	27200	6		102500	113000
43	10	CHEOY-LEE 44 MID	KTH	SA/CR	FBG	KL	IB	37D		13	3	27200	6		102500	113000
45	11	CHEOY-LEE 46	FB	TRWL	FBG	DS	IB	T120D	LEHM	14	8	43200	4	8	142500	156500
47	10	CHEOY-LEE 48 AFT	CUT	SA/CR	FBG	KL	IB	37D		13	9	32300	6	6	137500	151000
47	10	CHEOY-LEE 48 AFT	KTH	SA/CR	FBG	KL	IB	37D		13	9	32300	6	6	138000	151500
47	10	CHEOY-LEE 48 MID	CUT	SA/CR	FBG	KL	IB	37D		13	9	32300	6	6	137500	151000
47	10	CHEOY-LEE 48 MID	KTH	SA/CR	FBG	KL	IB	37D		13	9	32300	6	6	138000	151500
47	11	CLIPPER 48	SCH	SA/CR	FBG	KL	IB	37D		13		31000	6		136000	149000
47	11	CLIPPER 48	KTH	SA/CR	FBG	KL	IB	37D		13		31000	6		136500	150000
48		CHEOY-LEE 48	FB	MY	F/S	SV	IB	T350D	GM	15		37000	4		161500	177500
48		CHEOY-LEE 48	FB	MY	F/S	SV	IB	T550D	GM	15		37000	4		191000	210000
48		CHEOY-LEE 48 SPTYHT	FB	YTFS	F/S	SV	IB	T350D	GM	15		37000	4		147500	162500
48		CHEOY-LEE 48 SPTYHT	FB	YTFS	F/S	SV	IB	T550D	GM	15		37000	4		183000	201000
50		CHEOY-LEE 50	FB	TRWL	FBG	DS	IB	T120D		15	6	36000			139500	153500
51	9	CHEOY-LEE 52	KTH	MS	FBG	KL	IB	T120D	LEHM	16	5	67800	5	7	217000	238000

CONTINUED ON NEXT PAGE

CHEOY LEE SHIPYARDS LTD -CONTINUED See inside cover to adjust price for area

LOA FT	LOA IN	NAME AND/ OR MODEL	TOP/ RIG	BOAT TYPE	-HULL- MTL	-HULL- TP	TP	ENGINE # HP	ENGINE MFG	BEAM FT	BEAM IN	WGT LBS	DRAFT FT	DRAFT IN	RETAIL LOW	RETAIL HIGH
		1983 BOATS														
52		CHEOY-LEE		MY	FBG		IB	T210D	GM			51500			181500	199500
53		CHEOY-LEE/WITTHOLZ	CUT	SA/CR	FBG	KL	IB	D		14	6	45550	7	10	205500	226000
55		CHEOY-LEE 55	FB	MY	FBG	DS	IB	T210D	CAT	16	6	80000	5	4	250500	275000
55		CHEOY-LEE 55	FB	TRWL	FBG	DS	IB	T210D	CAT	16	6	80000	5	4	248000	272500
61		CHEOY-LEE CMY	FB	MY	FBG		IB	T210D	CAT						263000	289000
61	7	CHEOY-LEE 62	FB	TRWL	FBG	DS	IB	T210D	CAT	19		52T	6	7	365000	401000
63	4	CHEOY-LEE 63	KTH	MS	FBG	KC	IB	T260D	CAT	19		98500	6	6	473500	520500
66		CHEOY-LEE		MY	FBG		IB	T675D	GM			70000			347500	382000
66		CHEOY-LEE 66 SPTYHT	FB	YTFS	FBG	DV	IB	T350D	GM	18			5	3	391000	429500
66		LONG RANGE MY 66	FB	MY	FBG	DS	IB	T350D	GM	18		87000	5	3	343000	377000
70		CHEOY-LEE 70	FB	MY	FBG		IB	T650D		17	9	50T			458000	503000
		1982 BOATS														
27	11	CHEOY-LEE 28	FB	TRWL	FBG	DS	IB	80D	LEHM	10	9	14500	2	10	36100	40200
31	11	CHEOY-LEE 32	SLP	SA/CR	FBG	KL	IB	80D		10	6	11300	4	6	32900	36500
31	11	CHEOY-LEE 32	KTH	SA/CR	FBG	KL	IB	80D		10	6	11300	4	6	32900	36500
31	11	CHEOY-LEE 32	FB	TRWL	FBG	DS	IB	80D	LEHM	12		19000	4	5	49400	54200
31	11	CHEOY-LEE 32 AFT CBN	FB	TRWL	FBG	DS	IB	80D	LEHM	12		19000	4	5	55700	61200
32	11	CLIPPER 33	CUT	SA/CR	FBG	KL	IB	25D		10		12000	4		35000	38900
32	11	CLIPPER 33	KTH	SA/CR	FBG	KL	IB	25D		10		12000	4		35000	38900
34	10	CHEOY-LEE 35	SLP	SA/CR	FBG	KL	IB	25D		11	2	14300	5	4	42100	46800
34	10	CHEOY-LEE 35	KTH	SA/CR	FBG	KL	IB	25D		11	2	14300	5	4	42100	46800
34	11	CHEOY-LEE 35	FB	TRWL	FBG	DS	IB	120D	LEHM	12		21000	3	7	65400	71900
35	7	CLIPPER 36	CUT	SA/CR	FBG	KL	IB	25D		10	9	16250	5	3	48200	53000
35	7	CLIPPER 36	KTH	SA/CR	FBG	KL	IB	25D		10	9	16250	5	3	48200	53000
35	9	MIDSHIPMAN 36	SLP	SA/CR	FBG	KL	IB	D		11	6	15000	4		44900	49900
35	9	MIDSHIPMAN 36	KTH	SA/CR	FBG	KL	IB	D		11	6	15000	4		44900	49900
36	6	CHEOY-LEE 36	FB	TRWL	FBG	DS	IB	120D	LEHM	13		29600	3	6	86600	95200
37	11	CHEOY-LEE 38	SLP	SA/CR	FBG	KL	IB	35D		12		17500	5	8	55000	60500
37	11	CHEOY-LEE 38	KTH	SA/CR	FBG	KL	IB	35D		12		17500	5	8	55000	60500
40		CHEOY-LEE 40	FB	TRWL	FBG	DS	IB	T120D	LEHM	14		38000	4	8	124500	136500
40	9	CHEOY-LEE 41	SLP	SA/CR	FBG	KL	IB	35D		12	6	22000	6		73700	81000
40	9	CHEOY-LEE 41	YWL	SA/CR	FBG	KL	IB	35D		12	6	22000	6		73700	81000
40	9	CHEOY-LEE 41	KTH	SA/CR	FBG	KL	IB	35D		12	6	22000	6		73800	81100
40	11	PEDRICK 41	SLP	SA/CR	FBG	KL	IB	37D		12	9	21130	9		72400	79600
40	11	PEDRICK 41	YWL	SA/CR	FBG	KL	IB	37D		12	9	21130	9		72400	79600
42	5	CLIPPER 42	SCH	SA/CR	FBG	KL	IB	37D		12	1	23500	5	9	83300	91500
42	5	CLIPPER 42	KTH	SA/CR	FBG	KL	IB	37D		12	1	23500	5	9	83300	91600
42	9	CHEOY-LEE 43	CUT	MS	FBG	KL	IB	120D	LEHM	13	2	34000	5		105500	116000
42	9	CHEOY-LEE 43	KTH	MS	FBG	KL	IB	120D	LEHM	13	2	34000	5		105500	116000
43	10	CHEOY-LEE 44 AFT	CUT	SA/CR	FBG	KL	IB	37D		13	3	27200	6		97300	107000
43	10	CHEOY-LEE 44 AFT	KTH	SA/CR	FBG	KL	IB	37D		13	3	27200	6		97300	107000
43	10	CHEOY-LEE 44 MID	CUT	SA/CR	FBG	KL	IB	37D		13	3	27200	6		97300	107000
43	10	CHEOY-LEE 44 MID	KTH	SA/CR	FBG	KL	IB	37D		13	3	27200	6		97300	107000
45	11	CHEOY-LEE 46	FB	TRWL	FBG	DS	IB	T120D	LEHM	14	8	43200	4	8	136500	149500
47	10	CHEOY-LEE 48 AFT	CUT	SA/CR	FBG	KL	IB	37D		13	9	32300	6	6	130500	143000
47	10	CHEOY-LEE 48 AFT	KTH	SA/CR	FBG	KL	IB	37D		13	9	32300	6	6	130500	143500
47	10	CHEOY-LEE 48 MID	CUT	SA/CR	FBG	KL	IB	37D		13	9	32300	6	6	130500	143000
47	10	CHEOY-LEE 48 MID	KTH	SA/CR	FBG	KL	IB	37D		13	9	32300	6	6	130500	143500
47	11	CLIPPER 48	SCH	SA/CR	FBG	KL	IB	37D		13		31000	6		129000	141500
47	11	CLIPPER 48	KTH	SA/CR	FBG	KL	IB	37D		13		31000	6		129500	142000
48		CHEOY-LEE 48	FB	MY	F/S	SV	IB	T325D	GM	15		37000	4		151000	166000
48		CHEOY-LEE 48	FB	MY	F/S	SV	IB	T550D	GM	15		37000	4		182500	200500
48		CHEOY-LEE 48 SPTYHT	FB	YTFS	F/S	SV	IB	T325D	GM	15		37000	4		137500	151000
48		CHEOY-LEE 48 SPTYHT	FB	YTFS	F/S	SV	IB	T550D	GM	15		37000	4		175000	192500
51	6	CHEOY-LEE 50 TRI CBN	FB	TRWL	FBG	DS	IB	T120D	LEHM	15	6	62000	5	5	160500	176500
51	9	CHEOY-LEE 52	KTH	MS	FBG	KL	IB	T120D	LEHM	16	5	67800	5	7	205500	226000
53		CHEOY-LEE/WITTHOLZ	CUT	SA/CR	FBG	KL	IB	D		14	6	45550	7	10	195500	214500
55		CHEOY-LEE 55	FB	MY	FBG	DS	IB	T210D	CAT	16	6	80000	5	4	240000	264000
55		CHEOY-LEE 55	FB	TRWL	FBG	DS	IB	T210D	CAT	16	6	80000	5	4	238000	261500
61	7	CHEOY-LEE 62	FB	TRWL	FBG	DS	IB	T210D	CAT	19		52T	6	7	348500	383000
63	4	CHEOY-LEE 63	KTH	MS	FBG	KC	IB	T260D	CAT	19		98500	6	6	449000	493500
66		CHEOY-LEE 66 SPTYHT	FB	YTFS	FBG	DV	IB	T325D	GM	18		65000	5	3	298000	327500
66		LONG RANGE MY 66	FB	MY	FBG	DS	IB	T325D	GM	18		87000	5	3	327000	359500
70		FAST MOTOR YACHT	FB	MY	FBG	DV	IB	T650D	GM	17	9	50T	5		439500	483000
		1981 BOATS														
27	11	TRAWLER 28	FB	TRWL	FBG	DS	IB	80D	LEHM	10	3	14500	3	3	34700	38500
31	9	CORSAIRE 30		SDN	FBG	SV	IB	150		11	6				24200	26900
31	9	CORSAIRE 30		SDN	FBG	SV	IO	T		11	6		3		**	**
31	11	CHEOY-LEE 32	SLP	SA/CR	FBG	KL	IB	D		10	6	11300	4	6	31200	34600
31	11	CHEOY-LEE 32	KTH	SA/CR	FBG	KL	IB	D		10	6	11300	4	6	31200	34600
31	11	TRAWLER 32	FB	TRWL	FBG	DS	IB	80D	LEHM	12		19000	4	5	47800	52500
31	11	TRAWLER 32 AFT CABIN	FB	TRWL	FBG	DS	IB	80D	LEHM	12		19000	4	5	53400	58600
32	11	CLIPPER 33	CUT	SA/CR	FBG	KL	IB	D		10		12000	4		33200	36800
32	11	CLIPPER 33	KTH	SA/CR	FBG	KL	IB	D		10		12000	4		33200	36800
32	11	OFFSHORE 33	SLP	SA/CR	FBG	KL	IB	D		10	2	12480	3	8	34400	38300
32	11	OFFSHORE 33	KTH	SA/CR	FBG	KL	IB	D		10	2	12480	3	8	34400	38300
34	10	CHEOY-LEE 35	SLP	SA/CR	FBG	KL	IB	D		11	2	14300	5	4	40000	44400
34	10	CHEOY-LEE 35	KTH	SA/CR	FBG	KL	IB	D		11	2	14300	5	4	40000	44400
35		TRAWLER 35	FB	TRWL	FBG	DS	IB	120D	LEHM	12		23500	3	7	68600	75300
35	6	LUDERS 36	SLP	SA/RC	FBG	KL	IB	D		10	3	15000	5	3	42300	47000
35	6	LUDERS 36	YWL	SA/RC	FBG	KL	IB	D		10	3	15000	5	3	42300	47000
35	6	LUDERS 36	KTH	SA/RC	FBG	KL	IB	D		10	3	15000	5	3	42300	47000
35	7	CLIPPER 36	CUT	SA/CR	FBG	KL	IB	D		10	9	16250	5	3	46000	50600
35	7	CLIPPER 36	KTH	SA/CR	FBG	KL	IB	D		10	9	16250	5	3	46000	50600
35	9	MIDSHIPMAN 36	SLP	SA/CR	FBG	KL	IB	D		11	6	15000	4		42500	47300
35	9	MIDSHIPMAN 36	KTH	SA/CR	FBG	KL	IB	D		11	6	15000	4		42500	47300
36	6	TRAWLER 36	FB	TRWL	FBG	DS	IB	120D	LEHM	13		29600	3	6	82600	90700
36	6	TRAWLER 36	FB	TRWL	FBG	DS	IB	T 80D	LEHM	13		29600	3	6	80800	88800
36	6	TRAWLER MKII AFT CBN	FB	TRWL	FBG	DS	IB	T 80D	LEHM	13		29600	3	6	87000	95600
37	11	CHEOY-LEE 38	SLP	SA/CR	FBG	KL	IB	D		12		17500	5	8	52200	57400
37	11	CHEOY-LEE 38	KTH	SA/CR	FBG	KL	IB	D		12		17500	5	8	52300	57400
39	3	OFFSHORE 39	SLP	SA/CR	FBG	KL	IB	D		12	9	20300	6		62000	68200
39	10	CHEOY-LEE 40	KTH	SA/CR	FBG	KL	IB	D		13		22200	4	6	68000	74800
39	10	MIDSHIPMAN 40	SLP	SA/CR	FBG	KL	IB	D		13		22000	4	6	67500	74200
39	10	MIDSHIPMAN 40	KTH	SA/CR	FBG	KL	IB	D		13		22000	4	6	67600	74300
40		TRAWLER	FB	TRWL	FBG	DS	IB	T120D	LEHM	14		38000	4	8	118500	130000
40	9	CHEOY-LEE 41	SLP	SA/CR	FBG	KL	IB	D		12	6	22000	6		70200	77100
40	9	CHEOY-LEE 41	YWL	SA/CR	FBG	KL	IB	D		12	6	22000	6		70200	77100
40	9	CHEOY-LEE 41	KTH	SA/CR	FBG	KL	IB	D		12	6	22000	6		70200	77200
40	11	OFFSHORE 41	SLP	SA/CR	FBG	KL	IB	D		12	9	21130	6		68900	75700
40	11	OFFSHORE 41	YWL	SA/CR	FBG	KL	IB	D		12	9	21130	6		68900	75700
40	11	OFFSHORE 41	KTH	SA/CR	FBG	KL	IB	D		12	9	21130	6		69000	75800
41	9	CORSAIRE 42		SDN	FBG	SV	IB	T210		15					87300	95900
41	9	CORSAIRE 42		SDN	FBG	SV	IO	T D		15			4	8	**	**
42	5	CLIPPER 42	SCH	SA/CR	FBG	KL	IB	D		12	1	23500	5	9	79200	87100
42	5	CLIPPER 42	KTH	SA/CR	FBG	KL	IB	D		12	1	23500	5	9	79300	87100
42	9	MOTORSAILER 43	CUT	MS	FBG	KL	IB	120D	LEHM	13	3	36000	5		103000	113500
42	9	MOTORSAILER 43	KTH	MS	FBG	KL	IB	120D	LEHM	13	3	36000	5		103000	113500
43	3	ST-THOMIAN		YTFS	FBG	SV	IB	T185		14					**	**
43	3	ST-THOMIAN		YTFS	FBG	SV	IB	T D		14		29000	3	10	**	**
43	10	CHEOY-LEE 44	CUT	SA/CR	FBG	KL	IB	D		13	3	27200	6		92700	102000
43	10	CHEOY-LEE 44	KTH	SA/CR	FBG	KL	IB	D		13	3	27200	6		92700	102000
44		MIDNIGHT-LACE 44	FB	EXP	FBG	DV	IB	T210D		11		15400			77200	84900
45	11	TRAWLER 46	FB	TRWL	FBG	DS	IB	T120D	LEHM	14	8	49000	4	8	139000	152500
46	9	OFFSHORE 47	SLP	SA/CR	FBG	KL	IB	D		12	2	27000	6	6	109000	120000
46	9	OFFSHORE 47	YWL	SA/CR	FBG	KL	IB	D		12	2	27000	6	6	109000	120000
46	9	OFFSHORE 47	KTH	SA/CR	FBG	KL	IB	D		12	2	27000	6	6	109000	120000
47	10	CHEOY-LEE 48 AFT	CUT	SA/CR	FBG	KL	IB	D		13	9	32300	6	6	124500	136500
47	10	CHEOY-LEE 48 AFT	KTH	SA/CR	FBG	KL	IB	D		13	9	32300	6	6	124500	137000
47	10	CHEOY-LEE 48 MID	CUT	SA/CR	FBG	KL	IB	D		13	9	32300	6	6	124500	136500
47	10	CHEOY-LEE 48 MID	KTH	SA/CR	FBG	KL	IB	D		13	9	32300	6	6	124500	137000
47	11	CLIPPER 48	SCH	SA/CR	FBG	KL	IB	D		13		31000	6		123000	135000
47	11	CLIPPER 48	KTH	SA/CR	FBG	KL	IB	D		13		31000	6		123000	135500
48		MOTOR YACHT 48	FB	MY	F/S	SV	IB	T325D	GM	15		37000	4		162000	178000
48		MOTOR YACHT 48	FB	MY	F/S	SV	IB	T550D	GM	15		37000	4		194500	213500
48		SPORTFISHERMAN 48	FB	SF	F/S	SV	IB	T325D	GM	15		37000	4		147500	162000
48		SPORTFISHERMAN 48	FB	SF	F/S	SV	IB	T550D	GM	15		37000	4		188500	207000
50	4	TRAWLER 50 TRI CABIN	FB	TRWL	FBG	DS	IB	T120D	LEHM	15	7	67000	5	5	159500	175500
51	6	MIDSHIPMAN 52	KTH	MS	FBG	KC	IB	D		14	6	44500	5	6	168500	185500
51	9	MOTORSAILER 52	KTH	MS	FBG	KL	IB	T120D	LEHM	16	5	67800	5	7	195000	214000
52	6	MIDNIGHT-LACE 52	FB	EXP	FBG	DV	IB	T240D		13		19850			121000	133000
52	9	OFFSHORE 53	KTH	MS	FBG	KL	IB	D		15		60400	6		195000	214500
55		LONG RANGE MY	FB	MY	FBG	DS	IB	T225D	CAT	16	6	80000	5	4	232500	255000
55		TRAWLER 55	FB	TRWL	FBG	DS	IB	T225D	CAT	16	6	80000	5	4	229500	252500
61	7	TRAWLER 62	FB	TRWL	FBG	DS	IB	T225D	CAT	19		52T	6	7	335000	368500
65	8	YACHT FISHERMAN	FB	YTFS	FBG	DV	IB	T675D		18	6	65000			307500	337500
66		LONG RANGE MY	FB	MY	FBG	DS	IB	T325D	GM	18		87000	5	3	320000	351500
70		LONG RANGE MY	FB	MY	FBG	DV	IB	T650D	GM	17	9	50T	5		419000	460000
		1980 BOATS														
27	11	TRAWLER	FB	TRWL	FBG	DS	IB	80D	LEHM	10	9	14500	2	10	33300	37000
27	11	TRAWLER 28	FB	TRWL	FBG	DS	IB	80D	LEHM	10	9	14500	2	10	33300	37000
31	9	CORSAIRE		CR	FBG	DS	IB	150D		11	6				29800	33100
31	11	CHEOY-LEE 32	SLP	SA/CR	FBG	KL	IB	25D		10	6	11300	4	6	30000	33300
31	11	CHEOY-LEE 32	KTH	SA/CR	FBG	KL	IB	25D		10	6	11300	4	6	30000	33300
31	11	TRAWLER	FB	TRWL	FBG	DS	IB	80D-120D		12		19000	4	5	48500	53300
31	11	TRAWLER 32	FB	TRWL	FBG	DS	IB	80D	LEHM	12		19000	4	5	45900	50400

CONTINUED ON NEXT PAGE

LOA FT	IN	NAME AND/ OR MODEL	TOP/ RIG	BOAT TYPE	-HULL- MTL	TP	----ENGINE--- TP	# HP	MFG	BEAM FT	IN	WGT LBS	DRAFT FT	IN	RETAIL LOW	RETAIL HIGH
		1980 BOATS														
31	11	TRAWLER 32 AFT CABIN	FB	TRWL	FBG	DS	IB	80D	LEHM	12		19000	4	5	51400	56400
31	11	TRAWLER AFT CABIN	FB	TRWL	FBG	DS	IB	80D	LEHM	12		19000	4	5	48500	53300
32	11	CLIPPER 33	CUT	SA/CR	FBG	KL	IB	25D		10		12000	4		31900	35400
32	11	CLIPPER 33	KTH	SA/CR	FBG	KL	IB	25D		10		12000	4		31900	35400
32	11	OFFSHORE 33	SLP	SA/CR	FBG	KL	IB	25D		10	2	12480	3	8	33100	36800
32	11	OFFSHORE 33	KTH	SA/CR	FBG	KL	IB	25D		10	2	12480	3	8	33100	36800
34	10	CHEOY-LEE 35	SLP	SA/CR	FBG	KL	IB	25D		11	2	14300	5	4	38400	42700
34	10	CHEOY-LEE 35	KTH	SA/CR	FBG	KL	IB	25D		11	2	14300	5	4	38400	42700
35		TRAWLER	FB	TRWL	FBG	DS	IB	120D	LEHM	12		21000	3	7	60700	66700
35		TRAWLER 35	FB	TRWL	FBG	DS	IB	120D	LEHM	12		21000	3	7	60700	66700
35	6	LUDERS 36	SLP	SA/CR	FBG	KL	IB	25D		10	3	15000	5	3	40600	45100
35	6	LUDERS 36	YWL	SA/CR	FBG	KL	IB	25D		10	3	15000	5	3	40600	45100
35	6	LUDERS 36	KTH	SA/CR	FBG	KL	IB	25D		10	3	15000	5	3	40600	45100
35	6	LUDERS 36	SLP	SA/RC	FBG	KL	IB	25D		10	3	15000	5	3	40600	45100
35	6	LUDERS 36	YWL	SA/RC	FBG	KL	IB	25D		10	3	15000	5	3	40600	45100
35	6	LUDERS 36	KTH	SA/RC	FBG	KL	IB	25D		10	3	15000	5	3	40600	45100
35	7	CLIPPER 36	KTH	SA/CR	FBG	KL	IB	25D		10	9	16250	5	3	43700	48600
35	9	MIDSHIPMAN 36	SLP	SA/CR	FBG	KL	IB	D		11	6	15000	4		40900	45500
35	9	MIDSHIPMAN 36	KTH	SA/CR	FBG	KL	IB	D		11	6	15000	4		40900	45500
36	6	TRAWLER	FB	TRWL	FBG	DS	IB	120D	LEHM	13		29600	3	6	78800	86600
36	6	TRAWLER	FB	TRWL	FBG	DS	IB	T 80D	LEHM	13		29600	3	6	80100	88000
36	6	TRAWLER	FB	TRWL	FBG	DS	IB	T120D		13					60000	65900
36	6	TRAWLER 36	FB	TRWL	FBG	DS	IB	120D	LEHM	13		29600	3	6	78800	86600
36	6	TRAWLER 36	FB	TRWL	FBG	DS	IB	T 80D	LEHM	13		29600	3	6	77100	84700
36	6	TRAWLER MKII AFT CBN	FB	TRWL	FBG	DS	IB	T 80D	LEHM	13		29600	3	6	83000	91200
37	11	CHEOY-LEE 38	SLP	SA/CR	FBG	KL	IB	25D		12		17500	5	8	50000	55000
37	11	CHEOY-LEE 38	KTH	SA/CR	FBG	KL	IB	25D		12		17500	5	8	50000	55000
39	3	OFFSHORE 39	SLP	SA/CR	FBG	KL	IB	D		12	9	20300	6		59700	65600
39	9	MIDSHIPMAN 40	SLP	SA/CR	FBG	KL	IB	D		10	9	20000	6		60500	66500
39	10	CHEOY LEE 40	KTH	SA/CR	FBG	KL	IB	D		13		22200	4	6	65400	71900
39	10	MIDSHIPMAN 40	KTH	SA/CR	FBG	KL	IB	37D		13		27000	4	6	74300	81600
40		TRAWLER	FB	TRWL	FBG	DS	IB	T120D	LEHM	14	6	38000	4	8	111500	122500
40		TRAWLER 40	FB	TRWL	FBG	DS	IB	T120D	LEHM	14	6	38000	4	8	111500	122500
40	9	CHEOY-LEE 41	SLP	SA/CR	FBG	KL	IB	37D		12	6	22000	6		67300	73900
40	9	CHEOY-LEE 41	YWL	SA/CR	FBG	KL	IB	37D		12	6	22000	6		67300	73900
40	9	CHEOY-LEE 41	KTH	SA/CR	FBG	KL	IB	37D		12	6	22000	6		67300	73900
40	11	OFFSHORE 41	SLP	SA/CR	FBG	KL	IB	37D		12	9	21130	6		66100	72600
40	11	OFFSHORE 41	YWL	SA/CR	FBG	KL	IB	37D		12	9	21130	6		66100	72600
40	11	OFFSHORE 41	KTH	SA/CR	FBG	KL	IB	37D		12	9	21130	6		66100	72600
41	9	CORSAIRE		CR	FBG	DS	IB	T210D		15					87600	96300
42	5	CLIPPER 42	SLP	SA/CR	FBG	KL	IB	D		12	1	23500	5	9	76300	83800
42	5	CLIPPER 42	KTH	SA/CR	FBG	KL	IB	37D		12	1	23500	5	9	76000	83500
43	3	ST-THOMIAN		SF	FBG		IB	T185D		14					93300	102500
43	9	CHEOY-LEE 44	CUT	SA/CR	FBG	KL	IB	37D		13	3	27200	6		88300	97100
43	9	CHEOY-LEE 44	KTH	SA/CR	FBG	KL	IB	37D		13	3	27200	6		88300	97100
43	10	CHEOY LEE 44	SLP	SA/CR	FBG	KL	IB	D		13	2	27500	6		89700	98600
44	6	MIDNIGHT LACE 44		EXP	F/S	RB	IB	T240D	REN	11		15300	2	10	75500	83000
45	11	TRAWLER	FB	TRWL	FBG	DS	IB	T120D	LEHM	14	8	49200	4	8	130500	143500
45	11	TRAWLER 46	FB	TRWL	FBG	DS	IB	T120D	LEHM	14	8	49200	4	8	135000	148000
46	9	OFFSHORE 42	SLP	SA/CR	FBG	KL	IB	37D		12	2	28500	6	6	107000	117500
46	9	OFFSHORE 42	YWL	SA/CR	FBG	KL	IB	37D		12	2	28500	6	6	107000	117500
46	9	OFFSHORE 42	KTH	SA/CR	FBG	KL	IB	37D		12	2	28500	6	6	107000	117500
46	9	OFFSHORE 47	SLP	SA/CR	FBG	KL	IB	D		12	2	27000	6	6	105000	115500
46	9	OFFSHORE 47	SLP	SA/CR	FBG	KL	IB	37D		12	2	28500	6	6	107000	117500
46	9	OFFSHORE 47	YWL	SA/CR	FBG	KL	IB	D		12	2	27000	6	6	105000	115500
46	9	OFFSHORE 47	YWL	SA/CR	FBG	KL	IB	37D		12	2	28500	6	6	107000	117500
46	9	OFFSHORE 47	KTH	SA/CR	FBG	KL	IB	D		12	2	27000	6	6	105000	115500
46	9	OFFSHORE 47	KTH	SA/CR	FBG	KL	IB	37D		12	2	28500	6	6	107000	117500
47		CLIPPER 48		SA/CR	FBG	KL	IB	37D		13		32000	6		113500	125000
47	10	CHEOY-LEE 48	CUT	SA/CR	FBG	KL	IB	37D		13	5	32300	6	6	119000	130500
47	10	CHEOY-LEE 48	KTH	SA/CR	FBG	KL	IB	37D		13	5	32300	6	6	119000	131000
47	11	CLIPPER 48	SLP	SA/CR	FBG	KL	IB	D		13		31000	6		118500	130000
47	11	CLIPPER 48	KTH	SA/CR	FBG	KL	IB	37D		13		32000	6		119500	131000
48		MOTOR YACHT	FB	MY	FBG	SV	IB	T425D		15					144000	158000
48		MOTOR YACHT	FB	MY	FBG	SV	IB	T550D	GM	15		37000	4		155000	170500
48		MOTOR YACHT 48	FB	MY	FBG	SV	IB	T325D	GM	15		37000	4		154500	169500
48		SPORTFISHERMAN	FB	SF	FBG	SV	IB	T425D		15					163000	179500
48		SPORTFISHERMAN	FB	SF	FBG	SV	IB	T550D	GM	15		37000	4		183000	201000
48		SPORTFISHERMAN 48	FB	SF	FBG	SV	IB	T325D	GM	15		37000	4		140500	154500
49	2	TRAWLER/MOTORSAILER	KTH	MS	FBG	KL	IB	T120D	FORD	15	9	57500	5	7	160500	176500
51	6	MIDSHIPMAN 52	KTH	MS	FBG	CB	IB	120D		14	6	45000	5	6	163000	179500
51	6	MIDSHIPMAN 52	KTH	SA/CR	FBG	CB	IB	120D		14	6	45000	5	6	163000	179500
51	6	TRAWLER TRI CABIN	FB	TRWL	FBG	DS	IB	T120D	LEHM	15	7	67000	5	7	152000	167000
51	9	MOTOR SAILER 52	KTH	MS	FBG	KL	IB	T120D		16	5	68000	5	7	187500	206000
51	9	MOTORSAILER 52	KTH	MS	FBG	KL	IB	T120D		16	5	68000	5	7	187500	206000
52	6	MIDNIGHT LACE 52		EXP	F/S	RB	IB	T240D	REN	13		20000	3	2	113000	124500
52	9	OFFSHORE 53	KTH	MS	FBG	KL	IB	120D		15		60000	6		187500	206000
55		TRAWLER	FB	TRWL	FBG	DS	IB	T225D	CAT	16	6	80000	5	4	219500	241000
55		TRAWLER 55	FB	TRWL	FBG	DS	IB	T210D	CAT	16	6	80000	4	8	217500	239000
61	7	TRAWLER	FB	TRWL	FBG	DS	IB	T225D	CAT	19		52T	6	7	320000	351500
61	7	TRAWLER 62	FB	TRWL	FBG	DS	IB	T210D	CAT	19		52T	6	7	317000	348000
62		MIDNIGHT LACE 62		EXP	F/S	RB	IB	T320D	GM	14		31000	3	6	137000	150500
66		MOTOR YACHT	FB	MY	FBG	DS	IB	T280D	GM	18		80000	5	3	290000	318500
66		MOTOR YACHT	FB	MY	FBG	DS	IB	T325D	GM	18		80000	5	3	292500	321500
66		TRAWLER	FB	TRWL	FBG	DS	IB	T210D		18					312000	343000
70		MOTOR YACHT	FB	MY	FBG	DV	IB	T550D	GM	17	9	50T	5		392000	430500
70		MOTOR YACHT	FB	MY	FBG	DV	IB	T650D	GM	17	9	50T	5		399500	439000
		1979 BOATS														
27	11	TRAWLER	FB	TRWL	FBG	DS	IB	80D	LEHM	10	3	14500	3	3	31800	35300
31	11	TRAWLER	FB	TRWL	FBG	DS	IB	80D	LEHM	12		19000	3	3	43700	48600
31	11	TRAWLER AFT CABIN	FB	TRWL	FBG	DS	IB	80D	LEHM	12		19000	3	3	49400	54300
35		TRAWLER	FB	TRWL	FBG	DS	IB	120D	LEHM	12		23500	3	7	63400	69700
36	6	TRAWLER	FB	TRWL	FBG	DS	IB	120D	LEHM	13		29600	3	6	75300	82700
36	6	TRAWLER	FB	TRWL	FBG	DS	IB	T 80D	LEHM	13		29600	3	6	73400	80700
36	6	TRAWLER MKII AFT CBN	FB	TRWL	FBG	DS	IB	T 80D	LEHM	13		29600	3	6	79600	87400
40		TRAWLER	FB	TRWL	FBG	DS	IB	T120D	LEHM	14	6	38000	4	8	106500	117000
45	11	TRAWLER	FB	TRWL	FBG	DS	IB	T120D	LEHM	14	8	49000	4	8	126500	139000
48		SPORTFISHERMAN	FB	SF	FBG	DS	IB	T265D	GM	15		37000	4		130000	143000
51	6	TRAWLER TRI CABIN	FB	TRWL	FBG	DS	IB	T120D	LEHM	15	7	62000	5	5	140000	154000
51	9	TRAWLER/MOTORSAILER	KTH	MS	FBG	KL	IB	T120D	LEHM	16	5	67000	5	7	181000	199000
55		TRAWLER	FB	TRWL	FBG	DS	IB	T210D	CAT	17	2	80000	5	4	208000	228500
61	7	TRAWLER	FB	TRWL	FBG	DS	IB	T210D	CAT	19	3	52T	6	7	303000	333000
66		MOTOR YACHT	FB	MY	FBG	DS	IB	T210D	CAT	18		87000	5	3	284000	312500
70		MOTOR YACHT	FB	MY	FBG	DS	IB	T675D	GM	17	9	50T	5		383500	421500
		1978 BOATS														
27	11	TRAWLER		TRWL	FBG	DS	IB	80D		10	3				19600	21800
28		OFFSHORE 28	SLP	SA/CR	FBG	KC	IB	30	UNIV	9	2	7900	3	6	19300	21400
28		OFFSHORE 28 SHOAL	SLP	SA/CR	FBG	KL	IB	30	UNIV	9	2	7900	3	6	19300	21400
29	10	LUDERS 30	SLP	SA/RC	FBG	KL	IB	30	UNIV	9	1	10000	4	9	25100	27900
30		CRUISAIRE 30	SLP	MS	FBG	CB	IB	D		10	8	12000	6	9	30500	33900
30	10	OFFSHORE 31	SLP	SA/RC	FBG	KL	IB	30D		8	10	10750	3	9	27100	30100
30	10	OFFSHORE 31	KTH	SA/RC	FBG	KL	IB	30D		8	10	10750	3	9	27100	30100
31	11	CHEOY-LEE 32	SLP	SA/CR	FBG	KL	IB	25D		10	6	11300	4	6	28200	31300
31	11	CHEOY-LEE 32	KTH	SA/CR	FBG	KL	IB	25D		10	6	11300	4	6	28200	31300
31	11	TRAWLER		TRWL	FBG	DS	IB	120D		12		19000			48200	53000
32	11	CLIPPER 33	CUT	SA/CR	FBG	KL	IB	30	UNIV	10		12000	4		29900	33300
32	11	CLIPPER 33	KTH	SA/CR	FBG	KL	IB	30	UNIV	10		12000	4		29900	33300
32	11	OFFSHORE 33	SLP	SA/CR	FBG	KL	IB	30	UNIV	10	2	12480	3	8	31100	34500
32	11	OFFSHORE 33	KTH	SA/CR	FBG	KL	IB	30	UNIV	10	2	12480	3	8	31100	34500
34	6	TRAWLER		TRWL	FBG	DS	IB	T120D		13					48200	53000
34	10	CHEOY-LEE 35	SLP	SA/CR	FBG	KL	IB	25D-	35D	11	2	13000	5	4	33100	36900
34	10	CHEOY-LEE 35	KTH	SA/CR	FBG	KL	IB	25D-	35D	11	2	13000	5	4	33100	36900
35	6	LUDERS 36	SLP	SA/RC	FBG	KL	IB	25D		10	3	15000	5	3	38200	42500
35	6	LUDERS 36	YWL	SA/RC	FBG	KL	IB	25D		10	3	15000	5	3	38200	42500
35	6	LUDERS 36	KTH	SA/RC	FBG	KL	IB	25D		10	3	15000	5	3	38200	42500
35	8	CLIPPER 36	SCH	SA/CR	FBG	KL	IB	25D		10	9	16250	5	3	41200	45800
35	8	CLIPPER 36	SCH	SA/CR	FBG	KL	IB	35D		10	9	16250	5	3	41300	45900
35	8	CLIPPER 36	CUT	SA/CR	FBG	KL	IB	25D		10	9	16250	5	3	41200	45800
35	8	CLIPPER 36	CUT	SA/CR	FBG	KL	IB	35D		10	9	16250	5	3	41300	45900
35	8	CLIPPER 36	KTH	SA/CR	FBG	KL	IB	25D		10	9	16250	5	3	41200	45800
35	8	CLIPPER 36	KTH	SA/CR	FBG	KL	IB	35D		10	9	16250	5	3	41300	45900
35	9	MIDSHIPMAN 36	SLP	SA/CR	FBG	KL	IB	37D		11	6	15000	4		38500	42800
35	9	MIDSHIPMAN 36	KTH	SA/CR	FBG	KL	IB	37D		11	6	15000	4		38500	42800
36	6	TRAWLER		TRWL	FBG	DS	IB	T120D		13		30440			74900	82300
37	11	CHEOY-LEE 38	SLP	SA/CR	FBG	KL	IB	37D		12		17500	5	8	47500	52200
37	11	CHEOY-LEE 38	KTH	SA/CR	FBG	KL	IB	37D		12		17500	5	8	47500	52200
39	3	OFFSHORE 39	SLP	SA/RC	FBG	KL	IB	37D		12	8	20300	6		56000	61500
39	9	OFFSHORE 40	SLP	SA/CR	FBG	KL	IB	37D		10	9	20000	6		56800	62400
39	9	OFFSHORE 40	YWL	SA/CR	FBG	KL	IB	37D		10	9	20000	6		56800	62400
39	10	MIDSHIPMAN 40	KTH	SA/CR	FBG	KL	IB	37D		13		22000	4	6	60900	66900
40		TRAWLER		TRWL	FBG	DS	IB	T120D		14	6				77700	85300
40	11	OFFSHORE 41	SLP	SA/CR	FBG	KL	IB	37D		12	9	21130	6		62100	68300
40	11	OFFSHORE 41	YWL	SA/CR	FBG	KL	IB	37D		12	9	21130	6		62100	68300
40	11	OFFSHORE 41	KTH	SA/CR	FBG	KL	IB	37D		12	9	21130	6		62100	68300
41	9	CORSAIRE 42		CR	FBG	DS	IO	T210		15					45900	50400

CONTINUED ON NEXT PAGE

LOA FT	LOA IN	NAME AND/ OR MODEL	TOP/ RIG	BOAT TYPE	-HULL- MTL	-HULL- TP	ENGINE TP	ENGINE # HP	ENGINE MFG	BEAM FT	BEAM IN	WGT LBS	DRAFT FT	DRAFT IN	RETAIL LOW	RETAIL HIGH
		1978 BOATS														
41	9	CORSAIRE 42		CR	FBG	DS	IB	T210		15					65500	71900
42	5	CLIPPER 42	SCH	SA/CR	FBG	KL	IB	37D		12	1	23500	5	9	71500	78500
42	5	CLIPPER 42	KTH	SA/CR	FBG	KL	IB	37D		12	1	23500	5	9	71500	78500
43	3	ST-THOMIAN		SF	FBG	DS	IB	T185		14					75400	82800
43	8	OFFSHORE 44	KTH	SA/CR	FBG	KL	IB	105D		13		30000	5	6	88100	96800
43	10	CHEOY-LEE 44	SLP	SA/CR	FBG	KL	IB	37D		13	3	27500	6		83900	92200
43	10	CHEOY-LEE 44	KTH	SA/CR	FBG	KL	IB	37D		13	3	27500	6		83900	92200
45	11	TRAWLER		TRWL	FBG	DS	IB	T120D		14	8	49133			121000	133000
46	9	OFFSHORE 47	SLP	SA/CR	FBG	KL	IB	35D		12	2	27000	6	6	98300	108000
46	9	OFFSHORE 47	YWL	SA/CR	FBG	KL	IB	35D		12	2	27000	6	6	98300	108000
46	9	OFFSHORE 47	KTH	SA/CR	FBG	KL	IB	35D		12	2	27000	6	6	98300	108000
47	11	CLIPPER 48	SCH	SA/CR	FBG	KL	IB	35D		13		31000	6		110500	121500
47	11	CLIPPER 48	KTH	SA/CR	FBG	KL	IB	35D		13		31000	6		111000	122000
50	4	OFFSHORE 50	KTH	SA/CR	FBG	KL	IB	75D		13	2	34000	6	6	132500	145500
51	6	MIDSHIPMAN 52	KTH	MS	FBG	KC	IB	120D		14	6	44500	5	6	153000	168000
51	6	TRAWLER		TRWL	FBG	DS	IB	T120D		15	7				132000	145000
52	9	OFFSHORE 53	KTH	MS	FBG	KL	IB	120D		15		60000	6		176500	194000
55		TRAWLER		TRWL	FBG	DS	IB	T210D		16	6				172500	189500
61	11	TRAWLER		TRWL	FBG	DS	IB	T210D		18	6	78500			213000	234500
66		TRAWLER		TRWL	FBG	DS	IB	T210D		18					285500	313500
		1977 BOATS														
28		OFFSHORE 28	SLP	SA/CR	FBG	KC	IB	30	UNIV	9	2	7935	3	6	19100	21200
28		OFFSHORE 28	SLP	SA/CR	FBG	KC	IB	20D	WEST	9	2	7935	3	6	19200	21300
29	10	LUDERS 30	SLP	SA/RC	FBG	KL	IB	30	UNIV	9	1	9900	4	9	24200	26900
29	10	LUDERS 30	SLP	SA/RC	FBG	KL	IB	20D	WEST	9	1	9900	4	9	24400	27100
30	10	OFFSHORE 31	SLP	SA/RC	FBG	KL	IB	30	UNIV	8	10	10750	3	9	26300	29200
30	10	OFFSHORE 31	SLP	SA/RC	FBG	KL	IB	20D	WEST	8	10	10750	3	9	26400	29300
30	10	OFFSHORE 31	KTH	SA/RC	FBG	KL	IB	30	UNIV	8	10	10750	3	9	26300	29200
30	10	OFFSHORE 31	KTH	SA/RC	FBG	KL	IB	20D	WEST	8	10	10750	3	9	26400	29300
31	11	TRAWLER		TRWL	FBG	DS	IB			12		19000	3	6	**	**
32	11	CLIPPER 33	KTH	SA/CR	FBG	KL	IB	30	UNIV	10		12000	4		29100	32400
32	11	CLIPPER 33	KTH	SA/CR	FBG	KL	IB	25D	WEST	10		12000	4		29200	32500
32	11	OFFSHORE 33	SLP	SA/CR	FBG	KL	IB	30	UNIV	10	2	10500	3	8	25600	28400
32	11	OFFSHORE 33	SLP	SA/CR	FBG	KL	IB	25D	WEST	10	2	10500	3	8	25700	28500
32	11	OFFSHORE 33	KTH	SA/CR	FBG	KL	IB	30	UNIV	10	2	10500	3	8	25600	28400
32	11	OFFSHORE 33	KTH	SA/CR	FBG	KL	IB	25D	WEST	10	2	10500	3	8	25700	28500
34		TRAWLER	FB	TRWL	FBG	DS	IB	T120D	FORD	13		29000	3	6	65900	72400
35	6	LUDERS 36	SLP	SA/RC	FBG	KL	IB	25D	VLVO	10	3	15000	5	3	37200	41300
35	6	LUDERS 36	SLP	SA/RC	FBG	KL	IB	37D	WEST	10	3	15000	5	3	37400	41500
35	6	LUDERS 36	YWL	SA/RC	FBG	KL	IB	25D	VLVO	10	3	15000	5	3	37200	41300
35	6	LUDERS 36	YWL	SA/RC	FBG	KL	IB	37D	WEST	10	3	15000	5	3	37400	41500
35	6	LUDERS 36	KTH	SA/RC	FBG	KL	IB	25D	VLVO	10	3	15000	5	3	37200	41300
35	6	LUDERS 36	KTH	SA/RC	FBG	KL	IB	37D	WEST	10	3	15000	5	3	37400	41500
35	8	CLIPPER 36	SCH	SA/CR	FBG	KL	IB	25D	VLVO	10	3	16250	5	3	40100	44600
35	8	CLIPPER 36	SCH	SA/CR	FBG	KL	IB	37D	WEST	10	3	16250	5	3	40300	44700
35	8	CLIPPER 36	KTH	SA/CR	FBG	KL	IB	25D	VLVO	10	9	16250	5	3	40100	44600
35	8	CLIPPER 36	KTH	SA/CR	FBG	KL	IB	37D	WEST	10	3	16250	5	3	40300	44700
35	9	MIDSHIPMAN 36	SLP	SA/CR	FBG	KL	IB	37D	PERK	11	6	15000	4		37400	41500
35	9	MIDSHIPMAN 36	KTH	SA/CR	FBG	KL	IB	37D	PERK	11	6	15000	4		37400	41500
36		TRAWLER AFT CABIN	FB	TRWL	FBG	DS	IB	T120D	FORD	13		29600	3	6	70900	77900
36		TRAWLER AFT SALOON	FB	TRWL	FBG	DS	IB	T120D	FORD	13		29600	3	6	65000	71400
39	3	OFFSHORE 39	SLP	SA/RC	FBG	KL	IB	37D	PERK	12	9	20300	6		54200	59600
39	9	OFFSHORE 40	SLP	SA/CR	FBG	KL	IB	37D	PERK	10	9	20000	6		55000	60500
39	9	OFFSHORE 40	YWL	SA/CR	FBG	KL	IB	37D	PERK	10	9	20000	6		55000	60500
39	10	MIDSHIPMAN 40	SLP	SA/CR	FBG	KL	IB	37D	PERK	13	10	20000	4	6	55300	60800
39	10	MIDSHIPMAN 40	SLP	SA/CR	FBG	KL	IB	85D	PERK	13	10	20000	4	6	55900	61400
39	10	MIDSHIPMAN 40	KTH	SA/CR	FBG	KL	IB	37D	PERK	13	10	20000	4	6	55300	60800
39	10	MIDSHIPMAN 40	KTH	SA/CR	FBG	KL	IB	85D	PERK	13	10	20000	4	6	55900	61400
40		TRAWLER	FB	TRWL	FBG	DS	IB	T120D	FORD	14	6	38000	4	8	97700	107500
40		TRAWLER AFT CABIN	FB	TRWL	FBG	DS	IB	T160D	PERK	14	6	38000	4	8	99700	109500
40	11	OFFSHORE 41	SLP	SA/CR	FBG	KL	IB	37D	PERK	12	9	21100	6		60200	66100
40	11	OFFSHORE 41	SLP	SA/CR	FBG	KL	IB	37D	VLVO	12	9	21100	6		60500	66400
40	11	OFFSHORE 41	YWL	SA/CR	FBG	KL	IB	37D	PERK	12	9	21100	6		60200	66100
40	11	OFFSHORE 41	YWL	SA/CR	FBG	KL	IB	37D	VLVO	12	9	21100	6		60500	66400
40	11	OFFSHORE 41	KTH	SA/CR	FBG	KL	IB	37D	PERK	12	9	21100	6		60200	66100
40	11	OFFSHORE 41	KTH	SA/CR	FBG	KL	IB	37D	VLVO	12	9	21100	6		60500	66400
42		CORSAIRE 42		SPTCR	FBG	DS	IB	T120D		15					59700	65600
42	5	CLIPPER 42	SCH	SA/CR	FBG	KL	IB	37D	PERK	12	1	23500	5	9	69300	76100
42	5	CLIPPER 42	KTH	SA/CR	FBG	KL	IB	37D	PERK	12	1	23500	5	9	69300	76100
43	8	OFFSHORE 44	KTH	MS	FBG	KL	IB	106D	VLVO	13		32000	5	6	88700	97400
46	9	OFFSHORE 47	SLP	SA/CR	FBG	KL	IB	37D	PERK	12	2	27000	6	6	95500	105000
46	9	OFFSHORE 47	SLP	SA/CR	FBG	KL	IB	37D	WEST	12	2	27000	6	6	95900	105500
46	9	OFFSHORE 47	YWL	SA/CR	FBG	KL	IB	37D	PERK	12	2	27000	6	6	95500	105000
46	9	OFFSHORE 47	YWL	SA/CR	FBG	KL	IB	37D	WEST	12	2	27000	6	6	95900	105500
46	9	OFFSHORE 47	KTH	SA/CR	FBG	KL	IB	37D	PERK	12	2	27000	6	6	95500	105000
46	9	OFFSHORE 47	KTH	SA/CR	FBG	KL	IB	37D	WEST	12	2	27000	6	6	95900	105500
47		TRAWLER	FB	TRWL	FBG	DS	IB	T120D	LEHM	14		44000	4	8	112000	123000
47	11	CLIPPER 48	SCH	SA/CR	FBG	KL	IB	37D	PERK	13	6	31000	6		107000	117500
47	11	CLIPPER 48	KTH	SA/CR	FBG	KL	IB	37D	PERK	13	6	31000	6		107500	118500
47	11	CLIPPER 48	KTH	SA/CR	FBG	KL	IB	50D	PERK	13	6	31000	6		108000	118500
50		TRAWLER DC	FB	TRWL	FBG	DS	IB	T120D	FORD	15	7	55000	5	5	116500	128000
50		TRAWLER TRI CABIN	FB	TRWL	FBG	DS	IB	T120D	FORD	15	7	55000	5	5	130500	143500
50	4	OFFSHORE 50	KTH	SA/CR	FBG	KC	IB	75D	VLVO	13	2	34000	5	6	129000	141500
50	4	OFFSHORE 50	KTH	SA/CR	FBG	KL	IB	75D	VLVO	13	2	34000	6	6	129000	141500
51	6	MIDSHIPMAN 52	KTH	MS	FBG	KC	IB	120D	FORD	14	6	38000	5	6	143500	157500
51	6	TRAWLER		TRWL	FBG	DS	IB			15	7	55000	5	5	**	**
52	9	OFFSHORE 53	KTH	MS	FBG	KL	IB	120D	FORD	15		60400	6		172000	189000
55		TRAWLER	FB	TRWL	FBG	DS	IB	T210D	CAT	17	2	60000	5	4	143500	157500
62		TRAWLER	FB	TRWL	FBG	DS	IB	T210D	CAT	18	6	78500	6	6	204500	225000
65		TRAWLER	FB	TRWL	FBG	DS	IB	T210D	CAT	18		87000	6	6	245000	269500
		1976 BOATS														
28		OFFSHORE 28	SLP	SA/CR	FBG	KC	IB	30	UNIV	9	2	7935	3	6	18600	20700
29	10	LUDERS 30	SLP	SA/RC	FBG	KL	IB	30	UNIV	9	1	9900	4	9	23600	26200
30		CORSAIRE 30		CR	FBG	DS	IO	200		11	6	7811			15700	17800
30		CORSAIRE 30		CR	FBG	DS	IB	270		11	6	7811			15100	17100
30		CORSAIRE 30		SF	FBG	DS	IO	200		11	6	8393			17300	19600
30		CORSAIRE 30		SF	FBG	DS	IB	270		11	6	8393			14500	16500
32	11	CLIPPER 33	CUT	SA/CR	FBG	KL	IB	30	UNIV	10		12000	4		28400	31600
32	11	CLIPPER 33	KTH	SA/CR	FBG	KL	IB	30	UNIV	10		12000	4		28400	31600
32	11	OFFSHORE 33	SLP	SA/CR	FBG	KL	IB	30	UNIV	10	2	10500	3	8	25000	27700
32	11	OFFSHORE 33	KTH	SA/CR	FBG	KL	IB	30	UNIV	10	2	10500	3	8	25000	27700
34	6	TRAWLER	FB	TRWL	FBG	DS	IB	T120D	LEHM	13		27500	3	6	61800	67900
35	6	LUDERS 36	SLP	SA/RC	FBG	KL	IB	25D	VLVO	10	3	15000	5	3	36300	40300
35	6	LUDERS 36	YWL	SA/RC	FBG	KL	IB	25D	VLVO	10	3	15000	5	3	36300	40300
35	8	CLIPPER 36	SCH	SA/CR	FBG	KL	IB	25D	VLVO	10	9	16250	5	3	39100	43500
35	8	CLIPPER 36	CUT	SA/CR	FBG	KL	IB	25D	VLVO	10	9	16250	5	3	39100	43500
35	8	CLIPPER 36	KTH	SA/CR	FBG	KL	IB	25D	VLVO	10	9	16250	5	3	39100	43500
35	9	MIDSHIPMAN 36	KTH	SA/CR	FBG	KL	IB	37D	PERK	11	6	15000	4		36500	40500
36	6	TRAWLER	FB	TRWL	FBG	DS	IB	T120D	LEHM	13		30440	3	6	68900	75700
39	3	OFFSHORE 39	SLP	SA/RC	FBG	KL	IB	37D	PERK	12	9	20300	6		52900	58200
39	10	MIDSHIPMAN 40	SLP	SA/CR	FBG	KL	IB	37D	WEST	13	10	20000	4	6	54300	59700
39	10	MIDSHIPMAN 40	KTH	SA/CR	FBG	KL	IB	37D	WEST	13	10	20000	4	6	54300	59700
40		TRAWLER	FB	TRWL	FBG	DS	IB	T 80D		14		38000	4	8	94100	103500
40		TRAWLER	FB	TRWL	FBG	DS	IB	T120D	LEHM	14		38000	4	8	95000	104500
40		TRAWLER	FB	TRWL	FBG	DS	IB	T160D	PERK	14		38000	4	8	97000	106500
41		RICHARDS 41	SLP	SA/CR	FBG	KL	IB	50D	PERK	12	9	20000	6		57100	62800
41		RICHARDS 41	YWL	SA/CR	FBG	KL	IB	50D	PERK	12	9	20000	6		57100	62800
41		RICHARDS 41	KTH	SA/CR	FBG	KL	IB	50D	PERK	12	9	20000	6		57100	62800
42		CORSAIRE 42		SF	FBG	DS	IB	T120D		15		19968			57300	62900
42		CORSAIRE 42		SPTCR	FBG	DS	IB	T120D		15		19017			57100	62700
42	5	CLIPPER 42	SCH	SA/CR	FBG	KL	IB	37D	WEST	12	1	23500	5	9	68000	74700
42	5	CLIPPER 42	KTH	SA/CR	FBG	KL	IB	37D	WEST	12	1	23500	5	9	68000	74700
43	8	OFFSHORE 44	KTH	MS	FBG	KL	IB	63D	PERK	13		32000	5	6	85500	94000
46	9	OFFSHORE 47	SLP	SA/CR	FBG	KL	IB	50D	PERK	12	2	27000	6	6	93300	102500
46	9	OFFSHORE 47	YWL	SA/CR	FBG	KL	IB	50D	PERK	12	2	27000	6	6	93300	102500
46	9	OFFSHORE 47	KTH	SA/CR	FBG	KL	IB	50D	PERK	12	2	27000	6	6	93300	102500
47		TRAWLER	FB	TRWL	FBG	DS	IB	210D	CAT	14		44000	4	8	104500	114500
		IB T120D LEHM 107000 118000, IB T160D PERK 109500 120500, IB T210D CAT													111500	122500
47	11	CLIPPER 48	SCH	SA/CR	FBG	KL	IB	50D	PERK	13		31000	6		104500	115000
47	11	CLIPPER 48	KTH	SA/CR	FBG	KL	IB	50D	PERK	13		31000	6		105000	115500
50	4	OFFSHORE 50	KTH	SA/CR	FBG	KL	IB	63D	PERK	13	2	34000	6	6	125000	137500
51	6	MIDSHIPMAN 52	KTH	MS	FBG	KC	IB	120D	FORD	14	6	44450	5	6	145000	159500
51	6	TRAWLER	FB	TRWL	FBG	DS	IB	150D	CAT	15	7	55000	5	5	115500	126500
51	6	TRAWLER	FB	TRWL	FBG	DS	IB	T120D	LEHM	15	7	55000	5	5	117500	129000
51	6	TRAWLER	FB	TRWL	FBG	DS	IB	T160D	PERK	15	7	55000	5	5	119500	131500
52	9	OFFSHORE 53	KTH	MS	FBG	KL	IB	120D	FORD	15		60000	6		167500	184000
55		TRAWLER	FB	TRWL	FBG	DS	IB	T210D	CAT	16	6	70000	5	4	161000	177000
64	5	TRAWLER	FB	TRWL	FBG	DS	IB	T210D	CAT	18	6	87000	6	7	233500	256500
		1975 BOATS														
28		OFFSHORE 30	SLP	SAIL	FBG	KL	IB	25D	VLVO	9	2	7900	3	6	18400	20500
29	10	LUDERS 30	SLP	SA/RC	FBG	KL	IB	25D	VLVO	9	1	9900	4	9	23200	25800
30		CRUISAIRE 30	SLP	MS	FBG	CB	IB	37D	WEST	10	8	12000	6	9	28400	31600
30		CRUISAIRE 30	SLP	MS	FBG	KL	IB	37D	WEST	10	8	12000	3	11	28400	31600
30	10	OFFSHORE 31	SLP	SA/RC	FBG	KL	IB	25D	VLVO	8	10	10750	3	9	25200	28000
30	10	OFFSHORE 31	KTH	SA/RC	FBG	KL	IB	25D	VLVO	8	10	10750	3	9	25200	28000
31	6	ALDEN 32	SLP	MS	FBG	KL	IB	75D	VLVO	10	6	13500	4	6	31400	34900

 CONTINUED ON NEXT PAGE

LOA FT	LOA IN	NAME AND/ OR MODEL	TOP/ RIG	BOAT TYPE	-HULL- MTL	-HULL- TP	ENGINE TP	ENGINE # HP	ENGINE MFG	BEAM FT	BEAM IN	WGT LBS	DRAFT FT	DRAFT IN	RETAIL LOW	RETAIL HIGH
		1975 BOATS														
31	6	ALDEN 32	KTH	MS	FBG	KL	IB	75D	VLVO	10	6	13500	4	6	31400	34900
32	11	CLIPPER 33	CUT	SA/CR	FBG	KL	IB	36D	VLVO	10		12000	4		27900	31000
32	11	CLIPPER 33	KTH	SA/CR	FBG	KL	IB	36D	VLVO	10		12000	4		27900	31000
32	11	OFFSHORE 33	SLP	SA/CR	FBG	KL	IB	25D	VLVO	10	2	12480	3	8	28900	32200
32	11	OFFSHORE 33	KTH	SA/CR	FBG	KL	IB	25D	VLVO	10	2	12480	3	8	28900	32200
35	6	LUDERS 36 MKI	SLP	SA/RC	FBG	KL	IB	36D	VLVO	10	3	15000	5	3	35600	39500
35	6	LUDERS 36 MKI	YWL	SA/RC	FBG	KL	IB	36D	VLVO	10	3	15000	5	3	35600	39500
35	8	CLIPPER 36	SCH	SA/CR	FBG	KL	IB	36D	VLVO	10	9	16250	5	3	38300	42600
35	8	CLIPPER 36	KTH	SA/CR	FBG	KL	IB	36D	VLVO	10	9	16250	5	3	38300	42600
35	9	MIDSHIPMAN 36	KTH	SA/CR	FBG	KL	IB	37D	PERK	11	6	15000	4		35700	39600
36	6	TRAWLER	FB	TRWL	FBG	RB	IB	160D	PERK	13		30440	3	6	65000	71500
36	6	TRAWLER	FB	TRWL	FBG	RB	IB	T120D	LEHM	13		30440	3	6	66200	72700
39	3	OFFSHORE 39	SLP	SA/RC	FBG	KL	IB	36D	VLVO	12	9	20300			52000	57100
39	3	OFFSHORE 39	SLP	SA/RC	FBG	KL	IB	36D	WEST	12	9	20300			52100	57200
39	9	OFFSHORE 40	SLP	SA/CR	FBG	KL	IB	36D	VLVO	10	9	20000	6		52800	58000
39	9	OFFSHORE 40	YWL	SA/CR	FBG	KL	IB	36D	VLVO	10	9	20000	6		52800	58000
39	10	MIDSHIPMAN 40	KTH	SA/CR	FBG	KL	IB	36D	VLVO	13		20000	4	6	53000	58300
40		TRAWLER	FB	TRWL	FBG	RB	IB	T120D	LEHM	14		34857	4	8	84700	93100
40		TRAWLER	FB	TRWL	FBG	RB	IB	T160D	PERK	14		34857	4	8	86700	95200
42	5	CLIPPER 42	SCH	SA/CR	FBG	KL	IB	75D	VLVO	12	1	23500	5	9	67000	73600
42	5	CLIPPER 42	KTH	SA/CR	FBG	KL	IB	75D	VLVO	12	1	23500	5	9	67000	73600
43	8	OFFSHORE 44	KTH	MS	FBG	KL	IB	106D		13		29714	5	6	81400	89400
43	8	OFFSHORE 44 BOWSPRIT	KTH	MS	FBG	KL	IB	106D		13		29714	5	6	81400	89400
46	9	OFFSHORE 47	SLP	SA/CR	FBG	KL	IB	37D	WEST	12	2	27000	6	6	91500	100500
46	9	OFFSHORE 47	YWL	SA/CR	FBG	KL	IB	37D	WEST	12	2	27000	6	6	91500	100500
46	9	OFFSHORE 47	KTH	SA/CR	FBG	KL	IB	37D	WEST	12	2	27000	6	6	91500	100500
47		TRAWLER	FB	TRWL	FBG	RB	IB	T120D	LEHM	14		44000	4	8	103000	113000
47		TRAWLER	FB	TRWL	FBG	RB	IB	T160D	PERK	14		44000	4	8	105000	115500
47		TRAWLER	FB	TRWL	FBG	RB	IB	T210D	CAT	14		44000	4	8	107000	117500
48		CLIPPER 48	SCH	SA/CR	FBG	KL	IB	D							108000	118500
48		CLIPPER 48	KTH	SA/CR	FBG	KL	IB	D							109000	119500
50	4	OFFSHORE 50	KTH	SA/CR	FBG	KL	IB	75D	VLVO	13	2	34000	6	6	123000	135000
51	6	MIDSHIPMAN 52	KTH	MS	FBG	KL	IB	120D	FORD	14	6	44450	5	6	142000	156000
51	6	TRAWLER	FB	TRWL	FBG	RB	IB	T120D	LEHM	15	7	58583	5	5	115500	127000
51	6	TRAWLER	FB	TRWL	FBG	RB	IB	T160D	PERK	15	7	58583	5	5	117500	129500
51	6	TRAWLER	FB	TRWL	FBG	RB	IB	T210D	CAT	15	7	58583	5	5	120500	132500
52	9	OFFSHORE 53	KTH	MS	FBG	KL	IB	120D	FORD	15		60080	6		164000	180000
55		TRAWLER	FB	TRWL	FBG	RB	IB	T210D	CAT	16	6	71167	5	4	158000	173500
64	5	TRAWLER	FB	TRWL	FBG	RB	IB	T210D	CAT	18	6	87000	6	7	224000	246000
66		TRAWLER	FB	TRWL	FBG	RB	IB	400D		18		87000	5	3	231000	254000
		1974 BOATS														
25	7	OFFSHORE 26	SLP	SA/CR	FBG	KL	IB	D		8		6100	3	9	12800	14600
26	9	OFFSHORE 26 MARK II	SLP	SA/CR	FBG	KL	IB	D		7	9	7400	4	5	16100	18300
28		OFFSHORE 28	SLP	SAIL	FBG	KC	IB	25D	VLVO	9	2	7900	3	6	18100	20100
29	10	LUDERS 30	SLP	SA/RC	FBG		IB	25D	VLVO	9	1	9900	4	9	22800	25300
30		CRUISAIRE 30	SLP	MS	FBG	KC	IB	37D	WEST	10	8	12000	2	6	27800	30900
30		CRUISAIRE 30	SLP	MS	FBG	KL	IB	37D	WEST	10	8	12000	3	11	27800	30900
30	10	OFFSHORE 31	SLP	SA/RC	FBG	KL	IB	25D	VLVO	8	10	10750	3	9	24700	27400
30	10	OFFSHORE 31	KTH	SA/RC	FBG	KL	IB	25D	VLVO	8	10	10750	3	9	24700	27400
31	6	ALDEN 32	SLP	MS	FBG	KL	IB	75D	VLVO	10	6	13500	4	6	30800	34200
31	6	ALDEN 32	KTH	MS	FBG	KL	IB	75D	VLVO	10	6	13500	4	6	30800	34200
32	11	CLIPPER 33	CUT	SA/CR	FBG	KL	IB	36D	VLVO	10		12000	4		27300	30400
32	11	CLIPPER 33	KTH	SA/CR	FBG	KL	IB	36D	VLVO	10		12000	4		27300	30400
32	11	OFFSHORE 33	SLP	SA/CR	FBG	KL	IB	25D	VLVO	10	2	12480	3	8	28400	31500
32	11	OFFSHORE 33	KTH	SA/CR	FBG	KL	IB	25D	VLVO	10	2	12480	3	8	28400	31500
34	6	TRAWLER	HT	TRWL	FBG	DS	IB	T120D	FORD	13		29000	3	6	60300	66300
35	6	LUDERS 36 MKI	SLP	SA/RC	FBG	KL	IB	36D	VLVO	10	3	15000	5	3	34900	38700
35	8	CLIPPER 36	KTH	SA/CR	FBG		IB	36D	VLVO	10	9	16250	5	3	37600	41700
35	9	MIDSHIPMAN 36	KTH	SA/CR	FBG		IB	37D	PERK	11	6	15000	4		34900	38800
39	3	OFFSHORE 39	SLP	SA/RC	FBG	KL	IB	36D	VLVO	12	9	20300	6		50900	56000
39	3	OFFSHORE 39	SLP	SA/RC	FBG	KL	IB	36D	WEST	12	9	20300	6		51000	56100
39	9	OFFSHORE 40	SLP	SA/CR	FBG	KL	IB	36D	VLVO	10	9	20000	6		51700	56800
39	9	OFFSHORE 40	YWL	SA/CR	FBG	KL	IB	36D	VLVO	10	9	20000	6		51700	56800
39	10	MIDSHIPMAN 40	KTH	SA/CR	FBG	KL	IB	36D	VLVO	13		20000	4	6	51900	57100
40		TRAWLER	FB	TRWL	FBG	DS	IB	T120D	FORD	14		27000	4	8	65900	72400
40		TRAWLER	FB	TRWL	FBG	DS	IB	T145D	PERK	14		27000	4	8	67400	74000
42	5	CLIPPER 42	SCH	SA/CR	FBG		IB	75D	VLVO	12	1	23500	5	9	65600	72100
42	5	CLIPPER 42	KTH	SA/CR	FBG		IB	75D	VLVO	12	1	23500	5	9	65600	72100
43	8	OFFSHORE 44	KTH	MS	FBG	KL	IB	106D	VLVO	13		29714	5	6	79100	86900
43	8	OFFSHORE 44 BOWSPRIT	KTH	MS	FBG	KL	IB	106D	VLVO	13		29714	5	6	80500	88500
46	9	OFFSHORE 47	KTH	SA/CR	FBG	KL	IB	37D	WEST	12	2	27000	6	6	89700	98500
47		TRAWLER	FB	TRWL	FBG	DS	IB	150D	CAT	14		44000	4	8	95000	104500
		IB T120D FORD 98800 108500, IB T130D PERK 100000 110000, IB T145D FORD 99600 109500														
		IB T145D PERK 100500 110500, IB T210D CAT 102500 113000														
50	4	OFFSHORE 50	KTH	SA/CR	FBG	KL	IB	75D	VLVO	13	2	34000	6	6	120500	132500
51	6	MIDSHIPMAN 52	KTH	MS	FBG	KC	IB	120D	FORD	14	6	44450	5	6	139000	153000
51	6	TRAWLER	FB	TRWL	FBG		IB	150D	CAT	15	7	55000	5	5	106500	117000
		IB T120D FORD 108500 119000, IB T145D FORD 109000 120000, IB T145D PERK 109500 120500														
52	9	OFFSHORE 53	KTH	MS	FBG	KL	IB	120D	FORD	15		60080	6		160500	176500
55		TRAWLER	FB	TRWL	FBG	DS	IB	T210D	CAT	16	6	57000	5	4	123000	135000
64	5	TRAWLER	FB	TRWL	FBG	DS	IB	T210D	CAT	18	6	87000	6	7	215000	236000
		1973 BOATS														
25	7	OFFSHORE 26	SLP	SAIL	FBG	KL	IB	10D	VLVO	8		6100	3	10	12500	14200
26	9	OFFSHORE 26 MARK II	SLP	SA/CR	FBG	KL	IB	10D	VLVO	7	9	8000	4	5	17100	19500
28		OFFSHORE 28	SLP	SAIL	FBG	KC	IB	25D		9	2	7900	3	6	17300	19700
29	10	LUDERS 30	SLP	SA/RC	FBG	KL	IB	30	UNIV	9	1	9900	4	9	22200	24600
29	10	LUDERS 30	SLP	SA/RC	FBG	KL	IB	15D	VLVO	9	1	9900	4	9	22300	24800
30		CRUISAIRE 30	SLP	MS	FBG	KC	IB	50D	PERK	10	8	12000	2	6	27300	30300
30	10	OFFSHORE 31	SLP	SA/RC	FBG	KL	IB	25D		8	10	10750	3	9	24200	26900
30	10	OFFSHORE 31	KTH	SA/RC	FBG	KL	IB	25D		8	10	10750	3	9	24200	26900
31	6	ALDEN 32	SLP	MS	FBG	KL	IB	50D	PERK	10	6	13500	4	6	30200	33500
32	11	CLIPPER 33	CUT	SA/CR	FBG	KL	IB	30	UNIV	10		12000	4		26700	29700
32	11	CLIPPER 33	CUT	SA/CR	FBG	KL	IB	15D	VLVO	10		12000	4		26800	29800
32	11	OFFSHORE 33	SLP	SA/CR	FBG	KL	IB	25D		10	2	10500	3	8	23500	26100
32	11	OFFSHORE 33	KTH	SA/CR	FBG	KL	IB	25D		10	2	10500	3	8	23500	26100
34	6	TRAWLER		TRWL	FBG	DS	IB	T 80D	FORD	13		29000	3	6	59100	64900
35	6	CRUISAIRE 36	SLP	MS	FBG	KL	IB	50D	PERK	10	6	17500	5	2	39200	43600
35	6	LUDERS 36	SLP	SA/RC	FBG	KL	IB	30	UNIV	10	3	15000	5	3	33900	37600
35	6	LUDERS 36	SLP	SA/RC	FBG	KL	IB	15D	VLVO	10	3	15000	5	3	34000	37800
35	8	CLIPPER 36	KTH	SA/CR	FBG	KL	IB	30	UNIV	10	9	16250	5	3	36500	40500
35	8	CLIPPER 36	KTH	SA/CR	FBG	KL	IB	50D	PERK	10	9	16250	5	3	36800	40900
35	9	MIDSHIPMAN 36	KTH	SA/CR	FBG	KL	IB	37D		11	6	15000	4		34400	38200
35	10	OFFSHORE 36	SLP	SAIL	FBG	KL	IB	30	UNIV	10		15950	4	8	36000	40000
35	10	OFFSHORE 36	SLP	SAIL	FBG	KL	IB	15D	VLVO	10		15950	4	8	36200	40200
38	4	SIGMA 38	SLP	SA/RC	FBG	KL	IB			10	8	18000	5	10	43000	47800
39	9	OFFSHORE 40	SLP	SA/CR	FBG	KL	IB	50D	PERK	10	9	20000	6		50600	55700
39	10	MIDSHIPMAN 40	KTH	SA/CR	FBG	KL	IB	36D		13		20000	4	6	50900	56000
40		TRAWLER		TRWL	FBG	DS	IB	T145D	PERK	14		34857	4	8	79700	87600
40	9	RELIANT 41	SLP	SA/RC	FBG	KL	IB	30	UNIV	10	9	20700	5	9	53500	58800
40	9	RELIANT 41	SLP	SA/RC	FBG	KL	IB	50D	PERK	10	9	20700	5	9	54300	59600
42	5	CLIPPER 42	KTH	SA/CR	FBG	KL	IB	30	UNIV	12	1	23500	5	9	63000	69200
42	5	CLIPPER 42	KTH	SA/CR	FBG	KL	IB	50D	PERK	12	1	23500	5	9	63700	70000
44		OFFSHORE 44	KTH	MS	FBG	KL	IB	100D	PERK	13		30000	5	6	79500	87300
46	10	OFFSHORE 47	SLP	SA/CR	FBG	KL	IB	70	UNIV	12	2	27000	6	6	87500	96200
47		TRAWLER		TRWL	FBG	DS	IB	150D	CAT	14		44000	4	8	91300	100500
47		TRAWLER		TRWL	FBG	DS	IB	T160D	PERK	14		44000	4	8	97100	106500
50	4	OFFSHORE 50 CPT AFT	KTH	SA/CR	FBG	KL	IB	68D	VLVO	13	2	34000	6	6	118000	129500
50	4	OFFSHORE 50 CPT CTR	KTH	SA/CR	FBG	KL	IB	68D	VLVO	13	2	34000	6	6	118000	129500
55		TRAWLER		TRWL	FBG	DS	IB	T210D	CAT	16	6	71167	5	4	145000	159500
65		TRAWLER		TRWL	FBG	DS	IB	T210D	CAT	18	6	87000	6	7	210000	231000
		1972 BOATS														
26		FRISCO-FLYER	SLP	SA/RC	FBG		IB	10D	VLVO	7	4	6000	3	11	12200	13800
26	10	OFFSHORE 26	SLP	SA/CR	FBG		IB	10D	VLVO	7	8	6900	4	4	14300	16300
29	10	LUDERS 30	SLP	SA/RC	FBG		IB	30	UNIV	9	1	9900	4	9	21700	24100
30		CLIPPER 30	KTH	SA/CR	FBG		IB	50D	PERK	10	8	12000	2	6	26700	29700
30		CRUISAIRE	SLP	SA/CR	FBG	KC	IB	D		10	8	8537	2	6	19000	21100
30	9	OFFSHORE 31	KTH	SA/RC	FBG		IB	30	UNIV	8	10	10750	3	9	23600	26200
31	6	ALDEN 32	SLP	MS	FBG	KL	IB	68D		10	6	12500	4	6	27400	30500
32	10	OFFSHORE 33	SLP	SA/CR	FBG		IB	30	UNIV	10	3	12575	3	8	27400	30400
32	10	OFFSHORE 33	KTH	SA/CR	FBG		IB	30	UNIV	10	3	12575	3	8	27400	30400
32	11	CLIPPER 33	KTH	SA/CR	FBG		IB	30	UNIV	10		12000	4		26200	29100
32	11	OFFSHORE	KTH	SA/CR	FBG	KL	IB	D		10	2	10523	3	8	23100	25600
35	6	CRUISAIRE	YWL	SA/CR	FBG	KL	IB	D		10	6	12041	5	1	27400	30400
35	6	LUDERS 36	SLP	SA/RC	FBG		IB	30	UNIV	10	3	15000	5	3	33100	36800
35	7	CLIPPER 36	KTH	SA/CR	FBG		IB	30	UNIV	10	9	16250	5	3	35700	39600
36	10	CRUISEMASTER	KTH	SA/CR	FBG	KL	IB	D		11			4		38700	43000
38	4	SIGMA 38	SLP	SA/CR	FBG	KL	IB	30D		10	3	18000	5	10	42600	47400
39	9	OFFSHORE 40	SLP	SA/CR	FBG		IB	50D	PERK	10	9	20750	6		50800	55900
39	9	OFFSHORE 40	YWL	SA/CR	FBG		IB	50D	PERK	10	9	20750	6		50800	55900
40	9	RELIANT	SLP	SA/CR	FBG	KL	IB	70D		10	9	20700	5	9	53700	59000
42	5	CLIPPER 42	KTH	SA/CR	FBG		IB	50D	PERK	12	1	23500	5	9	62400	68500
43	8	OFFSHORE 44	KTH	MS	FBG		IB	50D	PERK	12	8	28000	5	6	73300	80600
46	9	LUDERS	KTH	SA/RC	FBG	KL	IB	D		12			6	8	88700	97500
46	9	OFFSHORE	KTH	SA/CR	FBG	KL	IB	50D		12		27000	6	8	86200	94700
50	4	OFFSHORE 50	KTH	SA/CR	FBG		IB	72D	PERK	13	2	34000	6	6	115000	126500

 CONTINUED ON NEXT PAGE

LOA FT	LOA IN	NAME AND/ OR MODEL	TOP/ RIG	BOAT TYPE	-HULL- MTL	-HULL- TP	ENGINE TP	ENGINE # HP	ENGINE MFG	BEAM FT	BEAM IN	WGT LBS	DRAFT FT	DRAFT IN	RETAIL LOW	RETAIL HIGH
1971 BOATS																
25		FRISCO-FLYER	SLP	SA/RC	FBG		IB	10D	VLVO	7	2	5500	3	11	10600	12000
25	7	OFFSHORE 26	SLP	SA/CR	FBG	KL	IB	10D	VLVO	8		6100	3	10	11900	13600
26	10	NEWELL-CADET	SLP	SA/CR	FBG	KL	IB	30D		7	8	6900	4	4	14200	16100
29	10	LUDERS 30	SLP	SA/RC	FBG	KL	IB	30	UNIV	9	1	9900	4	9	21200	23500
30		CLIPPER 30	KTH	SA/CR	FBG	KL	IB	50D	PERK	10	8	12000	2	6	26000	28900
30		CRUISAIRE 30	SLP	SA/CR	FBG	KC	IB	37D		10	8	12000	2	6	26000	28900
30	10	OFFSHORE 31	KTH	SA/RC	FBG	KL	IB	30	UNIV	8	10	10750	3	9	23000	25600
32	10	OFFSHORE 33	SLP	SA/CR	FBG	KL	IB	30	UNIV	10	3	12575	3	8	26700	29600
32	10	OFFSHORE 33	KTH	SA/CR	FBG	KL	IB	30	UNIV	10	3	12575	3	8	26700	29600
32	11	CLIPPER 33	KTH	SA/CR	FBG	KL	IB	30	UNIV	10		12000	4		25500	28300
35	6	LUDERS 36	SLP	SA/RC	FBG	KL	IB	30	UNIV	10	3	15000	5	3	32300	35900
35	7	CLIPPER 36	CUT	SA/CR	FBG	KL	IB	30	UNIV	10	9	16250	5	3	34800	38600
35	7	CLIPPER 36	KTH	SA/CR	FBG	KL	IB	30	UNIV	10	9	16250	5	3	34800	38600
36	10	CRUISEMASTER 37	SLP	SA/CR	FBG	KL	IB	D		11			4		37700	41900
36	10	CRUISEMASTER 37	KTH	SA/CR	FBG	KL	IB	D		11					37700	41900
38	4	SIGMA 38	SLP	SA/CR	FBG	KL	IB	30D		10	3	18100	5	11	41700	46300
39	9	OFFSHORE 40	SLP	SA/CR	FBG	KL	IB	50D	PERK	10	9	20000	6		48300	53100
39	9	OFFSHORE 40	YWL	SA/CR	FBG	KL	IB	50D	PERK	10	9	20000	6		48300	53100
40	9	RELIANT 41	YWL	SA/CR	FBG	KL	IB	37D		10	9	20700	5	9	51800	57000
42	5	CLIPPER 42	KTH	SA/CR	FBG	KL	IB	50D	PERK	12	1	23500	5	9	60800	66800
43	8	OFFSHORE 44	KTH	MS	FBG	KL	IB	50D	PERK	13		30000	5	6	74100	81400
47		GARDEN 47		TRWL	FBG	DS	IB	D		14			4	8	**	**
50	4	OFFSHORE 50	KTH	SA/CR	FBG	KL	IB	72D	PERK	13	2	34000	6	6	112500	123500
1970 BOATS																
26	10	NEWELL-CADET	SLP	SA/CR	FBG	KL		22		7	8	6900	4	4	13200	15000
26	10	OFFSHORE 27 II	SLP	SA/CR	FBG		IB	D		7	8	6900	4	4	13700	15600
29	10	LUDERS 30	SLP	SA/RC	FBG	KL	IB	D		9	2	9900	4	9	20800	23100
30	9	OFFSHORE 31	SLP	SA/RC	FBG	KL	IB	D		8	10	10750	3	9	22500	25000
30	9	OFFSHORE 31	KTH	SA/RC	FBG	KL	IB	D		8	10	10750	3	9	22500	25000
32	10	CLIPPER 33	KTH	SA/CR	FBG		IB	D		10		12000	4		24900	27700
35	6	CRUISAIRE 36	SLP	MS	FBG	KL	IB	D		10	7	16000	5	2	33700	37500
35	6	LUDERS 36	SLP	SA/RC	FBG	KL	IB	D		10	3	15000	5	3	31800	35400
35	6	LUDERS 36	YWL	SA/RC	FBG	KL	IB	D		10	3	15000	5	3	31800	35400
35	8	CLIPPER 36	KTH	SA/CR	FBG	KL	VD	36D	PERK	10	9	16250	5		34200	38000
38	4	SIGMA 38	SLP	SA/RC	FBG	KL	IB	D		10	3	18000	5	11	40600	45100
39	9	OFFSHORE 39	YWL	SAIL	FBG		IB	D		10	9	20000	6		47600	52300
39	9	OFFSHORE 40	SLP	SA/CR	FBG	KL	IB	D		10	9	20000	6		47600	52300
40	9	RELIANT 41	SLP	SA/RC	FBG	KL	IB	D		10	9	20700	5	9	50700	55700
40	9	RELIANT 41	YWL	SA/RC	FBG	KL	IB	D		10	9	20700	5	9	50700	55700
42	5	CLIPPER 42	KTH	SA/CR	FBG	KL	IB	D		12	1	23500	5	9	59600	65500
43	8	OFFSHORE 44	KTH	MS	FBG		IB	D		13		28000	5	6	70200	77100
50	4	OFFSHORE 50	KTH	SA/CR	FBG	KL	IB	D		13	2	34000	6	6	110000	121000
1969 BOATS																
26	10	NEWELL-CADET	SLP	SAIL	FBG	KL	IB	7D-	22D	7	9	6900	4	4	13300	15300
29	10	LUDERS 30	SLP	SA/CR	FBG	KL	IB	D	PALM	9	1	10000	4	9	20500	22800
29	10	LUDERS 30	SLP	SA/RC	FBG	KL	IB	D	PALM	9	1	10000	4	9	20500	22800
30	10	OFFSHORE 31	SLP	SA/RC	FBG	KL	IB	20D-	22D	8	10	11000	3	9	22500	25000
30	10	OFFSHORE 31	KTH	SA/RC	FBG	KL	IB	20D-	22D	8	10	11000	3	9	22500	25000
35	6	CRUISAIRE 36	SLP	MS	FBG	KL	IB	40D	PALM	10	7	16000	5	2	33000	36700
35	6	CRUISAIRE 36	SLP	MS	FBG	KL	IB	66D	PALM	10	7	16000	5	2	33200	36800
35	6	LUDERS 36	SLP	SA/RC	FBG	KL	IB	22D	PALM	10	3	15000	5	3	31000	34500
35	8	CLIPPER 36	KTH	SA/CR	FBG	KL	IB	20D	PALM	10	9	16250	5		33400	37200
35	8	CLIPPER 36	KTH	SA/CR	FBG	KL	IB	36D	PERK	10	9	16250	5		33500	37200
35	8	CLIPPER 36	KTH	SA/CR	FBG	KL	IB	36D	WEST	10	9	16250	5		33600	37300
38	4	SIGMA 38	SLP	SA/RC	FBG	KL	IB	22D	PALM	10	3	18000	5	11	39500	43900
39	9	OFFSHORE 40	SLP	SA/CR	FBG	KL	IB	22D	PALM	10	9	20000	6		46200	50800
39	9	OFFSHORE 40	YWL	SA/CR	FBG	KL	IB	22D	PALM	10	9	20000	6		46200	50800
40	9	RELIANT 41	SLP	SA/RC	FBG	KL	IB	22D	PALM	10	9	20700	5	9	49200	54100
40	9	RELIANT 41	SLP	SA/RC	FBG	KL	IB	36D	PERK	10	9	20700	5	9	49200	54100
40	9	RELIANT 41	YWL	SA/RC	FBG	KL	IB	22D	PALM	10	9	20700	5	9	49200	54100
40	9	RELIANT 41	YWL	SA/RC	FBG	KL	IB	36D	PERK	10	9	20700	5	9	49200	54100
50	4	OFFSHORE 50	KTH	SA/CR	FBG	KL	IB	66D	PALM	13	2	35000	6	6	108000	119000
1968 BOATS																
25	1	FLYER I	SLP	SA/RC	FBG	KL	IB	5D		7	3	6000	3	11	10700	12100
25	1	FLYER I TEAK	SLP	SA/RC	WD	KL	IB	5D		7	3	6000	3	11	10700	12100
25	1	FLYER III	SLP	SA/RC	FBG	KL	IB	8D	VLVO	7	3	6000	3	11	10700	12200
25	1	FLYER III TEAK	SLP	SA/RC	WD	KL	IB	8D	VLVO	7	3	6000	3	11	10700	12200
26	10	NEWELL-CADET	SLP	SAIL	FBG	KL	IB	30	UNIV	7	9	6900	4	4	12900	14600
26	10	NEWELL-CADET	SLP	SAIL	FBG	KL	IB	6D	VLVO	7	9	6900	4	4	13000	14800
28		ROZINANTE	YWL	SA/OD	FBG	KL	OB			6	4	6000	3	9	11200	12700
28		ROZINANTE	YWL	SA/OD	WD	KL	OB			6	4	6000	3	9	11200	12700
29	7	BERMUDA 30	SLP	SA/CR	FBG	KL	IB	30	UNIV	8	9	10000	3	8	20000	22200
29	7	BERMUDA 30	SLP	SA/CR	FBG	KL	IB	15D	VLVO	8	9	10000	3	8	20100	22300
29	7	BERMUDA 30	KTH	SA/CR	FBG	KL	IB	30	UNIV	8	9	10000	3	8	20000	22200
29	7	BERMUDA 30	KTH	SA/CR	FBG	KL	IB	15D	VLVO	8	9	10000	3	8	20100	22300
29	7	BERMUDA 30 TEAK	SLP	SA/CR	WD	KL	IB	30	UNIV	8	9	10000	3	8	20000	22200
29	7	BERMUDA 30 TEAK	SLP	SA/CR	WD	KL	IB	15D	VLVO	8	9	10000	3	8	20100	22300
29	7	BERMUDA 30 TEAK	KTH	SA/CR	WD	KL	IB	30	UNIV	8	9	10000	3	8	20000	22200
29	7	BERMUDA 30 TEAK	KTH	SA/CR	WD	KL	IB	15D	VLVO	8	9	10000	3	8	20100	22300
30	10	OFFSHORE 31	SLP	SA/RC	FBG	KL	IB	D		8	10	11000	3	9	22100	24500
30	10	OFFSHORE 31	KTH	SA/RC	FBG	KL	IB	D		8	10	11000	3	9	22100	24500
35	2	LION	SLP	SA/RC	FBG	KL	IB	30	UNIV	8	10	14500	5	6	29100	32300
35	2	LION	SLP	SA/RC	FBG	KL	IB	15D	VLVO	8	10	14500	5	6	29300	32500
35	2	LION TEAK	SLP	SA/RC	WD	KL	IB	30	UNIV	8	10	14500	5	6	29100	32300
35	2	LION TEAK	SLP	SA/RC	WD	KL	IB	15D	VLVO	8	10	14500	5	6	29300	32500
35	6	CRUISAIRE 36	SLP	MS	FBG	KL	IB	D		10	3	15000	5	3	30500	33900
35	6	ROBB 35	SLP	SA/RC	FBG	KL	IB	30	UNIV	10			4	7	13200	15000
35	6	ROBB 35	SLP	SA/RC	FBG	KL	IB	36D	PERK	10			4	7	27500	30500
35	6	ROBB 35	YWL	SA/RC	FBG	KL	IB	30	UNIV	10			4	7	13200	15000
35	6	ROBB 35	YWL	SA/RC	FBG	KL	IB	36D	PERK	10			4	7	27500	30500
35	10	OFFSHORE 36	SLP	SAIL	FBG	KL	IB	30	UNIV	10		15950	4	8	32100	35700
35	10	OFFSHORE 36	YWL	SAIL	FBG	KL	IB	30	UNIV	10		15950	4	8	32100	35700
35	10	OFFSHORE 36	YWL	SAIL	FBG	KL	IB	36D	PERK	10		15950	4	8	32300	35900
38	4	SIGMA 38	SLP	SA/RC	FBG	KL	IB	30	UNIV	10	3	18000	5	11	38300	42600
38	4	SIGMA 38	SLP	SA/RC	FBG	KL	IB	36D	PERK	10	3	18000	5	11	38700	43000
39	9	OFFSHORE 40	SLP	SA/CR	FBG	KL	IB	30	UNIV	10	9	20000	6		44300	49200
39	9	OFFSHORE 40	SLP	SA/CR	FBG	KL	IB	36D	PERK	10	9	20000	6		44800	49700
39	9	OFFSHORE 40	YWL	SA/CR	FBG	KL	IB	30	UNIV	10	9	20000	6		44300	49200
39	9	OFFSHORE 40	YWL	SA/CR	FBG	KL	IB	36D	PERK	10	9	20000	6		44800	49700
40	9	RELIANT 41	SLP	SA/RC	FBG	KL	IB	31D		10	9	20700	5	9	48400	53200
40	9	RELIANT 41	SLP	SA/RC	FBG	KL	IB	36D	PERK	10	9	20700	5	9	48200	53000
40	9	RELIANT 41	YWL	SA/RC	FBG	KL	IB	31D		10	9	20700	5	9	48400	53200
40	9	RELIANT 41	YWL	SA/RC	FBG	KL	IB	36D	PERK	10	9	20700	5	9	48200	53000
50	4	OFFSHORE 50	KTH	SA/CR	FBG	KL	IB	66D	PALM	13	2	35000	6	6	106000	116500
1967 BOATS																
25	1	FLYER I	SLP	SA/RC	FBG	KL	IB	5D		7	3	6000	3	11	10500	11900
25	1	FLYER I TEAK	SLP	SA/RC	WD	KL	IB	5D		7	3	6000	3	11	10500	11900
25	1	FLYER III	SLP	SA/RC	FBG	KL	IB	8D	VLVO	7	3	6000	3	11	10500	11900
25	1	FLYER III TEAK	SLP	SA/RC	WD	KL	IB	8D	VLVO	7	3	6000	3	11	10500	11900
26	10	NEWELL-CADET	SLP	SAIL	FBG	KL	IB	30	UNIV	7	9	7000	4	4	12800	14600
26	10	NEWELL-CADET	SLP	SAIL	FBG	KL	IB	6D	VLVO	7	9	7000	4	4	12900	14700
28		ROZINANTE	YWL	SA/OD	FBG	KL	OB			6	4	6000	3	9	11000	12500
28		ROZINANTE	YWL	SA/OD	WD	KL	OB			6	4	6000	3	9	11000	12500
29	7	BERMUDA 30	SLP	SA/CR	FBG	KL	IB	30	UNIV	8	9	10000	3	8	19600	21800
29	7	BERMUDA 30	SLP	SA/CR	FBG	KL	IB	15D	VLVO	8	9	10000	3	8	19700	21900
29	7	BERMUDA 30	KTH	SA/CR	FBG	KL	IB	30	UNIV	8	9	10000	3	8	19600	21800
29	7	BERMUDA 30	KTH	SA/CR	FBG	KL	IB	15D	VLVO	8	9	10000	3	8	19700	21900
29	7	BERMUDA 30 TEAK	SLP	SA/CR	WD	KL	IB	30	UNIV	8	9	10000	3	8	19600	21800
29	7	BERMUDA 30 TEAK	SLP	SA/CR	WD	KL	IB	15D	VLVO	8	9	10000	3	8	19700	21900
29	7	BERMUDA 30 TEAK	KTH	SA/CR	WD	KL	IB	30	UNIV	8	9	10000	3	8	19600	21800
29	7	BERMUDA 30 TEAK	KTH	SA/CR	WD	KL	IB	15D	VLVO	8	9	10000	3	8	19700	21900
31		OFFSHORE 31	SLP	SA/RC	FBG		IB	D				9915			19500	21700
31		OFFSHORE 31	KTH	SA/RC	FBG		IB	D				9915			19500	21700
35	2	LION	SLP	SA/RC	FBG	KL	IB	30	UNIV	8	10	14500	5	6	28600	31700
35	2	LION	SLP	SA/RC	FBG	KL	IB	15D	VLVO	8	10	14500	5	6	28700	31900
35	2	LION TEAK	SLP	SA/RC	WD	KL	IB	30	UNIV	8	10	14500	5	6	28600	31700
35	2	LION TEAK	SLP	SA/RC	WD	KL	IB	15D	VLVO	8	10	14500	5	6	28700	31900
35	6	ROBB 35	SLP	SA/RC	FBG	KL	IB	30	UNIV	10			4	7	12900	14700
35	6	ROBB 35	SLP	SA/RC	FBG	KL	IB	36D	PERK	10			4	7	27000	30000
35	6	ROBB 35	YWL	SA/RC	FBG	KL	IB	30	UNIV	10			4	7	12900	14700
35	6	ROBB 35	YWL	SA/RC	FBG	KL	IB	36D	PERK	10			4	7	27000	30000
35	10	OFFSHORE 36	SLP	SAIL	FBG		IB	30	UNIV	10		15950	4	8	31500	35000
35	10	OFFSHORE 36	SLP	SAIL	FBG		IB	36D	PERK	10		15950	4	8	31700	35300
35	10	OFFSHORE 36	YWL	SAIL	FBG		IB	30	UNIV	10		15950	4	8	31500	35000
35	10	OFFSHORE 36	YWL	SAIL	FBG		IB	36D	PERK	10		15950	4	8	31700	35300
40		OFFSHORE 40	SLP	SA/CR	FBG		IB	30	UNIV			20000			44100	49000
40		OFFSHORE 40	SLP	SA/CR	FBG		IB	36D	PERK			20000			44500	49500
40		OFFSHORE 40	YWL	SA/CR	FBG		IB	30	UNIV			20000			44100	49000
40		OFFSHORE 40	YWL	SA/CR	FBG		IB	36D	PERK			20000			44500	49500
40	9	RELIANT 41	SLP	SA/RC	FBG	KL	IB	31D	GRAY	10	9	21750	5	9	49000	53900
40	9	RELIANT 41	SLP	SA/RC	FBG	KL	IB	36D	PERK	10	9	21750	5	9	48900	53700
40	9	RELIANT 41	YWL	SA/RC	FBG	KL	IB	31D	GRAY	10	9	21750	5	9	49000	53900
40	9	RELIANT 41	YWL	SA/RC	FBG	KL	IB	36D	PERK	10	9	21750	5	9	48900	53700
50	4	ALDEN 50	KTH	SA/CR	FBG	KL	IB	62D	PERK	13	2	34000	6	6	103000	113500
1966 BOATS																
25	1	FLYER I	SLP	SA/RC	FBG	KL	IB	5D		7	3	6000	3	11	10300	11700
25	1	FLYER III	SLP	SA/RC	FBG	KL	IB	8D	VLVO	7	3	6000	3	11	10400	11800

CONTINUED ON NEXT PAGE

```
         LOA  NAME AND/              TOP/ BOAT  -HULL-  ----ENGINE---  BEAM    WGT   DRAFT RETAIL RETAIL
         FT IN OR MODEL              RIG  TYPE  MTL TP  TP # HP  MFG   FT IN   LBS   FT IN RETAIL RETAIL
         ----------------- 1966 BOATS -----------------------------------------------------------------
         26 10 NEWELL-CADET          SLP  SAIL  FBG KL IB    30  UNIV  7   9   7000  4  4  12600  14300
         26 10 NEWELL-CADET          SLP  SAIL  FBG KL IB    6D  VLVO  7   9   7000  4  4  12700  14500
         29  7 BERMUDA 30            SLP  SA/CR FBG KL IB    30  UNIV  8   9  10222  3  8  19700  21900
         29  7 BERMUDA 30            SLP  SA/CR FBG KL IB   15D  VLVO  8   9  10222  3  8  19800  22000
         29  7 BERMUDA 30            KTH  SA/CR FBG KL IB    30  UNIV  8   9  10222  3  8  19700  21900
         29  7 BERMUDA 30            KTH  SA/CR FBG KL IB   15D  VLVO  8   9  10222  3  8  19800  22000
         35  2 LION                  SLP  SA/RC FBG KL IB    30  UNIV  8  10  14500  5  6  28100  31200
         35  2 LION                  SLP  SA/RC FBG KL IB   15D  VLVO  8  10  14500  5  6  28200  31400
         35  6 ROBB 35               SLP  SA/RC FBG KL IB    30  UNIV 10      14500  4  7  28300  31400
         35  6 ROBB 35               SLP  SA/RC FBG KL IB   36D  PERK 10      14500  4  7  28500  31600
         35  6 ROBB 35               YWL  SA/RC FBG KL IB    30  UNIV 10      14500  4  7  28300  31400
         35  6 ROBB 35               YWL  SA/RC FBG KL IB   36D  PERK 10      14500  4  7  28500  31600

         40  9 RELIANT 41            SLP  SA/RC FBG KL IB   31D  GRAY 10   9  21225  5  9  47700  52400
         40  9 RELIANT 41            SLP  SA/RC FBG KL IB   36D  PERK 10   9  21225  5  9  47600  52300
         40  9 RELIANT 41            YWL  SA/RC FBG KL IB   31D  GRAY 10   9  21225  5  9  47700  52400
         40  9 RELIANT 41            YWL  SA/RC FBG KL IB   36D  PERK 10   9  21225  5  9  47600  52300
         ----------------- 1965 BOATS -----------------------------------------------------------------
         25  1 FLYER I               SLP  SA/RC FBG KL IB    5D        7   3   5500  3 11   9300  10600
         25  1 FLYER I TEAK          SLP  SA/RC WD  KL IB    5D        7   3   5500  3 11   9300  10600
         25  1 FLYER III             SLP  SA/RC FBG KL IB    8D  VLVO  7   3   5500  3 11   9350  10600
         25  1 FLYER III TEAK        SLP  SA/RC WD  KL IB    8D  VLVO  7   3   5500  3 11   9350  10600
         26 10 NEWELL-CADET          SLP  SAIL  FBG KL IB    30  UNIV  7   9   7000  4  4  12400  14100
         26 10 NEWELL-CADET          SLP  SAIL  FBG KL IB    8D  VLVO  7   9   7000  4  4  12600  14300
         28    ROZINANTE             YWL  SA/OD WD  KL OB          6   4   6000  3  9  10700  12100
         29  7 BERMUDA 30            SLP  SA/CR FBG KL IB    30  UNIV  8   9  10000  3  8  19000  21100
         29  7 BERMUDA 30            SLP  SA/CR FBG KL IB   15D  VLVO  8   9  10000  3  8  19100  21200
         29  7 BERMUDA 30            KTH  SA/CR FBG KL IB    30  UNIV  8   9  10000  3  8  19000  21100
         29  7 BERMUDA 30            KTH  SA/CR FBG KL IB   15D  VLVO  8   9  10000  3  8  19100  21200

         29  7 BERMUDA 30 TEAK       SLP  SA/CR WD  KL IB    30  UNIV  8   9  10000  3  8  19000  21100
         29  7 BERMUDA 30 TEAK       SLP  SA/CR WD  KL IB   15D  VLVO  8   9  10000  3  8  19100  21200
         29  7 BERMUDA 30 TEAK       KTH  SA/CR WD  KL IB    30  UNIV  8   9  10000  3  8  19000  21100
         29  7 BERMUDA 30 TEAK       KTH  SA/CR WD  KL IB   15D  VLVO  8   9  10000  3  8  19100  21200
         35  2 LION                  SLP  SA/RC FBG KL IB    30  UNIV  8  10  14200  5  6  27200  30200
         35  2 LION                  SLP  SA/RC FBG KL IB   15D  VLVO  8  10  14200  5  6  27300  30300
         35  2 LION TEAK             SLP  SA/RC WD  KL IB    30  UNIV  8  10  14200  5  6  27200  30200
         35  2 LION TEAK             SLP  SA/RC WD  KL IB   15D  VLVO  8  10  14200  5  6  27300  30300
         35  6 ROBB 35               SLP  SA/RC FBG KL IB    30  UNIV 10      12500  4  7  26200  29100
         35  6 ROBB 35               SLP  SA/RC FBG KL IB   36D  BENZ 10      12500  4  7  26200  29100
         35  6 ROBB 35               YWL  SA/RC WD  KL IB    30  UNIV 10      12500  4  7  26200  29100
         35  6 ROBB 35               YWL  SA/RC WD  KL IB   36D  BENZ 10      12500  4  7  26200  29100

         35 10 OFFSHORE 36           SLP  SAIL  FBG KL IB    30  UNIV 10      15950  4  8  30500  33900
         40  9 RELIANT 41            SLP  SA/RC FBG KL IB    30  UNIV 10   9  20700  5  9  45600  50200
         40  9 RELIANT 41            SLP  SA/RC FBG KL IB   36D  PERK 10   9  20700  5  9  46100  50700
         40  9 RELIANT 41            YWL  SA/RC FBG KL IB    31  UNIV 10   9  20700  5  9  45600  50200
         40  9 RELIANT 41            YWL  SA/RC FBG KL IB   36D  PERK 10   9  20700  5  9  46100  50700
         46 10 CALIFORNIA 32         SLP  SAIL      IB     D        10   9          6 10  84200  92500
         ----------------- 1963 BOATS -----------------------------------------------------------------
         29  7 BERMUDA 30            SLP  SA/CR WD  KL IB    D         8   9  10000  3  8  18900  21000
```

CHEVERTON BOATS

Call 1-800-327-6929 for BUC Personalized Evaluation Service
Or, for 1959 to 1960 boats, sign onto www.BUCValuPro.com

CHEYENNE BOAT MFG INC
COAST GUARD MFG ID- CYF

Call 1-800-327-6929 for BUC Personalized Evaluation Service
Or, for 1980 to 1984 boats, sign onto www.BUCValuPro.com

CHIEN HWA BOAT MFG & IND LTD
TAIPEI TAIWAN   COAST GUARD MFG ID- CBK See inside cover to adjust price for area

DIST MARIN YACHT SALES
SAN RAFAEL CA 94901

For more recent years, see the BUC Used Boat Price Guide, Volume 1 or Volume 2

```
         LOA  NAME AND/              TOP/ BOAT  -HULL-  ----ENGINE---  BEAM    WGT   DRAFT RETAIL RETAIL
         FT IN OR MODEL              RIG  TYPE  MTL TP  TP # HP   MFG  FT IN   LBS   FT IN  LOW   HIGH
         ----------------- 1983 BOATS -----------------------------------------------------------------
         33  6 CHIEN-HWA 34          FB   TRWL  FBG DS IB  120D-135D  11  9  16000  3  2  50700  55800
         33  6 CHIEN-HWA 34 SEDAN    FB   TRWL  FBG DS IB  120D-135D  11  9  16000  3  2  50700  55800
         33  6 CHIEN-HWA 34 SEDAN    FB   TRWL  FBG DS IB  T80D-T124D 11  9  16500  3  2  52900  60100
         34  5 CHIEN-HWA 35 DC       FB   TRWL  FBG DS IB  120D-135D  12     16500  3  2  53600  59800
         34  5 CHIEN-HWA 35 DC       FB   TRWL  FBG DS IB  T80D-T135D 12     17000  3  2  55800  64200
         38 10 CHIEN-HWA 39          FB   TRWL  FBG DS IB  120D LEHM  13  6  27000  3  8  82500  90700
         38 10 CHIEN-HWA 39          FB   TRWL  FBG DS IB  T120D LEHM 13  6  28500  3  8  90400  99300
         42  4 KROGEN 42             FB   TRWL  FBG DS IB  120D LEHM  15     39500  4  7 116000 127500
         ----------------- 1982 BOATS -----------------------------------------------------------------
         33  6 CHIEN-HWA 34          FB   TRWL  FBG DS IB  120D-135D  11  9  16000  3  2  48800  54600
         33  6 CHIEN-HWA 34          FB   TRWL  FBG DS IB  T80D-T124D 11  9  16000  3  2  49900  57700
         33  6 CHIEN-HWA 34 DC       FB   TRWL  FBG DS IB  120D-135D  11  9  16000  3  2  48800  54600
         33  6 CHIEN-HWA 34 DC       FB   TRWL  FBG DS IB  T80D-T124D 11  9  16500  3  2  50800  57700
         34  5 CHIEN-HWA 35 DC       FB   TRWL  FBG DS IB  120D-135D  12     16500  3  2  51500  57000
         34  5 CHIEN-HWA 35 DC       FB   TRWL  FBG DS IB  T80D-T135D 12     17000  3  2  53700  61700
         38 10 CHIEN-HWA 39          FB   TRWL  FBG DS IB  120D LEHM  13  6  27000  3  8  78800  86500
         38 10 CHIEN-HWA 39          FB   TRWL  FBG DS IB  T120D LEHM 13  6  28500  3  8  86300  94800
         42  4 KROGEN 42             FB   TRWL  FBG DS IB  120D LEHM  15     39500  4  7 111000 121500
         ----------------- 1981 BOATS -----------------------------------------------------------------
         33  6 CHIEN-HWA 34          FB   TRWL  FBG DS IB  120D LEHM  11  9  16000  3  2  47100  51800
         33  6 CHIEN-HWA 34 DC       FB   TRWL  FBG DS IB  120D LEHM  11  9  16000  3  2  47100  51800
         34  5 CHIEN-HWA 35 DC       FB   TRWL  FBG DS IB  120D-124D  12     16500  3  2  49500  55300
         34  5 CHIEN-HWA 35 DC       FB   TRWL  FBG DS IB  T80D-T124D 12     17000  3  2  51600  58200
         38 10 CHIEN-HWA 39          FB   TRWL  FBG DS IB  120D LEHM  13  6  28500  3  8  82200  90300
         42  4 KROGEN 42             FB   TRWL  FBG DS IB  120D LEHM  15     39500  4  7 105500 116000
         ----------------- 1980 BOATS -----------------------------------------------------------------
         33  6 CHIEN-HWA 34          FB   TRWL  FBG DS IB  120D LEHM  11  9  16000  3  2  44500  49500
         33  6 CHIEN-HWA 34 DC       FB   TRWL  FBG DS IB  120D LEHM  11  9  16000  3  2  45700  50200
         33  6 CHIEN-HWA 34 DC       FB   TRWL  FBG DS IB  T 80D LEHM 11  9  16000  3  2  46400  51000
         34  5 CHIEN-HWA 35 DC       FB   TRWL  FBG DS IB  120D-124D  12     16500  3  2  47900  53200
         34  5 CHIEN-HWA 35 DC       FB   TRWL  FBG DS IB  T80D-T124D 12     17000  3  2  49600  56100
         38 10 CHIEN-HWA 39          FB   TRWL  FBG DS IB  120D LEHM  13  6  27000  3  8  71600  78700
         38 10 CHIEN-HWA 39          FB   TRWL  FBG DS IB  T120D LEHM 13  6  28500  3  8  78400  86100
         42  4 KROGEN 42             FB   TRWL  FBG DS IB  120D LEHM  15     39500  4  7 100500 110500
```

CHIPPENDALE BOATS LTD

Call 1-800-327-6929 for BUC Personalized Evaluation Service
Or, for 1965 to 1972 boats, sign onto www.BUCValuPro.com

CHITA INC

Call 1-800-327-6929 for BUC Personalized Evaluation Service
Or, for 1983 boats, sign onto www.BUCValuPro.com

DENNIS CHOATE SAILBOATS
LONG BEACH CA 90813   COAST GUARD MFG ID- CFJ See inside cover to adjust price for area
                        FOR MORE RECENT YEARS SEE DENCHO MARINE INC

```
         LOA  NAME AND/              TOP/ BOAT  -HULL-  ----ENGINE---  BEAM    WGT   DRAFT RETAIL RETAIL
         FT IN OR MODEL              RIG  TYPE  MTL TP  TP # HP   MFG  FT IN   LBS   FT IN  LOW   HIGH
         ----------------- 1980 BOATS -----------------------------------------------------------------
         39  8 CHOATE 40             SLP  SA/RC F/S KL IB   30D       12  5  14000  6  9  40900  45500
         43  9 CHOATE 44             SLP  SA/RC KEV KL IB   40D       13  2  19000  7  6  61700  67800
```

CHOY SEAMAN & KUMALAE

Call 1-800-327-6929 for BUC Personalized Evaluation Service
Or, for 1968 to 1970 boats, sign onto www.BUCValuPro.com

CHRIS CRAFT BOATS
OMC COMPANY   See inside cover to adjust price for area
SARASOTA FL 34243   COAST GUARD MFG ID- CCB

For more recent years, see the BUC Used Boat Price Guide, Volume 1 or Volume 2

```
         LOA  NAME AND/              TOP/ BOAT  -HULL-  ----ENGINE---  BEAM    WGT   DRAFT RETAIL RETAIL
         FT IN OR MODEL              RIG  TYPE  MTL TP  TP # HP  MFG   FT IN   LBS   FT IN  LOW   HIGH
         ----------------- 1983 BOATS -----------------------------------------------------------------
         16 11 SCORPION 167BR        OP   RNBT  FBG DV OB           6   9   1455  2  8   2850   3300
         16 11 SCORPION 168BR        OP   RNBT  FBG DV IO  120-140  6   9   2620  2  8   2700   3300
         16 11 SCORPION 169S         OP   RNBT  FBG DV IO           6   9   2620  2  8   2700   3200
         16 11 SCORPION 169SL        OP   RNBT  FBG DV IO  120-140  6   9   2620  2  8   2800   3300
         17  3 170SC                 OP   RNBT  FBG TR OB           7   4   1210  2  4   2450   2850
```

LOA FT	LOA IN	NAME AND/ OR MODEL	TOP/ RIG	BOAT TYPE	-HULL- MTL	-HULL- TP	ENGINE TP	ENGINE # HP	ENGINE MFG	BEAM FT	BEAM IN	WGT LBS	DRAFT FT	DRAFT IN	RETAIL LOW	RETAIL HIGH
		1983 BOATS														
17	3	170SC	OP	RNBT	FBG	TR	IO	170-188		7	4	2475	2	7	2900	3350
17	3	SPRINT 170	OP	CTRCN	FBG	TR	IO	140		7	4	2225	2	5	2900	3350
17	11	SCORPION 182BR	OP	RNBT	FBG	DV	IO	185-200		7	8	2752	2	8	3250	3800
17	11	SCORPION 183S	OP	RNBT	FBG	DV	IO	185-200		7	8	2752	2	8	3200	3850
17	11	SCORPION 183SL	OP	RNBT	FBG	DV	IO	185-200		7	8	2752	2	8	3200	3850
17	11	SCORPION 184VF	OP	CTRCN	FBG	DV	OB			7	8	1900	2	8	3400	3950
18	6	190SC	OP	RNBT	FBG	TR	IO	198-260		7	8	2300	2	7	3000	3700
18	6	190SI	OP	CTRCN	FBG	TR	OB			7	8	1285	2	4	2650	3100
18	6	190SI	OP	CTRCN	FBG	TR	IO	198-260		7	8	2300	2	7	3350	4150
18	6	ELITE 190	OP	RNBT	FBG	TR	IO	198-260		7	8	2300	2	7	3150	3900
18	6	SPRINT 190	OP	CTRCN	FBG	TR	IO	170-200				2250	2	7	3350	3950
20	5	SCORPION 215WAC	OP	RNBT	FBG	DV	IO	170-230		8		2950	2	6	4150	5150
20	5	SCORPION 216WAC	OP	RNBT	FBG	DV	OB			8		1981	2	6	4650	5350
20	7	SCORPION 210BR	OP	RNBT	FBG	DV	IO	225-260		8		3348	2	8	4850	5750
20	7	SCORPION 210S	OP	RNBT	FBG	DV	IO	225-260		8		3239	2	8	4750	5650
20	7	SCORPION 210SL	OP	RNBT	FBG	DV	IO	225-260		8		3220	2	8	4700	5700
21	3	SCORPION 211VF	OP	RNBT	FBG	DV	IO	170-175		8		3160	2	6	4550	5450
21	3	SCORPION 211VF	OP	RNBT	FBG	DV	IO	225-260		8		3339	2	6	5000	6000
21	3	SCORPION 212VF	OP	UTL	FBG	DV	OB			8		2370	1	3	4900	5650
21	3	SCORPION 213VF	OP	CTRCN	FBG	DV	OB			8		2300	1	3	5350	6150
21	3	SCORPION 214VF	OP	CTRCN	FBG	DV	IO	198-260		8		3200	1	3	5100	6150
21	6	ELITE 220	OP	RNBT	FBG	TR	IO	260		7	10	2700	2	8	4400	5050
22	2	SCORPION 230S	OP	RNBT	FBG	DV	IO	260		8		3550	2	10	5350	6400
22	2	SCORPION 230SL	OP	RNBT	FBG	DV	IO	260		8		3570	2	10	5400	6450
25	4	CATALINA 251	OP	EXP	FBG	DV	IB	225-230		9	9	4600	2	3	10100	11500
26		CORINTHIAN BRDGE 263	OP	EXP	FBG	DV	IB	T225	MPC	10	6	6800	2	2	15200	17200
26		CORINTHIAN BRDGE 263	OP	EXP	FBG	DV	IB	T124D	VLVO	10	6	6800	2	2	20400	22600
26		CORINTHIAN BRDGE 266	OP	EXP	FBG	DV	IB	225	MPC	10	6	6800	2	2	13600	15500
26	4	SCORPION 260		RNBT	FBG	DV	IO	330		8					8900	10100
26	4	SCORPION 260		RNBT	FBG	DV	IO	T260		8					9700	11000
26	5	SCORPION 264AC	OP	EXP	FBG	DV	IO	260		8	6	4801	2	11	9050	10300
26	5	SCORPION 265WAC	OP	OPFSH	FBG	DV	IO	260		8	6	4501			9050	10300
26	5	STINGER 260SL	OP	SPTCR	FBG	DV	IO	T260	MRCR	8		5252			11000	12500
28	11	CATALINA 280	OP	EXP	FBG	DV	IB	225-230		10	8	6300	2	5	14600	16700
28	11	CATALINA 280	OP	EXP	FBG	DV	IB	124D	VLVO	10	8	6300	2	5	15600	17700
28	11	CATALINA 281	OP	EXP	FBG	DV	IB	T225-T230		10	8	7000	2	3	17200	19700
28	11	CATALINA 291 BRIDGE	FB	EXP	FBG	DV	IB	T230	MRCR	10	8	7800	2	3	18300	20400
28	11	CATALINA BRIDGE 291	FB	EXP	FBG	DV	IB	T225	MPC	10	8	7800	2	3	18300	20300
31	6	SCORPION 311VF	OP	CTRCN	FBG	DV	OB			8		4100	1	5	18900	21000
31	6	STINGER 312SL	OP	RACE	FBG	DV	IO	T330-T400		8		6854	3		15100	18100
33		COMMANDER BRIDGE 333	FB	SDN	FBG	DV	IB	T250-T340		12	4	13000	2	9	33600	39500
33		COMMANDER BRIDGE 333	FB	SDN	FBG	DV	IB	T235D	VLVO	12	4	14940	2	9	47000	51700
33		COMMANDER EXP 332	OP	EXP	FBG	DV	IB	T250-T340		12	4	11560	2	9	30500	35600
33		COMMANDER EXP 332	OP	EXP	FBG	DV	IB	T160D-T235D		12	4	13500	2	9	38000	44700
33		COMMANDER EXP 332	HT	EXP	FBG	DV	IB	T250-T340		12	4	12360	2	9	31000	36100
33		COMMANDER EXP 332	HT	EXP	FBG	DV	IB	T158D-T235D		12	4	14300	2	9	39200	46000
33		COMMANDER EXP 332	FB	EXP	FBG	DV	IB	T250-T340		12	4	12700	2	9	31200	36300
33		COMMANDER EXP 332	FB	EXP	FBG	DV	IO	T165D	VLVO	12	4	14640	2	9	29600	32900
33		COMMANDER EXP 332	FB	EXP	FBG	DV	IB	T235D	VLVO	12	4	14640	2	9	42000	46600
33		COMMANDER MID-CAB336	OP	EXP	FBG	DV	VD	T250-T340		12	4	12360	2	9	31000	36100
35	1	CATALINA 350	FB	DC	FBG	DV	IB	T235	MPC	13	1	17229	2	10	39800	44200
35	1	CATALINA 350	FB	DC	FBG	DV	IB	T260	MRCR	13	1	17229	3	2	40100	44600
36		COMMANDER 360	FB	SDNSF	FBG	DV	IB	T330	MPC	13		22600	3	2	55100	60500
		IB T340 MRCR 55300 60700, IB T300D CAT 71200 78300, IB T320D CUM													70800	77800
36		WEST INDIAN 361	FB	TRWL	FBG	SV	IB	120D	PERK	13		17500	2	10	50700	55800
36		WEST INDIAN 361	FB	TRWL	FBG	SV	IB	T 85D	PERK	13		17500	2	10	52700	57900
37	10	CATALINA 381	FB	DC	FBG	DV	IB	T330	MPC	14		21600	3		58500	64300
37	10	CATALINA 381	FB	DC	FBG	DV	IB	T340	MRCR	14		21600	3		58700	64500
37	10	CATALINA 381	FB	DC	FBG	DV	IB	T235D	VLVO	14		23600	3		69100	75900
37	10	CORINTHIAN 380	FB	SDNSF	FBG	DV	IB	T330	MPC	14		22500	3		60600	66500
37	10	CORINTHIAN 380	FB	SDNSF	FBG	DV	IB	T340	MRCR	14		22500	3		60700	66700
37	10	CORINTHIAN 380	FB	SDNSF	FBG	DV	IB	T235D	VLVO	14		24500	3		71200	78200
39		SCORPION 390SL	OP	RACE	FBG	DV	IO	T370	MRCR	9		9140	3	4	29200	32400
39		SCORPION 390SL	OP	RACE	FBG	DV	IO	T400	MRCR	9		8960	3	4	30200	33600
39		STINGER 390X	OP	RACE	FBG	DV	IO	T370	MRCR	9		8940	3	4	29200	32400
39		STINGER 390X	OP	RACE	FBG	DV	IO	T400	MRCR	9		8760	3	4	30200	33600
41		COMMANDER 410	HT	MY	FBG	DV	IB	T330	MPC	14		26565	3	4	78600	86400
41		COMMANDER 410	HT	MY	FBG	DV	IB	T340	MRCR	14		26565	3	4	78900	86700
41		COMMANDER 410	HT	MY	FBG	DV	IB	T286D	VLVO	14		29213	3	4	92700	102000
41		COMMANDER 410	FB	MY	FBG	DV	IB	T330	MPC	14		26565	3	4	78500	86300
41		COMMANDER 410	FB	MY	FBG	DV	IB	T340	MRCR	14		26565	3	4	78900	86700
41		COMMANDER 410	FB	MY	FBG	DV	IB	T286D	VLVO	14		29213	3	4	92700	102000
42		COMMANDER 421	F+T	SDNSF	FBG	DV	IB	T425D	GM	14		34750	3	11	112000	123000
42		COMMANDER 421	F+T	SDNSF	FBG	DV	IB	T500D	J&T	14		34750	3	11	119000	130500
		1982 BOATS														
17	6	SUPER-SPORT 170	OP	RNBT	FBG	SV	IB	250		6	10	2790			3850	4500
17	11	SCORPION 182BR	OP	RNBT	FBG	DV	IO	175-225		7	8	2600	2	8	3200	3850
17	11	SCORPION 183SL	OP	RNBT	FBG	DV	IO	175-225		7	8	2600	2	8	3300	3950
17	11	SCORPION 184VF	OP	CTRCN	FBG	DV	OB			7	8	2050	2	8	3500	4050
20	7	SCORPION 210S	OP	RNBT	FBG	DV	IO	225-260							5050	5800
20	7	SCORPION 210SL	OP	RNBT	FBG	DV	IO	225-228		8		3220	2	8	4700	5350
20	7	SCORPION 210SL	OP	RNBT	FBG	DV	IO	260		8		3270	2	8	4700	5850
21	3	SCORPION 211VF	OP	CBNCR	FBG	DV	IO	175-260		8			2	6	5700	6650
21	3	SCORPION 211VF	OP	UTL	FBG	DV	IO	175-260		8		3050	2	6	5050	5900
21	3	SCORPION 212VF	OP	UTL	FBG	DV	OB			8		2370	1	3	4800	5550
21	3	SCORPION 213VF	OP	CTRCN	FBG	DV	OB			8		2300	1	3	5250	6050
21	3	SCORPION 214VF	OP	CTRCN	FBG	DV	IO	260	MRCR	8		2980	1	3	5050	5800
22	2	SCORPION 230S	OP	RNBT	FBG	DV	IO	260-290		8		3550	2	10	5300	6550
22	2	SCORPION 230SL	OP	RNBT	FBG	DV	IO	260-290		8		3570	2	10	5300	6600
24		SCORPION 250		SPTCR	FBG	DV	IO			8	6				**	**
25	2	SCORPION 255CC	OP	CUD	FBG	DV	IO	260		8		3570	2	10	6800	8000
25	4	CATALINA 251	OP	EXP	FBG	DV	IB	225	MPC	9	9	4600	2	3	9700	11000
25	4	CATALINA 251	HT	EXP	FBG	DV	IB	225	MPC	9	9	4600	2	3	9700	11000
26		CORINTHIAN 263	FB	SDN	FBG	DV	IB	225	MPC	10	3	8750	2	8	16400	18600
26		CORINTHIAN 263	FB	SDN	FBG	DV	IB	124D	VLVO	10	3	9186	2	8	23300	25900
26	5	SCORPION 264AC	OP	EXP	FBG	DV	IO	260		8		5140	2	11	9150	10500
26	5	STINGER 260SL	OP	SPTCR	FBG	DV	IO	T260	MRCR	8		5140			10700	12200
28	11	CATALINA 280	OP	EXP	FBG	DV	IB	225	MPC	10	8	6300	2	5	14100	16100
28	11	CATALINA 280	OP	EXP	FBG	DV	IB	124D	VLVO	10	8	6300	2	5	15100	17100
28	11	CATALINA 280	HT	EXP	FBG	DV	IB	225	MPC	10	8	6300	2	5	14100	16100
28	11	CATALINA 280	HT	EXP	FBG	DV	IB	124D	VLVO	10	8	6300	2	5	15100	17100
28	11	CATALINA 281	OP	EXP	FBG	DV	IB	T225	MPC	10	8	7000	2	3	16600	18900
28	11	CATALINA 281	HT	EXP	FBG	DV	IB	T225	MPC	10	8	7000	2	3	16600	18900
31	6	SCORPION 311VF	OP	CTRCN	FBG	DV	OB			8		4100	1	5	18500	20500
31	6	STINGER 312SL	OP	RACE	FBG	DV	IO	T330-T370		8		4800	3		14700	17400
33		CONVERTIBLE 335	FB	SDN	FBG	DV	IB	T330	MPC	8		6800	3		27100	30100
33		CONVERTIBLE 335	FB	SDN	FBG	DV	IB	T221D	VLVO	8		6800	3		34400	38200
33		EXPRESS 332	OP	EXP	FBG	DV	IB	T250-T330		12	4	11560	2	9	29400	34100
33		EXPRESS 332	OP	EXP	FBG	DV	IB	T155D	VLVO	12	4	11500	2	9	33600	37400
33		SEDAN 333	FB	SDN	FBG	DV	IB	T250-T330		12	4	13000	2	9	32400	37100
33		SEDAN 333	FB	SDN	FBG	DV	IB	T221D	VLVO	12	4	11500	2	9	40100	44600
35	1	CATALINA 350	FB	DC	FBG	DV	IB	T235	MPC	13	1	17229	2	10	38400	42700
35	1	CATALINA 350	FB	DC	FBG	SV	IB	T250		13	1	17229			38600	42900
36		COMMANDER 360	FB	SDNSF	FBG	DV	IB	T330	MPC	13		20174	3	2	49500	54400
36		COMMANDER 360	FB	SDNSF	FBG	DV	IB	T300D	CAT	13		22174	3	2	62900	69100
36		COMMANDER 360	FB	SDNSF	FBG	DV	IB	T320D	CUM	13		22174	3	2	62500	68600
37	10	CATALINA 381	FB	DC	FBG	DV	IB	T221	VLVO	14		23600	3		59900	65800
37	10	CATALINA 381	FB	DC	FBG	DV	IB	T330	MPC	14		21600	3		56300	61900
37	10	CORINTHIAN 380	FB	SDNSF	FBG	DV	IB	T221	VLVO	14		22500	3		57500	63200
37	10	CORINTHIAN 380	FB	SDNSF	FBG	DV	IB	T330	MPC	14		22500	3		58200	64000
38		CATALINA 381	FB	DC	FBG	SV	IB	T300		14		21600			56400	61900
38		CORINTHIAN 380	FB	SDNSF	FBG	SV	IB	T300		14		22500			58300	64100
39		SCORPION 390SL	OP	RACE	FBG	DV	IO	T330	MRCR	9		8500	3	4	27900	30900
39		SCORPION 390SL	OP	RACE	FBG	DV	IO	T370	MRCR	9		8600	3	4	29000	32200
39		STINGER 390X	OP	RACE	FBG	DV	IO	T330	MRCR	9		8500	3	4	27200	30300
39		STINGER 390X	OP	RACE	FBG	DV	IO	T370	MRCR	9		8600	3	4	28400	31600
41		COMMANDER 410	HT	MY	FBG	DV	IB	T330	MPC	14		26565	3	4	75600	83100
41		COMMANDER 410	HT	MY	FBG	DV	IB	T286D	VLVO	14		29213	3	4	89200	98000
41		COMMANDER 410	HT	MY	FBG	SV	IB	T300		14		26565			74500	81800
41		COMMANDER 410	FB	MY	FBG	DV	IB	T330	MPC	14		26565	3	4	75500	83000
41		COMMANDER 410	FB	MY	FBG	DV	IB	T286D	VLVO	14		29213	3	4	89100	97900
		1981 BOATS														
17	6	SUPER-SPORT	OP	RNBT	FBG	SV	IB	250	MPC	6	10	2790	2	3	3700	4350
17	11	SCORPION 182	OP	RNBT	FBG	DV	IO	185	MRCR	7	8	2600	2	8	3100	3600
20	7	SCORPION 210S	OP	RNBT	FBG	DV	IO	228-260		8		3200	2	8	4450	5300
20	7	SCORPION 210SL	OP	RNBT	FBG	DV	IO	228-260		8		3250	2	8	4500	5350
21	3	SCORPION 211VF	OP	UTL	FBG	DV	IO	185	MRCR	8		3050	2	6	4850	5550
21	3	SCORPION 212VF	OP	UTL	FBG	DV	OB			8		2370	1	3	4700	5400
21	3	SCORPION 213VF	OP	CTRCN	FBG	DV	OB			8		2300	1	3	5100	5900
22	2	SCORPION 230S	OP	RNBT	FBG	DV	IO	260	MRCR	8		3550	2	10	5250	6000
22	2	SCORPION 230SL	OP	RNBT	FBG	DV	IO	260	MRCR	8		3570	2	10	5250	6050
25	4	CATALINA 251	OP	EXP	FBG	DV	IB	225	MPC	9	9	4600	2	3	9450	10700
25	4	CATALINA 251	HT	EXP	FBG	DV	IB	225	MPC	9	9	4600	2	3	9450	10700
25	4	CATALINA 252	OP	EXP	FBG	DV	IO	228	MRCR	9	9	4600	2	3	8000	9150
25	4	CATALINA 252	HT	EXP	FBG	DV	IO	228	MRCR	9	9	4600	2	3	8000	9150

 CONTINUED ON NEXT PAGE

LOA FT	IN	NAME AND/ OR MODEL	TOP/ RIG	BOAT TYPE	HULL MTL	HULL TP	ENGINE TP	# HP	MFG	BEAM FT	BEAM IN	WGT LBS	DRAFT FT	DRAFT IN	RETAIL LOW	RETAIL HIGH
		1981 BOATS														
26		CORINTHIAN 261		EXP	FBG	SV	IB	250		10	5				11200	12800
26		CORINTHIAN 262	FB	SDN	FBG	DV	IB	T225	MPC	10	3	8750	2	8	17400	19800
26		CORINTHIAN 262	FB	SDN	FBG	DV	IB	T124D	VLVO	10	3	9186	2	8	25600	28500
26	5	SCORPION 260SL	OP	RNBT	FBG	DV	IO	T260-T330		8		5140	2	11	9700	12100
28	11	CATALINA 280	OP	EXP	FBG	DV	IB	225	MPC	10	8	6300	2	5	13600	15500
28	11	CATALINA 280	OP	EXP	FBG	DV	IB	124D	VLVO	10	8	6300	2	5	14600	16600
28	11	CATALINA 280	OP	EXP	FBG	SV	IB	250		10	8				14500	16500
28	11	CATALINA 280	HT	EXP	FBG	DV	IB	225	MPC	10	8	6300	2	5	13600	15500
28	11	CATALINA 280	HT	EXP	FBG	DV	IB	124D	VLVO	10	8	6300	2	5	14600	16600
28	11	CATALINA 281	OP	EXP	FBG	DV	IB	T225	MPC	10	8	7000	2	3	16000	18200
28	11	CATALINA 281	HT	EXP	FBG	DV	IB	T225	MPC	10	8	7000	2	3	16000	18200
30	10	CATALINA 310	OP	SPTCR	FBG	DV	IB	T250	MPC	11	9	11704	2	3	23800	26400
30	10	CATALINA 310	OP	SPTCR	FBG	DV	IB	T124D	VLVO	11	9	11704	2	3	28800	32000
30	10	CATALINA 310	HT	SPTCR	FBG	DV	IB	T250	MPC	11	9	11704	2	3	23800	26400
30	10	CATALINA 310	HT	SPTCR	FBG	DV	IB	T124D	VLVO	11	9	11704	2	3	28800	32000
30	10	CATALINA 310	FB	SPTCR	FBG	DV	IB	T250	MPC	11	9	11704	2	3	23800	26400
30	10	CATALINA 310	FB	SPTCR	FBG	DV	IB	T124D	VLVO	11	9	11704	2	3	28800	32000
31	6	SCORPION 310		RNBT	FBG	DV	IO	T330		8					14900	16900
31	6	SCORPION 311SL	OP	CTRCN	FBG	DV	OB			8		4100	1	5	18100	20100
31	6	SCORPION 312SL	OP	RACE	FBG	DV	IO	T330-T370		8		6700	3		14700	17200
33		EXPRESS 332	OP	EXP	FBG	DV	IB	T260-T330		12	4	11050	2	9	28200	32900
33		EXPRESS 332	OP	EXP	FBG	DV	IB	T124D	VLVO	12	4	11500	2	9	31700	35200
33		EXPRESS 332	OP	EXP	FBG	SV	IB	T250		12	4				27600	30700
33		SEDAN 333	FB	SDN	FBG	DV	IB	T250	MPC	12	4		2	9	26700	29700
33		SEDAN 333	FB	SDN	FBG	DV	IB	T330	MPC	12	4	11500	2	9	32200	35800
33		SEDAN 333	FB	SDN	FBG	DV	IB	T221D	VLVO	12	4	11500	2	9	38800	43200
33	1	TRAWLER 334	FB	TRWL	FBG	DV	IB	124D	VLVO	12	5	12400	2	4	35500	39500
33	1	TRAWLER 334	FB	TRWL	FBG	SV	IB	203D		12	5				30600	34000
35	1	CATALINA 350		DC	FBG	SV	IB	T250		13	1				31000	34500
35	1	CATALINA 350	FB	DC	FBG	DV	IB	T235	MPC	13	1	17229	2	10	37100	41200
36		COMMANDER 360		SDNSF	FBG	SV	IB	T300		13					41600	46300
36		COMMANDER 360	FB	SDNSF	FBG	DV	IB	T330	MPC	13		20174	3	2	47800	52500
36		COMMANDER 360	FB	SDNSF	FBG	DV	IB	T250D	CUM	13		22174	3	2	57600	63300
37	10	CATALINA 381	FB	DC	FBG	DV	IB	T330	MPC	14		21600	3		54000	59400
37	10	CATALINA 381	FB	DC	FBG	DV	IB	T205D	CUM	14		23600	3		63800	70100
37	10	CATALINA 381	FB	DC	FBG	SV	IB	T300		14					49400	54300
37	10	CORINTHIAN 380	FB	SDNSF	FBG	DV	IB	T330	MPC	14		22500	3		55900	61400
37	10	CORINTHIAN 380	FB	SDNSF	FBG	SV	IB	T300		14					46100	50600
37	10	TRAWLER 382	FB	TRWL	FBG	DV	IB	T124D	VLVO	14		20700	3		55600	61100
38		TRAWLER 382	FB	TRWL	FBG	SV	IB	T203D		14					62000	68100
39		SCORPION 390SL	OP	RACE	FBG	DV	IO	T370	MRCR	9		8600	3	4	28500	31700
41		COMMANDER 410	HT	MY	FBG	DV	IB	T330	MPC	14		26565	3	4	72500	79700
41		COMMANDER 410	HT	MY	FBG	DV	IB	T286D	CUM	14		29213	3	4	86700	95200
41		COMMANDER 410	HT	MY	FBG	SV	IB	T300		14					58200	64000
41		COMMANDER 410	FB	MY	FBG	DV	IB	T330	MPC	14		26565	3	4	72500	79600
41		COMMANDER 410	FB	MY	FBG	DV	IB	T286D	CUM	14		29213	3	4	86600	95100
42	3	COMMANDER 420		SF	FBG	SV	IB	T425D		14					106000	116500
45		COMMANDER 451		MY	FBG	SV	IB	T325D		15					79300	87200
45	6	COMMANDER 450		SF	FBG	SV	IB	T425D		16					103000	113000
		1980 BOATS														
17	6	SUPER-SPORT	OP	RNBT	FBG	SV	IB	225	MPC	6	10	2790	2	3	3550	4150
20	7	SCORPION 210S	OP	RNBT	FBG	DV	IO	228-260		8		3200	2	8	4450	5300
20	7	SCORPION 210SL	OP	RNBT	FBG	DV	IO	228-260		8		3250	2	8	4500	5350
21	3	211VF	OP	UTL	FBG	DV	OB			8		2370			4600	5300
21	3	SCORPION 211VF	OP	UTL	FBG	DV	IO	170	MRCR	8		3050	2	6	4800	5550
21	3	SCORPION 212VF	OP	UTL	FBG	DV	OB			8		2370	1	3	4600	5300
21	3	SCORPION 213VF	OP	CTRCN	FBG	DV	OB			8		2300	1	3	5000	5750
22	2	SCORPION 230S	OP	RNBT	FBG	DV	IO	210-260		8		3550	2	10	5050	5900
22	2	SCORPION 230S	OP	RNBT	FBG	DV	IO	330	MRCR	8		3925	2	10	6200	7100
22	2	SCORPION 230SL	OP	RNBT	FBG	DV	IO	260	MRCR	8		3570	2	10	5250	6050
22	2	SCORPION 230SL	OP	RNBT	FBG	DV	IO	330	MRCR	8		3945	2	10	6200	7150
25	4	CATALINA	OP	EXP	FBG	DV	IB	225	MPC	9	9	4600	2	3	9100	10300
25	4	CATALINA	HT	EXP	FBG	DV	IB	225	MPC	9	9	4600	2	3	9100	10300
26		CORINTHIAN	FB	SDN	FBG	DV	IB	250	MPC	10	6	7950	2	2	14500	16400
26		CORINTHIAN	FB	SDN	FBG	DV	IB	T225	MPC	10	6	8750	2	2	16900	19200
26		CORINTHIAN	FB	SDN	FBG	DV	IB	T124D	VLVO	10	6	9186	2	2	24900	27700
26	5	SCORPION 260SL	OP	RNBT	FBG	DV	IO	330	MRCR	8		4615	2	11	8400	9650
26	5	SCORPION 260SL	OP	RNBT	FBG	DV	IO	T260	MRCR	8		5140	2	11	9700	11000
28	11	CATALINA	OP	EXP	FBG	DV	IB	225	MPC	10	8	6300	2	5	13200	14900
28	11	CATALINA	OP	EXP	FBG	DV	IB	T225	MPC	10	8	7000	2	3	15500	17600
28	11	CATALINA	HT	EXP	FBG	DV	IB	225	MPC	10	8	6300	2	5	13200	14900
28	11	CATALINA	HT	EXP	FBG	DV	IB	124D	VLVO	10	8	6300	2	5	14100	16100
28	11	CATALINA	HT	EXP	FBG	DV	IB	T225	MPC	10	8	7000	2	3	15500	17600
28	11	CATALINA EXPRESS	OP	EXP	FBG	DV	IB	124D	VLVO	10	8	6300	2	5	14100	16100
30	10	CATALINA	FB	SPTCR	FBG	DV	IB	T250	MPC	11	9	11704	2	3	23000	25500
30	10	CATALINA EXPRESS	FB	SPTCR	FBG	DV	IB	T124D	VLVO	11	9	11704	2	3	27900	31000
31	6	EXCALIBUR	OP	RACE	FBG	DV	IO	T330	MRCR	8		6700	3		14700	16700
31	6	EXCALIBUR 310	OP	RACE	FBG	DV	IO	T370	MRCR	8		6800	3		15100	17200
31	6	EXCALIBUR 311	OP	CTRCN	FBG	DV	OB			8		4100	1	5	17400	19800
33		EXPRESS	OP	EXP	FBG	DV	IB	T250-T330		11	6	11050	2	11	27200	31800
33	1	CATALINA	HT	SDN	FBG	DV	IB	T250	MPC	12	5	14800	2	4	31200	34700
33	1	CATALINA	FB	SDN	FBG	DV	IB	T250	MPC	12	5	14800	2	4	31200	34700
33	1	CATALINA SEDAN	HT	SDN	FBG	DV	IB	T145D	PERK	12	5	15714	2	4	40600	45100
33	1	CORINTHIAN	FB	SDN	FBG	DV	IB	T250	MPC	12	5	11976	2	4	29800	33100
35	1	CATALINA	FB	DC	FBG	DV	IB	T235	MPC	13	1	17229	2	10	35800	39700
35	1	CATALINA DOUBLE CBN	FB	DC	FBG	DV	IB	T145D	PERK	13	1	18145	2	10	46300	50800
36		COMMANDER	FB	SDNSF	FBG	DV	IB	T330	MPC	13		22600	3	2	48900	53700
36		COMMANDER	FB	SDNSF	FBG	DV	IB	T250D	CUM	13		25300	3	2	60500	66500
38		CATALINA DOUBLE CBN	FB	DC	FBG	DV	IB	T330	MPC	14		21600	3		52400	57600
38		CATALINA DOUBLE CBN	FB	DC	FBG	DV	IB	T203D	CUM	14		23300	3		61100	67100
38		CATALINA DOUBLE CBN	FB	DC	FBG	DV	IB	T252D	CAT	14		23450	3		64400	70800
38		CORINTHIAN	FB	SDN	FBG	DV	IB	T330	MPC	14		21900	3		53200	58500
		IB T124D VLVO 56400 62000, IB T203D CUM 62000 68200, IB T252D CAT 65400 71900														
39		SCORPION 390SL	OP	RACE	FBG	DV	IO	T370	MRCR			9785	3	4	29800	33200
41		COMMANDER	HT	MY	FBG	DV	IB	T330	MPC	14		29800	3	4	77300	84900
41		COMMANDER	HT	MY	FBG	DV	IB	T286D	CUM	14		32900	3	4	92100	101000
41		COMMANDER	FB	MY	FBG	DV	IB	T330	MPC	14		29800	3	4	77200	84800
41		COMMANDER	FB	MY	FBG	DV	IB	T286D	CUM	14		32900	3	4	92000	101000
42	4	COMMANDER	FB	YTFS	FBG	DV	IB	T425D	GM	14		33000	3	11	104000	114500
45		COMMANDER	HT	MY	FBG	DV	IB	T325D	GM	15		39400	4	2	102500	112500
45		COMMANDER	FB	MY	FBG	DV	IB	T325D	GM	15		39400	4	2	102000	112000
45	6	COMMANDER	FB	SDNSF	FBG	DV	IB	T425D	GM	16		38700	3	11	112500	123500
		1979 BOATS														
17	6	SUPER-SPORT	OP	RNBT	FBG	SV	IB	225	MPC	6	10	2790	2	2	3450	4000
20	7	SCORPION 210S	ST	RNBT	FBG	DV	IO	228-260		8		3200			4500	5300
21	11	LANCER	ST	RNBT	FBG	DV	IB	250	MPC	8		3650	2	3	5950	6850
22	2	SCORPION 230S	ST	RNBT	FBG	DV	IO	260	MRCR	8		3550			5250	6050
22	4	CUTLASS	ST	CUD	FBG	SV	IB	225	MPC	8		3400	2	3	5700	6550
24	2	LANCER	ST	EXP	FBG	DV	IO	250	MPC	8		5000	2	9	7450	8550
25	4	CATALINA	OP	EXP	FBG	DV	IB	225	MPC	9	9	4600	2	3	8700	10000
26	5	SCORPION 260SL	ST	RNBT	FBG	DV	IO	T260	MRCR	8		5140			9750	11100
28	11	CATALINA	OP	EXP	FBG	DV	IB	225	MPC	10	8	7125	2	5	13300	15100
28	11	CATALINA	OP	EXP	FBG	DV	IB	T225	MPC	10	8	8125	2	3	15700	17800
30	10	CATALINA	FB	SDNSF	FBG	DV	IB	T250	MPC	11	9	11704	2	3	22100	24600
31	6	EXCALIBUR	OP	RACE	FBG	DV	IO	T330	MRCR	8		5300	2	4	14600	16600
33	1	CATALINA	HT	SDN	FBG	DV	IB	T250	MPC	12	5	14800	2	4	30200	33500
33	1	CATALINA	FB	SDN	FBG	DV	IB	T250	MPC	12	5	14800	2	4	30200	33500
33	1	CORINTHIAN	FB	SDN	FBG	DV	IB	T250	MPC	12	5	11976	2	4	28800	32000
35	1	CATALINA	FB	DC	FBG	DV	IB	T235	MPC	13	1	17229	2	10	34500	38400
36		COMMANDER	FB	SDNSF	FBG	DV	IB	T330	MPC	13		22600	3	2	47200	51900
36		COMMANDER	FB	SDNSF	FBG	DV	IB	T250D	CUM	13		25300	3	2	58200	64000
38		CORINTHIAN	FB	SDN	FBG	DV	IB	T330	MPC	14		21900	3		51200	56200
38		CORINTHIAN	FB	SDN	FBG	DV	IB	T128D	GM	14		21900	3		54700	60200
41		COMMANDER	HT	MY	FBG	DV	IB	T330	MPC	14		29800	3	4	74300	81700
41		COMMANDER	HT	MY	FBG	DV	IB	T286D	CUM	14		32900	3	4	88600	97300
41		COMMANDER	FB	MY	FBG	DV	IB	T330	MPC	14		29800	3	4	74300	81600
41		COMMANDER	FB	MY	FBG	DV	IB	T286D	CUM	14		32900	3	4	88500	97200
42	4	COMMANDER	FB	YTFS	FBG	DV	IB	T425D	GM	14		33000	3	11	100000	110000
45		COMMANDER	HT	MY	FBG	DV	IB	T325D	GM	15		39400	4	2	98600	108500
45		COMMANDER	FB	MY	FBG	DV	IB	T325D	GM	15		39400	4	2	98100	108000
45	6	COMMANDER	FB	SDNSF	FBG	DV	IB	T425D	GM	16		38700	3	11	108000	119000
		1978 BOATS														
17	6	SUPER-SPORT	OP	RNBT	FBG	SV	IB	130-225		6	10	2790	2	2	3150	3850
17	7	LANCER	ST	RNBT	FBG	DV	IO	140	MRCR	7	3	2600	2	6	2950	3450
17	7	LANCER-STINGER	ST	RNBT	FBG	DV	IO	225	MPC	7	3	2600	2	6	2700	3150
18	9	CROOKED-ISLAND CAT	OP	UTL	FBG	DS	IB	11D	REN	9	4	1800	1	5	4100	4800
19	7	LANCER	ST	RNBT	FBG	DV	IO	140-225		7	7	2715	2	6	3450	4000
20	6	CUTLASS FRONTRUNNER	ST	RNBT	FBG	SV	IO	140-225		7	9	3100	2	5	4200	4900
21	11	LANCER	ST	RNBT	FBG	DV	IO	225	MPC	8		3650	2	8	4850	5550
21	11	LANCER	ST	RNBT	FBG	DV	IB	225	MPC	8			2	3	5500	6350
21	11	LANCER-STINGER	ST	RNBT	FBG	DV	IO	225	MPC	8		3800	2	8	5000	5750
22	3	CUTLASS	OP	OPFSH	FBG	SV	OB			8		2200	1	1	5000	5750
22	4	CUTLASS	OP	CUD	FBG	SV	IB	130-225		8		3400	2	3	5300	6300
22	4	CUTLASS	OP	OPFSH	FBG	SV	IB	130-225		8		3197	2	3	5100	6050
23	1	LANCER	ST	OVNTR	FBG	DV	IO	225-250		8		4000	2	8	5850	6800

LOA FT	LOA IN	NAME AND/ OR MODEL	TOP/ RIG	BOAT TYPE	HULL MTL	HULL TP	ENGINE TP	ENGINE # HP	ENGINE MFG	BEAM FT	BEAM IN	WGT LBS	DRAFT FT	DRAFT IN	RETAIL LOW	RETAIL HIGH
		1978 BOATS														
23	1	LANCER	ST	RNBT	FBG	DV	IO	225	MPC	8		3700	2	8	5200	5950
		IB 225 MPC 6100 7000, IO 250 MPC 5250 6000, IB 250 MPC 6100 7050														
24	2	LANCER	ST	EXP	FBG	DV	IO	225-250		8			2	9	7800	9050
25	4	CATALINA	OP	EXP	FBG	DV	IB	225	MPC	9	9	4600	2	3	8400	9650
25	4	CATALINA SPORTSMAN	OP	FSH	FBG	DV	IB	T130	MPC	9	9	5400	1	8	9800	11100
28	11	CATALINA	OP	EXP	FBG	DV	IB	225	MPC	10	8	7125	2	5	12800	14600
28	11	CATALINA	OP	EXP	FBG	DV	IB	T130	MPC	10	8	8125	2	3	13900	15800
28	11	CATALINA	HT	EXP	FBG	DV	IB	225	MPC	10	8	7125	2	5	12800	14600
28	11	CATALINA	HT	EXP	FBG	DV	IB	T130	MPC	10	8	8125	2	3	13900	15800
30	2	COMMANDER	FB	SDNSF	FBG	DV	IB	T225-T250		11	11	13500	2	8	21400	24100
30	2	COMMANDER	FB	SDNSF	FBG	DV	IB	T210D	REN	11	11	13500	2	8	31100	34500
30	2	COMMANDER SPORTSMAN	OP	CR	FBG	DV	IB	T225-T250		11	11	12300	2	8	20600	23200
30	2	COMMANDER SPORTSMAN	OP	CR	FBG	DV	IB	T210D	REN	11	11	12300	2	8	29200	32400
33	1	CATALINA	FB	SDN	FBG	DV	IB	T225-T250		12	5	14800	2	4	28700	32300
33	1	CORINTHIAN	FB	SDN	FBG	DV	IB	T225-T250		12	5	11976	2	4	27300	30900
35	1	CATALINA	FB	DC	FBG	DV	IB	T235	MPC	13	1	17229	2	10	33300	37000
36		COMMANDER	FB	SDNSF	FBG	DV	IB	T330	MPC	13		22600	3	2	45000	50000
36		COMMANDER	FB	SDNSF	FBG	DV	IB	T250D	CUM	13		25300	3	2	56100	61600
38		CORINTHIAN	FB	SDN	FBG	DV	IB	T330	MPC	14		21900	3		49300	54200
38		CORINTHIAN	FB	SDN	FBG	DV	IB	T140D		14		21900	3		53000	58200
41		COMMANDER	FB	MY	FBG	DV	IB	T330	MPC	14		29800	3	4	71500	78600
41		COMMANDER	FB	MY	FBG	DV	IB	T286D	CUM	14		32900	3	4	85200	93600
42	4	COMMANDER	FB	YTFS	FBG	DV	IB	T330	MPC	14		33000	3	11	78000	85700
42	4	COMMANDER	FB	YTFS	FBG	DV	IB	T325D	GM	14		33000	3	11	88500	97300
42	4	COMMANDER	FB	YTFS	FBG	DV	IB	T425D	GM	14		33000	3	11	96300	106000
45		COMMANDER A	HT	MY	FBG	DV	IB	T330	MPC	15		39400	4	2	78000	85700
45		COMMANDER A	HT	MY	FBG	DV	IB	T325D	GM	15		39400	4	2	87900	96500
45		COMMANDER A	FB	MY	FBG	DV	IB	T330	MPC	15	6	39400	4	2	73800	81100
45		COMMANDER A	FB	MY	FBG	DV	IB	T325D	GM	15	6	39400	4	2	83700	91900
45		COMMANDER B	HT	MY	FBG	DV	IB	T330	MPC	15	6	39400	4	2	76800	84400
45		COMMANDER B	HT	MY	FBG	DV	IB	T325D	GM	15	6	39400	4	2	86900	95500
45		COMMANDER B	FB	MY	FBG	DV	IB	T330	MPC	15	6	39400	4	2	78200	85900
45		COMMANDER B	FB	MY	FBG	DV	IB	T325D	GM	15	6	39400	4	2	88000	96700
45	6	COMMANDER	FB	SDNSF	FBG	DV	IB	T325D	GM	16		38700	3	11	93900	103000
45	6	COMMANDER	FB	SDNSF	FBG	DV	IB	T425D	GM	16		38700	3	11	104000	114500
55		CUSTOM	FB	YTFS	FBG	DV	IB	T655D		16	7		4	3	138000	151500
62		CUSTOM	HT	MY	AL	SV	IB	T655D		17	3	70000			223000	245500
70		CUSTOM	HT	MY	AL	SV	IB	T655D		17	3	78800			282500	310500
70		CUSTOM	HT	YTFS	AL	SV	IB	T655D		17	3	79000			283000	311000
74		CUSTOM	HT	MY	AL	SV	IB	T655D		18		52T			**	**
74		CUSTOM	HT	YTFS	AL	SV	IB	T655D		18		52T			**	**
		1977 BOATS														
17	6	SUPER-SPORT	OP	RNBT	FBG	SV	IB	225	CC	6	10	2505	2	1	3000	3500
17	7	LANCER	ST	RNBT	FBG	DV	IO	188-195		7	3	2140	2	6	2750	3200
18	9	CROOKED-ISLAND CAT	OP	UTL	FBG	DS	IB	11D	REN	9	4	1800	1	5	4000	4650
19	7	LANCER	ST	RNBT	FBG	DV	IO	225-233		7	7	2715	2	6	3650	4250
20	6	SPORTSMAN	ST	RNBT	FBG	DV	IO	195-233		7	9	3100	2	5	4400	5150
22	4	SPORTSMAN	OP	FSH	FBG	SV	OB			8		2200			4900	5650
22	4	SPORTSMAN	ST	FSH	FBG	SV	IB	195	CC	8		3197	2		5100	5850
23	1	LANCER	ST	OVNTR	FBG	DV	IO	233-250		8		4000	2	8	6450	7500
23	1	LANCER	ST	RNBT	FBG	DV	IO	233	MRCR	8		3700	2	9	5750	6600
23	1	LANCER	ST	RNBT	FBG	DV	IO	250	CC	8		3700	2	9	5800	6650
23	1	LANCER	ST	RNBT	FBG	DV	IB	250	CC	8		3700	2	3	5900	6800
25	4	EXPRESS CRUISER	OP	EXP	FBG	SV	IB	195	CC	9	9	4600	2	3	8000	9150
25	4	EXPRESS CRUISER	HT	EXP	FBG	SV	IB	195	CC	9	9	4600	2	3	8000	9150
25	4	SPORTSMAN	OP	FSH	FBG	SV	IB	T130	CC	9	9	4599	1	8	8500	9750
30	2	COMMANDER TOURNAMENT	FB	SF	FBG	DV	IB	T250	CC	11	11	13000	2	8	20600	22900
30	2	SPORTSMAN	OP	CR	FBG	DV	IB	T250	CC	11	11	12300	2	8	20200	22400
33	1	OFFSHORE	FB	OFF	FBG	SV	VD	T250	CC	12	5	11976	2	4	24000	26700
33	1	SPORTS SEDAN	HT	SDNSF	FBG	SV	IB	T250	CC	12	5	14800	2	4	26500	29400
33	1	SPORTS SEDAN	FB	SDNSF	FBG	SV	IB	T250	CC	12	5	14800	2	4	26500	29400
35	1		FB	DC	FBG	SV	IB	T235	CC	13		17229	3		32200	35800
35	2	CARIBBEAN	SLP	MS	FBG	KL	IB	42D	PERK	11		18000	4	8	38100	42300
35	2	CARIBBEAN	SLP	MS	FBG	KL	IB	45D	VLVO	11		18000	4	8	38200	42500
35	2	CARIBBEAN	KTH	MS	FBG	KL	IB	42D	PERK	11		18000	4	8	38100	42300
35	2	CARIBBEAN	KTH	MS	FBG	KL	IB	45D	VLVO	11		18000	4	8	38200	42500
36		COMMANDER TOURNAMENT	FB	SF	FBG	SV	IB	T330	CC	13		22600	3	2	43400	48200
36		COMMANDER TOURNAMENT	FB	SF	FBG	SV	IB	T215D	CUM	13		25300	3	2	53200	58500
41		COMMANDER	HT	FD	FBG	SV	IB	T330	CC	14		29800	3	4	69300	76200
41		COMMANDER	HT	FD	FBG	SV	IB	T286D	CUM	14		32900	3	4	82300	90400
41		COMMANDER	FB	FD	FBG	SV	IB	T330	CC	14		29800	3	4	69300	76100
41		COMMANDER	FB	FD	FBG	SV	IB	T286D	CUM	14		32900	3	4	82200	90300
42	4	COMMANDER TOURNAMENT	FB	SF	FBG	SV	IB	T320D	GM	14		33000	3	11	84000	92400
42	4	COMMANDER TOURNAMENT	FB	SF	FBG	SV	IB	T425D	GM	14		33000	3	11	91700	101000
45		COMMANDER	HT	FD	FBG	SV	IB	T320D	GM	15		39400	4	2	94700	104000
45		COMMANDER	FB	FD	FBG	SV	IB	T320D	GM	15		39400	4	2	94100	103500
45	6	COMMANDER TOURNAMENT	FB	SF	FBG	SV	IB	T320D	GM	16		38700	3	11	88200	96900
45	6	COMMANDER TOURNAMENT	FB	SF	FBG	SV	IB	T425D	GM	16		38700	3	11	98300	108000
55		COMMANDER	HT	FD	FBG	SV	IB	T425D	GM	16	5	57800	4		154000	169000
55		COMMANDER	FB	FD	FBG	SV	IB	T425D	GM	16	5	57800	4		150500	165500
55		CUSTOM TOURNAMENT	FB	YTFS	AL	SV	IB	T655D	GM	16	7	56800	4	3	158500	174500
62		CUSTOM	HT	FD	AL	SV	IB	T655D	GM	17	3	70000	4		219500	241500
62		CUSTOM	HT	MY	AL	SV	IB	T655D	GM	17	3	70000	4	6	219000	240500
68	4	CUSTOM	HT	FD	AL	SV	IB	T655D	GM	17	3	78800	4	10	263000	289000
70		CUSTOM	HT	FD	AL	SV	IB	T655D	GM	17	3	79000	4	10	274000	301500
70		CUSTOM	HT	YTFS	AL	SV	IB	T655D	GM	17	3	78800	4	10	274000	301000
74		CUSTOM	HT	FD	AL	DV	IB	T655D	GM	18		52T	5	11	**	**
74		CUSTOM	HT	MY	AL	DV	IB	T655D	GM	18		52T	5	11	**	**
74		CUSTOM	HT	YTFS	AL	DV	IB	T655D	GM	18		52T	5	11	**	**
		1976 BOATS														
16	5	SPORTSMAN	OP	RNBT	FBG	TR	OB			6	10	1400	2	4	2500	2900
16	5	SPORTSMAN	OP	RNBT	FBG	TR	IO	105-120		6	10	2150	2	4	2550	2950
17	7	5.4 METER XK	ST	RNBT	FBG	DV	IO	215-233		7	3	2140	2	6	2950	3500
17	7	LANCER	ST	RNBT	FBG	DV	IO	215-233		7	3	2140	2	6	2850	3350
18	9	CROOKED-ISLAND CAT	OP	UTL	FBG	DS	IB	11D	REN	9	4	1800	1	5	3850	4500
19	7	LANCER	ST	RNBT	FBG	DV	IO	215-233		7	7	2715	2	6	3750	4400
20	6	SPORTSMAN	ST	RNBT	FBG	SV	IO	215-233		7	9	3100	2	5	4550	5300
22	3	SPORTSMAN	OP	FSH	FBG	SV	OB			8		2200	2		4850	5600
22	4	TOURNAMENT	OP	OPFSH	FBG	SV	IB	215	CC	8		3197	2		4900	5650
22	9	6.9 METER XK	HT	RNBT	FBG	DV	IO	300	CC	7	8	3300	2	10	5750	6600
23	1	LANCER	ST	OVNTR	FBG	DV	IO	233-250		8		4000	2	8	6650	7750
23	1	LANCER	ST	RNBT	FBG	DV	IO	233	MRCR	8		3700	2	8	5900	6800
23	1	LANCER	ST	RNBT	FBG	DV	IO	250	CC	8		3700	2	8	6000	6900
23	1	LANCER	ST	RNBT	FBG	DV	IB	250	CC	8		3700	2	3	5700	6550
25	4	EXPRESS CRUISER	OP	EXP	FBG	SV	IB	200	CC	9	9	4600	2	3	7750	8900
25	4	TOURNAMENT	OP	OPFSH	FBG	SV	IB	T130	CC	9	9	4599	1	8	8100	9300
27	8	8 METER XK	OP	RNBT	FBG	DV	IO	T300	CC	7	10	4380	2	8	11700	13200
30	2	SPORTSMAN	OP	CR	FBG	DV	IB	T250	CC	11	11	12300	2	8	19500	21600
30	2	TOURNAMENT	FB	SF	FBG	DV	IB	T250	CC	11	11	13000	2	8	19900	22100
33	1	OFFSHORE	FB	OFF	FBG	SV	IB	T250	CC	12	5	11976	2	4	23200	25800
33	1	SPORTS SEDAN	HT	SDNSF	FBG	SV	IB	T250	CC	12	5	14800	2	4	25600	28400
33	1	SPORTS SEDAN	FB	SDNSF	FBG	SV	IB	T250	CC	12	5	14800	2	4	25600	28400
35	1		FB	DC	FBG	SV	IB	T235	CC	13		17229	3		31200	34600
35	2	CARIBBEAN	SLP	MS	FBG	KL	IB	42D	PERK	11		18000	4	8	36900	41000
35	2	CARIBBEAN	SLP	MS	FBG	KL	IB	45D	VLVO	11		18000	4	8	37000	41200
35	2	CARIBBEAN	KTH	MS	FBG	KL	IB	42D	PERK	11		18000	4	8	36900	41000
35	2	CARIBBEAN	KTH	MS	FBG	KL	IB	45D	VLVO	11		18000	4	8	37000	41200
36		TOURNAMENT	FB	SF	FBG	SV	IB	T330	CC	13		22600	3	2	41800	46500
36		TOURNAMENT	FB	SF	FBG	SV	IB	T215D	CUM	13		25300	3	2	51400	56400
41			HT	FD	FBG	SV	IB	T330	CC	14		29800	3	4	67000	73600
41			HT	FD	FBG	SV	IB	T286D	CUM	14		32900	3	4	79500	87300
41			FB	FD	FBG	SV	IB	T330	CC	14		29800	3	4	66900	73500
41			FB	FD	FBG	SV	IB	T286D	CUM	14		32900	3	4	79400	87200
42	4	TOURNAMENT	FB	SF	FBG	SV	IB	T320D	GM	14		33000	3	11	77700	85400
42	4	TOURNAMENT	FB	SF	FBG	SV	IB	T425D	GM	14		33000	3	11	84400	92700
45			HT	FD	FBG	SV	IB	T320D	GM	15		39400	4	2	91700	101000
45			FB	FD	FBG	SV	IB	T320D	GM	15		39400	4	2	91200	100000
45	6	TOURNAMENT	FB	SF	FBG	SV	IB	T425D	GM	16		38700	3	11	84200	92500
47			HT	FD	FBG	SV	IB	T350D	CUM	15		41500	3	9	103500	113500
47			FB	FD	FBG	SV	IB	T350D	CUM	15		41500	3	9	102500	112500
55		CUSTOM TOURNAMENT	FB	YTFS	AL	SV	IB	T655D	GM	16	7	56800	4	3	153000	168000
55		ENCLOSED FLUSH DECK	HT	FD	FBG	SV	IB	T425D	GM	16	5	57800	4		133500	146500
55		ENCLOSED FLUSH DECK	FB	FD	FBG	SV	IB	T425D	GM	16	5	57800	4		130500	143000
60			FB	MY	AL	SV	IB	T655D	GM	17	3	70000	4	6	200000	219500
60		ENCLOSED FLUSH DECK	HT	FD	FBG	SV	IB	T655D	GM	17	3		4		150500	165500
67	8	YACHT FISHERMAN PH	FB	YTFS	AL	SV	IB	T655D	GM	17	3	79000	4	10	253500	278500
68	4	ENCLOSED FLUSH DECK	FB	FDPH	AL	SV	IB	T655D	GM	17	3	80000	4	10	256000	281000
73	9	YACHT FISHERMAN	FB	YTFS	AL	SV	IB	T655D	GM	18		92000	5	11	**	**
74			FB	FDPH	AL	SV	IB	T655D	GM	18		92000	5	11	**	**
74			FB	MY	AL	SV	IB	T655D	GM	18		92000	5	11	**	**
		1975 BOATS														
16	5	SPORTSMAN	OP	RNBT	FBG	TR	OB			6	10	1400	2	2	2500	2900
16	5	SPORTSMAN	OP	RNBT	FBG	TR	IO	105	CC	6	10	2150	2	4	2650	3100
17	7	LANCER	OP	RNBT	FBG	DV	IO	215	CC	7	3	2140	2	6	3000	3500
19	1	DOLPHIN 19	OP	RNBT	FBG		IO	215	CC	7	4	2450			3500	4100

CONTINUED ON NEXT PAGE

LOA FT	LOA IN	NAME AND/ OR MODEL	TOP/ RIG	BOAT TYPE	-HULL- MTL	-HULL- TP	ENGINE TP	ENGINE # HP	ENGINE MFG	BEAM FT	BEAM IN	WGT LBS	DRAFT FT	DRAFT IN	RETAIL LOW	RETAIL HIGH
1975 BOATS																
19	3	XK-19	OP	RNBT	FBG	DV	IO	300	CC	7	4	2635	2	5	4150	4800
19	7	LANCER	OP	RNBT	FBG	DV	IO	215	CC	7	7	2715	2	6	3900	4500
19	7	LANCER RALLY	ST	RNBT	FBG	DV	IO	250	CC	7	7	2715	2	6	4000	4650
22	4	SPORTSMAN	OP	RNBT	FBG		IB	200	CC	8					5050	5800
22	4	TOURNAMENT 22	OP	SF	FBG	SV	IB	200	CC	8		3197	2		4750	5450
22	9	XK-22	OP	RNBT	FBG	DV	IO	300	CC	7	8	3300	2	10	5950	6850
23	1	LANCER	OP	RNBT	FBG	DV	IO	215	CC	8		3275	2	8	5600	6450
23	1	LANCER	ST	RNBT	FBG	DV	IB	235	CC	8		3695	2	3	5100	5850
23	1	LANCER RALLY	ST	RNBT	FBG	DV	IB	235	CC	8		3695	2	3	5900	6800
23	1	LANCER RALLY	ST	RNBT	FBG	DV	IO	250	CC	8		3275	2	8	5750	6600
25	4		OP	EXP	FBG		IB	200	CC	9	9	4200	2	3	7050	8100
25	4	TOURNAMENT	OP	SF	FBG	SV	IB	T130	CC	9	9	4599	1	8	7900	9100
26	7	8 METER	OP	RNBT	FBG	DV	IO	T300	CC	7	10	5225	2	8	11700	13300
30			OP	EXP	FBG		IB	T200	CC	10	6	8500	2	1	15500	17600
30			HT	EXP	FBG		IB	T200	CC	10	6	8500	2	1	15500	17600
30		30 EXPRESS CR	FB	EXP	FBG		IB	T200	CC	10	6	8500	2	1	15500	17600
30	2	TOURNAMENT	FB	SF	FBG	SV	IB	T235	CC	11	11	12000	2	8	18700	20800
33	1	COHO	FB	SDN	FBG		IB	T235	CC	12	4	11976	2	4	24800	27500
33	1	SPORTS SEDAN	HT	SDNSF	FBG		IB	T235	CC	12	4	12500	2	4	23400	26000
33	1	SPORTS SEDAN	FB	SDNSF	FBG		IB	T235	CC	12	4	12500	2	4	23400	26000
35	2	CARIBBEAN	SLP	MS	FBG	KL	IB	50D	PERK	11		18000	4	8	35900	39900
35	2	CARIBBEAN	SLP	MS	FBG	KL	IB	75D	VLVO	11		18000	4	8	36100	40100
35	2	CARIBBEAN	KTH	MS	FBG	KL	IB	50D	PERK	11		18000	4	8	35900	39900
35	2	CARIBBEAN	KTH	MS	FBG	KL	IB	75D	VLVO	11		18000	4	8	36100	40100
35	11		FB	DC	FBG		IB	T235	CC	13		17229	3		32000	35600
36		TOURNAMENT	FB	SF	FBG	SV	IB	T330	CC	13		22600	3	2	40400	44900
36		TOURNAMENT	FB	SF	FBG	SV	IB	T215D	CUM	13		25300	3	2	49600	54500
38		COHO	FB	SDN	FBG		IB	T300	CC	14		21925	3		43700	48600
38		COHO	FB	SDN	FBG		IB	T286D	CUM	14		21925	3		51000	56000
41			HT	FD	FBG		IB	T330	CC	14		29800	3	4	64700	71100
41			HT	FD	FBG		IB	T286D	CUM	14		32900	3	4	76800	84400
41			FB	FD	FBG		IB	T330	CC	14		29800	3	4	64600	71000
41			FB	FD	FBG		IB	T286D	CUM	14		32900	3	4	76700	84300
42	4	TOURNAMENT	FB	SF	FBG		IB	T330	CC	14		33000	3	11	66600	73200
42	4	TOURNAMENT	FB	SF	FBG		IB	T320D	GM	14		33000	3	11	75100	82500
42	4	TOURNAMENT	FB	SF	FBG		IB	T425D	GM	14		33000	3	11	81500	89600
45			HT	FD	FBG		IB	T320D	GM	15		39400	4	2	88600	97400
45			FB	FD	FBG		IB	T320D	GM	15		39400	4	2	88100	96900
45	6	TOURNAMENT	FB	SF	FBG		IB	T320D	GM	16		38700	3	11	73500	80800
45	6	TOURNAMENT	FB	SF	FBG		IB	T425D	GM	16		38700	3	11	81300	89300
47			HT	FD	FBG		IB	T350D	CUM	15		41500	3	9	99900	109500
47			FB	FD	FBG		IB	T350D	CUM	15		41500	3	9	99000	109000
55		ENCLOSED FD	HT	FD	FBG		IB	T425D	GM	16	5	57800	4		130500	143500
55		ENCLOSED FD	FB	FD	FBG		IB	T425D	GM	16	5	57800	4		127500	140000
55		TOURNAMENT		SF	FBG		IB	T655D	GM	16	7				120000	131500
60			FB	MY	AL		IB	T655D	GM	17	3	70000	4	6	194000	213000
60	4	ENCLOSED FD	HT	FDPH	AL		IB	T655D	GM	17	3	71000	4	8	201500	221000
60	4	ENCLOSED FD	FB	FDPH	AL		IB	T655D	GM	17	3	71000	4	8	199000	219000
67	8		FB	YTFS	AL		IB	T655D	GM	17	3	79000	4	10	245000	269000
68	4	ENCLOSED FD	FB	FDPH	AL		IB	T655D	GM	17	3	87200	4	10	260000	285500
72	9		FB	YTFS	AL		IB	T655D	GM	18	3	85000	5	3	**	**
73			FB	MY	AL		IB	T655D	GM	18	3	85000	5	3	**	**
73		ENCLOSED FD	FB	FDPH	AL		IB	T655D	GM	18	3	85000	5	3	**	**
1974 BOATS																
16		SEASPORT	ST	RNBT	FBG		IO	150	CC	7	1	1950			2600	3050
17	7	LANCER	OP	RNBT	FBG	DV	IO	150	CC	7	4	2140	2	6	3050	3550
18		XK-18	OP	RNBT	FBG		JT	400	CC	7		2500	1	6	3200	3750
19	1	DOLPHIN	ST	RNBT	FBG	TR	IO	200	CC	7	4	2450			3600	4200
19	4	XK-19	OP	RNBT	FBG	DV	IO	300	CC	7	5	2635	2	6	4400	5050
19	7	LANCER	ST	RNBT	FBG	DV	IO	200	CC	7	7	2715	2	6	4000	4650
22	4	TOURNAMENT FISHERMAN	OP	SF	FBG	SV	IO	200	CC	8		3197	2		6650	7650
22	9	XK-22	OP	RNBT	FBG		IO	300	CC	7	8	3300	2	10	6200	7150
23	1	LANCER	ST	RNBT	FBG		IO	200	CC	8		3275	2	8	5800	6650
23	1	LANCER	ST	RNBT	FBG		IB	235	CC	8		3695	2	4	5300	6100
25	4		OP	EXP	FBG		IB	200	CC	9	9	4200	2	3	6800	7850
25	4	TOURNAMENT FISHERMAN	OP	SF	FBG	SV	IB	T130	CC	9	9	4599	1	9	7650	8800
30			OP	EXP	FBG		IB	T200	CC	10	6	8500	2	1	15000	17000
30			FB	EXP	FBG		IB	T200	CC	10	6	8500	2	1	15000	17000
31			HT	SPTCR	FBG		IB	T235	CC	11	4	9828	2	8	17600	20000
31			FB	SPTCR	FBG		IB	T235	CC	11	4	9828	2	8	17600	20000
33	1		HT	SDNSF	FBG		IB	T235	CC	12	5	12500	2	4	22600	25100
33	1	COHO	FB	SDN	FBG		IB	T235	CC	12	5	11976	2	4	24000	26600
34		AQUA-HOME	HT	HB	FBG		IB	T200	CC	12	10	11296	3	6	27900	31000
35		CARIBBEAN	SLP	MS	FBG	KL	IB	75D	VLVO	11		18000	4	8	35100	39000
35	1		FB	DC	FBG		IB	T235	CC	13	1	17229	3		29000	32300
36		TOURNAMENT FISHERMAN	FB	SF	FBG	SV	IB	T300	CC	13		20000	3	2	36100	40100
36		TOURNAMENT FISHERMAN	FB	SF	FBG	SV	IB	T215D	CUM	13		23700	3	2	46100	50700
38		COHO	FB	SDN	FBG		IB	T300	CC	14	3	21925	3		41800	46400
41			HT	FD	FBG		IB	T300	CC	14		29800	3	4	62100	68300
41			FB	FD	FBG		IB	T300	CC	14		29800	3	4	62100	68200
41			FB	FD	FBG		IB	T286D	CUM	14		32900	3	4	74200	81600
45			HT	FD	FBG		IB	T320D	GM	15		27907	4	2	68000	74800
45			FB	FD	FBG		IB	T320D	GM	15		27907	4	2	67600	74300
45	6	TOURNAMENT FISHERMAN	FB	SF	FBG		IB	T320D	GM	16		30164	3	10	65900	72400
45	6	TOURNAMENT FISHERMAN	FB	SF	FBG		IB	T425D	GM	16		30164	3	10	75600	83100
47			HT	FD	FBG		IB	T350D	CUM	15		35480	4	1	86000	94500
47			FB	FD	FBG		IB	T350D	CUM	15		35480	4	1	85200	93700
55			HT	FD	FBG		IB	T425D	GM	16	6	51783	4		127000	139500
55			FB	FD	FBG		IB	T425D	GM	16	6	51783	4		124000	136500
60			FB	MY	AL		IB	T655D	GM	17	3	66000	4	3	178500	196000
60	5		HT	FDPH	AL		IB	T655D	GM	17	3	68500	4	8	189000	207500
60	5		FB	FDPH	AL		IB	T655D	GM	17	3	68500	4	8	187000	205500
68	6	ROAMER	FB	MY	AL		IB	T595D		17	3	94150	4	11	257000	282500
68	6	ROAMER	FB	MY	AL		IB	T655D		17	3	94150	4	11	260500	286500
73			FB	FDPH	AL		IB	T655D	GM	18		85000	5	6	**	**
1973 BOATS																
16		EXPLORER	OP	RNBT	FBG		IO	120	OMC	7	1		2	8	2550	2950
16		SEASPORT	ST	RNBT	FBG		IO	150	OMC	7	1	1950	2	8	2700	3150
17	7	LANCER	OP	RNBT	FBG	DV	IO	150	VLVO	7	4	2140	2	6	3350	3900
18		XK-18	OP	RNBT	FBG		JT	400	CC	7		2500	1	3	3100	3600
19		DOLPHIN	ST	RNBT	FBG	TR	IO	200	OMC	7	4	2450	2	8	3700	4300
19	4	XK-19	OP	RNBT	FBG	DV	IO	225	CC	7	5	2635	2	6	4050	4700
19	7	LANCER	ST	RNBT	FBG	DV	IO	200	CC	7	7	2715	2	6	4150	4850
22	9	XK-22	OP	RNBT	FBG		IO	225	CC	7	8	3300	2	10	5950	6850
23	1	LANCER	ST	RNBT	FBG		IO	200	VLVO	8		3275	2	8	6200	7150
23	1	LANCER	ST	RNBT	FBG		IB	225	CC	8		3695	2	8	5150	5900
25				EXP	FBG		IO	200	CC	9	9				9300	10600
25	5	TOURNAMENT FISHERMAN		SF	FBG		IB	T135	CC	9	9	4200	1	9	7100	8200
26			OP	EXP	FBG		IB	235	CC	10	2	5174	2	3	8000	9200
28	1	SPORTS EXPRESS	HT	EXP	FBG		IB	T235	CC	11	1	8236	2	7	12400	14100
28	1	SPORTS EXPRESS	FB	EXP	FBG		IB	T235	CC	11	1	8236	2	7	12400	14100
28	6		OP	EXP	FBG		IB	235	CC	10	6	6125	2		9900	11200
28	6		OP	EXP	FBG		IB	T200	CC	10	6	6125	2		11000	12500
28	6	COHO	FB	SDN	FBG		IB	T200	CC	10	6	7771	2	3	13200	15000
28	6	SPORTSMAN	HT	FSH	FBG		IB	235	CC	10	6	5875	2	3	9750	11100
28	6	SPORTSMAN	HT	FSH	FBG		IB	T200	CC	10	6	5875	2	3	10900	12400
28	6	SPORTSMAN	FB	FSH	FBG		IB	235	CC	10	6	5875	2	3	9750	11100
28	6	SPORTSMAN	FB	FSH	FBG		IB	T200	CC	10	6	5875	2	3	10900	12400
30			OP	EXP	FBG		IB	T200	CC	10	6	8500	2	1	14500	16400
30			FB	EXP	FBG		IB	T200	CC	10	6	8500	2	1	14500	16400
31			HT	SPTCR	FBG		IB	T235-T300		11	4	9828	2	8	17000	20200
31			FB	SPTCR	FBG		IB	T235-T300		11	4	9828	2	8	17000	20200
33			HT	SDNSF	FBG		IB	T235	CC	12	4	12500	2	4	21700	24100
33			FB	SDNSF	FBG		IB	T235	CC	12	4	12500	2	4	21700	24100
33		COHO	FB	SDN	FBG		IB	T235	CC	12	4	11976	2	4	23100	25600
34		AQUA-HOME	HT	HB	FBG		VD	T200	CC	12	10	11296	3		28000	31100
35			FB	DC	FBG		IB	T235	CC	13		17229			28000	31100
35		CARIBBEAN	SLP	MS	FBG	KL	IB	42D	PERK	11		18000	4	8	34000	37800
35		CARIBBEAN	KTH	MS	FBG	KL	IB	42D	PERK	11		18000	4	8	34000	37800
35		SALON	OP	DC	FBG		IB	T300	CC	13		17496	3		28800	32000
36		TOURNAMENT FISHERMAN	HT	SF	FBG		IB	T300	CC	13		22600	3	2	37600	41700
36		TOURNAMENT FISHERMAN	HT	SF	FBG		IB	T189D	CUM	13		22600	3	2	42300	47000
36		TOURNAMENT FISHERMAN	HT	SF	FBG		IB	T203D	CAT	13		22600	3	2	43100	47900
36		TOURNAMENT FISHERMAN	FB	SF	FBG		IB	T300	CC	13		22600	3	2	37600	41700
36		TOURNAMENT FISHERMAN	FB	SF	FBG		IB	T189D	CUM	13		22600	3	2	42300	47000
36		TOURNAMENT FISHERMAN	FB	SF	FBG		IB	T203D	CAT	13		22600	3	2	43100	47900
38		COHO	FB	SDN	FBG		IB	T300	CC	14	3	21925	3		40500	45000
38		COHO	FB	SDN	FBG		IB	T203D	CAT	14	3	23257	3		48400	53200
41			HT	FD	FBG		IB	T300	CC	14		29800	3	4	60200	66100
41			HT	FD	FBG		IB	T260D	GM	14		32900	3	4	71400	78500
41			HT	FD	FBG		IB	T280D	CUM	14		32900	3	4	71800	78900
41			FB	FD	FBG		IB	T300	CC	14		29800	3	4	60100	66100
41			FB	FD	FBG		IB	T260D	GM	14		32900	3	4	71300	78400
41			FB	FD	FBG		IB	T280D	CUM	14		32900	3	4	71700	78800
42		SPORTS CRUISER	HT	SDNSF	FBG		IB	T300	CC	13		21267	3	2	47400	52000

 CONTINUED ON NEXT PAGE

LOA FT	LOA IN	NAME AND/ OR MODEL	TOP/ RIG	BOAT TYPE	-HULL- MTL	-HULL- TP	ENGINE TP	ENGINE # HP	ENGINE MFG	BEAM FT	BEAM IN	WGT LBS	DRAFT FT	DRAFT IN	RETAIL LOW	RETAIL HIGH
		1973 BOATS														
42		SPORTS CRUISER	HT	SDNSF	FBG		IB	T260D	GM	13			3	2	73600	80900
42		SPORTS CRUISER	FB	SDNSF	FBG		IB	T300	CC	13			3	2	67500	74200
42		SPORTS CRUISER	FB	SDNSF	FBG		IB	T260D	GM	13			3	2	73500	80700
45			HT	FD	FBG		IB	T320D	GM	15		27907	4	2	65900	72400
45			HT	FD	FBG		IB	T350D	CUM	15		27907	4	2	67000	73600
45			FB	FD	FBG		IB	T320D	GM	15		27907	4	2	65500	72000
45			FB	FD	FBG		IB	T350D	CUM	15		27907	4	2	66600	73200
45	6	TOURNAMENT FISHERMAN	FB	SF	FBG		IB	T320D	GM	16		30164	3	11	63800	70100
		IB T350D CUM 66500 73000, IB T373D FORD 68600 75400, IB T425D GM													73200	80500
46		AQUA-HOME	HT	HB	FBG		VD	T230		15		16666	2	6	37600	41800
47			HT	FD	FBG		IB	T350D	CUM	15		35480	3	2	83300	91500
47			FB	FD	FBG		IB	T350D	CUM	15		35480	3	2	82600	90700
55			HT	FD	FBG		IB	T450	FORD	16	6	51783	3	9	123000	135000
55			HT	FD	FBG		IB	T390D	GM	16	6	51783	3	9	119000	130500
55			HT	FD	FBG		IB	T425D	GM	16	6	51783	3	9	123000	135000
55		ROAMER	HT	FD	AL		IB	T390D	GM	16		54500	4	6	112000	123000
55		ROAMER	HT	FD	AL		IB	T425D	GM	16		54500	4	6	116000	127500
55		ROAMER	FB	FD	AL		IB	T390D	GM	16		54500	4	6	109500	120000
55		ROAMER	FB	FD	AL		IB	T425D	GM	16		54500	4	6	113500	124500
57		CONSTELLATION	HT	MY	M/P		IB	T390D	GM	15		45732	4		98100	108000
57		CONSTELLATION	FB	MY	M/P		IB	T390D	GM	15		45732	4		96000	105500
60		ROAMER	HT	FD	AL		IB	T390D	GM	17	3	68500	4	8	151000	166000
		IB T425D GM 155500 171000, IB T480D GM 162500 178500, IB T595D GM													175000	192500
		IB T655D GM 181000 199000														
60		ROAMER	FB	FD	AL		IB	T390D	GM	17	3	68500	4	8	149500	164000
		IB T425D GM 154000 169000, IB T480D GM 160500 176500, IB T595D GM													173000	190500
		IB T655D GM 179500 197000														
60	10		HT	FD	FBG		IB	T655D	GM	18		78795	4	7	205500	226000
68	6	ROAMER	FB	MY	AL		IB	T595D	GM	17	3	94150	4	11	251500	276500
68	6	ROAMER	FB	MY	AL		IB	T655D	GM	17	3	94150	4	11	255500	280500
73		ROAMER	FB	MY	AL		IB	T655D	GM	18		85000	5	6	**	**
		1972 BOATS														
16		SEASPORT	ST	RNBT	FBG		IO	150	CC	7	1	1950			2850	3300
16		SEASPORT	ST	RNBT	FBG	TR	IO	140	CC	7	1	1950			2800	3300
17	7	LANCER CUSTOM	OP	RNBT	FBG	DV	IO	150	CC	7	4	2150	2	6	3300	3850
18		XK-18	OP	RNBT	FBG		JT	235-400		7		2250	1	6	2850	3350
19	1	DOLPHIN	ST	RNBT	FBG	TR	IO	200	CC	7	4	2450			3900	4550
19	4	XK-19	OP	RNBT	FBG	DV	IO	320	CC	7	5	2861	2	6	5150	5950
19	7	LANCER CUSTOM	ST	RNBT	FBG	DV	IO	200	CC	7	7	2626	2	6	4250	4950
22	9	XK-22	OP	RNBT	FBG	DV	IO	320	CC	7	8	4150	2	10	8050	9250
23	1	LANCER	ST	RNBT	FBG	DV	IB	235	CC	8		3900	2	4	5200	5950
23	1	LANCER OFFSHORE	ST	RNBT	FBG	DV	IO	200	CC	8		3900	2	8	7100	8150
26		CATALINA	OP	EXP	FBG		IB	235	CC	10	2	5174	2	3	7750	8900
26		CATALINA	HT	EXP	FBG		IB	235	CC	10	2	5174	2	3	7750	8900
28	1	COMMANDER	HT	EXP	FBG	DV	IB	T200-T235		11	1	8236	2	7	11700	13600
28	1	COMMANDER	FB	EXP	FBG	DV	IB	T200-T235		11	1	8236	2	7	11700	13600
28	6	CATALINA	OP	EXP	FBG		IB	230	CC	10	6	6125	2	3	9550	10800
28	6	CATALINA	OP	EXP	FBG		IB	T200	CC	10	6	7371	2	3	11300	12900
28	6	CATALINA	HT	EXP	FBG		IB	230	CC	10	6	7371	2	3	10300	11700
28	6	CATALINA	HT	EXP	FBG		IB	T200	CC	10	6	7371	2	3	11300	12900
28	6	CATALINA COHO	FB	SDN	FBG		IB	T200	CC	10	6	7771	2	3	12700	14500
28	6	CATALINA SPORTSMAN	HT	SF	FBG		IB	235	CC	10	6	5825	2	3	9400	10700
28	6	CATALINA SPORTSMAN	HT	SF	FBG		IB	T200	CC	10	6	7071	2	3	11200	12700
28	6	CATALINA SPORTSMAN	FB	SF	FBG		IB	235	CC	10	6	7071	2	3	10100	11500
28	6	CATALINA SPORTSMAN	FB	SF	FBG		IB	T200	CC	10	6	7071	2	3	11200	12700
31		CATALINA	OP	EXP	FBG		IB	T235	CC	11	7	10080	2	4	16600	18900
31		CATALINA	OP	EXP	FBG		IB	T145D	PERK	11	7	10080	2	4	21200	23600
31		CATALINA	HT	EXP	FBG		IB	T235	CC	11	7	10080	2	4	16600	18900
31		CATALINA	HT	EXP	FBG		IB	T145D	PERK	11	7	10080	2	4	21200	23600
31		CATALINA	FB	EXP	FBG		IB	T235	CC	11	7	10080	2	4	16600	18900
31		CATALINA	FB	EXP	FBG		IB	T145D	PERK	11	7	10080	2	4	21200	23600
31		COMMANDER	OP	EXP	FBG		IB	T235	CC	11	4	10190	2	4	16600	18800
31		COMMANDER	OP	EXP	FBG		IB	T145D	PERK	11	4	10190	2	4	21300	23600
31		COMMANDER	HT	EXP	FBG		IB	T235	CC	11	4	10190	2	4	16600	18800
31		COMMANDER	HT	EXP	FBG		IB	T145D	PERK	11	4	10190	2	4	21300	23600
31		COMMANDER	FB	EXP	FBG		IB	T235	CC	11	4	10190	2	4	16600	18800
31		COMMANDER	FB	EXP	FBG		IB	T145D	PERK	11	4	10190	2	4	21300	23600
31		COMMANDER	HT	SDN	FBG		IB	T235	CC	11	4	10550	2	4	18700	20800
31		COMMANDER	HT	SDN	FBG		IB	T145D	PERK	11	4	10550	2	4	24500	27200
31		COMMANDER	FB	SDN	FBG		IB	T235	CC	11	4	10550	2	4	18700	20800
31		COMMANDER	FB	SDN	FBG		IB	T145D	PERK	11	4	10550	2	4	24500	27200
31		COMMANDER	HT	SPTCR	FBG		IB	T235-T300		11	4	9828	2	8	16500	19600
31		COMMANDER	HT	SPTCR	FBG		IB	T145D	PERK	11	4	9828	2	8	20900	23200
31		COMMANDER	FB	SPTCR	FBG		IB	T235-T300		11	4	9828	2	8	16500	19600
31		COMMANDER	FB	SPTCR	FBG		IB	T145D	PERK	11	4	9828	2	8	20900	23200
33		CATALINA	OP	EXP	FBG		IB	T235	CC	12	4	10080	2	3	20100	22300
33		CATALINA	HT	EXP	FBG		IB	T235	CC	12	4	10080	2	3	20100	22300
33		CATALINA	FB	EXP	FBG		IB	T235	CC	12	4	10080	2	3	20100	22300
33		CATALINA COHO	FB	SDN	FBG		IB	T235	CC	12	4	11610	2	4	22200	24600
33		CATALINA COHO	FB	SDN	FBG		IB	T145D	PERK	12	4	11610	2	4	28300	31400
34		AQUA-HOME	HT	HB	FBG		IO	200	CC	12	10	11600	2	7	25600	28400
		IO T150 CC 28300 31400, VD T200 CC 29100 32300, JT T235 CC													30700	34100
34		AQUA-HOME	FB	HB	FBG		IO	T150-T235		12	10	12200	2	8	28300	32300
35		COMMANDER	HT	EXP	FBG		IB	T235	CC	13		14063	3		24900	27700
35		COMMANDER	HT	EXP	FBG		IB	T300	CC	13		14063	3		25500	28400
35		COMMANDER	HT	EXP	FBG		IB	T189D	CUM	13		14063	3		32200	35800
35		COMMANDER	FB	EXP	FBG		IB	T230	CC	13			3		23600	26200
35		COMMANDER	FB	EXP	FBG		IB	T300	CC	13			3		24300	27000
35		COMMANDER	FB	EXP	FBG		IB	T189D	CUM	13			3		31200	34700
35		COMMANDER SALON	OP	DC	FBG		IB	T235	CC	13		16086	3		26300	29200
35		COMMANDER SALON	OP	DC	FBG		IB	T300	CC	13		16086	3		26900	29900
35		COMMANDER SALON	OP	DC	FBG		IB	T189D	CUM	13		16086	3		34600	38500
35		COMMANDER SALON	HT	DC	FBG		IB	T235	CC	13		16086	3		26300	29200
35		COMMANDER SALON	HT	DC	FBG		IB	T300	CC	13		16086	3		26900	29900
35		COMMANDER SALON	HT	DC	FBG		IB	T189D	CUM	13		16086	3		34600	38500
35		COMMANDER SPORTS CR	HT	SDNSF	FBG		IB	T235	CC	13		16588	3		26600	29600
35		COMMANDER SPORTS CR	HT	SDNSF	FBG		IB	T300	CC	13		16588	3		27200	30200
35		COMMANDER SPORTS CR	HT	SDNSF	FBG		IB	T189D	CUM	13		16588	3		35300	39200
35		COMMANDER SPORTS CR	FB	SDNSF	FBG		IB	T235	CC	13		16588	3		26600	29600
35		COMMANDER SPORTS CR	FB	SDNSF	FBG		IB	T300	CC	13		16588	3		27200	30200
35		COMMANDER SPORTS CR	FB	SDNSF	FBG		IB	T189D	CUM	13		16588	3		35300	39200
35	2	CARIBBEAN	SLP	MS	FBG	KL	IB	42D	PERK	11		18000	4	8	33300	37000
35	2	CARIBBEAN	KTH	MS	FBG	KL	IB	42D	PERK	11		18000	4	8	33300	37000
38		COMMANDER	HT	SDN	FBG		IB	T300	CC	13		19605	3		38400	42700
38		COMMANDER	HT	SDN	FBG		IB	T260D	GM	13		19605	3		44100	49000
38		COMMANDER	FB	SDN	FBG		IB	T260D	GM	13		19605	3		44100	49000
41		COMMANDER	HT	MY	FBG		IB	T300	CC	14		21740	3	4	44600	49500
41		COMMANDER	HT	MY	FBG		IB	T260D	GM	14		21740	3	4	50700	55700
41		COMMANDER	HT	MY	FBG		IB	T280D	CUM	14		21740	3	4	51200	56300
41		COMMANDER	FB	MY	FBG		IB	T300	CC	14		21740	3	4	44500	49500
41		COMMANDER	FB	MY	FBG		IB	T260D	GM	14		21740	3	4	50600	55600
41		COMMANDER	FB	MY	FBG		IB	T280D	CUM	14		21740	3	4	51200	56200
42		COMMANDER SALON	OP	MY	FBG		IB	T300	CC	13		22407	3	2	49900	54900
42		COMMANDER SALON	OP	MY	FBG		IB	T260D	GM	13		22407	3	2	55700	61200
42		COMMANDER SALON	HT	MY	FBG		IB	T300	CC	13		22407	3	2	50200	55100
42		COMMANDER SALON	HT	MY	FBG		IB	T260D	GM	13		22407	3	2	56000	61500
42		COMMANDER SPORTS CR	HT	SDNSF	FBG		IB	T300	CC	13		21267	3	2	47900	52600
42		COMMANDER SPORTS CR	HT	SDNSF	FBG		IB	T258D	GM	13		21267	3	2	53200	58500
42		COMMANDER SPORTS CR	FB	SDNSF	FBG		IB	T300	CC	13		22193	3	2	48800	53600
42		COMMANDER SPORTS CR	FB	SDNSF	FBG		IB	T258D	GM	13		22193	3	2	54400	59700
42		CONSTELLATION	HT	MY	M/P		IB	T235	CC	13		20643	3		43700	48600
42		CONSTELLATION	HT	MY	M/P		IB	T300	CC	13		20643	3		46100	50700
45		COMMANDER	HT	MY	FBG		IB	T300	CC	15		27907	4	2	50000	55000
		IB T260D GM 55800 61300, IB T320D GM 60200 66200, IB T350D GM													62400	68500
45		COMMANDER	FB	MY	FBG		IB	T300	CC	15		27907	4	2	49800	54700
		IB T260D GM 55500 61000, IB T320D GM 59900 65800, IB T350D GM													62000	68100
45	6	COMMANDER TOURNAMENT	FB	SF	FBG		IB	T350	FORD	16		30164	3	11	57000	62600
		IB T320D GM 63900 70200, IB T350D CUM 66600 73200, IB T390D GM													70400	77300
46		AQUA-HOME	HT	HB	FBG		VD	T230	CC	15		16666	2	6	37200	41400
46		AQUA-HOME	HT	HB	FBG		IB	T145D	PERK	15		16666	2	6	44700	49700
46		AQUA-HOME	FB	HB	FBG		VD	T230	CC	15		16666	2	6	37200	41400
46		AQUA-HOME	FB	HB	FBG		IB	T145D	PERK	15		16666	2	6	44700	49700
47		COMMANDER	HT	DC	FBG		IB	T260D	GM	15		33000	3	2	63100	69300
47		COMMANDER	HT	DC	FBG		IB	T350D	CUM	15		33000	3	2	70600	77600
47		COMMANDER	FB	DC	FBG		IB	T260D	GM	15		33000	3	2	62600	68800
47		COMMANDER	FB	DC	FBG		IB	T350D	CUM	15		33000	3	2	70100	77000
47		COMMANDER COCKPIT	FB	MYCPT	FBG		IB	T260D	GM	15		33807	3	2	71500	78600
47		COMMANDER COCKPIT	FB	MYCPT	FBG		IB	T350D	CUM	15		33807	3	2	83100	91400
47		COMMANDER S C	HT	MY	FBG		IB	T260D	GM	15		32166	3	2	70900	77900
47		COMMANDER S C	HT	MY	FBG		IB	T350D	CUM	15		32166	3	2	80100	88000

 CONTINUED ON NEXT PAGE

CHRIS CRAFT BOATS -CONTINUED See inside cover to adjust price for area

LOA FT	IN	NAME AND/ OR MODEL	TOP/ RIG	BOAT TYPE	-HULL- MTL	TP	----ENGINE--- TP	# HP	MFG	BEAM FT	IN	WGT LBS	DRAFT FT	IN	RETAIL LOW	RETAIL HIGH
		1972 BOATS														
47		COMMANDER S C	FB	MY	FBG		IB	T260D	GM	15		33000	3	2	71600	78700
47		COMMANDER S C	FB	MY	FBG		IB	T350D	CUM	15		33000	3	2	80600	88500
55		COMMANDER	HT	MY	FBG		IB	T450	FORD	16	6	51783	3	9	110000	121000
55		COMMANDER	HT	MY	FBG		IB	T390D	GM	16	6	51783	3	9	104500	114500
55		COMMANDER	FB	MY	FBG		IB	T450	FORD	16	6	51783	3	9	107500	118000
55		COMMANDER	FB	MY	FBG		IB	T390D	GM	16	6	51783	3	9	102000	112000
55		ROAMER	HT	MY	AL		IB	T325D	GM	16		54500	4	6	94900	104500
55		ROAMER	HT	MY	AL		IB	T390D	GM	16		54500	4	6	102500	113000
57		CONSTELLATION	HT	MY	M/P		IB	T320D	GM	15		45732	4		84800	93100
57		CONSTELLATION	HT	MY	M/P		IB	T350D	CUM	15		45732	4		89500	98400
57		CONSTELLATION	HT	MY	M/P		IB	T390D	GM	15		45732	4		95200	104500
57		CONSTELLATION	FB	MY	M/P		IB	T320D	GM	15		45732	4		82900	91100
57		CONSTELLATION	FB	MY	M/P		IB	T350D	CUM	15		45732	4		87600	96200
57		CONSTELLATION	FB	MY	M/P		IB	T390D	GM	15		45732	4		93100	102500
60		ROAMER	HT	MY	AL		IB	T388D	CAT	17	3	68500	4	8	144000	158500
		IB T390D GM 145500 160000, IB T480D GM 156500 172000, IB T595D GM													168500	185000
60		ROAMER	FB	MY	AL		IB	T388D	CAT	17	3	68500	4	8	142000	156500
		IB T390D GM 144000 158000, IB T480D GM 154500 170000, IB T595D GM													166500	183000
60	10	COMMANDER	HT	MY	FBG		IB	T555D	GM	18		78795	4	7	188500	207500
68	6	ROAMER	FB	MY	AL		IB	T595D	GM	17	3	94150	4	11	244000	268000
		1971 BOATS														
16		SEASPORT	ST	RNBT	FBG	TR	IO	150	CC	7	1	1950			2950	3400
17	7	LANCER	OP	RNBT	FBG		OB			7	4	1200	2	6	2250	2600
17	7	LANCER	OP	RNBT	FBG		IO	150	CC	7	4	2150	2	6	3350	3900
17	7	LANCER CUSTOM	OP	RNBT	FBG		IO	150	CC	7	4	2150	2	6	3500	4100
17	11	XK-18 JET	OP	RNBT	FBG		JT	230-350		7		2150	1	3	2700	3150
19	1	DOLPHIN	ST	RNBT	FBG	TR	IO	200	CC	7	4	2450			4050	4700
19	4	XK-19	OP	RNBT	FBG	DV	VD	230	CC	7	5	2861			3050	3550
19	4	XK-19	OP	RNBT	FBG	DV	IO	350	CC	7	5	2861	2	6	5850	6750
19	7	LANCER	ST	RNBT	FBG	DV	IO	200	CC	7	7	2626	2	6	4300	5000
19	7	LANCER CUSTOM	ST	RNBT	FBG	DV	IO	200	CC	7	7	2626	2	6	4550	5250
22	1	CUTLASS CAVALIER	OP	RNBT	FBG		IB	230	CC	7	11	3608	2	1	4500	5200
22	9	XK-22	OP	RNBT	FBG	DV	IO	350	CC	7	8	4150	2	10	8950	10200
23	1	LANCER OFFSHORE	ST	RNBT	FBG		IO	200	CC	8		3900	2	8	7350	8450
25	1	LANCER	OP	RNBT	FBG		IO	T150	CC	9	8	4500	2	7	10200	11600
25	1	LANCER	HT	RNBT	FBG		IO	T150	CC	9	8	4500	2	7	10200	11600
25	1	LANCER SPORTSMAN	OP	CUD	FBG		IO	T150	CC	9	8	4600	2	7	11200	12700
26		CATALINA	OP	EXP	FBG		IB	230	CC	10	2	5174	2	3	7450	8600
26		CATALINA	HT	EXP	FBG		IB	230	CC	10	2	5174	2	3	7450	8600
26	2	PAWNEE	SLP	SA/RC	FBG	KL	IB	6D	WEST	8		4074	4		7000	8050
27		COMMANDER	OP	EXP	FBG		IB	T200	CC	10	3	7174	1	11	10500	12000
27		COMMANDER	HT	EXP	FBG		IB	T200	CC	10	3	7174	1	11	10500	12000
28	1	COMMANDER	HT	EXP	FBG	DV	IB	T200-T230		11	1	7733	2	7	11000	12800
28	1	COMMANDER	FB	EXP	FBG	DV	IB	T200-T230		11	1	7733	2	7	11000	12800
28	6	CATALINA	OP	EXP	FBG		IB	230	CC	10	6	6125	2	3	9300	10500
28	6	CATALINA	OP	EXP	FBG		IB	T200	CC	10	6	7371	2	3	11000	12500
28	6	CATALINA	HT	EXP	FBG		IB	230	CC	10	6	6125	2	3	9300	10500
28	6	CATALINA	HT	EXP	FBG		IB	T200	CC	10	6	7371	2	3	11000	12500
30		SEA-SKIFF	OP	EXP	L/P		IB	T200	CC	10	8	7815	2	2	13300	15100
30		SEA-SKIFF	HT	EXP	L/P		IB	T200	CC	10	8	7815	2	2	13300	15100
30	3	SHIELDS	SLP	SA/OD	FBG	KL	OB			6	5	4600	4	9	8250	9500
31		CATALINA	OP	EXP	FBG		IB	T230	CC	11	7	10300	2	4	16100	18300
31		CATALINA	OP	EXP	FBG		IB	T145D	PERK	11	7	10300	2	4	21100	23400
31		CATALINA	HT	EXP	FBG		IB	T230	CC	11	7	10300	2	4	16100	18300
31		CATALINA	HT	EXP	FBG		IB	T145D	PERK	11	7	10300	2	4	21100	23400
31		CATALINA	FB	EXP	FBG		IB	T230	CC	11	7	10300	2	4	16100	18300
31		CATALINA	FB	EXP	FBG		IB	T145D	PERK	11	7	10300	2	4	21100	23400
31		COMMANDER	OP	EXP	FBG		IB	T230	CC	11	4	10400	2	4	16100	18300
31		COMMANDER	OP	EXP	FBG		IB	T145D	PERK	11	4	10400	2	4	21100	23500
31		COMMANDER	HT	EXP	FBG		IB	T230	CC	11	4	10400	2	4	16100	18300
31		COMMANDER	HT	EXP	FBG		IB	T145D	PERK	11	4	10400	2	4	21100	23500
31		COMMANDER	FB	EXP	FBG		IB	T230	CC	11	4	10400	2	4	16100	18300
31		COMMANDER	FB	EXP	FBG		IB	T145D	PERK	11	4	10400	2	4	21100	23500
31		COMMANDER	HT	SDN	FBG		IB	T230	CC	11	4	10800	2	4	18100	20200
31		COMMANDER	HT	SDN	FBG		IB	T145D	PERK	11	4	10800	2	4	24300	27000
31		COMMANDER	FB	SDN	FBG		IB	T230	CC	11	4	10800	2	4	18100	20200
31		COMMANDER	FB	SDN	FBG		IB	T145D	PERK	11	4	10800	2	4	24300	27000
31		COMMANDER	HT	SPTCR	FBG		IB	T230-T300		11	4	9893	2	7	15900	18900
31		COMMANDER	HT	SPTCR	FBG		IB	T145D	PERK	11	4	9893	2	7	20600	22800
31		COMMANDER	FB	SPTCR	FBG		IB	T230-T300		11	4	9893	2	7	15900	18900
31		COMMANDER	FB	SPTCR	FBG		IB	T145D	PERK	11	4	9893	2	7	20600	22800
31		CONSTELLATION	OP	EXP	P/M		IB	T230	CC	10	8	8820	2		15400	17500
31		CONSTELLATION	HT	EXP	P/M		IB	T230	CC	10	8	8820	2		15400	17500
31		CONSTELLATION	FB	EXP	P/M		IB	T230	CC	10	8	8820	2		15400	17500
33		CATALINA	OP	EXP	FBG		IB	T230	CC	12	4	11229	2	3	19800	22000
33		CATALINA	HT	EXP	FBG		IB	T230	CC	12	4	11229	2	3	19800	22000
33		CATALINA	FB	EXP	FBG		IB	T230	CC	12	4	11229	2	3	19800	22000
33		CATALINA	FB	SDN	FBG		IB	T230	CC	12	4	12643	2	4	21800	24200
33		CATALINA	FB	SDN	FBG		IB	T145D	PERK	12	4	12643	2	4	28800	32000
33		SEA-SKIFF	OP	EXP	L/P		IB	T230	CC	11	10	9278	2	3	19200	21300
33		SEA-SKIFF	HT	EXP	L/P		IB	T230	CC	11	10	9278	2	3	19200	21300
33		SEA-SKIFF	FB	EXP	L/P		IB	T230	CC	11	10	9278	2	3	19200	21300
34		AQUA-HOME	HT	HB	FBG		IO	200	CC	12	10	11600	2	7	25400	28200
34		AQUA-HOME	HT	HB	FBG		IO	T150	CC	12	10	12200	2	8	28000	31200
34		AQUA-HOME	HT	HB	FBG		IB	T230	CC	12	10	12200	2	8	28600	31800
34		AQUA-HOME	FB	HB	FBG		IO	200	CC	12	10	11600	2	7	25400	28200
34		AQUA-HOME	FB	HB	FBG		IO	T150	CC	12	10	12200	2	8	28000	31200
34		AQUA-HOME	FB	HB	FBG		IB	T230	CC	12	10	12200	2	8	28600	31800
35		COMMANDER	HT	EXP	FBG		IB	T230	CC	13		14344	3		24200	26900
35		COMMANDER	HT	EXP	FBG		IB	T300	CC	13		14344	3		24900	27700
35		COMMANDER	HT	EXP	FBG		IB	T189D	CUM	13		14344	3		32000	35500
35		COMMANDER	FB	EXP	FBG		IB	T230	CC	13		14344	3		24200	26900
35		COMMANDER	FB	EXP	FBG		IB	T300	CC	13		14344	3		24900	27700
35		COMMANDER	FB	EXP	FBG		IB	T189D	CUM	13		14344	3		32000	35500
35		COMMANDER	FB	SPTCR	FBG		IB	T230	CC	13		17364	3		26200	29200
35		COMMANDER	FB	SPTCR	FBG		IB	T300	CC	13		17364	3		26900	29800
35		COMMANDER	FB	SPTCR	FBG		IB	T189D	CUM	13		17364	3		35600	39500
35		COMMANDER SALON	OP	DC	FBG		IB	T230	CC	13		16100	3		25400	28200
35		COMMANDER SALON	OP	DC	FBG		IB	T300	CC	13		16100	3		26000	28900
35		COMMANDER SALON	OP	DC	FBG		IB	T189D	CUM	13		16100	3		34000	37800
35		COMMANDER SALON	HT	DC	FBG		IB	T230	CC	13		16100	3		25400	28200
35		COMMANDER SALON	HT	DC	FBG		IB	T300	CC	13		16100	3		26000	28900
35		COMMANDER SALON	HT	DC	FBG		IB	T189D	CUM	13		16100	3		34000	37800
35	2	CARIBBEAN	SLP	MS	FBG	KL	IB	42D	PERK	11		18000	4	8	32600	36200
35	2	CARIBBEAN	KTH	MS	FBG	KL	IB	42D	PERK	11		18000	4	8	32600	36300
36		FUTURA SALON	FB	MY	PLY		IB	T230	CC	12	8	11672	2	5	25800	28700
37		APACHE	SLP	SA/RC	FBG	KL	IB			11	6	14280	5	9	27100	30100
38		COMMANDER	HT	EXP	FBG		IB	T300	CC	13		16954	3		33200	36900
38		COMMANDER	HT	EXP	FBG		IB	T258D	GM	13		19654	3		42600	47300
38		COMMANDER	FB	EXP	FBG		IB	T300	CC	13		16954	3		33200	36900
38		COMMANDER	FB	EXP	FBG		IB	T258D	GM	13		16954	3		38500	42800
38		COMMANDER	HT	SDN	FBG		IB	T300	CC	13		17736	3		34600	38400
38		COMMANDER	HT	SDN	FBG		IB	T258D	GM	13		17736	3		40000	44400
38		COMMANDER	FB	SDN	FBG		IB	T300	CC	13		17736	3		34600	38400
38		COMMANDER	FB	SDN	FBG		IB	T258D	GM	13		17736	3		40000	44400
38		CONSTELLATION SALON	FB	DC	MHG		IB	T230	CC	12	11	14880	2	11	30000	33300
38		REGAL-ROAMER	HT	SDN	AL		IB	T230	CC	12	10	16400	2	10	32600	36200
38		REGAL-ROAMER	HT	SDN	STL		IB	T230	CC	12	10	20500	3	1	38600	42900
38		REGAL-ROAMER	HT	SDN	AL		IB	T300	CC	12	10	16400	2	10	33000	36700
38		REGAL-ROAMER	HT	SDN	STL		IB	T300	CC	12	10	20500	3	1	39000	43300
38		REGAL-ROAMER	FB	SDN	AL		IB	T230	CC	12	10	16400	2	10	32600	36200
38		REGAL-ROAMER	FB	SDN	STL		IB	T230	CC	12	10	20500	3	1	38600	42900
38		REGAL-ROAMER	FB	SDN	AL		IB	T300	CC	12	10	16400	2	10	33000	36700
38		REGAL-ROAMER	FB	SDN	STL		IB	T300	CC	12	10	20500	3	1	39000	43300
38		RIVIERA-ROAMER	HT	EXP	AL		IB	T230	CC	12	10	16400	2	10	32400	36000
38		RIVIERA-ROAMER	HT	EXP	STL		IB	T230	CC	12	10	20400	3	1	38300	42600
38		RIVIERA-ROAMER	HT	EXP	AL		IB	T300	CC	12	10	16400	2	10	32800	36400
38		RIVIERA-ROAMER	HT	EXP	STL		IB	T300	CC	12	10	20400	3	1	38700	43000
38		RIVIERA-ROAMER	FB	EXP	AL		IB	T230	CC	12	10	16400	2	10	32400	36000
38		RIVIERA-ROAMER	FB	EXP	STL		IB	T230	CC	12	10	20400	3	1	38300	42600
38		RIVIERA-ROAMER	FB	EXP	AL		IB	T300	CC	12	10	16400	2	10	32800	36400
38		RIVIERA-ROAMER	FB	EXP	STL		IB	T300	CC	12	10	20400	3	1	38700	43000
40		CORINTHIAN		SDN	PLY		IB	T300	CC	14		24110	3		46500	51100
41		REGAL-ROAMER		SDN	AL		IB	T300	CC	15		22600	2	10	43200	48000
42		COMANCHE	SLP	SA/RC	FBG	KL	IB	30	UNIV	10	10	17641	6	6	39500	43900
42		COMANCHE	SLP	SA/RC	FBG	KL	IB	15D	VLVO	10	10	17641	6	6	39900	44300
42		COMANCHE	SLP	SA/RC	FBG	KL	IB	42D	PERK	10	10	17641	6	6	40000	44500
42		COMMANDER SALON DC	FB	DC	FBG		IB	T300	CC	13		22823	3	2	49500	54400
42		COMMANDER SALON DC	FB	DC	FBG		IB	T258D	GM	13		22823	3	2	55100	60600
42		COMMANDER SPORTS CR	HT	SDNSF	FBG		IB	T300	CC	13		22193	3	2	47700	52400
42		COMMANDER SPORTS CR	HT	SDNSF	FBG		IB	T258D	GM	13		22193	3	2	52900	58200
42		COMMANDER SPORTS CR	FB	SDNSF	FBG		IB	T300	CC	13		22193	3	2	47600	52300
42		COMMANDER SPORTS CR	FB	SDNSF	FBG		IB	T258D	GM	13		22193	3	2	52800	58000

 CONTINUED ON NEXT PAGE

LOA FT	IN	NAME AND/ OR MODEL	TOP/ RIG	BOAT TYPE	-HULL- MTL	TP	----ENGINE--- TP	# HP	MFG	BEAM FT	IN	WGT LBS	DRAFT FT	IN	RETAIL LOW	RETAIL HIGH
		1971 BOATS														
42		CONSTELLATION	HT	MY	M/P		IB	T230	CC	13			3		48500	53300
42		CONSTELLATION	HT	MY	M/P		IB	T300	CC	13			3		50400	55400
46		AQUA-HOME	HT	HB	FBG		IB	T230	CC	15		16666	2	6	36900	41100
46		AQUA-HOME	HT	HB	FBG		IB	T145D	PERK	15		16666	2	6	44400	49300
46		AQUA-HOME	FB	HB	FBG		IB	T230	CC	15		16666	2	6	36900	41100
46		AQUA-HOME	FB	HB	FBG		IB	T145D	PERK	15		16666	2	6	44400	49300
47		COMMANDER	HT	DC	FBG		IB	T300	CC	15		33000	3	2	55400	60800
		IB T258D GM 61000 67100, IB T280D CUM 62900 69100, IB T350D CUM													68600	75400
47		COMMANDER	FB	DC	FBG		IB	T300	CC	15		33000	3	2	55000	60400
		IB T258D GM 60600 66600, IB T280D CUM 62400 68600, IB T350D CUM													68100	74800
47		COMMANDER COCKPIT	FB	MYCPT	FBG		IB	T258D	GM	15		33000	3	2	68300	75100
47		COMMANDER COCKPIT	FB	MYCPT	FBG		IB	T350D	CUM	15		33000	3	2	76300	83900
47		COMMANDER S C	HT	MY	FBG		IB	T300	CC	15		33000	3	2	63000	69200
		IB T258D GM 69900 76800, IB T280D CUM 72200 79300, IB T350D CUM													78900	86700
47		COMMANDER S C	FB	MY	FBG		IB	T300	CC	15		33000	3	2	62500	68700
		IB T258D GM 69100 75900, IB T280D CUM 71600 78700, IB T350D CUM													81600	89700
55		COMMANDER	HT	MY	FBG		IB	T320D	CAT	16	6	52600	3	9	94200	103500
		IB T320D GM 94200 103500, IB T350D CUM 98000 107500, IB T390D GM													103000	113000
55		COMMANDER	FB	MY	FBG		IB	T320D	CAT	16	6	52600	3	9	92000	101000
		IB T320D GM 92000 101000, IB T350D CUM 95700 105000, IB T390D GM													100500	110500
57		CONSTELLATION	HT	MY	M/P		IB	T320D	CAT	15		46525	4		83600	91900
		IB T320D GM 83800 92000, IB T350D CUM 88400 97100, IB T390D GM													93800	103000
57		CONSTELLATION	FB	MY	M/P		IB	T320D	CAT	15		46525	4		81800	89900
		IB T320D GM 81900 90000, IB T350D CUM 86400 95000, IB T390D GM													91700	101000
58		RIVIERA-ROAMER	HT	MY	AL		IB	T320D	GM	17	3	68500	4	8	130500	143500
		IB T388D CAT 138500 152500, IB T390D GM 138500 152000, IB T480D GM													147500	162500
58		RIVIERA-ROAMER	FB	MY	AL		IB	T320D	GM	17	3	68500	4	8	128500	141500
		IB T388D CAT 136500 150000, IB T390D GM 136500 150000, IB T480D GM													146000	160500
60	10	COMMANDER	HT	MY	FBG		IB	T555D	GM	18		80235	4	7	181000	199000
60	10	COMMANDER ENCL AFT	HT	MY	FBG		IB	T555D	GM	18		80235	4	7	191500	210500
		1970 BOATS														
17		LANCER	OP	SKI	FBG	SV	IB	230	CC	7	2	2505	1	8	2300	2650
17	7	LANCER	OP	RNBT	FBG	DV	IO	150	CC	7	3	2150	2	6	3550	4150
19	3	XK-19	OP	RNBT	FBG	SV	IB	230	CC	7	4	2861	2	6	2950	3400
19	3	XK-19	OP	RNBT	FBG	SV	IO	310	CC	7	4	2861	2	6	5400	6200
19	4	CUSTOM SUPER SPORT	OP	RNBT	FBG		IB	230	CC	7	5	2861	2	6	2950	3450
19	7	LANCER	ST	RNBT	FBG	DV	IO	185	CC	7	7	2626	2	6	4600	5300
22	1	CUTLASS CAVALIER	OP	RNBT	FBG	SV	IB	230	CC	7	11	3608	2	1	4350	5050
23	1	LANCER OFFSHORE	OP	RNBT	FBG	DV	IO	200	CC	8		3900	2	8	7650	8800
23	1	LANCER PREMIER	OP	RNBT	FBG	DV	VD	300	CC	8		4625	2	7	5600	6450
25		CORINTHIAN SP		SPTCR	P/P	RB	IB	185		9	1	4700	2		6200	7100
25	1	LANCER	OP	RNBT	FBG	DV	IO	200	CC	9	8	4550	2	10	9700	11000
25	1	LANCER	OP	RNBT	FBG	DV	IO	T150	CC	9	8	5000	2	7	11300	12900
25	1	LANCER	HT	RNBT	FBG	DV	IO	200	CC	9	8	4550	2	10	9700	11000
25	1	LANCER	HT	RNBT	FBG	DV	IO	T150	CC	9	8	5000	2	7	11300	12900
25	1	LANCER	FB	SF	FBG	DV	IO	200	CC	9	8	5800	2	10	14200	16100
25	1	LANCER	FB	SF	FBG	DV	IO	T150	CC	9	8	5800	2	7	15400	17500
25	1	LANCER SPORTSMAN	HT	CUD	FBG	DV	IO	200	CC	9	8	4153	2	10	9900	11200
25	1	LANCER SPORTSMAN	HT	CUD	FBG	DV	IO	T150	CC	9	8	4601	2	7	11600	13200
26		CATALINA	OP	EXP	FBG	SV	IB	200-230		10	2	4883	2	3	6850	8050
26		CATALINA	HT	EXP	FBG	SV	IB	200-230		10	2	4883	2	3	6850	8050
26		FUTURA	OP	EXP	PLY	SV	IB	200	CC	9	6	4471	1	10	6450	7400
26	2	PAWNEE	SLP	SA/RC	FBG	KL	OB			8		4074	4		6450	7450
26	2	PAWNEE	SLP	SA/RC	FBG	KL	IB	6	WEST	8		4074	4		6600	7600
27		COMMANDER	OP	EXP	FBG	SV	IB	T200	CC	10	3	7174	1	11	10200	11600
27		COMMANDER	HT	EXP	FBG	SV	IB	T200	CC	10	3	7174	1	11	10200	11600
28		FUTURA CAVALIER	OP	EXP	PLY		IB	230	CC	10	2	5192	2	3	7950	9100
28		FUTURA CAVALIER	HT	EXP	PLY		IB	230	CC	10	2	5192	2	3	7950	9100
28	6	CATALINA	OP	EXP	FBG	SV	IB	230	CC	10	6	5918	2	3	8850	10100
28	6	CATALINA	HT	EXP	FBG	SV	IB	230	CC	10	6	5918	2	3	8850	10100
30		FUTURA	OP	EXP	PLY	SV	IB	T200	CC	10	8	7815	2	2	12900	14600
30		FUTURA	HT	EXP	PLY	SV	IB	T200	CC	10	8	7815	2	2	12900	14600
30		SEA-SKIFF	OP	EXP	L/P	SV	IB	T200	CC	10	8	7815	2	2	12900	14600
30		SEA-SKIFF	HT	EXP	L/P	SV	IB	T200	CC	10	8	7815	2	2	12900	14600
30	3	SHIELDS	SLP	SA/OD	FBG	KL	OB			6	5	4600	4	9	8100	9350
31		COMMANDER	OP	EXP	FBG	SV	IB	T230	CC	11	3	10389	2	4	15500	17700
31		COMMANDER	HT	EXP	FBG	SV	IB	T230	CC	11	3	10389	2	4	15500	17700
31		COMMANDER	FB	EXP	FBG	SV	IB	T230	CC	11	3	10389	2	4	15500	17700
31		COMMANDER	HT	SDN	FBG	SV	IB	T230	CC	11	3	10801	2	4	17200	19500
31		COMMANDER	FB	SDN	FBG	SV	IB	T230	CC	11	3	10801	2	4	17200	19500
31		COMMANDER	HT	SPTCR	FBG	SV	IB	T230-T300		11	3	9893	2	7	15400	18300
31		COMMANDER	FB	SPTCR	FBG	SV	IB	T230-T300		11	3	9893	2	7	15400	18300
31		CONSTELLATION	OP	EXP	P/M	SV	IB	T230	CC	10	8	8820	2		14900	17000
31		CONSTELLATION	HT	EXP	P/M	SV	IB	T230	CC	10	8	8820	2		14900	17000
31		CONSTELLATION	FB	EXP	P/M	SV	IB	T230	CC	10	8	8820	2		14900	17000
32		CHEROKEE	SLP	SA/RC	FBG	KL	IB	30	UNIV	9		8698	5	1	15800	18000
33		CATALINA	OP	EXP	FBG	SV	IB	T230	CC	12	4	10585	2	4	19100	21200
33		CATALINA	HT	EXP	FBG	SV	IB	T230	CC	12	4	10585	2	4	19100	21200
33		CATALINA	FB	EXP	FBG	SV	IB	T230	CC	12	4	10585	2	4	19100	21200
33		CATALINA	FB	SDN	FBG	SV	IB	T230	CC	12	4	11883	2	4	20800	23100
33		CATALINA	FB	SDN	FBG	SV	IB	T145D	PERK	12	4	11883	2	4	27600	30700
33		FUTURA CAVALIER	OP	EXP	PLY		IB	T230	CC	11	10	10200	2	3	19100	21200
33		FUTURA CAVALIER	HT	EXP	PLY		IB	T230	CC	11	10	10200	2	3	19100	21200
33		FUTURA CAVALIER	FB	EXP	PLY		IB	T230	CC	11	10	10200	2	3	19100	21200
33		SEA-SKIFF	OP	EXP	L/P	SV	IB	T230	CC	11	10	9278	2	3	18800	20800
33		SEA-SKIFF	HT	EXP	L/P	SV	IB	T230	CC	11	10	9278	2	3	18800	20800
33		SEA-SKIFF	FB	EXP	L/P	SV	IB	T230	CC	11	10	9278	2	3	18800	20800
33		SEA-SKIFF	HT	SDN	L/P		IB	T230	CC	11	10		2	3	18300	20400
33		SEA-SKIFF	FB	SDN	L/P		IB	T230	CC	11	10		2	3	18300	20400
34		AQUA-HOME	HT	HB	FBG	SV	IO	200	CC	12	10	10484	2	7	23000	25500
34		AQUA-HOME	HT	HB	FBG	SV	IO	T150	CC	12	10	10484	2	8	24800	27500
34		AQUA-HOME	FB	HB	FBG	SV	IO	200	CC	12	10	10484	2	7	23000	25500
34		AQUA-HOME	FB	HB	FBG	SV	IO	T150	CC	12	10	10484	2	8	24800	27500
35		COMMANDER	HT	EXP	FBG	SV	IB	T230	CC	13		14344	3		23500	26100
35		COMMANDER	HT	EXP	FBG	SV	IB	T300	CC	13		14344	3		24100	26800
35		COMMANDER	HT	EXP	FBG	SV	IB	T145D	PERK	13		14344	3		31000	34400
35		COMMANDER	FB	EXP	FBG	SV	IB	T230	CC	13		14344	3		23500	26100
35		COMMANDER	FB	EXP	FBG	SV	IB	T300	CC	13		14344	3		24100	26800
35		COMMANDER	FB	EXP	FBG	SV	IB	T145D	PERK	13		14344	3		31000	34400
35		COMMANDER	FB	SPTCR	FBG	SV	IB	T230	CC	13		17364	3		25400	28200
35		COMMANDER	FB	SPTCR	FBG	SV	IB	T300	CC	13		17364	3		26000	28900
35		COMMANDER	FB	SPTCR	FBG	SV	IB	T145D	PERK	13		17364	3		34600	38500
35		CORINTHIAN	HT	EXP	PLY		IB	T230	CC	11	7	12870	2	5	21700	24100
35		CORINTHIAN	FB	EXP	PLY		IB	T230	CC	11	7	12870	2	5	21700	24100
35		SEA-SKIFF	HT	SDN	L/P		IB	T230	CC	12	6	14320	2	7	24700	27500
35		SEA-SKIFF	FB	SDN	L/P		IB	T230	CC	12	6	14320	2	7	24700	27500
35	2	CARIBBEAN	SLP	MS	FBG	KL	IB	42D	PERK	11		18000	4	8	32000	35600
35	2	CARIBBEAN	KTH	MS	FBG	KL	IB	42D	PERK	11		18000	4	8	32100	35600
36		FUTURA SALON	FB	MY	PLY	SV	IB	T230	CC	12	8	11672	2	5	25100	27900
36		SEA-SKIFF	FB	MY	L/P		IB	T230	CC	12	8	12672	2	6	25900	28800
37		APACHE	SLP	SA/RC	FBG	KL	IB	30	UNIV	10	3	14280	5	9	26600	29600
37		APACHE	SLP	SA/RC	FBG	KL	IB	15D	VLVO	10	3	14280	5	9	26800	29800
38		COMMANDER	HT	EXP	FBG	SV	IB	T300	CC	13		16954	3		32300	35900
38		COMMANDER	HT	EXP	FBG	SV	IB	T258D	GM	13		16954	3		37500	41600
38		COMMANDER	FB	EXP	FBG	SV	IB	T300	CC	13		16954	3		32300	35900
38		COMMANDER	HT	SDN	FBG	SV	IB	T300	CC	13		17736	3		33600	37400
38		COMMANDER	HT	SDN	FBG	SV	IB	T197D	GM	13		17736	3		37600	41700
38		COMMANDER	HT	SDN	FBG	SV	IB	T258D	GM	13		17736	3		38900	43200
38		COMMANDER	FB	SDN	FBG	SV	IB	T300	CC	13		17736	3		33600	37400
38		CONSTELLATION	FB	DC	MHG	SV	IB	T230	CC	12	11	14880	2	11	29200	32400
38		REGAL-ROAMER	HT	SDN	AL	SV	IB	T230	CC	12	10	16400	2	10	31700	35200
38		REGAL-ROAMER	HT	SDN	AL	SV	IB	T300	CC	12	10	16400	2	10	32100	35700
38		REGAL-ROAMER	HT	SDN	STL	SV	IB	T300	CC	12	10	20500	3	1	37900	42200
38		REGAL-ROAMER	FB	SDN	AL	SV	IB	T230	CC	12	10	16400	2	10	31700	35200
38		REGAL-ROAMER	FB	SDN	AL	SV	IB	T300	CC	12	10	16400	2	10	32100	35700
38		REGAL-ROAMER	FB	SDN	STL	SV	IB	T300	CC	12	10	20500	3	1	37900	42200
38		RIVIERA-ROAMER	HT	EXP	AL	SV	IB	T230	CC	12	10	16400	2	10	31500	35000
38		RIVIERA-ROAMER	HT	EXP	AL	SV	IB	T300	CC	12	10	16400	2	10	31900	35500
38		RIVIERA-ROAMER	HT	EXP	STL	SV	IB	T300	CC	12	10	20400	3	1	37600	41800
38		RIVIERA-ROAMER	FB	EXP	AL	SV	IB	T230	CC	12	10	16400	2	10	31500	35000
38		RIVIERA-ROAMER	FB	EXP	AL	SV	IB	T300	CC	12	10	16400	2	10	31900	35500
38		RIVIERA-ROAMER	FB	EXP	STL	SV	IB	T300	CC	12	10	20400	3	1	37600	41800
40		CORINTHIAN SEA SKIFF		SDNSF	PLY		IB	300	CC	14		24110	3		43600	48400
41		REGAL-ROAMER	HT	SDN	AL	SV	IB	T300	CC	15		22600	2	10	42100	46800
41		REGAL-ROAMER	HT	SDN	AL	SV	IB	T258D	GM	15		22600	2	10	47900	52700
41		REGAL-ROAMER	FB	SDN	AL	SV	IB	T300	CC	15		22600	2	10	42000	46700
41		REGAL-ROAMER	FB	SDN	AL	SV	IB	T258D	GM	15		22600	2	10	47900	52600
42		COMANCHE	SLP	SA/RC	FBG	KL	IB	30	UNIV	10	10	17641	6	6	38800	43100

CONTINUED ON NEXT PAGE

LOA FT	LOA IN	NAME AND/ OR MODEL	TOP/ RIG	BOAT TYPE	-HULL- MTL	-HULL- TP	ENGINE TP	ENGINE # HP	ENGINE MFG	BEAM FT	BEAM IN	WGT LBS	DRAFT FT	DRAFT IN	RETAIL LOW	RETAIL HIGH
1970 BOATS																
42		COMANCHE	SLP	SA/RC	FBG	KL	IB	15D	VLVO	10	10	17641	6	6	39200	43500
42		COMANCHE	SLP	SA/RC	FBG	KL	IB	42D	PERK	10	10	17641	6	6	39300	43700
42		COMMANDER	OP	SPTCR	FBG	SV	IB	T300	CC	13		22193	3	2	44500	49500
42		COMMANDER	OP	SPTCR	FBG	SV	IB	T258D	GM	13		22193	3	2	49900	54800
42		COMMANDER SALON	OP	MY	FBG	SV	IB	T300	CC	13		22823	3	2	47700	52500
42		COMMANDER SALON	OP	MY	FBG	SV	IB	T258D	GM	13		22823	3	2	53100	58400
42		COMMANDER SALON	HT	MY	FBG	SV	IB	T300	CC	13		22823	3	2	48000	52700
42		COMMANDER SALON	HT	MY	FBG	SV	IB	T258D	GM	13		22823	3	2	53400	58700
46		AQUA-HOME	HT	HB	FBG	SV	IB	T230	CC	15		16666	2	6	35100	39000
46		AQUA-HOME	HT	HB	FBG	SV	IB	T145D	PERK	15		16666	2	6	42100	46800
46		AQUA-HOME	FB	HB	FBG	SV	IB	T230	CC	15		16666	2	6	35100	39000
46		AQUA-HOME	FB	HB	FBG	SV	IB	T145D	PERK	15		16666	2	6	42100	46800
47		COMMANDER 1 STRMAFT	HT	MY	FBG	SV	IB	T300	CC	15		31127	3	2	64600	71000
47		COMMANDER 1 STRMAFT	HT	MY	FBG	SV	IB	T258D	GM	15		31127	3	2	72000	79100
47		COMMANDER 2 STRMAFT	HT	MY	FBG	SV	IB	T300	CC	15		31127	3	2	65500	72000
47		COMMANDER 2 STRMAFT	HT	MY	FBG	SV	IB	T258D	GM	15		31127	3	2	72900	80100
47		COMMANDER W/COCKPIT	FB	YTFS	FBG	SV	IB	T258D	GM	15		31600	3	2	78800	86600
55		COMMANDER	HT	MY	FBG	SV	IB	T320D	GM	16	6	49300	3	9	85000	93400
55		COMMANDER	HT	MY	FBG	SV	IB	T375D	GM	16	6	49300	3	9	91800	101000
57		CONSTELLATION	HT	MY	M/P	SV	IB	T320D	GM	15		46525	4		80800	88800
58		RIVIERA-ROAMER	HT	MY	AL	SV	IB	T320D	GM	17	3	68500	4	8	126000	138500
58		RIVIERA-ROAMER	HT	MY	AL	SV	IB	T375D	GM	17	3	68500	4	8	132000	145000
60	10	COMMANDER	HT	MY	FBG	SV	IB	T478D	GM	18		80235	4	7	173000	190500
60	10	COMMANDER ENCL SALON	HT	MY	FBG	SV	IB	T478D	GM	18		83170	4	7	179500	197500
1969 BOATS																
17		CAVALIER	OP	SKI	FBG	SV	IB	200-230		7	2	2645	1	8	2300	2650
17		GRAND-PRIX	OP	SKI	M/P		IB	210		6	8	2618	1	7	2200	2550
17	7	LANCER CORSAIR	OP	RNBT	FBG	SV	IO	150	CC	7	4	2150	2	6	3750	4350
17	7	SPORT	OP	RNBT	FBG		IO	150		7	4	1950	2	3	3550	4150
19	4	COMMANDER SUPER SPT	OP	RNBT	FBG	SV	IB	230	CC	7	5	2861	2	6	2850	3350
19	7	LANCER CORSAIR	OP	RNBT	FBG		IO	185	CC	7	7	2810	2	6	4950	5700
20	4	SEA-V CORSAIR	OP	RNBT	FBG		IO	150		7	11				5400	6200
20	4	SEA-V CORSAIR	OP	RNBT	FBG		IB	185		7	11				3200	3700
20	4	SEA-V CORSAIR	OP	RNBT	FBG	SV	IB	185	CC	7	11	2725	2	2	3200	3700
22	1	CUTLASS CAVALIER	OP	RNBT	FBG	SV	IB	230	CC	7	11	3608	2	1	4200	4850
23	1	COMMANDER	OP	CUD	FBG	DV	IB	230-300		8		4325	2	7	5050	6250
23	1	LANCER CORSAIR	OP	RNBT	FBG	DV	IO	150-185		8		3910	2	8	7900	9100
25		CORINTHIAN		SPTCR	P/P		IB	185		9	1	4700	2		6000	6900
25	1	LANCER CORSAIR	FB	SF	FBG		IO	185	CC	9	8	5200	2	10	13500	15400
25	1	LANCER CORSAIR	FB	SF	FBG		IO	T150	CC	9	8	6300	2	3	16900	19200
26		CUTLASS	OP	RNBT	L/P		IB	210		10		3567	2		5550	6400
26		FUTURA CAVALIER	OP	EXP	PLY	SV	IB	200-230		10		5030	2	2	6750	7900
26		FUTURA CAVALIER	HT	EXP	PLY	SV	IB	200-230		10		5030	2	2	6750	7900
26	3	CAPITAN	SLP	SA/RC	FBG	KL	OB			8	2	4300	4		6700	7700
26	3	CAPRI 26	SLP	SAIL	FBG	KL	OB			8	2	4800	4		7450	8600
27		COMMANDER	HT	EXP	FBG	SV	IB	T200	CC	10	3	6436	1	10	9400	10700
27		COMMANDER	FB	EXP	FBG	SV	IB	T200	CC	10	3	6436	1	10	9400	10700
27		COMMANDER	OP	RNBT	FBG	SV	IB	230	CC	10	3	5915	2	2	7850	9050
27		COMMANDER	OP	RNBT	FBG	SV	IB	T200	CC	10	3	7174	1	10	9700	11000
27		COMMANDER	HT	RNBT	FBG	SV	IB	230	CC	10	3	5915	2	2	7850	9050
27		COMMANDER	HT	RNBT	FBG	SV	IB	T200	CC	10	3	7174	1	10	9700	11000
27		SEA-SKIFF	OP	EXP	L/P	RB	IB	230	CC	10	3	5370	2		7600	8750
27		SEA-SKIFF	HT	EXP	L/P	RB	IB	230	CC	10	3	5370	2		7600	8750
28		CLIPPER SEA SKIFF		SPTCR	L/P		IB	210		10	6		2	6	8900	10100
28	6	FUTURA CAVALIER	OP	EXP	PLY	SV	IB	230	CC	10	2	5192	2	3	8100	9300
28	6	FUTURA CAVALIER	HT	EXP	PLY	SV	IB	230	CC	10	2	5192	2	3	8100	9300
29	9	CORSAIR 29	FB	CR	FBG		IO	T210		11	6		1	6	19300	21400
30		CONSTELLATION		EXP	M/P		IB	T210		10	8	9110	2		13100	14900
30		FUTURA CAVALIER	OP	EXP	PLY	SV	IB	T200	CC	10	8	8640	2	2	12800	14500
30		FUTURA CAVALIER	HT	EXP	PLY	SV	IB	T200	CC	10	8	8640	2	2	12800	14500
30		SEA-SKIFF	OP	EXP	L/P		IB	T200	CC	10	8	7815	2	2	12500	14200
30		SEA-SKIFF	HT	EXP	L/P		IB	T200	CC	10	8	7815	2	2	12500	14200
30		SEASTRAKE	OP	EXP	L/P		IB	210	CC	10	7		2	2	10500	11900
30		SEASTRAKE	OP	EXP	L/P		IB	T185		10	7		2	2	11700	13300
30		SEASTRAKE	HT	EXP	L/P		IB	210		10	7		2	2	10500	11900
30		SEASTRAKE	HT	EXP	L/P		IB	T185		10	7		2	2	11700	13300
30	3	SHIELDS	SLP	SA/OD	FBG	KL	OB			6	5	4600	4	9	8000	9200
31		CLIPPER SEA SKIFF	HT	CBNCR	L/P	RB	IB	T210		11	6	9750	2	3	16400	18600
31		CLIPPER SEA SKIFF	FB	CBNCR	L/P	RB	IB	T210		11	6	9750	2	3	16400	18600
31		CLIPPER SEA SKIFF	HT	SPTCR	L/P	RB	IB	T210		11	6	9100	2	3	13000	14700
31		CLIPPER SEA SKIFF	FB	SPTCR	L/P	RB	IB	T210		11	6	9100	2	3	13000	14700
31		COMMANDER	OP	EXP	FBG	SV	IB	T230	CC	11	3	9682	2	4	14900	16900
31		COMMANDER	HT	EXP	FBG	SV	IB	T230	CC	11	3	9682	2	4	14900	16900
31		COMMANDER	FB	EXP	FBG	SV	IB	T230	CC	11	3	9682	2	4	14900	16900
31		COMMANDER	HT	SDN	FBG	SV	IB	T230	CC	11	3	11500	2	4	16800	19100
31		COMMANDER	FB	SDN	FBG	SV	IB	T230	CC	11	3	11500	2	4	16800	19100
31		COMMANDER SPORTS	HT	EXP	FBG	SV	IB	T230-T300		11	3	9320	2	4	14700	17800
31		COMMANDER SPORTS	FB	EXP	FBG	SV	IB	T230-T300		11	3	10018	2	4	14900	17800
31		CONSTELLATION	OP	EXP	M/P		IB	T230	CC	10	8	9670	2		14700	16700
31		CONSTELLATION	HT	EXP	M/P		IB	T230	CC	10	8	9670	2		14700	16700
31		CONSTELLATION	FB	EXP	M/P		IB	T230	CC	10	8	9670	2		14700	16700
31		SEA-SKIFF	OP	EXP	L/P	RB	IB	T230	CC	11	3	9180	2	1	14700	16700
31		SEA-SKIFF	HT	EXP	L/P	RB	IB	T230	CC	11	3		2	1	14900	16900
31		SEA-SKIFF	FB	EXP	L/P	RB	IB	T230	CC	11	3		2	1	14900	16900
32		CHEROKEE	SLP	SA/RC	FBG	KL	IB	30	UNIV	9		8698	5	1	15600	17700
33		FUTURA CAVALIER	OP	EXP	PLY	SV	IB	T230	CC	11	10	10200	2	3	18500	20500
33		FUTURA CAVALIER	HT	EXP	PLY	SV	IB	T230	CC	11	10	10200	2	3	18500	20500
33		FUTURA CAVALIER	FB	EXP	PLY	SV	IB	T230	CC	11	10	10200	2	3	18500	20500
33		SEA-SKIFF	OP	EXP	L/P		IB	T230	CC	11	10	9278	2	3	18200	20200
33		SEA-SKIFF	HT	EXP	L/P		IB	T230	CC	11	10	9278	2	3	18200	20200
33		SEA-SKIFF	FB	EXP	L/P		IB	T230	CC	11	10	9278	2	3	18200	20200
33		SEA-SKIFF	HT	SDN	L/P		IB	T230	CC	11	10		2	3	17400	19700
33		SEA-SKIFF	FB	SDN	L/P		IB	T230	CC	11	10		2	3	17400	19700
33		SEASTRAKE CAVALIER	OP	EXP	L/P		IB	T210	CC	11	10	9009	2	3	17500	19800
33		SEASTRAKE CAVALIER	HT	EXP	L/P		IB	T210	CC	11	10	9009	2	3	17500	19800
33	3		HT	HB	FBG		IO	185	CC	12		9900	2	5	22500	25000
33	3		HT	HB	FBG		IO	T150	CC	12		10430	2	8	25200	28000
34		AQUA-HOME	HT	HB	FBG		IO	200	CC	12	10	10484	2	7	23400	26000
34		AQUA-HOME	FB	HB	FBG		IO	200	CC	12	10	10484	2	7	23400	26000
35		COMMANDER	HT	EXP	FBG	SV	IB	T230	CC	13		13478	3		22200	24700
35		COMMANDER	HT	EXP	FBG	SV	IB	T300	CC	13		13994	3		23100	25700
35		COMMANDER	FB	EXP	FBG	SV	IB	T230	CC	13		13994	3		22500	25000
35		COMMANDER	FB	EXP	FBG	SV	IB	T300	CC	13		13994	3		23100	25700
35		COMMANDER	FB	SPTCR	FBG	SV	IB	T230	CC	13		13271	3		22100	24600
35		COMMANDER	FB	SPTCR	FBG	SV	IB	T300	CC	13		13890	3		23100	25700
35		CORINTHIAN SEA SKIFF	HT	EXP	PLY	RB	IB	T230	CC	11	7	12870	2	5	21000	23400
35		CORINTHIAN SEA SKIFF	FB	EXP	PLY	RB	IB	T230	CC	11	7	12870	2	5	21000	23400
35		SEA-SKIFF	HT	SDN	L/P	RB	IB	T230	CC	12	6	14320	2	7	23900	26600
35		SEA-SKIFF	FB	SDN	L/P	RB	IB	T230	CC	12	6	14320	2	7	23900	26600
36		CAVALIER	FB	DC	PLY	SV	IB	T230	CC	12	8	12672	2	5	24500	27200
36		CONSTELLATION	HT	EXP	M/P		IB	T230	CC	12		14870	2	8	25800	28600
36		CORVETTE	OP	SPTCR	M/P	DV	IB	T230	CC	12	5	15800	3		27500	30600
36		CORVETTE	OP	SPTCR	M/P	DV	IB	T300	CC	12	5	15800	3		28100	31200
36		CORVETTE	HT	SPTCR	M/P	DV	IB	T230	CC	12	5	16300	3		28000	31100
36		CORVETTE	HT	SPTCR	M/P	DV	IB	T300	CC	12	5	16300	3		28500	31700
36		CORVETTE	FB	SPTCR	M/P	DV	IB	T230	CC	12	5	16300	3		28000	31100
36		CORVETTE	FB	SPTCR	M/P	DV	IB	T300	CC	12	5	16300	3		28500	31700
36		SEA-SKIFF	FB	MY	L/P	RB	IB	T230	CC	12	8	12672	2	6	25300	28100
37		APACHE	SLP	SA/RC	FBG	KL	IB	30	UNIV	10	3	14280	5	9	26200	29100
38		COMMANDER	HT	EXP	FBG	SV	IB	T300	CC	13		16644	3		31100	34500
38		COMMANDER	HT	EXP	FBG	SV	IB	T197D	GM	13		19272	3		38500	42800
38		COMMANDER	HT	EXP	FBG	SV	IB	T258D	GM	13		19272	3		39800	44200
38		COMMANDER	FB	EXP	FBG	SV	IB	T300	CC	13		19272	3		34700	38600
38		COMMANDER	HT	SDN	FBG	SV	IB	T300	CC	13		18580	3		33900	37700
38		COMMANDER	HT	SDN	FBG	SV	IB	T197D	GM	13		21200	3		41600	46200
38		COMMANDER	HT	SDN	FBG	SV	IB	T258D	GM	13		21200	3		42900	47600
38		COMMANDER	FB	SDN	FBG	SV	IB	T300	CC	13		21200	3		37600	41800
38		CONSTELLATION SALON		MY	MHG		IB	T		13			2	11	**	**
38		REGAL-ROAMER	HT	SDN	AL	SV	IB	T230	CC	12	10	17400	2	10	32300	35800
38		REGAL-ROAMER	HT	SDN	AL	SV	IB	T300	CC	12	10	17400	2	10	32600	36300
38		REGAL-ROAMER	HT	SDN	STL	SV	IB	T300	CC	12	10	21400	3	1	38200	42500
38		REGAL-ROAMER	FB	SDN	AL	SV	IB	T230	CC	12	10	21400	2	10	37800	42000
38		REGAL-ROAMER	FB	SDN	AL	SV	IB	T300	CC	12	10	21400	2	10	38200	42500
38		REGAL-ROAMER	FB	SDN	STL	SV	IB	T300	CC	12	10	21400	3	1	38200	42500
38		RIVIERA-ROAMER	HT	EXP	AL	SV	IB	T230	CC	12	10	17300	2	10	32000	35500
38		RIVIERA-ROAMER	HT	EXP	AL	SV	IB	T300	CC	12	10	17300	2	10	32300	35900
38		RIVIERA-ROAMER	HT	EXP	STL	SV	IB	T300	CC	12	10	21300	3	1	37900	42100
38		RIVIERA-ROAMER	FB	EXP	AL	SV	IB	T230	CC	12	10	21300	2	10	37600	41700
38		RIVIERA-ROAMER	FB	EXP	AL	SV	IB	T300	CC	12	10	21300	2	10	37900	42100
38		RIVIERA-ROAMER	FB	EXP	STL	SV	IB	T300	CC	12	10	21300	3	1	37900	42100
40		CORINTHIAN SEA SKIFF	HT	SDNSF	PLY	RB	IB	T300	CC	14		21840	3		40100	44600
40		CORINTHIAN SEA SKIFF	HT	SDNSF	PLY	RB	IB	T258D	GM	14		24110	3		49200	54000
40		CORINTHIAN SEA SKIFF	FB	SDNSF	PLY	RB	IB	T300	CC	14		24110	3		43600	48400
40		CORINTHIAN SEA SKIFF	FB	SDNSF	PLY	RB	IB	T258D	GM	14		24110	3		49200	54000
41		CONSTELLATION	OP	DC	M/P		IB	T230	CC	13		19920	2	11	39100	43400

 CONTINUED ON NEXT PAGE

LOA FT	LOA IN	NAME AND/ OR MODEL	TOP/ RIG	BOAT TYPE	-HULL- MTL	-HULL- TP	ENGINE TP	ENGINE # HP	ENGINE MFG	BEAM FT	BEAM IN	WGT LBS	DRAFT FT	DRAFT IN	RETAIL LOW	RETAIL HIGH
1969 BOATS																
41		CONSTELLATION	OP	DC	M/P		IB	T300	CC	13		19920	2	11	40200	44700
41		CONSTELLATION	HT	DC	M/P		IB	T230	CC	13		20540	2	11	40000	44500
41		CONSTELLATION	HT	DC	M/P		IB	T300	CC	13		20540	2	11	41100	45700
41		REGAL-ROAMER	HT	SDN	AL	SV	IB	T300	CC	15		23700	2	10	42600	47300
41		REGAL-ROAMER	HT	SDN	AL	SV	IB	T258D	GM	15		23700	2	10	48000	52800
41		REGAL-ROAMER	FB	SDN	AL	SV	IB	T300	CC	15		23700	2	10	42500	47200
41		REGAL-ROAMER	FB	SDN	AL	SV	IB	T258D	GM	15		23700	2	10	48000	52700
42		COMANCHE	SLP	SA/RC	FBG	KL	IB	30	UNIV	10	10	17641	6	6	38200	42500
42		COMMANDER	OP	DC	FBG	SV	IB	T300	CC	13		22443	3	2	47000	51700
42		COMMANDER	OP	DC	FBG	SV	IB	T258D	GM	13		25621	3	2	56400	62000
42		COMMANDER	HT	DC	FBG	SV	IB	T300	CC	13		25621	3	2	51300	56400
42		COMMANDER	HT	DC	FBG	SV	IB	T258D	GM	13		25621	3	2	56700	62300
42		COMMANDER	FB	SPTCR	FBG	SV	IB	T300	CC	13		22443	3	2	43800	48600
42		COMMANDER	FB	SPTCR	FBG	SV	IB	T258D	GM	13		25621	3	2	53200	58400
45		CONSTELLATION	HT	MY	M/P		IB	T300	CC	13		27410	3	2	48000	52700
46			HT	HB	FBG		VD	T230	CC	15		17900	2	6	37900	42100
46			FB	HB	FBG		VD	T230	CC	15		17900	2	6	37900	42100
46		RIVIERA-ROAMER	HT	MY	AL	SV	IB	T300	CC	15		42276	3	7	64300	70700
46		RIVIERA-ROAMER	HT	MY	AL	SV	IB	T320D	GM	15		42276	3	7	74200	81500
46		RIVIERA-ROAMER	HT	MY	STL	SV	IB	T320D	GM	15		50512	3	11	86100	94600
47		COMMANDER 1 STRMAFT	HT	MY	FBG		IB	T300	CC	15		30451	3	2	61900	68000
47		COMMANDER 1 STRMAFT	HT	MY	FBG		IB	T258D	GM	15		33539	3	2	73900	81200
47		COMMANDER 2 STRMAFT	HT	MY	FBG		IB	T300	CC	15		30451	3	2	62900	69100
47		COMMANDER 2 STRMAFT	HT	MY	FBG		IB	T258D	GM	15		33539	3	2	74800	82200
47		COMMANDER W/COCKPIT	FB	YTFS	FBG		IB	T258D	GM	15		33539	3	2	78900	86700
57		CONSTELLATION	HT	MY	M/P		IB	T320D	GM	15		46525	4		79400	87200
58		RIVIERA-ROAMER	HT	MY	AL	SV	IB	T388D	CAT	17	3	56450	4	3	106500	117000
60	10	COMMANDER		MY	FBG		IB	T478D	GM	18			4	7	117500	129000
1968 BOATS																
17		GRAND-PRIX	OP	SKI	M/P		IB	210	CC	6	8	2618	1	7	2050	2450
17		SEA-SKIFF 283	OP	SKI	M/P		IB	185	CC	6	8	2523	1	7	2000	2400
17	7	CORSAIR SPORT-V	OP	RNBT	FBG		IO	150	CC	7	4	1950	2	3	3700	4300
17	10	CAVALIER	OP	SKI	PLY		IB	185		6	10	2011	1	6	1900	2250
18	4	SUPER-SPORT	OP	RNBT	M/P	TR	IB	210		6	5		1	8	2350	2700
19	7	LANCER CORSAIR	OP	RNBT	FBG		IO	150	CC	7	7	2626	2	6	4900	5650
20					WD		IB	300	FORD						**	**
20		GRAND-PRIX	OP	RNBT	M/P		IB	210-300		6	8	3400	1	7	3250	3900
20	4	SEA-V CORSAIR	OP	RNBT	FBG		IO	150	CC	8	2	2383	2	3	5400	6200
20	4	SEA-V CORSAIR	OP	RNBT	FBG		IB	185	CC	7	11	2725	2	2	3100	3600
22		CUTLASS CAVALIER	OP	RNBT	L/P		IB	210	CC	8		3337	1	9	3850	4450
22		SEA-HAWK SPORTSMAN	OP	EXP	L/P		IB	185		8		3470	1	11	3900	4500
23	6	CORSAIR LANCER	OP	EXP	FBG		IO	185	CC	8		3979	2	8	9200	10400
23	6	LANCER CORSAIR	OP	RNBT	FBG		IO	150-185		8		3927	2	8	8400	9700
23	6	LANCER CORSAIR	OP	RNBT	FBG		IO	T120		8		3927	2	8	9400	10700
25		CORINTHIAN SEA SKIFF	OP	SPTCR	P/P	RB	IB	185-210		9	1	4700	2		5800	6750
25		CORINTHIAN SEA SKIFF	HT	SPTCR	P/P	RB	IB	185-210		9	1	4700	2		5800	6750
25		SEA-HAWK CLIPPER	OP	EXP	L/P		IB	185		9	1	4500	2		5650	6500
25		SEA-HAWK SPORTSMAN		EXP	L/P		IB	185		9	1	4400	2		5550	6400
25		SEASTRAKE	OP	EXP	L/P		IB	185		9	6	4640	2		5800	6700
26		CUTLASS CAVALIER	OP	RNBT	L/P		IB	210	CC	10		3567	2		5400	6200
26		CUTLASS CAVALIER	OP	RNBT	L/P		IB	T185		10		3567	2		6250	7150
26		FUTURA CAVALIER	OP	EXP	PLY		IB	185-210		10		4300	2	2	5900	6900
26		FUTURA CAVALIER	HT	EXP	PLY		IB	185-210		10		4700	2	2	6200	7250
26	3	CAPITAN 26	SLP	SA/RC	FBG	KL	OB			8	2	4300	4		6650	7650
26	3	CAPRI	SLP	SAIL	FBG	KL	OB			8	2	4800	4		7400	8500
27		COMMANDER	OP	EXP	FBG		IB	210	CC	10	3	6290	1	10	7950	9150
27		COMMANDER	OP	EXP	FBG		IB	T185		10	3	6290	1	10	8900	10100
27		COMMANDER	HT	EXP	FBG		IB	210		10	3	7470	1	10	8900	10100
27		COMMANDER	HT	EXP	FBG		IB	T185		10	3	7470	1	10	9700	11000
27		COMMANDER SPORTS	ST	EXP	FBG		IB	210	CC	10	3	5330	1	10	7250	8350
27		COMMANDER SPORTS	ST	EXP	FBG		IB	T185		10	3	5330	1	10	8150	9400
27		COMMANDER SPORTS	HT	EXP	FBG		IB	210		10	3	6710	1	10	8250	9500
27		COMMANDER SPORTS	HT	EXP	FBG		IB	T185		10	3	6710	1	10	9200	10500
27		COMMANDER SPORTS	FB	EXP	FBG		IB	210		10	3	6710	1	10	8250	9500
27		COMMANDER SPORTS	FB	EXP	FBG		IB	T185		10	3	6710	1	10	9200	10500
27		FUTURA CAVALIER	OP	EXP	PLY		IB	185-210		10	3	5240	2	1	7050	8250
27		FUTURA CAVALIER	HT	EXP	PLY		IB	185-210		10	3	5240	2	1	7050	8250
27		SEA-SKIFF		EXP	L/P		IB	230		10	3	5370	2		7400	8500
27		SEASTRAKE CAVALIER	OP	EXP	L/P		IB	210	CC	10	3	4706	2		6850	7850
27		SEASTRAKE CAVALIER	HT	EXP	L/P		IB	210	CC	10	3	5310	2		7250	8350
28		CLIPPER SEA SKIFF	HT	SPTCR	L/P	RB	IB	210	CC	10	6	7850	2	6	9050	10300
28		CLIPPER SEA SKIFF	HT	SPTCR	L/P	RB	IB	T210	CC	10	6	7850	2	6	10000	11400
28		CLIPPER SEA SKIFF	FB	SPTCR	L/P	RB	IB	210	CC	10	6	8730	2	6	9550	10900
28		CLIPPER SEA SKIFF	FB	SPTCR	L/P	RB	IB	T210	CC	10	6	8730	2	6	10500	12000
28		CORINTHIAN SEA SKIFF	HT	SPTCR	PLY	RB	IB	210		10	1	7000	2	4	8350	9600
28		CORINTHIAN SEA SKIFF	FB	SPTCR	PLY	RB	IB	210		10	1	7000	2	4	8350	9600
28		CRUSADER CAVALIER	OP	EXP	MHG		IB	210		10	2	5858	1	11	7700	8850
28		CRUSADER CAVALIER	HT	EXP	MHG		IB	210		10	2	5858	1	11	7700	8850
28		SEA-HAWK SEA SKIFF	OP	EXP	L/P		IB	210		10	1	7000	2	4	8350	9600
28		SEA-HAWK SEA SKIFF	HT	EXP	L/P		IB	210		10	1	7000	2	4	8350	9600
28		SEA-HAWK SPORT	OP	EXP	L/P		IB	210		10	2	6200	2	1	7900	9100
28		SEA-HAWK SPORT	HT	EXP	L/P		IB	210		10	2	6200	2	1	7900	9100
28		SEA-HAWK SPORT	FB	EXP	L/P		IB	210		10	2	6200	2	1	7900	9100
28	6	FUTURA CAVALIER	OP	EXP	PLY		IB	230	CC	10	2	5192	2	3	7850	9000
28	6	FUTURA CAVALIER	HT	EXP	PLY		IB	230	CC	10	2	5192	2	3	7850	9000
30		CONSTELLATION	OP	EXP	M/P		IB	T210	CC	10	8	9110	2		12700	14400
30		CONSTELLATION	HT	EXP	M/P		IB	T210	CC	10	8	9110	2		12700	14400
30		CONSTELLATION	FB	EXP	M/P		IB	T210	CC	10	8	9110	2		12700	14400
30		CRUSADER CAVALIER	OP	EXP	M/P		IB	T210	CC	10	8	9100	2		12700	14400
30		CRUSADER CAVALIER	HT	EXP	M/P		IB	T210	CC	10	8	9100	2		12700	14400
30		FUTURA CAVALIER	OP	EXP	PLY		IB	210	CC	10	7	7170	2	1	10600	12000
30		FUTURA CAVALIER	OP	EXP	PLY		IB	T185		10	7	7170	2	1	11700	13200
30		FUTURA CAVALIER	HT	EXP	PLY		IB	210	CC	10	7	8350	2	1	11100	12600
30		FUTURA CAVALIER	HT	EXP	PLY		IB	T185		10	7	8350	2	1	12100	13800
30		SEASTRAKE CAVALIER	OP	EXP	L/P		IB	210		10	7	6300	2	2	10200	11600
30		SEASTRAKE CAVALIER	OP	EXP	L/P		IB	T185		10	7	6950	2	2	11600	13200
30		SEASTRAKE CAVALIER	HT	EXP	L/P		IB	210		10	7	6300	2	2	10200	11600
30		SEASTRAKE CAVALIER	HT	EXP	L/P		IB	T185		10	7	6950	2	2	11600	13200
30	3	SHIELDS	SLP	SA/OD	FBG	KL	OB			6	5	4600	4	9	7900	9050
31		CLIPPER SEA SKIFF	HT	CBNCR	L/P	RB	IB	T210		11	6	9750	2	3	15900	18100
31		CLIPPER SEA SKIFF	FB	CBNCR	L/P	RB	IB	T210		11	6	9750	2	3	15900	18100
31		CLIPPER SEA SKIFF	HT	SPTCR	L/P	RB	IB	T210		11	6	9100	2	3	12600	14300
31		CLIPPER SEA SKIFF	FB	SPTCR	L/P	RB	IB	T210		11	6	9100	2	3	12600	14300
31		COMMANDER	OP	EXP	FBG		IB	T210	CC	11	3	10660	2	4	14500	16500
31		COMMANDER	HT	EXP	FBG		IB	T210	CC	11	3	10660	2	4	14500	16500
31		COMMANDER	FB	EXP	FBG		IB	T210	CC	11	3	10660	2	4	14500	16500
31		COMMANDER SPORTS	HT	EXP	FBG		IB	T210-T300		11	3	10120	2	4	14300	17300
31		COMMANDER SPORTS	FB	EXP	FBG		IB	T210-T300		11	3	10820	2	4	14600	17500
31		CONSTELLATION	OP	EXP	M/P		IB	T230	CC	10	8	9670	2		14300	16200
32		CHEROKEE	SLP	SA/RC	FBG	KL	IB	30		9		8698	5	1	15400	17500
32		SEA-HAWK SEA SKIFF	HT	SPTCR	L/P		IB	T185-T210		11	2	10500	2		15600	18100
33		FUTURA CAVALIER	OP	EXP	PLY		IB	T210	CC	11	10	9009	2	3	16900	19200
33		FUTURA CAVALIER	HT	EXP	PLY		IB	T210	CC	11	10	9009	2	3	16900	19200
33		SEASTRAKE CAVALIER	OP	EXP	L/P		IB	T210	CC	11	10	9009	2	3	16900	19200
33		SEASTRAKE CAVALIER	HT	EXP	L/P		IB	T210	CC	11	10	9009	2	3	16900	19200
33	3		HT	HB	FBG		IO	185	CC	12		9900	2	5	22300	24800
33	3		HT	HB	FBG		IO	T150	CC	12		10430	2	8	25000	27800
35		CLIPPER SEA SKIFF	HT	CBNCR	L/P	RB	IB	T210	CC	11	7	12470	2	5	21600	24000
35		CLIPPER SEA SKIFF	FB	CBNCR	L/P	RB	IB	T210	CC	11	7	12470	2	5	21600	24000
35		COMMANDER	HT	EXP	FBG		IB	T210	CC	13		14420	3		21900	24400
35		COMMANDER	HT	EXP	FBG		IB	T300		13		14420	3		22700	25200
35		COMMANDER	FB	EXP	FBG		IB	T210	CC	13		14930	3		22200	24700
35		COMMANDER	FB	EXP	FBG		IB	T300		13		14930	3		23000	25500
35		COMMANDER	FB	SPTCR	FBG		IB	T230	CC	13		13271	3		21400	23800
35		CORINTHIAN SEA SKIFF	HT	EXP	PLY	RB	IB	185		11	7	13170	2	5	19400	21600
35		CORINTHIAN SEA SKIFF	HT	EXP	PLY	RB	IB	210		11	7	13170	2	5	19400	21600
35		CORINTHIAN SEA SKIFF	FB	EXP	PLY	RB	IB	185		11	7	13170	2	5	19400	21600
35		CORINTHIAN SEA SKIFF	FB	EXP	PLY	RB	IB	210		11	7	13170	2	5	19400	21600
35		SAIL YACHT	SLP	MS	FBG	KL	IB			11		18112	4	8	31100	34600
35		SEA-HAWK SEA SKIFF	HT	EXP	L/P		IB	T185		11	7	13170	2	5	20200	22500
35		SEA-HAWK SEA SKIFF	HT	EXP	L/P		IB	T210		11	7	13170	2	5	20400	22700
36		CAVALIER	FB	DCMY	PLY		IB	T210	CC	12	8	12340	2	6	24200	26900
36		CORVETTE	OP	SPTCR	M/P	DV	IB	T230	CC	12	5	16300	3		27300	30300
36		CORVETTE	HT	SPTCR	M/P	DV	IB	T230	CC	12	5	16300	3		27300	30300
36		CORVETTE	FB	SPTCR	M/P	DV	IB	T230	CC	12	5	16300	3		27300	30300
36		CRUSADER CAVALIER	HT	EXP	M/P		IB	T210	CC	12		14430	2	8	24600	27400
36		CRUSADER CAVALIER	FB	EXP	M/P		IB	T210	CC	12		14430	2	8	24600	27400
36		SEASTRAKE CAVALIER		MY	L/P		IB	T185		12	8	12340	2	6	24000	26700
36		SEASTRAKE CAVALIER		MY	L/P		IB	T210		12	8	12340	2	6	24200	26900
37		APACHE	SLP	SA/RC	FBG	KL	IB	30		10	3	14280	5	9	25900	28700
37		CONSTELLATION	HT	EXP	M/P		IB	T185		12	3	14000	2	10	25800	28600
37		CONSTELLATION	FB	EXP	M/P		IB	T185		12	3	14000	2	10	25800	28600
37		RIVIERA-ROAMER	HT	EXP	AL		IB	T210	CC	12	10	15540	2	10	27400	30500
37		RIVIERA-ROAMER	HT	EXP	STL		IB	T210	CC	12	10	19900	2	11	32500	36200
37		RIVIERA-ROAMER	HT	EXP	AL		IB	T300		12	10	15540	2	10	28000	31100

 CONTINUED ON NEXT PAGE

LOA FT	LOA IN	NAME AND/ OR MODEL	TOP/ RIG	BOAT TYPE	HULL MTL	HULL TP	ENGINE TP	ENGINE # HP	ENGINE MFG	BEAM FT	BEAM IN	WGT LBS	DRAFT FT	DRAFT IN	RETAIL LOW	RETAIL HIGH
		1968 BOATS														
37		RIVIERA-ROAMER	HT	EXP	STL		IB	T300		12	10	19900	2	11	33000	36700
37		RIVIERA-ROAMER	HT	EXP	AL		IB	T197D		12	10	15540	2	10	31100	34600
37		RIVIERA-ROAMER	HT	EXP	STL		IB	T197D		12	10	19900	2	11	36700	40700
37		RIVIERA-ROAMER	FB	EXP	AL		IB	T210	CC	12	10	16470	2	10	28500	31700
37		RIVIERA-ROAMER	FB	EXP	STL		IB	T210	CC	12	10	16470	2	11	28500	31700
37		RIVIERA-ROAMER	FB	EXP	AL		IB	T300		12	10	16470	2	10	29000	32300
37		RIVIERA-ROAMER	FB	EXP	STL		IB	T300		12	10	16470	2	11	29000	32300
38		COMMANDER	HT	EXP	FBG		IB	T300	CC	13		17840	3		31900	35500
38		COMMANDER	HT	EXP	FBG		IB	T197D		13		17840	3		35600	39600
38		COMMANDER	HT	EXP	FBG		IB	T258D		13		17840	3		36800	40900
38		COMMANDER	FB	EXP	FBG		IB	T300	CC	13		20470	3		35500	39500
38		COMMANDER	HT	SDN	FBG		IB	T300	CC	13		18580	3		33100	36800
38		COMMANDER	HT	SDN	FBG		IB	T197D		13		18580	3		36900	41000
38		COMMANDER	HT	SDN	FBG		IB	T258D		13		18580	3		38200	42400
38		COMMANDER	FB	SDN	FBG		IB	T300	CC	13		21200	3		36700	40700
38		COMMANDER	FB	SF	FBG		IB	T300	CC	13		22000	3		37600	41800
38		COMMANDER	FB	SF	FBG		IB	T197D		13		22000	3		41400	46100
38		COMMANDER	FB	SF	FBG		IB	T258D		13		22000	3		42700	47400
38		CORINTHIAN SEA SKIFF	HT	SDNSF	P/P	RB	IB	T210	CC	13		15800	2	10	28700	31900
38		CORINTHIAN SEA SKIFF	HT	SDNSF	P/P	RB	IB	T300		13		15800	2	10	29200	32400
38		CORINTHIAN SEA SKIFF	FB	SDNSF	P/P	RB	IB	T210	CC	13		16300	2	10	29400	32700
40		CONSTELLATION SALON		MY	M/P		IB	T210		13		21000	2	11	39600	44000
40		CORINTHIAN SEA SKIFF	HT	SDNSF	P/P	RB	IB	T210	CC	14		22200	3		39300	43700
40		CORINTHIAN SEA SKIFF	HT	SDNSF	P/P	RB	IB	T300		14		22200	3		39700	44100
40		CORINTHIAN SEA SKIFF	HT	SDNSF	P/P	RB	IB	T258D		14		22200	3		44900	49800
40		CORINTHIAN SEA SKIFF	FB	SDNSF	P/P	RB	IB	T210	CC	14		23750	3		41600	46200
40		CORINTHIAN SEA SKIFF	FB	SDNSF	P/P	RB	IB	T300		14		23750	3		42000	46600
40		CORINTHIAN SEA SKIFF	FB	SDNSF	P/P	RB	IB	T258D		14		23750	3		47700	52400
41		CONSTELLATION SALON	OP	DC	M/P		IB	T210		13		19000	2	11	37300	41400
41		CONSTELLATION SALON	OP	DC	M/P		IB	T300		13		19000	2	11	39000	43300
41		CONSTELLATION SALON	HT	DC	M/P		IB	T210		13		20000	2	11	38800	43100
41		CONSTELLATION SALON	HT	DC	M/P		IB	T300		13		20000	2	11	40500	45000
41		REGAL-ROAMER	HT	SDN	AL		IB	T300	CC	15		21500	2	10	38500	42800
41		REGAL-ROAMER	HT	SDN	STL		IB	T300	CC	15		26155	2	11	45000	50000
41		REGAL-ROAMER	HT	SDN	AL		IB	T258D		15		21500	2	10	43500	48400
41		REGAL-ROAMER	HT	SDN	STL		IB	T258D		15		26155	2	11	50300	55300
41		REGAL-ROAMER	FB	SDN	AL		IB	T300	CC	15		21500	2	10	38500	42700
41		REGAL-ROAMER	FB	SDN	STL		IB	T300	CC	15		26155	2	11	44900	49900
41		REGAL-ROAMER	FB	SDN	AL		IB	T258D		15		21500	2	10	43500	48300
41		REGAL-ROAMER	FB	SDN	STL		IB	T258D		15		26155	2	11	50300	55200
42		COMANCHE	SLP	SA/RC	FBG	KL	IB	30		10	10	19000	6	6	39400	43800
42		COMMANDER	OP	MY	FBG		IB	T300	CC	13		23940	3	1	47600	52300
42		COMMANDER	OP	MY	FBG		IB	T258D		13		23940	3	1	52500	57700
42		COMMANDER	HT	MY	FBG		IB	T300	CC	13		27120	3	1	51800	57000
42		COMMANDER	HT	MY	FBG		IB	T258D		13		27120	3	1	57100	62800
42		COMMANDER	FB	SDN	FBG		IB	T300	CC	13		22443	3	2	44700	49600
42		COMMANDER	FB	SDN	FBG		IB	T D	GM	13		22443	3	2	**	**
43		CORINTHIAN SEA SKIFF	OP	DC	P/P	RB	IB	T300	CC	13		24000	2	11	49700	54600
43		CORINTHIAN SEA SKIFF	OP	DC	P/P	RB	IB	T258D		13		24000	2	11	54900	60400
43		CORINTHIAN SEA SKIFF	HT	EXP	P/P	RB	IB	T300	CC	13		27000	2	11	51500	56500
43		CORINTHIAN SEA SKIFF	HT	EXP	P/P	RB	IB	T258D		13		27000	2	11	56300	61900
45		CONSTELLATION	HT	MY	M/P		IB	T300		13		27000	3	2	46700	51300
45		CONSTELLATION	HT	MY	M/P		IB	T258D		13		27000	3	2	50800	55900
46		RIVIERA-ROAMER 1 STR	HT	MY	AL		IB	T300	CC	15		30600	3	4	48000	52700
46		RIVIERA-ROAMER 1 STR	HT	MY	STL		IB	T300	CC	15		36715	3	5	54900	60300
46		RIVIERA-ROAMER 1 STR	HT	MY	AL		IB	T258D		15		30600	3	4	52900	58200
46		RIVIERA-ROAMER 1 STR	HT	MY	STL		IB	T258D		15		36715	3	5	60500	66500
46		RIVIERA-ROAMER 1 STR	HT	MY	AL		IB	T300D		15		30600	3	4	56000	61500
46		RIVIERA-ROAMER 1 STR	HT	MY	STL		IB	T300D		15		36715	3	5	63300	69600
46		RIVIERA-ROAMER 1 STR	HT	MY	AL		IB	T320D		15		30600	3	4	57400	63100
46		RIVIERA-ROAMER 1 STR	HT	MY	STL		IB	T320D		15		36715	3	5	64600	71000
46		RIVIERA-ROAMER 2 STR	HT	MY	AL		IB	T300		15		30600	3	4	48400	53200
46		RIVIERA-ROAMER 2 STR	HT	MY	STL		IB	T300		15		36715	3	5	55800	61300
46		RIVIERA-ROAMER 2 STR	HT	MY	AL		IB	T258D		15		30600	3	4	53600	58900
46		RIVIERA-ROAMER 2 STR	HT	MY	STL		IB	T258D		15		36715	3	5	61200	67300
46		RIVIERA-ROAMER 2 STR	HT	MY	AL		IB	T300D		15		30600	3	4	56600	62200
46		RIVIERA-ROAMER 2 STR	HT	MY	STL		IB	T300D		15		36715	3	5	64100	70400
46		RIVIERA-ROAMER 2 STR	HT	MY	AL		IB	T320D		15		30600	3	4	58000	63700
46		RIVIERA-ROAMER 2 STR	HT	MY	STL		IB	T320D		15		36715	3	5	65400	71900
47		COMMANDER 1 STRM AFT	HT	MY	FBG		IB	T300	CC	15		30451	3	2	48100	52900
47		COMMANDER 1 STRM AFT	HT	MY	FBG		IB	T258D		15		30451	3	2	52700	57900
47		COMMANDER 2 STRM AFT	HT	MY	FBG		IB	T300	CC	15		30451	3	2	49000	53800
47		COMMANDER 2 STRM AFT	HT	MY	FBG		IB	T258D		15		30451	3	2	53500	58800
52		CONSTELLATION	HT	MY	M/P		IB	T270D		14	4	40700	3	6	62800	69000
57		CONSTELLATION	HT	MY	M/P		IB	T300D	CAT	15		46650	4		74700	82100
57		CONSTELLATION	HT	MY	M/P		IB	T320D		15		46650	4		77500	85100
57	3	ROAMER	HT	MY	AL		IB	T300D	CAT	15		58600	3	8	97200	107000
57	3	ROAMER	HT	MY	STL		IB	T300D	CAT	15		68830	3	11	113500	124500
57	3	ROAMER	HT	MY	AL		IB	T320D		15		58600	3	8	99800	109500
57	3	ROAMER	HT	MY	STL		IB	T320D		15		68830	3	11	117500	129500
65			HT	MY	M/P		IB	T460D	CAT	16	10	69000	3	9	148000	162500
65			HT	MY	M/P		IB	T478D		16	10	69000	3	9	149000	163500
65		CONSTELLATION	HT	MY	M/P		IB	T460D	CAT	16	10	67000	3	9	143500	158000
65		CONSTELLATION	HT	MY	M/P		IB	T478D		16	10	67000	3	9	145000	159000
		1967 BOATS														
16		SPORT-V	OP	RNBT	FBG		IO	60		6	9	1450			2850	3350
16	1		OP	SKI	PLY		IB	185		6	10	2170			1700	2050
17		CUSTOM	OP	SKI	M/P		IB	185		6	8	2700	1	8	2050	2400
17		SUPER-SPORT	OP	RNBT	M/P		IB	210		6	8	2700	1	8	2200	2550
17	7	CORSAIR SPORT V	OP	SKI	FBG		OB			7	5	935			1800	2100
17	9	CORSAIR SPORT V	OP	SKI	FBG		IO	150		7	5	1950			3750	4350
18		CAVALIER CUSTOM	OP	UTL	MHG		IB	185		7	2	2415	1	11	2100	2500
18	4	SUPER-SPORT	OP	RNBT	M/P	TR	IB	210		6	5	2800	1	8	2350	2700
18	7	SEA-V-CORSAIR	OP	FSH	FBG		IO	150		7	7	2340			4950	5700
18	7	SPORTSMAN SEA SKIFF	OP	RNBT	FBG		IO	150		7	7	2315	2	4	4550	5250
20		SEA-V-CORSAIR	OP	RNBT	FBG		IO	150		7	11	2685			5750	6600
20		SEA-V-CORSAIR	OP	RNBT	FBG		IO	185		7	11	2685			5800	6650
20		SEA-V-CORSAIR	OP	RNBT	FBG		IB	185		7	11	2915			3050	3550
20		SPORTSMAN SEA SKIFF	OP	RNBT	FBG		IB	185		7	11	2925	2	3	3100	3600
20		SUPER-SPORT	OP	RNBT	M/P		IB	210		6	7	2747	1	10	2700	3150
20		SUPER-SPORT	OP	RNBT	M/P		IB	300		6	7	3203	1	10	3100	3600
21		SUPER-SPORT	OP	RNBT	M/P	TR	IB	210		7	6	3205	2		3350	3900
21		SUPER-SPORT	OP	RNBT	M/P	TR	IB	300		7	6	3650	2		3750	4350
22		CAVALIER DORY	OP	CTRCN	L/P		IB	185		8		3000	1	11	3400	4000
22		CUTLASS CAVALIER	OP	RNBT	L/P		IB	185		8		3200	1	11	3600	4200
22		SEA-HAWK SS SPORT	OP	EXP	L/P		IB	185-210		8		3470	1	11	3750	4400
22		SEA-SKIFF SPORTSMAN	OP	RNBT	L/P		IB	185		8			1	10	3800	4400
23	1	LANCER CORSAIR	OP	EXP	FBG	DV	IO	150-185		8		3960			9250	10600
23	1	LANCER CORSAIR	OP	RNBT	FBG	DV	IO	150-185		8		3610			8050	9300
23	1	LANCER CORSAIR	OP	RNBT	FBG	DV	IO	T120		8		3610			9150	10400
25		FUTURA CAVALIER	OP	EXP	PLY		IO	150		9	6	4640	2		11600	13100
25		FUTURA CAVALIER	OP	EXP	PLY		IB	185		9	6	4640	2		5650	6500
25		RANGER SEA-SKIFF	OP	RNBT	L/P		IB	185		9	1		2		5450	6250
25		RANGER SEA-SKIFF	HT	RNBT	L/P		IB	185		9	1		2		5450	6250
25		SEA-HAWK SS CLIPPER	OP	EXP	L/P		IB	185-210		9	1	4500	2		5450	6350
25		SEA-HAWK SS SPORT	OP	EXP	L/P		IB	185-210		9	1	4400	2		5400	6250
25		SEA-HAWK SS SPORT	HT	EXP	L/P		IB	185-210		9	1	4400	2		5400	6250
25		SEA-SKIFF SPORTSMAN	OP	RNBT	L/P		IB	185		9	1		2		5450	6250
25		SEASTRAKE CAVALIER	OP	EXP	L/P		IB	185		9	6	4640	2		5650	6500
25	11	CUTLASS CAVALIER	OP	CUD	L/P		IB	185		10		4070	2	6	5550	6350
25	11	CUTLASS CAVALIER	OP	CUD	L/P		IB	210		10		5020	2	6	6350	7300
25	11	CUTLASS CAVALIER	OP	CUD	L/P		IB	T185		10		5020	2	2	7100	8200
26	3	CAPITAN 26	SLP	SA/RC	FBG	KL	OB			8	2	4300	4		6550	7550
26	3	CAPRI	SLP	SAIL	FBG	KL	OB			8	2	4800	4		7300	8400
27		COMMANDER	OP	EXP	FBG		IB	185-210		10	3	5635	2	1	7150	8350
27		COMMANDER	OP	EXP	FBG		IB	T185		10	3	6759	1	10	8950	10200
27		COMMANDER	HT	EXP	FBG		IB	185-210		10	3	5635	2	1	7150	8350
27		COMMANDER	HT	EXP	FBG		IB	T185		10	3	6759	1	10	8950	10200
27		COMMANDER SPORTS	OP	EXP	FBG		IB	185-210		10	3	4525	2	1	6400	7500
27		COMMANDER SPORTS	OP	EXP	FBG		IB	T185		10	3	5649	1	10	8150	9350
27		COMMANDER SPORTS	HT	EXP	FBG		IB	185-210		10	3	4525	2	1	6400	7500
27		COMMANDER SPORTS	HT	EXP	FBG		IB	T185		10	3	5649	1	10	8150	9350
27		COMMANDER SPORTS	FB	EXP	FBG		IB	185-210		10	3	4525	2	1	6400	7500
27		COMMANDER SPORTS	FB	EXP	FBG		IB	T185		10	3	5649	1	10	8150	9350
27		FUTURA CAVALIER	OP	EXP	PLY		IB	185-210		10	3	5240	2	1	6850	8050
27		FUTURA CAVALIER	HT	EXP	PLY		IB	185-210		10	3	5240	2	1	6850	8050
27		SEASTRAKE CAVALIER	OP	EXP	L/P		IB	185-210		10	3	5240	2	1	6850	8050
27		SEASTRAKE CAVALIER	HT	EXP	L/P		IB	185-210		10	3	5240	2	1	6850	8050
28		CLIPPER SEA-SKIFF	HT	SPTCR	L/P	RB	IB	210		10	6	7850	2	6	8650	9950
28		CLIPPER SEA-SKIFF	FB	SPTCR	L/P	RB	IB	210		10	6	8730	2	6	9300	10600
28		CONSTELLATION	OP	EXP	M/P		IB	210		10	2		2	2	8250	9450
28		CONSTELLATION	HT	EXP	M/P		IB	210		10	2		2	2	8250	9450
28		CORINTHIAN SEA SKIFF	HT	SPTCR	PLY	RB	IB	210		10	1	7000	2	4	8100	9350
28		CORINTHIAN SEA SKIFF	HT	SPTCR	PLY	RB	IB	T185-T210		10	1	8000	2	2	9550	11100

 CONTINUED ON NEXT PAGE

LOA FT	LOA IN	NAME AND/ OR MODEL	TOP/ RIG	BOAT TYPE	-HULL- MTL	-HULL- TP	ENGINE TP	ENGINE # HP	ENGINE MFG	BEAM FT	BEAM IN	WGT LBS	DRAFT FT	DRAFT IN	RETAIL LOW	RETAIL HIGH
		1967 BOATS														
28		CORINTHIAN SEA SKIFF	FB	SPTCR	PLY	RB	IB	210		10	1	7000	2	4	8100	9350
28		CORINTHIAN SEA SKIFF	FB	SPTCR	PLY	RB	IB	T185-T210		10	1	8000	2	2	9550	11100
28		CRUSADER CAVALIER	OP	EXP	MHG		IB	210		10	2	5858	2	2	7450	8600
28		CRUSADER CAVALIER	OP	EXP	MHG		IB	T185		10	2	6633	1	11	8850	10100
28		CRUSADER CAVALIER	HT	EXP	MHG		IB	210		10	2	5858	2	2	7450	8600
28		CRUSADER CAVALIER	HT	EXP	MHG		IB	T185		10	2	6633	1	11	8850	10100
28		SEA-HAWK SEA SKIFF	OP	EXP	L/P		IB	210		10	1	7000	2	4	8100	9300
28		SEA-HAWK SEA SKIFF	OP	EXP	L/P		IB	T185-T210		10	1	8000	2	2	9550	11100
28		SEA-HAWK SEA SKIFF	HT	EXP	L/P		IB	210		10	1	7000	2	4	8100	9300
28		SEA-HAWK SEA SKIFF	HT	EXP	L/P		IB	T185-T210		10	1	8000	2	2	9550	11100
28		SEA-HAWK SS SPORT	OP	EXP	L/P		IB	210		10	2	6200	2	1	7650	8800
28		SEA-HAWK SS SPORT	OP	EXP	L/P		IB	T185-T210		10	2	7200	1	11	9150	10600
28		SEA-HAWK SS SPORT	HT	EXP	L/P		IB	210		10	2	6200	2	1	7650	8800
28		SEA-HAWK SS SPORT	HT	EXP	L/P		IB	T185-T200		10	2	7200	1	11	9150	10500
28		SEA-HAWK SS SPORT	FB	EXP	L/P		IB	210		10	2	6200	2	1	7650	8800
28		SEA-HAWK SS SPORT	FB	EXP	L/P		IB	T185-T200		10	2	7200	1	11	9150	10500
28		SEA-SKIFF SPORTSMAN	OP	RNBT	L/P		IB	210		10	2		2	2	8100	9300
28		SEA-SKIFF SPORTSMAN	HT	RNBT	L/P		IB	210		10	2		2	2	8100	9300
28		SEA-SKIFF SPORTSMAN	FB	RNBT	L/P		IB	210		10	2		2	2	8100	9300
30					WD		IB	T283	CC						**	**
30		CAPRI	SLP	SAIL	FBG	KC	IB	25		9	8	11740	3	9	20800	23100
30		CONSTELLATION	FB		M/P		IB	T210		10	8	8920	2	2	10400	11900
30		CONSTELLATION	OP	EXP	M/P		IB	T185-T210		10	8	8920	2	2	12000	13900
30		CONSTELLATION	HT	EXP	M/P		IB	T185-T210		10	8	8920	2	2	12000	13900
30		CONSTELLATION	FB	EXP	M/P		IB	T185		10	8	8920	2	2	12000	13600
30		CRUSADER CAVALIER	OP	EXP	MHG		IB	210		10	8	7850	2	2	10600	12000
30		CRUSADER CAVALIER	OP	EXP	MHG		IB	T185		10	8	8920	2		12000	13600
30		CRUSADER CAVALIER	HT	EXP	MHG		IB	210		10	8	7850	2	2	10600	12000
30		CRUSADER CAVALIER	HT	EXP	MHG		IB	T185		10	8	8920	2		12000	13600
30		FUTURA CAVALIER	OP	EXP	PLY		IB	210		10	7	6300	2	2	9950	11300
30		FUTURA CAVALIER	OP	EXP	PLY		IB	T185		10	7	6950	2	2	11200	12800
30		FUTURA CAVALIER	HT	EXP	PLY		IB	210		10	7	6300	2	2	9950	11300
30		FUTURA CAVALIER	HT	EXP	PLY		IB	T185		10	7	6950	2	2	11200	12800
30		SEASTRAKE CAVALIER	OP	EXP	L/P		IB	210		10	7	6300	2	2	9950	11300
30		SEASTRAKE CAVALIER	OP	EXP	L/P		IB	T185		10	7	6950	2	2	11200	12800
30		SEASTRAKE CAVALIER	HT	EXP	L/P		IB	210		10	7	6300	2	2	9950	11300
30		SEASTRAKE CAVALIER	HT	EXP	L/P		IB	T185		10	7	6950	2	2	11200	12800
30	3	SHIELDS	SLP	SA/OD	FBG	KL	OB			6	5	4600	4	9	7800	8950
31		COMMANDER	OP	EXP	FBG		IB	T185-T210		11	3	10500	2	4	13800	15900
31		COMMANDER	HT	EXP	FBG		IB	T185-T210		11	3	10500	2	4	13800	15900
31		COMMANDER SPORTS	HT	EXP	FBG		IB	T185-T300		11	3	9454	2	4	13400	16700
31		COMMANDER SPORTS	FB	EXP	FBG		IB	T185-T300		11	3	9454	2	4	13400	16700
32		CHEROKEE	SLP	SA/RC	FBG	KL	IB	30	UNIV	9		8698	5	1	15200	17300
32		CORINTHIAN SEA SKIFF	HT	EXP	PLY	RB	IB	T185-T210		11	2	11800	2		15500	17900
32		CORINTHIAN SEA SKIFF	FB	EXP	PLY	RB	IB	T185-T210		11	2	11800	2		15500	17900
32		SEA-HAWK SEA SKIFF	OP	EXP	L/P		IB	T185-T210		11	2	11800	2		15500	17900
32		SEA-HAWK SEA SKIFF	HT	EXP	L/P		IB	T185-T210		11	2	11800	2		15500	17900
32		SEA-HAWK SEA SKIFF	HT	SPTCR	L/P		IB	T185-T210		11	2	10500	2		15100	17500
33		FUTURA CAVALIER	OP	EXP	PLY		IB	T185-T210		11	10	10500	2	3	16600	19100
33		FUTURA CAVALIER	HT	EXP	PLY		IB	T185-T210		11	10	10500	2	3	16600	19100
33		RIVIERA-ROAMER	HT	EXP	STL		IB	T185-T300		12		15530	2	7	18900	21900
33		RIVIERA-ROAMER	FB	EXP	STL		IB	T185-T300		12		15530	2	7	18900	21900
33		SEASTRAKE CAVALIER	OP	EXP	L/P		IB	T185-T210		11	10	10500	2	3	16600	19100
33		SEASTRAKE CAVALIER	HT	EXP	L/P		IB	T185-T210		11	10	10500	2	3	16600	19100
35		COMMANDER		EXP	FBG		IB	T210		13		14420	3		21300	23600
35		CORINTHIAN SEA SKIFF	HT	EXP	PLY	RB	IB	T185		11	7	13170	2	5	19600	21800
35		CORINTHIAN SEA SKIFF	HT	EXP	PLY	RB	IB	T210		11	7	13170	2	5	19800	22000
35		CORINTHIAN SEA SKIFF	FB	EXP	PLY	RB	IB	T185		11	7	13170	2	5	19600	21800
35		CORINTHIAN SEA SKIFF	FB	EXP	PLY	RB	IB	T210		11	7	13170	2	5	19800	22000
35		SAIL YACHT	SLP	MS	FBG	KL	IB	60		11		18112	4	8	30800	34200
35		SAIL YACHT	SLP	MS	FBG	KL	IB	30D		11		18112	4	8	30900	34400
35		SEA-HAWK SEA SKIFF	HT	EXP	L/P		IB	T185		11	7	13170	2	5	19600	21800
35		SEA-HAWK SEA SKIFF	HT	EXP	L/P		IB	T210		11	7	13170	2	5	19800	22000
36		CAVALIER	OP	MY	PLY		IB	T185		12	8	12340	2	6	23400	26000
36		CAVALIER	OP	MY	PLY		IB	T210		12	8	12340	2	6	23700	26300
36		CONSTELLATION	HT	SDN	M/P		IB	T210		12		13558	2	10	24000	26600
36		CONSTELLATION	FB	SDN	M/P		IB	T210		12		13558	2	10	24000	26600
36		CRUSADER CAVALIER	HT	EXP	MHG		IB	T185		12		15300	2	8	24700	27400
36		CRUSADER CAVALIER	HT	EXP	MHG		IB	T210		12		15300	2	8	24800	27600
36		CRUSADER CAVALIER	FB	EXP	MHG		IB	T185		12		15300	2	8	24700	27400
36		CRUSADER CAVALIER	FB	EXP	MHG		IB	T210		12		15300	2	8	24800	27600
36		SEASTRAKE CAVALIER	OP	MY	L/P		IB	T185		12	8	12340	2	6	23400	26000
36		SEASTRAKE CAVALIER	OP	MY	L/P		IB	T210		12	8	12340	2	6	23700	26300
37		APACHE	SLP	SA/RC	FBG	KL	IB	30	UNIV	10	3	13022	5	9	23600	26200
37		CONSTELLATION	HT	EXP	M/P		IB	T185		12	3	14000	2	10	25200	28000
37		CONSTELLATION	HT	EXP	M/P		IB	T210		12	3	14000	2	10	25300	28100
37		CONSTELLATION	HT	EXP	M/P		IB	T300		12	3	14000	2	10	25800	28600
37		CONSTELLATION	FB	EXP	M/P		IB	T185		12	3	14000	2	10	25200	28000
37		CONSTELLATION	FB	EXP	M/P		IB	T210		12	3	14000	2	10	25300	28100
37		CONSTELLATION	FB	EXP	M/P		IB	T300		12	3	14000	2	10	25800	28600
37		RIVIERA-ROAMER	HT	EXP	AL		IB	T210		12	10	16470	2	10	27900	31000
37		RIVIERA-ROAMER	HT	EXP	STL		IB	T210		12	10	20330	2	11	32300	35900
37		RIVIERA-ROAMER	HT	EXP	AL		IB	T300		12	10	16470	2	10	28400	31500
37		RIVIERA-ROAMER	HT	EXP	STL		IB	T300		12	10	20330	2	11	32800	36400
37		RIVIERA-ROAMER	HT	EXP	AL		IB	T197D		12	10	16470	2	10	31600	35100
37		RIVIERA-ROAMER	HT	EXP	STL		IB	T197D		12	10	20330	2	11	36400	40400
37		RIVIERA-ROAMER	FB	EXP	AL		IB	T210		12	10	16470	2	10	27900	31000
37		RIVIERA-ROAMER	FB	EXP	STL		IB	T210		12	10	20330	2	11	32300	35900
37		RIVIERA-ROAMER	FB	EXP	AL		IB	T300		12	10	16470	2	10	28400	31500
37		RIVIERA-ROAMER	FB	EXP	STL		IB	T300		12	10	20330	2	11	32800	36400
37		RIVIERA-ROAMER	FB	EXP	AL		IB	T197D		12	10	16470	2	10	31600	35100
37		RIVIERA-ROAMER	FB	EXP	STL		IB	T197D		12	10	20330	2	11	36400	40400
38		COMMANDER	HT	EXP	FBG		IB	T210		13		17090	3		29800	33100
38		COMMANDER	HT	EXP	FBG		IB	T300		13		17090	3		30200	33600
38		COMMANDER	HT	EXP	FBG		IB	T258D		13		19805	3		38700	43000
38		COMMANDER	FB	EXP	FBG		IB	T210		13		17090	3		29800	33100
38		COMMANDER	FB	EXP	FBG		IB	T300		13		17090	3		30200	33600
38		COMMANDER	HT	SDN	FBG		IB	T210		13		17090	3		29900	33300
38		COMMANDER	HT	SDN	FBG		IB	T300		13		17090	3		30400	33800
38		COMMANDER	HT	SDN	FBG		IB	T258D		13		19805	3		39000	43300
38		COMMANDER	FB	SDN	FBG		IB	T210		13		17090	3		29900	33300
38		COMMANDER	FB	SDN	FBG		IB	T300		13		17090	3		30400	33800
38		COMMANDER	FB	SF	FBG		IB	T210		13		18690	3		31900	35500
38		COMMANDER	FB	SF	FBG		IB	T300		13		18690	3		32300	35900
38		COMMANDER	FB	SF	FBG		IB	T258D		13		21405	3		40900	45400
38		CONSTELLATION	OP	TCMY	M/P		IB	T185		13		16900	2	11	29500	32800
38		CONSTELLATION	OP	TCMY	M/P		IB	T210		13		16900	2	11	29600	32800
38		CONSTELLATION	OP	TCMY	M/P		IB	T300		13		16900	2	11	30000	33300
38		CONSTELLATION	HT	TCMY	M/P		IB	T185		13		16900	2	11	29500	32800
38		CONSTELLATION	HT	TCMY	M/P		IB	T210		13		16900	2	11	29600	32900
38		CONSTELLATION	HT	TCMY	M/P		IB	T300		13		16900	2	11	30000	33300
38		CORINTHIAN SEA SKIFF	HT	EXP	PLY	RB	IB	T210		13		15700	2	10	28000	31100
38		CORINTHIAN SEA SKIFF	HT	EXP	PLY	RB	IB	T300		13		15700	2	10	28400	31500
38		CORINTHIAN SEA SKIFF	HT	EXP	PLY	RB	IB	T197D		13		16300	2	10	32700	36300
38		CORINTHIAN SEA SKIFF	FB	EXP	PLY	RB	IB	T210		13		15700	2	10	28000	31100
38		CORINTHIAN SEA SKIFF	FB	EXP	PLY	RB	IB	T300		13		15700	2	10	28400	31500
38		ROAMER		OFF	STL	SV	IB	T300		12	9				20000	22200
40		CONSTELLATION SALON	OP	MY	M/P		IB	T210		13		21000	2	11	38600	42900
40		CONSTELLATION SALON	OP	MY	M/P		IB	T300		13		21360	2	11	39500	43900
40		CONSTELLATION SALON	HT	MY	M/P		IB	T210		13		21000	2	11	38700	43000
40		CONSTELLATION SALON	HT	MY	M/P		IB	T300		13		21360	2	11	39500	43900
40		CORINTHIAN SEA SKIFF	HT	SDNSF	PLY	RB	IB	T210		14		20300	3		35600	39600
		IB T300 36000 40000, IB T197D 45900 50400, IB T258D													47100	51800
40		CORINTHIAN SEA SKIFF	FB	SDNSF	PLY	RB	IB	T210		14		20300	3		35700	39600
		IB T300 36000 40000, IB T197D 45900 50400, IB T258D													47100	51800
41		REGAL-ROAMER	HT	SDN	AL		IB	T300		15		22600	2	10	39100	43400
41		REGAL-ROAMER	HT	SDN	STL		IB	T300		15		27255	3		46000	50500
41		REGAL-ROAMER	HT	SDN	AL		IB	T258D		15		22600	2	10	44000	48900
41		REGAL-ROAMER	HT	SDN	STL		IB	T258D		15		27255	3		50700	55700
41		REGAL-ROAMER	FB	SDN	AL		IB	T300		15		22600	2	10	39100	43400
41		REGAL-ROAMER	FB	SDN	STL		IB	T300		15		27255	3		45900	50500
41		REGAL-ROAMER	FB	SDN	AL		IB	T258D		15		22600	2	10	44000	48900
41		REGAL-ROAMER	FB	SDN	STL		IB	T258D		15		27255	3		50700	55700
42		COMMANDER	FB	DC	FBG		IB	T300		13		24000	3	2	47000	51600
42		COMMANDER	FB	DC	FBG		IB	T258D		13		24000	3	2	51800	56900
43		CORINTHIAN SEA SKIFF	OP	DC	M/P	RB	IB	T300		13		22600	2	11	47100	51800
43		CORINTHIAN SEA SKIFF	OP	DC	M/P	RB	IB	T258D		13		25700	2	11	55800	61300
45		CONSTELLATION	HT	MY	M/P		IB	T300		13		27000	3	2	45600	50100
45		CONSTELLATION	HT	MY	M/P		IB	T258D		13		28912	3	2	51600	56700
47		COMMANDER	HT	MY	FBG		IB	T300		15		27304	3	2	43800	48600
47		COMMANDER	HT	MY	FBG		IB	T258D		15		30304	3	2	51000	56100
47		COMMANDER 2 STRMS	HT	MY	FBG		IB	T300		15		27304	3	2	44800	49700
47		COMMANDER 2 STRMS	HT	MY	FBG		IB	T258D		15		30304	3	2	52100	57200

 CONTINUED ON NEXT PAGE

LOA FT	LOA IN	NAME AND/ OR MODEL	TOP/ RIG	BOAT TYPE	HULL MTL	HULL TP	ENGINE TP	ENGINE # HP	ENGINE MFG	BEAM FT	BEAM IN	WGT LBS	DRAFT FT	DRAFT IN	RETAIL LOW	RETAIL HIGH
		1967 BOATS														
48		CONSTELLATION	HT	MY	M/P		IB	T300		13		32000	3	1	49600	54500
48		CONSTELLATION	HT	MY	M/P		IB	T258D		13		32000	3	1	52800	58000
48		RIVIERA-ROAMER	HT	MY	AL		IB	T300		13		26498	3	2	54100	59400
48		RIVIERA-ROAMER	HT	MY	STL		IB	T300		13		31500	3	3	58800	64600
48		RIVIERA-ROAMER	HT	MY	STL		IB	T270D		13		31500	3	3	65200	71600
48		RIVIERA-ROAMER	FB	MY	AL		IB	T270D		3	2	26498			**	**
48		RIVIERA-ROAMER	FB	MY	AL		IB	T300D		13		26498	3	2	62500	68600
48		RIVIERA-ROAMER	FB	MY	STL		IB	T300D		13		31500	3	3	67100	73700
52		CONSTELLATION	HT	MY	M/P		IB	T270D		14	3	36000	3	8	57800	63500
57		CONSTELLATION	HT	MY	M/P		IB	T270D		15		48503	3	11	71900	79000
57		CONSTELLATION	HT	MY	M/P		IB	T300D		15		49037	3	11	77000	84600
57		CONSTELLATION	HT	MY	M/P		IB	T320D		15		49037	3	11	79700	87600
57	3	ROAMER	HT	MY	AL		IB	T270D		15		54400	3	8	82900	91100
57	3	ROAMER	HT	MY	STL		IB	T270D		15		63400	3	11	103000	113500
57	3	ROAMER	HT	MY	STL		IB	T300D		15		63400	3	11	106000	116500
57	3	ROAMER	FB	MY	AL		IB	T300D		15		54400	3	8	85100	93600
57	3	ROAMER	FB	MY	AL		IB	T320D		15		54400	3	8	87700	96400
57	3	ROAMER	FB	MY	STL		IB	T320D		15		63400	3	11	107000	117500
65			HT	MYDKH	M/P		IB	T460D		16	9	72000	4	4	149500	164500
65			HT	MYDKH	M/P		IB	T478D		16	9	73700	4	4	155000	170500
65		CONSTELLATION	HT	MYDKH	M/P		IB	T460D		16	9	72073	4	2	150000	164500
65		CONSTELLATION	HT	MYDKH	M/P		IB	T478D		16	9	73868	4	2	155500	170500
		1966 BOATS														
16		CORSAIR SPORTS	OP	RNBT	FBG		IO	120		6	9	1400			2950	3400
16		SPORT-V	OP	RNBT	FBG		IO	60-120		6	9	1450			3000	3500
17		SUPER-SPORT	OP	RNBT	M/P		IB	210		6	8		1	8	1750	2100
17	6	CORSAIR SPORTS	OP	EXP	FBG		IO	120							5000	5750
17	6	SPORT-V	OP	CBNCR	FBG		OB			7	6	1040			2000	2350
17	6	SPORT-V	OP	RNBT	FBG		OB			7	5	920			1800	2150
17	6	SPORT-V	OP	RNBT	FBG		IO	150		7	5	1935			4000	4650
18					WD		IB	185-210							**	**
18		CAVALIER CUSTOM	OP	UTL	MHG		IB	185-210		7	2	2415	1	11	2050	2450
18	2	SEA-SKIFF SPORTSMAN	OP	RNBT	FBG		IO	150		7	7		2	4	4900	5650
18	2	SEA-V	OP	RNBT	FBG		IO	150		7	9	2100			4500	5150
18	4	SUPER-SPORT	OP	RNBT	M/P		IB	210		6	5		1	8	2200	2550
20		SEA-SKIFF SPORTSMAN	OP	RNBT	FBG		IB	210		7	11		2	3	2850	3350
20		SEA-V	OP	RNBT	FBG		IO	150		7	11	2560			5800	6700
20		SEA-V	OP	RNBT	FBG		IB	185		7	11	2760			2900	3350
20		SUPER-SPORT	OP	RNBT	M/P		IB	210-300		6	7		1	10	2600	3150
21					WD		IB	280	GRAY						**	**
21		SUPER-SPORT	OP	RNBT	M/P		IB	210-300		7	6		2		3450	4150
22		CAVALIER DORY	OP	CTRCN	L/P		IB	185		8		3000	1	11	3300	3850
22		CUTLASS CAVALIER	OP	CUD	L/P		IB	185		8		3200	1	11	3450	4050
22		CUTLASS CAVALIER	OP	CUD	MHG		IB	210		8		3200	1	11	3500	4050
22		SEA-SKIFF SPORTSMAN	OP	RNBT	L/P		IB	185-210		8			1	10	3700	4300
23	1	LANCER CORSAIR	OP	RNBT	FBG	DV	IO	150		8		3750			8600	9900
24		RANGER SEA-SKIFF	OP	RNBT	L/P		IB	185		9		4100	2		4750	5450
24		RANGER SEA-SKIFF	HT	RNBT	L/P		IB	185		9		4100	2		4750	5450
24		SEA-SKIFF SPORTSMAN	OP	RNBT	L/P		IB	175		9	1	4100	2		4750	5450
24		SEA-SKIFF SPORTSMAN	HT	RNBT	L/P		IB	175		9	1	4100	2		4750	5450
25		FUTURA CAVALIER	OP	EXP	PLY		IO	150		9	6	3800	2		10500	12000
25		FUTURA CAVALIER	OP	EXP	PLY		IB	185		9	6	3800	2		4800	5500
25		RANGER SEA SKIFF	OP	RNBT	L/P		IB	185-210		9	1		2		5600	6500
25		RANGER SEA SKIFF	HT	RNBT	L/P		IB	185-210		9	1		2		5250	6100
25		SEASTRAKE CAVALIER	OP	EXP	L/P		IB	185		9	6	3800	2		4800	5500
25		SPORTSMAN SEA SKIFF	OP	RNBT	L/P		IB	185-210		9	1		2		4950	5750
26		CUTLASS CAVALIER	OP	CUD	L/P		IB	185-210		10		3500	2	6	5050	5900
26		CUTLASS CAVALIER	OP	CUD	L/P		IB	T185		10		3500	2	2	6000	6900
26	3	CAPITAN 26	SLP	SA/RC	FBG	KL	OB					3920			5950	6850
26	3	CAPRI	SLP	SAIL	FBG	KL	OB			8	2	3920	4		5950	6850
27		COMMANDER	OP	EXP	FBG	SV	IB	185-210		10	3		2	1	6900	8050
27		COMMANDER	OP	EXP	FBG	SV	IB	T185		10	3		2	1	7850	9050
27		COMMANDER	HT	EXP	FBG	SV	IB	185-210		10	3		2	1	6900	8050
27		COMMANDER	HT	EXP	FBG	SV	IB	T185		10	3		2	1	7850	9050
27		FUTURA CAVALIER	OP	EXP	PLY		IB	185-210		10	3	5240	2	1	6650	7800
27		FUTURA CAVALIER	HT	EXP	PLY		IB	185-210		10	3	5240	2	1	6650	7800
27		SEASTRAKE CAVALIER	OP	EXP	L/P		IB	185-210		10	3	5240	2	1	6650	7800
27		SEASTRAKE CAVALIER	HT	EXP	L/P		IB	185-210		10	3	5240	2	1	6650	7800
27	11	SEA-HAWK SEA SKIFF	OP	EXP	L/P		IB	210		10	1		2	2	8450	9700
27	11	SEA-HAWK SEA SKIFF	OP	EXP	L/P		IB	T185-T210		10	1		2	4	9400	10800
27	11	SEA-HAWK SEA SKIFF	HT	EXP	L/P		IB	210		10	1		2	2	8450	9700
27	11	SEA-HAWK SEA SKIFF	HT	EXP	L/P		IB	T185-T210		10	1		2	4	9400	10800
28		CONSTELLATION	OP	EXP	M/P		IB	210		10	2		2	2	8000	9200
28		CONSTELLATION	OP	EXP	M/P		IB	T185-T210		10	2		1	11	8900	10300
28		CONSTELLATION	HT	EXP	M/P		IB	210		10	2		2	2	8000	9200
28		CONSTELLATION	HT	EXP	M/P		IB	T185-T210		10	2		1	11	8900	10300
28		CRUSADER CAVALIER	OP	EXP	M/P		IB	210		10	2	5968	2	2	7300	8400
28		CRUSADER CAVALIER	OP	EXP	M/P		IB	T185		10	2	5968	1	11	8150	9400
28		CRUSADER CAVALIER	HT	EXP	M/P		IB	210		10	2	5968	2	2	7300	8400
28		CRUSADER CAVALIER	HT	EXP	M/P		IB	T185		10	2	5968	1	11	8150	9400
28		SEA-SKIFF SPORTSMAN	OP	RNBT	L/P		IB	210		10	2		2	2	7850	9050
28		SEA-SKIFF SPORTSMAN	OP	RNBT	L/P		IB	T185		10	2		1	11	8600	9900
28		SEA-SKIFF SPORTSMAN	HT	RNBT	L/P		IB	210		10	2		2	2	7850	9050
28		SEA-SKIFF SPORTSMAN	HT	RNBT	L/P		IB	T185		10	2		1	11	8600	9900
28		SEA-SKIFF SPORTSMAN	FB	RNBT	L/P		IB	210		10	2		2	2	7850	9050
28		SEA-SKIFF SPORTSMAN	FB	RNBT	L/P		IB	T185		10	2		1	11	8600	9900
30		CAPRI	SLP	SAIL	FBG	KC	IB	25		9	8	11740	3	9	20600	22900
30		CONSTELLATION	OP	EXP	M/P		IB	T185-T210		10	8	8920	2	2	12800	14500
30		CONSTELLATION	HT	EXP	M/P		IB	T185-T210		10	8	8920	2	2	12800	14500
30		CRUSADER	OP	EXP	M/P		IB	210		10	8		2	2	9600	10900
30		CRUSADER	OP	EXP	M/P		IB	T185		10	8		2	2	9600	10900
30		CRUSADER	HT	EXP	M/P		IB	210		10	8		2	2	9600	10900
30		CRUSADER	HT	EXP	M/P		IB	T185		10	8		2	2	9600	10900
30		DISPATCHER EN BRIDGE	HT	EXP	STL		IB	T185-T210		11	7	14425	2	6	14200	16400
30		DISPATCHER ROAMER	OP	EXP	STL		IB	T185-T210		11	7	13825	2	5	13900	16100
30		DISPATCHER ROAMER	HT	EXP	STL		IB	T185-T210		11	7	13825	2	5	13900	16100
30		FUTURA CAVALIER	OP	EXP	PLY		IB	210		10	7	6300	2	2	9650	11000
30		FUTURA CAVALIER	OP	EXP	PLY		IB	T185		10	7	6300	2	2	10700	12100
30		FUTURA CAVALIER	HT	EXP	PLY		IB	210		10	7	6300	2	2	9650	11000
30		FUTURA CAVALIER	HT	EXP	PLY		IB	T185		10	7	6300	2	2	10700	12100
30		SEASTRAKE CAVALIER	OP	EXP	L/P		IB	210		10	7	6300	2	2	9650	11000
30		SEASTRAKE CAVALIER	OP	EXP	L/P		IB	T185		10	7	6300	2	2	10700	12100
30		SEASTRAKE CAVALIER	HT	EXP	L/P		IB	210		10	7	6300	2	2	9650	11000
30		SEASTRAKE CAVALIER	HT	EXP	L/P		IB	T185		10	7	6300	2	2	10700	12100
30	3	SHIELDS	SLP	SA/OD	FBG	KL	OB			6	5	4600	4	9	7700	8900
31		COMMANDER	OP	EXP	FBG		IB	T185-T210		11	3		2	4	13100	15200
31		COMMANDER	HT	EXP	FBG		IB	T185-T210		11	3		2	4	13100	15200
32		CONSTELLATION	OP	EXP	M/P		IB	T185		11	6	12600	2	8	15300	17400
32		CONSTELLATION	HT	EXP	M/P		IB	T185		11	6	12600	2	8	15300	17400
32		CORINTHIAN SEA SKIFF	OP	EXP	PLY		IB	T185-T210		11	2		1	11	15100	17500
32		CORINTHIAN SEA SKIFF	HT	EXP	PLY		IB	T185-T210		11	2		1	11	15100	17500
32		SEA-HAWK SEA SKIFF	OP	EXP	L/P		IB	T185-T210		11	2		2		15100	17500
32		SEA-HAWK SEA SKIFF	HT	EXP	L/P		IB	T185-T210		11	2		2		15100	17500
32		SEA-SKIFF	HT	SPTCR	L/P		IB	T185-T210		11	2		2		13300	15400
32		SEA-SKIFF	FB	SPTCR	L/P		IB	T185-T210		11	2		2		13300	15400
33		FUTURA CAVALIER	OP	EXP	PLY		IB	T185-T210		11	10	10500	2	3	16100	18600
33		FUTURA CAVALIER	HT	EXP	L/P		IB	T185-T210		11	10	10500	2	3	16100	18600
33		RIVIERA-ROAMER	HT	EXP	STL		IB	T185-T300		12		14780	2	9	18000	21200
33		RIVIERA-ROAMER	FB	EXP	STL		IB	T185-T300		12		14780	2	9	18000	21200
33		SEASTRAKE CAVALIER	OP	EXP	L/P		IB	T185-T210		11	10	10500	2	3	16100	18600
33		SEASTRAKE CAVALIER	HT	EXP	PLY		IB	T185-T210		11	10	10500	2	3	16100	18600
35		CORINTHIAN SEA SKIFF	HT	EXP	PLY	RB	IB	T185		11	7	12500	2	4	18900	21000
35		CORINTHIAN SEA SKIFF	HT	EXP	PLY	RB	IB	T210		11	7	12500	2	4	19100	21200
35		CORINTHIAN SEA SKIFF	FB	EXP	PLY	RB	IB	T185		11	7	12500	2	4	18900	21000
35		CORINTHIAN SEA SKIFF	FB	EXP	PLY	RB	IB	T210		11	7	12500	2	4	19100	21200
35		SAIL YACHT	SLP	MS	FBG	KL	IB	60		11		18112	4	8	30500	33900
35		SAIL YACHT	SLP	MS	FBG	KL	IB	30D		11		18112	4	8	30700	34100
35		SEA-HAWK SEA SKIFF	HT	EXP	L/P		IB	T185		11	7		2	5	19900	22100
35		SEA-HAWK SEA SKIFF	HT	EXP	L/P		IB	T210		11	7		2	5	20100	22300
35		SEA-HAWK SEA SKIFF	FB	EXP	L/P		IB	T185		11	7		2	5	19900	22100
35		SEA-HAWK SEA SKIFF	FB	EXP	L/P		IB	T210		11	7		2	5	20100	22300
36		CAVALIER	FB	MY	PLY		IB	T185		12	8	12340	2	6	22900	25500
36		CAVALIER	FB	MY	PLY		IB	T210		12	8	12340	2	6	23200	25700
36		CONSTELLATION	HT	SDN	M/P		IB	T185		12			2	10	26000	28900
36		CONSTELLATION	HT	SDN	M/P		IB	T210		12			2	10	26200	29100
36		CONSTELLATION	FB	SDN	M/P		IB	T185		12			2	10	26000	28900
36		CONSTELLATION	FB	SDN	M/P		IB	T210		12			2	10	26200	29100
36		CRUSADER CAVALIER	HT	EXP	M/P		IB	T185		12		13000	2	8	22300	24700
36		CRUSADER CAVALIER	HT	EXP	M/P		IB	T210		12		13000	2	8	22400	24900
36		SEASTRAKE CAVALIER	FB	MY	L/P		IB	T185		12	8	12340	2	6	22900	25500
36		SEASTRAKE CAVALIER	FB	MY	L/P		IB	T210		12	8	12340	2	6	23200	25700
37		CONSTELLATION	HT	EXP	MHG		IB	T185		12	3		2	10	28100	31200
37		CONSTELLATION	HT	EXP	MHG		IB	T210		12	3		2	10	28200	31300
37		CONSTELLATION	HT	EXP	MHG		IB	T300		12	3		2	10	28700	31800
37		CONSTELLATION	FB	EXP	MHG		IB	T185		12	3		2	10	28100	31200

 CONTINUED ON NEXT PAGE

CHRIS CRAFT BOATS -CONTINUED See inside cover to adjust price for area

LOA FT	LOA IN	NAME AND/ OR MODEL	TOP/ RIG	BOAT TYPE	-HULL- MTL	-HULL- TP	ENGINE TP	ENGINE # HP	ENGINE MFG	BEAM FT	BEAM IN	WGT LBS	DRAFT FT	DRAFT IN	RETAIL LOW	RETAIL HIGH
		1966 BOATS														
37		CONSTELLATION	FB	EXP	MHG		IB	T210		12	3		2	10	28200	31300
37		CONSTELLATION	FB	EXP	MHG		IB	T300		12	3		2	10	28700	31800
37		RIVIERA-ROAMER	HT	EXP	AL		IB	T185		12	10	16470	2	10	27200	30200
37		RIVIERA-ROAMER	HT	EXP	STL		IB	T185		12	10	20830	2	11	32100	35600
37		RIVIERA-ROAMER	HT	EXP	AL		IB	T210		12	10	16470	2	10	27300	30300
37		RIVIERA-ROAMER	HT	EXP	STL		IB	T210		12	10	20830	2	11	32200	35700
37		RIVIERA-ROAMER	HT	EXP	AL		IB	T300		12	10	16470	2	10	27800	30900
37		RIVIERA-ROAMER	HT	EXP	STL		IB	T300		12	10	20830	2	11	32600	36300
37		RIVIERA-ROAMER	HT	EXP	AL		IB	T197D		12	10	16470	2	10	30900	34300
37		RIVIERA-ROAMER	HT	EXP	STL		IB	T197D		12	10	20830	2	11	36200	40200
37		RIVIERA-ROAMER	FB	EXP	AL		IB	T185		12	10	16470	2	10	27200	30200
37		RIVIERA-ROAMER	FB	EXP	STL		IB	T185		12	10	20830	2	11	32100	35600
37		RIVIERA-ROAMER	FB	EXP	AL		IB	T210		12	10	16470	2	10	27300	30300
37		RIVIERA-ROAMER	FB	EXP	STL		IB	T210		12	10	20830	2	11	32200	35700
37		RIVIERA-ROAMER	FB	EXP	AL		IB	T300		12	10	16470	2	10	27800	30900
37		RIVIERA-ROAMER	FB	EXP	STL		IB	T300		12	10	20830	2	11	32600	36300
37		RIVIERA-ROAMER	FB	EXP	AL		IB	T197D		12	10	16470	2	10	30900	34300
37		RIVIERA-ROAMER	FB	EXP	STL		IB	T197D		12	10	20830	2	11	36200	40200
38		COMMANDER	HT	EXP	FBG		IB	T210		13			3		27100	30100
38		COMMANDER	HT	EXP	FBG	SV	IB	T300		13			3		27400	30500
38		COMMANDER	HT	EXP	FBG	SV	IB	T258D		13			3		42500	47200
38		COMMANDER	FB	EXP	FBG	SV	IB	T210		13			3		27100	30100
38		COMMANDER	FB	EXP	FBG	SV	IB	T300		13			3		27400	30500
38		COMMANDER	FB	EXP	FBG	SV	IB	T258D		13			3		42500	47200
38		COMMANDER	HT	SDN	FBG	SV	IB	T210		13			3		35700	39600
38		COMMANDER	HT	SDN	FBG	SV	IB	T300		13			3		36000	40100
38		COMMANDER	HT	SDN	FBG	SV	IB	T258D		13			3		41700	46300
38		COMMANDER	FB	SDN	FBG	SV	IB	T210		13			3		35700	39600
38		COMMANDER	FB	SDN	FBG	SV	IB	T300		13			3		36100	40100
38		COMMANDER	FB	SDN	FBG	SV	IB	T258D		13			3		41700	46300
38		COMMANDER	FB	SF	FBG	SV	IB	T210		13			3		32500	36100
38		COMMANDER	FB	SF	FBG	SV	IB	T300		13			3		32900	36500
38		COMMANDER	FB	SF	FBG	SV	IB	T258D		13			3		44300	49200
38		CONSTELLATION	OP	TCMY	MHG		IB	T185		13			2	11	35300	39200
38		CONSTELLATION	OP	TCMY	MHG		IB	T210		13			2	11	35400	39300
38		CONSTELLATION	OP	TCMY	MHG		IB	T300		13			2	11	35700	39700
38		CONSTELLATION	HT	TCMY	MHG		IB	T185		13			2	11	35300	39200
38		CONSTELLATION	HT	TCMY	MHG		IB	T210		13			2	11	35400	39300
38		CONSTELLATION	HT	TCMY	MHG		IB	T300		13			2	11	35800	39700
38		CORINTHIAN SEA SKIFF	HT	EXP	PLY		IB	T210		13		16650	2	10	28600	31800
38		CORINTHIAN SEA SKIFF	HT	EXP	PLY		IB	T300		13		16650	2	10	29000	32200
38		CORINTHIAN SEA SKIFF	HT	EXP	PLY		IB	T197D		13		16650	2	10	32500	36100
38		CORINTHIAN SEA SKIFF	FB	EXP	PLY		IB	T210		13		16650	2	10	28600	31800
38		CORINTHIAN SEA SKIFF	FB	EXP	PLY		IB	T300		13		16650	2	10	29000	32200
38		CORINTHIAN SEA SKIFF	FB	EXP	PLY		IB	T197D		13		16650	2	10	32500	36100
38		CORINTHIAN SEA SKIFF		SF	WD		IB	T210		13		16650	2	10	28600	31800
38		CORINTHIAN SEA SKIFF		SF	WD		IB	T300		13		16650	2	10	29000	32200
38		CORINTHIAN SEA SKIFF		SF	WD		IB	T197D		13		16650	2	10	32500	36100
38		ROAMER OFFSHORE	HT	OFF	AL	SV	IB	T300		12	9	22280	2	10	36400	40400
38		ROAMER OFFSHORE	FB	OFF	AL	SV	IB	T300		12	9	22280	2	10	36400	40400
40		CONSTELLATION SALON	FB	MY	MHG		IB	T210		13			2	11	37400	41600
40		CONSTELLATION SALON	FB	MY	MHG		IB	T300		13			2	11	37700	41900
43		CONSTELLATION	HT	MY	M/P		IB	T210		13		22500	3		38800	43100
43		CORINTHIAN SEA SKIFF	OP	DC	PLY		IB	T300		13			2	11	46900	51600
43		CORINTHIAN SEA SKIFF	OP	DC	PLY		IB	T258D		13			2	11	54000	59400
43		CORINTHIAN SEA SKIFF	HT	DC	PLY		IB	T300		13			2	11	47300	52000
43		CORINTHIAN SEA SKIFF	HT	DC	PLY		IB	T258D		13			2	11	54500	59800
45		CONSTELLATION	HT	MY	MHG		IB	T300		13		27000	3	2	44100	49100
45		CONSTELLATION	HT	MY	MHG		IB	T258D		13		27000	3	2	48600	53400
47		COMMANDER		MY	FBG		IB	T300		15		27304			42700	47400
47		COMMANDER		MY	FBG		IB	T258D		15		27304			47200	51800
48		CONSTELLATION	HT	MY	MHG		IB	T300		13		32000	3	1	48200	53000
48		CONSTELLATION	HT	MY	MHG		IB	T258D		13		32000	3	1	51500	56600
48		RIVIERA-ROAMER	HT	MY	AL	SV	IB	T300		13		28560	3	2	54700	60100
48		RIVIERA-ROAMER	HT	MY	STL	SV	IB	T300		13		34000	3	3	60200	66200
48		RIVIERA-ROAMER	HT	MY	AL	SV	IB	T270D		13		28560	3	2	60800	66900
48		RIVIERA-ROAMER	HT	MY	STL	SV	IB	T270D		13		34000	3	3	66600	73200
48		RIVIERA-ROAMER	HT	MY	AL	SV	IB	T300D		13		28560	3	2	63500	69800
48		RIVIERA-ROAMER	HT	MY	STL	SV	IB	T300D		13		34000	3	3	69000	75800
52		CONSTELLATION	HT	MY	MHG		IB	T300		13		36000	3	8	56500	62100
		IB T270D 55900 61400, IB T280D 56400 61900, IB T300D													57400	63100
		IB T320D 58600 64300														
57		CONSTELLATION	HT	MY	MHG		IB	T270D		15		48503	3	11	70300	77300
		IB T280D 71800 78800, IB T300D 74500 81900, IB T320D													77100	84800
57	3	ROAMER	HT	MY	AL	SV	IB	T270D		15		50000	4	3	72600	79700
57	3	ROAMER	HT	MY	STL	SV	IB	T270D		15		60000	4	3	94500	104000
57	3	ROAMER	HT	MY	AL	SV	IB	T320D		15		50000	4	3	79300	87100
57	3	ROAMER	HT	MY	STL	SV	IB	T320D		15		60000	4	3	100000	110000
65			HT	MYDKH	WD		IB	T460D		16	9		4	4	134500	148000
65			HT	MYDKH	WD		IB	T478D		16	9		4	4	136500	150000
65		CONSTELLATION	HT	MYDKH	WD		IB	T460D		16	9		3	9	130500	143000
65		CONSTELLATION	HT	MYDKH	WD		IB	T478D		16	9		3	9	132000	145000
		1965 BOATS														
16		CORSAIR XL160 SPORTS	OP	RNBT	FBG		IO	120		6	9	1400			3050	3550
17		CUSTOM	OP	SKI	M/P		IB	185		6	8	2481	1	8	1800	2150
17		SUPER-SPORT	OP	RNBT	M/P		IB	210		6	8	2481	1	8	1900	2300
17	2	LUXURY LOUNGER	OP	RNBT	L/P		OB			6	5	920	1	8	1800	2100
17	2	TRADITIONAL	OP	RNBT	MHG		OB								2100	2500
17	6	CORSAIR XL175	OP	EXP	FBG		OB			7	6	1060			2000	2400
17	6	CORSAIR XL175 SPORTS	OP	EXP	FBG		IO	120-150							5200	6000
17	6	SUNLOUNGER COR XL175	OP	RNBT	FBG		OB					900			1750	2100
17	6	SUNLOUNGER COR XL175	OP	RNBT	FBG		IO	120-150		7	6	1540			3850	4450
18					WD		IB	185-283							**	**
18		CAVALIER CUSTOM	OP	UTL	PLY		IB	185-210		7	2	2415	1	11	1950	2350
18	2	LUXURY LOUNGER SKIFF	OP	RNBT	L/P		OB			7	5	1200			2350	2700
18	2	LUXURY RUNABOUT	OP	RNBT	L/P		OB			7	4	1200			2350	2700
18	2	SEA-V CORSAIR XL180	OP	RNBT	FBG		IO	120		7	4	2750			5150	5950
18	2	SEA-V SKIFF	OP	RNBT	L/P		IO	120		7	4	1850			4200	4900
18	4	SUPER-SPORT	OP	RNBT	M/P		IB	185-210		6	5	2605	1	8	2050	2500
19		GOLDEN-ARROW	OP	RNBT	PLY		IB	185-210		7	5	2271	1	11	2200	2600
19		SEA-SKIFF SPORTSMAN	OP	RNBT	L/P		IB	185		7	1	2570	1	11	2300	2650
20		HOLIDAY	OP	RNBT	M/P		IB	185		6	7	2747			2550	2950
20		LUXURY CRUISETTE		CUD	L/P		OB			7	4	1750			3650	4250
20		SEA-V CORSAIR XL200	OP	RNBT	FBG		IO	140-185		7	11	2750			6300	7300
20		SEA-V LUXURY CRUISER		CR	L/P		IO	140		7	4	2450			5850	6750
20		SEA-V LUXURY LOUNGER	FB	CR	L/P		IO	140		7	4	2250			5650	6450
20		SUPER-SPORT	OP	RNBT	M/P		IB	210-275		6	7	2747	1	10	2550	3050
20		TRADITIONAL	OP	RNBT	WD		OB								3550	4150
21		RANGER SEA-SKIFF	OP	RNBT	L/P		IB	185		7	7	2667	1	10	2800	3300
21		SEA-SKIFF SPORTSMAN	OP	RNBT	L/P		IB	185		7	7	2667	1	10	2800	3300
21		SUPER-SPORT	OP	RNBT	M/P		IB	210-275		7	6	3205	2		3150	3750
22		CAVALIER DORY	OP	CTRCN	L/P		IB	185		8		3000	1	11	3250	3750
22		CUTLASS CAVALIER	OP	CUD	PLY		IB	185-210		8		3200	1	11	3350	3950
22		SEA-SKIFF SPORTSMAN	OP	RNBT	L/P		IB	185-210		8		3470	1	10	3600	4200
23		SEA-V SKIFF	OP	RNBT	L/P		IO	165		8	9	3550			9000	10200
24		FUTURA CAVALIER	OP	EXP	PLY		IB	185		8		3500	2		4000	4600
24		RANGER SEA SKIFF	OP	RNBT	L/P		IB	185-210		9		4100	2		4650	5350
24		RANGER SEA SKIFF	HT	RNBT	L/P		IB	185-210		9		4100	2		4650	5350
24		SEA-SKIFF SPORTSMAN	OP	RNBT	L/P		IB	175-210		9	1	4100	2		4650	5350
24		SEA-SKIFF SPORTSMAN	HT	RNBT	L/P		IB	175-210		9	1	4100	2		4650	5350
24		SEASTRAKE CAVALIER	OP	EXP	L/P		IB	185		8		3500	2		4000	4600
25		FUTURA CAVALIER	OP	EXP	PLY		IB	185		9	6	3800	2		4650	5350
25		SEASTRAKE CAVALIER	OP	EXP	L/P		IB	185		9	6	3800	2		4650	5350
26	3	CAPRI	SLP	SAIL	FBG		OB			8	2		4		6600	7600
27		COMMANDER	OP	EXP	FBG		IB	185-210		10	3				6700	7850
27		COMMANDER	HT	EXP	FBG		IB	185-210		10	3				6700	7850
27		CONSTELLATION	OP	CBNCR	M/P		IB	185		10	2	5544	2	1	7750	8900
27		CONSTELLATION	HT	CBNCR	M/P		IB	185		10	2	5544	2	1	7750	8900
27		FUTURA CAVALIER	OP	EXP	PLY		IB	185		10	3	5017	2	1	6300	7250
27		FUTURA CAVALIER	HT	EXP	PLY		IB	185		10	3	5017	2	1	6300	7250
27		SEASTRAKE CAVALIER	OP	EXP	L/P		IB	185		10	3	5017	2	1	6300	7250
27		SEASTRAKE CAVALIER	HT	EXP	L/P		IB	185		10	3	5017	2	1	6300	7250
28		CONSTELLATION	OP	EXP	M/P		IB	210		10	2		2	2	7750	8900
28		CONSTELLATION	OP	EXP	M/P		IB	T185		10	2	5544	1	11	7750	8900
28		CONSTELLATION	OP	EXP	M/P		IB	T185-T210		10	2		2	2	8550	10000
28		CONSTELLATION	HT	EXP	M/P		IB	210		10	2		2	2	7750	8900
28		CONSTELLATION	HT	EXP	M/P		IB	T185		10	2	5544	1	11	7750	8900
28		CONSTELLATION	HT	EXP	M/P		IB	T185-T210		10	2		2	2	8550	10000
28		CORINTHIAN SEA-SKIFF	OP	EXP	L/P		IB	185		10		6443	2	3	7200	8300
28		CRUSADER CAVALIER	OP	EXP	MHG		IB	185-210							7650	8900
28		CRUSADER CAVALIER	OP	EXP	MHG		IB	T185							8550	9800
28		FUTURA CAVALIER	OP	EXP	PLY		IB	185		10	5	6114	2	2	7100	8150
28		SEA-SKIFF	OP	EXP	L/P		IB	210		10	1	8100	2	4	8250	9500

 CONTINUED ON NEXT PAGE

CHRIS CRAFT BOATS -CONTINUED See inside cover to adjust price for area

LOA FT	IN	NAME AND/ OR MODEL	TOP/ RIG	BOAT TYPE	-HULL- MTL	TP	----ENGINE--- TP	# HP	MFG	BEAM FT	IN	WGT LBS	DRAFT FT	IN	RETAIL LOW	RETAIL HIGH
		1965 BOATS														
28		SEA-SKIFF	OP	EXP	L/P		IB	T185		10	1	8100	2	1	9100	10400
28		SEA-SKIFF	HT	EXP	L/P		IB	210		10	1	8100	2	4	8250	9500
28		SEA-SKIFF	HT	EXP	L/P		IB	T185		10	1	8100	2	1	9100	10400
28		SEA-SKIFF SPORTSMAN	OP	RNBT	L/P		IB	185		10	2	7500	2		7700	8850
28		SEA-SKIFF SPORTSMAN	OP	RNBT	L/P		IB	T185		10	2	7500	2		8550	9800
28		SEA-SKIFF SPORTSMAN	HT	RNBT	L/P		IB	210		10	2	7500	2		7800	8950
28		SEA-SKIFF SPORTSMAN	HT	RNBT	L/P		IB	T185		10	2	7500	2		8550	9800
28		SEA-SKIFF SPORTSMAN	FB	RNBT	L/P		IB	210		10	2	7500	2		7800	8950
28		SEA-SKIFF SPORTSMAN	FB	RNBT	L/P		IB	T185		10	2	7500	2		8550	9800
30		CAPRI	SLP	SAIL	FBG	KC	IB	25	GRAY	9	9	11740	3	9	20500	22700
30		CONSTELLATION	OP	EXP	M/P		IB	T185		10	8	7731	2	2	10900	12300
30		CONSTELLATION	HT	EXP	M/P		IB	T185		10	8	7731	2	2	10900	12300
30		DISPATCHER ROAMER	OP	EXP	STL		IB	T185-T210		11	7				10500	12200
30		DISPATCHER ROAMER	HT	EXP	STL		IB	T185-T210		11	7				10500	12200
30		DISPATCHER ROAMER	FB	EXP	STL		IB	T185-T210		11	7				11200	13000
30		DISPATCHER ROAMER EN	FB	EXP	STL		IB	T185-T210		11	7				9800	11400
30		FUTURA CAVALIER	OP	EXP	PLY		IB	210		10	7	6300	2	2	9400	10700
30		FUTURA CAVALIER	OP	EXP	PLY		IB	T185		10	7	6300	2	2	10400	11800
30		FUTURA CAVALIER	HT	EXP	PLY		IB	210		10	7	6300	2	2	9400	10700
30		FUTURA CAVALIER	HT	EXP	PLY		IB	T185		10	7	6300	2	2	10400	11800
30		SEASTRAKE CAVALIER	OP	EXP	L/P		IB	T185		10	7	6300	2	2	10400	11800
30		SEASTRAKE CAVALIER	HT	EXP	L/P		IB	T185		10	7	6300	2	2	10400	11800
30	3	SHIELDS	SLP	SA/OD	FBG	KL	OB			6	5	4600	4	9	7650	8800
31		COMMANDER	OP	EXP	FBG		IB	T185		11	3		2	4	12700	14500
31		COMMANDER	HT	EXP	FBG		IB	T185		11	3		2	4	12700	14500
32		CONSTELLATION	OP	EXP	M/P		IB	T185-T210		11	6	12600	2	8	14900	17200
32		CONSTELLATION	HT	EXP	M/P		IB	T185-T210		11	6	12600	2	8	14900	17200
32		CORINTHIAN	HT	CR	L/P		IB	T185		11			2		12900	14700
32		RIVIERA ROAMER	HT	EXP	STL	SV	IB	T185		11	4	12100	2	5	14700	16700
32		SEA-HAWK	OP	EXP	L/P		IB	T185-T210		11	2	10700	2	1	14300	16500
32		SEA-HAWK	HT	EXP	L/P		IB	T185-T210		11	2	10700	2	1	14300	16500
32		SEA-SKIFF	HT	SPTCR	L/P		IB	T185-T210		11	2	10500	2	1	14300	16500
32		SEA-SKIFF	FB	SPTCR	L/P		IB	T185-T210		11	2	10500	2	1	14300	16500
33		FUTURA CAVALIER	OP	EXP	PLY		IB	T185-T210		11	10	10500	2	3	15600	18000
33		FUTURA CAVALIER	HT	EXP	PLY		IB	T185-T210		11	10	10500	2	3	15600	18000
33		RIVIERA-ROAMER	HT		STL		IB	T185-T210		12					13000	15000
33		RIVIERA-ROAMER	FB		STL		IB	T185-T210		12					13000	15000
33		SEASTRAKE CAVALIER	OP	EXP	L/P		IB	T185-T210		11	10	10500	2	3	15600	18000
33		SEASTRAKE CAVALIER	HT	EXP	L/P		IB	T185-T210		11	10	10500	2	3	15600	18000
34		CONSTELLATION	HT	EXP	M/P		IB	T185		12		11885	2	8	17400	19800
34		CONSTELLATION	FB	EXP	M/P		IB	T185		12		11885	2	8	17400	19800
34		CONSTELLATION	HT	SDN	M/P		IB	T185		12		12300	2	8	18900	21000
34		CONSTELLATION	FB	SDN	M/P		IB	T185		12		12300	2	8	18900	21000
35		CORINTHIAN SEA SKIFF	HT	EXP	PLY		IB	T185							19400	21500
35		CORINTHIAN SEA SKIFF	HT	EXP	PLY		IB	T210							19600	21700
35		SAIL YACHT	SLP	MS	FBG		IB	60		11		18112	4	8	30300	33600
35		SAIL YACHT	SLP	MS	FBG		IB	30D		11		18112	4	8	30400	33800
35		SEA-HAWK SEA SKIFF	HT	EXP	L/P		IB	T185		11	7	12500	2	4	18300	20400
35		SEA-HAWK SEA SKIFF	HT	EXP	L/P		IB	T210		11	7	12500	2	4	18500	20600
35		SEA-HAWK SEA SKIFF	FB	EXP	L/P		IB	T185		11	7	12500	2	4	18300	20400
35		SEA-HAWK SEA SKIFF	FB	EXP	L/P		IB	T210		11	7	12500	2	4	18500	20600
36		CAVALIER	FB	MY	PLY		IB	T185		12	8	12340	2	6	22500	25000
36		CAVALIER	FB	MY	PLY		IB	T210		12	8	12340	2	6	22700	25200
36		CHALLENGER	HT	EXP	M/P		IB	T185		12		15720	2	6	24000	26700
36		CHALLENGER	HT	EXP	M/P		IB	T210		12		15720	2	6	24100	26800
36		CHALLENGER	HT	SDN	M/P		IB	T185		12		16325	2	6	25000	27700
36		CHALLENGER	HT	SDN	M/P		IB	T210		12		16325	2	6	25100	27900
36		CONSTELLATION	HT	EXP	M/P		IB	T185		12		13172	2	8	22000	24400
36		CONSTELLATION	HT	EXP	M/P		IB	T210		12		13172	2	8	22100	24600
36		CONSTELLATION	FB	EXP	M/P		IB	T185		12		13172	2	8	22000	24400
36		CONSTELLATION	FB	EXP	M/P		IB	T210		12		13172	2	8	22100	24600
36		CONSTELLATION	HT	SDN	M/P		IB	T185		12		16325	2	10	25000	27700
36		CONSTELLATION	HT	SDN	M/P		IB	T210		12		16325	2	10	25100	27900
36		CONSTELLATION	FB	SDN	M/P		IB	T185		12		16325	2	10	25000	27700
36		CONSTELLATION	FB	SDN	M/P		IB	T210		12		16325	2	10	25100	27900
36		RIVIERA ROAMER	HT	EXP	AL		IB	T185		12		11900	2	10	21000	23300
36		RIVIERA ROAMER	HT	EXP	AL		IB	T D		12			2	10	**	**
36		SEASTRAKE CAVALIER	FB	MY	L/P		IB	T185		12	8	12340	2	6	22500	25000
36		SEASTRAKE CAVALIER	FB	MY	L/P		IB	T210		12	8	12340	2	6	22700	25200
37		CONSTELLATION	FB	EXP	M/P		IB	T185		12	3	16800	2	10	27200	30200
37		CONSTELLATION	FB	EXP	M/P		IB	T210		12	3	16800	2	10	27300	30300
37		CONSTELLATION	FB	EXP	M/P		IB	T275		12	3	16800	2	10	27600	30700
37		RIVIERA-ROAMER	HT	EXP	AL		IB	T185		12	10				26600	29600
37		RIVIERA-ROAMER	HT	EXP	STL		IB	T185		12	10				26600	29600
37		RIVIERA-ROAMER	HT	EXP	AL		IB	T210		12	10				26700	29700
37		RIVIERA-ROAMER	HT	EXP	STL		IB	T210		12	10				26700	29700
37		RIVIERA-ROAMER	HT	EXP	AL		IB	T275		12	10				27000	30000
37		RIVIERA-ROAMER	HT	EXP	STL		IB	T275		12	10				27000	30000
37		RIVIERA-ROAMER	HT	EXP	AL		IB	T196D		12	10				30600	34000
37		RIVIERA-ROAMER	HT	EXP	STL		IB	T196D		12	10				30600	34000
37		RIVIERA-ROAMER	FB	EXP	AL		IB	T185		12	10				26600	29600
37		RIVIERA-ROAMER	FB	EXP	STL		IB	T185		12	10				26600	29600
37		RIVIERA-ROAMER	FB	EXP	AL		IB	T210		12	10				26700	29700
37		RIVIERA-ROAMER	FB	EXP	STL		IB	T210		12	10				26700	29700
37		RIVIERA-ROAMER	FB	EXP	AL		IB	T275		12	10				27000	30000
37		RIVIERA-ROAMER	FB	EXP	STL		IB	T275		12	10				27000	30000
37		RIVIERA-ROAMER	FB	EXP	AL		IB	T196D		12	10				30600	34000
37		RIVIERA-ROAMER	FB	EXP	STL		IB	T196D		12	10				30600	34000
38		COMMANDER	HT		FBG		IB	T210		13					25800	28700
38		COMMANDER	HT		FBG		IB	T275		13					26000	28900
38		COMMANDER	HT		FBG		IB	T258D		13					40800	45400
38		COMMANDER	FB		FBG		IB	T210		13					25800	28700
38		COMMANDER	FB		FBG		IB	T275		13					26000	28900
38		COMMANDER	FB		FBG		IB	T258D		13					40800	45400
38		COMMANDER	HT	SDN	FBG		IB	T210		13					34900	38800
38		COMMANDER	HT	SDN	FBG		IB	T275		13					35200	39100
38		COMMANDER	HT	SDN	FBG		IB	T258D		13					40800	45400
38		COMMANDER	FB	SDN	FBG		IB	T210		13					35000	38800
38		COMMANDER	FB	SDN	FBG		IB	T275		13					35200	39100
38		COMMANDER	FB	SDN	FBG		IB	T258D		13					40800	45400
38		COMMANDER		SF	FBG		IB	T210		13					31800	35400
38		COMMANDER		SF	FBG		IB	T275		13					32000	35600
38		COMMANDER		SF	FBG		IB	T258D		13					43400	48300
38		CONSTELLATION SALON	FB	TCMY	M/P		IB	T185		13		18500	3		30400	33700
38		CONSTELLATION SALON	FB	TCMY	M/P		IB	T210		13		18500	3		30400	33800
38		CORINTHIAN SEA SKIFF	HT	EXP	PLY		IB	T210							28400	31500
38		CORINTHIAN SEA SKIFF	HT	EXP	PLY		IB	T275							28600	31800
38		CORINTHIAN SEA SKIFF	HT	EXP	PLY		IB	T197D							39800	44200
38		ROAMER OFFSHORE	HT	OFF	STL		IB	T280		13					18700	20800
38		ROAMER OFFSHORE	FB	OFF	STL		IB	T280		13					18700	20800
38		SEA-HAWK SEA SKIFF	HT	SDN	L/P		IB	T210		13		15700	2	10	27000	30000
38		SEA-HAWK SEA SKIFF	HT	SDN	L/P		IB	T275		13		15700	2	10	27200	30200
38		SEA-HAWK SEA SKIFF	HT	SDN	L/P		IB	T197D		13		15700	2	10	30800	34300
38		SEA-HAWK SEA SKIFF	FB	SDN	L/P		IB	T210		13		15700	2	10	27000	30000
38		SEA-HAWK SEA SKIFF	FB	SDN	L/P		IB	T275		13		15700	2	10	27200	30200
38		SEA-HAWK SEA SKIFF	FB	SF	L/P		IB	T210		13		15700	2	10	26800	29800
38		SEA-HAWK SEA SKIFF	FB	SF	L/P		IB	T275		13		15700	2	10	27100	30100
38		SEA-HAWK SEA SKIFF	FB	SF	L/P		IB	T197D		13		15700	2	10	30600	34000
43		CONSTELLATION	HT	MY	M/P		IB	T210		13		22500	3		38000	42200
		IB T275 40300 44700, IB T197D 42700 47500, IB T258D													46100	50600
46		CONSTELLATION	HT	MY	M/P		IB	T275		13		28437	3	2	42900	47600
46		CONSTELLATION	HT	MY	M/P		IB	T197D		13		28437	3	2	44600	49600
46		CONSTELLATION	HT	MY	M/P		IB	T258D		13		28437	3	2	48500	53300
48		RIVIERA-ROAMER	HT		AL		IB	T275		13					**	**
48		RIVIERA-ROAMER	HT		STL		IB	T275		13					**	**
48		RIVIERA-ROAMER	HT		AL		IB	T270D		13					**	**
48		RIVIERA-ROAMER	HT		STL		IB	T270D		13					**	**
48		RIVIERA-ROAMER	HT		AL		IB	T274D		13					**	**
48		RIVIERA-ROAMER	HT		STL		IB	T274D		13					**	**
52		CONSTELLATION	HT	MY	M/P		IB	T275		14	3	35271	3	8	53600	58800
		IB T270D 53700 59000, IB T270D CAT 53300 58600, IB T280D													54200	59500
		IB T320D 56400 61900														
57		CONSTELLATION	HT	MY	M/P		IB	T270D		15		48503	3	11	69000	75800
		IB T270D CAT 69000 75800, IB T280D 70400 77300, IB T320D													75600	83100
57		ROAMER		MY	AL		IB	T270D		15					81300	89300
57		ROAMER		MY	STL		IB	T270D		15					84200	92500
57		ROAMER		MY	AL		IB	T274D		15					81500	89500
57		ROAMER		MY	STL		IB	T274D		15					84400	92800
57		ROAMER		MY	AL		IB	T320D		15					83700	92000
57		ROAMER		MY	STL		IB	T320D		15					86900	95500
65			HT	MYDKH	M/P		IB	T460D		16	9	72073	4	4	145000	159500
65			HT	MYDKH	M/P		IB	T478D		16	9	72073	4	4	147000	161500
65		CONSTELLATION	HT	MYDKH	M/P		IB	T460D		16	9	72073	3	9	142500	156500

 CONTINUED ON NEXT PAGE

LOA FT	LOA IN	NAME AND/ OR MODEL	TOP/ RIG	BOAT TYPE	-HULL- MTL	-HULL- TP	ENGINE TP	ENGINE # HP	ENGINE MFG	BEAM FT	BEAM IN	WGT LBS	DRAFT FT	DRAFT IN	RETAIL LOW	RETAIL HIGH
		1965 BOATS														
65		CONSTELLATION	HT	MYDKH	M/P		IB	T478D		16	9	72073	3	9	144000	158500
		1964 BOATS														
17		CUSTOM	OP	SKI	M/P		IB	185		6	8	2481	1	8	1750	2100
17		SUPER-SPORT	OP	RNBT	WD		IB	210		6	8	2481			1850	2250
17	2	LUXURY LOUNGER	OP	RNBT	L/P		OB			6	6	920			1800	2150
17	2	TRADITIONAL	OP	RNBT	L/P		OB			6	6	950			1850	2200
17	6	CORSAIR LX-175	OP	RNBT	FBG	DV	IO	140		7	6				5100	5850
17	6	CORSAIR XL-175	OP	RNBT	FBG	DV	OB			7	6	860			1700	2050
17	6	CORSAIR XL-175 EXP	OP	RNBT	FBG	DV	OB			7	6	1060			2050	2450
17	6	SUNLOUNGER XL-175	OP	RNBT	FBG		OB			7	6	1540			2800	3250
17	6	SUNLOUNGER XL175	OP	RNBT	FBG		IO	140		7	6	900			3600	4200
18					WD		IB	165	CC						**	**
18	2	SEA-V LUXURY	OP	RNBT	L/P	DV	OB			7	4	1200			2300	2700
18	2	SEA-V LUXURY LOUNGER		RNBT	M/P		IO	110		7	4	1850	1	8	4450	5100
18	2	SEA-V LUXURY LOUNGER	OP	RNBT	L/P	DV	OB			7	4	1200			2400	2800
18	4	HOLIDAY	OP	RNBT	MHG		IB	185		6	5	2605	1	8	2000	2400
18	4	SUPER-SPORT	OP	RNBT	WD		IB	210		6	5				2000	2400
19		GOLDEN-ARROW CAVALER	OP	RNBT	PLY		IB	185-210		7	5	2271	1	11	2100	2500
19		SEA-SKIFF SPORTSMAN	OP	RNBT	L/P		IB	185		7		2233	1	11	2000	2400
20		HOLIDAY	OP	RNBT	M/P		IB	185		6	7	2747			2450	2850
20		LUXURY CRUISETTE		CUD	L/P		OB			7	4				4500	5200
20		SEA-V CRUISETTE	OP	RNBT	L/P	DV	IO	140		7	4	2250			5650	6500
20		SEA-V LUXURY SKIFF	OP	CR	L/P	DV	IO	140		7	4	2250			5850	6750
20		SUPER-SPORT	OP	RNBT	MHG		IB	210-275		6	7	2747			2500	2950
20		TRADITIONAL	OP	RNBT	L/P		OB			7	4	1350			3000	3500
20	2	SEA-V SUNLNG XL200	OP	RNBT	FBG	DV	IO	140		7	11	2700			6550	7500
21		CONTINENTAL	OP	RNBT	M/P		IB	185		7	6	3205	2		3050	3550
21		RANGER SEA-SKIFF	OP	RNBT	L/P		IB	185		7	7	2667	1	10	2900	3400
21		SEA-SKIFF SPORTSMAN	OP	RNBT	L/P		IB	185		7	7	2667	1	10	2600	3000
21		SUPER-SPORT	OP	RNBT	MHG		IB	210-275		7	6	3205			3050	3600
21	4	CORSAIR-CADET XL210	OP	CR	FBG		IO	140		7	10	3700			8950	10200
23		SEA-V CUSTOM	OP	CBNCR	L/P		IO	140		8	9		1	5	12900	14700
24		FUTURA CAVALIER	OP	EXP	PLY		IB	185		8		3500	2		3850	4500
24		RANGER SEA-SKIFF	OP	RNBT	L/P		IB	185-210		9		3397	2		4200	4900
24		SEA-SKIFF SPORTSMAN	OP	RNBT	L/P		IB	185-210		9		3397	2		3600	4250
24		SEASTRAKE CAVALIER	OP	EXP	L/P		IB	185		8		3500	2		3850	4500
26		FUTURA CAVALIER	OP	EXP	PLY		IB	185		9	4	4057	1	10	5000	5750
27		CONSTELLATION	OP		M/P		IB	185		10	2	5544	2	1	6450	7450
27		CONSTELLATION	OP		M/P		IB	T185		10	2	5544	1	11	7350	8450
27		CONSTELLATION	HT		M/P		IB	185		10	2	5544	2	1	6450	7450
27		CONSTELLATION	HT		M/P		IB	T185		10	2	5544	1	11	7350	8450
27		FUTURA CAVALIER	OP	EXP	PLY		IB	185		10	3	5017	2	1	6150	7050
27		SEASTRAKE CAVALIER	OP	EXP	L/P		IB	185		10	3	5017	2	1	6150	7050
28					WD		IB	T283	CHEV						**	**
28		CORINTHIAN SEA SKIFF	OP	EXP	L/P		IB	185-210		10		6443	2	3	7000	8200
28		CORINTHIAN SEA SKIFF	OP	EXP	L/P		IB	T185		10		6443	2	1	7900	9100
28		FUTURA CAVALIER	OP	EXP	PLY		IB	185		10	5	6114	2	2	6900	7900
28		FUTURA CAVALIER	OP	EXP	PLY		IB	T185		10	5	6114	2	1	7800	8950
28		SEA-SKIFF SPORTSMAN	OP	RNBT	L/P		IB	185-210		10	2	4691	2		6000	7050
28		SEA-SKIFF SPORTSMAN	OP	RNBT	L/P		IB	T185		10	2	4691	2		6950	8000
30		CAPRI	SLP	SAIL	FBG	KC	IB	25	GRAY	9	8	11740	3	9	20300	22600
30		CONSTELLATION	HT	EXP	M/P		IB	T185		10	8	7731	2	2	10600	12000
30		CONSTELLATION	FB	EXP	M/P		IB	T185		10	8	7731	2	2	10600	12000
31		FUTURA CAVALIER	OP	EXP	PLY		IB	185		10	6	6445	2	2	10200	11600
31		FUTURA CAVALIER	OP	EXP	PLY		IB	T185		10	6	6445	2		11400	13000
31		SEASTRAKE CAVALIER	OP	EXP	L/P		IB	T185		10	6	6445	2		11400	13000
32		CORINTHIAN SEA SKIFF	HT	SPTCR	L/P		IB	T185-T210		11		7738	2		11800	13700
32		CORINTHIAN SS CUSTOM	HT	CR	L/P		IB	T185-T210		11		9281	2		12000	13900
32		RIVIERA-ROAMER	HT	EXP	STL	SV	IB	T185-T210		11	4	12100	2	5	14300	16500
34		CONSTELLATION	HT		M/P		IB	T185-T210		12		11885	2	8	16900	19500
34		CONSTELLATION	FB		M/P		IB	T185-T210		12		11885	2	8	16900	19500
34		CONSTELLATION	HT	SDN	M/P		IB	T185-T210		12		12300	2	8	18400	20800
34		CONSTELLATION	FB	SDN	M/P		IB	T185-T210		12		12300	2	8	18400	20800
35		CORINTHIAN SS CUSTOM	HT	CR	L/P		IB	T185		11	7	10663	2		16400	18600
35		CORINTHIAN SS CUSTOM	HT	CR	L/P		IB	T210		11	7	10663	2		16600	18800
35		SAIL YACHT	SLP	MS	FBG	KL	IB	60	CC	11		18112	4	8	30100	33400
35		SAIL YACHT	SLP	MS	FBG	KL	IB	30D	WEST	11		18112	4	8	30300	33600
35	1	CAVALIER		MY	PLY		IB	T185		12	8	12310	2	6	19200	21300
36		CHALLENGER	HT	EXP	M/P		IB	T185		12		15720	2	8	23600	26200
36		CHALLENGER	HT	EXP	M/P		IB	T210		12		15720	2	8	23700	26400
36		CHALLENGER	HT	SDN	M/P		IB	T185		12		16325	2	8	24500	27200
36		CHALLENGER	HT	SDN	M/P		IB	T210		12		16325	2	8	24700	27400
36		RIVIERA-ROAMER	HT	EXP	AL	SV	IB	T185		12		11900	2	10	20600	22900
36		RIVIERA-ROAMER	HT	EXP	STL	SV	IB	T185		12		15400	2	11	23300	25900
36		RIVIERA-ROAMER	HT	EXP	AL	SV	IB	T210		12		11900	2	10	20700	23000
36		RIVIERA-ROAMER	HT	EXP	STL	SV	IB	T210		12		15400	2	11	23500	26100
36		RIVIERA-ROAMER	HT	EXP	AL	SV	IB	T275		12		11900	2	10	21100	23500
36		RIVIERA-ROAMER	HT	EXP	STL	SV	IB	T275		12		15400	2	11	23800	26500
36		RIVIERA-ROAMER	HT	EXP	AL	SV	IB	T181D		12		11900	2	10	23500	26100
36		RIVIERA-ROAMER	HT	EXP	STL	SV	IB	T181D		12		15400	2	11	26900	29900
37		CONSTELLATION	HT	MY	M/P		IB	T185		12	3	12893	2	10	22800	25400
37		CONSTELLATION	HT	MY	M/P		IB	T210		12	3	12893	2	10	23000	25500
37		CONSTELLATION	HT	MY	M/P		IB	T275		12	3	12893	2	10	23300	25900
37		CONSTELLATION	FB	MY	M/P		IB	T185		12	3	12893	2	10	22800	25400
37		CONSTELLATION	FB	MY	M/P		IB	T210		12	3	12893	2	10	23000	25500
37		CONSTELLATION	FB	MY	M/P		IB	T275		12	3	12893	2	10	23300	25900
38		CHALLENGER SALON	FB	TCMY	M/P		IB	T185		13		18500	2	10	29800	33100
38		CHALLENGER SALON	FB	TCMY	M/P		IB	T210		13		18500	2	10	29900	33200
38		COMMANDER	HT	MY	FBG		IB	T210		13		20000	3		31900	35400
38		COMMANDER	HT	MY	FBG		IB	T275		13		20000	3		32100	35700
38		COMMANDER	FB	MY	FBG		IB	T210		13		20000	3		31900	35400
38		COMMANDER	FB	MY	FBG		IB	T275		13		20000	3		32100	35700
38		ROAMER OFFSHORE	HT	OFF	STL	SV	IB	T275		12	9	21300	2	10	33700	37400
38		ROAMER OFFSHORE	HT	OFF	STL	SV	IB	T280		12	9	21300	2	10	33700	37400
38		SEA-HAWK SEA SKIFF	HT	SDN	L/P		IB	T210		13		15500	2	9	26200	29100
38		SEA-HAWK SEA SKIFF	HT	SDN	L/P		IB	T275		13		15500	2	9	26500	29400
38		SEA-HAWK SEA SKIFF	HT	SDN	L/P		IB	T181D		13		15500	2	9	29800	33100
42		CONSTELLATION	HT	MY	M/P		IB	T185		12	10	20697	3		35400	39400
		IB T210 36100 40100, IB T275 37700 41900, IB T181D													39400	43800
46		CONSTELLATION	HT	MY	M/P		IB	T275		13		28437	3	1	42100	46800
46		CONSTELLATION	HT	MY	M/P		IB	T180D	CAT	13		28437	3	1	43000	47800
46		CONSTELLATION	HT	MY	M/P		IB	T181D		13		28437	3	1	42800	47600
46		RIVIERA-ROAMER	HT	MY	STL	SV	IB	T275		13		24800	2	11	46400	51000
46		RIVIERA-ROAMER	HT	MY	STL	SV	IB	T270D		13		24800	2	11	53400	58700
46		RIVIERA-ROAMER	HT	MY	STL	SV	IB	T300D		13		24800	2	11	55600	61100
52		CONSTELLATION	HT	MY	M/P		IB	T275		14	3	35271	3	8	51900	57000
		IB T270D 52100 57300, IB T270D CAT 51800 56900, IB T321D													54900	60400
56		ROAMER	HT	MY	AL	SV	IB	T270D		15		41000	3	8	56400	62000
56		ROAMER	HT	MY	STL	SV	IB	T270D		15		50000	3	11	70200	77100
56		ROAMER	HT	MY	AL	SV	IB	T270D	CAT	15		41000	3	8	56400	62000
56		ROAMER	HT	MY	STL	SV	IB	T270D	CAT	15		50000	3	11	70200	77100
56		ROAMER	HT	MY	AL	SV	IB	T321D		15		41000	3	8	63400	69600
56		ROAMER	HT	MY	STL	SV	IB	T321D		15		50000	3	11	76500	84100
57		CONSTELLATION	HT	MY	M/P		IB	T270D		15		48503	3	11	67700	74400
57		CONSTELLATION	HT	MY	M/P		IB	T321D		15		48503	3	11	74400	81800
65			HT	MYDKH	M/P		IB	T460D	CAT	16	9	67580	4	4	133500	146500
65			HT	MYDKH	M/P		IB	T478D		16	9	67580	4	4	134500	147500
65		CONSTELLATION	HT	MYDKH	M/P		IB	T460D	CAT	16	9	72073	3	9	142000	156000
65		CONSTELLATION	HT	MYDKH	M/P		IB	T478D		16	9	72073	3	9	143000	157000
		1963 BOATS														
16	6	SKI-JET	OP	SKI	M/P		JT	185		6	8	2040	1		1750	2100
17	2	LUXURY SKIFF	OP	RNBT	L/P		OB			6	6	920			1800	2150
17	2	TRADITIONAL	OP	RNBT	L/P		OB			6	6	950			1850	2200
17	6	SUNLOUNGER T/D XL170		RNBT	FBG		IO	80-100							5550	6400
17	6	SUNLOUNGER XL-170	OP	RNBT	FBG		OB								2500	2900
17	6	XL-170		RNBT	FBG		OB								2500	2900
17	6	XL-170		RNBT	FBG		IO	80-100							5450	6250
17	6	XL-170 T/D		EXP	FBG		IO	80-100							5650	6450
18	4	HOLIDAY	OP	RNBT	M/P		IB	185		6	5	2354	1	8	1850	2200
19		GOLDEN-ARROW CAVALER	OP	RNBT	MHG		IB	185		7	5	2271	1	11	2050	2450
19		SEA-SKIFF SPORTSMAN		RNBT	WD		IB	185		7					2150	2500
20		CARAVELLE	OP	RNBT	M/P		IB	185-275		7	6	3139	1	11	2800	3300
20		CLUB-CRUISETT	OP	CR	L/P		OB			7	4	1490			3250	3750
20		HOLIDAY	OP	RNBT	M/P		IB	185-275		6	7	2641	1	11	2350	2800
20		LUXURY CRUISETTE	OP	CUD	L/P		IO	80-100		7	4	2220			6050	6950
20		LUXURY SKIFF	OP	RNBT	L/P		IO	80-100		7	4	2120			5700	6550
20		TRADITIONAL	OP	RNBT	L/P		OB			7	4	1350			3000	3500
20		TRADITIONAL	OP	RNBT	L/P		IO	80-100		7	4	1900			5500	6300
21		SEA-SKIFF SPORTSMAN		RNBT	WD		IB	185		7	7				3200	3700
23					WD		IB		CC						**	**
24		FIESTA CAVALIER	OP	EXP	MHG		IB	185		8		3500	2		3750	4350
24		RANGER SEA-SKIFF		RNBT	WD		IB	185		9					5350	6150
24		SEA-SKIFF SPORTSMAN		RNBT	WD		IB	185		9					4650	5350
26		FUTURA CAVALIER		EXP	MHG		IB	185		9	4	4057	1	10	4900	5600

CONTINUED ON NEXT PAGE

```
LOA  NAME AND/         TOP/ BOAT  -HULL- ----ENGINE---  BEAM   WGT   DRAFT RETAIL RETAIL
FT IN  OR MODEL        RIG  TYPE  MTL TP TP # HP MFG    FT IN  LBS   FT IN  LOW    HIGH
------------------ 1963 BOATS ---------------------------------------------------------
27   COMET ROAMER CUSTOM FB EXP  AL SV IB 185        10     6700   2     7000   8050
27   COMET ROAMER CUSTOM FB EXP  AL SV IB T185       10     6700   2     7800   8900
27   CONSTELLATION      OP CBNCR M/P  IB 185    10 2 6093   2  1   7600   8750
27   CONSTELLATION      OP CBNCR M/P  IB T185   10 2 6093   1 11   8350   9600
27   CORINTHIAN SEA-SKIFF  EXP  WD    IB 185        10            6300   7250
27   CORINTHIAN SEA-SKIFF  EXP  WD    IB T185       10            7200   8250
27   SILVER-COMET ROAMER   EXP  AL    IB 185        10            6300   7250
27   SILVER-COMET ROAMER   EXP  AL    IB T185       10            7200   8250
28   FUTURA CAVALIER    OP EXP  MHG   IB 185   10 5 6114   2  2   6700   7700
28   FUTURA CAVALIER    OP EXP  MHG   IB T185  10 5 6114   2  1   7600   8700
28   SEA-SKIFF SPORTSMAN   RNBT WD    IB 185-275 10 2       7100   8550
28   SEA-SKIFF SPORTSMAN   RNBT WD    IB T185  10 2        7900   9100

30   CONSTELLATION      OP CBNCR M/P  IB T185  10 8 8572   1 11  11900  13500
31   CORINTHIAN SS CUSTOM  CR   WD    IB T185  11           10700  12200
31   FUTURA CAVALIER    OP EXP  MHG   IB 185   10 6 6445   2  2   9900  11300
31   FUTURA CAVALIER    OP EXP  MHG   IB T185  10 6 6445   2    11100  12600
31   SEA-SKIFF             SPTCR WD   IB T185  11           10700  12200
32                      EXP  STL   IB T185  11 4          13600  15500
32   DELUXE             EXP  STL   IB T185  11 4          14200  16100
32   RIVIERA-ROAMER     OP EXP  STL SV IB T185 11 4 12100  2  5  13900  15800
34   CONSTELLATION      HT CBNCR M/P  IB T185  12   11951  2  8  18600  20700
34   CORINTHIAN SS CUSTOM  CR   WD    IB T185  11 7          14400  16300
35   SAIL YACHT         SLP MS   FBG KL IB 60  CC  11 18112 4  8  30000  33300
35   SAIL YACHT         SLP MS   FBG KL IB 30D WEST 11 18112 4 8  30200  33500

35  1 CAVALIER          FB MY   MHG   IB T185  12 8 12340  2  6  18900  21000
36   RIVIERA-ROAMER     FB EXP  AL SV IB T185  12   11900  2 10  20300  22500
36   RIVIERA-ROAMER     FB EXP  STL SV IB T185 12   15400  2 11  22900  25500
36   RIVIERA-ROAMER     FB EXP  AL SV IB T275  12   11900  2 10  20800  23100
36   RIVIERA-ROAMER     FB EXP  STL SV IB T275 12   15400  2 11  23500  26100
36   RIVIERA-ROAMER     FB EXP  AL SV IB T181D GM 12 11900 2 10  23100  25700
36   RIVIERA-ROAMER     FB EXP  STL SV IB T181D GM 12 15400 2 11  26500  29400
36   ROAMER             EXP  AL SV IB T185  12      2 10  23800  26500
36   ROAMER             EXP  STL SV IB T185 12      2 11  23800  26400
36   ROAMER             EXP  AL SV IB T275  12      2 10  24300  27100
36   ROAMER             EXP  STL SV IB T275 12      2 11  24400  27000
36   ROAMER             EXP  AL SV IB T181D GM 12   2 10  27700  30800

36   ROAMER             EXP  STL SV IB T181D GM 12  2 11  27700  30800
36   ROAMER DELUXE      EXP  AL SV IB T185  12      2 10  24500  27200
36   ROAMER DELUXE      EXP  STL SV IB T185 12      2 11  24600  27300
36   ROAMER DELUXE      EXP  AL SV IB T275  12      2 10  25000  27800
36   ROAMER DELUXE      EXP  STL SV IB T275 12      2  9  25000  27800
36   ROAMER DELUXE      EXP  AL SV IB T181D GM 12   2 10  28300  31400
36   ROAMER DELUXE      EXP  STL SV IB T181D GM 12  2  9  28300  31400
37   CONSTELLATION      HT MY   M/P  IB T185  12 3 16057  2  8  25700  28600
37   CONSTELLATION      HT MY   M/P  IB T275  12 3 16057  2  8  26200  29100
37   CONSTELLATION      OP TCMY M/P  IB T185  12 5 17940  2  8  27200  30200
37   CONSTELLATION      OP TCMY M/P  IB T275  12 5 17940  2  8  27600  30600

38   CORINTHIAN SS CUSTOM  CR   WD    IB T185  12           27100  30100
38   CORINTHIAN SS CUSTOM  CR   WD    IB T275  12           27400  30400
38   ROAMER OFFSHORE    HT OFF  STL SV VD T280 12 9 19800 2 10  31300  34800
42   CONQUEROR          OP TCMY M/P  IB T185  12 10 20297  3    36900  41100
42   CONQUEROR          OP TCMY M/P  IB T275  12 10 20297  3    40000  44500
42   CONQUEROR          OP TCMY M/P  IB T181D GM 12 10 20297 3  42100  46800
42   CONSTELLATION      HT MY   M/P  IB T185  12 10 20697  3    34900  38700
42   CONSTELLATION      HT MY   M/P  IB T275  12 10 20697  3    37100  41200
42   CONSTELLATION      HT MY   M/P  IB T181D GM 12 10 20697 3  39200  43600
42  5 CORINTHIAN SS CUSTOM  CR  WD   IB T185  13 2          33800  37600
     IB T275  35500 39500, IB T180D CAT  40600 45100, IB T181D GM  40100 44500

44   RIVIERA-ROAMER     HT MY   STL SV IB T275  13   24600 2 11  42900  47700
44   RIVIERA-ROAMER     HT MY   STL SV IB T235D 13   24600 2 11  47800  52500
44   RIVIERA-ROAMER     HT MY   STL SV IB T270D 13   24600 2 11  49500  54400
46   CONSTELLATION      HT MY   M/P  IB T275  13   28437  3  1  41400  46000
46   CONSTELLATION      HT MY   M/P  IB T180D CAT 13 28437 3  1  42000  46900
46   CONSTELLATION      HT MY   M/P  IB T181D GM 13  28437 3  1  42000  46700
52   CONSTELLATION      HT MY   M/P  IB T275  14 3 35271  3  8  54400  55400
     IB T270D  50700 55800, IB T270D CAT  50400 55400, IB T308D  52800 58000

56   ROAMER             OP MY   AL SV IB T270D     15 41000 3  8  53200  58500
56   ROAMER             OP MY   STL SV IB T270D    15 50000 3 11  66200  72700
56   ROAMER             OP MY   AL SV IB T270D CAT 15 41000 3  8  53200  58400
56   ROAMER             OP MY   STL SV IB T270D CAT 15 50000 3 11 66200  72700
56   ROAMER             OP MY   AL SV IB T308D     15 41000 3  8  58100  63900
56   ROAMER             OP MY   STL SV IB T308D    15 50000 3 11  70700  77700
57   CONSTELLATION      OP MY   STL SV IB T275     15 48503 3 11  67300  74000
     IB T270D  66700 73200, IB T270D CAT  66700 73300, IB T308D  71600 78700

60  6                  HT MY   M/P  IB T165D CAT 16 4 64972 3  9  80500  88500
60  6                  HT MY   M/P  IB T456D     16 4 64972 3  9 115500 127000
60  6                  HT MY   M/P  IB T460D     16 4 64972 3  9 116000 127500
65                     HT MY   M/P  IB T308D     16 9 67580 4  4 114500 126000
65                     HT MY   M/P  IB T456D     16 9 67580 4  4 130000 143000
65                     HT MY   M/P  IB T460D     16 9 67580 4  4 130500 143500
------------------ 1962 BOATS ---------------------------------------------------------
17  2 SEA-LANCER CUSTOM  OP RNBT L/P  OB     6 6 990   1950   2300
17  2 SEA-LANCER DELUXE  OP RNBT L/P  OB     6 6 1610  2900   3350
17  2 SEA-LANCER STD     OP RNBT L/P  OB     6 6 950   1900   2250
18                     WD   IB 185 CHEV              **     **
18   SEA-SKIFF SPORTSMAN  OP RNBT MHG IB 60        1850   2200
18   SEA-SKIFF SPORTSMAN  OP RNBT MHG IB 100       1950   2350
18   SEA-SKIFF SPORTSMAN  OP RNBT MHG IB 185       2200   2550
18  3 HOLIDAY           OP RNBT MHG IB 185  6 5   1  8  1900   2300
19                     WD   IB                    **     **
19  7                  OP SF   L/P  IO 80   7 4 1325  2700   3100
19  7                  OP SF   L/P  IO 80   7 4       7350   8400
19  7 CLUB-CRUISETTE    OP CUD  L/P  OB     7 4 1470  2950   3400

19  7 CLUB-CRUISETTE    OP CUD  L/P  IO 80  7 4       6450   7400
19  7 HOLIDAY           OP RNBT MHG IB 185-275 7 6  1 11  2200   2600
19 11 SEA-SKIFF SPORTSMAN  OP RNBT IB 100-185 7 6  1 10  2200   2750
20                     WD   IB 185 CC              **     **
21   CAVALIER          OP EXP  MHG IB 100-185 8 6 3372 1  8  3000   3700
21   CAVALIER SPORTSMAN   OP RNBT MHG IB 100-185 8 6 2955 1 8  2800   3450
22  7 HOLIDAY           OP RNBT MHG IB 185-275 8  1 10  4100   4850
23  3 RANGER SEA SKIFF     RNBT    IB 185          4350   5000
23  3 SPORTSMAN SEA SKIFF  RNBT    IB 100-185      4150   5000
24  8 CAVALIER 2 BERTH  OP EXP  MHG IB 100  9 4 3507 2  6  3750   4350
24  8 CAVALIER 2 BERTH  OP EXP  MHG IB 185  9 4      4000   4650
24  8 CAVALIER 4 BERTH  OP EXP  MHG IB 100-185 9 4 3807 1 8  3950   4900

25                     WD   IB 185 CC              **     **
25  5 CONSTELLATION     OP EXP  IB 185  9 4 4057  1 11  4950   5650
25  5 CAVALIER 4 BERTH  OP EXP  MHG IB 100  9 4      4250   4950
25  7 CAVALIER 4 BERTH  OP EXP  MHG IB 185  9 4 4057 1 10  4700   5400
26  7 SEA-SKIFF SPORTSMAN  OP RNBT IB 185-275 8 10 2  1  5850   7050
26  7 SEA-SKIFF SPORTSMAN  OP RNBT IB 185  8 10  1 11  5950   6800
27  7 SEA-SKIFF SPORTSMAN  OP RNBT IB 185  8 10  1 11  6700   7700
27   SILVER-COMET ROAMER  OP EXP AL SV IB 185 10 6400 2  7550   8650
27   SILVER-COMET ROAMER  OP EXP AL SV IB T185 10 6400 2  7550   8650
27  7                  FB SF   IB 185  9 4  1 11  8150   9350
27  7 CONSTELLATION     OP EXP  IB 185  10 2  3  7350   8450
27  7 CONSTELLATION     OP EXP  IB T100 10  1 10  7450   8600

27  7 CONSTELLATION     OP EXP  IB 185  10          8200   9450
29 11 CAVALIER CUSTOM   OP CR   MHG IB 185  10 6 6445 2   7650   8800
29 11 CAVALIER CUSTOM   OP CR   MHG IB 100  10 6 6445 2   7750   8900
29 11 CAVALIER CUSTOM   OP CR   MHG IB T185 10 6 6445 2   8600   9900
30  5 CORINTHIAN SS CUSTOM  CR   IB 100  10          8100   9300
30  5 CORINTHIAN SS CUSTOM  CR   IB 185  10          9150  10400
30  5 SEA-SKIFF         HT SPTCR  IB 100  9 9        8000   9200
30  5 SEA-SKIFF         HT SPTCR  IB 185  9 9        9000  10200
32                     WD   IB T225 CHRY             **     **
32   CONSTELLATION      HT CR   M/P IB T185 11 5 12600 2  5 13800  15700
32   CONSTELLATION SS CUSTOM HT EXP IB T185 11       12100  13800
32  1 RIVIERA DELUXE    HT EXP  STL SV IB T185 11 4 12100 13800  15700

32  1 ROAMER DELUXE     OP EXP  STL SV IB T185 11 4 11900 2 5 13700  15600
32  1 ROAMER STANDARD   OP EXP  STL SV IB T185 11 4 11900 2 10 13700 15600
33                     FB SF   IB 185  11          13800  15800
35  1 CAVALIER CUSTOM   FB MY   MHG IB T185 12 8 11741 6 18300  20400
35  9 RIVIERA DELUXE    HT EXP  AL SV IB T185 12 15400 2 11 19500 21700
35  9 RIVIERA DELUXE    HT EXP  STL SV IB T185 12 15400 2 11 20000 22200
35  9 RIVIERA DELUXE    HT EXP  AL SV IB T275 12 15400 2 9 22000  24500
35  9 RIVIERA DELUXE    HT EXP  STL SV IB T181D 12 15200 2 9 33500 35500
35  9 ROAMER DELUXE     OP EXP  AL SV IB T185 12 15200 2 9 19400  21600
35  9 ROAMER DELUXE     OP EXP  STL SV IB T185 12 15200 2 9 19900 22100
35  9 ROAMER DELUXE     OP EXP  AL SV IB T275 12 15200 2 9 31700  35300
35  9 ROAMER DELUXE     OP EXP  STL SV IB T181D 12 15200 2 9 31700 35300
35  9 ROAMER STANDARD   OP EXP  AL SV IB T185 12 15200 2 9 19400  21600
35  9 ROAMER STANDARD   OP EXP  STL SV IB T275 12 15200 2 9 19900 22100

35  9 ROAMER STANDARD   OP EXP  STL SV IB T181D 12 15200 2 9 23700 35300
36  3 ROAMER            EXP  STL SV IB T185 12 15200 2 9 23700  26300
36  4 CONSTELLATION     HT   IB T185  12      2  9 24200  26900
```

LOA FT IN	NAME AND/ OR MODEL	TOP/ RIG	BOAT TYPE	-HULL- MTL TP	----ENGINE--- TP # HP MFG	BEAM FT IN	WGT LBS	DRAFT FT IN	RETAIL LOW	RETAIL HIGH
					1962 BOATS					
36 4	CONSTELLATION	HT			IB T275	12		2 9	24600	27400
37	CORINTHIAN SS CUSTOM		CR		IB T185	12		2 8	26600	29600
37	CORINTHIAN SS CUSTOM		CR		IB T275	12		2 8	27000	30000
37 3	CONSTELLATION	FB	TCMY		IB T185	12 5		2 8	26900	29900
40 1		FB	SF		IB T185D				41700	46400
40 5		FB	SF		IB T275	13 2		3	35100	39100
41	CONQUEROR	FB	MY		IB T185	12 10		3	35000	38900
41	CONQUEROR	FB	MY		IB T275	12 10		3	36500	40500
41	CONQUEROR	FB	MY		IB T181D	12 10		3	42800	47600
42 5	CORINTHIAN SS CUSTOM		CR		IB T185				32800	36500
	IB T275 34500 38300, IB T180D				38700 43000, IB T181D				38700	43000
43 10	RIVIERA-ROAMER	HT	MY	STL SV	IB T275	13	24600	2 11	44600	49500
43 10	RIVIERA-ROAMER	HT	MY	STL SV	IB T235D	13	24600	2 11	49300	54200
44 7	CONSTELLATION	HT	MY		IB T275	13 1		3 1	37000	41100
44 7	CONSTELLATION	HT	MY		IB T181D	13 1		3 1	39600	44000
50 5	CONSTELLATION	HT	MY		IB T275	14 2		3 5	47400	52100
55 6	CONSTELLATION	HT	MY		IB T275	14 9		1 2	60600	66300
	IB T235D 58800 64600, IB T270D				63300 69600, IB T308D				67900	74600
56 1	ROAMER	HT	MY	STL SV	IB T235	15	50000	3 11	63700	70000
56 1	ROAMER	HT	MY	STL SV	IB T270D	15	50000	3 11	68200	75000
56 1	ROAMER	HT	MY	STL SV	IB T308D	15	50000	3 11	72900	80100
60 6			MY		IB T270	16 4		3 8	170000	186500
60 6			MY		IB T456D	16 4		3 8	98200	108000
60 6			MY		IB T460D	16 4		3 8	98400	108000
					1961 BOATS					
17	SEA-LANCER	OP	RNBT	L/P	OB	6 6	950		1900	2250
18	SEA-SKIFF	OP	UTL	WD	IB 185 CHEV	7		1 11	1700	2050
19	CAPRI	OP	RNBT	WD	IB 100	6 6		1 6	1800	2150
19	CAPRI	OP	RNBT	WD	IB 185	6 6		1 6	2000	2350
19	CLUB-CRUISETTE	OP	CUD	L/P	OB	7 1	1395		2750	3200
19	CONTINENTAL	OP	RNBT	WD	IB 100	6 6		1 6	1800	2150
19	CONTINENTAL	OP	RNBT	WD	IB 185	6 6		1 6	2000	2350
19	OFFSHORE	OP	RNBT	L/P	OB	7 1	1200		2450	2850
19 7				WD	IB 185 CC				**	**
20	SEA-SKIFF	OP	UTL	WD	IB 100-185	7 6		1 9	2250	2800
21	CAVALIER SPORTSMAN	OP	RNBT	MHG	IB 100-185	8 6	2665	1 8	2600	3200
21	CONTINENTAL	OP	RNBT	WD	IB 185-275	7 6		1 10	3100	3650
21	SEA-LANE	OP	SF	L/P	OB	8	1810		3900	4500
23	RANGER SS 2 SLEEPER		RNBT	WD	IB 185	8 4		1 11	4200	4850
23	SEA-SKIFF	OP	UTL	WD	IB 100-185	8 4		1 11	4000	4850
24	SPORTSMAN			WD	IB 185-275	8		1 11	4750	5500
24	SPORTSMAN			WD	IB T185	8		1 11	5200	5950
25	CAVALIER 2 BERTH	OP	EXP	MHG	IB 100	9 4	3750	1 8	3900	4550
25	CAVALIER 2 BERTH	OP	EXP	MHG	IB 185	9 4	3750	1 8	4200	4900
25	CAVALIER 4 BERTH	OP	EXP	MHG	IB 100	9 4	4055	1 8	4100	4800
25	CAVALIER 4 BERTH	OP	EXP	MHG	IB 185	9 4	4055	1 8	4500	5150
25	CAVALIER CUS 4 BERTH		CR	MHG	IB 100-185	9 4	4205	1 8	4200	5250
25	CONSTELLATION		CR	WD	IB 185	9 4		1 10	4800	5500
25	CONSTELLATION C DLX	OP	EXP	WD	IB 185	9 4		1 10	4800	5500
27	SEA-SKIFF	OP	UTL	WD	IB 185	8 9		2 1	6600	6900
27	SEA-SKIFF	OP	UTL	WD	IB T100	8 9		2 1	6100	7000
27	SEA-SKIFF	OP	UTL	WD	IB T185	8 9		2 1	6850	7850
28	CONSTELLATION		CR	WD	IB 185	10		2 2	7000	8050
28	CONSTELLATION		CR	WD	IB T100	10		2 2	7100	8150
28	CONSTELLATION		CR	WD	IB T185	10		2 2	7850	9000
28	CONSTELLATION		SF	WD	IB T185	10		2 2	7850	9000
30	CAVALIER	OP	EXP	MHG	IB 185	10 6		2 2	8350	9600
30	CAVALIER	OP	EXP	MHG	IB T100	10 6		2 2	8450	9700
30	CAVALIER	OP	EXP	MHG	IB T185	10 6		2 2	9500	10800
30	CAVALIER CUSTOM	OP	CBNCR	MHG	IB 185	10 6	5678	2	9400	10700
30	CAVALIER CUSTOM	OP	CBNCR	MHG	IB T100-T185	10 6	5678	2	9550	11500
30	SEA-SKIFF	HT	CR	WD	IB T100	9 9		2	7550	8650
30	SEA-SKIFF	HT	CR	WD	IB T185	9 9		2	8400	9650
30	SEA-SKIFF 4 SLEEPER	HT	CR	WD	IB T100	9 9		2 4	7550	8650
30	SEA-SKIFF 4 SLEEPER	HT	CR	WD	IB T185	9 9		2 4	8400	9650
30	SEA-SKIFF 4 SLPR		CR	WD	IB T100	9 9		2 4	7550	8650
30	SEA-SKIFF 4 SLPR		CR	WD	IB T185	9 9		2 4	8400	9650
31			EXP	STL	IB T185				11700	13300
31	RIVIERA	HT	CR	STL	IB T185				10500	11900
32	CONSTELLATION	HT	CR	STL	IB T185	11 5	12600	2 5	13700	15500
32	SEA-SKIFF 6 SLPR	HT	CR	WD	IB T185	11 2		2 2	11900	13500
32	SEA-SKIFF 6 SLPR CUS		SF	WD	IB T185	11 2		2 2	11900	13500
33	CONSTELLATION		SF	WD	IB T185	11		2 9	12000	13600
35			EXP	STL	IB T185				18000	20800
35			SF	STL	IB T185				15400	17500
35	REGAL-ROAMER		SDN	STL	IB T185				16800	19100
35	RIVIERA	HT	CR	STL	IB T185				16100	18300
36	CONSTELLATION		CR	WD	IB T185	12		2 8	23500	26100
36	CONSTELLATION		CR	WD	IB T275	12		2 8	24000	26700
36	SEA-SKIFF 6 SLPR	HT	CR	WD	IB T185	12		2 7	23500	26100
36	SEA-SKIFF 6 SLPR	HT	CR	WD	IB T275	12		2 7	24000	26700
36	SEA-SKIFF 6 SLPR CUS		CR	WD	IB T185	12		2 7	23500	26100
36	SEA-SKIFF 6 SLPR CUS		CR	WD	IB T275	12		2 7	24000	26700
40			SF	WD	IB T275	13 1		2 11	34600	38400
40			SF	WD	IB T181D	13 1		2 11	42500	47300
41	CONQUEROR	FB	DC	WD	IB T185	12 9		3	40300	44800
41	CONQUEROR	FB	DC	WD	IB T275	12 9		3	41600	46300
41	CONQUEROR	FB	DC	WD	IB T181D	12 9		3	46100	50600
41	CONSTELLATION		CR	WD	IB T185	12 9		3	28800	32200
41	CONSTELLATION		CR	WD	IB T275	12 9		3	29400	32700
41	CONSTELLATION		CR	WD	IB T181D	12 9		3	34900	38800
42	SEA-SKIFF 6 SLPR CUS		CR	WD	IB T185	13 2		2 10	33900	37700
42	SEA-SKIFF 6 SLPR CUS		CR	WD	IB T275	13 2		2 10	35300	39300
42	SEA-SKIFF 6 SLPR CUS		CR	WD	IB T181D	13 2		2 10	40100	44000
43			MY	STL	IB T275				34700	38500
45	CONSTELLATION	HT	CR	WD	IB T275	13	27000	3	36000	40000
45	CONSTELLATION	HT	CR	WD	IB T181D	13	27000	3	37800	41900
50	CONSTELLATION		CR	WD	IB T275	14			37600	41800
50	CONSTELLATION		CR	WD	IB T275	14		3 5	37600	41800
52			CR	STL	IB T235D				52300	57400
55	CONSTELLATION		CR	WD	IB T275	14 9		3 7	56500	62100
	IB T235D 55100 60600, IB T270D				58900 64700, IB T308D				62800	69000
66	CONSTELLATION		CR	WD	IB T308D	16 6		3 8	194500	214000
66	CONSTELLATION		CR	WD	IB T456D	16 6		3 8	199500	219500
					1960 BOATS					
17	SEA-LANCER	OP	RNBT		OB				2200	2600
18	CAVALIER CUS SPT	OP	UTL	MHG	OB	6 6			1800	2150
18	CONTINENTAL	OP	RNBT		IB 185				1950	2300
18	CONTINENTAL	OP	RNBT		IB 100				2100	2500
18	SEA-SKIFF	OP	UTL		IB 100	7			1700	2000
19	CAPRI	OP	RNBT		IB 185				2050	2450
19	CAPRI	OP	RNBT		IB 185				2250	2600
19	OFFSHORE FISH		FSH	L/P DV	IB	6 10	1200		2450	2850
19	THOMPSON OFFSHORE		FSH	WD	OB				2700	3100
20	SEA-SKIFF	OP	UTL		IB 100	7 6			2250	2750
21	CONTINENTAL	OP	RNBT		IB 185-275				3250	3850
21	SEA-LANE		CR	WD	OB				3850	4500
21 6	SEA-LANE		CR	L/P DV	OB	8	1700		3850	4450
23	CAVALIER 2 BERTH	OP	EXP	WD	IB 100-185	8 3			3950	4800
23	CAVALIER SPORTSMAN	OP	RNBT	WD	IB 100-185	8 3			3950	4800
23	RANGER SS 2 SLEEPER		CR	WD	IB 185	8 4			4150	4800
23	SEA-SKIFF	OP	UTL		IB 100-185	8 4			3950	4800
24	SPORTSMAN	OP	CR		IB 185-275				5200	5550
24	SPORTSMAN	OP	CR		IB T185				5200	5950
25	CAVALIER 2 BERTH	OP	EXP	WD	IB 100-185	8			4250	5300
25	CAVALIER 4 BERTH	OP	EXP	WD	IB 100-185	8			4250	5300
25	CAVALIER CUS 4 BERTH		CR	WD	IB 185				4700	5400
27	CONSTELLATION				IB T185				5950	6850
27	CONSTELLATION				IB T100				6050	7000
27	CONSTELLATION								6800	7850
27	SEA-SKIFF	OP	UTL		IB T185	8 10			5950	6850
27	SEA-SKIFF	OP	UTL		IB T185	8 10			6050	6950
27	SEA-SKIFF	OP	UTL		IB T185				6800	7800
27	SEMI-ENCLOSED	HT	CR		IB T185				5950	6800
27	SEMI-ENCLOSED	HT	CR		IB T100				6050	7000
27	SEMI-ENCLOSED	HT	CR		IB T185				6800	7850
30	CAVALIER 4 BERTH		EXP	WD	IB 185	10 6			8250	9500
30	CAVALIER 4 BERTH		EXP	WD	IB T100	10 6			8350	9600
30	CAVALIER 4 BERTH		EXP	WD	IB T185	9 9			9350	10600
30	SEA-SKIFF	OP	UTL		IB T100	9 9			7850	9050
30	SEA-SKIFF	OP	UTL		IB T185	9 9			8900	10100
30	SEA-SKIFF 4 SLEEPER	HT	CR		IB T100	9 9			7450	8600
30	SEA-SKIFF 4 SLEEPER	HT	CR		IB T185	9 9			8400	9650

LOA FT IN	NAME AND/OR MODEL	TOP/RIG	BOAT TYPE	HULL MTL	HULL TP	ENG TP	ENG #	HP	MFG	BEAM FT IN	WGT LBS	DRAFT FT IN	RETAIL LOW	RETAIL HIGH
													1960 BOATS	
31			EXP	STL		IB		T185					11600	13200
31	REGAL-ROAMER		SDN	STL		IB		T185					11300	12800
32	COMMANDER					IB		T185					12000	12500
32	CONSTELLATION	HT	CR		WD	IB		T185		11 5	12600		13500	15400
32	SEA-SKIFF 6 SLEEPER	HT	CR			IB		T185-T275		11 2			11800	14200
33			SF			IB		T185					12200	13800
33			SPTCR			IB		T185					13000	14700
35			EXP	STL		IB		T185					17500	19800
35			SF	STL		IB		T197D					23800	26400
35	REGAL-ROAMER		SDN	STL		IB		T185					16600	18900
36			EXP			IB		T185					22900	25400
36			EXP			IB		T275					23300	25900
36	6 SLEEPER	HT	CR			IB		T275					23300	25900
36	CONSTELLATION 6 SLPR	HT	SDN			IB		T185					23300	25800
36	CONSTELLATION 6 SLPR	HT	SDN			IB		T275					23300	26500
36	SEA-SKIFF 6 SLEEPER	HT	CR			IB		T185		12			23300	25800
40			EXP			IB		T185					30000	33300
40			EXP			IB		T275					30200	33600
40			EXP			IB		T275					39600	43900
40			SF			IB		T197D					33800	37600
40			SF			IB		T197D					40900	45400
40	CONQUEROR	FB	DC			IB		T185					44000	48900
40	CONQUEROR	FB	DC			IB		T275					44200	49100
40	CONQUEROR	FB	DC			IB		T197D					43000	47800
40	CONSTELLATION					IB		T185					28100	31200
40	CONSTELLATION					IB		T275					28300	31500
40	CONSTELLATION					IB		T197D					40200	44700
40	SEA-SKIFF	HT	CR			IB		T197D		12			39000	43400
40	SEA-SKIFF 6 SLEEPER	HT	CR			IB		T275		12			32100	35700
43			MY	STL		IB		T197D					42200	46900
43	REGAL-ROAMER		SDN	STL		IB		T197D					32000	35600
43			EXP			IB		T275					29800	33200
45			EXP			IB		T197D					32700	36300
45	CONSTELLATION	HT	CR		WD	IB		T275		13	27000		35700	39600
45	CONSTELLATION	HT	CR		WD	IB		T197D		13	27000		37700	41900
50			EXP			IB		T275					35700	39600
50			EXP			IB		T235D					42400	47100
50			EXP			IB		T300D					46500	51100
50	CONSTELLATION		CR		WD	IB		T275		14			36800	40900
50	CONSTELLATION		CR		WD	IB		T235D		14			40400	44900
50	CONSTELLATION		CR		WD	IB		T300D		14			42300	47000
52			MY	STL		IB		235D					59600	65400
55			EXP			IB		T235D					65300	71800
55			EXP			IB		T300D					69300	76100
55			EXP			IB		T336D					71600	78700
55	CONSTELLATION		CR		WD	IB		T336D		14 9			55000	60500
	IB T235D 53300 58600, IB T300D 60200 66100, IB T336D 63700 70000													
66	CONSTELLATION		CR		WD	IB		T300D		16 6			190500	209500
66	CONSTELLATION		CR		WD	IB		T336D		16 6			191500	210500
66	CONSTELLATION		CR		WD	IB		T504D		16 6			197500	217000
													1959 BOATS	
17	SEA-LANCER	OP	RNBT			OB							2250	2600
18				WD		IB		131	CC				**	**
18				WD		IB		283					**	**
18			CR	WD		OB							2150	2500
18	CAPRI	OP	RNBT		P/M	IB		100-131		6 7			1700	2100
18	CAPRI	OP	RNBT		P/M	IB		185		6 7			1850	2200
18	CONTINENTAL	OP	RNBT		P/M	IB		100-131		6 7			1700	2100
18	CONTINENTAL	OP	RNBT		P/M	IB		185		6 7			1850	2200
18	SEA-SKIFF	OP	RNBT		L/P	IB		60-95					1800	2250
18	SEA-SKIFF	OP	RNBT		L/P	IB		105					1900	2300
19				WD		IB		185-283					**	**
19	SILVER-ARROW		RNBT		P/M	IB		185		6 6			1950	2300
20	SPORTSMAN	OP	CR		P/M	IB		100-131		7			2100	2550
20	SPORTSMAN	OP	CR		P/M	IB		185		7			2300	2700
21				WD		IB		150	CHRY				**	**
21			CR	WD		OB							3850	4500
21	CAPRI	OP	RNBT		P/M	IB		185-275		7 8			3050	3600
21	CONTINENTAL	OP	RNBT		P/M	IB		185-275		7 6			3050	3600
21	SPORTSMAN CAVALIER		RNBT			IB		100					3050	3550
22	RANGER SS 2 SLEEPER		RNBT		L/P	IB		130-185					3250	3850
22	RANGER SS TRUNK CBN		CR		L/P	IB		130-185					3200	3800
22	SEA-SKIFF	OP			L/P	IB		95-185					3100	3800
23	CAVALIER		EXP	PLY		IB		185					4100	4800
24	SPORTSMAN	OP	CR		P/M	IB		185-275		8			4700	5400
24	SPORTSMAN	OP	CR		P/M	IB		T100-T185		8			4750	5850
25	CAVALIER	FB	SF	STL		IB		T185		9			5250	6050
25	CAVALIER SEMI-ENCL		EXP	PLY		IB		185					4650	5350
25	SEMI-ENCLOSED		CR	WD		IB		T100					4700	5400
25	SEMI-ENCLOSED		SF	STL		IB		T185		9			5250	6050
26	CONTINENTAL	OP	RNBT		P/M	IB		185-275		8 4			5000	6050
26	CONTINENTAL	OP	RNBT		P/M	IB		T185		8 4			5700	6550
26	SEA-SKIFF	OP			L/P	IB		130-185					5100	6150
26	SEA-SKIFF		FSH			IB		T 95-T105					5400	6350
26	SEA-SKIFF		FSH			IB		T185					6100	7000
26	SEA-SKIFF	OP	RNBT		L/P	IB		175					5000	5750
26	SEA-SKIFF 4 SLPR ENC	FB	CR			IB		T 95-T105					5400	6300
26	SEA-SKIFF 4 SLPR ENC	FB	CR			IB		T185					6100	7000
26 6				WD		IB		185	CC				**	**
27	CAVALIER		EXP	WD		IB		185					5900	6800
27	CONSTELLATION				P/M	IB		185		10			6000	6900
27	CONSTELLATION				P/M	IB		T100		10			6100	7050
27	CONSTELLATION				P/M	IB		185		10			6850	7900
28			SF	STL		IB		T225		10			7950	9100
28	SEMI-ENCLOSED	HT	SF	STL		IB		T225		10			7950	9100
30	CAVALIER		EXP	WD		IB		T100					8300	9550
30	CAVALIER		EXP	WD		IB		T185					9400	10700
30	SEA-SKIFF	OP			L/P	IB		T 95-T130					7000	8450
30	SEA-SKIFF	OP			L/P	IB		T185					7850	9050
30	SEA-SKIFF	OP	RNBT		L/P	IB		T175					8050	9250
30	SEA-SKIFF 2SLPR SEMI	HT	CR		L/P	IB		T 95-T130					7400	9000
30	SEA-SKIFF 2SLPR SEMI	HT	CR		L/P	IB		T175-T185					8250	9600
30	SEA-SKIFF 4SLPR SEMI	HT	CR		L/P	IB		T 95-T130					7400	9000
30	SEA-SKIFF 4SLPR SEMI	HT	CR		L/P	IB		T175-T185					8250	9600
31		FB	EXP	STL		IB		T225		11 3			11800	13500
31	CONSTELLATION				P/M	IB		T130-T185		9 11			9050	10700
32				WD		IB		T185	CHEV				**	**
32	COMMANDER				P/M	IB		T130-T185		11 1			10400	12300
33			SF		P/M	IB		T185		11 1			11800	13400
33			SPTCR			IB		T185					12900	14600
33	SPORT		SF		P/M	IB		T275		11			12400	14100
33	SPORT		SPTCR		P/M	IB		T275		11			13300	15100
35		FB	EXP	STL		IB		T275		12 1			18100	20100
35	CONSTELLATION			STL		IB		T185		11 1			15300	17400
35	REGAL-ROAMER		SDN	STL		IB		T275		12			18500	20500
35	REGAL-ROAMER		SDN	STL		IB		T275		12			17000	19300
35	RIVIERA	HT	SDN	STL		IB		T275		12			16200	18400
35	SEA-SKIFF 4SLPR SEMI	HT	CR		L/P	IB		T130					15400	17500
35	SEA-SKIFF 4SLPR SEMI	HT	CR		L/P	IB		T175					15800	17900
35	SEA-SKIFF 4SLPR SEMI	HT	CR		L/P	IB		T185					15800	18000
35	SEA-SKIFF 6SLPR SEMI	HT	CR		L/P	IB		T130					15400	17500
35	SEA-SKIFF 6SLPR SEMI	HT	CR		L/P	IB		T175					15800	17900
35	SEA-SKIFF 6SLPR SEMI	HT	CR		L/P	IB		T185					15800	18000
38				WD		IB		T200	CC				**	**
40			SF	STL		IB		T200		13 1			33500	37300
	IB T225 33600 37300, IB T275 33700 37500, IB T197D 41900 46600													
40	CONQUEROR	FB	DC		P/M	IB		T185		12 8			46500	51100
	IB T200 46500 51100, IB T275 46700 51300, IB T197D 44700 49700													
40	CONSTELLATION				P/M	IB		T185		12 8			30300	33700
40	CONSTELLATION				P/M	IB		T275		12 8			30300	33700
40	CONSTELLATION				P/M	IB		T197D		12 8			40500	45000
40	CONSTELLATION				P/M	IB		T275		12 8			30400	33800
40	SEA-SKIFF SEMI ENCL	HT	CR		L/P	IB		T200					30800	34300
40	SEA-SKIFF SEMI ENCL	HT	CR		L/P	IB		T275					30900	34300
40	SEA-SKIFF SEMI ENCL	HT	CR		L/P	IB		T197D					38100	42400
42	CONSTELLATION		CR		P/M	IB		T200		13			33400	37100
42	CONSTELLATION		CR		P/M	IB		T275		13			34300	38100
42	CONSTELLATION		CR		P/M	IB		T197D		13			39400	43800
42	REGAL-ROAMER		SDN	STL		IB		T200		13			41700	46400
42	RIVIERA	HT	CR	STL		IB		T200		13			33800	37500
42	ROYAL		DC	STL		IB		T275		13			42000	46600
50	CONSTELLATION		CR		P/M	IB		T200		14			35700	39700
	IB T225 35900 39900, IB T275 36300 40300, IB T235D 39600 44000													

LOA FT IN	NAME AND/ OR MODEL	TOP/ RIG	BOAT TYPE	HULL MTL TP	TP	ENGINE # HP	MFG	BEAM FT IN	WGT LBS	DRAFT FT IN	RETAIL LOW	RETAIL HIGH
						1959 BOATS						
50	CONSTELLATION	CR	P/M	IB		T300D		14			41500	46100
52		MY	STL	IB		T300		15			57100	62800
55	CONSTELLATION			IB		T275		14	6		58800	64600
55	CONSTELLATION			IB		T235D		14	6		56800	62500
55	CONSTELLATION			IB		T336D		14	6		68200	74900
55	CONSTELLATION	CR	P/M	IB		T200		14	6		46200	50800
55	CONSTELLATION	CR	P/M	IB		T300D		14	6		58700	64500
66	CONSTELLATION	CR	WD	IB		T300D		16	6		186500	205000
66	CONSTELLATION	CR	WD	IB		T336D		16	6		187500	206500
66	CONSTELLATION	CR	WD	IB		T504D		16	6		193500	212500
						1958 BOATS						
16	CAVALIER S-ENCL	HT	SPTCR	WD	IB	60					**	**
17	SEA-COASTER	OP	RNBT	WD	OB						2250	2650
18				WD	IB	130-134					**	**
18		CR		WD	OB						2150	2500
18	CONTINENTAL	OP	RNBT		IB	95-131					1900	2350
18	HOLIDAY	OP	RNBT		IB	95-131					1900	2350
18	SEA-SKIFF	OP			IB	60- 95					1700	2150
18	SEA-SKIFF	OP			IB	105					1850	2200
19				WD	IB	131	HERC				**	**
19	CAPRI	OP	RNBT		IB	95-131					2000	2500
19	CAVALIER		EXP	WD	OB						2400	2800
19	CAVALIER		EXP	WD	IB	60- 95					1850	2300
19	CAVALIER SEMI-ENCL	HT	CR	WD	OB						2450	2850
19	CAVALIER SEMI-ENCL	HT	CR	WD	IB	60- 95					1850	2300
19	SILVER-ARROW		RNBT		IB	131-215					2100	2600
20	SPORTSMAN	OP	CR		IB	95-215					2350	2900
21			CR	WD	OB						3850	4500
21	CAPRI	OP	RNBT		IB	130-300					3100	3800
21	CONTINENTAL	OP	RNBT		IB	130-300					3100	3800
22	CAVALIER 4 SLPR		EXP	WD	OB						6700	7700
22	CAVALIER 4 SLPR		EXP	WD	IB	60- 95					3000	3600
22	RANGER SS 2 SLEEPER		RNBT		IB	95-130					3100	3750
22	RANGER SS TRUNK CBN		CR		IB	95-130					3100	3700
22	SEA-SKIFF	OP			IB	95-130					3100	3700
22	4 CAVALIER 2 SLPR		EXP	WD	OB						7000	8050
22	4 CAVALIER 2 SLPR		EXP	WD	IB	60-105					3050	3700
23	CONTINENTAL	OP	RNBT		IB	130-300					4000	4900
24	SPORTSMAN				IB	130-300					4600	5500
25		FB	SF		IB	T105					4700	5400
25	CADET	FB	SDN		IB	95-175					4450	5500
25	CADET	FB	SDN		IB	T 95-T105					4850	5700
25	SEMI-ENCLOSED	HT	CR		IB	95-175					4250	5250
25	SEMI-ENCLOSED	HT	CR		IB	T 95-T105					4650	5400
25	SEMI-ENCLOSED	HT	SF		IB	T105					4700	5400
26			EXP		IB	130-175					5300	6350
26			EXP		IB	T 95-T130					5600	6800
26			EXP		IB	T175					6200	7150
26	CLIPPER	FB	SDN		IB	130-175					5400	6500
26	CLIPPER	FB	SDN		IB	T 95-T105					5750	6750
26	COMMUTER				IB	130-175					5100	6050
26	COMMUTER				IB	T 95-T130					5350	6500
26	COMMUTER				IB	T175					6000	6900
26	CONTINENTAL	OP	RNBT		IB	175-300					5000	6150
26	CONTINENTAL	OP	RNBT		IB	T105					5150	5950
26	CONTINENTAL	OP	RNBT		IB	T275					6150	7050
26	SEA-SKIFF	OP			IB	95-175					4900	6050
26	SEA-SKIFF 2 SLEEPER		FSH		IB	130-175					5100	6050
26	SEA-SKIFF 2 SLEEPER		FSH		IB	T 95-T105					5400	6300
26	SEA-SKIFF 2 SLPR TC		CR		IB	130-175					5100	6050
26	SEA-SKIFF 2 SLPR TC		CR		IB	T 95-T105					5350	6300
26	SEA-SKIFF 4 SLPR ENC	FB	CR		IB	130-175					5100	6050
26	SEA-SKIFF 4 SLPR ENC	FB	CR		IB	T 95-T105					5350	6300
28		FB	SF		IB	T185					7650	8800
28	CONSTELLATION				IB	T 95-T130					6900	8300
28	CONSTELLATION				IB	T175					7600	8700
28	SEMI-ENCLOSED		SF		IB	T185					7650	8800
30	SEA-SKIFF	OP			IB	130-175					6600	7850
30	SEA-SKIFF	OP			IB	T 95-T130					6950	8400
30	SEA-SKIFF	OP			IB	T175-T215					7700	9250
30	SEA-SKIFF 2SLPR SEMI	HT	CR		IB	130-175					7000	8350
30	SEA-SKIFF 2SLPR SEMI	HT	CR		IB	T 95-T130					7350	8900
30	SEA-SKIFF 2SLPR SEMI	HT	CR		IB	T175-T215					8200	9800
30	SEA-SKIFF 4 SLEEPER	FB	CR		IB	130-175					7000	8350
30	SEA-SKIFF 4 SLEEPER	FB	CR		IB	T 95-T130					7350	8900
30	SEA-SKIFF 4 SLEEPER	FB	CR		IB	T175-T215					8200	9800
30	SEA-SKIFF 4SLPR SEMI	HT	CR		IB	130-175					7000	8350
30	SEA-SKIFF 4SLPR SEMI	HT	CR		IB	T 95-T130					7350	8900
30	SEA-SKIFF 4SLPR SEMI	HT	CR		IB	T175-T215					8200	9800
31	CONSTELLATION				IB	T 95-T175					8850	10800
32			SDN		IB	T 95-T175					11500	14200
32	COMMANDER				IB	T 95-T175					10200	12200
33			SF		IB	T130-T275					11500	14300
33			SPTCR		IB	T130-T275					12300	15300
33	FUTURA		EXP		IB	T130-T250					13700	16800
35		FB	EXP		IB	T225					17500	19800
35	REGAL-ROAMER		SDN		IB	T225					16700	19000
35	RIVIERA	HT	CR		IB	T145					15400	17600
35	RIVIERA	HT	CR		IB	T225					16000	18200
35	SEA-SKIFF 4SLPR SEMI	HT	CR		IB	T 95					15000	17100
	IB T105	15100	17100,	IB T130			15300	17400,	IB T175			15700	17800
	IB T215	15900	18100									
36	SEASTRAKE CAVALIER		EXP	WD	IB	T185					22500	25000
36	SEASTRAKE CAVALIER		EXP	WD	IB	T210					22600	25100
38	CONSTELLATION 4 SLPR		MY		IB	T130					27100	30100
	IB T175	27400	30400,	IB T200			27500	30500,	IB T275			27700	30800
	IB T197D	36000	40000									
38	CONSTELLATION 6 SLPR		MY		IB	T130					27100	30100
	IB T175	27400	30400,	IB T200			27500	30500,	IB T275			27700	30800
	IB T151D	35400	39300,	IB T197D			36000	40000					
38	CORSAIR	FB	DC		IB	T130					27700	30700
	IB T175	27900	31000,	IB T200			28000	31100,	IB T225			28100	31200
40			SF		IB	T130					32500	36100
	IB T175	32800	36500,	IB T200			32900	36500,	IB T275			33100	36700
	IB T197D	40200	44600									
40	SEA-SKIFF		SDN		IB	T130					34800	38600
	IB T175	35100	39000,	IB T200			35100	39000,	IB T215			35100	39000
	IB T225	35200	39100,	IB T197D			41500	46100					
40	SEA-SKIFF SEMI ENCL	HT	CR		IB	T130					30200	33600
	IB T175	30500	33900,	IB T200			30600	34000,	IB T215			30600	34000
	IB T225	30600	34000,	IB T197D			37900	42100					
42	CONSTELLATION				IB	T200					37300	41400
42	CONSTELLATION				IB	T275					38300	42600
42	CONSTELLATION				IB	T197D					27200	30200
42	REGAL-ROAMER		SDN		IB	T225					38900	43200
42	RIVIERA	HT	CR		IB	T225					33100	36800
42	ROYAL		DC		IB	T275					37600	41800
48	CONSTELLATION	HT	MY	MHG	IB	T200		13	32000		37800	42000
	IB T275	40200	44600,	IB T197D			41400	46000,	IB T235D			43600	48400
55			WD		IB	300D	GM				**	**
55			WD		IB	300D GM					**	**
55	CONSTELLATION				IB	T200		14	6		48900	53800
	IB T275	57500	63100,	IB T235D			55300	60800,	IB T300D			62900	69100
56	SALON		MY		IB	T300D					58900	64700
65	CONSTELLATION				IB	T300D					138000	151500
						1957 BOATS						
17	SEA-LANCER	OP	RNBT	WD	OB						2300	2650
18				WD	IB	120	HERC				**	**
18		CR		WD	OB						2200	2550
18	CONTINENTAL	OP	RNBT		IB	95-131					1850	2350
18	HOLIDAY	OP	RNBT		IB	95-131					1850	2350
18	SEA-SKIFF				IB	60					1700	2050
18	SEA-SKIFF	OP			IB	95					1800	2150
19				WD	IB	120	CC				**	**
19				WD	IB	283	CC				**	**
19	CAPRI	OP	RNBT		IB	95-131					2000	2450
19	2			WD	IB	350	CHEV				**	**
20				WD	IB	120	HERC				**	**
20	CONTINENTAL	OP	RNBT		IB	175					2550	2950
20	SPORTSMAN	OP	RNBT		IB	95-175					2350	2950

```
LOA    NAME AND/          TOP/  BOAT  -HULL-  ----ENGINE---  BEAM   WGT  DRAFT RETAIL RETAIL
FT IN  OR MODEL           RIG   TYPE  MTL TP  TP # HP  MFG   FT IN  LBS  FT IN  LOW    HIGH
--------------------------- 1957 BOATS -----------------------------------------------------
20  SPORTSMAN          OP   RNBT        IB 215                            2550   3000
21                          CR    WD    OB                                3900   4500
21  CAPRI              OP   RNBT        IB 130-300   .                    3100   3800
21  CONTINENTAL        OP   RNBT        IB 130-300                        3100   3800
22  CAVALIER           OP   EXP   P/M   IB  95    8  2908   1 7           2650   3050
22  SEA-SKIFF          OP               IB  60- 95                        3000   3550
23  CONTINENTAL        OP   RNBT        IB 130-300                        4000   4850
24                     FB   SDN         IB 105                            4550   5200
24  CAVALIER                EXP         IB  95                            4750   5500
25  CADET              FB   SDN         IB  60-105                        4150   5100
25  CADET              FB   SDN         IB T 95-T105                      4850   5650
25  CAVALIER SEMI-ENCL      CR          IB T105                           4700   5400

25  SEMI-ENCLOSED      HT   CR          IB  60-105                        4100   4950
25  SEMI-ENCLOSED      HT   CR          IB T 95-T105                      4650   5400
26                          EXP         IB 130-175                        5300   6300
26                          EXP         IB T 95-T130                      5550   6750
26                          EXP         IB T175                           6150   7100
26  CLIPPER            FB   SDN         IB 130-175                        5350   6450
26  CLIPPER            FB   SDN         IB T 95-T105                      5700   6700
26  COMMUTER                            IB 130-175                        5050   6050
26  COMMUTER                            IB T 95-T130                      5350   6500
26  COMMUTER                            IB T175                           5950   6850
26  CONTINENTAL        OP   RNBT        IB 175-300                        4950   6100
26  CONTINENTAL        OP   RNBT        IB T105                           5150   5900

26  CONTINENTAL        OP   RNBT        IB T175                           5650   6500
26  SEA-SKIFF          OP               IB  95-175                        4850   6050
26  SEA-SKIFF 4 SLPR ENC FB  CR         IB 130-175                        5050   6050
26  SEA-SKIFF 4 SLPR ENC FB  CR         IB T 95-T105                      5350   6250
27                     FB   SDN         IB T 95                           6400   7350
27  CAVALIER                EXP         IB  105                           5400   6200
28                     FB   EXP         IB T130                           7200   8250
28                     FB   SDN         IB T 95-T105                      7350   8600
28  CONSTELLATION                       IB T 95-T130                      6850   8250
28  CONSTELLATION                       IB T175                           7550   8650
28  SEMI-ENCLOSED      HT   CR          IB T130                           7200   8250
30  CONSTELLATION                       IB T175                           7700   8800

30  SEA-SKIFF          OP               IB 130-175                        6550   7850
30  SEA-SKIFF          OP               IB T 95-T130                      6900   8350
30  SEA-SKIFF          OP               IB T175                           7700   8800
30  SEA-SKIFF 2SLPR SEMI HT  CR         IB 130-175                        6950   8300
30  SEA-SKIFF 2SLPR SEMI HT  CR         IB T 95-T130                      7350   8850
30  SEA-SKIFF 2SLPR SEMI HT  CR         IB T175                           8150   9350
30  SEA-SKIFF 4 SLEEPER FB   CR         IB 130-175                        6950   8300
30  SEA-SKIFF 4 SLEEPER FB   CR         IB T 95-T130                      7350   8850
30  SEA-SKIFF 4 SLEEPER FB   CR         IB T175                           8150   9350
30  SEA-SKIFF 4SLPR SEMI HT  CR         IB 130-175                        6950   8300
30  SEA-SKIFF 4SLPR SEMI HT  CR         IB T 95-T130                      7350   8850
30  SEA-SKIFF 4SLPR SEMI HT  CR         IB T175                           8150   9350

31  CONSTELLATION                       IB T 95-T175                      8700  10700
32                          EXP         IB T 95-T175                     12400  14900
32                          SDN         IB T 95-T175                     11400  14100
32  COMMANDER               SDN         IB T 95-T175                     10100  12200
33                          WD          IB T330  CHRY                      **     **
33  FUTURA                  EXP         IB T130-T250                     13600  16800
35                     HT   EXP         IB T145                          16800  19000
35                          SDN         IB T145                          15900  18100
35  SEA-SKIFF 4SLPR SEMI HT  CR         IB T 95                          15000  17000
    IB T105    15000 17000, IB T130    15200 17300, IB T175    15600 17700
    IB T215    15800 18000

35  SEA-SKIFF 6SLPR SEMI HT  CR         IB T 95                          15000  17000
    IB T105    15000 17000, IB T130    15200 17300, IB T175    15600 17700
35  SEMI-ENCL 6 SLPR        CR          IB T145                          15800  18000
38  CONSTELLATION 4 SLPR    MY          IB T130                          26800  29800
    IB T175    27200 30200, IB T200    27200 30300, IB T275    27500 30500
    IB T151D   35200 39100, IB T197D   35800 39800

38  CONSTELLATION 6 SLPR    MY          IB T130                          26800  29800
    IB T175    27200 30200, IB T200    27200 30300, IB T275    27500 30500
    IB T151D   35200 39100, IB T197D   35800 39800

38  CORSAIR            FB   DC          IB T130                          27400  30500
    IB T175    27700 30800, IB T200    27800 30900, IB T225    27900 31000

40                          SF          IB T130                          32200  35800
    IB T175    32500 36100, IB T200    32600 36200, IB T275    32700 36400
    IB T151D   39300 43600, IB T197D   39900 44300

40  SEA-SKIFF SEMI ENCL HT  CR          IB T130                          30000  33400
    IB T175    30300 33700, IB T200    30400 33700, IB T215    30400 33800
    IB T225    30400 33800, IB T400    31700 35200, IB T197D   37700 41900

40  SEA-SKIFF SEMI ENCL FB  CR          IB T130                          30000  33400
    IB T175    30300 33700, IB T200    30400 33800, IB T215    30400 33800
    IB T225    30400 33800, IB T400    31700 35300, IB T197D   37700 41900

42                     HT   EXP         IB T225                          27900  31000
42                          SDN         IB T225                          39000  43300
42  CONSTELLATION                       IB T200                          37100  41200
    IB T275    38200 42400, IB T151D   26000 28900, IB T197D   27100 30100

42  CORSAIR            FB   DC          IB T200                          35500  39400
    IB T275    37500 41600, IB T151D   38100 42300

48  CONSTELLATION      HT   MY   MHG    IB T200    13  32000             37300  41400
    IB T275    39800 44200, IB T151D   40300 44700, IB T197D   41000 45600
    IB T235D   43300 48100

55  CONQUEROR          FB   DC          IB T235D                         48800  53700
55  CONQUEROR          FB   DC          IB T300D                         56200  61800
55  CONSTELLATION                       IB T200    14  6                 47900  52700
    IB T275    56300 61900, IB T235D   53800 59200, IB T300D   61400 66700

56  SALON                   MY          IB T300D   14 11                 57400  63100
65  CONSTELLATION                       IB T300D                        137000 150500
--------------------------- 1956 BOATS -----------------------------------------------------
18                          WD          IB  95-120                         **     **
18                          WD          IB  327  CHEV                      **     **
18  CONTINENTAL        OP   RNBT        IB 105-131   6  7                1700   2100
18  HOLIDAY            OP   RNBT        IB 105-131   6  7                1700   2100
18  SEA-SKIFF ROUND    OP               IB  60                           1700   2050
19                          WD          IB 130-155                         **     **
19  CAPRI              OP   RNBT        IB  95-120   6  4                1700   2100
19  CAPRI              OP   RNBT        IB 131       6  4                1800   2150
20                          WD          IB 135-150                         **     **
20  CAVALIER                RNBT        IB  95                            2350   2750
20  CONTINENTAL        OP   RNBT        IB  95-175   7  6                2250   2750
20  CONTINENTAL        OP   RNBT        IB 215  INT  7  6                2400   2800

20  HOLIDAY            OP   RNBT        IB  95-175   7  6                2250   2750
20  HOLIDAY            OP   RNBT        IB 215  INT  7  6                2400   2800
20  SPORTSMAN          OP   CR          IB  95-131   7                   2050   2550
20  SPORTSMAN          OP   CR          IB 158-215   7                   2250   2650
21  CAPRI              OP   RNBT        IB 145-300   7  6                2950   3550
21  CAVALIER 4 BERTH        CR          IB  95                           2950   3400
22  SEA-SKIFF ROUND    OP               IB  60- 95                       2950   3550
23                     OP   EXP         IB  95-105   7  3                3700   4300
23  CONTINENTAL        OP   RNBT        IB 130-300   8                   3900   4750
24                     FB   SDN         IB  60-105   8  1                4300   5150
24  CAVALIER                EXP         IB  95                            4750   5450
24  CAVALIER           FB   EXP         IB 105                            4800   5500

24  CAVALIER SEMI-ENCL HT   CR          IB  95                            4500   5150
24  SEMI-ENCLOSED      HT   CR          IB  60-105   8  1                4300   5150
26                          WD          IB T130  CC                        **     **
26                     FB   SDN         IB  95-130   8  1                5000   6050
26                     FB   SDN         IB 175       8  1                5500   6300
26  CONTINENTAL        OP   RNBT        IB 175-300   8  4                4900   6050
26  CONTINENTAL        OP   RNBT        IB T105      8  4                5050   5800
26  CONTINENTAL        OP   RNBT        IB T275      8  4                6000   6900
26  SEA-SKIFF ROUND    OP               IB  60-130                       4800   5800
27                          WD          IB  95  CC                         **     **
27                     FB   SDN         IB T 95-T105 8  6                5650   6750
27                     FB   SDN         IB 175       8  6                6150   7100

27  CAVALIER           FB   SDN         IB T 95-T105 8  6                6300   7400
27  CAVALIER           HT   EXP         IB T 95                          6750   7500
27                     FB   EXP         IB T105                          5950   6850
27  SEMI-ENCLOSED      HT   CR          IB 130-175   8  6                5500   6550
27  SEMI-ENCLOSED      HT   CR          IB T 95-T105 8  6                5800   6800
28                     FB   EXP         IB T130                          7150   8250
```

LOA FT IN	NAME AND/ OR MODEL	TOP/ RIG	BOAT TYPE	HULL MTL TP TP#	HP	MFG	BEAM FT IN	WGT LBS	DRAFT FT IN	RETAIL LOW	RETAIL HIGH
\-\-\- 1956 BOATS \-\-\-											
28		FB	SDN		IB 130-175		8 6			6700	8050
28		FB	SDN		IB T 59		8 6			6650	7600
28		FB	SDN		IB T105		8 6			7250	8350
28	SEMI-ENCLOSED	HT	CR		IB T130					7150	8250
30	CONSTELLATION	FB			IB T 95-T130		9 8			6800	8250
30	CONSTELLATION	FB			IB T175		9 8			7550	8700
30	SEA-SKIFF	FB	CR		IB 95-145					6750	8050
30	SEA-SKIFF	FB	CR		IB T 95					7300	8400
30	SEA-SKIFF 4 SLPR RND	FB	CR		IB 95-145					6750	8050
30	SEA-SKIFF 4 SLPR RND	FB	CR		IB T 95					7300	8400
30	SEA-SKIFF ROUND	OP			IB 95-145					6350	7600
30	SEA-SKIFF ROUND	OP			IB T 95					6900	7900
30	SEA-SKIFF SEMI-ENCL	HT			IB 95-145					6350	7600
30	SEA-SKIFF SEMI-ENCL	HT			IB T 95					6900	7900
32	COMMANDER	FB			IB T 95-T175		11 1			10000	12000
33	FUTURA		EXP		IB T130-T250		10 10			13300	16300
35		HT	EXP		IB T200					17100	19400
35			SDN		IB T145					15800	18000
35	CONSTELLATION	FB			IB T130		11 1			14700	16700
35	CONSTELLATION	FB			IB T175		11 1			15000	17100
35	SEA-SKIFF 4 SLPR RND	FB	CR		IB T 95					14900	16900
35	SEA-SKIFF 4 SLPR RND	FB	CR		IB T105					14900	17000
35	SEA-SKIFF 4 SLPR RND	FB	CR		IB T130					15200	17200
35	SEA-SKIFF 6 SLPR RND	FB	CR		IB T 95					14900	16900
35	SEA-SKIFF 6 SLPR RND	FB	CR		IB T105					14900	17000
35	SEA-SKIFF 6 SLPR RND	FB	CR		IB T130					15200	17200
35	SEA-SKIFF SEMI-ENCL	HT			IB T 95					14200	16100
35	SEA-SKIFF SEMI-ENCL	HT			IB T105					14200	16200
35	SEA-SKIFF SEMI-ENCL	HT			IB T130					14400	16400
38		FB	SF	WD	IB T130	CC				**	**
38					IB T130		13			28000	31100
	IB T175 28300 31400, IB T200 28400 31500, IB T250 CHRY 28400 31500										
	IB T151D GM 37700 41900										
38	CONSTELLATION	FB			IB T		12 6			**	**
	IB T130 24000 26600, IB T175 24300 27000, IB T200 24300 27000										
	IB T250 CHRY 24400 27100, IB T151D GM 36400 40500										
38	CONSTELLATION 6 SLPR	FB	MY		IB T130		12 6			28700	31900
	IB T175 29000 32200, IB T200 29100 32300, IB T250 CHRY 29100 32400										
	IB T151D GM 36300 40300										
38	CORSAIR	FB	DC		IB T130		12 6			29100	32300
	IB T175 29400 32600, IB T200 CC 29400 32700, IB T200 CHRY 29400 32600										
40	SEA-SKIFF ROUND	FB	CR		IB T130					29900	33200
	IB T145 30000 33300, IB T200 30200 33600, IB T200 CHRY 30100 33500										
40	SEA-SKIFF SEMI-ENCL	HT			IB T130					27100	30100
40	SEA-SKIFF SEMI-ENCL	HT			IB T145					27200	30300
40	SEA-SKIFF SEMI-ENCL	HT			IB T200					27500	30500
42		HT	EXP		IB T225					27800	30900
42			SDN		IB T225					38900	43200
42	CONSTELLATION	FB			IB T200		13			38300	42600
42	CONSTELLATION	FB			IB T250 CHRY		13			39000	43300
42	CONSTELLATION	FB			IB T151D GM		13			26500	29400
42	CORSAIR	FB	DC		IB T200		13			39500	43800
42	CORSAIR	FB	DC		IB T250 CHRY		13			40600	45100
42	CORSAIR	FB	DC		IB T151D GM		13			41100	45600
46	CONSTELLATION	FB	MY	M/P	IB T200		13	28437		34900	38700
46	CONSTELLATION	FB	MY	M/P	IB T250 CHRY		13	28437		37400	41600
46	CONSTELLATION	FB	MY	M/P	IB T151D GM		13	28437		37300	41400
55	CONQUEROR	FB	DC		IB T200		14 6			47600	52300
	IB T250 CHRY 49600 54500, IB T235D GM 50200 55100, IB T300D GM 58200 63900										
55	CONSTELLATION	FB			IB T200		14 6			47000	51700
	IB T250 CHRY 52500 57700, IB T235D GM 52800 58100, IB T300D GM 60500 66500										
56	SALON		MY		IB T200		14 11			**	**
	IB T250 CHRY 47500 52200, IB T235D GM 47900 52600, IB T300D GM 56300 61800										
\-\-\- 1955 BOATS \-\-\-											
18				WD	IB	CC				**	**
	IB 55 HOME ** ** , IB 120-131 ** ** , IB 185-265 ** **										
18			RNBT	WD	IB 120	CC				1900	2300
18			RNBT		IB 131	CC				1950	2300
18	COBRA	OP	RACE		IB 95-131					1800	2250
18	CONTINENTAL	OP	RNBT		IB 60-95					1800	2200
18	CONTINENTAL	OP	RNBT		IB 105-131					1900	2300
18	HOLIDAY	OP	RNBT		IB 60-95					1800	2200
18	HOLIDAY	OP	RNBT		IB 105-131					1900	2300
18	SEA-SKIFF	OP			IB 60					1700	2050
18 6				WD	IB					**	**
19				WD	IB 115-156					**	**
19	CAPRI	OP	RNBT		IB 95-131					1950	2450
20				WD	IB 120-158					**	**
20	CONTINENTAL	OP	RNBT		IB 95-158					2350	2900
20	HOLIDAY	OP	RNBT		IB 95-158					2350	2900
21				WD	IB 130-200					**	**
21			RNBT	WD	IB 285	CADI				3200	3750
21	CAPRI	OP	RNBT		IB 130-200					3050	3700
21	COBRA	OP	RACE		IB 158-285					3100	3700
22	CAVALIER		CBNCR		IB 105					3050	3550
22	CONTINENTAL	OP	RNBT		IB 130-200					3150	3800
22	HOLIDAY	OP	RNBT		IB 130-200					3150	3800
22	SEA-SKIFF	OP			IB 60-95					2950	3550
23	EMPRESS 2 SLEEPER		CR		IB 60-105					3750	4500
24	CAVALIER		EXP		IB 95					4750	5450
25				WD	IB 185	CC				**	**
25	CONTINENTAL	OP	RNBT		IB 145-200					4400	5200
25	CONTINENTAL	OP	RNBT		IB 150D					8600	9900
25	CONTINENTAL	OP	RNBT		IB T105					4650	5350
25	EMPRESS 2 SLEEPER		CR		IB 95-145					4200	5100
26				WD	IB 185	INT				**	**
26		HT	SDN		IB 95-105					5100	5900
26		FB	SDN		IB 95-105					5100	5900
26	SEA-SKIFF	OP			IB 60-130					4750	5750
26	SEMI-ENCLOSED	HT	CR		IB 95-105					4850	5600
27		FB	SDN		IB 95-145					5650	6950
27		FB	SDN		IB T 95-T105					6350	7450
27	CAVALIER		EXP		IB T 95					5850	6750
27	EMPRESS 2 SLEEPER		CR		IB 130-145					5500	6450
27	EMPRESS 2 SLEEPER		CR		IB 150D					10500	11900
27	EMPRESS 2 SLEEPER		CR		IB T 95-T105					5850	6850
28				WD	IB	HERC				**	**
29			EXP		IB 130-145					6950	8100
29			EXP		IB T 95-T105					7300	8550
29			SDN		IB 130-145					7450	8700
29			SDN		IB T 95-T105					7900	9250
29	CAPITAN				IB 130-145					6950	8100
29	CAPITAN				IB T 95-T105					7300	8550
29	SEMI-ENCLOSED	HT	CR		IB 130-145					6450	7550
29	SEMI-ENCLOSED	HT	CR		IB T 95-T145					6850	8450
29	SPORTSMAN		CR		IB 130-145					6450	7550
29	SPORTSMAN		CR		IB 150D					11100	12600
29	SPORTSMAN		CR		IB T 95-T145					6850	8450
30	SEA-SKIFF		OP		IB 95-145					6350	7600
30	SEA-SKIFF		OP		IB 150D					10800	12200
30	SEA-SKIFF		OP		IB T 95					6850	7900
30	SEA-SKIFF 2 SLEEPER	FB	CR		IB 95-145					6750	8050
30	SEA-SKIFF 2 SLEEPER	FB	CR		IB 150D					11400	13000
30	SEA-SKIFF 2 SLEEPER	FB	CR		IB T 95					7300	8350
30	SEA-SKIFF 2SLPR SEMI	HT	CR		IB 95-145					6750	8050
30	SEA-SKIFF 2SLPR SEMI	HT	CR		IB 150D					11400	13000
30	SEA-SKIFF 2SLPR SEMI	HT	CR		IB T 95					7300	8350
33	COMMANDER				IB T130-T145					11400	13100
34	CAPITAN		SDN		IB T130-T145					14200	16400
35	SEA-SKIFF 4 SLEEPER	FB	CR		IB T 95					14900	16900
35	SEA-SKIFF 4 SLEEPER	FB	CR		IB T105					14900	16900
35	SEA-SKIFF 4 SLEEPER	FB	CR		IB T130					15100	17200
35	SEA-SKIFF 4SLPR SEMI	HT	CR		IB T 95					14900	16900
35	SEA-SKIFF 4SLPR SEMI	HT	CR		IB T105					14900	16900
35	SEA-SKIFF 4SLPR SEMI	HT	CR		IB T130					15100	17200
37	COMMANDER 4 SLEEPER				IB T145					24000	26700
	IB T190 24300 27000, IB T200 24300 27000, IB T 87D 26900 29900										
	IB T150D 27400 30400										

```
LOA   NAME AND/     TOP/ BOAT -HULL- ----ENGINE--- BEAM  WGT  DRAFT RETAIL RETAIL
FT IN OR MODEL      RIG  TYPE MTL TP TP # HP MFG   FT IN  LBS  FT IN  LOW    HIGH
------------------- 1955 BOATS --------------------------------------------------
37  COMMANDER 6 SLEEPER                 IB T145                         24000  26700
    IB T190  24300 27000, IB T200    24300 27000, IB T 87D             26900  29900
    IB T150D 27400 30400

37  CORVETTE            SPTCR           IB T145                         24300  27000
    IB T190  24500 27200, IB T200    24600 27300, IB T 87D             27300  30400
    IB T150D 27700 30800

40  SEA-SKIFF          FB  CR           IB T130                         29700  33000
    IB T145  29900 33200, IB T190    30100 33400, IB T200              30100  33400
    IB T150D 36900 40900

40  SEA-SKIFF SEMI ENCL HT  CR          IB T130                         29700  33000
    IB T145  29800 33200, IB T190    30000 33400, IB T200              30100  33400
    IB T150D 36000 40900

42                      EXP             IB T190                         27200  30200
42                      EXP             IB T200                         27400  30400
42                      EXP             IB T150D                        31700  35200
42  COMMANDER 4 SLEEPER                 IB T190                         35100  39000
42  COMMANDER 4 SLEEPER                 IB T200                         35200  39200
42  COMMANDER 4 SLEEPER                 IB T150D                        38900  43200
42  COMMANDER 6 SLEEPER                 IB T190                         35100  39000
42  COMMANDER 6 SLEEPER                 IB T200                         35200  39200
42  COMMANDER 6 SLEEPER                 IB T150D                        38900  43200
42  COMMODORE                           IB T190                         37300  41400
42  COMMODORE                           IB T200                         37400  41600
42  COMMODORE                           IB T150D                        26500  29400

45  CORSAIR                             IB T190                         27200  30300
45  CORSAIR                             IB T200                         27400  30400
45  CORSAIR                             IB T150D                        30600  33900
46  CONSTELLATION                       IB T200                         33900  37600
46  CONSTELLATION      MY   M/P         IB T190     13     28437        34200  38000
    IB T150D 37000 41100, IB T151D   37100 41200, IB T235D             42100  46800

53  CONQUEROR          MY               IB T190                         58100  63900
    IB T200  58400 64100, IB T150D   61900 68000, IB T151D             61900  68000
    IB T223D 64400 70800, IB R190    59300 65200, IB R200              59600  65500
    IB R150D 64500 70900

53  CONSTELLATION      **   **          IB T190                         **     **
    IB T200  **   **  , IB T150D     51500 56600, IB T151D             51600  56700
    IB T223D 55500 61000, IB R190    **   **  , IB R200                **     **
    IB R150D 57900 63600
-------------------- 1954 BOATS -------------------------------------------------
18                        WD          IB   95  CC                       **     **
18                        WD          IB  185  CC                       **     **
18                   UTL  WD          IB   95  HERC                     1800   2100
18                   UTL  WD          IB  350  CHEV                     2200   2550
18  RIVIERA          OP RNBT          IB   95-131                       1850   2300
18  SPORTSMAN        OP  CR           IB   95-120                       1800   2200
19                      RNBT WD       IB  158  HERC                     2150   2500
19  RACING           OP RNBT          IB  158                           2150   2500
20                      RNBT WD       IB  158  CC                       2500   2900
20  HOLIDAY          OP RNBT          IB   95-158                       2350   2900
20  RIVIERA          OP RNBT          IB  130-158                       2450   2900
20  SPORTSMAN        OP  CR           IB   95-158                       2300   2850

22                        WD          IB  130-285                       **     **
22                   OP EXP           IB   60-105                       2950   3550
22                   UTL  WD          IB  130  HERC                     3150   3650
22  CUSTOM           HT SDN           IB  130-158                       3150   3700
22  SPORTSMAN        OP  CR           IB   95-158                       3050   3700
24                   OP EXP           IB   95-145                       4750   5600
24  HOLIDAY          OP RNBT          IB  130-158                       4550   5300
24  HOLIDAY          OP RNBT          IB  150D                          9650   11000
26                   OP EXP           IB   95-145                       5100   6100
26                   OP EXP           IB  150D                          10600  12100
26                   FB SDN           IB  T 95-T105                     5550   6450
26                                    IB   95-105                       5050   5900

26  ENCLOSED         HT  CR           IB   95-105                       4850   5600
27                        WD          IB  T 95  HERC                    **     **
28  SUPER            OP EXP           IB  130-145                       6500   7550
28  SUPER            OP EXP           IB  T 95-T105                     6800   7950
28  SUPER ENCLOSED   HT  CR           IB  130-145                       6500   7550
28  SUPER ENCLOSED   HT  CR           IB  T 95-T105                     6800   7950
28  SUPER SEMI-ENCLOSED HT  CR        IB  130-145                       6500   7550
28  SUPER SEMI-ENCLOSED HT  CR        IB  150D                          12600  14400
28  SUPER SEMI-ENCLOSED HT  CR        IB  T 95-T105                     6800   7950
30                        SPTCR       IB  130-145                       6900   8050
30                        SPTCR       IB  T 95-T105                     7300   8500

31                        SDN         IB  130-145                       9400   10800
31                        SDN         IB  T 95-T105                     9900   11400
32                        WD          IB  T145  CC                      **     **
32                        EXP         IB  T 95-T145                     12300  14500
32  COMMANDER             SDN         IB  T 95-T145                     10100  11800
33  CAPITAN               SDN         IB  T 95-T145                     12400  14800
35                        SF          IB  T130                          14400  16400
35                        SF          IB  T145                          14500  16500
35                        SF          IB  T150D                         26500  29500
35                        SPTCR       IB  T130                          15100  17200
35                        SPTCR       IB  T145                          15300  17300
35                        SPTCR       IB  T150D                         27900  31000

35  COMMANDER                         IB  T130                          14400  16400
35  COMMANDER                         IB  T145                          14500  16500
36  COMMANDER                         IB  T130                          21300  23700
36  COMMANDER                         IB  T145                          21400  23800
36  COMMANDER                         IB  T150D                         24800  27500
36  COMMANDER 6 SLEEPER               IB  T130                          21300  23700
36  COMMANDER 6 SLEEPER               IB  T145                          21400  23800
36  COMMANDER 6 SLEEPER               IB  T150D                         24800  27500
36  CORVETTE          SPTCR           IB  T130                          21900  24400
36  CORVETTE          SPTCR           IB  T145                          22000  24500
36  CORVETTE          SPTCR           IB  T150D                         25500  28300

40                   FB  DC           IB  T130                          41700  46300
40                   FB  DC           IB  T130                          41800  46400
40                        EXP         IB  T130                          28600  31800
    IB T145  28700 31900, IB T160    28800 32000, IB T150D             37900  42100

43  COMMANDER                         IB  T160                          28700  31900
43  COMMANDER                         IB  T150D                         33900  37700
45                                    IB  T160                          25100  27900
45  CORSAIR W/SUN DECK                IB  T130                          26100  29000
    IB T145  26300 29200, IB T160    26500 29500, IB T150D             30300  33700

50  CATALINA         FB  DC           IB  T160                          **     **
50  CATALINA         FB  DC           IB  R145                          **     **
53  CONQUEROR W/SUN DECK MY           IB   160                          55200  60700
    IB 150D  58700 64500, IB T160    57500 63200, IB T150D             62000  68100
    IB T216D 64300 70700

53  CONSTELLATION                     IB  T160                          **     **
    IB T150D 51600 56700, IB T216D   55100 60600, IB R160              **     **
    IB R150D 57500 63200

55                   MY               IB  T160     14 11               42600  47400
    IB T150D 38500 42800, IB T216D   44100 48900, IB R160              44400  49400
    IB R150D 45700 50200

63                   MY               IB  T160                          188000 206500
    IB T216D 81700 89800, IB T265D   87900 96600, IB R160              188500 207000
    IB R216D 94700 104000
-------------------- 1953 BOATS -------------------------------------------------
18                        WD          IB  120  CC                       **     **
18                        WD          IB  131  CC                       1950   2300
18                   UTL  WD          IB   95-131                       1800   2250
18  RIVIERA          OP RNBT          IB   95-131                       1850   2300
18  SPORTSMAN        OP  CR           IB   95-120                       1800   2200
19                        WD          IB       CHRY                     **     **
19                        WD          IB       CADI                     **     **
19  HOLIDAY          OP RNBT          IB   95-120                       1950   2400
19  RACING           OP RNBT          IB  158                           2150   2500
20                        WD          IB   95                           **     **
20                   RNBT WD          IB   95-158                       2350   2900
20  RIVIERA          OP RNBT          IB  130-158                       2450   2900

20  SPECIAL SPORTSMAN OP RNBT         IB   95-158                       2350   2900
22                   OP EXP           IB   60-105                       2950   3550
22  CUSTOM           HT SDN           IB  130-158                       3150   3700
22  SPORTSMAN        OP  CR           IB   95-158                       3050   3700
```

CHRIS CRAFT BOATS -CONTINUED See inside cover to adjust price for area

LOA FT IN	NAME AND/ OR MODEL	TOP/ RIG	BOAT TYPE	-HULL- MTL	-HULL- TP	ENGINE TP	ENGINE # HP	ENGINE MFG	BEAM FT IN	WGT LBS	DRAFT FT IN	RETAIL LOW	RETAIL HIGH
	1953 BOATS												
24		OP	EXP			IB	95-145					4750	5600
24	HOLIDAY	OP	RNBT			IB	130-158					4550	5300
25	ENCLOSED	HT	CR			IB	95-105					4200	4900
26		HT	EXP			IB	95-145					5100	6100
26		HT	EXP			IB	T 95-T105					5550	6450
28				WD		IB	T105	HERC				**	**
28	SUPER DELUXE	HT	EXP			IB	130-145					6500	7550
28	SUPER DELUXE	HT	EXP			IB	T 95-T105					6800	7950
28	SUPER DELUXE ENCL	HT	CR			IB	130-145					6500	7550
28	SUPER DELUXE ENCL	HT	CR			IB	T 95-T105					6800	7950
28	SUPER DELUXE SEMI EN	HT	CR			IB	130-145					6500	7550
28	SUPER DELUXE SEMI EN	HT	CR			IB	T 95-T105					6800	7950
31		HT	SDN			IB	130-145					9400	10800
31		HT	SDN			IB	T 95-T105					9900	11400
32		OP	EXP			IB	T 95-T145					12300	14500
33	CAPITAN	HT	SDN			IB	T 95-T145					12400	14800
34		FB	DC			IB	T 95-T105					13900	15900
34	ENCLOSED	FB	DC			IB	T 95-T105					13900	15900
35	COMMANDER					IB	T105					14200	16100
35	COMMANDER					IB	T130					14400	16400
35	COMMANDER					IB	T145					14500	16500
40		FB	DC			IB	T130					41400	46100
40		FB	DC			IB	T145					41600	46200
40		OP	EXP			IB	T130					28000	31100
40		OP	EXP			IB	T145					28100	31300
40		OP	EXP			IB	T160					28200	31400
42	CHALLENGER					IB	T145					36600	40700
42	CHALLENGER					IB	T160					36900	41100
42	COMMANDER					IB	T145					34500	38300
42	COMMANDER					IB	T160					34800	38600
45		FB	DC			IB	T130					24400	27200
45		FB	DC			IB	T145					24600	27400
45		FB	DC			IB	T160					24800	27600
50	CATALINA		MY			IB	T160					37600	41800
50	CATALINA		MY			IB	R145					36100	40200
52	CONQUEROR		MY			IB	T160					47200	51900
52	CONQUEROR		MY			IB	T200D					61500	67500
52	CONQUEROR		MY			IB	R160					43200	48000
55			MY			IB	T160		14 11			41900	46500
55			MY			IB	T200D		14 11			41100	45700
55			MY			IB	R160		14 11			43700	48600
63			MY			IB	T160					184500	203000
	IB T200D 79900 87800, IB R160 185000 203000, IB R200											185000	203500
	1952 BOATS												
18	RIVIERA	OP	RNBT			IB	95-131					1850	2350
18	SPORTSMAN	OP	CR			IB	95-120					1800	2200
19				WD		IB	120	HERC				**	**
19			RNBT	WD		IB	158	CC				2150	2550
19	HOLIDAY	OP	RNBT			IB	95-120					2000	2450
19	RACING	OP	RNBT			IB	158					2150	2550
20	RIVIERA	OP	RNBT			IB	130-158					2450	2900
22				WD		IB	115-165					**	**
22		OP	EXP			IB	60-105					2950	3600
22			UTL			IB	145-158					3200	3750
22		OP	UTL	WD		IB	136	CC				3150	3650
22	CUSTOM	HT	SDN			IB	130-158					3150	3750
22	SPORTSMAN	OP	CR			IB	95-158					3050	3750
23	HOLIDAY	OP	RNBT			IB	130-158					4000	4700
24		OP	EXP			IB	95-145					4750	5600
25	ENCLOSED	HT	CR			IB	95-105					4200	4900
27	SUPER	OP	EXP			IB	130-145					5550	6450
27	SUPER	OP	EXP			IB	T 95-T105					5850	6850
27	SUPER ENCLOSED	HT	CR			IB	130-145					5550	6450
27	SUPER ENCLOSED	HT	CR			IB	T 95-T105					5850	6850
27	SUPER SEMI-ENCLOSED	HT	CR			IB	130-145					5550	6450
27	SUPER SEMI-ENCLOSED	HT	CR			IB	T 95-T105					5850	6850
28				WD		IB	T 95	CC				**	**
30		HT	SDN			IB	T145					8850	10000
31						IB	T145	CC				**	**
31		OP	EXP			IB	T 95-T145					10400	12400
32				WD		IB	T130	CC				**	**
32	SUPER ENCLOSED	HT	CR			IB	T 95-T145					10900	12800
34		FB	DC			IB	T 95-T105					13900	15900
34	ENCLOSED	HT	CR			IB	T 95-T105					13300	15200
34	ENCLOSED BRIDGE	HT	DC			IB	T 95-T105					13900	15900
35	COMMANDER					IB	T105					14200	16200
35	COMMANDER					IB	T130					14400	16400
35	COMMANDER					IB	T145					14600	16600
39		FB	DC			IB	T130					26000	28900
39		FB	DC			IB	T145					26100	29000
39	ENCLOSED BRIDGE	HT	DC			IB	T130					25900	28800
39	ENCLOSED BRIDGE	HT	DC			IB	T145					26000	28900
39	SALON		DC			IB	T130					25900	28800
39	SALON		DC			IB	T145					26000	28900
42				WD		IB	T175	CC				**	**
42		FB	DC			IB	T130					33400	37100
42		FB	DC			IB	T145					34000	37700
42	CHALLENGER					IB	T145					36900	41000
42	CHALLENGER					IB	T160					37200	41300
42	COMMANDER					IB	T145					34700	38500
42	COMMANDER					IB	T160					35000	38800
42	ENCLOSED	FB	DC			IB	T130					33400	37100
42	ENCLOSED	FB	DC			IB	T145					34000	37700
47	BUCCANEER	FB	DC			IB	T145					33900	37700
47	BUCCANEER	FB	DC			IB	T160					34700	38500
50	CATALINA	FB	DC			IB	T160					**	**
50	CATALINA	FB	DC			IB	R145					**	**
51				WD		IB	T300	SEAM				**	**
54			MY			IB	T160					59000	64900
54			MY			IB	T200D					66100	72600
54			MY			IB	R160					61000	67100
62			MY			IB	T160					160500	176500
	IB T200D 92500 101500, IB R160 161000 176500, IB R200D											103000	113500
	1951 BOATS												
18				WD		IB	131	CC				**	**
18			RNBT	WD		IB	95-131					1900	2350
18	RIVIERA	OP	RNBT			IB	95-131					1900	2350
18	SPORTSMAN	OP	CR			IB	95-120					1800	2200
19				WD		IB	120-158					**	**
19			RNBT	WD		IB						**	**
19		OP	RNBT	WD		IB	158	CC				2200	2550
19	HOLIDAY	OP	RNBT			IB	95-120					2000	2450
19	RACING	OP	RNBT			IB	158					2200	2550
20		OP	RNBT	WD		IB	158	HERC				2500	2950
20	RIVIERA	OP	RNBT			IB	130-158					2450	2950
22				WD		IB	130	CC				**	**
22		OP	EXP			IB	60-105					3000	3600
22	SPORTSMAN	OP	CR			IB	95-158					3050	3750
23	HOLIDAY	OP	RNBT			IB	130-158					4000	4700
24		OP	EXP			IB	95-145					4800	5650
25	ENCLOSED	HT	CR			IB	95-105					4200	4950
27	SUPER	OP	EXP			IB	130-145					5550	6500
27	SUPER	OP	EXP			IB	T 95-T105					5900	6900
27	SUPER ENCLOSED	HT	CR			IB	130-145					5550	6500
27	SUPER ENCLOSED	HT	CR			IB	T 95-T105					5900	6900
27	SUPER SEMI-ENCLOSED	HT	CR			IB	130-145					5550	6500
27	SUPER SEMI-ENCLOSED	HT	CR			IB	T 95-T105					5900	6900
28	HOLIDAY	OP	RNBT			IB	316					7200	8250
29	SUPER SEMI-ENCLOSED	HT	CR			IB	130-145					6500	7600
29	SUPER SEMI-ENCLOSED	HT	CR			IB	T 95-T145					6900	8550
31		OP	EXP			IB	130-145					10300	11700
31		OP	EXP			IB	T 95-T145					10400	12500
32	SUPER ENCLOSED	HT	CR			IB	130-145					10900	12400
32	SUPER ENCLOSED	HT	CR			IB	T 95-T145					10900	12800
34		FB	DC			IB	130-145					13800	15700
34		FB	DC			IB	T 95-T105					14000	16000
34	COMMANDER					IB	T 95-T145					12600	14800
34	ENCL0SED BRIDGE	HT	DC			IB	T 95					14000	15900
34	ENCLOSED	HT	CR			IB	130-145					13200	15000
34	ENCLOSED	HT	CR			IB	T 95-T105					13300	15200
34	ENCLOSED BRIDGE	HT	DC			IB	130-145					13800	15700
34	ENCLOSED BRIDGE	HT	DC			IB	T105					14100	16000
38		FB	DC			IB	T130					26700	29600
38		FB	DC			IB	T145					26800	29800
38	ENCLOSED BRIDGE	HT	DC			IB	T130					26600	29500

CONTINUED ON NEXT PAGE

CHRIS CRAFT BOATS   -CONTINUED   See inside cover to adjust price for area

LOA FT IN	NAME AND/ OR MODEL	TOP/ RIG	BOAT TYPE	HULL MTL TP	ENGINE TP # HP MFG	BEAM FT IN	WGT LBS	DRAFT FT IN	RETAIL LOW	RETAIL HIGH

------------------- 1951 BOATS -------------------

38	ENCLOSED BRIDGE	HT	DC		IB T145				26700	29700
38	SALON	HT	DC		IB T130				26600	29500
38	SALON	HT	DC		IB T145				26700	29700
42				WD	IB T240 FORD				**	**
42		FB	DC		IB T130				33700	37400
42		FB	DC		IB T145				34300	38100
42	CHALLENGER				IB T130				36900	40900
42	CHALLENGER				IB T145				37200	41300
42	CHALLENGER				IB T160				37500	41700
42	COMMANDER				IB T130				34600	38500
42	COMMANDER				IB T145				34900	38800
42	COMMANDER				IB T160				35200	39100
42	COMMANDER W/ENCL BR	HT	MY		IB T130				29500	32800
42	COMMANDER W/ENCL BR	HT	MY		IB T145				30200	33500
42	COMMANDER W/ENCL BR	HT	MY		IB T160				30700	34100
42	ENCLOSED	FB	DC		IB T130				33700	37400
42	ENCLOSED	FB	DC		IB T145				34300	38100
47	BUCCANEER	FB	DC		IB T130				33400	37200
47	BUCCANEER	FB	DC		IB T145				33600	37300
47	BUCCANEER	FB	DC		IB T160				33700	37500
50	CATALINA	FB	DC		IB T160				**	**
50	CATALINA	FB	DC		IB R145				**	**
54			MY		IB T160				59500	65400
54			MY		IB T200D				66400	73000
54			MY		IB R160				61500	67600
62			MY		IB T160				158000	173500
	IB T200D	93300 102500, IB R160			158500 174000, IB R200D				104000	114500

------------------- 1950 BOATS -------------------

18			RNBT	WD	IB CC				**	**
18			RNBT	WD	IB 105-120				1900	2300
18	RIVIERA	OP	RNBT		IB 95-131				1900	2350
18	SPORTSMAN	OP	CR		IB 60- 95				1750	2150
18	SPORTSMAN	OP	CR		IB 105				1850	2200
19				WD	IB 158 CC				**	**
19		OP	RACE		IB 158				2100	2450
19			RNBT	WD	IB 158 HERC				2200	2550
20			RNBT	WD	IB 158 CC				2550	2950
20	RIVIERA	OP	RNBT		IB 95-158				2400	2950
21		OP	EXP		IB 60-105				2900	3500
22				WD	IB 95-145				**	**
22	CUSTOM	HT	SDN		IB 105-145				3100	3750
22	SPORTSMAN	OP	CR		IB 95-145				3100	3750
23		OP	EXP		IB 60-145				3800	4700
23	HOLIDAY	OP	RNBT		IB 95-158				3950	4750
24	ENCLOSED	HT	CR		IB 60-105				4450	5250
25	SPORTSMAN	OP	CR		IB 145-225				4500	5350
25	SPORTSMAN	OP	CR		IB T 95-T145				4650	5750
26	SUPER	OP	EXP		IB 95-145				5150	6200
26	SUPER	OP	EXP		IB T 60-T105				5250	6550
26	SUPER ENCLOSED	HT	CR		IB 95-145				4950	5950
26	SUPER ENCLOSED	HT	CR		IB T 60-T105				5050	6300
26	SUPER SEMI-ENCLOSED	HT	CR		IB 95-145				4900	5950
26	SUPER SEMI-ENCLOSED	HT	CR		IB T 60-T105				5050	6300
28	SUPER ENCLOSED	HT	CR		IB 130-145				6550	7650
28	SUPER ENCLOSED	HT	CR		IB T 95-T145				6900	8450
28	SUPER SEMI-ENCLOSED	HT	CR		IB 130-145				6550	7650
28	SUPER SEMI-ENCLOSED	HT	CR		IB T 95-T145				6900	8450
30				WD	IB 95 CC				**	**
30				WD	IB T130 HERC				**	**
30		OP	EXP		IB 130-145				7750	9000
30		OP	EXP		IB T 95-T145				8150	10100
30		HT	SDN		IB 130-145				7550	8850
30		HT	SDN		IB T 95-T105				8100	9450
32	SUPER ENCLOSED	HT	CR		IB 130-145				10900	12400
32	SUPER ENCLOSED	HT	CR		IB T 95-T145				11000	12900
33	ENCLOSED DELUXE	HT	CR		IB 130-145				11800	13400
33	ENCLOSED DELUXE	HT	CR		IB T 95-T105				11900	13700
34		OP	EXP		IB T130-T145				15100	17400
34	COMMANDER				IB 130-145				12500	14300
34	COMMANDER				IB T 95-T145				12700	14900
36		HT	DC		IB T 95				22400	24900
	IB T105	22400 24900, IB T130			22600 25100, IB T145				22600	25100
36	QUARTERDECK		CR		IB T 95				21800	24200
	IB T105	21900 24300, IB T130			22000 24400, IB T145				22100	24500
36	SALON		CR		IB T 95				21800	24200
	IB T105	21900 24300, IB T130			22000 24400, IB T145				22100	24500
40			DC	WD	IB T 35D				39300	43700
40		OP	EXP		IB T130				27700	30700
40		OP	EXP		IB T145				27800	30900
40		OP	EXP		IB T160				27900	31000
40	CHALLENGER				IB T130				27720	30200
40	CHALLENGER				IB T145				27300	30300
40	CHALLENGER				IB T160				27400	30500
41		FB	DC		IB T 95				35400	39300
	IB T105	35500 39400, IB T130			35600 39500, IB T145				35900	39800
41	ENCLOSED BRIDGE	HT	DC		IB T 95				35400	39300
	IB T105	35500 39400, IB T130			35500 39500, IB T145				35800	39800
46		FB	DC	WD	IB T130	12			35800	39800
46		FB	DC	WD	IB T145	12			37400	41500
46		FB	DC	WD	IB T160	12			38800	43100
48		FB	DC		IB T130				34800	38600
	IB T145	34900 38800, IB T160			35100 39000, IB R130				33500	37200
	IB R145	33700 37500								
52			MY		IB T160				48100	52900
52			MY		IB T200D				62700	68900
52			MY		IB R160				44100	49000

------------------- 1949 BOATS -------------------

17	6			WD	IB 95 HERC				**	**
17	7 SPECIAL	OP	RNBT	WD	IB 95 CC				1750	2100
18			RNBT	WD	IB 158 HERC				2050	2450
18		OP	RNBT	WD	IB 95 CC				1900	2250
18	RIVIERA	OP	RNBT	WD	IB 60- 95				1800	2250
18	RIVIERA	OP	RNBT	WD	IB 105-131				1950	2350
18	SPORTSMAN	OP	CR	WD	IB 60- 95				1750	2150
18	SPORTSMAN	OP	CR	WD	IB 105				1850	2200
19		OP	RACE	WD	IB 95-131				1950	2400
19		OP	RACE	WD	IB 158				2100	2500
19			RNBT	WD	IB 95 HERC				2000	2400
20	CUSTOM	OP	RNBT	WD	IB 95-130	6	7	2635 1 9	2050	2550
20	CUSTOM	OP	RNBT	WD	IB 145-158	6	7	2635 1 9	2500	2600
21	DELUXE	OP	EXP	WD	IB 60- 95				2900	3500
22		OP	EXP	WD	IB 60-105				2900	3500
22			UTL	WD	IB 158-300				**	**
22	CUSTOM	HT	SDN	WD	IB 145 CC				3250	3750
22	SPORTSMAN	OP	CR	WD	IB 95-145				3100	3750
23		OP	EXP	WD	IB 60-130	7	8	3080 1 9	2800	3500
23		OP	EXP	WD	IB 145	7	8	3080 1 9	3050	3550
24		OP	EXP	WD	IB 60-145				4750	5700
24		OP	EXP	WD	IB T 60-T105				4900	5900
24	ENCLOSED W/DINETTE	HT	CR	WD	IB 60-105				4500	5300
25	SPORTSMAN	HT	CR	WD	IB 130	7	9	3846 2 1	3850	4500
25	SPORTSMAN	OP	CR	WD	IB 145-225	7	9	3846 2 1	3900	4800
25	SPORTSMAN	OP	CR	WD	IB T 95-T130	7	9	3846 2 1	4100	5050
25	SPORTSMAN	OP	CR	WD	IB T145	7	9	3846 2 1	4300	5250
26	SUPER	OP	EXP	WD	IB 95-145				5200	6250
26	SUPER	OP	EXP	WD	IB T 60-T105				5300	6600
26	SUPER DELUXE ENCLOSE	HT	CR	WD	IB 95-145				4950	6000
26	SUPER DELUXE ENCLOSE	HT	CR	WD	IB T 60-T105				5100	6350
26	SUPER DELUXE SEMI EN	HT	CR	WD	IB 95-145				4950	6000
26	SUPER DELUXE SEMI EN	HT	CR	WD	IB T 60-T105				5100	6350
28	SUPER DELUXE SEMI EN	HT	CR	WD	IB 95-145				6550	7700
28	SUPER DELUXE SEMI EN	HT	CR	WD	IB T 95-T145				6950	8550
30		OP	EXP	WD	IB 130-145				7800	9100
30		OP	EXP	WD	IB T 95-T145				8250	10200
30		HT	SDN	WD	IB 95-145	9	6	6150 2 1	7100	8750
30		HT	SDN	WD	IB T 95-145	9	6	6150 2 1	8000	9400
33	ENCLOSED DELUXE	HT	CR	WD	IB 130-145				11900	13500
33	ENCLOSED DELUXE	HT	CR	WD	IB T 95-T105				12000	13700
34				WD	IB T145 CC				**	**
34		OP	EXP	WD	IB T 95-T145	10	9	12000 2 6	14000	16400

148   CONTINUED ON NEXT PAGE   96th ed. - Vol. III

LOA FT IN	NAME AND/ OR MODEL	TOP/ RIG	BOAT TYPE	HULL MTL	HULL TP	ENGINE TP	#	HP	MFG	BEAM FT IN	WGT LBS	DRAFT FT IN	RETAIL LOW	RETAIL HIGH
\-	\-	\-	\-	\-	\-	\-	1949 BOATS \-							
34	COMMANDER			WD		IB		130-145					12600	14400
34	COMMANDER			WD		IB	T	95-T145					12700	15000
36	ENCLOSED	HT	DC	WD		IB	T	95		11 5	14200	2 6	20500	22800
	IB T105	20600	22900, IB T130					20800	23100, IB T145				20900	23200
36	QUARTERDECK		CR	WD		IB	T	95					21900	24300
	IB T105	21900	24300, IB T130					22000	24500, IB T145				22100	24600
36	SALON		CR	WD		IB	T	95					21900	24300
	IB T105	21900	24300, IB T130					22000	24500, IB T145				22100	24600
40		OP	EXP	WD		IB	T130			11 6	16200	2 6	28900	32100
	IB T145	29000	32300, IB T160					29100	32400, IB T225				29300	32600
	IB T316	29700	33000											
40	CHALLENGER			WD		IB	T130			11 6	16300	2 6	30700	34100
	IB T145	30800	34200, IB T160					30900	34300, IB T225				31100	34500
	IB T316	31400	34900											
40	ENCLOSED BRIDGE	HT	DC	WD		IB	T 95			11 6	16250	2 6	28900	32100
	IB T105	28900	32200, IB T130					29200	32400, IB T145				29300	32500
42				WD		IB	T210	CHRY					**	**
46		FB	DC	WD		IB	T130	12					36300	40400
46		FB	DC	WD		IB	T145	12					37900	42100
46		FB	DC	WD		IB	T160	12					39300	43700
46	ENCLOSED BRIDGE	HT	DC	WD		IB	T130	12			20000	2 8	33700	37400
46	ENCLOSED BRIDGE	HT	DC	WD		IB	T145	12			20000	2 8	35300	39300
46	ENCLOSED BRIDGE	HT	DC	WD		IB	T160	12			20000	2 8	36900	41000
52	CONQUEROR		MY	WD		IB	T160						48800	53600
	IB T225	44700	49700, IB T250					46800	51500, IB T316				50400	55400
	IB T200D	63200	69400, IB R160					44700	49700					
\-	\-	\-	\-	\-	1948 BOATS \-									
17	6		RNBT	WD		IB		95	HERC				1850	2200
18				WD		IB		185	CC				**	**
18			RNBT	WD		IB		105	CC				1950	2300
19				WD		IB		95	CC				**	**
19				WD		IB		158	CC				**	**
19		OP	RACE	WD		IB		95-121					1950	2400
19		OP	RACE	WD		IB		145					2100	2500
19			RNBT	WD		IB		158	CC				2250	2600
19		OP	RNBT	WD		IB		158	CC				2250	2600
20				WD		IB		158-270					**	**
20			RNBT	WD		IB		158	CC				2600	3000
20	CUSTOM	OP	RNBT	WD		IB		95-130		6 7	2635	1 9	2050	2550
20	CUSTOM	OP	RNBT	WD		IB		145		6 7	2635	1 9	2250	2600
22	CUSTOM	OP	SDN	WD		IB		95-130					3150	3750
22	SPORTSMAN	OP	CR	WD		IB		95-115					3150	3700
23		OP	EXP	WD		IB		60-115		7 8	3080	1 9	2850	3450
25				WD		IB		131-225					**	**
25		OP	EXP	WD		IB		95-160		8 2	4280	2	4100	5100
25		OP	EXP	WD		IB	T 95			8 2	4280	2	4550	5200
25	SPORTSMAN	OP	CR	WD		IB		130		7 9	3846	2 1	3900	4550
25	SPORTSMAN	OP	CR	WD		IB		160-225		7 9	3846	2 1	4000	4850
25	SPORTSMAN	OP	CR	WD		IB	T 95			7 9	3846	2 1	4150	4800
26				WD		IB		165	CC				**	**
26	ENCLOSED W/DINETTE	HT	CR	WD		IB		60- 92		8 1	4650	1 10	4450	5200
26	SEMI-ENCLOSED	HT	CR	WD		IB		60- 95		8 1	3850	1 10	3800	4600
26	SEMI-ENCLOSED	HT	CR	WD		IB		155		8 1	3850	1 10	4350	5000
26	SEMI-ENCLOSED	HT	CR	WD		IB	T 95			8 1	3850	1 10	4550	5200
27	SUPER DELUXE ENCLOSE	HT	CR	WD		IB		95-115		8 4	5158	1 10	5100	6050
30		HT	SDN	WD		IB		95-130		9 6	6150	2 1	7150	8650
30		HT	SDN	WD		IB	T 95			9 6	6150	2 1	8050	9250
33				WD		IB		145	HERC				**	**
33	ENCLOSED DELUXE	HT	CR	WD		IB		95-130					11900	13600
33	ENCLOSED DELUXE	HT	CR	WD		IB	T 92-T 95						12000	13700
34		OP	EXP	WD		IB	T 95-T130			10 9	11200	2 6	13800	16000
36	ENCLOSED	HT	DC	WD		IB	T 95			11 5	14200	2 6	20600	22900
36	ENCLOSED	HT	DC	WD		IB	T115			11 5	14200	2 6	20700	23000
36	ENCLOSED	HT	DC	WD		IB	T130			11 5	14200	2 6	20800	23100
40		OP	EXP	WD		IB	T 95			11 6	16200	2 6	28600	31700
	IB T130	28900	32100, IB T160					29100	32300, IB T225				29200	32500
40	CHALLENGER	HT	EXP	WD		IB	T 95			11 6	16200	2 6	29400	32700
	IB T130	29700	33000, IB T160					29900	33300, IB T225				30100	33500
	IB T316	30500	33900											
40	ENCLOSED BRIDGE	HT	DC	WD		IB	T 95			11 6	16250	2 6	28800	32000
40	ENCLOSED BRIDGE	HT	DC	WD		IB	T130			11 6	16250	2 6	29100	32300
46	ENCLOSED BRIDGE	HT	DC	WD		IB	T 95			12	20000	2 6	23600	26200
46	ENCLOSED BRIDGE	HT	DC	WD		IB	T130			12	20000	2 6	34200	38000
46	ENCLOSED BRIDGE	HT	DC	WD		IB	T160			12	20000	2 6	37100	41200
\-	\-	\-	\-	\-	1947 BOATS \-									
19			RNBT	WD		IB		158	CC				2250	2650
19			RNBT	WD		IB		158	HERC				2250	2650
20				WD		IB		130-158					**	**
20	CUSTOM	OP	RNBT	WD		IB		95		6 7	2635	1 9	2100	2500
21				WD		IB		125	CHRY				**	**
22				WD		IB		90-115					**	**
22	DELUXE	OP	UTL	WD		IB		60		7 3	2445	1 8	2300	2650
22	SPORTSMAN	OP	CR	WD		IB		115		7			3250	3750
23		OP	EXP	WD		IB		60-115		7 8	3080	1 9	2900	3500
25				WD		IB		345					**	**
25		OP	EXP	WD		IB		130-160		8 2	4280	2	4350	5150
25		OP	EXP	WD		IB	T 95			8 2	4280	2	4600	5300
25	SPORTSMAN	OP	CR	WD		IB		130		7 9	3846	2 1	3950	4600
25	SPORTSMAN	HT	CR	WD		IB		130		7 9	3846	2 1	3950	4600
26	ENCLOSED DELUXE	HT	CR	WD		IB		92		8 1	4650	1 10	4600	5250
26	SEMI-ENCLOSED	HT	CR	WD		IB		115		8 1	3850	1 10	4150	4800
27				WD		IB		130	CC				5750	6600
27	SUPER DELUXE ENCLOSE	HT	CR	WD		IB		115-130		8 4	5158	1 10	5300	6200
36	ENCLOSED CRUISER	HT	DC	WD		IB	T 95			11 5	14200	2 6	20600	22900
36	ENCLOSED CRUISER	HT	DC	WD		IB	T115			11 5	14200	2 6	20700	23000
36	ENCLOSED CRUISER	HT	DC	WD		IB	T130			11 5	14200	2 6	20800	23100
40	ENCLOSED BRIDGE	HT	DC	WD		IB	T 95			11 6	16250	2 6	**	**
46		FB	DC	WD		IB	T160	12			20500	2 8	38300	42500
46		FB	DCCPT	WD		IB	T160	HERC	12		22000	2 8	24900	27600
46	ENCLOSED BRIDGE	HT	DC	WD		IB	T130	12			20000	2 8	34800	38700
46	ENCLOSED BRIDGE	HT	DC	WD		IB	T160	12			20000	2 8	38100	42300
\-	\-	\-	\-	\-	1946 BOATS \-									
18				WD		IB		95	HERC				**	**
18	DELUXE	OP	UTL	WD		IB		92- 95		7 8	3080	1 9	2050	2450
20	CUSTOM	OP	RNBT	WD		IB		95-145		7 8	3080	1 9	2550	3000
22				WD		IB			CHRY				**	**
22				WD		IB		125-158					**	**
22	DELUXE	OP	UTL	WD		IB		60-130		7 3	2445	1 8	2300	2900
23		OP	EXP	WD		IB		60-130		7 8	3080	1 9	2900	3500
23	CUSTOM	OP	RNBT	WD		IB		130-160		6 8	3350	1 10	3150	3750
25		OP	EXP	WD		IB		95-160		8 2	4280	2	4200	5200
25		OP	EXP	WD		IB	T 92-T 95			8 2	4280	2	4650	5350
25	SPORTSMAN	OP	CR	WD		IB		130-160		7 9	3846	2 1	4000	4800
25	SPORTSMAN	OP	CR	WD		IB	T 95			7 9	3846	2 1	4250	4950
26	ENCLOSED W/DIN DLX	HT	CR	WD		IB		60- 95		8 1	4650		4550	5350
26	SEMI-ENCLOSED	HT	CR	WD		IB		60- 95		8 1	3850	1 10	3900	4750
26	SEMI-ENCLOSED	HT	CR	WD		IB		115-130		8 1	3850	1 10	4200	5000
26	SEMI-ENCLOSED	HT	CR	WD		IB	T 95			8 1	3850	1 10	4650	5350
27	SUPER DELUXE ENCLOSE	HT	CR	WD		IB		60- 95		8 4	5158	1 10	5200	6050
27	SUPER DELUXE ENCLOSE	HT	CR	WD		IB		115		8 4	5158	1 10	5400	6200
27	SUPER DELUXE ENCLOSE	HT	CR	WD		IB		130		8 4	5158	1 10	5500	6400
29		OP	EXP	WD		IB		130-160		8 8	6700	2 3	6900	8350
29		OP	EXP	WD		IB	T 95-T130			8 8	6700	2 3	7300	8850
30		HT	SDN	WD		IB		95-130		9 6	6150	2 1	7250	8750
30		HT	SDN	WD		IB	T 92-T 95			9 6	6150	2 1	8150	9400
33	ENCLOSED DELUXE	HT	CR	WD		IB		95			6150	2 1	10600	12100
33	ENCLOSED DELUXE	HT	CR	WD		IB		115-130					12100	13800
33	ENCLOSED DELUXE	HT	CR	WD		IB	T 92-T 95						12200	13900
34		OP	EXP	WD		IB	T 95-T130			10 9	11200	2 6	13900	16200
36	ENCLOSED BRIDGE	HT	DC	WD		IB	T 95			11 5	14200	2 6	20700	22900
36	ENCLOSED BRIDGE	HT	DC	WD		IB	T115			11 5	14200	2 6	20700	23000
36	ENCLOSED BRIDGE	HT	DC	WD		IB	T130			11 5	14200	2 6	20800	23100
36	ENCLOSED CRUISER	HT	DC	WD		IB	T 95			11 5	14200	2 6	20700	22900
36	ENCLOSED CRUISER	HT	DC	WD		IB	T115			11 5	14200	2 6	20800	23100
36	ENCLOSED CRUISER	HT	DC	WD		IB	T130			11 5	14200	2 6	20900	23200
40		OP	EXP	WD		IB	T 95			11 6	16200	2 6	28600	31700
	IB T130	28800	32000, IB T141					28800	32100, IB T160				29000	32300
40	CHALLENGER	HT	EXP	WD		IB	T 95			11 6	16300	2 6	29600	32800
	IB T130	29900	33200, IB T141					30000	33300, IB T160				30100	33400

LOA FT IN	NAME AND/ OR MODEL	TOP/ RIG	BOAT TYPE	-HULL- MTL	TP	TP	----ENGINE--- # HP	MFG	BEAM FT	IN	WGT LBS	DRAFT FT	IN	RETAIL LOW	RETAIL HIGH
1946 BOATS															
40	ENCLOSED BRIDGE	HT		WD		IB	130		11	6	16250	2	6	30000	33400
40	ENCLOSED BRIDGE	HT	DC	WD		IB	160		11	6	16250	2	6	28400	31600
	IB T 95 28800 32000, IB T115 28900 32100, IB T130													29100	32300
46	ENCLOSED BRIDGE	HT	DC	WD		IB	T 95		12		20000	2	8	24700	27500
	IB T130 35600 39500, IB T141 36800 40900, IB T160													38800	43100
1945 BOATS															
22	DELUXE	OP	UTL	MHG		IB			7	3	2670	1	7	**	**
23		OP	EXP	MHG		IB			7	8	3300	1	9	**	**
23	CUSTOM	OP	RNBT	MHG		IB			6	8	3350	1	10	**	**
25		OP	EXP	MHG		IB			8	2	4050	2		**	**
26	DELUXE ENCLOSED	HT	CR	MHG		IB			8	1	4500	1	8	**	**
26	SEMI-ENCLOSED	HT	CR	MHG		IB			8	1	3850	1	8	**	**
29		OP	EXP	MHG		IB			8	8	6700	2	3	**	**
30		HT	SDN	MHG		IB			9	6	6150	2	1	**	**
34		OP	EXP	MHG		IB			10	9	11200	2	6	**	**
40		OP	EXP	MHG		IB			11	6	16200	2	6	**	**
40	CHALLENGER	HT	EXP	MHG		IB			11	6	16300	2	6	**	**
40	ENCLOSED BRIDGE	HT	DC	MHG		IB			11	6	17000	2	6	**	**
1944 BOATS															
19	CUSTOM	OP	RNBT	MHG		IB			6	2	2650	1	6	**	**
22	DELUXE	OP	UTL	MHG		IB			7	3	2670	1	7	**	**
22	DELUXE	HT	UTL	MHG		IB			7	3	2670	1	7	**	**
23		OP	EXP	MHG		IB			7	8	3300	1	9	**	**
23	CUSTOM	OP	RNBT	MHG		IB			6	8	3350	1	10	**	**
24	CLIPPER	HT	CR	MHG		IB			7	8	3050	1	11	**	**
25		OP	EXP	MHG		IB			8	2	4050	2		**	**
26	DELUXE ENCLOSED	HT	CR	MHG		IB			8	1	4500	1	8	**	**
26	SEMI-ENCLOSED	HT	CR	MHG		IB			8	1	3850	1	8	**	**
29		OP	EXP	MHG		IB			8	8	6700	2	3	**	**
30		HT	SDN	MHG		IB			9	6	6150	2	1	**	**
32	DELUXE ENCLOSED	HT	CR	MHG		IB			10	5	8000	2	2	**	**
34		OP	EXP	MHG		IB			10	9	11200	2	6	**	**
35	DELUXE ENCLOSED	HT	CR	MHG		IB			11	3	11450	2	6	**	**
35	ENCLOSED BRIDGE	HT	DC	MHG		IB			11	3	13000	2	6	**	**
35	QUARTER DECK	HT	CR	MHG		IB			11	3	12300	2	6	**	**
40		OP	EXP	MHG		IB			11	6	16200	2	6	**	**
40	CHALLENGER	HT	EXP	MHG		IB			11	6	16300	2	6	**	**
40	ENCLOSED BRIDGE	HT	DC	MHG		IB			11	6	17000	2	6	**	**
45	ENCLOSED	FB	DC	MHG		IB			12		20500	2	8	**	**
45	ENCLOSED BRIDGE	HT	DC	MHG		IB			12		20000	2	8	**	**
55		HT	MY	MHG		IB			14	4	32700	3	4	**	**
1943 BOATS															
19	CUSTOM	OP	RNBT	MHG		IB			6	2	2650	1	6	**	**
22	DELUXE	OP	UTL	MHG		IB			7	3	2670	1	7	**	**
22	DELUXE	HT	UTL	MHG		IB			7	3	2670	1	7	**	**
23		OP	EXP	MHG		IB			7	8	3300	1	9	**	**
23	CUSTOM	OP	RNBT	MHG		IB			6	8	3350	1	10	**	**
25		OP	EXP	MHG		IB			8	2	4050	2		**	**
26	ENCLOSED	HT	CR	MHG		IB			8	1	4500	1	8	**	**
26	SEMI-ENCLOSED	HT	CR	MHG		IB			8	1	3850	1	8	**	**
30		HT	SDN	MHG		IB			9	6	6150	2	1	**	**
32	ENCLOSED DELUXE	HT	CR	MHG		IB			10	5	8000	2	2	**	**
34		OP	EXP	MHG		IB			10	9	11200	2	6	**	**
35	ENCLOSED DELUXE	HT	CR	MHG		IB			11	3	11450	2	6	**	**
35	QUARTERDECK	HT	CR	MHG		IB			11	3	12300	2	6	**	**
40		OP	EXP	MHG		IB			11	6	16200	2	6	**	**
40	CHALLENGER	HT	EXP	MHG		IB			11	6	16300	2	6	**	**
40	ENCLOSED BRIDGE	HT	DC	MHG		IB			11	6	17000	2	6	**	**
45		FB	DC	MHG		IB			12		20500	2	8	**	**
45	ENCLOSED BRIDGE	HT	DC	MHG		IB			12		20000	2	8	**	**
1942 BOATS															
17			RNBT	WD		IB		HERC						**	**
19	CUSTOM	OP	RNBT	MHG		IB	95-130		6	2	2650	1	6	1950	2450
19	CUSTOM	OP	RNBT	MHG		IB	145		6	2	2650	1	6	2150	2500
22				WD		IB								**	**
22				WD		IB	125	CC						**	**
22	NAVY TOP DELUXE	ST	UTL	MHG		IB	60- 95		7	3	2670	1	7	2600	3150
22	NAVY TOP DELUXE	ST	UTL	MHG		IB	130		7	3	2670	1	7	2800	3300
22	VENTED CABIN DELUXE	HT	UTL	MHG		IB	60- 95		7	3	2670	1	7	2600	3150
22	VENTED CABIN DELUXE]	HT	UTL	MHG		IB	130		7	3	2670	1	7	2800	3300
23		OP	EXP	MHG		IB	60- 95		9	8	3080	1	9	3500	4200
23	CUSTOM	OP	RNBT	MHG		IB	95-160		6	8	3350	1	10	3300	4050
23	CUSTOM	OP	RNBT	MHG		IB	T121		6	8	3350	1	10	3800	4400
25		OP	EXP	MHG		IB	95-160		8	1	4050	2		4400	5400
25		OP	EXP	MHG		IB	T 95		8	1	4050	2		4800	5550
26	ENCLOSED	HT	CR	MHG		IB	60- 95		8	1	4500	1	8	4750	5650
26	SEMI-ENCLOSED	HT	CR	MHG		IB	60- 95		8	1	3850	1	8	4200	5100
26	SEMI-ENCLOSED	HT	CR	MHG		IB	130		8	1	3850	1	8	4700	5400
26	SEMI-ENCLOSED	HT	CR	MHG		IB	T 60-T 95		8	1	3850	1	8	4600	5750
30		HT	SDN	MHG		IB	60- 95		9	6	6500	2	3	7200	8700
30		HT	SDN	MHG		IB	130		9	6	6500	2	3	7900	9100
30		HT	SDN	MHG		IB	T 60-T 95		9	6	6500	2	3	7850	9750
32	ENCLOSED DELUXE	HT	CR	MHG		IB	95-130		10	5	8000	2	2	9950	11300
32	ENCLOSED DELUXE	HT	CR	MHG		IB	T 95		10	5	8000	2	2	10300	11700
34		OP	EXP	MHG		IB	130-160		10	9	11200	2	6	14000	15900
34		OP	EXP	MHG		IB	T 95-T130		10	9	11200	2	6	14100	16400
35	ENCLOSED DELUXE	HT	CR	MHG		IB	95		11	3	11450	2	6	15300	17400
35	ENCLOSED DELUXE	HT	CR	MHG		IB	130		11	3	11450	2	6	15400	17500
35	ENCLOSED DELUXE	HT	CR	MHG		IB	T 95		11	3	11450	2	6	15500	17600
35	ENCLOSED QUARTERDECK	HT	CR	MHG		IB	95		11	3	11450	2	6	15300	17400
35	ENCLOSED QUARTERDECK	HT	CR	MHG		IB	130		11	3	12300	2	6	15900	18100
35	ENCLOSED QUARTERDECK	HT	CR	MHG		IB	T 95		11	3	12300	2	6	16000	18200
38	DELUXE	HT	SDN	MHG		IB	130		11	3	14600	2	8	23900	26600
	IB 160 24000 26700, IB T 95 24300 27000, IB T130													24600	27400
40		OP	EXP	MHG		IB	T 95		11	6	15600	2	6	28100	31200
40		OP	EXP	MHG		IB	T130		11	6	15600	2	6	28400	31600
40		OP	EXP	MHG		IB	T160		11	6	15600	2	6	28600	31800
40	CHALLENGER	HT	EXP	MHG		IB	T 95		11	6	16300	2	6	30000	33300
40	CHALLENGER	HT	EXP	MHG		IB	T130		11	6	16300	2	6	30300	33600
40	CHALLENGER	HT	EXP	MHG		IB	T160		11	6	16300	2	6	30500	33900
40	ENCLOSED BRIDGE	HT	DC	MHG		IB	T 95		11	6	17000	2	6	30000	33400
40	ENCLOSED BRIDGE	HT	DC	MHG		IB	T130		11	6	17000	2	6	30300	33700
40	ENCLOSED BRIDGE	HT	DC	MHG		IB	T160		11	6	17000	2	6	30600	33900
45		FB	DC	MHG		IB	T 95		12		20500	2	8	29400	32700
45		FB	DC	MHG		IB	T130		12		20500	2	8	38900	43200
45		FB	DC	MHG		IB	T160		12		20500	2	8	40200	44700
45	ENCLOSED BRIDGE	HT	DC	MHG		IB	T 95		12		20000	2	8	29000	32200
45	ENCLOSED BRIDGE	HT	DC	MHG		IB	T130		12		20000	2	8	38600	42800
45	ENCLOSED BRIDGE	HT	DC	MHG		IB	T160		12		20000	2	8	39900	44300
1941 BOATS															
18						IB	375	CHEV						**	**
19				WD		IB								**	**
19	CUSTOM	OP	RNBT	MHG		IB	95		6	2	2650	1	6	2000	2400
19	CUSTOM	OP	RNBT	MHG		IB	130		6	2	2650	1	6	2150	2550
22			UTL	WD		IB	175	HERC						3800	4400
22	DELUXE	OP	UTL	MHG		IB	60- 95		7	3	2670	1	7	2700	3250
22	DELUXE	OP	UTL	MHG		IB	130		7	3	2670	1	7	2900	3350
22	DELUXE	HT	UTL	MHG		IB	60- 95		7	3	2670	1	7	2700	3250
22	DELUXE	HT	UTL	MHG		IB	130		7	3	2670	1	7	2900	3350
23				WD		IB	125-255							**	**
23		OP	EXP	MHG		IB			7	8	3700	1	9	**	**
23	CUSTOM	OP	RNBT	MHG		IB	95-160		6	8	3350	1	10	3400	4150
23	CUSTOM	OP	RNBT	MHG		IB	T121		6	8	3350	1	10	3900	4500
25		OP	EXP	MHG		IB	95-160		8	1	4050	2		4500	5500
25		OP	EXP	MHG		IB	T 95		8	1	4050	2		4950	5700
25	ENCLOSED	HT	CR	MHG		IB	60- 95		8	1	3900	1	8	4200	5050
25	ENCLOSED DELUXE	HT	CR	MHG		IB	60- 95		8	1	4400	1	8	4700	5500
25	SPORTSMAN	OP	CR	MHG		IB	95-130		7	9	3200	1	11	3750	4600
25	SPORTSMAN	OP	CR	MHG		IB	160		7	9	3200	1	11	4100	4750
25	SPORTSMAN	OP	CR	MHG		IB	T 95		7	9	3200	1	11	4250	4950
26	ENCLOSED DELUXE	HT	CR	MHG		IB	60- 95		8	1	4500	1	8	4900	5750
26	SEMI-ENCLOSED	HT	CR	MHG		IB	60- 95		8	1	4500	1	8	4900	5750
26	SEMI-ENCLOSED	HT	CR	MHG		IB	130		8	1		1	8	5800	6700
26	SEMI-ENCLOSED	HT	CR	MHG		IB	T 60-T 95		8	1		1	8	5750	7050
27				WD		IB	250	CRUS						**	**
27	CUSTOM	OP	RNBT	MHG		IB	160-275		7	2	4950	2	4	5900	7350
27	CUSTOM	OP	RNBT	MHG		IB	350		7	2	4950	2	4	6750	7750
29		OP	EXP	MHG		IB	130-160		8	8	6700	2	3	7700	9050
29		OP	EXP	MHG		IB	T130		8	8	6700	2	3	8550	9800
30		HT	SDN	MHG		IB	60- 95		9	6	6500	2	3	7250	8700
30		HT	SDN	MHG		IB	130		9	6	6500	2	3	7950	9150
30		HT	SDN	MHG		IB	T 60-T 95		9	6	6500	2	3	7900	9800
30	SEMI-ENCLOSED	HT	CR	MHG		IB	60-130		9	6	5500	2	1	6750	8100
30	SEMI-ENCLOSED	HT	CR	MHG		IB	T 60-T 95		9	6	5500	2	1	7000	8650
31	ENCLOSED DELUXE	HT	CR	MHG		IB	95-130		10	5	8500	2	2	9200	10500
31	ENCLOSED DELUXE	HT	CR	MHG		IB	T 95		10	5	8500	2	2	9550	10800

CONTINUED ON NEXT PAGE

```
  LOA   NAME AND/       TOP/ BOAT  -HULL-  ----ENGINE---   BEAM   WGT  DRAFT RETAIL RETAIL
FT IN   OR MODEL        RIG  TYPE  MTL TP  TP # HP  MFG   FT IN  LBS  FT IN  LOW    HIGH
-------------------- 1941 BOATS --------------------------------------------------------
34                          WD    MHG   IB T 95    CHRY                           **     **
34                     OP  EXP   MHG   IB 130-160    10  9 11200  2  6 14400  15900
34     ENCLOSED BRIDGE  HT  DC    MHG   IB  95-130    11  3 11150  2  6 13800  15700
34     ENCLOSED BRIDGE  HT  DC    MHG   IB T 95       11  3 11150  2  6 13900  15800
34     ENCLOSED DELUXE  HT  CR    MHG   IB  95-130    11  3 10750  2  6 13600  15500
34     ENCLOSED DELUXE  HT  CR    MHG   IB T 95       11  3 10750  2  6 13800  15700
38     DELUXE           HT  SDN   MHG   IB 130        11  3 14600  2  8 24000  26700
       IB 160    24100  26800, IB T 95     24500 27200, IB T130       24800  27500

38     ENCLOSED BRIDGE  HT  DC    MHG   IB 160        11  3 15000  2  8 25100  27900
38     ENCLOSED BRIDGE  HT  DC    MHG   IB T 95       11  3 15000  2  8 25400  28200
38     ENCLOSED BRIDGE  HT  DC    MHG   IB T130       11  3 15000  2  8 25500  28300
40                          WD    MHG   IB T275                               **     **
40                     OP  EXP   MHG   IB T 95       11  6 15600  2  6 28300  31500
       IB T130   28600  31800, IB T160     28800 32000, IB T275       29100  32400

40     CHALLENGER       HT  EXP   MHG   IB T 95       11  6 16300  2  6 30200  33500
       IB T130   30500  33900, IB T160     30700 34100, IB T275       31000  34500

44     ENCLOSED BRIDGE  HT  DC    MHG   IB            12    18800  2  8    **     **
48     ENCLOSED BRIDGE  HT  DC    MHG   IB T130       12  8 29000  3  1 32900  36500
       IB T160   50300  55300, IB T110D    56000 61600, IB T165D       57000  62600

55                          HT  MY    MHG   IB T130       14    32700  3  4 37800  42000
       IB T160   38000  42200, IB T275     56400 61900, IB T165D       35600  39600

-------------------- 1940 BOATS --------------------------------------------------------
18                          WD    MHG   IB  60- 70                            **     **
19                          WD    MHG   IB 130-285                            **     **
19     CUSTOM           OP  RNBT  MHG   IB     95       6  2  2135  1  6  1800   2150
19     CUSTOM           OP  RNBT  MHG   IB    130       6  2  2135  1  6  1900   2300
22     DELUXE           OP  UTL   MHG   IB  60- 95      7  3  2360  1  7  2550   3100
22     DELUXE           OP  UTL   MHG   IB    130       7  3  2360  1  7  2800   3250
22     DELUXE           HT  UTL   MHG   IB  60- 95      7  3  2360  1  7  2550   3100
22     DELUXE           HT  UTL   MHG   IB    130       7  3  2360  1  7  2800   3250
23     CUSTOM           OP  RNBT  MHG   IB  95-160      6  8  3050  1 10  3250   4000
25                          WD    MHG   IB 160-165                            **     **
25                     HT  CR    MHG   IB  60- 95      8  1  3600  1  8  4050   4900
25                     HT  CR    MHG   IB    130       8  1  3600  1  8  4450   5100

25                     HT  CR    MHG   IB T 60        8  1  3600  1  8  4400   5050
25                     OP  EXP   MHG   IB  95-160      8  1  4300  2     4850   5900
25                     OP  EXP   MHG   IB    223       8  1  4300  2     5300   6100
25                     OP  EXP   MHG   IB T 95        8  1  4300  2     5300   6050
25     DELUXE ENCLOSED  HT  CR    MHG   IB     95       8  1  4400  1  8  4900   5650
25     ENCLOSED         HT  CR    MHG   IB  60- 95      8  1  4100  1  8  4550   5400
25     SPORTSMAN        OP  CR    MHG   IB  95-160      7  9  3985  1 11  4550   5550
25     SPORTSMAN        OP  CR    MHG   IB    223       7  9  3985  1 11  5000   5750
25     SPORTSMAN        OP  CR    MHG   IB T 95        7  9  3985  1 11  5000   5750
25     SPORTSMAN        HT  CR    MHG   IB  95-160      7  9  3985  1 11  4550   5550
25     SPORTSMAN        HT  CR    MHG   IB    223       7  9  3985  1 11  5000   5750
25     SPORTSMAN        HT  CR    MHG   IB T 95        7  9  3985  1 11  5000   5750

27                          WD    MHG   IB 250      CHRY                        **     **
27     CUSTOM           OP  RACE  MHG   IB 350               7  2  4360  2  4  6550   7550
27     CUSTOM           OP  RNBT  MHG   IB 160               7  2  4300  2  4  5600   6450
27     CUSTOM           OP  RNBT  MHG   IB 275               7  2  4300  2  4  6150   7100
28                          WD    MHG   IB  96      GRAY                        7750   8900
29                     ST  EXP   MHG   IB 130-160            8  8  6880  2  3  8000   9450
29                     ST  EXP   MHG   IB 275                8  8  6880  2  3  8950  10200
29                     ST  EXP   MHG   IB T 95-T130          8  8  6880  2  3  8400  10200
29     SPORTSMAN        ST  CR    MHG   IB 130-160            8  8  6300  2  3  7650   9050
29     SPORTSMAN        ST  CR    MHG   IB 275                8  8  6300  2  3  8500   9800
29     SPORTSMAN        ST  CR    MHG   IB T 95-T130          8  8  6300  2  3  8100   9850

30                     OP  SPTCR MHG   IB  95-130       9  6  5800  2  1  7000   8300
30                     OP  SPTCR MHG   IB T 60-T 95     9  6  5800  2  1  7200   8850
30     ENCLOSED         HT  CR    MHG   IB  95-130       9  6  6200  2  1  7150   8450
30     ENCLOSED         HT  CR    MHG   IB T160          9  6  6200  2  1  8800  10000
33                     HT  SPTCR MHG   IB  95-130      11  3 10250  2  6 12200  13900
33                     HT  SPTCR MHG   IB T 95-T130    11  3 10250  2  6 12300  14200
33     ENCLOSED         OP  CR    MHG   IB  95-130      11  3 11400  2  6 13600  15500
33     ENCLOSED         HT  CR    MHG   IB T 95         11  3 11400  2  6 13800  15700
33     ENCLOSED BRIDGE  HT  DC    MHG   IB  95-130      11  3 11500  2  6 13800  15700
33     ENCLOSED BRIDGE  HT  DC    MHG   IB T 95         11  3 11500  2  6 13900  15800
34                          WD    MHG   IB T200     PALM                        **     **

34                     ST  EXP   MHG   IB 130-275      10  9 11600  2  6 14200  16500
34                     ST  EXP   MHG   IB T 95-T160    10  9 11600  2  6 14300  16900
37     ENCLOSED         HT  DC    MHG   IB 130         11  3 14200  2  8 23500  26100
       IB 160    23600  26200, IB T 95     23800 26500, IB T130       24100  26800

37     ENCLOSED BRIDGE  HT  DC    MHG   IB 130         11  3 14200  2  8 23500  26100
       IB 160    23600  26200, IB T 95     23800 26500, IB T130       24100  26800

42     ENCLOSED         HT  DC    MHG   IB 130         11  6 16700  2  8 31600  35100
       IB 160    31800  35400, IB T 95     32600 36200, IB T130       33100  36800
       IB T160   33500  37200

42     ENCLOSED BRIDGE  HT  DC    MHG   IB 130         11  6 17800  2  8 32900  36600
       IB 160    33100  36800, IB T 95     33800 37600, IB T130       34400  38200
       IB T160   34700  38600

48     ENCLOSED BRIDGE  HT  DC    MHG   IB T130        12  8 29000  3  1 33900  37700
       IB T160   52000  57200, IB T275     57100 62700, IB T110D GM    56800  62400
       IB T165D GM 57900 63600

55     ENCLOSED BRIDGE  HT  MY    MHG   IB T130        14    32700  3  4 38000  42300
       IB T160   38300  42500, IB T275     58400 64200, IB T110D GM    30300  33600
       IB T165D GM 36900 41000

-------------------- 1939 BOATS --------------------------------------------------------
18                          WD    MHG   IB  60      CC                          **     **
18                          WD    MHG   IB 125      CC                          **     **
18                     RNBT WD    MHG   IB 130      HERC                       2450   2850
19                          WD    MHG   IB          CHEV                        **     **
19                          WD    MHG   IB 120-200                              **     **
19     CUSTOM           OP  RNBT  MHG   IB  95-135      6  2  2135  1  6  1900   2350
19     SPORTSMAN        OP  CR    MHG   IB  60- 95      6  7  2250  1  6  1850   2250
19     SPORTSMAN        OP  CR    MHG   IB 125          6  7  2250  1  6  2000   2400
21                          WD    MHG   IB  94      CC                          **     **
21     DELUXE           OP  UTL   MHG   IB  60- 95      7  1  2280  1  7  2400   2900
21     DELUXE           OP  UTL   MHG   IB 121          7  1  2280  1  7  2550   3000

21     DELUXE           HT  UTL   MHG   IB  60- 95      7  1  2280  1  7  2400   2900
21     DELUXE           HT  UTL   MHG   IB 121          7  1  2280  1  7  2550   3000
22                          WD    MHG   IB 150-158                              **     **
22     CUSTOM           OP  RNBT  MHG   IB  95-135      6  8  2975  1 10  3200   3750
24     DELUXE           OP  UTL   MHG   IB  95-135      7  9  3300  1 10  4100   4750
24     DELUXE           HT  UTL   MHG   IB  95-135      7  9  3300  1 10  3950   4750
24     SPORTSMAN        OP  CR    MHG   IB  95-212      7  9  3910  1 11  4950   5700
24     SPORTSMAN        OP  CR    MHG   IB T 95         7  9  3910  1 11  5000   5550
24     SPORTSMAN        OP  CR    MHG   IB  95-212      7  9  3910  1 11  4550   5450
24     SPORTSMAN        HT  CR    MHG   IB T 95         7  9  3910  1 11  4800   5550
24     UTILITY          OP  CR    MHG   IB  95-212      7  9  3900  1 11  4800   5550
24     UTILITY          OP  CR    MHG   IB T 95         7  9  3900  1 11  4800   5550

24   9                      WD    MHG   IB 318      CHRY                        **     **
25                     HT  CR    MHG   IB 130      HERC                        **     **
25     CLIPPER          HT  CR    MHG   IB  60- 95      8  1  4100  1  8  4900   5650
25     CLIPPER DELUXE   HT  CR    MHG   IB     95       8  1  4350  1  8  5300   6100
25     SEMI-ENCLOSED    HT  CR    MHG   IB  60-135      8  1  4265  1 10  5400   6200
25     SEMI-ENCLOSED    HT  CR    MHG   IB T 95         8  1  4265  1 10  5400   6200
27                          WD    MHG   IB 275      CC                          **     **
27     CUSTOM           OP  RACE  MHG   IB             7  2  4360  2  4  6600   7600
28   7                      ST  RNBT  MHG   IB 275               8  8  6000  2  3  7500   8650
28   7                      ST  EXP   MHG   IB 135               8  8  6000  2  3  8350   9600
28   7                      ST  EXP   MHG   IB 275               8  8  6000  2  3  8350   9600
28   7                      ST  EXP   MHG   IB T 95-T135         8  8  6000  2  3  7950   9700

28   7 CUSTOM SPORTSMAN ST  CR    MHG   IB 135               8  8  5000  2  3  7700   8050
28   7 CUSTOM SPORTSMAN ST  CR    MHG   IB 275               8  8  5000  2  3  7700   8850
28   7 CUSTOM SPORTSMAN ST  CR    MHG   IB T 95-T135         8  8  5000  2  3  7350   9100
29     ENCLOSED         HT  CR    MHG   IB  60-135           8  9  6000  2  1  7650   8900
29     ENCLOSED         HT  CR    MHG   IB T 60             8  9  6000  2  1  7650   8900
29     SINGLE CABIN     HT  CR    MHG   IB  60-135           8  6  6100  2  1  7750   8900
29     SINGLE CABIN     HT  CR    MHG   IB T 60             8  6  6100  2  1  7750   8900
33                          HT        MHG   IB 135      HERC                        **     **
33                     HT  SPTCR MHG   IB  95-135     11  3  9500  2  6 11900  13600
33                     HT  SPTCR MHG   IB T 95-T135    11  3  9500  2  6 12100  13800
33     ENCLOSED         HT  CR    MHG   IB  95-135     11  3  9950  2  6 12100  13800
33     ENCLOSED         HT  CR    MHG   IB T 95        11  3  9950  2  6 12300  13900

33     ENCLOSED BRIDGE  HT  DC    MHG   IB  95-135     11  3 10400  2  6 12700  14500
33     ENCLOSED BRIDGE  HT  DC    MHG   IB T 95        11  3 10400  2  6 12900  14600
```

LOA FT	LOA IN	NAME AND/ OR MODEL	TOP/ RIG	BOAT TYPE	-HULL- MTL	-HULL- TP	ENGINE TP	ENGINE # HP	ENGINE MFG	BEAM FT	BEAM IN	WGT LBS	DRAFT FT	DRAFT IN	RETAIL LOW	RETAIL HIGH
		1939 BOATS														
36					WD		IB	T 86	HERC						**	**
36		DOUBLE STATEROOM	HT	DC	MHG		IB	135		11	3	12280	2	8	19500	21700
36		DOUBLE STATEROOM	HT	DC	MHG		IB	T 95		11	3	12280	2	8	20200	22500
36		DOUBLE STATEROOM	HT	DC	MHG		IB	T135		11	3	12280	2	8	20600	22900
36		ENCLOSED BRIDGE	HT	DC	MHG		IB	135		11	3	12280	2	8	20800	23100
36		ENCLOSED BRIDGE	HT	DC	MHG		IB	T 95		11	3	12280	2	8	20200	22500
36		ENCLOSED BRIDGE	HT	DC	MHG		IB	T135		11	3	12280	2	8	20600	22900
41		CUSTOM	HT	EXP	MHG		IB	T135		11	6	17800	2	8	33900	37700
41		CUSTOM	HT	EXP	MHG		IB	T275		11	6	17800	2	8	34700	38500
41		DOUBLE STATEROOM	HT	DC	MHG		IB	135		11	6	15260	2	8	27500	30500
		IB D ** **, IB T 95 29200 32400, IB T135													29600	32900
41		ENCLOSED BRIDGE	HT	DC	MHG		IB	135		11	6	15260	2	8	29700	33000
		IB D ** **, IB T 95 29200 32400, IB T135													29600	32900
48		CUSTOM	HT	MY	MHG		IB	T135		12	8	29000	3	1	34800	38700
		IB T160 53200 58500, IB T275 58700 64500, IB T D													**	**
55		CUSTOM	HT	MY	MHG		IB	T135		14		32700	3	4	38400	42700
		IB T160 38800 43100, IB T275 60600 66600, IB T D													**	**
		1938 BOATS														
17					WD		IB								**	**
19					WD		IB								**	**
19					WD		IB	95-125							**	**
19		CUSTOM	OP	RNBT	MHG		IB	95-118		6	2	2135	1	6	1950	2400
19		CUSTOM	OP	RNBT	MHG		IB	128-148		6	2	2135	1	6	2050	2500
19		SPORTSMAN	OP	CR	MHG		IB	60		6	7	2250	1	6	1850	2200
19		SPORTSMAN	OP	CR	MHG		IB	95-118		6	7	2250	1	6	1950	2450
19		SPORTSMAN	OP	CR	MHG		IB	128		6	7	2250	1	6	2050	2450
21	4	DELUXE	OP	UTL	MHG		IB	55-110		7	1	2280	1	7	2500	3100
21	4	DELUXE	HT	UTL	MHG		IB	55-110		7	1	2280	1	7	2500	3100
22					WD		IB								**	**
22					WD		IB	95	CHRY						**	**
22		CUSTOM	OP	RNBT	MHG		IB	95-148		6	8	2975	1	10	3200	3900
24					WD		IB	90	CC						**	**
24		DELUXE	OP	UTL	MHG		IB	85-130		7	9	3710	1	10	4450	5300
24		DELUXE	OP	UTL	MHG		IB	T 55-T 85		7	9	3710	1	10	4550	5400
24		DELUXE	HT	UTL	MHG		IB	85-130		7	9	3710	1	10	4450	5300
24		DELUXE	HT	UTL	MHG		IB	T 55-T 85		7	9	3710	1	10	4550	5400
24		SPORTSMAN	OP	CR	MHG		IB	85-130		7	9	3910	1	11	4650	5500
24		SPORTSMAN	OP	CR	MHG		IB	T 55-T 85		7	9	3910	1	11	4700	5650
24		SPORTSMAN	HT	CR	MHG		IB	85-130		7	9	3910	1	11	4650	5500
24		SPORTSMAN	HT	CR	MHG		IB	T 55-T 85		7	9	3910	1	11	4700	5650
25					WD		IB	149-165							**	**
25		CLIPPER	HT	CR	MHG		IB	55- 85		8	1	4100	1	8	5000	5700
25		CLIPPER DELUXE	HT	CR	MHG		IB	85		8	1	4100	1	8	5450	6250
25		CUSTOM	OP	RNBT	MHG		IB	128-212		6	8	3685	1	11	4550	5550
25		SEMI-ENCLOSED	HT	CR	MHG		IB	55- 85		8	1	4265	1	10	4950	5800
26					WD		IB	115	CC						**	**
26		ENCLOSED	HT	CR	MHG		IB	55-130		8	8	5545	2	1	6300	7550
26		SINGLE CABIN	OP	CR	MHG		IB	55-110		8	8	5545	2	1	6600	7800
26		SINGLE CABIN	HT	CR	MHG		IB	55-110		8	8	5545	2	1	6800	8000
27		CUSTOM	OP	RNBT	MHG		IB	275		7	2	4700	2	4	6800	7850
27		SPECIAL	OP	RACE	MHG		IB	350		7	2	4360	2	4	7000	8050
28	7		ST	EXP	MHG		IB	130		8	8	5400	2	3	7400	8500
28	7		ST	EXP	MHG		IB	275		8	8	5400	2	3	8300	9550
28	7		ST	EXP	MHG		IB	T 95-T130		8	8	5400	2	3	7850	9600
28	7	CUSTOM SPORTSMAN	ST	CR	MHG		IB	130		8	8	5000	2	3	7100	8200
28	7	CUSTOM SPORTSMAN	ST	CR	MHG		IB	275		8	8	5000	2	3	8000	9200
28	7	CUSTOM SPORTSMAN	ST	CR	MHG		IB	T 95-T130		8	8	5000	2	3	7650	9350
29		ENCLOSED	HT	CR	MHG		IB	55- 85		9	6	5800	2	1	7350	8600
29		SINGLE CABIN	HT	CR	MHG		IB	55- 85		9	6	5800	2	1	7350	8600
31		ENCLOSED	HT	CR	MHG		IB	55-130		11	2	9240	2	5	10100	11600
31		ENCLOSED	HT	CR	MHG		IB	T 55-T 85		11	2	9240	2	5	10300	11800
31		SINGLE CABIN DECKHSE	HT	CR	MHG		IB	55-130		11	2	9540	2	5	9950	11600
31		SINGLE CABIN DECKHSE	HT	CR	MHG		IB	T 55-T 85		11	2	9540	2	5	10200	11800
31		SINGLE CABIN SPORTCR	HT	SPTCR	MHG		IB	55-130		11	2	8750	2	5	9900	11500
31		SINGLE CABIN SPORTCR	HT	SPTCR	MHG		IB	T 55-T 85		11	2	8750	2	5	10100	11700
33		ENCLOSED	HT	CR	MHG		IB	95		11	3	10000	2	6	12100	13800
33		ENCLOSED BRIDGE	HT	CR	MHG		IB	95		11	3	10000	2	6	12100	13800
35		DBL STATEROOM ENCLOS	HT	DC	MHG		IB	85		11		12640	2	8	16000	18200
		IB 110 16100 18300, IB 130 16100 18300, IB T 85													16200	18400
		IB T110 16300 18500, IB T130 16500 18800														
35		DOUBLE STATEROOM	OP	DC	MHG		IB	85		11		12040	2	8	15500	17600
		IB 110 15500 17700, IB 130 15600 17700, IB T 85													15700	17800
		IB T110 15800 18000, IB T130 16000 18200														
35		DOUBLE STATEROOM	HT	DC	MHG		IB	85		11		12040	2	8	15700	17800
		IB 110 15700 17900, IB 130 15800 17900, IB T 85													15900	18000
		IB T110 16000 18200, IB T130 16200 18400														
35		ENCLOSED BRIDGE	HT	DC	MHG		IB	85		11		13840	2	8	16700	19000
		IB 110 16800 19100, IB 130 16800 19100, IB T 85													16900	19200
		IB T110 17000 19300, IB T130 17100 19500														
36					WD		IB	T	CHRY						**	**
40		DBL STATEROOM ENCLOS	HT	DC	MHG		IB	85		11	6	15020	2	8	26400	29400
		IB 110 26600 29500, IB 130 26700 29600, IB T 85													27200	30200
		IB T110 27500 30500, IB T130 27700 30700														
40		ENCLOSED BRIDGE	HT	DC	MHG		IB	85		11	6	15020	2	8	29600	32900
		IB 110 29700 33000, IB 130 29800 33100, IB T 85													30100	33400
		IB T110 30300 33600, IB T130 30400 33800														
		1937 BOATS														
17					WD		IB								**	**
17		DELUXE	OP	RNBT			IB	55- 85		6	6	3910	1	6	2850	3400
19					WD		IB	130-225							**	**
19		CUSTOM	OP	RNBT	MHG		IB	85-110		6	2	2135	1	6	2000	2450
19		CUSTOM	OP	RNBT	MHG		IB	125		6	2	2135	1	6	2200	2550
19		SPECIAL	OP	RACE	MHG		IB	120		6	2	2135	1	5	2200	2550
19		SPECIAL	OP	RACE	MHG		IB	175		6	2	2135	1	5	2350	2750
21	4	DELUXE	OP	UTL			IB	55- 85		7	1	2340	1	7	2650	3200
21	4	DELUXE	OP	UTL			IB	110		7	1	2340	1	7	2850	3300
21	4	DELUXE	HT	UTL			IB	55-110		7	1	2790	1	7	2950	3650
22					WD		IB		CC						**	**
22					WD		IB	125-158							**	**
22		CUSTOM	OP	RNBT	MHG		IB	85-125		6	8	2975	1	10	3300	4000
22		CUSTOM	OP	RNBT	MHG		IB	152		6	8	2975	1	10	3550	4150
23					WD		IB	135	CC						**	**
24		CLIPPER	HT	CR	MHG		IB	55		8	1	4100	1	8	5200	5950
24		SPORTSMAN	OP	CR			IB	85-212		7	9	3910	1	11	5100	6200
24		SPORTSMAN	OP	CR			IB	T 55-T 85		7	9	3910	1	11	5350	6650
24		SPORTSMAN	HT	CR			IB	85-212		7	9	3910	1	11	5100	6050
24		SPORTSMAN	HT	CR			IB	T 55-T 85		7	9	3910			5350	6150
25		CLIPPER	HT	CR	MHG		IB	85		8	1	4100	1	8	5200	6000
25		CUSTOM	OP	RNBT	MHG		IB	125-212		6	8	3685	1	11	4750	5750
25		SEMI-ENCLOSED	HT	CR	MHG		IB	55-130		8	1	4500	1	10	5550	6900
25		SEMI-ENCLOSED	HT	CR	MHG		IB	T 55-T 85		8	1	4500	1	10	6000	7300
26			OP	SPTCR	MHG		IB	75-102		8	8	5000	2	1	6250	7350
26		ENCLOSED	HT	CR	MHG		IB	55-110		8	8	5000	2	1	5950	7150
26		ENCLOSED	HT	CR	MHG		IB	130		8	8	5000	2	1	6500	7500
26		SINGLE CABIN	OP	CR	MHG		IB	55-110		8	8	5000	2	1	6150	7350
26		SINGLE CABIN	HT	CR	MHG		IB	55-110		8	8	5000	2	1	6350	7600
27		CUSTOM	OP	RNBT	MHG		IB	275		7	2	4700	2	4	7050	8100
27		SPECIAL	OP	RACE	MHG		IB	350		7	2	4360	2	4	7250	8300
29		ENCLOSED	HT	CR	MHG		IB	55-130		9	6	7500	2	4	9150	10500
29		ENCLOSED	HT	CR	MHG		IB	T 55-T 85		9	6	7500	2	4	9200	10800
29		SINGLE CABIN	OP	CR	MHG		IB	55-130		9	6	7500	2	4	9350	10700
29		SINGLE CABIN	OP	CR	MHG		IB	T 55-T 85		9	6	7500	2	4	9400	11000
29		SINGLE CABIN	HT	CR	MHG		IB	55-130		9	6	7500	2	4	9450	10800
29		SINGLE CABIN	HT	CR	MHG		IB	T 55-T 85		9	6	7500	2	4	9500	11200
32			OP	SPTCR	MHG		IB	75-102		10	6	9000	2	5	10300	11800
32			OP	SPTCR	MHG		IB	T 55-T 75		10	6	9000	2	5	10300	11800
32		DOUBLE STATEROOM	OP	DC	MHG		IB	85-130		10	6	9000	2	5	11000	12500
32		DOUBLE STATEROOM	OP	DC	MHG		IB	T 55-T 85		10	6	9000	2	5	11000	12600
32		DOUBLE STATEROOM	HT	DC	MHG		IB	85-130		10	6	9000	2	5	11000	12500
32		DOUBLE STATEROOM	HT	DC	MHG		IB	T 55-T 88		10	6	9000	2	5	11000	12700
32		ENCLOSED	HT	CR	MHG		IB	85-130		10	6	9000	2	5	10300	11800
32		ENCLOSED	HT	CR	MHG		IB	T 55-T 85		10	6	9000	2	5	10400	11900
32		TRIPLE STATEROOM DKH	HT	TCMY	MHG		IB	85-130		10	6	9000	2	5	11000	12500
32		TRIPLE STATEROOM DKH	HT	TCMY	MHG		IB	T 55-T 85		10	6	9000	2	5	11000	12600
35					WD		IB	130	CC						**	**
35		DOUBLE STATEROOM	HT	DC	MHG		IB	85		11		14000	2	8	16000	18200
		IB 110 16100 18300, IB 130 16200 18400, IB T 85													16300	18600
		IB T110 16500 18700, IB T130 16600 18800														
35		ENCLOSED BRIDGE	HT	CR	MHG		IB	85		11		14000	2	8	17000	19300

 CONTINUED ON NEXT PAGE

CHRIS CRAFT BOATS   -CONTINUED   See inside cover to adjust price for area

```
LOA   NAME AND/    TOP/ BOAT  -HULL- ----ENGINE--- BEAM   WGT  DRAFT RETAIL RETAIL
FT IN  OR MODEL    RIG TYPE  MTL TP TP # HP  MFG   FT IN  LBS  FT IN  LOW    HIGH
------------------------ 1937 BOATS ----------------------------------------------
35  ENCLOSED BRIDGE    HT CR   MHG   IB  110      11   14000  2 8  17000  19300
    IB  130    17000  19300, IB T 85     17100  19500, IB T110    17200  19600
    IB T130    17300          19700

35  ENCLOSED DECKHOUSE HT DC   MHG   IB   85      11   14000  2 8  18000  20000
    IB  110    18000  20000, IB  130     18100  20100, IB T 85    18100  20100
    IB T110    18100  20100, IB T130     18200  20300

35  SPORT BRIDGE       OP SPTCR MHG  IB   85      11   14000  2 8  16800  19100
    IB  110    16900  19200, IB  130     16900  19200, IB T 85    17000  19300
    IB T110    17100  19400, IB T130     17200  19500

40                              WD   IB T135  CC                     **     **
40  DOUBLE STATEROOM   HT DC   MHG   IB   85    11 6  17000  2 8  28100  31200
    IB  110    28300  31400, IB  130     28400  31600, IB T 85    29000  32200
    IB T110    29300  32600, IB T130     29600  32900

40  ENCLOSED BRIDGE    HT DC   MHG   IB   85    11 6  17000  2 8  33900  37700
    IB  110    34000  37700, IB  130     34000  37800, IB T 85    34300  38100
    IB T110    34400  38200, IB T130     34500  38400
------------------------ 1936 BOATS ----------------------------------------------
18                              WD   IB   98  CC                     **     **
18  DELUXE             OP RNBT MHG   IB 55- 75  6        1 3   1950   2400
18  DOUBLE COCKPIT     OP RNBT MHG   IB 55- 75  5 10     1 6   2000   2500
18  STANDARD           OP UTL  MHG   IB 55- 75  6        1 3   1950   2400
19                              WD   IB 130  CC                      **     **
19  DOUBLE COCKPIT     OP RNBT MHG   IB 75- 93  6 2      1 6   2350   2750
19  SPECIAL            OP RACE MHG   IB 155     6 2      1 5   2450   2850
21                              WD   IB  90  CC                      **     **
21  DELUXE             OP UTL  MHG   IB 55- 93  6 6      1 4   3400   4150
21  STANDARD           OP UTL  MHG   IB 55      6 6      1 4   3400   4000
22                              WD   IB 125  CC                      **     **
22                     OP UTL  WD    IB       HERC                   **     **

22  CUSTOM             OP RNBT MHG   IB 93-152  6 8      1 10  3850   4700
23 6 SEA-SKIFF UTILITY OP CR   MHG   IB 55- 93  8 1      1 10  5750   6750
23 6 SEMI-ENCLOSED     HT CR   MHG   IB 55- 93  8 1      1 10  5750   6750
24  CLIPPER            HT CR   MHG   IB 55      8 1 3675 1 8   4850   5550
25                              WD   IB 150-300                      **     **
25  CUSTOM             OP RNBT MHG   IB 115-152 6 8      1 11  5600   6650
25  SINGLE CABIN       HT CR   MHG   IB 55- 75  8 1      1 10  5550   6450
25  STREAMLINE         HT CR   MHG   IB 55- 93  8 1      1 10  5550   6550
25  UTILITY            HT CR   MHG   IB 55- 93  8 1      1 10  5550   6550
27  CUSTOM             OP RNBT MHG   IB 250     7 2      2 4   7850   9050
28  ENCLOSED BRIDGE    HT CR   MHG   IB 55-115  9        2 3   8600  10000

28  SINGLE CABIN       HT CR   MHG   IB 55- 93  9        2 3   8600  10000
28  SINGLE CABIN       HT CR   MHG   IB T 55    9        2 3   8800  10000
29                              WD   IB                              **     **
30                     HT SPTCR MHG  IB 55- 92  9  6000 2 2   8500   9900
31                              WD   IB 90-105                       **     **
31                              WD   IB T100  KERM                   **     **
31  DOUBLE STATEROOM   HT DC   MHG   IB 55- 93  10 3     2 5   10200 11600
31  DOUBLE STATEROOM   HT DC   MHG   IB T 55-T 75 10 3   2 5   10200 11700
31  ENCLOSED BRIDGE    HT CR   MHG   IB 55- 93  10 3     2 5   9750  11100
31  ENCLOSED BRIDGE    HT CR   MHG   IB T 55-T 75 10 3   2 5   9750  11300
31  SINGLE CABIN       HT CR   MHG   IB 55- 93  10 3     2 5   9750  11100
31  SINGLE CABIN       HT CR   MHG   IB T 55-T 75 10 3   2 5   9950  11100

36                                   IB  95  CC
38  COMMUTER           OP CR   MHG   IB 250     9  9     2 5   30100 33400
38 2                   HT DC   MHG   IB  92     11 3     2 8   30600 34000
38 2                   HT DC   MHG   IB 108     11 3     2 8   30800 34200
38 2                   HT DC   MHG   IB T 92    11 3     2 8   31500 35000
38 2                   HT SF   MHG   IB  92     11 3     2 8   32000 35600
    IB  108    32100  35600, IB  152    32300  35800, IB 250    32400  36000
    IB T 92    32600  36300, IB T108     32800  36400

38 2 ENCLOSED BRIDGE   HT DC   MHG   IB  92     11 3     2 8   35200 39100
38 2 ENCLOSED BRIDGE   HT DC   MHG   IB 108     11 3     2 8   35100 39000
38 2 ENCLOSED BRIDGE   HT DC   MHG   IB T 92    11 3     2 8   35500 39400
38 2 ENCLOSED SALON    HT CR   MHG   IB  92     11 3     2 8   27600 30600
    IB  108    27600  30700, IB  152    27800  30900, IB T 92   28200  31300

38 2 OWNERS STATEROOM  HT DC   MHG   IB  92     11 3     2 8   31900 35500
38 2 OWNERS STATEROOM  HT DC   MHG   IB 108     11 3     2 8   32100 35600
38 2 OWNERS STATEROOM  HT DC   MHG   IB T 92    11 3     2 8   32700 36300
------------------------ 1935 BOATS ----------------------------------------------
18  DELUXE             OP RNBT MHG   IB  70     5 10 1900 1 6   1750   2100
18  DELUXE             OP RNBT MHG   IB  92     5 10 2000 1 6   1900   2250
18  DELUXE             OP UTL  MHG   IB  70      6   2170 1 3   1800   2150
19  DELUXE             OP RNBT MHG   IB 70- 92  6 2  2135 1 6   2050   2600
21                              WD   IB       CHRY                   **     **
21  DELUXE             OP UTL  MHG   IB 55- 70  6 6  2240 1 4   2550   3150
21  DELUXE             OP UTL  MHG   IB  92     6 6  2450 1 4   2850   3300
21  STANDARD           OP UTL  MHG   IB  55     6 6  2050 1 4   2450   2850
22  CUSTOM             OP RNBT MHG   IB  92     6 8  2525 1 10  3200   3700
22  CUSTOM             OP RNBT MHG   IB 125-150 6 8  2830 1 10  3550   4450
25  STREAMLINE         OP CR   MHG   IB 55- 70  7 9  3675 1 9   4850   5800

25  UTILITY            OP CR   MHG   IB 55- 92  7 9  3475        4650   5800
27  CUSTOM             OP RNBT MHG   IB 250     7 2  4700 2 4   7450   8600
30  DOUBLE STATEROOM   HT DC   MHG   IB 55- 92  9    6200 2 2   7850   9700
------------------------ 1934 BOATS ----------------------------------------------
18                              WD   IB   9  CC                      **     **
18  DELUXE             OP RNBT MHG   IB  67     5 10 1900 1 7   1800   2150
18  DELUXE             OP RNBT MHG   IB  85     5 10 2000 1 7   1950   2250
21                     OP UTL  MHG   IB 55- 85  6 6       1 5   3700   4450
21  CUSTOM             OP RNBT MHG   IB  85     6 6  2500 1 9   3000   3500
21  CUSTOM             OP RNBT MHG   IB 125     6 5  2800 1 10  3400   3950
24                     HT CR   MHG   IB 55- 85  7 9  3600 1 10  5000   5750
25                     HT UTL  MHG   IB 55- 85  7 9  3600 1 10  5000   5900
25  CUSTOM             OP RNBT MHG   IB 125-150 6 8  3800 1 11  5400   6550
26                              WD   IB 350  CC                      **     **
27                              WD   IB 330  MRCR                    **     **

27  CUSTOM             OP RNBT MHG   IB 250     7 2  4700 2 4   7800   8950
27  CUSTOM             OP RNBT MHG   IB 425     7 2  4700 2 4   9000  10200
30  DOUBLE STATEROOM   HT DC   MHG   IB 55- 85  9    6000 2 2   8850  10600
30  DOUBLE STATEROOM   HT DC   MHG   IB T 55    9    6700 2 2   9550  10800
31                     HT CR   MHG   IB  80               2     9950  11300
36                     HT CR   MHG   IB 106               2     24000 26600
38                     HT CR   MHG   IB 250               2     26800 29300
------------------------ 1933 BOATS ----------------------------------------------
22                     OP RNBT MHG   IB  82     6        1 10  4150   4800
22  CADET              OP RNBT MHG   IB 100     6        1 10  4200   4900
24                     OP RNBT MHG   IB 120     6  4     1 10  6600   7650
26                     OP RNBT MHG   IB 120-200 6 8      2     6950   8250
26                     OP SDN  MHG   IB 150-200 6 8      2     8100   9700
26  HYDROPLANE         OP SPTCR MHG  IB 200     6 8      2     7900   9100
30  COMMUTER           OP CR   MHG   IB 200     7 1      2 3   10800 12200
30  CUSTOM             OP RNBT MHG   IB 200     7 1      2 3   10600 12000
31  SINGLE CABIN       HT CR   MHG   IB  80     9 9      2 7   9950  11300
34  COMMUTER           HT CR   MHG   IB T200    9 9      2 8   18000 18000
36  SINGLE CABIN       HT CR   MHG   IB 106     10 8     2 8   26700 29700
38  COMMUTING          HT CR   MHG   IB 250     9 9      2 7   33400 37100
------------------------ 1932 BOATS ----------------------------------------------
17  STANDARD           OP RNBT MHG   IB  41  D  5 7      1 5   2050   2450
18                              WD   IB  60  CC                      **     **
18                              WD   IB 115  CC                      **     **
18  DELUXE             OP RNBT MHG   IB  85     5 10 2000 1 7   2150   2500
18  STANDARD           OP RNBT MHG   IB  85     5 10 1850 1 7   1900   2250
21                              WD   IB 150  PALM                    **     **
21  CUSTOM             OP RNBT MHG   IB 125     6 5  2800 1 10  3750   4350
21  DELUXE             OP RNBT MHG   IB  85     6 5  2500 1 9   3300   3850
21  STANDARD           OP RNBT MHG   IB  85     6 5  2500 1 9   3300   3850
22                              WD   IB  80  CHRY                    **     **
22                              WD   IB 300  CHRY                    **     **
22  STANDARD           OP RNBT MHG   IB  82     6        1 10  4400   5050

24  STANDARD           OP RNBT MHG   IB 120     6 4      1 10  6950   8000
25                              WD   IB 160  GRAY                    **     **
25  CUSTOM             OP RNBT MHG   IB 125-150 6 8  3800 1 11  5850   7200
25  CUSTOM             OP RNBT MHG   IB 200     6 8  4100 2     6550   7550
26  CUSTOM             OP RNBT MHG   IB 200-250 6 8      2     7800   9200
26  CUSTOM CONVERTIBLE HT SDN  MHG   IB 200-250 6 8      2     10500 12200
26  STANDARD           OP RNBT MHG   IB 120     6 8      2     7300   8350
26  STANDARD           OP RNBT MHG   IB 150     6 8      2     8500   9750
27  CUSTOM             OP RNBT MHG   IB 250     7 2  4700 2 4   8500   9800
28  CUSTOM             OP RNBT MHG   IB 200     7 2      2 3   11400 11900
30  CUSTOM             OP SDN  MHG   IB 200     7 1      2 2   11700 13300
31  SINGLE CABIN       HT CR   MHG   IB 200               2     10100 11500

34  COMMUTER           HT CR   MHG   IB T200    8 5      2 8   15900 18100
36  SINGLE CABIN       HT CR   MHG   IB         10 8     2 8    **     **
```

CHRIS CRAFT BOATS   -CONTINUED   See inside cover to adjust price for area

LOA FT IN	NAME AND/ OR MODEL	TOP/ RIG	BOAT TYPE	-HULL- MTL TP	TP	----ENGINE--- # HP MFG	BEAM FT IN	WGT LBS	DRAFT FT IN	RETAIL LOW	RETAIL HIGH
------------------ 1932 BOATS -------------------
38	COMMUTING	HT	CR	MHG	IB	250	9 9		2 7	34400	38200
------------------ 1931 BOATS -------------------
18				WD	IB	65-115				**	**
18	DELUXE	OP	RNBT	MHG	IB	85	5 10			2650	3100
18	STANDARD	OP	RNBT	MHG	IB	63	5 10			2600	3000
20				WD	IB	75 CHRY				**	**
22	STANDARD	OP	RNBT	MHG	IB	75	6		1 7	3300	3800
22	STANDARD	OP	RNBT	MHG	IB	75-125	6		1 10	4600	5500
24	DELUXE	HT	SDN	MHG	IB	125	6 4		1 10	7350	8450
24	STANDARD	OP	RNBT	MHG	IB	125-150	6 4		1 10	7350	8550
26				WD	IB	CC				**	**
26					IB	250 CC				**	**
26				WD	IB	300 CHRY				**	**
26	CONVERTIBLE	HT	SDN	MHG	IB	200	6 8		2	9400	10700
26	STANDARD	OP	RNBT	MHG	IB	125-200	6 8		2	7700	9400
27				WD	IB	125 CC				**	**
28				WD	IB	250 CC				**	**
28	ALL-WOOD	HT	SDN	MHG	IB	250	7		65	11900	13600
28	CUSTOM	OP	RNBT	MHG	IB	250	7		2 3	11200	12700
28	CUSTOM CONVERTIBLE	HT	SDN	MHG	IB	200-250	7		2 3	11700	13400
30	CUSTOM	OP	RNBT	MHG	IB		7		65	**	**
31	DELUXE	HT	DC	MHG	IB	70	9 9		2 5	11300	12800
31	DELUXE SINGLE CAB	HT	CR	MHG	IB	70	9 9		2 5	11300	12800
31	STANDARD	HT	DC	MHG	IB	70	9 9		2 5	9550	10900
31	STANDARD SINGLE CAB	HT	CR	MHG	IB	70	9 9		2 5	9150	10400
34	COMMUTER	HT	CR	MHG	IB	T200	8 5		2 2	16200	18400
36	CUSTOM SINGLE CAB	HT	CR	MHG	IB	250	10 8		3	28600	31800
36	DELUXE SINGLE CAB	HT	CR	MHG	IB	70	10 8		3	28200	31300
36	DELUXE SINGLE CAB	HT	CR	MHG	IB	106	10 8		3	28300	31500
36	ENCLOSED BRIDGE	HT	DC	MHG	IB	70	10 8		3	30400	33800
36	ENCLOSED BRIDGE	HT	DC	MHG	IB	106	10 8		3	30500	33900
36	OPEN BRIDGE	HT	DC	MHG	IB	70	10 8		3	26900	29900
36	OPEN BRIDGE	HT	DC	MHG	IB	106	10 8		3	27100	30100
38	COMMUTING	HT	CR	MHG	IB	250	9 9		2 7	35500	39500
48	CUSTOM	HT	MY	MHG	IB	T250	11 6		2 8	73600	80900
------------------ 1930 BOATS -------------------
17				WD	IB					**	**
18				WD	IB	40 GRAY				**	**
20		OP	RNBT	MHG	IB	75	6			3450	4000
22		OP	RNBT	MHG	IB	75-125	6			4800	5800
24				WD	IB	225 CHRY				**	**
24		OP	RNBT	MHG	IB	125	6 4			7750	8900
24		HT	SDN	MHG	IB	125	6 4			7750	8900
26				WD	IB	225-375				**	**
26		OP	RNBT	MHG	IB	125-200	6 8			8100	9900
26		OP	RNBT	MHG	IB	250 CC	6 8			8950	10200
26	CONVERTIBLE	HT	SDN	MHG	IB	200-250	6 8			9950	11700
26	DELUXE	HT	SDN	MHG	IB	155-250	6 8			9500	11500
28				WD	IB	250 CC				**	**
28	CONVERTIBLE	HT	SDN	MHG	IB	200-250	7			11800	13600
28	CUSTOM	OP	RNBT	MHG	IB	200-250	7			11400	13300
28	MAHOGANY CABIN	HT	SDN	MHG	IB	200	7			12200	13800
28	MAHOGNY CABIN	HT	SDN	MHG	IB	250 CC	7			12400	14000
30	CUSTOM	OP	RNBT	MHG	IB	250 CC	7 1			12100	13700
34	COMMUTER	HT	CR	MHG	IB	T200	8 5			16600	18900
38				WD	IB	300				**	**
38	COMMUTING	HT	CR	MHG	IB	250 CC	9 9			36800	40900
48		HT	MY	MHG	IB	T250 CC	11 6			76300	83800
------------------ 1929 BOATS -------------------
20				WD	IB	95 CHRY				**	**
22				WD	IB	85-106				**	**
22		OP	RNBT	MHG	IB	82-106	6	2790	1 10	4300	5150
24				WD	IB	CHRY				**	**
24				WD	IB	145-225				**	**
24		OP	RNBT	MHG	IB	106 CHRY	6 4	3100	1 10	5550	6400
24		HT	SDN	MHG	IB	106 CHRY	6 4	3275	1 10	5800	6650
26				WD	IB	130-275				**	**
26				WD	IB	300-360				**	**
26		OP	RNBT	MHG	IB	106 CHRY	6 8	3470	2	6650	7650
26		OP	RNBT	MHG	IB	200-225	6 8	3835	2	7850	9350
26		HT	SDN	MHG	IB	200-225	6 8	4120	2	9200	10500
26	DELUXE CABIN	HT	SDN	MHG	IB	200-225	6 8	4035	2	9100	10700
28				WD	IB					**	**
	IB CC **	**	, IB	115	CHRY	** ** , IB	225-275			12500	14300
28		OP	RNBT	MHG	IB	225 CC	7	4200	2 3	9350	10600
28		HT	SDN	MHG	IB	200 KERM	7	4225	2	9450	10800
28	CUSTOM	OP	RNBT	MHG	IB	200 KERM	7	4025	2 3	10300	10300
28	DELUXE CABIN	HT	SDN	MHG	IB	225 CC	7	4400	2 3	9850	11200
30	COMMUTER	HT	CR	MHG	IB	225 CC	7 4	4635	2 3	8450	9700
30	CUSTOM	OP	RNBT	MHG	IB	225 CC	7 4	4135	2 2	7950	9100
38				WD	IB	T400				**	**
38				WD	IB	200 CC				**	**
38		HT	SDN	MHG	IB	T115				38700	43000
38	COMMUTING	HT	CR	MHG	IB	225 CC	9 9	10200	2 10	30300	33700
------------------ 1928 BOATS -------------------
22				WD	IB					**	**
22				WD	IB	82-150				**	**
24				WD	IB	115-325				**	**
26				WD	IB					**	**
26				WD	IB	175-210				**	**
------------------ 1927 BOATS -------------------
22				WD	IB	85-185				**	**
26				WD	IB	141-275				**	**
------------------ 1926 BOATS -------------------
22				WD	IB	90 CHRY				**	**
26				WD	IB	GRAY				**	**
26				WD	IB	150-225				**	**
------------------ 1922 BOATS -------------------
18				WD	IB	CC				**	**

CHRISBANK CORP
HOLIDAY BOATS

Call 1-800-327-6929 for BUC Personalized Evaluation Service
Or, for 1959 to 1961 boats, sign onto www.BUCValuPro.com

CHRISIDON MARINE LTD
COAST GUARD MFG ID- CDD

Call 1-800-327-6929 for BUC Personalized Evaluation Service
Or, for 1977 boats, sign onto www.BUCValuPro.com

CHRISTENSEN YACHT CORP
WESTPORT CT 06880   See inside cover to adjust price for area

LOA FT IN	NAME AND/ OR MODEL	TOP/ RIG	BOAT TYPE	-HULL- MTL TP	TP	----ENGINE--- # HP MFG	BEAM FT IN	WGT LBS	DRAFT FT IN	RETAIL LOW	RETAIL HIGH
------------------ 1973 BOATS -------------------
21	X21		SAIL	FBG	OB		6 6	2400	3 6	3850	4500

HANS CHRISTIAN YACHTS AMERICA
ANNAPOLIS MD 21403-2524   See inside cover to adjust price for area

For more recent years, see the BUC Used Boat Price Guide, Volume 1 or Volume 2

LOA FT IN	NAME AND/ OR MODEL	TOP/ RIG	BOAT TYPE	-HULL- MTL TP	TP	----ENGINE--- # HP MFG	BEAM FT IN	WGT LBS	DRAFT FT IN	RETAIL LOW	RETAIL HIGH
------------------ 1983 BOATS -------------------
32 9	HANS-CHRISTIAN 33	CUT	SA/CR	FBG KL	IB	D	11 6	18000	5 6	61800	67900
32 9	HANSA 33	CUT	SA/CR	FBG KL	IB	D	11 6	17900	5 6	61500	67600
37 9	HANS-CHRISTIAN MKII	CUT	SA/CR	FBG KL	IB	D	12 6	27500	6	88600	97400
38	HANS-CHRISTIAN 38T	CUT	SA/CR	FBG KL	IB	D	12 4	26500	6	86300	94900
38 6	HANS-CHRISTIAN 39PH	CUT	SA/CR	FBG KL	IB	D	12 6	31500	6	104000	114500
42 6	HANS-CHRISTIAN 43T	CUT	SA/CR	FBG KL	IB	D	13	31500	6	108000	118500
42 7	HANS-CHRISTIAN 43T	KTH	SA/CR	FBG KL	IB	D	13	31500	6	108000	118500
43 9	HANSA 44PH	CUT	SA/CR	FBG KL	IB	D	14 7	44000	5 8	154500	169500
47 10	HANS-CHRISTIAN 48T	CUT	SA/CR	FBG KL	IB	110D YAN	14 3	44000	6	153500	168500
47 10	HANS-CHRISTIAN 48T	KTH	SA/CR	FBG KL	IB	110D YAN	14 3	44000	6	153500	168500
------------------ 1982 BOATS -------------------
32 9	HANS-CHRISTIAN 33	CUT	SA/CR	FBG KL	IB	35D VLVO	11 6	17900	5 6	58300	64100
37 9	HANS-CHRISTIAN MK II	CUT	SA/CR	FBG KL	IB	60D ISUZ	12 6	27500	6	83400	91600
38	HANS-CHRISTIAN 38T	CUT	SA/CR	FBG KL	IB	60D ISUZ	12 4	26500	6	81200	89300
38 6	HANS-CHRISTIAN 39 PH	CUT	SA/CR	FBG KL	IB	60D ISUZ	12 6	28000	6	97900	107500
42 7	HANS-CHRISTIAN 43T	CUT	SA/CR	FBG KL	IB	60D ISUZ	13	31500	6	101000	111000
42 7	HANS-CHRISTIAN 43T	KTH	SA/CR	FBG KL	IB	60D ISUZ	13	31500	6	101000	111000

LOA FT	IN	NAME AND/ OR MODEL	TOP/ RIG	BOAT TYPE	-HULL- MTL	TP	ENGINE TP	# HP	MFG	BEAM FT	IN	WGT LBS	DRAFT FT	IN	RETAIL LOW	RETAIL HIGH
		1982 BOATS														
42	7	HANS-CHRISTIAN MK II	CUT	SA/CR	FBG	KL	IB	60D	ISUZ	13		30000	6		98400	108000
42	7	HANS-CHRISTIAN MK II	KTH	SA/CR	FBG	KL	IB	60D	ISUZ	13		30000	6	2	98500	108000
43	9	HANS-CHRISTIAN 44 PH	KTH	SA/CR	FBG	KL	IB	120D	ISUZ	14	7	44000	5	8	145500	159500
		1981 BOATS														
32	9	HANS-CHRISTIAN 33	CUT	SA/CR	FBG	KL	IB	35D	VLVO	11	6	17900	5	6	55200	60700
37	9	HANS-CHRISTIAN MK II	CUT	SA/CR	FBG	KL	IB	60D	ISUZ	12	6	27500	6		79000	86800
38		HANS-CHRISTIAN 38T	CUT	SA/CR	FBG	KL	IB	60D	ISUZ	12	4	26500	6		77000	84600
38	6	HANS-CHRISTIAN 39 PH	CUT	SA/CR	FBG	KL	IB	60D	ISUZ	12	6	28000	6		92800	102000
42	7	HANS-CHRISTIAN 43T	CUT	SA/CR	FBG	KL	IB	60D	ISUZ	13		31500	6		95900	105500
42	7	HANS-CHRISTIAN 43T	KTH	SA/CR	FBG	KL	IB	60D	ISUZ	13		31500	6		95900	105500
42	7	HANS-CHRISTIAN MK II	CUT	SA/CR	FBG	KL	IB	60D	ISUZ	13		30000	6	2	93300	102500
42	7	HANS-CHRISTIAN ML II	KTH	SA/CR	FBG	KL	IB	60D	ISUZ	13		30000	6	2	93300	102500
43	9	HANS-CHRISTIAN 44 PH	KTH	SA/CR	FBG	KL	IB	120D	ISUZ	14	7	44000	5	8	137500	151500
		1980 BOATS														
16	7	B-J 17	GAF	SAIL	FBG	CB				4	8	380			1800	2150
20	6	WILDERNESS 21	SLP	SA/CR	FBG	KL				7	3	1870	4		4500	5150
26	9	FOX 25	SLP	SA/CR	FBG	KL				8		5000	3	1	12200	13900
29	6	WILDERNESS 30	SLP	SA/CR	FBG	KL	IB	16D	REN	9	5	8420	4	5	25000	27800
32	9	HANS-CHRISTIAN 33	CUT	SA/CR	FBG	KL	IB	35D	VLVO	11	6	17900	5	6	53200	58400
34		HANS-CHRISTIAN 34T	CUT	SA/CR	FBG	KL	IB	D		11		19400	5	10	56800	62400
37	9	HANS-CHRISTIAN 38 PH	KTH	SA/CR	FBG	KL	IB	D		12	6	27500	6		88100	96800
37	9	HANS-CHRISTIAN MK II	CUT	SA/CR	FBG	KL	IB	50D	VW	12	6	27500	6		76400	84000
37	9	HANS-CHRISTIAN MK II	KTH	SA/CR	FBG	KL	IB	D		13		29000	6	2	79800	87700
38		HANS-CHRISTIAN 38T	CUT	SA/CR	FBG	KL	IB	50D	VW	12	4	26500	6		74500	81900
38		HANS-CHRISTIAN 38T	KTH	SA/CR	FBG	KL	IB	D		12	4	26500	6		74600	82000
42	7	HANS-CHRISTIAN 43T	CUT	SA/CR	FBG	KL	IB	50D	NISS	13		31500	6		92800	102000
42	7	HANS-CHRISTIAN MK II	CUT	SA/CR	FBG	KL	IB	50D	NISS	13		29000	6	2	88600	97400
42	9	HANS-CHRISTIAN 43 PH	KTH	SA/CR	FBG	KL	IB	50D	PERK	14	6	38000	5	6	118500	130500
		1979 BOATS														
27	9	CHOATE 27	SLP	SA/RC	F/S	KL	OB			9	5	4000	5	4	10600	12000
27	9	CHOATE 27	SLP	SA/RC	F/S	KL	IB	7D	WEST	9	5	4000	5	4	11100	12600
33	2	CHOATE 33	SLP	SA/RC	F/S	KL	SD	12D	YAN	10	10	9330	5	10	27200	30200
34		HANS-CHRISTIAN 34	CUT	SA/CR	FBG	KL	SD	35D	VLVO	11		19400	5	10	54900	60400
36	3	WINDWARD-PASSAGE 36	KTH	SA/CR	F/S	KL	SD	70D	CHRY	11	4	20000	5		56700	62300
38		HANS-CHRISTIAN 38	CUT	SA/CR	FBG	KL	SD	70D	CHRY	12	4	26500	5	10	72400	79600
38		HANS-CHRISTIAN 38-2	CUT	SA/CR	FBG	KL	SD	70D	CHRY	13		27500	6		74500	81800
38		WINDWARD-PASSAGE 38	CUT	SA/CR	F/S	KL	SD	70D	CHRY	11	4	20000	5		58400	64200
38	8	CHOATE 39	SLP	SA/RC	F/S	KL	SD	20D	YAN	12	5	14000	6	6	44600	49500
40	8	CHOATE 41	SLP	SA/RC	F/S	KL	SD	25D	YAN	13	8	16000	7	2	54900	60400
42	7	HANS-CHRISTIAN 43	CUT	SA/CR	FBG	KL	SD	70D	CHRY	13		32000	6		91100	100000
48	2	CHOATE 48	SLP	SA/RC	F/S	KL	SD	50D	YAN	14		30000	9		112000	123000

CHRYSLER CORPORATION

MARINE PRODUCTS GROUP
DETROIT MI 48288 COAST GUARD MFG ID- CBC

See inside cover to adjust price for area

LOA FT	IN	NAME AND/ OR MODEL	TOP/ RIG	BOAT TYPE	-HULL- MTL	TP	ENGINE TP	# HP	MFG	BEAM FT	IN	WGT LBS	DRAFT FT	IN	RETAIL LOW	RETAIL HIGH
		1979 BOATS														
20		CHRYSLER 20	SLP	SA/OD	FBG	SK	OB			7	11	2200	1	11	2750	3200
22		CHRYSLER 22	SLP	SAIL	FBG	SK	OB			7	9	3000	1	11	3250	3800
22		CHRYSLER 22 POP TOP	SLP	SAIL	FBG	SK	OB			7	9	3000	1	11	3350	3900
22	3	CV 223	ST	CBNCR	FBG	DV	IO	195-265		8		3700			6450	7750
26		CHRYSLER 26	SLP	SAIL	FBG	KL	OB			8		5500	3	11	6350	7300
26		CHRYSLER 26	SLP	SAIL	FBG	KL	SD	8D		8		5500	3	11	6650	7650
26		CHRYSLER 26	SLP	SAIL	FBG	SK	OB			8		5000	2	3	5750	6600
26		CHRYSLER 26	SLP	SAIL	FBG	SK	SD	8D		8		5000	2	3	6100	7000
29	11	CHRYSLER 30	SLP	SA/CR	FBG	KL	IB			11		9800	4	11	12500	14200
		1978 BOATS														
16	2	SPORT-FURY B/R	ST	RNBT	FBG	TR	IO	140	VLVO	6	4	950			1950	2350
17	3	CONQUEROR 140	OP	RNBT	FBG	SV	IO	140-240		7	1	1100			2500	2900
17	3	COURIER 231	ST	RNBT	FBG	SV	IO	140-165		7	3	1400			2700	3100
18	2	SPORT-CROWN B/R	ST	RNBT	FBG	TR	IO	140-195		7		1350			2800	3250
18	6	CONQUEROR S-III	OP	RNBT	FBG	SV	IO	195-240		7	8	1157			2900	3500
18	6	CONQUEROR S-III	OP	RNBT	FBG	SV	IO	265	CHRY	7	8	1157			3150	3650
20		CHRYSLER 20	SLP	SA/OD	FBG	SK	OB			7	11	2400	1	11	2800	3250
20		COURIER 300	ST	RNBT	FBG	SV	IO	140-265		7	5	1800			3350	4100
21		CONQUEROR 21	ST	RNBT	FBG	SV	IO	195-265		8		1750			3600	4500
22		CHRYSLER 22	SLP	SAIL	FBG	KL	OB			7	9	3000	3	9	3200	3750
22		CHRYSLER 22	SLP	SAIL	FBG	SK	OB			7	9	3000	1	11	3150	3650
22		CHRYSLER 22 POP TOP	SLP	SAIL	FBG	SK	OB			7	9	3000	1	11	3250	3800
22	3	CV-223	ST	CBNCR	FBG	DV	IO	140-265		8		4000			6850	8250
22	3	CV-223	ST	CBNCR	FBG	DV	IO	T140		8		4000			7650	8800
22	3	CV-233	ST	CBNCR	FBG	DV	IO	195	CHRY	8		4000			6900	7900
22	3	CV-250	ST	CBNCR	FBG	DV	IO	140-165		8		4000			6850	7850
22	3	CV-250	ST	CBNCR	FBG	DV	IO	T140		8		4000			7650	8800
25		CV-250	ST	CBNCR	FBG	DV	IO	195-265		8		5088			10200	12000
25		CV-250	ST	CBNCR	FBG	DV	IO	T140	VLVO	8		5088			11200	12800
26		CHRYSLER 26	SLP	SAIL	FBG	KL	OB			8		5500	3	11	6100	7050
26		CHRYSLER 26	SLP	SAIL	FBG	KL	IB	8D	YAN	8		5500	3	11	6450	7400
26		CHRYSLER 26	SLP	SAIL	FBG	SK	OB			8		5000	2	3	5550	6400
26		CHRYSLER 26	SLP	SAIL	FBG	SK	IB	8D	YAN	8		5000	2	3	5900	6750
		1977 BOATS														
16	2	SPORT-FURY B/R	ST	RNBT	FBG	TR	IO	140	VLVO	6	4	850			1950	2300
17	3	CONQUEROR 135	OP	RNBT	FBG	DV	IO	140-195		7	1	1100			2550	2950
		JT 240 CHRY 3000 3500, IO 240 CHRY 2550 2950, JT 265 CHRY 3000 3500														
17	3	COURIER 231	ST	RNBT	FBG	*	IO	140	VLVO	7	3	1400			2700	3150
17	3	COURIER 231	ST	RNBT	FBG	SV	IO	165	MRCR	7	3	1400			2600	3000
18	2	SPORT-CROWN B/R	ST	RNBT	FBG	TR	IO	140-195		7		1300			2800	3250
18	3	CONQUEROR S-III	OP	RNBT	FBG	DV	IO	195-240		7	8	1157			2850	3450
18	3	CONQUEROR S-III	OP	RNBT	FBG	DV	JT	265	CHRY	7	8	1157			3450	4000
18	3	CONQUEROR S-III	OP	RNBT	FBG	DV	IO	265	CHRY	7	8	1157			3100	3600
20		CARVEL III	OP	CUD	FBG	SV	IO	195-265		7	5	2100			3650	4550
20		CARVEL III	HT	CUD	FBG	SV	IO	195-265		7	5	2100			3650	4550
20		COURIER 300	ST	RNBT	FBG	SV	IO	140-265		7	5	1840			3450	4150
21		CONQUEROR 21	ST	RNBT	FBG	DV	IO	195-240		8		1750			3650	4400
21		CONQUEROR 21	ST	RNBT	FBG	DV	JT	265	CHRY	8		1750			4300	5000
21		CONQUEROR 21	ST	RNBT	FBG	DV	IO	265	CHRY	8		1750			3900	4550
21	7	CHRYSLER 22	SLP	SAIL	FBG	KL	OB			7	9	3000	3	9	3100	3600
21	7	CHRYSLER 22	SLP	SAIL	FBG	SK	OB			7	9	3000	1	11	3100	3600
23		C-486	ST	CR	FBG	SV	IO	195-265		8		2885			5250	6350
23		C-486	ST	CR	FBG	SV	IO	T140	VLVO	8		2885			6300	7250
23		C-486	HT	CR	FBG	SV	IO	195-265		8		2885			5250	6350
23		C-486	HT	CR	FBG	SV	IO	T140	VLVO	8		2885			6300	7250
26		CHRYSLER 26	SLP	SAIL	FBG	SK	OB			8		5000	2	3	5350	6150
26		CHRYSLER 26	SLP	SAIL	FBG	SK	IB	8D	YAN	8		5000	2	3	5700	6550
		1976 BOATS														
16	2	SPORT-FURY B/R	OP	RNBT	FBG	TR	IO	130	VLVO	6	4				2500	2950
17	3	CONQUEROR 135	OP	RNBT	FBG	DV	IO	170-195							2900	3350
17	3	CONQUEROR 135	OP	RNBT	FBG	DV	JT	240	CHRY						3150	3650
17	3	CONQUEROR 135	OP	RNBT	FBG	DV	IO	240	CHRY						2900	3350
17	3	COURIER 231 B/R	ST	RNBT	FBG	SV	IO	165-170							2700	3350
18	2	SPORT-CROWN B/R	OP	RNBT	FBG	TR	IO	170-195		7					2950	3400
18	6	CONQUEROR S-III	OP	RNBT	FBG	DV	JT	265	CHRY						3550	4100
18	6	CONQUEROR S-III	OP	RNBT	FBG	DV	IO	265	CHRY						3400	3950
20		CARVEL III	OP	CUD	FBG	SV	IO	170-240							3850	4500
20		CARVEL III	HT	CUD	FBG	SV	IO	170-240							3850	4500
20		COURIER 300 B/R	ST	RNBT	FBG	SV	IO	195-240							3400	4100
21		CONQUEROR 21	OP	RNBT	FBG	DV	IO	195-240		8					3750	4500
21		CONQUEROR 21	OP	RNBT	FBG	DV	JT	265	CHRY	8					4100	4800
21		CONQUEROR 21	OP	RNBT	FBG	DV	IO	265	CHRY	8					4000	4650
22		CHRYSLER 22	SLP	SAIL	FBG	KL	OB			7	9	3000			3000	3500
22		CHRYSLER 22	SLP	SAIL	FBG	SK	OB			7	9	3000			3000	3500
23		C-486	HT	CR	FBG	SV	IO	265	CHRY						5900	6800
23		C-486	HT	CR	FBG	SV	IO	T130	VLVO						6700	7700
23		C-486	FB	CR	FBG	DV	IO	T130	VLVO						6700	7700
23		C-486	FB	CR	FBG	SV	IO	265	CHRY	8					5900	6800
23		COMMANDO 486	OP	SF	FBG	SV	IO	170-265		8					7100	8300
23		COMMANDO 486	OP	SF	FBG	SV	IO	T130	VLVO						8150	9350
		1975 BOATS														
16	2	SPORT-FURY B/R	ST	RNBT	FBG	TR	IO	130	VLVO	6	4	1491		11	2500	2950
16	4	CHARGER 186	ST	RNBT	FBG	DV	IO	130-170		6	10	1806	1		2900	3450
17		COURIER 231 W/T	ST	RNBT	FBG	DV	IO	130-170		7	3	2041	1	1	3250	3900
17	3	CONQUEROR 135	OP	RNBT	FBG	DV	IO	155-225		7	1	1900	1		3000	3700
18		SPORT-CROWN B/R	ST	RNBT	FBG	TR	IO	130-170		7		1941		11	3300	3950
18	6	CONQUEROR S-III	OP	RNBT	FBG	DV	JT	250	CHRY	7	8	2150	1	2	3750	4350
18	6	CONQUEROR S-III	OP	RNBT	FBG	DV	IO	250	CHRY	7	8	2150	1	2	3850	4450
20		CARVEL III	OP	CUD	FBG	DV	IO	170-225		7	5	2100	1	1	4000	4650
21	7	CHRYSLER 22	SLP	SAIL	FBG	SK	OB			7	9	2650	4	6	2650	3100
23		C-486	OP	CR	FBG	DV	IO	250	CHRY	8		3835			6950	7950
23		C-486	OP	CR	FBG	DV	IO	T130	VLVO	8		3975			8000	9200
23		COMMANDO 486	OP	SF	FBG	DV	IO	170	VLVO	8		2987	1	3	6650	7650
23		COMMANDO 486	OP	SF	FBG	DV	IO	250	CHRY	8		3975	1	3	8100	9300
		1974 BOATS														
16	2	SPORT-FURY B/R	OP	RNBT	FBG		IO	130	CHRY	6	4				2500	2900
16	4	CHARGER 186	OP	RNBT	FBG		IO	130-170		6	10				2650	3100
17		COURIER 231	ST	RNBT	FBG		IO	130-170		7	3				2850	3350
18		SPORT-CROWN B/R	ST	RNBT	FBG		IO	130-170		7					2900	3400
18	6	CONQUEROR S-III	OP	RNBT	FBG		JT	250	CHRY	7	8				3250	3800

 CONTINUED ON NEXT PAGE

LOA FT	LOA IN	NAME AND/ OR MODEL	TOP/ RIG	BOAT TYPE	HULL MTL	HULL TP	ENGINE TP	ENGINE # HP	ENGINE MFG	BEAM FT	BEAM IN	WGT LBS	DRAFT FT	DRAFT IN	RETAIL LOW	RETAIL HIGH
		1974 BOATS														
18	6	CONQUEROR S-III	OP	RNBT	FBG		IO	250	CHRY	7	8				3550	4150
20		CARVEL III	OP	CUD	FBG		IO	155-225		7	5				3950	4700
23		C-486	ST	CR	FBG		IO	250	CHRY	8					6200	7150
23		C-486	ST	CR	FBG		IO	T130	CHRY	8					6800	7800
		1973 BOATS														
16	2	SPORT-FURY B/R	OP	RNBT	FBG		IO	130	CHRY	6	4				2600	3000
16	4	CHARGER 186	OP	RNBT	FBG		IO	130-170		6	10				2750	3200
17		COURIER 231	ST	RNBT	FBG		IO	130-170		7	3				2950	3450
18		CROWN	ST	RNBT	FBG		IO	130-170		7					3000	3500
18		SPORT-CROWN B/R	ST	RNBT	FBG		IO	130-170		7					2950	3550
18	6	CONQUEROR S-III	OP	RNBT	FBG		JT	275	CHRY	7	8				3150	3650
18	6	CONQUEROR S-III	OP	RNBT	FBG		IO	275	CHRY	7	8				3850	4450
20		CARVEL II	OP	CUD	FBG		IO	155-225		7	5				3950	4900
20		CARVEL III	OP	CUD	FBG		IO	155-235		7	5				4150	4900
23		C-486	ST	CR	FBG		IO	235	CHRY	8					6350	7300
23		C-486	ST	CR	FBG		IO	T130	CHRY	8					7000	8050
23		COMMODORE II	OP	SPTCR	FBG		IO	225	CHRY	8					6400	7350
		1972 BOATS														
16	2	FURY DELUXE	OP	RNBT	FBG		IO	130	CHRY	6	4	655			1900	2300
16	2	SPORT-FURY DLX B/R	OP	RNBT	FBG		IO	130	CHRY	6	4	680			1950	2300
16	4	CHARGER 186	OP	RNBT	FBG		IO	130-170		6	10	1065			2400	2850
17		COURIER 231	ST	RNBT	FBG		IO	130-170		7	3	1270			2850	3350
18		CROWN DELUXE	ST	RNBT	FBG		IO	130-170		7		1344			3050	3600
18		SPORT-CROWN DLX B/R	ST	RNBT	FBG		IO	130-170		7		1224			3000	3550
20		CARVEL 300	OP	CR	FBG		IO	130-200		7	5	2030			4100	4900
23		CLIPPER 486	OP	CR	FBG		IO	200-260		8		2400			5650	6750
23		CLIPPER 486	OP	CR	FBG		IO	T130	CHRY	8		2400			6450	7400
23		COMMODORE II 486	OP	SPTCR	FBG		IO	200-260		8		2970			6300	7500
23		COMMODORE II 486	OP	SPTCR	FBG		IO	T130	CHRY	8		2970			7100	8150
24		CRUISE-LINER III	OP	CR	AL		IO	130-165		8					6700	7750
		1971 BOATS														
16		CHARGER 183	ST	RNBT	FBG		IO	130-160		6	10	880			2250	2650
16	2	FURY DELUXE	OP	RNBT	FBG		IO	82-130		6	4	655			2050	2450
16	2	FURY STD	OP	RNBT	FBG		IO	82-130		6	4	655			2000	2400
16	2	SPORT-FURY B/R	OP	RNBT	FBG		IO	82-130		6	4	680			1900	2350
16	2	SPORT-FURY DLX B/R	OP	RNBT	FBG		IO	82-130		6	4	680			2100	2500
17		COURIER 231	ST	RNBT	FBG		IO	130-170		7	3	1270			2950	3450
18		CROWN	ST	RNBT	FBG		IO	130-170		7		1344			3150	3700
18		CROWN DELUXE	ST	RNBT	FBG		IO	130-170		7		1344			3200	3750
18		SPORT-CROWN B/R	ST	RNBT	FBG		IO	130-170		7		1224			3050	3600
18		SPORT-CROWN DLX B/R	ST	RNBT	FBG		IO	130-170		7		1224			3150	3700
20		CARVEL 300	OP	CR	FBG		IO	130-200		7	5	2030			4250	5050
23		CLIPPER 486	OP	CR	FBG		IO	200-235		8		2400			5800	6800
23		CLIPPER 486	OP	CR	FBG		IO	T120-T130		8		2400			6650	7650
23		COMMODORE II 486	OP	SPTCR	FBG		IO	200-235		8		2970			6500	7600
23		COMMODORE II 486	OP	SPTCR	FBG		IO	T120-T130		8		2970			7350	8450
24		CRUISE-LINER III	OP	CR	AL		IO	130-165		8		2000			5700	6550
24		CRUISE-LINER III	OP	CR	AL		IO	T 82	CHRY	8		2000			6600	7600
		1970 BOATS														
16		CHARGER 183	ST	RNBT	FBG	TR	IO	120-160		6	10	1049			2450	2900
16	2	FURY	OP	RNBT	FBG	TR	IO	82-130		6	4	655			1950	2450
16	2	SPORT-FURY B/R	OP	RNBT	FBG	TR	IO	82-130		6	4	680			2000	2450
17		COURIER 229	ST	RNBT	FBG	TR	IO	120-160		7	3	1000			2850	3350
18		CROWN	ST	RNBT	FBG	TR	IO	130-170		7		1344			3300	3850
18		SPORT-CROWN B/R	ST	RNBT	FBG	TR	IO	130-170		7		1224			3200	3800
20		CARVEL 300	OP	CR	FBG	TR	IO	130-200		7	5	2030			4450	5200
23		CLIPPER 486	OP	CR	FBG	TR	IO	200-225		8		2400			6000	7000
23		CLIPPER 486	OP	CR	FBG	TR	IO	T130	CHRY	8		2400			6900	7900
23		COMMODORE II 486	OP	SPTCR	FBG	TR	IO	200-225		8		2970			6700	7800
23		COMMODORE II 486	OP	SPTCR	FBG	TR	IO	T130	CHRY	8		2970			7600	8700
24		CRUISE-LINER III	OP	CR	AL	SV	IO	130-175		8		2000			5900	6800
24		CRUISE-LINER III	OP	CR	AL	SV	IO	T 82	CHRY	8		2000			6800	7850
		1969 BOATS														
16		CHARGER 183		RNBT	FBG	TR	IO	130	VLVO	6	10				3250	3800
16		CHARGER 183	ST	RNBT	FBG	TR	IO	120-160		6	10				3050	3550
16	2	FURY	OP	RNBT	FBG	TR	IO	82-130		6	4				3050	3550
16	4	COURIER 229		RNBT	FBG	TR	IO	130	VLVO	7	2				3400	3950
16	4	POLARA 185		RNBT	AL	SV	IO	120	VLVO	6	11				3350	3900
16	4	POLARA 185	OP	RNBT	AL	SV	IO	120-130		6	11	760			2450	2850
17		CHESAPEAKE		RNBT	FBG	SV	IO	130	VLVO	7					3450	4050
17		COURIER 229 B/R	ST	RNBT	FBG	TR	IO	120-160		7	3				3350	3900
18		CHESAPEAKE	OP	CUD	FBG	SV	IO	120-130		7	6				3600	4200
19		POLARA 254		RNBT	AL	SV	IO	120	VLVO	7	2				4050	4700
19		POLARA 254	OP	RNBT	AL	SV	IO	120-150		7	2				3850	4500
19		WESTPORT	OP	RNBT	FBG	DV	IO	150-175		7	10				4100	4800
22	3	SOUTHWIND	HT	CR	FBG	DV	IO	175-225		7	10				7900	9250
22	3	SOUTHWIND	HT	CR	FBG	DV	IO	T130	CHRY	7	10				9000	10200
23		CLIPPER 486	OP	CR	FBG	TR	IO	175-235		8					7050	8300
23		CLIPPER 486	OP	CR	FBG	TR	IO	T120-T130		8					8000	9200
23		COMMODORE II 486	OP	SPTCR	FBG	TR	IO	175-235		8					7150	8400
23		COMMODORE II 486	OP	SPTCR	FBG	TR	IO	T120-T130		8					8100	9300
24		CRUISE-LINER III	OP	CR	AL	SV	IO	120-175		8					7400	8550
24		CRUISE-LINER III	OP	CR	AL	SV	IO	T 82	CHRY	8					8350	9600
24		CRUISE-LINER III		EXP	AL	SV	IO	120	VLVO	8					7700	8850
		1968 BOATS														
16		CHARGER 183	ST	RNBT	FBG	TR	IO	120-160		6	10	955			2550	2950
16	4	POLARA 185	OP	RNBT	AL	SV	IO	110-120		6	11	1540			3200	3700
17		COURIER 229	ST	RNBT	FBG	TR	IO	120-160		7	2	1480			3350	3950
18		CHESAPEAKE	OP	CUD	FBG	SV	IO	110-120		7	6	1780			4050	4700
19		POLARA 254	OP	RNBT	AL	SV	IO	120-160		7	2	1795			4150	4850
19		POLARA 254	OP	RNBT	AL	SV	IO	T 80		7	2	1795			5150	5900
19		WESTPORT 259	OP	RNBT	FBG	DV	IO	150-175		7	10	1840			4500	5200
22	3	SOUTHWIND	HT	CR	FBG	DV	IO	150-210		8		3550			7650	8900
22	3	SOUTHWIND	HT	CR	FBG	DV	IO	T120	CHRY	8		3550			8650	9950
23		CLIPPER 486	OP	CR	FBG	TR	IO	150-210		8					7250	8450
23		CLIPPER 486	OP	CR	FBG	TR	IO	T120		8					8250	9500
24		CRUISE-LINER III	OP	CR	AL		IO	110-175		8		1995			6250	7250
24		CRUISE-LINER III	OP	CR	AL		IO	T 80	CHRY	8		1995			7300	8350
		1967 BOATS														
16		CHARGER 183		RNBT	FBG		IO	110		6	10				3250	3750
16		CHARGER 183	ST	RNBT	FBG		IO	120-155				955			2600	3000
16	4	POLARA 185	OP	RNBT	AL		IO	80-120				1540			3200	3750
17		COURIER 229		RNBT	FBG		IO	110		7	3				3550	4150
17		COURIER 229	ST	RNBT	FBG		IO	120-160				1480			3500	4100
18		CHESAPEAKE	OP	CUD	FBG		IO	110-120				1780			4050	4700
19		CHARGER 283		RNBT	FBG		IO	150		7	5				4200	4900
19		POLARA 254		RNBT	AL		IB	110		7	2				1900	2250
19		POLARA 254	OP	RNBT	AL		IO	120-175				1795			4500	5250
19		WESTPORT	OP	RNBT	FBG		IO	110-150				1840			4550	5250
22	3	SOUTHWIND	HT	CR	FBG		IO	150-210				3550			7900	9200
22	3	SOUTHWIND	HT	CR	FBG		IO	T120				3550			9050	10300
23		CLIPPER 486		CR	FBG		IO	150		8					7500	8600
24		CRUISE-LINER III	OP	CR	AL		IO	120-175				1995			6500	7500
24		CRUISER-LINER III		CR	AL		IB	110		8					3650	4200
		1966 BOATS														
16		BEDFORD	OP	RNBT	FBG		IO	60- 90		6	3				3150	3700
16	4	MAYPORT	OP	RNBT	FBG		IO	90		6	3				3250	3800
16	4	MEDALLION II	OP	RNBT	AL		OB			7		6620			2350	2750
16	4	MEDALLION II	OP	RNBT	AL		IO	60-110		7					3450	4050
16	8	FLEETWOOD		RNBT	FBG		IO	120-150		6	7				3400	3950
18	3	RELIANT DLX		RNBT	AL		IO	90		7	2				3900	4500
19		WESTPORT	OP	RNBT	FBG		IO	110-150		7	10				4550	5250
19	5	SOVEREIGN		EXP	AL		IO	120-150		7	2				4550	5250
22	3	SOUTHWIND	HT	CR	FBG		IO	110-210		8					8850	10200
24		CRUISE-LINER III	OP	CR	AL		IO	120-150		8					8150	9400
		1965 BOATS														
16	4	MAYPORT DELUXE	OP	RNBT	FBG		IO	90							3550	4150
16	4	MAYPORT SPORT	OP	RNBT	FBG		IO	90							3450	4000
16	8	FLEETWOOD	OP	RNBT	FBG		IO	110-150							3700	4300
18		CHESAPEAKE	OP	CUD	FBG		IO	110-120							3950	4600
19	5	SOVEREIGN	HT	EXP	AL		IO	120-150							4900	5650
22	3	SOUTHWIND	HT	CR	FBG		IO	120-225							9150	10600
24		CRUISE-LINER II		CR	AL		OB								2350	2700
24		CRUISE-LINER II		CR	AL		IO	120-150							8400	9700
		1964 BOATS														
18		CHESAPEAKE	OP	CUD	FBG		IO	110							4100	4750
23	2	CRUISE-LINER I		CR	AL		IO	100							8300	9550
24		CRUISE-LINER II		CR	AL		OB								2350	2750
24		CRUISE-LINER II		CR	AL		IO	100							8700	10000
		1963 BOATS														
23	2	CRUISE-LINER I		CR	AL		IO	100							8600	9900
24		CRUISE-LINER II		CR	AL		OB								2350	2750
		1962 BOATS														
23	2	CRUISE-LINER		CR	AL		OB								1700	2000
23	2	CRUISE-LINER		CR	AL		IO	100							9000	10200
		1961 BOATS														
23		CRUISE-LINER		CR	AL		OB								1700	2000
		1960 BOATS														
23		CRUISE-LINER		CR	AL		OB								1700	2000

 CONTINUED ON NEXT PAGE

LOA FT	IN	NAME AND/ OR MODEL	TOP/ RIG	BOAT TYPE	-HULL- MTL	TP	ENGINE TP	# HP	MFG	BEAM FT	IN	WGT LBS	DRAFT FT	IN	RETAIL LOW	RETAIL HIGH
		1956 BOATS														
19		CRUISE-MASTER		CR	AL		IO								**	**

CHUNG HWA BOAT BLDG CO

TAIPEITER TAIWAN COAST GUARD MFG ID- CHB See inside cover to adjust price for area

For more recent years, see the BUC Used Boat Price Guide, Volume 1 or Volume 2

LOA FT	IN	NAME AND/ OR MODEL	TOP/ RIG	BOAT TYPE	-HULL- MTL	TP	ENGINE TP	# HP	MFG	BEAM FT	IN	WGT LBS	DRAFT FT	IN	RETAIL LOW	RETAIL HIGH
		1983 BOATS														
33	6	CHB 34 DC	FB	TRWL	FBG	DS	IB	120D-135D		11	9	17500	3	6	54100	59500
44	6	CHB 45 SDN	FB	TRWL	FBG	SV	IB	T120D	LEHM	14	10	29000	4		97600	107000
		IB T200D PERK 102000 112500, IB T210D CAT 105500 116000, IB T270D CUM 108000 119000														
44	10	CHB 45 DC	FB	TRWL	FBG	SV	IB	T120D	LEHM	15		27000	4	2	94100	103500
44	10	CHB 45 DC	FB	TRWL	FBG	SV	IB	T210D	CAT	15		28500	4	2	101000	111000
44	10	CHB 45 DC	FB	TRWL	FBG	SV	IB	T270D	CUM	15		30000	4	2	105500	116000
44	10	CHB 45 PH	FB	TRWL	FBG	SV	IB	T120D	LEHM	15	10	26500	4	2	93000	102000
44	10	CHB 45 PH	FB	TRWL	FBG	SV	IB	T200D	PERK	15	10	27000	4	2	97600	107500
44	10	CHB 45 PH	FB	TRWL	FBG	SV	IB	T210D	CAT	15	10	26500	4	2	97100	106500
		1982 BOATS														
33	6	CHB 34 DC	FB	TRWL	FBG	DS	IB	120D-165D		11	9	17500	3	6	52000	57700
44	6	CHB 45 SDN	FB	TRWL	FBG	SV	IB	T120D	LEHM	14	10	31500	4		98000	107500
		IB T165D PERK 100000 110000, IB T210D CAT 102000 112000, IB T270D CUM 103500 113500														
44	10	CHB 45 DC	FB	TRWL	FBG	SV	IB	T120D	LEHM	15		30500	4	2	96400	106000
44	10	CHB 45 DC	FB	TRWL	FBG	SV	IB	T210D	CAT	15		30500	4	2	100000	110000
44	10	CHB 45 DC	FB	TRWL	FBG	SV	IB	T270D	CUM	15		30500	4	2	102000	112000
44	10	CHB 45 PH	FB	TRWL	FBG	SV	IB	T120D	LEHM	15	10	26500	4	2	88800	97600
44	10	CHB 45 PH	FB	TRWL	FBG	SV	IB	T165D	PERK	15	10	26500	4	2	90900	99900
44	10	CHB 45 PH	FB	TRWL	FBG	SV	IB	T210D	CAT	15	10	26500	4	2	92600	102000
		1981 BOATS														
33	6	CHB 34 DC	FB	TRWL	FBG	DS	IB	120D	LEHM	11	9	17500	3	6	50000	54900
44	6	CHB 45 DC	FB	TRWL	FBG	DS	IB	T120D	LEHM	14	10	30500	4		93500	102500
44	6	CHB 45 DC	FB	TRWL	FBG	DS	IB	T160D	PERK	14	10	30700	4		95700	105000
44	6	CHB 45 PH	FB	TRWL	FBG	DS	IB	T120D	LEHM	14	10	31500	4		95800	105500
44	6	CHB 45 PH	FB	TRWL	FBG	DS	IB	T160D	PERK	14	10	31700	4		98100	108000
44	6	CHB 45 SDN	FB	TRWL	FBG	DS	IB	T120D	LEHM	14	10	31500	4		95400	105000
44	6	CHB 45 SDN	FB	TRWL	FBG	DS	IB	T160D	PERK	14	10	31700	4		97700	107500
		1980 BOATS														
33	6	CHB 34 DC	FB	TRWL	FBG	DS	IB	120D-160D		11	9	17500	3	6	48100	53300
44	6	CHB 45 DC	FB	TRWL	FBG	DS	IB	T120D	LEHM	14	10	30500	4		89200	98000
44	6	CHB 45 DC	FB	TRWL	FBG	DS	IB	T160D	PERK	14	10	30700	4		91300	100500
44	6	CHB 45 PH	FB	TRWL	FBG	DS	IB	T120D	LEHM	14	10	31500	4		91400	100500
44	6	CHB 45 PH	FB	TRWL	FBG	DS	IB	T160D	PERK	14	10	31700	4		93600	103000
44	6	CHB 45 SDN	FB	TRWL	FBG	DS	IB	T120D	LEHM	14	10	31500	4		91000	100000
44	6	CHB 45 SDN	FB	TRWL	FBG	DS	IB	T160D	PERK	14	10	31700	4		93200	102500
		1979 BOATS														
33	6	CHB 34 DC	FB	TRWL	FBG	DS	IB	120D	LEHM	11	9	17500	3	6	46500	51100
33	6	CHB 34 SDN	FB	TRWL	FBG	DS	IB	120D	LEHM	11	9	17500	3	6	46500	51100

CIGARETTE RACING TEAM LTD

OPA LOCA FL 33054 COAST GUARD MFG ID- CRT See inside cover to adjust price for area

For more recent years, see the BUC Used Boat Price Guide, Volume 1 or Volume 2

LOA FT	IN	NAME AND/ OR MODEL	TOP/ RIG	BOAT TYPE	-HULL- MTL	TP	ENGINE TP	# HP	MFG	BEAM FT	IN	WGT LBS	DRAFT FT	IN	RETAIL LOW	RETAIL HIGH
		1983 BOATS														
19	7	20	OP	RACE	FBG	DV	IO	280	MRCR	7	2	2450	1	5	6750	7800
24		24	OP	RACE	FBG	DV	IO	400	MRCR	7	10	5000	1	5	16700	19000
27		27	OP	RACE	FBG	DV	IO	400	MRCR	7	6	4200	1	6	17200	19500
27	10	28 SS	OP	RACE	FBG	DV	IO	T280	MRCR	8		5000	1	6	20600	22900
35		35	OP	RACE	FBG	DV	IO	T370	MRCR	8		7000	1	6	44500	49400
35		35	OP	RACE	FBG	DV	IO	T400	MRCR	8		7000	1	6	47500	52200
36		36	OP	RACE	FBG	DV	IO	T370	MRCR	9	3	7500	1	6	34200	38000
36		36	OP	RACE	FBG	DV	IO	T400	MRCR	9	3	7500	1	6	36000	40000
37	9	38	OP	RACE	FBG	DV	IO	T400	MRCR	8		10000	1	6	42900	47600
37	9	38	OP	RACE	FBG	DV	IO	T500		8		10000	1	6	48600	53400
41	3	41	OP	RACE	FBG	DV	IB	T210D	CAT	9	9	15500	3	9	117000	129000
41	3	ATTACK 41	OP	RACE	FBG	DV	IB	T260D	CAT	9	9	13500	3	9	113500	124500
		1982 BOATS														
19	7	20	OP	RACE	FBG	DV	IO	330	MRCR	7	2	2450	1	5	7500	8600
24		24	OP	RACE	FBG	DV	IO	330-370		7	10	5000	1	5	14300	17400
24		24	OP	RACE	FBG	DV	IO	400	MRCR	7	10	5000	1	5	16300	18600
24		SQUADRON 24	OP	RACE	FBG	DV	IO	400	MRCR			5000	1	6	12000	13700
27		SQUADRON 27	OP	RACE	FBG	DV	IO	400	MRCR	7	6	4200	1	6	12600	14300
27	10	28 SS	OP	RACE	FBG	DV	IO	T260-T330		8		5000	1	6	19700	24000
35		35	OP	RACE	FBG	DV	IO	T370	MRCR	8		7000	1	6	43500	48300
35		35	OP	RACE	FBG	DV	IO	T400	MRCR	8		7000	1	6	46400	51000
36		36	OP	RACE	FBG	DV	IO	T370	MRCR	9	3	7500	1	6	33400	37200
36		36	OP	RACE	FBG	DV	IO	T400	MRCR	9	3	7500	1	6	35200	39100
39		SQUADRON 39	OP	RACE	FBG	DV	IO	T370	MRCR	8		10000	1	6	33900	37600
39		SQUADRON 39	OP	RACE	FBG	DV	IO	T400	MRCR	8		10000	1	6	34900	38800
39		SQUADRON 39	OP	RACE	FBG	DV	IO	R400	MRCR	8		10000	1	6	40600	45100
41	3	41	OP	RACE	FBG	DV	IB	T210D	CAT	9	9	15500	3	9	112000	123000
41	3	ATTACK 41	OP	RACE	FBG	DV	IB	T260D	CAT	9	9	13500	3	9	108000	119000
		1981 BOATS														
19	7	20		RACE	FBG	DV	IO	280		7	2				9350	10600
24		24		RACE	FBG	DV	IO	330		7	10				10900	12400
27	6	SQUADRON 27	OP	RACE	FBG	DV	IO	T400	MRCR	7	9	4000	1	6	16600	18900
27	10	28 SS	OP	RACE	FBG	DV	IO	T260-T330		8		5000	1	6	19400	23500
27	10	28SS		RACE	FBG	DV	IO	T280		8					21600	24000
35		35	OP	RACE	FBG	DV	IO	T370	MRCR	8		9000	1	6	40300	44800
35		35	OP	RACE	FBG	DV	IO	T400	MRCR	8		9000	1	6	41700	46300
36		36	OP	RACE	FBG	DV	IO	T370	MRCR	9	4	8500	1	6	32000	35600
36		36	OP	RACE	FBG	DV	IO	T400	MRCR	9	4	8500	1	6	33300	37000
39	3	SQUADRON 39	OP	RACE	FBG	DV	IO	T400	MRCR	8		9000	2		34900	38800
41	3	41	OP	RACE	FBG	DV	IO	T210D	CAT	9	9	14500	3	2	60000	65900
		1980 BOATS														
19	7	20	OP	RACE	FBG	DV	IO	260	MRCR	7	2	2450	1	5	6250	7150
19	7	20	OP	RACE	FBG	DV	IO	330	MRCR	7	2	2450	1	5	7300	8400
19	7	CIGARETTE 20	OP	RACE	FBG	DV	OB			7	2	2450			14100	16000
19	7	CIGARETTE 20	OP	RACE	FBG	DV	IO	280		7	2				9250	10500
24		24	OP	RACE	FBG	DV	IO	330-370		7	10	3850	1	5	11600	14300
27	10	CIGARETTE 28 SS	OP	RACE	FBG	DV	IO	T280		8					21400	23800
27	10	CIGARETTE 28 STD	OP	RACE	FBG	DV	IO	T165		8					19400	21600
27	10	S-S 28	OP	RACE	FBG	DV	IO	T260-T330		8		5000	1	6	19300	23300
32		CIGARETTE 32	OP	RACE	FBG	DV	OB			8		6500			76400	84000
33		SQUADRON 12	OP	RACE	FBG	DV	IO	T370		9	3				24300	27000
35		35	OP	RACE	FBG	DV	IO	T370	MRCR	8		7000	1	6	42300	47000
35		35	OP	RACE	FBG	DV	IO	T400	MRCR	8		7000	1	6	44700	49700
35		35	OP	RACE	FBG	DV	IO	T475	MRCR	8		7000	1	6	52200	57300
36		36	OP	RACE	FBG	DV	IO	T370	MRCR	9	4	8500	1	6	31700	35300
		IO T400 MRCR 33000 36700, IO T475 MRCR 37100 41200, IO T210D CAT 32100 35700														
39		CIGARETTE 39	OP	RACE	FBG	DV	IO	T370		9	3				41600	46200
41	3	41	OP	RACE	FBG	DV	IO	T475	MRCR	9	9	14500	3	2	67100	73700
41	3	41	OP	RACE	FBG	DV	IO	T210D	CAT	9	9	14500	3	2	59500	65400
		1979 BOATS														
19	7	20	OP	RACE	FBG	DV	IO	280	MRCR	7	2	2450	1	5	6450	7400
19	7	20	OP	RACE	FBG	DV	IO	330	MRCR	7	2	2450	1	5	7300	8400
24		24	OP	RACE	FBG	DV	IO	330-370		7	10	3850	1	5	11600	14300
27	10	28	OP	RACE	FBG	DV	IO	T165	MRCR	8		4500	1	6	16500	18800
27	10	28	OP	RACE	FBG	DV	IO	T280	MRCR	8		4500	1	6	19200	21300
27	10	S-S 28	OP	RACE	FBG	DV	IO	T280-T330		8		5000	1	6	19600	23200
35		AWESOME 35	OP	RACE	FBG	DV	IO	T370	MRCR	8		7000	1	6	42300	47000
35		AWESOME 35	OP	RACE	FBG	DV	IO	T475	MRCR	8		7000	1	6	52100	57200
35		AWESOME 35	OP	RACE	FBG	DV	IO	T475D	REN	8		7000	1	6	55700	61200
35		MISTRESS 35	OP	RACE	FBG	DV	IO	T370	MRCR	8		7000	1	6	42300	47000
35		MISTRESS 35	OP	RACE	FBG	DV	IO	T475	MRCR	8		7000	1	6	52100	57200
35		MISTRESS 35	OP	RACE	FBG	DV	IO	T475D	REN	8		7000	1	6	55700	61200
36		36	OP	RACE	FBG	DV	IO	T370	MRCR	9	4	8500	1	6	31700	35200
36		36	OP	RACE	FBG	DV	IO	T475	MRCR	9	4	8500	1	6	37100	41200
36		36	OP	RACE	FBG	DV	IO	T240D		9	4	8500	1	6	32200	35800
36		ST-TROPEZ	OP	RACE	FBG	DV	IO	T370	MRCR	9	4	8500	1	6	31700	35200
36		ST-TROPEZ	OP	RACE	FBG	DV	IO	T475	MRCR	9	4	8500	1	6	37100	41200
36		ST-TROPEZ	OP	RACE	FBG	DV	IO	T240D		9	4	8500	1	6	32200	35800
39	4	39	OP	RACE	FBG	DV	IO	T370	MRCR	7	10	7800	1	6	45900	50500
39	4	39	OP	RACE	FBG	DV	IO	T475	MRCR	7	10	7800	1	6	53700	59000
45		SE		CR	FBG	DV	IO	T600		14	6				67500	74200
		1978 BOATS														
19	7	20	OP	RNBT	FBG	DV	IO	280	MRCR	7	2	2450	1	5	6650	7600
19	7	20	OP	RNBT	FBG	DV	IO	395	MRCR	7	2	2450	1	5	9450	10700
27	10	S-S 28	OP	RNBT	FBG	DV	IO	T165	MRCR	8		4800	1	6	16800	19100
27	10	S-S 28	OP	RNBT	FBG	DV	IO	T280	MRCR	8		4800	1	6	19500	21700
27	10	S-S 28	OP	RNBT	FBG	DV	IO	T395	MRCR	8		4800	1	6	22700	25200
27	10	STANDARD 28	OP	RNBT	FBG	DV	IO	T165	MRCR	8		4500	1	6	16400	18700
27	10	STANDARD 28	OP	RNBT	FBG	DV	IO	T280	MRCR	8		4500	1	6	19200	21400
35		AWESOME 35	OP	RNBT	FBG	DV	IO	T280	MRCR	8		7000	1	6	36000	40000

 CONTINUED ON NEXT PAGE

LOA		NAME AND/	TOP/	BOAT	-HULL-		----ENGINE---			BEAM		WGT	DRAFT		RETAIL	RETAIL
FT	IN	OR MODEL	RIG	TYPE	MTL	TP	TP	# HP	MFG	FT	IN	LBS	FT	IN	LOW	HIGH
		1978 BOATS														
35		AWESOME 35	OP	RNBT	FBG	DV	IO	T370	MRCR	8		7000	1	6	38700	43000
35		MISTRESS 35	OP	RNBT	FBG	DV	IO	T370	MRCR	8		7000	1	6	38700	43000
		1977 BOATS														
19	7	20	OP	RNBT	FBG	DV	IO	280	MRCR	7	2	2450	1	5	6700	7700
19	7	20	OP	RNBT	FBG	DV	IO	395	MRCR	7	2	2450	1	5	9550	10900
23	11	24	OP	RNBT	FBG	DV	IO	280	MRCR	7	10	4000	1	6	11100	12600
		IO 370 MRCR 12900 14700, IO T165 MRCR 11700 13300, IO T280 MRCR 13000 14800														
27	10	S-S 28	OP	RNBT	FBG	DV	IO	T165	MRCR	8		4800	1	6	17000	19300
27	10	S-S 28	OP	RNBT	FBG	DV	IO	T280	MRCR	8		4800	1	6	19600	21800
27	10	S-S 28	OP	RNBT	FBG	DV	IO	T395	MRCR	8		4800	1	6	22900	25500
27	10	STANDARD 28	OP	RNBT	FBG	DV	IO	T165-T188		8		4500	1	6	16700	19400
27	10	STANDARD 28	OP	RNBT	FBG	DV	IO	T280	MRCR	8		4500	1	6	19500	21600
27	10	STANDARD 28	OP	RNBT	FBG	DV	IO	T395	MRCR	8		4500	1	6	22500	25000
35		AWESOME 35	OP	RNBT	FBG	DV	IO	T280	MRCR	8		7000	1	6	36500	40600
35		AWESOME 35	OP	RNBT	FBG	DV	IO	T370	MRCR	8		7000	1	6	39300	43600
35		MISTRESS 35	OP	RNBT	FBG	DV	IO	T280	MRCR	8		7000	1	6	36500	40600
35		MISTRESS 35	OP	RNBT	FBG	DV	IO	T370	MRCR	8		7000	1	6	39300	43600
		1976 BOATS														
19	7	20		RNBT	FBG	DV	IO	280	MRCR	7	2	2450	1	5	6850	7900
19	7	20		RNBT	FBG	DV	IO	395	MRCR	7	2	2450	1	5	9750	11100
23	11	24		RNBT	FBG	DV	IO	T165-T188		7	10	4000	1	6	12000	13700
23	11	24		RNBT	FBG	DV	IO	T280	MRCR	7	10	4000	1	6	13200	15000
27	10	S-S 28		SPTCR	FBG	DV	IO	T165-T188		8		4800	1	6	19400	22000
27	10	S-S 28		SPTCR	FBG	DV	IO	T280	MRCR	8		4800	1	6	22000	24400
27	10	S-S 28		SPTCR	FBG	DV	IO	T395	MRCR	8		4800	1	6	25000	27800
27	10	STANDARD 28		OPFSH	FBG	DV	IO	T165	MRCR	8		4500	1	6	19500	21700
27	10	STANDARD 28		OPFSH	FBG	DV	IO	T280-T300		8		4500	1	6	22100	25300
35		AWESOME		SPTCR	FBG	DV	IO	T280	MRCR	8		7000	1	6	47100	51800
35		AWESOME		SPTCR	FBG	DV	IO	T395	MRCR	8		7000			51700	56800
		1975 BOATS														
19	11	20	OP	RNBT	FBG	DV	IO	300	CC	7		2450	1	5	7350	8450
23	11	24	OP	RNBT	FBG	DV	IO	T165-T188		7	10	4000	1	6	12300	14100
23	11	24	OP	RNBT	FBG	DV	IO	T280	MRCR	7	10	4000	1	6	13600	15500
27	10	28	OP	OPFSH	FBG	DV	IO	T165-T188		8		4500	1	6	20000	22800
27	10	28	OP	OPFSH	FBG	DV	IO	T280-T300		8		4500	1	6	22700	25900
27	10	28-SS	HT	SPTCR	FBG	DV	IO	T165-T188		8		4800	1	6	19900	22700
27	10	28-SS	HT	SPTCR	FBG	DV	IO	T280-T300		8		4800	1	6	22600	25700
27	10	28-SS	HT	SPTCR	FBG	DV	IO	T395	MRCR	8		4800	1	6	25700	28600
35		AWESOME	HT	SPTCR	FBG	DV	IO	T280	MRCR	8		7000	1	6	48400	53200
35		AWESOME	HT	SPTCR	FBG	DV	IO	T395	MRCR	8		7000	1	6	53400	58600
36		RACE	HT	RACE	FBG	DV	IO	T600	MRCR	9	10	7500			52400	57600
40		RACE	OP	RACE	FBG	DV	IO	T600	MRCR	9	10	8000			66700	73300
		1974 BOATS														
19	7	CIGARETTE 20			FBG		IO	300	CC	7	2	2450	1	5	7450	8600
19	7	CIGARETTE 20			FBG		JT	390	BERK	7	2	2450	1	5	6250	7200
23	11	CIGARETTE 24			FBG		IO	T165-T188		7	10	4000	1	6	12900	14800
27	10	CIGARETTE 28 SS			FBG		IO	T188-T300		8		4800	1	6	18900	22800
27	10	CIGARETTE 28 STD			FBG		IO	T165-T188		8		4500	1	6	17600	20100
27	10	CIGARETTE 28 STD			FBG		IO	T300	CC	8		4800	1	6	20500	22800
35		CIGARETTE 35			FBG		IO	T300	CC	8		6500	1	8	52000	57100
36		CIGARETTE 36		RACE	FBG		IO	T600	MRCR	9	4	7200	2		55500	61000
36		CIGARETTE 36 CUSTOM			FBG		IO	T390	MRCR	9	4	7500	2		46200	50800
40		CIGARETTE 40		RACE	FBG		IO	T600	MRCR	9	4	9000	2		67300	74000
40		CIGARETTE 40 CUSTOM			FBG		IO	T390	MRCR	9	4	9000	2		59700	65600
		1973 BOATS														
19	7	CIGARETTE 20			FBG		IO	320	CC	7	2	2450	1	5	8100	9300
23	11	CIGARETTE 24			FBG		IO	T165-T188		7	10	4000	1	6	13300	15200
27	10	CIGARETTE 28			FBG		IO	T165-T188		8		4500	1	6	18600	20800
27	10	CIGARETTE 28			FBG		IO	T320	CC	8		4500	1	6	21300	23700
27	10	CIGARETTE 28 SS			FBG		IO	T320	CC	8		4800	1	6	22100	24500
36		CIGARETTE 36		RACE	FBG		IO	T500	MRCR	9	4	7200	2		49700	54700
36		CIGARETTE 36 CUSTOM			FBG		IO	T390	MRCR	9	4	7500	2		47700	52500
		1972 BOATS														
23	8	CIGARETTE		RNBT	FBG	DV	IO	T165-T188		8			2		13600	15500
27	10	CIGARETTE		RNBT	FBG	DV	IO	T165		8			2	2	20800	23100
36		CIGARETTE		RACE	FBG	DV	IO	T505		9	6				45700	50200
		1971 BOATS														
24		CIGARETTE 24		RACE	FBG	DV	IO	T165	MRCR	7	10	3750	1	6	13600	15500
27	10	CIGARETTE 28		RACE	FBG	DV	IO	T165	MRCR	8		4500	1	6	20400	22700
36		CIGARETTE 36		RACE	FBG	DV	IO	T475	MRCR	9	5	9000	2	2	44800	49800

CIMMARON INC

COAST GUARD MFG ID- CIM

Call 1-800-327-6929 for BUC Personalized Evaluation Service
Or, for 1983 to 1985 boats, sign onto www.BUCValuPro.com

CLAIR YACHTS INC

Call 1-800-327-6929 for BUC Personalized Evaluation Service
Or, for 1976 boats, sign onto www.BUCValuPro.com

CLARK CUSTOM BOATS

COAST GUARD MFG ID- HLN

Call 1-800-327-6929 for BUC Personalized Evaluation Service
Or, for 1979 to 1983 boats, sign onto www.BUCValuPro.com

CLASSIC BOATS INC

ROSELLE IL 60172 COAST GUARD MFG ID- CSB See inside cover to adjust price for area

LOA		NAME AND/	TOP/	BOAT	-HULL-		----ENGINE---			BEAM		WGT	DRAFT		RETAIL	RETAIL
FT	IN	OR MODEL	RIG	TYPE	MTL	TP	TP	# HP	MFG	FT	IN	LBS	FT	IN	LOW	HIGH
		1980 BOATS														
17		SPORTWALK 170		RNBT	F/S	SV	IO	120	MRCR	7		2700			2850	3300
18	6	FALCHION 190	ST	RACE	F/S	SV	IO	260	MRCR	7		3000			3400	3950
18	6	SPORTCABIN 190	ST	CUD	F/S	SV	IO	140-228		7		3000			3400	4100
18	6	SPORTCABIN 190	ST	CUD	F/S	SV	IO	260	MRCR	7		3000			3650	4250
18	6	SUMMER-WINGS 190	ST	UTL	F/S	SV	IO	140-228		7		3000			3550	4300
18	6	SUMMER-WINGS 190	ST	UTL	F/S	SV	IO	260	MRCR	7		3000			3850	4450
20	8	SUNLOUNGER 211	ST	CUD	F/S	SV	IO	170-260		8		3850			5450	6550
23		FALCHION 230		RACE	F/S	SV	IO	T260	MRCR	8		4700			7950	9150
25		INTERCEPTOR 250	ST	CBNCR	F/S	SV	IO	198-260		8		5250			10300	12100
25		SPORTCRUISER 250	ST	SPTCR	F/S	SV	IO	198-260		8		5250			8550	10200
		1979 BOATS														
17	2	CLASSIC 183		RNBT	F/S	DV	IO	120-140		6	9				2350	2750
17	6	DAYTRIPPER 176		RNBT	F/S	DV	IO	120-228		7		2650			2900	3500
17	6	SUMMER 17.5		RNBT	F/S	DV	IO	120-228		7					2700	3300
17	6	SUMMER-WINGS 176		RNBT	F/S	DV	IO	120-228		7		2600			2850	3450
18	6	DAYTRIPPER 186		RNBT	F/S	DV	IO	140-260		7		3050			3300	4150
18	6	FALCHION 18.5		RACE	F/S	DV	IO	260		7		3200			3550	4150
18	6	SP CAB 18.5			F/S	DV	IO	140-260		7					3250	4050
18	6	SUMMER-WINGS 186		RNBT	F/S	DV	IO	140-260		7		3000			3300	4100
20	8	FALCHION 211		SPTCR	F/S	DV	IO	198-250		8		4100			5750	6800
20	8	SUNLOUNGER 211		OVNTR	F/S	DV	IO	198-250		8		4100			5750	6800
20	8	TC EDITION 211		SF	F/S	DV	IO	198-250		8		4100			6550	7700
25		FALCHION 250		SPTCR	F/S	DV	IO	228		8		5200			8650	9950
25		FALCHION 250		SPTCR	F/S	DV	IO	T165		8		5200			9450	10700
25		INTERCEPTOR 250		WKNDR	F/S	DV	IO	228		8		5200			8900	10100
25		INTERCEPTOR 250		WKNDR	F/S	DV	IO	T165		8		5200			9600	10900
25		TC EDITION 250		SF	F/S	DV	IO	228		8		5200			9900	11200
25		TC EDITION 250		SF	F/S	DV	IO	T165		8		5200			10700	12200
		1978 BOATS														
16	6	CLASSIC 170	ST	RNBT	F/S	DV	IO	120-170		6	8				2300	2700
17	2	CLASSIC 183	ST	RNBT	F/S	DV	IO	120-140		6	9				2350	2750
17	6	DAYTRIPPER 176	ST	RNBT	F/S	DV	IO	140	MRCR	7		2650			2900	3400
17	6	SUMMER-WINGS 176	ST	RNBT	F/S	DV	IO	140	MRCR	7		2600			2900	3350
18	3	CLASSIC 190	ST	RNBT	F/S	DV	IO	140-228		7	3				2900	3500
18	3	DAYTRIPPER 190	ST	CAMPR	F/S	DV	IO	140-228		7	3				2950	3600
18	6	DAYTRIPPER 186	ST	RNBT	F/S	DV	IO	198	MRCR	7		3050			3400	3950
18	6	FALCHION 18.5	ST	RACE	F/S	DV	IO	260	MRCR	7		3200			3600	4150
18	6	SPORTCABIN	ST	CUD	F/S	DV	IO	165-260		7		3200			3600	4450
18	6	SUMMER-WINGS 186	ST	RNBT	F/S	DV	IO	198	MRCR	7		3000			3350	3900
20	8	FALCHION 211	ST	SPTCR	F/S	DV	IO	240-260		8		4100			5850	6900
20	8	SUNLOUNGER 211	ST	OVNTR	F/S	DV	IO	185-260		8		4100			5700	6900
20	8	TC EDITION 211	ST	SF	F/S	DV	IO	185-260		8		4100			6500	7850
25		COMMAND BRIDGE 2411	FB	SDN	F/S	DV	IO	185-260		8		6050			9900	11800
25		FALCHION 250	ST	SPTCR	F/S	DV	IO	240-260		8		5200			8850	10200
25		FALCHION 250	ST	SPTCR	F/S	DV	IO	T120-T170		8		5200			9350	10800
25		INTERCEPTOR 250	ST	WKNDR	F/S	DV	IO	185-260		8		5200			8650	10400
25		INTERCEPTOR 250	ST	WKNDR	F/S	DV	IO	T120-T170		8		5200			9450	11000
25		SALON CRUISER 2411	HT	SDN	F/S	DV	IO	185-260		8		5800			9400	11200
25		SUNDECKER 2411	HT	SDN	F/S	DV	IO	185-260		8		5800			9850	11700
25		TC EDITION 250	ST	SF	F/S	DV	IO	185-260		8		5200			9700	11600
25		TC EDITION 250	ST	SF	F/S	DV	IO	T120-T170		8		5200			10600	12300
		1976 BOATS														
16	6	CLASSIC 170	ST	RNBT	FBG	DV	IO	120-165		6	8	1750			2250	2650
16	6	CLASSIC 170B	ST	RNBT	FBG	DV	OB			6	8				2950	3400

CLASSIC BOATS INC — CONTINUED

See inside cover to adjust price for area

LOA FT IN	NAME AND/ OR MODEL	TOP/ RIG	BOAT TYPE	-HULL- MTL TP	----ENGINE--- TP # HP	MFG	BEAM FT IN	WGT LBS	DRAFT FT IN	RETAIL LOW	RETAIL HIGH
					1976 BOATS						
17 2	CLASSIC 183	ST	RNBT	FBG TR	IO 120-140		6 9	2100		2550	3000
17 2	CLASSIC 183B	ST	RNBT	FBG TR	OB		6 9			2950	3400
18 3	CLASSIC 190	ST	RNBT	FBG DV	IO 140-233		7 3	2800		3300	4000
20 8	CLASSIC 210	ST	RNBT	FBG DV	IO 188-280		8	3700		5550	6850
25	2411 SALON	HT	CR	FBG DV	IO 188-255		8			8100	9750
25	2411B COMMAND	FB	CR	FBG DV	IO 188-255		8			8100	9750
25	INTERCEPTOR 250		CR	FBG DV	IO 188-255		8			8100	9750
25	INTERCEPTOR 250		CR	FBG DV	IO T120-T165		8			8950	10500
					1975 BOATS						
16 6	170-B	ST	RNBT	FBG DV	OB		6 8	1500	1	2750	3200
16 6	170-I/O	ST	RNBT	FBG DV	IO 120-165		6 8	1750	2 5	2350	2700
17 2	183-B W/T	ST	RNBT	FBG TR	OB		6 9	1750	1	3050	3550
17 2	183-IO W/T	ST	RNBT	FBG TR	IO 120-140		6 9	1950	2 5	2550	3000
17 10	18 SST LO-PRO	OP	RNBT	FBG SV	JT 390-454		7 4	1775		2850	3350
17 10	18SST SUPER	OP	RNBT	FBG DV	JT 390-454		7 2	1850		2850	3350
18 3	190-IO	ST	RNBT	FBG DV	IO 140-233		7 3	2200	2 5	3000	3650
18 3	190-IO	ST	RNBT	FBG DV	JT 390 CHEV		7 3	2200	2 5	3150	3650
20 8	210-IO	ST	SPTCR	FBG DV	IO 188-280		8	3700	2 7	5750	7100
24 6	250-IO	ST	CR	FBG DV	IO 188-255		8	4600	2 10	8250	9800
24 6	250-IO	ST	CR	FBG DV	IO T120-T233		8	4600	2 10	9100	10900
					1972 BOATS						
16 6	C-170			FBG	IO 120-165		6 8	1750		2450	2850
16 6	C-170B			FBG	OB		6 8			2900	3350
17 2	C-183			FBG	IO 120-165		6 9			2700	3150
17 2	C-183B			FBG	OB		6 9			2850	3350
18 3	C-190			FBG	IO 140-245		7 3			3350	4100
22	CLASSIC		CR	FBG DV	IO 165					6800	7800

CLASSIC BOATWORKS
COAST GUARD MFG ID- CDJ

Call 1-800-327-6929 for BUC Personalized Evaluation Service
Or, for 1980 to 1981 boats, sign onto www.BUCValuPro.com

CLASSIC PRODUCTS LTD
MISS CLASSIC

Call 1-800-327-6929 for BUC Personalized Evaluation Service
Or, for 1971 boats, sign onto www.BUCValuPro.com

CLAYTON MARINE INDUSTRIES INC
TOMS RIVER NJ
See inside cover to adjust price for area

LOA FT IN	NAME AND/ OR MODEL	TOP/ RIG	BOAT TYPE	-HULL- MTL TP	----ENGINE--- TP # HP	MFG	BEAM FT IN	WGT LBS	DRAFT FT IN	RETAIL LOW	RETAIL HIGH
					1963 BOATS						
27 11		EXP		WD	IB 215					7650	8800
27 11		SF		WD	IB 185					7400	8500
27 11	GAME-FISHER			WD	IB 185					7250	8300
36 8		SDN		WD	IB 230					25300	28100
					1962 BOATS						
27 11		EXP		WD	IB 215					7450	8600
27 11		EXP		WD	IB T185-T230					8200	9750
27 11		SF		WD	IB 215					7350	8450
27 11		SF		WD	IB T135-T215					7650	9550
27 11		SF		WD	IB T230					8400	9650
27 11	GAME-FISHER			WD	IB 215					7200	8300
27 11	GAME-FISHER			WD	IB T135-T215					7550	9400
27 11	GAME-FISHER			WD	IB T230					8250	9500
					1961 BOATS						
27 11	CUSTOM	SF		P/M	IB T125		10 9		2 1	7450	8550
35 11	EXP CR	EXP		P/M	IB T177		12 6		2 10	19100	21300
35 11	SPORT FISH	SF		P/M	IB T177		12 6		2 10	20200	22500
					1960 BOATS						
24	JERSEY SEA SKIFF			WD	IB 125-135					3800	4450
26	SEA-SKIFF			WD	IB 125-135					4850	5650
26	SEA-SKIFF			WD	IB T110					5300	6100
27	SEA-SKIFF CUSTOM	HT		WD	IB T170					6150	7050
34			EXP	WD	IB 125					16700	19000
34			EXP	WD	IB T225					18300	20300
34			SF	WD	IB T215					15900	18000
					1959 BOATS						
20	SKIFF			L/P	IB 95-109		7 6			1900	2300
23	SKIFF			L/P	IB 95-125		8 1			2950	3550
24	TRUNK CABIN SKIFF	CR		L/P	IB 177					3850	4450
26	SKIFF			L/P	IB 125-225		9			4750	5900
26	TWIN SKIFF			L/P	IB T109		9			5200	5950
34	SINGLE SCREW	SF		L/P	IB 225		10 6			14500	16500
34	TWIN SCREW	CR		L/P	IB T225		10 6			15200	17300
34	TWIN SCREW	SF		L/P	IB T225		10 6			15300	17400
					1958 BOATS						
20	SKIFF			WD	IB 95					1850	2200
26	SKIFF			WD	IB 95					4550	5250
					1957 BOATS						
20	SKIFF			WD	IB 95					1800	2150
23	TRUNK CABIN SKIFF	CR		WD	IB 125					3150	3700
26	SKIFF			WD	IB 95					4500	5150
26	SKIFF			WD	IB T185					5550	6350
34	SKIFF			WD	IB T215					16300	18500
					1956 BOATS						
20	SKIFF			WD	IB 95					1800	2150
26	SKIFF			WD	IB 95					4400	5100
					1955 BOATS						
20	SKIFF			WD	IB 95					1750	2100
26	SKIFF			WD	IB 95					4300	5000
					1954 BOATS						
20	SKIFF			WD	IB 95					1750	2050
					1953 BOATS						
24	TRUNK CABIN SKIFF	CR		WD	IB 95					3350	3900
					1952 BOATS						
24	TRUNK CABIN SKIFF	CR		WD	IB 95					3300	3850
26	SKIFF			WD	IB 95					4150	4800

CLEARWATER BAY MARINE WAYS
CLEARWATER FL 33515
See inside cover to adjust price for area

For more recent years, see the BUC Used Boat Price Guide, Volume 1 or Volume 2

LOA FT IN	NAME AND/ OR MODEL	TOP/ RIG	BOAT TYPE	-HULL- MTL TP	----ENGINE--- TP # HP	MFG	BEAM FT IN	WGT LBS	DRAFT FT IN	RETAIL LOW	RETAIL HIGH
					1983 BOATS						
16 6	SUN-CAT	CAT	SA/OD	CT			7 3		9	3500	4050
16 6	SUN-CAT CABIN CB	CAT	SAIL	FBG CB			7 3	1400	9	3300	3850
16 6	SUN-CAT CABIN KL	CAT	SAIL	FBG KL			7 3	1400	2	3200	3700
16 6	SUN-CAT OPEN CB	CAT	SAIL	FBG CB			7 3	1400	9	2550	2950
16 6	SUN-CAT OPEN KL	CAT	SAIL	FBG KL			7 3	1400	2	2400	2800
					1961 BOATS						
25 5	AMPHIBI-CON	SLP	SA/OD	P/C KC			7 9		2 4	4050	4700
27	MILLS 27	SLP	SA/CR	WD	CB OB					5450	6250
28 5	MOUNT-DESERT C-28	SLP	SA/CR	WD	CB OB		8 6			7300	8400
40	GULF-COAST	YWL	SA/CR	FBG	CB OB					22700	25200
					1960 BOATS						
24	MILLS 24	SLP	SA/OD	P/C KC						3400	3950
25 6	AMPHIBI-CON	SLP	SA/OD	P/C KC			7 9		2 4	3750	4350
28	C-28	SLP	SA/CR	P/C KC						6250	7150
					1959 BOATS						
24	MILLS 24-MORC		SA/CR	FLY			7 6		2	3400	3950
25 5	AMPHIBI-CON	SLP	SA/CR	WD			7 9		2 4	3650	4250
28 5	CONTROVERSY	SLP	SA/CR	WD	OB		8 6		4 8	7350	8450

CLEARWATER CUSTOM YACHTS
CLEARWATER FL 33520
COAST GUARD MFG ID- FCW See inside cover to adjust price for area

LOA FT IN	NAME AND/ OR MODEL	TOP/ RIG	BOAT TYPE	-HULL- MTL TP	----ENGINE--- TP # HP	MFG	BEAM FT IN	WGT LBS	DRAFT FT IN	RETAIL LOW	RETAIL HIGH
					1983 BOATS						
22	CLEARWATER 22	OP	CTRCN	FBG SV	OB		8	1800	10	3700	4300
24	CLEARWATER 24	OP	CTRCN	FBG DV	OB		8	3000	1 2	6100	7000
24	CLEARWATER 24	OP	EXP	FBG DV	OB		8	3000	1 2	6100	7000
33	OFFSHORE 33	SLP	SAIL	FBG KL IB	16D UNIV	11	13000	5	22600	25100
33	OFFSHORE 33	SLP	SAIL	FBG KL IB	16D UNIV	11	13000	5	22600	25100
33	OFFSHORE 33	CUT	SAIL	FBG KL IB	16D UNIV	11	13000	5	22600	25100
33	OFFSHORE 33 SHOAL	CAT	SAIL	FBG KL IB	16D UNIV	11	13000	4	22600	25100
33	OFFSHORE 33 SHOAL	SLP	SAIL	FBG KL IB	16D UNIV	11	13000	4	22600	25100
33	OFFSHORE 33 SHOAL	CUT	SAIL	FBG KL IB	16D UNIV	11	13000	4	22600	25100
33 9	WINGS 33	CAT	SAIL	FBG KL IB	16D UNIV	11	13000	5	22600	25100
39 9	WINGS 40	SLP	SA/RC	FBG KL IB	D	13	21000	5 2	43100	47900
39 9	WINGS 40	KTH	SA/RC	FBG KL IB	D	13	21000	5 2	43100	47900
40	OFFSHORE 40	SLP	SAIL	FBG KL IB	50D UNIV		22000	5 2	45700	50200
40	OFFSHORE 40	CUT	SAIL	FBG KL IB	50D UNIV		22000	5 2	45700	50200

96th ed. - Vol. III   CONTINUED ON NEXT PAGE   159

LOA FT IN	NAME AND/ OR MODEL	TOP/ RIG	BOAT TYPE	-HULL- MTL TP	TP	----ENGINE--- # HP MFG	BEAM FT IN	WGT LBS	DRAFT FT IN	RETAIL LOW	RETAIL HIGH
---	--- 1982 BOATS										
22	CLEARWATER 22	OP	CTRCN	FBG SV	OB	8		1800	10	3650	4250
24	CLEARWATER 24	OP	CTRCN	FBG DV	OB	8		3000	1 2	6000	6900
24	CLEARWATER 24	OP	EXP	FBG DV	OB	8		3000	1 2	6000	6900
33	OFFSHORE 33	SLP	SAIL	FBG KL	IB	16D UNIV 11		13000	5	21300	23600
33	OFFSHORE 33	CUT	SAIL	FBG KL	IB	16D UNIV 11		13000	5	21000	23400
33	OFFSHORE 33	KTH	SAIL	FBG KL	IB	16D UNIV 11		13000	5	20400	22700
33	OFFSHORE 33 SHOAL	SLP	SAIL	FBG KL	IB	16D UNIV 11		13000	4	21300	23600
33	OFFSHORE 33 SHOAL	CUT	SAIL	FBG KL	IB	16D UNIV 11		13000	4	21500	23900
33	OFFSHORE 33 SHOAL	KTH	SAIL	FBG KL	IB	16D UNIV 11		13000	4	21100	23400
33	WINGS 33	KTH	SAIL	FBG KL	IB	16D UNIV 11		13000	5	22400	24900
40	OFFSHORE 40	CUT	SAIL	FBG KL	IB	50D UNIV 13	3	21000	5 2	41200	45800

CLIPPER MARINE CORP
SANTA ANA CA 92705   COAST GUARD MFG ID- CLM See inside cover to adjust price for area

LOA FT IN	NAME AND/ OR MODEL	TOP/ RIG	BOAT TYPE	-HULL- MTL TP	TP	----ENGINE--- # HP MFG	BEAM FT IN	WGT LBS	DRAFT FT IN	RETAIL LOW	RETAIL HIGH
---	--- 1978 BOATS										
25 9	CLIPPER	SLP	SA/CR	FBG SK			8	2400	5 4	4200	4900
30	CLIPPER 9.3	SLP	SA/CR	FBG KL	IB	12D	8	5000		8850	10000
31 7	CLIPPER	SLP	SA/CR	FBG KL	IB	12D	8	7500		13200	15000
31 7	CLIPPER AFT CABIN	SLP	SA/CR	FBG KL	IB	12D	8	7700		13500	15400
---	--- 1977 BOATS										
20 11	CM21	SLP	SA/CR	FBG SK	OB		7 3	1650	4 10	2600	3050
22 8	CM23	SLP	SA/CR	FBG TK	OB		7 8	2100	2 2	3200	3750
25 9	CM26 MK II	SLP	SA/CR	FBG KL	OB		8	2400	5 4	3950	4600
26 8	CM27	SLP	SA/CR	FBG KC	OB		8	4400	5	6850	7900
30 7	CM9.3	SLP	SA/CR	FBG KL	OB		8	4400	3 6	7300	8400
31 7	CM32	SLP	SA/CR	FBG TK	IB	D	8	6500	3 11	11000	12500
31 7	CM32 AFT CBN	SLP	SA/CR	FBG TK	IB	D	8	5700	3 6	9650	11000
36 8	CM37	SLP	SA/CR	FBG TK	IB	D	10 10	14800	5 3	26100	29000
---	--- 1976 BOATS										
20 11	CM21	SLP	SAIL	FBG SK	OB		7 3	1650	7	2550	2950
22 8	CM23	SLP	SAIL	FBG TK	OB		7 8	2025	7	3050	3550
22 8	CM23	SLP	SAIL	FBG TK	OB		7 8	2025	1 7	3050	3550
23 7	CM4	SLP	SAIL	FBG KL	OB		7 11	2900	3 11	4050	4700
25 9	CM26 MK II	SLP	SAIL	FBG KL	OB		7 11	2600	4	4050	4750
25 9	CM26 MK II	SLP	SAIL	FBG SK	OB		7 11	2400	1 4	3850	4450
30	CM30	SLP	SAIL	FBG KL	OB		8	3700	3 6	5600	6800
30	CM30 DELUXE	SLP	SAIL	FBG KL	IB	D	8	3700	3 6	5800	6700
30	CM30 MK II	SLP	SAIL	FBG KL	IB	D	8	3700	3 6	6400	7350
31 7	CM32	SLP	SAIL	FBG KL	IB	D	8	5300	3 6	8600	9900
31 7	CM32	KTH	SAIL	FBG KL	IB	D	8	5300	3 6	8600	9900
---	--- 1975 BOATS										
20 11	MK-21	SLP	SAIL	FBG SK			7 3	1650	4 4	2450	2850
23 7	CM/4	SLP	SAIL	FBG KL			7 11	2900	3 11	3950	4550
23 7	CM/4C OR MK-23	SLP	SAIL	FBG KL			7 11	2550	3 11	3600	4150
23 7	CM/4C OR MK-23	SLP	SAIL	FBG SK			7 11	2000	5 4	3100	3600
25 9	MK-26	SLP	SAIL	FBG KL			7 11	2900	5 4	4350	5000
25 9	MK-26	SLP	SAIL	FBG SK			7 11	2400	5 4	3800	4450
30	CM-30	SLP	MS	FBG KL	OB		8	3500	2 8	5450	6250
30	CM-30	SLP	MS	FBG KL	IB	8D YAN	8	3500	2 8	5600	6400
---	--- 1974 BOATS										
20 11	MK-21	SLP	SAIL	FBG	OB		7 3	1650	7	2400	2800
20 11	MK-21 FD	SLP	SAIL	FBG	OB		7 6	1650	7	2400	2800
23 7	CM/4	SLP	SAIL	FBG	OB		7 11	2900	3 11	3850	4450
23 7	CM/4C	SLP	SAIL	FBG	OB		7 11	2000	1 6	3000	3500
23 7	CM/4C	SLP	SAIL	FBG	OB		7 11	2500	3 11	3450	4000
25 9	MK-21 FD	SLP	SAIL	FBG	OB		7 11	2650	1 4	3900	4450
25 9	MK-26	SLP	SAIL	FBG	OB		7 11	2400	1 4	3650	4250
25 9	MK-26	SLP	SAIL	FBG	OB		7 11	2650	4	3900	4550
25 9	MK-26 FD	SLP	SAIL	FBG	OB		7 11	2400	4	3650	4200
---	--- 1973 BOATS										
20 11	CLIPPER MK 21 CBN		SAIL	FBG	OB		7 3	1650		2350	2700
20 11	CLIPPER MK 21 FD		SAIL	FBG	OB		7 3	1650		2350	2700
24	CLIPPER CM/4 1/4 TON		SAIL	FBG	OB		7 11	2900		4150	4850
24	CLIPPER MK 23 CBN		SAIL	FBG	OB		7 11	2350		3300	3850
24	CLIPPER MK-23 FD		SAIL	FBG	OB		7 11	2350		3500	4050
25 9	CLIPPER MK 26 CBN		SAIL	FBG	OB		7 11	2400		3550	4100
25 9	CLIPPER MK 26 FD		SAIL	FBG	OB		7 11	2650		3800	4450
---	--- 1972 BOATS										
20 11	CLIPPER CBN MK 21		SAIL	FBG	OB		7 3	1650	4 4	2300	2700
20 11	CLIPPER FD MK 21		SAIL	FBG	OB		7 3	1650	4 4	2300	2700
25 9	CLIPPER CBN MK 26		SAIL	FBG	OB		7 11	2400	5 4	3450	4000
---	--- 1971 BOATS										
20 11	CLIPPER MK 21		SAIL	FBG KC	OB		7 3	1650	4 4	2250	2650

CLIPPERCRAFT MFG CO

Call 1-800-327-6929 for BUC Personalized Evaluation Service
Or, for 1959 boats, sign onto www.BUCValuPro.com

CLUETT & COMPANY INC

Call 1-800-327-6929 for BUC Personalized Evaluation Service
Or, for 1959 to 1967 boats, sign onto www.BUCValuPro.com

CLYDE BOAT WORKS

Call 1-800-327-6929 for BUC Personalized Evaluation Service
Or, for 1960 to 1961 boats, sign onto www.BUCValuPro.com

COASTAL MARINE COMPANY

Call 1-800-327-6929 for BUC Personalized Evaluation Service
Or, for 1971 boats, sign onto www.BUCValuPro.com

COASTAL PLASTICS INC
COAST GUARD MFG ID- CTP

Call 1-800-327-6929 for BUC Personalized Evaluation Service
Or, for 1977 to 1980 boats, sign onto www.BUCValuPro.com

COASTAL RECREATION INC
STANTON CA 90680   COAST GUARD MFG ID- LAY See inside cover to adjust price for area

LOA FT IN	NAME AND/ OR MODEL	TOP/ RIG	BOAT TYPE	-HULL- MTL TP	TP	----ENGINE--- # HP MFG	BEAM FT IN	WGT LBS	DRAFT FT IN	RETAIL LOW	RETAIL HIGH
---	--- 1983 BOATS										
16	BALBOA 16	SLP	SAIL	FBG KL	OB		7 5	1000	2 5	2200	2600
21 7	BALBOA 22R	SLP	SA/CR	FBG SK	OB		8	1980	1 3	3650	4250
21 7	BALBOA 22S	SLP	SA/CR	FBG KL	OB		8	2280	2 11	4000	4650
23 7	BALBOA 24	SLP	SA/CR	FBG KL	OB		8 4	2600	2 11	4850	5600
26 6	BALBOA 27	SLP	SA/RC	FBG KC	OB		8	4900	5 6	9950	11300
---	--- 1982 BOATS										
16	BALBOA 16	SLP	SAIL	FBG KL	OB		7 5	1000	2 5	2050	2450
21 7	BALBOA 22	SLP	SA/CR	FBG SK	OB		8	1980	1 3	3450	4000
21 7	BALBOA 22S	SLP	SA/CR	FBG KL	OB		8	2280	2 11	3750	4350
23 7	BALBOA 24	SLP	SA/CR	FBG KL	OB		8 4	2600	2 11	4600	5300
26 6	BALBOA 27	SLP	SA/CR	FBG KC	OB		8	4900	2 5	9400	10700
---	--- 1981 BOATS										
16	BALBOA 16	SLP	SAIL	FBG KL	OB		7 5	1000	2 5	1900	2300
21 7	BALBOA 21	SLP	SA/CR	FBG CB	OB		7 11	2000	4 7	3150	3700
21 7	BALBOA 22	SLP	SA/CR	FBG SK	OB		8	1980	1 3	3250	3750
21 7	BALBOA 22S	SLP	SA/CR	FBG KL	OB		8	2280	2 11	3550	4100
22 8	BALBOA 23	SLP	SA/CR	FBG CB	OB		8 11	2500	4 7	3950	4600
23 7	BALBOA 24	SLP	SA/CR	FBG KL	OB		8 4	2600	2 11	4050	4700
26 6	BALBOA 27	SLP	SA/CR	FBG KC	OB		8	4900	2 5	8850	10000
26 6	BALBOA 27	SLP	SA/CR	FBG KC	IB	9D	8	4900	2 5	8850	9950
---	--- 1980 BOATS										
21 7	BALBOA 21	SLP	SA/CR	FBG SK	OB		7 11	2000	1 3	3050	3500
21 7	BALBOA 22	SLP	SA/CR	FBG SK	OB		8	1980	1 3	3100	3600
22 8	BALBOA 23	SLP	SA/CR	FBG SK	OB		8 11	2500	1 3	3800	4400
26 6	BALBOA 27	SLP	SA/CR	FBG KC	OB		8	4900	2 5	8350	9600
26 6	BALBOA 27	SLP	SA/CR	FBG KC	IB	D	8		2 5	8300	9500
---	--- 1979 BOATS										
21 7	BALBOA 21	SLP	SA/CR	FBG SK	OB		7 11	2000	1	2900	3400
21 7	BALBOA 22	SLP	SA/CR	FBG SK	OB		8	1980	1 3	2950	3450
22 8	BALBOA 23	SLP	SA/CR	FBG SK	OB		8 11	2500	1 3	3650	4250
26 6	BALBOA 27	SLP	SA/CR	FBG KC	IB	D PETT	8	4600	2 5	7950	9150
---	--- 1978 BOATS										
21	AQUARIUS 21	SLP	SA/CR	FBG KC	IB	D	7 11	1900	4 7	3600	4200
21	AQUARIUS-PELICAN	SLP	SA/CR	FBG KC	OB		7 11	1900	4 7	2700	3150
22 8	AQUARIUS 7.0	SLP	SA/CR	-HBG KC	OB		7 11	2280	1 1	3300	3850
25 1	LA-PAZ 25	SLP	SA/CR	FBG KC	IB	25D	8	4600	2 8	7500	8600
25 7	BALBOA 26	SLP	SA/CR	FBG SK	OB		7 11	3600	5	5550	6350
25 7	BALBOA 26	SLP	SA/CR	FBG SK	OB		7 11	3600	1 10	5550	6350
26 6	BALBOA 8.2	SLP	SA/CR	FBG KC	IB	7D	8	4600	2 5	7650	8800

LOA FT	LOA IN	NAME AND/ OR MODEL	TOP/ RIG	BOAT TYPE	HULL MTL	HULL TP	ENGINE TP	# HP	ENGINE MFG	BEAM FT	BEAM IN	WGT LBS	DRAFT FT	DRAFT IN	RETAIL LOW	RETAIL HIGH
		1977 BOATS														
20		BALBOA	SLP	SAIL	FBG	SK	OB			7	1	1760	1	9	2450	2800
20		ENSENADA	SLP	SAIL	FBG	SK	OB			7	1	1600	1		2350	2700
21		AQUARIUS 21	SLP	SAIL	FBG	KC	OB			7	10	1900	1		2650	3050
22	8	AQUARIUS 23	SLP	SAIL	FBG	KC	OB			7	11	2280	1	1	3200	3700
25	1	LA-PAZ 25	SLP	MS	FBG	KL	IB	25D	VLVO	8		4600	2		7250	8300
25	7	BALBOA 26	SLP	SAIL	FBG	SK	OB			8		3600	1	10	5350	6150
26	6	BALBOA 8.2	SLP	SA/CR	FBG	KC	IB	7D	PETT	8		4600	2	2	7400	8500
		1976 BOATS														
20		BALBOA 20	SLP	SAIL	FBG	SK	OB			7	1	1700	1	9	2300	2700
20		ENSENADA 20	SLP	SAIL	FBG	SK	OB			7	1	1700	1		2350	2700
21		AQUARIUS 21	SLP	SAIL	FBG	KC	OB			7	11	1900	1		2550	2950
22	8	AQUARIUS 23	SLP	SAIL	FBG	KC				7	11	2280	1	1	3100	3600
25	1	LA-PAZ 25	SLP	MS	FBG	KL	IB	25D	VLVO	8		5500	2		8300	9500
25	7	BALBOA 26	SLP	SAIL	FBG	SK	OB			8		3600	1	10	5150	5950
26	6	BALBOA 27	SLP	SAIL	FBG	KC	IB	D		8		4600	2	2	7200	8250
		1975 BOATS														
20		BALBOA WE	SLP	SAIL	FBG	SK	OB			7	1	1760	4		2300	2700
20		ENSENADA 20	SLP	SAIL	FBG	SK	OB			7	1	1600	4		2200	2550
21		AQUARIUS 21	SLP	SAIL	FBG	KC	OB			7	10	1900	4	7	2500	2900
22	8	AQUARIUS 2-23	SLP	SAIL	FBG	KL	OB			7	11	2580	4	7	3250	3800
22	8	AQUARIUS 23	SLP	SAIL	FBG	KC				7	11	2280	4	7	3000	3500
25	1	LA-PAZ 25	SLP	SAIL	FBG	KL	IB	25D	VLVO	8		4600	2		6800	7800
25	7	BALBOA 26	SLP	SAIL	FBG	KL	IB	D		8			5		6750	7750
25	7	BALBOA 26	SLP	SAIL	FBG	SK	IB	D		8		3600	5		5450	6250
		1974 BOATS														
20		BALBOA 20	SLP	SAIL	FBG	SK	OB			7	1	1700	4		2200	2550
20		ENSENADA 20	SLP	SAIL	FBG	SK	OB			7	1	1600	4		2100	2500
21		AQUARIUS 21	SLP	SAIL	FBG	KC	OB			7	11	1900	4	7	2400	2800
22	8	AQUARIUS 2-23	SLP	SAIL	FBG	KL	OB			7	11	2800	4	7	3350	3900
22	8	AQUARIUS 23	SLP	SAIL	FBG	KC	OB			7	11	2280	4	7	2900	3400
25	1	LA-PAZ 25	SLP	SAIL	FBG	KL	IB	25D	VLVO	7	11	4600	2		6600	7600
25	7	BALBOA 26	SLP	SAIL	FBG	KL	OB			7	11	3600	5		4900	5600
		1973 BOATS														
20		BALBOA	SLP	SAIL	FBG	SK	OB			7	1	1700	1	9	2100	2500
20		ENSENADA	SLP	SAIL	FBG	SK	OB			7	1	1600	1		2050	2400
21		AQUARIUS	SLP	SAIL	FBG	KL	OB			7	10	1900	1		2350	2750
22	8	AQUARIUS	SLP	SAIL	FBG	KL	OB			7	11	2280	1	1	2850	3300
25	7	BALBOA	SLP	SAIL	FBG	KL	OB			8		4450	4	4	5800	6700
25	7	BALBOA	SLP	SAIL	FBG	SK	OB			8		3600	1	10	4750	5500
		1972 BOATS														
20		BALBOA	SLP	SAIL	FBG	SK	OB			7	1	1700	1	9	2050	2450
20		ENSENADA	SLP	SAIL	FBG	SK	OB			7	1	1600	1		2000	2350
21		AQUARIUS	SLP	SAIL	FBG	KC	OB			7	10	1900	1		2300	2700
22	8	AQUARIUS	SLP	SAIL	FBG	KC	OB			7	11	2280	1	1	2800	3250
22	8	AQUARIUS	SLP	SAIL	FBG	KL	OB			7	11	2580	3	8	3000	3500
25	7	BALBOA	SLP	SAIL	FBG	KL	OB			8		4450	4	4	5700	6550
25	7	BALBOA	SLP	SAIL	FBG	SK	OB			8		3600	1	10	4650	5350
		1971 BOATS														
20		BALBOA WE	SLP	SAIL	FBG	SK	OB			7	1	1760	4		2050	2450
20		ENSENADA	SLP	SAIL	FBG	SK	OB			7	1	1600	4		1950	2300
21		AQUARIUS	SLP	SAIL	FBG	KC	OB			7	10	1900	4	7	2300	2650
22	8	AQUARIUS	SLP	SAIL	FBG	KC	OB			7	11	2280	4	7	2700	3150
25	7	BALBOA	SLP	SAIL	FBG	KL	OB			8		3600	5		4600	5300
25	7	BALBOA	SLP	SAIL	FBG	SK	OB			8		3600	5		4600	5300
		1970 BOATS														
20		BALBOA WE	SLP	SAIL	FBG	SK	OB			7	1	1760	4		2000	2400
20		ENSENADA	SLP	SAIL	FBG	SK	OB			7	1	1600	4		1900	2250
21		AQUARIUS	SLP	SAIL	FBG	KC	OB			7	10	1900	4	7	2250	2600
22	8	AQUARIUS	SLP	SAIL	FBG	KC	OB			7	11	2280	4	7	2700	3100
25	7	BALBOA	SLP	SAIL	FBG	KL	OB			8		3600	5		4500	5200
25	7	BALBOA	SLP	SAIL	FBG	SK	OB			8		3600	5		4500	5200
		1969 BOATS														
20		BALBOA WE	SLP	SAIL	FBG	SK	OB			7	1	1760	4		2000	2350
20		ENSENADA	SLP	SAIL	FBG	SK	OB			7	1	1600	4		1900	2250
21		AQUARIUS	SLP	SAIL	FBG	KC	OB			7	10	1900	4	7	2200	2550
22	8	AQUARIUS	SLP	SAIL	FBG	KC	OB			7	11	2280	4	7	2650	3050
25	7	BALBOA	SLP	SAIL	FBG	KL	OB			8		3600	5		4450	5100
25	7	BALBOA	SLP	SAIL	FBG	SK	OB			8		3600	5		4450	5100

COASTAL YACHTS INC

COAST GUARD MFG ID- DGC

Call 1-800-327-6929 for BUC Personalized Evaluation Service
Or, for 1983 boats, sign onto www.BUCValuPro.com

COBALT BOATS

FIBERGLASS ENGINEERING INC
NEODESHA KS 66757 COAST GUARD MFG ID- FGE

See inside cover to adjust price for area

For more recent years, see the BUC Used Boat Price Guide, Volume 1 or Volume 2

LOA FT	LOA IN	NAME AND/ OR MODEL	TOP/ RIG	BOAT TYPE	HULL MTL	HULL TP	ENGINE TP	# HP	ENGINE MFG	BEAM FT	BEAM IN	WGT LBS	DRAFT FT	DRAFT IN	RETAIL LOW	RETAIL HIGH
		1983 BOATS														
17	2	CS7	ST	RNBT	FBG	DV	IO	185	OMC	7	5	2400	1	6	3650	4250
18	2	COBALT 18DV	ST	RNBT	FBG	DV	IO	185-198		7	5	2700	1	6	4100	4850
18	2	COBALT 18DV	ST	RNBT	FBG	DV	IO	200	OMC	7	5	2700	1	6	4150	4800
18	2	COBALT 18DV	ST	RNBT	FBG	DV	IO	200-260		7	5	2800	1	6	4500	5400
19		COBALT 19BR	ST	RNBT	FBG	DV	IO	225-260		7	7	2850	1	5	4900	5850
19		COBALT 19CD	ST	RNBT	FBG	DV	IO	225-260		7	7	2850	1	5	4850	5800
19		COBALT CM9	ST	RNBT	FBG	DV	IO	228-260		7	7	2800	1	5	4750	5700
19		COBALT CS9	ST	RNBT	FBG	DV	IO	225-260		7	7	2800	1	5	4800	5700
22	7	COBALT CM23	ST	CUD	FBG	DV	IO	260	MRCR	8		3900	1	6	8350	9600
22	7	COBALT CS23	ST	CUD	FBG	DV	IO	260		8		3900	1	6	7950	9450
22	7	COBALT CS23	ST	CUD	FBG	DV	IO	T185-T228		8		4700	1	6	9950	12000
22	7	COBALT CS23	ST	CUD	FBG	DV	IO	T260		8		4900	1	6	10900	12400
22	7	CONDESA	ST	CUD	FBG	DV	IO	260		8		4200	1	6	8500	10100
22	7	CONDESA	ST	CUD	FBG	DV	IO	T185-T228		8		5000	1	6	10400	12500
22	7	CONDESA	ST	CUD	FBG	DV	IO	T260		8		5200	1	6	11400	13600
		1982 BOATS														
17	2	C57	ST	RNBT	FBG	DV	IO	170-198		7	5	2450	1	6	3600	4450
17	2	C57	ST	RNBT	FBG	DV	IO	200		7	5	2450	1	6	3650	4500
18	2	COBALT 18DV	ST	RNBT	FBG	DV	IO	170-200		7	5	2700	1	6	4000	4900
18	2	COBALT 18DV	ST	RNBT	FBG	DV	IO	225-260		7	5	2800	1	6	4500	5400
18	2	COBALT 18TH	ST	RNBT	FBG	TR	IO	170-200		7	5	2605	1	3	3900	4800
18	2	COBALT 18TH	ST	RNBT	FBG	TR	IO	225-260		7	5	2700	1	3	4400	5300
19		COBALT 19BR	ST	RNBT	FBG	DV	IO	225-260		7	7	2800	1	5	4700	5750
19		COBALT 19CD	ST	RNBT	FBG	DV	IO	225-260		7	7	2800	1	5	4700	5750
22	7	CONDESA	ST	CUD	FBG	DV	IO	260		8		4500	1	6	8850	10100
22	7	CONDESA	ST	CUD	FBG	DV	IO	330	MRCR	8		4843	1	6	10100	11500
22	7	CONDESA	ST	CUD	FBG	DV	IO	T175-T260		8		5065	1	6	10700	13200
		1981 BOATS														
18	2	COBALT 18DV	ST	RNBT	FBG	DV	IO	170-185		7	5	2530	1	6	3800	4450
18	2	COBALT 18DV	ST	RNBT	FBG	DV	IO	198-230		7	5	2800	1	6	4100	5100
18	2	COBALT 18DV	ST	RNBT	FBG	DV	IO	260		7	5	2809	1	6	4400	5300
18	2	COBALT 18TH	ST	RNBT	FBG	TR	IO	170-200		7	5	2605	1	3	3850	4650
18	2	COBALT 18TH	ST	RNBT	FBG	TR	IO	225-260		7	5	2700	1	3	4300	5200
18	2	COBALT 18TH	ST	RNBT	FBG	TR	IO	815	MRCR	7	5	2580	1	3	**	**
19		COBALT 19BR	ST	RNBT	FBG	DV	IO	225-260		7	7	2900	1	5	4750	5650
19		COBALT 19CD	ST	RNBT	FBG	DV	IO	225-260		7	7	2900	1	5	4700	5650
22	7	CONDESA	ST	CUD	FBG	DV	IO	260		8		4500	1	6	8600	9900
		IO 330 MRCR 10000 11300, IO T185-T228 10200 12600, IO T260													11400	13000
		1980 BOATS														
16	8	COBALT 16SE	ST	RNBT	FBG	TR	IO	140-170		6	7	2500	1		3250	3800
16	8	COBALT 16SE	ST	RNBT	FBG	TR	IO	198-200		6	7	2800	1		3550	4150
18	2	COBALT 18DV	ST	RNBT	FBG	DV	IO	165-198		7	5	2523	1	6	3800	4700
		IO 200 4050 4950, IO 225-260 4400 5250, IO 290 VLVO													4850	5550
18	2	COBALT 18TH	ST	RNBT	FBG	TR	IO	165-198		7	5	2423	1	3	3700	4600
		IO 200 3950 4850, IO 225-260 4250 5150, IO 290 VLVO													4750	5450
19		COBALT 19BR	ST	RNBT	FBG	DV	IO	225-260		7	7	2900	1	5	4700	5600
19		COBALT 19BR	ST	RNBT	FBG	DV	IO	290	VLVO	7	7	2900	1	5	5150	5950
19		COBALT 19CD	ST	RNBT	FBG	DV	IO	225-260		7	7	2900	1	5	4700	5600
19		COBALT 19CD	ST	RNBT	FBG	DV	IO	290	VLVO	7	7	2900	1	5	5150	5900
22	7	COBALT CONDESA	ST	CUD	FBG	DV	IO	260-290		8		4200	1	6	8350	10000
22	7	COBALT CONDESA	ST	CUD	FBG	DV	IO	T260-T290		8		4200	1	6	9950	12000
22	7	CONDESA	ST	CUD	FBG	DV	IO	260		8		4500	1	6	8550	9800
		IO 330 MRCR 9900 11200, IO T165-T198 9850 12200, IO T228-T260													11000	12900
		1979 BOATS														
16	8	COBALT 16SE	ST	RNBT	FBG	TR	IO	140-170		6	7	2390	1		3150	3800
16	8	COBALT 16SE	ST	RNBT	FBG	TR	IO	198-200		6	7	2800	1		3550	4150
18	2	COBALT 18DV	ST	RNBT	FBG	DV	IO	165-200		7	5	2523	1	6	3800	4700
18	2	COBALT 18DV	ST	RNBT	FBG	DV	IO	228-260		7	5	2807	1	6	4150	5000
18	2	COBALT 18TH	ST	RNBT	FBG	TR	IO	165-170		7	2	2423	1	3	3600	4200
18	2	COBALT 18TH	ST	RNBT	FBG	TR	IO	198-260		7	2	2700	1	3	3900	4800
19		COBALT 19BR	ST	RNBT	FBG	DV	IO	228-260		7	7	2900	1	5	4500	5350
19		COBALT 19CD	ST	RNBT	FBG	DV	IO	228-260		7	7	2900	1	5	4500	5350
22	7	CONDESA	ST	CUD	FBG	DV	IO	260		8		4500	1	6	8550	9800
		IO 330 MRCR 9900 11200, IO T165-T198 9800 12200, IO T228-T260													11000	12900

CONTINUED ON NEXT PAGE

LOA FT	IN	NAME AND/ OR MODEL	TOP/ RIG	BOAT TYPE	-HULL- MTL	TP	----ENGINE--- TP	# HP	MFG	BEAM FT	IN	WGT LBS	DRAFT FT	IN	RETAIL LOW	RETAIL HIGH
		1978 BOATS														
16	8	COBALT 17	ST	RNBT	FBG	TR	IO	140-185		6	7	2500	1		3300	3850
18	2	COBALT 18	ST	RNBT	FBG	TR	IO	165-260		7	2	2700	1	3	3900	4850
19		COBALT 19BR	ST	RNBT	FBG	DV	IO	225-260		7	7	2900	1	5	4500	5400
19		COBALT 19CD	ST	RNBT	FBG	DV	IO	225-260		7	7	2900	1	5	4500	5400
22	7	CONDESA	ST	CUD	FBG	DV	IO	240-260		8		4500	1	6	8450	9900
22	7	CONDESA	ST	CUD	FBG	DV	IO	330	MRCR	8		4500	1	6	9450	10700
22	7	CONDESA	ST	CUD	FBG	DV	IO	T140-T260		8		5500	1	6	10700	13000
		1977 BOATS														
16	8	COBALT 17	ST	RNBT	FBG	TR	IO	140-190		6	7	2350	1		3200	3750
18	2	COBALT 18	ST	RNBT	FBG	TR	IO	165-235		7	2	2600	1	3	3850	4650
18	2	COBALT 18	ST	RNBT	FBG	TR	JT	320	HARD	7	2	2600	1	3	4650	5350
19		COBALT 19BR	ST	RNBT	FBG	DV	IO	175-235		8		2810	1	5	4550	5400
19		COBALT 19BR	ST	RNBT	FBG	DV	JT	320	HARD	8		2810	1	5	5350	6150
19		COBALT 19CD	ST	RNBT	FBG	DV	IO	175-235		8		2810	1	5	4500	5350
19		COBALT 19CD	ST	RNBT	FBG	DV	JT	320	HARD	8		2810	1	5	5300	6050
		1976 BOATS														
16	8	COBALT 17	OP	RNBT	FBG	TR	IO	140-190		6	7	2350	1		3300	3850
18	2	COBALT 18	OP	RNBT	FBG	TR	IO	165-235		7	2	2600	1	3	3950	4800
18	2	COBALT 18	OP	RNBT	FBG	TR	JT	290	OMC	7	2	2600	1	3	4500	5150
19		COBALT 19	OP	RNBT	FBG	DV	IO	165-235		7	7	2810	1	5	4500	5350
19		COBALT 19	OP	RNBT	FBG	DV	JT	290	OMC	7	7	2810	1	5	4950	5700
		1975 BOATS														
16	4	COBALT 16	OP	RNBT	FBG	TR	IO	140-190		6	7	2350	1		3350	3900
18		COBALT 18	OP	RNBT	FBG	TR	IO	165-235		7		2600	1	3	4000	4850
18		COBALT 18	OP	RNBT	FBG	TR	JT	290	OMC	7		2600	1	3	4200	4850
19		COBALT 19	OP	RNBT	FBG	DV	IO	165-235		7	7	2810	1	5	4650	5500
19		COBALT 19	OP	RNBT	FBG	DV	JT	290	OMC	7	7	2810	1	5	4750	5450
		1974 BOATS														
16	4	COBALT 16	OP	RNBT	FBG	TR	IO	140-165		6	7	2280			3400	4000
18		COBALT 16	OP	RNBT	FBG	TR	IO	188-225		7		2815			4400	5100
18		COBALT 16	OP	RNBT	FBG	TR	JT	245	OMC	7		2722			4100	4800
18		COBALT 18	OP	RNBT	FBG	TR	IO	165	OMC	7		2600			4100	4800
18		COBALT 18	OP	RNBT	FBG	TR	IO	245	OMC	7		2760			4500	5200
18		COBLAT 18	OP	RNBT	FBG	TR	IO	165	MRCR	7		2600			4100	4800
18		COBLAT 18	OP	RNBT	FBG	TR	JT	290	OMC	7		2722			4100	4800
19		COBALT 19 W/T	OP	RNBT	FBG	DV	IO	165		7	5				4750	5450
		IB 245 4050 4700, IO 290 5300 6100, IB 290													4100	4800
		1973 BOATS														
16	4	COBALT 16	OP	RNBT	FBG	TR	IO	120-165		6	7	2295			3500	4200
18		COBALT 18	OP	RNBT	FBG	TR	IO	140-165		7		2525			4200	4950
		IO 188-225 4550 5250, JT 245 OMC 3950 4600, IO 245 OMC													4650	5350
		1972 BOATS														
16	4				FBG	TR	IO	120-165		6	7	2295			3500	4150
18					FBG	TR	IO	140-165		7		2525			4200	5000
18					FBG	TR	IO	188-245		7		2815			4600	5400
		1971 BOATS														
16	4	COBALT TH16	OP	RNBT	FBG	TH	IO	120		6	7	1900			3400	3950
18		COBALT TH18	OP	RNBT	FBG	TH	IO	165		7		2100			4100	4750
		1970 BOATS														
16	5	COBALT GT200		SKI	FBG	SV	IO	210		7					3150	3700
16	5	COBALT GT200		SKI	FBG	SV	IB	220	CONQ	7			1		1950	2300
16	5	COBALT XV200		SKI	FBG	SV	IO	210		7					3150	3700
16	5	COBALT XV200		SKI	FBG	SV	IB	220	CONQ	7			1		1950	2300
18		COBALT GT500		SKI	FBG	SV	IO	210		7					4900	5600
18		COBALT GT500		SKI	FBG	SV	IB	220	CONQ	7			1		3050	3550
18		COBALT TH18		SKI	FBG	TR	IB	160	MRCR	7			1	10	3000	3450
18		COBALT TH18		SKI	FBG	TR	IO	210		7					4900	5600
18		COBALT XF100		RNBT	FBG	FL	IB	327		7					3350	3900
18		COBALT XV100		RNBT	FBG	SV	IB	327		7					3350	3900
18		COBALT XV500		SKI	FBG	SV	IB	220	CONQ	7			1		3050	3550
23		COBALT 23		RNBT	FBG	DV	IB	160	MRCR	8			2	10	5650	6500
23		COBALT 23		RNBT	FBG	DV	IO	T160		8					10100	11500

COBIA BOAT COMPANY

DIV OF MAVERICK BOAT CO
FT PIERCE FL 34946 COAST GUARD MFG ID- CBA

See inside cover to adjust price for area

For more recent years, see the BUC Used Boat Price Guide, Volume 1 or Volume 2

LOA FT	IN	NAME AND/ OR MODEL	TOP/ RIG	BOAT TYPE	-HULL- MTL	TP	----ENGINE--- TP	# HP	MFG	BEAM FT	IN	WGT LBS	DRAFT FT	IN	RETAIL LOW	RETAIL HIGH
		1983 BOATS														
16	11	CB166		BASS	FBG	DV	OB			7	7	900			1750	2100
17		MONTE-CARLO C17VBR		RNBT	FBG	DV	OB			6	11	1200			2350	2700
17		MONTE-CARLO C17VBR		RNBT	FBG	DV	IO	120		6	11				2250	2600
17	2	CB175		BASS	FBG	DV	OB			7	11	975			1900	2300
18		CENTAUR C18V		RNBT	FBG	DV	OB			6	11	1250			2450	2850
18		SPORTSTER C18VBR	ST	RNBT	FBG	DV	OB			6	11	1300			2500	2950
18		SPORTSTER C18VBR	ST	RNBT	FBG	DV	IO	120-185		6	11	1950			2300	2750
18		SUNSKIFF CU180	OP	CTRCN	FBG	DV	OB			6	11	1000			2000	2400
18	6	ODYSSEY 195	ST	RNBT	FBG	DV	OB			7	11	1450			2750	3250
18	6	ODYSSEY 195	ST	RNBT	FBG	DV	IO	140-200		7	11	2200			2750	3250
18	6	ODYSSEY 195CC	OP	CUD	FBG	DV	OB			7	11	1550			2900	3400
18	6	ODYSSEY 195CC	OP	CUD	FBG	DV	IO	140		7	11	2300			2900	3350
18	6	ODYSSEY 195SCL	OP	RNBT	FBG	DV	IO	170-198		7	11	2200			2750	3250
18	6	ODYSSEY 195XL	OP	RNBT	FBG	DV	IO	170		7	11	2200			2800	3250
20	7	SUNSKIFF CU210	OP	CTRCN	FBG	DV	OB			7	6	1510			3400	3950
21	6	ODYSSEY 228	ST	RNBT	FBG	DV	IO	185-260		8		3600			4450	5350
21	6	ODYSSEY 228SD	ST	RNBT	FBG	DV	IO		OMC	8		3300			**	**
21	6	TRITON 228	ST	FSH	FBG	DV	OB			8		2400			5100	5900
21	6	TRITON 228SD	ST	FSH	FBG	DV	IO		OMC	8		2850			**	**
21	8	SUNSKIFF CU220		CTRCN	FBG	DV	OB			8		2000			4500	5200
23	7	CARIBBEAN 248		FSH	FBG	DV	IO	198		8		4200			6250	7200
27		CARIBBEAN 288		FSH	FBG	DV	IO	260		10		4600			9000	10200
		1982 BOATS														
16		TORNADO C16TBR	ST	RNBT	FBG	TR	OB			7		975			1800	2150
16	1	CB166	OP	BASS	FBG	DV	OB			7	7	900			1700	2000
17		MONTE-CARLO C17VBR	ST	RNBT	FBG	DV	OB			6	11	1200			2300	2650
17		MONTE-CARLO C17VBR	ST	RNBT	FBG	DV	IO	120		6	11				2200	2550
17	2	CB175	OP	BASS	FBG	DV	OB			7	11	975			1900	2250
18		CENTAUR C18V	ST	RNBT	FBG	DV	OB			6	11	1250			2400	2800
18		SPORTSTER C18VBR	ST	RNBT	FBG	DV	OB			6	11	1300			2500	2900
18		SPORTSTER C18VBR	ST	RNBT	FBG	DV	IO	120-200		6	11	1950			2250	2700
18		SUNSKIFF CU180	OP	CTRCN	FBG	DV	OB			6	11	1000			2000	2350
18	6	ODYSSEY 195	ST	RNBT	FBG	DV	OB			7	11	1550			2850	3300
18	6	ODYSSEY 195	ST	RNBT	FBG	DV	IO	120-200		7	11	2300			2700	3200
19	3	RANGER C20VBR	ST	RNBT	FBG	DV	IO	140		7	9				2900	3400
20	7	CONDOR C21V	ST	RNBT	FBG	DV	OB			7	6	1850			3950	4600
20	7	SUNSKIFF CU210	OP	CTRCN	FBG	DV	OB			7	6	1510			3350	3900
21	6	ODYSSEY 228	ST	RNBT	FBG	DV	IO	170-260		8		3600			4350	5250
21	6	TRITON 228	ST	FSH	FBG	DV	OB			8		2400			5000	5750
21	8	SUNSKIFF CU220	OP	CTRCN	FBG	DV	OB			8		2000			4400	5050
23	7	CARIBBEAN 248	ST	FSH	FBG	DV	IO	198	MRCR	8		4200			6100	7000
23	7	CARIBBEAN 248	TT	FSH	FBG	DV	IO	330	MRCR	8		4200			6900	7900
27		CARIBBEAN 288	ST	FSH	FBG	DV	IO	T170-T230		10		4600			9400	11400
27		CARIBBEAN 288	ST	FSH	FBG	DV	IO	T260	OMC	10		4600			10400	11900
27		CARIBBEAN 288	HT	FSH	FBG	DV	IO	260	OMC	10		4600			8700	10000
27		CARIBBEAN 288	HT	FSH	FBG	DV	IO	T170-T230		10		4600			9400	11400
27		CARIBBEAN 288	HT	FSH	FBG	DV	IO	T260	OMC	10		4600			10400	11900
27		CARIBBEAN 288	FB	FSH	FBG	DV	IO	T170-T230		10		4600			9400	11400
27		CARIBBEAN 288	FB	FSH	FBG	DV	IO	T260	OMC	10		4600			10400	11900
27		CARIBBEAN 288	FB	FSH	FBG	DV	IO	T130D	VLVO	10		4600			12800	14500
		1981 BOATS														
16		TORNADO C16TBR	ST	RNBT	FBG	TR	OB			7		975			1800	2150
17		MONTE-CARLO C17VBR	ST	RNBT	FBG	DV	OB			6	11	1200			2250	2600
17		MONTE-CARLO C17VBR	ST	RNBT	FBG	DV	IO	120-170		6	11	1850			2000	2400
17	2	CB175	OP	BASS	FBG	DV	OB			7	11	975			1850	2200
18		CENTAUR C18V	ST	RNBT	FBG	DV	OB			6	11	1250			2350	2750
18		SPORTSTER C18VBR	ST	RNBT	FBG	DV	OB			6	11	1300			2450	2850
18		SPORTSTER C18VBR	ST	RNBT	FBG	DV	IO	120-200		6	11	1950			2250	2650
18		SUNSKIFF CU180	OP	CTRCN	FBG	DV	OB			6	11	1000			1950	2300
18	6	GULFWINDS 198			FBG	DV	IO	120		7	10				2600	3000
18	6	ODYSSEY 195	ST	RNBT	FBG	DV	IO	120-200		7	11	2300			2700	3150
19	3	RANGER C20VBR		RNBT	FBG	DV	OB			7	9	1600			2950	3450
19	3	RANGER C20VBR	ST	RNBT	FBG	DV	IO	120-260		7	9	2510			2850	3600
20	7	CONDOR C21V	ST	RNBT	FBG	DV	OB			7	6	1850			3900	4550
20	7	CONDOR C21V	ST	RNBT	FBG	DV	IO	120		7	6				3450	4000
20	7	SUNSKIFF CU210	OP	CTRCN	FBG	DV	OB			7	6	1510			3250	3800
21	6	GULFSTREAM 228		CR	FBG	DV	OB			8		2600			5250	6050
21	6	ODYSSEY 228	ST	RNBT	FBG	DV	IO	120-260		8		3600			4200	5150
21	6	TRITON 228	ST	FSH	FBG	DV	OB			8		2400			4900	5650
21	8	SUNSKIFF CU220	OP	CTRCN	FBG	DV	OB			8		2000			4250	4950
23	7	CARIBBEAN 248	ST	FSH	FBG	DV	IO			8		4200			**	**
23	7	CARIBBEAN 248	TT	FSH	FBG	DV	IO			8		4200			**	**
27		CARIBBEAN 288	ST	FSH	FBG	DV	IO	T140-T200		10		4600			9000	10900
27		CARIBBEAN 288	ST	FSH	FBG	DV	IO	T230-T260		10		4600			9900	11700
27		CARIBBEAN 288	ST	FSH	FBG	DV	IO	T D	VLVO	10		4600			**	**

 CONTINUED ON NEXT PAGE

LOA FT	IN	NAME AND/ OR MODEL	TOP/ RIG	BOAT TYPE	-HULL- MTL	TP	TP	----ENGINE--- # HP	MFG	BEAM FT	IN	WGT LBS	DRAFT FT	IN	RETAIL LOW	RETAIL HIGH
		1981 BOATS														
27		CARIBBEAN 288	HT	FSH	FBG	DV	IO	T140-T200		10		4600			9000	10900
27		CARIBBEAN 288	HT	FSH	FBG	DV	IO	T230-T260		10		4600			9900	11700
27		CARIBBEAN 288	HT	FSH	FBG	DV	IO	T D	VLVO	10		4600			**	**
27		CARIBBEAN 288	FB	FSH	FBG	DV	IO	T140-T200		10		4600			9000	10900
27		CARIBBEAN 288	FB	FSH	FBG	DV	IO	T230-T260		10		4600			9900	11700
27		CARIBBEAN 288	FB	FSH	FBG	DV	IO	T D	VLVO	10		4600			**	**
		1980 BOATS														
16		TORNADO 16		RNBT	FBG	TR	IO	120		7		1800			1900	2250
16		TORNADO 16TBR		RNBT	FBG	TR	OB			7		990			1800	2150
16		TORNADO C-16 W/T		RNBT	FBG	TR	IO	120		7					1850	2200
16	10	CHARGER C-16 W/T		RNBT	FBG	DV	IO	120		6	10	1725			1900	2300
17		MONTE-CARLO 17		RNBT	FBG	DV	IO	120		7		1900			2050	2450
17		MONTE-CARLO 17BR		RNBT	FBG	SV	OB			7		1300			2350	2700
17		MONTE-CARLO C-17 W/T		RNBT	FBG	DV	IO	120		6	11				2100	2500
18		CENTAUR		RNBT	FBG	SV	OB			7		1275			2350	2750
18		CENTAUR 18		RNBT	FBG	DV	IO	120		7		2000			2250	2600
18		CENTAUR C-18		RNBT	FBG	DV	IO	120		6	11				2300	2700
18		SPORTSTER		RNBT	FBG	DV	OB			7		1300			2400	2800
18		SPORTSTER 18		RNBT	FBG	DV	IO	120		7		2000			2300	2700
18		SPORTSTER C-18		RNBT	FBG	DV	IO	120		6	11				2350	2750
18		SPORTSTER C-18 W/T		RNBT	FBG	DV	OB			6	11	1130			2200	2550
19	3	RANGER		RNBT	FBG	DV	OB			7	9	1600			2900	3400
19	3	RANGER 20		RNBT	FBG	DV	IO	120		7	9	2200			2700	3150
19	3	RANGER C-20		RNBT	FBG	DV	IO	120		7	9				2850	3300
19	3	RANGER C-20 W/T		RNBT	FBG	DV	OB			7	9	1600			2900	3400
20	7	CONDOR		RNBT	FBG	SV	OB			7	6	1550			3350	3900
20	7	CONDOR 21		RNBT	FBG	DV	IO	120		7	6	2300			3000	3450
20	7	CONDOR C-21		RNBT	FBG	DV	IO	120		7	6				3400	3950
20	7	VANTAGE		CUD	FBG	DV	OB			7	6	1750			3700	4300
20	7	VANTAGE 21		CUD	FBG	DV	IO	120		7	6	2400			3200	3700
20	7	VANTAGE C-21CC		CUD	FBG	DV	OB			7	6	1800			3750	4350
20	7	VANTAGE C-21CC		CUD	FBG	DV	IO	120		7	6				3700	4300
21	1	GULFSTREAM 22		CUD	FBG	DV	IO	120		8		2800			3700	4300
21	1	GULFSTREAM C-22CC		CUD	FBG	DV	IO	120		8					3950	4600
21	5	CUDDY 228		CR	FBG	DV	OB			8		2400			4850	5600
21	5	CUDDY 228		CUD	FBG	DV	IO	120		8					4000	4650
22		CU-220		UTL	FBG	DV	OB			8		1800			3400	3950
22		ODYSSEY		CR	FBG	DV	IO	120		8		2700			3800	4400
22	1	GULFSTREAM		CUD	FBG	DV	OB			8		2750			5550	6400
22	1	GULFSTREAM C-22CC		CUD	FBG	DV	OB			8		2550			5300	6100
23	7	CARIBBEAN 24		CUD	FBG	DV	IO	120		8		3500			4900	5600
23	7	CARIBBEAN C-24CC		CUD	FBG	DV	OB			8		3200			6700	7700
23	7	CARIBBEAN C-24CC		CUD	FBG	DV	IO	120		8					5550	6350
23	9	CARIBBEAN		CUD	FBG	DV	OB			8		3200			6800	7800
		1979 BOATS														
16		TORNADO	ST	RNBT	FBG	TR	IO	140		7		1540			1750	2100
17		MONTE-CARLO	ST	RNBT	FBG	DV	OB			6	11	1060			1950	2300
17		MONTE-CARLO	ST	RNBT	FBG	DV	IO	140		6	11	2050			2150	2500
17	7	CU 170 UTILITY	OP	UTL	FBG	TR	OB			7	6	1000			1750	2100
18		CENTAUR	ST	RNBT	FBG	DV	OB			6	11	1130			2100	2500
18		CENTAUR	ST	RNBT	FBG	DV	IO	200		6	11	1750			2200	2550
18		SPORTSTER	ST	RNBT	FBG	DV	OB			6	11	1130			2100	2500
18		SPORTSTER	ST	RNBT	FBG	DV	IO	200		6	11	1750			2200	2550
18	7	CU 180 UTILITY	OP	UTL	FBG	DV	OB			7	6	1050			1800	2150
19	3	RANGER C20VBR	ST	RNBT	FBG	DV	OB			7	9	1600			2900	3350
19	3	RANGER C20VBR	ST	RNBT	FBG	DV	IO	260		7	9	2350			3000	3450
20	7	CONDOR C21V	ST	RNBT	FBG	DV	OB			7	6	1550			3300	3850
20	7	CONDOR C21V	ST	RNBT	FBG	DV	IO	230		7	6	2300			3100	3600
20	7	VANTAGE C21CC	ST	CUD	FBG	DV	OB			7	6	1800			3700	4300
20	7	VANTAGE C21CC	ST	CUD	FBG	DV	IO	230		7	6	2600			3450	4000
22	1	GULFSTREAM C22CC	ST	CUD	FBG	DV	OB			8		2550			5200	6000
22	1	GULFSTREAM C22CC	ST	CUD	FBG	DV	IO	260		8		3300			4600	5250
23	7	CARIBBEAN	ST	CUD	FBG	DV	OB			8		3200			6600	7600
23	7	CARIBBEAN	ST	CUD	FBG	DV	IO	500		8		3950			9300	10600
		1978 BOATS														
16		TORNADO C16TBR	ST	RNBT	FBG	TR	OB			7		1180			2050	2450
16		TORNADO C16TBR	ST	RNBT	FBG	TR	IO	120		7		2000			2000	2400
16		TORNADO C16TBR	ST	RNBT	FBG	TR	IO	130-140		7		2000			2150	2550
17		MONTE-CARLO C17VBR	ST	RNBT	FBG	DV	OB			7		1250			2250	2600
17		VIKING C17V	ST	RNBT	FBG	DV	OB			7		1200			2150	2500
18		CENTAUR C18V	ST	RNBT	FBG	DV	OB			7		1800			2950	3400
18		CENTAUR C18V	ST	RNBT	FBG	DV	IO	120-228		7		2000			2250	2800
18		SPORTSTER C18VBR	ST	RNBT	FBG	DV	OB			7		1350			2400	2800
18		SPORTSTER C18VBR	ST	RNBT	FBG	DV	IO	120-228		7		2000			2350	2900
19	3	RANGER C20VBR	ST	RNBT	FBG	DV	OB			7	9	1600			2850	3300
19	3	RANGER C20VBR	ST	RNBT	FBG	DV	IO	120-240		7	9	2250			2750	3400
		IO 260 MRCR 2950 3450, IO T120-T130 3300 4150, IO T140													3300	4150
20	7	CONDOR C21V	ST	RNBT	FBG	DV	OB			7	6	1550			3250	3800
20	7	CONDOR C21V	ST	RNBT	FBG	DV	IO	120-228		7	6	2450			3100	3800
20	7	VANTAGE C21CC	ST	CUD	FBG	DV	OB			7	6	1850			3750	4350
20	7	VANTAGE C21CC	ST	CUD	FBG	DV	IO	120-228		7	6	2450			3250	4000
22	1	GULFSTREAM C22CC	ST	CUD	FBG	DV	OB			8		2550			5150	5900
22	1	GULFSTREAM C22CC	ST	CUD	FBG	DV	IO	120-260		8		3150			4200	5150
22	1	GULFSTREAM C22CC	ST	CUD	FBG	DV	IO	T120-T140		8		3150			4850	5900
23	9	CARIBBEAN C24CC	ST	CUD	FBG	DV	OB			8		3200			6550	7550
23	9	CARIBBEAN C24CC	ST	CUD	FBG	DV	IO	120-260		8		3800			5250	6300
23	9	CARIBBEAN C24CC	ST	CUD	FBG	DV	IO	T120-T240		8		3800			5900	7200
		1977 BOATS														
16		TORNADO C16TBR	ST	RNBT	FBG	TR	OB			7		1180			2050	2400
16		TORNADO C16TBR	ST	RNBT	FBG	TR	IO	120-140		7		3125			2650	3250
18		CENTAUR C18V	ST	RNBT	FBG	DV	OB			6	11	1300			2300	2650
18		CENTAUR C18V	ST	RNBT	FBG	DV	IO	120-235		6	11	2000			2300	2850
18		CUTLASS C18TBR	ST	RNBT	FBG	TR	OB			7	6	1300			2350	2700
18		CUTLASS C18TBR	ST	RNBT	FBG	TR	IO	120-235		7	6	2000			2400	3000
18		SPORTSTER C18VBR	ST	RNBT	FBG	DV	OB			6	11	1300			2400	2800
18		SPORTSTER C18VBR	ST	RNBT	FBG	DV	IO	120-235		6	11	2000			2350	2900
19	3	RANGER C20VBR	ST	RNBT	FBG	DV	OB			7	9	1600			2800	3300
19	3	RANGER C20VBR	ST	RNBT	FBG	DV	IO	120-240		7	9	2250			2800	3450
19	3	RANGER C20VBR	ST	RNBT	FBG	DV	IO	T120-T130		7	9	2250			3350	4200
19	3	RANGER C20VBR	ST	RNBT	FBG	DV	IO	T140		7	9	2250			3350	4200
20	7	CONDOR C21V	ST	RNBT	FBG	DV	OB			7	6	1550			3200	3750
20	7	CONDOR C21V	ST	RNBT	FBG	DV	IO	120-235		7	6	2450			3150	3850
20	7	VANTAGE C21CC	ST	CUD	FBG	DV	OB			7	6	1850			3700	4300
20	7	VANTAGE C21CC	ST	CUD	FBG	DV	IO	120-235		7	6	2450			3300	4050
22	1	GULFSTREAM C22CC	ST	CUD	FBG	DV	OB			8		2552			5050	5800
22	1	GULFSTREAM C22CC	ST	CUD	FBG	DV	IO	120-240		8		3150			4250	5200
22	1	GULFSTREAM C22CC	ST	CUD	FBG	DV	IO	T120-T175		8		3150			4950	6000
23	7	CARIBBEAN C24CC	ST	CUD	FBG	DV	OB			8		3200			6450	7400
23	7	CARIBBEAN C24CC	ST	CUD	FBG	DV	IO	120-240		8		3800			5300	6300
23	7	CARIBBEAN C24CC	ST	CUD	FBG	DV	IO	T120-T240		8		3800			5950	7250
		1976 BOATS														
16		TORNADO C16TBR	ST	RNBT	FBG	TR	OB			7		1180			2000	2400
16		TORNADO C16TBR	ST	RNBT	FBG	TR	IO	120-175		7		1780			1950	2350
17		MONTE-CARLO C17VBR	ST	RNBT	FBG	DV	OB			7		1300			2250	2650
17		MONTE-CARLO C17VBR	ST	RNBT	FBG	DV	IO	120		7		1900			2200	2550
17		VIKING C17V	ST	RNBT	FBG	DV	OB			7		1300			2250	2650
17		VIKING C17V	ST	RNBT	FBG	DV	IO	120		7		1900			2200	2550
18		CENTAUR TW18V	ST	RNBT	FBG	DV	OB			7		1300			2300	2700
18		CENTAUR TW18V	ST	RNBT	FBG	DV	IO	120		7		1900			2350	2700
18		CUTLASS C18TBR	ST	RNBT	FBG	TR	OB			7		1350			2400	2750
18		CUTLASS C18TBR	ST	RNBT	FBG	TR	IO	120		7		2050			2400	2800
18		SPORTSTER C18VBR	ST	RNBT	FBG	DV	OB			7		1300			2300	2700
18		SPORTSTER C18VBR	ST	RNBT	FBG	DV	IO	120		7		2000			2350	2750
18		SPORTSTER TW18VBR	ST	RNBT	FBG	DV	OB			7		1300			2300	2700
18		SPORTSTER TW18VBR	ST	RNBT	FBG	DV	IO	120		7		1900			2350	2700
19	3	RANGER I C19VBR	ST	RNBT	FBG	DV	OB			7	6	1600			2800	3250
19	3	RANGER I C19VBR	ST	RNBT	FBG	DV	IO	120		7	6	2200			2750	3200
19	3	RANGER II C19VBR	ST	RNBT	FBG	DV	OB			7	8	1750			2950	3450
19	3	SEA-SKIPPER C19VF	OP	FSH	FBG	DV	OB			7	6	1600			2800	3250
20	7	CONDOR C21V	ST	RNBT	FBG	DV	OB			7	6	1550			3150	3700
20	7	CONDOR C21V	ST	RNBT	FBG	DV	IO	120		7	6	2450			3250	3750
20	7	CONDOR TW21V	ST	RNBT	FBG	DV	OB			7	6	1550			3150	3700
20	7	CONDOR TW21V	ST	RNBT	FBG	DV	IO	120		7	6	2450			3250	3750
20	7	VANTAGE C21CC	ST	CUD	FBG	DV	OB			7	6	1800			3550	4150
20	7	VANTAGE C21CC	ST	CUD	FBG	DV	IO	120		7	6	2700			3550	4150
20	7	VANTAGE TW21CC	ST	CUD	FBG	DV	OB			7	6	1800			3550	4150
20	7	VANTAGE TW21CC	ST	CUD	FBG	DV	IO	120		7	6	2700			3550	4150
22	1	GULFSTREAM C22CC	OP	CUD	FBG	DV	OB			8		2250			4600	5250
22	1	GULFSTREAM C22CC	OP	CUD	FBG	DV	IO	120		8		3300			4550	5250
22	1	GULFSTREAM C22CC	OP	CUD	FBG	DV	IO	T140		8		3300			5200	6000
22	1	GULFSTREAM C22CSV	ST	CUD	FBG	DV	IO	165		8		3900			5150	5900
22	1	GULFSTREAM C22CSV	ST	CUD	FBG	DV	IO	T140		8		3900			5750	6650
22	1	GULFWINDS C22CSV	ST	CR	FBG	DV	OB			8		3000			5550	6400
22	1	GULFWINDS C22CSV	ST	CR	FBG	DV	IO	120		8		3900			5100	5900
23	9	CARIBBEAN C24CC	ST	CUD	FBG	DV	OB			8		3000			6100	7000
23	9	CARIBBEAN C24CC	ST	CUD	FBG	DV	IO	120-165		8		3900			5600	6450
23	9	CARIBBEAN C24CC	ST	CUD	FBG	DV	IO	T190		8		3900			6300	7250

CONTINUED ON NEXT PAGE

LOA FT	LOA IN	NAME AND/ OR MODEL	TOP/ RIG	BOAT TYPE	-HULL- MTL	-HULL- TP	ENGINE TP	ENGINE # HP	ENGINE MFG	BEAM FT	BEAM IN	WGT LBS	DRAFT FT	DRAFT IN	RETAIL LOW	RETAIL HIGH
		1975 BOATS														
16		TORNADO 16TBR	ST	RNBT	FBG	TR	OB			7		1180	2	9	2000	2400
16		TORNADO 16TBR	ST	RNBT	FBG	TR	IO	120-140		7		2135	2	9	2250	2750
17		CUTLASS 17TBR	ST	RNBT	FBG	TR	OB			6	11	1300			2250	2600
17		CUTLASS 17TBR	ST	RNBT	FBG	TR	IO	120-245		6	11	2000			2300	2850
17		MONTE-CARLO 17VBR	ST	RNBT	FBG	DV	OB			7		1150			2000	2350
17		MONTE-CARLO 17VBR	ST	RNBT	FBG	DV	IO	120-175		7		1750			2200	2700
18		CENTAUR C18V	ST	RNBT	FBG	DV	OB			6	11	1300	3	9	2300	2700
18		CENTAUR C18V	ST	RNBT	FBG	DV	IO	120-245		6	11	2000	3	9	2450	3000
18		SPORTSTER 18VBR	ST	RNBT	FBG	DV	OB			6	11	1300	3	9	2300	2700
18		SPORTSTER 18VBR	ST	RNBT	FBG	DV	IO	120-245		6	11	2000	3	9	2450	3000
19	3	FISHERMAN 20VF	ST	OPFSH	FBG	DV	OB			7	6	1600	4	1	2750	3200
19	3	FISHERMAN 20VF	ST	OPFSH	FBG	DV	IO	130-245		7	6	2200	4	1	3250	3800
19	3	GULFWINDS 20CV	ST	CR	FBG	DV	OB			7	6	1750	4	1	2950	3450
19	3	GULFWINDS 20CV	ST	CR	FBG	DV	IO	130-245		7	6	2450	4	1	3250	3800
19	3	RANGER C20VBR	ST	RNBT	FBG	DV	OB			7	6	1600	4	1	2800	3250
19	3	RANGER C20VBR	ST	RNBT	FBG	DV	IO	130-245		7	6	2200	4	1	3000	3500
20	7	CONDOR C21V	ST	RNBT	FBG	DV	OB			7	6	1550	3	9	3150	3650
20	7	CONDOR C21V	ST	RNBT	FBG	DV	IO	130-245		7	6	2450	3	9	3450	4050
20	7	VANTAGE C21CC	ST	CUD	FBG	DV	OB			7	6	1900	4	7	3700	4250
20	7	VANTAGE C21CC	ST	CUD	FBG	DV	IO	130-245		7	6	2670	4	7	3800	4450
23	8	CARIBBEAN C24CC	ST	CUD	FBG	DV	IO	170-245		8		3750	5	4	5750	6600
23	8	CARIBBEAN C24CC	ST	CUD	FBG	DV	IO	T120-T140		8		3750	5	4	6250	7500
		1974 BOATS														
16	10	MONTE-CARLO C17VBR	ST	RNBT	FBG		OB			6	8	1150	1		1950	2350
16	10	MONTE-CARLO C17VBR	ST	RNBT	FBG		IO	140-188		6	8		1	5	2350	2700
17		CUTLASS C17TBR	ST	RNBT	FBG		OB			6	11	1300		10	2250	2600
17		CUTLASS C17TBR	ST	RNBT	FBG		IO	140-165		6	11		1	3	2350	2750
18	1	CENTAUR C18V	ST	RNBT	FBG		OB			6	11	1200	1	2	2150	2500
18	1	CENTAUR C18V	ST	RNBT	FBG		IO	140		6	11		1	8	2550	2950
18	1	SEA-QUEEN C18C	ST	RNBT	FBG		OB			6	11	1500	1	3	2550	2950
18	1	SEA-QUEEN C18C	ST	RNBT	FBG		IO	140		6	11		1	8	2700	3150
18	1	SPORTSTER C18VBR	ST	RNBT	FBG		OB			6	11	1300	1	2	2300	2700
18	1	SPORTSTER C18VBR	ST	RNBT	FBG		IO	140		6	11		1	8	2600	3050
19	3	C20VF	OP	FSH	FBG		OB			7	6	1500	1	6	2650	3050
19	3	C20VF	OP	FSH	FBG		IO	140		7	6		1	8	3150	3650
19	3	GULFWINDS C20CF	OP	CR	FBG		OB			7	6	1750	1	6	2950	3400
19	3	HOLIDAY C20VBR	OP	CR	FBG		OB			7	6	1500	1	6	2650	3050
19	3	HOLIDAY C20VBR	OP	CR	FBG		IO	140		7	6		1	8	3100	3600
20	7	CONDOR C21V	ST	RNBT	FBG		OB			7	6	1550	1	6	3100	3650
20	7	CONDOR C21V	ST	RNBT	FBG		IO	165		7	6		1	10	3850	4450
20	7	VANTAGE C21CC	ST	CUD	FBG		OB			7	6	1800	1	6	3500	4100
20	7	VANTAGE C21CC	ST	CUD	FBG		IO	165		7	6		2		4200	4850
23	8	CARIBBEAN C24CC	ST	CUD	FBG		IO	165		8			2		6250	7200
23	8	CARIBBEAN C24CC	ST	CUD	FBG		IO	T140		8			2		6950	7950
		1973 BOATS														
16	3	SEA-QUEEN C17C	ST	RNBT	FBG		OB			6	11	1200	1		2000	2400
16	10	MONTE-CARLO C17VBR	ST	RNBT	FBG		OB			6	8	1150	1	3	1950	2350
17		CUTLASS C17TBR	ST	RNBT	FBG		IO			6	11	1300	1	3	**	**
18		SPOILER C18SK	OP	RNBT	FBG		OB			6	11	1250	1		2250	2600
18	1	CENTAUR C18V	ST	RNBT	FBG		IO			6	11	1200	1	6	**	**
18	1	SPORTSTER C18VBR	ST	RNBT	FBG		IO			6	11	1300	1	6	**	**
19	3	GULFWINDS C20CV	ST	CR	FBG		OB			7	6	1750	1	6	2900	3400
20	7	C19F	OP	FSH	FBG		OB			7	6	1400	1		2800	3250
20	7	CONDOR C21V	ST	RNBT	FBG		IO			7	6	1550	1	9	**	**
20	7	VANTAGE C21CC	ST	CUD	FBG		IO			7	6	1800	1	9	**	**
23	9	CARIBBEAN C24CC	ST	CUD	FBG		IB			8		3750	2		**	**
		1972 BOATS														
16	3	SEA-QUEEN	ST	RNBT	FBG		OB			6	11	1000		6	1700	2050
16	10	MONTE-CARLO	ST	RNBT	FBG		OB			6	8	1010		8	1750	2100
18	1	C18VBR	ST	RNBT	FBG		OB			6	11	1240		8	2200	2550
18	1	CENTAUR			FBG		IO	245		6	11	1850		8	2700	3150
18	1	CENTAUR C18V	ST	RNBT	FBG		OB			6	11	1200		8	2150	2500
18	1	CENTAUR C18V	ST	RNBT	FBG		IO	120	OMC	6	11	1850		8	2550	3000
19				FSH	FBG		OB			7	6	1250		8	2300	2650
19	3	GULFWINDS C20CV	ST	CR	FBG		OB			7	6	1250		8	2300	2650
20	7	CONDOR			FBG		IO	245		7	6	2040	1		3550	4150
20	7	CONDOR C21V	ST	RNBT	FBG		OB			7	6	1290	1		2700	3150
20	7	CONDOR C21V	ST	RNBT	FBG		IO	165	OMC	7	6	2040	1		3400	3950
20	7	VANTAGE			FBG		IO	245		7	6	2360	1		3800	4400
20	7	VANTAGE C21CC	ST	CUD	FBG		OB			7	6	1610	1		3200	3700
20	7	VANTAGE C21CC	ST	CUD	FBG		IO	165	MRCR	7	6	2360	1		3800	4400
24		CARIBBEAN			FBG		IO	245		8	2	3250	1	6	5650	6450
24		CARIBBEAN C24CC	ST	CUD	FBG		IO	165	MRCR	8	2	3250	1	6	5750	6600
		1971 BOATS														
16	3	C17C	ST	RNBT	FBG		OB			6	11	1010		7	1700	2050
16	10	C17VBR	ST	RNBT	FBG		OB			6	8	1010		10	1750	2100
17	6	C18TBR	ST	RNBT	FBG		OB			7	2	1300		8	2250	2600
17	6	C18TC	ST	RNBT	FBG		OB			7	2	1350		9	2300	2700
18	1	C18V	ST	RNBT	FBG		OB			6	11	1240		10	2150	2500
18	1	C18V	ST	RNBT	FBG		IO	140	MRCR	6	11	1920	1	3	2750	3200
18	1	C18VBR	ST	RNBT	FBG		OB			6	11	1240		10	2250	2650
19		C19F	ST	FSH	FBG		OB			7	6	1240		7	2250	2650
19	3	C20CV	OP	FSH	FBG		OB			7	6	1610	1		2750	3200
20	7	C21CC	ST	CUD	FBG		OB			7	6	1610	1	3	3200	3700
20	7	C21CCV	ST	CUD	FBG		IO	155-235		7	6	2260	1	5	3800	4650
20	7	C21V	ST	RNBT	FBG		OB			7	6	1350	1		2750	3200
20	7	C21V	ST	RNBT	FBG		IO	155-165		7	6	2000	1	5	3450	4100
22	4	MOBILE MINI YACHT	HT	HB	FBG	TR	OB			8		3500	1	6	**	**
22	4	MOBILE MINI YACHT	HT	HB	FBG	TR	IO	155		8			1	6	**	**
23	8	C24CC	ST	CUD	FBG		IO	165-235		8		3000	2	10	5500	6500
27		C27CC		CUD	FBG		IO	T155-T215		9	10	4800	2	8	10700	13000
		1970 BOATS														
16	10	CUTLASS C17VBR	ST	RNBT	FBG	DV	IO	120	MRCR	6	9	1500	1	6	2350	2750
17	9	CUTLASS C18TBR	ST	RNBT	FBG	TR	OB			7	2	1000	1		1800	2150
17	9	CUTLASS C18TBR	ST	RNBT	FBG	TR	IO	120	MRCR	7	2	1800	1	2	2750	3200
17	9	CUTLASS C18TCC	ST	RNBT	FBG	TR	OB			7	2	1050	1		1850	2250
18	1	CUTLASS C18V	ST	RNBT	FBG	DV	OB			6	11	1022		10	1850	2200
18	1	CUTLASS C18V	ST	RNBT	FBG	DV	IO	120	MRCR	6	11	1700	1	6	2700	3150
19	3	CUTLASS C20CV	ST	RNBT	FBG	DV	OB			7	6	1300	1	10	2350	2750
19	3	CUTLASS C20CV	ST	RNBT	FBG	DV	IO	120	MRCR	7	6	2300	1	6	3450	4000
20	5	CUTLASS C21V	ST	RNBT	FBG	DV	OB			7	6	1500	1	2	3000	3450
20	5	CUTLASS C21V	ST	RNBT	FBG	DV	IO	120	MRCR	7	6	2500	1	6	3950	4600
22	4	CARIBBEAN K22TCC	ST	CUD	FBG	TR	IO	155	OMC			3300	1	6	5650	6450
22	4	MOBILE-MINI-YACHT	HT	CR	FBG	TR	OB			8		3300	1	6	5800	6700
22	4	MOBILE-MINI-YACHT	HT	CR	FBG	TR	IO	120	MRCR	8		3800	1	6	6200	7100
23	9	CARIBBEAN K24CC	ST	CUD	FBG	DV	IO	155	OMC	8		3500	1	9	6250	7200
27		CARIBBEAN K27CC	FB	CUD	FBG	DV	IO	T120	MRCR	9	11	4400	1	9	10300	11700
		1969 BOATS														
16	5	MONTE-CARLO G17 RNV	ST	RNBT	FBG		IO	120-140		6	8	850			1900	2250
18		SPOILER 3000		RNBT	FBG		OB			6	6	1225			2200	2550
18	1	RAIDER K-18 RNV		RNBT	FBG		IO	140-160		6	10	1022			2500	2900
18	1	SPORTSTER G18 RVO		RNBT	FBG		OB			6	11	1022			1850	2200
18	1	SPORTSTER G18 RVO		RNBT	FBG		IO	120-160		6	11	1022			2500	2900
18	3	CENTAUR T19		RNBT	FBG		IO	120-160		7	4	1350			2750	3200
18	3	CENTAUR T19	HT	RNBT	FBG		IO	120-160		7	4	1350			2750	3200
18	3	CENTAUR T19	FB	RNBT	FBG		IO	120-160		7	4	1350			2750	3200
18	3	CENTAUR T19 BRO		RNBT	FBG		OB			7	4	1350			2350	2750
18	3	CENTAUR T19 BRO	HT	RNBT	FBG		OB			7	4	1350			2350	2750
18	3	CENTAUR T19 BRO	FB	RNBT	FBG		OB			7	4	1350			2350	2750
19	3	CARIB CO G20		CBNCR	FBG		OB			7	6	1350			2450	2800
19	3	CARIB CV G20		CBNCR	FBG		IO	120-160		7	6	1450			3300	3900
19	3	CARIB CVO G20		CBNCR	FBG		OB			7	6	1450			2550	2950
19	3	CARIBBEAN G20 RVIO			FBG		IO	120-160		7	6	1300			2950	3450
19	3	CARIBBEAN G20 RVO			FBG		OB			7	6	1300			2350	2750
20	5	GULFWINDS G21 RNV			FBG		IO	120-210		7	6	1500			3400	4050
20	5	GULFWINDS G21 RNV	HT		FBG		IO	120-210		7	6	1500			3400	4050
20	5	GULFWINDS G21 RNV	FB		FBG		IO	120-210		7	6	1500			3400	4050
20	5	GULFWINDS G21 RNVO			FBG		OB			7	6	1500			2950	3450
20	5	GULFWINDS G21 RNVO	HT		FBG		OB			7	6	1500			2950	3450
20	5	GULFWINDS G21 RNVO	FB		FBG		OB			7	6	1500			2950	3450
22	4	MOBILE-MINI-YACHT	HT	CR	FBG		OB			8		3300			5800	6700
22	4	MOBILE-MINI-YACHT	HT	CR	FBG		IO	120		8		3800			6400	7350
24	8	VANTAGE CV K-24		CUD	FBG		IO	155-225		8		2475			5700	6900
24	8	VANTAGE CV K-24		CUD	FBG		IO	T120-T160		8		2475			6600	7850
24	8	VANTAGE CV K-24	HT	CUD	FBG		IO	155-225		8		2475			5700	6900
24	8	VANTAGE CV K-24	HT	CUD	FBG		IO	T120-T160		8		2475			6600	7850
24	8	VANTAGE CV K-24	FB	CUD	FBG		IO	155-225		8		2475			5700	6900
24	8	VANTAGE CV K-24	FB	CUD	FBG		IO	T120-T160		8		2475			6600	7850
27		CONDOR CV K-27			FBG		IO	155-250		9	11	4400			9900	12300
27		CONDOR CV K-27			FBG		IO	T120-T160		9	11	4400			11100	13300
27		CONDOR CV K-27	HT		FBG		IO	155-250		9	11	4400			9900	12300
27		CONDOR CV K-27	HT		FBG		IO	T120-T160		9	11	4400			11100	13300
27		CONDOR CV K-27	FB		FBG		IO	155-250		9	11	4400			9900	12300
27		CONDOR CV K-27	FB		FBG		IO	T120-T160		9	11	4400			11100	13300
		1968 BOATS														
16	1	CUTLASS		RNBT	FBG	TR	IO	80		5	11				2400	2800
16	5	MONTE-CARLO		RNBT	FBG		IO	120		6	8				2550	3000
18		HOLIDAY		RNBT	FBG	SV	OB			6	11	1022			1850	2200
18	1	G18RVI/O	OP		FBG		IO	160		6	10				2750	3200

 CONTINUED ON NEXT PAGE

LOA FT IN	NAME AND/ OR MODEL	TOP/ RIG	BOAT TYPE	-HULL- MTL TP	ENGINE TP # HP MFG	BEAM FT IN	WGT LBS	DRAFT FT IN	RETAIL LOW	RETAIL HIGH
					----- 1968 BOATS -----					
18	1 G18RVO	OP		FBG DV	OB	6 2	1022		1850	2200
18	1 HOLIDAY	RNBT	FBG	IO	120-160	6 11			3200	3700
18	1 PANTHER	RNBT	FBG	IO	155-160	6 10			3150	3700
18	3 RANGER T19R	RNBT	FBG TR	OB		7 4	1215		2200	2550
18	3 RANGER T19R	RNBT	FBG TR	IO	160	7 4			3350	3900
18	3 RANGER T19R	RNBT	FBG TR	IO	T 60	7 4			4100	4750
18	3 T194VI/O	OP	FBG TR	IO	T 60	7 4			3700	4300
18	3 T19RO	OP		FBG SV	OB	7 4	1215		2200	2550
19	3 G20CO	OP	RNBT	FBG SV	OB	7 6	1300		2350	2750
19	3 G20CVI/O	OP		FBG	IO	T 60	7 6		4350	5000
19	3 G20RO	OP	RNBT	FBG SV	OB	7 6	1150		2200	2550
19	3 G20RVI/O	OP		FBG	IO	T 60	7 6		4350	5000
19	3 TRADEWINDS		CBNCR FBG SV	IO	160	7 6			3850	4500
19	3 TRADEWINDS		CBNCR FBG SV	IO	T 60	7 6			4700	5400
19	3 TRADEWINDS		RNBT FBG SV	IO	160	7 6			3800	4450
19	3 TRADEWINDS		RNBT FBG SV	IO	T 60	7 6			4600	5300
19	3 TRADEWINDS G20CVO		RNBT FBG SV	OB		7 6	1295		2350	2750
19	3 TRADEWINDS G20RVO		CBNCR FBG SV	OB		7 6	1150		2150	2500
20	5 TRADEWINDS		RNBT FBG DV	IO	210	7 6			4500	5200
20	5 TRADEWINDS		RNBT FBG DV	IO	T 60	7 6			5200	5950
23	8 VANTAGE	CR	FBG	IO	155-160	8			7550	8650
23	9 G24CV		FBG	IO	150				7150	8250
23	9 G24RV		FBG	IO	120				7150	8200
26	8 NAVIGATOR	CR	FBG	IO	T120-T210	9 11			13100	16100
					----- 1967 BOATS -----					
16	T17R	RNBT	FBG TR	IO	80	5 11			2450	2850
16	5 MONTE-CARLO G17	RNBT	FBG DV	IO	110	6 5			2600	3050
18	1 G18RV10	RNBT	FBG	IO	120	7 6			3450	4000
18	1 G18RVO		FBG	OB		7 6			3450	3150
18	4 T19R		FBG	OB					2750	3200
18	4 T19R	RNBT	FBG TR	IO	120	7 4			3450	4000
19	1 TRADEWINDS G20	RNBT	FBG DV	OB		7 6	1300		2350	2750
19	4 G20CVO		FBG	OB					3400	4000
19	4 G20RV10		CBNCR FBG	IO	120	7 6			4000	4650
19	4 G20RVO		FBG	OB					2900	3400
23	9 G24CV		FBG	IO	150				7400	8500
23	9 G24RV		FBG	IO	120				7400	8500

COBRA BOAT SALES
JET KING

Call 1-800-327-6929 for BUC Personalized Evaluation Service
Or, for 1972 boats, sign onto www.BUCValuPro.com

COBRA BOATS INC

Call 1-800-327-6929 for BUC Personalized Evaluation Service
Or, for 1977 boats, sign onto www.BUCValuPro.com

COBRA CATAMARANS INT'L
PETER FLETCHER & SONS   COAST GUARD MFG ID- 3013

Call 1-800-327-6929 for BUC Personalized Evaluation Service
Or, for 1982 boats, sign onto www.BUCValuPro.com

COBRA MARINE CORPORATION
COAST GUARD MFG ID- CDH

Call 1-800-327-6929 for BUC Personalized Evaluation Service
Or, for 1977 boats, sign onto www.BUCValuPro.com

COBURN & SARGENT

Call 1-800-327-6929 for BUC Personalized Evaluation Service
Or, for 1969 boats, sign onto www.BUCValuPro.com

CODDINGTON YACHTS INC
COAST GUARD MFG ID- CVG

Call 1-800-327-6929 for BUC Personalized Evaluation Service
Or, for 1979 boats, sign onto www.BUCValuPro.com

COLEMAN SALING MFG CO INC
COAST GUARD MFG ID- CSM

Call 1-800-327-6929 for BUC Personalized Evaluation Service
Or, for 1970 to 1973 boats, sign onto www.BUCValuPro.com

COLONIAL BOAT WORKS

Call 1-800-327-6929 for BUC Personalized Evaluation Service
Or, for 1959 boats, sign onto www.BUCValuPro.com

COLONIAL CRUISERS
DIV OF THE JADE CORP
MILLVILLE NJ 08332   COAST GUARD MFG ID- CLL   See inside cover to adjust price for area

LOA FT IN	NAME AND/ OR MODEL	TOP/ RIG	BOAT TYPE	-HULL- MTL TP	ENGINE TP # HP MFG	BEAM FT IN	WGT LBS	DRAFT FT IN	RETAIL LOW	RETAIL HIGH
					----- 1970 BOATS -----					
45	BOSTONIAN COCKPIT	MYCPT	WD	SV IB	T300 CHRY 14	4 29000	3 2		32000	35500
45	CHARLESTONIAN	SF	WD	SV IB	T300 CHRY 14	4 29000	3 2		31100	34500
	IB T300 INT	31100	34500, IB T325 MRCR	32200	35800, IB T283D GM				36200	40200
	IB T290D GM	36500	40500, IB T300D CUM	36800	40900					
45	PHILADELPHIAN	MY	WD	SV IB	T300 CHRY 14	4 29000	3 2		31100	34500
	IB T300 INT	31100	34600, IB T325 MRCR	31900	35500, IB T283D GM				36200	40200
	IB T290D GM	36400	40500, IB T300D CUM	36700	40800					
57	TRENTONIAN	MY	WD	SV IB	T290D GM 16	46000	4		47100	51800
	IB T300D CUM	47900	52700, IB T350D GM	52000	57100, IB T370D CUM				53600	58900
	IB T525D GM	61300	67400							
					----- 1969 BOATS -----					
38	GEORGETONIAN	SDN	WD	SV IB	T210 CHRY 13		2 8		21100	23500
	IB T250	21200	23600, IB T260	21300	23600, IB T300				21400	23800
	IB T165D GM	24400	27100, IB T180D GM	24500	27200					
38	MIAMIAN	SF	WD	SV IB	T210 CHRY 13		2 8		19600	21800
	IB T250	19700	21900, IB T260	19800	22000, IB T300				19900	22100
	IB T165D GM	25600	28500, IB T180D GM	25800	28600					
45	BOSTONIAN	MY	WD	SV IB	T300 CHRY 14 4		3 2		30500	33900
	IB T325	31300	34800, IB T215D GM	32900	36500, IB T283D GM				35400	39400
45	CHARLESTONIAN	SF	WD	SV IB	T300 CHRY 14 4		3 2		30100	33400
	IB T325	31200	34600, IB T215D GM	31400	34900, IB T283D GM				35000	38900
45	PHILADELPHIAN	MY	WD	SV IB	T300 CHRY 14 4		3 2		31500	35000
	IB T325	32300	35900, IB T215D GM	33600	37300, IB T283D GM				36200	40300
					----- 1968 BOATS -----					
38	GEORGETONIAN	SDN	WD		IB T210 13		2 8		20500	22800
38	GEORGETONIAN	SDN	WD		IB T290 13		2 8		20700	23000
38	GEORGETONIAN	SDN	WD		IB T300 13		2 8		20700	23000
38	MIAMIAN	SF	WD		IB T210 13		2 8		19000	21200
38	MIAMIAN	SF	WD		IB T290 13		2 8		19200	21400
38	MIAMIAN	SF	WD		IB T300 13		2 8		19300	21400
45	BOSTONIAN	MY	WD		IB T290 14 4		3 2		29300	32500
	IB T300	29600	32900, IB T215D	31800	35400, IB T283D				34300	38100
45	CHARLESTONIAN	SF	WD		IB T290 14 4		3 2		28700	31900
	IB T300	29200	32400, IB T215D	30400	33800, IB T283D				33900	37700
45	PHILADELPHIAN	MY	WD		IB T290 14 4		3 2		30200	33600
	IB T300	30600	34000, IB T215D	32600	36200, IB T283D				35200	39100
45	PRINCETONIAN	SDN	WD		IB T290 14 4		3 2		23900	26500
	IB T300	24100	26800, IB T215D	25400	28200, IB T283D				27600	30700
					----- 1967 BOATS -----					
45	BOSTONIAN		WD		IB T290		3		22400	24900
45	CHARLESTONIAN	SF	WD		IB T280 14 2		3		27500	30500
45	CHARLESTONIAN	SF	WD		IB T300		3		28300	31500
45	CHARLESTONIAN	SF	WD		IB T283D				32900	36600
45	PHILADELPHIAN		WD		IB T290				23300	25800

LOA FT IN	NAME AND/OR MODEL	TOP/RIG	BOAT TYPE	HULL MTL TP	ENGINE TP # HP	MFG	BEAM FT IN	WGT LBS	DRAFT FT IN	RETAIL LOW	RETAIL HIGH
1967 BOATS											
45	PHILADELPHIAN			WD	IB T300					23000	25500
45	PHILADELPHIAN		DC	WD	IB T280		14 2		3 2	29000	32200
45	PHILADELPHIAN		MY	WD	IB T215D					26600	29500
1966 BOATS											
38 11		FB	DC	WD RB	IB T225		12 10		2 10	17300	19700
					IB T280					17400	19800
					IB T290					17400	19800
					IB T300					17500	19900
43 6			SF	WD RB	IB T280		14 4		3	27800	30800
					IB T290					27900	31000
					IB T300					28000	31100
					IB T216D					30800	34300
43 9			MY	WD RB	IB T280		14 4		3 2	28700	31900
					IB T290					28800	32000
					IB T300					28900	32100
					IB T216D					32000	35500
53 4			MY	WD RB	IB T216D		16 2		3 6	43900	48800
					IB T280D					44600	49500
					IB T300D					45700	50200
					IB T370D					47700	52500
1965 BOATS											
38	CAVALERO		DC	WD	IB T225					17400	19700
38	CAVALERO		DC	WD	IB T280					17500	19900
38	CHESAPEAKE		SPTCR	WD	IB T225					10500	11900
38	CHESAPEAKE		SPTCR	WD	IB T280					10600	12100
38	CHESAPEAKE	FB	SPTCR	WD	IB T225					10800	12200
38	CHESAPEAKE	FB	SPTCR	WD	IB T280					10900	12400
42	CAPRICE		SPTCR	WD	IB T225	CHRY				20800	23100
					IB T280					21500	23900
					IB T130D					21100	23500
					IB T195D					23200	25700
					IB T215D					23600	26300
					IB T300D					24800	27600
42	CAPRICE	HT	SPTCR	WD	IB T225	CHRY				20900	23200
					IB T280					21500	23900
					IB T130D					21200	23500
					IB T195D					23200	25800
					IB T215D					23700	26300
					IB T300D					24900	27600
42	CRITERION			WD	IB T225	CHRY				26000	28900
					IB T225	GRAY				26000	28900
					IB T280					26600	29600
					IB T130D					18100	20100
					IB T195D					19000	21100
					IB T215D					19400	21600
42	CRITERION		MY	WD	IB T225	CHRY				23300	25900
					IB T225	GRAY				23300	25900
					IB T280					23800	26400
					IB T130D					27800	30800
					IB T195D					28100	31200
					IB T215D					28400	31600
53	CANADIAN		MY	WD	IB T280					40600	45100
					IB T195D					41900	46500
					IB T280D					39400	43800
					IB T300D					40000	44400
					IB T370D					42000	46600
1964 BOATS											
38	CAVALERO		SPTCR	WD	IB T225					11800	13400
38	CAVALERO		SPTCR	WD	IB T280					11900	13500
38	CHESAPEAKE		SPTCR	WD	IB T225					8550	9800
38	CHESAPEAKE		SPTCR	WD	IB T280					8700	10000
38	CHESAPEAKE	FB	SPTCR	WD	IB T225					10500	11900
38	CHESAPEAKE	FB	SPTCR	WD	IB T280					10600	12000
42	CAPRICE		SPTCR	WD	IB T225					20300	22600
					IB T280					20900	23200
					IB T130D					20600	22900
					IB T195D					22600	25100
					IB T215D					23000	25600
					IB T300D					24600	27300
42	CRITERION		MY	WD	IB T225					22700	25200
					IB T225	GRAY				22700	25200
					IB T280					23100	25700
					IB T130D					27000	30000
					IB T195D					27400	30400
					IB T215D					27600	30700
53	CANADIAN		MY	WD	IB T280					39500	43900
					IB T370					44000	48800
					IB T195D					40500	45000
					IB T280D					38400	42700
					IB T300D					39000	43300
1963 BOATS											
38	CAVALERO		DC	WD	IB T225					16500	18700
42	CAPRICE		SF	WD	IB T225					13700	15600
					IB T280					14100	16000
					IB T130D					24500	27200
					IB T181D					25400	28200
42	CARAVEL		DC	WD	IB T225					22900	25400
					IB T280					23300	25800
					IB T130D					22900	25400
					IB T181D					23100	25700
42	CRITERION		MY	WD	IB T225					22200	24600
					IB T225	GRAY				22200	24600
					IB T280					22500	25100
					IB T130D					26300	29200
					IB T181D					26500	29400
53	CANADIAN		MY	WD	IB T280					38600	42900
					IB T181D					39000	43300
					IB T235D					40200	44600
					IB T280D					37500	41600
1962 BOATS											
41 7	CAPRICE		SF	WD	IB T225					13400	15200
					IB T280					13600	15400
					IB T130D					24200	26900
					IB T181D					24500	27300
41 7	CARAVEL		DC	WD	IB T225					22100	24600
					IB T280					22400	24900
					IB T130D					22300	24800
					IB T181D					22300	24700
41 10	CRITERION		MY	WD	IB T225					21800	24200
					IB T280					21900	24300
					IB T130D					25800	28700
					IB T181D					25800	28600
1961 BOATS											
32			EXP	WD	IB 170		11 2		2 3	6800	7800
32			SDN	WD	IB 170		11 2		2 3	6600	7600
35			EXP	WD	IB T170		11 8		2 8	10100	11500
35			SDN	WD	IB T170		11 8		2 8	10800	12200
36			SF	WD	IB T170		11 8		2 8	12200	13800
38			EXP	WD	IB T170		12 4		2 10	14000	15900
38			SDN	WD	IB T170		12 4		2 10	17400	19800
39			SF	WD	IB T170		12 4		2 10	15500	17600
41			SDN	WD	IB T170		13		3	20300	22500
41			SF	WD	IB T170		13		3	19900	22100
41	CUSTOM		DC	WD	IB T170		13		3	21500	23900
41	CUSTOM		SPTCR	WD	IB T170		13		3	10600	12100
41	FISHERMAN	FB	DC	WD	IB T170		13		3	21600	24000
42			MY	WD	IB T188		13		3	22100	24600
1960 BOATS											
30			EXP	WD	IB T170					5900	6800
30			SDN	WD	IB T170					5900	6800
34			EXP	WD	IB T170					9350	10600
34			SDN	WD	IB T170					9150	10300
34	CUSTOM		SPTCR	WD	IB T170					8300	9550
34	GULFSTREAM CUSTOM		CR	WD	IB T170					8400	9650
38			EXP	WD	IB T170					13100	14900
38			SDN	WD	IB T170					16400	18700
39	CUSTOM		SPTCR	WD	IB T170					12300	14000
41			DC	WD	IB T170					20500	22800
41			SDN	WD	IB T170					19700	21800
41	CUSTOM		SPTCR	WD	IB T170					13400	15300
42			MY	WD	IB T170					20300	22500
1959 BOATS											
24			EXP	P/C	IB 170		8 8			2250	2600
24			UTL	P/C	IB 170		8 8			2100	2450
33			EXP	WD	IB T170					8050	9250
33			SDN	WD	IB T170					8500	8700
33			SDN	WD	IB T170					11600	13100
37			EXP	WD	IB T170					10600	12100
37	CUSTOM	FB	SPTCR	WD	IB T170					14600	16600
39		FB	DC	WD	IB T170					20200	22400
41		FB	DC	WD	IB T170						
41	CUSTOM		SPTCR	P/C	IB T170		13 6			9800	11200
1958 BOATS											
33			EXP	WD	IB T125					7650	8800
33			SDN	WD	IB T125					7150	8200
33	CUSTOM		SPTCR	WD	IB T125					6700	7700
37			EXP	WD	IB T150					11300	12800
37			SDN	WD	IB T150					11800	13400
37	CUSTOM		SPTCR	WD	IB T150					10200	11500
1957 BOATS											
33			EXP	WD	IB T125					7500	8650
33			SDN	WD	IB T125					7050	8100
33	CUSTOM		SPTCR	WD	IB T125					6550	7550
37			EXP	WD	IB T150					11200	12700
37			SDN	WD	IB T150					11600	13200
37	CUSTOM	FB	SDN	WD	IB T150						
1956 BOATS											
32			EXP	WD	IB T125					6550	7500
32			SDN	WD	IB T125					6400	7350
37			EXP	WD	IB T150					11000	12500
37			SDN	WD	IB T150					11500	13000
37	CUSTOM	FB	SPTCR	WD	IB T150					9900	11200
1955 BOATS											
30			EXP	WD	IB T125					5350	6150
37			SDN	WD	IB T150					10900	12400
37		FB	SDN	WD	IB T175					11400	12900
1954 BOATS											
35		FB	CR	WD SV	IB T115	CHRY	11 7		2 10	8350	9550
35			EXP	WD SV	IB T115	CHRY	11 7		2 10	8650	9950
35			SDN	WD SV	IB T115	CHRY	11 7		2 10	9300	10600
1953 BOATS											
34		HT	SPTCR	WD	IB 115	CHRY				6900	7900
34	WANDERER	HT	SDN	WD	IB 115	CHRY				7400	8500

LOA FT	LOA IN	NAME AND/ OR MODEL	TOP/ RIG	BOAT TYPE	-HULL- MTL	-HULL- TP	ENGINE TP	ENGINE # HP	ENGINE MFG	BEAM FT	BEAM IN	WGT LBS	DRAFT FT	DRAFT IN	RETAIL LOW	RETAIL HIGH
		1952 BOATS														
33			HT	SPTCR	WD	SV	IB								**	**

COLUMBIA YACHT

DIV OF WHITTAKER CORP
CHESAPEAKE VA 23320 COAST GUARD MFG ID- CLY

See inside cover to adjust price for area

LOA FT	LOA IN	NAME AND/ OR MODEL	TOP/ RIG	BOAT TYPE	-HULL- MTL	-HULL- TP	ENGINE TP	ENGINE # HP	ENGINE MFG	BEAM FT	BEAM IN	WGT LBS	DRAFT FT	DRAFT IN	RETAIL LOW	RETAIL HIGH
		1979 BOATS														
25	1	COLUMBIA 7.6 METER	SLP	SA/CR	FBG	KL	OB			9	2	4500	3	6	5850	6700
25	1	COLUMBIA 7.6 METER	SLP	SA/CR	FBG	KL	IB	8D	YAN	9	2	4500	3	6	6300	7200
27	2	COLUMBIA 8.3 METER	SLP	SA/CR	FBG	KL	OB			9	4	7300	4	4	11400	13000
27	2	COLUMBIA 8.3 METER	SLP	SA/CR	FBG	KL	IB	30	UNIV	9	4	7300	4	4	11600	13200
27	2	COLUMBIA 8.3 METER	SLP	SA/CR	FBG	KL	IB	13D-	15D	9	4	7300	4	4	11700	13400
28	7	COLUMBIA 8.7 METER	SLP	SA/CR	FBG	KL	IB	30	UNIV	10		8500	4	8	14700	16700
28	7	COLUMBIA 8.7 METER	SLP	SA/CR	FBG	KL	IB	13D-	15D	10		8500	4	8	14800	16800
31	6	COLUMBIA 9.6 METER	SLP	SA/CR	FBG	KL	IB	13D-	15D	10	2	10500	5	6	20500	22800
35	2	COLUMBIA 10.7 METER	SLP	SA/CR	FBG	KL	IB	22D	YAN	11	4	13900	5	5	27300	30400
39		COLUMBIA 11.8 METER	SLP	SA/CR	FBG	KC	IB	50D	PERK	12	4	23500	4	6	45900	50400
39		COLUMBIA 11.8 METER	SLP	SA/CR	FBG	KL	IB	50D	PERK	12	4	23500			45900	50400
39		COLUMBIA 11.8 METER	CUT	SA/CR	FBG	KC	IB	50D	PERK	12	4	23500	4	6	45900	50400
39		COLUMBIA 11.8 METER	CUT	SA/CR	FBG	KL	IB	50D	PERK	12	4	23500			45900	50400
		1978 BOATS														
22	7	COLUMBIA T-23	SLP	SA/CR	FBG	KL	OB			7	11	2700	1	11	3050	3550
25	2	COLUMBIA 7.6 METER	SLP	SA/CR	FBG	KL	OB			9	2	4500	3	6	5700	6550
25	2	COLUMBIA 7.6 METER	SLP	SA/CR	FBG	KL	IB	8D	YAN	9	2	4500	3	6	6150	7050
25	10	COLUMBIA T-26	SLP	SA/CR	FBG	KL	OB			8		4225	2	1	5700	6550
27	2	COLUMBIA 8.3 METER	SLP	SA/CR	FBG	KL	OB			9	4	7300	4	4	11100	12600
27	2	COLUMBIA 8.3 METER	SLP	SA/CR	FBG	KL	IB	30	UNIV	9	4	7300	4	4	11300	12800
27	2	COLUMBIA 8.3 METER	SLP	SA/CR	FBG	KL	IB	13D-	15D	9	4	7300	4	4	11400	13000
28	7	COLUMBIA 8.7 METER	SLP	SA/CR	FBG	KL	IB	30	UNIV	10		8500	4	8	14200	16200
28	7	COLUMBIA 8.7 METER	SLP	SA/CR	FBG	KL	IB	13D-	15D	10		8500	4	8	14300	16300
31	6	COLUMBIA 9.6 METER	SLP	SA/CR	FBG	KL	IB	13D-	15D	10	2	10500	5	6	20000	22200
35	2	COLUMBIA 10.7 METER	SLP	SA/CR	FBG	KL	IB	22D	YAN	11	4	13900	5	5	26500	29500
		1977 BOATS														
22	7	COLUMBIA T-23	SLP	SAIL	FBG	KL	OB			7	11	2700	1	11	2950	3450
25	7	COLUMBIA 26-K	SLP	SAIL	FBG	KL	OB			8	6	5900	4	4	7600	8750
25	10	COLUMBIA T-26	SLP	SAIL	FBG	KL	IB			8		4225	2	1	5750	6600
27	2	COLUMBIA 8.3	SLP	SAIL	FBG	KL				9	4	7300	4	4	9000	10200
28	7	COLUMBIA 8.7	SLP	SAIL	FBG	KL	IB	10	UNIV	10		8500	4	8	13800	15700
28	7	COLUMBIA 8.7	SLP	SAIL	FBG	KL	IB	10D	VLVO	10		8500	4	8	13900	15800
31	6	COLUMBIA	SLP	SA/CR	FBG	KL	IB			10	2	10500	5	6	19400	21600
31	6	COLUMBIA-PAYNE 9.6	SLP	SA/CR	FBG	KL	IB	10D	VLVO	10	2	10500	5	6	19400	21600
		1976 BOATS														
22	7	COLUMBIA T-23	SLP	SAIL	FBG	KL	OB			7	11	2700	1	11	2900	3350
25	7	COLUMBIA 26K	SLP	SAIL	FBG	KL	OB			8	6	5900	4	4	7450	8550
25	7	COLUMBIA 26K SH	SLP	SAIL	FBG	KL	OB			8	6	6600	3	2	8400	9650
25	10	COLUMBIA T-26	SLP	SAIL	FBG	KL	OB			8		4225	2	1	5400	6200
28	7	COLUMBIA 8.7	SLP	SAIL	FBG	KL	IB	10	UNIV	10		8000	4	8	12600	14400
31	6	COLUMBIA 9.6	SLP	SA/CR	FBG	KL	IB	10D	VLVO	10	2	10500	5	6	19000	21100
32	1	COLUMBIA 32	SLP	SAIL	FBG	KL	IB	30	UNIV	9	6	9450	5	5	17100	19500
32	1	COLUMBIA 32	SLP	SAIL	FBG	KL	IB	23D	VLVO	9	6	9450	5	5	17100	19500
32	1	COLUMBIA 32 SH	SLP	SAIL	FBG	KL	IB	30	UNIV	9	6	11500	4	3	21000	23300
32	1	COLUMBIA 32 SH	SLP	SAIL	FBG	KL	IB	23D	VLVO	9	6	11500	4	3	21000	23300
35	2	COLUMBIA 35	SLP	SAIL	FBG	KL	IB	30	UNIV	10		11350	5	6	20700	23000
35	2	COLUMBIA 35	SLP	SAIL	FBG	KL	IB	23D	VLVO	10		11350	5	6	20900	23200
35	3	CORONADO 35	SLP	SAIL	FBG	KL	IB	30	UNIV	10	1	13000	5	6	23500	26100
35	3	CORONADO 35	SLP	SAIL	FBG	KL	IB	23D	VLVO	10	1	13000	5	6	23700	26300
35	3	CORONADO 35	KTH	SAIL	FBG	KL	IB	30	UNIV	10	1	13000	5	6	23500	26100
35	3	CORONADO 35	KTH	SAIL	FBG	KL	IB	23D	VLVO	10	1	13000	5	6	23700	26300
35	3	CORONADO 35 SH	SLP	SAIL	FBG	KL	IB	30	UNIV	10	1	15260	3	9	27300	30300
35	3	CORONADO 35 SH	SLP	SAIL	FBG	KL	IB	23D	VLVO	10	1	15260	3	9	27500	30500
35	3	CORONADO 35 SH	KTH	SAIL	FBG	KL	IB	30	UNIV	10	1	15260	3	9	27300	30300
35	3	CORONADO 35 SH	KTH	SAIL	FBG	KL	IB	23D	VLVO	10	1	15260	3	9	27500	30500
40	6	COLUMBIA 41	SLP	SAIL	FBG	KL	IB	50D	PERK	11	3	19500	6	3	38600	42900
40	6	COLUMBIA 41	KTH	SAIL	FBG	KL	IB	50D	PERK	11	3	19500	6	3	38600	42900
40	6	COLUMBIA 41 SH	SLP	SAIL	FBG	KC	IB	50D	PERK	11	3	20700	4	11	40100	44600
40	6	COLUMBIA 41 SH	KTH	SAIL	FBG	KC	IB	50D	PERK	11	3	20700	4	11	40100	44600
45	3	COLUMBIA 45	SLP	SAIL	FBG	KL	IB	50D	PERK	12	4	25000	7	3	51900	57000
45	3	COLUMBIA 45	SLP	SAIL	FBG	KL	IB	85D	PERK	12	4	25000	7	3	52200	57300
45	3	COLUMBIA 45	KTH	SAIL	FBG	KL	IB	50D	PERK	12	4	25000	7	3	51900	57000
45	3	COLUMBIA 45	KTH	SAIL	FBG	KL	IB	85D	PERK	12	4	25000	7	3	52200	57300
45	3	COLUMBIA 45 SH	SLP	SAIL	FBG	KL	IB	50D	PERK	12	4	27000	5	3	53800	59100
45	3	COLUMBIA 45 SH	SLP	SAIL	FBG	KL	IB	85D	PERK	12	4	27000	5	3	54000	59400
45	3	COLUMBIA 45 SH	KTH	SAIL	FBG	KL	IB	50D	PERK	12	4	27000	5	3	53800	59100
45	3	COLUMBIA 45 SH	KTH	SAIL	FBG	KL	IB	85D	PERK	12	4	27000	5	3	54000	59400
		1975 BOATS														
22	7	COLUMBIA T23	SLP	SAIL	FBG	KL	OB			7	11	2900	1	11	3000	3450
25	7	COLUMBIA 26K	SLP	SAIL	FBG	KL	OB			8	6	5900	4	4	7250	8350
25	7	COLUMBIA 26KSH	SLP	SAIL	FBG	KL	OB			8	6	6600	3	2	8200	9450
25	10	COLUMBIA T26	SLP	SAIL	FBG	KL	OB			8		4400	2	1	5500	6300
28		CORONADO 28	SLP	SAIL	FBG	KL	OB			8	6	6800	4	10	10000	11400
28		CORONADO 28	SLP	SAIL	FBG	KL	IB			8	6	6800	4	10	10200	11600
32	1	COLUMBIA 32	SLP	SAIL	FBG	KL	IB			9	6	9450	5	5	16700	19000
32	1	COLUMBIA 32	SLP	SAIL	FBG	KL	IB	D		9	6		5	5	19000	21100
35	2	COLUMBIA 35	SLP	SAIL	FBG	KL	IB			10		11350	5	6	20200	22500
35	2	COLUMBIA 35	SLP	SAIL	FBG	KL	IB	D		10		11350	5	6	20400	22700
35	3	CORONADO 35	SLP	SAIL	FBG	KL	IB			10	1	13000	5	6	23000	25600
35	3	CORONADO 35	SLP	SAIL	FBG	KL	IB	D		10	1	15260	5	6	26900	29900
35	3	CORONADO 35 SH	SLP	SAIL	FBG	KL	IB			10	1	15260	3	9	26700	29600
35	3	CORONADO 35 SH	SLP	SAIL	FBG	KL	IB	D		10	1	15260	3	9	26900	29900
40	6	COLUMBIA 41RD	SLP	SAIL	FBG	KL	IB	D		11	3	19500	6	4	38500	42700
40	6	COLUMBIA 41RD SH	SLP	SAIL	FBG	KL	IB	D		11	3	20700	4	11	39400	43800
40	6	CORONADO 41FD	SLP	SAIL	FBG	KL	IB	D		11	3	19500	6	3	37200	41400
40	6	CORONADO 41FD SH	SLP	SAIL	FBG	KL	IB	D		11	3	20700	4	11	39400	43800
43	2	COLUMBIA 43	SLP	SAIL	FBG	KL	VD	D		12	4	22200	6	11	44400	49300
43	2	COLUMBIA 43 SH	SLP	SAIL	FBG	KL	VD	D		12	4	23500	4	11	46300	50800
45	3	COLUMBIA 45 RD	SLP	SAIL	FBG	KL	IB	50D	PERK	12	4	25000	7	3	50700	55800
45	3	COLUMBIA 45RD SH	SLP	SAIL	FBG	KL	IB	50D	PERK	12	4	27000	5	3	52600	57800
45	3	COLUMBIA 45TC	SLP	SAIL	FBG	KL	IB	85D	PERK	12	4	23000	7	3	49100	54000
45	3	COLUMBIA 45TC SH	SLP	SAIL	FBG	KL	IB	85D	PERK	12	4	25000	5	3	51000	56000
45	3	CORONADO 45	SLP	SAIL	FBG	KL	IB	D	PERK	12	4	23000	7	3	48900	53700
45	3	CORONADO 45 SH	SLP	SAIL	FBG	KL	IB	D	PERK	12	4	25000	4	11	50800	55800
		1974 BOATS														
22	7	COLUMBIA 23	SLP	SAIL	FBG	KL	OB			7	11	2300	1	11	2500	2900
25	7	COLUMBIA MK II	SLP	SAIL	FBG	KL	OB			8	6	5900	4	4	7100	8200
25	7	COLUMBIA MK II	SLP	SAIL	FBG	KL	IB	6D	PETT	8	6	5900	4	4	7400	8550
30		COLUMBIA 30	SLP	SAIL	FBG	KL	OB			9	6	10500	5	9	17000	19300
30		COLUMBIA 30	SLP	SAIL	FBG	KL	IB	20D	FARY	9	6	10500	5	9	17100	19500
33	7	COLUMBIA 34 MK II	SLP	SAIL	FBG	KL	OB			10		12000	5	6	20700	23000
33	7	COLUMBIA 34 MK II	SLP	SAIL	FBG	KL	IB	20D	FARY	10		12000	5	6	20900	23200
36	2	COLUMBIA 36 MK II		SAIL	FBG		OB			10	6	13200	5	3	23000	25500
36	2	COLUMBIA 36 MK II		SAIL	FBG		IB	20D	FARY	10	6	13200	5	3	23300	25900
40	6	COLUMBIA 41	SLP	MS	FBG	KL	IB	50D	PERK	11	3	20500	6	4	38200	42400
43	9	COLUMBIA 43 MK II	SLP	SAIL	FBG	KL	IB	50D	PERK	12	4	22200	7		44200	49100
45	3	COLUMBIA 45 CTR CPT	SLP	SA/CR	FBG	KL	IB	D		12	4	25000	7	3	50000	54900
45	3	COLUMBIA 45 CTR CPT	KTH	SA/CR	FBG	KL	IB	D		12	4	25000	7	3	50000	54900
52		COLUMBIA 52	SLP	SAIL	FBG	KL	IB	50D	PERK	13		38000	8		85200	93600
55	7	COLUMBIA 56 CTR CPT	KTH	MS	FBG	KL	IB	D		13			8		120000	132000
		1973 BOATS														
22	7	COLUMBIA 23	SLP	SAIL	FBG	KL	OB			7	11	2300	1	11	2450	2850
25	7	COLUMBIA 26 MKII	SLP	SAIL	FBG	KL	OB			8	6	5900	4	4	7000	8000
30		COLUMBIA 30	SLP	SAIL	FBG	KL	IB	27	PALM	9	6	10500	5	9	16700	19000
30		COLUMBIA 30	SLP	SAIL	FBG	KL	IB	20D	ALBN	9	6	10500	5	9	16800	19100
33	7	COLUMBIA 34 MKII	SLP	SAIL	FBG	KL	IB	27	PALM	10		12000	5	6	20400	22700
33	7	COLUMBIA 34 MKII	SLP	SAIL	FBG	KL	IB	20D	ALBN	10		12000	5	6	20500	22700
40	6	COLUMBIA 41	SLP	SAIL	FBG	KL	IB	20D	ALBN	11	3	20500	6	4	37300	41500
43	9	COLUMBIA 43 MKIII	SLP	SAIL	FBG	KL	IB	27	PALM	12	4	22000	7		42600	47400
43	9	COLUMBIA 43 MKIII	SLP	SAIL	FBG	KL	IB	50D	PERK	12	4	22000	7		43100	47900
45	3	COLUMBIA	SLP	SA/CR	FBG	KL	IB	50D	PERK	12	4	25000	7	3	48800	53600
45	3	COLUMBIA	SLP	SA/CR	FBG	KL	IB	85D	PERK	12	4	25000	7	3	49000	53900
45	3	COLUMBIA	KTH	SA/CR	FBG	KL	IB	50D	PERK	12	4	25000	7	3	48800	53600
45	3	COLUMBIA	KTH	SA/CR	FBG	KL	IB	85D	PERK	12	4	25000	7	3	49000	53900
52		COLUMBIA 52	SLP	SAIL	FBG	KL	IB	50D	PERK	13		38000	8		83600	91900
		1972 BOATS														
22		COLUMBIA 22	SLP	SAIL	FBG	KL	OB			7	9	3000	3	2	2800	3250
25	7	COLUMBIA 26	SLP	SAIL	FBG	KL	OB			8	6	5900	4	4	6850	7850
27	7	COLUMBIA 28	SLP	SAIL	FBG		OB			8	6	7000	4	10	9500	10800
30	1	COLUMBIA 30	SLP	SAIL	FBG	KL	IB	30	UNIV	9	6	10500	5	9	16400	18700
33	7	COLUMBIA 34	SLP	SAIL	FBG	KL	IB	27D	PALM	10		12000	5	6	20100	22300
35	9	COLUMBIA 36		SAIL	FBG		IB	30	UNIV	10	6	13000	5	3	21800	24200
38	7	COLUMBIA 39	SLP	SAIL	FBG	KL	IB	27D	PALM	11	3	18500	6	3	31800	35400
43	3	COLUMBIA 43	SLP	SAIL	FBG	KL	IB	27D	PALM	12	4	22000	6	11	41400	46000
45	3	COLUMBIA 45	SLP	SAIL	FBG	KL	IB	50D	PERK	12	4	25000	7	3	47800	52500
50		COLUMBIA 50	SLP	SAIL	FBG		IB	30	UNIV	12	1	34000	6	7	67700	74400
50		COLUMBIA 50	YWL	SAIL	FBG		IB	30	UNIV	12	1	34000	6	7	67700	74400
51	10	COLUMBIA 52	SLP	SAIL	FBG	KL	IB	50D	PERK	13		38000	8		80800	88800

 CONTINUED ON NEXT PAGE

LOA FT	IN	NAME AND/ OR MODEL	TOP/ RIG	BOAT TYPE	-HULL- MTL	TP	ENGINE TP	# HP	MFG	BEAM FT	IN	WGT LBS	DRAFT FT	IN	RETAIL LOW	RETAIL HIGH
		1972 BOATS														
56	6	COLUMBIA 57	SLP	SAIL	FBG	KL	IB	85D	PERK	13		45000	8		131000	144000
56	6	COLUMBIA 57	YWL	SAIL	FBG	KL	IB	85D	PERK	13		45000	8		131000	144000
		1971 BOATS														
22		COLUMBIA 22	SLP	SAIL	FBG	CB	OB			7	9	3385	2	6	3000	3500
22		COLUMBIA 22	SLP	SAIL	FBG	KL	OB			7	9	3000	3	2	2750	3200
25	7	COLUMBIA 26	SLP	SAIL	FBG	CB	OB			8	6	5950	3	2	6750	7750
25	7	COLUMBIA 26	SLP	SAIL	FBG	KL	OB			8	6	5900	4	4	6650	7650
27	7	COLUMBIA 28	SLP	SAIL	FBG		OB			8	6	7000	4	10	9300	10600
33	7	COLUMBIA 34	SLP	SAIL	FBG	CB	IB	22D		10		13000	3	9	21100	23400
33	7	COLUMBIA 34	SLP	SAIL	FBG	KL	IB	22D		10		12000	5	6	19500	21700
35	9	COLUMBIA 36	SLP	SAIL	FBG		IB	22D		10	6	13200	5	3	21700	24100
35	9	COLUMBIA 36	YWL	SAIL	FBG		IB	22D		10	6	13200	5	3	21700	24100
38	7	COLUMBIA 39	SLP	SAIL	FBG	CB	IB	22D		11	3	17000	4	6	29000	32300
38	7	COLUMBIA 39	SLP	SAIL	FBG	KL	IB	22D		11	3	16000	6		27700	30800
43	3	COLUMBIA 43	SLP	SAIL	FBG	CB	IB	22D		12	4	23500	4	11	41800	46400
43	3	COLUMBIA 43	SLP	SAIL	FBG	KL	IB	22D		12	4	22000	6	11	40300	44800
50		COLUMBIA 50	SLP	SAIL	FBG		IB	37D		12	1	34000	6	7	66500	73100
50		COLUMBIA 50	YWL	SAIL	FBG		IB	37D		12	1	34000	6	7	66500	73100
51	7	COLUMBIA 52	SLP	SAIL	FBG	KL	IB	37D		12	8	36000	7	6	76300	83900
56	6	COLUMBIA 57	SLP	SAIL	FBG	KL	IB	85D		13		45000	8		128000	140500
56	6	COLUMBIA 57	YWL	SAIL	FBG	KL	IB	85D		13		45000	8		128000	140500
		1970 BOATS														
21	8	COLUMBIA 21	SLP	SA/OD	FBG	KL	OB			7	7	1700	3	3	1800	2150
22		COLUMBIA 22	SLP	SA/OD	FBG	KL	OB			7	9	2200	3	2	2200	2550
25	7	COLUMBIA 26	SLP	SA/OD	FBG	KL	OB			8	6	5500	4	4	6050	6950
27	7	COLUMBIA 28	SLP	SA/OD	FBG	KL	OB			8	6	5800	4	10	7400	8500
27	7	COLUMBIA 28	SLP	SA/OD	FBG	KL	IB	16D-	22D	8	6	5800	4	10	7650	8800
35	9	COLUMBIA 36	SLP	SA/OD	FBG	KL	IB	20D	ALBN	10	6	12000	5	2	19400	21600
35	9	COLUMBIA 36	SLP	SA/OD	FBG	KL	IB	32D	PALM	10	6	12000	5	2	19500	21600
35	9	COLUMBIA 36	YWL	SA/OD	FBG	KL	IB	20D	ALBN	10	6	12000	5	2	19400	21600
35	9	COLUMBIA 36	YWL	SA/OD	FBG	KL	IB	32D	PALM	10	6	12000	5	2	19500	21600
43	3	COLUMBIA 43	SLP	SAIL	FBG	KL	IB	22D	PALM	12	4	18900	6	11	36200	40300
43	3	COLUMBIA 43	SLP	SAIL	FBG	KL	IB	40D	PERK	12	4	18900	6	11	36300	40300
50		COLUMBIA 50	SLP	SA/OD	FBG	KL	IB	50	UNIV	12	1	32000	6	7	63400	69700
50		COLUMBIA 50	SLP	SA/OD	FBG	KL	IB	40D	WEST	12	1	32000	6	7	64000	70300
50		COLUMBIA 50	YWL	SA/OD	FBG	KL	IB	50	UNIV	12	1	32000	6	7	63400	69700
50		COLUMBIA 50	YWL	SA/OD	FBG	KL	IB	40D	WEST	12	1	32000	6	7	64000	70300
56	6	COLUMBIA 57	SLP	SAIL	FBG	KL	IB	85D	PERK	13		45000	7	11	124500	137000
56	6	COLUMBIA 57	YWL	SAIL	FBG	KL	IB	85D	PERK	13		45000	7	11	124500	137000
		1969 BOATS														
22		COLUMBIA 22	SLP	SAIL	FBG	KL	OB			7	9	2200	3	2	2100	2500
25	7	COLUMBIA 26 MARK II	SLP	SAIL	FBG	KL	OB			8	6	4400	4	4	4700	5400
27	7	COLUMBIA 28	SLP	SAIL	FBG	KL	OB			8	6	5800	4	4	7200	8300
27	7	COLUMBIA 28	SLP	SAIL	FBG	KL	IB	30	UNIV	8	6	5800	4	4	7350	8450
30	6	COLUMBIA 31	SLP	SAIL	FBG	CB	IB	30	UNIV	9	10	8500	7		12500	14200
35	9	COLUMBIA 36	SLP	SAIL	FBG	KL	IB	30	UNIV	10	6	12000	5	5	19000	21100
35	9	COLUMBIA 36	YWL	SAIL	FBG	KL	IB	30	UNIV	10	6	12000	5	5	19000	21100
39	2	COLUMBIA 40	SLP	SA/CR	FBG	KC	IB	30D		10	8	8400	4	6	16400	18700
39	2	COLUMBIA 40	YWL	SA/CR	FBG	KC	IB	30D		10	8	8400	4	6	16400	18700
50		COLUMBIA 50 CUS INT	SLP	SAIL	FBG	KL	IB	70	UNIV	12	1	32000	6	7	67800	74500
50		COLUMBIA 50 CUS INT	YWL	SAIL	FBG	KL	IB	70	UNIV	12	1	32000	6	7	62100	68200
50		COLUMBIA 50 STD INT	SLP	SAIL	FBG	KL	IB	70	UNIV	12	1	32000	6	7	56400	61900
50		COLUMBIA 50 STD INT	YWL	SAIL	FBG	KL	IB	70	UNIV	12	1	32000	6	7	62100	68200
56	6	COLUMBIA 57	SLP	SA/CR	FBG	KL	IB	85D	PERK	13		42000	8		119000	131000
56	6	COLUMBIA 57	YWL	SA/CR	FBG	KL	IB	85D	PERK	13		42000	8		119000	131000
		1968 BOATS														
22		COLUMBIA 22 STD	SLP	SAIL	FBG	KL	OB			7	9	2200	3	4	1900	2250
22		COLUMBIA 22 W/DIN	SLP	SAIL	FBG	KL	OB			7	9	2200	3	4	2250	2600
24		CONTENDER	SLP	SAIL	FBG	KL				7	10		3	3	2600	3050
24	4	CHALLENGER	SLP	SAIL	FBG	KL				8			3	4	2650	3050
25	2	COLUMBIA 25		SAIL	FBG		OB			8	2	5100	4		5150	5950
27	7	COLUMBIA 28	SLP	SAIL	FBG	KL	OB			8	6	5800	4	4	7050	8150
27	7	COLUMBIA 28	SLP	SAIL	FBG	KL	IB	30D		8	6	5800	4	4	7400	8500
30	6	COLUMBIA 31	SLP	SAIL	FBG	KC	IB	30D		9	10	8500	3	1	12300	14000
35	9	COLUMBIA 36	SLP	SAIL	FBG	KL	IB	20D		10	6	12000	5	6	18800	20900
35	9	COLUMBIA 36	SLP	SAIL	FBG	KL	IB	30D		10	6	12000	5	6	18800	20900
35	9	COLUMBIA 36	YWL	SAIL	FBG	KL	IB	20D		10	6	12000	5	6	18800	20900
35	9	COLUMBIA 36	YWL	SAIL	FBG	KL	IB	30D		10	6	12000	5	6	18800	20900
39	2	COLUMBIA 40	SLP	SAIL	FBG	KC	IB	30D		10	8	19200	4	6	30500	33900
39	2	COLUMBIA 40	YWL	SAIL	FBG	KC	IB	30D		10	8	19200	4	6	30500	33900
50		COLUMBIA 50 CUSTOM	SLP	SAIL	FBG	KL	IB	47D		12	1	32000	6	7	68500	75300
50		COLUMBIA 50 CUSTOM	SLP	SAIL	FBG	KL	IB	55D		12	1	32000	6	7	68700	75500
50		COLUMBIA 50 CUSTOM	SLP	SAIL	FBG	KL	IB	70D		12	1	32000	6	7	69000	75800
50		COLUMBIA 50 CUSTOM	YWL	SAIL	FBG	KL	IB	47D		12	1	32000	6	7	61200	67300
50		COLUMBIA 50 CUSTOM	YWL	SAIL	FBG	KL	IB	55D		12	1	32000	6	7	61300	67400
50		COLUMBIA 50 CUSTOM	YWL	SAIL	FBG	KL	IB	70D		12	1	32000	6	7	61400	67500
50		COLUMBIA 50 STD	SLP	SAIL	FBG	KL	IB	47D		12	1	32000	6	7	54000	59300
50		COLUMBIA 50 STD	SLP	SAIL	FBG	KL	IB	55D		12	1	32000	6	7	54000	59300
50		COLUMBIA 50 STD	SLP	SAIL	FBG	KL	IB	70D		12	1	32000	6	7	53900	59200
50		COLUMBIA 50 STD	YWL	SAIL	FBG	KL	IB	47D		12	1	32000	6	7	61200	67300
50		COLUMBIA 50 STD	YWL	SAIL	FBG	KL	IB	55D		12	1	32000	6	7	61300	67400
50		COLUMBIA 50 STD	YWL	SAIL	FBG	KL	IB	70D		12	1	32000	6	7	61400	67500
		1967 BOATS														
22		COLUMBIA 22	SLP	SAIL	FBG	KL	OB					2200			1850	2250
22		COLUMBIA 22 W/DIN	SLP	SAIL	FBG	KL	OB					2200			2200	2550
24		CONTENDER		SAIL	FBG		OB					3600			3200	3750
24		CONTENDER		SAIL	FBG		IB	8D				3600			3550	4150
24	4	CHALLENGER		SAIL	FBG		OB					3930			3600	4200
24	4	CHALLENGER		SAIL	FBG		IB	8D-	30D			3930			3950	4800
24	4	COLUMBIA 24		SAIL	FBG		OB					4050			3700	4300
24	4	COLUMBIA 24		SAIL	FBG		IB	8D-	30D			4050			4050	4950
26		COLUMBIA 26		SAIL	FBG		OB					5200			5550	6350
26		COLUMBIA 26		SAIL	FBG		IB	7D-	30D			5200			5800	6850
28	6	COLUMBIA 29 MARK II		SAIL	FBG		IB	30D				8400			11600	13100
28	6	DEFENDER		SAIL	FBG		IB	30D				8400			10600	12100
30	6	COLUMBIA 31	SLP	SAIL	FBG	CB	IB	30D				8500			12100	13800
32	5	COLUMBIA 5.5		SAIL	FBG		OB					4500			6450	7400
32	5	SABRE		SAIL	FBG		OB					5200			7550	8700
34		COLUMBIA 34		SAIL	FBG		IB	15D-	30D			10000			14800	16900
38	11	COLUMBIA 38		SAIL	FBG	CB	IB	30D				16500			26500	29400
38	11	COLUMBIA 38		SAIL	FBG	KL	IB	20D				14000			23300	25900
38	11	COLUMBIA 38		SAIL	FBG	KL	IB	30D				14000			23400	26000
39	2	COLUMBIA 40	SLP	SAIL	FBG	CB	IB	30D				18200			28800	32000
39	3	CONSTELLATION		SAIL	FBG	CB	IB	20D							34600	38400
39	3	CONSTELLATION		SAIL	FBG	CB	IB	30D							34700	38500
39	3	CONSTELLATION		SAIL	FBG	KL	IB	20D				15000			25000	27800
39	3	CONSTELLATION		SAIL	FBG	KL	IB	30D				15000			25100	27900
43		CONCORD	SLP	SAIL	FBG	KL	IB	30D							37500	41700
50		COLUMBIA 50	SLP	SAIL	FBG		IB	35D				27500			57600	63300
50		COLUMBIA 50	SLP	SAIL	FBG		IB	40D				27500			57600	63300
50		COLUMBIA 50	SLP	SAIL	FBG		IB	72D				27500			57900	63600
50		COLUMBIA 50	YWL	SAIL	FBG		IB	35D				27500			57600	63300
50		COLUMBIA 50	YWL	SAIL	FBG		IB	40D				27500			57600	63300
50		COLUMBIA 50	YWL	SAIL	FBG		IB	72D				27500			57900	63600
		1966 BOATS														
22		COLUMBIA 22	SLP	SAIL	FBG	KL	OB			7	9	2200	3	2	1850	2200
22		COLUMBIA 22 W/DIN	SLP	SAIL	FBG	KL	OB			7	9	2200	3	2	2100	2500
24		CONTENDER	SLP	SAIL	FBG	KL	OB			7	10	3600	3	3	3150	3650
24		CONTENDER	SLP	SAIL	FBG	KL	IB	8D-	30D	7	10		3	3	4250	5150
24	4	CHALLENGER	SLP	SAIL	FBG	KL	OB			8		3200	3	4	2950	3450
24	4	CHALLENGER	SLP	SAIL	FBG	KL	IB	8D-	30D	8			3	4	4400	5100
24	4	COLUMBIA 24	SLP	SAIL	FBG	KL	OB			8		4050	3	4	3650	4250
24	4	COLUMBIA 24	SLP	SAIL	FBG	KL	IB	8D		8		4050	3	4	3950	4600
24	4	COLUMBIA 24	SLP	SAIL	FBG	KL	IB	30D		8			3	4	4750	5450
26		COLUMBIA 26	SLP	SAIL	FBG	KL	OB			8		5200	3	5	5450	6250
26		COLUMBIA 26	SLP	SAIL	FBG	KL	IB	8D-	30D	8			3	5	6500	7600
28	6	COLUMBIA 29	SLP	SAIL	FBG	KL	IB	30D		8		8400	4		11300	12900
28	6	DEFENDER	SLP	SAIL	FBG	KL	IB	30D		8		8400	4		10500	11900
30	6	COLUMBIA 31	SLP	SAIL	FBG	CB	IB	30D		9	10	8500			11900	13500
32	5	COLUMBIA 5.5	SLP	SAIL	FBG	KL	OB			6	3	4500	4	4	6350	7300
32	5	SABRE	SLP	SAIL	FBG	KL	OB			6	3	5200	4	4	7450	8550
33	1	CARIBBEAN	SLP	SA/CR	FBG	KC	IB	D		9	10		3	6	15300	17400
34		COLUMBIA 34		SAIL	FBG		IB	30D				10000			14600	16600
38	11	COLUMBIA 38		SAIL	FBG	CB	IB	30D				16500			26100	29000
38	11	COLUMBIA 38		SAIL	FBG	KL	IB	30D				14000			23000	25600
39	2	COLUMBIA 40	SLP	SAIL	FBG	CB	IB	30D		10	8	19200	4	6	29400	32700
39	2	CONSTELLATION		SAIL	FBG	CB	IB	30D				15000			24600	27300
39	2	CONSTELLATION		SAIL	FBG	KL	IB	30D				15000			24600	27300
43		CONCORD	SLP	SAIL	FBG	KL	IB	30D							36900	41000
50		COLUMBIA 50	SLP	SAIL	FBG	KL	IB	70D		12	6	27500	6	7	56900	62600
50		COLUMBIA 50	YWL	SAIL	FBG	KL	IB	70D		12	6	27500	6	7	56900	62600
		1965 BOATS														
22		COLUMBIA 22	SLP	SAIL	FBG	KL	OB					2200			1950	2300
22		COLUMBIA 22	SLP	SAIL	FBG	KL	IB	8D				2200			2450	2850
22		COLUMBIA 22	SLP	SAIL	FBG	KL	IB	30D							2900	3400
24		CONTENDER		SAIL	FBG		OB								2500	2900
24		CONTENDER		SAIL	FBG		IB	8D-	30D						4150	5100

 CONTINUED ON NEXT PAGE

COLUMBIA YACHT (continued)

LOA FT IN	NAME AND/ OR MODEL	TOP/ RIG	BOAT TYPE	HULL MTL	HULL TP	ENG TP	# HP	MFG	BEAM FT IN	WGT LBS	DRAFT FT IN	RETAIL LOW	RETAIL HIGH
1965 BOATS													
24 4	CHALLENGER		SAIL	FBG		OB						2300	2700
24 4	CHALLENGER		SAIL	FBG		IB	8D- 30D					3950	4800
24 4	COLUMBIA 24		SAIL	FBG		OB						2800	3250
24 4	COLUMBIA 24		SAIL	FBG		IB	8D- 30D					4650	5600
26	COLUMBIA 26		SAIL	FBG		OB						4400	5050
26	COLUMBIA 26		SAIL	FBG		IB	8D- 30D					6400	7500
28 6	COLUMBIA 29 4 BERTH		SAIL	FBG		OB						8250	9500
28 6	COLUMBIA 29 4 BERTH		SAIL	FBG		IB	8D- 30D					10700	12200
28 6	COLUMBIA 29 6 BERTH		SAIL	FBG		OB						8650	9900
28 6	COLUMBIA 29 6 BERTH		SAIL	FBG		IB	8D- 30D					11100	12700
28 6	DEFENDER		SAIL	FBG		OB						8200	9400
28 6	DEFENDER		SAIL	FBG		IB	8D- 30D					10600	12100
30 6	COLUMBIA 31	SLP	SAIL	FBG	CB	IB	8D- 30D			8500		11700	13300
32 5	COLUMBIA 5.5		SAIL	FBG		OB						11900	13600
32 5	SABRE		SAIL	FBG		OB						9850	11200
32 5	SABRE		SAIL	FBG		IB	8D- 30D					15100	17200
33 1	COLUMBIA 33		SAIL	FBG		IB	8D- 30D					15100	17200
39 2	COLUMBIA 40	SLP	SAIL	FBG	CB	IB	30D			19200		29000	32200
1964 BOATS													
24 4	CHALLENGER		SAIL	FBG		OB						2550	2950
24 4	COLUMBIA 24		SAIL	FBG		OB						2550	2950
26	COLUMBIA 26		SAIL	FBG		OB						4350	5000
28 6	COLUMBIA 29		SAIL	FBG		OB						8250	9500
32 5	5.5-METER		SAIL	FBG		OB						10700	12200
39 2	COLUMBIA 40	SLP	SAIL	FBG	CB	IB	30D			19200		28600	31800
1963 BOATS													
24 4	CHALLENGER		SAIL	FBG		OB						2500	2900
24 4	COLUMBIA 24		SAIL	FBG		OB						2500	2900
26	COLUMBIA 26		SAIL	FBG		OB						4250	4950
28 6	COLUMBIA 29		SAIL	FBG		OB						8150	9400
32 5	5.5-METER		SAIL	FBG		OB						10600	12100

COLUMBIAN FIBERGLASS INC
COAST GUARD MFG ID- CFG

Call 1-800-327-6929 for BUC Personalized Evaluation Service
Or, for 1967 to 1977 boats, sign onto www.BUCValuPro.com

COLVIN MFG
MILES POINT VA 23114   See inside cover to adjust price for area

LOA FT IN	NAME AND/ OR MODEL	TOP/ RIG	BOAT TYPE	HULL MTL	HULL TP	ENG TP	# HP	MFG	BEAM FT IN	WGT LBS	DRAFT FT IN	RETAIL LOW	RETAIL HIGH
1971 BOATS													
25		KTH	SA/CR	AL	KL	IB	8D		7 6	6000		8600	9900
28		KTH	SA/CR	AL	KL	IB	8D		8 3	6000	2 3	9850	11200
33 4		SCH	SA/CR	AL	KL	IB	10D		9 11	14100	4	23100	25600
33 4		KTH	SA/CR	AL	KL	IB	10D		9 11	14100	4	23300	25900
36		KTH	SA/CR	AL	KL	IB	10D		10	11000	3 6	19500	21700
42		SCH	SA/CR	AL	KL	IB	10D		11 4	18200	3 10	33100	36800
1970 BOATS													
25		KTH	SA/CR	AL	KL	IB	D		7 6	6000	3	8500	9750
25		KTH	SA/CR	STL	KL	IB	D		7 6		3	8500	9750
28		KTH	SA/CR	AL	KL	IB	D		8 3	6000	2 8	9700	11000
28		KTH	SA/CR	STL	KL	IB	D		8 3		2 8	9700	11000
31		SCH	SA/CR	AL	KL	IB	D		9 3	10800	3 6	18200	20200
31		SCH	SA/CR	STL	KL	IB	D		9 3		3 6	18200	20200
33 4		SCH	SA/CR	AL	KL	IB	D		9 11	14100	4	22500	25000
33 4		SCH	SA/CR	STL	KL	IB	D		9 11		4	22400	24900
33 4		KTH	SA/CR	AL	KL	IB	D		9 11	14100	4	22700	25300
33 4		KTH	SA/CR	STL	KL	IB	D		9 11		4	22600	25100
36		KTH	SA/CR	AL	KL	IB	D		10	11000	3 6	19100	21200
36		KTH	SA/CR	STL	KL	IB	D		10		3 6	19500	21700
41 1		KTH	SA/CR	AL	KL	IB	D		12 4	27200	4 7	42300	47000
41 1		KTH	SA/CR	STL	KL	IB	D		12 4		4 7	42300	47000
1969 BOATS													
25	25	KTH	SA/CR	STL	KL	IB	D		7 6	6000	3	8250	9500
28	28	KTH	SA/CR	STL	KL	IB	D		8 3	6000	2 8	9500	10800
31	31	SCH	SA/CR	STL	KL	IB	D		9 3	10800	3 6	17400	19700
33 4	34	SCH	SA/CR	STL	KL	IB	D		9 11	14100	4	22000	24400
33 4	34	KTH	SA/CR	STL	KL	IB	D		9 11	14100	4	22200	24600
36	36	KTH	SA/CR	STL	KL	IB	D		10	11000	3 6	18700	20800
41 1	41	KTH	SA/CR	STL	KL	IB	D		12 4	27200	4 7	41300	45900
1968 BOATS													
25		KTH	SA/CR	STL	KL	IB	35D		7 6	6000	3	9050	10300
28		KTH	SA/CR	STL	KL	IB	35D		8 3	6000	2 8	9950	11300
31		KTH	SA/CR	STL	KL	IB	35D		9 3	10800	3 6	18400	20500
31		SCH	SA/CR	STL	KL	IB	35D		9 3	10800	3 6	18400	20500
33 4		SCH	SA/CR	STL	KL	IB	35D		9 11	14100	4	22800	25300
33 4		KTH	SA/CR	STL	KL	IB	35D		9 11	14100	4	22900	25500
36		KTH	SA/CR	STL	KL	IB	35D		10	11000	3 7	18800	20900
41 1		SCH	SA/CR	STL	KL	IB	35D		12 4	27200	4 7	45000	45000
41 1		KTH	SA/CR	STL	KL	IB	35D		12 4	27200	4 7	42100	46800
41 3		SCH	SA/CR	STL	KL	IB	35D		11 5		3 10	40600	45200
1967 BOATS													
25		KTH	SA/CR	STL	KL	IB	4D		7 6			8350	9600
28		KTH	SA/CR	STL	KL	IB	4D		8 3		2 8	9550	10800
31		SCH	SA/CR	STL	KL	IB	4D		9 3		3 6	17600	20000
33 4		SCH	SA/CR	STL	KL	IB	4D		9 11		4	22200	24700
33 4		KTH	SA/CR	STL	KL	IB	4D		9 11		4	22400	24900
36		KTH	SA/CR	STL	KL	IB	4D		10		3 6	18400	20400
41 1		KTH	SA/CR	STL	KL	IB	35D		12 4		4 7	42100	45800
1966 BOATS													
28		KTH	SA/CR	STL	KL	IB	5D		7 10	6000	2 8	9350	10600
33 2		SCH	SA/CR	STL	KL	IB	14D		9 11	14100	3 6	22200	24700
33 2		KTH	SA/CR	STL	KL	IB	14D		9 11	14100	3 6	22200	24400
36		KTH	SA/CR	STL	KL	IB	18D		10	11000	3 1	18100	20100
41		SCH	SA/CR	STL	KL	IB	30D		12 3	27200	4 6	38800	43100
41		KTH	SA/CR	STL	KL	IB	30D		12 3	27200	4 6	40400	44800
1965 BOATS													
26	SHARPIE	KTH	SAIL	STL	KL	IB	5D		7 10		2 8	8550	9850
28		KTH	SAIL	STL	KL	IB	5D		7 10		2 8	9200	10400
33 2		KTH	SAIL	STL	KL	IB	14D		9 11		3 6	22000	24400
36		SCH	SAIL	STL	KL	IB	18D		10		3 1	17400	19800
41		SCH	SAIL	STL	KL	IB	30D		12 3		4 6	38100	42300
66 2		SCH	SAIL	STL	KL	IB	58D		19 3		7	149500	164500

COMAR S P A
FORLI ITALY 47100   COAST GUARD MFG ID- CDF See inside cover to adjust price for area

COMAR USA INC
IRVINGTON NJ 07111

For more recent years, see the BUC Used Boat Price Guide, Volume 1 or Volume 2

LOA FT IN	NAME AND/ OR MODEL	TOP/ RIG	BOAT TYPE	HULL MTL	HULL TP	ENG TP	# HP	MFG	BEAM FT IN	WGT LBS	DRAFT FT IN	RETAIL LOW	RETAIL HIGH
1977 BOATS													
30	COMET 30	SLP	SAIL	FBG	KL	IB	D		10	7040	5 6	13600	15400
1976 BOATS													
30	COMET 910	SLP	SA/CR	FBG	KL	IB	12D	FARY	10	7040	5 6	13100	14900
30	COMET 910 SHOAL	SLP	SA/CR	FBG	KL	IB	12D	FARY	10	7040	4 6	13100	14900

COMARCO INC

Call 1-800-327-6929 for BUC Personalized Evaluation Service
Or, for 1961 boats, sign onto www.BUCValuPro.com

COMMAND YACHTS INT'L LTD
COAST GUARD MFG ID- ZCK

Call 1-800-327-6929 for BUC Personalized Evaluation Service
Or, for 1975 to 1976 boats, sign onto www.BUCValuPro.com

COMMERCIAL WORK BOATS
MIAMI FL 33178   COAST GUARD MFG ID- UUV See inside cover to adjust price for area

For more recent years, see the BUC Used Boat Price Guide, Volume 1 or Volume 2

LOA FT IN	NAME AND/ OR MODEL	TOP/ RIG	BOAT TYPE	HULL MTL	HULL TP	ENG TP	# HP	MFG	BEAM FT IN	WGT LBS	DRAFT FT IN	RETAIL LOW	RETAIL HIGH
1983 BOATS													
26 9	OFFSHORE 27	HT	OFF	FBG	DS	IB	85D	PERK	10 3		2	22800	25300
39	MAGELLAN 39	SLP	MS	FBG	KL	IB	130D	PERK	12		2	48800	53600
40 3	OFFSHORE 40	HT	TRWL	FBG	DS	IB	130D	PERK	14		3	80300	88300
40 3	OFFSHORE 40	HT	TRWL	FBG	DS	IB	300D	CAT	14		3	84100	92400
40 3	OFFSHORE 40	HT	TRWL	FBG	DS	IB	T300D	CAT	14		3	93300	102500
40 3	OFFSHORE 40	FB	TRWL	FBG	DS	IB	T130D	PERK	14		3	85900	94400

LOA FT IN	NAME AND/ OR MODEL	TOP/ RIG	BOAT TYPE	HULL MTL	TP	ENG TP	# HP	MFG	BEAM FT IN	WGT LBS	DRAFT FT IN	RETAIL LOW	RETAIL HIGH
1982 BOATS													
26 9	OFFSHORE 27	HT	OFF	FBG	DS	IB	85D-225D		10 3		2	21900	25800
39	MAGELLAN 39	SLP	MS	FBG	KL	IB	130D	PERK	12		3	46200	50700
40 3	OFFSHORE 40	FB	SF	FBG	DS	IB	T300D	CAT	14		3	85000	93400
40 3	OFFSHORE 40	HT	TRWL	FBG	DS	IB	130D	PERK	14		3	76700	84300
40 3	OFFSHORE 40	HT	TRWL	FBG	DS	IB	300D	CAT	14		3	80300	88200
40 3	OFFSHORE 40	FB	TRWL	FBG	DS	IB	T130D	PERK	14		3	82100	90200
1981 BOATS													
26 9	OFFSHORE 27	HT	OFF	FBG	DS	IB	85D-130D		10 3		2	21000	24400
40 3	OFFSHORE 40	HT	TRWL	FBG	DS	IB	130D	PERK	14		3	73100	80300
40 3	OFFSHORE 40	HT	TRWL	FBG	DS	IB	300D	CAT	14		3	76500	84100
1979 BOATS													
38 9	GLOBEMASTER 39	SLP	MS	FBG	KL	IB	62D	PERK	11 11	14500	3 8	30000	33400
38 9	GLOBEMASTER 39	SLP	MS	FBG	KL	IB	130D	PERK	11 11	14500	3 8	30000	33300
38 9	GLOBEMASTER 39	CUT	MS	FBG	KL	IB	62D	PERK	11 11	14500	3 8	30000	33100
38 9	GLOBEMASTER 39	CUT	MS	FBG	KL	IB	130D	PERK	11 11	14500	3 8	29900	33200
38 9	GLODEMASTER 39	KTH	MS	FBG	KL	IB	62D	PERK	11 11	14500	4	31100	34500
38 9	GLOBEMASTER 39	KTH	MS	FBG	KL	IB	130D	PERK	11 11	14500	4	30700	34100
41 3	LINDSEY 41	FB	TRWL	FBG	DS	VD	160D	PERK	14 6	20000	3 3	62500	68700
41 3	LINDSEY 41	FB	TRWL	FBG	DS	VD	T 85D	PERK	14 6	20000	3 3	64900	71300
1978 BOATS													
26 9	LINDSEY 27	OP	OFF	FBG	DS	IB	80D-130D		10 3		2	18700	21800
38 9	LINDSEY 39	SLP	MS	FBG	KL	IB	65D	FORD	11 11	14500	3 6	29100	32400
38 9	LINDSEY 39	SLP	MS	FBG	KL	IB	115D	WEST	11 11	14500	3 6	29200	32500
38 9	LINDSEY 39	SLP	MS	FBG	KL	IB	120D	LEHM	11 11	14500	3 6	29100	32300
38 9	LINDSEY 39	KTH	MS	FBG	KL	IB	65D	FORD	11 11	14500	3 6	30100	33400
38 9	LINDSEY 39	KTH	MS	FBG	KL	IB	115D	WEST	11 11	14500	3 6	29800	33200
38 9	LINDSEY 39	KTH	MS	FBG	KL	IB	120D	LEHM	11 11	14500	3 6	29700	33000
39 11	LINDSEY WORKBOAT	HT	UTL	FBG	DS	IB	120D	LEHM	14		3	52800	58000

```
     IB  128D GM   52800  58000,  IB  130D PERK  53300  58600,  IB  210D CAT   54200  59500
     IB  257D GM   54200  59600,  IB  T   D FORD    **     **,  IB T128D GM    55700  61200
     IB T130D PERK 56600  62200,  IB T160D PERK  57200  62900,  IB T210D CAT   58100  63900
     IB T257D GM   58300  64100
```

LOA FT IN	NAME AND/ OR MODEL	TOP/ RIG	BOAT TYPE	HULL MTL	TP	ENG TP	# HP	MFG	BEAM FT IN	WGT LBS	DRAFT FT IN	RETAIL LOW	RETAIL HIGH
40	LINDSEY 40	HT	TRWL	FBG	DS	VD	120D	FORD	12	14000	3	48200	53000
40	LINDSEY 40	HT	TRWL	FBG	DS	VD	225D	CAT	12	14000	3	50200	55100
40	LINDSEY 40	HT	TRWL	FBG	DS	VD	T 65D	FORD	12	14000	3	50400	55300
40	LINDSEY 40	FB	TRWL	FBG	DS	VD	120D	FORD	12	14000	3	48200	53000
40	LINDSEY 40	FB	TRWL	FBG	DS	VD	225D	CAT	12	14000	3	50200	55200
40	LINDSEY 40	FB	TRWL	FBG	DS	VD	T 65D	FORD	12	14000	3	50400	55400

COMMODORE BOATS

Call 1-800-327-6929 for BUC Personalized Evaluation Service
Or, for 1956 to 1971 boats, sign onto www.BUCValuPro.com

COMMODORE CORPORATION

Call 1-800-327-6929 for BUC Personalized Evaluation Service
Or, for 1963 boats, sign onto www.BUCValuPro.com

COMMODORE YACHT CORP
ST JAMES FL 33956   COAST GUARD MFG ID- XYV See inside cover to adjust price for area

For more recent years, see the BUC Used Boat Price Guide, Volume 1 or Volume 2

LOA FT IN	NAME AND/ OR MODEL	TOP/ RIG	BOAT TYPE	HULL MTL	TP	ENG TP	# HP	BEAM FT IN	WGT LBS	DRAFT FT IN	RETAIL LOW	RETAIL HIGH
1983 BOATS												
25 10	COMMODORE 26	SLP	SA/CR	FBG	KL	OB		7 11	4225	2 1	5850	6750
1982 BOATS												
25 10	COMMODORE 26	SLP	SA/CR	FBG	KL	OB		7 11	4500	2 1	5850	6750
25 10	COMMODORE 26	SLP	SA/CR	FBG	KL	IB	D	7 11		2 1	6050	6950
1981 BOATS												
25 10	COMMODORE 26	SLP	SA/CR	FBG	KL	OB		7 11	4225	2 1	5200	5950
25 10	COMMODORE 26	SLP	SA/CR	FBG	KL	IB	7D REN	7 11	4225	2 1	5500	6350
1980 BOATS												
25 10	COMMODORE 26	SLP	SA/CR	FBG	KL	OB		7 11	4225	2 1	4950	5700
25 10	COMMODORE 26	SLP	SA/CR	FBG	KL	IB	7D REN	7 11	4225	2 1	5250	6050

COMPASS YACHT MFG
COAST GUARD MFG ID- CYM

Call 1-800-327-6929 for BUC Personalized Evaluation Service
Or, for 1979 boats, sign onto www.BUCValuPro.com

COMPASS YACHTS PTY LTD
DIV OF COMPASS CHARTERS

Call 1-800-327-6929 for BUC Personalized Evaluation Service
Or, for 1979 to 1981 boats, sign onto www.BUCValuPro.com

COMPODYNE CORPORATION
COAST GUARD MFG ID- BNU
FORMERLY FORCE ENGINEER

Call 1-800-327-6929 for BUC Personalized Evaluation Service
Or, for 1976 to 1986 boats, sign onto www.BUCValuPro.com

COMPOSITE TECHNOLOGY INC
ISLAND YACHT CORP
LEAGUE CITY TX 77573   COAST GUARD MFG ID- CTE See inside cover to adjust price for area
FORMERLY PLASTREND

LOA FT IN	NAME AND/ OR MODEL	TOP/ RIG	BOAT TYPE	HULL MTL	TP	ENG TP	# HP	MFG	BEAM FT IN	WGT LBS	DRAFT FT IN	RETAIL LOW	RETAIL HIGH
1982 BOATS													
25 8	PETERSON 36	SLP	SA/RC	FBG	KL	IB	D		8 7	3900	5	10200	11500
33 11	PETERSON 34	SLP	SA/RC	FBG	KL	IB	D		11 3	10800	3 3	30500	33900
37 10	PETERSON 38	SLP	SAIL	FBG	KL	IB	D		12 1		7 1	58700	64600
1981 BOATS													
34	PETERSON 34	SLP	SA/RC	FBG	KL	IB	D		11 3	10200	5 7	27200	30200
1977 BOATS													
22	PT-1/4	SLP	SAIL	FBG	KL	IB			7	2000	4 3	4950	5700
25 8	PETERSON 1/4 TON	SLP	SA/RC	FBG	KL	IB	D		9	3900	5	8150	9350
33 11	PETERSON 34	SLP	SAIL	FBG	KL	IB			11 2	10800	6 3	24400	27100
33 11	PETERSON 34	SLP	SAIL	FBG	KL	IB	12D- 25D		11 2	10800	6 3	24500	27300
35 8	CARTER 36	SLP	SAIL	FBG	KL	IB			11 8	14200	6 3	33300	37000
40 10	CARTER TWO TON	SLP	SA/RC	FBG	KL	IB	D		12 2	18800	6 10	53500	58800
1976 BOATS													
22	PT-1/4	SLP	SAIL	FBG	KC	OB			7	2000	5 1	3750	4400
25 8	PETERSON 1/4 TON	SLP	SAIL	FBG	KL	IB	15D	WEST	8 7	3900	5 7	8000	9200
30	PETERSON 30 1/2 TON	SLP	SAIL	F/S	KL	IB	30D		10 2	7800	5 7	16600	18900
31 9	PT-32	SLP	SAIL	FBG	KL	IB	25	UNIV	9 10	10400	6 3	22200	24700
33 11	PETERSON 34	SLP	SAIL	FBG	KL	IB	30	UNIV	11	10800	6 3	23600	26200
33 11	PETERSON 34	SLP	SAIL	FBG	KL	IB	12D	YAN	11	10800	6 3	23700	26400
35 10	CARTER 36	SLP	SAIL	FBG	KL	IB	30D	PISC	11 8	14200	6 3	32500	36100
41	CARTER-TWO-TON	SLP	SAIL	FBG	KL	IB	55D	WEST	12 2	18800	6 10	52500	57700
1975 BOATS													
22	PT-1/4	SLP	SAIL	FBG	KC	OB			7	2000	5 1	3650	4250
22	PT-1/4	SLP	SAIL	FBG	KC	OB			7	2000	5 1	3650	4250
25 8	PETERSON 1/4 TON	SLP	SAIL	FBG	KL	IB	6D	WEST	8 7	3900	5 7	7600	8750
31 9	PT-32	SLP	SAIL	FBG	KL	IB	25	UNIV	9 10	10200	5 7	21200	23500
35 8	CARTER 36	SLP	SAIL	FBG	KL	IB	27D	GM	11 8	14200	6 3	31300	34800
40 10	CARTER-TWO-TON	SLP	SAIL	FBG	KL	IB	35D	WEST	12 2	18800	6 10	50400	55400
1974 BOATS													
22	PT-1/4		SAIL	FBG	KC	OB			7	2000	5 1	3550	4150
22	PT-1/4		SAIL	FBG	KC	OB			7	2000	5 1	3550	4150
31 9	PT-32	SLP	SAIL	FBG	KL	IB	30	UNIV	9 10	10400	5 7	21100	23300
35 8	CARTER 36	SLP	SAIL	FBG	KL	IB	27D	PISC	11 8	14200	6 3	30500	33900
1973 BOATS													
22	PT-1/4	SLP	SAIL	FBG	KL	OB			7	2000	2 4	3500	4050
22	PT-1/4	SLP	SAIL	FBG	KL	OB	D		7	2000	2 4	4450	5100
30	PT MK II	SLP	SAIL	FBG	KL	IB	15D	VLVO	9 9	10400	4 2	20700	23000
31 9	PT 32	SLP	SAIL	FBG	KL	IB	25	UNIV	9 10	10400	5 7	20500	22800
40	PT 40	SLP	SAIL	FBG	KL	IB	30D		11	16000	5 6	41200	45700
1972 BOATS													
22	MUSTANG PT 22	SLP	SAIL	FBG	KC	IB	8D		7	2000	2 4	4350	5000
22	MUSTANG PT 22	SLP	SA/CR	FBG	KC				7	2000	2 4	3400	3900
26	TEMPEST	SLP	SAIL	FBG		IB			7 6	1035	5	2500	2900
26 9	INTERNATIONAL SOLING		SAIL	FBG		OB			6		4 3	2400	4850
30	PT 30-MARK II	SLP	SAIL	FBG		IB	18D	VLVO	9 9	10400	4 2	20300	22500
40	PT 40	SLP	SA/CR	FBG	KL	IB	30D		11	16000	5 6	40200	44700
1971 BOATS													
22	INTERNATL-TEMPEST	SLP	SA/OD	FBG	KL	IB			6	1020	3 2	2450	2850
22	MUSTANG PT 22	SLP	SAIL	FBG	KC	IB	8D		7	2000	2 4	4200	4900
26 9	INTERNATIONAL SOLING		SAIL	FBG		IB			6 3	2200	4 1	4100	4750
30	PT 30-MK-II	SLP	SAIL	FBG		IB	30	UNIV	9 9	10400	5 6	19800	22000
39 8	PT 40	SLP	SA/RC	FBG	KL	IB	30D		11	16000	5 6	43200	48000

COMPOSITE TECHNOLOGY INC   -CONTINUED   See inside cover to adjust price for area

LOA FT IN	NAME AND/ OR MODEL	TOP/ RIG	BOAT TYPE	-HULL- MTL TP	----ENGINE--- TP # HP MFG	BEAM FT IN	WGT LBS	DRAFT FT IN	RETAIL LOW	RETAIL HIGH
	------- 1970 BOATS									
22	INTERNATL-TEMPEST	SLP	SA/OD	FBG KL		6 6	480	3 7	1950	2350
22	MUSTANG	SLP	SA/OD	FBG KC		6 6	3250	2 4	3250	3800
22	MUSTANG		SAIL	FBG	IB 8D	7	2000	2 4	4150	4850
26 9	INTERNATIONAL SOLING		SAIL	FBG	OB	6 3	2200	4 3	4050	4700
30 1	PT 30		SAIL	FBG	IB 12D	9 3	9070	5 6	16700	19000
40	PT 40		SAIL	FBG	IB 25D GRAY	11	16000	5 6	38600	42900
	------- 1969 BOATS									
21 11	TEMPEST	SLP	SA/OD	FBG KL OB		6 6	1035	3 7	2350	2750
22	MUSTANG		SAIL	FBG	IB 8D	7	2000	5	4100	4750
26 9	INTERNATIONAL SOLING		SAIL	FBG	OB	6 3	2200	4 3	3950	4600
40	PT 40		SAIL	FBG	IB 25D GRAY	11	16000	5 6	38000	42200
	------- 1967 BOATS									
22	MUSTANG	SLP	SA/OD	FBG KC		7	1950	2 4	3100	3600
22	TEMPEST	SLP	SA/OD	FBG KL		6 6	1020	3 7	2350	2700
	------- 1965 BOATS									
22	MUSTANG	SLP	SAIL	FBG KC		7 8		7	3100	3600

JOSEPH L CONBOY ASSOC
COAST GUARD MFG ID- JCN

Call 1-800-327-6929 for BUC Personalized Evaluation Service
Or, for 1961 to 1983 boats, sign onto www.BUCValuPro.com

CONCORDIA YACHT INC
S DARTMOUTH MA 02748   COAST GUARD MFG ID- CNC See inside cover to adjust price for area

For more recent years, see the BUC Used Boat Price Guide, Volume 1 or Volume 2

LOA FT IN	NAME AND/ OR MODEL	TOP/ RIG	BOAT TYPE	-HULL- MTL TP	----ENGINE--- TP # HP MFG	BEAM FT IN	WGT LBS	DRAFT FT IN	RETAIL LOW	RETAIL HIGH
	------- 1974 BOATS									
17 8		GAF	SAIL	FBG CB		5 5	1800		4000	4650
17 8		SLP	SAIL	FBG CB		5 5	1800		4000	4650
18 2	SANDERLING	CAT	SA/OD	FBG CB OB		8 6		1 7	2350	2750
22 2	MARSHALL		SAIL	FBG	OB	10 2	5660		12600	14300
	------- 1972 BOATS									
17 8		SLP	SA/OD	WD CB OB		5	1000		2800	3250
18 2	SANDERLING	CAT	SA/OD	FBG CB OB		8 6		1 7	2250	2650
22 2	MARSHALL		SAIL	FBG	OB	10 2	5660		12000	13700
24		CR	WD	SV OB		7	720		2400	2800
30		CR	WD	SV OB		8 6	7000		20100	22400
31	CONCORDIA	SLP	SA/CR	WD KL IB	31D	9 4	14000		36900	41000
39 10	CONCORDIA	YWL	SA/CR	WD KL IB	31D	10 3	18000		53000	58300
41	CONCORDIA	YWL	SA/CR	WD KL IB	31D	10 3	21000		59800	65800
	------- 1970 BOATS									
17 8	CONCORDIA	SLP	SA/OD	WD CB OB		5	1000	3	2700	3150
31	CONCORDIA	SLP	SA/CR	WD KL IB	31D	9 4	14000	5	35100	39000
39 10	CONCORDIA	YWL	SA/CR	WD KL IB	31D	10 3	18000	5 8	50200	55200
	------- 1969 BOATS									
17 8	CONCORDIA	SLP	SA/OD	WD CB OB		5	1000	3	2650	3100
31	CONCORDIA 31	SLP	SA/CR	WD KL IB	31D	9 4	14000	5	34400	38200
39 10	CONCORDIA	YWL	SA/CR	WD KL IB	31D	10 3	18000	5 8	49600	54500
	------- 1968 BOATS									
17 8	CONCORDIA	SLP	SAIL	WD CB OB		5	1000	1 6	2600	3050
39 10	CONCORDIA	YWL	SAIL	MHG KL IB	31D	10 3	18314	5 8	52500	57700
	------- 1967 BOATS									
17 8	CONCORDIA	SLP	SAIL	WD CB OB		5	1000	1 6	3100	3600
31	CONCORDIA 31	SLP	SA/CR	WD KL IB	31D	9 4		5	25800	28600
39 10	CONCORDIA	YWL	SAIL	WD IB	31D		18314		51600	56800
	------- 1966 BOATS									
39 10	CONCORDIA	YWL	SAIL	WD IB	31D				53300	58600
41	CONCORDIA 41	YWL	SAIL	WD IB	31D				55000	60400
	------- 1965 BOATS									
39 10	CONCORDIA	YWL	SAIL	WD KL IB	31D	10 3		5 8	52800	58000
41	CONCORDIA 41	YWL	SAIL	WD KL IB	31D	10 3		5 10	54500	59900
	------- 1963 BOATS									
39 10	CONCORDIA	YWL	SAIL	WD IB	D			5 8	52200	57400
	------- 1962 BOATS									
39 10	CONCORDIA		SAIL	WD IB	D	10 3		5 8	51900	57000
	------- 1961 BOATS									
39 10	CONCORDIA		SAIL	WD IB	D	10 3		5 8	51700	56800
	------- 1960 BOATS									
39 10	CONCORDIA	YWL	SA/CR	P/M KL IB	D	10 3		5 8	51600	56700
39 10	CONCORDIA		SAIL	WD IB	D	10 3		5 8	51700	56800
41	CONCORDIA 41	SLP	SA/CR	P/M KL IB	D	10 3		5 10	53400	58700
	------- 1959 BOATS									
39 10	CONCORDIA	YWL	SAIL	WD CB IB	D	10 3		5 8	51700	56800
41	CONCORDIA 41	SLP	SAIL	P/M KL IB	D	10 3		5 10	53500	58800
	------- 1958 BOATS									
39 10	CONCORDIA		SAIL	WD IB	D	10 3		5 8	51900	57100
	------- 1957 BOATS									
39 10	CONCORDIA		SAIL	WD IB	D				52300	57500
	------- 1956 BOATS									
39 10	CONCORDIA		SAIL	WD IB	D				52700	57900
	------- 1955 BOATS									
39 10	CONCORDIA		SAIL	WD IB	D				53200	58500
	------- 1954 BOATS									
39 10	CONCORDIA		SAIL	WD IB	D				53800	59200

CONDOR YACHTS LTD
CORNWALL ENGLAND   See inside cover to adjust price for area

LOA FT IN	NAME AND/ OR MODEL	TOP/ RIG	BOAT TYPE	-HULL- MTL TP	----ENGINE--- TP # HP MFG	BEAM FT IN	WGT LBS	DRAFT FT IN	RETAIL LOW	RETAIL HIGH
	------- 1980 BOATS									
31 4	CONDOR 32	SLP	SA/CR	FBG KL IB	23D VLVO	9 7	9800	4 10	13400	15200
37 4	CONDOR 37	SLP	SA/CR	FBG KL IB	35D VLVO	11 9	15933	6 9	23100	25700
	------- 1979 BOATS									
31 9	CONDOR 32	SLP	SA/CR	FBG KL IB	23D VLVO	9 8	10000	5	13100	14900
37 4	CONDOR 37	CUT	SA/CR	FBG KL IB	23D VLVO	11 9	17227	6 9	23600	26200

CONQUEST MARINE INTERNATIONAL

Call 1-800-327-6929 for BUC Personalized Evaluation Service
Or, for 1981 boats, sign onto www.BUCValuPro.com

CONQUEST YACHT BUILDERS INC

Call 1-800-327-6929 for BUC Personalized Evaluation Service
Or, for 1981 boats, sign onto www.BUCValuPro.com

CONSOLIDATED MARINE CORP
COCOA FL 32922   See inside cover to adjust price for area

LOA FT IN	NAME AND/ OR MODEL	TOP/ RIG	BOAT TYPE	-HULL- MTL TP	----ENGINE--- TP # HP MFG	BEAM FT IN	WGT LBS	DRAFT FT IN	RETAIL LOW	RETAIL HIGH
	------- 1971 BOATS									
34 2	PEMBROKE		CUD	FBG DV	IB T225 CHRY	11 11	12500	2 8	31500	35000
34 2	PEMBROKE		SF	FBG DV	IB T225 CHRY	11 11	12500	2 8	31000	34500
36 10	SEA-CHAMP	HT	HB	FBG TR	215	13	10000	2 3	14700	16700
39 10	AVENGER		DC	FBG DV	IB T300 CHRY	13 10	23000	3 6	57900	63400
39 10	AVENGER		SF	FBG DV	IB T300 CHRY	13 10	23000	3 6	56800	62400
45 6	CAPRI XL	HT	FB	FBG TR	T215	13	14000	2 3	16800	19000
	------- 1968 BOATS									
44	CAPRI XL		HB	STL DV	IO 185	12	14000	1 6	16700	19000
	------- 1949 BOATS									
39	FAMILY CRUISER		SDN	WD RB	IB				**	**
50		FB	SF	WD	IB T D				**	**
	------- 1946 BOATS									
39	PLAYBOAT		HT	DC	WD	IB T				**	**
39	PLAYBOAT		HT	SDN	WD	IB T				**	**
42		HT	DC	WD	IB T CHRY	11		2 10	**	**
52		FB	MY	WD	IB R200D GM	13		3 6	72900	80100
60		FB	MY	WD	IB T200D GM	15		4	88500	97300
	------- 1939 BOATS									
42		FB	SF	WD	IB T200 SCRI	11		3	27000	30000
	------- 1937 BOATS									
42				WD	IB T				**	**
42	PLAYBOAT		HT	DC	WD	IB T115 SPEE				46200	50700
	------- 1936 BOATS									
39			HT	CR	WD	IB				**	**
	------- 1932 BOATS									
47			HT	DC	WD	IB 180 SPEE				52600	57800
	------- 1931 BOATS									
50			HT	DC	MHG	IB 180 SPEE	11 6		3 6	**	**
	------- 1925 BOATS									
34 9					WD	IB 155				**	**
45					WD	IB 225 PALM				**	**

```
 LOA  NAME AND/        TOP/ BOAT  -HULL- ----ENGINE--- BEAM   WGT  DRAFT RETAIL RETAIL
FT IN  OR MODEL        RIG  TYPE  MTL TP TP # HP MFG  FT IN   LBS  FT IN  LOW    HIGH
------------------- 1917 BOATS -----------------------------------------------------------
52                         WD   IB  195D                          **     **
```

CONSUL MARINE INC
COAST GUARD MFG ID- COM

Call 1-800-327-6929 for BUC Personalized Evaluation Service
Or, for 1983 to 1984 boats, sign onto www.BUCValuPro.com

CONTENDER BOATS INC
COAST GUARD MFG ID- XBE

Call 1-800-327-6929 for BUC Personalized Evaluation Service
Or, for 1980 boats, sign onto www.BUCValuPro.com

CONTESSA YACHTS LTD
HAMPSHIRE ENGLAND   See inside cover to adjust price for area

For more recent years, see the BUC Used Boat Price Guide, Volume 1 or Volume 2

```
 LOA  NAME AND/        TOP/ BOAT  -HULL- ----ENGINE--- BEAM   WGT  DRAFT RETAIL RETAIL
FT IN  OR MODEL        RIG  TYPE  MTL TP TP # HP MFG  FT IN   LBS  FT IN  LOW    HIGH
------------------- 1979 BOATS -----------------------------------------------------------
27  8 CONTESSA 28      SLP SA/CR FBG KL IB     D       9  5   4 10 17000  19300
32    CONTESSA 32      SLP SA/CR FBG KL IB     D       9  6   5  6 27500  30600
```

CONTEST YACHTS
1671 GD MEDEMBLIK HOLLA COAST GUARD MFG ID- HLY See inside cover to adjust price for area

CONTEST YACHTS
STAMFORD CT 06902
                    FORMERLY CONYPLEX

For more recent years, see the BUC Used Boat Price Guide, Volume 1 or Volume 2

```
 LOA  NAME AND/        TOP/ BOAT  -HULL- ----ENGINE--- BEAM   WGT  DRAFT RETAIL RETAIL
FT IN  OR MODEL        RIG  TYPE  MTL TP TP # HP MFG  FT IN   LBS  FT IN  LOW    HIGH
------------------- 1983 BOATS -----------------------------------------------------------
24  9 CONTEST 250C     SLP SAIL F/S KL SD   8D VLVO  9      3788  4 11  9800  11200
27 11 CONTEST 28A      SLP SAIL F/S KL SD  15D VLVO  9  4   6570  4  7 20200  22400
27 11 CONTEST 28B      SLP SAIL F/S KL SD  15D VLVO  9  4   6173  5  4 19100  21300
31  2 CONTEST 31HTA    SLP SAIL F/S KL SD  25D VLVO 10  4  11157  4  9 38500  42800
31  2 CONTEST 31HTB    SLP SAIL F/S KL SD  25D VLVO 10  4  10509  5  9 36300  40300
31 10 CONTEST 32CSA    SLP SAIL F/S KL SD  25D VLVO 10 11  14300  4  3 50000  54900
31 10 CONTEST 32CSA    KTH SAIL F/S KL SD  25D VLVO 10 11  14300  4  3 50000  54900
31 10 CONTEST 32CSB    SLP SAIL F/S KL SD  25D VLVO 10 11  13860  5  3 48500  53300
31 10 CONTEST 32CSB    KTH SAIL F/S KL SD  25D VLVO 10 11  13860  5  3 48500  53300
34 11 CONTEST 35A      SLP SAIL F/S KL SD  35D VLVO 11  8  15180  5  5 54500  59900
34 11 CONTEST 35B      SLP SAIL F/S KL SD  35D VLVO 11  8  14879  6  3 53500  58800
37  3 CONTEST 38SA     KTH SAIL F/S KL SD  35D VLVO 12     19285  5  5 71000  78000

37  3 CONTEST 38SB     KTH SAIL F/S KL SD  35D VLVO 12     18603  6  5 69000  75800
39  9 CONTEST 40       KTH SAIL F/S KL SD  61D VLVO 12  8  25297  5 11 95700 105500
42  7 CONTEST 42       KTH SAIL F/S KL IB  52D VLVO 13  1  27403  6  1 109500 120000
48  3 CONTEST 48       KTH SAIL F/S KL IB  72D VLVO 14  2  37881  6  1 159500 175000
------------------- 1982 BOATS -----------------------------------------------------------
27 11 CONTEST 28A      SLP SAIL F/S KL IB  13D VLVO  9  4   6570  4  7 19100  21300
27 11 CONTEST 28B      SLP SAIL F/S KL IB  13D VLVO  9  4   6173  5  4 17600  20000
31  2 CONTEST 31HTA    SLP SAIL F/S KL IB  25D VLVO 10  4  11157  4  9 36200  40200
31  2 CONTEST 31HTB    SLP SAIL F/S KL IB  25D VLVO 10  4  10509  5  9 34100  38000
31 10 CONTEST 32CSA    KTH SAIL F/S KL IB  25D VLVO 10 11  14300  4  3 47300  52000
31 10 CONTEST 32CSB    KTH SAIL F/S KL IB  25D VLVO 10 11  13860  5  3 45900  50400
34 11 CONTEST 35A      SLP SAIL F/S KL IB  36D VLVO 11  8  15180  5  5 51300  56400
34 11 CONTEST 35B      SLP SAIL F/S KL IB  36D VLVO 11  8  14879  6  3 50400  55400
37  3 CONTEST 385A     KTH SAIL F/S KL IB  36D VLVO 12     19285  6  5 66900  73500
37  3 CONTEST 385B     KTH SAIL F/S KL IB  36D VLVO 12     18603  6  5 65000  71400
42  7 CONTEST 42       KTH SAIL F/S KL IB  52D VLVO 13  1  27403  6  1 103500 113500
48  3 CONTEST 48       KTH SAIL F/S KL IB  72D VLVO 14  2  37881  6  1 151000 166000
------------------- 1979 BOATS -----------------------------------------------------------
27 11 CONTEST 28       SLP SA/CR FBG KL IB 13D VLVO  9  4   6570  5  4 16200  18400
29  7 CONTEST 30       SLP SA/CR FBG KL IB 25D VLVO 10  3   9100  5  8 24400  27100
31  6 CONTEST 32       SLP SA/CR FBG KL IB 25D VLVO 10  4  11450  5  9 32300  35900
34    CONTEST 34       SLP SA/CR FBG KL IB 25D VLVO 11  2  16315  5  9 47000  51700
36    CONTEST 36       SLP SA/CR FBG KL IB 25D VLVO 11  2  17957  6  3 52500  57700
36    CONTEST 36       KTH SA/CR FBG KL IB 25D VLVO 11  2  17957  6  3 52600  57800
42  7 CONTEST 42       SLP SA/CR FBG KL IB 52D VLVO 13  1  27403  6  9 86900  95500
42  7 CONTEST 42       KTH SA/CR FBG KL IB 52D VLVO 13  1  27403  6  9 89500  98400
48  3 CONTEST 48       KTH SA/CR FBG KL IB 75D VLVO 14  2  36000  6  5 129000 141500
------------------- 1978 BOATS -----------------------------------------------------------
24  8 CONTEST 25       SLP SA/CR FBG KL IB    D      8  3   5160  4  1 10200  11600
27 11 CONTEST 28       SLP SA/CR FBG KL IB 13D VLVO  9  4   6600  4  7 15700  17800
29  7 CONTEST 30       SLP SA/CR FBG KL IB 13D VLVO 10  3   9100  4  7 23500  26100
31  2 CONTEST 32       SLP SA/CR FBG KL IB 25D VLVO 10  4  11157  4  9 30100  33500
34    CONTEST 34       SLP SA/CR FBG KL IB 25D VLVO 11  2  16315  5  9 44800  49800
36    CONTEST 36       SLP SA/CR FBG KL IB 25D VLVO 11  2  17957  4  4 50600  55600
36    CONTEST 36       KTH SA/CR FBG KL IB 25D VLVO 11  2  17957  4  4 50700  55700
42  7 CONTEST 42       SLP SA/CR FBG KL IB 52D VLVO 13  1  27403  6  1 83400  91700
42  7 CONTEST 42       KTH SA/CR FBG KL IB 52D VLVO 13  1  27403  6  1 86100  94600
48  3 CONTEST 48       KTH SA/CR FBG KL IB 75D VLVO 14  2  36000  6  5 124000 136000
------------------- 1977 BOATS -----------------------------------------------------------
24  8 CONTEST 25       SLP SA/CR FBG KL IB  6D- 15D  8  3   5200  4  1  9800  11300
27 11 CONTEST 28 SHOAL SLP SA/CR FBG KL IB 10D- 25D  9  4   6570  4  7 15000  17200
29  7 CONTEST 30       SLP SA/CR FBG KL IB 13D- 25D 10  3   9100  4  7 22700  25300
31  2 CONTEST 32       SLP SA/CR FBG KL IB 25D- 36D 11  2  11157  4  9 29100  32400
34    CONTEST 34       SLP SA/CR FBG KL IB 25D- 36D 11  2  16000  5  2 42500  47300
36    CONTEST 36       SLP SA/CR FBG KL IB 36D VLVO 11  2  17957  4 11 48900  53700
36    CONTEST 36       SLP SA/CR FBG KL IB 36D VLVO 11  2  17957  4 11 49000  53800
36    CONTEST 36       KTH SA/CR FBG KL IB 25D VLVO 11  2  17957  4 11 49000  53800
42  6 CONTEST 42       KTH SA/CR FBG KL IB 52D VLVO 13  1  26455  6  7 81100  89200
48  3 CONTEST 48       KTH SA/CR FBG KL IB 75D VLVO 14  2  36000  5  4 119000 131000
------------------- 1976 BOATS -----------------------------------------------------------
24  8 CONTEST 25       SLP SAIL FBG KL OB           8  3   5200  4  1  9000  10200
24  8 CONTEST 25       SLP SAIL FBG KL OB  5D- 10D  8  3   5200  4  1  9400  10900
28    CONTEST 28       SLP SAIL FBG KL IB  10D VLVO  9  4   6600  4  5 14700  16700
29  7 CONTEST 30       SLP SAIL FBG KL IB  10D VLVO 10  3   9100  4  9 22000  24400
31  2 CONTEST 31       SLP SAIL FBG KL IB  25D VLVO 10  4  11157  4  9 28200  31400
34    CONTEST 34       SLP SAIL FBG KL IB  25D VLVO 11  2  16500  5  9 42400  47100
36    CONTEST 36       SLP SAIL FBG KL IB  25D VLVO 11  2  18000  4 11 47800  52500
48  3 CONTEST 48       KTH SAIL FBG KL IB  75D VLVO 14  2  38000  5  9 117500 129000
------------------- 1975 BOATS -----------------------------------------------------------
27    CONTEST 27       SLP SAIL FBG KL IB  12D VLVO  9      6000  4  5 12400  14100
30    CONTEST 30       SLP SAIL FBG KL IB  16D VLVO 10  3   9100  4  9 21600  24000
31    CONTEST 31       SLP SAIL FBG KL IB  16D VLVO 10  4   9850  4  9 24100  26800
32  9 CONTEST 33       SLP SAIL FBG KL IB  36D VLVO 11  2  11575  5  3 29000  32300
36    CONTEST 36       SLP SAIL FBG KL IB  36D VLVO 11  2  18000  4 11 46300  50900
38    CONTEST 38       SLP SAIL FBG KL IB  36D VLVO 11  3  17000  6  6 46800  51500
48    CONTEST 48       KTH SAIL FBG KL IB  75D VLVO 14  2  32000  6  6 105500 115500
------------------- 1974 BOATS -----------------------------------------------------------
23  7 KRAMER 24 1/4 TON SLP SAIL FBG  OB            7 11   3000  4  5  4700   5400
27    CONTEST 27       SLP SAIL FBG    OB  10D VLVO  9      5730  4  5 11700  13300
31  2 CONTEST 31 HT    SLP SA/CR FBG KL IB          10  4   9850  4  5 23500  26100
31  4 CONTEST 31       SLP SAIL FBG KL IB  25D VLVO  9  4   8380  4  7 20100  22400
32  8 CONTEST 33       SLP SAIL FBG KL IB  25D VLVO 10  4   9370  5  3 23000  25500
36    CONTEST 36       KTH SAIL FBG KL IB          11  2  18000  4 11 44300  49300
38    CONTEST 38       SLP SAIL FBG KL IB  36D VLVO 11  3  17000  6  6 45000  50000
39  9 CONTEST 40       YWL SAIL FBG KL IB  36D VLVO 11  3  17190  6  6 49500  54400
39  9 CONTEST 40       YWL SAIL FBG KL IB  54D VLVO 11  3  17500  6  6 50400  55400
42    NORTH-SEA        HT  TRWL FBG DS IB  175     13       3  6 100500 110500
42    NORTH-SEA        HT  TRWL FBG DS IB  T125    13       3  6 102000 112000

50    NORTH-SEA        HT  TRWL FBG DS IB  175     14  5   4  2 178500 196500
50    NORTH-SEA        HT  TRWL FBG DS IB  T100    14  5   4  2 180500 198500
65    NORTH-SEA        HT  TRWL FBG DS IB  220     16  3     7 547000 601000
65    NORTH-SEA        HT  TRWL FBG DS IB  T100    16  3     7 542500 596500
------------------- 1973 BOATS -----------------------------------------------------------
23  7 KRAMER 24 1/4 TON SLP SAIL FBG  OB            7 11   3000  4  3  4550   5250
27    CONTEST 27       SLP SAIL FBG KL IB  10D VLVO  9      6160  4  5 12300  14000
31  4 CONTEST 31       SLP SAIL FBG KL IB  10D VLVO 10  4   8380  4  7 19600  21800
32  8 CONTEST 33       SLP SAIL FBG KL IB  25D VLVO 10  4   9370  5  3 22400  24900
38    CONTEST 38       SLP SAIL FBG KL IB  36D VLVO 11  2  16850  6  6 43500  48300
39  9 CONTEST 40       YWL SAIL FBG KL IB  53D VLVO 11  3  17190  6  6 48600  53500
61    NORTH-SEA        HT  TRWL STL DS IB  175     15       6    383000 421000
66    ATLANTIC         MY  STL     IB T135D 16           7    524500 576500
72    PACIFIC          MY  STL     IB                          **     **
------------------- 1972 BOATS -----------------------------------------------------------
27  5 CONTEST 27       SLP SAIL FBG KL IB 12D- 17D  8  1   5906  5  4 11500  13200
31  4 CONTEST 31       SLP SAIL FBG KL IB 12D- 15D 10  4   8820  4  7 19200  22400
32  3 CONTEST 33       SLP SAIL FBG KL IB 12D- 15D 10  4   9370  4  6 21800  24300
39  9 CONTEST 40       YWL SAIL FBG KL IB  52D VLVO 11  3  16755  6  1 46600  51200
```

LOA FT IN	NAME AND/ OR MODEL	TOP/ RIG	BOAT TYPE	-HULL- MTL TP	----ENGINE--- TP # HP MFG	BEAM FT IN	WGT LBS	DRAFT FT IN	RETAIL LOW	RETAIL HIGH
				1971 BOATS						
25	CONTEST 25	SLP	SAIL	FBG KL	8D	7 3	4400	3 11	7300	8400
27 4	CONTEST 27	SLP	SAIL	FBG KL	IB 12D- 17D	8 1	5732	4 1	10900	12500
30	CONTEST 30	SLP	SAIL	FBG KL	IB 12D- 15D	9 3	8820	4 4	19100	21200
32 8	CONTEST 33	SLP	SAIL	FBG KL	IB 12D- 15D	10 4	9370	4 6	21500	23800
39 9	CONTEST 40	YWL	SAIL	FBG KL	IB 52D VLVO	11 3	16755	6 1	45600	50100
45	CALYPSO 45	KTH	MS	FBG KL	IB D	13		4 6	78400	86200
				1970 BOATS						
25	CONTEST 25	SLP	SAIL	FBG KL	8D	7 3	4400	3 11	7200	8250
27 4	CONTEST 27	SLP	SAIL	FBG KL	IB 7D- 12D	8 1	5500	4 1	10300	11700
29 11	CONTEST 30	SLP	SAIL	FBG KL	IB 30 UNIV	9 4	9000	4 4	19000	21100
29 11	CONTEST 30	SLP	SAIL	FBG KL	IB 15D VLVO	9 4	9000	4 4	19100	21200
34 11	CONTEST 35	SLP	SAIL	FBG KL	IB 30 UNIV	10 6	11000	4 8	25200	28000
34 11	CONTEST 35	SLP	SAIL	FBG KL	IB 15D VLVO	10 6	11000	4 8	25300	28100
40	SEVEN-SEAS		MS	FBG KL	IB 85D FORD	11 6	22000	4 6	52400	57600
				1969 BOATS						
23 7	CONTEST 24	SLP	SAIL	FBG KL		7 6		2 5	4850	5550
25	CONTEST 25	SLP	SAIL	FBG KL	IB 8D	7 3	4400	3 11	7100	8150
29	CONTEST 29	SLP	SAIL	FBG KL	IB 12D	8 3	8500	4 3	17000	19300
34 11	CONTEST 35	SLP	SAIL	FBG KL	IB 36D	10 6	11000	4 8	25000	27800
38	CONTEST 38	SLP	SAIL	FBG KL	IB 85D	11 2		5 9	45800	50300
38	CONTEST 38	YWL	SAIL	FBG KL	IB 85D	11 2		5 9	45800	50300
40	SEVEN-SEAS 40	KTH	SAIL	FBG KL	IB 85D	11 6	22000	4 6	53800	59100
45	CALYPSO 45	KTH	SAIL	FBG KL	IB 110D	13	32000	5 2	77800	85500
				1968 BOATS						
24	CONTEST 24	SLP	SAIL	FBG	OB	7 6	3600	2 5	4950	5700
25	CONTEST 25	SLP	SAIL	FBG KL	IB 8D	7 3	4400	3 11	7000	8050
27	CONTEST 27	SLP	SAIL	FBG	IB 8D	8 1	5500	4 1	9800	11100
29	CONTEST 29	SLP	SAIL	FBG KL	IB 12D	8 3	8500	4 3	16700	19000
30	CONTEST 30	SLP	SAIL	FBG	IB 30D	9 4	9000	4 4	18800	20900
34 11	CONTEST 35	SLP	SAIL	FBG	IB 15D	10 6	11000	4 8	24500	27200
40	SEVEN-SEAS		MS	FBG	IB 85D	11 6	22000	4 6	49700	54700
45	CALYPSO 45		SAIL	FBG	IB 110D	12 6	31350	5 2	72100	79300
				1967 BOATS						
25	CONTEST 25	SLP	SAIL	FBG	OB				5500	6300
29	CONTEST 29	SLP	SAIL	FBG	OB				8900	10100
29	CONTEST 29	SLP	SAIL	FBG	OB 5D- 12D				14700	16700
29 7	TRINTELLA 30		SAIL	FBG	OB				12300	13900
29 7	TRINTELLA 30		SAIL	FBG	IB 10D				17500	19900
				1966 BOATS						
25	CONTEST 25	SLP	SAIL	FBG	OB				5450	6250
25	CONTEST 25	SLP	SAIL	FBG	OB 5D				6950	8000
29	CONTEST 29	SLP	SAIL	FBG	OB 8				8800	10000
29	CONTEST 29	SLP	SAIL	FBG	IB 8				14900	17000
29	CONTEST 29	SLP	SAIL	FBG	IB 5D- 12D				14500	16600
29 7	TRINTELLA 30		SAIL	FBG	OB				12200	13800
29 7	TRINTELLA 30		SAIL	FBG	IB 10D				17400	19700

CONTINENTAL BOAT CO
SQUALL KING   COAST GUARD MFG ID- CTL

Call 1-800-327-6929 for BUC Personalized Evaluation Service
Or, for 1959 to 1979 boats, sign onto www.BUCValuPro.com

CONTINENTAL MARINE CORP LTD

Call 1-800-327-6929 for BUC Personalized Evaluation Service
Or, for 1965 to 1966 boats, sign onto www.BUCValuPro.com

CONTINENTAL PLASTICS CORP
COSTA MESA CA   See inside cover to adjust price for area

LOA FT IN	NAME AND/ OR MODEL	TOP/ RIG	BOAT TYPE	-HULL- MTL TP	----ENGINE--- TP # HP MFG	BEAM FT IN	WGT LBS	DRAFT FT IN	RETAIL LOW	RETAIL HIGH
				1968 BOATS						
26 4	LUDERS 16	SLP	SA/OD	FBG KL		5 9	2950	4	5500	6300
				1967 BOATS						
24	GLADIATOR 24		SAIL	FBG	OB		3850		6150	7100
24	GLADIATOR 24		SAIL	FBG	OB 8D		4150		7250	8300
24	LAPWORTH 24		SAIL	FBG	OB		4350		6900	7950
24	LAPWORTH 24		SAIL	FBG	IB 8D		4580		7900	9100
26 4	LUDERS 16	SLP	SA/OD	FBG	OB		2950		5550	6400
29 11	GLADIATOR 29		SAIL	FBG	OB		7200		14800	16800
29 11	GLADIATOR 29		SAIL	FBG	OB 8D		7550		15700	17800
30	GLADIATOR 30		SAIL	FBG	IB		7500		15400	17500
30	GLADIATOR 30		SAIL	FBG	IB 8D- 22D		7725		16000	18200
				1966 BOATS						
24	GLADIATOR	SLP	SA/OD	FBG KL	OB	7 6	3850	4	6100	7000
24	LAPWORTH 24	SLP	SA/CR	FBG KL		7 6	4350	4	6850	7850
26 4	LUDERS 16	SLP	SA/OD	FBG KL		5 9	2950	4	5350	6150
29 11	GLADIATOR 29	SLP	SAIL	FBG KL			7200		13100	14900
				1965 BOATS						
24	GLADIATOR		SAIL	FBG	OB				6800	7800
24	LAPWORTH	SLP	SA/OD	FBG KL		7 6			6150	7050
24	SPARTAN	SLP	SAIL	FBG KL					6800	7800
26 4	LUDERS 16	SLP	SA/OD	FBG KL		5 9			5400	6200
				1964 BOATS						
24	GLADIATOR 24		SAIL	FBG	OB				5600	6450
24	LAPWORTH 24 CUSTOM		SAIL	FBG					7850	9000
24	LAPWORTH 24 SPARTON		SAIL	FBG	OB				6800	7800
				1960 BOATS						
17	COMMANDER	RNBT	FBG DV	OB		6	725		2750	3200
17	COMMANDER DLX	RNBT	FBG DV	OB		6	725		3000	3450
17	CRUISER DLX	CR	FBG DV	OB		6	800		3100	3650
17	FISHERMAN	FSH	FBG DV	OB		6	635		2400	2800
17	FISHERMAN DLX	FSH	FBG DV	OB		6	635		2650	3100

CONWAY POWERBOATS LTD

Call 1-800-327-6929 for BUC Personalized Evaluation Service
Or, for 1979 to 1980 boats, sign onto www.BUCValuPro.com

COOPER YACHT SALES LTD
VANCOUVER BC CANADA V6H COAST GUARD MFG ID- CEL See inside cover to adjust price for area
FORMERLY COOPER ENTERPRISES LTD

For more recent years, see the BUC Used Boat Price Guide, Volume 1 or Volume 2

LOA FT IN	NAME AND/ OR MODEL	TOP/ RIG	BOAT TYPE	-HULL- MTL TP	----ENGINE--- TP # HP MFG	BEAM FT IN	WGT LBS	DRAFT FT IN	RETAIL LOW	RETAIL HIGH
				1983 BOATS						
31 6	COOPER 316	SLP	SA/CR	F/S KL	SD 17D VLVO	10 11	10500	5 5	37000	41100
31 6	COOPER 316 PH	SLP	SA/CR	FBG KL	IB D	10 11	10500	5 5	37000	41100
35 3	COOPER 353	SLP	SA/CR	F/S KL	SD 23D VLVO	12	12500	5 10	47400	52100
35 3	COOPER 353 PH	SLP	SA/CR	FBG KL	IB D	12	12500	5 10	44500	49500
36 7	BANNER 37	SLP	SA/RC	FBG KL	IB D	12	13500	5 10	52800	58000
36 7	BANNER 37	SLP	SA/RC	FBG KL	IB 23D VLVO	12	13500	5 10	49400	54300
36 9	SEA BIRD 37 CC	SLP	SA/CR	FBG KL	IB D	11 6	18000	4	63700	70000
36 9	SEA BIRD 37 CC	CUT	SA/CR	FBG KL	IB D	11 6	18000	4	63700	70000
36 9	SEA BIRD 37 CC	KTH	SA/CR	FBG KL	IB D	11 6	18000	4	63700	70000
36 9	SEA BIRD 37 PH	SLP	MS	FBG KL	IB D	11 6	18000	4	63600	69900
36 9	SEA BIRD 37 PH	CUT	MS	FBG KL	IB D	11 6	18000	4	63600	69800
36 9	SEA BIRD 37 PH	KTH	MS	FBG KL	IB D	11 6	18000	4	63700	70000
36 10	SEA BIRD 37	SLP	SA/CR	F/S KL	IB 46D LEHM	11 8	18000	4	63900	70300
36 10	SEA BIRD 37 MS	SLP	SA/CR	F/S KL	IB 46D LEHM	11 8	18000	4	64400	70300
41 6	COOPER 416	SLP	SA/CR	F/S KL	IB D	14	24000	6 7	89400	98300
41 6	COOPER 416 PH	SLP	SA/CR	FBG KL	IB D	14	24000	6 7	90000	99000
47 8	MAPLE LEAF 48	SLP	SA/CR	F/S KL	IB 80D LEHM	14	34000	6 6	123500	135500
48 6	MAPLE LEAF 48 CC	SLP	SA/CR	FBG KL	IB D	14	34000	6 6	127000	139500
48 6	MAPLE LEAF 48 CC	CUT	SA/CR	FBG KL	IB D	14	34000	6 6	127000	139500
50 8	MAPLE LEAF 50	SLP	SA/RC	F/S KL	IB 80D LEHM	15	38500	8	144500	152500
50 8	COOPER 508	SLP	SA/RC	F/S KL	IB 80D LEHM	15	38500	8	145000	159000
50 8	COOPER 508 PH	SLP	SA/CR	FBG KL	IB D	15	38300	8	137000	150500
54 5	MAPLE LEAF 54	SLP	SA/CR	F/S KL	IB 120D LEHM	14 9	42000	7 2	170500	187500
54 5	MAPLE LEAF 54 CC	SLP	SA/CR	F/S KL	IB D	14 9	42000	7 2	179500	197500
54 5	MAPLE LEAF 54 CC	CUT	SA/CR	F/S KL	IB D	14 9	42000	7 2	179500	197500
56 4	MAPLE LEAF 56	SLP	SA/CR	F/S KL	IB 120D LEHM	14 9	44000	7 2	89400	218500
56 4	MAPLE LEAF 56	SLP	SA/CR	F/S KL	IB 120D LEHM	14 9	44000	7 2	234500	257500
				1982 BOATS						
31 6	COOPER 316	SLP	SA/CR	F/S KL	IB D VLVO	10 11	10500	5 5	35100	39000
35 3	COOPER 353	SLP	SA/CR	F/S KL	IB 23D VLVO	12	12250	5 10	41400	46000
36 10	SEA BIRD 37	SLP	MS	F/S KL	IB 45D LEHM	11	18000	4	60600	66600
36 10	SEA BIRD 37	CUT	MS	F/S KL	IB 45D LEHM	11	18000	4	60600	66600
36 10	SEA BIRD 37	SLP	SA/CR	F/S KL	IB 45D LEHM	11	18000	4	60600	66600
36 10	SEA BIRD 37	CUT	SA/CR	F/S KL	IB 45D LEHM	11	18000	4	60600	66600
36 10	SEA BIRD 37	KTH	SA/CR	F/S KL	IB 45D LEHM	11	18000	4	60600	66600
41 6	COOPER 416	SLP	SA/CR	F/S KL	IB 80D LEHM	14	24000	6 7	84700	93100
47 8	MAPLE LEAF 48	SLP	SA/CR	F/S KL	IB 80D LEHM	14 7	34000	6 6	117000	128500
50 8	COOPER 508	SLP	SA/RC	F/S KL	IB 80D LEHM	15	38300	8	137000	150500
50 8	COOPER 508 SHOAL	SLP	SA/RC	F/S KL	IB 80D LEHM	15	38300	8	137000	150500
54 5	MAPLE LEAF 54	SLP	SA/CR	F/S KL	IB 120D LEHM	14 9	42000	7 2	170500	187500

LOA FT IN	NAME AND/ OR MODEL	TOP/ RIG	BOAT TYPE	MTL	-HULL- TP	TP #	ENGINE HP	MFG	BEAM FT IN	WGT LBS	DRAFT FT IN	RETAIL LOW	RETAIL HIGH
						1981 BOATS							
35 3	COOPER 353	SLP	SA/CR	F/S	KL	IB	23D	VLVO	12	13250	5 10	42200	46800
36 9	SEA BIRD 37	CUT	SA/CR	F/S	KL	IB	42D	PERK	11 6	18000	4	57100	62700
36 9	SEA BIRD 37	KTH	SA/CR	F/S	KL	IB	42D	PERK	11 6	18000	4	57100	62700
41 6	COOPER 416	SLP	SA/CR	F/S	KL	IB	42D	PERK	14	24000	6 7	79900	87800
47 8	MAPLE LEAF 48	SLP	SA/CR	F/S	KL	IB	80D	PERK	14 7	34000	6 6	110500	121500
54 5	MAPLE LEAF 54	SLP	SA/CR	F/S	KL	IB	120D	PERK	14 9	42000	7 2	161000	177000
						1980 BOATS							
35 3	COOPER 353	SLP	SA/CR	F/S	KL	IB	23D	VLVO	12	12250	5 10	37700	41900
37	SEABIRD 37	CUT	SA/CR	F/S	KL	IB	42D	PERK	11 6	18000	4	55200	60600
41 6	COOPER 416	SLP	SA/CR	F/S	KL	IB	42D	PERK	14	24000	6 7	76900	84500
47 8	MAPLE-LEAF 48	SLP	SA/CR	F/S	KL	IB	80D	PERK	14 9	34000	6 6	106500	117000
54 5	MAPLE-LEAF 54	SLP	SA/CR	F/S	KL	IB	120D	PERK	14 9	42000	7 2	155000	170000
						1978 BOATS							
36 9	SEABIRD 37	KTH	SA/CR	F/S	KL	IB	50D	PERK	11 6	18000	4	51700	56800
47 8	MAPLE-LEAF 48	SLP	SA/CR	F/S	KL	IB	120D	FORD	14 8	36000	6 6	103800	113500
54 3	MAPLE-LEAF 54	SLP	SA/CR	F/S	KL	IB	120D	FORD	14 11	44000	7	146000	160500

COPLAND BOATS
COAST GUARD MFG ID- CPP

COPLAND BOATS U S

Call 1-800-327-6929 for BUC Personalized Evaluation Service
Or, for 1966 to 1986 boats, sign onto www.BUCValuPro.com

CORBIN LES BATEAUX INC
NAPIERVILLE QUE CANADA   COAST GUARD MFG ID- ZCJ See inside cover to adjust price for area

For more recent years, see the BUC Used Boat Price Guide, Volume 1 or Volume 2

LOA FT IN	NAME AND/ OR MODEL	TOP/ RIG	BOAT TYPE	MTL	-HULL- TP	TP #	ENGINE HP	MFG	BEAM FT IN	WGT LBS	DRAFT FT IN	RETAIL LOW	RETAIL HIGH
						1983 BOATS							
38 9	CORBIN AFT CPT	CUT	SA/CR	F/S	KL	IB	33D	WEST	12 2	22000	5 6	73600	80800
						1982 BOATS							
20	CORBIN 600		OPFSH	FBG	DS	IB	15D		8	2740		3550	4150
20	CORBIN 600 PH		OPFSH	FBG	DS	IB	15D		8	2740		3550	4150
23	CORBIN 700		OPFSH	FBG	DS	IB	20D		8	2960		4500	5200
23	CORBIN 700		TRWL	FBG	DS	IB	20D		8	2960		4500	5200
23	CORBIN 700 PH		PH	FBG	DS	IB	20D		8	2960		4500	5200
26	CORBIN 800		OPFSH	FBG	DS	IB	30D		8	3840		4800	5550
26	CORBIN 800		PH	FBG	DS	IB	30D		8	3840		4800	5550
26	CORBIN 800		TRWL	FBG	DS	IB	30D		8	3840		4800	5550
38 6	CORBIN AFT CPT	CUT	SA/CR	F/S	KL	IB	33D	WEST	12 1	22800	5 6	70700	77600
						1981 BOATS							
38 9	CORBIN 30 CTR CPT	KTH	SA/CR	FBG	KL	IB	D		12 2	21500	5 6	64700	71100
38 9	CORBIN 39	CUT	SA/CR	FBG	KL	IB	D		12 2	21500	5 6	64300	70700
38 9	CORBIN 39 CTR CPT	CUT	SA/CR	FBG	KL	IB	D		12 2	21500	5 6	64300	70700
38 9	CORBIN AFT CPT	CUT	SA/CR	F/S	KL	IB	40D	PATH	12 2	22000	5 6	65200	71700
38 9	CORBIN CTR CPT	KTH	SA/CR	F/S	KL	IB	40D	PATH	12 2	22000	5 6	65700	72100
						1980 BOATS							
38 9	CORBIN AFT CPT	CUT	SA/CR	F/S	KL	IB	40D	PATH	12 2	22000	5 6	62100	68300
38 9	CORBIN CTR CPT	KTH	SA/CR	F/S	KL	IB	40D	PATH	12 2	22000	5 6	62700	68900
						1979 BOATS							
38 9	CORBIN CRUISER AFT	CUT	SA/CR	F/S	KL	IB	D	VLVO	12 11	22000	5 6	59900	65800
38 9	CORBIN CRUISER AFT	CUT	SA/CR	F/S	KL	IB	40D	PATH	12 11	22000	5 6	59700	65600
38 9	CORBIN CTR CPT	KTH	SA/CR	F/S	KL	IB	D	VLVO	12 11	22000	5 6	60500	66500
38 9	CORBIN CTR CPT	KTH	SA/CR	F/S	KL	IB	40D	PATH	12 11	22000	5 6	60300	66300
38 9	CORBIN TALL RIG AFT	CUT	SA/CR	F/S	KL	IB	D	VLVO	12 11	22000	5 6	59900	65800
38 9	CORBIN TALL RIG AFT	CUT	SA/CR	F/S	KL	IB	40D	PATH	12 11	22000	5 6	59700	65600

CORINTHIAN YACHT CORP
TARPON SPRINGS FL 34689   See inside cover to adjust price for area

LOA FT IN	NAME AND/ OR MODEL	TOP/ RIG	BOAT TYPE	MTL	-HULL- TP	TP #	ENGINE HP	MFG	BEAM FT IN	WGT LBS	DRAFT FT IN	RETAIL LOW	RETAIL HIGH
						1970 BOATS							
41	CORINTHIAN 41	KTH	SA/CR	FBG	TR	IB	50D	PERK	23 9	14000	2 2	33800	37500
						1969 BOATS							
41	CORINTHIAN 41	SLP	SAIL	FBG	TR	IB	50D	PERK	23 9	14000	2 2	33300	36900
						1968 BOATS							
41 7	CORINTHIAN 41	KTH	SA/CR	FBG	TM	IB	50D	PERK	23 9	14000	2 2	48400	53100
						1967 BOATS							
40	CORINTHIAN 40	KTH	SAIL	FBG	TM	IB	50D	PERK	23 9	14000	2 2	42800	47600

CORMED MARINE INC
COAST GUARD MFG ID- CDB

Call 1-800-327-6929 for BUC Personalized Evaluation Service
Or, for 1977 to 1979 boats, sign onto www.BUCValuPro.com

CORONADO YACHTS
DIV OF WHITTAKER CORP
COSTA MESA CA 92626   COAST GUARD MFG ID- CNY   See inside cover to adjust price for area
ALSO SEE COLUMBIA YACHTS CO MARINE

LOA FT IN	NAME AND/ OR MODEL	TOP/ RIG	BOAT TYPE	MTL	-HULL- TP	TP #	ENGINE HP	MFG	BEAM FT IN	WGT LBS	DRAFT FT IN	RETAIL LOW	RETAIL HIGH
						1974 BOATS							
22 7	CORONADO 23 MK II		SAIL	FBG		OB			7 11	2500	1 11	3150	3700
26 8	CORONADO 27		SAIL	FBG		IB			8 6	6250	4 5	8650	9950
26 8	CORONADO 27		SAIL	FBG		IB	6D	PETT	8 6	6250	4 5	9050	10300
28	CORONADO 28		SAIL	FBG		OB			8 6	6800	4 10	10000	11400
28	CORONADO 28		SAIL	FBG		IB	27	PALM	8 6	6800	4 10	10100	11500
31 11	CORONADO 32 MK II		SAIL	FBG		IB	27	PALM	9 5	12000	5 10	19400	21600
31 11	CORONADO 32 MK II		SAIL	FBG		IB	20D	FARY	9 5	12000	5 10	19400	21600
35 3	CORONADO 35	SLP	SAIL	FBG	KL	IB	27	PALM	10 1	13000	5 6	21000	23300
35 3	CORONADO 35	SLP	SAIL	FBG	KL	IB	27	PALM	10 1	13000	5 6	21200	23500
35 3	CORONADO 35	KTH	SAIL	FBG	KL	IB	27	PALM	10 1	13000	5 6	21000	23300
35 3	CORONADO 35	KTH	SAIL	FBG	KL	IB	20D	FARY	10 1	13000	5 6	21200	23500
40 6	CORONADO 41	SLP	SAIL	FBG	KL	IB	50D	PERK	11 3	19500	6 3	35100	39000
40 6	CORONADO 41	KTH	MS	FBG	KL	IB	50D	PERK	11 3	19500	6 3	35100	39000
45 3	CORONADO 45		SAIL	FBG	KL	IB	50D	PERK	12 4	23000	7 3	48600	53400
						1973 BOATS							
26 8	CORONADO 27	SLP	SAIL	FBG		OB			8 6	6250	4 5	8450	9700
26 8	CORONADO 27	SLP	SAIL	FBG		IB	5D	PETT	8 6	6250	4 5	8850	10000
29 11	CORONADO 30	SLP	SAIL	FBG		IB	27-30		10 1	8500	5	13000	14800
31 11	CORONADO 32	SLP	SAIL	FBG		IB	27	PALM	9 5	12000	5 10	19200	21300
31 11	CORONADO 32	SLP	SAIL	FBG		IB	20D	ALBN	9 5	12000	5 10	19200	21300
35 3	CORONADO 35	SLP	SAIL	FBG		IB	27	PALM	10 1	13000	5 6	20500	22800
35 3	CORONADO 35	SLP	SAIL	FBG		IB	22D	ALBN	10 1	13000	5 6	20600	22900
35 3	CORONADO 35	KTH	SAIL	FBG		IB	27	PALM	10 1	13000	5 6	20500	22800
35 3	CORONADO 35	KTH	SAIL	FBG		IB	22D	ALBN	10 1	13000	5 6	20600	22900
40 6	CORONADO 41	SLP	SAIL	FBG		IB	50D	PERK	11 3	19500	6 3	33700	37500
40 6	CORONADO 41	KTH	SAIL	FBG		IB	50D	PERK	11 3	19500	6 3	34200	38000
40 6	CORONADO 41	KTH	SAIL	FBG		IB	30D	UNIV	11 3	19500	6 3	33700	37500
40 6	CORONADO 41	KTH	SAIL	FBG		IB	50D	PERK	11 3	19500	6 3	34200	38000
						1972 BOATS							
22 7	CORONADO 23		SAIL	FBG		OB			7 9	3100	3 3	3550	4100
25	CORONADO 25		SAIL	FBG		OB			8	4950	3 8	5950	6850
26 8	CORONADO 27		SAIL	FBG		OB			8 6	6250	4 5	8250	9500
26 8	CORONADO 27		SAIL	FBG		IB	D	WEST	8 6	6250	4 5	8650	9950
29 11	CORONADO 30		SAIL	FBG		IB			10 1	8500	5 3	12600	14400
29 11	CORONADO 30		SAIL	FBG		IB	D	PALM	10 1	8500	5 3	12800	14600
35 3	CORONADO 35		SAIL	FBG		IB			10 1	13000	5 6	19900	22100
35 3	CORONADO 35		SAIL	FBG		IB	D	PALM	10 1	13000	5 6	20200	22500
40 6	CORONADO 41		SAIL	FBG		IB	30	UNIV	11 3	19500	6 3	33000	36600
						1971 BOATS							
22 7	CORONADO 23		SAIL	FBG	CB	OB			7 9	3485	2 6	3800	4400
22 7	CORONADO 23		SAIL	FBG	KL	OB			7 9	3100	3 3	3450	4050
25	CORONADO 25		SAIL	FBG		OB			8	4950	3 8	5850	6700
25	CORONADO 25		SAIL	FBG	CB	OB			8	4300	2 6	5100	5900
26 8	CORONADO 27		SAIL	FBG		OB			8 6	6250	4 5	8100	9300
26 8	CORONADO 27		SAIL	FBG	CB	OB			8 6	6250	4 5	8100	9300
29 11	CORONADO 30		SAIL	FBG		IB	22D		10 1	8500	5 3	12600	14400
35 3	CORONADO 35		SAIL	FBG		IB	22D		10 1	13000	5 6	19700	21800
34 8	CORONADO 35 SHOAL		SAIL	FBG		IB	22D		10 1	14000	3 8	21100	23400
						1970 BOATS							
22 7	CORONADO 23	SLP	SAIL	FBG	CB	OB			7 9	2485	2 6	2900	3350
22 7	CORONADO 23	SLP	SAIL	FBG	KL	OB			7 9	2300	3 3	2750	3200
25	CORONADO 25	SLP	SAIL	FBG	CB	OB			8	4300	2 6	5200	6000
25	CORONADO 25	SLP	SAIL	FBG	KL	OB			8	4950	3 8	5500	6300
26 6	CORONADO 27	SLP	SAIL	FBG	CB	OB			8 6	6250	4 5	7900	9100
26 6	CORONADO 27	SLP	SAIL	FBG	KL	OB	6D		8 6	6250	4 5	8250	9500
29 11	CORONADO 30	SLP	SAIL	FBG	KL	IB	6D	PALM	10 1	8500	5 3	12300	14000
34	CORONADO 34	SLP	SAIL	FBG	KL	IB	20D- 22D		10	10500	5	15500	17600
						1969 BOATS							
21	AURORA	SLP	SAIL	SA/OD	FBG	KL	OB		6 4	1800	3 3	2350	2700
21	VICTORY 21	SLP	SAIL	SA/OD	FBG	KL	OB		6 4	1350	3	2000	2350

CORONADO YACHTS -CONTINUED See inside cover to adjust price for area

LOA FT	IN	NAME AND/ OR MODEL	TOP/ RIG	BOAT TYPE	-HULL- MTL	TP	----ENGINE--- TP	# HP	MFG	BEAM FT	IN	WGT LBS	DRAFT FT	IN	RETAIL LOW	RETAIL HIGH
		1969 BOATS														
22	6	CORONADO 22	SLP	SAIL	FBG	KL	OB			7	10	2450	3	5	2800	3300
25		AVALON 25	SLP	SA/CR	FBG	KC	IB	9D		8			2	6	5550	6400
25		CORONADO 25	SLP	SAIL	FBG	KL	OB			8		4300	3	8	4900	5650
29	11	CORONADO 30	SLP	SAIL	FBG	KL	IB	30D	ALBN	10	1	7700	5	2	11000	12500
34		CORONADO 34	SLP	SAIL	FBG	KL	IB	30	UNIV	10		10500	5		15200	17200
34		CORONADO 34	SLP	SAIL	FBG	KL	IB	30D		10		10500	5		15300	17400

CORONET BOATS LTD

BOTVED BOATS
WOODSTOCK CANADA COAST GUARD MFG ID- ZCA

See inside cover to adjust price for area

LOA FT	IN	NAME AND/ OR MODEL	TOP/ RIG	BOAT TYPE	-HULL- MTL	TP	----ENGINE--- TP	# HP	MFG	BEAM FT	IN	WGT LBS	DRAFT FT	IN	RETAIL LOW	RETAIL HIGH
		1977 BOATS														
31		CORONET AFT CABIN		CR	FBG		IB			10	4	9000	3	3	**	**
31		CORONET SEAFARER		CR	FBG		IB			10	4	8000	3	3	**	**
		1976 BOATS														
31	8	CORONET AFT CABIN	ST	CR	FBG	DV	IB	106D	VLVO	10	4	9000	3	3	20000	22300
31	8	CORONET AFT CABIN	ST	CR	FBG	SV	IB	160D	PERK	10	4	9000	3	3	19500	21600
31	8	CORONET AFT CABIN	HT	CR	FBG	DV	IB	106D	VLVO	10	4	9000	3	3	20100	22300
31	8	CORONET AFT CABIN	HT	CR	FBG	SV	IB	160D	PERK	10	4	9000	3	3	19500	21600
31	8	CORONET SEAFARER	HT	CR	FBG	DV	IO	T165-T170		10	4	8000	3	3	17300	19900
31	8	CORONET SEAFARER	HT	CR	FBG	SV	IO	T120-T130		10	4	8000	3	3	16900	19500
31	8	CORONET SEAFARER	FB	CR	FBG	DV	IO	T165-T170		10	4	8000	3	3	17300	19900
31	8	CORONET SEAFARER	FB	CR	FBG	SV	IO	T120-T130		10	4	8000	3	3	16900	19500
		1975 BOATS														
31		CORONET AFT CABIN	OP	CR	FBG		IB	D		10	4	9000	3	3	**	**
		1974 BOATS														
17				RNBT	FBG		IO	115	VLVO	6	11	1400		6	2350	2750
21				CR	FBG		IO	170	VLVO	7	8	2850	1	3	4750	5450
21				CR	FBG		IO	T130	VLVO	7	8	3000	1	4	5700	6600
21		PLAYMATE CTRCN	OP	RNBT	FBG		IO	130	VLVO	7	8	2700	1	2	4450	5100
24			OP	CBNCR	FBG		IO	170	VLVO	8		4400	1	7	7950	9100
24			OP	CBNCR	FBG		IO	T130	VLVO	8		4400	1	7	9150	10400
24		FAMILY	HT	CBNCR	FBG		IO	170	VLVO	8		4600	1	4	8200	9450
24		FAMILY	HT	CBNCR	FBG		IO	T106-T130		8		4800	1	4	9750	11100
24		FAMILY	FB	CBNCR	FBG		IO	170	VLVO	8		5000	1	8	8850	10100
24		FAMILY	FB	CBNCR	FBG		IO	T130	VLVO	8		5200	1	8	10300	11700
24		MIDI	OP	SPTCR	FBG		IO	170	VLVO	8		4000	1	7	7100	8150
24		MIDI	OP	SPTCR	FBG		IO	T130	VLVO	8		4000	1	7	8050	9300
27	4	SEAFARER		EXP	FBG		IB	330	CHRY	10	4	6700	2	6	10400	11800
27	4	SEAFARER		EXP	FBG		IO	T170	VLVO	10	4	6614	1	7	13100	14900
27	4	SEAFARER		EXP	FBG		IO	T106D	VLVO	10	4	6800	2		15500	17700
31		TRI-CABIN		CR	FBG		IB	160		10	4		3	2	13100	14900
31		TRI-CABIN		CR	FBG		IB	T106		10	4		3	2	13600	15400
32		DEEPSEA	FB	SDN	FBG		IO	T170	VLVO	10		10000	2	6	22400	24900
32		DEEPSEA	FB	SDN	FBG		IB	T225	CHRY	10		11000	3		19400	21500
32		OCEANFARER	FB	SDN	FBG		IO	T170	VLVO	10	9	9800	1	7	22600	25100
32		OCEANFARER	FB	SDN	FBG		IB	T225	CHRY	10	9	10000	2	6	19200	21300
44		TRI-CABIN		TCMY	FBG		IB	T250		14	8		4		45600	50100
		1973 BOATS														
17		RUNABOUT	OP	RNBT	FBG	DV	IO	115		6	11	1400		6	2300	2700
21				CR	FBG		IO	170	VLVO	7	8	2850	1	3	4900	5650
21				CR	FBG		IO	T130	VLVO	7	8	3000	1	4	5900	6800
21		PLAYMATE CTRCN	OP	RNBT	FBG		IO	130	VLVO	7	8	2700	1	2	4600	5250
24			OP	CBNCR	FBG		IO	170	VLVO	8		4400	1	7	8200	9450
24			OP	CBNCR	FBG		IO	T130	VLVO	8		4400	1	7	9500	10800
24		FAMILY	HT	CBNCR	FBG		IO	170	VLVO	8		4600	1	4	8500	9800
24		FAMILY	HT	CBNCR	FBG		IO	T130	VLVO	8		5200	1	8	10600	12100
24		MIDI	OP	SPTCR	FBG		IO	170	VLVO	8		4000	1	7	7350	8450
24		MIDI	OP	SPTCR	FBG		IO	T130	VLVO	8		4000	1	7	8350	9600
27	4	SEAFARER		EXP	FBG		IB	330	CHRY	10	4	6700	2	6	10000	11300
27	4	SEAFARER		EXP	FBG		IO	T106-T170		10	4	6800	2		13100	15300
32		DEEPSEA	FB	SDN	FBG		IO	T170	VLVO	10		10000	2	6	23100	25700
32		DEEPSEA	FB	SDN	FBG		IB	T225	CHRY	10		11000	3		18800	20900
32		DEEPSEA	FB	SDN	FBG		IB	T165D	PERK	10		11700	3		26500	29400
32		OCEANFARER	FB	SDN	FBG		IB	T170-T225		10	9	9800	1	7	17300	20700
32		OCEANFARER	FB	SDN	FBG		IB	T165D	PERK	10	9	10500	2	6	25700	28500
		1972 BOATS														
17			OP		FBG	DV	IO	115		6	11				2250	2650
21				CR	FBG		IO	130-210		7	8	2850	1	2	5050	6000
21				CR	FBG		IO	T130	VLVO	7	8	3000	1	4	6100	7000
21		PLAYMATE CTRCN	OP	RNBT	FBG		IO	130-170		7	8	2700	1	2	4700	5450
24			OP	CBNCR	FBG		IO	170	VLVO	8		4400	1	7	8500	9800
24			OP	CBNCR	FBG		IO	T130	VLVO	8		4400	1	7	9850	11200
24		FAMILY	HT	CBNCR	FBG		IO	170	VLVO	9	3	4600	1	4	9200	10400
24		FAMILY	HT	CBNCR	FBG		IO	T130	VLVO	9	3	4600	1	4	10400	11800
24		MIDI	OP	SPTCR	FBG		IO	170	VLVO	8		4000	1	7	7600	8750
24		MIDI	OP	SPTCR	FBG		IO	T120-T170		8		4000	1	7	8300	10000
27		SEAFARER		EXP	FBG		VD	330	CHRY	10	4	6700	2		9450	10700
27		SEAFARER		EXP	FBG		IO	T170	VLVO	10	4	6614	1	7	13700	15500
32		OCEANFARER	FB	SDN	FBG		IO	T170-T210		10	9	9800	1	7	24000	27600
32		OCEANFARER	FB	SDN	FBG		IB	T225	CHRY	10	9	10000	2		17500	19900
32		OCEANFARER	FB	SDN	FBG		IO	T100D	VLVO	10	9	10000	1	11	27200	30200
33			HT	HB	FBG	DV	IO	T170		11					25800	28600
33			HT	HB	FBG	DV	IO	T170D		11					20900	23200
		1971 BOATS														
21				CR	FBG		IO	130-210		7	8	2547	1	2	4950	5800
21				CR	FBG		IO	T130	VLVO	7	8	2547	1	2	5850	6750
21		PLAYMATE CTRCN	OP	RNBT	FBG		IO	130-170		7	8		1	2	4850	5650
24			OP	CBNCR	FBG		IO	170-210		8		4400	1	7	8950	10300
24			OP	CBNCR	FBG		IO	T130	VLVO	8		4400	1	7	10200	11600
24		MIDI	OP	SPTCR	FBG		IO	170	VLVO	8			1	7	7900	9100
24		MIDI	OP	SPTCR	FBG		IO	T130-T170		8			1	7	9050	10400
24	3	FAMILY	HT	CBNCR	FBG		IO	170-210		9	3	4600	1	7	9700	11200
24	3	FAMILY	HT	CBNCR	FBG		IO	T130	VLVO	9	3	4600	1	7	10900	12400
24	3	FAMILY	HT	CBNCR	FBG		IO	T102D	VLVO	9	3	4600	1	7	14400	16400
27	4	SEAFARER		EXP	FBG		IO	T170	VLVO	10	4		1	7	14000	16000
27	4	SEAFARER		EXP	FBG		IO	T102D	VLVO	10	4		1	7	16800	19100
32		OCEANFARER	FB	SDN	FBG		IO	T165-T210		10	9	9259	2	8	24400	28500
32		OCEANFARER	FB	SDN	FBG		IO	T102D	VLVO	10	9	9259	2	8	27300	30400
33		WAYFARER		HB	FBG		IO	T170		11					25900	29400
		1970 BOATS														
21		DAYCRUISER		CR	FBG	DV	IO	130-165		7	8	2547	1	2	5100	5900
21		DAYCRUISER		CR	FBG	DV	IO	T130	VLVO	7	8	2547	1	2	6050	6950
21		PLAYMATE CTRCN	OP	RNBT	FBG	DV	IO	130-170		7	8		1	2	5050	5800
24			OP	CBNCR	FBG	DV	IO	170-185		8			1	7	9200	10500
24			OP	CBNCR	FBG	DV	IO	T130		8			1	7	10300	11700
24			FB	CR	FBG	DV	IO	T120	VLVO	8		3965	1	7	9250	10500
24		FAMILY	HT	CBNCR	FBG	DV	IO	106-170		8			1	7	9150	10700
24		FAMILY	HT	CBNCR	FBG	DV	IO	T130	VLVO	8			1	7	10700	12100
24		FAMILY	HT	CBNCR	FBG	DV	IO	T130D		8			1	7	15500	17600
27		SEAFARER		EXP	FBG	DV	IO	T160-T170		10	4		1	6	14000	16200
27		SEAFARER		EXP	FBG	DV	IO	T106D	VLVO	10	4		1	6	17400	19700
32		OCEANFARER	FB	SDN	FBG	DV	IO	T160-T185		10	9		2	8	25300	28900
32		OCEANFARER	FB	SDN	FBG	DV	IO	T106D	VLVO	10	9		2	8	29800	33100
32		OCEANFARER	FB	SDN	FBG	DV	IB	T160D-T225D		10	9	9259	2	8	22500	27500
33		WAYFARER		HB	FBG		IB	T165	VLVO	11					25800	28600
		1969 BOATS														
18		FJORDLING	OP	RNBT	FBG	DV	IO	120	VLVO			1800			3250	3750
21				CR	FBG		IO	150-165		7	8		1	2	5550	6400
21				CR	FBG		IO	T130	VLVO	7	8		1	2	6500	7500
21				RNBT	FBG	DV	IO	T130	VLVO	7	8	2547	1	2	5950	6850
24			OP	CBNCR	FBG		IO	150-165		8		4400	1	7	9750	11200
24			OP	CBNCR	FBG		IO	T120-T130		8			1	7	11100	12600
24			FB	CR	FBG		IO	T130		8			1	7	9900	11200
24			FB	CR	FBG	DV	IO	T120		8			1	7	9850	11200
24			OP	WKNDR	FBG		IO	160	MRCR	8			1	7	9000	10200
24			OP	WKNDR	FBG	DV	IO	T120	VLVO	8			1	7	10300	11700
27		SEAFARER		EXP	FBG	DV	IO	T150-T165		10	4		1	6	14700	16700
27		SEAFARER		EXP	FBG	DV	IO	T 92D		10	4		1	6	18500	20500
32		OCEANFARER	FB	SDN	FBG		IB	T160	MRCR	10	9		2	8	14700	16700
		IO T165-T185 26200 29700, IB T225 15600 17800, IB T130D													21900	24300
32		OCEANFARER	FB	SDN	FBG	DV	IB	T150	VLVO	10	9		2	8	14500	16500
		1968 BOATS														
21				CR	FBG		IO	120-160		7	8	2547	1	2	5250	6300
21				CR	FBG		IO	T120		7	8	2547	1	2	6100	7400
21		EXPLORER	OP	EXP	FBG		IO	150	VLVO	7	8	2975	1	2	5850	6750
24			OP	CBNCR	FBG		IO	150-185		8		4400	1	7	10100	11500
24			OP	CBNCR	FBG		IO	T120		8		4400	1	7	11100	13200
24			OP	WKNDR	FBG		IO	150-185		8			1	7	9450	10700
24			OP	WKNDR	FBG		IO	T120		8			1	7	10200	12100
30		OCEANFARER	FB	SDN	FBG		IO	T150-T185		10	9	9259	1	7	21400	24000
		1966 BOATS														
33		WAYFARER	HT	HB	AL		IO	210		12			2	6	22800	25300
33		WAYFARER	HT	HB	STL		IO	210		12			2	6	20400	22600

 CONTINUED ON NEXT PAGE

CORONET BOATS LTD   -CONTINUED   See inside cover to adjust price for area

LOA FT IN	NAME AND/ OR MODEL	TOP/ RIG	BOAT TYPE	HULL MTL TP	ENGINE TP # HP MFG	BEAM FT IN	WGT LBS	DRAFT FT IN	RETAIL LOW	RETAIL HIGH
----- 1965 BOATS										
27	SEAFARER		EXP	WD	IB T110	9 8		2 3	6800	7800
----- 1964 BOATS										
18 3		ST	RNBT	WD	IO 110				3400	3950
18 3			SDN	WD	IO 110				3450	4000
18 3	VIKING	ST	CR	WD	IO 110				3450	4000
22 2	EXPLORER	ST	EXP	WD	IO 110				6600	7550
27 2	SEAFARER SEVEN	ST	EXP	WD	IO T110				17000	19300
----- 1963 BOATS										
18			CNV	WD	IO 80-100				3950	4600
18		HT	SDN	WD	IO 80-100				3450	4050
18	VIKING	ST	CR	WD	IO 80-100				3450	4050
22	EXPLORER	OP	EXP	WD	OB				2650	3050
22	EXPLORER	OP	EXP	WD	IO 80-100				6750	7750
27	SEAFARER		EXP	WD	TO 80				16000	18100
27	SEAFARER		EXP	WD	IO T100				17400	19800
----- 1962 BOATS										
21 6			RNBT	WD	IB 100				2300	2650
21 6			SDN	WD	IB 100				2250	2650
21 6	VIKING	ST	CR	WD	IB 80				2250	2600
22			RNBT	WD	OB				3550	4100
22			SDN	WD	OB				1950	2350
22	EXPLORER	OP	EXP	WD	OB				2700	3100
25 6			EXP	WD	IB 100				5550	6400
25 6			SDN	WD	IB 100				5700	6550
25 6	EXPLORER	OP	EXP	WD	IB 100				5550	6400
29 6	SEAFARER		EXP	WD	IB T 80				8250	9500
----- 1961 BOATS										
22	EXPLORER	OP	EXP	PLY	OB		7 9	1650	2000	2350
22	EXPLORER	OP	EXP	PLY	IB 80		7 9		2250	2650
22 6		OP	CNV	WD	OB			1 10	2450	2850
22 6		OP	CNV	WD	IB 80				3350	3900
22 6		HT	CNV	WD	OB				2700	3100
----- 1960 BOATS										
18	SEDAN DAY CRUISER		SDN	F/W DV	IO 80		7 4	1 3	4000	4650
21	EXPLORER		CR	F/W DV	OB		8	1450	2000	2350
21	EXPLORER		CR	F/W DV	IO 80		8	1 3	7350	8450
----- 1959 BOATS										
20	EXPLORER		CR	PLY	OB		8		1950	2350

CORONET BOATS OF N AMERICA
CORONET BOATS INTERNATIONAL

Call 1-800-327-6929 for BUC Personalized Evaluation Service
Or, for 1983 to 1986 boats, sign onto www.BUCValuPro.com

CORRECT CRAFT INC
ORLANDO FL 32809   COAST GUARD MFG ID- CTC See inside cover to adjust price for area

For more recent years, see the BUC Used Boat Price Guide, Volume 1 or Volume 2

LOA FT IN	NAME AND/ OR MODEL	TOP/ RIG	BOAT TYPE	HULL MTL TP	ENGINE TP # HP MFG	BEAM FT IN	WGT LBS	DRAFT FT IN	RETAIL LOW	RETAIL HIGH
----- 1983 BOATS										
16 6	MUSTANG 165	OP	RNBT	FBG SV	IB 220 PCM	5 11	1600	1 9	4350	5000
17 9	SKI-TIQUE 179	OP	SKI	FBG SV	IB 220-280	6 4	2200	1 9	5350	6300
18 9	SKI-NAUTIQUE 2001	OP	SKI	FBG SV	IB 250-330	7	2350	2 2	6250	7650
19	BAREFOOT-NAUTIQUE	OP	SKI	FBG DV	IB 250-330	6 10	2750	2 2	6900	8350
19	SOUTHWIND	OP	SKI	FBG DV	IB 250-330	6 10	2500	2 2	6500	7900
19 3	MARTINIQUE	OP	RNBT	FBG DV	IB 250-330	7	2600	2 2	7050	8550
19 3	RIVIERA	OP	RNBT	FBG DV	IB 250-330	7	3100	2 4	7850	9550
19 11	SOUTHWIND BOWRIDER	OP	RNBT	FBG DV	IB 250-330	7 6	2800	2 3	7900	9500
23	CUDDY-NAUTIQUE	OP	FSH	FBG DV	IB 250-330	8	4200	2 6	14000	16400
23	CUDDY-NAUTIQUE DLX	OP	FSH	FBG DV	IB 250-330	8	4200	2 6	14200	16700
23	FISH-NAUTIQUE	ST	OPFSH	FBG DV	IB 250-330	8	3790	2 6	13100	15300
23	SEA-NAUTIQUE	HT	PH	FBG DV	IB 250-330	8	4000	2 6	13500	15800
23 5	SAN-JUAN	HT	CR	FBG DV	IB 255	8	3250	2 10	12000	13600
23 5	SAN-JUAN	FB	CR	FBG DV	IB 255	8	3250	2 10	12000	13600
23 5	SAN-JUAN	OP	RNBT	FBG DV	IB 255	8	3250	2 10	12000	13600
----- 1982 BOATS										
16 6	MUSTANG	OP	RNBT	FBG SV	IB 170-230	5 11	1600	1 9	4400	5050
17 9	SKI-TIQUE	OP	SKI	FBG SV	IB 170-230	6 4	2200	1 9	5350	6150
18 9	SKI-NAUTIQUE	OP	SKI	FBG SV	IB 220-280	7	2350	2 2	5950	7500
19	BAREFOOT-NAUTIQUE	OP	SKI	FBG DV	IB 220-280	6 10	2750	2 2	6550	7700
19	BAREFOOT-NAUTIQUE	OP	SKI	FBG DV	IB 350 PCM	6 10	2750	2 2	7150	8200
19	SOUTHWIND	OP	SKI	FBG DV	IB 220-280	6 10	2500	2 2	6150	7250
19	SOUTHWIND	OP	SKI	FBG DV	IB 350 PCM	6 10	2500	2 2	6750	7800
19 3	MARTINIQUE	OP	RNBT	FBG DV	IB 220-280	7	2600	2 2	6700	7850
19 3	MARTINIQUE	OP	RNBT	FBG DV	IB 350 PCM	7	2600	2 2	7300	8400
19 3	RIVIERA	OP	RNBT	FBG DV	IB 220-350	7	3100	2 4	7500	9300
19 11	SOUTHWIND BOWRIDER	OP	RNBT	FBG DV	IB 220-280	7 6	2600	2 3	7200	8800
19 11	SOUTHWIND BOWRIDER	OP	RNBT	FBG DV	IB 350 PCM	7 6	2800	2 3	8100	9350
23	CUDDY-NAUTIQUE	OP	FSH	FBG DV	IB 220-350	8	4200	2 6	13400	15900
23	CUDDY-NAUTIQUE DLX	OP	FSH	FBG DV	IB 220-350	8	4200	2 6	13600	16200
23	FISH-NAUTIQUE	ST	OPFSH	FBG DV	IB 220-350	8	3790	2 6	12400	14900
23	FISH-NAUTIQUE	ST	OPFSH	FBG DV	IB 170 OMC	8	3790	2 6	14500	16500
23	SEA-NAUTIQUE	OP	PH	FBG DV	IB 255 PCM	8	4000	2 6	12900	14700
23	SEA-NAUTIQUE	HT	PH	FBG DV	IB 230-350	8	4000	2 6	12900	15400
23 5	SAN-JUAN	HT	CR	FBG DV	IB 220-350	8	4400	2 10	14200	16900
23 5	SAN-JUAN	HT	CR	FBG DV	IB T220 PCM	8	4400	2 10	15800	17900
23 5	SAN-JUAN	FB	CR	FBG DV	IB T220 PCM	8	4750	2 10	15100	17900
23 5	SAN-JUAN	FB	CR	FBG DV	IB 220-350	8	4750	2 10	16700	18900
23 5	SAN-JUAN	OP	RNBT	FBG DV	IB 220-350	8	4400	2 10	14200	16900
23 5	SAN-JUAN	OP	RNBT	FBG DV	IB T220 PCM	8	4400	2 10	15800	17900
----- 1981 BOATS										
16 6	SKI-TIQUE	OP	SKI	FBG SV	IB 220 PCM	5 11	1600	1 9	3650	4250
17 9	SKI-NAUTIQUE	OP	SKI	FBG SV	IB 220-250	6 4	2100	1 9	4750	5550
19	BAREFOOT-NAUTIQUE	OP	RNBT	FBG DV	IB 220-250	6 10	2750	2 2	6500	7500
19	BAREFOOT-NAUTIQUE	OP	RNBT	FBG DV	IB 350 PCM	6 10	2750	2 2	7050	8100
19 3	MARTINIQUE	OP	RNBT	FBG DV	IB 220-350	7	2600	2 2	7000	8700
19 3	RIVIERA	OP	RNBT	FBG DV	IB 255 PCM	7 4	3200	2 2	8100	9300
19 11	SOUTHWIND BOWRIDER	OP	RNBT	FBG DV	IB 220-350	7 6	2450	2 3	6700	8350
23	CUDDY-NAUTIQUE	OP	FSH	FBG DV	IB 220-350	8	4200	2 6	12800	15300
23	CUDDY-NAUTIQUE	OP	FSH	FBG DV	IB 145D REN	8	4200	2 6	18500	20500
23	CUDDY-NAUTIQUE DLX	OP	FSH	FBG DV	IB 220-350	8	4200	2 6	13000	15500
23	CUDDY-NAUTIQUE DLX	OP	FSH	FBG DV	IB 145D REN	8	4200	2 6	17500	19800
23	FISH-NAUTIQUE	ST	OPFSH	FBG DV	IB 220-350	8	3790	2 6	11900	14300
23	FISH-NAUTIQUE	ST	OPFSH	FBG DV	IB 145D REN	8	3790	2 6	16300	18500
23	SEA-NAUTIQUE		FSH	FBG DV	IB 255 PCM	8	3790	2 6	12000	13600
23 5	SAN-JUAN	HT	CR	FBG DV	IB 220-350	8	4400	2 10	13600	16100
23 5	SAN-JUAN	HT	CR	FBG DV	IB T220 PCM	8	4400	2 10	15100	17100
23 5	SAN-JUAN	FB	CR	FBG DV	IB 220-350	8	5000	2 10	15100	18000
23 5	SAN-JUAN	FB	CR	FBG DV	IB T220 PCM	8	5000	2 10	15900	18100
23 5	SAN-JUAN	OP	RNBT	FBG DV	IB 220-350	8	4400	2 10	13600	16200
23 5	SAN-JUAN	OP	RNBT	FBG DV	IB T220 PCM	8	4400	2 10	15100	17200
----- 1980 BOATS										
16 6	SKI-TIQUE	OP	SKI	FBG SV	IB 220-280	5 11	1600	1 9	3350	4100
17 9	SKI-NAUTIQUE	OP	SKI	FBG SV	IB 220-330	6 4	2100	1 9	4600	5400
19	BAREFOOT-NAUTIQUE	OP	RNBT	FBG DV	IB 220-330	6 10	2750	2 2	6200	7300
19	BAREFOOT-NAUTIQUE	OP	RNBT	FBG DV	IB 350 PCM	6 10	2750	2 2	6750	7900
19 3	MARTINIQUE	OP	RNBT	FBG DV	IB 220-330	7	3000	2 2	6700	8350
19 11	SOUTHWIND BOWRIDER	OP	RNBT	FBG DV	IB 220-350	7 6	2450	2 3	6400	8000
23	CUDDY-NAUTIQUE	OP	FSH	FBG DV	IB 220-350	8	4200	2 6	12300	14600
23	CUDDY-NAUTIQUE	OP	FSH	FBG DV	IB 145D REN	8	4200	2 6	17300	19600
23	CUDDY-NAUTIQUE DLX	OP	CUD	FBG DV	IB 260	8			11400	13000
23	CUDDY-NAUTIQUE DLX	OP	FSH	FBG DV	IB 220-350	8	4200	2 6	12500	14800
23	CUDDY-NAUTIQUE DLX	OP	FSH	FBG DV	IB 145D REN	8			17500	19800
23	FISH-NAUTIQUE	ST	OPFSH	FBG DV	IB 220-350	8	3790	2 6	11400	13700
23	FISH-NAUTIQUE	ST	OPFSH	FBG DV	IB 145D REN	8	3790	2 6	16300	18500
23	SEA-NAUTIQUE		FSH	FBG DV	IB 255 PCM	8	3790	2 6	12000	13600
23 5	SAN-JUAN	HT	CR	FBG DV	IB 220-350	8	4400	2 10	13000	15500
23 5	SAN-JUAN	HT	CR	FBG DV	IB T220-T225	8	4400	2 10	14500	16400
23 5	SAN-JUAN	FB	CR	FBG DV	IB 220-350	8	5000	2 10	14700	17100
23 5	SAN-JUAN	FB	CR	FBG DV	IB T220-T225	8	5000	2 10	15900	18100
23 5	SAN-JUAN	OP	RNBT	FBG DV	IB 220-350	8	4400	2 10	13000	15500
23 5	SAN-JUAN	OP	RNBT	FBG DV	IB T220-T225	8	4400	2 10	14500	16400
----- 1979 BOATS										
16 6	SKI-TIQUE	OP	SKI	FBG SV	IB 220-225	5 11	1600	1 9	3350	3900
16 6	SKI-TIQUE	OP	SKI	FBG SV	IB 230 OMC	5 11	1600	1 9	3700	4300
17	AMERICAN-SKIER	OP	SKI	FBG SV	IB 220-225	6 4	2000	1 9	4000	4700
17	AMERICAN-SKIER	OP	SKI	FBG SV	IB 230 OMC	6 4	2000	1 9	4400	5050
17	MUSTANG	OP	SKI	FBG SV	IB 220-225	6 4	2000	1 9	4050	4750
17	MUSTANG	OP	SKI	FBG SV	IB 230 OMC	6 4	2000	1 9	4450	5100
17 9	SKI-NAUTIQUE	OP	SKI	FBG SV	IB 250-260	6 4	2100	1 9	4450	5500
18 2	SOUTHWIND	ST	RNBT	FBG DV	IB 250-260	6 10	2750	2 2	5800	6550
19	BAREFOOT-NAUTIQUE	ST	RNBT	FBG DV	IB 250-260	6 10	2750	1 5	**	**
19 11	SOUTHWIND	ST	RNBT	FBG DV	IB 250-260	7 6	2450	2 3	6700	7350
19 11	SOUTHWIND B/R	ST	RNBT	FBG DV	IB 250-260	7 6	2450	2 3	6350	7700
23	CUDDY-NAUTIQUE	OP	CUD	FBG DV	IB 230	8			11800	12700
23	FISH-NAUTIQUE	ST	OPFSH	FBG DV	IB 250-260	8	3790	2 6	11000	12900
23 5	SAN-JUAN	HT	CR	FBG DV	IB 250-260	8	4400	2 10	12500	14700

```
LOA NAME AND/           TOP/ BOAT -HULL- ----ENGINE--- BEAM   WGT DRAFT RETAIL RETAIL
FT IN OR MODEL          RIG TYPE MTL TP TP # HP MFG  FT IN  LBS  FT IN  LOW   HIGH
----------------- 1979 BOATS -------------------------------------------------------
23 5 SAN-JUAN           HT  CR   FBG DV IB T225 PCM   8      4400 2  6  13900 15800
23 5 SAN-JUAN           FB  CR   FBG DV IB 250-260    8      5000 2 10  13900 16200
23 5 SAN-JUAN           FB  CR   FBG DV IB T225 PCM   8      5000 2  6  15200 17300
23 5 SAN-JUAN           ST  RNBT FBG DV IB 250-260    8      4400 2 10  12500 14700
23 5 SAN-JUAN           ST  RNBT FBG DV IB T225 PCM   8      4400 2  6  13900 15800
----------------- 1978 BOATS -------------------------------------------------------
16 6 SKI-TIQUE          OP  SKI  FBG SV IB 225-230 5 11 1600 1  9  3250  3750
17   AMERICAN-SKIER     OP  SKI  FBG SV IB 225-230 6  4 2000 1  8  3850  4500
17   MUSTANG            OP  SKI  FBG SV IB 225-230 6  4 2000 1  8  3900  4550
17 9 MARTINIQUE         OP  SKI  FBG SV IB 250-260 6  4 2200 1  9  4600  5300
17 9 SKI-NAUTIQUE       OP  SKI  FBG SV IB 250-260 6  4 2100 1  9  4200  4950
18 2 SOUTHWIND          ST  RNBT FBG DV IB 250-260 7  3 2300 2  3  5150  5950
19 11 FISH-TIQUE        ST  OPFSH FBG DV IB 250-260 7 6 2500 2     5850  6750
19 11 SOUTHWIND         ST  RNBT FBG DV IB 250-260 7  6 2450 2  3  5800  6700
19 11 SOUTHWIND B/R     ST  RNBT FBG DV IB 250-260 7  6 2450 2  3  6100  7000
20 11 CUDDY DELUXE      ST  CUD  FBG DV IB 250-260 8    3400 2  6  8650 10000
23   CUDDY-NAUTIQUE     ST  CUD  FBG DV IB 250-260 8             10500 11900
23   FISH-NAUTIQUE      ST  OPFSH FBG DV IB 250-260 8   3790 2  6 10600 12000

23 5 SAN-JUAN           HT  CR   FBG DV IB 250-260    8      4400 2 10  12000 13700
23 5 SAN-JUAN           HT  CR   FBG DV IB T225 FORD  8      4400 2  6  13300 15100
23 5 SAN-JUAN           FB  CR   FBG DV IB 250-260    8      5000 2 10  13300 15200
23 5 SAN-JUAN           FB  CR   FBG DV IB T225 FORD  8      5000 2  6  14600 16600
23 5 SAN-JUAN           ST  RNBT FBG DV IB 250-260    8      4400 2 10  12000 13700
23 5 SAN-JUAN           ST  RNBT FBG DV IB T225 FORD  8      4400 2  6  13300 15100
----------------- 1977 BOATS -------------------------------------------------------
16 6 MUSTANG            OP  RNBT FBG SV IB 215 PCM  5 10 1700 1  9  3400  3950
16 6 MUSTANG            OP  RNBT FBG SV IB 230 OMC  5 10 1700 1  9  3700  4300
16 6 SKI-TIQUE          OP  SKI  FBG SV IB 215 PCM  5 11 1600 1  9  3100  3600
16 6 SKI-TIQUE          OP  SKI  FBG SV IB 230 OMC  5 11 1600 1  9  3400  3950
17   AMERICAN-SKIER     OP  SKI  FBG SV IB 215 PCM  6  4 2000 1  8  3700  4300
17   AMERICAN-SKIER     OP  SKI  FBG SV IB 230 OMC  6  4 2000 1  8  4000  4650
17   MUSTANG            OP  SKI  FBG SV IB 215 PCM  6  4 2000 1  8  3750  4350
17   MUSTANG            OP  SKI  FBG SV IB 230 OMC  6  4 2000 1  8  4050  4700
17 9 MARTINIQUE         OP  RNBT FBG SV IB 255-260  6  4 2200 2  1  4400  5400
17 9 SKI-NAUTIQUE       OP  SKI  FBG SV IB 255-260  6  4 2100 1  9  4050  5050
18   CARIBE             ST  RNBT FBG DV IO 175-235  7  6 2400 2  3  4800  5750
18   SOUTHWIND          ST  RNBT FBG DV IO 255-260  7  3 2300 2  3  4900  6000

19 11 FISH-TIQUE        OP  OPFSH FBG DV IB 255-260 7  6 2800 2  3  6000  7250
20 2 CARIBE             ST  RNBT FBG DV IO 175-235  7  6 2600 2  3  6150  7350
20 2 MARAUDER           ST  RNBT FBG DV IB 255-260  7  6 2400 2  3  6450  7800
20 2 SOUTHWIND          ST  RNBT FBG DV IB 255-260  7  6 2450 2  3  6500  7850
20 2 SOUTHWIND B/R      ST  RNBT FBG DV IB 255-260  7  6 2600 2  3  6700  8100
20 9 CUDDY DELUXE       ST  CUD  FBG DV IO 175-190  8    2800 2  3  7150  8300
   IB 215-230    7250 8700, IO 233-235  7400  8500, IB 255-260  7300 8800

23 5 FISH-NAUTIQUE      OP  OPFSH FBG DV IB 255-260 8    4000 2 10 10800 12600
23 5 SAN-JUAN           HT  CR   FBG DV IB 255-260  8    4000 2 10 10700 12600
23 5 SAN-JUAN           HT  CR   FBG DV IB T215 PCM 8    4000 2 10 11900 13500
23 5 SAN-JUAN           FB  CR   FBG DV IB 255-260  8    4000 2 10 10700 12600
23 5 SAN-JUAN           FB  CR   FBG DV IB T215 PCM 8    4000 2 10 11900 13500
23 5 SAN-JUAN           OP  RNBT FBG DV IB 255-260  8    4000 2 10 10800 12600
23 5 SAN-JUAN           OP  RNBT FBG DV IB T215 PCM 8    4000 2 10 11900 13500
----------------- 1976 BOATS -------------------------------------------------------
16 3 SEPARATOR          OP  RNBT FBG SV IB 225      6  9      2  6  3550  4100
16 6 MUSTANG            OP  RNBT FBG SV IB 220-230 5 10 1700 1  9  3300  3800
16 6 SKI-TIQUE          OP  SKI  FBG SV IB 220-230 5 11 1600 1  9  3000  3450
17   MUSTANG            OP  RNBT FBG SV IB 220-230 6  4 2000 1  8  3800  4400
17 9 MARTINIQUE         OP  RNBT FBG SV IB 255-260 6  4 2200 1  9  4200  4900
17 9 SKI-NAUTIQUE       OP  SKI  FBG SV IB 255-260 6  4 2100 1  9  3900  4550
18 2 CARIBE             ST  RNBT FBG DV IO 188 MRCR 7 3 2300 2  3  4800  5500
18 2 SOUTHWIND          ST  RNBT FBG DV IB 255-260 7  3 2300 2  3  4750  5450
19 9 MARAUDER           OP  RNBT FBG DV IB 255-260 7  5 2750 2  3  5750  6600
19 11 SOUTHWIND         ST  RNBT FBG DV IB 255-260 7  6 2450 2  3  5350  6150
19 11 SOUTHWIND B/R     ST  RNBT FBG DV IB 255-260 7  6 2450 2  3  5600  6450
19 11 TOBAGO FISHERMAN  ST  FSH  FBG DV IB 255-260 7  6 2350 2     5200  6000

20   CARIBE             ST  RNBT FBG DV IO 188 MRCR 7 3 2300 2  3  5850  6700
20 11 CUDDY             ST  CUD  FBG DV IO 188 MRCR 8   3340       8250  9500
   IB 220-230    7850 9050, IO 233 MRCR 8450 9700, IB 255-260 7900 9100

23   SPORT FISHERMAN    OP  SF   FBG    IB                         **    **
23 5 SAN-JUAN           HT  CR   FBG DV IB 255-260  8    4400 2 10 11100 12600
23 5 SAN-JUAN           HT  CR   FBG DV IB T220 FORD 8   4400 2  6 12200 13900
23 5 SAN-JUAN           FB  CR   FBG DV IB 255-260  8    4400 2 10 11100 12600
23 5 SAN-JUAN           FB  CR   FBG DV IB T220 FORD 8   4400 2  6 12200 13900
23 5 SAN-JUAN           ST  RNBT FBG DV IB 255-260  8    4400 2 10 11100 12600
23 5 SAN-JUAN           ST  RNBT FBG DV IB T220 FORD 8   4400 2  6 12200 13900
----------------- 1975 BOATS -------------------------------------------------------
16 2 SEPARATOR          OP  RNBT FBG SV IO 188 MRCR 6 9 2200 2  6  4150  4800
16 2 SEPARATOR          OP  RNBT FBG SV IO 255-260  6 9 2200 2  6  4500  5250
16 6 MUSTANG            OP  RNBT FBG SV IB 220-230 5 10 1700 1  9  3150  3650
16 6 SKIER              OP  SKI  FBG SV IB 220-230 5 11 1600 1  9  2850  3300
17   MUSTANG            OP  RNBT FBG SV IB 220-230 6  4 2000 1  8  3650  4250
17 8 FREEPORT           ST  RNBT FBG TR IB 220-260 6  4 1800 1 11  3650  4300
17 9 MARTINIQUE         OP  RNBT FBG SV IB 220-260 6  4 2200 1  9  4000  4700
17 9 SKI-NAUTIQUE       OP  SKI  FBG SV IB 220-260 6  4 2100 1  9  3700  4350
18 2 SOUTHWIND          ST  RNBT FBG DV IO 188 MRCR 7 3 2300 2  3  4950  5650
   IB 220 FORD 4550 5200, IO 225 5050 5800, IB 230-260 4550 5300

19 9 MARAUDER           OP  RNBT FBG SV IB 255-260  7 5 2750 1 11  5550  6350
19 11 SOUTHWIND B/R     ST  RNBT FBG DV IO 188 MRCR 7 6 2450 2  3  5700  6050
   IB 220 FORD 5200 6000, IO 225 5800 6650, IB 230-260 5250 6050

19 11 TOBAGO FISHERMAN  ST  FSH  FBG DV IO 188 MRCR 7 6 2350 2     6100  7000
   IB 220 FORD 4950 5700, IO 225 6200 7150, IB 230-260 5000 5800

20   FREEPORT           ST  RNBT FBG TR IB 220-260  7 6 2450       6000  7000
20 2 SOUTHWIND          ST  RNBT FBG DV IO 188 MRCR 7 6 2450 2  3  6300  7200
   IB 220 FORD 5950 6850, IO 225 6450 7400, IB 230-260 5950 6900

23 5 SAN-JUAN           HT  CR   FBG DV IB 188-225  8    4400 2  6 11900 13700
   IB 255-330 10700 12400, IO T165 MRCR 13200 15000, IO T165 OMC 13100 14900
   IB T165 CORR 11600 13200

23 5 SAN-JUAN           FB  CR   FBG DV IB 188-225  8    5000 2  8 13100 15000
   IB 255-330 11800 13600, IO T165 MRCR 14500 16400, IO T165 OMC 14400 16300
   IB T165 CORR 12700 14500
----------------- 1974 BOATS -------------------------------------------------------
16 3 SEPARATOR          OP  RNBT FBG    IO 165-188 CORR 6 10 2200     **    **
16 3 SEPARATOR          OP  RNBT FBG    IO 255-260 CORR 6 10 2200   4300  5050
16 6                        SKI  FBG    IB 225 CORR    5 11 1600       **    **
16 6                        SKI  FBG    IB 225 CORR    5 11 1600     3000  3500
16 6 MUSTANG            OP  RNBT FBG    IB 225 OMC     5 11 1750       **    **
16 6 MUSTANG            OP  RNBT FBG    IB 225 OMC     5 11 1750     3350  3900
17   MUSTANG            OP  RNBT FBG    IB 225 CORR    6  4 2000       **    **
17   MUSTANG            OP  RNBT FBG    IB 225 CORR    6  4 2000     3750  4350
17 8 T-18 B/R           ST  RNBT FBG    IO 120-140 CORR 7 2 1800     4300  5000
17 9 MARTINIQUE         OP  RNBT FBG    IB 225 CHRY    6  4 2200       **    **
17 9 MARTINIQUE         OP  RNBT FBG    IB 225-250 CORR 6 4 2200     4100  4800

17 9 SKI-NAUTIQUE       OP  SKI  FBG    IB 225 CORR    6  4 2100       **    **
17 9 SKI-NAUTIQUE       OP  SKI  FBG    IB 225 CHRY    6  4 2100     3500  4350
17 9 SKI-NAUTIQUE       OP  SKI  FBG    IB 225-250 CORR 6 4 2100     3800  4450
18 2 SOUTHWIND          ST  RNBT FBG    IB 225 CORR    7  3 2300       **    **
   IO 165-188 5050 5850, IB 225 MRCR 5200 6000, IO 225 OMC 5150 5950
   IB 225 4250 5300, IO 225 5300 6050, IB 250 4300 5350
   IO 255 MRCR 5400 6200, IB 330 CHRY 4600 5300

19 9 MARAUDER           OP  RNBT FBG    IB     CORR    7  5 2750       **    **
19 9 MARAUDER           OP  RNBT FBG    IB 250-330 CORR 7 5 2750     5250  6400
19 9 MARAUDER           HT  RNBT FBG    IB     CORR    7  5 2750       **    **
19 9 MARAUDER           HT  RNBT FBG    IB 250-330 CORR 7 5 2750     5250  6400
19 11 FREEPORT          ST  RNBT FBG    IB     CORR    7  6 2450       **    **
   IO 165-188 5500 6400, IO 225 5850 6750, IB 225 OMC 5500 6300
   IB 225 4700 5700, IO 245 OMC 5750 6600, JT 250 CHRY 5500 6350
   IB 250 4700 5850, IO 255 MRCR 5900 6800, JT 330 CHRY 5500 6350
   IB 330 CHRY 5000 5750

19 11 SOUTHWIND         ST  RNBT FBG    IB     CORR    7  6 2450       **    **
   IO 165-188 5850 6750, IO 225 6150 6950, IO 225 OMC 5800 6550
   IB 225 4950 6100, IO 245 OMC 6050 6950, JT 250 CHRY 5800 6650
   IB 250 4950 6150, IO 255 MRCR 6150 7050, JT 330 CHRY 5800 6650
   IB 330 CHRY 5250 6050

19 11 SOUTHWIND B/R     ST  RNBT FBG    IB     CORR    7  6 2450       **    **
   IO 165-188 6100 7050, IO 225 MRCR 6400 7350, IO 225 OMC 6050 6950
   IB 225 5250 6400, IO 245 OMC 6300 7250, IB 250 5200 6500
   IO 255 MRCR 6450 7400, IB 330 CHRY 5500 6350

19 11 TOBAGO FISHERMAN  OP  OPFSH FBG   IO     CORR    7  6 2350       **    **
19 11 TOBAGO FISHERMAN  OP  FSH  FBG    IO 165        7  6 2350     6250  7150
19 11 TOBAGO FISHERMAN  OP  FSH  FBG    IB 225        7  6 2350     4750  5800
```

LOA FT	LOA IN	NAME AND/ OR MODEL	TOP/ RIG	BOAT TYPE	-HULL- MTL	-HULL- TP	ENGINE TP	ENGINE # HP	ENGINE MFG	BEAM FT	BEAM IN	WGT LBS	DRAFT FT	DRAFT IN	RETAIL LOW	RETAIL HIGH
		1974 BOATS														
23	5	SAN-JUAN	HT	CR	FBG		IB		CORR	8		4400			**	**
		IO 165 MRCR 12200 13900, IO 165 OMC 12200 13900, IB 165-330													10100	12000
		IB T155 CHRY 11000 12500, IO T165 MRCR 13600 15500, IO T165 OMC													13500	15400
		IB T165 11200 12700														
23	5	SAN-JUAN	FB	CR	FBG		IB		CORR	8		4400			**	**
		IO 165 MRCR 12200 13900, IO 165 OMC 12200 13900, IB 165-330													10100	12000
		IB T155 CHRY 11000 12500, IO T165 MRCR 13600 15500, IO T165 OMC													13500	15400
		IB T165 11200 12700														
		1973 BOATS														
16	3	SEPARATOR	OP	RNBT	FBG		IO	165-188		3		2200			3800	4450
16	3	SEPARATOR	OP	RNBT	FBG		IB	235	HOLM	3		2200			3050	3550
16	6			SKI	FBG		IB	215-220		2	10	1600			2350	2700
16	6			SKI	FBG		IB	225	OMC	2	10	1600			2550	2950
16	6	MUSTANG	OP	RNBT	FBG		IB	215-220		2	10	1700			2600	3000
16	6	MUSTANG	OP	RNBT	FBG		IB	225	OMC	2	10	1700			2850	3300
17	8	T-18 B/R	OP	RNBT	FBG		IO	120-140		6	6	1800			4200	4900
17	9	MARTINIQUE	OP	RNBT	FBG		IB	215-255		6	4	2200			3700	4550
17	9	SKI-NAUTIQUE	OP	SKI	FBG		IB	215-235		6	4	2100			3400	4250
17	9	SKI-NAUTIQUE	OP	SKI	FBG		IB	250	CHRY	6	4	2100			3400	3950
17	9	SKI-NAUTIQUE	OP	SKI	FBG		IB	250-255		6	4	2100			3700	4300
19	9	MARAUDER	OP	RNBT	FBG		IB	235-330		7	5	2750			5100	6150
19	11	SOUTHWIND	ST	RNBT	FBG		IO	165-188		7	6	2450			6000	6950
		IB 215-220 4800 5550, IO 225 MRCR 6150 7100, IO 225 OMC													6150	7050
		IB 225-235 4800 5800, IO 245 OMC 6200 7150, JT 250 CHRY													5450	6250
		IB 250 4800 5850, IO 255 MRCR 6350 7300, IB 255													4850	5600
		JT 330 CHRY 5450 6250, IB 330 CHRY 5050 5800														
19	11	TOBAGO FISHERMAN	OP	FSH	FBG		IO	165		7	6	2350			6450	7400
19	11	TOBAGO FISHERMAN	OP	FSH	FBG		IB	215-225		7	6	2350			4600	5550
20		FREEPORT	ST	RNBT	FBG		IB	215-235		7	6	2450			5450	6600
		JT 250 CHRY 6150 7050, IB 250-255 5450 6650, JT 330 CHRY													6150	7050
		IB 330 CHRY 5700 6550														
23	5	SAN-JUAN	HT	CR	FBG		IO	165		8		4400			12600	14300
		IB 225-255 8550 10200, IB 330 CHRY 10100 11400, IB T155 CHRY													10600	12000
		IO T165 14100 16000														
23	5	SAN-JUAN	FB	CR	FBG		IO	165		8					11100	12600
		IB 225-330 8550 10200, IB T155 CHRY 9350 10600, IO T165													12600	14300
		1972 BOATS														
16	3	SEPARATOR	OP	RNBT	FBG		IB	165-188		6	10	2200	2	6	3350	3900
16	3	SEPARATOR	OP	RNBT	FBG		VD	235	HOLM	6	10	2200	2	6	3400	3950
16	6			SKI	FBG		IB	150-200		5	11	1600	1	7	2400	2900
16	6			SKI	FBG		IB	210-235		5	11	1600	1	7	2750	3200
16	6	MUSTANG	OP	RNBT	FBG		IB	200	CHRY	5	11	1700	1	7	2750	3200
16	6	MUSTANG	OP	RNBT	FBG		IB	210-235		5	11	1700	1	7	3050	3500
17	4	SOUTHWIND	ST	RNBT	FBG		JT	200	CHRY	7	3	2250	2	3	4350	5000
		IB 200 CHRY 3700 4300, JT 210 OMC 4400 5050, IB 210 OMC													4000	4650
		JT 220 CONQ 4400 5050, IB 220 CONQ 3750 4400, JT 225 CHRY													4400	5050
		IB 225 CHRY 3700 4300, JT 235 HOLM 4400 5050, IB 235 HOLM													3800	4400
17	6	SKI-NAUTIQUE	OP	SKI	FBG		IB	210-250		6	4	2050	1	9	3400	4000
17	9	MARTINIQUE	OP	RNBT	FBG		IB	210-235		6	4	2200	1	9	3750	4350
19	9	MARAUDER	OP	RNBT	FBG		IB	235-300		7	5	2790	2		4900	5950
19	11	FREEPORT	ST	RNBT	FBG		IB	210-235		7	6	2450	2	6	4650	5350
19	11	SOUTHWIND	ST	RNBT	FBG		IO	155-165		7	6	2450	2	6	6150	7100
		IB 210-220 5100 5850, JT 225 CHRY 5200 6000, IB 225-235													4850	5600
		JT 250-290 5250 6000														
19	11	TOBAGO FISHERMAN	OP	FSH	FBG		IO	155-165		7	6	2250	2	6	6450	7500
19	11	TOBAGO FISHERMAN	OP	FSH	FBG		IB	200-235		7	6	2250	2	6	4250	5250
23	5	SAN-JUAN	HT	CR	FBG		IO	155-165		8		4400	2	10	12900	14800
		IB 225-300 9400 11100, IO T155 OMC 14400 16400, IB T155 CHRY													10200	11500
		IO T165 MRCR 14500 16500														
23	5	SAN-JUAN	FB	CR	FBG		IO	155-165		8			2	10	11500	13100
		IB 225-300 8200 9850, IO T155 OMC 12800 14600, IB T155 CHRY													9050	10300
		IO T165 MRCR 13000 14800														
		1971 BOATS														
16	3	SEPARATOR	OP	RNBT	FBG		IB	351	HOLM	6	10	2200	2	6	3650	4250
16	6			SKI	FBG		IB	150-200		5	11	1600	1	7	2350	2750
16	6			SKI	FBG		IB	210-235		5	11	1600	1	7	2650	3100
16	6	MUSTANG	OP	RNBT	FBG		IB	200		5	11	1700	1	7	2650	3150
16	6	MUSTANG	OP	RNBT	FBG		IB	210-235		5	11	1700	1	7	2900	3400
17	4	FREEPORT		RNBT	FBG	DV	IO	160		7	3		2	3	5250	6050
17	4	SWINGER		RNBT	FBG	DV	IO	155-165		7	3		2	3	5250	6050
17	6	SKI-NAUTIQUE	OP	SKI	FBG		IB	210-351		6	4	2050	1	9	3300	4000
17	9	MARTINIQUE	OP	RNBT	FBG		IB	210-235		6	4	2200	1	9	3600	4200
19	9	MARAUDER	OP	RNBT	FBG		IB	250-351		7	5	2790	2		4750	5850
19	11	FREEPORT	ST	RNBT	FBG		IB	210-235		7	6	2450	2	6	4450	5150
19	11	SOUTHWIND	ST	RNBT	FBG		IO	155-165		7	6	2450	2	6	6350	7350
19	11	SOUTHWIND	ST	RNBT	FBG		IB	210-235		7	6	2450	2	3	4900	5650
19	11	TOBAGO FISHERMAN	OP	FSH	FBG		IO	155-165		7	6	2250	2	6	6650	7750
19	11	TOBAGO FISHERMAN	OP	FSH	FBG		IB	200-235		7	6	2250	2	6	4100	5050
23	5	SAN-JUAN	HT	CR	FBG		IO	155-165		8		4400	2	10	13300	15200
		IB 225-351 9100 10800, IO T155 OMC 14900 16900, IB T155 CHRY													9750	11100
		IO T165 MRCR 15000 17100														
23	5	SAN-JUAN	FB	CR	FBG		IO	155-165		8			2	10	11800	13500
		IB 225-351 9100 10800, IO T155 OMC 13300 15100, IB T155 CHRY													9750	11100
		IO T165 MRCR 13400 15200														
		1970 BOATS														
16	1	MUSTANG	OP	RNBT	FBG	SV	IB	200	CHRY	5	11	1600	1	7	2400	2800
16	1	MUSTANG	OP	RNBT	FBG	SV	IB	210-235		5	11	1600	1	7	2650	3100
16	1	SKIER		SKI	FBG	SV	IB	150-200		5	11	1500	1	7	2050	2500
16	1	SKIER		SKI	FBG	SV	IB	210-235		5	11	1500	1	7	2400	2800
16	3	SEPARATOR	OP	RNBT	FBG	DV	IB	351	HOLM	6	10	2200	2	6	3500	4100
16	3	TORINO		RNBT	FBG	DV	IO	160		6	9		3		4350	5050
16	3	TORINO		RNBT	FBG	DV	IB	235	HOLM	6	10		3		2800	3300
17	1	BARRACUDA	OP	RNBT	FBG	DV	IB	235	HOLM	6	10	2400	1	8	3450	4050
17	1	BARRACUDA	OP	RNBT	FBG	SV	IB	210-225		6	10	2400	1	8	3650	4250
17	4	FREEPORT	ST	RNBT	FBG	DV	IO	155-165		7	3	2250	2	3	5350	6250
17	4	FREEPORT	ST	RNBT	FBG	DV	IB	200	CHRY	7	3	2250	2	3	3450	4000
17	4	FREEPORT	ST	RNBT	FBG	DV	IB	210-235		7	3	2250	2	3	3700	4300
17	4	SWINGER			FBG		IO	120-165		7	3	2100	2	3	4950	5800
17	4	SWINGER			FBG	DV	IB	150-200		7	3	2100	2	3	3100	3650
17	4	SWINGER			FBG	DV	IB	210-235		7	3	2100	2	3	3400	3950
17	6	SKI-NAUTIQUE	OP	SKI	FBG	SV	IB	210-351		6	4	2050	1	9	3150	3850
17	9	MARTINIQUE	OP	RNBT	FBG		IB	210-235		6	4	2200	1	6	3500	4050
18	10	MARAUDER	OP	RNBT	FBG	SV	IB	250-351		7	5	2790	2		4600	5400
19	11	FISHERMAN		FSH	FBG	DV	IO	155-165		7	6	2250	2	6	6850	7950
19	11	FISHERMAN		FSH	FBG	DV	IB	200-235		7	6	2250	2	6	3900	4850
19	11	SOUTHWIND	ST	RNBT	FBG	DV	IO	155-165		7	6	2450	2	6	6550	7600
19	11	SOUTHWIND	ST	RNBT	FBG	DV	IB	210-235		7	6	2450	2	3	4500	5200
23	5	SAN-JUAN	HT	CR	FBG	DV	IO	155-165		8		4400	3		13700	15600
		IB 225-351 8650 10400, IO T155 OMC 15300 17400, IB T155 CHRY													9400	10700
		IO T165 MRCR 15400 17600														
		1969 BOATS														
16	1			SKI	FBG		IB	155	CHRY	5	11	1500	1	7	1950	2350
16	1	MUSTANG		RNBT	FBG		IB	165-210		5	11		1	7	2450	2850
16	1	MUSTANG	OP	RNBT	FBG		IB	200	CHRY	5	11	1600	1	7	2350	2700
16	1	MUSTANG SS		RNBT	FBG		IB	210	INT	5	11		1	7	2700	3150
16	1	SKYLARK		RNBT	FBG		IB	155		5	11		1	7	2400	2800
16	3	SPOILER			FBG		IB	351	HOLM	6	10	2200	2	6	3200	3750
16	3	TORINO		RNBT	FBG	DV	IO	210		6	10		2	6	4650	5350
16	3	TORINO		RNBT	FBG	DV	IB	210		6	10		2	6	2700	3150
16	3	TORINO		RNBT	FBG	DV	IO	235	HOLM	6	10	2170	2	6	5300	6100
17	1	BARRACUDA	OP	RNBT	FBG		IB	225	CHRY	6	10	2400	1	8	3300	3800
17	1	BARRACUDA DLX		RNBT	FBG		IB	235		6	10		1	8	3200	3750
17	1	BARRACUDA SS		RNBT	FBG		IB	250		6	10		1	8	3250	3750
17	4	FREEPORT		RNBT	FBG	DV	IO	120	OMC	7	3				5500	6350
17	4	FREEPORT		RNBT	FBG	DV	IB	210		7	3		2	3	3350	3900
17	4	FREEPORT	ST	RNBT	FBG	DV	IO	160-200		7	3	2250	2	3	5600	6550
17	4	FREERORT		RNBT	FBG	DV	IO	165		7	3		2	6	5600	6450
17	4	SWINGER			FBG		IB	155	CHRY	7	3	2100	2	3	2950	3450
17	6	SKI-NAUTIQUE		SKI	FBG		IB	250		6	4	2050	1	9	2900	3350
17	6	SKI-NAUTIQUE	OP	SKI	FBG		IB	225	CHRY	6	4	2050	1	9	2800	3250
18	10	MARAUDER	OP	RNBT	FBG		IB	300	CHRY	7	5	2790	2		4250	4950
18	10	WILDCAT		RNBT	FBG		IB	225-325		7	5		2		3650	4550
19	6	SOUTHWIND		CR	FBG	DV	IO	120	OMC	8					7150	8250
19	6	SOUTHWIND		CR	FBG	DV	IO	T120		8					8200	9400
19	11			FSH	FBG		IO	160	MRCR	7	6	2250	2	6	7150	8250
19	11			FSH	FBG		IB	200	CHRY	7	6	2250	2	6	3800	4400
19	11			FSH	FBG		VD	200	CHRY	7	6	2250	2	6	3800	4400
19	11	SOUTHWIND		RNBT	FBG	DV	IO	225		7	6		2	6	7100	8150
19	11	SOUTHWIND		RNBT	FBG	DV	IB	250		7	6		2	3	4200	4850

CONTINUED ON NEXT PAGE

CORRECT CRAFT INC -CONTINUED See inside cover to adjust price for area

LOA FT	IN	NAME AND/ OR MODEL	TOP/ RIG	BOAT TYPE	-HULL- MTL	TP	----ENGINE--- TP	# HP	MFG	BEAM FT	IN	WGT LBS	DRAFT FT	IN	RETAIL LOW	RETAIL HIGH
		1969 BOATS														
19	11	SOUTHWIND	ST	RNBT	FBG	DV	IO	160	MRCR	7	6	2450	2	6	6800	7800
19	11	SOUTHWIND	ST	RNBT	FBG	DV	IB	225	CHRY	7	6	2450	2	3	4050	4750
20	2	RIVIERA		RNBT	FBG		IB	225	CHRY	8			2		4900	5650
20	3	RIVIERA		RNBT	FBG		IB	325		8			2		5250	6050
23	5	SAN-JUAN		CR	FBG	DV	IO	160	OMC	8					12500	14200
23	5	SAN-JUAN		CR	FBG	DV	IO	T160	OMC	8					14100	16000
23	5	SAN-JUAN	HT	CR	FBG	DV	IO	160	MRCR	8		4400	3		14200	16200
23	5	SAN-JUAN	HT	CR	FBG	DV	IB	225-300		8		4400	2	10	8300	9700
23	5	SAN-JUAN	HT	CR	FBG	DV	IO	T160	MRCR	8		4400	2	7	15900	18100
23	5	SAN-JUAN		RNBT	FBG	DV	IO	225		8			3		11900	13500
23	5	SAN-JUAN		RNBT	FBG	DV	IB	325		8			3		7500	8600
		1968 BOATS														
16	1	MUSTANG	OP	RNBT	FBG		IB	165-210		5	11	1600	1	7	2250	2700
16	1	MUSTANG SS	OP	RNBT	FBG		IB	210	INT	5	11	1700	1	7	2350	2750
16	1	SKYLARK	OP	SKI	FBG		IB	155	UNIV	5	11	1600	1	7	2000	2400
16	3	TORINO			FBG		IB	165	INT	6	10	2170	2	6	2650	3100
		VD 165 INT 2650 3100, IB 210 INT 2700 3150, VD 210 INT													2700	3150
17	1	BARRACUDA	OP	RNBT	FBG		IB	210-235		6	10	2400	1	8	3150	3700
17	1	BARRACUDA SS	OP	RNBT	FBG		IB	235	CHRY	6	10	2500	1	8	3250	3750
17	4	FREEPORT	ST	RNBT	FBG		IO	120-160		7	3	2250	2	6	5750	6650
		IO 165 INT 5800 6650, IB 165 INT 3150 3700, VD 165 INT													3150	3700
		IB 210 3200 3750														
17	6	SKI-NAUTIQUE	OP	SKI	FBG		IB	210-250		6	4	2050	1	9	2700	3200
18	10	WILDCAT	OP	SKI	FBG		IB	235-300		7	5	2650	2		3700	4450
19	11	SOUTHWIND	ST	RNBT	FBG		IO	120-160		7	6	2450	2	6	7000	8100
		IO 165 INT 7050 8100, IB 165 INT 3900 4550, VD 165 INT													3900	4550
		IO 210 INT 7150 8250, IO 210 OMC 7100 8150, IB 210													3900	4600
		IO 225 MRCR 7250 8350, IB 235-250 3950 4650														
20	3	RIVIERA	OP	RNBT	FBG		IB	235-300		8		2900	2		5150	6100
23	5	SAN-JUAN	HT	CR	FBG		IO	155-165		8		4400	3		14700	16800
		IO 210 INT 14900 17000, IO 210 OMC 14900 16900, IB 210													8000	9250
		IO 225 MRCR 15000 17100, IB 235-300 8050 9350, IO T160 MRCR													16600	18800
		IO T165 INT 16600 18800, IO T165 OMC 16500 18700, IB T165 INT													8900	10100
		1967 BOATS														
16	1	MUSTANG		RNBT	FBG		IB	70		5	11				1850	2200
16	1	MUSTANG	OP	RNBT	FBG		IO	60				1600			4500	5150
16	1	MUSTANG	OP	RNBT	FBG		IB	165-210				1600			2300	2700
16	1	MUSTANG SS	OP	RNBT	FBG		IB	190-210				1700			2400	2800
16	1	SKYLARK	OP	SKI	FBG		IB	155-202				1600			2050	2500
17	1	AL-TYLL	OP	SKI	FBG		IB	155-202				2250			2900	3450
17	1	BARRACUDA	OP	RNBT	FBG		IB	210-235				2400			3250	3750
17	1	BARRACUDA SS	OP	RNBT	FBG		IB	210-235				2500			3300	3850
17	4	FREEPORT		RNBT	FBG		IO	120		7	3				5950	6850
17	6	SKI-NAUTIQUE	OP	SKI	FBG		IB	210-250		6	4	2050			2650	3100
18	10	WILDCAT	OP	SKI	FBG		IB	220-290				2650			3650	4350
19	6	SOUTHWIND		RNBT	FBG		IO	120		8					7450	8550
19	6	SOUTHWIND		RNBT	FBG		IO	T 60		8					8400	9650
20	3	RIVIERA	OP	RNBT	FBG		IO	220-290				2900			9300	11400
20	3	RIVIERA	HT	RNBT	FBG		IO	220-290				2900			9300	11400
23	5	SAN-JUAN	HT	CR	FBG		IO	150-225				4400			15200	17600
23	5	SAN-JUAN	HT	CR	FBG		IO	T150				4400			17100	19400
23	5	SAN-JUAN	HT	CR	FBG		IB	T150-T210				4400			8400	9900
		1966 BOATS														
16	1	AMERICAN	OP	SKI	FBG		IB	190							1950	2350
16	1	MUSTANG	OP	RNBT	FBG		IO	60		5	11				4600	5300
		IB 70 1800 2150, IB 100 1900 2300, IB 165													2200	2550
16	1	SKYLARK	OP	SKI	FBG		IB	140-155							1850	2250
16	1	TAHOE ONE SIXTY	OP	RNBT	FBG		IB	210							2350	2750
16	5	STAR-FLITE	OP	RNBT	FBG		IB	210							2400	2800
17	1	AL-TYLL	OP	SKI	FBG		IB	155-202							2800	3300
17	1	SPORTSMAN	OP	RNBT	FBG		IO	110		6	9		1	7	5850	6700
17	1	SPORTSMAN	OP	RNBT	FBG		IB	140		6	9		1	7	2700	3150
17	6	BARRACUDA	OP	RNBT	FBG		IB	210							3100	3600
17	6	SKI-NAUTIQUE	OP	SKI	FBG		IB	210-215		6	4	2050			2550	2950
18	9	CLEARWATER	OP	FSH	FBG		IO	155-200							7300	8500
18	9	GRAND-PRIX		RNBT	FBG		IB	280-310							3400	4000
18	9	MARAUDER	OP	RNBT	FBG		IB	300							3400	4000
18	9	SPORTSMAN	OP	RNBT	FBG		IB	140							3150	3700
		IO 150 6750 7750, IB 155 3200 3750, IO 210													6900	7900
		IB 220 3300 3850														
18	9	TOURNAMENT	OP	SKI	FBG		IB	250							3200	3750
18	10	WILDCAT	OP	SKI	FBG		IB	235-280							3200	3800
20	2	DEBONNAIRE	OP	RNBT	FBG		IB	250-290							4350	5100
20	2	DEBONNAIRE CUSTOM	HT	RNBT	FBG		IB	300-310							4450	5150
20	2	RIVIERA	OP	RNBT	FBG		IB	220-235							4800	5500
20	2	SPORTSMAN	OP	RNBT	FBG		IO	150							8500	9800
20	2	SPORTSMAN	OP	RNBT	FBG		IO	210							8700	10000
20	2	SPORTSMAN	OP	RNBT	FBG		IB	210-220							4250	4950
23	5	SAN-JUAN	HT	CR	FBG		IO	150-225							13800	16000
23	5	SAN-JUAN	HT	CR	FBG		IO	T150							15700	17900
23	5	SAN-JUAN	HT	CR	FBG		IB	T235							7400	8550
		1965 BOATS														
16	1	AMERICAN	OP	SKI	FBG		IB	190							1900	2250
16	1	MUSTANG	OP	RNBT	FBG		IO	60							5000	5750
		IB 70 1700 2050, IB 100-120 1950 2450, IB 140-165													2200	2600
16	1	SKYLARK	OP	SKI	FBG		IB	140-150							1800	2150
16	1	STAR-FLITE	OP	RNBT	FBG		IB	210							2300	2700
16	1	TAHOE ONE SIXTY	OP	RNBT	FBG		IB	160							2250	2600
16	6	BARRACUDA	OP	RNBT	FBG		IB	210		6	9		1	7	2650	3100
16	6	CLASSIC	OP	SKI	FBG		IB	210							2650	3100
16	6	SPORTSMAN	OP	RNBT	FBG		IO	110							6150	7050
16	6	SPORTSMAN	OP	RNBT	FBG		IB	110-140							2550	3100
17	6	SKI-NAUTIQUE	OP	SKI	FBG		IB	210		6	4	2050			2450	2850
18	9	CLEARWATER	OP	FSH	FBG		IO	155-200							7500	8800
18	9	SPORTSMAN	OP	RNBT	FBG		IB	140							3050	3550
		IO 150 6950 8000, IB 155 3100 3600, IO 210-220													7100	8250
18	9	TOURNAMENT	OP	SKI	FBG		IB	220-240							3050	3600
18	10	GRAND-PRIX		RNBT	FBG		IB	280					7	5	3250	3800
18	10	MARAUDER	OP	RNBT	FBG		IB	300							3300	3850
18	10	MARAUDER	OP	RNBT	FBG		IB	400							3800	4400
18	10	WILDCAT	OP	SKI	FBG		IB	235-290							3100	3700
20	3	DEBONNAIRE	OP	RNBT	FBG		IB	240-290							4150	4950
20	3	DEBONNAIRE CUSTOM	HT	RNBT	FBG		IB	310							4350	5000
20	3	SPORTSMAN	OP	RNBT	FBG		IO	150							8950	10200
20	3	SPORTSMAN	OP	RNBT	FBG		IO	210							9100	10300
20	3	SPORTSMAN	OP	RNBT	FBG		IB	210-220							4150	4950
		1964 BOATS														
16		AMERICAN DELUXE	OP	SKI	FBG		IB	140-160							1700	2100
16		COMPACT DLX	OP	SKI	WD		IB	140-160							1700	2100
16		STAR-FLITE	OP	RNBT	FBG		IB	190-210							2200	2550
16		TAHOE ONE SIXTY	OP	RNBT	FBG		IB	160							2150	2500
17		CLASSIC	OP	SKI	FBG		IB	120-190							2450	3050
17		CLASSIC	OP	SKI	FBG		IB	215							2650	3100
17	6	SKI-NAUTIQUE	OP	SKI	FBG		IB	190-220		6	4	2050			2350	2750
18		AQUA-SKIER-DELUXE	OP	SKI	WD		IB	190-280							3000	3550
18		TOURNAMENT	OP	SKI	WD		IB	190-260							2600	3150
19		COLLEGIAN	OP	FSH	FBG		IB	220-310							3000	3650
19		GRAND-PRIX		RNBT	FBG		IB	310							3250	3800
19		GRAND-PRIX		RNBT	FBG		IB	400							3650	4250
20		DEBONNAIRE	OP	FSH	FBG		IB	120-220							3600	4450
20		DEBONNAIRE DELUXE	OP	RNBT	FBG		IB	220-280							3950	4700
		1963 BOATS														
16	1	AMERICAN	OP	SKI	FBG		IO	85							4550	5250
16	1	AMERICAN	OP	SKI	FBG		JT	100							1900	2250
16	1	ATOM-SKIER-DELUXE	OP	SKI	WD		IB	225							1800	2100
16	1	ATOM-SPECIAL	OP	SKI	WD		IO	100							4550	5250
16	1	STAR-FLITE	OP	RNBT	FBG		IB	140-160							2000	2350
16	1	TAHOE ONE SIXTY	OP	RNBT	FBG		IB	160							2100	2500
16	6	CLASSIC	OP	SKI	FBG		IO	100							6200	7150
		IB 100-138 2250 2750, IB 160 2400 2800, JT 185													2850	3300
		IB 185-215 2450 2950														
17				RNBT	FBG		OB								2250	2600
17	4	TOURNAMENT	OP	SKI	WD		IB	138-185							2500	3000
17	6	SKI-NAUTIQUE	OP	SKI	FBG		IB	185-215		6	4	2050			2300	2700
18		AQUA-SKIER-DELUXE	OP	SKI	WD		IB	135-178							2600	3150
18		AQUA-SKIER-DELUXE	OP	SKI	WD		JT	185							3100	3600
18		AQUA-SKIER-DELUXE	OP	SKI	WD		IB	185-280							2700	3250
18		DELUXE	OP	RNBT	WD		OB								2600	3050
18		MONTEREY	OP	CR	WD		OB								2150	2550
18		MONTEREY	OP	CR	WD		IB	70							2350	2700
19	6	BONIFAY	OP	CR	WD		OB								3050	3550
19	6	BONIFAY	OP	CR	WD		IO	100							8500	9750
19	6	BONIFAY	OP	CR	WD		IB	135-178							3050	3650
19	6	BONIFAY	OP	CR	WD		JT	185							3550	4150

CONTINUED ON NEXT PAGE

LOA FT IN	NAME AND/ OR MODEL	TOP/ RIG	BOAT TYPE	-HULL- MTL TP	TP	# HP	ENGINE MFG	BEAM FT IN	WGT LBS	DRAFT FT IN	RETAIL LOW	RETAIL HIGH
1963 BOATS												
19 6	SANIBEL-ISLANDER	OP	RNBT	WD	IO	100					8200	9450
	IB 111-178 3050		3800, JT	185		3650	4250, IB 185-225				3250	3850
20	COLLEGIAN	OP	FSH	WD	IB	225-280					3700	4400
20 2	DEBONNAIRE	OP	RNBT	FBG	IB	225-280					3850	4550
23	VACATIONER	OP	EXP	WD	IO	100					16300	18500
23	VACATIONER	OP	EXP	WD	IB	135-185					6250	7350
1962 BOATS												
16	ATOM-SKIER	OP	SKI	WD	IB	135					1700	2000
17 6	DELUXE	OP	RNBT	WD	OB						2600	3000
17 6	MONTEREY	OP	CR	WD	OB						2100	2500
17 6	MONTEREY	OP	CR	WD	IB	70					2250	2600
18	AQUA-SKIER-DELUXE	OP	SKI	WD	IB	138					2550	2950
18	INTERNATIONAL	OP	SKI	WD	IB	225-240					2650	3100
18	PANTHER DELUXE	OP	RNBT	WD	IB	70					2400	2800
18	STAR-FLITE	OP	RNBT	WD	IB	225-240					2800	3250
18	TOURNAMENT	OP	SKI	WD	IB	111-135					2450	2950
20	BONIFAY	OP	CR	WD	OB						3250	3800
20	BONIFAY	OP	CR	WD	IB	70					3200	3700
20	COLLEGIAN	OP	FSH	WD	IB	225-300					3600	4350
20	SANIBEL-ISLANDER	OP	RNBT	WD	IB	111-135					3450	4150
1961 BOATS												
17 3	PANTHER DELUXE	OP	RNBT	PLY	IB	70		6 10		1 8	2100	2500
17 6	AQUA-SKIER-DELUXE	OP	SKI	PLY	IB	135		6 2		1 7	2150	2500
17 6	INTERNATIONAL	OP	SKI	PLY	IB	215		6 2		1 7	2300	2650
17 6	MONTEREY	OP	CR	WD	IB	70		6 10		1 8	2000	2400
17 6	STAR-FLITE	OP	RNBT	PLY	IB	135		6 2		1 7	2300	2650
18	TOURNAMENT	OP	SKI	WD	IB	111					2400	2800
19	COLLEGIAN	OP	FSH	PLY	IB	135		6 10		1 7	2500	2900
19 6	BONIFAY	OP	CR	WD	OB			7 5	1050		2350	2700
19 6	BONIFAY	OP	CR	PLY	IB	70		7 5		1 7	2650	3100
19 6	SANIBEL-ISLANDER	OP	RNBT	PLY	IB	135		7 5		1 7	2950	3450
1960 BOATS												
17 6	AQUA-SPECIAL	OP	SKI	WD	IB	135					2350	2750
17 6	DELUXE	OP	RNBT	WD	OB						2600	3050
17 6	INTERNATIONAL	OP	SKI	WD	IB	215					2450	2900
17 6	MONTEREY	OP	CR	WD	OB						2100	2500
17 6	MONTEREY	OP	CR	WD	IB	70					2100	2500
17 6	PANTHER DELUXE	OP	RNBT	WD	IB	70					2350	2750
17 6	PANTHER SPECIAL	OP	RNBT	WD	IB	70					2100	2500
18	STAR-FLITE	OP	RNBT	WD	IB	135					2550	2950
19	COLLEGIAN	OP	FSH	WD	IB	135					2600	3000
20	BONIFAY	OP	CR	WD	OB						3300	3800
20	BONIFAY	OP	CR	WD	IB	70					3050	3550
20	SANIBEL-ISLANDER	OP	RNBT	WD	IB	135					3450	4000
1959 BOATS												
17	STAR-FLITE	OP	RNBT	WD	IB	135					2350	2750
17 6	AQUA-SKIER	OP	SKI	WD	IB	135					2350	2700
17 6	DELUXE	OP	RNBT	WD	OB						2600	3050
17 6	INTERNATIONAL	OP	SKI	WD	IB	115					2250	2650
17 6	MONTEREY	OP	CR	WD	OB						2150	2500
17 6	MONTEREY	OP	CR	WD	IB	70					2050	2450
17 6	PANTHER DELUXE	OP	RNBT	WD	IB	70					2350	2700
17 6	PANTHER SPECIAL	OP	RNBT	WD	IB	70					2050	2450
18	COLLEGIAN	OP	FSH	WD	IB	135					2400	2750
19	BONIFAY	OP	CR	WD	OB						2500	2900
19	BONIFAY	OP	CR	WD	IB	70					2350	2750
20	DEBONNAIRE	OP	RNBT	WD	IB	135					3350	3900
1958 BOATS												
17	MONTEREY	OP	CR	WD	IB	75					1950	2350
17	PANTHER		UTL	WD	IB	60					1900	2250
18	AQUA-SKIER	OP	SKI	WD	IB	75					2150	2500
18	COLLEGIAN	OP	RNBT	WD	IB	115					2400	2750
18	INTERNATIONAL SKIER	OP	SKI	WD	IB	185					2450	2850
1957 BOATS												
17			UTL	WD	IB	75					1950	2300
18	AQUA-SKIER	OP	SKI	WD	IB	75					2050	2450
18	COLLEGIAN	OP	RNBT	WD	IB	115					2350	2700
20	DEBONNAIRE	OP	RNBT	WD	IB	115					3200	3700
22			RNBT	WD	IB	115					3850	4450
22	VACATIONER DELUXE	OP	CR	WD	IB	135					3850	4500
27	BISCAYNE		SF	WD	IB	135					8150	9350
1956 BOATS												
18	AQUA-SKIER	OP	SKI	WD	IB	75					2050	2450
18	COLLEGIAN	OP	RNBT	WD	IB	115					2350	2700
20	DEBONNAIRE	OP	RNBT	WD	IB	115					3150	3650
24	VACATIONER	OP	EXP	WD	IB	115					5450	6250
26	BISCAYNE SPORTSTER		SPTCR	WD	IB	135					7300	8400
27	BELLWOOD		EXP	WD	IB	T100					9050	10300
30	DEL-RAY		EXP	WD	IB	135					13100	14800
1955 BOATS												
17 2	AQUA-SKIER	OP	SKI	WD	IB	60					1850	2200
18	COMMUTER	OP	RNBT	WD	IB	115					2300	2650
19	HURRICANE		RNBT	WD	IB	60					2250	2600
21			EXP	WD	IB	100					3400	4000
21	CLEARWATER	OP	FSH	WD	IB	75					3350	3900
24	VACATIONER	OP	EXP	WD	IB	115					5350	6150
26	NORTHPORT		SDN	WD	IB	115					9500	10800
28	MARATHON		EXP	WD	IB	115					9950	11300
34	CHESAPEAKE	HT	SDN	WD	IB	T115					22800	25400
34	KEY-WESTER	ST	EXP	WD	IB	T150					23900	26500
38	CORVETTE		HT	WD	IB	T175					36500	40500
38	SAN-JUAN	HT	EXP	WD	IB	T150					37000	41100
42			SF	WD	IB	T200					32300	35900
44	MIAMIAN	FB	CR	WD	IB	T100D					43000	47800
50	SOUTHWIND	HT	FD	WD	IB	T200D					**	**
1954 BOATS												
17 2	AQUA-SKIER	OP	SKI	WD	IB	60					1800	2150
18	COMMUTER	OP	RNBT	WD	IB	115					2250	2650
21	BOCA-RATON		UTL	WD	IB	115					3450	4050
21	POMPANO		RNBT	WD	IB	115					3500	4050
24	VACATIONER	OP	EXP	WD	IB	115					5300	6050
28	GULFSTREAM		FSH	WD	IB	115					8600	9900
28	MARATHON		EXP	WD	IB	115					9850	11200
34	CHESAPEAKE	HT	SDN	WD	IB	T115					22500	25000
34	KEY-WESTER	ST	EXP	WD	IB	T150					23500	26100
42	MIAMIAN	FB	CR	WD	IB	T100D					54800	60200
42	ROYAL-PALM FD	FB	EXP	WD	IB	T100D					46600	51200
50	SOUTHWIND	HT	FD	WD	IB	T200D					**	**
1953 BOATS												
17			RNBT	WD	IB						**	**
18			FSH	WD	IB						**	**
18	AQUA-SKIER	OP	SKI	WD	IB						**	**
21			EXP	WD	IB						**	**
25			EXP	WD	IB	125					6400	7350
28		FB		WD	IB						**	**
33	GULFSTREAM		FSH	WD	IB	T225					17500	19900
36			SDN	WD	IB						**	**
42	ROYAL-PALM FD	FB	EXP	WD	IB	T175					40400	44800
50	SOUTHWIND	HT	FD	WD	IB	T235D					**	**
52	CARIBBEAN		CR	WD	IB	T220D					68700	75500
1952 BOATS												
18	DART	OP	RNBT	WD	IB	60					2000	2350
21			EXP	WD	IB	135					3400	3950
25			EXP	WD	IB	175					6550	7550
28		FB	CR	WD	IB	T135					10500	11900
42	ROYAL-PALM FD	FB	EXP	WD	IB	T175					40000	44400
52	CARIBBEAN		CR	WD	IB	T175					62400	68600
1951 BOATS												
35			EXP	WD	IB	T135					24100	26800
1950 BOATS												
18		OP	RNBT	WD	IB						**	**
18		OP	UTL	WD	IB						**	**
19 6		OP	RACE	WD	IB						**	**
19 6		OP	UTL	WD	IB						**	**
19 6	DELUXE	OP	RNBT	WD	IB	100					2450	2850
21		HT	CUD	WD	IB						**	**
21		OP	UTL	WD	IB						**	**
25		HT	CBNCR	WD	IB						**	**
25		HT	FSH	WD	IB						**	**
28		HT	CR	WD	IB						**	**
28		FB	CR	WD	IB						**	**
28			FSH	WD	IB						**	**
28		HT	SDN	WD	IB	100					9900	11200
33		HT	SDN	WD	IB						**	**
36		HT	EXP	WD	IB						**	**
1949 BOATS												
18		OP	RNBT	WD	IB						**	**
19 6		OP	RNBT	WD	IB						**	**
21		OP	RNBT	WD	IB						**	**
25		OP	EXP	WD	OB		8 10				8100	9300
27		OP	RNBT	WD	IB						**	**
32		HT	SDN	WD	IB						**	**

LOA FT IN	NAME AND/ OR MODEL	TOP/ RIG	BOAT TYPE	-HULL- MTL TP TP	----ENGINE--- # HP MFG	BEAM FT IN	WGT LBS	DRAFT FT IN	RETAIL LOW	RETAIL HIGH
					1949 BOATS					
32		HT	SDN	WD	IB T				**	**

CORSA MARINE LTD
MIAMI FL 33054   COAST GUARD MFG ID- MPB See inside cover to adjust price for area

For more recent years, see the BUC Used Boat Price Guide, Volume 1 or Volume 2

LOA FT IN	NAME AND/ OR MODEL	TOP/ RIG	BOAT TYPE	-HULL- MTL TP TP	----ENGINE--- # HP MFG	BEAM FT IN	WGT LBS	DRAFT FT IN	RETAIL LOW	RETAIL HIGH
					1983 BOATS					
25 6	8-METER SF	FSH	FBG	DV OB	8		1560		7900	9100
25 6	8-METER SF	FSH	FBG	DV IO	260	8			7550	8650
25 6	8-METER SF	FSH	FBG	DV IB T185	8			9800	11100
25 6	8-METER SS	RNBT	FBG	DV OB	7 4	1410		7750	8900
25 6	8-METER SS	RNBT	FBG	DV IO	260	7 4			6450	7400
30	9-METER SF	FSH	FBG	DV OB	8		1900		18900	20900
30	9-METER SF	FSH	FBG	DV IB T185	8			12300	14000
30	9-METER SF	RNBT	FBG	DV IB T185	8			9450	10800
31	9-METER SS	FSH	FBG	DV IO T260	8			11500	13000
31	9-METER SS	RNBT	FBG	DV OB	8		1900		20800	23100
41	12-METER	OFF	FBG	DV OB	9 2	7990			**	**
41	12-METER	SF	FBG	DV OB	9 2	8250			**	**
41	12-METER SF	SF	FBG	DV IO T330	9 2				33500	37200
41	12-METER SF	SF	FBG	DV IB T340	9 2				46100	50600
41	12-METER SS	SPTCR	FBG	DV IO T330	9 2				29900	33300
41	12-METER SS	SPTCR	FBG	DV IB T340	9 2				43600	48400
53 3	CORSA 533	SPTCR	FBG	DV OB	13		9900		**	**
53 3	CORSA 533	SPTCR	FBG	DV IO	13				**	**
53 3	CORSA 533	SPTCR	FBG	DV IB	13				**	**
					1982 BOATS					
25 6	8-METER SF	FSH	FBG	DV OB	8		1560		7700	8850
25 6	8-METER SF	FSH	FBG	DV IO	260	8			7300	8400
25 6	8-METER SS	RNBT	FBG	DV OB	7 4	1410		7550	8650
25 6	8-METER SS	RNBT	FBG	DV IO	260	7 4			6300	7200
26	8-METER	FSH	FBG	DV IB T185	8			9550	10800
30	9-METER SF	FSH	FBG	DV OB	8		1900		18700	20800
30	9-METER SF	FSH	FBG	DV IB T185	8			11800	13400
30	9-METER SF	SF	FBG	DV IB T185	8			9950	11300
31	9-METER SS	RNBT	FBG	DV OB	8		1900		20600	22900
31	9-METER SS	RNBT	FBG	DV IO T260	8			10300	11600
41	12-METER SF	SF	FBG	DV OB	9 2	3500			**	**
41	12-METER SF	SF	FBG	DV IO T330	9 2				32200	35800
41	12-METER SF	SF	FBG	DV IB T340	9 6				42200	47300
41	12-METER SS	SPTCR	FBG	DV OB	9 2	3950			**	**
41	12-METER SS	SPTCR	FBG	DV IO T330	9 2				29200	32400
41	12-METER SS	SPTCR	FBG	DV IB T340	9 6				40900	45400
53 3	CORSA 533	SPTCR	FBG	DV OB	13		9900		**	**
53 3	CORSA 533	SPTCR	FBG	DV IO	13				**	**
53 3	CORSA 533	SPTCR	FBG	DV IB T650D	13				97900	107500
					1981 BOATS					
26	SPRINT 8-METER	OP		FBG	DV IO	370 MRCR			7550	8700
26	SPRINT 8-METER	OP		FBG	DV IO T260	MRCR			7900	9100
30	OPEN SPORTFISHERMAN	OP	FSH	FBG	DV OB	8	4500		17400	19700
30	OPEN SPORTFISHERMAN	FB	FSH	FBG	DV OB	8	4500		17500	19800
30	SPRINT 9-METER	OP	OVNTR	FBG	DV IO T260-T330	8	6400	1 6	9450	11500
40	12-METER	OP	SPTCR	FBG	DV IO T400	MRCR	9 6	9000	1 8	23400	26000
					1980 BOATS					
26	8-METER	CR		FBG	DV IO T260	7	5000		6900	7950
26	SPRINT	CR		FBG	DV OB	8	4000		11300	12800
30	9-METER	OVNTR	FBG	DV IO T350	8	6500		10200	11600
30	OPEN FISHERMAN	OPFSH	FBG	DV OB	8	5000		16600	18900
30	OPEN FISHERMAN	OPFSH	FBG	DV IB T350	8	5000		10100	11500
30	OPEN FISHERMAN	OP	OPFSH	FBG	DV IB 330	8			10900	12300
30	SPRINT	RACE	FBG	DV IO T330	8	6000		9400	10700
40	12-METER	CR		FBG	DV IB T400	9 6			36100	40100
40	12-METER	SF		FBG	DV IB T350D	9 6	10000		38700	43000
40	12-METER	WKNDR	FBG	DV IO T400	9 6	10000		24100	26800
40	12-METER SPORT FISH	SF		FBG	DV IO T350	9 6	10000		24600	27300
53	SPORT CRUISER	CR		FBG	DV IO T650	11	18000		67900	74700
53	SPORT CRUISER	CR		FBG	DV IO T650D	11	18000		95800	105500
					1979 BOATS					
30	9-METER	OP	OVNTR	FBG	DV IO T330-T370	8	6400	1 6	9850	11700
30	OPEN SPORT FISHERMAN	OP	OPFSH	FBG	DV OB	8		1 6	16300	18500
30	OPEN SPORT FISHERMAN	OP	OPFSH	FBG	DV IO T330-T370	8		1 6	10400	12500
30	SPRINT 9-METER	OP	RACE	FBG	DV IO T330-T370	8	6400	1 6	9450	11600
40	12-METER	OP	WKNDR	FBG	DV IO T400	MRCR	9 6	9000	1 8	23100	25700
					1978 BOATS					
30	OPEN SPORT FISHERMAN	TT	OPFSH	FBG	DV OB	8	4500	1 6	16000	18200
30	OPEN SPORT FISHERMAN	TT	OPFSH	FBG	DV IB T250	8	4500	1 6	9350	10600
30	PLEASURE	OP	OVNTR	FBG	DV IO T330-T370	8	6400	1 6	9850	11600
30	SPRINT PLEASURE	OP	OVNTR	FBG	DV IO T330-T370	8	6400	1 6	9850	11600
30	SPRINT RACER	OP	OFF	FBG	DV IO T	MRCR	8	5400	1 6	**	**
40	PLEASURE	OP	WKNDR	FBG	DV IO T450	MRCR	9 6	9000	1 8	25000	27800
40	RACER	OP	OFF	FBG	DV IO T	MRCR	9 6	8000	1 8	**	**
					1977 BOATS					
30	9-METER	OP	RNBT	FBG	DV IO T280	MRCR	8	6200		7600	8750
30	9-METER	OP	RNBT	FBG	DV IO T350	MRCR	8	6200		8450	9700
30	9-METER	OP	RNBT	FBG	DV IO T395	MRCR	8	6200		9500	10800
40	12-METER	OP	RNBT	FBG	DV IO T350	MRCR	9 6	9000		19400	21600
40	12-METER	OP	RNBT	FBG	DV IO T475	MRCR	9 6	9000		23300	25900
					1976 BOATS					
30	9 METER	OP	RACE	FBG	DV IO T395	MRCR	8	5980	1 5	9850	11200
30	9 METER	OP	RNBT	FBG	DV IO T280	MRCR	8	6400	1 6	7650	8800
39 10	12 METER	OP	RACE	FBG	DV IO T625	MRCR	9 4	8200	1 11	20900	32200
40 3	12 METER	OP	RNBT	FBG	DV IO T450	MRCR	9 6	9000	1 8	23300	25900
40 3	12 METER	OP	RNBT	FBG	DV IO T600	MRCR	9 6	9000	1 8	30200	33500
					1975 BOATS					
30	9 METER	OP	RNBT	FBG	DV IO T280	MRCR	8	6700	2 6	7800	9000
30	9 METER	OP	RNBT	FBG	DV IO T395	MRCR	8	6850	2 6	9600	10900
40 6	12 METER	OP	RNBT	FBG	DV IO T400	MRCR	9 6	9500	2 9	22900	25400

CORSON BOAT CO
COAST GUARD MFG ID- CBT

Call 1-800-327-6929 for BUC Personalized Evaluation Service
Or, for 1981 to 1986 boats, sign onto www.BUCValuPro.com

CORVETTE BOAT
PACIFIC DYNAMICS

Call 1-800-327-6929 for BUC Personalized Evaluation Service
Or, for 1961 to 1965 boats, sign onto www.BUCValuPro.com

COUGAR CUSTOM BOATS & EQUIP
COAST GUARD MFG ID- ZCZ

Call 1-800-327-6929 for BUC Personalized Evaluation Service
Or, for 1983 to 1989 boats, sign onto www.BUCValuPro.com

COUGAR HOLDINGS LIMITED
SOUTHAMPTON ENGLAND   See inside cover to adjust price for area

For more recent years, see the BUC Used Boat Price Guide, Volume 1 or Volume 2

LOA FT IN	NAME AND/ OR MODEL	TOP/ RIG	BOAT TYPE	-HULL- MTL TP TP	----ENGINE--- # HP MFG	BEAM FT IN	WGT LBS	DRAFT FT IN	RETAIL LOW	RETAIL HIGH
					1982 BOATS					
58	BIG-CAT	FB	MY	AL CT	IB T D GM	22 10	40000	4	**	**

COVE YACHTS
DIV OF BEAR TRAILER & M COAST GUARD MFG ID- CJY

Call 1-800-327-6929 for BUC Personalized Evaluation Service
Or, for 1980 boats, sign onto www.BUCValuPro.com

COWELL BOAT WORKS

Call 1-800-327-6929 for BUC Personalized Evaluation Service
Or, for 1959 to 1961 boats, sign onto www.BUCValuPro.com

COX MARINE LTD

Call 1-800-327-6929 for BUC Personalized Evaluation Service
Or, for 1967 to 1993 boats, sign onto www.BUCValuPro.com

COYOTE MARINE CORP
COAST GUARD MFG ID- HCN

Call 1-800-327-6929 for BUC Personalized Evaluation Service
Or, for 1978 to 1985 boats, sign onto www.BUCValuPro.com

CRAFTLINE INDUSTRIES

Call 1-800-327-6929 for BUC Personalized Evaluation Service
Or, for 1961 to 1972 boats, sign onto www.BUCValuPro.com

CRAWFORD BOAT BUILDING
COAST GUARD MFG ID- RDB
FORMERLY ROGER CRAWFORD BOAT BUILDING

Call 1-800-327-6929 for BUC Personalized Evaluation Service
Or, for 1980 to 2008 boats, sign onto www.BUCValuPro.com

CREEKMORE BOATS
DIV OF WINDSONG SAILBOATS INC   See inside cover to adjust price for area
MEDLEY FL 33178   COAST GUARD MFG ID- WSN

LOA FT IN	NAME AND/ OR MODEL	TOP/ RIG	BOAT TYPE	-HULL- MTL TP	----ENGINE--- TP # HP MFG	BEAM FT IN	WGT LBS	DRAFT FT IN	RETAIL LOW	RETAIL HIGH
1977 BOATS										
21	CREEKMORE 21	SLP	SA/RC	FBG DB OB		8	2750	1	3100	3600
21	CREEKMORE 21	SLP	SA/RC	FBG KL OB		8	2750	3 6	3100	3600
23	CREEKMORE 23	SLP	SA/RC	FBG KL OB		8	3200	3 6	3750	4400
27	CREEKMORE 27	SLP	SA/RC	FBG KC OB		10 1	5700	2 6	8050	9250
27	CREEKMORE 27	SLP	SA/RC	FBG KL OB		10 1	5700	4 6	8050	9250
34	CREEKMORE 34	CUT	SA/CR	FBG KL IB	25D VLVO	11 6	16000	5	24600	27300
39 8	CREEKMORE 39	CUT	SA/CR	FBG KL IB	40D PERK	13	25000	5 6	36000	40000
1974 BOATS										
36	UDELL ONE DESIGN	SLP	SA/OD	FBG KL		6 4		4 4	12600	14300
1973 BOATS										
36	UDELL ONE DESIGN	SLP	SA/OD	FBG KL		6 6		4 4	12300	13900
1972 BOATS										
36	UDELL ONE DESIGN	SLP	SA/OD	FBG KL		6 6		4 4	12000	13600
1971 BOATS										
36	UDELL ONE DESIGN	SLP	SA/OD	FBG KL		6 6		4 4	11700	13300
1968 BOATS										
36 4	UDELL ONE DESIGN	SLP	SA/OD	F/W KL		6 6		4 4	11400	12900

RAYMOND CREEKMORE
MIAMI FL 33133   See inside cover to adjust price for area

LOA FT IN	NAME AND/ OR MODEL	TOP/ RIG	BOAT TYPE	-HULL- MTL TP	----ENGINE--- TP # HP MFG	BEAM FT IN	WGT LBS	DRAFT FT IN	RETAIL LOW	RETAIL HIGH
1970 BOATS										
36	UDELL ONE DESIGN	SLP	SA/OD	FBG KL IB	D	6 6		4 4	4950	5650
1969 BOATS										
30	CREEKMORE 30	SLP	SA/CR	FBG KL IB	D	8 5		4 7	10400	11800
36 4	UDELL-ONE-DESIGN	SLP	SA/OD	FBG KL IB	D	6 6		4 4	4850	5600
38	CREEKMORE 38	SLP	SA/CR	FBG KC IB	D	10 7			23800	26400
38	CREEKMORE 38	SLP	SA/CR	FBG KL IB	D	10 7		4	23800	26400
45	CREEKMORE 45	SLP	SA/CR	FBG KC IB	D	12 9			40700	45200
45	CREEKMORE 45	SLP	SA/CR	FBG KL IB	D	12 9		4 6	40700	45200
1967 BOATS										
30	CREEKMORE 30	SLP	SA/CR	FBG KL IB	D	8 5		4	10100	11500
38	CREEKMORE 38	SLP	SA/CR	FBG KL IB	D	10 7		5 3	23200	25800
45	CREEKMORE 45	YWL	SA/CR	FBG CB IB	D	12 9		5 2	39700	44100
1965 BOATS										
30	CREEKMORE 30	SLP	SAIL	FBG KL IB	D	8 5		4	9950	11300
36 8	CREEKMORE 36	SLP	SAIL	FBG KC IB	D	10		4	20000	22200
42	CREEKMORE 42	SLP	SAIL	FBG KC IB	D	11 9		4 6	30200	33600
1959 BOATS										
36		SLP	SA/CR	FBG CB IB	D	9 8		3 5	18100	20200

CRENCO INC
CASTOLDI   COAST GUARD MFG ID- CRE

Call 1-800-327-6929 for BUC Personalized Evaluation Service
Or, for 1975 boats, sign onto www.BUCValuPro.com

CRESTLINER
A M F
SANFORD FL 32771   COAST GUARD MFG ID- CRL   See inside cover to adjust price for area

LOA FT IN	NAME AND/ OR MODEL	TOP/ RIG	BOAT TYPE	-HULL- MTL TP	----ENGINE--- TP # HP MFG	BEAM FT IN	WGT LBS	DRAFT FT IN	RETAIL LOW	RETAIL HIGH
1982 BOATS										
18 6	CRUSADER 1850	ST	RNBT	FBG DV OB		7 7	2090		2350	2700
18 6	CRUSADER 1855	ST	RNBT	FBG DV IO	140-185	7 7			3450	4050
18 6	RAMPAGE SL 1875	ST	RNBT	FBG DV IO	140-198	7 7	2650		3300	3900
20 2	CRUSADER 2055	ST	CUD	FBG DV IO	170-260	7 7	2784		4200	5200
20 2	CRUSADER 2085	ST	CBNCR	FBG DV IO	170-260	7 7	3320		5050	6200
20 2	CRUSADER 2085	ST	CUD	FBG DV IO	198-260	7 7	3320		4800	5750
20 2	RAMPAGE SL 2075	ST	CUD	FBG DV IO	170-260	7 7	2335		3800	4500
20 2	RAMPAGE SL 2075	ST	CUD	FBG DV IO	260	7 7	2335		4100	4800
24 2	CRUSADER 2465	OP	CUD	FBG DV IO	260	8	4100		7300	8400
24 2	CRUSADER 2465	OP	CUD	FBG DV IO	T170	8	5100		9250	10500
24 2	RAMPAGE CRUS 2475	OP	SPTCR	FBG DV IO	T170-T260	8	5305		9000	10200
24 2	RAMPAGE CRUS 2475	OP	SPTCR	FBG DV IO	T170-T260	8	5305		9450	11400
25 10	RAMPAGE CRUS 2675	OP	SPTCR	FBG DV IO	T170 OMC	8	5305		10200	11600
25 10	RAMPAGE CRUS 2675	OP	SPTCR	FBG DV IO	T260	8	6050		11900	13600
1981 BOATS										
17 1	NORDIC 1856	OP	RNBT	AL SV IO	120-140	6 10	1225		2000	2400
17 3	CRUSADER 1755	OP	RNBT	FBG DV IO	170-200	7 2	2500		2750	3400
17 3	CRUSADER 1775	OP	RNBT	FBG DV IO	140	7 2			2750	3200
17 3	RAMPAGE CRUS 1775	OP	RNBT	FBG DV IO	170-200	7 2	2500		2850	3500
17 5	CRUSADER 1840	OP	RNBT	FBG DV OB		7 3	1550		1800	2150
17 8	CRUSADER 1845	OP	RNBT	FBG DV IO	140-230	7 3			3050	3800
19 4	CRUSADER 1945	OP	RNBT	FBG DV IO	170-260	7 10	3125		3800	4750
19 4	CRUSADER 2065	ST	CUD	FBG DV IO	OMC	7 10	2335		3400	4200
19 4	CRUSADER 2065	ST	CUD	FBG DV IO	185-260	7 10	2335		**	**
20 2	CRUSADER 2085	ST	CBNCR	FBG DV IO	OMC	7 7	3320		**	**
20 2	CRUSADER 2085	ST	CBNCR	FBG DV IO	185-260	7 7	3320		5050	6100
20 2	RAMPAGE SL 2075	ST	CUD	FBG DV IO	OMC	7 7			**	**
20 2	RAMPAGE SL 2075	ST	CUD	FBG DV IO	185-260	7 7	2335		3800	4700
20 5	NORDIC 2051	OP	RNBT	AL DV OB		7 8	1550		2100	2500
20 5	NORDIC 2056	OP	RNBT	AL SV IO	OMC	7 8	2800		**	**
20 5	NORDIC 2056	OP	RNBT	AL SV IO	170-200	7 8	2800		4050	4800
20 5	NORDIC 2066	OP	RNBT	AL DV IO	140	7 8			4050	4700
20 5	NORSEMAN 2081	OP	CBNCR	AL DV OB		7 8	1850		2450	2850
20 5	NORSEMAN 2086	OP	CBNCR	AL DV IO	OMC	7 8	2850		**	**
20 5	NORSEMAN 2086	OP	CBNCR	AL DV IO	170-200	7 8	2850		4650	5400
21 6	CRUSADER 2265	OP	CUD	FBG DV IO	185-260	8	3725		5600	6700
21 6	CRUSADER 2265	OP	CUD	FBG DV IO	T170-T185	8	4150		6800	7900
21 6	CRUSADER 2285	OP	CBNCR	FBG DV IO	185-260	8			6800	7800
21 6	CRUSADER 2285	OP	CBNCR	FBG DV IO	T170-T185	8	4400		7800	9000
21 8	NORSEMAN 2086	OP	CBNCR	AL DV IO	140	7 10			6800	7800
24 2	CRUSADER 2465	OP	CUD	FBG DV IO	198-260	8	4100		6950	8250
24 2	CRUSADER 2465	OP	CUD	FBG DV IO	T170-T185	8	5100		9100	10400
24 2	RAMPAGE CRUS 2475	OP	SPTCR	FBG DV IO	260	8	4100		7200	8250
24 2	RAMPAGE CRUS 2475	OP	SPTCR	FBG DV IO	330 MRCR	8	4100		7850	9050
24 2	RAMPAGE CRUS 2475	OP	SPTCR	FBG DV IO	T260	8	5305		9900	11300
24 4	CRUSADER 2485	OP	EXP	FBG DV IO	260 MRCR	8	4400		7650	8800
24 4	CRUSADER 2485	OP	EXP	FBG DV IO	T170-T185	8	5450		9600	11000
24 4	CRUSADER 2485 EXP	OP	EXP	FBG DV IO	260 OMC	8	4400		7550	8700
25 11	CRUSADER 2655	FB	CR	FBG DV IO	260	8			10800	12300
25 11	CRUSADER 2685	FB	CR	FBG DV IO	260-330	8	5850		10000	12300
25 11	CRUSADER 2685	FB	CR	FBG DV IO	T170-T260	8	6850		11900	14500
25 11	RAMPAGE CRUS 2655		EXP	FBG DV IO	T170	8			11000	12500
25 11	RAMPAGE CRUS 2675	OP	SPTCR	FBG DV IO	T260	8	6050		11800	13400
25 11	RAMPAGE CRUS 2695	OP	SPTCR	FBG DV IO	T260 MRCR	8	6050		11800	13500
1980 BOATS										
17 3	CRUSADER 775	OP	RNBT	FBG DV IO	140-185	7 2	2163		2650	3250
17 3	CRUSADER 775	OP	RNBT	FBG DV IO	198-200	7 2	2447		2850	3350
17 5	CRUSADER 880	OP	RNBT	FBG DV OB		7 3	1550		1750	2100
17 8	CRUSADER 885	OP	RNBT	FBG DV IO	140-185	7 3	2438		2900	3550
17 8	CRUSADER 885	OP	RNBT	FBG DV IO	198-230	7 3	2722		3100	3750
19 4	CRUSADER 2055	OP	RNBT	FBG DV IO	170-228	7 10	3002		3850	4500
19 4	CRUSADER 2055	OP	RNBT	FBG DV IO	230-260	7 10	3269		4150	5000
19 4	CRUSADER 995 B/R	OP	RNBT	FBG DV IO	170-228	7 10	2852		3600	4350
19 4	CRUSADER 995 B/R	OP	RNBT	FBG DV IO	230-260	7 10	3119		3900	4650
19 4	CRUSADER 995 CUDDY	OP	RNBT	FBG DV IO	170-228	7 10	2802		3550	4450
19 4	CRUSADER 995 CUDDY	OP	RNBT	FBG DV IO	230-260	7 10	3069		3850	4600
20 5	NORDIC 20	OP	RNBT	AL SV OB		7 8	1550		2050	2450
20 5	NORDIC 20	OP	RNBT	AL SV IO	140-200	7 8	2800		4000	4750

LOA FT	LOA IN	NAME AND/ OR MODEL	TOP/ RIG	BOAT TYPE	-HULL- MTL	-HULL- TP	ENGINE TP	ENGINE # HP	ENGINE MFG	BEAM FT	BEAM IN	WGT LBS	DRAFT FT	DRAFT IN	RETAIL LOW	RETAIL HIGH
		1980 BOATS														
21	6	CRUSADER 2255	OP	CBNCR	FBG	DV	IO	185-260		8		3887			6250	7550
21	6	CRUSADER 2255	OP	CBNCR	FBG	DV	IO	T120-T170		8		4174			7350	8850
21	6	CRUSADER 2255	OP	CUD	FBG	DV	IO	185-260		8		3637			5450	6600
21	6	CRUSADER 2255	OP	CUD	FBG	DV	IO	T120-T170		8		3924			6450	7750
21	6	CRUSADER 2255 FF	OP	FSH	FBG	DV	IO	185-260		8		3762			5850	7150
21	6	CRUSADER 2255 FF	OP	FSH	FBG	DV	IO	T120-T170		8		4049			6950	8400
21	8	NORSEMAN II	OP	CR	AL	SV	IO	140-200		7	10	2913			4700	5800
23	6	CRUSADER 2455	OP	CUD	FBG	DV	IO	185-260		8		4187			6700	8050
23	6	CRUSADER 2455	OP	CUD	FBG	DV	IO	T165-T170		8		4780			8200	9450
24	4	CRUSADER 2455 EXP	OP	EXP	FBG	DV	IO	260		8		4400			7550	8700
24	4	CRUSADER 2455 EXP	OP	EXP	FBG	DV	IO	T170-T200		8		5450			9500	10900
25	11	CRUSADER 2655 COM BR	FB	CR	FBG	DV	IO	260		8		5850			9950	11300
25	11	CRUSADER 2655 COM BR	FB	CR	FBG	DV	IO	T170-T260		8		6850			11700	14200
25	11	RAMPAGE CRUS 2655	OP	SPTCR	FBG	DV	IO	T170-T228		8		5454			10100	12600
25	11	RAMPAGE CRUS 2655	OP	SPTCR	FBG	DV	IO	T230-T260		8		5988			11200	13100
		1979 BOATS														
17	3	CRUSADER 775	ST	RNBT	FBG	DV	IO	140-185		7	2	2163			2600	3250
17	3	CRUSADER 775	ST	RNBT	FBG	DV	IO	198-200		7	2	2447			2850	3350
17	5	CRUSADER 880	ST	RNBT	FBG	DV	OB			7	3	1550			1750	2050
17	8	CRUSADER 885	ST	RNBT	FBG	DV	IO	140-185		7	3	2438			2900	3550
17	8	CRUSADER 885	ST	RNBT	FBG	DV	IO	198-230		7	3	2722			3100	3750
19		NORDIC 19	ST	RNBT	AL	SV	IO	120-170		7	3	1887			2750	3300
19		NORSEMAN DAY CR	ST	CR	AL	SV	IO	120-140		7	3	2087			2950	3450
19	3	CRUSADER 995	ST	RNBT	FBG	DV	IO	170-228		7	7	2802			3500	4350
19	3	CRUSADER 995	ST	RNBT	FBG	DV	IO	230-260		7	7	3069			3750	4500
19	4	CRUSADER 2055	ST	CUD	FBG	DV	IO	170-200		7	8	3002			3800	4700
19	4	CRUSADER 2055	ST	CUD	FBG	DV	IO	225-260		7	8	3215			4250	5000
19	4	CRUSADER 995 B/R	ST	RNBT	FBG	DV	IO	170-228		7	8	2852			3550	4450
19	4	CRUSADER 995 B/R	ST	RNBT	FBG	DV	IO	230-260		7	8	3119			3850	4600
21	6	CRUSADER 2255	ST	CUD	FBG	DV	IO	185-260		7	9	3887			5600	7000
21	6	CRUSADER 2255	ST	CUD	FBG	DV	IO	290	VLVO	7	9				6350	7300
21	6	CRUSADER 2255	ST	CUD	FBG	DV	IO	T120-T170		7	9	4174			6650	7700
21	6	CRUSADER 2255 FF	ST	FSH	FBG	DV	IO	185-250		7	9	3762			5800	6950
		IO 260 MRCR 6100 7000, IO 260 OMC 6100 7050, IO 260-290													6700	8000
		IO T120-T170 6900 8300														
21	8	NORDIC 22	ST	RNBT	AL	SV	IO	140-198		7	8	2463			4000	5000
21	8	NORDIC 22	ST	RNBT	AL	SV	IO	200	OMC	7	8	2809			4350	5000
21	8	NORSEMAN	ST	CUD	AL	SV	IO	140-200		7	8	2663			4400	5450
21	8	NORSEMAN II	ST	CR	AL	SV	IO	140-200		7	8	2913			4650	5750
23	6	CRUSADER 2455	ST	CUD	FBG	DV	IO	185-250		8		4187			6700	8000
		IO 260 7000 8650, IO 290 VLVO 7800 8950, IO 130D VLVO													8300	9500
		IO T120-T170 7800 9450														
23	6	CRUSADER II	ST	CR	FBG	DV	IO	185-250		8		4287			6800	8150
		IO 260 MRCR 7100 8200, IO 260 OMC 7150 8200, IO 260-290													8300	9800
		IO T120-T170 7900 9600														
23	6	CRUSADER II	HT	CR	FBG	DV	IO	185-250		8		4287			6800	8150
		IO 260 MRCR 7100 8200, IO 260 OMC 7150 8200, IO 260-290													8300	9800
		IO T120-T170 7900 9600														
25	11	RAMPAGE CRUS 2655	ST	SPTCR	FBG	DV	IO	T170-T200		8		5454			10100	12400
25	11	RAMPAGE CRUS 2655	ST	SPTCR	FBG	DV	IO	T225-T260		8		5880			11300	13400
		1978 BOATS														
17	4	CRUSADER 775	ST	RNBT	FBG	SV	IO	140-198		7	3	2450			2850	3400
17	4	MUSKIE 775	ST	RNBT	FBG	TR	IO	120-185		7	1	2400			2800	3250
17	8	CRUSADER 775 B/R	ST	RNBT	FBG	SV	IO	140-198		7	4	2590			3000	3550
19		NORDIC 19	ST	RNBT	AL	SV	IO	120-170		7	4	2150			2950	3450
19		NORSEMAN DAY CR	ST	CR	AL	DV	OB			7	4	1675			1850	2200
19		NORSEMAN DAY CR	ST	CR	AL	DV	IO	120-140		7	4	2425			3200	3750
19	3	CRUSADER 990	ST	RNBT	FBG	SV	OB			7	9	1660			1900	2250
19	3	CRUSADER 995	ST	RNBT	FBG	SV	IO	165-260		7	9	2975			3700	4550
19	4	CRUSADER 2055	ST	CUD	FBG	DV	IO	170-260		7	11	3575			4450	5350
19	4	CRUSADER 995 B/R	ST	RNBT	FBG	SV	IO	165-260		7	11	3350			4050	4950
21	6	CRUSADER 2255	OP	CBNCR	FBG	DV	IO	185-260		8					6700	8050
21	6	CRUSADER 2255	OP	CBNCR	FBG	DV	IO	T120-T170		8		5000			8400	9700
21	6	CRUSADER 2255	ST	CUD	FBG	DV	IO	185-260		8		3825			5650	6800
21	6	CRUSADER 2255	ST	CUD	FBG	DV	IO	T120-T170		8		4550			7150	8300
21	6	CRUSADER 2255 FF	ST	FSH	FBG	DV	IO	185-260		8		4175			6350	7650
21	6	CRUSADER 2255 FF	ST	FSH	FBG	DV	IO	T120-T170		8		4750			7850	9050
21	9	NORDIC 22	ST	RNBT	AL	DV	IO	140-198		7	10	2790			4400	5150
21	9	NORSEMAN	ST	CUD	AL	DV	IO	140-198		7	10	3225			5050	5850
21	9	NORSEMAN II	ST	CR	AL	DV	IO	140-198		7	10	3400			5200	6050
23	6	CRUSADER 2455	ST	CUD	FBG	DV	IO	198-260		8		4300			6900	8200
23	6	CRUSADER 2455	ST	CUD	FBG	DV	IO	T120-T170		8		4850			8300	9600
23	6	CRUSADER II	OP	CR	FBG	DV	IO	198-260		8		5200			8100	9550
23	6	CRUSADER II	OP	CR	FBG	DV	IO	T120-T170		8		5750			9550	10900
		1977 BOATS														
17	4	CRUSADER 775	ST	RNBT	FBG	SV	IO	140-190		7	3	2450			2900	3400
17	4	MUSKIE 775	ST	RNBT	FBG	TR	IO	120-175		7	1	2400			2800	3300
19		NORDIC 19	ST	RNBT	AL	SV	IO	120-170		7	4	2150			3000	3500
19		NORSEMAN DAY CR	ST	CR	AL	DV	OB			7	4	1500			1700	2000
19		NORSEMAN DAY CR	ST	CR	AL	DV	IO	120-140		7	4	2425			3250	3800
19	3	CRUSADER 990	ST	RNBT	FBG	SV	OB			7	9	1660			1850	2200
19	3	CRUSADER 995	ST	RNBT	FBG	SV	IO	165-235		7	9	2975			3750	4500
21	6	CRUSADER 2255	ST	CUD	FBG	DV	IO	165-235		8		4550			6550	7700
21	6	CRUSADER 2255	ST	CUD	FBG	DV	IO	T120-T170		8		4550			7250	8400
21	9	NORDIC 22	ST	RNBT	AL	DV	IO	140-190		7	10	3050			4700	5450
21	9	NORSEMAN II	ST	CR	AL	DV	IO	120-190		7	10	3400			5300	6150
23	6	CRUSADER 2455	ST	CUD	FBG	DV	IO	188-235		8		4850			7700	9000
23	6	CRUSADER 2455	ST	CUD	FBG	DV	IO	T120-T170		8		4850			8450	9750
23	6	CRUSADER II	ST	CR	FBG	DV	IO	188-235		8		5750			9000	10400
23	6	CRUSADER II	ST	CR	FBG	DV	IO	T120-T170		8		5750			9700	11100
		1976 BOATS														
17	1	CRUSADER 775	ST	RNBT	FBG	SV	IO	140-190		7	3	2450			2950	3450
17	5	MUSKIE 775	OP	RNBT	FBG	TR	IO	120-165		7	1	2400			2900	3400
19		NORDIC 19	ST	RNBT	AL	DV	IO	120-165		7	4	2150			3050	3600
19		NORSEMAN DAY CR	FB	CR	AL	DV	IO	120-140		7	4	2425			3350	3900
19	3	CRUSADER 990	ST	RNBT	FBG	SV	OB			7	9	1600			1800	2100
19	3	CRUSADER 995	ST	RNBT	FBG	SV	IO	165-235		7	9	2975			3800	4600
21	10	NORSEMAN II	OP	CR	AL	DV	IO	140-190		7	10	3400			5450	6300
23	6	CRUSADER 2455	ST	CUD	FBG	DV	IO	175-235		8		4222			7000	8250
23	6	CRUSADER 2455	ST	CUD	FBG	DV	IO	T120-T190		8		4222			7800	9000
23	6	CRUSADER II	OP	CR	FBG	DV	IO	175-235		8		5372			8550	10000
23	6	CRUSADER II	OP	CR	FBG	DV	IO	T120-T190		8		5372			9400	10700
		1975 BOATS														
16	7	MUSKIE 775	OP	RNBT	FBG	TR	IO	120-140		6	6	1936			2450	2900
17	1	CRUSADER 775	OP	RNBT	FBG	SV	IO	140-175		7	2	2040			2750	3350
17	1	CRUSADER 775	OP	RNBT	FBG	SV	IO	188-190		7	2	2297			2950	3400
18	4	MUSKIE 885	OP	RNBT	FBG	TR	IO	120-165		7		2075			2900	3500
19		NORSEMAN	OP	RNBT	AL	DV	IO	120-165		7	4	1884			3000	3600
19		NORSEMAN DAY CR	HT	CR	AL	DV	IO	120-140		7	4	2237			3300	3850
19	3	CRUSADER 990	OP	RNBT	FBG	SV	OB			7	9	1600			1750	2100
19	3	CRUSADER 995	OP	RNBT	FBG	SV	IO	165-245		7	9	2867			3850	4750
23	6	CRUSADER 2455		CUD	FBG	SV	IO	188-245		8		3607			6500	7900
23	6	CRUSADER 2455		CUD	FBG	SV	IO	T120-T165		8		3886			7600	9250
23	6	CRUSADER II	OP	CR	FBG	SV	IO	188-235		8		4757			8050	9750
23	6	CRUSADER II	OP	CR	FBG	SV	IO	T120-T165		8		5036			9300	11000
		1974 BOATS														
16	7	MUSKIE 775	OP	RNBT	FBG		IO	120-165		6	6	1690		8	2350	2750
17		TIGER-MUSKIE 17	ST	RNBT	AL		IO	120-165		7	1	1790		9	2600	3050
17	1	CRUSADER 775	OP	RNBT	FBG		IO	120-165		7	3	2065	1	1	2850	3350
17	1	CRUSADER 775	OP	RNBT	FBG	DV	IO	188		7	3	2065	1	1	2900	3350
18	4	MUSKIE 885	OP	RNBT	FBG		IO	120-188		7		1900		10	2900	3400
19		NORSEMAN	OP	RNBT	AL		IO	120-165		7	4	2080		11	3200	3750
19		NORSEMAN DAY CR	OP	CR	AL		IO	120-165		7	4	2080		11	3300	3850
19	3	CRUSADER 995	OP	RNBT	FBG		IO	165-245		7	9	2525	1	3	3700	4500
23	6	CRUSADER 2455	OP	CUD	FBG		IO	165-245		8		3800	1	4	6950	8150
23	6	CRUSADER 2455	OP	CUD	FBG		IO	T120-T165		8		3800	1	4	7750	8950
		1973 BOATS														
17		CRUSADER 17	ST	RNBT	FBG		IO	120-188		7	3	2065			2950	3450
17		CRUSADER 17	ST	RNBT	FBG		JT	245	OMC	7	3	2065			2750	3150
17		MUSKIE 17	OP	RNBT	FBG		IO	120-165		7	1	1845			2750	3200
17		TIGER-MUSKIE 17	ST	RNBT	AL		IO	120-165		7	1	1790			2700	3150
19		CRUSADER 19	ST	RNBT	FBG		IO	140-245		7	9	2525			3800	4600
19		NORSEMAN	ST	RNBT	AL		IO	120-165		7	4	2000			3250	3800
19		NORSEMAN DAY CR	OP	CR	AL		IO	120-165		7	4	2080			3400	4000
23		CRUSADER 23	ST	CUD	FBG		IO	165-255		8		3800			6950	8300
23		CRUSADER 23	ST	CUD	FBG		IO	T120-T165		8					7900	9150
		1972 BOATS														
17		CRUSADER 17	ST	RNBT	FBG		IO	120-188		7	3	2065			3050	3600
17		MUSKIE 17	OP	RNBT	FBG		IO	120-165		7	1	1845			2850	3350
17		NORDIC 17	ST	RNBT	AL		IO	120-140		6	10	1730			2700	3150
19		CRUSADER 19	ST	RNBT	FBG		IO	140-245		7	9	2525			3900	4750
19		NORSEMAN	ST	RNBT	AL		IO	120-188		7	4	2000			3300	4000
19		NORSEMAN DAY CR	OP	CR	AL		IO	120-165		7	4	2080			3450	4150
19		TIGER-MUSKIE 19	OP	RNBT	AL		IO	120-188		7		1930			3250	3800
23		CRUSADER 23	ST	CUD	FBG		IO	165-270		8		3800			7200	8700
23		CRUSADER 23	ST	CUD	FBG		IO	T120-T165		8		3800			8050	9350

CONTINUED ON NEXT PAGE

LOA FT	LOA IN	NAME AND/ OR MODEL	TOP/ RIG	BOAT TYPE	-HULL- MTL	-HULL- TP	ENGINE TP	ENGINE # HP	ENGINE MFG	BEAM FT	BEAM IN	WGT LBS	DRAFT FT	DRAFT IN	RETAIL LOW	RETAIL HIGH
		1971 BOATS														
16	4	APOLLO 16	ST	RNBT	FBG		IO	120-140		6	11	1740			2700	3150
17		TIGER-MUSKIE 17	ST	RNBT	AL		IO	120-140		7	1	1790			2900	3350
17	2	MUSKIE 17	ST	RNBT	FBG		IO	120-140		7	1	1845			2950	3450
18	1	CHARGER 18	ST	RNBT	FBG		IO	120-165		7	3	2065			3350	3900
19		NORSEMAN	OP	CR	AL		IO	120-140		7	4	2080			3650	4250
19		NORSEMAN	ST	RNBT	AL		IO	120-165		7	4	2000			3500	4100
23	1	CRESTLINER 23			FBG		IO	165-215		8		3000			6100	7050
23	1	CRESTLINER 23			FBG		IO	T165	MRCR	8		3000			6950	8000
		1970 BOATS														
16	4	BUCCANEER 16	ST	RNBT	FBG	DV	IO	160		6	1	1360			2350	2750
17		TIGER-MUSKIE 17	ST	RNBT	AL	TR	IO	140		7	1	1400			2700	3150
17	1	NORDIC 17	OP	RNBT	AL	DV	IO	140		6	10	1350			2650	3050
17	2	MUSKIE 17	ST	RNBT	FBG	TR	IO	140		7	1	1410			2750	3200
18	1	RAIDER 18	OP	RNBT	AL	DV	IO	160		7	3	1515			3100	3600
18	1	VIKING 18	ST	CR	AL	DV	IO	140		7	3	1615			3200	3700
19		NORSEMAN	OP	CR	AL	DV	IO	140		7	4	1750			3500	4100
19		NORSEMAN	ST	RNBT	AL	DV	IO	160		7	4	1560			3350	3900
		1969 BOATS														
16	4	BUCCANEER 16	ST	RNBT	FBG	DV	IO	160	MRCR	6	2	1310			2400	2800
17	1	NORDIC 17	OP	RNBT	AL	DV	IO	120		6	10	1300			2700	3150
17	1	TIGER-MUSKIE 17	ST	RNBT	AL	TR	IO	120		7	1	1450			2850	3300
17	2	MUSKIE 17	ST	RNBT	FBG	TR	IO	120		7	1	1410			2850	3300
17	8	RAIDER 18	OP	RNBT	FBG	DV	IO	160	MRCR			1515			3100	3600
17	8	VIKING 18	OP	CR	FBG	DV	IO	120		7	3	1515			3100	3600
19		NORSEMAN	OP	CR	AL	DV	IO	120		7	2	1950			3750	4350
19		NORSEMAN	ST	RNBT	AL	DV	IO	160	MRCR	7	2	1510			3350	3900
19		PIRATE 19	ST	CUD	FBG		IO	160	MRCR	7	11	2700			4700	5450
		1968 BOATS														
16	4	BUCCANEER V268	ST	RNBT	FBG	SV	IO	120-210		6	8	1310	1	4	2550	3100
17	1	NORDIC V178	ST	RNBT	AL	SV	IO	120		6	10	1300	1	4	2800	3250
17	8	RAIDER V288	ST	RNBT	FBG	SV	IO	120-210		7	3	1600	1	4	3250	3900
17	9	VIKING CV288	OP	CR	FBG		IO	120-210		7	3	1515	1	4	3250	3900
19		NORSEMAN	ST	RNBT	AL	SV	IO	120-160		7	4	1060	1	4	3400	3950
19		NORSEMAN DAY CR	OP	CR	AL	SV	IO	120		7	4	1300	1		3500	4100
19		PIRATE 19	ST	CUD	FBG	SV	IO	120-210		7	11	2700	1	8	4850	5700
		1967 BOATS														
16	4	DEL-RIO IMPERIAL	OP	RNBT	FBG		IO	120				1410			2700	3100
17	1	NORDIC 17	ST	RNBT	AL		IO	120				1250			2900	3400
17	7	RAIDER	ST	RNBT	FBG		IO	120-160				1700			3400	3950
19		NORSEMAN	ST	RNBT	AL		IO	120-160				1460			3700	4350
19		NORSEMAN DAY CR	OP	CR	AL		IO	120				1700			3850	4450
19		PIRATE 19	OP	CUD	FBG		IO	120-160				2700			4950	5750
		1966 BOATS														
16	4	DEL-RIO		RNBT	FBG		IO	60		6	7				3000	3500
16	4	FLYING-CREST IMPERIA		RNBT	AL		IO	60	MRCR	6	3	910			2300	2700
17	1	NORDIC 17	OP	RNBT	AL		IO	110-120		6	10	1250			2950	3400
17	2	RAIDER	ST	RNBT	FBG		IO	110-150		7					3850	4500
17	3	MARAUDER		RNBT	FBG		IO	60		7					3900	4550
19		NORSEMAN	ST	RNBT	AL		IO	110-150		7	4	1460			3750	4350
19		NORSEMAN DAY CR	OP	CR	AL		IO	110-150		7	4	1700			3950	4650
19		PIRATE 19		CUD	FBG	DV	IO	150		7	10	2700			5150	5950
		1965 BOATS														
17	2	RAIDER 17	OP	RNBT	FBG		IO	110-150							4050	4750
17	2	RAIDER EXPRESS 17	OP	EXP	FBG		IO	110-120							4100	4750
20	3	VIKING 20	OP	CR	FBG		IO	110-150							6300	7250
		1964 BOATS														
17	2	RAIDER	ST	RNBT	FBG		IO	80-110							4200	4900
18	2	CAPTAINS-GIG	OP	CR	FBG		IO	100							4950	5700
18	4	BLUEWATER	OP	CR	FBG		IO	80-110							5000	5750
18	4	BLUEWATER	HT	EXP	FBG		IO	100-110							4950	5700
20	2	VIKING 20	OP	CR	FBG		OB								1900	2300
20	2	VIKING 20	OP	CR	FBG		IO	110							6450	7450
		1963 BOATS														
18	2	CAPTAINS-GIG	OP	CR	FBG		IB	100							1700	2050
18	4	BLUEWATER	OP	CR	FBG		IO	100							5200	5950
18	4	BLUEWATER	HT	EXP	FBG		IO	100							5100	5900
20	2	EMPRESS	OP	CR	FBG		OB								1900	2300
20	2	EMPRESS	OP	CR	FBG		IO	100							6700	7650
20	2	VIKING 20	OP	CR	FBG		OB								1900	2300
20	2	VIKING 20	OP	CR	FBG		IO	100							6700	7650
		1962 BOATS														
18		BLUEWATER	OP	CR	FBG		IO	100							5250	6050
18		WILDWIND		RNBT	AL		IO	100							5100	5900
20		EMPRESS	OP	CR	FBG		OB								1900	2250
20		EMPRESS	OP	CR	FBG		IO	100							6850	7850
20		VIKING 20	OP	CR	FBG		OB								1900	2250
20		VIKING 20	OP	CR	FBG		IO	100							6850	7850

CRESTLINER INC

LITTLE FALLS MN 56345 COAST GUARD MFG ID- CRL See inside cover to adjust price for area

For more recent years, see the BUC Used Boat Price Guide, Volume 1 or Volume 2

LOA FT	LOA IN	NAME AND/ OR MODEL	TOP/ RIG	BOAT TYPE	-HULL- MTL	-HULL- TP	ENGINE TP	ENGINE # HP	ENGINE MFG	BEAM FT	BEAM IN	WGT LBS	DRAFT FT	DRAFT IN	RETAIL LOW	RETAIL HIGH
		1983 BOATS														
16	2	EXPLORER 16	OP	BASS	AL	DV	OB			6	4	850	3	2	2300	2650
16	2	NORTHSTAR 16	OP	FSH	AL	DV	OB			6	4	800			2100	2500
16	2	NORTHSTAR 16 SF	OP	FSH	AL	DV	OB			6	4	800			2200	2550
16	4	APOLLO 660	OP	RNBT	FBG	SV	OB			6	11	1050			2800	3250
17	3	CRUSADER 770 C/B	OP	RNBT	FBG	SV	OB			7	2	1300			3450	4000
17	3	CRUSADER 775 C/B	OP	RNBT	FBG	SV	IO	170-200		7	2	2500			3400	4050
18		CRUSADER 180 O/B	OP	RNBT	FBG	SV	OB			7	2	1560			4050	4700
18		CRUSADER 180 O/B	OP	RNBT	FBG	SV	IO	170-200		7	2	2525			3600	4200
18		FISH-HAWK 18	OP	BASS	AL	RB	OB			6	5	675			2000	2350
18		NORDIC 18 GLF	OP	FSH	AL	DV	OB			6	10	925			2650	3100
18		NORDIC 18 GLF	OP	FSH	AL	DV	IO	120-140		6	10	925			2700	3150
18		NORDIC 18 OPEN BOW	OP	FSH	AL	DV	OB			6	10	1150			3200	3700
18		NORDIC 18 OPEN BOW	OP	RNBT	AL	DV	IO	120-140		6	10	1150			2600	3000
18		NORDIC 18 SF	OP	FSH	AL	DV	OB			6	10	1150			3200	3700
18		NORDIC 18 SF	OP	FSH	AL	DV	IO	120-140		6	10	1150			2750	3200
19		NORDIC 19 CLOSED BOW	OP	RNBT	AL	DV	OB			7	4	1350			3750	4350
19		NORDIC 19 CLOSED BOW	OP	RNBT	AL	DV	IO	140-188		7	4	2015			3400	4000
19		NORDIC 19 OPEN BOW	OP	RNBT	AL	DV	OB			7	4	1380			3850	4450
19		NORDIC 19 OPEN BOW	OP	RNBT	AL	DV	IO	140-188		7	4	2100			3450	4100
19		NORDIC 19 SF	OP	FSH	AL	DV	OB			7	4	1380			3850	4450
19		NORDIC 19 SF	OP	FSH	AL	DV	IO	140-188		7	4	2100			3750	4450
20	2	CRUSADER 200	OP	CUD	FBG	SV	IO	185-260		7	7	2976			5050	6150
20	2	CRUSADER 200	OP	RNBT	FBG	SV	IO	185-260		7	7	2784			4650	5700
21	8	NORDIC 22	OP	RNBT	AL	DV	IO		OMC	7	8	2540			**	**
21	8	NORDIC 22	OP	RNBT	AL	DV	IO	170-200		7	8	2540			4850	5600
21	8	NORDIC 22 TRIDENT	OP	CUD	AL	DV	IO		OMC	7	8	1800			**	**
21	8	NORDIC 22 TRIDENT	OP	CUD	AL	DV	IO	170-200		7	8	1800			4500	5200
		1982 BOATS														
16	2	EXPLORER 16	OP	BASS	AL	RB	OB			6	4	850			2250	2600
16	2	EXPLORER I	OP	FSH	AL	DV	OB			6	4	720			1900	2250
16	2	NORTHSTAR 16	OP	RNBT	AL	DV	OB			6	4	800			2050	2450
16	2	NORTHSTAR 16 SF	OP	RNBT	AL	DV	OB			6	4	720			1900	2250
16	4	NORDIC 660	OP	RNBT	FBG	DV	OB			6	11	1050			2750	3150
17	1	NORDIC 18	OP	RNBT	AL	SV	IO	120-140		6	10	1225			2350	2750
17	1	NORDIC 18 OP BOW	OP	RNBT	AL	SV	OB			6	10	1150			3000	3500
17	1	NORDIC 18 SF	OP	FSH	AL	DV	OB			6	10	1225			3150	3650
17	3	CRUSADER 770 CL BOW	OP	RNBT	FBG	DV	OB			7	2	1300			3350	3900
17	3	CRUSADER 775 CL BOW	OP	RNBT	FBG	DV	IO	170-200		7	2	2500			3350	3950
18		CRUSADER 180 CL BOW	OP	RNBT	FBG	SV	OB			7	2	1560			3950	4600
18		CRUSADER 180 CL BOW	OP	RNBT	FBG	SV	IO	170-230		7	2	2525			3500	4200
18		CRUSADER 180 CL BOW	OP	RNBT	FBG	SV	IO	260	MRCR	7	2	2525			3750	4350
18		FISH-HAWK 18	OP	BASS	AL	RB	OB			6	5	675			1950	2300
18		GREAT-LAKES NORDIC	OP	RNBT	AL	DV	OB			6	10	1150			3100	3600
18		NORDIC 18 SF	OP	RNBT	AL	DV	OB			6	10	1150			3100	3600
19		NORDIC 19	OP	RNBT	AL	DV	IO	140		7	4	2100			3400	3950
19		NORDIC 19	OP	RNBT	AL	DV	IO	170-185		7	8	2850			4100	4800
19		NORDIC 19 CL BOW	OP	RNBT	AL	DV	OB			7	4	1380			3700	4300
19	4	CRUSADER 200 CUDDY	OP	CUD	FBG	DV	IO	185-260		7	10	3320			4850	5850
19	4	CRUSADER 200 RNBT	OP	RNBT	FBG	DV	IO	185-230		7	10	2835			4050	4850
19	4	CRUSADER 200 RNBT	OP	RNBT	FBG	DV	IO	260		7	10	2835			4550	5250
19	4	RAMPAGE CRUSADER 200	OP	RNBT	FBG	DV	IO	185-260		7	10	2835			4400	5400
20	5	NORDIC 2056	OP	RNBT	AL	DV	OB			7	8	1550			4900	5600
20	5	NORDIC 2056	OP	RNBT	AL	SV	IO	170-200		7	8	2800			4650	5400
21	8	NORDIC 22	OP	RNBT	AL	DV	IO		OMC	7	8	2800			**	**
21	8	NORDIC 22	OP	RNBT	AL	DV	IO	170-198		7	8	2800			4950	5750
21	9	NORDIC 22	OP	RNBT	AL	DV	IO	200	OMC	7	8	2800			5000	5750

CRI CAT

Call 1-800-327-6929 for BUC Personalized Evaluation Service
Or, for 1982 boats, sign onto www.BUCValuPro.com

CRIPE EQUIPMENT CO
SYLVAN PONTOON

Call 1-800-327-6929 for BUC Personalized Evaluation Service
Or, for 1961 boats, sign onto www.BUCValuPro.com

CRITCHFIELD MARINE INC
HASTINGS FL 32145-0716   COAST GUARD MFG ID- CHM See inside cover to adjust price for area

For more recent years, see the BUC Used Boat Price Guide, Volume 1 or Volume 2

LOA FT IN	NAME AND/ OR MODEL	TOP/ RIG	BOAT TYPE	-HULL- MTL TP	TP	---ENGINE--- # HP MFG	BEAM FT IN	WGT LBS	DRAFT FT IN	RETAIL LOW	RETAIL HIGH
_____ 1973 **BOATS** _____											
16 11	T-17			FBG	OB		7 10	1230		1700	2050
18 3	SDV-186			FBG	IO		7	2030		**	**
18 3	V-186			FBG	OB		7	1230		1750	2100
20	C-20			FBG	OB		7 7	1610		2450	2850
20	R-20			FBG	OB		7 7	1420		2250	2600
20	SDC-20			FBG	IO		7 7	2410		**	**
22 10	SDC-23			FBG	IO		8	3315		**	**
22 10	SDR-23			FBG	IO		8	3200		**	**
22 10	V-23			FBG	OB		8	2600		4000	4700
24 9	SDC-25			FBG	IO		8	3300		**	**
_____ 1972 **BOATS** _____											
16 11	T-17			FBG	OB		7 10	1230		1700	2000
18 3	SDV-186			FBG	IO		7	2030		**	**
18 3	V-186			FBG	OB		7	1230		1750	2100
20	C-20			FBG	OB		7 7	1610		2450	2850
20	R-20			FBG	OB		7 7	1420		2250	2600
20	SDC-20			FBG	IO		7 7	2410		**	**
20	SDR-20			FBG	IO		7 7	2220		**	**
22 10	SDC-23			FBG	IO		8	3315		**	**
22 10	SDR-23			FBG	IO		8	3200		**	**
24 9	SDC-25			FBG	IO		8	3300		**	**
_____ 1971 **BOATS** _____											
16 11	T-17			FBG	OB		7 10	1230		1700	2000
17 9	TC-185			FBG	OB		6 9	1450		1950	2350
18 3	SDV-186			FBG	IO	120-130	7	2030		3850	4500
20	C-20			FBG	OB		7 7	1610		2450	2850
20	F-20			FBG	OB		7 7	1220		1950	2300
20	R-20			FBG	OB		7 7	1420		2250	2600
20	SDC-20		CBNCR	FBG	IO	120-130	7 7	2410		4500	6000
20	SDR-20			FBG	IO	120-130	7 7	2220		4500	5150
22 10	SDC-23		CBNCR	FBG	IO	155-170	8	3315		7900	9150
22 10	SDR-23			FBG	IO	155-170	8	3200		6550	7600
24 2	SDC-24		CBNCR	FBG	IO	210-215	8	3565		9400	10700
_____ 1970 **BOATS** _____											
16	SDR-165		RNBT	FBG RB	IO	120	6 6	1760		3200	3750
16 10	SDT-17			FBG	IO	120	7 10			3600	4200
16 10	T-17	OP	RNBT	FBG TR	OB		7 10	1230		1700	2050
17 9	SDT-185			FBG TR	IO	120	6 9	2150		3900	4500
17 9	T-185	OP	RNBT	FBG TR	OB		6 9	1350		1900	2250
17 9	TC-185		CBNCR	FBG	OB		6 9	1450		1950	2350
18 3	R-18	OP		FBG DV	OB		7	1230		1750	2100
18 3	RX-18			FBG	OB		7	1190		1700	2050
18 3	SDR-18		RNBT	FBG DV	IO	120	7	2030		4100	4750
20	C-20			FBG DV	OB		7 7	1610		2450	2850
20	CX-20			FBG	OB		7 7	1560		2400	2800
20	R-20	OP		FBG DV	OB		7 7	1420		2250	2600
20	SDC-20		CBNCR	FBG DV	IO	120	7 7	1610		4700	5400
20	SDR-20		RNBT	FBG DV	IO	120	7 7	2220		4650	5350
22 10	SDC-23		CBNCR	FBG DV	IO	155-160	8	3315		8150	9450
22 10	SDR-23		CR	FBG DV	IO	155-160	8	3200		7100	8250
22 10	V-23		CR	FBG DV	OB		8	2250		3550	4150
27 7	SDC-28			FBG DV	IO	160	10			15800	17900
_____ 1969 **BOATS** _____											
16 1	SDV-165		RNBT	FBG	IO	125	6 6			3350	3900
16 10	SDT-17		RNBT	FBG TR	IO	125	7 6	1950	2 1	4000	4650
16 10	T-17		RNBT	FBG TR	OB		7 6	1230		1700	2050
16 10	TC-17		CBNCR	FBG	OB		7 6	1500		2000	2350
17	SDT-17		RNBT	FBG TR	IO	120	7 6	1950	2 1	4050	4700
18 2	R-18		RNBT	FBG DV	OB		7 8	1230	2 3	1800	2100
18 3	SDR-18		RNBT	FBG DV	IO	150	7	1950	2 3	4150	4850
20 2	C-20		CBNCR	FBG DV	OB		7 7	1600	2 4	2450	2850
20 2	R-20		RNBT	FBG DV	OB		7 7	1620	2 4	2500	2900
20 2	SDC-20		CBNCR	FBG DV	IO	150	7 7			6150	7050
20 2	SDR-20		RNBT	FBG DV	IO	120-150	7 7	2250	2 4	4900	5700
22 10	SDC-23		CBNCR	FBG DV	IO	160 MRCR	8	3600	3 1	9100	10300
22 10	SDC-23		CR	FBG DV	IO	160 OMC	8	3600	3 1	8000	9150
22 10	SDR-23		CR	FBG DV	IO	160 OMC	8	3300	3 1	7500	8650
22 10	SDR-23		RNBT	FBG DV	IO	160-225	8	3300	3 1	7150	8350
28 10	SDC-29			FBG DV	IO	160	9 8		3 5	15000	17000
_____ 1968 **BOATS** _____											
16 1	SDV-165		RNBT	FBG	IO	120	6 6			3450	4050
16 10			RNBT	FBG	IO	120	7 6			4150	4850
16 10	T-17	OP	RNBT	FBG TR	OB		7 6	1230	2 1	1700	2050
18 3	R-18	OP	RNBT	FBG SV	OB		7	1230	2 3	1800	2100
18 3	SDR-18	OP	RNBT	FBG SV	IO	120-160	7	1950	2 3	4300	5000
20 2	C-20	OP	CBNCR	FBG SV	OB		7 7	1610	2 4	2450	2900
20 2	R-20		RNBT	FBG SV	OB		7 7	1420	2 4	2250	2650
20 2	SDC-20		CBNCR	FBG	IO	120-160	7 7			6550	7550
20 2	SDR-20	OP	RNBT	FBG SV	IO	120-160	7 7	2250	2 4	5050	5850
22 10	CRUISEABOUT SDR-23		CBNCR	FBG	IO	155-160	8	3200	3 1	8550	9850
22 10	SDC-23		CBNCR	FBG	IO	155-160	8	3600	3 1	9400	10700

CROCE & LOFTHOUSE SAILCRAFT
C & L BOATWORKS   COAST GUARD MFG ID- CLS
FOR NEWER MODELS SEE C & L BOATWORKS

Call 1-800-327-6929 for BUC Personalized Evaluation Service
Or, for 1964 to 1973 boats, sign onto www.BUCValuPro.com

CROCKER

LOA FT IN	NAME AND/ OR MODEL	TOP/ RIG	BOAT TYPE	-HULL- MTL TP	TP	---ENGINE--- # HP MFG	BEAM FT IN	WGT LBS	DRAFT FT IN	RETAIL LOW	RETAIL HIGH
_____ 1947 **BOATS** _____											
23	STONE-HORSE		CUT	SAIL	IB		7	4500	4	8000	9200
_____ 1942 **BOATS** _____											
37			KTH	SAIL WD	KL IB		11		5	26200	29100
_____ 1939 **BOATS** _____											
32					IB					**	**
_____ 1932 **BOATS** _____											
37			KTH	SAIL WD	KL IB		11		5	36700	40800

CRON HOUSEBOAT CO
COAST GUARD MFG ID- CRH

Call 1-800-327-6929 for BUC Personalized Evaluation Service
Or, for 1968 to 1996 boats, sign onto www.BUCValuPro.com

CROSBY

Call 1-800-327-6929 for BUC Personalized Evaluation Service
Or, for 1914 boats, sign onto www.BUCValuPro.com

CROSBY AEROMARINE COMPANY

Call 1-800-327-6929 for BUC Personalized Evaluation Service
Or, for 1957 to 1973 boats, sign onto www.BUCValuPro.com

CROSBY YACHT YARD INC
OSTERVILLE MA 02655   COAST GUARD MFG ID- CRY See inside cover to adjust price for area

For more recent years, see the BUC Used Boat Price Guide, Volume 1 or Volume 2

LOA FT IN	NAME AND/ OR MODEL	TOP/ RIG	BOAT TYPE	-HULL- MTL TP	TP	---ENGINE--- # HP MFG	BEAM FT IN	WGT LBS	DRAFT FT IN	RETAIL LOW	RETAIL HIGH
_____ 1983 **BOATS** _____											
21 6	TUG BOAT	HT	PH	FBG DS	IB	50D PERK	10	8000	2 9	25300	28100
21 6	YACHT-CLUB LAUNCH	OP	LNCH	FBG DS	IB	50D PERK	10	7740	2 9	17400	19800
21 6	YACHT-CLUB LAUNCH	OP	LNCH	FBG DS	IB	52D WEST	10	7740	2 9	17000	19300
24	CROSBY-STRIPER	OP	CTRCN	FBG SV	IB	170 MRCR	8 5	5200	2 2	**	**
24	CROSBY-STRIPER	OP	CUD	FBG SV	IB	170 MRCR	8 5	5200	2 2	**	**
26 6	CRUISING TUG BOAT	HT	TRWL	FBG DS	IB	50D WEST	10 4	11000	3	42500	47300
26 6	EASTERN-RIG	HT	TRWL	FBG DS	IB	50D PERK	10 4	11000	3	42500	47500
26 6	TOUR TUG LAUNCH	OP	PH	FBG DS	IB	50D WEST	10 4		3	42900	47700
26 6	YACHT CLUB LAUNCH	OP	LNCH	FBG DS	IB	50D PERK	10 4	11000	3	29700	33000
26 6	YACHT-CLUB LAUNCH	OP	LNCH	FBG DS	IB	50D WEST	10 4	11000	3	30000	33300

CROSBY YACHT YARD INC   -CONTINUED   See inside cover to adjust price for area

LOA FT IN	NAME AND/ OR MODEL	TOP/ RIG	BOAT TYPE	-HULL- MTL TP	----ENGINE--- TP # HP MFG	BEAM FT IN	WGT LBS	DRAFT FT IN	RETAIL LOW	RETAIL HIGH

--------------------- 1983 BOATS --------------------

29 4	CANYON 30	FB	FSH	FBG DS IB		11 5	12000	2 9	**	**
29 4	CANYON 30	FB	FSH	FBG DS IB T		11 5	12000	2 9	**	**
29 4	CANYON 30	OP	SF	FBG SV IB T200D PERK	11 5	12000	2 3	68500	75200
29 4	CANYON 30	OP	SPTCR	FBG SV IB T340 MRCR	11 5	12000	2 3	49100	54000
29 4	HAWK 29	ST	CUD	FBG DS IB 300D CAT	11 5	12000	2 9	64600	71000
29 4	HAWK 29	ST	CUD	FBG DS IB T340 MRCR	11 5	12000	2 9	49100	54000
29 4	HAWK 29	ST	CUD	FBG DS IB T200D PERK	11 5	12000	2 9	68700	75500
29 4	HAWK 29	OP	RNBT	FBG DS IB T340 MRCR	11 4	12000	2 9	48100	52900
29 4	HAWK 29	OP	RNBT	FBG DS IB T200D PERK	11 4	12000	2 9	67100	73700
29 4	HAWK 29	OP	RNBT	FBG SV IB 300D CAT	11 5	12000	2	63300	69600
29 4	HAWK 29	OP	SF	FBG SV IB T200D PERK	11 5	12000	2	68500	75200

--------------------- 1982 BOATS --------------------

21 6	YACHT CLUB LAUNCH	OP	LNCH	FBG DS IB 36D PERK	10	7740	2 9	16200	18400
26 6	TOUR TUG LAUNCH	HT	LNCH	FBG DS IB 36D PERK	10 4	11000	3	28100	31200
29 4	CANYON 30	ST	FSH	FBG DV IB T330 MRCR	11 4	12000	2 3	51600	56900
29 4	CANYON 30	ST	FSH	FBG DV IB T200D PERK	11 4	12000	2 3	65900	72500

--------------------- 1981 BOATS --------------------

21 6	TUG BOAT	HT	PH	FBG DS IB 50D PERK	10	8000	2 9	23400	26000
21 6	YACHT CLUB LAUNCH	OP	LNCH	FBG DS IB 50D PERK	10	7740	2 9	16100	18200
26 6	CRUISING TUG BOAT	HT	TRWL	FBG DS IB 65D PERK	10 4	11000	3	39700	44100
26 6	TUG BOAT	HT	PH	FBG DS IB 130D PERK	10 4	14000	3 2	53400	58700
26 6	TUG BOAT	HT	PH	FBG DS IB T130D PERK	10 4	15000	3 4	59000	64800

--------------------- 1980 BOATS --------------------

21 6	TUG BOAT	HT	PH	FBG DS IB 50D PERK	10	8000	2 9	22500	25000
21 6	YACHT CLUB LAUNCH	OP	LNCH	FBG DS IB 50D PERK	10	7740	2 9	15500	17600
26 6	CRUISING TUG BOAT	HT	TRWL	FBG DS IB 65D PERK	10 4	11000	3	38200	42500
26 6	TUG BOAT	HT	PH	FBG DS IB 130D PERK	10 4	14000	3 2	51300	56400
26 6	TUG BOAT	HT	PH	FBG DS IB T130D PERK	10 4	15000	3 4	56700	62400

--------------------- 1979 BOATS --------------------

21 6	TUG BOAT	HT	PH	FBG DS IB 50D PERK	10	8000	2 9	21700	24100
21 6	YACHT CLUB LAUNCH	OP	LNCH	FBG DS IB 50D PERK	10	7740	2 9	14900	16900
26 6	CRUISING TUG BOAT	HT	TRWL	FBG DS IB 65D PERK	10 4	11000	3	36800	40900
26 6	TUG BOAT	HT	PH	FBG DS IB 130D PERK	10 4	14000	3 2	49400	54300
26 6	TUG BOAT	HT	PH	FBG DS IB T130D PERK	10 4	15000	3 4	54600	60000

--------------------- 1978 BOATS --------------------

| 25 | WIANNO-SR KNOCKABOUT | GAF | SA/OD | P/M KC OB | 8 | 3900 | 2 6 | 12400 | 14100 |

--------------------- 1976 BOATS --------------------

| 25 | WIANNO-SR KNOCKABOUT | GAF | SA/OD | P/M KC OB | 8 | 3900 | 2 6 | 11500 | 13100 |

--------------------- 1975 BOATS --------------------

| 25 | WIANNO-SR KNOCKABOUT | GAF | SA/OD | P/M KC OB | 8 | 3900 | 2 6 | 11200 | 12800 |

--------------------- 1974 BOATS --------------------

| 25 | WIANNO-SR KNOCKABOUT | GAF | SA/OD | P/M KC OB | 8 | 3900 | 2 6 | 10900 | 12400 |

--------------------- 1973 BOATS --------------------

| 25 | WIANNO-SR KNOCKABOUT | GAF | SA/OD | P/M KC OB | 8 | 3900 | 2 6 | 10600 | 12100 |

--------------------- 1972 BOATS --------------------

| 25 | WIANNO-SR KNOCKABOUT | GAF | SA/OD | P/M KC OB | 8 | 3900 | 2 6 | 10300 | 11800 |

--------------------- 1971 BOATS --------------------

| 25 | WIANNO-SR KNOCKABOUT | GAF | SA/OD | P/M KC OB | 8 | 3900 | 2 6 | 10100 | 11500 |

--------------------- 1970 BOATS --------------------

| 24 | CROSBY-STRIPER | OP | EXP | WD SV IB 150 PALM | 8 4 | 5000 | 2 2 | ** | ** |
| 25 | WIANNO-SR KNOCKABOUT | GAF | SA/OD | WD KC OB | 8 | 3850 | 2 6 | 9750 | 11100 |

--------------------- 1969 BOATS --------------------

| 25 | WIANNO-SR | | GAF | SA/OD WD KC OB | 8 | 3850 | 2 6 | 9550 | 10900 |

--------------------- 1968 BOATS --------------------

| 24 | CROSBY-STRIPER | OP | EXP | WD IB 125 CHRY | 8 4 | 5200 | 2 2 | ** | ** |
| 25 | WIANNO-SR KNOCKABOUT | GAF | SA/OD | WD KC OB | 8 | 3850 | 2 6 | 9150 | 10400 |

--------------------- 1967 BOATS --------------------

| 24 | CROSBY-STRIPER | OP | EXP | WD IB 125 | 8 4 | 5200 | 2 2 | ** | ** |
| 25 | WIANNO-SR KNOCKABOUT | GAF | SA/OD | WD KC OB | 8 | 3850 | 2 6 | 9000 | 10300 |

--------------------- 1966 BOATS --------------------

| 24 | CROSBY-STRIPER | OP | EXP | WD IB 125 | 8 4 | 5200 | 2 2 | ** | ** |
| 25 | WIANNO-SR KNOCKABOUT | GAF | SA/OD | WD KC OB | 8 | 3850 | 2 6 | 8900 | 10100 |

--------------------- 1965 BOATS --------------------

| 24 | CROSBY-STRIPER | OP | EXP | WD IB 125-150 | 8 4 | 5200 | 2 2 | ** | ** |
| 25 | WIANNO-SR KNOCKABOUT | GAF | SA/OD | WD KC OB | 8 | 3850 | 2 6 | 8800 | 10000 |

--------------------- 1964 BOATS --------------------

| 24 | CROSBY-STRIPER | OP | EXP | WD IB 120-135 | 8 4 | 5200 | 2 2 | ** | ** |
| 25 | WIANNO-SR KNOCKABOUT | GAF | SA/OD | WD KC OB | 8 | 3850 | 2 6 | 8650 | 9900 |

--------------------- 1961 BOATS --------------------

24	CROSBY-STRIPER	CR	P/M	IB 120	8 4		2 2	**	**
25	WIANNO-SR-KNOCKABOUT	GAF	SA/OD	WD KC OB	8	3850	2 6	8500	9800
28	SUPER-STRIPER	CR	P/M	IB T177	9 8		2 4	18600	20600
31	ALBACORE	CR	P/M	IB T135	10 6		2 6	19500	21700
34	TUNA	CR	P/M	IB T135	11 2		2 6	25200	28000
43	MARLIN	CR	P/M	IB T150D	12 8		3	61800	67900

--------------------- 1960 BOATS --------------------

24	CROSBY-STRIPER	SPTCR	WD	IB 120	8 4		2 2	**	**
27 9	DOLPHIN	SPTCR	WD	IB 225	9 6		2 2	14800	16800
28	SUPER-STRIPER	SPTCR	WD	IB T177	9 8		2 4	18300	20300
30 10	ALBACORE	SPTCR	WD	IB T135	10 6		2 6	19000	21100
34	TUNA	SPTCR	WD	IB T225	11 2		2 6	24900	27700
42 8	MARLIN	SPTCR	WD	IB T150D	12 8		3	56400	62000

--------------------- 1959 BOATS --------------------

24	CROSBY-STRIPER	FSH		OB	8 4			6900	7900
24	CROSBY-STRIPER	SPTCR	P/M	IB 150	8 4			**	**
27 9	DOLPHIN	SPTCR	P/M	IB 225	9 6		2 2	14900	17000
30 10	ALBACORE	SPTCR	P/M	IB T135	10 6		2 6	18900	21000
34	TUNA	SPTCR	P/M	IB T225	11 2		2 6	24500	27200
42 8	MARLIN	SPTCR	P/M	IB T150	12 8		3	49300	54100

--------------------- 1954 BOATS --------------------

21	CROSBY 21	SLP	SAIL	WD KC	6 5		2	4800	5550
24	CROSBY-STRIPER	OP	EXP	MHG IB	8 4	5200	2	**	**
25	WIANNO-SR KNOCKABOUT	GAF	SA/OD	WD KC OB	8	3850	2 6	9050	10300
29 4		SF	MHG	IB T100 GRAY	10		2 4	15700	17900
34	TUNA CRUISER	HT	FSH	MHG IB T CHRY	11 2	11944	2 6	**	**

--------------------- 1952 BOATS --------------------

24	CROSBY-STRIPER	OP	EXP	WD IB	8 4	5200	2	**	**
24	CROSBY-STRIPER	OP	UTL	WD IB	8 4	5200	2	**	**
34	TUNA CRUISER	OP	FSH	WD IB T CHRY	11 2		2 6	**	**

--------------------- 1950 BOATS --------------------

21	CROSBY 21	SLP	SAIL	WD KC	6 5		2	5150	5900
24	CROSBY-STRIPER	OP	UTL	WD IB 87-104	8	5200	1 10	**	**
25	WIANNO-SR KNOCKABOUT	GAF	SA/OD	WD KC OB	8	3850	2 6	9700	11000

N A CROSS

Call 1-800-327-6929 for BUC Personalized Evaluation Service
Or, for 1969 to 1974 boats, sign onto www.BUCValuPro.com

CROWN CUSTOM FIBERGLASS INC
COAST GUARD MFG ID- CGL

Call 1-800-327-6929 for BUC Personalized Evaluation Service
Or, for 1980 boats, sign onto www.BUCValuPro.com

CROWN MARINE INC
COAST GUARD MFG ID- CWN

Call 1-800-327-6929 for BUC Personalized Evaluation Service
Or, for 1974 to 1978 boats, sign onto www.BUCValuPro.com

CROWNLINE INC
COAST GUARD MFG ID- CRN

Call 1-800-327-6929 for BUC Personalized Evaluation Service
Or, for 1960 to 1967 boats, sign onto www.BUCValuPro.com

CRUIS ALONG INC
SOLOMONS MD 20688   COAST GUARD MFG ID- CSA See inside cover to adjust price for area
                           FORMERLY M M DAVIS & SONS INC

LOA FT IN	NAME AND/ OR MODEL	TOP/ RIG	BOAT TYPE	-HULL- MTL TP	----ENGINE--- TP # HP MFG	BEAM FT IN	WGT LBS	DRAFT FT IN	RETAIL LOW	RETAIL HIGH

--------------------- 1974 BOATS --------------------

| 31 | | | SDN | WD | IB T215 | 12 6 | 9219 | 2 6 | 8550 | 9800 |
| 36 | | | SDN | WD | IB T215 | 12 6 | 14000 | 2 7 | 14500 | 16500 |

--------------------- 1973 BOATS --------------------

31			FB	SDNSF WD	IB 250-330	12 6	9219	2 6	7200	8500
31			FB	SDNSF WD	IB T215-T330	12 6	11122	2 6	8800	10600
36			FB	SDN WD	IB T215 WAUK	12 6	14000	2 7	13700	15600
	IB T225 CHRY 13800			15600, IB T250 CHRY 13900	15800, IB T255 WAUK		14200		16100	
	IB T330 CHRY 14600			16500						

| 38 | YACHT | | | DCMY WD SV IB T330 | 13 6 | 20000 | 2 6 | 19300 | 21400 |

--------------------- 1972 BOATS --------------------

36	SIERRA			SDN WD	IB T225 CHRY 12 6 12400	2 6	12500		14200	
	IB T250 CHRY 12600			14400, IB T280 CHRY 12800	14500, IB T330 CHRY		13100		14900	
	IB T375 CHRY 13400			15200						

| 36 | SIERRA | | | FB SDN WD | IB T225 CHRY 12 6 | 2 6 | 12000 | | 13700 | |
| | IB T250 CHRY 12100 | | | 13800, IB T280 CHRY 12300 | 14000, IB T330 CHRY | | 12600 | | 14300 | |

186   CONTINUED ON NEXT PAGE   96th ed. - Vol. III

CRUIS ALONG INC   -CONTINUED   See inside cover to adjust price for area

LOA FT IN	NAME AND/ OR MODEL	TOP/ RIG	BOAT TYPE	HULL MTL TP	ENGINE TP # HP	MFG	BEAM FT IN	WGT LDS	DRAFT FT IN	RETAIL LOW	RETAIL HIGH
1972 BOATS											
36	SIERRA	FB	SDN	WD	IB T375	CHRY	12 6		2 6	13000	14700
38			DCMY	WD	IB T225	CHRY	13 6	20000	2 6	18300	20300
38					IB T250	CHRY				18300	20300
38					IB T280	CHRY				18400	20400
38					IB T330	CHRY				18600	20700
38					IB T375	CHRY				18800	20900
1970 BOATS											
36	ELDORADO		EXP	MHG SV	IB T225	CHRY	12 6	11000	3	10300	11700
36	ELDORADO		EXP	MHG SV	IB T260	CHRY	12 6	11000	3	10400	11900
36	ELDORADO		EXP	MHG SV	IB T300	CHRY	12 6	11000	3	10600	12000
36	SIERRA		SDN	MHG SV	IB T225	CHRY	12 6	11000	3	10400	11800
36	SIERRA		SDN	MHG SV	IB T260	CHRY	12 6	11000	3	10500	12000
36	SIERRA		SDN	MHG SV	IB T300	CHRY	12 6	11000	3	10700	12200
38			DC	MHG SV	IB T225	CHRY	13 6	20000	3 6	16700	18900
38			DC	MHG SV	IB T260	CHRY	13 6	20000	3 6	16700	19000
38			DC	MHG SV	IB T300	CHRY	13 6	20000	3 6	16800	19100
1969 BOATS											
33	ELDORADO		EXP	WD SV	IB 210	CHRY	12 6	11000	2 6	8050	9250
33	SIERRA		SDN	WD SV	IB 210	CHRY	12 6	11000	2 6	8400	9650
36	ELDORADO		EXP	MHG SV	IB T210	CHRY	12 6	11000	3	9950	11300
36	ELDORADO		EXP	MHG SV	IB T260	CHRY	12 6	11000	3	10100	11500
36	ELDORADO		EXP	MHG SV	IB T300	CHRY	12 6	11000	3	10200	11600
36	SIERRA		SDN	WD SV	IB 210	CHRY	12 6	13000	2 6	10800	12300
36	SIERRA		SDN	MHG SV	IB T210	CHRY	12 6	11000	3	10000	11400
36	SIERRA		SDN	MHG SV	IB T260	CHRY	12 6	11000	3	10200	11600
36	SIERRA		SDN	MHG SV	IB T300	CHRY	12 6	11000	3	10400	11800
38			DC	MHG SV	IB T210	CHRY	13 6	20000	3 6	16100	18300
38			DC	MHG SV	IB T260	CHRY	13 6	20000	3 6	16200	18400
38			DC	MHG SV	IB T300	CHRY	13 6	20000	3 6	16300	18500
38	DC MOTOR YACHT		DCMY	WD	IB 210	CHRY	13 6	20000	2 6	15300	17400
38	SEDAN CRUISER		SDN	WD SV	IB 210	CHRY	13 6	20000	2 6	15100	17200
38	SPORTFISH		SF	WD SV	IB 210	CHRY	13 6	20000	2 6	15100	17200
38	SPORTFISH CRUISER	FB	SF	WD SV	IB 210	CHRY	13 6	20000	2 6	15200	17300
1968 BOATS											
33	ELDORADO		EXP	WD	IB T210-T290		12 6	11000	2 6	8300	9950
33	ELDORADO	FB	EXP	WD	IB T210-T290		12 6	11000	2 6	8300	9950
33	SIERRA		SDN	WD	IB T210-T290		12 6	11000	2 6	8900	10700
33	SIERRA	FB	SDN	WD	IB T210-T290		12 6	11000	2 6	9000	10700
36	ELDORADO		EXP	WD	IB T210	CHRY	12 6	13000	2 6	11100	12600
36	SIERRA		SDN	WD	IB T210	CHRY	12 6	13000	2 6	11100	12600
36	SIERRA		SDN	WD	IB T235		12 6	13000	2 6	11200	12800
36	SIERRA		SDN	WD	IB T300		12 6	13000	2 6	11500	13100
36	SIERRA	FB	SDN	WD	IB T210	CHRY	12 6	13000	2 6	11200	12700
36	SIERRA	FB	SDN	WD	IB T235		12 6	13000	2 6	11300	12800
36	SIERRA	FB	SDN	WD	IB T300		12 6	13000	2 6	11500	13100
38			DCMY	WD	IB T210	CHRY	13 6	20000	2 6	15300	17400
38			DCMY	WD	IB T300		13 6	20000	2 6	15600	17700
1967 BOATS											
33	ELDORADO		EXP	WD	IB T210-T290					8000	9550
33	ELDORADO	FB	EXP	WD	IB T210-T290					8050	9600
33	SIERRA		SDN	WD	IB T210-T290					7800	9500
33	SIERRA	FB	SDN	WD	IB T210-T290					7800	9600
38			DC	WD	IB T210			20000		15000	17000
38					IB T290					15100	17200
38					IB T320					15200	17300
38					IB T216D					19600	21800
38		HT	DC	WD	IB T210					15000	17000
38					IB T290					15100	17200
38					IB T320					15200	17300
38					IB T216D					19600	21800
38		FB	DC	WD	IB T210					15000	17100
38					IB T290					15200	17200
38					IB T320					15300	17400
38					IB T216D					19700	21900
1966 BOATS											
33	ELDORADO		EXP	WD SV	IB T220		12 6		2 6	7800	8950
33	ELDORADO		SDN	WD SV	IB T220		12 6		2 6	7550	8650
1962 BOATS											
26	CLIPPER 26			WD	IB 188-225					2150	2600
29	CLIPPER 29			WD	IB T188-T225					4150	4950
29	GULFSTREAM 29			WD	IB T188-T225					4150	4950
29	VENTURER 29			WD	IB T188-T225					4150	4950
33	ELDORADO			WD	IB T188-T225					5600	6550
33	GULFSTREAM 33			WD	IB T188-T225					5600	6550
1961 BOATS											
25	COURIER	CR		PLY	IB 135-225		8 11		1 11	1900	2350
25	COURIER	CR		PLY	IB T135-T225		8 11		1 11	2200	2700
29	CLIPPER	CR		P/M	IB 225		10 9		1 9	3800	4400
29	CLIPPER	CR		P/M	IB T135-T225		10 9		1 9	3950	4900
29	GULFSTREAM	SF		P/M	IB 225-240		10 9		1 9	3450	4050
29	GULFSTREAM	SF		P/M	IB T135-T188		10 9		1 9	3600	4450
29	GULFSTREAM	SF		P/M	IB T215-T225		10 9		1 9	3900	4550
29	SPORTSMAN	CR		P/M	IB 225		10 9		1 9	3800	4400
33	BLUEWATER	CR		P/M	IB T170-T225		12 6		2 6	5700	6800
33	ELDORADO CUSTOM	CR		WD	IB T170-T225		12 6		2 6	5700	6800
33	GULFSTREAM	SF		P/M	IB T170-T225		12 6		2 6	5350	6350
33	SPORTSMAN	CR		P/M	IB T170-T225		12 6		2 6	5700	6800
1960 BOATS											
28	CLIPPER			WD	IB 225-240					2900	3400
28	CLIPPER			WD	IB T109-T135					2950	3550
28	CLIPPER			WD	IB T185-T215					3200	3850
28	GULFSTREAM			WD	IB 225-240					2900	3400
28	GULFSTREAM			WD	IB T109-T135					2950	3550
28	GULFSTREAM			WD	IB T185-T215					3200	3850
31	BLUEWATER			WD	IB T109-T188					4150	5100
31	BLUEWATER			WD	IB T225-T240					4500	5250
31	BLUEWATER		SDN	WD	IB T109					4550	5200
31	BLUEWATER		SDN	WD	IB T188-T240					4950	6000
31	CUSTOM			WD	IB T109-T188					4150	5100
31	CUSTOM			WD	IB T240					4550	5250
31	GULFSTREAM			WD	IB T109-T188					4150	5100
31	GULFSTREAM			WD	IB T240					4550	5250
33	BLUEWATER	CR		P/M	IB T170-T240		12 6		2 6	5650	6750
33	ELDORADO		SDN	P/M	IB T170-T240		12 6		2 6	5950	7250
33	ELDORADO CUSTOM	CR		WD	IB T170-T240		12 6		2 6	5600	6800
33	ELDORADO GULFSTREAM	FB	SF	P/M	IB T170-T240		12 6		2 6	5250	6300
1959 BOATS											
28	CLIPPER		EXP	P/M	IB 120-225		10 1			2750	3450
28	CLIPPER		EXP	P/M	IB T95-T135		10 1			2950	3600
28	GULFSTREAM			P/M	IB 109-170		10 1			2650	3200
28	GULFSTREAM			P/M	IB 225		10 1			2850	3300
28	GULFSTREAM			P/M	IB T95-T135		10 1			2850	3500
28	GULFSTREAM	FB	CR	P/M	IB T135		10 1			3050	3550
31			SDN	P/M	IB 225		10 10			4400	5100
31			SDN	P/M	IB T109-T170		10 10			4400	5450
31			SDN	P/M	IB T225		10 10			5000	5750
31	BLUEWATER		EXP	P/M	IB 225		10 10			4700	5400
31	BLUEWATER		EXP	P/M	IB T109-T170		10 10			4750	5700
31	BLUEWATER		EXP	P/M	IB T225		10 10			5150	5950
31	BLUEWATER	FB	EXP	P/M	IB T135		10 10			4850	5550
31	CUSTOM		EXP	P/M	IB 225		10 10			4700	5400
31	CUSTOM		EXP	P/M	IB T109-T170		10 10			4750	5700
31	CUSTOM		EXP	P/M	IB T225		10 10			5150	5950
1958 BOATS											
26 9			EXP	WD	IB 109-136					2150	2600
26 9			EXP	WD	IB 225					2350	2750
26 9			EXP	WD	IB T109					2400	2800
26 9	BIMINI			WD	IB 109-136					1900	2300
26 9	BIMINI			WD	IB 225					2100	2450
26 9	BIMINI			WD	IB T95-T109					2100	2550
26 9	BIMINI			WD	IB T125					2250	2600
31	CUSTOM			WD	IB 150-225					3850	4550
31	CUSTOM			WD	IB T109-T136					4000	4700
31	CUSTOM			WD	IB T225					4300	5000
1957 BOATS											
26 9			EXP	WD	IB 100-135					2100	2550
26 9			EXP	WD	IB T100					2350	2750
26 9	BIMINI			WD	IB 100-135					1850	2300
26 9	BIMINI			WD	IB T100					2100	2500
1956 BOATS											
21 7	ROVER			WD	OB					4850	5600
21 7	SEAFARER			WD	OB					4850	5600
21 7	TROLLER			WD	OB					5600	5600
26 9			EXP	WD	IB 100-135					2050	2500
1955 BOATS											
26 9			EXP	WD	IB 100-135					2050	2500
1954 BOATS											
18 11	BUCCANEER			WD	OB					4150	4800
25 11			EXP	WD	IB 100-135					1850	2300
1949 BOATS											
21	CONVERTER			WD	IO						
21	CONVERTER	OP	EXP	PLY	OB		6 9	1500	1 6	5650	6500
1930 BOATS											
45	P L RHODES DESIGN	HT	MY		IB		11 6		3 6	**	**

CRUISE BOATS INC
OPA LOCKA FL 33054   COAST GUARD MFG ID- CCX See inside cover to adjust price for area
FORMERLY CRUISE CRAFT INC

LOA FT IN	NAME AND/ OR MODEL	TOP/ RIG	BOAT TYPE	-HULL- MTL TP	TP	----ENGINE--- # HP	MFG	BEAM FT IN	WGT LBS	DRAFT FT IN	RETAIL LOW	RETAIL HIGH
					1980 BOATS							
16 7	OPEN FISHERMAN	OP	CTRCN	FBG SV	OB			7 4	1000		1750	2100
18 6	BOW RIDER	OP	RNBT	FBG SV	OB			7 4	1200		2200	2600
18 6	CABIN CRUISER	OP	CBNCR	FBG SV	OB			7 4	1400		2450	2850
18 6	SKIPPER	OP	RNBT	FBG SV	OB			7 4	1200		2200	2600
20	CUDDY FISHERMAN	OP	FSH	FBG DV	OB			8	2200		3550	4100
20	CUDDY FISHERMAN	OP	FSH	FBG DV	IO	140		8			3900	4500
20	OPEN FISHERMAN	OP	CTRCN	FBG DV	OB			8	2200		3550	4100
20 9	BOW RIDER	OP	RNBT	FBG DV	OB			7 8	1600		2950	3450
20 9	CABIN CRUISER	OP	RNBT	FBG DV	OB			7 8	1900		3400	3950
20 9	SKIPPER	OP	RNBT	FBG DV	OB			7 8	1600		2950	3450
20 9	SKIPPER	OP	RNBT	FBG DV	IO	140		7 8			3200	3750
22	CUDDY FISHERMAN	OP	FSH	FBG DV	OB			8	2650		4650	5350
22	OPEN FISHERMAN	OP	CTRCN	FBG DV	OB			8	2400		4300	5000
23 4	SLOPE DECK	OP	CUD	FBG DV	OB			8	3200		5700	6550
23 4	SLOPE DECK	OP	CUD	FBG DV	IO			8			**	**
					1979 BOATS							
17	OPEN FISHERMAN	OP	OFSH	FBG SV	OB			7 4	1000		1750	2100
18 6	BOW RIDER	OP	RNBT	FBG SV	OB			7 4	1200		2200	2550
18 6	BOW RIDER	OP	RNBT	FBG SV	IO	120		7 4			2250	2650
18 6	CABIN CRUISER		CUD	FBG SV	OB			7 4	1400		2450	2850
18 6	SKIPPER		CUD	FBG SV	OB			7 4	1200		2200	2550
18 6	SKIPPER		CUD	FBG SV	IO	120		7 4			2050	2450
20	CUDDY CABIN		CUD	FBG SV	OB			8	2100	11	3400	3950
20	CUDDY CABIN		CUD	FBG SV	IO	140		8			3650	4250
20	OPEN FISHERMAN	OP	OFSH	FBG SV	OB			8	2400		3650	4250
20 9	BOW RIDER		RNBT	FBG SV	OB			7 8	1600		2950	3400
20 9	CABIN CRUISER		CUD	FBG SV	OB			7 8	1950		3400	3950
20 9	SKIPPER		RNBT	FBG SV	OB			7 8	1600		2950	3400
20 9	SKIPPER		RNBT	FBG SV	IO	140		7 8			3200	3750
22	CUDDY CABIN		CUD	FBG SV	OB			8	2800		4750	5450
22	CUDDY CABIN		CUD	FBG SV	IO	140		8			3350	3850
22	OPEN FISHERMAN	OP	OFSH	FBG SV	OB			8	2800		4750	5450
22	OPEN FISHERMAN	OP	OFSH	FBG SV	IO	140		8			3850	4450
23	CUDDY CABIN		CUD	FBG SV	IO	185		8			4700	5400
23	SLOPE DECK		CUD	FBG SV	OB			8	2900		5150	5900
23	SLOPE DECK		CUD	FBG SV	IO	185		8			4700	5400
					1978 BOATS							
18 6	BOW RIDER	OP	RNBT	FBG SV	OB			7 4	1200		2150	2500
18 6	CABIN CRUISER		CUD	FBG SV	OB			7 4	1400		2400	2800
18 6	CABIN CRUISER		CUD	FBG SV	IO	140		7 4	1400		2100	2450
18 6	SKIPPER		RNBT	FBG SV	OB			7 4	1200		2150	2500
18 6	SKIPPER		RNBT	FBG SV	IO	140		7 4	1200		2000	2350
18 6	V-HULL FISH	OP	FSH	FBG SV	OB			7 4	1000		1800	2150
19	V-HULL FISH	OP	FSH	FBG DV	OB			8	1750		2850	3300
20	CUDDY CABIN		CUD	FBG DV	OB			8	2100		3350	3900
20	CUDDY CABIN		CUD	FBG DV	IO	140		8	3000		3650	4250
20	V-HULL FISH	OP	FSH	FBG DV	OB			8	2400		3600	4200
20 9	BOW RIDER	OP	RNBT	FBG DV	OB			7 8	1600		2900	3350
20 9	BOW RIDER	OP	RNBT	FBG DV	IO	175		7 8	2377		3150	3650
20 9	CABIN CRUISER		CUD	FBG DV	OB			7 8	1950		3350	3900
20 9	CABIN CRUISER		CUD	FBG DV	IO	175		7 8	1950		3050	3550
20 9	SKIPPER		RNBT	FBG DV	OB			7 8	1600		2900	3350
20 9	SKIPPER		RNBT	FBG DV	IO	175		7 8	2377		3150	3650
					1977 BOATS							
16 7	CENTER CONSOLE 17	OP	OPFSH	FBG SV	OB			7 4	1000		1700	2000
18 6	BOW RIDER 19	ST	RNBT	FBG SV	OB			7 4	1200		2100	2500
18 6	BOW RIDER 19	ST	RNBT	FBG SV	IO	140		7 4			2300	2700
18 6	SHELTER CABIN 19	ST	CR	FBG SV	OB			7 4	1400		2400	2750
18 6	SHELTER CABIN 19	ST	CR	FBG SV	IO	140		7 4			2350	2750
18 6	SKIPPER 19	ST	RNBT	FBG SV	OB			7 4	1200		2100	2500
18 6	SKIPPER 19	ST	RNBT	FBG SV	IO	140		7 4			2300	2700
19	CENTER CONSOLE 19	OP	OPFSH	FBG DV	OB			8	1750		2800	3300
20	CENTER CONSOLE 20	OP	OPFSH	FBG DV	OB			8	2400		3550	4150
20	CUDDY CABIN 20	OP	CUD	FBG DV	OB			8	3050		3850	4500
20	CUDDY CABIN 20	OP	CUD	FBG DV	IO	175		8			3800	4400
20 9	BOW RIDER 21	ST	RNBT	FBG DV	OB			8	1600		2850	3350
20 9	BOW RIDER 21	ST	RNBT	FBG DV	IO	175		8			3400	3950
20 9	SHELTER CABIN 21	ST	CR	FBG DV	OB			8	1950		3350	3850
20 9	SHELTER CABIN 21	ST	CR	FBG DV	IO	175		8			3800	4450
20 9	SKIPPER 21	ST	RNBT	FBG DV	OB			8	1600		2850	3350
20 9	SKIPPER 21	ST	RNBT	FBG DV	IO	175		8			3400	3950
23	CUDDY CABIN 23		CUD	FBG DV	IO	175	OMC	8	3400		4750	5500
23	SLOPE DECK 23		CR	FBG DV	OB			8	2500		4500	5200
23	SLOPE DECK 23		CR	FBG DV	IO	175	OMC	8	3400		4750	5500
					1976 BOATS							
16 9	OPEN FISHERMAN 1700	OP	FSH	FBG SV	OB			6 9	1050	7	1750	2100
18 6	BOW RIDER 1900	ST	RNBT	FBG SV	OB			7 4	1200	7	2100	2500
18 6	BOW RIDER 1900	ST	RNBT	FBG SV	IO	120-140		7 4	1950	6	2400	2900
18 6	CABIN CRUISER 1900	ST	CR	FBG SV	OB			7 4	1400	6	2350	2750
18 6	SKIPPER 1900	ST	RNBT	FBG SV	OB			7 4	1200	7	2100	2500
18 6	SKIPPER 1900	ST	RNBT	FBG SV	IO	120-140		7 4	1950	6	2400	2900
20	CUDDY CABIN 2000	ST	CUD	FBG DV	OB			8	2100	10	3300	3800
20	CUDDY CABIN 2000	ST	CUD	FBG DV	IO	120-175		8	3050	10	3850	4650
20	OPEN FISHERMAN 2000	OP	OPFSH	FBG DV	OB			8	2400	10	3550	4100
20	OPEN FISHERMAN 2000	OP	OPFSH	FBG DV	IO	120-175		8		10	4050	4950
20 9	BOW RIDER 2100	ST	RNBT	FBG DV	OB			8	1600	7	2850	3300
20 9	BOW RIDER 2100	ST	RNBT	FBG DV	IO	120-175		8	2550	9	3450	4200
20 9	CABIN CRUISER	ST	CR	FBG DV	OB			8	1950	8	3300	3850
20 9	CABIN CRUISER	ST	CR	FBG DV	IO	120-175		8	2900	8	3900	4700
23	CUDDY CABIN 2300	ST	CUD	FBG DV	IO	120-175		8	3400		4900	5800
					1975 BOATS							
16 9	1700	OP	OPFSH	FBG SV	OB			6 9	1050		1750	2050
18 6	1900 B/R	ST	W/T	FBG SV	OB			7 4	1200		2050	2450
18 6	1900 B/R	ST	W/T	FBG SV	IO	120		7 4	1950		2400	2900
18 6	1900 B/R	ST	W/T	FBG DV	IO	130-140		7 4	1950		2600	3000
18 6	1900 CABIN CR	ST	CR	FBG SV	OB			7 4	1400		2350	2750
18 6	1900 SKIPPER	ST	W/T	FBG SV	OB			7 4	1200		2050	2450
18 6	1900 SKIPPER	ST	W/T	FBG SV	IO	120		7 4	1950		2400	2900
18 6	1900 SKIPPER	ST	W/T	FBG DV	IO	130-140		7 4	1950		2600	3000
20	2000	ST	CUD	FBG DV	OB			8	2100		3250	3800
20	2000	ST	CUD	FBG DV	IO	120-175		8	3050		4000	4850
20	2000	ST	CR	FBG DV	OB			8	2400	2 11	3500	4100
20 9	2100 CABIN CR	ST	CR	FBG DV	OB			8	1950		3250	3800
20 9	2100 CABIN CR	ST	CR	FBG DV	OB			8	2900		4000	4900
20 9	2100B/R	ST	W/T	FBG DV	OB			8	1600		2800	3250
20 9	2100B/R	ST	W/T	FBG DV	IO	120-175		8	1550		3200	3900

CRUISE-A-HOME INC
EVERETT WA 98201   COAST GUARD MFG ID- CAH See inside cover to adjust price for area

LOA FT IN	NAME AND/ OR MODEL	TOP/ RIG	BOAT TYPE	-HULL- MTL TP	TP	----ENGINE--- # HP	MFG	BEAM FT IN	WGT LBS	DRAFT FT IN	RETAIL LOW	RETAIL HIGH
					1980 BOATS							
31	CAPRICE 31	HT	HB	FBG SV	IB	T225		12			31000	34000
31	CRUSADER 31	HT	HB	FBG SV	IB	T225		12			30500	33900
40	CORSAIR 40	HT	HB	FBG SV	IB	T225		12			33600	37300
40	CORSAIR CUD 40	HT	HB	FBG SV	IB	T225		12			35600	39600
					1978 BOATS							
31		FB	HB	FBG SV	IB	T350		11 8	10000	3	29600	32900
31	CAPRICE 31	FB	HB	FBG DV	VD	325	OMC	11 8	14000	3	33400	37100
	IO 330 MRCR	34900		38800,	VD	200D-210D	34500		39200,	IO T165	MRCR	34400 38200
	VD T225-T260	35300		39500								
31		FB	HB	FBG SV	IB	T225		11 8	10000	3	27800	30800
31	CRUSADER 31	FB	HB	FBG DV	VD	325	OMC	11 8	14000	3	32500	36100
	IO 330 MRCR	34000		37800,	VD	200D-210D	33800		38400,	IO T165	MRCR	33600 37300
	VD T225-T260	34500		38700								
39 11		FB	HB	FBG SV	IB	T225		12	14000	3	32200	35700
39 11		FB	HB	FBG SV	IB	T250		12	14000	3	32300	35900
39 11	CORSAIR 40	FB	HB	FBG SV	VD	325	OMC	12	19000	2 10	39800	44200
	IO 330 MRCR	40300		44800,	VD	200D CHRY	43800		48700,	VD 210D	CAT	44800 49700
	IO T165 MRCR	39400		44300,	VD	T225 OMC	41800		46800,	VD T260	OMC	42100 46800
	VD T325 OMC	43400		48300,	VD	T105D CHRY	47100		51700,	VD T135D	CHRY	47800 52500
	VD T200D CHRY	49600		54500								
					1977 BOATS							
31	CRUISE-A-HOME		FB	HB	FBG	SV	OB	325	OMC	12	14000	3	26600	29500
	VD 200D-225D	27700		32000,	IO	T165 MRCR	27400		30500,	VD T225-T250		28500 31900
39 11	CRUISE-A-HOME		FB	HB	FBG SV	VD	325	OMC	12	14000	3	31300	34800
	VD 200D CHRY	35400		39300,	VD	225 CAT	36600		40700,	IO T165	MRCR	31400 34900
	VD T225 OMC	33200		36900,	VD	T250 OMC	33400		37100,	VD T100D CHRY		37900 42100
	VD T130D CHRY	38700		43000,	VD	T200D CHRY	40600		45200				

LOA FT	IN	NAME AND/ OR MODEL	TOP/ RIG	BOAT TYPE	-HULL- MTL	TP	TP	----ENGINE--- # HP	MFG	BEAM FT	IN	WGT LBS	DRAFT FT	IN	RETAIL LOW	RETAIL HIGH
		1976 BOATS														
31		CRUISE-A-HOME	FB	HB	FBG	SV	VD	330	CC	12		10000	3		25400	28200
31		CRUISE-A-HOME	FB	HB	FBG	SV	IO	T165	MRCR	12		10000	3		26800	29700
31		CRUISE-A-HOME	FB	HB	FBG	SV	VD	T230	OMC	12		10000	3		27800	30900
31		CRUISE-A-HOME FWC	FB	HB	FBG	SV	VD	330	CC	12		10000	3		25900	28800
		VD 100D-225D 26200 31600, IO T165 MRCR 27500 30600, VD T230 OMC													28700	31900
39	11	CRUISE-A-HOME	FB	HB	FBG	SV	VD	330	CC	12		14000	3		30000	33300
39	11	CRUISE-A-HOME	FB	HB	FBG	SV	IO	T165	MRCR	12		14000	3		30700	34200
39	11	CRUISE-A-HOME	FB	HB	FBG	SV	VD	T230	OMC	12		14000	3		32500	36100
39	11	CRUISE-A-HOME FWC	FB	HB	FBG	SV	VD	330	CC	12		14000	3		30700	34100
		VD 225D CAT 36200 40200, IO T165 MRCR 31400 34900, VD T230 OMC													33300	37000
		VD T100D NISS 37400 41600, VD T165D PERK 40500 45000														
		1975 BOATS														
31		CRUISE-A-HOME	FB	HB	FBG	SV	IB	350	MRCR	11	8	10000	3		25300	28200
31		CRUISE-A-HOME	FB	HB	FBG	SV	IO	T165	MRCR	11	8	10000	3		26500	29500
31		CRUISE-A-HOME	FB	HB	FBG	SV	IB	T225	OMC	11	8	10000	3		27500	30500
31		CRUISE-A-HOME FWC	FB	HB	FBG	SV	IB	350	MRCR	11	8	10000	3		26000	28800
		IB 225D CAT 28200 31300, IO T165 MRCR 27200 30200, IB T225 OMC													28400	31500
		IB T100D CHRY 29300 32500														
39	11	CRUISE-A-HOME	FB	HB	FBG	SV	IB	350	MRCR	12		14000	3		29500	32800
		IO T165 MRCR 30400 33800, IB T225 OMC 31700 35200, IB T225D CAT													41700	46300
39	11	CRUISE-A-HOME FWC	FB	HB	FBG	SV	IB	350	MRCR	12		14000	3		30200	33600
		IB 225D CAT 35400 39400, IO T165 MRCR 31100 34500, IB T225 OMC													32500	36100
		IB T100D CHRY 36600 40700														
		1974 BOATS														
31		CRUISE-A-HOME		HB	FBG		IO	T165	OMC	11	8	10000	3		26600	29600
31		CRUISE-A-HOME		HB	FBG		VD	T225	OMC	11	8	10000	3		27700	30800
40		CRUISE-A-HOME		HB	FBG		VD	225D	CAT	12		14000	3		36800	40900
40		CRUISE-A-HOME		HB	FBG		VD	T225	OMC	12		14000	3		34000	37800
40		CRUISE-A-HOME		HB	FBG		VD	T100D	NISS	12		14000	3		38100	42300
		1973 BOATS														
31		CRUISE-A-HOME	FB	HB	FBG	SV	VD	325		11	8	10000	3		24900	27700
39	11	CRUISE-A-HOME	FB	HB	FBG	SV	VD	325		12		14000	3		29400	32600

CRUISERS YACHTS

DIV OF KCS INTERNATIONAL INC
OCONTO WI 54153 COAST GUARD MFG ID- CRS

See inside cover to adjust price for area

For more recent years, see the BUC Used Boat Price Guide, Volume 1 or Volume 2

LOA FT	IN	NAME AND/ OR MODEL	TOP/ RIG	BOAT TYPE	-HULL- MTL	TP	TP	----ENGINE--- # HP	MFG	BEAM FT	IN	WGT LBS	DRAFT FT	IN	RETAIL LOW	RETAIL HIGH
		1983 BOATS														
20	3	BEACHCOMBER 206	ST	CUD	FBG	DV	IO	170-260		7	9	3300			4600	5550
20	3	HOLIDAY 20 207	ST	CUD	FBG	DV	IO	170-260		7	9	3500			4750	5800
20	3	HOLIDAY 20 207	HT	CUD	FBG	DV	IO	170-260		7	9	3500			4750	5800
22		BARON 222	ST	RNBT	FBG	DV	IO	185-260		8		3500			5050	5900
22		BARON 222SX	ST	RNBT	FBG	DV	IO	198-260		8		3500			5200	6200
22		HOLIDAY 22 224	ST	CR	FBG	DV	IO	198-260		8		3650			5550	6600
22		SEA-DEVIL 22 221	ST	FSH	FBG	DV	SE	155	OMC	8		3200			7150	8200
22		SEA-DEVIL 22 221	ST	FSH	FBG	DV	IO	170-188		8		3500			5600	6600
24	8	HOLIDAY 25 254	ST	CR	FBG	DV	IO	200-260		8		4500			7200	8550
24	8	HOLIDAY 25 254	ST	CR	FBG	DV	IO	T170	MRCR	8		4500			8100	9300
24	8	HOLIDAY 25 254-4	ST	CR	FBG	DV	IO	198	MRCR	8		4500			7250	8300
24	8	HOLIDAY 25 254-6	ST	CR	FBG	DV	IO	198-260		8		4500			7500	8800
24	8	HOLIDAY 25 254-6	ST	CR	FBG	DV	IO	T170	MRCR	8		4500			8350	9600
24	8	SEA-DEVIL 25 251	ST	FSH	FBG	DV	IO	185-200		8		4000			7100	8250
24	8	SEA-DEVIL 25 251	ST	FSH	FBG	DV	SE	205	OMC	8		4000			9600	10900
24	8	SEA-DEVIL 25 251	ST	FSH	FBG	DV	IO	228-260		8		4000			7300	8600
24	8	SEA-DEVIL 25 251	ST	FSH	FBG	DV	SE	T115	OMC	8		4000			9600	10900
26	1	BAR-HARBOR 264 III	ST	CR	FBG	DV	IO	260-330		9	11	6500			10900	13100
26	1	BAR-HARBOR 264 III	ST	CR	FBG	DV	IO	T170-T188		9	11	6500			11500	13200
26	1	VEE-SPORT 266 III	ST	SPTCR	FBG	DV	IO	T170-T260		9	11	6600	3		11600	14200
28	8	VILLA-VEE 288 III	FB	SDN	FBG	DV	IB	T170-T230		10	8	9500	2	9	21800	25500
28	8	VILLA-VEE 288 III	FB	SDN	FBG	DV	IB	T124D	VLVO	10	8	9500	2	9	30200	33600
32	10	ULTRA-VEE 336 II	OP	SPTCR	FBG	DV	IB	T260-T350		11	10	13000	2	9	34000	39600
32	10	ULTRA-VEE 336 II	OP	SPTCR	FBG	DV	IB	T235D	VLVO	11	10	13000	2	9	42700	47400
32	10	ULTRA-VEE 336 III	OP	SPTCR	FBG	DV	IB	T158D	VLVO	11	10	13000	2	9	40100	44600
		1982 BOATS														
20	3	BEACHCOMBER 206	ST	CUD	FBG	DV	IO	170-260		7	9	3300			4500	5450
20	3	HOLIDAY 20 207	ST	CUD	FBG	DV	IO	170-260		7	9	3500			4700	5650
20	3	HOLIDAY 20 207	HT	CUD	FBG	DV	IO	170-260		7	9	3500			4700	5650
22		BARON 222	ST	RNBT	FBG	DV	IO	170-260		8		3500			4950	5850
22		BARON 222SX	ST	RNBT	FBG	DV	IO	185-260		8		3500			5050	6050
22		HOLIDAY 22 224	ST	CR	FBG	DV	IO	198-260		8		3650			5400	6450
22		SEA-DEVIL 22 221	ST	FSH	FBG	DV	IO		OMC	8		3600			**	**
22		SEA-DEVIL 22 221	ST	FSH	FBG	DV	IO	170-185		8		3600			5600	6450
24	8	HOLIDAY 25 254	ST	CR	FBG	DV	IO	198-260		8		4500			7200	8350
24	8	HOLIDAY 25 254	ST	CR	FBG	DV	IO	130D	VLVO	8		4500			8350	9600
24	8	HOLIDAY 25 254	ST	CR	FBG	DV	IO	T170	MRCR	8		4500			8050	9250
24	8	HOLIDAY 254	ST	CR	FBG	DV	IO	200	OMC	8		4300			6950	8000
24	8	SEA-DEVIL 25 251	ST	FSH	FBG	DV	IO		OMC	8		4000			**	**
24	8	SEA-DEVIL 25 251	ST	FSH	FBG	DV	IO	170-185		8		4000			6900	8000
26	1	BAR-HARBOR 264	ST	CR	FBG	DV	IO			9	11	6500			**	**
		IO 170-260 10100 12100, IO 330 MRCR 11300 12800, IO T170 OMC													11200	12700
		IB T170 MRCR 13600 15400														
26	1	VEE-SPORT	HT	SPTCR	FBG	DV	IO	T170	OMC	9	11	6600	3		11300	12900
		IB T170 MRCR 18100 20100, IO T198 MRCR 11600 13200, IB T228 MRCR													18600	20600
		IO T230-T260 11800 14200														
26	1	VEE-SPORT 266	ST	SPTCR	FBG	DV	IO	170-260		9	11	6600	3		10200	12200
26	1	VEE-SPORT 266	ST	SPTCR	FBG	DV	IO	T170-T260		9	11	6600	3		11300	13900
26	1	VEE-SPORT 266	ST	SPTCR	FBG	DV	IO	T130D	VLVO	9	11	6600	3		14300	16300
28	8	VILLA-VEE 288	FB	SDN	FBG	DV	IB	T170-T228		10	8	9500	2	9	20800	24300
28	8	VILLA-VEE 288	FB	SDN	FBG	DV	IB	T130D	VLVO	10	8	9500	2	9	29300	32600
		1981 BOATS														
16	7	RALLY 170 B/R	ST	RNBT	FBG	DV	IO	120-185		7		2340			2550	2950
16	7	RALLY 170SX B/R	ST	RNBT	FBG	DV	IO	170-200		7		2340			2600	3100
18	6	RALLY 190 B/R	ST	RNBT	FBG	DV	IO	140-230		7	6	2650			3150	3700
18	6	RALLY 190SX B/R	ST	RNBT	FBG	DV	IO	170-260		7	6	2650			3200	3950
18	6	RALLY 190SXB/R	ST	RNBT	FBG	DV	IO	185	MRCR	7	6	2650			3200	3750
18	11	SEA-DEVIL 192	OP	CTRCN	FBG	SV	OB			7	6	1600			3250	3800
20	3	BEACHCOMBER 206	ST	CUD	FBG	DV	OB			7	9	2200			4800	5550
20	3	BEACHCOMBER 206	ST	CUD	FBG	DV	IO	170-260		7	9	3300			4450	5400
20	3	HOLIDAY 20 207	ST	CUD	FBG	DV	IO	170-260		7	9	3500			4600	5550
20	3	SEA-DEVIL 201	ST	FSH	FBG	DV	IO	170-230		8		3300			4750	5800
21	1	BONANZA 216	ST	CUD	FBG	SV	OB			8		2200			5100	5900
22		BARNEGAT 220	ST	CUD	FBG	DV	IO	170-260		8		3600			5250	6300
22		BARON 222	ST	RNBT	FBG	DV	IO	170-260		8		3500			4850	5700
22		BARON 222SX	ST	RNBT	FBG	DV	IO	198-260		8		3500			5050	6000
22		HOLIDAY 22 224	ST	CR	FBG	DV	IO	198-260		8		3650			5300	6350
22		SEA-DEVIL 221	ST	FSH	FBG	DV	IO	170-260		8		3600			5500	6650
24	8	HOLIDAY 25	ST	CR	FBG	DV	IO	198-260		8		4500			7100	8450
24	8	HOLIDAY 25	ST	CR	FBG	DV	IO	130D	VLVO	8		4500			8200	9450
24	8	HOLIDAY 25	ST	CR	FBG	DV	IO	T140-T170		8		4500			7800	9100
25	8	BAR-HARBOR 257	ST	CR	FBG	DV	IO	130D	VLVO			4600			8550	9850
25	8	BAR-HARBOR 257	ST	CR	FBG	SV	IO	198-260				4600			7750	9350
26	1	CHALET-VEE 260	FB	CR	FBG	DV	IO	260-330		9	11	6400	3	3	10400	12500
26	1	CHALET-VEE 260	FB	CR	FBG	DV	IO	T170	MRCR	9	11	6900	2	10	11500	13000
26	1	VEE-SPORT 266	ST	SPTCR	FBG	DV	IO	T170-T260		9	11	6600	3		10800	13400
26	1	VEE-SPORT 266	ST	SPTCR	FBG	DV	IO	T130D	VLVO	9	11	6600	3		14100	16000
26	1	VEE-SPORT 266 SP ED	ST	SPTCR	FBG	DV	IO	T170-T260		9	11	6600	3		11300	13900
28	8	VILLA-VEE 288	FB	SDN	FBG	DV	IB	T170-T228		10	8	9500	2	9	19900	23400
28	8	VILLA-VEE 288	FB	SDN	FBG	DV	IB	T130D	VLVO	10	8	9500	2	9	28200	31300
		1980 BOATS														
16	7	RALLY 170 B/R	ST	RNBT	FBG	DV	IO	120-170		7		2340			2550	3100
18	6	RALLY 190 B/R	ST	RNBT	FBG	DV	IO	120-230		7	6	2650			3100	3850
18	11	SPORTSMAN 192 UTL	OP	CTRCN	FBG	SV	OB			7	6	1600			3200	3700
20	3	BEACHCOMBER 206	ST	CUD	FBG	DV	OB			7	9	2200			4750	5450
20	3	BEACHCOMBER 206	ST	CUD	FBG	DV	IO	140-230		7	9	3300			4400	5350
20	3	BEACHCOMBER 206	ST	CUD	FBG	DV	IO	260		7	9	3300			4650	5650
20	3	BEACHCOMBER UTL 201	ST	CUD	FBG	DV	IO	140-230		7	9	3300			4350	5300
20	3	BEACHCOMBER UTL 201	ST	CUD	FBG	DV	IO	260		7	9	3300			4600	5600
20	3	HOLIDAY 20 207	ST	CUD	FBG	DV	IO	170-230		7	9	3500			4600	5450
20	3	HOLIDAY 20 207	ST	CUD	FBG	DV	IO	260		7	9	3500			4800	5750
20	3	HOLIDAY 20 207	HT	CUD	FBG	DV	IO	170-230		7	9	3500			4600	5450
20	3	HOLIDAY 20 207	HT	CUD	FBG	DV	IO	260		7	9	3500			4800	5750
21	1	BONANZA 216	ST	CUD	FBG	SV	OB			8		2200			5050	5800
21	1	BONANZA 216	HT	CUD	FBG	SV	OB			8		2200			5050	5800
21	1	BONANZA 216-C	ST	CAMPR	FBG	SV	IO	170-230		8		3300			4700	5550
21	1	BONANZA 216-C	ST	CAMPR	FBG	SV	IO	260		8		3300			4900	5850
21	1	BONANZA 216-C	HT	CAMPR	FBG	SV	IO	170-230		8		3300			4700	5550
21	1	BONANZA 216-C	HT	CAMPR	FBG	SV	IO	260		8		3300			4900	5850
22		BARNEGAT 220	ST	CUD	FBG	DV	IO	170-230		8		3600			5300	6400

CONTINUED ON NEXT PAGE

LOA FT	LOA IN	NAME AND/ OR MODEL	TOP/ RIG	BOAT TYPE	HULL MTL	HULL TP	ENGINE TP	# HP	MFG	BEAM FT	BEAM IN	WGT LBS	DRAFT FT	DRAFT IN	RETAIL LOW	RETAIL HIGH
		1980 BOATS														
22		BARNEGAT 220	ST	CUD	FBG	DV	IO	260		8		3600			5500	6650
22		BARNEGAT 220	HT	CUD	FBG	DV	IO	170-230		8		3600			5300	6300
22		BARNEGAT 220	HT	CUD	FBG	DV	IO	260		8		3600			5500	6650
22		BARNEGAT 220-C	ST	CAMPR	FBG	DV	IO	170-260		8		3600			5200	6450
22		BARNEGAT 220-C	HT	CAMPR	FBG	DV	IO	170-260		8		3600			5200	6450
22		BARNEGAT UTILITY 221	ST	CUD	FBG	DV	IO	170-230		8		3600			5050	6100
22		BARNEGAT UTILITY 221	ST	CUD	FBG	DV	IO	260		8		3600			5300	6400
22		BARNEGAT UTILITY 221	HT	CUD	FBG	DV	IO	170-230		8		3600			5050	6000
22		BARNEGAT UTILITY 221	HT	CUD	FBG	DV	IO	260		8		3600			5300	6400
22		HOLIDAY 22 224	ST	CR	FBG	DV	IO	198-260		8		3650			5250	6500
24	8	GRAN-BATEAU 246	ST	CR	FBG	DV	IO	198-260		8		4300			6900	8550
24	8	GRAN-BATEAU 246	ST	CR	FBG	DV	IO	130D	VLVO	8		4300			7850	9050
24	8	GRAN-BATEAU 246	ST	CR	FBG	DV	IO	T140-T170		8		5100			8550	10100
24	8	GRAN-BATEAU 246	HT	CR	FBG	DV	IO	198-260		8		4300			6900	8550
24	8	GRAN-BATEAU 246	HT	CR	FBG	DV	IO	130D	VLVO	8		4300			7850	9050
24	8	GRAN-BATEAU 246	HT	CR	FBG	DV	IO	T140-T170		8		5100			8550	10100
24	8	GRAN-BATEAU FD 249	ST	CR	FBG	DV	IO	198-260		8		4300			6700	8300
24	8	GRAN-BATEAU FD 249	ST	CR	FBG	DV	IB	130D	VLVO	8		4300			9950	11300
24	8	GRAN-BATEAU FD 249	ST	CR	FBG	DV	IO	T140-T170		8		5100			8300	9850
24	8	GRAN-BATEAU FD 249	HT	CR	FBG	DV	IO	198-260		8		4300			6700	8300
24	8	GRAN-BATEAU FD 249	HT	CR	FBG	DV	IB	130D	VLVO	8		4300			9950	11300
24	8	GRAN-BATEAU FD 249	HT	CR	FBG	DV	IO	T140-T170		8		5100			8300	9850
25	8	BAR-HARBOR 257	ST	CR	FBG	SV	IO	198-260				4600			7700	9450
25	8	BAR-HARBOR 257	HT	CR	FBG	SV	IO	198-260				4600			7700	9450
26	1	CHALET-VEE 260	FB	CR	FBG	DV	IO	260-330		9	11	6400	3	3	10300	12400
26	1	CHALET-VEE 260	FB	CR	FBG	DV	IO	T170	MRCR	9	11	6900	2	10	11400	12900
26	1	VEE-SPORT 266	ST	SPTCR	FBG	DV	IO	T170-T260		9	11	6600	3		11100	13500
28	8	VILLA-VEE 288	FB	SDN	FBG	DV	IB	T225-T228		10	8	9500	2	9	20200	22400
		1979 BOATS														
17	2	RALLY 174 B/R	ST	RNBT	FBG	SV	OB			6	9	1400			2750	3200
17	2	RALLY 174 B/R	ST	RNBT	FBG	SV	IO	140-170		6	9	2300			2400	2950
17	2	RALLY 174-SS	ST	RNBT	FBG	SV	IO	140-170		6	9	2300			2650	3250
18	11	RALLY 194 B/R	ST	RNBT	FBG	SV	OB			7	6	1600			3150	3700
18	11	RALLY 194 B/R	ST	RNBT	FBG	SV	IO	140-230		7	6	2800			3150	3800
18	11	RALLY 194-SS B/R	ST	RNBT	FBG	SV	IO	140-230		7	6	2800			3450	4150
18	11	RALLY 194-SS B/R	ST	RNBT	FBG	SV	IO	260		7	6	2800			3500	4300
18	11	SPORTSMAN 192	OP	CTRCN	FBG	SV	OB			7	6	1600			3150	3650
20	3	BEACHCOMBER 206	ST	CUD	FBG	DV	OB			7	9	2200			4800	5550
20	3	BEACHCOMBER 206	ST	CUD	FBG	DV	IO	170-230		7	9	3300			4450	5250
20	3	BEACHCOMBER 206	ST	CUD	FBG	DV	IO	260		7	9	3300			4700	5600
20	3	BEACHCOMBER 206-C	ST	CAMPR	FBG	DV	OB			7	9	2200			4700	5400
20	3	BEACHCOMBER 206-C	ST	CAMPR	FBG	DV	IO	170-230		7	9	3300			4400	5150
20	3	BEACHCOMBER 206-C	ST	CAMPR	FBG	DV	IO	260		7	9	3300			4650	5550
20	3	BEACHCOMBER UTL 201	ST	CUD	FBG	DV	OB			7	9	2200			4600	5300
20	3	BEACHCOMBER UTL 201	ST	CUD	FBG	DV	IO	170-230		7	9	3300			4250	5100
20	3	BEACHCOMBER UTL 201	ST	CUD	FBG	DV	IO	260		7	9	3300			4600	5400
20	3	BEACHCOMBER-HOLIDAY	ST	CUD	FBG	DV	IO	170-230		7	9	3500			4550	5400
20	3	BEACHCOMBER-HOLIDAY	ST	CUD	FBG	DV	IO	260		7	9	3500			4800	5750
21	1	BONANZA 216	ST	CUD	FBG	SV	OB			8		2200			5100	5850
21	1	BONANZA 216	ST	CUD	FBG	SV	IO	170-230		8		3300			4700	5500
21	1	BONANZA 216	ST	CUD	FBG	SV	IO	260		8		3300			4950	5850
21	1	BONANZA 216	HT	CUD	FBG	SV	OB			8		2200			5100	5850
21	1	BONANZA 216	HT	CUD	FBG	SV	IO	170-230		8		3300			4700	5500
21	1	BONANZA 216	HT	CUD	FBG	SV	IO	260		8		3300			4950	5850
21	1	BONANZA 216-C	ST	CAMPR	FBG	SV	OB			8		2200			5000	5750
21	1	BONANZA 216-C	ST	CAMPR	FBG	SV	IO	170-230		8		3300			4650	5450
21	1	BONANZA 216-C	ST	CAMPR	FBG	SV	IO	260		8		3300			4900	5850
21	1	BONANZA 216-C	HT	CAMPR	FBG	SV	OB			8		2200			5000	5750
21	1	BONANZA 216-C	HT	CAMPR	FBG	SV	IO	170-230		8		3300			4650	5450
21	1	BONANZA 216-C	HT	CAMPR	FBG	SV	IO	260		8		3300			4900	5850
21	1	BONANZA UTILITY 211	ST	CUD	FBG	SV	OB			8		2200			4850	5600
21	1	BONANZA UTILITY 211	ST	CUD	FBG	SV	IO	170-260		8		3300			4650	5750
21	1	BONANZA UTILITY 211	HT	CUD	FBG	SV	OB			8		2200			4850	5600
21	1	BONANZA UTILITY 211	HT	CUD	FBG	SV	IO	170-260		8		3300			4650	5750
22		BARNEGAT 220	ST	CUD	FBG	DV	OB			8		2500			5750	6600
22		BARNEGAT 220	ST	CUD	FBG	DV	IO	198-260		8		3600			5300	6550
22		BARNEGAT 220	HT	CUD	FBG	DV	OB			8		2500			5750	6600
22		BARNEGAT 220	HT	CUD	FBG	DV	IO	198-260		8		3600			5300	6550
22		BARNEGAT 220-C	ST	CAMPR	FBG	DV	IO	198-260		8		3600			5200	6450
22		BARNEGAT 220-C	HT	CAMPR	FBG	DV	IO	198-260		8		3600			5200	6450
22		BARNEGAT UTILITY 221	ST	CUD	FBG	DV	IO	198-260		8		3600			5100	6300
22		BARNEGAT UTILITY 221	HT	CUD	FBG	DV	IO	198-260		8		3600			5100	6300
22	4	MACKINAC 227	ST	CBNCR	FBG	SV	IO	198-260				4200			6600	8100
22	4	MACKINAC 227	HT	CBNCR	FBG	SV	IO	198-260				4200			6600	8100
24	8	GRAN-BATEAU 246	ST	CR	FBG	DV	IO	198-260		8		4300			6900	8450
24	8	GRAN-BATEAU 246	ST	CR	FBG	DV	IO	T140		8		5100			8550	10000
24	8	GRAN-BATEAU 246	HT	CR	FBG	DV	IO	198-260		8		4300			6900	8450
24	8	GRAN-BATEAU 246	HT	CR	FBG	DV	IO	T140-T170		8		5100			8550	10000
24	8	GRAN-BATEAU FD 248	ST	CR	FBG	DV	IB	255	MRCR	8		4300			7550	8650
24	8	GRAN-BATEAU FD 248	ST	CR	FBG	DV	IB	130D	VLVO	8		4300			9600	10900
24	8	GRAN-BATEAU FD 248	HT	CR	FBG	DV	IB	255	MRCR	8		4300			7550	8650
24	8	GRAN-BATEAU FD 248	HT	CR	FBG	DV	IB	130D	VLVO	8		4300			9600	10900
24	8	GRAN-BATEAU FD 249	ST	CR	FBG	DV	IO	198-260		8		4300			6700	8200
24	8	GRAN-BATEAU FD 249	ST	CR	FBG	DV	IO	T140-T170		8		5100			8400	9800
24	8	GRAN-BATEAU FD 249	HT	CR	FBG	DV	IO	198-260		8		4300			6700	8250
24	8	GRAN-BATEAU FD 249	HT	CR	FBG	DV	IO	T140-T170		8		5100			8400	9750
24	8	VENTURER 241	ST	CUD	FBG	DV	IO	198-260		8		4200			6700	8200
24	8	VENTURER 241	ST	CUD	FBG	DV	IO	T140-T170		8		5000			8300	9800
24	8	VENTURER 241-S	HT	SDN	FBG	DV	IO	198-260		8		4400			7150	8800
24	8	VENTURER 241-S	HT	SDN	FBG	DV	IO	T140		8		5200			8900	10400
25	8	BAR-HARBOR 257	ST	CR	FBG	SV	IO	198-260				4600			7700	9450
25	8	BAR-HARBOR 257	HT	CR	FBG	SV	IO	198-260				4600			7700	9450
26	1	CHALET-VEE 260	FB	CR	FBG	DV	IO	260-330		9	11	6900			10800	13300
26	1	CHALET-VEE 260	FB	CR	FBG	DV	IO	T170	MRCR	9	11	7500			12000	13600
28	8	VILLA-VEE 288	FB	SDN	FBG	DV	IB	T225-T228		10	8	9500			19400	21500
		1978 BOATS														
17	2	RALLY 174 B/R	ST	RNBT	FBG	SV	OB			6	9	1320			2600	3050
17	2	RALLY 174 B/R	ST	RNBT	FBG	SV	IO	140-170		6	9	1970			2350	2750
17	2	RALLY 174-SS	ST	RNBT	FBG	SV	IO	140-185		6	9	2075			2400	2850
17	2	RALLY 175	ST	RNBT	FBG	SV	IO	140-170		6	9	1970			2350	2750
17	2	RALLY 175-SS	ST	RNBT	FBG	SV	IO	140-175		6	9	2075			2400	2850
18	11	RALLY 194 B/R	ST	RNBT	FBG	SV	OB			7	6	1465			2950	3400
18	11	RALLY 194 B/R	ST	RNBT	FBG	SV	IO	140-228		7	6	2145			2900	3600
18	11	RALLY 194-SS B/R	ST	RNBT	FBG	SV	IO	170-260		7	6	2250			2950	3700
18	11	SPORTSMAN 192	OP	UTL	FBG	SV	OB			7	6	1600			2850	3300
20	3	BEACHCOMBER 206	ST	CUD	FBG	DV	OB			7	9	1955			4450	5100
20	3	BEACHCOMBER 206	ST	CUD	FBG	DV	IO	170-240		7	9	2800			4000	4900
20	3	BEACHCOMBER 206	ST	CUD	FBG	DV	IO	255-260		7	9	2800			4450	5150
20	3	BEACHCOMBER 206-C	ST	CAMPR	FBG	DV	OB			7	9	2055			4500	5150
20	3	BEACHCOMBER 206-C	ST	CAMPR	FBG	DV	IO	170-240		7	9	2900			4050	4900
20	3	BEACHCOMBER 206-C	ST	CAMPR	FBG	DV	IO	255-260		7	9	2900			4500	5150
20	3	BEACHCOMBER UTL 201	ST	CUD	FBG	DV	OB			7	9	1955			4200	4850
20	3	BEACHCOMBER UTL 201	ST	CUD	FBG	DV	IO	170-240		7	9	2800			3900	4750
20	3	BEACHCOMBER UTL 201	ST	CUD	FBG	DV	IO	255-260		7	9	2800			4350	5000
21	1	BONANZA 216	ST	CUD	FBG	SV	OB			8		2115			4850	5600
21	1	BONANZA 216	ST	CUD	FBG	SV	IO	170-240		8		2960			4400	5300
21	1	BONANZA 216	ST	CUD	FBG	SV	IO	255-260		8		2960			4800	5550
21	1	BONANZA 216	HT	CUD	FBG	SV	OB			8		2115			4850	5550
21	1	BONANZA 216	HT	CUD	FBG	SV	IO	170-240		8		2960			4400	5300
21	1	BONANZA 216	HT	CUD	FBG	SV	IO	255-260		8		2960			4800	5550
21	1	BONANZA 216-C	ST	CAMPR	FBG	SV	OB			8		2215			4950	5700
21	1	BONANZA 216-C	ST	CAMPR	FBG	SV	IO	170-260		8		3060			4500	5600
21	1	BONANZA 216-C	HT	CAMPR	FBG	SV	OB			8		2215			4950	5700
21	1	BONANZA 216-C	HT	CAMPR	FBG	SV	IO	170-260		8		3060			4500	5600
21	1	BONANZA UTILITY 211	ST	CUD	FBG	SV	OB			8		2115			4750	5450
21	1	BONANZA UTILITY 211	ST	CUD	FBG	SV	IO	170-240		8		2960			4350	5250
21	1	BONANZA UTILITY 211	ST	CUD	FBG	SV	IO	255-260		8		2960			4750	5450
21	1	BONANZA UTILITY 211	HT	CUD	FBG	SV	OB			8		2115			4750	5450
21	1	BONANZA UTILITY 211	HT	CUD	FBG	SV	IO	170-240		8		2960			4350	5250
21	1	BONANZA UTILITY 211	HT	CUD	FBG	SV	IO	255-260		8		2960			4750	5450
22		BARNEGAT 220	ST	CUD	FBG	DV	IO	185-260		8		3350			4950	6200
22		BARNEGAT 220	HT	CUD	FBG	DV	IO	185-260		8		3350			4950	6200
22		BARNEGAT 220-C	ST	CAMPR	FBG	DV	IO	185-260		8		3450			5050	6300
22		BARNEGAT 220-C	HT	CAMPR	FBG	DV	IO	185-260		8		3450			5050	6300
22		BARNEGAT UTILITY 221	ST	CUD	FBG	DV	IO	185-260		8		3350			4950	6150
22		BARNEGAT UTILITY 221	HT	CUD	FBG	DV	IO	185-240		8		3350			4950	5900
22		BARNEGAT UTILITY 221	HT	CUD	FBG	DV	IO	255-260		8		3350			5350	6150
22	4	MACKINAC 227	ST	CBNCR	FBG	SV	IO	185-260				3660			5950	7400
22	4	MACKINAC 227	HT	CBNCR	FBG	SV	IO	185-260				3660			5950	7400
24	8	GRAN-BATEAU 246	ST	CR	FBG	DV	IO	185-260		8		4340			6900	8500
24	8	GRAN-BATEAU 246	ST	CR	FBG	DV	IO	T140-T170		8		4740			8150	9450
24	8	GRAN-BATEAU 246	HT	CR	FBG	DV	IO	185-260		8		4340			6900	8500
24	8	GRAN-BATEAU 246	HT	CR	FBG	DV	IO	T140-T170		8		4740			8150	9450
24	8	GRAN-BATEAU FD 248	ST	CR	FBG	DV	IB	228	MRCR	8		4340			7200	8300
24	8	GRAN-BATEAU FD 248	HT	CR	FBG	DV	IB	228	MRCR	8		4340			7200	8300

CONTINUED ON NEXT PAGE

CRUISERS YACHTS -CONTINUED See inside cover to adjust price for area

LOA FT	LOA IN	NAME AND/ OR MODEL	TOP/ RIG	BOAT TYPE	HULL MTL	HULL TP	ENGINE TP	ENGINE # HP MFG	BEAM FT	BEAM IN	WGT LBS	DRAFT FT	DRAFT IN	RETAIL LOW	RETAIL HIGH
		1978 BOATS													
24	8	GRAN-BATEAU FD 249	ST	CR	FBG	DV	IO	185-260	8		4340			6750	8350
24	8	GRAN-BATEAU FD 249	ST	CR	FBG	DV	IO	T140-T170	8		4740			8050	9300
24	8	GRAN-BATEAU FD 249	HT	CR	FBG	DV	IO	185-260	8		4340			6750	8350
24	8	GRAN-BATEAU FD 249	HT	CR	FBG	DV	IO	T140-T170	8		4740			8050	9300
24	8	VENTURER 241	ST	CUD	FBG	DV	IO	185-260	8		4100			6550	8100
24	8	VENTURER 241	ST	CUD	FBG	DV	IO	T140-T170	8		4500			7800	9050
24	8	VENTURER 241	HT	CUD	FBG	DV	IO	185-260	8		4100			6550	8100
24	8	VENTURER 241	HT	CUD	FBG	DV	IO	T140-T170	8		4500			7800	9050
24	8	VENTURER 241-C	ST	CAMPR	FBG	DV	IO	185-260	8		4200			6650	8250
24	8	VENTURER 241-C	ST	CAMPR	FBG	DV	IO	T140-T170	8		4600			7900	9200
24	8	VENTURER 241-S	HT	SDN	FBG	DV	IO	185-260	8		4500			7250	8950
24	8	VENTURER 241-S	HT	SDN	FBG	DV	IO	T140-T170	8		4900			8500	9900
25	8	BAR-HARBOR 257	ST	CR	FBG	SV	IO	185-260			4460			7550	9300
25	8	BAR-HARBOR 257	ST	CR	FBG	SV	IO	T140-T170			4860			8900	10300
25	8	BAR-HARBOR 257	HT	CR	FBG	SV	IO	185-260			4460			7550	9300
25	8	BAR-HARBOR 257	HT	CR	FBG	SV	IO	T140-T170			4860			8900	10300
25	8	SEAFARER 258	FB	CBNCR	FBG	SV	IO	225-260			5000			10200	11900
25	8	SEAFARER 258	FB	CBNCR	FBG	SV	IO	T140-T170			5400			11200	12800
28	8	VILLA-VEE 288	FB	CR	FBG	DV	IB	T225-T228	10	8	9500			16900	19200
		1977 BOATS													
16	5	RALLY 163 B/R	ST	RNBT	FBG	TR	OB		6	6	1195			2350	2750
17	2	RALLY 174 B/R	ST	RNBT	FBG	DV	OB		6	9	1320			2550	3000
17	2	RALLY 174 B/R	ST	RNBT	FBG	DV	IO	140-175	6	9	1970			2400	2800
17	2	RALLY 175	ST	RNBT	FBG	DV	OB		6	9	1320			2550	3000
17	2	RALLY 175	ST	RNBT	FBG	DV	IO	140-175	6	9	1970			2400	2800
18	11	RALLY 190-SS B/R	ST	RNBT	FBG	DV	IO	170-235	7	6	2220			3000	3600
18	11	RALLY 194 B/R	ST	RNBT	FBG	DV	OB		7	6	1465			2900	3350
18	11	RALLY 194 B/R	ST	RNBT	FBG	DV	IO	140-190	7	6	2145			2950	3450
18	11	RALLY 195	ST	RNBT	FBG	DV	OB		7	6	1465			2900	3350
18	11	RALLY 195	ST	RNBT	FBG	DV	IO	140-190	7	6	2145			2950	3450
18	11	RALLY 195-SS	ST	RNBT	FBG	DV	IO	170-235	7	6	2220			3000	3600
18	11	SPORTSMAN 192	OP	OPFSH	FBG	DV	OB		7	6	1600			3050	3550
20	3	BEACHCOMBER 206	ST	CUD	FBG	DV	IO	170-235	7	9	2800			4000	4800
20	3	BEACHCOMBER 206-C	ST	CAMPR	FBG	DV	IO	170-235	7	9	2950			4150	4950
21	1	BONANZA 216	ST	CUD	FBG	DV	OB		8		2115			4900	5600
21	1	BONANZA 216	ST	CUD	FBG	DV	IO	170-235	8		2960			4500	5350
21	1	BONANZA 216-C	ST	CAMPR	FBG	SV	OB		8		2215			4900	5650
21	1	BONANZA 216-C	ST	CAMPR	FBG	SV	IO	170-235	8		3060			4550	5400
21	1	BONANZA UTILITY 211	ST	CUD	FBG	DV	OB		8		2115			4650	5350
21	1	BONANZA UTILITY 211	ST	CUD	FBG	DV	IO	170-235	8		2960			4400	5200
22		BARNEGAT 220	ST	CUD	FBG	DV	IO	170-235	8		3350			5050	5950
22		BARNEGAT 220	HT	CUD	FBG	DV	IO	170-235	8		3350			5050	5950
22		BARNEGAT 220-C	ST	CAMPR	FBG	DV	IO	170-235	8		3450			5150	6050
22		BARNEGAT 220-C	HT	CAMPR	FBG	DV	IO	170-235	8		3450			5150	6050
22	4	MACKINAC 227	ST	CBNCR	FBG	SV	IO	170-235			3660			6050	7150
24	8	GRAN-BATEAU 246	ST	CR	FBG	DV	IO	188-235	8		4340			7000	8200
24	8	GRAN-BATEAU 246	ST	CR	FBG	DV	IO	T120-T170	8		4340			7650	9000
24	8	GRAN-BATEAU 246	HT	CR	FBG	DV	IO	188-235	8		4340			7000	8200
24	8	GRAN-BATEAU 246	HT	CR	FBG	DV	IO	T120-T170	8		4340			7650	9000
24	8	GRAN-BATEAU FD 249	ST	CR	FBG	DV	IO	188-235	8		4380			7000	8250
24	8	GRAN-BATEAU FD 249	ST	CR	FBG	DV	IO	T120-T170	8		4380			7700	9050
24	8	GRAN-BATEAU FD 249	HT	CR	FBG	DV	IO	188-235	8		4380			7000	8250
24	8	GRAN-BATEAU FD 249	HT	CR	FBG	DV	IO	T120-T170	8		4380			7700	9050
24	8	VENTURER 241	ST	CUD	FBG	DV	IO	188-235	8		4100			6700	7900
24	8	VENTURER 241	ST	CUD	FBG	DV	IO	T120-T170	8		4100			7350	8700
24	8	VENTURER 241-S	HT	SDN	FBG	DV	IO	188-235	8		4500			7400	8750
24	8	VENTURER 241-S	HT	SDN	FBG	DV	IO	T120-T170	8		4500			8100	9500
25	8	BAR-HARBOR 257	ST	CR	FBG	SV	IO	188-235	8		4560			7550	9000
25	8	BAR-HARBOR 257	ST	CR	FBG	SV	IO	T120-T170	8		4560			8250	9900
25	8	SEAFARER 258	FB	CBNCR	FBG	SV	IO	188-235	8		5000			9900	11500
		1976 BOATS													
16	2	RALLY 175	ST	RNBT	FBG	DV	OB		6	9	1320			2500	2950
16	2	RALLY 175	ST	RNBT	FBG	DV	IO	120-140	6	9	1970			2350	2700
16	5	RALLY 163	ST	RNBT	FBG	TR	OB		6	6	1195			2350	2700
17	2	RALLY 174 B/R	ST	RNBT	FBG	DV	OB		6	9	1320			2550	2950
17	2	RALLY 174 B/R	ST	RNBT	FBG	DV	IO	120-140	6	9	1970			2450	2850
17	6	NOR'WESTER	OP	UTL	FBG	TR	OB		7	3	1275			2400	2800
18	8	RALLY 193	ST	RNBT	FBG	TR	OB		7	5	1375			2700	3150
18	8	RALLY 193	ST	RNBT	FBG	TR	IO	120-190	7	5	2055			2900	3400
18	8	VACATIONER CAMP 196C	ST	CUD	FBG	TR	OB		7	5	1735			3150	3700
18	8	VACATIONER CAMP 196C	ST	CUD	FBG	TR	IO	140-175	7	5	2410			3200	3750
18	11	ENDURO 195	ST	RNBT	FBG	DV	OB		7	6	1465			2850	3300
18	11	ENDURO 195	ST	RNBT	FBG	DV	IO	120-190	7	6	2145			3050	3550
18	11	ENDURO BOWRIDER 194	ST	RNBT	FBG	DV	OB		7	6	1465			2850	3300
18	11	ENDURO BOWRIDER 194	ST	RNBT	FBG	DV	IO	120-190	7	6	2145			3050	3550
18	11	ENDURO BWRIDER 194SS	ST	RNBT	FBG	DV	IO	175-190	7	6	2250			3050	3600
18	11	ENDURO SPEC ED 195SS	ST	RNBT	FBG	DV	IO	175-190	7	6	2250			3050	3600
18	11	RALLY 190	ST	RNBT	FBG	DV	OB		7	6	1465			2850	3350
18	11	RALLY 190	ST	RNBT	FBG	DV	IO	120-190	7	6	2125			3000	3500
21	1	BONANZA	ST	CUD	FBG	SV	OB		8		2200			4850	5600
21	1	BONANZA	ST	CUD	FBG	SV	IO	165-235	8		3045			4650	5500
21	1	BONANZA	HT	CUD	FBG	SV	OB		8		2200			4850	5600
21	1	BONANZA	HT	CUD	FBG	SV	IO	165-235	8		3045			4650	5500
21	1	BONANZA 216	ST	CUD	FBG	SV	OB		8		2115			4850	5600
21	1	BONANZA 216	ST	CUD	FBG	SV	IO	165-235	8		2960			4650	5450
21	1	BONANZA 216	HT	CUD	FBG	SV	OB		8		2115			4850	5550
21	1	BONANZA 216	HT	CUD	FBG	SV	IO	165-235	8		2960			4650	5450
21	1	BONANZA UTILITY 211	ST	CUD	FBG	SV	OB		8		2115			4650	5350
21	1	BONANZA UTILITY 211	ST	CUD	FBG	SV	IO	165-235	8		2960			4550	5350
21	1	BONANZA UTILITY 211	HT	CUD	FBG	SV	OB		8		2115			4650	5350
21	1	BONANZA UTILITY 211	HT	CUD	FBG	SV	IO	165-235	8		2960			4550	5350
22		BARNEGAT 220	ST	CUD	FBG	DV	IO	165-235	8		3350			5150	6100
22		BARNEGAT 220	HT	CUD	FBG	DV	IO	165-235	8		3350			5150	6100
22	4	MACKINAC 227	ST	CBNCR	FBG	SV	IO	165-235			3660			6200	7300
22	4	MACKINAC 227	HT	CBNCR	FBG	SV	IO	165-235			3660			6200	7300
22	4	MARLIN CAMPER 226C	ST	CUD	FBG	TR	IO	165-235	8		3355			5250	6200
22	4	MARLIN CAMPER 226C	HT	CUD	FBG	TR	IO	165-235	8		3355			5250	6200
24	8	GRAN-BATEAU 246	ST	CR	FBG	DV	IO	188-235	8		4340			7250	8500
24	8	GRAN-BATEAU 246	ST	CR	FBG	DV	IO	T120-T165	8		4340			7900	9300
24	8	GRAN-BATEAU 246	HT	CR	FBG	DV	IO	188-235	8		4340			7250	8500
24	8	GRAN-BATEAU 246	HT	CR	FBG	DV	IO	T120-T165	8		4340			7900	9300
24	8	GRAN-BATEAU FD 249	ST	CR	FBG	DV	IO	188-235	8		4340			7100	8350
24	8	GRAN-BATEAU FD 249	ST	CR	FBG	DV	IO	T120-T165	8		4340			7750	9150
24	8	GRAN-BATEAU FD 249	HT	CR	FBG	DV	IO	188-235	8		4340			7100	8350
24	8	GRAN-BATEAU FD 249	HT	CR	FBG	DV	IO	T120-T165	8		4340			7750	9150
25	8	BAR-HARBOR 257	ST	CR	FBG	SV	IO	188-235	8		4460			7650	9100
25	8	BAR-HARBOR 257	ST	CR	FBG	SV	IO	T120-T165	8		4460			8350	10000
25	8	BAR-HARBOR 257	HT	CR	FBG	SV	IO	188-235	8		4460			7650	9100
25	8	BAR-HARBOR 257	HT	CR	FBG	SV	IO	T120-T165	8		4460			8350	10000
		1975 BOATS													
16	5	RALLY 163 W/T	OP	RNBT	FBG	TR	OB		6	6	1195			2300	2700
17		RALLY 173	OP	RNBT	FBG	DV	OB		6	8	1130			2250	2600
17	2	RALLY 174 B/R	OP	RNBT	FBG	DV	IO	120	6	8				2550	2950
17	2	RALLY 175	OP	RNBT	FBG	DV	OB		6	8	1320			2500	2900
17	6	NOR'WESTER	OP	UTL	FBG	TR	OB		7	3	1275			2350	2750
18	8	EXPLORER 191	OP	CUD	FBG	TR	OB		7	5	1590			2950	3450
18	8	ROGUE 193	ST	RNBT	FBG	TR	OB		7	5	1375			2700	3100
18	8	ROGUE 193	ST	RNBT	FBG	TR	IO	140-190	7	5	2055			3000	3500
18	8	VACATIONER CAMP 196C	ST	CUD	FBG	TR	OB		7	5	1735			3150	3650
18	8	VACATIONER CAMP 196C	ST	CUD	FBG	TR	IO	140-165	7	5	2410			3300	3850
18	11	ENDURO 195	ST	RNBT	FBG	DV	OB		7	6	1735			3150	3700
18	11	ENDURO 195	ST	RNBT	FBG	DV	IO	140-190	7	6	2410			3300	3850
18	11	ENDURO BOWRIDER 194	ST	RNBT	FBG	DV	OB		7	6	1465			2850	3300
18	11	ENDURO BOWRIDER 194	ST	RNBT	FBG	DV	IO	140-190	7	6	2145			3100	3650
21	1	BONANZA	ST	CUD	FBG	SV	OB		8		2115			4850	5600
21	1	BONANZA	ST	CUD	FBG	SV	IO	165-233	8		2960			4800	5700
21	1	BONANZA 216	ST	CUD	FBG	SV	OB		8		2115			4600	5250
21	1	BONANZA 216	ST	CUD	FBG	SV	IO	165-233	8		2960			4650	5450
22		BARNEGAT 220	ST	CUD	FBG	DV	IO	165-233	8		3350			5350	6300
22	4	MACKINAC 227	ST	CBNCR	FBG	SV	IO	165-233	8		3360			6050	7150
22	4	MARLIN 226	ST	CUD	FBG	TR	IO	165-233	8		3355			5350	6300
22	4	MARLIN CAMPER 226	ST	CUD	FBG	TR	IO	165-233	8		3355			5550	6550
24	8	GRAN-BATEAU 246	ST	CR	FBG	DV	IO	188-233	8		4340			7400	8700
24	8	GRAN-BATEAU 246	ST	CR	FBG	DV	IO	T120-T165	8		4340			8100	9500
25	8	BAR-HARBOR 257	ST	CR	FBG	DV	IO	188-233	8		4460			7900	9400
25	8	BAR-HARBOR 257	ST	CR	FBG	DV	IO	T120-T140	8		4460			8600	10100
25	8	BAR-HARBOR 257	ST	CR	FBG	SV	IO	T165 MRCR			4460			9350	10600
25	8	SEAFARER 268	FB	CBNCR	FBG	SV	IO	188-233	8	7	5030			10600	12400
25	8	SEAFARER 268	FB	CBNCR	FBG	SV	IO	T120-T165	8	7	5030			11400	13000
		1974 BOATS													
16	5	RALLY 163 W/T	OP	RNBT	FBG	TR	OB		6	5	1095			2100	2450
17	2	RALLY 174 B/R	OP	RNBT	FBG	DV	OB		6	8	1195			2350	2700
17	2	RALLY 174 B/R	OP	RNBT	FBG	DV	IO	120-140	6	8				2600	3050
17	6	NOR'WESTER	OP	UTL	FBG	TR	OB		7	3	1275			2350	2750
18	8	EXPLORER	OP	UTL	FBG		OB		7	5	1525			2650	3100
18	8	ROGUE 193	ST	RNBT	FBG		OB		7	5	1375			2650	3100
18	8	ROGUE 193	ST	RNBT	FBG		IO	120-165	7	5	2055			3100	3700

CONTINUED ON NEXT PAGE

LOA FT	LOA IN	NAME AND/ OR MODEL	TOP/ RIG	BOAT TYPE	-HULL- MTL	-HULL- TP	ENGINE TP	ENGINE # HP	ENGINE MFG	BEAM FT	BEAM IN	WGT LBS	DRAFT FT	DRAFT IN	RETAIL LOW	RETAIL HIGH
		1974 BOATS														
18	8	ROGUE 193	ST	RNBT	FBG		IO	188	MRCR	7	5	2390			3350	3900
18	8	VACATIONER CAMPER	ST	CUD	FBG		OB			7	5	1735			3100	3600
18	8	VACATIONER CAMPER	ST	CUD	FBG		IO	120-188		7	5	2300			3350	4150
18	11	ENDURO	ST	B/R	FBG		OB			7	4	1465			2800	3300
18	11	ENDURO	ST	B/R	FBG		IO	120-165		7	4	2035			2950	3550
18	11	ENDURO	ST	B/R	FBG		IO	188	MRCR	7	4	2390			3250	3800
18	11	ENDURO	ST	RNBT	FBG		OB			7	4	1465			2800	3250
18	11	ENDURO	ST	RNBT	FBG		IO	120-165		7	4	2035			3100	3700
18	11	ENDURO	ST	RNBT	FBG		IO	188	MRCR	7	4	2390			3350	3900
21	1	BONANZA	ST	CAMPR	FBG		OB			8		2185			4800	5500
21	1	BONANZA	ST	CAMPR	FBG		IO	165-225		8		3180			5100	6250
21	1	BONANZA	HT	CAMPR	FBG		OB			8					4350	5000
21	1	BONANZA	HT	CAMPR	FBG		IO	165-225		8					4650	5400
21	1	BONANZA	ST	CR	FBG		OB			8		2010			4550	5200
21	1	BONANZA	ST	CR	FBG		IO	165-225		8		3105			5000	6050
21	1	BONANZA	HT	CR	FBG		OB			8					4050	4700
21	1	BONANZA	HT	CR	FBG		IO	165-225		8					5000	5800
22		MACKINAC	ST	CBNCR	FBG		IO	165-225				3475			6250	7600
22		MACKINAC	HT	CBNCR	FBG		IO	165-225							6450	7500
22	4	MARLIN	ST	CR	FBG		IO	165-225		8		3325			5600	6800
22	4	MARLIN	HT	CR	FBG		IO	165-225		8					5950	6900
22	4	MARLIN CAMPER	ST	CUD	FBG		IO	165-225		8		3400			5700	6850
22	4	MARLIN CAMPER	HT	CUD	FBG		IO	165-225		8					5800	6750
24	8	GRAN-BATEAU		CR	FBG		IO	188-225		8		3500			6600	7950
24	8	GRAN-BATEAU		CR	FBG		IO	T120-T165		8		4050			8000	9850
25	8	SEAFARER	ST	CBNCR	FBG		IO	188-225				4540			10500	12100
25	8	SEAFARER	ST	CBNCR	FBG		IO	T120-T165				4950			11800	14300
25	8	SEAFARER	HT	CBNCR	FBG		IO	188-225							10500	12000
25	8	SEAFARER	HT	CBNCR	FBG		IO	T120-T165							11100	12700
25	8	SEAFARER	FB	CBNCR	FBG		IO	188-225				4850			10900	12900
25	8	SEAFARER	FB	CBNCR	FBG		IO	T120-T165				5400			12500	14700
		1973 BOATS														
16		ANTIGUA	ST	RNBT	FBG		OB			6	5	950			1800	2150
16		ANTIGUA	ST	RNBT	FBG		IO	120-140		6	5	1615			2250	2650
17		CHARGER	ST	RNBT	FBG		OB			6	8	965			1900	2250
17		CHARGER	ST	RNBT	FBG		IO	120-140		6	8	1630			2450	2850
17	6	NOR'WESTER	OP	UTL	FBG		OB			7	3	1045			1950	2300
18	8	CRUSADER	ST	RNBT	FBG		OB			7	5	1230			2450	2850
18	8	CRUSADER	ST	RNBT	FBG		IO	120-188		7	5	1980			3150	3900
18	8	EXPLORER	OP	UTL	FBG		OB			7	5	1500			2600	3050
18	8	VACATIONER	ST	CBNCR	FBG		OB			7	5	1490			2750	3200
18	8	VACATIONER	ST	CBNCR	FBG		IO	120-188		7	5	2240			3550	4300
18	8	VACATIONER CAMPER	ST	CUD	FBG		OB			7	5	1550			2850	3350
18	8	VACATIONER CAMPER	ST	CUD	FBG		IO	120-188		7	5	2300			3450	4300
18	11	CHALLENGER	ST	RNBT	FBG		OB			7	4	1180			2400	2800
18	11	CHALLENGER	ST	RNBT	FBG		IO	120-188		7	4	1880			3100	3650
18	11	CHALLENGER	ST	RNBT	FBG		JT	245	OMC	7	4	1880			2850	3300
21	1	BONANZA	ST	CAMPR	FBG		OB			8		2185			4800	5500
21	1	BONANZA	ST	CAMPR	FBG		IO	165-225		8		3180			5250	6500
21	1	BONANZA	HT	CAMPR	FBG		OB			8					4300	5000
21	1	BONANZA	HT	CAMPR	FBG		IO	165-225		8					4800	5650
21	1	BONANZA	ST	CR	FBG		OB			8		2010			4550	5200
21	1	BONANZA	ST	CR	FBG		IO	165-225		8		3105			5150	6450
21	1	BONANZA	HT	CR	FBG		OB			8					4050	4700
21	1	BONANZA	HT	CR	FBG		IO	165-225		8					5150	6050
22		MACKINAC	ST	CBNCR	FBG		IO	165-225				3475			6450	7850
22		MACKINAC	HT	CBNCR	FBG		IO	165-225							6650	7800
22	4	MARLIN	ST	CR	FBG		IO	165-225		8		3325			5800	7000
22	4	MARLIN	HT	CR	FBG		IO	165-225		8		3936			6500	7600
22	4	MARLIN CAMPER	ST	CUD	FBG		IO	165-225		8		3400			5850	7150
22	4	MARLIN CAMPER	HT	CUD	FBG		IO	165-225		8					6000	7050
25	8	SEAFARER	ST	CBNCR	FBG		IO	188-255				4200			10400	12300
25	8	SEAFARER	ST	CBNCR	FBG		IO	T120-T165				4600			11700	14200
25	8	SEAFARER	HT	CBNCR	FBG		IO	188-255							10800	12600
25	8	SEAFARER	HT	CBNCR	FBG		IO	T120-T165							11500	13100
		1972 BOATS														
16		ANTIGUA	ST	RNBT	FBG		OB			6	5	950			1800	2150
16		ANTIGUA	ST	RNBT	FBG		IO	100-140		6	5	1615			2300	2700
17		CHARGER	ST	RNBT	FBG		OB			6	8	965			1850	2250
17		CHARGER	ST	RNBT	FBG		IO	100-140		6	8	1630			2500	2950
17	6	BARBADOS	ST	CUD	FBG		OB			7	3	1255			2400	2800
17	6	BARBADOS C	ST	CAMPR	FBG		OB			7	3	1280			2450	2850
17	6	NOR'WESTER	OP	UTL	FBG		OB			7	3	1045			1950	2300
18	8	CHALLENGER	ST	RNBT	FBG		IO	120-188		7	4	1880			3150	3700
18	8	CRUSADER	ST	RNBT	FBG		OB			7	5	1230			2450	2850
18	8	CRUSADER	ST	RNBT	FBG		IO	120-188		7	5	1980			3250	4000
18	8	VACATIONER	ST	CBNCR	FBG		OB			7	5	1490			2750	3200
18	8	VACATIONER	ST	CBNCR	FBG		IO	120-188		7	5	2240			3650	4550
18	8	VACATIONER CAMPER	ST	CUD	FBG		OB			7	5	1550			2850	3300
18	8	VACATIONER CAMPER	ST	CUD	FBG		IO	120-188		7	5	2300			3550	4400
18	11	CHALLENGER		RNBT	FBG	SV	OB			7	4	1130			2300	2700
21	1	ADVENTURER	ST	RNBT	FBG		IO	140-225		8		2875			4850	6050
21	1	BONANZA	ST	CAMPR	FBG		OB			8		2185			4800	5500
21	1	BONANZA	ST	CAMPR	FBG		IO	155-225		8		3180			5400	6650
21	1	BONANZA	ST	CR	FBG		OB			8		2010			4550	5200
21	1	BONANZA	ST	CR	FBG		IO	155-225		8		3105			5300	6450
22		MACKINAC	ST	CBNCR	FBG		IO	155-225		8		3475			6650	8100
22	4	MARLIN	ST	CR	FBG		IO	155-225		8		3325			5950	7250
22	4	MARLIN CAMPER	ST	CUD	FBG		IO	155-225		8		3400			6000	7350
25	8	COMMODORE	ST	CBNCR	FBG		IO	165-225				4100			10500	12300
25	8	COMMODORE	ST	CBNCR	FBG		IO	T120-T140				4600			12100	13700
		1971 BOATS														
16		ANTIGUA	ST	RNBT	FBG		OB			6	5	950			1800	2150
17		CHARGER	ST	RNBT	FBG		OB			6	8	965			1850	2200
17		CHARGER	ST	RNBT	FBG		IO	120-140		6	8	1630			2600	3050
17	6	BARBADOS	ST	CUD	FBG		OB			7	3	1255			2400	2800
17	6	BARBADOS C	ST	CAMPR	FBG		OB			7	3	1280			2450	2800
17	6	NOR'WESTER	OP	UTL	FBG		OB			7	3	1045			1950	2300
18	8	CRUSADER	ST	RNBT	FBG		OB			7	5	1230			2450	2850
18	8	CRUSADER	ST	RNBT	FBG		IO	120-215		7	5	1980			3350	4150
18	8	VACATIONER	ST	CBNCR	FBG		OB			7	5	1490			2750	3200
18	8	VACATIONER	ST	CBNCR	FBG		IO	120-165		7	5	2240			3800	4550
18	8	VACATIONER	ST	CBNCR	FBG		IO	215	OMC	7	5	2480			4100	4750
18	8	VACATIONER CAMPER	ST	CUD	FBG		OB			7	5	1550			2850	3300
18	8	VACATIONER CAMPER	ST	CUD	FBG		IO	120-165		7	5	2300			3700	4400
18	8	VACATIONER CAMPER	ST	CUD	FBG		IO	215	OMC	7	5	2540			3950	4600
21	1	ADVENTURER	ST	RNBT	FBG		IO	140-165		8		2875			5000	5950
21	1	ADVENTURER	ST	RNBT	FBG		IO	215		8		3240			5500	6300
21	1	BONANZA	ST	CAMPR	FBG		IO	140-165		8		3050			5450	6450
21	1	BONANZA	ST	CAMPR	FBG		IO	215		8		3425			6000	6900
21	1	BONANZA	ST	CR	FBG		OB			8		2010			4550	5200
21	1	BONANZA	ST	CR	FBG		IO	140-165		8		2975			5350	6350
21	1	BONANZA	ST	CR	FBG		IO	215		8		3340			5900	6750
21	1	BONANZA	HT	CR	FBG		IO	140-165		8		3050			5450	6450
21	1	BONANZA	HT	CR	FBG		IO	215		8		3425			6000	6900
21	1	BONANZA	FB	CR	FBG		IO	155-215		8		3425			5850	7000
22		MACKINAC	ST	CBNCR	FBG		IO	155-215		8		3475			6850	8450
22	4	MARLIN	ST	CR	FBG		IO	155-215		8		3325			6150	7550
22	4	MARLIN	HT	CR	FBG		IO	155-215		8		3400			6200	7650
22	4	MARLIN	FB	CR	FBG		IO	155-215		8		3775			6700	8000
22	4	MARLIN CAMPER	ST	CUD	FBG		IO	155-215		8		3400			6200	7650
		1970 BOATS														
16	2	ANTIGUA	ST	RNBT	FBG	TR	OB			6	5	950			1800	2150
16	2	ANTIGUA	ST	RNBT	FBG	TR	IO	120-140		6	5	1615			2500	2900
17		NASSAU	ST	RNBT	FBG	DV	OB			6	8	965			1850	2200
17		NASSAU	ST	RNBT	FBG	DV	IO	120-140		6	8	1630			2700	3150
17	6	BAHAMA	ST	RNBT	FBG	TR	OB			7	3	1155			2250	2650
17	6	BARBADOS	ST	CUD	FBG	TR	OB			7	3	1255			2400	2800
17	6	BARBADOS	ST	CUD	FBG	TR	IO	120-140		7	3	2015			3250	3800
17	6	BARBADOS C	ST	CAMPR	FBG	TR	OB			7	3	1280			2450	2800
17	6	BARBADOS C	ST	CAMPR	FBG	TR	IO	120-140		7	3	2040			3250	3800
17	6	NOR'WESTER	OP	UTL	FBG	TR	OB			7	3	1045			1950	2300
18	8	CRUSADER	HT		FBG	TR	IO	120-210		7	5	2180			3500	4400
18	8	CRUSADER	HT		FBG	TR	IO	215	MRCR	7	5	2420			3800	4450
18	8	CRUSADER	ST	RNBT	FBG	TR	IO	120-210		7	5	1980			3450	4300
18	8	CRUSADER	ST	RNBT	FBG	TR	IO	215	MRCR	7	5	2220			3750	4350
21	1	BONANZA	ST	CR	FBG	SV	OB			8		2125			4700	5400
21	1	BONANZA	ST	CR	FBG	SV	IO	140-215		8		2865			5400	6650
21	1	BONANZA	HT	CR	FBG	SV	IO	140-215		8		3065			5650	6950
22		MACKINAC	ST	CBNCR	FBG	SV	IO	155-215		8		3475			7100	8550
22	4	MARLIN	ST	CR	FBG	TR	OB			8		2475			5600	6450
22	4	MARLIN	ST	CR	FBG	TR	IO	155-215		8		3325			6350	7650
22	4	MARLIN	HT	CR	FBG	TR	IO	155-215		8		3525			6600	7950
		1969 BOATS														
16		ANTIGUA	ST	RNBT	FBG	TR	OB			6	5	900			1700	2000
16		ANTIGUA	ST	RNBT	FBG	TR	IO	120		6	5	1595			2500	2950
17	3	NASSAU	ST	RNBT	FBG	SV	OB			6	7	920			1800	2150

CONTINUED ON NEXT PAGE

LOA FT IN	NAME AND/ OR MODEL	TOP/ RIG	BOAT TYPE	HULL MTL	TP	TP	ENGINE # HP MFG	BEAM FT IN	WGT LBS	DRAFT FT IN	RETAIL LOW	RETAIL HIGH
----- 1969 BOATS -----												
17 6	BAHAMA	ST	RNBT	FBG	TR	OB		7 3	1100		2150	2500
17 6	BARBADOS		CAMPR	FBG	TR	OB		7 3	1250		2400	2750
17 6	BARBADOS	ST	CUD	FBG	TR	OB		7 3	1235		2350	2750
17 6	BARBADOS	ST	CUD	FBG	TR	IO	OMC	7 3	2015		**	**
17 6	BARBADOS	ST	CUD	FBG	TR	IO	120-160	7 3	2015		3350	4050
17 6	COHO FISHING BOAT	OP	FSH	FBG		OB		7 3	1000		1950	2300
17 6	NOR'WESTER		RNBT	FBG	TR	OB		7 3	1050		2050	2450
18 6	CRUSADER	ST	RNBT	FBG	TR	IO	120-160	7 8	1985		3600	4300
21 1	BONANZA		CR	FBG		IO	225	8			6000	6900
21 1	BONANZA	ST	CR	FBG	SV	IO	155-225	8	3000		5700	7050
22	MACKINAC	ST	CBNCR	FBG	SV	IO	155-210		3550		7450	8900
22 3	MARLIN	ST	CR	FBG	TR	IO	155-225	8	3350		6550	8050
----- 1968 BOATS -----												
16	ANTIGUA	ST	RNBT	FBG	TR	OB		6 5	900		1700	2050
16	ANTIGUA	ST	RNBT	FBG	TR	IO	80-160	6 5	1595		2600	3050
17 6	BAHAMA	ST	RNBT	FBG	TR	OB		7 3	1085		2150	2500
17 6	BAHAMA	ST	RNBT	FBG	TR	IO	120-160	7 3	1780		3250	3800
17 6	BARBADOS	OP	CUD	FBG	TR	OB		7 3	1250		2400	2800
17 6	BARBADOS	OP	CUD	FBG	TR	IO	120-160	7 3	2015		3450	4050
21 1	BONANZA		CR	FBG	SV	IO	120-200	8	3000		5950	6900
22	MACKINAC	OP	CBNCR	FBG	SV	IO	120-210	8	3800		8050	9450
----- 1967 BOATS -----												
17 3	BERMUDA	OP	RNBT	FBG		IO			1025		2000	2350
17 3	BERMUDA	OP	RNBT	FBG		IO	120		1725		3200	3700
17 6	BAHAMA	ST	RNBT	FBG		OB			1110		2200	2550
17 6	BAHAMA	ST	RNBT	FBG		IO	120-160		2030		3550	4150
17 6	CARIBBEAN	ST	RNBT	FBG		OB			1030		2000	2400
17 6	CARIBBEAN	ST	RNBT	FBG		IO	120-160		1950		3500	4100
20 10	BONANZA		CR	FBG		IO	120-200		3000		6000	7000
22	MACKINAC	OP	CBNCR	FBG		IO	120-160		3800		8350	9650
----- 1966 BOATS -----												
17	ADVENTURER	ST	RNBT	WD		OB		6 9			2150	2500
17	BERMUDA	OP	RNBT	FBG		OB		6 9			1950	2350
17	BERMUDA	OP	RNBT	FBG		IO	110-120	6 9			3250	3900
17	BERMUDA DELUXE	OP	RNBT	FBG		OB		6 9			2300	2700
17	BERMUDA DELUXE	OP	RNBT	FBG		IO	110-120	6 9			3500	4150
18	BAHAMA	ST	RNBT	FBG		OB		7 3			2350	2750
18	BAHAMA	ST	RNBT	FBG		IO	110-150	7 3			3750	4500
18	BAHAMA DELUXE	ST	RNBT	FBG		OB		7 3			2650	3100
18	BAHAMA DELUXE	ST	RNBT	FBG		IO	110-150	7 3			4000	4750
18	COMMANDER	OP	RNBT	WD		OB		7 1			2500	2900
20	EXPLORER	ST	UTL	WD		OB		8			1950	2350
20	EXPLORER	ST	UTL	WD		IO	110-150	8			5900	6800
20	GLACIER	ST	CUD	WD		OB		8			4800	5500
20	GLACIER	ST	CUD	WD		IO	110-150	8			5600	6500
20	VACATIONER	OP	CR	WD		OB		8			3500	4050
20	VACATIONER	OP	CR	WD		IO	110-150	8			5250	6050
21	OLYMPIC	ST	CBNCR	WD		IO	110-150	8			6800	7850
22	MACKINAC	OP	CBNCR	FBG		IO	110-150	8			8350	9600
23	NAVIGATOR	OP	CR	WD		IO	150-225	8			8100	9500
23	PATHFINDER	ST	CAMPR	WD		IO	150	8			7400	8500
23	SEQUOIA	HT	CBNCR	WD		IO	110-150	8			6900	7950
25	BARNEGAT	HT	CUD	WD		IO	150-225	8			10100	11900
----- 1965 BOATS -----												
17 3	ADVENTURER	ST	RNBT	WD		IO	90-110				2200	2550
17 3	ADVENTURER	ST	RNBT	WD		IO	90-110				3650	4200
17 3	BERMUDA	OP	RNBT	FBG		IO					2150	2500
17 3	BERMUDA	OP	RNBT	FBG		IO	90-120				3650	4200
17 11	COMMANDER	OP	RNBT	WD		OB					2500	2900
17 11	RAINIER	OP	CUD	WD		OB					3150	3700
19	YOSEMITE	OP	CBNCR	WD		OB					2350	2700
19	YOSEMITE	OP	CBNCR	WD		IO	110-150				4700	5400
20 3	EXPLORER	ST	UTL	WD		OB					1950	2350
20 3	EXPLORER	ST	UTL	WD		IO	110-150				5950	6900
20 3	GLACIER	ST	CUD	WD		OB					4950	5650
20 3	GLACIER	ST	CUD	WD		IO	110-150				5850	6700
20 3	VACATIONER	OP	CR	WD		OB					3550	4150
20 3	VACATIONER	OP	CR	WD		IO	110-150				5300	6150
21	OLYMPIC	ST	CBNCR	WD		OB					4300	5000
21	OLYMPIC	ST	CBNCR	WD		IO	110-150				6950	8000
22 8	NAVIGATOR	OP	CR	WD		IO	150-225				8250	9650
23	ALBACORE	OP	OPFSH	WD		IO	110-150				7850	9050
23	SEQUOIA	HT	CBNCR	WD		IO	110-150				7100	8200
24 10	BARNEGAT	HT	CUD	WD		IO	150-225				10500	12400
----- 1964 BOATS -----												
17 3	ADVENTURER	ST	RNBT	WD		OB					2200	2550
17 3	ADVENTURER	ST	RNBT	WD		IO	80-110				3750	4350
17 11			CAMPR	WD		OB					2900	3400
17 11	COMMANDER	OP	RNBT	WD		OB					2500	2900
17 11	COMMANDER	OP	RNBT	WD		IO	110				4150	4800
20 3			CAMPR	WD		OB					3500	4050
20 3	VACATIONER	OP	CR	WD		OB					3600	4150
20 3	VACATIONER	OP	CR	WD		IO	110-140				5500	6350
22 8	NAVIGATOR	OP	CR	WD		IO	140-225				8500	10000
24 10	BARNEGAT			WD		IO	190-225				11200	13000
24 10	BARNEGAT			WD		IO	T110				12200	13800
----- 1963 BOATS -----												
17 11	BOBTAIL COMMANDER	ST	CR	WD		IO	100-110				3800	4450
17 11	COMMANDER 300	ST	RNBT	WD		OB					2500	2900
17 11	COMMANDER 302	OP	RNBT	WD		OB					2500	2900
17 11	SEACAMPER 18	OP	CUD	WD		OB					3150	3700
20 3	BOBTAIL VACATION CBN	ST	CR	WD		IO	110				6050	7000
20 3	BOBTAIL VACATIONER	ST	CR	WD		IO	100-140				5700	6550
20 3	SEACAMPER	OP	CUD	WD		OB					5000	5750
20 3	VACATIONER	OP	CR	WD		OB					3600	4200
24 10	BARNEGAT 25	ST	CAMPR	WD		IO	195-225				10800	12500
----- 1962 BOATS -----												
17 11	COMMANDER V 302-M	OP	RNBT	WD		OB					2500	2900
20 3	VACATIONER V 502M	OP	CR	WD		OB					3650	4250
----- 1961 BOATS -----												
17 7	COMMANDER 302		UTL	L/P		OB		7 1	900		1700	2000
17 7	HOLIDAY 350		RNBT	L/P		OB		7 1	900		1800	2150
17 7	ROYAL-COMMANDER		CR	L/P		OB		7 1	1000		1950	2350
20 3	1502		UTL	L/P		IB	85	7 11			1950	2350
20 3	CRUISETTE 1570		CR	L/P		IB	85	7 11			1800	2150
20 3	ROYAL-VACATIONER		CR	L/P		OB		7 11	1215		3050	3550
20 3	VACATIONER 502		UTL	L/P		OB		7 11	1115		2400	2800
----- 1960 BOATS -----												
17	COMMANDER	OP	RNBT	WD		OB					2200	2550
17	HOLIDAY	OP	RNBT	WD		OB					2200	2550
20	SUPER-VACATIONER	OP		WD		OB					2900	3400
----- 1959 BOATS -----												
18 8	VACATIONER DLX 502		RNBT	L/P		OB		7 2	880		1850	2200
19	ROYAL-VACATIONER 570		CR	L/P		OB		7 3	1300		2550	3000
19	VACATIONER 196C	ST	CUD	WD		OB					3300	3850
----- 1958 BOATS -----												
18	VACATIONER		RNBT	WD		OB					2500	2950
22			RNBT	WD		OB					6500	7450

CRUISING BOATS OF AMERICA INC

Call 1-800-327-6929 for BUC Personalized Evaluation Service
Or, for 1972 boats, sign onto www.BUCValuPro.com

CRUISING CONSULTANTS INC
NEWPORT BEACH CA 92663   COAST GUARD MFG ID- CXS See inside cover to adjust price for area

LOA FT IN	NAME AND/ OR MODEL	TOP/ RIG	BOAT TYPE	HULL MTL	TP	TP	ENGINE # HP MFG	BEAM FT IN	WGT LBS	DRAFT FT IN	RETAIL LOW	RETAIL HIGH
----- 1979 BOATS -----												
36 11	CREALOCK 37	SLP	SA/CR	FBG	KL	IB	24D VLVO 10 10	15350	5 4	52900	58100
36 11	CREALOCK 37	CUT	SA/CR	FBG	KL	IB	24D VLVO 10 10	15350	5 4	52900	58100
36 11	CREALOCK 37	YWL	SA/CR	FBG	KL	IB	24D VLVO 10 10	15350	5 4	52900	58100
----- 1978 BOATS -----												
36 8	CREALOCK 37	SLP	SA/CR	FBG	KL	IB	24D VLVO 10 9	15000	5 4	49700	54600

CRUISING YACHTS INT'L INC
HOUSTON TX 77077   COAST GUARD MFG ID- CYI See inside cover to adjust price for area
                        FORMERLY CRUISING YACHTS INTERNATIONAL

For more recent years, see the BUC Used Boat Price Guide, Volume 1 or Volume 2

LOA FT IN	NAME AND/ OR MODEL	TOP/ RIG	BOAT TYPE	HULL MTL	TP	TP	ENGINE # HP MFG	BEAM FT IN	WGT LBS	DRAFT FT IN	RETAIL LOW	RETAIL HIGH
----- 1982 BOATS -----												
42 6	SLOCUM 43	CUT	SA/CR	FBG	KL	IB	50D PERK 12 11	28104	6 4	97300	107000

CRUIZON BOAT WORKS
COSTA MESA CA 92627

See inside cover to adjust price for area

LOA FT IN	NAME AND/ OR MODEL	TOP/ RIG	BOAT TYPE	-HULL- MTL TP TP	----ENGINE--- # HP MFG	BEAM FT IN	WGT LBS	DRAFT FT IN	RETAIL LOW	RETAIL HIGH
--------- 1967 BOATS ---------
38 5	CRUISER FISH		CR	F/W IB	T100D	13 3		3	32000	35600
45 5	CRUISER FISH		CR	F/W IB	T185D	15 5		3 4	36400	40500
55 6	CRUISER FISH		CR	F/W IB	T200D	17 6		4	66900	73500
--------- 1965 BOATS ---------
36			CR	F/W IB		13		2 10	**	**
38			CR	F/W IB		13 3		2 11	**	**
42			CR	F/W IB		15 6		3 1	**	**
45			CR	F/W IB		15 6		3 3	**	**
50			CR	F/W IB		17		3 6	**	**
55			CR	F/W IB		17 6		3 8	**	**

CRUSADER BOATS
DIV OF GRANTS FEBERGLASS INC
MOORE HAVEN FL 33471-80 COAST GUARD MFG ID- GFY

See inside cover to adjust price for area

For more recent years, see the BUC Used Boat Price Guide, Volume 1 or Volume 2

LOA FT IN	NAME AND/ OR MODEL	TOP/ RIG	BOAT TYPE	-HULL- MTL TP TP	----ENGINE--- # HP MFG	BEAM FT IN	WGT LBS	DRAFT FT IN	RETAIL LOW	RETAIL HIGH
--------- 1980 BOATS ---------
34	CRUSADER 34	FB	SF	FBG SV IB	260D CAT 12			3 2	41100	45700

CRUSADER BOATS
MARATHON FL 33050

See inside cover to adjust price for area

LOA FT IN	NAME AND/ OR MODEL	TOP/ RIG	BOAT TYPE	-HULL- MTL TP TP	----ENGINE--- # HP MFG	BEAM FT IN	WGT LBS	DRAFT FT IN	RETAIL LOW	RETAIL HIGH
--------- 1982 BOATS ---------
34	CRUSADER		SF	FBG IB	D CUM 12				**	**

CRYSTALINER CORP
COSTA MESA CA 92627

See inside cover to adjust price for area

For more recent years, see the BUC Used Boat Price Guide, Volume 1 or Volume 2

LOA FT IN	NAME AND/ OR MODEL	TOP/ RIG	BOAT TYPE	-HULL- MTL TP TP	----ENGINE--- # HP MFG	BEAM FT IN	WGT LBS	DRAFT FT IN	RETAIL LOW	RETAIL HIGH
--------- 1983 BOATS ---------
29 5	CRYSTALINER 29		UTL	FBG SV IB	T270	11		2 6	27200	30300
33 2	CRYSTALINER 33		SF	FBG SV IB	T270	11		2 6	40200	44600
43	CRYSTALINER 43		FSH	FBG SV IB	310D	14			129500	142000
--------- 1982 BOATS ---------
29 5	CRYSTALINER 29		UTL	FBG SV IB	216D	11			32100	35600
29 5	CRYSTALINER 29		UTL	FBG SV IB	T270	11			26200	29100
33 2	CRYSTALINER 33		SF	FBG SV IB	216D	11			44200	49200
33 2	CRYSTALINER 33		SF	FBG SV IB	T270	11			38600	42900
43	CRYSTALINER 43		FSH	FBG SV IB	310D	14			123500	136000
--------- 1981 BOATS ---------
29 5	RESCUE	OP	UTL	FBG SV IB	210D-286D	11 11000		2 6	31300	35900
29 5	RESCUE	OP	UTL	FBG SV IB	T270-T350	11 11000		2 6	26000	30000
33 2	SPORT FISHER	FB	SF	FBG SV IB	215-286	11 13000		2 6	37600	42200
	IB 210D-260D 45600	51700, IB T270-T350		40200 46100, IB T140D GM					52900	58100
--------- 1959 BOATS ---------
27	CRYSTALINER		CR	FBG	325	9 2			9500	10800
33	CRYSTALINER	CUT	SA/CR	FBG KC OB		9 10		4 9	21100	23500
33	CRYSTALINER	YWL	SA/CR	FBG KC OB		9 10		4 9	21100	23500

CSI MARINE
SONIC
STUART FL 34996   COAST GUARD MFG ID- CSI
FORMERLY AMERICAN INDUSTRIES INC

See inside cover to adjust price for area

For more recent years, see the BUC Used Boat Price Guide, Volume 1 or Volume 2

LOA FT IN	NAME AND/ OR MODEL	TOP/ RIG	BOAT TYPE	-HULL- MTL TP TP	----ENGINE--- # HP MFG	BEAM FT IN	WGT LBS	DRAFT FT IN	RETAIL LOW	RETAIL HIGH
--------- 1983 BOATS ---------
24 2	SONIC OPEN FISHERMAN	OP	OFF	FBG DV IO	330 MRCR	8			7900	9050
24 2	SONIC OPEN FISHERMAN	OP	OFF	FBG DV IO	T185-T260	8			7750	9600
24 2	SONIC OPEN FISHERMAN	OP	OPFSH	FBG DV OB		8			8850	10000
24 2	SONIC S	OP	OFF	FBG DV OB		8			6450	7400
24 2	SONIC S	OP	OFF	FBG DV IO	330 MRCR	8			7900	9050
24 2	SONIC S	OP	OFF	FBG DV IO	T185-T260	8			7750	9600
24 2	SONIC S	OP	OFF	FBG DV OB		8			6450	7400
24 2	SONIC SE	OP	OFF	FBG DV IO	330 MRCR	8			8600	9900
24 2	SONIC SE	OP	OFF	FBG DV IO	370 MRCR	8			8600	9900
24 2	SONIC SE	OP	OFF	FBG DV IO	T185-T260	8			7750	9600
24 2	SONIC SS/IO	OP	OFF	FBG DV OB		8			6450	7400
24 2	SONIC SS/IO	OP	OFF	FBG DV IO	330 MRCR	8			7900	9050
24 2	SONIC SS/IO	OP	OFF	FBG DV IO	T185-T260	8			7750	9600
24 2	SONIC SS/OB	OP	OFF	FBG DV OB		8			6450	7400
24 2	SONIC SS/OB	OP	OFF	FBG DV IO	330 MRCR	8			7900	9050
24 2	SONIC SS/OB	OP	OFF	FBG DV IO	T185-T260	8			7750	9600
33 4	SONIC RS		OFF	FBG DV OB		8 2			22300	24800
33 4	SONIC RS		OFF	FBG DV IO	T HAWK	8 2			**	**
33 4	SONIC RS		OFF	FBG DV IO	T330-T400	8 2			25200	29900
33 4	SONIC SE		OFF	FBG DV OB		8 2			27000	30000
33 4	SONIC SE		OFF	FBG DV IO	T330-T400	8 2			28600	33200
33 4	SONIC SE		OFF	FBG DV IO	R	8 2			**	**
--------- 1981 BOATS ---------
20 6	SONIC 21	OP	RNBT	FBG DV JT		7 10 1200			3050	3550
20 6	SONIC 21	OP	RNBT	FBG DV IO		7 10 2000			**	**
20 6	SONIC 21	OP	RNBT	FBG DV IO	198-260 BERK	7 10 2000			3950	4850
20 6	SONIC 21	OP	RNBT	FBG DV JT	320-333	7 10 2000			5550	6400
24 2	SONIC 24	OP	OPFSH	FBG DV OB		8 2400		1 8	6250	7150
24 2	SONIC 24	OP	OPFSH	FBG DV IO	260	8 3500		1 8	7500	8600
	JT 333 CHEV 9800	11100, IO T185-T228		6850 8100, IO T260-T330					11000	12500
24 2	SONIC 24S	OP	CUD	FBG DV OB		8		1 8	8850	10000
24 2	SONIC 24S	OP	CUD	FBG DV IO	260	8 3950		1 8	7700	8900
	IO T260 10500	11900	IO 330 MRCR 8450	9750, JT 333 CHEV 9500	10800, IO T185-T228				8350	9900
24 2	SONIC 24SE	OP	OVNTR	FBG DV OB		8		1 8	9950	11300
24 2	SONIC 24SE	OP	OVNTR	FBG DV IO	260	8 3950		1 8	7700	8900
	IO T260 10500	11900	IO 330 MRCR 8450	9750, JT 333 CHEV 9500	10800, IO T185-T228				8350	9900
24 2	SONIC 24SS	OP	RACE	FBG DV OB		8 2800			7050	8100
24 2	SONIC 24SS	OP	RACE	FBG DV IO	260	8 3450		1 8	6600	7550
	IO T260 9800	11100	IO 330 MRCR 7250	8350, JT 333 CHEV 8600	9900, IO T185-T228				7150	8500
33 4	SONIC 33 RS	OP	OFF	FBG DV OB		8 2 5000			17300	19700
33 4	SONIC 33 RS	OP	OFF	FBG DV IO	T330-T400	8 2 7000			25600	30100
--------- 1980 BOATS ---------
21	SONIC 21	OP	RNBT	FBG SV IO		7 10 1200			3050	3550
21	SONIC 21	OP	RNBT	FBG SV IO	170	7 10			5250	6050
24	SONIC S	OP	CUD	FBG SV IO		8 3000			7300	8350
24	SONIC S	OP	CUD	FBG SV IO	330	8			8350	9600
24	SONIC SE	OP	OVNTR	FBG SV IO	330	8			8350	9600
24	SONIC SF	OP	SF	FBG SV OB		8 2600			6450	7450
24	SONIC SF	OP	SF	FBG SV IO	260	8 3500			7950	9100
24	SONIC SS	OP	RACE	FBG SV IO		8 3000			7300	8350
--------- 1979 BOATS ---------
20 6	SONIC 21	OP	RNBT	FBG DV IO	170-188	7 10 1300		2 4	3150	3650
20 6	SONIC 21	OP	RNBT	FBG DV IO	260 MRCR	7 10 2000		2 4	3850	4750
20 6	SONIC 21	OP	RNBT	FBG DV JT	320-650	7 10 2400		2 4	5000	6150
20 6	SONIC 21 OPEN BOW	OP	RNBT	FBG DV IO	188-260	7 10 1300		2 4	3150	3650
20 6	SONIC 21 OPEN BOW	OP	RNBT	FBG DV JT	320-650	7 10 2400		2 4	5250	6400
24 2	SONIC 24 OF	OP	OPFSH	FBG DV OB		8 3600			7550	8700
24 2	SONIC 24 OF	OP	OPFSH	FBG DV IO	260 MRCR	8 3800			8600	9900
24 2	SONIC 24 OF	OP	OPFSH	FBG DV IO	330 MRCR	8 3800			10500	11900
24 2	SONIC 24 OF	OP	OPFSH	FBG DV IO	T260 MRCR	8 4700			9900	11900
24 2	SONIC 24 S	OP	CUD	FBG DV IO	260	8 4000		3	7700	8850
	IO 330 MRCR 8450	9750, JT 333 CHEV 8850		10000, IO T170-T260					9750	11800
	JT T333 CHEV 11900	13500
24 2	SONIC 24 SE	OP	OVNTR	FBG DV IO	260	8 3000		1 6	7200	8250
24 2	SONIC 24 SE	OP	OVNTR	FBG DV IO		8 4000		3	7700	8850
	IO 330 MRCR 8450	9700, JT 333 CHEV 8850		10000, IO T170-T260					9750	11800
	JT T333 CHEV 11900	13500
24 2	SONIC 24 SS	OP	RACE	FBG DV IO	260	8 4000		3	7200	8300
	IO 330 MRCR 7900	9050, JT 333 CHEV 8800		10000, IO T170-T260					9150	11000

CSI MARINE -CONTINUED

See inside cover to adjust price for area

LOA FT IN	NAME AND/ OR MODEL	TOP/ RIG	BOAT TYPE	-HULL- MTL TP	TP	# HP MFG	BEAM FT IN	WGT LBS	DRAFT FT IN	RETAIL LOW	RETAIL HIGH
					1979 BOATS						
24	2 SONIC 24 SSO	OP	RACE	FBG DV	OB	8		3000	1 6	7200	8250
24	2 SONIC 24 SST	OP	RACE	FBG DV	JT	650 CHEV	8	4200	3	9250	10500
					1977 BOATS						
20	6 SONIC 21		RNBT	FBG DV	JT	320-535	7 10	2000		4700	5400

CUSTOM BOAT WORKS
CALYPSO   COAST GUARD MFG ID- CTD

Call 1-800-327-6929 for BUC Personalized Evaluation Service
Or, for 1979 boats, sign onto www.BUCValuPro.com

CUSTOM CRAFT MARINE
MOLDED FIBERGLASS BODY CO
BUFFALO NY

See inside cover to adjust price for area

LOA FT IN	NAME AND/ OR MODEL	TOP/ RIG	BOAT TYPE	-HULL- MTL TP	TP	# HP MFG	BEAM FT IN	WGT LBS	DRAFT FT IN	RETAIL LOW	RETAIL HIGH
					1963 BOATS						
16	DEVIL-RAY MKD MSTR			FBG	IO					**	**
16	6 DELTA-RAY DR 17			FBG	IO					**	**
16	6 SUN-RAY SM 17			FBG	IO					**	**
					1962 BOATS						
16	6	HT		FBG	IO					**	**
16	6 BAHAMIAN CUS FULL HT	HT		FBG	OB					1800	2100
16	6 BAHAMIAN CUS HALF HT	HT		FBG	OB					1800	2100
16	6 DELTA-RAY	HT		FBG	OB					1800	2100
16	6 DELTA-RAY BAHAMIAN			FBG	OB					1800	2100
16	6 DELTA-RAY BAHAMIAN	EXP		FBG	OB					1950	2300
16	6 DELTA-RAY CAT	HT		FBG	OB					1800	2100
16	6 DELTA-RAY CAT	EXP		FBG	OB					1950	2300
16	6 DELTA-RAY CAT	RNBT		FBG	OB					1800	2150
16	6 DELTA-RAY SPTSMN DLX			FBG	OB					1800	2100
16	6 KEY-WEST	HT		FBG	IO					**	**
16	6 KEY-WEST	EXP		FBG	IO					**	**
16	6 KEY-WEST STD			FBG	IO					**	**
16	6 MIAMIAN			FBG	OB					1800	2100
16	6 SUN-RAY MIAMIAN	HT		FBG	OB					1800	2100
16	6 SUN-RAY MIAMIAN		EXP	FBG	OB					1950	2300
					1961 BOATS						
16	6 DELTA-RAY			FBG	OB		6 10	695		2000	2350
16	6 DELTA-RAY	HT	RNBT	FBG	OB		6 10	660		1900	2250
16	6 DELTA-RAY CUSTOM		RNBT	FBG	OB		6 10	645		1850	2200
16	6 DELTA-RAY SPORT		RNBT	FBG	OB		6 10	638		1850	2200
16	6 DELTA-RAY SPT		RNBT	FBG	OB		6 10	640		1800	2100
16	6 DELTA-RAY SPT CUS		RNBT	FBG	OB		6 10	640		1900	2250
16	6 SUN-RAY	HT		FBG	OB		6 10	625		1800	2150
16	6 SUN-RAY		EXP	FBG	OB		6 10	675		1950	2300
16	6 SUN-RAY SPORT		RNBT	FBG	OB		6 10	600		1750	2050
					1960 BOATS						
17	SEA-RAY SENIOR	HT		FBG	OB					1850	2250
17	SEA-RAY SENIOR		RNBT	FBG	OB					1900	2250
22	VICTORY		EXP	WD	IB					**	**
22	VICTORY		SDN	WD	IB					**	**
22	VICTORY TWIN TRUNK		CR	WD	IB					**	**

CUSTOM FIBERGLASS MFG
COAST GUARD MFG ID- CFM

Call 1-800-327-6929 for BUC Personalized Evaluation Service
Or, for 1978 to 1993 boats, sign onto www.BUCValuPro.com

CUSTOM LINE INC
COAST GUARD MFG ID- CWY

Call 1-800-327-6929 for BUC Personalized Evaluation Service
Or, for 1980 to 1984 boats, sign onto www.BUCValuPro.com

CUSTOM MARINE

Call 1-800-327-6929 for BUC Personalized Evaluation Service
Or, for 1976 to 1977 boats, sign onto www.BUCValuPro.com

CUSTOM MARINE
DIV OF SAVANNAH DIST CO COAST GUARD MFG ID- CMN

Call 1-800-327-6929 for BUC Personalized Evaluation Service
Or, for 1977 to 1984 boats, sign onto www.BUCValuPro.com

CUSTOM YACHTS & ACCESSORIES

Call 1-800-327-6929 for BUC Personalized Evaluation Service
Or, for 1971 to 1972 boats, sign onto www.BUCValuPro.com

CUSTOMFLEX INC
TOLEDO OH 43607   COAST GUARD MFG ID- CTF See inside cover to adjust price for area

For more recent years, see the BUC Used Boat Price Guide, Volume 1 or Volume 2

LOA FT IN	NAME AND/ OR MODEL	TOP/ RIG	BOAT TYPE	-HULL- MTL TP	TP	# HP MFG	BEAM FT IN	WGT LBS	DRAFT FT IN	RETAIL LOW	RETAIL HIGH
					1983 BOATS						
18	INTERLAKE	SLP	SA/OD	FBG CB	OB		6 3	650	8	2950	3400
20	HIGHLANDER	SLP	SA/OD	FBG CB	OB		6 8	830	8	3500	4100
					1982 BOATS						
18	INTERLAKE	SLP	SA/OD	FBG CB	OB		6 3	650	8	2750	3200
20	HIGHLANDER	SLP	SA/OD	FBG CB	OB		6 8	830	8	3300	3850
					1981 BOATS						
18	INTERLAKE	SLP	SA/OD	FBG CB	OB		6 3	650	8	2600	3000
20	HIGHLANDER	SLP	SA/OD	FBG CB	OB		6 8	830	8	3100	3600
					1980 BOATS						
20	HIGHLANDER	SLP	SA/OD	FBG CB	OB		6 8	830	8	3000	3450
					1979 BOATS						
18	INTERLAKE	SLP	SA/OD	FBG CB	OB		6 3	650	8	2400	2800
19	FLYING-SCOT	SLP	SA/OD	FBG CB	OB		6 9	675	8	2500	2950
					1978 BOATS						
18	INTERLAKE	SLP	SA/OD	FBG CB	OB		6 3	650	8	2350	2700
19	FLYING-SCOT	SLP	SA/OD	FBG CB	OB		6 9	675	8	2450	2850
19	1 C 5.8	SLP	SA/OD	FBG CB	OB		6 8	1150	8	3050	3550
					1977 BOATS						
18	INTERLAKE	SLP	SA/OD	FBG CB	OB		6 3	650	8	2250	2600
19	FLYING-SCOT	SLP	SA/OD	FBG CB	OB		6 9	775	8	2500	2900
19	1 C5.8	SLP	SAIL	FBG CB	OB		6 8	1250	8	3100	3600
					1976 BOATS						
18	INTERLAKE	SLP	SA/OD	FBG CB	OB		6 3	650	8	2200	2550
19	FLYING-SCOT	SLP	SA/OD	FBG CB	OB		6 9	775	8	2450	2800
					1975 BOATS						
18	INTERLAKE	SLP	SA/OD	FBG CB	OB		6 3	650	8	2050	2450
19	FLYING-SCOT	SLP	SA/OD	FBG CB	OB		6 9	850	8	2450	2850
19	1 MALLARD	SLP	SAIL	FBG DB	OB		6 8	850	8	2450	2850
					1974 BOATS						
18	INTERLAKE	SLP	SA/OD	FBG CB	OB		6 3	650	8	2000	2400
19	FLYING-SCOT	SLP	SA/OD	FBG CB	OB		6 9	775	8	2300	2700
19	1 MALLARD	SLP	SAIL	FBG DB	OB		6 8	1150	8	2700	3150
					1973 BOATS						
18	INTERLAKE	SLP	SA/OD	FBG CB	OB		6 3	650	8	1950	2350
19	FLYING-SCOT	SLP	SA/OD	FBG CB	OB		6 9	820	8	2300	2650
19	1 MALLARD	SLP	SAIL	FBG CB	OB		6 8	1150	8	2650	3100
					1972 BOATS						
18	INTERLAKE	SLP	SA/OD	FBG CB	OB		6 3	650		1900	2300
19	FLYING-SCOT	SLP	SA/OD	FBG CB	OB		6 9	900	6	2350	2700
19	1 MALLARD	SLP	SAIL	FBG KC	OB		6 8	1150	8	2600	3000
					1971 BOATS						
18	INTERLAKE	SLP	SA/OD	FBG CB	OB		6 3	650	8	1900	2250
19	FLYING-SCOT	SLP	SAIL	FBG CB	OB		7	820	6	2200	2550
19	1 MALLARD	SLP	SAIL	FBG KC	OB		6 8	1150	8	2550	2950
					1970 BOATS						
18	INTERLAKE	SLP	SA/OD	FBG CB	OB		6 3	650	8	1850	2200
19	FLYING-SCOT	SLP	SA/OD	FBG CB	OB		7 1	805	8	2100	2500
19	1 MALLARD	SLP	SA/OD	FBG KC	OB		6 8	1150	8	2500	2900
					1969 BOATS						
18	INTERLAKE	SLP	SA/OD	FBG CB	OB		6 3	650	8	1800	2150
19	FLYING-SCOT	SLP	SA/OD	FBG CB	OB		7 1	850	8	2150	2500
					1968 BOATS						
18	INTERLAKE	SLP	SA/OD	FBG CB	OB		6 3	650	8	1800	2150
19	FLYING-SCOT	SLP	SA/OD	FBG CB	OB		7 1	850	8	2100	2500

LOA FT IN	NAME AND/ OR MODEL	TOP/ RIG	BOAT TYPE	-HULL- MTL TP	----ENGINE--- TP # HP MFG	BEAM FT IN	WGT LBS	DRAFT FT IN	RETAIL LOW	RETAIL HIGH
					1967 BOATS					
18	INTERLAKE	SLP	SA/OD	FBG CB	OB	6 3	650	8	1750	2100
19	FLYING-SCOT	SLP	SA/OD	FBG CB	OB	7 1	850	8	2050	2450
24	CRESCENT	SLP	SA/OD	FBG KL	OB	7	2650	4 1	4700	5350
					1966 BOATS					
18	INTERLAKE	SLP	SA/OD	FBG CB	OB	6 3	650	8	1750	2100
19	FLYING-SCOT	SLP	SA/OD	F/S CB	OB	6 9	850	8	2050	2450
24	CRESCENT	SLP	SA/OD	FBG KL	OB	7 6	2650	4 2	4650	5350
					1965 BOATS					
18	INTERLAKE	SLP	SA/OD	FBG CB	OB	6 3	650	4 6	1750	2100
19	FLYING-SCOT	SLP	SA/OD	FBG CB	OB	6 9	850	8	2050	2400
					1961 BOATS					
18	INTERLAKE		SA/OD	FBG CB	OB	6 3	650	8	1750	2050
19	FLYING-SCOT	SLP	SA/OD	FBG CB	OB	6 9	850	8	2000	2400
					1960 BOATS					
18	INTERLAKE	SLP	SA/OD	FBG CB	OB	6 3	650	8	1750	2050
19	FLYING-SCOT	SLP	SA/OD	FBG CB	OB	6 9	850	8	2000	2400
					1959 BOATS					
18	INTERLAKE	SLP	SAIL	FBG CB	OB	6 3	650	8	1750	2050

CUTHBERTSON & CASSIAN LTD

Call 1-800-327-6929 for BUC Personalized Evaluation Service
Or, for 1967 boats, sign onto www.BUCValuPro.com

CUTTER DIVISION
BRUNSWICK CORPORATION

Call 1-800-327-6929 for BUC Personalized Evaluation Service
Or, for 1957 to 1963 boats, sign onto www.BUCValuPro.com

CYCLONE MARINE CORP
COAST GUARD MFG ID- CMI

Call 1-800-327-6929 for BUC Personalized Evaluation Service
Or, for 1981 to 1987 boats, sign onto www.BUCValuPro.com

CYGNUS MARINE LIMITED

Call 1-800-327-6929 for BUC Personalized Evaluation Service
Or, for 1980 boats, sign onto www.BUCValuPro.com

D S YACHT SALES LTD
COAST GUARD MFG ID- ZCW

Call 1-800-327-6929 for BUC Personalized Evaluation Service
Or, for 1979 to 1985 boats, sign onto www.BUCValuPro.com

JACK DANIEL YACHTS LTD
PACIFIC MARINE TRADING   COAST GUARD MFG ID- PTD
FORMERLY PACIFIC MARINE TRADING CO INC

Call 1-800-327-6929 for BUC Personalized Evaluation Service
Or, for 1980 to 1982 boats, sign onto www.BUCValuPro.com

DANYACHTS
DIV OF BAESS BOATS INC   COAST GUARD MFG ID- KBA

SCANDINAVIAN YACHT MARINE SER

Call 1-800-327-6929 for BUC Personalized Evaluation Service
Or, for 1969 to 1984 boats, sign onto www.BUCValuPro.com

DAR-VAN MANUFACTURING INC
PLAY BUOY PONTOONS   COAST GUARD MFG ID- DVN

Call 1-800-327-6929 for BUC Personalized Evaluation Service
Or, for 1971 to 1978 boats, sign onto www.BUCValuPro.com

DARGEL BOAT WORKS INC
COAST GUARD MFG ID- DBW

Call 1-800-327-6929 for BUC Personalized Evaluation Service
Or, for 1960 to 2008 boats, sign onto www.BUCValuPro.com

DARRAGH LTD

Call 1-800-327-6929 for BUC Personalized Evaluation Service
Or, for 1980 to 1987 boats, sign onto www.BUCValuPro.com

DAVIDSON BROS BOATBLDG LTD

Call 1-800-327-6929 for BUC Personalized Evaluation Service
Or, for 1982 to 1983 boats, sign onto www.BUCValuPro.com

DAVIS BOATS

Call 1-800-327-6929 for BUC Personalized Evaluation Service
Or, for 1959 boats, sign onto www.BUCValuPro.com

DAVIS INTERNATIONAL YACHTS
COAST GUARD MFG ID- DMU

BRYAN YACHT SALES

Call 1-800-327-6929 for BUC Personalized Evaluation Service
Or, for 1980 boats, sign onto www.BUCValuPro.com

DAWN BOAT CORP
NEW YORK NY 10473   See inside cover to adjust price for area

LOA FT IN	NAME AND/ OR MODEL	TOP/ RIG	BOAT TYPE	-HULL- MTL TP	----ENGINE--- TP # HP MFG	BEAM FT IN	WGT LBS	DRAFT FT IN	RETAIL LOW	RETAIL HIGH
					1939 BOATS					
52		HT	MY	WD	IB				**	**
					1938 BOATS					
56 6				WD	IB T225D GM				**	**
					1937 BOATS					
60	PILOT HOUSE	MY		WD	IB T D GM				**	**
					1932 BOATS					
30		HT	CR	WD	VD				**	**
45		HT	CR	WD	IB				**	**
50		HT	MY	WD	VD				**	**
60		HT	MY	WD	IB				**	**
					1931 BOATS					
45		HT	CR	WD	IB T100 LATH				48800	53600
48		FB	CR	WD	IB				**	**
					1930 BOATS					
46				WD	IB 200 PALM				**	**
48				WD	IB				**	**
					1929 BOATS					
42		HT	MY	WD	IB T				**	**

DAWN-CRAFT
JOHN E CLABBURN & CO LTD

Call 1-800-327-6929 for BUC Personalized Evaluation Service
Or, for 1979 boats, sign onto www.BUCValuPro.com

DAWSON YACHT CORP
DIV OF ALEXANDER DAWSON INC   See inside cover to adjust price for area
LAS VEGAS NV 89030   COAST GUARD MFG ID- DYC

LOA FT IN	NAME AND/ OR MODEL	TOP/ RIG	BOAT TYPE	-HULL- MTL TP	----ENGINE--- TP # HP MFG	BEAM FT IN	WGT LBS	DRAFT FT IN	RETAIL LOW	RETAIL HIGH
					1978 BOATS					
25 7	DAWSON 26	KTH	SA/CR	FBG SK	IB 8D YAN	8	4750	1 8	9750	11100
					1977 BOATS					
25 7	DAWSON 26	SLP	SA/CR	FBG SK	IB 8D YAN	8	4700	1 8	9400	10700
25 7	DAWSON 26	KTH	SA/CR	FBG SK	IB 8D YAN	8	4700	1 8	9400	10700

DAWSON YACHT CORP

-CONTINUED   See inside cover to adjust price for area

LOA FT IN	NAME AND/ OR MODEL	TOP/ RIG	BOAT TYPE	-HULL- MTL TP	TP	----ENGINE--- # HP MFG	BEAM FT IN	WGT LBS	DRAFT FT IN	RETAIL LOW	RETAIL HIGH
					1976 BOATS						
25 7	DAWSON 26	SLP	SAIL	FBG SK	IB	10 UNIV	8	3875	1 8	7250	8300
25 7	DAWSON 26	SLP	SAIL	FBG SK	IB	7D- 25D	8	3875	1 8	7550	8900
25 7	DAWSON 26	KTH	SAIL	FBG SK	IB	10 UNIV	8	3875	1 8	7250	8300
25 7	DAWSON 26	KTH	SAIL	FBG SK	IB	7D- 25D	8	3875	1 8	7550	8900
					1975 BOATS						
25 7	DAWSON 26	SLP	SA/CR	FBG SK	IB	D	8	3875	1 8	7350	8450
25 7	DAWSON 26	KTH	SA/CR	FBG SK	IB	D	8	3875	1 8	7350	8450

DAYTONA BOAT CO
COAST GUARD MFG ID- DYL

Call 1-800-327-6929 for BUC Personalized Evaluation Service
Or, for 1980 boats, sign onto www.BUCValuPro.com

DAYTONA MARINA & BOAT WORKS
DAYTONA BEACH FL 32014   See inside cover to adjust price for area

LOA FT IN	NAME AND/ OR MODEL	TOP/ RIG	BOAT TYPE	-HULL- MTL TP	TP	----ENGINE--- # HP MFG	BEAM FT IN	WGT LBS	DRAFT FT IN	RETAIL LOW	RETAIL HIGH
					1972 BOATS						
37	DAYTONA		SF	WD SV	IB	T280	12 7			54900	60300
65	DAYTONA		SF	WD SV	IB	T280	12 7			**	**
65	DAYTONA		SF	WD SV	IB	T280D	12 7			211500	232500
					1971 BOATS						
37	DAYTONA		SF	F/W	IB	T			3	**	**
41	DAYTONA		SF	F/W	IB	T	13 6		3 4	**	**
43	DAYTONA				IB	T	13 9		3 6	**	**
48 2	DAYTONA		SF	F/W	IB	T	15 4		3 9	**	**
50	DAYTONA			FBG	IB	T	15 7		3 9	**	**
					1970 BOATS						
37	DAYTONA		SF	F/W SV	IB	T	12 6		3	**	**
41	DAYTONA		SF	F/W SV	IB	T	13 9		3 4	**	**
43	DAYTONA				IB	T	13 9		3 6	**	**
48 2	DAYTONA		SF	F/W SV	IB	T	15 4		3 9	**	**
50	DAYTONA			FBG	IB	T	15 7		3 9	**	**
					1969 BOATS						
37	DAYTONA 37		SF	FBG SV	IB	T	12 6		3	**	**
37	DAYTONA 37		SF	WD SV	IB	T	12 6		3	**	**
41	DAYTONA 41		SF	FBG SV	IB	T	13 9		3 4	**	**
41	DAYTONA 41		SF	WD SV	IB	T	13 9		3 4	**	**
43	DAYTONA 43				IB	T	13 9		3 6	**	**
48	DAYTONA 48		SF	FBG SV	IB	T	15 4		3 9	**	**
48	DAYTONA 48		SF	WD SV	IB	T	15 4		3 9	**	**
50	DAYTONA 50			FBG	IB	T	15 7		3 9	**	**
					1968 BOATS						
37	DAYTONA		SF	F/W	IB	T	12 6		3	**	**
41	DAYTONA		SF	F/W	IB	T	13		3 4	**	**
45	DAYTONA		SF	F/W	IB	T	15		3 6	**	**
48	DAYTONA		SF	F/W	IB	T	15		3 6	**	**

DE SILVA BOATS
COAST GUARD MFG ID- DSA

Call 1-800-327-6929 for BUC Personalized Evaluation Service
Or, for 1961 to 1977 boats, sign onto www.BUCValuPro.com

DEACONS BOAT CENTRE

Call 1-800-327-6929 for BUC Personalized Evaluation Service
Or, for 1971 to 1985 boats, sign onto www.BUCValuPro.com

JOHN L DEAN & COMPANY

Call 1-800-327-6929 for BUC Personalized Evaluation Service
Or, for 1966 boats, sign onto www.BUCValuPro.com

DECKERT MARINE ENT
INFINITY YACHTS
FORT WALTON BEACH FL 32 COAST GUARD MFG ID- NAN   See inside cover to adjust price for area

LOA FT IN	NAME AND/ OR MODEL	TOP/ RIG	BOAT TYPE	-HULL- MTL TP	TP	----ENGINE--- # HP MFG	BEAM FT IN	WGT LBS	DRAFT FT IN	RETAIL LOW	RETAIL HIGH
					1980 BOATS						
39	INFINITY 388		SF	FBG DV	IB	T350	13 8	18500		89500	98400
39	INFINITY 388 DIVE		SF	FBG DV	IB	T210D	13 8	18500		104500	114500
					1979 BOATS						
38 8	INFINITY 388		SF	FBG DV	IB	T350	13 8	18500		84300	92700
38 8	INFINITY 388		SF	FBG DV	IB	T D	13 8	18500		**	**
38 8	INFINITY 388 DIVE		SF	FBG DV	IB	T210	13 8	18500		82100	90200
					1978 BOATS						
38 8	INFINITY 388	FB	SF	FBG DV	IB	T350	13 8	18500		81100	89100
38 8	INFINITY 388	FB	SF	FBG DV	IB	T D	13 8	18500		**	**
38 8	INFINITY 388 D	OP	SF	FBG DV	IB	T350	13 8	18000		76600	84100
38 8	INFINITY 388 D	OP	SF	FBG DV	IB	T	13 8	18000		**	**
					1977 BOATS						
38 8	INFINITY 388	FB	SF	FBG DV	IB	T350	13 8	18500		77700	85400
38 8	INFINITY 388	FB	SF	FBG DV	IB	T D	13 8	18500		**	**
38 8	INFINITY 388 D	OP	SF	FBG DV	IB	T350	13 8	18000		73400	80600
38 8	INFINITY 388 D	OP	SF	FBG DV	IB	T	13 8	18000		**	**
					1976 BOATS						
38 8	INFINITY 388	FB	SF	FBG DV	IB	T350 MRCR	13 8	18000	2 6	73000	80200
38 8	INFINITY 388	FB	SF	FBG DV	IB	T210D CAT	13 8	18500	3	88800	97600
38 8	INFINITY 388	FB	SF	FBG DV	IB	T210D GM	13 8	18500	3	86800	95400
					1975 BOATS						
38 8	INFINITY 388	FB	SF	FBG DV	IB	T225D	13 8	18000		84000	92400
38 8	INFINITY 388 D	OP	SF	FBG DV	IB	T350	13 8	18000		67600	74300
38 8	INFINITY 388 D	OP	SF	FBG DV	IB	T D	13 8	18500		**	**

DEERFOOT YACHTS
FT LAUDERDALE FL 33302   See inside cover to adjust price for area

For more recent years, see the BUC Used Boat Price Guide, Volume 1 or Volume 2

LOA FT IN	NAME AND/ OR MODEL	TOP/ RIG	BOAT TYPE	-HULL- MTL TP	TP	----ENGINE--- # HP MFG	BEAM FT IN	WGT LBS	DRAFT FT IN	RETAIL LOW	RETAIL HIGH
					1982 BOATS						
62	DEERFOOT 62	SLP	SA/CR AL	KL IB		85D PERK	14 6	49700	5 9	369000	405500
62 3	DEERFOOT 62	SLP	SA/CR AL	KL IB	T	D VW	14 6	49700	5 9	375000	412000
62 3	DEERFOOT 62	KTH	SA/CR AL	KL IB		85D PERK	14 6	49700	5 9	369000	406500
62 3	DEERFOOT 62	KTH	SA/CR AL	KL IB	T	D VW	14 6	49700	5 9	375000	412000
68	DEERFOOT 70	SLP	SA/CR FBG	KL IB		83D GM	14 3	60000	8 6	415500	456500
68	DEERFOOT 70	CUT	SA/CR FBG	KL IB		83D GM	14 3	60000	8 6	415500	456500
68	DEERFOOT 70	KTH	SA/CR FBG	KL IB		83D GM	14 3	60000	8 6	415500	456500

DEFEVER PASSAGEMAKER TRWL
A BANGOR PUNTA COMPANY
DIV OF JENSEN MARINE
COSTA MESA CA 92626   COAST GUARD MFG ID- PAS   See inside cover to adjust price for area

For more recent years, see the BUC Used Boat Price Guide, Volume 1 or Volume 2

LOA FT IN	NAME AND/ OR MODEL	TOP/ RIG	BOAT TYPE	-HULL- MTL TP	TP	----ENGINE--- # HP MFG	BEAM FT IN	WGT LBS	DRAFT FT IN	RETAIL LOW	RETAIL HIGH
					1980 BOATS						
42 7	DEFEVER TRI-CABIN	FB	TRWL	FBG DS	IB	T120D LEHM	14	52000	4 5	107500	118500
49	DEFEVER PILOT HOUSE		TRWL	FBG DS	IB	T120D	15	60000		111000	122000
58	OFFSHORE SEDAN		TRWL	FBG DS	IB	T250D	18	85000		205500	226000
					1979 BOATS						
42 7	PASSAGEMAKER TRI-CBN	FB	TRWL	FBG DS	IB	T120D LEHM	14	52000	4 5	104500	114500
49	PASSAGEMAKER PH		TRWL	FBG DS	IB	T120D LEHM	15	60000		107000	117500
58	PASSAGEMAKER SDN		TRWL	FBG DS	IB	T250D	18	85000		196000	215500
					1978 BOATS						
42 7	PASSAGEMAKER TRI-CBN	FB	TRWL	FBG DS	IB	T120D LEHM	14	52000	4 5	99700	109500
					1977 BOATS						
39 6	PASSAGEMAKER		FB	TRWL	FBG DS IB		130D PERK	13 8	26500	4 2	64000	70300
					1976 BOATS						
34	PASSAGEMAKER		FB	TRWL	FBG DS IB		130D PERK	13 3	19259	3	50400	55400
39 6	PASSAGEMAKER		FB	TRWL	FBG DS IB		130D PERK	13 8	26465	4 2	61300	67400
					1975 BOATS						
34	PASSAGEMAKER DC	FB	TRWL	FBG DS	IB	130D	12 3	19300	3 4	48900	53700
39 6	PASSAGEMAKER TRI-CBN	FB	TRWL	FBG DS	IB	130D PERK	13 8	26500	4 2	58900	64800
39 6	PASSAGEMAKER TRI-CBN	FB	TRWL	FBG DS	IB	T130D PERK	13 8	26500	4 2	62400	68600
					1974 BOATS						
34	PASSAGEMAKER DC	FB	TRWL	FBG DS	IB	120D	12 3	19300	3 4	47800	52500
39 6	PASSAGEMAKER TRI-CBN	FB	TRWL	FBG DS	IB	120D	13 8	26500	4 2	56200	61700
39 6	PASSAGEMAKER TRI-CBN	FB	TRWL	FBG DS	IB	T120D	13 8	26500	4 2	59000	64800
49 11	PASSAGEMAKER TRI-CBN		TRWL	FBG DS	IB	200D	14 6		5 10	87400	96100
52	PASSAGEMAKER		TRWL	F/W DS	IB	T185D	15 9			121500	133500

LOA FT IN	NAME AND/ OR MODEL	TOP/ RIG	BOAT TYPE	HULL MTL	HULL TP	ENG TP	#	HP	MFG	BEAM FT IN	WGT LBS	DRAFT FT IN	RETAIL LOW	RETAIL HIGH
1973 BOATS														
38	PASSAGEMAKER		TRWL	FBG	DS	IB		120D		13 8		4	43600	48400
39 6	PASSAGEMAKER		TRWL	FBG	DS	IB		120D		13 8	26500	4 2	54100	59400
49 11	PASSAGEMAKER		TRWL	F/W	DS	IB		200D		14 6		5 10	106500	117000
53 11	PASSAGEMAKER		TRWL	WD	DS	IB		T200D		16 11	60083	4 9	116000	127500
1972 BOATS														
38	PASSAGEMAKER		TRWL	WD	DS	IB		120D		13 8	23158	4	43600	48400
38	PASSAGEMAKER		TRWL	WD	DS	IB		210D		13 8	23158	4	44200	49100
49 11	PASSAGEMAKER		TRWL	WD	DS	IB		125D		14 6	60000	5 10	100500	110500
53 11	PASSAGEMAKER	HT	TRWL	WD	DS	IB		T125D		16 11	60083	4 9	103500	113500
53 11	PASSAGEMAKER	HT	TRWL	WD	DS	IB		T260D		16 11	60083	4 9	122500	134500
53 11	PASSAGEMAKER	FB	TRWL	WD	DS	IB		T125D		16 11	60083	4 9	102000	112000
53 11	PASSAGEMAKER	FB	TRWL	WD	DS	IB		T260D		16 11	60083	4 9	120000	132000
1971 BOATS														
38	PASSAGEMAKER		TRWL	FBC	DS	IB		120D		13 8		4	40600	45100
45 7	PASSAGEMAKER		TRWL	WD	DS	IB		200D		14 6		5 9	81000	89000
49 11	PASSAGEMAKER		TRWL	STL	DS	IB		445D		15		5 11	104500	114500
49 11	PASSAGEMAKER		TRWL	WD	DS	IB		T200D		14 6		5 9	105000	115500
53 8	PASSAGEMAKER		TRWL	FBG	DS	IB		T200D		16 9		4 9	104000	114000
53 8	PASSAGEMAKER		TRWL	WD	DS	IB		T200D		16 9		4 9	103500	114000
53 8	PASSAGEMAKER		TRWL	FBG	DS	IB		T280D		16 9		4 9	107500	118500
53 8	PASSAGEMAKER		TRWL	WD	DS	IB		T280D		16 9		4 9	107500	118500

DELANY SPORTING GOODS

Call 1-800-327-6929 for BUC Personalized Evaluation Service
Or, for 1960 to 1961 boats, sign onto www.BUCValuPro.com

DELHI MANUFACTURING CORP

TERRY BOATS
DIV OF WOODSTREAM CORP   COAST GUARD MFG ID- DEM

Call 1-800-327-6929 for BUC Personalized Evaluation Service
Or, for 1961 to 1982 boats, sign onto www.BUCValuPro.com

DELL QUAY DORIES

BOSUN MARINE MARKETING   COAST GUARD MFG ID- DQU
DELL QUAY MARINE LTD

Call 1-800-327-6929 for BUC Personalized Evaluation Service
Or, for 1983 to 1986 boats, sign onto www.BUCValuPro.com

DELLWIHK CRUISERS

Call 1-800-327-6929 for BUC Personalized Evaluation Service
Or, for 1965 to 1979 boats, sign onto www.BUCValuPro.com

DELTA COUNTRY BOATS

COAST GUARD MFG ID- DCN

Call 1-800-327-6929 for BUC Personalized Evaluation Service
Or, for 1980 boats, sign onto www.BUCValuPro.com

DELTA MARINE & FIBERGLASS INC

COAST GUARD MFG ID- DEL

Call 1-800-327-6929 for BUC Personalized Evaluation Service
Or, for 1977 to 1983 boats, sign onto www.BUCValuPro.com

DELTA MFG CO INC

COAST GUARD MFG ID- DLT

Call 1-800-327-6929 for BUC Personalized Evaluation Service
Or, for 1979 to 1980 boats, sign onto www.BUCValuPro.com

DERECKTOR SHIPYARDS

MAMARONECK NY 10543   COAST GUARD MFG ID- DBY See inside cover to adjust price for area

LOA FT IN	NAME AND/ OR MODEL	TOP/ RIG	BOAT TYPE	HULL MTL	HULL TP	ENG TP	#	HP	MFG	BEAM FT IN	WGT LBS	DRAFT FT IN	RETAIL LOW	RETAIL HIGH
1968 BOATS														
40	PT40	SLP	SA/CR	FBG	KL	IB				11		5 6	30900	34400
1964 BOATS														
47	CLASS B	SLP	SA/RC	AL									**	**

DESIGN UNLIMITED

Call 1-800-327-6929 for BUC Personalized Evaluation Service
Or, for 1966 to 1968 boats, sign onto www.BUCValuPro.com

SAMUAL S DEVLIN BOATBUILDING

COAST GUARD MFG ID- XDK

Call 1-800-327-6929 for BUC Personalized Evaluation Service
Or, for 1982 to 1993 boats, sign onto www.BUCValuPro.com

DEWORLD ENTERPRISES INC

TAIPEI TAIWAN   See inside cover to adjust price for area

LOA FT IN	NAME AND/ OR MODEL	TOP/ RIG	BOAT TYPE	HULL MTL	HULL TP	ENG TP	#	HP	MFG	BEAM FT IN	WGT LBS	DRAFT FT IN	RETAIL LOW	RETAIL HIGH
1981 BOATS														
42 8	CAPE-HORN 43	CUT	SA/CR	F/S	KL	IB		D	PERK	12 6	24600	6 2	73900	81300
42 8	POLARIS 43	CUT	SA/CR	F/S	KL	IB		D	PERK	12 6	24600	6 2	73900	81300

DIAMOND MARINE CORP

COAST GUARD MFG ID- DMW

Call 1-800-327-6929 for BUC Personalized Evaluation Service
Or, for 1979 to 1982 boats, sign onto www.BUCValuPro.com

DICKERSON BOATBUILDERS INC

TRAPPE MD 21673   COAST GUARD MFG ID- DBB See inside cover to adjust price for area

For more recent years, see the BUC Used Boat Price Guide, Volume 1 or Volume 2

LOA FT IN	NAME AND/ OR MODEL	TOP/ RIG	BOAT TYPE	HULL MTL	HULL TP	ENG TP	#	HP	MFG	BEAM FT IN	WGT LBS	DRAFT FT IN	RETAIL LOW	RETAIL HIGH
1983 BOATS														
37	DICKERSON 37 AFT	SLP	SA/CR	F/S	KL	VD		50D	PERK	11 6	15960	4 6	47800	52500
37	DICKERSON 37 AFT	CUT	SA/CR	F/S	KL	VD		50D	PERK	11 6	15960	4 6	47800	52500
37	DICKERSON 37 CTR	KTH	SA/CR	F/S	KL	VD		50D	PERK	11 6	15960	4 6	47800	52500
50	DICKERSON 50 AFT	SLP	SA/CR	F/S	KC	VD		62D	PERK	13 8	33900	5 2	140000	154000
50	DICKERSON 50 AFT	SLP	SA/CR	F/S	KL	VD		62D	PERK	13 8	33900	6 6	140000	154000
50	DICKERSON 50 AFT	CUT	SA/CR	F/S	KC	VD		62D	PERK	13 8	33900	5 2	137500	151000
50	DICKERSON 50 AFT	CUT	SA/CR	F/S	KL	VD		62D	PERK	13 8	33900	6 6	137500	151000
50	DICKERSON 50 AFT	KTH	SA/CR	F/S	KC	VD		62D	PERK	13 8	33900	5 2	143000	157000
50	DICKERSON 50 AFT	KTH	SA/CR	F/S	KL	VD		62D	PERK	13 8	33900	6 6	143000	157000
1982 BOATS														
32	CRUISER		CR	FBG	SV	IO		128		10 4			14200	16100
32	WORKBOAT		UTL	FBG	SV	IO				10 4			**	**
37	DICKERSON 37	KTH	SA/CR	FBG	KL	IB		37D	PERK	11 6	15950	4 6	44100	49000
39 8	CRUISER		CR	FBG	SV	IO		200		12 6			26600	29500
39 8	WORKBOAT		UTL	FBG	SV	IO				12 6			**	**
41	DICKERSON 41	CUT	SA/CR	FBG	KC	IB		50D	WEST	12 6	24500	4 6	71700	78800
41	DICKERSON 41	CUT	SA/CR	FBG	KC	IB		50D	WEST	12 6	24500	4 6	71700	78800
41	DICKERSON 41	KTH	SA/CR	FBG	KC	IB		50D	WEST	12 6	24500	4 6	71900	79000
41	DICKERSON 41	KTH	SA/CR	FBG	KC	IB		50D	WEST	12 6	24500	4 6	71900	79000
50	DICKERSON 50	KTH	SA/CR	FBG	KC	IB		85D	PERK	13 8	33900	5 2	134500	148000
50	DICKERSON 50	KTH	SA/CR	FBG	KC	IB		85D	PERK	13 8	33900	6 6	143000	148000
1981 BOATS														
32 3	CHOPTANK-CANNONBALL		UTL	FBG	SV	IO		140		10 3			15000	17000
32 3	WAVERLY-ISLAND-JR		CR	FBG	SV	IO		140		10 3			14700	16700
36	DICKERSON 36	SLP	SA/CR	FBG	KL	IB		30D	WEST	10 5	14500	4	33400	37100
36	DICKERSON 36	CUT	SA/CR	FBG	KL	IB		30D	WEST	10 5	14500	4	33400	37100
36	DICKERSON 36	KTH	SA/CR	FBG	KL	IB		30D	WEST	10 5	14500	4	33400	37100
37	DICKERSON 37	KTH	SA/CR	FBG	KL	IB		40D	WEST	14	15350	4 6	40300	44800
41	DICKERSON 41	CUT	SA/CR	FBG	KC	IB		50D	WEST	12 6	24500	4 6	67200	73900
41	DICKERSON 41	CUT	SA/CR	FBG	KC	IB		50D	WEST	12 6	24500	4 6	67200	73900
41	DICKERSON 41	KTH	SA/CR	FBG	KC	IB		50D	WEST	12 6	24500	4 6	67300	73900
41	DICKERSON 41	KTH	SA/CR	FBG	KC	IB		50D	WEST	12 6	24500	4 6	67300	73900
42	WAVERLY-ISLAND-SR		CR	FBG	SV	IO		140		13		6	35100	39100

LOA FT	LOA IN	NAME AND/ OR MODEL	TOP/ RIG	BOAT TYPE	-HULL- MTL	-HULL- TP	ENGINE TP	ENGINE # HP	ENGINE MFG	BEAM FT	BEAM IN	WGT LBS	DRAFT FT	DRAFT IN	RETAIL LOW	RETAIL HIGH
		1980 BOATS														
32		WORKBOAT/CRUISER	HT	UTL	FBG	DV	IB	D	PERK	10	2		2	9	**	**
36		DICKERSON 36	SLP	SA/CR	FBG	KL	IB	30D	WEST	10	5	14500	4		31700	35300
36		DICKERSON 36	CUT	SA/CR	FBG	KL	IB	30D	WEST	10	5	14500	4		31700	35300
36		DICKERSON 36	KTH	SA/CR	FBG	KL	IB	30D	WEST	10	5	14500	4		31700	35300
37		DICKERSON 37	KTH	SA/CR	FBG	KL	IB	40D	WEST	11	1	14430	4	6	36400	40400
41		DICKERSON 41	KTH	SA/CR	FBG	KC	IB	50D	WEST	12	6	24500			64000	70300
41		DICKERSON 41	KTH	SA/CR	FBG	KL	IB	50D	WEST	12	6	24500	4	6	64000	70300
42		WORKBOAT/CRUISER	HT	UTL	FBG	DV	IB	D	PERK	13			3	2	**	**
		1979 BOATS														
29	10	CHESAPEAKE 30	SLP	SA/CR	FBG	KC	IB	D		12		14000	3		25800	28700
36	2	DICKERSON 36	SLP	SA/CR	FBG	KL	IB	30D	WEST	10	5	13500	4		28800	32000
36	2	DICKERSON 36	SLP	SA/CR	FBG	KL	IB	40D	WEST	10	5	13500	4		28900	32100
36	2	DICKERSON 36	CUT	SA/CR	FBG	KL	IB	30D	WEST	10	5	13500	4		28800	32000
36	2	DICKERSON 36	CUT	SA/CR	FBG	KL	IB	40D	WEST	10	5	13500	4		28900	32100
36	2	DICKERSON 36	KTH	SA/CR	FBG	KL	IB	30D	WEST	10	5	13500	4		28800	32000
36	2	DICKERSON 36	KTH	SA/CR	FBG	KL	IB	40D	WEST	10	5	13500	4		28900	32100
41		DICKERSON 41	KTH	SA/CR	FBG	KL	IB	40D	WEST	12	6	24000	4	6	59100	65000
41		DICKERSON 41	KTH	SA/CR	FBG	KL	IB	60D	WEST	12	6	24000	4	6	59500	65400
41		DICKERSON 41 PH	KTH	SA/CR	FBG	KL	IB	40D	WEST	12	6	24000	4	6	61500	67600
41		DICKERSON 41 PH	KTH	SA/CR	FBG	KL	IB	60D	WEST	12	6	24000	4	6	61800	67900
		1978 BOATS														
29	10	CHESAPEAKE 30	SLP	SA/CR	FBG	CB	IB	30	UNIV	12		11400	3		19800	22000
29	10	CHESAPEAKE 30	SLP	SA/CR	FBG	CB	IB	D	WEST	12		11400	3		20000	22200
36	2	DICKERSON 36	SLP	SA/CR	FBG	KL	IB	30	UNIV	10	5	13000	4		26400	29300
36	2	DICKERSON 36	SLP	SA/CR	FBG	KL	IB	40D	WEST	10	5	13000	4		26900	29800
36	2	DICKERSON 36	KTH	SA/CR	FBG	KL	IB	30	UNIV	10	5	13000	4		26400	29300
36	2	DICKERSON 36	KTH	SA/CR	FBG	KL	IB	40D	WEST	10	5	13000	4		26900	29800
41		DICKERSON 41	SLP	SA/CR	FBG	KL	IB	37D	WEST	12	6	24000	4	6	57800	63600
41		DICKERSON 41	KTH	SA/CR	FBG	KL	IB	37D	WEST	12	6	24000	4	6	57900	63600
		1977 BOATS														
30		SEIDELMANN 30	SLP	SA/RC	FBG	KC	IB	30	UNIV	12		9400	3	6	15500	17600
30		SEIDELMANN 30	SLP	SA/RC	FBG	KC	IB	30D		12		9400	3	6	15600	17700
36		DICKERSON DOUBLE CBN	KTH	SA/CR	FBG	KL	IB	30	UNIV	10	6	12000	4		24200	26900
36		DICKERSON DOUBLE CBN	KTH	SA/CR	FBG	KL	IB	37D	WEST	10	6	12000	4		24600	27400
36		DICKERSON SINGLE CBN	KTH	SA/CR	FBG	KL	IB	30	UNIV	10	6	12000	4		22500	25000
36		DICKERSON SINGLE CBN	KTH	SA/CR	FBG	KL	IB	37D	WEST	10	6	12000	4		23000	25600
41		DICKERSON	KTH	SA/CR	FBG	KL	IB	40D	WEST	12	6	23000	4	6	54300	59700
41		DICKERSON	KTH	SA/CR	FBG	KL	IB	53D	WEST	12	6	23000	4	6	54500	59900
		1976 BOATS														
28	4	DICKERSON	SLP	SA/CR	FBG	CB	IB	D		8	9	7000	6	5	11000	12500
36		DICKERSON DOUBLE CBN	KTH	SA/CR	FBG	KL	IB	30	UNIV	10	5	12000	4		23400	26000
36		DICKERSON DOUBLE CBN	KTH	SA/CR	FBG	KL	IB	37D	WEST	10	5	12000	4		23800	26400
36		DICKERSON SINGLE CBN	KTH	SA/CR	FBG	KL	IB	30	UNIV	10	5	12000	4		21800	24200
36		DICKERSON SINGLE CBN	KTH	SA/CR	FBG	KL	IB	37D	WEST	10	5	12000	4		22200	24700
41		DICKERSON	KTH	SA/CR	FBG	KL	IB	37D	WEST	12	6	23000	4	6	52400	57600
41		DICKERSON	KTH	SA/CR	FBG	KL	IB	53D	WEST	12	6	23000	4	6	52700	57900
		1975 BOATS														
36		DICKERSON DOUBLE CBN	KTH	SA/CR	FBG	KL	IB	30	UNIV	10	5	12000	4		22700	25200
36		DICKERSON DOUBLE CBN	KTH	SA/CR	FBG	KL	IB	D		10	5	12000	4		22900	25500
36		DICKERSON SINGLE CBN	KTH	SA/CR	FBG	KL	IB	30	UNIV	10	5	12000	4		21000	23400
36		DICKERSON SINGLE CBN	KTH	SA/CR	FBG	KL	IB	D		10	5	12000	4		21400	23700
41	6	DICKERSON	KTH	SA/CR	FBG	KL	IB	40D	WEST	12	6	23000	4	6	52000	57100
41	6	DICKERSON	KTH	SA/CR	FBG	KL	IB	53D	WEST	12	6	23000	4	6	52200	57300
		1974 BOATS														
35		DICKERSON	KTH	SA/CR	P/M	KL	IB	30	UNIV	10	5	12000	4		20200	22400
35		DICKERSON DC	KTH	SA/CR	P/M	KL	IB	30	UNIV	10	5	12000	4		20200	22400
36		DICKERSON	KTH	SA/CR	FBG	KL	IB	30	UNIV	10	6	12000	4		20400	22700
36		DICKERSON	KTH	SA/CR	P/M	KL	IB	30	UNIV	10	5	12000	4		21300	23600
36		DICKERSON DC	KTH	SA/CR	FBG	KL	IB	30	UNIV	10	6	12000	4		22100	24500
40		DICKERSON	KTH	SA/CR	P/M	KL	IB	40D	WEST	12		18000	4	6	38800	43100
40		DICKERSON DC	KTH	SA/CR	P/M	KL	IB	40D	WEST	12		18000	4	6	41500	46100
41	6	DICKERSON	KTH	SA/CR	FBG	KL	IB	40D	WEST	12		23000	4	6	50500	55500
41	6	DICKERSON DC	KTH	SA/CR	FBG	KL	IB	40D	WEST	12		23000	4	6	50500	55500
		1973 BOATS														
35		DICKERSON	KTH	SA/CR	P/M	KL	IB	30	UNIV	10	5	12000	4		19100	21200
35		DICKERSON DC	KTH	SA/CR	P/M	KL	IB	30	UNIV	10	5	12000	4		20500	22700
36		DICKERSON	KTH	SA/CR	FBG	KL	IB	30	UNIV	10	6	12000	4		19900	22100
36		DICKERSON	KTH	SA/CR	P/M	KL	IB	30	UNIV	10	5	12000	4		19900	22100
36		DICKERSON DC	KTH	SA/CR	FBG	KL	IB	30	UNIV	10	6	12000	4		21600	24000
36		DICKERSON DC	KTH	SA/CR	P/M	KL	IB	30	UNIV	10	5	12000	4		21600	24000
40		DICKERSON	KTH	SA/CR	P/M	KL	IB	40D	WEST	12		18000	4	6	37800	42000
40		DICKERSON		TRWL	P/M		IB	130D	FORD	12	9	28000	4		46600	51200
40		DICKERSON DC	KTH	SA/CR	P/M	KL	IB	40D	WEST	12		18000	4	6	40600	45100
40		OFFSHORE DC		TRWL	WD	RB	IB	120D		12	9	28000			46500	51100
41		DICKERSON	KTH	SA/CR	P/M		IB	40D	WEST	12		18000	4	6	39700	44100
41		DICKERSON DC	KTH	SA/CR	P/M	KL	IB	40D	WEST	12		18000	4	6	42500	47300
42		OFFSHORE DC		TRWL	WD	RB	IB	120D		12	9	29753			50300	55300
		1972 BOATS														
25		DICKERSON		OFF	P/M		IB	110		9			2		3800	4400
25		DICKERSON		OFF	P/M		IB	400		9			2		4700	5350
35		DICKERSON	KTH	SA/CR	P/M		IB	30	UNIV	10	5	12000	4		19300	21400
36		DICKERSON	KTH	SA/CR	FBG		IB	30	UNIV	10	6	12000	4		20300	22600
40		DICKERSON	KTH	SA/CR	P/M		IB	37D	WEST	12		18000	4	6	38300	42600
40		DICKERSON		TRWL	P/M		IB	130D	FORD	12	9	28000	4		44400	49300
42		DICKERSON OFFSHORE		TRWL	P/M		IB	200		13		29753	4		44600	49600
42		DICKERSON OFFSHORE		TRWL	P/M		IB	T130D		13		29753	4		51100	56100
		1971 BOATS														
35		DICKERSON	KTH	SA/CR	P/M		IB	30	UNIV	10	5	12000	4		19100	21300
40		DICKERSON	KTH	SA/CR	P/M		IB	37D	WEST	12		18000	4	6	37700	41900
40		DICKERSON		TRWL	P/M		IB	130D	FORD	12	9	28000	4		42800	47600
		1970 BOATS														
35		DICKERSON 35	KTH	SA/CR	P/M	KL	IB	30	UNIV	10	6	12000	4		18400	20400
35		DICKERSON 35 DBL CBN	KTH	SA/CR	P/M	KL	IB	30	UNIV	10	6	12000	4		19100	21300
40		DICKERSON 40	KTH	SA/CR	P/M	KL	IB	37D	WEST	12		18000	4	6	36300	40300
40		DICKERSON 40 DBL CBN	KTH	SA/CR	P/M	KL	IB	37D	WEST	12		18000	4	6	38000	42200
40		DICKERSON OFFSHORE		TRWL	WD	RB	IB	125D		12	6	24000	4		36500	40500
		1969 BOATS														
35		DICKERSON 35	KTH	SA/CR	P/M	KL	IB	25D		10	5	12000	4		18800	20900
40		DICKERSON 40	KTH	SA/CR	P/M	KL	IB	35D		12		16000	4	6	33700	37500
		1968 BOATS														
35		DICKERSON	KTH	SA/CR	P/M	KL	IB	25D		10	5	13206	4		20100	22400
40		DICKERSON	KTH	SA/CR	P/M	KL	IB	35D		12		18000	4	6	36200	40200
		1967 BOATS														
35		DICKERSON		SA/CR	WD	CB	IB	D		10		13206	4		21300	23700
35		DICKERSON		SA/CR	WD	KL	IB	D		10		13206	4		20400	22600
35		DICKERSON 35	KTH	SA/CR	P/M	KL	IB	25D		10	5		4		20700	23000
35		DICKERSON 35 DC	KTH	SA/CR	P/M	KL	IB	25D		10	5		4		22500	25000
35		DICKERSON SINGLE CBN		SA/CR	WD	CB	IB	D		10		13206	4		19700	21800
35		DICKERSON SINGLE CBN		SA/CR	WD	KL	IB	D		10		13206	4		18900	21000
		1966 BOATS														
35		DICKERSON		SA/CR	WD	CB	IB	D		10		13206	3		21200	23600
35		DICKERSON		SA/CR	WD	KL	IB	D		10		13206	4		20300	22500
35		DICKERSON SINGLE CBN		SA/CR	WD	CB	IB	D		10		13206	3		19600	21700
35		DICKERSON SINGLE CBN		SA/CR	WD	KL	IB	D		10		13206	4		18800	20900
		1965 BOATS														
35		DICKERSON		SA/CR	WD	CB	IB	D		10		13206	4		20200	22500
35		DICKERSON		SA/CR	WD	KL	IB	D		10		13206	4		21300	23600
35		DICKERSON SINGLE CBN		SA/CR	WD	CB	IB	D		10		13206	4		18700	20800
35		DICKERSON SINGLE CBN		SA/CR	WD	KL	IB	D		10		13206	4		19500	21700
		1964 BOATS														
33		DICKERSON	KTH	SA/CR	WD		IB	D				10523			14500	16500
35		DICKERSON 35		SA/CR	WD		IB	D		10		13206	4		19900	22100
		1963 BOATS														
32		DICKERSON	KTH	SA/CR	WD		IB	25D		10		9825	4		13100	14900
35		DICKERSON	YWL	SA/CR	WD		IB	25D		10		13206	4		19900	22100
35		DICKERSON	KTH	SA/CR	WD		IB	25D		10		13206	4		19900	22100
		1962 BOATS														
32		DICKERSON 32	KTH	SA/CR	WD		IB	25D		10		9825	4		13100	14900
35		DICKERSON 35	YWL	SA/CR	WD		IB	25D		10		13206	4		20000	22200
35		DICKERSON 35	KTH	SA/CR	WD		IB	25D		10		13206	4		20000	22200
		1961 BOATS														
29		DICKERSON	SLP	SA/CR	P/M	KL	OB			9		7000	3		9250	10500
32		DICKERSON	KTH	SA/CR	P/M	KC	OB			10		6537			8850	10000
		1960 BOATS														
26	6	DICKERSON 26	SLP	SA/CR	WD	KL				8	6		4	3	5700	6550
29		DICKERSON	SLP	SA/CR	WD		OB					7000			9300	10600
32		DICKERSON	KTH	SA/CR	WD		OB					6537			8900	10100
32		DICKERSON 32	KTH	SA/CR	WD	KL				10			4		**	**
		1959 BOATS														
26	6	DICKERSON	SLP	SA/CR	P/M	KL	OB			8	6	3587	3		4550	5200
32		DICKERSON	KTH	SA/CR	P/M	KL	OB			10		6537	4		9000	10200
35		SIMPLISSIMA	KTH	SA/CR	P/M	KL	OB			10		8699	3	9	13300	15100
		1952 BOATS														
34	9	SIMPLISSIMA	KTH	SA/CR	WD	KC	IB		UNIV	9	7	13206			22200	24700

DISCOVERY ENTERPRISES LTD

Call 1-800-327-6929 for BUC Personalized Evaluation Service
Or, for 1979 boats, sign onto www.BUCValuPro.com

DITCHBURN

Call 1-800-327-6929 for BUC Personalized Evaluation Service
Or, for 1912 to 1927 boats, sign onto www.BUCValuPro.com

DIXIE MARINE INC
NEWTON NC 28658   COAST GUARD MFG ID- BKW See inside cover to adjust price for area
FORMERLY SPORTSMAN TRAILERS INC

For more recent years, see the BUC Used Boat Price Guide, Volume 1 or Volume 2

LOA FT IN	NAME AND/ OR MODEL		TOP/ RIG	BOAT TYPE	-HULL- MTL TP	----ENGINE--- TP # HP MFG	BEAM FT IN	WGT LBS	DRAFT FT IN	RETAIL LOW	RETAIL HIGH
				1983 BOATS							
17	CUSTOM 170		OP	RNBT	FBG DV	IO 120 MRCR	6 8	1875		1700	2050
17	DELUXE 170		OP	RNBT	FBG DV	IO 120-140	6 8	1875		1950	2350
17	FISH-ABOUT 171		OP	FSH	FBG DV	IO 140 MRCR	6 8	1875		1800	2150
18	1 188-X		OP	RNBT	FBG DV	IO 120-185	7 1	2200		2200	2550
18	1 CLASSIC 187		OP	RNBT	FBG DV	IO 140-198	7 2	2000		1950	2350
18	1 SUNCRUISER 187		OP	RNBT	FBG DV	IO 170-198	7 2	2000		2000	2400
19	299		OP	SKI	FBG DV	IB 250 PCM	7 7	2700		3300	3850
19	PERFORMER 199		OP	SKI	FBG DV	IO 170-198	7 7	2700		2450	2900
19	PERFORMER 199		OP	SKI	FBG DV	IO 260	7 7	2700		2650	3050
21	1 721			CBNCR	FBG DV	IO 170-260	8	3300		4050	5000
21	1 721			CUD	FBG DV	IO 170 MRCR	8	3300		3800	4400
21	1 821		OP	FSH	FBG DV	IO 140-188	8	2100		3150	3700
21	1 FAMILY CRUISER 521		OP	CBNCR	FBG DV	IO 140-188	8	3300		4050	4750
21	1 FAMILY CRUISER 521		OP	CUD	FBG DV	IO 170 MRCR	8	3300		3800	4400
21	1 WALKAROUND 821		OP	FSH	FBG DV	IO 170 MRCR	8	3300		4050	4750
21	1 WALKAROUND OFF 821		OP	FSH	FBG DV	OB	8	2100		2850	3300
				1982 BOATS							
18	188X-D		OP	RNBT	FBG DV	IO 140-170	7	1600		1700	2050
18	1 187		OP	RNBT	FBG DV	IO 140-198	7 2	1900		1850	2250
19	196		OP	FSH	FBG DV	IO 198	7 8	1300		2100	2450
19	199		OP	SKI	FBG DV	IO 198-260	7 7	2700		2450	2850
21	1 421		OP	CUD	FBG SV	OB	8	1550		2250	2600
21	1 521		OP	FSH	FBG SV	IO	8	1550		2250	2600
21	1 521		OP	FSH	FBG SV	IO 140-260	8	3300		3950	4550
21	1 721		OP	CR	FBG SV	IO 140 MRCR	8	2200		2950	3400
21	1 721		OP	CR	FBG SV	IO 140-260	8	3300		3650	4250
				1981 BOATS							
18	188X-D		OP	RNBT	FBG DV	IO 145 VLVO	7	1600		1800	2100
18	1 187		OP	RNBT	FBG SV	IO 120-260	7 2	1900		1950	2400
18	1 189		OP	RNBT	FBG SV	IO 120-260	7 2	1900		1950	2400
19	196			FSH	FBG	IO 198	7 8			2600	3050
19	199		OP	SKI	FBG DV	IO 198-200	7 7	2150		2100	2500
19	199		OP	SKI	FBG DV	IO 260	7 7	2150		2250	2650
19	7 195			CR	FBG	IO 165	7 8			2550	2950
21	1 421		OP	CUD	FBG SV	OB	8	1550		2200	2550
21	1 421		OP	CUD	FBG SV	IO 140-200	8	2200		2850	3500
21	1 421		OP	CUD	FBG SV	IO 260	8	2200		3100	3600
21	1 421		OP	CUD	FBG SV	IO 140D	8	2200		4150	4850
21	1 521		OP	FSH	FBG SV	OB	8	1650		2300	2700
21	1 521		OP	FSH	FBG SV	IO 140-200	8	2200		3050	3700
21	1 521		OP	FSH	FBG SV	IO 260	8	2200		3300	3800
21	1 521		OP	FSH	FBG SV	IO 140D	8	2200		5350	6100
21	1 721		OP	CR	FBG SV	IO 140-200	8	2200		2900	3500
21	1 721		OP	CR	FBG SV	IO 260	8	2200		3100	3600
21	1 721		OP	CR	FBG SV	IO 140D VLVO	8	2200		3950	4600
				1980 BOATS							
18	1 187		OP	RNBT	FBG SV	IO 120-200	7 2	1900		1800	2250
18	1 187		OP	RNBT	FBG SV	IO 260	7 2	1900		1950	2350
18	1 189		OP	RNBT	FBG SV	IO 120-200	7 2	1900		1800	2250
18	1 189		OP	RNBT	FBG SV	IO 260	7 2	1900		1950	2350
19	199		OP	SKI	FBG DV	IO 198-200	7 7	2150		2050	2450
19	199		OP	SKI	FBG SV	IO 260	7 7	2150		2250	2600
19	7 195		OP	RNBT	FBG SV	IO 120-260	7 8	2150		2200	2750
19	7 196		OP	FSH	FBG SV	IO 120-200	7 8	2150		2400	2950
19	7 196		OP	FSH	FBG SV	IO 260	7 8	2150		2600	3000
21	DIXIE 321			RNBT	FBG SV	IO 165	8			3200	3700
21	1 421		OP	CUD	FBG SV	OB	8	1550		2150	2500
21	1 421		OP	CUD	FBG SV	IO 140-200	8	2200		2800	3400
	IO 260	3050	3550, IO		130D VLVO	3800	4450, IO	140D MRCR		4100	4750
21	1 521		OP	FSH	FBG SV	OB	8	1650		2250	2650
21	1 521		OP	FSH	FBG SV	IO 140-200	8	2200		3000	3600
21	1 521		OP	FSH	FBG SV	IO 260	8	2200		3250	3750
21	1 521		OP	FSH	FBG SV	IO 130D-140D	8	2200		4900	6050
				1979 BOATS							
18	1 187		OP	RNBT	FBG SV	IO 120-230	7 2	1900		1800	2250
18	1 187		OP	RNBT	FBG SV	IO 260	7 2	1900		1950	2350
18	1 189		OP	RNBT	FBG SV	IO 120-230	7 2	1900		1800	2250
18	1 189		OP	RNBT	FBG SV	IO 260	7 2	1900		1950	2350
19	7 195		OP	RNBT	FBG SV	IO 140-260	7 8	2150		2200	2750
19	7 196		OP	FSH	FBG SV	IO 140-230	7 8	2150		2400	2900
19	7 196		OP	FSH	FBG SV	IO 260	7 8	2150		2600	3000
21	1 321		OP	FSH	FBG SV	OB	8	1550		2050	2450
21	1 321		OP	FSH	FBG SV	IO 165-260	8	2200		3050	3750
21	1 421		OP	CUD	FBG SV	IO 165-260	8	2200		2850	3500
21	1 521		OP	FSH	FBG SV	OB	8	1650		2200	2600
21	1 521		OP	FSH	FBG SV	IO 165-260	8	2200		3000	3750
				1978 BOATS							
18	1 TEQUILA 187		ST	RNBT	FBG SV	IO 140	7 2	1840		1800	2100
18	1 TEQUILA 187		ST	RNBT	FBG SV	IO 140	7 2	1840		1900	2300
18	1 TEQUILA 189			RNBT	FBG SV	IO 140	7 2			1800	2150
20	GULFCRUISER 195			RNBT	FBG SV	OB	7 8	2150		2450	2850
20	GULFCRUISER 195			RNBT	FBG SV	IO 165	7 8			2700	3150
21	1 GULFSTREAM 421F		ST	CUD	FBG DV	IB 165	8	2700		3250	3800
21	1 GULFSTREAM 421F		ST	CUD	FBG DV	IO 198	8	2700		3150	3700
21	1 GULFSTREAM 421F		ST	CUD	FBG SV	OB	8	1430		1900	2250
21	1 GULFSTREAM 421F		ST	CUD	FBG SV	IO 165	8	2700		3150	3650
21	1 WHITEWATER 321		OP	FSH	FBG SV	OB	8	1550		2000	2400
21	1 WHITEWATER 321		OP	FSH	FBG SV	IO 165-250	8	2530		3250	3950
				1977 BOATS							
17	4 280		ST	RNBT	FBG TR	IO 140-190	7	2100		1800	2200
17	4 280		ST	RNBT	FBG TR	IO 233-235	7	2100		1900	2350
18	1 183		ST	RNBT	FBG SV	IO 140-190	7 2	1840		1800	2150
18	1 183		ST	RNBT	FBG SV	IO 233-235	7 2	1840		1900	2250
18	1 187		ST	RNBT	FBG SV	IO 140-190	7 2	1840		1900	2300
18	1 187		ST	RNBT	FBG SV	IO 233-235	7 2	1840		2000	2350
18	1 318		ST	FSH	FBG SV	IO 140 MRCR	7 2	1840		1950	2300
18	1 318		ST	FSH	FBG SV	IO 140 OMC	7 2	1840		1900	2300
18	1 318		ST	FSH	FBG SV	IO 140-235	7 2	1840		2000	2450
21	1 221		ST	RNBT	FBG SV	OB	8	1550		2000	2350
21	1 221		ST	RNBT	FBG SV	IO 165-235	8	2530		2950	3550
21	1 321		ST	RNBT	FBG SV	OB	8	1550		2000	2350
21	1 321		ST	FSH	FBG SV	IO 165-235	8	2530		3250	3900
21	1 421		ST	CUD	FBG SV	IO 165-235	8	2700		3200	3800
				1976 BOATS							
17	4 280 B/R		ST	RNBT	FBG TR	IO 140-190	7	2100		1850	2250
17	4 280 B/R		ST	RNBT	FBG TR	IO 233-235	7	2100		1950	2350
18	1 183 W/T		ST	RNBT	FBG SV	IO 140-190	7 2	1840		1850	2200
18	1 183 W/T		ST	RNBT	FBG SV	IO 233-235	7 2	1840		1950	2300
18	1 187 B/R		ST	RNBT	FBG SV	IO 140-190	7 2	1840		1850	2250
18	1 187 B/R		ST	RNBT	FBG SV	IO 233-235	7 2	1840		1950	2350
21	1 221 B/R		ST	RNBT	FBG SV	OB		1700		2150	2500
21	1 221 B/R		ST	RNBT	FBG SV	IO 165-235	8	2530		3050	3650
21	1 321		ST	SF	FBG SV	OB		1700		3050	3650
21	1 321		ST	SF	FBG SV	IO 165-235	8	2530		3550	4300
22	7 DIXIE 223		ST	SF	FBG SV	IO 165-275	8	3200		4500	5450
				1975 BOATS							
17	4 280		OP	RNBT	FBG TR	IO 140-165	7	2100		1900	2300
18	1 183		OP	RNBT	FBG SV	IO 140-225	7 2	1800		1900	2300
18	1 183-S		OP	RNBT	FBG SV	IO 140-225	7 2	1800		2000	2400
18	1 188		OP	RNBT	FBG SV	IO 188-245	7 2	1800		2000	2450
21	1 221		OP	RNBT	FBG SV	IO 165-245	8	2530		3100	3750
22	7 223		OP	RNBT	FBG SV	IO 165-245	8	3200		3800	4550
				1974 BOATS							
18	1 183		OP	RNBT	FBG SV	IO 120	7 2	1800		1950	2300
21	1 221		OP	RNBT	FBG SV	IO 235	8	2530		3300	3850
22	7 223		OP	RNBT	FBG SV	IO 155	8	3200		3950	4550
				1973 BOATS							
17	2 180		OP	RNBT	FBG SV	IO 120	6 11	1650	2	1800	2150
17	2 280		OP	RNBT	FBG TR	IO 140-155	7	2100	2	2050	2400
18	1 183		OP	RNBT	FBG SV	IO 140	7 2	1800	2 6	2050	2400
19	1 192		OP	RNBT	FBG SV	IO 155	7 6	2175	2	2450	2800
21	1 221		OP	RNBT	FBG SV	IO 165	8	2530		3300	3850
22	7 223		OP	RNBT	FBG SV	IO 165	8	3200		4050	4750
				1972 BOATS							
16	4 169			RNBT	FBG SV	IO 130-140	6 4		2 3	1800	2150
17	2 177			RNBT	FBG DV	IO 235-245	6 11		2 7	2100	2500
17	2 180			RNBT	FBG DV	IO 120-155	6 11		2 4	1950	2350

LOA FT IN	NAME AND/ OR MODEL	TOP/ RIG	BOAT TYPE	MTL	-HULL- TP	TP	----ENGINE--- # HP	MFG	BEAM FT IN	WGT LBS	DRAFT FT IN	RETAIL LOW	RETAIL HIGH
--------------------- 1972 BOATS ---
17 4	280		RNBT	FBG	SV	IO	120		7		2 7	2000	2400
17 4	280		RNBT	FBG	SV	IO	245		7		2 7	2200	2550
19 1	192		RNBT	FBG	DV	IO	155-245		7 6		2 11	2750	3350
21 1	221		RNBT	FBG	DV	IO	235		8		2 11	3850	4500
22 7	223		CR	FBG	DV	IO	235-245		8		3	5100	5900
--------------------- 1971 BOATS ---
19 1	192		RNBT	FBG		IB	155-235		7 6			1900	2350
22 7	223		CR	FBG		IB	155-260		8			3300	3900
--------------------- 1970 BOATS ---
16 4	168		RNBT	FBG		IO	130	VLVO	6 4	1430		1800	2150
17 1	S/S 177		RNBT	FBG	SV	IO	235	HOLM	6 11	1830	1 8	2150	2500
17 1	S/S 177		RNBT	FBG	SV	IO	155	OMC	6 11	1830		2050	2450
17 2	180			FBG	DV	IO	120	OMC	6 11	1650	1 8	1850	2250
17 2	180			FBG	DV	IO	120-155		6 11	1650	1 8	2000	2400
17 2	180		RNBT	FBG	DV	IO	120	MRCR	6 11	1650	1 8	2000	2350
17 4	280		RNBT	FBG	TR	IO	140		7	1750	1 6	2100	2450
19 1	192			FBG	DV	IO	155-160		7 6	2175	1 10	2600	3050
19 1	192		RNBT	FBG	DV	IO	120	MRCR	7 6	2175	1 10	2650	3100
22 7	233			FBG	DV	IO	160	MRCR	8	3200	1 10	4550	5250
22 7	233		CR	FBG	DV	IO	155	OMC	8	3200	1 10	4750	5450
--------------------- 1969 BOATS ---
16 4	168		RNBT	FBG		IO	110-120		6 4	1430	1 8	1850	2200
17 1	177S/S		RNBT	FBG	SV	IO	155-225		6 11	1830	1 8	2150	2650
17 2	177	OP	RNBT	FBG	SV	IO	225	HOLM	6 11	1830	1 8	2300	2700
17 2	180		RNBT	FBG	DV	IO	120	MRCR	6 11	1650	1 8	2050	2450
17 2	180		RNBT	FBG	DV	IO	120	OMC	6 11	1650	1 8	2050	2400
17 2	180		RNBT	FBG	DV	IO	120-155		6 11	1650	1 8	2250	2600
19 1	192		RNBT	FBG	DV	IO	120-160		7 6	2175		2550	3000
19 1	192	OP	RNBT	FBG	SV	IO	155	OMC	7 6	1850	2 2	2550	3000
22 7	223		SF	FBG	DV	IO	155-160		8	3200	2 2	5550	6450
22 7	223	OP	SF	FBG	DV	IO	155	MRCR	8	3200	2 2	5600	6400
--------------------- 1968 BOATS ---
16 4	168	OP	RNBT	FBG	TR	IO	110-120		6 4		2 2	2200	2600
17 1	177S/S	OP	RNBT	FBG	SV	IO	155-225		6 8	1830	2 4	2200	2700
17 2	180	OP	RNBT	FBG	DV	IO	120-155		6 8	1600	2 4	2050	2450
19 1	192	OP	RNBT	FBG	SV	IO	120	MRCR	7 6	1850	2 4	2650	3100
19 1	192	OP	RNBT	FBG	SV	IO	155-160		7 6		2 4	3100	3600
22 7	223		FSH	FBG		IO	155-160		8	3200	2 4	5450	6250
--------------------- 1967 BOATS ---
17 1	177		RNBT	FBG		IO	200		6 9		1 8	2350	2750
17 1	176		RNBT	FBG		IO	110-120		6 9		1 8	2300	2700
17 1	177		RNBT	FBG		IO	150		6 9		1 8	2350	2700
19 2	191		RNBT	FBG		IO	120		7 6		1 10	3200	3750
22 7	223		RNBT	FBG		IO	150-160		8		1 10	5450	6250
--------------------- 1966 BOATS ---
17 1	176		RNBT	FBG		IO	110		6 9	1530		2200	2550
19 2	191		RNBT	FBG		IO	100		7 6	1850		2850	3350
22 7	223		CR	FBG		IO	150		8	3200		5450	6250
--------------------- 1965 BOATS ---
21 7	223		RNBT	FBG		IB	140		8		2 4	2150	2550

DOCKRELL YACHTS LTD
PARSIPPANY NJ 07054   COAST GUARD MFG ID- JLD See inside cover to adjust price for area

For more recent years, see the BUC Used Boat Price Guide, Volume 1 or Volume 2

LOA FT IN	NAME AND/ OR MODEL	TOP/ RIG	BOAT TYPE	MTL	-HULL- TP	TP	----ENGINE--- # HP	MFG	BEAM FT IN	WGT LBS	DRAFT FT IN	RETAIL LOW	RETAIL HIGH
--------------------- 1983 BOATS ---
22	DOCKRELL 22	SLP	SA/CR	FBG	KC	OB			7 6	2150	1 4	2400	2750
22	DOCKRELL 22	SLP	SA/CR	FBG	KC	IB			7 6	2150	1 4	2650	3050
27	DOCKRELL 27	CUT	SA/CR	FBG	KL	OB			8	7000	3	9500	10800
27	DOCKRELL 27	CUT	SA/CR	FBG	KL	IB	15D	YAN	8	7000	3	9800	11200
37	DOCKRELL 37	CUT	SA/CR	FBG	KC	OB			10 2	11500	3 9	22900	25500
--------------------- 1982 BOATS ---
17	DOCKRELL 17	SLP	SA/CR	FBG	SK	IB	6D	SEAG	7 4	1100	10	2350	2700
22	DOCKRELL 22	SLP	SA/CR	FBG	KC	OB			7 6	2150	1 4	2250	2650
22	DOCKRELL 22	SLP	SA/CR	FBG	KC	IB	6D	SEAG	7 6	2150	1 4	2750	3200
27	DOCKRELL 27	CUT	SA/CR	FBG	KL	OB			8	7000	3	8950	10200
27	DOCKRELL 27	CUT	SA/CR	FBG	KL	IB	15D	YAN	8	7000	3	9300	10600
37	DOCKRELL 37	CUT	SA/CR	FBG	KC	OB			10 2	11500	3 9	21600	24000
--------------------- 1981 BOATS ---
22	DOCKRELL 22	SLP	SA/CR	FBG	KC	OB			7 6	2150	1 4	2100	2450
22	DOCKRELL 22	SLP	SA/CR	FBG	KC	IB	6D	SEAG	7 6	2150	1 4	2600	3050
27	DOCKRELL 27	CUT	SA/CR	FBG	KL	OB			8	7000	3	8350	9600
27	DOCKRELL 27	CUT	SA/CR	FBG	KL	IB	15D	YAN	8	7000	3	8650	9950
37	DOCKRELL 37	CUT	SA/CR	FBG	KC	IB	24D	PANT	10 2	11500	3 9	20800	23100
--------------------- 1980 BOATS ---
17	DOCKRELL 17	SLP	SAIL	FBG	CB	IB	D		7 4	1100	3	2300	2650
22	DOCKRELL 22	SLP	SA/CR	FBG	KC	IB	D		7 6	2150	4	2550	2950
27	DOCKRELL 27	CUT	SA/CR	FBG	KL	IB	D		8	7000	3	8250	9450
37	DOCKRELL 37	CUT	SA/CR	FBG	KC	IB	D		10 2	11500	3 9	19800	22000
--------------------- 1979 BOATS ---
22	DOCKRELL 22	SLP	SA/CR	FBG	SK	OB			7 6	2200	4	1950	2300
27	DOCKRELL 27	CUT	SA/CR	FBG	KL	IB	D		8	7000	3	7900	9100
37	DOCKRELL 37	CUT	SA/CR	FBG	KC	IB	D		10 2	12000	3 9	19800	22000
--------------------- 1978 BOATS ---
22	DOCKRELL 22	SLP	SA/CR	FBG	KL	OB			7 6	2150	3	1850	2200
22	DOCKRELL 22	SLP	SA/CR	FBG	KL	IB	D		7 6	2150	3	2350	2700
22	DOCKRELL 22	SLP	SA/CR	FBG	SK	OB			7 6	2150	3	1850	2200
22	DOCKRELL 22	SLP	SA/CR	FBG	SK	IB	D		7 6	2150	1 4	2350	2700
27	DOCKRELL 27	CUT	SA/CR	FBG	KL	IB	D	PETT	8	7000	4	7650	8750
27	DOCKRELL 27 SHOAL	CUT	SA/CR	FBG	KL	IB	D	PETT	8	7000	4	7650	8750
37	DOCKRELL 37	CUT	SA/CR	FBG	KC	IB	D		10 2	11500	3 9	18600	20700
--------------------- 1977 BOATS ---
22	DOCKRELL 22	SLP	SA/CR	FBG	KL	IB	D		7 6	2150	3	1800	2150
22	DOCKRELL 22	SLP	SA/CR	FBG	KL	OB			7 6	2150	3	2050	2550
22	DOCKRELL 22	SLP	SA/CR	FBG	SK	OB			7 6	2150	3	1800	2150
22	DOCKRELL 22	SLP	SA/CR	FBG	SK	IB	D		7 6	2150	1 4	2300	2650
27	CRUISING CUTTER	CUT	SA/CR	FBG	KL	OB			8	7000	4	7150	8200
27	CRUISING CUTTER	CUT	SA/CR	FBG	KL	IB	D	PETT	8	7000	4	7350	8500
--------------------- 1976 BOATS ---
22	DOCKRELL 22	SLP	SAIL	FBG	KL	OB			7 6	2200	3	1750	2100
22	DOCKRELL 22	SLP	SAIL	FBG	KL	IB	D		7 6	2200	3	2000	2600
22	DOCKRELL 22	SLP	SAIL	FBG	SK	OB			7 6	2200	1 4	1750	2100
27	CRUISING CUTTER	CUT	SAIL	FBG	KL	IB	8D	PETT	8	7000	4	7100	8150
--------------------- 1975 BOATS ---
27	CRUISING CUTTER	CUT	SAIL	FBG	KL	IB	7D	PETT	8	7000	4	6900	7900
--------------------- 1974 BOATS ---
28	D-28	SLP	SAIL	FBG	KL				8		4	4950	5700
28	DOCKRELL 28	SLP	SAIL	FBG	KL	IB	D		8 6	8000	4	8150	9350

THE DODGE BOAT CO
HORACE DODGE BOAT&PLANE CORP

Call 1-800-327-6929 for BUC Personalized Evaluation Service
Or, for 1924 to 1939 boats, sign onto www.BUCValuPro.com

HUGH DOHERTYS KING HARBOR BTS

Call 1-800-327-6929 for BUC Personalized Evaluation Service
Or, for 1961 boats, sign onto www.BUCValuPro.com

DOLPHIN BOATS INC
COAST GUARD MFG ID- DFL

Call 1-800-327-6929 for BUC Personalized Evaluation Service
Or, for 1971 to 2008 boats, sign onto www.BUCValuPro.com

DOMINATOR MARINE PRODUCTS
COAST GUARD MFG ID- DNT

Call 1-800-327-6929 for BUC Personalized Evaluation Service
Or, for 1980 boats, sign onto www.BUCValuPro.com

DONZI MARINE CORP
DIV AMERICAN MARINE HLDNGS INC
SARASOTA FL 34243   COAST GUARD MFG ID- DMR   See inside cover to adjust price for area

For more recent years, see the BUC Used Boat Price Guide, Volume 1 or Volume 2

LOA FT IN	NAME AND/ OR MODEL	TOP/ RIG	BOAT TYPE	MTL	-HULL- TP	TP	----ENGINE--- # HP	MFG	BEAM FT IN	WGT LBS	DRAFT FT IN	RETAIL LOW	RETAIL HIGH
--------------------- 1982 BOATS ---
18	2-PLUS-3	OP	RNBT	FBG	DV	IO	255	VLVO	7 2	2450	2 3	5500	6300
20 3	HORNET II	OP	RNBT	FBG	DV	IO	260	MRCR	7 10	3400	2 3	6300	7250
20 3	HORNET II	OP	RNBT	FBG	DV	IO	290	VLVO	7 10	3400	2 4	6900	7900
20 3	HORNET II	OP	RNBT	FBG	DV	IO	330	MRCR	7 10	3800	2 4	7600	8750
22 8	2-PLUS-3	OP	RNBT	FBG	DV	IO	260	MRCR	7 2	3000	2 3	6350	7300
22 8	2-PLUS-3	OP	RNBT	FBG	DV	IO	290-330		7 2	3500	2 3	7550	8700

DONZI MARINE CORP -CONTINUED See inside cover to adjust price for area

LOA FT	LOA IN	NAME AND/ OR MODEL	TOP/ RIG	BOAT TYPE	HULL MTL	HULL TP	ENGINE TP	ENGINE # HP	ENGINE MFG	BEAM FT	BEAM IN	WGT LBS	DRAFT FT	DRAFT IN	RETAIL LOW	RETAIL HIGH
		1982 BOATS														
22	8	CRITERION	OP	RNBT	FBG	DV	IO	330	MRCR	7	2	3600	2	4	7350	8450
		1981 BOATS														
16	7	SKI SPORTER		RNBT	FBG	DV	IO	280		7					4600	5300
18		2-PLUS-3	OP	RNBT	FBG	DV	IO	260	MRCR	7		2250	1		4950	5650
18		2-PLUS-3	OP	RNBT	FBG	DV	IO	330	MRCR	7		2250	1		5850	6750
20	3	HORNET II	OP	RNBT	FBG	DV	IO	260	MRCR	7	10	3000	1		5750	6600
20	3	HORNET II	OP	RNBT	FBG	DV	IO	330	MRCR	7	10	3000	1		6550	7550
21	1	GT-21		RNBT	FBG	DV	IO	330		7	8				6800	7800
22	8	2-PLUS-3	OP	RNBT	FBG	DV	IO	260	MRCR	7	2	2900			6100	7050
22	8	2-PLUS-3	OP	RNBT	FBG	DV	IO	330	MRCR	7	2	2900			6900	7950
22	8	CRITERION	OP	RNBT	FBG	DV	IO	330	MRCR	7	2	3700	1	8	7350	8450
		1980 BOATS														
16	8	SKI-SPORTER	OP	RNBT	FBG	DV	IO	265	CHRY	7		2150	1		4150	4850
16	8	SKI-SPORTER	OP	RNBT	FBG	DV	IO	280	VLVO	7		2150	1		4650	5350
18		2-PLUS-3	OP	RNBT	FBG	DV	IO	260-265		7		2250	1		5050	5800
18		2-PLUS-3	OP	RNBT	FBG	DV	IO	280-330		7		2250	1		5550	6900
18		X-18	OP	RNBT	FBG	DV	IO	260-265		7		2250	1		4400	5350
18		X-18	OP	RNBT	FBG	DV	IO	280-330		7		2250	1		4900	6000
20	3	HORNET II	OP	RNBT	FBG	DV	IO	260-280		7	10	3000	1		5700	7050
20	3	HORNET II	OP	RNBT	FBG	DV	IO	330	MRCR	7	10	3000	1		6500	7450
21	2	G-T 21	OP	RNBT	FBG	DV	IO	265-280		7	9	2900	1	3	5400	6650
21	2	G-T 21	OP	RNBT	FBG	DV	IO	330	MRCR	7	9	2900	1	3	6100	7000
22	8	CRITERION	OP	RNBT	FBG	DV	IO	280-330		7	2	3700	1	8	7000	8400
22	8	CRITERION II	OP	RNBT	FBG	DV	IO	330	MRCR	7	2	3500	1	8	7050	8100
22	8	F-22	OP	RNBT	FBG	DV	IO	260-280		7	2	2900	1	8	5600	6950
22	8	F-22	OP	RNBT	FBG	DV	IO	330	MRCR	7	2	2900	1	8	6350	7300
		1979 BOATS														
16	8	SKI-SPORTER	OP	RNBT	FBG	DV	IO	265	CHRY	7		2150	1		4150	4800
16	8	SKI-SPORTER	OP	RNBT	FBG	DV	IO	280	VLVO	7		2150	1		4650	5350
18		2-PLUS-3	OP	RNBT	FBG	DV	IO	260-265		7		2250	1		4800	5550
18		2-PLUS-3	OP	RNBT	FBG	DV	IO	280-330		7		2250	1		5350	6600
18		X-18	OP	RNBT	FBG	DV	IO	260-265		7		2250	1		4600	5300
18		X-18	OP	RNBT	FBG	DV	IO	280-330		7		2250	1		5050	6250
20	3	HORNET II	OP	RNBT	FBG	DV	IO	260-280		7	10	3000	1		5700	7050
20	3	HORNET II	OP	RNBT	FBG	DV	IO	330	MRCR	7	10	3000	1		6500	7450
21	2	G-T 21	OP	RNBT	FBG	DV	IO	265-280		7	9	2900	1	3	5400	6650
21	2	G-T 21	OP	RNBT	FBG	DV	IO	330	MRCR	7	9	2900	1	3	6100	7000
22	8	CRITERION	OP	RNBT	FBG	DV	IO	280-330		7	2	3700	1	8	6950	8350
22	8	F-22	OP	RNBT	FBG	DV	IO	260-280		7	2	3200			5950	7300
22	8	F-22	OP	RNBT	FBG	DV	IO	330	MRCR	7	2	3200			6650	7650
		1978 BOATS														
16	8	BABY	OP	RNBT	FBG	DV	OB			7		1650	1		3300	3800
16	8	SKI-SPORTER	OP	RNBT	FBG	DV	IO	225-265		7		2300	1		4050	5000
16	8	SKI-SPORTER	OP	RNBT	FBG	DV	IO	300	CC	7		2300	1		4700	5450
18		2-PLUS-3	OP	RNBT	FBG	DV	IO	225-265		7		2400	1		4850	5800
18		2-PLUS-3	OP	RNBT	FBG	DV	IO	300	CC	7		2400	1		5400	6200
18		X-18	OP	RNBT	FBG	DV	IO	260-300		7		2400	1		4750	5950
20	3	HORNET II	OP	RNBT	FBG	DV	IO	260-300		7	10	3200	1		5950	7300
20	3	HORNET II	OP	RNBT	FBG	DV	IO	330	MRCR	7	10	3200	1		6750	7750
21	2	G-T 21	OP	RNBT	FBG	DV	IO	265-300		7	9	3500	1	3	6100	7350
21	2	G-T 21	OP	RNBT	FBG	DV	IO	330	MRCR	7	9	3500	1	3	6800	7800
24	2	EL-PESCADOR	OP	OPFSH	FBG	DV	IO	T170-T265		8		4200	1	8	10100	11900
24	2	EL-PESCADOR	OP	OPFSH	FBG	DV	IO	T300	CC	8		4200	1	8	11200	12700
24	2	SPIRIT	OP	CUD	FBG	DV	IO	T170-T300		8		5300	1	8	11300	14000
24	2	SPITFIRE	OP	RNBT	FBG	DV	IO	T260-T300		8		4200	1	8	9300	11300
		1977 BOATS														
16	8	SKI-SPORTER 16	OP	RNBT	FBG	DV	IO	130-225		7		2200	2	6	4100	4750
16	8	SKI-SPORTER 16	OP	RNBT	FBG	DV	IO	300	CC	7		2200	2	6	4700	5400
18		2-PLUS-3	OP	RNBT	FBG	DV	IO	130-280		7		2350	2	6	4900	6100
18		2-PLUS-3	OP	RNBT	FBG	DV	IO	300	CC	7		2350	2	6	5450	6250
18		X-18	OP	RNBT	FBG	DV	IO	225-280		7		2350	2	6	4500	5600
18		X-18	OP	RNBT	FBG	DV	IO	300	CC	7		2350	2	6	5200	5950
20	3	HORNET II	OP	RNBT	FBG	DV	IO	225-280		7	11	3100	2	6	5700	7050
20	3	HORNET II	OP	RNBT	FBG	DV	IO	300	CC	7	11	3100	2	6	6350	7300
21	2	G-T 21	OP	RNBT	FBG	DV	IO	225-280		7	9	3250	2	6	5600	6950
21	2	G-T 21	OP	RNBT	FBG	DV	IO	300	CC	7	9	3250	2	6	6250	7150
24	2	DORAL 24	OP	CUD	FBG	DV	IO	T130-T225		8		4000	2	9	9400	10800
24	2	DORAL 24	OP	CUD	FBG	DV	IO	T300	CC	8		4000	2	9	10500	11900
24	2	EL-PESCADOR	OP	OPFSH	FBG	DV	IO	T130-T225		8		4500	2	9	10700	12300
24	2	EL-PESCADOR	OP	OPFSH	FBG	DV	IO	T300	CC	8		4500	2	9	11900	13500
24	2	SPIRIT	ST	CUD	FBG	DV	IO	T130-T225		8		5100	2	9	11100	12700
24	2	SPIRIT	ST	CUD	FBG	DV	IO	T300	CC	8		5100	2	9	12200	13900
24	2	SPITFIRE	OP	RNBT	FBG	DV	IO	T225	COMM	8		5100	2	9	10200	11600
24	2	SPITFIRE	OP	RNBT	FBG	DV	IO	T300	CC	8		5100	2	9	11400	13000
		1976 BOATS														
16	7	BABY 16	OP	RNBT	FBG	DV	OB			7		1050	1		2250	2600
16	7	SKI-SPORTER 16	OP	RNBT	FBG	DV	IO	130	VLVO	7		1900	1		3850	4500
16	7	SKI-SPORTER 16	OP	RNBT	FBG	DV	IO	300	CC	7		1900	1		4500	5200
18		2-PLUS-3	OP	RNBT	FBG	DV	IO	188-233		7		2250	2	3	4700	5550
18		2-PLUS-3	OP	RNBT	FBG	DV	IO	280-300		7		2250	2	3	5200	6300
18		2-PLUS-3	OP	RNBT	FBG	DV	JT	330	BERK	7		2250	2	3	5300	6050
18		X-18	OP	RNBT	FBG	DV	IO	188-233		7		2250	2	3	4500	5300
18		X-18	OP	RNBT	FBG	DV	IO	280-300		7		2250	2	3	4950	6000
18		X-18	OP	RNBT	FBG	DV	JT	330	BERK	7		2250	2	3	5050	5800
19	3	HORNET 19	OP	RNBT	FBG	DV	IO	188-233		7	10	2700	2	3	5700	6750
19	3	HORNET 19	OP	RNBT	FBG	DV	IO	280-300		7	10	2700	2	3	6500	7500
19	3	ST-TROPEZ	OP	RNBT	FBG	DV	IO	188-233		7	10	2700	2	3	5700	6700
19	3	ST-TROPEZ	OP	RNBT	FBG	DV	IO	300	CC	7	10	2700	2	3	6450	7450
21	2	G-T	OP	RNBT	FBG	DV	IO	188-280		7	9	2900	2	6	5350	6650
21	2	G-T	OP	RNBT	FBG	DV	IO	300	CC	7	9	2900	2	6	6000	6900
21	2	G-T	OP	RNBT	FBG	DV	JT	330	BERK	7	9	2900	2	6	5800	6650
24	2	DORAL 24	OP	CUD	FBG	DV	IO	280-300		8		4000	2	9	8900	10400
24	2	DORAL 24	OP	CUD	FBG	DV	IO	T165-T170		8		4000	2	9	9400	11100
24	2	DORAL 24	OP	CUD	FBG	DV	IO	T300	CC	8		4000	2	9	10800	12200
24	2	EL-PESCADOR	OP	OPFSH	FBG	DV	IO	280-300		8		4000	2	9	9350	10900
24	2	EL-PESCADOR	OP	OPFSH	FBG	DV	IO	T165-T170		8		4000	2	9	9800	11600
24	2	EL-PESCADOR	OP	OPFSH	FBG	DV	IO	T300	CC	8		4000	2	9	11400	12900
24	2	SPIRIT	OP	CUD	FBG	DV	IO	280-300		8		4500	2	9	9650	11200
24	2	SPIRIT	OP	CUD	FBG	DV	IO	T165-T170		8		4500	2	9	10100	11900
24	2	SPIRIT	OP	CUD	FBG	DV	IO	T300	CC	8		4500	2	9	11600	13100
24	2	SPITFIRE	OP	RNBT	FBG	DV	IO	280-300		8		4500	2	9	9050	10500
24	2	SPITFIRE	OP	RNBT	FBG	DV	IO	T165-T170		8		4500	2	9	9450	11200
24	2	SPITFIRE	OP	RNBT	FBG	DV	IO	T300	CC	8		4500	2	9	10800	12300
		1975 BOATS														
16		SKI-SPORTER 16	OP	RNBT	FBG	DV	IO	130-250				1050			3000	3600
16	8	SKI-SPORTER 16	OP	RNBT	FBG	DV	OB			7		1050	1		2250	2600
18		2-PLUS-3	OP	RNBT	FBG	DV	IO	188-250		7		2250	1		4800	5850
18		2-PLUS-3	OP	RNBT	FBG	DV	IO	300	CC	7		2250	1		5650	6500
18		2-PLUS-3	OP	RNBT	FBG	DV	JT	390	BERK	7		2250	1		5050	5850
18		X-18	OP	RNBT	FBG	DV	IO	188-250		7		2250	1		4650	5600
18		X-18	OP	RNBT	FBG	DV	IO	300	CC	7		2250	1		5400	6200
18		X-18	OP	RNBT	FBG	DV	JT	390	BERK	7		2250	1		4850	5550
19	3	HORNET 19	OP	RNBT	FBG	DV	IO	188-250		7	10	2700	1		6150	7350
19	3	HORNET 19	OP	RNBT	FBG	DV	IO	300	CC	7	10	2700	1		6950	8000
19	3	HORNET 19	OP	RNBT	FBG	DV	JT	390	BERK	7	10	2700	1		6300	7250
19	3	ST-TROPEZ 19	OP	RNBT	FBG	DV	IO	188-250		7	10	2600	2	3	5550	6700
19	3	ST-TROPEZ 19	OP	RNBT	FBG	DV	IO	300	CC	7	10	2600	2	3	6350	7300
19	3	ST-TROPEZ 19	OP	RNBT	FBG	DV	JT	390	BERK	7	10	2600	2	3	5750	6600
21	2	G-T 21	OP	RNBT	FBG	DV	IO	188-280		7	9	2900	1	3	5550	6900
21	2	G-T 21	OP	RNBT	FBG	DV	IO	300	CC	7	9	2900	1	3	6200	7100
21	2	G-T 21	OP	RNBT	FBG	DV	JT	390	BERK	7	9	2900	1	3	5550	6400
24	2	DORAL 24	OP	RNBT	FBG	DV	IO	188-300		8		3450	2	9	7500	9350
24	2	DORAL 24	OP	RNBT	FBG	DV	IO	T130-T280		8		3450	2	9	8800	10700
24	2	DORAL 24	OP	RNBT	FBG	DV	IO	T300	CC	8		3450	2	9	9800	11200
24	2	EL-PESCADOR	OP	RNBT	FBG	DV	IO	188-280		8		3450	1	8	6950	8550
		IO 300 CC 7600 8750, IO T130-T280 8200 10200, IO T300 CC													9350	10600
24	2	SPITFIRE MK XXIV	OP	RNBT	FBG	DV	IO	235-300		8		3450	2	9	7400	9200
24	2	SPITFIRE MK XXIV	OP	RNBT	FBG	DV	IO	T165-T255		8		3450	2	9	8350	10200
24	2	SPITFIRE MK XXIV	OP	RNBT	FBG	DV	IO	T280-T300		8		3450	2	9	9350	11000
		1974 BOATS														
16	8	BABY			FBG		OB			7		1050		9	1950	2350
16	8	BABY			FBG		IO	235-265		7					4550	5500
18		2-PLUS-3			FBG		IO	235	CC	7		2250	1	2	5100	5850
		IO 245-285 5650 7050, JT 290 OLDS 5150 5900, IO 320 CC													6700	7700
18		X-18			FBG		JT	290	OLDS	7					4900	5650
18		X-18			FBG		IO	300	CC	7		2300	1	2	5400	6200
19	2	HORNET			FBG		JT	290	OLDS	7	10				6300	7250
19	2	HORNET			FBG		IO	300	CC	7	10	2700	1	2	7100	8150
19	2	HORNET			FBG		IO	325	MRCR	7	10				8050	9250
21	1	G-T 21			FBG		JT	290	OLDS	7	9				5900	6800
21	1	G-T 21			FBG		IO	300	CC	7	9	2900	1	3	6350	7300
21	1	G-T 21			FBG		IO	325	MRCR	7	9				7550	8650
23	10	BABY			FBG		IO	T188-T320		8		4500	1	4	10100	11900
24	2	DORAL 24	OP	RNBT	FBG	DV	IO	188		8		3450			7500	8600
24	2	DORAL 24	OP	RNBT	FBG	DV	IO	T320		8		3450			10500	11900

 CONTINUED ON NEXT PAGE

```
  LOA NAME AND/          TOP/ BOAT   -HULL- ----ENGINE--- BEAM  WGT  DRAFT RETAIL RETAIL
  FT IN OR MODEL         RIG  TYPE   MTL TP TP # HP  MFG  FT IN  LBS FT IN  LOW   HIGH
-------------------- 1973 BOATS ----------------------------------------------------
  16  8 BABY 16               FBG    OB           7        1050 1      1950   2350
  16  8 SKI-SPORTER      SKI  FBG    IO 185-235   7        1050 1      3050   3800
  16  8 SKI-SPORTER      SKI  FBG    IO 255-265   7        1050 1      3400   4050
  18  2-PLUS-3                FBG    IO 185-265   7        2250 2  3    5100   6350
      IO 285  CRUS  5750 6600, IO 320  CC   6350 7300, JT  390 BERK    4600   5300

  18    CORSICAN 18           FBG    IO 185-265   7        2300 2  3    4750   5950
      IO 285  CRUS  5400 6200, IO 320  CC   5950 6800, JT  390 BERK    4250   4950

  19  3 HORNET                FBG    IO 185-265   7 10     2700 2  3    6450   7900
      IO 285-320   7150 8850, IO 325  MRCR 7800 9000, JT  390 BERK    5650   6500

  19  3 ST-TROPEZ             FBG    IO 185-265   7        2700 2  3    5600   6900
      IO 285  CRUS  6250 7150, IO 320-325   6800 7900, JT  390 BERK    4950   5700

  21  2 G-T 21                FBG    IO 185-265   7  9     2900 2  6    5900   7200
  21  2 G-T 21                FBG    IO 285-325   7  9     2900 2  6    6450   8050
  21  2 G-T 21                FBG    JT  390 BERK 7  9     2900 2  6    5050   5800
-------------------- 1972 BOATS ----------------------------------------------------
  16  8 BABY 16          RNBT FBG    OB           7        1050 1      2200   2550
  16  8 SKI-SPORTER      SKI  FBG    IO 185-255   7        2150 2  3    4300   5350
  16  8 SKI-SPORTER      SKI  FBG    IO 260-285   7        2150 2  3    4700   5700
  16  8 SKI-SPORTER      SKI  FBG    IO 320  CC   7        2150 2  3    5500   6350
  18    2-PLUS-3              FBG    IO 188-265   7        2250 2  3    5250   6550
  18    2-PLUS-3              FBG    IO 285  CRUS 7        2250 2  3    5950   6850
  18    2-PLUS-3              FBG    IO 320  CC   7        2250 2  3    6550   7550
  18    2-PLUS-3         RNBT FBG    IO 185  WAUK 7        2250 2  3    5400   6200
  18    CORSICAN              FBG    IO 188-265   7        2300 2  3    4900   6150
  18    CORSICAN              FBG    IO 285  CRUS 7        2300 2  3    5550   6400
  18    CORSICAN              FBG    IO 320  CC   7        2300 2  3    6150   7050
  18    CORSICAN         RNBT FBG    IO 185  WAUK 7        2300 2  3    5050   5800

  19  3 HORNET                FBG    IO 188-265   7 10     2700 2  3    6650   8200
  19  3 HORNET                FBG    IO 285-320   7 10     2700 2  3    7350   9150
  19  3 HORNET                FBG    IO 325  MRCR 7 10     2700 2  3    8100   9300
  19  3 HORNET           RNBT FBG    IO 185  WAUK 7 10     2700 2  3    6750   7750
  19  3 ST-TROPEZ             FBG    IO 188-265   7 10     2700 2  3    6150   7600
  19  3 ST-TROPEZ             FBG    IO 285-320   7 10     2700 2  3    6800   8500
  19  3 ST-TROPEZ             FBG    IO 325  MRCR 7 10     2700 2  3    7500   8600
  19  3 ST-TROPEZ        RNBT FBG    IO 185  WAUK 7 10     2700 2  3    6250   7200
  21  2 G-T 21                FBG    IO 188-265   7  9     2900 2  6    6100   7400
  21  2 G-T 21                FBG    IO 285-325   7  9     2900 2  6    6650   8300
  21  2 G-T 21           RNBT FBG    IO 185  WAUK 7  9     2900 2  6    6100   7000
-------------------- 1971 BOATS ----------------------------------------------------
  16  8 BABY             RNBT FBG    OB           7        1050 1      2150   2550
  16  8 SKI-SPORTER      SKI  FBG    IO 235-260   7        2150 2  3    4650   5550
  18    2-PLUS-3              FBG    IO 235-260   7        2250 2  3    5600   6700
  18    2-PLUS-3         RNBT FBG    IO 235  CRUS 7        2250 2  3    5800   6650
  18    CORSICAN              FBG    IO 235-260   7        2300 2  3    5250   6250
  18    CORSICAN         RNBT FBG    IO 235  CRUS 7        2300 2  3    5400   6200
  19  3 HORNET                FBG    IO 235-260   7 10     2700 2  3    7100   8400
  19  3 HORNET           RNBT FBG    IO 235  CRUS 7 10     2700 2  3    7200   8250
  19  3 ST-TROPEZ             FBG    IO 235-260   7 10     2700 2  3    6550   7750
  19  3 ST-TROPEZ        RNBT FBG    IO 235  CRUS 7 10     2700 2  3    6650   7650
  21  2 G-T 21                FBG    IO 235-260   7  9     2900 2  6    6450   7600
  21  2 G-T 21           RNBT FBG    IO 235  CRUS 7  9     2900 2  6    6500   7450

  23    SEVEN-METER           FBG    IO 260  HOLM 8        4500 2  6   10000  11300
  23    SEVEN-METER           FBG    IO T260 CRUS 8        4500 2  6   11400  13000
  23    SEVEN-METER      RNBT FBG    IO 260  CRUS 8        4500 2  6    9900  11200
  23    SEVEN-METER      RNBT FBG    IO T235 CRUS 8        4500 2  6   11000  12500
-------------------- 1970 BOATS ----------------------------------------------------
  16  8 SKI-SPORTER      SKI  FBG DV IO 165-210   7        2150 2  3    4600   5400
  16  8 SKI-SPORTER      SKI  FBG DV IB 235  HOLM 7        2150 2  3    2900   3400
  18    2-PLUS-3         RNBT FBG DV IO 165-235   7        2250 2  3    5700   6850
  18    2-PLUS-3         RNBT FBG DV IB 300  HOLM 7        2250 2  3    3800   4400
  18    2-PLUS-3         RNBT FBG DV IB 400  HOLM 7        2250 2  3    4400   5100
  18    CORSICAN         RNBT FBG DV IO 165-235   7        2300 2  3    5350   6400
  18    CORSICAN         RNBT FBG DV IB 300  HOLM 7        2300 2  3    3550   4150
  18    CORSICAN         RNBT FBG DV IB 400  HOLM 7        2300 2  3    4100   4750
  19  3 HORNET           RNBT FBG DV IO 235  HOLM 7 10     2700 2  3    7450   8550
      IB 300  HOLM  4750 5500, IB 400  HOLM  5350 6150, IB 500 HOLM    6300   7250

  21  2 G-T 21           RNBT FBG DV IO 235-290   7  9     2850 2  6    6650   8150
  21  2 G-T 21           RNBT FBG DV IB 300  HOLM 7  9     2850 2  6    4200   4850
  21  2 G-T 21           RNBT FBG DV IB 400  HOLM 7  9     2850 2  6    4700   5400
  23    SEVEN-METER 23   RNBT FBG DV IO 210-235   8        4500 2  4    9950  11400
  23    SEVEN-METER 23   RNBT FBG DV IO T165-T235 8        4500 2  4   10900  12900
-------------------- 1969 BOATS ----------------------------------------------------
  16  8 BABY             RNBT FBG    IB 210       7        1050 2  3    2250   2600
  16  8 SKI-SPORTER      SKI  FBG DV IO 200-210   7        1800 1      4400   5100
  16  8 SKI-SPORTER      SKI  FBG DV IO 225  HOLM 7        1800 1      4500   5200
  16  8 SKI-SPORTER      SKI  FBG DV IO 165  INT  7        1800 1      2550   2950
  16  8 SKI-SPORTER      SKI  FBG SV IO 165  INT  7        1800 1      4250   4950
  18    2-PLUS-3         RNBT FBG DV IO 160-210   7        2000 1      5550   6550
      IO 225  HOLM  5800 6650, IB 225-300   3300 4050, IB 400 HOLM    4000   4650

  18    BABY             RNBT FBG    IB 210       7        3800 2  3    4600   5250
  18    CORSICAN              FBG DV IO 200-225   7        2000 1      5100   5950
  18    CORSICAN              FBG DV IO 225  HOLM 7        2000 1      3100   3550
  18    CORSICAN         RNBT FBG DV IO 225  HOLM 7        2000 1      3100   3600
  18    CORSICAN         RNBT FBG DV IB 400  HOLM 7        2000 1      3700   4300
  19  3 BABY             RNBT FBG    IB 225       7        2000 1      7050   8100
  19  3 HORNET                FBG DV IO 225-271   7 10     2700 2  4    7500   9100
  23    BABY                  CR   FBG IB 335      8        7050 2  5    9100  10300
  23    BABY                  CR   FBG IO 225      7        8050 2  5   19100  21200
  23    SEVEN-METER           CR   FBG DV IO 225  HOLM 8   3800 1  3    9650  11000
  23    SEVEN-METER           CR   FBG DV IB 300-400 8     4500 1      7500   9000
  23    SEVEN-METER           CR   FBG DV IO T120-T225 8   4500 1     11900  14000
-------------------- 1968 BOATS ----------------------------------------------------
  16  8 BABY             OP   SKI FBG SV IO 120-200 7      1500 1      4000   4800
  16  8 BABY             OP   SKI FBG SV IO 210      7     1500 1      4150   4850
  18    BABY             OP   SKI FBG VD IO 210-225  7     1500 1      2250   2650
  18    BABY             OP   SKI FBG SV IO 120-200  7     1650 1      4700   5550
  18    BABY             OP   SKI FBG SV IO 210      7     1650 1      4850   5550
  18    BABY             OP   SKI FBG SV IO 210-225  7     1650 1      2600   3050
  19  3 HORNET           RNBT FBG    VD 320-335     7 10   3000 2  3    4900   5650
  19  3 LITRE 7               FBG    IB 225-335     7      3000        7550   8750
  19  3 LITRE 7               FBG    IB 225-335     7      3000        4150   5100
  19  3 ST-TROPEZ             FBG    IO T120-T160   7      3000        8850  10100
  19  3 ST-TROPEZ        CTRCN FBG SV IO 155-210    7 10   2600 2  3    7550   8900
  23    BABY                  CR   FBG IB 165  MRCR 8      2700 1  3    4750   5450

  28    SPORTSMAN        SF   FBG    IB T250-T325  10       7700 1  5  11300  13500
  28    SPORTSMAN        SF   FBG    IB T425       10       7700 1  5  12900  14700
-------------------- 1967 BOATS ----------------------------------------------------
  16  8 BABY                  FBG    IO 120-210    7        1500        4150   5050
  18  8 DONZI 16         SKI  FBG    IO 110        7             1      5300   6100
  18    2-PLUS-3         SKI  FBG    IO 165        7             1      6700   7700
  19  3 BABY                  FBG    IO 120-210    7        1650        4950   5850
  19  3 BABY                  FBG    IO 150-210    7        2600        7150   8400
  19  3 HORNET                FBG    IO 320        7        3000        9350  10600
  19  3 HORNET           RNBT FBG    IB 320        7 11          1      4700   5400
  19  3 ST-TROPEZ        FSH  FBG    IO 110        7 10          1      8650   9900
  23    BABY                  FBG    IO 160-200    7             1      9000  10300
  23    BABY                  FBG    IO 225-335    7             1      4550   5450
  23    BABY                  FBG    IO T120-T160  7             1     10100  11500

  28    BABY                  FBG    IB T250-T325          7700       10700  12900
  28    BABY                  FBG    IB T425              7700       12400  14100
  28    DONZI 28         RNBT FBG    IB T250       10  6         1  5   9200  10500
-------------------- 1966 BOATS ----------------------------------------------------
  16  7 BABY             RNBT FBG    IO 110        7             1      5550   6600
  16  7 BABY             SKI  FBG    IO 165        7             1      5500   6350
  18  7 BABY             RNBT FBG    IO 165-200    7             1      6700   7800
  19  2 HORNET T-LITRE   RNBT FBG    IO 290-325    7 10          1      9850  12000
  19  2 HORNET T-LITRE   RNBT FBG    IO 433        7 10          1     15000  17000
  19  2 ST-TROPEZ        OPFSH FBG   IO 110-200    7 10          1      9000  10400
  28    BABY             CR   FBG    IO T250-T290         20900       24400
  28    BABY             CR   FBG    IB T425              26100       29000
-------------------- 1965 BOATS ----------------------------------------------------
  16  7 BABY                  FBG    IO 165-230            5750        6900
  16  7 BABY                  FBG    IO 110                5900        6800
  19  2 BABY                  FBG    IO 325               10200       11600
  28    DONZI            EXP  FBG    IB T210       10  6       2  6    8700  10000
  35    DONZI            CR   FBG    IB T390       12  6       2  6   20200  22500
```

DORCHESTER SHIPBUILDING CORP

Call 1-800-327-6929 for BUC Personalized Evaluation Service
Or, for 1965 boats, sign onto www.BUCValuPro.com

DORSETT MARINE
AMERICAN MARINE IND INC
SANTA CLARA CA   COAST GUARD MFG ID- DST   See inside cover to adjust price for area

FT	IN	NAME AND/ OR MODEL	TOP/ RIG	BOAT TYPE	HULL MTL	HULL TP	ENG TP	# HP	MFG	BEAM FT	IN	WGT LBS	DRAFT FT	IN	RETAIL LOW	RETAIL HIGH
		——— 1970 BOATS ———														
16		DX 416 SK		SKI	FBG		OB								1750	2100
16	6	CATALINA		CBNCR	FBG	DV	OB			6	8	1025	3	8	2400	2750
16	6	CATALINA		CBNCR	FBG	RB	IO	130	VLVO	6	8	1025			2750	3200
16	6	DAYTONA STD	OP	UTL	FBG	DV	OB			6	8	990			2300	2650
16	6	DAYTONA STD	OP	UTL	FBG	DV	IO	120-160		6	8	1030			2650	3100
16	6	DAYTONA STD	OP	UTL	FBG	DV	IO	165	VLVO	6	8	1030			2900	3400
17	5	EL-REY STD	OP	UTL	FBG	DV	OB			6	8	1423			3050	3550
17	5	EL-REY STD	OP	UTL	FBG	DV	IO	120		6	8				3050	3500
17	5	EL-REY STD	OP	UTL	FBG	DV	IO	130-160		6	8				3250	3800
17	5	EL-REY STD	OP	UTL	FBG	DV	IO	165	VLVO	6	8	1423			3500	4100
18		NEWPORT TRI-V			FBG	TR	OB								3050	3500
18		NEWPORT TRI-V			FBG	TR	IO	120-155							3300	4050
18	2	SAN-JUAN		CBNCR	FBG	DV	OB			7	5	1456			3300	3800
18	2	SAN-JUAN		CBNCR	FBG	SV	IO	160	MRCR	7	5				3750	4350
19		HOLIDAY TRI-V			FBG	TR	IO	120-215							3650	4500
19		SAN-JUAN		CBNCR	FBG	DV	IO	120-165		7	5	1456			4050	5000
20		MONTEREY		CUD		RB	IO	155	MRCR	8					4800	5550
20		RESORTER		UTL		DV	IO	120	MRCR	8					5050	5800
23		FARALLON		CR	FBG	DV	IO	155-215		8		3000			7450	8750
23		FARALLON		CR	FBG	DV	IO	T120-T155		8		3000			8550	10400
		——— 1969 BOATS ———														
16	6	CATALINA		CR	FBG	SV	OB			6	8	1025	3	8	2400	2750
16	6	DAYTONA		RNBT	FBG	SV	OB			6	8	990	3	8	2350	2700
16	6	DAYTONA		RNBT	FBG	SV	IO	120-160		6	8	1030			2650	3100
17	5	EL-REY		RNBT	FBG	SV	OB			6	8	1423	3	8	3200	3700
17	5	EL-REY		RNBT	FBG	SV	IO	120-160		6	8	1423	3	8	3200	3700
18	2	SAN-JUAN		CR	FBG	SV	IO	120-160		7	5	1456			3700	4350
20		MONTEREY			FBG	SV	IO	160	MRCR	8					4750	5450
23		FARALLON		CR	FBG		IO	160-225		8		3000			7750	9100
23		FARALLON		CR	FBG		IO	T120	MRCR	8		3000			8950	10200
23		FARALLON OFFSHORE		OFF	FBG		IO	160-225		8		2700			7300	8600
23		FARALLON OFFSHORE		OFF	FBG		IO	T120	MRCR	8		2700			8400	9650
		——— 1968 BOATS ———														
16	6	CATALINA	OP		FBG		OB			6	8	1025			2400	2800
16	6	DAYTONA	OP		FBG	SV	OB			6	8	990			2300	2700
16	6	DAYTONA	OP		FBG	SV	IO	120-160		6	8	1030			2550	3000
17	3	EL-REY	OP		FBG		OB			6	8	1200			2750	3200
17	3	EL-REY	OP		FBG		IO	120-160		6	8	1260			2950	3500
18	3	SAN-JUAN		CR	FBG		OB			6	6	1247			2950	3400
18	3	SAN-JUAN		CR	FBG		IO	120-160		6	6	1456			3500	4100
18	3	SAN-JUAN OFFSHORE		OFF	FBG		IO	120-160		6	6	1456			3500	4100
23		FARALLON		CR	FBG		IO	160-225		8		3700			9300	10700
23		FARALLON OFFSHORE		OFF	FBG		IO	160-225		8		3250			8400	9900
28		CALIFORNIAN		EXP	FBG		IB	T190-T250		9	6	6800			11000	13100
28		CALIFORNIAN SPORT		SPTCR	FBG		IB	T190-T250		9	6	7100			11200	13300
		——— 1967 BOATS ———														
16	6	CATALINA			FBG		OB					1025			2400	2800
16	6	DAYTONA			FBG		OB			6	8	990			2300	2700
16	6	DAYTONA			FBG		IO	110		6	8	1030			2650	3050
16	6	DAYTONA 4+2			FBG		OB			6	8	1100			2550	2950
16	6	DAYTONA 4+2			FBG		IO	120-160		6	8	1140			2750	3200
16	6	EL-REY			FBG		OB			6	8	1200			2700	3150
16	6	EL-REY			FBG		IO	120-160		6	8	1260			2850	3350
17	3	EL-TIGRE			FBG		OB			6	8	1383			3100	3600
17	3	EL-TIGRE			FBG		IO	120-160		6	8	1423			3200	3750
18	3	SAN-JUAN		CR	FBG		OB			7	5	1247			2950	3400
18	3	SAN-JUAN		CR	FBG		IO	120-160		7	5	1456			4000	4650
18	3	SAN-JUAN OFFSHORE		OFF	FBG		IO	120-160		7	5	1456			4000	4650
23		FARALLON		CR	FBG		IO	160-225		8		3700			9550	11100
23		FARALLON OFFSHORE		OFF	FBG		IO	160-225		8		3250			8700	10200
28		CALIFORNIA	HT	EXP	FBG		IB	220-280				6800			9650	11300
28		CALIFORNIA	HT	EXP	FBG		IB	170D				6800			14000	15900
28		CALIFORNIA	HT	EXP	FBG		IB	T180-T250				6800			10600	12700
28		CALIFORNIA SPORT	HT		FBG		IB	220-280				7100			9850	11600
28		CALIFORNIA SPORT	HT		FBG		IB	170D				7100			14500	16500
28		CALIFORNIA SPORT	HT		FBG		IB	T180-T250				7100			10800	12900
28		CALIFORNIAN		EXP	FBG		IB	220-280		9	6	6800	2	3	9600	11300
28		CALIFORNIAN		EXP	FBG		IB	170D		9	6	6800	2	3	13900	15800
28		CALIFORNIAN		EXP	FBG		IB	T180-T250		9	6	6800	2	3	10500	12600
28		CALIFORNIAN SPORT		SPTCR	FBG		IB	220-280		9	6	7100	2	3	9800	11500
28		CALIFORNIAN SPORT		SPTCR	FBG		IB	170D		9	6	7100	2	3	14400	16400
28		CALIFORNIAN SPORT		SPTCR	FBG		IB	T180-T250		9	6	7100	2	3	10700	12800
		——— 1966 BOATS ———														
16	6	CATALINA		CR	FBG		OB			6	8	860			2000	2400
16	6	CATALINA		CR	FBG		OB	110-120		6	8				3000	3450
16	6	DAYTONA		SKI	FBG		OB			6	8	775			1850	2150
16	6	DAYTONA		SKI	FBG		OB	110-150		6	8				2800	3250
16	6	EL-REY		RNBT	FBG		OB			6	8	800			1900	2250
16	6	EL-REY		RNBT	FBG		OB	110-150		6	8				3000	3550
17	2	EL-TIGRE		RNBT	FBG		OB								2550	2950
17	2	EL-TIGRE		RNBT	FBG		OB	110-150							3250	3800
18	3	SAN-JUAN		CR	FBG		OB								2950	3450
18	3	SAN-JUAN		CR	FBG		IO	120-150		7	5				4100	4750
18	3	SAN-JUAN OFFSHORE		OFF	FBG		IO	110-150		7	5				4100	4800
23		FARALLON		CR	FBG		IO	110-225		8					8950	10300
23		FARALLON OFFSHORE		OFF	FBG		IO	150-225		8					8500	10000
		——— 1965 BOATS ———														
16		600 CUSTOM			FBG		IO	90-150							1950	2450
16		CATALINA			FBG		OB								2000	2400
16		CATALINA			FBG		IO	110-150							2300	2700
16		DAYTONA			FBG		IO	110							1900	2250
16		DAYTONA			FBG		IO	120-150							2000	2400
16		DAYTONA		CNV	FBG		IO	90-150							2500	2950
16		EL-REY			FBG		OB								1850	2200
16		EL-REY			FBG		IO	90-150							2250	2600
17	2	EL-TIGRE			FBG		OB								2600	3050
17	2	EL-TIGRE			FBG		IO	110-225							3200	3950
17	4	700 CUSTOM			FBG		OB								2400	2800
17	4	700 CUSTOM			FBG		IO	110-150							3150	3800
17	4	FLEETWOOD			FBG		OB								2850	3300
17	4	FLEETWOOD			FBG		IO	110-150							3200	4000
17	4	FLEETWOOD		CNV	FBG		OB								2550	2950
17	4	FLEETWOOD		CNV	FBG		IO	110-225							3850	4800
17	7	SEA-HAWK			FBG		OB								3000	3500
18	2	SAN-JUAN			FBG		OB								3050	3550
18	2	SAN-JUAN			FBG		IO	110-150							3950	4650
20	4	SAN-JUAN			FBG		IO	110-150							3150	3650
20	4	SAN-JUAN			FBG		IO	110-150							5650	6500
22		FARALLON 22			FBG		IO	110-225							8100	9550
22		MONTAUK			FBG		IO	110-150							8100	9350
23		FARALLON			FBG		IO	120-225							9200	10700
23		FARALLON		CR	FBG		IO	60D							13300	15100
23		FARALLON OFFSHORE		OFF	FBG		IO	120-225							8850	10300
23		FARALLON OFFSHORE		OFF	FBG		IO	60D							**	**
		——— 1964 BOATS ———														
16		CATALINA			FBG		OB								2000	2350
16		CATALINA			FBG		IO	80-160							2350	2800
16		DAYTONA			FBG		IO	80-110							2000	2400
16		DAYTONA			FBG		IO	120							1950	2350
16		DAYTONA			FBG		IO	120-160							2100	2500
16		DAYTONA LUXURY			FBG		IO	80-160							2150	2550
16		EL-REY			FBG		OB								1800	2150
16		EL-REY			FBG		IO	80-160							2250	2650
17	4	FLEETWOOD			FBG		OB								2650	3050
17	4	FLEETWOOD			FBG		IO	110-160							3350	3950
17	7	SEA-HAWK II			FBG		JT								**	**
18	2	SAN-JUAN			FBG		OB								3100	3600
18	2	SAN-JUAN			FBG		IO	110-160							4050	4750
20	5	FARALLON			FBG		IO	140-160							5750	6600
		——— 1963 BOATS ———														
16		CATALINA			FBG		OB								1800	2150
16		CATALINA			FBG		OB	80-120							2600	3000
16		DAYTONA		CNV	FBG		IO	80							2700	3150
16		DAYTONA		CNV	FBG		IO	100							2700	3150
16		DAYTONA		CNV	FBG		IO	100-110							3000	3500
16		DAYTONA		UTL	FBG		IO	80							3150	3700
16		DAYTONA		UTL	FBG		IO	100							3150	3700
16		DAYTONA		UTL	FBG		IO	100-110							3450	4000
16		DAYTONA LUXURY			FBG		IO	80							2000	2400
16		DAYTONA LUXURY			FBG		IO	100							2200	2550
16		DAYTONA LUXURY			FBG		IO	100-110							2500	2900
16		EL-REY			FBG		OB								1700	2000
16		EL-REY			FBG		IO	80							2100	2500
16		EL-REY			FBG		IO	100							2250	2650
16		EL-REY			FBG		IO	100-110							2500	2900

DORSETT MARINE (continued)

LOA FT IN	NAME AND/OR MODEL	TOP/RIG	BOAT TYPE	MTL	TP	TP	#	HP	MFG	BEAM FT IN	WGT LBS	DRAFT FT IN	RETAIL LOW	RETAIL HIGH
1963 BOATS														
17 4	FLEETWOOD	EXP		FBG		OB							2550	3000
17 4	FLEETWOOD	EXP		FBG		IO		80-120					3600	4500
17 4	FLEETWOOD	UTL		FBG		OB							2700	3150
17 4	FLEETWOOD	UTL		FBG		IO		80-120					3750	4400
17 4	FLEETWOOD OFFSHORE	OFF		FBG		OB							2550	3000
17 4	FLEETWOOD OFFSHORE	OFF		FBG		IO		80-120					3600	4500
17 7	SEA-HAWK			FBG		JT		150					1750	2050
18 10	SAN-JUAN	EXP		FBG		OB							3150	3650
18 10	SAN-JUAN	EXP		FBG		IO		80-120					4800	5800
20 5	FARALLON	EXP		FBG		OB							4850	5600
20 5	FARALLON	EXP		FBG		IO		100-120					6200	7450
1962 BOATS														
16 8	CATALINA	CR		FBG		OB							2250	2650
16 8	CATALINA	RNBT		FBG		IO		80-100					3500	4050
16 8	EL-REY	RNBT		FBG		OB							2550	2950
16 8	EL-REY	RNBT		FBG		IO		80-100					3500	4050
16 8	LEXINGTON	RNBT		FBG		OB							2550	2950
16 8	LEXINGTON	RNBT		FBG		IO		80-100					3500	4050
16 8	LEXINGTON	ST RNBT		FBG		OB							2550	2950
16 8	LEXINGTON	ST RNBT		FBG		IO		80-100					3500	4050
18 10	CHESAPEAKE	RNBT		FBG		OB							3200	3700
18 10	CHESAPEAKE	RNBT		FBG		IO		80-100					4850	5550
18 10	MONTEREY	CR		FBG		JT		100					1750	2100
18 10	SAN-JUAN	CR		FBG		OB							3050	3550
18 10	SAN-JUAN	CR		FBG		IO		80-100					4950	5700
20 5	FARALLON	CR		FBG		OB							3950	4600
20 5	FARALLON	CR		FBG		IO		80-100					6400	7400
1961 BOATS														
16 8	CATALINA	CBNCR		FBG		OB				5 8	815		1950	2350
16 8	EL-REY DLX	RNBT		FBG		OB				6 7	755		1850	2200
16 8	LEXINGTON LUXURY	RNBT		FBG		OB				6 7	720		1750	2100
16 8	LEXINGTON SPORT	RNBT		FBG		OB				6 7	685		1700	2000
18 10	SAN-JUAN	CBNCR		FBG		OB				6 10	1350		3250	3750
20 5	FARALLON	CBNCR		FBG		OB				7 7	1800		4550	5250
1960 BOATS														
17	CATALINA	CR		FBG		OB							2300	2700
17	EL-REY	CR		FBG		OB							2600	3000
17	LEXINGTON LUXURY	RNBT		FBG		OB							2600	3000
17	LEXINGTON SPORT	RNBT		FBG		OB							2600	3000
19	SAN-JUAN	CR		FBG		OB							3100	3600
20	FARALLON LUXURY	CR		FBG		OB							3900	4550
1959 BOATS														
17	CATALINA	CR		FBG		OB				6 6	850		2100	2450
17	EL-REY	RNBT		FBG		OB				6 6	675		1700	2000
19	SAN-JUAN	CR		FBG		OB				7 6	1500		3550	4100
19	SANTA-CRUIS	RNBT		FBG		OB				7 6	1300		3200	3700
20	FARALLON	CR		FBG		OB				7 11	1900		4650	5300
1958 BOATS														
17	EL-REY SPORT	RNBT		FBG		OB							2600	3050
1957 BOATS														
17	EL-REY SPORT	RNBT		FBG		OB							2600	3050

JOHN DORY BOAT WORKS INC
COAST GUARD MFG ID- JDB

Call 1-800-327-6929 for BUC Personalized Evaluation Service
Or, for 1974 to 1979 boats, sign onto www.BUCValuPro.com

DORY U S A LTD
DELL QUAY DORY
HUNTINGTON STA NY   COAST GUARD MFG ID- DRY   See inside cover to adjust price for area

LOA FT IN	NAME AND/OR MODEL	TOP/RIG	BOAT TYPE	MTL	TP	TP	#	HP	MFG	BEAM FT IN	WGT LBS	DRAFT FT IN	RETAIL LOW	RETAIL HIGH
1974 BOATS														
17 1	DELL-QUAY DORY 17			FBG		OB				7 2	800		4050	4700
1973 BOATS														
17 2	DELL-QUAY DORY 17			FBG		OB				7 2	800		4050	4750

DOUGLAS MARINE CORP
DOUGLAS MI 49406   COAST GUARD MFG ID- DUX   See inside cover to adjust price for area

For more recent years, see the BUC Used Boat Price Guide, Volume 1 or Volume 2

LOA FT IN	NAME AND/OR MODEL	TOP/RIG	BOAT TYPE	MTL	TP	TP	#	HP	MFG	BEAM FT IN	WGT LBS	DRAFT FT IN	RETAIL LOW	RETAIL HIGH
1983 BOATS														
17 7	SKATER 18	OP	RNBT	F/S	TH	OB				7 11	1475	11	5150	5900
17 7	SKATER 18	OP	RNBT	F/S	TH	IO		260		7 11	2050	1 5	4700	5400
17 7	SKATER 18 "S"	OP	RNBT	F/S	TH	OB				7 11	900	9	3450	4000
1982 BOATS														
17 7	SKATER 18	OP	RNBT	F/S	TH	OB				7 11	1200	11	4250	4950
1981 BOATS														
17 7	SKATER 18	OP	RNBT	F/S	TH	OB				7 11	850	11	3100	3600
17 7	SKATER 18	OP	RNBT	F/S	TH	IO		260		7 11	1075	11	3750	4350
1980 BOATS														
17 7	SKATER 18	OP	RNBT	F/S	TH	OB				7 11	1050	11	3650	4200
17 7	SKATER 18	OP	RNBT	F/S	TH	IO		260		7 11	1050	11	3700	4300
1979 BOATS														
17 7	SKATER 18	OP	RNBT	FBG	TH	OB				7 11	1050	6	3550	4150
17 7	SKATER 18	OP	RNBT	FBG	TH	IO		260		7 11		6	4500	5200

DOUGLAS MARINE CRAFT

Call 1-800-327-6929 for BUC Personalized Evaluation Service
Or, for 1970 boats, sign onto www.BUCValuPro.com

DOUGLASS & MCLEOD INC
GRAND RIVER OH 44045   COAST GUARD MFG ID- DMC   See inside cover to adjust price for area
SEE ALSO TARTAN MARINE COMPANY

LOA FT IN	NAME AND/OR MODEL	TOP/RIG	BOAT TYPE	MTL	TP	TP	#	HP	MFG	BEAM FT IN	WGT LBS	DRAFT FT IN	RETAIL LOW	RETAIL HIGH
1979 BOATS														
17	THISTLE	SLP	SA/OD	FBG	CB					6	515	9	2650	3050
20	HIGHLANDER	SLP	SA/OD	FBG	CB					6 8	830	8	3150	3650
22	D-&-M	SLP	SA/CR	FBG	KL	OB				8 5	4000	3 6	7150	8250
1978 BOATS														
17	THISTLE	SLP	SA/OD	FBG	CB					6	515	9	2500	2950
20	HIGHLANDER	SLP	SA/OD	FBG	CB					6 8	830	8	3050	3550
22	D-&-M 22	SLP	SA/CR	FBG	KL	OB				8 5	3900	3 6	6750	7750
1977 BOATS														
17	THISTLE	SLP	SA/OD	FBG	CB					6	515	9	2500	2900
20	HIGHLANDER	SLP	SA/OD	FBG	CB					6 8	830	8	2900	3400
22	D-&-M 22	SLP	SA/RC	FBG	KL					8 5	4000	3 6	6650	7600
1976 BOATS														
22	D-&-M 22	SLP	SA/RC	FBG	KL					8 5	4000	3 6	6450	7400
1975 BOATS														
17	THISTLE	SLP	SA/OD	FBG	CB					6	515	9	2300	2700
22	D-&-M 22	SLP	SA/RC	FBG	KL					8 5	4000	3 6	6250	7200
1974 BOATS														
17	THISTLE	SLP	SA/OD	FBG	CB					6	515	9	2250	2600
20	HIGHLANDER	SLP	SA/OD	FBG	CB					6 8	830	8	2700	3100
22	D-&-M 22	SLP	SA/RC	FBG	KL					8 5	4000	3 6	6050	6950
1973 BOATS														
17	THISTLE	SLP	SA/OD	FBG	CB					6	515	9	2150	2500
22	D-&-M 22	SLP	SA/RC	FBG	KL					8 5	4000	3 6	5850	6750
1972 BOATS														
17	THISTLE	SLP	SA/OD	FBG	CB					6	515	9	2050	2450
20	HIGHLANDER	SLP	SA/OD	FBG	CB					6 8	830	8	2550	2950
21 11	D-&-M 22	SLP	SA/RC	FBG	KC					8 5			5850	6750
1971 BOATS														
17	THISTLE	SLP	SA/OD	FBG	CB					6	515	9	2000	2400
20	HIGHLANDER	SLP	SA/OD	FBG	CB					6 8	830	8	2450	2850
27	TARTAN 27	SLP	SA/CR	FBG	KC	IB			D	8 8	6875	3 2	12600	14300
27	TARTAN 27	YWL	SA/CR	FBG	KC	IB			D	8 8	6875	3 2	12600	14300
30 1	TARTAN 30	SLP	SA/CR	FBG	KL	IB			D	10	8750	4 11	17400	19800
34 5	TARTAN 34	SLP	SA/CR	FBG	KC	IB			D	10 6	11200	3 11	22700	25200
34 5	TARTAN 34	YWL	SA/CR	FBG	KC	IB			D	10 6	11200	3 11	22700	25200
37	BLACK-WATCH	SLP	SA/CR	FBG	KC	IB			D	10 6	15700	5 1	31300	34800
37	BLACK-WATCH	YWL	SA/CR	FBG	KC	IB			D	10 6	15700	5 1	31300	34800
37	TARTAN 37	SLP	SA/CR	FBG	KC	IB			D	10 6	13800	3 10	28000	31100
37	TARTAN 37	YWL	SA/CR	FBG	KC	IB			D	10 6	13800	3 10	27900	31000
37	TARTAN 37	YWL	SA/CR	FBG	KC	IB			D	10 6	13800	3 10	27900	31000
37	TARTAN 37	YWL	SA/CR	FBG	KL	IB			D	10 6	13800	6 1	27800	30900
1970 BOATS														
17	THISTLE	SLP	SA/OD	FBG	CB					6	500	9	1950	2300
20	HIGHLANDER	SLP	SA/OD	FBG	CB					6 8	830	8	2450	2850
27	TARTAN 27	SLP	SA/CR	FBG	KC	IB		30	UNIV	8 7		3 2	10300	11700

LOA FT	LOA IN	NAME AND/ OR MODEL	TOP/ RIG	BOAT TYPE	-HULL- MTL	-HULL- TP	ENGINE TP	# HP	ENGINE MFG	BEAM FT	BEAM IN	WGT LBS	DRAFT FT	DRAFT IN	RETAIL LOW	RETAIL HIGH
		1970 BOATS														
27		TARTAN 27	YWL	SA/CR	FBG	KC	IB	30	UNIV	8	7		3	2	10300	11700
34	5	TARTAN 34	SLP	SA/CR	FBG	KC	IB	D		10	2	11200	3	11	22200	24600
34	5	TARTAN 34	YWL	SA/CR	FBG	KC	IB	D		10	2	11200	3	11	22200	24600
37		BLACK-WATCH	SLP	SA/CR	FBG	KC	IB	D		10	6	15700	5	1	30600	34000
37		BLACK-WATCH	YWL	SA/CR	FBG	KC	IB	D		10	6	15700	5	1	30500	33900
37		TARTAN 37	SLP	SA/CR	FBG	KC	IB	D		10	6	13800	5	1	27400	30400
37		TARTAN 37	SLP	SA/CR	FBG	KL	IB	D		10	6	13800	5	1	27200	30200
37		TARTAN 37	YWL	SA/CR	FBG	KC	IB	D		10	6	13800	5	1	27300	30400
37		TARTAN 37	YWL	SA/CR	FBG	KL	IB	D		10	6	13800	5	1	27200	30200
		1969 BOATS														
17		THISTLE	SLP	SA/OD	FBG	CB				6		500		9	1900	2250
20		HIGHLANDER	SLP	SA/OD	FBG	CB				6	8			8	2650	3050
27		TARTAN 27	SLP	SA/CR	FBG	CB	IB	30D		8	8	7400	3	2	13000	14700
27		TARTAN 27	YWL	SA/CR	FBG	CB	IB	30D		8	8	7400	3	2	13000	14700
34	5	TARTAN 34	SLP	SA/CR	FBG	KC	IB	30D		10	2	11200	3	10	22300	24700
34	5	TARTAN 34	YWL	SA/CR	FBG	KC	IB	30D		10	2	11200	3	10	22300	24700
37		BLACK-WATCH T37	SLP	SA/CR	FBG	KL	IB	30D		10	6	15700	3	10	29700	33000
37		BLACK-WATCH T37	YWL	SA/CR	FBG	KL	IB	30D		10	6	15700	3	10	29700	33000
37		TARTAN 37	SLP	SA/CR	FBG	KC	IB	30D		10	6	15700	3	10	29900	33200
37		TARTAN 37	SLP	SA/CR	FBG	KL	IB	30D		10	6	15700	3	10	29700	33000
		1968 BOATS														
17		THISTLE	SLP	SA/OD	FBG	CB				6		500			1750	2100
20		HIGHLANDER	SLP	SA/OD	FBG	CB				6	8	800			2350	2700
27		TARTAN 27	SLP	SA/CR	FBG	KC	IB	30D		8	7	6875	3	2	12200	13800
27		TARTAN 27	YWL	SA/CR	FBG	KC	IB	30D		8	7	6875	3	2	12200	13800
34	5	TARTAN 34	SLP	SA/CR	FBG	KL	IB	30D		10	2	11200	3	11	22300	24800
34	5	TARTAN 34	YWL	SA/CR	FBG	KL	IB	30D		10	2	11200	3	11	22300	24800
37		BLACK-WATCH	SLP	SA/CR	FBG	KL	IB	30D		10	6	15700	5	2	32500	36100
37		BLACK-WATCH	YWL	SA/CR	FBG	KL	IB	30D		10	6	15700	5	2	32500	36100
37		TARTAN 37	SLP	SA/CR	FBG	KL	IB	30D		10	6	15700	5	1	28500	31600
37		TARTAN 37	YWL	SA/CR	FBG	KL	IB	30D		10	6	15700	5	1	28500	31600
		1967 BOATS														
20		HIGHLANDER	SLP	SA/OD	FBG	CB				6	8	830		8	2300	2700
27		TARTAN 27	SLP	SA/OD	FBG	KC	IB	D		8	8	6875	3	2	11800	13500
27		TARTAN 27	YWL	SA/OD	FBG	KC	IB	D		8	8	6875	3	2	11800	13500
37		BLACK-WATCH	SLP	SA/CR	FBG	KL	IB	35D		10	6		5	1	32200	35800
37		BLACK-WATCH	YWL	SA/CR	FBG	KC	IB	35D		10	6		5	1	32300	35900
		1966 BOATS														
17		THISTLE	SLP	SA/OD	FBG	CB				6		515		9	1750	2050
17		THISTLE	SLP	SA/OD	WD	CB				6		515		9	1750	2050
20		HIGHLANDER	SLP	SA/OD	FBG	CB				6	8	830		8	2300	2650
20		HIGHLANDER	SLP	SA/OD	PLY	CB				6	8	830		8	2300	2650
27		TARTAN	YWL	SA/OD	FBG	KC	IB	D		8	8	6875	3	2	11700	13300
37		BLACK-WATCH	SLP	SA/CR	FBG	KL	IB	35D		10	6		5	1	31700	35300
37		BLACK-WATCH	YWL	SA/CR	FBG	KL	IB	35D		10	6		5	1	31700	35200
		1965 BOATS														
17		THISTLE	SLP	SA/OD	F/W	CB				6		515		9	1700	2050
20		HIGHLANDER	SLP	SA/OD	FBG	CB				6	8	830	4	10	2250	2650
27		TARTAN 27	SLP	SA/CR	FBG	KC	IB	30D		8	7		3	2	11000	12500
27		TARTAN 27	YWL	SA/CR	FBG	KC	IB	30D		8	7		3	2	11000	12500
		1961 BOATS														
17		THISTLE	SLP	SA/OD	FBG	CB				6		515			1700	2000
17		THISTLE	SLP	SA/OD	MHG	CB				6		515			1700	2000
20		HIGHLANDER	SLP	SA/OD	FBG	CB				6	8	830			2250	2600
20		HIGHLANDER	SLP	SA/OD	MHG	CB				6	8	830			2250	2600
		1960 BOATS														
17		THISTLE	SLP	SA/OD	PLY	CB				6		515		9	1700	2000
20		HIGHLANDER	SLP	SA/OD	PLY	CB				6	8	830		8	2250	2600
		1959 BOATS														
17		THISTLE	SLP	SA/OD	PLY	CB				6		515		9	1700	2000
20		HIGHLANDER	SLP	SA/OD	PLY	CB				6	8	830		8	2250	2600

DOWN EAST DORIES

COAST GUARD MFG ID- DED

Call 1-800-327-6929 for BUC Personalized Evaluation Service
Or, for 1970 to 1980 boats, sign onto www.BUCValuPro.com

DOWN EAST YACHTS INC

SANTA ANA CA 92705 COAST GUARD MFG ID- AAY See inside cover to adjust price for area

LOA FT	LOA IN	NAME AND/ OR MODEL	TOP/ RIG	BOAT TYPE	-HULL- MTL	-HULL- TP	ENGINE TP	# HP	ENGINE MFG	BEAM FT	BEAM IN	WGT LBS	DRAFT FT	DRAFT IN	RETAIL LOW	RETAIL HIGH
		1981 BOATS														
34		DOWNEAST 34		TRWL	FBG	DS	IB	85D		12	3	20500			65500	71900
35	6	DOWNEASTER 32	CUT	SA/CR	FBG	KL	IB	D		11		17900	4	9	37700	41900
38		DOWNEASTER 38	SCH	SA/CR	FBG	KL	IB	32D	UNIV	11	10	19500	4	11	42800	47500
38		DOWNEASTER 38	CUT	SA/CR	FBG	KL	IB	32D	UNIV	11	10	19500	4	11	42700	47500
38		DOWNEASTER 38	KTH	SA/CR	FBG	KL	IB	32D	UNIV	11	10	19500	4	11	43100	47900
39	8	DOWNEAST 40		TRWL	FBG	DS	IB	130D		13	8	27000			94000	103500
41	9	DOWNEASTER 41	SLP	SA/CR	FBG	KL	IB	65D	FORD	11	10	19500	4	11	50700	55800
41	9	DOWNEASTER 41	CUT	SA/CR	FBG	KL	IB	65D	FORD	11	10	19500	4	11	50700	55700
45		DOWNEASTER 45	SCH	SA/CR	FBG	KL	IB	52D	PERK	14		39000	6	4	83400	91700
45		DOWNEASTER 45	SCH	SA/CR	FBG	KL	IB	85D	PERK	14		39000	6	4	83800	92100
45		DOWNEASTER 45	CUT	SA/CR	FBG	KL	IB	52D	PERK	14		39000	6	4	83400	91700
45		DOWNEASTER 45	CUT	SA/CR	FBG	KL	IB	85D	PERK	14		39000	6	4	83800	92100
45		DOWNEASTER 45	KTH	SA/CR	FBG	KL	IB	52D	PERK	14		39000	6	4	83500	91800
45		DOWNEASTER 45	KTH	SA/CR	FBG	KL	IB	85D	PERK	14		39000	6	4	83900	92100
		1980 BOATS														
32		DOWNEASTER 32	CUT	SA/CR	FBG	KL	IB	24D	UNIV	11		17000	4	9	33900	37700
34		DOWNEASTER 34	FB	TRWL	FBG	DS	IB	65D	LEHM	12	3	20500	3	4	62900	69100
38		DOWNEASTER 38	CUT	SA/CR	FBG	KL	IB	32D	UNIV	11	10	19500	4	11	40800	45300
38		DOWNEASTER 38	KTH	SA/CR	FBG	KL	IB	32D	UNIV	11	10	19500	4	11	41000	45600
39	8	DOWNEAST TRAWLER 40	FB	TRWL	FBG	DS	IB	130D	PERK	13	8	27000	4		90900	99900
39	8	DOWNEAST TRAWLER 40	FB	TRWL	FBG	DS	IB	T130D	PERK	13	8	27000	4		96900	106500
41	9	DOWNEASTER 41	SLP	SA/CR	FBG	KL	IB	65D	LEHM	11	10	20500	5		49900	54800
45		DOWNEASTER 45	CUT	SA/CR	FBG	KL	IB	65D	PERK	14		39000	6	2	79800	87700
45		DOWNEASTER 45	KTH	SA/CR	FBG	KL	IB	65D	PERK	14		39000	6	2	79900	87800
		1979 BOATS														
32		DOWNEASTER 32	CUT	SA/CR	FBG	KL	IB	D		11		17000	4	9	32600	36200
32		DOWNEASTER 32	KTH	SA/CR	FBG	KL	IB	D		11		17000	4	9	32600	36200
38		DOWNEASTER 38	SCH	SA/CR	FBG	KL	IB	D		11	10	19500	4	11	39300	43700
38		DOWNEASTER 38	CUT	SA/CR	FBG	KL	IB	D		11	10	19500	4	11	39300	43700
38		DOWNEASTER 38	KTH	SA/CR	FBG	KL	IB	D		11	10	19500	4	11	39500	43800
45		DOWNEASTER 45	SCH	SA/CR	FBG	KL	IB	D		14		39000	6		77200	84900
45		DOWNEASTER 45	CUT	SA/CR	FBG	KL	IB	D	PERK	14		39000	6		76900	84500
45		DOWNEASTER 45	KTH	SA/CR	FBG	KL	IB	D	PERK	14		39000	6		76900	84600
		1978 BOATS														
32		DOWNEASTER 32	SLP	SA/CR	FBG	KL	IB	D		11		17000	4	9	31400	34900
32		DOWNEASTER 32	KTH	SA/CR	FBG	KL	IB	D		11		17000	4	9	31400	34900
38		DOWNEASTER 38	SCH	SA/CR	FBG	KL	IB	D		11	10	19500	4	11	37900	42100
38		DOWNEASTER 38	CUT	SA/CR	FBG	KL	IB	D		11	10	19500	4	11	37900	42100
38		DOWNEASTER 38	KTH	SA/CR	FBG	KL	IB	D		11	10	19500	4	11	38000	42200
45		DOWNEASTER 45	SCH	SA/CR	FBG	KL	IB	D	PERK	14		39000	5	11	74100	81500
45		DOWNEASTER 45	KTH	SA/CR	FBG	KL	IB	D	PERK	14		39000	5	11	74200	81500
		1977 BOATS														
32		DOWNEASTER 32	CUT	SA/CR	FBG	KL	IB	12D-	24D	11		16000	4	9	28600	31800
32		DOWNEASTER 32	KTH	SA/CR	FBG	KL	IB	12D-	24D	11		16000	4	9	28600	31800
38		DOWNEASTER 38	SCH	SA/CR	FBG	KL	IB	24D	FARY	12		19500	4	11	36400	40500
38		DOWNEASTER 38	SCH	SA/CR	FBG	KL	IB	32D	FARY	12		19500	4	11	36500	40600
38		DOWNEASTER 38	CUT	SA/CR	FBG	KL	IB	24D	FARY	12		19500	4	11	36400	40500
38		DOWNEASTER 38	CUT	SA/CR	FBG	KL	IB	32D	FARY	12		19500	4	11	36500	40600
38		DOWNEASTER 38	KTH	SA/CR	FBG	KL	IB	24D	FARY	12		19500	4	11	36500	40600
38		DOWNEASTER 38	KTH	SA/CR	FBG	KL	IB	32D	FARY	12		19500	4	11	36600	40700
45		DOWNEASTER 45	SCH	SA/CR	FBG	KL	IB	55D	PERK	14		40000	6		72300	79400
45		DOWNEASTER 45	SCH	SA/CR	FBG	KL	IB	85D	PERK	14		40000	6		72500	79700
45		DOWNEASTER 45	KTH	SA/CR	FBG	KL	IB	55D	PERK	14		40000	6		72300	79400
45		DOWNEASTER 45	KTH	SA/CR	FBG	KL	IB	85D	PERK	14		40000	6		72500	79700
		1976 BOATS														
32		DOWNEASTER 32	CUT	SA/CR	FBG	KL	IB	12D-	24D	11		17000	4	9	29400	32700
32		DOWNEASTER 32	KTH	SA/CR	FBG	KL	IB	12D-	24D	11		17000	4	9	29400	32700
38		DOWNEASTER 38	SCH	SA/CR	FBG	KL	IB	24D	FARY	11	10	19500	4	11	35300	39200
38		DOWNEASTER 38	SCH	SA/CR	FBG	KL	IB	32D	FARY	11	10	19500	4	11	35400	39300
38		DOWNEASTER 38	CUT	SA/CR	FBG	KL	IB	24D	FARY	11	10	19500	4	11	35300	39200
38		DOWNEASTER 38	CUT	SA/CR	FBG	KL	IB	32D	FARY	11	10	19500	4	11	35400	39300
38		DOWNEASTER 38	KTH	SA/CR	FBG	KL	IB	24D	FARY	11	10	19500	4	11	35400	39300
38		DOWNEASTER 38	KTH	SA/CR	FBG	KL	IB	32D	FARY	11	10	19500	4	11	35400	39400
		1975 BOATS														
38		DOWNEASTER 38	SCH	SA/CR	FBG	KL	IB	24D	FARY	11	10	19500	4	11	34300	38100
38		DOWNEASTER 38	SCH	SA/CR	FBG	KL	IB	32D	FARY	11	10	19500	4	11	34300	38200
38		DOWNEASTER 38	CUT	SA/CR	FBG	KL	IB	24D	FARY	11	10	19500	4	11	34300	38100
38		DOWNEASTER 38	CUT	SA/CR	FBG	KL	IB	32D	FARY	11	10	19500	4	11	34300	38200
38		DOWNEASTER 38	KTH	SA/CR	FBG	KL	IB	24D	FARY	11	10	19500	4	11	34300	38100
38		DOWNEASTER 38	KTH	SA/CR	FBG	KL	IB	32D	FARY	11	10	19500	4	11	34400	38200

206 96th ed. - Vol. III

DRAKE CRAFT BOATS
OXNARD CA 93030   See inside cover to adjust price for area

LOA FT IN	NAME AND/ OR MODEL	TOP/ RIG	BOAT TYPE	-HULL- MTL TP	TP	----ENGINE--- # HP MFG	BEAM FT IN	WGT LBS	DRAFT FT IN	RETAIL LOW	RETAIL HIGH
--- 1967 BOATS ---											
31	CUSTOM		PLY	IB			11 4		2	**	**
42	CUSTOM		PLY	IB			14		2 6	**	**
53	CUSTOM		PLY	IB			16 9		3	**	**
55	CUSTOM		PLY	IB			16 9		3	**	**
60	CUSTOM		PLY	IB			19 6		3 4	**	**
65	CUSTOM		PLY	IB			19 6		4	**	**
75	CUSTOM		PLY	IB			22 6		4	**	**

DREADNOUGHT BOATWORKS INC
CARPINTERIA CA 93013   COAST GUARD MFG ID- DRD See inside cover to adjust price for area

LOA FT IN	NAME AND/ OR MODEL	TOP/ RIG	BOAT TYPE	-HULL- MTL TP	TP	----ENGINE--- # HP MFG	BEAM FT IN	WGT LBS	DRAFT FT IN	RETAIL LOW	RETAIL HIGH
--- 1982 BOATS ---											
21	MONTEREY 21		TRWL	FBG DS	IB	13D 8				7800	8950
21	MONTEREY 21 PH	HT	TRWL	F/S DS	IB	18D 8		3500	1 8	7950	9150
32	TAHITI	KTH	SA/CR	FBG KL	IB	10D SABB 10	9	19980	4 8	32300	35800
--- 1981 BOATS ---											
21	MONTEREY 21		TRWL	F/S DS	IB	13D 8				7500	8600
21	MONTEREY 21 PH	HT	TRWL	F/S DS	IB	18D 8		3500	1 8	7650	8800
32	TAHITI	KTH	SA/CR	FBG KL	IB	10D SABB 10	9	19980	4 8	30400	33800
--- 1980 BOATS ---											
21	MONTEREY 21		TRWL	FBG DS	IB	13D 8				7200	8300
32	TAHITI	KTH	SA/CR	FBG KL	IB	D 10	4	20000	4 8	29000	32200
--- 1979 BOATS ---											
21	MONTEREY	OP	LNCH	FBG DS	IB	8D SABB 8		2800	1 7	7950	9150
21	MONTEREY 21 PH	HT	TRWL	FBG DS	IB	8D SABB 8		3500	1 9	6800	7800
32	TAHITI	CUT	SA/CR	FBG KL	IB	18D- 25D 10	9	19980	4 8	27800	30900
32	TAHITI	KTH	SA/CR	FBG KL	IB	18D- 25D 10	9	19980	4 8	27800	30900
--- 1978 BOATS ---											
21	MONTEREY 21	HT	FSH	FBG RB	IB	8D SABB 8		3500	1 9	6550	7500
21	MONTEREY 21 PH	HT	TRWL	FBG RB	IB	8D SABB 8		3500	1 9	6550	7500
32	TAHITI	CUT	SA/CR	FBG KL	IB	10D SABB 10	9	19980	4 9	26800	29800
32	TAHITI	KTH	SA/CR	FBG KL	IB	10D SABB 10	9	19980	4 9	26800	29800
--- 1975 BOATS ---											
32	TAHITI	CUT	SA/CR	FBG KL	IB	30 UNIV 10	9	19980	4 9	24400	27100
32	TAHITI	KTH	SA/CR	FBG KL	IB	25D VLVO 10	9	19980	4 9	24400	27100
--- 1974 BOATS ---											
32	TAHITI	KTH	SA/CR	FBG KL	IB	18D SABB 10	9	19500	4 9	23200	25700

DREAMBOAT MFG CO
Call 1-800-327-6929 for BUC Personalized Evaluation Service
Or, for 1959 to 1961 boats, sign onto www.BUCValuPro.com

DREYER BOAT YARD
COAST GUARD MFG ID- FCF

Call 1-800-327-6929 for BUC Personalized Evaluation Service
Or, for 1983 to 2000 boats, sign onto www.BUCValuPro.com

DRIFT-R-CRUZ HOUSEBOATS INC
GALLATIN TN 37066   COAST GUARD MFG ID- DRC See inside cover to adjust price for area
ALSO SEE THUNDERBIRD PROD PACKERMAKER

LOA FT IN	NAME AND/ OR MODEL	TOP/ RIG	BOAT TYPE	-HULL- MTL TP	TP	----ENGINE--- # HP MFG	BEAM FT IN	WGT LBS	DRAFT FT IN	RETAIL LOW	RETAIL HIGH
--- 1966 BOATS ---											
30	DRIFT-R-CRUZ	HT	HB	FBG	OB	11			1	2350	2700
39	3 DRIFT-R-CRUZ	HT	HB	FBG	OB	12 1			1 1	8850	10100
	IB 150	9550	10900,	IB	210	9650 11000, IB T150				10100	11500
	IB T210	10300	11700								

DRIFTER MARINE ENT INC
COAST GUARD MFG ID- DRZ

Call 1-800-327-6929 for BUC Personalized Evaluation Service
Or, for 1983 to 1984 boats, sign onto www.BUCValuPro.com

DRISCOLL CUSTOM BOATS
COAST GUARD MFG ID- DCS

Call 1-800-327-6929 for BUC Personalized Evaluation Service
Or, for 1978 to 1979 boats, sign onto www.BUCValuPro.com

FRED J DRIVER

Call 1-800-327-6929 for BUC Personalized Evaluation Service
Or, for 1965 boats, sign onto www.BUCValuPro.com

DRUMMOND YACHTS INC
DANIA FL 33004   COAST GUARD MFG ID- DRU See inside cover to adjust price for area

LOA FT IN	NAME AND/ OR MODEL	TOP/ RIG	BOAT TYPE	-HULL- MTL TP	TP	----ENGINE--- # HP MFG	BEAM FT IN	WGT LBS	DRAFT FT IN	RETAIL LOW	RETAIL HIGH
--- 1978 BOATS ---											
19	190V		CTRCN	FBG DV	IO	140	7 8			3400	4000
20	3 223	ST	CUD	FBG DV	IO	140-255	8			4700	5650
20	3 223	ST	CUD	FBG DV	IO	106D-130D	8	4000	2	6150	7450
20	3 223	ST	CUD	FBG DV	IO	175D	8			7000	8050
23	6 HAWK 240	OP	CUD	FBG DV	IO	175-265	8			6250	7700
	IO 92D-130D	7900	9050,	IO	235D	9150 10400, IO T140-T175				6900	8350
23	6 HAWK 240	HT	CUD	FBG DV	IO	175-265	8			6250	7750
	IO 92D-130D	7900	9050,	IO	235D	9150 10400, IO T140-T175				6900	8350
23	6 HAWK 240	FB	SF	FBG DV	IO	175-265	8			7750	9450
23	6 HAWK 240	FB	SF	FBG DV	IO	92D-130D	8			10200	11600
23	6 HAWK 240	FB	SF	FBG DV	IO	T140-T175	8			8450	10200
26	6 270	HT	SF	FBG DV	IO	155-255	8 6			15300	18100
	IO 230D-300D	24600	28400,	IO	T175-T190	16500 19100, IOT130D-175D			2	24500	30000
26	6 270	FB	SF	FBG DV	IO	155-255	8 6			15300	18100
	IO 230D-300D	24600	28500,	IO	T175-T235	16500 19300, IOT106D-175D			2	24500	30000
--- 1977 BOATS ---											
19	190V	OP	CTRCN	FBG DV	OB		7 6			2550	2950
19	190V	OP	CR	FBG DV	OB	130-190	7 6			3600	4200
21	6 223V	HT	CR	FBG SV	IO	140-165	8	3300		4800	5550
21	6 223V	HT	CR	FBG DV	IO	106D VLVO	8	3800		6450	7450
23	6 241V	HT	CR	FBG DV	IO	175-225	8			7000	8200
	IO 235 OMC	7150	8200,	IB	235 OMC	7100 8200, IO 106D VLVO				8200	9450
	IO 150D GM	8900	10100,	IO	150D-200D	9700 11600, IO 210D REN				9400	10700
	IO T130-T140	8050	9250,	IO	T 75D VLVO	9700 11000					
--- 1976 BOATS ---											
18	DRUMMOND	OP	CTRCN	FBG FL	OB		7 8			1500	1800
19	DRUMMOND	OP	RNBT	FBG FL	OB		7 8	1500		2050	2450
19	DRUMMOND		FSH	FBG DV	JT	130	7 8	3000		3600	4150
19	DRUMMOND		FSH	FBG DV	IO	130	7 8	3000		3850	4450
19	SUPER-SPORT	OP	RNBT	FBG DV	IO		7 8	1800		2400	2800
22	223-V RAISED CBN CNV	ST	CR	FBG SV	IO	140-165	8	3750	2	5550	6400
22	223-V RAISED CBN CNV	ST	CR	FBG DV	IO	106D VLVO	8	4000	2	7000	8050
24	241-V CTR CNSOLE CBN	ST	CR	FBG DV	IO	175-225	8	4000	2	7500	8750
	IO 235 OMC	7650	8800,	IB	235 OMC	7100 8200, IO 106D-115D				8500	9800
	IO 150D GM	9450	10700,	IO	150D-200D	9750 11500, IO 210D REN				9950	11300
	IB 210D REN	10300	11700,	IO	T120-T140	8200 9850, IO T150D VLVO				11400	12900
24	241-V RAISED CBN CNV	ST	CR	FBG DV	IO	175-225	8	4600	2	7250	8450
	IO 235 OMC	7400	8500,	IB	235 OMC	6900 7900, IO 106D-115D				8500	10200
	IO 150D GM	9250	10500,	IO	150D-200D	9450 11200, IO 210D REN				9700	11000
	IB 210D REN	10000	11400,	IO	T120-T140	7950 9550, IO T150D VLVO				11100	12600
28	DRUMMOND		SF	FBG DV	IO	170	8	7500		13700	15600
28	DRUMMOND		SF	FBG DV	IO	170D	8	7500		18600	20600
--- 1975 BOATS ---											
18	DRUMMOND 180	OP	OPFSH	FBG FL	OB		7 6	1500	2	2050	2400
18	DRUMMOND 180	OP	UTL	FBG FL	OB		7 6	1500	2	1950	2300
19	DRUMMOND 190V	OP	OPFSH	FBG DV	OB		7 8	3000	2	2850	3300
19	DRUMMOND 190V	OP	OPFSH	FBG DV	IO	130-165	7 8	3000	2	4150	4800
19	DRUMMOND 190V	OP	OPFSH	FBG DV	JT	170 VLVO	7 8	3000	2	3550	4100
19	DRUMMOND 190V	OP	OPFSH	FBG DV	IO	170-235	7 8	3000	2	4150	4850
22	DRUMMOND 223V	OP	CR	FBG DV	IO	165-170	7 8	4000	2	5350	5800
	JT 225 COMM	4600	5300,	IO	105D-120D	6350 7450, JT 150D GM				6500	7450
	IO 150D-210D	6700	8300								
24	DRUMMOND 244		CR	FBG DV	IO	165	8	4800	2	7800	8950
24	DRUMMOND 244		CR	FBG DV	IO	T170	8	4800	2	8550	9850

DRUMMOND YACHTS INC — CONTINUED

LOA FT IN	NAME AND/ OR MODEL	TOP/ RIG	BOAT TYPE	HULL MTL	HULL TP	ENG TP	# HP	MFG	BEAM FT IN	WGT LBS	DRAFT FT IN	RETAIL LOW	RETAIL HIGH
1975 BOATS													
27	DRUMMOND 270	EXP		FBG		IO	225		8		2	14600	16600
27	DRUMMOND 270	EXP		FBG		IO	T170		8		2	15500	17600
27	DRUMMOND 270	RNBT		FBG		IO	225		8		2	13600	15400
27	DRUMMOND 270	RNBT		FBG		IO	T170		8		2	14300	16300
27	DRUMMOND 270	SF		FBG		IO	225		8		2	16700	18900
27	DRUMMOND 270	SF		FBG		IO	T170		8		2	18000	20000
28	DRUMMOND 280V	OP	CNV	FBG	DV	IO	T106D	VLVO	8	7500	2	22800	25400
28	DRUMMOND 280V	OP	CNV	FBG	DV	IB	T170D		8	7500	2	20300	22500
28	DRUMMOND 280V	TT	CNV	FBG	DV	IO	T106D	VLVO	8	7500	2	22800	25400
28	DRUMMOND 280V	TT	CNV	FBG	DV	IB	T170D		8	7500	2	20300	22500
28	DRUMMOND 280V	FB	CR	FBG	DV	IO	T106D	VLVO	8	8500	2	18200	20200
28	DRUMMOND 280V	FB	CR	FBG	DV	IB	T170D		8	8500	2	19300	21400
28	DRUMMOND 290		SF	FBG	DV	IO	T170		8			15800	18000
28	DRUMMOND 290		SF	FBG	DV	IO	T170D		8			22800	25400
1974 BOATS													
19	DRUMMOND 190-V			FBG		OB			7 10		1 2	2550	2950
19	DRUMMOND 190-V			FBG		IO	130-140		7 10		1 2	3600	4200
22	DRUMMOND 223-V		CBNCR	FBG		IO	165	OMC	8		1 2	6600	7600
22	DRUMMOND 223-V		CBNCR	FBG		IO	100D-112D		8		1 2	9300	10700
22	DRUMMOND 223-V	SPORT FB		FBG		IO	165	OMC	8		1 2	5400	6200
22	DRUMMOND 223-V	SPORT FB		FBG		IO	100D-112D		8		1 2	6800	7900
29	DRUMMOND 290-V	HT		FBG		IO	112D	GM	8		1 2	21600	24000
29	DRUMMOND 290-V	HT		FBG		IO	T170	VLVO	8		1 2	16700	18900
29	DRUMMOND 290-V	HT		FBG		IO	T100D-T106D		8		1 2	22400	25000
29	DRUMMOND 290-V	FB		FBG		IO	112D	GM	8		1 2	21600	24000
29	DRUMMOND 290-V	FB		FBG		IO	T170	VLVO	8		1 2	16700	18900
29	DRUMMOND 290-V	FB		FBG		IO	T100D-T106D		8		1 2	22400	25000
29	DRUMMOND 290-V		CNV	FBG		IO	112D	GM	8		1 2	24100	26800
29	DRUMMOND 290-V		CNV	FBG		IO	T170	VLVO	8		1 2	19500	21700
29	DRUMMOND 290-V		CNV	FBG		IO	T100D-T106D		8		1 2	27100	30100
1973 BOATS													
19	DRUMMOND 19-V		SF	FBG		IO	130-140		7 10		1 2	3750	4350
19	DRUMMOND 19-V		SF	FBG		IO	100D-112D		7 10		1 2	5800	6800
22	DRUMMOND 223-V		CBNCR	FBG		IO	140-170		8	3750	2	6800	8250
22	DRUMMOND 223-V		CBNCR	FBG		IO	100D-112D		8	4000	2	9600	11200
29	DRUMMOND 29-V		CBNCR	FBG		IO	225	OMC	8	6800	2	17200	19600

IO T170 VLVO 19600 21800, IOT100D-T106D 24600 27800, IO T224D GM 29200 32400

LOA FT IN	NAME AND/ OR MODEL	TOP/ RIG	BOAT TYPE	HULL MTL	HULL TP	ENG TP	# HP	MFG	BEAM FT IN	WGT LBS	DRAFT FT IN	RETAIL LOW	RETAIL HIGH
29	DRUMMOND 29-V	HT	CR	FBG		IO	225	OMC	8	7000	2	14300	16200

IO T170 VLVO 16300 18500, IOT100D-T106D 20200 22800, IO T224D GM 24100 26800

LOA FT IN	NAME AND/ OR MODEL	TOP/ RIG	BOAT TYPE	HULL MTL	HULL TP	ENG TP	# HP	MFG	BEAM FT IN	WGT LBS	DRAFT FT IN	RETAIL LOW	RETAIL HIGH
29	DRUMMOND 290-V	FB	SF	FBG		IO	225	OMC	8	7500	2	16700	19000

IO T170 VLVO 19200 21300, IOT100D-T106D 26300 29700, IO T224D GM 31000 34500

LOA FT IN	NAME AND/ OR MODEL	TOP/ RIG	BOAT TYPE	HULL MTL	HULL TP	ENG TP	# HP	MFG	BEAM FT IN	WGT LBS	DRAFT FT IN	RETAIL LOW	RETAIL HIGH
1972 BOATS													
19	DRUMMOND 19-V			FBG		OB			7 8		1	2500	2950
19	DRUMMOND 190 SS			FBG		OB			7 8	2000	1	2500	2950
19	DRUMMOND 190 SS			FBG		IO	130-170		7 8	2650	2	3800	4500
19	DRUMMOND 190 SS			FBG		IO	75D-100D		7 8	2650	2	4800	5750
19	DRUMMOND 190-C			FBG		OB			7 8		1	2500	2950
22	DRUMMOND 223		CBNCR	FBG		IO	140-170		8	3750	2	7050	8350
22	DRUMMOND 223		CBNCR	FBG		IO	100D	CHRY	8	3750	2	9550	10800
27	DRUMMOND 270	HT	CBNCR	FBG		IO	T170	VLVO	8 6		2	20800	23100
27	DRUMMOND 270	HT	CBNCR	FBG		IO	T100D	CHRY	8 6		2	29500	32800
27	DRUMMOND 270	FB	EXP	FBG		IO	T170	VLVO	8 6		2	17400	19800
27	DRUMMOND 270	FB	EXP	FBG		IO	T100D	CHRY	8 6		2	23900	26500

DU PONT INC
SUBSIDIARY OF SAFTI CRAFT

Call 1-800-327-6929 for BUC Personalized Evaluation Service
Or, for 1953 to 1962 boats, sign onto www.BUCValuPro.com

DUCKWORTH BOAT WORKS INC
COAST GUARD MFG ID- ESM

Call 1-800-327-6929 for BUC Personalized Evaluation Service
Or, for 1978 to 1979 boats, sign onto www.BUCValuPro.com

DUFFY & DUFFY CUSTOM YACHTS
BROOKLIN ME 04616   COAST GUARD MFG ID- DUJ See inside cover to adjust price for area
FORMERLY DUFFY & DUFFY FIBERGLASS BOATS

For more recent years, see the BUC Used Boat Price Guide, Volume 1 or Volume 2

LOA FT IN	NAME AND/ OR MODEL	TOP/ RIG	BOAT TYPE	HULL MTL	HULL TP	ENG TP	# HP	BEAM FT IN	WGT LBS	DRAFT FT IN	RETAIL LOW	RETAIL HIGH
1983 BOATS												
35	DUFFY 35	HT	CR	FBG	DV	IB	D	11 10	8000	3 3	**	**
41	DUFFY 41	HT	CR	FBG	DS	IB	D	13 10	26000	4 2	**	**
50 2	DUFFY 50	HT	TRWL	FBG	DS	IB	D	16 3	52000	5 9	**	**
1982 BOATS												
34 7	DUFFY 34 PH	HT	CR	FBG	DS	IB		11 4	8000	3	**	**
41	DUFFY 41 PH	HT	CR	FBG	DS	IB		13 10	26000	4 2	**	**
50 2	DUFFY 50	HT	TRWL	FBG	DS	IB		16 3	52000	5 9	**	**
1981 BOATS												
34 7	DUFFY 34		FSH	FBG	DS	IB	100	11 4			55900	61400
41	DUFFY 41		FSH	FBG	DS	IB	175	13 10			**	**
50 2	DUFFY		TRWL	FBG	DS	IB	350	16 3			249000	273500
1980 BOATS												
34 7	DUFFY & DUFFY 34		FSH	FBG		IB	140D	11 4			69900	76800
50 2	DUFFY & DUFFY 50		TRWL	FBG		IB	350	16 3			238000	261500
1979 BOATS												
34 7	DUFFY 34	HT	FSH	FBG	RB	IB	140D GM	11 4	16000	3	79400	87300
50 2	DUFFY 50	HT	TRWL	FBG	DS	IB	350	16 3	48000	5 9	205000	225000
1978 BOATS												
34 6		HT	FSH	FBG	DV	IB	D FORD	11 4	6000	3	**	**
34 6		HT	FSH	FBG	DV	IB	D GM	11 4	6000	3	**	**
34 6		HT	FSH	FBG	DV	IB	160D PERK	11 4	6000	3	43700	48500

DUFFY ELECTRIC BOAT CO
COSTA MESA CA 92627   COAST GUARD MFG ID- DFF See inside cover to adjust price for area
FORMERLY DUFFIELD MARINE

For more recent years, see the BUC Used Boat Price Guide, Volume 1 or Volume 2

LOA FT IN	NAME AND/ OR MODEL	TOP/ RIG	BOAT TYPE	HULL MTL	HULL TP	ENG TP	# HP	BEAM FT IN	WGT LBS	DRAFT FT IN	RETAIL LOW	RETAIL HIGH
1981 BOATS												
18 1	EDISON-ELECTRIC	LNCH				EL	10	6 5			**	**
20	DUFFIELD 20	FSH		FBG	RB	OB	40	7 2			4250	4950
26	ZAP 26	SLP	SA/RC	FBG	KL	OB		9 4	3200	5 9	9950	11300
49 6	DUFFIELD 50	SLP	SA/RC	FBG	KL	IB	D	13 3	15500	8	112500	123500
1976 BOATS												
16	EDISON 16	LNCH		FBG		EL	4	6 6			**	**
20	EDISON 20	LNCH		FBG		EL	4	6 10			**	**

DUFOUR YACHTS
PERIGNY FRANCE 17185   COAST GUARD MFG ID- DUF See inside cover to adjust price for area

DUFOUR YACHTS USA INC
ANNAPOLIS MD 21403

For more recent years, see the BUC Used Boat Price Guide, Volume 1 or Volume 2

LOA FT IN	NAME AND/ OR MODEL	TOP/ RIG	BOAT TYPE	HULL MTL	HULL TP	ENG TP	# HP	MFG	BEAM FT IN	WGT LBS	DRAFT FT IN	RETAIL LOW	RETAIL HIGH
1983 BOATS													
25 1	DUFOUR 25	SLP	SA/CR	FBG	CB	OB			8 11	3940	2 6	9300	10600
25 1	DUFOUR 25	SLP	SA/CR	FBG	KL	OB			8 11	3940	4 4	9300	10600
25 1	DUFOUR 25	SLP	SA/CR	FBG	KL	SD	8D	VLVO	8 11	3940	4 4	10000	11400
27 2	DUFOUR 28	SLP	SA/CR	FBG	CB	SD	17D	VLVO	9 7	6160	4 11	16300	18600
27 2	DUFOUR 28 TALL RIG	SLP	SA/CR	FBG	KL	SD	17D	VLVO	9 7	6160	7	16800	19100
30 6	DUFOUR/FRERS 31	SLP	SA/CR	FBG	KL	SD	17D	VLVO	10 8	8360	5 7	24000	26700
30 6	DUFOUR/FRERS 31CS	SLP	SA/RC	FBG	KL	SD	17D	VLVO	10 8	8360	5 7	24000	26700
34 11	VALENTIJN AFT	SLP	SA/CR	FBG	KL	IB	25D	VLVO	11 2	10560	6	29500	32800
34 11	VALENTIJN AFT CS	SLP	SA/CR	FBG	KL	IB	25D	VLVO	11 2	10560	6	29900	33300
34 11	VALENTIJN OFF	SLP	SA/CR	FBG	KL	IB	25D	VLVO	11 2	10579	6	29600	32900
34 11	VALENTIJN OFF CS	SLP	SA/CR	FBG	KL	IB	25D	VLVO	11 2	10579	6	30000	33300
38 5	FRERS 39	SLP	SA/CR	FBG	KC	IB	50D	PERK	12	14960	6	42600	47300
38 5	FRERS 39	SLP	SA/CR	FBG	KL	IB	50D	PERK	12 6	14960	6 7	41300	45900
38 5	FRERS 39CS	SLP	SA/CR	FBG	KL	IB	50D	PERK	12 6	14960	6 7	46300	50900
40 1	VALENTIJN 40	SLP	SA/CR	FBG	AL	IB	85D	PERK	12 1	19845	6 9	57200	62800
45 3	DUFOUR 46 KETCH	KTH	SA/CR	FBG	KL	IB	85D	PERK	13 1	26400	6 11	79700	87600
1982 BOATS													
25 1	DUFOUR 1800	SLP	SA/CR	FBG	KL	IB	8D	VLVO	7	4500	4	10700	12100
25 1	DUFOUR 1800 CS	SLP	SA/CR	FBG	KL	IB	8D	VLVO	7	4500	4	10700	12100
25 1	DUFOUR 1800 DL	SLP	SA/CR	FBG	CB	IB	8D	VLVO	7	4500	4 4	9550	10900
25 1	DUFOUR 25	SLP	SA/CR	FBG	KL	IB	D		8 9	3940	3 3	9300	10900

DUFOUR YACHTS -CONTINUED See inside cover to adjust price for area

LOA FT	LOA IN	NAME AND/ OR MODEL	TOP/ RIG	BOAT TYPE	-HULL- MTL	-HULL- TP	TP	ENGINE # HP	ENGINE MFG	BEAM FT	BEAM IN	WGT LBS	DRAFT FT	DRAFT IN	RETAIL LOW	RETAIL HIGH
		1982 BOATS														
27	2	DUFOUR 2800	SLP	SA/CR	FBG	KL	IB	8D-	13D	9	7	6160	4	10	15600	17800
27	2	DUFOUR 2800 CS	SLP	SA/RC	FBG	KL	IB	8D-	13D	9	7	6165	5	3	15600	17800
27	2	DUFOUR 2800 DL	SLP	SA/CR	FBG	CB	IB	8D-	13D	9	7	6160	4	11	15600	17800
27	2	DUFOUR 2800 SHOAL	SLP	SA/CR	FBG	KL	IB	8D-	13D	9	7	6160	3	10	15600	17800
30	7	DUFOUR/FRERS 30	SLP	SA/CR	FBG	KL	IB	13D	VLVO	10	5	8380	4	4	22800	25300
30	7	DUFOUR/FRERS 30CS	SLP	SA/RC	FBG	KL	IB	13D	VLVO	10	5	8380	4	4	22800	25300
31	2	DUFOUR 31 AFT CBN	SLP	SA/CR	FBG	KL	IB	13D-	23D	10	6	9260	5	8	25300	28100
31	2	DUFOUR 31 SHOAL	SLP	SA/CR	FBG	KL	IB	13D	VLVO	10	6	9260	4	9	25300	28100
31	2	DUFOUR 31 TALL RIG	SLP	SA/CR	FBG	KL	IB	13D-	23D	10	6	9260	5	8	25300	28100
34	9	DUFOUR 4800	SLP	SA/CR	FBG	KL	IB	23D	VLVO	11	2	10579	4	9	28200	31300
34	9	DUFOUR 4800 CS	SLP	SA/CR	FBG	KL	IB	23D	VLVO	11		8250	4	9	22100	24500
34	9	DUFOUR-VALENJIN 35	SLP	SA/CR	FBG	KL	IB			11	2	10579	4	9	28000	31100
35	9	DUFOUR 35 AFT CBN	SLP	SA/CR	FBG	KL	IB	23D	VLVO	11	5	13885	6		36500	40500
35	9	DUFOUR 35 SHOAL	SLP	SA/CR	FBG	KL	IB	23D	VLVO	11	5	13885	5	6	36500	40500
35	9	DUFOUR 35 SHOAL	SLP	SA/CR	FBG	KL	IB	35D	VLVO	11	5	13885	5	6	36600	40600
35	9	DUFOUR 35 TALL RIG	SLP	SA/CR	FBG	KL	IB	23D	VLVO	11	5	13885	6		36500	40500
35	9	DUFOUR 35 TALL RIG	SLP	SA/CR	FBG	KL	IB	35D	VLVO	11	5	13885	6		36600	40600
39	2	DUFOUR A9000 AFT CBN	SLP	SA/RC	AL	KL	IB	50D	PERK	12	11	19845	6	9	52200	57400
45	4	DUFOUR 12000 CT	KTH	SA/CR	FBG	KL	IB	85D	PERK	13	1	26450	6	11	75800	83300
		1981 BOATS														
20		DUFOUR T7	SLP	SA/CR	FBG	KL	IB	D		7					6600	7600
24	1	DUFOUR 1800 CS	SLP	SA/CR	FBG	KL	IB	8D	VLVO	7		4500	4		9700	11000
25	1	DUFOUR 1800	SLP	SA/CR	FBG	KL	IB	8D	VLVO	7		4500	4		10200	11500
27	2	DUFOUR 2800	SLP	SA/CR	FBG	KL	IB	8D-	13D	9	7	6160	4	10	14700	17000
27	2	DUFOUR 2800 CS	SLP	SA/RC	FBG	KL	IB	8D-	13D	9	7	6165	5	3	14800	16800
27	2	DUFOUR 2800 DL	SLP	SA/CR	FBG	CB	IB	8D-	13D	9	7	6160	2	11	14700	17500
27	2	DUFOUR 2800 SHOAL	SLP	SA/CR	FBG	KL	IB	8D-	13D	9	7	6160	3	10	14800	16800
29	3	DUFOUR 29	SLP	SA/CR	FBG	KL	IB	13D	VLVO	9	8	7260	5	6	18600	20700
29	3	DUFOUR 29 SHOAL	SLP	SA/CR	FBG	KL	IB	13D	VLVO	9	8	7260	4	1	18700	20700
31	2	DUFOUR 31 AFT CBN	SLP	SA/CR	FBG	KL	IB	13D	VLVO	10	6	9260	5	8	24000	26600
31	2	DUFOUR 31 SHOAL	SLP	SA/CR	FBG	KL	IB	13D	VLVO	10	6	9260	4	9	24000	26600
31	2	DUFOUR 31 TALL RIG	SLP	SA/CR	FBG	KL	IB	13D-	23D	10	6	9260	5	8	24000	26600
31	2	DUFOUR 31.AFT CBN	SLP	SA/CR	FBG	KL	IB	23D	VLVO	10	6	9260	5	8	25300	28100
34	9	DUFOUR 4800 AFT CBN	SLP	SA/CR	FBG	KL	IB	23D	VLVO	11	2	10579	4	9	26700	29700
34	9	DUFOUR 4800 CS	SLP	SA/CR	FBG	KL	IB	23D	VLVO	11	2	10579	4	9	26700	29700
35	9	DUFOUR 35 AFT CABIN	SLP	SA/CR	FBG	KL	IB	23D	VLVO	11	5	13885	6		34600	38400
35	9	DUFOUR 35 SHOAL	SLP	SA/CR	FBG	KL	IB	23D	VLVO	11	5	13885	5		34600	38400
35	9	DUFOUR 35 SHOAL	SLP	SA/CR	FBG	KL	IB	35D	VLVO	11	5	13885	5	6	36700	40800
35	9	DUFOUR 35 TALL RIG	SLP	SA/CR	FBG	KL	IB	23D	VLVO	11	5	13885	6		34600	38400
35	9	DUFOUR 35 TALL RIG	SLP	SA/CR	FBG	KL	IB	35D	VLVO	11	5	13885	6		32600	36200
39	2	DUFOUR A9000 AFT CBN	SLP	SA/RC	AL	KL	IB	50D	PERK	12	11	19845	6	9	49500	54400
45	4	DUFOUR 12000 CT	KTH	SA/CR	FBG	KL	IB	85D	PERK	13	1	26450	6	11	71900	79000
		1980 BOATS														
25	1	DUFOUR 1800	SLP	SA/RC	FBG	KL	IB			8	10	3969	4	3	8400	9650
27	2	DUFOUR 2800	SLP	SA/CR	FBG	KL	IB	8D-	13D	9	7	6160	4	10	14200	16200
27	2	DUFOUR 2800 CS	SLP	SA/RC	FBG	KL	IB	8D-	13D	9	7	6165	5	3	14200	16200
27	2	DUFOUR 2800 DL	SLP	SA/CR	FBG	CB	IB	8D	VLVO	9	7		2	11	14800	16800
27	2	DUFOUR 2800 DL	SLP	SA/CR	FBG	KL	IB	8D	VLVO	9	7		4	11	14800	16800
27	2	DUFOUR 2800 SHOAL	SLP	SA/CR	FBG	KL	IB	8D	VLVO	9	7	6160	3	10	14200	16200
29	3	DUFOUR 29	SLP	SA/CR	FBG	KL	IB	13D	VLVO	9	8	7260	5	6	17500	19900
29	3	DUFOUR 29 SHOAL	SLP	SA/CR	FBG	KL	IB	13D	VLVO	9	8	7260	4	1	17600	20000
31	2	DUFOUR 31 AFT CABIN	SLP	SA/CR	FBG	KL	IB	13D	VLVO	10	6	9260	5	8	23500	26100
31	2	DUFOUR 31 SHOAL	SLP	SA/CR	FBG	KL	IB	13D	VLVO	10	6	9260	4	9	22900	25400
31	2	DUFOUR 31 TALL RIG	SLP	SA/CR	FBG	KL	IB	13D-	23D	10	6	9260	5	8	22800	25600
35	9	DUFOUR 35 AFT CABIN	SLP	SA/CR	FBG	KL	IB	23D	VLVO	11	5	13885	6		33700	37400
35	9	DUFOUR 35 SHOAL	SLP	SA/CR	FBG	KL	IB	23D	VLVO	11	5	13885	5		33100	36800
35	9	DUFOUR 35 TALL RIG	SLP	SA/CR	FBG	KL	IB	23D	VLVO	11	5	13885	6		33000	36700
35	9	DUFOUR 35 TALL RIG	SLP	SA/CR	FBG	KL	IB	36D	VLVO	11	5	13885	6		33400	37100
39	5	DUFOUR A9000	SLP	SA/RC	AL	KL	IB	36D	VLVO	12	11	19800	6	8	48000	52700
45	4	DUFOUR 12000 CT	KTH	SA/CR	FBG	KL	IB	83D	PERK	13	1	26450	6	11	69100	76000
		1979 BOATS														
27	3	DUFOUR 2800	SLP	SA/CR	FBG	KL	IB	13D	VLVO	9	7	6064	4	11	13200	15000
27	3	DUFOUR 2800 CS	SLP	SA/CR	FBG	KL	IB	13D	VLVO	9	7	6064	5	4	14600	16600
27	3	DUFOUR 2800 SHOAL	SLP	SA/CR	FBG	KL	IB	13D	VLVO	9	7	6064	3	11	13100	14900
29	4	DUFOUR 29	SLP	SA/CR	FBG	KL	IB	13D-	23D	9	8	7275	5	3	17000	19400
29	4	DUFOUR 29 SHOAL	SLP	SA/CR	FBG	KL	IB	13D-	23D	9	8	7275	4	5	17000	19400
30	10	DUFOUR 31	SLP	SA/CR	FBG	KL	IB	13D-	23D	10	6	9240	5	8	22200	24700
30	10	DUFOUR 31 SHOAL	SLP	SA/CR	FBG	KL	IB	13D-	23D	10	6	9240	4	9	22300	24800
35		DUFOUR 35	SLP	SA/CR	FBG	KL	IB	25D	VLVO	11	3	13860	6		32200	35700
35		DUFOUR 35	SLP	SA/CR	FBG	KL	IB	35D	VLVO	11	3	13860	6		32200	35800
44	10	DUFOUR 12000 CT	KTH	SA/CR	FBG	KL	IB	83D	PERK	13		26400	6	10	65700	72200
		1978 BOATS														
24	3	DUFOUR 24	SLP	SA/CR	FBG	KL	OB			8	3	2984	3	10	5600	6450
24	3	DUFOUR 24	SLP	SA/CR	FBG	KL	IB	8D-	13D	8	3	2984	3	10	6300	7350
24	3	DUFOUR 24 SHOAL	SLP	SA/CR	FBG	KL	OB			8	3	2984	2	6	5650	6500
24	3	DUFOUR 24 SHOAL	SLP	SA/CR	FBG	KL	IB	8D-	13D	8	3	2984	2	6	6300	7400
27	3	DUFOUR 2800	SLP	SA/CR	FBG	KL	IB	13D	VLVO	9	7	6064	4	11	13200	15000
27	3	DUFOUR 2800 SHOAL	SLP	SA/CR	FBG	KL	IB	13D	VLVO	9	7	6064	3	11	13300	15100
29	4	SOUVERAINE	SLP	SA/CR	FBG	KL	IB	13D-	23D	9	8	7275	5	3	16500	18800
29	4	SOUVERAINE SHOAL	SLP	SA/CR	FBG	KL	IB	13D-	23D	9	8	7275	4	5	16600	18900
30	10	DUFOUR 31	SLP	SA/CR	FBG	KL	IB	13D-	25D	10	6	9240	5	8	21600	24000
30	10	DUFOUR 31 SHOAL	SLP	SA/CR	FBG	KL	IB	13D-	25D	10	6	9240	4	9	21600	24100
33	7	DUFOUR 34	SLP	SA/CR	FBG	KL	IB	D		10	9	11000	5	10	25300	28100
35		DUFOUR 35	SLP	SA/CR	FBG	KL	IB	25D	VLVO	11	3	12600	6		28600	31700
35		DUFOUR 35	SLP	SA/CR	FBG	KL	IB	35D	VLVO	11	3	12600	6		28600	31800
35		DUFOUR 35 SHOAL	SLP	SA/CR	FBG	KL	IB	25D	VLVO	11	3	12600	5		28600	31800
35		DUFOUR 35 SHOAL	SLP	SA/CR	FBG	KL	IB	35D	VLVO	11	3	12600	5		28700	31900
44	9	DUFOUR 12000 CT	KTH	SA/CR	FBG	KL	IB	73D	PERK	13		24640	6	8	61400	67500
44	9	DUFOUR 12000 CT	KTH	SA/CR	FBG	KL	IB	86D	VLVO	13		24640	6	8	61900	68000
44	9	DUFOUR 12000 CT	KTH	SA/CR	FBG	KL	IB	125D	VLVO	13		24640	6	8	62300	68400
44	9	DUFOUR 12000 CT SHL	KTH	SA/CR	FBG	KL	IB	73D	PERK	13		24640	5	5	61400	67500
44	9	DUFOUR 12000 CT SHL	KTH	SA/CR	FBG	KL	IB	86D	VLVO	13		24640	5	5	61900	68000
44	9	DUFOUR 12000 CT SHL	KTH	SA/CR	FBG	KL	IB	125D	VLVO	13		24640	5	5	62300	68400
		1977 BOATS														
24	11	DUFOUR 24	SLP	SA/CR	FBG	KL	OB			8	2	3000	2	6	5700	6550
24	11	DUFOUR 24	SLP	SA/CR	FBG	KL	IB	5D-	10D	8	2	3000	2	6	6250	7300
27	3	DUFOUR 27	SLP	SA/CR	FBG	KL	IB	9D-	10D	9	2	5000	5	2	10600	12100
29	4	SOUVERAINE D-29	SLP	SA/CR	FBG	KL	IB	10D	VLVO	9	8	7275	5	3	16100	18300
29	4	SOUVERAINE SHOAL	SLP	SA/CR	FBG	KL	IB	10D	VLVO	9	8	7275	4	5	16100	18300
30	4	ARPEGE	SLP	SA/RC	FBG	KL	IB	10D-	25D	9	11	7200	4	5	16100	18400
30	10	DUFOUR 31	SLP	SA/CR	FBG	KL	IB	10D-	30D	10	6	8400	5	8	19100	21300
30	10	DUFOUR 31 SHOAL	SLP	SA/CR	FBG	KL	IB	10D-	30D	10	6	8400	4	9	19100	21300
33	7	DUFOUR 34	SLP	SA/CR	FBG	KL	IB	25D	VLVO	10	9	10000	5	10	22400	24900
35		DUFOUR 35	SLP	SA/CR	FBG	KL	IB	25D	VLVO	11	3	12600	6		27800	30900
35		DUFOUR 35	SLP	SA/CR	FBG	KL	IB	30D	REN	11	3	12600	6		27800	30900
35		DUFOUR 35	SLP	SA/CR	FBG	KL	IB	36D	VLVO	11	3	12600	6		27900	31000
41		SORTILEGE 41	SLP	SA/CR	FBG	KL	IB	D		12	5	18734	6		44300	49200
41		SORTILEGE 41	KTH	SA/CR	FBG	KL	IB	D		12	5	18734	6		44300	49200
		1976 BOATS														
24	3	DUFOUR 24	SLP	SA/CR	FBG	KL	OB			8	3	2984	2	6	5300	6100
24	11	MON-PETIT-BATEAU	SLP	SA/CR	FBG	KL	IB	D		8	2	3000	3	10	6150	7050
27	3	DUFOUR 27	SLP	SA/CR	FBG	KL	IB	10D	VLVO	9	2	5000	5	2	10400	11800
29	4	DUFOUR 29	SLP	SA/CR	FBG	KL	IB	10D	VLVO	9	8	7275	5	3	15700	17800
30	4	ARPEGE	SLP	SA/CR	FBG	KL	IB	25D		9	11	8000	4	5	17500	19900
30	10	DUFOUR 31	SLP	SA/CR	FBG	KL	IB	10D	VLVO	10	6	8400	5	8	18900	20900
33	7	DUFOUR 34	SLP	SA/CR	FBG	KL	IB	25D	VLVO	10	9	10000	5	10	21900	24300
35		DUFOUR 35	SLP	SA/CR	FBG	KL	IB	25D	VLVO	11	3	12600	6		27100	30200
41		DUFOUR 41	KTH	SA/CR	FBG	KL	IB	D		12	5	20000	5	9	45600	50100
		1975 BOATS														
23		DUFOUR 1300	SLP	SA/CR	FBG	KL				8	10	2900	5		4750	5450
24	3	DUFOUR 24	SLP	SA/CR	FBG	KL	OB			8	3	2984	2	6	5200	6000
27		SAFARI 27	SLP	SA/CR	FBG	KL	IB	10D	VLVO	9	2	5400	4	4	10800	12300
27	3	DUFOUR 27	SLP	SA/CR	FBG	KL	IB	10D	VLVO	9	2	5000	5	2	10100	11500
30	4	ARPEGE	SLP	SA/CR	FBG	KL	IB	10D		9	11	8000	4	5	17100	19400
30	10	DUFOUR 31	SLP	SA/CR	FBG	KL	IB	25D	VLVO	10	6	8400	5	8	18500	20500
33	7	DUFOUR 34	SLP	SA/CR	FBG	KL	IB	25D	VLVO	10	9	10000	5	10	21400	23700
35		DUFOUR 35	SLP	SA/CR	FBG	KL	IB	25D	VLVO	11	3	12600	6		26500	29500
41		DUFOUR 41	SLP	SA/CR	FBG	KL	IB	43D		12	5	17000	5	9	39700	44100
41		DUFOUR 41	YWL	SA/CR	FBG	KL	IB	43D		12	5	17000	5	9	39700	44100
		1974 BOATS														
27		SAFARI 27	SLP	SA/CR	FBG	KL	IB	10D		9	2	5400	4	4	10600	12100
27	3	DUFOUR 27	SLP	SA/CR	FBG	KL	IB	10D		9	2	5000	5	2	9900	11300
30	4	ARPEGE	SLP	SA/CR	FBG	KL	IB	25D		9	11	7200	4	5	15100	17200
33	7	DUFOUR 34	SLP	SA/CR	FBG	KL	IB	25D		10	9	10000	5	11	20900	23300
35		DUFOUR 35	SLP	SA/CR	FBG	KL	IB	25D		11	3	12600	6		26000	28900
41		DUFOUR 41 CTR CPT	SLP	SA/CR	FBG	KL	IB	43D		12	5	17000	5	9	38900	43200
41		DUFOUR 41 CTR CPT	YWL	SA/CR	FBG	KL	IB	43D		12	5	17000	5	9	38900	43200
41		DUFOUR 41 CTR CPT	KTH	SA/CR	FBG	KL	IB	43D		12	5	17000	5	9	38900	43200
		1973 BOATS														
27		SAFARI	SLP	SAIL	FBG		OB			9	2				8950	10200
27		SAFARI	SLP	SAIL	FBG		IB	10D	VLVO	9	2	6000	4	4	11600	13200
27	2	DUFOUR 27	SLP	SAIL	FBG		IB	D	VLVO	9	10	4000	5	1	7850	9000
30	4	ARPEGE		SAIL	FBG		IB	25D	VLVO	9	11	8000	4	5	16500	18700
30	4	ARPEGE	SLP	SAIL	FBG		IB	10D	VLVO	9	2	7600	4	5	15600	17700
35	3	DUFOUR 35	SLP	SAIL	FBG		IB	25D	VLVO	11	4	10000	5	11	20500	22800
41		DUFOUR 41	SLP	SAIL	FBG		IB	43D	PERK	12		20000	5	9	42100	46800
		1972 BOATS														
26	9	SOLING	SLP	SA/OD	FBG	KL	IB	D		6	3	2000	4	3	4350	5000
27		SAFARI	SLP	SAIL	FBG		OB			9	2		4	4	8650	9950
27		SAFARI	SLP	SAIL	FBG		IB	7D	VLVO	9	2	6000	4	4	11300	12800
30	4	ARPEGE		SAIL	FBG		IB	15D	VLVO	9	11	8000	4	5	16100	18300

CONTINUED ON NEXT PAGE

DUFOUR YACHTS -CONTINUED

See inside cover to adjust price for area

LOA FT IN	NAME AND/ OR MODEL	TOP/ RIG	BOAT TYPE	-HULL- MTL TP	TP	----ENGINE--- # HP	MFG	BEAM FT IN	WGT LBS	DRAFT FT IN	RETAIL LOW	RETAIL HIGH
				1972 BOATS								
30 4	ARPEGE	SLP	SAIL	FBG	IB	10D	VLVO	9 11	8000	4 5	16100	18300
41	DUFOUR 41	SLP	SAIL	FBG	IB	43D	PERK	12 5	20000	5 9	41200	45800
				1971 BOATS								
21 4	SYLPHE	SLP	SA/CR	FBG KL	IB	D		7 10	2000	3 5	4050	4700
26 9	SOLING	SLP	SA/OD	FBG CB	IB	D		6 2	2207		4550	5250
27	SAFARI	SLP	SA/CR	FBG KL	IB	12D		9 12		4 4	11900	13550
30 4	ARPEGE	SLP	SA/CR	FBG KL	IB	15D		9 10	6600	4 5	12900	14700
41	DUFOUR 41	SLP	SA/CR	FBG KL	IB	D		12 4		5 9	34900	38800
				1970 BOATS								
21 5	SULPHE	SLP	SA/CR	FBG KL	IB	D		7 10	2200	3 5	4150	4850
26 9	SOLING	SLP	SA/OD	FBG KL	IB	D		6 3	2200	4 3	4450	5100
30 4	ARPEGE	SLP	SA/CR	FBG KL	IB	D		9 11	6600	4 5	12600	14300
				1969 BOATS								
21 6	SYLPHE	SLP	SAIL	FBG KL	IB	D		7 11	2200	3 5	4050	4750
30 4	ARPEGE	SLP	SAIL	FBG KL	IB	D		9 10	7700	4 7	14400	16400
				1968 BOATS								
30 4	ARPEGE	SLP	SAIL	FBG KL	IB	D	VLVO	9 11		4 6	14600	16600

DUO MARINE
A BANGOR PUNTA COMPANY
GOSHEN IN 46526

See inside cover to adjust price for area

LOA FT IN	NAME AND/ OR MODEL	TOP/ RIG	BOAT TYPE	-HULL- MTL TP	TP	----ENGINE--- # HP	MFG	BEAM FT IN	WGT LBS	DRAFT FT IN	RETAIL LOW	RETAIL HIGH
			1974 BOATS									
16 3	CHALLENGER 16			FBG	IO	120-140		6 7	1365		2200	2550
16 11	RANGER 17			FBG	OB			6 11	950		2100	2500
16 11	ROAMER 17			FBG	OB			6 11	1000		2250	2600
16 11	VAGABOND 17			FBG	IO	120-165		6 11	1655		2600	3200
18 2	CHALLENGER 18			FBG	OB			6 4	1080		2450	2850
18 2	CHALLENGER 18			FBG	IO	140-165		7	1695		2900	3400
	JT 185	2800	3250, IO	188	MRCR	2950	3450, JT	350			2850	3350
20 3	CHALLENGER 20			FBG	IO	165-188		7 11	2135		4350	5050
20 3	CHALLENGER 20			FBG	JT	255-350		7 11	2135		4050	4750
20 4	VAGABOND 20			FBG	IO	140-188		7 6	2475		4500	5250
20 4	VAGABOND 20			FBG	JT	255-350		7 6	2475		4200	4900
			1973 BOATS									
16 11	RANGER 17	OP	RNBT	FBG TR	OB			6 11	950		2100	2500
16 11	ROAMER 17	OP	RNBT	FBG TR	OB			6 11	1000		2250	2600
16 11	VAGABOND 17	OP	RNBT	FBG TR	IO	120		6 11		2 3	2700	3100
20 4	CAPITAN 20		RNBT	FBG TR	IO	165		7 6		2 6	4250	4950
20 4	VAGABOND 20	OP	RNBT	FBG TR	IO	140		7 6		2 6	4250	4900
			1972 BOATS									
17	GYPSY 3V7			FBG	IO	120-140		6 10	1700		2800	3250
17	PLAYMATE 3V7			FBG	OB			6 10	1000		2200	2600
17	ROAMER 3V7			FBG	OB			6 10	1050		2300	2700
19 2	COMMODORE DV190			FBG	IO	155-170		7 6	2150		3800	4500
20 5	VAGABOND 3V20			FBG	IO	155-170		7 6	2285		4650	5400
			1971 BOATS									
16 6	AVENGER DV175			FBG	IO	120-140		7	1685		2800	3250
16 6	VOYAGER DV175			FBG	OB			7	950		2050	2400
17	GYPSY 3V7			FBG	IO	120-140		6 10	1700		2900	3350
17	ROAMER 3V7			FBG	OB			6 10	1000		2200	2600
19 2	COMMODORE DV190			FBG	IO	120-235		7 6	2150		3950	4750
20 5	VAGABOND 3V20			FBG	IO	120-235		7 6	1985		4550	5350
			1970 BOATS									
16 6	AVENGER DV175		RNBT	FBG DV	IO	120-140		7	1485		2900	3350
16 6	VOYAGER DV175	OP	RNBT	FBG DV	OB			7	950		2050	2450
17	HUGGER 3V7		RNBT	FBG TR	IO	120-140		6 10	1500		2950	3450
17	MYSTRY 17	OP	RNBT	FBG TH	OB			7 6	775		1750	2050
17	PLAYMATE 3V7	OP	RNBT	FBG TR	OB			6 10	1000		2250	2600
19 2	COMMODORE DV190		RNBT	FBG DV	IO	120-215		7 6	1850		3900	4700
20 5	VAGABOND 3V20		RNBT	FBG TR	IO	120-215		7 6	1985		4700	5550
			1969 BOATS									
17 9	DV-180YO		RNBT	FBG DV	IO	120	OMC	6 9	1550		3200	3750
20 6	DV-200YO		RNBT	FBG DV	IO	120	OMC	7 7	1850		4800	5500
			1968 BOATS									
17	3V-7	OP	RNBT	FBG TR	OB			6 10	850		1900	2250
17 3	DV-180	OP	RNBT	FBG SV	OB			6 9	1015		2300	2650
17 3	DV-180	OP	RNBT	FBG SV	IB	185		6 9			1750	2050
20	DV-200	OP	RNBT	FBG SV	OB			7 7	1300		3150	3650
20	DV-200	OP	RNBT	FBG SV	IB	120-185		7 7			2550	3150
			1967 BOATS									
16 2	DV-170		CBNCR	FBG	IO	60-120		6 6	1250		2750	3200
17 9	DV-180		RNBT	FBG	OB			6 9			2450	2850
17 9	DV-180		CBNCR	FBG	IO	120-185		6 9	1800		3850	4550
17 9	DV-180		RNBT	FBG	OB			6 9	1015		2350	2700
17 9	DV-180		RNBT	FBG	IO	120-185		6 9	1500		3450	4050
20 6	DV-200		CBNCR	FBG	OB			7 7			3200	3750
20 6	DV-200		CBNCR	FBG	IO	120-200		7 7	2100		6050	7050
20 6	DV-200		RNBT	FBG	OB			7 7	1300		3200	3750
20 6	DV-200		RNBT	FBG	IO	120-200		7 7	1800		5100	6000
			1966 BOATS									
16 2	DV-170		RNBT	FBG	IO	60-120		6 6	1250		2850	3300
16 2	F-107		RNBT	FBG	IO	60- 80		6 4	975		2550	2950
16 4	DV 160			FBG	IO	60- 80		6 6			2850	3300
17 3	DV-180		CBNCR	FBG	OB			6 9			2100	2500
17 3	DV-180		RNBT	FBG	OB			6 9	1015		2300	2650
17 9	DV-180		CBNCR	FBG	IO	120-185		6 9	1800		3900	4650
17 9	DV-180		RNBT	FBG	IO	120-185		6 9	1500		3500	4150
20	DV-200		CBNCR	FBG	OB			7 7			3150	3650
20	DV-200		RNBT	FBG	OB			7 7	1300		3150	3650
20 6	DV-200		CBNCR	FBG	IO	120-200		7 7	210		11000	12500
20 6	DV-200		RNBT	FBG	IO	120-200		7 7	1800		5250	6100
			1965 BOATS									
17 3	DV-108			FBG	OB						2100	2500
17 3	DV-108			FBG DV	IO						**	**
			1961 BOATS									
16	VOLARE		RNBT	FBG CT	OB			7 3	900		1950	2350
			1960 BOATS									
16	VOLARE		RNBT	FBG CT	OB			7 3	950		2100	2500
16 6	AVENGER DV175		RNBT	FBG DV	OB			7	850		1900	2250
16 6	DV-175YO		RNBT	FBG DV	IO	120		7	1350		3850	4500
17	3V7YO		RNBT	FBG TR	IO	120		6 10	1400		4000	4650
17	HUGGER 3V7		RNBT	FBG TR	OB			6 10	900		2050	2450
17 3	DV-180		RNBT	FBG DV	IO			7	1065		2450	2850
17 9	DV-180YO		RNBT	FBG DV	IO	120	MRCR	6 9	1550		4400	5050
20 6	DV-200YO		RNBT	FBG DV	IO	120	MRCR	7 7	1850		6450	7450
21 4	DV-200		RNBT	FBG DV	OB			7 7	1350		3450	4000

DURA NAUTIC INC
GREENTOWN PA 18426

COAST GUARD MFG ID- DNU See inside cover to adjust price for area

For more recent years, see the BUC Used Boat Price Guide, Volume 1 or Volume 2

LOA FT IN	NAME AND/ OR MODEL	TOP/ RIG	BOAT TYPE	-HULL- MTL TP	TP	----ENGINE--- # HP	MFG	BEAM FT IN	WGT LBS	DRAFT FT IN	RETAIL LOW	RETAIL HIGH
				1983 BOATS								
16	RANGER 16	OP	CTRCN	AL	SV OB			5 10	625		1750	2050
16	RANGER 16	OP	UTL	AL	SV OB			5 10	625		1700	2050
				1982 BOATS								
16	RANGER 16	OP	CTRCN	AL	SV OB			5 10	625		1700	2000
16	RANGER 16	OP	UTL	AL	SV OB			5 10	625		1700	2000
				1978 BOATS								
19 2	SPORTSMAN		RNBT	AL	IO	140-225		7 8			2950	3550
				1975 BOATS								
18	SPORTSMAN 18	OP	RNBT	AL	SV OB			7 1	900		2400	2800
				1973 BOATS								
16 1	SPORTSMAN 16			AL	OB			6 5	700	4	1700	2050
				1972 BOATS								
16 2	SPORTSMAN			AL	OB			5 8	850		2050	2450

DURACRAFT MARINE CORP
COLUMBIA SC 29203

COAST GUARD MFG ID- DCA See inside cover to adjust price for area

For more recent years, see the BUC Used Boat Price Guide, Volume 1 or Volume 2

LOA FT IN	NAME AND/ OR MODEL	TOP/ RIG	BOAT TYPE	-HULL- MTL TP	TP	----ENGINE--- # HP	MFG	BEAM FT IN	WGT LBS	DRAFT FT IN	RETAIL LOW	RETAIL HIGH
				1972 BOATS								
16	DURAFLITE SPORTSMAN	OP	FSH	AL	IO	120		5 8			2900	3400
16	DURAFLITE W/T	OP	RNBT	AL	DV IO	120		5 8			3300	3850
16	DURAFLITE W/T	OP	RNBT	AL	SV IO	120		5 8			3300	3850
18	SPORTSMAN W/T	OP	RNBT	AL	DV IO			6 8	850		1750	2050
18	WALK THRU	OP	RNBT	AL	DV IO	120-160		6 8			4450	5150
18	WALK THRU	OP	RNBT	AL	TR IO			7 6	926		1850	2200
18	WALK THRU	OP	RNBT	AL	TR OB			7 6			4750	5500
18	WALK THRU	OP	RNBT	AL	TR IO	120-160		7 6			5500	6350
20	CLYDSDALE		CUD	AL	OB			7			2750	3150
20	PINTO	OP	CUD	AL	SV OB			7			2750	3150
23	THOROUGHBRED		CUD	AL	IO	165		7 8			10000	11400
24	CUTTER		CUD	AL	SV IB	215		8			7850	9050
26	THOROUGHBRED		CUD	AL	TR IO	165		7 8			13500	15400

LOA FT	LOA IN	NAME AND/ OR MODEL	TOP/ RIG	BOAT TYPE	HULL MTL	HULL TP	ENGINE TP	ENGINE # HP	ENGINE MFG	BEAM FT	BEAM IN	WGT LBS	DRAFT FT	DRAFT IN	RETAIL LOW	RETAIL HIGH
		1972 BOATS														
28		CUTTER		CUD	AL	SV	IB	T165		10					15200	17200
29		BOOMER	OP	RNBT	AL	TR	IO	165		8					17100	19500
32		CUTTER		DCMY	AL	SV	IB	T140D		11					46100	50600
36		CUTTER		DCMY	AL	SV	IB	T200D		12					63500	69800
40		CUTTER		DCMY	AL	SV	IB	T200D		13					84300	92600
		1971 BOATS														
16		DURAFLITE		RNBT	AL		IO	120		6	1	650			2150	2500
16		SPORTSMAN		RNBT	AL		IO	120		6	1	650			2500	2900
18				RNBT	AL	DV	IO	160		6	6	800			3600	4200
18				RNBT	AL	SV	OB			6	6	925			1850	2200
18		SPORTSMAN		RNBT	AL		OB			6	6	850			1700	2050
		1970 BOATS														
16				RNBT	AL	DV	IO	120		6	2				3650	4250
16	3	SPORTSMAN		RNBT	AL	RB	IO	120		6	2	680			2600	3000
16	6	DURAFLITE		RNBT	AL	RB	IO	120		6	2	680			2750	3200
17		DURAFLITE		RNBT	AL	RB	IO	160		6	8	850			3300	3800
17		SPORTS		RNBT	AL	RB	IO	120		6	8	800			3250	3750
18				RNBT	AL	TR	IO	120		7	6				5050	5800
18		SPORTSMAN		RNBT	AL	SV	IO	120		6	8				4700	5450
18	11			RNBT	AL	DV	OB			6	8	800			1700	2000
18	11			RNBT	AL	DV	IO	160		6	8	875			4450	5100
18	11	DURAFLITE		RNBT	AL	RB	OB			6	8	825			1750	2050
18	11	DURAFLITE		RNBT	AL	RB	IO	160		6	8	875			4100	4750
18	11	SPORTSMAN		RNBT	AL	RB	OB			6	8	825			1750	2050
		1969 BOATS														
16	3	SPORTSMAN 16	OP	FSH	AL	RB	IO	120		6	2	680			2750	3150
16	6	DURAFLITE 16	OP	RNBT	AL	RB	IO	120		6	2	680			2850	3300
17		DURAFLITE 17	OP	RNBT	AL	RB	IO	160		6	8	850			3400	3950
17		SPORTSMAN 17	OP	RNBT	AL	RB	IO	120		6	8	800			3350	3900
18	11	DEEP V 18	OP	RNBT	AL	DV	OB			6	8	800			1800	2150
18	11	DEEP V 18	OP	RNBT	AL	DV	IO	160		6	8	875			4600	5250
18	11	DURAFLITE 18	OP	RNBT	AL	RB	OB			6	8	825			1750	2050
18	11	DURAFLITE 18	OP	RNBT	AL	RB	IO	160		6	8	875			4250	4900
18	11	SPORTSMAN 18	OP	FSH	AL	RB	OB			6	8	825			1750	2050
34		AQUA-VILLA 34	HT	HB	AL	PN	OB			10		5500	2	6	6600	7600
		1968 BOATS														
16	3	SPORTSMAN	OP	FSH	AL	SV	IO	80		6	2	680			2800	3250
16	6	DURAFLITE	OP	RNBT	AL	SV	IO	120		6	2	680			2950	3400
17		DURAFLITE	OP	RNBT	AL	SV	IO	120-160		6	8	850			3450	4050
18		CLIPPER	HT	CR	AL	SV	OB			6	8	1050			2050	2450
18		CLIPPER	HT	CR	AL	SV	IO	120		6	8	1070			4050	4750
18		SPORTSMAN	OP	RNBT	AL	SV	OB			6	8				1900	2250
18	11	DURAFLITE	OP	RNBT	AL	SV	OB			6	8	825			1750	2100
18	11	DURAFLITE	OP	RNBT	AL	SV	IO	120-160		6	8	875			4300	5050
18	11	V-I-P	OP	RNBT	AL	SV	IO	120-160		6	8	875			4700	5450
19		CLIPPER	HT	CR	AL	SV	IO	120-160		6	8	1385			4700	5450
25		CATALINA	HT	EXP	AL	SV	OB			8		1785			4900	5650
25		CATALINA	HT	EXP	AL	SV	IO	160		8		1895			9650	11000
34		AQUA-VILLA	ST	HB	AL	PN	OB			10		5500	2	6	6600	7550
		1967 BOATS														
16	3	SPORTSMAN	OP	RNBT	AL	SV	IO	80		5	2	680			2600	3050
16	6	DURAFLITE	OP	RNBT	AL	SV	IO	120		5	2	680			2750	3200
17		DURAFLITE	OP	RNBT	AL	SV	IO	120-160		5	8	850			3250	3850
18		CLIPPER	HT	CBNCR	AL	SV	OB			5	8	1050			2100	2450
18		CLIPPER	HT	CBNCR	AL	SV	IO	120		5	8	1070			4000	4650
18		SPORTSMAN	OP	RNBT	AL	SV	OB			5	8				1900	2250
18	11	DURAFLITE	OP	RNBT	AL	SV	OB			5	8	825			1750	2100
18	11	DURAFLITE	OP	RNBT	AL	SV	IO	120-160		5	8	875			4250	5000
18	11	V-I-P	OP	RNBT	AL	SV	IO	120-160				875			5150	5950
19		CLIPPER	HT	CBNCR	AL	SV	IO	120-160		6	8	1385			5150	5950
25		EXPRESS		EXP	AL		IB	120		8					7350	8450
34		AQUA-VILLA	ST	HB	AL	PN	OB			10		5500			6550	7500
		1966 BOATS														
16	3	DURAFLITE	OP	RNBT	AL		IO	110		6	2	680			2950	3450
16	3	DURAFLITE	OP	RNBT	AL	SV	IO	120		6	2	680			2950	3450
16	3	SPORTSMAN	OP	RNBT	AL	SV	IO	60		6	2	680			2950	3450
17		DURAFLITE	OP	RNBT	AL	SV	IO	120-150		6	8	850			3700	4350
18		CLIPPER	HT	CBNCR	AL	SV	OB			6	8	1050			2100	2500
18		CLIPPER	HT	CBNCR	AL	SV	IO	120-150		6	8	1070			4600	5300
18		DURAFLITE	OP	RNBT	AL	SV	OB			6	8	825			1700	2050
18		DURAFLITE	OP	RNBT	AL	SV	IO	120-150		5	8	875			3900	4550
18		SPORTSMAN	OP	RNBT	AL	SV	OB			6	8				1900	2250
19		CLIPPER	OP	CBNCR	AL	SV	IO	120-150		8		1385			6050	7000
19		CLIPPER	OP	RNBT	AL	SV	OB			8		1325			2650	3050
		1965 BOATS														
16	3	DURAFLITE	OP	RNBT	AL	SV	IO	90-120		5	2	680			2800	3250
17		DURAFLITE	OP	RNBT	AL	SV	IO	90-120		5	8	850			3500	4050
18		DURAFLITE	OP	RNBT	AL	SV	OB			5	8	825			1700	2050
18		DURAFLITE	OP	RNBT	AL	SV	IO	110-150		5	8	875			4000	4700
19		CLIPPER	OP	CBNCR	AL	SV	IO	150		6	8	1385			5500	6350
19		CLIPPER	HT	CBNCR	AL	SV	IO	120-150		6	8	1385			5500	6350
		1964 BOATS														
18		DURAFLITE 18	OP	RNBT	AL	SV	OB			5	8	825			1700	2050

DURATECH MFG CORP

COAST GUARD MFG ID- DUT

Call 1-800-327-6929 for BUC Personalized Evaluation Service
Or, for 1959 to 1969 boats, sign onto www.BUCValuPro.com

DURBECK'S INC

HOLMES BEACH FL 33510 COAST GUARD MFG ID- DBK See inside cover to adjust price for area

For more recent years, see the BUC Used Boat Price Guide, Volume 1 or Volume 2

LOA FT	LOA IN	NAME AND/ OR MODEL	TOP/ RIG	BOAT TYPE	HULL MTL	HULL TP	ENGINE TP	ENGINE # HP	ENGINE MFG	BEAM FT	BEAM IN	WGT LBS	DRAFT FT	DRAFT IN	RETAIL LOW	RETAIL HIGH
		1983 BOATS														
45	10	D46 TRAWLER	HT	TRWL	FBG	DS	IB	135D	PERK	15		62500	5	3	234000	257500
46	9	D46 FLUSH DECK	CUT	SA/CR	FBG	KL	IB	85D	PERK	13	8	35825	5	1	103000	113500
46	9	D46 FLUSH DECK	KTH	SA/CR	FBG	KL	IB	85D	PERK	13	8	35825	5	1	103500	113500
46	9	D46 GREAT CABIN	CUT	SA/CR	FBG	KL	IB	85D	PERK	13	8	37375	5	2	105000	115500
46	9	D46 GREAT CABIN	KTH	SA/CR	FBG	KL	IB	85D	PERK	13	8	37375	5	2	105000	115500
46	9	D46 WORLD CRUISING	CUT	SA/CR	FBG	KL	IB	85D	PERK	13	8	38925	5	3	107000	117500
46	9	D46 WORLD CRUISING	KTH	SA/CR	FBG	KL	IB	85D	PERK	13	8	38925	5	3	107000	117500
48		SNAPPER D 48	HT	TRWL	FBG	DS	IB	131D	GM	15		65000	5	6	163500	180000
50	9	D50 FISHERMAN	KTH	SA/CR	FBG	KL	IB	85D	PERK	13	10	45000	5	3	133000	146000
50	9	D50 FLUSH DECK	CUT	SA/CR	FBG	KL	IB	85D	PERK	13	10	44600	5	1	132500	145500
50	9	D50 FLUSH DECK	KTH	SA/CR	FBG	KL	IB	85D	PERK	13	10	44600	5	1	132500	145500
50	9	D50 GREAT CABIN	CUT	SA/CR	FBG	KL	IB	85D	PERK	13	10	46450	5	2	134000	147000
50	9	D50 GREAT CABIN	KTH	SA/CR	FBG	KL	IB	85D	PERK	13	10	46450	5	2	134000	147000
50	9	D50 WORLD CRUISING	CUT	SA/CR	FBG	KL	IB	85D	PERK	13	10	48300	5	3	135500	149000
50	9	D50 WORLD CRUISING	KTH	SA/CR	FBG	KL	IB	85D	PERK	13	10	48300	5	3	135500	149000
62		D620 WORLD CRUISING	KTH	SA/CR	FBG	KL	IB	120D	WEST	13	11	54700	5	3	243500	267500
		1982 BOATS														
45	10	D46 TRAWLER	HT	TRWL	FBG	DS	IB	130D	PERK	15		62500	5	3	223500	245500
46	9	D46 FLUSH DECK	CUT	SA/CR	FBG	KL	IB	60D	PERK	13	8	37000	5	1	98100	108000
46	9	D46 FLUSH DECK	KTH	SA/CR	FBG	KL	IB	60D	PERK	13	8	37000	5	1	98300	108000
46	9	D46 GREAT CABIN	CUT	SA/CR	FBG	KL	IB	60D	PERK	13	8	38000	5	2	99200	109000
46	9	D46 GREAT CABIN	KTH	SA/CR	FBG	KL	IB	60D	PERK	13	8	38000	5	2	99400	109000
46	9	D46 RAISED DK DODGER	CUT	SA/CR	FBG	KL	IB	60D	PERK	13	8	39000	5	3	99800	109500
46	9	D46 RAISED DK DODGER	KTH	SA/CR	FBG	KL	IB	60D	PERK	13	8	39000	5	3	100000	110000
46	9	D46 WORLD CRUISING	CUT	SA/CR	FBG	KL	IB	60D	PERK	13	8	39000	5	3	101000	111000
46	9	D46 WORLD CRUISING	KTH	SA/CR	FBG	KL	IB	60D	PERK	13	8	39000	5	3	101000	111000
48		SNAPPER D 48	HT	TRWL	FBG	DS	IB	131D	GM	15		65000	5	6	156000	171500
50	9	D50 FISHERMAN	KTH	SA/CR	FBG	KL	IB	85D	PERK	13	10	45000	5	1	125000	137500
50	9	D50 FLUSH DECK	CUT	SA/CR	FBG	KL	IB	85D	PERK	13	10	45000	5	3	117500	129500
50	9	D50 FLUSH DECK	KTH	SA/CR	FBG	KL	IB	85D	PERK	13	10	45000	5	3	118000	129500
50	9	D50 GREAT CABIN	CUT	SA/CR	FBG	KL	IB	85D	PERK	13	10	46600	5	2	126000	138500
50	9	D50 GREAT CABIN	KTH	SA/CR	FBG	KL	IB	85D	PERK	13	10	46600	5	2	126000	138500
50	9	D50 RAISED DECK	CUT	SA/CR	FBG	KL	IB	85D	PERK	13	10	48600	5	3	127500	140000
50	9	D50 RAISED DECK	KTH	SA/CR	FBG	KL	IB	85D	PERK	13	10	48600	5	3	127500	140500
50	9	D50 WORLD CRUISING	CUT	SA/CR	FBG	KL	IB	85D	PERK	13	10	45000	5	3	132000	145000
50	9	D50 WORLD CRUISING	KTH	SA/CR	FBG	KL	IB	85D	PERK	13	10	45000	5	3	132000	145000
		1981 BOATS														
41		D38	CUT	SA/CR	FBG	KL	IB	37D	PERK	11	4	19200	5		53500	58800
41		D38	KTH	SA/CR	FBG	KL	IB	37D	PERK	11	4	19200	5		53700	59000
45	10	D46 TRAWLER	HT	TRWL	FBG	DS	IB	130D	PERK	15		62500	5	3	213000	234500
46	9	D 46 WORLD CRUISING	CUT	SA/CR	FBG	KL	IB	85D	PERK	13	8	39000	5	3	95100	104500
46	9	D 46 WORLD CRUISING	KTH	SA/CR	FBG	KL	IB	85D	PERK	13	8	39000	5	3	95200	104500
46	9	D46 FLUSH DECK	CUT	SA/CR	FBG	KL	IB	60D	PERK	13	8	37000	5	1	92300	101500
46	9	D46 FLUSH DECK	KTH	SA/CR	FBG	KL	VD	60D	PERK	13	8	37000	5	1	92400	101500
46	9	D46 GREAT CABIN	CUT	SA/CR	FBG	KL	IB	85D	PERK	13	8	38000	5	2	93600	103000
46	9	D46 GREAT CABIN	KTH	SA/CR	FBG	KL	IB	85D	PERK	13	8	38000	5	2	93700	103000
46	9	D46 RAISED DK DODGER	CUT	SA/CR	FBG	KL	IB	85D	PERK	13	8	39000	5	3	94100	103500
46	9	D46 RAISED DK DODGER	KTH	SA/CR	FBG	KL	IB	85D	PERK	13	8	39000	5	3	94300	103500
48		SNAPPER D 48	HT	TRWL	FBG	DS	IB	131D	GM	15		65000	5	6	149000	164000
50	9	D 50 WORLD CRUISING	CUT	SA/CR	FBG	KL	IB	85D	PERK	13	10	45000	5	3	117500	129000
50	9	D 50 WORLD CRUISING	KTH	SA/CR	FBG	KL	IB	85D	PERK	13	10	45000	5	3	117500	129000

CONTINUED ON NEXT PAGE

LOA FT	LOA IN	NAME AND/ OR MODEL	TOP/ RIG	BOAT TYPE	HULL MTL	HULL TP	ENGINE TP	#	HP	MFG	BEAM FT	BEAM IN	WGT LBS	DRAFT FT	DRAFT IN	RETAIL LOW	RETAIL HIGH
		1980 BOATS															
41		D38	CUT	SA/CR	FBG	KL	IB		37D	PERK	11	4	19200	5		51100	56200
41		D38	KTH	SA/CR	FBG	KL	IB		37D	PERK	11	4	19200	5		51200	56300
45	10	D46 TRAWLER	HT	TRWL	FBG	DS	IB		130D	PERK	15		62500	5	3	203500	224000
46	9	D46 FLUSH DECK	CUT	SA/CR	FBG	KL	IB		60D	PERK	13	8	37000	5	1	88100	96800
46	9	D46 FLUSH DECK	KTH	SA/CR	FBG	KL	IB		60D	PERK	13	8	37000	5	1	88200	96900
46	9	D46 GREAT CABIN	CUT	SA/CR	FBG	KL	IB		85D	PERK	13	8	38000	5	2	89300	98200
46	9	D46 GREAT CABIN	KTH	SA/CR	FBG	KL	IB		85D	PERK	13	8	38000	5	2	89400	98200
46	9	D46 RAISED DK DODGER	CUT	SA/CR	FBG	KL	IB		85D	PERK	13	8	39000	5	3	89600	98500
46	9	D46 RAISED DK DODGER	KTH	SA/CR	FBG	KL	IB		85D	PERK	13	8	39000	5	3	89900	98800
46	9	D46 RAISED DK PH	CUT	SA/CR	FBG	KL	IB		85D	PERK	13	8	39000	5	3	91100	100000
46	9	D46 RAISED DK PH	KTH	SA/CR	FBG	KL	IB		85D	PERK	13	8	39000	5	3	90800	99800
48		SNAPPER D 48	HT	TRWL	FBG	DS	IB		131D	GM	15		65000	5	6	142500	156500
		1979 BOATS															
41		D38	CUT	SA/CR	FBG	KL	IB		37D	PERK	11	4	19200	5		49200	54000
41		D38	KTH	SA/CR	FBG	KL	IB		37D	PERK	11	4	19200	5		49200	54100
45	10	D46 TRAWLER	HT	TRWL	FBG	DS	IB		130D	PERK	15		62500	5	3	195000	214000
46	9	D46 FLUSH DECK	CUT	SA/CR	FBG	KL	IB		60D	PERK	13	8	37000	5	1	84700	93100
46	9	D46 FLUSH DECK	KTH	SA/CR	FBG	KL	IB		60D	PERK	13	8	37000	5	1	84800	93200
46	9	D46 GREAT CABIN	CUT	SA/CR	FBG	KL	IB		85D	PERK	13	8	38000	5	2	85900	94400
46	9	D46 GREAT CABIN	KTH	SA/CR	FBG	KL	IB		85D	PERK	13	8	38000	5	2	86000	94500
46	9	D46 RAISED DK DODGER	CUT	SA/CR	FBG	KL	IB		85D	PERK	13	8	39000	5	3	86200	94700
46	9	D46 RAISED DK DODGER	KTH	SA/CR	FBG	KL	IB		85D	PERK	13	8	39000	5	3	86500	95000
46	9	D46 RAISED DK PH	CUT	SA/CR	FBG	KL	IB		85D	PERK	13	8	39000	5	3	87500	96200
46	9	D46 RAISED DK PH	KTH	SA/CR	FBG	KL	IB		85D	PERK	13	8	39000	5	3	87300	96000
48		SNAPPER D 48	HT	TRWL	FBG	DS	IB		131D	GM	15		65000	5	6	136500	150000
		1978 BOATS															
36		VANCOUVER 36	SLP	SA/CR	FBG	KL	VD		35D	VLVO	11		18000	5		38200	42400
41		D38	CUT	SA/CR	FBG	KL	IB		37D	PERK	11	4	19200	5		47600	52400
41		D38	KTH	SA/CR	FBG	KL	IB		37D	PERK	11	4	19200	5		47700	52400
45	10	D46 TRAWLER	HT	TRWL	FBG	DS	IB		130D		15		62500	5	3	186000	204500
46	9	D46 FLUSH DECK	KTH	SA/CR	FBG	KL	IB		60D	PERK	13	8	37000	4	11	81700	89800
46	9	D46 RAISED DECK	CUT	SA/CR	FBG	KL	IB		85D	PERK	13	8	39000	5	2	83700	92000
46	9	D46 RAISED DECK	KTH	SA/CR	FBG	KL	IB		85D	PERK	13	8	39000	5	2	83800	92000
48		D48	FB	MY	FBG	DS	IB		130D	PERK	15		65000			132000	145000
48		SNAPPER D48	HT	TRWL	FBG	DS	IB		131D	GM	15		65000	5	6	130000	143000
52		D52 PH	FB	TRWL	FBG	DS	IB		250D	CUM			53664			144000	158500
		1977 BOATS															
37		CAROLINA-CAT	CAT	SA/CR	FBG	CT	IB	T	25D		17	1	13000	2		39400	43700
37		CAROLINA-CAT	KTH	SA/CR	FBG	CT	IB	T	25D		17	1	13000	2		39400	43700
41		D38	CUT	SA/CR	FBG	KL	IB		37D	PERK	11	4	19200	5		46000	50600
41		D38	CUT	SA/CR	FBG	KL	IB		50D		11	4	19200	5		46400	51000
41		D38	KTH	SA/CR	FBG	KL	IB		37D	PERK	11	4	19200	5		46100	50600
41		D38	KTH	SA/CR	FBG	KL	IB		50D		11	4	19200	5		46500	51100
41		D41 TRAWLER		TRWL	FBG	DS	IB		130D		15			5	3	92900	102000
45	10	D46 TRAWLER	HT	TRWL	FBG	DS	IB		130D	PERK	15		62500	5	3	179000	196500
46	9	D46 AFT CABIN	SLP	SA/CR	FBG	KL	IB		60D	PERK	13	8	35000	4	11	77100	84700
46	9	D46 AFT CABIN	SCH	SA/CR	FBG	KL	IB		60D	PERK	13	8	35000	4	11	77100	84700
46	9	D46 AFT CABIN	CUT	SA/CR	FBG	KL	IB		60D	PERK	13	8	35000	4	11	77100	84700
46	9	D46 AFT CABIN	KTH	SA/CR	FBG	KL	IB		60D	PERK	13	8	35000	4	11	77100	84800
46	9	D46 FLUSH DECK	SLP	SA/CR	FBG	KL	IB		60D	PERK	13	8	35000	4	11	77100	84700
46	9	D46 FLUSH DECK	SCH	SA/CR	FBG	KL	IB		60D	PERK	13	8	35000	4	11	77100	84700
46	9	D46 FLUSH DECK	CUT	SA/CR	FBG	KL	IB		60D	PERK	13	8	35000	4	11	77100	84700
46	9	D46 FLUSH DECK	KTH	SA/CR	FBG	KL	IB		60D	PERK	13	8	35000	4	11	77100	84800
46	9	D46 RAISED DECK	CUT	SA/CR	FBG	KL	IB		85D	PERK	13	8	39000	5	2	80900	88900
46	9	D46 RAISED DECK	KTH	SA/CR	FBG	KL	IB		85D	PERK	13	8	39000	5	2	80900	88900
48		SNAPPER D48	HT	FSH	FBG	DS	IB		130D	GM	15		65000	5	6	122000	134000
		1976 BOATS															
37		CAROLINA-CAT	CAT	SA/CR	FBG	CT	IB	T	25D		17	1	13000	2		38100	42400
37		CAROLINA-CAT	KTH	SA/CR	FBG	CT	IB	T	25D		17	1	13000	2		38100	42400
37		D 37		TRWL	FBG	DS	IB		130D		13					65000	71500
38		DURBECK D 38	KTH	SA/CR	FBG	KL	IB		50D		11	4	19200	5		39600	44000
40		D 40		TRWL	FBG	DS	IB		130D		13					94600	104000
41		DURBECK 38	CUT	SA/CR	FBG	KL	IB		37D	PERK	11	4	19200	5		44100	49000
41		DURBECK 38	KTH	SA/CR	FBG	KL	IB		37D	PERK	11	4	19200	5		44100	49000
45	10	D 46		TRWL	FBG	DS	IB		150D	PERK	15					137000	150500
45	10	D 46	HT	TRWL	FBG	DS	IB		130D	PERK	15		62500	5	3	138000	151500
46	9	D 46	CUT	MS	FBG	KL	IB		85D	PERK	13	8	37000	4	11	76700	84300
46	9	D 46	KTH	MS	FBG	KL	IB		85D	PERK	13	8	37000	4	11	76700	84300
46	9	D 46	KTH	SA/CR	FBG	KL	IB		60D	PERK	13	8	35000	4	11	74700	82100
48		D 48	HT	TRWL	FBG	DS	IB		200D		15	3	65000	5	6	170500	187500
		1975 BOATS															
45		DURBECK D 45		TRWL	FBG	DS	IB		120D	FORD	15		62500	5	3	138000	151500
46	9	DURBECK D 46	KTH	SA/CR	FBG	KL	IB		60D	PERK	13	8	35000	4	11	72600	79700
48		SNAPPER D48	HT	TRWL	FBG	DS	IB		200D		15	3		5	6	116000	127500
		1974 BOATS															
46	9	DURBECK 46K	KTH	SA/CR	FBG	KL	IB		50D		13	8	35000	4	11	70800	77800
48		DURBECK 48T	HT	TRWL	FBG	DS	IB		130D		15	3	65000	5	6	155500	171000
52		DURBECK 52T		TRWL	FBG	DS	IB		200D		15	3				128000	140500
53		DURBECK 53	KTH	SA/CR	FBG	KL	IB		125D		15		57000	5	3	111000	122000
65				MY	FBG	SV	IB		T500D		16	6				400000	439500
		1973 BOATS															
46	9	DURBECK 46	KTH	SA/CR	FBG	KL	IB		45		13	8	35000	4	11	68300	75100
48		D48	HT	TRWL	FBG	DS	IB		130D		15	3	65000	5	6	106500	117000
52		D52		TRWL	FBG	DS	IB		200D		15	3				123500	135500
53		DURBECK 53	KTH	SA/CR	FBG	KL	IB		125		15		57000	5	3	107000	117500
65		D65		MY	FBG	SV	IB		T500D		16	6				383500	421500

DUSKY MARINE INC

DANIA FL 33004 COAST GUARD MFG ID- DUS See inside cover to adjust price for area

For more recent years, see the BUC Used Boat Price Guide, Volume 1 or Volume 2

LOA FT	LOA IN	NAME AND/ OR MODEL	TOP/ RIG	BOAT TYPE	HULL MTL	HULL TP	ENGINE TP	# HP	MFG	BEAM FT	BEAM IN	WGT LBS	DRAFT FT	DRAFT IN	RETAIL LOW	RETAIL HIGH
		1983 BOATS														
16	6	DUSKY 17	OP	OPFSH	FBG	SV	OB			7	3	1200		6	1800	2100
20	3	DUSKY 20	OP	OPFSH	FBG	DV	OB			8		2000	1		4600	5300
20	3	DUSKY 20	OP	OPFSH	FBG	DV	SE	115	OMC	8		3000	1	1	5550	6400
20	3	DUSKY 20	OP	OPFSH	FBG	DV	IO	170-200		8		3000	1	1	6350	7350
20	3	DUSKY 20	OP	OPFSH	FBG	DV	SE	205	OMC	8		3000	1	1	5550	6400
20	3	DUSKY 20	OP	OPFSH	FBG	DV	IB	220-225		8		3000	1	1	7650	8800
		IO 230 OMC 6550 7500, IB 255-270 7550 8950, IB 135D PERK 11800 13400														
		IO 155D VLVO 10000 11400, IB 158D VLVO 10900 12400, IB 165D PERK 12300 14000														
20	3	DUSKY 20	OP	OPFSH	FBG	DV	SE	T115	OMC	8		3000	1	1	5550	6400
22	6	DUSKY 226CC	OP	CUD	FBG	DV	OB			8		2800	1	2	4850	5600
22	6	DUSKY 226CC	OP	CUD	FBG	DV	IO	170-200		8		3900	2	8	6250	7250
22	6	DUSKY 226CC	OP	CUD	FBG	DV	SE	205	OMC	8		3900	2	8	6150	7100
22	6	DUSKY 226CC	OP	CUD	FBG	DV	IB	220-225		8		3900	2	8	7900	9100
		IO 230 OMC 6400 7350, IB 255 COMM 7850 9000, IO 260 OMC 6500 7500														
		IB 270-350 8000 9650, IB 135D PERK 11500 13000, IO 155D VLVO 7900 9050														
		IB 158D VLVO 10700 12200, IB 165D-235D 11800 14000														
22	6	DUSKY 226CC	OP	CUD	FBG	DV	SE	T115	OMC	8		3900	2	8	6150	7100
22	6	DUSKY 226CSS	OP	CUD	FBG	DV	OB			8		2800	1	2	5300	6100
22	6	DUSKY 226CSS	OP	CUD	FBG	DV	IO	170-200		8			2	8	5850	6750
22	6	DUSKY 226CSS	OP	CUD	FBG	DV	SE	205	OMC	8			2	8	**	**
22	6	DUSKY 226CSS	OP	CUD	FBG	DV	IB	220-225		8			2	8	7400	8500
		IO 230 OMC 5950 6850, IB 255 COMM 7300 8400, IO 260 OMC 6100 7000														
		IB 270-350 7500 9050, IB 135D PERK 10900 12400, IO 155D VLVO 7450 8550														
		IB 158D VLVO 10100 11500, IB 165D-235D 11200 13300														
22	6	DUSKY 226CSS	OP	CUD	FBG	DV	SE	T115	OMC	8			2	8	**	**
23	3	DUSKY 23	OP	OPFSH	FBG	DV	OB			8		2800	1	2	5300	6050
23	3	DUSKY 23	OP	OPFSH	FBG	DV	IO	170-200		8		3500	2	8	6350	7350
23	3	DUSKY 23	OP	OPFSH	FBG	DV	SE	205	OMC	8		3500	2	8	6200	7100
23	3	DUSKY 23	OP	OPFSH	FBG	DV	IB	220-225		8		3500	2	8	7650	8750
		IO 230 OMC 6500 7450, IB 255 COMM 7550 8650, IO 260 OMC 6650 7600														
		IB 270-350 7700 9300, IO 155D VLVO 9650 10900, IB 158D VLVO 10400 11900														
		IB 165D-235D 11600 13700														
23	3	DUSKY 23	OP	OPFSH	FBG	DV	SE	T115	OMC	8		3500	2	8	6200	7100
23	3	DUSKY 233FC	OP	CTRCN	FBG	DV	OB			8		2800	1	2	5300	6050
23	3	DUSKY 233FC	OP	CTRCN	FBG	DV	SE	205	OMC	8		3500	2	8	6200	7100
23	3	DUSKY 233FC	OP	CTRCN	FBG	DV	IB	220-350		8		3500	2	8	7650	9300
23	3	DUSKY 233FC	OP	CTRCN	FBG	DV	IB	158D	VLVO	8		3500	2	8	10400	11900
23	3	DUSKY 233FC	OP	CTRCN	FBG	DV	IB	165D-235D		8		3500	2	8	11600	13700
23	3	DUSKY 233FC	OP	CTRCN	FBG	DV	SE	T115	OMC	8		3500	2	8	6200	7100
25	6	DUSKY 25	OP	OPFSH	FBG	DV	OB			8		3000	1	2	6700	7700
25	6	DUSKY 25	OP	OPFSH	FBG	DV	IO	170-200		8		4700	2	9	8550	10000
25	6	DUSKY 25	OP	OPFSH	FBG	DV	SE	205	OMC	8		4700	2	9	8000	9200
25	6	DUSKY 25	OP	OPFSH	FBG	DV	IB	220-225		8		4700	2	9	10500	11900
		IO 230 OMC 9000 10200, IB 255 COMM 9600 10900, IO 260 OMC 8100 9300														
		IB 270 CRUS 9750 11100, IB 350 CRUS 11300 12900, IO 155D VLVO 14600 16600														
		IB 165D-235D 13800 16500, IB 300D CAT 16700 18900														
25	6	DUSKY 25	OP	OPFSH	FBG	DV	SE	T115-T205		8		4700	2	9	8000	9200
25	6	DUSKY 256CC	OP	CUD	FBG	DV	OB			8					7450	8550
25	6	DUSKY 256CC	OP	CUD	FBG	DV	IO	170-200		8					7600	8900
25	6	DUSKY 256CC	OP	CUD	FBG	DV	SE	205	OMC	8					7250	8350
25	6	DUSKY 256CC	OP	CUD	FBG	DV	IB	220-225		8					9850	11200
		IO 230 OMC 7900 9100, IB 255 COMM 9950 11300, IO 260 OMC 8150 9350														

CONTINUED ON NEXT PAGE

```
LOA   NAME AND/       TOP/ BOAT  -HULL- ----ENGINE--- BEAM    WGT  DRAFT RETAIL RETAIL
FT IN  OR MODEL       RIG  TYPE  MTL TP TP # HP   MFG  FT IN   LBS  FT IN  LOW    HIGH
-------------------------- 1983 BOATS -----------------------------------------------
25  6 DUSKY 256CC     OP  CUD   FBG DV IB 270-350    8               10200  12200
      IO  155D VLVO 9200 10400, IB 165D-235D 13300 16000, IB 300D CAT 16400  18600

25  6 DUSKY 256CSS    OP  CUD   FBG DV SE T115-T205  8                7300   8400
25  6 DUSKY 256CSS    OP  CUD   FBG DV OB            8                7900   9100
25  6 DUSKY 256CSS    OP  CUD   FBG DV IO 170-200    8                7850   9200
25  6 DUSKY 256CSS    OP  CUD   FBG DV SE  205  OMC  8                7500   8600
25  6 DUSKY 256CSS    OP  CUD   FBG DV IB 220-225    8               10200  11500
      IO  230  OMC 8200  9400, IB  255  COMM 10300 11700, IO  260  OMC 8400   9650
      IB  270-350 10500 12600, IO  155D VLVO 9400 10700, IB 165D-235D 13600  16300
      IB  300D CAT 16600 18900

25  6 DUSKY 256CSS    OP  CUD   FBG DV SE T115  OMC  8                7450   8600
25  6 DUSKY 256CSS    OP  CUD   FBG DV IB T165 CRUS  8               11200  12700
25  6 DUSKY 256CSS    OP  CUD   FBG DV SE T205  OMC  8                7450   8550
25  6 DUSKY 256FAC    OP  CR    FBG DV OB            8                7600   8750
25  6 DUSKY 256FAC    OP  CR    FBG DV SE  205  OMC  8                7400   8500
25  6 DUSKY 256FAC    OP  CR    FBG DV IB 220-350    8                9800  12200
25  6 DUSKY 256FAC    OP  CR    FBG DV IB 165D-235D  8               13000  15700
25  6 DUSKY 256FAC    OP  CR    FBG DV SE T115-T205  8                7400   8500
25  6 DUSKY 256FC     OP  OPFSH FBG DV OB            8      3100 1 2  6800   7800
25  6 DUSKY 256FC     OP  OPFSH FBG DV SE  205  OMC  8      3100 1 2  6800   7800
25  6 DUSKY 256FC     OP  OPFSH FBG DV IB 220-270    8      3100 1 2  8300   9900
      IB  350  CRUS 9350 10600, IB 165D-235D 10500 13000, IB 300D CAT 13700  15600

25  6 DUSKY 256FC     OP  OPFSH FBG DV SE T115-T205  8      3100 1 2  6800   7800
25 11 DUSKY 26        OP  SF    FBG SV OB           11 3 6000  2 9  11900  13600
25 11 DUSKY 26        OP  SF    FBG SV IB T     OMC 11 3 7500  2 9    **     **
25 11 DUSKY 26        OP  SF    FBG SV IB T165-T270 11 3 7500  2 9  17600  21200
25 11 DUSKY 26        OP  SF    FBG SV IB T350 CRUS 11 3 7500  2 9  20100  22300
25 11 DUSKY 26        OP  SF    FBG SV IBT135D-T235D 11 3 7500 2 9  26400  32000
-------------------------- 1982 BOATS -----------------------------------------------
16  6 DUSKY 17            OPFSH FBG SV OB            7 3 1225         1750   2100
16  6 DUSKY 17        OP  OPFSH FBG SV OB            7 3 1200      6  1750   2050
20  3 DUSKY 20        OP  OPFSH FBG DV IO            8   2000   1 1  4500   5200
20  3 DUSKY 20        OP  OPFSH FBG DV IB 200  OMC   8   3000   1 1  6250   7200
20  3 DUSKY 20        OP  OPFSH FBG DV IB 220-255    8   3000   2 6  7350   8450
20  3 DUSKY 203           OPFSH FBG DV OB            8   2000      6  4500   5200
20  3 DUSKY 203           OPFSH FBG DV IO 185        8                5150   5900
20  3 DUSKY 203           OPFSH FBG DV IB 225        7 3 3200         7100   8200
22  6 DUSKY 226CC         CUD   FBG DV OB            8   2500         4450   5150
22  6 DUSKY 226CC         CUD   FBG DV IB 225        8   3700         7200   8250
22  6 DUSKY 226CC     OP  CUD   FBG DV OB            8   2800   1 2  5000   5750
22  6 DUSKY 226CC     OP  CUD   FBG DV IB 270  CRUS  8   3900   2 8  7650   8800

22  6 DUSKY 226CSS        CUD   FBG DV OB            8   2500         4750   5450
22  6 DUSKY 226CSS        CUD   FBG DV IB 225        8   3600         7050   8100
22  6 DUSKY 226CSS    OP  CUD   FBG DV OB            8   2800   1 2  5000   5750
23  3 DUSKY 23        OP  OPFSH FBG DV IB            8   3500   1 2  5200   5950
23  3 DUSKY 23        OP  OPFSH FBG DV IB 255  COMM  8   3500   2 8  7200   8300
23  3 DUSKY 23        OP  OPFSH FBG DV IB 148D VLVO  8   3500   2 9 10400  11800
23  3 DUSKY 233           OPFSH FBG DV OB            8   2700         5050   5800
23  3 DUSKY 233           OPFSH FBG DV IO 200        8                5950   6800
23  3 DUSKY 233           OPFSH FBG DV IB 225        8   3700         7450   8600
25  6 DUSKY 25        OP  OPFSH FBG DV IB            8   3000   1 2  6600   7550
25  6 DUSKY 25        OP  OPFSH FBG DV IB 240-270    8   4700     2 10000  11400
25  6 DUSKY 25        OP  OPFSH FBG DV IB 200D PERK  8               12200  13900

25  6 DUSKY 25        OP  OPFSH FBG DV IO T260D VLVO 8   6000   2   20600  22900
25  6 DUSKY 256           OPFSH FBG DV OB            8   3000         7500   7550
25  6 DUSKY 256           OPFSH FBG DV IB 230        8                7800   8950
25  6 DUSKY 256           OPFSH FBG DV IB 255        8   4200         9550  10800
25  6 DUSKY 256CC         CUD   FBG DV IB            8   3125         6500   7500
25  6 DUSKY 256CC         CUD   FBG DV IB 255        8   4500        10000  11400
25  6 DUSKY 256CC     OP  CUD   FBG DV OB            8                7550   8650
25  6 DUSKY 256CC     OP  CUD   FBG DV IB 225-270    8                9500  11200
25  6 DUSKY 256CC     OP  CUD   FBG DV IB 300D CAT   8               15800  18000
25  6 DUSKY 256CSS        CUD   FBG DV IB            8   3125         6850   7900
25  6 DUSKY 256CSS        CUD   FBG DV IB 255        8   4400         9850  11200
25  6 DUSKY 256CSS    OP  CUD   FBG DV OB            8                7550   8650

25  6 DUSKY 256CSS    OP  CUD   FBG DV IB 255-270    8                9700  11500
25  6 DUSKY 256CSS    OP  CUD   FBG DV IB 200D PERK  8               13600  15500
25  6 DUSKY 256CSS    OP  CUD   FBG DV IB T165D CR   8  8            14000  15900
25  6 DUSKY 256FC         OPFSH FBG DV IB            8   3125         6700   7700
25  6 DUSKY 256FC         OPFSH FBG DV IB 255        8   4500         9850  11200
25  6 DUSKY 256FC     OP  OPFSH FBG DV IB            8   3100   1 2  6650   7650
25  6 DUSKY 256FC     OP  OPFSH FBG DV IB 255  COMM  8   3100   1 2  8050   9250
25 11 DUSKY 26        TT  SF    FBG SV IB T225      11 3             12100  13700
25 11 DUSKY 26        TT  SF    FBG SV IB T270 CRUS 11 3        2 5 13300  15200
25 11 DUSKY 26        TT  SF    FBG SV IB T145D REN 11 3        2 5 17400  19700
32    DUSKY 32            FBG   DV IB T225          11               24100  26800
-------------------------- 1981 BOATS -----------------------------------------------
16  6 DUSKY 17        OP  OPFSH FBG SV OB            7 3 1200      6  1700   2050
20  3 DUSKY 20        OP  OPFSH FBG DV IO            8   2000   1 1  4450   5100
20  3 DUSKY 20        OP  OPFSH FBG DV IO 200  OMC   8   3000   1 1  6150   7100
20  3 DUSKY 20        OP  OPFSH FBG DV IB 220-255    8   3000   2 6  7050   8100
22  6 DUSKY 226CC     OP  CUD   FBG DV OB            8   2800   1 2  4750   5450
22  6 DUSKY 226CC     OP  CUD   FBG DV IB 270  CRUS  8   3900   2 8  7350   8450
22  6 DUSKY 226CSS    OP  CUD   FBG DV OB            8   2800   1 2  5100   5850
23  3 DUSKY 23        OP  OPFSH FBG DV OB            8   2800   1 2  5100   5850
23  3 DUSKY 23        OP  OPFSH FBG DV IB 255  COMM  8   3500   2 8  6900   7950
23  3 DUSKY 23        OP  OPFSH FBG DV IB 148D VLVO  8   3000   2 9 10000  11400
25  6 DUSKY 25        OP  OPFSH FBG DV OB            8   3000   1 2  6450   7400

25  6 DUSKY 25        OP  OPFSH FBG DV IB 240-270    8   4700     2  9600  10900
25  6 DUSKY 25        OP  OPFSH FBG DV IB 200D PERK  8               11800  13400
25  6 DUSKY 25        OP  OPFSH FBG DV IO T260D VLVO 8   6000   2   20300  22500
25  6 DUSKY 256CC     OP  CUD   FBG DV IB            8                7600   8750
25  6 DUSKY 256CC     OP  CUD   FBG DV IB 225-270    8                9150  10500
25  6 DUSKY 256CC     OP  CUD   FBG DV IB 300D CAT   8               15200  17300
25  6 DUSKY 256CSS    OP  CUD   FBG DV OB            8                7600   8750
25  6 DUSKY 256CSS    OP  CUD   FBG DV IB 255-270    8                9300  10900
25  6 DUSKY 256CSS    OP  CUD   FBG DV IB 200D PERK  8               13100  14900
25  6 DUSKY 256FC     OP  OPFSH FBG DV IB 255  COMM  8   3100   1 2  6550   7550
25  6 DUSKY 256FC     OP  OPFSH FBG DV IB T165D CR   8               16200  18400
25 11 DUSKY 26        TT  SF    FBG SV IB T270 CRUS 11 3        2 5 12800  14500
25 11 DUSKY 26        TT  SF    FBG SV IB T145D REN 11 3        2 5 16700  18900
-------------------------- 1980 BOATS -----------------------------------------------
20  3 DUSKY 20        OP  OPFSH FBG DV OB            8   2000   1 1  4400   5050
20  3 DUSKY 20        OP  OPFSH FBG DV IO            8   3000   1 1  6100   7000
20  3 DUSKY 20        OP  OPFSH FBG DV IB   D FORD   8   3830        **      **
22  6 DUSKY 226CC     OP  OPFSH FBG DV IO            8   2800   1 2  4850   5550
22  6 DUSKY 226CC     OP  OPFSH FBG DV IO 230  OMC   8   3900   1 3  6400   7400
22  6 DUSKY 226CC     OP  OPFSH FBG DV IB 270  CRUS  8   3900   2 8  7050   8100
22  6 DUSKY 226CSS    OP  OPFSH FBG DV IO            8   2775   1 2  4800   5550
22  6 DUSKY 226CSS    OP  OPFSH FBG DV IB 225  COMM  8   3800   1 2  6700   7700
22  6 DUSKY 226CSS    OP  OPFSH FBG DV JT  255  COMM 8   3800   1 2  7250   8350
22  6 DUSKY 226CSS    OP  OPFSH FBG DV IB 160D PERK  8   3800   1 2 10300  11700
23  3 DUSKY 23        OP  OPFSH FBG DV OB            8   2800   1 2  5050   5800

23  3 DUSKY 23        OP  OPFSH FBG DV IO 200  OMC   8   3500   1 3  6100   7000
      IB  225-255 6600 8050, IO  260  OMC 6300 7250, IB 270-350 6750   8200
25  6 DUSKY 25        OP  OPFSH FBG DV IB 225-270    8   3000   1 2  6400   7350
25  6 DUSKY 25        OP  OPFSH FBG DV IB            8   4000   2 8  8200   9800
      IB  350  CRUS 9150 10400, IB 200D PERK 11000 12500, IB 240D REN 13100  14900
25  6 DUSKY 256CC     OP  OPFSH FBG DV IO            8                7150   8200
25  6 DUSKY 256CC     OP  OPFSH FBG DV IO 260  OMC   8                7700   8850
25  6 DUSKY 256CC     OP  OPFSH FBG DV IO 200D PERK  8               11600  13200
25  6 DUSKY 256CC     TT  OPFSH FBG DV IO 200D PERK  8               11300  12800
25  6 DUSKY 256CSS    OP  OPFSH FBG DV IO            8                7150   8200
25  6 DUSKY 256CSS    OP  OPFSH FBG DV IB 255-350    8                8250  10000
25  6 DUSKY 256CSS    OP  OPFSH FBG DV IB 200D PERK  8               11400  12900
25  6 DUSKY 256CSS    TT  OPFSH FBG DV IB 200D PERK  8               11400  12900
25  6 DUSKY 25TT      TT  OPFSH FBG DV IB            8   3300   1 3  6650   7600
25 11 DUSKY 26        TT  SF    FBG SV IB T255  COMM 11 3 8000  2 6 16500  18800
25 11 DUSKY 26        TT  SF    FBG SV IB T145D REN 11 3 8600  2 6 25300  28100
25 11 DUSKY 26        TT  SF    FBG SV IB T240D REN 11 3 9400  2 7 29800  33200
-------------------------- 1979 BOATS -----------------------------------------------
20  3 DUSKY 20        OP  OPFSH FBG DV OB            8   2000         4250   4950
20  3 DUSKY 20        OP  OPFSH FBG DV IO 185-200    8   3000   1 1  6100   7000
      IB  220-225 6450 7400, IO  230  OMC 6200 7150, JT  255  COMM 7000   8050
      IB  255-270 6350 7550
22  6 DUSKY 23        OP  OPFSH FBG DV OB            8   2500         4450   5100
22  6 DUSKY 23        OP  OPFSH FBG DV IO 200  OMC   8   3500   1 3  5850   6750
      IB  220-225 6200 7100, IO  260  OMC 5950 6850, JT  255  COMM 6600   7600
      IB  255  COMM 6100 7000, IO 200D-240D 6100 7000, IB 270-350 6250   7550
      IB  124D-145D 8800 10700, IB 200D-240D 10100 12400, IB 300D CAT 12200  13900
22  6 DUSKY 23        TT  OPFSH FBG DV IO            8   2800   1 2  4800   5500
22  6 DUSKY 23        TT  OPFSH FBG DV IO 200  OMC   8   3800   1 4  6200   7150
```

```
  LOA  NAME AND/       TOP/ BOAT  -HULL-   ----ENGINE---  BEAM   WGT  DRAFT RETAIL RETAIL
FT IN   OR MODEL       RIG  TYPE  MTL TP TP # HP   MFG    FT IN  LBS  FT IN  LOW    HIGH
------------------- 1979 BOATS ------------------------------------------------------------
22  6 DUSKY 23          TT  OPFSH FBG DV IB 220   CRUS   8      3800  2  9  6550   7500
      JT  225 COMM  6950 8000, IO  230 OMC   6300  7250, JT 255 COMM    6950   8000
      IO  260 OMC   6450 7400, IB  270 CRUS  6600  7600, IB 200D-240D  10600  12900
      IB  350D CAT 14500 16500

22  6 DUSKY 23CC        OP  OPFSH FBG DV OB           8         2900  1  2  4900   5650
22  6 DUSKY 23CC        OP  OPFSH FBG DV IO 200  OMC  8         3900  1  3  6350   7300
      IB  220-225  6650 7650, IO  230 OMC   6400  7350, JT 255 COMM    7100   8150
      IB  255 COMM  6600 7600, IO  260 OMC  6550  7550, IB 270-350     6750   8100
      IB  200D-240D 10700 13000, IB 250D CAT 12800 14500

22  6 DUSKY 23CCTT      TT  OPFSH FBG DV OB           8         3200  1  3  5250   6000
22  6 DUSKY 23CCTT      TT  OPFSH FBG DV IO 200  OMC  8         4200  1  4  6700   7700
      IB  220-225  7050 8100, IO  230 OMC   6800  7800, JT 255 COMM    7450   8600
      IB  255 COMM  6950 8000, IO  260 OMC  6900  7950, ID 270-350     7100   8550
      IB  200D-240D 11100 13500, IB 250D CAT 13200 15000

25  6 DUSKY 25          OP  OPFSH FBG DV OB           8         3000  1  2  6300   7250
25  6 DUSKY 25          OP  OPFSH FBG DV IO 200  OMC  8         4000  1  3  7500   8600
      IB  220-225  7950 9150, IO  230 OMC   7650  8800, JT 255 COMM    8400   9650
      IB  255 COMM  8000 9200, IO  260 OMC  7850  9050, IB 270-350     8200  10000
      IB  200D-240D 11600 14400, IB 250D CAT 14000 15900

25  6 DUSKY 25TT        TT  OPFSH FBG DV OB           8         3300  1  3  6550   7550
25  6 DUSKY 25TT        TT  OPFSH FBG DV IB 220-225   8         4300  2  9  8300   9550
      IO  230 OMC   8000 9200, JT  255 COMM 8850 10000, IB 255 COMM    8350   9600
      IO  260 OMC   8200 9450, IB  270-350  8500 10400, IB 200D-240D  12200  15000
      IB  250D CAT 14600 16600

25 11 DUSKY 26          TT  OPFSH FBG SV IB T220-T350 11 3     7500  2  5 15100  18600
      IBT124D-T145D 22100 25800, IBT200D-T240D 25600 30700, IB T250D CAT 30500 33900

25 11 DUSKY 26          TT  OPFSH FBG SV IB T220-T350 11 3     8000  2  6 15700  19400
      IBT124D-T145D 23300 27000, IBT200D-T240D 26700 31900, IB T250D CAT 31600 35100
------------------- 1978 BOATS ------------------------------------------------------------
20    DUSKY 20          OP  OPFSH FBG DV OB           8         2000  1        4150   4800
20    DUSKY 20          OP  OPFSH FBG DV IB           8         2000  1          **     **
20    DUSKY 20          OP  OPFSH FBG DV IO 140-235   8         2000  1        4900   5850
20    DUSKY 20          OP  OPFSH FBG DV JT 240  HARD 8         2000  1        5550   6350
22  6 DUSKY 23          OP  OPFSH FBG DV OB           8         2500  1  2     4400   6050
22  6 DUSKY 23          OP  OPFSH FBG DV IO 175-190   8         2500  1  2     4800   5550
      IB  225 COMM  4750 5450, IO  235 OMC   4950  5700, JT 240 HARD    5250   6050
      IB  255 COMM  4800 5500, JT  200D CHRY 7900  9050, IB 200D CHRY   7900   9050

22  6 DUSKY 23CC CUDDY  OP  OPFSH FBG DV IO 175-190   8         2700  1  2     5000   5750
      IB  225       4950 5900, IO  235 OMC   5150  5900, JT 240 HARD    5450   6250
      IB  250-255   5200 5950, JT  324 HARD  5450  6250, JT 200D CHRY   8100   9300
      IB  200D CHRY 8100 9300

25 11 DUSKY 26 CUDDY    OP  OPFSH FBG SV IO T225  COMM 11 3                    9900  11200
25 11 DUSKY 26 CUDDY    OP  OPFSH FBG SV IB T225-T255 11 3                     9750  11400
25 11 DUSKY 26 CUDDY    OP  OPFSH FBG SV IB T200D CHRY 11 3                   15000  17100
25 11 DUSKY 26 CUDDY    TT  OPFSH FBG SV IO T225  COMM 11 3                    9900  11200
25 11 DUSKY 26 CUDDY    TT  OPFSH FBG SV IB T225-T255 11 3                     9750  11400
25 11 DUSKY 26 CUDDY    TT  OPFSH FBG SV IB T200D CHRY 11 3                   15000  17100
------------------- 1977 BOATS ------------------------------------------------------------
16  6 DUSKY 17          OP  OPFSH FBG SV JT 140  OMC  7 3      2000      8     2750   3200
20    DUSKY 20          OP  OPFSH FBG DV OB           8        1800  1        3850   4450
20    DUSKY 20          OP  OPFSH FBG DV IO 140-225   8        1800  1        4800   5700
20    DUSKY 20          OP  OPFSH FBG DV JT 240-324   8        1800  1        5550   5950
22  6 DUSKY 23          OP  OPFSH FBG DV OB           8        2500  1  2     4300   5000
22  6 DUSKY 23          OP  OPFSH FBG DV IO 165-225   8        2500  1  2     4850   5750
      IB  230 OMC   4750 5450, IO  235 OMC   5000  5750, JT 240-324     5050   5800
      JT  200D CHRY 7600 8750, IB  200D CHRY 7600  8750

26    DUSKY 26          OP  OPFSH FBG DV IB T230  OMC  11 3    7500  2  5 14100  16000
26    DUSKY 26          OP  OPFSH FBG DV IB T200D CHRY 11 3    7500  2  5 21700  24200
26    DUSKY 26          TT  OPFSH FBG DV IB T230  OMC  11 3    7500  2  5 14100  16000
26    DUSKY 26          TT  OPFSH FBG DV IB T200D CHRY 11 3    7500  2  5 21700  24200
------------------- 1976 BOATS ------------------------------------------------------------
16  6 DUSKY 17          OP  OPFSH FBG SV JT 140  OMC  7 3      2000      8     2600   3050
20    DUSKY 20          OP  OPFSH FBG DV OB           8        2800  1        4100   4750
20    DUSKY 20          OP  OPFSH FBG DV IO 140-225   8        2800  1        6000   7100
20    DUSKY 20          OP  OPFSH FBG DV JT 240-324   8        2800  1        5900   6750
22  6 DUSKY 23          OP  OPFSH FBG DV OB           8        3500  1  2     4250   4950
22  6 DUSKY 23          OP  OPFSH FBG DV IO 165-225   8        3500  2  6     6100   7150
      IB  230 OMC   5550 6350, IO  235 OMC   6250  7200, JT 240-324     5800   6700
      JT  200D CHRY 9350 10700, IB 200D CHRY 8850 10100

26    DUSKY 26          OP  OPFSH FBG DV IB T230  OMC  11 3    7500  2  5 13500  15400
26    DUSKY 26          OP  OPFSH FBG DV IB T200D CHRY 11 3    7500  2  5 21000  23300
26    DUSKY 26          TT  OPFSH FBG DV IB T230  OMC  11 3    7500  2  5 13500  15400
26    DUSKY 26          TT  OPFSH FBG DV IB T200D CHRY 11 3    7500  2  5 21000  23300
------------------- 1975 BOATS ------------------------------------------------------------
16  6 DUSKY 17 JET      OP  OPFSH FBG SV JT 140  OMC  7 3      2000      8     2500   2950
20    DUSKY 20          OP  OPFSH FBG SV OB           8        1800  1        3750   4400
20    DUSKY 20          OP  OPFSH FBG SV JT 140  OMC  8        1800  1        4550   5250
      IO  140-165  5100 5850, JT  185 OMC    4700  5400, JT 225 COMM    4750   5450
      IO  225 OMC   5250 6050, JT  245 OMC   4750  5450

22  6 DUSKY 23          OP  OPFSH FBG DV OB           8        2500  1  2     4200   4900
22  6 DUSKY 23          OP  OPFSH FBG DV IO 165  OMC  8        2500  1  2     5150   5950
      JT  225 COMM  4700 5400, IO  235 OMC   5300  6050, JT 245 OMC     4700   5400
      IO  245 OMC   5350 6150, JT  255-290   4700  5400

26    DUSKY 26          OP  OPFSH FBG DV IO T230  OMC  11 3    7500  2  5 15800  18000
26    DUSKY 26          OP  OPFSH FBG SV IO T225-T230 11 3     7500  2  5 15700  18000
26    DUSKY 26          OP  SF    FBG SV IO T225  COMM 11 3    7500  2  5 17200  19600
------------------- 1974 BOATS ------------------------------------------------------------
20    DUSKY 20          OP  OPFSH FBG DV OB           8        1800  1        3750   4350
20    DUSKY 20          OP  OPFSH FBG DV IO 215       8        1800  1        5650   6500
      IB  215       4100 4800, IO  235       5750  6600, IB 235         4150   4800

22  6 DUSKY 23          OP  OPFSH FBG DV OB           8        2500  1  2     4200   4900
22  6 DUSKY 23          OP  OPFSH FBG DV IO 235       8              1  2     6350   7300
22  6 DUSKY 23          OP  OPFSH FBG DV IB 235       8              1  2     4700   5400
------------------- 1973 BOATS ------------------------------------------------------------
20    DUSKY 20          OP  OPFSH FBG DV OB           8        1800  1        3750   4350
20    DUSKY 20          OP  OPFSH FBG DV IO 165       8              1        5700   6550
```

THE DUTCH CRAFT CO
COAST GUARD MFG ID- DTC

Call 1-800-327-6929 for BUC Personalized Evaluation Service
Or, for 1966 to 1973 boats, sign onto www.BUCValuPro.com

DYNACAT
COAST GUARD MFG ID- DYR

Call 1-800-327-6929 for BUC Personalized Evaluation Service
Or, for 1980 to 1985 boats, sign onto www.BUCValuPro.com

DYNAMAGLAS BOATS
DIV OF O'NEILL ASSOC INC   See inside cover to adjust price for area
SARASOTA FL 33580   COAST GUARD MFG ID- DYB

```
  LOA  NAME AND/       TOP/ BOAT  -HULL-   ----ENGINE---  BEAM   WGT  DRAFT RETAIL RETAIL
FT IN   OR MODEL       RIG  TYPE  MTL TP TP # HP   MFG    FT IN  LBS  FT IN  LOW    HIGH
------------------- 1979 BOATS ------------------------------------------------------------
16    DORY             OP  DGY   FBG FL OB           7                      2450   2850
16  8 V170 CLOSED DECK OP  RNBT  FBG SV OB           7                      2650   3050
16  8 V170 OPFSH       OP  RNBT  FBG SV OB           7          950        2650   3050
18  6 T200             OP  RNBT  FBG TR OB           6 8       1350        3750   4350
18  6 T200             OP  RNBT  FBG TR IO           6 8                     **     **
19    V190             OP  RNBT  FBG SV OB           7         1325        3750   4350
19    V190             OP  RNBT  FBG SV IO 120-200   7         2400        2500   3100
19    V190             OP  RNBT  FBG SV IO 225-260   7         2400        2750   3300
19    V190             OP  RNBT  FBG SV IO 330  MRCR 7         2400        3200   3700
21    V220             OP  CUD   FBG SV OB           8                      7550   8650
21    V220             OP  CUD   FBG SV IO 120-250   8         3500        4250   5250
21    V220             OP  CUD   FBG SV IO 255-330   8         3500        4700   5800

24  2 V240             OP  CUD   FBG SV IO 140-260   8                     5750   7100
24  2 V240             OP  CUD   FBG SV IO 330  MRCR 8                     6550   7550
24  2 V240             OP  CUD   FBG SV IO 130D-145D 8                     7500   9000
```

DYNASTY BOAT CORPORATION
COAST GUARD MFG ID- OFF
FORMERLY OFFSHORE MARINE INDUSTRIES

Call 1-800-327-6929 for BUC Personalized Evaluation Service
Or, for 1983 to 1995 boats, sign onto www.BUCValuPro.com

E O TAIWAN ENT U S A
WEBSTER NY 14580   COAST GUARD MFG ID- ETE See inside cover to adjust price for area

LOA FT IN	NAME AND/ OR MODEL	TOP/ RIG	BOAT TYPE	-HULL- MTL TP TP	----ENGINE--- # HP MFG	BEAM FT IN	WGT LBS	DRAFT FT IN	RETAIL LOW	RETAIL HIGH
	---------------- 1982 BOATS									
31 9	EO-32	CUT	SA/CR	FBG KL IB	D	10 10	11500	4 10	35900	39800
35 10	EO-36	CUT	SA/CR	FBG KL IB	D	11 6	22500	5 6	66800	73400
	---------------- 1981 BOATS									
31 9	EO32	CUT	SA/CR	FBG KL IB	20D YAN	10 10	11500	4 10	34100	37800
35 10	EO36 MKII	CUT	SA/CR	FBG KL IB	47D LEHM	11 6	23000	5 6	64600	71000
	---------------- 1980 BOATS									
31 9	EO-32	CUT	SA/CR	FBG KL IB	20D YAN	10 10	11500	4 10	32400	36000
35 10	EO-36 MK II	CUT	SA/CR	FBG KL IB	47D LEHM	11 6	23000	5 6	61400	67500
	---------------- 1979 BOATS									
31 9	EO-32	SLP	SA/CR	FBG KL IB	D	10 10		4 10	30900	34400
35 10	EO-36	CUT	SA/CR	FBG KL IB	D	11 6	22000	5 6	57000	62600
	---------------- 1978 BOATS									
35 10	EO-36	CUT	SA/CR	FBG KL IB	D	11 6	22000	5 6	54500	59900
40 11	EO-41	KTH	SA/CR	FBG KL IB	D	12 2	28000	6 2	75100	82600
42	EO-42	CUT	SA/CR	FBG KL IB	D	12 2	29000	6	72500	79700

E X E FIBERCRAFT LTD
EXETER ONTARIO CANADA   See inside cover to adjust price for area

LOA FT IN	NAME AND/ OR MODEL	TOP/ RIG	BOAT TYPE	-HULL- MTL TP TP	----ENGINE--- # HP MFG	BEAM FT IN	WGT LBS	DRAFT FT IN	RETAIL LOW	RETAIL HIGH
	---------------- 1982 BOATS									
16	NORDICA 16 STANDARD	SLP	SA/OD	FBG KL OB		6 2	925	1 8	3100	3650
19 6	FISHERMAN 20	CAT	SAIL	FBG KL IB	6D BMW	6 2	1700	2	6250	7200
19 6	NORDICA 20	SLP	SA/OD	FBG KL OB		7 8	2520	3 3	5600	6400
19 6	NORDICA 20	SLP	SA/OD	FBG KL IB	6D BMW	7 8	2520	3 3	7350	8400
29 11	NORDICA 29	SLP	SA/OD	FBG KL IB	17D VLVO	9 6	10350	5 1	27000	30000
	---------------- 1981 BOATS									
16	NORDICA 16 STANDARD	SLP	SA/OD	FBG KL OB		6 2	925	1 8	3000	3450
19 6	FISHERMAN 20	CAT	SAIL	FBG KL IB	7D BMW	6 2	1700	2	6000	6900
19 6	NORDICA 20	SLP	SA/OD	FBG KL OB		7 8	2520	3 3	5350	6150
19 6	NORDICA 20	SLP	SA/OD	FBG KL IB	7D BMW	7 8	2520	3 3	7050	8100
	---------------- 1980 BOATS									
19 6	FISHERMAN 20		SAIL	FBG KL OB	12D BMW	7 8	1700	2	5800	6700
19 6	NORDICA 20	SLP	SA/OD	FBG KL OB		7 8	2520		5100	5900
19 6	NORDICA 20	SLP	SA/OD	FBG KL IB	7D BMW	7 8	2520	3 3	6750	7750
19 6	NORDICA 20 SPEC ED	SLP	SA/OD	FBG KL IB	8D REN	7 8	2520		6750	7800
	---------------- 1979 BOATS									
19 6	NORDICA 20	SLP	SA/OD	FBG KL OB		7 8	2520		4900	5650
19 6	NORDICA 20	SLP	SA/OD	FBG KL IB	6 WEST	7 8	2520		5300	6100
19 6	NORDICA 20	SLP	SA/OD	FBG KL IB	7D REN	7 8	2520		6500	7500
	---------------- 1978 BOATS									
19 6	NORDICA 20	SLP	SA/OD	FBG KL OB		7 8	2520	3 3	4800	5500
19 6	NORDICA 20	SLP	SA/OD	FBG KL IB	6 WEST	7 8	2520	3 3	5150	5900
	---------------- 1977 BOATS									
19 6	NORDICA 20	SLP	SA/CR	FBG KL OB		7 8	2500	3 3	4600	5300
19 6	NORDICA 20	SLP	SA/CR	FBG KL IB	7 WEST	7 8	2500	3 3	4950	5700
	---------------- 1976 BOATS									
19 6	NORDICA 20	SLP	SAIL	FBG KL OB		7 8	2520	3 3	4500	5200
19 6	NORDICA 20	SLP	SAIL	FBG KL IB	6 WEST	7 8	2520	3 3	4850	5600

EAGLE PACIFIC BOATS
COAST GUARD MFG ID- XUU

Call 1-800-327-6929 for BUC Personalized Evaluation Service
Or, for 1979 boats, sign onto www.BUCValuPro.com

EAGLE TRAWLER YACHTS
MILLER YACHT SALES INC   See inside cover to adjust price for area
S TOMS RIVER NJ 08753   COAST GUARD MFG ID- ETY

For more recent years, see the BUC Used Boat Price Guide, Volume 1 or Volume 2

LOA FT IN	NAME AND/ OR MODEL	TOP/ RIG	BOAT TYPE	-HULL- MTL TP TP	----ENGINE--- # HP MFG	BEAM FT IN	WGT LBS	DRAFT FT IN	RETAIL LOW	RETAIL HIGH
	---------------- 1983 BOATS									
39 11	EAGLE DBL CBN	FB	TRWL	FBG DS IB	120D LEHM	14		4	112500	123500
39 11	EAGLE SEDAN	FB	TRWL	FBG DS IB	120D LEHM	14		4	112500	123500
39 11	EAGLE SEDAN	FB	TRWL	FBG DS IB	T120D LEHM	14		4	118500	130000
	---------------- 1982 BOATS									
39 11	EAGLE DBL CBN	FB	TRWL	FBG DS IB	120D LEHM	14		4	107500	118000
39 11	EAGLE DBL CBN	FB	TRWL	FBG DS IB	T120D LEHM	14		4	113000	124000
39 11	EAGLE SEDAN	FB	TRWL	FBG DS IB	120D LEHM	14		4	107500	118000
39 11	EAGLE SEDAN	FB	TRWL	FBG DS IB	T120D LEHM	14		4	113000	124000
	---------------- 1981 BOATS									
39 11	EAGLE DBL CBN	FB	TRWL	FBG DS IB	120D LEHM	14		4	102500	112500
39 11	EAGLE DBL CBN	FB	TRWL	FBG DS IB	T120D LEHM	14		4	107500	118500
39 11	EAGLE SEDAN	FB	TRWL	FBG DS IB	120D LEHM	14		4	102500	112500
39 11	EAGLE SEDAN	FB	TRWL	FBG DS IB	T120D LEHM	14		4	107500	118500
39 11	EAGLE TRAWLER DC		TRWL	FBG DS IB	128D	14			102500	112500
39 11	EAGLE TRAWLER SEDAN		TRWL	FBG DS IB	128D	14			102500	112500
	---------------- 1980 BOATS									
34 6	EAGLE 35 DBL CBN		TRWL	FBG DS IB	128D	13			61600	67700
34 6	EAGLE 35 PH		TRWL	FBG DS IB	128D	13			61600	67700
39 11	EAGLE CBN	FB	TRWL	FBG DS IB	120D LEHM	14		4	103000	113000
39 11	EAGLE DBL CBN	FB	TRWL	FBG DS IB	120D LEHM	14		4	97800	107500
39 11	EAGLE SEDAN	FB	TRWL	FBG DS IB	120D LEHM	14		4	97800	107500
39 11	EAGLE SEDAN	FB	TRWL	FBG DS IB	T120D LEHM	14		4	103000	113000
	---------------- 1979 BOATS									
34 6	EAGLE DBL CBN	FB	TRWL	FBG DS IB	128D FORD	13		3 6	59300	65200
34 6	EAGLE PILOTHOUSE	FB	TRWL	FBG DS IB	128D FORD	13		3 6	59300	65200
35	MAINE-COASTER 35	SF		FBG DS IB	D GM	12		3	**	**
35	SPORT FISHERMAN	SF		FBG DS IB	D CHRY	12		3	**	**
	IB D FORD **	**	, IB	D PERK	** ** , IB		D VLVO		**	**
39 11	EAGLE DBL CBN	FB	TRWL	FBG DS IB	128D FORD	14		4	93500	103000
	IB 160D PERK 94700 104000, IB		185D CUM		94200 103500, IB		T128D FORD		98400	108000
	---------------- 1978 BOATS									
39 11	EAGLE SEDAN	FB	TRWL	FBG DS IB	128D FORD	14		4	93500	103000
	IB 160D PERK 94700 104000, IB		185D CUM		94200 103500, IB		T128D FORD		98400	108000
34 6	EAGLE DBL CBN	FB	TRWL	FBG DS IB	120D FORD	13		3 6	57400	63100
34 6	EAGLE PILOTHOUSE	FB	TRWL	FBG DS IB	120D FORD	13		3 6	57400	63100
39 11	EAGLE DBL CBN	FB	TRWL	FBG DS IB	120D FORD	14		4	94800	104000
	IB 160D PERK 95800 105000, IB		185D CUM		95000 104500, IB		T120D FORD		98900	108500
	---------------- 1977 BOATS									
39 11	EAGLE SEDAN	FB	TRWL	FBG DS IB	120D FORD	14		4	83900	92200
	IB 160D PERK 85400 93900, IB		185D CUM		85100 93500, IB		T120D FORD		88900	97700
34 6	EAGLE DBL CBN	FB	TRWL	FBG DS IB	120D FORD	13		3 6	57100	62800
34 6	EAGLE PILOTHOUSE	FB	TRWL	FBG DS IB	120D FORD	13		3 6	53500	58800
39 11	EAGLE DBL CBN	FB	TRWL	FBG DS IB	120D FORD	14		4	90800	99800
	IB 160D PERK 91700 101000, IB		185D CUM		91000 100000, IB		T120D FORD		94700	104000
	---------------- 1976 BOATS									
39 11	EAGLE SEDAN	FB	TRWL	FBG DS IB	120D FORD	14		4	80400	88300
	IB 160D PERK 81800 89900, IB		185D CUM		81500 89600, IB		T120D FORD		85200	93600
34 6	EAGLE PILOTHOUSE	FB	TRWL	FBG DS IB	128D LEHM	14	22000	3 6	64300	70700
39 11	EAGLE 40 DBL CBN	FB	TRWL	FBG DS IB	160D PERK	14	34000	4	104500	114500
39 11	EAGLE DBL CBN	FB	TRWL	FBG DS IB	160D PERK	14	34000	4	105000	115500
39 11	EAGLE DBL CBN	FB	TRWL	FBG DS IB	185D CUM	14	34000	4	104500	114500
39 11	EAGLE DBL CBN	FB	TRWL	FBG DS IB	T120D LEHM	14	34000	4	102500	112500
39 11	EAGLE SEDAN	FB	TRWL	FBG DS IB	128D LEHM	14	34000	4	92400	101500
	IB 160D PERK 93700 103000, IB		185D CUM		93500 102500, IB		T128D FORD		102500	113000
	---------------- 1975 BOATS									
34 6	EAGLE PILOTHOUSE	FB	TRWL	FBG DS IB	128D FORD	13		3 6	51500	56600
39 11	EAGLE DBL CBN	FB	TRWL	FBG DS IB	128D FORD	14		4	83700	92000
	IB 160D PERK 84500 92800, IB		185D CUM		83800 92100, IB		T128D FORD		87500	96100
39 11	EAGLE SEDAN	FB	TRWL	FBG DS IB	128D FORD	14		4	74100	81400
	IB 160D PERK 75400 82800, IB		185D CUM		75100 82500, IB		T128D FORD		78700	86400
	---------------- 1974 BOATS									
34 6	EAGLE PILOTHOUSE	FB	TRWL	FBG DS IB	128D FORD	13		3 6	50100	55000
39 11	EAGLE DBL CBN	FB	TRWL	FBG DS IB	128D FORD	14		4	79200	87100
	IB 160D PERK 80000 87900, IB		185D CUM		79500 87300, IB		T128D FORD		83000	91200
39 11	EAGLE SEDAN	FB	TRWL	FBG DS IB	128D FORD	14		4	72500	79700
	IB 160D PERK 73700 81000, IB		185D CUM		73300 80600, IB		T128D FORD		76700	84300
49 8	EAGLE	FB	TRWL	FBG DS IB	T160D PERK	15 2	47860	4 6	118000	129500
	---------------- 1973 BOATS									
34 6	EAGLE PILOTHOUSE	FB	TRWL	FBG DS IB	128D FORD	13	22000	3 6	58900	64700
39 11	EAGLE DBL CBN	FB	TRWL	FBG DS IB	T128D FORD	14	34000	4	94800	104000

LOA FT IN	NAME AND/ OR MODEL	TOP/ RIG	BOAT TYPE	HULL MTL TP TP	ENGINE # HP MFG	BEAM FT IN	WGT LBS	DRAFT FT IN	RETAIL LOW	RETAIL HIGH
					---- 1973 BOATS ----					
39 11	EAGLE SEDAN	FB	TRWL	FBG DS IB	T128D FORD	14	34000	4	87700	96400
49 8	EAGLE	FB	TRWL	FBG DS IB	T160D PERK	15 2	47860	4 6	113500	125000
					---- 1972 BOATS ----					
34 6	EAGLE PILOTHOUSE	FB	TRWL	FBG DS IB	128D FORD	13	22000	3 6	57600	63200
39 11	EAGLE DBL CBN	FB	TRWL	FBG DS IB	128D FORD	14	34000	4	87700	96400
39 11	EAGLE DBL CBN	FB	TRWL	FBG DS IB	T210D	14	34000	4	90000	98900
39 11	EAGLE SEDAN	FB	TRWL	FBG DS IB	128D FORD	14	34000	4	80800	88800
39 11	EAGLE SEDAN	FB	TRWL	FBG DS IB	T210D	14	34000	4	90000	98900
49 8	EAGLE	FB	TRWL	FBG DS IB	T128D	15 2	47860	4 6	107000	117500
49 8	EAGLE	FB	TRWL	FBG DS IB	T256D	15 2	47860	4 6	117000	128500
					---- 1971 BOATS ----					
34 10	EAGLE	FB	TRWL	FBG DS IB	128D FORD	12	22000	3 9	57400	63100
39 11	EAGLE	FB	TRWL	FBG DS IB	T128D FORD	14		4	71500	78600
47 10	EAGLE	FB	TRWL	FBG DS IB T	D CUM	15 11	42615	4 8	**	**
					---- 1970 BOATS ----					
39 11	EAGLE	FB	TRWL	FBG DS IB	T128D FORD	14		4	69100	76000

EAST/WEST CUSTOM BOATS INC
COAST GUARD MFG ID- EWV

Call 1-800-327-6929 for BUC Personalized Evaluation Service
Or, for 1983 to 1984 boats, sign onto www.BUCValuPro.com

EASTERLY YACHTS
HALTER MARINE SERVICES INC
PEARLINGTON MS   COAST GUARD MFG ID- EAS   See inside cover to adjust price for area

LOA FT IN	NAME AND/ OR MODEL	TOP/ RIG	BOAT TYPE	HULL MTL TP	ENGINE TP # HP MFG	BEAM FT IN	WGT LBS	DRAFT FT IN	RETAIL LOW	RETAIL HIGH
					---- 1979 BOATS ----					
38	EASTERLY 38	SLP	SA/CR FBG KL IB	40D WEST	10 10	13500	5 3	33700	37400
					---- 1978 BOATS ----					
26 4	LUDERS 16	SLP	SA/OD FBG IB	D	5 9	2800	4	5650	6500
38	EASTERLY 38	SLP	SA/CR FBG KL IB	23D VLVO	10 10	13500	5 3	32000	35600
38	EASTERLY 38	KTH	SA/CR FBG KL IB	23D VLVO	10 10	13500	5 3	33400	37100
					---- 1977 BOATS ----					
26 4	LUDERS 16	SLP	SA/OD FBG IB	D	5 9	2800	4	5400	6250
30	EASTERLY	SLP	SA/CR FBG KL IB	30D	9 1	7000	4	14700	16800
33	EASTERLY	SLP	SA/CR FBG KL IB	12D	10 6	10500	5 3	23000	25600
38	EASTERLY	SLP	SA/CR FBG KL IB	30D	10 10	12000	5 3	28000	31100
					---- 1976 BOATS ----					
26 4	LUDERS 16	SLP	SA/OD FBG IB	D	5 9	2800	4	5200	6000
30	EASTERLY	SLP	SA/CR FBG KL IB	30D	9 1	7000	4	14200	16100
36	EASTERLY 36	SLP	SA/CR FBG KL IB	30D	10 10	12000	5 3	25400	28200
36	EASTERLY 36 AFT CBN	SLP	SA/CR FBG KL IB	25D	10 10	14000	5 3	28900	32100
					---- 1975 BOATS ----					
26 4	LUDERS 16	SLP	SA/OD FBG IB	D	5 9	2800	4	5050	5800
30	EASTERLY	SLP	SAIL FBG KL IB	30 UNIV	9 1	7000	4	13600	15500
36	EASTERLY	SLP	SAIL FBG KL IB	30 UNIV	10 10	12000	5 3	24800	27500
36	EASTERLY AFT CBN	SLP	SAIL FBG KL IB	25D WEST	10 10	14000	5 3	27900	31000
					---- 1974 BOATS ----					
26 4	LUDERS 16	SLP	SAIL FBG OB		5 9	2800	4	4600	5300
30	EASTERLY 30	SLP	SAIL FBG KL IB	30 UNIV	9 1	7000	4	13600	15400
36	EASTERLY 36	SLP	SAIL FBG KL IB	30 UNIV	10 10	12000	5 3	24000	26600
36	EASTERLY 36	SLP	SAIL FBG KL IB	25D WEST	10 10	12000	5 3	22800	25300
36	EASTERLY 36 AFT CBN	SLP	SAIL FBG KL IB	25D WEST	10 10	12000	5 3	25200	28000
					---- 1973 BOATS ----					
26 4	LUDERS 16	SLP	SA/OD FBG OB		5 9	2800	4	4500	5150
30	EASTERLY 30	SLP	SAIL FBG KL IB	30D	9 1	7200	4	13300	15200
36	EASTERLY 36	SLP	SAIL FBG KL IB	30D	10 10	12000	5 3	23600	26200
					---- 1972 BOATS ----					
30	EASTERLY 30	SLP	SA/CR FBG KL IB	30D	9 1	7200	4	13000	14800
36	EASTERLY 36	SLP	SA/CR FBG KL IB	30D	10 10	12000	5 3	22900	25400
					---- 1971 BOATS ----					
30 1	EASTERLY 30	SLP	SA/CR FBG OB		9 1			11200	12700
30 1	EASTERLY 30	SLP	SA/CR FBG IB	30 UNIV	9 1	7200	4	12600	14300
36	EASTERLY 36	SLP	SA/CR FBG IB	30 UNIV	10 10	11760	5 3	22100	24600
					---- 1970 BOATS ----					
30 1	EASTERLY 30	SLP	SA/CR FBG KL IB	30D	9 1	7200	4	12600	14300
					---- 1969 BOATS ----					
30 1	EASTERLY 30	SLP	SA/CR FBG KL IB	30D	9 1	7200	4	12300	14000

EASTERN SEA SKIFFS INC

Call 1-800-327-6929 for BUC Personalized Evaluation Service
Or, for 1958 to 1967 boats, sign onto www.BUCValuPro.com

EASTPORT YACHT MFG

Call 1-800-327-6929 for BUC Personalized Evaluation Service
Or, for 1979 to 1982 boats, sign onto www.BUCValuPro.com

EASTWOOD MARINE LTD

Call 1-800-327-6929 for BUC Personalized Evaluation Service
Or, for 1977 to 1978 boats, sign onto www.BUCValuPro.com

EBBTIDE CORP
WHITE BLUFF TN 37187   COAST GUARD MFG ID- ETC See inside cover to adjust price for area

For more recent years, see the BUC Used Boat Price Guide, Volume 1 or Volume 2

LOA FT IN	NAME AND/ OR MODEL	TOP/ RIG	BOAT TYPE	HULL MTL TP	ENGINE TP # HP MFG	BEAM FT IN	WGT LBS	DRAFT FT IN	RETAIL LOW	RETAIL HIGH
					---- 1982 BOATS ----					
16 5	MONTEGO		RNBT	FBG DV IO	140	6 10			2250	2600
16 5	MONTEGO		RNBT	FBG SV OB		6 10	1000		1700	2050
16 8	DYAN-TRAK 166SS		RNBT	FBG SV OB		7	1100		1900	2250
16 8	DYNA-TRAK 166		BASS	FBG SV OB		7	1050		1800	2150
16 9	CAPTIVA 17		RNBT	FBG TR IO		7 1	1250		2150	2500
17 9	CAPTIVA 17		RNBT	FBG TR IO	140	7 1			2600	3050
17 5	RIVIERA 17		RNBT	FBG TR IO	170	7 2			2750	3200
17 11	DYNA-TRAK 176		BASS	FBG SV OB		7 2	1075		1900	2250
17 11	DYNA-TRAK 176SS		RNBT	FBG SV OB		7 2	1100		1950	2350
17 11	DYNA-TRAK 178		RNBT	FBG SV OB		7 2	1100		1950	2300
17 11	DYNA-TRAK 180		SKI	FBG SV OB		7 2	1100		1950	2300
18 4	CATALINA 18		RNBT	FBG SV OB		7 8	1530		2550	3000
18 4	CATALINA 18		RNBT	FBG DV IO	198	7 8			3050	3500
					---- 1981 BOATS ----					
16 8	DYNA-TRAK 166		BASS	FBG SV OB		7	1050		1750	2100
16 8	DYNA-TRAK 166SS		FSH	FBG SV OB		7	1100		1850	2150
16 9	CAPTIVA 16		RNBT	FBG TR IO	140	7	1250		2250	2950
16 9	CAPTIVA 17		RNBT	FBG TR OB		7 1			2050	2450
17 5	RIVIERA 17		RNBT	FBG TR IO	198	7 1			2700	3150
17 11	DYNA-TRAK 176		BASS	FBG SV OB		7 2	1075		1850	2200
18 4	CATALINA 18		RNBT	FBG SV OB		7 8	1530		2500	2900
18 4	CATALINA 18		RNBT	FBG DV IO	198	7 8			3000	3450
					---- 1980 BOATS ----					
16 8	DYNA-TRAK 166	OP	BASS	FBG SV OB		7	1050		1700	2050
16 8	DYNA-TRAK 166SS	OP	BASS	FBG SV OB		7	1100		1800	2150
16 9	CAPTIVA	ST	RNBT	FBG TR OB		7 1	1250		2000	2400
16 9	CAPTIVA	ST	RNBT	FBG TR IO	120-170	7 1	2050		2400	2850
17 5	RIVIERA	ST	RNBT	FBG TR IO	170-190	7 2	2400		2750	3250
17 5	RIVIERA 17	ST	RNBT	FBG TR IO	165	7 2			2650	3100
17 11	DYNA-TRAK 176	OP	BASS	FBG SV OB		7 2	1075		1850	2200
17 11	DYNA-TRAK 176SS	OP	BASS	FBG SV OB		7 2	1100		1850	2200
17 11	DYNA-TRAK 180	OP	RNBT	FBG SV OB		7 2	1075		1850	2200
18 4	CATALINA	ST	RNBT	FBG TR IO	170-260	7 8	2550		3100	3900
18 4	CATALINA	ST	RNBT	FBG SV OB		7 8	1550		2500	2900
					---- 1979 BOATS ----					
16 8	DYNA-TRAK 166	OP	BASS	FBG SV OB		7	1050		1700	2000
16 8	DYNA-TRAK 166SS	OP	FSH	FBG SV OB		7	1100		1750	2100
16 9	CAPTIVA	ST	RNBT	FBG TR OB		7 1	1250		2000	2350
16 9	CAPTIVA	ST	RNBT	FBG TR IO	140-170	7 1	2050		2450	2850
17 5	RIVIERA	ST	RNBT	FBG TR IO	165-198	7 2	2400		2750	3250
17 11	DYNA-TRAK 176	OP	BASS	FBG SV OB		7 2	1075		1800	2150
18 4	CATALINA	ST	RNBT	FBG DV IO	185-198	7 8	2550		3100	3650
					---- 1978 BOATS ----					
16 9	CAPTIVA	ST	RNBT	FBG TR IO	130-140	7 1	1250		1950	2300
16 9	CAPTIVA	ST	RNBT	FBG TR IO	165-198	7 2	2400		2550	3000
17 5	RIVIERA	ST	RNBT	FBG TR		7 2	2400		2750	3250
17 11	DYNA-TRAK 176	ST	RNBT	FBG SV OB		7 2	1075		1750	2100
					---- 1977 BOATS ----					
16 9	CAPTIVA	ST	RNBT	FBG TR IO		7 1			1700	2050
16 9	CAPTIVA	ST	RNBT	FBG TR IO	140 MRCR	6 10	2000		2400	2800
17 5	RIVIERA	ST	RNBT	FBG TR IO	165-175	7 2	2400		2800	3250
17 6	SUPER-BASS-BANDIT C	OP	BASS	FBG TR OB		6 6	1025		1750	2100

EBBTIDE CORP -CONTINUED See inside cover to adjust price for area

LOA FT	IN	NAME AND/ OR MODEL	TOP/ RIG	BOAT TYPE	HULL MTL	HULL TP	ENGINE TP	# HP	MFG	BEAM FT	BEAM IN	WGT LBS	DRAFT FT	DRAFT IN	RETAIL LOW	RETAIL HIGH
		1976 BOATS														
17	5	RIVIERA	ST	RNBT	FBG	TR	IO	165		7	2	2400			2900	3350
		1975 BOATS														
17	5	RIVIERA	OP	RNBT	FBG	TR	IO	165	MRCR	7	2	2400	2	3	3000	3450

EBKO INDUSTRIES INC

HASTINGS NE 68902 COAST GUARD MFG ID- EBK See inside cover to adjust price for area

For more recent years, see the BUC Used Boat Price Guide, Volume 1 or Volume 2

LOA FT	IN	NAME AND/ OR MODEL	TOP/ RIG	BOAT TYPE	HULL MTL	HULL TP	ENGINE TP	# HP	MFG	BEAM FT	BEAM IN	WGT LBS	DRAFT FT	DRAFT IN	RETAIL LOW	RETAIL HIGH
		1983 BOATS														
16	2	CIMMARON 1621	ST	RNBT	FBG	SV	OB			6	8	910			1850	2200
16	2	CIMMARON 1621	ST	RNBT	FBG	SV	IO	120-170		6	8	1800			2350	2700
16	3	CIMMARON 1631	ST	RNBT	FBG	DV	OB			6	9	910			1850	2200
16	3	CIMMARON 1631	ST	RNBT	FBG	DV	IO	120-170		6	9	1850			2350	2950
16	3	CIMMARON 1631	ST	RNBT	FBG	SV	OB			6	9	910			1850	2200
16	3	CIMMARON 1631	ST	RNBT	FBG	SV	IO	120-170		6	9	1800			2350	2750
16	3	EBKO V163	ST	RNBT	FBG	SV	OB			6	9	915			1850	2200
16	3	SCORPION	ST	RNBT	FBG	SV	IO	120-170		6	9	1850			2350	2800
17		CIMMARON 1721	ST	RNBT	FBG	SV	OB			6	8	1020			2100	2500
17		CIMMARON 1721	ST	RNBT	FBG	SV	IO	120-170		6	8	1900			2500	2950
17	3	EBKO V173	ST	RNBT	FBG	SV	OB			7	7	1170			2400	2800
17	3	SEVILLE	ST	RNBT	FBG	DV	IO	200-230		7	7	2010			3000	3550
17	3	SEVILLE	ST	RNBT	FBG	SV	IO	170-230		7	7	2010			2850	3400
17	3	SEVILLE SS	ST	RNBT	FBG	DV	IO	170-198		7	7	2010			2850	3450
17	3	SEVILLE SS	ST	RNBT	FBG	DV	IO	200		7	7	2010			2850	3550
17	3	SEVILLE SS	ST	RNBT	FBG	DV	IO	225-230		7	7	2010			3150	3650
18	3	BIARRITZ	ST	RNBT	FBG	DV	IO	170-200		7	7	2430			3250	4000
18	3	BIARRITZ	ST	RNBT	FBG	DV	IO	225-260		7	7	2430			3500	4250
18	3	BIARRITZ SS	ST	RNBT	FBG	DV	IO	170-200		7	7	2430			3300	4100
18	3	BIARRITZ SS	ST	RNBT	FBG	DV	IO	225-260		7	7	2430			3600	4350
18	3	BIARRITZ SS	ST	RNBT	FBG	SV	IO	170		7	7	2210			3150	3650
18	3	BIARRITZ SS	ST	RNBT	FBG	SV	IO	260		7	7	2210			3350	3900
18	6	COBRA	ST	RNBT	FBG	DV	IO	170-230		8		2750			3650	4400
18	6	COBRA	ST	RNBT	FBG	DV	IO	260		8		2750			3900	4600
18	6	COBRA SS	ST	RNBT	FBG	DV	IO	198-230		8		2600			3650	4500
18	6	COBRA SS	ST	RNBT	FBG	DV	IO	260		8		2600			3850	4700
18	7	CIMMARON 1821	ST	RNBT	FBG	DV	IO	120-170				1900			2900	3550
18	7	CIMMARON V1821	ST	RNBT	FBG	SV	IO	120-170		7	7	2000			3050	3550
20	3	LE-BARON	ST	RNBT	FBG	DV	IO	198-260		8		3200			4600	5500
		1982 BOATS														
16	2	CIMMARON 1621	ST	RNBT	FBG	SV	OB					910			1800	2150
16	2	CIMMARON 1621	ST	RNBT	FBG	SV	IO	120-170				1800			2350	2700
16	2	FIREBIRD	ST	RNBT	FBG	SV	IO	120-170		6	8	1800			2300	2750
16	2	STILETTO	OP	RNBT	FBG	TR	IO	170-185		6	8	1800			2300	2700
16	2	V162	ST	RNBT	FBG	SV	OB			6	8	910			1800	2150
16	11	CAPRI	ST	RNBT	FBG	TR	IO	140-185		6	8	2050			2500	2950
16	11	ROGUE 1730	ST	RNBT	FBG	TR	OB			6	8	1150			2300	2700
17		CIMMARON 1721	ST	RNBT	FBG	SV	OB								2050	2450
17		CIMMARON 1721	ST	RNBT	FBG	SV	IO	120-185				1920			2600	3050
17	3	SEVILLE	ST	RNBT	FBG	DV	IO	170-200		7	7	2010			2750	3250
17	3	V173	ST	RNBT	FBG	DV	OB			6	8	1170			2350	2750
18	6	COBRA	ST	RNBT	FBG	DV	IO	170-260		8		2750			3600	4450
20	3	LE-BARON	ST	RNBT	FBG	DV	IO	228-260		8		3200			4600	5400
		1981 BOATS														
16	2	FIREBIRD	ST	RNBT	FBG	SV	IO	120-170		6	8	1925			2350	2700
16	2	STILETTO	OP	RNBT	FBG	TR	IO	170-185		6	8	1800			2250	2650
16	2	V162	ST	RNBT	FBG	SV	OB			6	8	1020			1950	2350
16	11	CAPRI	ST	RNBT	FBG	TR	IO	140-185		6	8	2050			2500	2950
16	11	ROGUE 1730	ST	RNBT	FBG	TR	OB			6	8	1150			2300	2650
17	3	SEVILLE	ST	RNBT	FBG	DV	IO	170		7	7	2010			2700	3150
17	3	V173	ST	RNBT	FBG	DV	OB			6	8	1170			2350	2700
17	7	SEVILLE	ST	RNBT	FBG	DV	IO	185-200		7	7	2010			2800	3250
18	6	COBRA	ST	RNBT	FBG	DV	IO	170-260		8		2750			3500	4350
18	6	COBRA BOW RIDER	ST	RNBT	FBG	DV	IO	170-260		8		2750			3500	4350
20	3	LE-BARON	ST	RNBT	FBG	DV	IO	228-260		8		2750			4050	4900
20	3	LE-BARON BOW RIDER	ST	RNBT	FBG	DV	IO	228-260		8		2750			4050	4900
		1980 BOATS														
16	2	FIREBIRD	ST	RNBT	FBG	SV	IO	120-140		6	8	1925			2300	2700
16	2	FIREBIRD	ST	RNBT	FBG	TR	IO	120	MRCR	6	8	1925			2300	2700
16	2	SSV16	ST	RNBT	FBG	SV	OB			6	8	1020			1950	2300
16	2	STILETTO	OP	RNBT	FBG	SV	IO	120-185		6	8				2200	2600
16	2	STILETTO	OP	RNBT	FBG	TR	IO	120-185		6	8	1800			2250	2650
16	11	CAPRI	ST	RNBT	FBG	TR	IO	140-185		6	8	2050			2450	2900
16	11	ROGUE 1730	ST	RNBT	FBG	TR	OB			6	8	1150			2250	2600
18	1	EXECUTIVE	ST	RNBT	FBG	TR	IO	198	MRCR	7	1	2650			3150	3650
18	6	COBRA	ST	RNBT	FBG	DV	IO	165-260		8		2750			3450	4300
18	6	COBRA BOW RIDER	ST	RNBT	FBG	DV	IO	165-260		8		2750			3450	4300
20	3	LE-BARON	ST	RNBT	FBG	DV	IO	185-260		8		3200			4350	5250
20	3	LE-BARON BOW RIDER	ST	RNBT	FBG	DV	IO	185-260		8		3200			4350	5050
		1979 BOATS														
16	2	MARQUIS 1650	ST	RNBT	FBG	DV	IO	140	MRCR	6	6	1520			2000	2350
16	11	CAPRI 1750	ST	RNBT	FBG	TR	IO	140-170		6	8	2050			2450	2900
16	11	ROGUE 1730	ST	RNBT	FBG	TR	OB			6	8	1150			2250	2600
18	1	EXECUTIVE 1850	ST	RNBT	FBG	TR	IO	165-230		7	1	2600			3050	3700
18	1	T-181	ST	RNBT	FBG	TR	IO	165-230		7	1	2650			3100	3750
18	6	COBRA V-186	ST	RNBT	FBG	DV	IO	165-260		8		2750			3450	4300
18	6	COBRA V-186 B/R	ST	RNBT	FBG	DV	IO	165-260		8		2750			3450	4300
20	3	LE-BARON	ST	RNBT	FBG	DV	IO	185-260		8		3200			4250	5300
20	3	LE-BARON B/R	ST	RNBT	FBG	DV	IO	185-260		8		3200			4250	5300
		1978 BOATS														
16	2	MARQUIS	ST	RNBT	FBG	DV	IO	140	MRCR	6	6	1520			2000	2350
17		CAPRI	ST	RNBT	FBG	TR	IO	140-185		6	9	2050			2500	2950
17		ROGUE 1730	ST	RNBT	FBG	TR	OB			6	9	1090			2050	2450
18	3	EXECUTIVE	ST	RNBT	FBG	TR	IO	165-260		7	2	2600			3150	3900
20	3	LE-BARON B/R	ST	RNBT	FBG	DV	IO	198-260		8		3050			4200	5150
20	3	LE-BARON CLASSIC	ST	RNBT	FBG	DV	IO	198-260		8		3050			4200	5150
		1977 BOATS														
16	2	MARQUIS 1650	ST	RNBT	FBG	DV	IO	140	MRCR	6	6	1520			2000	2400
16	8	SURFMASTER 1700	ST	RNBT	FBG	TR	OB			6	6	970			1850	2200
16	11	CAPRI 1750	ST	RNBT	FBG	SV	IO	140-175		6	9	2050			2500	2950
18	3	EXECUTIVE 1850	ST	RNBT	FBG	TR	IO	165-235		7	2	2600			3150	3850
20	3	LE-BARON	ST	RNBT	FBG	DV	IO	188-235		8		3050			4250	5050
		1976 BOATS														
16	2	MARQUIS 1650	ST	RNBT	FBG	DV	IO	140	MRCR	6	6	1520			2050	2450
16	8	SURFMASTER 1700	ST	RNBT	FBG	TR	OB			6	6	970			1800	2150
16	8	SURFMASTER 1700 STD	OP	RNBT	FBG	TR	OB			6	6	940			1750	2100
18	3	EXECUTIVE 1850	ST	RNBT	FBG	TR	IO	165-235		7	2	2600			3250	3900
		1975 BOATS														
16	2	MARQUIS 1650	ST	RNBT	FBG	DV	IO	140	MRCR	6	6	1520			2200	2550
16	8	SURFMASTER 1700	ST	W/T	FBG	TR	OB			6	6	970			1800	2150
18	3	EXECUTIVE 1850	ST	W/T	FBG	TR	IO	165-188		7	2	2600			3350	3950
		1974 BOATS														
16	2	ENDURO		RNBT	FBG	SV	IO	120-140		6	5	800			1700	2050
16	2	SURFMASTER W/T		RNBT	FBG	SV	OB			6	5	950			1750	2050
16	2	SURFMASTER W/T		RNBT	FBG	SV	IO	120-140		6	5	950			1800	2150
16	2	SURFMASTER W/T DLX		RNBT	FBG	SV	OB			6	5	975			1800	2100
16	2	SURFMASTER W/T DLX		RNBT	FBG	SV	IO	120-140		6	5	975			1800	2150
17	9	TWISTER		RNBT	FBG	SV	JT	390		6	7				2800	3250
18	1	SURFMASTER W/T		RNBT	FBG	SV	IO	165-188		7	2				2950	3500
18	1	SURFMASTER W/T		RNBT	FBG	SV	JT	245		7	2				2950	3450

EDEL CANADA

REXDALE ONTARIO CANADA See inside cover to adjust price for area

LOA FT	IN	NAME AND/ OR MODEL	TOP/ RIG	BOAT TYPE	HULL MTL	HULL TP	ENGINE TP	# HP	MFG	BEAM FT	BEAM IN	WGT LBS	DRAFT FT	DRAFT IN	RETAIL LOW	RETAIL HIGH
		1982 BOATS														
17	9	EDEL 540	SLP	SA/RC	FBG	KL	IB		D	8		1711	2	4	4950	5700
21	10	EDEL 665	SLP	SA/RC	FBG	KL	IB		D	8	3	3484	3	3	6600	7600
28	5	EDEL 820	SLP	SA/CR	FBG	KL	IB		D	9	10	6340	4	5	14300	16300
		1981 BOATS														
17	9	EDEL-HI-TECH 540	SLP	SA/RC	FBG	KL	IB		D	8		1213	2	4	4200	4850
21	10	EDEL-HI-TECH 665	SLP	SA/RC	FBG	KL	IB		D	8	3	2403	3	3	4950	5700
27	10	EDEL-HI-TECH 820	SLP	SA/CR	FBG	KL	IB		D	9	8	7050	4	4	14900	16900
		1980 BOATS														
17	8	EDEL 540	SLP	SA/RC	FBG	KL	IB		D	8		1213	2	3	4050	4700
21	10	EDEL 665	SLP	SA/RC	FBG	KL	IB		D	8		2403	3	3	4750	5450

EDEY & DUFF LTD
MATTAPOISETT MA 02739   COAST GUARD MFG ID- EAD See inside cover to adjust price for area

For more recent years, see the BUC Used Boat Price Guide, Volume 1 or Volume 2

LOA FT IN	NAME AND/ OR MODEL	TOP/ RIG	BOAT TYPE	-HULL- MTL TP	----ENGINE--- TP # HP MFG	BEAM FT IN	WGT LBS	DRAFT FT IN	RETAIL LOW	RETAIL HIGH
--- 1982 BOATS ---
21 6	DOVEKIE	CAT	SA/CR	F/S LB IB	D	6 8	600	4	4850	5600
23 4	STONE-HORSE	CUT	SA/CR	F/S KL IB	7D WEST	7 1	4500	3 6	12500	14200
40	BIRD-OF-DAWNING	YWL	SA/CR	F/S LB IB	D	9 10	16300	2	66300	72800
--- 1981 BOATS ---
21 6	DOVEKIE	CAT	SA/CR	F/S LB IB	D	6 8	600	4	4600	5300
23 4	STONE-HORSE	CUT	SA/CR	F/S KL IB	7D	7 1	4500	3 6	11700	13200
40	BIRD-OF-DAWNING	YWL	SA/CR	F/S LB IB	D	9 10	16300	2	62300	68500
--- 1980 BOATS ---
21 6	DOVEKIE	CAT	SA/CR	F/S LB IB	D	5 6	500	3	4150	4850
23 4	STONE-HORSE	CUT	SA/CR	F/S KL IB	7D WEST	7 1	4500	3 6	11200	12800
--- 1979 BOATS ---
21 5	DOVEKIE	CAT	SA/CR	F/S LB ID	D	6 8	600	4	4200	4850
23 4	STONE-HORSE	SLP	SA/CR	F/S KL OB		7 1	4500	3 6	9850	11200
23 4	STONE-HORSE	SLP	SA/CR	F/S KL IB	7D WEST	7 1	4500	3 6	10800	12300
--- 1978 BOATS ---
23 4	STONE-HORSE	SLP	SA/CR	F/S KL OB		7 1	4500	3 6	9500	10800
23 4	STONE-HORSE	SLP	SA/CR	F/S KL IB	7D WEST	7 1	4500	3 6	10400	11800
23 4	STONE-HORSE	CUT	SA/CR	F/S KL OB		7 1	4500	3 6	9500	10800
23 4	STONE-HORSE	CUT	SA/CR	F/S KL IB	7D WEST	7 1	4500	3 6	10400	11800
--- 1977 BOATS ---
23 4	STONE-HORSE	SLP	SAIL	F/S KL IB	5D WEST	7 1	4490	3 7	9950	11300
--- 1976 BOATS ---
23 4	STONE-HORSE	SLP	SAIL	F/S KL OB		7 1	4490	3 7	8900	10100
23 4	STONE-HORSE	SLP	SAIL	F/S KL IB	5D WEST	7 1	4490	3 7	9650	11000
--- 1975 BOATS ---
23 4	STONE-HORSE	SLP	SAIL	F/S KL OB		7 1	4490	3 7	8550	9800
23 4	STONE-HORSE	SLP	SAIL	F/S KL IB	5D WEST	7 1	4490	3 7	9350	10600
--- 1974 BOATS ---
23 4	STONE-HORSE	SLP	SAIL	F/S KL OB		7 1	4490	3 7	8300	9550
23 4	STONE-HORSE	SLP	SAIL	F/S KL IB	5D WEST	7 1	4490	3 7	9150	10400
--- 1973 BOATS ---
23 4	STONE-HORSE	SLP	SAIL	F/S KL IB	8D WEST	7 1	4490	3 7	9000	10300
--- 1972 BOATS ---
23 4	STONE-HORSE	SLP	SA/CR	FBG KL IB	8D	7 1	4490	3 7	8650	9950
--- 1971 BOATS ---
23 4	STONE-HORSE	SLP	SAIL	FBG KL IB	30D	7 1	4490	3 5	9000	10200
--- 1970 BOATS ---
23 4	STONE-HORSE	SLP	SAIL	FBG KL IB	6D WEST	7 1	4490	3 5	8350	9550

EDMONDS YACHT SALES INC
EDMONDS WA 98020-7214   COAST GUARD MFG ID- EYS See inside cover to adjust price for area

LOA FT IN	NAME AND/ OR MODEL	TOP/ RIG	BOAT TYPE	-HULL- MTL TP	----ENGINE--- TP # HP MFG	BEAM FT IN	WGT LBS	DRAFT FT IN	RETAIL LOW	RETAIL HIGH
--- 1978 BOATS ---
36 9	PERRY DC	FB	TRWL	FBG DS IB	120D LEHM	12 8	18950	3 9	55200	60600
--- 1977 BOATS ---
37	PERRY	FB	TRWL	FBG DS IB	120D FORD	12 8	18950	3 9	53300	58600

EDSON BOAT COMPANY
ANCHOR DIVISION
DIV MARR'S LEISURE PROD COAST GUARD MFG ID- ZAI

Call 1-800-327-6929 for BUC Personalized Evaluation Service
Or, for 1983 to 1989 boats, sign onto www.BUCValuPro.com

EDWARDS BOAT YARD

Call 1-800-327-6929 for BUC Personalized Evaluation Service
Or, for 1961 boats, sign onto www.BUCValuPro.com

EGG HARBOR YACHTS
EGG HARBOR CITY NJ 0821 COAST GUARD MFG ID- EGH See inside cover to adjust price for area

For more recent years, see the BUC Used Boat Price Guide, Volume 1 or Volume 2

LOA FT IN	NAME AND/ OR MODEL	TOP/ RIG	BOAT TYPE	-HULL- MTL TP	----ENGINE--- TP # HP MFG	BEAM FT IN	WGT LBS	DRAFT FT IN	RETAIL LOW	RETAIL HIGH
--- 1983 BOATS ---
25 10	OPEN FISHERMAN	TT	CTRCN	FBG SV IB	350 CRUS	9 10	6400	1 8	18300	20300
33	EXPRESS FISHERMAN	TT	FSH	FBG SV IB	T350 CRUS	13 2	17000	2 5	50900	55900
33	EXPRESS FISHERMAN	TT	FSH	FBG SV IB	IBT235D-T300D	13 2	17500	2 5	66500	76900
33	TOURNAMENT FISHERMAN	FB	SDNSF	FBG SV IB	T350 CRUS	13 2	17000	2 5	50900	55900
33	TOURNAMENT FISHERMAN	FB	SDNSF	FBG SV IB	IBT235D-T300D	13 2	17500	2 5	66400	76800
36	TOURNAMENT FISHERMAN	FB	SDNSF	FBG SV IB	T350 CRUS	13 3	20000	2 9	60200	66200
	IB T270D CUM	69700	66600, IB T300D CAT	72400	79500, IB T300D J&T				71500	78500
40	MOTOR YACHT	FB	MY	FBG SV IB	T350 CRUS	14 1	30000	2 11	101500	111500
	IB T410 J&T	105000	115000, IB T270D CUM	111500	122500, IB T300D CAT				116000	127000
40	TOURNAMENT FISHERMAN	FB	SDNSF	FBG SV IB	T350 CRUS	14	28000	3	95900	105500
40	TOURNAMENT FISHERMAN	FB	SDNSF	FBG SV IB	T410D J&T	14	28900	3	117000	128500
40	TOURNAMENT FISHERMAN	FB	SDNSF	FBG SV IB	T450D J&T	14	28900	3	120500	132000
46 8	TOURNAMENT FISHERMAN	FB	SDNSF	FBG SV IB	T450D J&T	15	42000	4	127000	139500
46 8	TOURNAMENT FISHERMAN	FB	SDNSF	FBG SV IB	T600D J&T	15	42000	4	139500	153500
48 2	GOLDEN EGG	FB	SDNSF	FBG SV IB	T570D J&T	15	44000	4	140000	154000
48 2	GOLDEN EGG	FB	SDNSF	FBG SV IB	T600D J&T	15	44000	4	141500	155500
48 2	GOLDEN EGG	FB	SDNSF	FBG SV IB	T570D J&T	15	44000	4	140000	160500
48 2	GOLDEN-EGG	FB	SDNSF	FBG SV IB	T570D J&T	15	44000	4	140000	154000
48 2	GOLDEN-EGG	FB	SDNSF	FBG SV IB	T600D J&T	15	44000	4	142000	156000
48 2	GOLDEN-EGG	FB	SDNSF	FBG SV IB	T675D J&T	15	44000	4	146500	161000
--- 1982 BOATS ---
33	SEDAN CRUISER	FB	SDN	FBG SV IB	T350 CRUS	13 2	16700	2 5	51600	56700
33	SEDAN CRUISER	FB	SDN	FBG SV IB	IBT235D-T300D	13 2	17200	2 5	68400	79800
33	TOURNAMENT FISHERMAN	FB	SDNSF	FBG SV IB	T350 CRUS	13 2	16700	2 5	48400	53200
33	TOURNAMENT FISHERMAN	FB	SDNSF	FBG SV IB	IBT235D-T300D	13 2	17200	2 5	63100	73100
36	SEDAN CRUISER	FB	SDN	FBG SV IB	T350 CRUS	13 3	17000	2 9	54200	59600
	IB T270D CUM	63100	69300, IB T300D CAT	65900	72400, IB T300D J&T				65000	71500
36	TOURNAMENT FISHERMAN	FB	SDNSF	FBG SV IB	T350 CRUS	13 3	17000	2 9	52600	57800
	IB T270D CUM	60600	66600, IB T300D CAT	63200	69400, IB T300D J&T				62300	68500
40	MOTOR YACHT	FB	MY	FBG SV IB	T350 CRUS	14	24000	2 11	80200	88100
	IB T270D CUM	94000	103500, IB T300D CAT	98100	108000, IB T300D J&T				96400	106000
	IB T410D J&T	103500	113500							
40	SEDAN CRUISER	FB	SDN	FBG SV IB	T350 CRUS	14	20000	2 9	69400	76300
40	SEDAN CRUISER	FB	SDN	FBG SV IB	T310D J&T	14	24000	2 9	91700	101000
40	SEDAN CRUISER	FB	SDN	FBG SV IB	T410D J&T	14	24000	2 9	98200	108000
40	TOURNAMENT FISHERMAN	FB	SDNSF	FBG SV IB	T350 CRUS	14	20000	2 9	69400	76200
40	TOURNAMENT FISHERMAN	FB	SDNSF	FBG SV IB	T310D J&T	14	24000	2 9	91600	100500
40	TOURNAMENT FISHERMAN	FB	SDNSF	FBG SV IB	T410D J&T	14	24000	2 9	98100	108000
43	SEDAN CRUISER	FB	SDN	FBG SV IB	T GM	14 6			**	**
43	TOURNAMENT FISHERMAN	SF		FBG SV IB	T GM	14 6			**	**
46 8	SEDAN CRUISER	FB	SDN	FBG SV IB	T410D J&T	15	38000	4	111000	122000
46 8	SEDAN CRUISER	FB	SDN	FBG SV IB	T460D J&T	15	38000	4	114000	125000
46 8	TOURNAMENT FISHERMAN	FB	SDNSF	FBG SV IB	T410D J&T	15	38000	4	113500	125000
46 8	TOURNAMENT FISHERMAN	FB	SDNSF	FBG SV IB	T460D J&T	15	38000	4	117000	129000
48 2	GOLDEN-EGG	FB	SDNSF	FBG SV IB	T570D J&T	15	42000	4	132500	145500
48 2	GOLDEN-EGG	FB	SDNSF	FBG SV IB	T675D J&T	15	42000	4	138500	152000
48 2	SEDAN CRUISER	FB	SDN	FBG SV IB	T570D J&T	15	42000	4	128500	141500
48 2	SEDAN CRUISER	FB	SDN	FBG SV IB	T675D J&T	15	42000	4	134000	147500
50	MOTOR YACHT	FB	MY	FBG SV IB		17			**	**
--- 1981 BOATS ---
33	SEDAN CRUISER	FB	SDN	FBG SV IB	T270 CRUS	13 2	15000	2 6	46100	50700
33	SEDAN CRUISER	FB	SDN	FBG SV IB	T260D CAT	13 2	15000	2 6	63400	69600
33	SEDAN CRUISER	FB	SDN	FBG SV IB	T270 CRUS	13 2	15000	2 6	42900	47600
36	TOURNAMENT FISHERMAN	FB	SDN	FBG SV IB	270D CUM	13 3	17000	2 9	53000	58300
36	SEDAN CRUISER	FB	SDN	FBG SV IB	T350 CRUS	13 3	17000	2 9	50400	55200
36	SEDAN CRUISER	FB	SDN	FBG SV IB	T350 CRUS	13 3	17000	2 9	50100	55100
36	TOURNAMENT FISHERMAN	FB	SDNSF	FBG SV IB	T GM	13 3	17000	2 9	**	**
40	SEDAN CRUISER	FB	SDN	FBG SV IB	T350 CRUS	14	20000	2 9	66100	72700
40	SEDAN CRUISER	FB	SDN	FBG SV IB	T284D GM	14	20000	2 9	76400	82400
40	SEDAN CRUISER	FB	SDN	FBG SV IB	T325D GM	14	20000	2 9	77100	84700
40	TOURNAMENT FISHERMAN	FB	SDNSF	FBG SV IB	T350 CRUS	14	20000	2 9	66100	72600
40	TOURNAMENT FISHERMAN	FB	SDNSF	FBG SV IB	T325D GM	14	20000	2 9	77000	84600
48 2	GOLDEN-EGG	FB	YTFS	FBG SV IB	T550D GM	15	42000	4	116500	128000
--- 1980 BOATS ---
33	SEDAN CRUISER	FB	SDN	FBG SV IB	T270 CRUS	13 2	15000	2 6	43700	48600
33	SEDAN CRUISER	FB	SDN	FBG SV IB	T185D PERK	13 2	16000	2 6	58800	64700
33	TOURNAMENT FISHERMAN	FB	SDNSF	FBG SV IB	T270 CRUS	13 2	15000	2 6	41100	45400
33	TOURNAMENT FISHERMAN	FB	SDNSF	FBG SV IB	T185D PERK	13 2	16000	2 6	54500	59900
36	SEDAN CRUISER	FB	SDN	FBG SV IB	T350 CRUS	13 3	17000	2 9	49300	54100
36	SEDAN CRUISER	FB	SDN	FBG SV IB	T225D GM	13 3	18000	2 9	56500	62100

LOA FT	IN	NAME AND/ OR MODEL	TOP/ RIG	BOAT TYPE	-HULL- MTL	TP	TP	----ENGINE--- # HP	MFG	BEAM FT	IN	WGT LBS	DRAFT FT	IN	RETAIL LOW	RETAIL HIGH
		1980 BOATS														
36		TOURNAMENT FISHERMAN	FB	SDNSF	FBG	SV	IB	T350	CRUS	13	3	17000	2	9	47800	52600
36		TOURNAMENT FISHERMAN	FB	SDNSF	FBG	SV	IB	T225D	GM	13	3	18000	2	9	54400	59800
40		SEDAN CRUISER	FB	SDN	FBG	SV	IB	T350	CRUS	14		20000	2	9	63100	69300
40		SEDAN CRUISER	FB	SDN	FBG	SV	IB	T310D	GM	14		21000	2	9	75300	82700
40		SEDAN CRUISER	FB	SDN	FBG	SV	IB	T410D	GM	14		21000	2	9	81000	89000
40		TOURNAMENT FISHERMAN	FB	SDNSF	FBG	SV	IB	T350	CRUS	14		20000	2	9	63000	69300
40		TOURNAMENT FISHERMAN	FB	SDNSF	FBG	SV	IB	T310D	GM	14		21000	2	9	75200	82600
40		TOURNAMENT FISHERMAN	FB	SDNSF	FBG	SV	IB	T410D	GM	14		21000	2	9	80900	88900
46	8	TOURNAMENT FISHERMAN	FB	YTFS	FBG	SV	IB	T410D	GM	15		38000	4		99300	109000
46	8	TOURNAMENT FISHERMAN	FB	YTFS	FBG	SV	IB	T425D	GM	15		38000	4		100500	110500
48	2	GOLDEN-EGG	FB	YTFS	FBG	SV	IB	T510D	GM	15		42000	4	4	108500	119500
		1979 BOATS														
33		SEDAN CRUISER	FB	SDN	FBG	SV	IB	T270-T350		13	2		2	6	35200	41400
33		SEDAN CRUISER	FB	SDN	FBG	SV	IB	T185D	PERK	13	2		2	6	49100	53900
33		TOURNAMENT FISHERMAN	FB	SDNSF	FBG	SV	IB	T270-T350		13	2		2	6	36400	42200
33		TOURNAMENT FISHERMAN	FB	SDNSF	FBG	SV	IB	T185D	PERK	13	2		2	6	47700	52500
36		SEDAN CRUISER	FB	SDN	FBG	SV	IB	T350	CRUS	13	3	17000	2	9	47300	52000
36		SEDAN CRUISER	FB	SDN	FBG	SV	IB	T216D	GM	13	3	17000	2	9	51900	57100
36		TOURNAMENT FISHERMAN	FB	SDNSF	FBG	SV	IB	T350	CRUS	13	3	17000	2	9	45900	50500
36		TOURNAMENT FISHERMAN	FB	SDNSF	FBG	SV	IB	T216D	GM	13	3	17000	2	9	50000	54900
40		SEDAN CRUISER	FB	SDN	FBG	SV	IB	T350	CRUS	14		20000	2	9	60300	66200
40		SEDAN CRUISER	FB	SDN	FBG	SV	IB	T265D	GM	14		20000	2	9	67600	74300
40		SEDAN CRUISER	FB	SDN	FBG	SV	IB	T325D	GM	14		20000	2	9	70200	77200
40		TOURNAMENT FISHERMAN	FB	SDNSF	FBG	SV	IB	T350	CRUS	14		20000	2	9	60200	66200
40		TOURNAMENT FISHERMAN	FB	SDNSF	FBG	SV	IB	T265D	GM	14		20000	2	9	67500	74200
40		TOURNAMENT FISHERMAN	FB	SDNSF	FBG	SV	IB	T325D	GM	14		20000	2	9	70100	77100
46	8	TOURNAMENT FISHERMAN	FB	YTFS	FBG	SV	IB	T325D	GM	15		38000	4		89600	98400
46	8	TOURNAMENT FISHERMAN	FB	YTFS	FBG	SV	IB	T435D	GM	15		38000	4		96600	106000
48	2	GOLDEN-EGG	FB	MY	FBG	SV	IB	T510D	GM	15		42000	4	4	113000	124000
		1978 BOATS														
33		SEDAN CRUISER	FB	SDN	FBG	SV	IB	T250	CHRY	13	2	15000	2	6	39700	44100
33		SEDAN CRUISER	FB	SDN	FBG	SV	IB	T185D	PERK	13	2	15000	2	6	52800	58000
36		SEDAN CRUISER	FB	SDN	FBG	SV	IB	T330	CHRY	13	3	17000	2	9	44000	48900
36		SEDAN CRUISER	FB	SDN	FBG	SV	IB	T250D	GM	13	3	17000	2	9	50900	55900
36		TOURNAMENT FISHERMAN	FB	SDNSF	FBG	SV	IB	T330	CHRY	13	3	17000	2	9	42700	47500
36		TOURNAMENT FISHERMAN	FB	SDNSF	FBG	SV	IB	T250D	GM	13	3	17000	2	9	48800	53600
40		SEDAN CRUISER	FB	SDN	FBG	SV	IB	T330	CHRY	14		20000	2	9	56500	62100
40		SEDAN CRUISER	FB	SDN	FBG	SV	IB	T284D	GM	14		20000	2	9	65400	71800
40		SEDAN CRUISER	FB	SDN	FBG	SV	IB	T335D	GM	14		20000	2	9	67600	74300
40		TOURNAMENT FISHERMAN	FB	SDNSF	FBG	SV	IB	T330	CHRY	14		20000	2	9	56500	62100
40		TOURNAMENT FISHERMAN	FB	SDNSF	FBG	SV	IB	T284D	GM	14		20000	2	9	65300	71700
40		TOURNAMENT FISHERMAN	FB	SDNSF	FBG	SV	IB	T335D	GM	14		20000	2	9	67500	74200
46	8	TOURNAMENT FISHERMAN	FB	YTFS	FBG	SV	IB	T335D	GM	15		38000	3	8	86200	94700
46	8	TOURNAMENT FISHERMAN	FB	YTFS	FBG	SV	IB	T350D	GM	15		38000	3	8	87000	95600
48	3	GOLDEN-EGG	FB	MY	FBG	SV	IB	T550D	GM	15	4	42000	3	8	110500	121500
48	3	TOURNAMENT FISHERMAN	FB	YTFS	FBG	SV	IB	T335D	GM	15	4	42000	3	8	90900	99900
48	3	TOURNAMENT FISHERMAN	FB	YTFS	FBG	SV	IB	T425D	GM	15	4	42000	3	8	95600	105000
		1977 BOATS														
30	7	CONVERTIBLE SEDAN	HT	SDN	FBG	SV	IB	T220-T250		11	6	11000	2	9	28800	32700
30	7	CONVERTIBLE SEDAN	FB	SDN	FBG	SV	IB	T220-T250		11	6	11000	2	9	28800	32700
30	7	SEDAN FISHERMAN	FB	SDNSF	FBG	SV	IB	T220-T250		11	6	11000	2	9	26500	29900
33		SEDAN FISHERMAN	FB	SDNSF	FBG	SV	IB	T225-T280		13	2	13000	2	6	33900	38800
33		SEDAN FISHERMAN	FB	SDNSF	FBG	SV	IB	T185D-T210D		13	2	13000	2	6	42900	48700
36		SEDAN FISHERMAN	FB	SDNSF	FBG	SV	IB	T280	CHRY	13	3	20000	2	9	44100	49000
		IB T330 CHRY 44800 49700, IB T330 MPC 44900 49900, IB T350 CRUS 46000 50500														
		IB T197D GM 50200 55200, IB T210D CAT 51200 56200, IB T210D CUM 50400 55400														
		IB T250D CUM 51500 56500														
40		SEDAN FISHERMAN	FB	SDNSF	FBG	SV	IB	T330	CHRY	14		20000	2	9	54100	59500
		IB T330 MPC 54300 59700, IB T350 CRUS 55200 60600, IB T197D GM 59700 65600														
		IB T210D CAT 61400 67400, IB T210D CUM 59800 65700, IB T240D GM 61000 67000														
		IB T250D GM 61300 67400, IB T325D GM 64200 70600														
40	7	MOTOR YACHT	HT	MY	FBG	SV	IB	T330	CHRY	14	1	22000	2	11	59000	64900
		IB T330 MPC 59200 65100, IB T350 CRUS 60200 66200, IB T210D CAT 65400 71900														
		IB T240D GM 65400 71900														
40	7	MOTOR YACHT	FB	MY	FBG	SV	IB	T330	CHRY	14	1	22000	2	11	59000	64800
		IB T330 MPC 59200 65000, IB T350 CRUS 60200 66100, IB T210D CAT 65400 71900														
		IB T240D GM 65400 71900														
46	8	SEDAN FISHERMAN	FB	SDNSF	FBG	SV	IB	T240D	GM	15		38000	3	8	82700	90900
		IB T307D CUM 84700 93100, IB T325D GM 85700 94200, IB T340D CUM 86000 94500														
		IB T425D GM 90100 99000														
		1976 BOATS														
30	7	CONVERTIBLE SEDAN	HT	SDN	FBG	SV	IB	T220-T250		11	6	11000	2	9	27700	31400
30	7	CONVERTIBLE SEDAN	FB	SDN	FBG	SV	IB	T220-T250		11	6	11000	2	9	27700	31400
30	7	SEDAN FISHERMAN	FB	SDNSF	FBG	SV	IB	T220-T250		11	6	11000	2	9	25400	28700
33		SEDAN FISHERMAN	FB	SDNSF	FBG	SV	IB	T225-T280		13	2	13000	2	6	32600	37200
33		SEDAN FISHERMAN	FB	SDNSF	FBG	SV	IB	T185D-T210D		13	2	13000	2	6	41400	46900
36		SEDAN FISHERMAN	FB	SDNSF	FBG	SV	IB	T280	CHRY	13	3	20000	2	9	42300	47000
		IB T330 CHRY 42900 47700, IB T330 MPC 43000 47800, IB T350 CRUS 43600 48500														
		IB T210D CAT 49100 53900, IB T210D CUM 48300 53100, IB T216D GM 48600 53400														
		IB T250D GM 49500 54400														
40		SEDAN FISHERMAN	FB	SDNSF	FBG	SV	IB	T330	CHRY	14		20000	2	9	51900	57000
		IB T330 MPC 52100 57200, IB T350 CRUS 52900 58100, IB T210D CAT 58800 64700														
		IB T210D CUM 57300 63000, IB T216D GM 57800 63500, IB T250D GM 58800 64600														
		IB T310D GM 61000 67000, IB T350D GM 62700 68900														
40	7	MOTOR YACHT	HT	MY	FBG	SV	IB	T330	CHRY	14	1	22000	2	11	56600	62200
		IB T330 MPC 56800 62400, IB T350 CRUS 57800 63500, IB T210D CAT 62800 69000														
		IB T310D GM 65800 72300, IB T350D GM 67800 74500														
40	7	MOTOR YACHT	FB	MY	FBG	SV	IB	T330	CHRY	14	1	22000	2	11	56600	62200
		IB T330 MPC 56800 62400, IB T350 CRUS 57700 63400, IB T210D CAT 62700 69000														
		IB T310D GM 65800 72300, IB T350D GM 67800 74500														
46	8	SEDAN FISHERMAN	FB	SDNSF	FBG	SV	IB	T310D	GM	15		38000	3	8	81600	89600
		IB T320D CUM 81700 89700, IB T350D GM 83100 91300, IB T400D CUM 84800 93200														
		IB T435D GM 86800 95400														
		1975 BOATS														
30	7	CONVERTIBLE SEDAN	HT	SDN	FBG	SV	IB	T220-T250		11	6	11000	2	9	26600	30200
30	7	CONVERTIBLE SEDAN	FB	SDN	FBG	SV	IB	T220-T250		11	6	11000	2	9	26600	30200
30	7	SEDAN FISHERMAN	FB	SDNSF	FBG	SV	IB	T220-T250		11	6	11000	2	9	24400	27600
33		SEDAN FISHERMAN	FB	SDNSF	FBG	SV	IB	T225-T280		13	2	13000	2	6	31300	35800
33		SEDAN FISHERMAN	FB	SDNSF	FBG	SV	IB	T185D-T210D		13	2	13000	2	6	40100	45300
36		SEDAN	FB	SDN	FBG	SV	IB	T280	CHRY	13	3	20000	2	4	41500	46100
36		SEDAN	FB	SDN	FBG	SV	IB	T330	CHRY	13	3	20000	2	4	42200	46900
36		SEDAN	FB	SDN	FBG	SV	IB	T350	CRUS	13	3	20000	2	4	42900	47700
40		SEDAN FISHERMAN	FB	SDNSF	FBG	SV	IB	T330	CHRY	14		20000	2	9	49800	54800
		IB T350 CRUS 50800 55800, IB T174D GM 54400 59800, IB T210D CUM 55100 60500														
		IB T216D GM 55500 61000, IB T225D CAT 57000 62600														
40	7	MOTOR YACHT	HT	MY	FBG	SV	IB	T330	CHRY	14	1	22000	2	11	54400	59700
40	7	MOTOR YACHT	HT	MY	FBG	SV	IB	T350	CRUS	14	1	22000	2	11	55500	61000
40	7	MOTOR YACHT	HT	MY	FBG	SV	IB	T174D	GM	14	1	22000	2	11	57900	63600
40	7	MOTOR YACHT	FB	MY	FBG	SV	IB	T330	CHRY	14	1	22000	2	11	54300	59700
40	7	MOTOR YACHT	FB	MY	FBG	SV	IB	T350	CRUS	14	1	22000	2	11	55400	60900
40	7	MOTOR YACHT	FB	MY	FBG	SV	IB	T174D	GM	14	1	22000	2	11	57900	63600
46	8	SEDAN FISHERMAN	FB	SDNSF	FBG	SV	IB	T174D	GM	15		38000	3	8	74200	81600
		IB T320D CUM 78300 86100, IB T320D GM 78600 86400, IB T370D CUM 80200 88100														
		IB T425D GM 82800 91000														
		1974 BOATS														
30	7		FB	SDNSF	FBG	SV	IB	T220-T250		11	6	11000	2	9	23500	26500
33			FB	SDNSF	FBG	SV	IB	T225-T280		13	2	13000	2	6	30100	34400
33			FB	SDNSF	FBG	SV	IB	T185D	PERK	13	2	13000	2	6	39000	43400
38	6		FB	SDNSF	FBG	SV	IB	T330	CHRY	14		20000	2	9	44200	49100
		IB T350 CRUS 45600 50100, IB T210D CUM 49400 54200, IB T216D GM 49800 54700														
		IB T225D CAT 51100 56200, IB T265D GM 51100 56200														
40	7		HT	MY	FBG	SV	IB	T330		14	2	22000	2	10	52500	57700
46	8		FB	SDNSF	FBG	SV	IB	T265D	GM	15		38000	3	8	78400	86200
		IB T320D CUM 84500 92800, IB T325D GM 85100 93500, IB T370D CUM 89900 98700														
		IB T370D GM 89900 98800														
		1973 BOATS														
30	7		FB	SDNSF	FBG	SV	IB	T220-T250		11	6	11000	2	9	22600	25500
33			FB	SDNSF	FBG	SV	IB	T225-T280		13	2	13000	2	6	28900	33000
33			FB	SDNSF	FBG	SV	IB	T185D	PERK	13	2	13000	2	6	38000	42200
38	6		FB	SDN	FBG	SV	IB	225D	CAT	14		20000	2	9	44600	49500
		IB T330 CHRY 42700 47500, IB T350 CRUS 43600 48400, IB T210D CUM 47700 52500														
		IB T216D GM 48100 52900, IB T265D GM 49500 54400														
46	8		FB	SDNSF	FBG	SV	IB	T265D	GM	15		38000	3	8	75500	83000
		IB T350D GM 84500 92900, IB T370D CUM 86500 95100, IB T400D GM 89600 98500														
		1972 BOATS														
33			FB	SDNSF	FBG	SV	IB	T220-T280		13	2	13000	2	6	27700	31800
33			FB	SDNSF	FBG	SV	IB	T160D-T185D		13	2	13000	2	6	36300	41200

 CONTINUED ON NEXT PAGE

```
EGG HARBOR YACHTS           -CONTINUED    See inside cover to adjust price for area
   LOA  NAME AND/                TOP/ BOAT  -HULL- ----ENGINE--- BEAM  WGT  DRAFT RETAIL RETAIL
   FT IN OR MODEL                RIG  TYPE  MTL TP TP # HP MFG  FT IN  LBS  FT IN  LOW    HIGH
------------------------- 1972 BOATS -----------------------------------------------------
38  6                            FB   SDN   FBG SV IB T320  CRUS 14    20000  2  9  41600  46200
    IB T330  CHRY 41200   45800, IB T210D CUM   46300  50900, IB T216D GM   46700  51300
    IB T220D BARR 46800   51400, IB T300D BARR  48800  53700

43  3                            FB   SDN   MHG SV IB T277  SEA  14  4 32000  3  6  68500  75300
    IB T320  CRUS 69800   76700, IB T330  CHRY  69800  76600, IB T220D BARR  73600  80900
    IB T255D GM   74900   82400, IB T283D GM    76000  83600, IB T300D BARR  76700  84300
    IB T300D CUM  76500   84100, IB T350D GM    78800  86600, IB T370D CUM   79400  87300
    IB T400D GM   81000   89000

43  6                            HT   MY    MHG SV IB T277  SEA  14 10 32000  3  6  63100  69400
    IB T320  CRUS 65400   71800, IB T330  CHRY  65500  71900, IB T220D BARR  68700  75500
    IB T255D GM   70800   77800, IB T283D GM    73600  80900, IB T300D BARR  74200  81500
    IB T300D CUM  72900   80100, ID T350D GM    78000  85700, IB T370D CUM   79100  86900
    IB T400D GM   80300   88200

43  6                            FB   MY    MHG SV IB T277  SEA  14 10 32000  3  6  63000  69200
    IB T320  CHRY 64500   70800, IB T320  CRUS  66300  72900, IB T330  CHRY  65900  72400
    IB T220D BARR 69600   76500, IB T255D GM    71600  78700, IB T283D GM    73400  80600
    IB T300D BARR 73900   81200, IB T300D CUM   73700  81000, IB T350D GM    76700  84300
    IB T370D CUM  77800   85400, IB T400D GM    80000  88000

48                               FB   SDN   MHG SV IB T277  SEA  14  8 37000  3  6  83000  91200
    IB T300  CHRY 84000   92300, IB T320  CRUS  84800  93200, IB T220D BARR  87300  95900
    IB T255D GM   89000   97800, IB T283D GM    90200  99200, IB T300D BARR  91000 100000
    IB T300D CUM  91000   99900, IB T350D GM    93000 102000, IB T370D CUM   93800 103000
    IB T400D GM   95000  104500

48  3                            HT   MY    MHG SV IB T277  SEA  14 10 37000  3  6  68300  75000
    IB T320  CRUS 69600   76400, IB T330  CHRY  69600  76500, IB T220D BARR  72800  80000
    IB T255D GM   72900   80100, IB T283D GM    76300  83800, IB T300D BARR  76600  84200
    IB T300D CUM  76600   84100, IB T350D GM    81700  89800, IB T370D CUM   82200  90300
    IB T400D GM   84700   93000

48  3                            FB   MY    MHG SV IB T277  SEA  14 10 37000  3  6  67800  74500
    IB T320  CRUS 70000   76900, IB T330  CHRY  70100  77100, IB T220D BARR  72300  79400
    IB T255D GM   73100   80400, IB T283D GM    75900  83400, IB T300D BARR  77300  84900
    IB T300D CUM  76200   83700, IB T350D GM    79100  86900, IB T370D CUM   80600  88500
    IB T400D CUM  83100   91400

------------------------- 1971 BOATS -----------------------------------------------------
33                               FB   SDNSF FBG    IB T215-T265 13  2 13000  2  6  26600  30300
33                               FB   SDNSF FBG    IB T170D BARR 13  2 13000  2  6  35600  39600
37                               HT   DC    MHG    IB T225  CHRY 13  2 19000  3  3  36200  40200
    IB T260  CRUS 36700   40800, IB T265  PALM  36500  40500, IB T277  SEA   36600  40600
    IB T300  CHRY 36700   40700, IB T320  CRUS  37300  41400, IB T135D GM   40000  44400
    IB T160D PERK 40900   45400, IB T170D BARR  40400  44900, IB T185D CUM   40500  45000
    IB T190D GM   40800   45300, IB T215D GM    41300  45900, IB T220D BARR  41400  46000

37                               FB   DC    MHG    IB T225  CHRY 13  2 19000  3  3  36200  40200
    IB T260  CRUS 36700   40800, IB T265  PALM  36500  40500, IB T277  SEA   36600  40600
    IB T300  CHRY 36700   40700, IB T320  CRUS  37300  41400, IB T135D GM   40000  44400
    IB T160D PERK 40900   45400, IB T170D BARR  40400  44900, IB T185D CUM   40500  45000
    IB T190D GM   40800   45300, IB T215D GM    41300  45900, IB T220D BARR  41400  46000

37                               HT   EXP   MHG    IB T225  CHRY 13  2 17000  3  3  33400  37200
    IB T260  CRUS 34000   37700, IB T265  PALM  33800  37500, IB T277  SEA   33900  37600
    IB T300  CHRY 34000   37700, IB T320  CRUS  34500  38400, IB T135D GM   36900  40900
    IB T160D PERK 37900   42100, IB T170D BARR  37400  41600, IB T185D CUM   37500  41700
    IB T190D GM   37800   42000, IB T215D GM    38300  42600, IB T220D BARR  38400  42700

37                               FB   EXP   MHG    IB T225  CHRY 13  2 17000  3  3  33400  37200
    IB T260  CRUS 34000   37700, IB T265  PALM  33800  37500, IB T277  SEA   33900  37600
    IB T300  CHRY 34000   37700, IB T320  CRUS  34500  38400, IB T135D GM   36900  40900
    IB T160D PERK 37900   42100, IB T170D BARR  37400  41600, IB T185D CUM   37500  41700
    IB T190D GM   37800   42000, IB T215D GM    38300  42600, IB T220D BARR  38400  42700

37                               HT   SDN   MHG    IB T225  CHRY 13  2 17000  3  3  33300  37000
    IB T260  CRUS 33900   37600, IB T265  PALM  33700  37400, IB T277  SEA   33800  37500
    IB T300  CHRY 33900   37700, IB T320  CRUS  34500  38400, IB T135D GM   36900  41000
    IB T160D PERK 38100   42300, IB T170D BARR  37600  41800, IB T185D CUM   37800  42000
    IB T190D GM   38100   42300, IB T215D GM    38700  43000, IB T220D BARR  38700  43000

37                               FB   SDN   MHG    IB T225  CHRY 13  2 17000  3  3  33400  37100
    IB T260  CRUS 33900   37700, IB T265  PALM  33700  37500, IB T277  SEA   33900  37600
    IB T300  CHRY 33900   37700, IB T320  CRUS  34600  38400, IB T135D GM   36900  41000
    IB T160D PERK 38100   42300, IB T170D BARR  37600  41800, IB T185D CUM   37800  42000
    IB T190D GM   38100   42300, IB T215D GM    38700  43000, IB T220D BARR  38700  43000

37                               HT   SDNSF MHG    IB T225  CHRY 13  2 17000  3  3  33400  37100
    IB T260  CRUS 34000   37700, IB T265  PALM  33800  37500, IB T277  SEA   33800  37600
    IB T300  CHRY 33900   37700, IB T320  CRUS  34500  38400, IB T135D GM   36900  40900
    IB T160D PERK 42100   42100, IB T170D BARR  37400  41500, IB T185D CUM   37500  41700
    IB T190D GM   37800   42000, IB T215D GM    38300  42600, IB T220D BARR  38400  42700

37                               FB   SDNSF MHG    IB T225  CHRY 13  2 17000  3  3  33400  37100
    IB T260  CRUS 37700   37700, IB T265  PALM  33800  37500, IB T277  SEA   33800  37600
    IB T300  CHRY 33900   37700, IB T320  CRUS  34500  38400, IB T135D GM   36900  40900
    IB T160D PERK 42100   42100, IB T170D BARR  37400  41500, IB T185D CUM   37500  41700
    IB T190D GM   37800   42000, IB T215D GM    38300  42600, IB T220D BARR  38400  42700

37                               HT   SF    MHG    IB T225  CHRY 13  2 17000  3  3  33400  37200
    IB T260  CRUS 34000   37700, IB T265  PALM  33800  37500, IB T277  SEA   33800  37600
    IB T300  CHRY 33900   37700, IB T320  CRUS  34500  38400, IB T135D GM   36900  40900
    IB T160D PERK 37900   42100, IB T170D BARR  37400  41500, IB T185D CUM   37500  41700
    IB T190D GM   37800   42000, IB T215D GM    38300  42600, IB T220D BARR  38400  42700

37                               FB   SF    MHG    IB T225  CHRY 13  2 17000  3  3  33400  37200
    IB T260  CRUS 33800   37700, IB T265  PALM  33800  37500, IB T277  SEA   33900  37600
    IB T300  CHRY 33900   37700, IB T320  CRUS  34500  38400, IB T135D GM   36900  40900
    IB T160D PERK 37900   42100, IB T170D BARR  37400  41500, IB T185D CUM   37500  41700
    IB T190D GM   37800   42000, IB T215D GM    38300  42600, IB T220D BARR  38400  42700

37  DELUXE                       HT   SDN   MHG    IB T225  CHRY 13  2 17000  3  3  34300  38200
    IB T260  CRUS 34900   38800, IB T265  PALM  34700  38600, IB T277  SEA   34700  38600
    IB T300  CHRY 34900   38800, IB T320  CRUS  35500  39500, IB T135D GM   37800  42000
    IB T160D PERK 39000   43300, IB T170D BARR  38500  42800, IB T185D CUM   38600  42900
    IB T190D GM   38900   43200, IB T215D GM    39400  43800, IB T220D BARR  39400  44000

37  DELUXE                       FB   SDN   MHG    IB T225  CHRY 13  2 17000  3  3  34300  38100
    IB T260  CRUS 34900   38700, IB T265  PALM  34700  38500, IB T277  SEA   34800  38600
    IB T300  CHRY 34900   38800, IB T320  CRUS  35500  39400, IB T135D GM   37800  42000
    IB T160D PERK 39000   43300, IB T170D BARR  38500  42800, IB T185D CUM   38600  42900
    IB T190D GM   38900   43200, IB T215D GM    39400  43800, IB T220D BARR  39600  44000

43  3                            FB   SDNSF MHG    IB T277  SEA  14  4 32000  3  6  61300  67400
    IB T300  CHRY 62700   68800, IB T320  CRUS  64200  70500, IB T220D BARR  66000  72500
    IB T255D GM   68600   75400, IB T283D GM    70700  77700, IB T300D CUM   71800  78900

43  6                            HT   MY    MHG    IB T277  SEA  14 10 32000  3  6  62000  68200
    IB T300  CHRY 61800   67900, IB T320  CRUS  64300  70700, IB T220D BARR  66300  72900
    IB T255D GM   68300   75300, IB T283D GM    70000  76900, IB T300D CUM   72000  79100
    IB T350D GM   75300   82700, IB T370D GM    76300  83900

43  6                            FB   MY    MHG    IB T277  SEA  14 10 32000  3  6  61800  66800
    IB T300  CHRY 61700   67800, IB T320  CRUS  62900  69100, IB T220D BARR  66100  72700
    IB T255D GM   68200   74900, IB T283D GM    70800  77800, IB T300D CUM   71700  78800
    IB T350D GM   74900   82400, IB T370D GM    76100  83600

48                               FB   SF    WD     IB T277  SEA  14  8 37000  3  6  65200  71600
    IB T300  CHRY 65500   72000, IB T320  CRUS  66300  72900, IB T220D BARR  68500  74700
    IB T255D GM   69200   76000, IB T280D GM    70300  77200, IB T300D CUM   71200  78200
    IB T350D GM   75000   82400, IB T370D CUM   76700  84300

48  3                            HT   MY    WD     IB T277  SEA  14 10 37000  3  6  66600  73200
    IB T300  CHRY 67100   73800, IB T320  CRUS  68000  74700, IB T220D BARR  69400  76300
    IB T255D GM   71100   78100, IB T280D GM    72600  79800, IB T300D CUM   73900  81200
    IB T350D GM   77800   85500, IB T370D CUM   79400  87200

48  3                            FB   MY    WD     IB T277  SEA  14 10 37000  3  6  66200  72800
    IB T300  CHRY 66700   73300, IB T320  CRUS  67500  74200, IB T220D BARR  69000  75900
    IB T255D GM   70600   77500, IB T280D GM    72000  79100, IB T300D CUM   73300  80500
    IB T350D GM   77100   84800, IB T370D CUM   78600  86400

------------------------- 1970 BOATS -----------------------------------------------------
37                               HT   DC    MHG    IB T225  CHRY 13  2 19000  3  3  35400  38900
    IB T260  CRUS 35500   39400, IB T265  PALM  35300  39200, IB T277  SEA   35400  39300
    IB T300  CHRY 35500   39400, IB T320  CRUS  36000  40000, IB T135D GM   38600  42900
    IB T160D PERK 39500   43900, IB T170D BARR  39100  43400, IB T185D CUM   39200  43500
    IB T190D GM   39400   43800, IB T215D GM    39900  44400, IB T220D BARR  40000  44500

37                               FB   DC    MHG    IB T225  CHRY 13  2 19000  3  3  35000  38900
    IB T260  CRUS 35500   39400, IB T265  PALM  35300  39200, IB T277  SEA   35400  39300
    IB T300  CHRY 35500   39400, IB T320  CRUS  36000  40000, IB T135D GM   38600  42900
    IB T160D PERK 39500   43900, IB T170D BARR  39100  43400, IB T185D CUM   39200  43500
    IB T190D GM   39400   43800, IB T215D GM    39900  44400, IB T220D BARR  40000  44500
```

```
  LOA  NAME AND/               TOP/ BOAT  -HULL- ----ENGINE--- BEAM   WGT  DRAFT RETAIL RETAIL
  FT IN  OR MODEL              RIG TYPE   MTL TP TP # HP  MFG  FT IN  LBS  FT IN  LOW   HIGH
--------------------- 1970 BOATS -------------------------------------------------------------
  37                           HT   EXP   MHG   IB T225  CHRY 13  2 17000  3  3  32300  35900
       IB T260  CRUS  32800  36500, IB T265  PALM 32600  36300, IB T277  SEA   32700  36400
       IB T300  CHRY  32800  36500, IB T320  CRUS 33400  37100, IB T135D GM    35600  39600
       IB T160D PERK  36600  40700, IB T170D BARR 36200  40200, IB T185D CUM   36300  40300
       IB T190D GM    36500  40600, IB T215D GM   37000  41200, IB T220D BARR  37100  41300

  37                           FB   EXP   MHG   IB T225  CHRY 13  2 17000  3  3  32300  35900
       IB T260  CRUS  32800  36500, IB T265  PALM 32600  36300, IB T277  SEA   32700  36400
       IB T300  CHRY  32800  36500, IB T320  CRUS 33400  37100, IB T135D GM    35600  39600
       IB T160D PERK  36600  40700, IB T170D BARR 36200  40200, IB T185D CUM   36300  40300
       IB T190D GM    36500  40600, IB T215D GM   37000  41200, IB T220D BARR  37100  41300

  37                           HT   SDN   MHG   IB T225  CHRY 13  2 17000  3  3  32700  36300
       IB T260  CRUS  32700  36400, IB T265  PALM 32500  36100, IB T277  SEA   32700  36400
       IB T300  CHRY  32700  36400, IB T320  CRUS 33400  37100, IB T135D GM    35700  39600
       IB T160D PERK  36800  40800, IB T170D BARR 36300  40300, IB T185D CUM   36500  40600
       IB T190D GM    36800  40800, IB T215D GM   37300  41500, IB T220D BARR  37400  41600

  37                           FB   SDN   MHG   IB T225  CHRY 13  2 17000  3  3  32200  35800
       IB T260  CRUS  32800  36400, IB T265  PALM 32600  36200, IB T277  SEA   32800  36400
       IB T300  CHRY  32800  36400, IB T320  CRUS 33400  37100, IB T135D GM    35700  39600
       IB T160D PERK  36800  40800, IB T170D BARR 36300  40400, IB T185D CUM   36500  40600
       IB T190D GM    36800  40800, IB T215D GM   37300  41500, IB T220D BARR  37400  41600

  37                           HT   SDNSF MHG   IB T225  CHRY 13  2 17000  3  3  32300  35900
       IB T260  CRUS  32800  36500, IB T265  PALM 32600  36300, IB T277  SEA   32700  36400
       IB T300  CHRY  32800  36500, IB T320  CRUS 33400  37100, IB T135D GM    35600  39600
       IB T160D PERK  36600  40700, IB T170D BARR 36200  40200, IB T185D CUM   36300  40300
       IB T190D GM    36500  40600, IB T215D GM   37000  41200, IB T220D BARR  37100  41300

  37                           FB   SDNSF MHG   IB T225  CHRY 13  2 17000  3  3  32300  35900
       IB T260  CRUS  32800  36500, IB T265  PALM 32600  36300, IB T277  SEA   32700  36400
       IB T300  CHRY  32800  36500, IB T320  CRUS 33400  37100, IB T135D GM    35600  39600
       IB T160D PERK  36600  40700, IB T170D BARR 36200  40200, IB T185D CUM   36300  40300
       IB T190D GM    36500  40600, IB T215D GM   37000  41200, IB T220D BARR  37100  41300

  37                           HT   SF    MHG   IB T225  CHRY 13  2 17000  3  3  32300  35900
       IB T260  CRUS  32800  36500, IB T265  PALM 32600  36300, IB T277  SEA   32700  36400
       IB T300  CHRY  32800  36500, IB T320  CRUS 33400  37100, IB T135D GM    35600  39600
       IB T160D PERK  36600  40700, IB T170D BARR 36200  40200, IB T185D CUM   36300  40300
       IB T190D GM    36500  40600, IB T215D GM   37000  41200, IB T220D BARR  37100  41300

  37                           FB   SF    MHG   IB T225  CHRY 13  2 17000  3  3  32300  35900
       IB T260  CRUS  32800  36500, IB T265  PALM 32600  36300, IB T277  SEA   32700  36400
       IB T300  CHRY  32800  36500, IB T320  CRUS 33400  37100, IB T135D GM    35600  39600
       IB T160D PERK  36600  40700, IB T170D BARR 36200  40200, IB T185D CUM   36300  40300
       IB T190D GM    36500  40600, IB T215D GM   37000  41200, IB T220D BARR  37100  41300

  37  DELUXE                   HT   SDN   MHG   IB T225  CHRY 13  2 17000  3  3  32700  36300
       IB T260  CRUS  33800  37500, IB T265  PALM 33600  37300, IB T277  SEA   33600  37300
       IB T300  CHRY  33800  37600, IB T320  CRUS 34400  38200, IB T135D GM    36600  40700
       IB T160D PERK  37700  41900, IB T170D BARR 37300  41400, IB T185D CUM   37300  41500
       IB T190D GM    37600  41800, IB T215D GM   38200  42400, IB T220D BARR  38300  42600

  37  DELUXE                   FB   SDN   MHG   IB T225  CHRY 13  2 17000  3  3  33200  36900
       IB T260  CRUS  33700  37500, IB T265  PALM 33600  37300, IB T277  SEA   33600  37300
       IB T300  CHRY  33800  37500, IB T320  CRUS 34300  38200, IB T135D GM    36600  40700
       IB T160D PERK  37700  41900, IB T170D BARR 37200  41400, IB T185D CUM   37300  41500
       IB T190D GM    37600  41800, IB T215D GM   38200  42400, IB T220D BARR  38300  42600

  43                           HT   MY    MHG   IB T277  SEA  14 10 32000  3     58700  64500
       IB T300  CHRY  59500  65400, IB T320  CRUS 60700  66700, IB T220D BARR  63900  70200
       IB T255D GM    65800  72300, IB T280D GM   67200  73800, IB T300D CUM   68100  74900

  43                           FB   MY    MHG   IB T277  SEA  14 10 32000  3     58600  64400
       IB T300  CHRY  59400  65300, IB T320  CRUS 60600  66500, IB T220D BARR  63700  70000
       IB T255D GM    65600  72100, IB T280D GM   67000  73600, IB T300D CUM   66900  74600

  43                           FB   SDNSF MHG   IB T277  SEA  14 10 32000  3     58900  64700
       IB T300  CHRY  60100  66000, IB T320  CRUS 61500  67600, IB T220D BARR  63400  69700
       IB T255D GM    65800  72300, IB T280D GM   67600  74300, IB T300D CUM   68800  75600

  43  TWIN AFT STATEROOM       HT   MY    MHG   IB T277  SEA  14 10 32000  3     57700  63400
       IB T300  CHRY  58400  64200, IB T320  CRUS 59400  65300, IB T220D BARR  63000  69200
       IB T255D GM    64400  70700, IB T280D GM   65500  72000, IB T300D CUM   66200  72800

  43  TWIN AFT STATEROOM       FB   MY    MHG   IB T277  SEA  14 10 32000  3     57600  63300
       IB T300  CHRY  58200  64000, IB T320  CRUS 59200  65400, IB T220D BARR  62900  69100
       IB T255D GM    64300  70600, IB T280D GM   65400  71800, IB T300D CUM   66100  72600

--------------------- 1969 BOATS -------------------------------------------------------------
  37                           FB   DC    MHG RB IB T210 CHRY 13  2 18000  3  3  32500  36100
       IB T220       32600  36300, IB T238       32700  36400, IB T265  PALM   32900  36500
       IB T280       33000  36700, IB T290  CHRY 33000  36600, IB T290  CRUS   33300  37000
       IB T130D GM   35900  39900, IB T160D PERK 36900  41000, IB T215D GM     37300  41400

  37                           HT   EXP   MHG RB IB T210 CHRY 13  2 18000  3  3  32500  36100
       IB T220       32600  36300, IB T238       32700  36400, IB T265  PALM   32900  36500
       IB T280       33000  36700, IB T290  CHRY 33000  36600, IB T290  CRUS   33300  37000
       IB T130D GM   35900  39900, IB T160D PERK 36900  41000, IB T215D GM     37300  41400

  37                           FB   EXP   MHG   IB T238  CHRY 13  2 18000  3  3  32500  36100
       IB T220       32600  36300, IB T238       32700  36400, IB T265  PALM   32900  36500
       IB T280       33000  36700, IB T290  CHRY 33000  36600, IB T290  CRUS   33300  37000
       IB T130D GM   35900  39900, IB T160D PERK 36900  41000, IB T215D GM     37300  41400

  37                           HT   SDN   MHG RB IB T265 PALM 13  2 18000  3  3  32900  36500
       IB T220       33000  36700, IB T265  PALM 33300  37000, IB T280        33400  37100
       IB T290  CHRY 37100  41300, IB T290  CRUS 37200  41300, IB T130D GM    36300  40300
       IB T160D PERK 37400  41600, IB T215D GM   37900  42100

  37                           FB   SDN   MHG   IB T238  CHRY 13  2 18000  3  3  32900  36500
       IB T220       33000  36700, IB T238       33100  36800, IB T265  PALM   33300  37000
       IB T280       33400  37100, IB T290  CHRY 33400  37100, IB T290  CRUS   33700  37400
       IB T130D GM   36300  40300, IB T160D PERK 37400  41600, IB T215D GM     37900  42100

  37                           HT   SDNSF MHG RB IB T210 CHRY 13  2 18000  3  3  32500  36100
       IB T220       32600  36300, IB T238       32700  36400, IB T265  PALM   32900  36500
       IB T280       33000  36600, IB T290  CHRY 33000  36600, IB T290  CRUS   33300  37000
       IB T130D GM   35900  39900, IB T160D PERK 36900  41000, IB T215D GM     37300  41400

  37                           FB   SDNSF MHG   IB T210  CHRY 13  2 18000  3  3  32500  36100
       IB T220       32600  36300, IB T238       32700  36400, IB T265  PALM   32900  36500
       IB T280       33000  36600, IB T290  CHRY 33000  36600, IB T290  CRUS   33300  37000
       IB T130D GM   35900  39900, IB T160D PERK 36900  41000, IB T215D GM     37300  41400

  37                           HT   SF    MHG RB IB T210 CHRY 13  2 18000  3  3  32500  36100
       IB T220       32600  36300, IB T238       32700  36400, IB T265  PALM   32900  36500
       IB T280       33000  36600, IB T290  CHRY 33000  36600, IB T290  CRUS   33300  37000
       IB T130D GM   35900  39900, IB T160D PERK 36900  41000, IB T215D GM     37300  41400

  37                           FB   SF    MHG RB IB T210 CHRY 13  2 18000  3  3  32500  36100
       IB T220       32600  36300, IB T238       32700  36400, IB T265  PALM   32900  36500
       IB T280       33000  36600, IB T290  CHRY 33000  36600, IB T290  CRUS   33300  37000
       IB T130D GM   35900  39900, IB T160D PERK 36900  41000, IB T215D GM     37300  41400

  43                           HT   MY    MHG RB IB T277 SEA  14 10 25000  3     47800  52500
       IB T320  CRUS 49600  54500, IB T215D GM   52200  57300, IB T283D CUM    55900  61400
       IB T300D CUM  56700  62300

  43                           FB   SF    MHG RB IB T277 SEA  14 10 25000  3     47400  52100
       IB T320  CRUS 49800  54800, IB T215D GM   51200  56300, IB T283D CUM    55700  61200
       IB T300D CUM  56700  62300

--------------------- 1968 BOATS -------------------------------------------------------------
  37                           FB   DC    MHG   IB T210  CHRY 13  2 18000  3  3  31500  35000
       IB T265  PALM 34700  38500, IB T130D GM   45700  50200, IB T160D PERK   46600  51200
       IB T215D GM   46700  51300

  37                           HT   EXP   MHG   IB T210  CHRY 13  2 18000  3  3  31500  35000
       IB T265  PALM 26900  29900, IB T130D GM   44500  49400, IB T160D PERK   45900  50400
       IB T215D GM   46000  50500

  37                           FB   EXP   MHG   IB T210  CHRY 13  2       3  3  26500  29500
       IB T265  PALM 26900  29900, IB T130D GM   44500  49400, IB T160D PERK   45900  50400
       IB T215D GM   46000  50500

  37                           HT   SDN   MHG   IB T210  CHRY 13  2 18000  3  3  31900  35400
       IB T265  PALM 29200  32400, IB T130D GM   44500  49500, IB T160D PERK   46100  50700
       IB T215D GM   46500  51100

  37                           FB   SDN   MHG   IB T210  CHRY 13  2 18000  3  3  28800  32000
       IB T265  PALM 29200  32400, IB T130D GM   44500  49500, IB T160D PERK   46100  50700
       IB T215D GM   46500  51100

  37                           HT   SDNSF MHG   IB T210  CHRY 13  2 18000  3  3  31500  35000
```

```
  LOA   NAME AND/                TOP/ BOAT -HULL- ----ENGINE---  BEAM   WGT  DRAFT RETAIL RETAIL
FT IN   OR MODEL                 RIG TYPE MTL TP TP # HP  MFG   FT IN   LBS  FT IN  LOW   HIGH
------------------- 1968 BOATS ------------------------------------------------------------------
37                               HT   SDNSF MHG    IB T265 PALM 13  2         3  3  29200  32400
        IB T130D GM     45700  50200, IB T160D PERK  46600  51200, IB T215D GM     46700  51300

37                               FB   SDNSF MHG    IB T210 CHRY 13  2         3  3  28800  32000
        IB T265  PALM   29200  32400, IB T130D GM   45700  50200, IB T160D PERK  46600  51200
        IB T215D GM     46700  51300

37                               HT   SF  MHG    IB T210 CHRY 13  2 18000  3  3  31500  35000
        IB T265  PALM   29600  32900, IB T130D GM   43800  48700, IB T160D PERK  44700  49700
        IB T215D GM     44800  49800

37                               FB   SF  MHG    IB T210 CHRY 13  2         3  3  29300  32500
        IB T265  PALM   29600  32900, IB T130D GM   43800  48700, IB T160D PERK  44700  49700
        IB T215D GM     42200  46900

43  6                            HT   MY  MHG    IB T277 SEA  14 10 25000  3     46800  51400
        IB T320  CRUS   48500  53300, IB T215D GM   51100  56200, IB T283D GM     54600  60000
        IB T300D CUM    55400  60800

43  6                            FB   SF  MHG    IB T277 SEA  14  4 25000  3     46600  51300
        IB T320  CRUS   49000  53800, IB T215D GM   50500  55500, IB T283D GM     54700  60100
        IB T300D CUM    55700  61200
------------------- 1967 BOATS ------------------------------------------------------------------
37                               HT   EXP MHG    IB T210 CHRY 13  2         3  3  25800  28600
        IB T220  CRUS   26100  29000, IB T238 GRAY 26000  28800, IB T265  PALM  26100  29000
        IB T280  GRAY   26200  29100, IB T290      26200  29100, IB T290  CRUS  26500  29400
        IB T130D GM     43200  48000, IB T160D PERK 44100  49000, IB T215D GM   44200  49100

37                               FB   EXP MHG    IB T210 CHRY 13  2         3  3  25800  28600
        IB T220  CRUS   26100  29000, IB T238 GRAY 26000  28800, IB T265  PALM  26100  29000
        IB T280  GRAY   26200  29100, IB T290      26200  29100, IB T290  CRUS  26500  29400
        IB T130D GM     43200  48000, IB T160D PERK 44100  49000, IB T215D GM   44200  49100

37                               HT   SDN MHG    IB T210 CHRY 13  2         3  3  28000  31100
        IB T220  CRUS   28300  31400, IB T238 GRAY 28200  31300, IB T265  PALM  28300  31500
        IB T280  GRAY   28500  31600, IB T290      28400  31600, IB T290  CRUS  28800  31900
        IB T130D GM     43200  48000, IB T160D PERK 44300  49200, IB T215D GM   44600  49600

37                               FB   SDN MHG    IB T210 CHRY 13  2         3  3  28000  31100
        IB T220  CRUS   28300  31400, IB T238 GRAY 28200  31300, IB T265  PALM  28400  31500
        IB T280  GRAY   28500  31600, IB T290      28400  31600, IB T290  CRUS  28800  32000
        IB T130D GM     43200  48000, IB T160D PERK 44300  49200, IB T215D GM   44600  49600

37                               HT   SDNSF MHG    IB T210 CHRY 13  2         3  3  28000  31100
        IB T220  CRUS   28300  31400, IB T238 GRAY 28200  31300, IB T265  PALM  28300  31500
        IB T280  GRAY   28400  31600, IB T290 CHRY 28400  31600, IB T290  CRUS  28700  31900
        IB T130D GM     43900  48800, IB T160D PERK 44800  49700, IB T215D GM   44800  49800

37                               FB   SDNSF MHG    IB T210 CHRY 13  2         3  3  28000  31100
        IB T220  CRUS   28300  31400, IB T238 GRAY 28200  31300, IB T265  PALM  28300  31500
        IB T280  GRAY   28400  31600, IB T290 CHRY 28400  31600, IB T290  CRUS  28700  31900
        IB T130D GM     43900  48800, IB T160D PERK 44800  49700, IB T215D GM   44800  49800

37                               HT   SF  MHG    IB T210 CHRY 13  2         3  3  28400  31600
        IB T220  CRUS   28700  31900, IB T238 GRAY 28600  31800, IB T265  PALM  28700  31900
        IB T280  GRAY   28800  32000, IB T290 CHRY 28800  32000, IB T290  CRUS  29100  32300
        IB T130D GM     42500  47300, IB T160D PERK 43400  48200, IB T215D GM   43500  48400

37                               FB   SF  MHG    IB T210 CHRY 13  2         3  3  28400  31600
        IB T220  CRUS   28700  31900, IB T238 GRAY 28600  31800, IB T265  PALM  28700  31900
        IB T280  GRAY   28800  32000, IB T290 CHRY 28800  32000, IB T290  CRUS  29100  32300
        IB T130D GM     42500  47300, IB T160D PERK 43400  48200, IB T215D GM   43500  48400

43  6                            HT   DC  MHG    IB T320 CRUS 14 10         3     50900  56000
43  6                            HT   DC  MHG    IB T258D GM  14 10         3     67500  74100
43  6                            FB   SDNSF MHG    IB T283D GM 14 10        3     67900  74600
------------------- 1966 BOATS ------------------------------------------------------------------
37                               HT   EXP MHG    IB T210 CC   13  2         3  3  25100  27900
        IB T210  CHRY   25000  27800, IB T225 PALM 25200  28000, IB T238  GRAY  25200  28000
        IB T275  CC     25400  28300, IB T277 SEA  25400  28300, IB T280  GRAY  25500  28300
        IB T140D GM     42100  46700, IB T216D GM   42900  47700

37                               FB   EXP MHG    IB T210 CC   13  2         3  3  25100  27900
        IB T210  CHRY   25000  27800, IB T225 PALM 25200  28000, IB T238  GRAY  25200  28000
        IB T275  CC     25400  28300, IB T277 SEA  25400  28300, IB T280  GRAY  25500  28300
        IB T140D GM     42100  46800, IB T216D GM   42900  47700

37                               HT   SDN MHG    IB T210 CC   13  2         3  3  27300  30300
        IB T210  CHRY   27200  30200, IB T225 PALM 27300  30400, IB T238  GRAY  27400  30500
        IB T275  CC     27600  30700, IB T277 SEA  27600  30700, IB T280  GRAY  27700  30700
        IB T140D GM     42200  46800, IB T216D GM   43400  48200

37                               FB   SDN MHG    IB T210 CC   13  2         3  3  27300  30300
        IB T210  CHRY   27200  30200, IB T225 PALM 27300  30400, IB T238  GRAY  27400  30500
        IB T275  CC     27600  30700, IB T277 SEA  27600  30700, IB T280  GRAY  27700  30700
        IB T140D GM     42200  46800, IB T216D GM   43400  48200

37                               HT   SDNSF MHG    IB T210 CC  13  2         3  3  27300  30300
        IB T210  CHRY   27200  30200, IB T225 PALM 27300  30400, IB T238  GRAY  27400  30400
        IB T275  CC     27600  30700, IB T277 SEA  27600  30700, IB T280  GRAY  27600  30700
        IB T140D GM     42700  47500, IB T216D GM   43600  48500

37                               FB   SDNSF MHG    IB T210 CC  13  2         3  3  27300  30300
        IB T210  CHRY   27200  30200, IB T225 PALM 27300  30400, IB T238  GRAY  27400  30400
        IB T275  CC     27600  30700, IB T277 SEA  27600  30700, IB T280  GRAY  27600  30700
        IB T140D GM     42800  47500, IB T216D GM   43600  48500

37                               HT   SF  MHG    IB T210 CC   13  2         3  3  27700  30800
        IB T210  CHRY   27600  30700, IB T225 PALM 27700  30900, IB T238  GRAY  27800  30900
        IB T275  CC     28000  31100, IB T277 SEA  28000  31100, IB T280  GRAY  28000  31100
        IB T140D GM     41400  46100, IB T216D GM   42300  47000

37                               FB   SF  MHG    IB T210 CC   13  2         3  3  27700  30800
        IB T210  CHRY   27600  30700, IB T225 PALM 27700  30800, IB T238  GRAY  27800  30900
        IB T275  CC     28000  31100, IB T277 SEA  28000  31100, IB T280  GRAY  28000  31100
        IB T140D GM     41400  46100, IB T216D GM   42300  47000

47                               HT   MY  MHG    IB T300D CUM 13  2         3  3  73300  80500
------------------- 1965 BOATS ------------------------------------------------------------------
37                               FB   EXP MHG    IB T210 CHRY 13  2         3  3  24400  27100
37                               FB   SDN MHG    IB T210 CC   13  2         3  3  26600  29500
        IB T210  CHRY   26500  29400, IB T238 GRAY 26700  29600, IB T250  CHRY  26700  29600
        IB T275         26900  29800, IB T277      26900  29800, IB T280  GRAY  26900  29800
        IB T280  GRAY   26900  29800, IB T290 CHRY 26900  29800, IB T130D GM    40900  45400
        IB T195D GM     41900  46500

37                               HT   SF  MHG    IB T210 CHRY 13  2         3  3  26900  29900
37                               FB   SF  MHG    IB T210 CC   13  2         3  3  26900  29900
37                               FB   SF  MHG    IB T290 CHRY 13  2         3  3  27200  30300
37                               FB   SF  MHG    IB T130D GM  13  2         3  3  40300  44700
46  8                            HT   DC  MHG    IB T290 CHRY 14  3 32000  3 10  50700  55700
------------------- 1964 BOATS ------------------------------------------------------------------
37                               HT   EXP MHG    IB T210 CHRY 13  2         3  3  23800  26400
        IB T215  GRAY   23900  26500, IB T220      23900  26500, IB T225  PALM  23900  26600
        IB T225  PALM   23900  26600, IB T238 GRAY 23900  26600, IB T250  CHRY  23900  26600
        IB T260  CHRY   24000  26600, IB T260      24000  26700, IB T280  GRAY  24100  26800
        IB T280  GRAY   24200  26800, IB T290      24200  26800, IB T310  GRAY  24400  27100
        IB T130D GM     39900  44300, IB T195D GM  40500  45000

37                               FB   EXP MHG    IB T210 CHRY 13  2         3  3  23800  26400
        IB T215  GRAY   23900  26500, IB T220      23900  26500, IB T225  PALM  23900  26600
        IB T225  PALM   23900  26600, IB T238 GRAY 23900  26600, IB T250  CHRY  23900  26600
        IB T260  CHRY   24000  26600, IB T260      24000  26700, IB T280  GRAY  24100  26800
        IB T280  GRAY   24200  26800, IB T290      24200  26800, IB T310  GRAY  24400  27100
        IB T130D GM     39900  44300, IB T195D GM  40500  45000

37                               HT   SDN MHG    IB T210 CHRY 13  2         3  3  25800  28700
        IB T215  GRAY   25900  28800, IB T220      25900  28800, IB T225  PALM  25900  28800
        IB T225  PALM   26000  28900, IB T238 GRAY 26000  28900, IB T250  CHRY  26100  29000
        IB T260  CHRY   26100  29000, IB T260      26100  29000, IB T280  GRAY  26200  29100
        IB T280  GRAY   26300  29200, IB T290      26200  29200, IB T310  GRAY  26500  29400
        IB T130D GM     39900  44300, IB T195D GM  40800  45400

37                               FB   SDN MHG    IB T210 CHRY 13  2         3  3  25800  28700
        IB T215  GRAY   25900  28800, IB T220      25900  28800, IB T225  PALM  25900  28800
        IB T225  PALM   26000  28900, IB T238 GRAY 26000  28900, IB T250  CHRY  26100  29000
        IB T260  CHRY   26100  29000, IB T260      26100  29000, IB T280  GRAY  26200  29100
        IB T280  GRAY   26300  29200, IB T290      26200  29200, IB T310  GRAY  26500  29400
        IB T130D GM     39900  44300, IB T195D GM  40800  45400

37                               HT   SF  MHG    IB T210 CHRY 13  2         3  3  26200  29100
        IB T215  GRAY   26300  29100, IB T220      26300  29100, IB T225  PALM  26400  29300
        IB T225  PALM   26300  29300, IB T238 GRAY 26400  29300, IB T250  CHRY  26500  29400
        IB T260  CHRY   26400  29300, IB T260      26500  29400, IB T280  GRAY  26500  29400
        IB T280  GRAY   26600  29500, IB T290 CHRY 26600  29500, IB T310       26800  29800
```

EGG HARBOR YACHTS -CONTINUED

LOA FT IN	NAME AND/OR MODEL	TOP/RIG	BOAT TYPE	HULL MTL TP	ENGINE TP # HP MFG	BEAM FT IN	WGT LBS	DRAFT FT IN	RETAIL LOW	RETAIL HIGH
1964 BOATS										
37		HT	SF	MHG	IB T130D GM	13 2		3 3	39300	39600
37		HT	SF	MHG	IB T195D GM	13 2		3 3	39900	44300
37		FB	SF	MHG	IB T210 CHRY	13 2		3 3	26200	29100

```
     IB T215 GRAY 26300 29200, IB T220 GRAY 26300 29200, IB T225 GRAY 26300 29300
     IB T225 PALM 26300 29300, IB T238 GRAY 26400 29300, IB T250 CHRY 26400 29300
     IB T260 CHRY 26400 29300, IB T260 GRAY 26500 29400, IB T280 CHRY 26500 29400
     IB T280 GRAY 26600 29500, IB T290 CHRY 26600 29500, IB T310 GRAY 26800 29800
     IB T130D GM  39300 43600, IB T195D GM 39900 44300
```

LOA FT IN	NAME AND/OR MODEL	TOP/RIG	BOAT TYPE	HULL MTL TP	ENGINE TP # HP MFG	BEAM FT IN	WGT LBS	DRAFT FT IN	RETAIL LOW	RETAIL HIGH
1963 BOATS										
37		HT	EXP	MHG	IB T210 CHRY	13 2		3 3	23200	25800
37		HT	EXP	MHG	IB T225 GRAY	13 2		3 3	23300	25900
37		HT	EXP	MHG	IB T280 CHRY	13 2		3 3	23600	26200
37		FB	EXP	MHG	IB T210 CHRY	13 2		3 3	23200	25800
37		FB	EXP	MHG	IB T225 GRAY	13 2		3 3	23300	25900
37		FB	EXP	MHG	IB T280 GRAY	13 2		3 3	23600	26200
37		HT	SF	MHG	IB T210 CHRY	13 2		3 3	25600	28400
37		HT	SF	MHG	IB T225 GRAY	13 2		3 3	25700	28600
37		HT	SF	MHG	IB T280 GRAY	13 2		3 3	25900	28800
37		FB	SF	MHG	IB T210 CHRY	13 2		3 3	25600	28400
37		FB	SF	MHG	IB T225 GRAY	13 2		3 3	25700	28600
37		FB	SF	MHG	IB T280 GRAY	13 2		3 3	25900	28800
37	CONVERTIBLE	HT	SDN	MHG	IB T210 CHRY	13 2		3 3	25200	28000
37	CONVERTIBLE	HT	SDN	MHG	IB T225 GRAY	13 2		3 3	25300	28100
37	CONVERTIBLE	HT	SDN	MHG	IB T280 GRAY	13 2		3 3	25600	28500
37	CONVERTIBLE	FB	SDN	MHG	IB T210 CHRY	13 2		3 3	25200	28000
37	CONVERTIBLE	FB	SDN	MHG	IB T225 GRAY	13 2		3 3	25300	28100
37	CONVERTIBLE	FB	SDN	MHG	IB T280 GRAY	13 2		3 3	25600	28500
1962 BOATS										
36	EGG-HARBOR	HT	EXP	MHG	IB T210 CHRY	12 8		3 3	20900	23200
36	EGG-HARBOR	HT	SDN	MHG	IB T210 CHRY	12 8		3 3	23000	25500
36	EGG-HARBOR	FB	SDN	MHG	IB T210 CHRY	12 8		3 3	23000	25500
36	EGG-HARBOR	HT	SF	MHG	IB T210 CHRY	12 8		3 3	22300	24800
36	EGG-HARBOR	FB	SF	MHG	IB T210 CHRY	12 8		3 3	22300	24800
1961 BOATS										
36		HT	EXP	MHG	IB T177	12 8		3 3	20300	22500
36		HT	SDN	MHG	IB T225	12 8		3 3	22600	25100
36		FB	SDN	MHG	IB T225	12 8		3 3	22600	25100
36		FB	SF	MHG	IB T225	12 8		3 3	22000	24400
1960 BOATS										
31			SF	MHG	IB T155				11600	13100
31	SPORT FISH		SF	P/M	IB 125	11		2 6	10700	12200
31	SPORT FISH		SF	P/M	IB 125	11		2 6	12100	13800
36			EXP	MHG	IB T177				20500	22800
36			EXP	MHG	IB T275				21100	23400
36	CRUISER		CR	P/M	IB	12 3		3 3	**	**
36	CRUISER		CR	P/M	IB 125	12 3		3 3	19300	21400
1959 BOATS										
31	EGG-HARBOR		SF	MHG	IB T130				11100	12600
31	EGG-HARBOR		SF	P/M	IB T225	11			11900	13500
36			EXP	MHG	IB T177				20100	22400
36	EGG-HARBOR		EXP	MHG	IB T225				20400	22700
36	EGG-HARBOR		SPTCR	P/M	IB T225	12 3			19600	21800
1958 BOATS										
30	TWIN		SPTCR	MHG	IB T125				10500	12000
1957 BOATS										
29			SPTCR	MHG	IB T 95				9000	10200
30			SF	MHG	IB T135				9600	10900
34			SPTCR	MHG	IB T125				16200	18400
1956 BOATS										
31			SF	MHG	IB T135				10600	12000
1955 BOATS										
30			SF	MHG	IB T135				9350	10600
1954 BOATS										
29 5			SF	MHG	IB T135	9 6		2 5	9250	10500
1953 BOATS										
29 5			SF	MHG	IB T135	9 6		2 5	9100	10300
1952 BOATS										
30		HT	SF	MHG	IB T135	9 6		2 5	8650	9950
1951 BOATS										
30			SF	MHG	IB T135				8850	10100
1950 BOATS										
29	JERSEY-SEA SKIFF	HT	SF	MHG	IB 104 CHRY	9 6			7650	8800
1949 BOATS										
28	SEA SKIFF		HT	SF	MHG	IB 110 CHRY				6650	7650

EICHENLAUB BOAT CO
COAST GUARD MFG ID- EBC

Call 1-800-327-6929 for BUC Personalized Evaluation Service
Or, for 1961 to 1977 boats, sign onto www.BUCValuPro.com

WILLIAM EICKHOLT & ASSOC INC
SEATTLE WA 98148   See inside cover to adjust price for area

For more recent years, see the BUC Used Boat Price Guide, Volume 1 or Volume 2

LOA FT IN	NAME AND/OR MODEL	TOP/RIG	BOAT TYPE	HULL MTL TP	ENGINE TP # HP MFG	BEAM FT IN	WGT LBS	DRAFT FT IN	RETAIL LOW	RETAIL HIGH
1982 BOATS										
34 6	BRISE 35	CUT	SA/CR	FBG KL	IB D	11	19500	5 6	57800	63500
41 6	KINGS-LEGEND 41	SLP	SA/CR	FBG KL	IB 45D VW	11 4	20000	5 10	76900	84500
50 4	FD-12 METER	CUT	SA/CR	FBG KL	IB 61D LEHM	14 3	35175	6 6	118500	130500
1981 BOATS										
34 6	BRISE 35	CUT	SA/CR	FBG KL	IB D	11	19500	5 6	54400	59800
37 11	HOLLMAN 38	SLP	SA/RC	FBG KL	IB D	11 6	12000	6	38500	42800
41 6	KINGS-LEGEND 41	SLP	SA/CR	FBG KL	IB D	11 4	20000	5 10	72600	79800
51	FD 12 METER	SLP	SA/CR	FBG KL	IB D	14 6	35000	6 6	119000	131000

EL MAR BOAT CO
DIV OF MILSMITH IND INC COAST GUARD MFG ID- ELM

Call 1-800-327-6929 for BUC Personalized Evaluation Service
Or, for 1973 to 1977 boats, sign onto www.BUCValuPro.com

ELCO BOAT DIVISION
BAYONNE NJ   COAST GUARD MFG ID- ELC See inside cover to adjust price for area

LOA FT IN	NAME AND/OR MODEL	TOP/RIG	BOAT TYPE	HULL MTL TP	ENGINE TP # HP MFG	BEAM FT IN	WGT LBS	DRAFT FT IN	RETAIL LOW	RETAIL HIGH
1949 BOATS										
36		FB	SDN	WD	IB T210				31800	35300
40		FB	SDN	WD	IB T225 PALM				50400	55400
1948 BOATS										
27			EXP	WD	IB 125				10800	12200
30			EXP	WD	IB T185				15500	17600
35			SDN	WD	IB T155				26700	29700
40		FB	SDN	WD	IB T225				50300	55300
48		FB	SDN	WD	IB T215				58200	63900
1947 BOATS										
27		HT	EXP	WD	IB T115				12200	13900
27 6			CR	WD	IB 125 CHRY				11500	13100
30			EXP	WD	IB T185				15400	17500
35		FB	SDN	WD	IB T158				26500	29500
40		FB	SDN	WD	IB T175				50200	55100
1946 BOATS										
27			CR	WD	IB 115				10900	12400
35		FB	SDN	WD	IB T158				26300	29200
1941 BOATS										
30	MARINETTE	HT	CBNCR	WD	IB				**	**
30	MARINETTE	HT	DC	WD	IB				**	**
32	ELCOETTE	HT	CR	WD	IB	10 1		2 4	**	**
32	ELCOETTE	OP	FSH	WD	IB				**	**
34	CRUISETTE	HT	CBNCR	WD	IB				**	**
39	CRUISETTE	HT	DC	WD	IB				**	**
39	CRUISETTE	HT	TCMY	WD	IB				**	**
44	CRUISETTE	HT	CBNCR	WD	IB				**	**
44	CRUISETTE	HT	DC	WD	IB				**	**
57		HT	MY	WD	IB	15 9		3 4	**	**
1940 BOATS										
35		FB	SDN	WD	IB T135				25300	28100
42		FB	SDN	WD	IB T135				65300	71800
1939 BOATS										
30	ELCOETTE	HT	CR	WD	IB				**	**
30	MARINETTE	HT	CBNCR	WD	IB				**	**
30	MARINETTE	HT	DC	WD	IB				**	**
34	CRUISETTE	HT	CBNCR	WD	IB				**	**
34	CRUISETTE	HT	DC	WD	IB				**	**
39	CRUISETTE	HT	DC	WD	IB				**	**
39	CRUISETTE	HT	TCMY	WD	IB				**	**
39 5				WD	IB T125 CHRY				**	**

LOA FT IN	NAME AND/ OR MODEL	TOP/ RIG	BOAT TYPE	-HULL- MTL TP	TP	----ENGINE--- # HP	MFG	BEAM FT IN	WGT LBS	DRAFT FT IN	RETAIL LOW	RETAIL HIGH
						1939 BOATS						
41	CRUISETTE	HT	TCMY	WD	IB						**	**
44		FB	SDN	WD	IB	T145					60900	66900
50		FB	DC	WD	IB	T200					**	**
53		HT	TCMY	WD	IB						**	**
						1938 BOATS						
34				WD	IB	T 95	NORD				**	**
						1937 BOATS						
30	MARINETTE	HT	CR	WD RB	IB						**	**
31				WD	IB	210	CHEV				**	**
32	CRUISETTE	HT	DC	WD	IB						**	**
35		FB	SDN	WD	IB	T175					25600	28500
38	CRUISETTE	HT	CNV	WD	IB						**	**
41	CRUISETTE	HT	CNV	WD	IB						**	**
48		HT	TCMY	WD	IB	T					**	**
53			MY	WD	TR	T225					107000	117500
						1935 BOATS						
32			SDN	WD	IB	T110					17100	19400
35			SDN	WD	IB	T135					25100	27900
42		HT	DC	WD	DS IB	T125	CHRY				61600	67700
						1934 BOATS						
31	VEEDETTE 31	HT	CR	WD	IB						**	**
38		HT	DC	WD	IB						**	**
42		HT	MY	WD	IB						**	**
						1933 BOATS						
30	VEEDETTE 30	HT	CR	WD	IB						**	**
31	VEEDETTE 31	HT	RNBT	WD	IB						**	**
32	CRUISETTE 32	HT	CR	WD	IB						**	**
35			SDN	WD	IB	T145					25400	28300
50		HT	MY	WD	IB	T					**	**
						1932 BOATS						
24	MARINETTE 24	HT	CNV	MHG	IB						**	**
27	MARINETTE 27	HT	CNV	MHG	IB						**	**
30	VEEDETTE 30	HT	DC	MHG	IB						**	**
30	VEEDETTE 305	HT	DC	MHG	IB						**	**
31	VEEDETTE 31	HT	CR	MHG	IB						**	**
32				MHG	IB		FORD				**	**
33				MHG	IB	110	CHRY				**	**
35	CRUISETTE	HT	CNV	MHG	IB						**	**
38		HT	MY	MHG	IB						**	**
42		HT	MY	MHG	IB						**	**
50		HT	MY	MHG	IB						**	**
						1931 BOATS						
24	MARINETTE 24	HT	CNV	MHG	IB		ELCO				**	**
27	MARINETTE 24	HT	CNV	MHG	IB		ELCO				**	**
30	VEEDETTE 30	HT	DC	MHG	IB	80	ELCO		12800			14600
30	VEEDETTE 30	HT	DC	MHG	IB	100	ELCO		14500			16400
31	VEEDETTE 31	HT	CR	MHG	IB		ELCO				**	**
35			SDN	MHG	IB	T145			26200			29100
38		HT		MHG	IB		ELCO				**	**
42		HT		MHG	IB		ELCO				**	**
50		HT		MHG	IB		ELCO				**	**
						1930 BOATS						
35			SDN	WD	IB	T145					26900	29900
44			MY	WD	IB	T135					61200	67200
						1929 BOATS						
34		HT	SDN	WD	DS IB	135	CHRY				23000	25600
37				WD	IB	78D	FORD				**	**
38	6			WD	IB	250					**	**
40			SDN	WD	IB	T185					68800	75600
						1928 BOATS						
33			CR	WD	IB	125					21100	23400
						1927 BOATS						
27	RAISED DECK			WD	IB	125					10400	11800
50				WD	IB	130D	FORD				**	**
						1917 BOATS						
50				WD	IB	120					**	**
						1915 BOATS						
16				WD	IB	22					**	**

ELEGANT MOTORS INC

Call 1-800-327-6929 for BUC Personalized Evaluation Service
Or, for 1979 to 1986 boats, sign onto www.BUCValuPro.com

JOHN W ELFREY CO
COAST GUARD MFG ID- JWE

Call 1-800-327-6929 for BUC Personalized Evaluation Service
Or, for 1980 boats, sign onto www.BUCValuPro.com

ELIMINATOR BOATS
MIRA LOMA CA 91752   COAST GUARD MFG ID- ELB See inside cover to adjust price for area

For more recent years, see the BUC Used Boat Price Guide, Volume 1 or Volume 2

LOA FT IN	NAME AND/ OR MODEL	TOP/ RIG	BOAT TYPE	-HULL- MTL TP	TP	----ENGINE--- # HP	MFG	BEAM FT IN	WGT LBS	DRAFT FT IN	RETAIL LOW	RETAIL HIGH
						1982 BOATS						
18	2 BUBBLE-DECK	OP	SKI	SV	JT			6 8	850		**	**
18	9 SPRINT	OP	SKI	DV	JT			6 8	900		**	**
20	6 FORMULA	OP	SPTCR	DV	IO			7 8			**	**
20	6 FORMULA B/R	OP	SPTCR	DV	IO			7 8			**	**
20	10 DAYTONA	OP	SKI	TH	OB			7 9	1150		3250	3800
21	3 DAYCRUISER	OP	CR	DV	OB						6550	7550

ELITE BOATS
PERRY FL 32347   COAST GUARD MFG ID- ELE See inside cover to adjust price for area

LOA FT IN	NAME AND/ OR MODEL	TOP/ RIG	BOAT TYPE	-HULL- MTL TP	TP	----ENGINE--- # HP	MFG	BEAM FT IN	WGT LBS	DRAFT FT IN	RETAIL LOW	RETAIL HIGH
						1977 BOATS						
16	10 ELITE 1700-T	OP	RNBT	FBG	IO	120-140		6 10			2550	3000
16	10 ELITE 1700-T DLX	OP	RNBT	FBG	OB			6 10	900		2000	2350
17	9 ELITE 1800-T	OP	RNBT	FBG	IO	120-175		7 1			2850	3350
17	9 ELITE 1800-T DLX	OP	RNBT	FBG	OB			7 1	1150		2550	2950
18	2 ELITE 1800-V	OP	RNBT	FBG	IO	120-175		7 1			2950	3450
18	2 ELITE 1800-V DLX	OP	RNBT	FBG	OB			7 1	1000		2300	2700

ELITE CRAFT INC

Call 1-800-327-6929 for BUC Personalized Evaluation Service
Or, for 1980 to 1990 boats, sign onto www.BUCValuPro.com

ELLIOTT BAY STEAM LAUNCH CO
ELLIOTT BAY COMPANY   COAST GUARD MFG ID- EBQ

Call 1-800-327-6929 for BUC Personalized Evaluation Service
Or, for 1983 to 1985 boats, sign onto www.BUCValuPro.com

ELLIS BOAT COMPANY
SOUTHWEST HARBOR ME 046 COAST GUARD MFG ID- RDL See inside cover to adjust price for area

For more recent years, see the BUC Used Boat Price Guide, Volume 1 or Volume 2

LOA FT IN	NAME AND/ OR MODEL	TOP/ RIG	BOAT TYPE	-HULL- MTL TP	TP	----ENGINE--- # HP	MFG	BEAM FT IN	WGT LBS	DRAFT FT IN	RETAIL LOW	RETAIL HIGH
						1983 BOATS						
20	ELLIS 20	OP	UTL	FBG	DS OB			7 6	1200	11	2250	2650
28	4 ELLIS 28 BASSBOAT	HT	FSH	FBG	IB			9 4		3	**	**
28	4 ELLIS 28 CRUISER	HT	WKNDR	FBG	DS IB	85D	PERK	9 4		3	65100	71500
28	4 ELLIS 28 WORKBOAT	HT	UTL	FBG	DS IB	85D	PERK	9 4		3	49600	54500
						1982 BOATS						
20	ELLIS 20	OP	UTL	FBG	FL OB			7 5	1500	1	3050	3550
20	1 ELLIS 20		UTL	FBG	DS OB			7 6	1200	11	2250	2600
28	ELLIS 28		WKNDR	FBG	RB IB	85D	PERK	9 6	6000	3	41500	46100
28	ELLIS 28 CRUISER		WKNDR	FBG	DS IB	85D	PERK	9 6	12000		83900	92300
						1981 BOATS						
20	ELLIS 20	OP	UTL	FBG	DS OB			7 6	1200	11	2200	2550
28	4 ELLIS 28 CRUISER	HT	WKNDR	FBG	DS IB	85D	PERK	9 6		3	60300	66300
28	4 ELLIS 28 WORKBOAT	HT	UTL	FBG	DS IB	85D	PERK	9 6		3	45800	50300
28	4 WEEKENDER	HT	OVNTR	FBG	IB	85D	PERK	9 6	5500	3	34500	38300
28	4 WORKBOAT	HT	FSH	FBG	IB	125D	PERK	9 6	5500	3	38300	42500

EMERALD BAY TRADING CO LTD

Call 1-800-327-6929 for BUC Personalized Evaluation Service
Or, for 1980 boats, sign onto www.BUCValuPro.com

ENDEAVOUR YACHT CORP

CLEARWATER FL 34620   COAST GUARD MFG ID- ECR See inside cover to adjust price for area

For more recent years, see the BUC Used Boat Price Guide, Volume 1 or Volume 2

LOA FT IN	NAME AND/ OR MODEL	TOP/ RIG	BOAT TYPE	-HULL- MTL TP	----ENGINE--- TP # HP MFG	BEAM FT IN	WGT LBS	DRAFT FT IN	RETAIL LOW	RETAIL HIGH
			1983 BOATS							
37 5	ENDEAVOUR 37	SLP	SA/CR FBG	KL IB	50D PERK 11 7	21000	4 6	52400	57600
37 5	ENDEAVOUR 37	KTH	SA/CR FBG	KL IB	50D PERK 11 7	21000	4 6	52400	57600
40	ENDEAVOUR 40	SLP	SA/CR FBG	KL IB	50D PERK 13	25000	5	65100	71600
40	ENDEAVOUR 40	KTH	SA/CR FBG	KL IB	50D PERK 13	25000	5	65100	71600
43	ENDEAVOUR 43	CUT	SA/CR FBG	KL IB	62D PERK 14	33000	5 5	83800	92100
43	ENDEAVOUR 43	KTH	SA/CR FBG	KL IB	62D PERK 14	33000	5 5	83800	92100
			1982 BOATS							
32 4	ENDEAVOUR 32	SLP	SA/CR FBG	KL IB	20D YAN 10	11700	4 2	26800	29800
37 5	ENDEAVOUR 37	SLP	SA/CR FBG	KL IB	50D PERK 11 7	21000	4 6	49000	53900
37 5	ENDEAVOUR 37	KTH	SA/CR FBG	KL IB	50D PERK 11 7	21000	4 6	49100	53900
40	ENDEAVOUR 40	SLP	SA/CR FBG	KL IB	50D PERK 13	25000	5	60900	67000
40	ENDEAVOUR 40	KTH	SA/CR FBG	KL IB	50D PERK 13	25000	5	61000	67000
43	ENDEAVOUR 43	CUT	SA/CR FBG	KL IB	62D PERK 14	33000	5 5	78400	86200
43	ENDEAVOUR 43	KTH	SA/CR FBG	KL IB	62D PERK 14	33000	5 5	78500	86200
			1981 BOATS							
32 4	ENDEAVOUR 32	SLP	SA/CR FBG	KL IB	20D YAN 10	11700	4 2	25100	27900
37 5	ENDEAVOUR 37	SLP	SA/CR FBG	KL IB	50D PERK 11 7	20000	4 6	43900	48800
37 5	ENDEAVOUR 37	KTH	SA/CR FBG	KL IB	50D PERK 11 7	20000	4 6	43900	48800
40	ENDEAVOUR 40	SLP	SA/CR FBG	KL IB	50D PERK 13	25000	5	57100	62700
40	ENDEAVOUR 40	KTH	SA/CR FBG	KL IB	50D PERK 13	25000	5	57100	62700
43	ENDEAVOUR 43	CUT	SA/CR FBG	KL IB	62D PERK 14	33000	5 5	73400	80700
43	ENDEAVOUR 43	KTH	SA/CR FBG	KL IB	62D PERK 14	33000	5 5	73500	80700
			1980 BOATS							
32 4	ENDEAVOUR	SLP	SA/CR FBG	KL IB	20D YAN 10	11700	4 2	23900	26500
37 5	ENDEAVOUR	SLP	SA/CR FBG	KL IB	50D PERK 11 7	20000	4 6	41800	46400
37 5	ENDEAVOUR	KTH	SA/CR FBG	KL IB	50D PERK 11 7	20000	4 6	41800	46400
43	ENDEAVOUR	CUT	SA/CR FBG	KL IB	62D PERK 14	33000	5 3	69800	76700
43	ENDEAVOUR	KTH	SA/CR FBG	KL IB	62D PERK 14	33000	5 3	69800	76700
			1979 BOATS							
32 4	ENDEAVOUR	SLP	SA/CR FBG	KL IB	20D YAN 10	11700	4 2	22800	25400
37 5	ENDEAVOUR	SLP	SA/CR FBG	KL IB	50D PERK 11 7	20000	4 6	40000	44400
37 5	ENDEAVOUR	KTH	SA/CR FBG	KL IB	50D PERK 11 7	20000	4 6	40000	44400
43	ENDEAVOUR	CUT	SA/CR FBG	KL IB	62D PERK 14	33000	5 3	66900	73500
43	ENDEAVOUR	KTH	SA/CR FBG	KL IB	62D PERK 14	33000	5 3	66900	73500
			1978 BOATS							
32 4	ENDEAVOUR	SLP	SA/CR FBG	KC IB	20D YAN 10	11700	3 6	21900	24400
32 4	ENDEAVOUR	SLP	SA/CR FBG	KL IB	20D YAN 10	11700	4 2	21900	24400
37 5	ENDEAVOUR	SLP	SA/CR FBG	KL IB	50D PERK 11 7	20000	4 6	38400	42700
37 5	ENDEAVOUR	KTH	SA/CR FBG	KL IB	50D PERK 11 7	20000	4 6	38400	42700
			1977 BOATS							
32	ENDEAVOUR	SLP	SA/CR FBG	KC IB	12D- 20D 9 9	11700	3 6	21100	23400
32	ENDEAVOUR	SLP	SA/CR FBG	KL IB	12D- 20D 9 9	11700	4 2	21100	23400
37 5	ENDEAVOUR	SLP	SA/CR FBG	KL IB	50D PERK 11 7	19000	4 6	35500	39400
37 5	ENDEAVOUR	KTH	SA/CR FBG	KL IB	50D PERK 11 7	19000	4 6	35500	39400
			1976 BOATS							
32	ENDEAVOUR	SLP	SAIL FBG	CB IB	12D YAN 9 9	11700	3 6	20400	22600
			1975 BOATS							
32	ENDEAVOUR	SLP	SAIL FBG	CB IB	12D YAN 9 9	11700	3 6	19700	21900
			1971 BOATS							
25 9	ENDEAVOR	SLP	SA/OD FBG	KL	7		4	4650	5350
			1970 BOATS							
25 9	ENDEAVOR	SLP	SA/OD FBG	KL	7		4	4600	5300

ENSIGN YACHTS

CORINTHIAN SERVICES INC
FT LAUDERDALE FL 33334 COAST GUARD MFG ID- ENN   See inside cover to adjust price for area

LOA FT IN	NAME AND/ OR MODEL	TOP/ RIG	BOAT TYPE	-HULL- MTL TP	----ENGINE--- TP # HP MFG	BEAM FT IN	WGT LBS	DRAFT FT IN	RETAIL LOW	RETAIL HIGH
			1981 BOATS							
37	BILLFISHER 37	FB	FBG DV	IB	T270D CAT 14	22000	3 6	88500	97200
37	CHARTER BOAT		SF	FBG SV IB	T225 14			58500	64300
37	CHARTER BOAT	FB	FBG DV	IB	210D CAT 14	19000	3 6	71000	78000
37	COMMERCIAL FISHERMAN	FSH	FBG SV	IB	225 14			52200	57400
37	COMMERCIAL FISHERMAN	HT	FSH	FBG DV IB	210D CAT 14	18000	3 6	67900	74600
37	DIVE BOAT		UTL	FBG DV IB	225 14			***	***
37	DIVE BOAT	FB	UTL	FBG DV IB	210D CAT 14	19000	3 6	62500	68700
37	SEDAN CRUISER		SDN	FBG SV IB	T150 14			56600	62200
37	SEDAN CRUISER	FB	SDN	FBG DV IB	T130D LEHM 14	22000	3 6	82200	90300
37	WORK BOAT		HT	UTL	FBG DV IB	210D CAT 14	18000	3 6	59900	65800
			1980 BOATS							
37	BILLFISHER 37	FB	SF	FBG DV IB	T270D CAT 14	22000	3 6	84400	92700
37	CHARTER BOAT	FB	SF	FBG DV IB	210D CAT 14	19000	3 6	67700	74400
37	COMMERCIAL FISHERMAN	HT	FSH	FBG DV IB	210D CAT 14	18000	3 6	64700	71200
37	COMMERCIAL FISHERMAN	HT	FSH	FBG DV IB	225D 14	15000		55800	61400
37	DIVE BOAT	FB	UTL	FBG DV IB	210D CAT 14	19000	3 6	59800	65700
37	DIVE BOAT	FB	UTL	FBG SV IB	225D 14	16000		53100	58300
37	SEDAN CRUISER	FB	SDN	FBG DV IB	T130D LEHM 14	22000	3 6	78400	86200
37	SEDAN CRUISER	FB	SDN	FBG SV IB	275D 14	17400		64300	70600
37	WORK BOAT	HT	UTL	FBG DV IB	210D CAT 14	18000	3 6	57800	63500
			1979 BOATS							
37	BILLFISHER	FB	SF	FBG DV IB	T250D CAT 14	22000	3 6	79600	87500
37	COMMERCIAL FISHERMAN	HT	FSH	FBG DV IB	210D CAT 14	18000	3 6	61900	68000
37	DIVE BOAT	FB	UTL	FBG DV IB	210D CAT 14	19000	3 4	57700	63400
37	SEDAN CRUISER	HT	SDN	FBG DV IB	T120D LEHM 14	22000	3 6	74600	82000
37	WORK BOAT	HT	UTL	FBG DV IB	210D CAT 14	18000	3 5	55300	60700
			1978 BOATS							
36 5	SPORT FISHERMAN	HT	SF	FBG DV VD	T120D FORD 14		3	63000	69200
36 5	SPORT FISHERMAN	HT	SF	FBG DV VD	T225D CAT 14		3	66200	72800
36 5	SPORT FISHERMAN	HT	SF	FBG DV VD	T450D CAT 14		3	78700	86500
			1977 BOATS							
36 5	ENSIGN 36		FSH	FBG DV IB	225D 14		3	50700	55700
36 5	ENSIGN 36		FSH	FBG DV IB	350D 14		3	52500	57700
			1976 BOATS							
36 5	SEDAN CRUISER	HT	SDN	FBG DV VD	225D CAT 14		3	58600	64400
			1975 BOATS							
36 5	SPORT FISHERMAN	TT	SF	FBG DV VD	T450D CAT 14		3	69500	76400
			1974 BOATS							
36 5	FLORIDIAN 36		SDN	FBG DV VD	D 14		3	**	**
36 5	FLORIDIAN 36		SF	FBG KL VD	D 14		3	**	**
			1973 BOATS							
36 5	SEDAN CRUISER	HT	SDN	FBG DV VD	225D CAT 14		3	52100	57300

ENTERPRISE BOAT CO INC

CORWIN SERIES
RANCHO CORDOVA CA 95670 COAST GUARD MFG ID- ENT   See inside cover to adjust price for area

For more recent years, see the BUC Used Boat Price Guide, Volume 1 or Volume 2

LOA FT IN	NAME AND/ OR MODEL	TOP/ RIG	BOAT TYPE	-HULL- MTL TP	----ENGINE--- TP # HP MFG	BEAM FT IN	WGT LBS	DRAFT FT IN	RETAIL LOW	RETAIL HIGH
			1983 BOATS							
16	16EIO	ST	RNBT FBG	TR IO	120-170	6 8	1850	11	2050	2500
16	16EOB	ST	RNBT FBG	TR OB		6 8	1150	9	2100	2500
16 10	E17CIO	ST	CR FBG	TR IO	120 OMC	7 3	2150	1 6	2500	2950
16 10	E17CIO	ST	CR FBG	TR IO	140-230	7 3	2450	1 2	2700	3300
16 10	E17COB	ST	CR FBG	TR OB		7 3	1700	1	2900	3350
16 10	E17FRIO	ST	RNBT FBG	TR IO	120-230	7 3	2150	1 6	2550	2950
16 10	E17FROB	ST	RNBT FBG	TR OB		7 3	1400	1 6	2500	3050
16 10	E17IO	ST	RNBT FBG	TR IO	120-230	7 3	2200	1 6	2500	3050
16 10	E17OB	ST	RNBT FBG	TR OB		7 3	1400	1 6	2500	2850
17	17VBRIO	ST	RNBT FBG	SV IO	120-230	7 3	2100	1 6	2500	3050
17	17VBROB	ST	RNBT FBG	SV OB		7 3	1300	1 6	2400	2750
18 1	181VIO	OP	RNBT FBG	DV IO	170-230	7 4	1200	1 6	2300	2750
20 2	202DVIO	ST	RNBT FBG	DV IO	120-230	7 4	2500	1 2	3100	3750
20 2	202DVIO	ST	RNBT FBG	DV IO	170 OMC	7 4	2500	1 2	3150	3700
20 2	202DVOB	ST	RNBT FBG	DV OB		7 4	1650	1 2	3100	3600
			1982 BOATS							
16	16EIO	ST	RNBT FBG	TR IO	140 OMC	6 8	1850		2050	2400
16	16EOB	ST	RNBT FBG	TR OB		6 8	1150		2050	2450
16 10	E17CIO	ST	CR FBG	TR IO	140 OMC	7 3	2450		2650	3050
16 10	E17COB	ST	CR FBG	TR OB		7 3	1700		2800	3300
16 10	E17FRIO	ST	RNBT FBG	TR IO	170 OMC	7 3	2150		2450	2850
16 10	E17FROB	ST	RNBT FBG	TR OB		7 3	1400		2450	2850
16 10	E17IO	ST	RNBT FBG	TR IO	170 OMC	7 3	2200		2500	2900
16 10	E17OB	ST	RNBT FBG	TR OB		7 3	1400		2450	2850
17	17VBRIO	ST	RNBT FBG	SV IO	170 OMC	7 3	2100		2450	2850
17	17VBROB	ST	RNBT FBG	SV OB		7 3	1300		2350	2700
17	17VIO	ST	RNBT FBG	DV IO	170 OMC	7 3	2000		2400	2800
17	17VOB	ST	RNBT FBG	DV OB		7 3	1150		2100	2500
18 1	181VIO	ST	RNBT FBG	DV IO	170 OMC	7 4	1200		2250	2600
20 2	202DVIO	ST	RNBT FBG	DV IO	170 OMC	7 4	2500		3100	3600
20 2	202DVOB	ST	RNBT FBG	DV OB		7 4	1650		3050	3550
			1981 BOATS							
16	16EIO	ST	RNBT FBG	TR IO	140 OMC	6 8	1850	11	2000	2350
16 10	17CIO	ST	CR FBG	TR IO	140	7 3			2600	3050
16 10	E17FRIO	ST	RNBT FBG	TR IO	170-185	7 3	2150	1 6	2400	2850
16 10	E17FROB	ST	RNBT FBG	TR OB		7 3	1800	1	2950	3450

LOA FT IN	NAME AND/ OR MODEL	TOP/ RIG	BOAT TYPE	-HULL- MTL TP	----ENGINE--- TP # HP MFG	BEAM FT IN	WGT LBS	DRAFT FT IN	RETAIL LOW	RETAIL HIGH
					1981 BOATS					
16 10	E17IO	ST	RNBT	FBG TR IO	170-185	7 3	2300	1 6	2500	2900
16 10	E170B	ST	RNBT	FBG TR OB		7 3	1800	1	2900	3350
17	17VIO	ST	RNBT	FBG DV IO	170-185	7 3	2000	1 6	2350	2900
17	17VOB	ST	RNBT	FBG DV OB		7 3	1600	1	2700	3100
18 1	181VIO	ST	RNBT	FBG DV IO	170 OMC	7 4	1200		2200	2550
20 2	202DVIO	ST	RNBT	FBG DV IO	170-185	7 4	2500	1 2	3050	3600
20 2	202DVOB	ST	RNBT	FBG DV OB		7 4	1650	1	3000	3450
					1980 BOATS					
16	16EIO	ST	RNBT	FBG TR IO	140 OMC	6 8	1850	11	2000	2350
16	16EOB	ST	RNBT	FBG TR OB		6 8	1200	9	2050	2450
16 10	E17CIO	ST	CR	FBG TR IO	140 OMC	7 3	2450	1 2	2600	3000
16 10	E17COB	ST	CR	FBG TR OB		7 3	1800	1	2850	3300
16 10	E17FRIO	ST	RNBT	FBG TR IO	140 OMC	7 3	2150	1 6	2400	2750
16 10	E17FROB	ST	RNBT	FBG TR OB		7 3	1800	1	2900	3400
16 10	E17IO	ST	RNBT	FBG TR IO	140 OMC	7 3	2300	1 6	2450	2850
16 10	E170B	ST	RNBT	FBG TR OB		7 3	1800	1	2850	3300
17	17VIO	ST	RNBT	FBG DV IO	140 OMC	7 3	2000	1 6	2350	2700
17	17VOB	ST	RNBT	FBG DV OB		7 3	1600	1	2650	3050
20 2	202DVIO	ST	RNBT	FBG DV IO	185 OMC	7 4	2500	1 2	3050	3555
20 2	202DVOB	ST	RNBT	FBG DV OB		7 4	1650	1	2950	3400
					1979 BOATS					
16	16EIO	ST	RNBT	FBG TR IO	140 OMC	6 8	2000	11	2050	2450
16	16EOB	ST	RNBT	FBG TR OB		6 8	1600	9	2650	3100
16 10	17CIO	ST	CR	FBG TR IO	140 OMC	7 3	2400	1 2	2550	2950
16 10	17COB	ST	CR	FBG TR OB		7 3	2100	1	3100	3600
16 10	E17FRIO	ST	RNBT	FBG TR IO	185 OMC	7 3	2300	1 6	2500	2900
16 10	E17FROB	ST	RNBT	FBG TR OB		7 3	1800	1	2850	3300
16 10	E17IO	ST	RNBT	FBG TR IO	185 OMC	7 3	2300	1 6	2500	2900
16 10	E170B	ST	RNBT	FBG TR OB		7 3	1800	1	2800	3250
17	17VIO	ST	RNBT	FBG DV IO	185 OMC	7 3	2100	1 6	2400	2800
17	17VOB	ST	RNBT	FBG DV OB		7 3	1600	1	2600	3000
20 2	202DVIO	ST	RNBT	FBG SV IO	185 OMC	7 4	2500	1 2	3050	3550
20 2	202DVOB	ST	RNBT	FBG SV OB		7 4	2000	1	3300	3850
					1978 BOATS					
16	16EFRIO	ST	RNBT	FBG TR IO	120	6 8	1900	10	2050	2450
16	16EFRIO	ST	RNBT	FBG TR IO	130-170	6 8	1900	10	2250	2850
16	16EFROB	ST	RNBT	FBG TR OB		6 8	1500	8	2450	2850
16	16EIO	ST	RNBT	FBG TR IO	120	6 8	2000	11	2100	2500
16	16EIO	ST	RNBT	FBG TR IO	130-170	6 8	2000	11	2300	2650
16	16EOB	ST	RNBT	FBG TR OB		6 8	1600	9	2600	3050
16 10	17CIO	HT	CR	FBG TR IO	120-198	7 3	2400	1 2	2600	3200
16 10	17CIO	HT	CR	FBG TR IO	200-240	7 3	2400	1 2	2800	3350
16 10	17CIO	HT	CR	FBG TR JT	360-460	7 3	2400	1 2	3150	3650
16 10	17COB	HT	CR	FBG TR OB		7 3	2100	1	3050	3500
16 10	E170B	ST	RNBT	FBG TR OB		7 3	1800	1	2750	3200
16 10	E17FRIO	ST	RNBT	FBG TR IO	120-200	7 3	2300	1 6	2500	3150
	IO 225 OMC 2550	2950, IO 225-240			2800	3250, JT 360-460			3250	3750
16 10	E17FROB	ST	RNBT	FBG TR OB		7 3	1800	1	2800	3250
16 10	E17IO	ST	RNBT	FBG TR IO	120-200	7 3	2300	1 6	2500	3150
	IO 225 OMC 2550	2950, IO 225-240			2800	3250, JT 360-460			3250	3750
20 2	202DVIO	ST	RNBT	FBG DV IO	140-200	7 4	2500	1 2	3050	3750
20 2	202DVIO	ST	RNBT	FBG DV IO	225-240	7 4	2500	1 2	3100	3850
20 2	202DVIO	ST	RNBT	FBG DV JT	360-460	7 4	2500	1 2	3800	4450
20 2	202DVOB	ST	RNBT	FBG DV OB		7 4	2000	1	3250	3800
					1977 BOATS					
16	16EFRIO	ST	UTL	FBG TR IO	140 OMC	6 8	1850		2200	2550
16	16EFROB	ST	UTL	FBG TR OB		6 8	1100		1800	2150
16	16EIO B/R	ST	UTL	FBG TR IO	140 OMC	6 8	1900		2050	2450
16	16EOB B/R	ST	UTL	FBG TR OB		6 8	1150		1900	2250
16 10	17CIO	HT	CR	FBG TR IO	140 OMC	7 3	2350		2600	3000
16 10	17COB	HT	CR	FBG TR OB		7 3	1650		2550	2950
16 10	E17IO	ST	UTL	FBG TR IO	185 OMC	7 3	2250		2700	3150
16 10	E17FROB	ST	RNBT	FBG TR OB		7 3	1300		2050	2450
16 10	E17IO B/R	ST	RNBT	FBG TR IO	185 OMC	7 3	2300		2550	2950
16 10	E170B B/R	ST	RNBT	FBG TR OB		7 3	1350		2250	2600
20 2	202DVIO	ST	RNBT	FBG SV IO	185 OMC	7 4	2450		3100	3600
20 2	202DVOB	ST	RNBT	FBG SV OB		7 4	1450		2550	2950

ENTERPRISE BOATS INC
COAST GUARD MFG ID- ENB

Call 1-800-327-6929 for BUC Personalized Evaluation Service
Or, for 1978 boats, sign onto www.BUCValuPro.com

ENTERPRISE YACHT CORPORATION

Call 1-800-327-6929 for BUC Personalized Evaluation Service
Or, for 1967 to 1971 boats, sign onto www.BUCValuPro.com

ENTERPRISE YACHTS
SANTA ANA CA 92704   COAST GUARD MFG ID- ENY See inside cover to adjust price for area

LOA FT IN	NAME AND/ OR MODEL	TOP/ RIG	BOAT TYPE	-HULL- MTL TP	----ENGINE--- TP # HP MFG	BEAM FT IN	WGT LBS	DRAFT FT IN	RETAIL LOW	RETAIL HIGH
					1972 BOATS					
20 6	NEWPORT	SLP	SA/OD	FBG KL OB		7 6	2500	3 4	3800	4400
27	NEWPORT 27	SLP	SAIL	FBG KL IB	D	9 2	6000	4 3	11500	13100
30	NEWPORT 30	SLP	SAIL	FBG KL IB	D	10 6	7500	4 9	15500	17700
41	NEWPORT 41	SLP	SAIL	FBG KL IB	D	11 3	18000	6 3	41200	45800
					1971 BOATS					
20 6	NEWPORT	SLP	SA/OD	FBG KL OB		7 6	2500	3 4	3700	4300
27	NEWPORT 27	SLP	SAIL	FBG KL IB	30 UNIV	9 2	6000	4 3	10700	12200
30	NEWPORT 30	SLP	SAIL	FBG KL IB	30 UNIV	10 6	7500	4 9	15100	17100
41	NEWPORT 41	SLP	SAIL	FBG KL IB	65 UNIV	11 3	18000	6 3	39800	44200
					1970 BOATS					
20 6	NEWPORT 20	SLP	SA/OD	FBG KL OB		7 6	2500	3 4	3650	4250
27	NEWPORT 27	SLP	SAIL	FBG KL OB		9 2	5000	4 3	8850	10100
30	NEWPORT 30	SLP	SAIL	FBG KL IB	30 UNIV	10 6	7500	4 9	14800	16800
41	NEWPORT 41	SLP	SAIL	FBG KL IB	65 UNIV	11 3	18000	6 3	39000	43300
41	NEWPORT 41	SLP	SAIL	FBG KL IB	50D PERK	11 3	18000	6 3	39400	43800
					1969 BOATS					
20 6	NEWPORT	SLP	SA/OD	FBG KL OB		7 6	2500	3 4	3550	4150
27	NEWPORT 27	SLP	SAIL	FBG KL IB	D	9 2	6000	4 3	10900	12400
30	NEWPORT 30	SLP	SAIL	FBG KL IB	D	10 6	7500	4 9	14600	16600
41	NEWPORT 41	SLP	SAIL	FBG KL IB	D	11 3	18000	6 3	38800	43100

EQUITABLE EQUIPMENT CO INC
EQUITY

Call 1-800-327-6929 for BUC Personalized Evaluation Service
Or, for 1961 to 1972 boats, sign onto www.BUCValuPro.com

ERAS

Call 1-800-327-6929 for BUC Personalized Evaluation Service
Or, for 1959 boats, sign onto www.BUCValuPro.com

ERIC MARINE

Call 1-800-327-6929 for BUC Personalized Evaluation Service
Or, for 1982 boats, sign onto www.BUCValuPro.com

ERICSON YACHTS INC
FULLERTON CA 92631   COAST GUARD MFG ID- PCS See inside cover to adjust price for area

For more recent years, see the BUC Used Boat Price Guide, Volume 1 or Volume 2

LOA FT IN	NAME AND/ OR MODEL	TOP/ RIG	BOAT TYPE	-HULL- MTL TP	----ENGINE--- TP # HP MFG	BEAM FT IN	WGT LBS	DRAFT FT IN	RETAIL LOW	RETAIL HIGH
					1983 BOATS					
25 5	ERICSON 25	SLP	SAIL	FBG KL OB		9 3	5000	4 11	10500	12000
25 5	ERICSON 25 SHOAL	SLP	SAIL	FBG KL OB		9 3	5000	3 11	11000	12000
25 5	ERICSON 25	SLP	SAIL	FBG KL IB	8D YAN	9 3	5000	4 11	11200	12800
25 5	ERICSON 25 SHOAL	SLP	SAIL	FBG KL IB	8D YAN	9 3	5000	3 11	11200	12800
28 6	ERICSON 28	SLP	SAIL	FBG KL IB	11D UNIV	10 6	7500	5	18600	20600
28 6	ERICSON 28 SHOAL	SLP	SAIL	FBG KL IB	11D UNIV	10 6	7500	4	18600	20600
29 11	ERICSON 30	SLP	SAIL	FBG KL IB	16D UNIV	10 6	9000	5 10	22500	25000
29 11	ERICSON 30 SHOAL	SLP	SAIL	FBG KL IB	16D UNIV	10 6	9125	4	22800	25300
33 6	ERICSON 33	SLP	SAIL	FBG KL IB	21D UNIV	11 2	9500	5 11	23900	26500
33 6	ERICSON 33 SHOAL	SLP	SAIL	FBG KL IB	21D UNIV	11 2	13000	4 3	24300	26900
35 6	ERICSON 35	SLP	SAIL	FBG KL IB	21D UNIV	11 10	13000	6 1	33200	36900
35 6	ERICSON 35 SHOAL	SLP	SAIL	FBG KL IB	21D UNIV	11 10	13000	4 11	33200	36900
35 9	ERICSON 36	SLP	SAIL	FBG KL IB	21D UNIV	11 10	11600	6 3	30000	33300
37 8	ERICSON 38	SLP	SAIL	FBG KL IB	32D UNIV	12	14900	6	40200	44700
37 8	ERICSON 38 SHOAL	SLP	SAIL	FBG KL IB	32D UNIV	12	14900	4 11	40200	44700

ERICSON YACHTS INC -CONTINUED See inside cover to adjust price for area

LOA FT	LOA IN	NAME AND/ OR MODEL	TOP/ RIG	BOAT TYPE	-HULL- MTL	-HULL- TP	ENGINE TP	ENGINE # HP	ENGINE MFG	BEAM FT	BEAM IN	WGT LBS	DRAFT FT	DRAFT IN	RETAIL LOW	RETAIL HIGH
		1983 BOATS														
37	8	ERICSON 381	SLP	SAIL	FBG	KL	IB	32D	UNIV	12		14400	6	6	39100	43400
37	8	ERICSON 381 SHOAL	SLP	SAIL	FBG	KL	IB	32D	UNIV	12		14400	4	1	39100	43400
		1982 BOATS														
25	5	ERICSON 25	SLP	SAIL	FBG	KL	OB			9	3	5000	4	11	9850	11200
25	5	ERICSON 25	SLP	SAIL	FBG	KL	IB	15	OMC	9	3	5000	4	11	10200	11600
25	5	ERICSON 25	SLP	SAIL	FBG	KL	IB	8D	VLVO	9	3	5000	4	11	10500	11900
25	5	ERICSON 25 SHOAL	SLP	SAIL	FBG	KL	OB			9	3	5000	3	11	9850	11200
25	5	ERICSON 25 SHOAL	SLP	SAIL	FBG	KL	IB	15	OMC	9	3	5000	3	11	10200	11600
25	5	ERICSON 25 SHOAL	SLP	SAIL	FBG	KL	IB	8D	VLVO	9	3	5000	3	11	10500	11900
28	6	ERICSON 28	SLP	SAIL	FBG	KL	IB	11D	UNIV	10	6	7500	5		17000	19300
28	6	ERICSON 28 SHOAL	SLP	SAIL	FBG	KL	IB	11D	UNIV	10	6	7500	4		17000	19300
29	11	ERICSON 30	SLP	SAIL	FBG	KL	IB	16D	UNIV	10	6	9000	5	10	21000	23400
29	11	ERICSON 30 SHOAL	SLP	SAIL	FBG	KL	IB	16D	UNIV	10	6	9125	4		21300	23700
33	6	ERICSON 33	SLP	SAIL	FBG	KL	IB	21D	UNIV	11	2	9500	5	11	22400	24800
34	8	ERICSON 35	SLP	SAIL	FBG	KL	IB	24D	UNIV	10		11600	4	11	27500	30600
35	6	ERICSON 35	SLP	SAIL	FBG	KL	IB	21D	UNIV	11	4	13000	4	11	31100	34500
35	7	ERICSON 36	SLP	SAIL	FBG	KL	IB	24D	UNIV	11	10	11600	6	3	28100	31200
37	8	ERICSON 38	SLP	SAIL	FBG	KL	IB	32D	UNIV	12		14850	4	11	37500	41700
		1981 BOATS														
25	5	ERICSON 25+	SLP	SAIL	FBG	KL	OB			9	3	5000	4	11	9300	10600
25	5	ERICSON 25+	SLP	SAIL	FBG	KL	IB	15	OMC	9	3	5000	4	11	9550	10800
25	5	ERICSON 25+	SLP	SAIL	FBG	KL	IB	8D	VLVO	9	3	5000	4	11	9800	11200
25	5	ERICSON 25+ SHOAL	SLP	SAIL	FBG	KL	OB			9	3	5000	3	11	9300	10600
25	5	ERICSON 25+ SHOAL	SLP	SAIL	FBG	KL	IB	15	OMC	9	3	5000	3	11	9550	10800
25	5	ERICSON 25+ SHOAL	SLP	SAIL	FBG	KL	IB	8D	VLVO	9	3	5000	3	11	9800	11200
28	6	ERICSON 28+	SLP	SAIL	FBG	KL	IB	11D	UNIV	10	6	7500	5		15900	18100
28	6	ERICSON 28+ SHOAL	SLP	SAIL	FBG	KL	IB	11D	UNIV	10	6	7500	4		15900	18100
29	11	ERICSON 30+	SLP	SAIL	FBG	KL	IB	16D	UNIV	10	6	9000	5	10	19700	21900
29	11	ERICSON 30+ SHOAL	SLP	SAIL	FBG	KL	IB	16D	UNIV	10	6	9125	4		20000	22200
30	11	INDEPENDENCE 31	SLP	SA/CR	FBG	KL	IB	16D	UNIV	10	5	11400	4	11	25100	27900
30	11	INDEPENDENCE 31	CUT	SA/CR	FBG	KL	IB	16D	UNIV	10	5	11400	4	11	25100	27900
34	8	ERICSON 35	SLP	SAIL	FBG	KL	IB	24D	UNIV	10		11600	4	11	25800	28700
36	7	ERICSON 36	SLP	SAIL	FBG	KL	IB	24D	UNIV	11	10	11600	6	3	27100	30100
37	8	ERICSON 38	SLP	SAIL	FBG	KL	IB	36D	UNIV	12		14000	4	11	33500	37200
		1980 BOATS														
25	5	ERICSON 25+	SLP	SAIL	FBG	KL	OB			9	3	5000	3	11	8850	10000
25	5	ERICSON 25+	SLP	SAIL	FBG	KL	IB	15	OMC	9	3	5000	3	11	9100	10400
25	5	ERICSON 25+	SLP	SAIL	FBG	KL	IB	8D	VLVO	9	3	5000	3	11	9400	10700
29	11	ERICSON 30+	SLP	SAIL	FBG	KL	IB	16D	UNIV	10	5	9000	4		19000	21100
30	11	INDEPENDENCE 31	SLP	SA/CR	FBG	KL	IB	16D-	30D	10	5	11400	4	11	23800	26500
30	11	INDEPENDENCE 31	CUT	SA/CR	FBG	KL	IB	16D-	30D	10	5	11400	4	11	23800	26500
34	8	ERICSON 35	SLP	SAIL	FBG	KL	IB	24D	UNIV	10		11600	4	11	24500	27200
37	8	ERICSON 38	SLP	SAIL	FBG	KL	IB	36D	UNIV	12		14000	4	11	31900	35400
		1979 BOATS														
22	11	ERICSON 23	SLP	SA/OD	FBG	KL	OB			7	11	3100	3	8	4750	5450
25	5	ERICSON 25+	SLP	SAIL	FBG	KL	OB			9	3	5000	4	11	8350	9600
25	5	ERICSON 25+	SLP	SAIL	FBG	KL	IB			9	3	5000	4	11	8700	9950
25	5	ERICSON 25+ SHOAL	SLP	SAIL	FBG	KL	OB			9	3	5000	3	11	8350	9600
25	5	ERICSON 25+ SHOAL	SLP	SAIL	FBG	KL	IB			9	3	5000	3	11	8700	9950
26	9	ERICSON 27	SLP	SAIL	FBG	KL	OB			9		7000	3	11	12600	14300
26	9	ERICSON 27	SLP	SAIL	FBG	KL	IB			9		7000	3	11	12900	14600
28	7	ERICSON 29	SLP	SAIL	FBG	KL	OB			9	3	8500	4	4	16200	18400
30		ERICSON 30	SLP	SAIL	FBG	KL	IB			10	5	8990	5	9	18000	20000
30		ERICSON 30 SHOAL	SLP	SAIL	FBG	KL	IB			10	5	8990	4		18000	20000
30	11	INDEPENDENCE 31	SLP	SAIL	FBG	KL	OB			10	5	11400	4	11	22700	25200
30	11	INDEPENDENCE 31	SLP	SAIL	FBG	KL	IB	D		10	5	11400	4	11	22800	25400
30	11	INDEPENDENCE 31	CUT	SAIL	FBG	KL	OB			10	5	11400	4	11	22700	25200
30	11	INDEPENDENCE 31	CUT	SAIL	FBG	KL	IB	D		10	5	11400	4	11	22800	25400
33	8	ERICSON 34T	SLP	SAIL	FBG	KL	IB	D		10	11	11600	6	2	23200	25800
34	8	ERICSON 35	SLP	SAIL	FBG	KL	IB	D		10		12500	4	11	25200	28000
36		ERICSON 36C	SLP	SAIL	FBG	KL	IB	D		12		17200	5	6	34500	38300
36		INDEPENDENCE 36	KTH	SA/CR	FBG	KL	IB	D		12		16000	5	6	32400	36000
39		ERICSON 39B	SLP	SAIL	FBG	KL	IB	D		11	4	19000	5	11	41100	45700
		1978 BOATS														
22	11	ERICSON 23	SLP	SA/OD	FBG	KL	OB			7	11	3200	1	11	4700	5400
24	8	ERICSON 25	SLP	SAIL	FBG	KC	OB			8		5400	2		8400	9650
24	8	ERICSON 25	SLP	SAIL	FBG	KC	IB	30	UNIV	8		5400	2		8850	10100
24	8	ERICSON 25	SLP	SAIL	FBG	KC	IB	8D	YAN	8		5400	2		9100	10300
24	8	ERICSON 25	SLP	SAIL	FBG	KL	OB			8		5300	3	10	8250	9450
24	8	ERICSON 25	SLP	SAIL	FBG	KL	IB	30	UNIV	8		5300	3	10	8600	9900
24	8	ERICSON 25	SLP	SAIL	FBG	KL	IB	8D	YAN	8		5300	3	10	8950	10100
26	9	ERICSON 27	SLP	SAIL	FBG	KL	OB			9		6600	3	11	11400	12900
26	9	ERICSON 27	SLP	SAIL	FBG	KL	IB	30	UNIV	9		7000	3	11	12400	14100
26	9	ERICSON 27	SLP	SAIL	FBG	KL	IB	8D	YAN	9		7000	3	11	12500	14200
28	7	ERICSON 29	SLP	SAIL	FBG	KL	IB	30	UNIV	9	3	8500	4	4	15700	17900
28	7	ERICSON 29	SLP	SAIL	FBG	KL	IB	8D-	13D	9	3	8500	4	4	15900	18000
30		ERICSON 30	SLP	SA/RC	FBG	KL	IB	30	UNIV	10	5	8990	5	10	16900	19200
30		ERICSON 30	SLP	SA/RC	FBG	KL	IB	12D	YAN	10	5	8990	5	10	17000	19300
30	11	ERICSON CRUISING 31	SLP	SA/CR	FBG	KL	IB	30	UNIV	10	5	11400	4	11	21900	24300
30	11	ERICSON CRUISING 31	SLP	SA/CR	FBG	KL	IB	20D	WEST	10	5	11400	4	11	21900	24400
30	11	ERICSON CRUISING 31	CUT	SA/CR	FBG	KL	IB	30	UNIV	10	5	11400	4	11	21900	24300
30	11	ERICSON CRUISING 31	CUT	SA/CR	FBG	KL	IB	20D	WEST	10	5	11400	4	11	21900	24400
31	7	ERICSON 32	SLP	SAIL	FBG	KL	IB	30	UNIV	9	8	8800	4	11	16700	19000
31	7	ERICSON 32	SLP	SAIL	FBG	KL	IB	15D-	25D	9	8	8800	4	11	16700	19000
33	8	ERICSON 34	SLP	SA/RC	FBG	KL	IB	30	UNIV	10	11	10000	5	11	19200	21300
33	8	ERICSON 34T	SLP	SAIL	FBG	KL	IB	30	UNIV	10	11	10700	5	11	20500	22800
33	8	ERICSON 34T	SLP	SAIL	FBG	KL	IB	15D-	22D	10	11	10700	5	11	20600	22900
34	8	ERICSON 35	SLP	SA/RC	FBG	KL	IB	30	UNIV	10		11600	4	11	22400	24900
34	8	ERICSON 35	SLP	SA/RC	FBG	KL	IB	20D-	25D	10		11600	4	11	22500	25100
36		ERICSON CRUISING 36	SLP	SA/CR	FBG	KL	IB	30	UNIV	12		16000	5		30700	34200
36		ERICSON CRUISING 36	SLP	SA/CR	FBG	KL	IB	20D		12		16000	5		31000	34400
36		ERICSON CRUISING 36	KTH	SA/CR	FBG	KL	IB	30	UNIV	12		16000	5		30700	34200
36		ERICSON CRUISING 36	KTH	SA/CR	FBG	KL	IB	20D		12		16000	5		31000	34400
39		ERICSON 39B	SLP	SA/CR	FBG	KL	IB	50D	PERK	11	4	19000	5	11	39400	43700
		1977 BOATS														
22	11	ERICSON 23	SLP	SA/OD	FBG	KL	OB			7	11	3200	1	11	4500	5200
24	8	ERICSON 25	SLP	SAIL	FBG	KC	OB			8		5400	2		8100	9300
24	8	ERICSON 25	SLP	SAIL	FBG	KC	IB	D		8		5400	2		8800	10000
24	8	ERICSON 25	SLP	SAIL	FBG	KL	OB			8		5300	3	10	7950	9100
24	8	ERICSON 25	SLP	SAIL	FBG	KL	IB	D		8		5300	3	10	8550	9850
26	9	ERICSON 27	SLP	SAIL	FBG	KL	OB			9		6600	3	11	10900	12400
26	9	ERICSON 27	SLP	SAIL	FBG	KL	IB	30	UNIV	9		7000	3	11	11900	13500
28	7	ERICSON 29	SLP	SAIL	FBG	KL	IB	30	UNIV	9	3	8500	4	4	15200	17200
30	11	ERICSON CRUISING 31	SLP	SA/CR	FBG	KL	IB	20D	WEST	10	5	11400	4	11	21100	23500
30	11	ERICSON CRUISING 31	CUT	SA/CR	FBG	KL	IB	20D	WEST	10	5	11400	4	11	21100	23500
31	7	ERICSON 32	SLP	SAIL	FBG	KL	IB	30	UNIV	9	8	8800	4	11	16100	18300
34	8	ERICSON 35	SLP	SAIL	FBG	KL	IB	30	UNIV	10		11600	4	11	21500	23900
34	8	ERICSON 35	SLP	SAIL	FBG	KL	IB	25D	WEST	10		11600	4	11	21700	24200
36		ERICSON CRUISING 36	CUT	SA/CR	FBG	KL	IB	20D	WEST	12		16000	5		29900	33200
36		ERICSON CRUISING 36	KTH	SA/CR	FBG	KL	IB	20D	WEST	12		16000	5		29900	33200
37	5	ERICSON 37	SLP	SAIL	FBG	KL	IB	30	UNIV	11	4	16000	5	9	30700	34100
37	5	ERICSON 37	SLP	SAIL	FBG	KL	IB	25D	WEST	11	4	16000	5	9	31100	34600
37	5	ERICSON 37	SLP	SAIL	FBG	KL	IB	37D	PERK	11	4	16000	5	9	31000	34500
39		ERICSON 39	SLP	SAIL	FBG	KL	IB	30	UNIV	11	4	19000	5	11	37400	41500
39		ERICSON 39	SLP	SAIL	FBG	KL	IB	25D	WEST	11	4	19000	5	11	37900	42100
39		ERICSON 39	SLP	SAIL	FBG	KL	IB	37D	PERK	11	4	19000	5	11	37800	42000
39		ERICSON 39B	SLP	SA/CR	FBG	KL	IB	50D	PERK	11	4	19000	5	11	37900	42100
		1976 BOATS														
22	11	ERICSON 23	SLP	SA/OD	FBG	KL				7	11	3200	1	11	4350	5000
22	11	ERICSON 23 SPECIAL	SLP	SAIL	FBG	KC				7	11	3200	1	11	4350	5000
22	11	ERICSON 23 SPECIAL	SLP	SAIL	FBG	KL				7	11	3100	3	8	4200	4900
24	8	ERICSON 25	SLP	SAIL	FBG	KC				8		5400	2		7650	8800
24	8	ERICSON 25	SLP	SAIL	FBG	KL				8		5300	3	10	7500	8650
26	9	ERICSON 27	SLP	SAIL	FBG	KL				9		6600	3	11	10000	11400
26	9	ERICSON 27	SLP	SAIL	FBG	KL	IB	30	UNIV	9		7000	3	11	11500	13100
28	7	ERICSON 29	SLP	SAIL	FBG	KL	IB	30	UNIV	9	3	8500	4	4	14600	16600
31	7	ERICSON 32	SLP	SAIL	FBG	KL	IB	30	UNIV	9	8	8800	4	11	15500	17600
34	8	ERICSON 35	SLP	SAIL	FBG	KL	IB	30	UNIV	10		11600	4	11	20800	23100
34	8	ERICSON 35	SLP	SAIL	FBG	KL	IB	25D	WEST	10		11600	4	11	21000	23300
36		ERICSON CRUISING 36	CUT	SA/CR	FBG	KL	IB	20D	WEST	12		16000	5	6	28800	32000
36		ERICSON CRUISING 36	KTH	SA/CR	FBG	KL	IB	20D	WEST	12		16000	5	6	28800	32000
37	5	ERICSON 37	SLP	SAIL	FBG	KL	IB	30	UNIV	11	4	16000	5	9	29700	32900
		IB 25D WEST 30000 33400, IB 37D PERK 30000 33300, IB 37D WEST													30200	33500
39		ERICSON 39	SLP	SAIL	FBG	KL	IB	30	UNIV	11	4	19000	5	11	36100	40100
		IB 25D WEST 36600 40700, IB 37D PERK 36500 40600, IB 37D WEST													36800	40800
39		ERICSON 39B	SLP	SAIL	FBG	KL	IB	D	PERK	11	4	19000	5	11	36500	40600
45	10	ERICSON 46	SLP	SAIL	FBG	KL	IB	D	PERK	13	3	31500	7	2	65600	72100
		1975 BOATS														
22	11	ERICSON 23	SLP	SA/OD	FBG	KL				7	11	3200	1	11	4150	4850
24	8	ERICSON 25	SLP	SAIL	FBG	KC				8		5500	2		7600	8700
24	8	ERICSON 25	SLP	SAIL	FBG	KL				8		5400	3	10	7450	8550
26	9	ERICSON 27	SLP	SAIL	FBG	KL	OB			9		6600	3	11	10200	11600
26	9	ERICSON 27	SLP	SAIL	FBG	KL	IB	30	UNIV	9		7000	3	11	11100	12700
28	7	ERICSON 29	SLP	SAIL	FBG	KL	OB			9	3	8500	4	4	14000	16000
28	7	ERICSON 29	SLP	SAIL	FBG	KL	IB	30	UNIV	9	3		4	4	13000	14800
31	7	ERICSON 32	SLP	SAIL	FBG	KL	IB	30	UNIV	9	8	8800	4	11	15000	17100
34	8	ERICSON 35	SLP	SAIL	FBG	KL	IB	30	UNIV	10		11600	4	11	20200	22400

CONTINUED ON NEXT PAGE

ERICSON YACHTS INC -CONTINUED See inside cover to adjust price for area

LOA FT	IN	NAME AND/ OR MODEL	TOP/ RIG	BOAT TYPE	-HULL- MTL	TP	TP	#	HP	MFG	BEAM FT	IN	WGT LBS	DRAFT FT	IN	RETAIL LOW	RETAIL HIGH
		1975 BOATS															
34	8	ERICSON 35	SLP	SAIL	FBG	KL	IB		35D	PERK	10		11600	4	11	20300	22600
36		ERICSON CRUISING 36	CUT	SA/CR	FBG	KL	IB		20D		12		16000	5		27900	31000
37	5	ERICSON 37	SLP	SAIL	FBG	KL	IB		30	UNIV	11	4	16000	5	9	28700	31900
37	5	ERICSON 37	SLP	SAIL	FBG	KL	IB		55D	WEST	11	4	16000	5	9	29400	32600
39		ERICSON 39	SLP	SAIL	FBG	KL	IB		30	UNIV	11	4	19000	5	11	35000	38900
39		ERICSON 39	SLP	SAIL	FBG	KL	IB		55D	WEST	11	4	19000	5	11	35800	39800
39		ERICSON 39	CUT	SAIL	FBG	KL	IB		30	UNIV	11	4	19000	5	11	35000	38900
39		ERICSON 39	KTH	SAIL	FBG	KL	IB		30	UNIV	11	4	19000	5	11	35000	38900
39		ERICSON CRUISING 39B	SLP	SA/CR	FBG	KL	IB		50D	PERK	5	11	19000	11	4	35500	39400
39		ERICSON CRUISING 39B	CUT	SA/CR	FBG	KL	IB		50D	PERK	5	11	19000	11	4	35500	39400
39		ERICSON CRUISING 39B	KTH	SA/CR	FBG	KL	IB		50D	PERK	5	11	19000	11	4	35500	39400
45	10	ERICSON 46	SLP	SAIL	FBG	KL	IB		50D	PERK	13	3	31500	7	2	63400	69600
		1974 BOATS															
24	8	ERICSON 25	SLP	SAIL	FBG		OB				8		5400	2		7350	8450
26	9	ERICSON 27	SLP	SAIL	FBG		OD				9		6600	3	11	9950	11300
28	7	ERICSON 29	SLP	SAIL	FBG		OB				9	3	8500	4	4	13600	15500
31	7	ERICSON 32	SLP	SAIL	FBG		IB		30	UNIV	9	8	8800	4	11	14600	16600
34	8	ERICSON 35	SLP	SAIL	FBG		IB		30	UNIV	10		11600	4	11	19600	21800
37	5	ERICSON 37	SLP	SAIL	FBG		IB		30	UNIV	11	4	16000	5	9	27900	31000
39		ERICSON 39		SAIL	FBG		IB		30	UNIV	11	4	19000	5	11	34000	37800
45	10	ERICSON 46	SLP	SAIL	FBG		IB		50D	PERK	13	3	31500	7	2	61600	67700
		1973 BOATS															
24	8	ERICSON 25	SLP	SAIL	FBG	KC	OB				8		5400	2		7200	8250
26	9	ERICSON 27	SLP	SAIL	FBG		OB				9		6600	3	11	9700	11000
26	9	ERICSON 27	SLP	SAIL	FBG		IB		30	UNIV	9		6600	3	11	9950	11300
28	7	ERICSON 29	SLP	SAIL	FBG		OB				9	3	8500	4	4	13300	15100
28	7	ERICSON 29	SLP	SAIL	FBG		IB		30	UNIV	9	3	8500	4	4	13500	15300
31	7	ERICSON 32	SLP	SAIL	FBG		IB		30	UNIV	9	8	8000	4	11	13000	14700
34	8	ERICSON 35	SLP	SAIL	FBG		IB		30	UNIV	10		11600	4	11	19100	21200
34	8	ERICSON 35	SLP	SAIL	FBG		IB		25D	WEST	10		11600	4	11	19300	21400
37	5	ERICSON 37	SLP	SAIL	FBG		IB		30	UNIV	11	4	16000	5	9	27200	30300
39		ERICSON 39	SLP	SAIL	FBG		IB		30	UNIV	11	4	19000	5	11	33200	36900
		IB 25D WEST 33600 37400, IB 37D WEST 33800 37500, IB 50D PERK														33600	37400
45	10	ERICSON 46	SLP	SAIL	FBG		IB		40D	PERK	13	3	31500	7	2	60000	66000
		1972 BOATS															
22	7	ERICSON 23	SLP	SA/OD	FBG	KL	OB				7	6		3	6	2500	2900
26	9	ERICSON 27	SLP	SAIL	FBG		OB				9		6600	3	11	9500	10800
26	9	ERICSON 27	SLP	SAIL	FBG		IB		30	UNIV	9		6600	3	11	9750	11100
28	7	ERICSON 29	SLP	SAIL	FBG		OB				9	3	8500	4	4	13000	14800
28	7	ERICSON 29	SLP	SAIL	FBG		IB		30	UNIV	9	3	8500	4	4	13200	15000
30	3	ERICSON 30	SLP	SA/OD	FBG	KL	IB		D		9	6		4	10	10800	12200
31	7	ERICSON 32	SLP	SAIL	FBG		IB		30	UNIV	9	8	8800	4	11	14000	15900
34	8	ERICSON 35	SLP	SAIL	FBG		IB		30	UNIV	10		11600	4	11	18900	21100
39		ERICSON 39	SLP	SAIL	FBG		IB		30	UNIV	11	4	19000	5	11	32500	36100
39		ERICSON 39	SLP	SAIL	FBG		IB		25D	WEST	11	4	19000	5	11	33000	36600
45	10	ERICSON 46	SLP	SAIL	FBG		IB		55D	PERK	13	3	31500	7	2	58900	64800
45	10	ERICSON 46	KTH	SAIL	FBG		IB		55D	PERK	13	3	31500	7	2	58900	64800
		1971 BOATS															
22	7	ERICSON 23	SLP	SA/OD	FBG	KL	OB				7	6	2700	3	6	3300	3850
26	9	ERICSON 27	SLP	SAIL	FBG		OB				9	6	6600	3	11	9400	10700
26	9	ERICSON 27	SLP	SAIL	FBG		IB		30	UNIV	9	6		3	11	8350	9600
28	7	ERICSON 29	SLP	SAIL	FBG		OB				9	3	8500	4	4	12800	14600
28	7	ERICSON 29	SLP	SAIL	FBG		IB		D		9	3		4	4	11600	13200
30	3	ERICSON 30	SLP	SA/OD	FBG	KL	IB		D		9	6	7800	4	10	12100	13800
31	7	ERICSON 32	SLP	SAIL	FBG		IB		30	UNIV	9	8	8800	4	11	13700	15600
34	8	ERICSON 35	SLP	SAIL	FBG		IB		30	UNIV	10		11600	4	11	18600	20700
39		ERICSON 39	SLP	SAIL	FBG		IB		30	UNIV	11	5	19000	6		31900	35500
41	4	ERICSON 41	SLP	SAIL	FBG		IB		30	UNIV	10	8	17800	5	11	34000	37700
		1970 BOATS															
22	7	ERICSON 23	SLP	SA/OD	FBG	KL	IB		D		7	6		3	6	2850	3300
22	7	ERICSON 23	SLP	SAIL	FBG	KL	IB		D		7	6	2700	3	6	3900	4500
25	9	ERICSON 26	SLP	SAIL	FBG	KL	IB		D		7	9	4400	4	3	6200	7150
28	7	ERICSON 29	SLP	SAIL	FBG		IB		D		9	3		4	6	11500	13000
30	3	ERICSON 30	SLP	SAIL	FBG	KL	IB		30	UNIV	9	6	7800	4	10	11900	13500
31	7	ERICSON 32	SLP	SAIL	FBG	KL	IB		30	UNIV	9	8	8800	4	11	13500	15400
34	8	ERICSON 35	SLP	SAIL	FBG	KL	IB		30	UNIV	10		11600	4	11	18300	20400
41	4	ERICSON 41	SLP	SAIL	FBG	KL	IB		30	UNIV	10	8	17800	5	11	33500	37200
41	4	ERICSON 41	SLP	SAIL	FBG	KL	IB		30D	WEST	10	8	17800	5	11	34000	37800
		1969 BOATS															
22	7	ERICSON 23	SLP	SAIL	FBG	KL	IB		D		7	6	2700	3	6	3850	4450
25	9	ERICSON 26	SLP	SAIL	FBG	KL	IB		D		7	9	4400	4	3	6150	7050
30	3	ERICSON 30	SLP	SAIL	FBG	KL	IB		15D		9	6	7400	5		11200	12700
31	9	ERICSON 32	SLP	SA/CR	FBG	KL	IB		35D		9	6	8400	5		12800	14500
41	4	ERICSON 41	SLP	SA/CR	FBG	KL	IB		D		10		18750	5	11	34700	38600
		1968 BOATS															
22	7	ERICSON 23	SLP	SA/OD	FBG	KL	IB		D		7	6	2700	3	6	3800	4400
25	9	ERICSON 26	SLP	SAIL	FBG	KL	IB		D		7	9	4400	4	3	6100	7000
25	9	PACER	SLP	SAIL	FBG	KL	IB		D		7	9	4200	4	3	5850	6700
30	3	ERICSON 30	SLP	SAIL	FBG	KL	IB		D		9	6	7400	5		11100	12600
32	3	ERICSON 32	SLP	SAIL	FBG	KL	IB		D		6	3	4600	4	3	6750	7750
34	9	ERICSON 34	SLP	SAIL	FBG	KL	IB		D		9	8	12000	4	11	18700	20800
41	4	ERICSON 41	SLP	SAIL	FBG	KL	IB		D		10	8	18750	6		34400	38200
		1967 BOATS															
25	9	ERICSON 26	SLP	SA/CR	FBG		IB		D		7	9		4	3	7950	9150
25	9	PACER	SLP	SA/CR	FBG		IB		D		7	9		4	3	6650	7650
30	3	ERICSON 30	SLP	SA/CR	FBG		IB		D		9	6		4	11	13200	15000
32	3	ERICSON 32	SLP	SA/CR	FBG		IB		D		6	3		4	3	14600	16600
34	9	ERICSON 35	SLP	SA/CR	FBG		IB		D		9	8		4	11	19800	22000
41	4	ERICSON 41	SLP	SA/CR	FBG		IB		D					5	10	39400	43800
		1966 BOATS															
32	3	ERICSON 32	SLP	SA/CR	FBG	KL	IB		D		6	3	4500	4	3	6500	7450
34	8	ERICSON 35	SLP	SA/CR	FBG	KL	IB		D		10		11600	4	11	17500	19900
		1965 BOATS															
32	3	SCROPION 32	SLP	SA/OD	FBG	KL	IB		D		6	3		4	4	14500	16500
34	9	ERICSON	YWL	SAIL		KL	IB		30D		9	8		5	2	19700	21900

NILS ERIKSON BOAT WORKS

Call 1-800-327-6929 for BUC Personalized Evaluation Service
Or, for 1967 to 1972 boats, sign onto www.BUCValuPro.com

TERRY ERSKINE YACHTS

PLYMOUTH DEVON ENGLAND COAST GUARD MFG ID- TEY See inside cover to adjust price for area

LOA FT	IN	NAME AND/ OR MODEL	TOP/ RIG	BOAT TYPE	-HULL- MTL	TP	TP	#	HP	MFG	BEAM FT	IN	WGT LBS	DRAFT FT	IN	RETAIL LOW	RETAIL HIGH
		1982 BOATS															
26		GOLDEN-HIND 26	SLP	SA/CR	FBG	KL	IB		10D	BUKH	8	2	5700	2	6	15500	17600
26		GOLDEN-HIND 26	SLP	SA/CR	WD	KL	IB		10D	BUKH	8	2		2	6	15500	17600
26		GOLDEN-HIND 26	CUT	SA/CR	FBG	KL	IB		10D	BUKH	8	2	5700	2	6	15500	17600
26		GOLDEN-HIND 26	CUT	SA/CR	WD	KL	IB		10D	BUKH	8	2		2	6	15500	17600
31	6	GOLDEN-HIND 31	SLP	SA/CR	FBG	KL	IB		12D	LIST	9		11600	3	8	33000	36600
31	6	GOLDEN-HIND 31	SLP	SA/CR	WD	KL	IB		12D	LIST	9			3	8	33000	36600
31	6	GOLDEN-HIND 31	CUT	SA/CR	FBG	KL	IB		12D	LIST	9		11600	3	8	33000	36600
31	6	GOLDEN-HIND 31	CUT	SA/CR	WD	KL	IB		12D	LIST	9			3	8	33000	36600
31	6	GOLDEN-HIND 31	KTH	SA/CR	FBG	KL	IB		12D	LIST	9		11600	3	8	33000	36600
31	6	GOLDEN-HIND 31	KTH	SA/CR	WD	KL	IB		12D	LIST	9			3	8	33000	36600
33		DULCIBELLA 33	SLP	SA/CR	WD	KL	IB		D		10	6		6	6	32800	36400
33		DULCIBELLA 33	CUT	SA/CR	WD	KL	IB		D		10	6		6	6	32800	36400
33		DULCIBELLA 33	KTH	SA/CR	WD	KL	IB		D		10	6		6	6	32800	36400
39		GOLDEN-HIND 39	SLP	SA/CR	STL	KL	IB		30D	LIST	10	8	17380	4	8	54200	59500
39		GOLDEN-HIND 39	CUT	SA/CR	STL	KL	IB		30D	LIST	10	8	17380	4	8	54200	59500
39		GOLDEN-HIND 39	KTH	SA/CR	STL	KL	IB		30D	LIST	10	8	17380	4	8	54200	59500
		1981 BOATS															
26		GOLDEN-HIND 26	SLP	SA/CR	FBG	TK	IB		10D	BUKH	8	2	5700	2	6	14600	16500
26		GOLDEN-HIND 26	SLP	SA/CR	STL	TK	IB		10D	BUKH	8	2	5700	2	6	14600	16500
26		GOLDEN-HIND 26	SLP	SA/CR	WD	TK	IB		10D	BUKH	8	2	5700	2	6	14600	16500
26		GOLDEN-HIND 26	CUT	SA/CR	FBG	TK	IB		10D	BUKH	8	2	5700	2	6	14600	16500
26		GOLDEN-HIND 26	CUT	SA/CR	STL	TK	IB		10D	BUKH	8	2	5700	2	6	14600	16500
26		GOLDEN-HIND 26	CUT	SA/CR	WD	TK	IB		10D	BUKH	8	2	5700	2	6	14600	16500
31	6	GOLDEN-HIND 31	SLP	SA/CR	FBG	KL	IB		12D	LIST	9		11600	3	8	31000	34500
31	6	GOLDEN-HIND 31	SLP	SA/CR	STL	KL	IB		12D	LIST	9		11600	3	8	31000	34500
31	6	GOLDEN-HIND 31	SLP	SA/CR	WD	KL	IB		12D	LIST	9		11600	3	8	31000	34500
31	6	GOLDEN-HIND 31	CUT	SA/CR	FBG	KL	IB		12D	LIST	9		11600	3	8	31000	34500
31	6	GOLDEN-HIND 31	CUT	SA/CR	STL	KL	IB		12D	LIST	9		11600	3	8	31000	34500
31	6	GOLDEN-HIND 31	CUT	SA/CR	WD	KL	IB		12D	LIST	9		11600	3	8	31000	34500
31	6	GOLDEN-HIND 31	KTH	SA/CR	FBG	KL	IB		12D	LIST	9		11600	3	8	31000	34500
31	6	GOLDEN-HIND 31	KTH	SA/CR	STL	KL	IB		12D	LIST	9		11600	3	8	31000	34500
31	6	GOLDEN-HIND 31	KTH	SA/CR	WD	KL	IB		12D	LIST	9		11600	3	8	31000	34500
39		GOLDEN-HIND 39	SLP	SA/CR	STL	KL	IB		30D	LIST	10	8	17380	4	4	50900	56000
39		GOLDEN-HIND 39	CUT	SA/CR	STL	KL	IB		30D	LIST	10	8	17380	4	4	50900	56000
39		GOLDEN-HIND 39	KTH	SA/CR	STL	KL	IB		30D	LIST	10	8	17380	4	4	51000	56000
		1980 BOATS															
26		GOLDEN-HIND 26	SLP	SA/CR	FBG	TK	IB		10D	BUKH	8	2	5700	2	6	13900	15800
26		GOLDEN-HIND 26	SLP	SA/CR	STL	TK	IB		10D	BUKH	8	2	5700	2	6	13900	15800
26		GOLDEN-HIND 26	SLP	SA/CR	WD	TK	IB		10D	BUKH	8	2	5700	2	6	13900	15800
26		GOLDEN-HIND 26	CUT	SA/CR	FBG	TK	IB		10D	BUKH	8	2	5700	2	6	13900	15800
26		GOLDEN-HIND 26	CUT	SA/CR	STL	TK	IB		10D	BUKH	8	2	5700	2	6	13900	15800
26		GOLDEN-HIND 26	CUT	SA/CR	WD	TK	IB		10D	BUKH	8	2	5700	2	6	13900	15800
31	6	GOLDEN-HIND 31	SLP	SA/CR	FBG	KL	IB		20D	LIST	9		11600	3	8	29600	32900
31	6	GOLDEN-HIND 31	SLP	SA/CR	WD	KL	IB		20D	LIST	9		11600	3	8	29600	32900

LOA FT IN	NAME AND/ OR MODEL	TOP/ RIG	BOAT TYPE	-HULL- MTL TP	TP	----ENGINE--- # HP MFG	BEAM FT IN	WGT LBS	DRAFT FT IN	RETAIL LOW	RETAIL HIGH
						1980 BOATS					
31 6	GOLDEN-HIND 31	CUT	SA/CR	FBG KL	IB	20D LIST 9		11600	3 8	29600	32900
31 6	GOLDEN-HIND 31	CUT	SA/CR	WD KL	IB	20D LIST 9		11600	3 8	29600	32900
31 6	GOLDEN-HIND 31	KTH	SA/CR	FBG KL	IB	20D LIST 9		11600	3 8	29600	32900
31 6	GOLDEN-HIND 31	KTH	SA/CR	WD KL	IB	20D LIST 9		11600	3 8	29600	32900
39	GOLDEN-HIND 39	SLP	SA/CR	STL KL	IB	36D LIST 10 8		17380	4 4	48800	53600
39	GOLDEN-HIND 39	CUT	SA/CR	STL KL	IB	36D LIST 10 8		17380	4 4	48800	53600
39	GOLDEN-HIND 39	KTH	SA/CR	STL KL	IB	36D LIST 10 8		17380	4 4	48800	53600
						1979 BOATS					
31 6	GOLDEN-HIND 31	SLP	SA/CR	F/W KL	IB	20D LIST 9		11600	3 8	28500	31700
31 6	GOLDEN-HIND 31	SLP	SA/CR	FBG KL	IB	20D LIST 9		11600	3 7	28500	31700
31 6	GOLDEN-HIND 31	SLP	SA/CR	F/W TK	IB	20D LIST 9		11600		28500	31700
31 6	GOLDEN-HIND 31	SLP	SA/CR	FBG TK	IB	20D LIST 9		11600		28500	31700
31 6	GOLDEN-HIND 31	CUT	SA/CR	F/W KL	IB	20D LIST 9		11600	3 7	28500	31700
31 6	GOLDEN-HIND 31	CUT	SA/CR	FBG KL	IB	20D LIST 9		11600	3 7	28500	31700
31 6	GOLDEN-HIND 31	CUT	SA/CR	F/W TK	IB	20D LIST 9		11600		28500	31700
31 6	GOLDEN-HIND 31	CUT	SA/CR	FBG TK	IB	20D LIST 9		11600		28500	31700
31 6	GOLDEN-HIND 31	KTH	SA/CR	F/W KL	IB	20D LIST 9		11600	3 7	28500	31700
31 6	GOLDEN-HIND 31	KTH	SA/CR	FBG KL	IB	20D LIST 9		11600	3 7	28500	31700
31 6	GOLDEN-HIND 31	KTH	SA/CR	F/W TK	IB	20D LIST 9		11600		28500	31700
31 6	GOLDEN-HIND 31	KTH	SA/CR	FBG TK	IB	20D LIST 9		11600		28500	31700
39	GOLDEN-HIND 39	SLP	SA/CR	STL KL	IB	30D LIST 10 8		17380	4 4	47000	51700
39	GOLDEN-HIND 39	SLP	SA/CR	STL TK	IB	30D LIST 10 8		17380		47000	51700
39	GOLDEN-HIND 39	CUT	SA/CR	STL KL	IB	30D LIST 10 8		17380	4 4	47000	51700
39	GOLDEN-HIND 39	CUT	SA/CR	STL TK	IB	30D LIST 10 8		17380		47000	51700
39	GOLDEN-HIND 39	KTH	SA/CR	STL KL	IB	30D LIST 10 8		17380	4 4	47000	51700
39	GOLDEN-HIND 39	KTH	SA/CR	STL TK	IB	30D LIST 10 8		17380		47000	51700
						1978 BOATS					
31 6	GOLDEN-HIND 31	SLP	SA/CR	F/W KL	IB	20D LIST 9		11600	3 8	27500	30500
31 6	GOLDEN-HIND 31	SLP	SA/CR	FBG KL	IB	20D LIST 9		11600	3 8	27500	30500
31 6	GOLDEN-HIND 31	CUT	SA/CR	F/W KL	IB	20D LIST 9		11600	3 8	27500	30500
31 6	GOLDEN-HIND 31	CUT	SA/CR	FBG KL	IB	20D LIST 9		11600	3 8	27500	30500
31 6	GOLDEN-HIND 31	KTH	SA/CR	F/W KL	IB	20D LIST 9		11600	3 8	27500	30500
31 6	GOLDEN-HIND 31	KTH	SA/CR	FBG KL	IB	20D LIST 9		11600	3 8	27500	30500
39	GOLDEN-HIND 39	SLP	SA/CR	STL KL	IB	30D LIST 10 8		17380	4 4	44800	49800
						1977 BOATS					
31 6	GOLDEN-HIND 31	SLP	SA/CR	F/W KL	IB	20D LIST 9		11600	3 8	26500	29500
31 6	GOLDEN-HIND 31	SLP	SA/CR	FBG KL	IB	20D LIST 9		11600	3 8	26500	29500
31 6	GOLDEN-HIND 31	CUT	SA/CR	F/W KL	IB	20D LIST 9		11600	3 8	26500	29500
31 6	GOLDEN-HIND 31	CUT	SA/CR	FBG KL	IB	20D LIST 9		11600	3 8	26500	29500
31 6	GOLDEN-HIND 31	KTH	SA/CR	F/W KL	IB	20D LIST 9		11600	3 8	26500	29500
31 6	GOLDEN-HIND 31	KTH	SA/CR	FBG KL	IB	20D LIST 9		11600	3 8	26500	29500
						1976 BOATS					
31 6	GOLDEN-HIND 31	SLP	SAIL	FBG KL	IB	20D LIST 9		11600	3 7	25700	28600
31 6	GOLDEN-HIND 31	SLP	SAIL	WD KL	IB	20D LIST 9		11600	3 7	25700	28600
31 6	GOLDEN-HIND 31	CUT	SAIL	FBG KL	IB	20D LIST 9		11600	3 7	25700	28600
31 6	GOLDEN-HIND 31	CUT	SAIL	WD KL	IB	20D LIST 9		11600	3 7	25700	28600
31 6	GOLDEN-HIND 31	KTH	SAIL	FBG KL	IB	20D LIST 9		11600	3 7	25700	28600
31 6	GOLDEN-HIND 31	KTH	SAIL	WD KL	IB	20D LIST 9		11600	3 7	25700	28600

ESCAPADE MARINE INC
SUNCHASER   COAST GUARD MFG ID- SSR

Call 1-800-327-6929 for BUC Personalized Evaluation Service
Or, for 1973 to 1980 boats, sign onto www.BUCValuPro.com

ESSBOATS

Call 1-800-327-6929 for BUC Personalized Evaluation Service
Or, for 1967 to 1968 boats, sign onto www.BUCValuPro.com

ESSEX BAY BOAT CO INC
COAST GUARD MFG ID- ESI

Call 1-800-327-6929 for BUC Personalized Evaluation Service
Or, for 1983 to 1986 boats, sign onto www.BUCValuPro.com

ESSEX CO LTD
COAST GUARD MFG ID- ESX

Call 1-800-327-6929 for BUC Personalized Evaluation Service
Or, for 1974 to 1978 boats, sign onto www.BUCValuPro.com

EUROPEAN YACHTS LTD

Call 1-800-327-6929 for BUC Personalized Evaluation Service
Or, for 1978 boats, sign onto www.BUCValuPro.com

KENNETH EVANS & PARTNERS LTD

Call 1-800-327-6929 for BUC Personalized Evaluation Service
Or, for 1970 boats, sign onto www.BUCValuPro.com

P EVANSON YACHT CO INC
COAST GUARD MFG ID- PEB

Call 1-800-327-6929 for BUC Personalized Evaluation Service
Or, for 1954 to 1984 boats, sign onto www.BUCValuPro.com

EVINRUDE MOTORS
DIV OUTBOARD MARINE CORP
MILWAUKEE WI 53216   COAST GUARD MFG ID- TBT   See inside cover to adjust price for area

LOA FT IN	NAME AND/ OR MODEL	TOP/ RIG	BOAT TYPE	-HULL- MTL TP	TP	----ENGINE--- # HP MFG	BEAM FT IN	WGT LBS	DRAFT FT IN	RETAIL LOW	RETAIL HIGH
						1970 BOATS					
16 2	EXPLORER 155		RNBT	FBG TR	IO	155 OMC	7 1	1925		2650	3050
16 2	SPORTSMAN 155		RNBT	FBG TR	IO	155 OMC	7 1	1950		2650	3100
19 1	DOLPHIN 210		RNBT	FBG TR	IO	210 OMC	7 4	2450		3700	4300
19 1	ROGUE 120		FSH	FBG TR	IO	120 OMC	7 4	2050		3550	4150
19 1	ROGUE 210		RNBT	FBG TR	IO	210 OMC	7 4	2450		3600	4200
						1969 BOATS					
16 2	SPORTSMAN		RNBT	FBG TR	IO	120-155 OMC	7 1	1850		2800	3250
16 2	SPORTSMAN 120		RNBT	FBG TR	IO	120 OMC	7 1	1850	1 2	2500	2950
16 2	SPORTSMAN 155		RNBT	FBG TR	IO	155 OMC	7 1	1950	1 4	2850	3350
19 1	ROGUE		FSH	FBG TR	IO	120 OMC	7 4	2050	1	3650	4250
19 1	ROGUE		RNBT	FBG TR	IO	210 EVIN	7 4	2450		3800	4400
19 1	ROGUE		SF	FBG TR	IO	120 EVIN	7 4	2050		4000	4650
19 1	ROGUE II		RNBT	FBG	IO	210 OMC	7 4	2450	11	3750	4400
						1968 BOATS					
16 3	SPORTSMAN	OP	RNBT	FBG TR	IO	120-155	7 4	1800	8	2750	3300
19	ROGUE	OP	RNBT	FBG TR	IO	210	7 4	2300	10	3650	4250
19	ROGUE II	OP	RNBT	FBG TR	IO	210	7 4	2300	10	3950	4550
						1967 BOATS					
16 3	SPORTSMAN 120		RNBT	FBG	IO	120	7 1		11	2900	3400
16 3	SPORTSMAN 155		RNBT	FBG	IO	155	7 1		11	2950	3400
16 3	SPORTSMAN 90		RNBT	FBG	IO	90	7 1		11	2900	3400
19 1	ROGUE 200		RNBT	FBG	IO	200	7 4		1	4000	4650
						1966 BOATS					
16 3	SPORTSMAN 16		RNBT	FBG	IO	90-150	7 1			3150	3650
16 3	SWEET 16		RNBT	FBG	IO	90	7 1			2850	3350
19 1	ROGUE		RNBT	FBG	IO	150-200	7 4			4050	4800
						1965 BOATS					
16 3	SPORT 16			FBG	IO	90				3000	3500
16 3	SWEET 16			FBG	IO	90				2900	3400
						1964 BOATS					
16 2	SPORT 16			FBG	IO	88				2950	3450
16 2	SWEET 16			FBG	IO	88				3100	3600

EVOLUTION YACHTS

Call 1-800-327-6929 for BUC Personalized Evaluation Service
Or, for 1980 to 1981 boats, sign onto www.BUCValuPro.com

EXCALIBUR MARINE CORP
SARASOTA FL 33580   COAST GUARD MFG ID- NAP See inside cover to adjust price for area

For more recent years, see the BUC Used Boat Price Guide, Volume 1 or Volume 2

LOA FT IN	NAME AND/ OR MODEL	TOP/ RIG	BOAT TYPE	-HULL- MTL TP	TP	----ENGINE--- # HP MFG	BEAM FT IN	WGT LBS	DRAFT FT IN	RETAIL LOW	RETAIL HIGH
						1983 BOATS					
26 10	EXCALIBUR 27	OP	OFF	FBG DV	OB	7			1 11	8400	9650
26 10	EXCALIBUR 27	OP	OFF	FBG DV	IO	330-370	7		1 11	6250	7650
26 10	EXCALIBUR 27	OP	OFF	FBG DV	IO	400 MRCR	7		1 11	7000	8050
26 10	EXCALIBUR 27	OP	UTL	FBG DV	OB	7			1 11	8250	9450

LOA FT IN	NAME AND/ OR MODEL	TOP/ RIG	BOAT TYPE	-HULL- MTL TP TP	----ENGINE--- # HP MFG	BEAM FT IN	WGT LBS	DRAFT FT IN	RETAIL LOW	RETAIL HIGH
------- 1983 BOATS -------
30 6	EXCALIBUR-CAT 30		OFF	FBG CT OB		9 10		1	13600	15500
30 6	EXCALIBUR-CAT 30		OFF	FBG CT IO	T330 MRCR	9 10		1	13500	15300
31 6	EXCALIBUR 31	OP	OFF	FBG DV OB		8		2 4	14900	17000
31 6	EXCALIBUR 31	OP	OFF	FBG DV IO	T330-T400	8		2 4	14700	17600
32 8	EXCALIBUR 32	OP	OFF	FBG DV IO	T330-T400	9 6	8200	2 6	18200	21400
37 6	EXCALIBUR 38	OP	OFF	FBG DV IO	T330 MRCR	8	7800	1 11	24200	26900
37 6	EXCALIBUR 38	OP	OFF	FBG DV IO	T370 MRCR	8	7800	1 11	25300	28100
37 6	EXCALIBUR 38	OP	OFF	FBG DV IO	T400 MRCR	8	7800	1 11	26300	29200
39 3	EXCALIBUR-HAWK 40	OP	OFF	FBG DV IO	T330 MRCR	9		2 2	24900	27700
	IO T370 MRCR 26100	29100, IO T400 MRCR 27300	30400, IO T475 MRCR	30800	34200
	IO T500 32000	35500, IB T300D CAT 63400 69700
41 6	EXCALIBUR-EAGLE 42		OFF	FBG DV IO	T400 MRCR	9		2 6	32300	35900
41 6	EXCALIBUR-EAGLE 42		OFF	FBG DV IO	T300D	9		2 6	46800	51400
------- 1982 BOATS -------
26 10	EXCALIBUR 27	OP	OFF	FBG DV OB		7		1 11	8200	9450
26 10	EXCALIBUR 27	OP	OFF	FBG DV IO	330-370	7		1 11	6100	7500
26 10	EXCALIBUR 27	OP	UTL	FBG DV IO	330	7		1 11	8050	9300
27	SPEEDSTER		SPTCR	FBG DV IO	330	7			6500	7450
31 6	EXCALIBUR 31	OP	OFF	FBG DV OB		8		2 4	14600	16600
32 8	EXCALIBUR 32	OP	OFF	FBG DV IO	T330-T370	9 6	8200	2 6	17400	20300
32 8	EXCALIBUR 32	OP	UTL	FBG DV OB		9 6	5700	2 2	15300	17400
37 6	EXCALIBUR 38	OP	OFF	FBG DV IO	T370 MRCR	8	7800	1 11	24700	27400
39 3	EXCALIBUR-HAWK 40	OP	OFF	FBG DV IO	T370 MRCR	9		2 2	25500	28300
70	EXCALIBUR 70		MY	FBG DV IB	T400	16			215500	237000
------- 1981 BOATS -------
23 6	EXCALIBUR 24		OFF	FBG DV OB		6 8			4300	5000
26 10	EXCALIBUR 27	OP	OFF	FBG DV OB		7		1 11	8100	9300
26 10	EXCALIBUR 27	OP	OFF	FBG DV IO	330 MRCR	7		1 11	6000	6900
26 10	EXCALIBUR 27	OP	OFF	FBG DV IO	370 MRCR	7		1 11	6400	7350
26 10	EXCALIBUR 27	OP	OFF	FBG DV IO	T370 MRCR	7		1 11	8300	9500
26 10	EXCALIBUR 27	OP	UTL	FBG DV OB		7		1 11	7900	9100
31	EXCALIBUR 31	OP	OFF	FBG DV OB		7		1 11	13800	15600
32 8	EXCALIBUR 32	OP	OFF	FBG DV IO	T330-T370	9 6	8200	2 6	17100	20000
32 8	EXCALIBUR 32	OP	UTL	FBG DV OB		9 6	5700	2 2	15000	17100
37 6	EXCALIBUR 38	OP	OFF	FBG DV IO	T370 MRCR	8	7800	1 11	24200	26900
39 3	EXCALIBUR-HAWK 40	OP	OFF	FBG DV IO	T370 MRCR	9		2 2	25100	27800
70	EXCALIBUR 70		MY	FBG DV IB	T400	16			206500	227000
------- 1980 BOATS -------
24	EXCALIBUR		OFF	FBG DV OB		6 8	2500		4550	5200
24	EXCALIBUR 24	OP	OFF	FBG DV IO	330 MRCR	6 8	3400	2 2	4600	5250
27	EXCALIBUR 27	OP	OFF	FBG DV OB		6 8	2400	1 10	8250	9500
27	EXCALIBUR 27	OP	OFF	FBG DV IO	330 MRCR	6 8	3600	2 2	6050	6950
27	EXCALIBUR 27	OP	UTL	FBG DV OB		6 8	2300	1 10	8100	9300
31 6	EXCALIBUR 31	OP	OFF	FBG DV OB		8	4500	2 2	13600	15500
31 6	EXCALIBUR 31-K		RNBT	KEV DV IO	T370	8			11000	12500
31 6	EXECUTIONER	OP	OFF	FBG DV IO	T475 MRCR	8	6250	2	15600	17800
32 8	EXCALIBUR 32	OP	OFF	FBG DV IO	T330 MRCR	9 6	8200	2 4	16900	19300
32 8	EXCALIBUR 32	OP	UTL	FBG DV OB		9 6	5700	2 2	14800	16800
38	EXCALIBUR 38	OP	OFF	FBG DV IO	T370 MRCR	8	7800	2 5	25000	27800
------- 1979 BOATS -------
23 6	EXCALIBUR	OP	RACE	FBG DV OB		6 8	2300		4050	4700
23 6	EXCALIBUR	OP	RACE	FBG DV IO	330	6 8	2300		3400	3950
31 6	EXCALIBUR	OP	RACE	FBG DV IO	T330	8			11500	13000
32	EXCALIBUR	OP	SF	FBG DV IO	T330	9 6	8500		15600	17700
32	EXCALIBUR	OP	SF	FBG DV IO	T D	9 6	8500		**	**
------- 1978 BOATS -------
23 6	EXCALIBUR	OP	RACE	FBG DV OB		6 8	2472	1 6	4250	4950
23 6	EXCALIBUR	OP	RACE	FBG DV IO	265 CHRY	6 8	3750	1 6	4000	4650
	JT 325 FORD 4700	5350, IO 330 MRCR 4450	5150, IO 375 MRCR	4950	5650
	IO T170 MRCR 4400	5050
31 5	EXCALIBUR	OP	RACE	FBG DV IB	T260-T330	8	6500	2 4	10700	12900
32 6	EXCALIBUR	OP	RACE	FBG DV IB	T330 CHRY	9 6	8500	2 9	16900	19200
	VD T300 CHRY 16800	19100, IO T330 MRCR 13300	15200, VD T330 MRCR	17300	19700
	IB T200D CHRY 21100	23400
------- 1977 BOATS -------
23 6	EXCALIBUR	OP	RACE	FBG DV IO	280-300	6 8	3000		3600	4300
	JT 325 FORD 3850	4450, IO 375-400	4450	5150, IO T170 MRCR	3850	4450
	IO T300 CRUS 4650	5300
32	EXCALIBUR		RACE	FBG DV IO	T	9 3			**	**
32	EXCALIBUR		RACE	FBG DV IB	T	9 3			**	**
32	EXCALIBUR		SF	FBG DV IO	T	9 3			**	**
32	EXCALIBUR		SF	FBG DV IB	T	9 3			**	**
------- 1966 BOATS -------
22	EXCALIBUR 22	SLP	SA/CR	FBG KL IB	D	6 6		4	3250	3800
26	EXCALIBUR 26	CUT	SA/RC	FBG KL IB	D	7 9		4 8	5850	6750
34	EXCALIBUR 34	CUT	SA/CR	FBG KL IB	D	9 8		5 9	21900	24300

EXPLORER BOATS
DIV OF RENT-A-CRUISE OF COAST GUARD MFG ID- RNT

Call 1-800-327-6929 for BUC Personalized Evaluation Service
Or, for 1972 to 1973 boats, sign onto www.BUCValuPro.com

EXPLORER YACHTS INC

Call 1-800-327-6929 for BUC Personalized Evaluation Service
Or, for 1981 to 1997 boats, sign onto www.BUCValuPro.com

EXPRESS YACHTING
MIDLAND ONTARIO CANADA   See inside cover to adjust price for area

For more recent years, see the BUC Used Boat Price Guide, Volume 1 or Volume 2

LOA FT IN	NAME AND/ OR MODEL	TOP/ RIG	BOAT TYPE	-HULL- MTL TP TP	----ENGINE--- # HP MFG	BEAM FT IN	WGT LBS	DRAFT FT IN	RETAIL LOW	RETAIL HIGH
------- 1983 BOATS -------
20	EXPRESS 20	SLP	SAIL	FBG KL OB		7 10	2000	3 11	4950	5700
26 8	NIAGARA 26	SLP	SAIL	FBG KL OB		8 4	4000	4	10700	12100
26 8	NIAGARA 26	SLP	SAIL	FBG KL SD	VLVO	8 4	4000	4	11000	12500
30	EXPRESS 30	SLP	SAIL	FBG KL IB	15D	10	6600	5 6	19000	21100
30	EXPRESS 30 M	SLP	SAIL	FBG KL IB		9 10	6200	5 4	17200	19600
30	EXPRESS 30 SHOAL	SLP	SAIL	FBG KL IB	15D	10	6600	4	19100	21200
35	EXPRESS 35	SLP	SAIL	FBG KL IB	D	11 6	10600	6 6	30300	33700

F L TRIPP & SONS
ANGLER
WESTPORT PT MA 02791   COAST GUARD MFG ID- TRP   See inside cover to adjust price for area

For more recent years, see the BUC Used Boat Price Guide, Volume 1 or Volume 2

LOA FT IN	NAME AND/ OR MODEL	TOP/ RIG	BOAT TYPE	-HULL- MTL TP TP	----ENGINE--- # HP MFG	BEAM FT IN	WGT LBS	DRAFT FT IN	RETAIL LOW	RETAIL HIGH
------- 1983 BOATS -------
18 3	ANGLER 18	OP	OPFSH	FBG OB		7	1500	10	3500	4050
22 2	COMPLEAT-ANGLER	ST	CUD	FBG OB		7 10	2500	10	4950	5700
22 2	COMPLEAT-ANGLER	ST	CUD	FBG IB	200 OMC	7 10	4000	2 2	14900	16900
22 2	COMPLEAT-ANGLER	OP	OPFSH	FBG OB		7 10	2200	10	4550	5200
22 2	COMPLEAT-ANGLER	OP	OPFSH	FBG IB	200 OMC	7 10	3700	2 2	14500	16500
------- 1982 BOATS -------
18 3	ANGLER 18	OP	OPFSH	FBG RB OB		7 2	1500	10	3400	3950
22 2	COMPLEAT-ANGLER	ST	CUD	FBG RB OB		7 10	2500	10	4850	5600
22 2	COMPLEAT-ANGLER	ST	CUD	FBG RB IB	200 OMC	7 10	4000	2 2	14200	16100
22 2	COMPLEAT-ANGLER	OP	OPFSH	FBG RB OB		7 10	2200	10	4450	5100
22 2	COMPLEAT-ANGLER	OP	OPFSH	FBG RB IB	200 OMC	7 10	3700	2 2	13800	15700
------- 1981 BOATS -------
18 3	ANGLER 18	OP	OPFSH	FBG RB OB		7 2	1500	10	3300	3850
22 2	COMPLEAT-ANGLER	ST	CUD	FBG RB OB		7 10	2500	10	4800	5500
22 2	COMPLEAT-ANGLER	ST	CUD	FBG RB IB	200 OMC	7 10	4000	2 2	13600	15500
22 2	COMPLEAT-ANGLER	OP	OPFSH	FBG RB OB		7 10	2200	10	4300	5000
22 2	COMPLEAT-ANGLER	OP	OPFSH	FBG RB IB	200 OMC	7 10	3700	2 2	13300	15100
------- 1980 BOATS -------
18 3	ANGLER 18	OP	OPFSH	FBG RB OB		7 2	1500	10	3250	3750
22 2	COMPLEAT-ANGLER	ST	CUD	FBG RB OB		7 10	2500	10	4700	5400
22 2	COMPLEAT-ANGLER	ST	CUD	FBG RB IB	200 OMC	7 10	4000	2 2	13000	14800
22 2	COMPLEAT-ANGLER	OP	OPFSH	FBG RB OB		7 10	2200	10	4200	4900
22 2	COMPLEAT-ANGLER	OP	OPFSH	FBG RB IB	200 OMC	7 10	3700	2 2	12700	14400
------- 1979 BOATS -------
18 3	ANGLER 18	OP	OPFSH	FBG RB OB		7 2	1500	10	3150	3700
22 2	COMPLEAT-ANGLER	ST	CUD	FBG RB OB		7 10	2500	10	4600	5300
22 2	COMPLEAT-ANGLER	ST	CUD	FBG RB IB	220 OMC	7 10	4000	2 2	12500	14200
22 2	COMPLEAT-ANGLER	OP	OPFSH	FBG RB OB		7 10	2200	10	4150	4800
22 2	COMPLEAT-ANGLER	OP	OPFSH	FBG RB IB	220 OMC	7 10	3700	2 2	12300	14000
------- 1978 BOATS -------
18 3	ANGLER 18	OP	OPFSH	FBG OB		7 2	1500	10	3100	3600
22 2	COMPLEAT-ANGLER	ST	CUD	FBG RB OB		7 10	2500	10	4500	5200
22 2	COMPLEAT-ANGLER	ST	CUD	FBG RB IB	190 OMC	7 10	4000	2 2	12000	13600
22 2	COMPLEAT-ANGLER	OP	OPFSH	FBG RB OB		7 10	2200	10	4100	4750
22 2	COMPLEAT-ANGLER	OP	OPFSH	FBG RB IB	190 OMC	7 10	3700	2 2	11700	13300

F L TRIPP & SONS (continued)

LOA FT IN	NAME AND/OR MODEL	TOP/RIG	BOAT TYPE	HULL MTL	HULL TP	ENG TP	# HP	MFG	BEAM FT IN	WGT	DRAFT FT IN	RETAIL LOW	RETAIL HIGH
			1977 BOATS										
18 3	ANGLER 18	OP	OPFSH	FBG	RB	OB			7 2	1500	10	3050	3550
22 2	ANGLER 22	OP	CUD	FBG	RB	OB			7 10	2500	10	4500	5150
22 2	ANGLER 22	OP	OPFSH	FBG	RB	OB			7 10	2000	10	3750	4350
22 2	COMPLEAT-ANGLER	OP	CUD	FBG	RB	IB	190	PALM	7 10	4000	2 2	11200	12700
22 2	COMPLEAT-ANGLER	OP	OPFSH	FBG	RB	IB	190	PALM	7 10	3500	2 2	10500	11900
			1976 BOATS										
18 3	ANGLER 18	OP	OPFSH	FBG	RB	OB			7 2	1500	10	3000	3500
22 2	ANGLER 22	OP	CUD	FBG	RB	OB			7 10	2700	10	4700	5400
22 2	ANGLER 22	OP	CUD	FBG	RB	IB	190		7 10	2700	2 2	8250	9500
22 2	ANGLER 22	OP	OPFSH	FBG	RB	OB			7 10	2500	10	4450	5100
22 2	ANGLER 22	OP	OPFSH	FBG	RB	IB	190		7 10	2500	2 2	8150	9350

FABBRO MARINE GROUP

PENSACOLA FL 32523   COAST GUARD MFG ID- FAB See inside cover to adjust price for area
FORMERLY FABUGLAS COMPANY INC

LOA FT IN	NAME AND/OR MODEL	TOP/RIG	BOAT TYPE	HULL MTL	HULL TP	ENG TP	# HP	MFG	BEAM FT IN	WGT LBS	DRAFT FT IN	RETAIL LOW	RETAIL HIGH
			1977 BOATS										
16	FISHERMAN 160	OP	BASS	FBG	TR	OB			5 9	850		1900	2250
16	TRIDENT 160	ST	RNBT	FBG	TR	OB			5 9	850		1900	2250
17	TRIDENT 170	ST	RNBT	FBG	TR	OB			7 1	1250		2750	3200
17	TRIDENT 170	ST	RNBT	FBG	TR	IO	140-175		7 1	2100		2600	3100
17 6	CORINTHIAN 1750	ST	RNBT	FBG	DV	IO	170-190		7 1	2500		2950	3450
18 2	COMMODORE 182	ST	RNBT	FBG	SV	OB			7 2	1250		2850	3300
18 11	CORINTHIAN 1900	ST	RNBT	FBG	DV	IO	188-235		7 2	2800		3450	4150
18 11	CORINTHIAN 1900	ST	RNBT	FBG	DV	JT	320	BERK	7 2	2750		4000	4650
			1976 BOATS										
16	FISHERMAN 160	OP	BASS	FBG	TR	OB			5 9	850		1850	2200
16	TRIDENT 160	ST	RNBT	FBG	TR	OB			5 9	850		1850	2200
17	TRIDENT 170	OP	RNBT	FBG	TR	IO	140-165		7 1	2100		2700	3150
17	TRIDENT 170	ST	RNBT	FBG	TR	OB			7 1	1250		2750	3150
18 2	COMMODORE 182	OP	RNBT	FBG	SV	OB			7 2	1250		2800	3300
18 11	CORINTHIAN 1900	ST	RNBT	FBG	DV	IO	233-235		7 2	2750	3	3600	4200
18 11	CORINTHIAN 1900	ST	RNBT	FBG	DV	JT	330	BERK	7 2	2750	1 6	3850	4450
			1975 BOATS										
16	160 FISHERMAN	OP	BASS	FBG	TR	OB			5 9	850		1850	2200
16	TRIDENT 160	OP	RNBT	FBG	TR	OB			5 9	850		1850	2200
17	TRIDENT 170	OP	RNBT	FBG	TR	OB			7 1	1250		2700	3150
17	TRIDENT 170	OP	RNBT	FBG	TR	IO	140-165		7 1	2100		2750	3250
18 2	COMMODORE 182	OP	RNBT	FBG	SV	OB			7 2	1250		2800	3250
18 10	EXPERIMENTAL	OP	RNBT	FBG	DV	IO	190-235					3600	4350
18 10	EXPERIMENTAL	OP	RNBT	FBG	DV	IB	330					3450	4050
18 11	CORINTHIAN	OP	RNBT	FBG	DV	IO	188-235		7 2	2700		3600	4400
18 11	CORINTHIAN	OP	RNBT	FBG	DV	JT	330	BERK	7 2	2750		3700	4300
			1974 BOATS										
17	TRIDENT 170	OP	RNBT	FBG	TR	OB			7 1	1050		2350	2700
17	TRIDENT 170	OP	RNBT	FBG	TR	IO	140-165		7 1	2000		2800	3350
18 2	COMMODORE 182	OP	RNBT	FBG	SV	OB			7 2	1100		2500	2900
			1973 BOATS										
17	TRIDENT 170	OP	RNBT	FBG	TR	OB			7 1	1050		2350	2700
17	TRIDENT 170	OP	RNBT	FBG	TR	IO	140-165		7 1	2000		2900	3450
17 1	TROPHY 172 GT	OP	RNBT	FBG		JT	330	BERK	7	2500		2950	3450
18 2	COMMODORE 182	OP	RNBT	FBG	SV	OB			7 2	1100		2500	2900
			1972 BOATS										
17	TRIDENT 170			FBG		OB			7 1	900		2000	2350
17	TRIDENT 170			FBG		IO	120-165		7 1	1750		2700	3150
17 1	TROPHY 172			FBG		IO	235	OMC	7	1850		2900	3350
17 1	TROPHY 172 GT			FBG		IO	330	BERK	7	2150		4000	4650
18 2	COMMODORE 182			FBG		OB			7 2	1000		2300	2700
18 2	COMMODORE 182			FBG		IO	120-165		7 2	1850		3000	3500
			1971 BOATS										
17	TRIDENT 170			FBG		OB			7 1	900		2000	2350
17	TRIDENT 170			FBG		IO	120-165		7 1	1750		2750	3250
17 1	TROPHY 172			FBG		OB			7	1000		2250	2600
17 1	TROPHY 172			FBG		IO	140-165		7	1850		2850	3300
17 1	TROPHY 172 GT			FBG		IO	165-235		7	1850		2900	3450
18 2	COMMODORE 182			FBG		OB			7 2	1000		2300	2700
21 10	TRIDENT 220			FBG		IO	165		7 9	2900		5600	6400
21 10	TRIDENT 220		CBNCR	FBG		OB	165	MRCR	7 9	1800		4450	5100
			1970 BOATS										
17	TRIDENT 170		RNBT	FBG	TR	IO	120		6 10	1700		2900	3350
17	TRIDENT 170	OP	RNBT	FBG	TR	OB			6 10	900		2000	2400
17 1	TROPHY 172		RNBT	FBG	SV	IO	120-155		7	1800		3000	3500
17 1	TROPHY 172		RNBT	FBG	SV	IO	215	MRCR	7	2000		3300	3800
17 1	TROPHY 172	OP	RNBT	FBG	SV	OB			7	1000		2250	2600
17 6	TRIDENT		RNBT	FBG	SV	OB			7	1000		2300	2650
18 2	COMMODORE 182		RNBT	FBG	SV	IO	120-165		7 2	1800		3250	3850
18 2	COMMODORE 182	OP	RNBT	FBG	SV	OB			7 2	1000		2300	2700
21 10	TRIDENT 220		CBNCR	FBG	TR	OB			7 9	1800		4450	5100
21 10	TRIDENT 220		CBNCR	FBG	TR	IO	155-215		7 9	3000		6750	8150
21 10	TRIDENT 220		RNBT	FBG	SV	IO	155-210		7 9	3000		5800	6950
21 10	TRIDENT 220	OP	RNBT	FBG	TR	OB			7 9	1800		4450	5100
			1969 BOATS										
17	TRIDENT 170		RNBT	FBG	TR	OB			6 10	900		2000	2400
17	TRIDENT 170		RNBT	FBG	TR	IO	120-140		6 10	1700		3000	3500
17 1	TRIUMPH 172		RNBT	FBG	SV	OB			7	1000		2250	2650
17 1	TRIUMPH 172		RNBT	FBG	SV	IO	120-160		7	1800		3100	3650
18 2	COMMODORE		CR	FBG		OB			7 2	1200		2650	3100
18 2	COMMODORE		CR	FBG	SV	IO	120-160		7 2	2000		3600	4200
18 2	COMMODORE 182		RNBT	FBG		OB			7 2	1200		2200	2500
18 2	COMMODORE 182		RNBT	FBG	SV	IO	120-160		7 2	1700		3300	3900
21 10	TRIDENT 220		RNBT	FBG		OB			7 9	1800		4450	5150
21 10	TRIDENT 220		RNBT	FBG	TR	IO	155-225		7 9	3000		6000	7400
			1968 BOATS										
17	TRIDENT 170	OP	RNBT	FBG	TR	OB			6 10	900		2000	2400
17	TRIDENT 170	OP	RNBT	FBG	TR	IO	120		6 10	1700		3100	3600
18 2	COMMODORE		CR	FBG		OB			7 2	1200		2650	3100
18 2	COMMODORE		CR	FBG	SV	IO	120-155		7 2	2000		3750	4350
18 2	COMMODORE 182	OP	RNBT	FBG		OB			7 2	1200		2100	2500
18 2	COMMODORE 182	OP	RNBT	FBG	SV	IO	120-160		7 2	1700		3450	4000
21 10	TRIDENT 220			FBG		OB			7 9	1700		4200	4900
21 10	TRIDENT 220			FBG		IO	155-210		7 9	3000		6250	7400
			1967 BOATS										
16 7	BUCCANEER			FBG		OB			6 8	825	3 7	1800	2150
16 7	BUCCANEER			FBG		IO	80-160		6 8		3 7	3000	3500
16 7	PORTOFINO CUST	RNBT		FBG		OB			6 2	775		1750	2050
17	TRIDENT 170			FBG		OB			6 10	900	3 10	2000	2400
17	TRIDENT 170			FBG		IO	80-160		6 10		3 10	3150	3650
17	TRIDENT 170 DLX	RNBT		FBG		OB			6 10	900		2000	2450
18 2	COMMODORE CUSTOM			FBG		OB			7 2	900	4	2100	2500
18 2	COMMODORE CUSTOM			FBG		IO	80-160		7 2		4	3450	4050
18 2	COMMODORE CUSTOM	CR		FBG		OB			7 2	1200		2650	3100
18 2	COMMODORE CUSTOM	CR		FBG		IO	80-160		7 2			4050	4750
18 2	COMMODORE W/T	RNBT		FBG		OB			7 2	900		2100	2500
18 2	TRIDENT 182			FBG		OB			7 2	1050	4 5	2300	2800
18 2	TRIDENT 182			FBG		IO	80-160		7 2		4 5	3650	4250
			1966 BOATS										
16 7	BUCCANEER	RNBT		FBG		OB			6 8	825		**	**
16 7	BUCCANEER	RNBT		FBG		IO	110-120		6 8			3500	4200
16 7	PORTOFINO	RNBT		FBG		OB			6 2	775		1750	2050
16 7	SEA-GULL DELUXE	RNBT		FBG		OB			6 8			2550	2950
16 7	VIKING	RNBT		FBG		OB			6 8			2550	2950
16 7	VIKING	RNBT		FBG		IO	110-120		6 2			3400	3950
18 2	COMMODORE	CR		FBG		OB			7 2	1200		2650	3100
18 2	COMMODORE	CR		FBG		OB			7 2			**	**
18 2	COMMODORE	CR		FBG		IO	110-150		7 2			4200	4900
18 2	COMMODORE			FBG		OB			7 2	900		2150	2500
18 2	COMMODORE	RNBT		FBG		IO			7 2			**	**
18 2	COMMODORE	RNBT		FBG		IO	110-150		7 2			4400	5100
			1965 BOATS										
16 7	BUCCANEER			FBG		IO						2250	2600
16 7	BUCCANEER			FBG		IO						**	**
16 7	PORTOFINO			FBG		OB						3400	3950
16 7	PORTOFINO			FBG		IO	110-150					2250	2600
16 7	SEA-GULL THRIFTLINE			FBG		OB						1850	2200
16 7	VIKING			FBG		OB						2050	2400
16 7	VIKING			FBG		OB						**	**
16 7	VIKING			FBG		IO	110-120					3200	3750
18 2	COMMODORE			FBG		OB						2350	2700
18 2	COMMODORE			FBG		OB						**	**
18 2	COMMODORE			FBG		IO	110-150					3800	4400
18 2	COMMODORE	CR		FBG		OB						2600	3000
18 2	COMMODORE	CR		FBG		IO						**	**
18 2	COMMODORE	CR		FBG		IO	110-150					4350	5050
			1964 BOATS										
16 7	CUTLASS CUSTOM			FBG		OB						2300	2650
16 7	VIKING CUSTOM			FBG		OB						1900	2250
16 7	VIKING CUSTOM			FBG		IO						**	**
16 7	VIKING CUSTOM			FBG		IO	110					3400	3950

LOA FT IN	NAME AND/ OR MODEL	TOP/ RIG	BOAT TYPE	-HULL- MTL TP	----ENGINE--- TP # HP MFG	BEAM FT IN	WGT LBS	DRAFT FT IN	RETAIL LOW	RETAIL HIGH
1964 BOATS										
18 2	COMMODORE	CR	FBG	OB					2600	3000
18 2	COMMODORE	CR	FBG	IO					**	**
18 2	COMMODORE	CR	FBG	IO 110					4500	5200
18 2	COMMODORE CUSTOM		FBG	OB					2350	2750
18 2	COMMODORE CUSTOM		FBG	IO					**	**
18 2	COMMODORE CUSTOM		FBG	IO 110					3900	4550
1963 BOATS										
16 7	CUTLASS		FBG	OB					2300	2650
16 7	VIKING		FBG	OB					1950	2300
18 2	COMMODORE		FBG	OB					2350	2750
18 2	COMMODORE CUSTOM	CR	FBG	OB					2600	3000
1961 BOATS										
18 2	COMMODORE	CR	FBG	OB		7 2	1300		2900	3350
18 2	COMMODORE	RNBT	FBG	OB		7 2	900		2200	2550

FAENOE YACHTYARDS LTD
FORMERLY SKAERBAEK BADEBYGGERI

Call 1-800-327-6929 for BUC Personalized Evaluation Service
Or, for 1970 to 1986 boats, sign onto www.BUCValuPro.com

FAIR WEATHER MARINE INC
SAN PEDRO CA 90731   See inside cover to adjust price for area

For more recent years, see the BUC Used Boat Price Guide, Volume 1 or Volume 2

LOA FT IN	NAME AND/ OR MODEL	TOP/ RIG	BOAT TYPE	-HULL- MTL TP	----ENGINE--- TP # HP MFG	BEAM FT IN	WGT LBS	DRAFT FT IN	RETAIL LOW	RETAIL HIGH
1977 BOATS										
28	SKIPJACK 28	FB	CR	FBG DV	IO T225	8	6600		8500	9750

FAIRCHILD YACHTS
COAST GUARD MFG ID- FCH

Call 1-800-327-6929 for BUC Personalized Evaluation Service
Or, for 1978 boats, sign onto www.BUCValuPro.com

FAIRHAVEN MARINE INC
COAST GUARD MFG ID- FHV
SEE SURF HUNTER CORP

Call 1-800-327-6929 for BUC Personalized Evaluation Service
Or, for 1973 to 1984 boats, sign onto www.BUCValuPro.com

FAIRLINE BOATS PLC
HILTON HEAD NC 29925   COAST GUARD MFG ID- ZFA See inside cover to adjust price for area

FAIRLINE BOATS
OUNDLE ENGLAND PE8 5PA

For more recent years, see the BUC Used Boat Price Guide, Volume 1 or Volume 2

LOA FT IN	NAME AND/ OR MODEL	TOP/ RIG	BOAT TYPE	-HULL- MTL TP	----ENGINE--- TP # HP MFG	BEAM FT IN	WGT LBS	DRAFT FT IN	RETAIL LOW	RETAIL HIGH
1980 BOATS										
22 1	HOLIDAY 22		CBNCR	FBG SV	IO 185	8			10200	11600
28 5	MIRAGE 29		CBNCR	FBG SV	IO 260	10 2			25200	28000
28 5	MIRAGE 29		CBNCR	FBG SV	IO T140-T200	10 2			26000	29000
32 2	SEDAN 32		SDN	FBG SV	IO T200-T260	10 10			36400	42700
1979 BOATS										
22 1	HOLIDAY 22	ST	CBNCR	FBG SV	IO 120-290	8	4000	1 4	11000	13700
28 6	MIRAGE 29	HT	CBNCR	FBG SV	IO 228-290	10 2	8000	2	26800	31400
	IO 130D VLVO	31200	34600,	IO T140-T290	28200	34200, IO T130D VLVO			38600	42900
32 2	SEDAN	HT	SDN	FBG SV	IO T170-T260	10 10	10700	2	36500	43800
32 2	SEDAN	HT	SDN	FBG SV	IO T130D VLVO	10 10	10700	2	43300	48100
32 2	SEDAN	FB	SDN	FBG SV	IO T170-T260	10 10	10700	2	36500	43800
32 2	SEDAN	FB	SDN	FBG SV	IO T130D VLVO	10 10	10700	2	43300	48100
1978 BOATS										
22 1	HOLIDAY 22	ST	CR	FBG SV	IO 175-235	8	4000	1 4	10100	11700
28 6	MIRAGE 29	HT	CR	FBG SV	IO 235 OMC	10	7260	2	21800	24200
28 6	MIRAGE 29	HT	CR	FBG DV	IO T175 OMC	10	7260	2	23300	25900
32 2	SEDAN	FB	SDN	FBG DV	IO T235 OMC	10 10	8000	2	37700	41800
1977 BOATS										
22 1	HOLIDAY	OP	CR	FBG SV	IO 175-235	8	4000	1 4	10100	11700
28 6	MIRAGE	HT	CR	FBG SV	IO 235-240	10 2	7260	2	22200	24900
	IO 61D- 89D	22300	24900,	IO T130-T240	23000	28200, IO T 61D-T89D			24300	28500
29 6	MIRAGE	HT	CR	FBG SV	IO	MRCR 10 2	7260	2	**	**

FAIRLINER
AMERICAN MARINE IND INC   See inside cover to adjust price for area
TACOMA WA 98421   COAST GUARD MFG ID- FAL

LOA FT IN	NAME AND/ OR MODEL	TOP/ RIG	BOAT TYPE	-HULL- MTL TP	----ENGINE--- TP # HP MFG	BEAM FT IN	WGT LBS	DRAFT FT IN	RETAIL LOW	RETAIL HIGH
1976 BOATS										
31 4	FAIRLINER 3200	HT	SDN	FBG SV	IB T215-T255	10 10	12000	1 8	22600	25900
31 4	FAIRLINER 3200	HT	EXP	FBG SV	IB T215-T255	10 10	12000	1 8	20900	23800
31 4	FAIRLINER 3230	FB	CR	FBG SV	IB T215-T255	10 10	12000	1 8	20900	23800
31 4	FAIRLINER 3250	FB	SF	FBG SV	IB T215-T255	10 10	12000	1 8	21000	23900
1975 BOATS										
31 4	FAIRLINER 3200	HT	SDN	FBG	IB T255	10 10	12000	1 8	22400	24900
31 4	FAIRLINER 3200	HT	SDN	FBG SV	IB T255	10 10	12000	1 8	21700	24200
31 4	FAIRLINER 3220	HT	EXP	FBG	IB T255	10 10	12000	1 8	20100	22300
31 4	FAIRLINER 3220	HT	EXP	FBG SV	IB T215-T255	10 10	12000	1 8	20600	22900
31 4	FAIRLINER 3230	FB	CR	FBG	IB T255	10 10	12000	1 8	20100	22300
31 4	FAIRLINER 3250	FB	SF	FBG	IB T255	10 10	12000	1 8	20600	22900
31 4	FAIRLINER 3250	FB	SF	FBG SV	IB T215	10 10	12000	1 8	20100	22300
1974 BOATS										
31 4	FAIRLINER 3200	HT	SDN	FBG	IB T270-T350	10 10	12000	1 8	21800	25700
31 4	FAIRLINER 3200	HT	SDN	FBG SV	IB T220 CRUS	10 10	12000	1 8	20000	23300
31 4	FAIRLINER 3220	HT	EXP	FBG	IB T270-T350	10 10	12000	1 8	20000	23300
31 4	FAIRLINER 3220	HT	EXP	FBG SV	IB T220 CRUS	10 10	12000	1 8	19400	21500
31 4	FAIRLINER 3230	FB	CR	FBG	IB T270-T350	10 10	12000	1 8	20000	23300
31 4	FAIRLINER 3230	FB	CR	FBG SV	IB T220 CRUS	10 10	12000	1 8	19400	21500
31 4	FAIRLINER 3250	HT	SF	FBG	IB T350 CRUS	10 10	12000	1 8	20900	23200
31 4	FAIRLINER 3250	HT	SF	FBG	IB T270 CRUS	10 10	12000	1 8	19900	22100
31 4	FAIRLINER 3250	FB	SF	FBG SV	IB T220 CRUS	10 10	12000	1 8	19400	21600
1972 BOATS										
28	FASTBACK	CR	FBG DV	IB 225		11 2		2 8	9800	11100
28	FASTBACK	CR	FBG DV	IB T330		11 2		2 8	12100	13700
28	SPORT	SDN	FBG DV	IB 225		11 2		2 8	10900	12400
28	SPORT	SDN	FBG DV	IB T330		11 2		2 8	13000	14700
28	SPORT FISHERMAN	SF	FBG DV	IB 225		11 2		2 8	9800	11200
28	SPORT FISHERMAN	SF	FBG DV	IB T330		11 2		2 8	12100	13700
32 7	CONVERTABLE	SDN	FBG DV	IB 225		11 2		2 8	16600	18800
32 7	CONVERTABLE	SDN	FBG DV	IB T330		11 2		2 8	20600	22900
32 7	FASTBACK	CR	FBG DV	IB T225-T330		11 2		2 8	18500	21500
32 7	SPORT	SDN	FBG DV	IB 225		11 2		2 8	18100	20100
32 7	SPORT	SDN	FBG DV	IB T330		11 2		2 8	20600	22900
36 11	CHINOOK	CR	FBG DV	IB T330		12 4		3 1	30800	34200
36 11	CONVERTABLE	SDN	FBG DV	IB T330		12 4		3 1	30000	33300
36 11	FASTBACK	SDN	FBG DV	IB T330		12 4		3 1	27900	31000
36 11	FASTBACK	CR	FBG DV	IB 225		12 4		3 1	30100	33500
1971 BOATS										
28	FAIRLINER	SF	FBG	IB T225 CHRY		11 4		2 8	9450	10700
28	FAIRLINER	SF	FBG	IB T225 CHRY		11 4		2 8	10700	12100
28	FAIRLINER FASTBACK		FBG	IB 225 CHRY		11 4		2 8	9350	10600
28	FAIRLINER FASTBACK		FBG	IB T225 CHRY		11 4		2 8	10500	12000
32 7	FAIRLINER	SDN	FBG	IB 225 CHRY		11 4		2 8	15900	18100
32 7	FAIRLINER	SDN	FBG	IB T225 CHRY		11 4		2 8	18100	20100
32 7	FAIRLINER FASTBACK		FBG	IB 225 CHRY		11 4		2 8	15400	17500
32 7	FAIRLINER FASTBACK		FBG	IB T225 CHRY		11 4		2 8	16600	18900
32 7	FAIRLINER SPORT	SDN	FBG	IB 225 CHRY		11 4		2 8	17100	19400
32 7	FAIRLINER SPORT	SDN	FBG	IB T225 CHRY		11 4		2 8	19200	21300
36 11	CHINOOK		F/W	IB T300 CHRY		12 4		3 1	28600	30600
36 11	FAIRLINER		SDN	IB T300 CHRY		12 4		3 1	29600	31700
1970 BOATS										
27	FASTBACK	EXP	F/W	IB 225		10 3			8300	9500
27	HIGHLINER	FSH	F/W	IB 225		10 3			7500	8650
31		SDN	WD	IB T225 CHRY		10 10			15600	17700
31		FB	SDN	WD	IB T225		10 10		15600	17700
31 6	FASTBACK	EXP	FBG	IB T225-T300		11			16700	19400
34	HIGHLINER	FSH	F/W	IB 260		11			13000	14700
34		SDN	WD	IB T210-T300		11			21100	24400
34	FASTBACK	EXP	F/W	IB 225		11			21500	23900
36		CNV	F/W	IB T250		12 4			24700	27500
36		SDN	WD	IB T300 CHRY		12 4			25200	28000

FAIRLINER -CONTINUED See inside cover to adjust price for area

LOA FT	LOA IN	NAME AND/ OR MODEL	TOP/ RIG	BOAT TYPE	HULL MTL	HULL TP	ENGINE TP	ENGINE # HP	ENGINE MFG	BEAM FT	BEAM IN	WGT LBS	DRAFT FT	DRAFT IN	RETAIL LOW	RETAIL HIGH
		1970 BOATS														
36		CHINOOK			WD		IB	T300	CHRY	12	4				25200	28000
43	8	CUSTOM 440		FSH	F/W		IB	T260		14					**	**
		1969 BOATS														
27	3	FASTBACK 270		CR	PLY	DV	IB	225	CHRY	10	3	6500	2		8350	9600
28		FASTBACK 280		CR	PLY	DV	IB	260	CRUS	10	9	7000	2	2	9050	10300
28		FASTBACK 280		CR	PLY	DV	IB	T225	CHRY	10	9	8000	2	2	10500	11900
31		FASTBACK		CR	F/W		IB	250		10	10		2	2	12900	14700
31		FASTBACK		CR	F/W		IB	T250		10	10		2	2	14100	16000
31		FASTBACK 310	FB		PLY	DV	IB	260	CRUS	10	10	8800	2	2	11000	12500
31		FASTBACK 310	FB		PLY	DV	IB	T225	CHRY	10	10	9600	2	2	12200	13900
31		FASTBACK 310		EXP	PLY	DV	IB	260	CRUS	10	10	8800	2	2	13200	15000
31		FASTBACK 310		EXP	PLY	DV	IB	T225	CHRY	10	10	9600	2	2	14600	16600
31		FASTBACK 310		SDN	PLY	DV	IB	250-260		10	10	8800	2	2	12700	14500
31		FASTBACK 310		SDN	PLY	DV	IB	T210-T225		10	10	9600	2	2	14100	16300
31		FASTBACK 310	FB	SDN	PLY	DV	IB	260	CRUS	10	10	8800	2	2	12700	14500
31		FASTBACK 310	FB	SDN	PLY	DV	IB	T225	CHRY	10	10	9600	2	2	14300	16300
34		FASTBACK 340		EXP	PLY	DV	IB	T225	CHRY	11		9800	2	3	19600	21700
34		FASTBACK 340	FB	EXP	PLY	DV	IB	T225	CHRY	11		9800	2	3	19600	21700
34		FASTBACK 340		SDN	PLY	DV	IB	T225	CHRY	11		9800	2	3	19000	21100
34		FASTBACK 340	FB	SDN	PLY	DV	IB	T225	CHRY	11		9800	2	3	19000	21100
36				SDN	WD	DV	IB	T260	CRUS	12	4	14000	2	6	24500	27200
36			FB	SDN	WD	DV	IB	T260	CRUS	12	4	14000	2	6	24500	27200
36		SPACE-SEDAN		SDN	WD	DV	IB	T260	CRUS	12	4	14000	2	6	24500	27200
		1968 BOATS														
26	6	FASTBACK		EXP	WD		IB	210-260		10	3	6400	2		7650	9050
28				SDN	WD		IB	250-260		10	9	7000			9350	10700
28				SDN	WD		IB	T210-T260		10	9	8000			10900	13000
28		FASTBACK		EXP	WD		IB	250-260		10	9	7000	2	2	8500	9850
28		FASTBACK		EXP	WD		IB	T210-T260		10	9	8000	2	2	10000	11800
31				SDN	WD		IB	250-260		10	10	8600	2	2	12100	13900
31				SDN	WD		IB	T210-T260		10	10	9600	2	2	13600	16100
31		FASTBACK		EXP	WD		IB	250-260		10	10	8600	2	2	12500	14300
31		FASTBACK		EXP	WD		IB	T210-T260		10	10	9600	2	2	13900	16400
34				SDN	WD		IB	T210-T320		11		10500	2	3	18400	21600
34		FASTBACK	HT	EXP	WD		IB	T210-T320		11		10200	2	3	19100	22200
36				SDN	WD		IB	T250	CRUS	12	4				23400	26000
36				SDN	WD		IB	T260		12	4				23400	26000
36				SDN	WD		IB	T320		12	4				23900	26600
36		SPACE-SEDAN	FB	SDN	WD		IB	T250	CRUS	12	4	15000	2	6	24400	27100
36		SPACE-SEDAN	FB	SDN	WD		IB	T260		12	4	15000	2	6	24400	27100
36		SPACE-SEDAN	FB	SDN	WD		IB	T320		12	4	15000	2	6	25000	27700
37				TCMY	WD		IB	T250	CRUS	13		17000	2	6	26200	29100
37				TCMY	WD		IB	T260		13		17000	2	6	26100	29000
37				TCMY	WD		IB	T320		13		17900	2	6	27400	30500
		1967 BOATS														
26	6	DELUXE	OP	EXP	F/W		IB	210		10	4	6000	2		7100	8150
26	6	EXPRESS CR 260		EXP	PLY		IO	150		10	4		2		14400	16300
28				CR	F/W		IB	210-250		10	9	7700	2	2	8450	9900
28				CR	F/W		IB	T210		10	9	7700	2	2	9500	10800
28				EXP	F/W		IB	210-250		10	9	7700	2	2	8450	9900
28				EXP	F/W		IB	T210-T250		10	9	7700	2	2	9500	11100
28				SDN	F/W		IB	250		10	9	7700	2	2	9400	10700
28				SDN	F/W		IB	T210-T250		10	9	7700	2	2	10400	12200
28			FB	SDN	F/W		IB	T210-T250		10	9	7700	2	2	10400	12200
28	5	EXPRESS CR 280		EXP	PLY		IO	150		10	9		2	2	16500	18800
31				EXP	F/W		IB	250		10	10	8600	2	2	12100	13700
31				EXP	F/W		IB	T210-T250		10	10	8600	2	2	13100	15300
31				SDN	F/W		IB	250				8600			11800	13400
31				SDN	F/W		IB	T210-T250				8600			13000	15300
33	9			EXP	F/W		IB	T210-T250		11		9600	2	3	17400	20200
33	9		FB	EXP	F/W		IB	T210-T250		11		9600	2	3	17400	20200
33	9			SDN	F/W		IB	T210-T250		11		9600	2	3	16700	19500
33	9		FB	SDN	F/W		IB	T210-T250		11		9600	2	3	16700	19500
36			FB	SDN	F/W		IB	T250		12	4	14000	2	6	22900	25400
37				FD	F/W		IB	T250		13		16000	2	6	24300	27000
		1966 BOATS														
27	9	GOLDEN-ALBACORE	FB	SF	F/W		IB	250							8150	9400
27	9	GOLDEN-GULL		CR	F/W		IB	250							8100	9300
28	7	GOLDEN-FALCON		CR	F/W		IB	210							9200	10500
28	7	GOLDEN-FALCON		CR	F/W		IB	T210-T250							10100	11800
28	7	GOLDEN-FALCON	FB	CR	F/W		IB	T210-T250							10100	11800
28	7	GOLDEN-FALCON		EXP	F/W		IB	210-250							8950	10400
28	7	GOLDEN-FALCON		EXP	F/W		IB	T210-T250							9850	11500
28	7	GOLDEN-FALCON		SDN	F/W		IB	250							9200	10400
28	7	GOLDEN-FALCON	FB	SDN	F/W		IB	T210-T250							10200	11900
28	7	GOLDEN-SAILFISH		SF	F/W		IB	T210							9500	10800
31		GOLDEN-ALBATROSS		CR	F/W		IB	250-290							11600	13400
31		GOLDEN-ALBATROSS		CR	F/W		IB	T210-T250							12400	14400
31		GOLDEN-MARLIN		SF	F/W		IB	T250							11900	13500
33	9	GOLDEN-EAGLE	FB		F/W		IB	T250							18900	21000
33	9	GOLDEN-EAGLE		CR	F/W		IB	T210-T250							16000	18500
33	9	GOLDEN-EAGLE		SDN	F/W		IB	T210-T250							18200	20600
33	9	GOLDEN-EAGLE	FB	SDN	F/W		IB	T250							18500	20600
37		CONDOR		DC	F/W		IB	T250							28800	32000
37		GOLDEN-CONDOR		FD	F/W		IB	T250							**	**
		1965 BOATS														
27				EXP	F/W		IB	250							6950	8000
27				SF	F/W		IB	250							6650	7650
30				EXP	F/W		IB	250							11700	13300
30				EXP	F/W		IB	T250							12700	14500
30				SF	F/W		IB	T250							11000	12500
33			HT	EXP	F/W		IB	T250							16200	18400
33			FB	EXP	F/W		IB	T250							16200	18400
33			HT	SDN	F/W		IB	T250							15600	17700
33			FB	SDN	F/W		IB	T250							15600	17700
37				DC	F/W		IB	T250							28100	31200
37				FD	F/W		IB	T250							**	**
		1964 BOATS														
24	8	JETHAWK 4 SL			WD		IO	250							12400	14000
24	8	JETHAWK 4 SL			WD		IB	250							4850	5600
27				EXP	WD		IB	250							6700	7700
31		6 SLEEPER		CBNCR	WD		IB	250							12800	14500
31		6 SLEEPER		CBNCR	WD		IB	T250							14500	16500
33	9	FAIRLINER 6 SL			WD		IB	T250							17200	19500
36		FAIRLINER 6 SL			WD		IB	T250							21100	23400
		1963 BOATS														
27		F1			WD		IB	225-230							5750	6600
30		F1			WD		IB	225							9300	10600
30		F2			WD		IB	T225-T230							10100	11500
32		F2			WD		IB	T225-T230							10300	12700
32		F2FB			WD		IB	T225							11900	13500
32		F2SF			WD		IB	T225							11300	12900
		1962 BOATS														
26		F			WD		IB	215-230							5300	6150
29		F			WD		IB	225-280							8050	9500
29		F 2			WD		IB	T215-T280							9000	10700
31		S			WD		IB	T215-T280							10200	12000
31		S			WD		IB	T 85D							12700	14400
31		S F			WD		IB	T215-T280							10200	12000
31		S F			WD		IB	T 85D							12700	14400
31		S F L			WD		IB	T215-T280							10200	12000
31		S F L			WD		IB	T 85D							12700	14400
		1961 BOATS														
23	10	JETHAWK		CR	WD		IB	170-225		8	2		1	10	3800	4450
27	11	VISCOUNT		CR	WD		IB	170-225		9	3		2		6500	7750
34		ELECTRA		CR	WD		IB	170		10	11		2	2	12900	14600
34		ELECTRA		CR	WD		IB	225		10	11		2	2	13000	14800
34		ELECTRA		CR	WD		IB	T225		10	11		2	2	13900	15800
		1960 BOATS														
23	10	FAIRLINER 24		CR	PLY		IB	135-225		8	2		1	10	3650	4350
24		FAIRLINER 24		CR	WD		IB	135-225							3700	4400
26	10	FAIRLINER 27		CR	PLY		IB	135-225		9	3		2		5800	7050
27		FAIRLINER 27		CR	WD		IB	135-225							5900	7200
32		FAIRLINER 32		CR	WD		IB	T135-T225							10600	12800
32	3	FAIRLINER 32		CR	PLY		IB	T135-T225		10	11		2	2	11000	13300
		1959 BOATS														
25	10	GOLDEN-ARROW		CR	WD		IB	275		8	10				5600	6450
		1949 BOATS														
26		FAIRLINER	HT	SDN	WD		IB								**	**
		1948 BOATS														
27		FAIRLINER		CR	WD		IB	135							5000	5750
		1947 BOATS														
27		FAIRLINER		CR	WD		IB	145							5050	5800
		1946 BOATS														
26			HT	SDN	WD		VD								**	**
30			HT	SDN	WD		IB								**	**
35			FB	SDN	WD		IB								**	**

FAIRWAYS MARINE

DAVID SKELLON YACHTS LTD
SOUTHAMPTON ENGLAND   COAST GUARD MFG ID- DSK

See inside cover to adjust price for area

ATALANTA LTD DISTRIBUTOR
WARREN RI 02885

LOA FT	LOA IN	NAME AND/ OR MODEL	TOP/ RIG	BOAT TYPE	-HULL- MTL	-HULL- TP	ENGINE TP	#	HP	MFG	BEAM FT	BEAM IN	WGT LBS	DRAFT FT	DRAFT IN	RETAIL LOW	RETAIL HIGH
		1981 BOATS															
31	3	FISHER 31	SLP	MS	FBG	KL	IB		35D	VLVO	10	4	14000	4	3	50900	55900
31	3	FISHER 31	KTH	MS	FBG	KL	IB		35D	VLVO	10	4	14000	4	3	50900	55900
32		SEEKER 32/33		TRWL	FBG	DS	IB		50D		11					36800	40900
37		FISHER 37 IV AFT CBN	KTH	MS	FBG	KL	IB		80D	FORD	12		28000	5	3	94800	104000
37		FISHER 37 IV AFT CPT	KTH	MS	FBG	KL	IB		80D	FORD	12		28000	5	3	94800	104000
38		EXPLORER 38	KTH	SA/CR	FBG	KL	IB		D		12		23500	5		83500	91800
38		SEEKER 38		TRWL	FBG	DS	IB		85D		12					93300	102500
43	5	SEASTREAM 43	KTH	MS	FBG	KL	IB		80D	BENZ	14		28000	6		114000	125000
45	8	FISHER 46	KTH	MS	FBG	KL	IB		120D	FORD	15		50000	6	6	166000	182500
		1980 BOATS															
25	3	FISHER 5 TONNER	KTH	MS	FBG	KL	IB		25D	VLVO	9	4	9000	3	9	30500	33900
25	3	POTTER 25	HT	PH	FBG	DS	IB		25D	VLVO	9	4	9000	3	9	22200	24700
25	3	POTTER DAYSAILER	KTH	MS	FBG	KL	IB		25D	VLVO	9	4	9000	3	9	27000	30000
30		FISHER 30	KTH	MS	FBG	KL	IB		36D	VLVO	9	6	13000	4	3	46000	50500
30		FISHER 31	CUT	MS	FBG	KL	IB		36D	VLVO	10	4	13000	4	3	46000	50500
34	4	FISHER 10 TONNER	KTH	MS	FBG	KL	IB		36D	VLVO	11	3	21000	4	9	70700	77700
37		FISHER 37 AFT CBN	KTH	MS	FBG	KL	IB		80D	FORD	12		28000	5	3	87800	96500
37		FISHER 37 AFT CPT	KTH	MS	FBG	KL	IB		80D	FORD	12		28000	5	3	94700	104000
37	9	TRAWLER 38	HT	TRWL	FBG	DS	IB	T	80D	FORD	13	9	20000	3	9	65700	72200
45	8	FISHER 46	KTH	MS	FBG	KL	IB		120D	FORD	15		50000	6	6	160000	175500
46		GUERNSEYMAN	HT	TRWL	FBG	DS	IB	T	120D	FORD	15		50000	6	6	144500	159000
		1979 BOATS															
25	3	FISHER 25	KTH	MS	FBG	KL	IB		25D	VLVO	9	4	9000	3	9	28800	32000
25	3	POTTER 25	HT	PH	FBG	DS	IB		25D	VLVO	9	4	9000	3	9	21400	23800
25	3	POTTER DAYSAILER	KTH	MS	FBG	KL	IB		25D	VLVO	9	4	9000	3	9	26900	29900
28		CATFISHER 28	KTH	MS	FBG	CT	IB		42D	BENZ	13	1	7600	3	5	26000	28900
30		FISHER 30	KTH	MS	FBG	KL	IB		36D	VLVO	9	4	13000	4	3	37700	41900
30		NORTHEASTER 30	KTH	MS	FBG	KL	IB		36D	VLVO	10	4	13000	4	3	50600	55600
34	4	FISHER 34	KTH	MS	FBG	KL	IB		36D-	85D	11	3	19500	4	9	64100	70500
37		FISHER 37 AFT CBN	KTH	MS	FBG	KL	IB		80D	FORD	12		28000	5	3	91800	101000
37		FISHER 37 AFT CPT	KTH	MS	FBG	KL	IB		80D	FORD	12		28000	5	3	85100	93500
37	9	TRAWLER 38	HT	TRWL	FBG	DS	IB	T	80D	FORD	13	9	30000	3	9	87800	96400
37	9	TRAWLER 38	HT	TRWL	FBG	DS	IB	T	120D	FORD	13	9	30000	3	9	88600	97300
37	9	TRAWLER 38	HT	TRWL	FBG	DS	IB	T	212D	FORD	13	9	30000	3	9	91300	100500
45	8	FISHER 46	KTH	MS	FBG	KL	IB		120D	FORD	15		50000	6	6	155000	170000
		1978 BOATS															
25	3	FISHER 25 PH	KTH	MS	FBG	KL	IB		25D	VLVO	9	4	9000	3	9	31100	34600
25	3	FREEWARD 25	SLP	SAIL	FBG	KL	IB		25D	VLVO	9	4	9000	3	9	27000	30000
25	3	POTTER 25	HT	PH	FBG	DS	IB		25D	VLVO	9	4	9000	3	9	20600	22900
25	3	POTTER DAYSAILER	KTH	MS	FBG	KL	IB		25D	VLVO	9	4	9000	3	9	22900	25500
25	3	POTTER LINESMAN	HT	PH	FBG	DS	IB		25D	VLVO	9	4	10080	3	9	23100	25600
28		CATFISHER 28	KTH	MS	FBG	CT	IB		42D	BENZ	13	1	7600	3	5	25300	28100
30		FISHER 30	KTH	MS	FBG	KL	IB		36D	VLVO	9	6	13000	4	3	42800	47500
30		NORTHEASTER 30 PH	KTH	MS	FBG	KL	IB		36D	VLVO	10	4	13000	4	3	42800	47500
34	4	FISHER 34 PH	KTH	MS	FBG	KL	IB		60D	LEHM	11	3	19500	4	9	62300	68500
36	6	TRAWLER 37 PH	HT	TRWL	FBG	DS	IB		120D	FORD	13	6	30000	3	6	77800	85500
37		FISHER 37 AFT CBN	KTH	MS	FBG	KL	IB		80D	FORD	12		28000	5	3	85300	93800
37		FISHER 37 AFT CBN&DC	KTH	MS	FBG	KL	IB		80D	FORD	12		28000	5	3	92300	101500
37		FISHER 37 AFT CPT	KTH	MS	FBG	KL	IB		80D	FORD	12		28000	5	3	80400	88300
37		FISHER 37 AFT CPT&DC	KTH	MS	FBG	KL	IB		80D	FORD	12		28000	5	3	85300	93800
38		TRAWLER 38	HT	TRWL	FBG	DS	IB	T	120D	FORD	13	6	30000	3	6	86500	95000
45	8	FISHER 46 PH	KTH	MS	FBG	KL	IB		120D	FORD	15		50000	6	6	150500	165000
		1977 BOATS															
25	3	FISHER 25	KTH	MS	FBG	KL	IB		25D	VLVO	9	4	9000	3	9	26300	29200
25	3	FREEWARD 25	SLP	SAIL	FBG	KL	IB		25D	VLVO	9	4	9000	3	9	26300	29200
25	3	POTTER 25	HT	PH	FBG	DS	IB		25D-	36D	9	4	9000	3	9	19800	22200
28		CATFISHER 28	SLP	MS	FBG	CT	IB		42D		13	1	7600	3	5	24600	27300
28		CATFISHER 28	KTH	MS	FBG	CT	IB		42D		13	1	7600	3	5	24600	27300
30		FISHER 30	KTH	MS	FBG	KL	IB		36D	VLVO	9	6	13000	4	3	41600	46300
30		NORTHEASTER 30	KTH	MS	FBG	KL	IB		36D	VLVO	10	4	13000	4	3	41600	46300
34	4	FISHER 34	KTH	MS	FBG	KL	IB		60D	FORD	11	3	19500	4	9	60700	66700
37		FISHER 37 AFT CBN	KTH	MS	FBG	KL	IB		80D	FORD	12		30000	5	3	90900	99900
37		FISHER 37 AFT CPT	KTH	MS	FBG	KL	IB		80D	FORD	12		30000	5	3	85600	94100
45	8	FISHER 46	KTH	MS	FBG	KL	IB		120D	FORD	15		50000	6	6	146500	161000
		1976 BOATS															
25		FREEWARD 25	SLP	SAIL	FBG	KL	IB		25D	VLVO	9	4	10000	3	9	28800	32000
25		POTTER 25	HT	PH	FBG	DS	IB		25D	VLVO	9	4	10000	3	9	20900	23300
25	3	FISHER 25	KTH	MS	FBG	KL	IB		25D	VLVO	9	4	10000	3	9	29000	32200
30		FISHER 30	KTH	MS	FBG	KL	IB		36D	VLVO	9	6	14000	4	3	43900	48800
30		NORTHEASTER 30	KTH	MS	FBG	KL	IB		36D	VLVO	10	4	14000	4	3	43900	48800
37		FISHER 37 AFT CABIN	KTH	MS	FBG	KL	IB		80D	FORD	12		30000	5	3	88900	97700
37		FISHER 37 AFT COCKPT	KTH	MS	FBG	KL	IB		80D	FORD	12		30000	5	3	83400	91600
46		FISHER 46	KTH	MS	FBG	KL	IB		95D		15		56000	6	6	151500	166500
46		FISHER 46	KTH	MS	FBG	KL	IB		120D	PERK	15		56000	6	6	151500	166500
		1975 BOATS															
25	3	FISHER 25	KTH	MS	FBG	KL	IB		25D	VLVO	9	4	9000	3	9	25100	27800
30		FISHER 30	KTH	MS	FBG	KL	IB		36D	VLVO	9	6	13000	4	3	39700	44100
30		NORTHEASTER 30	KTH	MS	FBG	KL	IB		36D	VLVO	10	4	13000	4	3	39700	44100
37		FISHER 37	KTH	MS	FBG	KL	IB		80D	FORD	12		30000	5	3	84200	92500

FALCON BOATS

FALCON BOATS   COAST GUARD MFG ID- WXH
FORMERLY W I HUDSON CO

Call 1-800-327-6929 for BUC Personalized Evaluation Service
Or, for 1975 to 1976 boats, sign onto www.BUCValuPro.com

FALCON POWERBOAT COMPANY

Call 1-800-327-6929 for BUC Personalized Evaluation Service
Or, for 1982 boats, sign onto www.BUCValuPro.com

FALES YACHTS INC

NEWPORT RI 02840

See inside cover to adjust price for area

For more recent years, see the BUC Used Boat Price Guide, Volume 1 or Volume 2

LOA FT	LOA IN	NAME AND/ OR MODEL	TOP/ RIG	BOAT TYPE	-HULL- MTL	-HULL- TP	ENGINE TP	#	HP	MFG	BEAM FT	BEAM IN	WGT LBS	DRAFT FT	DRAFT IN	RETAIL LOW	RETAIL HIGH
		1982 BOATS															
32		SEEKER 32/33		TRWL	FBG	DS	IB		50D		11		17500			41400	46000
38		EXPLORER 38	KTH	SA/CR	FBG	KL	IB		D		12		23500	5		60200	66200
38		SEEKER 38		TRWL	FBG	DS	IB		85D		12		23500			71800	78900
		1981 BOATS															
32		SEEKER 32/33		TRWL	FBG	DS	IB		50D		11					33900	37700
38		EXPLORER 38	KTH	SA/CR	FBG	KL	IB		D		12		23500	5		56700	62300
38		SEEKER 38		TRWL	FBG	DS	IB		85D		12					66900	73500
		1980 BOATS															
32		SEEKER		TRWL	FBG	DS	IB		50D		11		17000			37300	41500
38		EXPLORER 38	KTH	SA/CR	FBG	KL	IB		D		12		23000	5		53200	58500
38		SEEKER		TRWL	FBG	DS	IB		85D		12		23000			64200	70500
		1979 BOATS															
31	8	FALES	SLP	SA/CR	FBG	KL	IB		D		11		17000	3	6	34800	38700
31	8	SEEKER	FB	TRWL	FBG	DV	IB		50D	PERK	11		17000	3	6	35600	39500
38		FALES 38	CUT	SA/CR	FBG	KL	IB		D		12		23000	5		51100	56200
38		FALES 38	KTH	SA/CR	FBG	KL	IB		D		12		23000	5		51200	56200
38		SEEKER	FB	TRWL	FBG	DV	IB		85D	PERK	12		23000	4	3	61800	67900
38		SEEKER	FB	TRWL	FBG	DV	IB	T	50D	PERK	12		23000	4	3	64000	70300
		1978 BOATS															
31	8	NAVIGATOR	SLP	MS	FBG	KL	IB		50D	PERK	11		17000	3	6	33500	37300
31	8	SEEKER	FB	TRWL	FBG	DV	IB		50D	PERK	11		17000	3	6	34200	38000
31	8	SOUNDER	HT	TRWL	FBG	DV	IB		50D	PERK	11		17000	3	6	34200	38000
35	7	EXPLORER	CUT	SA/CR	FBG	KL	IB		50D	PERK	11		17000	3	6	35200	39200
38		EXPLORER	CUT	SA/CR	FBG	KL	IB		85D	PERK	12		23500	5		50200	55100
38		NAVIGATOR	KTH	MS	FBG	KL	IB		85D	PERK	12		23000	5		49400	54200
38		SEEKER	FB	TRWL	FBG	DV	IB		85D	PERK	12		23000	4	3	59100	64900
38		SEEKER	FB	TRWL	FBG	DV	IB	T	50D	PERK	12		23000	4	3	61200	67200
41	8	EXPLORER	SLP	SA/CR	FBG	KL	IB		85D	PERK	12		23500	5		56700	62300
41	8	EXPLORER	KTH	SA/CR	FBG	KL	IB		85D	PERK	12		23000	5		56000	61500
		1977 BOATS															
31	8	NAVIGATOR	SLP	MS	FBG	KL	IB		50D	PERK	11		17000	3	6	32400	36000
31	8	SEEKER	FB	TRWL	FBG	KL	IB		50D	PERK	11		17000	3	6	33000	36600
35	7	EXPLORER	CUT	SA/CR	FBG	KL	IB		50D	PERK	11		17000	3	6	34100	37800
38		NAVIGATOR	KTH	MS	FBG	KL	IB		85D	PERK	12		23000	5		48000	52700
38		NAVIGATOR	KTH	MS	FBG	KL	IB	T	50D	PERK	12		23000	5		48300	53100
38		SEEKER	FB	TRWL	FBG	KL	IB		85D	PERK	12		23000	4	3	56600	62200
38		SEEKER	FB	TRWL	FBG	KL	IB	T	50D	PERK	12		23000	4	3	58600	64400
41	8	EXPLORER	SLP	SA/CR	FBG	KL	IB		85D	PERK	12		23500	5		54800	60200
41	8	EXPLORER	KTH	SA/CR	FBG	KL	IB		85D	PERK	12		23500	5		54800	60200
		1976 BOATS															
31	8	NAVIGATOR 32/33	SLP	MS	FBG	KL	IB		50D	PERK	10	6	17000	3	6	31400	34900
31	8	SEEKER 32/33	FB	TRWL	FBG	KL	IB		50D	PERK	10	6	17000	3	6	30400	33800
31	8	SOUNDER 32/33	FB	TRWL	FBG	KL	IB		50D	PERK	10	6	17000	3	6	29700	33000
38		NAVIGATOR	KTH	MS	FBG	KL	IB		85D	PERK	12		22750	5		46100	50600
38		NAVIGATOR	KTH	MS	FBG	KL	IB	T	50D	PERK	12		22750	5		46600	51300

234
CONTINUED ON NEXT PAGE
96th ed. - Vol. III

LOA FT IN	NAME AND/ OR MODEL	TOP/ RIG	BOAT TYPE	-HULL- MTL TP TP	# HP	MFG	BEAM FT IN	WGT LBS	DRAFT FT IN	RETAIL LOW	RETAIL HIGH
---- 1976 BOATS ----											
38	SEEKER	FB	TRWL	FBG DV IB	85D	PERK	12	22750	5	54100	59500
38	SEEKER	FB	TRWL	FBG KL IB	T 50D	PERK	12	22750	5	56100	61600
38	SOUNDER	FB	TRWL	FBG DV IB	85D	PERK	12	22750	5	53500	58800
38	SOUNDER	FB	TRWL	FBG DV IB	T 50D	PERK	12	22750	5	55400	60900
---- 1975 BOATS ----											
31 8	SEEKER 32/33	SLP	MS	FBG DV IB	50D	PERK	11	17000	3 6	30500	33900
31 8	SEEKER 32/33	FB	TRWL	FBG DV IB	50D	PERK	11	17000	3 6	31200	34600
31 8	SOUNDER 32/33	FB	TRWL	FBG DV IB	50D	PERK	11	17000	3 6	30400	33800
38	NAVIGATOR	KTH	MS	FBG KL IB	85D	PERK	12	22750	5	44300	49200
38	NAVIGATOR	KTH	MS	FBG KL IB	T 50D	PERK	12	23000	5	45700	50200
38	SEEKER	FB	TRWL	FBG DV IB	85D	PERK	12	22750	5	52000	57200
38	SEEKER	FB	TRWL	FBG DV IB	T 50D	PERK	12		5	54000	59400
38	SOUNDER	FB	TRWL	FBG DV IB	85D	PERK	12	22750	5	51300	56400
38	SOUNDER	FB	TRWL	FBG DV IB	T 50D	PERK	12		5	53400	58700
---- 1974 BOATS ----											
30	CARIB TRAWLER	FB	TRWL	FBG DV IB	50D	PERK	10 6	15000	3 6	25600	28500
30	NAVIGATOR 30	FB	TRWL	FBG DV IB	50D	PERK	10	15000	3 6	26600	29500
30	NAVIGATOR 30	FB	TRWL	FBG DV IB	50D	PERK	10 6	15000	3 6	25600	28500
31 8	NAVIGATOR 32/33	SLP	MS	FBG KL IB	50D	PERK	11	15000	3 6	26300	29200
31 8	SEEKER 32/33	FB	TRWL	FBG KL IB	50D	PERK	11	15000	3 6	26900	29900

FALLS CITY FLYING SERVICE
MARINETTE

Call 1-800-327-6929 for BUC Personalized Evaluation Service
Or, for 1959 to 1961 boats, sign onto www.BUCValuPro.com

FALMOUTH BOAT CONST LTD
TUFNOL INDUSTRIES LTD

Call 1-800-327-6929 for BUC Personalized Evaluation Service
Or, for 1979 to 1985 boats, sign onto www.BUCValuPro.com

FAMCO BOAT CO INC

Call 1-800-327-6929 for BUC Personalized Evaluation Service
Or, for 1961 boats, sign onto www.BUCValuPro.com

FANTASY BOATS INC
COAST GUARD MFG ID- FAN

Call 1-800-327-6929 for BUC Personalized Evaluation Service
Or, for 1975 to 1976 boats, sign onto www.BUCValuPro.com

FAR EAST YACHT BLDRS INC

LOA FT IN	NAME AND/ OR MODEL	TOP/ RIG	BOAT TYPE	-HULL- MTL TP TP	# HP	MFG	BEAM FT IN	WGT LBS	DRAFT FT IN	RETAIL LOW	RETAIL HIGH
---- 1973 BOATS ----											
32 8	CARIBBEAN 33	KTH	SAIL	FBG KL IB	D		9 3		4 8	21600	24000
---- 1972 BOATS ----											
32	MARINER	KTH	SAIL	FBG KL IB	50D	PERK				21500	23900
---- 1971 BOATS ----											
31	MARINER	KTH	SAIL	FBG KL IB	50D	PERK				17200	19500
32	MARINER	KTH	SA/CR	FBG KL IB	D		9 10		3 9	21000	23400
35 10	MARINER	KTH	SA/CR	FBG KL IB	D		10 9		5	31000	34500
40	MARINER	KTH	SA/CR	FBG KL IB	D		11 6		5 9	40600	45100
---- 1970 BOATS ----											
31	MARINER 31	KTH	SA/CR	FBG BB IB	D		9 9		3 9	16800	19100
32	MARINER 32	KTH	SAIL	FBG IB	40D	PERK	9 9		5 8	20700	23000
40	MARINER 40	KTH	SA/CR	FBG BB IB	D		11 5		5 8	39800	44300
---- 1969 BOATS ----											
30 10	MARINER	KTH	SAIL	FBG IB	40D	PERK				16600	18800
---- 1968 BOATS ----											
30 10	MARINER	KTH	SAIL	FBG IB	50D	PERK				16400	18600
39 11			SAIL	WD IB	30	UNIV				28100	31200
---- 1967 BOATS ----											
34 6	MARINER 35	KTH	SAIL	MHG IB	55D			19000		29300	32500
40	MARINER 40	KTH	SAIL	WD IB	25D		11 6	24000	6	38000	42200
---- 1966 BOATS ----											
29 5	HERRESHOFF 30	KTH	SAIL	WD IB	30D					11700	13300
30 10	MARINER 31	KTH	SAIL	FBG IB	30D	PERK				16000	18200
34 6	GARDEN 35	KTH	SAIL	WD IB	30D-	36D				28900	32100
39 11	SPARKMAN-&-STEPHENS		SAIL	WD IB	30D					37600	41700
40	MARINER 40	KTH	SAIL	WD IB	36					27700	30800
40	MARINER 40		SAIL	WD IB	60D					38000	42200
---- 1965 BOATS ----											
35	GARDEN 35	KTH	SAIL	MHG KL IB	30D		10 1		5 4	28700	31800
40	MARINER 40	KTH	SAIL	WD IB	36D					37500	41600
40	MARINER 40	KTH	SAIL	WD IB	60D					37700	41900
40	MARINER 40 TEAK	KTH	SAIL	WD IB	36D					37500	41600
40	MARINER 40 TEAK	KTH	SAIL	WD IB	60D					37700	41900
---- 1964 BOATS ----											
29 5	HERRESHOFF 30	KTH	SAIL	WD IB	30D					11500	13100
34 6	GARDEN 35	KTH	SAIL	WD IB	30D-	36D				28500	31700
39 11	SPARKMAN-&-STEPHENS	KTH	SAIL	WD IB	30D					37100	41200

FAR EAST YACHT SPECIALISTS

Call 1-800-327-6929 for BUC Personalized Evaluation Service
Or, for 1971 boats, sign onto www.BUCValuPro.com

FAR WEST YACHTS

Call 1-800-327-6929 for BUC Personalized Evaluation Service
Or, for 1980 to 1981 boats, sign onto www.BUCValuPro.com

FARALLON BOATS
FORMERLY FARALLON PLASTICS

For more recent years, see the BUC Used Boat Price Guide, Volume 1 or Volume 2

LOA FT IN	NAME AND/ OR MODEL	TOP/ RIG	BOAT TYPE	-HULL- MTL TP TP	# HP	MFG	BEAM FT IN	WGT LBS	DRAFT FT IN	RETAIL LOW	RETAIL HIGH
---- 1981 BOATS ----											
26 2	FARALLON 25	OP	FSH	FBG DV IB	225	MPC	8	5000	2 6	15800	18000
26 2	FARALLON 25	HT	FSH	FBG DV IB	225-250		8	5000	2 6	15800	18300
26 2	FARALLON 25	HT	FSH	FBG DV IO	260	VLVO	8	5000	2 6	14800	16800
26 2	FARALLON 25	HT	FSH	FBG DV IB	124D	VLVO	8	5000	2 6	18700	20800
26 2	FARALLON 25	HT	OFF	FBG DV IB	225-250		8	5000	2 6	15500	17900
26 2	FARALLON 25	HT	OFF	FBG DV IO	260	VLVO	8	5000	2 6	13800	15700
26 2	FARALLON 25	HT	OFF	FBG DV IB	124D	VLVO	8	5000	2 6	18000	20000
28 2	FARALLON 27	OP	FSH	FBG DV IB	250	MPC	9 8	6500	2 6	19400	21600
28 2	FARALLON 27	HT	FSH	FBG DV IB	216D	GM	9 8	6500	2 6	24500	27200
28 2	FARALLON 27	HT	FSH	FBG DV IB	250	MPC	9 8	6500	2 6	19400	21600
28 2	FARALLON 27	HT	FSH	FBG DV IB	216D	GM	9 8	6500	2 6	24500	27200

HARRISON FARRELL

Call 1-800-327-6929 for BUC Personalized Evaluation Service
Or, for 1959 to 1961 boats, sign onto www.BUCValuPro.com

FARRINGTON MARINE INC
COAST GUARD MFG ID- FDR

Call 1-800-327-6929 for BUC Personalized Evaluation Service
Or, for 1982 to 1986 boats, sign onto www.BUCValuPro.com

FASTNET MARINE LTD

Call 1-800-327-6929 for BUC Personalized Evaluation Service
Or, for 1974 to 1975 boats, sign onto www.BUCValuPro.com

FAY BOW BOAT COMPANY
FAY & BOWEN ENGINE CO

Call 1-800-327-6929 for BUC Personalized Evaluation Service
Or, for 1907 to 1927 boats, sign onto www.BUCValuPro.com

FEADSHIP INC
FT LAUDERDALE FL 33316

See inside cover to adjust price for area

LOA FT IN	NAME AND/ OR MODEL	TOP/ RIG	BOAT TYPE	-HULL- MTL TP	TP	----ENGINE--- # HP MFG	BEAM FT IN	WGT LBS	DRAFT FT IN	RETAIL LOW	RETAIL HIGH
75		--- 1957 BOATS --- MY	AL		IB	T175D GM				**	**
48		--- 1956 BOATS --- FB	CR	STL DS	IB	T325D GM				110000	121000
72		MY	STL		IB	T216D GM				**	**
24	5 BABY-WEEKENDER	--- 1954 BOATS --- SLP	SAIL				6 6		3 3	2950	3400
30		HT	EXP	MHG	IB	T100 GRAY				17000	19300
45		KTH	SA/CR	STL KL	IB	CHRY				49800	54700
60		FB	FD	WD	IB	T D GM				**	**
60	CORONET	FB	MY	WD	IB		15		4 3	**	**
27		--- 1953 BOATS --- SLP	SA/RC							3450	4050
30	DUTCH-GIRL	OP	EXP	STL	IB					**	**
45		KTH	3A/CR	KC	IB		12 10		4 6	50500	55500
55	CAPRI	FB	YTFS	STL	IB	T D GM				**	**
71		FB	MY	STL	IB	T D GM				**	**

FEADSHIP-HOLLAND
2110 AB AERDENHOUT NETHERLANDS

See inside cover to adjust price for area

LOA FT IN	NAME AND/ OR MODEL	TOP/ RIG	BOAT TYPE	-HULL- MTL TP	TP	----ENGINE--- # HP MFG	BEAM FT IN	WGT LBS	DRAFT FT IN	RETAIL LOW	RETAIL HIGH
35 6		--- 1959 BOATS --- EXP	STL		IB	T165	11 4			49900	54900
40 5		EXP	STL		IB	T185D	11 6			108500	119000
40 7		CR	STL		IB	T200	11 6			80800	88800
45 1		SF	STL		IB	T165	13 3			98800	108500
50 6	MONTEREY	CR	STL		IB	T200	14 10			157500	173000
55	COLUMBIA	CR	STL		IB					**	**
60	HEAD-SEAL	CR	STL		IB	D	15			**	**
61	FLORIDIAN	CR	STL		IB	D				**	**
65 1	GLADYS	CR	STL		IB	D	16 6			**	**
70 4	FLUSHDECK	CR	STL		IB	D	16 1			**	**
75	FLUSHDECK	CR	STL		IB	D				**	**

FEATHER CRAFT INC
COAST GUARD MFG ID- FEA

Call 1-800-327-6929 for BUC Personalized Evaluation Service
Or, for 1958 to 1971 boats, sign onto www.BUCValuPro.com

FEATHERSTONE MARINE CORP

Call 1-800-327-6929 for BUC Personalized Evaluation Service
Or, for 1971 to 1972 boats, sign onto www.BUCValuPro.com

TOM FEXAS INTERNATIONAL
STUART FL 33490

See inside cover to adjust price for area

LOA FT IN	NAME AND/ OR MODEL	TOP/ RIG	BOAT TYPE	-HULL- MTL TP	TP	----ENGINE--- # HP MFG	BEAM FT IN	WGT LBS	DRAFT FT IN	RETAIL LOW	RETAIL HIGH
44	MARRATOOKA 44	--- 1982 BOATS --- TRWL	FBG	DS	IB	T 80D	15	42000		113500	125000
48	FULL-CRY 48	SF	FBG	DS	IB	T240D	12	19000		82300	90500
60	MERIDIAN 60	TRWL	FBG	DS	IB	T210D	18	75000		207000	227500
60	WARRIOR 60	SF	FBG	SV	IB	T D	17 6	66000		**	**
44	MARRATOOKA 44	--- 1981 BOATS --- TRWL	FBG	DS	IB	T 80D	15	42000		108000	119000
60	MERIDIAN 60	TRWL	FBG	DS	IB	T210D	17	75000		193000	212000
65	MYSTIC 65	SF	FBG	DV	IB	T575D	18 6			305000	335500
44	MARRATOOKA 44	--- 1980 BOATS --- TRWL	FBG	DS	IB	T 80D	15	42000		103500	113500
60	MERIDIAN 60	TRWL	FBG	DS	IB	T210D	17	75000		184500	202500
65	MYSTIC 65	SF	FBG	SV	IB	T575D	18 6			292000	321000

FIBER GLASS ENGRG
TEMPO

Call 1-800-327-6929 for BUC Personalized Evaluation Service
Or, for 1959 boats, sign onto www.BUCValuPro.com

FIBERCRAFT PRODUCTS CORP
NORTH MIAMI FL 33181

See inside cover to adjust price for area

LOA FT IN	NAME AND/ OR MODEL	TOP/ RIG	BOAT TYPE	-HULL- MTL TP	TP	----ENGINE--- # HP MFG	BEAM FT IN	WGT LBS	DRAFT FT IN	RETAIL LOW	RETAIL HIGH
18 3	FC-183	--- 1967 BOATS ---	FBG	SV	OB		7 5	1800	1 10	3300	3800
18 3	FC-183		FBG	SV	IO	120-155	7 5	1800	1 10	3750	4400
18 6	FC T-186		FBG	TR	OB		7 2		1 4	3300	3850
18 6	FC T-186		FBG	TR	IO	120-160	7 2		1 4	3750	4350
22 8	FC 23	RNBT	FBG		IO	155-225	8	2400	1 10	6300	7450
22 8	FC 23	RNBT	FBG		IO	T120	8	2400	1 10	7350	8400
22 8	FC-23	OVNTR	FBG		IO	155-225	8	2400	1 10	6700	7900
22 8	FC-23	OVNTR	FBG		IO	T120	8		1 10	7750	8900
18 4	FIBERCRAFT 18	--- 1965 BOATS --- RNBT	FBG		OB		7 2	1200		2500	2900
20	FIBERCRAFT 20	RNBT	FBG		OB		8	1400		3850	4500
23	FIBERCRAFT 23	RNBT	FBG		OB		8	1600		470	5450
28	FIBERCRAFT 28	RNBT	FBG		IB		11 5		3	**	**
18 2	OCEAN	--- 1963 BOATS --- RNBT	FBG		OB					2050	2450
18 2	OCEAN	RNBT	FBG		IB					**	**
20	SEA-VEE 21	UTL	FBG		OB					3600	4200
20	SEA-VEE 21	UTL	FBG		IB					**	**
18 2	FLYER	--- 1962 BOATS --- RNBT	FBG		OB					2050	2450
20	SEA-VEE	CR	FBG		OB					4100	4800
20	SEA-VEE	RNBT	FBG		OB					4000	4650
20	DELUXE 21	--- 1961 BOATS --- CBNCR	FBG		OB		7 11	1600		4400	5050
20	FAMILY 21	RNBT	FBG		OB		7 11	1500		4100	4800
21	CRUISER	CR	FBG		IB	80	7 11			2550	2950
21	RUNABOUT	RNBT	FBG		IB	80	7 11			2500	2900
20	CRUISER	--- 1960 BOATS --- CR	FBG	DV	OB		7 11	1200		3450	4000
20	RUNABOUT	RNBT	FBG	DV	OB		7 11	1100		3200	3750
20	HARD TOP	--- 1959 BOATS --- HT	CR	FBG		OB		7 11	975		2900	3400
20	HARD TOP	HT	CR	FBG	OB		7 11			**	**
20	RUNABOUT	RNBT	FBG		IB		7 11	975		2900	3400
20	RUNABOUT	RNBT	FBG		IB		7 11			**	**

FIBERFORM
BAYLINER MARINE CORP
SPOKANE WA 99214   COAST GUARD MFG ID- FBF

See inside cover to adjust price for area

LOA FT IN	NAME AND/ OR MODEL	TOP/ RIG	BOAT TYPE	-HULL- MTL TP	TP	----ENGINE--- # HP MFG	BEAM FT IN	WGT LBS	DRAFT FT IN	RETAIL LOW	RETAIL HIGH
16 2	LASER 1601	--- 1982 BOATS --- ST	RNBT	FBG DV	OB		6 6	923		2200	2550
16 5	WAIKIKI 1701	OP	SKI	FBG DV	OB		6 8	840		2000	2350
16 9	SURFSTAR 1702	ST	RNBT	FBG TR	OB		7 2	1130		3050	3500
18 1	ISLANDER 1855 B/R	ST	RNBT	FBG DV	IO	120-175	7 10	1700		2350	2900
18 1	ISLANDER 1855 B/R	ST	RNBT	FBG DV	IO	225-228	7 10	1700		2600	3000
18 1	ISLANDER 1855 C/B	ST	RNBT	FBG DV	IO	120-175	7 10	1600		2350	2850
18 1	ISLANDER 1855 C/B	ST	RNBT	FBG DV	IO	225-228	7 10	1600		2550	2950
18 1	OPEN BOW 1882	ST	RNBT	FBG DV	OB		7 10	1350		3150	3700
18 1	RUNABOUT 1881	ST	RNBT	FBG DV	OB		7 10	1250		3000	3450
18 1	RUNABOUT 1883	ST	RNBT	FBG DV	IO	170	7 10	1600		2350	2700
18 4	SS185	OP	RNBT	FBG DV	IO	120-140	6 10	1400		2050	2450
18 4	SS185	OP	RNBT	FBG DV	IO	175 VLVO	6 10	1400		2250	2600
19	COUGAR 1955	OP	SKI	FBG DV	IO	170-175	7 6	1600		2350	2850
19	COUGAR 1955	OP	SKI	FBG DV	IO	225-260	7 6	1600		2550	3100
19 2	CATALINA 1955	ST	RNBT	FBG DV	IO	120-228	7 10	2170		2650	3250
19 2	CATALINA 1955	ST	RNBT	FBG DV	IO	260	7 10	2170		2900	3500
20	CUDDY 2007	HT	CUD	FBG DV	IO	170-185	7 10	2050		3150	3700
20	SANTA-CATALINA 2009	HT	CUD	FBG DV	IO	170-185	7 10	2150		3200	3800
20 1	BIMINI 2055 CUDDY	ST	CUD	FBG DV	IO	140-175	7 10	2150		3250	3950
20 1	BIMINI 2055 CUDDY	ST	CUD	FBG DV	IO	225-260	7 10	2150		3500	4300
20 1	BIMINI 2055 EXP	ST	EXP	FBG DV	IO	28-175	7 10	2400		3400	4150
20 1	BIMINI 2055 EXP	ST	EXP	FBG DV	IO	225-228	7 10	2400		3700	4300
20 1	BIMINI 2055 OPEN SPT	OP	SPTCR	FBG DV	IO	140-175	7 10	2150		3250	4000
20 1	BIMINI 2055 OPEN SPT	OP	SPTCR	FBG DV	IO	225-260	7 10	2150		3550	4300
20 1	CRUISER 2008		CR	FBG DV	OB		7 10	2150		5000	5750

```
LOA  NAME AND/        TOP/ BOAT  -HULL-  ----ENGINE--- BEAM   WGT DRAFT RETAIL RETAIL
FT IN OR MODEL        RIG  TYPE  MTL TP TP # HP  MFG   FT IN  LBS FT IN  LOW   HIGH
----------------- 1982 BOATS ----------------------------------------------------
20 1 SOUNDER 2010          FSH  FBG DV IO  170       7 10  2000         3350   3900
21 2 SPORTSMAN 2101        SF   FBG DV IO  170       7 10  2550         4300   5000
21 2 SPORTSMAN 2102   OP   SF   FBG DV OB            7 10  2450         5900   6750
22   BAJA 2355        FB   CBNCR FBG DV IO 170-228   8    3350         5200   6300
22   BAJA 2355        FB   CBNCR FBG DV IO 260       8    3350         5450   6500
22   EXPRESS 2350     ST   OVNTR FBG DV IO 170-230   8    2800         4150   5150
22   EXPRESS 2350     ST   OVNTR FBG DV IO 260       8    2800         4450   5350
22   SUN-BLAZER 2355  HT   OVNTR FBG DV IO 170-260   8    2800         4150   5150
24 2 BERMUDA 2555     ST   CR   FBG DV IO  170-228   8    3340         5250   6400
24 2 BERMUDA 2555     ST   CR   FBG DV IO  260       8    3340         5550   6600
24 2 BERMUDA 2555     ST   CR   FBG DV IO  T145-T175 8    3340         6250   7250
24 2 BERMUDA 2575     ST   CR   FBG DV IO  260   OMC 8    3340         5500   6350

24 2 HARDTOP 2500     HT   CR   FBG DV IO  198       8    2600         4650   5350
24 2 SUN-BLAZER 2555  HT   CBNCR FBG DV IO 185-260   8    3400         6150   7600
24 2 SUN-BLAZER 2555  HT   CBNCR FBG DV IO T145-T185 8    3400         7200   8350
24 2 SUNBRIDGE 2575        EXP  FBG DV IO  198       8         5400    6200
25 7 BAJA 2650        FB   CBNCR FBG DV IB 225      10    4950        10800  12300
25 7 BAJA 2650        FB   CBNCR FBG DV IB 260      10    4950         9850  11200
25 7 SEA-BLAZER 2700       EXP  FBG DV IB 225      10    4400         9000  10200
25 7 SEA-BLAZER 2700       EXP  FBG DV IB 260      10    4400         7600   8750
26 2 BAJA 2600        FB   CBNCR FBG DV IO 198       8    3910         8500   9750
26 2 RIVIERA 2655     ST   CR   FBG DV IO  185-198   8    3550         6400   7450
26 2 RIVIERA 2655     ST   CR   FBG DV IO  260       8    3550         6900   8100
26 2 RIVIERA 2655     ST   CR   FBG DV IO  T145-T175 8    3550         8450   8950

28 1 CORONADO 2855    FB   SDN  FBG DV IO  260      10    5900  1 6  11900  13700
     IO T175-T260  13000  15400, VD T350     16600 18900, IOT130D-T155D 15400  18500

28 1 CRUISER 2850     FB   CR   FBG DV IB  330      10    5900  1 6  13700  15600
28 1 SPORT FISHERMAN 2875 FB  SF  FBG DV IO  260     10    5460        12000  13700
28 1 SPORT FISHERMAN 2875 FB  SF  FBG DV IO  330     10    5460  1 6  13400  15200
31 7 CRUISER 3200     FB   SF   FBG DV IB  T228     11  9 8800        20800  23100
33 5 CRUISER 3300     FB   MY   FBG DV IB  T225     13  4 14070  2 8  33700  37600
33 5 TRI-CABIN 3450   FB   TCMY FBG DV IB  T250     13  4 13600  2 8  31900  35400
----------------- 1981 BOATS ----------------------------------------------------
16 2 LASER 1610       ST   RNBT FBG DV OB            6  6   940         2200   2550
16 5 WAIKIKI 1701     OP   SKI  FBG SV OB            6  8   840         1950   2300
16 9 SURFSTAR 1702    ST   RNBT FBG TR OB            7  2  1330         3000   3450
18 1 OPEN BOW 1882    ST   RNBT FBG DV IO            7 10  1350         3100   3600
18 1 OPEN BOW 1884    ST   RNBT FBG DV IO       OMC  7 10  1700          **     **
18 1 OPEN BOW 1884    ST   RNBT FBG DV IO  120-200   7 10  1700         2350   2900
18 1 OPEN BOW 1884    ST   RNBT FBG DV IO  225-230   7 10  1700         2550   3000
18 1 RUNABOUT 1881    ST   RNBT FBG DV OB            7 10  1250         2950   3400
18 1 RUNABOUT 1883    ST   RNBT FBG DV IO  120-200   7 10  1600         2300   2850
18 1 RUNABOUT 1883    ST   RNBT FBG DV IO  225-230   7 10  1600         2500   2900
18 4 SS184           OP   RNBT FBG DV IO  120   MRCR 6 10  1300         1950   2350
18 4 SS184           OP   RNBT FBG DV IO  120   OMC  6 10  1300         1950   2300

18 4 SS184           OP   RNBT FBG DV IO  120-200   6 10  1300         2100   2550
18 4 SS185           OP        FBG DV IO  198   MRCR 6 10  1400         2000   2350
18 4 SS185           OP   RNBT FBG DV IO  120   MRCR 6 10  1400         2000   2400
18 4 SS185           OP   RNBT FBG DV IO  120   OMC  6 10  1400         2000   2350
18 4 SS185           OP        FBG DV IO  120-200   6 10  1400         2150   2600
19   COUGAR 1901     OP   SKI  FBG DV IO  170-200   7    1060         2200   2750
19   COUGAR 1901     OP   SKI  FBG DV IO  225-260   7    1060         2400   2950
19   COUGAR 1901     OP   SKI  FBG DV JT  460  PANT 7  6  1060         3150   3700
20   CUDDY 2007      HT   CUD  FBG DV IO  170-185   7 10  2050         3100   3650
20   SANTA-CATALINA 2009 HT CUD FBG DV IO 170-185   7 10  2150         3150   3750
20 1 CRUISER 2006    ST   CR   FBG DV IO  140-200   7 10  2400         3350   4150
20 1 CRUISER 2006    ST   CR   FBG DV IO  225-260   7 10  2400         3650   4400

20 1 CRUISER 2006    HT   CR   FBG DV IO  260  VLVO 7 10  2400         3800   4400
20 1 CRUISER 2008    ST   CR   FBG DV OB            7 10  2150         4900   5650
20 1 CUDDY 2007      ST   CUD  FBG DV IO  140-200   7 10  2050         3150   3900
20 1 CUDDY 2007      ST   CUD  FBG DV IO  225-260   7 10  2050         3400   4150
20 1 CUDDY 2007      HT   CUD  FBG DV IO  140-200   7 10  2050         3150   3900
20 1 CUDDY 2007      HT   CUD  FBG DV IO  225-260   7 10  2050         3400   4150
20 1 SANTA-CATALINA 2009 ST CUD FBG DV IO 140-200   7 10  2150         3200   3950
20 1 SANTA-CATALINA 2009 ST CUD FBG DV IO 225-260   7 10  2150         3450   4200
20 1 SANTA-CATALINA 2009 HT CUD FBG DV IO 140-200   7 10  2150         3200   3950
20 1 SANTA-CATALINA 2009 HT CUD FBG DV IO 225-260   7 10  2150         3450   4200
20 1 SOUNDER 2010    ST   FSH  FBG DV IO  120-200   7 10  2000         3250   4050
20 1 SOUNDER 2010    ST   FSH  FBG DV IO  225-260   7 10  2000         3550   4150

21 2 CUDDY 2200      ST   CUD  FBG DV IO  140-200   7 10  2100         3400   4150
21 2 CUDDY 2200      ST   CUD  FBG DV IO  225-260   7 10  2100         3650   4350
21 2 CUDDY 2200      HT   CUD  FBG DV IO  140-200   7 10  2100         3400   4150
21 2 CUDDY 2200      HT   CUD  FBG DV IO  225-260   7 10  2100         3650   4450
21 2 SPORTSMAN 2101  ST   SF   FBG DV IO  140-230   7 10  2550         4200   5250
21 2 SPORTSMAN 2101  ST   SF   FBG DV IO  260       7 10  2550         4550   5450
21 2 SPORTSMAN 2101  ST   SF   FBG DV IO  130D VLVO 7 10  2550         6050   6750
21 2 SPORTSMAN 2102  OP   SF   FBG DV OB            7 10  2450         5800   6650
22   BAJA 2300       FB   CBNCR FBG DV IO 170-230   8    3350         5100   6200
22   BAJA 2300       FB   CBNCR FBG DV IO 260       8    3350         5350   6400
22   EXPRESS 2350    ST   OVNTR FBG DV IO 170-230   8    2800         4100   5100
22   EXPRESS 2350    ST   OVNTR FBG DV IO 260       8    2800         4400   5250

22   EXPRESS 2350    HT   OVNTR FBG DV IO 185-230   8    2800         4100   5100
22   EXPRESS 2350    HT   OVNTR FBG DV IO 260       8    2800         4400   5250
22   SUN-BLAZER 2375 HT   OVNTR FBG DV IO 170-230   8    2800         4100   5100
22   SUN-BLAZER 2375 HT   OVNTR FBG DV IO 260       8    2800         4400   5250
24 2 BERMUDA 2550    ST   OFF  FBG DV IO  185-260   8    3340         5500   6450
24 2 BERMUDA 2550    ST   OFF  FBG DV IO  T120-T200 8    3340         5800   7200
24 2 BERMUDA 2550    ST   CR   FBG DV IO  T225-T230 8    3340         6400   7350
24 2 BERMUDA 2575    ST   CR   FBG DV IO  170-230   8    3340         5150   6250
     IO 260     5450   6450, IO T120-T200    5850    7250, IO T225-T230    6450   7400

24 2 EXPRESS 2502    ST   EXP  FBG DV IO  185-260   8    3400         5250   6550
24 2 EXPRESS 2502    ST   EXP  FBG DV IO  T120-T200 8    3400         5900   7300
24 2 EXPRESS 2502    ST   EXP  FBG DV IO  T225-T230 8    3400         6500   7450
24 2 EXPRESS 2502    HT   EXP  FBG DV IO  185-260   8    3400         5400   6500
24 2 EXPRESS 2502    HT   EXP  FBG DV IO  T120-T200 8    3400         5900   7300
24 2 EXPRESS 2502    HT   EXP  FBG DV IO  T225-T230 8    3400         6500   7450
24 2 SEDAN 2501      FB   SDN  FBG DV IO  185-260   8    3500         5400   6750
24 2 SEDAN 2501      FB   SDN  FBG DV IO  T120-T200 8    3500         6050   7450
24 2 SEDAN 2501      FB   SDN  FBG DV IO  T225-T230 8    3500         6600   7600
24 8 HARDTOP 2500    HT   CR   FBG DV IO  185-230   8    2600         4700   5800
     IO 260     5100   6000, IO 130D VLVO   5450   6300, IO T120-T198    5400   6600

25 7 BAJA 2650       FB   CBNCR FBG DV VD 250-255  10    4950        10500  11900
     IO 260     9700  11200, VD 325-330    10700  12100, IO 130D VLVO  11800  13400
     IO T140-T200 10000  11900

25 7 SEA-BLAZER 2700 ST   EXP  FBG DV VD 250-255  10    4400         8900  10100
     IO 260     7500   8750, VD 325-330     9350  10600, IO 130D VLVO   7700   8900
     IO T140-T200  7850   9750, IO T225-T230 8800 10000

26 2 BAJA 2600       FB   CBNCR FBG DV IO 185-260   8    3910         8300   9900
26 2 BAJA 2600       FB   CBNCR FBG DV IO 130D VLVO 8    3910        10300  11700
26 2 BAJA 2600       FB   CBNCR FBG DV IO T120-T230 8    3910         8850  10600
26 2 RIVIERA 2620    ST   CR   FBG DV IO  185-230   8    3550         6300   7650
     IO 260     6800   7950, IO T120-T185    6950   8700, IO T198-T230   7700   9350

28 1 CRUISER 2850    FB   CR   FBG DV IO  260      10    5900  1 6  10600  12200
     VD 325-330  13200  15000, IB 130D VLVO 13400 15200, IO T170  MRCR  11300  12800
     IB T170   OMC 13500  15400, IO T185-T200 11500 13400, IO T225  VLVO 12100  13700
     VD T225   OMC 14300  16200, IO T228  MRCR 12000 13600, VD T228  MRCR 14100  16100
     IO T230   OMC 12000  13600, IO T250-T255 14600 16600, IB T130D VLVO 16700  18900

28 1 SPORT FISHERMAN 2875 FB SF FBG DV OB          10    5460  1 6  11800  14300
     VD 325-330  12900  14700, IB 130D VLVO 12800 14600, IO T170  MRCR  12600  14300
     IB T170   OMC 13300  15100, IO T185-T200 12800 14900, IO T225  VLVO 13500  15400
     VD T225   OMC 14100  16000, IO T228  MRCR 13400 15200, VD T228  MRCR 14000  15900
     IO T230   OMC 13400  15200, IO T255     14300 16400, IB T130D VLVO 16400  18900

31 7 CRUISER 3200    FB   SF   FBG DV IB  260      11  9         18300  20300
31 7 CRUISER 3200    FB   SF   FBG DV IB  T145-T255 11  9 8800        18900  22300
31 7 CRUISER 3200    FB   SF   FBG DV IB  T140D VLVO 11  9 8800        23800  26400
33 5 CRUISER 3300    FB   SF   FBG DV IB  T210-T240 13  4 12300        32700  36300
33 5 CRUISER 3300    FB   MY   FBG DV IB  T225-T330 13  4 14070  2 8  42300  38100
33 5 CRUISER 3300    FB   MY   FBG DV IB  T200D VLVO 13  4 14070  2 8  43600  46600
33 5 CRUISER 3300    FB   TCMY FBG DV IB  T225-T330 13  4 15370  2 8  31800  35000
33 5 CRUISER 3450    FB   TCMY FBG DV IB  T200D VLVO 13  4 15370  2 8  40400  44000
33 5 TRI-CABIN 3450  FB   TCMY FBG DV IB  T210-T250 13  4 13600        30000  33800
----------------- 1980 BOATS ----------------------------------------------------
16 2 LASER 1610      ST   RNBT FBG DV OB            6  6   940         2150   2500
16 5 WAIKIKI         OP   SKI  FBG SV OB            6  8   840         1900   2300
16 9 SURFSTAR 1702   ST   RNBT FBG TR OB            7  2  1330         2950   3400
17 1 SS-163          ST   RNBT FBG SV IO  120-140   6  6         1750   2100
18 1 OPEN BOW 1882   ST   RNBT FBG DV IO            7 10  1350         3050   3550
18 1 OPEN BOW 1884   ST   RNBT FBG DV IO  120-200   7 10  1700         2300   2900
18 1 OPEN BOW 1884   ST   RNBT FBG DV IO  225-230   7 10  1700         2550   2950
18 1 RUNABOUT 1881   ST   RNBT FBG DV OB            7 10  1250         2900   3350
```

LOA FT	IN	NAME AND/ OR MODEL	TOP/ RIG	BOAT TYPE	-HULL- MTL	TP	TP	----ENGINE--- # HP	MFG	BEAM FT	IN	WGT LBS	DRAFT FT	IN	RETAIL LOW	RETAIL HIGH
		1980 BOATS														
18	1	RUNABOUT 1883	ST	RNBT	FBG	DV	IO	120-200		7	10	1600			2300	2850
18	1	RUNABOUT 1883	ST	RNBT	FBG	DV	IO	225-230		7	10	1600			2500	2900
18	4	SS184	OP	RNBT	FBG	DV	IO	120	MRCR	6	10	1300			1950	2350
18	4	SS184	OP	RNBT	FBG	DV	IO	120	OMC	6	10	1300			1950	2300
18	4	SS184	OP	RNBT	FBG	DV	IO	120-200		6	10	1300			2050	2550
18	4	SS185	OP	RNBT	FBG	DV	IO	120	MRCR	6	10	1400			2000	2350
18	4	SS185	OP	RNBT	FBG	DV	IO	120	OMC	6	10	1400			1950	2350
18	4	SS185	OP	RNBT	FBG	DV	IO	120-200		6	10	1400			2150	2600
19		COUGAR 1901	OP	SKI	FBG	DV	IO	170-200		7	6	1060			2150	2700
19		COUGAR 1901	OP	SKI	FBG	DV	IO	225-260		7	6	1060			2350	2900
19		COUGAR 1901	OP	SKI	FBG	DV	JT	460	PANT	7	6	1060			3050	3550
20	1	CRUISER 2006	ST	CR	FBG	DV	IO	140-200		7	10	2400			3350	4100
20	1	CRUISER 2006	ST	CR	FBG	DV	IO	225-260		7	10	2400			3600	4350
20	1	CRUISER 2006	HT	CR	FBG	DV	OB			7	10	2150			4850	5550
20	1	CRUISER 2006	HT	CR	FBG	DV	IO	140-200		7	10	2400			3350	4100
20	1	CRUISER 2006	HT	CR	FBG	DV	IO	225-260		7	10	2400			3600	4350
20	1	CRUISER 2008	ST	CR	FBG	DV	OB			7	10	2150			4850	5550
20	1	CUDDY 2007	ST	CUD	FBG	DV	IO	140-200		7	10	2050			3100	3850
20	1	CUDDY 2007	ST	CUD	FBG	DV	IO	225-260		7	10	2050			3400	4100
20	1	CUDDY 2007	HT	CUD	FBG	DV	IO	140-200		7	10	2050			3100	3850
20	1	CUDDY 2007	HT	CUD	FBG	DV	IO	225-260		7	10	2050			3400	4100
20	1	SANTA-CATALINA 2009	ST	CUD	FBG	DV	IO	140-200		7	10	2150			3150	3900
20	1	SANTA-CATALINA 2009	ST	CUD	FBG	DV	IO	225-260		7	10	2150			3450	4200
20	1	SANTA-CATALINA 2009	HT	CUD	FBG	DV	IO	140-200		7	10	2150			3150	3900
20	1	SANTA-CATALINA 2009	HT	CUD	FBG	DV	IO	225-260		7	10	2150			3450	4200
21	2	CUDDY 2200	ST	CUD	FBG	DV	IO	140-200		7	10	2100			3350	4150
21	2	CUDDY 2200	ST	CUD	FBG	DV	IO	225-260		7	10	2100			3600	4400
21	2	CUDDY 2200	HT	CUD	FBG	DV	IO	140-200		7	10	2100			3350	4150
21	2	CUDDY 2200	HT	CUD	FBG	DV	IO	225-260		7	10	2100			3600	4400
21	2	SPORTSMAN 2101	ST	SF	FBG	DV	IO	140-240		7	10	2550			4150	5200
21	2	SPORTSMAN 2101	ST	SF	FBG	DV	IO	260		7	10	2550			4500	5400
21	2	SPORTSMAN 2101	ST	SF	FBG	DV	IO	130D	VLVO	7	10	2550			6000	6900
21	2	SPORTSMAN 2102	ST	SF	FBG	DV	OB			7	10	2450			5700	6550
22		BAJA 2300	FB	CBNCR	FBG	DV	IO	185-240		8		3350			5050	6150
22		BAJA 2300	FB	CBNCR	FBG	DV	IO	260		8		3350			5300	6350
22		EXPRESS 2350	ST	EXP	FBG	DV	IO	185-240		8		2800			4050	5050
22		EXPRESS 2350	ST	EXP	FBG	DV	IO	260		8		2800			4350	5250
22		EXPRESS 2350	HT	EXP	FBG	DV	IO	185-240		8		2800			4050	5050
22		EXPRESS 2350	HT	EXP	FBG	DV	IO	260		8		2800			4350	5250
22		SUN-BLAZER 2375	HT	OVNTR	FBG	DV	IO	185-230		8		2800			4100	5050
22		SUN-BLAZER 2375	HT	OVNTR	FBG	DV	IO	260		8		2800			4350	5250
24	2	BERMUDA 2550	ST	CR	FBG	DV	IO	185-265		8		3340			5150	6400
24	2	BERMUDA 2550	ST	CR	FBG	DV	IO	T120-T200		8		3340			5800	7150
24	2	BERMUDA 2550	ST	CR	FBG	DV	IO	T225-T230		8		3340			6400	7350
24	2	BERMUDA 2575		CR	FBG	DV	IO	185-260		8		3340			5150	6400
24	2	BERMUDA 2575		CR	FBG	DV	IO	T120-T200		8		3340			5800	7150
24	2	BERMUDA 2575		CR	FBG	DV	IO	T225-T230		8		3340			6400	7350
24	2	EXPRESS 2502	ST	EXP	FBG	DV	IO	185-265		8		3400			5200	6500
24	2	EXPRESS 2502	ST	EXP	FBG	DV	IO	T120-T200		8		3400			5850	7250
24	2	EXPRESS 2502	ST	EXP	FBG	DV	IO	T225-T230		8		3400			6450	7400
24	2	EXPRESS 2502	HT	EXP	FBG	DV	IO	185-265		8		3400			5200	6450
24	2	EXPRESS 2502	HT	EXP	FBG	DV	IO	T120-T200		8		3400			5850	7250
24	2	EXPRESS 2502	HT	EXP	FBG	DV	IO	T225-T230		8		3400			6450	7400
24	2	SEDAN 2501	FB	SDN	FBG	DV	IO	185-265		8		3500			5350	6650
24	2	SEDAN 2501	FB	SDN	FBG	DV	IO	T120-T200		8		3500			6000	7350
24	2	SEDAN 2501	FB	SDN	FBG	DV	IO	T225-T230		8		3500			6550	7500
24	8	CUDDY 2500	ST	CUD	FBG	DV	IO	185-240		8		2600			4700	5750
		IO 260-265 5050 5950, IO 130D VLVO 5400 6200, IO T120-T198													5350	6500
		IO T200-T230 5900 6900														
24	8	CUDDY 2500	HT	CUD	FBG	DV	IO	185-240		8		2600			4700	5750
		IO 260-265 5050 5950, IO 130D VLVO 5400 6200, IO T120-T198													5350	6500
		IO T200-T230 5900 6900														
25	7	BAJA 2650	FB	CBNCR	FBG	DV	IO	240	CHRY	10		4950			9550	10800
		VD 250-255 9900 11400, IO 260-265 9600 11100, VD 325-330													10200	11600
		IO 130D VLVO 11700 13300, IO T140-T240 9950 11800														
25	7	SEA-BLAZER 2700	ST	EXP	FBG	DV	IO	240	CHRY	10		4400			7300	8350
		VD 250-255 8250 9700, IO 260-265 7400 8650, VD 325-330													8950	10200
		IO 130D VLVO 7650 8800, IO T140-T200 7750 9650, IO T225-T240													8650	9900
26	2	BAJA 2600	FB	CBNCR	FBG	DV	IO	185-265		8		3910			8250	9800
26	2	BAJA 2600	FB	CBNCR	FBG	DV	IO	130D	VLVO	8		3910			10200	11600
26	2	BAJA 2600	FB	CBNCR	FBG	DV	IO	T120-T230		8		3910			8700	10500
26	2	RIVIERA 2620	ST	CR	FBG	DV	IO	185-240		8		3550			6200	7550
		IO 260-265 6750 7900, IO T120-T185 6900 8550, IO T195-T240													7600	9300
		IO T260 8050 9550														
28	1	CRUISER 2850	FB	CR	FBG	DV	IO	260-265		10		5900	1	6	10500	12100
		VD 325-330 12600 14300, IB 130D VLVO 12900 14700, IO T170-T200													11200	13200
		IO T225 VLVO 12000 13600, VD T225 13500 15500, IO T228 MRCR													11900	13500
		VD T228 MRCR 13500 15400, IO T230-T240 11900 13700, VD T250-T255													13800	15900
		IB T130D VLVO 16000 18200														
28	1	EXECUTIVE 2875	FB	SF	FBG	DV	IO	260-265		10		5460	1	6	11700	13400
		VD 325-330 12400 14000, IB 130D VLVO 12400 14100, IO T170-T200													12500	14800
		IO T225 VLVO 13400 15200, VD T225 13300 15300, IO T228 MRCR													13300	15100
		VD T228 MRCR 13300 15100, IO T230-T240 13300 15300, VD T250-T255													13600	15700
		IB T130D VLVO 15600 17800														
31	7	CRUISER 3200	FB	SF	FBG	DV	IB	T225-T255		11	9	8800			19100	21600
31	7	CRUISER 3200	FB	SF	FBG	DV	IB	T140D	VLVO	11	9	8800			22900	25400
33	5	CRUISER 3300	FB	MY	FBG	DV	IB	T225-T330		13	4	14070	2	8	30900	36500
33	5	CRUISER 3300	FB	MY	FBG	DV	IB	T200D	VLVO	13	4	14070	2	8	40400	44800
33	5	CRUISER 3450	FB	TCMY	FBG	DV	IB	T250-T330		13	4	15370	2	8	30400	35100
33	5	CRUISER 3450	FB	TCMY	FBG	DV	IB	T200D	VLVO	13	4	15370	2	8	38900	43200
		1979 BOATS														
16		COLUMBIA	ST	RNBT	FBG	DV	OB			6	6	940			2100	2500
16	5	WAIKIKI	OP	SKI	FBG	SV	OB			6	8	840			1900	2250
16	9	SURFSTAR 1702	ST	RNBT	FBG	TR	OB			7	2	1330			2900	3350
18	1	OPEN BOW 1882	ST	RNBT	FBG	DV	OB			7	10	1350			3050	3500
18	1	OPEN BOW 1884	ST	RNBT	FBG	DV	IO	120-200		7	10	1700			2300	2900
18	1	OPEN BOW 1884	ST	RNBT	FBG	DV	IO	225-230		7	10	1700			2550	2950
18	1	RUNABOUT 1881	ST	RNBT	FBG	DV	OB			7	10	1250			2850	3300
18	1	RUNABOUT 1883	ST	RNBT	FBG	DV	IO	120-200		7	10	1600			2250	2850
18	1	RUNABOUT 1883	ST	RNBT	FBG	DV	IO	225-230		7	10	1600			2500	2900
18	4	SS184	OP	RNBT	FBG	DV	IO	120	MRCR	6	10	1300			1950	2300
18	4	SS184	OP	RNBT	FBG	DV	IO	120	OMC	6	10	1300			1950	2300
18	4	SS184	OP	RNBT	FBG	DV	IO	120-170		6	10	1300			2050	2450
18	4	SS185	OP	RNBT	FBG	DV	IO	120	MRCR	6	10	1400			2000	2350
18	4	SS185	OP	RNBT	FBG	DV	IO	120	OMC	6	10	1400			1950	2350
18	4	SS185	OP	RNBT	FBG	DV	IO	120-170		6	10	1400			2150	2500
19		COUGAR 1901	OP	SKI	FBG	DV	IO	170-198		7	6	1060			2150	2550
19		COUGAR 1901	OP	SKI	FBG	DV	IO	200-260		7	6	1060			2300	2850
19		COUGAR 1901	OP	SKI	FBG	DV	JT	460	PANT	7	6	1060			2900	3400
19	2	OFFSHORE 1900	ST	CUD	FBG	DV	IO	140-200		7	10	2170			2750	3450
19	2	OFFSHORE 1900	ST	CUD	FBG	DV	IO	225-260		7	10	2170			3000	3650
20	1	CRUISER 2006	ST	CR	FBG	DV	IO	140-200		7	10	2400			3300	4100
20	1	CRUISER 2006	ST	CR	FBG	DV	IO	225-260		7	10	2400			3600	4350
20	1	CRUISER 2006	HT	CR	FBG	DV	OB			7	10	2150			4800	5500
20	1	CRUISER 2006	HT	CR	FBG	DV	IO	140-200		7	10	2400			3300	4100
20	1	CRUISER 2006	HT	CR	FBG	DV	IO	225-260		7	10	2400			3600	4350
20	1	CRUISER 2008	ST	CR	FBG	DV	OB			7	10	2150			4800	5500
20	1	CUDDY 2007	ST	CUD	FBG	DV	IO	140-200		7	10	2050			3100	3850
20	1	CUDDY 2007	ST	CUD	FBG	DV	IO	225-260		7	10	2050			3350	4100
20	1	CUDDY 2007	HT	CUD	FBG	DV	IO	140-200		7	10	2050			3100	3850
20	1	CUDDY 2007	HT	CUD	FBG	DV	IO	225-260		7	10	2050			3350	4100
20	1	OPEN BOW 2002	ST	RNBT	FBG	DV	OB			7	10	1600			3900	4500
20	1	OPEN BOW 2004	ST	RNBT	FBG	DV	IO	140-200		7	10	1950			2950	3650
20	1	OPEN BOW 2004	ST	RNBT	FBG	DV	IO	225-260		7	10	1950			3200	3850
20	1	OPEN BOW 2004	HT	RNBT	FBG	DV	IO	140-200		7	10	1950			2950	3650
20	1	OPEN BOW 2004	HT	RNBT	FBG	DV	IO	225-260		7	10	1950			3200	3850
20	1	RUNABOUT 2001	ST	RNBT	FBG	DV	OB			7	10	1500			3700	4300
20	1	RUNABOUT 2003	ST	RNBT	FBG	DV	IO	140-200		7	10	1850			2900	3600
20	1	RUNABOUT 2003	ST	RNBT	FBG	DV	IO	225-260		7	10	1850			3150	3800
20	1	RUNABOUT 2003	HT	RNBT	FBG	DV	IO	140-200		7	10	1850			2900	3600
20	1	RUNABOUT 2003	HT	RNBT	FBG	DV	IO	225-260		7	10	1850			3150	3800
20	1	SANTA-CATALINA 2005	ST	RNBT	FBG	DV	IO	140-200		7	10	2000			2950	3650
20	1	SANTA-CATALINA 2005	ST	RNBT	FBG	DV	IO	225-260		7	10	2000			3200	3900
20	1	SANTA-CATALINA 2005	HT	RNBT	FBG	DV	IO	140-200		7	10	2000			2950	3650
20	1	SANTA-CATALINA 2005	HT	RNBT	FBG	DV	IO	225-260		7	10	2000			3200	3900
20	1	SANTA-CATALINA 2009	ST	CUD	FBG	DV	IO	140-200		7	10	2150			3150	3900
20	1	SANTA-CATALINA 2009	ST	CUD	FBG	DV	IO	225-260		7	10	2150			3450	4150
20	1	SANTA-CATALINA 2009	HT	CUD	FBG	DV	IO	140-200		7	10	2150			3150	3900
20	1	SANTA-CATALINA 2009	HT	CUD	FBG	DV	IO	225-260		7	10	2150			3450	4150
21	2	CUDDY 2200	ST	CUD	FBG	DV	IO	140-200		7	10	2100			3350	4150
21	2	CUDDY 2200	ST	CUD	FBG	DV	IO	225-260		7	10	2100			3600	4350

 CONTINUED ON NEXT PAGE

LOA FT	LOA IN	NAME AND/ OR MODEL	TOP/ RIG	BOAT TYPE	-HULL- MTL	-HULL- TP	ENGINE TP	ENGINE # HP	ENGINE MFG	BEAM FT	BEAM IN	WGT LBS	DRAFT FT	DRAFT IN	RETAIL LOW	RETAIL HIGH
		1979 BOATS														
21	2	CUDDY 2200	HT	CUD	FBG	DV	IO	140-200		7	10	2100			3350	4150
21	2	CUDDY 2200	HT	CUD	FBG	DV	IO	225-260		7	10	2100			3600	4350
21	2	SPORTSMAN 2101	ST	SF	FBG	DV	IO	140-240		7	10	2550			4150	5200
21	2	SPORTSMAN 2101	ST	SF	FBG	DV	IO	255-260		7	10	2550			4650	5350
21	2	SPORTSMAN 2101	ST	SF	FBG	DV	IO	130D	VLVO	7	10	2550			6000	6900
21	2	SPORTSMAN 2102	ST	SF	FBG	DV	OB			7	10	2450			5650	6450
21	8	2000 W/T		CUD	FBG	DV	IO	200	VLVO	7	10	2150	3		3700	4300
22		BAJA 2300	FB	CBNCR	FBG	DV	IO	185-260		8		3350			5050	6300
22		EXPRESS 2350	ST	EXP	FBG	DV	IO	185-240		8		2800			4050	5050
22		EXPRESS 2350	ST	EXP	FBG	DV	IO	255-260		8		2800			4500	5200
22		EXPRESS 2350	HT	EXP	FBG	DV	IO	185-240		8		2800			4050	5050
22		EXPRESS 2350	HT	EXP	FBG	DV	IO	255-260		8		2800			4500	5200
24	2	BERMUDA 2550	ST	CR	FBG	DV	IO	185-265		8		3340			5150	6350
		IO 130D VLVO 6300 7200, IO T120-T200 5750 7150, IO T225-T230													6350	7300
24	2	EXPRESS 2502	ST	EXP	FBG	DV	IO	185-265		8		3400			5200	6450
24	2	EXPRESS 2502	ST	EXP	FBG	DV	IO	T120-T200		8		3400			5850	7250
24	2	EXPRESS 2502	ST	EXP	FBG	DV	IO	T225-T230		8		3400			6450	7400
24	2	EXPRESS 2502	HT	EXP	FBG	DV	IO	185-265		8		3400			5200	6450
24	2	EXPRESS 2502	HT	EXP	FBG	DV	IO	T120-T200		8		3400			5850	7250
24	2	EXPRESS 2502	HT	EXP	FBG	DV	IO	T225-T230		8		3400			6450	7400
24	2	SEDAN 2501	FB	SDN	FBG	DV	IO	185-265		8		3500			5350	6650
24	2	SEDAN 2501	FB	SDN	FBG	DV	IO	T120-T200		8		3500			6000	7350
24	2	SEDAN 2501	FB	SDN	FBG	DV	IO	T225-T230		8		3500			6550	7500
24	8	CUDDY 2500	ST	CUD	FBG	DV	IO	185-240		8		2600			4700	5750
		IO 255-265 5150 5950, IO 130D VLVO 5400 6200, IO T120-T198													5350	6500
		IO T200-T230 5850 6900														
24	8	CUDDY 2500	HT	CUD	FBG	DV	IO	185-240		8		2600			4700	5750
		IO 255-265 5150 5950, IO 130D VLVO 5400 6200, IO T120-T198													5350	6500
		IO T200-T230 5850 6900														
25	7	BAJA 2650	FB	CBNCR	FBG	DV	IO	240	CHRY	10		4950			9550	10800
		VD 250 9500 11000, IO 255 VLVO 9750 11100, VD 255 MRCR													9550	10800
		IO 260-265 9600 10900, VD 325-330 9800 11200, IO 130D VLVO													11700	13300
		IO T140-T240 9950 11800														
25	7	SEA-BLAZER 2700	ST	EXP	FBG	DV	IO	240	CHRY	10		4400			7300	8350
		VD 250 7900 9300, IO 255 VLVO 7500 8600, VD 255 MRCR													7950	9150
		IO 260-265 7400 8550, VD 325-330 8500 9750, IO 130D VLVO													7650	8800
		IO T140-T200 7750 9650, IO T225-T240 8600 9900														
26	2	BAJA 2600	FB	CBNCR	FBG	DV	IO	185-265		8		3910			8200	9800
26	2	BAJA 2600	FB	CBNCR	FBG	DV	IO	130D	VLVO	8		3910			10200	11500
26	2	BAJA 2600	FB	CBNCR	FBG	DV	IO	T120-T230		8		3910			8700	10500
28	1	CRUISER 2800	FB	CBNCR	FBG	DV	IO	255-265		10		5900			13200	15000
		VD 325-330 14000 15900, IO 130D VLVO 14500 16400, IO T170-T200													13400	15400
		IO T225 VLVO 13700 15500, VD T225 14100 16200, IO T228 MRCR													13500	15400
		VD T228 MRCR 14100 16100, IO T230-T240 13500 15400, VD T250-T255													14100	16300
		IO T130D VLVO 18700 20800														
28	1	EXECUTIVE 2850	FB	CR	FBG	DV	IO	255-265		10		5900	1	6	10500	12000
		VD 320-330 12100 13700, IB 130D VLVO 12400 14100, IO T170-T200													11200	13200
		IO T225 VLVO 11900 13600, VD T225 12900 14900, IO T228 MRCR													11800	13500
		VD T228 MRCR 13000 14700, IO T230-T240 11800 13600, VD T250-T255													13200	15200
		IB T130D VLVO 15400 17500														
28	1	EXECUTIVE 2875	FB	SF	FBG	DV	IO	190-265		10		5460	1	6	11000	13300
		VD 325-330 11800 13500, IB 130D VLVO 11900 13500, IB T130 VLVO													11500	13000
		IO T170-T200 12400 14800, IO T225 VLVO 13300 15200, VD T225													12700	14700
		IO T228 MRCR 13200 15000, VD T228 MRCR 12800 14500, IO T230-T240													13200	15200
		VD T250 13000 15000														
28	1	SPORT FISHERMAN 2825	FB	SDNSF	FBG	DV	IO	255-265		10		5460			11700	13300
		VD 325-330 11800 13400, IO 130D VLVO 12000 13600, IO T170-T200													12400	14700
		IO T225 VLVO 13300 15100, VD T225 12600 14500, IO T228 MRCR													13200	15000
		VD T228 MRCR 12700 14400, IO T230-T240 13200 15200, VD T250-T255													12900	14900
		IO T130D VLVO 15100 17100														
33	5	EXECUTIVE 3300	FB	MY	FBG	DV	IB	T225-T330		13	4	14070	2	8	29600	35000
33	5	EXECUTIVE 3300	FB	MY	FBG	DV	IB	T200D	VLVO	13	4	14070	2	8	38800	43100
33	5	EXECUTIVE 3450	FB	TCMY	FBG	DV	IB	T250-T330		13	4	15370	2	8	29200	33600
33	5	EXECUTIVE 3450	FB	TCMY	FBG	DV	IB	T200D	VLVO	13	4	15370	2	8	37400	41600
		1978 BOATS														
16		COLUMBIA	OP	RNBT	FBG	SV	OB			6	6	940		9	2050	2450
16	3	SS163	OP	RNBT	FBG	DV	IO	140	VLVO	6	6	1300		10	1700	2050
16	5	WAIKIKI	OP	SKI	FBG	SV	OB			6	8	840		8	1850	2200
18	1	OPEN BOW	ST	RNBT	FBG	DV	OB			7	10	1350		10	3000	3500
18	1	OPEN BOW	ST	RNBT	FBG	DV	IO	120-225		7	10	1700		11	2350	2900
18	1	RUNABOUT	ST	RNBT	FBG	DV	OB			7	10	1250		10	2800	3300
18	1	RUNABOUT	ST	RNBT	FBG	DV	IO	120-225		7	10	1600		11	2300	2850
18	4	SS184	OP	RNBT	FBG	DV	IO	120		6	10	1400		10	2000	2400
		IO 140 MRCR 2000 2400, IO 140 OMC 2000 2350, IO 140-170													2150	2550
18	4	SS185	OP	RNBT	FBG	DV	IO	120		6	10	1600		10	2050	2450
		IO 140 MRCR 2100 2450, IO 140 OMC 2050 2450, IO 140-170													2250	2600
19	2	OFFSHORE	ST	OFF	FBG	DV	IO	140-195		6	10	2170	1		2550	3150
19	2	OFFSHORE	ST	OFF	FBG	DV	IO	198-255		7	10	2170	1		2850	3400
19	2	OFFSHORE	HT	OFF	FBG	DV	IO	140-200		6	10	2170	1		2550	3200
19	2	OFFSHORE	HT	OFF	FBG	DV	IO	225-240		6	10	2170	1		2650	3250
19	2	OFFSHORE	HT	OFF	FBG	DV	IO	255	VLVO	6	10	2170	1		2950	3400
20	1	CRUISER 2006	ST	CR	FBG	DV	IO	120-200		7	10	2400	1		3350	4150
20	1	CRUISER 2006	ST	CR	FBG	DV	IO	225-240		7	10	2400	1		3450	4200
20	1	CRUISER 2006	ST	CR	FBG	DV	IO	255	VLVO	7	10	2400	1		3750	4350
20	1	OPEN BOW	ST	RNBT	FBG	DV	OB			7	10	1600		10	3850	4450
20	1	OPEN BOW	ST	RNBT	FBG	DV	IO	120-200		7	10	1950	1		2950	3650
20	1	OPEN BOW	ST	RNBT	FBG	DV	IO	225-240		7	10	1950	1		3050	3750
20	1	OPEN BOW	ST	RNBT	FBG	DV	IO	255	VLVO	7	10	1950	1		3350	3900
20	1	RUNABOUT	ST	RNBT	FBG	DV	OB			7	10	1500		10	3650	4250
20	1	RUNABOUT	ST	RNBT	FBG	DV	IO	120-200		7	10	1850	1		2900	3600
20	1	RUNABOUT	ST	RNBT	FBG	DV	IO	225-240		7	10	1850	1		3000	3700
20	1	RUNABOUT	ST	RNBT	FBG	DV	IO	255	VLVO	7	10	1850	1		3300	3800
20	1	SANTA-CATALINA 2005	ST	RNBT	FBG	DV	IO	120-200		7	10	2000	1		3000	3700
20	1	SANTA-CATALINA 2005	ST	RNBT	FBG	DV	IO	225-240		7	10	2000	1		3050	3750
20	1	SANTA-CATALINA 2005	ST	RNBT	FBG	DV	IO	255	VLVO	7	10	2000	1		3350	3900
21	2	CUDDY	HT	CUD	FBG	DV	IO	140-200		7	10	2100	1	1	3350	4150
21	2	CUDDY	HT	CUD	FBG	DV	IO	225-240		7	10	2100	1	1	3450	4250
21	2	CUDDY	HT	CUD	FBG	DV	IO	255	VLVO	7	10	2100	1	1	3750	4400
21	2	CUDDY 2102	ST	CUD	FBG	DV	IO	140-200		7	10	2100	1	1	3350	4150
21	2	CUDDY 2102	ST	CUD	FBG	DV	IO	225-240		7	10	2100	1	1	3450	4250
21	2	CUDDY 2102	ST	CUD	FBG	DV	IO	255	VLVO	7	10	2100	1	1	3750	4400
21	2	SPORTSMAN 2101	ST	SF	FBG	DV	IO	140-240		7	10	2550	1	1	4200	5250
21	2	SPORTSMAN 2101	ST	SF	FBG	DV	IO	255	VLVO	7	10	2550	1	1	4700	5350
22		BAJA 2202	HT	CBNCR	FBG	DV	IO	185-255		8		3350	1	2	5100	6350
22		BAJA 2202	FB	CBNCR	FBG	DV	IO	185-255		8		3350	1	2	5100	6350
22		WESTPORTER	ST	CR	FBG	DV	IO	185-240		8		3000	1	2	4250	5250
22		WESTPORTER	ST	CR	FBG	DV	IO	255	VLVO	8		3000	1	2	4700	5400
22		WESTPORTER	HT	CR	FBG	DV	IO	185-240		8		3000	1	2	4250	5250
22		WESTPORTER	HT	CR	FBG	DV	IO	255	VLVO	8		3000	1	2	4700	5400
24	2	BERMUDA	ST	CR	FBG	DV	IO	185-265		8		2780	1	4	4650	5800
24	2	BERMUDA	ST	CR	FBG	DV	IO	T120-T225		8		2780	1	4	5300	6600
24	2	BERMUDA-FLYER	OP	CR	FBG	DV	IO	185-265		8		3040	1	4	4900	6100
24	2	BERMUDA-FLYER	OP	CR	FBG	DV	IO	T120-T225		8		3040	1	4	5500	6900
24	2	EXPRESS	ST	EXP	FBG	DV	IO	185-265		8		3400	1	4	5250	6500
24	2	EXPRESS	ST	EXP	FBG	DV	IO	T120-T170		8		3400	1	4	5850	7100
24	2	EXPRESS	ST	EXP	FBG	DV	IO	T185-T225		10		4950	1	6	7950	9350
24	2	SEDAN 2501	FB	SDN	FBG	DV	IO	185-265		8		3500	1	4	5400	6700
24	2	SEDAN 2501	FB	SDN	FBG	DV	IO	T120-T225		8		3500	1	4	6050	7400
25	7	BAJA 2650	FB	CBNCR	FBG	DV	IO	240		10		4950	1	6	9600	10900
		VD 250 OMC 9300 10600, IO 255 VLVO 9800 11100, VD 255 MRCR													9200	10400
		IO 265 CHRY 9700 11000, VD 325-330 9450 10700, IO T140-T185													10000	11600
		VD T190 OMC 9850 11200, IO T195-T200 10100 11800, IO T225 OMC													10200	11500
		IO T225 VLVO 10500 11900, VD T225 9600 11200, IO T228 MRCR													10200	11600
		VD T228 MRCR 9650 11000, IO T240 10300 11700, VD T250-T255													9600	11300
25	7	SEA-BLAZER	ST	EXP	FBG	DV	IO	120-240		10		4400	1	6	6750	8400
26	2	BAJA 2601	FB	CBNCR	FBG	DV	IO	185-265		8		3910	1	4	8300	9850
26	2	BAJA 2601	FB	CBNCR	FBG	DV	IO	T120-T225		8		3910	1	4	8850	10400
28	1	CRUISER	FB	CBNCR	FBG	DV	IO	255-265		10		5900	1	6	13300	15100
		VD 325-330 13400 15200, IO T170-T185 13500 15300, VD T190 OMC													13700	15500
		IO T195-T200 13500 15500, IO T225 OMC 13600 15400, IO T225 VLVO													13800	15600
		VD T225 13500 15600, IO T228 MRCR 13600 15500, VD T228 MRCR													13600	15400
		IO T240 13700 15500, VD T250-T255 13600 15600														
28	1	EXECUTIVE 2850	FB	CR	FBG	DV	IO	T225	OMC	10		5900	1	6	11900	13500
28	1	EXECUTIVE 2875	FB	SF	FBG	DV	IO	T225	OMC	10		5460	1	6	13200	15000
28	1	SPORT FISHERMAN 2825	FB	SDNSF	FBG	DV	IO	255-265		10		5460	1	6	11800	13400
		VD 325-330 11300 12800, VD 200D CHRY 12800 14500, IO T170-T185													12500	14400
		VD T190 OMC 11800 13500, IO T195-T200 12800 14800, IO T225 OMC													13200	15000
		IO T225 VLVO 13400 15200, VD T225 12100 13900, IO T228 MRCR													13300	15100

CONTINUED ON NEXT PAGE

```
       LOA  NAME AND/              TOP/ BOAT -HULL- ----ENGINE--- BEAM  WGT DRAFT RETAIL RETAIL
       FT IN  OR MODEL             RIG TYPE MTL TP TP # HP MFG    FT IN LBS FT IN LOW   HIGH
       ------------------ 1978 BOATS --------------------------------------------------------
       28 1 SPORT FISHERMAN 2825 FB SDNSF FBG DV VD T228 MRCR 10      5460 1 6 12200 13800
       28 1 SPORT FISHERMAN 2825 FB SDNSF FBG DV IO T240      10      5460 1 6 13500 15300
       28 1 SPORT FISHERMAN 2825 FB SDNSF FBG DV VD T250-T255 10      5460 1 6 12400 14300
       29 9 EXECUTIVE 3000      FB MY    FBG DV IB T228 MRCR 11 6 10000 2 8 20000 22200
       33 5 EXECUTIVE 3300      FB MY    FBG DV IB T228 MRCR 13 4 12300 2 8 27600 30600
       33 5 EXECUTIVE 3400      FB MY    FBG DV IB T228 MRCR 13 4 12600 2 8 27700 30800
       33 5 EXECUTIVE 3450      FB TCMY  FBG DV IB T255 MRCR 13 4 13600 2 8 27000 30000
       ------------------ 1977 BOATS --------------------------------------------------------
       16   COLUMBIA     ST RNBT FBG SV OB          6 6  910    2000 2350
       16 3 MONTEREY     ST RNBT FBG SV OB          6 6 1100    2400 2800
       16 9 BOWRIDER     ST RNBT FBG TR IO 120      7 2         1800 2150
       16 9 BOWRIDER     ST RNBT FBG TR IO 130-200  7 2         1950 2350
       16 9 SURFRIDER    ST RNBT FBG TR OB          7 2 1400    2950 3450
       16 9 SURFRIDER    ST RNBT FBG TR IO 120      7 2         1850 2250
       16 9 SURFRIDER    ST RNBT FBG TR IO 130-200  7 2         2000 2450
       17   WAIKIKI      OP SKI  FBG DV OB          6 8  860    1950 2300
       18 4 ISLANDER     ST RNBT FBG DV OB          6 10 1150   2650 3050
       18 4 MONTEREY     ST RNBT FBG DV IO 120      6 10        2100 2500
       18 4 MONTEREY     ST RNBT FBG DV IO 130-225  6 10        2250 2750

       19 2 BIMINI       ST CBNCR FBG TR IO 120-200 7 9 2337    3050 3800
       19 2 BIMINI       ST CBNCR FBG TR IO 225-240 7 9 2337    3350 3950
       19 2 ISLANDER     ST RNBT FBG DV OB          7 10 1400   3150 3650
       19 2 MONTEREY     ST RNBT FBG DV IO 120-188  7 10        2550 3150
            IO 190 OMC 2600   3000, IO 190 VLVO 2750  3200, VD 190 OMC  2850 3300
            IO 200 VLVO 2750  3200, IO 225 VLVO 2800  3300, VD 225 OMC  2850 3350
            IO 233 MRCR 2700  3150, VD 233 MRCR 2750  3150, IO 235-240  2700 3350
            VD 250-330 2900   3600

       19 2 OFFSHORE     ST CUD FBG DV IO 120-188   7 10 2170   2850 3450
            IO 190 OMC 2850   3300, IO 190 VLVO 3000  3500, VD 190 OMC  2950 3400
            IO 200 VLVO 3050  3500, IO 225 VLVO 3100  3600, VD 225 OMC  2950 3450
            IO 233 MRCR 2950  3450, VD 233 MRCR 2800  3250, IO 235-240  2950 3650
            VD 250-330 3000   3700

       19 2 OFFSHORE     HT CUD FBG DV IO 120-188   7 10 2170   2850 3450
            IO 190 OMC 2850   3300, IO 190 VLVO 3000  3500, VD 190 OMC  2950 3400
            IO 200 VLVO 3050  3500, IO 225 VLVO 3100  3600, VD 225 OMC  2950 3450
            IO 233 MRCR 2950  3450, VD 233 MRCR 2800  3250, IO 235-240  2950 3650
            VD 250-330 3000   3700

       19 2 SANTA-CATALINA ST RNBT FBG DV IO 165-188 7 10 1800  2550 3000
            IO 190 OMC 2550   3000, IO 190 VLVO 2750  3150, VD 190 OMC  2850 3300
            IO 200 VLVO 2750  3200, VD 225 OMC 2850   3300, IO 233 MRCR 2700 3100
            VD 233 MRCR 2700  3150, IO 235-240 2650   3300, IO 250      2900 3350
            VD 255 VLVO 2900  3400, VD 255 MRCR 2750  3150, IO 325-330  3050 3550

       19 2 SURFRIDER    ST RNBT FBG TR IO 120-200  7 9 1879    2550 3200
       19 2 SURFRIDER    ST RNBT FBG TR IO 225-240  7 9 1879    2800 3350
       21 2 CUDDY        HT CUD FBG DV IO 120-188   7 10 2250   3600 4200
            IO 190 OMC 3550   4100, IO 190 VLVO 3700  4300, VD 190 OMC  3600 4200
            IO 200 VLVO 3750  4350, IO 225 VLVO 3800  4400, VD 225 OMC  3650 4250
            IO 233 MRCR 3650  4250, VD 233 MRCR 3500  4050, IO 235-240  3650 4500
            IO 250 OMC 3650   4250, IO 255 MRCR 3750  4350, IO 255 VLVO 3950 4550
            VD 255 MRCR 3500  4050, VD 325-330 3850   4500

       21 2 CUDDY 2102   ST CUD FBG DV IO 120-188   7 10 2250   3500 4250
            IO 190 OMC 3550   4100, IO 190 VLVO 3700  4300, VD 190 OMC  3600 4200
            IO 200 VLVO 3750  4350, IO 225 VLVO 3800  4400, VD 225 OMC  3650 4250
            IO 233 MRCR 3650  4250, VD 233 MRCR 3500  4050, IO 235-240  3650 4500
            IO 250 OMC 3650   4250, IO 255 MRCR 3750  4350, IO 255 VLVO 3950 4550
            VD 255 MRCR 3500  4050, VD 325-330 3850   4500

       22 2 BAJA 2202    HT CBNCR FBG DV IO 165-188 8   3350    5200 6000
            IO 190 OMC 5200   5950, IO 190 VLVO 5400  6200, VD 190 OMC  4750 5450
            IO 200 VLVO 5400  6200, IO 225 VLVO 5450  6300, VD 225 OMC  4800 5500
            IO 233 MRCR 5300  6100, VD 233 MRCR 4650  5350, IO 235-240  5300 6350
            IO 250 OMC 4800   5550, IO 255 MRCR 5400  5900, IO 255 VLVO 5600 6450
            VD 255-330 4650   5750, IO T120-T170 5900  7150

       22 2 BAJA 2202    FB CBNCR FBG DV IO 165-188 8   3350    5200 6000
            IO 190 OMC 5200   5950, IO 190 VLVO 5400  6200, VD 190 OMC  4750 5450
            IO 200 VLVO 5400  6200, IO 225 VLVO 5450  6300, VD 225 OMC  4800 5500
            IO 233 MRCR 5300  6100, VD 233 MRCR 4650  5350, IO 235-240  5300 6350
            IO 250 OMC 4800   5550, IO 255 MRCR 5400  5900, IO 255 VLVO 5600 6450
            VD 255-330 4650   5750, IO T120-T170 5900  7150

       22 2 CHINOOK      HT CBNCR FBG DV IO 165-188 8   3260    5100 5900
            IO 190 OMC 5100   5850, IO 190 VLVO 5300  6050, VD 190 OMC  4700 5400
            IO 200 VLVO 5300  6100, IO 225 VLVO 5400  6200, VD 225 OMC  4700 5400
            IO 233 MRCR 5250  6000, VD 233 MRCR 4550  5250, IO 235-240  5200 6250
            IO 250 OMC 4750   5450, IO 255 MRCR 5300  5800, IO 255 VLVO 5550 6350
            VD 255-330 4600   5650, IO T120-T170 5800  7050

       22 2 CHINOOK      FB CBNCR FBG DV IO 140-188 8   3260    5100 5900
            IO 190 OMC 5100   5850, IO 190 VLVO 5300  6050, VD 190 OMC  4700 5400
            IO 200 VLVO 5300  6100, IO 225 VLVO 5400  6200, VD 225 OMC  4700 5400
            IO 233 MRCR 5250  6000, VD 233 MRCR 4550  5250, IO 235-240  5200 6250
            IO 250 OMC 4750   5450, IO 255 MRCR 5300  5800, IO 255 VLVO 5550 6350
            VD 255-330 4600   5650, IO T120-T140 5800  7050

       22 2 WESTPORTER   HT CR FBG DV IO 140-188    8   3250    4600 5450
            IO 190 OMC 4600   5300, IO 190 VLVO 4750  5500, VD 190 OMC  4700 5400
            IO 200 VLVO 4800  5500, IO 225 VLVO 4850  5600, VD 225 OMC  4700 5400
            IO 233-240 4700   5650, IO 250 OMC 4750  5650, IO 255       4800 5750
            VD 325 OMC 5250   6350, IO T120-T170 5250

       24 2 BAJA COMMAND BRIDGE FB CBNCR FBG DV IO 165-188 8 3700 6500 7500
            IO 190 OMC 6500   7450, IO 190 VLVO 6700  7700, VD 190 OMC  5800 6650
            IO 200 VLVO 6700  7700, IO 225 VLVO 6800  7800, VD 225 OMC  5800 6700
            IO 233 MRCR 6650  7600, VD 233 MRCR 5650  6500, IO 235-240  6600 7850
            IO 250 OMC 5850   6700, IO 255 MRCR 6750  7750, IO 255 VLVO 6950 7950
            VD 255-330 5700   6950, IO T120-T235 7200  9000, IO T240-T255 7950 9350

       24 2 BERMUDA 2400 ST CR FBG DV IO 165-188    8   2780    4700 5450
            IO 190 OMC 4700   5450, IO 190 VLVO 4900  5600, VD 190 OMC  4800 5500
            IO 200 VLVO 4900  5650, IO 225 VLVO 5000  5750, VD 225 OMC  4850 5550
            IO 233 MRCR 4850  5600, VD 233 MRCR 4700  5400, IO 235-240  4850 5800
            IO 250 OMC 4850   5600, IO 255 MRCR 4950  5700, IO 255 VLVO 5150 5900
            VD 255-330 4700   5850, IO T120-T200 5350  6700, IO T225-T255 5950 7150

       24 2 BERMUDA 2425 HT CR FBG DV IO 165-188    8   2940    4850 5600
            IO 190 OMC 4850   5600, IO 190 VLVO 5050  5800, VD 190 OMC  4950 5650
            IO 200 VLVO 5050  5900, IO 225 VLVO 5150  5900, VD 225 OMC  5000 5800
            IO 233 MRCR 5000  5750, VD 233 MRCR 4850  5550, IO 235-240  5000 6000
            IO 250 OMC 5000   5750, IO 255 MRCR 5100  5850, IO 255 VLVO 5300 6050
            VD 255-330 4850   6050, IO T120-T200 5500  6850, IO T225-T255 6100 7300

       24 2 BERMUDA 2450 HT CR FBG DV IO 165-188    8   3020    4950 5700
            IO 190 OMC 4950   5700, IO 190 VLVO 5150  5900, VD 190 OMC  5000 5750
            IO 200 VLVO 5150  6000, IO 225 VLVO 5250  6000, VD 225 OMC  5050 5800
            IO 233 MRCR 5100  5850, VD 233 MRCR 4900  5650, IO 235-240  5050 6050
            IO 250 OMC 5100   5850, IO 255 MRCR 5200  5950, IO 255 VLVO 5350 6150
            VD 255-330 4950   6100, IO T120-T200 5600  6950, IO T225-T255 6200 7400

       24 2 BERMUDA-FLYER 2475 OP CR FBG DV IO 165-188 8 2980    4900 5650
            IO 190 OMC 4900   5650, IO 190 VLVO 5100  5850, VD 190 OMC  4950 5700
            IO 200 VLVO 5100  5950, IO 225 VLVO 5200  5950, VD 225 OMC  5000 5800
            IO 233 MRCR 5050  5800, VD 233 MRCR 4850  5600, IO 235-240  5000 6000
            IO 250 OMC 5050   5800, IO 255 MRCR 5150  5900, IO 255 VLVO 5300 6100
            VD 255-330 4900   6050, IO T120-T200 5550  6900, IO T225-T255 6150 7350

       24 2 CHINOOK      FB CBNCR FBG DV IO 165-188 8   3500    6250 7200
            IO 190 OMC 6250   7200, IO 190 VLVO 6450  7450, VD 190 OMC  5600 6400
            IO 200 VLVO 6450  7450, IO 225 VLVO 6500  7550, VD 225 OMC  5600 6450
            IO 233 MRCR 6400  7350, VD 233 MRCR 5450  6250, IO 235-240  6350 7600
            IO 250 OMC 5650   6500, IO 255 MRCR 6500  7500, IO 255 VLVO 6700 7700
            VD 255-330 5500   6700, IO T120-T200 6950  8550, IO T225-T255 7600 9050

       24 2 CRUISER      HT CR FBG DV IO 165-188    8   3175    5100 5900
            IO 190 OMC 5850   5850, IO 190 VLVO 5300  6050, VD 190 OMC  5150 5950
            IO 200 VLVO 6100  6100, IO 225 VLVO 5400  6150, VD 225 OMC  5200 6000
            IO 233 MRCR 6000  6000, VD 233 MRCR 5050  5800, IO 235-240  5200 6250
            IO 250 OMC 5250   6000, IO 255 MRCR 5350  5950, IO 255 VLVO 5550 6350
            VD 255-330 5100   6300, IO T120-T200 5750  7150, IO T225-T255 6350 7600

       24 2 CUDDY        ST CUD FBG DV IO 165-188   8   2600    4600 5300
            IO 190 OMC 4600   5300, IO 190 VLVO 5450  5450, VD 190 OMC  4650 5350
            IO 200 VLVO 4750  5450, IO 225 VLVO 5550  5550, VD 225 OMC  4700 5400
            IO 233 MRCR 4700  5400, VD 233 MRCR 4550  5250, IO 235-240  4700 5650
            IO 250 OMC 4700   5400, IO 255 MRCR 5500  5500, IO 255 VLVO 5000 5700
            VD 255-330 4600   5700, IO T120-T200 5200  6500, IO T225-T255 5800 6950

       24 2 CUDDY        HT CUD FBG DV IO 165-188   8   2600    4600 5300
            IO 190 OMC 4600   5300, IO 190 VLVO 5300          VD 190 OMC  4650 5350
            IO 200 VLVO 4750  5450, IO F225 VLVO 4850         VD 225 OMC  4700 5400
```

```
LOA   NAME AND/        TOP/ BOAT   -HULL- ----ENGINE--- BEAM  WGT  DRAFT RETAIL RETAIL
FT IN  OR MODEL        RIG  TYPE   MTL TP TP # HP  MFG   FT IN LBS  FT IN  LOW   HIGH
-------------------- 1977 BOATS ------------------------------------------------------
24 2 CUDDY              HT  CUD  FBG DV IO 233 MRCR  8       2600        4700  5400
     VD  233 MRCR 4550   5250, IO 235-240   4700 5650, VD 250 OMC    4700  5400
     IO  255 MRCR 4800   5500, IO 255 VLVO  5000 5750, VD 255-330    4600  5700
     IO T120-T200 5200   6500, IO T225-T255 5800 6950

25 7 BAJA COMMAND BRIDGE  FB  CBNCR FBG DV IO 188-240 10   4410       9000 10500
     VD  250 OMC  8250   9450, IO 255 MRCR  9200 10400, IO 255 VLVO  9350 10600
     VD  255-330 8100    9650, IO T140-T188 9500 11100, IO T190 OMC  9500 10800
     IO T190 VLVO 9800  11200, VD T190 OMC  8850 10100, IO T200 VLVO 9850 11200
     IO T225 VLVO 9950  11300, VD T225 OMC  8900 10100, IO T233 MRCR 9750 11100
     VD T233 MRCR 8600   9900, IO T235-T240 9700 11400, VD T250 OMC  8950 10200
     IO T255 VLVO 10200 11600, VD T255 MRCR 8650 9900

25 7 CHINOOK            FB  CBNCR FBG DV IO 188-240 10   4200       8650 10200
     VD  250 OMC  8000   9200, IO 255 MRCR  8900 10100, IO 255 VLVO  9050 10300
     VD  255-330 7850    9350, IO T140-T188 9300 10800, IO T190 OMC  9300 10600
     IO T190 VLVO 9550  10800, VD T190 OMC  9800       , IO T200 VLVO 9600 10900
     IO T225 VLVO 9700  11000, VD T225 OMC  8600 9850, IO T233 MRCR  9500 10800
     VD T233 MRCR 8350   9600, IO T235-T240 9450 11100, VD T250 OMC  8650  9900
     IO T255 VLVO 9950  11300, VD T255 MRCR 8400 9650

25 7 OPEN 26            ST  RNBT  FBG DV IO 188-240 10   3800       6100  7400
     VD  250 OMC  6750   7750, IO 255 MRCR  6450 7400, IO 255 VLVO  6550  7550
     VD  255-330 6650    8200, IO T140-T188 6800 8200, IO T190 OMC  7100  8150
     IO T190 VLVO 7350   8400, VD T190 OMC  7650 8800, IO T200 VLVO 7400  8500
     IO T225 VLVO 7600   8750, VD T225 OMC  7900 9100, IO T233 MRCR 7450  8600
     VD T233 MRCR 7700   8850, IO T235-T240 7450 8950, VD T250 OMC  8050  9250
     IO T255 VLVO 7950   9150, VD T255 MRCR 7850 9000

26 2 BAJA COMMAND BRIDGE  FB  CBNCR FBG DV IO 165-225 8   3700       8150  9600
     IO  233 MRCR 8250   9500, VD 233 MRCR  7550 8650, IO 235-240   8250  9650
     VD  250 OMC  7650   8800, IO 255 MRCR  8350 9550, IO 255 VLVO  8450  9750
     VD  255-330 7550    8950, IO T120-T255 8650 10700

26 2 CHINOOK            FB  CBNCR FBG DV IO 165-225 8   3600       8050  9500
     IO  233 MRCR 8150   9350, VD 233 MRCR  7450 8550, IO 235-240   8150  9550
     VD  250 OMC  7550   8700, IO 255 MRCR  8200 9450, IO 255 VLVO  8350  9600
     VD  255-330 7450    8850, IO T120-T255 8550 10500

26 2 OFFSHORE COMMAND BR  FB  CR  FBG DV IO 165-225 8   3800       6450  7950
     IO  233 MRCR 6900   7900, VD 233 MRCR  6750 7750, IO 235-240   6850  8100
     VD  250 OMC  6900   7950, IO 255 MRCR  7050 8100, IO 255 VLVO  7150  8200
     VD  255-330 6850    8450, IO T120-T188 7250 9050, IO T190-T235 7850  9700
     VD T240-T255 8600  10000

28 1 CRUISER 2800       FB  CBNCR FBG DV IO 188-255 10   5500       12300 14900
     VD  325-330 12500 14200, IO T165-T188 13300 15100, IO T190 OMC  13300 15100
     IO T190 VLVO 13400 15300, VD T190 OMC 12700 14400, IO T200 VLVO 13500 15300
     IO T225 VLVO 13600 15400, VD T225 OMC 12800 14500, IO T233 MRCR 13400 15300
     VD T233 MRCR 12600 14400, IO T235-T240 13400 15500, VD T250 OMC  12800 14500
     IO T255 VLVO 13700 15600, VD T255-T330 12700 14800

28 1 SEDAN CB           FB  SDN  FBG DV IO 188-255 10   5300       10700 13100
     VD  325-330 12100 13700, IO T165-T188 12300 14200, IO T190 OMC  12500 14200
     IO T190 VLVO 12700 14400, VD T190 OMC 12500 14200, IO T200 VLVO 12700 14400
     IO T225 VLVO 12700 14500, VD T225 OMC 12600 14300, IO T233 MRCR 12600 14400
     VD T233 MRCR 12400 14100, IO T235-T240 12600 14600, VD T250 OMC  12600 14300
     IO T255 VLVO 12900 14600, VD T255-T330 12500 14600

28 1 SPORT FISHERMAN 2825  FB  SDNSF FBG DV IO 188-255 10   5240    11000 13400
     VD  325-330 10700 12100, IO T165-T188 12400 14500, IO T190 OMC  13000 14500
     IO T190 VLVO 12900 14700, VD T190 OMC 11200 12800, IO T200 VLVO 13100 14900
     IO T225 VLVO 13500       , VD T225 OMC 11600 13200, IO T233 MRCR 13400 15300
     VD T233 MRCR 11600 13200, IO T235-T240 13400 15600, VD T250 OMC  11900 13500
     IO T255 VLVO 13900 15800, VD T255-T330 11800 14500
-------------------- 1976 BOATS ------------------------------------------------------
16   COLUMBIA          ST  RNBT FBG SV OB         6  6   835      1800  2150
16 3 CUSTOM            OP  RNBT FBG    OB         6  6            2050  2450
16 3 CUSTOM            ST  RNBT FBG    IO 130 VLVO 6  6           1700  2000
16 3 MONTEREY          ST  RNBT FBG DV OB         6  6  1045      2300  2650
16 3 MONTEREY          ST  RNBT FBG DV IO 130 VLVO 6  6           1700  2000
16 9 BIMINI            HT  RNBT FBG TR IO 120     7  2            1900  2250
16 9 BIMINI            HT  RNBT FBG TR IO 130-200 7  2            2000  2450
16 9 BOWRIDER          ST  RNBT FBG TR OB         7  2  1320      2000  2450
16 9 BOWRIDER          OP  RNBT FBG TR IO 120     7  2            2800  3250
16 9 BOWRIDER          ST  RNBT FBG TR IO 130-200 7  2            1850  2250
16 9 KINGFISHER        OP  FSH  FBG TR OB         7  2  1200      2550  3000
16 9 SURFRIDER         ST  RNBT FBG TR OB         7  2  1314      2800  3250

16 9 SURFRIDER         ST  RNBT FBG TR IO 120     7  2            1850  2250
16 9 SURFRIDER         ST  RNBT FBG TR IO 130-200 7  2            2000  2450
18 4 CUSTOM            OP  RNBT FBG DV IO 120-190 6 10            2200  2700
18 4 CUSTOM            OP  RNBT FBG DV IO 200-235 6 10            2350  2800
18 4 CUSTOM            OP  RNBT FBG DV JT 245 OMC 6 10            2500  2950
18 4 ISLANDER          OP  RNBT FBG DV OB         6 10  1085      2500  2900
18 4 MONTEREY          ST  RNBT FBG DV OB         6 10  1225      2750  3200
18 4 MONTEREY          ST  RNBT FBG DV IO 120-190 6 10            2200  2700
18 4 MONTEREY          ST  RNBT FBG DV IO 200-235 6 10            2350  2800
18 4 MONTEREY          ST  RNBT FBG DV JT 245 OMC 6 10            2500  2950
19 2 BIMINI            HT  CR   FBG TR IO 120-200 7  9            2700  3400
19 2 BIMINI            HT  CR   FBG TR IO 225-240 7  9            3000  3550

19 2 BIMINI            HT  CR   FBG TR JT 245-455 7  9            2900  3550
19 2 BOWRIDER          ST  RNBT FBG TR IO 120-200 7  9  1839      2600  3250
19 2 BOWRIDER          ST  RNBT FBG TR IO 225-235 7  9            2800  3450
19 2 BOWRIDER          ST  RNBT FBG TR JT 225-290 7  9            2950  3450
19 2 CONTINENTAL       HT  CR   FBG DV IO 120-200 7 10            2750  3450
     IO 225 VLVO 3000  3500, VD 230 OMC  2700 3150, IO 233 MRCR  2900  3550
     VD 233 MRCR 2550  2950, IO 235 OMC  2850 3300, IO 240 VLVO  3050  3550
     JT 245 OMC  2900  3400, JT 255-260  2550 3150, JT 290-455   2900  3400

19 2 CUSTOM            OP  RNBT FBG DV IO 120-200 7  9            2600  3250
     IO 225 VLVO 2850  3350, VD 230 OMC  2750 3200, IO 233 MRCR  2750  3200
     VD 233 MRCR 2600  3000, IO 235-240  2700 3400, JT 245 OMC   2950  3450
     VD 255-260 2600   3100, JT 290-455  2950 3450

19 2 ISLANDER          OP  RNBT FBG DV OB         7 10  1300      2950  3450
19 2 KINGFISHER        OP  FSH  FBG DV OB         7 10  1300      2950  3400
19 2 MONTEREY          ST  RNBT FBG DV IO 120-190 7 10            2500  3100
     IO 200-225 3200   3800, VD 230 OMC  2650 3050, IO 233 MRCR  2600  3050
     VD 233 MRCR 2500  2900, IO 235-240  2600 3050, JT 245 OMC   2800  3250
     VD 255-260 2500   3100, JT 290-455  2800 3250

19 2 OFFSHORE          ST  RNBT FBG DV IO 120-200 7 10            2750  3400
     IO 225 VLVO 3000  3500, VD 230 OMC  2850 3300, IO 233 MRCR  2850  3350
     VD 233 MRCR 2700  3150, IO 235-240  2850 3300, JT 245 OMC   3100  3600
     VD 255-260 2700   3350, JT 290      3100 3600

19 2 SANTA-CATALINA    ST  RNBT FBG DV IO 165-200 7 10            2700  3350
     IO 225 VLVO 2950  3450, VD 230 OMC  2800 3250, IO 233 MRCR  2700  3300
     VD 233 MRCR 2650  3100, IO 235-240  2800 3300, JT 245 OMC   3050  3550
     VD 255-260 2700   3300, JT 290-455  3050 3600

19 2 SURFRIDER         ST  RNBT FBG TR IO 120-190 7  9            2600  3250
19 2 SURFRIDER         ST  RNBT FBG TR IO 200-235 7  9            2800  3350
19 2 SURFRIDER         ST  RNBT FBG TR JT 245-290 7  9            2950  3450
21 2 CUDDY             OP  CUD  FBG DV IO 120-200 7 10            3550  4350
     IO 225 VLVO 3800  4450, VD 230 OMC  3450 4000, IO 233 MRCR  3700  4300
     VD 233 MRCR 3300  3800, IO 235-240  3650 4500, JT 245 OMC   3700  4300
     IO 255 MRCR 3750  4400, VD 255-260  3300 4050, JT 290-455   4300  4300

21 2 KOOTENAY          HT  CR   FBG DV IO 120-200 7 10            3300  4050
     IO 200-225 3550   4200, VD 230 OMC  3500 4000, IO 233 MRCR  3450  4000
     VD 233 MRCR 3350  3900, IO 235-240  3450 4250, JT 245 OMC   3450  4000
     VD 255-260 3600   4150, JT 290-455  4100

21 2 SAN-JUAN          HT  CR   FBG DV IO 120-235 7 10            3900  4850
     IO 240 VLVO 4250  4950, JT 245 OMC  4050 4700, IO 255 MRCR  4100  4750
     JT 290-455 4050   4700

21 2 SPORTSMAN         ST  CR   FBG DV IO 120-200 7 10            3600  4450
     IO 225-240 3900   4600, JT 245 OMC  3750 4350, IO 255 MRCR  3850  4450
     JT 290-455 3750   4350

22 8 CUDDY             ST  CUD  FBG DV IO 140-225 7 10            3900  4500
     IO 230 OMC  3400  3950, VD 233 MRCR 3650 4200, VD 233 MRCR  3300  3800
     IO 235-240 3650   4000, JT 245 OMC  3600 4200, IO 255 MRCR  3750  4400
     VD 255-260 3300   4000, JT 290-455  3650 4250

22 8 SANTA-CATALINA    ST  CUD  FBG DV IO 165-225 7 10            4250  5250
     IO 230 OMC  4100  4750, IO 233 MRCR 5100 5250, VD 233 MRCR  3900  4550
     IO 235-240 4400   5350, JT 245 OMC  4400 5100, IO 255 MRCR  4500  5150
     VD 255-260 3900   4750, JT 290-455  4400 5050

22 8 SITKA             HT  CR   FBG DV IO 140-225 7 10            4450  5450
     VD 230 OMC  4550  5250, IO 233 MRCR 4600 5300, VD 233 MRCR  4400  5050
```

96th ed. - Vol. III   CONTINUED ON NEXT PAGE   241

```
  LOA  NAME AND/       TOP/ BOAT  -HULL-  ----ENGINE--- BEAM   WGT  DRAFT RETAIL RETAIL
  FT IN  OR MODEL      RIG TYPE   MTL TP TP # HP  MFG   FT IN  LBS  FT IN  LOW    HIGH
-------------------- 1976 BOATS ------------------------------------------------------
 22  8 SITKA            HT  CR    FBG DV IO 235-240  7 10                    4600   5500
      JT  245  OMC 4500 5200, IO 255  MRCR 4700  5400, VD 255-260            4450   5300
      JT 290-455   4550 5200
 22  8 SITKA            FB  CR    FBG DV IO 165-225  7 10                    4750   5750
      VD  230  OMC 4550 5250, IO 233  MRCR 4850  5600, VD 233  MRCR          4400   5050
      IO 235-240   4850 5850, IO 255  MRCR 4950  5700, VD 255-260            4450   5300
 22  8 WESTPORTER       HT  CR    FBG DV IO 140-240  7 10                    5000   6150
      JT  245  OMC 5100 5850, IO 255  MRCR 5200  6000, JT 290-455            5050   5800
 24  2 BAJA COMMAND BRIDGE FB CBNCR FBG DV IO 175-225  8                     6500   7850
      VD  230  OMC 5450 6300, IO 233  MRCR 6650  7650, VD 233  MRCR          5300   6100
      IO 235-240   6600 7900, IO 255  MRCR 6750  7750, VD 255-260            5350   6350
      IO  280  MRCR 6900 7950, VD 350  MRCR 5550  6400, IO T120-T235         7250   9050
      IO T240  VLVO 8000 9200
 24  2 BERMUDA 2400      ST  CR    FBG DV IO 165-225  8                      5100   6200
      VD  230  OMC 4900 5650, IO 233  MRCR 5300  6050, VD 233  MRCR          4750   5500
      IO 235-240   5250 6300, IO 255  MRCR 5350  6150, VD 255-260            4800   5700
      IO  280  MRCR 5500 6350, VD 350  MRCR 5050  5850, IO T120-T200         5800   7200
      IO T225-T240 6400 7500
 24  2 BERMUDA 2425      HT  CR    FBG DV IO 165-225  8                      5150   6250
      VD  230  OMC 5000 5750, IO 233  MRCR 5300  6100, VD 233  MRCR          4850   5600
      IO 235-240   5300 6350, IO 255  MRCR 5400  6200, VD 255-260            4900   5800
      IO  280  MRCR 5550 6400, VD 350  MRCR 5150  5900, IO T120-T200         5950   7300
      IO T225-T240 6500 7600
 24  2 BERMUDA 2450          CR    FBG DV IO 165-225  8                      5100   6200
      VD  230  OMC 4900 5650, IO 233  MRCR 5300  6050, VD 233  MRCR          4750   5500
      IO 235-240   5250 6300, IO 255  MRCR 5350  6150, VD 255-260            4800   5700
      IO  280  MRCR 5500 6350, VD 350  MRCR 5050  5850, IO T120-T200         5800   7200
      IO T225-T240 6400 7500
 24  2 BERMUDA-FLYER 2475 OP  CR   FBG DV IO 165-225  8                      5100   6200
      IB  230  OMC 4900 5650, VD 230  OMC  4900  5650, IO 233  MRCR          5300   6050
      IB  233  MRCR 4750 5500, IO 233  MRCR 4750  5500, IO 235-240           5250   6300
      IB  255  MRCR 5350 6150, IB 255  MRCR 4800  5500, VD 255  MRCR         4800   5500
      IB  260  OMC 4950 5700, IO 260  OMC  4950  5700, IO 280  MRCR          5500   6350
      IB  350  MRCR 5050 5800, VD 350  MRCR 5050  5850, IO T120-T200         5800   7200
      IO T225-T240 6400 7500
 24  2 CHINOOK COMMAND BR FB  CR   FBG DV IO 175-225  8                      5100   6200
      IB  230  OMC 4900 5650, VD 230  OMC  4900  5650, IO 233  MRCR          5300   6050
      IB  233  MRCR 4750 5500, IO 233  MRCR 4750  5500, IO 235-240           5250   6300
      IB  255  MRCR 5350 6150, IB 255  MRCR 4800  5500, VD 255  MRCR         4800   5500
      IB  260  OMC 4950 5700, IO 260  OMC  4950  5700, IO 280  MRCR          5500   6350
      IB  350  MRCR 5050 5800, VD 350  MRCR 5050  5850, IO T120-T200         5800   7200
      IO T225-T240 6400 7500
 24  2 CONTINENTAL       HT  CR    FBG DV IO 165-225  8                      4850   5900
      VD  230  OMC 4650 5350, IO 233  MRCR 5000  5750, VD 233  MRCR          4550   5150
      IO 235-240   4950 5950, IO 255  MRCR 5100  5900, VD 255-260            4550   5400
      IO  280  MRCR 5300 6050, VD 350  MRCR 4750  5500, IO T120-T200         5550   6900
      IO T225-T240 6100 7150
 24  2 CRUISER           HT  CR    FBG DV IO 165-225  8                      5350   6500
      VD  230  OMC 5150 5900, IO 233  MRCR 5500  6350, VD 233  MRCR          4950   5700
      IO 235-240   5500 6600, IO 255  MRCR 5600  6450, VD 255-260            5000   5950
      IO  280  MRCR 5750 6600, VD 350  MRCR 5300  6050, IO T120-T235         6100   7650
      IO T240  VLVO 6750 7750
 24  2 CUDDY             ST  CUD   FBG DV IO 165-225  8                      4650   5700
      IB  230  OMC 4500 5200, VD 230  OMC  4500  5200, IO 235-240            4850   5550
      IB  233  MRCR 4400 5050, VD 233  MRCR 4400  5050, VD 255  MRCR         4800   5800
      IB  255  MRCR 4950 5650, IB 255  MRCR 4400  5050, IB 360  MRCR         5050   5850
      IB  260  OMC 4550 5250, VD 260-350  4550  5350, IB 360  MRCR           4700   5400
      IO T120-T200 5350 6700, IO T225-T240  5950  6950
 24  2 EXECUTIVE         OP  CUD   FBG DV IO 165-225  8                      4650   5700
      VD  230  OMC 4500 5200, IO 233  MRCR 4850  5550, VD 233  MRCR          4400   5050
      IO 235-240   4800 5800, IO 255  MRCR 4950  5650, VD 255-260            4400   5250
      IO  280  MRCR 5100 5850, VD 350  MRCR 4650  5350, IO T120-T200         5350   6700
      IO T225-T240 5950 6950
 24  2 KINGFISHER        OP  CUD   FBG DV OB         8                       8600   9900
 26  2 CHINOOK           FB CBNCR  FBG DV IO 175-225  8                      9000  10600
      VD  230  OMC 7900 9050, IO 233  MRCR 9200 10500, VD 233  MRCR          7800   8950
      IO 235-240   9200 10600, IO 255  MRCR 9300 10500, VD 255-260          7800   9100
      IO  280  MRCR 9400 10700, VD 350  MRCR 7950  9150, IO T120-T240        9550  11500
 26  2 CRUISER           HT  CR    FBG DV IO 175-255  8                      6550   8150
      IO  280  MRCR 7300 8400, IO T120-T165 7300  8900, IO T170-T225        7950   9800
      VD T230  OMC 7800 9000, IO T233  MRCR 8400  9650, VD T233  MRCR        7600   8750
      IO T235-T240 8350 9950, VD T255-T350  7650  9200
 26  2 OFFSHORE COMMAND BR FB CR   FBG DV IO 175-225  8                      6550   8000
      VD  230  OMC 6450 7400, IO 233  MRCR 6950  7950, VD 233  MRCR          6350   7300
      IO 235-240   6900 8150, IO 255  MRCR 7100  8150, VD 255-260           6450   7550
      IO  280  MRCR 7300 8400, VD 350  MRCR 7000  8050, IO T120-T165         7300   8900
      IO T170-T240 7950 9950
 28  1 CRUISER           FB  CR    FBG DV IO 175-280 10                     11800  14400
      IO T140-T225 12900 15900, VD T230  OMC 12900 14600, IO T233  MRCR    13900  15800
      VD T233  MRCR 12700 14500, IO T235-T240 13900 16100, IO T255-T260     13000  15000
 28  1 HARDTOP           HT  CR    FBG DV IO 175-280 10                     10300  12700
      IO T140-T200 11300 13900, VD T225  VLVO 12500 14200, VD T230  OMC     11600  13200
      IO T233  MRCR 12500 14200, VD T233  MRCR 11500 13100, IO T235-T240    12500  14500
      VD T255-T260 11700 13600
 28  1 HARDTOP COMMAND BR HT  CR   FBG DV IO 175-280 10                      9550  11900
      IO T140-T200 10600 13000, VD T225  VLVO 11800 13400, VD T230  OMC     11000  13300
      IO T233  MRCR 11800 13400, VD T233  MRCR 10900 12400, IO T235-T240    11800  13600
      VD T255-T260 11100 12800
 28  1 SPORT FISHERMAN   FB  CR    FBG DV IO 175-280 10                      9600  11900
      IO T140-T225 10800 13400, VD T230  OMC 11000 12500, IO T233  MRCR    11800  13400
      VD T233  MRCR 10900 12400, IO T235-T240 11800 13700, IO T255-T260     11200  12900
-------------------- 1975 BOATS ------------------------------------------------------
 16    COLUMBIA          OP  RNBT  FBG SV OB  120    6  6  835    11        1800   2150
 16    COLUMBIA          OP  RNBT  FBG SV IO  120  MRCR 6 6 1345  11        1700   2050
 16    COLUMBIA          OP  RNBT  FBG SV IO 130-140    6  6 1345  11       1850   2200
 16  3 CUSTOM            OP  RNBT  FBG DV IO  120    6  6 1045  11           2050   2400
 16  3 CUSTOM            OP  RNBT  FBG DV IO 130-140    6  6 1555  11        1750   2100
 16  3 CUSTOM            OP  RNBT  FBG DV OB  120    6  6 1045             2450   2850
 16  3 MONTEREY          OP  RNBT  FBG DV IO  120    6  6 1555  11           1950   2300
 16  3 MONTEREY          OP  RNBT  FBG DV IO 130-140    6  6 1555  11        2100   2500
 16  9 BIMINI            HT  RNBT  FBG TR IO 120-170    7  2 2193  1         2400   3000
 16  9 BOWRIDER          OP  RNBT  FBG TR OB 120-170    7  2 1320  1         2800   3250
 16  9 BOWRIDER          OP  RNBT  FBG TR IO 120-170    7  2 1830  1         2250   2750
 16  9 KINGFISHER        OP  RNBT  FBG TR OB 120-170    7  2 1200  1         2550   3000
 16  9 KINGFISHER        OP  RNBT  FBG TR IO 120-170    7  2 1710  1         2150   2700
 16  9 SURFRIDER         OP  RNBT  FBG TR OB 120-170    7  2 1314  1         2750   3200
 16  9 SURFRIDER         OP  RNBT  FBG TR IO 120-170    7  2 1824  1         2250   2750
 18  4 CUSTOM            OP  RNBT  FBG DV IO 120-190    6 10 1225  1         2500   2900
 18  4 CUSTOM            OP  RNBT  FBG DV IO 233-235    6 10 1735  1         2300   2900
 18  4 CUSTOM            OP  RNBT  FBG DV JT 245-330    6 10 2125  1         2700   3100
 18  4 CUSTOM            OP  RNBT  FBG DV OB  120    6 10 1225  1            2500   2900
 18  4 ISLANDER          OP  RNBT  FBG DV OB  120    6 10 1085  1            2500   2900
 18  4 MONTEREY          OP  RNBT  FBG DV IO 120-190    6 10 1225  1         2450   3000
 18  4 MONTEREY          OP  RNBT  FBG DV IO 233-235    6 10 1735  1         2250   3200
 18  4 MONTEREY          OP  RNBT  FBG DV JT 245-330    6 10 2125  1         2800   3250
 19  2 BIMINI            HT  CR    FBG TR IO 120-200    7  9 2847  1         3450   4250
      IO  225  VLVO 3700 4350, VD 225-230  3200  3900, IO 233  MRCR         3900   4500
      VD  233  MRCR 3200 3750, IO 235  OMC  3850  4500, JT 245  OMC         3600   4150
      VD 255-260   3250 3950, JT 290-330  3600  4150
 19  2 BOWRIDER          OP  CR    FBG TR IO 120-200    7  9 2349  1         3000   3700
      IO  225  VLVO 3250 3800, VD 225-230  3000  3650, IO 233  MRCR         3400   3950
      VD  233  MRCR 2950 3350, IO 235  OMC  3350  3900, JT 245  OMC         3350   3900
      VD 255-260   3000 3700, JT 290-330  3350  3900
 19  2 CONTINENTAL       HT  CR    FBG DV IO 120-200    7 10 2315  1         3100   3850
      IO  225  VLVO 3350 3900, VD 225-230  2900  3550, IO 233  MRCR         3500   4050
      VD  233  MRCR 2900 3350, IO 235  OMC  3500  4050, JT 245  OMC         3250   3800
      VD 255-260   2900 3550, JT 290-330  3250  3800
 19  2 CUSTOM            OP  RNBT  FBG DV IO 120-200    7 10 2175  1         2750   3450
      IO  225  VLVO 3050 3550, VD 225-230  2700  3050, IO 233  MRCR         3100   3600
      VD  233  MRCR 2750 3200, IO 235  OMC  3050  3550, JT 245  OMC         3050   3550
```

```
 LOA  NAME AND/              TOP/ BOAT  -HULL- ----ENGINE--- BEAM   WGT  DRAFT RETAIL RETAIL
 FT IN OR MODEL              RIG TYPE   MTL TP TP # HP  MFG  FT IN  LBS  FT IN  LOW   HIGH
------------------ 1975 BOATS ------------------------------------------------------------
 19  2 CUSTOM               OP  RNBT  FBG DV VD 255-260     7 10  2465  1      2750  3400
 19  2 CUSTOM               OP  RNBT  FBG DV JT 290-330     7 10  2465  1      3100  3600
 19  2 ISLANDER             OP  RNBT  FBG DV OB            7 10  1300  1      2900  3400
 19  2 KINGFISHER           OP  RNBT  FBG TR IO 120-200    7  9  2281  1      2950  3650
       IO  225  VLVO  3200  3750, VD 225-230    2950  3600, IO  233  MRCR     3350  3900
       VD  233  MRCR  2950  3450, IO  235  OMC  3300  3850, JT  245  OMC      3300  3850
       VD 255-260    2950  3650, JT 290-330     3300  3850

 19  2 KINGFISHER V         OP  RNBT  FBG DV OB            7 10  1300  1      2950  3450
 19  2 MONTEREY             OP  RNBT  FBG DV IO 120-200    7 10  2175  1      3050  3750
       IO  225  VLVO  3300  3850, VD 225-230    2950  3600, IO  233  MRCR     3350  3900
       VD  233  MRCR  2950  3450, IO  235  OMC  3350  3850, JT  245  OMC      3350  3900
       VD 255-260    2950  3650, JT 290-330     3350  3900

 19  2 SANTA-CATALINA       OP  RNBT  FBG DV IO 165-200    7 10  2355  1      3050  3750
       IO  225  VLVO  3300  3800, VD 225-230    2950  3600, IO  233  MRCR     3350  3900
       VD  233  MRCR  2950  3450, IO  235  OMC  3300  3850, JT  245  OMC      3300  3850
       VD 255-260    2950  3650, JT 290-330     3300  3850

 19  2 SURFRIDER            OP  RNBT  FBG TR IO 120-200    7  9  2389  1      3000  3750
       IO  225  VLVO  3300  3800, VD 225-230    3000  3650, IO  233  MRCR     3400  3950
       VD  233  MRCR  3000  3500, IO  235  OMC  3400  3950, JT  245  OMC      3400  3900
       VD 255-260    3050  3700, JT 290-330     3400  3900

 21  2 CUDDY                OP  CUD   FBG DV IO 120-200    7 10  2475  1 1    3900  4800
       IO  225  VLVO  4200  4850, VD 225-230    3550  4300, IO  233  MRCR     4300  5000
       VD  233  MRCR  3550  4150, IO  235  OMC  4250  4950, JT  245  OMC      3950  4600
       VD 255-260    3600  4400, JT 290-330     3950  4600

 21  2 KOOTENAY             HT  CR    FBG DV IO 120-200    7 10  2485  1 1    3900  4800
       IO  225  VLVO  4200  4900, VD 225-230    3550  4350, IO  233  MRCR     4300  5000
       VD  233  MRCR  3550  4150, IO  235  OMC  4250  4950, JT  245  OMC      3950  4600
       VD 255-260    3600  4350, JT 290-330     3950  4600

 21  2 SANTA-CATALINA       OP  RNBT  FBG DV IO 165-200    7 10  2635  1 1    3850  4700
       IO  225  VLVO  4100  4800, VD 225-230    3650  4450, IO  233  MRCR     4100  4800
       VD  233  MRCR  3650  4250, IO  235  OMC  4100  4750, JT  245  OMC      4050  4700
       VD 255-260    3700  4500, JT 290-330     4050  4700

 21  2 SPORTSMAN            HT  CR    FBG DV IO 120-225    7 10  2710  1 1    4100  5100
 21  2 SPORTSMAN            HT  CR    FBG DV IO 233-235    7 10  3000  1 1    4550  5200
 21  2 SPORTSMAN            HT  CR    FBG DV JT 245-330    7 10  3000  1 1    4150  4800
 22  8 CUDDY                OP  CUD   FBG DV IO 140-200    7 10  2820  1 2    4600  5500
       IO  225  VLVO  4850  5600, VD 225-230    4050  4900, IO  233  MRCR     4900  5600
       VD  233  MRCR  4050  4750, IO  235  OMC  4850  5600, JT  245  OMC      4500  5150
       VD 255-260    4100  4950, JT 290-330     4500  5150

 22  8 SAN-JUAN             HT  CR    FBG DV IO 140-235    7 10  3490  1 2    5250  6400
 22  8 SAN-JUAN             HT  CR    FBG DV JT 245-330    7 10  3670  1 2    5650  5800
 22  8 SITKA                HT  CR    FBG DV IO 140-200    7 10  3570  1 2    5350  6350
       IO  225  VLVO  5600  6450, VD 225-230    4750  5650, IO  233  MRCR     5650  6500
       VD  233  MRCR  4750  5450, IO  235  OMC  5650  6500, JT  245  OMC      5150  5900
       VD 255-260    4800  5700, JT 290-330     5150  5900

 22  8 SITKA                FB  CR    FBG DV IO 165-200    7 10  3690  1 2    5450  6500
       IO  225  VLVO  5750  6600, VD 225-230    4850  5750, IO  233  MRCR     5800  6650
       VD  233  MRCR  4850  5600, IO  235  OMC  5750  6650, VD 255-260        4900  5800

 22  8 WESTPORTER           HT  CR    FBG DV IO 140-235    7 10  3540  1 2    5300  6450
 22  8 WESTPORTER           HT  CR    FBG DV JT 245-330    7 10  3720  1 2    5100  5900
 24  2 BAJA COMMAND BRIDGE  FB  CBNCR FBG SV IO 175-200    8    4600  1 3     8050  9600
       IO  225  VLVO  8400  9700, VD 225-230    6150  7250, IO  233  MRCR     8250  9500
       VD  233  MRCR  6150  7100, IO  235  OMC  8250  9450, VD 255-350        6200  7350
       IO T120-T170  10600

 24  2 CONTINENTAL          HT  CR    FBG DV IO 165-200    8    3555  1 3     5800  6900
       IO  225  VLVO  6100  7000, VD 225-230    5200  6150, IO  233  MRCR     6150  7100
       VD  233  MRCR  5200  5950, IO  235  OMC  6150  7050, IO 255-350        5200  6300
       IO T120-T170  6700  8150

 24  2 CRUISER              HT  CR    FBG DV IO 165-200    8    3890  1 3     6200  7350
       IO  225  VLVO  6500  7450, VD 225-230    5500  6500, IO  233  MRCR     6550  7550
       VD  233  MRCR  5550  6350, IO  235  OMC  6550  7500, IO 255-350        5550  6700
       IO T120-T170  7100  8600

 24  2 CUDDY                OP  CUD   FBG DV IO 165-200    8    3215  1 3     5450  6500
       IO  225  VLVO  5750  6600, VD 225-230    4850  5750, IO  233  MRCR     5800  6650
       VD  233  MRCR  4850  5600, IO  235  OMC  5750  6600, IO 255-350        4900  5900
       IO T120-T170  6300  7700

 24  2 EXECUTIVE            OP  CUD   FBG DV IO 165-200    8    3300  1 3     5500  6600
       IO  225  VLVO  5800  6700, VD 225-230    4750  5650, IO  233  MRCR     5700  6550
       VD  233  MRCR  4800  5500, IO  235  OMC  5650  6500, IO 255-350        4800  5800
       IO T120-T170  6200  7600

 24  2 WESTPORTER           HT  CR    FBG DV IO 165-200    8    3790  1 3     6050  7200
       IO  225  VLVO  6350  7300, VD 225-230    5300  6300, IO  233  MRCR     6300  7250
       VD  233  MRCR  5350  6350, IO  235  OMC  6300  7250, IO 255-350        5350  6450
       IO T120-T170  6850  8300

 26  2 CRUISER              HT  CR    FBG SV IO 175-200    8    4550  1 3     7600  9000
       IO  225  VLVO  8000  9200, VD 225-230    6750  7900, IO  233  MRCR     7950  9150
       VD  233  MRCR  6800  7800, IO  235  OMC  7950  9150, IO 255-350        6900  8450
       IO T120-T170  8350 10300

 26  2 OFFSHORE COMMANDER B FB  CR    FBG SV IO 175-200    8    4700  1 3     7800  9300
       IO  225  VLVO  8250  9500, VD 225-230    6950  8100, IO  233  MRCR     8200  9400
       VD  233  MRCR  7000  8000, IO  235  OMC  8200  9400, IO 255-350        7100  8700
       IO T120-T170  8550 10600

 28  1 CRUISER              HT  CR    FBG DV IO 188-200    10   6200  1 3    12300 14200
       IO  225  VLVO 12800 14250, VD 225-230   10900 12500, IO  233  MRCR    12100 14500
       VD  233  MRCR 10900 12400, IO  235  OMC 12700 14500, IO 255-350       11100 13300
       IO T120-T200 12900 16000, VD T225  VLVO 14400 16400, IO T225-T230     13100 14100
       IO T233  MRCR 14300 16300, VD T233  MRCR 12300 13900, IO T235  OMC    14300 16300
       VD T255-T260 12500 14400

 28  1 CRUISER              FB  CR    FBG DV IO 188-200    10   6500  1 3    11300 13000
       IO  225  VLVO 11600 13200, VD 225-230    9950 11400, IO  233  MRCR    11600 13200
       VD  233  MRCR 10000 11400, IO  235  OMC 11600 13200, IO 255-350       10100 12200
       IO T120-T200 11900 14800, VD T225  VLVO 13400 15200, IO T225-T230     13100 13100
       IO T233  MRCR 13300 15100, VD T233  MRCR 11400 13000, IO T235  OMC    13300 15100
       VD T255-T260 11600 13400

 28  1 HARDTOP              HT  CR    FBG DV IO 188-200    10   6200  1 3     9750 11200
       IO  225  VLVO 10000 11400, VD 225-230    8550  9950, IO  233  MRCR    10100 11400
       VD  233  MRCR  8600  9900, IO  235  OMC 10100 11400, IO 255-350        8850 10700
       IO T120-T190 10500 12900, VD T200  VLVO 11600 13100, IO T225  VLVO    13100 13500
       VD T225-T230 10100 11700, IO T235  OMC 11900 13500, IO T233  MRCR     10200 11600
       VD T235  OMC 11900 12000

 28  1 HARDTOP COMMANDER    FB  CR    FBG DV IO 188-200    10   6400  1 3    11200 12900
       IO  225  VLVO 11600 13300, VD 225-230    9900 11300, IO  233  MRCR    11600 13100
       VD  233  MRCR  9950 11300, IO  235  OMC 11600 13100, IO 255-350       10100 12100
       IO T120-T200 11800 14700, VD T225  VLVO 13300 15100, IO T225-T230     13000 13000
       IO T233  MRCR 13300 15100, VD T233  MRCR 11400 12900, IO T235  OMC    13200 15100
       VD T255-T260 11600 13400

 28  1 SPORT-FISHERMAN      FB  CR    FBG DV IO 188-200    10   6140  1 3    11000 12700
       IO  225  VLVO 11400 13000, VD 225-230    9700 11100, IO  233  MRCR    11100 12600
       VD  233  MRCR  9750 11100, IO  235  OMC 11300 12900, IO 255-350        9900 11900
       IO T120-T200 11600 14500, VD T225  VLVO 13100 14900, IO T225-T230     13100 14800
       IO T233  MRCR 13100 15100, VD T233  MRCR 11200 12700, IO T235  OMC    13100 14800
       VD T255-T260 11400 13200
-------------------- 1974 BOATS ---------------------------------------------------------
 16  1 COLUMBIA             ST  RNBT  FBG    OB            6  6   835         1800  2100
 16  1 CUSTOM               OP  RNBT  FBG    OB            6  8  1075         2300  2700
 16  1 MONTEREY             OP  RNBT  FBG    OB            6  8  1100         2350  2750
 16  1 MONTEREY             OP  RNBT  FBG    IO 120        6  8              1800  2100
 16  1 MONTEREY             OP  RNBT  FBG    IO 130-140    6  8              1950  2300
 16  9                      B/R RNBT  FBG    OB            7  2              3050  3550
 16  9                      B/R RNBT  FBG    IO 120        7  2  1500        1950  2300
 16  9                      B/R RNBT  FBG    IO 130-190    7  2  1500        2100  2500
 16  9 SURFRIDER            ST  RNBT  FBG    OB            7  2  1500        3050  3550
 16  9 SURFRIDER            ST  RNBT  FBG    IO 120        7  2  1500        1950  2450
 16  9 SURFRIDER            ST  RNBT  FBG    IO 130-140    7  2  1500        2250  2650
 17    WAIKIKI              OP  SKI   FBG    OB            6  8   760         1700  2000

 18  5 CUSTOM               OP  RNBT  FBG    OB            7  1  1265         2800  3250
 18  5 CUSTOM               OP  RNBT  FBG    IO 120-188    7  1              2300  2800
 18  5 CUSTOM               OP  RNBT  FBG    IO 225  OMC   7  1              2350  2700
 18  5 CUSTOM               OP  RNBT  FBG    IO 225  VLVO  7  1              2500  2900
 18  5 MONTEREY             OP  RNBT  FBG    OB            7  1  1290         2850  3300
 18  5 MONTEREY             OP  RNBT  FBG    IO 120-200    7  1              2600  3100
 18  5 MONTEREY             OP  RNBT  FBG    IO 225  OMC   7  1              2600  3000
 18  5 MONTEREY             OP  RNBT  FBG    IO 225  VLVO  7  1              2800  3250
```

FIBERFORM   -CONTINUED   See inside cover to adjust price for area

```
LOA   NAME AND/     TOP/ BOAT -HULL- ----ENGINE--- BEAM  WGT DRAFT RETAIL RETAIL
FT IN  OR MODEL     RIG  TYPE MTL TP TP # HP  MFG  FT IN  LBS FT IN  LOW    HIGH
------------------------- 1974 BOATS -----------------------------------------
18  6                  B/R  FBG  OB              7 10 1510  3200  3700
18  6                  B/R  FBG  IO 120-190      7 10       2650  3250
18  6                  B/R  FBG  IO 200-225      7 10       2850  3350
18  6 BIMINI      ST   CR   FBG  IO 120-190      7 10       2800  3450
18  6 BIMINI      ST   CR   FBG  IO 200-225      7 10       3000  3600
18  6 SURFRIDER   ST   RNBT FBG  OB              7 10 1510  3200  3700
18  6 SURFRIDER   ST   RNBT FBG  IO 120-190      7 10       2700  3350
18  6 SURFRIDER   ST   RNBT FBG  IO 200-225      7 10       2900  3450
19  2 CONTINENTAL HT   CR   FBG  IO 120-200      7 10       2950  3650
19  2 CONTINENTAL HT   CR   FBG  IO 225          7 10       3000  3750
19  2 CONTINENTAL HT   CR   FBG  JT 245-330      7 10       2700  3150

19  2 CUSTOM      OP   RNBT FBG  IO 120-225      7 10       2800  3450
19  2 CUSTOM      OP   RNBT FBG  JT 245-330      7 10       2450  2950
19  2 MALIBU      OP   SKI  FBG  IO 165-190      7          2350  2900
19  2 MALIBU      OP   SKI  FBG  IO 200-225      7          2500  3000
19  2 MALIBU      OP   SKI  FBG  JT 245-330      7          2350  2700
19  2 MONTEREY    ST   RNBT FBG  IO 120-200      7 10       2800  3500
19  2 MONTEREY    ST   RNBT FBG  IO 225          7 10       2900  3600
19  2 MONTEREY    ST   RNBT FBG  JT 245-330      7 10       2750  3200
19  2 SANTA-CATALINA OP RNBT FBG IO 165-225      7 10       3150  3850
19  2 SANTA-CATALINA OP RNBT FBG JT 245-330      7 10       3100  3600
21  2                  CUD  FBG  IO 120-200      7 10       3800  4650
21  2                  CUD  FBG  IO 225          7 10       3850  4750

21  2                  CUD  FBG  JT 245-330      7 10       3400  3950
21  2 CONTINENTAL HT   CR   FBG  IO 120-200      7 10       3650  4450
21  2 CONTINENTAL HT   CR   FBG  IO 225          7 10       3700  4550
21  2 CONTINENTAL HT   CR   FBG  JT 245-330      7 10       3250  3800
21  2 KOOTENAY    HT   CR   FBG  IO 120-225      7 10       3800  4750
21  2 KOOTENAY    HT   CR   FBG  JT 245-330      7 10       3400  3950
21  2 SANTA-CATALINA        FBG  IO 165-225      7 10       3700  4600
21  2 SANTA-CATALINA        FBG  JT 245-330      7 10       3450  4000
21  2 SPORTSMAN   HT   CR   FBG  IO 120-225      7 10       4250  5200
21  2 SPORTSMAN   HT   CR   FBG  JT 245-330      7 10       3750  4350
22  8                  CUD  FBG  IO 140-200      7 10 1910  4000  4900
22  8                  CUD  FBG  IO 225          7 10 1910  4100  5000

22  8                  CUD  FBG  JT 245-330      7 10 1910  3550  4150
22  8 SAN-JUAN    HT   CR   FBG  IO 140-225      7 10       5050  6100
22  8 SAN-JUAN    HT   CR   FBG  JT 245-330      7 10       4400  5050
22  8 SITKA       FB   CR   FBG  IO 140-225      7 10       5050  6150
22  8 SITKA       FB   CR   FBG  JT 245-330      7 10       4450  5100
22  8 WESTPORTER  HT   CR   FBG  IO 140-225      7 10       5150  6250
22  8 WESTPORTER  HT   CR   FBG  JT 245-330      7 10  10   4500  5150
24    CONTINENTAL HT   CR   FBG  IO 165-225      8          5400  6550
24    CONTINENTAL HT   CR   FBG  JT 245-330      8          4700  5400
24    CONTINENTAL      CR   FBG  IO 165-225      8          6100  7450
24  2                  CR   FBG  JT 245-330      8          5450  6650
24  2                  CR   FBG  IO T120-T190    8          4750  5500

24  2                  CR   FBG  IO T120-T190    8          6200  7550
24  2                  CUD  FBG  IO 165-225      8  2900    5300  6400
24  2                  CUD  FBG  JT 245-330      8  2900    4650  5350
24  2                  CUD  FBG  IO T120-T190    8  2900    6000  7350
24  2 BAJA       FB CBNCR FBG  IO 170-225        8  3700    7300  8550
24  2 BAJA       FB CBNCR FBG  JT 245-330        8  3700    5400  6200
24  2 BAJA       FB CBNCR FBG  IO T120-T190      8  3700    7900  9550
24  2 WESTPORTER HT   CR   FBG  IO 165-225       8          5450  6650
24  2 WESTPORTER HT   CR   FBG  JT 245-330       8          4750  5500
24  2 WESTPORTER HT   CR   FBG  IO T120-T170     8          6200  7550
26  2                  CR   FBG  IO 170-225      8          7050  8850
      JT 245-300 6150  7300, IO T120-T165 7800  9500, IO T170-T225 8500 10500
26  2 OFFSHORE   FB   OFF  FBG  IO 170-225       8          7350  8850
26  2 OFFSHORE   FB   OFF  FBG  JT 245-330       8          6350  7550
26  2 OFFSHORE   FB   OFF  FBG  IO T120-T190     8          8050  9950
28  1              HT       FBG  IO 170-225      8         11300 13400
      JT 245-330 9100 10800, IO T120-T190 12100 15000, IO T200-T225 13500 15700
      IB T106D VLVO 11800 13400
28  1              FB       FBG  IO 170-225      9         11300 13400
      JT 245-330 9100 10800, IO T120-T188 12100 15000, IO T200-T225 13500 15700
      IO T106D VLVO 14400 16400
28  1              CR       FBG  IO 188-225      9         10900 12900
      JT 245-330 9300 11100, IO T120-T190 11600 14200, IO T200-T225 12800 14900
      IO T106D VLVO 13200 15000
28  1              FB CR    FBG  IO 188-225      9         10900 12900
      JT 245-330 9300 11100, IO T120-T190 11600 14200, IO T200-T225 12800 14900
      IO T106D VLVO 13200 15000
------------------------- 1973 BOATS -----------------------------------------
16    COLUMBIA    ST   RNBT FBG  OB              6 6   835  1800  2100
16    COLUMBIA    ST   RNBT FBG  IO 130   VLVO   6 8        1700  2050
16    COLUMBIA    ST   RNBT FBG                  6 8        1850  2200
16  1 MONTEREY    OP   RNBT FBG  OB              6 8  1100  1700  2050
16  1 MONTEREY    OP   RNBT FBG  IO 100-120      6 8        1850  2200
16  1 MONTEREY    OP   RNBT FBG  IO 130-140      6 8        2300  2700
16  1 VOYAGER     ST   RNBT FBG  OB              6 8  1075  1700  2050
16  1 VOYAGER     ST   RNBT FBG  IO 100-120      6 8        1850  2200
16  1 VOYAGER     ST   RNBT FBG  IO 130-140      6 8        2300  2700
16  6                  B/R  FBG  OB              7 3  1300  2700  3150
16  6                  B/R  FBG  IO 100-120      7 3        1900  2300
16  6                  B/R  FBG  IO 130-140      7 3        2050  2450

16  6 SURFRIDER   ST   RNBT FBG  OB              7 3  1200  2550  2950
16  6 SURFRIDER   ST   RNBT FBG  IO 100-120      7 3        2050  2450
16  6 SURFRIDER   ST   RNBT FBG  IO 130-140      7 3        2250  2600
17    WAIKIKI     OP   SKI  FBG  OB              6 8   760  1700  2000
18  5 MONTEREY    OP   RNBT FBG  OB              7 1  1290  2350  2800
18  5 MONTEREY    OP   RNBT FBG  IO 100-165      7 1        2450  3000
18  5 MONTEREY    OP   RNBT FBG  IO 170-246      7 1        2600  3050
18  5 VOYAGER     ST   CR   FBG  OB              7 1  1265  2750  3200
18  5 VOYAGER     ST   CR   FBG  IO 100-165      7 1        2450  3100
18  5 VOYAGER     ST   CR   FBG  IO 170-246      7 1        2700  3150
18  6 BEACHCOMBER OP   CR   FBG  OB              7 10 1510  3150  3650
18  6 BEACHCOMBER OP   CR   FBG  IO 100-225      7 10       2850  3550
18  6 BEACHCOMBER ST   CR   FBG  IO 246    FIBF  7 10       3100  3600
18  6 BIMINI      ST   CR   FBG  IO 100-225      7 10       2850  3550
18  6 BIMINI      ST   CR   FBG  IO 246    FIBF  7 10       3100  3600
18  6 SURFRIDER   ST   RNBT FBG  OB              7 10 1510  3150  3700
18  6 SURFRIDER   ST   RNBT FBG  IO 100-225      7 10       2750  3450
18  6 SURFRIDER   ST   RNBT FBG  IO 246    FIBF  7 10       3000  3750
19  2 CONTINENTAL HT   CR   FBG  IO 100-225      7 10       3000  3750
      JT 245 OMC 2600 3000, IO 246 FIBF 3250 3750, JT 330 BERK 2600 3000
19  2 MALIBU      OP   SKI  FBG  IO 165-225      7          2400  3000
      JT 245 OMC 2250 2650, IO 246 FIBF 2600 3000, JT 330 BERK 2250 2650
19  2 MONTEREY    ST   RNBT FBG  IO 100-225      7 10       2900  3600
      JT 245 OMC 2650 3100, IO 246 FIBF 3100 3600, JT 330 BERK 2650 3100
19  2 SANTA-CATALINA OP RNBT FBG IO 100-225      7 10       2900  3600
      JT 245 OMC 2650 3100, IO 246 FIBF 3100 3600, JT 330 BERK 2650 3100
19  2 VOYAGER     ST   CR   FBG  IO 100-225      7 10       3000  3750
      JT 245 OMC 2600 3000, IO 246 FIBF 3250 3750, JT 330 BERK 2600 3000
21  2 CONTINENTAL HT   CR   FBG  IO 100-188      7 10       3700  4550
      IO 225 4100 4800, JT 245 OMC 3150 3650, IO 246 FIBF 3950 4600
      JT 330 BERK 3150 3650
21  2 KOOTENAY    HT   CR   FBG  IO 100-225      7 10       3850  4700
      JT 245 OMC 3250 3750, IO 246 FIBF 4100 4750, JT 330 BERK 3250 3800
21  2 SANTA-CATALINA       FBG  IO 100-225       7 10       3750  4600
      JT 245 OMC 3300 3850, IO 246 FIBF 4000 4650, JT 330 BERK 3300 3850
21  2 SPORTSMAN   HT   CR   FBG  IO 100-225      7 10       4350  5250
      JT 245 OMC 3600 4150, IO 246 FIBF 4550 5250, JT 330 BERK 3550 4150
21  2 VOYAGER     ST   CUD  FBG  IO 100-225      7 10       3850  4750
      JT 245 OMC 3250 3800, IO 246 FIBF 4100 4800, JT 330 BERK 3250 3800
22  8 SAN-JUAN    HT   CR   FBG  IO 140-225      7 10       5150  6200
      JT 245 OMC 4150 4850, IO 246 FIBF 5350 6150, JT 330 BERK 4150 4850
22  8 SITKA       FB   CR   FBG  IO 140-225      7 10       5200  6200
      JT 245 OMC 4200 4900, IO 246 FIBF 5450 6250, JT 330 BERK 4200 4900
22  8 WESTPORTER  HT   CR   FBG  IO 120-225      7 10       5200  6350
      JT 245 OMC 4300 5000, IO 246 FIBF 5500 6300, JT 330 BERK 4250 4950
24    CONTINENTAL HT   CR   FBG  IO 165-225      8          5600  6600
```

          CONTINUED ON NEXT PAGE

```
   LOA  NAME AND/        TOP/ BOAT -HULL- ----ENGINE--- BEAM  WGT  DRAFT RETAIL RETAIL
   FT IN OR MODEL        RIG  TYPE MTL TP TP # HP  MFG  FT IN LBS  FT IN  LOW   HIGH
-------------------- 1973 BOATS ------------------------------------------------
24    CONTINENTAL        HT   CR   FBG  JT  245  OMC   8                 4550  5200
   IO 246-255   5800     6700, JT  330  BERK 4550  5200, IO T120-T170    6300  7700

24  2                         CR   FBG  IO  165-225    8                 5650  6700
   JT  245  OMC   4600   5300, IO 246-255   5900  6800, JT  330  BERK    4650  5300
   IO T120-T170  6400    7800

24  2 CATALINA          ST    CR   FBG  IO  165-225    8                 5650  6700
   JT  245  OMC   4600   5300, IO 246-255   5900  6800, JT  330  BERK    4650  5300
   IO T120-T170  6400    7800

24  2 SAN-JUAN          HT    CR   FBG  IO  165-225    8                 5650  6700
   JT  245  OMC   4600   5300, IO 246-255   5900  6800, JT  330  BERK    4650  5300
   IO T120-T170  6400    7800

26  2                         CR   FBG  IO  188-246    8                 7300  8900
   IO T120-T165  8050    9800, IO T170-T246  8900  10700, IOT100D-T106D 10800 12300

26  2                    FB   CR   FBG  IO  188-246    8                 7300  8900
   IO T120-T165  8050    9800, IO T170-T246  8900  10700, IOT100D-T106D 10800 12300

28  1                         CR   FBG  IO  188   MRCR 10               11500 13100
   IO  225  MRCR 11800   13500, IO  225  OMC  11800 13400, VD  225  MRCR  8850 10100
   IO  246  FIBF 12000   13700, VD 246-325        9000 10700, IO T120-T188 12200 15000
   IO T225  MRCR 13700   15500, IO T225  OMC  13600 15500, VD T225  MRCR 10100 11500
   IO T246  FIBF 14000   15900, IO T246-T255 10300 11800, IO T100D CHRY 13900 15800
   VD T100D CHRY 12000   13600, IO T106D VLVO 13800 15700, VD T106D VLVO 11900 13600

28  1                    FB   CR   FBG  IO  188   MRCR 10               11500 13100
   IO  225  MRCR 11800   13500, IO  225  OMC  11800 13400, VD  225  MRCR  8850 10100
   IO  246  FIBF 12000   13700, VD 246-325        9000 10700, IO T120-T188 12200 15000
   IO T225  MRCR 13700   15500, IO T225  OMC  13600 15500, VD T225  MRCR 10100 11500
   IO T246  FIBF 14000   15900, IO T246-T255 10300 11800, IO T100D CHRY 13900 15800
   VD T100D CHRY 12000   13600, IO T106D VLVO 13800 15700, VD T106D VLVO 11900 13600

28  1                    SDN  FBG  IO  188   MRCR 10                    12200 13900
   IO  225  MRCR 12700   14400, IO  225  OMC  12700 14400, VD  225  MRCR  9500 10800
   IO  246  FIBF 13000   14700, VD 246-325        9650 11700, IO T120-T188 13100 16300
   IO T225  MRCR 14400   16400, IO T225  OMC  14400 16300, VD T225  MRCR 10700 12200
   IO T246  FIBF 14500   16500, IO T246-T255 10700 12200, IO T100D CHRY 16200 18400
   VD T100D CHRY 14000   15900, IO T106D VLVO 16300 18500, VD T106D VLVO 14000 15900

28  1                    FB   SDN  FBG  IO  188   MRCR 10               12200 13900
   IO  225  MRCR 13000   14400, IO  225  OMC  12700 14400, VD  225  MRCR  9500 10800
   IO  246  FIBF 13000   14700, VD 246-325        9650 11700, IO T120-T188 13100 16300
   IO T225  MRCR 14400   16400, IO T225  OMC  14400 16300, VD T225  MRCR 10700 12200
   IO T246  FIBF 14500   16500, IO T246-T255 10700 12200, IO T100D CHRY 16200 18400
   VD T100D CHRY 14000   15900, IO T106D VLVO 16300 18500, VD T106D VLVO 14000 15900

28  1                    FB   SF   FBG  IO  188   MRCR 10               12700 14400
   IO  225  MRCR 13100   14900, IO  225  OMC  13100 14900, VD  225  MRCR  8550  9850
   IO  246  FIBF 13300   15100, VD 246-325        8700 10500, IO T120-T188 13500 16600
   IO T225  MRCR 15200   17300, IO T225  OMC  15200 17300, VD T225  MRCR 10000 11400
   IO T246  FIBF 15600   17700, IO T246-T255 10200 11700, IO T100D CHRY 16500 18800
   VD T100D CHRY 13400   13400, IO T106D VLVO 16500 18700, VD T106D VLVO 11600 13200
-------------------- 1972 BOATS ------------------------------------------------
16    COLUMBIA             ST   RNBT FBG  OB             6  6   835        1750  2100
16  1 CHELAN MONTEREY      ST   RNBT FBG  OB             6  8  1100        2350  2700
16  1 CHELAN MONTEREY      ST   RNBT FBG  IO  100-120    6  8             1800  2200
16  1 CHELAN MONTEREY      ST   RNBT FBG  IO  130-140    6  8             2000  2400
16  1 CHELAN VOYAGER       ST   RNBT FBG  OB             6  8  1075        2300  2700
16  1 CHELAN VOYAGER       ST   RNBT FBG  IO  100-120    6  8             1700  2050
16  1 CHELAN VOYAGER       ST   RNBT FBG  IO  130-140    6  8             1850  2200
16  6                           B/R  FBG  OB             7  3  1390        2850  3300
16  6                           B/R  FBG  IO  100-120    7  3             1950  2350
16  6                           B/R  FBG  IO  130-170    7  3             2200  2600
16  6 SURFRIDER            ST   RNBT FBG  OB             7  3  1325        2750  3200

16  6 SURFRIDER            ST   RNBT FBG  IO  100-120    7  3             2100  2550
16  6 SURFRIDER            ST   RNBT FBG  IO  130-170    7  3             2300  2550
17    WAIKIKI              OP   SKI  FBG  OB             6  8   760        1700  2000
18  5 YELLOWSTONE MONTEREY OP   RNBT FBG  OB             7  1  1290        2800  3250
18  5 YELLOWSTONE MONTEREY OP   RNBT FBG  IO  100-165    7  1             2500  3100
18  5 YELLOWSTONE MONTEREY OP   RNBT FBG  IO  170-245    7  1             2700  3150
18  5 YELLOWSTONE VOYAGER  OP   CR   FBG  OB             7  1  1265        2750  3200
18  5 YELLOWSTONE VOYAGER  OP   CR   FBG  IO  100-165    7  1             2550  3200
18  5 YELLOWSTONE VOYAGER  OP   CR   FBG  IO  170-245    7  1             2750  3200
18  6 BEACHCOMBER          OP   CR   FBG  OB             7 10  1510        3150  3650
18  6 BEACHCOMBER          OP   CR   FBG  IO  100-165    7 10             2950  3650
18  6 BIMINI               ST   CR   FBG  OB             7 10  1750        3450  4000

18  6 BIMINI               ST   CR   FBG  IO  100-170    7 10             2950  3700
18  6 SURFRIDER            ST   RNBT FBG  OB             7 10  1510        3150  3650
18  6 SURFRIDER            ST   RNBT FBG  IO  100-165    7 10  1510        2700  3350
19  2 CONTINENTAL          HT   CR   FBG  IO  100-245    7 10             3100  3800
19  2 CONTINENTAL          HT   CR   FBG  JT  260  BERK  7 10             2500  2900
19  2 MALIBU               OP   SKI  FBG  IO  140-245    7 10             2700  3350
19  2 MALIBU               OP   SKI  FBG  JT  260  BERK  7 10             2300  2700
19  2 MONTEREY             ST   RNBT FBG  IO  100-245    7 10             3000  3700
19  2 MONTEREY             ST   RNBT FBG  JT  260  BERK  7 10             2550  2950
19  2 SANTA-CATALINA       OP   RNBT FBG  IO  100-245    7 10             3000  3700
19  2 SANTA-CATALINA       OP   RNBT FBG  JT  260  BERK  7 10             2550  2950

19  2 VOYAGER              ST   CR   FBG  IO  100-245    7 10             3100  3850
19  2 VOYAGER              ST   CR   FBG  JT  260  BERK  7 10             2500  2900
21  2 CONTINENTAL          HT   CR   FBG  IO  100-225    7 10             3600  4450
   IO  245  OMC   3850     4500, JT  260  BERK 2900  3350, IO T120-T130     4900  6050
21  2 KOOTENAY             HT   CR   FBG  IO  100-245    7 10             3750  4650
21  2 KOOTENAY             HT   CR   FBG  JT  260  BERK  7 10             3000  3450
21  2 SAN-JUAN             HT   CR   FBG  IO  100-245    7 10             4450  5350
21  2 SAN-JUAN             HT   CR   FBG  JT  260  BERK  7 10             3400  3950
21  2 SITKA                HT   CR   FBG  IO  100-245    7 10             4050  4950
21  2 SITKA                HT   CR   FBG  JT  260  BERK  7 10             3150  3700
21  2 SPORTSMAN            HT   CR   FBG  IO  100-245    7 10             4200  5150
21  2 SPORTSMAN            HT   CR   FBG  JT  260  BERK  7 10             3250  3800
21  2 VOYAGER              ST   CUD  FBG  IO  100-245    7 10             4000  4900
21  2 VOYAGER              ST   CUD  FBG  JT  260  BERK  7 10             3150  3650
21  2 WESTPORTER           HT   CR   FBG  IO  100-245    7 10             4550  5500
21  2 WESTPORTER           HT   CR   FBG  JT  260  BERK  7 10             3500  4100

24  2                           CR   FBG  IO  165-245    8                5850  6950
   JT  260  BERK  4450     5100, IO 325  MRCR 6800  7800, IO T120-T245     6600  8100
24  2 CATALINA             ST   CR   FBG  IO  165-245    8                5850  6950
   JT  260  BERK  4450     5100, IO 325  MRCR 6800  7800, IO T120-T245     6600  8100
24  2 CONTINENTAL          HT   CR   FBG  IO  165-245    8                5550  6600
   JT  260  BERK  4200     4850, IO 325  MRCR 6500  7500, IO T120-T245     6350  7800
24  2 SAN-JUAN             HT   CR   FBG  IO  165-245    8                6100  7250
   JT  260  BERK  4650     5300, IO 325  MRCR 7050  8100, IO T120-T245     6800  8400

28  1 KONA                 HT   SDN  FBG  IO  188   MRCR 10              12600 14400
   VD  215  MRCR  9050    10300, IO  225  OMC  13100 14900, VD  270  MRCR  9500 10800
   IO  325  MRCR 14500    16500, VD  325  MRCR  9900 11200, IO T120-T170 13500 16700
   VD T215  MRCR 13700    15500, IO T225  OMC  14900 16900, IO T100D CHRY 16800 19000
   VD T100D CHRY 13600    15500, IO T106D VLVO 16800 19100, VD T106D VLVO 13700 15500

28  1 KONA                 FB   SDN  FBG  VD  215   MRCR 10               9050 10300
   IO  225  OMC  13100    14900, VD  270  MRCR  9500 10800, IO  325  MRCR 14500 16500
   VD  325  OMC   9900    11200, IO T120-T170 13500 16700, VD T215  MRCR 14500 16500
   IO T225  OMC  14900    16900, IO T100D CHRY 16800 19000, VD T215  MRCR 13700 15500
   IO T106D VLVO 16800    19100, IO T106D VLVO 15500
-------------------- 1971 BOATS ------------------------------------------------
16  1 CHELAN-MONTEREY           RNBT FBG  OB            6  8   790   1 2  1700  2000
16  1 SURFRIDER                 RNBT FBG  OB            7  2   975   1 2  1850  2200
16  6 SURFRIDER                 RNBT FBG  IO  130       7  2   975   1 2  2100  2450
16  6 SURFRIDER                 RNBT FBG  IO  170       7  2   975   1 2  2350  2750
18  3 YELLOWSTONE-MONTEREY      RNBT FBG  OB            7  2   980   1 2  2250  2650
18  3 YELLOWSTONE-MONTEREY      RNBT FBG  IO  170-200   7  2   980   1 2  2600  2900
18  3 YELLOWSTONE-VOYAGER       RNBT FBG  OB            7  2   990   1 2  2300  2650
18  3 YELLOWSTONE-VOYAGER       RNBT FBG  IO  170       7  2   990   1 2  2500  2950
18  6 SURFRIDER                 RNBT FBG  IO  170-235   7 10  1130   1 2  2550  2950
18  6 SURFRIDER                 RNBT FBG  IO  170-235   7 10  1130   1 2  2700  3100
19  3 COEUR-D'ALENE CONT    HT  RNBT FBG  IO  170-235   8         1 3  3200  3900
19  3 COEUR-D'ALENE M           RNBT FBG  IO  170-235   8         1 3  3400  3950

19  3 COEUR-D'ALENE V           RNBT FBG  IO  170       8         1 3  3000  3500
19  3 COEUR-D'ALENE V           RNBT FBG  IO  235       8         1 3  3350  3800
21  2 KOOTENAY                  RNBT FBG  IO  210       8         1 3  4050  4700
21  2 KOOTENAY                  RNBT FBG  IO T170       8         1 3  4950  5700
21  2 PEND-OREILLE CONT     HT  RNBT FBG  IO  210       8         1 3  4200  4900
21  2 PEND-OREILLE CONT     HT  RNBT FBG  IO T170       8         1 3  4950  5700
21  2 PEND-OREILLE SAN JUA      RNBT FBG  IO  210       8         1 3  4750  5450
21  2 PEND-OREILLE SAN JUA      RNBT FBG  IO T170       8         1 3  4950  5700
```

LOA FT IN	NAME AND/OR MODEL	TOP/RIG	BOAT TYPE	HULL MTL TP	ENGINE TP # HP MFG	BEAM FT IN	WGT LBS	DRAFT FT IN	RETAIL LOW	RETAIL HIGH
	---- 1971 BOATS ----									
21 2	PEND-OREILLE SPORT	RNBT	FBG	IO	210	8		1 3	4500	5200
21 2	PEND-OREILLE SPORT	RNBT	FBG	IO	T170	8		1 3	4950	5700
21 2	PEND-OREILLE VOYAGER	RNBT	FBG	IO	210	8		1 3	3700	4300
21 2	PEND-OREILLE VOYAGER	RNBT	FBG	IO	T170	8		1 3	4950	5700
21 2	SANTA-CATALINA	RNBT	FBG	IO	210	8		1 3	4100	4750
21 2	SANTA-CATALINA	RNBT	FBG	IO	T170	8		1 3	4950	5700
24 2	PACIFICA	CR	FBG	IO	235	8		1 6	6400	7350
24 2	PACIFICA	CR	FBG	IO	T215	8		1 6	7100	8150
24 2	PACIFICA-CATALINA	RNBT	FBG	IO	235	8		1 6	5750	6600
24 2	PACIFICA-CATALINA	RNBT	FBG	IO	T215	8		1 6	6800	7800
24 2	PACIFICA-CONTINENTAL HT	RNBT	FBG	IO	235	8		1 6	5950	6850
24 2	PACIFICA-CONTINENTAL HT	RNBT	FBG	IO	T215	8		1 6	6800	7800
24 2	PACIFICA-SAN-JUAN	CR	FBG	IO	235	8		1 6	6050	6950
24 2	PACIFICA-SAN-JUAN	CR	FBG	IO	T215	8		1 6	7100	8150
24 2	SANTA-CATALINA	RNBT	FBG	IO	235	8		1 6	6200	7100
24 2	SANTA-CATALINA	RNBT	FBG	IO	T215	8		1 6	6800	7800

FIBERGLASS BOAT CO

Call 1-800-327-6929 for BUC Personalized Evaluation Service
Or, for 1960 to 1965 boats, sign onto www.BUCValuPro.com

FIBERGLASS CONCEPTS INC
COAST GUARD MFG ID- FXN

Call 1-800-327-6929 for BUC Personalized Evaluation Service
Or, for 1981 boats, sign onto www.BUCValuPro.com

FIBERGLASS FABRICATORS INC
SUPER SPORT BOATS   COAST GUARD MFG ID- FGF

Call 1-800-327-6929 for BUC Personalized Evaluation Service
Or, for 1971 to 1979 boats, sign onto www.BUCValuPro.com

FIBERGLASS UNLIMITED
COAST GUARD MFG ID- FGD

Call 1-800-327-6929 for BUC Personalized Evaluation Service
Or, for 1968 to 1980 boats, sign onto www.BUCValuPro.com

FIBERKING INC
BOMBER & COMMANDER BOAT COAST GUARD MFG ID- FBK

Call 1-800-327-6929 for BUC Personalized Evaluation Service
Or, for 1978 to 1993 boats, sign onto www.BUCValuPro.com

FIBERTECH INT'L CORP
COAST GUARD MFG ID- FNT

Call 1-800-327-6929 for BUC Personalized Evaluation Service
Or, for 1978 to 1980 boats, sign onto www.BUCValuPro.com

FIBRA BOATS INC
MIAMI FL   See inside cover to adjust price for area

LOA FT IN	NAME AND/OR MODEL	TOP/RIG	BOAT TYPE	HULL MTL TP	ENGINE TP # HP MFG	BEAM FT IN	WGT LBS	DRAFT FT IN	RETAIL LOW	RETAIL HIGH
	---- 1970 BOATS ----									
19 10	DUAL-CATH		FBG	TR IO	80	7 1		1 6	5700	6550
20 2	V-20	CR	FBG	DV IO	130 VLVO	8	3000	2 2	7150	8250
22	CHEETAH FXL		FBG	SV IO	200	8		1 8	9300	10600
23 6	ISLANDER-BIMINI	CR	FBG	DV IO	210 OMC	8	4150	2 4	10500	12000
23 6	V-24	CR	FBG	DV IO	155 OMC	8	3900	2 4	9950	11300
25 11	VOYAGER	HT	HB FBG	IO	130	7		2 2	**	**
27 6	ISLANDER-NASSAU	SF	FBG	SV IO	210	10	6000	2 3	19800	22000
27 6	V-28	CR	FBG	DV IO	200 CHRY	10	5000	2 8	15600	17800
	---- 1968 BOATS ----									
20 2	CAPRI V-20	CR	FBG	IO	120-200	8	3000	2 2	7400	9050
23 4	RIVIERA V-24	CR	FBG	IO	165-200	8	4000	2 2	10800	12300
23 4	RIVIERA V-24	CR	FBG	IO	T110	8	4450	2 2	12900	14700

FIBRE GLASS BOAT CORP
WOODSON

Call 1-800-327-6929 for BUC Personalized Evaluation Service
Or, for 1964 to 1970 boats, sign onto www.BUCValuPro.com

FIBRO TECNICA, SA

Call 1-800-327-6929 for BUC Personalized Evaluation Service
Or, for 1982 boats, sign onto www.BUCValuPro.com

FINISH LINE INC
COAST GUARD MFG ID- FNS

Call 1-800-327-6929 for BUC Personalized Evaluation Service
Or, for 1976 to 1980 boats, sign onto www.BUCValuPro.com

FINLANDER BOATS INC

Call 1-800-327-6929 for BUC Personalized Evaluation Service
Or, for 1959 to 1961 boats, sign onto www.BUCValuPro.com

FINN CRAFT CORP

Call 1-800-327-6929 for BUC Personalized Evaluation Service
Or, for 1970 to 1972 boats, sign onto www.BUCValuPro.com

FINNYACHT USA

Call 1-800-327-6929 for BUC Personalized Evaluation Service
Or, for 1980 to 1989 boats, sign onto www.BUCValuPro.com

FINO-MONZA MARINE INC
MONZA   See inside cover to adjust price for area
DANIA FL 33004   COAST GUARD MFG ID- MNA

LOA FT IN	NAME AND/OR MODEL	TOP/RIG	BOAT TYPE	HULL MTL TP	ENGINE TP # HP MFG	BEAM FT IN	WGT LBS	DRAFT FT IN	RETAIL LOW	RETAIL HIGH
	---- 1974 BOATS ----									
19		OP	FBG	DV IO	320	7 8			28500	31600
19	TUNNEL	OP	FBG	TH OB		7 6	1600		4150	4850
26		OP	FBG	DV IO	T320	8			78200	85900
	---- 1973 BOATS ----									
20	MONZA 20		FBG	DV IO	188-235	7 8	3000	2 4	28300	32300
	IO 300 CHEV 31900 35500, IO 350 CHEV 36200 40200, JT 390 OLDS								24400	27100
26	DOMANI 26		FBG	DV IO	T165 CHEV	8	5000	2 9	67600	74300
	IO T290-T350 78200 94200, IO T390 OLDS 92500 101500, IB T450 CHEV								61400	67500
26	MONZA 26		FBG	DV IO	T165 CHEV	8	4700	2 9	65600	72100
26	PRIMO		FBG	DV IO	T300-T375	8	4600	2 9	76400	94800
26	PRIMO		FBG	DV IO	T415 CHEV	8	4600	2 9	94100	103500
30	FINO		FBG	IB	T375-T400	9 4	11000	2 3	102500	115000
	---- 1972 BOATS ----									
19 4	MONZA 19		FBG	IO	188 MRCR	7 8	3000	2 4	26000	28900
19 4	MONZA 19		FBG	IO	320 CC	7 8	3000	2 4	30900	34300
19 4	MONZA 19		FBG	JT	390-450	7 8	3000	2 4	20900	23200
26	MONZA V26		FBG	DV IO	320-325	8	5000	2 9	69700	77100
26	MONZA V26		FBG	DV IO	T165-T188	8	5000	2 9	69900	78500
26	MONZA V26		FBG	DV IO	T320 CC	8	5000	2 9	84600	92900
	---- 1971 BOATS ----									
30 3	SPORT FINO DLX		FBG	VD	325-390				77100	87100
	---- 1970 BOATS ----									
30 2	FINO		FBG	SV IB	325	9 2	8000	2 6	67000	73600

FISH-N-SKI MARINE PROD INC

Call 1-800-327-6929 for BUC Personalized Evaluation Service
Or, for 1971 boats, sign onto www.BUCValuPro.com

FISHER CRAFT
BYRON CA 94514   COAST GUARD MFG ID- FSV See inside cover to adjust price for area

For more recent years, see the BUC Used Boat Price Guide, Volume 1 or Volume 2

LOA FT IN	NAME AND/ OR MODEL	TOP/ RIG	BOAT TYPE	-HULL- MTL TP	----ENGINE--- TP # HP MFG	BEAM FT IN	WGT LBS	DRAFT FT IN	RETAIL LOW	RETAIL HIGH
					1983 BOATS					
28 9	FISHER-CRAFT	HT	HB	FBG SV	IO 138 VLVO	11 10	7500	1 5	**	**
28 9	FISHER-CRAFT	FB	HB	FBG SV	IO 138-260	11 10	7500	1 5	**	**
					1982 BOATS					
28 9	FISHER-CRAFT	HT	HB	FBG SV	IO 145-260	11 10	7500	1 5	**	**
28 9	FISHER-CRAFT	FB	HB	FBG SV	IO 145-260	11 10	7500	1 5	**	**
					1981 BOATS					
28 9	FISHER CRAFT 29	HT	HB	FBG SV	IO 145 VLVO	11 10	7500	1 5	**	**
28 9	FISHER-CRAFT	HT	HB	FBG SV	IO 200-260	11 10	7500	1 5	**	**
28 9	FISHER-CRAFT	FB	HB	FBG SV	IO 145-260	11 10	7500	1 5	**	**

FISHER MARINE
DIV OF BRUNSWICK MARINE GROUP
TOPEKA IN 46571   COAST GUARD MFG ID- FMC   See inside cover to adjust price for area

For more recent years, see the BUC Used Boat Price Guide, Volume 1 or Volume 2

LOA FT IN	NAME AND/ OR MODEL	TOP/ RIG	BOAT TYPE	-HULL- MTL TP	----ENGINE--- TP # HP MFG	BEAM FT IN	WGT LBS	DRAFT FT IN	RETAIL LOW	RETAIL HIGH
					1971 BOATS					
21 4	OUTRAGE	OP	FSH	FBG	OB	7 4	1600		3150	3700

FISHIN' SKI-BARGE
KNOXVILLE AR 72845   COAST GUARD MFG ID- SKB See inside cover to adjust price for area

For more recent years, see the BUC Used Boat Price Guide, Volume 1 or Volume 2

LOA FT IN	NAME AND/ OR MODEL	TOP/ RIG	BOAT TYPE	-HULL- MTL TP	----ENGINE--- TP # HP MFG	BEAM FT IN	WGT LBS	DRAFT FT IN	RETAIL LOW	RETAIL HIGH
					1983 BOATS					
16 6	SUN-CAT	CAT	SA/OD	FBG CT		7 3		9	2350	2750
18 11	BARRACUDA	OP	UTL	FBG SV	OB	7	800		2100	2500
18 11	BARRACUDA FSH	OP	UTL	FBG SV	OB	7	900		2400	2750
18 11	BARRACUDA I	OP	UTL	FBG SV	OB	7	825		2050	2450
18 11	BARRACUDA I DELUXE	OP	UTL	FBG SV	OB	7	830		2200	2600
18 11	BARRACUDA III	OP	UTL	FBG SV	OB	7	825		2300	2700
18 11	BARRACUDA III DLX	OP	UTL	FBG SV	OB	7	855		2300	2650
18 11	BARRACUDA PLAYTHING	OP	UTL	FBG SV	OB	7	880		2350	2700
19 8	MARLIN	OP	UTL	FBG RB	OB	7 10	900		2350	2700
19 8	MARLIN FSH	OP	UTL	FBG RB	OB	7 10	1000		2600	3000
19 8	MARLIN I	OP	UTL	FBG RB	OB	7 10	920		2400	2750
19 8	MARLIN I DELUXE	OP	UTL	FBG RB	OB	7 10	935		2400	2800
19 8	MARLIN III	OP	UTL	FBG RB	OB	7 10	925		2400	2800
19 8	MARLIN III DLX	OP	UTL	FBG RB	OB	7 10	950		2450	2850
19 8	MARLIN PLAYTHING	OP	UTL	FBG RB	OB	7 10	975		2550	2950
23 7	WORKMASTER 24	OP	UTL	FBG RB	OB	7 10	1700		4800	5550
					1982 BOATS					
18 11	BARRACUDA	OP	UTL	FBG SV	OB	7	800		2050	2450
18 11	BARRACUDA FSH	OP	UTL	FBG SV	OB	7	900		2350	2700
18 11	BARRACUDA I	OP	UTL	FBG SV	OB	7	825		2100	2500
18 11	BARRACUDA I DELUXE	OP	UTL	FBG SV	OB	7	830		2200	2550
18 11	BARRACUDA III	OP	UTL	FBG SV	OB	7	825		2200	2550
18 11	BARRACUDA III DLX	OP	UTL	FBG SV	OB	7	855		2250	2600
18 11	BARRACUDA PLAYTHING	OP	UTL	FBG SV	OB	7	880		2300	2700
19 8	MARLIN	OP	UTL	FBG RB	OB	7 10	900		2300	2700
19 8	MARLIN FSH	OP	UTL	FBG RB	OB	7 10	1000		2550	2950
19 8	MARLIN I	OP	UTL	FBG RB	OB	7 10	920		2350	2700
19 8	MARLIN I DELUXE	OP	UTL	FBG RB	OB	7 10	935		2400	2750
19 8	MARLIN III	OP	UTL	FBG RB	OB	7 10	925		2350	2750
19 8	MARLIN III DLX	OP	UTL	FBG RB	OB	7 10	950		2400	2800
19 8	MARLIN PLAYTHING	OP	UTL	FBG RB	OB	7 10	975		2500	2900
23 7	WORKMASTER 24	OP	UTL	FBG RB	OB	7 10	1700		4750	5450
					1981 BOATS					
16 6	SUN-CAT	CAT	SA/OD	FBG CT		7 3			2050	2450
18 11	BARRACUDA	OP	FSH	FBG SV	OB	7	900		2600	3050
18 11	BARRACUDA	OP	UTL	FBG SV	OB	7	800		2000	2400
18 11	BARRACUDA EXPRESS	OP	RNBT	FBG SV	OB	7	910		2650	3100
18 11	BARRACUDA I	OP	UTL	FBG SV	OB	7	825		2050	2450
18 11	BARRACUDA II	OP	UTL	FBG SV	OB	7	830		2100	2500
18 11	BARRACUDA III	OP	UTL	FBG SV	OB	7	825		2150	2500
18 11	BARRACUDA III DLX	OP	UTL	FBG SV	OB	7	855		2200	2550
18 11	BARRACUDA PLAYTHING	OP	UTL	FBG SV	OB	7	880		2300	2650
19 8	MARLIN	OP	FSH	FBG RB	OB	7 10	1000		2950	3400
19 8	MARLIN	OP	UTL	FBG RB	OB	7 10	900		2300	2650
19 8	MARLIN EXPRESS	OP	RNBT	FBG RB	OB	7 10	1010		2950	3450
19 8	MARLIN I	OP	UTL	FBG RB	OB	7 10	920		2350	2700
19 8	MARLIN II	OP	UTL	FBG RB	OB	7 10	915		2300	2700
19 8	MARLIN III	OP	UTL	FBG RB	OB	7 10	925		2350	2750
19 8	MARLIN III DLX	OP	UTL	FBG RB	OB	7 10	950		2400	2750
19 8	MARLIN PLAYTHING	OP	UTL	FBG RB	OB	7 10	975		2450	2850
23 7	WORKMASTER 24	OP	UTL	FBG RB	OB	7 10	1700		4700	5400
					1980 BOATS					
18 11	BARRACUDA	OP	FSH	FBG SV	OB	7	900		2600	3000
18 11	BARRACUDA	OP	UTL	FBG SV	OB	7	800		2000	2350
18 11	BARRACUDA EXPRESS	OP	RNBT	FBG SV	OB	7	910		2600	3050
18 11	BARRACUDA III	OP	UTL	FBG SV	OB	7	825		2050	2450
18 11	BARRACUDA III DLX	OP	UTL	FBG SV	OB	7	855		2200	2550
18 11	BARRACUDA PLAYTHING	OP	UTL	FBG SV	OB	7	880		2250	2600
19 8	MARLIN	OP	FSH	FBG RB	OB	7 10	1000		2900	3350
19 8	MARLIN	OP	UTL	FBG RB	OB	7 10	900		2250	2600
19 8	MARLIN EXPRESS	OP	RNBT	FBG RB	OB	7 10	1010		2950	3400
19 8	MARLIN III	OP	UTL	FBG RB	OB	7 10	925		2300	2700
19 8	MARLIN III DLX	OP	UTL	FBG RB	OB	7 10	950		2350	2750
19 8	MARLIN PLAYTHING	OP	UTL	FBG RB	OB	7 10	975		2400	2800
23 7	WORKMASTER 24	OP	UTL	FBG RB	OB	7 10	1700		4600	5300
					1979 BOATS					
18 11	BARRACUDA	OP	UTL	FBG SV	OB	7	800		1950	2350
18 11	BARRACUDA EXPRESS	OP	RNBT	FBG SV	OB	7	910		2600	3000
18 11	BARRACUDA III	OP	UTL	FBG SV	OB	7	825		2050	2400
18 11	BARRACUDA III DLX	OP	FSH	FBG SV	OB	7	855		2450	2850
18 11	BARRACUDA PLAYTHING	OP	UTL	FBG SV	OB	7	880		2200	2600
19 8	MARLIN	OP	UTL	FBG RB	OB	7 10	900		2200	2600
19 8	MARLIN EXPRESS	OP	RNBT	FBG RB	OB	7 10	1010		2900	3350
19 8	MARLIN III	OP	UTL	FBG RB	OB	7 10	925		2300	2650
19 8	MARLIN III DLX	OP	FSH	FBG RB	OB	7 10	950		2750	3200
19 8	MARLIN PLAYTHING	OP	UTL	FBG RB	OB	7 10	975		2400	2750
23 7	WORKMASTER 24	OP	UTL	FBG RB	OB	7 10	1700		4550	5250
					1978 BOATS					
16 6	SUN-CAT	CAT	SA/OD	FBG BB		7 3	1850	9	3300	3850
18 11	BARRACUDA	OP	UTL	FBG SV	OB	7	800		1950	2300
18 11	BARRACUDA EXPRESS	OP	RNBT	FBG SV	OB	7	910		2550	2950
18 11	BARRACUDA III	OP	UTL	FBG SV	OB	7	825		2000	2400
18 11	BARRACUDA III DLX	OP	FSH	FBG SV	OB	7	855		2400	2800
19 8	MARLIN	OP	UTL	FBG RB	OB	7 10	900		2200	2550
19 8	MARLIN EXPRESS	OP	RNBT	FBG RB	OB	7 10	1010		2850	3350
19 8	MARLIN III	OP	UTL	FBG RB	OB	7 10	925		2250	2650
19 8	MARLIN III DLX	OP	FSH	FBG RB	OB	7 10	950		2700	3150
23 7	WORKMASTER 24	OP	UTL	FBG RB	OB	7 10	1700		4500	5150
					1977 BOATS					
16 6	SUN-CAT	CAT	SA/OD	FBG BB		7 3	1100	9	2400	2800
18 11	BARRACUDA	OP	UTL	FBG SV	OB	7	900	5	2200	2600
18 11	BARRACUDA EXPRESS	OP	RNBT	FBG SV	OB	7	1045	5	2850	3300
18 11	BARRACUDA III	OP	UTL	FBG SV	OB	7	955	5	2650	3050
18 11	BARRACUDA III DLX	OP	BASS	FBG SV	OB	7	980	5	2700	3150
19 8	MARLIN	OP	UTL	FBG RB	OB	7 10	950	5	2300	2650
19 8	MARLIN EXPRESS	OP	RNBT	FBG RB	OB	7 10	1095	5	3050	3550
19 8	MARLIN III	OP	FSH	FBG RB	OB	7 10	1005	5	2800	3300
19 8	MARLIN III DLX	OP	BASS	FBG RB	OB	7 10	1030	5	2900	3350
23 7	WORKMASTER	OP	UTL	FBG RB	OB	7 10	1700		4450	5100
					1976 BOATS					
16 6	SUN-CAT	CAT	SA/OD	FBG BB		7 3	1100	9	2300	2700
18 11	BARRACUDA	OP	UTL	FBG SV	OB	7	900	5	2100	2550
18 11	BARRACUDA EXPRESS	OP	RNBT	FBG SV	OB	7	1045	5	2800	3300
18 11	BARRACUDA III	OP	UTL	FBG SV	OB	7	955	5	2600	3000
18 11	BARRACUDA III DLX	OP	UTL	FBG SV	OB	7	980	5	2650	3100
19 8	MARLIN	OP	UTL	FBG RB	OB	7 10	950	5	2300	2650
19 8	MARLIN EXPRESS	OP	RNBT	FBG RB	OB	7 10	1095	5	3000	3500
19 8	MARLIN III	OP	FSH	FBG RB	OB	7 10	1005	5	2800	3250
19 8	MARLIN III DLX	OP	BASS	FBG RB	OB	7 10	1030	5	2850	3300

LOA FT IN	NAME AND/ OR MODEL	TOP/ RIG	BOAT TYPE	-HULL- MTL TP	TP	----ENGINE--- # HP MFG	BEAM FT IN	WGT LBS	DRAFT FT IN	RETAIL LOW	RETAIL HIGH
				1975 BOATS							
16 6	SUN-CAT	CAT	SA/OD	FBG BB	OB	7 3	1100	9	2300	2650
18 11	BARRACUDA	OP	UTL	FBG SV	OB	7	900	5	2200	2550
18 11	BARRACUDA EXPRESS	OP	EXP	FBG SV	OB	7	1045	5	2800	3250
18 11	BARRACUDA II	OP	OPFSH	FBG SV	OB	7	955	5	2600	3000
18 11	BARRACUDA III	OP	OPFSH	FBG SV	OB	7	955	5	2600	3000
19 8	MARLIN	OP	UTL	FBG RB	OB	7 10	950	5	2250	2650
19 8	MARLIN EXPRESS	OP	EXP	FBG RB	OB	7 10	1095	5	3000	3450
19 8	MARLIN II	OP	OPFSH	FBG RB	OB	7 10	1005	5	2800	3250
19 8	MARLIN III	OP	OPFSH	FBG RB	OB	7 10	1005	5	2800	3250
				1974 BOATS							
16 6	SUN-CAT	CAT	SA/OD	FBG BB	OB	7 3	1100	9	2200	2600
18 11	BARRACUDA	OP	FSH	FBG SV	OB	7	850	6	2250	2600
18 11	BARRACUDA	OP	UTL	FBG SV	OB	7	850	6	2000	2400
18 11	BARRACUDA EXPRESS	OP	RNBT	FBG SV	OB	7	850	6	2350	2750
18 11	BARRACUDA II	OP	FSH	FBG SV	OB	7	850	6	2400	2800
18 11	BARRACUDA III	OP	FSH	FBG SV	OB	7	850	6	2400	2800
19 8	MARLIN		FSH	FBG	OB	7 10	950	6	2650	3050
19 8	MARLIN	OP	UTL	FBG RB	OB	7 10	950	6	2250	2600
19 8	MARLIN EXPRESS	OP	RNBT	FBG RB	OB	7 10	950	6	2650	3050
19 8	MARLIN II	OP	FSH	FBG RB	OB	7 10	950	6	2650	3050
19 8	MARLIN III	OP	FSH	FBG RB	OB	7 10	950	6	2650	3050
				1973 BOATS							
16 6	SUN-CAT	CAT	SA/OD	FBG BB	OB	7 3	1100	2 7	2150	2500
18 11	BARRACUDA	OP	UTL	FBG SV	OB	7	850	6	2000	2400
18 11	BARRACUDA EXPRESS	OP	RNBT	FBG SV	OB	7	850	6	2350	2700
18 11	BARRACUDA FISHER	OP	OPFSH	FBG SV	OB	7	850	6	2350	2700
18 11	BARRACUDA II	OP	FSH	FBG SV	OB	7	850	6	2350	2700
18 11	BARRACUDA III	OP	FSH	FBG SV	OB	7	850	6	2350	2700
19 8	MARLIN	OP	UTL	FBG SV	OB	7 10	950	6	2250	2600
19 8	MARLIN EXPRESS	OP	RNBT	FBG SV	OB	7 10	950	6	2650	3050
19 8	MARLIN FISHER	OP	OPFSH	FBG SV	OB	7 10	950	6	2600	3050
19 8	MARLIN II	OP	FSH	FBG SV	OB	7 10	950	6	2800	3250
19 8	MARLIN III	OP	FSH	FBG RB	OB	7 10	950	6	2450	2850
23 7	WORKMASTER	OP	UTL	FBG RB	OB	7 10	1700		4300	5000
				1972 BOATS							
16 6	SUN-CAT	CAT	SA/OD	FBG BB	OB	7 3	1100	9	2050	2450
18 11	BARRACUDA	OP	UTL	FBG SV	OB	7	900	5	2150	2500
18 11	BARRACUDA EXPRESS	OP	EXP	FBG SV	OB	7	1045	5	2750	3200
18 11	BARRACUDA FISHER	OP	OPFSH	FBG SV	OB	7	955	5	2750	3100
18 11	BARRACUDA II	OP	OPFSH	FBG SV	OB	7	955	5	2500	2900
18 11	BARRACUDA III	OP	OPFSH	FBG SV	OB	7	955	5	2500	2900
19 8	MARLIN	OP	UTL	FBG RB	OB	7 10	950	5	2250	2600
19 8	MARLIN EXPRESS	OP	EXP	FBG RB	OB	7 10	1095	5	2950	3450
19 8	MARLIN FISHER	OP	OPFSH	FBG RB	OB	7 10	1005	5	2850	3350
19 8	MARLIN II	OP	OPFSH	FBG RB	OB	7 10	1005	5	2700	3100
19 8	MARLIN III	OP	OPFSH	FBG RB	OB	7 10	1005	5	2700	3100
				1971 BOATS							
16 6	SUN-CAT	CAT	SA/OD	FBG BB	OB	7 3	1100	9	2050	2400
18 11	BARRACUDA EXPRESS	OP	EXP	FBG SV	OB	7	1045	5	2750	3200
18 11	BARRACUDA II	OP	OPFSH	FBG SV	OB	7	955	5	2450	2850
18 11	BARRACUDA III	OP	OPFSH	FBG SV	OB	7	955	5	2650	3100
19 8	MARLIN EXPRESS	OP	EXP	FBG RB	OB	7 10	1005	5	2750	3200
19 8	MARLIN II	OP	OPFSH	FBG RB	OB	7 10	1005	5	2650	3050
19 8	MARLIN III	OP	OPFSH	FBG RB	OB	7 10	1005	5	2850	3300
				1970 BOATS							
18 11	BARRACUDA EXPRESS	OP	EXP	FBG SV	OB	7	1045	5	2750	3200
18 11	BARRACUDA II	OP	OPFSH	FBG SV	OB	7	955	5	2400	2800
18 11	BARRACUDA III	OP	OPFSH	FBG SV	OB	7	955	5	2750	3200
19 8	MARLIN EXPRESS	OP	EXP	FBG RB	OB	7 10	1095	5	2950	3450
19 8	MARLIN II	OP	OPFSH	FBG RB	OB	7 10	1005	5	2650	3100
19 8	MARLIN III	OP	OPFSH	FBG RB	OB	7 10	1005	5	2850	3300
				1969 BOATS							
18 11	BARRACUDA EXPRESS	OP	EXP	FBG SV	OB	7	1045	5	2750	3200
18 11	BARRACUDA II	OP	OPFSH	FBG SV	OB	7	955	5	2500	2900
18 11	BARRACUDA III	OP	OPFSH	FBG SV	OB	7	955	5	2650	3100
				1968 BOATS							
18 11	BARRACUDA EXPRESS	OP	EXP	FBG SV	OB	7	1045	5	2800	3250
18 11	BARRACUDA II	OP	OPFSH	FBG SV	OB	7	955	5	2500	2900
18 11	BARRACUDA III	OP	OPFSH	FBG SV	OB	7	955	5	2700	3100

FJORD PLAST LTD
FJORD PLAST (UK) LTD   See inside cover to adjust price for area
HAMPSHIRE ENGLAND

FJORD MOTOR SAILERS
ST PETERSBURG FL

For more recent years, see the BUC Used Boat Price Guide, Volume 1 or Volume 2

LOA FT IN	NAME AND/ OR MODEL	TOP/ RIG	BOAT TYPE	-HULL- MTL TP	TP	----ENGINE--- # HP MFG	BEAM FT IN	WGT LBS	DRAFT FT IN	RETAIL LOW	RETAIL HIGH
				1979 BOATS							
21 4	FJORD 21		CR	FBG DV	IO	170	8 2			4950	5700
21 4	FJORD 21		CR	FBG DV	IO	T140	8 2			5450	6300
21 4	FJORD 21	OP	SPTCR	FBG DV	IO	170	8 2	2560		5100	5850
21 4	FJORD 21	OP	SPTCR	FBG DV	IO	T140	8 2	2560		5700	6550
21 4	FJORD 21	HT	SPTCR	FBG DV	IO	170	8 2			5100	5850
21 4	FJORD 21	HT	SPTCR	FBG DV	IO	T140	8 2			5700	6550
23 8	FJORD 24	OP	SPTCR	FBG DV	IO	T140-T170	9 7	4746		10000	11400
25 8	FJORD		SPTCR	FBG DV	IB	130-140	9 5			10800	12300
28 2	FJORD	KTH	SA/CR	FBG KL	IB	D	10		4 7	23200	25700
30 3	FJORD	FB	CR	FBG DV	IO	T106				16300	18600
30 3	FJORD	FB	CR	FBG DV	IO	T225				19000	21100
				1978 BOATS							
28	FJORD CS 28	CUT	SA/CR	FBG KL	IB	20D	6 4	9700	4 7	30900	34400
33	FJORD MS 33	CUT	MS	FBG KL	IB	47D	10 11	15400	4 5	50500	55500
				1977 BOATS							
28	FJORD CS 28	CUT	SA/CR	FBG KL	IB	20D	6 4	9700	4 7	29800	33200
33	FJORD MS 33	CUT	MS	FBG KL	IB	47D	10 11	15400	4 5	48800	53600
				1976 BOATS							
33	FJORD MS 33	CUT	MS	FBG KL	IB	47D	10 11	15400	4 5	47500	52200
				1975 BOATS							
33 2	FJORD MS33	CUT	MS	FBG KL	IB	47D PERK	10 11	14000	4 5	41600	46200
				1973 BOATS							
20	NORDIC		CUD	FBG RB	IB	25D	6 7			5650	6450
21	NORDIC		CUD	FBG RB	IB	25D	6 3			5750	6650
21 4	FJORD 21	OP	WKNDR	FBG DV	IO	170	8 2	2560		5450	6250
23	NORDIC	OP	DC	FBG DV	IO	170	8 2	2563		6050	6950
23	NORDIC		CUD	FBG RB	IB	25D		7		6600	7600
23 8	FJORD 24	OP	DC	FBG DV	IO	T130	9 7	4114		10800	12300
23 8	FJORD 24	OP	WKNDR	FBG DV	IO	T130	9 7	5170		11500	13000
32	FJORD 32		CR	FBG DV	IO	170	10 8			23400	26000
34			SDN	FBG DV	IB	T145D	12 2			39500	43900
38	FJORD 38		MY	FBG DV	IB	T175D	12 4			56300	61800
38	FJORD 38		SDN	FBG DV	IB	T175D	12 4			55200	60700
				1972 BOATS							
16	FJORD TRIFOIL 100	OP	RNBT	FBG TR	OB		6			1850	2200
16	FJORD TRIFOIL 100 GT	OP	RNBT	FBG TR	OB		6	770		1950	2350
18	FJORD TRIFOIL 120	OP	RNBT	FBG TR	OB		7	1210		3150	3650
18 8	FJORD WING SSP	OP	SPTCR	FBG DV	IO	170	7 2	2035	2 6	3900	4550
18 8	FJORDWING	HT	RNBT	FBG DV	IO		7 2	2400		4900	5600
18 8	FJORDWING SSP	OP	SPTCR	FBG DV	IO	210	7 2	2035	2 6	3950	4600
21 4	FJORD 21	OP	WKNDR	FBG DV	IO	T115-T170	8 2	2563	2 7	6350	7400
21 4	FJORD 21 DELUXE	OP	DC	FBG DV	IO	T115-T170	8 2	2563	2 7	7050	8200
23 8	FJORD 24	OP	CBNCR	FBG DV	IO	T130	9 7	5170	2 9	12600	14300
23 8	FJORD 24	OP	CR	FBG DV	IO	T120	9 7	4746	2 9	11000	12500
23 8	FJORD 24	OP	DC	FBG DV	IO	T130-T210	9 7	4114	2 9	11100	12900
23 8	FJORD 24	OP	WKNDR	FBG DV	IO	T130-T210	9 7	5170	2 9	11800	13700
25 6	FJORD 1/4 TON	SLP	SA/RC	FBG KL	IB	D	8 2	6300	4	15200	17300
26	1/4 TON CUP RACER	SLP	SA/RC	FBG KL	IB	D	8 2	6300		15500	17600
29 7	FJORD 30	HT	CBNCR	FBG DV	IB	T130	10 11	8250	2 9	16600	18900
29 7	FJORD 30	HT	CBNCR	FBG DV	IB	T170-T210	10 11	8250	2 9	23900	26800
29 7	FJORD 30	OP	WKNDR	FBG DV	IB	T130	10 11	8250	2 9	13200	15100
29 7	FJORD 30	OP	WKNDR	FBG DV	IB	T170-T210	10 11	8250	2 9	19300	22000
29 7	FJORD CABIN		CR	FBG DV	IB	600	10 11		2 9	15900	18100
29 7	FJORD CABIN		WKNDR	FBG DV	IB	600	10 11		2 9	14500	16500
30 5	FJORD 1/2 TON	SLP	SA/RC	FBG KL	IB	D	9 4	8158	5	22500	25000
31	1/2 TON CUP RACER	SLP	SA/RC	FBG KL	IB	D	9 4	8158		22600	25100
33	FJORD MS 33	CUT	MS	FBG KL	IB	50D	10 6	17000	4 5	46800	51500
33	FJORD MS33	SLP	MS	FBG KL	IB	50D	10 6	17000	4 5	46900	51500
34	FJORD 34	FB	DC	FBG DV	IB	T185D	12 2	11969	2 11	33800	37500
34	FJORD 34	FB	DC	FBG DV	IB	T420D	12 2	11969	2 11	41900	46400
34	FJORD 34	FB	SF	FBG DV	IB	T185D	12 2	11351	2 11	32700	36400
34	FJORD 34	FB	SF	FBG DV	IB	T420D	12 2	11351	2 11	40700	45200
38	FJORD 38	FB	DC	FBG DV	IB	700	13	16774	2 6	39400	43800
38	FJORD 38	FB	DC	FBG DV	IB	700D	13	16774	2 6	42500	47200
38	FJORD 38	FB	SF	FBG DV	IB	700D	13	15139	2 6	46600	51200
38	FJORD 38	FB	SF	FBG DV	IB	T185D	13	15139	2 6	42000	46600
53 6	FJORD	FB	DC	FBG KL	IB	200D	14 9	72000	7	150000	164500
53 6	FJORD MS 54	CUT	MS	FBG KL	IB	200D	14 9	72000	7	142000	156000
54	FJORD	FB	SF	FBG DV	IB	700	15	43627	5	104500	115000
54	FJORD	FB	SF	FBG DV	IB	T185D	15	43627	5	96900	106500

FJORD PLAST LTD — CONTINUED   See inside cover to adjust price for area

LOA FT	IN	NAME AND/OR MODEL	TOP/RIG	BOAT TYPE	HULL MTL	HULL TP	ENG TP	#	HP	MFG	BEAM FT	IN	WGT LBS	DRAFT FT	IN	RETAIL LOW	RETAIL HIGH
1972 BOATS																	
54		FJORD	TRWL		FBG	DV	IB		500D		15			5		115000	126500
54		FJORD	TRWL		FBG	DV	IB		T185D		15			5		111000	122000
1971 BOATS																	
16		FJORD ALI 16	OP	RNBT	FBG		IO				6	1	600			**	**
17	1	FJORDLING	HT	RNBT	FBG	DV	OB				7		1210			3050	3550
17	1	FJORDLING	HT	RNBT	FBG	DV	IO				7		600			**	**
18	8	FJORDWING	HT	RNBT	FBG		OB				7	2	2024			4550	5250
18	8	FJORDWING	HT	RNBT	FBG		IO				7	2	2024			**	**
18	8	FJORDWING SSP	OP	SPTCR	FBG		OB				7	2	2035			4500	5200
18	8	FJORDWING SSP	OP	SPTCR	FBG		IO				7	2	2035			**	**
21	4	FJORD 21	OP	WKNDR	FBG	DV	IO				8	2	2560			**	**
21	4	FJORD 21	OP	WKNDR	FBG	DV	IB				8	2	2560			**	**
21	4	FJORD 21 DELUXE	OP	DC	FBG	DV	IO				8	2	2563			**	**
21	4	FJORD 21 DELUXE	OP	DC	FBG	DV	IB				8	2	2563			**	**
23	8	FJORD 24	OP	DC	FBG		IO		170	VLVO	9	7	4114			10600	12100
23	8	FJORD 24	OP	WKNDR	FBG		IO		170	VLVO	9	7	5170			11400	12900
23	8	FJORD 24 ATTACHE	OP	CBNCR	FBG		IO		170	VLVO	9	7	5170			12100	13700
25	8	CONSUL	HT	EXP	FBG		IO		T130	VLVO	10	5	5940			14300	16200
29	7	FJORD 30	HT	CBNCR	FBG		IO		T170	VLVO	10	11	8250			25000	27800
29	7	FJORD 30	OP	WKNDR	FBG		IO		T170	VLVO	10	11	8250			20000	22200
30		DIPLOMAT	HT	CBNCR	FBG		IO		T170	VLVO	11	3	8250			25800	28600
33		FJORD MS 33	SLP	MS	FBG		IB		107D	PERK	10	6	14000			37800	42000
34		FJORD 34	HT	DC	FBG	DV	IB	T	D	PERK	12	2	11969			**	**
34		FJORD 34	FB	DC	FBG	DV	IB	T	D	PERK	12	2	11969			**	**
34		FJORD 34	FB	SF	FBG	DV	IB	T	D	PERK	12	2	11351			**	**
38		FJORD 38	FB	DC	FBG	DV	IB	T	D	PERK	12	2	16774			**	**
38		FJORD 38	FB	SF	FBG	DV	IB	T	D	PERK	12	2	15139			**	**
39	9	FJORD 40	HT	TCMY	FBG		IB	T		VLVO	13	6	20781			**	**
53	6	FJORD	KTH	MS	FBG	KL	IB		D	PERK	14	9	72000	7		145000	159000
53	6	FJORD	FB	MY	FBG		IB		D	PERK	14	9	70000	7		**	**
56		FJORD 56	FB	MY	AL		IB	T	D	CUM	16		48581			**	**
75	6	FJORD 75	FB	MY	FBG		IB	T	D	CAT	17	9				**	**
75	6	FJORD 75	FB	MY	FBG		IB	T	D	CUM	17	9				**	**
1970 BOATS																	
30		DIPLOMAT	HT	CBNCR	FBG	SV	IO		210		11	3	6000	2	6	21400	23800

A/S FJORD PLAST
Call 1-800-327-6929 for BUC Personalized Evaluation Service
Or, for 1972 to 1980 boats, sign onto www.BUCValuPro.com

FLAGSHIP YACHTS LTD
Call 1-800-327-6929 for BUC Personalized Evaluation Service
Or, for 1978 boats, sign onto www.BUCValuPro.com

FLARE FIBERGLASS BOAT COMPANY
Call 1-800-327-6929 for BUC Personalized Evaluation Service
Or, for 1960 to 1964 boats, sign onto www.BUCValuPro.com

FLEITZ BROS
Call 1-800-327-6929 for BUC Personalized Evaluation Service
Or, for 1960 boats, sign onto www.BUCValuPro.com

FLETCHER INTL SPORTSBTS LTD
Call 1-800-327-6929 for BUC Personalized Evaluation Service
Or, for 1980 to 1987 boats, sign onto www.BUCValuPro.com

FLIPPER SCOW A/S
NORDIC OFFSHORE CRUISING YCHT

Call 1-800-327-6929 for BUC Personalized Evaluation Service
Or, for 1977 to 1982 boats, sign onto www.BUCValuPro.com

FLOATING BOATS INC
Call 1-800-327-6929 for BUC Personalized Evaluation Service
Or, for 1973 boats, sign onto www.BUCValuPro.com

FLORIDA BAY BOAT CO
COAST GUARD MFG ID- FBQ

Call 1-800-327-6929 for BUC Personalized Evaluation Service
Or, for 1981 to 1987 boats, sign onto www.BUCValuPro.com

FLORIDA FIBERGLASS PROD INC
PLASTI-CRUISER

Call 1-800-327-6929 for BUC Personalized Evaluation Service
Or, for 1959 boats, sign onto www.BUCValuPro.com

FLORIDA MARINE PROD INC
MITCHELL BTS & SURFRIDE COAST GUARD MFG ID- MBP

Call 1-800-327-6929 for BUC Personalized Evaluation Service
Or, for 1967 to 1979 boats, sign onto www.BUCValuPro.com

FLORIDA SOUTHEAST YTS INC
Call 1-800-327-6929 for BUC Personalized Evaluation Service
Or, for 1974 to 1977 boats, sign onto www.BUCValuPro.com

FLORIDA-CAROLINA BOAT BLDG
PERFECTION BOATS   COAST GUARD MFG ID- PFT

Call 1-800-327-6929 for BUC Personalized Evaluation Service
Or, for 1967 to 1971 boats, sign onto www.BUCValuPro.com

FLOTILLA CORPORATION
FLEET CRAFT   COAST GUARD MFG ID- FTC

Call 1-800-327-6929 for BUC Personalized Evaluation Service
Or, for 1959 to 1976 boats, sign onto www.BUCValuPro.com

FLYING FINN
Call 1-800-327-6929 for BUC Personalized Evaluation Service
Or, for 1959 to 1962 boats, sign onto www.BUCValuPro.com

FLYING SCOT INC
DEER PARK MD 21550   COAST GUARD MFG ID- GDB See inside cover to adjust price for area
FORMERLY GORDON DOUGLASS BOAT CO INC

For more recent years, see the BUC Used Boat Price Guide, Volume 1 or Volume 2

LOA FT	IN	NAME AND/OR MODEL	TOP/RIG	BOAT TYPE	HULL MTL	HULL TP	ENG TP	# HP	MFG	BEAM FT	IN	WGT LBS	DRAFT FT	IN	RETAIL LOW	RETAIL HIGH
1983 BOATS																
19		FLYING-SCOT	SLP	SA/OD	F/S	CB	OB			6	9	850		8	3500	4050
1982 BOATS																
19		FLYING-SCOT	SLP	SA/OD	F/S	CB	OB			6	9	850		8	3300	3850
1981 BOATS																
19		FLYING-SCOT	SLP	SA/OD	F/S	CB	OB			6	9	850		8	3150	3650
1980 BOATS																
19		FLYING-SCOT	SLP	SA/OD	F/S	CB	OB			6	9	850		8	3000	3500
1979 BOATS																
19		FLYING-SCOT	SLP	SA/OD	FBG	CB	OB			6	9	675		8	2650	3050
1978 BOATS																
19		FLYING-SCOT	SLP	SA/OD	F/S	CB	OB			6	9	675		8	2550	2950
1977 BOATS																
19		FLYING-SCOT	SLP	SA/OD	FBG	CB	OB			6	9	850		8	2700	3150
1976 BOATS																
19		FLYING-SCOT	SLP	SA/OD	F/S	CB	OB			6	9	850		8	2600	3000

LOA FT IN	NAME AND/OR MODEL	TOP/RIG	BOAT TYPE	HULL MTL TP TP	ENGINE # HP MFG	BEAM FT IN	WGT LBS	DRAFT FT IN	RETAIL LOW	RETAIL HIGH
1975 BOATS										
19	FLYING-SCOT	SLP	SA/OD	FBG CB OB		6 9	850	8	2500	2950
1974 BOATS										
19	FLYING-SCOT	SLP	SA/OD	FBG CB OB		6 9	850	8	2450	2850
1973 BOATS										
19	FLYING-SCOT	SLP	SA/OD	FBG CB OB		6 9	850	4	2400	2750
1972 BOATS										
19	DOUGLASS	SLP	SA/OD	FBG CB		6 9	850		2300	2650
19	FLYING-SCOT	SLP	SA/OD	FBG CB		6 9	850	4	2400	2800
1971 BOATS										
19	FLYING-SCOT	SLP	SA/OD	FBG CB		6 9	850	4	2300	2650
1970 BOATS										
19	FLYING-SCOT	SLP	SA/OD	FBG CB		6 9	850	4	2250	2650
1969 BOATS										
19	FLYING-SCOT	SLP	SA/OD	FBG CB		6 9	850	4	2200	2600
1968 BOATS										
19	FLYING-SCOT	SLP	SA/OD	FBG CB		6 9	850	4	2200	2550
1967 BOATS										
19	FLYING-SCOT	SLP	SA/OD	FBG CB		6 9	850	4	2150	2500
1966 BOATS										
19	FLYING-SCOT	SLP	SA/OD	FBG CB		6 9	850	4	2100	2500
1965 BOATS										
19	FLYING-SCOT	SLP	SA/OD	FBG CB		6 9	850	4	2050	2450
1961 BOATS										
19	FLYING-SCOT	SLP	SA/OD	FBG CB		6 9	850	4	2050	2400
1960 BOATS										
19	FLYING-SCOT	SLP	SA/OD	FBG CB		6 9	850	4	2050	2400
1959 BOATS										
19	FLYING-SCOT	SLP	SA/OD	FBG CB		6 9	850	4	2050	2450

FOREIGN ADVISORY SERVICE CORP

Call 1-800-327-6929 for BUC Personalized Evaluation Service
Or, for 1959 boats, sign onto www.BUCValuPro.com

FORESAIL MARINE
COAST GUARD MFG ID- BSR

Call 1-800-327-6929 for BUC Personalized Evaluation Service
Or, for 1973 to 1976 boats, sign onto www.BUCValuPro.com

FORMOSA BOAT BLDG CO
PLAYA DEL REY CA   See inside cover to adjust price for area

LOA FT IN	NAME AND/OR MODEL	TOP/RIG	BOAT TYPE	HULL MTL TP TP	ENGINE # HP MFG	BEAM FT IN	WGT LBS	DRAFT FT IN	RETAIL LOW	RETAIL HIGH
1982 BOATS										
29 7	FORMOSA 30	KTH	SA/CR	FBG KL IB	D	10 6	10800	3 6	26500	29400
34	FORMOSA 34	SLP	SA/RC	FBG KL IB	D	11 10	13600	5 6	33700	37400
34	FORMOSA 35	CUT	SA/CR	FBG KL IB	D	11	18300	5 6	44400	49300
35 4	FORMOSA 37	CUT	SA/CR	FBG KL IB	D	11	18000	5	44200	49100
36 6	FORMOSA 36	KTH	SA/CR	FBG KL IB	D	11 3		4 5	43100	47900
40 2	FORMOSA 40	TRWL		FBG DV IB		14	27000		71400	78500
40 11	FORMOSA 41	KTH	SA/CR	FBG KL IB	D	12 2	28000	6 2	72400	79500
41 6	FORMOSA 42	TRWL		FBG DV IB	T120D	14	28000		75300	82800
41 10	FORMOSA 43	SLP	SA/RC	FBG KC IB	D	12 7	24800	6 7	69300	76100
42 8	FORMOSA 44	CUT	SA/RC	FBG KL IB	D	13	34810	6 4	86900	95500
45	FORMOSA 46	CUT	SA/CR	FBG KL IB	D	12 11	30700	6 4	89000	97800
46 5	FORMOSA 47	KTH	SA/CR	FBG KL IB	D	14	30864	7 5	95300	104500
1980 BOATS										
50 10	FORMOSA 51	KTH	SA/CR	FBG KL IB	D	14 1	52000	6 2	140500	154500
55 6	FORMOSA 56	KTH	SA/CR	FBG KL IB	D	15 9	47300	7 8	182500	200500
20	SUPER-CAT	CAT	SA/OD	FBG CT		12		6	1950	2300
20	SUPER-CAT	SLP	SAIL	FBG CT		12	450	6	1950	2300
1979 BOATS										
20	SUPER-CAT	SLP	SAIL	FBG CT		12	450	6	1900	2250

FORMULA BOATWORKS LLC
NOANK CT 06340   COAST GUARD MFG ID- FMU See inside cover to adjust price for area
FORMERLY FORMULA YACHTS INC

For more recent years, see the BUC Used Boat Price Guide, Volume 1 or Volume 2

LOA FT IN	NAME AND/OR MODEL	TOP/RIG	BOAT TYPE	HULL MTL TP TP	ENGINE # HP MFG	BEAM FT IN	WGT LBS	DRAFT FT IN	RETAIL LOW	RETAIL HIGH
1983 BOATS										
25 5	EVELYN 25.5	SLP	SAIL	F/S KL IB		9	4300	4 5	10100	11500
25 5	EVELYN 25.5	SLP	SAIL	F/S KL IB	D	9	4300	4 5	10900	12400
26	EVELYN 26	SLP	SA/OD	F/S DB OB		9 6	4500	1	10900	12300
26	EVELYN 26	SLP	SA/OD	F/S KL OB		9 6	4500	4 6	10400	11800
32	EVELYN 32	SLP	SAIL	F/S KL OB		9 8	4500	6	12600	14430
1982 BOATS										
25 5	EVELYN 25.5	SLP	SAIL	F/S KL IB		9	4300	4 5	9500	10800
25 5	EVELYN 25.5	SLP	SAIL	F/S KL IB		9	4300	4 5	9900	11300
26	EVELYN 26	SLP	SA/OD	F/S DB OB		9 6	4500	1	10200	11600
26	EVELYN 26	SLP	SA/OD	F/S KL OB		9	4300	4 6	9750	11100
1981 BOATS										
26	EVELYN 26	SLP	SA/OD	F/S KL OB		9 6	4200	1	9050	10300
1980 BOATS										
26	EVELYN 26	SLP	SA/OD	F/S KL OB		9 5	4200	1	8550	9800

FORT MYERS YHT & SHIPBLDG INC
FORT MYERS FL 33901   COAST GUARD MFG ID- FMW See inside cover to adjust price for area

For more recent years, see the BUC Used Boat Price Guide, Volume 1 or Volume 2

LOA FT IN	NAME AND/OR MODEL	TOP/RIG	BOAT TYPE	HULL MTL TP TP	ENGINE # HP MFG	BEAM FT IN	WGT LBS	DRAFT FT IN	RETAIL LOW	RETAIL HIGH
1983 BOATS										
34 8	NIGHTWIND 35	SLP	SA/RC	FBG KC IB	25 UNIV 11	6	12500	2 9	62600	68800
42	BREWER 12.8	CUT	SA/RC	FBG KC IB	61D LEHM 13	6	25000	4 3	118500	130500
42	BREWER 42	KTH	SA/CR	FBG KL IB	67D LEHM 13	6	24000	5	116000	127500
1982 BOATS										
42	WHITBY 42	KTH	SAIL	FBG KL IB	80D LEHM 13		23500	5	108000	119000

FORTIER BOATS INC
SOMERSET MA 02725   COAST GUARD MFG ID- FDF See inside cover to adjust price for area

For more recent years, see the BUC Used Boat Price Guide, Volume 1 or Volume 2

LOA FT IN	NAME AND/OR MODEL	TOP/RIG	BOAT TYPE	HULL MTL TP TP	ENGINE # HP MFG	BEAM FT IN	WGT LBS	DRAFT FT IN	RETAIL LOW	RETAIL HIGH
1983 BOATS										
26 10	FORTIER 26	OP	CR	FBG DV IB	255 MRCR 10		6500	2 6	26400	29300
26 10	FORTIER 26	OP	CR	FBG DV IB	165D PERK 10		6500	2 6	33600	37400
33 5	FORTIER 33	OP	CR	FBG DV IB					**	**
33 5	FORTIER 33	FB	CR	FBG DV IB					**	**
1982 BOATS										
26 10	FORTIER 26	OP	CR	FBG DV IB	255 MRCR 10		6500	2 6	25200	28000
26 10	FORTIER 26	OP	CR	FBG DV IB	160D PERK 10		6500	2 6	31300	35700
33 5	FORTIER 33	OP	CR	FBG DV IB					**	**
33 5	FORTIER 33	FB	CR	FBG DV IB					**	**
1981 BOATS										
26 10	FORTIER 26	OP	CR	FBG DV IB	255 MRCR 10		6500	2 6	24200	26800
26 10	FORTIER 26	OP	CR	FBG DV IB	160D PERK 10		6500	2 6	30900	34300
33 5	FORTIER 33	OP	CR	FBG DV IB					**	**
33 5	FORTIER 33	FB	CR	FBG DV IB					**	**
1980 BOATS										
26 10	FORTIER 26	OP	CR	FBG DV IB	255 MRCR 10		6500	2 6	23100	25700
26 10	FORTIER 26	OP	CR	FBG DV IB	160D PERK 10		6500	2 6	29700	33000
1978 BOATS										
26 6	FORTIER 26	OP	CR	FBG DV IO	255 MRCR 10		6500	2 6	20200	22500

FOUNTAIN POWERBOATS INC
WASHINGTON NC 27889   COAST GUARD MFG ID- FGQ See inside cover to adjust price for area
FORMERLY FOUNTAIN & GARBRECHT INC

For more recent years, see the BUC Used Boat Price Guide, Volume 1 or Volume 2

LOA FT IN	NAME AND/OR MODEL	TOP/RIG	BOAT TYPE	HULL MTL TP TP	ENGINE # HP MFG	BEAM FT IN	WGT LBS	DRAFT FT IN	RETAIL LOW	RETAIL HIGH
1983 BOATS										
33	10M SPORT BOAT	OP	OFF	F/S SV IO	T330-T370 8	4	7000	1 6	23300	27800
33	10M SPORT BOAT	OP	OFF	F/S SV IO	T400-T475 8	4	7000	1 6	26400	31400
1981 BOATS										
32	FEVER 33	OP	OFF	F/S SV IO	T330 8		7000		19300	21400

FOUR WINDS YACHT CORP
COAST GUARD MFG ID- FWC

Call 1-800-327-6929 for BUC Personalized Evaluation Service
Or, for 1976 boats, sign onto www.BUCValuPro.com

FOUR WINNS INC
CADILLAC MI 49601   COAST GUARD MFG ID- GFN See inside cover to adjust price for area
                         FOR OLDER MODELS SEE SAF-T-MATE

For more recent years, see the BUC Used Boat Price Guide, Volume 1 or Volume 2

LOA FT IN	NAME AND/ OR MODEL	TOP/ RIG	BOAT TYPE	MTL	-HULL- TP	TP	----ENGINE--- # HP	MFG	BEAM FT IN	WGT LBS	DRAFT FT IN	RETAIL LOW	RETAIL HIGH
1983 BOATS
16 7	MARQUISE 170	ST	RNBT	FBG	DV	IO	120	MRCR	7 2	1780		2300	2650
16 7	MARQUISE 170 BROUGHM	ST	RNBT	FBG	DV	IO	120-185		7 2	1780		2300	2700
18	MARQUISE 180	ST	CUD	FBG	DV	OB			7 7	1600		1800	2150
18	MARQUISE 180	ST	CUD	FBG	DV	IO	120-200		7 7	2500		3100	3650
18	MARQUISE 180	ST	RNBT	FBG	DV	IO	120-230		7 7	2800		2800	3400
18	MARQUISE 180	ST	RNBT	FBG	DV	IO	260	OMC	7 7	2200		3050	3550
18	MARQUISE 180 BROUGHM	ST	RNBT	FBG	DV	IO	120-228		7 7	2200		2850	3450
18	MARQUISE 180 SPORT	ST	CUD	FBG	DV	OB			7 7	1600		1900	2250
18	MARQUISE 180 SPORT	ST	CUD	FBG	DV	IO	140-185		7 7	2500		3150	3750
20 4	LIBERATOR 204	OP	CUD	FBG	DV	IO	185-260		8	2830		4550	5500
20 4	SANTARA 204	ST	CUD	FBG	DV	IO	140-185		8	2800		4500	5600
20 4	SANTARA 204	ST	CUD	FBG	DV	IO	198-260		8	3180		4900	5850
20 4	SANTARA 204 SPORT	ST	CUD	FBG	DV	IO	120-260		8	2900		4550	5550
22 5	SANTARA 225	ST	CUD	FBG	DV	IO	198-260		8	3640		5850	7000
22 5	SANTARA 225 SPORT	ST	CUD	FBG	DV	IO	198-260		8	3640		6100	7300
1982 BOATS
16 7	MARQUISE 170	ST	RNBT	FBG	DV	IO	120-170		7 2	1780		2250	2650
16 7	MARQUISE 170 BROUGHM	ST	RNBT	FBG	DV	IO	120-170		7 2	1800		2300	2700
18	MARQUISE 180	ST	CUD	FBG	DV	OB						2000	2400
18	MARQUISE 180	ST	CUD	FBG	DV	IO	140-185		7 7	2500		2950	3450
18	MARQUISE 180	ST	RNBT	FBG	DV	IO	140-185		7 7	2200		2750	3200
18	MARQUISE 180 BROUGHM	ST	RNBT	FBG	DV	IO	140-185		7 7	2200		2800	3300
18	MARQUISE 180 SPORT	ST	CUD	FBG	DV	OB						2300	2650
18	MARQUISE 180 SPORT	ST	CUD	FBG	DV	IO	140-185					3150	3700
20 4	SANTARA 204	ST	CUD	FBG	DV	IO	170-200		8	2800		4400	5500
20 4	SANTARA 204 SPORT	ST	CUD	FBG	DV	IO	170-200		8	2900		4500	5200
1981 BOATS
16 7	MARQUISE 170	ST	RNBT	FBG	DV	IO	120-170		7 2	1800		2200	2550
16 7	MARQUISE 170 BROUGHM	ST	RNBT	FBG	DV	IO	120-170		7 2	1800		2250	2650
18	MARQUISE 180	ST	CUD	FBG	DV	IO	140-185		7 7	2500		3000	3500
18	MARQUISE 180	ST	RNBT	FBG	DV	IO	140-185		7 7	2200		2700	3150
18	MARQUISE 180 BROUGHM	ST	RNBT	FBG	DV	IO	140-185		7 7	2200		2750	3250
20 4	SANTARA 204	ST	CUD	FBG	DV	IO	170-198		8	3180		4700	5400
1980 BOATS
16 7	MARQUISE 170	ST	RNBT	FBG	DV	IO	120-170		7 2	1800		2150	2550
16 7	MARQUISE 170 BROUGHM	ST	RNBT	FBG	DV	IO	120-170		7 2	1800		2250	2600
18	MARQUISE 180	ST	CUD	FBG	DV	IO	140-198		7 7	2500		2950	3500
18	MARQUISE 180	ST	RNBT	FBG	DV	IO	140-198		7 7	2200		2650	3150
18	MARQUISE 180 BROUGHM	ST	RNBT	FBG	DV	IO	140-198		7 7	2200		2750	3250
20 4	SANTARA 204	ST	CUD	FBG	DV	IO	170-228		8	3180		4650	5450
1979 BOATS
16 7	MARQUISE 170	OP	RNBT	FBG	DV	IO	120-170		7 2	1780		2200	2650
18	MARQUISE 180	OP	RNBT	FBG	DV	IO	140-170		7 7	2200		2700	3250
18	MARQUISE 180	OP	RNBT	FBG	DV	IO	198-200		7 7	2600		3000	3450
1978 BOATS
16 4	SIROCCO	OP	RNBT	FBG	DV	IO			6 5	1690		**	**
16 4	SIROCCO	OP	RNBT	FBG	DV	IO	120		6 5	1690		1950	2300
16 7	MARQUISE 170	OP	RNBT	FBG	DV	IO	120-165		6 5	1780		2200	2600
16 8	CORDOVA	OP	RNBT	FBG	TR	IO	120		6 5	1580		1900	2300
17	CANDIA 170	OP	RNBT	FBG	TR	IB			7 3	1800		**	**
18	MARQUISE 180	OP	RNBT	FBG	DV	IO	140-228		7 7	2200		2700	3300
18 7	NASSAU	OP	RNBT	FBG	TR	IO	140		7 5	2190		2750	3200
19 2	CANDIA 190	OP	RNBT	FBG	TR	IO			7 8	2200		**	**
1977 BOATS
16 2	SIROCCO	OP	RNBT	FBG	DV	IO	120-140		6 5			2250	2650
16 10	CORDOVA	OP	RNBT	FBG	TR	IO	120-140		6 9			2400	2750
18	MARQUISE	OP	RNBT	FBG	DV	OB			7 8	1675		1750	2100
18	MARQUISE	OP	RNBT	FBG	DV	IO	140-235		7 8			3000	3650
18 7	NASSAU	OP	RNBT	FBG	TR	OB			7 5	1685		1800	2100
18 7	NASSAU	OP	RNBT	FBG	TR	IO	140-235		7 5			3100	3800
1976 BOATS
17	COMMODORE	OP	RNBT	FBG	TR	IO	120		6 9			2450	2850
18	ADMIRAL II	OP	RNBT	FBG	TR	IO	165		7 3			3000	3500
18	SEAFARER	OP	RNBT	FBG	SV	IO	165		7			2950	3400

FOX BOATWORKS

Call 1-800-327-6929 for BUC Personalized Evaluation Service
Or, for 1981 to 2000 boats, sign onto www.BUCValuPro.com

FREEDOM BOAT WORKS
N FREEDOM WI 53951   COAST GUARD MFG ID- FBY See inside cover to adjust price for area

LOA FT IN	NAME AND/ OR MODEL	TOP/ RIG	BOAT TYPE	MTL	-HULL- TP	TP	----ENGINE--- # HP	MFG	BEAM FT IN	WGT LBS	DRAFT FT IN	RETAIL LOW	RETAIL HIGH
1983 BOATS
17 7	MIRAGE	SAIL	CDR	DB					2 11	80		1900	2300

FREEDOM YACHTS INC
MIDDLETOWN RI 02842   COAST GUARD MFG ID- FYC See inside cover to adjust price for area

For more recent years, see the BUC Used Boat Price Guide, Volume 1 or Volume 2

LOA FT IN	NAME AND/ OR MODEL	TOP/ RIG	BOAT TYPE	MTL	-HULL- TP	TP	----ENGINE--- # HP	MFG	BEAM FT IN	WGT LBS	DRAFT FT IN	RETAIL LOW	RETAIL HIGH
1982 BOATS
25 8	FREEDOM 25	SLP	SA/CR	F/S	KL	OB			8 6	3800	4 5	8400	9650
28 4	FREEDOM 28	KTH	SA/CR	F/S	KC	IB	15D	YAN	9 4	7000	2 6	19000	21100
33	FREEDOM 33	KTH	SA/CR	F/S	KC	IB	22D	YAN	11	12000	3 6	35300	39200
33	FREEDOM 33	KTH	SA/CR	F/S	KC	IB	22D	YAN	11	12000	4 6	35300	39200
39	FREEDOM 39	SCH	SA/CR	F/S	KC	IB	50D	PERK	12	19500	5 5	60100	66000
40	FREEDOM 40 AFT CPT	KTH	SA/CR	F/S	KL	IB	50D	PERK	12	20000	4 3	64200	70500
44	FREEDOM 44 AFT CPT	KTH	SA/CR	F/S	KL	IB	50D	PERK	12	25000	6	86800	95300
1981 BOATS
28 4	FREEDOM 28	KTH	SA/CR	F/S	KC	IB	15D	YAN	9 4	7000	2 6	17500	19900
33	FREEDOM 33	KTH	SA/CR	F/S	KC	IB	22D	YAN	11	12000	3 6	33200	36900
40	FREEDOM 40 AFT CPT	KTH	SA/CR	F/S	KC	IB	50D	PERK	12	22000	4 3	64400	70700
40	FREEDOM 40 CTR CPT	KTH	SA/CR	F/S	KC	IB	50D	PERK	12	22000	4 3	64400	70700
44	FREEDOM 44 AFT CPT	KTH	SA/CR	F/S	KL	IB	50D	PERK	12	25000	8	81600	89700
1980 BOATS
28 4	FREEDOM 28	KTH	SA/CR	F/S	KC	IB	15D	YAN	9 4	7000	2 6	16700	19000
33	FREEDOM 33	KTH	SA/CR	F/S	KC	IB	22D	YAN	11	12000	3 6	31700	35200
40	FREEDOM 40 AFT CPT	KTH	SA/CR	F/S	KC	IB	50D	PERK	12	22000	4 3	61300	67400
40	FREEDOM 40 CTR CPT	KTH	SA/CR	F/S	KC	IB	50D	PERK	12	22000	4 3	61300	67400
1979 BOATS
28 4	FREEDOM 28	KTH	SAIL	F/S	KC	IB	15D	YAN	9 4	7000	2 6	16100	18200
33	FREEDOM 33	KTH	SAIL	F/S	KC	IB	15D	YAN	11	11000	3	28000	31100
40	FREEDOM 40 AFT CPT	KTH	SAIL	F/S	KC	IB	50D	PERK	12	22000	4	58900	64800
40	FREEDOM 40 CTR CPT	KTH	SAIL	F/S	KC	IB	50D	PERK	12	22000	4	58900	64800
1978 BOATS
30 6	ETCHELLS 22	SLP	SA/OD	FBG	KL	IB			6 11		4 6	13600	15400
40	FREEDOM 40	CUT	SA/CR	FBG	KL	IB	38D		12	21000	4 6	55100	60600
40	FREEDOM 40	KTH	SA/CR	FBG	KC	IB	38D		12	21000	3 6	55200	60600
1977 BOATS
25 8	BONITO	SF	FBG	SV	IO		255		11 1		2 2	10200	11600
30 6	ETCHELLS 22	SLP	SA/OD	FBG	KL	IB		D	6 11	3400	4 6	7650	8750
40	FREEDOM 40	CUT	SAIL	FBG	KC	IB	50D		12	22000	3 4	55100	60600
40	FREEDOM 40	KTH	SAIL	FBG	KC	IB	50D		12	22000	3 4	55200	60600
1976 BOATS
25 8	BONITO	SF	FBG	SV	IO		255		11 1		2 2	10400	11800
30 6	ETCHELLS 22	SLP	SA/OD	FBG	KL	IB		D	6 11	3400	4 6	7400	8500
1975 BOATS
30 6	ETCHELLS 22	SLP	SA/OD	FBG	KL	IB		D	6 11	3400	4 6	7200	8250
37 4	FREEDOM 38	CUT	SA/CR	FBG	KL	IB	75D	PERK	14	32000	6 4	64300	70700
44 6	FREEDOM 45	KTH	SA/CR	FBG	KL	IB		PERK	13	26000	5 8	68700	75500
1974 BOATS
30 6	ETCHELLS 22	SLP	SA/OD	FBG	KL	IB		D	6 11	3400	4 6	7000	8050

FREEPORT POINT SHIPYARD INC

Call 1-800-327-6929 for BUC Personalized Evaluation Service
Or, for 1961 to 1966 boats, sign onto www.BUCValuPro.com

FREESTYLE CATAMARANS INC
COAST GUARD MFG ID- GSN
FORMERLY GLENMORE SAILBOATS INC

Call 1-800-327-6929 for BUC Personalized Evaluation Service
Or, for 1976 to 1982 boats, sign onto www.BUCValuPro.com

FRERS AND CIBILS
BUENOS AIRES ARGENTIA   See inside cover to adjust price for area

For more recent years, see the BUC Used Boat Price Guide, Volume 1 or Volume 2

LOA FT IN	NAME AND/ OR MODEL	TOP/ RIG	BOAT TYPE	-HULL- MTL TP	TP #	----ENGINE--- HP MFG	BEAM FT IN	WGT LBS	DRAFT FT IN	RETAIL LOW	RETAIL HIGH
			--- 1980 BOATS ---								
36 9	F&C 37	SLP	MS	FBG KL	IB	28D VLVO	11 8	12100	4 9	48600	53400
36 9	F&C 37	SLP	SA/CR	FBG KL	IB	28D VLVO	11 8	12100	4 9	48600	53400
36 9	F&C 37'	SLP	MS	FBG KL	IB	43D VLVO	11 8	12100	4 9	48800	53600
36 9	F&C 37'	SLP	SA/CR	FBC KL	IB	43D VLVO	11 8	12100	4 9	48800	53600
			--- 1974 BOATS ---								
43 7	F&C 44	SLP	SA/CR	F/S KL	IB	48D PERK	12 6	21400	5 5	85200	93600
43 7	F&C 44	KTH	SA/CR	F/S KL	IB	48D PERK	12 6	21400	5 5	86200	94700
43 7	F&C 44'	SLP	SA/CR	F/S KL	IB	48D PERK	12 6	21400	6 7	85200	93600
43 7	F&C 44'	KTH	SA/CR	F/S KL	IB	48D PERK	12 6	21400	6 7	86200	94700

FRIEND SHIP MFG CO
COAST GUARD MFG ID- FDS

Call 1-800-327-6929 for BUC Personalized Evaluation Service
Or, for 1970 to 1979 boats, sign onto www.BUCValuPro.com

FRIENDSHIP

Call 1-800-327-6929 for BUC Personalized Evaluation Service
Or, for 1980 to 1993 boats, sign onto www.BUCValuPro.com

FRITZMEIER BOOTSBAU
FRANCONIA ENTERPRISES LTD

Call 1-800-327-6929 for BUC Personalized Evaluation Service
Or, for 1975 to 1980 boats, sign onto www.BUCValuPro.com

FROG CRAFT
COAST GUARD MFG ID- FGZ

Call 1-800-327-6929 for BUC Personalized Evaluation Service
Or, for 1982 boats, sign onto www.BUCValuPro.com

L E FRY

Call 1-800-327-6929 for BUC Personalized Evaluation Service
Or, for 1909 to 1925 boats, sign onto www.BUCValuPro.com

FT DODGE INC

Call 1-800-327-6929 for BUC Personalized Evaluation Service
Or, for 1959 to 1961 boats, sign onto www.BUCValuPro.com

FUJI YACHTS
DIV OF TOKIWA INTERNATIONAL   See inside cover to adjust price for area
YOKOSUKA JAPAN 238   COAST GUARD MFG ID- FUJ

U S DISTRIBUTOR
NEWPORT BEACH CA

LOA FT IN	NAME AND/ OR MODEL	TOP/ RIG	BOAT TYPE	-HULL- MTL TP	TP #	----ENGINE--- HP MFG	BEAM FT IN	WGT LBS	DRAFT FT IN	RETAIL LOW	RETAIL HIGH
			--- 1982 BOATS ---								
31 6	FUJI 32	KTH	SA/CR	FBG KL	IB	50D PERK	9 10	13115	3 8	37600	41800
34 7	FUJI 35	KTH	SA/CR	FBG KL	IB	50D PERK	10	16302	5	49400	54300
39 2	FUJI 40	SLP	SA/RC	FBG KL	IB	50D PERK	12 8	27007	6	88800	97500
45	FUJI 45	KTH	SA/CR	FBG KL	IB	85D PERK	12 8	30500	5 6	110500	121500
			--- 1981 BOATS ---								
31 6	FUJI 32	SLP	SA/CR	FBG KL	IB	D	9 10	13115	3 8	35400	39300
34 7	FUJI 35	SLP	SA/CR	FBG KL	IB	D	10	16302	5	46700	51300
34 7	FUJI 35	CUT	SA/CR	FBG KL	IB	D	10	16302	5	46700	51300
34 7	FUJI 35	KTH	SA/CR	FBG KL	IB	D	10	16302	5	46700	51300
39 2	FUJI 40	SLP	SA/CR	FBG KL	IB	D	12 8	27000	6	84000	92300
45	FUJI 45AC	KTH	SA/CR	FBG KL	IB	D	12 8	30500	5 6	104000	114500
45	FUJI 45CC	KTH	SA/CR	FBG KL	IB	D	12 8	30500	5 6	104000	114500
			--- 1980 BOATS ---								
32	FUJI 32	SLP	SA/CR	FBG KL	IB	D	9 10	13115	3 8	33700	37400
32	FUJI 32	CUT	SA/CR	FBG KL	IB	D	9 10	13115	3 8	33700	37400
32	FUJI 32	KTH	SA/CR	FBG KL	IB	D	9 10	13115	3 8	33700	37400
34 7	FUJI 35	SLP	SA/CR	FBG KL	IB	D	10	16302	5	44100	49000
34 7	FUJI 35	CUT	SA/CR	FBG KL	IB	D	10	16302	5	44100	49000
34 7	FUJI 35	KTH	SA/CR	FBG KL	IB	D	10	16302	5	44100	49000
39 2	FUJI 40	SLP	SA/CR	FBG KL	IB	40D PERK	12 8	27000	6	79600	87500
45	FUJI 45AC	KTH	SA/CR	FBG KL	IB	60D PERK	12 8	34000	5 6	104000	114500
45	FUJI 45CC	KTH	MS	FBG KL	IB	80D PERK	12 8	33500	5 6	103500	114000
49	FUJI 49 CUSTOM	KTH	SA/CR	AL KL	IB	D	14	35000	6	120500	132500
60	FUJI CUSTOM 60CC	KTH	MS	F/S KL	IB	160D GM	14	51000	7	322000	354000
			--- 1979 BOATS ---								
25 5	FUJI 2260	SLP	SA/CR	FBG KL	IB	D	9 10	3250	5	7400	8500
29 5	FUJI 2300	SLP	SA/CR	FBG KL	IB	D	10	5800	5 6	13900	15800
31 6	FUJI 32	SLP	SA/CR	FBG KL	IB	D	9 10	13115	3 8	32500	36100
31 6	FUJI 32	KTH	SA/CR	FBG KL	IB	D	9 10	13115	3 8	32500	36100
34 7	FUJI 35	SLP	SA/CR	FBG KL	IB	D	10	16302	5	42400	47100
34 7	FUJI 35	KTH	SA/CR	FBG KL	IB	D	10	16302	5	42400	47100
39 2	F415 40	SLP	SA/CR	FBG KL	IB	D	12 8	27000	6	77200	84800
45	F415 45 MKII	SLP	SA/CR	FBG KL	IB	D	12 8	30500	5 6	95600	105000
45	FUJI 45	KTH	SA/CR	MBL KL	IB	D	12 8	30500	5 6	95600	105000
			--- 1978 BOATS ---								
31 6	FUJI 32	CUT	SA/CR	FBG KL	IB	D	9 10	13115	3 8	31300	34800
31 6	FUJI 32	KTH	SA/CR	FBG KL	IB	D	9 10	13115	3 8	31300	34800
34 7	FUJI 35	KTH	SA/CR	FBG KL	IB	D	10	16302	5	40900	45400
34 7	FUJI 35	KTH	SA/CR	FBG KL	IB	D	10	16302	5	40900	45400
39	FUJI 40	SLP	SA/CR	FBG KL	IB	D	12 8	27000	6	73800	81100
39	FUJI 40	CUT	SA/CR	FBG KL	IB	D	12 8	27000	6	73800	81100
45	FUJI 45 CTR-CPT	KTH	SA/CR	FBG KL	IB	D	12 8	30500	5 6	97000	106500
45	FUJI 45 MK II	KTH	SA/CR	FBG KL	IB	D	12 8	30500	5 6	87300	95900
			--- 1977 BOATS ---								
31 6	FUJI 32	SLP	SA/CR	FBG KL	IB	25D VLVO	9 10	13115	3 8	30300	33600
34 7	FUJI 35	CUT	SA/CR	FBG KL	IB	37D PERK	10	16302	5	39400	43800
34 7	FUJI 35	KTH	SA/CR	FBG KL	IB	37D PERK	10	16302	5	39400	43800
45	FUJI 45	KTH	SA/CR	FBG KL	IB	75D WEST	12 8	30500	5 6	89400	98200
45	FUJI 45 AFT COCKPIT	KTH	SA/CR	FBG KL	VD	40D PISC	12 8	30500	5 6	88600	97400
			--- 1976 BOATS ---								
31 10	FUJI 32	CUT	SA/CR	FBG KL	IB	36D	9 9	13115	3 8	29300	32500
31 10	FUJI 32	KTH	SA/CR	FBG KL	IB	36D	9 9	13115	3 8	29300	32500
34 7	FUJI 35	CUT	SA/CR	FBG KL	IB	36D	10	16302	5	38300	42600
34 7	FUJI 35	KTH	SA/CR	FBG KC	IB	36D	10	16302	5	38300	42600
43 9	ALDEN 44	KTH	SA/CR	FBG KL	IB	D	12 8	27000	6	78300	86000
45	FUJI 45	KTH	SA/CR	FBG KL	IB	75D	12 8	30500	5 6	86400	94900
			--- 1975 BOATS ---								
34 7	FUJI 35	KTH	SAIL	FBG KL	IB	25D- 36D	10	16302	5	37200	41300
45	FUJI 45	KTH	SAIL	FBG KL	IB	75D WEST	12 8	30500	5 6	84100	92400
			--- 1974 BOATS ---								
34 7	FUJI 35	KTH	SAIL	FBG KL	IB	36D PERK	10	16302	5	36100	40100
43	FUJI 43	KTH	MS	FBG KL	IB	85D PERK	12 8	25000	5	69400	76300

FULLERS

Call 1-800-327-6929 for BUC Personalized Evaluation Service
Or, for 1965 to 1966 boats, sign onto www.BUCValuPro.com

R FUNG CO LTD
HONG KONG CHINA   See inside cover to adjust price for area

LOA FT IN	NAME AND/ OR MODEL	TOP/ RIG	BOAT TYPE	-HULL- MTL TP	TP #	----ENGINE--- HP MFG	BEAM FT IN	WGT LBS	DRAFT FT IN	RETAIL LOW	RETAIL HIGH
			--- 1966 BOATS ---								
22	GB22	KTH	SA/CR	WD KL			7 3			4700	5400
29 10	SEA-SAILER		MS	WD KL	IB	40D	10 2		4 6	30600	33900
32	DL32		CR	WD	IB	130D	11		2	20800	23100
34 3	OFFSHORE	SLP	SA/CR	WD KL	IB	D	10 6		4 6	35500	39400
36 9	WANDERBIRD	KTH	SA/CR	WD KL	IB	40D	10 6		5	46700	51400
42	DL42		CR	WD	IB	T200D	13		2 9	48000	52700

LOA FT IN	NAME AND/ OR MODEL	TOP/ RIG	BOAT TYPE	-HULL- MTL TP TP	----ENGINE--- # HP MFG	BEAM FT IN	WGT LBS	DRAFT FT IN	RETAIL LOW	RETAIL HIGH
	1965 BOATS									
22	GRAND-BANKS	KTH	SAIL	WD KL		7 3			4650	5350
32	DRAGON-LADY 32	CR		WD	IB 125	11		2	11800	13400
42	DRAGON-LADY 42	CR		WD	IB T130	13		2 9	37300	41500

FUZZY SPECIALTIES
COAST GUARD MFG ID- FYY

Call 1-800-327-6929 for BUC Personalized Evaluation Service
Or, for 1983 to 1992 boats, sign onto www.BUCValuPro.com

G D B MARINE

Call 1-800-327-6929 for BUC Personalized Evaluation Service
Or, for 1979 boats, sign onto www.BUCValuPro.com

G S B DISTRIBUTING INC

Call 1-800-327-6929 for BUC Personalized Evaluation Service
Or, for 1980 boats, sign onto www.BUCValuPro.com

G-CAT INTERNATIONAL INC
COAST GUARD MFG ID- GAT

Call 1-800-327-6929 for BUC Personalized Evaluation Service
Or, for 1976 to 1986 boats, sign onto www.BUCValuPro.com

GALAXIE BOAT WORKS INC
COAST GUARD MFG ID- GBW

Call 1-800-327-6929 for BUC Personalized Evaluation Service
Or, for 1973 to 2008 boats, sign onto www.BUCValuPro.com

GALAXY BOAT MFG CO INC
COLUMBIA SC 29240   COAST GUARD MFG ID- GAL See inside cover to adjust price for area

For more recent years, see the BUC Used Boat Price Guide, Volume 1 or Volume 2

LOA FT IN	NAME AND/ OR MODEL	TOP/ RIG	BOAT TYPE	-HULL- MTL TP TP	----ENGINE--- # HP MFG	BEAM FT IN	WGT LBS	DRAFT FT IN	RETAIL LOW	RETAIL HIGH
	1979 BOATS									
16 4	APOLLO 720	OP	RNBT	FBG TR	IO 120	7	1900		2050	2450
16 9	SATELLITE 700	OP	RNBT	FBG DV	IO 120	6 11	1900		2100	2450
17 9	VENUS 800	OP	RNBT	FBG DV	OB	7 2	1300		1800	2100
17 9	VENUS 800	OP	RNBT	FBG DV	IO 120	7 2	1950		2300	2700
18 3	SUNLINER 820	OP	RNBT	FBG TR	IO 120	7	2000		2350	2750
19 2	STARLINER 1000	OP	RNBT	FBG DV	IO 120	7 6	2000		2600	3000
19 2	STARLINER 1000-V	OP	RNBT	FBG DV	OB	7 4	1500		2100	2500
20 5	JUPITER 2000	OP	RNBT	FBG DV	IO 120	8			2550	3000
	1978 BOATS									
16 4	APOLLO 720	OP	RNBT	FBG TR	IO 120	7	1900		2050	2450
16 9	JAGUAR 700 B/R	OP	RNBT	FBG DV	IO 120 MRCR	6 11	1900		2100	2500
16 9	JAGUAR 700V	OP	RNBT	FBG DV	IO 120 MRCR	6 11	1900		2050	2450
17 9	VENUS 800	OP	RNBT	FBG DV	OB	7 2	1300		1750	2100
17 9	VENUS 800	OP	RNBT	FBG DV	IO 120 MRCR	7 2	1950		2300	2700
18 3	SUNLINER 820	OP	RNBT	FBG TR	IO 120 MRCR	7	2000		2350	2750
19 2	STARLINER 1000 B/R	OP	RNBT	FBG DV	OB	7 6	1500		2100	2500
19 2	STARLINER 1000 B/R	OP	RNBT	FBG DV	IO 120 MRCR	7 6	2000		2550	3000
19 2	STARLINER 1000V	OP	RNBT	FBG DV	OB	7 6	1500		2050	2400
19 2	STARLINER 1000V	OP	RNBT	FBG DV	IO 120 MRCR	7 6	2000		2550	2950
19 2	STARLINER LTD 1000BR	OP	RNBT	FBG DV	IO 120 MRCR	7 6	2000		2650	3100
19 2	STARLINER LTD 1000V	OP	RNBT	FBG DV	IO 120 MRCR	7 6	2000		2600	3050
20 3	TOM-CAT 2000 B/R	OP	RNBT	FBG DV	IO 120 MRCR	7 9	2500		2850	3300
20 3	TOM-CAT 2000 CC	OP	CUD	FBG DV	IO 120 MRCR	7 11	2500		2950	3450
20 3	TOM-CAT 2000V	OP	RNBT	FBG DV	IO 120 MRCR	7 9	2500		2800	3250
	1975 BOATS									
16 4	APOLLO	OP	RNBT	FBG	IO 188	7	1000		1700	2050
16 10	SATELLITE	OP	RNBT	FBG	IO 120-188	6 10	1050		1750	2150
17 8	SUNLINER	OP	RNBT	FBG	IO 120-188	7	1100		2000	2400
18 8	PANTHER	OP	RNBT	FBG	OB	7 2	1225		1700	2000
18 8	PANTHER	OP	RNBT	FBG	IO 120	7 2	1225		2300	2700
18 8	PANTHER	OP	RNBT	FBG	IO 255	7 2	1225		2500	2900
18 8	PANTHER W/T	OP	RNBT	FBG	OB	7 2	1225		1700	2000
18 8	PANTHER W/T	OP	RNBT	FBG	IO 120	7 2	1225		2300	2700
18 8	PANTHER W/T	OP	RNBT	FBG	IO 255	7 2	1225		2500	2900

C C GALBRAITH & SONS INC
Call 1-800-327-6929 for BUC Personalized Evaluation Service
Or, for 1950 to 1961 boats, sign onto www.BUCValuPro.com

GALE FORCE
Call 1-800-327-6929 for BUC Personalized Evaluation Service
Or, for 1982 boats, sign onto www.BUCValuPro.com

GALION YACHTS
Call 1-800-327-6929 for BUC Personalized Evaluation Service
Or, for 1969 to 1974 boats, sign onto www.BUCValuPro.com

GALLART SHIPYARDS
BARCELONA SPAIN   See inside cover to adjust price for area

For more recent years, see the BUC Used Boat Price Guide, Volume 1 or Volume 2

LOA FT IN	NAME AND/ OR MODEL	TOP/ RIG	BOAT TYPE	-HULL- MTL TP TP	----ENGINE--- # HP MFG	BEAM FT IN	WGT LBS	DRAFT FT IN	RETAIL LOW	RETAIL HIGH
	1983 BOATS									
36	GALLART 10.50 MP		CR	FBG DV	IB T235D	12	15000		54400	59800
36	GALLART 36		CBNCR	FBG DV	IB T250D GM	12 9	19000	3 9	67000	73600
44	GALLART 13.50 MP		CR	FBG DV	IB T340D	13	26000		88800	97600
44	GALLART 13.50 MS		MY	FBG DS	IB 600D	14	25000		94000	103500
44	GALLART 44		CBNCR	FBG DV	IB T500D	13 5	25000	4 2	103000	113500
44	GALLART 44	SLP	MS	FBG KL	SD T 61D VLVO	19 2	26000	5 6	138000	151500
	1980 BOATS									
35	GALLART 10.50		CR	FBG SV	IB 400D	13 2			46000	50500
45	GALLART 13.50		CR	FBG SV	IB 600D	13 5			77200	84900
	1979 BOATS									
35	GALLART		CR	FBG DV	IB T200D	12 5			44700	49700
44	GALLART 13.50	SLP	MS	FBG KL	IB T 70D	14	25387		111000	122000
45	GALLART		CR	FBG DV	IB T300D	14			72200	79400
	1978 BOATS									
34 6	GALLART 10.5 MP	FB	MY	FBG DV	IB T200D VLVO	11 10	15873	3 8	46500	51100
34 6	GALLART 10.5 MP-2	FB	MY	FBG DV	IB T200D CUM	11 10	15873	3 8	46700	51400
44 4	GALLART 13.5 MP	SLP	MS	FBG KL	IB T 70D PERK	14 2	25000	5 9	105500	116000
44 4	GALLART 13.5 MP-2	FB	MY	FBG DV	IB T300D GM	13	27558	3 9	88800	97500
44 4	GALLART 13.5 MP-3	FB	MY	FBG DV	IB T300D VLVO	13	27558	3 9	82200	90300
	1976 BOATS									
34 2	GALLART 10.5 MP		CR	FBG DV	IB T200D VLVO	12	14500	3	37600	41800
43 4	GALLART 13.5 MP		DC	FBG DV	IB T270	12	14500	3	55200	60600
43 4	GALLART 13.5 MP		DC	FBG DV	IB T325	12	14500	3	56500	62100
43 4	GALLART 13.5 MP		DC	FBG DV	IB T300D VLVO	13 2	23000	3	80600	88600
55	GALLART 19M		MY	FBG DV	IB T450	17		4 6	109500	120000
55	GALLART 19M		MY	FBG DV	IB T650	17		4 6	117500	129000
	1975 BOATS									
43 4	GALLART 13.5 MP		DC	FBG DV	IB T250	13	23000	3 10	64700	71100
	1974 BOATS									
40	GALLART 12 MP		CR	FBG DV	IO 488	13		3	45700	50200
	1972 BOATS									
40	GALLART 40		SF	WD	IB T210	13 1		1 10	44500	49500
40	GALLART 40		SF	WD	IB T210D	13 1		1 10	55700	61200
	1968 BOATS									
23 7	CUTLASS	SLP	SAIL	WD KL		7		4	7200	8300
27	CUTLASS MAJOR	SLP	SAIL	FBG KL		8 8		4 7	10700	12200
27	CUTLASS MAJOR	SLP	SAIL	WD KL		8 8		4 7	10700	12200
	1967 BOATS									
30 3	CARLSON 30	SLP	SA/OD	WD KL		9		5 2	9150	10400

GALLATIN BOAT WORKS INC
COAST GUARD MFG ID- GLT

Call 1-800-327-6929 for BUC Personalized Evaluation Service
Or, for 1970 to 1974 boats, sign onto www.BUCValuPro.com

GALLEON INDUSTRIES INC
Call 1-800-327-6929 for BUC Personalized Evaluation Service
Or, for 1970 boats, sign onto www.BUCValuPro.com

GAMBLER MARINE
COAST GUARD MFG ID- GAN

Call 1-800-327-6929 for BUC Personalized Evaluation Service
Or, for 1983 to 1984 boats, sign onto www.BUCValuPro.com

GANNON YACHTS
PETALUMA CA 94952   COAST GUARD MFG ID- GCB See inside cover to adjust price for area

LOA FT IN	NAME AND/ OR MODEL	TOP/ RIG	BOAT TYPE	-HULL- MTL TP	TP	#	--ENGINE--- HP	MFG	BEAM FT IN	WGT LBS	DRAFT FT IN	RETAIL LOW	RETAIL HIGH
							1979 BOATS						
39 3	FREYA 39	CUT	SA/CR	FBG	KL	IB	30D	YAN	11 3	23000	6	70800	77800

THE GARWOOD BOAT CO
ALGONAC MI   See inside cover to adjust price for area

For more recent years, see the BUC Used Boat Price Guide, Volume 1 or Volume 2

LOA FT IN	NAME AND/ OR MODEL	TOP/ RIG	BOAT TYPE	-HULL- MTL TP	TP	#	--ENGINE--- HP	MFG	BEAM FT IN	WGT LBS	DRAFT FT IN	RETAIL LOW	RETAIL HIGH
							1948 BOATS						
22				WD	IB			CHRY				**	**
							1946 BOATS						
16		OP	UTL	WD	IB							**	**
17 6	DOUBLE COCKPIT	OP	RNBT	WD	IB		93-115		6 3			2150	2600
17 6	DOUBLE COCKPIT	OP	RNBT	WD	IB		150	GRAY	6 3			2350	2750
18 6		OP	UTL	WD	IB							**	**
19				WD	IB		115	CHRY				**	**
19 5		OP	RNBT	WD	IB							**	**
22 6		HT	SDN	WD	IB							**	**
22 6		OP	UTL	WD	IB							**	**
22 6	STREAMLINER	OP	RNBT	WD	IB							**	**
25 11		HT	OVNTR	WD	IB		T	GRAY				**	**
25 11		HT	OVNTR	WD	IB		T115	CHRY				8600	9900
27 6		OP	RNBT	WD	IB							**	**
							1941 BOATS						
18 6	CABIN-SKIPPER	CBNCR		WD	IB			CHRY				**	**
19 6				WD	IB		150	CHRY				**	**
19 6	DELUXE	RNBT		WD	IB			GRAY				**	**
20 6				WD	IB		117	CHRY				**	**
20 6	CABIN-ROYALE	CBNCR		WD	IB		110	CHRY				3950	4600
20 6	VACATIONER	RNBT		WD	IB		110	CHRY				4050	4700
22 6		RNBT		WD	VD		117	CHRY				6100	7000
24				WD	IB		225	SCRI				**	**
24 6	AMERICAN	RNBT		WD	IB		110	CHRY				6000	6900
24 6	CABIN-ARISTOCRAT	CBNCR		WD	IB		143	CHRY				6750	7750
24 6	OVERNITER	RNBT		WD	IB		110	CHRY				6000	6900
28 6		RNBT		WD	IB		316	SCRI				10500	11900
30	COMMODORE	RNBT		WD	IB		143	CHRY				11400	13000
							1940 BOATS						
20 6				WD	IB			CHRY				**	**
28				WD	IB		316	SCRI				**	**
							1939 BOATS						
16		OP	RNBT	MHG	IB							**	**
19				WD	IB		95-125					**	**
							1938 BOATS						
19				WD	IB		135	CC				**	**
							1937 BOATS						
16		OP	RNBT	WD	IB							**	**
18				WD	IB		62	GRAY				**	**
18		OP	UTL	WD	IB							**	**
18		HT	UTL	WD	IB							**	**
19	2 COCKPITS	OP	RNBT	WD	IB		110					3000	3500
20		OP	UTL	WD	IB							**	**
22				WD	IB		270	CHRY				**	**
22		OP	RNBT	WD	IB							**	**
24		OP	UTL	WD	IB				7 7			**	**
24		HT	UTL	WD	IB				7 7			**	**
25		OP	RNBT	WD	IB		316		7 2			8000	9200
26		HT	CR	WD	IB							**	**
32		HT	CR	WD	IB				10 3			**	**
33		OP	RNBT	WD	IB							**	**
							1936 BOATS						
18				WD	IB		115-125					**	**
19				WD	IB		230	OMC				**	**
20				WD	IB		90	CHRY				**	**
							1935 BOATS						
16				WD	IB		300	CHRY				**	**
22 4		RNBT		WD	IB		145	CC	6 8			5200	6000
							1934 BOATS						
22				WD	IB		125	CHRY				**	**
							1932 BOATS						
18 2		RNBT		WD	IB				5 8			**	**
							1931 BOATS						
28				WD	IB		202	SCRI				**	**
28		RNBT		WD	IB		425		7 2		2 3	11700	13300
33				WD	IB		600					**	**
40	COMMUTING	HT	MY	WD	IB		425					65700	72200
40	COMMUTING	HT	MY	WD	IB		T200					65600	72000
							1930 BOATS						
28				WD	IB		225	SCRI				**	**
30				WD	IB		T500	CHEV				**	**
							1928 BOATS						
22				WD	IB		195	OMC				**	**
28				WD	IB			CHRY				**	**
	IB 125 CHRY **		** , IB	300	CHRY		**	** , IB	550	CHEV		**	**
							1927 BOATS						
26				WD	IB		225	SCRI				**	**
28				WD	IB		380	CHRY				**	**
33				WD	IB		600					**	**
							1926 BOATS						
33				WD	IB		550					**	**

GAVIN-SUMMERHILL CUST YTS INC
COAST GUARD MFG ID- GVN

Call 1-800-327-6929 for BUC Personalized Evaluation Service
Or, for 1979 to 1980 boats, sign onto www.BUCValuPro.com

GDANSK BOAT YARD

Call 1-800-327-6929 for BUC Personalized Evaluation Service
Or, for 1972 to 1974 boats, sign onto www.BUCValuPro.com

GEMICO CORPORATION
COAST GUARD MFG ID- GMC

Call 1-800-327-6929 for BUC Personalized Evaluation Service
Or, for 1968 to 1974 boats, sign onto www.BUCValuPro.com

GEMINI BOATS INC

Call 1-800-327-6929 for BUC Personalized Evaluation Service
Or, for 1969 to 1970 boats, sign onto www.BUCValuPro.com

GEMINI MARINE INC
COAST GUARD MFG ID- GEM

Call 1-800-327-6929 for BUC Personalized Evaluation Service
Or, for 1970 to 1974 boats, sign onto www.BUCValuPro.com

GEMINI PRODUCTS INC
COAST GUARD MFG ID- GPT

Call 1-800-327-6929 for BUC Personalized Evaluation Service
Or, for 1979 to 1982 boats, sign onto www.BUCValuPro.com

GENERAL BOATS CORPORATION

EDENTON NC 27932   COAST GUARD MFG ID- GBX See inside cover to adjust price for area

For more recent years, see the BUC Used Boat Price Guide, Volume 1 or Volume 2

LOA FT IN	NAME AND/ OR MODEL	TOP/ RIG	BOAT TYPE	-HULL- MTL TP	TP	----ENGINE--- # HP	MFG	BEAM FT IN	WGT LBS	DRAFT FT IN	RETAIL LOW	RETAIL HIGH
----- 1983 BOATS -----
22	RHODES 22	SLP	SAIL	FBG	KC	OB		8	2500	1 8	4950	5650
----- 1982 BOATS -----
22	RHODES 22	SLP	SAIL	FBG	KC	OB		8	2500	1 8	4650	5350
----- 1981 BOATS -----
22	RHODES 22	SLP	SAIL	FBG	KC	OB		8	2500	1 8	4400	5050
----- 1980 BOATS -----
22	RHODES-CONTINENTAL	SLP	SAIL	FBG	KC	OB		8	2500	1 8	4150	4800
----- 1979 BOATS -----
22	RHODES-CONTINENTAL	SLP	SAIL	FBG	KC	OB		8	2500	1 8	4000	4650
----- 1978 BOATS -----
22	RHODES-CONTINENTAL	SLP	SAIL	FBG	KC	OB		8	2500	1 8	3850	4450
----- 1977 BOATS -----
22	RHODES-CONTINENTAL	SLP	SAIL	FBG	KC	OB		8	2500	1 8	3700	4300
----- 1976 BOATS -----
22	RHODES-CONTINENTAL	SLP	SAIL	FBG	KC	OB		8	2500	1 8	3600	4200
----- 1975 BOATS -----
22	RHODES CONTINENTAL	SLP	SAIL	FBG	KC	OB		8	2000	4 6	3050	3500
----- 1974 BOATS -----
22	RHODES DELUXE	SLP	SAIL	FBG	KC	OB		8	2000	1 6	3100	3600
22	RHODES-CONTINENTAL	SLP	SAIL	FBG	KC	OB		8	2000	1 6	2800	3250
----- 1973 BOATS -----
22	RHODES DELUXE	SLP	SAIL	FBG	KC	OB		8	2000	1 6	3150	3650
22	RHODES-CONTINENTAL	SLP	SAIL	FBG	KC	OB		8	2000	1 6	2600	3050
----- 1972 BOATS -----
22	RHODES-CONTINENTAL	SLP	SAIL	FBG	KC	OB		8	1850	4	2700	3150
----- 1971 BOATS -----
22	RHODES-CONTINENTAL	SLP	SAIL	FBG	KC	OB		8	1850	4	2650	3050
----- 1970 BOATS -----
22	RHODES-CONTINENTAL	SLP	SA/OD	FBG	KC	OB		8	1600	1 6	2400	2800
----- 1969 BOATS -----
17 3	PICNIC 17	SLP	SAIL	FBG	KC	JT	5	6 8	800	1 1	1800	2150
----- 1968 BOATS -----
17 3	PICNIC 17	SLP	SAIL	FBG	KC	JT		6 8	800	1	1900	2250
----- 1967 BOATS -----
17 3	PICNIC 17	SLP	SAIL	FBG	KC	JT	4	6 8		1	2350	2750

GENERAL DEVELOPMENT CO

Call 1-800-327-6929 for BUC Personalized Evaluation Service
Or, for 1965 boats, sign onto www.BUCValuPro.com

GENERAL FIBERGLASS CORP

SKIMMAR BOATS   COAST GUARD MFG ID- GFH
FORMERLY AERO NAUTICAL INC

Call 1-800-327-6929 for BUC Personalized Evaluation Service
Or, for 1969 to 1979 boats, sign onto www.BUCValuPro.com

GENERAL FIBERGLASS PROD CORP

FIBERCRAFT

Call 1-800-327-6929 for BUC Personalized Evaluation Service
Or, for 1968 to 1970 boats, sign onto www.BUCValuPro.com

GENERAL MARINE CORP

COAST GUARD MFG ID- XSW

Call 1-800-327-6929 for BUC Personalized Evaluation Service
Or, for 1979 boats, sign onto www.BUCValuPro.com

GENERAL PROPULSION

GLASSJET

Call 1-800-327-6929 for BUC Personalized Evaluation Service
Or, for 1967 to 1973 boats, sign onto www.BUCValuPro.com

GEORGETOWN YACHT BASIN INC

Call 1-800-327-6929 for BUC Personalized Evaluation Service
Or, for 1959 to 1960 boats, sign onto www.BUCValuPro.com

GEORGIAN STEEL BOATS

DIV OF ABICON LIMITED   COAST GUARD MFG ID- GSB

Call 1-800-327-6929 for BUC Personalized Evaluation Service
Or, for 1966 to 1979 boats, sign onto www.BUCValuPro.com

GERRARD BOAT CO

COAST GUARD MFG ID- GBV

Call 1-800-327-6929 for BUC Personalized Evaluation Service
Or, for 1977 to 1983 boats, sign onto www.BUCValuPro.com

GIACOMO COLOMBO

Call 1-800-327-6929 for BUC Personalized Evaluation Service
Or, for 1980 to 1996 boats, sign onto www.BUCValuPro.com

GIBSON BOAT CO

TULSA OK 74136   COAST GUARD MFG ID- GCW See inside cover to adjust price for area

For more recent years, see the BUC Used Boat Price Guide, Volume 1 or Volume 2

LOA FT IN	NAME AND/ OR MODEL	TOP/ RIG	BOAT TYPE	-HULL- MTL TP	TP	----ENGINE--- # HP	MFG	BEAM FT IN	WGT LBS	DRAFT FT IN	RETAIL LOW	RETAIL HIGH
----- 1983 BOATS -----
20 9	GBC 9080101	OP	UTL	KEV	TR	IO	220D	SAAB 6	2175	7	3200	3750
21	GBC 9080601	OP	OPFSH	KEV	TR	IO	160	OMC 7	2900	8	2000	2400
23	GBC 9080801	OP	UTL	KEV	TR	IO	220D	SAAB 7	3000	8	4200	4850
24	GBC 9080501	OP	UTL	KEV	TR	IO	220D	SAAB 7 6	3100	7	4550	5250
25	GBC 9080401	FB	UTL	KEV	TR	IO	220D	SAAB 7 6	3175	9	4650	5350
29	GBC 9080301	FB	UTL	KEV	DV	IO	T220D	SAAB 8 9	6100	1	10500	11900
36	GBC 9080701	FB	HB	FBG	DV	IO	T220D	SAAB 14	9600	2 9	40600	45100
49	GBC 9080901	FB	HB	FBG	DV	IO	T220D	SAAB 16	10300	2 9	51200	56200

GIBSON FIBERGLASS PROD INC

GOODLETTSVILLE TN 37072 COAST GUARD MFG ID- GBN See inside cover to adjust price for area

For more recent years, see the BUC Used Boat Price Guide, Volume 1 or Volume 2

LOA FT IN	NAME AND/ OR MODEL	TOP/ RIG	BOAT TYPE	-HULL- MTL TP	TP	----ENGINE--- # HP	MFG	BEAM FT IN	WGT LBS	DRAFT FT IN	RETAIL LOW	RETAIL HIGH
----- 1983 BOATS -----
36	GIBSON 36	HT HB		FBG	SV	IO	138	VLVO 12			22200	24700
	IO 200 VLVO	22400	24900, IO	225	VLVO	25000, IO 260	VLVO	22900	25500
	IO 130D VLVO	24100	26800, IO	T138	VLVO	23900	26500, VD T220	CRUS	24700	27500
	VD T225 CHRY	24100	26800, VD	T270	CRUS	25000	27800
42	GIBSON 42	HT HB		FBG	SV	IO	138	VLVO 12			27100	30100
	IO 130D VLVO	40100	44500, IO	T138	VLVO	28800	32000, VD T220	CRUS	29200	32400
	VD T225 CHRY	28600	31800, VD	T270	CRUS	29400	32700
42	LAZYCRUZ 42	HT HB		FBG	SV	IO	138	VLVO 12			27100	30100
42	LAZYCRUZ 42	HT HB		FBG	SV	IO	130D	VLVO 12			40100	44500
42	LAZYCRUZ 42	HT HB		FBG	SV	IO	T138	VLVO 12			28800	32000
44	GIBSON 44	HT HB		FBG	SV	IO	138	VLVO 14			30800	34200
	IO 130D VLVO	43700	48600, IO	T138	VLVO	32300	35900, VD T270	CRUS	32700	36300
	VD T225 CHRY	32700	36300
44	GIBSON 44 EXECUTIVE	HT HB		FBG	SV	IO	130D	VLVO 14			43700	48600
	IO T138 VLVO	32300	35900, VD	T270	CRUS	32700	36300, VD T330	CHRY	32700	36300
	VD T350 CRUS	33700	37500
50	GIBSON 50	HT HB		FBG	SV	IO	138	VLVO 14			39500	43800
	IO 130D VLVO	49800	54700, IO	T138	VLVO	40900	45400, VD T270	CRUS	40900	45400
	VD T330 CHRY	40900	45500, VD	T350	CRUS	41900	46500
50	GIBSON 50 EXECUTIVE	HT HB		FBG	SV	IO	130D	VLVO 14			49800	54700
	IO T138 VLVO	40900	45400, VD	T270	CRUS	40900	45400, VD T330	CHRY	40900	45500
	VD T350 CRUS	41900	46500

```
GIBSON FIBERGLASS PROD INC    -CONTINUED      See inside cover to adjust price for area
  LOA  NAME AND/           TOP/ BOAT  -HULL-  ----ENGINE---  BEAM   WGT  DRAFT RETAIL RETAIL
  FT IN  OR MODEL           RIG  TYPE  MTL TP TP # HP  MFG   FT IN  LBS  FT IN  LOW    HIGH
------------------- 1983 BOATS ---------------------------------------------------------
  50   LAZYCRUZ 50          HT   HB   FBG SV IO  138   VLVO 14                 39500  43800
  50   LAZYCRUZ 50          HT   HB   FBG SV IO  130D  VLVO 14                 49800  54700
  50   LAZYCRUZ 50          HT   HB   FBG SV IO T138   VLVO 14                 40900  45400
------------------- 1982 BOATS ---------------------------------------------------------
  36   GIBSON 36            HT   HB   FBG SV IB  220        12   10500  2  4   20000  22200
  42   GIBSON 42            HT   HB   FBG SV IO  145        12   14000  2  4   21700  24100
  42   GIBSON 42            HT   HB   FBG SV IB T220       12   14000  2  4   22800  25300
  42   GIBSON 42 EXECUTIVE  HT   HB   FBG SV IB  220        12   15125  2  4   23100  25700
  50   GIBSON 50            HT   HB   FBG SV IO T145       14   20000  2  4   32700  36300
  50   GIBSON 50            HT   HB   FBG SV IB T270       14   20000  2  4   32800  36500
  50   GIBSON 50 EXECUTIVE  HT   HB   FBG SV IB T270       14   20000  2  4   32800  36500
------------------- 1981 BOATS ---------------------------------------------------------
  36   GIBSON 36            HT   HB   FBG SV VD  220        12   10500  2  4   19900  22200
  36   GIBSON 36 EXECUTIVE  HT   HB   FBG SV IO  330        12   11500  2  4   21800  24300
  36   GIBSON 36 EXECUTIVE  HT   HB   FBG SV VD T220       12   11500  2  4   22100  24500
  42   GIBSON 42            HT   HB   FBG SV VD T220       12   14000  2  4   22900  25400
  42   LAZYCRUZ 42          HT   HB   FBG SV IO  145        12          2  4   25800  28700
  50   GIBSON 50            HT   HB   FBG SV VD T270       14   20000  2  4   32200  35800
  50   GIBSON 50 EXECUTIVE  HT   HB   FBG SV VD T270       14   20000  2  4   32200  35800
------------------- 1980 BOATS ---------------------------------------------------------
  36   GIBSON 36 EXECUTIVE  HT   HB   FBG SV IO  330   MRCR 12   11500  2  4   21500  23900
       VD T220   CRUS 22100  24600, VD T220   PCM   21700  24100, VD T225   CHRY 21500  23900
       VD T270   CRUS 22400  24900, VD T270   PCM   21900  24400

  36   GIBSON 36 EXECUTIVE  FB   HB   FBG SV IO  330   MRCR 12   11500  2  4   21500  23900
       VD T220   CRUS 22100  24600, VD T220   PCM   21700  24100, VD T225   CHRY 21500  23900
       VD T270   CRUS 22400  24900, VD T270   PCM   21900  24400

  36   GIBSON 36 STANDARD   HT   HB   FBG SV VD  220   CRUS 12   10500  2  4   19900  22100
       VD  220   PCM  19600  21800, VD  225   CHRY 19600  21700, VD  270   CRUS 20000  22200
       VD  270   PCM  19800  21900, IO  330   MRCR 20400  22600, VD T220   CRUS 21300  23700
       VD T220   PCM  20900  23200, VD T225   CHRY 20700  23000, VD T270   CRUS 21600  24000
       VD T270   PCM  21100  23500

  36   GIBSON 36 STANDARD   FB   HB   FBG SV VD  220   CRUS 12   10500  2  4   19900  22100
       VD  220   PCM  19600  21800, VD  225   CHRY 19600  21700, VD  270   CRUS 20000  22200
       VD  270   PCM  19800  21900, IO  330   MRCR 20400  22600, VD T220   CRUS 21300  23700
       VD T220   PCM  20900  23200, VD T225   CHRY 20700  23000, VD T270   CRUS 21600  24000
       VD T270   PCM  21100  23500

  42   GIBSON 42 EXECUTIVE  HT   HB   FBG SV VD T220   CRUS 12   15125  2  4   24200  26900
       VD T220   PCM  23900  26500, VD T225   CHRY 23700  26400, VD T270   CRUS 24500  27200
       VD T270   PCM  24100  26700

  42   GIBSON 42 EXECUTIVE  FB   HB   FBG SV VD T220   CRUS 12   15125  2  4   25300  28100
       VD T220   PCM  24900  27600, VD T225   CHRY 24700  27500, VD T270   CRUS 25500  28300
       VD T270   PCM  25100  27900

  42   GIBSON 42 STANDARD   HT   HB   FBG SV VD T220   CRUS 12   14000  2  4   22900  25400
       VD T220   PCM  22500  25000, VD T225   CHRY 22400  24800, VD T270   CRUS 22900  25400
       VD T270   PCM  22700  25200

  42   GIBSON 42 STANDARD   FB   HB   FBG SV VD T220   CRUS 12   14000  2  4   23500  26200
       VD T220   PCM  23200  25700, VD T225   CHRY 23000  25600, VD T270   CRUS 23800  26400
       VD T270   PCM  23400  26000

  50   GIBSON 50 EXECUTIVE  HT   HB   FBG SV VD  270   CRUS 14   20000  2  4   31600  35100
       VD  270   PCM  31400  34900, VD  350   CRUS 32000  35600, VD  350   PCM  31800  35300

  50   GIBSON 50 EXECUTIVE  FB   HB   FBG SV VD  270   CRUS 14   20000  2  4   34400  38200
       VD  270   PCM  34200  38000, VD  350   CRUS 34800  38700, VD  350   PCM  34600  38400

  50   GIBSON 50 STANDARD   HT   HB   FBG SV VD  270   CRUS 14   20000  2  4   29800  33100
       VD  270   PCM  29700  33000, VD  350   CRUS 30300  33700, VD  350   PCM  30100  33400

  50   GIBSON 50 STANDARD   FB   HB   FBG SV VD  270   CRUS 14   20000  2  4   32500  36200
       VD  270   PCM  32400  36000, VD  350   CRUS 33100  36700, VD  350   PCM  32800  36500
------------------- 1979 BOATS ---------------------------------------------------------
  36   GIBSON               HT   HB   FBG SV VD  220   PALM 12   10500  2  4   19300  21500
       VD  225   CHRY 19300  21400, IO  228   MRCR 18800  20900, VD  270   PALM 19500  21600
       IO  330   MRCR 20100  22300, VD T220   PALM 21700  24100, VD T225   CHRY 21600  24000
       VD T270   PALM 21600  24000

  42   GIBSON               HT   HB   FBG SV VD T220   PALM 12   14000  2  4   22200  24600
  42   GIBSON               HT   HB   FBG SV VD T225   CHRY 12   14000  2  4   22000  24500
  42   GIBSON               HT   HB   FBG SV VD T270   PALM 12   14000  2  4   22400  24900
  50   GIBSON               HT   HB   FBG SV VD T270   PALM 14   20000  2  4   31300  34800
  50   GIBSON               HT   HB   FBG SV VD T350   PALM 14   21000  2  4   34000  37800
  50   GIBSON EXEC          HT   HB   FBG SV VD T270   PALM 14   21000  2  4   33200  36900
  50   GIBSON EXEC          HT   HB   FBG SV VD T350   PALM 14   22000  2  4   36000  40000
------------------- 1978 BOATS ---------------------------------------------------------
  36   GIBSON               HT   HB   FBG SV IB  225        12    9600  2  4   17300  19600
  36   GIBSON               HT   HB   FBG SV IB T270       12    9600  2  4   19500  21600
  42   GIBSON               HT   HB   FBG SV IB T225       12   13000  2  4   20600  22900
  42   GIBSON               HT   HB   FBG SV IB T270       12   13000       2  4   20800  23100
  50   GIBSON               HT   HB   FBG SV IB T270       14   20000  2  4   30900  34300
------------------- 1975 BOATS ---------------------------------------------------------
  30   GIBSON               HT   HB   FBG SV IO  225        12    8600  1  7   16800  19000
  36   GIBSON               HT   HB   FBG SV IO  225   MRCR 12    9600  1  7   16500  18700
  36   GIBSON               HT   HB   FBG SV IO T225   MRCR 12    9600  1  7   18600  20600
  36   GIBSON               FB   HB   FBG SV IO  225   MRCR 12    9600  1  7   16500  18700
  36   GIBSON               FB   HB   FBG SV IO T225   MRCR 12    9600  1  7   18600  20600
  42   GIBSON               HT   HB   FBG SV IO  225   MRCR 12   13000  1  7   18900  21000
  42   GIBSON               HT   HB   FBG SV IO T225   MRCR 12   13000  1  7   20000  22200
  42   GIBSON               HT   HB   FBG SV IO  225   MRCR 12   14000  1  7   20700  23100
  42   GIBSON               FB   HB   FBG SV IO T225   MRCR 12   14000  1  7   22000  24400
------------------- 1974 BOATS ---------------------------------------------------------
  30   GIBSON                    HB   FBG     IO  225   CHRY 12    8600  1  7   17400  19700
  30   GIBSON                    HB   FBG     IO T225   CHRY 12    8600  1  7   19500  21600
  30   GIBSON               FB   HB   FBG     IO  225   CHRY 12    8600  1  7   17400  19700
  30   GIBSON               FB   HB   FBG     IO T225   CHRY 12    8600  1  7   19500  21600
  36   GIBSON                    HB   FBG     IO  225   CHRY 12    9600  1  7   17400  19800
  36   GIBSON                    HB   FBG     IO T225   CHRY 12    9600  1  7   19600  21800
  36   GIBSON               FB   HB   FBG     IO  225   CHRY 12    9600  1  7   17400  19800
  36   GIBSON               FB   HB   FBG     IO T225   CHRY 12    9600  1  7   19600  21800
  42   GIBSON                    HB   FBG     IO  225   CHRY 12   14000  1  7   20900  23200
  42   GIBSON                    HB   FBG     IO T225   CHRY 12   14000  1  7   22100  24500
  42   GIBSON               FB   HB   FBG     IO  225   CHRY 12   14000  1  7   21300  23600
  42   GIBSON               FB   HB   FBG     IO T225   CHRY 12   14000  1  7   22500  25000
------------------- 1973 BOATS ---------------------------------------------------------
  30   GIBSON 30                 HB   FBG     IO  225   CHRY 12               1  7   18700  21100
  30   GIBSON 30                 HB   FBG     IO T225   CHRY 12               1  7   20800  23100
  36   GIBSON 36                 HB   FBG     IO  255   CHRY 12               1  7   21300  23700
  36   GIBSON 36                 HB   FBG     IO T225   CHRY 12               1  7   22500  25000
  36   GIBSON 36                 HB   FBG     IO T225   CHRY 12               1  7   22800  25200
  42   GIBSON                    HB   FBG     IO  225   CHRY 12               1  7   25000  27800
  42   GIBSON                    HB   FBG     IO T225   CHRY 12               1  7   26500  29400
  42   GIBSON                    HB   FBG     IO T225   CHRY 12               1  7   26500  29400
------------------- 1972 BOATS ---------------------------------------------------------
  30   GIBSON                    HB   FBG     IO  215   MRCR 12    8600            1  7   17500  19300
       IO  225   CHRY 17100  19400, VD  225   CHRY 18800  20900, IO  270   MRCR       17500  19900
       IO T155-T225      20000  22900

  30   GIBSON               FB   HB   FBG     IO  215   MRCR 12                     1  7   18700  20800
       IO  225   CHRY 18800  20900, VD  225   CHRY 18800  20900, IO  270   MRCR       19300  21400
       IO T155-T225      20000  22900

  36   GIBSON                    HB   FBG     IO  215   MRCR 12    9600            1  7   17100  19400
       IO  225   CHRY 17100  19400, VD  225   CHRY 17500  19900, IO  270   MRCR       17500  19900
       IO  280   CHRY 18100  20100, IO  300   CHRY 18400  20500, IO T155   OMC        18700  20800
       IO T225   CHRY 19300  21400

  36   GIBSON               FB   HB   FBG     IO  215   MRCR 12                     1  7   20800  23100
       IO  225   CHRY 20900  23200, VD  225   CHRY 21400  23800, IO  270   MRCR       21300  23700
       IO  280   CHRY 21400  23800, IO  300   CHRY 21800  24200, IO T155   OMC        21700  24100
       IO T225   CHRY 22300  24800

  42   GIBSON                    HB   FBG     IO T215   MRCR 12   14000            1  7   21600  24000
       IO T225   CHRY 21700  24100, VD T225   CHRY 21600  24000, IO T270   MRCR       22400  24900

  42   GIBSON                    HB   FBG     IO T215   MRCR 12                     1  7   26700  29700
       IO T225   CHRY 26800  29800, VD T225   CHRY 26800  29800, IO T270   MRCR       27600  30600
------------------- 1971 BOATS ---------------------------------------------------------
  30   GIBSON 30                 HB   FBG     IO  225        12    8000  1  7   16000  18200
  36   GIBSON 36                 HB   FBG     IO  225        12   10000  1  7   17200  18400
  42   GIBSON 42                 HB   FBG     IO T225       12   12000  1  7   19300  21500
```

GIDLEY-CREW

GLANDER BOATS INC
TAVERNIER FL 33070   COAST GUARD MFG ID- GLB See inside cover to adjust price for area

For more recent years, see the BUC Used Boat Price Guide, Volume 1 or Volume 2

LOA FT IN	NAME AND/ OR MODEL	TOP/ RIG	BOAT TYPE	-HULL- MTL TP	----ENGINE--- TP # HP MFG	BEAM FT IN	WGT LBS	DRAFT FT IN	RETAIL LOW	RETAIL HIGH
				1983 BOATS						
23	CAY	SLP	SAIL	FBG KL IB	D	8	6800	3	8650	9950
33	TAVANA	SLP	SAIL	FBG KC IB	D 10	12900	3	18900	21000
33	TAVANA	YWL	SAIL	FBG KC IB	D 10	12900	3	18900	21000
				1982 BOATS						
23	CAY	SLP	SAIL	FBG KL IB	D	8	6800	3	8150	9350
33	TAVANA	SLP	SAIL	FBG KC IB	D 10	12900	3	17500	19900
33	TAVANA	YWL	SAIL	FBG KC IB	D 10	12900	3	17500	19900
				1981 BOATS						
23	CAY	SLP	SAIL	FBG KL IB	D	8	6800	3	7650	8800
33	TAVANA	SLP	SAIL	FBG KC IB	D 10	12900	3	16500	18800
33	TAVANA	YWL	SAIL	FBG KC IB	D 10	12900	3	16500	18800
				1980 BOATS						
23	CAY	SLP	SAIL	FBG KL IB	D	8	6500	3	6950	8000
33	TAVANA	SLP	SAIL	FBG KC IB	D 10	12500	3	15300	17400
33	TAVANA	YWL	SAIL	FBG KC IB	D 10	12500	3	15300	17400
				1979 BOATS						
23	CAY	SLP	SAIL	FBG KL IB	6D VLVO 8	6500	3	6550	7550
33	TAVANA	SLP	SAIL	FBG KC IB	36D VLVO 10	12500	3	14400	16400
33	TAVANA	YWL	SAIL	FBG KC IB	36D VLVO 10	12500	3	14400	16400
				1978 BOATS						
23	CAY KIT	SLP	SAIL	FBG KL IB	13D 8	6800	3	6700	7750
33	TAVANA KIT	SLP	SAIL	FBG KC IB	25D 10	12000	3	13400	15200
33	TAVANA KIT	YWL	SAIL	FBG KC IB	25D 10	12000	3	13400	15200
				1977 BOATS						
23	2 CAY KIT	SLP	SA/CR	FBG KL IB	D	8	6800	3	6550	7550
33	TAVANA KIT	SLP	SA/CR	FBG KC IB	D 10	12000	3	12800	14600
33	TAVANA KIT	YWL	SA/CR	FBG KC IB	D 10	12000	3	12800	14600
				1976 BOATS						
27	6 CAY KIT	SLP	SAIL	FBG KL IB	D	8	6800	3	6850	7900
33	TAVANA KIT	SLP	MS	FBG CB IB	D 10	12000	3	12300	14000
33	TAVANA KIT	YWL	MS	FBG CB IB	D 10	12000	3	12300	14000
				1975 BOATS						
23	9 CAY KIT	SLP	SAIL	FBG KL IB	D	8	6800	3	6250	7150
33	TAVANA KIT	SLP	SAIL	FBG CB IB	D 10	12000	3	12000	13600
33	TAVANA KIT	YWL	SAIL	FBG CB IB	D 10	12000	6 3	12000	13600
				1974 BOATS						
23	9 CAY	SLP	SAIL	FBG KL IB	15D VLVO 8	6800	3	6050	6950
33	TAVANA	SLP	SAIL	FBG CB IB	30D VLVO 10	12500	3	12100	13800
33	TAVANA	YWL	SAIL	FBG CB IB	30D VLVO 10	12500	3	12100	13800
				1973 BOATS						
23	9 CAY	SLP	SAIL	FBG KL IB	15D 8	6800	3	5900	6750
33	TAVANA	SLP	SAIL	FBG CB IB	30D VLVO 10	12000	3	11400	12900
33	TAVANA	YWL	SAIL	FBG CB IB	30D VLVO 10	12000	3	11400	12900
				1972 BOATS						
23	CAY	SLP	SA/RC	FBG KL IB	D	8		3	5500	6300
33	TAVANA	SLP	SAIL	FBG IB	D 10	12000	3	11100	12600
33	TAVANA	YWL	SAIL	FBG IB	D 10	12000	3	11100	12600
				1971 BOATS						
23	CAY	SLP	SAIL	FBG KL IB	D	8		3	5350	6150
33	TAVANA	SLP	SAIL	FBG IB	D 10	12000	3	10900	12400
33	TAVANA	YWL	SAIL	FBG IB	D 10	12000	3	10900	12400
				1970 BOATS						
22	9 CAY	SLP	SAIL	FBG KL IB	30D 8	6000	3	4850	5600
33	TAVANA	SLP	SA/OD	FBG KC IB	D 10	12000	3	10700	12200
33	TAVANA	YWL	SA/OD	FBG KC IB	D 10	12000	3	10700	12200
				1969 BOATS						
22	9 CAY		SA/OD	FBG KL IB	D	8	6000	3	4700	5400
33	TAVANA	SLP	SAIL	FBG KC IB	D 10	12000	3	10500	12000
33	TAVANA	YWL	SAIL	FBG KC IB	D 10	12000	3	10500	12000
				1968 BOATS						
33	TAVANA	SLP	SA/CR	FBG	OB	10	12000	3	10400	11900
33	TAVANA	YWL	SA/CR	FBG	OB	10	12000	3	10400	11900
				1967 BOATS						
23	CAY	SLP	SA/OD	FBG KL IB	D	8	6000	3	4450	5100
33	TAVANA	SLP	SA/CR	FBG	OB	10	12000	3	10300	11700
33	TAVANA	YWL	SA/CR	FBG	OB	10	12000	3	10300	11700
				1966 BOATS						
23	CAY	SLP	SA/OD	FBG KL IB	D	8	6000	3	4400	5050
33	TAVANA	SLP	SA/OD	FBG KC IB	D 10	12000	3	10200	11600
				1965 BOATS						
23	CAY	SLP	SAIL	FBG KL	8	6000	3	4150	4850
33	TAVANA	SLP	SA/CR	FBG KC IB	D 10	12000	3	10200	11500
33	TAVANA	YWL	SA/CR	FBG KC IB	D 10	12000	3	10200	11500
				1961 BOATS						
22	9 CAY	SLP	SA/OD	FBG KL IB	D	8	6000	3	4250	4950
33	TAVANA	SLP	SA/CR	FBG CB IB	D 10	12000	3	10000	11400
33	TAVANA	YWL	SA/CR	FBG CB IB	D 10	12000	3	10000	11400
				1960 BOATS						
23	CAY	SLP	SA/CR	FBG	OB	8 2	6000	3	4100	4800

GLAS BOOTSBAU
Call 1-800-327-6929 for BUC Personalized Evaluation Service
Or, for 1977 boats, sign onto www.BUCValuPro.com

GLAS-PLY INC
KIRKLAND WA 98034   COAST GUARD MFG ID- GPL See inside cover to adjust price for area

For more recent years, see the BUC Used Boat Price Guide, Volume 1 or Volume 2

LOA FT IN	NAME AND/ OR MODEL	TOP/ RIG	BOAT TYPE	-HULL- MTL TP	----ENGINE--- TP # HP MFG	BEAM FT IN	WGT LBS	DRAFT FT IN	RETAIL LOW	RETAIL HIGH
				1983 BOATS						
16	1 GP-1700 SL	ST	RNBT	FBG SV OB	6 6	1060		2250	2600
16	1 GP-1700 SL	ST	RNBT	FBG SV IO	120 VLVO 6 6	1740		2650	3100
16	1 GPRV-1700 X	ST	RNBT	FBG SV OB	6 6	1060		1850	2200
17	3 GP-1800 FM	OP	FSH	FBG SV OB	6 10	1095		2200	2550
17	3 GP-1800 SL	ST	RNBT	FBG SV OB	6 10	1095		2350	2700
17	3 GP-1870 SL	OP	RNBT	FBG SV IO	120 VLVO 6 10	1890		3050	3500
17	3 GPV-1800 X	ST	RNBT	FBG SV OB	6 10	1095		2000	2350
18	2 GP-1900 SL	OP	SKI	FBG SV OB	7	1360		2650	3050
18	2 GP-1900 SL	ST	RNBT	FBG SV IO	120 VLVO 7	1900		3100	3600
19	4 GP-2100	ST	CUD	FBG SV OB	7 10	1995		3550	4150
19	4 GP-2100	ST	RNBT	FBG SV IO	120 VLVO 7 10	2785		4600	5300
19	4 GP-2100	ST	RNBT	FBG SV OB	7 10	1515		3000	3450
19	4 GP-2100 FM	OP	FSH	FBG SV OB	7 10	1750		3300	3850
19	4 GP-2100 SL	ST	RNBT	FBG SV IO	120 VLVO 7 10	2625		4250	4950
19	4 GPV-2100 X	ST	CUD	FBG SV OB	7 10	1700		3250	3750
19	4 GPV-2100 X	ST	CUD	FBG SV OB	7 10	1500		2950	3450
19	4 GPV-2181 SL	ST	CUD	FBG SV IO	120 VLVO 7 10	2800		4650	5350
19	4 GPV-2181 SL	ST	RNBT	FBG SV OB	7 10	2650		4300	5000
21	GPV-2200 FM	OP	FSH	FBG SV OB	7 10	2235		4600	5300
21	GPV-2210	ST	CUD	FBG SV OB	8	2560		5000	5750
21	GPV-2280 OV	ST	CUD	FBG SV OB	8	2758		5200	6000
21	4 GP-2200 SL	ST	RNBT	FBG SV OB	8	2235		4700	5400
21	4 GP-2200 SL	ST	CUD	FBG SV IO	138 VLVO 8	3285		5600	6450
21	4 GP-2210	ST	RNBT	FBG SV IO	138 VLVO 8	3615		5900	6800
21	4 GP-2210 FB	FB	SPTCR	FBG SV IO	138 VLVO 8	3668		6350	7300
23	2 GP-2280 OV	ST	CUD	FBG SV IO	138 VLVO 8	3615		6650	7650
23	2 GP-2400	ST	RNBT	FBG SV OB	8	2330		5250	6000
23	2 GP-2400 SL	ST	CUD	FBG SV IO	138 VLVO 8	3190		6000	6900
23	2 GP-2410	ST	CUD	FBG SV OB	8	3800		7150	8250
23	2 GP-2410 FB	FB	SPTCR	FBG SV IO	138 VLVO 8	3698		7000	8050
23	2 GPV-2400	ST	CUD	FBG SV OB	8	2330		5250	6000
24	GP-2510	HT	CUD	FBG SV IO	138 VLVO 8	3896		7600	8750
24	GP-2580	HT	CUD	FBG SV IO	138 VLVO 8	3915		7650	8750
24	GPV-2500	ST	CUD	FBG SV OB	8	2990		6600	7600
24	GPV-2580	HT	CUD	FBG SV OB	8	3050		6700	7750
26	4 GP-2600	HT	SDN	FBG SV IB	260 VLVO 10	7000	2 6	18000	20000
26	4 GP-2600	FB	SDN	FBG SV IB	260 VLVO 10	7400	2 6	18000	20700
27	7 GP-2800	FB	SDN	FBG SV IB	260 VLVO 10 11	9000	2 5	18000	20000
28	GP-2881 CRUISER	HT	SDN	FBG DV IB	260 VLVO 10 11	9500		19200	21300
28	GP-2881 SPORT FISH	HT	SDN	FBG DV IO	260 VLVO 10 11	8000		17300	19600
35		KTH	MS	FBG SV IB	D 12 4	16500	4 2	53800	59200
36	LRC 36	FB	TRWL	FBG SV IB	D 12 3	20000	4 11	**	**
39	LRC 39	FB	TRWL	FBG SV IB	D 12 3	22000	4 11	**	**
42	LRC 42	FB	TRWL	FBG SV IB	D 12 3	24000	4 11	**	**
				1982 BOATS						
16	1 GP-1700 SL	ST	RNBT	FBG SV OB	6 6	1060		2200	2550
16	1 GP-1700 SL	ST	RNBT	FBG SV IO	125 VLVO 6 6	1740		2600	3050
16	1 GPRV-1700 X	ST	RNBT	FBG SV OB	6 6	1060		1800	2150
17	3 GP-1800 FM	OP	FSH	FBG DV OB	6 10	1095		2100	2500
17	3 GP-1800 SL	ST	RNBT	FBG DV OB	6 10	1095		2300	2650
17	3 GP-1870 SL	OP	RNBT	FBG DV IO	125 VLVO 6 10	1890		2950	3450
17	3 GPV-1800 X	ST	RNBT	FBG DV OB	6 10	1095		1950	2300
18	2 GP-1900 SL	OP	SKI	FBG DV OB	7	1360		2600	3000
18	2 GP-1900 SL	OP	SKI	FBG DV IO	125 VLVO 7	1900		3050	3500

96th ed. - Vol. III   CONTINUED ON NEXT PAGE   257

GLAS-PLY INC -CONTINUED See inside cover to adjust price for area

LOA FT	LOA IN	NAME AND/ OR MODEL	TOP/ RIG	BOAT TYPE	-HULL- MTL	-HULL- TP	ENGINE TP	ENGINE # HP	ENGINE MFG	BEAM FT	BEAM IN	WGT LBS	DRAFT FT	DRAFT IN	RETAIL LOW	RETAIL HIGH
		1982 BOATS														
19	4	GP-2100	ST	CUD	FBG	DV	OB			7	10	1995			3500	4050
19	4	GP-2100	ST	CUD	FBG	DV	IO	125	VLVO	7	10	2785			4500	5200
19	4	GP-2100	ST	RNBT	FBG	DV	OB			7	10	1515			2950	3400
19	4	GP-2100 FM	OP	FSH	FBG	DV	OB			7	10	1750			3250	3750
19	4	GP-2100 SL	ST	RNBT	FBG	DV	IO	125	VLVO	7	10	2625			4150	4850
19	4	GPV-2100 X	ST	CUD	FBG	DV	OB			7	10	1700			3150	3700
19	4	GPV-2100 X	ST	RNBT	FBG	DV	OB			7	10	1500			2900	3400
19	4	GPV-2181 SL	ST	CUD	FBG	DV	IO	125	VLVO	7	10	2800			4550	5200
19	4	GPV-2181 SL	ST	RNBT	FBG	DV	IO	125	VLVO	7	10	2650			4200	4850
21		GPV-2200 FM	OP	FSH	FBG	DV	OB			7	10	2235			4550	5200
21		GPV-2210	ST	CUD	FBG	DV	OB			8		2560			4900	5650
21		GPV-2280 OV	ST	CUD	FBG	DV	OB			8		2758			5100	5900
21	4	GP-2200 SL	ST	RNBT	FBG	DV	OB			8		2235			4600	5300
21	4	GP-2200 SL	ST	RNBT	FBG	DV	IO	145	VLVO	8		3285			5500	6300
21	4	GP-2210	ST	CUD	FBG	DV	IO	145	VLVO	8		3615			5800	6650
21	4	GP-2210 FB	FB	SPTCR	FBG	DV	IO	145	VLVO	8		3668			6200	7150
21	4	GP-2280 OV	ST	CUD	FBG	DV	IO	145	VLVO	8		3615			6500	7500
23	2	GP-2400	ST	RNBT	FBG	DV	OB			8		2330			5150	5900
23	2	GP-2400 SL	ST	RNBT	FBG	DV	IO	145	VLVO	8		3190			5850	6750
23	2	GP-2410	ST	CUD	FBG	DV	IO	145	VLVO	8		3800			7000	8050
23	2	GP-2410 FB	FB	SPTCR	FBG	DV	IO	145	VLVO	8		3698			6850	7900
23	2	GPV-2400	ST	CUD	FBG	DV	OB			8		2330			5150	5900
24		GP-2510	HT	CUD	FBG	DV	IO	145	VLVO	8		3896			7450	8550
24		GP-2580	HT	CUD	FBG	DV	IO	145	VLVO	8		3915			7450	8600
24		GPV-2500	ST	CUD	FBG	DV	OB			8		2990			6500	7450
24		GPV-2580	ST	CUD	FBG	DV	OB			8		3050			6600	7600
26	4	GP-2600	HT	SDN	FBG	DV	IB	260	VLVO	10		7000	2	6	16900	19100
26	4	GP-2600	FB	SDN	FBG	DV	IB	260	VLVO	10		7400	2	6	17400	19800
27	7	GP-2800	FB	SDN	FBG	DV	IO	260	VLVO	10	11	9000	2	5	17200	19600
28		GP-2881 CRUISER	HT	SDN	FBG	DV	IO	260	VLVO	10	11	9500			18700	20800
28		GP-2881 SPORT FISH	HT	SDN	FBG	DV	IO	260	VLVO	10	11	8000			16900	19200
29	6	GP-3050	FB	CR	FBG	DV	IB	T165		10	11				21300	23700
		1981 BOATS														
16	1	GP-1700 SL	ST	RNBT	FBG	SV	OB			6	6	1060			2100	2500
16	1	GP-1700 SL	ST	RNBT	FBG	SV	IO	120	VLVO	6	6	1740			2550	3000
16	1	GPRV-1700 X	ST	RNBT	FBG	SV	OB			6	6	1060			1800	2150
17	3	GP-1800 FM	OP	FSH	FBG	DV	OB			6	10	1095			2050	2450
17	3	GP-1800 SL	ST	RNBT	FBG	DV	OB			6	10	1095			2250	2600
17	3	GP-1870 SL	OP	RNBT	FBG	DV	IO	120	MRCR	6	10	1890			2750	3200
17	3	GPV-1800 X	ST	RNBT	FBG	DV	OB			6	10	1095			1950	2300
18	2	GP-1900 SL	OP	SKI	FBG	DV	OB			7		1360			2550	2950
18	2	GP-1900 SL	OP	SKI	FBG	DV	IO	140	MRCR	7		1900			2850	3300
18	2	GPV-1900 X	ST	RNBT	FBG	DV	OB			7		1100			2200	2550
19	4	GP-2100	ST	CUD	FBG	DV	OB			7	10	1995			3450	4000
19	4	GP-2100	ST	CUD	FBG	DV	IO	140	MRCR	7	10	2785			4250	4900
19	4	GP-2100	ST	RNBT	FBG	DV	OB			7	10	1515			2900	3350
19	4	GP-2100 FM	OP	FSH	FBG	DV	OB			7	10	1750			3200	3700
19	4	GP-2100 SL	ST	RNBT	FBG	DV	IO	140	MRCR	7	10	2625			3950	4600
19	4	GPV-2100 X	ST	CUD	FBG	DV	OB			7	10	1700			3100	3650
19	4	GPV-2100 X	ST	RNBT	FBG	DV	OB			7	10	1500			2850	3350
19	4	GPV-2181 SL	ST	CUD	FBG	DV	IO	140	MRCR	7	10	2800			4250	4950
19	4	GPV-2181 SL	ST	RNBT	FBG	DV	IO	140	MRCR	7	10	2650			3950	4600
21		GPV-2200 FM	OP	FSH	FBG	DV	OB			7	10	2235			4450	5150
21		GPV-2210	ST	CUD	FBG	DV	OB			8		2560			4850	5550
21		GPV-2280 OV	ST	CUD	FBG	DV	OB			8		2758			5050	5800
21	4	GP-2200 SL	ST	RNBT	FBG	DV	OB			8		2235			4550	5250
21	4	GP-2200 SL	ST	RNBT	FBG	DV	IO	170	MRCR	8		3285			5250	6050
21	4	GP-2210	ST	CUD	FBG	DV	IO	170	MRCR	8		3615			5500	6300
21	4	GP-2210 FB	FB	SPTCR	FBG	DV	IO	170	MRCR	8		3668			5950	6850
21	4	GP-2280 OV	ST	CUD	FBG	DV	IO	170	MRCR	8		3615			6300	7250
23	2	GP-2400	ST	RNBT	FBG	DV	OB			8		2330			5050	5800
23	2	GP-2400 SL	ST	RNBT	FBG	DV	IO	170	MRCR	8		3190			5600	6450
23	2	GP-2410	ST	CUD	FBG	DV	IO	170	MRCR	8		3800			6750	7750
23	2	GP-2410 FB	FB	SPTCR	FBG	DV	IO	170	MRCR	8		3698			6600	7600
23	2	GPV-2400	ST	CUD	FBG	DV	OB			8		2330			5050	5800
24		GP-2500		CUD	FBG	DV	IO	170		8					7150	8250
24		GP-2510	HT	CUD	FBG	DV	IO	170	MRCR	8		3896			7150	8250
24		GP-2580	HT	CUD	FBG	DV	IO	185	MRCR	8		3915			7200	8300
24		GPV-2500	ST	CUD	FBG	DV	OB			8		2990			6400	7350
24		GPV-2580	ST	CUD	FBG	DV	OB			8		3050			6500	7450
26		GP-2600	HT	SDN	FBG	DV	IO	260		10					13500	15400
26	4	GP-2600	HT	SDN	FBG	DV	IB	255	MRCR	10		7000	2	6	16000	18200
26	4	GP-2600	FB	SDN	FBG	DV	IB	255	MRCR	10		7400	2	6	16600	18800
27	6	GP-2800	HT	SDN	FBG	DV	IB	T165		10	11				20700	23000
27	7	GP-2800	HT	SDN	FBG	DV	IB	255	MRCR	10	11	8500	2	5	19400	21500
27	7	GP-2800	HT	SDN	FBG	DV	IO	350		10	11				18200	20200
27	7	GP-2800	FB	SDN	FBG	DV	IB	255	MRCR	10	11	9000	2	5	20000	22200
28		GP-2881 CRUISER	HT	SDN	FBG	DV	IB	255	MRCR	10	11	9500			21300	23600
28		GP-2881 SPORT FISH	HT	SDN	FBG	DV	IB	255	MRCR	10	11	8000			19600	21700
29	6	GP-3050	FB	CR	FBG	DV	IB	T165		10	11				20400	22700
		1980 BOATS														
16	1	GP-1700		RNBT	FBG	RB	IO	120		6	5				2350	2750
16	1	GP-1700		RNBT	FBG	RB	IO	240		6	5				2550	3000
16	1	GP-1700	ST	RNBT	FBG	SV	OB			6	6				1700	2050
16	1	GP-1700SL	ST	RNBT	FBG	SV	IO	140	VLVO	6	6	1740			2550	2950
17		GP-1870		RNBT	FBG	DV	OB			6	10	1095			2000	2400
17		GP-1870		RNBT	FBG	DV	IO	120		6	10	1890			2700	3150
17		GP-1870FM		FSH	FBG	DV	OB			6	10	1095			2000	2400
17	2	GP-1800	ST	RNBT	FBG	DV	IO	120-170		6	10				2650	3150
17	3	GP-1800	ST	RNBT	FBG	DV	OB			6	10				2050	2450
17	3	GP-1800FM	OP	FSH	FBG	DV	OB			6	10				2050	2400
17	3	GP-1870SL	OP	RNBT	FBG	DV	IO	130	BMW	6	10	1890			2950	3450
18	1	GP-1900		RNBT	FBG	DV	IO	120		7					2850	3350
18	1	GP-1900		RNBT	FBG	DV	IO	290		7					3350	3900
18	2	GP-1900SL	OP	SKI	FBG	DV	OB			7					2500	2900
18	2	GP-1900SL	OP	SKI	FBG	DV	IO	170	MRCR	7		2025			2900	3400
19	4	GP-2100		FSH	FBG	DV	IO	120-170		7	10				4450	5200
19	4	GP-2100	ST	RNBT	FBG	DV	OB			7	10				2850	3300
19	4	GP-2100 CUTTY	ST	CUD	FBG	DV	OB			7	10				3250	3800
19	4	GP-2100 CUTTY	ST	CUD	FBG	DV	IO	120-230		7	10				4100	4950
19	4	GP-2100FB	FB	SPTCR	FBG	DV	IO	170	MRCR	7	10	1995			3600	4150
19	4	GP-2100FM	OP	FSH	FBG	DV	OB			7	10				3150	3650
19	4	GP-2100SL	ST	RNBT	FBG	DV	IO	190	BMW	7	10	1995			3750	4350
21		GP-2200FM		FSH	FBG	DV	OB			8		2235			4400	5050
21		GP-2280		CUD	FBG	DV	OB			8		2758			4950	5700
21		GP-2280		CUD	FBG	DV	IO	170		8		3615			5750	6600
21	4	GP-2200		RNBT	FBG	DV	IO	170-260		8					5050	6100
21	4	GP-2200FM	OP	FSH	FBG	DV	IO	140	VLVO	8		3615			6300	7250
21	4	GP-2200SL	ST	RNBT	FBG	DV	OB			8					4500	5150
21	4	GP-2200SL	ST	RNBT	FBG	DV	IO	190	BMW	8		3615			5800	6700
21	4	GP-2210		CUD	FBG	DV	OB			8		2560			4900	5600
21	4	GP-2210 CUTTY	ST	CUD	FBG	DV	IO	170-260		8		3615			5850	6900
21	4	GP-2210FB	FB	SPTCR	FBG	DV	IO	200	VLVO	8		3615			6050	7000
21	4	GP-2280 CUTTY	ST	CUD	FBG	DV	IO	190	BMW	8		3615			6100	7050
23		GP-2400	ST	RNBT	FBG	DV	IO	170		8		3195			5550	6350
23		GP-2410		CUD	FBG	DV	OB			8		2995			6000	6900
23	2	GP-2400		CUD	FBG	DV	OB			8		2995			6050	6950
23	2	GP-2400	ST	RNBT	FBG	DV	OB			8					5000	5700
23	2	GP-2400	ST	RNBT	FBG	DV	IO	170-260		8					5550	6700
23	2	GP-2400SL	ST	RNBT	FBG	DV	IO	190	BMW	8		3800			6550	7500
23	2	GP-2410 CUTTY	ST	CUD	FBG	DV	IO	220	BMW	8		3800			7050	8100
23	2	GP-2410 EXPRESS	HT	EXP	FBG	DV	IO	228	MRCR	8		3800			6800	7800
23	2	GP-2410FB	FB	SPTCR	FBG	DV	IO	225	VLVO	8		3800			7000	8050
24		GP-2500		CUD	FBG	DV	OB			8		3295			6750	7800
24		GP-2500 CUTTY		CUD	FBG	DV	IO	170-260		8					7100	8500
24		GP-2510		CUD	FBG	DV	IO	170		8		3896			7100	8150
24		GP-2510 CUTTY	HT	CUD	FBG	DV	IO	260	VLVO	8		3915			7650	8800
24		GP-2580		CUD	FBG	DV	IO	170		8		3996			7250	8300
24		GP-2580 CUTTY	HT	CUD	FBG	DV	IO	220	BMW	8		3915			7500	8600
26		GP-2600		CR	FBG	DV	IO	260		9					12200	13900
26		GP-2600		CR	FBG	DV	IO	T200		9					13200	15000
26	4	GP-2600	HT	SDN	FBG	DV	IB	T170	MRCR	10		6200	2	6	15400	17500
26	4	GP-2600	FB	SDN	FBG	DV	IB	270	CRUS	10		6350	2	6	14700	16700
27	7	GP-2800	HT	SDN	FBG	DV	IB	T130D	VLVO	10	11	8500	2	5	28200	31300
27	7	GP-2800	FB	SDN	FBG	DV	IB	T270	CRUS	10	11	8500	2	5	21500	23900
27	10	GP-2800		CR	FBG	DV	IO	350		10	11				16500	18800
27	10	GP-2800		CR	FBG	DV	IO	T260		10	11				17400	19800
29	1	GP-3050	HT	SDN	FBG	DV	IB	T220	CRUS	10	11	8500	2	8	23000	25600
29	6	GP-3000	FB	CR	FBG	DV	IB	305		10	11				19200	21300
29	6	GP-3000		SDN	FBG	DV	IB	305		10	11				20900	23200
		1979 BOATS														
16	1	GP-16SL		RNBT	FBG	DV	OB			6	6	1060			1900	2250
16	1	GP-5SL		RNBT	FBG	DV	IO	120		6	6				2400	2750
17	2	GP-171SL/FM		FSH	FBG	DV	IO	120		6	10				2850	3300
17	2	GP-17FM		FSH	FBG	DV	OB			6	10	1290			2300	2700
17	2	GP-17SL		RNBT	FBG	DV	OB			6	10	1095			2000	2400

CONTINUED ON NEXT PAGE

LOA FT IN	NAME AND/OR MODEL	TOP/RIG	BOAT TYPE	HULL MTL TP	TP	ENGINE # HP	MFG	BEAM FT IN	WGT LBS	DRAFT FT IN	RETAIL LOW	RETAIL HIGH
	1979 BOATS											
18 1	GP-5.5 METER SS	RNBT	FBG	DV	OB			7	1360		2500	2900
18 1	GP-5.5 METER SS	RNBT	FBG	DV	OB	170		8 4			3250	3800
19 4	CUTTY GP-191SL	CUD	FBG	DV	IO	170		7 10			4150	4800
19 4	CUTTY GP-19SL	CUD	FBG	DV	OB			7 10	1995		3350	3900
19 4	GP-191FM	FSH	FBG	DV	IO	170		7 10			4500	5150
19 4	GP-191SL	RNBT	FBG	DV	IO	170		7 10			3900	4500
19 4	GP-19FM	FSH	FBG	DV	OB			7 10	1750		3100	3600
19 4	GP-19SL	RNBT	FBG	DV	OB			7 10	1510		2800	3250
21 4	CUTTY GP-21SL	CUD	FBG	DV	OB			8	2560		4800	5550
21 4	GP-2100SL	OP RNBT	FBG	DV	IO	170		8			5050	5800
21 4	GP-21FM	FSH	FBG	DV	OB			8	2430		4650	5350
21 4	GP-21SL	RNBT	FBG	DV	OB			8	2235		4400	5050
21 4	GP-2280SL	CR	FBG	DV	IO	170		8			5650	6500
23 2	CUTTY GP-23SL	CUD	FBG	DV	OB			8	2995		5950	6850
23 2	GP-2300SL	CUD	FBG	DV	IO	200		8			6600	7600
23 2	GP-2300SL	RNBT	FBG	DV	IO	200		8			5600	6450
23 2	GP-23SL	RNBT	FBG	DV	OB			8	2330		4900	5650
23 2	GP-7.5B	CR	FBG	DV	IO	200		8			6350	7300
27 6	GP-9FB	CR	FBG	DV	IO	T228		10 11			16800	19100
29 6	GP 3050	FB CR	FBG	DV	IB	T165	VLVO	10 11		2 5	19000	21200
	1978 BOATS											
16 1	OPEN 16	OP RNBT	FBG	SV	IO			6 6	1060		**	**
17 3	OPEN 171	OP RNBT	FBG	DV	OB			6 10			2000	2400
17 3	OPEN 171	OP RNBT	FBG	DV	IO	140	MRCR	6 10	1890		2750	3200
18 2	OPEN 5.5	OP RNBT	FBG	DV	OB			7	1360		2450	2850
18 4	OPEN 5.5	OP RNBT	FBG	DV	IO	170	MRCR	7	2025		3050	3550
19 4	6.5 METER	FB EXP	FBG	DV	IO	170	MRCR	7 10	2785		4250	4950
19 4	CUTTY 191	OP CUD	FBG	DV	OB			7 10			3200	3700
19 4	CUTTY 191	OP CUD	FBG	DV	IO	170	MRCR	7 10	2785		4250	4950
19 4	FISHING-MACHINE 191	OP CTRCN	FBG	DV	OB			7 10			3000	3500
19 4	OPEN 191	OP RNBT	FBG	DV	OB			7 10			2750	3200
19 4	OPEN 191	OP RNBT	FBG	DV	IO	170	MRCR	7 10	2785		4100	4750
19 4	VIP 191	OP RNBT	FBG	DV	OB			7 10			2750	3200
19 4	VIP 191	OP RNBT	FBG	DV	IO	170	MRCR	7 10	2785		4100	4750
21 4	7 METER	FB EXP	FBG	DV	IO	198	MRCR	8	3615		5900	6800
21 4	CUTTY 2280	OP CUD	FBG	DV	OB			8			4850	5600
21 4	CUTTY 2280	HT OVNTR	FBG	DV	IO	198	MRCR	8	3615		5900	6800
21 4	CUTTY OV 2280	HT OVNTR	FBG	DV	IO	198	MRCR	8	3615		5900	6800
21 4	EXPRESS 2100	HT EXP	FBG	DV	IO	198-260		8	3615		5900	7100
21 4	OPEN 2100	OP RNBT	FBG	DV	OB			8			4350	5000
21 4	VIP 2100	OP RNBT	FBG	DV	IO	198-260		8			5600	6700
21 4	OPEN 2100	OP RNBT	FBG	DV	IO	198	MRCR	8	3615		5600	6450
23 2	7.5 METER	FB EXP	FBG	DV	IO	228	MRCR	8	3195		6100	7000
23 2	CABIN 2300	HT CBNCR	FBG	DV	IO	228	MRCR	8	3195		6850	7850
23 2	CUTTY 2300	OP CUD	FBG	DV	IO	228	MRCR	8	3195		6100	7000
23 2	EXPRESS 2300	HT EXP	FBG	DV	IO	228-260		8	3195		6100	7200
23 2	OPEN 2300	OP RNBT	FBG	DV	OB			8			4850	5550
23 2	OPEN 2300	OP RNBT	FBG	DV	IO	228	MRCR	8	3195		5750	6600
23 2	VIP 2300	OP RNBT	FBG	DV	IO	228	MRCR	8	3195		5750	6600
27 10	SEDAN 9M	FB SDN	FBG	DV	VD	T228	MRCR	10 11	8500	2 5	19300	21400
27 10	SEDAN 9M	FB SDN	FBG	DV	IO	T330		10 11	8500	2 5	20000	22300
	1977 BOATS											
17 3	OPEN 17	OP RNBT	FBG	DV	OB			6 10	1180		2100	2500
17 3	OPEN 171	OP RNBT	FBG	DV	OB	120-170		6 10	1831		2750	3400
18 1	OPEN 18	OP RNBT	FBG	DV	OB			7 2	1350		2400	2800
18 1	OPEN 181	OP RNBT	FBG	DV	IO	120-190		7 2	2000		3100	3850
18 1	OPEN 181	OP RNBT	FBG	DV	IO	200-255		7 2	2000		3350	4150
19 2	CUTTY 19	OP CUD	FBG	DV	OB			7 8	1890		3150	3650
19 2	CUTTY 19	HT CUD	FBG	DV	OB			7 8	1890		3150	3650
19 2	CUTTY 191	OP CUD	FBG	DV	IO	120-200		7 8	2550		4000	4950
19 2	CUTTY 191	HT CUD	FBG	DV	IO	120-200		7 8	2550		4000	4950
19 2	OPEN 19	OP RNBT	FBG	DV	OB			7 8	1612		2850	3300
19 2	OPEN 19	HT RNBT	FBG	DV	OB			7 8	1612		2850	3300
19 2	OPEN 191	OP RNBT	FBG	DV	IO	120-200		7 8	2350		3700	4600
19 2	OPEN 191	HT RNBT	FBG	DV	IO	120-200		7 8	2350		3700	4600
19 2	VIP 19	OP RNBT	FBG	DV	OB			7 8	1742		3000	3500
19 2	VIP 19	HT RNBT	FBG	DV	OB			7 8	1742		3000	3500
19 2	VIP 191	OP RNBT	FBG	DV	IO	120-200		7 8	2480		3800	4700
19 2	VIP 191	HT RNBT	FBG	DV	IO	120-200		7 8	2480		3800	4700
21 4	CABIN 2100	HT CBNCR	FBG	DV	IO	120-240		8	3455		6300	7800
21 4	CABIN 2100	HT CBNCR	FBG	DV	IO	255	VLVO	8	3455		6900	7900
21 4	CUTTY 2100	OP CUD	FBG	DV	OB			8			4800	5500
21 4	CUTTY 2100	OP CUD	FBG	DV	IO	120-240		8	3355		5650	7000
21 4	CUTTY 2100	OP CUD	FBG	DV	IO	255	VLVO	8	3355		6150	7100
21 4	EXPRESS 2100	HT EXP	FBG	DV	IO	120-255		8	3700		6050	7550
21 4	OPEN 2100	OP RNBT	FBG	DV	OB			8			4250	4950
21 4	OPEN 2100	OP RNBT	FBG	DV	IO	120-240		8	2855		4850	6050
21 4	OPEN 2100	OP RNBT	FBG	DV	IO	255	VLVO	8	2855		5350	6150
21 4	VIP 2100	OP RNBT	FBG	DV	IO	120-240		8	3055		5050	6250
21 4	VIP 2100	OP RNBT	FBG	DV	IO	255	VLVO	8	3055		5550	6350
23 2	CABIN 2300	HT CBNCR	FBG	DV	IO	140-255		8	3950		7900	9750
23 2	CABIN 2300	HT CBNCR	FBG	DV	IO	T120-T140		8	3950		8900	10600
23 2	CUTTY 2300	OP CUD	FBG	DV	OB			8			5250	6000
23 2	CUTTY 2300	OP CUD	FBG	DV	IO	140-255		8	3840		6850	8450
23 2	CUTTY 2300	OP CUD	FBG	DV	IO	T120-T140		8	3840		7700	9250
23 2	EXPRESS 2300	HT EXP	FBG	DV	IO	140-255		8	3950		7000	8650
23 2	EXPRESS 2300	HT EXP	FBG	DV	IO	T120-T140		8	3950		7850	9400
23 2	OPEN 2300	OP RNBT	FBG	DV	OB			8			4800	5500
23 2	OPEN 2300	OP RNBT	FBG	DV	IO	165-255		8	3340		5850	7300
23 2	OPEN 2300	OP RNBT	FBG	DV	IO	T120-T140		8	3340		6600	8000
23 2	VIP 2300	OP RNBT	FBG	DV	IO	165-255		8	3640		6250	7700
23 2	VIP 2300	OP RNBT	FBG	DV	IO	T120-T140		8	3640		7000	8400
27 10	CRUISER 2300	FB CR	FBG	DV	IO	255	MRCR	10 11	8500	2 5	15600	17800
	VD 255-330 15300 18000, IO T200-T225 16900 19600, VD T230-T233 17000 19300											
	IO T240 VLVO 17500 19900, IO T255 VLVO 18100 20100, VD T255-T260 17100 19700											

GLASCO MARINE
COAST GUARD MFG ID- GCM

Call 1-800-327-6929 for BUC Personalized Evaluation Service
Or, for 1968 to 1979 boats, sign onto www.BUCValuPro.com

GLASCRAFTER
COAST GUARD MFG ID- GXS

Call 1-800-327-6929 for BUC Personalized Evaluation Service
Or, for 1978 boats, sign onto www.BUCValuPro.com

GLASS MAGIC BOATS INC

Call 1-800-327-6929 for BUC Personalized Evaluation Service
Or, for 1958 to 1963 boats, sign onto www.BUCValuPro.com

GLASS MASTER'S INC
COAST GUARD MFG ID- GIN

Call 1-800-327-6929 for BUC Personalized Evaluation Service
Or, for 1983 to 1984 boats, sign onto www.BUCValuPro.com

GLASSCO

Call 1-800-327-6929 for BUC Personalized Evaluation Service
Or, for 1960 boats, sign onto www.BUCValuPro.com

GLASSMASTER CO MARINE DIV
LEXINGTON SC 29072   COAST GUARD MFG ID- GPC See inside cover to adjust price for area

For more recent years, see the BUC Used Boat Price Guide, Volume 1 or Volume 2

LOA FT IN	NAME AND/OR MODEL	TOP/RIG	BOAT TYPE	HULL MTL TP	TP	ENGINE # HP	MFG	BEAM FT IN	WGT LBS	DRAFT FT IN	RETAIL LOW	RETAIL HIGH
	1983 BOATS											
16 1	PLAYMATE 600XSD	ST	RNBT	FBG TR	OB			6 3	900		4300	5000
16 3	BASSMATE VI 600F	ST	BASS	FBG TR	OB			5 10	760		3650	4250
16 3	SUPER-SPORT 600D	OP	RNBT	FBG DV	OB			6 5	855		4100	4750
16 4	SUPER-BASSMATE 640SB	OP	BASS	FBG TR	OB			6 8	960		4600	5300
16 5	CADET 650BS	OP	RNBT	FBG TR	OB			6 11	1050		5000	5750
16 5	CADET 650EBS	OP	RNBT	FBG DV	OB			6 11	1050		5000	5750
17 5	CITATION 700EC	ST/	RNBT	FBG DV	IO	120-170		7 11	1800		2450	2900
17 5	DAYTONA 700ESD	ST	RNBT	FBG DV	IO	120-185		6 11	1890		2450	2900
17 5	DAYTONA 700SD	ST	RNBT	FBG DV	OB			6 11	1810		2400	2850
17 5	PATRIOT 750BS	ST	RNBT	FBG DV	OB			6 11	1150		4950	5700
17 5	PATRIOT 750EBS	ST	RNBT	FBG DV	OB			6 11	1150		5000	6350
17 5	PATRIOT 750EBS	ST	RNBT	FBG DV	IO	120-185		6 11	1930		2450	2900
18	TARPON 800XESD	ST	RNBT	FBG TR	IO	120-230		7	2000		2600	3200

GLASSMASTER CO MARINE DIV -CONTINUED See inside cover to adjust price for area

LOA FT	LOA IN	NAME AND/ OR MODEL	TOP/ RIG	BOAT TYPE	-HULL- MTL	-HULL- TP	ENGINE TP	ENGINE # HP	ENGINE MFG	BEAM FT	BEAM IN	WGT LBS	DRAFT FT	DRAFT IN	RETAIL LOW	RETAIL HIGH
		1983 BOATS														
18		TARPON 800XSD	ST	RNBT	FBG	TR	OB			7		1260			6000	6900
18	5	CHIEF 850EC	ST	RNBT	FBG	TR	IO	120-230		7		2150			2750	3350
18	5	SUPREME 850BS	ST	RNBT	FBG	DV	OB			7	3	1370			6450	7450
18	5	SUPREME 850EBS	ST	RNBT	FBG	DV	IO	140-230		7	3	2150			2850	3450
21		REGENCY 210EFSD	ST	FSH	FBG	DV	IO	140-260		7	11	2850			4750	5800
21		REGENCY 210ESD	ST	CUD	FBG	DV	IO	140-260		7	11	2650			4350	5350
21		REGENCY 210ESS	OP	CUD	FBG	DV	IO	140-260		7	11	2650			4350	5350
21		REGENCY 210EWF	ST	FSH	FBG	DV	IO	140-260		7	11	2900			4800	5900
21		REGENCY 210FSD	ST	FSH	FBG	DV	OB			7	11	2070			9650	11000
21		REGENCY 210SD	ST	RNBT	FBG	DV	OB			7	11	1870			8950	10200
21		REGENCY 210WF	OP	FSH	FBG	DV	OB			7	11	2120			9850	11200
21		REGENCY EFRD	ST	RNBT	FBG	DV	IO	140-260		7	11	2875			4350	5300
24	3	HERITAGE 244ESD	ST	FSH	FBG	DV	IO	185-260		7	11	4020			7200	8600
24	3	HERITAGE 244ESD	ST	FSH	FBG	DV	IO	T120-T170		7	11	4020			7950	9250
		1982 BOATS														
16	1	PLAYMATE 600XD	ST	RNBT	FBG	TR	OB			6	3	900			4150	4850
16	1	PLAYMATE 600XESD	ST	RNBT	FBG	TR	IO	120		6	3	1595			1900	2250
16	1	PLAYMATE 600XSD	ST	RNBT	FBG	TR	OB			6	3	900			4150	4850
16	3	BASSMATE VI 600F	OP	BASS	FBG	TR	OB			5	10	760			3550	4100
16	3	SUPER-SPORT 600D	OP	RNBT	FBG	DV	OB			6	5	855			4000	4650
16	4	SUPER-BASSMATE 640SB	OP	BASS	FBG	TR	OB			6	8	960			4450	5150
16	5	CADET 650BS	OP	RNBT	FBG	TR	OB			6	11	1050			4900	5650
16	5	CADET 650EBS	OP	RNBT	FBG	DV	IO		OMC	7	11	1800			**	**
16	5	CADET 650EBS	OP	RNBT	FBG	DV	IO	120-170		7	11	1800			2400	2800
17	5	CITATION 700EC	ST	RNBT	FBG	DV	IO		OMC	6	11	1890			**	**
17	5	CITATION 700EC	ST	RNBT	FBG	DV	IO	120-185		6	11	1890			2400	2850
17	5	DAYTONA 700ESD	ST	RNBT	FBG	DV	IO		OMC	6	11	1810			**	**
17	5	DAYTONA 700ESD	ST	RNBT	FBG	DV	IO	120-185		6	11	1810			2350	2750
17	5	DAYTONA 700SD	ST	RNBT	FBG	DV	OB			6	11	1000			4850	5550
17	5	PATRIOT 750BS	ST	RNBT	FBG	DV	OB			6	11	1150			5400	6200
17	5	PATRIOT 750EBS	ST	RNBT	FBG	DV	IO		OMC	6	11	1930			**	**
17	5	PATRIOT 750EBS	ST	RNBT	FBG	DV	IO	120-185		6	11	1930			2400	2850
18		TARPON 800XESD	ST	RNBT	FBG	TR	IO		OMC	7		2000			**	**
18		TARPON 800XESD	ST	RNBT	FBG	TR	IO	140-230		7		2000			2550	3100
18		TARPON 800XSD	ST	RNBT	FBG	TR	OB			7		1260			5850	6700
18	5	SUPREME 850BS	ST	RNBT	FBG	DV	OB			7	3	1370			6300	7250
18	5	SUPREME 850EBS	ST	RNBT	FBG	DV	IO		OMC	7	3	2150			**	**
18	5	SUPREME 850EBS	ST	RNBT	FBG	DV	IO	140-230		7	3	2150			2750	3350
21		GULFSTREAM	ST	RNBT	FBG	DV	IO		OMC	7	11	2875	4	10	**	**
21		GULFSTREAM	ST	RNBT	FBG	DV	IO	140-260		7	11	2875	4	10	4200	5200
21		REGENCY 210EFSD	ST	FSH	FBG	DV	IO		OMC	7	11	2850			**	**
21		REGENCY 210EFSD	ST	FSH	FBG	DV	IO	140-260		7	11	2850			4700	5700
21		REGENCY 210ESD	ST	CUD	FBG	DV	IO		OMC	7	11	2650			**	**
21		REGENCY 210ESD	ST	CUD	FBG	DV	IO	140-260		7	11	2650			4200	5200
21		REGENCY 210ESS	OP	CUD	FBG	DV	IO		OMC	7	11	2650			**	**
21		REGENCY 210ESS	OP	CUD	FBG	DV	IO	140-260		7	11	2650			4200	5200
21		REGENCY 210EWF	ST	FSH	FBG	DV	IO		OMC	7	11	2900			**	**
21		REGENCY 210EWF	ST	FSH	FBG	DV	IO	140-260		7	11	2900			4700	5750
21		REGENCY 210FSD	ST	FSH	FBG	DV	OB			7	11	2070			9400	10700
21		REGENCY 210SD	ST	RNBT	FBG	DV	OB			7	11	1870			8600	9900
21		REGENCY 210WF	OP	FSH	FBG	DV	OB			7	11	2120			9550	10900
24	3	HERITAGE 244ESD	ST	FSH	FBG	DV	IO	185-260		7	11	4020			7050	8400
24	3	HERITAGE 244ESD	ST	FSH	FBG	DV	IO	T	OMC	7	11	4020			**	**
24	3	HERITAGE 244ESD	ST	FSH	FBG	DV	IO	T120-T170		7	11	4020			7750	9050
		1981 BOATS														
16	1	PLAYMATE 600XD	ST	RNBT	FBG	TR	OB			6	3	900			3900	4550
16	1	PLAYMATE 600XESD	ST	RNBT	FBG	TR	IO	120		6	3	1595			1850	2250
16	1	PLAYMATE 600XSD	ST	RNBT	FBG	TR	OB			6	3	900			4200	4900
16	3	BASSMATE VI 600F	OP	BASS	FBG	TR	OB			5	10	760			3450	4000
16	3	BASSMATE VI 600F	ST	BASS	FBG	TR	OB			5	10	760			3450	4000
16	3	SUPER-SPORT 600D	OP	RNBT	FBG	DV	OB			6	5	855			3900	4500
16	4	SUPER-BASSMATE 640SB	OP	BASS	FBG	TR	OB			6	8	960			4350	5000
17	5	CITATION 700EC	ST		FBG	DV	IO	120-185		6	11	1890			2300	2700
17	5	DAYTONA 700ESD	ST	RNBT	FBG	DV	IO	120-185		6	11	1810			2350	2750
17	5	DAYTONA 700SD	ST	RNBT	FBG	DV	OB			6	11	1000			4700	5400
17	5	PATRIOT 750BS	ST	RNBT	FBG	DV	OB			6	11	1150			5250	6000
17	5	PATRIOT 750EBS	ST	RNBT	FBG	DV	IO	120-185		6	11	1930			2400	2800
18		TARPON 800XESD	ST	RNBT	FBG	TR	IO	140-230		7		2000			2500	3050
18		TARPON 800XSD	ST	RNBT	FBG	TR	OB			7		1260			5700	6550
18	5	SUPREME 850BS	ST	RNBT	FBG	DV	OB			7	3	1370			6150	7050
18	5	SUPREME 850EBS	ST	RNBT	FBG	DV	IO	140-230		7	3	2150			2750	3300
21		REGENCY 210EFSD	ST	FSH	FBG	DV	IO	140-260		7	11	2850			4600	5600
21		REGENCY 210ESD	ST	CUD	FBG	DV	IO	140-260		7	11	2650			4150	5150
21		REGENCY 210ESD	OP		FBG	DV	IO	140-260		7	11	2650			3950	4900
21		REGENCY 210ESS	ST		FBG	DV	IO	140-260		7	11	2650			3950	4900
21		REGENCY 210EWF	ST	FSH	FBG	DV	IO	140-260		7	11	2900			4650	5650
21		REGENCY 210FSD	ST	FSH	FBG	DV	OB			7	11	2070			9150	10400
21		REGENCY 210SD	ST	RNBT	FBG	DV	OB			7	11	1870			8400	9650
24	3	HERITAGE 244ESD	ST		FBG	DV	IO	185-260		7	11	4020			6300	7550
24	3	HERITAGE 244ESD	ST		FBG	DV	IO	T120-T170		7	11	4020			6950	8100
		1980 BOATS														
16	1	PLAYMATE 600XD	ST	RNBT	FBG	TR	OB			6	3	900			3800	4450
16	1	PLAYMATE 600XESD	ST	RNBT	FBG	TR	IO	120		6	3	1595			1850	2200
16	1	PLAYMATE 600XSD	ST	RNBT	FBG	TR	OB			6	3	900			4100	4800
16	3	BASSMATE VI 600F	OP	BASS	FBG	TR	OB			5	10	760			3400	3950
16	3	BASSMATE VI 600F	ST	BASS	FBG	TR	OB			5	10	760			3400	3950
16	3	SUPER-SPORT 600D	OP	RNBT	FBG	DV	OB			6	5	855			3800	4400
16	4	SUPER-BASSMATE 640SB	OP	BASS	FBG	TR	OB			6	8	960			4200	4900
17	5	CITATION 700EC	ST		FBG	DV	IO	120-185		6	11	1890			2250	2700
17	5	DAYTONA 700ESD	ST	RNBT	FBG	DV	IO	120-185		6	11	1810			2300	2700
17	5	DAYTONA 700SD	ST	RNBT	FBG	DV	OB			6	11	1000			4600	5300
17	5	PATRIOT 750BS	ST	RNBT	FBG	DV	OB			6	11	1150			5100	5900
17	5	PATRIOT 750EBS	ST	RNBT	FBG	DV	IO	120-185		6	11	1930			2350	2800
18		TARPON 800XESD	ST	RNBT	FBG	TR	IO	140-230		7		2000			2500	3050
18		TARPON 800XSD	ST	RNBT	FBG	TR	OB			7		1260			5600	6400
18	5	SUPREME 850BS	ST	RNBT	FBG	DV	OB			7	3	1370			6000	6900
18	5	SUPREME 850EBS	ST	RNBT	FBG	DV	IO	140-230		7	3	2150			2700	3300
21		REGENCY 210EFSD	ST	FSH	FBG	DV	IO	140-260		7	11	2850			4550	5550
21		REGENCY 210ESD	ST	CUD	FBG	DV	IO	140-260		7	11	2650			4100	5100
21		REGENCY 210ESS	OP		FBG	DV	IO	140-260		7	11	2650			3900	4850
21		REGENCY 210ESS	ST		FBG	DV	IO	140-260		7	11	2650			3900	4850
21		REGENCY 210EWF	ST	FSH	FBG	DV	IO	140-260		7	11	2900			4600	5600
21		REGENCY 210FSD	ST	FSH	FBG	DV	OB			7	11	2070			8950	10200
21		REGENCY 210SD	ST	RNBT	FBG	DV	OB			7	11	1870			8250	9450
24	3	HERITAGE 244ESD	ST		FBG	DV	IO	185-260		7	11	4020			6250	7500
24	3	HERITAGE 244ESD	ST		FBG	DV	IO	T120-T170		7	11	4020			6900	8050
		1979 BOATS														
16	1	PLAYMATE 600XD	ST	RNBT	FBG	TR	OB			6	3	900			3750	4350
16	1	PLAYMATE 600XESD	ST	RNBT	FBG	TR	IO	120		6	3	1595			1850	2200
16	1	PLAYMATE 600XSD	ST	RNBT	FBG	TR	OB			6	3	900			4050	4700
16	3	BASSMATE VI 600F	OP	BASS	FBG	TR	OB			5	10	760			3300	3850
16	3	BASSMATE VI 600F	ST	BASS	FBG	TR	OB			5	10	760			3300	3850
16	3	SUPER-SPORT 600D	OP	RNBT	FBG	DV	OB			6	5	855			3700	4350
16	4	SUPER-BASSMATE 640SB	OP	BASS	FBG	TR	OB			6	8	960			4150	4800
17	5	DAYTONA 700ESD	ST	RNBT	FBG	DV	IO	120-170		6	11	1810			2300	2700
17	5	DAYTONA 700SD	ST	RNBT	FBG	DV	OB			6	11	1000			4500	5200
17	5	PATRIOT 750BS	ST	RNBT	FBG	DV	OB			6	11	1150			5000	5750
17	5	PATRIOT 750EBS	ST	RNBT	FBG	DV	IO	120-170		6	11	1930			2350	2750
18		TARPON 800SD	ST	RNBT	FBG	TR	OB			7		1260			5450	6300
18		TARPON 800XESD	ST	RNBT	FBG	TR	IO	140-230		7		2000			2500	3050
18	5	SUPREME 850BS	ST	RNBT	FBG	DV	OB			7	3	1370			5900	6750
18	5	SUPREME 850EBS	ST	RNBT	FBG	DV	IO	140-230		7	3	2150			2700	3250
18	5	SUPREME FSH 850EFSD	ST	FSH	FBG	DV	IO	140-230		7	3	2175			2950	3550
21		REGENCY 210EFSD	ST	FSH	FBG	DV	IO	140-260		7	11	2850			4550	5550
21		REGENCY 210ESD	ST	CUD	FBG	DV	IO	140-260		7	11	2650			4100	5100
21		REGENCY 210FSD	ST	FSH	FBG	DV	OB			7	11	2070			8700	10000
21		REGENCY 210SD	ST	RNBT	FBG	DV	OB			7	11	1870			8050	9250
		1978 BOATS														
16	1	PLAYMATE 600XESD	ST	RNBT	FBG	TR	IO	120		6	3	1595			1850	2250
16	1	PLAYMATE 600XSD	ST	RNBT	FBG	TR	OB			6	3	900			3800	4450
16	3	BASSMATE VI 600F	OP	BASS	FBG	TR	OB			5	10	760			3250	3800
16	3	SUPER-SPORT 600D	OP	RNBT	FBG	DV	OB			6	5	855			3650	4250
16	4	SUPER-BASSMATE 640SB	OP	BASS	FBG	TR	OB			6	8	960			4050	4700
17	5	DAYTONA 700ESD	ST	RNBT	FBG	DV	IO	120-170		6	11	1810			2350	2700
17	5	DAYTONA 700SD	ST	RNBT	FBG	DV	OB			6	11	1000			4400	5100
17	5	PATRIOT 750BS	ST	RNBT	FBG	DV	OB			6	11	1150			5000	5700
17	5	PATRIOT 750EBS	ST	RNBT	FBG	DV	IO	120-175		6	11	1930			2350	2800
18		TARPON 800XESD	ST	RNBT	FBG	TR	IO	140-198		7		2000			2500	3000
18		TARPON 800XSD	ST	RNBT	FBG	TR	OB			7		1260			5350	6150
18		TARPON 800XSD	ST	RNBT	FBG	TR	IO	140	MRCR	7		2000			2500	2950
18	5	SUPREME 850ESD	ST	RNBT	FBG	DV	IO	140-240		7	3	2150			2700	3300
18	5	SUPREME FSH 850EFSD	ST	FSH	FBG	DV	IO	140-240		7	3	2175			2950	3600
19	2	SHARK 900XESD	ST	RNBT	FBG	TR	IO	140-240		7	3	2295			2950	3550
19	2	SHARK 900XSD	ST	RNBT	FBG	TR	OB			7	3	1515			6400	7350
19	2	SHARK CRUISER 900XEC	ST	CR	FBG	TR	IO	140-170		7	3	2435			3100	3650
21		REGENCY 210ESD	ST	CUD	FBG	DV	IO	140-240		7	11	2650			4150	4950

 CONTINUED ON NEXT PAGE

GLASSMASTER CO MARINE DIV -CONTINUED See inside cover to adjust price for area

LOA FT	IN	NAME AND/ OR MODEL	TOP/ RIG	BOAT TYPE	-HULL- MTL	TP	ENGINE TP	# HP	MFG	BEAM FT	IN	WGT LBS	DRAFT FT	IN	RETAIL LOW	RETAIL HIGH
		1977 BOATS														
16	1	PLAYMATE 600XD	ST	RNBT	FBG	TR	OB			6	3	900			3650	4250
16	1	PLAYMATE 600XESD	ST	RNBT	FBG	TR	IO	120		6	3	1595			1900	2250
16	1	PLAYMATE 600XSD	ST	RNBT	FBG	TR	OB			6	3	900			3850	4500
16	3	BASSMATE VI 600F	OP	BASS	FBG	TR	OB			5	10	760			3200	3700
16	3	SUPER-SPORT 600D	ST	RNBT	FBG	DV	OB			6	5	855			3600	4200
17	5	DAYTONA 700ESD	ST	RNBT	FBG	DV	IO	120-170		6	11	1810			2350	2750
17	5	DAYTONA 700SD	ST	RNBT	FBG	DV	OB			6	11	1000			4350	5000
17	5	PATRIOT 750BS	ST	RNBT	FBG	DV	OB			6	11	1150			4900	5650
17	5	PATRIOT 750EBS	ST	RNBT	FBG	DV	IO	120-170		6	11	1930			2400	2850
18		TARPON 800ESD	ST	RNBT	FBG	TR	IO	140-190		7		2000			2550	3000
18		TARPON 800XSD	ST	RNBT	FBG	TR	OB			7		1260			5300	6100
18	5	SUPREME 850ESD	ST	RNBT	FBG	DV	IO	140-235		7	3	2150			2750	3350
18	5	SUPREME FSH 850EFSD	ST	FSH	FBG	DV	IO	140-235		7	3	2175			3000	3650
19		GULFSTREAM 900ESD	ST	RNBT	FBG	DV	IO	140-235		7		2050			2750	3300
19		GULFSTREAM 900SD	ST	RNBT	FBG	DV	OB			7		1245			5400	6200
19	2	SHARK 900XESD	ST	RNBT	FBG	TR	IO	140-235		7	3	2295			3000	3600
19	2	SHARK 900XSD	ST	RNBT	FBG	TR	OB			7	3	1515			6300	7200
19	2	SHARK CRUISER 900XEC	HT	CR	FBG	TR	IO	140-170		7	3	2435			3150	3700
		1976 BOATS														
16	1	PLAYMATE 600XD	OP	RNBT	FBG	TR	OB			6	3	900			3450	4000
16	1	PLAYMATE 600XED	OP	RNBT	FBG	TR	IO	120		6	3	1595			2000	2350
16	1	PLAYMATE 600XESD	OP	RNBT	FBG	TR	IO	120		6	3	1595			2000	2350
16	1	PLAYMATE 600XSD	OP	RNBT	FBG	TR	OB			6	3	900			3950	4600
16	3	BASSMATE VI 600F	OP	BASS	FBG	TR	OB			5	10	760			3150	3650
16	3	SUPER-SPORT 600D	OP	RNBT	FBG	DV	OB			6	5	855			3550	4100
17	5	DAYTONA 700D	OP	RNBT	FBG	DV	OB			6	11	1000			4250	4950
17	5	DAYTONA 700ED	OP	RNBT	FBG	DV	IO	140-165		6	11	1000			1950	2350
17	5	DAYTONA 700ESD	OP	RNBT	FBG	DV	IO	140-165		6	11	1000			2050	2450
17	5	PATRIOT 750BS	OP	RNBT	FBG	DV	OB			6	11	1150			4850	5550
18		TARPON 800XD	OP	RNBT	FBG	TR	OB			7		1185			4700	5400
18		TARPON 800XED	OP	RNBT	FBG	TR	IO	140-190		7		1905			2500	2950
18		TARPON 800XESD	OP	RNBT	FBG	TR	IO	140-190		7		1905			2650	3100
18		TARPON 800XSD	OP	RNBT	FBG	TR	OB			7		1185			5300	6100
18	5	SUPREME 850ESD	OP	RNBT	FBG	DV	IO	140-235		7	3	2050			2800	3350
18	5	SUPREME FSH 850EFSD	OP	FSH	FBG	DV	IO	140-190		7	3	2075			3000	3550
19		GULFSTREAM 900ED	OP	RNBT	FBG	DV	IO	140-235		7		2050			2750	3350
19		GULFSTREAM 900ESD	OP	RNBT	FBG	DV	IO	140-235		7		2050			2850	3450
19		GULFSTREAM 900FD	OP	RNBT	FBG	DV	OB			7		1245			5350	6150
19	2	SHARK 900XD	OP	RNBT	FBG	TR	OB			7	3	1515			5900	6800
19	2	SHARK 900XED	OP	RNBT	FBG	TR	IO	140-235		7	3	2295			3000	3650
19	2	SHARK 900XESD	OP	RNBT	FBG	TR	IO	140-235		7	3	2295			3100	3800
19	2	SHARK 900XSD	OP	RNBT	FBG	TR	OB			7	3	1515			6450	7450
19	2	SHARK CRUISER 900XEC	HT	CR	FBG	TR	IO	140-165		7	3	2435			3250	3800
		1975 BOATS														
16	1	PLAYMATE 600XD	OP	RNBT	FBG	TR	OB			6	3	840			3250	3800
16	1	PLAYMATE 600XP	OP	RNBT	FBG	TR	OB			6	3	840			3250	3800
16	1	PLAYMATE 600XSD	OP	RNBT	FBG	TR	OB			6	3	840			3750	4350
16	3	BASSMATE VI 600F	OP	BASS	FBG	TR	OB			5	10	725			3000	3450
17	1	SUPER-SPORT 600D	OP	RNBT	FBG	DV	OB			6	5	800			3400	3950
17	5	DAYTONA 700D	OP	RNBT	FBG	DV	OB			6	11	930			3950	4600
17	5	DAYTONA 700ED	OP	RNBT	FBG	DV	IO	140-188		6	11	1665			2400	2850
17	5	DAYTONA 700P	OP	RNBT	FBG	DV	OB			6	11	930			3950	4600
18		TARPON 800 XP	OP	RNBT	FBG	TR	OB			7		1060			4300	5000
18		TARPON 800XD	OP	RNBT	FBG	TR	OB			7		1060			4300	5000
18		TARPON 800XED	OP	RNBT	FBG	TR	IO	140-175		7		1665			2500	3100
18		TARPON 800XED	OP	RNBT	FBG	TR	IO	188-190		7		2100			2800	3250
18		TARPON 800XESD	OP	RNBT	FBG	TR	IO	140-175				1665			2550	3200
18		TARPON 800XESD	OP	RNBT	FBG	TR	IO	188-190				2100			2850	3350
18		TARPON 800XSD	OP	RNBT	FBG	TR	OB			7		1060			4950	5700
18	5	SUPREME 850ESD	OP	RNBT	FBG	DV	IO	140-175		7	3	2050			2850	3450
18	5	SUPREME 850ESD	OP	RNBT	FBG	DV	IO	188-190		7	3	2365			3100	3600
18	5	SUPREME 850ESD	OP	RNBT	FBG	DV	JT	290	OMC	7	3	2295			3150	3700
18	5	SUPREME 850SD	OP	RNBT	FBG	DV	OB			7	3	1300			5350	6150
19		GULFSTREAM 900D	OP	RNBT	FBG	DV	OB			7		1200			5100	5900
19		GULFSTREAM 900ED	OP	RNBT	FBG	DV	IO	140-175		7		1950			2850	3450
19		GULFSTREAM 900ED	OP	RNBT	FBG	DV	IO	188-190		7		2265			3100	3600
19		GULFSTREAM 900ED	OP	RNBT	FBG	DV	JT	290	OMC	7		2150			3100	3600
19		GULFSTREAM 900FP	OP	RNBT	FBG	DV	OB			7		1200			5100	5900
19	2	SHARK 900XD	OP	RNBT	FBG	TR	OB			7	3	1450			5750	6600
19	2	SHARK 900XED	OP	RNBT	FBG	TR	IO	140-175		7	3	2150			3000	3600
19	2	SHARK 900XED	OP	RNBT	FBG	TR	IO	188-235		7	3	2465			3250	3800
19	2	SHARK 900XESD	OP	RNBT	FBG	TR	IO	140-175		7	3	2150			3150	3750
19	2	SHARK 900XESD	OP	RNBT	FBG	TR	IO	188-235		7	3	2465			3400	4000
19	2	SHARK 900XP	OP	RNBT	FBG	TR	OB			7	3	1450			5750	6600
19	2	SHARK 900XSD	OP	RNBT	FBG	TR	OB			7	3	1450			6300	7200
19	2	SHARK CRUISER 900XEC	HT	CR	FBG	TR	IO	140-165		7	3	2300			3250	3900
		1974 BOATS														
16	1	PLAYMATE 600XD	OP	RNBT	FBG		OB			6	3	840			3250	3800
16	1	PLAYMATE 600XED	OP	RNBT	FBG		IO	100-120		6	3	1500			1950	2350
16	1	PLAYMATE 600XESD	OP	RNBT	FBG		IO	100-120		6	3	1500			2050	2500
16	1	PLAYMATE 600XP	OP	RNBT	FBG		OB			6	3	840			3100	3600
16	1	PLAYMATE 600XSD	OP	RNBT	FBG		OB			6	3	840			3850	4450
16	3	BASSMATE VI 600F	OP	BASS	FBG		OB					750			3050	3550
16	3	SUPER-SPORT 600D	OP	RNBT	FBG		OB			6	5	800			3250	3800
17	5	DAYTONA 700D	OP	RNBT	FBG		OB			6	11	930			3950	4600
17	5	DAYTONA 700ED	OP	RNBT	FBG		IO	120-165		6	11	1665			2500	2950
17	5	DAYTONA 700P	OP	RNBT	FBG		OB			6	11	930			3850	4500
18		TARPON 800XD	OP	RNBT	FBG		OB			7		1060			4400	5050
18		TARPON 800XED	OP	RNBT	FBG		IO	120-165		7		1785			2600	3100
18		TARPON 800XED	OP	RNBT	FBG		IO	188	MRCR	7		2075			2800	3250
18		TARPON 800XED	OP	RNBT	FBG		JT	245	OMC	7		2055			2750	3150
18		TARPON 800XESD	OP	RNBT	FBG		IO	120-165		7		1785			2750	3250
18		TARPON 800XESD	OP	RNBT	FBG		IO	188	MRCR	7		2075			2950	3450
18		TARPON 800XESD	OP	RNBT	FBG		JT	245	OMC	7		2055			2850	3350
18		TARPON 800XP	OP	RNBT	FBG		OB			7		1060			4150	4800
18		TARPON 800XSD	OP	RNBT	FBG		OB			7		1060			4950	5650
19		GULFSTREAM 900D	OP	RNBT	FBG		OB			7		1200			5150	5900
19		GULFSTREAM 900ED	OP	RNBT	FBG		IO	120-165		7		1950			2950	3550
19		GULFSTREAM 900ED	OP	RNBT	FBG		IO	188	MRCR	7		2240			3150	3700
19		GULFSTREAM 900ED	OP	RNBT	FBG		JT	245	OMC	7		2220			3050	3550
19		GULFSTREAM 900FP	OP	RNBT	FBG		OB			7		1200			5050	5800
19	2	SHARK 900SD	OP	RNBT	FBG		OB			7	3	1450			5750	6600
19	2	SHARK 900XEC	OP	CR	FBG		IO	140-165		7	3	2300			3350	4000
19	2	SHARK 900XED	OP	RNBT	FBG		IO	140-165		7	3	2150			3050	3650
19	2	SHARK 900XED	OP	RNBT	FBG		IO	188-225		7	3	2440			3300	3850
19	2	SHARK 900XED	OP	RNBT	FBG		JT	245	OMC	7	3	2420			3150	3650
19	2	SHARK 900XESD	OP	RNBT	FBG		OB			7	3	1450			6350	7300
19	2	SHARK 900XESD	OP	RNBT	FBG		IO	140-225		7	3	2150			3250	4050
19	2	SHARK 900XESD	OP	RNBT	FBG		JT	245	OMC	7	3	2420			3300	3850
19	2	SHARK 900XP	OP	RNBT	FBG		OB			7	3	1450			5550	6400
		1973 BOATS														
16	1	PLAYMATE 600XD	OP	RNBT	FBG		OB			6	3	840			3250	3750
16	1	PLAYMATE 600XED	OP	RNBT	FBG		IO	100-120		6	3	1500			2000	2400
16	1	PLAYMATE 600XESD	OP	RNBT	FBG		IO	100-120		6	3	1500			2150	2550
16	1	PLAYMATE 600XP	OP	RNBT	FBG		OB			6	3	840			3050	3550
16	1	PLAYMATE 600XSD	OP	RNBT	FBG		OB			6	3	840			3850	4450
16	3	SUPER-SPORT 600D	OP	RNBT	FBG		OB			6	5	800			3250	3750
17	5	DAYTONA 700D	OP	RNBT	FBG		OB			6	11	930			3950	4550
17	5	DAYTONA 700ED	OP	RNBT	FBG		IO	120-165		6	11	1665			2550	3050
17	5	DAYTONA 700P	OP	RNBT	FBG		OB			6	11	930			3800	4450
18		TARPON 800XD	OP	RNBT	FBG		OB			7		1060			4250	4900
18		TARPON 800XED	OP	RNBT	FBG		IO	120-165		7		1785			2650	3200
18		TARPON 800XED	OP	RNBT	FBG		IO	188	MRCR	7		2075			2900	3400
18		TARPON 800XED	OP	RNBT	FBG		JT	245	OMC	7		2055			2600	3050
18		TARPON 800XESD	OP	RNBT	FBG		IO	120-165		7		1785			2850	3400
18		TARPON 800XESD	OP	RNBT	FBG		IO	188	MRCR	7		2075			3050	3550
18		TARPON 800XESD	OP	RNBT	FBG		JT	245	OMC	7		2055			2750	3200
18		TARPON 800XP	OP	RNBT	FBG		OB			7		1060			4000	4700
18		TARPON 800XSD	OP	RNBT	FBG		OB			7		1060			5000	5750
19		GULFSTREAM 900D	OP	RNBT	FBG		OB			7		1200			5100	5850
19		GULFSTREAM 900ED	OP	RNBT	FBG		IO	120-165		7		1950			3050	3650
19		GULFSTREAM 900ED	OP	RNBT	FBG		IO	188	MRCR	7		2240			3250	3800
19		GULFSTREAM 900ED	OP	RNBT	FBG		JT	245	OMC	7		2220			2900	3400
19		GULFSTREAM 900FP	OP	RNBT	FBG		OB			7		1200			5000	5750
19	2	SHARK 900XD	OP	RNBT	FBG		OB			7	3	1450			5700	6500
19	2	SHARK 900XEC	OP	CR	FBG		IO	140-165		7	3	2300			3500	4150
19	2	SHARK 900XED	OP	RNBT	FBG		IO	140-165		7	3	2150			3150	3800
19	2	SHARK 900XED	OP	RNBT	FBG		IO	188-225		7	3	2440			3400	4000
19	2	SHARK 900XED	OP	RNBT	FBG		JT	245	OMC	7	3	2420			3050	3500
19	2	SHARK 900XP	OP	RNBT	FBG		OB			7	3	1450			5500	6300
19	2	SHARK 900XSD	OP	RNBT	FBG		OB			7	3	1450			6350	7300
19	2	SHARK 900XSD	OP	RNBT	FBG		IO	140-225		7	3	2150			3350	4200
19	2	SHARK 900XSD	OP	RNBT	FBG		JT	245	OMC	7	3	2420			3200	3700
		1972 BOATS														
16	1	PLAYMATE 600XD	OP	RNBT	FBG		OB			6	3	840			3400	3950
16	1	PLAYMATE 600XED	OP	RNBT	FBG		IO	90-100		6	3	1400			2100	2550
16	1	PLAYMATE 600XP	OP	RNBT	FBG		OB			6	3	840			3300	3850
17	5	DAYTONA 700D	OP	RNBT	FBG		OB			6	11	930			3900	4550

CONTINUED ON NEXT PAGE

LOA FT	IN	NAME AND/OR MODEL	TOP/RIG	BOAT TYPE	HULL MTL	HULL TP	ENG TP	HP	MFG	BEAM FT	IN	WGT LBS	RETAIL LOW	RETAIL HIGH
		1972 BOATS												
17	5	DAYTONA 700ED	OP	RNBT	FBG		IO	120-165		6	11	1665	2650	3150
17	5	DAYTONA 700P	OP	RNBT	FBG		OB			6	11	930	3800	4400
18		TARPON 800XD	OP	RNBT	FBG		OB			7		1060	4500	5200
18		TARPON 800XED	OP	RNBT	FBG		IO	120-165		7		1785	2855	3400
18		TARPON 800XED	OP	RNBT	FBG		IO	188	MRCR	7		2100	3100	3600
18		TARPON 800XP	OP	RNBT	FBG		OB			7		1060	4400	5050
19		GULFSTREAM 900ED	OP	RNBT	FBG		IO	120-188		7		1950	3150	3700
19		GULFSTREAM 900FP	OP	RNBT	FBG		OB			7		1200	5000	5750
19	2	SHARK 900XD	OP	RNBT	FBG		OB			7	3	1450	5850	6750
19	2	SHARK 900XEC	OP	CR	FBG		IO	140-165		7	3	2300	3600	4300
19	2	SHARK 900XED	OP	RNBT	FBG		IO	140-165		7	3	2150	3400	4000
19	2	SHARK 900XED	OP	RNBT	FBG		IO	188-225		7	3	2460	3650	4250
19	2	SHARK 900XP	OP	RNBT	FBG		OB			7	3	1450	5750	6600
		1971 BOATS												
17	5	DAYTONA 700D	OP	RNBT	FBG		OB			6	11	930	3850	4450
17	5	DAYTONA 700ED	OP	RNBT	FBG		IO	120-165		6	11	1665	2750	3350
18		TARPON 800XD	OP	RNBT	FBG		OB			7		1060	4500	5150
18		TARPON 800XED	OP	RNBT	FBG		IO	120-165		7		1785	2950	3500
18		TARPON 800XP	OP	RNBT	FBG		OB			7		1060	4350	5000
19		GULFSTREAM 900ED	OP	RNBT	FBG		IO	120-165		7		1950	3250	3800
19		GULFSTREAM 900FP	OP	RNBT	FBG		OB			7		1200	5000	5750
19	2	SHARK 900XEC	OP	CR	FBG		IO	140-165		7	3	2300	3700	4400
19	2	SHARK 900XED	OP	RNBT	FBG		IO	140-215		7	3	2150	3500	4350
		1970 BOATS												
17	3	TARPON 700XD	OP	RNBT	FBG	TR	OB			6	10	1040	4200	4900
17	3	TARPON 700XED	OP	RNBT	FBG	TR	IO	120-160		6	10	1765	2850	3350
17	5	DAYTONA 700D	OP	RNBT	FBG	SV	OB			6	11	930	3850	4450
17	5	DAYTONA 700ED	OP	RNBT	FBG	DV	IO	120-160		6	11	1665	2850	3300
19		GULFSTREAM 900E	OP	RNBT	FBG	DV	IO	120-160		7		1950	3350	3900
19		GULFSTREAM 900F	OP	FSH	FBG	SV	OB			7		1200	5000	5750
19	2	SHARK 900XEC	OP	CR	FBG	TR	IO	140-155		7	3	2300	3850	4450
19	2	SHARK 900XED	OP	RNBT	FBG	TR	IO	140-155		7	3	2150	3600	4200
		1969 BOATS												
16	1	DEL-RAY 600	OP	RNBT	FBG	DV	OB			6	11	865	3450	4000
16	1	FASTBACK 600E	OP	RNBT	FBG	DV	IO	120		6	11	1595	2600	3050
17	3	TARPON 700X	OP	RNBT	FBG	TR	OB			6	10	1040	4200	4900
17	3	TARPON 700XE	OP	RNBT	FBG	TR	IO	120		6	10	1765	2950	3400
17	5	DAYTONA 700	OP	RNBT	FBG	DV	OB			6	11	930	3850	4450
17	5	DAYTONA 700E	OP	RNBT	FBG	DV	IO	120		6	11	1665	2900	3400
19		GULFSTREAM 900E	OP	RNBT	FBG	DV	IO	120		7		1950	3450	4000
19		GULFSTREAM 900F	OP	FSH	FBG	DV	OB			7		1200	5000	5750
19	2	SHARK 900XE B/R	OP	CR	FBG	DV	IO	120		7	3	2150	3850	4450
19	2	SHARK 900XEC	OP	CR	FBG	TR	IO	120		7	3	2300	3950	4600
		1968 BOATS												
16	1	DEL-RAY 600	OP	RNBT	FBG	SV	IO	120	MRCR	6	10	700	2800	3300
16	1	FASTBACK 600E	OP	RNBT	FBG	SV	IO			6	10	1300	2450	2850
17	1	DAYTONA 700	OP	RNBT	FBG	SV	OB			6	10	930	3800	4400
17	1	DAYTONA 700E	OP	RNBT	FBG	SV	IO	120-160		6	10	1540	2850	3350
17	3	TARPON 700X	OP	RNBT	FBG	TR	OB			6	10	1050	4250	4950
17	3	TARPON 700XE	OP	RNBT	FBG	TR	IO	120-160		6	10	1660	2950	3450
19		GULFSTREAM 900E	OP	RNBT	FBG	SV	IO	120-160		7		1810	3450	4050
19		GULFSTREAM 900F	OP	FSH	FBG	SV	OB			7		1200	5000	5750
19	2	SHARK 900XE B/R	OP	CR	FBG	TR	IO	120-160		7	3	2200	4000	4650
19	2	SHARK 900XEC	OP	CR	FBG	TR	IO	120-160		7	3	2350	4150	4850
		1967 BOATS												
16	1	DEL-RAY 600	OP	RNBT	FBG		OB			6	9	700	2800	3300
16	1	FASTBACK 600E		RNBT	FBG		IO	80		6	9		2900	3350
16	1	FASTBACK 600E	OP	RNBT	FBG		IO	120		6	9	1300	2500	2900
17	1	DAYTONA 700	OP	RNBT	FBG		OB			6	10	930	3800	4400
17	1	DAYTONA 700E		RNBT	FBG		IO	80		6	10		3200	3700
17	1	DAYTONA 700E	OP	RNBT	FBG		IO	120-160		6	10	1540	2950	3450
17	3	TARPON 700X	OP	RNBT	FBG		OB			6	10		4250	4950
17	3	TARPON 700XE	OP	RNBT	FBG	TR	IO	80		6	10	1050	3250	3750
17	3	TARPON 700XE		RNBT	FBG		IO	120		6	10		3050	3550
19		GULFSTREAM 900E	OP	RNBT	FBG		IO	120-160		7		1660	3600	4200
19		GULFSTREAM 900F	OP	FSH	FBG		IO			7		1810	5000	5750
19	2	SHARK 900XE B/R	OP	CR	FBG		IO	120-160		7	3	2200	4150	4850
		1966 BOATS												
16	1	DEL-RAY 600	OP	RNBT	FBG		OB			6	9	700	2800	3300
16	1	FASTBACK 600E	OP	RNBT	FBG		IO	110-120		6	10		3000	3500
16	3	TARPON 600X	OP	RNBT	FBG		OB			6	9		3550	4150
17	1	DAYTONA 700	OP	RNBT	FBG		OB			6	10	900	3700	4300
17	1	DAYTONA 700E	OP	RNBT	FBG		IO	110-165		6	10		3300	3900
17	1	DAYTONA 700F	OP	FSH	FBG		IO						**	**
19		GULFSTREAM 900	OP	RNBT	FBG		OB			7		2100	7250	8300
19		GULFSTREAM 900E	OP	RNBT	FBG		IO	110-200		7			3900	4650
19		GULFSTREAM 900F	OP	FSH	FBG		OB			7			5350	6100
24		MARINER 2400	OP	CR	FBG		IO	150-225		8			9500	11000
24		MARINER 2400	OP	CR	FBG		IO	T110-T200		8			10500	12200
		1965 BOATS												
16	1	DEL-RAY 600	OP	RNBT	FBG		OB						3550	4100
16	1	DEL-RAY 600E FASTBK	OP	RNBT	FBG		IO						**	**
16	1	DEL-RAY 600E FASTBK	OP	RNBT	FBG		IO	110-120					3300	4100
17	1	DAYTONA 700	OP	RNBT	FBG		OB						4350	5000
17	1	DAYTONA 700E	OP	RNBT	FBG		IO						**	**
17	1	DAYTONA 700E	OP	RNBT	FBG		IO	110-120					3450	4250
17	1	DAYTONA 700F	OP	FSH	FBG		OB						4600	5250
19		GULFSTREAM 900	OP	RNBT	FBG		OB						5400	6200
19		GULFSTREAM 900E	OP	RNBT	FBG		IO						**	**
19		GULFSTREAM 900E	OP	RNBT	FBG		IO	110-150					4100	5000
19		GULFSTREAM 900F	OP	FSH	FBG		OB						5350	6100
24		MARINER 2400 DLX	OP	CR	FBG		IO	140-225					9750	11300
24		MARINER 2400 DLX	OP	CR	FBG		IO	T110-T120					10800	12800
24		MARINER 2400F	OP	FSH	FBG		IO	140-225					10200	11800
24		MARINER 2400F	OP	FSH	FBG		IO	T110-T120					11400	13400
		1964 BOATS												
16	1	FASTBACK VF	OP	RNBT	FBG		IO			6	9		**	**
16	1	MALABAR V	OP	RNBT	FBG		IO			6	9	700	2800	3300
17	1	CAPE-CORAL VE	OP	CR	FBG		IO	110-120		6	10	1540	3250	3750
17	1	CAPE-SABLE VE	OP	CR	FBG		OB			6	10		4350	5000
17	1	CRUISETTE VC	OP	RNBT	FBG		OB			6	10	1000	4050	4700
17	1	DAYTONA V	OP	RNBT	FBG		OB			6	10	930	3800	4400
17	1	FISHERMAN VF	OP	FSH	FBG		OB			6	10	930	3750	4350
17	1	MELBOURNE V	OP	FSH	FBG		OB			6	10	930	3800	4400
19		GULFSTREAM VE	OP	RNBT	FBG		IO	110-150		7			4200	4900
19		KEY-WESTER VE	OP	RNBT	FBG		OB			7		1200	5200	6000
19		LARGO V	OP	RNBT	FBG		OB			7		1200	4850	5550
		1963 BOATS												
16	1			FSH	FBG		OB						3550	4100
16	1			SKI	FBG		OB						3450	4050
16	1			SKI	FBG		IO						3250	3800
16	1	CRUISETTE	OP	RNBT	FBG		IO	80					3950	4600
16	1	CRUISETTE	OP	RNBT	FBG		IO	80					3700	4300
16	1	DEL-RAY	OP	RNBT	FBG		IO	80					3150	3650
16	1	DEL-RAY	OP	RNBT	FBG		IO						3550	3900
16	1	DEL-RAY	HT	RNBT	FBG		IO	80					3550	4100
16	1	DEL-RAY	HT	RNBT	FBG		IO						3550	4050
16	1	SPECIAL			FBG		IO						3500	4050
19		CAPE-CODDER	OP	RNBT	FBG		IO						5400	6200
19		CAPE-CODDER	OP	RNBT	FBG		IO	80-110					4450	5100
19		VENETIAN	OP	CR	FBG		OB						5350	6150
19		VENETIAN	OP	CR	FBG		IO	80-110					4600	5300
		1962 BOATS												
16	1			OVNTR	FBG		OB						3500	4050
16	1			RNBT	FBG		OB						3550	4100
16	1	CRUISETTE 6317C	OP	RNBT	FBG		OB						3550	4100
19		C		CR	FBG		OB						5350	6150
19		GULFSTREAM		RNBT	FBG		OB						5400	6200
		1961 BOATS												
16	1	6117		UTL	FBG		OB			6	8	700	2750	3200
16	1	6117-C		CR	FBG		OB			6	8	800	3150	3700
19		6119		UTL	FBG		OB			6	11	1050	3950	4600
19		6119-C		CR	FBG		OB			6	11	1300	5300	6100
		1960 BOATS												
16				RNBT	FBG		OB						3550	4100
16		6017		RNBT	FBG	RB	OB			16		600	2500	2900
16		6017C		CR	FBG	RB	OB			16		650	2600	3050
16		C		CR	FBG		OB						3450	4050
		1959 BOATS												
16				UTL	FBG		OB						3450	4000
18	9	OFFSHORE		OFF	FBG		OB			7	9	900	3900	4550

GLASSPAR BOATS

DIV LARSON INDUSTRIES INC
LITTLE FALLS MN 56345   COAST GUARD MFG ID- LAR
See inside cover to adjust price for area

LOA FT	IN	NAME AND/OR MODEL	TOP/RIG	BOAT TYPE	HULL MTL	HULL TP	ENG TP	HP	MFG	BEAM FT	IN	WGT LBS	RETAIL LOW	RETAIL HIGH
		1978 BOATS												
17	2	CUTLAS 17	ST	RNBT	FBG	TR	IO	120-165		6	10	2248	1750	2150
17	3	FLYING-V 17V	ST	RNBT	FBG	SV	IO	140-200		7	2	1968	1750	2150
17	3	FLYING-V 17V	ST	RNBT	FBG	SV	IO	225	OMC	7	2	1968	1700	2050

LOA FT	IN	NAME AND/ OR MODEL	TOP/ RIG	BOAT TYPE	-HULL- MTL	TP	ENGINE TP	# HP	MFG	BEAM FT	IN	WGT LBS	DRAFT FT	IN	RETAIL LOW	RETAIL HIGH
		1978 BOATS														
17	3	FLYING-V 17V	ST	RNBT	FBG	SV	IO	225	VLVO	7	2	1968			1850	2200
18		GRENADA 18V	ST	RNBT	FBG	SV	IO	140	MRCR	6	11	2260			1800	2150
18		GRENADA 18V	ST	RNBT	FBG	SV	IO	140	OMC	6	11	2260			1800	2150
18		GRENADA 18V	ST	RNBT	FBG	SV	IO	140-250		6	11	2260			1900	2400
18	1	SEAFAIR SEDAN	ST	CAMPR	FBG	SV	OB			7	4	1400			1700	2000
18	1	SEAFAIR SEDAN	ST	CAMPR	FBG	SV	IO	140-185		7	4	2300			1950	2450
18	3	CHALLENGER	ST	RNBT	FBG		OB			7	2	1600			1900	2250
18	3	CHALLENGER	ST	RNBT	FBG		IO	140-198		7	2	2400			1950	2450
18	3	CHALLENGER	ST	RNBT	FBG		IO	200-250		7	2	2400			2100	2550
19	1	CUTLAS 19	ST	RNBT	FBG	TR	OB			7	7	1705			2000	2400
19	1	CUTLAS 19	ST	RNBT	FBG	TR	IO	140-200		7	7	2660			2300	2800
19	1	CUTLAS 19	ST	RNBT	FBG	TR	IO	225-250		7	7	2660			2350	2850
21	2	TOBAGO 21	ST	CR	FBG	DV	IO	165-198		7	10	2845			3050	3550
21	2	TOBAGO 21	ST	CR	FBG	DV	IO	200-250		7	10	3185			3450	4000
21	2	TOBAGO 21	HT	CR	FBG	DV	IO	185-250		7	10				3300	4100
21	5	BIMINI 21	ST	CUD	FBG	DV	IO	165-250		8		3010			3200	3950
23	2	BERMUDA 23	ST	CUD	FBG	DV	IO	140-198		8		4350			4600	5400
23	2	BERMUDA 23	ST	CUD	FBG	DV	IO	T170-T250		8		4350			5150	6400
23	2	BERMUDA 23	HT	EXP	FBG	DV	IO	140-198		8		4729			4900	5750
23	2	BERMUDA 23	HT	EXP	FBG	DV	IO	T170-T250		8		4729			5450	6750
23	2	ROTUMA DAY 23	ST	CR	FBG	DV	IO	140-198		8		3315			3750	4550
23	2	ROTUMA DAY 23	ST	CR	FBG	DV	IO	T170-T200		8		3315			4400	5400
23	2	ROTUMA DAY 23	ST	CR	FBG	DV	IO	T225-T250		8		3315			4500	5550
23	2	SKIPPER 23	FB	CR	FBG	DV	IO	140		8					3850	4600
23	2	SKIPPER 23	FB	CR	FBG	DV	IO	T170-T200		8					4450	5450
23	2	SKIPPER 23	FB	CR	FBG	DV	IO	T225-T250		8					4550	5600
25	10	GRAND-BAHAMA 26	HT	CR	FBG	DV	IO	140-198		8		5519			6050	7200
25	10	GRAND-BAHAMA 26	HT	CR	FBG	DV	IO	T170-T250		8		5519			7150	8750
		1977 BOATS														
17	2	CUTLAS 17	ST	RNBT	FBG	TR	IO	130-170		6	9				1700	2050
17	4	FLYING-V 17V	ST	RNBT	FBG	SV	IO	130-225		6	6				1700	2100
17	4	TONGA 17DV	ST	RNBT	FBG	DV	IO	170-233		6	7				1750	2150
17	4	TONGA 17DV	ST	RNBT	FBG	DV	JT	245-320		6	7				2050	2450
18		GRENADA 18V	ST	RNBT	FBG	SV	OB			6	9				1700	2000
18		GRENADA 18V	ST	RNBT	FBG	SV	IO	130-235		6	9				1900	2400
19	1	CUTLAS 19	ST	RNBT	FBG	TR	OB			7	6				1900	2250
19	1	CUTLAS 19	ST	RNBT	FBG	TR	IO	140-170		7	6				2250	2750
19	1	CUTLAS 19	ST	RNBT	FBG	TR	IO	225-280		7	6				2450	2900
21	2	TOBAGO 21	ST	CR	FBG	DV	IO	165-233		7	6				3250	4050
21	2	TOBAGO 21	HT	CR	FBG	DV	IO	175-233		7	6				3250	4050
21	5	BIMINI 21	ST	CUD	FBG	DV	IO	165-233		8					3200	3950
23	2	BERMUDA 23	ST	CUD	FBG	DV	IO	188-233		7	10				4550	5450
23	2	BERMUDA 23	ST	CUD	FBG	DV	IO	T130-T140		7	10				5300	6050
23	2	BERMUDA 23	HT	EXP	FBG	DV	IO	188-233		7	10				4950	5900
23	2	BERMUDA 23	HT	EXP	FBG	DV	IO	T130-T140		7	10				5700	6550
23	2	ROTUMA DAY 23	ST	CR	FBG	DV	IO	188-233		7	10				3900	4750
23	2	ROTUMA DAY 23	ST	CR	FBG	DV	IO	T130-T140		7	10				4650	5350
		1976 BOATS														
17	2	CUTLAS 17	ST	RNBT	FBG	TR	IO	120		6	10	2260			1750	2100
17	2	CUTLAS 17	ST	RNBT	FBG	TR	IO	130-165		6	10	2260			1900	2250
17	3	FLYING-V 17V	ST	RNBT	FBG	SV	IO	130-225		7	2	1990			1800	2250
17	3	FLYING-V 17V	ST	RNBT	FBG	SV	IO	230	VLVO	7	2	1990			1950	2300
17	4	TONGA 17DV	ST	RNBT	FBG	DV	IO	140-165		6	9	2307			1800	2150
17	4	TONGA 17DV	ST	RNBT	FBG	DV	IO	170-233		6	9	2307			1950	2400
18		GRENADA 18V	ST	RNBT	FBG	SV	IO	130-225		6	11	2282			2000	2450
19	1	CUTLAS 19	ST	RNBT	FBG	TR	OB			7	7				1900	2250
19	1	CUTLAS 19	ST	RNBT	FBG	TR	IO	140-225		7	7	2680			2350	2900
19	1	CUTLAS 19	ST	RNBT	FBG	TR	IO	230-233		7	7	2680			2550	2950
21	2	TOBAGO 21	ST	CR	FBG	DV	IO	175-233		7	10	3640			3700	4600
21	3	TOBAGO 21	ST	CR	FBG	SV	IO	165-225		7	10	2845			3150	3850
21	3	TOBAGO 21	ST	CR	FBG	SV	IO	230-233		7	10	2845			3400	3950
21	5	BIMINI 21	ST	CUD	FBG	DV	IO	165-233		8		3005			3300	4100
23	2	BERMUDA 23	ST	CUD	FBG	DV	IO	188-233		8		4350			4800	5700
23	2	BERMUDA 23	ST	CUD	FBG	DV	IO	T140		8		4350			5300	6100
23	2	BERMUDA 23	ST	EXP	FBG	DV	IO	188-233		8		4729			5050	6050
23	2	BERMUDA 23	ST	EXP	FBG	DV	IO	T140		8		4729			5600	6450
23	2	ROTUMA DAY 23	ST	CR	FBG	DV	IO	188-233		8		3315			3950	4800
23	2	ROTUMA DAY 23	ST	CR	FBG	DV	IO	T140		8		3315			4500	5200
		1975 BOATS														
16	1	CUTLAS 160	ST	UTL	FBG	TR	IO	120	MRCR	6	5	1896			1700	2000
16	1	CUTLAS 160	ST	UTL	FBG	TR	IO	130-140		6	5	1896			1800	2150
16	1	CUTLAS 165	ST	UTL	FBG	TR	IO	120	MRCR	6	6	1871			1700	2000
16	1	CUTLAS 165	ST	UTL	FBG	TR	IO	130-170		6	6	1871			1800	2150
17	2	CUTLAS 170	ST	RNBT	FBG	TR	IO	120-165		6	10	2004			1750	2150
17	2	CUTLAS 170	ST	RNBT	FBG	TR	IO	170-188		6	10	2004			1850	2200
17	3	V-175	ST	RNBT	FBG	DV	IO	170-266		6	7	1880			1750	2200
17	4	SPORT V175	ST	RNBT	FBG	DV	IO	120-165		6	7	2131			1750	2100
17	4	SPORT V175	ST	RNBT	FBG	DV	IO	170-233		6	7	2131			1900	2350
18		GRENADA 18V	ST	RNBT	FBG	SV	IO	120		6	11	1945			1800	2150
		IO 130-200 1900 2300, IO 225 MRCR 1900 2250, IO 225 OMC 1850 2200														
		IO 225-233 2000 2400														
18		GRENADA B/R 18V	ST	UTL	FBG	SV	IO	120		6	11	1998			2050	2400
18		GRENADA B/R 18V	ST	UTL	FBG	SV	IO	130-233		6	11	1998			2200	2700
19	2	CUTLAS 191	ST	RNBT	FBG	TR	OB			7	7	1516			1800	2150
19	2	CUTLAS 191	ST	RNBT	FBG	TR	IO	120-200		7	7	2470			2350	2900
19	2	CUTLAS 191	ST	RNBT	FBG	TR	IO	225-233		7	7	2470			2400	2950
21	2	V-210	HT	CR	FBG	DV	IO	165-233		7	10	3640			3800	4700
21	2	V-212	ST	SPTCR	FBG	DV	IO	165-233		7	10	2845			3400	4150
21	5	V-215	ST	CUD	FBG	DV	IO	165-233		8		3005			3400	4200
23	2	V-230		SPTCR	FBG	DV	IO	165-233		8		3315			4100	5050
23	2	V-230		SPTCR	FBG	DV	IO	T140		8		3315			4750	5450
23	2	V-231	ST	CUD	FBG	DV	IO	188-233		8		4350			4900	5850
23	2	V-231	ST	CUD	FBG	DV	IO	T140		8		4350			5450	6250
23	2	V234	HT	CR	FBG	DV	IO			8		4729			**	**
		1974 BOATS														
16	3	SPEC ED V-165	ST	RNBT	FBG		IO	165		6	11	1848			1700	2000
17	3	CUTLAS 170	ST	RNBT	FBG	TR	IO	120-170		6	11	1825			1750	2150
17	5	SPORT V-175	ST	RNBT	FBG	SV	IO	140-170		7	4	1796			1800	2200
17	5	SPORT V-175	ST	RNBT	FBG	SV	IO	188	MRCR	7	4	2224			2000	2400
17	5	V-175	ST	RNBT	FBG	SV	IO	140-170		7	4	1779			1800	2200
17	5	V-175	ST	RNBT	FBG	SV	IO	188	MRCR	7	4	2207			2000	2400
18	3	CUTLAS 190	ST	RNBT	FBG	TR	IO	140-170		7	5	2269			2150	2600
18	3	CUTLAS 190	ST	RNBT	FBG	TR	IO	188	MRCR	7	5	2697			2400	2800
19	7	DON-TWENTY	ST	SKI	FBG	DV	JT	275	CHRY	7	2	2545			2400	2750
19	7	DON-TWENTY	ST	SKI	FBG	DV	IO	275	CHRY	7	2	2598			2650	3050
20		V-200	ST	RNBT	FBG	DV	IO	165-188		7	4	2324			2600	3250
21	3	V-210	HT	CR	FBG	DV	IO	188-225		8		3200			3700	4400
21	3	V-211	OP	SPTCR	FBG	DV	IO	188-225		8		3100			3750	4500
21	5	V-215	ST	CUD	FBG	DV	IO	165-170		8		2465			3150	3650
21	5	V-215	ST	CUD	FBG	DV	IO	188	MRCR	8		2775			3400	3950
23	3	V-230	ST	SPTCR	FBG	DV	IO	188-225		8		3475			4500	5300
23	3	V-230	ST	SPTCR	FBG	DV	IO	T140		8		3644			5200	6000
23	3	V-231	ST	CUD	FBG	DV	IO	188-225		8		3475			4250	5100
23	3	V-231	ST	CUD	FBG	DV	IO	T140		8		3644			5000	5750
		1973 BOATS														
16	4	CUTLAS 175	ST	RNBT	FBG	TR	IO	120-140		7	5	1925			1800	2150
16	4	CUTLAS 175	ST	RNBT	FBG	TR	IO	165	MRCR	7	5	2065			1900	2250
16	4	CUTLAS 175/MT	ST	RNBT	FBG	TR	IO	120	OMC	7	5	1955			1750	2100
16	4	CUTLAS 175/PT	ST	RNBT	FBG	TR	IO	120	OMC	7	5	1955			1800	2150
16	8	CITATION	ST	RNBT	FBG	SV	IO	120-165		7	1	1820			1750	2150
16	8	CITATION MT	ST	RNBT	FBG	SV	IO	120	OMC	7	1	1850			1700	2050
16	8	CITATION PT	ST	RNBT	FBG	SV	IO	120	OMC	7	1	1850			1750	2100
17	5	V-175	ST	RNBT	FBG		IO	188	MRCR	7	4	2188			2050	2450
17	5	V-175	ST	RNBT	FBG	SV	IO	140-170		7	4	1940			1950	2400
18	3	CUTLAS 190	ST	RNBT	FBG	TR	OB			7	5	1500			1700	2000
18	3	CUTLAS 190	ST	RNBT	FBG	TR	IO	140-188		7	5	2265			2250	2800
20		COMMANDANT	ST	RNBT	FBG	SV	IO	140-188		7	4	2021			2500	3100
20		CONSORT	ST	CUD	FBG	SV	IO	165-188		7	4	2213			2700	3250
21	5	BARON	ST	RNBT	FBG	DV	IO	165-188		8		2865			3400	4050
21	5	BARON	ST	RNBT	FBG	DV	IO	225		8		3235			3700	4350
		1972 BOATS														
16	3	CUTLAS 1600	ST	RNBT	FBG	TR	IO	130	VLVO	6	3	1668			1700	2000
16	4	CUTLAS	ST	RNBT	FBG		IO	120		7	5	2000			1900	2250
16	4	CUTLAS	ST	RNBT	FBG		IO	130	CHRY	7	5	2000			1900	2250
16	4	CUTLAS	ST	RNBT	FBG		IO	130-155		7	5	2000			2000	2400
16	8	CITATION	ST	RNBT	FBG	SV	IO	120		7	1	1920			1850	2200
16	8	CITATION	ST	RNBT	FBG	SV	IO	130	CHRY	7	1	1920			1850	2200
16	8	CITATION	ST	RNBT	FBG	SV	IO	130-140		7	1	1920			1950	2350
16	8	CITATION CLOSED BOW	ST	RNBT	FBG	SV	IO	120		7	1	1865			1800	2150
16	8	CITATION CLOSED BOW	ST	RNBT	FBG	SV	IO	130	CHRY	7	1	1865			1800	2150
16	8	CITATION CLOSED BOW	ST	RNBT	FBG	SV	IO	130-155		7	1	1865			1950	2300
17	5	SUPER SPORT V-175	ST	RNBT	FBG	DV	IO	120		7	4	1940			2000	2350
17	5	SUPER SPORT V-175	ST	RNBT	FBG	DV	IO	130	CHRY	7	4	1940			2000	2350
17	5	SUPER SPORT V-175	ST	RNBT	FBG	DV	IO	130-225		7	4	1940			2100	2500
18	3	CUTLAS	ST	RNBT	FBG	TR	OB			7	5	1500			1700	2000
18	3	CUTLAS	ST	RNBT	FBG	TR	IO	120-225		7	5	2265			2300	2850
20		NEWPORT	ST	CR	FBG	DV	IO	140-225		7	4	2213			2800	3400

CONTINUED ON NEXT PAGE

LOA FT IN	NAME AND/ OR MODEL	TOP/ RIG	BOAT TYPE	-HULL- MTL TP	TP	# HP	MFG	BEAM FT IN	WGT LBS	DRAFT FT IN	RETAIL LOW	RETAIL HIGH
			---- 1972 BOATS									
20	SEALINER	ST	RNBT	FBG	DV	IO 120-225		7 4	2021		2600	3200
			---- 1971 BOATS									
16 4	CUTLAS	ST	RNBT	FBG		IO 120-140		7 5	2000		1950	2350
16 8	CITATION	ST	RNBT	FBG	SV	IO 120-140		7 1	1865		1900	2300
17 2	FLYING-V	ST	RNBT	FBG	SV	IO 120-215		7 4	2040		2100	2500
18 3	CUTLAS	ST	CAMPR	FBG	TR	IO 120-215		7 5	2330		2450	2900
18 3	CUTLAS	ST	RNBT	FBG	TR	OB		7 5	1500		1700	2000
18 3	CUTLAS	ST	RNBT	FBG	TR	IO 120-215		7 5	2330		2450	2800
20	NEWPORT	ST	CR	FBG	DV	OB		7 4	1454		1800	2150
20	NEWPORT	ST	CR	FBG	DV	IO 120-215		7 4	2213		2900	3400
20	SEALINER	ST	RNBT	FBG	DV	IO 120-215		7 4	2021		2700	3250
23 2	RAIDER	HT	CR	FBG	DV	IO 155-215		8	4000		5300	6050
			---- 1970 BOATS									
16	REGATTA 165	SLP	SA/OD	FBG	LB	OB		5 8	450		1700	2050
16 4	CUTLAS	ST	RNBT	FBG	TR	IO 120		7 2	2000		2000	2350
16 8	CITATION	ST	RNBT	FBG	SV	IO 120		7 1	1865		1950	2300
16 8	CITATION STANDARD	OP	RNBT	FBG	SV	IO 120		7 1	1865		1950	2300
17 2	FLYING-V	ST	RNBT	FBG	DV	IO 120-215		7 4	2040		2200	2650
18 2	SEAFARER	ST	CUD	FBG	SV	OB		7 2	1520		1700	2000
18 2	SEAFARER	ST	CUD	FBG	SV	IO 120-215		7 5	2380		2600	3100
18 2	SEAFARER SUNLINER	ST	RNBT	FBG	SV	IO 120-215		7 5	2110		2400	2850
18 3	CUTLAS	ST	CAMPR	FBG	TR	IO 120-215		7 2	2330		2500	3000
18 3	CUTLAS	ST	RNBT	FBG	TR	OB		7 2	1500		1700	2000
18 3	CUTLAS	ST	RNBT	FBG	TR	IO 120-215		7 2	2330		2450	2950
20 2	COMMODORE CHARGER	ST	CR	FBG	DV	IO 120-215		7 10	2660		3450	4150
21 3	CRUISER HOME	HT	FH	FBG	TR	IO 155-215		7 5	2900		**	**
23 2	RAIDER	HT	CR	FBG	DV	IO 155-215		8	4200		5650	6650
			---- 1969 BOATS									
16	REGATTA 165	SLP	SA/OD	FBG	LB	OB		5 8	450		1700	2000
16 3	CUTLAS 16	ST	RNBT	FBG	SV	IO 120	MRCR	7 5	1885		2050	2400
16 8	CITATION	ST	RNBT	FBG	SV	IO 120	MRCR	7 1	1685		1900	2300
16 8	GLASSPAR 16	ST	RNBT	FBG	SV	IO 120	MRCR	7 1	1665		1900	2300
17 2	FLYING-V 175	ST	RNBT	FBG	DV	IO 120	MRCR	7 4	1835		2150	2500
18 2	SEAFARER	ST	CUD	FBG	DV	IO 120	MRCR	7 5	2010		2450	2850
18 2	SEAFARER SUNLINER	ST	RNBT	FBG	SV	IO 120	MRCR	7 5	1910		2350	2750
18 4	CUTLAS 18	ST	RNBT	FBG	TR	OB		7 2	1500		1700	2000
18 4	CUTLAS 18	ST	RNBT	FBG	TR	IO 120	MRCR	7 2	2160		2450	2850
20 2	CHARGER	ST	CR	FBG		IO 120	MRCR	7 10	2660		3600	4200
			---- 1968 BOATS									
16 3	CUTLAS	ST	RNBT	FBG	TR	IO 120		7 5	1885	3 1	2100	2500
16 8	CITATION	OP	RNBT	FBG	SV	IO 120-165		7 1	1685	3 4	2000	2450
17 2	FLYING-V	OP	RNBT	FBG		IO 120-200		7 4	1835	3 5	2250	2700
18 2	SEAFAIR SEDAN	OP	SDN	FBG		IO 120-200		7 5	2010	3 5	2500	3050
18 2	SEAFAIR SEDAN	OP	SDN	FBG		IO 210		7 5	2238	3 5	2700	3150
18 2	SEAFAIR SUNLINER	OP	RNBT	FBG	SV	IO 120-210		7 5	1910	3 5	2450	3050
20 2	CHARGER	OP	CR	FBG	SV	IO 120-155		7 10	2000	4 3	3250	3750
20 2	CHARGER	ST	CR	FBG	SV	IO 160-210		7 10	2742	4 3	3800	4650
			---- 1967 BOATS									
16 2	CITATION CUSTOM	OP	RNBT	FBG	SV	IO 120-200		6 11			2200	2650
17 2	FLYING-V CUSTOM	OP	RNBT	FBG	SV	IO 120-200		7 4			2400	2850
17 6	SEAFAIR SEDAN	OP	SDN	FBG	SV	IO 120-200		7 1			2550	3000
17 6	SEAFAIR SUNLINER	OP	RNBT	FBG		IO 120-200		7 1			2500	3000
20 2	COMMODORE CHARGER	OP	CR	FBG		IO 120-225		7 10			3500	4200
			---- 1966 BOATS									
16	FLYING-V 1600	OP	RNBT	FBG		IO 110-150		7			2100	2500
16	GOLD-CUP 16-60	ST	RNBT	FBG		IO 60-120					2050	2450
16 9	CITATION	OP	RNBT	FBG		IO 110-120		6 11			2200	2600
16 9	CITATION CUSTOM	OP	RNBT	FBG		IO 110-120		6 11			2300	2850
17 2	FLYING-V	OP	RNBT	FBG		IO 110-150		7 4			2400	2800
17 2	FLYING-V CUSTOM	OP	RNBT	FBG		IO 110-150		7 4			2500	2950
17 6	SEAFAIR SEDAN	OP	SDN	FBG		IO 110-150		7 1			2600	3050
17 6	SEAFAIR SUNLINER	OP	RNBT	FBG		IO 110-150		7 1			2600	3050
21 1	NEWPORTER	OP	CR	FBG		IO 150-225		7 8			4700	5550
			---- 1965 BOATS									
16	SUPER G CUSTOM	OP	RNBT	FBG		IO 110-165					2150	2650
17 2	FLYING-V CUSTOM	OP	RNBT	FBG		IO 110-165					2500	3100
17 2	FLYING-V STANDARD	OP	RNBT	FBG		IO 110-165					2400	2950
17 6	SEAFAIR SEDAN	OP	SDN	FBG		IO 110-165					2700	3300
17 6	SEAFAIR SUNLINER	OP	RNBT	FBG		IO 110-165					2700	3300
21 1	NEWPORTER	OP	CR	FBG		IO 140-225					4900	5800
			---- 1964 BOATS									
16	SUPER G	OP	RNBT	FBG		IO 80-160					2250	2600
17 6	SEAFAIR CUSTOM	OP	SDN	FBG		IO 80-140					2850	3350
17 6	SEAFAIR DELUXE	OP	SDN	FBG		IO 80-140					2700	3200
17 6	SEAFAIR SPORTSMAN	OP	RNBT	FBG		IO 80-140					2600	3100
17 6	SEAFAIR SUNLINER CUS	OP	RNBT	FBG		OB					1800	2150
17 6	SEAFAIR SUNLINER CUS	OP	RNBT	FBG		IO 80-140					2950	3450
17 6	SEAFAIR SUNLINER DLX	OP	RNBT	FBG		IO 80-140					2800	3300
21 1	NEWPORTER	OP	CR	FBG		IO 140-160					5050	5850
			---- 1963 BOATS									
16	CITATION CUSTOM	OP	RNBT	FBG		IO 80					2350	2750
16	CITATION STANDARD	OP	RNBT	FBG		IO 80					2250	2600
17 6	SEAFAIR CUSTOM	OP	SDN	FBG		IO 80-110					2900	3350
17 6	SEAFAIR SPORTSMAN	OP	RNBT	FBG		IO 80-110					2800	3250
17 6	SEAFAIR STD		SDN	FBG		IO 80-110					2900	3350
17 6	SEAFAIR SUNLINER	OP	RNBT	FBG		OB					1750	2050
17 6	SEAFAIR SUNLINER	OP	RNBT	FBG		IO 80-110					2950	3450
21 1	VENTURA CUSTOM	OP	CR	FBG		OB					2400	2800
21 1	VENTURA CUSTOM	OP	CR	FBG		IO 100-170					5350	6250
21 1	VENTURA STANDARD	OP	CR	FBG		OB					2050	2450
21 1	VENTURA STANDARD	OP	CR	FBG		IO 100-170					5050	5900
			---- 1962 BOATS									
17 5	SEAFAIR PHAETON	ST	CR	FBG		IO 80					2750	3200
17 5	SEAFAIR SEDAN	OP	SDN	FBG		IO 80					2750	3200
17 5	SEAFAIR SUNLINER	OP	RNBT	FBG		IO 80					2750	3200
17	MERIDIAN	OP	CR	FBG		IB 170					1800	2150
21 1	VENTURA	OP	CR	FBG		OB					2250	2650
			---- 1960 BOATS									
19	CLUB MARINER		CBNCR	FBG	SV	OB		7 4	1500		1700	2050
19	CLUB-MARINER			FBG		OB					1800	2150
19	MARINER		RNBT	FBG		OB					1800	2150
19	SPORT-MARINER	HT	CR	FBG		OB					1800	2150
			---- 1959 BOATS									
19	SPORT-MARINER		CR	FBG		OB					1800	2150
			---- 1958 BOATS									
19	CLUB-MARINER		CR	FBG		OB					1800	2150
19	MARINER		CNV	FBG		OB					1800	2150
19	SPORT-MARINER		CR	FBG		OB					1800	2150

GLASTECH ENGINEERING CO

Call 1-800-327-6929 for BUC Personalized Evaluation Service
Or, for 1974 boats, sign onto www.BUCValuPro.com

GLASTEX COMPANY

SEA STAR
MONMOUTH IL 61462   COAST GUARD MFG ID- GTX   See inside cover to adjust price for area

LOA FT IN	NAME AND/ OR MODEL	TOP/ RIG	BOAT TYPE	-HULL- MTL TP	TP	# HP	MFG	BEAM FT IN	WGT LBS	DRAFT FT IN	RETAIL LOW	RETAIL HIGH
			---- 1982 BOATS									
17	BASS B780		BASS	FBG	DV	OB		6 11	790		1700	2000
17	SKI/BASS B780		BASS	FBG	DV	OB		6 11	795		1700	2000
17 7	MACH I V888		RNBT	FBG	DV	IO 140		7 2	2200		4000	4650
17 7	MACH I V888 CB		RNBT	FBG	DV	IO 140		7 2	2100		3900	4550
17 7	SPOILER V888		RNBT	FBG	DV	OB		7 2	1200		2550	3000
17 7	SPOILER V888		RNBT	FBG	DV	IO 140		7 2	2200		3700	4300
17 7	SPOILER V888 CB		RNBT	FBG	DV	OB		7 2	1200		2450	2850
17 7	SPOILER V888 CB		RNBT	FBG	DV	IO 140		7 2	2100		3650	4200
19 11	BAHAMA V2096		RNBT	FBG	DV	IO 170		8	2800		5300	6100
19 11	BERMUDA VBR2096		RNBT	FBG	DV	IO 170		8	2850		5400	6200
19 11	TAHITIAN VC2096		CR	FBG	DV	IO 170		8	2850		5600	6450
21 6	CARIBBEAN V2296		CR	FBG	DV	IO 185		8	3100		6850	7900
22 4	ISLANDER T2295		CR	FBG	TR	IO 198		8	3850		8350	9600
25 2	ENCOUNTER V2596		CR	FBG	DV	IO 260		8	4685		11400	12900
			---- 1981 BOATS									
16 1	CAPRI T681		RNBT	FBG	TR	OB		6 11	1000		2000	2350
16 1	CAPRI T681		RNBT	FBG	TR	IO 120		6 11			3300	3850
16 1	V681 FD		RNBT	FBG	TR	IO 120		6 11			3000	3450
17 7	MACH I V888		RNBT	FBG	TR	IO 140		7 4			4000	4650
17 7	SPOILER V888		RNBT	FBG	DV	OB		7 2	1200		2450	2850
17 7	SPOILER V888		RNBT	FBG	DV	IO 140		7 2			3700	4300
18	APOLLO T886		RNBT	FBG	TR	OB		7 4	1300		2650	3100
18	APOLLO T886		RNBT	FBG	TR	IO		7 4			4000	4650
19 11	BERMUDA VBR2096		RNBT	FBG	DV	IO 165		8			5200	5950
19 11	TAHITIAN VC2096		CR	FBG	DV	IO 165		8			5450	6250
21 6	CARIBBEAN V2296		CR	FBG	DV	IO 165		8			7550	8650
25 2	ENCOUNTER V2596		CR	FBG	DV	IO 185		8			10700	12100
			---- 1980 BOATS									
16 1	CAPRI T681		RNBT	FBG	TR	IO 120-170		6 11			3150	3650
16 1	CAPRI T681 W/T		RNBT	FBG	TR	OB		6 11	1000		1950	2350

LOA FT IN		NAME AND/ OR MODEL	TOP/ RIG	BOAT TYPE	-HULL- MTL TP	----ENGINE--- TP # HP MFG	BEAM FT IN	WGT LBS	DRAFT FT IN	RETAIL LOW	RETAIL HIGH
						1980 BOATS					
17	7	SPOILER V888		RNBT	FBG DV	IO 140	7 4			3800	4400
17	7	SPOILER V888		RNBT	FBG DV	IO 260	7 4			4150	4800
17	7	SPOILER V888 W/T		RNBT	FBG DV	OB	7 2	1200		2450	2800
18		APOLLO T886		RNBT	FBG TR	IO 165	7 2			3900	4550
18		APOLLO T886		RNBT	FBG TR	IO 260	7 4			4200	4900
18		APOLLO T886 W/T		RNBT	FBG TR	OB	7 2	1300		2600	3050
19	11	BERMUDA VBR2096		RNBT	FBG DV	IO 165-260	8			5100	6200
19	11	TAHITIAN VC2096		CR	FBG DV	IO 165-260	8			5350	6550
21	6	CARIBBEAN V2296		CR	FBG DV	IO 185-260	8			7400	8850
25	2	ENCOUNTER V2596		CR	FBG DV	IO 185	8			10500	11900
25	2	ENCOUNTER V2596		CR	FBG DV	IO T260	8			12900	14600
						1979 BOATS					
16	1	CAPRI T681	OP	RNBT	FBG TR	OB	6 9	1000		1950	2300
16	1	CAPRI T681	OP	RNBT	FBG TR	IO 120-140	6 9	1900		3100	3650
17	7	MACH I V887		RNBT	FBG DV	IO 140-235	7 2			3850	4550
17	7	MACH I V888	ST	RNBT	FBG DV	IO 140-250	7 2	2300		3750	4600
17	7	MONTEGO V887		RNBT	FBG DV	IO 140	7 2			3550	4100
17	7	MONTEGO V887		RNBT	FBG DV	IO 235	7 2			3900	4550
17	7	SPOILER V888	OP	RNBT	FBG DV	OB	7 2	1200		2400	2800
17	7	SPOILER V888	OP	RNBT	FBG DV	IO 140-250	7 2	2300		3750	4600
18		APOLLO T886	OP	RNBT	FBG TR	OB	7 2	1300		2600	3000
18		APOLLO T886	OP	RNBT	FBG TR	IO 165-250	7 2	2300		3850	4700
19	11	BAHAMA V2096	ST	RNBT	FBG DV	IO 165-260	8	2850		4950	6050
19	11	BERMUDA VBR2096	ST	RNBT	FBG DV	IO 165-260	8	2850		5200	6350
19	11	TAHITIAN VC2096	ST	CUD	FBG DV	IO 165-260	8	2850		5250	6450
21	6	CARIBBEAN V2296	ST	CUD	FBG DV	IO 185-260	8	3100		6450	7750
22	4	ISLANDER T2295		CR	FBG DV	IO 225	8			7750	8900
22	4	ISLANDER T2295		CR	FBG DV	IO T170	8			8550	9850
						1978 BOATS					
16	1	CAPRI T681	OP	RNBT	FBG TR	OB	6 9	1000		1900	2300
16	1	CAPRI T681	OP	RNBT	FBG TR	IO 120-140	6 9	1800		3000	3500
17	7	MACH I V887	ST	RNBT	FBG SV	IO 140-228	7 2	2200		3650	4450
17	7	MACH I V888	ST	RNBT	FBG SV	IO 140-228	7 2	2300		3750	4550
17	7	MONTEGO B887	OP	RNBT	FBG DV	IO 140-228	7 2	2200		3650	4400
17	7	SPOILER V888	OP	RNBT	FBG SV	OB	7 2	1200		2350	2750
17	7	SPOILER V888	OP	RNBT	FBG DV	IO 140-228	7 2	2200		3700	4450
18		APOLLO T886	OP	RNBT	FBG TR	OB	7 2	1300		2550	2950
18		APOLLO T886	OP	RNBT	FBG TR	IO 165-185	7 2	2300		3850	4450
19	11	BAHAMA V2096	ST	RNBT	FBG DV	IO 165-240	8	2700		4950	5850
19	11	TAHITI VC2096	ST	RNBT	FBG DV	IO 165-240	8	2850		5050	6000
21	6	CARIBBEAN V2296	ST	CUD	FBG DV	IO 198-240	8	3100		6500	7500
						1977 BOATS					
16	1	BIMINI V680	OP	RNBT	FBG DV	OB	6 9	890		1700	2000
16	1	BIMINI V680	OP	RNBT	FBG DV	IO 140	6 9	1736		3000	3450
16	1	CAPRI T681	OP	RNBT	FBG TR	OB	6 9	968		1850	2200
16	1	CAPRI T681	OP	RNBT	FBG TR	IO 120-140	6 9	1862		3100	3600
17	7	SPOILER V888	OP	RNBT	FBG DV	OB	7 2	1200		2250	2700
17	7	SPOILER V888	OP	RNBT	FBG DV	IO 140-235	7 2	2190		3650	4450
18		APOLLO T886	OP	RNBT	FBG TR	OB	7 2	1280		2500	2900
18		APOLLO T886	OP	RNBT	FBG TR	IO 165-190	7 2	2334		3900	4500
19	11	BAHAMA V2096	OP	RNBT	FBG DV	IO 165-235	8	2700		5000	5850
19	11	CHESAPEAKE F2096	OP	FSH	FBG DV	IO 165-235	8	2600		5300	6200
21	6	CARIBBEAN V2296	ST	CUD	FBG DV	IO 188-235	8	3074		6450	7500
22	4	ISLANDER T2295	OP	CR	FBG DV	IO 233-235	8	3850		9000	9200
						1976 BOATS					
16		SURFER V680	OP	RNBT	FBG DV	OB	6 8	890		1700	2000
16		SURFER V680	OP	RNBT	FBG DV	IO 120-140	6 8	1736		3000	3500
16	1	CAPRI T681	OP	RNBT	FBG TR	OB	6 9	968		1900	2250
16	1	CAPRI T681	OP	RNBT	FBG TR	IO 120-140	6 9	1862		3100	3650
16	1	SKIPPER T682	OP	RNBT	FBG TR	OB	6 9	968		1750	2100
17	1	PLAYMATE T785	OP	RNBT	FBG TR	IO 140-175	7 1	2079		3550	4300
17	4	MONTEGO V887	OP	RNBT	FBG DV	IO 140-188	7 3	2084		3600	4250
17	4	SPOILER V888BR	OP	RNBT	FBG DV	OB	7 3	1290		2450	2850
17	4	SPOILER V888BR	OP	RNBT	FBG DV	IO 140-188	7 3	2240		3700	4400
18		APOLLO T886	OP	RNBT	FBG TR	OB	7 2	1330		2550	2950
18		APOLLO T886	OP	RNBT	FBG TR	IO 165-190	7 2	2334		3950	4600
18		HOOKER B880	OP	BASS	FBG SV	OB	6 8	1058		2100	2500
19	6	V2096	OP	CUD	FBG DV	IO 188 MRCR	8	2880		5300	6100
21	4	CARIBBEAN V2296	OP	CUD	FBG DV	IO 188-235	8	3074		6500	7550
22	4	ISLANDER T2295	ST	CR	FBG DV	IO 233 MRCR	8	3850		8100	9300
22	4	ISLANDER V2295	ST	CR	FBG DV	IO 235 OMC	8	3850		8050	9250
						1975 BOATS					
16		SURFER V680	OP	RNBT	FBG DV	IO 120-140	6 8	1736		3050	3550
16	1	CAPRI T681	OP	RNBT	FBG TR	OB	6 9	968		1800	2150
16	1	CAPRI T681	OP	RNBT	FBG TR	IO 120-140	6 9	1862		3200	3700
17	1	PLAYMATE T785	OP	RNBT	FBG TR	OB	7 1	1010		1950	2300
17	1	PLAYMATE T785	OP	RNBT	FBG TR	IO 140-165	7 1	2079		3550	4150
17	4	MONTEGO V887	OP	RNBT	FBG DV	IO 140-165	7 2	2334		3900	4550
18		APOLLO T886	OP	RNBT	FBG TR	OB	7 2	1250		2400	2800
18		APOLLO T886	OP	RNBT	FBG TR	IO 165	7 2	2334		4000	4700
18		HOOKER B880	OP	BASS	FBG TR	OB	6 8	1058		2100	2450
21	6	CARIBBEAN V2296	ST	CUD	FBG DV	IO 188-235	8	3074		6600	7750
22	4	ISLANDER T2295	ST	CR	FBG DV	IO 188-235	8	3850		8150	9500
						1974 BOATS					
16		JAVELIN V-680			FBG	IO 120-140	6 8	1760		2950	3450
16	1	CAPRI T-681			FBG	OB	6 9	920		1700	2050
16	1	CAPRI T-681			FBG	IO 120-140	6 9	1970		3200	3750
17	1	PLAYMATE T-785			FBG	OB	7 1	975		1850	2200
17	1	PLAYMATE T-785			FBG	IO 140-165	7 1	2068		3550	4150
17	4	MONTEGO V-887			FBG	IO 140-165	7 2	1958		3550	4150
18		APOLLO T-886			FBG	OB	7 2	1190		2300	2650
18		APOLLO T-886			FBG	IO 140-165	7 2	2160		3800	4450
18	1	HOOKER B-880			FBG	OB	7	1060		2000	2400
21	6	CARIBBEAN V-2296			FBG	IO 188-225	8	3440		7000	8150
						1973 BOATS					
16		JAVELIN V-680			FBG	IO 120-140	6 8			3150	3650
16	1	CAPRI T-681			FBG	OB	6 9	920		1700	2000
16	1	CAPRI T-681			FBG	IO 120-140	6 9	1970		3300	3850
17	3	ELECTRA T-784			FBG	OB	7			1850	2200
17	3	ELECTRA T-784			FBG	IO 140-165	7	1960		3550	4150
17	6	FURY 1905		RNBT	FBG DV	OB	7	915		1800	2150
17	6	FURY 1905		RNBT	FBG DV	IO 120	7	1860		3650	4250
18		APOLLO T-886			FBG	OB	7 2	1190		2300	2650
18		APOLLO T-886			FBG	IO 140-165	7 2	2160		3950	4600
21	6	CARIBBEAN V-2296			FBG	IO 188-225	8	3440		7050	8200
						1972 BOATS					
17	3	ELECTRA 1784			FBG	OB	7	945		1800	2150
17	3	ELECTRA 1784			FBG	IO 120-188	7	1930		3600	4300
17	6	FURY 1905			FBG	OB	7	915		1750	2100
17	6	FURY 1905			FBG	IO 120-165	7	1860		3600	4250
18		APOLLO 1886			FBG	OB	7 2	1160		2250	2600
18		APOLLO 1886			FBG	IO 120-188	7 2	2130		4050	4800
						1969 BOATS					
16	1	GALAXIE 1703		RNBT	FBG	OB	6 5			1800	2150
17	3	ELECTRA 1802		RNBT	FBG TR	OB	6 10			2400	2750
17	3	ELECTRA 1802		RNBT	FBG TR	IO 120	6 10			4000	5050
17	6	FURY 1905		RNBT	FBG	OB	7			2350	2750
17	6	FURY 1905		RNBT	FBG SV	IO 120	7	1860		4200	4850
18	9	FLEETWOOD 2084		CR	FBG SV	IO 120	7			5700	6550
						1961 BOATS					
16	8	SPORTSMAN		RNBT	FBG	OB	6 3			2450	2850
19	2	CONTINENTAL		RNBT	FBG	OB	6 10			2750	3200
19	2	VOYAGER		RNBT	FBG	OB	6 10			2300	2650
						1960 BOATS					
17	7	CRUISETTE 800 DLX		CR	FBG RB	IO 80	6 10			6100	7050

GLASTRON BOATS

DIV OF GENMAR INDUSTRIES INC   See inside cover to adjust price for area
LITTLE FALLS MN 56345   COAST GUARD MFG ID- GLA

For more recent years, see the BUC Used Boat Price Guide, Volume 1 or Volume 2

LOA FT IN		NAME AND/ OR MODEL	TOP/ RIG	BOAT TYPE	-HULL- MTL TP	----ENGINE--- TP # HP MFG	BEAM FT IN	WGT LBS	DRAFT FT IN	RETAIL LOW	RETAIL HIGH
						1983 BOATS					
17	6	SSV-177	OP	RNBT	FBG SV	IO 140-185	6 11	1100		1950	2350
17	6	SSV184	ST	RNBT	FBG SV	IO 140-188		1200		2250	2650
17	6	SX180	ST	RNBT	FBG SV	IO 170-188		1200		2250	2650
18	2	CUX18	OP	RACE	FBG SV	IO 260 MRCR		950		2450	2850
18	8	SSV-194	OP	RNBT	FBG SV	IO 170-200	7 4	1230		2400	2950
18	8	SSV-194	ST	RNBT	FBG SV	IO 170-200	7 4	1230		2650	3100
18	8	SX-190	OP	RNBT	FBG SV	IO 170-228	7 4	1250		2550	3100
18	8	V197	ST	RNBT	FBG SV	IO 228-260		1200		2600	3050
18	10	V195	ST	RNBT	FBG SV	IO 170-260		1200		2700	3150
19	3	SV191	ST	RNBT	FBG SV	IO 170-228		1350		2800	3350
19	3	SV191	ST	RNBT	FBG SV	IO 260 MRCR		1750		3100	3500
20	7	SEA-FURY V-216	OP	OPFSH	FBG DV	OB	8	2030		2450	2850
20	7	V-217	OP	CR	FBG DV	IO 170-260	8	2320		3500	4350
23	1	SCIMITAR	HT	RNBT	FBG DV	IO 260 MRCR	7 7	1850		3700	4300
23	5	CV-23	OP	RACE	FBG DV	IO 260 MRCR	7 8	1400		3700	4300

LOA FT	LOA IN	NAME AND/ OR MODEL	TOP/ RIG	BOAT TYPE	-HULL- MTL	-HULL- TP	ENGINE TP	ENGINE # HP	ENGINE MFG	BEAM FT	BEAM IN	WGT LBS	DRAFT FT	DRAFT IN	RETAIL LOW	RETAIL HIGH
		1982 BOATS														
16	4	SSV-164	OP	RNBT	FBG	SV	IO	120	OMC	8		880			1800	2150
17	1	SSV-173		RNBT	FBG	SV	IO	140		6	11	1100			1900	2250
17	1	SSV-177	OP	RNBT	FBG	SV	IO	140-185		6	11	1100			1900	2300
17	7	C-537	OP	RNBT	FBG	DV	IO	170		6	6	752			1900	2250
18	2	CVZ-18	OP	RACE	FBG	DV	IO	198	MRCR	7	6	950			2200	2600
18	2	SS-18	OP	RACE	FBG	DV	IO	228-260		7	6	1050			2300	2800
18	2	SSCVX-18	OP	RACE	FBG	DV	IO	185	MRCR	7	6	1050			2200	2550
18	8	SSV-194	OP	RNBT	FBG	SV	IO	170-228		7	4	1230			2350	2900
18	8	SSV-194	OP	RNBT	FBG	SV	IO	260		7	4	1230			2600	3050
18	8	SX-190	OP	RNBT	FBG	SV	IO	228-260		7	4	1250			2500	3050
18	11	V-195		RNBT	FBG	DV	IO	170		7	3	1435			2450	2850
20	4	INTIMIDATOR	OP	RNBT	FBG	DV	IO	260	MRCR	7	4	1400			2900	3350
20	7	SEA-FURY V-216	OP	OPFSH	FBG	DV	OB			8		2030			2400	2800
20	7	V-217	OP	CR	FBG	DV	IO	170-260		8		2320			3400	4250
22	1	V-225		SPTCR	FBG	DV	IO	170		7	7	2275			3600	4200
23	1	SCIMITAR	HT	RNBT	FBG	DV	IO	260	MRCR	7	7	1850			3600	4200
23	5	CV-23	OP	RACE	FBG	DV	IO	260	MRCR	7	8	1400			3600	4200
24	4	SEAFURY V-243	OP	FSH	FBG	DV	OB			8		2650			3400	3950
25	7	V-266		CR	FBG	DV	IO	260		8		3485			6300	7250
27	4	CV-27	OP	CR	FBG	DV	IO	T185-T260		7	10	2925			8350	9900
		1981 BOATS														
17	1	SSV-173	OP	RNBT	FBG	SV	IO	140-185		6	11	1100			1850	2250
17	1	SSV-177	OP	RNBT	FBG	SV	IO	140-170		6	11	1100			1850	2250
17	1	SSV-177	OP	RNBT	FBG	SV	IO	185	MRCR	6	11				2400	2800
17	7	C-537	OP	RNBT	FBG	DV	IO	170		6	7	752			1850	2200
18	2	CVX-18	OP	RACE	FBG	DV	IO	185	MRCR	7	6	1050			2150	2550
18	2	CVX-18	OP	RACE	FBG	DV	IO	260	MRCR	7	6	1050			2350	2750
18	2	CVZ-18	OP	RACE	FBG	DV	IO	185-198		7	6	950			2150	2550
18	2	CVZ-18	OP	RNBT	FBG	DV	IO	228	MRCR	7	6	950			2350	2700
18	8	SSV-194	OP	RNBT	FBG	SV	IO	170-228		7	3	1230			2350	2850
18	8	SSV-194	OP	RNBT	FBG	SV	IO	260		7	4	1230			2550	3000
18	8	SX-190	OP	RNBT	FBG	SV	IO	170-228		7	4	1250			2350	2850
18	8	SX-190	OP	RNBT	FBG	SV	IO	260		7	4	1250			2550	3000
18	11	V-195	OP	RNBT	FBG	DV	IO	170-228		7	3	1467			2400	2950
18	11	V-195	OP	RNBT	FBG	DV	IO	260		7	3	1467			2650	3100
20	4	INTIMIDATOR	OP	RNBT	FBG	DV	IO	260	MRCR	7	4	1400			2850	3300
20	7	SEA-FURY V-216	OP	OPFSH	FBG	DV	OB			8		2030			2350	2700
20	7	V-217	OP	CR	FBG	DV	IO	170-260		8		2320			3350	4200
22	1	AVENTURA V-225	OP	SPTCR	FBG	DV	IO	170	OMC	7	7	2275			3500	4100
22	1	AVENTURA V-225	OP	SPTCR	FBG	DV	IO	198-228		7	7				4500	5150
22	1	V-225	OP	RNBT	FBG	SV	IO	170-260		7	7	2275			3350	4150
22	1	V-225	OP	SPTCR	FBG	DV	IO	185-260		7	7	2275			3550	4400
23	1	SCIMITAR	HT	RNBT	FBG	DV	IO	260	MRCR	7	7	1850			3550	4100
23	5	CV-23	OP	RACE	FBG	DV	IO	260	MRCR	7	8	1400			3550	4150
24	4	SEAFURY V-243	OP	FSH	FBG	DV	OB			8		2650			3300	3850
25	7	AVENTURA V-266S	OP	CR	FBG	DV	IO	260		8		3405			6100	7050
25	7	AVENTURA V-266T	OP	CR	FBG	DV	IO	T170	MRCR	8		3405			6700	7700
27	4	CV-27	OP	CR	FBG	DV	IO	T185-T260		7	10	2925			8200	9750
27	4	CV-27	OP	CR	FBG	SV	IO	T170	OMC	7	10	2925			8000	9200
		1980 BOATS														
16	4	SSV-164	OP	RNBT	FBG	SV	IO	120-140		6	7				2200	2700
16	4	SSV-168	OP	RNBT	FBG	SV	IO	120-140		6	7				2200	2700
16	10	CVX-16SS	OP	RACE	FBG	DV	IO	140		6	8				2150	2500
17	1	SSV-173	OP	RNBT	FBG	SV	IO	140-170		6	11				2350	2900
17	1	SSV-177	OP	RNBT	FBG	SV	IO	140-170		6	11				2350	2900
18		CVX-18		RNBT	FBG	DV	IO	230		7	3	1050			2250	2650
18		CVZ-18 B/R		RNBT	FBG	DV	IO	230		7	3	950			2250	2600
18	2	CVX-18	OP	RACE	FBG	DV	IO	198-228		7	6				2700	3200
18	2	CVZ-18	OP	RACE	FBG	DV	IO	198-228		7	6				2700	3200
18	2	V-184		RNBT	FBG		IO	185-200		7	1	1050			2150	2550
18	11	V-194	OP	RNBT	FBG	DV	IO	198-228		7	3				2850	3350
18	11	V-194	OP	RNBT	FBG	DV	IO	260		7	3				3000	3700
18	11	V-195	OP	RNBT	FBG	DV	IO	198-228		7	3				2850	3350
18	11	V-195	OP	RNBT	FBG	DV	IO	260		7	3				3000	3700
18	11	V-198	OP	RNBT	FBG	DV	IO	198-228		7	3				2850	3350
18	11	V-198	OP	RNBT	FBG	DV	IO	260		7	3				3000	3700
20	1	CVX-20 JET	OP	RACE	FBG	DV	JT		BERK	7	6				**	**
20	3	SPRINT CVX-20	OP	RACE	FBG	DV	OB			7	6				2550	2950
20	4	INTIMIDATOR	OP	RNBT	FBG	DV	IO	260	MRCR	7	4				3350	3900
20	7	AVENTURA V-210	OP	CR	FBG	DV	IO	198-260		8					4550	5600
20	7	AVENTURA V-214	OP	CUD	FBG	DV	IO	198-260		8					4550	5600
20	7	SEA-FURY V-215	OP	OPFSH	FBG	DV	OB			8					2600	3050
20	7	SEA-FURY V-216	OP	OPFSH	FBG	DV	OB			8					2600	3050
20	7	SEA-FURY V-218	OP	OPFSH	FBG	DV	OB			8					2600	3050
20	7	SEA-FURY V-219	OP	OPFSH	FBG	DV	IO	198-260		8					4750	5900
21		V-210		CR	FBG	DV	IO	225		8		2280			3500	4050
21		V-214		CUD	FBG	DV	IO	230		8		1910			3300	3850
22		V-225		SPTCR	FBG	DV	IO	230		7	7	2275			3600	4200
22	1	AVENTURA V-225	OP	SPTCR	FBG	DV	IO	198-228		7	7				4450	5200
22	1	AVENTURA V-225	OP	SPTCR	FBG	DV	IO	D	VLVO	7	7				**	**
22	1	V-225		RNBT	FBG	DV	IO	185		7	7				4150	4800
22	11	AVENTURA V-235	OP	CR	FBG	DV	IO	228-260		8					5100	6200
22	11	AVENTURA V-235	OP	CR	FBG	DV	IO	D	VLVO	8					**	**
22	11	V-235		RNBT	FBG	DV	IO	200		8					5000	5750
23	3	SCIMITAR	HT	RNBT	FBG	DV	IO	260		7	7				5150	6150
23	5	CV-23	OP	RACE	FBG	DV	IO	260		7	8				4950	5900
24	4	SEAFURY V-243	OP	FSH	FBG	DV	OB			8					3700	4300
25	7	AVENTURA V-264	OP	CR	FBG	DV	IO	260		8					6950	8150
25	7	AVENTURA V-264	OP	CR	FBG	DV	IO	T140-T170		8					7500	8600
25	7	AVENTURA V-266	OP	CR	FBG	DV	IO	260		8					6950	8150
25	7	AVENTURA V-266	OP	CR	FBG	DV	IO	D	VLVO	8					**	**
25	7	AVENTURA V-266	OP	CR	FBG	DV	IO	T140-T170		8					7500	8600
25	7	SEA-FURY V-265	OP	OPFSH	FBG	DV	IO	260		8					7250	8500
25	7	SEA-FURY V-265	OP	OPFSH	FBG	DV	IO	D	VLVO	8					**	**
25	7	SEA-FURY V-265	OP	OPFSH	FBG	DV	IO	T140-T170		8					7800	8950
25	7	V-266		CR	FBG	DV	IO	T198-T260		8					7700	9500
27	4	CV-27		CR	FBG	DV	IO	T198		7	10				9800	11200
27	4	CV-27	OP	RACE	FBG	DV	IO	T260		7	10				9650	11100
		1979 BOATS														
17	1	SSV-173	ST	RNBT	FBG	SV	IO	120-170		6	11	1745			2200	2550
17	1	SSV-177	ST	RNBT	FBG	SV	IO	120	MRCR	6	11	1775			2200	2550
17	1	SSV-177 XL	ST	RNBT	FBG	SV	IO	140-170		6	11	1775			2200	2600
18	1	SSV-189	ST	RNBT	FBG	SV	IO	165-198		7	4	2155			2650	3100
18	2	CVX-18	OP	RACE	FBG	DV	IO	198	MRCR	7	6	1050			2150	2500
18	2	CVZ-18	OP	RACE	FBG	DV	IO	198	MRCR	7	6	950			2150	2500
18	2	V-184	OP	RNBT	FBG	DV	IO	165-200		7	1				2650	3300
18	11	V-194 XL	ST	RNBT	FBG	DV	IO	165-230		7	3	2110			2700	3350
18	11	V-194 XL	ST	RNBT	FBG	DV	IO	260	MRCR	7	3	2110			2950	3400
18	11	V-195 XL	ST	RNBT	FBG	DV	IO	165-200		7	3	2185			2750	3400
18	11	V-195 XL	ST	RNBT	FBG	DV	IO	228-230		7	3	2185			3000	3500
20	1	CVX-20 DELUXE	OP	RACE	FBG	DV	JT	320	BERK	7	6	1225			3350	3900
20	7	AVENTURA V-210	OP	CR	FBG	DV	IO	140-260		8					4450	5350
20	7	AVENTURA V-213	OP	CUD	FBG	DV	IO	140-220		8					4450	5250
20	7	AVENTURA V-214	ST	CUD	FBG	DV	IO	140-230		8		2585			3500	4300
20	7	SEA-FURY V-215	OP	OPFSH	FBG	DV	OB			8					2550	3000
20	7	SEA-FURY V-216	OP	OPFSH	FBG	DV	OB			8		2220			2400	2750
20	7	SEA-FURY V-218	OP	OPFSH	FBG	DV	OB			8					2550	3000
20	7	SEA-FURY V-219	OP	OPFSH	FBG	DV	IO	140-200		8					4700	5650
22	1	AVENTURA V-225	ST	SPTCR	FBG	DV	IO	140-230		7	8	3225			4450	5200
23	5	CV-23	OP	RACE	FBG	DV	IO	260	MRCR	7	8	1400			3500	4100
23	5	CV-23	OP	RACE	FBG	DV	JT	320	BERK	7	8	1400			4300	5000
25	7	AVENTURA V-266	OP	CR	FBG	DV	IO	198-260		8					6600	8000
25	7	AVENTURA V-266	OP	CR	FBG	DV	IO	T140-T200		8					7300	9100
27	4	CV-27	OP	RACE	FBG	DV	IO	T198	MRCR	7	10	2925			7400	8500
27	4	CV-27	OP	RACE	FBG	DV	IO	T260	MRCR	7	10	2925			8100	9300
		1978 BOATS														
16	10	CVX-16SS	OP	RACE	FBG	DV	IO	140		6	8	1450			1800	2150
17	1	SSV-172	ST	RNBT	FBG	SV	IO	120	MRCR	6	11	1670			2150	2500
17	1	SSV-173	ST	RNBT	FBG	SV	IO	140-170		6	11	1745			2200	2650
17	1	SSV-177	ST	RNBT	FBG	SV	IO	140-170		6	11	1775			2250	2650
18	1	SSV-189	ST	RNBT	FBG	SV	IO	165-198		7	4	2155			2650	3250
18	2	CVX-18	OP	RACE	FBG	DV	IO	198	MRCR	7	6	1875			2500	2900
18	2	CVX-18	OP	RACE	FBG	DV	IO	225	OMC	7	6				2750	3200
18	2	CVZ-18 B/R	OP	RACE	FBG	DV	IO	198	MRCR	7	6	1950			2500	2950
18	2	CVZ-18 B/R	OP	RACE	FBG	DV	IO	225	OMC	7	6				2750	3200
18	11	SEA-RIDER V-194	ST	RNBT	FBG	DV	IO	165-198		7	3	2110			2750	3350
18	11	SEA-RIDER V-195	ST	RNBT	FBG	DV	IO	165-198		7	3	2185			2800	3400
20	1	CVX-20 DELUXE	OP	RACE	FBG	DV	JT	320	BERK	7	6	2075			3550	4100
20	5	SEA-FURY V-209	ST	OPFSH	FBG	DV	IO	140-198		8		2585			3700	4600
20	6	SEA-FURY V-202	ST	OPFSH	FBG	DV	OB			8		1710			1900	2250
20	6	SEA-FURY V-208	ST	OPFSH	FBG	DV	OB			8		1895			2050	2450
20	7	AVENTURA V-210	HT	CR	FBG	DV	IO	140	MRCR	8		2955			3800	4450
20	7	AVENTURA V-210	HT	CR	FBG	DV	IO	185-228		8					4500	5250
20	7	AVENTURA V-214	ST	CUD	FBG	DV	IO	140-170		8		2585			3550	4200
20	7	AVENTURA V-214	ST	CUD	FBG	DV	IO	185-198		8					4500	5200
22	1	BAL-HARBOR V-225	ST	SPTCR	FBG	DV	IO	190-228		7	7	3125			4250	5200

 CONTINUED ON NEXT PAGE

LOA FT	LOA IN	NAME AND/ OR MODEL	TOP/ RIG	BOAT TYPE	-HULL- MTL	-HULL- TP	ENGINE TP	ENGINE # HP	ENGINE MFG	BEAM FT	BEAM IN	WGT LBS	DRAFT FT	DRAFT IN	RETAIL LOW	RETAIL HIGH
		1978 BOATS														
23	5	CV-23	OP	RACE	FBG	DV	IO	228	MRCR	7	8	2325			3750	4350
23	5	CV-23	OP	RACE	FBG	DV	IO	240-260		7	8				4900	5600
23	5	CV-23	OP	RACE	FBG	DV	JT	320	BERK	7	8	2250			4450	5150
23	5	CV-23	HT	RACE	FBG	DV	IO	260	MRCR	7	8	2625			4050	4750
		1977 BOATS														
16	9	STARFLITE T-179	ST	RNBT	FBG	TR	IO	120-130		6	10	1700			2150	2600
16	10	CVX-16SS	OP	RACE	FBG	DV	IO	140		6	7	1425			1800	2150
17	1	BAYFLITE V-174	ST	RNBT	FBG	DV	IO	120-140		6	11	1650			2200	2650
17	1	SSV-177	ST	RNBT	FBG	SV	IO	130-170				1675			2400	2900
18	1	SSV-189	ST	RNBT	FBG	SV	IO	165-190		7	4	2155			2700	3300
18	2	CVX-18	OP	RACE	FBG	DV	IO	188-190		7	6	1875			2500	2900
18	2	V-184	ST	RNBT	FBG	DV	IO	165-190		7	1	2050			2600	3150
18	11	SEA-RIDER V-195	ST	RNBT	FBG	DV	IO	165-190		7	3	2185			2850	3450
20	1	CVX-20	OP	RACE	FBG	DV	JT	320	BERK	7	6	1875			3300	3800
20	1	CVX-20 DELUXE	OP	RACE	FBG	DV	JT	320	BERK	7	6	2075			3400	3950
20	8	GULFSTREAM V-212	ST	SPTCR	FBG	DV	IO	188-235		7	7	2650			3600	4250
21	5	SIERRA T-215	ST	CUD	FBG	TR	IO	188-235		7	8	3450			4500	5250
22	1	BAL-HARBOR V-225	ST	SPTCR	FBG	DV	IO	190-235		7	7	3125			4300	5250
23	5	CV-23	OP	RACE	FBG	DV	JT	320	BERK	7	6	2250			4200	4900
		1976 BOATS														
16	6	CV-16 SS	OP	SKI	FBG	SV	IO	130	GLAS	6	7	1350			1750	2100
16	6	CV-16 V8	OP	SKI	FBG	SV	IO	140-155		6	7	1450			1800	2200
16	9	STARFLITE T-179	ST	RNBT	FBG	TR	IO	120-140		6	10	1700			2200	2600
17	1	BAYFLITE V-174	ST	RNBT	FBG	DV	IO	120-140		6	11	1650			2250	2650
17	8	SWINGER T-187	ST	RNBT	FBG	TR	IO	165-190		7	1	2050			2600	3100
17	8	SWINGER T-187	HT	RNBT	FBG	TR	IO	165-190		7	1	2050			2600	3100
17	11	CVC-18	OP	RACE	FBG	SV	JT	455	BERK	6	9	2100			2800	3300
18	2	CRESTFLITE V-184	ST	RNBT	FBG	DV	IO	165-190		7		2050			2650	3250
18	2	CRESTFLITE V-184	HT	RNBT	FBG	DV	IO	165-190		7		2050			2650	3100
18	11	CV-19 SS	OP	SKI	FBG	SV	JT	455	BERK	7	4	2050			3100	3600
18	11	SEA-RIDER V-195	ST	RNBT	FBG	DV	IO	165-190		7	3	2150			2900	3500
19	3	GULFCRUISER T-197	ST	RNBT	FBG	TR	IO	188-190		7	4	2400			3150	3650
20	1	CVX-20	OP	RACE	FBG	SV	JT	455	BERK	7	6	1925			3200	3700
20	2	GULFSTREAM V-204	ST	SPTCR	FBG	DV	IO	165-188		7	6	2550			3450	4200
20	2	GULFSTREAM V-204	ST	SPTCR	FBG	DV	IO	225	VLVO	7	6	2750			3850	4500
20	2	GULFSTREAM V-205	ST	SPTCR	FBG	DV	IO	140-188		7	5	2550			3400	4250
20	2	GULFSTREAM V-205	HT	SPTCR	FBG	DV	IO	140-188		7	5	2550			3400	4250
20	8	SIERRA V-212	ST	CR	FBG	DV	IO	188-233		7	8	2650			3700	4450
21	5	VAGABOND T-215	ST	SPTCR	FBG	TR	IO	188-190		7	8	3450			4600	5300
21	5	VAGABOND T-215	HT	SPTCR	FBG	TR	IO	188-190		7	8	3450			4600	5300
22	1	BAL-HARBOR V-225	ST	SPTCR	FBG	DV	IO	225-235		7	7	3225			4750	5450
22	1	BAL-HARBOR V-225	HT	SPTCR	FBG	DV	IO	225-235		7	7	3225			4750	5450
23	4	CV-23	OP	RACE	FBG	SV	JT	455	BERK	7	8	3530			5150	5900
24	9	CARIBBEAN V-250	ST	SPTCR	FBG	DV	IO	190-235		8		3775			5900	7250
24	9	CARIBBEAN V-250	ST	SPTCR	FBG	DV	IO	T170	GLAS	8		4375			7400	8500
24	9	CARIBBEAN V-253	HT	SPTCR	FBG	DV	IO	190-235		8		3950			6100	7450
24	9	CARIBBEAN V-253	HT	SPTCR	FBG	DV	IO	T170	GLAS	8		4550			7550	8700
24	9	CARIBBEAN V-254	FB	SPTCR	FBG	DV	IO	225-233		8		4600			7050	8150
24	9	CARIBBEAN V-254	FB	SPTCR	FBG	DV	IO	T170	GLAS	8		5100			8150	9350
		1975 BOATS														
16	6	CV-16SS	OP	SKI	FBG	SV	IO	130-155		6	7	1350	3	4	1800	2250
16	9	STARFLITE V-179	ST	RNBT	FBG	TR	IO	130-140		6	10	1625	3	2	2250	2700
17	1	BAYFLITE V-174	ST	RNBT	FBG	DV	IO	130-140		6	8	1675	3	3	2300	2650
17	8	SWINGER V-187	ST	RNBT	FBG	TR	IO	165-170		7	1	2150	3	6	2750	3200
18	1	CV-18SS	OP	SKI	FBG	SV	IO	200	GLAS	6	9	2075	3	3	2600	3000
18	1	CV-18SS	OP	SKI	FBG	SV	JT	330	BERK	6	9	2075	3	3	2700	3150
18	1	CVC-18	OP	RACE	FBG		JT	330	BERK	6	9		3	11	2850	3300
18	2	CRESTFLITE V-184	ST	RNBT	FBG	DV	IO	165-200		7		2050	3	7	2750	3300
18	2	CRESTFLITE V-184	ST	RNBT	FBG	DV	JT	330	BERK	7		2150	3	7	2950	3400
18	11	CV-19SS	OP	SKI	FBG	SV	JT	330	BERK	7	4	2050	3	2	2950	3450
19	3	GULFCRUISER V-197	ST	RNBT	FBG	TR	IO	188-200		7	4	2400	4	1	3250	3750
20	2	GULFSTREAM V-205	ST	SPTCR	FBG	DV	IO	188-200		7	5	2725	5	4	3700	4300
20	3	GULFSTREAM V-204	ST	SPTCR	FBG	DV	IO	188-200		7	6	2725	4	7	3750	4350
20	8	SIERRA V-212	ST	CR	FBG	DV	IO	188-225		7	7	2650	4	2	3800	4500
20	8	SIERRA V-212	ST	CR	FBG	DV	JT	330	BERK	7	7	2575	4	2	3550	4150
21	2	CV-21 JET	OP	SKI	FBG	SV	JT	330	BERK	7	2	2300	3	6	3400	3950
21	5	VAGABOND V-215	ST	SPTCR	FBG	DV	IO	188-200		7	8	3450	4	11	4750	5450
22	1	BAL-HARBOR V-225	ST	SPTCR	FBG	DV	IO	188-225		7	7	3200	5	8	4700	5450
22	1	BAL-HARBOR V-225	ST	SPTCR	FBG	DV	IO	T130	GLAS	7	7	3425	5	8	5500	6350
23		GLASTRON	SLP	SAIL	FBG	KC				7	11	2800	2		5450	6250
24	9	CARIBBEAN V-250	ST	SPTCR	FBG	DV	IO	190-225		8		3703	5	8	6050	7300
24	9	CARIBBEAN V-250	ST	SPTCR	FBG	DV	IO	T165-T170		8		4625	5	8	7850	9050
24	9	CARIBBEAN V-253	HT	SPTCR	FBG	DV	IO	190-225		8		3878	5	8	6200	7500
24	9	CARIBBEAN V-253	HT	SPTCR	FBG	DV	IO	T165-T170		8		4800	5	8	8050	9250
24	9	CARIBBEAN V-254	FB	SPTCR	FBG	DV	IO	225	GLAS	8		4575	5	8	7150	8200
24	9	CARIBBEAN V-254	FB	SPTCR	FBG	DV	IO	T165-T170		8		5350	5	8	8700	10000
26	6	GLASTRON	SLP	SAIL	FBG	KC				7	11	3500	2	3	7300	8400
		1974 BOATS														
16	6	CV-16SS	OP	RNBT	FBG		IO	130-140		6	5	775			1700	2000
16	10	STARFLITE V-179	ST	RNBT	FBG		IO	130-140		6	10	1200			2050	2450
17	1	BAYFLITE V174	ST	RNBT	FBG		IO	130-140		6	11	1025			2050	2400
17	8	SWINGER V-187	ST	RNBT	FBG		IO	130-165		7	1	1300			2350	2750
17	8	SWINGER V-187	HT	RNBT	FBG		IO	130-165		7	1	1300			2350	2750
18	1	CV-18SS	OP	RNBT	FBG		IO	200	GLAS	6	9				2950	3400
18	1	CV-18SS	OP	RNBT	FBG		JT	225	BERK	6	9				2850	3300
18	2	CRESTFLITE V-184	ST	RNBT	FBG		IO	165-200		7	1	1300			2450	2900
18	2	CRESTFLITE V-184	ST	RNBT	FBG		JT	225	BERK	7	1	1300			2450	2850
18	2	CRESTFLITE V-184	HT	RNBT	FBG		IO	165-200		7	1	1300			2450	2900
18	2	CRESTFLITE V-184	HT	RNBT	FBG		JT	225	BERK	7	1	1300			2450	2850
18	11	CV-19SS	OP	RNBT	FBG		JT	225	BERK	7	5	1200			2650	3050
19	3	GULFCRUISER V-197	ST	RNBT	FBG		IO	200	GLAS	7	4	1475			2850	3300
20	8	SIERRA V-212	ST	CR	FBG		IO	165-188		7	8	1725			3300	3900
20	8	SIERRA V-212	ST	CR	FBG		JT	225	BERK	7	8	1725			3000	3450
20	8	SIERRA V-212	ST	CR	FBG		IO	225	GLAS	7	8	1725			3400	3950
21	2	CV-21	OP	SKI	FBG		JT	225	BERK	4	8	1450			2450	2850
21	5	VAGABOND V-215	ST	SPTCR	FBG		IO	188-200		7	9	2525			4050	4750
21	5	VAGABOND V-215	HT	SPTCR	FBG		IO	188-200		7	9	2525			4050	4750
22	2	BAL-HARBOR V-225	ST	SPTCR	FBG		IO	188-225		7	8				5000	5800
22	2	BAL-HARBOR V-225	HT	SPTCR	FBG		IO	188-225		7	8				5000	5800
24	9	CARIBBEAN V-250	ST	SPTCR	FBG		IO	190-225		8	1	3100			5650	6650
24	9	CARIBBEAN V-250	ST	SPTCR	FBG		IO	T165	GLAS	8	1	3100			6550	7500
24	9	CARIBBEAN V-253	HT	SPTCR	FBG		IO	190-225		8	1	3300			5850	6900
24	9	CARIBBEAN V-253	HT	SPTCR	FBG		IO	T165	GLAS	8	1	3300			6750	7750
24	9	CARIBBEAN V-254	FB	SPTCR	FBG		IO	225	GLAS	8	1	3500			6200	7150
24	9	CARIBBEAN V-254	FB	SPTCR	FBG		IO	T165	GLAS	8	1	3500			6950	7950
		1973 BOATS														
16	10	STARFLITE V-179	ST	RNBT	FBG		IO	130-140		6	10	1200			2150	2500
17	1	BAYFLITE V174	ST	RNBT	FBG		IO	130-140		6	11	1025			2100	2500
17	8	SWINGER V-187	ST	RNBT	FBG		IO	165-170		7	1	1300			2450	2850
17	8	SWINGER V-187	HT	RNBT	FBG		IO	165-170		7	1				3000	3500
18	2	CRESTFLITE V-184	ST	RNBT	FBG		IO	165-190		7	1	1300			2550	3000
18	2	CRESTFLITE V-184	ST	RNBT	FBG		JT	220	GLAS	7	1	1300			2350	2750
18	2	CRESTFLITE V-184	HT	RNBT	FBG		IO	165-190		7	1				3100	3650
18	2	CRESTFLITE V-184	HT	RNBT	FBG		JT	220	GLAS	7	1				2800	3250
18	11	CV-19SS	OP	SKI	FBG		IO	190	GLAS	7	5	1200			2650	3100
18	11	CV-19SS	OP	SKI	FBG		JT	250	BERK	7	5	1200			2450	2850
19	3	GULFCRUISER V-197	ST	RNBT	FBG		IO	190	GLAS	7	4	1475			2900	3400
20	8	SIERRA V-212	ST	CR	FBG		IO	170-190		7	8	1725			3400	4000
20	8	SIERRA V-212	ST	CR	FBG		JT	220	GLAS	7	8	1725			2850	3350
21	2	CV-21	OP	SKI	FBG		JT	250	BERK	6	6	1450			2650	3100
21	4	VAGABOND V-214	ST	SPTCR	FBG		IO	170		7	7	2605	4		4150	4850
21	7	VAGABOND V-215	ST	SPTCR	FBG		IO	188-190		7	9	2800			4500	5200
21	7	VAGABOND V-215	HT	SPTCR	FBG		IO	188-190		7	9				5000	5750
		1972 BOATS														
16	6	CV-16SS	OP	SKI	FBG		IO	130	GLAS	6	4	1350	2	3	1950	2300
16	8	BAYFLITE V-164	OP	RNBT	FBG		IO	130-140		6	1	1500	2	11	2250	2600
17	9	SWINGER V-177	OP	RNBT	FBG		IO	130-170		7	1	1743	3	4	2750	3200
18		V-184	ST	RNBT	FBG		IO	165-210		7	1	1740	3	2	2800	3350
18		V-184	ST	RNBT	FBG		JT	260	BERK	7	1	1740	3	2	2400	2800
18	11	CV-19SS	OP	SKI	FBG		IO	210	GLAS	7		2070	2	9	3100	3600
18	11	CV-19SS	OP	SKI	FBG		JT	260-270		7		2070	2	9	2600	3000
19	1	GULFCRUISER V-197	ST	RNBT	FBG		IO	165-170		7	1	2030	3	5	3200	3700
20	9	SIERRA V-212	ST	CR	FBG		IO	165-210		7		2000	4	1	3500	4150
20	9	SIERRA V-212	ST	CR	FBG		JT	260	BERK	7		2000	4	1	2750	3200
20	10	CV-21	OP	SKI	FBG		JT	270	BERK	6	11	2300	3	2	2900	3350
21	4	VAGABOND V-214	ST	SPTCR	FBG		IO	165-210		7	7	2605	4		4300	5050
21	4	VAGABOND V-215	ST	SPTCR	FBG		OB			7	7	2800	4		2600	3050
23	6	CARIBBEAN V-234	ST	SPTCR	FBG		IO	165-210		7	5	3025	5		5300	6200
23	6	CARIBBEAN V-234	ST	SPTCR	FBG		IO	T130-T140		7	5	3025	5		6050	6950
		1971 BOATS														
16	6	BAYFLITE V-164	OP	RNBT	FBG		IO	120-140		6	5	1515	2	11	2300	2700
17	4	SWINGER V-177	OP	RNBT	FBG		IO	120-155		7		1600	3	4	2650	3100
17	6	CRESTFLITE V-174	OP	RNBT	FBG		IO	120-170		6	10	1535	3	4	2600	3050
17	6	CRESTFLITE V-175	OP	RNBT	FBG		JT	265	BERK	6	10	1535	3	4	2150	2500
18	11	CV-19	OP	SKI	FBG		IO	165-170		7	2	1200			2750	3200
18	11	CV-19	OP	SKI	FBG		JT	265	BERK	7	2	1200			2250	2600
19	2	GULFCRUISER V-197	ST	RNBT	FBG		IO	140-170		7	3	2030	3	5	3350	3900

CONTINUED ON NEXT PAGE

LOA FT	IN	NAME AND/ OR MODEL	TOP/ RIG	BOAT TYPE	HULL MTL	TP	ENGINE TP	# HP	MFG	BEAM FT	IN	WGT LBS	DRAFT FT	IN	RETAIL LOW	RETAIL HIGH
1971 BOATS																
20		GULFSTREAM V-204	OP	SPTCR	FBG		IO	165-215		7	6	1985	3	11	3600	4250
20		GULFSTREAM V-205	OP	SPTCR	FBG		JT	265	BERK	7	6	1985	3	11	2650	3050
20	9	SIERRA V-210	OP	CR	FBG		IO	165-170		7	8	2000	4	1	3850	4450
20	9	SIERRA V-212	ST	CR	FBG		IO	165-170		7	8	2000			3850	4450
20	9	SIERRA V-213		CR	FBG		JT	265	BERK	7	8	2100			2800	3300
20	10	CV-21	OP	SKI	FBG		JT	265-365		6	11	1200		3	2500	2900
21	5	VAGABOND V-214	ST	SPTCR	FBG		IO	165-215		7	8	2605	4		4550	5250
23	6	CARIBBEAN V-234	ST	SPTCR	FBG		IO	165-215		8		3025	5		5600	6500
23	6	CARIBBEAN V-234	ST	SPTCR	FBG		IO	T120-T140		8		3025	5		6350	7350
1970 BOATS																
16		BAYFLITE V-164	OP	RNBT	FBG	DV	IO	120-140		6	5	1505			2400	3000
17	4	SWINGER V-177	OP	RNBT	FBG	TR	IO	120		7		1600			2750	3200
17	4	SWINGER V-177	OP	RNBT	FBG	TR	IO	130-155		7					3200	3750
17	6	CRESTFLITE V-174	OP	RNBT	FBG	DV	IO	120-160		6	10	1510			2650	3300
17	6	CRESTFLITE V-174	OP	RNBT	FBG	DV	IO	1/0	VLVO	6	10	1530			2900	3350
17	6	CRESTFLITE V-174	OP	RNBT	FBG	DV	JT	327	BERK	6	10				2400	2750
19	2	GULFCRUISER V-197	ST	RNBT	FBG	TR	IO	140	MRCR	7	3	1855			3350	3850
19	2	GULFSTREAM V-197	ST	RNBT	FBG	TR	IO	155-210		7	3	2290			3600	4450
20		GULFSTREAM V-204	OP	SPTCR	FBG	DV	IO	140	MRCR	7	6	2055			3750	4350
20		GULFSTREAM V-204	OP	SPTCR	FBG	DV	IO	155-215		7	6				4150	5100
21	5	VAGABOND V-214	ST	SPTCR	FBG	TR	IO	140-210		7	8	2605			4650	5650
23	6	CARIBBEAN V-234	ST	SPTCR	FBG	DV	IO	155	OMC	8		3082			5800	6700
23	6	CARIBBEAN V-234	ST	SPTCR	FBG	DV	IO	160-215		8		3475			6350	7400
23	6	CARIBBEAN V-234	ST	SPTCR	FBG	DV	IO	T120-T140		8		3475			7100	8200
1969 BOATS																
16	2	BAYFLITE V-164	OP	RNBT	FBG	TR	IO	120	MRCR	6		1277			2200	2550
17	4	SWINGER V-177	OP	RNBT	FBG	TR	IO	120	MRCR	7		1450			2750	3200
17	7	CRESTFLITE V-174	OP	RNBT	FBG	DV	IO	120	MRCR	6	10	1400			2700	3150
20		GULFCRUISER V-205	OP	RNBT	FBG	DV	IO	120	MRCR	7	6	1970			3650	4250
20		GULFSTREAM V-204	OP	SPTCR	FBG	DV	IO	120	MRCR	7	6	1750			3650	4250
21	5	VAGABOND V-214	ST	SPTCR	FBG	TR	IO	120	MRCR	7	8	1850			4150	4800
23	6	CARIBBEAN V-234	ST	SPTCR	FBG		IO	155	OMC	8		2425			5300	6100
23	6	CARIBBEAN V-234	ST	SPTCR	FBG	DV	IO	T155	OMC	8		2425			6100	7000
1968 BOATS																
16	4	BAYFLITE V-164	OP	RNBT	FBG		IO	120	MRCR	6	6	1277			2350	2750
17	4	SWINGER V-177	OP	RNBT	FBG	TR	IO	120	MRCR	7		1450			2800	3300
17	7	CRESTFLITE V-174	OP	RNBT	FBG		IO	120-160		6	10	1400			2800	3300
20		GULFCRUISER V-205	OP	RNBT	FBG		IO	120-160		7	6	1970			3800	4450
20		GULFSTREAM V-204	OP	SPTCR	FBG		IO	120-210		7	6	1750			3800	4500
23	6	CARIBBEAN V-234	ST	SPTCR	FBG		IO	155-210		8		2425			5500	6400
23	6	CARIBBEAN V-234	ST	SPTCR	FBG		IO	T120		8		2425			6350	7300
1967 BOATS																
16	2	BAYFLITE V-164	OP	RNBT	FBG		IO	120		6	9	1310			2500	2900
17	4	SWINGER V-177	OP	RNBT	FBG		IO	120		7		1480			2950	3400
17	7	CRESTFLITE V-174	OP	RNBT	FBG		IO	120-160		6	10	1425			2900	3400
20		GULFCRUISER V-205	OP	RNBT	FBG		IO	120-160		7	6	2750			4650	5350
20		GULFSTREAM V-204	OP	SPTCR	FBG		IO	120-225		7	6	1800			3950	4750
20		SPORTSMAN V-203		RNBT	FBG		IO	225		7	6	1700			3900	4500
23	6	CARIBBEAN V-234	ST	SPTCR	FBG		IO	155-200		8		2425			5700	6600
23	6	CARIBBEAN V-234	ST	SPTCR	FBG		IO	T120		8		2425			6550	7550
1966 BOATS																
16	6	BAYFLITE V-164	OP	RNBT	FBG		IO	90-120		6	8				3250	3750
17	7	CRESTFLITE V-174	OP	RNBT	FBG		IO	110-200		6	10				3550	4250
17	7	CRESTFLITE V-174 SS	OP	RNBT	FBG		IO	110-200		6	10				3800	4500
20		GULFCRUISER V-205	ST	RNBT	FBG		IO			6	10				**	**
20		GULFSTREAM V-204	OP	SPTCR	FBG		IO	110-200		7	6				4700	5550
20		GULFSTREAM V-204	OP	SPTCR	FBG		IO	T 60-T120		7	6				5650	6500
20		GULFSTREAM V-204	OP	SPTCR	FBG		IO	110-225		7	6				4850	5700
20		GULFSTREAM V-204 SS	OP	SPTCR	FBG		IO	310		7	6				5650	6500
20		GULFSTREAM V-204 SS	OP	SPTCR	FBG		IO	T 60-T120		7	6				5750	6600
23	6	CARIBBEAN V-234	ST	SPTCR	FBG		IO	150-225		8					7300	8550
23	6	CARIBBEAN V-234	ST	SPTCR	FBG		IO	310		8					8150	9350
23	6	CARIBBEAN V-234	ST	SPTCR	FBG		IO	T 60-T120		8					8200	9400
1965 BOATS																
16	5	FUTURA 500 V164	OP	RNBT	FBG		IO	90-120							3450	4300
17	3	CRESTFLITE V-174	OP	RNBT	FBG		IO	110-165							3650	4300
18	7	GULFCRUISER V-195	ST	RNBT	FBG		IO	110-225							4200	5100
18	7	GULFCRUISER V-195	ST	RNBT	FBG		IO	T110-T120							5100	6300
20		GULFSTREAM V-204	OP	SPTCR	FBG		IO	110-225							5100	6050
20		GULFSTREAM V-204	OP	SPTCR	FBG		IO	T110-T120							6050	7400
23	6	CARIBBEAN V-234	ST	SPTCR	FBG		IO	140-225							7650	9000
23	6	CARIBBEAN V-234	ST	SPTCR	FBG		IO	310	MRCR						8550	9850
23	6	CARIBBEAN V-234	ST	SPTCR	FBG		IO	T110-T150							8600	10300
1964 BOATS																
16	5	FUTURA 500 V164	OP	RNBT	FBG		IO	80-110							3600	4200
17	3	CRESTFLITE	OP	RNBT	FBG		IO	110-140							3800	4400
18	7	GULFCRUISER V-195	OP	RNBT	FBG		IO	110-225							4400	5250
18	7	GULFCRUISER V-195	OP	RNBT	FBG		IO	T110							5300	6050
18	7	GULFSTREAM V-194	OP	RNBT	FBG		IO	110-225							4500	5350
18	7	GULFSTREAM V-194	OP	CR	FBG		IO	T110							5450	6250
1963 BOATS																
16		BAYFLITE	OP	RNBT	FBG		IO	100-110							3650	4250
17	3	CRESTFLITE	OP	RNBT	FBG		IO	100-110							3900	4550
18	7	GULFSTREAM V-194	OP	CR	FBG		IO	100-110							4650	5300
1962 BOATS																
25	8	EXPLORER	OP	RNBT	FBG		IB	135							3750	4350

GLASWAY INC
TUFFY BOATS   COAST GUARD MFG ID- TUF

Call 1-800-327-6929 for BUC Personalized Evaluation Service
Or, for 1977 to 1986 boats, sign onto www.BUCValuPro.com

GLEN-COE BOAT
COAST GUARD MFG ID- JET

Call 1-800-327-6929 for BUC Personalized Evaluation Service
Or, for 1974 boats, sign onto www.BUCValuPro.com

GLENDALE CORP PLASTICS DIV
DIV GLENDALE MOBILE HOM COAST GUARD MFG ID- GDP

Call 1-800-327-6929 for BUC Personalized Evaluation Service
Or, for 1970 to 1974 boats, sign onto www.BUCValuPro.com

GLENMORE BOATS LTD
COAST GUARD MFG ID- ZGB

Call 1-800-327-6929 for BUC Personalized Evaluation Service
Or, for 1973 to 1982 boats, sign onto www.BUCValuPro.com

GLOBE YACHT BUILDING CO LTD
TAIPEI TAIWAN   See inside cover to adjust price for area

LOA FT	IN	NAME AND/ OR MODEL	TOP/ RIG	BOAT TYPE	HULL MTL	TP	ENGINE TP	# HP	MFG	BEAM FT	IN	WGT LBS	DRAFT FT	IN	RETAIL LOW	RETAIL HIGH
1983 BOATS																
37	4	GY 38-PH	CUT	SA/CR	FBG	KL	IB		D	11	8	32000	6		72200	79400
37	4	GY 38-PH	KTH	SA/CR	FBG	KL	IB		D	11	8	32000	6		72600	79800
41	1	GY 41-CC	KTH	SA/CR	FBG	KL	IB		D	12	2	31000	6	3	75500	83000
1982 BOATS																
37	4	GY 38-PH	CUT	SA/CR	FBG	KL	IB		D	11	8	32000	6		68000	74800
37	4	GY 38-PH	KTH	SA/CR	FBG	KL	IB		D	11	8	32000	6		68300	75100
41	1	GY 41-CC	KTH	SA/CR	FBG	KL	IB		D	12	2	31000	6	3	71000	78100
1981 BOATS																
37	4	GY 38-PH	CUT	SA/CR	FBG	KL	IB		D	11	8	32000	6		64100	70400
37	4	GY 38-PH	KTH	SA/CR	FBG	KL	IB		D	11	8	32000	6		64300	70600
37	4	GY 38-TC	CUT	SA/CR	FBG	KL	IB		D	11	8	32000	6		64100	70400
37	4	GY 38-TC	KTH	SA/CR	FBG	KL	IB		D	11	8	32000	6		64300	70600
41	1	GY 41-AC	SCH	SA/CR	FBG	KL	IB		D	12	2	32500	6	3	68600	75600
41	1	GY 41-AC	KTH	SA/CR	FBG	KL	IB		D	12	2	32500	6	3	68800	75600
41	1	GY 41-CC	KTH	SA/CR	FBG	KL	IB		D	12	2	32500	6	3	68800	75600
45	9	GY 46-CC	CUT	SA/CR	FBG	KL	IB		D	13	4	40000	5	8	86200	94800
45	9	GY 46-CC	KTH	SA/CR	FBG	KL	IB		D	13	4	40000	5	8	88000	96700
1980 BOATS																
37	4	GY 38-PH	CUT	SA/CR	FBG	KL	IB		D	11	8	32000	6		61100	67200
37	4	GY 38-PH	KTH	SA/CR	FBG	KL	IB		D	11	8	32000	6		61400	67500
37	4	GY 38-TC	CUT	SA/CR	FBG	KL	IB		D	11	8	32000	6		61100	67200
37	4	GY 38-TC	KTH	SA/CR	FBG	KL	IB		D	11	8	32000	6		61400	67500
41	1	GY 41-AC	SCH	SA/CR	FBG	KL	IB		D	12	2	32500	6	3	65400	71900
41	1	GY 41-AC	KTH	SA/CR	FBG	KL	IB		D	12	2	32500	6	3	65700	72200
41	1	GY 41-CC	KTH	SA/CR	FBG	KL	IB		D	12	2	32500	6	3	65700	72200
45	9	GY 46-CC	CUT	SA/CR	FBG	KL	IB		D	13	4	40000	5	8	82200	90300
45	9	GY 46-CC	KTH	SA/CR	FBG	KL	IB		D	13	4	40000	5	8	84000	92300

GLOUCESTER YACHTS INC

GLOUCESTER VA 23061   COAST GUARD MFG ID- GYI See inside cover to adjust price for area

For more recent years, see the BUC Used Boat Price Guide, Volume 1 or Volume 2

LOA FT IN	NAME AND/ OR MODEL	TOP/ RIG	BOAT TYPE	-HULL- MTL TP	----ENGINE--- TP # HP MFG	BEAM FT IN	WGT LBS	DRAFT FT IN	RETAIL LOW	RETAIL HIGH
			1983 BOATS							
19 3	GLOUCESTER 19	SLP	SA/CR	FBG KC	OB	7 6	1600	1	2300	2700
19 3	GLOUCESTER 20	SLP	SA/CR	FBG KC	OB	7 6	1600	1	2550	2950
21 8	GLOUCESTER 22	SLP	SA/CR	FBG KC	OB	8	2300	1 8	3150	3700
22 10	GLOUCESTER 23	SLP	SA/CR	FBG KC	OB	8	2500	1 11	3500	4100
26 8	GLOUCESTER 27	SLP	SA/CR	F/S KL	SD 8D VLVO	8	5300	3 8	8600	9900

GODFREY MARINE

AQUA-PATIO HURRICANE & SANPAN   See inside cover to adjust price for area
ELKHART IN 46516   COAST GUARD MFG ID- GDY
FORMERLY GODFREY CONVEYOR COMPANY

For more recent years, see the BUC Used Boat Price Guide, Volume 1 or Volume 2

LOA FT IN	NAME AND/ OR MODEL	TOP/ RIG	BOAT TYPE	-HULL- MTL TP	----ENGINE--- TP # HP MFG	BEAM FT IN	WGT LBS	DRAFT FT IN	RETAIL LOW	RETAIL HIGH
			1983 BOATS							
17 1	CYPRUS SD176	OP	RNBT	FBG TR	IO 120-170	7 2	2070		2850	3350
17 1	GENEVA SD176	OP	RNBT	FBG TR	IO 120-170	7 2	2070		2850	3350
18 10	CYPRUS SD196	OP	RNBT	FBG TR	OB	7 6	1500		2150	2500
18 10	CYPRUS SD196	OP	RNBT	FBG TR	IO 140-230	7 6	2500		3550	4300
18 10	GENEVA SD196	OP	RNBT	FBG TR	OB	7 6	1500		2150	2500
18 10	GENEVA SD196	OP	RNBT	FBG TR	IO 140-230	7 6	2500		3550	4300
18 10	TAHOE SD196	OP	RNBT	FBG TR	IO 140-230	7 6	2500		3550	4300
			1982 BOATS							
17 1	CYPRUS SD176	OP	RNBT	FBG TR	IO 120-170	7 2	2070		2800	3300
17 1	GENEVA SD176	OP	RNBT	FBG TR	IO 120-170	7 2	2070		2800	3300
17 1	TAHOE SD176	OP	RNBT	FBG TR	IO 120-170	7 2	2070		2750	3250
18 10	CYPRUS SD196	OP	RNBT	FBG TR	OB	7 6	1500		2150	2500
18 10	CYPRUS SD196	OP	RNBT	FBG TR	IO 140-230	7 6	2500		3500	4250
18 10	GENEVA SD196	OP	RNBT	FBG TR	OB	7 6	1500		2000	2400
18 10	GENEVA SD196	OP	RNBT	FBG TR	IO 140-230	7 6	2500		3450	4150
18 10	TAHOE SD196	OP	RNBT	FBG TR	IO 140-230	7 6	2500		3500	4250
			1981 BOATS							
18 10	CYPRUS	OP	RNBT	FBG TR	IO 140-230	7 6	2500		3500	4200
18 10	GENEVA	OP	RNBT	FBG TR	OB	7 6	1500		2050	2450
18 10	GENEVA	OP	RNBT	FBG TR	IO 140-230	7 6	2500		3350	4100
18 10	PLACID	OP	RNBT	FBG TR	OB	7 6	1500		2000	2400
18 10	PLACID	OP	RNBT	FBG TR	IO 140-230	7 6	2500		3300	4050
18 10	TAHOE	OP	RNBT	FBG TR	IO 140-230	7 6	2500		3500	4200
19	HURRICANE SD-196	OP	RNBT	FBG TR	IO 185	7 8			3500	4100
			1972 BOATS							
24	CAMP-N-CRUISE SANPAN		CAMPR	AL PN	OB	8	1450	9	2200	2550
28	CAMP-N-CRUISE SANPAN		CAMPR	AL PN	OB	8	1600	9	7400	8500
			1971 BOATS							
23 8	CAMP-N-CRUISE		CAMPR	AL PN	OB	8	1400	9	2100	2500
27 8	CAMP-N-CRUISE		CAMPR	AL PN	OB	8	1550	9	7250	8300
30	WEEKENDER	HT	HB	AL PN	OB	8			4200	4850
			1970 BOATS							
23	CAMP-N-CRUISE SANPAN		CAMPR	AL PN	OB	8	1500	9	2250	2600
27	CAMP-N-CRUISE SANPAN		CAMPR	AL PN	OB	8	1850	9	6350	7300
30	WEEKENDER	HT	HB	AL PN	OB	8	2200	9	**	**
			1969 BOATS							
28	WEEKENDER	HT	HB	AL PN	OB	8	2100	9	**	**
30	SANPAN	HT	HB	AL PN	OB	8		6	4150	4800
			1968 BOATS							
28	WEEKENDER	HT	HB	AL PN	OB	8	2100	9	**	**
			1967 BOATS							
28	WEEKENDER	HT	HB	AL PN	OB	10	2100	7	**	**

GOLDEN ERA BOATS INC

COAST GUARD MFG ID- GEB

Call 1-800-327-6929 for BUC Personalized Evaluation Service
Or, for 1980 to 1994 boats, sign onto www.BUCValuPro.com

GOLDEN VIKING INDUSTRIES

Call 1-800-327-6929 for BUC Personalized Evaluation Service
Or, for 1970 boats, sign onto www.BUCValuPro.com

GOLDEN WAVE SHIPYARD LTD

KOWLOON HONG KONG   See inside cover to adjust price for area

For more recent years, see the BUC Used Boat Price Guide, Volume 1 or Volume 2

LOA FT IN	NAME AND/ OR MODEL	TOP/ RIG	BOAT TYPE	-HULL- MTL TP	----ENGINE--- TP # HP MFG	BEAM FT IN	WGT LBS	DRAFT FT IN	RETAIL LOW	RETAIL HIGH
			1983 BOATS							
38	GOLDEN-WAVE GW38	SLP	SA/CR	FBG KL	IB D UNIV	11 9		6	67200	73800
42	GOLDEN-WAVE GW42	CUT	SA/CR	FBG KL	VD 40D PERK	12 8	25000	6 2	91400	100500
47 10	GOLDEN-WAVE GW48	SLP	SA/CR	FBG KL	IB 60D PERK	15 1	34000	6 6	129500	142000
47 10	GOLDEN-WAVE GW48	KTH	SA/CR	FBG KC	IB D PERK	15 10	34000	11	129500	142500
55 9	GOLDEN-WAVE GW55	SLP	SA/RC	FBG KL	IB 85D PERK	16	48000	9 3	249000	273500
			1982 BOATS							
38	GOLDEN-WAVE GW38	SLP	SA/CR	FBG KL	IB D UNIV	11 9		6	63200	69500
42	GOLDEN-WAVE GW42	CUT	SA/CR	FBG KL	VD 40D PERK	12 8	25000	6 2	86000	94500
47 10	GOLDEN-WAVE GW48	KTH	SA/CR	FBG KC	IB D PERK	15 10	34000	11	122000	134000
47 10	GOLDEN-WAVE GW48	SLP	SA/CR	FBG KL	IB 60D PERK	15 1	34000	6 6	121500	133500
			1981 BOATS							
42	GOLDEN-WAVE GW42	CUT	SA/CR	FBG KL	VD 50D PERK	12 8	23000	6 2	77100	84800
47 10	GOLDEN-WAVE GW48	SLP	SA/CR	FBG KL	IB D PERK	15 1	34000	6 6	114500	126000

GOLDLINE CORPORATION

COAST GUARD MFG ID- GLC

Call 1-800-327-6929 for BUC Personalized Evaluation Service
Or, for 1974 boats, sign onto www.BUCValuPro.com

GOMAN BOAT LTD

Call 1-800-327-6929 for BUC Personalized Evaluation Service
Or, for 1982 boats, sign onto www.BUCValuPro.com

GOODELL YACHT CORP

COAST GUARD MFG ID- GDL

Call 1-800-327-6929 for BUC Personalized Evaluation Service
Or, for 1973 to 1974 boats, sign onto www.BUCValuPro.com

GOODHUE & HAWKINS

Call 1-800-327-6929 for BUC Personalized Evaluation Service
Or, for 1927 boats, sign onto www.BUCValuPro.com

GORDON PAYNE LTD

Call 1-800-327-6929 for BUC Personalized Evaluation Service
Or, for 1970 to 1971 boats, sign onto www.BUCValuPro.com

GP MARINE

Call 1-800-327-6929 for BUC Personalized Evaluation Service
Or, for 1981 boats, sign onto www.BUCValuPro.com

GRADY-WHITE BOATS INC

GREENVILLE NC 27835-152 COAST GUARD MFG ID- NTL See inside cover to adjust price for area

For more recent years, see the BUC Used Boat Price Guide, Volume 1 or Volume 2

LOA FT IN	NAME AND/ OR MODEL	TOP/ RIG	BOAT TYPE	-HULL- MTL TP	----ENGINE--- TP # HP MFG	BEAM FT IN	WGT LBS	DRAFT FT IN	RETAIL LOW	RETAIL HIGH
			1983 BOATS							
18 11	BLUEFISH 197	OP	RNBT	FBG SV	IO 170 MRCR	7 10	2550	1 4	4200	4900
18 11	TARPON 190	OP	RNBT	FBG SV	OB	7 10	1900	1 4	4900	5650
20 4	FISHERMAN 204	OP	CTRCN	FBG SV	OB	8	1995	1 2	6900	7950
20 4	GULFSTREAM 205	OP	CUD	FBG SV	IO 170-230	8	3000	1 2	6500	7850
20 4	GULFSTREAM 205	OP	CUD	FBG SV	IO 260	8	3000	1 2	6900	8300
20 4	ISLANDER 206	OP	CUD	FBG SV	SE 155-205	8	2780	1 2	6500	9500
20 4	OVERNIGHTER 204-C	OP	OVNTR	FBG SV	OB	8	3220	1 2	7400	8500
22	BAHAMA 222	OP	FSH	FBG DV	SE 205 OMC	8	3260	1 2	10600	12100
22	BIMINI 220	OP	SPTCR	FBG SV	OB	8	2700	1 2	9500	10800

LOA FT	IN	NAME AND/ OR MODEL	TOP/ RIG	BOAT TYPE	-HULL- MTL	TP	----ENGINE--- TP	# HP	MFG	BEAM FT	IN	WGT LBS	DRAFT FT	IN	RETAIL LOW	RETAIL HIGH
		1983 BOATS														
22		PACIFIC 221	OP	SPTCR	FBG	SV	IO	170-230		8		3560	1	3	8000	9850
22		PACIFIC 221	OP	SPTCR	FBG	SV	IO	260		8		3740	1	3	8650	10300
22		PACIFIC 221	OP	SPTCR	FBG	SV	IO	130D-155D		8		3740	1	3	10300	11700
22		SEAFARER 226	OP	CUD	FBG	SV	OB			8		2730	1	2	10200	11600
22		SEAFARER 227	OP	CUD	FBG	SV	IO	170-260		8		3590	1	2	8050	10000
22		SEAFARER 227	OP	CUD	FBG	SV	IO	130D-155D		8		3590	1	2	10000	11700
22		SEAFARER 228	OP	CUD	FBG	SV	SE		OMC	8		3290	1	2	**	**
22		SEAFARER 228	OP	CUD	FBG	SV	SE	205	OMC	8		3290	1	2	11400	13000
22		TOURNAMENT 223	OP	SF	FBG	DV	OB			8		2600	1	2	9300	10600
22		TOURNAMENT 223	TT	SF	FBG	DV	OB			8		3560	1	2	11100	12600
22		TOURNAMENT 224	OP	SF	FBG	DV	IO	170-230		8		2380	1	2	7200	8650
22		TOURNAMENT 224	OP	SF	FBG	DV	IO	260		8		2380	1	2	7600	9150
22		TOURNAMENT 224	OP	SF	FBG	DV	IO	130D-155D		8		2380	1	2	10300	12100
22		TOURNAMENT 224	TT	SF	FBG	DV	IO	170-260		8		3450	1	2	9000	11100
22		TOURNAMENT 224	TT	SF	FBG	DV	IO	130D	VLVO	8		3450	1	2	12200	13900
22		TOURNAMENT 224	TT	SF	FBG	SV	IO	185-188		8		3450	1	2	9000	10300
22		TOURNAMENT 224	TT	SF	FBG	SV	IO	155D	VLVO	8		3450	1	2	12500	14200
22		TOURNAMENT 225	OP	SF	FBG	DV	SE	205	OMC	8		3160	1	2	10400	11900
22		TOURNAMENT 225	TT	SF	FBG	DV	SE	205	OMC	8		4075	1	2	11600	13200
24	1	CARIBBEAN 242	OP	SF	FBG	DV	SE	205	OMC	8		3820	1	4	13500	15400
24	1	OFFSHORE 240	OP	SF	FBG	DV	OB			8		3025	1	4	11400	13000
24	1	TOURNAMENT 243	OP	SF	FBG	SV	OB			8		2800	1	4	10700	12200
24	1	TOURNAMENT 243	TT	SF	FBG	SV	OB			8		2800	1	4	10700	12200
24	1	TOURNAMENT 244	OP	SF	FBG	SV	IO	198-260		8		3600	1	4	10400	12600
24	1	TOURNAMENT 244	OP	SF	FBG	SV	IO	130D-155D		8		3600	1	4	13800	16000
24	1	TOURNAMENT 244	TT	SF	FBG	SV	IO	198-260		8		3600	1	4	10400	12600
24	1	TOURNAMENT 244	TT	SF	FBG	SV	IO	130D-155D		8		3600	1	4	13800	16000
24	1	TOURNAMENT 245	OP	SF	FBG	SV	SE	205	OMC	8		3360	1	4	12400	14100
24	1	TOURNAMENT 245	TT	SF	FBG	SV	SE	205	OMC	9	6	3360	1	4	12400	14100
24	1	WEEKENDER 241	OP	SF	FBG	DV	IO	228-230		8		4150	1	4	11600	13900
24	1	WEEKENDER 241	OP	SF	FBG	DV	IO	260		8		4460	1	4	12500	14600
24	1	WEEKENDER 241	OP	SF	FBG	DV	IO	130D-155D		8		4460	1	4	15800	18300
25	4	KINGFISH 254	OP	SF	FBG	DV	IO	260		9	6	5500	1	7	16100	18300
25	4	KINGFISH 254	OP	SF	FBG	DV	IO	T170-T188		9	6	5100	1	7	16100	19800
25	4	KINGFISH 254 DLX	TT	SF	FBG	DV	IO	260		9	6	5100	1	7	15100	17500
25	4	KINGFISH 254 DLX	TT	SF	FBG	DV	IO	T170		9	6	5100	1	7	16100	18300
25	4	KINGFISH DLX 254	TT	SF	FBG	DV	IO	T175-T188		9	6	5100	1	7	16600	18900
25	4	SAILFISH 255	OP	SF	FBG	DV	OB			9	6	5130	1	7	16200	18400
25	4	SAILFISH 255 DLX	TT	SF	FBG	DV	OB			9	6	5100	1	7	16200	18400
25	4	SWORDFISH 252	OP	SF	FBG	SV	IO	T120	OMC	9	6	4365	1	7	14100	16100
25	4	SWORDFISH 252	OP	SF	FBG	SV	SE	T155	OMC	9	6	5130	1	7	16200	18400
25	4	SWORDFISH 252	TT	SF	FBG	SV	IO	T120	OMC	9	6	4365	1	7	14100	16100
25	4	SWORDFISH 252	TT	SF	FBG	SV	SE	T155	OMC	9	6		1	7	14100	16000
25	4	TROPHY 257	OP	SF	FBG	SV	OB			9	6	4075	1	7	14700	16700
25	4	TROPHY 257	TT	SF	FBG	SV	OB			9	6	4075	1	7	14700	16700
25	4	TROPHY 258	OP	SF	FBG	SV	IO	260		9	6	5500	1	7	15900	18200
25	4	TROPHY 258	OP	SF	FBG	SV	IO	T170-T188		9	6	5500	1	7	16900	19600
25	4	TROPHY 258	TT	SF	FBG	SV	IO	260		9	6	5500	1	7	15900	18400
25	4	TROPHY 258	TT	SF	FBG	SV	IO	T170-T188		9	6	5500	1	7	16900	19700
25	4	TROPHY 259	OP	SF	FBG	SV	SE	155-205		9	6	5130	1	7	16200	18400
25	4	TROPHY 259	TT	SF	FBG	SV	SE	155-205		9	6	5130	1	7	16200	18400
		1982 BOATS														
18	11	ATLANTIC 196	OP	RNBT	FBG	SV	IO	120-230		7	10	2500	1	4	4050	5000
18	11	ATLANTIC 196	OP	RNBT	FBG	SV	IO	260		7	10	2500	1	4	4400	5350
18	11	BLUEFISH 197	OP	RNBT	FBG	SV	IO	120-230		7	10	2550	1	4	4100	5050
18	11	BLUEFISH 197	OP	RNBT	FBG	SV	IO	260		7	10	2550	1	4	4450	5350
18	11	SPORTSMAN 195	OP	RNBT	FBG	SV	OB			7	10	1800	1	2	4700	5400
18	11	TARPON 190	OP	RNBT	FBG	SV	OB			7	10	1900	1	2	4850	5550
20	4	FISHERMAN 204	OP	CTRCN	FBG	SV	OB			8		1995	1	2	6800	7800
20	4	GULFSTREAM 205	OP	CUD	FBG	SV	IO	120-230		8		3000	1	2	6350	7700
20	4	GULFSTREAM 205	OP	CUD	FBG	SV	IO	260		8		3000	1	2	6750	8100
20	4	OVERNIGHTER 204-C	OP	OVNTR	FBG	SV	OB			8		2220	1	2	7250	8350
21	2	CHESAPEAKE 212	OP	CUD	FBG	SV	IO	120-230		8		2850	1	2	6450	7800
21	2	CHESAPEAKE 212	OP	CUD	FBG	SV	IO	260		8		2850	1	2	6850	8200
22		BAHAMA 222	OP	FSH	FBG	DV	IO		OMC	8		3260	1	2	**	**
22		BIMINI 220	OP	SPTCR	FBG	SV	OB			8		2700	1	2	9350	10600
22		PACIFIC 221	OP	SPTCR	FBG	SV	IO	170-260		8		3740	1	3	8100	10100
22		PACIFIC 221	OP	SPTCR	FBG	SV	IO	130D	VLVO	8		3740	1	3	10000	11400
22		SEAFARER 226	OP	SF	FBG	DV	OB			8		2800			10200	11600
22		SEAFARER 227	OP	SF	FBG	DV	IO	170-260		8		3660			9150	11200
22		SEAFARER 227	OP	SF	FBG	DV	IO	130D	VLVO	8		3660			12400	14000
22		SEAFARER 227	HT	SF	FBG	DV	IO	170-260		8					9200	11300
22		SEAFARER 227	HT	SF	FBG	DV	IO	130D	VLVO	8					12200	13900
22		SEAFARER 228	OP	SF	FBG	DV	IO			8		3360			**	**
22		TOURNAMENT 223	OP	SF	FBG	DV	OB			8		2600	1	2	9100	10400
22		TOURNAMENT 223	TT	SF	FBG	DV	OB			8		3560	1	2	10900	12400
22		TOURNAMENT 224	OP	SF	FBG	DV	IO	170-230		8		2380	1	2	7050	8500
22		TOURNAMENT 224	OP	SF	FBG	DV	IO	260		8		2380	1	2	7450	8950
22		TOURNAMENT 224	OP	SF	FBG	DV	IO	130D	VLVO	8		2380	1	2	10100	11500
22		TOURNAMENT 224	TT	SF	FBG	DV	IO	170-260		8		3450	1	2	8800	10800
22		TOURNAMENT 224	TT	SF	FBG	DV	IO	130D	VLVO	8		3450	1	2	12000	13600
22		TOURNAMENT 225	OP	SF	FBG	DV	IO		OMC	8		3160	1	2	**	**
22		TOURNAMENT 225	TT	SF	FBG	DV	IO		OMC	8		4075	1	2	**	**
24	1	CARIBBEAN 242	OP	SF	FBG	DV	IO		OMC	8		3820	1	4	**	**
24	1	OFFSHORE 240	OP	SF	FBG	DV	OB			8		3025	1	4	11200	12700
24	1	WEEKENDER 241	OP	SF	FBG	DV	IO	228-260		8		4250	1	4	11600	14300
24	1	WEEKENDER 241	OP	SF	FBG	DV	IO	130D	VLVO	8		4460	1	4	15400	17500
25	4	KINGFISH 254	OP	SF	FBG	DV	IO	260		9	6	5100	1	7	14800	17100
25	4	KINGFISH 254	OP	SF	FBG	DV	IO	T170-T185		9	6	5100	1	7	15800	18100
25	4	KINGFISH 254 DLX	TT	SF	FBG	DV	IO	260		9	6	5100	1	7	14800	17100
25	4	KINGFISH 254 DLX	TT	SF	FBG	DV	IO	T170-T185		9	6	5100	1	7	15800	18100
25	4	SAILFISH 255	OP	SF	FBG	DV	OB			9	6	4075	1	7	14500	16400
25	4	SAILFISH 255 DLX	TT	SF	FBG	DV	OB			9	6	5100	1	7	15900	18000
25	4	SWORDFISH 252	OP	SF	FBG	SV	IO		OMC	9	6	5130	1	7	**	**
25	4	SWORDFISH 252	TT	SF	FBG	SV	IO		OMC	9	6		1	7	**	**
25	4	WAHOO 256	OP	SF	FBG	SV	IB	260-330		9	6		1	7	13700	16200
25	4	WAHOO 256	OP	SF	FBG	SV	IB	180D	PCM	9	6		1	7	26400	29300
25	4	WAHOO DLX TOWER	TT	SF	FBG	SV	IO	180-260		9	6		1	7	12300	14900
25	4	WAHOO DLX TOWER	TT	SF	FBG	SV	IB	330	GM	9	6		1	7	14300	16200
		1981 BOATS														
18	11	ATLANTIC 196	OP	RNBT	FBG	SV	IO	120-230		7	10	2500	1	4	3900	4800
18	11	ATLANTIC 196	OP	RNBT	FBG	SV	IO	260		7	10	2500	1	4	4250	5050
18	11	BLUEFISH 197	OP	RNBT	FBG	SV	IO	120-230		7	10	2550	1	4	4000	4950
18	11	BLUEFISH 197	OP	RNBT	FBG	SV	IO	260		7	10	2550	1	4	4350	5300
18	11	HOLIDAY 193	OP	RNBT	FBG	SV	OB			7	10	1850		11	4650	5350
18	11	RIVIERA 194	OP	RNBT	FBG	SV	IO	120-230		7	10	2500	1	4	4050	5000
18	11	RIVIERA 194	OP	RNBT	FBG	SV	IO	260		7	10	2500	1	4	4450	5200
18	11	SPORTSMAN 195	OP	RNBT	FBG	SV	OB			7	10	1800		11	4650	5350
18	11	TARPON 190	OP	RNBT	FBG	SV	OB			7	10	1850		11	4750	5450
19	1	ANGLER 192	OP	RNBT	FBG	SV	IO	120-230		8		2360	1	2	3950	4900
19	8	DOLPHIN 200	OP	CUD	FBG	DV	OB			8		2000	1	2	5150	5900
19	8	MARLIN 201	OP	CUD	FBG	DV	IO	140-230		8		2685	1	2	4600	5550
19	8	MARLIN 201	OP	CUD	FBG	DV	IO	260		8		2685	1	2	4850	5900
20	4	FISHERMAN 204	OP	CTRCN	FBG	SV	OB			8		1990	1	2	6650	7650
20	4	GULFSTREAM 205	OP	CUD	FBG	SV	IO	120-230		8		3000	1	2	6250	7550
20	4	GULFSTREAM 205	OP	CUD	FBG	SV	IO	260		8		3000	1	2	6650	8000
20	4	OVERNIGHTER 204-C	OP	CUD	FBG	SV	OB			8		2220	1	2	7150	8200
21	2	CHESAPEAKE 212	OP	CUD	FBG	SV	IO	120-230		8		2850	1	2	6350	7650
21	2	CHESAPEAKE 212	OP	CUD	FBG	SV	IO	260		8		2850	1	2	6750	8100
22		BIMINI 220	OP	SPTCR	FBG	SV	OB			8		2900	1	3	9600	10900
22		PACIFIC 221	OP	SPTCR	FBG	SV	IO	170-260		8		3740	1	3	7950	9900
22		PACIFIC 221	OP	SPTCR	FBG	SV	IO	130D-155D		8		3740	1	3	9850	11500
24	1	OFFSHORE 240	OP	SF	FBG	DV	OB			8		3225	1	4	11600	13200
24	1	WEEKENDER 241	OP	SF	FBG	DV	IO	228-260		8		4460	1	4	11800	14100
24	1	WEEKENDER 241	OP	SF	FBG	DV	IO	130D-155D		8		4460	1	4	15200	17600
24	1	WEEKENDER 241	OP	SF	FBG	DV	IO	T170-T185		8		4460	1	4	12900	14700
25	4	KINGFISH 254	OP	SF	FBG	DV	IO	260		9	6	5100	1	7	14500	16800
25	4	KINGFISH 254	OP	SF	FBG	DV	IO	T170-T185		9	6	5100	1	7	15500	17800
25	4	KINGFISH 254 DLX	TT	SF	FBG	DV	IO	260-365		9	6	5100	1	7	14900	17100
25	4	KINGFISH 254 DLX	TT	SF	FBG	DV	IO	T170-T185		9	6	5100	1	7	15900	18200
25	4	SAILFISH 255	OP	SF	FBG	DV	OB			9	6	4300	1	7	14600	16500
25	4	SAILFISH 255 DLX	TT	SF	FBG	DV	IO	260-365		9	6	5100	1	7	14300	17100
25	4	SAILFISH 255 DLX	TT	SF	FBG	DV	IO	T170-T185		9	6	5100	1	7	15100	17400
25	4	WAHOO 256	OP	SF	FBG	SV	IB	260	CHRY	9	6				13000	14800
		IB 260 MRCR 13100 14900, IB 260-330 15000 17000, IB 130D-155D													18600	21300
		IB 180D 25300 28200														
25	4	WAHOO 256 DLX TOWER	TT	SF	FBG	SV	IB	255-454		9	6	5180	2	4	14900	17000
25	4	WAHOO 256 DLX TOWER	TT	SF	FBG	SV	IB	130D-155D		9	6	5180	2	4	18600	21300
25	4	WAHOO 256 DLX TOWER	TT	SF	FBG	SV	IB	180D							25200	28000
		1980 BOATS														
18	11	ATLANTIC 196	OP	RNBT	FBG	SV	IO	120-230		7	10	2500	1	4	3950	4800
18	11	ATLANTIC 196	OP	RNBT	FBG	SV	IO	260		7	10	2500	1	4	4350	5100
18	11	HOLIDAY 193	OP	RNBT	FBG	SV	OB			7	10	1850		11	4700	5400
18	11	RIVIERA 194	OP	RNBT	FBG	SV	IO	120-230		7	10	2500	1	4	3950	4800

 CONTINUED ON NEXT PAGE

GRADY-WHITE BOATS INC -CONTINUED See inside cover to adjust price for area

LOA FT	LOA IN	NAME AND/ OR MODEL	TOP/ RIG	BOAT TYPE	-HULL- MTL	-HULL- TP	ENGINE TP	ENGINE # HP MFG	BEAM FT	BEAM IN	WGT LBS	DRAFT FT	DRAFT IN	RETAIL LOW	RETAIL HIGH
		1980 BOATS													
18	11	RIVIERA 194	OP	RNBT	FBG	SV	IO	260	7	10	2500	1	4	4350	5100
18	11	SPORTSMAN 195	OP	RNBT	FBG	SV	OB		7	10	1800		11	4600	5250
18	11	TARPON 190	OP	RNBT	FBG	SV	OB		7	10	1850		11	4600	5300
19	1	ANGLER 192		RNBT	FBG	SV	IO	260	8					4300	5000
19	1	ANGLER 192	OP	RNBT	FBG	SV	IO	120-230	8		2360	1	2	3900	4850
19	8	DOLPHIN 200	OP	CUD	FBG	DV	OB		8		2000	1	2	5100	5850
19	8	MARLIN 201	OP	CUD	FBG	DV	IO	140-230	8		2685	1	2	4550	5500
19	8	MARLIN 201	OP	CUD	FBG	DV	IO	260	8		2685	1	2	4800	5850
20	4	FISHERMAN 204	OP	CTRCN	FBG	SV	OB		8		1990	1	2	6550	7550
20	4	GULFSTREAM 205	OP	CUD	FBG	SV	IO	140-230	8		3000	1	2	6200	7500
20	4	GULFSTREAM 205	OP	CUD	FBG	SV	IO	260	8		3000	1	2	6600	7900
20	4	OVERNIGHTER 204-C	OP	CUD	FBG	SV	OB		8		2220	1	2	7050	8100
21	2	CHESAPEAKE 212	OP	CUD	FBG	SV	IO	140-230	8		2850	1	2	6300	7600
21	2	CHESAPEAKE 212	OP	CUD	FBG	SV	IO	260	8		2850	1	2	6650	8000
24	1	OFFSHORE 240	OP	SF	FBG	DV	OB		8		3225	1	4	11400	13000
24	1	WEEKENDER 241	OP	SF	FBG	DV	IO	228-260	8		4460	1	4	11700	14000
24	1	WEEKENDER 241	OP	SF	FBG	DV	IO	130D VLVO	8		4460	1	4	15000	17100
24	1	WEEKENDER 241	OP	SF	FBG	DV	IO	T140-T170	8		4460	1	4	12700	15000
25	4	KINGFISH 254	OP	SF	FBG	DV	IO	260	9	6	5100	1	7	14400	16700
25	4	KINGFISH 254	OP	SF	FBG	DV	IO	T140-T170	9	6	5100	1	7	15100	17500
25	4	SAILFISH 255	OP	SF	FBG	DV	OB		9	6	4300	1	7	14300	16300
		1979 BOATS													
16	10	DUKE 175	OP	RNBT	FBG	SV	OB		6	9	1190	1		3100	3650
16	10	PACER 174	OP	RNBT	FBG	SV	IO	120-170	6	9	2100	1	1	2950	3650
16	10	SPRINT 173	OP	RNBT	FBG	SV	OB		6	9	1200	1		3150	3650
18	4	ADVENTURER 183 B/R	OP	RNBT	FBG	SV	OB		7	6	1450	1		3800	4400
18	4	CHALLENGER 185	OP	RNBT	FBG	SV	OB		7	6	1390	1		3650	4250
18	4	ROGUE 184	OP	RNBT	FBG	SV	IO	120-230	7	6	2260	1	2	3550	4400
18	4	ROGUE 184	OP	RNBT	FBG	SV	IO	260	7	6	2260	1	2	3850	4700
19	1	ANGLER 192	OP	RNBT	FBG	SV	IO	120-230	8		2360	1	2	3900	4850
19	8	DOLPHIN 200	OP	CUD	FBG	DV	OB		8		2000	1	2	5050	5800
19	8	MARLIN 201	OP	CUD	FBG	DV	IO	140-230	8		2685	1	2	4550	5500
19	8	MARLIN 201	OP	CUD	FBG	DV	IO	260	8		2685	1	2	4800	5800
19	8	SEVILLE 203	ST	CUD	FBG	DV	IO	170-230	8		2820	1	2	4700	5650
19	8	SEVILLE 203	ST	CUD	FBG	DV	IO	260	8		2820	1	2	4950	5950
20	4	FISHERMAN 204	OP	CTRCN	FBG	SV	OB		8		1990	1	2	6450	7450
20	4	GULFSTREAM 205	OP	CUD	FBG	SV	IO	140-230	8		3000	1	2	6200	7500
20	4	GULFSTREAM 205	OP	CUD	FBG	SV	IO	260	8		3000	1	2	6550	7900
20	4	OVERNIGHTER 204-C	OP	CUD	FBG	SV	OB		8		2220	1	2	6950	7950
21	2	CHESAPEAKE 212	OP	CUD	FBG	SV	IO	140-230	8		2850	1	2	6300	7600
21	2	CHESAPEAKE 212	OP	CUD	FBG	SV	IO	260	8		2850	1	2	6650	8000
21	2	NASSAU 212-C	OP	CR	FBG	SV	IO	140-230	8		2800	1	2	6200	7500
21	2	NASSAU 212-C	OP	CR	FBG	SV	IO	260	8		2800	1	2	6600	7950
24	1	OFFSHORE 240	OP	SF	FBG	DV	OB		8		3225	1	4	11300	12800
24	1	WEEKENDER 241	OP	SF	FBG	DV	IO	228-260	8		4460	1	4	11700	13900
24	1	WEEKENDER 241	OP	SF	FBG	DV	IO	T140-T170	8		4460	1	4	12700	15000
25	4	KINGFISH 254	OP	SF	FBG	DV	IO	260-330	9	6	5100	1	7	14400	17600
25	4	KINGFISH 254	OP	SF	FBG	DV	IO	T140-T170	9	6	5100	1	7	15100	17500
		1978 BOATS													
16	10	DUKE 175	OP	RNBT	FBG	SV	OB		6	9	1190	1		3100	3600
16	10	PACER 174	OP	RNBT	FBG	SV	IO	120-170	6	9	2100	1	1	2950	3650
16	10	SPRINT 173	OP	RNBT	FBG	SV	OB		6	9	1200	1		3100	3600
18	4	ADVENTURER 183 B/R	OP	RNBT	FBG	SV	OB		7	6	1450	1		3750	4350
18	4	CHALLENGER 185	OP	RNBT	FBG	SV	OB		7	6	1390	1		3650	4250
18	4	ROGUE 184	OP	RNBT	FBG	SV	IO	120-240	7	6	2260	1	2	3550	4350
18	4	ROGUE 184	OP	RNBT	FBG	SV	IO	260 MRCR	7	6	2260	1	2	3850	4500
19	1	ANGLER 192	OP	RNBT	FBG	SV	IO	120-198	8		2360	1	2	3950	4800
19	1	ANGLER 192	OP	RNBT	FBG	SV	IO	200-260	8			1	2	4300	5000
19	8	DOLPHIN 200	OP	CUD	FBG	DV	OB		8		2000	1	2	4950	5700
19	8	MARLIN 201	OP	CUD	FBG	DV	IO	140-260	8		2685	1	2	4550	5600
19	8	SEVILLE 203	ST	CUD	FBG	SV	IO	170-260	8		2820	1	2	4700	5750
20	4	GULFSTREAM 205	OP	CUD	FBG	SV	IO	140-260	8		3000	1	2	6250	7600
20	4	HATTERAS 204	OP	CTRCN	FBG	SV	OB		8		1990	1	2	6400	7350
20	4	HATTERAS 204-C	OP	OVNTR	FBG	SV	OB		8		2220	1	2	6850	7900
21	2	CHESAPEAKE 212	OP	CUD	FBG	SV	IO	140-198	8		2850	1	2	6300	7800
21	2	CHESAPEAKE 212	OP	CUD	FBG	SV	IO	200-260	8			1	2	7000	8050
21	2	NASSAU 212-C	OP	CR	FBG	SV	IO	140-198	8		2800	1	2	6250	7700
21	2	NASSAU 212-C	OP	CR	FBG	SV	IO	200-260	8			1	2	6950	8000
25	4	KINGFISH 254	OP	SF	FBG	DV	IO	255-330	9	6	5100	1	7	14700	16700
25	4	KINGFISH 254	OP	SF	FBG	DV	IO	T140-T200	9	6		1	7	13500	16600
		1977 BOATS													
16	10	DUKE 175	OP	RNBT	FBG	SV	OB		6	9	1190	1		3050	3550
16	10	PACER 174	OP	RNBT	FBG	SV	IO	120-140	6	9	2100	1	1	3000	3500
16	10	SPRINT 173	OP	RNBT	FBG	SV	OB		6	9	1200	1		3100	3600
18	4	ADVENTURER 183 B/R	OP	RNBT	FBG	SV	OB		7	6	1450	1		3700	4300
18	4	CHALLENGER 185	OP	RNBT	FBG	SV	OB		7	6	1390	1		3600	4200
18	4	ROGUE 184	OP	RNBT	FBG	SV	IO	120-235	7	6	2250	1	2	3600	4300
19	1	ANGLER 192	OP	RNBT	FBG	SV	IO	120-235	8		2360	1	2	4000	4950
19	8	DOLPHIN 200	OP	CUD	FBG	SV	OB		8		2000	1	2	4950	5650
19	8	MARLIN 201	OP	CUD	FBG	SV	IO	120-235	8		2685	1	2	4650	5550
20	4	GULFSTREAM 205	OP	CUD	FBG	SV	IO	120-235	8		3000	1	2	6300	7250
20	4	HATTERAS 204	OP	CTRCN	FBG	SV	OB		8		1990	1	2	6300	7250
20	4	HATTERAS 204-C	OP	OVNTR	FBG	SV	OB		8		2220	1	2	6800	7800
21	2	CHESAPEAKE 212	OP	CUD	FBG	SV	IO	120-190	8		2850	1	2	6400	7900
21	2	CHESAPEAKE 212	OP	CUD	FBG	SV	IO	233-235	8			1	2	7000	8050
21	2	NASSAU 212-C	OP	CR	FBG	SV	IO	120-190	8		2800	1	2	6350	7800
21	2	NASSAU 212-C	OP	CR	FBG	SV	IO	233-235	8			1	2	6950	8000
		1976 BOATS													
16	10	DUKE 175	OP	RNBT	FBG	SV	OB		6	9	1190	1		3050	3550
16	10	PACER 174	OP	RNBT	FBG	SV	IO	120-140	6	9	2100	1	1	3100	3600
16	10	SPRINT 173	OP	RNBT	FBG	SV	OB		6	9	1200	1		3050	3550
18	4	ADVENTURER 183 B/R	OP	RNBT	FBG	SV	OB		7	6	1450	1		3700	4300
18	4	BARON 186	OP	RNBT	FBG	SV	IO	120-235	7	6	2240	1	2	3700	4500
18	4	BARON 186	OP	RNBT	FBG	SV	JT	290 OMC	7	6	2240	1	2	4150	4850
18	4	CHALLENGER 185	OP	RNBT	FBG	SV	OB		7	6	1390	1		3600	4150
18	4	ROGUE 184	OP	RNBT	FBG	SV	IO	120-235	7	6	2250	1	2	3700	4500
18	4	ROGUE 184	OP	RNBT	FBG	SV	JT	290 OMC	7	6	2250	1	2	4150	4850
19	1	ANGLER 192	OP	RNBT	FBG	SV	IO	120-235	8		2360	1	2	4100	5000
19	1	ANGLER 192	OP	RNBT	FBG	SV	JT	290 OMC	8		2360	1	2	4650	5300
19	1	ATLANTIC 191-C	OP	WKNDR	FBG	SV	OB		8		1740		10	4300	5000
19	1	SPORTSMAN 191	OP	RNBT	FBG	SV	OB		8		1495		10	3900	4500
20	4	GULFSTREAM 205	OP	CUD	FBG	SV	IO	120-235	8		3000	1	2	6500	7700
20	4	GULFSTREAM 205	OP	CUD	FBG	SV	JT	290 OMC	8		3000	1	2	6650	7650
20	4	HATTERAS 204	OP	CTRCN	FBG	SV	OB		8		2100	1	2	6500	7450
20	4	HATTERAS 204-C	OP	CUD	FBG	SV	OB		8		2220	1	2	6700	7750
21	2	CHESAPEAKE 212	OP	CUD	FBG	SV	IO	120-235	8		2620	1	2	6300	7500
21	2	CHESAPEAKE 212	OP	CUD	FBG	SV	JT	290 OMC	8		2620	1	2	6450	7400
21	2	NASSAU 212-C	OP	CR	FBG	SV	IO	120-235	8		2800	1	2	6500	7750
21	2	NASSAU 212-C	OP	CR	FBG	SV	JT	290 OMC	8		2800	1	2	6650	7650
		1975 BOATS													
16	6	STING-RAY 166	OP	RNBT	FBG	SV	OB		6	7	990		10	2550	2950
18	4	ADVENTURER 183 B/R	OP	RNBT	FBG	SV	OB		7	6	1450	1		3650	4250
18	4	BARON 186	OP	RNBT	FBG	SV	IO	120-235	7	6	2240	1	2	3800	4650
		JT 245 OMC 4000 4650, IO 245 OMC 4000 4650, JT 290 OMC												4000	4650
18	4	CHALLENGER 185	OP	RNBT	FBG	SV	OB		7	6	1390	1		3550	4150
18	4	ROGUE 184 W/T	OP	RNBT	FBG	SV	IO	120-235	7	6	2260	1	2	3850	4650
		JT 245 OMC 4000 4650, IO 245 OMC 4000 4700, JT 290 OMC												4000	4650
19	1	ANGLER 192	OP	RNBT	FBG	SV	IO	120-235	8		2360	1	2	4250	5150
		JT 245 OMC 4450 5100, IO 245 OMC 4500 5150, JT 290 OMC												4450	5100
19	1	ATLANTIC 191-C	OP	WKNDR	FBG	SV	OB		8		1740		10	4250	4950
19	1	SPORTSMAN 191	OP	RNBT	FBG	SV	OB		8		1495		10	3850	4500
20	4	HATTERAS 204	OP	CTRCN	FBG	SV	OB		8		2100	1	2	6450	7400
20	4	HATTERAS 204	OP	OVNTR	FBG	SV	OB		8		2220	1	2	6650	7650
21	2	CHESAPEAKE 212	OP	CUD	FBG	SV	IO	120-235	8		2620	1	2	6500	7750
		JT 245 OMC 6200 7100, IO 245 OMC 6750 7750, JT 290 OMC												6200	7100
21	2	NASSAU 212-C	OP	CR	FBG	SV	IO	120-235	8		2800	1	2	6750	8000
		JT 245 OMC 6400 7350, IO 245 OMC 7000 8050, JT 290 OMC												6400	7350
		1974 BOATS													
16	6	STING-RAY 166	OP	RNBT	FBG		OB		6	7	975			2500	2900
17	1	CAPRI 171	OP	RNBT	FBG		OB		7		1220			3100	3600
18	4	ADVENTURER 183 B/R	OP	RNBT	FBG		OB		7	6	1420			3600	4200
18	4	ROGUE 184	OP	RNBT	FBG		IO	120-225	7	6	2240			3950	4650
18	4	ROGUE 184	OP	RNBT	FBG		JT	245 OMC	7	6				3800	4400
18	4	ROGUE 184	OP	RNBT	FBG		IO	245 OMC	7	6				4050	4750
19	1	ANGLER 192	OP	RNBT	FBG		IO	120-225	8		2360			4450	5350
19	1	ANGLER 192	OP	RNBT	FBG		JT	245 OMC	8					4350	5000
19	1	ANGLER 192	OP	RNBT	FBG		IO	245 OMC	8					4700	5400
19	1	ATLANTIC 191C	OP	WKNDR	FBG		OB		8		1620			4050	4700
19	1	SPORTSMAN 191	OP	RNBT	FBG		OB		8		1495			3850	4450
21	2	CHESAPEAKE 212	OP	CUD	FBG		IO	120-188	8		2800			6950	8650
		IO 225 OMC 7600 8750, JT 245 OMC 6550 7500, IO 245 OMC												7700	8850
21	2	NASSAU 212-C	OP	CR	FBG		IO	120-225	8		2800			6950	8650
21	2	NASSAU 212-C	OP	CR	FBG		JT	245 OMC	8					6500	7450
21	2	NASSAU 212-C	OP	CR	FBG		IO	245 OMC	8					7650	8750

96th ed. - Vol. III CONTINUED ON NEXT PAGE 271

GRADY-WHITE BOATS INC -CONTINUED See inside cover to adjust price for area

LOA FT	IN	NAME AND/ OR MODEL	TOP/ RIG	BOAT TYPE	-HULL- MTL	TP	----ENGINE--- TP	# HP	MFG	BEAM FT	IN	WGT LBS	DRAFT FT	IN	RETAIL LOW	RETAIL HIGH
		1973 BOATS														
16	6	STING-RAY 166	OP	RNBT	FBG		OB			6	7	975			2500	2900
17	1	CAPRI 171	OP	RNBT	FBG		OB			7		1220			3100	3600
18	4	ADVENTURER 183 B/R	OP	RNBT	FBG		OB			7	6	1420			3600	4150
18	4	ROGUE 184	OP	RNBT	FBG		IO	120-225		7	6	2240			4050	4800
18	4	ROGUE 184	OP	RNBT	FBG		JT	245	OMC	7	6				3650	4250
18	4	ROGUE 184	OP	RNBT	FBG		IO	245	OMC	7	6				4200	4900
19	1	ANGLER 192	OP	RNBT	FBG		IO	120-225		8		2360			4600	5500
19	1	ANGLER 192	OP	RNBT	FBG		JT	245	OMC	8					4150	4800
19	1	ANGLER 192	OP	RNBT	FBG		IO	245	OMC	8					4850	5600
19	1	ATLANTIC 191-C	OP	WKNDR	FBG		OB			8		1620			4000	4650
19	1	SPORTSMAN 191	OP	RNBT	FBG		OB			8		1495			3800	4450
21	2	CHESAPEAKE 212	OP	CUD	FBG		IO	120-188		8		2800			7200	8950
		IO 225 OMC 7850 9000, JT 245 OMC 6300 7250, IO 245 OMC 7950 9150														
21	2	NASSAU 212-C	OP	CR	FBG		IO	120-225		8		2800			7200	8950
21	2	NASSAU 212-C	OP	CR	FBG		JT	245	OMC	8					6250	7150
21	2	NASSAU 212-C	OP	CR	FBG		IO	245	OMC	8					7900	9050
		1972 BOATS														
16	6	STING-RAY 166	OP	RNBT	FBG		OB			6	7	920			2350	2750
17	1	CAPRI 171	OP	RNBT	FBG		OB			7		1230			3100	3600
18	4	ADVENTURER 183 B/R	OP	RNBT	FBG		OB			7	6	1390			3550	4100
18	4	ROGUE 184	OP	RNBT	FBG		IO	120-245		7	6	2310			4250	5050
19	1	ANGLER 192	OP	RNBT	FBG		IO	120-165		8					4800	5550
19	1	ATLANTIC 191-C	OP	WKNDR	FBG		OB			8		1590			3950	4600
19	1	SPORTSMAN 191	OP	RNBT	FBG		OB			8		1485			3800	4400
21	2	CHESAPEAKE 212	OP	CUD	FBG		IO	120-245		8					7950	9450
21	2	NASSAU 212-C	OP	CR	FBG		IO	120-245		8					7850	9350
		1971 BOATS														
16	6	STING-RAY	OP	RNBT	FBG		OB			6	7	920			2350	2750
17	1	CAPRI 171	OP	RNBT	FBG		OB			7		1230			3100	3600
18	2	RIVIERA 182	OP	RNBT	FBG		IO	120-165		7	3	2110			4100	4800
19	1	ANGLER 192	OP	RNBT	FBG		IO	120-165		8		2320			4850	5600
19	1	ATLANTIC 191-C	OP	WKNDR	FBG		OB			8		1590			3950	4600
19	1	SPORTSMAN 191	OP	RNBT	FBG		OB			8		1485			3800	4400
21	2	CHESAPEAKE 1002	OP	CUD	FBG		IO	120-235		8		2470			7200	8500
21	2	NASSAU 212-C	OP	CR	FBG		IO	120-235		8		2670			7450	8850
		1970 BOATS														
16	6	STING-RAY	OP	RNBT	FBG	SV	OB			6	7	920			2350	2750
17	1	CAPRI 171	OP	RNBT	FBG	TR	OB			7		1230			3100	3600
18	2	RIVIERA 182	OP	RNBT	FBG	DV	IO	120-165		7	3	2110			4250	4950
19	1	ATLANTIC 191-C	OP	WKNDR	FBG	SV	OB			8		1590			3950	4600
19	1	SPORTSMAN 191	OP	RNBT	FBG	SV	OB			8		1485			3800	4400
21	2	CHESAPEAKE 1002	OP	CUD	FBG		IO	120-215		8		2470			7400	8750
21	2	NASSAU 212-C	OP	CR	FBG		IO	120-215		8		2670			7700	9100
		1969 BOATS														
16	6	PAMLICO 1116	OP	RNBT	FBG		OB			6	7				4950	5650
17	1	CAPRI 1174	ST	RNBT	FBG		IO	120-160		6	10				3850	4500
17	1	CAPRI 1175	ST	RNBT	FBG		OB			6	10	1200			3050	3550
18	1	JUNIPER 1195	OP	RNBT	FBG		IO	120-160		7	3				4450	5150
19	1	STRIPER CABIN 1119C	OP	CBNCR	FBG		OB			8		1740			4200	4900
21	4	NASSAU CABIN 1121C	OP	CBNCR	WD		IO	120-160		8					9400	10700
21	4	SHOWAN CUDDY 1121	OP	CUD	WD		IO	120-160		8					8950	10200
		1968 BOATS														
16	5	PAMLICO	OP	RNBT	WD		OB			6	3	740		7	1750	2100
16	5	PAMLICO	OP	RNBT	WD		IO	85		6	3				3450	4000
16	5	PAMLICO CAPRI	OP	RNBT	WD		OB			6	3	740		7	2150	2500
16	5	PAMLICO CAPRI	OP	RNBT	WD		IO	85		6	3				3450	4000
16	6	RIVIERA	OP	RNBT	FBG		OB			6	3	750		7	1950	2300
16	6	RIVIERA	OP	RNBT	FBG		IO	80		6	3	1225		7	2950	3450
17	4	HATTERAS	OP	OVNTR	WD		OB			7	2	980		10	2600	3000
17	4	HATTERAS 174-0	OP	CR	WD		IO	110		7	2				4600	5300
17	4	HATTERAS CAPRI	OP	CR	WD		OB			7	2	960		9	2750	3200
17	4	HATTERAS CAPRI	OP	CR	WD		IO	110		7	2				4600	5300
17	4	HATTERAS DELUXE	OP	CR	WD		OB			7	2	960		9	2350	2700
17	4	HATTERAS DELUXE	OP	CR	WD		IO	110		7	2				4600	5300
19	1	STRIPER		CBNCR	WD		IO	140		7	10				5450	6250
19	3	PACIFIC 191	OP	CR	WD		OB			7	7	1290		11	3450	4000
19	3	PACIFIC 191	OP	CR	WD		IO	110-200		7	7			11	5300	6100
19	3	PACIFIC-CAPRI	OP	CR	WD		OB			7	7			11	4800	5500
19	3	PACIFIC-CAPRI	OP	CR	WD		IO	120-200		7	7			11	5350	6400
19	6	STRIPER		CBNCR	FBG		OB			8		1150		11	3150	3650
19	6	STRIPER	OP	CBNCR	FBG		OB			8		1440		11	3800	4400
20	4	ATLANTIC	OP	CR	WD		OB			8		1310	1	5	4500	5200
20	4	ATLANTIC	OP	CR	WD		IO	120-200		8			1	5	7000	8450
20	4	ATLANTIC 204-W	OP	WKNDR	WD		OB			8		1385	2	3	4700	5400
20	4	ATLANTIC 204-W	OP	WKNDR	WD		IO	120-200		8			2	3	7850	9200
20	4	ATLANTIC-ADVENTURER	OP	CR	WD		IO	195		8					7500	8650
20	4	ATLANTIC-CAPRI	OP	CR	WD		IO	120-200		8			1		7450	8900
21	4	BIMINI	OP	CR	FBG		IO	120-200		8					9250	10800
21	4	BIMINI CUTTY	OP	CR	FBG		IO	120-200		8					8600	10200
22	2	CHESAPEAKE 222	OP	RNBT	WD		OB			8		1800	2	5	4750	5450
22	2	CHESAPEAKE 222	OP	RNBT	WD		IO	120-200		8			2	5	9550	11000
22	2	CHESAPEAKE 222	OP	RNBT	WD		IB	210	CHRY	8			2	5	5250	6000
22	2	CHESAPEAKE 222C	OP	CBNCR	WD		OB			8		1975	1	8	5100	5900
22	2	CHESAPEAKE 222C	OP	CBNCR	WD		IO	120-200		8			1	8	11800	13500
26	9	BAHAMA CUSTOM	OP	CR	WD		IB	195		9	8		1	11	10900	12400
26	9	BAHAMA CUSTOM	FB	CR	WD		IB	195		9	8		1	11	10900	12400
26	11	CATALINA CUSTOM	FB	CBNCR	WD		IB	210	CHRY	10	5	6200	2		12200	13900
26	11	CATALINA CUSTOM	FB	CBNCR	WD		IB	T160		10	5	6200	2		13100	14900
27	6	MARLIN 275	HT	CUD	FBG		IB	T290		10	9				13900	15800
27	6	MARLIN 275 SPORTSMAN	FB	CUD	FBG		IB	T290		10	9				13900	15800
30		CATALINA CUSTOM	FB	CBNCR	WD		IB	290	CHRY	11	3	8350	2	4	19400	21600
30		CATALINA CUSTOM	FB	CBNCR	WD		IB	T195		11	3	8350	2	4	20400	22700
33	4	CARIBBEAN CUSTOM	FB	CR	WD		IB	T210		12		9600	2	3	23300	25900
		1967 BOATS														
16	5	PAMLICO	OP	RNBT	WD		OB					740			1950	2300
16	7	RIVIERA	OP	RNBT	FBG		OB								4950	5700
17	4	HATTERAS	OP	OVNTR	WD		OB					980			2600	3000
17	4	HATTERAS CAPRI	OP	CR	WD		OB								4150	4850
17	4	HATTERAS DELUXE	OP	CR	WD		OB					960			2550	2950
19	1	STRIPER		CBNCR	FBG		OB								4750	5450
19	1	STRIPER	OP	CBNCR	FBG		OB								4750	5450
19	3	PACIFIC 191	OP	CR	WD		OB					1290			3200	3700
19	3	PACIFIC 191	OP	CR	WD		IO	80-200							5200	6150
19	3	PACIFIC-CAPRI	OP	CR	WD		OB					1290			3700	4350
19	3	PACIFIC-CAPRI	OP	CR	WD		IO	80-200							5600	6550
20	4	ATLANTIC			WD		OB					1310			4550	5200
20	4	ATLANTIC			WD		IO	80-200							7150	8350
20	4	ATLANTIC 204-W	OP	WKNDR	WD		OB					1385			4700	5450
20	4	ATLANTIC 204-W	OP	WKNDR	WD		IO	80-200							8100	9500
20	4	ATLANTIC-ADVENTURER	OP	CR	WD		IB	195							3550	4150
20	4	ATLANTIC-CAPRI	OP	CR	WD		OB					1310			4550	5200
20	4	ATLANTIC-CAPRI	OP	CR	WD		IO	80-200							7400	8700
22	2	CHESAPEAKE 222		RNBT	WD		OB								7000	8050
22	2	CHESAPEAKE 222		RNBT	WD		IO	80-185							9950	11400
22	2	CHESAPEAKE 222		RNBT	WD		IB	195							5150	5900
22	2	CHESAPEAKE 222		RNBT	WD		IO	200							10100	11500
22	2	CHESAPEAKE 222C	OP	CBNCR	WD		OB								7050	8100
22	2	CHESAPEAKE 222C	OP	CBNCR	WD		IO	80-200							12200	14000
26	11	BAHAMA CUSTOM	OP	CR	WD		IB	195				4700			8600	9900
26	11	CATALINA CUSTOM	FB	CBNCR	WD		IB	220				6200			11800	13400
26	11	CATALINA CUSTOM	FB	CBNCR	WD		IB	T157							13100	14900
27	6	MARLIN 275	HT	CUD	FBG		IB	T250							12800	14500
27	6	MARLIN 275	FB	CUD	FBG		IB	T250							12800	14500
27	6	MARLIN 275 SPORTSMAN	FB	CUD	FBG		IB	T250				8500			14100	16000
27	6	MARLIN 275 W/CONV TP	FB	CUD	FBG		IB	T250				8500			14400	16400
30		CATALINA CUSTOM	FB	CBNCR	WD		IB	290				9000			19200	21300
30		CATALINA CUSTOM	FB	CBNCR	WD		IB	T195							20400	22700
33	4	CARIBBEAN CUSTOM	FB	CR	WD		IB	T195				9600			22800	25300
		1966 BOATS														
16	5	PAMLICO	OP	RNBT	L/P		OB			6	3	740			1950	2300
16	5	PAMLICO CAPRI	OP	RNBT	L/P		OB								2050	2450
16	7	RIVIERA	OP	RNBT	FBG		OB			6	3	648			1700	2050
17	4	HATTERAS	OP	OVNTR	L/P		OB			7		980			2600	3000
17	4	HATTERAS CAPRI	OP	CR	L/P		OB			7					4200	4850
17	4	HATTERAS DELUXE	OP	CR	L/P		OB			7		960			2550	2950
19	3	PACIFIC 191	OP	CR	L/P		OB			7	7	1290			3450	4050
19	3	PACIFIC 191	OP	CR	L/P		IO	110-200		7	7				5400	6650
19	3	PACIFIC-CAPRI	OP	CR	L/P		OB			7	7				4800	5550
19	3	PACIFIC-CAPRI	OP	CR	L/P		IO	110-200		7	7				5750	7100
19	3	STRIPER	OP	CBNCR	FBG		OB			7	7				4800	5500
19	3	STRIPER	OP	CBNCR	FBG		IO			7	7				**	**
19	3	STRIPER	OP	CBNCR	FBG		IO	110-200		7	7				5750	6950
20	4	ATLANTIC		RNBT	L/P		OB			8		1310			4550	5200
20	4	ATLANTIC		RNBT	L/P		IO	110-200		8					8100	9650
20	4	ATLANTIC 204-W	OP	WKNDR	L/P		OB			8					7150	8200
20	4	ATLANTIC 204-W	OP	WKNDR	L/P		IO	110-200		8					8400	10000
20	4	ATLANTIC-ADVENTURER	OP	CR	L/P		IB	195		8			1	5	3550	4100
20	4	ATLANTIC-CAPRI	OP	CR	L/P		OB			8					7150	8200

 CONTINUED ON NEXT PAGE

LOA FT	IN	NAME AND/ OR MODEL	TOP/ RIG	BOAT TYPE	-HULL- MTL TP	----ENGINE--- TP # HP MFG	BEAM FT IN	WGT LBS	DRAFT FT IN	RETAIL LOW	RETAIL HIGH
				1966 BOATS							
20	4	ATLANTIC-CAPRI	OP	CR	L/P	IO 110-200	8			7900	9450
22	2	CHESAPEAKE 222		RNBT	L/P	OB	8	1600		4300	4950
22	2	CHESAPEAKE 222		RNBT	L/P	IO 110-200	8			10200	11900
22	2	CHESAPEAKE 222		RNBT	L/P	IB 220 GRAY	8	1600 1 8		3600	4150
22	2	CHESAPEAKE 222C	OP	CBNCR	L/P	OB	8			7100	8150
22	2	CHESAPEAKE 222C	OP	CBNCR	L/P	IO 110-200	8			12600	14700
26	11	BAHAMA CUSTOM	OP	CR	L/P	IB 195	9 5		2	10200	11500
26	11	CATALINA CUSTOM	HT	CBNCR	L/P	IB 220	10 5		2	11900	13500
26	11	CATALINA CUSTOM	HT	CBNCR	L/P	JT T150	10 5		2	13200	15000
27	6	MARLIN 275	HT	CUD	FBG	IB T250				12300	14000
27	6	MARLIN 275	FB	CUD	FBG	IB T250				14000	15900
27	6	MARLIN 275 SPORTSMAN	FB	CUD	FBG	IB T250				11400	12900
27	6	MARLIN 275 W/CONV TP	FB	CUD	FBG	IB T250				11700	13200
27	7	GULFSTREAM		CR	L/P	IB T150	10		2	11400	13000
27	7	GULFSTREAM	HT	CR	L/P	IB T150	10		2	11500	13100
27	9	GULFSTREAM	SF	L/P		IB T150	10		2	11500	13100
33	4	CARIBBEAN CUSTOM	FB	CR	WD	IB T220	12		2	22900	25400
				1965 BOATS							
16	5	PAMLICO	OP	RNBT	WD	OB				1800	2150
16	5	PAMLICO CAPRI	OP	RNBT	WD	OB				2350	2750
17	4	HATTERAS	OP	OVNTR	WD	OB				4200	4850
17	4	HATTERAS CAPRI	OP	CR	WD	OB				5000	5700
17	4	HATTERAS DELUXE	OP	CR	WD	OB				4000	4650
17	4	HATTERAS STANDARD	OP	CR	WD	OB				3600	4200
19	3	PACIFIC 191	OP	CR	WD	OB				4150	4800
19	3	PACIFIC 191	OP	CR	WD	IO 110-140				5500	6500
19	3	PACIFIC 191	OP	CR	WD	IO 150				5200	5950
19	3	PACIFIC 191	OP	CR	WD	IO 150-160				6100	7000
19	3	PACIFIC-CAPRI	OP	CR	WD	OB				5000	5750
19	3	PACIFIC-CAPRI	OP	CR	WD	IO 110-140				5950	7050
19	3	PACIFIC-CAPRI	OP	CR	WD	IO 150				5650	6500
19	3	PACIFIC-CAPRI	OP	CR	WD	IO 150-160				6500	7500
19	3	PACIFIC-HOLIDAY	OP	CR	WD	OB				5350	6150
19	3	PACIFIC-HOLIDAY	OP	CR	WD	IO 110-140				6150	7250
19	3	PACIFIC-HOLIDAY	OP	CR	WD	IO 150				4650	5350
19	3	PACIFIC-HOLIDAY	OP	CR	WD	IO 150-160				6700	7750
20	4	ATLANTIC		WD		OB				7150	8250
20	4	ATLANTIC		WD		IO 110-160				7650	8800
20	4	ATLANTIC	OP	CAMPR	WD	OB				7150	8250
20	4	ATLANTIC	OP	CAMPR	WD	IO 110-160				7500	8650
20	4	ATLANTIC 204-W	OP	WKNDR	WD	OB				7150	8250
20	4	ATLANTIC 204-W	OP	WKNDR	WD	IO 110-160				8650	10000
20	4	ATLANTIC-ADVENTURER	OP	CR	WD	IB 160-175				3250	3850
20	4	ATLANTIC-CAPRI	OP	CR	WD	OB				7150	8250
20	4	ATLANTIC-CAPRI	OP	CR	WD	IO 110-160				7900	9150
22	2	CHESAPEAKE 222		RNBT	WD	OB				7000	8050
22	2	CHESAPEAKE 222		RNBT	WD	IO 110-160				10600	12100
22	2	CHESAPEAKE 222C	OP	CBNCR	WD	OB				7100	8150
22	2	CHESAPEAKE 222C	OP	CBNCR	WD	IO 110-160				13000	14800
22	4	VEE LIFT	OP	CR	WD	OB				9500	10800
22	4	VEE LIFT	OP	CR	WD	IO				**	**
22	4	VEE LIFT	OP	CR	WD	IO 110-160				11800	13400
24	9	CATALINA CUSTOM	HT	CBNCR	WD	IB 215-220				7050	8100
24	9	CATALINA CUSTOM 2500	OP	CR	WD	IB 215-220				7200	8300
24	9	NASSAU	OP	CBNCR	WD	IB 195				7050	8100
27	7	GULFSTREAM	HT	CR	WD	IB T150-T160				10400	11900
27	7	GULFSTREAM	HT	CR	WD	IB 238-240				11000	12600
27	7	GULFSTREAM	FB	CR	WD	IB T150-T160				10500	12000
27	7	GULFSTREAM	FB	CR	WD	IB 238-240				11000	12700
27	7	GULFSTREAM CUSTOM	FB	CR	WD	IB T150-T160				10300	11700
27	7	GULFSTREAM CUSTOM	FB	CR	WD	IB 238-240				10900	12500
27	9	BAHAMA		CR	WD	IB 175				9950	11300
27	9	BAHAMA CRUISMASTER		CR	WD	IB 175				10300	11800
33	4	CARIBBEAN CUSTOM	FB	CR	WD	IB T190-T220				22500	25300
				1964 BOATS							
16	5	PAMLICO	OP	RNBT	WD	OB				1800	2150
16	5	PAMLICO CAPRI	OP	RNBT	WD	OB				2350	2750
17	4	HATTERAS	OP	OVNTR	WD	OB				4200	4900
17	4	HATTERAS CAPRI	OP	CR	WD	OB				5000	5750
17	4	HATTERAS DELUXE	OP	CR	WD	OB				4050	4700
17	4	HATTERAS STANDARD	OP	CR	WD	OB				3650	4200
19	3	PACIFIC 191	OP	CR	WD	OB				4150	4800
19	3	PACIFIC 191	OP	CR	WD	IO 110-160				5650	6600
19	3	PACIFIC-CAPRI	OP	CR	WD	OB				5000	5750
19	3	PACIFIC-CAPRI	OP	CR	WD	IO 110-160				6100	7150
19	3	PACIFIC-HOLIDAY	OP	CR	WD	OB				5350	6150
19	3	PACIFIC-HOLIDAY	OP	CR	WD	IO 110-160				6450	7450
20	4	ATLANTIC		WD		OB				7200	8250
20	4	ATLANTIC		WD		IO 110-160				7900	9450
20	4	ATLANTIC	OP	CAMPR	WD	OB				7200	8250
20	4	ATLANTIC	OP	CAMPR	WD	IO 110-160				7750	9250
20	4	ATLANTIC 204-W	HT	CBNCR	WD	OB				7200	8300
20	4	ATLANTIC 204-W	OP	WKNDR	WD	IO 110-160				9050	10700
20	4	ATLANTIC-ADVENTURER	OP	CR	WD	IB 160-175				3150	3700
20	4	ATLANTIC-CAPRI	OP	CR	WD	OB				7200	8250
20	4	ATLANTIC-CAPRI	OP	CR	WD	IO 110-160				8200	9800
22	2	CHESAPEAKE 222		RNBT	WD	OB				7050	8100
22	2	CHESAPEAKE 222		RNBT	WD	IO 110-160				11000	12900
22	2	CHESAPEAKE 222C	OP	CBNCR	WD	OB				7100	8200
22	4	VEE LIFT	OP	CR	WD	OB				9550	10800
22	4	VEE LIFT	OP	CR	WD	IO 110-160				12200	14200
24	9	CATALINA CUSTOM	HT	CBNCR	WD	IB 215-220				6800	7800
24	9	CATALINA CUSTOM 2500	OP	CR	WD	IB 215-220				6950	8000
27	7	GULFSTREAM	HT	CR	WD	IB 238-240				10100	11400
27	7	GULFSTREAM	FB	CR	WD	IB 238-240				10600	12100
27	7	GULFSTREAM CUSTOM	FB	CR	WD	IB T150-T160				10100	11400
27	7	GULFSTREAM CUSTOM	FB	CR	WD	IB T150-T160				10600	12100
33	4	CARIBBEAN CUSTOM	FB	CR	WD	IB T190-T220				21800	24500
				1963 BOATS							
16	5	PAMLICO	OP	RNBT	WD	OB				2100	2500
17	4	HATTERAS	HT	CR	WD	OB				4250	4900
17	4	HATTERAS	OP	OVNTR	WD	OB				4200	4900
17	4	HATTERAS CAPRI	OP	CR	WD	OB				5000	5750
17	4	HATTERAS DELUXE	OP	CR	WD	OB				4050	4700
17	4	HATTERAS STANDARD	OP	CR	WD	OB				3650	4250
19	3	PACIFIC 191	HT	CR	WD	OB				4850	5600
19	3	PACIFIC 191	OP	CR	WD	IO 80-140				6150	7100
19	3	PACIFIC DELUXE	OP	CR	WD	OB				4200	4850
19	3	PACIFIC DELUXE	OP	CR	WD	IO 80-140				5750	6900
19	3	PACIFIC-HOLIDAY	OP	CR	WD	OB				5550	6350
19	3	PACIFIC-HOLIDAY	OP	CR	WD	IO 80-140				6600	7750
20	4	ATLANTIC		WD		OB				7200	8300
20	4	ATLANTIC		WD		IO 80-140				8150	9400
20	4	ATLANTIC	OP	CAMPR	WD	OB				7200	8300
20	4	ATLANTIC	OP	CAMPR	WD	IO 80-140				8000	9200
20	4	ATLANTIC	HT	CBNCR	WD	OB				7200	8300
20	4	ATLANTIC 204-W	OP	WKNDR	WD	IO 80-140				10400	11900
20	4	ATLANTIC 204-W	OP	WKNDR	WD	OB				7200	8300
20	4	ATLANTIC-ADVENTURER	OP	CR	WD	IB 135-150				2950	3500
22	2	CHESAPEAKE 222		RNBT	WD	OB				7050	8100
22	2	CHESAPEAKE 222		RNBT	WD	IO 80-140				11400	12900
22	2	CHESAPEAKE 222 C	OP	CBNCR	WD	OB				7150	8200
22	2	CHESAPEAKE 222 C	OP	CBNCR	WD	IO 80-140				13900	15800
24	9	CATALINA CUSTOM	OP	CBNCR	WD	IB 215				6550	7550
24	9	CATALINA CUSTOM 2500	OP	CR	WD	IB 215				6700	7700
27	7	GULFSTREAM CUSTOM	FB	CR	WD	IB 210-215				9550	10900
27	7	GULFSTREAM CUSTOM	FB	CR	WD	IB T145-T150				10100	11600
27	7	GULFSTREAM OPEN MODE	OP	CR	WD	IB 210-215				9550	10900
27	7	GULFSTREAM OPEN MODE	OP	CR	WD	IB T145-T150				10100	11600
				1962 BOATS							
16	5	PAMLICO	OP	RNBT	WD	OB				2150	2500
17	4	CAPRI 171	OP	RNBT	WD	OB				4900	5650
17	4	HATTERAS	OP	CR	WD	OB				4250	4950
17	4	HATTERAS	OP	OVNTR	WD	IO 80-100				5900	6750
17	4	HATTERAS DELUXE	OP	CR	WD	OB				4250	4950
17	4	HATTERAS DELUXE	OP	CR	WD	IO 80-100				5400	6200
19	3	PACIFIC DELUXE	OP	CR	WD	OB				4900	5600
19	3	PACIFIC DELUXE	OP	CR	WD	IO 80-100				6350	7300
19	3	PACIFIC-HOLIDAY HC	OP	CR	WD	OB				4900	5600
19	3	PACIFIC-HOLIDAY HC	OP	CR	WD	IO 80-100				6350	7300
20	4	ATLANTIC 204	OP	RNBT	WD	OB				7300	8350
20	4	ATLANTIC 204	OP	RNBT	WD	IO 80-100				9200	10500
20	4	ATLANTIC 204-VC	OP	CAMPR	WD	OB				7250	8300
20	4	ATLANTIC 204-VC	OP	CAMPR	WD	IO 80-100				8250	9300
20	4	ATLANTIC W	OP	WKNDR	WD	OB				7250	8300
20	4	ATLANTIC W	OP	WKNDR	WD	IO 80-100				9600	10900

```
GRADY-WHITE BOATS INC          -CONTINUED      See inside cover to adjust price for area
 LOA   NAME AND/        TOP/ BOAT   -HULL-  ----ENGINE--- BEAM    WGT   DRAFT RETAIL RETAIL
FT IN  OR MODEL         RIG  TYPE   MTL TP  TP # HP  MFG  FT IN   LBS   FT IN  LOW    HIGH
--------------------- 1962 BOATS --------------------------------------------------------
27  7  GULFSTREAM            CR     WD      IB T135                            9800   11100
--------------------- 1961 BOATS --------------------------------------------------------
16  6  PAMLICO 166      OP   RNBT   L/P     OB         6  3   640            1750   2100
17  4  HATTERAS         OP   CBNCR  L/P     OB         7  2   910            2500   2900
17  4  HATTERAS         OP   CBNCR  L/P     IO  80     7  2            8     4450   5100
17  4  HATTERAS 174     OP   RNBT   L/P     OB         7  2   885            2450   2850
17  4  HATTERAS 174     OP   RNBT   L/P     IO  80     7  2            8     5250   6050
20  4  ATLANTIC         OP   CBNCR  L/P     OB         8      1385          4800   5550
20  4  ATLANTIC         OP   CBNCR  L/P     IO  80     8               8    11300  12900
20  4  ATLANTIC 204     OP   RNBT   L/P     OB         8      1150          4100   4750
20  4  ATLANTIC 204     OP   RNBT   L/P     IO  80     8               8     9550  10900
```

GRAFTON BOAT COMPANY INC
STEEL KING

Call 1-800-327-6929 for BUC Personalized Evaluation Service
Or, for 1959 to 1965 boats, sign onto www.BUCValuPro.com

GRAHAM-PRAMS

Call 1-800-327-6929 for BUC Personalized Evaluation Service
Or, for 1959 to 1961 boats, sign onto www.BUCValuPro.com

GRAMPIAN MARINE LTD INC
TORONTO ONTARIO CANADA   COAST GUARD MFG ID- GRM See inside cover to adjust price for area

For more recent years, see the BUC Used Boat Price Guide, Volume 1 or Volume 2

```
 LOA   NAME AND/        TOP/ BOAT   -HULL-  ----ENGINE--- BEAM    WGT   DRAFT RETAIL RETAIL
FT IN  OR MODEL         RIG  TYPE   MTL TP  TP # HP  MFG  FT IN   LBS   FT IN  LOW    HIGH
--------------------- 1977 BOATS --------------------------------------------------------
23  3  GRAMPIAN 23      SLP  SA/CR  FBG KC  OB         7 11  3200  2  4  3650   4200
23  3  GRAMPIAN 23      SLP  SA/CR  FBG KL  OB         7 11  3200  3  1  3650   4200
26     DISCOVERY 79     SLP  SA/CR  FBG KL  OB         8  4  5100  3  9  6600   7550
26     DISCOVERY 79     SLP  SA/CR  FBG KL  IB 14 VLVO 8  4  5100  3  9  6750   7750
26     DISCOVERY 79     SLP  SA/CR  FBG KL  IB         8  4  5100  3  9  6900   7900
28     GRAMPIAN 28      SLP  SA/CR  FBG KL  IB 30 UNIV 9  6  6900  4 10  9900  11200
28     GRAMPIAN 28      SLP  SA/CR  FBG KL  IB 7D VLVO 9  6  6900  4 10 10100  11400
28     GRAMPIAN 28 SHOAL SLP SA/CR  FBG KL  IB 30      9  6  6900  3  6 10100  11400
28     GRAMPIAN 28 SHOAL SLP SA/CR  FBG KL  IB 7D VLVO 9  6  6900  3  6 10100  11400
29  9  GRAMPIAN 30      SLP  SA/CR  FBG KL  IB 30 UNIV 9  6  8600  4  8 13000  14800
29  9  GRAMPIAN 30      SLP  SA/CR  FBG KC  IB 20D YAN 9  6  8600  4  8 13100  14900

29  9  GRAMPIAN 30      SLP  SA/CR  FBG KL  IB 30 UNIV 9  6  8600  3  3 13000  14800
29  9  GRAMPIAN 30      SLP  SA/CR  FBG KL  IB 20D YAN 9  6  8600  3  3 13100  14900
29  9  GRAMPIAN 30      CUT  SA/CR  FBG KL  IB 30 UNIV 9  6  8600  4  8 13000  14800
29  9  GRAMPIAN 30      CUT  SA/CR  FBG KC  IB 20D YAN 9  6  8600  4  8 13100  14900
29  9  GRAMPIAN 30      CUT  SA/CR  FBG KL  IB 30 UNIV 9  6  8600  3  3 13000  14800
29  9  GRAMPIAN 30      CUT  SA/CR  FBG KC  IB 20D YAN 9  6  8600  3  3 13100  14900
33  7  GRAMPIAN 34      KTH  SA/CR  FBG KL  IB 30 UNIV 10    12000  5   19000  21100
33  7  GRAMPIAN 34      KTH  SA/CR  FBG KL  IB D       10    12000  5   19100  21100
33  9  GRAMPIAN 2-34    SLP  SA/CR  FBG KC  IB 30 UNIV 10    12000      19100  21100
33  9  GRAMPIAN 2-34    SLP  SA/CR  FBG KL  IB D       10    12000      19100  21100
33  9  GRAMPIAN 2-34    SLP  SA/CR  FBG KC  IB 30 UNIV 10    12000  5   19000  21100
33  9  GRAMPIAN 2-34    SLP  SA/CR  FBG KL  IB D       10    12000  5   19100  21100

46     GRAMPIAN 46      YWL  SA/CR  FBG KC  IB 55D     12    25000  4 11 51600  56700
--------------------- 1976 BOATS --------------------------------------------------------
23  3  GRAMPIAN 23      SLP  SAIL   FBG KC  OB         8      3200  2  5  3500   4050
23  3  GRAMPIAN 23      SLP  SAIL   FBG KL  OB         8      3200  2  5  3500   4050
26     GRAMPIAN 26      SLP  SAIL   FBG KC  OB         8  4   5600  3     7000   8050
26     GRAMPIAN 26      SLP  SAIL   FBG KC  IB 14 VLVO 8  4   5600  3     7150   8250
26     GRAMPIAN 26      SLP  SAIL   FBG KC  IB 5D WEST 8  4   5600  3     7350   8400
26     GRAMPIAN 26      SLP  SAIL   FBG KL  OB         8  4   5600  4  3  7000   8050
26     GRAMPIAN 26      SLP  SAIL   FBG KL  IB 14 VLVO 8  4   5600  4  3  7150   8250
26     GRAMPIAN 26      SLP  SAIL   FBG KL  IB 5D WEST 8  4   5600  4  3  7350   8400
28     GRAMPIAN 28      SLP  SAIL   FBG KL  IB 30 UNIV 9  6   6900  4  6  9500  10800
28     GRAMPIAN 28      SLP  SAIL   FBG KL  IB 30 UNIV 9  6   6900  4  6  9650  10900
28     GRAMPIAN 28      SLP  SAIL   FBG KL  IB 10D VLVO 9 6   6900  4  6  9750  11100

29  9  GRAMPIAN 30      SLP  SAIL   FBG KC  OB         9  6   8600  3  3 12500  14200
29  9  GRAMPIAN 30      SLP  SAIL   FBG KC  IB 30 UNIV 9  6   8600  3  3 12600  14300
29  9  GRAMPIAN 30      SLP  SAIL   FBG KC  IB 15D VLVO 9 6   8600  3  3 12700  14400
29  9  GRAMPIAN 30      SLP  SAIL   FBG KL  OB         9  6   8600  4  8 12500  14200
29  9  GRAMPIAN 30      SLP  SAIL   FBG KL  IB 30 UNIV 9  6   8600  4  8 12600  14300
29  9  GRAMPIAN 30      SLP  SAIL   FBG KL  IB 15D VLVO 9 6   8600  4  8 12700  14400
33  7  GRAMPIAN 34      SLP  SAIL   FBG KL  IB 30 UNIV 10    12000  5   18300  20400
33  7  GRAMPIAN 34      SLP  SAIL   FBG KL  IB 15D VLVO 10   12000  5   18400  20400
33  7  GRAMPIAN 34      SLP  SAIL   FBG KL  IB 30 UNIV 10    12000  5   18300  20400
33  7  GRAMPIAN 34      SLP  SAIL   FBG KL  IB 15D VLVO 10   12000  5   18400  20400
33  7  GRAMPIAN 34      KTH  SAIL   FBG KC  IB 30 UNIV 10    12000      18300  20400
33  7  GRAMPIAN 34      KTH  SAIL   FBG KC  IB 15D VLVO 10   12000      18400  20400

33  7  GRAMPIAN 34      KTH  SAIL   FBG KL  IB 30 UNIV 10    12000      18300  20400
33  7  GRAMPIAN 34      KTH  SAIL   FBG KL  IB 15D VLVO 10   12000      18400  20400
33  9  GRAMPIAN 2-34    SLP  SAIL   FBG KC  IB 30 UNIV 10    12000      18300  20400
33  9  GRAMPIAN 2-34    SLP  SAIL   FBG KL  IB 30 UNIV 10    12000      18300  20400
33  9  GRAMPIAN 2-34    SLP  SAIL   FBG KL  IB 15D VLVO 10   12000      18400  20400
46     GRAMPIAN 46      SLP  SAIL   FBG KC  IB 85      12    25000  4 11 49300  54100
46     GRAMPIAN 46      YWL  SAIL   FBG KC  IB 85      12    25000  4 11 49300  54100
--------------------- 1975 BOATS --------------------------------------------------------
23  3  GRAMPIAN 23      SLP  SAIL   FBG KC            8      3200  5  4  3400   3950
23  3  GRAMPIAN 23      SLP  SAIL   FBG KL            8      3200  5  4  3400   3950
26     GRAMPIAN 26      SLP  SAIL   FBG KC            8      5800  6  6  6600   7550
26     GRAMPIAN 26      SLP  SAIL   FBG KL            8  4   5800  4  3  6600   7550
28     GRAMPIAN 28      SLP  SAIL   FBG KC  OB         9  6  6900  4  6  9250  10500
28     GRAMPIAN 28      SLP  SAIL   FBG KC  IB 15 VLVO 9  6  6900  4  6  9350  10600
28     GRAMPIAN 28      SLP  SAIL   FBG KC  IB 10D VLVO 9 6  6900  4  6  9450  10700
28     GRAMPIAN 28      SLP  SAIL   FBG KL  OB         9  6  6900  4  6  9250  10500
28     GRAMPIAN 28      SLP  SAIL   FBG KL  IB 15 VLVO 9  6  6900  4  6  9350  10600
28     GRAMPIAN 28      SLP  SAIL   FBG KL  IB 10D VLVO 9 6  6900  4  6  9450  10700
29  9  GRAMPIAN 30      SLP  SAIL   FBG KC  OB         9  6  8600  3  3 12100  13800
29  9  GRAMPIAN 30      SLP  SAIL   FBG KC  IB 30 UNIV 9  6  8600  3  3 12200  13900

29  9  GRAMPIAN 30      SLP  SAIL   FBG KC  OB 25D VLVO 9 6  8600  3  3 12300  14000
29  9  GRAMPIAN 30      SLP  SAIL   FBG KL  OB         9  6  8600  4  8 12100  13800
29  9  GRAMPIAN 30      SLP  SAIL   FBG KL  IB 30 UNIV 9  6  8600  4  8 12200  13900
29  9  GRAMPIAN 30      SLP  SAIL   FBG KL  IB 25D VLVO 9 6  8600  4  8 12300  14000
33  7  GRAMPIAN 34      SLP  SAIL   FBG KL  OB        10     12000  5   17100  19500
33  7  GRAMPAIN 34      SLP  SAIL   FBG KL  IB 25D VLVO 10   12000  5   17300  19700
33  9  GRAMPIAN 2-34    SLP  SAIL   FBG KC  IB        10     12000      17500  19800
33  9  GRAMPIAN 2-34    SLP  SAIL   FBG KL  IB 25D VLVO 10   12000      17300  19700
33  9  GRAMPIAN 2-34    SLP  SAIL   FBG KC  IB        10     12000  5   17500  19800
33  9  GRAMPIAN 2-34    SLP  SAIL   FBG KL  IB 25D VLVO 10   12000  5   17300  19700

33  9  GRAMPIAN 2-34    KTH  SAIL   FBG KC  IB        10     12000      17100  19500
33  9  GRAMPIAN 2-34    KTH  SAIL   FBG KL  IB 25D VLVO 10   12000      17300  19700
33  7  GRAMPIAN 34      SLP  SAIL   FBG KC  IB        10     12000      17500  19800
33  7  GRAMPIAN 34      SLP  SAIL   FBG KL  IB 25D VLVO 10   12000      18000  20000
33  7  GRAMPIAN 34      KTH  SAIL   FBG KC  IB        10     12000      17500  19800
33  7  GRAMPIAN 34      KTH  SAIL   FBG KL  IB 25D VLVO 10   12000  5  2 17100  19700
--------------------- 1974 BOATS --------------------------------------------------------
23  3  GRAMPIAN 23           SAIL   FBG KC  OB         8      3200          3300   3850
23  3  GRAMPIAN 23           SAIL   FBG KL  OB         8      3200          3300   3850
26     GRAMPIAN 26           SAIL   FBG KC  OB         8      2600  4  3    3150   3750
26     GRAMPIAN 26           SAIL   FBG KC  IB 30 UNIV 8  4         4  3    6400   7350
26     GRAMPIAN 26           SAIL   FBG KC  IB 10D VLVO 8 4               4  3    6450   7350
26     GRAMPIAN 26           SAIL   FBG KL  OB         8      2600          3250   3750
26     GRAMPIAN 26           SAIL   FBG KL  IB 30 UNIV 8  4               6400   7350
26     GRAMPIAN 26           SAIL   FBG KL  IB 10D VLVO 8 4               6650   7650
29  9  GRAMPIAN 30           SAIL   FBG KC  OB         9  6   8600  4  8 11800  13500
29  9  GRAMPIAN 30           SAIL   FBG KC  IB 30 UNIV 9  6   8600  4  8 11800  13500
29  9  GRAMPIAN 30           SAIL   FBG KC  IB 25D VLVO 9 6   8600  4  8 11900  13600

29  9  GRAMPIAN 30           SAIL   FBG KL  OB         9  6   8600  4  8 11800  13400
29  9  GRAMPIAN 30           SAIL   FBG KL  IB 30 UNIV 9  6   8600  4  8 11800  13400
29  9  GRAMPIAN 30           SAIL   FBG KL  IB 25D VLVO 9 6   8600  4  8 11900  13600
33  7  GRAMPIAN 34           SAIL   FBG KC  IB        10     12000      16900  19300
33  7  GRAMPIAN 34           SAIL   FBG KC  IB 25D VLVO 10   12000      16900  19300
33  7  GRAMPIAN 34           SAIL   FBG KL  IB        10     12000      16900  19200
33  7  GRAMPIAN 34           SAIL   FBG KL  IB 30 UNIV 10    12000      16900  19200
33  7  GRAMPIAN 34           SAIL   FBG KL  IB 25D VLVO 10   12000      16900  19200
33  7  GRAMPIAN 34      KTH  SAIL   FBG KL  IB 30 UNIV 10    12000      16900  19200
33  7  GRAMPIAN 34      KTH  SAIL   FBG     IB 25D VLVO 10   12000      16900  19300
--------------------- 1973 BOATS --------------------------------------------------------
23  3  GRAMPIAN 23           SAIL   FBG KC  OB         8      3200          3200   3750
23  3  GRAMPIAN 23           SAIL   FBG KL  OB         8      3200          3200   3750
26     GRAMPIAN 26           SAIL   FBG KC  OB         8  4   2600  4  3    3150   3650
26     GRAMPIAN 26           SAIL   FBG KC  IB 30 UNIV 8  4         4  3    6250   7150
```

GRAMPIAN MARINE LTD INC — CONTINUED

LOA FT IN	NAME AND/ OR MODEL	TOP/ RIG	BOAT TYPE	HULL MTL TP TP	ENGINE # HP MFG	BEAM FT IN	WGT LBS	DRAFT FT IN	RETAIL LOW	RETAIL HIGH
1973 BOATS										
26	GRAMPIAN 26	SAIL	FBG KC IB		10D VLVO	8 4		4 3	6500	7450
26	GRAMPIAN 26	SAIL	FBG KL OB			8 4	2600	4 3	3150	3650
26	GRAMPIAN 26	SAIL	FBG KL IB		30 UNIV	8 4		4 3	6250	7150
26	GRAMPIAN 26	SAIL	FBG KL IB		10D VLVO	8 4		4 3	6450	7450
29 9	GRAMPIAN 30	SAIL	FBG KC OB			9 6	8600	4 8	11500	13100
29 9	GRAMPIAN 30	SAIL	FBG KC IB		30 UNIV	9 6	8600	4 8	11600	13100
29 9	GRAMPIAN 30	SAIL	FBG KC IB		25D VLVO	9 6	8600	4 8	11700	13200
29 9	GRAMPIAN 30	SAIL	FBG KL OB			9 6	8600	4 8	11500	13100
29 9	GRAMPIAN 30	SAIL	FBG KL IB		30 UNIV	9 6	8600	4 8	11600	13100
29 9	GRAMPIAN 30	SAIL	FBG KL IB		25D VLVO	9 6	8600	4 8	11700	13200
33 7	GRAMPIAN 34	SAIL	FBG KC IB		30 UNIV	10	12000	5	16500	18700
33 7	GRAMPIAN 34	SAIL	FBG KC IB		25D VLVO	10	12000	5	16500	18800
33 7	GRAMPIAN 34	SAIL	FBG KL IB		30 UNIV	10	12000	5	16500	18700
33 7	GRAMPIAN 34	SAIL	FBG KL IB		25D VLVO	10	12000	5	16500	18800
33 7	GRAMPIAN 34	KTH SAIL	FBG IB		30 UNIV	10	12000	5	16500	18700
33 7	GRAMPIAN 34	KTH SAIL	FBG IB		25D VLVO	10	12000	5	16500	18800
1972 BOATS										
23 4	GRAMPIAN 23	SAIL	FBG OB			8	3100	2 5	3100	3600
26	GRAMPIAN 26	SAIL	FBG IB			8 4	5600	3	6300	7250
26	GRAMPIAN 26	SAIL	FBG IB		PALM	8 4		3	6100	7000
29 11	GRAMPIAN 30	SAIL	FBG IB		30 UNIV	9 6	8600	3 3	11400	12900
34 3	GRAMPIAN 34	SAIL	FBG IB		35D VLVO	12	12000	4 6	16300	18500
1971 BOATS										
22 4	GRAMPIAN 22	SAIL	FBG OB			7	1892	3 9	2050	2450
26	GRAMPIAN 26	SAIL	FBG OB			8 4	5600	4 3	6200	7100
29 9	GRAMPIAN 30	SAIL	FBG OB			9 6	8600	3 3	11100	12600
46	US 46	YWL	FBG CB IB		58	12	25000	4 11	42600	47300
1970 BOATS										
22 3	GRAMPIAN 22	SLP SA/OD	FBG KL OB			7 6	1800	3 9	1950	2350
26 1	GRAMPIAN 26	SLP SAIL	FBG KC OB			8 4	5600	3 9	6100	7050
26 3	GRAMPIAN 29	SLP SAIL	FBG KC IB		20	8 4	8600	3 3	10900	12300
29 10	GRAMPIAN 30	SLP SA/RC	FBG CB IB		UNIV	9 6	8600	3 3	11000	12500
30 11	CLASSIC 31	SLP SAIL	FBG KL IB		30 UNIV	8 5	10000	4 9	13000	14800
30 11	CLASSIC 31	CUT SAIL	FBG KL IB		30 UNIV	8 5	10000	4 9	13000	14800
30 11	CLASSIC 31	KTH SAIL	FBG KL IB		30 UNIV	8 5	10000	4 9	13000	14800
1969 BOATS										
22	GRAMPIAN 22	SLP SAIL	FBG KL OB			7	1850	3 9	1950	2300
26	GRAMPIAN 26	SLP SAIL	FBG KC			8 4		3 9	5600	6450
26	GRAMPIAN 26	SLP SAIL	FBG KL OB			8 4	5500	3 9	5900	6800
30 11	CLASSIC 31	SLP SAIL	FBG KL IB		25 UNIV	8 5	10000	4 9	12800	14600
30 11	CLASSIC 31	KTH SAIL	FBG KL IB		25 UNIV	8 5	10000	4 9	12800	14600
30 11	CLASSIC 31 CUTTER	CUT SAIL	FBG KL IB		25 UNIV	8 5	10000	4 9	12800	14600
1968 BOATS										
22 4	CLASSIC 22	SLP SAIL	FBG KL OB			7	1892	3 9	2000	2350
30 11	CLASSIC 31	SLP SAIL	FBG KL OB			8 5	9937	4 6	12600	14300
30 11	CLASSIC 31	KTH SAIL	FBG KL OB			8 5	9937	4 6	12600	14300
30 11	CLASSIC 31 CUT MSTHD	CUT SAIL	FBG KL OB			8 5	9937	4 6	12500	14200
30 11	CLASSIC CUT DBL HD	CUT SAIL	FBG KL OB			8 5	9937	4 6	12700	14400
37 4	CLASSIC 37	SLP SAIL	FBG KL OB			10 2	16000	5 10	21100	23400
37 4	CLASSIC 37	YWL SAIL	FBG KL OB			10 2	16000	5 10	21100	23400
1967 BOATS										
22 4	CLASSIC 22	SLP SAIL	FBG KL OB			7	1892	3 9	1950	2350
27	EAGLE	SLP SA/CR	FBG KL OB			8 5		3 10	6200	7100
30 11	CLASSIC 31	SLP SAIL	FBG KL OB			8 5	9937	4 6	12500	14200
30 11	CLASSIC 31	KTH SAIL	FBG KL OB			8 5	9937	4 6	12500	14200
30 11	CLASSIC 31 DBL HEAD	CUT SAIL	FBG KL OB			8 5	9937	4 6	12500	14200
30 11	CLASSIC 31 MASTHEAD	CUT SAIL	FBG KL OB			8 5	9937	4 6	12500	14200
32	TRIANGLE	KTH SA/CR	FBG CB OB			10			9700	11000
32	TRIANGLE	KTH SA/CR	FBG KL OB			10		3 5	9700	11000
37 4	CLASSIC 37	SLP SAIL	FBG KL OB			10 2	16000	5 10	20900	23300
37 4	CLASSIC 37	YWL SAIL	FBG KL OB			10 2	16000	5 10	20900	23300
41 11	U-S-41	YWL SA/CR	FBG CB OB			12			34100	37900
41 11	U-S-41	YWL SA/CR	FBG KL OB			12		4 11	34100	37900
1966 BOATS										
22 4	CLASSIC 22	SLP SAIL	FBG KL OB			7		3 9	2400	2800
27	EAGLE	SLP SA/CR	FBG KL IB		25	8 5		3 9	6550	7550
30 11	CLASSIC 31	SLP SAIL	FBG KL IB		30	8 5		4 6	11800	13400
30 11	CLASSIC 31	KTH SAIL	FBG IB		30	8 5		4 6	11800	13400
30 11	CLASSIC 31 CUT MSTHD	CUT SAIL	FBG IB		30	8 5		4 6	11700	13300
30 11	CLASSIC CUT DBL HD	CUT SAIL	FBG KL IB		30	8 5		4 6	12000	13600
32	TRIANGLE	SLP SA/CR	FBG KC IB		60	10		3 5	8150	9400
37 4	CLASSIC 37	SLP SAIL	FBG KL IB		30	10 2		5 10	12700	14400
37 4	CLASSIC 37	YWL SAIL	FBG KL IB		30	10 2		5 10	12700	14400
41 10	U-S-41	YWL SA/CR	FBG KC IB		60	12		5	30300	33600
1965 BOATS										
27	EAGLE	SAIL	FBG IB						6550	7500
31	CLASSIC 31	SLP SAIL	FBG IB						11800	13400
31	CLASSIC 31	CUT SAIL	FBG IB						11800	13400
31	CLASSIC 31	KTH SAIL	FBG IB						11800	13400
32	TRIANGLE 32	SAIL	FBG IB						8150	9350
37	WALTON 37	SAIL	FBG IB						12400	14100
41	U-S-YACHTS 41	SAIL	FBG IB						21200	23600
1963 BOATS										
20	TRIANGLE 20	SAIL	FBG OB						1850	2200
27	EAGLE	SLP SAIL	FBG OB						6150	7100
32	TRIANGLE 32	YWL SAIL	FBG OB						9200	10400
1961 BOATS										
20 6	TRIANGLE	SLP SAIL	FBG CB OB			6		1 6	1900	2250
20 6	TRIANGLE 20	SLP SA/OD	FBG CB OB			6			1900	2250

GRAND BAHAMA YACHTS LTD

NEWPORT BEACH CA 92663   COAST GUARD MFG ID- GBU See inside cover to adjust price for area

LOA FT IN	NAME AND/ OR MODEL	TOP/ RIG	BOAT TYPE	HULL MTL TP TP	ENGINE # HP MFG	BEAM FT IN	WGT LBS	DRAFT FT IN	RETAIL LOW	RETAIL HIGH
1979 BOATS										
38	GRAND-BAHAMA			FBG IB	T185	13			36100	40100
38	GRAND-BAHAMA			FBG IB	T270	13			36400	40500
42	COMMODORE BY TAYANA	TRWL		FBG DS IB	T120	14 7			59500	65400
42	COMMODORE BY TAYANA	TRWL		FBG DS IB	T160	14 7			60200	66200

GRAND BANKS YACHTS LTD

NEWPORT RI 02840   COAST GUARD MFG ID- GND See inside cover to adjust price for area
ALSO AMERICAN MARINE PTE

For more recent years, see the BUC Used Boat Price Guide, Volume 1 or Volume 2

LOA FT IN	NAME AND/ OR MODEL	TOP/ RIG	BOAT TYPE	HULL MTL TP TP	ENGINE # HP MFG	BEAM FT IN	WGT LBS	DRAFT FT IN	RETAIL LOW	RETAIL HIGH
1983 BOATS										
31 11	GRAND BANKS 32	FB	TRWL	FBG DS IB	120D LEHM	11 6	17000	3 8	109000	120000
36 4	GRAND BANKS 36	FB	TRWL	FBG DS IB	120D LEHM	12	23300	3 11	108500	119500
36 4	GRAND BANKS 36	FB	TRWL	FBG DS IB	128D GM	12	23300	3 11	109500	120500
36 4	GRAND BANKS 36	FB	TRWL	FBG DS IB	T120D LEHM	12	23300	3 11	113000	124000
41 10	GRAND BANKS 42	FB	TRWL	FBG DS IB	D	13 7	34000	4	**	**
41 10	GRAND BANKS 42	FB	TRWL	FBG DS IB	120D LEHM	13 7	34000	4 2	163500	179500
41 10	GRAND BANKS 42	FB	TRWL	FBG DS IB	T120D LEHM	13 7	34000	4 2	169500	186000
41 10	GRAND BANKS 42 E	FB	TRWL	FBG DS IB	120D LEHM	13 7	34000	4 2	181500	199500
	IB 210D CAT 169500 186500, IB T120D LEHM 179500 197000, IB T128D GM 177500 195000									
41 10	GRAND BANKS 42 MY	FB	TRMY	FBG DS IB	D	13 7	34000	4 2	**	**
41 10	GRAND BANKS 42 SC	FB	TRWL	FBG DS IB	120D LEHM	13 7	34000	4 2	150000	165000
	IB T120D LEHM 164500 181000, IB T128D GM 167500 184000, IB T210D CAT 178000 195500									
50 6	GRAND BANKS 49	FB	TRWL	FBG DS IB	210D CAT	15 5	60000	5 2	207000	227500
	IB 310D GM 212500 233500, IB T120D LEHM 210500 231500, IB T128D GM 211000 231500									
1982 BOATS										
31 11	GRAND BANKS 32	FB	TRWL	FBG DS IB	120D LEHM	11 6	17000	3 8	104000	114000
36 4	GRAND BANKS 36	FB	TRWL	FBG DS IB	120D LEHM	12	23000	3 11	102500	112500
36 4	GRAND BANKS 36	FB	TRWL	FBG DS IB	128D GM	12	23300	3 11	103500	113500
36 4	GRAND BANKS 36	FB	TRWL	FBG DS IB	T120D LEHM	12	23300	3 11	106500	117000
41 10	GRAND BANKS 42	FB	TRWL	FBG DS IB	120D LEHM	13 7	34000	4 2	154000	169500
41 10	GRAND BANKS 42	FB	TRWL	FBG DS IB	120D LEHM	13 7	34000	4 2	160000	176000
41 10	GRAND BANKS 42 E	FB	TRWL	FBG DS IB	120D LEHM	13 7	34000	4 2	171500	188500
	IB 210D CAT 160500 176000, IB T120D LEHM 169500 186000, IB T128D GM 167500 184000									
41 10	GRAND BANKS 42 MY	FB	TRMY	FBG DS IB	D	13 7	34000	4 2	**	**
41 10	GRAND BANKS 42 SC	FB	TRWL	FBG DS IB	120D LEHM	13 7	34000	4 2	142000	156000
	IB T120D LEHM 155500 171000, IB T128D GM 158000 174000, IB T210D CAT 168000 184500									
50 6	GRAND BANKS 49	FB	TRWL	FBG DS IB	210D CAT	15 5	60000	5 2	196000	215500
	IB 310D GM 201000 221000, IB T120D LEHM 199500 219000, IB T128D GM 199500 219000									
51	GRAND BANKS 49	FB	TRWL	FBG DS IB	T120D LEHM	15 5	60000	5 1	199500	219500
1981 BOATS										
31 11	GRAND BANKS 32	FB	TRWL	FBG DS IB	120D LEHM	11 6	17000	3 9	98400	108000
36 4	GRAND BANKS 36	FB	TRWL	FBG DS IB	120D LEHM	12	23000	3 11	100000	110000
36 4	GRAND BANKS 36	FB	TRWL	FBG DS IB	T120D LEHM	12	23300	3 11	102500	112500
41 10	GRAND BANKS 42 E	FB	TRWL	FBG DS IB	120D LEHM	13 7	34000	4 2	151500	166500
	IB 210D CAT 150500 165500, IB T120D LEHM 157500 172500, IB T128D GM 157000 173000									
41 10	GRAND BANKS 42 SC	FB	TRWL	FBG DS IB	120D LEHM	13 7	34000	4 2	142500	157000

LOA FT	LOA IN	NAME AND/ OR MODEL	TOP/ RIG	BOAT TYPE	-HULL- MTL	-HULL- TP	TP	ENGINE # HP	ENGINE MFG	BEAM FT	BEAM IN	WGT LBS	DRAFT FT	DRAFT IN	RETAIL LOW	RETAIL HIGH
		1981 BOATS														
41	10	GRAND BANKS 42 SC	FB	TRWL	FBG	DS	IB	T120D	LEHM	13	7	34000	4	2	148000	163000
41	10	GRAND BANKS 42 SC	FB	TRWL	FBG	DS	IB	T128D	GM	13	7	34000	4	2	148500	163500
41	10	GRAND BANKS 42 SC	FB	TRWL	FBG	DS	IB	T210D	CAT	13	7	34000	4	2	157500	173500
50	6	GRAND BANKS 49	FB	TRWL	FBG	DS	IB	210D	CAT	15	5	60000	5	2	184000	202500
		IB 310D GM 189000 207500, IB T120D LEHM 187500 206000, IB T128D GM													187500	206000
		1980 BOATS														
31	11	GRAND BANKS 32	FB	TRWL	FBG	DS	IB	120D	LEHM	11	6	17000	3	9	93000	102000
36	4	GRAND BANKS 36	FB	TRWL	FBG	DS	IB	120D	LEHM	12	2	23000	3	11	90200	99200
36	4	GRAND BANKS 36	FB	TRWL	FBG	DS	IB	T120D		12	2	23000	3	11	93100	102500
41	10	GRAND BANKS 42	FB	TRWL	FBG	DS	IB	T120D	LEHM	13	7	34000	4	2	141000	154500
41	10	GRAND BANKS 42	FB	TRWL	FBG	DS	IB	T210D	CAT	13	7	34000	4	2	146000	160500
41	10	GRAND BANKS 42 E	FB	TRWL	FBG	DS	IB	T120D	LEHM	13	7	34000	4	2	143500	157500
41	10	GRAND BANKS 42 E	FB	TRWL	FBG	DS	IB	T210D	CAT	13	7	34000	4	2	149000	164000
41	10	GRAND BANKS 42 SC	FB	TRWL	FBG	DS	IB	T120D	LEHM	13	7	34000	4	2	142500	156500
41	10	GRAND BANKS 42 SC	FB	TRWL	FBG	DS	IB	T210D	CAT	13	7	34000	4	2	148000	162500
50	6	GRAND BANKS 49	FB	TRWL	FBG	DS	IB	T120D	LEHM	15	5	55000	5		160000	185000
50	6	GRAND BANKS 49	FB	TRWL	FBG	DS	IB	T210D	CAT	15	5	55000	5		176500	194000
		1979 BOATS														
31	11	GRAND BANKS 32	FB	TRWL	FBG	DS	IB	120D	LEHM	11	6	17000	3	9	87600	96300
36	4	GRAND BANKS 36	FB	TRWL	FBG	DS	IB	120D	LEHM	12	2	23300	3	11	85200	93600
36	4	GRAND BANKS 36	FB	TRWL	FBG	DS	IB	T120D	LEHM	12	2	23300	3	11	87800	96500
41	10	GRAND BANKS 42	FB	TRWL	FBG	DS	IB	120D	LEHM	13	7	34000	4	2	127000	139500
		IB 210D CAT 129500 142000, IB T120D LEHM 131500 144500, IB T210D CAT													136500	150000
49		GRAND BANKS 49	FB	TRWL	FBG	DS	IB	T120D		15	6	55000			158500	174000
50	6	GRAND BANKS 50	FB	TRWL	FBG	DS	IB	T210D		15	5				151000	165500
50	6	GRAND BANKS 50	FB	TRWL	FBG	DS	IB	T300D		15	5				158000	173500
		1978 BOATS														
31	11	GRAND BANKS 32	FB	TRWL	FBG	DS	IB	120D	LEHM	11	6	17000	3	9	82300	90500
36	4	GRAND BANKS 36	FB	TRWL	FBG	DS	IB	120D	LEHM	12	2	23300	3	11	79500	87400
36	4	GRAND BANKS 36	FB	TRWL	FBG	DS	IB	T120D	LEHM	12	2	23300	3	11	81900	90100
41	10	GRAND BANKS 42	FB	TRWL	FBG	DS	IB	120D	LEHM	13	7	34000	4	2	118500	130000
41	10	GRAND BANKS 42	FB	TRWL	FBG	DS	IB	T120D	LEHM	13	7	34000	4	2	123000	135000
		1977 BOATS														
31	11	GRAND BANKS 32	FB	TRWL	FBG	DS	IB	120D	LEHM	11	6	17000	3	9	77300	84900
36	4	GRAND BANKS 36	FB	TRWL	FBG	DS	IB	120D	LEHM	12	2	23300	3	11	74200	81500
36	4	GRAND BANKS 36	FB	TRWL	FBG	DS	IB	T120D	LEHM	12	2	23300	3	11	76400	84000
41	10	GRAND BANKS 42	FB	TRWL	FBG	DS	IB	120D	LEHM	13	7	34000	4	2	110500	121500
41	10	GRAND BANKS 42	FB	TRWL	FBG	DS	IB	T120D	LEHM	13	7	34000	4	2	114500	126000
		1976 BOATS														
31	11	GRAND BANKS 32	FB	TRWL	FBG	DS	IB	128D		11	6	17000	3	9	72500	79700
36	4	GRAND BANKS 36	FB	TRWL	FBG	DS	IB	T134D		12	2	23300	3	11	71700	78800
41	10	GRAND BANKS 42	FB	TRWL	FBG	DS	IB	T134D		13	7	34000	4	2	107500	118000
48		GRAND BANKS 48	FB	TRWL	WD	DS	IB	T134D		15	5	49550	4	6	160000	175500
50		GRAND BANKS 50	FB	TRWL	WD	DS	IB	T134D		16		59300	5		133500	147000
		1975 BOATS														
31	11	GRAND BANKS 32	FB	TRWL	FBG	DS	IB	120D	FORD	11	6	17000	3	9	68300	75100
32	9	LAGUNA 10 METRE	FB	EXP	FBG	DS	IB	T275D	AMML	11	9	17000	2	3	71900	79000
36	4	GRAND BANKS 36	FB	TRWL	FBG	DS	IB	130D	AMML	12	2	23300	3	11	64500	70900
36	4	GRAND BANKS 36	FB	TRWL	FBG	DS	IB	T130D	AMML	12	2	23300	3	11	66900	73500
37	9	LAGUNA 11 5 METRE	FB	EXP	FBG	DS	IB	T275D	AMML	14	5	23000	3		70200	77200
41	10	GRAND BANKS 42	FB	TRWL	FBG	DS	IB	130D	AMML	13	7	34000	4	2	96300	106000
41	10	GRAND BANKS 42	FB	TRWL	FBG	DS	IB	T130D	AMML	13	7	34000	4	2	100000	110000
44	9	ALASKAN 45	HT	MY	P/M	DS	IB	130D	AMML	14		34000	4	3	108500	119500
44	9	ALASKAN 45	HT	MY	P/M	DS	IB	T130D	AMML	14		34000	4	3	112000	123500
48	6	GRAND BANKS 48	FB	TRWL	P/M	DS	IB	130D	AMML	15	5	49550	4	6	142000	156000
48	6	GRAND BANKS 48	FB	TRWL	P/M	DS	IB	T130D	AMML	15	5	49550	4	6	146500	161000
50	11	GRAND BANKS 50	FB	TRWL	P/M	DS	IB	T130D	AMML	16		59300	5		124000	136000
53		ALASKAN 53	HT	MY	P/M	DS	IB	T130D	AMML	15	2	58500	5	2	149500	164000
63		ALASKAN 63	HT	MY	WD	DS	IB	T480D		21	3	84T			**	**
		1974 BOATS														
31	11	GRAND BANKS 32	FB	TRWL	FBG	DS	IB	128D	FORD	11	6	17000	3	9	64700	71100
32	9	LAGUNA 10 METRE	FB	EXP	FBG		IB	T280D	AMML	11	9	17000	2	3	68200	75000
36	4	GRAND BANKS 36	FB	TRWL	FBG	DS	IB	T128D	FORD	12	2	23300	3	11	62500	68700
37	9	LAGUNA 11 5 METRE	FB	EXP	FBG		IB	T280D	AMML	14	5	23000	3		65900	72400
41	10	GRAND BANKS 42	FB	TRWL	FBG	DS	IB	T128D	FORD	13	7	34000	4	2	93600	103000
48	6	GRAND BANKS 48	FB	TRWL	MHG		IB	T128D	FORD	15	5	49500	4	6	131500	144500
48	7	ALASKAN 49	HT	MY	WD		IB	T128D	FORD	15	1	57000	5	2	115500	127000
50	11	GRAND BANKS 50	FB	TRWL	MHG	DS	IB	T185D	AMML	16		59300	5		120000	132000
54	9	ALASKAN 55	HT	MY	WD		IB	T185D	AMML	17	1	91000	5	6	217500	239000
62		GRAND BANKS 62 DC	FB	TRWL	MHG	DS	IB	T250D		20	10	69T	6		471500	518000
76		ALASKAN 76 DC	HT	MY	MHG	DS	IB	T210D		20	6	97T	6	8	**	**
		1973 BOATS														
31	11	GRAND BANKS 32	FB	TRWL	WD	DS	IB	128D	FORD	11	6	17000	3	9	61400	67500
32	9	LAGUNA 10 METRE	FB	EXP	FBG		IB	T275D	AMML	11	9	17000	2	3	64500	70900
36	4	GRAND BANKS 36	FB	TRWL	FBG	DS	IB	128D	FORD	12	2	23300	3	11	56700	62300
37	9	LAGUNA 11 5 METRE	FB	EXP	FBG		IB	T275D	AMML	14	5	23000	3		61700	67700
41	10	GRAND BANKS 42	FB	TRWL	WD		IB	T128D	FORD	13	7	34000	4	2	82700	90900
43	9	LAGUNA 13 4 METRE	FB	EXP	FBG	DS	IB	T300D		16	2	21083	3	4	74000	81400
48	6	GRAND BANKS 48	FB	TRWL	WD		IB	T128D	FORD	15	5	49550	4	6	123500	135500
48	7	ALASKAN 49	HT	MY	WD		IB	T128D	FORD	15	1	57000	5	2	108500	119000
50	11	GRAND BANKS 50	FB	TRWL	WD		IB	T210D	AMML	16		59300	5		113000	124500
54	9	ALASKAN 55	HT	MY	WD		IB	T210D	AMML	17	1	91000	5	6	206000	226000
62		GRAND BANKS 62 DC	FB	TRWL	WD	DS	IB	T230D		20	10	69T	6		440000	483000
76		ALASKAN 76 DC	HT	MY	WD	DS	IB	T210D		20	6	97T	6	8	**	**
		1972 BOATS														
31	11	GRAND BANKS 32	FB	TRWL	WD	DS	IB	120D	FORD	11	6	17000	3	9	58400	64200
32	9	LAGUNA 10 METRE	FB	EXP	WD		IB	T275D	AMML	11	9	17000	2	3	61400	67500
36	4	GRAND BANKS 36	FB	TRWL	WD	DS	IB	120D	FORD	12	2	23300	3	11	53500	58800
36	4	GRAND BANKS 36	FB	TRWL	WD	DS	IB	T120D	FORD	12	2	23300	3	11	55100	60500
37	9	LAGUNA 11 5 METRE	FB	EXP	WD		IB	T275D	AMML	14	5	23000	3	2	58100	63800
41	10	GRAND BANKS 42	FB	TRWL	WD	DS	IB	D	CAT	13	7	34000	4	2	**	**
41	10	GRAND BANKS 42	FB	TRWL	WD	DS	IB	T120D	FORD	13	7	34000	4	2	82600	90700
48	7	ALASKAN 49	HT	MY	WD		IB	T120D	FORD	15	1	57000	5	2	101500	112000
48	7	ALASKAN 49	HT	MY	WD		IB	T230D	CAT	15	1	57000	5	2	106000	116500
50	11	GRAND BANKS 50	FB	TRWL	WD	DS	IB	T128D	FORD	16		59300	5		102000	112500
50	11	GRAND BANKS 50	FB	TRWL	WD	DS	IB	T210D	AMML	16		59300	5		108000	119000
54	9	ALASKAN 55	HT	MY	WD		IB	T230D	CAT	17	1	91000	5	6	196500	216000
62		ALASKAN 62 DC	FB	MY	WD	DS	IB	T250D		18	6	68T	5	6	409000	449500
62		GRAND BANKS 62 DC	FB	TRWL	WD	DS	IB	T230D	CAT	20	10	69T	6		414000	454500
76		ALASKAN 76 DC	FB	MY	WD	DS	IB	T460D		20	6	97T	6	8	**	**
		1971 BOATS														
31	11	GRAND BANKS 32	FB	TRWL	WD	DS	IB	120D	FORD	11	6	17000	3	9	55900	61400
32	9	LAGUNA 10 METRE	FB	EXP	WD		IB	T275D	AMML	11	9	17000	2	3	58800	64600
36	4	GRAND BANKS 36	FB	TRWL	WD	DS	IB	120D	FORD	12	2	23300	3	11	50600	55600
36	4	GRAND BANKS 36	FB	TRWL	WD	DS	IB	T120D	FORD	12	2	23300	3	11	52100	57300
41	10	GRAND BANKS 42	FB	TRWL	WD		IB	230D	CAT	13	7	34000	4	2	76600	84100
41	10	GRAND BANKS 42	FB	TRWL	WD		IB	T120D	FORD	13	7	34000	4	2	77600	85300
48	7	ALASKAN 49	HT	MY	WD		IB	T120D	FORD	15	1	57000	5	2	96100	105500
48	7	ALASKAN 49	HT	MY	WD		IB	T230D	CAT	15	1	57000	5	2	100500	110000
50	11	GRAND BANKS 50	FB	TRWL	WD		IB	T120D	FORD	16		59300	5		95500	105000
50	11	GRAND BANKS 50	FB	TRWL	WD		IB	T230D	CAT	16		59300	5		102500	112500
54	9	ALASKAN 55	HT	MY	WD		IB	T230D	CAT	17	1	91000	5	6	185500	203500
		1970 BOATS														
31	11	GRAND BANKS 32	FB	TRWL	WD	DS	IB	120D	FORD	11	6	17000	3	9	53700	59000
36	4	GRAND BANKS 36	FB	TRWL	WD	DS	IB	T120D	FORD	12	2	23300	3	11	49500	54400
41	10	GRAND BANKS 42	FB	TRWL	WD	RB	IB	T120D	FORD	13	7	34000	4	2	73900	81200
45	7	ALASKAN 46	HT	MY	MHG	RB	IB	T120D	FORD	14	4	40000	4	9	75900	83400
49	6	ADMIRALTY 50	SLP	MS	WD	KL	IB	120D	FORD	14	4	35506	4	6	91700	100500
50	11	GRAND BANKS 50	FB	TRWL	WD		IB	T370D	DAY	16		59300	5		106500	117000
55		ALASKAN 55	HT	MY	WD	RB	IB	T370D	DAY	17		91000	5		189500	208500
56	8	GRAND BANKS 57	FB	TRWL	WD	RB	IB	T370D	DAY	18		84000	5	6	185500	204000
		1969 BOATS														
31	11	GRAND BANKS 32	FB	TRWL	MHG	DS	IB	120D	FORD	11	6	17000	3	9	51900	57100
36	4	GRAND BANKS 36	FB	TRWL	MHG	DS	IB	120D	FORD	12	2	23300	3	11	46200	50800
36	4	GRAND BANKS 36	FB	TRWL	MHG	DS	IB	225D	GM	12	2	23300	3	11	46400	51000
36	4	GRAND BANKS 36	FB	TRWL	MHG	DS	IB	T120D	FORD	12	2	23300	3	11	47600	52300
41	10	GRAND BANKS 42	FB	TRWL	MHG	SV	IB	120D	FORD	13	7	34000	4	2	67900	74600
41	10	GRAND BANKS 42	FB	TRWL	MHG	SV	IB	600D		13	7	34000	4	2	76400	83900
45	7	ALASKAN 46	HT	MY	MHG	SV	IB	120D	FORD	14	4	40000	4	9	77800	85500
45	7	ALASKAN 46	HT	MY	MHG	SV	IB	T120D	FORD	14	4	40000	4	9	72400	79600
50	11	GRAND BANKS 50	FB	TRWL	MHG	SV	IB	740D		16		59300	5		102000	112000
50	11	GRAND BANKS 50	FB	TRWL	MHG	SV	IB	T120D	FORD	16		59300	5		86500	95000
56	8	GRAND BANKS 57	FB	TRWL	MHG	SV	IB	240D		18		84000	5	6	156000	171500
56	8	GRAND BANKS 57	FB	TRWL	MHG	SV	IB	740D		18		84000	5	6	183000	201500
		1968 BOATS														
31	11	GRAND BANKS 32	FB	TRWL	MHG	DS	IB	120D	FORD	11	6	17000	3	9	50400	55400
36	4	GRAND BANKS 36	FB	TRWL	MHG	DS	IB	120D	FORD	12	2	23300	3	11	43800	48700
		IB 150D DAY 43500 48400, IB 225D DAY 44000 48900, IB T120D FORD													45600	50100
41	10	GRAND BANKS 42	FB	TRWL	MHG	DS	IB	120D	FORD	13	7	34000	4	2	65600	72100
		IB 225D DAY 66500 73100, IB T120D FORD 68100 74800, IB T225D DAY													70000	76900
		IB T300D 72200 79300														
45	7	ALASKAN 46	HT	MY	MHG		IB	T120D	FORD	14	4	40000	4	9	69400	76300
50	11	GRAND BANKS 50	FB	TRWL	MHG	DS	IB	T240D		16		59300	5		91400	100500
56	8	GRAND BANKS 57	FB	TRWL	MHG	DS	IB	T240D		18		85000	5	6	161500	177500
		1967 BOATS														
31	11	GRAND BANKS 32	FB	TRWL	MHG	DS	IB	120D	FORD	11	6	17000	3	9	49200	54000
36	4	GRAND BANKS 36	FB	TRWL	MHG	DS	IB	120D	FORD	12	2	23300	3	11	42200	46900
		IB 150D DAY 42000 46700, IB 225D DAY 42400 47100, IB T120D FORD													43500	48300
41	10	GRAND BANKS 42	FB	TRWL	MHG	DS	IB	120D	FORD	13	7	34000	4	2	63200	69400
		IB 150D DAY 63400 69700, IB 300D CUM 65100 71500, IB T120D FORD													65600	72100

CONTINUED ON NEXT PAGE

LOA FT	LOA IN	NAME AND/ OR MODEL	TOP/ RIG	BOAT TYPE	-HULL- MTL	-HULL- TP	ENGINE TP	ENGINE # HP	ENGINE MFG	BEAM FT	BEAM IN	WGT LBS	DRAFT FT	DRAFT IN	RETAIL LOW	RETAIL HIGH
		1967 BOATS														
41	10	GRAND BANKS 42	FB	TRWL	MHG	DS	IB	T150D	DAY	13	7	34000	4	2	66000	72500
41	10	GRAND BANKS 42	FB	TRWL	MHG	DS	IB	T225D	DAY	13	7	34000	4	2	67400	74100
41	10	GRAND BANKS 42	FB	TRWL	MHG	DS	IB	T300D	CUM	13	7	34000	4	2	69400	76200
50	11	GRAND BANKS 50	FB	TRWL	MHG	DS	IB	T240D		16		59300	5		88000	96700
56	8	GRAND BANKS 57	FB	TRWL	MHG	DS	IB	T240D		18		85000	5	6	155000	170000
		1966 BOATS														
31	11	GRAND BANKS 32	FB	TRWL	MHG	DS	IB	86D		11	6	17000	3	8	44600	49500
36	4	GRAND BANKS 36		TRWL	MHG	DS	IB	86D		12	2	23300	3	11	39600	44000
41	10	GRAND BANKS 42	FB	TRWL	MHG	DS	IB	86D		13	7	34000	4	2	60800	66800
		1965 BOATS														
36	4	GRAND BANKS 36		TRWL	WD	DS	IB	T 86		12	2	23300	3	11	34400	38300

GRAND PRIX BOAT BLDG INC

COAST GUARD MFG ID- GPE

Call 1-800-327-6929 for BUC Personalized Evaluation Service
Or, for 1976 to 1979 boats, sign onto www.BUCValuPro.com

GRANDY BOAT COMPANY

SEATTLE WA See inside cover to adjust price for area

LOA FT	LOA IN	NAME AND/ OR MODEL	TOP/ RIG	BOAT TYPE	-HULL- MTL	-HULL- TP	ENGINE TP	ENGINE # HP	ENGINE MFG	BEAM FT	BEAM IN	WGT LBS	DRAFT FT	DRAFT IN	RETAIL LOW	RETAIL HIGH
		1967 BOATS														
50		RAISED DECK		SF	P/C		IB	T370D		16	6				80100	88000
		1963 BOATS														
28		GRANDY 28			WD		IB	180							6200	7150
32		GRANDY 32		DC	WD		IB								**	**
32		GRANDY 32		EXP	WD		IB								**	**
32		GRANDY 32		SDN	WD		IB								**	**
32		GRANDY 32		SF	WD		IB								**	**
32		GRANDY 32 MARLINEER			WD		IB								**	**
36		GRANDY 36			WD		IB	T260							22900	25400
40		GRANDY 40			WD		IB	T275							30900	34300
44		MARLINEER			WD		IB								**	**
		1962 BOATS														
28		GRANDY 28			WD		IB	180							6050	6950
32		GRANDY 32			WD		IB								**	**
40		GRANDY 40			WD		IB	T275							30200	33500
44		GRANDY 44 MARLINEER			WD		IB								**	**
		1961 BOATS														
28		GRANDY 28		CR	WD		IB	180		9	10				6000	6900
32		MARLINEER		CR	WD		IB			11					**	**
36		MARLINEER		CR	WD		IB			12	9				**	**
40		MARLINEER		CR	WD		IB	T275		12	9				29300	32600
		1960 BOATS														
28		GRANDY 28		CBNCR	WD		IB	225							6900	7900
35		GRANDY 36		CBNCR	WD		IB	T225							16700	18900
35		GRANDY 36		CBNCR	WD		IB	T225		12	6		3		16700	19000
36		GRANDY 36		CBNCR	WD		IB	275							**	**
36		GRANDY 36		CBNCR	WD		IB	275		12	6		3		**	**
		1953 BOATS														
20		ALBATROSS	HT	CBNCR	PLY		IB								**	**
		1950 BOATS														
36		DREAMLINER	HT	CR	WD		IB								**	**
		1949 BOATS														
28		GRANDY 28		CBNCR	WD		IB	35							5000	5750

GRAVES MARINE SALES

HILTON HEAD ISLA SC COAST GUARD MFG ID- GVS See inside cover to adjust price for area

LOA FT	LOA IN	NAME AND/ OR MODEL	TOP/ RIG	BOAT TYPE	-HULL- MTL	-HULL- TP	ENGINE TP	ENGINE # HP	ENGINE MFG	BEAM FT	BEAM IN	WGT LBS	DRAFT FT	DRAFT IN	RETAIL LOW	RETAIL HIGH
		1979 BOATS														
51		GRAVES 51	FB	SF	F/W	SV	IB	T650D	GM	16			3	6	297000	326000
		1975 BOATS														
37		GRAVES 37	FB	SF	F/W	SV	IB	T225		14			3		72700	79900
37		GRAVES 37	FB	SF	F/W	SV	IB	T370		14			3		75800	83300
41		GRAVES 41	FB	SF	F/W	SV	IB	T370		15			3		114500	126000
45		GRAVES 45	FB	SF	F/W	SV	IB	T370		16			3	6	136500	150000
45		GRAVES 45	FB	SF	F/W	SV	IB	T400		16			3	6	142500	156500
48		GRAVES 48	FB	SF	F/W	SV	IB	T370		16	8		4		146000	160500
48		GRAVES 48	FB	SF	F/W	SV	IB	T400		16	8		4		149500	164500
52		GRAVES 52	FB	SF	F/W	SV	IB	T400		17	4		4		196500	216000
52		GRAVES 52	FB	SF	F/W	SV	IB	T650		17	4		4		238000	261500
56		GRAVES 56	FB	SF	F/W	SV	IB	T400		17	8		4	2	242000	266000
56		GRAVES 56	FB	SF	F/W	SV	IB	T650		17	8		4	2	242500	266500
60		GRAVES 60	FB	SF	F/W	SV	IB	T525		18			4	6	242000	266000
60		GRAVES 60	FB	SF	F/W	SV	IB	T650		18			4	6	262000	287500
65		GRAVES 65	FB	SF	F/W	SV	IB	T525		18	6		4	6	**	**
65		GRAVES 65	FB	SF	F/W	SV	IB	T650		18	6		4	6	**	**

GRAVES YACHT YARDS

MARBLEHEAD MA 01945 COAST GUARD MFG ID- GRG See inside cover to adjust price for area

LOA FT	LOA IN	NAME AND/ OR MODEL	TOP/ RIG	BOAT TYPE	-HULL- MTL	-HULL- TP	ENGINE TP	ENGINE # HP	ENGINE MFG	BEAM FT	BEAM IN	WGT LBS	DRAFT FT	DRAFT IN	RETAIL LOW	RETAIL HIGH
		1973 BOATS														
29	10	INTERNATIONAL	SLP	SA/OD	WD	KL	OB			5	10	2400	3	10	7000	8050
		1972 BOATS														
29	10	INTERNATIONAL	SLP	SA/OD	FBG	KL	OB			5	10	2400	3	10	6850	7850
		1971 BOATS														
29	8	CONSTELLATION	SLP	SA/OD	FBG	KL				8			4	8	12000	13600
29	8	CONSTELLATION	SLP	SAIL	FBG	KL	IB			8		6000	4	8	16800	19100
29	10	INTERNATIONAL	SLP	SA/OD	FBG	KL				5	10	2400	3	10	7150	8250
		1970 BOATS														
29	8	CONSTELLATION 30	SLP	SA/OD	FBG	KL	OB			8		6000	4	8	16300	18500
29	10	INTERNATIONAL	SLP	SA/OD		KL				5	10	2400	3	10	7000	8050
		1969 BOATS														
24		INTERNATIONAL	SLP	SA/OD	PLY	KC				4	2	1000	2	8	3700	4300
29	8	CONSTELLATION	SLP	SA/CR	FBG	KL	OB			8		6000	4	8	15900	18100
29	8	CONSTELLATION	SLP	SA/OD	FBG	KL				8			4	8	11400	13000
29	8	CONSTELLATION WKNDR	SLP	SAIL	FBG	KL	OB			8		6000	4	8	15900	18100
29	10	INTERNATIONAL	SLP	SA/OD		KL				5	10	2400	3	10	6900	7900
		1968 BOATS														
29	7	CONSTELLATION WKNDR	SLP	SAIL	FBG	KL	OB			8		6000	4	8	16900	19200
		1967 BOATS														
24		INTERNATIONAL	SLP	SA/OD	PLY	KL				4	2	900	2	9	3650	4250
29	7	CONSTELLATION		SA/CR	FBG		OB								16700	19000
29	7	CONSTELLATION WKNDR		SAIL	FBG		OB								16700	18900
29	10	INTERNATIONAL	SLP	SA/OD	PLY	KL				5	10	2400	3	10	7000	8050
		1966 BOATS														
20	1	BARNEGAT	SLP	SA/OD	PLY	KL	IB	6		7			3	7	5350	6200
24		INTERNATIONAL	SLP	SA/OD	WD	KL	OB								3650	4250
29	8	CONSTELLATION		SA/CR	FBG		OB								16500	18700
29	8	CONSTELLATION WKNDR		SAIL	FBG		OB								16500	18700
29	10	INTERNATIONAL	SLP	SA/OD	WD	KL	OB			5	10	2400	3	10	6550	7550
		1965 BOATS														
20	1	BARNEGAT 20	SLP	SA/OD	PLY	KL	IB	6		7			3	7	5300	6100
24		INTERNATIONAL	SLP	SA/OD	PLY	KL	OB								3600	4200
29	8	CONSTELLATION 30	SLP	SAIL	FBG		OB								16300	18500
29	10	INTERNATIONAL	SLP	SA/OD	PLY	KL	OB			5	10	2400	3	10	6500	7500
		1964 BOATS														
20	1	BARNEGAT	SLP	SA/OD	PLY	KL	IB	6		7			3	7	5250	6050
24		INTERNATIONAL	SLP	SA/OD	PLY	KL	OB								3600	4150
29	5	CONSTELLATION		SAIL	FBG		IB								16100	18300
29	10	INTERNATIONAL	SLP	SA/OD	PLY	KL	OB			5	10	2400	3	10	6450	7400
		1963 BOATS														
20	1	BARNEGAT	SLP	SA/OD	PLY	KL	IB	6		7			3	7	5250	6000
24		INTERNATIONAL	SLP	SA/OD	PLY	KL	OB								3550	4150
29	10	INTERNATIONAL	SLP	SA/OD	PLY	KL	OB			5	10	2400	3	10	6450	7450
		1962 BOATS														
20	1	BARNEGAT 20	SLP	SA/OD	PLY	KL	IB	6		7			3	7	5200	6000
24		INTERNATIONAL	SLP	SA/OD	PLY	KL	OB								3550	4100
29	10	INTERNATIONAL	SLP	SA/OD	PLY	KL	OB			5	10	2400	3	10	6450	7400
		1961 BOATS														
19		LIGHTNING	SLP	SA/OD	PLY	CB				6	6	700		5	2650	3050
20	1	BARNEGAT 20	SLP	SA/OD	PLY	KL	IB	6		7			3	7	5200	6000
24		INTERNATIONAL	SLP	SA/OD	PLY	KL				4	2		2	10	8000	9200
29	10	INTERNATIONAL	SLP	SA/OD	PLY	KL				5	10	2400	3	10	6700	7700
40		EXPLORER	KTH	SA/CR	P/M	KC	OB			11	2		2	8	52100	57300
		1960 BOATS														
19		LIGHTNING	SLP	SA/OD	PLY	CB				6	6	700		5	2650	3050
20	1	BARNGATTER	SLP	SA/CR	PLY	KL				7			2	7	4200	4900
24		INTERNATIONAL	SLP	SA/OD	PLY	KL				4	2		3		8000	9200
29	10	INTERNATIONAL	SLP	SA/OD	PLY	KL				5	10	2400	3	10	6700	7700
40		EXPLORER	KTH	SA/CR	PLY	KC	IB	6		11	2		2	8	52700	57900
		1959 BOATS														
19		LIGHTNING	SLP	SA/OD	PLY	CB	IB	6		6	6				5250	6000
20	1	HEADER	SLP	SAIL	PLY	KL	OB			7			2	7	4250	4900
24		INTERNATIONAL	SLP	SA/OD	PLY	KL				4	2		2	8	8050	9250

 CONTINUED ON NEXT PAGE

GRAVES YACHT YARDS — CONTINUED — 1959 BOATS

LOA FT IN	NAME AND/OR MODEL	TOP/RIG	BOAT TYPE	HULL MTL	HULL TP	ENG TP	ENG #	ENG HP	ENG MFG	BEAM FT IN	WGT LBS	DRAFT FT IN	RETAIL LOW	RETAIL HIGH
29 10	INTERNATIONAL	SLP	SA/OD	PLY	KL					5 10	2400	3 10	6700	7700
40	EXPLORER	KTH	SA/CR	PLY	KC	IB	6			11 2		2 8	52800	58000

GREAT BAY BOAT WORKS INC
COAST GUARD MFG ID- GBE

Call 1-800-327-6929 for BUC Personalized Evaluation Service
Or, for 1975 to 1978 boats, sign onto www.BUCValuPro.com

GREAT MIDWEST YACHT CO
COAST GUARD MFG ID- GRU

Call 1-800-327-6929 for BUC Personalized Evaluation Service
Or, for 1976 to 1994 boats, sign onto www.BUCValuPro.com

GREAVETTE BOAT CORP LTD

Call 1-800-327-6929 for BUC Personalized Evaluation Service
Or, for 1932 to 1978 boats, sign onto www.BUCValuPro.com

HENRY C GREBE & CO INC
CHICAGO IL 60618   COAST GUARD MFG ID- HCG See inside cover to adjust price for area

LOA FT IN	NAME AND/OR MODEL	TOP/RIG	BOAT TYPE	HULL MTL	HULL TP	ENG TP	ENG #	ENG HP	ENG MFG	BEAM FT IN	WGT LBS	DRAFT FT IN	RETAIL LOW	RETAIL HIGH
1967 BOATS														
60		FD		WD		IB		T350D	GM				97200	107000
1966 BOATS														
45	VR45	MY		WD		IB		T195		14		3 4	49300	54100
50	VR50	MY		WD		IB		T280		15		3 6	66600	73200
55	VR55	MY		WD		IB		T280		15 8		3 9	85900	94400
57	VR57	MY		WD		IB		T280		16 2		4	92000	101000
60	VR60	MY		WD		IB		T350		16 6		4	83800	92100
65	VR65	MY		WD		IB		T530		17		4 6	201000	221000
1963 BOATS														
57		MY		WD		IB		T350D	GM				89800	98700
1961 BOATS														
48	GREBE 48	CR		P/M		IB				13 10		3 4	**	**
54	GREBE 54	CR		P/M		IB				15		3 6	**	**
65	GREBE 65	MY		P/M		IB				16		4 6	**	**
65	GREBE 75	MY		P/M		IB				18		5 6	**	**
1959 BOATS														
47 10	GREBE 47	FB	CR	P/M		IB		T225		13 10			51600	56700
54	GREBE 54	FB	CR	P/M		IB		T235		14 6			61500	67600
65	GREBE 65	MY		P/M		IB		T235		16			152000	167000
73	GREBE 73	MY		P/M		IB		T235		17			**	**
1952 BOATS														
53 9		FB	MY	MHG		IB		T200D	GM	13 10		3 6	63700	70000
1950 BOATS														
65		FD		WD		IB		T200D					78000	85700
1947 BOATS														
65		FB	MY	WD		IB		T D					**	**
1941 BOATS														
71		FB	MY	WD		IB		T D					**	**
1939 BOATS														
60		FB	MY	WD		IB		T D					**	**
1937 BOATS														
62		FB	MY	WD		IB		T D					**	**
1931 BOATS														
46		HT	MY	WD		IB		T					**	**

RAY GREENE & CO INC
TOLEDO OH 43609   COAST GUARD MFG ID- RAG See inside cover to adjust price for area
                         FOR MORE RECENT YEARS SEE REBEL INDUSTRIES INC

LOA FT IN	NAME AND/OR MODEL	TOP/RIG	BOAT TYPE	HULL MTL	HULL TP	ENG TP	ENG HP	ENG MFG	BEAM FT IN	WGT LBS	DRAFT FT IN	RETAIL LOW	RETAIL HIGH
1975 BOATS													
23 7	KITTIWAKE 24	SLP	SA/CR	FBG	KL	OB			7 6	3700	2 10	3300	3850
1974 BOATS													
23 7	KITTIWAKE	SLP	SAIL	FBG		OB			7 5	3700	2 10	3250	3750
1973 BOATS													
23 7	KITTIWAKE	SLP	SAIL	FBG		OB			7 5	3700	2 10	3150	3650
24	CLIPPER	SLP	SAIL	FBG	KL	OB			6 7	3600	4	3100	3650
25 7	NEW-HORIZONS	SLP	SAIL	FBG	KC	IB	30		7 9	6030	3	5900	6800
1972 BOATS													
23 7	KITTIWAKE	SLP	SAIL	FBG		OB			7 5	3600	2 10	3000	3500
24	CLIPPER	SLP	SAIL	FBG		OB			6 7	3600	4	3050	3550
25 7	NEW-HORIZONS	SLP	SAIL	FBG		IB	30	UNIV	7 9	6030	3	5750	6650
1971 BOATS													
24	CLIPPER I	SLP	SAIL	FBG		OB			6 8	3600	3 9	3000	3500
25 7	NEW-HORIZONS	SLP	SAIL	FBG		IB	30	UNIV	7 9	6030	3	5650	6500
1970 BOATS													
24	CLIPPER ONE	SLP	SAIL	FBG	KL	OB			6 7	3000	3 9	2550	2950
25 7	NEW-HORIZONS	SLP	SAIL	FBG	KC	IB	30	UNIV	8	6000	3	5550	6350
1968 BOATS													
24	CLIPPER	SLP	SAIL	FBG	KL	OB			6 8	4000	3 9	3150	3650
25 5	NEW-HORIZONS	SLP	SAIL	FBG	KC	IB	30		7 9	6056	3	5400	6200
1967 BOATS													
24	CLIPPER ONE	SLP	SAIL	FBG		OB						2900	3350
25 7	NEW-HORIZONS	SLP	SAIL	FBG		IB	30					5350	6150
1966 BOATS													
24	CLIPPER ONE	SLP	SAIL	FBG	KL	OB			6 8	3000	3 9	2400	2800
25 7	NEW-HORIZONS	SLP	SAIL	FBG	KL	IB	30		7 9	6000	3	5250	6050
1965 BOATS													
24	CLIPPER	SLP	SAIL	FBG		OB						2850	3300
25 5	NEW-HORIZONS	SLP	SAIL	FBG		IB	30					5200	6000
1964 BOATS													
24	CLIPPER	SLP	SAIL	FBG		OB						2850	3300
25 5	NEW-HORIZONS	SLP	SAIL	FBG		IB	30					5200	5950
1963 BOATS													
25 5	NEW-HORIZONS	SLP	SAIL	FBG		IB	30					5150	5950
1962 BOATS													
25 5	NEW-HORIZONS	SLP	SAIL	FBG		IB	30					5150	5900
1961 BOATS													
26	NEW-HORIZONS	SLP	SAIL	FBG	KC	OB			7 9			3700	4300
1960 BOATS													
25 3	NEW-HORIZONS	SLP	SAIL	FBG		OB						3050	3550
1959 BOATS													
26	NEW-HORIZONS	SLP	SAIL	FBG	KC	OB			7 9		3	3750	4350
1958 BOATS													
26	NEW-HORIZONS	SLP	SA/CR	FBG		OB						3750	4350

GREENWICH SHIPYARD LTD

Call 1-800-327-6929 for BUC Personalized Evaluation Service
Or, for 1980 boats, sign onto www.BUCValuPro.com

GREENWICH YACHT COMPANY
GREENWICH N J   See inside cover to adjust price for area

LOA FT IN	NAME AND/OR MODEL	TOP/RIG	BOAT TYPE	HULL MTL	HULL TP	ENG TP	ENG HP	ENG MFG	BEAM FT IN	WGT LBS	DRAFT FT IN	RETAIL LOW	RETAIL HIGH
1966 BOATS													
42	DOUBLE CABIN	FB	DC	WD		IB	T280				3	59100	64900
42	MOTOR YACHT	MY		WD		IB	T280				3	58000	63700
48	MOTOR YACHT	MY		WD		IB	T280				3	79100	85300
54	MOTOR YACHT	MY		WD		IB	T320				3	88600	97300
1963 BOATS													
27 3	DELUXE		EXP	WD		IB	T195-215					7900	9200
27 3	DELUXE		EXP	WD		IB	T195-T215					9050	10500
27 3	DELUXE		SPTCR	WD		IB	T195-215					7600	8850
27 3	DELUXE		SPTCR	WD		IB	T195-T215					8700	10200
27 3	SEA-CRUISER DELUXE			WD		IB	T195-215					7350	8550
27 3	SEA-CRUISER DELUXE			WD		IB	T195-T215					8450	9950
27 3	SEA-CRUISER STANDARD			WD		IB	T195-215					6450	7500
27 3	SEA-CRUISER STANDARD			WD		IB	T195-T215					7550	8850
27 3	STANDARD		EXP	WD		IB	T195-215					7400	8600
27 3	STANDARD		EXP	WD		IB	T195-T215					8450	9900
27 3	STANDARD		SPTCR	WD		IB	T195-215					6750	7850
27 3	STANDARD		SPTCR	WD		IB	T195-T215					7800	9150
36 8	DELUXE		EXP	WD		IB	T195					35300	39200
36 8	DELUXE		EXP	WD		IB	T215					35400	39400
36 8	DELUXE		SDN	WD		IB	T195					37900	42100
36 8	DELUXE		SDN	WD		IB	T215					38000	42300
36 8	STANDARD		EXP	WD		IB	T195					31500	35000
36 8	STANDARD		EXP	WD		IB	T215					31600	35100
36 8	STANDARD		SDN	WD		IB	T195					33900	37700

LOA FT	IN	NAME AND/ OR MODEL	TOP/ RIG	BOAT TYPE	HULL MTL	HULL TP	ENGINE TP	# HP	MFG	BEAM FT	BEAM IN	WGT LBS	DRAFT FT	DRAFT IN	RETAIL LOW	RETAIL HIGH
		1963 BOATS														
36	8	STANDARD		SDN	WD		IB	T215							34100	37800
41	4			DC	WD		IB	T215							52200	57400
41	4			DC	WD		IB	T280							53900	59300
45	2		FB	DC	WD		IB	T225							73500	80800
45	2		FB	DC	WD		IB	T280							73700	81000
45	2			MY	WD		IB	T225							56300	61800
45	2			MY	WD		IB	T280							56900	62500
45	2			SPTCR	WD		IB	T225							39400	43800
45	2			SPTCR	WD		IB	T280							42200	46900
50				MY	WD		IB								**	**
		1962 BOATS														
36	1	NEWPORT 6S		EXP	WD		IB	T188							29500	32800
40	3	FAIRFIELD AFT CABIN		CR	WD		IB	T215							42400	47100
44	1	CUMBERLAND		FD	WD		IB	T225							56900	62500
44	1	FAIRFIELD AFT CABIN		CR	WD		IB	T225							41300	45900
48	3	CUMBERLAND		FD	WD		IB	T280							68200	74900
		1961 BOATS														
36				EXP	WD		IB	T188		11	7		2	9	28400	31600
36				SDN	WD		IB	T188		11	7		2	9	31100	34500
43			FB	DC	WD		IB	T225		13	4		3	4	53000	58300
43				MY	WD		IB	T225		13	4		3	4	59800	65700
43				SDN	WD		IB	T225		13	4		3	4	40800	45400
		1960 BOATS														
34	1	GREENWICH		EXP	WD		IB	T190							20500	22800
34	1	NEWPORT		CR	WD		IB	T190							18500	20600
34	1	NEWPORT COHANSEY		EXP	WD		IB	T190							20500	22800
43		GREENWICH-FAIRFIELD			WD		IB								**	**

GREENWICH YACHT SALES

Call 1-800-327-6929 for BUC Personalized Evaluation Service
Or, for 1967 boats, sign onto www.BUCValuPro.com

GREGOR BOATS

FRESNO CA 93722 COAST GUARD MFG ID- GBC See inside cover to adjust price for area

For more recent years, see the BUC Used Boat Price Guide, Volume 1 or Volume 2

LOA FT	IN	NAME AND/ OR MODEL	TOP/ RIG	BOAT TYPE	HULL MTL	HULL TP	ENGINE TP	# HP	MFG	BEAM FT	BEAM IN	WGT LBS	DRAFT FT	DRAFT IN	RETAIL LOW	RETAIL HIGH
		1983 BOATS														
16	6	FISH-MASTER F-6B	OP	BASS	AL	SV	OB			5	10	715			1750	2050
18	6	R-186 RIVER BOAT	OP	UTL	AL	SV	OB			7	6	795			1850	2200
18	6	RJ-186	OP	UTL	AL	SV	JT	235		7	6	1490			2350	2700
18	6	RJ-186 RIVER BOAT	OP	UTL	AL	SV	JT	130	CHEV	7	6	1490			2200	2550
20	6	R-206 RIVER BOAT	OP	UTL	AL	SV	OB			7	6	860			1900	2300
20	6	RJ-206	OP	UTL	AL	SV	JT	235		7	6	1555			2650	3050
20	6	RJ-206 RIVER BOAT	OP	UTL	AL	SV	JT	130	CHEV	7	6	1555			2450	2850
24	6	R-246 RIVER BOAT	OP	UTL	AL	SV	OB			7	6	1050			3150	3650
24	6	RJ-246	OP	UTL	AL	SV	JT	235		7	6	1990			3550	4150
24	6	RJ-246 RIVER BOAT	OP	UTL	AL	SV	JT	130	CHEV	7	6	1990			3300	3850
		1982 BOATS														
16	6	FISH-MASTER F-6B	OP	BASS	AL	SV	OB			5	10	715			1700	2050
18	6	R-186 RIVER BOAT	OP	UTL	AL	SV	OB			7	6	795			1800	2150
18	6	RJ-186	OP	UTL	AL	SV	JT	235		7	6	1490			2250	2600
18	6	RJ-186 RIVER BOAT	OP	UTL	AL	SV	JT	130	CHEV	7	6	1490			2050	2450
20	6	R-206 RIVER BOAT	OP	UTL	AL	SV	OB			7	6	860			1900	2250
20	6	RJ-206	OP	UTL	AL	SV	JT	235		7	6	1555			2500	2900
20	6	RJ-206 RIVER BOAT	OP	UTL	AL	SV	JT	130	CHEV	7	6	1555			2350	2750
24	6	R-246 RIVER BOAT	OP	UTL	AL	SV	OB			7	6	1050			3100	3600
24	6	RJ-246	OP	UTL	AL	SV	JT	235		7	6	1990			3400	3950
24	6	RJ-246 RIVER BOAT	OP	UTL	AL	SV	JT	130	CHEV	7	6	1990			3150	3650
		1981 BOATS														
18	6	R-186 RIVER BOAT	OP	UTL	AL	SV	OB			7	6	795			1800	2150
18	6	RJ-186	OP	UTL	AL	SV	JT	235		7	6	1490			2150	2500
18	6	RJ-186 RIVER BOAT	OP	UTL	AL	SV	JT	130	CHEV	7	6	1490			1950	2350
20	6	R-206 RIVER BOAT	OP	UTL	AL	SV	OB			7	6	860			1850	2200
20	6	RJ-206	OP	UTL	AL	SV	JT	235		7	6	1555			2400	2800
20	6	RJ-206 RIVER BOAT	OP	UTL	AL	SV	JT	130	CHEV	7	6	1555			2300	2650
24	6	R-246 RIVER BOAT	OP	UTL	AL	SV	OB			7	6	1050			3050	3550
24	6	RJ-246	OP	UTL	AL	SV	JT	235		7	6	1990			3250	3800
24	6	RJ-246 RIVER BOAT	OP	UTL	AL	SV	JT	130	CHEV	7	6	1990			3050	3550
		1980 BOATS														
18	6	R-186 RIVER BOAT	OP	UTL	AL	SV	OB			7	6	797			1750	2100
18	6	RJ-186 RIVER BOAT	OP	UTL	AL	SV	JT	140	CHEV	7	6	1490			1900	2250
20	6	R-206 RIVER BOAT	OP	UTL	AL	SV	OB			7	6	860			1850	2200
20	6	RJ-206 RIVER BOAT	OP	UTL	AL	SV	JT	140	CHEV	7	6	1555			2200	2550
24	6	R-246 RIVER BOAT	OP	UTL	AL	SV	OB			7	6	980			2850	3300
24	6	RJ-246 RIVER BOAT	OP	UTL	AL	SV	JT	140	CHEV	7	6	1990			2900	3400
		1979 BOATS														
18	6	R-186 RIVER BOAT	OP	UTL	AL	SV	OB			7	6	797			1750	2100
18	6	RJ-186 RIVER BOAT	OP	UTL	AL	SV	JT	240		7	6	1490			1950	2300
20	6	R-206 RIVER BOAT	OP	UTL	AL	SV	OB			7	6	860			1800	2150
20	6	RJ-206 RIVER BOAT	OP	UTL	AL	SV	JT	240		7	6	1555			2200	2550
24	6	R-246 RIVER BOAT	OP	UTL	AL	SV	OB			7	6	980			2800	3250
24	6	RJ-246 RIVER BOAT	OP	UTL	AL	SV	JT	240		7	6	1990			3000	3500
		1978 BOATS														
18	6	R-186 RIVER BOAT	OP	UTL	AL	SV	OB			7	6	795			1700	2050
18	6	RJ-186	OP	UTL	AL	SV	JT	140	HAM	7	6	1490			1750	2100
18	6	RJ-186	OP	UTL	AL	SV	JT	240	HAM	7	6	1490			1850	2200
20	6	R-206 RIVER BOAT	OP	UTL	AL	SV	OB			7	6	860			1800	2150
20	6	RJ-206	OP	UTL	AL	SV	JT	140	HAM	7	6	1555			1950	2350
20	6	RJ-206	OP	UTL	AL	SV	JT	240	HAM	7	6	1555			2050	2450
24	6	D-246 RIVER BOAT	OP	UTL	AL	SV	OB			7	6	980			2800	3250
24	6	RJ-246	OP	UTL	AL	SV	JT	140-240		7	6	1990			2700	3350
		1977 BOATS														
18	6	R-186	OP	UTL	AL	FL	OB			7	6	795			1700	2050
20	6	R-206	OP	UTL	AL	FL	OB			7	6	860			1800	2100
24	6	R-246	OP	UTL	AL	FL	OB			7	6	980			2750	3200
27		CON-27	HT	HB	AL	PN	OB			10		3100			**	**
27		CON-27	HT	HB	AL	PN	IO	120	MRCR	10		3900			**	**
31		CON-31	HT	HB	AL	PN	OB			10		3350			5450	6300
31		CON-31	HT	HB	AL	PN	IO	120	MRCR	10		4150			11400	12900
		1976 BOATS														
18	6	R-186	OP	UTL	AL	SV	OB			7	6	795			1700	2000
20	6	R-206	OP	UTL	AL	SV	OB			7	6	860			1750	2100
24	6	R-246	OP	UTL	AL	SV	OB			7	6	980			2750	3150
27		CON-27	HT	HB	AL	PN	OB			10		3100			**	**
27		CON-27	HT	HB	AL	PN	IO	120	MRCR	10		3100			**	**
31		CON-31	HT	HB	AL	PN	OB			10		3350			5400	6200
31		CON-31	HT	HB	AL	PN	IO	120	MRCR	10		3350			7800	8950
		1975 BOATS														
20	6	R-206	OP	UTL	AL	SV	OB			7	6	860			1750	2100
24	6	R-246	OP	UTL	AL	SV	OB			7	6	980			2700	3150
27		CON-27	HT	HB	AL	PN	OB			10		3100			**	**
27		CON-27	HT	HB	AL	PN	IO	120	MRCR	10		3900			**	**
31		CON-31	HT	HB	AL	PN	OB			10		3350			5400	6200
31		CON-31	HT	HB	AL	PN	IO	120	MRCR	10		4150			11100	12700
		1974 BOATS														
27		CON-27	HT	HB	AL	PN	OB					3100			**	**
27		CON-27	HT	HB	AL	PN	IO	120	MRCR			3900			**	**
31		CON-31	HT	HB	AL	PN	OB					3350			5350	6150
31		CON-31	HT	HB	AL	PN	IO	120	MRCR			4150			11000	12500
		1973 BOATS														
27		CON-27	HT	HB	AL	PN	OB			10		3100			**	**
31		CON-31	HT	HB	AL	PN	IO	120		10		4150			11000	12400
		1972 BOATS														
27		CON-27	HT	HB	AL	PN	OB			10		3100			**	**
31		CON-31	HT	HB	AL	PN	OB			10		4150			8450	9700
		1971 BOATS														
27		CON-27		HB	AL	PN	OB			10		3100		9	**	**
27		CON-27		HB	AL	PN	IO	120		10		3700		11	**	**
31		CON-31		HB	AL	PN	OB			10		3350		10	5200	6000
31		CON-31		HB	AL	PN	IO	120		10		4000	1		10300	11700

GREW BOATS

PENTANGUISHENE ONTARIO COAST GUARD MFG ID- ZGR See inside cover to adjust price for area

LOA FT	IN	NAME AND/ OR MODEL	TOP/ RIG	BOAT TYPE	HULL MTL	HULL TP	ENGINE TP	# HP	MFG	BEAM FT	BEAM IN	WGT LBS	DRAFT FT	DRAFT IN	RETAIL LOW	RETAIL HIGH
		1981 BOATS														
16	6	1600		RNBT	FBG	DV	OB			7		1450			3100	3600
17	6	1800		RNBT	FBG	DV	OB			7		1550			3250	3800
17	6	1850		RNBT	FBG	DV	IO	165		7					1700	2000
19	6	2000		RNBT	FBG	DV	IO	185		7	7				2300	2650
20	3	2100		RNBT	FBG	DV	IO	185		7	10				2600	3050
22	10	SPORTSMAN 2350		RNBT	FBG	DV	IO	188		8					3450	4000
22	10	WEEKENDER 2400		RNBT	FBG	DV	IO	188		8					3450	4000
		1980 BOATS														
17	6	CHALLENGER 1850		RNBT	FBG	DV	IO	228		7					1750	2050
19	6	SEVILLE 2000		RNBT	FBG	DV	IO	140-228		7	7				2250	2700
21	5	ADVENTURER 2100		RNBT	FBG	DV	IO	170-260		7	10				2700	3300
21	5	OFFSHORE 2150		RNBT	FBG	DV	IO	170-260		7	10				2700	3300

CONTINUED ON NEXT PAGE

LOA FT IN	NAME AND/ OR MODEL	TOP/ RIG	BOAT TYPE	-HULL- MTL TP	----ENGINE--- TP # HP MFG	BEAM FT IN	WGT LBS	DRAFT FT IN	RETAIL LOW	RETAIL HIGH
				1980 BOATS						
22 10	OFFSHORE 2450		RNBT	FBG DV	IO 188				3400	3950
22 10	OFFSHORE 2450		RNBT	FBG DV	IO 330				3950	4600
22 10	SPORTSMAN 2350		RNBT	FBG DV	IO 188-260	8			3400	4100
22 10	WEEKENDER 2400		RNBT	FBG DV	IO 188-260				3400	4100
				1979 BOATS						
16 2	GREW 163	OP	RNBT	FBG DV	OB	6 6	1250		2600	3050
17 6	GREW 178	ST	RNBT	FBG DV	IO 170-230	7	2200		1750	2150
19 6	GREW 198	ST	RNBT	FBG DV	IO 165-230	7 7	2700		2200	2750
19 6	GREW 205 B/R	ST	RNBT	FBG DV	IO 228 MRCR	7 7	2920		2350	2750
19 6	GREW 206	ST	CUD	FBG DV	IO 165-230	7 7	2920		2350	2950
20 3	GREW 215	ST	CUD	FBG DV	IO 260 MRCR	7 10	3100		2950	3450
22 10	GREW 230	ST	CUD	FBG DV	IO 185-230	8	3450		3450	4250
22 10	GREW 230	ST	CUD	FBG DV	IO 260	8	3450		3650	4400
22 10	GREW 238	ST	WKNDR	FBG DV	IO 185-230	8	3550		3600	4400
22 10	GREW 238	ST	WKNDR	FBG DV	IO 260	8	3550		3800	4550
25 4	CHRIS-CRAFT-CATALINA	OP	EXP	FBG DV	IB 225 CC	9 9		2 3	7100	8150
				1978 BOATS						
16 2	GREW 163	OP	RNBT	FBG SV	OB	6 6	1250		2600	3000
17 6	GREW 178	ST	RNBT	FBG DV	IO 170-225	7	2200		1750	2100
19 6	GREW 204	ST	RNBT	FBG DV	IO 165-240	7 7	2700		2200	2700
19 6	GREW 205	ST	RNBT	FBG DV	IO 165-240	7 7	2920		2300	2750
19 6	GREW 206	ST	RNBT	FBG DV	IO 185-240	7 7	2920		2350	2850
20 3	GREW 215	ST	CUD	FBG DV	IO 198-260	7 10	3100		2850	3450
22 10	GREW 245	ST	CUD	FBG DV	IO 198-260	8	3550		3600	4350
22 10	GREW 245	ST	CUD	FBG DV	IO T140-T170	8	3550		4050	4700
22 10	GREW 245	HT	CUD	FBG DV	IO 198-260	8	3550		3600	4350
22 10	GREW 245	HT	CUD	FBG DV	IO T140-T170	8	3550		4050	4700
25 4	CATALINA	OP	EXP	FBG DV	IB 225 CC	9 9		2 3	6750	7750
25 4	GREW 255	ST	WKNDR	FBG DV	IO 228-260	9 8	6000	2 6	6550	7650
25 4	GREW 255	ST	WKNDR	FBG DV	IO T165-T198	9 8	6000	2 6	7150	8450
25 4	GREW 255	HT	WKNDR	FBG DV	IO 228-260	9 8	6000	2 6	6550	7650
25 4	GREW 255	HT	WKNDR	FBG DV	IO T165-T198	9 8	6000	2 6	7150	8450
25 4	GREW 255	FB	WKNDR	FBG DV	IO 228-260	9 8	6000		7200	8400
25 4	GREW 255	FB	WKNDR	FBG DV	IO T165-T198	9 8	6000		7900	9350

M H GRINNEL

Call 1-800-327-6929 for BUC Personalized Evaluation Service
Or, for 1961 to 1965 boats, sign onto www.BUCValuPro.com

AL GROVER'S

GROVER BUILT BOATS   See inside cover to adjust price for area
FREEPORT NY 11520   COAST GUARD MFG ID- ALX

For more recent years, see the BUC Used Boat Price Guide, Volume 1 or Volume 2

LOA FT IN	NAME AND/ OR MODEL	TOP/ RIG	BOAT TYPE	-HULL- MTL TP	----ENGINE--- TP # HP MFG	BEAM FT IN	WGT LBS	DRAFT FT IN	RETAIL LOW	RETAIL HIGH
				1982 BOATS						
26 10	GROVERBUILT FSHSKIFF	HT	CUD	FBG DV	IB 80D LEHM	9	6000	2	15300	17300

GRUMMAN BOATS

DIV OF OMC ALUMINUM BOAT GROUP   See inside cover to adjust price for area
LEBANON MO 65536   COAST GUARD MFG ID- GBM

For more recent years, see the BUC Used Boat Price Guide, Volume 1 or Volume 2

LOA FT IN	NAME AND/ OR MODEL	TOP/ RIG	BOAT TYPE	-HULL- MTL TP	----ENGINE--- TP # HP MFG	BEAM FT IN	WGT LBS	DRAFT FT IN	RETAIL LOW	RETAIL HIGH
				1983 BOATS						
16 10	GRUMMAN 5.0 CTRCN	OP	BASS	AL DV	OB	7 6	853		2250	2650
16 10	GRUMMAN 5.0 S/CON	OP	BASS	AL DV	OB	7 6	853		2250	2600
				1982 BOATS						
16 10	GRUMMAN 5.0 CTRCN	OP	BASS	AL DV	OB	7 6	853		2200	2550
16 10	GRUMMAN 5.0 S/CON	OP	BASS	AL DV	OB	7 6	853		2200	2550
				1981 BOATS						
17	GRUMMAN 5.0 CONSOLE	OP	CTRCN	AL DV	OB	7 1	800		2000	2350
				1966 BOATS						
19	CUSTOM		AL		OB				2350	2700
20	20 GUIDE CUS		AL		OB				2450	2900
				1965 BOATS						
16 4	HAWK		SAIL	FBG	OB				1950	2300
19 7	RESOLUTE		SAIL	FBG	OB				3700	4300
19 7	SPORTSTER G-19			AL	OB				2400	2750
19 7	SPORTSTER G-19			AL	IB				**	**
				1964 BOATS						
16 4	HAWK		SAIL	FBG	OB				1950	2300
17 2	SPORTABOUT			FBG	IO 80				3200	3700
18 6	SPORTSTER G-19			AL	OB				2300	2650
				1963 BOATS						
16 4	PEARSON HAWK		SAIL	FBG	OB				1950	2300
18 6	SPORTSTER G-19			AL	OB				2300	2650
				1962 BOATS						
17	P 17 SPORTABOUT			AL	IO				**	**
18 6	G 19 SPORTSTER			AL	OB				2300	2650
18 6	G 19 SPORTSTER			AL	IO				**	**
				1961 BOATS						
18 6	SPORTSTER G-19			UTL	AL	IO	7 2		**	**
18 6	SPORTSTER G-19			UTL	AL	IO 80	7 2		5000	5750
				1960 BOATS						
19	SPORTSTER G-19			RNBT	AL	OB			2350	2750

GRUMMAN CRUISERS

DIV OF GRUMMAN ALLIED IND INC

Call 1-800-327-6929 for BUC Personalized Evaluation Service
Or, for 1966 to 1968 boats, sign onto www.BUCValuPro.com

GULF COAST SAILBOATS INC

DIV OF LOUVER-LOK   See inside cover to adjust price for area
HOUSTON TX 77087   COAST GUARD MFG ID- GCS

LOA FT IN	NAME AND/ OR MODEL	TOP/ RIG	BOAT TYPE	-HULL- MTL TP	----ENGINE--- TP # HP MFG	BEAM FT IN	WGT LBS	DRAFT FT IN	RETAIL LOW	RETAIL HIGH
				1980 BOATS						
18	GULF-COAST 18	SLP	SA/OD	FBG CB	OB	6 2	900	10	2950	3400
20	GULF-COAST 20	SLP	SA/OD	FBG CB	OB	6 11	1150	10	3450	4050
20 8	GULF-COAST 21	SLP	SAIL	FBG KC	OB	7 4	1650	1 7	4150	4800
23	GULF-COAST 23	SLP	SAIL	FBG KC	OB	7 4	1960	1 7	4800	5500
				1979 BOATS						
18	GULF-COAST 18	SLP	SA/OD	FBG CB	OB	6 2	900	10	2800	3300
20	GULF-COAST 20	SLP	SA/OD	FBG CB	OB	6 11	1150	10	3300	3850
20 8	GULF-COAST 21	SLP	SAIL	FBG KC	OB	7 4	1710	1 7	4050	4700
20 8	GULF-COAST 21	SLP	SAIL	FBG SK	OB	7 4	1650	1	3950	4600
23	GULF-COAST 23	SLP	SAIL	FBG KC	OB	7 4	1960	1 7	4600	5250
23	GULF-COAST 23	SLP	SAIL	FBG KL	OB	7 4	2300	3 6	5000	5750
23	GULF-COAST 23	SLP	SAIL	FBG SK	OB	7 4	1900	1	4500	5200
26	GULF-COAST 26	SLP	SA/CR	FBG KC	OB	7 11	4800	5 10	10400	11800
26	GULF-COAST 26	SLP	SA/CR	FBG KL	OB	7 11	4800	5 10	10300	11700
				1978 BOATS						
18	GULF-COAST 18	SLP	SA/CR	FBG CB	OB	6 2	900	10	2700	3150
18	GULF-COAST 18-II	SLP	SA/CR	FBG KC	OB	7 1	1450	1 7	3400	3950
18	GULF-COAST 18-II	SLP	SA/CR	FBG SK	OB	7 1	1450	1 1	3400	3950
20	GULF-COAST 20	SLP	SA/OD	FBG CB	OB	6 11	1150	10	3250	3750
20 8	GULF-COAST 21	SLP	SAIL	FBG KC	OB	7 4	1710	1 7	3850	4450
20 8	GULF-COAST 21	SLP	SAIL	FBG SK	OB	7 4	1650	1	3800	4400
23	GULF-COAST 23	SLP	SAIL	FBG KC	OB	7 4	1900	1 7	4250	4950
23	GULF-COAST 23	SLP	SAIL	FBG KL	OB	7 4	2300	3 6	4800	5550
23	GULF-COAST 23	SLP	SAIL	FBG SK	OB	7 4	1900	1	4250	4950
25 11	GULF-COAST 26	SLP	SAIL	FBG KC	OB	7 11	4500	5 5	9500	10600
28 6	GULF-COAST 29	SLP	SAIL	FBG KC	OB	9	5600	4 6	12700	14400
28 6	GULF-COAST 29	SLP	SAIL	FBG KL	OB	9	5600	4 6	12900	14600
				1977 BOATS						
28 6	GULF-COAST 29	SLP	SAIL	FBG KC	IB	10D- 20D UNIV	9	5600	4 6	13000	14800
32	GULF-COAST 32	SLP	SAIL	FBG KC	IB	D	9	9000	4	22300	24800
45	GULF-COAST 45	KTH	SAIL	FBG KC	IB	D	10 11	20000	5 10	63100	69400
				1977 BOATS						
18	GULF-COAST 18	SLP	SA/OD	FBG CB	OB	6 2	900	10	2650	3050
18	GULF-COAST 18-II	SLP	SA/CR	FBG KC	OB	7 1	1450	1 7	3300	3850
18	GULF-COAST 18-II	SLP	SA/CR	FBG SK	OB	7 1	1450	1 1	3300	3850
20	GULF-COAST 20	SLP	SA/CR	FBG CB	OB	6 11	1100	10	3050	3550
20 8	GULF-COAST 21	SLP	SA/CR	FBG KC	OB	7 4	1710	1 7	3700	4350
20 8	GULF-COAST 21	SLP	SA/CR	FBG SK	OB	7 4	1650	1	3650	4250
23	GULF-COAST 23	SLP	SA/CR	FBG KC	OB	7 4	1900	1 7	4150	4850
23	GULF-COAST 23	SLP	SA/CR	FBG KL	OB	7 4	2300	3 6	4650	5350
23	GULF-COAST 23	SLP	SA/CR	FBG SK	OB	7 4	1900	1	4150	4850
26	GULF-COAST 26	SLP	SA/CR	FBG KC	OB	8	4800	10	9650	10800
26	GULF-COAST 26	SLP	SA/CR	FBG KC	IB	10D- 20D	8	4800	1 9	10100	11700
26	GULF-COAST 26	SLP	SA/CR	FBG KL	OB	8	4800	4 4	9600	10900

LOA FT IN	NAME AND/ OR MODEL	TOP/ RIG	BOAT TYPE	-HULL- MTL TP	----ENGINE--- TP # HP MFG	BEAM FT IN	WGT LBS	DRAFT FT IN	RETAIL LOW	RETAIL HIGH
1977 BOATS
26	GULF-COAST 26	SLP	SA/CR	FBG KL IB	10D- 20D	8	4800	4 4	10100	11600
28 6	GULF-COAST 29	SLP	SA/CR	FBG KL OB		9	5600	4 4	12200	13800
28 6	GULF-COAST 29	SLP	SA/CR	FBG KL IB	30 UNIV	9	5600	4 4	12400	14100
28 6	GULF-COAST 29	SLP	SA/CR	FBG KL IB	10D- 20D	9	5600	4 4	12500	14300
1976 BOATS
18	GULF-COAST 18	SLP	SA/OD	FBG CB OB		5 10	900	10	2550	2950
18	GULF-COAST 18-II	SLP	SA/CR	FBG KC OB		7 1	1450	1 7	3200	3700
18	GULF-COAST 18-II	SLP	SA/CR	FBG SK OB		7 1	1450	1 1	3200	3700
20	GULF-COAST 20	SLP	SA/OD	FBG CB OB		6 2	1100	10	2950	3450
20 8	GULF-COAST 21	SLP	SAIL	FBG KC OB		7 4	1650	1 7	3500	4100
20 8	GULF-COAST 21	SLP	SAIL	FBG SK OB		7 4	1650	1	3500	4100
23	GULF-COAST 23	SLP	SAIL	FBG KC OB		7 4	1960	1 7	4000	4650
23	GULF-COAST 23	SLP	SAIL	FBG KL OB		7 4	2300	3 6	4450	5150
23	GULF-COAST 23	SLP	SAIL	FBG SK OB		7 4	1900	1	3950	4600
26	GULF-COAST 26	SLP	SAIL	FBG KC OB		8	4500	1 9	8600	9900
26	GULF-COAST 26	SLP	SAIL	FBG KC IB	10D- 20D	8	4500	1 9	9250	10700
26	GULF-COAST 26	SLP	SAIL	FBG KL OB		8	4175	4 4	8000	9200
26	GULF-COAST 26	SLP	SAIL	FBG KL IB	10D- 20D	8	4175	4 4	8550	9950
28 6	GULF-COAST 29	SLP	SAIL	FBG KC OB		9	5600	4 4	11800	13400
28 6	GULF-COAST 29	SLP	SAIL	FBG KC IB	30 UNIV	9	5600	4 4	12000	13700
28 6	GULF-COAST 29	SLP	SAIL	FBG KC IB	10D- 20D	9	5600	4 4	12100	13900
28 6	GULF-COAST 29	SLP	SAIL	FBG KL OB		9	5600	4 4	11700	13300
28 6	GULF-COAST 29	SLP	SAIL	FBG KL IB	30 UNIV	9	5600	4 4	11900	13500
28 6	GULF-COAST 29	SLP	SAIL	FBG KL IB	10D- 20D	9	5600	4 4	12000	13800
1975 BOATS
18	GULF COAST 18	SLP	SAIL	FBG SK OB		6 2	900	3 6	2450	2850
18	GULF COAST 18 II	SLP	SAIL	FBG SK OB		7 1	1450	3 6	3100	3650
20	GULF COAST 20	SLP	SAIL	FBG CB OB		6 11	1150	4 4	2900	3400
20	GULF COAST 20 W/4	SLP	SAIL	FBG SK OB		6 11	1375	4 4	3150	3700
21	GULF COAST 21	SLP	SAIL	FBG SK OB		7 4	1650	5	3450	4000
22	GULF COAST 22	SLP	SAIL	FBG KC OB		7 3	2250	3 6	4150	4800
23	GULF COAST 23	SLP	SAIL	FBG SK OB		7 4	1900	5	3800	4450
25 11	GULF OOAST 26	SLP	SAIL	FBG KC OB		7 11	4500	5 5	8300	9550
28 6	GULF COAST 29	SLP	SAIL	FBG KL OB		9	5600	4 4	11300	12900
32	GULF COAST 32	SLP	SAIL	FBG KL IB	D	9	9000	4	20000	22200
45	GULF COAST 45	KTH	SAIL	FBG KC IB	D	10 11	20000	5 10	57400	63000
1974 BOATS
18	GULF-COAST 18	SLP	SA/OD	FBG CB OB		6 2	1000	4 8	2500	2950
20	GULF-COAST 20	SLP	SA/OD	FBG CB OB		6 11	1150	4 4	2850	3350
21	GULF-COAST 21	SLP	SAIL	FBG SK OB		7 4	1700	5	3400	3950
22 5	GULF-COAST 22	SLP	SAIL	FBG KL OB		7 4	2200	3 8	4000	4600
23	GULF-COAST 23	SLP	SAIL	FBG SK OB		7 4	2000	5	3800	4400
25 11	GULF-COAST 26	SLP	SAIL	FBG KL OB		7 11	4500	5 5	8000	9200
28 6	GULF-COAST 29	SLP	SAIL	FBG KL OB		9	5600	4 6	11100	12600
1973 BOATS
18	GULF-COAST 18	SLP	SA/OD	FBG CB OB		6 2	1000	4 8	2450	2850
20	GULF-COAST 20	SLP	SA/OD	FBG CB OB		6 11	1150	4 4	2800	3250
21	GULF-COAST 21	SLP	SAIL	FBG SK OB		7 4	1500	5	3150	3650
23	GULF-COAST 23	SLP	SAIL	FBG KL OB		7 4	2000	5	3700	4300
25 11	GULF-COAST 26	SLP	SAIL	FBG KC OB		7 11	4500	5 5	7800	8950
28 6	GULF-COAST 29	SLP	SAIL	FBG KL OB		9	5600	4 6	10800	12200
45	GULF-COAST 45	KTH	SAIL	FBG KC OB		10 11	20000	5 10	54000	59400
1972 BOATS
18	GULF-COAST 18	SLP	SA/OD	FBG CB OB		6 2	900	3 10	2300	2650
20	GULF-COAST 20	SLP	SA/OD	FBG CB OB		7		4	2750	3200
22	GULF-COAST 22	SLP	SA/CR	FBG KL OB		6 10	2100	3	4000	4700
23	GULF-COAST 23	SLP	SAIL	FBG OB		7 4	1900	5	3550	4100
26 2	GULF-COAST 26	SLP	SAIL	FBG OB		8			8150	9400
28 6	GULF-COAST 29	SLP	SAIL	FBG OB		9		4 4	10500	11900
45	GULF-COAST 45	YWL	SA/CR	FBG KC IB	6- 30	12	20000	5 1	50000	54900
1971 BOATS
16	GULF-COAST 16	SLP	SAIL	FBG CB OB		6	750	9	1850	2200
18	GULF-COAST 18	SLP	SAIL	FBG CB OB		6 1	800	9	2100	2500
19 11	GULF-COAST 20	SLP	SAIL	FBG CB OB		6 8	1100	10	2600	3000
20	GULF-COAST 20 W/4	SLP	SAIL	FBG CB OB		6 10	1100	10	2600	3000
22	GULF-COAST 22	SLP	SAIL	FBG KC OB		7 3	2100	3	3550	4100
22 7	GULF-COAST 23	SLP	SAIL	FBG CB OB		7 3	1900	2	3400	3950
25 6	GULF-COAST 26	SLP	SAIL	FBG KL OB		8	4300	4 4	6900	7950
28 10	GULF-COAST 29	SLP	SAIL	FBG KL IB	30	9	5600	4 11	10500	11900
45	GULF-COAST 45	SLP	SAIL	FBG KC IB	30	12 2	20000	5 1	49200	54100
1970 BOATS
18	GULF-COAST 18	SLP	SA/OD	FBG CB OB		6 1	800	9	2050	2450
20	GULF-COAST 20	SLP	SAIL	FBG CB OB		6 10	1100	10	2550	2950
22	GULF-COAST 22	SLP	SAIL	FBG KC OB		7	2100	3	3500	4050
25 6	GULF-COAST 26	SLP	SAIL	FBG KL OB		8	4300	4 4	6800	7800
28 10	GULF-COAST 29	SLP	SAIL	FBG KL IB	30	9	5600	4 11	10200	11600

GULF MARINE

Call 1-800-327-6929 for BUC Personalized Evaluation Service
Or, for 1969 to 1971 boats, sign onto www.BUCValuPro.com

GULF TRAWLER YACHTS INC
COAST GUARD MFG ID- GTY

Call 1-800-327-6929 for BUC Personalized Evaluation Service
Or, for 1977 to 1978 boats, sign onto www.BUCValuPro.com

GULF-CRAFT INC

Call 1-800-327-6929 for BUC Personalized Evaluation Service
Or, for 1966 to 1967 boats, sign onto www.BUCValuPro.com

GULFSTAR INC
ST PETERSBURG FL 33714   COAST GUARD MFG ID- GFS See inside cover to adjust price for area

For more recent years, see the BUC Used Boat Price Guide, Volume 1 or Volume 2

LOA FT IN	NAME AND/ OR MODEL	TOP/ RIG	BOAT TYPE	-HULL- MTL TP	----ENGINE--- TP # HP MFG	BEAM FT IN	WGT LBS	DRAFT FT IN	RETAIL LOW	RETAIL HIGH
1983 BOATS
36 1	GULFSTAR 36	SLP	SA/CR	FBG KL IB	50D PERK	12	15000	4 10	47800	52500
38 4	GULFSTAR 38	MY	FBG SV IB	B 85D PERK	12 5	19000	3 3	104000	114000
39 7	GULFSTAR 40 SAILMSTR	SLP	SA/CR	FBG KL IB	50D PERK	12 1	20000	4 10	68100	74800
44 8	GULFSTAR 44 MK II	SLP	SA/CR	FBG KL IB	50D PERK	13	26000	5	92900	102000
49	GULFSTAR 49	MY	FBG DS IB	T350D PERK	15 2	39000	5 7	155000	170000
50	GULFSTAR 50 SAILMSTR	SLP	SA/CR	FBG KL IB	135D PERK	14 6	42000	5 6	139500	153500
60 6	GULFSTAR 60	SLP	SA/CR	FBG KL IB	135D PERK	14	57500	6	297000	326500
62 12	GULFSTAR 62 SAILMSTR	SLP	SA/CR	FBG KL IB	135D PERK	16 3	67500	6 9	345000	379500
1982 BOATS
39 8	SAILMASTER	SLP	SA/CR	FBG KL IB	50D PERK	12	19000	5 1	62500	68700
44 4	CRUISING SAILBOAT	SLP	SA/CR	FBG KL IB	62D PERK	13 2	26000	5	87200	95800
44 4	CRUISING SAILBOAT	KTH	SA/CR	FBG KL IB	62D PERK	13 3	26000	5	87200	95800
48 11	COCKPIT MOTOR YACHT	FB	MYCPT	FBG DS IB	T310D GM	15	40500	3 7	149500	164500
48 11	MOTOR YACHT	FB	MY	FBG DS IB	T290D	15	40500		162500	179000
48 11	MOTOR YACHT	FB	MY	FBG DS IB	T310D GM	15	40500	3 7	166500	183000
48 11	MOTOR YACHT	FB	MY	FBG DS IB	T390D J&T	15	40500	3 7	181500	199500
49	SAILMASTER	SLP	SA/CR	FBG KL IB	135D PERK	14 7	38500	5 6	122000	134000
49	SAILMASTER	KTH	SA/CR	FBG KL IB	135D PERK	14 7	38500	5 6	122000	134000
60 6	SAILING AUX SHOAL	SLP	SA/CR	FBG KL IB	135D PERK	16	55400		291000	320000
60 6	SAILING AUX SHOAL	SLP	SA/CR	FBG KL IB	165D PERK	16	55400		287000	315500
60 6	SAILING AUX SHOAL	SLP	SA/CR	FBG KL IB	200D PERK	16	55400		287500	316000
60 6	SAILING AUX SHOAL	KTH	SA/CR	FBG KC IB	135D PERK	16	55400	6	276000	303500
60 6	SAILING AUX SHOAL	KTH	SA/CR	FBG KC IB	165D PERK	16	55400	6	276500	304000
60 6	SAILING AUX SHOAL	KTH	SA/CR	FBG KC IB	200D PERK	16	55400	6	277000	304500
60 6	SAILING AUX SHOAL	KTH	SA/CR	FBG KL IB	135D PERK	16	55400		276000	303500
60 6	SAILING AUX SHOAL	KTH	SA/CR	FBG KL IB	165D PERK	16	55400		276500	304000
60 6	SAILING AUX SHOAL	KTH	SA/CR	FBG KL IB	200D PERK	16	55400		277000	304500
60 6	SAILING AUXILIARY	SLP	SA/CR	FBG KL IB	135D PERK 16		55400		271000	298000
60 6	SAILING AUXILIARY	SLP	SA/CR	FBG KL IB	165D PERK 16		55400		271500	298500
60 6	SAILING AUXILIARY	SLP	SA/CR	FBG KL IB	200D PERK 16		55400		262500	288500
60 6	SAILING AUXILIARY	SLP	SA/CR	FBG KL IB	135D PERK 16		55400		271500	298500
60 6	SAILING AUXILIARY	KTH	SA/CR	FBG KC IB	135D PERK 16		55400	6	276500	303500
60 6	SAILING AUXILIARY	KTH	SA/CR	FBG KC IB	165D PERK 16		55400	6	276500	304000
60 6	SAILING AUXILIARY	KTH	SA/CR	FBG KC IB	200D PERK 16		55400	6	277000	304500
60 6	SAILING AUXILIARY	KTH	SA/CR	FBG KL IB	135D PERK 16		55400		276000	303500
60 6	SAILING AUXILIARY	KTH	SA/CR	FBG KL IB	165D PERK 16		55400		276500	304000
60 6	SAILING AUXILIARY	KTH	SA/CR	FBG KL IB	200D PERK 16		55400		277000	304500
62 2	CRUISING SAILBOAT	SLP	SA/CR	FBG KL IB	200D	16 3	60000		299000	328500
1981 BOATS
38 4	GULFSTAR 38	MY	FBG SV IB	200D	12 5	18000		86500	95100
39 7	SAILMASTER	KTH	SA/CR	FBG KL IB	50D PERK	12 1	19000	4 9	59200	65100
39 8	SAILMASTER	SLP	SA/CR	FBG KL IB	50D PERK	12 1	19000		59200	65100
44 4	CRUISING SAILBOAT	SLP	SA/CR	FBG KL IB	65D PERK	13 2	26000	5	82700	90900
44 4	CRUISING SAILBOAT	KTH	SA/CR	FBG KL IB	65D PERK	13 3	26000	5 6	82700	90900
47 5	GULFSTAR 47	SLP	SA/CR	FBG KL IB	D	13 10	38000	5 6	108000	118500

LOA FT	LOA IN	NAME AND/ OR MODEL	TOP/ RIG	BOAT TYPE	HULL MTL	HULL TP	ENGINE TP	ENGINE # HP	ENGINE MFG	BEAM FT	BEAM IN	WGT LBS	DRAFT FT	DRAFT IN	RETAIL LOW	RETAIL HIGH
		1981 BOATS														
47	5	GULFSTAR 47	KTH	SA/CR	FBG	KL	IB	D		13	10	38000	5	6	108000	118500
48	11	MOTOR YACHT	FB	MY	FBG	DS	IB	T290D	GM	15		40500	3	7	155000	170500
60	6	SAILING AUXILIARY	SLP	SA/CR	FBG	KC	IB	135D	PERK	16		55400	6		261500	287500
60	6	SAILING AUXILIARY	SLP	SA/CR	FBG	KL	IB	135D	PERK	16		55400	6		261500	287500
60	6	SAILING AUXILIARY	KTH	SA/CR	FBG	KC	IB	135D	PERK	16		55400	6		261500	287500
60	6	SAILING AUXILIARY	KTH	SA/CR	FBG	KL	IB	135D	PERK	16		55400	6		261500	287500
		1980 BOATS														
38	4	MOTOR CRUISER	FB	MY	FBG	SV	IB	200D	PERK	12	5	18000	3	3	83600	91800
38	4	MOTOR CRUISER	FB	MY	FBG	SV	IB	T 85D	PERK	12	5	18000	3	3	86700	95300
38	4	MOTOR CRUISER	FB	MY	FBG	SV	IB	T115D	PERK	12	5	18000	3	3	88000	96700
39	7	SAILMASTER	SLP	SA/CR	FBG	KL	IB	50D	PERK	12	1	19000	4	9	56800	62400
44	5	MOTOR CRUISER	FB	MY	FBG	SV	IB	T130D	PERK	14	6	28400	4		105500	116000
44	5	MOTOR CRUISER	FB	MY	FBG	SV	IB	T200D	PERK	14	6	28400	4		98300	108000
44	8	CRUISING SAILBOAT	SLP	SA/CR	FBG	KL	IB	62D	PERK	13	2	26000	5	6	80500	88400
44	8	CRUISING SAILBOAT	KTH	SA/CR	FBG	KL	IB	62D	PERK	13	2	26000	5	6	80500	88400
47	5	SAILMASTER	SLP	SA/CR	FBG	KL	IB	130D	PERK	13	10	38000	5	6	104000	114000
47	5	SAILMASTER	KTH	SA/CR	FBG	KL	IB	130D	PERK	13	10	38000	5	6	104000	114000
50		CRUISING SAILBOAT	SLP	SA/CR	FBG	KL	IB	85D	PERK	13	8	35000	6		114000	125500
50		CRUISING SAILBOAT	KTH	SA/CR	FBG	KL	IB	85D	PERK	13	8	35000	6		114000	125500
		1979 BOATS														
37		CRUISING SAILBOAT	SLP	SA/CR	FBG	KL	IB	50D	PERK	11	10	19500	4	9	51100	56100
44	5	MOTOR CRUISER	FB	MY	FBG	SV	IB	T130D	PERK	14	6		4		117500	129000
44	5	MOTOR CRUISER	FB	MY	FBG	SV	IB	T160D	PERK	14	6		4		119000	130500
47		SAILMASTER	SLP	SA/CR	FBG	KL	IB	130D	PERK	13	10	38000	5	6	99600	109500
47		SAILMASTER	KTH	SA/CR	FBG	KL	IB	130D	PERK	13	10	38000	5	6	99700	109500
		1978 BOATS														
37		CRUISING SAILBOAT	SLP	SA/CR	FBG	KL	IB	50D	PERK	11	10	19500	4	9	49600	54500
40	2	RACER/CRUISER	SLP	SA/RC	FBG	KC	IB	50D	PERK	11	4	24000	3	11	69700	76600
42	7	CRUISING SAILBOAT	SLP	SA/CR	FBG	KL	IB	50D	PERK	11	10	23000	5		66000	72500
42	7	CRUISING SAILBOAT	KTH	SA/CR	FBG	KL	IB	50D	PERK	11	10	23000	5		66000	72500
44	5	MOTOR CRUISER	FB	MY	FBG	SV	IB	T130D	PERK	14	6		3	6	112500	123500
44	5	MOTOR CRUISER	FB	MY	FBG	SV	IB	T160D	PERK	14	6		3	6	113500	125000
47		SAILMASTER	SLP	SA/CR	FBG	KL	IB	130D	PERK	14	2	38000	5	6	96700	106500
47		SAILMASTER	KTH	SA/CR	FBG	KL	IB	130D	PERK	14	2	38000	5	6	96800	106500
50		CRUISING SAILBOAT	SLP	SA/CR	FBG	KL	IB	62D	PERK	13	8	35000	6		107000	117500
50		CRUISING SAILBOAT	KTH	SA/CR	FBG	KL	IB	62D	PERK	13	8	35000	6		107000	117500
		1977 BOATS														
37		AFT COCKPIT	SLP	SA/CR	FBG	KL	IB	50D	PERK	11	10	17000	4	9	42900	47600
37		CENTER COCKPIT	SLP	SA/CR	FBG	KL	IB	50D	PERK	11	10	21000	4	9	51300	56400
40	2	CUSTOM	SLP	SA/RC	FBG	KC	IB	50D	PERK	11	4	24000	3	11	67900	74600
42	7	MARK-II	SLP	SA/CR	FBG	KL	IB	50D	PERK	11	10	22000	5		62700	68800
42	7	MARK-II	KTH	SA/CR	FBG	KL	IB	50D	PERK	11	10	22000	5		62700	68800
43	4	MARK-II TRAWLER	FB	TRWL	FBG	SV	IB	T130D	PERK	13	11		3	6	99500	109500
43	4	MARK-II TRAWLER	FB	TRWL	FBG	SV	IB	T160D	PERK	13	11		3	6	100500	110500
50		MARK-II	SLP	SA/CR	FBG	KL	IB	62D	PERK	13	8	34000	5	9	103500	113500
50		MARK-II	KTH	SA/CR	FBG	KL	IB	62D	PERK	13	8	34000	5	9	103500	113500
		1976 BOATS														
36	3	MARK-II TRAWLER	FB	TRWL	FBG	SV	IB	T 62D	PERK	12		16000	3		49100	53900
37		CRUISING SAILBOAT	SLP	SA/CR	FBG	KL	IB	50D	PERK	11	10	17000	4	9	41800	46500
42		MOTOR SAILER	KTH	MS	FBG	KL	IB	62D	PERK	12			4	9	73000	80200
42	7	CRUISING SAILBOAT	SLP	SA/CR	FBG	KL	IB	50D	PERK	11	10	22000	5		61100	67200
42	7	CRUISING SAILBOAT	KTH	SA/CR	FBG	KL	IB	50D	PERK	11	10	22000	5		61100	67200
43	4	MARK-II TRAWLER	FB	TRWL	FBG	SV	IB	T130D	PERK	13	11	21000	3	6	66700	73300
43	4	MARK-II TRAWLER	FB	TRWL	FBG	SV	IB	T160D	PERK	13	11	21000	3	6	67500	74200
50		CRUISING SAILBOAT	SLP	SA/CR	FBG	KL	IB	62D	PERK	13	8	34000	5	9	101000	110500
50		CRUISING SAILBOAT	KTH	SA/CR	FBG	KL	IB	62D	PERK	13	8	34000	5	9	101000	110500
51	8	MOTOR SAILER	KTH	MS	FBG	KL	IB	130D	PERK	13	11		5		121000	133000
53	2	MARK-II TRAWLER	FB	TRWL	FBG	SV	IB	T130D	PERK	15		42000	4	6	94400	104000
53	2	MARK-II TRAWLER	FB	TRWL	FBG	SV	IB	T160D	PERK	15		42000	4	6	95700	105000
62		MOTOR SAILER	KTH	MS	FBG	KL	IB	D	PERK	15			6		241500	265500
62		MOTOR SAILER	KTH	MS	FBG	KL	IB	185D	PERK	15			6		242000	266000
		1975 BOATS														
36	3	MARK-II TRAWLER	FB	TRWL	FBG	SV	IB	T 62D	PERK	12		16000	3		47300	52000
36	3	MARK-II TRAWLER	FB	TRWL	FBG	SV	IB	T 85D	PERK			16000			47400	52100
41		SAILING AUXILIARY	SLP	SA/CR	FBG	KL	IB	50D	PERK	12		22000	5		57100	62700
41		SAILING AUXILIARY	KTH	SA/CR	FBG	KL	IB	50D	PERK	12		22000	5		57100	62700
43	4	MARK-II TRAWLER	FB	TRWL	FBG	SV	IB	T130D	PERK	13	11	21000	3	6	64000	70400
43	7	MOTOR SAILER	SLP	MS	FBG	KL	IB	130D	PERK	14		22500	3	6	63500	69700
43	7	MOTOR SAILER	SLP	MS	FBG	KL	IB	185D	PERK	14		22500	3	6	63900	70200
43	7	MOTOR SAILER	KTH	MS	FBG	KL	IB	130D	PERK	14		22500	3	6	63500	69800
43	7	MOTOR SAILER	KTH	MS	FBG	KL	IB	185D	PERK	14		22500	3	6	63900	70200
50		SAILING AUXILIARY	SLP	SA/CR	FBG	KL	IB	85D	PERK	13	8	32500	5	6	97500	107000
50		SAILING AUXILIARY	KTH	SA/CR	FBG	KL	IB	85D	PERK	13	8	32500	5	6	97500	107000
53	2	MARK-II TRAWLER	FB	TRWL	FBG	SV	IB	T130D	PERK	15		42000	4	6	90500	99400
53	2	MOTOR SAILER	SLP	MS	FBG	KL	IB	130D	PERK	15		44000	4	6	129000	142000
53	2	MOTOR SAILER	SLP	MS	FBG	KL	IB	225D	PERK	15		44000	4	6	130000	142500
53	2	MOTOR SAILER	KTH	MS	FBG	KL	IB	130D	PERK	15		44000	4	6	129000	142000
53	2	MOTOR SAILER	KTH	MS	FBG	KL	IB	225D	PERK	15		44000	4	6	130000	143000
		1974 BOATS														
36	3	GULFSTAR 36	FB	TRWL	FBG	SV	IB	T 85D	PERK	12		16000	3		46200	50800
41		GULFSTAR 41	SLP	SA/CR	FBG	KL	IB	50D	PERK	12		22000	4	10	55900	61400
41		GULFSTAR 41	KTH	SA/CR	FBG	KL	IB	50D	PERK	12		22000	4	10	55900	61400
43	4	GULFSTAR 43	FB	TRWL	FBG	SV	IB	160D	PERK	13	11	21000	3	6	59100	64900
43	4	GULFSTAR 43	FB	TRWL	FBG	SV	IB	185D	PERK	13	11	21000	3	6	59400	65300
43	4	GULFSTAR 43	FB	TRWL	FBG	SV	IB	T130D	PERK	13	11	21000	3	6	61900	68000
43	7	GULFSTAR 44	SLP	MS	FBG	KL	IB	130D	PERK	14		22500	3	6	62200	68300
43	7	GULFSTAR 44	SLP	MS	FBG	KL	IB	160D	PERK	14		22500	3	6	62400	68600
53	2	GULFSTAR 53	KTH	MS	FBG	KL	IB	130D	PERK	15		32000	4	6	119500	131500
53	2	GULFSTAR 53	KTH	MS	FBG	KL	IB	160D	PERK	15		32000	4	6	120000	132000
53	2	GULFSTAR 53	KTH	MS	FBG	KL	IB	216D	GM	15		32000	4	6	121000	133000
		1973 BOATS														
36	3	GULFSTAR 36	FB	TRWL	FBG	SV	IB	T 85D	PERK	12		16000	3		44000	48900
41		GULFSTAR 41	SLP	SA/CR	FBG	KL	IB	50D	PERK	12		22000	4	10	54900	60300
41		GULFSTAR 41	KTH	SA/CR	FBG	KL	IB	50D	PERK	12		22000	4	10	54900	60300
43	4	GULFSTAR 43	FB	TRWL	FBG	KL	IB	T130D	PERK	13	11	21000	3	6	59900	65800
43	4	GULFSTAR 44	SLP	MS	FBG	KL	IB	130D	PERK	14		22500	3	6	60500	66400
43	4	GULFSTAR 44	KTH	MS	FBG	KL	IB	130D	PERK	14		22500	3	6	60500	66500
53	1	GULFSTAR 53	KTH	MS	FBG	KL	IB	160D	PERK	15		32000	4		117000	128500
		1972 BOATS														
36	3	GULFSTAR 36	SLP	MS	FBG	KL	IB	80D	FORD	12			3		34300	38100
36	3	GULFSTAR 36	KTH	MS	FBG	KL	IB	80D	FORD	12		18800	3		41600	46200
36	3	GULFSTAR 36	HT	TRWL	FBG	SV	IB	80D	FORD	12			3		46500	51100
		IB 128D FORD 47800 52500, IB 185D PERK 48200 53000, IB T 85D PERK													49400	54300
36	3	GULFSTAR 36	FB	TRWL	FBG	SV	IB	80D	FORD	12			3		46500	51100
		IB 128D FORD 47800 52500, IB 185D PERK 48200 53000, IB T 80D FORD													48900	53700
43	4	GULFSTAR 43		TRWL	FBG	SV	IB	T130D	PERK	13	11	23875	3	6	62000	68100
43	4	GULFSTAR 43	HT	TRWL	FBG	SV	IB	D	CAT	13	11	21000	3	6	**	**
		IB 128D FORD 54300 59700, IB 185D PERK 55300 60800, IB T 80D FORD													80700	88600
		IB T128D FORD 81800 89900														
43	4	GULFSTAR 43	FB	TRWL	FBG	SV	IB	D	CAT	13	11		3	6	**	**
		IB 128D FORD 78900 86700, IB 185D PERK 79900 87800, IB T 80D FORD													80400	88400
		IB T128D FORD 81600 89600														
44		GULFSTAR 44	KTH	MS	FBG	KL	IB	120D	FORD	14		22500	3	6	61000	67100
53		GULFSTAR 53	SLP	MS	FBG	KL	IB	D		15		59500	4		128500	141000
53		GULFSTAR 53	KTH	MS	FBG	KL	IB	D		15		59500	4		128500	141000
		1971 BOATS														
36	3	GULFSTAR SALON	SLP	MS	FBG	KL	IB	80D	FORD						33400	37100
36	3	GULFSTAR SALON	SLP	MS	FBG	KL	IB	128D	FORD						33700	37400
43	4	GULFSTAR 43	SLP	MS	FBG	KL	IB	120		13	11	21000	3	6	54700	60100
43	4	GULFSTAR 43	KTH	MS	FBG	KL	IB	120		13	11	21000	3	6	54700	60100
53		GULFSTAR 53	SLP	MS	FBG	KL	IB	120		15		59500	4		124000	136500
53		GULFSTAR 53	KTH	MS	FBG	KL	IB	120		15		59500	4		124000	136500

GULFSTREAM INT'L INC

W PALM BEACH FL

See inside cover to adjust price for area

LOA FT	LOA IN	NAME AND/ OR MODEL	TOP/ RIG	BOAT TYPE	HULL MTL	HULL TP	ENGINE TP	ENGINE # HP	ENGINE MFG	BEAM FT	BEAM IN	WGT LBS	DRAFT FT	DRAFT IN	RETAIL LOW	RETAIL HIGH
		1974 BOATS														
57		GULFSTREAM SHRIMPER			WD		IB	250D	CAT	17	1		4	6	118500	130500
57		TRAWLER		MY	WD		IB	333D		17	2				123000	135000
57		TRAWLER		MY	WD		IB	T333D		17	2				136000	149000
65		TRAWLER		MY	WD		IB	343D		21					196500	216000
65		TRAWLER		MY	WD		IB	T343D		21					226500	249000
75		TRAWLER		MY	WD		IB	343D		23					**	**
75		TRAWLER		MY	WD		IB	T343D		23					**	**
		1973 BOATS														
57		GULFSTREAM SHRIMPER			WD		IB	250D	CAT	17	6	94000	4	6	128000	140500
65		TRAWLER		MY	WD	SV	IB	T343D		21					217500	239000
75		TRAWLER		MY	WD	SV	IB	T343D		23					**	**
		1972 BOATS														
57		GULFSTREAM SHRIMPER			WD		IB	190		18		59000	4	6	88700	97400
57		GULFSTREAM SHRIMPER			WD		IB	250D	CAT	18		59000	4	6	96000	105500
		1971 BOATS														
43			SLP	MS	FBG		IB	D	LEHM						68700	75500

GULL MARINE

Call 1-800-327-6929 for BUC Personalized Evaluation Service
Or, for 1969 to 1970 boats, sign onto www.BUCValuPro.com

H & H SAILCRAFT
DIV OF DYNAMIC PLASTICS COAST GUARD MFG ID- DYP

Call 1-800-327-6929 for BUC Personalized Evaluation Service
Or, for 1972 to 1992 boats, sign onto www.BUCValuPro.com

H M S MARINE CORP
MERRICK NY 11566   See inside cover to adjust price for area

LOA FT IN	NAME AND/ OR MODEL	TOP/ RIG	BOAT TYPE	-HULL- MTL TP	----ENGINE--- TP # HP MFG	BEAM FT IN	WGT LBS	DRAFT FT IN	RETAIL LOW	RETAIL HIGH
				1975 BOATS						
16 7	ISLANDS 17	SLP	SA/OD	FBG CB		6 3		7	1750	2050
22 8	ISLAND 23	SLP	SAIL	FBG KC		7 10		2	3600	4200
22 8	ISLAND 23	SLP	SAIL	FBG KL		7 10		3 6	3600	4200

H-BOAT U S A
WINDOVER SAILS INC   COAST GUARD MFG ID- WSV
FORMERLY WINDOVER SAILS INC

Call 1-800-327-6929 for BUC Personalized Evaluation Service
Or, for 1980 to 1983 boats, sign onto www.BUCValuPro.com

HACKER BOAT COMPANY
HACKERCRAFT   See inside cover to adjust price for area
MADISON CT 06443

LOA FT IN	NAME AND/ OR MODEL	TOP/ RIG	BOAT TYPE	-HULL- MTL TP	----ENGINE--- TP # HP MFG	BEAM FT IN	WGT LBS	DRAFT FT IN	RETAIL LOW	RETAIL HIGH
				1957 BOATS						
26		OP	RNBT	WD	IB				**	**
				1954 BOATS						
20		OP	RNBT	MHG	IB				**	**
20		OP	UTL	MHG	IB				**	**
22		OP	EXP	MHG	IB				**	**
23		OP	RNBT	MHG	IB				**	**
23		OP	UTL	MHG	IB				**	**
26		OP	RNBT	MHG	IB	8			**	**
26		OP	UTL	MHG	IB	8			**	**
				1951 BOATS						
23				WD	IB 160 CHRY				**	**
				1949 BOATS						
25		OP	RNBT	WD	IB 325				4800	5500
25		OP	UTL	WD	IB 225 SCRI				3550	4150
28 6		OP	EXP	WD	IB T CHRY				**	**
				1948 BOATS						
22				WD	IB 238 GRAY				**	**
25				WD	IB 400 FORD				**	**
26				WD	IB SCRI				**	**
				1946 BOATS						
16				WD	IB 60 GRAY				**	**
				1941 BOATS						
34				WD	IB 450 KERM				**	**
				1937 BOATS						
23				WD	IB 115 CHRY				**	**
				1934 BOATS						
27				WD	IB HOLM				**	**
				1932 BOATS						
27				WD	IB 330 CHRY				**	**
32	CUSTOM 3 COCKPITS	OP	RNBT	MHG	IB KERM				**	**
				1931 BOATS						
24		OP	RNBT	MHG	IB				**	**
26		OP	RNBT	MHG	IB 225 KERM				6300	7200
28		OP	RNBT	MHG	IB 225 KERM				6200	7150
30	TWO COCKPITS	OP	RNBT	MHG	IB 225 KERM				5650	6450
35	COMMUTER	HT	CR	MHG	IB T CHRY				**	**
38	COMMUTER	HT	CR	MHG	IB T				**	**
				1930 BOATS						
19				WD	IB GRAY				**	**
23				WD	IB 125 GRAY				**	**
24 4			RNBT	WD	IB 145 CC	6 6			5550	6350
26				WD	IB 225 KERM				**	**
28				WD	IB 200-225				**	**
30				WD	IB 225-288				**	**
30			RNBT	WD	IB PALM	6 11			**	**
				1929 BOATS						
24				WD	IB 190 INT				**	**
26				WD	IB GRAY				**	**
26				WD	IB 225 KERM				**	**
29				WD	IB 140 CHRY				**	**
				1928 BOATS						
26	APBA			WD	IB				**	**
				1927 BOATS						
26				WD	IB 225				**	**
				1926 BOATS						
21				WD	IB 125 SCRI				**	**
26				WD	IB 225 KERM				**	**
				1925 BOATS						
33				WD	IB 225				**	**

MONROE B HALL & ASSOCIATES

Call 1-800-327-6929 for BUC Personalized Evaluation Service
Or, for 1969 boats, sign onto www.BUCValuPro.com

HALLBERG-RASSY VARV A B
ELLOS SWEDEN SE-474 31   COAST GUARD MFG ID- HRV See inside cover to adjust price for area
                         FOR OLDER MODELS SEE XAX CORPORATION

For more recent years, see the BUC Used Boat Price Guide, Volume 1 or Volume 2

LOA FT IN	NAME AND/ OR MODEL	TOP/ RIG	BOAT TYPE	-HULL- MTL TP	----ENGINE--- TP # HP MFG	BEAM FT IN	WGT LBS	DRAFT FT IN	RETAIL LOW	RETAIL HIGH
				1983 BOATS						
25 9	HALLBERG-RASSY 26	SLP	SA/CR	FBG KL SD	8D VLVO 8 8	5500		4 6	24100	26800
28 8	HALLBERG-RASSY 29	SLP	SA/CR	FBG KL SD	17D VLVO 9 2	8360		4 10	39900	44300
30 6	HALLBERG-RASSY 94 MS	SLP	SA/CR	FBG KL IB	35D VLVO 10 6	11440		3 9	56100	61700
30 7	HALLBERG-RASSY 312	SLP	SA/CR	FBG KL IB	23D VLVO 9 10	10780		5 5	52700	58000
34 3	HALLBERG-RASSY 352	SLP	SA/CR	FBG KL IB	61D VLVO 10 11	14740		5 5	71000	78000
37 6	HALLBERG-RASSY 38	SLP	SA/CR	FBG KL IB	61D VLVO 11 4	18700		5 8	91500	100500
41 11	HALLBERG-RASSY 42	SLP	SA/CR	FBG KL IB	61D VLVO 12 5	25300		6 9	129500	142500
41 11	HALLBERG-RASSY 42 SH	SLP	SA/CR	FBG KL IB	61D VLVO 12 5	25300		5 8	129500	142500
49 1	HALLBERG-RASSY 49	SLP	SA/CR	FBG KL IB	72D VLVO 14 6	39700		7 3	208000	229000
				1978 BOATS						
30 9	MONSUN 31	SLP	SA/CR	FBG KL IB	25D VLVO 9 5	9250		4 7	35200	39100
34 6	RASMUS 35	SLP	SA/CR	FBG KL IB	75D VLVO 10 4	12500		4 3	47900	52600
34 6	RASMUS 35	KTH	SA/CR	FBG KL IB	75D VLVO 10 4	12500		4 3	47900	52600
41	HALLBERG-RASSY 41	KTH	SA/CR	FBG KL IB	75D VLVO 11 10	22500		6 1	92100	101000
				1977 BOATS						
30 9	MONSUN 31	SLP	SA/CR	FBG KL IB	25D VLVO 9 5	8800		4 7	32300	35900
34 6	RASMUS 35	SLP	SA/CR	FBG KL IB	75D VLVO 10 4	13500		4 3	49700	54600
34 6	RASMUS 35	KTH	SA/CR	FBG KL IB	75D VLVO 10 4	13500		4 3	49700	54600
41	HALLBERG-RASSY 41	KTH	SA/CR	FBG KL IB	75D VLVO 11 10	21600		5 9	86800	95400

HALLETT BOATS
BARRON BOATS INC.   COAST GUARD MFG ID- BAR

Call 1-800-327-6929 for BUC Personalized Evaluation Service
Or, for 1967 to 2008 boats, sign onto www.BUCValuPro.com

HALLMARK MARINE CORP
COAST GUARD MFG ID- HMB

Call 1-800-327-6929 for BUC Personalized Evaluation Service
Or, for 1974 to 1977 boats, sign onto www.BUCValuPro.com

BENJAMIN HALLOCK

Call 1-800-327-6929 for BUC Personalized Evaluation Service
Or, for 1932 boats, sign onto www.BUCValuPro.com

HALMAN MANUFACTURING COMPANY
DIV OF VORTEX PLASTICS LTD
BEAMSVILLE ONTARIO CANA COAST GUARD MFG ID- ZHL See inside cover to adjust price for area

For more recent years, see the BUC Used Boat Price Guide, Volume 1 or Volume 2

LOA FT IN	NAME AND/ OR MODEL	TOP/ RIG	BOAT TYPE	-HULL- MTL TP	TP # HP	ENGINE MFG	BEAM FT IN	WGT LBS	DRAFT FT IN	RETAIL LOW	RETAIL HIGH
	---------------- 1981 BOATS										
19 8	NORDIC-HALMAN 20	SLP	SAIL	FBG KL	OB		7 9	2500	2 10	3650	4250
27 4	HORIZON 27	SLP	SA/RC	FBG KL	SD	7D VLVO	9 6	6200	4	11800	13500
	---------------- 1980 BOATS										
19 8	NORDIC-HALMAN 20	SLP	SAIL	FBG KL	OB		7 9	2500	2 10	3550	4100

HALMATIC LIMITED
DIV OF HUNTING GROUP
HAVANT HAMP ENGLAND COAST GUARD MFG ID- HMT See inside cover to adjust price for area

For more recent years, see the BUC Used Boat Price Guide, Volume 1 or Volume 2

LOA FT IN	NAME AND/ OR MODEL	TOP/ RIG	BOAT TYPE	-HULL- MTL TP	TP # HP	ENGINE MFG	BEAM FT IN	WGT LBS	DRAFT FT IN	RETAIL LOW	RETAIL HIGH
	---------------- 1983 BOATS										
29 6	HALMATIC 30 MKII	SLP	SA/CR	FBG KL	SD	17D VLVO	9 6	10300	4 6	31300	34700
	---------------- 1979 BOATS										
28 3	HALMATIC 8.80	SLP	MS	FBG TK	IB	30D WATE	9	8440	3	19800	22100
29 6	HALMATIC 30	SLP	SA/CR	FBG KL	IB	13D VLVO	9 6	10080	4 6	24800	27500
33	NICHOLSON 32 MK XI	SLP	SA/CR	FBG KL	IB	30D WATE	9 3	14560	5 6	38300	42600
	---------------- 1972 BOATS										
22	INTERNATL-TEMPEST	SLP	SA/OD	FBG KL			6 6	1020	3 7	1900	2250
	---------------- 1969 BOATS										
33	DARING 5.5	SLP	SA/OD	FBG KL			6 5		4 5	10800	12300
	---------------- 1967 BOATS										
33	DARING 5.5	SLP	SA/OD	FBG KL			6 5		4 9	11200	12700

HALTER MARINE INC
PEARLINGTON MS COAST GUARD MFG ID- XXM See inside cover to adjust price for area

LOA FT IN	NAME AND/ OR MODEL	TOP/ RIG	BOAT TYPE	-HULL- MTL TP	TP # HP	ENGINE MFG	BEAM FT IN	WGT LBS	DRAFT FT IN	RETAIL LOW	RETAIL HIGH
	---------------- 1980 BOATS										
24	COASTAL-FISHERMAN	OP	CTRCN	FBG DV	IB	130D VLVO		8000	1 8	13700	15500
31	COASTAL-FISHERMAN	OP	CUD	FBG DV	IB	192D-197D		8000	2 6	18500	20700
31	COASTAL-FISHERMAN	HT	CUD	FBG DV	IB	197D-265D		8000	2 6	18600	21700
	---------------- 1979 BOATS										
31	COASTAL-FISHERMAN	HT	CUD	FBG DV	IB	OMC		8000	2 6	**	**
31	COASTAL-FISHERMAN	HT	CUD	FBG DV	IB	197D-274D		8000	2 6	17500	21300

HALTER MARINE SERVICES INC
HALMAR
NEW ORLEANS LA 70189 See inside cover to adjust price for area

LOA FT IN	NAME AND/ OR MODEL	TOP/ RIG	BOAT TYPE	-HULL- MTL TP	TP # HP	ENGINE MFG	BEAM FT IN	WGT LBS	DRAFT FT IN	RETAIL LOW	RETAIL HIGH
	---------------- 1971 BOATS										
38	HALMAR 3L	SF	AL	SV	IB	T250D GM	13	16000	3 2	21800	24300
44	HALMAR 44	SF	AL	SV	IB	T350D GM	14 4	30000	3 6	40200	44700
55	HALMAR 55	SF	AL	SV	IB	T500D GM	15 3	45000	4 6	60400	66400
65	HALMAR 65	HB	AL	SV	IB	T900D GM	20	60000	3 6	82700	90900

HALVORSEN GOWLAND PTY LTD

Call 1-800-327-6929 for BUC Personalized Evaluation Service
Or, for 1977 boats, sign onto www.BUCValuPro.com

LARS HALVORSEN SONS PTY LTD

Call 1-800-327-6929 for BUC Personalized Evaluation Service
Or, for 1972 to 1973 boats, sign onto www.BUCValuPro.com

HAMMOND BOAT CO
AUSTIN TX 78762 COAST GUARD MFG ID- RRH See inside cover to adjust price for area

For more recent years, see the BUC Used Boat Price Guide, Volume 1 or Volume 2

LOA FT IN	NAME AND/ OR MODEL	TOP/ RIG	BOAT TYPE	-HULL- MTL TP	TP # HP	ENGINE MFG	BEAM FT IN	WGT LBS	DRAFT FT IN	RETAIL LOW	RETAIL HIGH
	---------------- 1983 BOATS										
17	CORDOBA SL V1725	OP	RNBT	FBG DV	IO	120 MRCR	7	2050		3150	3700
17	GRANADA V1750 SPORT	OP	RNBT	FBG DV	IO	120-170	7	2050		3150	3700
17	GRANADA V175OSL	OP	RNBT	FBG DV	IO	120-170	7	2050		3150	3700
17 6	CONTENDER V1800	OP	RNBT	FBG DV	OB		7 1	1275		4000	4700
17 6	CONTENDER V1850	OP	RNBT	FBG DV	IO	170-198	7 1	2000		3250	3850
19 4	EL-DORADO V1950SL	OP	RNBT	FBG DV	IO	198-260	7 6	2700		4400	5350
19 4	ESPADA V1925SL	OP	RNBT	FBG DV	IO	198-260	7 6	2400		4150	4800
19 4	MONTE-CARLO V1930SL	OP	RNBT	FBG DV	IO	170-260	7 6	2250		3950	4950
19 4	SEVILLE V1975SL	OP	CUD	FBG DV	IO	198-260	7 6	2700		4600	5550
19 4	ST-TROPEZ V1940SPORT	OP	RNBT	FBG DV	IO	198-260	7 6	2700		4400	5350
19 4	ST-TROPEZ V1940XL	OP	RNBT	FBG DV	IO	198-260	7 6	2700		4550	5450
21	CHALLENGER MII V2100	OP	CUD	FBG DV	OB		7 7	1500		5800	6650
21	CHALLENGER MII V2150	OP	CUD	FBG DV	IO	260 MRCR	7 7	2700		5750	6650
21	CHALLENGER MKIIV2100	OP	CUD	FBG DV	IO	198-200	7 7	2700		5500	6300
	---------------- 1982 BOATS										
17	CORDOBA SPORT V1725	ST	RNBT	FBG DV	IO	120-170	7	2050		3100	3600
17	GRANADA V1750	ST	RNBT	FBG DV	IO	120-170	7	2100		3150	3650
17	GRANADA V1750SL	ST	RNBT	FBG DV	IO	120-140	7	2100		3150	3650
17	MARBELLA V1740XL	ST	RNBT	FBG DV	IO	140-170	7	2100		3450	4050
17	MARSEILLE V1730	ST	RNBT	FBG DV	IO	140	7			3100	3600
17 6	CONTENDER V-1800	ST	RNBT	FBG DV	OB		7 1	1175		3700	4300
17 6	CONTENDER V-1850	ST	RNBT	FBG DV	IO	140 OMC	7 1	1175		2600	3050
17 6	CONTENDER V-1850	ST	RNBT	FBG DV	IO	140-198	7 1	2250		3350	4100
17 6	CONTENDER V1850	ST	RNBT	FBG DV	IO	228 MRCR	7 1	2460		3700	4300
19 4	ESPADA SPORT V1925	ST	RNBT	FBG DV	IO	170-198	7 6	2700		4200	4900
19 4	ESPADA SPORT V1925	ST	RNBT	FBG DV	IO	260	7 6	2700		4600	5350
19 4	MONTE-CARLO V1930	ST	RNBT	FBG DV	IO	170-198	7 6	2250		3800	4550
19 4	MONTE-CARLO V1930SL	ST	RNBT	FBG DV	IO	170-198	7 6	2250		3800	4550
19 4	ESPADA SPORT V-1975	ST	CUD	FBG DV	IO	170-198	7 6	2750		4450	5250
19 4	SEVILLE SPORT V-1975	ST	CUD	FBG DV	IO	260	7 6	2750		4700	5800
19 4	SEVILLE SPORT V1975	ST	CUD	FBG DV	IO	260 MRCR	7 6	2750		4850	5600
19 4	ST-TROPEZ V-1940	ST	RNBT	FBG DV	IO	170-198	7 6	2700		4200	4950
19 4	ST-TROPEZ V-1940	ST	RNBT	FBG DV	IO	260	7 6	2700		4600	5350
19 4	ST-TROPEZ XL V-1940	ST	RNBT	FBG DV	IO	170-198	7 6	2700		4250	5050
19 4	ST-TROPEZ XL V-1940	ST	RNBT	FBG DV	IO	260	7 6	2700		4550	5450
21	CHALLENGER V-2100	ST	RACE	FBG DV	OB		7 7	1600		6000	6900
21	CHALLENGER V-2150	ST	RACE	FBG DV	IO	260 MRCR	7 7	2750		5350	6150
	---------------- 1981 BOATS										
17	CORDOBA 1700		RNBT	FBG DV	OB		7	1500		4400	5050
17	CORDOBA SPORT V1725	ST	RNBT	FBG DV	IO	140-185	6 11	2050		2950	3450
17	CORDOBA V1725XL	ST	RNBT	FBG DV	IO	140-185	6 11	2050		2950	3500
17	GRANADA 1750		RNBT	FBG DV	OB	170	7			3100	3600
17	GRANADA V1700	ST	RNBT	FBG DV	OB		6 11	1500		3100	3600
17	GRANADA V1750 SPORT		RNBT	FBG DV	IO	170	7			3100	3600
17	MARBELLA V1740	ST	RNBT	FBG DV	IO	140-185	6 11	2050		2950	3650
17	MARBELLA V1740XL	ST	RNBT	FBG DV	IO	140-185	6 11	2050		3150	3700
19 4	EL-DORADO 1950		RNBT	FBG DV	IO	170-198	7 6			4450	5100
19 4	ESPADA SPORT V1925	ST	RNBT	FBG DV	IO	170-198	7 6	2700		4050	4800
19 4	ESPADA SPORT V1925	ST	RNBT	FBG DV	IO	260 MRCR	7 6	2700		4400	5100
19 4	ESPADA SPT LUX V1925	ST	RNBT	FBG DV	IO	170-260	7 6	2700		4100	5100
19 4	ESPADA V1925XL	ST	RNBT	FBG DV	IO	170-198	7 6	2700		4150	4900
19 4	ESPADA V1925XL	ST	RNBT	FBG DV	IO	260 MRCR	7 6	2700		4500	5200
19 4	MONTE-CARLO V1930	ST	RNBT	FBG DV	IO	170-198	7 6	2250		3800	4550
19 4	SEVILLE SPORT V-1975	ST	CUD	FBG DV	IO	170-260	7 6	2750		4400	5450
19 4	SEVILLE V-1975	ST	CUD	FBG DV	IO	170-260	7 6	2750		4350	5350
19 4	ST-TROPEZ LUX V-1940	ST	RNBT	FBG DV	IO	170-260	7 6	2700		4200	5250
19 4	ST-TROPEZ SPT V1940	ST	RNBT	FBG DV	IO	170-198	7 6	2700		4200	5250
19 4	ST-TROPEZ V-1940	ST	RNBT	FBG DV	IO	170 OMC	7 6	2700		4150	4850
19 4	ST-TROPEZ XL V-1940	ST	RNBT	FBG DV	IO	170-260	7 6	2700		4250	5450
21	CHALLENGER L3E	ST	RACE	FBG DV	OB		7 7	2700		5200	6000
21	CHALLENGER V-2100	ST	RACE	FBG DV	OB		7 7	1600		5850	6750
21	CHALLENGER V-2150	ST	RACE	FBG DV	IO	260 MRCR	7 7	2700		5200	5900
21	CHALLENGER XL V-2100	ST	RACE	FBG DV	OB		7 7	1600		5950	6850
21	CHALLENGER XL V-2150	ST	RACE	FBG DV	IO	260 MRCR	7 7	2700		5200	6000
	---------------- 1980 BOATS										
17	CORDOBA V-1725	OP	RNBT	FBG DV	IO	165	6 11	1960		2950	3400
17	CORDOBA XL V-1725	OP	RNBT	FBG DV	IO	165	6 11	1960		2950	3450
17	GRANADA V-1750	OP	RNBT	FBG DV	OB		6 11	1500		4300	5000
17	GRANADA V-1750	OP	RNBT	FBG DV	IO	165	6 11	2050		3000	3500
17	MARBELLA V-1740	OP	RNBT	FBG DV	IO	165	6 11	2050		3000	3500
17	MARBELLA XL V-1740	OP	RNBT	FBG DV	IO	165	6 11	2050		3050	3550
19 4	EL-DORADO V-1950	OP	RNBT	FBG DV	IO	260	7 6	2700		4450	5100

284   CONTINUED ON NEXT PAGE   96th ed. - Vol. III

LOA FT IN	NAME AND/ OR MODEL	TOP/ RIG	BOAT TYPE	-HULL- MTL TP	----ENGINE--- TP # HP MFG	BEAM FT IN	WGT LBS	DRAFT FT IN	RETAIL LOW	RETAIL HIGH
					--- 1980 BOATS ---					
19 4	ESPADA V-1925	OP	RNBT	FBG DV	IO 260	7 6	2700		4400	5050
19 4	ESPADA XL V-1925	OP	RNBT	FBG DV	IO 260	7 6	2700		4450	5150
19 4	SEVILLE V-1975		RNBT	FBG DV	IO 260	7 6	2750		4500	5200
19 4	ST-TROPEZ V-1950	OP	RNBT	FBG DV	IO 260	7 6	2700		4500	5150
19 4	ST-TROPEZ XL V-1950	OP	RNBT	FBG DV	IO 260	7 6	2700		4550	5250
21 4	CHALLENGER V-2150		RNBT	FBG DV	IO 260	7 7	2700		5350	6150
					--- 1979 BOATS ---					
17	CORDOBA V-1725	ST	RNBT	FBG DV	IO 165-185	7	2140		3100	3600
17	GRANADA V-1700	OP	RNBT	FBG DV	OB	7	1500		4250	4950
17	GRANADA V-1750	ST	RNBT	FBG DV	IO 165-185	7	2250		3200	3700
19 4	EL-DORADO V-1900	OP	RNBT	FBG DV	OB	7 6	1500		4600	5250
19 4	EL-DORADO V-1950	ST	RNBT	FBG DV	IO 228-260	7 6	2700		4250	5100
19 4	ESPADA V-1925	ST	RNBT	FBG DV	IO 228-260	7 6	2700		4200	5050
19 4	ESPADA XL V-1925	ST	RNBT	FBG DV	IO 228-260	7 6	2700		4250	5100
19 4	SEVILLE V-1975	ST	RNBT	FBG DV	IO 228-260	7 6	2750		4350	5200
19 4	ST-TROPEZ V-1940	ST	RNBT	FBG DV	IO 228-260	7 6	2700		4350	5200
19 4	ST-TROPEZ XL V-1940	ST	RNBT	FBG DV	IO 228-260	7 6	2700		4400	5250
21 4	CHALLENGER V-2150	ST	RNBT	FBG DV	IO 260 MRCR	7 6	2900		5500	6350
					--- 1978 BOATS ---					
17	CORDOBA	OP	RNBT	FBG SV	IO 165	6 11	2050		3050	3550
17	GRANADA	OP	RNBT	FBG SV	IO 165	6 11	2150		3100	3600
19	ESPADA	OP	RNBT	FBG SV	IO 225	7 5	2600		4100	4750
19	SEVILLE	OP	RNBT	FBG SV	IO 225	7 5	2700		4200	4850
19 4	EL-DORADO	OP	RNBT	FBG SV	OB	7 6	1500		4400	5050
19 4	EL-DORADO	OP	RNBT	FBG SV	IO 228-250	7 6			4250	5050
19 4	EL-DORADO ELITE	OP	RNBT	FBG SV	OB	7 6	1500		4650	5350
19 4	EL-DORADO ELITE	OP	RNBT	FBG SV	IO 228-250	7 6			4250	5050
19	ESPADA V-1925	OP	RNBT	FBG SV	IO 225	7 6	2650		4250	4950
					--- 1977 BOATS ---					
16	PORTO-FINE	OP	RNBT	FBG TR	IO 120	6 2			2750	3200
17	CORDOBA	OP	RNBT	FBG SV	IO 140	6 11	2050		3050	3550
17	CORDOBA ELITE	OP	RNBT	FBG SV	IO 165	6 11	2050		3100	3600
19	SEVILLE		RNBT	FBG SV	IO 190	7 5	2700		4150	4850
19	SEVILLE ELITE		RNBT	FBG SV	IO 235	7 5	2700		4300	5000
19 4	ELDORADO-ELITE V1950	OP	RNBT	FBG SV	IO 233 MRCR	7 5	2700		4450	5100
					--- 1976 BOATS ---					
17	GRANADA V-1700	OP	RNBT	FBG SV	OB	7			4100	4750
17	GRANADA V-1750	OP	RNBT	FBG SV	IO 140-165	7	1950		3100	3750
19 4	EL-DORADO V-1950	OP	RNBT	FBG SV	IO 188-233	7 6	2650		4400	5250

HAMPTON SHIPYARDS

COLUMBIA
EAST QUOGUE NY 11942   COAST GUARD MFG ID- HPN   See inside cover to adjust price for area

LOA FT IN	NAME AND/ OR MODEL	TOP/ RIG	BOAT TYPE	-HULL- MTL TP	----ENGINE--- TP # HP MFG	BEAM FT IN	WGT LBS	DRAFT FT IN	RETAIL LOW	RETAIL HIGH
					--- 1968 BOATS ---					
30		SF	WD	IB	200	11 6		2 6	8500	9750
30		SF	WD	IB	T265	11 6		2 6	9850	11200
34		SF	WD	IB	T200-T265	12 6		2 10	15000	17500
38		SF	WD	IB	T200	13 6		3 1	28200	31300
38		SF	WD	IB	T300	13 6		3 1	28600	31700
					--- 1967 BOATS ---					
30 2 4	SLEEPER CUSTOM	HT	EXP	WD	IB 200				9550	10800
30 2 4	SLEEPER CUSTOM	HT	EXP	WD	IB T250				11000	12500
30 2 4	SLEEPER CUSTOM	FB	EXP	WD	IB 200				9550	10800
30 2 4	SLEEPER CUSTOM	FB	EXP	WD	IB T250				11000	12500
30 2	CUSTOM		SDN	WD	IB 200				9050	10300
30 2	CUSTOM		SDN	WD	IB T250				10700	12200
30 2	CUSTOM	FB	SDN	WD	IB 200				9050	10300
30 2	CUSTOM	FB	SDN	WD	IB T250				10700	12200
30 2	FAMILY		SF	WD	IB 200				8200	9450
30 2	FAMILY		SF	WD	IB T250				9450	10700
30 2	FAMILY SPORT	FB		WD	IB 200				8150	9400
30 2	FAMILY SPORT	FB		WD	IB T250				9400	10700
30 8	RAISED DECK	FB	SF	WD	IB T200-T250				10000	11700
34 6	FAMILY		SF	WD	IB T200-T250				15200	17400
34 6	FAMILY SPORT	FB		WD	IB T200-T250				19500	21800
34 6	MULTI	FB	SDN	WD	IB T200				18700	20800
34 6	MULTI CABIN		SDN	WD	IB T200				18700	20800
34 6	RAISED DECK		FSH	WD	IB T200				15300	17300
34 6	RAISED DECK	FB	SF	WD	IB T200				15200	17300
34 6	TWIN CABIN	HT	EXP	WD	IB T200				17500	19900
34 6	TWIN CABIN	FB	EXP	WD	IB T200				17500	19900
38 2	DELUXE		SDN	WD	IB T250				31200	34700
38 2	RAISED DECK		SF	WD	IB T250				29300	32500
41		SF	WD	IB					**	**
44		SF	WD	IB					**	**
					--- 1966 BOATS ---					
30 2 4	SLEEPER CUSTOM	FB	EXP	WD	IB 200				9200	10400
30 2 4	SLEEPER CUSTOM	FB	EXP	WD	IB 250				9400	10700
30 2 4	SLEEPER CUSTOM	FB	EXP	WD	IB T250				10500	12200
30 2 6	SLEEPER CUSTOM	FB	EXP	WD	IB 200				9350	10600
30 2 6	SLEEPER CUSTOM	FB	EXP	WD	IB 250				9550	10800
30 2 6	SLEEPER CUSTOM	FB	EXP	WD	IB T250				10700	12200
30 2	CUSTOM	FB	SDN	WD	IB 200				8600	9900
30 2	CUSTOM	FB	SDN	WD	IB 250				9050	10300
30 2	CUSTOM	FB	SDN	WD	IB T250				10300	11800
30 2	FAMILY SPORT	FB		WD	IB 200				7850	9050
30 2	FAMILY SPORT	FB		WD	IB 250				8100	9300
30 2	FAMILY SPORT	FB		WD	IB T250				9100	10400
30 8	RAISED DECK	FB	SF	WD	IB T200-T250				9700	11300
34 6	MULTI	FB	SDN	WD	IB T200-T250				18000	20400
34 6	RAISED DECK	FB	SF	WD	IB T200-T250				14700	17000
					--- 1965 BOATS ---					
30 2	CUSTOM	HT	EXP	WD	IB 230				9100	10300
30 2	CUSTOM	HT	EXP	WD	IB 170D				14000	15900
30 2	CUSTOM	HT	EXP	WD	IB T230				10100	11500
30 2	CUSTOM		EXP	WD	IB 23				8450	9700
30 2	CUSTOM	FB	EXP	WD	IB 170D				14000	15900
30 2	CUSTOM	FB	EXP	WD	IB T230				10100	11500
30 2	CUSTOM		SDN	WD	IB 230				8500	9800
30 2	CUSTOM		SDN	WD	IB 170D				17200	19600
30 2	CUSTOM		SDN	WD	IB T230				9900	11300
30 2	CUSTOM	FB	SDN	WD	IB 230				8500	9800
30 2	CUSTOM	FB	SDN	WD	IB 170D				17200	19600
30 2	CUSTOM	FB	SDN	WD	IB T230				9900	11300
30 2	FAMILY SPORT	FB		WD	IB 230				7700	8850
30 2	FAMILY SPORT	FB		WD	IB 170D				11500	13000
30 2	FAMILY SPORT	FB		WD	IB T230				8550	9850
30 8	RAISED DECK	FB	SF	WD	IB T230				9500	10800
30 8	RAISED DECK	FB	SF	WD	IB T170D				17200	19500
34 6	DELUXE		SDN	WD	IB 230				28400	31600
34 6	DELUXE		SDN	WD	IB T170D				17200	19500
34 6	DELUXE	FB	SDN	WD	IB T230				28400	31600
34 6	RAISED DECK		FSH	WD	IB T250				14500	16400
34 6	RAISED DECK		FSH	WD	IB T170D				21900	24300
34 6	RAISED DECK	FB	SF	WD	IBT170D-T250D				24800	29000
34 6	TWIN CABIN	HT	EXP	WD	IB T170D				16500	18700
34 6	TWIN CABIN	HT	EXP	WD	IB T170D				27300	30400
34 6	TWIN CABIN	FB	EXP	WD	IBT170D-T230D				27300	31500
38 2		FB	DC	WD	IB T250				26200	29100
38 2		FB	DC	WD	IB T250D				31800	35300
38 2			SDN	WD	IB T250				29600	32800
38 2			SDN	WD	IB T217D				33300	37000
38 2		FB	SDN	WD	IB T250				29600	32800
38 2		FB	SDN	WD	IB T217D				33300	37000
38 2	RAISED DECK	FB	SF	WD	IB T250				27700	30800
38 2	RAISED DECK	FB	SF	WD	IB T217D				35500	39500
42			SF	WD	IB T280D				41800	46500
44			MY	WD	IB T280D				46500	51100
					--- 1963 BOATS ---					
30			SDN	WD	IB 175-260				7450	9150
30			SDN	WD	IB T178-T225				8500	10300
30 4	SLEEPER CUSTOM	HT	EXP	WD	IB 175-260				7800	9400
30 4	SLEEPER CUSTOM	HT	EXP	WD	IB T178-T225				8650	10300
30 6	SLEEPER CUSTOM	HT	EXP	WD	IB 175-260				8100	9800
30 6	SLEEPER CUSTOM	HT	EXP	WD	IB T178-T225				9050	10700
30	FAMILY		SF	WD	IB 175-260				6900	8300
30	FAMILY		SF	WD	IB T178-T225				7600	9050
36 8	CUSTOM DELUXE		SDN	WD	IB T280				20400	22700
36 8	DELUXE		SDN	WD	IB T280				21100	23500
					--- 1962 BOATS ---					
30 2	COLUMBIA 4 SLEEPER	HT	EXP	WD	IB 175-225				7900	9350
30 2	COLUMBIA 4 SLEEPER	HT	EXP	WD	IB T178-T225				8500	10400
30 2	COLUMBIA 4 SLEEPER		SF	WD	IB 175-225				6850	8100
30 2	COLUMBIA 4 SLEEPER		SF	WD	IB T178-T225				7500	8950
30 2	COLUMBIA 6 SLEEPER	HT	EXP	WD	IB 175-225				7900	9350

LOA FT IN	NAME AND/ OR MODEL	TOP/ RIG	BOAT TYPE	-HULL- MTL TP	TP	----ENGINE--- # HP MFG	BEAM FT IN	WGT LBS	DRAFT FT IN	RETAIL LOW	RETAIL HIGH
---	--- ---	1962	BOATS	---							
30 2	COLUMBIA 6 SLEEPER	HT	EXP	WD	IB	T178-T225				8850	10400
30 2	COLUMBIA 6 SLEEPER		SDN	WD	IB	175-225				7400	8850
30 2	COLUMBIA 6 SLEEPER		SDN	WD	IB	T178-T225				8450	10200
36 8			SDN	WD	IB	T210				20300	22600
36 8			SDN	WD	IB	T215				20300	22600
36 8			SDN	WD	IB	T225				20400	22600
36 8			SF	WD	IB	T210				19700	21900
36 8			SF	WD	IB	T215				19700	21900
36 8			SF	WD	IB	T225				19800	22100
---	--- ---	1961	BOATS	---							
28	COLUMBIA		CR	P/M	IB	135	10 3		2 2	5500	6300
30	COLUMBIA		SF	P/M	IB	135	10 6		2 2	6450	7450
34	COLUMBIA		SF	P/M	IB	135	11 6		2 4	11600	13200
35	HAMPTON		CR	P/M	IB	135				13400	15200
38	COLUMBIA		CF	P/M	IB	135	12 6		2 5	24400	27100
---	--- ---	1960	BOATS	---							
28	COLUMBIA		CR	P/M	IB	170-225	10 3		2 2	5550	6600
28	HAMPTON		SF	P/M	IB	190-225	9 6		2 2	5600	6550
30	COLUMBIA		SDN	WD	IB	225				7300	8350
---	--- ---	1958	BOATS	---							
27	COLUMBIA		EXP	WD	IB	125				4350	5000

HANCOCK & LANE LTD

Call 1-800-327-6929 for BUC Personalized Evaluation Service
Or, for 1980 to 1983 boats, sign onto www.BUCValuPro.com

WILLIAM HAND

Call 1-800-327-6929 for BUC Personalized Evaluation Service
Or, for 1931 to 1937 boats, sign onto www.BUCValuPro.com

TED HANES MARINE & CABLE

Call 1-800-327-6929 for BUC Personalized Evaluation Service
Or, for 1969 boats, sign onto www.BUCValuPro.com

CHARLES HANKINS
COAST GUARD MFG ID- CHS

Call 1-800-327-6929 for BUC Personalized Evaluation Service
Or, for 1959 to 1988 boats, sign onto www.BUCValuPro.com

JOHN HANNA

See inside cover to adjust price for area

LOA FT IN	NAME AND/ OR MODEL	TOP/ RIG	BOAT TYPE	-HULL- MTL TP	TP	----ENGINE--- # HP MFG	BEAM FT IN	WGT LBS	DRAFT FT IN	RETAIL LOW	RETAIL HIGH
---	--- ---	1952	BOATS	---							
30	TAHITI	KTH	SAIL	WD	IB	50 GRAY				12100	13800
---	--- ---	1938	BOATS	---							
28	GULFWIND		SAIL	WD	IB	29 GRAY				19000	21100

HANNAY MARINE LTD

Call 1-800-327-6929 for BUC Personalized Evaluation Service
Or, for 1970 boats, sign onto www.BUCValuPro.com

HARBOR BOAT BUILDING COMPANY

Call 1-800-327-6929 for BUC Personalized Evaluation Service
Or, for 1946 to 1973 boats, sign onto www.BUCValuPro.com

HARBOR CRAFT
DIV OF HOLIDAY RAMBLER CORP   See inside cover to adjust price for area
NAPPANEE IN 46550   COAST GUARD MFG ID- HHD

For more recent years, see the BUC Used Boat Price Guide, Volume 1 or Volume 2

LOA FT IN	NAME AND/ OR MODEL	TOP/ RIG	BOAT TYPE	-HULL- MTL TP	TP	----ENGINE--- # HP MFG	BEAM FT IN	WGT LBS	DRAFT FT IN	RETAIL LOW	RETAIL HIGH
---	--- ---	1983	BOATS	---							
20 2	VACATIONER 200	ST	CUD	FBG DV	IO	188 MRCR	7 7	3856		5250	6050
24 2	TARGA 240	ST	SPTCR	FBG DV	IO	T188-T260	8	7065		12800	15600
24 2	VACATIONER 240	ST	CUD	FBG DV	IO	188-260	8	6185		9850	11700
25 10	TARGA 260	ST	SPTCR	FBG DV	IO	T188 MRCR	8	7810		13900	15800
25 10	TARGA 260	ST	SPTCR	FBG DV	IO	T260 MRCR	8	8140		15300	17400
---	--- ---	1974	BOATS	---							
46	HARBOR-HOUSE	FB	HB	AL	TR	IB T325 MRCR	13 6	20500		34000	37800
46	HARBOR-HOUSE	FB	HB	AL	TR	IB T225D CAT	13 6	23000		43300	48100
---	--- ---	1973	BOATS	---							
46	HARBOR-HOUSE	FB	HB	AL	TR	IB 255 MRCR	13 6	20500	3	31200	34700
46	HARBOR-HOUSE	FB	HB	AL	TR	IB T255 WAUK	13 6	20500	3	33000	36600
46	HARBOR-HOUSE	FB	HB	AL	TR	IB T210D CAT	13 6	20500	3	40700	45200

HARBOR MASTER BOATS
DIV OF E M G INC   See inside cover to adjust price for area
GALLATIN TN 37066   COAST GUARD MFG ID- EVX
                          FORMERLY BOATING CORP OF AMERICA

For more recent years, see the BUC Used Boat Price Guide, Volume 1 or Volume 2

LOA FT IN	NAME AND/ OR MODEL	TOP/ RIG	BOAT TYPE	-HULL- MTL TP	TP	----ENGINE--- # HP MFG	BEAM FT IN	WGT LBS	DRAFT FT IN	RETAIL LOW	RETAIL HIGH
---	--- ---	1983	BOATS	---							
34	HARBOR-MASTER 3400		CR	FBG SV	IB	T220	13	16000		27000	30000
37 2	HARBOR-MASTER 375		HT	HB	FBG SV	IB	200	12		37400	41500
43 5	HARBOR-MASTER-435		HT	HB	FBG SV	IB	260	14	19000	2 4	43400	48200
48	HARBOR-MASTER 480		HT	HB	FBG SV	IB	330	14	25000		69700	76500
---	--- ---	1982	BOATS	---							
34	HARBOR-MASTER 3400		CR	FBG SV	IB	T220	13	1 16000		25800	28700
37 2	HARBOR-MASTER 375		HT	HB	FBG SV	IB	200	12		29700	33000
37 2	HARBOR-MASTER 375		HT	HB	FBG SV	IB	T170	12		30800	34200
43 6	HARBOR-MASTER 435		HT	HB	FBG SV	IO	260	14		68400	75200
43 6	HARBOR-MASTER 435		HT	HB	FBG SV	IB	T170	14		69100	75900
48	HARBOR-MASTER 480		HT	HB	FBG SV	IB	330	14		51600	56700
48	HARBOR-MASTER 480		HT	HB	FBG SV	IB	330	14	25000		68400	75200
---	--- ---	1981	BOATS	---							
34	HARBOR-MASTER 3400		FB	CR	FBG DV	IB	T220-T330	13	1 25000	3 4	31700	36300
34	HARBOR-MASTER 3400		FB	CR	FBG DV	IBT130D-T215D	13	1 25000	3 4	42900	47900
37 2	HARBOR-MASTER 375		HT	HB	FBG SV	IO	T70 MRCR	12	12000	2 6	12900	14600
	IO 228 MRCR	29300		32600, IO	260	VLVO	13800	15700, IO	330	MRCR	30900	34300
	IO 130D VLVO	33200		36900, VD	155	CRUS	30500	33900, IO	T170	MRCR	25800	28700
	VD T170 MRCR	25500		28400, VD	T220	CRUS	30900	34300, IO	T228	MRCR	31000	34500
	VD T228 MRCR	30500		33900, VD	T255	MRCR	30600	34000, IO	T260	VLVO	32400	36000
	VD T270 CRUS	31100		34600, VD	T330	MRCR	34100	37900, VD	T330	MRCR	31300	34800
	VD T350 CRUS	32200		35800								
37 2	HARBOR-MASTER 375		FB	HB	FBG SV	IO	170 MRCR	12		2 6	29100	32300
	IO 228 MRCR	29300		32600, IO	260	VLVO	30000	33400, IO	330	MRCR	14700	16700
	VD T155 CRUS	30500		33900, IO	T170	MRCR	30600	34000, VD	T170	MRCR	30300	33600
	VD T220 CRUS	37900		42100, IO	T228	MRCR	30400	34500, VD	T228	CRUS	30500	33900
	VD T255 MRCR	34000		37900, VD	T260	VLVO	32400	36000, VD	T270	CRUS	31100	34600
	VD T330 MRCR	34100		37900, VD	T330	MRCR	31300	34800, VD	T350	CRUS	32200	35800
	IO T130D VLVO	42300		47000								
43 5	HARBOR-MASTER 435		HT	HB	FBG SV	IO	260	VLVO	14	16000	2 6	25100	27900
	VD T155 CRUS	30100		33500, VD	T170	MRCR	30200	33600, VD	T228	MRCR	30600	34100
	VD T228 MRCR	30100		33500, VD	T255	MRCR	30200	33600, VD	T330	MRCR	33700	37500
43 5	HARBOR-MASTER 435		FB	HB	FBG SV	IO	228	MRCR	14	16000	2 6	24400	27200
	IO 330 MRCR	26000		28900, VD	T155	CRUS	30100	33500, VD	T170	MRCR	30200	33600
	VD T170 MRCR	29900		33200, VD	T220	CRUS	30500	33900, VD	T228	MRCR	30100	33500
	VD T255 MRCR	30200		33600, VD	T260	MRCR	32900	35600, VD	T270	CRUS	31100	34600
43 6	HARBOR-MASTER 435		HT	HB	FBG SV	IO	228	MRCR	14	16000	2 6	24300	27000
	IO 330 MRCR	68500		75300, IO	130D	VLVO	81700	89700, IO	T170	MRCR	25200	28000
	VD T220 CRUS	68500		75300, IO	T260	VLVO	70000	77000, VD	T270	CRUS	68700	75500
	VD T330 MRCR	69000		75800, VD	T350	CRUS	69900	76800, IO	T130D	VLVO	84600	93000
43 6	HARBOR-MASTER 435		FB	HB	FBG SV	IO	260	VLVO	14		3	67700	74400
	IO 130D VLVO	81700		89700, IO	T228	MRCR	68700	75500, VD	T330	MRCR	71700	78800
	VD T330 MRCR	69000		75800, VD	T350	CRUS	44800	49800, IO	T130D	VLVO	84600	93000
---	--- ---	1980	BOATS	---							
34	HARBOR-MASTER 3400		FB	CR	FBG DV	IB	T220-T330	13	25000	3 4	30400	34800
34	HARBOR-MASTER 3400		FB	CR	FBG DV	IBT120D-T215D	13	25000	3 4	41400	46100
34	HARBOR-MASTER S/3500		CR	FBG DV	IB	T255	13	17000		24800	27500

```
  LOA  NAME AND/           TOP/ BOAT  -HULL- ----ENGINE--- BEAM      WGT   DRAFT  RETAIL RETAIL
 FT IN OR MODEL            RIG TYPE   MTL TP TP # HP  MFG  FT IN     LBS   FT IN   LOW    HIGH
------------------- 1980 BOATS --------------------------------------------------------------
 35    HARBOR-MASTER 35    HT  HB     FBG SV IO  170       12                9450  10700
    SD 220           9450  10700, IB T200       9850  11200, IO T330        11400  13000

 37  2 HARBOR-MASTER 375   HT  HB     FBG SV IO  170  MRCR 12     12000  2 6 12700  14400
    IO  228  MRCR  28900  32100, IO  260  VLVO 13600  15400, IO  330  MRCR 30400  33800
    IO  120D VLVO  32600  36200, VD T155  CRUS 30000  33300, IO T170  MRCR 25400  28300
    VD T170  MRCR  25100  27900, VD T220  CRUS 30400  33700, IO T228  MRCR 30500  33900
    VD T228  MRCR  30000  33300, VD T255  MRCR 30100  33400, IO T260  VLVO 31900  35400
    VD T270  CRUS  30600  34000, IO T330  MRCR 33500  37300, VD T330  MRCR 30800  34300
    VD T350  CRUS  31700  35300

 37  2 HARBOR-MASTER 375   FB  HB     FBG SV IO  170  MRCR 12            2 6 28700  31800
    IO  228  MRCR  28900  32100, IO  260  VLVO 29500  32800, IO  330  MRCR 14400  16400
    VD T155  CRUS  30000  33300, IO T170  MRCR 30100  33400, VD T170  MRCR 29800  33100
    VD T220  CRUS  37300  41400, IO T228  MRCR 30500  33900, VD T228  MRCR 30000  33300
    VD T255  MRCR  30100  33400, IO T260  VLVO 31900  35400, VD T270  CRUS 30600  34000
    IO T330  MRCR  33500  37300, VD T330  MRCR 30800  34300, VD T350  CRUS 31700  35300
    IO T120D VLVO  41500  46100

 38    DRIFTER 38          HT  HB     STL FL IO  120       12 10             20200  22500
 38    DRIFTER 38          HT  HB     STL FL IO T330       12 10             24000  26700
 40    DRIFTER 40          HT  HB     STL SV IO  170       12                53500  58800
 40    DRIFTER 40          HT  HB     STL SV IO T330       12                57600  63300
 40    HARBOR-MASTER 40    HT  HB     FBG SV VD  170       12    6           53300  58600
    IO  228          53700  59000, IB T200       54300  59700, IO T350      58700  64500

 43    DRIFTER 43          HT  HB     STL FL IO  120       12 10             29000  32200
 43    DRIFTER 43          HT  HB     STL FL VD  170       12 10             28900  32100
 43    DRIFTER 43          HT  HB     STL FL IO T330       12 10             34000  37700
 43  5 HARBOR-MASTER 435   HT  HB     FBG SV IO  260  VLVO 14    16000  2 6 24700  27500
    VD T155  CRUS  29600  32900, IO T170  MRCR 29700  33000, IO T228  MRCR 30200  33500
    VD T228  MRCR  29600  32900, VD T255  MRCR 29700  33000, IO T330  MRCR 33200  36900

 43  5 HARBOR-MASTER 435   FB  HB     FBG SV IO  228  MRCR 14    16000  2 6 24100  26700
    IO  330  MRCR  25600  28400, VD T155  CRUS 29600  32900, IO T170  MRCR 29700  33000
    VD T170  MRCR  29400  32700, VD T220  CRUS 30000  33300, VD T228  MRCR 29600  32900
    VD T255  MRCR  29700  33000, IO T260  VLVO 31500  35000, VD T270  CRUS 30200  33600

 43  6 HARBOR-MASTER 435   HT  HB     FBG SV IO  228  MRCR 14    16000  2 6 23900  26600
    IO  330  MRCR  67400  74100, VD T170  MRCR 24800  27600, VD T220  CRUS 67400  74100
    VD T260  VLVO  68900  75700, VD T270  CRUS 67700  74400, VD T330  MRCR 67900  74600
    VD T350  CRUS  68800  75600

 43  6 HARBOR-MASTER 435   FB  HB     FBG SV IO  260  VLVO 14            3   66600  73200
    IO T228  MRCR  67600  74300, IO T330  MRCR 70600  77600, VD T330  MRCR 67900  74600
    VD T350  CRUS  44100  49000

 47    DRIFTER 47          HT  HB     STL SV VD  170       13  2            35400  39300
    IO  228          35700  39700, IB T220       36800  40900, IO T330      40400  44900

 48    DRIFTER 48          HT  HB     STL FL IO  120       12 10             48600  53400
 48    DRIFTER 48          HT  HB     STL FL VD  170       12 10             48500  53300
 48    DRIFTER 48          HT  HB     STL FL IO T330       12 10             53000  58300
 48    HARBOR-MASTER 48    HT  HB     FBG SV IB  220       14                49900  54800
 48    HARBOR-MASTER 48    HT  HB     FBG SV IO  330       14                50000  54900
 48    HARBOR-MASTER 48    HT  HB     FBG SV IO T330       14                53000  58300
 52    DRIFTER 52          HT  HB     STL SV SD  170       14 10             81400  89500
    IO  330          83600  91800, IB T220       83100  91300, IO T330      87200  95800

 53    DRIFTER 53          HT  HB     STL FL IO  179       12 10             79500  87400
 53    DRIFTER 53          HT  HB     STL FL SD  228       12 10             79400  87300
 53    DRIFTER 53          HT  HB     STL FL IO T330       12 10             85100  93500
------------------- 1979 BOATS --------------------------------------------------------------
 35    HARBOR-MASTER       HT  HB     FBG SV IO  260  VLVO 12    12000  1 6 19200  21300
 35    HARBOR-MASTER       HT  HB     FBG SV VD  270  CRUS 12    12000  1 6 20000  22200
 35    HARBOR-MASTER       HT  HB     FBG SV VD  270  CRUS 12    12000  1 6 20200  22500
 35    HARBOR-MASTER       FB  HB     FBG SV VD T228  MRCR 12    12000  1 6 19600  21800
 35    HARBOR-MASTER       FB  HB     FBG SV VD T255  MRCR 12    12000  1 6 19700  21900
 38    DRIFTER             HT  HB     STL FL IO  120  MRCR 12 10 14000  1 3 22300  24800
    IO  170  MRCR  22300  24800, IO  228  MRCR 22600  25100, IO T120  MRCR 23400  26000

 40    DRIFTER             HT  HB     STL SV IO  228  MRCR 12    15000  1 6 24300  27000
 40    HARBOR-MASTER       HT  HB     FBG SV IO  228  MRCR 12  4 14000  1 6 19400  21600
    IO  330  MRCR  20600  22900, IO T170  MRCR 20400  22600, VD T228  MRCR 20300  22500
    VD T255  MRCR  20400  22600

 40    HARBOR-MASTER       FB  HB     FBG SV IO  330  MRCR 12  4 14000  1 6 20600  22900
    VD T228  MRCR  20300  22500, VD T255  MRCR 20400  22600, VD T330  MRCR 21100  23500

 43    DRIFTER             HT  HB     STL FL IO  120  MRCR 12 10 16000  1 3 24200  26900
    IO  170  MRCR  24300  27000, IO  228  MRCR 24500  27200, IO T170  MRCR 25700  28500

 43    DRIFTER             FB  HB     STL FL IO T170  MRCR 12 10 16000  1 3 25700  28500
 43    DRIFTER             FB  HB     STL FL IO T228  MRCR 12 10 16000  1 3 26100  29000
 47    DRIFTER             HT  HB     STL SV IO  228  MRCR 13  2 17000  1 4 24200  26700
 47    DRIFTER             HT  HB     STL SV IO  330  MRCR 13  2 17000  1 6 24700  26700
 47    DRIFTER             FB  HB     STL SV VD T228  MRCR 13  2 17000  1 6 23700  26300
 47    DRIFTER             FB  HB     STL SV VD T255  MRCR 13  2 17000  1 6 23800  26400
 48    DRIFTER             HT  HB     STL FL IO  170  MRCR 12 10 18000  1 3 26100  29000
 48    DRIFTER             HT  HB     STL FL IO  228  MRCR 12 10 18000  1 6 26300  29300
 48    DRIFTER             HT  HB     STL FL IO  330  MRCR 12 10 18000  1 3 27800  30900
 48    HARBOR-MASTER       HT  HB     FBG SV VD T255  MRCR 14    20000  2   38800  43100
 48    HARBOR-MASTER       FB  HB     FBG SV VD T330  MRCR 14    20000  2   39600  43900
 52    DRIFTER             HT  HB     STL SV VD  228  MRCR 14 10 20000  2   36800  40900

 52    DRIFTER             FB  HB     STL SV IO T228  MRCR 14 10 20000  2   36800  40900
 53    DRIFTER             FB  HB     STL FL IO  120  MRCR 12 10 19000  1 3 27600  30700
 53    DRIFTER             FB  HB     STL FL IO T120  MRCR 12 10 19000  1 3 27600  30700
------------------- 1978 BOATS --------------------------------------------------------------
 38    DRIFTER 38          HT  HB     STL FL OB         12 10 14000  1 4 20900  23300
    IO  120  MRCR  27400  30400, IO  120  OMC  27300  30400, IO  170  MRCR 27400  30500
    IO  198  MRCR  27500  30600, IO  225  OMC  27600  30600, IO  228  MRCR 27600  30700
    IO  240  OMC   27700  30700, IO  330  MRCR 29100  32300, IO T120  MRCR 28700  31900
    IO T120  OMC   28600  31800, IO T170  MRCR 28800  32000, IO T198  MRCR 29000  32200
    IO T225  OMC   29100  32300, IO T228  MRCR 29300  32500, IO T240  OMC  29300  32500
    IO T330  MRCR  32200  35800

 38    DRIFTER 38          HT  HB     STL FL OB         12 10 14000  1 4 20900  23300
    IO  120  MRCR  27400  30400, IO  120  OMC  27300  30400, IO  170  MRCR 27400  30500
    IO  198  MRCR  27500  30600, IO  225  OMC  27600  30600, IO  228  MRCR 27600  30700
    IO  240  OMC   27700  30700, IO  330  MRCR 29100  32300, IO T120  MRCR 29000  31900
    IO T120  OMC   28600  31800, IO T170  MRCR 28800  32000, IO T198  MRCR 29000  32200
    IO T225  OMC   29100  32300, IO T228  MRCR 29300  32500, IO T240  OMC  29300  32500
    IO T330  MRCR  32200  35800

 40    DRIFTER V-400       HT  HB     STL SV OB         12    14000  1 6 17100  19400
    IO  120  MRCR  23700  26400, IO  120  OMC  23700  26300, IO  170  MRCR 23800  26400
    IO  198  MRCR  23900  26500, IO  225  OMC  23900  26600, IO  228  MRCR 24000  26700
    IO  240  OMC   24000  26700, IO  330  MRCR 25500  28300, IO T120  MRCR 25100  27900
    IO T120  OMC   25000  27800, IO T170  MRCR 25200  28100, IO T198  MRCR 25400  28300
    VD T198  MRCR  25000  27800, IO T225  OMC  25500  28300, IO T228  MRCR 25400  28100
    VD T228  MRCR  25100  27900, IO T240  OMC  25600  28500, IO T255  MRCR 25600  28500
    VD T305  MRCR  26600  29500, IO T330  MRCR 28500  31700, IO T330  MRCR 25900  28800
    VD T350  OMC   27200  30200, VD T454  OMC  30500  33900

 40    DRIFTER V-400       HT  HB     STL SV OB         12    14000  1 6 17100  19400
    IO  120  MRCR  23700  26400, IO  120  OMC  23700  26300, IO  170  MRCR 23800  26400
    IO  198  MRCR  23900  26500, IO  225  OMC  23900  26600, IO  228  MRCR 24000  26700
    IO  240  OMC   24000  26700, IO  330  MRCR 25500  28300, IO T120  MRCR 25100  27900
    IO T120  OMC   25000  27800, IO T170  MRCR 25200  28100, IO T198  MRCR 25400  28300
    VD T198  MRCR  25000  27800, IO T225  OMC  25500  28300, IO T228  MRCR 25400  28100
    VD T228  MRCR  25100  27900, IO T240  OMC  25600  28500, IO T255  MRCR 25600  28500
    VD T305  MRCR  26600  29500, IO T330  MRCR 28500  31700, IO T330  MRCR 25900  28800
    VD T350  OMC   27200  30200, VD T454  OMC  30500  33900

 40    HARBOR-MASTER       HT  HB     FBG SV IO  228  MRCR 14  4 18000  1 6 40900  45400
    IO  330  MRCR  42300  47000, IO T170  MRCR 42400  46700, IO T198  MRCR 40400  46900
    VD T198  MRCR  48000  52800, IO T228  MRCR 42500  47200, VD T228  MRCR 48100  52900
    IO  240  MRCR  42500  47200, VD T255  MRCR 48800  53000, VD T305  OMC  49000  54600
    IO T330  MRCR  45900  50500, VD T330  MRCR 48900  53800, IO T350  OMC  49800  54700
    VD T454  OMC   53100  58300

 40    HARBOR-MASTER       HT  HB     FBG SV VD  198  MRCR 14  4 20000  1 6 51900  57000
    IO  228  MRCR  46300  51200, VD T170  MRCR 51900  57100, IO T170  MRCR 52000  57000
    VD  305  OMC   52300  57500, IO  330  MRCR 48500  53300, VD  330  MRCR 52400  57500
    VD  350  OMC   53500  58300, VD  454  OMC  54200  59600, IO T330  MRCR 52500  57500
    VD T198  MRCR  48400  53100, IO T228  MRCR 48600  53500, IO T240  OMC  48700  53500
    IO T330  MRCR  51100  56200

 43    DRIFTER 43          HT  HB     STL FL OB         12 10 15000  1 4 17200  19600
    IO  120  MRCR  19100  21200, IO  120  OMC  19000  21100, IO  170  MRCR 19200  21200
    IO  198  MRCR  19200  21300, IO  225  OMC  19200  21400, IO  228  MRCR 19300  21500
    IO  240  OMC   19300  21500, IO  330  MRCR 20500  22800, IO T120  MRCR 20100  22400
    IO T120  OMC   20000  22200, IO T170  MRCR 20200  22500, IO T198  MRCR 20400  22700
    IO T225  OMC   20500  22800, IO T228  MRCR 20200  22500, IO T240  OMC  20700  23000
    IO T330  MRCR  23100  25700
```

```
 LOA  NAME AND/              TOP/ BOAT  -HULL- ----ENGINE--- BEAM   WGT  DRAFT RETAIL RETAIL
FT IN  OR MODEL               RIG TYPE  MTL TP TP # HP  MFG  FT IN  LBS  FT IN  LOW    HIGH
--------------------- 1978 BOATS ------------------------------------------------------------
43     DRIFTER 43             FB   HB    STL FL OB              12 10 15000  1  4  17200  19600
   IO  120  MRCR  19100  21200, IO  120  OMC   19000  21100, IO  170  MRCR  19100  21200
   IO  198  MRCR  19200  21300, IO  225  OMC   19200  21400, IO  228  MRCR  19300  21500
   IO  240  OMC   19300  21500, IO  330  MRCR  20500  22800, IO T120  MRCR  20100  22400
   IO T120  OMC   20000  22300, IO T170  MRCR  20200  22500, IO T198  MRCR  20400  22700
   IO T225  OMC   20500  22800, IO T228  MRCR  20700  23000, IO T240  OMC   20700  23000
   IO T330  MRCR  23100  25700

47     DRIFTER V-470          HT   HB    STL SV OB              13  2 18000  1  8  26200  29100
   IO  120  MRCR  27500  30600, IO  120  OMC   27500  30500, IO  170  MRCR  27600  30700
   IO  198  MRCR  27700  30700, IO  225  OMC   27700  30800, IO  228  MRCR  27800  30900
   IO  240  OMC   27800  30900, IO  330  MRCR  29200  32500, IO T120  MRCR  28900  32100
   IO T120  OMC   28800  32000, IO T170  MRCR  29000  32200, IO T198  MRCR  29100  32400
   VD T198  MRCR  28800  32000, IO T225  OMC   29200  32500, IO T228  MRCR  29400  32700
   VD T228  MRCR  28900  32100, IO T240  OMC   29400  32700, VD T255  MRCR  29000  32200
   VD T305  OMC   30400  33700, IO T330  MRCR  32300  35900, VD T330  MRCR  29700  33000
   VD T350  OMC   31000  34400, VD T454  OMC   34200  38000

47     DRIFTER V-470          FB   HB    STL SV OB              13  2 18000  1  8  26200  29100
   IO  120  MRCR  27500  30600, IO  120  OMC   27500  30500, IO  170  MRCR  27600  30700
   IO  198  MRCR  27700  30700, IO  225  OMC   27700  30800, IO  228  MRCR  27800  30900
   IO  240  OMC   27800  30900, IO  330  MRCR  29200  32500, IO T120  MRCR  28900  32100
   IO T120  OMC   28800  32000, IO T170  MRCR  29000  32200, IO T198  MRCR  29100  32400
   VD T198  MRCR  28800  32000, IO T225  OMC   29200  32500, IO T228  MRCR  29400  32700
   VD T228  MRCR  28900  32100, IO T240  OMC   29400  32700, VD T255  MRCR  29000  32200
   VD T305  OMC   30400  33700, IO T330  MRCR  32300  35900, VD T330  MRCR  29700  33000
   VD T350  OMC   31000  34400, VD T454  OMC   34200  38000

47     HARBOR-MASTER          HT   HB    FBG SV IB T198         14                  35800  39700
47     HARBOR-MASTER          HT   HB    FBG SV IB T330         14                  36700  40700
48     DRIFTER 48             HT   HB    STL FL OB              12 10 17000  1  6  19700  21900
   IO  120  MRCR  20700  23000, IO  120  OMC   20700  23000, IO  170  MRCR  20800  23100
   IO  198  MRCR  20800  23200, IO  225  OMC   20900  23200, IO  228  MRCR  21000  23300
   IO  240  OMC   21000  23300, IO  330  MRCR  22100  24600, IO T120  MRCR  21800  24200
   IO T120  OMC   21700  24100, IO T170  MRCR  21900  24300, IO T198  MRCR  22000  24400
   IO T225  OMC   22100  24600, IO T228  MRCR  22300  24800, IO T240  OMC   22300  24800
   IO T330  MRCR  24900  27700

48     DRIFTER 48             FB   HB    STL FL OB              12 10 17000  1  6  19700  21900
   IO  120  MRCR  20700  23000, IO  120  OMC   20700  23000, IO  170  MRCR  20800  23100
   IO  198  MRCR  20800  23200, IO  225  OMC   20900  23200, IO  228  MRCR  21000  23300
   IO  240  OMC   21000  23300, IO  330  MRCR  22100  24600, IO T120  MRCR  21800  24200
   IO T120  OMC   21700  24100, IO T170  MRCR  21900  24300, IO T198  MRCR  22000  24400
   IO T225  OMC   22100  24600, IO T228  MRCR  22300  24800, IO T240  OMC   22300  24800
   IO T330  MRCR  24900  27700

48     HARBOR-MASTER          HT   HB    FBG SV IO  330  MRCR 14     28000  2  4  82100  90200
   IO T228  MRCR  82200  90400, VD T228  MRCR  81700  89800, VD T255  MRCR  81800  89900
   VD T305  OMC   83000  91200, IO T330  MRCR  85100  93500, VD T330  MRCR  82500  90700
   VD T350  OMC   83800  92100, VD T454  OMC   87000  95600

48     HARBOR-MASTER          FB   HB    FBG SV IO  330  MRCR 14     28000  2  4  82100  90200
   IO T228  MRCR  82200  90400, VD T228  MRCR  81700  89800, VD T255  MRCR  81800  89900
   VD T305  OMC   83000  91200, IO T330  MRCR  85100  93500, VD T330  MRCR  82500  90700
   VD T350  OMC   83800  92100, VD T454  OMC   87000  95600

52     DRIFTER V-520          HT   HB    STL SV OB              14 10 20000  2     32600  36300
   IO  120  MRCR  34200  38000, IO  120  OMC   34100  37900, IO  170  MRCR  34200  38000
   IO  198  MRCR  34300  38100, IO  225  OMC   34400  38200, IO  228  MRCR  34500  38300
   IO  240  OMC   34500  38300, IO  330  MRCR  36200  40200, IO T120  MRCR  35700  39700
   IO T120  OMC   35600  39600, IO T170  MRCR  35800  39800, IO T198  MRCR  36000  40000
   VD T198  MRCR  35700  39600, IO T225  OMC   36100  40200, IO T228  MRCR  36300  40400
   VD T228  MRCR  35700  39700, IO T240  OMC   36400  40400, VD T255  MRCR  35900  39800
   VD T305  OMC   37000  41100, IO T330  MRCR  39700  44100, VD T330  MRCR  36700  40700
   VD T350  OMC   38200  42400, VD T454  OMC   41900  46500

52     DRIFTER V-520          FB   HB    STL SV OB              14 10 20000  2     32600  36300
   IO  120  MRCR  34200  38000, IO  120  OMC   34100  37900, IO  170  MRCR  34200  38000
   IO  198  MRCR  34300  38100, IO  225  OMC   34400  38200, IO  228  MRCR  34500  38300
   IO  240  OMC   34500  38300, IO  330  MRCR  36200  40200, IO T120  MRCR  35700  39700
   IO T120  OMC   35600  39600, IO T170  MRCR  35800  39800, IO T198  MRCR  36000  40000
   VD T198  MRCR  35700  39600, IO T225  OMC   36100  40200, IO T228  MRCR  36300  40400
   VD T228  MRCR  35700  39700, IO T240  OMC   36400  40400, VD T255  MRCR  35900  39800
   VD T305  OMC   37400  41600, IO T330  MRCR  39700  44100, VD T330  MRCR  36700  40700
   VD T350  OMC   38200  42400, VD T454  OMC   41900  46500

53     DRIFTER 53             HT   HB    STL FL OB              12 10 19000  1  6  24100  26800
   IO  120  MRCR  25700  28500, IO  120  OMC   25600  28500, IO  170  MRCR  25700  28600
   IO  198  MRCR  25800  28700, IO  225  OMC   25900  28800, IO  228  MRCR  26000  28900
   IO  240  OMC   26000  28900, IO  330  MRCR  27700  30700, IO T120  MRCR  27200  30300
   IO T120  OMC   27100  30100, IO T170  MRCR  27400  30400, IO T198  MRCR  27500  30600
   IO T225  OMC   27600  30700, IO T228  MRCR  27800  30900, IO T240  OMC   27900  31000
   IO T330  MRCR  31200  34600

53     DRIFTER 53             FB   HB    STL FL OB              12 10 19000  1  6  24100  26800
   IO  120  MRCR  25700  28500, IO  120  OMC   25600  28500, IO  170  MRCR  25700  28600
   IO  198  MRCR  25800  28700, IO  225  OMC   25900  28800, IO  228  MRCR  26000  28900
   IO  240  OMC   26000  28900, IO  330  MRCR  27700  30700, IO T120  MRCR  27200  30300
   IO T120  OMC   27100  30100, IO T170  MRCR  27400  30400, IO T198  MRCR  27500  30600
   IO T225  OMC   27600  30700, IO T228  MRCR  27800  30900, IO T240  OMC   27900  31000
   IO T330  MRCR  31200  34600
--------------------- 1977 BOATS ------------------------------------------------------------
38     DRIFTER 38             HT   HB    STL FL OB              12 10 14000  1  3  20700  23000
   IO  120  MRCR  21700  24100, IO  165  MRCR  21800  24200, IO  170  MRCR  21800  24200
   IO  233  MRCR  22000  24500, IO  255  MRCR  22200  24700, IO T120  MRCR  22800  25400
   IO T165  MRCR  22900  25500, IO T170  MRCR  22900  25500, IO T233  MRCR  23400  26000
   IO T255  MRCR  23800  26400

38     DRIFTER 38             FB   HB    STL FL OB              12 10 14000  1  3  20700  23000
   IO  120  MRCR  21700  24100, IO  165  MRCR  21800  24200, IO  170  MRCR  21800  24200
   IO  233  MRCR  22000  24500, IO  255  MRCR  22200  24700, IO T120  MRCR  22800  25400
   IO T165  MRCR  22900  25500, IO T170  MRCR  22900  25500, IO T233  MRCR  23400  26000
   IO T255  MRCR  23800  26400

40     HARBOR-MASTER          HT   HB    FBG SV IO  255  MRCR 12  4 20000  1  6  51800  56900
   IO T165  MRCR  52700  57900, IO T233  MRCR  53200  58500, VD T233  MRCR  52700  57900
   IO T255  MRCR  53600  58900, VD T255  MRCR  52700  58000

40     HARBOR-MASTER          FB   HB    FBG SV IO  255  MRCR 12  4 20000  1  6  51800  56900
   IO T165  MRCR  52700  57900, IO T233  MRCR  53200  58500, VD T233  MRCR  52700  57900
   IO T255  MRCR  53600  58900, VD T255  MRCR  52700  58000

43     DRIFTER 43             HT   HB    STL FL OB              12 10 16000  1  3  22500  25000
   IO  120  MRCR  23600  26200, IO  165  MRCR  23600  26300, IO  170  MRCR  23600  26300
   IO  233  MRCR  23900  26500, IO  255  MRCR  24100  26700, IO T120  MRCR  24900  27700
   IO T165  MRCR  25000  27800, IO T170  MRCR  25000  27800, IO T233  MRCR  25500  28300
   IO T255  MRCR  25900  28700

43     DRIFTER 43             FB   HB    STL FL OB              12 10 16000  1  3  22500  25000
   IO  120  MRCR  23600  26200, IO  165  MRCR  23600  26300, IO  170  MRCR  23600  26300
   IO  233  MRCR  23900  26500, IO  255  MRCR  24100  26700, IO T120  MRCR  24900  27700
   IO T165  MRCR  25000  27800, IO T170  MRCR  25000  27800, IO T233  MRCR  25500  28300
   IO T255  MRCR  25900  28700

45   5 DRIFTER V-450          HT   HB    STL SV OB              13  2 18000  1  8  28700  31900
   IO  120  MRCR  30000  33400, IO  165  MRCR  30100  33400, IO  170  MRCR  30100  33400
   IO  233  MRCR  30300  33700, IO  255  MRCR  30500  33900, IO T120  MRCR  31400  34800
   IO T165  MRCR  31400  34900, IO T170  MRCR  31400  34900, IO T233  MRCR  31900  35500
   IO T255  MRCR  32300  35900

45   5 DRIFTER V-450          FB   HB    STL SV OB              13  2 18000  1  8  28700  31900
   IO  120  MRCR  30000  33400, IO  165  MRCR  30100  33400, IO  170  MRCR  30100  33400
   IO  233  MRCR  30300  33700, IO  255  MRCR  30500  33900, IO T120  MRCR  31400  34800
   IO T165  MRCR  31400  34900, IO T170  MRCR  31400  34900, IO T233  MRCR  31900  35500
   IO T255  MRCR  32300  35900

48     DRIFTER 48             HT   HB    STL FL OB              12 10 18000  1  3  24100  26800
   IO  120  MRCR  25400  28200, IO  165  MRCR  25500  28300, IO  170  MRCR  25500  28300
   IO  233  MRCR  25700  28600, IO  255  MRCR  25900  28800, IO T120  MRCR  26700  29700
   IO T165  MRCR  26800  29800, IO T170  MRCR  26800  29800, IO T233  MRCR  27300  30400
   IO T255  MRCR  27700  30700

48     DRIFTER 48             FB   HB    STL FL OB              12 10 18000  1  3  24100  26800
   IO  120  MRCR  25400  28200, IO  165  MRCR  25500  28300, IO  170  MRCR  25500  28300
   IO  233  MRCR  25700  28600, IO  255  MRCR  25900  28800, IO T120  MRCR  26700  29700
   IO T165  MRCR  26800  29800, IO T170  MRCR  26800  29800, IO T233  MRCR  27300  30400
   IO T255  MRCR  27700  30700

50     DRIFTER V-500          HT   HB    STL SV OB              14 10 24000  2     53600  58900
   IO  255  MRCR  54900  60400, IO T120  MRCR  55800  61300, IO T165  MRCR  55900  61400
   IO T170  MRCR  55900  61400, IO T233  MRCR  56400  61900, IO T255  MRCR  56400  62000

50     DRIFTER V-500          FB   HB    STL SV OB              14 10 24000  2     53600  58900
   IO  255  MRCR  54900  60400, IO T120  MRCR  55800  61300, IO T165  MRCR  55900  61400
   IO T170  MRCR  55900  61400, IO T233  MRCR  56400  61900, IO T255  MRCR  56400  62000
```

 CONTINUED ON NEXT PAGE

```
 LOA  NAME AND/              TOP/ BOAT  -HULL-  ----ENGINE---   BEAM   WGT   DRAFT RETAIL RETAIL
FT IN  OR MODEL              RIG  TYPE  MTL TP TP # HP MFG  FT IN  LBS  FT IN  LOW   HIGH
------------------ 1977 BOATS ----------------------------------------------------------
 52    HARBOR-MASTER         HT  HB   STL SV IO T233      14        2      80600  88600
 52    HARBOR-MASTER         HT  HB   STL SV IO T330      14        2      83800  92100
 53    DRIFTER 53            HT  HB   STL FL OB        12 10 20000  1  3   30200  33500
       IO 120  MRCR  31700  35200, IO  165  MRCR  31800  35300, IO  170  MRCR  31800  35300
       IO 233  MRCR  32100  35600, IO  255  MRCR  32300  35800, IO T120  MRCR  33300  37000
       IO T165 MRCR  33300  37100, IO T170  MRCR  33400  37100, IO T233  MRCR  33900  37700
       IO T255 MRCR  34300  38100

 53    DRIFTER 53            FB  HB  -STL FL OB        12 10 20000  1  3   30200  33500
       IO 120  MRCR  31700  35200, IO  165  MRCR  31800  35300, IO  170  MRCR  31800  35300
       IO 233  MRCR  32100  35600, IO  255  MRCR  32300  35800, IO T120  MRCR  33300  37000
       IO T165 MRCR  33300  37100, IO T170  MRCR  33400  37100, IO T233  MRCR  33900  37700
       IO T255 MRCR  34300  38100
------------------ 1976 BOATS ----------------------------------------------------------
 38    DRIFTER               HT  HB   STL FL OB        12 10 14000  1  3   20400  22700
       IO 120  MRCR  21800  24200, IO  165  MRCR  21800  24300, IO T120  MRCR  22800  25400

 38    DRIFTER               FB  HB   STL FL IO  255   MRCR 12 10 14000  1  3   21900  24400
 40    HARBOR-MASTER         HT  HB   FBG SV IO  255   MRCR 12  6 15000  1  6   26400  26300
       IO T165 MRCR  24600  27300, VD T165  PCM  40700  45300, VD T215  PCM  40900  45500
       VD T233 MRCR  41000  45500, IO T255  MRCR  41900  46500, VD T255  MRCR  41100  45600
       VD T255 PCM   41100  45600

 40    HARBOR-MASTER         FB  HB   FBG SV IO  255   MRCR 12  6 18000  1  6   40100  44600
       IO T165 MRCR  41000  45600, VD T215  PCM  40900  45500, VD T233  MRCR  41000  45500
       IO T255 MRCR  41900  46500, VD T255  MRCR  41100  45600

 43    DRIFTER               HT  HB   STL FL OB        12 10 16000  1  3   22200  24700
       IO 165  MRCR  23400  26000, IO  255  MRCR  23800  26400, IO T165  MRCR  24700  27500

 43    DRIFTER               FB  HB   STL FL IO T255   MRCR 12 10 16000  1  3   25600  28400
 48    DRIFTER               FB  HB   STL FL OB        12 10 18000  1  3   23800  26500
 48    DRIFTER               HT  HB   STL FL IO  255   MRCR 12 10 18000  1  3   25600  28400
 48    DRIFTER               HT  HB   STL FL IO T165   MRCR 12 10 18000  1  3   26500  29500
 48    DRIFTER               FB  HB   STL FL IO T255   MRCR 12 10 18000  1  3   27300  30400
 53    DRIFTER               HT  HB   STL FL OB        12 10 20000  1  3   29900  33200
 53    DRIFTER               HT  HB   STL FL IO  255   MRCR 12 10 20000  1  3   31900  35400
 53    DRIFTER               HT  HB   STL FL IO T165   MRCR 12 10 20000  1  3   33000  36600
 53    DRIFTER               FB  HB   STL FL IO T255   MRCR 12 10 20000  1  3   33900  37700
------------------ 1975 BOATS ----------------------------------------------------------
 38    DRIFTER               HT  HB   STL FL OB        12 10 14000  1  3   20200  22500
       IO 120  MRCR  21600  24000, IO  165  MRCR  21600  24000, IO  225  MRCR  21800  24200

 38    DRIFTER               FB  HB   STL FL IO T165   MRCR 12 10 14000  1  3   22700  25200
 40    HARBOR-MASTER         FB  HB   FBG SV IO  255   MRCR 12  6 17000  1  6   34200  38000
       IO T165 MRCR  35200  39100, IO T225  MRCR  35600  39500, VD T225  MRCR  35100  39000
       IO T233 MRCR  35700  39600, VD T233  MRCR  35100  39000, IO T255  MRCR  36000  40000
       VD T255 MRCR  35200  39100

 40    HARBOR-MASTER         FB  HB   FBG SV IO T225   MRCR 12  6 17000  1  6   35600  39500
 40    HARBOR-MASTER         FB  HB   FBG SV VD T225   MRCR 12  6 17000  1  6   35100  39000
 43    DRIFTER               HT  HB   STL FL OB        12 10 16000  1  3   22000  24400
       IO 165  MRCR  23100  25700, IO  225  MRCR  23300  25900, IO  255  MRCR  23500  26100
       IO T165 MRCR  24500  27200, IO T225  MRCR  24900  27600

 43    DRIFTER               HT  HB   STL FL IO T165   MRCR 12 10 16000  1  3   24500  27200
 48    DRIFTER               HT  HB   STL FL OB        12 10 18000  1  3   23600  26200
       IO 225  MRCR  25100  27900, IO  255  MRCR  25300  28100, IO T165  MRCR  26200  29100
       IO T225 MRCR  26600  29600

 48    DRIFTER               HT  HB   STL FL IO  255   MRCR 12 10 18000  1  3   25300  28100
 48    DRIFTER               HT  HB   STL FL IO T225   MRCR 12 10 18000  1  3   26600  29600
 53    DRIFTER               HT  HB   STL FL OB        12 10 20000  1  3   29500  32800
       IO 225  MRCR  31300  34800, IO  255  MRCR  33100  36800, IO T165  MRCR  32600  36300
       IO T225 MRCR  33100  36800

 53    DRIFTER               FB  HB   STL FL IO  255   MRCR 12 10 20000  1  3   31600  35100
 53    DRIFTER               FB  HB   STL FL IO T225   MRCR 12 10 20000  1  3   33100  36800
------------------ 1974 BOATS ----------------------------------------------------------
 38    DRIFTER 38            HT  HB   STL    OB        12 10 14000  1  3   20000  22200
       IO 120  MRCR  21400  23700, IO  165  MRCR  21400  23800, IO  165  WAUK  21400  23800
       IO 215  WAUK  21500  23900, IO  225  MRCR  21600  24000, IO  255  MRCR  21800  24200
       IO T120 MRCR  24800  27600

 43    DRIFTER 43            HT  HB   STL    OB        12 10 16000  1  3   21800  24200
       IO 120  MRCR  22800  25400, IO  165  MRCR  22900  25400, IO  165  WAUK  22900  25400
       IO 215  WAUK  23000  25600, IO  225  MRCR  23100  25600, IO  255  MRCR  23300  25900
       IO T165 MRCR  26900  29900, IO T165  WAUK  26900  29900, IO T225  MRCR  27300  30300

 48    DRIFTER 48            HT  HB   STL    OB        12 10 18000  1  3   23300  25900
       IO 120  MRCR  24600  27300, IO  165  MRCR  24600  27400, IO  165  WAUK  23400  25900
       IO 215  WAUK  24800  27300, IO  225  MRCR  24800  27600, IO  255  MRCR  25100  27800
       IO T215 WAUK  28900  32100, IO T255  MRCR  29400  32700
------------------ 1973 BOATS ----------------------------------------------------------
 38    DRIFTER 38            HT  HB   STL    OB        12 10 14000  1  3   20200  22400
       IO 120  MRCR  21200  23500, IO  165  MRCR  21200  23500, IO  165  WAUK  21200  23500
       IO T120 MRCR  22100  24600

 43    DRIFTER 43            HT  HB   STL    OB        12 10 16000  1  3   21600  24000
       IO 120  MRCR  22900  25400, IO  165  WAUK  22900  25500, IO  215  WAUK  22900  25300
       IO 225  MRCR  22900  25400, IO  255  MRCR  23100  25600, IO T225  MRCR  24400  27100

 48    DRIFTER 48            HT  HB   STL    OB        12 10 18000  1  3   23100  25700
       IO 225  MRCR  24600  27300, IO  255  MRCR  24800  27600, IO T    MRCR  26100  29000
       IO T    WAUK  26100  29000
------------------ 1972 BOATS ----------------------------------------------------------
 43    DRIFTER               HT  HB   STL    IO  120   MRCR 12 10 12000  1  3    3700   4300
       IO 165  MRCR   3700   4300, IO  188  MRCR   3650   4250, IO  225  MRCR   3900   4500
       IO 270  MRCR   3950   4550, IO T120  MRCR   4050   4700, IO T165  MRCR   4450   5100
       IO T188 MRCR   4450   5150, IO T225  MRCR   4800   5500

 45    DRIFTER               HT  HB   STL    IO  165   MRCR 12 10 13000  1  3    4200   4900
       IO 188  MRCR   4200   4900, IO  225  MRCR   4450   5150, IO  270  MRCR   4900   5400
       IO T120 MRCR   5300   6050, IO T188  MRCR   5500   6300, IO T225  MRCR   5800   6650

 47    DRIFTER               HT  HB   STL    IO  165   MRCR 12 10 14000  1  3    5950   6850
       IO 188  MRCR   6050   6950, IO  225  MRCR   6200   7100, IO  270  MRCR   6600   7600
       IO T188 MRCR   7500   8600, IO T188  MRCR   7600   8750, IO T225  MRCR   7900   9050
       IO T325 MRCR   9850  11200
------------------ 1971 BOATS ----------------------------------------------------------
 43    1 DRIFTER 43          HT  HB   STL    IO  120        12       9700     11     **     **
       IO 165        **     **, IO  215       **     **, IO  270       **     **     **
       IO T120       **     **, IO T165       **     **, IO T215       **     **     **

 45    1 DRIFTER 45          HT  HB   STL    IO  120        12 10 10400    11     **     **
       IO 165        **     **, IO  215       **     **, IO  270       **     **     **
       IO T120       **     **, IO T165       **     **, IO T215       **     **     **

 47    1 DRIFTER 47          HT  HB   STL    IO  120        12 10 11100    11     **     **
       IO 165        **     **, IO  215       **     **, IO  270       **     **     **
       IO T165       **     **, IO T215       **     **     **
------------------ 1970 BOATS ----------------------------------------------------------
 40    6 DRIFTER 41 SD       HT  HB   STL FL OB           12       8400    11     **     **
 40    6 DRIFTER 41 SD       HT  HB   STL FL OB  120      12       8400    11     **     **
 45    1 DRIFTER 45 CD       HT  HB   STL SV OB  120      12 10 10400    11     **     **
       IO 165        **     **, IO  215       **     **, IO  270       **     **     **
       IO T210       **     **, IO T215       **     **

 45    1 DRIFTER 45 SD       HT  HB   STL SV OB           12 10 10400    11     **     **
 45    1 DRIFTER 45 SD       HT  HB   STL SV IO  120      12 10 10700    11     **     **
 45    1 DRIFTER 45 SD       HT  HB   STL SV IO  165      12 10 10700    11     **     **
 47    1 DRIFTER 47 CD       HT  HB   STL SV IO  120      12 10 11100    11     **     **
       IO 165        **     **, IO  215       **     **, IO  270       **     **     **
       IO T215       **     **
------------------ 1969 BOATS ----------------------------------------------------------
 40    2 REGAL 40            HT  HB   STL FL OB           12       8400    2 10   **     **
       IO 120  MRCR   **     **, IO  160  MRCR   **     **, IO  250  MRCR   **     **     **
       IO T120 MRCR   **     **, IO T160  MRCR   **     **

 44    2 IMPERIAL 44         HT  HB   STL FL OB           12 10  9600    2 10   **     **
       IO 120  MRCR   **     **, IO  160  MRCR   **     **, IO  250  MRCR   **     **     **
       IO T120 MRCR   **     **, IO T160  MRCR   **     **

 45    5 CLIPPER 45          HT  HB   STL SV IO  160  MRCR 12 10 10600    2 10   **     **
       IO 250  MRCR   **     **, IO T120  MRCR   **     **, IO T160  MRCR   **     **

 45    5 DRIFTER 45          HT  HB   STL    IO  160  MRCR 12 10 11100    2 10   **     **
------------------ 1968 BOATS ----------------------------------------------------------
 32    2 SPORTSMAN 32        HT  HB   STL SV OB                             **     **
 36    1 REGAL 36            HT  HB   STL FL OB           10 10  5900    10     **     **
```

LOA FT IN	NAME AND/ OR MODEL	TOP/ RIG	BOAT TYPE	-HULL- MTL TP	----ENGINE--- TP # HP MFG	BEAM FT IN	WGT LBS	DRAFT FT IN	RETAIL LOW	RETAIL HIGH

------- 1968 BOATS -------

38	2	REGAL 38		HT HB	STL FL IO	120		10 10	6400	10	**	**
38	2	REGAL 38		HT HB	STL FL IO	160		10 10	6400	10	**	**
41	10	DRIFTER 41		HT HB	STL FL OB			12 10	8400	10	**	**
44	2	DRIFTER ALL ELEC 44	HT HB	STL FL IO	120		12 10	8400	10	**	**
44	2	IMPERIAL 44		HT HB	STL FL IO	120		12 10	9000	10	**	**
44	2	IMPERIAL 44		HT HB	STL FL IO	160		12 10	9000	10	**	**
45	2	CLIPPER 45		HT HB	STL DV IO	120		12 10	10400	10	**	**
		IO 160	**	** , IO	225		**	** , IO T120		**	**
		IO T160	**	**							
45	2	DRIFTER ALL ELEC 45	HT HB	STL DV IO	160		12 10	10400	10	**	**

------- 1967 BOATS -------

32	2	SPORTSMAN		HT HB	STL	OB			4600		**	**
38	4	REGAL		HT HB	STL	IO	120		6400		**	**
		IO 160	**	** , IO	225		**	** , IO T120		18300	20300
		IO T160	18300	20400							
41	5	IMPERIAL		HT HB	STL	OB			8400		**	**
44	4	IMPERIAL		HT HB	STL	IO	120		9000		**	**
		IO 160	**	** , IO	225		**	** , IO T120		57100	62700
		IO T160	57100	62800							

------- 1966 BOATS -------

32	2	SPORTSMAN		HT HB	STL	OB					**	**
36	2	REGAL		HT HB	STL	OB					1950	2350
38	4	REGAL		HT HB	STL	IO	110				16700	19000
38	4	REGAL		HT HB	STL	IO	T110				18200	20200
41	5	IMPERIAL		HT HB	STL	OB					**	**
44	4	IMPERIAL		HT HB	STL	IO	110				55800	61400
		IO 120	55800	61400, IO	150		55900	61400, IO	210		56000	61500
		IO T110	56700	62300								

------- 1961 BOATS -------

22	9	DRIFTER 23		HT HB	FBG	OB			9 8		**	**
22	9	DRIFTER 23		HT HB	PLY	OB			9 8		**	**
22	9	DRIFTER 23		HT HB	STL	OB			9 8		**	**
26	9	DRIFTER 27		HT HB	FBG	OB			9 8		**	**
26	9	DRIFTER 27		HT HB	PLY	OB			9 8		**	**
26	9	DRIFTER 27		HT HB	STL	OB			9 8		**	**
32		DRIFTER 32		HT HB	FBG	OB			11		**	**
32		DRIFTER 32		HT HB	PLY	OB			11		**	**
32		DRIFTER 32		HT HB	STL	OB			11		**	**

HARBOUR YACHTS INC
WESTMINSTER CA   COAST GUARD MFG ID- GMY See inside cover to adjust price for area

LOA FT IN	NAME AND/ OR MODEL	TOP/ RIG	BOAT TYPE	-HULL- MTL TP	----ENGINE--- TP # HP MFG	BEAM FT IN	WGT LBS	DRAFT FT IN	RETAIL LOW	RETAIL HIGH

------- 1972 BOATS -------

37	GRAN-MARINER		FBG	IB T225 CHRY 13		16500	2 1	35100	39000
	IB T106D VLVO 37900	42100, IB T160D PERK	39800	44200, IB T185D CUM	39400	43800
37	GRAN-MARINER	FB	FBG	IB T225 CHRY 13		17000	2 1	35900	39900
	IB T106D VLVO 38700	43000, IB T160D PERK	40600	45100, IB T185D CUM	40200	44700
43	GRAN-MARINER	DC	FBG	IB T225 CHRY 13		18000	2 1	49000	53800
	IB T106D VLVO 46900	51600, IB T160D PERK	54800	60300, IB T185D CUM	56200	61700
43	GRAN-MARINER	FB DC	FBG	IB T225 CHRY 13		18500	2 1	49800	54700
	IB T106D VLVO 47800	52500, IB T160D PERK	55700	61200, IB T185D CUM	57000	62700

------- 1971 BOATS -------

37	GRAN-MARINER 37		FBG	IB 210D GM 13	16500	2 1	35800	39800
37	GRAN-MARINER 37		FBG	IB T225 CHRY 13	16500	2 1	33900	37700
37	GRAN-MARINER 37		FBG	IB T185D CUM 13	16500	2 1	38100	42300
37	GRAN-MARINER 37	FB	FBG	IB 210D GM 13		2 1	34800	38700
37	GRAN-MARINER 37	FB	FBG	IB T225 CHRY 13		2 1	32500	36100
37	GRAN-MARINER 37	FB	FBG	IB T185D CUM 13		2 1	37100	41200
43	GRAN-MARINER 43		FBG	IB 210D GM 13	18000	2 1	46400	51000
43	GRAN-MARINER 43		FBG	IB T225 CHRY 13	18000	2 1	46200	50700
43	GRAN-MARINER 43		FBG	IB T185D CUM 13	19500	2 1	52500	57700
43	GRAN-MARINER 43	FB	FBG	IB 210D GM 13		2 1	40300	44800
43	GRAN-MARINER 43	FB	FBG	IB T225 CHRY 13		2 1	38600	42900
43	GRAN-MARINER 43	FB	FBG	IB T185D CUM 13		2 1	44600	48900

------- 1970 BOATS -------

32	GRAN-MARINER	DC	FBG SV IB	225 CHRY 12	12000	1 9	18900	21000
32	GRAN-MARINER	HT HB	FBG SV IB	225 CHRY 12	12000	1 9	32800	36500
37	GRAN-MARINER	DC	FBG SV IB	225 CHRY 13	14000	1 9	27900	31000
37	GRAN-MARINER	HT HB	FBG SV IB	225 CHRY 13	14000	1 9	32700	36300
43	GRAN-MARINER 43	DC	FBG SV IB T170D CUM 13	16000	1 9	41400	46000
43	GRAN-MARINER 43	HT HB	FBG SV IB	225 CHRY 13	16000	1 9	40800	45300
43	GRAN-MARINER 43	FB HB	FBG SV IB	225 CHRY 13	16000	1 9	33200	36800
43	GRAN-MARINER 43	FB HB	FBG SV IB T173D CUM 13	16000	1 9	40800	45400

------- 1969 BOATS -------

| 43 | GRAN-MARINER | CR | FBG | IB T225 13 | 16000 | 1 10 | 40300 | 44800 |
| 43 | GRAN-MARINER | UTL | FBG | IB T250 13 | 14500 | | 31200 | 34700 |

HARCRAFT BOAT WORKS
HAWTHORNE CA   See inside cover to adjust price for area

LOA FT IN	NAME AND/ OR MODEL	TOP/ RIG	BOAT TYPE	-HULL- MTL TP	----ENGINE--- TP # HP MFG	BEAM FT IN	WGT LBS	DRAFT FT IN	RETAIL LOW	RETAIL HIGH

------- 1965 BOATS -------

26	6	HARCRAFT 26		SF	WD	IB 210	11		1 7	6700	7700
30	4	HARCRAFT 30	FB	CBNCR WD	IB T420	13		1 10	15700	17800
30	4	HARCRAFT 30		SF	WD	IB 210	13		1 10	10200	11500
32		HARCRAFT 32	FB	CBNCR WD	IB T420	14		2 2	20100	22400
33	4	MARLIN		SF	WD	IB T420	14		2 3	16600	18900

HARDIN INT'L CO LTD
KAOHSIUNG TAIWAN ROC   COAST GUARD MFG ID- HCL See inside cover to adjust price for area

EAST WEST YACHTS US DIST
MARINA DEL REY CA

LOA FT IN	NAME AND/ OR MODEL	TOP/ RIG	BOAT TYPE	-HULL- MTL TP	----ENGINE--- TP # HP MFG	BEAM FT IN	WGT LBS	DRAFT FT IN	RETAIL LOW	RETAIL HIGH

------- 1982 BOATS -------

41	10	HARDIN 42	FB DC	FBG DS IB 120D	14 1	32000	4	83700	92000
41	10	HARDIN 42	FB SDN	FBG DS IB 200D MDS	14 1	32000	4	83100	91300
44	6	HARDIN 45 XL	KTH SA/CR	FBG KL IB 60D MDS	13 4	32000	5 6	93600	103000
45	2	HARDIN 45	KTH SA/CR	FBG KL IB 60D MDS	13 4	32000	5 6	96600	106000
45	2	HARDIN 45	KTH SA/CR	FBG KL IB 65D	13 4	32000	5 6	95700	105000
45	2	HARDIN 45XL	KTH SA/CR	FBG KL IB 65D	13 4	32000	5 6	98800	108000

------- 1981 BOATS -------

40		SEA WOLF	KTH SA/CR	FBG KL IB D	12		6	67200	73800
41	10	HARDIN 42	FB SDN	FBG DS IB 200D FORD	14 1	32000	4	78700	86500
41	10	HARDIN 45	FB TRWL	FBG DS IB 120D	14 2			79200	87000
44	6	HARDIN 44 CHARTER	KTH SA/CR	FBG KL IB 60D PISC	13 4	32000	5 6	88600	97300
45	2	HARDIN 45	KTH SA/CR	FBG KL IB 65D FORD	13 4	32000	5 6	91500	100500
50	10	FORCE 50	KTH SA/CR	FBG KL IB 80D FORD	14 1	52000	6 2	142500	157000

------- 1980 BOATS -------

40		SEA-WOLF	KTH SA/CR	FBG KL IB 50D PISC	12	27000	6	64000	70400
41	10	HARDIN 42	FB SDN	FBG DS IB 200D FORD	14 1	32000	4	75200	82600
44	6	HARDIN 44 CHARTER	KTH SA/CR	FBG KL IB 60D FORD	13 4	32000	5 6	84600	92900
45	2	HARDIN 45	KTH SA/CR	FBG KL IB 65D FORD	13 4	32000	5 6	87400	96000
50	10	FORCE 50	KTH SA/CR	FBG KL IB 80D FORD	14 1	52000	6	136000	149500

------- 1979 BOATS -------

38	10	COASTER	FB TRWL	FBG DS IB 120D	14	24679	3 10	53800	59100
38	10	COASTER	FB TRWL	FBG DS IB T120D	14	24679	3 10	57100	62700
40		SEA-WOLF	KTH SA/CR	FBG KL IB 50D PISC	12	27000	6	61600	67700
44		VOYAGER 44	KTH SA/CR	FBG KL IB D	13	30000	6	77000	84600
44	6	BOUNTY 44	KTH SA/CR	FBG KL IB 67D PISC	13 4	32000	6	81400	89400
44	6	HARDIN 44	KTH SA/CR	FBG KL IB D	13 4	31000	5 6	80200	88100
50	10	FORCE 50	KTH SA/CR	FBG KL IB D	14 1	52000	6 2	131000	144000

------- 1978 BOATS -------

32	9	HARDIN 33	KTH SA/CR	FBG KL IB 27D PISC	10	15000	5 2	32400	36000
36	9	SEA-BIRD	KTH SA/CR	FBG KL IB 40D PISC	11	18000	4	39500	43900
40		SEA-WOLF	KTH SA/CR	FBG KL IB 40D PISC	12	27000	6	59200	65100
44	6	VOYAGER 44	KTH SA/CR	FBG KL IB 60D PISC	13	32000	6	78300	86100
50	10	FORCE 50	KTH SA/CR	FBG KL IB 80D LEHM	14	52000	6	126000	138500

------- 1977 BOATS -------

32	9	HARDIN 33	KTH SA/CR	FBG KL IB D	10	14000	5 2	29300	32500
36	9	SEA-BIRD	SLP SA/CR	FBG KL IB 59D FORD	11	18300	4	38800	43100
36	9	SEA-BIRD	KTH SA/CR	FBG KL IB 59D FORD	11	18300	4	38900	43200
40		SEA-WOLF	KTH SA/CR	FBG KL IB D	12	27000	6	57500	63200
44	6	VOYAGER 44	KTH SA/CR	FBG KL IB 59D FORD	13	32000	6	75600	83100
50	10	FORCE 50	KTH SA/CR	FBG KL IB D	14 1	52000	6 2	122000	134000

------- 1976 BOATS -------

36	9	SEA-BIRD	SLP SA/CR	FBG KL IB 50D PERK	11	18000	4	36800	40900
36	9	SEA-BIRD	KTH SA/CR	FBG KL IB 50D PERK	11	18000	4	36900	41000
40		SEA-WOLF	KTH SA/CR	FBG KL IB 50D PERK	12	27000	6	55300	60800
44	6	VOYAGER 44	KTH SA/CR	FBG KL IB 80D PERK	13 4	31000	6	72300	79500
50	10	FORCE 50	KTH SA/CR	FBG KL IB D	14 1	52000	6 2	118000	129500

```
LOA   NAME AND/          TOP/ BOAT  -HULL-  ----ENGINE---  BEAM   WGT  DRAFT RETAIL RETAIL
FT IN  OR MODEL          RIG  TYPE  MTL TP TP # HP  MFG   FT IN  LBS  FT IN  LOW   HIGH
------------------- 1975 BOATS ---------------------------------------------------------
32  9 HARDIN 33          SLP SA/CR FBG KL IB      D         10       14000  5  2 27500 30600
32  9 HARDIN 33          KTH SA/CR FBG KL IB      D         10       14000  5  2 27500 30600
36  9 SEA-BIRD           SLP SA/CR FBG KL IB      D         11  6    18000  4    35800 39800
36  9 SEA-BIRD           KTH SA/CR FBG KL IB      D         11  6    18000  4    35900 39900
44  6 VOYAGER 44         KTH SA/CR FBG KL IB      D         13  4    31000  6    70100 77000
------------------- 1974 BOATS ---------------------------------------------------------
36  9 SEA-BIRD           KTH SA/CR FBG KL IB  45D          11  6    18000  4    35000 38900
38 10 COASTER            FB  TRWL  FBG DS IB T120D FORD    14       24679  3 10 46400 51000
40    SEA-WOLF           KTH SA/CR FBG KL IB      D         12       27000  6    52600 57800
44    VOYAGER 44         KTH SA/CR FBG KL IB      D         13       30000  5 11 65500 72000
50 10 FORCE 50           KTH SA/CR FBG KL IB  80D          14       52000  6  2 111000 122000
------------------- 1973 BOATS ---------------------------------------------------------
36  9 SEA-BIRD           SLP SA/CR FBG KL IB  50D          11  6    18000  4    34000 37800
38 10 COASTER            FB  TRWL  FBG DS IB T120D         14       24679  3 10 44100 49100
40    SEA-WOLF           KTH SA/CR FBG KL IB  50D          12       27000  6    51200 56300
50 10 FORCE 50           KTH SA/CR FBG KL IB  80D          14  1    52000  6  2 108000 119000
```

HARGRAVE YACHT SALES INC
W PALM BEACH FL 33401   See inside cover to adjust price for area

```
LOA   NAME AND/          TOP/ BOAT  -HULL-  ----ENGINE---  BEAM   WGT  DRAFT RETAIL RETAIL
FT IN  OR MODEL          RIG  TYPE  MTL TP TP # HP  MFG   FT IN  LBS  FT IN  LOW   HIGH
------------------- 1982 BOATS ---------------------------------------------------------
64  2 HARGRAVE 64        SF   FBG DV IB              16  4       4  6  **    **
65  2 HARGRAVE 65        MY   FBG DV IB              16  4       4  9  **    **
------------------- 1980 BOATS ---------------------------------------------------------
50    HARGRAVE 50        SF   FBG DV IB              15  6          **    **
64  2 HARGRAVE 64        SF   FBG DV IB              16  4          **    **
65  2 HARGRAVE 65        MY   FBG DV IB              16  4          **    **
------------------- 1979 BOATS ---------------------------------------------------------
50    HARGRAVE           SF   FBG    IB              15  6          **    **
64  2 HARGRAVE           SF   FBG    IB              16  4          **    **
65  2 HARGRAVE           MY   FBG    IB              16  4          **    **
------------------- 1977 BOATS ---------------------------------------------------------
50    HARGRAVE 50        SF   FBG    IB              15  6       3  9  **    **
64  2 HARGRAVE 64        SF   FBG    IB              16  4       4  6  **    **
65  2 HARGRAVE 65        MY   FBG    IB              16  4       4  9  **    **
------------------- 1976 BOATS ---------------------------------------------------------
50    HARGRAVE 50        SF   FBG    IB              15  6       3  9  **    **
64  2 HARGRAVE 64        SF   FBG    IB              16  4       4  6  **    **
65  2 HARGRAVE 65        MY   FBG    IB              16  4       4  9  **    **
------------------- 1974 BOATS ---------------------------------------------------------
50                   FB  SF   FBG    IB T  D        16     15000  3  9  **    **
50    HULL               SF   FBG    IB T  D        16     15000  3  9  **    **
64  2 ASSEM          FB  SF   FBG    IB T  D        17     18000  4  6  **    **
64  2 HULL               MY   FBG    IB T  D        17     18000  4  6  **    **
64  2 HULL               SF   FBG    IB T  D        17     18000  4  6  **    **
64  2 HULL&DECK          MY   FBG    IB T  D        17     18000  4  6  **    **
------------------- 1973 BOATS ---------------------------------------------------------
50                       SF   FBG    IB T  D        16     15000  3  9  **    **
50                   FB  SF   FBG    IB T  D        16            3  9  **    **
64  2                    SF   FBG    IB T  D        17     18000  4  6  **    **
64  2 ASSEM          FB  SF   FBG    IB T  D        17            4  6  **    **
------------------- 1972 BOATS ---------------------------------------------------------
50                       SF   FBG    IB T  D        16     15000  3  9  **    **
50                   FB  SF   FBG    IB T  D        16            3  9  **    **
64  2                    SF   FBG    IB T  D        17     18000  4  6  **    **
64  2 ASSEM          FB  SF   FBG    IB T  D        17            4  6  **    **
```

HARLEY BOAT COMPANY
FIBERFLOAT CORPORATION   See inside cover to adjust price for area
BARTOW FL 33830   COAST GUARD MFG ID- HDH

For more recent years, see the BUC Used Boat Price Guide, Volume 1 or Volume 2

```
LOA   NAME AND/          TOP/ BOAT  -HULL-  ----ENGINE---  BEAM   WGT  DRAFT RETAIL RETAIL
FT IN  OR MODEL          RIG  TYPE  MTL TP TP # HP  MFG   FT IN  LBS  FT IN  LOW   HIGH
------------------- 1983 BOATS ---------------------------------------------------------
17 11 FREEDOM 18         OP  RNBT  KEV SV IO  170  OMC   6 11  1350         2050  2450
26  7 MINICUDDY          OP  CTRCN KEV SV OB        8  5  1750         3350  3900
26  7 MINICUDDY          OP  CTRCN KEV SV IO 170-205  8  5  2450  1  1 6600  7850
      IO  260      7500  8600, IO  85D PATH  5450   6300, IO 165D VLVO 8250 9500
26  7 OPEN FISHERMAN     OP  CTRCN KEV SV OB        8  5  1700         3350  3900
26  7 OPEN FISHERMAN     OP  CTRCN KEV SV IO 170-205  8  5  2450  1  1 6400  7600
26  7 OPEN FISHERMAN     OP  CTRCN KEV SV IO  260    8  5  2650  1  1 7250  8350
26  7 OPEN FISHERMAN     OP  CTRCN KEV SV IO 165D VLVO 8  5  2850  1  4 8050  9250
26  7 RAISED CUDDY       ST  CUD   KEV SV OB        8  4  2150  1  1 3450  4050
26  7 RAISED CUDDY       ST  CUD   KEV SV IO  205  OMC   8  4  2650  1  2 6450  7450
      IO  260      7200  8250, IO  165D VLVO  6850   7900, IO T115 OMC  7100 8150
      IO T170      8100  9300, IO T 85D PATH  8000   9200, IO T165D VLVO 11200 12700
```

HARLING AND RINGSTAD

Call 1-800-327-6929 for BUC Personalized Evaluation Service
Or, for 1959 to 1963 boats, sign onto www.BUCValuPro.com

HARMONIE SHIPYARD INC

Call 1-800-327-6929 for BUC Personalized Evaluation Service
Or, for 1982 to 1984 boats, sign onto www.BUCValuPro.com

HARMONY BOATS
COAST GUARD MFG ID- DWP

Call 1-800-327-6929 for BUC Personalized Evaluation Service
Or, for 1980 to 1983 boats, sign onto www.BUCValuPro.com

HARMONY MARINE INC
WAYNE H COLONEY CO   COAST GUARD MFG ID- HRT

Call 1-800-327-6929 for BUC Personalized Evaluation Service
Or, for 1979 to 1981 boats, sign onto www.BUCValuPro.com

HARRIS CUTTYHUNK BOATS INC
W FALMOUTH MA 02574   COAST GUARD MFG ID- HCH See inside cover to adjust price for area

```
LOA   NAME AND/          TOP/ BOAT  -HULL-  ----ENGINE---  BEAM   WGT  DRAFT RETAIL RETAIL
FT IN  OR MODEL          RIG  TYPE  MTL TP TP # HP  MFG   FT IN  LBS  FT IN  LOW   HIGH
------------------- 1983 BOATS ---------------------------------------------------------
22    CUTTYHUNK 22       OP  CTRCN FBG SV OB        7  7       1  4 3200  3750
22    CUTTYHUNK 22       OP  CTRCN FBG SV IO  120  7  7       1  4 7000  8050
      IB  125  VLVO 8000 9200, IO 138-140  7250  8350, IB 36D- 50D 10900 13200
22    CUTTYHUNK 22       HT  CUD   FBG SV OB        7  7       1  4 3950  4550
22    CUTTYHUNK 22       HT  CUD   FBG SV IO  120  7  7       1  4 7500  8500
      IB  125  VLVO 9050 10300, IO 138-140  7600  8750, IB 36D- 50D 11700 14200
22    CUTTYHUNK 22       HT  PH    FBG    IB  125  VLVO 7  7  1  4 6200  7150
22    CUTTYHUNK 22       HT  PH    FBG    IB  140  OMC  7  7  1  4 5300  6100
22    CUTTYHUNK 22       HT  PH    FBG    IB  36D- 50D  7  7  1  4 24100 27600
22    CUTTYHUNK 22       HT  PH    FBG SV OB        7  7       1  4 2750  3200
22    CUTTYHUNK 22       HT  PH    FBG SV IO 120-140  7  7     1  4 5350  6400
27 10 CUTTYHUNK 28       FB  CR    FBG SV IB  170  MRCR 10  1 9430 2 11 24700 27400
27 10 CUTTYHUNK 28       FB  CR    FBG SV IB  85D-165D 10 1 9430 2 11 33400 38900
27 10 CUTTYHUNK 28       TT  SF    FBG SV IB  170  MRCR 10  1 9430 2 11 24700 27400
27 10 CUTTYHUNK 28       TT  SF    FBG SV IB  85D-165D 10 1 9430 2 11 33400 38900
27 10 CUTTYHUNK 28       HT  TRWL  FBG SV IB  170  MRCR 10  1 9430 2 11 27100 30100
27 10 CUTTYHUNK 28       HT  TRWL  FBG SV IB  85D PERK 10 1 9430 2 11 34500 38400
27 10 CUTTYHUNK 28       HT  TRWL  FBG SV IB 135D-200D 10 1 9430 2 11 39200 46600
27 10 CUTTYHUNK 28       FB  TRWL  FBG SV IB  170  MRCR 10  1 9430 2 11 27100 30100
27 10 CUTTYHUNK 28       FB  TRWL  FBG SV IB  85D PERK 10 1 9430 2 11 34500 38400
27 10 CUTTYHUNK 28       FB  TRWL  FBG SV IB 135D-200D 10 1 9430 2 11 39200 46600
------------------- 1982 BOATS ---------------------------------------------------------
22    CUTTYHUNK 22       OP  CTRCN FBG SV OB        7  7       1  4 3150  3650
22    CUTTYHUNK 22       OP  CTRCN FBG SV IO  120  7  7       1  4 6850  7850
      IB  125  VLVO 7650 8800, IO  140  6850  8150, IB 33D- 50D 10400 12700
22    CUTTYHUNK 22       HT  CUD   FBG SV OB        7  7       1  4 3800  4400
22    CUTTYHUNK 22       HT  CUD   FBG SV IO  120  7  7       1  4 7250  8300
      IB  125  VLVO 8550 9850, IO  140  7250  8550, IB 33D- 50D 11200 13600
22    CUTTYHUNK 22       HT  PH    FBG    IB  125  VLVO 7  7  1  4 5950  6850
22    CUTTYHUNK 22       HT  PH    FBG    IO  140  OMC  7  7  1  4 5200  5950
22    CUTTYHUNK 22       HT  PH    FBG    IO  33D- 50D  7  7  1  4 23100 26600
22    CUTTYHUNK 22       HT  PH    FBG SV OB        7  7       1  4 2700  3100
22    CUTTYHUNK 22       HT  PH    FBG SV IO 120-140  7  7     1  4 5250  6250
27 10 CUTTYHUNK 28       FB  CR    FBG SV IB  170  MRCR 10  1 9430 2 11 23600 26200
```

LOA FT IN	NAME AND/ OR MODEL	TOP/ RIG	BOAT TYPE	-HULL- MTL TP	TP	----ENGINE--- # HP	MFG	BEAM FT IN	WGT LBS	DRAFT FT IN	RETAIL LOW	RETAIL HIGH
---------------- 1982 BOATS ----------------
27 10	CUTTYHUNK 28	FB	CR	FBG SV	IB	85D-165D		10 1	9430	2 11	32100	37400
27 10	CUTTYHUNK 28	TT	SF	FBG SV	IB	170	MRCR	10 1	9430	2 11	23600	26200
27 10	CUTTYHUNK 28	TT	SF	FBG SV	IB	85D-165D		10 1	9430	2 11	32100	37400
27 10	CUTTYHUNK 28	HT	TRWL	FBG SV	IB	170	MRCR	10 1	9430	2 11	25900	28800
27 10	CUTTYHUNK 28	HT	TRWL	FBG SV	IB	85D PERK		10 1	9430	2 11	33200	36900
27 10	CUTTYHUNK 28	HT	TRWL	FBG SV	IB	135D-200D		10 1	9430	2 11	37600	44800
27 10	CUTTYHUNK 28	FB	TRWL	FBG SV	IB	170	MRCR	10 1	9430	2 11	25900	28800
27 10	CUTTYHUNK 28	FB	TRWL	FBG SV	IB	85D PERK		10 1	9430	2 11	33200	36900
27 10	CUTTYHUNK 28	FB	TRWL	FBG SV	IB	135D-200D		10 1	9430	2 11	37600	44800

HARRIS TAYLOR MARINE & IND LTD
PEGASUS YACHTS
FORMERLY RYDGEWAY MARINE LTD

Call 1-800-327-6929 for BUC Personalized Evaluation Service
Or, for 1978 to 1994 boats, sign onto www.BUCValuPro.com

HARRIS YACHTS INC
NEWBURYPORT MA   COAST GUARD MFG ID- DFH See inside cover to adjust price for area

LOA FT IN	NAME AND/ OR MODEL	TOP/ RIG	BOAT TYPE	-HULL- MTL TP	TP	----ENGINE--- # HP	MFG	BEAM FT IN	WGT LBS	DRAFT FT IN	RETAIL LOW	RETAIL HIGH
---------------- 1980 BOATS ----------------
36	HARRIS COMM FISH	HT	CR	F/S SV	IB	T250D	CAT	12	14000	3 5	43800	48600
36	HARRIS EXPRESS FISH	TT	SF	F/S SV	IB	T250D	CAT	12 3	17000	3	48800	53600
36	HARRIS MARLIN	TT	OPFSH	F/S SV	IB	T250D	CAT	12 3	16500	2 10	46700	51300
36	HARRIS SPORT FISH	F+T	SF	F/S SV	IB	T250D	CAT	12 3	18000	3	50300	55300
---------------- 1978 BOATS ----------------
35 10	HARRIS 36	F+T	EXP	F/S SV	IB	T330	CHRY	12 3	16000	2 9	36900	41000
35 10	HARRIS 36	F+T	EXP	F/S SV	IB	T225D	CAT	12 3	17000	2 10	49400	54300
35 10	HARRIS 36	F+T	SF	F/S SV	IB	T330	CHRY	12 3	16500	2 9	37200	41300
35 10	HARRIS 36	F+T	SF	F/S SV	IB	T200D	GM	12 3	14000	3 2	41600	46300
35 10	HARRIS 36	F+T	SF	F/S SV	IB	T225D	CAT	12 3	17500	2 10	48800	53700
---------------- 1977 BOATS ----------------
35 10	HARRIS 36	F+T	SF	F/S SV	IB	T225D	CAT	12 3	17000	2 10	46400	51000
35 10	HARRIS 36 COMMERCIAL	HT	FSH	F/S SV	IB	225D	CAT	12	13000	3 3	35100	39000
35 10	HARRIS 36 FISH	TT	EXP	F/S SV	IB	T225D	CAT	12 3	16200	2 10	46400	51000
---------------- 1976 BOATS ----------------
35 10	HARRIS 35	FB	SF	F/S SV	IB	T225D	CAT	12 3	17000	2 10	44200	49100
35 10	HARRIS 35 FSH	FB	EXP	F/S SV	IB	T225D	CAT	12 3	17000	2 10	45700	50200

HARRISKAYOT
DIV OF HARRISKAYOT INC
FORT WAYNE IN 46808   COAST GUARD MFG ID- KAY See inside cover to adjust price for area
FORMERLY KAYOT

For more recent years, see the BUC Used Boat Price Guide, Volume 1 or Volume 2

LOA FT IN	NAME AND/ OR MODEL	TOP/ RIG	BOAT TYPE	-HULL- MTL TP	TP	----ENGINE--- # HP	MFG	BEAM FT IN	WGT LBS	DRAFT FT IN	RETAIL LOW	RETAIL HIGH
---------------- 1983 BOATS ----------------
30	8330-1 DELUXE	HT	HB	AL PN	OB			8	4000		3850	4500
30	8330-1 ECONOMY	HT	HB	AL PN	OB			8	4000		3400	3950
34	8334-1	HT	HB	AL PN	OB						6500	7500
39	8339-2	HT	HB	AL PN	OB						12400	14100
39	8339-2	HT	HB	AL PN	IO	140	OMC				13300	15100
41	8341-2	HT	HB	AL PN	OB						7800	8950
41	8341-2	HT	HB	AL PN	IO	140	OMC				14600	16600
51	8351-2	HT	HB	AL PN	OB						16800	19100
51	8351-2	HT	HB	AL PN	IO	140	OMC				19900	22200
---------------- 1980 BOATS ----------------
17	MONTEGO K-170	OP		FBG TR	IO			7 9	1250		2300	2650
17	MONTEGO K-170	OP		FBG TR	IO	120		7 9			2150	2500
20	MONTEREY K-200	OP		FBG TR	IO			7 9	1400		2850	3350
20	MONTEREY K-200	OP		FBG TR	IO	120		7 9			3750	4350
36	AMBASSADOR	HT	HB	AL PN	OB			12			9800	11100
36	AMBASSADOR	HT	HB	STL PN	OB			12			8400	9650
36	AMBASSADOR	HT	HB	AL PN	IO	120		12			12000	13600
36	AMBASSADOR	HT	HB	STL PN	IO	120		12			10500	12000
41	AMBASSADOR	HT	HB	AL PN	OB			13 11			7400	8500
41	AMBASSADOR	HT	HB	AL PN	IO	120		13 11			13800	15700
46	ROYAL-AMBASSADOR	HT	HB	AL PN	OB			13 11			14600	16600
46	ROYAL-AMBASSADOR	HT	HB	STL PN	OB			13 6			13300	15200
46	ROYAL-AMBASSADOR	HT	HB	AL PN	IO	120		13 11			19400	21500
46	ROYAL-AMBASSADOR	HT	HB	STL PN	IO	120		13 6			17400	19700
---------------- 1979 BOATS ----------------
36	AMBASSADOR	HT	HB	STL PN	OB			12			8250	9500
36	AMBASSADOR	HT	HB	STL PN	IO	120		12			10400	11800
46	ROYAL-AMBASSADOR	HT	HB	STL PN	OB			13 6			13200	14900
46	ROYAL-AMBASSADOR	HT	HB	STL PN	IO	120		13 6			17100	19400
---------------- 1978 BOATS ----------------
39	AMBASSADOR 39	HT	HB	AL PN	IO	120		13 5	12000		11400	12900
46	AMBASSADOR 46	HT	HB	AL PN	IO	120		13 5	16300		16200	18400
---------------- 1977 BOATS ----------------
37 6	AMBASSADOR	HT	HB	STL PN	OB			12	12000		9150	10400
37 6	AMBASSADOR	HT	HB	STL PN	IO	140	MRCR	12	12000		10200	11600
46	AMBASSADOR	HT	HB	STL PN	IO	120		12	12000		11800	13400
46	ROYAL-AMBASSADOR	HT	HB	STL PN	OB			14	16300		13100	14900
46	ROYAL-AMBASSADOR	HT	HB	STL PN	IO	120		14	16300		14700	16700
46	ROYAL-AMBASSADOR	HT	HB	STL PN	IO	140	MRCR	14	16300		14700	16700
---------------- 1976 BOATS ----------------
35	ROYAL-VISTA	HT	HB	STL PN	OB			12	7200		6550	7550
40	ROYAL-CAPRI	HT	HB	STL PN	OB			12	10450		7500	8650
46	ROYAL-VOYAGER	HT	HB	STL PN	OB			14	14500		11900	13500
---------------- 1975 BOATS ----------------
40	ROYAL-CAPRI 10	HT	HB	AL RB	OB			12	10450		8250	9450
40	ROYAL-CAPRI 10	HT	HB	STL RB	OB			12	10450		7150	8250
40	ROYAL-CAPRI 6	HT	HB	AL RB	OB			12	10450		8250	9450
40	ROYAL-CAPRI 6	HT	HB	STL RB	OB			12	10450		7150	8250
---------------- 1974 BOATS ----------------
33	ROYAL-VISTA	HT	HB	AL PN	OB			12	6300		6200	7100
33	ROYAL-VISTA	HT	HB	STL PN	OB			12	6300		6100	7000
40	ROYAL-CAPRI 100	HT	HB	AL PN	OB			12	10450		7300	8400
40	ROYAL-CAPRI 200	HT	HB	STL PN	OB			12	10450		7450	8550
---------------- 1973 BOATS ----------------
30	CAPRICE	HT	HB	STL PN	OB			10	6300		5600	6450
30	CAPRICE AL	HT	HB	AL PN	OB			10	5500		5250	6050
40	ROYAL-CAPRI III	HT	HB	AL PN	OB			12	10000		8050	9250
40	ROYAL-CAPRI III	HT	HB	STL PN	OB			12	10450		7300	8400
---------------- 1972 BOATS ----------------
30	CAPRICE	HT	HB	AL PN	OB			10	4800		4350	5000
30	CAPRICE	HT	HB	STL PN	OB			10	6450		5700	6550
40	ROYAL-CAPRI II	HT	HB	STL CT				12	10500		6900	7950
---------------- 1971 BOATS ----------------
30	CAPRICE 30	HT	HB	STL CT	OB			10	6900		5700	6550
34	CAPRI 34	HT	HB	AL CT				10	6000	1 8	5600	6400
34	CAPRI 34	HT	HB	STL CT				10	7400	1 8	6050	6950
38 6	ROYAL 39	HT	SF	STL CT				10	8800	1 8	6200	7150
38 6	ROYAL-CAPRI 39	HT	HB	AL CT				10	7000	1 8	5800	6700
40 2	ROYAL-CAPRI 40	HT	HB	STL	OB			10	10450		6900	7900
40 2	ROYAL-VOYAGER	HT	HB	FBG	IO	T165	MRCR	12	13500	2 9	11700	13300
40 2	ROYAL-VOYAGER	HT	HB	FBG	IO	T215	MRCR	12	13500	2 5	11800	13400
---------------- 1970 BOATS ----------------
34 10	CAPRI	HT	HB	AL PN	OB			12			6550	7550
34 10	CAPRI	HT	HB	STL PN	OB			12			5950	6850
40 10	ROYAL-CAPRI	HT	HB	AL PN	OB			12			6700	7700
40 10	ROYAL-CAPRI	HT	HB	STL PN	OB			12			5950	6800
41	ROYAL-VOYAGER	HT	HB	FBG SV	OB			14			6150	7050
---------------- 1969 BOATS ----------------
31	CAPRI	HT	HB	AL				10	4200	1 2	3350	3900
31	CAPRI	HT	HB	STL				10	6500	1 2	5900	6250
31	VISTA	HT	HB	AL				10	3800	1 1	2750	3200
31	VISTA	HT	HB	STL				10	5650	1 1	4650	5350
36	1936	HT	HB	STL PN	IO			10	8150		7350	8450
36	1936AL	HT	HB	AL PN	IO			10	5900		6350	7250
36	ROYAL-CAPRI	HT	HB	AL	OB			10	4800	1 3	3900	4500
36	ROYAL-CAPRI	HT	HB	STL				10	7500	1 3	5600	6450
---------------- 1968 BOATS ----------------
31	CAPRI	HT	HB	AL PN	OB			10	5000	10	4500	5150
31	CAPRI	HT	HB	STL PN	OB			10	6500	10	5600	6400
31	VISTA	HT	HB	AL PN	OB			10	3800	10	2750	3200
31	VISTA	HT	HB	STL PN	OB			10	5650	10	4850	5550
36	ROYAL-CAPRI	HT	HB	AL PN	OB			10	6300	10	5650	6500
36	ROYAL-CAPRI	HT	HB	STL PN	OB			10	8000	10	6150	7050
---------------- 1967 BOATS ----------------
31	CAPRI	HT	HB	AL	OB			10		10	3600	4200
31	CAPRI	HT	HB	STL	OB			10		10	3200	3750
31	VISTA	HT	HB	AL	OB			8		10	3600	4200
31	VISTA	HT	HB	STL	OB			8		10	3200	3750
---------------- 1966 BOATS ----------------
31	CAPRI	HT	HB	AL	OB			10		10	4100	4750
31	CAPRI	HT	HB	STL	OB			10		10	3700	4300

LOA FT IN	NAME AND/ OR MODEL	TOP/ RIG	BOAT TYPE	-HULL- MTL TP	----ENGINE--- TP # HP	MFG	BEAM FT IN	WGT LBS	DRAFT FT IN	RETAIL LOW	RETAIL HIGH
--- 1966 BOATS ---
31	VISTA	HT	HB	AL	OB	10				3100	3600
31	VISTA	HT	HB	STL	OB	10				2750	3200
--- 1965 BOATS ---
31	CAPRI IV	HT	HB	STL	OB					3200	3700
--- 1964 BOATS ---
31	CAPRI III	HT	HB	AL	OB					3550	4150
31	CAPRI III	HT	HB	STL	OB					3150	3700
--- 1963 BOATS ---
31	CAPRI II	HT	HB	STL	OB	4800				3600	4200
--- 1962 BOATS ---
31	CASA-CAPRI	HT	HB	STL	OB					3150	3650

HARSTAD TRAWLER CO
CLIPPER MARINE CORP   COAST GUARD MFG ID- HRD

Call 1-800-327-6929 for BUC Personalized Evaluation Service
Or, for 1976 to 1978 boats, sign onto www.BUCValuPro.com

HARSTIL INDUSTRIES INC
COAST GUARD MFG ID- HRS

Call 1-800-327-6929 for BUC Personalized Evaluation Service
Or, for 1960 to 1986 boats, sign onto www.BUCValuPro.com

HARTGE YACHT YARD
COAST GUARD MFG ID- HBK

Call 1-800-327-6929 for BUC Personalized Evaluation Service
Or, for 1959 to 1963 boats, sign onto www.BUCValuPro.com

HARTLEY MARINE LTD

Call 1-800-327-6929 for BUC Personalized Evaluation Service
Or, for 1979 to 1982 boats, sign onto www.BUCValuPro.com

HARTSILL INDUSTRIES

Call 1-800-327-6929 for BUC Personalized Evaluation Service
Or, for 1971 boats, sign onto www.BUCValuPro.com

HARTWELL BOAT BUILDERS LTD
DEVON ENGLAND   See inside cover to adjust price for area

LOA FT IN	NAME AND/ OR MODEL	TOP/ RIG	BOAT TYPE	-HULL- MTL TP	----ENGINE--- TP # HP	MFG	BEAM FT IN	WGT LBS	DRAFT FT IN	RETAIL LOW	RETAIL HIGH
--- 1969 BOATS ---
31 6	GOLDEN-HIND	SLP	SA/CR	FBG TK	IB 21D LIST	9	11600	3 8		17100	19400
--- 1968 BOATS ---
31 6	GOLDEN-HIND	SLP	SAIL	F/W KL	IB 10D SABB	9	11600	3 8		18400	20400
--- 1967 BOATS ---
31	GOLDEN-HIND 31	SLP	SA/CR	PLY KL	OB	8 10		3 6		12200	13800

HENRY HARVEY & SONS INC
HARVEY CRAFT

Call 1-800-327-6929 for BUC Personalized Evaluation Service
Or, for 1959 boats, sign onto www.BUCValuPro.com

HARVEY MARINE
DIV OF THE HARVEY CORP   COAST GUARD MFG ID- HVY

Call 1-800-327-6929 for BUC Personalized Evaluation Service
Or, for 1959 to 1979 boats, sign onto www.BUCValuPro.com

HATTERAS YACHTS
DIV OF BRUNSWICK CORP   See inside cover to adjust price for area
NEW BERN NC 28560   COAST GUARD MFG ID- HAT

For more recent years, see the BUC Used Boat Price Guide, Volume 1 or Volume 2

LOA FT IN	NAME AND/ OR MODEL	TOP/ RIG	BOAT TYPE	-HULL- MTL TP	----ENGINE--- TP # HP	MFG	BEAM FT IN	WGT LBS	DRAFT FT IN	RETAIL LOW	RETAIL HIGH
--- 1983 BOATS ---
32 8	FLYBRIDGE FISHERMAN	FB	SDNSF	FBG DV	IB T300		12	18000		49800	54700
32 8	SPORT FISHERMAN	OP	SF	FBG DV	IB T300		12	17200		49000	53800
32 8	SPORT FISHERMAN	OP	SF	FBG DV	IBT300D-T305D		12	19100		73400	80700
36 6	CONVERTIBLE	FB	SDNSF	FBG DV	IB T300		13 7	26500		75000	82400
36 6	CONVERTIBLE	FB	SDNSF	FBG DV	IB T275D	GM	13 7	26500		87500	96200
36 6	CONVERTIBLE	FB	SDNSF	FBG DV	IB T375D	GM	13 7	26500		92700	102000
36 6	SPORT FISHERMAN	OP	SF	FBG DV	IB T300		13 7	25000		71700	78800
36 6	SPORT FISHERMAN	OP	SF	FBG DV	IB T275D	GM	13 7	25000		83900	92200
36 6	SPORT FISHERMAN	OP	SF	FBG DV	IB T375D	GM	13 7	25000		89100	97900
37	CONVERTIBLE	FB	SDNSF	FBG DV	IB T390D	GM	14	29000	3 3	102500	112500
42 6	LONG RANGE CRUISER	FB	LRPH	FBG DS	IB T140D	GM	14 6	35000	3 10	121000	133000
43 1	DOUBLE CABIN	HT	DC	FBG SV	IB T284D	GM	14	34000	3 5	123500	135500
43 1	DOUBLE CABIN	FB	DC	FBG SV	IB T390D	GM	14	34000	3 5	132000	145000
43 1	TRIPLE CABIN	HT	DC	FBG SV	IB T284D	GM	14	34000	3 5	127500	140000
43 1	TRIPLE CABIN	FB	DC	FBG SV	IB T390D	GM	14	34000	3 5	136000	149500
43 8	CONVERTIBLE	FB	SF	FBG SV	IB T435D	GM	14 6	37000	4 2	141500	155500
43 2	CONVERTIBLE	FB	SF	FBG SV	IB T435D	GM	14 6	37000	4 2	147000	162000
43 8	CONVERTIBLE HIGHPERF	FB	SF	FBG SV	IB T500D	GM	14 6	37000	4 2	147000	162000
46 2	CONVERTIBLE	FB	SF	FBG SV	IB T435D	GM	14 9	41000	4 2	149000	164000
46 2	CONVERTIBLE HIGHPERF	FB	SF	FBG SV	IB T650D	S&S	14 9	41000	4 2	164000	180000
48 8	COCKPIT YACHT	FB	MYCPT	FBG SV	IB T285D	GM	15	45000	3 11	146500	161000
48 8	COCKPIT YACHT	FB	MYCPT	FBG SV	IB T425D	GM	15	45000	3 11	161000	177000
48 8	MOTOR YACHT	FB	MY	FBG SV	IB T285D	GM	15	45000	3 11	149000	164000
48 8	MOTOR YACHT	FB	MY	FBG SV	IB T425D	GM	15	45000	3 11	159500	175500
50	CONVERTIBLE	FB	YTFS	FBG SV	IB T550D	GM	16 4	54000	4 6	180000	198000
50	CONVERTIBLE HIGHPERF	FB	YTFS	FBG SV	IB T650D	S&S	16 4	54000	4 6	188500	207500
53 1	EXTENDED DECKHOUSE	FB	MY	FBG SV	IB T462D	GM	15 10	57000		209500	230000
53 1	MOTOR YACHT	FB	MY	FBG SV	IB T450D	GM	15 10	55000	4	203000	223000
55 8	CONVERTIBLE	FB	YTFS	FBG SV	IB T650D	GM	17 6	68000	4 10	284000	312000
55 8	CONVERTIBLE HIGHPERF	FB	YTFS	FBG SV	IB T825D	GM	17 6	68000	4 10	308500	339000
56 3	MOTOR YACHT	HT	MY	FBG SV	IB T550D	GM	18 2	74000	4 11	290500	319000
56 3	MOTOR YACHT	FB	MY	FBG SV	IB T550D	GM	18 2	74000	4 11	285000	313000
60 11	CONVERTIBLE	FB	YTFS	FBG SV	IB T650D	GM	18	82000	4 11	330000	362500
60 11	CONVERTIBLE HIGHPERF	FB	YTFS	FBG SV	IB T825D	GM	18	82000	4 11	374500	412000
60 11	CONVERTIBLE HIGHPERF	FB	YTFS	FBG SV	IB T975D	S&S	18	82000	4 11	390500	429000
61 3	COCKPIT YACHT	HT	MYCPT	FBG SV	IB T650D	GM	18 2	81000	4 11	354000	389000
61 3	COCKPIT YACHT	FB	MYCPT	FBG SV	IB T650D	GM	18 2	81000	4 11	351000	386000
61 3	MOTOR YACHT	HT	MY	FBG SV	IB T650D	GM	18 2	82000	4 11	344000	378000
61 3	MOTOR YACHT	FB	MY	FBG SV	IB T650D	GM	18 2	82000	4 11	341500	375000
64 1	MOTOR YACHT	HT	MY	FBG SV	IB T650D	GM	18	95000	5	417000	458000
64 1	MOTOR YACHT	FB	MY	FBG SV	IB T650D	GM	18	95000	5	417000	458000
65	LONG RANGE CRUISER	FB	LRPH	FBG SV	IB T174D	GM	17 11	52T	5	381000	418500
65	SAIL YACHT	SLP	SA/CR	FBG KC	IB T175D	GM	17 2	56T	13 10	414500	455500
70 2	MOTOR YACHT	FB	MYDKH	FBG SV	IB T650D	GM	18 7	54T	5	498000	547500
72	MOTOR YACHT	FB	MY	FBG DV	IB T675D	GM				**	**
77	COCKPIT MOTOR YACHT	FB	MYCPT	FBG DV	IB T675D	GM				**	**
77	COCKPIT MOTORYACHT	FB	MYCPT	FBG DV	IB T	GM				**	**
77	MOTOR YACHT	FB	MY	FBG DV	IB T675D	GM				**	**
--- 1982 BOATS ---
32 8	SPORT FISHERMAN	OP	SF	FBG SV	IB T340	MRCR	12		2	35200	39100
32 8	SPORT FISHERMAN	FB	SF	FBG SV	IB T	D CAT	12		2	**	**
32 8	SPORT FISHERMAN	FB	SF	FBG SV	IB T340	MRCR	12		2	35200	39100
32 8	SPORT FISHERMAN	FB	SF	FBG SV	IB T	D CAT	12		2	**	**
37	CONVERTIBLE	FB	SDNSF	FBG DV	IB T390D	GM	14	29000	3 3	97800	107500
42 6	LONG RANGE CRUISER	FB	LRPH	FBG DS	IB T112D	GM	14 6	35000	3 10	114500	126000
43 1	DOUBLE CABIN	HT	DC	FBG SV	IB T285D	GM	14	34000	3 5	120000	132000
43 1	DOUBLE CABIN	FB	DC	FBG SV	IB T340D	GM	14	34000	3 5	124500	136700
43 1	TRIPLE CABIN	HT	TCMY	FBG SV	IB T285D	GM	14	34000	3 5	125500	137500
43 1	TRIPLE CABIN	FB	TCMY	FBG SV	IB T340D	GM	14	34000	3 5	130000	143000
43 8	CONVERTIBLE	FB	SF	FBG SV	IB T450D	GM	14 6	37000	4 2	134000	147000
43 8	CONVERTIBLE	FB	SF	FBG SV	IB T500D	GM	14 6	37000	4 2	139000	153000
43 8	CONVERTIBLE ALT ARRG	FB	SF	FBG SV	IB T450D	GM	14 6	37000	4 2	141500	155500
43 8	CONVERTIBLE ALT ARRG	FB	SF	FBG SV	IB T500D	GM	14 6	37000	4 2	146000	160500
46 2	CONVERTIBLE	FB	SF	FBG SV	IB T450D	GM	14 9	41000	4 2	143500	157500
46 2	CONVERTIBLE	FB	SF	FBG SV	IB T650D	GM	14 9	41000	4 2	158500	174000
48 8	COCKPIT YACHT	FB	MYCPT	FBG SV	IB T285D	GM	15	45000	3 11	150500	165500
48 8	COCKPIT YACHT	FB	MYCPT	FBG SV	IB T425D	GM	15	45000	3 11	154500	170000
48 8	MOTOR YACHT	FB	MY	FBG SV	IB T285D	GM	15	45000	3 11	141500	155500
48 8	MOTOR YACHT	FB	MY	FBG SV	IB T425D	GM	15	45000	3 11	151500	166500
50	CONVERTIBLE	FB	SF	FBG SV	IB T550D	GM	16 4	54000	4 6	180000	197500

LOA FT	IN	NAME AND/ OR MODEL	TOP/ RIG	BOAT TYPE	-HULL- MTL	TP	TP	----ENGINE--- # HP	MFG	BEAM FT	IN	WGT LBS	DRAFT FT	IN	RETAIL LOW	RETAIL HIGH
		1982 BOATS														
50		CONVERTIBLE	FB	SF	FBG	SV	IB	T650D	GM	16	4	54000	4	6	189500	208000
53		YACHT FISHERMAN	FB	YTFS	FBG	SV	IB	T450D	GM	15	10	57000	4		192500	211500
53	1	MOTOR YACHT	FB	MY	FBG	SV	IB	T450D	GM	15	10	55000	4		194500	214000
55	8	CONVERTIBLE	FB	SF	FBG	SV	IB	T650D	GM	17	6	68000	4	10	272000	299000
56	3	MOTOR YACHT	HT	MY	FBG	SV	IB	T625D	GM	18	2	74000	4	11	289500	318000
58	2	COCKPIT YACHT	FB	MYCPT	FBG	SV	IB	T550D	GM	15	10	78000	4	9	306500	336500
58	4	YACHT FISHERMAN	FB	YTFS	FBG	SV	IB	T450D	GM	15	10	62500	4	9	228500	251000
60	11	CONVERTIBLE	FB	SF	FBG	SV	IB	T825D	GM	18		82000	4	11	332500	365500
60	11	CONVERTIBLE	FB	SF	FBG	SV	IB	T975D	GM	18		82000	4	11	351000	385500
60	11	CONVERTIBLE	FB	YTFS	FBG	SV	IB	T650D	GM	18		82000	4	11	315000	346000
60	11	CONVERTIBLE	FB	YTFS	FBG	SV	IB	T925D	GM	18	2	83000	5		353000	388000
61	3	COCKPIT MOTOR YACHT	FB	MYCPT	FBG	SV	IB	T650D	GM	18	2	81000	4	11	319500	351000
61	3	MOTOR YACHT	HT	MY	FBG	SV	IB	T650D	GM	18	2	82000	4	11	328500	361000
64	1	MOTOR YACHT	HT	MY	FBG	SV	IB	T650D	GM	18	4	95000	5		398000	437000
65		LONG RANGE CRUISER	FB	LRPH	FBG	DB	IB	T174D	GM	17	11	52T	5		364000	400000
65		SAIL YACHT	SLP	SA/CR	FBG	KC	IB	T115D	GM	17	2	56T	13	10	389500	428000
70	2	MOTOR YACHT	HT	MY	FBG	SV	IB	T650D	GM	18	7	54T	5		475500	522500
70	2	MOTOR YACHT EXT DECK	HT	MYDKH	FBG	SV	IB	T650D	GM	18	7	54T	5		479000	526500
		1981 BOATS														
37		SPORT FISHERMAN	FB	SDN	FBG	SV	IB	T284D	GM	14		29000	3	3	88700	97400
37		SPORT FISHERMAN	FB	SDN	FBG	SV	IB	T390D	GM	14		29000	3	3	94400	103500
42	6	LONG RANGE CRUISER	FB	LRPH	FBG	DS	IB	T112D	GM	14	6	35000	3	10	109000	120000
43	1	DOUBLE CABIN	HT	DC	FBG	SV	IB	T284D	GM	14		34000	3	5	114000	125500
43	1	DOUBLE CABIN	HT	DC	FBG	SV	IB	T390D	GM	14		34000	3	5	122500	134500
43	1	DOUBLE CABIN	FB	DC	FBG	SV	IB	T284D	GM	14		34000	3	5	114000	125500
43	1	DOUBLE CABIN	FB	DC	FBG	SV	IB	T390D	GM	14		34000	3	5	122000	134000
43	8	CONVERTIBLE ALT ARRG	FB	SF	FBG	SV	IB	T450D	GM	14	6	37000	4	2	132000	145000
43	8	SPORT FISHERMAN	FB	SDN	FBG	SV	IB	T450D	GM	14	6	37000	4	2	125500	138000
46	2	SPORT FISHERMAN	FB	SDN	FBG	SV	IB	T450D	GM	14	9	41000	4	2	131000	144000
48	8	COCKPIT YACHT	FB	MYCPT	FBG	SV	IB	T285D	GM	15		45000	3	11	134500	147500
48	8	COCKPIT YACHT	FB	MYCPT	FBG	SV	IB	T425D	GM	15		45000	3	11	147500	162000
48	8	MOTOR YACHT	FB	MY	FBG	SV	IB	T285D	GM	15		45000	3	11	135000	148000
48	8	MOTOR YACHT	FB	MY	FBG	SV	IB	T425D	GM	15		45000	3	11	144500	158500
48	10	LONG RANGE CRUISER	FB	LRPH	FBG	DS	IB	T112D	GM	16	6	54000	4	6	140000	153500
50		SPORT FISHERMAN	FB	SDN	FBG	SV	IB	T550D	GM	16	4	54000	4	6	171500	188500
53		YACHT FISHERMAN	FB	YTFS	FBG	SV	IB	T450D	GM	15	10	57000	4		184000	202000
53	1	MOTOR YACHT	FB	MY	FBG	SV	IB	T450D	GM	15	10	55000	4		186500	204500
53	7	CONVERTIBLE	FB	SDN	FBG	SV	IB	T650D	GM	16		61000	4		240500	264500
55	8	SPORT FISHERMAN	FB	SDN	FBG	SV	IB	T650D	GM	17	6	68000	4	10	260500	286000
56	3	MOTOR YACHT	HT	MY	FBG	SV	IB	T550D	GM	18	2	74000	4	11	264500	291000
56	3	MOTOR YACHT	FB	MY	FBG	SV	IB	T550D	GM	18	2	74000	4	11	259500	285000
58	2	COCKPIT MOTOR YACHT	HT	MYCPT	FBG	SV	IB	T550D	GM	15	10	73000	4	9	275000	302000
58	2	COCKPIT MOTOR YACHT	FB	MYCPT	FBG	SV	IB	T550D	GM	15	10	73000	4	9	270500	297500
58	2	LONG RANGE CRUISER	FB	LRPH	FBG	DS	IB	T115D	GM	17	11	90000	4	10	248500	273000
58	2	LONG RANGE CRUISER	FB	LRPH	FBG	DS	IB	T174D	GM	17	11	90000	4	10	261500	287500
58	3	MOTOR YACHT	HT	MY	FBG	SV	IB	T550D	GM	15	10	78000	4	9	283000	311000
58	4	YACHT FISHERMAN	FB	YTFS	FBG	SV	IB	T450D	GM	15	10	62500	4	9	217500	239000
60	11	CONVERTIBLE	FB	SDN	FBG	SV	IB	T650D	GM	18		82000	4	11	297500	326500
61	3	COCKPIT YACHT	HT	MYCPT	FBG	SV	IB	T650D	GM	18	2	81000	4	11	322000	354000
61	3	COCKPIT YACHT	FB	MYCPT	FBG	SV	IB	T650D	GM	18	2	81000	4	11	319500	351000
61	3	MOTOR YACHT	HT	MY	FBG	SV	IB	T650D	GM	18	2	82000	4	11	313000	344000
61	3	MOTOR YACHT	FB	MY	FBG	SV	IB	T650D	GM	18	2	82000	4	11	311000	341500
64	1	MOTOR YACHT	HT	MY	FBG	SV	IB	T650D	GM	18	4	95000	5		379000	416500
64	1	MOTOR YACHT	FB	MY	FBG	SV	IB	T650D	GM	18	4	95000	5		379000	416500
65		LONG RANGE CRUISER	FB	LRPH	FBG	SV	IB	T174D	GM	17	11	52T	5		347500	381500
70	2	MOTOR YACHT	HT	MY	FBG	SV	IB	T650D	GM	18	7	54T	5		453000	497500
70	2	MOTOR YACHT	FB	MY	FBG	SV	IB	T650D	GM	18	7	54T	5		453000	497500
70	2	MOTOR YACHT	HT	MYDKH	FBG	SV	IB	T650D	GM	18	7	54T	5		453000	497500
70	2	MOTOR YACHT	FB	MYDKH	FBG	SV	IB	T650D	GM	18	7	54T	5		453000	497500
		1980 BOATS														
37		CONVERTIBLE	FB	SDN	FBG	SV	IB	T284D	GM	14		29000	3	3	84600	92900
37		CONVERTIBLE	FB	SDN	FBG	SV	IB	T390D	GM	14		29000	3	3	90000	98900
42	6	LONG RANGE CRUISER	FB	LRPH	FBG	DS	IB	T112D	GM	14	6	35000	3	10	104000	114500
43	1	DOUBLE CABIN	HT	DC	FBG	SV	IB	T284D	GM	14		34000	3	5	109000	119500
43	1	DOUBLE CABIN	HT	DC	FBG	SV	IB	T325D	GM	14		34000	3	5	112000	123000
43	1	DOUBLE CABIN	FB	DC	FBG	SV	IB	T284D	GM	14		34000	3	5	109000	119500
43	1	DOUBLE CABIN	FB	DC	FBG	SV	IB	T325D	GM	14		34000	3	5	111500	122500
43	8	CONVERTIBLE	FB	CNV	FBG	SV	IB	T325D	GM	14	6	41000			123500	135500
43	8	CONVERTIBLE	FB	SDN	FBG	SV	IB	T425D	GM	14	6	37000	4	2	121000	132500
46	2	CONVERTIBLE	FB	SDN	FBG	SV	IB	T425D	GM	14	9	41000	4	2	124000	136500
48	10	LONG RANGE CRUISER	FB	LRPH	FBG	DS	IB	T112D	GM	16	6	54000	4	6	133500	147000
50		CONVERTIBLE	FB	SDN	FBG	SV	IB	T550D	GM	16	4	54000	4	6	174000	191000
53		YACHT FISHERMAN	FB	YTFS	FBG	SV	IB	T425D	GM	15	10	57000	4		172000	189000
53	1	MOTOR YACHT	FB	MY	FBG	SV	IB	T425D	GM	15	10	55000	4		175000	192500
53	7	CONVERTIBLE	FB	SDN	FBG	SV	IB	T650D	GM	16		61000	4		229500	252000
55	8	CONVERTIBLE	FB	SDN	FBG	SV	IB	T650D	GM	17	6	68000	4	10	249500	274000
58	2	COCKPIT MOTOR YACHT	HT	MYCPT	FBG	SV	IB	T550D	GM	15	10	73000	4	9	262500	288500
58	2	COCKPIT MOTOR YACHT	FB	MYCPT	FBG	SV	IB	T550D	GM	15	10	73000	4	9	258000	283500
58	2	LONG RANGE CRUISER	FB	LRPH	FBG	DS	IB	T115D	GM	17	11	90000	4	10	237000	260500
58	2	LONG RANGE CRUISER	FB	LRPH	FBG	DS	IB	T174D	GM	17	11	90000	4	10	249500	274500
58	3	MOTOR YACHT	HT	MY	FBG	SV	IB	T425D	GM	15	10	78000			251000	276000
58	3	MOTOR YACHT	HT	MY	FBG	SV	IB	T550D	GM	15	10	78000	4	9	270500	297000
58	3	MOTOR YACHT	FB	MY	FBG	SV	IB	T550D	GM	15	10	78000	4	9	266500	293000
58	4	YACHT FISHERMAN	FB	YTFS	FBG	SV	IB	T425D	GM	15	10	62500	4	9	203000	223000
60	11	CONVERTIBLE	FB	SDN	FBG	SV	IB	T650D	GM	18		82000	4	11	284500	313000
61	3	MOTOR YACHT	HT	MY	FBG	SV	IB	T650D	GM	18	2	82000	4	11	298500	328500
61	3	MOTOR YACHT	FB	MY	FBG	SV	IB	T650D	GM	18	2	82000	4	11	296500	326000
64	1	MOTOR YACHT	HT	MY	FBG	SV	IB	T650D	GM	18	4	95000	5		361500	397500
64	1	MOTOR YACHT	FB	MY	FBG	SV	IB	T650D	GM	18	4	95000	5		361500	397500
70	2	MOTOR YACHT	HT	MY	FBG	SV	IB	T650D	GM	18	7	54T	5		432000	475000
70	2	MOTOR YACHT	FB	MY	FBG	SV	IB	T650D	GM	18	7	54T	5		432000	475000
70	2	MOTOR YACHT	HT	MYDKH	FBG	SV	IB	T650D	GM	18	7	54T	5		432000	474500
70	2	MOTOR YACHT	FB	MYDKH	FBG	SV	IB	T650D	GM	18	7	54T	5		432000	474500
		1979 BOATS														
37		CONVERTIBLE	FB	SDN	FBG	SV	IB	T284D	GM	14		29000	3	3	80800	88700
37		CONVERTIBLE	FB	SDN	FBG	SV	IB	T325D	GM	14		29000	3	3	82600	90700
42	6	LONG RANGE CRUISER	FB	LRPH	FBG	DS	IB	T112D	GM	14	6	36000	3	10	101500	111500
43	1	DOUBLE CABIN	HT	DC	FBG	SV	IB	T284D	GM	14		34000	3	5	104000	114500
43	1	DOUBLE CABIN	HT	DC	FBG	SV	IB	T325D	GM	14		34000	3	5	107000	117500
43	1	DOUBLE CABIN	HT	DC	FBG	SV	IB	T410D	GM	14		34000	3	5	113000	124000
43	8	CONVERTIBLE	FB	SDN	FBG	SV	IB	T425D	GM	14	6	41000	4	2	124000	136500
46	2	CONVERTIBLE	FB	SDN	FBG	SV	IB	T425D	GM	14	9	40000	4	2	117500	129000
48	10	LONG RANGE CRUISER	FB	LRPH	FBG	DS	IB	T112D	GM	16	6	55000	4	6	128500	141500
53		YACHT FISHERMAN	FB	YTFS	FBG	SV	IB	T425D	GM	15	10	55000	4		161500	177500
53	1	MOTOR YACHT	FB	MY	FBG	SV	IB	T425D	GM	15	10	55000	4		167500	184000
53	7	CONVERTIBLE	FB	SDN	FBG	SV	IB	T550D	GM	16		61000	4		208500	229000
53	7	CONVERTIBLE	FB	SDN	FBG	SV	IB	T650D	GM	16		61000	4		219500	241000
58	2	COCKPIT MOTOR YACHT	HT	MYCPT	FBG	DS	IB	T550D	GM	15	10	73000	4	9	251000	276000
58	2	LONG RANGE CRUISER	FB	LRPH	FBG	DS	IB	T115D	GM	17	11	90000	4	10	226500	249000
58	2	LONG RANGE CRUISER	FB	LRPH	FBG	DS	IB	T284D	GM	17	11	90000	4	10	259000	284500
58	3	MOTOR YACHT	HT	MY	FBG	SV	IB	T550D	GM	15	10	78000	4	9	258500	284000
58	3	MOTOR YACHT	FB	MY	FBG	SV	IB	T550D	GM	15	10	78000	4	9	254500	280000
58	4	YACHT FISHERMAN	FB	YTFS	FBG	DS	IB	T425D	GM	15	10	62500	4	9	194500	213500
60	11	CONVERTIBLE	FB	SDN	FBG	SV	IB	T650D	GM	18		73000	4	11	263500	290000
64	1	MOTOR YACHT	HT	MY	FBG	SV	IB	T650D	GM	18	4	95000	5		345500	379500
64	1	MOTOR YACHT	FB	MY	FBG	SV	IB	T650D	GM	18	4	95000	5		345500	379500
70	2	MOTOR YACHT	HT	MY	FBG	SV	IB	T650D	GM	18	7	54T	5		413000	453500
70	2	MOTOR YACHT	FB	MY	FBG	SV	IB	T650D	GM	18	7	54T	5		413000	453500
70	2	MOTOR YACHT	HT	MYDKH	FBG	SV	IB	T650D	GM	18	7	54T	5		412500	453500
70	2	MOTOR YACHT	FB	MYDKH	FBG	SV	IB	T650D	GM	18	7	54T	5		412500	453500
		1978 BOATS														
37		CONVERTIBLE	FB	SDN	FBG	SV	IB	T330	MPC	14		32000	3	3	72600	79800
		IB T245D GM 81900 90000, IB T256D CUM 82000 90100, IB T284D GM													83300	91600
38	4	DOUBLE CABIN	FB	DC	FBG	SV	IB	T330	MPC	13	7	33000	3	5	83300	91600
38	4	DOUBLE CABIN	FB	DC	FBG	SV	IB	T284D	GM	13	7	33000	3	5	92600	102000
42	6	LONG RANGE CRUISER	FB	LRPH	FBG	DS	IB	T112D	GM	14	6	41000	3	10	107000	117500
42	6	LONG RANGE CRUISER	FB	LRPH	FBG	DS	IB	T115D	LEHM	14	6	41000	3	10	107000	117500
42	8	CONVERTIBLE	FB	SDN	FBG	SV	IB	T325D	GM	13	10	42000	3	5	118000	130000
42	8	CONVERTIBLE	FB	SDN	FBG	SV	IB	T374D	CUM	13	10	42000	3	5	120000	132000
43	1	DOUBLE CABIN	HT	DC	FBG	SV	IB	T257D	GM	14		39000	3	5	108000	119000
43	1	DOUBLE CABIN	HT	DC	FBG	SV	IB	T325D	CUM	14		39000	3	5	112000	123000
43	1	DOUBLE CABIN	FB	DC	FBG	SV	IB	T257D	GM	14		39000	3	5	108000	118500
43	1	DOUBLE CABIN	FB	DC	FBG	SV	IB	T325D	CUM	14		39000	3	5	112000	123000
46	2	CONVERTIBLE	FB	SDN	FBG	SV	IB	T421D	CUM	14	9	46000	4	2	120000	132000
46	2	CONVERTIBLE	FB	SDN	FBG	SV	IB	T425D	GM	14	9	46000	4	2	120500	132500
48	10	LONG RANGE CRUISER	FB	LRPH	FBG	DS	IB	T112D	GM	16	6	60000	4	6	127500	140000
48	10	LONG RANGE CRUISER	FB	LRPH	FBG	DS	IB	T115D	LEHM	16	6	60000	4	6	127500	140000
52	11	YACHT FISHERMAN	FB	YTFS	FBG	SV	IB	T425D	GM	15	10	55000	4		154000	169500
53		MOTOR YACHT	HT	MY	FBG	SV	IB	T425D	GM	15	10	57000	4		163500	179500
53		MOTOR YACHT	FB	MY	FBG	SV	IB	T425D	GM	15	10	57000	4		162500	179000
53	7	CONVERTIBLE	FB	SDN	FBG	SV	IB	T550D	GM	16		61000	4		199500	219000
53	7	CONVERTIBLE	FB	SDN	FBG	SV	IB	T650D	GM	16		61000	4		209500	230500
58	2	COCKPIT MOTOR YACHT	FB	MYCPT	FBG	SV	IB	T550D	GM	15	10	73000	4	9	236000	259000
58	2	LONG RANGE CRUISER	FB	LRPH	FBG	DS	IB	T115D	GM	17	11	90000	4	10	216500	238000
58	2	LONG RANGE CRUISER	FB	LRPH	FBG	DS	IB	T174D	GM	17	11	90000	4	10	228500	251000
58	3	MOTOR YACHT	HT	MY	FBG	SV	IB	T425D	GM	15	10	78000	4	9	229500	252500

 CONTINUED ON NEXT PAGE

LOA FT	IN	NAME AND/ OR MODEL	TOP/ RIG	BOAT TYPE	-HULL- MTL	TP	TP	----ENGINE--- # HP	MFG	BEAM FT	IN	WGT LBS	DRAFT FT	IN	RETAIL LOW	RETAIL HIGH
		1978 BOATS														
58	3	MOTOR YACHT	HT	MY	FBG	SV	IB	T550D	GM	15	10	78000	4	9	247000	271500
58	3	MOTOR YACHT	FB	MY	FBG	SV	IB	T425D	GM	15	10	78000	4	9	226500	249000
58	3	MOTOR YACHT	FB	MY	FBG	SV	IB	T550D	GM	15	10	78000	4	9	243500	268000
58	4	YACHT FISHERMAN	FB	YTFS	FBG	SV	IB	T425D	GM	15	10	62500	4		185500	204000
60	11	CONVERTIBLE	FB	SDN	FBG	SV	IB	T650D	GM	18		73000	4	9	252500	277500
64	1	MOTOR YACHT	HT	MY	FBG	SV	IB	T650D	GM	18	4	97000	5		337500	371000
64	1	MOTOR YACHT	FB	MY	FBG	SV	IB	T650D	GM	18	4	97000	5		337500	371000
70	2	MOTOR YACHT	HT	MY	FBG	SV	IB	T650D	GM	18	7	52T	5		388500	427000
70	2	MOTOR YACHT	FB	MY	FBG	SV	IB	T650D	GM	18	7	52T	5		388500	427000
70	2	MOTOR YACHT EXT DKH	HT	MYDKH	FBG	SV	IB	T650D	GM	18	7	53T	5		394500	433500
70	2	MOTOR YACHT EXT DKH	FB	MYDKH	FBG	SV	IB	T650D	GM	18	7	53T	5		394500	433500
		1977 BOATS														
31	9	EXPRESS CRUISER	HT	EXP	FBG	SV	IB	T330	CC	11	10	15000	3	1	34000	37800
31	9	EXPRESS CRUISER	HT	EXP	FBG	SV	IB	T203D	CAT	11	10	15000	3	1	45600	50100
31	9	EXPRESS CRUISER	FB	EXP	FBG	SV	IB	T330	CC	11	10	15000	3	1	34000	37800
31	9	EXPRESS CRUISER	FB	EXP	FBG	SV	IB	T203D	CAT	11	10	15000	3	1	45600	50100
31	9	SPORT CRUISER	FB	SPTCR	FBG	SV	IB	T330	CC	11	10	15000	3	1	34100	37800
31	9	SPORT CRUISER	FB	SPTCR	FBG	SV	IB	T203D	CAT	11	10	15000	3	1	45600	50200
36	1	CONVERTIBLE	FB	SDN	FBG	SV	IB	T330	CC	12	9	19000	3	5	47100	51700
36	1	CONVERTIBLE	FB	SDN	FBG	SV	IB	T203D	CAT	12	9	19000	3	5	53000	58300
36	1	CONVERTIBLE	FB	SDN	FBG	SV	IB	T250D	CUM	12	9	19000	3	5	53700	59000
38	4	DOUBLE CABIN	FB	DC	FBG	SV	IB	T330	CC	13	7	30000	3	5	73400	80700
38	4	DOUBLE CABIN	FB	DC	FBG	SV	IB	T284D	GM	13	7	30000	3	5	82200	90300
42	6	LONG RANGE CRUISER	FB	LRPH	FBG	DS	IB	T112D	GM	14	6	40000	3	10	100500	110500
42	6	LONG RANGE CRUISER	FB	LRPH	FBG	DS	IB	T115D	LEHM	14	6	40000	3	10	100500	110500
42	8	CONVERTIBLE	FB	SDN	FBG	SV	IB	T325D	CUM	13	10	31000	3	5	89700	98600
42	8	CONVERTIBLE	FB	SDN	FBG	SV	IB	T325D	GM	13	10	31000	3	5	90000	98900
42	8	CONVERTIBLE	FB	SDN	FBG	SV	IB	T374D	CUM	13	10	31000	3	5	92100	101000
43	1	DOUBLE CABIN	HT	DC	FBG	SV	IB	T257D	GM	14		34000	3	5	93700	103000
43	1	DOUBLE CABIN	HT	DC	FBG	SV	IB	T325D	CUM	14		34000	3	5	97500	107000
43	1	DOUBLE CABIN	FB	DC	FBG	SV	IB	T257D	GM	14		34000	3	5	93600	103000
43	1	DOUBLE CABIN	FB	DC	FBG	SV	IB	T325D	CUM	14		34000	3	5	97300	107000
46	2	CONVERTIBLE	FB	SDN	FBG	SV	IB	T421D	CUM	14	9	38500	4	2	105000	115500
46	2	CONVERTIBLE	FB	SDN	FBG	SV	IB	T425D	GM	14	9	38500	4	2	105500	116000
48	10	LONG RANGE CRUISER	FB	LRPH	FBG	DS	IB	T112D	GM	16	6	59000	4	6	121000	133000
48	10	LONG RANGE CRUISER	FB	LRPH	FBG	DS	IB	T115D	LEHM	16	6	59000	4	6	121500	133500
53	1	MOTOR YACHT	FB	MY	FBG	SV	IB	T425D	GM	15	10	55000	4		154000	169000
53	7	CONVERTIBLE	FB	SDN	FBG	SV	IB	T490D	GM	16		61000	4		184500	203000
53	7	CONVERTIBLE	FB	SDN	FBG	SV	IB	T650D	GM	16		61000	4		201000	220500
58	2	LONG RANGE CRUISER	FB	LRPH	FBG	DS	IB	T115D	GM	17	11	90000	4	10	207500	228000
58	2	LONG RANGE CRUISER	FB	LRPH	FBG	DS	IB	T174D	GM	17	11	90000	4	10	218500	240500
58	3	MOTOR YACHT	HT	MY	FBG	SV	IB	T425D	GM	15	10	78000	4		220000	242000
58	3	MOTOR YACHT	FB	MY	FBG	SV	IB	T425D	GM	15	10	78000	4		217000	238500
58	4	YACHT FISHERMAN	FB	YTFS	FBG	SV	IB	T425D	GM	15	10	62500	4		177500	195000
64	1	MOTOR YACHT	HT	MY	FBG	SV	IB	T650D	GM	18	4	95000	5		316500	347500
64	1	MOTOR YACHT	FB	MY	FBG	SV	IB	T650D	GM	18	4	95000	5		316500	347500
70	2	MOTOR YACHT	HT	MY	FBG	SV	IB	T650D	GM	18	7	50T	5		366000	402500
70	2	MOTOR YACHT	FB	MY	FBG	SV	IB	T650D	GM	18	7	50T	5		366000	402500
70	2	MOTOR YACHT EXT DKH	HT	MYDKH	FBG	SV	IB	T650D	GM	18	7	50T	5		368000	404500
70	2	MOTOR YACHT EXT DKH	FB	MYDKH	FBG	SV	IB	T650D	GM	18	7	50T	5		368000	404500
		1976 BOATS														
31	9	EXPRESS CRUISER	HT	EXP	FBG	SV	IB	T330	CC	11	10	15000	3	1	32700	36300
31	9	EXPRESS CRUISER	HT	EXP	FBG	SV	IB	T203D	CAT	11	10	15000	3	1	43500	48300
31	9	EXPRESS CRUISER	FB	EXP	FBG	SV	IB	T330	CC	11	10	15000	3	1	32700	36300
31	9	EXPRESS CRUISER	FB	EXP	FBG	SV	IB	T203D	CAT	11	10	15000	3	1	43500	48300
31	9	SPORT CRUISER	FB	SPTCR	FBG	SV	IB	T330	CC	11	10	15000	3	1	32700	36300
31	9	SPORT CRUISER	FB	SPTCR	FBG	SV	IB	T203D	CAT	11	10	15000	3	1	43500	48300
36	1	CONVERTIBLE	FB	SDN	FBG	SV	IB	T330	CC	12	9	19000	3		44700	49700
36	1	CONVERTIBLE	FB	SDN	FBG	SV	IB	T203D	CAT	12	9	19000	3		50800	55900
38	4	DOUBLE CABIN	FB	DC	FBG	SV	IB	T330	CC	13	7	30000	3	5	70400	77400
38	4	DOUBLE CABIN	FB	DC	FBG	SV	IB	T284D	GM	13	7	30000	3	5	78800	86600
42	6	LONG RANGE CRUISER	FB	LRPH	FBG	DS	IB	T115D	LEHM	14	6	40000	3	7	96500	106000
42	6	LONG RANGE CRUISER	FB	LRPH	FBG	DS	IB	T128D	GM	14	6	40000	3	7	96900	106500
42	8	CONVERTIBLE	FB	SDN	FBG	SV	IB	T325D	CUM	13	10	31000	3	5	86000	94500
42	8	CONVERTIBLE	FB	SDN	FBG	SV	IB	T325D	GM	13	10	31000	3	5	86300	94900
42	8	CONVERTIBLE	FB	SDN	FBG	SV	IB	T374D	CUM	13	10	31000	3	5	88300	97000
43	1	DOUBLE CABIN	HT	DC	FBG	SV	IB	T284D	GM	14		34000	3	5	91400	100500
43	1	DOUBLE CABIN	HT	DC	FBG	SV	IB	T325D	CUM	14		34000	3	5	93500	102500
43	1	DOUBLE CABIN	FB	DC	FBG	SV	IB	T284D	GM	14		34000	3	5	91200	100000
43	1	DOUBLE CABIN	FB	DC	FBG	SV	IB	T325D	CUM	14		34000	3	5	93300	102500
46	2	CONVERTIBLE	FB	SDN	FBG	SV	IB	T425D	GM	14	9	38500	4	2	101500	111500
48	9	YACHT FISHERMAN	FB	YTFS	FBG	SV	IB	T320D	GM	14	7	43500	3	7	102000	112000
48	9	YACHT FISHERMAN	FB	YTFS	FBG	SV	IB	T425D	GM	14	7	43500	3	7	108000	119000
48	10	LONG RANGE CRUISER	FB	LRPH	FBG	DS	IB	T115D	LEHM	16	6	59000	4	2	116500	128000
48	10	LONG RANGE CRUISER	FB	LRPH	FBG	DS	IB	T128D	GM	16	6	59000	4	2	116500	128000
53	1	MOTOR YACHT	FB	MY	FBG	SV	IB	T320D	GM	15	10	55000	4		137000	150500
53	1	MOTOR YACHT	FB	MY	FBG	SV	IB	T425D	GM	15	10	55000	4		147500	162000
53	7	CONVERTIBLE	FB	SDN	FBG	SV	IB	T480D	GM	16		61000	4		176000	193500
53	7	CONVERTIBLE	FB	SDN	FBG	SV	IB	T650D	GM	16		61000	4		192500	211500
58	2	LONG RANGE CRUISER	FB	LRPH	FBG	DS	IB	T115D	GM	17	11	90000	4	10	199000	218500
58	2	LONG RANGE CRUISER	FB	LRPH	FBG	DS	IB	T174D	GM	17	11	90000	4	10	209500	230500
58	4	YACHT FISHERMAN	FB	YTFS	FBG	SV	IB	T425D	GM	15	10	62500	4		170000	187000
58	5	TRIPLE CABIN	HT	TCMY	FBG	SV	IB	T425D	GM	15	10	63000	4		179000	197000
58	5	TRIPLE CABIN	HT	TCMY	FBG	SV	IB	T480D	GM	15	10	63000	4		187000	205500
58	5	TRIPLE CABIN	FB	TCMY	FBG	SV	IB	T425D	GM	15	10	63000	4		177000	194500
58	5	TRIPLE CABIN	FB	TCMY	FBG	SV	IB	T480D	GM	15	10	63000	4		184500	203000
64	1	MOTOR YACHT	HT	MY	FBG	SV	IB	T650D	GM	18	4	95000	5		303500	333500
64	1	MOTOR YACHT	FB	MY	FBG	SV	IB	T650D	GM	18	4	95000	5		303500	333500
70	2	MOTOR YACHT	HT	MY	FBG	SV	IB	T650D	GM	18	7	50T	5		351000	386000
70	2	MOTOR YACHT	FB	MY	FBG	SV	IB	T650D	GM	18	7	50T	5		351000	386000
70	2	MOTOR YACHT	HT	MYDKH	FBG	SV	IB	T650D	GM	18	7	50T	5		350500	385500
70	2	MOTOR YACHT	FB	MYDKH	FBG	SV	IB	T650D	GM	18	7	50T	5		350500	385500
		1975 BOATS														
31	9	EXPRESS CRUISER	HT	EXP	FBG	SV	IB	T330	CC	11	10	17200	3	1	32700	36300
31	9	EXPRESS CRUISER	HT	EXP	FBG	SV	IB	T203D	CAT	11	10	17200	3	1	46700	51300
31	9	EXPRESS CRUISER	FB	EXP	FBG	SV	IB	T330	CC	11	10	17200	3	1	32700	36300
31	9	EXPRESS CRUISER	FB	EXP	FBG	SV	IB	T203D	CAT	11	10	17200	3	1	46700	51300
31	9	SPORT CRUISER	FB	SPTCR	FBG	SV	IB	T330	CC	11	10	17200	3	1	32700	36300
31	9	SPORT CRUISER	FB	SPTCR	FBG	SV	IB	T203D	CAT	11	10	17200	3	1	46800	51400
36	1	CONVERTIBLE	FB	SDN	FBG	SV	IB	T330	CC	12	9	21200	3		46100	50600
36	1	CONVERTIBLE	FB	SDN	FBG	SV	IB	T203D	CAT	12	9	21200	3		52200	57300
38	4	DOUBLE CABIN	FB	DC	FBG	SV	IB	T330	CC	13	7	30000	3	5	67600	74300
38	4	DOUBLE CABIN	FB	DC	FBG	SV	IB	T174D	GM	13	7	30000	3	5	72600	79800
42	8	CONVERTIBLE	FB	SDN	FBG	SV	IB	T174D	GM	13	10	31000	3	5	77100	84700
		IB T286D CUM 81000 89000, IB T325D GM 82900 91100, IB T374D CUM													84800	93200
43	1	DOUBLE CABIN	HT	DC	FBG	SV	IB	T330	CC	14		34000	3	5	79600	87500
		IB T174D GM 82300 90500, IB T286D CUM 87500 96200, IB T325D GM													90000	98900
43	1	DOUBLE CABIN	FB	DC	FBG	SV	IB	T330	CC	14		34000	3	5	79400	87300
		IB T174D GM 82300 90400, IB T286D CUM 87400 96000, IB T325D GM													89800	98700
46	2	CONVERTIBLE	FB	SDN	FBG	SV	IB	T320D	GM	14	9	38500	4	2	92400	101500
46	2	CONVERTIBLE	FB	SDN	FBG	SV	IB	T374D	CUM	14	9	38500	4	2	94400	103500
46	2	CONVERTIBLE	FB	SDN	FBG	SV	IB	T425D	GM	14	9	38500	4	2	97200	107000
48	9	YACHT FISHERMAN	FB	YTFS	FBG	SV	IB	T320D	GM	14	7	43500	3	7	98000	107500
48	9	YACHT FISHERMAN	FB	YTFS	FBG	SV	IB	T425D	GM	14	7	43500	3	7	103500	114000
53	1	MOTOR YACHT	FB	MY	FBG	SV	IB	T320D	GM	15	10	55000	4		131000	144000
53	1	MOTOR YACHT	FB	MY	FBG	SV	IB	T425D	GM	15	10	55000	4		141000	155000
53	7	CONVERTIBLE	FB	SDN	FBG	SV	IB	T425D	GM	16		61000	4		163500	179500
53	7	CONVERTIBLE	FB	SDN	FBG	SV	IB	T480D	GM	16		61000	4		169000	185500
58	2	LONG RANGE CRUISER	FB	LRPH	FBG	DS	IB	T115D	GM	17	11	90000	4	10	191000	209500
58	2	LONG RANGE CRUISER	FB	LRPH	FBG	DS	IB	T255D	GM	17	11	90000	4	10	214000	235500
58	4	YACHT FISHERMAN	FB	YTFS	FBG	SV	IB	T425D	GM	15	10	62500	4		163500	179500
58	5	TRIPLE CABIN	HT	TCMY	FBG	SV	IB	T425D	GM	15	10	63000	4		169500	186000
58	5	TRIPLE CABIN	HT	TCMY	FBG	SV	IB	T480D	GM	15	10	63000	4		177000	194500
58	5	TRIPLE CABIN	FB	TCMY	FBG	SV	IB	T425D	GM	15	10	63000	4		167500	184000
58	5	TRIPLE CABIN	FB	TCMY	FBG	SV	IB	T480D	GM	15	10	63000	4		174500	192000
58	5	TRIPLE CBN ENCL AFT	HT	TCMY	FBG	SV	IB	T425D	GM	15	10	63000	4		174500	191500
58	5	TRIPLE CBN ENCL AFT	HT	TCMY	FBG	SV	IB	T480D	GM	15	10	63000	4		182000	200000
58	5	TRIPLE CBN ENCL AFT	FB	TCMY	FBG	SV	IB	T425D	GM	15	10	63000	4		172000	189000
58	5	TRIPLE CBN ENCL AFT	FB	TCMY	FBG	SV	IB	T480D	GM	15	10	63000	4		179500	197500
64	1	MOTOR YACHT	HT	MY	FBG	SV	IB	T650D	GM	18	4	95000	5		291500	320000
64	1	MOTOR YACHT	FB	MY	FBG	SV	IB	T650D	GM	18	4	95000	5		291500	320000
70	2	MOTOR YACHT	HT	MY	FBG	SV	IB	T650D	GM	18	7	50T	5		337000	370500
70	2	MOTOR YACHT	FB	MY	FBG	SV	IB	T650D	GM	18	7	50T	5		337000	370500
70	2	MOTOR YACHT	HT	MYDKH	FBG	SV	IB	T650D	GM	18	7	50T	5		337000	370000
70	2	MOTOR YACHT	FB	MYDKH	FBG	SV	IB	T650D	GM	18	7	50T	5		337000	370000
		1974 BOATS														
31	9		FB	SPTCR	FBG	SV	IB	T330	CC	11	10	17200	3	1	31400	34900
31	9		FB	SPTCR	FBG	SV	IB	T203D	CAT	11	10	17200	3	1	45000	50000
36	1	CONVERTIBLE	FB	SDN	FBG		IB	T300	CC	12	9	19000	3		40800	45300
36	1	CONVERTIBLE	FB	SDN	FBG		IB	T203D	CAT	12	9	19000	3		47100	51800
36	1	CONVERTIBLE	FB	SDN	FBG		IB	T216D	CUM	12	9	19000	3		46700	51300
38	4		FB	DC	FBG		IB	T300	CC	13	7	30000	3	4	64700	71100
38	4		FB	DC	FBG		IB	T203D	CAT	13	7	30000	3	4	71500	78600
38	4		FB	DC	FBG		IB	T260D	GM	13	7	30000	3	4	71900	79100

 CONTINUED ON NEXT PAGE

LOA FT	LOA IN	NAME AND/ OR MODEL	TOP/ RIG	BOAT TYPE	-HULL- MTL	-HULL- TP	ENGINE TP	ENGINE # HP	ENGINE MFG	BEAM FT	BEAM IN	WGT LBS	DRAFT FT	DRAFT IN	RETAIL LOW	RETAIL HIGH
		1974 BOATS														
38	4	CONVERTIBLE	FB	SDN	FBG		IB	T300	CC	13	7	29000	3	2	62900	69100
38	4	CONVERTIBLE	FB	SDN	FBG		IB	T260D	GM	13	7	29000	3	2	70200	77100
42	8	CONVERTIBLE	FB	SDN	FBG		IB	T300	CC	13	10	31000	3	5	70400	77400
42	8	CONVERTIBLE	FB	SDN	FBG		IB	T260D	GM	13	10	31000	3	5	77100	84800
42	8	CONVERTIBLE	FB	SDN	FBG		IB	T286D	CUM	13	10	31000	3	5	77900	85600
43	1		HT	DC	FBG		IB	T300	CC	14		34000	3	5	79000	86800
43	1		HT	DC	FBG		IB	T260D	GM	14		34000	3	5	86700	95200
43	1		HT	DC	FBG		IB	T286D	CUM	14		34000	3	5	88200	96900
43	1		FB	DC	FBG		IB	T300	CC	14		34000	3	5	78800	86600
43	1		FB	DC	FBG		IB	T260D	GM	14		34000	3	5	86400	95000
43	1		FB	DC	FBG		IB	T286D	CUM	14		34000	3	5	87900	96600
45	2	CONVERTIBLE	FB	SDN	FBG		IB	T320D	GM	14	7	37000	3	6	85400	93900
45	2	CONVERTIBLE	FB	SDN	FBG		IB	T425D	GM	14	7	37000	3	6	90000	99000
46	2	CONVERTIBLE	FB	SDN	FBG	SV	IB	T320D	GM	14	9	38500	4	2	88700	97500
46	2	CONVERTIBLE	FB	SDN	FBG	SV	IB	T425D	GM	14	9	38500	4	2	93400	102500
48	9		FB	YTFS	FBG		IB	T320D	GM	14	7	43500	3	7	96200	105500
48	9		FB	YTFS	FBG		IB	T425D	GM	14	7	43500	3	7	106000	116500
53	1		FB	MY	FBG	SV	IB	T320D	GM	15	10	55000	4		126000	138500
53	1		FB	MY	FBG	SV	IB	T425D	GM	15	10	55000	4		136000	149500
53	7	CONVERTIBLE	FB	SDN	FBG	SV	IB	T425D	GM	16		61000	4		157000	172500
53	7	CONVERTIBLE	FB	SDN	FBG	SV	IB	T478D	GM	16		61000	4		162000	178000
58	4	YACHT FISHERMAN	FB	YTFS	FBG		IB	T320D	GM	15	10	62500	4		142500	156500
58	4	YACHT FISHERMAN	FB	YTFS	FBG		IB	T425D	GM	15	10	62500	4		158000	174000
58	5	TRIPLE CABIN	HT	TCMY	FBG		IB	T320D	GM	15	10	63000	4		151000	166000
58	5	TRIPLE CABIN	HT	TCMY	FBG		IB	T425D	GM	15	10	63000	4		166000	182500
58	5	TRIPLE CABIN	HT	TCMY	FBG		IB	T478D	GM	15	10	63000	4		173500	190500
58	5	TRIPLE CABIN	FB	TCMY	FBG		IB	T320D	GM	15	10	63000	4		150000	164500
58	5	TRIPLE CABIN	FB	TCMY	FBG		IB	T425D	GM	15	10	63000	4		163500	180000
58	5	TRIPLE CABIN	FB	TCMY	FBG		IB	T478D	GM	15	10	63000	4		171000	187500
70	2		HT	MY	FBG		IB	T650D	GM	18	7	50T	5		326500	358500
70	2		FB	MY	FBG		IB	T650D	GM	18	7	50T	5		326500	358500
		1973 BOATS														
36	1	CONVERTIBLE	FB	SDN	FBG		IB	T300	CC	12	9	19000	3		39300	43700
36	1	CONVERTIBLE	FB	SDN	FBG		IB	T225D	CAT	12	9	19000	3		46000	50600
38	4		FB	DC	FBG		IB	T300	CC	13	7	30000	3	5	62300	68400
		IB T225D CAT 69400 76300, IB T280D GM 69900 76800, IB T283D GM													70000	76900
38	4	CONVERTIBLE	FB	SDN	FBG		IB	T300	CC	13	7	29000	3	2	60500	66500
38	4	CONVERTIBLE	FB	SDN	FBG		IB	T280D	GM	13	7	29000	3	2	68200	75000
42	8	CONVERTIBLE	FB	SDN	FBG		IB	T300	CC	13	10	31000	3	5	67800	74500
42	8	CONVERTIBLE	FB	SDN	FBG		IB	T280D	GM	13	10	31000	3	5	75000	82400
42	8	CONVERTIBLE	FB	SDN	FBG		IB	T320D	CUM	13	10	31000	3	5	76200	83800
43	1		HT	DC	FBG		IB	T300	CC	14		34000	3	5	76100	83600
		IB T280D GM 84700 93100, IB T283D GM 84900 93300, IB T320D CUM													87100	95700
43	1		FB	DC	FBG		IB	T300	CC	14		34000	3	5	75800	83300
		IB T280D GM 84500 92800, IB T283D GM 84600 93000, IB T320D CUM													86800	95400
45	2	CONVERTIBLE	FB	SDN	FBG		IB	T350D	GM	14	7	37000	3	6	83300	91600
45	2	CONVERTIBLE	FB	SDN	FBG		IB	T400D	GM	14	7	37000	3	6	85500	93900
48	9		FB	YTFS	FBG		IB	T350D	GM	14	7	43500	3	7	95000	104500
48	9		FB	YTFS	FBG		IB	T400D	GM	14	7	43500	3	7	99700	109500
53	1		FB	MY	FBG		IB	T400D	GM	15	10	55000	4		128000	141000
53	1		FB	MY	FBG	SV	IB	T350D	GM	15	10	55000	4		123500	135500
53	1		FB	MY	FBG	SV	IB	T400D	GM	15	10	55000	4		128000	140500
53	7	CONVERTIBLE	FB	SDN	FBG	SV	IB	T400D	GM	16		61000	4		148500	163500
53	7	CONVERTIBLE	FB	SDN	FBG	SV	IB	T525D	GM	16		61000	4		160500	176000
58	4	YACHT FISHERMAN	FB	YTFS	FBG		IB	T350D	GM	15	10	62500	4		141500	155500
58	4	YACHT FISHERMAN	FB	YTFS	FBG		IB	T400D	GM	15	10	62500	4		148500	163500
58	5	TRIPLE CABIN	HT	TCMY	FBG		IB	T350D	GM	15	10	63000	4		149500	164000
58	5	TRIPLE CABIN	HT	TCMY	FBG		IB	T400D	GM	15	10	63000	4		156000	171500
58	5	TRIPLE CABIN	HT	TCMY	FBG		IB	T525D	GM	15	10	63000	4		173000	190000
58	5	TRIPLE CABIN	FB	TCMY	FBG		IB	T350D	GM	15	10	63000	4		147500	162500
58	5	TRIPLE CABIN	FB	TCMY	FBG		IB	T400D	GM	15	10	63000	4		154000	169500
58	5	TRIPLE CABIN	FB	TCMY	FBG		IB	T525D	GM	15	10	63000	4		170000	187000
70	2		HT	MY	FBG		IB	T620D	GM	18	7	50T	5		312500	343500
70	2		FB	MY	FBG		IB	T620D	GM	18	7	50T	5		312500	343500
		1972 BOATS														
31	4		HT	EXP	FBG		IB	T230	CC	12	5	13500	2	4	25100	27900
31	4		FB	EXP	FBG		IB	T230	CC	12	5	13700	2	4	25200	28000
36	1	CONVERTIBLE	FB	SDN	FBG		IB	T300	CC	12	9	19000	3		37900	42100
36	1	CONVERTIBLE	FB	SDN	FBG		IB	T225D	CAT	12	9	19000	3		43900	48800
38	4		HT	DC	FBG		IB	T300	CC	13	7	23000	3	5	48000	52800
38	4		HT	DC	FBG		IB	T220D	GM	13	7	23000	3	5	53200	58500
38	4		HT	DC	FBG		IB	T283D	GM	13	7	23000	3	5	55000	60400
38	4		FB	DC	FBG		IB	T300	CC	13	7	23000	3	4	48000	52800
38	4		FB	DC	FBG		IB	T220D	GM	13	7	23000	3	4	53200	58500
38	4		FB	DC	FBG		IB	T283D	GM	13	7	23000	3	4	55000	60400
38	4	CONVERTIBLE	FB	SDN	FBG		IB	T300	CC	13	7	22000	3	4	46400	51000
38	4	CONVERTIBLE	FB	SDN	FBG		IB	T283D	GM	13	7	22000	3	4	53400	58700
42	8	CONVERTIBLE	FB	SDN	FBG		IB	T300	CC	13	10	26500	3	5	58300	64000
42	8	CONVERTIBLE	FB	SDN	FBG		IB	T260D	GM	13	10	26500	3	5	64500	70800
42	8	CONVERTIBLE	FB	SDN	FBG		IB	T280D	CUM	13	10	26500	3	5	65000	71400
43	1		HT	DC	FBG		IB	T300	CC	14		34000	3	5	73300	80600
		IB T280D GM 81700 89700, IB T283D GM 81900 90000, IB T320D CUM													84000	92300
43	1		FB	DC	FBG		IB	T300	CC	14		34000			73100	80300
		IB T280D GM 81400 89500, IB T283D GM 81600 89700, IB T320D CUM													83700	91900
44	8		OP	TCMY	FBG		IB	T280D	GM	14	7	32000	3	6	76000	83500
44	8		OP	TCMY	FBG		IB	T350D	GM	14	7	32000	3	6	81100	89100
44	8		OP	TCMY	FBG		IB	T400D	GM	14	7	32000	3	6	84900	93300
44	8		HT	TCMY	FBG		IB	T280D	GM	14	7	32000	3	6	77600	85300
44	8		HT	TCMY	FBG		IB	T350D	GM	14	7	32000	3	6	82400	90600
44	8		HT	TCMY	FBG		IB	T400D	GM	14	7	32000	3	6	86200	94700
44	8		FB	TCMY	FBG		IB	T280D	GM	14	7	32000	3	6	77300	85000
44	8		FB	TCMY	FBG		IB	T350D	GM	14	7	32000	3	6	82000	90200
44	8		FB	TCMY	FBG		IB	T400D	GM	14	7	32000	3	6	85700	94200
45	2	CONVERTIBLE	FB	SDN	FBG		IB	T350D	GM	14	7	32000	3	6	74700	82100
45	2	CONVERTIBLE	FB	SDN	FBG		IB	T370D	GM	14	7	32000	3	6	75500	82900
48	9		FB	YTFS	FBG		IB	T320D	GM	14	7	36000	3	7	82400	90500
48	9		FB	YTFS	FBG		IB	T400D	GM	14	7	36000	3	7	87700	96300
53	1		FB	MY	FBG		IB	T350D	GM	15	10	55000	4		118500	130500
53	1		FB	MY	FBG	SV	IB	T350D	GM	15	10	55000	4		118500	130000
53	1		FB	MY	FBG	SV	IB	T400D	GM	15	10	55000	4		123000	135000
53	7	CONVERTIBLE	FB	SDN	FBG	SV	IB	T400D	GM	16		61000	4		143500	157500
53	7	CONVERTIBLE	FB	SDN	FBG	SV	IB	T525D	GM	16		61000	4		154500	170000
58	4	YACHT FISHERMAN	FB	YTFS	FBG		IB	T350D	GM	15	10	62500	4		136500	150000
58	4	YACHT FISHERMAN	FB	YTFS	FBG		IB	T400D	GM	15	10	62500	4		143500	157500
58	5	TRIPLE CABIN	HT	TCMY	FBG		IB	T350D	GM	15	10	53000	4		129500	142000
58	5	TRIPLE CABIN	HT	TCMY	FBG		IB	T400D	GM	15	10	63000	4		150500	165500
58	5	TRIPLE CABIN	HT	TCMY	FBG		IB	T525D	GM	15	10	63000	4		166500	183000
58	5	TRIPLE CABIN	FB	TCMY	FBG		IB	T350D	GM	15	10	63000	4		142000	156000
58	5	TRIPLE CABIN	FB	TCMY	FBG		IB	T400D	GM	15	10	63000	4		148500	163000
58	5	TRIPLE CABIN	FB	TCMY	FBG		IB	T525D	GM	15	10	63000	4		164000	180000
70	2		HT	MY	FBG		IB	T555D	GM	18	7	90000	5		285000	313000
70	2		FB	MY	FBG		IB	T555D	GM	18	7	90000	5		285000	313000
		1971 BOATS														
31	4		HT	EXP	FBG		IB	T230	CC	12	5	13500	2	4	24100	26800
31	4		FB	EXP	FBG		IB	T230	CC	12	5	13500	2	4	24100	26800
36	1	CONVERTIBLE	FB	SDN	FBG		IB	T300	CC	12	9	17000	3		34500	38300
36	1	CONVERTIBLE	FB	SDN	FBG		IB	T205D	CAT	12	9	17000	3		39300	43600
38	4		HT	DC	FBG		IB	T300	CC	13	7	23000	3	4	46400	50900
38	4		HT	DC	FBG		IB	T181D	GM	13	7	23000	3	4	50600	55500
38	4		HT	DC	FBG		IB	T260D	GM	13	7	23000	3	4	52400	57600
38	4	CONVERTIBLE	FB	SDN	FBG		IB	T300	CC	13	7	22000	3	2	44400	49300
38	4	CONVERTIBLE	FB	SDN	FBG		IB	T260D	GM	13	7	22000	3	2	50900	55900
40	9	CONVERTIBLE	FB	SDN	FBG		IB	T300	CC	14		23000	2	11	49700	54700
40	9	CONVERTIBLE	FB	SDN	FBG		IB	T260D	GM	14		23000	2	11	55900	61400
40	11	TWIN CABIN	HT	DCMY	FBG		IB	T300	CC	14		24500	3		51900	57000
40	11	TWIN CABIN	HT	DCMY	FBG		IB	T260D	GM	14		24500	3		58500	64300
40	11	TWIN CABIN W/EXT HT	HT	DCMY	FBG		IB	T300	CC	14		24500	3		54100	59400
40	11	TWIN CABIN W/EXT HT	HT	DCMY	FBG		IB	T260D	GM	14		24500	3		60400	66300
42	8	CONVERTIBLE	FB	SDN	FBG		IB	T300	CC	13	10	26500	3	5	56200	61800
42	8	CONVERTIBLE	FB	SDN	FBG		IB	T260D	GM	13	10	26500	3	5	62200	68400
42	8	CONVERTIBLE	FB	SDN	FBG		IB	T370D	CUM	13	10	26500	3	5	66100	72600
43	1		HT	DC	FBG		IB	T300	CC	14		27000	3	5	59500	65400
43	1		HT	DC	FBG		IB	T260D	GM	14		27000	3	5	66300	72800
44	8		HT	TCMY	FBG		IB	T260D	GM	14	7	32000	3	6	72300	79500
44	8		HT	TCMY	FBG		IB	T320D	GM	14	7	32000	3	6	76100	83600
44	8		FB	TCMY	FBG		IB	T260D	GM	14	7	32000	3	6	73500	80700
44	8		FB	TCMY	FBG		IB	T320D	GM	14	7	32000	3	6	77100	84800
44	8	TWIN CABIN W/EXT HT	HT	TCMY	FBG		IB	T260D	GM	14	7	32000	3	6	75100	82500
44	8	TWIN CABIN W/EXT HT	HT	TCMY	FBG		IB	T320D	GM	14	7	32000	3	6	78800	86600
45	1	CONVERTIBLE	FB	SDN	FBG		IB	T320D	GM	14	7	32000	3	6	70700	77700
45	1	CONVERTIBLE	FB	SDN	FBG		IB	T370D	GM	14	7	32000	3	6	72600	79800
53	1		FB	MY	FBG	SV	IB	T320D	GM	15	10	55000	4		111000	122000
53	1		FB	MY	FBG	SV	IB	T370D	GM	15	10	55000	4		115500	127000

 CONTINUED ON NEXT PAGE

HATTERAS YACHTS -CONTINUED See inside cover to adjust price for area

LOA FT	LOA IN	NAME AND/ OR MODEL	TOP/ RIG	BOAT TYPE	HULL MTL	HULL TP	ENGINE TP	ENGINE # HP	ENGINE MFG	BEAM FT	BEAM IN	WGT LBS	DRAFT FT	DRAFT IN	RETAIL LOW	RETAIL HIGH
		1971 BOATS														
53	7	CONVERTIBLE	FB	SDN	FBG	SV	IB	T370D	GM	16		61000	4		135500	149000
53	7	CONVERTIBLE	FB	SDN	FBG	SV	IB	T480D	GM	16		61000	4		145500	160000
58	4	YACHT FISHERMAN	FB	YTFS	FBG		IB	T320D	GM	15	10	49000	4		108500	119000
58	4	YACHT FISHERMAN	FB	YTFS	FBG		IB	T370D	GM	15	10	62500	4		134500	147500
58	5	TRIPLE CABIN	HT	TCMY	FBG		IB	T320D	GM	15	10	63000	4		134500	148000
58	5	TRIPLE CABIN	HT	TCMY	FBG		IB	T370D	GM	15	10	63000	4		141000	155000
58	5	TRIPLE CABIN	HT	TCMY	FBG		IB	T480D	GM	15	10	63000	4		155000	170500
58	5	TRIPLE CABIN	FB	TCMY	FBG		IB	T320D	GM	15	10	63000	4		133000	146500
58	5	TRIPLE CABIN	FB	TCMY	FBG		IB	T370D	GM	15	10	63000	4		139500	153000
58	5	TRIPLE CABIN	FB	TCMY	FBG		IB	T480D	GM	15	10	63000	4		153000	168000
70	2		HT	MY	FBG		IB	T555D	GM	18	7	90000	5		275000	302000
70	2		FB	MY	FBG		IB	T555D	GM	18	7	90000	5		275000	302000
		1970 BOATS														
31	4		HT	EXP	FBG		IB	T225		12	5	13500	2	4	23100	25700
36	1	CONVERTIBLE	HT	SDN	FBG		IB	T300		12	9	15000	3		31400	34900
36	1	CONVERTIBLE	HT	SDN	FBG		IB	T180D	GM	12	9	15000	3		34400	38200
36	1	CONVERTIBLE	HT	SDN	FBG		IB	T220D	GM	12	9	15000	3		35400	39300
36	1	CONVERTIBLE	FB	SDN	FBG		IB	T300		12	9	15000	3		31400	34900
36	1	CONVERTIBLE	FB	SDN	FBG		IB	T180D	GM	12	9	15000	3		34400	38200
36	1	CONVERTIBLE	FB	SDN	FBG		IB	T220D	GM	12	9	15000	3		35400	39300
38	4		HT	DC	FBG		IB	T300		13	7	19000	3	4	37900	42100
38	4		HT	DC	FBG		IB	T216D	GM	13	7	19000	3	4	42600	47400
38	4		HT	DC	FBG		IB	T283D	GM	13	7	19000	3	4	44400	49400
38	4	CONVERTIBLE	FB	SDN	FBG		IB	T300		13	7	19000	3	4	38000	42200
38	4	CONVERTIBLE	FB	SDN	FBG		IB	T216D	GM	13	7	19000	3	4	42900	47700
38	4	CONVERTIBLE	FB	SDN	FBG		IB	T283D	GM	13	7	19000	3	4	44700	49600
40	9	CONVERTIBLE	HT	SDN	FBG		IB	T300		14		21000	2	11	44600	49600
40	9	CONVERTIBLE	HT	SDN	FBG		IB	T283D	GM	14		21000	2	11	51500	56600
40	9	CONVERTIBLE	FB	SDN	FBG		IB	T300		14		21000	2	11	44600	49500
40	9	CONVERTIBLE	FB	SDN	FBG		IB	T283D	GM	14		21000	2	11	51500	56600
40	11	TWIN CABIN	HT	DCMY	FBG		IB	T300		14		21500	3		46700	51300
40	11	TWIN CABIN	HT	DCMY	FBG		IB	T216D	GM	14		21500	3		50900	56000
40	11	TWIN CABIN	HT	DCMY	FBG		IB	T283D	GM	14		21500	3		53700	59000
44	8		HT	TCMY	FBG		IB	T283D	GM	14	7	32000	3	6	72500	79700
44	8		HT	TCMY	FBG		IB	T350D	GM	14	7	32000	3	6	76900	84500
45	1	CONVERTIBLE	FB	SDN	FBG		IB	T350D	GM	14	7	32000	3	6	69300	76200
45	1	CONVERTIBLE	FB	SDN	FBG		IB	T375D	GM	14	7	32000	3	6	70200	77200
53	1		FB	MY	FBG	SV	IB	T350D	GM	15	10	55000	4		109500	120000
53	7	CONVERTIBLE	FB	SDN	FBG	SV	IB	T350D	GM	16		61000	4		129000	142000
53	7	CONVERTIBLE	FB	SDN	FBG	SV	IB	T375D	GM	16		61000	4		131500	144500
53	7	CONVERTIBLE	FB	SDN	FBG	SV	IB	T500D	GM	16		61000	4		142000	156500
		1969 BOATS														
27	10		HT	EXP	FBG	SV	IB	T110	CHRY	12	5	12000	2	4	16900	19200
27	10		FB	EXP	FBG	SV	IB	T110	CHRY	12	5	12000	2	4	16900	19200
27	10		FB	SF	FBG	SV	IB	T110	CHRY	12	5	12000	2	4	18100	20100
31	4		HT	EXP	FBG	SV	IB	T110-T290		12	5	13500	2	4	20700	25700
34	2	CONVERTIBLE	FB	SDN	FBG	SV	IB	T300	CHRY	12	6	15000	3		31200	34700
34	2	CONVERTIBLE	FB	SDN	FBG	SV	IB	T180D	GM	12	6	15000	3		42700	47500
38	4		HT	DC	FBG	SV	IB	T300	CHRY	13	7	19000	3	2	36600	40600
38	4		HT	DC	FBG	SV	IB	T216D	GM	13	7	19000	3	2	41300	45900
38	4		HT	DC	FBG	SV	IB	T283D	GM	13	7	19000	3	2	43000	47800
38	4	CONVERTIBLE	FB	SDN	FBG	SV	IB	T300	CHRY	13	7	19000	3	2	36700	40800
38	4	CONVERTIBLE	FB	SDN	FBG	SV	IB	T216D	GM	13	7	19000	3	2	41500	46100
38	4	CONVERTIBLE	FB	SDN	FBG	SV	IB	T283D	GM	13	7	19000	3	2	43300	48100
40	9	CONVERTIBLE	FB	SDN	FBG	SV	IB	T300	CHRY	10	2	21000	2	11	53200	58400
40	9	CONVERTIBLE	FB	SDN	FBG	SV	IB	T216D	GM	10	2	21000	2	11	57800	63600
40	9	CONVERTIBLE	FB	SDN	FBG	SV	IB	T283D	GM	10	2	21000	2	11	59700	65600
40	11	TWIN CABIN	HT	DCMY	FBG	SV	IB	T300	CHRY	14		21500	3		44600	49600
40	11	TWIN CABIN	HT	DCMY	FBG	SV	IB	T216D	GM	14		21500	3		49300	54200
40	11	TWIN CABIN	HT	DCMY	FBG	SV	IB	T283D	GM	14		21500	3		51900	57100
44	8	TRIPLE CABIN	HT	TCMY	FBG	SV	IB	T283D	GM	14	7	32000	3	6	68000	74700
44	8	TRIPLE CABIN	HT	TCMY	FBG	SV	IB	T350D	GM	14	7	32000	3	6	70600	77600
45	2	CONVERTIBLE	FB	SDN	FBG	SV	IB	T350D	GM	14	7	24000	3	6	59100	64900
50		CONVERTIBLE	FB	SDN	FBG	SV	IB	T350D	GM	15	10	42000	4		107000	118000
50		CONVERTIBLE	FB	SDN	FBG	SV	IB	T530D	GM	15	10	42000	4		119500	131500
50	3		HT	MY	FBG	SV	IB	T350D	GM	15	7	42000	4		110000	121000
50	3		FB	MY	FBG	SV	IB	T350D	GM	15	7	42000	4		109500	120500
50	3		FB	YTFS	FBG	SV	IB	T350D	GM	15	7	42000	4		103500	113500
		1968 BOATS														
27	10		HT	EXP	FBG		IB	T110	CHRY	12	5	12000	2	4	16300	18500
27	10		FB	EXP	FBG		IB	T110	CHRY	12	5	12000	2	4	16300	18500
27	10		FB	SF	FBG		IB	T110	CHRY	12	5	12000	2	4	17200	19500
31	4		HT	EXP	FBG		IB	T110-T290		12	5	13500	2	4	20000	24700
34	2	CONVERTIBLE	FB	SDN	FBG		IB	T290	CHRY	12	6	15000	3		29900	33200
34	2	CONVERTIBLE	FB	SDN	FBG		IB	T170D	GM	12	6	15000	3		41600	46200
38	4		HT	DC	FBG		IB	T290	CHRY	13	7	19000	3	5	35400	39300
38	4		HT	DC	FBG		IB	T216D	GM	13	7	19000	3	5	40000	44500
38	4		HT	DC	FBG		IB	T283D	GM	13	7	19000	3	5	41600	46300
38	4	CONVERTIBLE	HT	SDN	FBG		IB	T290	CHRY	13	7	19000	3	5	35500	39400
38	4	CONVERTIBLE	HT	SDN	FBG		IB	T216D	GM	13	7	19000	3	5	40200	44700
38	4	CONVERTIBLE	HT	SDN	FBG		IB	T283D	GM	13	7	19000	3	5	41900	46500
40	9	CONVERTIBLE	FB	SDN	FBG		IB	T290	CHRY	14		21000	2	11	41600	46200
40	9	CONVERTIBLE	FB	SDN	FBG		IB	T216D	GM	14		21000	2	11	46700	51300
40	9	CONVERTIBLE	FB	SDN	FBG		IB	T283D	GM	14		21000	2	11	48300	53100
40	11	TWIN CABIN	HT	DCMY	FBG		IB	T290	CHRY	14		21500	3		43100	47800
40	11	TWIN CABIN	HT	DCMY	FBG		IB	T216D	GM	14		21500	3		48000	52700
40	11	TWIN CABIN	HT	DCMY	FBG		IB	T283D	GM	14		21500	3		50400	55300
44	8		HT	TCMY	FBG		IB	T283D	GM	14	7	32000	3	6	66900	73500
44	8		HT	TCMY	FBG		IB	T350D	GM	14	7	32000	3	6	71200	78200
44	8		FB	TCMY	FBG		IB	T283D	GM	14	7	32000	3	6	67700	74300
44	8		FB	TCMY	FBG		IB	T350D	GM	14	7	32000	3	6	71700	78800
44	8	TWIN CABIN W/EXT HT	HT	TCMY	FBG		IB	T283D	GM	14	7	32000	3	6	68900	75700
44	8	TWIN CABIN W/EXT HT	HT	TCMY	FBG		IB	T350D	GM	14	7	32000	3	6	73000	80200
50			HT	MY	FBG		IB	T350D	GM	15		42000	4		106500	117000
50			FB	MY	FBG		IB	T350D	GM	15		42000	4		106000	116500
50		CONVERTIBLE	FB	SDN	FBG		IB	T350D	GM	15		42000	4		104000	114000
50		CONVERTIBLE	FB	SDN	FBG		IB	T530D	GM	15		42000	4		116000	127500
50	3		FB	YTFS	FBG		IB	T350D	GM	15	7	42000	4		100000	110000
		1967 BOATS														
27	10		HT	EXP	FBG		IB	T210	CHRY	12	5	12000	2	4	16700	18900
27	10		FB	EXP	FBG		IB	T210	CHRY	12	5	12000	2	4	16700	18900
27	10		FB	SF	FBG		IB	T210	CHRY	12	5	12000	2	4	17300	19700
31	4		HT	EXP	FBG		IB	T210-T290		12	5	13500	2	4	20500	23800
34	2	CONVERTIBLE	FB	SDN	FBG		IB	T290	CHRY	12	6	15000	3		28800	32000
34	2	CONVERTIBLE	FB	SDN	FBG		IB	T170D	GM	12	6	15000	3		40900	45400
40	9	CONVERTIBLE	FB	SDN	FBG		IB	T290	CHRY	14		21000	2	11	40400	44800
40	9	CONVERTIBLE	FB	SDN	FBG		IB	T216D	GM	14		21000	2	11	44900	49900
40	9	CONVERTIBLE	FB	SDN	FBG		IB	T283D	GM	14		21000	2	11	47100	51700
40	11	TWIN CABIN	HT	DCMY	FBG		IB	T290	CHRY	14		21500	3		41800	46400
40	11	TWIN CABIN	HT	DCMY	FBG		IB	T216D	GM	14		21500	3		46600	51200
40	11	TWIN CABIN	HT	DCMY	FBG		IB	T283D	GM	14		21500	3		48900	53700
44	8		HT	TCMY	FBG		IB	T283D	GM	14	7	32000	3	6	65900	72400
44	8		HT	TCMY	FBG		IB	T350D	GM	14	7	32000	3	6	70000	76900
50		CONVERTIBLE	FB	SDN	FBG		IB	T350D	GM	15	10	42000	4		100500	110500
50		CONVERTIBLE	FB	SDN	FBG		IB	T530D	GM	15	10	42000	4		112500	123500
50	3		HT	MY	FBG		IB	T350D	GM	15	7	42000	4		103000	113000
50	3		FB	MY	FBG		IB	T350D	GM	15	7	42000	4		102500	112500
50	3		FB	YTFS	FBG		IB	T350D	GM	15	7	42000	4		97100	106500
		1966 BOATS														
27	10		HT	EXP	FBG		IB	T210	CHRY	12	5	12000	2	4	16100	18300
27	10		FB	EXP	FBG		IB	T210	CHRY	12	5	12000	2	4	16100	18300
27	10		FB	SF	FBG		IB	T210-T290		12	5		2	4	12400	14900
27	10		FB	SF	FBG		IB	T130D	GM	12	5		2	4	20000	22200
34	2		OP	DC	FBG		IB	T290	CHRY	12	6	14000	3		25800	28600
34	2		FB	DC	FBG		IB	T290	CHRY	12	6	14000	3		25800	28600
34	2		FB	SDN	FBG		IB	T210-T290		12	6	13000	3		25600	29200
34	2	CONVERTIBLE	FB	SDN	FBG		IB	T290	CHRY	12	6	13000	3		27200	30200
34	2	CONVERTIBLE	FB	SDN	FBG		IB	T140D	GM	12	6	15000	3		39300	43700
40	9	CONVERTIBLE	FB	SDN	FBG		IB	T290	CHRY	14		17000	3		33600	37300
40	9	CONVERTIBLE	FB	SDN	FBG		IB	T216D	GM	14		19000	3		40700	45300
40	9	CONVERTIBLE	FB	SDN	FBG		IB	T283D	GM	14		19000	3		42500	47200
40	11	TWIN CABIN	HT	DCMY	FBG		IB	T290	CHRY	14		19500	3		37700	41900
40	11	TWIN CABIN	HT	DCMY	FBG		IB	T216D	GM	14		19500	3		41900	46500
40	11	TWIN CABIN	HT	DCMY	FBG		IB	T283D	GM	14		19500	3		44400	49300
50	3		HT	MY	FBG		IB	T350D	GM	15	7	42000	4		99900	110000
50	3		FB	YTFS	FBG		IB	T350D	GM	15	7	42000	4		94300	103500
		1965 BOATS														
27	10		HT	EXP	FBG		IB	T210	CHRY			12900	2	4	15800	18000
27	10		FB	EXP	FBG		IB	T210	CHRY	12	5	12000	2	4	15500	17600
27	10		FB	SF	FBG		IB	T210-T290		12	5	12000	2	4	16300	19100
27	10		FB	SF	FBG		IB	T140D	GM	12	5	12000	2	4	28600	31800
34	2		OP	DC	FBG		IB	T210-T290		12	6	14000	3		24000	27600
34	2		OP	DC	FBG		IB	T130D	GM	12	6	17000	3		39500	43800
34	2		FB	DC	FBG		IB	T210-T290		12	6	14000	3		24000	27600
34	2		FB	DC	FBG		IB	T130D	GM	12	6	17000	3		39500	43800
34	2		HT	EXP	FBG		IB	T210-T290		12	6	12000	3		22900	26400
34	2		HT	EXP	FBG		IB	T130D	GM	12	6	12000	3		32100	35700
34	2		HT	SDN	FBG		IB	T210-T290		12	6	13000	3		24700	27700

CONTINUED ON NEXT PAGE

LOA FT IN	NAME AND/ OR MODEL	TOP/ RIG	BOAT TYPE	-HULL- MTL TP	----ENGINE--- TP # HP MFG	BEAM FT IN	WGT LBS	DRAFT FT IN	RETAIL LOW	RETAIL HIGH
				--- 1965 BOATS ---						
34 2		FB	SDN	FBG	IB T210-T290	12 6	13000	3	24700	28600
34 2		FB	SDN	FBG	IB T130D GM	12 6	15000	3	38400	42700
34 2		FB	SPTCR	FBG	IB T210-T290	12 6	13000	3	23500	27000
34 2		FB	SPTCR	FBG	IB T130D CHRY	12 6	13000	3	33500	37200
34 2		HT	SDN	FBG	IB T290 CHRY	12 6	13000	3	26600	29500
34 2	CONVERTIBLE	HT	SDN	FBG	IB T130D-T140D	12 6	13000	3	35800	43000
34 2	DELUXE	FB	SF	FBG	IB T210-T290	12 6	15000	3	24600	27400
34 2	DELUXE	FB	SF	FBG	IB T130D GM	12 6	15000	3	36200	40300
40 9	CONVERTIBLE	FB	SDN	FBG	IB T290 CHRY	14	17000	2 11	32700	36300
	IB T195D GM 39200		43500,	IB T280D GM	41200 45800,	IB T370D GM			44100	49000
40 11		HT	DC	FBG	IB T290 CHRY	14	19500	3	36400	40400
40 11		HT	DC	FBG	IB T195D GM	14	19500	3	39800	44200
40 11		HT	DC	FBG	IB T280D GM	14	19500	3	42600	47400
40 11		FB	DC	FBG	IB T290 CHRY	14	19500	3	36400	40400
40 11		FB	DC	FBG	IB T195D GM	14	19500	3	39700	44100
40 11		FB	DC	FBG	IB T280D GM	14	19500	3	42600	47300
40 11	TWIN CABIN	HT	DCMY	FBG	IB T290 CHRY	14	19500	3	36700	40800
	IB T216D GM 40800		45300,	IB T283D GM	43200 48000,	IB T370D CUM			46900	51600
50 3		HT	MY	FBG	IB T350D GM	15 7	42000	4	97000	106500
50 3		FB	MY	FBG	IB T350D GM	15 7	42000	4	96500	106000
50 3		FB	YTFS	FBG	IB T350D GM	15 7	42000	4	91600	100500
				--- 1964 BOATS ---						
34 2		OP	DC	FBG	IB T210-T290	12 6	14000	3	23200	26600
34 2		OP	DC	FBG	IB T130D GM	12 6	17000	3	38900	43300
34 2		FB	DC	FBG	IB T210-T290	12 6	14000	3	23200	26600
34 2		FB	DC	FBG	IB T130D GM	12 6	17000	3	38900	43300
34 2		HT	EXP	FBG	IB T210-T290	12 6	13000	3	22600	26000
34 2		HT	EXP	FBG	IB T130D GM	12 6	15000	3	35800	39700
34 2		HT	SDN	FBG	IB T210 CHRY	12 6	13000	3	23800	26400
34 2		FB	SPTCR	FBG	IB T210-T290	12 6	13000	3	22700	26100
34 2		FB	SPTCR	FBG	IB T130D GM	12 6	15000	3	35800	39800
34 2	CONVERTIBLE	HT	SDN	FBG	IB T290 CHRY	12 6	15000	3	25800	28700
34 2	CONVERTIBLE	HT	SDN	FBG	IB T130D CHRY	12 6	13000	3	35400	39300
34 2	CONVERTIBLE	FB	SDN	FBG	IB T210-T290	12 6	13000	3	23800	27600
34 2	CONVERTIBLE	FB	SDN	FBG	IB T130D GM	12 6	13000	3	35400	39300
34 2	DELUXE	FB	SF	FBG	IB T210-T290	12 6	13000	3	22600	26000
34 2	DELUXE	FB	SF	FBG	IB T130D GM	12 6	15000	3	35800	39700
40 9	CONVERTIBLE	FB	SDN	FBG	IB T290 CHRY	14	19000	2 11	31900	35400
40 9	CONVERTIBLE	FB	SDN	FBG	IB T181D GM	14	19000	2 11	37900	42100
40 9	CONVERTIBLE	FB	SDN	FBG	IB T283D GM	14	19000	2 11	40300	44800
40 11		OP	DC	FBG	IB T290 CHRY	14	19500		35400	39300
40 11		OP	DC	FBG	IB T181D GM	14	19500	2 11	38200	42400
40 11		OP	DC	FBG	IB T283D GM	14	19500	2 11	41500	46200
40 11		HT	DC	FBG	IB T290 CHRY	14	19500	2 11	35500	39400
40 11		HT	DC	FBG	IB T181D GM	14	19500	2 11	38300	42600
				--- 1963 BOATS ---						
34 2		HT	EXP	FBG	IB T210-T280	12 6	14000	3	21800	25000
34 2		HT	EXP	FBG	IB T130D GM	12 6	15000	3	35900	39900
34 2		FB	SPTCR	FBG	IB T210-T280	12 6	14000	3	21900	25000
34 2		FB	SPTCR	FBG	IB T130D GM	12 6	15000	3	35400	39300
40		HT	CR	FBG	IB T280 CHRY	14	17000	3	30000	33300
40		HT	CR	FBG	IB T181D GM	14	19000	2 10	36400	40500
40		HT	SDN	FBG	IB T181D GM	14	19000	2 10	36500	40500
40		FB	SF	FBG	IB T280 CHRY	14	17000	2 10	30000	33300
40		FB	SF	FBG	IB T181D GM	14	19000	2 10	36400	40500
40 9		HT	SDN	FBG	IB T280 CHRY	14	17000	2 10	31600	35100
40 9		FB	YTFS	FBG	IB T280 CHRY	14	17000	2 10	30900	34300
40 9		FB	YTFS	FBG	IB T181D GM	14	19000	2 10	36100	40100
40 11		OP	DCFD	FBG	IB T280 CHRY	14	19500	2 11	33400	38200
40 11		OP	DCFD	FBG	IB T181D GM	14	19500	2 11	37300	41400
40 11		HT	DCFD	FBG	IB T280 CHRY	14	19500	2 11	34500	38300
40 11		HT	DCFD	FBG	IB T181D GM	14	19500	2 11	37400	41500
				--- 1962 BOATS ---						
34 2		HT	EXP	FBG	IB T280 CHRY	12 6	11500	3	21300	23600
34 2		HT	EXP	FBG	IB T130D GM	12 6	11500	3	30400	33700
34 2		FB	EXP	FBG	IB T280 CHRY	12 6	11500	3	21300	23600
34 2		FB	EXP	FBG	IB T130D GM	12 6	11500	3	30400	33700
34 2			SDN	FBG	IB T280 CHRY	12 6	11500	3	22700	25200
34 2			SDN	FBG	IB T130D GM	12 6	11500	3	32800	36400
34 2			SF	FBG	IB T280 CHRY	12 6	11500	3	21300	23600
34 2			SF	FBG	IB T130D GM	12 6	11500	3	30400	33700
40 11		OP	DCFD	FBG	IB T280 CHRY	14	19500	2 11	33700	37300
40 11		OP	DCFD	FBG	IB T181D GM	14	19500	2 11	36400	40500
40 11		HT	DCFD	FBG	IB T280 CHRY	14	19500	2 11	33700	37400
40 11		HT	DCFD	FBG	IB T181D GM	14	19500	2 11	36500	40600
41 9		HT	EXP	FBG	IB T280 CHRY		19500		37300	41500
41 9		HT	SDN	FBG	IB T280 CHRY		19500		35400	39300
41 9		FB	SF	FBG	IB T280 CHRY		19500		35300	39200
41 9		FB	SF	FBG	IB T181D GM	14	19500		35800	39800
41 9	CONVERTIBLE		YTFS	FBG	IB T181D GM		19500		35400	38900
41 9	CONVERTIBLE	FB	YTFS	FBG	IB T280 CHRY		19500		35800	39700
				--- 1961 BOATS ---						
33 8		FB	EXP	FBG	IB T185-T275	12 6	11500	3	19200	22400
34 2		FB	EXP	FBG	IB T130D GM	12 6	11500	3	30100	33500
40 8		CR	FBG		IB T180	14	19500	2 10	32300	35800
40 8		CR	FBG		IB T275 CC	14	19500	2 10	32800	36500
40 8	CONVERTIBLE	SF	FBG		IB T180	12	19500	2 10	34600	38500
40 8	CONVERTIBLE	SF	FBG		IB T275 CC	12	19500	2 10	35800	39800
40 8	CONVERTIBLE	SF	FBG		IB T215D GM	12	19500	2 10	39500	43900
				--- 1960 BOATS ---						
40	CONVERTIBLE	SF	FBG		IB T225				34400	38200
40	CONVERTIBLE	SF	FBG		IB T275 CC				34500	38400
40	SPORT FISHERMAN	SF	FBG		IB T225	14		2 11	33000	36700

HAWKLINE BOAT COMPANY
COAST GUARD MFG ID- HAX

Call 1-800-327-6929 for BUC Personalized Evaluation Service
Or, for 1977 to 1985 boats, sign onto www.BUCValuPro.com

HAZELWOOD YACHTS
DIV OF ACME BUILDING CO

Call 1-800-327-6929 for BUC Personalized Evaluation Service
Or, for 1979 to 1982 boats, sign onto www.BUCValuPro.com

HEATING ASSURANCE INC

Call 1-800-327-6929 for BUC Personalized Evaluation Service
Or, for 1960 to 1966 boats, sign onto www.BUCValuPro.com

JACK A HELMS COMPANY
IRMO SC 29063   COAST GUARD MFG ID- JAH See inside cover to adjust price for area

For more recent years, see the BUC Used Boat Price Guide, Volume 1 or Volume 2

LOA FT IN	NAME AND/ OR MODEL	TOP/ RIG	BOAT TYPE	-HULL- MTL TP	----ENGINE--- TP # HP MFG	BEAM FT IN	WGT LBS	DRAFT FT IN	RETAIL LOW	RETAIL HIGH
				--- 1983 BOATS ---						
23 11	HELMS 24	SLP	SA/CR	FBG KL OB		8 10	4000	4	5300	6100
23 11	HELMS 24 SHOAL	SLP	SA/CR	FBG KL OB		8 10	4100	4 11	5400	6250
23 11	HELMS 24 SHOAL	SLP	SA/CR	FBG KL IB	8D YAN	8 10	4400	4 11	6400	7350
26 10	HELMS 27	SLP	SA/CR	FBG KL IB	T 15D YAN	9 8	6200	4 3	10400	11900
32	HELMS 32	SLP	SA/CR	FBG KL IB	15D YAN	10 6	9500	4 10	16400	18600
				--- 1982 BOATS ---						
23 11	HELMS 24	SLP	SA/CR	FBG KL OB		8 10	4000	4	5000	5750
23 11	HELMS 24	SLP	SA/CR	FBG KL SD	15 OMC	8 10	4200	4	5500	6300
23 11	HELMS 24	SLP	SA/CR	FBG KL IB	8D YAN	8 10	4400	4	6000	6900
23 11	HELMS 24 SHOAL	SLP	SA/CR	FBG KL OB		8 10	4100	4 11	5200	6000
23 11	HELMS 24 SHOAL	SLP	SA/CR	FBG KL SD	15 OMC	8 10	4400	4 11	5700	6600
23 11	HELMS 24 SHOAL	SLP	SA/CR	FBG KL IB	8D YAN	8 10	4400	4 11	6250	7200
26 10	HELMS 27	SLP	SA/CR	FBG KL IB	T 15D YAN	9 8	6200	4 3	9800	11200
29 11	HELMS 30	SLP	SA/CR	FBG KL IB		9 4	8100	4 6	12900	14700
				--- 1981 BOATS ---						
23 11	HELMS 24	SLP	SA/CR	FBG KL OB		8 10	4000	4	4700	5400
23 11	HELMS 24	SLP	SA/CR	FBG KL SD	15 OMC	8 10	4000	4	4950	5650
23 11	HELMS 24	SLP	SA/CR	FBG KL IB	8D YAN	8 10	4000	4	5200	5950
26 10	HELMS 27	SLP	SA/CR	FBG KL OB		9 6	6200	4 3	8650	9850
26 10	HELMS 27	SLP	SA/CR	FBG KL IB	T 15D YAN	9 8	6200	4 3	9300	10600
29 11	HELMS 30	SLP	SA/CR	FBG KL OB		9 4		4 6	9400	10700
				--- 1980 BOATS ---						
23 11	HELMS 24	SLP	SA/CR	FBG KL OB		8 10	4000	4	4500	5200
23 11	HELMS 24	SLP	SA/CR	FBG KL SD	15 OMC	8 10	4000	4	4700	5400
23 11	HELMS 24	SLP	SA/CR	FBG KL IB	11D UNIV	8 10	4000	4	5000	5750
24 11	HELMS 25	SLP	SA/CR	FBG KL KC		8	3950	6	4600	5300
26 10	HELMS 27	SLP	SA/CR	FBG KL SD	15 OMC	9 6	6200	4 3	8150	9400

LOA FT IN	NAME AND/ OR MODEL		TOP/ RIG	BOAT TYPE	-HULL- MTL TP	TP	----ENGINE--- # HP MFG	BEAM FT IN	WGT LBS	DRAFT FT IN	RETAIL LOW	RETAIL HIGH
			1980 BOATS									
26 10	HELMS 27		SLP	SA/CR	FBG KL	OB	11D UNIV	9 6	6200	4 3	8350	9600
29 11	HELMS 30		SLP	SA/CR	FBG KL	IB	15 OMC	9 4	8000	4 6	11500	13000
29 11	HELMS 30		SLP	SA/CR	FBG KL	IB T	11D-T16D	9 4	8000	4 6	11700	13300
			1979 BOATS									
23 11	HELMS-DOLPHIN		SLP	SA/CR	FBG KL	OB	8 10		4000	4	4250	4900
23 11	HELMS-DOLPHIN		SLP	SA/CR	FBG KL	SD	15 OMC	8 10	4000	4	4500	5200
23 11	HELMS-DOLPHIN		SLP	SA/CR	FBG KL	IB	8D REN	8 10	4000	4	4700	5400
23 11	HELMS-DOLPHIN SHOAL		SLP	SA/CR	FBG KL	OB	8 10		4000	3	4400	5050
23 11	HELMS-DOLPHIN SHOAL		SLP	SA/CR	FBG KL	SD	15 OMC	8 10	4000	3	4600	5300
23 11	HELMS-DOLPHIN SHOAL		SLP	SA/CR	FBG KL	IB	8D REN	8 10	4000	3	4800	5500
24 11	HELMS-DOLPHIN		SLP	SA/CR	FBG KC	OB	8		3950	1 8	4550	5200
26 10	HELMS-DOLPHIN		SLP	SA/CR	FBG KL	OB	9 6		5900	4 3	7300	8400
26 10	HELMS-DOLPHIN		SLP	SA/CR	FBG KL	SD	15 OMC	9 6	5900	4 3	7450	8600
26 10	HELMS-DOLPHIN		SLP	SA/CR	FBG KL	IB	8D	9 6	5900	4 3	7600	8750
29 11	HELMS-DOLPHIN		SLP	SA/CR	FBG KL	IB	12D- 16D	9 4	8000	4 6	11100	12600
			1978 BOATS									
23 10	HELMS 24		SLP	SA/CR	F/S KL	OB	8 10		3900	4	4000	4650
23 10	HELMS 24		SLP	SA/CR	F/S KL	OB	8D	8 10	3900	4	4500	5200
24 11	HELMS 25		SLP	SA/CR	F/S KC	OB	8		3950	1 8	4350	5000
28	HELMS 28		SLP	SA/CR	FBG KL	IB	D	9 2	6450	4 3	8350	9550
30	HELMS 30		SLP	SA/CR	F/S KL	IB	8D- 16D	9 2	8100	5	10800	12300
			1977 BOATS									
23 10	HELMS 24		SLP	SA/CR	F/S KL	OB	8 10		3500	3 9	3500	4100
23 10	HELMS 24		SLP	SA/CR	F/S KL	OB	10 UNIV	8 10	3500	3 9	3700	4300
23 10	HELMS 24		SLP	SA/CR	F/S KL	OB	8D YAN	8 10	3500	3 9	3950	4600
24 11	HELMS 25		SLP	SA/CR	F/S KC	OB	8		3950	1 8	4150	4850
30	HELMS 30		SLP	SA/CR	F/S KL	IB	9 2		8100	5	10400	11800
30	HELMS 30		SLP	SA/CR	F/S KL	IB	8D- 27D	9 2	8100	5	10500	11900
			1976 BOATS									
23 10	HELMS 24		SLP	SA/CR	FBG KL		8 10		3500	3 9	3400	3950
24 11	HELMS 25		SLP	SA/CR	FBG KC		8		4200	1 8	4150	4850
28	HELMS 28		SLP	SA/CR	FBG KL	IB	10D	9 2	6450	4 3	7750	9900
30	HELMS 30		SLP	SA/CR	FBG KL	IB	30D	9 2	8800	5	11100	12600
			1975 BOATS									
24 11	HELMS 25		SLP	SAIL	FBG KC	OB	8		3950	6	3900	4550
30	HELMS 30		SLP	SA/CR	FBG KL	IB	D	9 2	8800	5	10700	12200
			1974 BOATS									
24 11	HELMS 25		SLP	SAIL	FBG KC	OB	8		4000	5	3850	4500
30 1	HELMS 30 MK2		SLP	SAIL	FBG KL	IB	27D PALM	9 2	8800	4 6	10500	11900
			1973 BOATS									
24 11	HELMS 25		SLP	SAIL	FBG KC	OB	8		3550	1 8	3400	3950
			1972 BOATS									
25	HELMS 25		SLP	SA/CR	FBG KC	OB	8			1 8	3750	4350

HELTON BOAT WORKS INC

Call 1-800-327-6929 for BUC Personalized Evaluation Service
Or, for 1961 boats, sign onto www.BUCValuPro.com

HENDERSON MFG CO INC

Call 1-800-327-6929 for BUC Personalized Evaluation Service
Or, for 1921 to 1985 boats, sign onto www.BUCValuPro.com

HENDERSON PLASTIC ENGRG CORP
TEAL CRAFT

Call 1-800-327-6929 for BUC Personalized Evaluation Service
Or, for 1960 boats, sign onto www.BUCValuPro.com

HENRIQUES YACHTS INC
BAYVILLE NJ 08721   COAST GUARD MFG ID- HEH See inside cover to adjust price for area

For more recent years, see the BUC Used Boat Price Guide, Volume 1 or Volume 2

LOA FT IN	NAME AND/ OR MODEL		TOP/ RIG	BOAT TYPE	-HULL- MTL TP	TP	----ENGINE--- # HP MFG	BEAM FT IN	WGT LBS	DRAFT FT IN	RETAIL LOW	RETAIL HIGH
			1983 BOATS									
35 4	MAINE-COASTER CHARTR	HT	FSH	FBG SV	IB	235D VLVO	12		14000	3	62000	68200
35 4	MAINE-COASTER CHARTR	FB	FSH	FBG SV	IB	235D VLVO	12		14000	3	59400	65300
35 4	MAINE-COASTER CHARTR	FB	FSH	FBG SV	IB	280D GM	12		14000	3	60600	66600
35 4	MAINE-COASTER CHARTR	FB	FSH	FBG SV	IO	300D VLVO	12		14000	3	56100	61600
35 4	MAINE-COASTER COMM	HT	FSH	FBG SV	IB	235D VLVO	12		14000	3	56800	62400
35 4	MAINE-COASTER COMM	HT	FSH	FBG SV	IB	300D VLVO	12		14000	3	58300	64100
35 4	MAINE-COASTER COMM	HT	FSH	FBG SV	IB	310D GM	12		14000	3 2	61300	67400
35 4	MAINE-COASTER SPT	FB	FSH	FBG SV	IB	235D VLVO	12		14000	3	52400	57500
	IB 300D VLVO 55600 61100, IB T 40D 53100 58400, IB T200D PERK 59200 65000											
	IB T205D GM 56700 62300											
44	MAINE-COASTER CHARTR	FB	SF	FBG DV	IB	T300D VLVO	14 8	37000	4	121500	133500
44	MAINE-COASTER CHARTR	FB	SF	FBG DV	IB	T310D GM	14 8	37000	4	124000	136000
44	MAINE-COASTER CHARTR	FB	SF	FBG DV	IB	T355D CAT	14 8	37000	4	130500	143500
			1982 BOATS									
35 4	MAINE-COASTER CHARTR	HT	FSH	FBG SV	IB	200D PERK	12		14000	3	61500	67600
35 4	MAINE-COASTER CHARTR	HT	FSH	FBG SV	IB	235D VLVO	12		14000	3	62000	68100
35 4	MAINE-COASTER CHARTR	FB	FSH	FBG SV	IB	286D VLVO	12		14000	3	62700	68900
35 4	MAINE-COASTER COMM	HT	FSH	FBG SV	IB		12		14000	3 2	**	**
	IB 200D PERK 54400 59800, IB 235D VLVO 52300 57400, IB 286D VLVO 53200 58500											
	IB 310D GM 58900 64700											
35 4	MAINE-COASTER SPT	FB	SF	FBG SV	IB	235D VLVO	12		13500	3	50300	55300
	IB 286D VLVO 53100 58400, IB 310D GM 53000 58200, IB T160D PERK 55500 60900											
	IB T200D PERK 56900 62500, IB T205D GM 56400 62000											
			1981 BOATS									
35 4	MAINE-COASTER	HT	FSH	FBG SV	IB		12		14000	3 2	**	**
	IB 286 VLVO 47000 51700, IB 200D PERK 55700 61200, IB 230D VLVO 54900 60400											
	IB 230D VLVO 54900 60400, IB 286D VLVO 55700 61200, IB 310D GM 56600 62200											
35 4	MAINE-COASTER	FB	SF	FBG SV	IB	230D VLVO	12		13500	3	48300	53100
	IB 286D VLVO 51100 56100, IB 310D GM 50900 56000, IB T120D FORD 50700 55700											
	IB T160D PERK 53300 58600, IB T200D PERK 54700 60100											
			1980 BOATS									
35 4	MAINE-COASTER	FB	SF	FBG SV	IB	220D	12		14000	3	47900	52600
	IB 230D VLVO 46700 51400, IB 310D GM 49000 53900, IB T120D FORD 48800 53600											
	IB T250D CUM 53600 58900											
			1979 BOATS									
35 4	MAINE-COASTER	FB	SF	FBG SV	IB	220D VLVO	12		13500	3 1	44500	49500
	IB 300D GM 47300 51900, IB T120D FORD 47200 51900, IB T140D VLVO 47300 51900											
	IB T200D CUM 49900 54900											
35 4	MAINE-COASTER LOBSTR	TRWL	FBG SV	IB	220D VLVO	12		12000	3 1	51500	56600
35 4	MAINE-COASTER LOBSTR	TRWL	FBG SV	IB	300D GM	12		13000	3 1	55800	61300

HERITAGE BOAT WORKS INC
HOOD RIVER OR 47031   COAST GUARD MFG ID- HRG See inside cover to adjust price for area

For more recent years, see the BUC Used Boat Price Guide, Volume 1 or Volume 2

LOA FT IN	NAME AND/ OR MODEL		TOP/ RIG	BOAT TYPE	-HULL- MTL TP	TP	----ENGINE--- # HP MFG	BEAM FT IN	WGT LBS	DRAFT FT IN	RETAIL LOW	RETAIL HIGH
			1983 BOATS									
20	HERITAGE		OP		FBG		10D BMW	8	5260	2 6	12600	14300
20	HERITAGE		SLP	SAIL	FBG CB	IB	10D BMW	8	5260	2 6	6850	7900
20	HERITAGE		SLP	SAIL	FBG KL	IB	10D BMW	8	5260	3 6	6850	7900
20	HERITAGE CRUISING		CAT	SA/CR	FBG KL	IB	12D SAAB	8	5260	3 6	6900	7950
22	BENFORD 22		SLP	SAIL	FBG		7D BMW		4000	3	5450	6250
26	YANKEE 26		SLP	SAIL	FBG	IB	6D BMW	8 8	5335	4 9	7950	9150
30	BEDFORD 30		SLP	SAIL	FBG	IB	23D VLVO		10975		18000	20100
30	BENFORD 30		SLP	SAIL	FBG	IB	23D VLVO		10975		18000	20100
30 1	YANKEE 30		SLP	SAIL	FBG	IB	10D BMW	9	10000		16100	18100
			1982 BOATS									
20	HERITAGE CRUISING		CAT	SA/CR	FBG KL	IB	12D SAAB	8	5260	3 6	6500	7450
26	YANKEE 26		SLP	SAIL	FBG	IB	6D BMW	8 8	5335	4 9	7450	8600
30 1	YANKEE 30		SLP	SAIL	FBG KL	IB	10D BMW	9	10000		15000	17000
			1981 BOATS									
20	HERITAGE		SLP	CR	FBG		12D BMW	8	5260	2 6	11700	13300
20	HERITAGE		SLP	SAIL	FBG CB	IB	12D BMW	8	5260	2 6	6100	7000
20	HERITAGE		SLP	SAIL	FBG KL	IB	12D BMW	8	5260	3 6	6100	7000
20	HERITAGE CRUISING		CAT	SA/CR	FBG KL	IB	12D SABB	8	5260	3 6	6100	7000
25 6	COLUMBIA GILNETTER		OP	FSH	FBG DS	IB	35D BMW	7 6	10400		11800
26	YANKEE 26		SLP	SAIL	FBG	IB	7D BMW	8 8	5335	4 9	7050	8100
30 1	YANKEE 30		SLP	SAIL	FBG	IB	12D BMW	9	10000		14100	16100
			1980 BOATS									
16 8	SALLY-JAY		SLP	SAIL	FBG KL		5 10	3300	3	3000	3500
20	HERITAGE		SLP	CR	FBG		12D FARY	8	5260	2 6	11400	13000
20	HERITAGE		SLP	SAIL	FBG CB	IB	12D FARY	8	5260	2 6	5850	6700
20	HERITAGE		SLP	SAIL	FBG KL	IB	12D FARY	8	5260	3 6	5850	6700

LOA FT IN	NAME AND/ OR MODEL	TOP/ RIG	BOAT TYPE	HULL MTL	HULL TP	TP #	ENGINE HP	ENGINE MFG	BEAM FT IN	WGT LBS	DRAFT FT IN	RETAIL LOW	RETAIL HIGH
1980 BOATS													
20	HERITAGE CRUISING	CAT	SA/CR	FBG	KL	IB	12D	SABB	8	5260	3 6	5850	6700
1979 BOATS													
20	CRUISING CAT	GAF	SA/CR	FBG	KC	IB	10D- 12D		8	5600	2 6	5950	6900
20	CRUISING CAT	GAF	SA/CR	FBG	KL	IB	10D- 12D		8	5600	3 6	5950	6900
20	CRUISING CAT	SLP	SA/CR	FBG	KC	IB	10D- 12D		8	5600	2 6	5950	6900
20	CRUISING CAT	SLP	SA/CR	FBG	KL	IB	10D- 12D		8	5600	3 6	5950	6900
20	CRUISING CAT LUG	GAF	SA/CR	FBG	KC	IB	10D- 12D		8	5600	2 6	5950	6900
20	CRUISING CAT LUG	GAF	SA/CR	FBG	KL	IB	10D- 12D		8	5600	3 6	5950	6900
20	HERITAGE POCKET YT	CR	F/S	DV		IB	10D	SABB	8	4100	2 3	8900	10100
20	HERITAGE POCKET YT	CR	FBG	DV		IB	10D	SABB	8	4100	2 3	8900	10100
20	HERITAGE POCKET YT	CR	F/S	DV		IB	12D	FARY	8	4100	2 3	9200	10400
20	HERITAGE POCKET YT	CR	FBG	DV		IB	12D	FARY	8	4100	2 3	9150	10400

HERITAGE MARINE INC
LONG BEACH CA 90806   COAST GUARD MFG ID- HLK   See inside cover to adjust price for area

LOA FT IN	NAME AND/ OR MODEL	TOP/ RIG	BOAT TYPE	HULL MTL	HULL TP	TP #	ENGINE HP	ENGINE MFG	BEAM FT IN	WGT LBS	DRAFT FT IN	RETAIL LOW	RETAIL HIGH
1982 BOATS													
27	NOR'SEA 27	SLP	SA/CR	FBG	KL	IB	15D	YAN	8	8000	3 6	29900	33300
1979 BOATS													
25 7	NOR-SEA PH CR	SLP	SA/CR	FBG	KL	IB	15D	YAN	8	5500	3 6	17000	19400
27	NOR-SEA 27	SLP	SA/CR	FBG	KL	IB	15D	YAN	8	7000	3 6	23000	25500
27	NOR-SEA 27	SLP	SA/CR	FBG	KL	IB T	15D	YAN	8	7000	3 6	23800	26500
1978 BOATS													
27	NOR-SEA 27 OR 4 TON	SLP	SA/CR	FBG	KL	IB	8D- 9D		8	7000	3 6	22100	24600
27	NOR-SEA 27 OR 4 TON	CUT	SA/CR	FBG	KL	IB	8D- 9D		8	7000	3 6	22100	24600
1977 BOATS													
27	NOR-SEA 27	SLP	SA/CR	FBG	KL	IB	10D	FARY	8	7000	3 6	21500	23900
1976 BOATS													
27	NOR-SEA 27	SLP	SAIL	FBG	KL	IB	10D	FARY	8	7000	3 6	21000	23400
1965 BOATS													
18 8	PAGAN	CUT	SAIL	WD	KL	IB			6 2		2 6	4900	5600
18 8	PILOT II	SCH	SAIL	WD	KL	IB			6 2		2 6	4900	5600
31	PHANTOM	MS		WD	KL	IB	D		10		6	31200	34700
32	TAHITI	SLP	SAIL	WD	KL	IB			10		5	19100	21200

HERITAGE YACHT BLDRS CO
Call 1-800-327-6929 for BUC Personalized Evaluation Service
Or, for 1974 to 1976 boats, sign onto www.BUCValuPro.com

HERITAGE YACHT COMPANY
Call 1-800-327-6929 for BUC Personalized Evaluation Service
Or, for 1968 boats, sign onto www.BUCValuPro.com

HERITAGE YACHT CORP
CLEARWATER FL 33520   COAST GUARD MFG ID- HYA   See inside cover to adjust price for area

LOA FT IN	NAME AND/ OR MODEL	TOP/ RIG	BOAT TYPE	HULL MTL	HULL TP	TP #	ENGINE HP	ENGINE MFG	BEAM FT IN	WGT LBS	DRAFT FT IN	RETAIL LOW	RETAIL HIGH
1980 BOATS													
36	WEST-INDIAN	TRWL	FBG	SV		IB	130D		13	17500		56300	61900
46	WEST-INDIAN	TRWL	FBG	SV		IB	D		15	30000		**	**
1979 BOATS													
30	WEST-INDIAN	FB	TRWL	FBG	DS	IB	62D		12 8	14500		39800	44200
33	WEST-INDIES 33	SLP	SA/CR	FBG	KL	IB	D		11 5	12500	4 3	26200	29100
36	WEST-INDIAN	FB	TRWL	FBG	DS	IB	130D		13	17500		53800	59100
36 5	WEST-INDIES 36	SLP	SA/CR	FBG	KC	IB	D		12	17000	4	35300	39300
36 5	WEST-INDIES 36	KTH	SA/CR	FBG	KL	IB	D		12	17000	4	35300	39300
37	HERITAGE ONE TON	SLP	SA/RC	FBG	KL	IB	D		11 10	13000	6 6	28400	31500
38	WEST-INDIES 38	SLP	SA/CR	FBG	KC	IB	D		12	20000	4	41700	46300
38	WEST-INDIES 38	KTH	SA/CR	FBG	KC	IB	D		12	20000	4	41700	46400
46	WEST-INDIES 46	SLP	SA/CR	FBG	KC	IB	D		15	27500	4 2	66500	73100
46	WEST-INDIES 46	KTH	SA/CR	FBG	KL	IB	D		15	27500	4 2	66500	73100
48	WEST-INDIAN	FB	TRWL	FBG	DS	IB	D		15	30000		**	**
1978 BOATS													
27	SUPER 27	SLP	SA/CR	FBG	KC	IB	D		10	8000	5 6	17200	19500
30	WEST-INDIAN	FB	TRWL	FBG	DS	IB	62D- 85D		12 8	14500	2 10	38400	42700
33	WEST-INDIES 33	SLP	SA/CR	FBG	KL	IB	25D	YAN	11 4	12500	3 6	25200	28000
36	WEST-INDIAN	FB	TRWL	FBG	DS	IB	130D	PERK	13	17500	3 4	51800	56900
36	WEST-INDIAN	FB	TRWL	FBG	DS	IB	160D		13	17500		51800	57000
36 5	WEST-INDIES 36	SLP	SA/CR	FBG	KL	IB	50D	PERK	12	17000	4	34000	37800
37	HERITAGE ONE TON	SLP	SA/RC	FBG	KL	IB	22D	YAN	11 10	13500	6 6	28200	31300
38	WEST-INDIES AFT CPT	SLP	SA/CR	FBG	KL	IB	50D	PERK	12	20000	4	39100	43500
38	WEST-INDIES AFT CPT	KTH	SA/CR	FBG	KL	IB	50D	PERK	12	20000	4	40100	44500
38	WEST-INDIES CTR CPT	SLP	SA/CR	FBG	KL	IB	50D	PERK	12	20000	4	41000	45500
38	WEST-INDIES CTR CPT	KTH	SA/CR	FBG	KL	IB	50D	PERK	12	20000	4	41000	44500
42	WEST-INDIES 42	SLP	SA/CR	FBG	KL	IB	50D	PERK	13 6	25500	5	53100	58300
42	WEST-INDIES 42	KTH	SA/CR	FBG	KL	IB	50D	PERK	13 6	25500	5	53100	58400
46	WEST-INDIES 46	SLP	SA/CR	FBG	KL	IB	62D	PERK	15	27000	4 2	63200	69500
46	WEST-INDIES 46	KTH	SA/CR	FBG	KC	IB	62D	PERK	15	27000	4 2	63200	69500
48	WEST-INDIAN	FB	TRWL	FBG	DS	IB	D	PERK	13 7	30000	4	**	**
1977 BOATS													
26	HERITAGE QUARTER TON	SLP	SA/RC	FBG	KL	IB	5D		9 6	4700	5 1	9450	10800
27 8	WEST-INDIES 28	SLP	SA/CR	FBG	KC	IB	5D		11 1	7000	3 2	14200	16200
30	WEST-INDIES 30	SLP	SA/CR	FBG	KC	IB	10D		11 3	10500	3 9	21600	24000
33	WEST-INDIES 33	SLP	SA/CR	FBG	KC	IB	25D		11 4	12500	3 6	24400	27100
36	WEST-INDIAN SEDAN	FB	TRWL	FBG	DS	IB	130D	PERK	13	17500	2 10	49600	54500
36	WEST-INDIAN SEDAN	FB	TRWL	FBG	DS	IB T	85D	PERK	13	17500	4 10	51800	57100
36 5	WEST-INDIES 36	SLP	SA/CR	FBG	KL	IB	50D	PERK	12	17000	4	32800	36500
36 5	WEST-INDIES 36	KTH	SA/CR	FBG	KC	IB	50D	PERK	12	17000	4	32900	36500
37	HERITAGE ONE TON	SLP	SA/RC	FBG	KL	IB	22D	YAN	11 10	13000	6 6	26400	29300
38	WEST-INDIES 38 TC	SLP	SA/CR	FBG	KL	IB	50D	PERK	12	20000	4	38700	43000
44	TRAWLER		TRWL	FBG	DS	IB T	D		13 7			**	**
46	WEST-INDIES 46 TC	KTH	SA/CR	FBG	KC	IB	62D	PERK	15	27000	4 6	61100	67100
48	WEST-INDIAN	FB	TRWL	FBG	DS	IB	D		15	30000	4	**	**
1976 BOATS													
26	HERITAGE QUARTER TON	SLP	SA/RC	FBG	KL	IB	5D		9 6	4700	5 1		10500
27 8	WEST-INDIES 28	SLP	SA/CR	FBG	KC	IB	5D		11 1	7000	3 2	13800	15700
30	WEST-INDIES 30	SLP	SA/CR	FBG	KC	IB	10D		11 3	10500	3 9	20900	23300
34	UTILITY WORK BOAT		TRWL	FBG	DS	IB	130D-150D		13	17825		49100	54400
36 3	WEST-INDIES 36	SLP	SA/CR	FBG	KL	IB	23D		12	17000	4	31700	35200
36 3	WEST-INDIES 36	KTH	SA/CR	FBG	KC	IB	23D		12	17000	4	31700	35200
37	HERITAGE ONE TON	SLP	SA/RC	FBG	KL	IB	10D		11 10	13500	6 6	26200	29200
38	WEST-INDIES 38	SLP	SA/CR	FBG	KL	IB	23D		12	18400	4	35000	38900
38	WEST-INDIES 38	KTH	SA/CR	FBG	KC	IB	23D		12	18400	4 1	35000	38900
44	UTILITY WORK BOAT		TRWL	FBG	DS	IB	225		13 7			70500	77500
44	UTILITY WORK BOAT		TRWL	FBG	DS	IB T	D		13 7			**	**
44	WEST-INDIES 44	SLP	SA/CR	FBG	KL	IB	39D		14	24500	5	52200	57300
44	WEST-INDIES 44	KTH	SA/CR	FBG	KL	IB	39D		14	24500	5	52200	57300
1975 BOATS													
26	HERITAGE QUARTER TON	SLP	SA/RC	FBG	KL	IB	5D	PETT	9 6	4700	5 1	8950	10200
27 8	WEST-INDIES	SLP	SA/CR	FBG	KC	IB	5D	PETT	11 1	7000	3 2	13400	15200
29	HERITAGE HALF TON	SLP	SA/CR	FBG	KC	IB			9 10	7000	3 3	13500	15300
33	WEST-INDIES	SLP	SA/CR	FBG	KC	IB	10D	VLVO	11 3	10500	3 9	20300	22600
33	HERITAGE 3/4 TON	SLP	SA/RC	FBG	KC	IB	D		10 4	10000	3 6	20200	20700
33	HERITAGE 3/4 TON	SLP	SA/RC	FBG	KC	IB	D		10 4	10000	3 6	18600	20700
36 3	WEST-INDIES	SLP	SA/CR	FBG	KL	IB	23D	VLVO	12	17000	4	30800	34200
36 3	WEST-INDIES	KTH	SA/CR	FBG	KC	IB	23D	VLVO	12	17000	4	30800	34200
37	HERITAGE ONE TON	SLP	SA/RC	FBG	KL	IB	10D	VLVO	11 10	13500	6 6	25500	28300
38	WEST-INDIES	SLP	SA/CR	FBG	KL	IB	23D	VLVO	12	18400	4	34000	37800
38	WEST-INDIES	KTH	SA/CR	FBG	KC	IB	23D	VLVO	12	18400	4 1	34000	37800
44	WEST-INDIES	KTH	SA/CR	FBG	KL	IB	39D		14	24500	5	50700	55700

TED HERMANN'S BOAT SHOP
COAST GUARD MFG ID- THB

Call 1-800-327-6929 for BUC Personalized Evaluation Service
Or, for 1966 to 1979 boats, sign onto www.BUCValuPro.com

HERO BOAT OR A/S

Call 1-800-327-6929 for BUC Personalized Evaluation Service
Or, for 1980 boats, sign onto www.BUCValuPro.com

HALSEY C HERRESHOFF INC
BRISTOL RI 02809   See inside cover to adjust price for area

For more recent years, see the BUC Used Boat Price Guide, Volume 1 or Volume 2

LOA FT IN	NAME AND/ OR MODEL	TOP/ RIG	BOAT TYPE	-HULL- MTL TP	----ENGINE--- TP # HP MFG	BEAM FT IN	WGT LBS	DRAFT FT IN	RETAIL LOW	RETAIL HIGH
			1983 BOATS							
25	ALERION 25	SLP	SA/OD	FBG KL	IB D	7 3	4800	3 7	16600	18800
33	STREAKER	SLP	SA/OD	WD KL	IB D	8	5200	6	20900	23200
			1982 BOATS							
25	ALERION 25	SLP	SAIL	FBG KL	IB D	7 3	4800	3 7	15600	17700
33	STREAKER	SLP	SA/RC	WD KL	IB D	8	5200	6	19700	21800
			1981 BOATS							
25	ALERION 25	SLP	SAIL	FBG KL	IB D	7 3	4800	3 7	14700	16700
33	STREAKER	SLP	SA/RC	WD KL	IB D	8	5200	6	18700	20800

HERRE COAST GUARD MFG ID- HRF
FORMERLY NATHANIEL HERRESHOFF nside cover to adjust price for area

LOA FT IN	NAME AND/ OR MODEL	TOP/ RIG	BOAT TYPE	-HULL- MTL TP	----ENGINE--- TP # HP MFG	BEAM FT IN	WGT LBS	DRAFT FT IN	RETAIL LOW	RETAIL HIGH
			1938 BOATS							
44	FISH-ISLAND		SAIL	WD	IB 50 GRAY				106500	117000
64		SCH	SAIL	WD	IB T250 CHRY				338500	372000
			1932 BOATS							
23	KNOCKABOUT	SLP	SA/OD	WD KL					11200	12800
			1915 BOATS							
48		MY		WD	IB 160D PERK				89000	97900
			1905 BOATS							
43			SAIL	WD					796000	874500
43	NEW-YORK 30	SLP	SAIL	WD	IB 40 UNIV				407000	447500

HEWES MANUFACTURING CO INC
COAST GUARD MFG ID- HMC
FORMERLY HEWES BOAT CO

Call 1-800-327-6929 for BUC Personalized Evaluation Service
Or, for 1961 to 2008 boats, sign onto www.BUCValuPro.com

HEWES MARINE COMPANY INC
HEWESCRAFT   COAST GUARD MFG ID- HEW

Call 1-800-327-6929 for BUC Personalized Evaluation Service
Or, for 1963 to 2008 boats, sign onto www.BUCValuPro.com

HEWSON MARINE INC
COAST GUARD MFG ID- HWS
SEE SABRE CORP

Call 1-800-327-6929 for BUC Personalized Evaluation Service
Or, for 1969 to 1974 boats, sign onto www.BUCValuPro.com

HIDDEN HARBOR BOAT WORKS
BRADENTON FL 34203   COAST GUARD MFG ID- HHW See inside cover to adjust price for area

For more recent years, see the BUC Used Boat Price Guide, Volume 1 or Volume 2

LOA FT IN	NAME AND/ OR MODEL	TOP/ RIG	BOAT TYPE	-HULL- MTL TP	----ENGINE--- TP # HP MFG	BEAM FT IN	WGT LBS	DRAFT FT IN	RETAIL LOW	RETAIL HIGH
			1983 BOATS							
35 6	MEYERS 35	CUT	SA/RC	F/S CT	OB	18	4500	1 6	56300	61800
36	VANCOUVER 36	CUT	SA/CR	F/S KL	SD 35D VLVO	11	18000	5	78500	86300
48	CYGNET 48	CUT	SA/CR	F/S CB	SD 120D LEHM	13 6	38000	4 8	140500	154500
51 9	ARGOSEA 50	FB	MY	F/S SV	IB T225D LEHM	16 5	39000	3 11	124500	136500
			1982 BOATS							
36	VANCOUVER 36	CUT	SA/CR	F/S KL	VLVO	11	18000	5	74300	81700
44 3	HIDDEN-HARBOR 44	FB	TRWL	F/S DS	IB T160D GM	14 7	48000	4 6	137500	151500
44 3	HIDDEN-HARBOR 44 PH	MY	F/S DS	IB T160D GM		14 7	48000	4 6	137500	151500
47 3	MASON 48	CUT	SA/CR	F/S CB	IB 80D LEHM	13 6	42000	4 8	142500	156500
47 3	MASON 48	KTH	SA/CR	F/S CB	IB 80D LEHM	13 6	42000	4 8	152500	167500
56	HIDDEN-HARBOR	FB	MY	F/S DS	IB T D	16 6	95000	7	**	**
			1981 BOATS							
36	VANCOUVER 36	CUT	SA/CR	F/S KL	IB 35D VLVO	11	18000	5	70500	77500
44 1	HIDDEN-HARBOR 44	FB	TRWL	F/S DS	IB T100D GM	14 7	48000	4 6	129000	142000
			1977 BOATS							
33	AMERICANA		MY	FBG SV	IB 250	11			24500	27300
33	AMERICANA		MY	FBG SV	IB D	11			**	**
41	NORTH-CAPE	CUT	SA/CR	FBG KL	IB 50D	13	25000	5	83800	92100
45	AMERICANA		MY	FBG SV	IB T185	16			63200	69500
45	AMERICANA		MY	FBG SV	IB T	16			**	**
52	AMERICANA		MY	FBG SV	IB T225	16			94000	103500
52	AMERICANA		MY	FBG SV	IB T D	16			**	**
56	AMERICANA PH	FB	TRWL	FBG DS	IB T280	16 6	95000	7	175500	192500
56	AMERICANA PH	FB	TRWL	FBG DS	IB T D	16 6	95000	7	**	**
			1976 BOATS							
33	AMERICANA		MY	FBG SV	IB 250	11			23500	26200
33	AMERICANA		MY	FBG SV	IB D	11			**	**
38		CUT	SAIL	FBG KL	IB 80D	12	24000	5	72100	79300
38		KTH	SAIL	FBG KL	IB 80D	12	24000	5	76000	83600
45	AMERICANA		MY	FBG SV	IB T185	16			60600	66600
45	AMERICANA		MY	FBG SV	IB T	16			**	**
52	AMERICANA		MY	FBG SV	IB T225	16			90100	99000
52	AMERICANA		MY	FBG SV	IB T D	16			**	**
56	AMERICANA PH	FB	TRWL	FBG DS	IB T280	16 6	95000	7	168000	184500
56	AMERICANA PH	FB	TRWL	FBG DS	IB T D	16 6	95000	7	**	**
			1975 BOATS							
40		CUT	SA/CR	FBG KL	IB 45	13	29000	4 10	84200	92600

HIGGINS INC
NEW ORLEANS LA   COAST GUARD MFG ID- HGS See inside cover to adjust price for area

LOA FT IN	NAME AND/ OR MODEL	TOP/ RIG	BOAT TYPE	-HULL- MTL TP	----ENGINE--- TP # HP MFG	BEAM FT IN	WGT LBS	DRAFT FT IN	RETAIL LOW	RETAIL HIGH
			1963 BOATS							
18	MANDALAY 18	RNBT	WD	IB 240					1700	2050
25 3	CATALINA 25	CR	WD	IB 215					5200	6000
27 3	CAPRI 27	CR	WD	IB 215					7050	8100
28 2	TAHITI 28	CR	WD	IB T170					8500	9750
			1962 BOATS							
25 3	CATALINA	CR	WD	IB 185					5050	5800
27 3	CAPRI	CR	WD	IB 188					6800	7800
28 2	TAHITI	CR	WD	IB T170					8300	9500
			1961 BOATS							
25 3	CATALINA	CR	WD	IB 188	9		1 6	4950	5650
27	CAPRI	CR	WD	IB 188	10 3		2 1	6550	7550
33	CHANDELEUR	SF	WD	IB 225	11 4		2 6	12100	13800
			1960 BOATS							
17 7	MANDALAY	RNBT	PLY	OB	6 8		1 6	3700	4300
24	ANTIGUA	SF	WD	IB 109				3950	4600
24	TAHITI	SF	WD	OB				10900	12400
26	GRANADA	CR	WD	IB 135				5600	6450
			1959 BOATS							
23	MAGNUM	CR	WD	IB 220				3400	3950
26	MAGNUM	CR	WD	IB 220				5800	6650
30	MAGNUM	CR	WD	IB 220				8500	9750
			1958 BOATS							
23		EXP	WD	IB 220				3700	4350
26		EXP	WD	IB 220				5150	5950
30		EXP	WD	IB 220				9400	10700
			1957 BOATS							
24		EXP	WD	IB 125				3600	4200
26		EXP	WD	IB 135				4800	5500
			1956 BOATS							
23		EXP	WD	IB 125				3500	4050
26		EXP	WD	IB 135				4700	5400
			1955 BOATS							
23		CR	WD	IB 125				3050	3550
			1950 BOATS							
23		EXP	WD	IB				**	**
23		RNBT	WD	IB				**	**
26	SPORTS SPEEDSTER	HT	SDN	WD	IB 115-125				5600	6500
26		SPTCR	WD	IB 115-145				4200	5050
26		SPTCR	WD	IB T 92 CHRY				4550	5250
31	DELUXE	FB	CBNCR	WD	IB CHRY 11 1		2	**	**
			1949 BOATS							
23		OP	EXP	WD	IB				**	**
26		HT	SDN	WD	IB				**	**
34	P-T-COMMANDO	HT	SDN	WD	IB				**	**
			1947 BOATS							
23		RNBT	WD	IB	8			**	**
25		SDN	WD	IB 115				4500	5150

LOA FT	IN	NAME AND/ OR MODEL	TOP/ RIG	BOAT TYPE	-HULL- MTL	TP	ENGINE TP	# HP	MFG	BEAM FT	IN	WGT LBS	DRAFT FT	IN	RETAIL LOW	RETAIL HIGH
		1941 BOATS														
23				RNBT	WD		IB	95							2650	3100

HILINER MARINE CORP

SO DARTMOUTH MA 02748 COAST GUARD MFG ID- HMC See inside cover to adjust price for area

LOA FT	IN	NAME AND/ OR MODEL	TOP/ RIG	BOAT TYPE	-HULL- MTL	TP	ENGINE TP	# HP	MFG	BEAM FT	IN	WGT LBS	DRAFT FT	IN	RETAIL LOW	RETAIL HIGH
		1982 BOATS														
22		HI-LINER 222		CTRCN	FBG	DV	OB			8		2100	1	2	6700	7700
		1974 BOATS														
22	2			FSH	FBG		OB			8		2500	2	6	7150	8250
22	2	GYPSY			FBG		IO	165-245		8		2810	2	6	4200	5050
22	2	SPORTSMAN			FBG		IO	165-245		8		2695	2	6	4100	4950
		1973 BOATS														
21	6	GYPSY			FBG		IO	155-245		8		2810	2	6	4150	5050
21	6	SPORTSMAN			FBG		IO	155-245		8		2695	2	6	4050	4950
		1972 BOATS														
21	6	ADVENTURER			FBG		IO	155-245		8		2650	2	6	4150	5050
21	6	GYPSY			FBG		IO	155-245		8		2810	2	6	4350	5200
21	6	SPORTSMAN			FBG		IO	155-245		8		2695	2	6	4200	5100
21	6	SWINGER			FBG		IO	188-245		8		2900	2	6	4500	5300
		1971 BOATS														
21	6	ADVENTURER 222			FBG		IO	155-235		8		2850	2	6	4450	5250
21	6	GYPSY 222			FBG		IO	155-235		8		3000	2	6	4700	5550
21	6	SPORTSMAN 222			FBG		IO	155-235		8		2850	2	6	4650	5500
21	6	SWINGER 222			FBG		IO	155-235		8		2900	2	6	4600	5450
		1970 BOATS														
21				FSH	FBG	DV	IO	200-235		8		2650	2	6	5000	5850
21				FSH	FBG	DV	IO	290	HOLM	8		2650	2	6	5500	6300
21		GYPSY		CR	FBG	DV	IO	200-235		8		3000	2	6	5050	5900
21		GYPSY		CR	FBG	DV	IO	290	HOLM	8		3000	2	6	5500	6300
21		SPORTSMAN		RNBT	FBG	DV	IO	200-290		8		2850	2	6	4700	5850
		1969 BOATS														
21		HILINER 21	OP		FBG	DV	IO	200	HOLM	7	11	2600	1	2	4500	5200
21		HILINER 21	OP		FBG	DV	IB	200	HOLM	7	11	2600	1	2	2850	3350
21		HILINER 21		CR	FBG	DV	IO	200	HOLM	7	11	2800	1	2	4950	5700
21		HILINER 21		CR	FBG	DV	IB	200	HOLM	7	11	2800	1	2	3000	3500
21		HILINER 21		SF	FBG	DV	IO	200	HOLM	7	11	2400	1	2	5050	5800
21		HILINER 21		SF	FBG	DV	IB	200	HOLM	7	11	2400	1	2	2750	3200
		1966 BOATS														
17	1	CLIPPER		RNBT	MHG		OB			6	6	1000			2750	3200

HILUX INTERNATIONAL INC

Call 1-800-327-6929 for BUC Personalized Evaluation Service
Or, for 1980 boats, sign onto www.BUCValuPro.com

HINCKLEY YACHTS

S W HARBOR ME 04679 COAST GUARD MFG ID- THC See inside cover to adjust price for area
FORMERLY HENRY R HINCKLEY & CO

For more recent years, see the BUC Used Boat Price Guide, Volume 1 or Volume 2

LOA FT	IN	NAME AND/ OR MODEL	TOP/ RIG	BOAT TYPE	-HULL- MTL	TP	ENGINE TP	# HP	MFG	BEAM FT	IN	WGT LBS	DRAFT FT	IN	RETAIL LOW	RETAIL HIGH
		1983 BOATS														
40	9	BERMUDA 40	SLP	SA/CR	FBG	KC	IB	40D	WEST	11	9	20000	4	3	166500	183000
40	9	BERMUDA 40	YWL	SA/CR	FBG	KC	IB	40D	WEST	11	9	20000	4	3	166500	183000
42	9	SOU'WESTER 42	SLP	SA/CR	FBG	KC	IB	40D	WEST	12	6	20500	5		182000	200000
42	9	SOU'WESTER 42	YWL	SA/CR	FBG	KC	IB	40D	WEST	12	6	20500	5		182000	200000
59	3	SOU'WESTER 59	KTH	SA/CR	FBG	KC	IB	135D	PERK	15	6	63000	6	6	513000	564000
		1982 BOATS														
40	9	BERMUDA 40	SLP	SA/CR	FBG	KC	IB	40D	WEST	11	9	20000	4	3	158000	173500
40	9	BERMUDA 40	YWL	SA/CR	FBG	KC	IB	40D	WEST	11	9	20000	4	3	158000	173500
41	9	SOU'WESTER 42	KTH	SA/RC	FBG	KC	IB	D		12	6	20500	4	9	166000	182500
42	9	SOU'WESTER 42	SLP	SA/CR	FBG	KC	IB	40D	WEST	12	6	22000	5		179500	197500
42	9	SOU'WESTER 42	YWL	SA/CR	FBG	KC	IB	40D	WEST	12	6	22000	5		179500	197500
48	6	HINCKLEY 49	KTH	SA/RC	FBG	KC	IB	D		13	5	38000			288500	317000
58	8	SOU'WESTER 59	CUT	SA/RC	FBG	KC	IB	D		15	6	63000	6	1	477000	524500
59	8	SOU'WESTER 59	KTH	SA/CR	FBG	KC	IB	130D	PERK	15	6	63000	6	6	493500	542000
		1981 BOATS														
40	9	BERMUDA 40	SLP	SA/CR	FBG	KC	IB	40D	WEST	11	9	20000	4	3	149500	164500
40	9	BERMUDA 40	YWL	SA/CR	FBG	KC	IB	40D	WEST	11	9	20000	4	3	149500	164500
41	9	SOU'WESTER 42	SLP	SA/CR	FBG	KC	IB	40D	WEST	12	6	20500	4	9	157000	173000
42	10	HINCKLEY 43	SLP	SA/CR	FBG	KC	IB	50D	WEST	12	4	25500	4	4	185500	204000
50	8	SOU'WESTER 50A	YWL	SA/CR	FBG	KC	IB	80D	LEHM	13		36600	5	9	283500	312000
50	8	SOU'WESTER 50A	YWL	SA/CR	FBG	KC	IB	120D	LEHM	13		36600	5	9	284000	312000
50	8	SOU'WESTER 50B	YWL	SA/CR	FBG	KC	IB	80D	LEHM	13		36600	5	9	300000	329500
50	8	SOU'WESTER 50B	YWL	SA/CR	FBG	KC	IB	120D	LEHM	13		36600	5	9	300500	330000
50	8	SOU'WESTER 50C	YWL	SA/CR	FBG	KC	IB	80D	LEHM	13		36600	5	9	313500	344500
50	8	SOU'WESTER 50C	YWL	SA/CR	FBG	KC	IB	120D	LEHM	13		36600	5	9	314000	345000
50	8	SOU'WESTER 50D	YWL	SA/CR	FBG	KC	IB	80D	LEHM	13		36600	5	9	328500	361000
50	8	SOU'WESTER 50D	YWL	SA/CR	FBG	KC	IB	120D	LEHM	13		36600	5	9	329000	361500
58	8	SOU'WESTER 59	KTH	SA/CR	FBG	KC	IB	95D	PERK	15	6	62000	6	1	451000	496000
		1980 BOATS														
40	9	BERMUDA 40	SLP	SA/CR	FBG	KC	IB	40D	WEST	11	9	20000	4	3	144000	158500
40	9	BERMUDA 40	YWL	SA/CR	FBG	KC	IB	40D	WEST	11	9	20000	4	3	144000	158500
42	10	HINCKLEY 43	SLP	SA/CR	FBG	KC	IB	50D	WEST	12	4	25500	4	4	178500	196500
48	6	HINCKLEY 49	KTH	SA/CR	FBG	KC	IB	120D	LEHM	13	5	38000	5	8	264000	290000
50	8	SOU'WESTER 50A	YWL	SA/CR	FBG	KC	IB	80D	LEHM	13		36600	5	9	273000	300000
50	8	SOU'WESTER 50A	YWL	SA/CR	FBG	KC	IB	120D	LEHM	13		36600	5	9	295000	324000
50	8	SOU'WESTER 50B	YWL	SA/CR	FBG	KC	IB	80D	LEHM	13		36600	5	9	287500	316000
50	8	SOU'WESTER 50B	YWL	SA/CR	FBG	KC	IB	120D	LEHM	13		36600	5	9	295000	324000
50	8	SOU'WESTER 50C	YWL	SA/CR	FBG	KC	IB	80D	LEHM	13		36600	5	9	301500	331500
50	8	SOU'WESTER 50C	YWL	SA/CR	FBG	KC	IB	120D	LEHM	13		36600	5	9	295000	324000
50	8	SOU'WESTER 50D	YWL	SA/CR	FBG	KC	IB	80D	LEHM	13		36600	5	9	317000	348000
50	8	SOU'WESTER 50D	YWL	SA/CR	FBG	KC	IB	120D	LEHM	13		36600	5	9	295000	324000
64	8	HINCKLEY 64	KTH	SA/CR	FBG	KC	IB	148D	CAT	16		65000	5	9	718500	790000
		1979 BOATS														
40	9	BERMUDA 40	SLP	SA/CR	FBG	KC	IB	40D	WEST	11	9	20000	4	3	139500	153500
40	9	BERMUDA 40	YWL	SA/CR	FBG	KC	IB	40D	WEST	11	9	20000	4	3	139500	153500
42	10	HINCKLEY 43 MK II	SLP	SA/CR	FBG	KC				12	4	26000	4	4	170500	187500
48	6	HINCKLEY 49A	KTH	SA/CR	FBG	KC	IB	120D	LEHM	13	5	38000	5	8	256000	281000
48	6	HINCKLEY 49B	KTH	SA/CR	FBG	KC	IB	120D	LEHM	13	5	38000	5	8	256000	281000
50	8	SOU'WESTER 50A	YWL	SA/CR	FBG	KC	IB	80D	LEHM	13		36600	5	9	256500	282000
50	8	SOU'WESTER 50A	YWL	SA/CR	FBG	KC	IB	120D	LEHM	13		36600	5	9	285500	313500
50	8	SOU'WESTER 50B	YWL	SA/CR	FBG	KC	IB	80D	LEHM	13		36600	5	9	281500	309000
50	8	SOU'WESTER 50B	YWL	SA/CR	FBG	KC	IB	120D	LEHM	13		36600	5	9	285500	313500
50	8	SOU'WESTER 50C	YWL	SA/CR	FBG	KC	IB	80D	LEHM	13		36600	5	9	293000	322000
50	8	SOU'WESTER 50C	YWL	SA/CR	FBG	KC	IB	120D	LEHM	13		36600	5	9	285500	313500
50	8	SOU'WESTER 50D	YWL	SA/CR	FBG	KC	IB	80D	LEHM	13		36600	5	9	310500	341000
50	8	SOU'WESTER 50D	YWL	SA/CR	FBG	KC	IB	120D	LEHM	13		36600	5	9	285500	313500
64	8	HINCKLEY 64	KTH	SA/CR	FBG	KC	IB	D		16		65000	5	9	694500	763000
		1978 BOATS														
40	9	BERMUDA 40 MK III	SLP	SA/CR	FBG	KC	IB	35D	WEST	11	9	20000	4	3	135500	148500
40	9	BERMUDA 40 MK III	YWL	SA/CR	FBG	KC	IB	35D	WEST	11	9	20000	4	3	135500	148500
42	10	HINCKLEY 43	SLP	SA/CR	FBG	KC	VD	40D	WEST	12	4	25500	4	4	167500	184500
48	6	HINCKLEY 49	KTH	SA/CR	FBG	KC	IB	120D	LEHM	13	5	35000	5	8	241500	265000
50	8	SOU'WESTER 50A	YWL	SA/CR	FBG	KC	IB	80D	LEHM	13		36600	5	9	250500	275500
50	8	SOU'WESTER 50A	YWL	SA/CR	FBG	KC	IB	120D	LEHM	13		36600	5	9	251000	275500
50	8	SOU'WESTER 50B	YWL	SA/CR	FBG	KC	IB	80D	LEHM	13		36600	5	9	269500	296500
50	8	SOU'WESTER 50B	YWL	SA/CR	FBG	KC	IB	120D	LEHM	13		36600	5	9	270000	296500
50	8	SOU'WESTER 50C	YWL	SA/CR	FBG	KC	IB	80D	LEHM	13		36600	5	9	283000	310500
50	8	SOU'WESTER 50C	YWL	SA/CR	FBG	KC	IB	120D	LEHM	13		36600	5	9	282500	310500
50	8	SOU'WESTER 50D	YWL	SA/CR	FBG	KC	IB	80D	LEHM	13		36600	5	9	304500	335000
50	8	SOU'WESTER 50D	YWL	SA/CR	FBG	KC	IB	120D	LEHM	13		36600	5	9	304500	334500
64	8	HINCKLEY 64	YWL	SA/CR	FBG	KC	IB	T120D	LEHM	16		60000	5	9	629500	692000
		1977 BOATS														
40	9	BERMUDA 40 CUSTOM	YWL	SAIL	FBG	KC	IB	35D	WEST	11	9	19000	4	1	127500	140000
40	9	BERMUDA 40 MARK II	YWL	SAIL	FBG	KC	IB	35D	WEST	11	9	19500	4	1	129500	142500
40	9	BERMUDA 40 MARK III	SLP	SAIL	FBG	KC	IB	35D	WEST	11	9	20000	4	1	131500	145000
40	9	BERMUDA 40 MARK III	YWL	SAIL	FBG	KC	IB	35D	WEST	11	9	20000	4	1	131500	145000
42	10	HINCKLEY 43	SLP	SA/CR	F/S	KC	VD	40D	WEST	12	4	25500	4	4	163000	179500
48	6	HINCKLEY 49 AFT CBN	KTH	SA/CR	FBG	KC	IB	120D	LEHM	13	5	38000	5	5	242000	265500
48	6	HINCKLEY 49 PORT CBN	KTH	SA/CR	FBG	KC	IB	120D	LEHM	13	5	38000	5	5	242000	265500
48	6	HINCKLEY 49 STBD CBN	KTH	SA/CR	FBG	KC	IB	120D	LEHM	13	5	38000	5	5	242000	265500
50	8	SOU'WESTER 50A	YWL	SA/CR	FBG	KC	IB	80D	LEHM	13		36600	5	9	257000	282500
50	8	SOU'WESTER 50A	YWL	SA/CR	FBG	KC	IB	120D	LEHM	13		36600	5	9	269000	296000
50	8	SOU'WESTER 50B	YWL	SA/CR	FBG	KC	IB	80D	LEHM	13		36600	5	9	272000	298500
50	8	SOU'WESTER 50B	YWL	SA/CR	FBG	KC	IB	120D	LEHM	13		36600	5	9	269000	296000
50	8	SOU'WESTER 50C	YWL	SA/CR	FBG	KC	IB	80D	LEHM	13		36600	5	9	279500	307000
50	8	SOU'WESTER 50C	YWL	SA/CR	FBG	KC	IB	120D	LEHM	13		36600	5	9	269000	296000
		1976 BOATS														
40	9	BERMUDA 40 MKIII	YWL	SAIL	FBG	KC	IB	35D	WEST	11	9	20000	4	1	128500	141500
40	9	BERMUDA CUSTOM MKII	YWL	SAIL	FBG	KC	IB	35D	WEST	11	9	19500	4	1	126500	139000
42	10	HINCKLEY-HOOD 43	SLP	SAIL	FBG	KC	VD	40D	WEST	12	4	25500	4	4	159500	175000
48	6	HINCKLEY 49	KTH	SAIL	FBG	KC	IB	120D	LEHM	13	5	35000	5	5	229000	252000
50	8	SOU'WESTER DC 50A	YWL	SAIL	FBG	KC	IB	80D	LEHM	13		36600	5	9	250500	275500

 CONTINUED ON NEXT PAGE

LOA FT	LOA IN	NAME AND/ OR MODEL	TOP/ RIG	BOAT TYPE	-HULL- MTL	-HULL- TP	ENGINE TP	ENGINE # HP	ENGINE MFG	BEAM FT	BEAM IN	WGT LBS	DRAFT FT	DRAFT IN	RETAIL LOW	RETAIL HIGH
		1976 BOATS														
50	8	SOU'WESTER DC 50A	YWL	SAIL	FBG	KC	IB	120D	LEHM	13		36600	5	9	250500	275000
50	8	SOU'WESTER TC 50B	YWL	SAIL	FBG	KC	IB	80D	LEHM	13		36600	5	9	266500	292500
50	8	SOU'WESTER TC 50B	YWL	SAIL	FBG	KC	IB	120D	LEHM	13		36600	5	9	266000	292000
50	8	SOU'WESTER TC 50C	YWL	SAIL	FBG	KC	IB	80D	LEHM	13		36600	5	9	271000	298000
50	8	SOU'WESTER TC 50C	YWL	SAIL	FBG	KC	IB	120D	LEHM	13		36600	5	9	270500	297500
		1975 BOATS														
35	9	PILOT 35	SLP	SAIL	FBG	KL	IB	35D	WEST	9	6	13500	5	6	88000	96700
40	9	BERMUDA 40 MK II	SLP	SAIL	FBG	KC	IB	35D	WEST	11	9	19500	8	9	122500	135000
40	9	BERMUDA 40 MK II	YWL	SAIL	FBG	KC	IB	35D	WEST	11	9	19500			122500	135000
40	9	BERMUDA 40 MK III	SLP	SAIL	FBG	KC	IB	35D	WEST	11	9	19500	8	9	124500	137000
40	9	BERMUDA 40 MK III	YWL	SAIL	FBG	KC	IB	35D	WEST	11	9	19500	8	9	124500	137000
41	2	COMPETITION 41	SLP	SAIL	FBG	KL	IB	35D	WEST	10	3	18500	6	2	121500	133500
48	5	SOU'WESTER 48	SLP	SAIL	FBG	KC	IB	80D	FORD	13		36000	9	9	224000	246000
48	5	SOU'WESTER 48	YWL	SAIL	FBG	KC	IB	80D	FORD	13		36000	9	9	224000	246000
48	6	HINCKLEY 49	KTH	SAIL	FBG	KC	IB	120D	FORD	13	5	38000	10		230500	253500
		1974 BOATS														
40	9	BERMUDA 40	YWL	SAIL	FBG	KC	IB	35D	WEST	11	9	19000	4	1	119000	131000
40	9	BERMUDA 40 MARK III	YWL	SAIL	FBG	KC	IB	35D	WEST	11	9	20000	8	7	123000	135500
41	2	COMPETITION 41	SLP	SAIL	FBG	KL	IB	35D	WEST	10	3	19000	6	2	121000	133000
41	2	COMPETITION 41	YWL	SAIL	FBG	KL	IB	35D	WEST	10	3	19000	6	2	121000	133000
48	5	HINCKLEY	SLP	SAIL	FBG	KC	IB	35D	WEST	13		34000	5	3	214000	235000
48	5	HINCKLEY	YWL	SAIL	FBG	KC	IB	35D	WEST	13		34000	5	3	214000	235000
48	6	HINCKLEY 49	KTH	SAIL	FBG	KC	IB	120D	FORD	13	5	38000	5	5	226000	248000
		1973 BOATS														
26		ROUSTABOUT		UTL	FBG	RB	IB	40		8	2		3		16400	18700
30	5	SOUTH-WESTER CUSTOM	SLP	SA/OD	FBG	KL	IB	D		6	5		4	9	42300	47000
35	9	PILOT 35	SLP	SAIL	FBG	KL	IB	30	UNIV	9	6	13500	5		83200	91500
35	9	PILOT 35	SLP	SAIL	FBG	KL	IB	35D	WEST	9	6	13500	5		84300	92600
35	9	PILOT 35	YWL	SAIL	FBG	KL	IB	30	UNIV	9	6	13500	5		83200	91400
35	9	PILOT 35	YWL	SAIL	FBG	KL	IB	35D	WEST	9	6	13500	5		84200	92600
37	6	HINCKLEY 38	SLP	SAIL	FBG	KL	IB	30	UNIV	10	6	17500	6		104000	114500
37	6	HINCKLEY 38	SLP	SAIL	FBG	KL	IB	35D	WEST	10	6	17500	6		105500	116000
40	9	BERMUDA 40	YWL	SAIL	FBG	KC	IB	35D	WEST	11	9	19000	4	1	117000	128500
40	9	BERMUDA 40 MARK III	YWL	SAIL	FBG	KL	IB	35D	WEST	11	9	20000	8	7	121000	133000
41	2	COMPETITION 41	SLP	SAIL	FBG	KL	IB	30	UNIV	10	3	19000	6	2	116500	128000
41	2	COMPETITION 41	SLP	SAIL	FBG	KL	IB	35D	WEST	10	3	19000	6	2	118500	130500
41	2	COMPETITION 41	YWL	SAIL	FBG	KL	IB	30	UNIV	10	3	19000	6	2	116500	128000
41	2	COMPETITION 41	YWL	SAIL	FBG	KL	IB	35D	WEST	10	3	19000	6	2	118500	130500
48	5	HINCKLEY	SLP	SAIL	FBG	KC	IB	35D	WEST	13		34000	5	3	210000	230500
48	5	HINCKLEY	YWL	SAIL	FBG	KC	IB	35D	WEST	13		34000	5	3	210000	230500
48	6	HINCKLEY 49	KTH	SAIL	FBG	KC	IB	120D	FORD	13	5	38000	5	5	221500	243500
		1972 BOATS														
26		ROUSTABOUT		UTL	FBG	RB	IB	40- 45		8	2		3		15800	18000
26		YACHT CLUB		UTL	FBG	RB	IB	40- 45		8	2		3		15800	18000
30	3	SHIELDS	SLP	SA/OD	FBG	KL	OB			6	6	4600	4	9	27300	30300
35	9	PILOT 35	SLP	SAIL	FBG	KL	IB	30	UNIV	9	6	13500	5		81500	89500
35	9	PILOT 35	SLP	SAIL	FBG	KL	IB	35D	WEST	9	6	13500	5		82500	90700
35	9	PILOT 35	YWL	SAIL	FBG	KL	IB	30	UNIV	9	6	13500	5		81500	89500
35	9	PILOT 35	YWL	SAIL	FBG	KL	IB	35D	WEST	9	6	13500	5		82500	90600
37	6	HINCKLEY 38	SLP	SAIL	FBG	KL	IB	25	UNIV	10	6	17500	6		102000	112000
37	6	HINCKLEY 38	SLP	SAIL	FBG	KL	IB	35D	WEST	10	6	17500	6		103500	113500
40	9	BERMUDA 40	YWL	SAIL	FBG	KC	IB	35D	WEST	11	9	19000	4	1	114500	126000
40	9	BERMUDA 40 MARK III	YWL	SAIL	FBG	KC	IB	35D	WEST	11	9	20000	8	7	118500	130000
41	3	COMPETITION	SLP	SAIL	FBG	KL	IB	30	UNIV	10	3	19000	6	2	114500	125500
41	3	COMPETITION	SLP	SAIL	FBG	KL	IB	35D	WEST	10	3	19000	6	2	116500	128000
41	3	COMPETITION	YWL	SAIL	FBG	KL	IB	30	UNIV	10	3	19000	6	2	114500	125500
41	3	COMPETITION	YWL	SAIL	FBG	KL	IB	35D	WEST	10	3	19000	6	2	116500	128000
48	5	HINCKLEY	SLP	SAIL	FBG	KC	IB	35D	WEST	13		34000	5	3	205500	226000
48	5	HINCKLEY	YWL	SAIL	FBG	KC	IB	35D	WEST	13		34000	5	3	205500	226000
48	5	HINCKLEY	KTH	SAIL	FBG	KC	IB	35D	WEST	13		38000	5	3	214000	235500
		1971 BOATS														
26		ROUSTABOUT		UTL	FBG	RB	IB	40- 45		8	2		3		15200	17300
26		YACHT-CLUB		UTL	FBG		IB	40- 45		8	2		3		15200	17300
35	9	PILOT 35	SLP	SAIL	FBG	KL	IB	30	UNIV	9	6	13500	5		79600	87500
35	9	PILOT 35	YWL	SAIL	FBG	KL	IB	30	UNIV	9	6	13500	5		79600	87500
37	6	HINCKLEY 38	SLP	SAIL	FBG	KL	IB	25	UNIV	10	6	17500	6		99400	109000
40	9	BERMUDA 40	YWL	SAIL	FBG	KC	IB	35D	WEST	11	9	19000	4	1	111500	122500
41	3	COMPETITION 41	SLP	SAIL	FBG	KL	IB	30	UNIV	10	3	19000	6	2	111500	122500
41	3	COMPETITION 41	YWL	SAIL	FBG	KL	IB	30	UNIV	10	3	19000	6	2	111500	122500
48	5	HINCKLEY 48	SLP	SAIL	FBG	KC	IB	35D	WEST	13		34000	5	3	200500	220000
48	5	HINCKLEY 48	YWL	SAIL	FBG	KC	IB	35D	WEST	13		34000	5	3	200500	220000
		1970 BOATS														
35	9	PILOT 35	SLP	SAIL	FBG	KL	IB	30	UNIV	9	6	13500	5		77700	85400
35	9	PILOT 35	YWL	SAIL	FBG	KL	IB	30	UNIV	9	6	13500	5		77600	85300
37	6	HINCKLEY 38	SLP	SAIL	FBG	KL	IB	30	UNIV	10	6	17500	5	9	97000	106500
40	9	BERMUDA 40	YWL	SAIL	FBG	KC	IB	35D	WEST	11	9	19000	4	1	109000	119500
41	3	COMPETITION 41	SLP	SAIL	FBG	KL	IB	30	UNIV	10	4	18500	6	3	107000	117500
48	5	HINCKLEY 48	SLP	SAIL	FBG	KC	IB	35D	WEST	13		36500	5	3	200500	220500
48	5	HINCKLEY 48	YWL	SAIL	FBG	KC	IB	35D	WEST	13		36500	5	3	200500	220500
		1969 BOATS														
35	9	PILOT 35	SLP	SAIL	FBG	KL	IB	30	UNIV	9	6	13500	5		75800	83300
35	9	PILOT 35	YWL	SAIL	FBG	KL	IB	30	UNIV	9	6	13500	5		75800	83300
37	6	HINCKLEY 38	SLP	SAIL	FBG	KL	IB	30	UNIV	10	6		5	9	91300	100500
40	9	BERMUDA 40	YWL	SAIL	FBG	KC	IB	35D	WEST	11	9	19000	4	1	106500	117000
41	3	COMPETITION	SLP	SAIL	FBG	KL	IB	42	UNIV	10	3		6	1	81900	89900
41	3	HINCKLEY 41	SLP	SAIL	FBG	KL	IB	42	UNIV	10	3	18500	6	1	105000	115000
41	3	HINCKLEY 41	YWL	SAIL	FBG	KL	IB	42	UNIV	10	3	18500	6	1	105000	115000
48	5	HINCKLEY 48	SLP	SAIL	FBG	KC	IB	35D	WEST	13		36500	5	3	196000	215500
48	5	HINCKLEY 48	YWL	SAIL	FBG	KC	IB	35D	WEST	13		36500	5	3	196000	215500
		1968 BOATS														
35	9	PILOT 35	SLP	SAIL	FBG	KL	IB	25		9	6	13500	5		73700	80900
35	9	PILOT 35	YWL	SAIL	FBG	KL	IB	25		9	6	13500	5		73600	80900
40	9	BERMUDA 40	YWL	SAIL	FBG	KC	IB	30		11	9	19000	4	1	102500	112500
41	3	HINCKLEY 41	SLP	SAIL	FBG	KL	IB	42		10	3	18500	6	1	102500	113000
48	3	HINCKLEY 48	SLP	SAIL	FBG	KC	IB	35		13		36500	5	2	188500	207000
48	3	HINCKLEY 48	YWL	SAIL	FBG	KC	IB	35		13		36500	5	2	188500	207000
		1967 BOATS														
35	9	PILOT 35 STD	SLP	SAIL	FBG	KL	IB	30		9	6	13500	5		72200	79300
35	9	PILOT 35 STD	YWL	SAIL	FBG	KL	IB	30		9	6	13500	5		72100	79300
35	9	PILOT 35 STD	YWL	SAIL	FBG	KL	IB	35D		9	6	13500	5		72900	80100
40	9	BERMUDA 40 CUSTOM	YWL	SAIL	FBG	KL	IB	30		11	9	19000	4	1	100500	110500
40	9	BERMUDA 40 CUSTOM	YWL	SAIL	FBG	KL	IB	35D		11	9	19000	4	1	102000	112000
41	3	HINCKLEY 41 CUSTOM	SLP	SAIL	FBG	KL	IB	30		10	3	18500	6	1	100500	110500
41	3	HINCKLEY 41 CUSTOM	SLP	SAIL	FBG	KL	IB	35D		10	3	18500	6	1	102000	112000
41	3	HINCKLEY 41 CUSTOM	YWL	SAIL	FBG	KL	IB	30		10	3	18500	6	1	100500	110500
41	3	HINCKLEY 41 CUSTOM	YWL	SAIL	FBG	KL	IB	35D		10	3	18500	6	1	102000	112000
48	5	HINCKLEY 48	SLP	SAIL	FBG	KL	IB	35D		13		36000	5	2	187000	205500
48	5	HINCKLEY 48	YWL	SAIL	FBG	KL	IB	35D		13		36000	5	2	187000	205500
		1966 BOATS														
30	5	SOUTH-WESTER CUSTOM	SLP	SA/CR	FBG	KL	IB	25		8	10		4	6	31600	35100
35	9	PILOT 35 CUSTOM	SLP	SAIL	FBG	KL	IB	25		9	6	13500	5		75200	82600
35	9	PILOT 35 CUSTOM	SLP	SAIL	FBG	KL	IB	30D		9	6	13500	5		75700	83200
35	9	PILOT 35 CUSTOM	YWL	SAIL	FBG	KL	IB	25		9	6	13500	5		75100	82500
35	9	PILOT 35 CUSTOM	YWL	SAIL	FBG	KL	IB	30D		9	6	13500			75600	83100
35	9	PILOT 35 STD	SLP	SAIL	FBG	KL	IB	25		9	6	13500	5		66400	72900
35	9	PILOT 35 STD	SLP	SAIL	FBG	KL	IB	30D		9	6	13500	5		67300	73900
35	9	PILOT 35 STD	YWL	SAIL	FBG	KL	IB	25		9	6	13500	5		66400	73000
35	9	PILOT 35 STD	YWL	SAIL	FBG	KL	IB	30D		9	6	13500	5		67300	74000
40	9	BERMUDA 40 CUSTOM	YWL	SAIL	FBG	KC	IB	42		11	9	19000	4	1	99000	109000
40	9	BERMUDA 40 CUSTOM	YWL	SAIL	FBG	KC	IB	30D		11	9	19000	4	1	100000	110000
41	3	HINCKLEY 41 CUSTOM	SLP	SAIL	FBG	KL	IB	42		10	3	18500	6	1	99000	109000
41	3	HINCKLEY 41 CUSTOM	SLP	SAIL	FBG	KL	IB	30D		10	3	18500	6	1	100500	110000
		1965 BOATS														
30	5	SOUTH-WESTER CUSTOM	SLP	SA/CR	FBG	KL	IB	25							31100	34500
35	9	PILOT 35 CUSTOM	SLP	SAIL	FBG		IB	25							59300	65200
35	9	PILOT 35 CUSTOM	SLP	SAIL	FBG		IB	30D							84000	92300
35	9	PILOT 35 CUSTOM	YWL	SAIL	FBG		IB	25							59200	65100
35	9	PILOT 35 CUSTOM	YWL	SAIL	FBG		IB	30D							83900	92200
35	9	PILOT 35 STD	SLP	SAIL	FBG		IB	25							53000	58200
35	9	PILOT 35 STD	SLP	SAIL	FBG		IB	30D							74600	82000
35	9	PILOT 35 STD	YWL	SAIL	FBG		IB	25							53000	58200
35	9	PILOT 35 STD	YWL	SAIL	FBG		IB	30D							74700	82100
40	9	BERMUDA 40 CUSTOM	YWL	SAIL	FBG		IB	42							74200	81500
40	9	BERMUDA 40 CUSTOM	YWL	SAIL	FBG		IB	30D							113000	124500
41	3	HINCKLEY 41 CUSTOM	SLP	SAIL	FBG		IB	42							76300	83800
41	3	HINCKLEY 41 CUSTOM	SLP	SAIL	FBG		IB	30D							114500	126000
		1964 BOATS														
30	5	SOUTH-WESTER CUSTOM	SLP	SA/CR	FBG	KL	IB	30							30600	34000
35	9	PILOT 35 CUSTOM	SLP	SAIL	FBG		IB	25							58800	64700
35	9	PILOT 35 STD	SLP	SAIL	FBG		IB	25							52200	57400
40	9	BERMUDA 40 CUSTOM	YWL	SAIL	FBG		IB	30							76300	83800
40	9	BERMUDA 40 STD	YWL	SAIL	FBG		IB	30							70000	76900
41	3	HINCKLEY CUSTOM	CUT	SAIL	FBG		IB	30							80300	88200
41	3	HINCKLEY STANDARD	CUT	SAIL	FBG		IB	30							70100	77000
		1963 BOATS														
30	5	SOUTH-WESTER	SLP	SA/CR	FBG		IB	25							30200	33600
35	9	PILOT CUSTOM		SAIL	FBG		IB	25							58100	63900
35	9	PILOT STANDARD		SAIL	FBG		IB	25							51600	56700
35	9	PILOT STANDARD		SAIL	FBG		IB	30D							77200	84800
40	9	BERMUDA 40		SAIL	FBG		IB	30							72300	79500
40	9	BERMUDA 40		SAIL	FBG		IB	30D							110500	121500

 CONTINUED ON NEXT PAGE

LOA FT	IN	NAME AND/ OR MODEL	TOP/ RIG	BOAT TYPE	-HULL- MTL	TP	TP	ENGINE # HP	MFG	BEAM FT	IN	WGT LBS	DRAFT FT	IN	RETAIL LOW	RETAIL HIGH
		1962 BOATS														
30	3	SOUTH-WESTER JR	SLP	SA/CR	FBG		OB								30900	34300
40	9	BERMUDA 40	YWL	SAIL	FBG		OB								76700	84300
		1961 BOATS														
30	3	SOUTH-WESTER JR	SLP	SA/CR	FBG	KL	OB			8	9		4	7	30600	34000
40	9	BERMUDA	YWL	SAIL	FBG	CB	OB			11	9				76200	83700
		1960 BOATS														
30	3	SOUTH-WESTER JR	SLP	SA/CR	FBG		OB								30400	33800
30	3	SOUTH-WESTER JR	SLP	SA/CR	WD		OB								30300	33600
40	9	BERMUDA 40	YWL	SAIL	FBG		OB								75800	83300
62		HINCKLEY 62		CR	WD		IB	T240D		15	10		4	6	191000	209500
		1959 BOATS														
30	3	SOUTH-WESTER JR	SLP	SA/CR	WD		OB								30100	33500
35	2	HINCKLEY-PILOT		SAIL	WD		OB								59700	65600
39		SOUTH-WESTER SR		SAIL	WD		OB								77900	85700
41	11	HINCKLEY 42		SAIL	WD		OB								113500	124500
		1958 BOATS														
30	3	SOUTH-WESTER JR	SLP	SA/CR	WD		OB								30100	33400
39		SOUTH-WESTER SR		SAIL	WD		OB								77800	85500
		1957 BOATS														
30	3	SOUTH-WESTER JR	SLP	SA/CR	WD		OB								30100	33400
35	2	PILOT		SAIL	WD		OB								59900	65800
36		HINCKLEY 36	SLP	SAIL	WD		OB								52500	57700
36		HINCKLEY 36	YWL	SAIL	WD		OB								52500	57700
40	6	OWENS	CUT	SAIL	WD		OB								74500	81900
		1956 BOATS														
33		PILOT		SAIL	WD		OB								48900	53800
36		HINCKLEY 36 CUSTOM	YWL	SAIL	WD		OB								52600	57800
36		HINCKLEY 36 SPECIAL	YWL	SAIL	WD		OB								52600	57800
36		HINCKLEY 36 STD	YWL	SAIL	WD		OB								52600	57800
40	6	HINCKLEY-OWENS	CUT	SAIL	WD		OB								74600	82000
		1955 BOATS														
36		HINCKLEY 36 CUSTOM	YWL	SAIL	WD		OB								52800	58000
36		HINCKLEY 36 SPECIAL	YWL	SAIL	WD		OB								52800	58100
36		HINCKLEY 36 STD	YWL	SAIL	WD		OB								52800	58000
		1954 BOATS														
34	2	SOUTH-WESTER	SLP	SA/CR	WD		OB								54200	59500
36		HINCKLEY 36 CUSTOM	YWL	SAIL	WD		OB								53100	58400
36		HINCKLEY 36 STD	YWL	SAIL	WD		OB								53100	58400
40	6	HINCKLEY-OWENS	CUT	SAIL	WD		OB								75300	82700
		1953 BOATS														
34	2	SOUTH-WESTER	SLP	SA/CR	WD		OB								54600	60000
36		HINCKLEY 36	SLP	SAIL	WD		OB								53300	58600
36		HINCKLEY 36	YWL	SAIL	WD		OB								53300	58600
40	6	HINCKLEY-OWENS	CUT	SAIL	WD		OB								75800	83300
		1952 BOATS														
20		HINCKLEY ROUSTABOUT		UTL	WD		IB	45							4650	5350
23	9	BEETLE 24		CR	FBG		IB	100							8700	10000
34	2	SOUTH-WESTER	SLP	SA/CR	WD		OB								55200	60600
35	9	HINCKLEY 25	SLP	SAIL	WD		OB								53700	59000
40	6	OWENS 40	CUT	SAIL	WD		OB								76400	84000
		1951 BOATS														
20		ROUSTABOUT		UTL	WD		IB	45							4600	5250
34	2	SOUTH-WESTER	SLP	SA/CR	WD		OB								55900	61400
40	6	OWENS	CUT	SAIL	WD		OB								77700	85400
		1950 BOATS														
20		ROUSTABOUT		UTL	WD		IB	40							4500	5150
29	2	HINCKLEY 21 CUSTOM	SLP	SAIL	WD		OB								23600	26200
29	2	HINCKLEY 21 STD	SLP	SAIL	WD		OB								23600	26200
34	2	CUSTOM	SLP	SAIL	WD		OB								56900	62500
34	2	SOUTH-WESTER	SLP	SA/CR	WD		OB								56900	62600
34	2	SOUTH-WESTER STD	SLP	SA/CR	WD		OB								56900	62600
40		HINCKLEY	SLP	SAIL	WD		OB								79500	87300
40		HINCKLEY	YWL	SAIL	WD		OB								79500	87300
40	6	OWENS	CUT	SAIL	WD		OB								79100	87000
45		HINCKLEY 32	SLP	SAIL	WD		IB								159500	175500
		1949 BOATS														
29	3	HINCKLEY 21	SLP	SAIL	WD		IB								39900	44400
34	2	SOUTH-WESTER	SLP	SA/CR	WD		IB			9					81900	90000
		1948 BOATS														
34	2	SOUTH-WESTER	SLP	SA/CR	WD		OB								59700	65600
34	2	SOUTH-WESTER	YWL	SA/CR	WD		OB								59700	65600
		1947 BOATS														
34	2	SOUTH-WESTER	SLP	SA/CR	WD		OB								60800	66800
34	2	SOUTH-WESTER	YWL	SA/CR	WD		OB								60700	66800
		1946 BOATS														
28	6	HINCKLEY 21	SLP	SAIL	WD		OB								24900	27700
28	6	HINCKLEY 21	YWL	SAIL	WD		OB								24900	27700
34	2	SOUTH-WESTER	SLP	SA/CR	WD		OB								62200	68300
34	2	SOUTH-WESTER	YWL	SA/CR	WD		OB								62100	68300
40	9	HINCKLEY 28	SLP	SAIL	WD		OB								87400	96000
40	9	HINCKLEY 28	YWL	SAIL	WD		OB								87400	96000
45	9	HINCKLEY 32	SLP	SAIL	WD		IB	25							159500	175500
45	9	HINCKLEY 32	YWL	SAIL	WD		IB	25							159500	175500

HINTERHOELLER YACHTS

NIAGARA ON THE LAKE ONT COAST GUARD MFG ID- ZHY See inside cover to adjust price for area

For more recent years, see the BUC Used Boat Price Guide, Volume 1 or Volume 2

LOA FT	IN	NAME AND/ OR MODEL	TOP/ RIG	BOAT TYPE	-HULL- MTL	TP	TP	ENGINE # HP	MFG	BEAM FT	IN	WGT LBS	DRAFT FT	IN	RETAIL LOW	RETAIL HIGH
		1983 BOATS														
26		NONSUCH 26	CAT	SA/CR	FBG	KL	IB	21D		10	6	8500	3	9	30300	33600
30	4	NONSUCH 30	CAT	SA/CR	F/S	KL	IB	29D-	33D	11	10	11500	4	11	42200	46900
30	4	NONSUCH 30 SHOAL	CAT	SA/CR	F/S	KL	IB	29D	WEST	11	10	11500	3	11	42500	47200
30	4	NONSUCH ULTRA 30	CAT	SA/CR	F/S	KL	IB	33D	WEST	11	10	11500	3	11	42500	47200
30	4	NONSUCH ULTRA 30	CAT	SA/CR	F/S	KL	VD	33D	WEST	11	10	11500	4	11	42400	47100
30	4	NONSUCH ULTRA 30 SHL	CAT	SA/CR	F/S	KL	VD	29D	WEST	11	10	11500	3	11	42300	47100
31	3	NIAGARA 31	SLP	SA/RC	FBG	KL	VD	21D-	27D	10	4	8500	5		30000	33300
35	1	NIAGARA 35	SLP	SA/CR	F/S	KL	VD	29D	WEST	11	5	15000	5	2	49800	54800
35	1	NIAGARA 35	SLP	SA/CR	F/S	KL	VD	33D	WEST	11	5	15000	5	2	49900	54800
36		NONSUCH 36	CAT	SA/CR	F/S	KL	IB	52D	WEST	12	8	16800	5	6	60200	66100
36		NONSUCH 36	CAT	SA/CR	F/S	KL	VD	58D	WEST	12	8	17000	5	6	60800	66900
36		NONSUCH 36	KTH	SA/CR	F/S	KL	VD	52D	WEST	12	8	17000	5	6	60800	66800
36		NONSUCH 36	KTH	SA/CR	F/S	KL	VD	58D	WEST	12	8	17000	5	6	60800	66900
36	3	FRERS F3	SLP	SA/RC	F/S	KL	IB	29D	WEST	11	10	10900	6	9	40700	45200
		1982 BOATS														
26		NONSUCH 26	CAT	SA/CR	FBG	KL	IB	14D		10	6	8700	3	9	29100	32400
26		NONSUCH 26	CAT	SA/CR	FBG	KL	SD	21D	WEST	10	6	8500	4	6	28600	31700
26		NONSUCH 26	CAT	SA/CR	FBG	KL	IB	21D	WEST	10	6	8700	3	9	29300	32600
30	4	NONSUCH 30	CAT	SA/CR	F/S	KL	IB	29D-	33D	11	10	11500	3	11	39800	44300
31	3	NIAGARA 31	SLP	SA/RC	FBG	KL	IB	21D	WEST	10	4	8500	5		28200	31300
35	1	NIAGARA 35	SLP	SA/CR	F/S	KL	IB	29D	WEST	11	5	15000	5	2	47100	51800
35	1	NIAGARA 35	SLP	SA/CR	F/S	KL	IB	33D	WEST	11	5	15000	5	2	47200	51800
36	3	FRERS F3	SLP	SA/RC	F/S	KL	IB	29D	WEST	11	10	10900	6	9	38300	42500
		1981 BOATS														
26		NONSUCH 26	CAT	SA/CR	FBG	KL	SD	13D	WEST	10	6	7300	4	6	22700	25200
26		NONSUCH 26	CAT	SA/CR	FBG	KL	VD	21D	UNIV	10	6	8500	4	6	26900	29900
30	4	NONSUCH 30	CAT	SA/CR	F/S	KL	VD	27D-	33D	11	10	11500	4	11	37500	41700
31	3	NIAGARA 31	SLP	SA/RC	FBG	KL	VD	21D-	27D	10	4	8500	5		26500	29500
35	1	NIAGARA 35	SLP	SA/CR	F/S	KL	VD	27D	WEST	11	5	15000	5	2	43800	48700
35	1	NIAGARA 35	SLP	SA/CR	F/S	KL	VD	33D	WEST	11	5	15000	5	2	43900	48800
35	1	NIAGARA 35	SLP	SA/CR	F/S	KL	SD	35D	VLVO	11	5	14000	5	2	41200	45800
36	3	F 3	SLP	SA/RC	F/S	KL	SD	27D	WEST	11	10	10900	6	9	36000	40000
36	3	F 3	SLP	SA/RC	F/S	KL	SD	33D	WEST	11	11	10900	6	9	36000	40000
		1980 BOATS														
24		SHARK	SLP	SA/RC	FBG	KL	OB			6	10	2200	3		6300	7250
26	8	NIAGARA 26	SLP	SA/CR	FBG	KL	OB			8	4	4000	4		10500	11900
26	8	NIAGARA 26	SLP	SA/CR	FBG	KL	SD	15	OMC	8	4	4000	4		10800	12300
30	4	NONSUCH 30	CAT	SA/CR	F/S	KL	SD	23D-	35D	11	10	10500	4	11	32500	36200
31	3	NIAGARA 31	SLP	SA/RC	FBG	KL	SD	14D	VLVO	10	4	8500	5		25300	28100
31	3	NIAGARA 31	SLP	SA/RC	FBG	KL	IB	20D	WEST	10	4	8500	5		25300	28100
35	1	NIAGARA 35	SLP	SA/CR	F/S	KL	SD	23D	VLVO	11	5	14000	5	2	39200	43600
35	1	NIAGARA 35	SLP	SA/CR	F/S	KL	SD	35D	VLVO	11	5	14000	5	2	39300	43700
35	1	NIAGARA 35	SLP	SA/CR	F/S	KL	IB	37D	WEST	11	5	14000	5	2	39400	43800
		1979 BOATS														
26	8	NIAGARA 26	SLP	SA/CR	F/S	KL	OB			8	4	4000	4		10100	11400
26	8	NIAGARA 26	SLP	SA/CR	FBG	KL	SD	15	OMC	8	4	4000	4		10400	11800
30	4	NONSUCH 30	CAT	SA/CR	F/S	KL	SD	23D	VLVO	11	10	10500	4	11	31300	34800
35	1	NIAGARA 35	SLP	SA/CR	F/S	KL	SD	23D	VLVO	11	5	14000	5	2	37700	41900
35	1	NIAGARA 35	SLP	SA/CR	F/S	KL	SD	35D	VLVO	11	5	14000	5	2	37800	42000
35	1	NIAGARA 35	SLP	SA/CR	F/S	KL	IB	35D	WEST	11	5	14000	5	2	37900	42100
		1972 BOATS														
24		SHARK 24	SLP	SA/OD	FBG	KL				6	11	2100	3		4750	5500
		1971 BOATS														
24		SHARK	SLP	SAIL	FBG		OB			6	10	2200	3		4800	5500
27	4	C-&-C 27	SLP	SAIL	FBG		IB	30	UNIV	9	2	6000	4	3	13400	15300
30		C-&-C 30	SLP	SAIL	FBG		IB	30	UNIV	10	1	8500	5		20000	22200
34	7	C-&-C 35	SLP	SAIL	FBG		IB	30	UNIV	10	7	10500	5	3	24400	27100
		1970 BOATS														
24		SHARK		SA/OD	FBG	KL	OB			6	10	2200	3		4700	5400
25	1	H R-25		SAIL	FBG	KL	OB			8		3400	3	6	6800	7800
30	4	REDWING 30		SAIL	FBG	KL	IB	30	UNIV	8	10	7458	4	6	17000	19300
34		REDWING 34	SLP	SA/CR	FBG	KL		30		10	6	10000	5	3	22600	25200

 CONTINUED ON NEXT PAGE

HINTERHOELLER YACHTS

-CONTINUED See inside cover to adjust price for area

```
LOA   NAME AND/       TOP/ BOAT  -HULL-  ----ENGINE---  BEAM   WGT  DRAFT  RETAIL RETAIL
FT IN OR MODEL        RIG  TYPE  MTL TP  TP # HP  MFG   FT IN  LBS  FT IN  LOW    HIGH
----------------- 1969 BOATS ------------------------------------------------------------
24    SHARK           SLP SA/OD FBG KL              6 10  2200  3      4600   5300
28  4 HR 28           SLP SAIL  FBG KL              8  7        4     12200  13800
30  4 REDWING         SLP SA/CR FBG KL              8 10  7458  4  6  15400  17500
----------------- 1968 BOATS ------------------------------------------------------------
21  9 REDWING 30      SLP SAIL  FBG KL OB           8  9        4  6   7800   8950
24    SHARK           SLP SA/OD FBG KL              6 11        3      4850   5600
28  4 HT-28           SLP SAIL  FBG KL OB           8  6        4     13100  14900
30    NIAGARA 30      SLP SAIL  FBG KL OB           8  6        4  2  12800  14600
----------------- 1967 BOATS ------------------------------------------------------------
20  1 CYGNUS          SLP SA/OD F/S CB             7       825  8      2350   2750
20  1 CYGNUS          SLP SA/OD F/G KL             7       825  2  6   2350   2750
24    SHARK           SLP SA/OD FBG KL              6 11  2100  3      4400   5050
28  3 H R 25          SLP SA/CR FBG KL OB           8  5        4     13000  14700
28  3 H R 25          SLP SA/CR FBG KL IB 30        8  5        4     14600  16600
30    NIAGARA 30      SLP SA/CR FBG KL OB           8         4  3  12700  14400
35  8 INVADER         SLP SA/CR FBG KL IB 30       10  3      4 10  23600  26200
----------------- 1966 BOATS ------------------------------------------------------------
20    CYGNUS          SLP SA/OD FBG CB             6 10   825  8      2350   2750
20    CYGNUS          SLP SA/OD FBG KL             6 10   825  2  6   2350   2750
24    SHARK           SLP SA/OD FBG KL              6 11  2100  3      4300   5000
28  3 SEAHORSE        SLP SA/CR FBG KL OB           6 11        4     12800  14600
35  8 INVADAR         SLP SA/CR FBG KL IB          10  2      4 10  23400  26000
----------------- 1965 BOATS ------------------------------------------------------------
20    CYGNUS          SLP SAIL FBG CB              7            11   3500   4100
20    CYGNUS          SLP SAIL FBG KL              7            11   3500   4100
24    SHARK           SLP SAIL FBG KL              6 11      2  6   6200   7150
28  3 HR28            SLP SAIL FBG KC              8  5      3  4  11600  13200
35  8 INVADER         SLP SAIL FBG KL             10  3      4 10  22400  24900
```

HIPTIMCO MARINE

HIP SHING TIMBER CO INC
KOWLOON HONG KONG   COAST GUARD MFG ID- HTM   See inside cover to adjust price for area

```
LOA   NAME AND/       TOP/ BOAT  -HULL-  ----ENGINE---  BEAM   WGT  DRAFT  RETAIL RETAIL
FT IN OR MODEL        RIG  TYPE  MTL TP  TP # HP  MFG   FT IN  LBS  FT IN  LOW    HIGH
----------------- 1982 BOATS ------------------------------------------------------------
17 10 H 18            OP  RNBT FBG FL OB            7  4 1300  1      2600   3050
17 10 L 18            OP  RNBT FBG FL IB  140 OMC   7  4 1300  1      2650   3100
17 11 GLASKIF 18      OP  RNBT FBG RB OB            7  3 1300  1      2600   3050
17 11 GLASKIF 18      OP  RNBT FBG RB IB  140 OMC   7  3 1300  1      2650   3100
17 11 GLASKIF 18      HT  RNBT FBG RB OB            7  3 1950  1      3450   4000
17 11 GLASKIF 18      HT  RNBT FBG RB IB  140 OMC   7  3 1950  1      3000   3500
19 10 20 BRIDGE DECK  HT  EXP  FBG FL OB            8    2700  1      4500   5150
19 10 20 BRIDGE DECK  HT  EXP  FBG FL IB  140 OMC   8    2700  1      4000   4650
19 10 20 DAY CRUISER  HT  CR   FBG FL OB            8    2700  1      4500   5150
19 10 20 DAY CRUISER  HT  CR   FBG FL IB  140 OMC   8    2700  1      4100   4750
25    GLASKIF 25      HT  CR   FBG RB IB  80D LEHM  8  9 9000  1  7 19800  22000
25    GLASKIF 25      FB  CR   FBG RB IB  80D LEHM  8  9 9000  1  7 19800  22000

25    GLASKIF B/D 25  HT  EXP  FBG RB IB  80D  LEHM  8  9 6000  1  7 12800  14600
29 11 30 SPORTFISHERMAN FB SF  FBG RB IB 120D  LEHM 11   9000  2  3 21900  24300
29 11 GLASKIF 30      HT  EXP  FBG RB IB 120D  LEHM 11   9000  2  3 24600  27300
39 11 DIAMOND-RING    FB  TRWL FBG DS IB T120D LEHM 13  6 29500 3 10 91700 101000
39 11 GOLDEN-CROWN    FB  TRWL FBG DS IB  120D LEHM 13  6 28000 3 10 82500  90600
39 11 GOLDEN-CROWN    FB  TRWL FBG DS IB T120D LEHM 13  6 29500 3 10 85800  94300
39 11 PEARL-DELTA     FB  TRWL FBG DS IB T120D LEHM 13  6 29500 3 10 94600 104000
49  8 50 CRUISER      FB  CR   FBG FL IB 210D  CAT  15  2 40000 3   114000 125000
----------------- 1980 BOATS ------------------------------------------------------------
17 10 H 18            OP  RNBT FBG FL OB            7  4 1300  1      2550   2950
17 10 L 18            OP  RNBT FBG FL IB            7  4 1300  1       **     **
17 11 GLASKIF 18      OP  RNBT FBG RB OB            7  3 1300  1      2550   2950
17 11 GLASKIF 18      OP  RNBT FBG RB IB            7  3 1300  1       **     **
17 11 GLASKIF 18      HT  RNBT FBG RB OB            7  3 1950  1      3350   3900
17 11 GLASKIF 18      HT  RNBT FBG RB IB            7  3 1950  1       **     **
19 10 20 BRIDGE DECK  HT  EXP  FBG FL OB            8    2700  1      4350   5000
19 10 20 BRIDGE DECK  HT  EXP  FBG FL IB            8    2700  1       **     **
19 10 20 DAY CRUISER  HT  CR   FBG FL OB            8    2700  1      4350   5000
19 10 20 DAY CRUISER  HT  CR   FBG FL IB            8    2700  1       **     **
25    GLASKIF 25      HT  CR   FBG RB IB  80D LEHM  8  9 9000  1  7 18300  20400
25    GLASKIF 25      FB  CR   FBG RB IB  80D LEHM  8  9 9000  1  7 18300  20400

25    GLASKIF B/D 25  HT  EXP  FBG RB IB  80D  LEHM  8  9 6000  1  7 11900  13500
29 11 30 SPORTFISHERMAN FB SF  FBG RB IB 120D  LEHM 11   9000  2  3 20200  22500
29 11 GLASKIF 30      HT  EXP  FBG RB IB 120D  LEHM 11   9000  2  3 22700  25200
49  8 50 CRUISER      FB  CR   FBG FL IB 210D  CUT  15  2 40000 3   103000 113000
----------------- 1967 BOATS ------------------------------------------------------------
17  8 GLASKIF 180         RNBT FBG    OB            7  4  950       1850   2200
17  8 HIPTIMCO 180        RNBT FBG    IO   80       7  4 1000    1 6 2800   3250
17 10 H-18                RNBT FBG    OB            7  4         1 6 1950   2300
17 10 H-18                RNBT FBG    IO   80       7  4 1000    1 6 2800   3250
19 10 H-20                RNBT FBG    OB            8        1200     2450   2850
19 10 H-20                RNBT FBG    IO   80       8            1 8 4250   4950
19 10 H-20C               EXP  FBG    OB            8        2400     3950   4550
19 10 H-20C               EXP  FBG    IO   80       8            1 8 4400   5100
19 10 H-20D               CR   FBG    OB            8        2400     3950   4550
19 10 H-20D               CR   FBG    IO   80       8            1 8 4500   5150
24    MORCY          SLP SAIL WD CB                7  5         2 9 1900   2250
24  9 GLASKIF 250     HT  FBG        IB   210       8  9         1 7 4600   5250

24  9 GLASKIF 250         CR   FBG    IB   210       8  9        1 7 4850   5550
24  9 GLASKIF 250         CR   FBG    IO T 80       8  9        1 7 10600  12000
24  9 GLASKIF 250         FSH  FBG    IB   210       8  9        1 7 5300   6100
24  9 GLASKIF 250         FSH  FBG    IO T 80       8  9        1 7 12200  13900
24 10 GLASKIF 280     HT   FBG        IB   210      10  6        1 7 9750   11100
27 10 GLASKIF 280     HT   FBG        IB   210      10  6        2 3 7000   8050
30    NIMBLE         SLP SAIL WD TM              18             2 2 7800   8950
35    LODESTAR       KTH SAIL WD TM              20             2 6 15100  17200
39  6 HIPTIMCO 400    MY   FBG        IB   135      13  6        3 10 31400 34900
40    VICTRESS       KTH SAIL WD TM              22             2 9 23200  25800
----------------- 1966 BOATS ------------------------------------------------------------
17 10                RNBT  FBG    IO   110       7  4 1250       2750   3200
17 10                CBNCR FBG    OB             8    1250       2350   2950
19 10                CR    FBG    OB             8    1300       2600   3050
19 10                RNBT  FBG    OB             8     870       1850   2200
24    GLASKIF    SLP SA/CR WD CB                7  6         2 9 1900   2250
24  7                CR    FBG    IO   110       8  9        2 3 9900   11200
26  7 DAY CRUISER       EXP  FBG   IB   177      10  8        2 3 5850   6750
26  7                CR    FBG    IB   177      10  8        2 3 6200   7150
30                   SAIL PLY TM               18             2 2 7600   8750
34  7                SDN   L/P    IB   420      18             2 6 19300  21500
35                   SAIL PLY TM               20             3 6 14900  16900
----------------- 1965 BOATS ------------------------------------------------------------
19 10                RNBT  FBG    OB             8     850       1800   2150
23 10 SEA SKIFF     HT CR  WD     IB   210       8  7        1 6 3700   4350
27 10 DAY CR        OP CR  WD     IB   210      10  4        2 3 6600   7600
33 10                SDN   WD     IB   440      12             2 10 16200 18400
```

HO HSING FRP CO LTD

TAINAN TAIWAN   COAST GUARD MFG ID- HHG   See inside cover to adjust price for area

```
LOA   NAME AND/              TOP/ BOAT  -HULL-  ----ENGINE---  BEAM   WGT  DRAFT  RETAIL RETAIL
FT IN OR MODEL               RIG  TYPE  MTL TP  TP # HP  MFG   FT IN  LBS  FT IN  LOW    HIGH
----------------- 1983 BOATS ---------------------------------------------------------------------
32  3 NANTUCKET-ISLAND 331   SLP SAIL FBG KL IB  30D YAN 11 1 12665 5 3 41400 46000
37  7 NANTUCKET-ISLAND 38    SLP SAIL FBG KL IB  30D YAN 12 2 17518 5 3 63200 69400
37  7 NANTUCKET-ISLAND 38    KTH SAIL FBG KL IB  30D YAN 12 2 17518 5 6 63200 69400
```

HOBIE CAT COMPANY

HOBIE CATAMARANS
OCEANSIDE CA 92056   COAST GUARD MFG ID- CCM   See inside cover to adjust price for area
FORMERLY COAST CATAMARAN CORP

For more recent years, see the BUC Used Boat Price Guide, Volume 1 or Volume 2

```
LOA   NAME AND/       TOP/ BOAT  -HULL-  ----ENGINE---  BEAM   WGT  DRAFT  RETAIL RETAIL
FT IN OR MODEL        RIG  TYPE  MTL TP  TP # HP  MFG   FT IN  LBS  FT IN  LOW    HIGH
----------------- 1983 BOATS ------------------------------------------------------------
16  7 HOBIE 16        SLP SAIL F/S CT             7 11  340  10   2550   3000
17    HOLDER 17       SLP SA/OD FBG SK            7  3  950  1  8  3600   4200
17    HOLDER 17 DS    SLP SA/OD FBG SK            7  3  925  1  8  3550   4150
18    HOBIE 18        SLP SA/OD F/S CT            8     400       3100   3600
20  4 HOLDER 20       SLP SA/OD FBG DB            7 10 1160  4  2  4150   4850
33    HOBIE 33        SLP SA/OD FBG SK            8    4000  5  5  6850   7850
----------------- 1982 BOATS ------------------------------------------------------------
16  7 HOBIE 16        SLP SA/OD F/S CT            7 11  340  10   2450   2850
18    HOBIE 18        SLP SA/OD F/S CT            8     400       2900   3400
33    HOBIE 33        SLP SA/OD FBG SK            8    3800  5  6  5750   6650
----------------- 1981 BOATS ------------------------------------------------------------
16  7 HOBIE 16        SLP SA/OD F/S CT            7 11  340  10   2350   2700
18    HOBIE 18        SLP SA/OD F/S CT            8     400       2800   3250
```

LOA FT IN	NAME AND/ OR MODEL	TOP/ RIG	BOAT TYPE	-HULL- MTL TP	----ENGINE--- TP # HP MFG	BEAM FT IN	WGT LBS	DRAFT FT IN	RETAIL LOW	RETAIL HIGH
					---- 1980 BOATS ----					
16 7	HOBIE 16	CAT	SA/OD	F/S CT		7 11	340	10	2250	2600
16 7	HOBIE 16	SLP	SA/OD	F/S CT		7 11	340	10	2250	2600
18	HOBIE 18	SLP	SA/OD	F/S CT		8	400		2700	3150
					---- 1979 BOATS ----					
16	HOBIE 16	SLP	SA/OD	F/S CT		7 11	340	10	2050	2450
18	HOBIE 18	SLP	SA/OD	F/S CT		8	375		2500	2900
					---- 1978 BOATS ----					
16 7	HOBIE 16	SLP	SA/OD	F/S CT		7 11	340	10	1950	2300
16 7	HOBIE 16 SE	SLP	SA/OD	F/S CT		7 11	340	10	2250	2600
18	HOBIE 18	SLP	SA/OD	F/S CT		8	375		2400	2800
					---- 1977 BOATS ----					
16 7	HOBIE 16	SLP	SA/OD	F/S CT		7 11	340	10	2000	2400
18	HOBIE 18	SLP	SA/OD	F/S CT		8	375		2350	2750
					---- 1976 BOATS ----					
16 7	HOBIE-CAT 16	SLP	SA/OD	F/S CT		7 11	325	10	1900	2250
					---- 1975 BOATS ----					
16 7	HOBIE 16	SLP	SA/OD	FBG CT		7 11	325	10	1900	2250
					---- 1974 BOATS ----					
16	HOBIE-CAT 16		SA/OD	FBG CT		7 11	315	10	1750	2050
					---- 1973 BOATS ----					
16	HOBIE-CAT 16		SA/OD	FBG CT		7 11	315	10	1700	2000
					---- 1972 BOATS ----					
16 7	HOBIE-CAT 16		SA/OD	FBG CT		7 11	315	10	1700	2050

HODGDON BROTHERS

HENRIK AAS
E BOOTHBAY ME 04544   COAST GUARD MFG ID- HGB   See inside cover to adjust price for area

LOA FT IN	NAME AND/ OR MODEL	TOP/ RIG	BOAT TYPE	-HULL- MTL TP	----ENGINE--- TP # HP MFG	BEAM FT IN	WGT LBS	DRAFT FT IN	RETAIL LOW	RETAIL HIGH
					---- 1976 BOATS ----					
33 5	INTERNATL-ONE-DESIGN	SLP	SA/OD	FBG KL	IB D	6 9	7120	5 4	16600	18800
33 5	INTERNATL-ONE-DESIGN	SLP	SA/OD	WD KL	IB D	6 9	7120	5 4	16500	18700
					---- 1975 BOATS ----					
33 5	INTERNATL-ONE-DESIGN	SLP	SA/OD	FBG KL	IB D	6 9	7120	5 4	16000	18200
33 5	INTERNATL-ONE-DESIGN	SLP	SA/OD	WD KL	IB D	6 9	7120	5 4	15600	17700
					---- 1961 BOATS ----					
21 4	HODGDON-BROS 21	SLP	SAIL	WD KL		5 9		3 5	2550	2950
27 5	CRUISER		CR	WD	IB 110	8 9		2 8	13200	15000
27 5	SPORTSMAN		CR	WD	IB 110	8 9		2 8	11100	12600
32 5	CRUISER		CR	WD	IB	11 2		3	**	**
					---- 1960 BOATS ----					
21 4	HODGDON-BROTHERS 21	SLP	SAIL	WD KL		5 9		3 5	2550	2950
27 5	CRUISER		CR	WD	IB 110-177	8 9		2 8	13000	15500
27 5	SPORTSMAN			WD	IB 110-177	8 9		2 8	10900	13400
					---- 1959 BOATS ----					
20 2	LOBSTER BOAT		FSH	P/M	IB 60	7 3			4600	5300
21 4		SLP	SAIL	P/C KL		5 9		3 5	2550	2950
27 5	LOBSTER BOAT		FSH	P/M	IB 60	8 9			10400	11900
					---- 1933 BOATS ----					
63			KTH	MS	IB 185D GM				375500	412500

HOFMANN & PITCAIRN INC

Call 1-800-327-6929 for BUC Personalized Evaluation Service
Or, for 1965 boats, sign onto www.BUCValuPro.com

HOLBROOK MARINE INC

Call 1-800-327-6929 for BUC Personalized Evaluation Service
Or, for 1966 to 1969 boats, sign onto www.BUCValuPro.com

HOLIDAY BOATS
COAST GUARD MFG ID- HDY

Call 1-800-327-6929 for BUC Personalized Evaluation Service
Or, for 1960 to 1967 boats, sign onto www.BUCValuPro.com

HOLIDAY MANSION

DIV OF MOHAWK INC
SALINA KS 67401   COAST GUARD MFG ID- HMH   See inside cover to adjust price for area

For more recent years, see the BUC Used Boat Price Guide, Volume 1 or Volume 2

LOA FT IN	NAME AND/ OR MODEL	TOP/ RIG	BOAT TYPE	-HULL- MTL TP	----ENGINE--- TP # HP MFG	BEAM FT IN	WGT LBS	DRAFT FT IN	RETAIL LOW	RETAIL HIGH
					---- 1983 BOATS ----					
39 3	BARRACUDA AFT CBN	HT	CR	FBG SV SE	205 OMC 12	17000	1 7		**	**
39 3	BARRACUDA AFT CBN	HT	CR	FBG SV IO	225 VLVO 12	17000	1 7		22700	25200
	IO 260 VLVO 22800	25300, IO 130D VLVO 26300 29200, IO T138 VLVO 23300 25900								
	IO T200 VLVO 23400	26000, VD T220 CRUS 38500 42800, IO T260 VLVO 23800 26500								
	IO T130D VLVO 27800	30900								
39 3	BARRACUDA AFT CBN	FB	CR	FBG SV SE	205 OMC 12	18000	1 7		**	**
39 3	BARRACUDA AFT CBN	FB	CR	FBG SV IO	225 VLVO 12	18000	1 7		23600	26300
	IO 260 VLVO 23800	26400, IO 130D VLVO 27400 30400, IO T138 VLVO 24200 26900								
	IO T200 VLVO 24400	27100, VD T220 CRUS 40100 44500, IO T260 VLVO 24800 27600								
	IO T130D VLVO 28900	32100								
39 3	COASTAL-BARRACUDA	HT	HB	FBG TR SE	205 OMC 12	15000	1 7		25700	28600
	IO 225 VLVO 25800	28700, IO 260 VLVO 26200 29100, IO 130D VLVO 26500 29400								
	IO T138 VLVO 27400	30500, IO T200 VLVO 27800 30900, VD T228 MRCR 27000 30000								
	IO T130D VLVO 29200	32400								
39 3	COASTAL-BARRACUDA	FB	HB	FBG TR SE	205 OMC 12	15000	1 7		25900	28700
	IO 225 VLVO 25900	28800, IO 260 VLVO 26300 29200, IO 130D VLVO 26500 29400								
	IO T138 VLVO 27600	30600, IO T200 VLVO 27900 31000, VD T228 MRCR 27100 30100								
	IO T130D VLVO 29200	32400								
					---- 1982 BOATS ----					
35 3	BARRACUDA	HT	CR	FBG TR IO	225 VLVO 12	15000	1 7		20000	22200
	IO 330 MRCR 20400	22700, IO 130D VLVO 22300 24800, IO T140 VLVO 20300 22600								
	IO T200 VLVO 20800	23100, VD T228 MRCR 25300 28100								
35 3	BARRACUDA	FB	CR	FBG TR IO	225 VLVO 12	15000	1 7		19100	21300
	IO 330 MRCR 20400	22700, IO T200 VLVO 21000 23300, VD T228 MRCR 21000 23300								
35 3	SUPER-BARRACUDA	HT	HB	FBG DV OB	12	14000			22100	24500
35 3	SUPER-BARRACUDA	HT	HB	FBG TR IO	225 VLVO 12	15000	1 7		25400	28200
	IO 330 MRCR 26700	29700, IO 130D VLVO 25500 28300, IO T140 VLVO 27000 30000								
	IO T200 VLVO 27400	30400, VD T228 MRCR 26300 29200								
35 3	SUPER-BARRACUDA	FB	HB	FBG TR IO	225 VLVO 12	15000	1 7		26400	29400
	IO 330 MRCR 26700	29700, IO 130D VLVO 25500 28300, IO T145 VLVO 27000 30000								
	IO T200 VLVO 27100	30100, VD T228 MRCR 30700 34200								
39 3	COASTAL-BARRACUDA	FB	HB	FBG TR OB	12	16000	1 6		23900	26600
	IO 225 VLVO 26600	29500, IO 130D VLVO 26000 28900, IO T200 VLVO 28500 31700								
	IB T228 MRCR 28200	31400								
43	NAUTICA	HT	HB	FBG DV IO	225 14	17000			27500	30500
43	NAUTICA	HT	HB	FBG DV IB	225 14	17000			27400	30500
					---- 1981 BOATS ----					
35 3	BARRACUDA	HT	CR	FBG TR IO	225 VLVO 12	15000	1 7		15900	18100
	IO 330 MRCR 19800	22100, IO 130D VLVO 19000 21100, IO T140 VLVO 22100 24600								
	IO T200 VLVO 20300	22600, VD T228 MRCR 23900 26600								
35 3	BARRACUDA	FB	CR	FBG TR IO	225 VLVO 12	15000	1 7		19300	21400
	IO 330 MRCR 19700	21900, IO 130D VLVO 26300 26200, IO T140 VLVO 21900 24300								
	IO T200 VLVO 20300	22600, VD T228 MRCR 21200 23500								
35 3	SUPER-BARRACUDA	HT	HB	FBG TR IO	225 VLVO 12	15000	1 7		29500	32700
	IB 225 18200	20300, IO 330 MRCR 26700 29600, IO 130D VLVO 28400 31600								
	IO T140 VLVO 23800	26400, IO T200 VLVO 27000 30000, VD T228 MRCR 26200 29100								
35 3	SUPER-BARRACUDA	FB	HB	FBG TR IO	225 VLVO 12	15000	1 7		25400	28200
	IO 330 MRCR 26900	29900, IO 130D VLVO 23200 25800, IO T140 VLVO 24100 26800								
	IO T200 VLVO 27100	30100, VD T228 MRCR 29100 32400								
39 3	COASTAL-BARRACUDA	FB	HB	FBG TR IO	225 VLVO 12	16000	1 7		26100	29000
39 3	COASTAL-BARRACUDA	FB	HB	FBG TR IO	225 VLVO 12	16000	1 8		28100	31200
39 3	COASTAL-BARRACUDA	FB	HB	FBG TR IB T228	MRCR 12	16500	1 9		27800	30900
43	NAUTICA	HT	HB	FBG DV IO	225 14				38300	42600
43	NAUTICA	HT	HB	FBG DV IB	225 14				38400	42600
56	CROWN-ROYAL	FB	CR	F/S CT IB T130D	14	40000	2 2		51900	57900
56	CROWN-ROYAL	MY		FBG CT IB T140	14				74200	81500
					---- 1980 BOATS ----					
35 3	BARRACUDA	HT	CR	FBG TR IO	225 VLVO 12	15000	1 7		19200	21300
	IO 330 MRCR 19700	21900, IO 130D VLVO 21500 23900, IO T140 VLVO 19600 21800								
	IO T200 VLVO 20000	22200, VD T228 MRCR 22900 25500								

```
      LOA  NAME AND/        TOP/ BOAT  -HULL-  ----ENGINE---  BEAM   WGT  DRAFT RETAIL RETAIL
      FT IN  OR MODEL       RIG TYPE   MTL TP TP # HP MFG   FT IN   LBS  FT IN  LOW    HIGH
--------------------- 1980 BOATS ------------------------------------------------------------
 35  3 BARRACUDA            FB  CR    FBG TR IO  225 VLVO 12         15000  1 7  19200 21300
      IO  330  MRCR  19700  21900, IO 130D VLVO  21500 23900, IO T140 VLVO  19600 21800
      IO T200  VLVO  20000  22200, VD T228 MRCR  23000 25500

 35  3 SUPER-BARRACUDA      HT  HB    FBG TR IO  225 VLVO 12         15000  1 7  25000 27700
      IO  330  MRCR  26300  29200, IO 130D VLVO  25000 27800, IO T140 VLVO  26500 29500
      IO T200  VLVO  26900  29800, VD T228 MRCR  25800 28600

 35  3 SUPER-BARRACUDA      FB  HB    FBG TR IO  225 VLVO 12         15000  1 7  24900 27700
      IO  330  MRCR  26200  29200, IO 130D VLVO  25000 27800, IO T140 VLVO  26500 29400
      IO T200  VLVO  26800  29800, VD T228 MRCR  25800 28600

 56    CROWN-ROYAL               CR    FBG CT IO  130      14                     42800 47500
 56    CROWN-ROYAL          FB  CR    F/S CT IB T130D      14         40000  2 2  49600 54500
--------------------- 1979 BOATS ------------------------------------------------------------
 35  3 BARRACUDA            HT  CR    FBG TR IO  225 VLVO 12         15000  1 7  19200 21300
      IO  228  MRCR  19100  21300, IO  330  MRCR  19700 21900, IO T140 VLVO  19600 21800
      IO T200  VLVO  20000  22200, VD T228 MRCR  22000 24400

 35  3 BARRACUDA            FB  CR    FBG TR IO  225 VLVO 12         15000  1 7  19200 21400
      IO  228  MRCR  19200  21300, IO  330  MRCR  19700 21900, IO T140 VLVO  19600 21800
      IO T200  VLVO  20000  22200, VD T228 MRCR  22000 24500

 35  3 SUPER-BARRACUDA      HT  HB    FBG TR IO  225 VLVO 12         15000  1 7  24600 27300
      IO  228  MRCR  24200  26900, IO  330  MRCR  25900 28800, IO T140 VLVO  26100 29000
      IO T200  VLVO  26500  29400, VD T228 MRCR  25400 28300

 35  3 SUPER-BARRACUDA      FB  HB    FBG TR IO  225 VLVO 12         15000  1 7  24500 27300
      IO  228  MRCR  24200  26900, IO  330  MRCR  25900 28700, IO T140 VLVO  26100 29000
      IO T200  VLVO  26400  29400, VD T228 MRCR  25400 28200
--------------------- 1978 BOATS ------------------------------------------------------------
 33    WANDERER II          HT  HB    FBG PN OB       12          7200  1 3  12400 14100
 35  3 BARRACUDA            HT  CR    FBG TR IO  225 VLVO 12       12000  1 7  18000 20000
      IO  228  MRCR  17600  19900, IO T140 VLVO  18500 20500, IO T200 VLVO  18900 21000

 35  3 BARRACUDA            FB  CR    FBG TR IO  225 VLVO 12       12000  1 7  18000 20000
      IO  228  MRCR  17600  19900, IO T140 VLVO  18500 20500, IO T200 VLVO  18900 21000

 42    PENTHOUSE            HT  HB    FBG PN OB       12          9900  1 4  13500 15300
 48    EXECUTIVE            HT  HB    FBG PN OB       12         12200  1 6  14400 16400
 56    CROWN-ROYAL 300      HT  HB    F/S CT VD 225 CHRY 12      20000  2 8  33800 37500
      VD  260  CHRY  33800  37600, VD 105D CHRY  36100 40200, VD 130D CHRY  36400 40500
      VD 200D  CHRY  37300  41400, IO T130 VLVO  35600 39500, IO T170 VLVO  35700 39700

 56    CROWN-ROYAL 300      FB  HB    F/S CT VD 225 CHRY 12      20000  2 8  34100 37900
      VD  260  CHRY  34200  38000, VD 105D CHRY  36200 40200, VD 130D CHRY  36500 40600
      VD 200D  CHRY  37300  41500, IO T130 VLVO  35900 39900, IO T170 VLVO  36000 40000

 56    CROWN-ROYAL 400      HT  HB    F/S CT VD 225 CHRY 12      20000  2 8  34200 38000
      VD  260  CHRY  34200  38000, VD 105D CHRY  36500 40600, VD 130D CHRY  36800 40900
      VD 200D  CHRY  37600  41800, IO T130 VLVO  36000 40000, IO T170 VLVO  36100 40100

 56    CROWN-ROYAL 400      FB  HB    F/S CT VD 225 CHRY 12      20000  2 8  34500 38300
      VD  260  CHRY  34500  38300, VD 105D CHRY  36600 40600, VD 130D CHRY  36800 40900
      VD 200D  CHRY  37700  41800, IO T130 VLVO  36300 40300, IO T170 VLVO  36400 40500

 56    CROWN-ROYAL 500      HT  HB    F/S CT VD 225 CHRY 12      20000  2 8  34700 38600
      VD  260  CHRY  34800  38700, VD 105D CHRY  37100 41200, VD 130D CHRY  37300 41500
      VD 200D  CHRY  38200  42400, IO T130 VLVO  36700 40800, IO T170 VLVO  36800 40900

 56    CROWN-ROYAL 500      FB  HB    F/S CT VD 225 CHRY 12      20000  2 8  35000 38900
      VD  260  CHRY  35000  38900, VD 105D CHRY  37100 41200, VD 130D CHRY  37400 41500
      VD 200D  CHRY  38200  42400, IO T130 VLVO  36900 41000, IO T170 VLVO  37000 41100

 56    CROWN-ROYAL 600&700  HT  HB    F/S CT VD 225 CHRY 12      20000  2 8  35000 38900
      VD  260  CHRY  35100  39000, VD 105D CHRY  37400 41500, VD 130D CHRY  37600 41800
      VD 200D  CHRY  38400  42700, IO T130 VLVO  37000 41100, IO T170 VLVO  37100 41200

 56    CROWN-ROYAL 600&700  FB  HB    F/S CT VD 225 CHRY 12      20000  2 8  35300 39200
      VD  260  CHRY  35300  39200, VD 105D CHRY  37300 41400, VD 130D CHRY  37600 41800
      VD 200D  CHRY  38400  42700, IO T130 VLVO  37200 41400, IO T170 VLVO  37300 41500
--------------------- 1977 BOATS ------------------------------------------------------------
 33    WANDERER II          HT  HB    FBG PN         12          7200  1 3  12300 13900
 42    BARRACUDA            HT  CR    FBG    IO  225 CHRY 12     12000  1 2  18200 20200
 42    PENTHOUSE            HT  HB    FBG PN         12          9900  1 4  13300 15200
 48    EXECUTIVE            HT  HB    FBG PN         12         12200  1 6  14200 16200
 56    CROWN-ROYAL 300      HT  HB    F/S CT VD 225 CHRY 12      20000  2 8  33400 37100
      VD  260  CHRY  33400  37100, VD 105D CHRY  35700 39700, VD 130D CHRY  36000 40000
      VD 200D  CHRY  36800  40900, IO T130 VLVO  35100 39000, IO T170 VLVO  35300 39200

 56    CROWN-ROYAL 300      FB  HB    F/S CT VD 225 CHRY 12      20000  2 8  33700 37500
      VD  260  CHRY  33800  37500, VD 105D CHRY  35800 39700, VD 130D CHRY  36100 40100
      VD 200D  CHRY  36900  41000, IO T130 VLVO  35500 39400, IO T170 VLVO  35600 39600

 56    CROWN-ROYAL 400      HT  HB    F/S CT VD 225 CHRY 12      20000  2 8  33800 37500
      VD  260  CHRY  33800  37600, VD 105D CHRY  36100 40100, VD 130D CHRY  36400 40400
      VD 200D  CHRY  37200  41300, IO T130 VLVO  35600 39600, IO T170 VLVO  35700 39700

 56    CROWN-ROYAL 400      FB  HB    F/S CT VD 225 CHRY 12      20000  2 8  34100 37800
      VD  260  CHRY  34100  37900, VD 105D CHRY  36100 40100, VD 130D CHRY  36400 40400
      VD 200D  CHRY  37200  41400, IO T130 VLVO  35900 39900, IO T170 VLVO  36000 40000

 56    CROWN-ROYAL 500      HT  HB    F/S CT VD 225 CHRY 12      20000  2 8  34300 38100
      VD  260  CHRY  34400  38200, VD 105D CHRY  36700 40700, VD 130D CHRY  36900 41000
      VD 200D  CHRY  37700  41900, IO T130 VLVO  36200 40300, IO T170 VLVO  36300 40400

 56    CROWN-ROYAL 500      FB  HB    F/S CT VD 225 CHRY 12      20000  2 8  34600 38400
      VD  260  CHRY  34600  38500, VD 105D CHRY  36600 40700, VD 130D CHRY  36900 41000
      VD 200D  CHRY  37700  41900, IO T130 VLVO  36500 40600, IO T170 VLVO  36600 40700

 56    CROWN-ROYAL 600&700  HT  HB    F/S CT VD 225 CHRY 12      20000  2 8  34600 38400
      VD  260  CHRY  34700  38500, VD 105D CHRY  36900 41000, VD 130D CHRY  37200 41300
      VD 200D  CHRY  38000  42200, IO T130 VLVO  36600 40600, IO T170 VLVO  36600 40700

 56    CROWN-ROYAL 600&700  FB  HB    F/S CT VD 225 CHRY 12      20000  2 8  34800 38700
      VD  260  CHRY  34900  38800, VD 105D CHRY  36900 40900, VD 130D CHRY  37100 41300
      VD 200D  CHRY  38000  42200, IO T130 VLVO  36800 40900, IO T170 VLVO  36800 41000
--------------------- 1976 BOATS ------------------------------------------------------------
 33    WANDERER II          HT  HB    FBG PN OB       12          6200  10   10400 11800
 42    PENTHOUSE            HT  HB    FBG PN OB       12          8900  1    11500 13100
 48    EXECUTIVE 300        HT  HB    FBG PN OB       12         11200  1 3  12200 13800
 56    CROWN-ROYAL 300      HT  HB    F/S CT VD 225 CHRY 12      20000  2 8  32900 36500
      VD  300  CHRY  33100  36800, VD 105D CHRY  35200 39100, VD 130D CHRY  35500 39400
      IO T130  VLVO  34600  38500, IO T170 VLVO  34700 38600

 56    CROWN-ROYAL 300      FB  HB    F/S CT VD 225 CHRY 12      20000  2 8  33200 36900
      VD  300  CHRY  33400  37100, VD 105D CHRY  35300 39200, VD 130D CHRY  35600 39500
      IO T130  VLVO  35000  38900, IO T170 VLVO  35100 39000

 56    CROWN-ROYAL 400      HT  HB    F/S CT VD 225 CHRY 12      20000  2 8  33300 37000
      VD  300  CHRY  33500  37200, VD 105D CHRY  35600 39500, VD 130D CHRY  35900 39800
      IO T130  VLVO  35100  39000, IO T170 VLVO  35200 39100

 56    CROWN-ROYAL 400      FB  HB    F/S CT VD 225 CHRY 12      20000  2 8  33600 37300
      VD  300  CHRY  33800  37500, VD 105D CHRY  35600 39500, VD 130D CHRY  35900 39900
      IO T130  VLVO  35400  39300, IO T170 VLVO  35500 39400

 56    CROWN-ROYAL 500      HT  HB    F/S CT VD 225 CHRY 12      20000  2 8  33700 37600
      VD  300  CHRY  34000  37800, VD 105D CHRY  36200 40200, VD 130D CHRY  36400 40400
      IO T130  VLVO  35700  39700, IO T170 VLVO  35800 39800

 56    CROWN-ROYAL 500      FB  HB    F/S CT VD 225 CHRY 12      20000  2 8  34100 37900
      VD  300  CHRY  34300  38100, VD 105D CHRY  36100 40100, VD 130D CHRY  36400 40500
      IO T130  VLVO  36000  40000, IO T170 VLVO  36100 40100

 56    CROWN-ROYAL 600      HT  HB    F/S CT VD 225 CHRY 12      20000  2 8  34100 37900
      VD  300  CHRY  34300  38100, VD 105D CHRY  36400 40500, VD 130D CHRY  36700 40700
      IO T130  VLVO  36000  40000, IO T170 VLVO  36100 40100

 56    CROWN-ROYAL 600      FB  HB    F/S CT VD 225 CHRY 12      20000  2 8  34400 38200
      VD  300  CHRY  34600  38400, VD 105D CHRY  36400 40400, VD 130D CHRY  36700 40700
      IO T130  VLVO  36300  40300, IO T170 VLVO  36300 40400

 56    CROWN-ROYAL 700      HT  HB    F/S CT VD 225 CHRY 12      20000  2 8  34100 37900
      VD  300  CHRY  34300  38100, VD 105D CHRY  36400 40500, VD 130D CHRY  36700 40700
      IO T130  VLVO  36000  40000, IO T170 VLVO  36100 40100

 56    CROWN-ROYAL 700      FB  HB    F/S CT VD 225 CHRY 12      20000  2 8  34400 38200
      VD  300  CHRY  34600  38400, VD 105D CHRY  36400 40400, VD 130D CHRY  36700 40700
      IO T130  VLVO  36300  40300, IO T170 VLVO  36300 40400
--------------------- 1975 BOATS ------------------------------------------------------------
 33    WANDERER II          HT  HB    FBG PN OB       12          6200  10   10300 11700
 42    PENTHOUSE            HT  HB    FBG PN OB       12          8900  1    11400 13000
 42    PENTHOUSE            HT  HB    FBG PN IO  130 VLVO 12      8900  1    13100 14900
 48    EXECUTIVE 300        HT  HB    FBG PN OB       12         11200  1 3  11600 13200
 48    EXECUTIVE 300        HT  HB    FBG PN IO  130 VLVO 12     11200  1 3  13000 14700
```

LOA FT IN	NAME AND/OR MODEL	TOP/RIG	BOAT TYPE	HULL MTL	HULL TP	ENG TP	#	HP	MFG	BEAM FT IN	WGT LBS	DRAFT FT IN	RETAIL LOW	RETAIL HIGH
1975 BOATS														
48	EXECUTIVE 300	HT	HB	FBG	PN	IO		T130	CHRY	12	11200	1 3	13800	15700
48	EXECUTIVE 400	HT	HB	FBG	PN	OB				12	11200	1 3	12200	13800
48	EXECUTIVE 400	HT	HB	FBG	PN	IO		130	VLVO	12	11200	1 3	13500	15300
48	EXECUTIVE 400	HT	HB	FBG	PN	IO		T130	CHRY	12	11200	1 3	14400	16300
48	EXECUTIVE 500	HT	HB	FBG	PN	OB				12	11200	1 3	12300	14000
48	EXECUTIVE 500	HT	HB	FBG	PN	IO		130	VLVO	12	11200	1 3	13600	15500
48	EXECUTIVE 500	HT	HB	FBG	PN	IO		T130	CHRY	12	11200	1 3	14500	16500
56	CROWN-ROYAL 300	HT	HB	FBG	CT	VD		100D	NISS	14	16000	1 6	26400	29300
56	CROWN-ROYAL 300	HT	HB	FBG	CT	IO		T130	CHRY	14	16000	1 6	25400	28300
56	CROWN-ROYAL 300	HT	HB	FBG	CT	IO		T170	VLVO	14	16000	1 6	26100	29000
56	CROWN-ROYAL 300	FB	HB	FBG	CT	VD		100D	NISS	14	16000	1 6	26500	29400
56	CROWN-ROYAL 300	FB	HB	FBG	CT	IO		T130	CHRY	14	16000	1 6	25800	28600
56	CROWN-ROYAL 300	FB	HB	FBG	CT	IO		T170	VLVO	14	16000	1 6	26400	29300
56	CROWN-ROYAL 400	HT	HB	FBG	CT	VD		100D	NISS	14	16000	1 6	26700	29700
56	CROWN-ROYAL 400	HT	HB	FBG	CT	IO		T130	CHRY	14	16000	1 6	25800	28600
56	CROWN-ROYAL 400	HT	HB	FBG	CT	IO		T170	VLVO	14	16000	1 6	26400	29300
56	CROWN-ROYAL 400	FB	HB	FBG	CT	VD		100D	NISS	14	16000	1 6	26700	29700
56	CROWN-ROYAL 400	FB	HB	FBG	CT	IO		T130	CHRY	14	16000	1 6	26100	29000
56	CROWN-ROYAL 400	FB	HB	FBG	CT	IO		T170	VLVO	14	16000	1 6	26700	29700
56	CROWN-ROYAL 500	HT	HB	FBG	CT	VD		100D	NISS	14	16000	1 6	27100	30200
56	CROWN-ROYAL 500	HT	HB	FBG	CT	IO		T130	CHRY	14	16000	1 6	26300	29200
56	CROWN-ROYAL 500	HT	HB	FBG	CT	IO		T170	VLVO	14	16000	1 6	26900	29900
56	CROWN-ROYAL 500	FB	HB	FBG	CT	VD		100D	NISS	14	16000	1 6	27100	30100
56	CROWN-ROYAL 500	FB	HB	FBG	CT	IO		T130	CHRY	14	16000	1 6	26500	29500
56	CROWN-ROYAL 500	FB	HB	FBG	CT	IO		T170	VLVO	14	16000	1 6	27100	30100
56	CROWN-ROYAL 600	HT	HB	FBG	CT	VD		100D	NISS	14	16000	1 6	27400	30400
56	CROWN-ROYAL 600	HT	HB	FBG	CT	IO		T130	CHRY	14	16000	1 6	26500	29400
56	CROWN-ROYAL 600	HT	HB	FBG	CT	IO		T170	VLVO	14	16000	1 6	27100	30100
56	CROWN-ROYAL 600	FB	HB	FBG	CT	VD		100D	NISS	14	16000	1 6	27300	30300
56	CROWN-ROYAL 600	FB	HB	FBG	CT	IO		T130	CHRY	14	16000	1 6	26700	29700
56	CROWN-ROYAL 600	FB	HB	FBG	CT	IO		T170	VLVO	14	16000	1 6	27300	30400
1974 BOATS														
33	WANDERER II		HB	FBG		OB				10	6200	10	10200	11500
39	PENTHOUSE		HB	FBG		OB				10	7100	11	10800	12300
39	PENTHOUSE		HB	FBG		IO		T120	MRCR	12		11	28300	31400
39	PENTHOUSE		HB	FBG		IO		T170	CHRY	12		11	28400	31500
41	5TH-AVENUE	HT	HB	FBG		OB				12	8900	1	11900	13600
41	5TH-AVENUE	HT	HB	FBG		IO		T 90	OMC	12		1	24400	27100
41	5TH-AVENUE	HT	HB	FBG		IO		T130	CHRY	12		1	24600	27300
47	EXECUTIVE		HB	FBG		OB				12	11000	1 5	12000	13700
47	EXECUTIVE		HB	FBG		IO		T 90	OMC	12		1 5	39300	43700
47	EXECUTIVE		HB	FBG		IO		T130	CHRY	12		1 5	20300	22500
51	CROWN-ROYAL CAT	HT	HB	FBG		IO		T130	CHRY	12 9	14000	1 6	19800	22000
51	CROWN-ROYAL CAT	FB	HB	FBG		IO		T130	CHRY	12 9	14000	1 6	21100	23400
54	CROWN-ROYAL		HB	FBG	CT	IO		T185		14		1 8	60600	66600
1973 BOATS														
33	WANDERER II		HB	STL		OB				10	6200	10	9800	11100
39	PENTHOUSE		HB	STL		OB				10	7100	11	10400	11800
39	PENTHOUSE		HB	STL		IO		T120	MRCR	12		11	24100	26700
41	5TH-AVENUE		HB	STL		OB				12	8900	1	12500	14200
41	5TH-AVENUE	HT	HB	STL		IO		T130	CHRY	12		1	21800	24200
47	EXECUTIVE		HB	STL		OB				12	11000	1 5	**	**
47	EXECUTIVE		HB	STL		IO		T130	CHRY	12		1 5	**	**
51	CROWN-ROYAL CAT	HT	HB	STL		IO		T130	CHRY	12 9	14000	1 6	19600	21800
1972 BOATS														
33	WANDERER II		HB	STL		OB				10	6200	10	9700	11000
39	PENTHOUSE		HB	STL		OB				10	7100	11	10300	11700
39	PENTHOUSE		HB	STL		IO		T120	MRCR	12		11	23900	26500
41	5TH-AVENUE		HB	STL		OB				10	8900	1	12400	14100
41	5TH-AVENUE	HT	HB	STL		IO		T 90	OMC	10		1	21500	23900
41	5TH-AVENUE	HT	HB	STL		IO		T130	CHRY	10		1	21600	24000
47	EXECUTIVE		HB	STL		OB				12	11000	1 5	**	**
47	EXECUTIVE		HB	STL		IO		T 90	OMC	12		1 5	**	**
47	EXECUTIVE		HB	STL		IO		T130	CHRY	12		1 5	**	**
51	CROWN-ROYAL CAT	HT	HB	STL		IO		T130	CHRY	12 9	14000	1 6	19500	21600
1971 BOATS														
28	WANDERER II		HB	STL		OB				10	6200	10	**	**
39	PENTHOUSE		HB	AL		OB				10	7100	11	10500	11900
39	PENTHOUSE		HB	STL		OB				10	6500	11	9400	10700
41	5TH-AVENUE	HT	HB	AL		OB				10	8900	1	11600	13200
41	5TH-AVENUE	HT	HB	STL		OB				10	8900	1	12300	14000
47	EXECUTIVE		HB	AL		IO		T 80	OMC	12	13987	1 3	20000	22200
51	EXECUTIVE CAT		HB	STL		IO		T130	CHRY	12	15000	1 5	**	**
51	4 CROWN-ROYAL		HB			IO		T130	CHRY	11 9	14000	1 6	20100	22400
1970 BOATS														
28	WANDERER II	HT	HB	AL	PN	OB				10	5000	10	**	**
28	WANDERER II	HT	HB	STL	PN	OB				10	5000	10	**	**
31	WANDERER	HT	HB	AL	PN	OB					4100	11	5400	6200
39	PENTHOUSE	HT	HB	AL	PN	OB				10	6500	11	9600	10900
39	PENTHOUSE	HT	HB	STL	PN	OB				10	6500	11	9700	11000
39	PENTHOUSE	HT	HB	STL	PN	IO		120		12	7300	1 1	12400	14100
39	PENTHOUSE	HT	HB	STL	PN	IO		T 80		10		1 1	24500	27200
42	5TH-AVENUE	HT	HB	AL	PN	OB				10	7200	1 1	8000	9200
42	5TH-AVENUE	HT	HB	STL	PN	OB				10	7200	1 1	10700	12100
42	RENTAL BOAT	HT	HB	STL	PN	OB				12	8000	1	11600	13200
42	RENTAL BOAT	HT	HB	STL	PN	IO		120		12	8000	1	13400	15200
48	EXECUTIVE	HT	HB	AL	PN	IO		T 80	OMC	12	11500	1 3	14100	16000
48	EXECUTIVE	HT	HB	AL	PN	IO		T 80	OMC	12	11500	1 3	**	**
51	EXECUTIVE CAT	HT	HB	AL	PN	IO		T130	CHRY	12	15000	1 5	20700	22900
51	3 CROWN-ROYAL	HT	HB	STL	TR			130		13 1	15000	1 6	**	**
1969 BOATS														
31	WANDERER I	HT	HB	STL	PN	OB				8	4100	11	5350	6150
31	WANDERER I	HT	HB	STL	PN	OB				10	4500	10	6300	7250
39	PENTHOUSE	HT	HB	STL	PN	OB				10	7000	11	10300	11700
	OB 10700 12200, IO 120 — 12000 13700, IO 120												12300	14000
	IO T 80 13200 15000													
42	FIFTH-AVENUE	HT	HB	STL	PN	IO				10	7200	1	12300	14000
42	RENTAL BOAT	HT	HB	STL	PN	IO				12	8000	1	11600	13200
42	RENTAL BOAT	HT	HB	STL	PN	IO		120		12	8000	1	13300	15100
47	EXECUTIVE	HT	HB	STL	PN	IO		T 80		12	11500	1 3	**	**
47	EXECUTIVE	HT	HB	STL	PN	IB		T290	OMC	12	11000	1 1	**	**
1968 BOATS														
31	WANDERER I		HB	STL	PN	OB				10	4500	11	6250	7200
39	PENTHOUSE		HB	STL	PN	OB				10	7000	11	10200	11600
47	EXECUTIVE		HB	STL	PN	IB		T290	OMC	12	11000	1	**	**
1967 BOATS														
31	WANDERER I		HB	STL	PN	OB				10	4500	11	6200	7150
39	PENTHOUSE		HB	STL	PN	OB				10	7000	11	10200	11600
47	EXECUTIVE		HB	STL	PN	IB		T290	OMC	12	11000	11	**	**
1966 BOATS														
28	WANDERER		HB	STL	PN	OB				8	3500		**	**
36	PENTHOUSE		HB	STL	PN	OB				10	7000		10100	11500
1965 BOATS														
28	WANDERER		HB	STL	PN	OB				8	3500		**	**
36	PENTHOUSE		HB	STL	PN	OB				10	7000		10100	11400

HOLIDAY YACHT SALES INC

Call 1-800-327-6929 for BUC Personalized Evaluation Service
Or, for 1965 boats, sign onto www.BUCValuPro.com

HOLIDAY YACHTS INC

Call 1-800-327-6929 for BUC Personalized Evaluation Service
Or, for 1959 to 1968 boats, sign onto www.BUCValuPro.com

HOLLAND ARK CO

Call 1-800-327-6929 for BUC Personalized Evaluation Service
Or, for 1966 to 1967 boats, sign onto www.BUCValuPro.com

HOLLAND BOAT B V
NEPTUNUS SHIPYARD B V

Call 1-800-327-6929 for BUC Personalized Evaluation Service
Or, for 1980 to 1983 boats, sign onto www.BUCValuPro.com

HOLLAND BOATS LTD
COAST GUARD MFG ID- ZHO

Call 1-800-327-6929 for BUC Personalized Evaluation Service
Or, for 1979 boats, sign onto www.BUCValuPro.com

HOLLAND'S BOAT SHOP
COAST GUARD MFG ID- HLG

Call 1-800-327-6929 for BUC Personalized Evaluation Service
Or, for 1982 to 1983 boats, sign onto www.BUCValuPro.com

HOLLANDIA YACHTS INC
CONTEST YACHTS
MAMARONECK NY 10543   COAST GUARD MFG ID- HLH   See inside cover to adjust price for area

LOA FT IN	NAME AND/ OR MODEL	TOP/ RIG	BOAT TYPE	-HULL- MTL TP	ENGINE TP # HP MFG	BEAM FT IN	WGT LBS	DRAFT FT IN	RETAIL LOW	RETAIL HIGH
			1970 BOATS							
23 7	CONTEST 24	SLP	SA/CR FBG KL			7 6	3600	2 5	5800	6650
40	CONTEST 40	YWL	SA/CR FBG KL	36		11 6	15400	4 9	38900	43200

JOHN HOLMES INC

Call 1-800-327-6929 for BUC Personalized Evaluation Service
Or, for 1967 boats, sign onto www.BUCValuPro.com

HONNOR MARINE UK LTD
DARTINGTON   See inside cover to adjust price for area
TOTNES DEVON ENGLAND TQ COAST GUARD MFG ID- HNR

For more recent years, see the BUC Used Boat Price Guide, Volume 1 or Volume 2

LOA FT IN	NAME AND/ OR MODEL	TOP/ RIG	BOAT TYPE	-HULL- MTL TP	ENGINE TP # HP MFG	BEAM FT IN	WGT LBS	DRAFT FT IN	RETAIL LOW	RETAIL HIGH
			1983 BOATS							
18 9	LUGGER	YWL	SAIL FBG CB OB			6 3	850	10	4450	5100
21 6	DRIFTER	YWL	SAIL FBG BB IB		6D BMW	7 3	2000	2	10000	11400
21 6	DRIFTER	YWL	SAIL FBG CB OB			7 3	2000	2	7900	9100
21 9	COASTER	YWL	SAIL FBG CB OB			6 7	1060	1	5950	6850
21 9	LONGBOAT	YWL	SAIL FBG CB OB			6 7	880	1	5600	6450
			1982 BOATS							
18 9	LUGGER	YWL	SAIL FBG CB OB			6 3	850	10	4150	4800
21 6	DRIFTER	YWL	SAIL FBG BB IB		6D BMW	7 3	2000	2	9450	10700
21 6	DRIFTER	YWL	SAIL FBG CB OB			7 3	2000	2	7450	8550
21 9	COASTER	YWL	SAIL FBG CB OB			6 7	1060	1	5600	6450
21 9	LONGBOAT	YWL	SAIL FBG CB OB			6 7	880	1	5250	6050
			1981 BOATS							
18 9	LUGGER	YWL	SAIL FBG CB OB			6 3	850	10	3900	4500
21 6	DRIFTER	YWL	SAIL FBG BB IB			7 3	2000	2	7000	8050
21 6	DRIFTER	YWL	SAIL FBG BB IB		6D BMW	7 3	2000	2	8950	10200
21 9	COASTER	YWL	SAIL FBG CB OB			6 7	1060	1	5300	6050
21 9	LONGBOAT	YWL	SAIL FBG CB OB			6 7	880	1	4950	5700
			1980 BOATS							
18 9	LUGGER	YWL	SAIL FBG CB OB			6 3	850		3700	4300
21 6	DRIFTER	YWL	SAIL FBG BB IB			7 3	2000	2	6700	7650
21 6	DRIFTER	YWL	SAIL FBG BB IB		6D BMW	7 3	2000	2	8450	9700
21 9	COASTER	YWL	SAIL FBG CB OB			6 7	1060		5050	5800
21 9	LONGBOAT	YWL	SAIL FBG CB OB			6 7	880		4750	5450
			1979 BOATS							
18	DRIVER	YWL	SAIL FBG KL IB		D	6 1	730	1 5	6100	7050
18 9	LUGGER	YWL	SAIL FBG CB OB			6 3	850	10	3600	4150
21 6	DRIFTER	YWL	SAIL FBG KL IB			7 3	2000	2	6400	7400
21 6	DRIFTER	YWL	SAIL FBG KL IB		8D SAAB	7 3	2000	2	8200	9400
21 9	COASTER	YWL	SAIL FBG CB OB			6 7	1060	1	4850	5550
21 9	LONGBOAT	YWL	SAIL FBG CB OB			6 7	880	1	4600	5250
			1978 BOATS							
18	DRIVER	YWL	SAIL FBG KL IB		3D- 6D	6 1	730	1 5	5300	6250
18 9	LUGGER	YWL	SAIL FBG CB OB			6 3	850	10	3450	4000
21 6	DRIFTER	YWL	SA/CR FBG KL IB			7 3	2000	2	6200	7100
21 6	DRIFTER	YWL	SA/CR FBG KL IB		10D SABB	7 3	2000	2	8000	9150
21 9	CUDDY LONGBOAT	YWL	SA/CR FBG CB OB			6 7	1060	1	4650	5350
21 9	OPEN LONGBOAT	YWL	SAIL FBG CB OB			6 7	880	1	4400	5100
			1977 BOATS							
18	DRIVER	YWL	SAIL FBG KL IB		3D- 5D	6 1	800	1 5	5250	6100
18 9	LUGGER	YWL	SAIL FBG CB OB		3D WATE	6 3	850	10	5300	6100
21 9	CRUISER LONGBOAT	YWL	SAIL FBG CB OB			6 7	1200	1	4700	5450
21 9	OPEN LONGBOAT	YWL	SAIL FBG CB OB			6 7	1050	1	4500	5200
			1975 BOATS							
18	DRIVER	YWL	SAIL FBG KL IB		3D- 5D	6 1	800	1 5	4900	5750
18 9	LUGGER	YWL	SAIL FBG CB OB			6 3	850	10	3150	3650
21 9	LONGBOAT CRUISER	YWL	SAIL FBG CB OB			6 7	1200	1	4500	5150
21 9	LONGBOAT OPEN	YWL	SAIL FBG CB OB			6 7	1050	1	4200	4900
30	OCEAN-BIRD	SLP	SAIL FBG TM IB		33D	22 7	8000	2 3	35300	39200
			1974 BOATS							
18 9	DRASCOMBE LUGGER	YWL	SA/OD FBG CB OB			6 3	850	4	3050	3550
21 9	DRASCOMBE LONG BOAT		SAIL FBG CB OB			6 7	1100	4 2	4150	4850
30	OCEAN-BIRD		SAIL FBG TM IB		39D WATE	22 9	7200	2 9	33400	37100
			1973 BOATS							
18 9	DRASCOMBE LUGGER	YWL	SA/OD FBG CB OB			6 3	850	4	2950	3450
21 9	DRASCOMBE LONG BOAT		SAIL FBG CB OB			6 7	1100	4 2	4050	4700
30	OCEAN-BIRD		SAIL FBG TM IB		D		7200	2 9	32600	36200
			1972 BOATS							
18 9	DRASCOMBE LUGGER	YWL	SA/OD FBG CB			6 3	1000		3100	3650
18 9	DRASCOMBE LUGGER	YWL	SA/OD FBG CB IB			6 3		10	5850	6700
21 9	DRASCOMBE LONGBOAT	YWL	SA/OD FBG CB			6 7	1300		4250	4950
21 9	DRASCOMBE LONGBT CR	YWL	SAIL FBG CB IB			6 7		1	7850	9000
21 9	DRASCOMBE OP LONGBT	YWL	SAIL FBG CB			6 7			6050	6950
30	OCEAN BIRD	SLP	SA/CR FBG TM IB		33	22 7	8000	2 3	32800	36400
			1971 BOATS							
18 9	DRASCOMBE LUGGER	YWL	SAIL FBG CB OB			6 3		10	2700	3150
21 9	DRASCOMBE LONGBOAT	YWL	SAIL FBG CB OB			6 10		1	3750	4350
30	OCEAN-BIRD	SLP	SA/CR FBG TM IB			22 7	7200	2 2	31200	34700
			1970 BOATS							
18 9	DRASCOMBE LUGGER	YWL	SAIL FBG CB			6 3		10	2650	3100
30	OCEAN-BIRD	SLP	SA/CR FBG TM			22 7		2 2	29600	32900

HOOKS YACHT & MARINE INC

Call 1-800-327-6929 for BUC Personalized Evaluation Service
Or, for 1982 boats, sign onto www.BUCValuPro.com

HORIZON ENTERPRISES

Call 1-800-327-6929 for BUC Personalized Evaluation Service
Or, for 1970 to 1972 boats, sign onto www.BUCValuPro.com

HORIZON MFG INC
COAST GUARD MFG ID- HFB

Call 1-800-327-6929 for BUC Personalized Evaluation Service
Or, for 1979 boats, sign onto www.BUCValuPro.com

HORIZON YACHT & MARINE CO
CLEARWATER FL 33520   COAST GUARD MFG ID- HXY See inside cover to adjust price for area

For more recent years, see the BUC Used Boat Price Guide, Volume 1 or Volume 2

LOA FT IN	NAME AND/ OR MODEL	TOP/ RIG	BOAT TYPE	-HULL- MTL TP	ENGINE TP # HP MFG	BEAM FT IN	WGT LBS	DRAFT FT IN	RETAIL LOW	RETAIL HIGH
			1982 BOATS							
25 10	HORIZON 26	SLP	SA/CR FBG KL OB			7 11	4225	2 1	7150	8200
38 7	HORIZON 39	SLP	SA/CR FBG KC IB		42D PATH	11 2	18700	4	41000	45600
39 7	HORIZON 39	KTH	SA/CR FBG KC IB		42D PATH	11 2	18700	4	43000	47800
			1981 BOATS							
38 7	HORIZON 39	SLP	SA/CR FBG KC IB		50D PATH	11 2	18700	4	38600	42900
39 7	HORIZON 39	KTH	SA/CR FBG KC IB		50D PATH	11 2	18700	4	40600	45100
			1980 BOATS							
38 7	HORIZON 39	SLP	SA/CR FBG KC IB		50D PATH	11 2	18700	4	36900	41000

HOTFOOT BOATS
COAST GUARD MFG ID- ZHV

Call 1-800-327-6929 for BUC Personalized Evaluation Service
Or, for 1983 to 1987 boats, sign onto www.BUCValuPro.com

HOULTON BOAT CO

Call 1-800-327-6929 for BUC Personalized Evaluation Service
Or, for 1980 to 1981 boats, sign onto www.BUCValuPro.com

HOWIE CRAFT INC
COAST GUARD MFG ID- HWC

Call 1-800-327-6929 for BUC Personalized Evaluation Service
Or, for 1975 to 1986 boats, sign onto www.BUCValuPro.com

HUCKINS YACHT CORP
FAIRFORM-FLYER
JACKSONVILLE FL 32210   COAST GUARD MFG ID- HNS

See inside cover to adjust price for area

For more recent years, see the BUC Used Boat Price Guide, Volume 1 or Volume 2

LOA FT IN	NAME AND/OR MODEL	TOP/RIG	BOAT TYPE	HULL MTL	HULL TP	ENG TP	# HP	MFG	BEAM FT IN	WGT LBS	DRAFT FT IN	RETAIL LOW	RETAIL HIGH
1983 BOATS													
58	KIRKLINE 58	FB	SF	F/S	DV	IB	T450D	CUM	16 3	40000	3 6	282000	309500
74	FAIRFORM FLYER	HT	SPTCR	F/S	SV	IB	T	D	17 6	80000	4 4	**	**
1980 BOATS													
48	CEDAN	FB	SDN	F/S	SV	IB	T400D	J&T	16		3 10	160000	175500
48	SPORT CRUISER		SPTCR	F/W	SV	IB	T	D	16			**	**
53	OFFSHORE		OFF	F/W	SV	IB	T325D		15 1			221000	242500
54	SPORT CRUISER		SPTCR	F/W	SV	IB	T	D	16			**	**
56	SPORTSMAN		SF	F/W	SV	IB	T350D		15 1			273500	300500
58	OFFSHORE		CR	F/W	SV	IB	T325D		15 1			252500	277500
60	OFFSHORE		CR	F/W	SV	IB	T480D		15 1			253000	278000
65	OUT-ISLANDER		CR	F/W	SV	IB	T460D		17 4			623500	685000
65	SPORT CRUISER		SPTCR	F/W	SV	IB	T650D		17 4			405500	445500
72	MOTOR YACHT		MY	F/W	SV	IB	T650D		20			**	**
72	MOTOR YACHT		MY	F/S	SV	IB	T800D	MTI			5	**	**
72	SPORTSMAN		SF	F/W	SV	IB	T650D		19 5			**	**
76	MOTOR YACHT		MY	F/W	SV	IB	T650D		19 5			**	**
76	SPORTSMAN		SF	F/W	SV	IB	T650D		19 5			**	**
1979 BOATS													
54	SPORTSMAN		SDN	F/S	SV	IB	T400D	J&T	16		4	242500	266500
1978 BOATS													
54	SPORTSMAN		EXP	F/S	SV	IB	T500D	GM	16		4	236500	260000
1977 BOATS													
78	MOTOR YACHT		MY	F/S		IB	T650D		19 5		3 10	**	**
1975 BOATS													
36	SPORTS FISHERMAN	FB	SF			IB	T225D	CAT	13		2 10	85500	94000
50	SPORTS FISHERMAN	FB	SF	FBG		IB	T425D	GM	14		3 9	172000	189000
1974 BOATS													
65	OFF SHORE	FB	OFF	F/W		IB	T500D	CAT	17 4		4 4	310500	341000
1973 BOATS													
40	SPORTSMAN	FB	SDN	F/W	SV	IB	T225D		12 1		2 4	134000	147500
50 6	ATLANTIC	FB	CR	F/W	SV	IB	T370D	CUM	15 1		3 4	124000	136500
58 8	LINWOOD	FB	CR	F/W	SV	IB	T370D	CUM	16 1		3 10	205500	226000
76	SPORTSMAN		SF	F/W	SV	IB	T595D		19 5		5 2	**	**
1972 BOATS													
53 6	CORINTHIAN	FB	CR	F/W		IB	T	GM	15 1		3 6	**	**
58	SPORTSMAN	FB	SF	F/W		IB	T		16 1		3 10	**	**
1971 BOATS													
40	SPORTSMAN		SF	F/W		IB	T215D		12 1		3 4	119500	131500
40	SPORTSMAN		SF	F/W		IB	T300D		12 1		2 4	124000	136500
46 3			SDN	F/W		IB	T283D		13 11		2 8	86500	95100
46 3			SDN	F/W		IB	T370D		13 11		2 8	97700	107500
50 6	ATLANTIC		CR	F/W		IB	T283D		15 1		3 4	105000	115500
50 6	ATLANTIC		CR	F/W		IB	T370D		15 1		3 4	115500	127000
50 6	LINWOOD		CR	F/W		IB	T283D		15 1		3 4	105000	115500
50 6	SPORTSMAN		SF	F/W		IB	T283D		14 3		3 4	125000	137000
50 6	SPORTSMAN		SF	F/W		IB	T370D		14 3		3 4	141500	155500
53 6	ATLANTIC		SF	F/W		IB	T350D		15 1		3 6	176000	193500
53 6	ATLANTIC		SF	F/W		IB	T370D		15 1		3 6	178000	195500
53 6	CORINTHIAN		CR	F/W		IB	T350D		15 1		3 6	142000	156000
53 6	CORINTHIAN		CR	F/W		IB	T370D		15 1		3 6	144000	158000
53 6	LINWOOD		CR	F/W		IB	T350D		15 1		3 6	142000	156000
53 6	LINWOOD		CR	F/W		IB	T370D		15 1		3 6	144000	158000
53 6	SPORTSMAN		SF	F/W		IB	T370D		15 1		2 4	178000	195500
56 10	CORINTHIAN		CR	F/W		IB	T350D		15 1		3 8	175500	193000
56 10	CORINTHIAN		CR	F/W		IB	T370D		15 1		3 8	177500	195000
56 10	LINWOOD		CR	F/W		IB	T350D		15 1		4	175500	193000
56 10	LINWOOD		CR	F/W		IB	T370D		15 1		4	177500	195000
56 10	OUT-ISLANDER		CR	F/W		IB	T350D		15 1		4 1	175500	193000
56 10	OUT-ISLANDER		CR	F/W		IB	T370D		15 1		4 1	177500	195000
56 10	SPORTSMAN		SF	F/W		IB	T350D		15 1		3 8	189500	208000
56 10	SPORTSMAN		SF	F/W		IB	T370D		15 1		3 8	191500	210500
58	LINWOOD		CR	F/W		IB	T350D		15 1		4	180000	197500
58	LINWOOD		CR	F/W		IB	T370D		15 1		4	182500	200500
58	OUT-ISLANDER		CR	F/W		IB	T350D		15 1		4	180000	197500
58	OUT-ISLANDER		CR	F/W		IB	T370D		15 1		4	182500	200500
60	SPORTSMAN		SF	F/W		IB	T370D		16 1		4	188000	206500
60	SPORTSMAN		SF	F/W		IB	T595D		16 1		4	210500	231500
61 10	ATLANTIC		CR	F/W		IB	T350D		16 1		4	191000	209500
61 10	ATLANTIC		CR	F/W		IB	T595D		16 1		4	226000	248500
65	CORINTHIAN		CR	F/W		IB	T525D		16 1		4 2	415000	456000
65	CORINTHIAN		CR	F/W		IB	T595D		16 1		4 2	420500	462500
65	OFFSHORE		OFF	F/W		IB	T525D		16 1		4 4	263500	289500
65	OFFSHORE		OFF	F/W		IB	T595D		16 1		4 4	268000	294500
65	SEAFARER		CR	F/W		IB	T525D		16 1		4 4	450500	456000
65	SEAFARER		CR	F/W		IB	T595D		16 1		4 4	420500	462500
65	SPORTSMAN		SF	F/W		IB	T525D		16 1		4 4	254000	279000
65	SPORTSMAN		SF	F/W		IB	T595D		16 1		4 4	259000	285000
72	SPORTSMAN		SF	F/W		IB	T525D		19 5		4 10	**	**
72	SPORTSMAN		SF	F/W		IB	T595D		19 5		4 10	**	**
77	SPORTSMAN		SF	F/W		IB	T595D		19 5		5	**	**
1970 BOATS													
40	SPORTSMAN		SF	F/W	SV	IB	T215D	GM	12 1		2 4	115500	126500
46 3			SDN	F/W	SV	IB	T283D	GM	13 11		2 8	83700	92000
50 6	ATLANTIC		DC	F/W	SV	IB	T283D	GM	15 1		3 4	122500	134500
50 6	LINWOOD		DC	F/W	SV	IB	T283D	GM	15 1		3 4	122500	134500
50 6	SPORTSMAN		SF	F/W	SV	IB	T283D	GM	14 3		3 4	120000	132000
53 6	ATLANTIC		DC	F/W	SV	IB	T350D	GM	15 1		3 6	**	**
53 6	CORINTHIAN		DC	F/W	SV	IB	T350D	GM	15 1		3 6	**	**
53 6	LINWOOD		DC	F/W	SV	IB	T350D	GM	15 1		3 6	**	**
53 6	SPORTSMAN		SF	F/W	SV	IB	T350D	GM	15 1		3 6	168500	185000
56 10	CORINTHIAN		DC	F/W	SV	IB	T350D	GM	15 1		4	182000	200000
56 10	LINWOOD		DC	F/W	SV	IB	T350D	GM	15 1		4	182000	200000
56 10	OUT-ISLANDER		DC	F/W	SV	IB	T350D	GM	15 1		4	182000	200000
56 10	SPORTSMAN		SF	F/W		IB	T350D	GM	15 1		3 8	179500	197500
58	LINWOOD		DC	F/W		IB	T350D	GM	15 1		4	185000	203500
58	OUT-ISLANDER		DC	F/W		IB	T350D	GM	15 1		4	185000	203500
61 10	ATLANTIC		DC	F/W		IB	T350D	GM	16 1		4	183500	202000
65	OFFSHORE		CR	F/W		IB	T530D	GM	16 1		4 4	387000	425000
65	SEAFARER		CR	F/W		IB	T530D	GM	16 1		4 4	400000	439500
72 8	SPORTSMAN		SF	F/W		IB	T555D	GM	19 5		4 10	**	**
77 1	SPORTSMAN		SF	F/W		IB	T555D	GM	19 5		5	**	**
1969 BOATS													
40	SPORTSMAN 40	FSH	SF	F/W		IB	T290	CHRY	12 1		2 4	76200	83700
40	SPORTSMAN 40	FSH	SF	F/W		IB	T215D	GM	12 1		2 4	74700	82100
46 3	A OR B		SDN	F/W		IB	T300	CHRY	13 11		2 8	81000	89000
46 3	A OR B		SDN	F/W		IB	T283D	GM	13 11		2 8	91300	100500
46 3	A OR B		SDN	F/W		IB	T370D	CUM	13 11		2 8	94700	104000
50 6	LINWOOD 50		CR	F/W		IB	T283D	GM	15 1		3 4	98400	108000
50 6	SPORTSMAN 50A		FSH	F/W		IB	T283D	GM	14 3		3 4	125500	138000
50 6	SPORTSMAN 50A		FSH	F/W		IB	T350D	GM	14 3		3 4	135500	149000
50 6	SPORTSMAN 50B	FB	FSH	F/W		IB	T350D	GM	14 3		3 4	136500	150000
53 6	ATLANTIC 53		CR	F/W		IB	T350D	GM	15 1		3 6	130500	143000
53 6	CORINTHIAN 53		CR	F/W		IB	T350D	GM	15 1		3 6	130500	143000
53 6	LINWOOD 53 A OR B		CR	F/W		IB	T350D	GM	15 1		3 6	135500	149000
53 6	LINWOOD 53C		CR	F/W		IB	T350D	GM	15 1		3 6	132000	145000
53 6	SPORTSMAN 53		FSH	F/W		IB	T370D	CUM	15 1		3 6	170000	187000
56 10	CORINTHIAN 56	HT	CR	F/W		IB	T350D	GM	15 1		3 8	161000	177000
56 10	LINWOOD 56A		CR	F/W		IB	T350D	GM	15 1		3 8	158500	174500
56 10	LINWOOD 56B	FB	CR	F/W		IB	T350D	GM	15 1		4	160000	176000
56 10	OUT-ISLANDER 56		CR	F/W		IB	T350D	GM	15 1		4	161000	176500
56 10	SPORTSMAN 56		FSH	F/W		IB	T350D	GM	15 1		4	161000	177000
58	LINWOOD 58		DC	F/W		IB	T350D	GM	15 1		4	178000	195500
58	OUT-ISLANDER 58		CR	F/W		IB	T350D	GM	15 1		4	180500	198500
61 10	ATLANTIC 60A		CR	F/W		IB	T350D	GM	16 1		4	177500	195000
61 10	ATLANTIC 60A		CR	F/W		IB	T530D	GM	16 1		4	205500	226000
61 10	ATLANTIC	FB		F/W	SV	IB	T530D	GM	16 1		4	**	**
65	OFFSHORE 65A		OFF	F/W	SV	IB	T530D	GM	16 1		4 4	244500	268500
65	OFFSHORE 65B		OFF	F/W	SV	IB	T530D	GM	16 1		4 4	249000	273500
65	SEAFARER 65A		CR	F/W	SV	IB	T530D	GM	16 1		4 4	387000	425000
65	SEAFARER 65B		CR	F/W	SV	IB	T530D	GM	16 1		4 4	382500	420000
1968 BOATS													
40	SPORTSMAN 40		SF	WD		IB	T215		12 1		2 9	82700	90900
40	SPORTSMAN 40		SF	WD		IB	T290		12 1		2 9	83200	91500
46 3			SDN	WD		IB	T283		13 11		2 8	71900	79000
46 3			SDN	WD		IB	T290		13 11		2 8	71500	78000
50 6	ATLANTIC 50		MY	WD		IB	T283D		14 3		3 4	117000	128500

LOA FT	LOA IN	NAME AND/ OR MODEL	TOP/ RIG	BOAT TYPE	HULL MTL	HULL TP	ENGINE TP	ENGINE # HP	ENGINE MFG	BEAM FT	BEAM IN	WGT LBS	DRAFT FT	DRAFT IN	RETAIL LOW	RETAIL HIGH
		1968 BOATS														
50	6	SPORTSMAN 50		SF	WD		IB	T283D		14	3		3	4	113000	124500
50	6	SPORTSMAN 50		SF	WD		IB	T350D		14	3		3	4	125000	137500
53	6	ATLANTIC 53		MY	WD		IB	T350D		15	1		3	6	156500	172000
53	6	CORINTHIAN 53		MY	WD		IB	T350D		15	1		3	6	156500	172000
53	6	LINWOOD 53		MY	WD		IB	T350D		15	1		3	6	156500	172000
56	10	CORINTHIAN 56		MY			IB	T350D		15	1		3	8	169500	186500
56	10	LINWOOD 56		MY	WD		IB	T350D		15	1		4		179000	197000
56	10	OUT-ISLANDER 56		MY	WD		IB	T350D		15	1		4		169500	186500
56	10	SPORTSMAN 56		SF	WD		IB	T350		15	1		3	8	157500	173500
58		LINWOOD 58		MY	WD		IB	T350D		15	1		4		172500	189500
58		OUT-ISLANDER 58		MY	WD		IB	T350D		15	1		4		172500	189500
61	10	ATLANTIC 60		MY	WD		IB	T350D		16	1		4		196500	216000
61	10	ATLANTIC 60		MY	WD		IB	T530D		16	1		4		222000	244000
65		OFFSHORE 65		MY	WD		IB	T530D		16	1		4	4	265500	292000
65		SEAFARER 65		MY	WD		IB	T530D		16	1		4	4	265500	292000
		1967 BOATS														
40		SPORTSMAN 40		YTFS	P/M		IB	T215		12	1		2	4	109500	120500
46	3	SEDAN CR 46		SDN	P/M		IB	T283		13	11		2	8	69300	76200
50	6	ATLANTIC 50		CR	P/M		IB	T283D		14	3		3	4	89800	98600
50	6	SPORTSMAN 50		YTFS	P/M		IB	T283D		14	3		3	4	112500	123500
50	6	SPORTSMAN 50		YTFS	P/M		IB	T350D		14	3		3	4	122000	134000
53	6	ATLANTIC 53		CR	P/M		IB	T350D		15	1		3	6	125000	137500
53	6	CORINTHIAN 53		CR	P/M		IB	T350D		15	1		3	6	125000	137500
53	6	LINWOOD 53		CR	P/M		IB	T350D		15	1		3	6	125000	137500
56	10	CORINTHIAN 56		CR	P/M		IB	T350D		15	1		3	8	154000	169500
56	10	LINWOOD 56		CR	P/M		IB	T350D		15	1		4		162000	178000
56	10	OUT-ISLANDER 56		CR	P/M		IB	T350D		15	1		4		154000	169500
56	10	SPORTSMAN 56		YTFS	P/M		IB	T350D		15	1		4		166000	182500
58		LINWOOD 58		CR	P/M		IB	T350D		15	1		4		158000	173500
61	10	ATLANTIC 60		CR	P/M		IB	T350D		16	1		4		165500	182000
65		OFFSHORE 65		CR	P/M		IB	T530D		16	1		4		344000	378000
65		SEAFARER 65		CR	P/M		IB	T530D		16	1		4	4	344000	378000
		1966 BOATS														
34	10	SPORTSMAN 34		CR	P/M		IB	T140		12	3		2	4	35900	39900
40		SPORTSMAN 40		CR	P/M		IB	T216		12	1		2	4	71100	78100
40	8	PISCATORY 40		CR	P/M		IB	T175		12	1		2	6	72100	79200
43	4	SPORTSMAN 543		SF	P/M		IB	T215		13	8		2	6	95200	104500
43	11	DOGHOUSE 43		CR	P/M		IB	T265		13	11		2	8	74800	82200
46	3	GRAND-MANAN 46		CR	P/M		IB	T280		13	11		2	6	73000	80200
46	3	SEDAN CR 46		SDN	P/M		IB	T265		13	11		2	8	66600	73100
46	3	SPORTSMAN 46		CR	P/M		IB	T265		13	11		2	8	72800	79900
48	1	CORINTHIAN 48		CR	P/M		IB	T216		13	8		2	10	83800	92100
50	6	SPORTSMAN 50		CR	P/M		IB	T280D		14	3		3	4	89800	98700
53		ATLANTIC		CR	FBG		IB	T370D	CUM	15	1		3	6	118000	130000
53	5	LINWOOD 53		CR	P/M		IB	T350D		14	3		3	4	120500	132500
53	6	OFFSHORE 53		CR	P/M		IB	T280D		15	1		3	6	116000	127500
56	10	CORINTHIAN 56		CR	P/M		IB	T350D		15	1		4		150000	164500
58		LINWOOD 58		CR	P/M		IB	T350D		15	1		4		153500	169000
60	10	LINWOOD 60		CR	P/M		IB	T350D		16	1		4		153500	168500
61	10	ATLANTIC 60		CR	P/M		IB	T350D		16	1		4		160500	176000
65		OFFSHORE 65		CR	P/M		IB	T350D		16	1		4	6	323000	354500
75		HUCKINS 75		CR	P/M		IB	T700D		19	8		5		**	**
		1965 BOATS														
40		SPORTSMAN 40		SF	WD		IB	181		12	1		2	4	73200	80500
40	8	PISCATORY 40		SF	WD		IB	181		12	11		2	6	76600	84200
43	4	SPORTSMAN 43		SF	WD		IB	270		13	8		2	6	84000	92300
43	11	DOGHOUSE 43		SF	WD		IB	240		13	11		2	8	52500	57700
46	1	SPORTSMAN 46		SF	WD		IB	270		13	8		2	8	70600	77600
46	3	GRAND-MANAN 46		SDN	WD		IB	280		13	11		2	8	60700	66800
46	3	SEDAN		SDN	WD		IB	270		13	11		2	8	60600	66600
48	1	NEPTUNE 48		SDN	WD		IB	270		13	8		2	8	61000	67000
50	6	SPORTSMAN 50		SF	WD		IB	270		14	3		3	4	86100	94600
53	5	NEPTUNE 53		MY	WD		IB	270		14	3		3	4	122500	134500
53	6	BAHAMIAN 53		MY	WD		IB	270		15	1		3	4	116000	127000
53	6	CARIBBEAN 53		MY	WD		IB	270		15	1		3	8	116000	127000
53	6	LINWOOD 53		MY	WD		IB	270		15	1		3	8	116000	127000
53	6	OFFSHORE 53		MY	WD		IB	270		15	1		3	6	116000	127000
56	10	OUT-ISLANDER		MY	WD		IB	270		15	1		3	8	134000	147000
61	10	CARIBBEAN 60		MY	WD		IB	320		16	1		3	9	290000	319000
65		OFFSHORE 65		MY	WD		IB	320		16	1		3	9	264500	290500
65		SEAFARER 65		MY	WD		IB	320		16	1		3	9	264500	290500
		1961 BOATS														
34		GURNET 34		CR	P/M		IB	270		11	1		2	2	25800	28700
34		MENEMSHA 34		CR	P/M		IB	270		11	1		2	2	27300	30300
34		PRO-BONO 34		CR	P/M		IB	270		11	1		2	2	29700	33000
34		SPORTSMAN 34		SPTCR	P/M		IB	270		11	1		2	2	24700	27500
36		SPORTSMAN 36		SF	P/M		IB	354		12	1		2	6	43900	48800
40		SPORTSMAN 40		SPTCR	P/M		IB	302		12	1		2	4	47000	51600
40	8	PISCATORY 40		SPTCR	P/M		IB	302		13	11		2	6	34200	38000
43	4	SPORTSMAN 43		SF	P/M		IB	302		13	8		2	4	78500	86300
43	10	DOGHOUSE 43		CR	P/M		IB	302		13	11		2	6	58200	63900
45	5	GRAND-MANAN 46		CR	P/M		IB	450		13	11		2	6	57400	63100
46	1	SPORTSMAN 46		SF	P/M		IB	302		13	8		2	6	64200	70500
48	1	CORINTHIAN 48		CR	P/M		IB	450		13	8		2	6	77300	84900
48	1	NEPTUNE 48		CR	P/M		IB	302		13	8		2	6	71500	78600
48	1	SEAFARER 48		CR	P/M		IB	450		13	8		2	8	69600	76500
50	6	GRAND-MANAN 50		CR	P/M		IB	302		14	3		3	4	93900	103000
50	6	PISCATORY 50		SF	P/M		IB	460		14	3		3	4	84500	92800
50	6	SPORTSMAN 50		SPTCR	P/M		IB	460		14	3		3	4	55100	60600
53	5	NEPTUNE 53		CR	P/M		IB	460		14	3		3	4	100500	110000
53	6	ATLANTIC 53		CR	P/M		IB	460		15			3	4	100500	110500
53	6	BAHAMIAN 53		CR	P/M		IB	460		15			3	4	97500	107000
53	6	CARIBBEAN 53		CR	P/M		IB	460		15			3	4	106000	116500
53	6	CORINTHIAN 53		CR	P/M		IB	460		15			3	4	106000	116500
53	6	LINWOOD 53		CR	P/M		IB	460		15			3	4	103500	114000
53	6	OCEANIC 53		CR	P/M		IB	460		15			3	4	103500	114000
53	6	OFFSHORE 53		CR	P/M		IB	460		15			3	4	94800	104000
60	8			FD	MHG		IB	T350D	GM						135000	148500
60	10	ATLANTIC 60		CR	P/M		IB	616		16	1		3	6	127000	139500
60	10	CARIBBEAN 60		CR	P/M		IB	460		16	1		3	6	118500	130000
60	10	LINWOOD 60		CR	P/M		IB	616		16	1		3	6	134500	147500
60	10	PACIFIC 60		CR	P/M		IB	616		16	1		3	6	119000	131000
64		OFFSHORE 64		CR	P/M		IB	616		16	1		3	8	160000	176000
64		SEAFARER 64		CR	P/M		IB	616		16	1		3	8	160000	176000
		1960 BOATS														
34		GURNET 34		CR	WD		IB	T135-T275		11	1		2	2	26500	30500
34		MENEMSHA 34		CR	WD		IB	T135-T275		11	1		2	2	28000	32000
34		PRO-BONO 34		CR	WD		IB	T135-T275		11			2	2	28100	32200
34		SPORTSMAN 34		CR	WD		IB	T135-T275		11	1		2	2	29000	33100
40		SPORTSMAN 40		CR	WD		IB	T225		12	1		2	4	61400	67400
40		SPORTSMAN 40		CR	WD		IB	T197D		12	1		2	4	78400	86100
40	8	PISCATORY 40		CR	WD		IB	T225		13	11		2	6	56800	62400
40	8	PISCATORY 40		CR	WD		IB	T151D		13	11		2	6	70000	76900
43	10	DOGHOUSE 43		CR	WD		IB	T225		13	11		2	6	62300	68500
43	10	DOGHOUSE 43		CR	WD		IB	T197D		13	11		2	6	76800	84400
45	5	GRAND-MANAN 46		CR	WD		IB	T225		13	11		2	6	56500	62100
45	5	GRAND-MANAN 46		CR	WD		IB	T275		13	11		2	6	57300	63000
46	1	SPORTSMAN 46		CR	WD		IB	T225		13	8		2	6	62100	68200
46	1	SPORTSMAN 46		CR	WD		IB	T300D		13	8		2	6	61500	67500
48	1	CORINTHIAN 48		CR	WD		IB	T225		13	8		2	6	77200	84800
48	1	CORINTHIAN 48		CR	WD		IB	T180D		13	8		2	6	71700	78800
48	1	NEPTUNE 48		CR	WD		IB	T225		13	8		2	6	70900	77900
48	1	NEPTUNE 48		CR	WD		IB	T300D		13	8		2	6	75400	82900
48	1	SEAFARER 48		CR	WD		IB	T225		13	8		2	8	69600	76500
48	1	SEAFARER 48		CR	WD		IB	T197D		13	8		2	8	72200	79300
50	6	GRAND-MANAN 50		CR	WD		IB	T197D		14	3		3	6	74700	82100
50	6	GRAND-MANAN 50		CR	WD		IB	T235D		14	3		3	6	73900	81200
50	6	PISCATORY 50		CR	WD		IB	T197D		14	3		3	6	67400	74100
50	6	PISCATORY 50		CR	WD		IB	T300D		14	3		3	6	78700	86500
50	6	SPORTSMAN 50		CR	WD		IB	T197D		14	3		3	6	69400	76200
50	6	SPORTSMAN 50		CR	WD		IB	T300D		14	3		3	6	81000	89000
53	5	ATLANTIC 53		CR	WD		IB	T235D		14	3		3	6	97000	106500
53	5	ATLANTIC 53		CR	WD		IB	T300D		14	3		3	6	101500	111500
53	5	BAHAMIAN 53		CR	WD		IB	T235D		14	3		3	6	94100	103500
53	5	BAHAMIAN 53		CR	WD		IB	T300D		14	3		3	6	98800	108500
53	5	CORINTHIAN 53		CR	WD		IB	T235D		14	3		3	6	102500	112500
53	5	CORINTHIAN 53		CR	WD		IB	T300D		14	3		3	6	107000	118000
53	5	LINWOOD 53		CR	WD		IB	T235D		14	3		3	6	100000	110000
53	5	LINWOOD 53		CR	WD		IB	T300D		14	3		3	6	105000	115500
53	5	NEPTUNE 53		CR	WD		IB	T235D		14	3		3	6	88600	97400
53	5	NEPTUNE 53		CR	WD		IB	T300D		14	3		3	6	93100	102500
53	5	OCEANIC 53		CR	WD		IB	T235D		14	3		3	6	100000	110000
53	5	OCEANIC 53		CR	WD		IB	T300D		14	3		3	6	105000	115500
53	5	OFFSHORE 53		CR	WD		IB	T235D		14	3		3	6	91500	100500
53	5	OFFSHORE 53		CR	WD		IB	T300D		14	3		3	6	96000	105500
60		ATLANTIC 60		CR	WD		IB	T235D		15			3	8	107000	118000
60		ATLANTIC 60		CR	WD		IB	T300D		15			3	8	116000	127500

 CONTINUED ON NEXT PAGE

LOA FT IN	NAME AND/ OR MODEL	TOP/ RIG	BOAT TYPE	-HULL- MTL	TP	----ENGINE--- IB TP	# HP	MFG	BEAM FT IN	WGT LBS	DRAFT FT IN	RETAIL LOW	RETAIL HIGH
						--- 1960 BOATS ---							
60	CARIBBEAN 60	CR	WD		IB	T235D			15		3 8	99700	109500
60	CARIBBEAN 60	CR	WD		IB	T300D			15		3 8	108000	119000
60	PACIFIC 60	CR	WD		IB	T235D			15		3 8	100500	110500
60	PACIFIC 60	CR	WD		IB	T300D			15		3 8	109500	120000
60 8		FD	MHG		IB	T350D		GM				132500	145500
64	OFFSHORE 64	CR	WD		IB	T300D			16 1		3 8	148500	163000
64	OFFSHORE 64	CR	WD		IB	T460D			16 1		3 8	168500	185000
64	SEAFARER 64	CR	WD		IB	T300D			16 1		3 8	148500	163000
64	SEAFARER 64	CR	WD		IB	T460D			16 1		3 8	168500	185000
						--- 1958 BOATS ---							
53 7	CORINTHIAN	FB	WD		IB	T258D		GM				101500	111500
						--- 1955 BOATS ---							
45 10		FD	MHG		IB	T			13 8	48000	2 6	**	**
						--- 1954 BOATS ---							
34	GURNET	OP	WKNDR	MHG	IB	T		CHRY				**	**
34	MENEMSHA	FB	SF	MHG	IB	T		CHRY				**	**
34	PRO-BONO	HT	CBNCR	MHG	IB	T		CHRY				**	**
40	DOGHOUSE	FB	TCMY	MHG	IB	T						**	**
40	ORTEGA	FB	SDN	MHG	IB	T						**	**
40	SPORTSMAN	FB	SF	MHG	IB	T						**	**
45	GRAND-MANAN	FB	SDN	MHG	IB	T						**	**
45	NEPTUNE	HT	TCMY	MHG	IB	T						**	**
45	SPORTSMAN	FB	SF	MHG	IB	T						**	**
48	OFFSHORE	FB	MY	MHG	IB	T	D					**	**
48	SEAFARER	HT	MY	MHG	IB	T	D					**	**
52	LINWOOD	FB	MY	MHG	IB	T						**	**
52	OFFSHORE	FB	MY	MHG	IB	T	D					**	**
						--- 1953 BOATS ---							
34	GURNET	OP	WKNDR	WD	IB	T		CHRY				**	**
34	MENEMSHA	FB	SF	WD	IB	T		CHRY				**	**
34	PRO-BONO	HT	CBNCR	WD	IB	T		CHRY				**	**
40	DOGHOUSE	FB	TCMY	WD	IB	T		CHRY				**	**
40	ORTEGA	HT	SDN	WD	VD	T		CHRY				**	**
40	ORTEGA	FB	SDN	WD	VD	T		CHRY				**	**
40	SPORTSMAN	FB	SF	WD	IB	T		CHRY				**	**
45	GRAND-MANAN	HT	SDN	WD	IB	T		CHRY				**	**
45	GRAND-MANAN	FB	SDN	WD	IB	T		CHRY				**	**
45	NEPTUNE	FB	TCMY	WD	IB	T		CHRY				**	**
45	NEPTUNE	FB	TCMY	WD	IB	T	D	GM				**	**
45	SPORTSMAN	FB	SF	WD	IB	T		CHRY				**	**
45	SPORTSMAN	FB	SF	WD	IB	T	D	GM				**	**
48	SEAFARER	HT	MY	WD	IB	T	D	GM				**	**
52	BAHAMIAN	FB	MY	WD	IB	T	D	GM				**	**
52	LINWOOD	FB	MY	WD	IB	T	D	GM				**	**
52	OFFSHORE	FB	MY	WD	IB	T	D					**	**
58	CARIBBEAN	FB	MY	WD	IB	T	D	GM				**	**
60	FAIRFORM-FLYER	FB	MY	MHG	IB	T300D		CUM	15	32000	3 6	76600	84200
						--- 1952 BOATS ---							
34	GURNET	OP	WKNDR	WD	IB	T						**	**
34	PRO-BONO	HT	CBNCR	WD	IB	T						**	**
34 6	MENEMSHA	FB	SF	WD	IB	T225		CHRY				25000	27700
40	DOGHOUSE	FB	TCMY	WD	IB	T						**	**
40	ORTEGA	HT	SDN	WD	VD	T						**	**
40	SPORTSMAN	FB	SF	WD	IB	T						**	**
45	GRAND-MANAN	HT	SDN	WD	IB	T225		CHRY				48900	53700
45	NEPTUNE	FB	TCMY	WD	IB	T						**	**
45	NEPTUNE	FB	TCMY	WD	IB	T	D					**	**
45	SPORTSMAN	FB	SF	WD	IB	T						**	**
45	SPORTSMAN	FB	SF	WD	IB	T	D					**	**
48	SEAFARER	HT	MY	WD	IB	T	D					**	**
52	OCEANIC	FB	MY	WD	IB	T	D					**	**
52	OFFSHORE	FB	MY	WD	IB	T	D					**	**
58	CARIBBEAN	FB	MY	WD	IB	T	D					**	**
						--- 1950 BOATS ---							
40	ORTEGA	HT	DC	WD	VD	T		CHRY				**	**
						--- 1949 BOATS ---							
33	ORTEGA	HT	CBNCR	WD	IB	T						**	**
40	DOGHOUSE	HT	MYDKH	WD	IB	T		12				**	**
						--- 1947 BOATS ---							
50		FB	CR	WD	IB	T247D		GM				61700	67900
						--- 1946 BOATS ---							
28			SF	WD	IB							**	**
34			SF	WD	IB							**	**
36	FAIRFORM-FLYER	HT	CR	WD	IB							**	**
38	FAIRFORM-FLYER	HT	CR	WD	IB							**	**
40	FAIRFORM-FLYER	HT	CR	WD	IB							**	**
45	FAIRFORM-FLYER	HT	CR	WD	IB							**	**
48	FAIRFORM-FLYER	HT	CR	WD	IB							**	**
52	FAIRFORM-FLYER	HT	CR	WD	IB							**	**
						--- 1941 BOATS ---							
32	FAIRFORM-FLYER	HT	SDN	WD	IB	T						**	**
						--- 1940 BOATS ---							
38				WD	IB	T115		CHRY				**	**
						--- 1937 BOATS ---							
36		FB	CR	WD	IB	T						**	**
						--- 1932 BOATS ---							
45	FAIRFORM-FLYER	HT	OFF		IB	T200		KERM 11			2 8	42900	47600

HUDSON BOAT LTD
RANCHO PALOS VERDE CA 90732   See inside cover to adjust price for area

LOCUST HILL CORP
WINCHESTER VA 22601

For more recent years, see the BUC Used Boat Price Guide, Volume 1 or Volume 2

LOA FT IN	NAME AND/ OR MODEL	TOP/ RIG	BOAT TYPE	-HULL- MTL	TP	----ENGINE--- TP	# HP	MFG	BEAM FT IN	WGT LBS	DRAFT FT IN	RETAIL LOW	RETAIL HIGH
						--- 1982 BOATS ---							
43 7	SEA-WOLF 44	KTH	SA/RC	FBG	KL	IB	D		13 4	30000	6	67700	74400
50 10	FORCE 50 CTR CPT	KTH	SA/RC	FBG	KL	IB	D		14 2	52000	6	119500	131500
50 10	FORCE 50 PH	KTH	SA/RC	FBG	KL	IB	D		14 2	52000	6	117500	129000
59 9	SEA-WOLF 59 CTR CPT	KTH	SA/RC	FBG	KC	IB	D		15 6	65000	5 3	270000	297000
59 9	SEA-WOLF 59 PH	KTH	SA/RC	FBG	KL	IB	D		15 6	65000	5 3	262500	288500
						--- 1981 BOATS ---							
38 10	HUDSON-COASTER	FB	TRWL	FBG	DS	IB	120D	LEHM 14		28000	3 10	74500	81800
38 10	HUDSON-COASTER	FB	TRWL	FBG	DS	IB	T	D	LEHM 14	28000	3 10	**	**
50 10	FORCE 50 PH	KTH	SA/CR	FBG	KL	IB	80D	LEHM 14	1	52000	6 2	110000	122000
						--- 1980 BOATS ---							
38 10	HUDSON-COASTER 39	FB	TRWL	FBG	DS	IB	120D	LEHM 14		28000	3 10	71200	78200
						--- 1979 BOATS ---							
38 10	HUDSON-COASTER	FB	TRWL	FBG	DS	IB	120D		14	28000	3 10	68100	74800
38 10	HUDSON-COASTER	FB	TRWL	FBG	DS	IB	T120		14	28000	3 10	63500	69800
43 7	SEA-WOLF 44	KTH	SA/CR	FBG	KL	IB	D		13	32000	6	60500	66500
50 10	FORCE 50 CTR CPT	KTH	SA/CR	FBG	KL	IB	D		14	52000	6 6	102500	112500
50 10	FORCE 50 PH	KTH	SA/CR	FBG	KL	IB	D		14	52000	6 6	102500	112500
56	FORCE 55 CTR CPT	KTH	SA/CR	FBG	KL	IB	D		15 3	61000	6 9	150500	165000
56	FORCE 55 PH	KTH	SA/CR	FBG	KL	IB	D		15 3	61000	6 9	150500	165000

HULLMASTER BOATS LTD
COAST GUARD MFG ID- ZHB

Call 1-800-327-6929 for BUC Personalized Evaluation Service
Or, for 1975 to 1977 boats, sign onto www.BUCValuPro.com

HULLS UNLIMITED EAST INC
COAST GUARD MFG ID- HUE

Call 1-800-327-6929 for BUC Personalized Evaluation Service
Or, for 1974 to 1977 boats, sign onto www.BUCValuPro.com

HUNTER BOATS LTD
AQUALITY CRAFT
ORILLA ONTARIO CANADA   See inside cover to adjust price for area

LOA FT IN	NAME AND/ OR MODEL	TOP/ RIG	BOAT TYPE	-HULL- MTL	TP	----ENGINE--- TP	# HP	MFG	BEAM FT IN	WGT LBS	DRAFT FT IN	RETAIL LOW	RETAIL HIGH
						--- 1970 BOATS ---							
33	EXPRESS 33	EXP	MHG	RB	IB	T210		CHRY	11 6	14000	3 1	27100	30100
35		EXP	MHG		IB	T210			11 6		2 8	33300	36900
37		SDN	MHG		IB	T210			11		2 6	40200	44700
38		SDN	MHG		IB	T210			12		2 11	46000	50600
38		SDN	MHG		IB	T200D			12		2 11	61500	67600
38		FB	SDN	MHG	IB	T210			12		3	45700	50200
39		TCMY	MHG		IB	T210			11 9		3	58000	63800
40		FD	MHG		IB	T250			13		3	69100	75900
45		MY	MHG		IB	T290			12 9		3	80500	88500

HUNTER BOATS LTD (continued)

LOA FT	LOA IN	NAME/MODEL	TOP/RIG	BOAT TYPE	HULL MTL	HULL TP	ENG TP	# HP	MFG	BEAM FT	BEAM IN	WGT LBS	DRAFT FT	DRAFT IN	RETAIL LOW	RETAIL HIGH
		1969 BOATS														
33		EXPRESS		EXP	WD	RB	IB	T210	CHRY	11	6	14000	3	1	26100	29000
35				EXP	MHG	RB	IB	T210	CHRY	11	6	15000	2	8	29700	33000
37				SDN	MHG	RB	IB	T210		11			2	6	38900	43200
37		SEDAN		SDN	WD	RB	IB	195	CHRY	11		15000	3	2	37400	41600
38				SDN	MHG		IB	T200D		12			2	11	59500	65400
38				SDN	MHG	RB	IB	T210	CHRY	12		18000	2	11	44000	48900
38			FB	SF	MHG		IB	T210		12			3		43800	48600
39				TCMY	MHG	RB	IB	T210	CHRY	11	9	22000	3		55900	61500
40				FD	MHG	RB	IB	T250	MRCR	13		28000	3		66800	73400
45				MY	MHG	RB	IB	T290	CHRY	12	9	32000	3		78600	86400
45		MOTOR YACHT		MY	WD	RB	IB	290	CHRY	12	6	32000	3	4	57900	63700
		1968 BOATS														
35			FB	EXP	MHG		IB	T210	CHRY	11	6	15000	2	8	28600	31800
37				SDN	MHG		IB	T210	CHRY	11		15000	2	6	37800	42000
38		DELUXE		SDN	MHG		IB	T210	CHRY	12		18000	2	11	42700	47400
39			FB	TCMY	MHG		IB	T210	CHRY	11	9	22000	3		54300	59700
45			FB	TCMY	MHG		IB	T290	CHRY	12	9	32000	3		82600	90800
		1967 BOATS														
33				EXP	MHG		IB	T195		11	6		2	8	24200	26800
35				EXP	MHG		IB	T195		11	6		2	9	29600	32900
37				SDN	MHG		IB	T195		11			2	9	36500	40500
38		DELUXE		SDN	MHG		IB	T195		12			2	9	41400	46000
39				TCMY	MHG		IB	T210		11	9		2	10	52800	58100
45				MY	MHG		IB	T290		12	9		3		73400	80700
		1966 BOATS														
33				EXP	WD		IB	T210		11	6		2	8	23500	26100
35				EXP	WD		IB	T210		11	6		2	8	28600	31800
35				EXP	WD		IB	T290		11	6		2	8	29400	32700
35				SDN	WD		IB	T210		11			2	9	27700	30700
35				SDN	WD		IB	T290		11			2	9	28600	31700
37				SDN	WD		IB	T210		11			2	9	35500	39500
39				TCMY	WD		IB	T210		11	9		2	8	51500	56500
39				TCMY	WD		IB	T290		11	9		2	8	51800	56900
45				MY	WD		IB	T290		12	6		2	8	72800	80000
45				MY	WD		IB	T300D		12	6		2	8	78500	86200
		1965 BOATS														
31				SDN	WD		IB	195							15000	17000
33				EXP	WD		IB	T195							22600	25100
35				EXP	WD		IB	T195							27800	30900
35				SDN	WD		IB	T195							26900	29900
37				SDN	WD		IB	T195							34700	38600
38				EXP	WD		IB	T195							39700	44100
39				TCMY	WD		IB	T195							50100	55100
44			FB	DC	WD		IB	T195							51900	57000
		1964 BOATS														
31				SDN	WD		IB	195							14500	16400
33				EXP	WD		IB	T195-T260							21800	25000
35				EXP	WD		IB	T195							26800	29800
35				EXP	WD		IB	T260							27400	30400
35				SDN	WD		IB	T195							26000	28900
37				SDN	WD		IB	T195							33800	37600
38				EXP	WD		IB	T195							38700	43000
39				EXP	WD		IB	T260							38900	43300
39				TCMY	WD		IB	T195							48800	53700
39				TCMY	WD		IB	T260							49000	53900
44			FB	DC	WD		IB	T195							50500	55500
44			FB	DC	WD		IB	T260							53900	59200
		1963 BOATS														
31				CR	WD		IB	125							12500	14200
33				CR	WD		IB	260							18300	20400
33				CR	WD		IB	T195							19100	21200
35				SDN	WD		IB	T195							25100	27800
37				CR	WD		IB	T195							33100	36800
38				CR	WD		IB	T195							37700	41900
39				TCMY	WD		IB	T195							47700	52400
44				CR	WD		IB	T195							47000	51600
		1962 BOATS														
31				CR	WD		IB	110							12200	13900
31				CR	WD		IB	T110							12600	14300
33				CR	WD		IB	177							17400	19800
35				CR	WD		IB	177							22600	25100
37				CR	WD		IB	T110							31600	35200
38				CR	WD		IB	T177							36800	40800
44				CR	WD		IB	T177							45700	50200
		1961 BOATS														
31				CR	WD		IB	110		9	6		2	4	11600	13200
33				CR	WD		IB	T185	CC	11	3		2	5	18100	20100
35				CR	WD		IB	T110		11			2		22200	24700
37				CR	WD		IB	220		11	2		2	7	30100	33500
37	6			CR	WD		IB	275		11	6		2	6	34900	38800
44				CR	WD		IB	275		12			3		43800	48300
		1960 BOATS														
31				CR	WD		IB	110-177							11700	13400
33				CR	WD		IB	177							16700	19000
33				CR	WD		IB	T177							17300	19700
35				CR	WD		IB	T110							21800	24200
35				CR	WD		IB	T177							22300	24800
37				CR	WD		IB	T110							30300	33700
37				CR	WD		IB	T177							30900	34300
37	6			CR	WD		IB	T177							43200	48000
44				CR	WD		IB	T177							43600	48500
44				CR	WD		IB	T225								
		1959 BOATS														
30		TRUNK CABIN		CR	P/M		IB	109		9	6				9450	10700
35		TRUNK CABIN		CR	P/M		IB	109		11					21400	23800
36		TRUNK CABIN		CR	P/M		IB	T150		11					26700	29600
37		TRUNK CABIN	FB	CR	P/M		IB	T225		11	6				29300	32600
42		TRUNK CABIN	FB	CR	P/M		IB	T225		12					43000	47800
		1958 BOATS														
36				SDN	WD		IB	T150							26600	29600
38				CR	WD		IB	T228							34100	37900
		1957 BOATS														
23				CR	WD		IB	215							3900	4550
34			FB	EXP	WD		IB	165							19700	21900
36				SDN	WD		IB	T150							26200	29100
		1956 BOATS														
30				SDN	WD		IB	225							10300	11800
34				SDN	WD		IB	T120							18700	20800
		1955 BOATS														
36				SDN	WD		IB	T150							25500	28300
		1954 BOATS														
30			HT	EXP	MHG	RB	IB	115	GRAY	9	6				9850	11200
34				SDN	WD		IB	T150							18600	20600
36				SDN	WD		IB	T150							25100	27900
40				SDN	WD		IB	T135							46900	51600
42			FB	TCMY	MHG	RB	IB	T150	GRAY	12	6				41400	46000
		1953 BOATS														
34				EXP	WD		IB	T115							18800	20900
		1952 BOATS														
30				CR	WD		IB	T115							9300	10600
34				SDN	WD		IB	T135							17500	19900
		1951 BOATS														
30				CR	WD		IB	T115							9200	10400
34				SDN	WD		IB	T115							17100	19400
		1950 BOATS														
30				CR	WD		IB	T115							9100	10300
34				SDN	WD		IB	T115							16900	19200
		1949 BOATS														
34				SDN	WD		IB	T115							16700	19000
36		ZIMMER		CR	WD		IB	T100	PACK	11	6		3		22800	25300
		1948 BOATS														
34				SDN	WD		IB	T115							16500	18800
		1947 BOATS														
34				SDN	WD		IB	T115							16400	18600
		1941 BOATS														
28				CR	WD		IB	115							6800	7850
32				CR	WD		IB	115							11900	13600
		1940 BOATS														
28				CR	WD		IB	96							6900	7900
		1939 BOATS														
32				SDN	WD		IB	96							11900	13500
		1915 BOATS														
38					WD		IB	125	CHRY						**	**

HUNTER MARINE CORP

ST AUGUSTINE FL 32084   COAST GUARD MFG ID- HUN   See inside cover to adjust price for area

For more recent years, see the BUC Used Boat Price Guide, Volume 1 or Volume 2

LOA FT	LOA IN	NAME/MODEL	TOP/RIG	BOAT TYPE	HULL MTL	HULL TP	ENG TP	# HP	MFG	BEAM FT	BEAM IN	WGT LBS	DRAFT FT	DRAFT IN	RETAIL LOW	RETAIL HIGH
		1983 BOATS														
19	8	HUNTER 20	SLP	SA/CR	FBG	CB	OB			7		1700	1	3	2800	3250
22	3	HUNTER 22	SLP	SA/CR	FBG	KL	OB			7	11	3400	1	2	4650	5300
22	3	HUNTER 22	SLP	SA/CR	FBG	SK	OB			7	11	3200	1	11	4450	5100

LOA FT IN	NAME AND/OR MODEL	TOP/ RIG	BOAT TYPE	HULL MTL	TP	ENGINE TP # HP MFG	BEAM FT IN	WGT LBS	DRAFT FT IN	RETAIL LOW	RETAIL HIGH
1983 BOATS											
25	HUNTER 25	SLP	SA/CR	FBG	KL	OB	8	4400	3 11	6600	7600
25	HUNTER 25 SHOAL	SLP	SA/CR	FBG	KL	OB	8	4400	2 11	6600	7600
27 2	HUNTER 27	SLP	SA/CR	FBG	KL	IB D	9 3	7000	4 3	12300	14000
27 2	HUNTER 27 SHOAL	SLP	SA/CR	FBG	KL	IB D	9 3	7000	3 3	12300	14000
30	HUNTER 30	SLP	SA/CR	FBG	KL	IB D	10 2	9700	5 3	18600	20700
30	HUNTER 30 SHOAL	SLP	SA/CR	FBG	KL	IB D	10 2	9700	4	18600	20700
31 4	HUNTER 31	SLP	SA/CR	FBG	KL	IB D	10 11	9000	5 3	17000	19400
34 5	HUNTER 34	SLP	SA/CR	FBG	KL	IB 21D WEST	11 7	10900	5 6	21000	23400
34 5	HUNTER 34 SHOAL	SLP	SA/CR	FBG	KL	IB 21D WEST	11 7	11120	4 3	21400	23800
37	HUNTER 37	SLP	SA/CR	FBG	KL	IB D	11 11	17800	5 1	34300	38200
37	HUNTER 37 SHOAL	SLP	SA/CR	FBG	KL	IB D	11 11	17800	4	34300	38200
53 10	HUNTER 54	SLP	SA/CR	FBG	KL	IB 50D PERK	11 4	20500	6	103000	113000
1982 BOATS											
22 3	HUNTER 22	SLP	SA/CR	FBG	SK	OB	7 11	3200	1 11	4100	4800
25	HUNTER 25	SLP	SA/CR	FBG	KL	OB	8	4400	3 11	6200	7150
25	HUNTER 25 SHOAL	SLP	SA/CR	FBG	KL	OB	8	4400	2 11	6200	7150
27 2	HUNTER 27	SLP	SA/CR	FBG	KL	IB D	9 3	7000	4 3	11600	13100
27 2	HUNTER 27 SHOAL	SLP	SA/CR	FBG	KL	IB D	9 3	7000	3 3	11600	13100
30	HUNTER 30	SLP	SA/CR	FBG	KL	IB D	10 2	9700	5 3	17000	19400
30	HUNTER 30 SHOAL	SLP	SA/CR	FBG	KL	IB D	10 2	9700	4	17000	19400
32 8	HUNTER 33	SLP	SA/CR	FBG	KL	IB D	10 2	10600	5 3	19000	21100
32 8	HUNTER 33 SHOAL	SLP	SA/CR	FBG	KL	IB D	10 2	10600	4	19000	21100
35 11	HUNTER 36	SLP	SA/CR	FBG	KL	IB D	11 1	13500	4 11	24600	27400
37	HUNTER 37	SLP	SA/CR	FBG	KL	IB D	11 11	17800	5 1	32100	35700
37	HUNTER 37 SHOAL	SLP	SA/CR	FBG	KL	IB D	11 11	17800	4	32100	35700
53 10	HUNTER 54	SLP	SA/CR	FBG	KL	IB 50D PERK	11 4	20500	6	96600	106000
1981 BOATS											
22 3	HUNTER 22	SLP	SA/CR	FBG	SK	OB	7 11	2600	1 11	3300	3850
25	HUNTER 25	SLP	SA/RC	FBG	KL	OB	8	4400	3 11	5800	6700
27 2	HUNTER 27	SLP	SA/CR	FBG	KL	IB D	9 3	7000	4 3	10800	12300
27 2	HUNTER 27 SHOAL	SLP	SA/CR	FBG	KL	IB D	9 3	7000	3 3	10800	12300
30	HUNTER 30	SLP	SA/CR	FBG	KL	IB D	10 2	9700	5 3	16000	18100
30	HUNTER 30 SHOAL	SLP	SA/CR	FBG	KL	IB D	10 2	9700	4	16000	18100
32 8	HUNTER 33	SLP	SA/CR	FBG	KL	IB D	10 2	10600	5 3	17600	20000
32 8	HUNTER 33 SHOAL	SLP	SA/CR	FBG	KL	IB D	10 2	10600	4	17600	20000
35 11	HUNTER 36	SLP	SA/CR	FBG	KL	IB D	11 1	13500	4 11	23100	25600
37	HUNTER 37	SLP	SA/CR	FBG	KL	IB D	11 11	17800	5 1	30100	33400
37	HUNTER 37 SHOAL	SLP	SA/CR	FBG	KL	IB D	11 11	17800	4	30100	33400
53 10	HUNTER 54	SLP	SA/CR	FBG	KL	IB 50D PERK	11 4	19500	6	90300	99200
1980 BOATS											
25	HUNTER 25	SLP	SA/RC	FBG	KL	OB	8	4400	3 11	5550	6350
27	HUNTER 27	SLP	SA/CR	FBG	KL	IB 8D REN	9 3	7000	4 3	10200	11600
27	HUNTER 27 SHOAL	SLP	SA/CR	FBG	KL	IB 8D REN	9 3	7000	3 3	10200	11600
30	HUNTER 30	SLP	SA/CR	FBG	KL	IB 15D YAN	10 2	9700	5 3	15200	17200
30	HUNTER 30 SHOAL	SLP	SA/CR	FBG	KL	IB 15D YAN	10 2	9700	4	15200	17200
32 8	HUNTER 33	SLP	SA/CR	FBG	KL	IB 15D YAN	10 2	10600	5 3	16700	19000
32 8	HUNTER 33 SHOAL	SLP	SA/CR	FBG	KL	IB 15D YAN	10 2	10600	4	16700	19000
36	HUNTER 36	SLP	SA/CR	FBG	KL	IB	11 1	13500	4 11	22000	24400
37	HUNTER 37	CUT	SA/CR	FBG	KL	IB 30D YAN	11 10	15500	5 1	25400	28300
37	HUNTER 37 SHOAL	CUT	SA/CR	FBG	KL	IB 30D YAN	11 10	15500	4	25400	28300
1979 BOATS											
25	HUNTER 25	SLP	SA/CR	FBG	KL	OB	8	4400	3 11	5300	6100
25	HUNTER 25 SHOAL	SLP	SA/CR	FBG	KL	OB	8	4400	2 11	5300	6100
27	HUNTER 27	SLP	SA/CR	FBG	KL	IB 8D REN	9 3	7000	3 3	9750	11100
27	HUNTER 27 SHOAL	SLP	SA/CR	FBG	KL	IB 8D REN	9 3	7000	3 3	9750	11100
30	HUNTER 30	SLP	SA/CR	FBG	KL	IB 15D YAN	10 2	9700	5 3	14500	16500
30	HUNTER 30 SHOAL	SLP	SA/CR	FBG	KL	IB 15D YAN	10 2	9700	4	14500	16500
32 8	HUNTER 33	SLP	SA/CR	FBG	KL	IB 15D YAN	10 2	10600	5 3	16000	18200
32 8	HUNTER 33 SHOAL	SLP	SA/CR	FBG	KL	IB 15D YAN	10 2	10600	4	16000	18200
37	HUNTER 37	CUT	SA/CR	FBG	KL	IB 30D YAN	11 10	15500	5 1	24400	27100
37	HUNTER 37 SHOAL	CUT	SA/CR	FBG	KL	IB 30D YAN	11 10	15500	4	24400	27100
1978 BOATS											
25	HUNTER 25	SLP	SAIL	FBG	KL	OB	8	4400	3 11	5100	5850
25	HUNTER 25 SHOAL	SLP	SAIL	FBG	KL	OB	8	4400	2 11	5100	5850
27	HUNTER 27	SLP	SA/CR	FBG	KL	IB 8D YAN	9 3	7000	3 3	9450	10700
27	HUNTER 27 SHOAL	SLP	SA/CR	FBG	KL	IB 8D YAN	9 3	7000	3 3	9450	10700
30	HUNTER 30	SLP	SA/CR	FBG	KL	IB 12D YAN	10 2	9700	5 3	13900	15800
30	HUNTER 30 SHOAL	SLP	SA/CR	FBG	KL	IB 12D YAN	10 2	9700	4	13900	15800
32 8	HUNTER 33	SLP	SA/CR	FBG	KL	IB 20D YAN	10 2	10600	5 3	15400	17500
32 8	HUNTER 33 SHOAL	SLP	SA/CR	FBG	KL	IB 20D YAN	10 2	10600	4	15400	17500
37	HUNTER 37	SLP	SA/CR	FBG	KC	IB 30D YAN	11 11	15500	4 3	23400	26000
1977 BOATS											
24 11	HUNTER 25	SLP	SAIL	FBG	KL	OB	8	4400	3 11	4850	5600
24 11	HUNTER 25	SLP	SAIL	FBG	KL	OB	8	4400	2 11	5250	6050
27	HUNTER 27	SLP	SAIL	FBG	KL	IB 8D YAN	9 3	7000	3 3	9100	10300
30	HUNTER 30	SLP	SAIL	FBG	KL	IB 12D YAN	10 2	9700	5 3	13400	15200
33	HUNTER 33	SLP	SAIL	FBG	KL	IB 20D YAN		10600		14800	16800
1976 BOATS											
24 11	HUNTER 25	SLP	SAIL	FBG	KL	OB	8	4400	3 11	4650	5350
24 11	HUNTER 25	SLP	SAIL	FBG	KL	OB D YAN	8	4400	3 11	5100	5850
24 11	HUNTER 25 SHOAL	SLP	SAIL	FBG	KL	OB	8	4400	2 11	4650	5350
24 11	HUNTER 25 TC SHOAL	SLP	SAIL	FBG	KL	OB D YAN	8	4400	2 11	4750	5450
24 11	HUNTER 25 TC SHOAL	SLP	SAIL	FBG	KL	IB	8	4400	2 11	5150	5900
24 11	HUNTER 25 TRUNK CBN	SLP	SAIL	FBG	KL	OB	8	4400	3 11	4750	5450
24 11	HUNTER 25 TRUNK CBN	SLP	SAIL	FBG	KL	OB D YAN	8	4400	3 11	5150	5900
27	HUNTER 27	SLP	SAIL	FBG	KL	IB 8D YAN	9 3	6500	3 3	7750	9950
30	HUNTER 30	SLP	SAIL	FBG	KL	IB 12D YAN	10 2	9700	4	13000	14700
1975 BOATS											
24 11	HUNTER 25 POP-TOP	SLP	SAIL	FBG	KL	OB	8	4400	3 11	4600	5300
24 11	HUNTER 25 STANDARD	SLP	SAIL	FBG	KL	OB	8	4400	3 11	4550	5200
27	HUNTER 27	SLP	SAIL	FBG	KL	IB	9 3	6500	3 11	7500	8650
27	HUNTER 27	SLP	SAIL	FBG	KC	IB 8D YAN	9 3	6500	3 11	7750	8950
30	HUNTER 30	SLP	SAIL	FBG	KL	IB 12D YAN	10 2	9700	7 2	12600	14300
1974 BOATS											
24 11	HUNTER 25	SLP	SAIL	FBG	KL	OB	8	3850	3 11	3850	4500
24 11	HUNTER 25 SHOAL	SLP	SAIL	FBG	KL	OB	8	3850	2 11	3850	4500
30	HUNTER 30	SLP	SAIL	FBG	KC	IB 12D YAN	10	9700	5	12200	13900

HAINES HUNTER
COAST GUARD MFG ID- WWT

WORLD-WIDE TECHNICAL SERVICES

Call 1-800-327-6929 for BUC Personalized Evaluation Service
Or, for 1983 boats, sign onto www.BUCValuPro.com

HURLEY MARINE LTD
PLYMPTON ENGLAND   COAST GUARD MFG ID- HYM See inside cover to adjust price for area

HURLEY YACHTS LTD
PARSIPPANY NJ 07054

LOA FT IN	NAME AND/OR MODEL	TOP/ RIG	BOAT TYPE	HULL MTL	TP	ENGINE TP # HP MFG	BEAM FT IN	WGT LBS	DRAFT FT IN	RETAIL LOW	RETAIL HIGH
1974 BOATS											
17	HURLEY	SLP	SA/CR	FBG			6 6	1200	3	1800	2150
23 9	HURLEY 24/70	SLP	SA/CR	FBG	KL		7 5		4 1	5600	6400
24	HURLEY 24	SLP	SAIL	FBG	KL	IB D	7 8	4500	4	5800	6700
27	HURLEY	CUT	SAIL	FBG		OB	8	7000	4	10400	11800
27	HURLEY	CUT	SAIL	FBG		IB 7D PETT	8	7000	4	10600	12100
30	HURLEY 30/90	SLP	SA/CR	FBG	KL		9 9		4 9	14200	14600
38	HURLEY 38 TAILWIND	SLP	SA/CR	FBG	KL		11 10		6	14700	16700
1973 BOATS											
17	H17		SAIL	FBG		OB	6 6	1200	3	1750	2050
18 6	H18		SAIL	FBG		OB	6 8	2350	3 3	2600	3000
20	H20		SAIL	FBG		OB	7 1	2450	2 6	2700	3150
22	H22		SAIL	FBG		OB	7 5	4300	3 6	4650	5350
24	H24		SAIL	FBG		OB	7 8	4900	3 6	5600	6400
24	H24		SAIL	FBG		IB 7 PETT	7 8	4900	3 6	5650	6650
27	H27		SAIL	FBG		OB	8	6720	4	9600	10900
27	H27		SAIL	FBG		IB 10 VLVO	8	6720	4	9750	11100
1972 BOATS											
17 3	SILHOUETTE MK III	SLP	SA/CR	FBG	KL		6 7	1500	2 2	1900	2300
18 6	HURLEY 18	SLP	SA/CR	FBG	KL		6 8	2350	3 2	2500	2900
20	HURLEY 20	SLP	SA/CR	FBG	KL		7 1	2450	2 6	2650	3100
22	HURLEY 22	SLP	SA/CR	FBG	KL		7 5	4300	3 6	4550	5200
22	HURLEY 22	SLP	SA/CR	FBG	TK		7 5	4300	3 6	4550	5200
27	HURLEY 27	SLP	SA/CR	FBG	KL	IB 10	8	6000	4	8300	9550
1971 BOATS											
18 6	HURLEY 18	SLP	SA/CR	FBG	KL	OB	6 8		3	2400	2800
20	HURLEY 20	SLP	SA/CR	FBG	KL	OB	7 1		3	2500	2900
20	HURLEY 20	SLP	SA/CR	FBG	TK	OB	7 1		2	2500	2900
22	HURLEY 22	SLP	SA/CR	FBG	KL		7 5		3 2	4050	4700
22	HURLEY 22	SLP	SA/CR	FBG	TK		7 5		3 2	4050	4700
31	HURLEY 31	YWL	SA/CR	FBG	KL	IB 37		16000		25100	27900
1970 BOATS											
18 6	HURLEY 18	SLP	SAIL	FBG	KL		6 8		3	2350	2750
20	HURLEY 20	SLP	SAIL	FBG	KL		7 1		3	2500	2950
20	HURLEY 20	SLP	SAIL	FBG	TK		7 1		2	2500	2950
22	HURLEY 22	SLP	SAIL	FBG	TK		7 5		3 9	3450	4000
22	HURLEY 22	SLP	SAIL	FBG	TK		7 5		3	3450	4000

HURLEY MARINE LTD — CONTINUED

LOA FT IN	NAME AND/ OR MODEL	TOP/ RIG	BOAT TYPE	HULL MTL	HULL TP	ENG TP	ENG #	ENG HP	ENG MFG	BEAM FT IN	WGT LBS	DRAFT FT IN	RETAIL LOW	RETAIL HIGH
1969 BOATS														
20	HURLEY 20	SLP	SAIL	FBG	KL	OB				7 1	2450	2 6	2500	2900
22	HURLEY 22	SLP	SAIL	FBG	KL	OB				7 5	4300	2 6	4200	4900
1968 BOATS														
17 3	SILHOUETTE MKIII	SLP	SA/CR	FBG	KL					6 7		2 1	2200	2550
18	HURLEY 18	SLP	SA/CR	FBG	KL					6 8		3 3	2200	2550
20	HURLEY 20	SLP	SA/CR	FBG	KL					7 1		2 7	2600	3050
22	HURLEY 22	SLP	SA/CR	FBG	KL					7 6		2 6	4200	4900
1967 BOATS														
17 3	HURLEY 17	SLP	SA/CR	FBG	KL	OB				7		1 11	1700	2050
17 3	SILHOUETTE MK III	SLP	SA/CR	FBG	TK					6 7		1 9	2200	2550
18	HURLEY 18	SLP	SA/CR	FBG	KL					6 8		3 3	2200	2550
20	HURLEY 20	SLP	SA/CR	FBG	KL	OB				7 3		1 11	2600	3000
20	HURLEY 20	SLP	SA/CR	FBG	TK					7 1		2 6	2600	3000
22	HURLEY 22	SLP	SA/CR	FBG	KL					7 5		3 9	4150	4850
22	HURLEY 22	SLP	SA/CR	FBG	KL	OB				7 5		3 9	4150	4850

HUROMIC METAL IND LTD
GODERICH ONTARIO CANADA   See inside cover to adjust price for area

LOA FT IN	NAME AND/ OR MODEL	TOP/ RIG	BOAT TYPE	HULL MTL	HULL TP	ENG TP	ENG HP	ENG MFG	BEAM FT IN	WGT LBS	DRAFT FT IN	RETAIL LOW	RETAIL HIGH
1982 BOATS													
35 8	GODERICH 35	CUT	SA/CR	STL	KL	IB	23D	VLVO	11 6	16900	4 9	29100	32300
35 8	GODERICH 35 PILOT	CUT	SA/CR	STL	KL	IB	23D	VLVO	11 6	16900	4 9	34900	38700
37	GODERICH 37	CUT	SA/CR	STL	KL	IB	23D	VLVO	11 6	17400	4 10	32800	36400
37	GODERICH 37	CUT	SA/CR	STL	KL	IB	23D	VLVO	11 6	17400	4 10	33200	36800
40 9	GODERICH 41 AFT CPT	CUT	SA/CR	STL	KL	IB	35D	VLVO	12 7	23600	5 10	42500	47300
40 9	GODERICH 41 AFT CPT	KTH	SA/CR	STL	KL	IB	35D	VLVO	12 7	23600	5 10	47400	52100
40 9	GODERICH 41 CTR CPT	CUT	SA/CR	STL	KL	IB	35D	VLVO	12 7	23600	5 10	47400	52000
40 9	GODERICH 41 CTR CPT	KTH	SA/CR	STL	KL	IB	35D	VLVO	12 7	23600	5 10	47400	52100
40 9	GODERICH 41 PLT HSE	CUT	SA/CR	STL	KL	IB	35D	VLVO	12 7	23600	5 10	44700	49700
40 9	GODERICH 41 PLT HSE	KTH	SA/CR	STL	KL	IB	35D	VLVO	12 7	23600	5 10	47400	52100
1981 BOATS													
35 8	GODERICH 35	CUT	SA/CR	STL	KL	IB	23D	VLVO	11 6	16900	4 9	30100	33500
35 8	GODERICH 35 PILOT	CUT	SA/CR	STL	KL	IB	23D	VLVO	11 6	16900	4 9	30100	33500
37	GODERICH 37	CUT	SA/CR	STL	KL	IB	23D	VLVO	11 6	17400	4 10	30900	34300
37	GODERICH 37	KTH	SA/CR	STL	KL	IB	23D	VLVO	11 6	17400	4 10	31300	34800
40 9	GODERICH 41 AFT CPT	CUT	SA/CR	STL	KL	IB	35D	VLVO	12 7	23600	5 10	42400	47100
40 9	GODERICH 41 AFT CPT	KTH	SA/CR	STL	KL	IB	35D	VLVO	12 7	23600	5 10	44500	49500
40 9	GODERICH 41 CTR CPT	CUT	SA/CR	STL	KL	IB	35D	VLVO	12 7	23600	5 10	42400	47100
40 9	GODERICH 41 CTR CPT	KTH	SA/CR	STL	KL	IB	35D	VLVO	12 7	23600	5 10	44500	49500
40 9	GODERICH 41 PLT HSE	CUT	SA/CR	STL	KL	IB	35D	VLVO	12 7	23600	5 10	42400	47100
40 9	GODERICH 41 PLT HSE	KTH	SA/CR	STL	KL	IB	35D	VLVO	12 7	23600	5 10	44500	49500
1980 BOATS													
35 7	GODERICH 35	CUT	SA/CR	STL	KL	IB	23D	VLVO	11 6	17000	4 9	28900	32100
35 8	GODERICH 35	CUT	SA/CR	STL	KL	IB	23D	VLVO	11 6	16800	4 9	28600	31800
37	GODERICH 37	CUT	SA/CR	STL	KL	IB	23D	VLVO	11 6	17000	4 9	28900	32100
37	GODERICH 37	KTH	SA/CR	STL	KL	IB	23D	VLVO	11 6	17000	4 9	29300	32500
40 9	GODERICH 41	CUT	SA/CR	STL	KL	IB	35D	VLVO	12 7	23500	5 10	40200	44700
40 9	GODERICH 41	KTH	SA/CR	STL	KL	IB	35D	VLVO	12 7	23500	5 10	42300	47000
40 9	GODERICH 41 CTR CPT	CUT	SA/CR	STL	KL	IB	35D	VLVO	12 7	23600	5 10	40300	44800
40 9	GODERICH 41 CTR CPT	KTH	SA/CR	STL	KL	IB	35D	VLVO	12 7	23600	5 10	42400	47100
1979 BOATS													
35 8	GODERICH 35	CUT	SA/CR	STL	KL	IB	23D	VLVO	11 6	16850	4 10	27600	30600
37	GODERICH 37	KTH	SA/CR	STL	KL	IB	23D	VLVO	11 6	17300	4 10	28500	31700
40 9	GODERICH 41 AFT CPT	CUT	SA/CR	STL	KL	IB	35D	VLVO	12 7	23600	5 10	39000	43300
40 9	GODERICH 41 AFT CPT	CUT	SA/CR	STL	KL	IB	35D	VLVO	12 7	23600	5 10	38400	42700
40 9	GODERICH 41 AFT CPT	KTH	SA/CR	STL	KL	IB	35D	VLVO	12 7	23600	5 10	40500	45000
40 9	GODERICH 41 CTR CPT	CUT	SA/CR	STL	KL	IB	35D	VLVO	12 7	23600	5 10	39000	43300
40 9	GODERICH 41 CTR CPT	CUT	SA/CR	STL	KL	IB	35D	VLVO	12 7	23600	5 10	38400	42700
40 9	GODERICH 41 CTR CPT	KTH	SA/CR	STL	KL	IB	35D	VLVO	12 7	23600	5 10	40500	45000
40 9	GODERICH 41 MS	SLP	MS	STL	KL	IB	35D	VLVO	12 7	23600	5 10	39000	43300
40 9	GODERICH 41 MS	CUT	MS	STL	KL	IB	35D	VLVO	12 7	23600	5 10	38400	42600
1978 BOATS													
35 8	GODERICH 35	CUT	SA/CR	STL	KL	IB	23D	VLVO	11 6	17000	4 9	26800	29700
37	GODERICH 37	KTH	SA/CR	STL	KL	IB	23D	VLVO	11 6	17500	4 9	27700	30700
40	GODERICH 41	SLP	MS	STL	KL	IB	35D	VLVO	12 6	23750	5 4	36800	40800
40	GODERICH 41	CUT	SA/CR	STL	KL	IB	35D	VLVO	12 6	23750	5 4	36500	40500
40	GODERICH 41	SLP	SA/CR	STL	KL	IB	35D	VLVO	12 6	23750	5 4	36800	40900
40	GODERICH 41	CUT	SA/CR	STL	KL	IB	35D	VLVO	12 6	23750	5 4	36500	40500
40	GODERICH 41	YWL	SA/CR	STL	KL	IB	35D	VLVO	12 6	23750	5 4	36800	40900
40	GODERICH 41	KTH	SA/CR	STL	KL	IB	35D	VLVO	12 6	23750	5 4	38600	42900

HURRICANE PRECISION IND INC

Call 1-800-327-6929 for BUC Personalized Evaluation Service
Or, for 1969 to 1970 boats, sign onto www.BUCValuPro.com

HURST ENTERPRISES
COAST GUARD MFG ID- HST

Call 1-800-327-6929 for BUC Personalized Evaluation Service
Or, for 1977 boats, sign onto www.BUCValuPro.com

HUSTLER POWERBOATS
GLOBAL MARINE PERFORMANCE INC
CALVERTON NY 11933   COAST GUARD MFG ID- HUX
ALSO HUSTLER INDUSTRIES   See inside cover to adjust price for area

For more recent years, see the BUC Used Boat Price Guide, Volume 1 or Volume 2

LOA FT IN	NAME AND/ OR MODEL	TOP/ RIG	BOAT TYPE	HULL MTL	HULL TP	ENG TP	ENG HP	ENG MFG	BEAM FT IN	WGT LBS	DRAFT FT IN	RETAIL LOW	RETAIL HIGH
1983 BOATS													
26 6	HUSTLER 26		SPTCR	FBG	DV	OB	260	MRCR	8	4200	3	11700	13200
26 6	HUSTLER 260		SPTCR	FBG	DV	OB			8	2500	1 6	25500	28400
31 10	HUSTLER 320	OP	SPTCR	FBG	DV	OB			8	3000	1 6	43300	48100
31 10	HUSTLER 32SE	OP	OFF	FBG	DV	IO	T370	MRCR	8	6500	3	25400	28200
31 10	HUSTLER 32SS	OP	SPTCR	FBG	DV	IO	T330	MRCR	8	6500	3	23700	26400
1982 BOATS													
31 10	HUSTLER 320	OP	SPTCR	FBG	DV	OB			8	2800	1 6	42200	46900
31 10	HUSTLER 320	OP	SPTCR	FBG	DV	IO	T260		8	6500		21800	24300
31 10	HUSTLER 32SE	OP	OFF	FBG	DV	IO	T370	MRCR	8	6500	3	24800	27500
31 10	HUSTLER 32SS	OP	SPTCR	FBG	DV	IO	T330	MRCR	8	6500	3	23100	25700
1981 BOATS													
32	HUSTLER 32		CR	FBG	DV	IO	T260		8			22000	24500
32	HUSTLER 320		SPTCR	FBG	DV	OB			8			46600	51200
1980 BOATS													
32	HUSTLER 32		CR	FBG	DV	OB			8			44900	49900
32	HUSTLER 32		CR	FBG	DV	IO	T260-T370		8			21800	26300

HUTCHINS CO INC
CLEARWATER FL 33765   COAST GUARD MFG ID- ABV   See inside cover to adjust price for area

For more recent years, see the BUC Used Boat Price Guide, Volume 1 or Volume 2

LOA FT IN	NAME AND/ OR MODEL	TOP/ RIG	BOAT TYPE	HULL MTL	HULL TP	ENG TP	BEAM FT IN	WGT LBS	DRAFT FT IN	RETAIL LOW	RETAIL HIGH
1983 BOATS											
16	COM-PAC	SLP	SAIL	FBG	KL	OB	6	1100	1 6	3050	3500
19	COM-PAC	SLP	SA/CR	FBG	KL	OB	7	2000	2	4250	4950
22 9	COM-PAC	SLP	SA/CR	FBG	KL	OB	7 10	3000	2 3	5900	6800
1982 BOATS											
16	COM-PAC	SLP	SAIL	FBG	KL	OB	6	1100	1 6	2850	3350
19	COM-PAC	SLP	SA/CR	FBG	KL	OB	7	2000	2	4000	4650
22 9	COM-PAC	SLP	SA/CR	FBG	KL	OB	7 10	3000	2 3	5550	6400
1981 BOATS											
16	COM-PAC	SLP	SAIL	FBG	KL	OB	6	1100	1 6	2750	3200
19	COM-PAC	SLP	SA/CR	FBG	KL	OB	7	2000	2	3750	4400
22 9	COM-PAC	SLP	SA/CR	FBG	KL	OB	7 10	2900	2 3	5100	5850
1980 BOATS											
16	COM-PAC	SLP	SAIL	FBG	KL	OB	6	1100	1 6	2600	3000
22 9	COM-PAC	SLP	SA/CR	FBG	KL	OB	7 10	2900	2 3	4850	5600
1979 BOATS											
16	COM-PAC	SLP	SAIL	FBG	KL	OB	6	1100	1 6	2500	2900
22 11	COM-PAC	SLP	SA/CR	FBG	KL	OB	8	2600	2 4	4350	5000
1978 BOATS											
16	COM-PAC	SLP	SAIL	FBG	KL	OB	6	1100	1 6	2400	2800
1977 BOATS											
16	COM-PAC	SLP	SAIL	FBG	KL	OB	6	1100	1 6	2300	2700
1976 BOATS											
16	COM-PAC	SLP	SAIL	FBG	KL	OB	6	1100	1 6	2250	2600

HUTCHINSON
See inside cover to adjust price for area

LOA FT IN	NAME AND/ OR MODEL	TOP/ RIG	BOAT TYPE	HULL MTL	HULL TP	ENG TP	ENG HP	ENG MFG	BEAM FT IN	WGT LBS	DRAFT FT IN	RETAIL LOW	RETAIL HIGH
1931 BOATS													
35						IB	180	NORB				**	**

LOA FT IN	NAME AND/ OR MODEL	TOP/ RIG	BOAT TYPE	-HULL- MTL TP	TP	----ENGINE--- # HP MFG	BEAM FT IN	WGT LBS	DRAFT FT IN	RETAIL LOW	RETAIL HIGH
						--- 1930 BOATS ---					
26				IB		300 CHRY				**	**
40			SDN	IB		151 CHRY	8			752000	826500
						--- 1914 BOATS ---					
30				IB		100 CHRY				**	**

HUTCHINSONS BOAT WORKS INC

Call 1-800-327-6929 for BUC Personalized Evaluation Service
Or, for 1937 to 1966 boats, sign onto www.BUCValuPro.com

HY-RYDER INC
DIV OF HI-PLASTICS INC   COAST GUARD MFG ID- HPL

Call 1-800-327-6929 for BUC Personalized Evaluation Service
Or, for 1977 to 1982 boats, sign onto www.BUCValuPro.com

HYDRA-SPORTS INC
DIV OF GENMAR   See inside cover to adjust price for area
SARASOTA FL 34243   COAST GUARD MFG ID- HSX

For more recent years, see the BUC Used Boat Price Guide, Volume 1 or Volume 2

LOA FT IN	NAME AND/ OR MODEL	TOP/ RIG	BOAT TYPE	-HULL- MTL TP	TP	----ENGINE--- # HP MFG	BEAM FT IN	WGT LBS	DRAFT FT IN	RETAIL LOW	RETAIL HIGH
				--- 1983	BOATS ---						
16 3	1600	OP	CTRCN	KEV	SV	OB	7 5	1240		2250	2650
16 3	1600 CC	OP	CTRCN	FBG	SV	OB	7 5	1240		2000	2400
17 6	1800 CC	OP	CTRCN	FBG	SV	OB	7 5	1320		2200	2600
17 6	1800 SS	OP	CTRCN	KEV	SV	OB	7 5	1320		2400	2800
17 9	PL 150	OP	RNBT	KEV	SV	OB	6 9	850		1700	2000
20 6	2100 CC	OP	CTRCN	FBG	SV	OB	8	2100		4650	5350
20 6	2100 CD	OP	CUD	FBG	SV	OB	8	2600		5300	6050
23 10	2400 CC	OP	CTRCN	FBG	SV	OB	8	2400		5950	6650
23 10	2400 CD	OP	CUD	FBG	SV	OB	8	2900		7050	8100
23 10	2400 CD	OP	CUD	FBG	SV	IO	170 MRCR	8	3900		8050	9300
23 10	2400 CD	OP	CUD	FBG	SV	IO D VLVO	8	3900		**	**
23 10	2400 CD	OP	CUD	FBG	SV	IO T185 MRCR	8	3900		9200	10400
25	2500 WA	OP	CUD	FBG	SV	IO	8	2900		**	**
				--- 1982	BOATS ---						
16 3	1600	OP	CTRCN	KEV	SV	OB	7 5	1240		2200	2550
16 3	1600 CC	OP	CTRCN	FBG	SV	OB	7 5	1240		2000	2350
17 6	1800 CC	OP	CTRCN	FBG	SV	OB	7 5	1320		2200	2550
17 6	1800 SS	OP	CTRCN	KEV	SV	OB	7 5	1320		2350	2700
20 6	2100 CC	OP	CTRCN	FBG	SV	OB	8	2100		4550	5250
20 6	2100 CD	OP	CUD	FBG	SV	OB	8	2600		5200	5950
23 10	2400 CC	OP	CTRCN	FBG	SV	OB	8	2400		5850	6700
23 10	2400 CD	OP	CUD	FBG	SV	OB	8	2900		6900	7950
23 10	2400 CD	OP	CUD	FBG	SV	IO	170 MRCR	8	3900		7900	9050
23 10	2400 CD	OP	CUD	FBG	SV	IO D VLVO	8	3900		**	**
23 10	2400 CD	OP	CUD	FBG	SV	IO T185 MRCR	8	3900		8950	10200
				--- 1979	BOATS ---						
17 3	1700 CC	OP	CTRCN	FBG	SV	OB	7 2		10	2950	3400
19	1900 CC	OP	CTRCN	FBG	SV	OB	7 4	1000	1	1700	2000
20 6	2100 CC	OP	CTRCN	FBG	SV	OB	8		1	5200	6000
23 10	2400 CC	OP	CTRCN	FBG	SV	OB	8		1	9100	10300
23 10	2400 CD	OP	CUD	FBG	SV	OB	8		1	8250	9500
				--- 1978	BOATS ---						
17 2	SUN	OP	RNBT	FBG	TR	OB	6 3			2950	3400
17 3	168-SX	OP	BASS	FBG	SV	OB	6 3			2900	3400
17 3	168-VEE	OP	BASS	FBG	SV	OB	6 3			2900	3400
17 3	170HP	OP	BASS	FBG	TR	OB	6 3			2900	3400
17 3	SKI	OP	SKI	FBG	TR	OB	6 2			2900	3350
18 2	180HP	OP	BASS	FBG	TR	OB	6 7			2900	3350
18 3	178-SX	OP	BASS	FBG	SV	OB	6 9			2900	3400
18 3	178-VEE	OP	BASS	FBG	SV	OB	6 9			2900	3400
19 2	ADVANTAGE	ST	RNBT	KEV	SV	IO	170-250	7 11			4000	4850
				--- 1977	BOATS ---						
19 2	ADVANTAGE	OP	RNBT	KEV	SV	IO		7 11	2300	1 4	**	**

HYDRO-TECHNOLOGY
COAST GUARD MFG ID- HTQ

Call 1-800-327-6929 for BUC Personalized Evaluation Service
Or, for 1983 to 1989 boats, sign onto www.BUCValuPro.com

HYDRODYNE BOATS CO INC
COAST GUARD MFG ID- THI

Call 1-800-327-6929 for BUC Personalized Evaluation Service
Or, for 1983 to 1996 boats, sign onto www.BUCValuPro.com

HYDROFOIL MARINE SALES
COAST GUARD MFG ID- HYC

Call 1-800-327-6929 for BUC Personalized Evaluation Service
Or, for 1973 to 1974 boats, sign onto www.BUCValuPro.com

HYDROSTREAM
DIV OF W E PIPKORN MFG CO   See inside cover to adjust price for area
NEW BRGHTN MN 55112   COAST GUARD MFG ID- HSP

For more recent years, see the BUC Used Boat Price Guide, Volume 1 or Volume 2

LOA FT IN	NAME AND/ OR MODEL	TOP/ RIG	BOAT TYPE	-HULL- MTL TP	TP	----ENGINE--- # HP MFG	BEAM FT IN	WGT LBS	DRAFT FT IN	RETAIL LOW	RETAIL HIGH
				--- 1983	BOATS ---						
16 6	VAMP	OP	RNBT	F/S	DV	OB	7			2550	2950
16 6	VENTURA	OP	RNBT	F/S	DV	OB	7			2150	2500
17 1	VARMINT	OP	BASS	F/S	DV	OB	7			2200	2550
17 1	VECTOR	OP	RNBT	F/S	DV	OB	7 5			2450	2800
17 9	VIKING	OP	RNBT	F/S	DV	OB	7 5			2750	3200
20	VEGAS	OP	RNBT	F/S	DV	OB	7 5			3300	3850
20	VENUS	OP	CUD	F/S	DV	OB	7 5			4250	4950
20	VOYAGER	OP	RNBT	F/S	DV	OB	7 5			3650	4250
20	VULTURE	OP	RNBT	F/S	DV	OB	7 5			3200	3700
				--- 1982	BOATS ---						
16 6	VAMP	OP	RNBT	F/S	DV	OB	7			2500	2900
16 6	VENTURA	OP	RNBT	F/S	DV	OB	7			2050	2450
17 1	VARMINT	OP	BASS	F/S	DV	OB	7			2150	2500
17 1	VECTOR	OP	RNBT	F/S	DV	OB	7 5			2350	2750
17 9	VIKING	OP	RNBT	F/S	DV	OB	7 5			2700	3150
20	VENUS	OP	CUD	F/S	DV	OB	7 5			4150	4800
20	VOYAGER	OP	RNBT	F/S	DV	OB	7 5			3500	4100
20	VULTURE	OP	RNBT	F/S	DV	OB	7 5			3050	3550
				--- 1981	BOATS ---						
16 6	VAMP	OP	RNBT	F/S	DV	OB	7			2450	2900
16 6	VENTURA	OP	RNBT	F/S	DV	OB	7			2000	2400
17 1	VARMINT	OP	BASS	F/S	DV	OB	7			2050	2450
17 1	VECTOR	OP	RNBT	F/S	DV	OB	7 5			2300	2700
17 9	VIKING	OP	RNBT	F/S	DV	OB	7 5			2600	3050
20	VENUS	OP	CUD	F/S	DV	OB	7 5			4000	4650
20	VULTURE	OP	RNBT	F/S	DV	OB	7 5			3200	3750
				--- 1980	BOATS ---						
16 6	VAMP	OP	RNBT	F/S	DV	OB	7			2400	2800
16 6	VENTURA	OP	RNBT	F/S	DV	OB	7			1950	2350
17 1	VARMINT	SF	FBG	DV	OB		7 4			1950	2300
17 1	VECTOR	OP	RNBT	F/S	DV	OB	7 5			2250	2600
17 9	VIKING	OP	RNBT	F/S	DV	OB	7 5			2550	3000
20	VENUS	OP	CUD	F/S	DV	OB	7 5			3950	4550
20	VULTURE	OP	RNBT	F/S	DV	OB	7 5			3150	3650
				--- 1979	BOATS ---						
16 6	VAMP B/R	OP	RNBT	F/S	DV	OB	7			2400	2750
16 6	VENTURA	OP	RNBT	F/S	DV	OB	7			1900	2300
17 1	VARMINT	OP	BASS	F/S	DV	OB	7 4			1950	2350
17 1	VECTOR	OP	RNBT	F/S	DV	OB	7 5			2250	2550
17 9	VIKING	OP	RNBT	F/S	DV	OB	7 5			2500	2900
20	VENUS	OP	CUD	F/S	DV	OB	7 5			3850	4500
20	VULTURE	OP	RNBT	F/S	DV	OB	7 5			3050	3550
				--- 1978	BOATS ---						
16 6	VAMP B/R	OP	RNBT	F/S	DV	OB	7			2250	2650
16 6	VENTURA	OP	RNBT	F/S	DV	OB	7			1950	2300
17 1	VARMINT	OP	BASS	F/S	DV	OB	7 4			1950	2300
17 1	VECTOR	OP	RNBT	F/S	SV	OB	7 5			2150	2500
17 9	VIKING	OP	RNBT	F/S	SV	OB	7 5			2500	2900
20	VULTURE	OP	RNBT	F/S	SV	OB	7 5			3000	3500
				--- 1977	BOATS ---						
20 1	VULTURE	OP	RNBT	F/S	SV	OB	7 5	850		1700	2000

HYDROSWIFT INC

LUDLOW TOWNLEY CO INC   COAST GUARD MFG ID- HYD

Call 1-800-327-6929 for BUC Personalized Evaluation Service
Or, for 1959 to 1977 boats, sign onto www.BUCValuPro.com

I M P BOATS

INTERNATIONAL MARINE PRODUCTS
IOLA KS 66749   COAST GUARD MFG ID- XMP   See inside cover to adjust price for area

For more recent years, see the BUC Used Boat Price Guide, Volume 1 or Volume 2

LOA FT	LOA IN	NAME AND/ OR MODEL	TOP/ RIG	BOAT TYPE	-HULL- MTL	-HULL- TP	ENGINE TP	ENGINE # HP	ENGINE MFG	BEAM FT	BEAM IN	WGT LBS	DRAFT FT	DRAFT IN	RETAIL LOW	RETAIL HIGH
		1983 BOATS														
16		CHEROKEE BR	OP	RNBT	FBG	SV	IO	120	MRCR	7		1800			1900	2300
17	4	SHAWNEE	OP	RNBT	FBG	SV	IO	120-200		7	5	2050			2350	2750
17	6	APACHE	ST	RNBT	FBG	DV	IO	120-185		7		2200			2350	2750
18	2	NAVAJO BR	ST	RNBT	FBG	DV	IO	170-260		7	8	3200			3200	3950
18	6	COMANCHE	ST	RNBT	FBG	SV	IO	170-260		7	7	2960			3050	3800
20	2	AZTEC 202 BR	ST	RNBT	FBG	DV	IO	170-260		7	8	3140			3500	4350
20	2	AZTEC 202 CC	ST	CUD	FBG	DV	IO	228-260		7	8	3360			3950	4750
20	2	AZTEC 202 HT	HT	RNBT	FBG	DV	IO	170-260		7	8	3290			3650	4500
20	2	AZTEC 202CC	ST	CUD	FBG	DV	IO	170-200		7	8	3360			3850	4550
20	2	AZTEC WT	ST	RNBT	FBG	DV	IO	170-260		7	8	3140			3550	4350
23	2	INCA 232 CC	HT	CBNCR	FBG	DV	IO	228-260		8		4760			6950	8150
23	2	INCA 232 CC	HT	CBNCR	FBG	DV	IO	T140-T260		8		4760			7500	9250
23	2	INCA 232 CCFB	FB	CUD	FBG	DV	IO	228-260		8		4510			5900	6950
23	2	INCA 232 CCFB	FB	CUD	FBG	DV	IO	T140-T185		8		4510			6400	7450
23	2	INCA 232 CCHT	HT	CUD	FBG	DV	IO	228-260		8		4260			5650	6650
23	2	INCA 232 CCHT	HT	CUD	FBG	DV	IO	T140-T260		8		4260			6150	7600
23	2	INCA 232 CCO	ST	CUD	FBG	DV	IO	228-260		8		4110			5500	6450
23	2	INCA 232 CCO	ST	CUD	FBG	DV	IO	T140-T260		8		4110			6000	7450
23	2	INCA 232CCO	ST	CUD	FBG	SV	IO	T170-T185		8		4000			5900	6850
25	4	X-254	ST	CUD	FBG	DV	IO	228-260		8		5210			7250	8550
25	4	X-254	ST	CUD	FBG	DV	IO	T170-T260		8		5210			7950	9900
26	9	KANSA	ST	SPTCR	FBG	DV	IO	260		8		6600			9300	10500
26	9	KANSA	ST	SPTCR	FBG	DV	IO	T140-T230		8		6600			9550	11700
26	9	KANSA	ST	SPTCR	FBG	DV	IO	T260		8		6600			10600	12000
		1982 BOATS														
16		CHEROKEE BR	OP	RNBT	FBG	SV	IO	120	OMC	7		1800			1850	2200
17	4	SHAWNEE BR	OP	RNBT	FBG	SV	IO	120	OMC	7	6	2050			2300	2650
17	4	SHAWNEE WT	OP	RNBT	FBG	SV	IO	120	OMC	7	6	2050			2300	2650
17	6	APACHE	ST	RNBT	FBG	DV	IO	140-185		7		2200			2300	2700
18	2	NAVAJO BR	ST	RNBT	FBG	DV	IO	170-260		7	8	3200			3100	3850
18	6	COMANCHE	ST	RNBT	FBG	SV	IO	140-260		7	7	2960			3000	3700
20	2	AZTEC 202 BR	ST	RNBT	FBG	DV	IO	170-260		7	8	3140			3500	4300
20	2	AZTEC 202 CC	ST	CUD	FBG	DV	IO	228-260		7	8	3360			3900	4650
20	2	AZTEC 202 HT	HT	RNBT	FBG	DV	IO	170-260		7	8	3290			3550	4400
20	2	AZTEC WT	ST	RNBT	FBG	DV	IO	170-260		7	8	3140			3400	4200
23	2	INCA 232 CC	HT	CBNCR	FBG	DV	IO	170-260		8		4760			6650	7950
23	2	INCA 232 CC	HT	CBNCR	FBG	DV	IO	T140-T260		8		4760			7350	9050
23	2	INCA 232 CCFB	FB	CUD	FBG	DV	IO	228-260		8		4510			5750	6750
23	2	INCA 232 CCFB	FB	CUD	FBG	DV	IO	T140-T170		8		4510			6250	7250
23	2	INCA 232 CCHT	HT	CUD	FBG	DV	IO	170-260		8		4260			5400	6500
23	2	INCA 232 CCHT	HT	CUD	FBG	DV	IO	T140-T260		8		4260			6000	7450
23	2	INCA 232 CCO	ST	CUD	FBG	DV	IO	170-260		8		4110			5250	6300
23	2	INCA 232 CCO	ST	CUD	FBG	DV	IO	T140-T260		8		4110			5850	7250
25	4	X-254	ST	CUD	FBG	DV	IO	170-260		8		5210			6850	8350
25	4	X-254	ST	CUD	FBG	DV	IO	T170-T260		8		5210			7750	9650
26	9	KANSA	ST	SPTCR	FBG	DV	IO	170-260		8		6600			8450	10300
26	9	KANSA	ST	SPTCR	FBG	DV	IO	T140-T230		8		6600			9350	11400
26	9	KANSA	ST	SPTCR	FBG	DV	IO	T260		8		6600			10300	11800
		1981 BOATS														
17	6	APACHE 17		RNBT	FBG	DV	IO	140		7	8				2400	2750
18	2	NAVAJO W/T		RNBT	FBG	SV	IO	200		7	8				2500	2900
18	6	COMANCHE		RNBT	FBG	SV	IO	200		7	7				3000	3450
20	2	AZTEC 20		CR	FBG	SV	IO	200		7	8				3600	4200
20	2	AZTEC 20 W/T		RNBT	FBG	SV	IO	200		7	8				3500	4050
23	2	INCA 23	FB	CR	FBG	SV	IO	240		8					5100	5900
23	2	INCA 23		CUD	FBG	SV	IO	240		8					5100	5900
25	4	X-254		RNBT	FBG	DV	IO	260		8					6450	7450
26	9	KANSA 26		EXP	FBG	SV	IO	260		8					8450	9700
		1980 BOATS														
17	6	APACHE	ST	RNBT	FBG	DV	IO	140-170		7		2200			2250	2650
18	2	NAVAJO BR	ST	RNBT	FBG	DV	IO	198-260		7	8	3200			3050	3750
18	6	COMANCHE	ST	RNBT	FBG	SV	IO	140-260		7	10	2960			2950	3700
20	2	AZTEC 202 BR	ST	RNBT	FBG	DV	IO	198-260		7	8	3140			3450	4200
20	2	AZTEC 202 CC	ST	CUD	FBG	DV	IO	228-260		7	8	3360			3800	4550
20	2	AZTEC 202 HT	HT	RNBT	FBG	DV	IO	198-260		7	8	3290			3500	4250
20	2	AZTEC HT	HT	CR	FBG	DV	IO	225		7	8				3650	4200
20	2	AZTEC WT	ST	RNBT	FBG	DV	IO	198-260		7	8	3140			3350	4100
23	2	INCA		CR	FBG	DV	OB			8					2750	3200
23	2	INCA	HT	CR	FBG	DV	OB			8					2750	3200
23	2	INCA		CUD	FBG	DV	IO	240		8					5100	5850
23	2	INCA	FB	CUD	FBG	DV	OB			8					2750	3200
23	2	INCA	FB	CUD	FBG	DV	IO	240		8					5100	5850
23	2	INCA		SF	FBG	DV	OB			8					2700	3150
23	2	INCA 232 CC	HT	CBNCR	FBG	DV	IO	228-260		8		4760			6600	7750
23	2	INCA 232 CC	HT	CBNCR	FBG	DV	IO	T140-T260		8		4760			7150	8800
23	2	INCA 232 CCFB	FB	CUD	FBG	DV	IO	228-260		8		4510			5650	6600
23	2	INCA 232 CCFB	FB	CUD	FBG	DV	IO	T140-T170		8		4510			6100	7050
23	2	INCA 232 CCHT	HT	CUD	FBG	DV	IO	228-260		8		4260			5400	6300
23	2	INCA 232 CCHT	HT	CUD	FBG	DV	IO	T140-T260		8		4260			5850	7250
23	2	INCA 232 CCO	ST	CUD	FBG	DV	IO	228-260		8		4110			5250	6150
23	2	INCA 232 CCO	ST	CUD	FBG	DV	IO	T140-T260		8		4110			5750	7100
25	4	X-254	ST	CUD	FBG	DV	OB			8					3900	4550
25	4	X-254	ST	CUD	FBG	DV	IO	228-260		8		5210			6900	8450
25	4	X-254	ST	CUD	FBG	DV	IO	T170-T260		8		5210			7550	9400
25	4	X-254		SPTCR	FBG	DV	IO	T240-T260		8					7600	8950
26	9	KANSA	ST	SPTCR	FBG	DV	OB			8					4900	5650
26	9	KANSA	ST	SPTCR	FBG	DV	IO	260		8		6600			8850	10100
26	9	KANSA	ST	SPTCR	FBG	DV	IO	T140-T230		8		6600			9150	11100
26	9	KANSA	ST	SPTCR	FBG	DV	IO	T260		8		6600			10100	11500
		1979 BOATS														
17	6	APACHE	ST	RNBT	FBG	DV	IO	140-170		7		2200			2250	2650
18	2	NAVAJO II 182 BR	ST	RNBT	FBG	DV	IO	198-260		7	8	3200			3050	3750
18	2	NAVAJO II 182 WT	ST	RNBT	FBG	DV	IO	198-260		7	8	3050			2950	3650
18	2	PAWNEE BR	ST	RNBT	FBG	TR	IO	198-260		7	8	3310			3100	3800
20	2	AZTEC 202 BR	ST	RNBT	FBG	DV	IO	198-260		7	8	3140			3450	4200
20	2	AZTEC 202 CC	ST	CUD	FBG	DV	IO	228-260		7	8	3360			3800	4550
20	2	AZTEC 202 HT	HT	RNBT	FBG	DV	IO	198-260		7	8	3290			3500	4250
20	2	AZTEC WT	ST	RNBT	FBG	DV	IO	198-260		7	8	3140			3350	4100
23	2	INCA 232 CC	HT	CBNCR	FBG	DV	IO	228-260		8		4760			6600	7750
23	2	INCA 232 CC	HT	CBNCR	FBG	DV	IO	T140-T260		8		4760			7150	8800
23	2	INCA 232 CCFB	FB	CUD	FBG	DV	IO	228-260		8		4510			5600	6600
23	2	INCA 232 CCFB	FB	CUD	FBG	DV	IO	T140-T170		8		4510			6100	7050
23	2	INCA 232 CCHT	HT	CUD	FBG	DV	IO	228-260		8		4260			5400	6300
23	2	INCA 232 CCHT	HT	CUD	FBG	DV	IO	T140-T260		8		4260			5850	7250
23	2	INCA 232 CCO	ST	CUD	FBG	DV	IO	228-260		8		4110			5250	6150
23	2	INCA 232 CCO	ST	CUD	FBG	DV	IO	T140-T260		8		4110			5700	7100
25	4	X-250	ST	CUD	FBG	DV	IO	260		8		4010			6000	6900
25	4	X-250 SPORT	ST	SPTCR	FBG	DV	IO	228-260		8		5210			6900	8150
25	4	X-250 SPORT	ST	SPTCR	FBG	DV	IO	T170-T260		8		5210			7550	9400
26	9	KANSA	OP	SPTCR	FBG	DV	IO	260		8		5800			8100	9300
26	9	KANSA	OP	SPTCR	FBG	DV	IO	T170-T230		8		5800			8650	10500
26	9	KANSA	OP	SPTCR	FBG	DV	IO	T260		8		5800			9500	10800
		1978 BOATS														
17	6	APACHE	ST	RNBT	FBG	DV	IO	140-170		7		2200	1	6	2250	2650
18	2	NAVAJO II 182 BR	ST	RNBT	FBG	DV	IO	170-260		7	8	3200	1	8	3050	3750
18	2	NAVAJO II 182 WT	ST	RNBT	FBG	DV	IO	170-260		7	8	3050	1	8	2950	3650
18	2	PAWNEE B/R	ST	RNBT	FBG	TR	IO	170-260		7	8	3310	1	8	3100	3850
20	2	AZTEC 202 BR	ST	RNBT	FBG	DV	IO	170-260		7	8	3140	1	8	3450	4250
20	2	AZTEC 202 CCO	ST	CUD	FBG	DV	IO	225-260		7	8	3590	1	8	3950	4750
20	2	AZTEC 202 HT	HT	RNBT	FBG	DV	IO	170-260		7	8	3290	1	8	3500	4300
20	2	AZTEC WT	ST	RNBT	FBG	DV	IO	170-260		7	8	3140	1	8	3350	4150
23	2	INCA 232 CC	HT	CBNCR	FBG	DV	IO	228-260		8		4760	2		6650	7800
23	2	INCA 232 CC	HT	CBNCR	FBG	DV	IO	T140-T260		8		4760	2		7200	8850
23	2	INCA 232 CCO	ST	CUD	FBG	DV	IO	198-260		8		4110	2		5200	6200
23	2	INCA 232 CCO	ST	CUD	FBG	DV	IO	T140-T260		8		4110	2		5750	7150
23	2	INCA FB	FB	CUD	FBG	DV	IO	228-260		8		4510	2		5650	6650
23	2	INCA FB	FB	CUD	FBG	DV	IO	T140-T260		8		4510	2		6150	7600
23	2	INCA HT	HT	CUD	FBG	DV	IO	198-260		8		4260	2		5350	6350
23	2	INCA HT	HT	CUD	FBG	DV	IO	T140-T260		8		4260	2		5900	7300
25	4	X-250	ST	CUD	FBG	DV	IO	228-260		8		4010	2		5900	6950
25	4	X-250 SPORT	ST	SPTCR	FBG	DV	IO	228-260		8		4010	2		5900	6950
25	4	X-250 SPORT	ST	SPTCR	FBG	DV	IO	T170-T260		8		5210	2		7600	9500
		1977 BOATS														
17	6	APACHE 176WT	ST	RNBT	FBG	DV	IO	140-170		7		2200			2300	2700
18	2	NAVAJO II 182BR	ST	RNBT	FBG	DV	IO	170-235		7	8	3200			3100	3700
18	2	NAVAJO II 182WT	ST	RNBT	FBG	DV	IO	170-235		7	8	3050			3000	3600
18	2	PAWNEE	ST	RNBT	FBG	TR	IO	170-235		7	8	3310			3150	3800
20	2	AZTEC 202BR	ST	RNBT	FBG	DV	IO	170-235		7	8				3500	4200

CONTINUED ON NEXT PAGE

LOA FT	LOA IN	NAME AND/ OR MODEL	TOP/ RIG	BOAT TYPE	-HULL- MTL	-HULL- TP	TP	ENGINE # HP	ENGINE MFG	BEAM FT	BEAM IN	WGT LBS	DRAFT FT	DRAFT IN	RETAIL LOW	RETAIL HIGH
1977 BOATS																
20	2	AZTEC 202CCO	ST	CUD	FBG	DV	IO	170-235		7	8	3360			3750	4500
20	2	AZTEC 202HT	HT	RNBT	FBG	DV	IO	170-235		7	8	3290			3550	4250
20	2	AZTEC 202WT	ST	RNBT	FBG	DV	IO	170-235		7	8	3140			3450	4150
23	2	INCA 232CC	HT	CBNCR	FBG	DV	IO	233-280		8		4760			6800	8050
23	2	INCA 232CC	HT	CBNCR	FBG	DV	IO	T140-T235		8		4760			7350	8750
23	2	INCA 232CCFB	FB	CUD	FBG	DV	IO	233-280		8		4510			5750	6850
23	2	INCA 232CCFB	FB	CUD	FBG	DV	IO	T140-T235		8		4510			6250	7450
23	2	INCA 232CCHT	HT	CUD	FBG	DV	IO	188-280		8		4260			5450	6600
23	2	INCA 232CCHT	HT	CUD	FBG	DV	IO	T140-T235		8		4260			6000	7200
23	2	INCA 232CCO	ST	CUD	FBG	DV	IO	188-280		8		4110			5300	6400
23	2	INCA 232CCO	ST	CUD	FBG	DV	IO	T140-T235		8		4110			5850	7000
25	4	SPORT-X-250 X254	ST	RACE	FBG	DV	IO	233-280		8		5210			6600	7850
25	4	SPORT-X-250 X254	ST	RACE	FBG	DV	IO	T170-T235		8		5210			7150	8600
25	4	X-250 X254	ST	CUD	FBG	DV	IO	233-280		8		4010			6000	7200
1976 BOATS																
18	2	NAVAJO II 182WT	ST	RNBT	FBG	DV	IO	175-235		7	8	2700			2850	3450
18	2	PAWNEE	ST	RNBT	FBG	TR	IO	175-235		7	8	3100			3100	3750
20	1	AZTEC 201CCO	ST	CUD	FBG	DV	IO	175-235		7	8	3120			3650	4400
20	1	AZTEC 201HT	HT	CR	FBG	DV	IO	175-235		7	8	3100			3650	4400
20	1	AZTEC 201WT	ST	RNBT	FBG	DV	IO	175-235		7	8	2900			3350	4050
23	2	INCA 232CC	HT	CBNCR	FBG	DV	IO	190-300		8		4350			6350	7900
23	2	INCA 232CC	HT	CBNCR	FBG	DV	IO	T140-T190		8		4350			7050	8200
23	2	INCA 232CCFB	FB	CUD	FBG	DV	IO	188-300		8		4100			5400	6750
23	2	INCA 232CCFB	FB	CUD	FBG	DV	IO	T140-T190		8		4100			6000	6950
23	2	INCA 232CCHT	HT	CUD	FBG	DV	IO	188-300		8		3850			5150	6450
23	2	INCA 232CCHT	HT	CUD	FBG	DV	IO	T140-T190		8		3850			5750	6700
23	2	INCA 232CCO	ST	CUD	FBG	DV	IO	188-280		8		3700			5000	6100
23	2	INCA 232CCO	ST	CUD	FBG	DV	IO	300	CC	8		3700			5450	6300
23	2	INCA 232CCO	ST	CUD	FBG	DV	IO	T140-T190		8		3700			5600	6500
25	6	X-250 X256	ST	CUD	FBG	DV	IO	233-300		8		4800			6950	8500
25	6	X-250 X256	ST	CUD	FBG	DV	IO	T188-T235		8		4800			7700	9250
25	6	X-250 X256	ST	CUD	FBG	DV	IO	T300	CC	8		4800			8950	10200
1975 BOATS																
16	8	CHEROKEE 16	OP	RNBT	FBG	TR	IO	140-190		7	2	2200			2350	2750
17	6	X-176	OP	RNBT	FBG	DV	IO	188-245		7		2200			2450	3000
18	2	PAWNEE B/R	OP	RNBT	FBG	TR	IO	175-245		7	8	3100			3200	3900
18	8	NAVAJO II	OP	RNBT	FBG	DV	IO	175-245		7	8				3200	3900
20	2	AZTEC	OP	CUD	FBG	DV	IO	175-245		7	8	3120	1	6	3800	4600
20	2	AZTEC	OP	RNBT	FBG	DV	IO	175-245		7	8	2900	1	6	3500	4200
20	2	AZTEC	HT	RNBT	FBG	DV	IO	175-245		7	8	3100	1	6	3650	4400
23	2	INCA	HT	CR	FBG	DV	IO	225		8		3700			5250	6050
IO 225 5900 6800, IO 225D 8000 9200, IO T190															5850	6750
23	2	INCA	FB	CR	FBG	DV	IO	225		8		4100			5650	6500
23	2	INCA	FB	CR	FBG	DV	IO	T190		8		4100			6250	7200
23	2	INCA	HT	CUD	FBG	DV	IO	225		8		3856			5400	6200
23	2	INCA	HT	CUD	FBG	DV	IO	T190		8		3856			6000	6900
23	2	INCA	FB	SF	FBG	DV	IO	225		8		4100			6450	7450
23	2	INCA	FB	SF	FBG	DV	IO	T190		8		4100			7150	8250
24	6	X-246	OP	CUD	FBG	DV	IO	300		7	8	4200	2		6550	7550
24	6	X-246	OP	CUD	FBG	DV	IO	T300		7	8	4200	2		7800	8950
1974 BOATS																
16	8	CHEROKEE W/T	OP	RNBT	FBG	TR	IO	140-165		7	2	2200	2	7	2400	2800
17	6	X-176		RNBT	FBG	DV	IO	188-245		7		2200			2550	3100
18	2	PAWNEE B/R	OP	RNBT	FBG	TR	IO	165-245		7	8	3100	2	11	3300	4050
20	2	AZTEC	OP	CUD	FBG	DV	IO	165-245		7	8	3120	3		3950	4800
20	2	AZTEC WT	ST	RNBT	FBG	DV	IO	165-245		7	8	2900	3		3600	4350
23	2	INCA	HT	CR	FBG	DV	IO	188		8		3700			5350	6150
23	2	INCA	HT	CR	FBG	DV	IO	T245		8		3700			6350	7300
23	2	INCA	HT	CUD	FBG	DV	IO	188		8		3850			5500	6350
23	2	INCA	HT	CUD	FBG	DV	IO	T245		8		3850			6500	7450
23	2	INCA	FB	SF	FBG	DV	IO	188		8		4100			6600	7600
23	2	INCA	FB	SF	FBG	DV	IO	T245		8		4100			7700	8850
24	6	X-246		CUD	FBG	DV	IO	T165-T250		7	10	4200			7000	8600
1973 BOATS																
16	2	COMANCHE	OP	RNBT	FBG		JT	390	OLDS	6	6				2150	2500
16	8	CHEROKEE 16	OP	RNBT	FBG		IO	140-170		7	2	2200			2500	2900
16	8	CHEROKEE 16	OP	RNBT	FBG		JT	390	OLDS	7	2	2200			2350	2700
18	2	PAWNEE B/R	OP	RNBT	FBG		IO	140-245		7	8				2800	3450
18	2	PAWNEE B/R	OP	RNBT	FBG		IO	270	CHRY	7	8				3100	3600
18	2	PAWNEE B/R	OP	RNBT	FBG		JT	390	OLDS	7	8				2550	3000
20	2	AZTEC	OP	CUD	FBG		IO	165-270		7	8				4100	5100
20	2	AZTEC	OP	CUD	FBG		JT	390	OLDS	7	8				3350	3900
20	2	AZTEC	OP	RNBT	FBG		IO	165-270		7	8				3950	4950
20	2	AZTEC	OP	RNBT	FBG		JT	390	OLDS	7	8				3450	4000
20	2	AZTEC	HT	RNBT	FBG		IO	165-270		7	8				3950	4950
20	2	AZTEC	HT	RNBT	FBG		JT	390	OLDS	7	8				3450	4000
23	2	INCA	HT	CBNCR	FBG		OB			8		4050			2600	3050
23	2	INCA	HT	CBNCR	FBG		IO	140-270		8					6450	7800
23	2	INCA	HT	CBNCR	FBG		IO	T140-T245		8					7200	8650
23	2	INCA	HT	CBNCR	FBG		IO	T270	CHRY	8					7900	9100
23	2	INCA	HT	CR	FBG		IO	165-270		8					5700	6900
23	2	INCA	HT	CR	FBG		IO	T140-T245		8					6400	7700
23	2	INCA	HT	CR	FBG		IO	T270	CHRY	8					7000	8050
23	2	INCA	FB	CR	FBG		IO	165-270		8					5700	6900
23	2	INCA	FB	CR	FBG		IO	T140-T245		8					6400	7700
23	2	INCA	FB	CR	FBG		IO	T270	CHRY	8					7000	8050
23	2	INCA	HT	CUD	FBG		IO	165-270		8					5700	6900
23	2	INCA	HT	CUD	FBG		JT	390	OLDS	8					4600	5300
23	2	INCA	HT	CUD	FBG		IO	T140	MRCR	8					6400	7350
24	6	X-246	ST	CUD	FBG		OB			7	10	4200			2750	3200
24	6	X-246	ST	CUD	FBG		JT	390	OLDS	7	10				6450	7400
24	6	X-246	ST	CUD	FBG		IO	T	CHRY	7	10				**	**
24	6	X-246	ST	CUD	FBG		IO	T188-T270		7	10				9000	10900
1972 BOATS																
16	8	CHEROKEE W/T	OP	RNBT	FBG		IO	140-245		7	2	2200			2600	3150
18	2	PAWNEE B/R	OP	RNBT	FBG		IO	155-245		7	8				2900	3550
18	2	SANTEE	OP	RNBT	FBG		IO	155-245		7	4				2800	3450
18	2	SANTEE	HT	RNBT	FBG		IO	155-245		7	4	2700			3150	3850
20	2	AZTEC	OP	CUD	FBG		IO	155-245		7	8				4200	5100
20	2	AZTEC	HT	RNBT	FBG		IO	155-245		7	8				4050	4900
20	2	AZTEC WT	OP		FBG		IO	155-245		7	8				4000	4850
23	2	INCA	HT	CBNCR	FBG		IO	155-270		8		4050			6800	8250
IO 325 MRCR 7750 8900, IO T140-T245 7450 8950, IO T270															8150	9400
IO T325 MRCR 9400 10700																
23	2	INCA	HT	CR	FBG		IO	155-270		8					5900	7150
23	2	INCA	HT	CR	FBG		IO	325	MRCR	8	2	3750			6600	7600
23	2	INCA	HT	CR	FBG		IO	T140-T188		8					6600	7700
23	2	INCA	HT	CUD	FBG		IO	155-270		8					5900	7150
IO 325 MRCR 6700 7700, IO T140-T245 6600 7950, IO T270															7250	8350
IO T325 MRCR 8250 9500																
23	2	INCA	FB	SF	FBG		IO	155-270		8					6700	8150
23	2	INCA	FB	SF	FBG		IO	325	MRCR	8					7700	8800
23	2	INCA	FB	SF	FBG		IO	T140-T188		8					7550	8800
24	6	X-246	ST	CUD	FBG		IO	155-270		7	10				8250	10000
24	6	X-246	ST	CUD	FBG		IO	325	MRCR	7	10				9300	10600
24	6	X-246	ST	CUD	FBG		IO	T140-T270		7	10				9150	11300
1971 BOATS																
16	2	COMANCHE		RNBT	FBG	DV	IO	155-200		6	4	1900	2	3	2300	2700
16	8	CHEROKEE		RNBT	FBG	TR	IO	155-215		7	2		2	3	2650	3150
17		NAVAJO		RNBT	FBG	DV	IO	155-225		6	4	2000	2	3	2450	2950
18	2	PAWNEE		RNBT	FBG	TR	IO	165-215		7	8		2	5	3050	3600
18	2	SANTEE		RNBT	FBG	DV	IO	155-225		7	4	2500	2	5	3150	3750
20	2	AZTEC	OP	RNBT	FBG	DV	IO	165-225		7	8	2700			3800	4550
20	2	AZTEC	HT	RNBT	FBG	DV	IO	165		7	8		2	5	4250	4900
20	2	AZTEC CRUISER		SDN	FBG	DV	IO	165-225		7	8	3000	2	5	4250	5050
20	2	AZTEC W/T		RNBT	FBG	DV	IO	165		7	8		2	5	4250	4900
23	2	INCA		CBNCR	FBG	DV	IO	210		8			2	10	6950	8000
23	2	INCA		CBNCR	FBG	DV	IO	T215		8			2	10	7900	9100
23	2	INCA W/T	OP	CR	FBG	DV	IO	210		8			2	10	6200	7100
23	2	INCA W/T	OP	CR	FBG	DV	IO	T225		8			2	10	7050	8150
23	2	INCA W/T	HT	CR	FBG	DV	IO	210		8			2	10	6200	7100
1970 BOATS																
16	2	COMANCHE		RNBT	FBG	DV	IO	200		6	4	1900			2400	2800
17		NAVAJO		RNBT	FBG	DV	IO	225		6	4	2000			2600	3050
18	2	OCEANIC		RNBT	FBG	DV	IO	225		7	4	2500			3350	3900
20	1	AZTEC		RNBT	FBG	DV	IO	225		7	7	2700			4000	4650
20	1	AZTEC CRUISER		CR	FBG	DV	IO	225		7	7	3000			4500	5150
23	2	INCA		CR	FBG	DV	IO	225		8					6400	7400
1969 BOATS																
16	2	COMMANCHE	OP	RNBT	FBG	DV	IO	120	MRCR	6	4	1900	2	3	2400	2800
16	8	CHEROKEE	OP	RNBT	FBG	TR	IO	120	MRCR	7	2	2200	2	3	2850	3300
17		NANAJO	OP	RNBT	FBG	DV	OB			6	4	9856			7300	8400
17		NAVAJO	OP	RNBT	FBG	DV	IO	120	MRCR	6	4	2000	2	3	2600	3000
18	2	OCEANIC 18	OP	RNBT	FBG	DV	IO	225	MRCR	6	4	2500	3	7	3250	3750
18	2	SANTEE		RNBT	FBG	DV	IO	155	MRCR	7	4	2500	2	5	3350	3900
20	2	AZTEC	HT	CR	FBG	DV	IO	120	MRCR	7	8	3000	2	5	4550	5200
20	2	AZTEC	OP	RNBT	FBG	DV	IO	155	MRCR	7	8	2700	2	5	4050	4700
23	2	INCA	HT	CR	FBG	DV	IO	160	MRCR	8		2940	2	10	5400	6200

CONTINUED ON NEXT PAGE

LOA FT IN	NAME AND/ OR MODEL		TOP/ RIG	BOAT TYPE	-HULL- MTL TP TP	----ENGINE--- # HP MFG	BEAM FT IN	WGT LBS	DRAFT FT IN	RETAIL LOW	RETAIL HIGH
						1968 BOATS					
16	2	COMANCHE	OP	RNBT	FBG DV IO	120-200	6 4	1900		2500	2950
17		NAVAJO	OP	RNBT	FBG DV IO		6 4	1970		**	**
17		NAVAJO	OP	RNBT	FBG DV IO	120-225	6 4	1970		2650	3250
18	2	OCEANIC	OP	RNBT	FBG DV IO		7 4			**	**
18	2	OCEANIC	OP	RNBT	FBG DV IO	120-225	7 4	2600		3500	4250
18	2	OCEANIC	HT	RNBT	FBG DV IO		7 4			**	**
18	2	OCEANIC	HT	RNBT	FBG DV IO	120-255	7 4	2600		3500	4400
20	2	AZTEC	OP	CR	FBG DV IO		7 7			**	**
20	2	AZTEC	OP	CR	FBG DV IO	120-255	7 7	2800		4450	5450
20	2	AZTEC	HT	CR	FBG DV IO		7 7			**	**
20	2	AZTEC	HT	CR	FBG DV IO	120-225	7 7	2800		4450	5300
20	2	AZTEC	HT	RNBT	FBG DV IO		7 7			**	**
20	2	AZTEC	HT	RNBT	FBG DV IO	120-225	7 7	2800		4250	5100
23	2	INCA	OP	CR	FBG DV IB	155-225	8	2940	2 7	2850	3350
23	2	INCA	OP	CR	FBG DV IB	T120-T160	8	2940	2 7	3050	3750
						1967 BOATS					
16		APACHE	OP	RNBT	FBG DV IO		6	845		**	**
16		APACHE	OP	RNBT	FBG DV IO	80-225	6			2650	3250
16	2	COMANCHE	OP	RNBT	FBG DV IO	120-225	6 5	1900		2600	3150
17		NAVAJO	OP	RNBT	FBG DV IO		6 4	1970		**	**
17		NAVAJO	OP	RNBT	FBG DV IO	120-225	6 4	1970		2750	3350
18	2	OCEANIC	OP	RNBT	FBG DV IO		7 4			**	**
18	2	OCEANIC	OP	RNBT	FBG DV IO	120-225	7 4	2600		3650	4400
18	2	OCEANIC	HT	RNBT	FBG DV IO		7 4			**	**
18	2	OCEANIC	HT	RNBT	FBG DV IO	120-225	7 4	2600		3650	4400
20	2	AZTEC	OP	CR	FBG DV IO		7 7			**	**
20	2	AZTEC	OP	CR	FBG DV IO	120-225	7 7	2800		4600	5450
20	2	AZTEC	HT	CR	FBG DV IO		7 7			**	**
20	2	AZTEC	HT	CR	FBG DV IO	120-225	7 7	2800		4600	5450
20	2	AZTEC	HT	RNBT	FBG DV IO		7 7			**	**
20	2	AZTEC	HT	RNBT	FBG DV IO	120-225	7 7	2800		4450	5250
						1966 BOATS					
16		APACHE	OP	RNBT	FBG DV IO		5 11			**	**
16		APACHE	OP	RNBT	FBG DV IO	90-150	5 11			2800	3300
16		APACHE STANDARD	OP	RNBT	FBG IO		5 11			**	**
16		APACHE STANDARD	OP	RNBT	FBG IO	90-150	5 11			2700	3250
17		NAVAJO	OP	RNBT	FBG DV IO		6 4			**	**
17		NAVAJO	OP	RNBT	FBG DV IO	90-225	6 4			2950	3600
18	2	OCEANIC	OP	RNBT	FBG DV IO		6 11			**	**
18	2	OCEANIC	OP	RNBT	FBG DV IO	90-225	6 11			3300	4000
18	2	OCEANIC	OP	RNBT	FBG IO	310	6 11			4050	4700
20	2	AZTEC	OP	CR	FBG IO		7 7			**	**
20	2	AZTEC	OP	CR	FBG IO	90-225	7 7			5100	6050
20	2	AZTEC	OP	CR	FBG IO	310	7 7			5950	6800
20	2	AZTEC	HT	CR	FBG IO		7 7			**	**
20	2	AZTEC	HT	CR	FBG IO	90-225	7 7			5100	6050
20	2	AZTEC	HT	CR	FBG IO	310	7 7			5950	6800
20	2	AZTEC	HT	RNBT	FBG IO		7 7			**	**
20	2	AZTEC	HT	RNBT	FBG IO	90-225	7 7			4950	5850
20	2	AZTEC	HT	RNBT	FBG IO	310	7 7			5700	6550
						1965 BOATS					
16		APACHE	OP	RNBT	FBG IO	90				3050	3550
16		APACHE	OP	RNBT	FBG DV IO	90-120				3050	3600
17		NAVAJO	OP	RNBT	FBG DV IO					**	**
17		NAVAJO	OP	RNBT	FBG DV IO	90-225				3250	3950
18	2	OCEANIC	OP	RNBT	FBG IO					**	**
18	2	OCEANIC	OP	RNBT	FBG IO	90-225				3450	4200
20	1	AZTEC	HT	CR	FBG DV IO	150				5350	6150
20	1	AZTEC	OP	RNBT	FBG DV IO	150				5150	5900

IMAGE BOAT COMPANY
COAST GUARD MFG ID- KRG

Call 1-800-327-6929 for BUC Personalized Evaluation Service
Or, for 1980 to 1985 boats, sign onto www.BUCValuPro.com

IMPERIAL MARINE CORP

Call 1-800-327-6929 for BUC Personalized Evaluation Service
Or, for 1960 to 1961 boats, sign onto www.BUCValuPro.com

IMPERIAL YACHT COMPANY
SAN DIEGO CA 92106   See inside cover to adjust price for area
TA CHIAO BROS YACHT BLDG CO
TAIPEI TAIWAN

LOA FT IN	NAME AND/ OR MODEL	TOP/ RIG	BOAT TYPE	-HULL- MTL TP TP	----ENGINE--- # HP MFG	BEAM FT IN	WGT LBS	DRAFT FT IN	RETAIL LOW	RETAIL HIGH
					1977 BOATS					
36 11	EQUINOX	FB	SF	FBG DV IB	D	12 6		3 10	**	**
40 7	SEAHAWK 42	FB	TRWL	FBG DS IB	T D	12 6	28000	3 6	**	**
40 8	C-T 41	KTH	SA/CR	FBG KL IB	61D VLVO	12 2	28100	6	73400	80700
41 9	IMPERIAL 42	FB	TRWL	FBG DS IB	T120D LEHM	14 4	33000	4 6	77000	84700
46 7	PERRY 47	CUT	SA/CR	FBG KL IB	D	13 6	36400	6 4	88300	97000
52 10	IMPERIAL 53	FB	TRWL	FBG DV IB	D	16 3	62000	4 6	**	**

IMPERIAL YACHT COMPANY WEST
IMPERIAL WORLDWIDE IND INC   See inside cover to adjust price for area
LONG BEACH CA 90813
FORMERLY MARINER MARINE INDUSTRIES

LOA FT IN	NAME AND/ OR MODEL	TOP/ RIG	BOAT TYPE	-HULL- MTL TP TP	----ENGINE--- # HP MFG	BEAM FT IN	WGT LBS	DRAFT FT IN	RETAIL LOW	RETAIL HIGH
					1981 BOATS					
31 10	MARINER 32	KTH	SA/CR	FBG KL IB	50D PERK	10	12400	3 8	23400	26000
35 10	MARINER 36	CUT	SA/CR	FBG KL IB	50D PERK	11	21000	5	38900	43200
35 10	MARINER 36	KTH	SA/CR	FBG KL IB	50D PERK	11	21000	5	38900	43200
36	MARINER 36	FB	MY	FBG SV IB	T130D ISUZ	12 5	16200	2 11	57500	64300
40 4	MARINER 40	KTH	SA/CR	FBG KL IB	50D PERK	11 5	26500	5 8	52100	57200
47 11	MARINER 48	KTH	SA/RC	FBG KL IB	75D VLVO	13 6	36000	6 5	81900	90000
47 11	MARINER 48	KTH	SA/RC	FBG KL IB	85D PERK	13 6	36000	6 5	81700	89800
50	MARINER 50	CUT	MS	FBG KL IB	185D PERK	15	36000	4 6	91800	101000

IMPERIAL YACHTS

Call 1-800-327-6929 for BUC Personalized Evaluation Service
Or, for 1974 boats, sign onto www.BUCValuPro.com

INDEPENDENCE CHERUBINI CO
ANNAPOLIS MD 21403-1328 COAST GUARD MFG ID- CVJ See inside cover to adjust price for area
FORMERLY CHERUBINI BOAT CO INC

For more recent years, see the BUC Used Boat Price Guide, Volume 1 or Volume 2

LOA FT IN	NAME AND/ OR MODEL	TOP/ RIG	BOAT TYPE	-HULL- MTL TP TP	----ENGINE--- # HP MFG	BEAM FT IN	WGT LBS	DRAFT FT IN	RETAIL LOW	RETAIL HIGH
					1983 BOATS					
44	CHERUBINI 44	KTH	SA/CR FBG KC IB	50D BMW	12	28000	4 10	193500	212500
48 9	CHERUBINI 48	SCH	SA/CR FBG KL IB	75D BMW	13	37000	5	241500	265500
					1982 BOATS					
44	CHERUBINI 44	KTH	SA/CR FBG KC IB	50D BMW	12	28000	4 10	183500	201500
48 9	CHERUBINI 48	SCH	SA/CR FBG KL IB	75D BMW	13	37000	5	229500	252000
					1981 BOATS					
44	CHERUBINI 44	KTH	SA/CR FBG KL IB	D	12	28000	4 9	176500	194000
44	CHERUBINI 44	KTH	SA/CR WD IB	D	12	28600	4 9	176500	194000
48 8	CHERUBINI 48	SCH	SA/CR FBG KL IB	D	13	35000	5	213500	235000
48 8	CHERUBINI 48	SCH	SA/CR WD IB	D	13	35000	5	213500	235000
					1980 BOATS					
44	CHERUBINI 47	KTH	SA/CR FBG KL IB	50D WEST	12	28000	4 10	167000	183500
47	CHERUBINI 47	KTH	SA/CR FBG KL IB	D	12 6	34000	4 9	202000	222000
48	CHERUBINI 47	SCH	SA/CR FBG KL IB	58D WEST	13	36000	5	200000	219500
					1979 BOATS					
44	CHERUBINI 44	KTH	SA/CR FBG KL IB	50D WEST	12	28000	4 10	160000	175500
					1978 BOATS					
44	CHERUBINI	CUT	SA/CR FBG KC IB	40D WEST	12	28000	4 10	143000	157500
44	CHERUBINI 44	KTH	SA/CR FBG KC IB	40D WEST	12	28000	4 10	153000	168000

INDEPENDENT YACHTS LTD
COAST GUARD MFG ID- ZIY

Call 1-800-327-6929 for BUC Personalized Evaluation Service
Or, for 1981 boats, sign onto www.BUCValuPro.com

INDIAN RIVER BOAT MFG CO
DIV OF DAYTONA MARINE I COAST GUARD MFG ID- JHR

Call 1-800-327-6929 for BUC Personalized Evaluation Service
Or, for 1982 to 1984 boats, sign onto www.BUCValuPro.com

INDUSTRIAL FIBER GLASS PROD
PERE MARQUETTE DIVISION

Call 1-800-327-6929 for BUC Personalized Evaluation Service
Or, for 1959 to 1970 boats, sign onto www.BUCValuPro.com

INDUSTRIAL SHIPPING CO LTD

Call 1-800-327-6929 for BUC Personalized Evaluation Service
Or, for 1962 to 1968 boats, sign onto www.BUCValuPro.com

INDUSTRIES ESPADON INC
COAST GUARD MFG ID- ZIE

Call 1-800-327-6929 for BUC Personalized Evaluation Service
Or, for 1982 to 1983 boats, sign onto www.BUCValuPro.com

INITIAL MARINE CORP INC
SANFORD FL 32771   COAST GUARD MFG ID- VMP See inside cover to adjust price for area
                          FORMERLY VELOCITY MARINE INC

For more recent years, see the BUC Used Boat Price Guide, Volume 1 or Volume 2

LOA FT IN	NAME AND/ OR MODEL	TOP/ RIG	BOAT TYPE	-HULL- MTL TP	TP	ENGINE # HP	MFG	BEAM FT IN	WGT LBS	DRAFT FT IN	RETAIL LOW	RETAIL HIGH
1983 BOATS
30	VELOCITY 30		SF	FBG DV	OB			8	3000	2	38400	42700
30	VELOCITY 30		SPTCR	FBG DV	OB			8	3000	2	39500	43900
30	VELOCITY 30		SPTCR	FBG DV	IO	T330		8		2	14800	16800
30	VELOCITY-COMPETITOR		RNBT	FBG DV	OB			8	3000	2	38600	42900
30	VELOCITY-COMPETITOR		RNBT	FBG DV	IO	T370		8		2	13500	15300
38	VELOCITY 38		OFF	F/W DV	OB			8		2	**	**
38	VELOCITY 38		RACE	F/W DV	IO	T400		8		2	29400	32700
40	VELOCITY 40		OFF	F/W DV	OB			9	6		**	**
40	VELOCITY 40		OFF	F/W DV	IO	T400		9	6		35300	39200
42	VELOCITY 42		OFF	F/W DV	OB			9	6		**	**
1982 BOATS
30	SPORT CRUISER		OFF	FBG DV	IO	T330-T370		8	6500	2	15300	18700
30	SPORT CRUISER		OVNTR	FBG DV	OB			8	3500	2	37500	41700
30	SPORT CRUISER		OVNTR	FBG DV	IO	400	MRCR	8	5500	2	13000	14800
30	SS SPECIAL		OFF	FBG DV	OB			8	3500	2	38000	42200
34	COMPETITOR		OFF	F/W DV	OB			8	4000	2	38600	42900
34	COMPETITOR		OFF	F/W DV	IO	R		8	4000	2	**	**
38	COMPETITOR		OFF	F/W DV	IO	T400		8	4500	2	32800	36400
40	SPORT CRUISER		OFF	F/W DV	OB			9	6		**	**
40	SPORT CRUISER		OFF	F/W DV	IO	T400		9	6		34000	37700
42	SPORT CRUISER		OFF	F/W DV	OB			9	6		**	**
1981 BOATS
30	VELOCITY		CR	FBG DV	OB			8	3000	2	37800	42000
30	VELOCITY	OP	SPTCR	FBG DV	OB			8	3000	2	37800	42000
30	VELOCITY	OP	SPTCR	FBG DV	IO	T260	MRCR	8		2	13200	15000
30	VELOCITY	OP	SPTCR	FBG DV	IO	T330-T370		8	6500	2	14800	18100
30	VELOCITY	OP	SPTCR	FBG DV	IO	T240D	REN	8		2	21900	24300
30	VELOCITY COMP		RNBT	FBG DV	IO	T370		8		2	12800	14600
30	VELOCITY COMPETITOR	OP	RACE	FBG DV	OB			8	6800		36800	40900
30	VELOCITY COMPETITOR	OP	RACE	FBG DV	IO	T330		8		2	14400	16300
30	VELOCITY SC		CR	FBG DV	IO	T330		8	6800	2	15200	17300
30	VELOCITY-COMPETITOR	OP	RACE	FBG DV	OB			8	3000	2	36800	40900
30	VELOCITY-COMPETITOR	OP	RACE	FBG DV	IO	T330	MRCR	8	6000	2	12000	13600
30	VELOCITY-SS TURBO	OP	RACE	FBG DV	IO	T475	MRCR	8		2	17300	19700
1980 BOATS
30	VELOCITY		CR	FBG DV	OB			8			37000	41100
30	VELOCITY		CR	FBG DV	IO			8			**	**
1979 BOATS
30	VELOCITY 30	OP	RACE	FBG DV	OB			8	3000	2	35400	39300
30	VELOCITY 30	OP	RACE	FBG DV	IO	T330	MRCR	8	6000	2	11600	13100
30	VELOCITY 30	OP	RNBT	FBG DV	OB			8	3000	2	35400	39300
30	VELOCITY 30	OP	RNBT	FBG DV	IO	T330-T370		8	6500	2	11100	13600

INLAND PLASTICS CORP

Call 1-800-327-6929 for BUC Personalized Evaluation Service
Or, for 1966 to 1968 boats, sign onto www.BUCValuPro.com

INLAND SEAS BOAT CO
SANDUSKY OH 44870   See inside cover to adjust price for area

LOA FT IN	NAME AND/ OR MODEL	TOP/ RIG	BOAT TYPE	-HULL- MTL TP	TP	ENGINE # HP	MFG	BEAM FT IN	WGT LBS	DRAFT FT IN	RETAIL LOW	RETAIL HIGH
1971 BOATS
30	GLASS-CLIPPER	FB	EXP	AL SV	IB	T320		11	3	11000	12700	14400
30	GLASS-CLIPPER	FB	EXP	STL SV	IB	T320		11	3	11000	12600	14300
30	GLASS-CLIPPER		SDN	AL SV	IB	T320		11	3	11000	13800	15700
30	GLASS-CLIPPER		SDN	STL SV	IB	T320		11	3	11000	13800	15700
34	GLASS-CLIPPER	FB	EXP	AL SV	IB	T320		13	6	18000	20200	22500
34	GLASS-CLIPPER	FB	EXP	STL SV	IB	T320		13	6	18000	20200	22500
34	GLASS-CLIPPER		SDN	AL SV	IB	T320		13	6	18000	20500	22800
34	GLASS-CLIPPER		SDN	STL SV	IB	T320		13	6	18000	20500	22800
38	GLASS-CLIPPER	FB	EXP	AL SV	IB	T320		14		24000	29400	32700
38	GLASS-CLIPPER	FB	EXP	STL SV	IB	T320		14		24000	29400	32700
38	GLASS-CLIPPER DECKHO		DC	AL SV	IB	T320		14		24000	28600	31800
38	GLASS-CLIPPER DECKHO		DC	STL SV	IB	T320		14		24000	28600	31800
38	GLASS-CLIPPER SALON		DC	AL SV	IB	T320		14		24000	28600	31800
38	GLASS-CLIPPER SALON		DC	STL SV	IB	T320		14		24000	28600	31800
42	GLASS-CLIPPER	FB	EXP	AL SV	IB	T320		14	9	28000	38400	42700
42	GLASS-CLIPPER	FB	EXP	STL SV	IB	T320		14	9	28000	38400	42700
42	GLASS-CLIPPER DECKHO		DC	AL SV	IB	T320		14	9	28000	37900	42100
42	GLASS-CLIPPER DECKHO		DC	STL SV	IB	T320		14	9	28000	37900	42100
42	GLASS-CLIPPER SALON		DC	AL SV	IB	T320		14	9	28000	37800	42200
44	GLASS-CLIPPER TRI CB		TCMY	AL	IB	T320		15	3		32200	35800
44	GLASS-CLIPPER TRI CB		TCMY	STL	IB	T320		15	3		32200	35800
60	SPECIAL		MY	AL	IB						**	**
60	SPECIAL		MY	STL	IB						**	**
1970 BOATS
29	CONTINENTAL		STL		IB	250-320		11			9850	11400
29	CONTINENTAL	FB	STL		IB	T135-T215		11			10100	12000
29	CONTINENTAL		STL		IB	215		11			9750	11100
31	CONTINENTAL	FB	STL		IB	T135-T215		11	2		10300	12100
33	DELUXE	FB	STL		IB	T215-T250		11	6		18100	20400
36	DECKHOUSE DLX		STL		IB	T250		12	6		21000	23300
36	DECKHOUSE DLX		STL		IB	T300		12	6		21200	23600
36	DELUXE	FB	STL		IB	T250		12	6		21100	23400
36	DELUXE	FB	STL		IB	T300		12	6		21300	23700
39	DECKHOUSE DLX		AL		IB	T320		14	3		30200	33600
39	DECKHOUSE DLX		STL		IB	T320		14	3		30200	33600
39	DELUXE	FB	AL		IB	T320		14	3		30300	33700
39	DELUXE	FB	STL		IB	T320		14	3		30300	33700
39	SALON DELUXE		AL		IB	T320		14	3		30200	33600
39	SALON DELUXE		STL		IB	T320		14	3		30200	33600
41	DECKHOUSE DLX		AL		IB	T320		14	8		36700	40700
41	DECKHOUSE DLX		STL		IB	T320		14	8		36700	40700
41	DELUXE	FB	AL		IB	T320		14	8		36800	40800
41	DELUXE	FB	STL		IB	T320		14	8		36800	40800
41	SALON DELUXE		AL		IB	T320		14	8		36700	40700
41	SALON DELUXE		STL		IB	T320		14	8		36700	40700
43	CONQUEROR		TCMY	AL	IB	T320		14	11		39200	43500
43	CONQUEROR		TCMY	STL	IB	T320		14	11		39200	43500
43	DECKHOUSE DLX		STL	AL	IB	T320		14	10		35300	39200
43	DECKHOUSE DLX		STL		IB	T320		14	10		35300	39200
43	SALON DELUXE		STL		IB	T320		14	10		35300	39200
47 10	CONQUEROR		TCMY	AL	IB	T258D		15	3		47500	52200
47 10	CONQUEROR		TCMY	STL	IB	T258D		15	3		47500	52200
55	CONQUEROR		TCMY	AL	IB	T320D		15	4		68700	75500
55	CONQUEROR		TCMY	STL	IB	T320D		15	4		68700	75500
1969 BOATS
27	CONTINENTAL		OVNTR	STL SV	IB	210	CHRY	9	8	3	5700	6550
27	CONTINENTAL		SPTCR	STL SV	IB	210	CHRY	9	8	3	5550	6400
28	CONTINENTAL		EXP	STL SV	IB	210	CHRY	11		3	7850	9000
28	CONTINENTAL	FB	EXP	STL SV	IB	210	CHRY	11		3	6900	7950
28	STEEL-CLIPPER 28		UTL	STL SV	IB	T135	CHRY	10	8	3	7650	8700
30	CONTINENTAL	FB	EXP	STL SV	IB	T135	CHRY	11	2	3	10500	12000
32	CONTINENTAL	FB	EXP	STL SV	IB	T220	CHRY	11	2	3	12700	14400
34	STEEL-CLIPPER 34	FB	EXP	STL SV	IB	T220	CHRY	12	6	3 4	18600	20700
34	STEEL-CLIPPER 34		SDN	STL SV	IB	T220	CHRY	12	6	3 4	16600	18900

LOA FT	LOA IN	NAME AND/ OR MODEL	TOP/ RIG	BOAT TYPE	-HULL- MTL	-HULL- TP	ENGINE TP	ENGINE # HP	ENGINE MFG	BEAM FT	BEAM IN	WGT LBS	DRAFT FT	DRAFT IN	RETAIL LOW	RETAIL HIGH
		1969 BOATS														
35		DELUXE	FB	EXP	STL	SV	IB	T210	CHRY	12	6				20100	22300
37		STEEL-CLIPPER 37		EXP	STL	SV	IB	T220	CHRY	13	6		3	6	25400	28300
37		STEEL-CLIPPER 37		SDN	STL	SV	IB	T230	CHRY	13	6		3	6	24400	27200
38		DELUXE	FB	EXP	STL	SV	IB	T280	CHRY	14	8				26000	28900
40		STEEL-CLIPPER 40		EXP	STL	SV	IB	T300	CHRY	13	9		3	10	24000	26600
40		STEEL-CLIPPER 40		SDN	STL	SV	IB	T300D	CUM	13	9		3	10	36400	40400
41		DELUXE	FB	EXP	STL	SV	IB	T280	CHRY	14	8				34100	37800
42		CONQUERER		DC	STL	SV	IB	T280	CHRY	14	8				35100	39000
48		DELUXE		TCMY	STL	SV	IB	T300	CHRY	15					38300	42500
		1968 BOATS														
27		STEEL-CLIPPER		SDN	STL		IB	220	CHRY	10			3		6900	7950
28		STEEL-CLIPPER		EXP	STL		IB	T220	CHRY	10	8		3		7550	8700
28		STEEL-CLIPPER	OP	RNBT	STL		IB	T220	CHRY	10	8		3		6850	7850
30		STEEL-CLIPPER		EXP	STL		IB	T200	CHRY	11			3	2	10600	12100
32		STEEL-CLIPPER		EXP	STL		IB	T220	CHRY	11	8		3	4	12500	14200
34		STEEL-CLIPPER	HT	EXP	STL		IB	T220	CHRY	12	6		3	4	17500	19900
34		STEEL-CLIPPER		SDN	STL		IB	230	CHRY	12	6		3	4	15100	17100
37		STEEL-CLIPPER		EXP	STL		IB	T230	CHRY	13	6		3	6	24600	27400
37		STEEL-CLIPPER		SDN	STL		IB	T230	CHRY	13	6		3	6	24100	26800
40		STEEL-CLIPPER		EXP	STL		IB	T300	CHRY	13	9		3	10	23200	25800
40		STEEL-CLIPPER		SDN	STL		IB	T D	CUM	13	9		3	10	**	**
42		STEEL-CLIPPER		DCMY	STL		IB	T		13	9		3	10	**	**
48		STEEL-CLIPPER		TCMY	STL		IB	T		14			4		**	**
		1967 BOATS														
27				OVNTR	STL		IB	210-320							5350	6500
27		SPORT			STL		IB	210-320							4950	6050
28			FB		STL		IB	210-320							6250	7600
28			FB		STL		IB	T111-T135							6450	7550
28			FB		STL		IB	T210-T220							7050	8150
28				UTL	STL		IB	210-320							6150	7500
28				UTL	STL		IB	T111-T135							6300	7450
28				UTL	STL		IB	T210-T220							6950	8100
30			FB		STL		IB	T111-T220							8850	10500
32			FB		STL		IB	T210-T290							9850	11700
34			FB		STL		IB	T210-T290							16600	19200
34		DINETTE DECKHOUSE			STL		IB	T210-T290							16500	19100
37			FB		STL		IB	T280							24700	27500
		IB T290 24800 27500, IB T300 24800 27600, IB T320													24900	27700
37		DIN DKHSE & SALON			STL		IB	T280							24600	27400
		IB T290 24700 27400, IB T300 24700 27500, IB T320													24800	27600
40			FB		STL		IB	T280							24300	27000
		IB T290 24300 27000, IB T300 24300 27000, IB T300 PALM													24300	27000
		IB T320 24500 27200														
40		DIN DKHSE & SALON			STL		IB	T280							24200	26900
		IB T290 24200 26900, IB T300 24300 27000, IB T300 PALM													24300	27000
		IB T320 24400 27100														
42		CONQUEROR			STL		IB	T280							32500	36200
		IB T290 32700 36300, IB T300 32900 36500, IB T300 PALM													32900	36500
		IB T320 33200 36900														
46				TCMY	STL		IB	T280							32400	36000
		IB T290 33000 36600, IB T300 33500 37200, IB T300 PALM													33500	37200
		IB T320 34600 38400														
		1966 BOATS														
27				OVNTR	STL		IB	210-320							5200	6350
27			HT	OVNTR	STL		IB	210-320							5200	6350
27		SPORT			STL		IB	210-320							4750	5850
27		SPORT	FB		STL		IB	210-320							4750	5850
28			FB		STL		IB	210-320							6050	7400
28			FB		STL		IB	T111-T135							6200	7350
28			FB		STL		IB	T210-T220							6850	7900
28			HT	CR	STL		IB	210-320							6150	7500
28			HT	CR	STL		IB	T111-T135							6350	7450
28			HT	CR	STL		IB	T210-T220							6950	8050
28				UTL	STL		IB	210-320							5950	7300
28				UTL	STL		IB	T111-T135							6100	7250
28				UTL	STL		IB	T210-T220							6750	7850
30			FB		STL		IB	T111-T220							8450	10200
32			FB		STL		IB	T210-T290							9450	11300
34			FB		STL		IB	T210-T290							15400	18000
34		DECKHOUSE			STL		IB	T210-T290							15900	18400
34		DECKHOUSE	FB		STL		IB	T210-T290							16600	19000
37			FB		STL		IB	T280							24000	26600
		IB T290 24000 26700, IB T300 24000 26700, IB T320													24100	26800
37		DECKHOUSE			STL		IB	T280							24300	27000
		IB T290 24400 27100, IB T300 24400 27100, IB T320													24500	27300
37		DECKHOUSE	FB		STL		IB	T280							24600	27300
		IB T290 24600 27400, IB T300 24700 27400, IB T320													24800	27500
40			FB		STL		IB	T280							23200	25800
		IB T290 23300 25900, IB T300 22200 24700, IB T300 PALM													24100	26800
		IB T320 23400 26000														
40		DECKHOUSE			STL		IB	T280							23700	26400
		IB T290 23800 26400, IB T300 23800 26500, IB T300 PALM													23800	26500
		IB T320 23900 26600														
40		DECKHOUSE	FB		STL		IB	T280							24100	26700
		IB T290 24100 26800, IB T300 23300 25900, IB T300 PALM													25200	28000
		IB T320 24300 26900														
42		CONQUEROR			STL		IB	T280							31600	35100
		IB T290 31800 35300, IB T300 31900 35500, IB T300 PALM													31900	35500
		IB T320 32200 35800														
46				TCMY	STL		IB	T280							31500	35000
		IB T290 32000 35600, IB T300 32600 36200, IB T300 PALM													32600	36200
		IB T320 33600 37400														
		1965 BOATS														
28			FB		STL		IB	210-310							5800	7100
28			FB		STL		IB	T111-T135							5950	7100
28			FB		STL		IB	T210-T220							6600	7650
28				UTL	STL		IB	210-310							5700	7000
28				UTL	STL		IB	T111-T135							5850	7000
28				UTL	STL		IB	T210-T220							6500	7550
28			FB	UTL	STL		IB	210-310							5700	7000
28			FB	UTL	STL		IB	T111-T135							5850	7000
28			FB	UTL	STL		IB	T210-T220							6500	7550
30			FB		STL		IB	T111-T280							8150	10000
30				UTL	STL		IB	T111-T220							8450	10500
30				UTL	STL		IB	T240-T280							9400	10900
30			FB	UTL	STL		IB	T111-T220							8450	10500
30			FB	UTL	STL		IB	T260-T280							9500	10900
32			FB		STL		IB	T210-T280							9150	10900
32		DECKHOUSE STD			STL		IB	T210-T280							9150	10900
32		STANDARD	FB	MYDKH	STL		IB	T210-T280							**	**
34			FB		STL		IB	T210-T280							15400	17800
34		DECKHOUSE STD			STL		IB	T210-T280							15400	17700
34		STANDARD	FB	MYDKH	STL		IB	T210-T280							15400	18200
36			FB		STL		IB	T260							18300	20300
36			FB		STL		IB	T280							18400	20400
36			FB		STL		IB	T300							18500	20500
36		DECKHOUSE STD			STL		IB	T260							18200	20300
36		DECKHOUSE STD			STL		IB	T280							18300	20400
36		DECKHOUSE STD			STL		IB	T300							18400	20500
36		STANDARD	FB	MYDKH	STL		IB	T260							17300	19700
36		STANDARD	FB	MYDKH	STL		IB	T280							17400	19700
36		STANDARD	FB	MYDKH	STL		IB	T300							17500	19800
40			FB		STL		IB	T280							23100	25700
40			FB		STL		IB	T300							23200	25700
40			FB		STL		IB	T195D							30400	33700
40		DECKHOUSE STD			STL		IB	T280							23000	25600
40		DECKHOUSE STD			STL		IB	T300							23100	25700
40		DECKHOUSE STD			STL		IB	T195D							30300	33600
40		STANDARD	FB	MYDKH	STL		IB	T280							24700	27400
40		STANDARD	FB	MYDKH	STL		IB	T300							24300	27000
40		STANDARD	FB	MYDKH	STL		IB	T195D							33100	36800
42		CONQUEROR			STL		IB	T280							30800	34200
42		CONQUEROR			STL		IB	T300							31100	34500
42		CONQUEROR			STL		IB	T195D							23600	26300
46				TCMY	STL		IB	T280							30700	34100
46				TCMY	STL		IB	T300							31700	35200

 CONTINUED ON NEXT PAGE

LOA FT IN	NAME AND/ OR MODEL	TOP/ RIG	BOAT TYPE	HULL MTL	TP	ENGINE TP # HP	MFG	BEAM FT IN	WGT LBS	DRAFT FT IN	RETAIL LOW	RETAIL HIGH
						1965 BOATS						
46			TCMY	STL	IB	T195D					31600	35100
						1964 BOATS						
28		FB		STL	IB	210-310					5650	6850
28		FB		STL	IB	T111-T135					5750	6850
28		FB		STL	IB	T210-T220					6400	7450
28			UTL	STL	IB	210-310					5550	6750
28			UTL	STL	IB	T111-T135					5650	6750
28			UTL	STL	IB	T210-T220					6350	7350
28		FB	UTL	STL	IB	210-310					5550	6750
28		FB	UTL	STL	IB	T111-T135					5650	6750
28		FB	UTL	STL	IB	T210-T220					6350	7350
30		FB		STL	IB	T111-T280					7850	9650
30			UTL	STL	IB	T111-T220					8150	10200
30			UTL	STL	IB	T260-T280					9150	10500
30		FB	UTL	STL	IB	T111-T220					8150	10200
30		FB	UTL	STL	IB	T260-T280					9150	10500
32		FB		STL	IB	T210-T310					8050	10000
32	DECKHOUSE STD			STL	IB	T210-T310					8800	10800
32	DECKHOUSE STD	FB		STL	IB	T210-T310					9450	11400
34		FB		STL	IB	T210-T310					14900	17300
34	DECKHOUSE STD			STL	IB	T210-T310					14800	17200
34	STANDARD	FB		STL	IB	T210-T310					14900	17800
36		FB		STL	IB	T260					17500	19800
	IB T280	17500	19900,	IB	T300	18000	20000, IB T300 PALM				18000	20000
	IB T310	18100	20100									
36	DECKHOUSE STD			STL	IB	T260					17400	19800
	IB T280	17500	19900,	IB	T300	17600	20000, IB T300 PALM				17600	20000
	IB T310	18000	20000									
36	STANDARD	FB	MYDKH	STL	IB	T260					16900	19200
	IB T280	16900	19200,	IB	T300	17000	19300, IB T300 PALM				17000	19300
	IB T310	17000	19400									
40		FB		STL	IB	T280					22400	24900
	IB T300	22500	25000,	IB	T300	PALM T280 22500	25000, IB T310				22500	25000
	IB T195D	29600	32800									
40	DECKHOUSE STD			STL	IB	T280					22300	24800
	IB T300	22400	24900,	IB	T300	PALM T280 22400	24900, IB T310				22500	24900
	IB T195D	29400	32700									
40	STANDARD	FB	MYDKH	STL	IB	T280					24000	26700
	IB T300	24100	26800,	IB	T300	PALM T280 24100	26800, IB T310				24100	26800
	IB T195D	32200	35800									
42	CONQUEROR			STL	IB	T280					30000	33300
	IB T300	30300	33600,	IB	T300	PALM T280 30300	33600, IB T310				30400	33800
	IB T195D	23000	25600									
						1963 BOATS						
26		FB		STL	IB	210-300					4200	5200
26		FB		STL	IB	T111-T135					4500	5400
26		FB		STL	IB	T210-T215					5050	5800
26			UTL	STL	IB	210-300					3700	4550
26			UTL	STL	IB	T111-T135					3850	4700
26			UTL	STL	IB	T210-T215					4450	5100
29		FB		STL	IB	225-300					7450	8750
29		FB		STL	IB	T111-T225					7600	9350
29		FB		STL	IB	T280					8400	9650
29			UTL	STL	IB	225-300					7400	8750
29			UTL	STL	IB	T111-T225					7450	9350
29			UTL	STL	IB	T280					8400	9650
29	DECKHOUSE STD			STL	IB	225-300					7450	8750
29	DECKHOUSE STD			STL	IB	T111-T225					7600	9350
29	DECKHOUSE STD			STL	IB	T280					8400	9650
31	4	FB		STL	IB	225-300					7750	9100
31	4	FB		STL	IB	T210-T300					8350	10000
31	4	FB		STL	IB	T195D					12200	13900
31	4 DECKHOUSE STD			STL	IB	225-300					7750	9100
31	4 DECKHOUSE STD			STL	IB	T210-T300					8350	10000
31	4 DECKHOUSE STD			STL	IB	T195D					12100	13800
33		FB		STL	IB	225-300					13300	15200
33		FB		STL	IB	T210-T300					13700	16200
33		FB		STL	IB	T195D					17000	19300
33	DECKHOUSE STD			STL	IB	225-300					13300	15200
33	DECKHOUSE STD			STL	IB	T210-T300					13700	16200
33	DECKHOUSE STD			STL	IB	T195D					17000	19300
36		FB		STL	IB	T225					16900	19200
	IB T260	17000	19300,	IB	T275	17100	19400, IB T275 CHRY				17000	19300
	IB T280	17100	19400,	IB	T300	17200	19500, IB T195D				20100	22400
36	DECKHOUSE STD			STL	IB	T225					16900	19200
	IB T260	17000	19300,	IB	T275	17000	19300, IB T280				17000	19400
	IB T300	17100	19500,	IB	T195D	20100	22300					
40		FB		STL	IB	T225					21800	24200
	IB T225 CHRY	21700	24100,	IB	T260	21800	24200, IB T275				21800	24300
	IB T275 CHRY	21800	24200,	IB	T280	21900	24300, IB T300				21900	24400
	IB T195D	28800	32000									
40	DECKHOUSE STD			STL	IB	T225					21700	24100
	IB T260	21700	24200,	IB	T275	21800	24200, IB T275 CHRY				21700	24100
	IB T280	21800	24200,	IB	T300	21900	24300, IB T195D				28700	31900
44	DECKHOUSE STD			STL	IB	T225					18300	20400
	IB T260	18500	20500,	IB	T275	18200	20200, IB T280				18600	20600
	IB T300	18800	20900,	IB	T195D	21100	23400					
44	SPECIAL DECKHOUSE			STL	IB	T225					21700	24100
	IB T260	22000	24400,	IB	T275	21200	23600, IB T275 CHRY				21500	23900
	IB T280	22200	24600,	IB	T300	22300	24800, IB T195D				24400	27100
46			TCMY	STL	IB	T225					26600	29500
	IB T260	28100	31300,	IB	T275	28900	32100, IB T275 CHRY				28900	32100
	IB T280	29200	32400,	IB	T300	30200	33500, IB T195D				30000	33300
						1962 BOATS						
25 11		FB	CR	STL	IB	177					4350	5000
25 11			OVNTR	STL	IB	177					4200	4900
25 11			UTL	STL	IB	177					3500	4100
29		FB	CR	STL	IB	215					7250	8300
29			OVNTR	STL	IB	177					7150	8200
29			UTL	STL	IB	177					7000	8050
29	DECKHOUSE	FB	DC	STL	IB	177					7100	8150
31	4	FB	CR	STL	IB	215					7850	9050
31	4 DECKHOUSE	FB	DC	STL	IB	177					8300	9500
33		FB	CR	STL	IB	275					13600	15500
33	DECKHOUSE	FB	DC	STL	IB	275					13900	15700
36		FB	CR	STL	IB	T215					13900	15800
36	DECKHOUSE	FB	DC	STL	IB	T215					15700	17800
40		FB	CR	STL	IB	T215					19900	22100
40	DECKHOUSE	FB	DC	STL	IB	T215					29100	32400
44	DECKHOUSE	FB	DC	STL	IB	T275					24300	27000
46	SALON		TCMY	STL	IB	T275					28300	31400
						1961 BOATS						
26			UTL	STL	IB	177		8			3350	3900
28		FB	CR	STL	IB	177		10			5150	5900
28			OVNTR	STL	IB	177		10			5200	6000
28			UTL	STL	IB	177		10			4950	5650
31		FB	CR	STL	IB	215		10	8		7400	8500
31	DECKHOUSE	FB	DC	STL	IB	177		10	8		7650	8800
33		FB	DC	STL	IB	275		11	4		13300	15100
33	DECKHOUSE	FB	DC	STL	IB	275		11	4		13500	15400
33	DELUXE		FSH	STL	IB	275		11	4		11000	12500
36		FB	CR	STL	IB	T215		12			13900	15800
36	DECKHOUSE	FB	DC	STL	IB	T215		12			15600	17800
36	DELUXE		FSH	STL	IB	T215		12			14000	15900
40		FB	CR	STL	IB	T215		12	6		21000	23300
40	DECKHOUSE	FB	DC	STL	IB	T215		12	6		30000	33300
40	DELUXE		SF	STL	IB	T215		12	6		22600	25100
44		FB	CR	STL	IB	T275		13			19000	21100
44	DECKHOUSE	FB	DC	STL	IB	T275		13			30500	33900
44	DELUXE		FSH	STL	IB	T275		13			**	**
46	SALON		TCMY	STL	IB	T275		13	6		36300	40300
						1960 BOATS						
24			OVNTR	STL	IB	109					3150	3650
24			UTL	STL	IB	109					2550	3000
25 11		FB	CR	STL	IB	T109					4450	5100
25 11			OVNTR	STL	IB	T109					4550	5250
25 11			UTL	STL	IB	215					3450	4000
29		FB	CR	STL	IB	215					6900	7950

LOA FT IN	NAME AND/ OR MODEL	TOP/ RIG	BOAT TYPE	HULL MTL	HULL TP	ENG TP	#	HP	MFG	BEAM FT IN	WGT LBS	DRAFT FT IN	RETAIL LOW	RETAIL HIGH
1960 BOATS														
29		FB	MYDKH	STL		IB		215					7500	8600
32		FB	MYDKH	STL		IB		T225					**	**
36		FB	MYDKH	STL		IB		T225					15300	17400
42		FB	MYDKH	STL		IB		T225					27700	30700
42		FB	TCMY	STL		IB		T225					27700	30800
1959 BOATS														
24	STEEL-MATE		UTL	STL		IB		109		8			2450	2850
26	STEEL-CLIPPER	FB	EXP	STL		IB		T109					4450	5100
26	STEEL-CLIPPER		OVNTR	STL		IB		T109		8			4400	5050
26	STEEL-MATE	FB	CR	STL		IB		215		8			4150	4850
28	STEEL-CLIPPER	FB	EXP	STL		IB		215		9 6			5350	6100
31	STEEL-CLIPPER	FB	EXP	STL		IB		T225		10 8			8600	9850
35	STEEL-CLIPPER	FB	EXP	STL		IB		T225		11 8			15000	17000
40	STEEL-CLIPPER	FB	EXP	STL		IB		T225		12			20900	23300
1958 BOATS														
40		HT	EXP	STL		IB		T225					18500	20600
1957 BOATS														
26	STEEL-CLIPPER	FB	EXP	STL		IB		215					4250	4950
1956 BOATS														
31	STEEL-CLIPPER	FB	EXP	STL		IB		T225					8200	9450
1955 BOATS														
26	STEEL-CLIPPER		EXP	STL		IB		T215					4800	5500
32		HT	EXP	STL		IB		T					**	**
1954 BOATS														
22	STEEL-CLIPPER		SPTCR	STL		IB							**	**
25			EXP	STL		IB							**	**
32	STEEL-CLIPPER	HT	EXP	STL		IB							**	**
1953 BOATS														
23			EXP	STL		IB							**	**
25			DC	STL		IB		155					2700	3150
25			EXP	STL		IB		T145					3900	4550
32		HT	CR	STL		IB							**	**
1952 BOATS														
32	STEEL-CLIPPER	FB		STL		IB		105					6050	6950
1951 BOATS														
23			CR	STL		IB		75					2400	2750
1950 BOATS														
18	STEEL-CLIPPER	OP	EXP	STL		OB							4050	4700
23	STEEL-CLIPPER		CR	STL		IB		60					2350	2700
1949 BOATS														
22	STEEL-CLIPPER	HT	CR	STL		IB		60					2100	2500
22	STEEL-CLIPPER	HT	SDN	STL		IB		60					2300	2700

INTEGRITY MARINE CORP
COAST GUARD MFG ID- XFE

Call 1-800-327-6929 for BUC Personalized Evaluation Service
Or, for 1979 boats, sign onto www.BUCValuPro.com

INTER OCEANIC YACHT CO

Call 1-800-327-6929 for BUC Personalized Evaluation Service
Or, for 1970 boats, sign onto www.BUCValuPro.com

INTERCONTINENTAL YACHTS
SEATTLE WA 98109   See inside cover to adjust price for area
SEE ALSO HANS CHRISTIAN YACHTS INC

LOA FT IN	NAME AND/ OR MODEL	TOP/ RIG	BOAT TYPE	HULL MTL	HULL TP	ENG TP	#	HP	MFG	BEAM FT IN	WGT LBS	DRAFT FT IN	RETAIL LOW	RETAIL HIGH
1981 BOATS														
37 9	INTERCONTINENTAL 38	SLP	SA/RC	FBG	KL	IB			D	11 2	16500	6 5	37100	41200
42	INTERCONTINENTAL 42	SLP	SA/RC	FBG	KL	IB			D	12	19000	6 10	49800	54700
46 4	INTERCONTINENTAL 46	SLP	SA/RC	FBG	KL	IB			D	13 2	28000	7 5	74900	82400
50	INTERCONTINENTAL 50	SLP	SA/RC	FBG	KL	IB			D	13 6	34000	7 10	96400	106000
65 7	INTERCONTINENTAL 20M	SLP	SA/RC	FBG	KL	IB			D	11 2	26880	9	148000	162500
66 6	INTERCONTINENTAL 66	SLP	SA/RC	FBG	KL	IB			D	14 2	40000	8 4	133500	146500

INTERMARINE AGENCY
COAST GUARD MFG ID- XTR

Call 1-800-327-6929 for BUC Personalized Evaluation Service
Or, for 1972 to 1974 boats, sign onto www.BUCValuPro.com

INTERNATIONAL BOAT & YCHT BLD

Call 1-800-327-6929 for BUC Personalized Evaluation Service
Or, for 1965 boats, sign onto www.BUCValuPro.com

INTERNATIONAL MARINE CORP
BOSTON MA   See inside cover to adjust price for area

LOA FT IN	NAME AND/ OR MODEL	TOP/ RIG	BOAT TYPE	HULL MTL	HULL TP	ENG TP	#	HP	MFG	BEAM FT IN	WGT LBS	DRAFT FT IN	RETAIL LOW	RETAIL HIGH
1963 BOATS														
35	INTERNATIONAL 35		SAIL	WD		OB							35700	39700
40 2	INTERNATIONAL 40		SAIL	WD		OB							44800	49700
1962 BOATS														
35	INTERNATIONAL 35		SAIL	WD		OB							35600	39600
36	INTERNATIONAL 36		SAIL	WD		OB							36200	40200
40 2	INTERNATIONAL 40		SAIL	WD		OB							44700	49700
1961 BOATS														
35	INTERNATIONAL 35	SLP	SA/CR	WD	KL	OB				10 6		4 8	35800	39800
36	INTERNATIONAL 36	SLP	SA/CR	WD	CB	OB				10 6			36300	40300
36	INTERNATIONAL 36	YWL	SA/CR	WD	CB	OB				10 6			36300	40300
40 2	INTERNATIONAL 40	SLP	SA/CR	WD	CB	OB				11 6			44800	49800
40 2	INTERNATIONAL 40	YWL	SA/CR	WD	CB	OB				11 6			44800	49800
46	INTERNATIONAL 46	SLP	MS	WD	KL					13 6		5	**	**
46	INTERNATIONAL 46	KTH	MS	WD	KL					13 6		5	**	**
1960 BOATS														
28	SAMURAI	SLP	SA/CR	WD	KL	OB				9 2	9500	3 11	22300	25700
31	DAIMYO	SLP	SA/CR	WD	KL	OB				9 5	10500	4	26900	29900
35	KAPPA-SAN	SLP	SA/CR	WD	KL	OB				10	14100	4 8	35900	39900
1959 BOATS														
28	SAMURAI	SLP	SAIL	WD	KL	OB				9 2		3 11	22900	25400
36	KAPPA	SLP	SAIL	WD	KL	OB							36400	40400
36	KAPPA	YWL	SAIL	WD	KC	OB							36400	40400

INTERNATIONAL MARINE INC
INGLEWOOD CA 90302   COAST GUARD MFG ID- HMS See inside cover to adjust price for area
FORMERLY H M S MARINE INC

For more recent years, see the BUC Used Boat Price Guide, Volume 1 or Volume 2

LOA FT IN	NAME AND/ OR MODEL	TOP/ RIG	BOAT TYPE	HULL MTL	HULL TP	ENG TP	#	HP	MFG	BEAM FT IN	WGT LBS	DRAFT FT IN	RETAIL LOW	RETAIL HIGH
1983 BOATS														
19	WEST-WIGHT-POTTER	SLP	SAIL	FBG	CB	OB				7 6	1250	3 7	4100	4800
1982 BOATS														
19	WEST-WIGHT-POTTER	SLP	SAIL	FBG	CB	OB				7 6	1100	11	3650	4250
1981 BOATS														
19	WEST-WIGHT-POTTER	SLP	SAIL	FBG	CB	OB				7 6	1100	11	3450	4050
1978 BOATS														
18 3	H-M-S 18	SLP	SAIL	FBG	CB	OB				7 6	1400	1	3500	4050
1977 BOATS														
18 3	HMS 18	SLP	SAIL	FBG	KC	OB				7 6	1400	3 11	3400	3950
1976 BOATS														
18 3	H-M-S-EIGHTEEN	SLP	SAIL	FBG	KC	OB				7 6	1400	1	3300	3850
1975 BOATS														
18 3	HMS 18	SLP	SAIL	FBG	KL	OB				7 6	1400	3 11	3250	3800
1974 BOATS														
18 3	H-M-S	SLP	SAIL	FBG	KL	OB				7 6	1400	3 11	3200	3700
1973 BOATS														
18	H-M-S 18	SLP	SAIL	FBG	KL	OB				7 10	1350	3 6	3050	3550
1972 BOATS														
18 3	H-M-S 18	SLP	SA/CR	FBG	KC	OB				7 10	1350	9	3000	3500
1971 BOATS														
18	H-M-S 18	SLP	SA/OD	FBG	KC	OB				7 10	1500	4	3100	3600

INTERNATIONAL MARINE SERV

Call 1-800-327-6929 for BUC Personalized Evaluation Service
Or, for 1972 to 1977 boats, sign onto www.BUCValuPro.com

INTERNATIONAL ONE-O-ONE

Call 1-800-327-6929 for BUC Personalized Evaluation Service
Or, for 1978 boats, sign onto www.BUCValuPro.com

INTERNATIONAL YACHT
DICKSON TN 37055　　　　　　　　　　See inside cover to adjust price for area

LOA FT IN	NAME AND/ OR MODEL	TOP/ RIG	BOAT TYPE	HULL MTL TP	TP	ENGINE # HP MFG	BEAM FT IN	WGT LBS	DRAFT FT IN	RETAIL LOW	RETAIL HIGH
1972 BOATS											
16 4	CUSTOM	RNBT	FBG	OB			6 8	850		2200	2600
16 5	SPRINT SS		FBG	OB			6 2	790		1750	2100
16 9		RNBT	FBG	OB			6 10	1100		2450	2850
16 9		RNBT	FBG	IO	120-165		6 10	2000	1 10	3000	3500
16 9		RNBT	FBG TR	OB			6 10	1150		2550	2950
16 9 SS		SKI	FBG TR	OB			6 10	1150		2500	2950
16 9 SS		SKI	FBG TR	IO	120-165		6 10	2000	1 10	2800	3300
17 6		B/R	FBG	OB			7 2	1150		2600	3000
17 6		B/R	FBG	IO	120-165		7 2	2000	2	3050	3600
17 6		RNBT	FBG	OB			7 2	1100		2500	2900
17 6		RNBT	FBG	IO	120-165		7 2	2000	2	3200	3750
17 7		RNBT	FBG TR	OB			7 2	1250		2750	3200
17 7		RNBT	FBG TR	IO	120-165		7 2	2000	2	3200	3800
17 7		WKNDR	FBG	OB			7 2	1450		3050	3550
17 7		WKNDR	FBG	IO	120-140		7 2			3250	3800
18 9		CAMPR	FBG	OB			7 4	1300		2950	3400
18 9		CAMPR	FBG	IO	120-225		7 4	2200	2 2	3750	4500
21		CUD	FBG	OB			7 8	1950		4600	5250
21		CUD	FBG	IO	120-225		7 8	2600	2 4	5250	6150
23 9 240		HT	FBG	IO	155-225		8	4000	2 11	7800	9150
23 9 240		FB	FBG	IO	155-225		8	4500	2 11	8550	10000
23 9 240 OFFSHORE		OFF	FBG	IO	155-225		8	3700	2 11	7750	9100
28 2 280	IO T155-T188 19600		FB	FBG	VD	225-280	10 4	8000	3	11900	13900
	VD T225 13300		22500, IO T225	MRCR		20900 23200, IO T225	OMC			20900	23200
28 2 280	IO T155-T188 18700		EXP	FBG	VD	225-280	10 4	8000	3	11900	13900
	VD T225 13300		21200, IO T225	MRCR		19600 21800, IO T225	OMC			19600	21800
1971 BOATS											
21		CUD	FBG	OB			7 8	1950	2 4	4600	5250
21		CUD	FBG	IO	120-215		7 8	2600	2 4	5400	6300
23		CNV	FBG	IO	155-215		8	3500	2 11	8400	9850
23		HT CR	FBG	IO	155-215		8	4000	2 11	8150	10100
23		FB CR	FBG	IO	155-215		8	4200	3	8450	9900
23 SKIFF		CNV	FBG	IO	155-215		8	3800	3	9050	10500
23 SKIFF		FB CR	FBG	IO	155-215		8	4500	3	9000	10400
23 SPORTTIME 23			FBG	IO	120-140		8	3000	2 10	6350	7350
23 YACHT 23		FB SDN	FBG	IO	155-215		8	4500	3	9000	10400
28 6 SLEEPER		FB CR	FBG	IB	225-330		10 4	8000	3	11400	13600
28 6 SLEEPER		FB CR	FBG	IB	T215-T225		10 4	8000	3	12600	14500
1970 BOATS											
21		CUD	FBG	IO	120-215		7 8		2 4	5600	6600
23		CNV	FBG	OB			8			6850	7900
23		CNV	FBG	IO	155-215		8		2	9050	10500
23		CNV	FBG	IO	T120		8		2	10200	11000
23		HT CR	FBG	IO	155-215		8		2	8850	10200
23		HT CR	FBG	IO	T120		8		2	9800	11100
23		FB CR	FBG	IO	155-215		8		2	8850	10200
23		FB CR	FBG	IO	T120		8		2	9800	11100
23 YACHT 23 FAMILY		CR	FBG	IO	155-215		8		2	8850	10200
23 YACHT 23 FAMILY		CR	FBG	IO	T120		8		2	9800	11100
1969 BOATS											
20 INTERNATIONAL 20		OP	RNBT	FBG DV	OB		8	2000	2	4400	5050
20 INTERNATIONAL 20 CBN			RNBT	FBG DV	OB	120 MRCR	8	2000	2	4800	5500
23 INTERNATIONAL 23		OP	RNBT	FBG DV	OB		8	2500	2	6050	6950
23 INTERNATIONAL 23		HT	RNBT	FBG DV	OB		8	3200	2	7250	8300
23 INTERNATIONAL 23		HT	RNBT	FBG DV	IB	150	8		2	3650	4200
23 INTERNATIONAL 23		FB	RNBT	FBG DV	OB		8	3450	2	7600	8750
23 INTERNATIONAL 23		FB	RNBT	FBG DV	IB	150	8		2	3650	4200
23 INTERNATIONAL 23		FB	SF	FBG DV	IO	140 MRCR	8	3450	2	9050	10300
23 INTERNATIONAL 23 DLX			RNBT	FBG DV	OB		8	2750	2	6500	7450
23 INTERNATIONAL CVST			RNBT	FBG SV	IO	140 MRCR	8	2500	2	6100	7050
23 INTERNATIONAL DLX			RNBT	FBG SV	IB	150	8		2	3650	4200
23 INTERNATIONAL DLX		OP	RNBT	FBG SV	IO	140 MRCR	8	2750	2	6400	7400
23 INTERNATIONAL DLX		HT	SDN	FBG SV	IO	140 MRCR	8	3200	2	7450	8550
25 4 INTERNATIONAL 26			CBNCR	FBG DV	IB	175	8		2 6	6150	7100
25 4 INTERNATIONAL 26			CBNCR	FBG SV	IO	155 MRCR	8	4000	2	12000	13600
1968 BOATS											
20 INTERNATIONAL 20			CNV	FBG	IO	120-225	8			5850	6950
20 INTERNATIONAL 20			CNV	FBG	IO	T 80	8			7050	8100
23 INTERNATIONAL 23		HT	CR	FBG	IO	120-210	8	3800	2	8650	10700
23 INTERNATIONAL 23		HT	CR	FBG	IO	225	8	4250	2	9650	11000
23 INTERNATIONAL 23		HT	CR	FBG	IO	T120-T160	8	4600	2	11200	13100
23 INTERNATIONAL 23		ST	OVNTR	FBG	IO	120-185	8	3300	2	7850	9650
23 INTERNATIONAL 23		ST	OVNTR	FBG	IO	210-225	8	3650	2	8550	10100
23 INTERNATIONAL 23		ST	OVNTR	FBG	IO	T120-T160	8	4100	2	10300	12100
23 INTERNATIONAL 23		FB	SF	FBG	IO	120-210	8	4300	2	10900	13400
23 INTERNATIONAL 23		FB	SF	FBG	IO	225	8	4750	2	12000	13700
23 INTERNATIONAL 23		FB	SF	FBG	IO	T120-T160	8	5100	2	13700	16100
1967 BOATS											
23 INTERNATIONAL 23		HT	CR	FBG	IO	150-225		4000		9400	10900
23 INTERNATIONAL 23		HT	CR	FBG	IO	T110-T120		4000		10500	11900
23 INTERNATIONAL 23		ST	OVNTR	FBG	IO	150-225		3500		8450	10900
23 INTERNATIONAL 23		ST	OVNTR	FBG	IO	T110-T120		3500		9600	10900
23 INTERNATIONAL FAM		FB	SF	FBG	IO	150-225		4500		11700	13500
23 INTERNATIONAL FAM		FB	SF	FBG	IO	T110-T120		4500		12900	14700
1966 BOATS											
23 INTERNATIONAL 23		OP		FBG	IO	150-225	8			7500	8850
23 INTERNATIONAL 23		OP		FBG	IO	T110-T150	8			8550	9900
23 INTERNATIONAL 23		HT		FBG	IO	150-225	8			7500	8850
23 INTERNATIONAL 23		HT		FBG	IO	T110-T150	8			8550	9900
23 INTERNATIONAL 23		FB		FBG	IO	150-225	8			7500	8850
23 INTERNATIONAL 23		FB		FBG	IO	T110-T150	8			8550	9900

INTERNATIONAL YACHT & BT BLDR

Call 1-800-327-6929 for BUC Personalized Evaluation Service
Or, for 1968 to 1970 boats, sign onto www.BUCValuPro.com

INTERNATIONAL YACHT CORP
HELSEN
CLEARWATER FL 33520　　　COAST GUARD MFG ID- XNT　　　See inside cover to adjust price for area

LOA FT IN	NAME AND/ OR MODEL	TOP/ RIG	BOAT TYPE	HULL MTL TP	TP	ENGINE # HP MFG	BEAM FT IN	WGT LBS	DRAFT FT IN	RETAIL LOW	RETAIL HIGH
1977 BOATS											
20 3	INTERNATIONAL STREAK	SLP	SAIL	FBG KC	OB		6 6	1000	6	3000	3500
20 6	INTERNATIONAL	SLP	SAIL	FBG KC	OB		7 4	1750	1 2	3950	4600
22 2	INTERNATIONAL	SLP	SAIL	FBG KC	OB		8	2500	1 2	5250	6050
22 6	INTERNATIONAL	SLP	SAIL	FBG KL	OB		8	2500	1 3	5600	6450
22 6	INTERNATIONAL	SLP	SAIL	FBG KC	OB		8	2700	1 2	5600	6450
23 9	INTERNATIONAL	SLP	SAIL	FBG KC	OB		8	3090	1 4	6600	7550
23 9	INTERNATIONAL	SLP	SAIL	FBG KC	IB	10 UNIV	8	3090	1 4	7000	8000
23 9	INTERNATIONAL	SLP	SAIL	FBG KC	IB	8D VLVO	8	3090	1 4	7500	8600
23 9	INTERNATIONAL	SLP	SAIL	FBG KL	OB		8	3090	2 6	6600	7550
23 9	INTERNATIONAL	SLP	SAIL	FBG KL	IB	10 UNIV	8	3090	2 6	7000	8000
23 9	INTERNATIONAL	SLP	SAIL	FBG KL	IB	8D VLVO	8	3090	2 6	7500	8600
23 9	INTERNATIONAL-HMS	CUT	MS	FBG KC	IB	10 UNIV	8	3200	1 4	7150	8250
23 9	INTERNATIONAL-HMS	CUT	MS	FBG KC	IB	8D VLVO	8	3200	1 4	7650	8800
23 9	INTERNATIONAL-HMS	CUT	MS	FBG KL	IB	10 UNIV	8	3200	2 6	7150	8250
23 9	INTERNATIONAL-HMS	CUT	MS	FBG KL	IB	8D VLVO	8	3200	2 6	7650	8800
30	INTERNATIONAL	SLP	SA/CR	FBG IB	IB	30 UNIV	11 4	10000	4 2	27700	30800
30	INTERNATIONAL	SLP	SA/CR	FBG IB	IB	23D	11 4	10000	4 2	27900	31000
1976 BOATS											
20 1	HELSEN 11 20 DELUXE	SLP	SAIL	FBG KC	OB		7 4	2000	1 2	4600	5250
20 1	HELSEN 11 20-F	SLP	SAIL	FBG KC	OB		7 4	2000	1 2	3600	4200
20 3	HELSEN-STREAKER	SLP	SAIL	FBG KC	OB		6 6	1000	6	2900	3350
22	HELSEN 11 22	SLP	SAIL	FBG KC	OB		8	2500	1 2	5500	6300
22	HELSEN 11 22-E	SLP	SAIL	FBG KC	OB		8	2500	1 2	4600	5300
23 6	22 1/2 SHOAL KEEL	SLP	SAIL	FBG KL	OB		8	3200	2 6	6100	7000
23 6	CLUB-RACER SHOAL KL	SLP	SAIL	FBG KL	IB	10 UNIV	8	3200	2 6	6100	7000
23 6	CLUB-RACER SHOAL KL	SLP	SAIL	FBG KL	IB	7D- 9D	8	3200	2 6	6600	7650
23 6	ELITE SHOAL KEEL	SLP	SAIL	FBG KL	IB	10 UNIV	8	3500	2 6	7500	8650
23 6	ELITE SHOAL KEEL	SLP	SAIL	FBG KL	IB	7D- 9D	8	3500	2 6	8050	9400
23 6	H-M-S 23	SLP	SAIL	FBG KC	IB	10 UNIV	8	3200	1 4	8150	9400
23 6	H-M-S 23	SLP	SAIL	FBG KC	IB	7D- 9D	8	3200	1 4	8800	10000
23 6	H-M-S 23 SHOAL KEEL	SLP	SAIL	FBG KL	IB	10 UNIV	8	3200	2 6	8500	9800
23 6	H-M-S 23 SHOAL KEEL	SLP	SAIL	FBG KL	IB	7D- 9D	8	3200	2 6	9200	10400
23 6	INTERNATIONAL	SLP	SAIL	FBG KL	IB		8	3200	1 4	6250	7200

LOA FT IN	NAME AND/OR MODEL	TOP/ RIG	BOAT TYPE	HULL MTL	TP	TP	ENGINE # HP	MFG	BEAM FT IN	WGT LBS	DRAFT FT IN	RETAIL LOW	RETAIL HIGH
1976 BOATS													
23 6	INTL 23 CLUB RACER	SLP	SAIL	FBG	KC	IB	10	UNIV	8	3200	1 4	5700	6550
23 6	INTL 23 CLUB RACER	SLP	SAIL	FBG	KC	IB	7D-	9D	8	3200	1 4	6250	7250
23 6	INTL 23 CR SHOAL KL	SLP	SAIL	FBG	KL	IB	10	UNIV	8	3200	2 6	6500	7450
23 6	INTL 23 CR SHOAL KL	SLP	SAIL	FBG	KL	IB	7D-	9D	8	3200	2 6	7050	8100
23 6	INTL 23 CRUISER	SLP	SAIL	FBG	KC	IB	10	UNIV	8	3200	1 4	6100	7050
23 6	INTL 23 CRUISER	SLP	SAIL	FBG	KC	IB	7D-	9D	8	3200	1 4	6650	7700
23 6	INTL 23 ELITE	SLP	SAIL	FBG	KC	IB	10	UNIV	8	3500	1 4	7200	8250
23 6	INTL 23 ELITE	SLP	SAIL	FBG	KC	IB	7D-	9D	8	3500	1 4	7750	8900
1975 BOATS													
20 1	HELSEN 20	SLP	SAIL	FBG	KC	OB			7 4	2000	4 6	3950	4600
20 3	HELSEN-STREAKER	SLP	SAIL	FBG	CB	OB			6 6	1000	4	2800	3250
22	HELSEN 22	SLP	SAIL	FBG	KC	OB			8	2200	4 6	4500	5200
1974 BOATS													
22	HELSEN 22	SLP	SAIL	FBG	KC	OB			8	2200	4 6	4400	5050
1973 BOATS													
22	HELSEN 22	SLP	SAIL	FBG	KC	OB			8	2000		4000	4650

INTERNATIONAL YACHT SALES

Call 1-800-327-6929 for BUC Personalized Evaluation Service
Or, for 1960 to 1963 boats, sign onto www.BUCValuPro.com

INTERNATIONAL YACHT SERVICES

COAST GUARD MFG ID- NYV

Call 1-800-327-6929 for BUC Personalized Evaluation Service
Or, for 1980 to 1982 boats, sign onto www.BUCValuPro.com

INTERNATIONAL YACHTS INC

COAST GUARD MFG ID- GEY

Call 1-800-327-6929 for BUC Personalized Evaluation Service
Or, for 1979 to 1980 boats, sign onto www.BUCValuPro.com

INTREPID YACHTS

E TAUNTON MA 02718   COAST GUARD MFG ID- CPD See inside cover to adjust price for area

For more recent years, see the BUC Used Boat Price Guide, Volume 1 or Volume 2

LOA FT IN	NAME AND/OR MODEL	TOP/ RIG	BOAT TYPE	HULL MTL	TP	TP	ENGINE # HP	MFG	BEAM FT IN	WGT LBS	DRAFT FT IN	RETAIL LOW	RETAIL HIGH
1983 BOATS													
40	INTREPID 40 AFT CPT	SLP	SA/CR	FBG	KL	IB	50D	PERK	12 7	20000	5 8	71500	78500
40	INTREPID 40 CTR CPT	SLP	SA/CR	FBG	KL	IB	50D	PERK	12 7	20000	5 8	75900	83400
1982 BOATS													
40	INTREPID 40	SLP	SA/CR	FBG	KL	IB	50D	PERK	12 7	20000	5 8	69900	76800
1981 BOATS													
27 7	INTREPID 9 METER	SLP	SA/RC	FBG	KL	IB	D		9 9	7700	4 10	22100	24500
29 6	INTREPID 9 METER	SLP	SA/RC	FBG	KL	IB	D		9 9	7700	4 10	23100	25600
1980 BOATS													
29 7	INTREPID 9 METER	SLP	SA/CR	FBG	KL	IB	13D	VLVO	9 9	7700	4 10	22000	24500
35 1	INTREPID 35	SLP	SA/RC	FBG	KL	IB	D		10 2	13600	5 6	40100	44600
1979 BOATS													
28	INTREPID 28	SLP	SA/CR	FBG	KL	IB	12D	YAN	9 6	7500	4 10	20200	22400
29 7	INTREPID 9 METER	SLP	SA/CR	FBG	KL	IB	15D	VLVO	9 9	7700	4 10	21500	23900
29 7	INTREPID 9 METER SHL	SLP	SA/CR	FBG	KL	IB	15D	VLVO	9 9	7700	3 6	21500	23900
35 1	INTREPID 35	SLP	SA/CR	FBG	KL	IB	23D	VLVO	10 2	13600	5 6	38400	42700

INVADER MARINE

Call 1-800-327-6929 for BUC Personalized Evaluation Service
Or, for 1968 to 1971 boats, sign onto www.BUCValuPro.com

INVADER MARINE INC

GIDDINGS TX 78942   COAST GUARD MFG ID- ILP See inside cover to adjust price for area
FORMERLY INVADER BOATS INC

For more recent years, see the BUC Used Boat Price Guide, Volume 1 or Volume 2

LOA FT IN	NAME AND/OR MODEL	TOP/ RIG	BOAT TYPE	HULL MTL	TP	TP	ENGINE # HP	MFG	BEAM FT IN	WGT LBS	DRAFT FT IN	RETAIL LOW	RETAIL HIGH
1983 BOATS													
16 1	INVADER 16V B/R	ST	RNBT	FBG	SV	IO	120	MRCR	6 5	1790		2400	2800
17 1	INVADER 17 SPORT	ST	RNBT	FBG	SV	IO	120	VLVO	7 7	1900		3050	3500
17 3	INVADER 17V B/R	ST	RNBT	FBG	DV	IO	140-200		7	2500		3200	3750
17 3	INVADER 17V C/B	ST	RNBT	FBG	DV	IO	138	VLVO	7	2500		3350	3900
18 8	INVADER 19 B/R	ST	RNBT	FBG	DV	IO	170-260		7 7	2800		3850	4750
20 3	INVADER 20 B/R	ST	RNBT	FBG	DV	IO	170-260		7 8	3000		4150	5100
20 3	INVADER 20 CC	ST	CUD	FBG	DV	IO	170-260		7 8	3000		4350	5300
1982 BOATS													
16 1	INVADER 16V B/R	ST	RNBT	FBG	SV	IO	120-140		6 5	1790		2350	2700
17 3	INVADER 17V B/R	ST	RNBT	FBG	DV	IO	140-200		7	2500		3100	3700
17 3	INVADER 17V C/B	ST	RNBT	FBG	DV	IO	165	MRCR	7	2500		3150	3650
18 8	INVADER 19 B/R	ST	RNBT	FBG	DV	IO	170-260		7 7	2800		3750	4650
1981 BOATS													
16 1	INVADER 16V B/R	ST	RNBT	FBG	SV	IO	120-140		6 5	1790		2300	2700
16 6	INVADER 16 W/T	ST	RNBT	FBG	TR	IO	120		6 10			2700	3100
17 3	INVADER 17V B/R	ST	RNBT	FBG	DV	IO	140-200		7	2500		3050	3650
17 3	INVADER 17V C/B	ST	RNBT	FBG	DV	IO	165	MRCR	7	2500		3100	3600
18 1	INVADER 18 W/T	ST	RNBT	FBG	TR	IO	165		7			3050	3550
18 8	INVADER 19 B/R	ST	RNBT	FBG	DV	IO	170-260		7 7	2800		3700	4600
20 3	INVADER 20 B/R	ST	RNBT	FBG	DV	OB			7 8	1800		3400	3950
20 3	INVADER 20 B/R	ST	RNBT	FBG	DV	IO	170-260		7 8	3000		3950	4900
20 3	INVADER 20 CC	ST	CUD	FBG	DV	OB			7 8	2200		3950	4550
20 3	INVADER 20 CC	ST	CUD	FBG	DV	IO	170-260		7 8	3000		4150	5100
21 8	INVADER 22 CC	ST	CUD	FBG	DV	IO	198-260		8	3600		5250	6250
1980 BOATS													
16 1	INVADER 16V B/R	ST	RNBT	FBG	SV	IO	120-140		6 5	1790		2300	2700
16 6	INVADER 16T B/R	ST	RNBT	FBG	TR	IO	120-170		6 10	1958		2500	2950
17 3	INVADER 17V B/R	ST	RNBT	FBG	DV	IO	140-200		7	2500		3050	3600
17 3	INVADER 17V C/B	ST	RNBT	FBG	DV	IO	165	MRCR	7	2500		3050	3550
18 1	INVADER 18 B/R	ST	RNBT	FBG	TR	IO	165-200		7	2563		3250	3800
18 8	INVADER 19 B/R	ST	RNBT	FBG	DV	IO	170-260		7 7	2800		3650	4550
20 3	INVADER 20 B/R	ST	RNBT	FBG	DV	OB			7 8	1800		3350	3900
20 3	INVADER 20 B/R	ST	RNBT	FBG	DV	IO	170-260		7 8	3000		3950	4850
20 3	INVADER 20 CC	ST	CUD	FBG	DV	OB			7 8	2200		3850	4450
20 3	INVADER 20 CC	ST	CUD	FBG	DV	IO	170-260		7 8	3000		4100	5050
21 8	INVADER 22 CC	ST	CUD	FBG	DV	IO	198-260		8	3600		5200	6200
1979 BOATS													
16 6	INVADER 16 B/R	ST	RNBT	FBG	TR	IO	120-170		6 10	1958		2500	2950
17 3	INVADER 17 B/R	ST	RNBT	FBG	DV	IO	140-200		7	2500		3050	3600
18 1	INVADER 18 B/R	ST	RNBT	FBG	TR	IO	165-200		7	2563		3200	3800
18 8	INVADER 19 B/R	ST	RNBT	FBG	DV	IO	170-260		7 7	2700			4500
18 8	INVADER 19 C/B	ST	RNBT	FBG	DV	IO	165-200		7	2700		3550	4400
20 3	INVADER 20 B/R	ST	RNBT	FBG	DV	OB			7 8	1800		3250	3800
20 3	INVADER 20 B/R	ST	RNBT	FBG	DV	IO	170-260		7 8	3000		3950	4850
20 3	INVADER 20 CC	ST	CUD	FBG	DV	OB			7 8	2200		3750	4350
20 3	INVADER 20 CC	ST	CUD	FBG	DV	IO	170-260		7 8	3000		4100	5050
21 7	INVADER 22 CC	ST	CUD	FBG	DV	IO	198-260		8	3600		5150	6150
1978 BOATS													
16 6	INVADER 16 B/R	ST	RNBT	FBG	TR	IO	120-170		6 10	1958		2550	2950
17 3	INVADER 17B	ST	RNBT	FBG	DV	IO	140-198		7	2433		3000	3550
17 3	INVADER 17C	ST	RNBT	FBG	DV	IO	140-198		7	2133		2800	3300
18 1	INVADER 18 B/R	ST	RNBT	FBG	DV	IO	165-198		7	2563		3250	3800
18 8	INVADER 19 B/R	ST	RNBT	FBG	DV	IO	165-240		7 7	2760		3650	4350
20 3	INVADER 20 B/R	ST	RNBT	FBG	DV	IO	165-240		7 8			3650	4250
20 3	INVADER 20 CC	ST	CUD	FBG	DV	IO	170-240		7 8	3000		3900	4550
21 7	INVADER 22 B/R	ST	RNBT	FBG	DV	IO	198-240		8	3600		4950	5750
1977 BOATS													
16 6	INTRUDER	ST	RNBT	FBG	TR	IO	120		6 10	1945		2550	3000
16 6	INTRUDER-ELITE	ST	RNBT	FBG	DV	IO	140-175		6 10	2115		2700	3150
17 3	AQUARIUS	ST	RNBT	FBG	DV	IO	140-190		7	2610		3100	3700
17 3	AQUARIUS B/R	ST	RNBT	FBG	DV	IO	140-190		7	2610		2900	3450
18 1	EXECUTIVE	ST	RNBT	FBG	TR	IO	165-190		7	2460		3200	3750
18 1	EXECUTIVE-ELITE	ST	RNBT	FBG	DV	IO	165-190		7	2670		3350	3950
18 8	CONTINENTAL	ST	RNBT	FBG	DV	IO	165-235		7 7	2960		3850	4600
20 1	STARMAKER 241	ST	CUD	FBG	DV	IO	165-240		7 10	3240		4450	5300
21 7	STARMAKER 259	ST	CUD	FBG	DV	IO	188-265		8	3550		5200	6300
1976 BOATS													
16 6	INTRUDER	ST	RNBT	FBG	TR	IO	120-170		6 10	1980		2650	3100
16 6	INTRUDER-ELITE	ST	RNBT	FBG	DV	IO	140-175		6 10	1980		2650	3100
17 3	AQUARIUS	ST	RNBT	FBG	DV	IO	140-190		7	2140		2900	3450
17 3	AQUARIUS B/R	ST	RNBT	FBG	DV	IO	140-190		7	2350		3050	3650
18 1	EXECUTIVE	ST	RNBT	FBG	TR	IO	165-190		7	2480		3300	3900
18 1	EXECUTIVE-ELITE	ST	RNBT	FBG	DV	IO	165-190		7	2480		3300	3900
18 8	CONTINENTAL	ST	RNBT	FBG	DV	IO	165-235		7 7	2640		3650	4500
1975 BOATS													
16 2	INTRUDER	ST	RNBT	FBG	TR	IO	120-175		6 8	1960		2650	3100
16 2	INTRUDER ELITE	ST	RNBT	FBG	DV	IO	120-175		6 8	1960		2650	3100
17 3	AQUARIUS	ST	RNBT	FBG	DV	IO	140-190		7	2400		3150	3750

LOA FT IN	NAME AND/ OR MODEL	TOP/ RIG	BOAT TYPE	-HULL- MTL TP TP	----ENGINE--- # HP MFG	BEAM FT IN	WGT LBS	DRAFT FT IN	RETAIL LOW	RETAIL HIGH
----------------- 1975 BOATS -----------------
18 1	EXECUTIVE	ST	RNBT	FBG TR IO	165 MRCR	7	2528		3300	3800
18 1	EXECUTIVE ELITE	ST	RNBT	FBG TR IO	165-190	7	2528		3500	4100
18 8	CONTINENTAL	ST	RNBT	FBG DV IO	165-233	7 7	2760		3850	4650
----------------- 1974 BOATS -----------------
16 2	EXECUTIVE		RNBT	FBG	IO	140 MRCR		1862		2600	3050
16 2	INTRUDER SPEC DLX	ST	RNBT	FBG	IO	120-140		1862		2550	3050
17 7	CONVINCER DLX		RNBT	FBG	IO	140-165		2150		3150	3700
17 7	CONVINCER SP DLX		RNBT	FBG	IO	140-165		2150		3150	3650
17 7	EXECUTIVE		RNBT	FBG	IO	165		2175		3200	3700
19	CONTINENTAL		RNBT	FBG	IO	165-225		2210		3550	4300
----------------- 1973 BOATS -----------------
16 2	INTRUDER DLX	ST	RNBT	FBG	IO	120-140	6 4	1862		2600	3100
16 2	INTRUDER SPEC DLX	ST	RNBT	FBG	IO	120-140	6 4	1862		2750	3200
17 7	CONVINCER DLX		RNBT	FBG	IO	140-165	7 1	2090		3150	3800
17 7	CONVINCER JT		RNBT	FBG	JT	245 UMC	7 1	2250		3100	3600
17 7	CONVINCER SP DLX		RNBT	FBG	IO	140-165	7 1	2090		3250	3750
----------------- 1972 BOATS -----------------
16 2	INTRUDER DLX	ST	RNBT	FBG	IO	120-140	6 4	1862		2650	3150
16 2	INTRUDER SPEC DLX	ST	RNBT	FBG	IO	120-140	6 4	1862		2850	3300
17 7	PURT-NER DLX			FBG	IO	140-165	7 1	2090		3150	3800
17 7	PURT-NER SPEC DLX			FBG	IO	140-165	7 1	2090		3250	3750
----------------- 1971 BOATS -----------------
17 4	BWV DELUXE	OP		FBG TR IO	120 MRCR	7		3 5	3300	3850
22 6	23		CR	FBG IO	210		8	2 2	5000	5750
----------------- 1970 BOATS -----------------
17 4	BWV			FBG TR IO	120 MRCR	7		3 5	3400	3950
----------------- 1963 BOATS -----------------
16 8	INVADER 100	ST	RNBT	FBG	IO	100			4500	5200

INVADER MARINE LLC
HESPERIA CA 92345   COAST GUARD MFG ID- SKP See inside cover to adjust price for area
FORMERLY SKIPJACK INTERNATIONAL

For more recent years, see the BUC Used Boat Price Guide, Volume 1 or Volume 2

LOA FT IN	NAME AND/ OR MODEL	TOP/ RIG	BOAT TYPE	-HULL- MTL TP TP	----ENGINE--- # HP MFG	BEAM FT IN	WGT LBS	DRAFT FT IN	RETAIL LOW	RETAIL HIGH
----------------- 1983 BOATS -----------------
20 5	SKIPJACK 20	OP	CR	FBG DV IO	170-228	7 10	3200		6650	8100
20 5	SKIPJACK 20	OP	CR	FBG DV IO	260	7 10	3200		7000	8450
23 10	SKIPJACK 24	OP	CR	FBG DV IO	225-260	8	4000		9900	11600
23 10	SKIPJACK 24	OP	CR	FBG DV IO	165D VLVO	8	4000		11900	13500
23 10	SKIPJACK 24	OP	CR	FBG DV IO	T138 VLVO	8	4000		11000	12500
23 10	SKIPJACK 24	FB	CR	FBG DV IO	225-260	8	4600		11000	12800
23 10	SKIPJACK 24	FB	CR	FBG DV IO	165D VLVO	8	4600		12900	14700
23 10	SKIPJACK 24	FB	CR	FBG DV IO	T138 VLVO	8	4600		12100	13700
25	SKIPJACK 25	HT	CBNCR	FBG DV IO	225-330	8	5200		15000	18000
25	SKIPJACK 25	HT	CBNCR	FBG DV IO	165D VLVO	8	5200		19600	21800
25	SKIPJACK 25	HT	CBNCR	FBG DV IO	T138 VLVO	8	5200		16000	18200
25	SKIPJACK 25	HT	SPTCR	FBG DV IO	225-330	8	5000		12200	15100
25	SKIPJACK 25	HT	SPTCR	FBG DV IO	165D VLVO	8	5000		14200	16100
25	SKIPJACK 25	HT	SPTCR	FBG DV IO	T138 VLVO	8	5000		13300	15100
28	SKIPJACK 28	FB	PH	FBG DV IO	T170-T260	8	6600		18900	23000
28	SKIPJACK 28	FB	PH	FBG DV IO	IOT130D-165D	8	6600		23100	27400
28	SKIPJACK 28	FB	SPTCR	FBG DV IO	T170-T260	8	6600		17100	21300
28	SKIPJACK 28	FB	SPTCR	FBG DV IO	IOT130D-T165D	8	6600		20300	24000
----------------- 1982 BOATS -----------------
20 5	SKIPJACK 20	OP	CR	FBG DV IO	170-228	7 10	3200		6500	7900
20 5	SKIPJACK 20	OP	CR	FBG DV IO	260	7 10	3200		6850	8250
23 10	SKIPJACK 24	OP	CR	FBG DV IO	225-260	8	4000		9700	11300
23 10	SKIPJACK 24	OP	CR	FBG DV IO	155D VLVO	8	4000		11500	13000
23 10	SKIPJACK 24	OP	CR	FBG DV IO	T145 VLVO	8	4000		10800	12200
23 10	SKIPJACK 24	FB	CR	FBG DV IO	225-260	8	4600		10800	12500
23 10	SKIPJACK 24	FB	CR	FBG DV IO	155D VLVO	8	4600		12600	14300
23 10	SKIPJACK 24	FB	CR	FBG DV IO	T145 VLVO	8	4600		11800	13400
25	SKIPJACK 25	HT	CBNCR	FBG DV IO	225-330	8	5200		14700	17600
25	SKIPJACK 25	HT	CBNCR	FBG DV IO	155D VLVO	8	5200		19100	21200
25	SKIPJACK 25	HT	CBNCR	FBG DV IO	T145 VLVO	8	5200		15700	17800
25	SKIPJACK 25	HT	SPTCR	FBG DV IO	225-330	8	5000		12000	14800
25	SKIPJACK 25	HT	SPTCR	FBG DV IO	155D VLVO	8	5000		13700	15600
25	SKIPJACK 25	HT	SPTCR	FBG DV IO	T145 VLVO	8	5000		13000	14800
28	SKIPJACK 28	FB	PH	FBG DV IO	T170-T260	8	6600		18500	22500
28	SKIPJACK 28	FB	PH	FBG DV IO	IOT130D-T155D	8	6600		22600	26300
28	SKIPJACK 28	FB	SPTCR	FBG DV IO	T170-T228	8	6600		16700	20300
28	SKIPJACK 28	FB	SPTCR	FBG DV IO	T260	8	6600		18600	21000
28	SKIPJACK 28	FB	SPTCR	FBG DV IO	IOT130D-T155D	8	6600		19800	23000
----------------- 1971 BOATS -----------------
20 5	SKIPJACK 20	OP	CR	FBG SV IO	165	7 10			7800	8950
20 5	SKIPJACK 20	OP	CR	FBG SV IO	165	7 10			7800	8950
23 10	SKIPJACK 24	OP	CR	FBG SV IO	165	8			11100	12700
23 10	SKIPJACK 24	FB	CR	FBG SV IO	165	8			11100	12700

INVERNESS MARINE
Call 1-800-327-6929 for BUC Personalized Evaluation Service
Or, for 1982 to 1984 boats, sign onto www.BUCValuPro.com

INVERTED CHINE BOATS INC
COAST GUARD MFG ID- NVC

Call 1-800-327-6929 for BUC Personalized Evaluation Service
Or, for 1980 to 1984 boats, sign onto www.BUCValuPro.com

IRVING SAILBOATS
Call 1-800-327-6929 for BUC Personalized Evaluation Service
Or, for 1967 boats, sign onto www.BUCValuPro.com

IRWIN COMPETITION YACHTS
DIV IRWIN YACHT & MARINE CORP   See inside cover to adjust price for area
CLEARWATER FL 33520   COAST GUARD MFG ID- XYW

LOA FT IN	NAME AND/ OR MODEL	TOP/ RIG	BOAT TYPE	-HULL- MTL TP TP	----ENGINE--- # HP MFG	BEAM FT IN	WGT LBS	DRAFT FT IN	RETAIL LOW	RETAIL HIGH
----------------- 1980 BOATS -----------------
21	FREESPIRIT 21 MINI	SLP	SA/CR	FBG KL		8	1800		3450	4050
----------------- 1979 BOATS -----------------
20 8	MINI-TON	SLP	SA/RC	FBG DB		8	1900		3400	3950
20 8	MINI-TON	SLP	SA/RC	FBG KL		8	1900		3400	3950

IRWIN YACHTS INTERNATIONAL INC
IRWIN YACHTS   See inside cover to adjust price for area
TREASURE ISLAND FL 3370 COAST GUARD MFG ID- XYM
FORMERLY IRWIN YACHT & MARINE CORP

For more recent years, see the BUC Used Boat Price Guide, Volume 1 or Volume 2

LOA FT IN	NAME AND/ OR MODEL	TOP/ RIG	BOAT TYPE	-HULL- MTL TP TP	----ENGINE--- # HP MFG	BEAM FT IN	WGT LBS	DRAFT FT IN	RETAIL LOW	RETAIL HIGH
----------------- 1983 BOATS -----------------
31 3	CITATION 31	SLP	SA/RC	FBG KC IB	15D YAN	11	9300	4	22900	25500
31 3	CITATION 31	SLP	SA/RC	FBG KL IB	15D YAN	11	9300	6	22600	25100
31 3	CITATION 31 SHOAL	SLP	SA/RC	FBG KL IB	15D YAN	11	9300	4	22300	24800
34 3	CITATION 34	SLP	SA/RC	FBG KC IB	15D- 23D	11	11500	4	28700	31900
34 3	CITATION 34	SLP	SA/RC	FBG KL IB	15D- 23D	11	11500	6	28400	31600
34 3	CITATION 34 SHOAL	SLP	SA/RC	FBG KL IB	15D- 23D	11	11500	5 4	28100	31300
40 9	CITATION 41	SLP	SA/RC	FBG KL IB	30D YAN	13	17500	7 3	52200	57400
41 8	IRWIN 41	KTH	SA/CR	FBG KL IB	62D PERK	13	25000	4 6	67500	74200
45 6	IRWIN 46	KTH	SA/CR	FBG KL IB	62D PERK	13	33000	4 8	89500	98300
45 6	IRWIN 46	KTH	SA/CR	FBG KL IB	62D PERK	13	33000	6 1	89500	98300
45 6	IRWIN 46 SHOAL	KTH	SA/CR	FBG KL IB	62D PERK	13	33000	4 8	88400	97200
55 8	IRWIN 52	KTH	SA/CR	FBG KC IB	85D PERK	15	44500	5 5	130000	143000
55 8	IRWIN 52	KTH	SA/CR	FBG KC IB	135D PERK	15	44500	5 3	130000	143000
55 8	IRWIN 52	KTH	SA/CR	FBG KL IB	85D PERK	15	46500	6 10	132000	145000
55 8	IRWIN 52	KTH	SA/CR	FBG KL IB	135D PERK	15	46500	6 10	132000	145000
55 8	IRWIN 52 SHOAL	KTH	SA/CR	FBG KL IB	85D PERK	15	46500	5 3	130500	143500
55 8	IRWIN 52 SHOAL	KTH	SA/CR	FBG KL IB	135D PERK	15	46500	5 3	130500	143500
65 6	IRWIN 65	KTH	SA/CR	FBG KL IB	135D PERK	17	78500	8 6	307500	338000
65 6	IRWIN 65	KTH	SA/CR	FBG KL IB	200D PERK	17	78500	8 6	308500	338500
65 6	IRWIN 65 SHOAL	KTH	SA/CR	FBG KL IB	135D PERK	17	78500	5 9	305500	336000
65 6	IRWIN 65 SHOAL	KTH	SA/CR	FBG KL IB	200D PERK	17	78500	5 9	306000	336500
----------------- 1982 BOATS -----------------
30	CITATION 30	SLP	SA/RC	FBG KC IB	15D YAN	10	10400	4	23600	26200
30	CITATION 30	SLP	SA/RC	FBG KL IB	15D YAN	10	10400	5 4	23600	26200
31 3	CITATION 31	SLP	SA/RC	FBG KC IB	15D YAN	11	9300	4	21600	24000
31 3	CITATION 31	SLP	SA/RC	FBG KL IB	15D YAN	11	9300	6	21300	23700
31 3	CITATION 31 SHOAL	SLP	SA/RC	FBG KL IB	15D YAN	11	9300	4	21000	23300

IRWIN YACHTS INTERNATIONAL INC -CONTINUED See inside cover to adjust price for area

LOA FT	LOA IN	NAME AND/ OR MODEL	TOP/ RIG	BOAT TYPE	-HULL- MTL	-HULL- TP	ENGINE TP	ENGINE # HP	ENGINE MFG	BEAM FT	BEAM IN	WGT LBS	DRAFT FT	DRAFT IN	RETAIL LOW	RETAIL HIGH
		1982 BOATS														
34	3	CITATION 34	SLP	SA/RC	FBG	KC	IB	15D-	23D	11	3	11500	4		27000	30100
34	3	CITATION 34	SLP	SA/RC	FBG	KL	IB	15D-	23D	11	3	11500	5	4	26700	29700
34	3	CITATION 34 SHOAL	SLP	SA/RC	FBG	KL	IB	15D-	23D	11	3	11500	4		26400	29400
37		IRWIN 37 MK V	SLP	SA/RC	FBG	KC	IB	50D	PERK	11	6	20000	4		47100	51800
37		IRWIN 37 MK V	SLP	SA/RC	FBG	KL	IB	50D	PERK	11	6	20000	5	6	47300	51900
37		IRWIN 37 MK V	KTH	SA/RC	FBG	KC	IB	50D	PERK	11	6	20000	4		46600	51200
37		IRWIN 37 MK V	KTH	SA/RC	FBG	KL	IB	50D	PERK	11	6	20000	5	6	46600	51300
37		IRWIN 37 MK V SHOAL	SLP	SA/RC	FBG	KL	IB	50D	PERK	11	6	20000	4		46300	50800
37		IRWIN 37 MK V SHOAL	KTH	SA/RC	FBG	KL	IB	50D	PERK	11	6	20000	4		47400	52100
39	9	CITATION 40	SLP	SA/RC	FBG	KC	IB	23D	YAN	12	2	16890	4	3	46100	50600
39	9	CITATION 40	SLP	SA/RC	FBG	KC	IB	30D	YAN	12	2	16890	4	3	46200	50800
39	9	CITATION 40	SLP	SA/RC	FBG	KL	IB	23D	YAN	12	2	16890	6	3	47300	52000
39	9	CITATION 40	SLP	SA/RC	FBG	KL	IB	30D	YAN	12	2	16890	6	3	47400	52100
39	9	CITATION 40 SHOAL	SLP	SA/RC	FBG	KL	IB	23D	YAN	12	2	16890	4	3	44700	49700
39	9	CITATION 40 SHOAL	SLP	SA/RC	FBG	KL	IB	30D	YAN	12	2	16890	4	3	44900	49800
45	6	IRWIN 46	KTH	SA/CR	FBG	KC	IB	62D	PERK	13	6	33000	4	8	84200	92500
45	6	IRWIN 46	KTH	SA/CR	FBG	KL	IB	62D	PERK	13	6	33000	6	1	84200	92500
45	6	IRWIN 46 SHOAL	KTH	SA/CR	FBG	KL	IB	62D	PERK	13	6	33000	4	8	83200	91400
55	8	IRWIN 52	KTH	SA/CR	FBG	KC	IB	85D	PERK	15	5	44500	5	3	122500	134500
55	8	IRWIN 52	KTH	SA/CR	FBG	KC	IB	135D	PERK	15	5	44500	5	3	122500	134500
55	8	IRWIN 52	KTH	SA/CR	FBG	KL	IB	85D	PERK	15	5	46500	6	10	124500	136500
55	8	IRWIN 52	KTH	SA/CR	FBG	KL	IB	135D	PERK	15	5	46500	6	10	124500	137000
55	8	IRWIN 52 SHOAL	KTH	SA/CR	FBG	KL	IB	85D	PERK	15	5	46500	5	3	123000	135500
55	8	IRWIN 52 SHOAL	KTH	SA/CR	FBG	KL	IB	135D	PERK	15	5	46500	5	3	123000	135500
65	6	IRWIN 65	KTH	SA/CR	FBG	KL	IB	135D	PERK	17	4	78500	8	6	289500	318000
65	6	IRWIN 65	KTH	SA/CR	FBG	KL	IB	200D	PERK	17	4	78500	8	6	290000	318500
65	6	IRWIN 65 SHOAL	KTH	SA/CR	FBG	KL	IB	135D	PERK	17	4	78500	5	9	287500	316000
65	6	IRWIN 65 SHOAL	KTH	SA/CR	FBG	KL	IB	200D	PERK	17	4	78500	5	9	288000	316500
		1981 BOATS														
30		CITATION 30	SLP	SA/RC	FBG	KC	IB	15D	YAN	10	2	10400	4		22400	24800
30		CITATION 30	SLP	SA/RC	FBG	KL	IB	15D	YAN	10	2	10400	5	4	22500	25000
30		CITATION 30 SHOAL	SLP	SA/RC	FBG	KL	IB	15D	YAN	10	2	10400	4		21700	24100
34	3	CITATION 34	SLP	SA/RC	FBG	KC	IB	15D-	20D	11	3	11500	4		25100	27900
34	3	CITATION 34	SLP	SA/RC	FBG	KL	IB	15D-	20D	11	3	11500	5	4	25800	28600
34	3	CITATION 34 SHOAL	SLP	SA/RC	FBG	KL	IB	15D-	20D	11	3	11500	4		24500	28000
37		IRWIN 37 MK V	SLP	SA/RC	FBG	KC	IB	50D	PERK	11	6	20000	4		43600	48500
37		IRWIN 37 MK V	SLP	SA/RC	FBG	KL	IB	50D	PERK	11	6	20000	5	6	43600	48500
37		IRWIN 37 MK V	KTH	SA/RC	FBG	KC	IB	50D	PERK	11	6	20000	4		43600	48500
37		IRWIN 37 MK V	KTH	SA/RC	FBG	KL	IB	50D	PERK	11	6	20000	5	6	43600	48500
37		IRWIN 37 MK V SHOAL	SLP	SA/RC	FBG	KL	IB	50D	PERK	11	6	20000	4		43600	48500
37		IRWIN 37 MK V SHOAL	KTH	SA/RC	FBG	KL	IB	50D	PERK	11	6	20000	4		43600	48500
39	9	CITATION 40	SLP	SA/RC	FBG	KC	IB	20D	YAN	12	2	16890	4	3	42800	47600
39	9	CITATION 40	SLP	SA/RC	FBG	KC	IB	30D	YAN	12	2	16890	4	3	43000	47800
39	9	CITATION 40	SLP	SA/RC	FBG	KL	IB	20D	YAN	12	2	16890	6	3	44100	49000
39	9	CITATION 40	SLP	SA/RC	FBG	KL	IB	30D	YAN	12	2	16890	6	3	44300	49200
39	9	CITATION 40 SHOAL	SLP	SA/RC	FBG	KL	IB	20D	YAN	12	2	16890	4	3	41900	46600
39	9	CITATION 40 SHOAL	SLP	SA/RC	FBG	KL	IB	30D	YAN	12	2	16890	4	3	42100	46700
42	6	AVANTI 42	SLP	SA/CR	FBG	KC	IB	62D	PERK	13	4	26000	4	4	63100	69300
42	6	AVANTI 42 SHOAL	SLP	SA/CR	FBG	KL	IB	62D	PERK	13	4	26000	4	[illegible]	62300	68500
45	6	IRWIN 46	KTH	SA/CR	FBG	KC	IB	62D	PERK	13	6	33000	4	8	79200	87000
45	6	IRWIN 46	KTH	SA/CR	FBG	KL	IB	62D	PERK	13	6	33000	6	1	79300	87100
45	6	IRWIN 46 SHOAL	KTH	SA/CR	FBG	KL	IB	62D	PERK	13	6	33000	4	8	78200	85900
55	8	IRWIN 52	KTH	SA/CR	FBG	KC	IB	85D	PERK	15	5	44500	5	3	115500	126500
55	8	IRWIN 52	KTH	SA/CR	FBG	KC	IB	135D	PERK	15	5	44500	5	3	115500	127000
55	8	IRWIN 52	KTH	SA/CR	FBG	KL	IB	85D	PERK	15	5	46500	6	10	117000	128500
55	8	IRWIN 52	KTH	SA/CR	FBG	KL	IB	135D	PERK	15	5	46500	6	10	117500	129000
55	8	IRWIN 52 SHOAL	KTH	SA/CR	FBG	KL	IB	85D	PERK	15	5	46500	5	3	116000	127500
55	8	IRWIN 52 SHOAL	KTH	SA/CR	FBG	KL	IB	135D	PERK	15	5	46500	5	3	116000	127500
65	6	IRWIN 65	KTH	SA/CR	FBG	KL	IB	135D	PERK	17	4	78500	8	6	271000	297500
65	6	IRWIN 65	KTH	SA/CR	FBG	KL	IB	200D	PERK	17	4	78500	8	6	271500	298000
65	6	IRWIN 65 SHOAL	KTH	SA/CR	FBG	KL	IB	135D	PERK	17	4	78500	5	9	272500	299500
65	6	IRWIN 65 SHOAL	KTH	SA/CR	FBG	KL	IB	200D	PERK	17	4	78500	5	9	273000	300000
		1980 BOATS														
30		CITATION 30	SLP	SA/RC	FBG	KC	IB	15D	YAN	10	2	10400	4		21200	23500
30		CITATION 30	SLP	SA/RC	FBG	KL	IB	15D	YAN	10	2	10400	5	4	21900	24300
30		CITATION 30 SHOAL	SLP	SA/RC	FBG	KL	IB	15D	YAN	10	2	10400	4		20600	22800
34	3	CITATION 34	SLP	SA/RC	FBG	KC	IB	15D-	20D	11	3	11500	4		24000	26700
34	3	CITATION 34	SLP	SA/RC	FBG	KL	IB	15D-	20D	11	3	11500	5	4	24700	27400
34	3	CITATION 34 SHOAL	SLP	SA/RC	FBG	KL	IB	15D-	20D	11	3	11500	4		23300	26000
37		IRWIN 37 MK V	SLP	SA/RC	FBG	KC	IB	50D	PERK	11	6	20000	4		41900	46600
37		IRWIN 37 MK V	SLP	SA/RC	FBG	KL	IB	50D	PERK	11	6	20000	5	6	42000	46700
37		IRWIN 37 MK V	KTH	SA/RC	FBG	KC	IB	50D	PERK	11	6	20000	4		41900	46600
37		IRWIN 37 MK V	KTH	SA/RC	FBG	KL	IB	50D	PERK	11	6	20000	5	6	42000	46700
37		IRWIN 37 MK V SHOAL	SLP	SA/RC	FBG	KL	IB	50D	PERK	11	6	20000	4		41000	45600
37		IRWIN 37 MK V SHOAL	KTH	SA/RC	FBG	KL	IB	50D	PERK	11	6	20000	4		41000	45600
39	9	CITATION 39	SLP	SA/RC	FBG	KC	IB	22D	YAN	12	2	16890	4	3	40900	45400
39	9	CITATION 39	SLP	SA/RC	FBG	KC	IB	30D	YAN	12	2	16890	4	3	41000	45500
39	9	CITATION 39	SLP	SA/RC	FBG	KL	IB	22D	YAN	12	2	16890	6	3	42300	47000
39	9	CITATION 39	SLP	SA/RC	FBG	KL	IB	30D	YAN	12	2	16890	6	3	42400	47100
39	9	CITATION 39 SHOAL	SLP	SA/RC	FBG	KL	IB	22D	YAN	12	2	16890	4	3	40000	44500
39	9	CITATION 39 SHOAL	SLP	SA/RC	FBG	KL	IB	30D	YAN	12	2	16890	4	3	40100	44600
45	6	IRWIN 46	KTH	SA/CR	FBG	KC	IB	62D	PERK	13	6	33000	4	8	75700	83200
45	6	IRWIN 46	KTH	SA/CR	FBG	KL	IB	62D	PERK	13	6	33000	6	1	75600	83000
45	6	IRWIN 46 SHOAL	KTH	SA/CR	FBG	KL	IB	62D	PERK	13	6	33000	4	8	74700	82100
55	8	IRWIN 52	KTH	SA/CR	FBG	KC	IB	85D	PERK	15	5	44500	5	6	110000	121000
55	8	IRWIN 52	KTH	SA/CR	FBG	KL	IB	85D	PERK	15	5	46500	7		112000	123000
55	8	IRWIN 52 SHOAL	KTH	SA/CR	FBG	KL	IB	85D	PERK	15	5	46500	5	6	110500	121500
		1979 BOATS														
30		CITATION 30	SLP	SA/RC	FBG	KC	IB	15D	YAN	10	2	10400	4		20600	22900
30		CITATION 30	SLP	SA/RC	FBG	KL	IB	15D	YAN	10	2	10400	5	4	20700	23000
30		CITATION 30 SHOAL	SLP	SA/RC	FBG	KL	IB	15D	YAN	10	2	10400	4		20000	22200
34	3	CITATION 34	SLP	SA/RC	FBG	KL	IB	15D	YAN	11	3	11500	4		23100	25600
37		IRWIN 37 MK III	SLP	SA/CR	FBG	KC	IB	50D	PERK	11	6	20000	4		40300	44700
37		IRWIN 37 MK III	SLP	SA/CR	FBG	KL	IB	50D	PERK	11	6	20000	5	6	40400	44900
37		IRWIN 37 MK III	CUT	SA/CR	FBG	KC	IB	50D	PERK	11	6	20000	4		40200	44700
37		IRWIN 37 MK III	CUT	SA/CR	FBG	KL	IB	50D	PERK	11	6	20000	5	6	40400	44900
37		IRWIN 37 MK III	KTH	SA/CR	FBG	KC	IB	50D	PERK	11	6	20000	4		40300	44700
37		IRWIN 37 MK III	KTH	SA/CR	FBG	KL	IB	50D	PERK	11	6	20000	5	6	40400	44900
37		IRWIN 37 MK III SHOA	SLP	SA/CR	FBG	KL	IB	50D	PERK	11	6	20000	4		39500	43900
37		IRWIN 37 MK III SHOA	CUT	SA/CR	FBG	KL	IB	50D	PERK	11	6	20000	4		39500	43900
37		IRWIN 37 MK III SHOA	KTH	SA/CR	FBG	KL	IB	50D	PERK	11	6	20000	4		39500	43900
39	9	CITATION 39	SLP	SA/RC	FBG	KL	IB	20D	YAN	12	2	16890	4	3	39400	43800
43	6	IRWIN 44	KTH	SA/CR	FBG	KC	IB	62D	PERK	13	4	30500	4	4	61600	67700
43	6	IRWIN 44	KTH	SA/CR	FBG	KL	IB	62D	PERK	13	4	30500	5	9	61800	67900
43	6	IRWIN 44 SHOAL	KTH	SA/CR	FBG	KL	IB	62D	PERK	13	4	30500	4	4	61000	67000
55	8	IRWIN 52	KTH	SA/CR	FBG	KC	IB	85D	PERK	15	5	44500	5	3	106000	116000
55	8	IRWIN 52	KTH	SA/CR	FBG	KL	IB	85D	PERK	15	5	46500	6	10	107000	117500
55	8	IRWIN 52 SHOAL	KTH	SA/CR	FBG	KL	IB	85D	PERK	15	5	46500	5	3	107000	117500
		1978 BOATS														
25	4	IRWIN 10/4	SLP	SA/CR	FBG	CB	IB	8D		10	4	7000	2	9	11000	12500
28	5	IRWIN 28 MK IV	SLP	SA/CR	FBG	KC	IB	8D		9		7800	3		14000	15900
28	5	IRWIN 28 MK IV	SLP	SA/CR	FBG	KL	IB	8D		9		7800	4	6	13900	15800
30		CITATION 30	SLP	SA/RC	FBG	KC	IB	15D	YAN	10	2	10400	4	1	19700	21900
30		CITATION 30	SLP	SA/RC	FBG	KL	IB	15D	YAN	10	2	10400	5	4	19600	21800
30		CITATION 30 SHOAL	SLP	SA/RC	FBG	KL	IB	15D	YAN	10	2	10400	4		19600	21800
34	3	CITATION 34	SLP	SA/RC	FBG	KC	IB	15D	YAN	11	3	11500	4		22200	24700
34	3	CITATION 34	SLP	SA/RC	FBG	KL	IB	15D	YAN	11	3	11500	5	4	22200	24700
34	3	CITATION 34 SHOAL	SLP	SA/RC	FBG	KL	IB	15D	YAN	11	3	11500	4		22200	24700
37		IRWIN 37 MK III	SLP	SA/CR	FBG	KC	IB	40D	PERK	11	6	20000	4		38500	42800
37		IRWIN 37 MK III	SLP	SA/CR	FBG	KL	IB	40D	PERK	11	6	20000	5	6	38500	42800
37		IRWIN 37 MK III	KTH	SA/CR	FBG	KC	IB	40D	PERK	11	6	20000	4		38500	42800
37		IRWIN 37 MK III	KTH	SA/CR	FBG	KL	IB	40D	PERK	11	6	20000	5	6	38500	42800
37		IRWIN 37 MK III SHOA	SLP	SA/CR	FBG	KL	IB	40D	PERK	11	6	20000	4		38500	42800
37		IRWIN 37 MK III SHOA	KTH	SA/CR	FBG	KL	IB	40D	PERK	11	6	20000	4		38500	42800
39	9	CITATION 39	SLP	SA/RC	FBG	KC	IB	20D	YAN	12	2	16890	4	3	38000	42200
39	9	CITATION 39	SLP	SA/RC	FBG	KL	IB	20D	YAN	12	2	16890	6	3	38000	42200
39	9	CITATION 39 SHOAL	SLP	SA/RC	FBG	KL	IB	20D	YAN	12	2	16890	4	3	38000	42200
42	6	IRWIN 42	SLP	SA/CR	FBG	KC	IB	62D		13	4	29000	4	6	59200	65100
42	6	IRWIN 42	SLP	SA/CR	FBG	KL	IB	62D		13	4	29000	5	9	59200	65100
43	6	IRWIN 44	KTH	SA/CR	FBG	KC	IB	62D	PERK	13	4	30500	4	4	59400	65200
43	6	IRWIN 44	KTH	SA/CR	FBG	KL	IB	62D	PERK	13	4	30500	5	9	59500	65400
43	6	IRWIN 44 SHOAL	KTH	SA/CR	FBG	KL	IB	62D	PERK	13	4	30500	4	4	58900	64800
55	8	IRWIN 52	KTH	SA/CR	FBG	KC	IB	85D	PERK	15	5	44500	5	3	102000	112000
55	8	IRWIN 52	KTH	SA/CR	FBG	KL	IB	85D	PERK	15	5	46500	6	10	103000	113000
		1977 BOATS														
25	4	IRWIN 10/4	SLP	SA/CR	FBG	CB	IB	10	UNIV	10	4	7000	2	9	10500	11900
25	4	IRWIN 10/4	SLP	SA/CR	FBG	CB	IB	8D	YAN	10	4	7000	2	9	10700	12200
28	5	IRWIN 28 MK IV	SLP	SA/CR	FBG	KC	IB	10	UNIV	9		7800	3		13400	15200
28	5	IRWIN 28 MK IV	SLP	SA/CR	FBG	KC	IB	8D	YAN	9		7800	3		13500	15400
28	5	IRWIN 28 MK IV	SLP	SA/CR	FBG	KL	IB	10	UNIV	9		7800	4	6	13300	15200
28	5	IRWIN 28 MK IV	SLP	SA/CR	FBG	KL	IB	8D	YAN	9		7800	4	6	13500	15300
30		IRWIN 30	SLP	SA/CR	FBG	KC	IB	30	UNIV	10	2	9200	4	3	16500	18700
30		IRWIN 30	SLP	SA/CR	FBG	KC	IB	20D	YAN	10	2	9200	4	3	16600	18800
30		IRWIN 30	SLP	SA/CR	FBG	KL	IB	30	UNIV	10	2	9200	5		16300	18500
30		IRWIN 30	SLP	SA/CR	FBG	KL	IB	20D	YAN	10	2	9200	5		16400	18600
30		IRWIN 30 SHOAL	SLP	SA/CR	FBG	KL	IB	30	UNIV	10	2	9200	3	11	16600	18900
30		IRWIN 30 SHOAL	SLP	SA/CR	FBG	KL	IB	20D	YAN	10	2	9200	3	11	16700	19000

 CONTINUED ON NEXT PAGE

LOA FT	LOA IN	NAME AND/ OR MODEL	TOP/ RIG	BOAT TYPE	-HULL- MTL	-HULL- TP	ENGINE TP	ENGINE # HP	ENGINE MFG	BEAM FT	BEAM IN	WGT LBS	DRAFT FT	DRAFT IN	RETAIL LOW	RETAIL HIGH
		1977 BOATS														
32	6	IRWIN 32 1/2	SLP	SA/CR	FBG	KL	IB	30	UNIV	10		13000	3	11	23800	26500
32	6	IRWIN 32 1/2	KTH	SA/CR	FBG	KL	IB	30	UNIV	10		13000	3	11	23800	26500
32	6	IRWIN 32 1/2 SHOAL	SLP	SA/CR	FBG	KL	IB	40D	PERK	10		13000	3	11	23900	26500
32	6	IRWIN 32 1/2 SHOAL	KTH	SA/CR	FBG	KL	IB	40D	PERK	10		13000	3	11	23900	26500
33		IRWIN 33 MK II	SLP	SA/CR	FBG	KC	IB	30	UNIV	11	2	10150	4		19000	21100
33		IRWIN 33 MK II	SLP	SA/CR	FBG	KL	IB	30		11	2	10150	3	11	19000	21100
37		IRWIN 37 MK III	SLP	SA/CR	FBG	KC	IB	40D	PERK	11	6	22000	4		40400	44900
37		IRWIN 37 MK III	SLP	SA/CR	FBG	KL	IB	40D	PERK	11	6	22000	5	6	40700	45200
37		IRWIN 37 MK III	KTH	SA/CR	FBG	KC	IB	40D	PERK	11	6	22000	4		40400	44900
37		IRWIN 37 MK III	KTH	SA/CR	FBG	KL	IB	40D	PERK	11	6	22000	5	6	40600	45100
37		IRWIN 37 MK III SHOA	SLP	SA/CR	FBG	KL	IB	40D	PERK	11	6	22000	4		39700	44100
37		IRWIN 37 MK III SHOA	KTH	SA/CR	FBG	KL	IB	40D	PERK	11	6	22000	4		39700	44200
40	2	IRWIN 38	SLP	SA/CR	FBG	KC	IB	22D	YAN	10	6	15800	3	9	32100	35700
42	6	IRWIN 42	SLP	SA/CR	FBG	KC	IB	60D	STAR	13	4	29000	4	6	57400	63000
42	6	IRWIN 42	SLP	SA/CR	FBG	KL	IB	60D	STAR	13	4	29000	5	9	57600	63300
42	6	IRWIN 42	KTH	SA/CR	FBG	KC	IB	60D	STAR	13	4	29000	4	6	57600	63200
42	6	IRWIN 42	KTH	SA/CR	FBG	KL	IB	60D	STAR	13	4	29000	5	9	57800	63500
42	6	IRWIN 42 SHOAL	SLP	SA/CR	FBG	KL	IB	60D	STAR	13	4	29000	4	6	56600	62200
42	6	IRWIN 42 SHOAL	KTH	SA/CR	FBG	KL	IB	60D	STAR	13	4	29000	4	6	56800	62400
55	8	IRWIN 52	KTH	SA/CR	FBG	KC	IB	85D	PERK	15	5	44500	5	3	98300	108000
55	8	IRWIN 52	KTH	SA/CR	FBG	KL	IB	85D	PERK	15	5	46500	6	10	99900	109500
55	8	IRWIN 52 SHOAL	KTH	SA/CR	FBG	KL	IB	85D	PERK	15	5	46500	5	3	98900	108500
		1976 BOATS														
25	4	IRWIN 10/4	SLP	SA/CR	FBG	CB	IB	8D-	15D	10	4	7000	2	9	10400	11900
25	5	IRWIN 25	SLP	SA/RC	FBG	KC	OB			8		7000	5	8	10000	11400
28	5	IRWIN 28 MK IV	SLP	SA/CR	FBG	KC	IB	8D-	15D	9		7800	3		13100	14900
28	5	IRWIN 28 MK IV	SLP	SA/CR	FBG	KL	IB	8D-	15D	9		7800	4	6	13000	14900
30		IRWIN 30	SLP	SA/CR	FBG	KL	IB	30	UNIV	10	2	10000	5		17200	19500
30		IRWIN 30	SLP	SA/CR	FBG	KL	IB	20D	YAN	10	2	10000	5		17300	19600
30		IRWIN 30 SHOAL	SLP	SA/CR	FBG	KC	IB	30	UNIV	10	2	10000	4	3	17600	20000
30		IRWIN 30 SHOAL	SLP	SA/CR	FBG	KC	IB	20D	YAN	10	2	10000	4	3	18100	20100
30		IRWIN 30 SHOAL	SLP	SA/CR	FBG	KL	IB	30	UNIV	10	2	10000	3	11	17400	19700
30		IRWIN 30 SHOAL	SLP	SA/CR	FBG	KL	IB	20D	YAN	10	2	10000	3	11	17500	19800
30		IRWIN CUSTOM 1/2 TON	SLP	SA/RC	FBG	DB	IB	10	UNIV	10	3	7300	3	6	12500	14300
32	6	IRWIN 32 1/2	SLP	SA/CR	FBG	KL	IB	30	UNIV	10		13000	3	11	23100	25600
32	6	IRWIN 32 1/2	SLP	SA/CR	FBG	KL	IB	40D	PERK	10		13000	3	11	23100	25700
32	6	IRWIN 32 1/2	KTH	SA/CR	FBG	KL	IB	30	UNIV	10		13000	3	11	23100	25700
32	6	IRWIN 32 1/2	KTH	SA/CR	FBG	KL	IB	40D	PERK	10		13000	3	11	23100	25700
33		IRWIN 33 MK II	SLP	SA/CR	FBG	KL	IB	30	UNIV	11	2	10950	5	6	19400	21600
33		IRWIN 33 MK II SHOAL	SLP	SA/CR	FBG	KC	IB	30	UNIV	11	2	10950	4		19800	21900
33		IRWIN 33 MK II SHOAL	SLP	SA/CR	FBG	KL	IB	30	UNIV	11	2	10950	3	11	19600	21800
37		IRWIN 37 MK II	SLP	SA/CR	FBG	KL	IB	40D	PERK	11	6	20000	5	6	35900	39800
37		IRWIN 37 MK II	KTH	SA/CR	FBG	KL	IB	40D	PERK	11	6	20000	5	6	35900	39900
37		IRWIN 37 MK II SHOAL	SLP	SA/CR	FBG	KC	IB	40D	PERK	11	6	20000	5	6	36300	40300
37		IRWIN 37 MK II SHOAL	SLP	SA/CR	FBG	KL	IB	40D	PERK	11	6	20000	5	6	36100	40100
37		IRWIN 37 MK II SHOAL	KTH	SA/CR	FBG	KC	IB	40D	PERK	11	6	20000	5	6	36300	40300
37		IRWIN 37 MK II SHOAL	KTH	SA/CR	FBG	KL	IB	40D	PERK	11	6	20000	5	6	36100	40100
42	6	IRWIN 42	SLP	SA/CR	FBG	KL	IB	60D	PERK	13	4	29000	5	9	54800	60200
42	6	IRWIN 42	KTH	SA/CR	FBG	KL	IB	60D	PERK	13	4	29000	5	9	55000	60400
42	6	IRWIN 42 SHOAL	SLP	SA/CR	FBG	KC	IB	60D	PERK	13	4	29000	4	6	55600	61100
42	6	IRWIN 42 SHOAL	SLP	SA/CR	FBG	KL	IB	60D	PERK	13	4	29000	4	6	55200	60700
42	6	IRWIN 42 SHOAL	KTH	SA/CR	FBG	KC	IB	60D	PERK	13	4	29000	4	6	55700	61200
42	6	IRWIN 42 SHOAL	KTH	SA/CR	FBG	KL	IB	60D	PERK	13	4	29000	4	6	55300	60800
44		WINDWARD 44	SLP	SA/CR	FBG	KL	IB	D		13	4	31500	6	6	60900	67000
44		WINDWARD 44 SHOAL	SLP	SA/CR	FBG	KL	IB	D		13	4	30000	4	4	59400	65300
55	8	IRWIN 52	KTH	SA/CR	FBG	KC	IB	85D	PERK	15	5	44500	5	3	95100	104500
55	8	IRWIN 52	KTH	SA/CR	FBG	KL	IB	85D	PERK	15	5	46500	6	10	96100	105500
		1975 BOATS														
23		IRWIN 23	SLP	SA/RC	FBG	CB	OB			8		3200	2	5	3700	4300
25	4	IRWIN 10/4	SLP	SA/CR	FBG	CB	IB	D		10	4	7000	2	9	10200	11600
25	5	IRWIN 25	SLP	SA/RC	FBG	KC	OB			8		5400	2	8	7300	8350
25	5	IRWIN 25	SLP	SA/RC	FBG	KL		D		8		5400	4		6700	7750
28	5	IRWIN 28 MK IV	SLP	SA/CR	FBG	KC	IB	30	UNIV	9		7800	3		12600	14300
28	5	IRWIN 28 MK IV	SLP	SA/CR	FBG	KL	IB	30	UNIV	9		7800	4	6	12600	14300
29	11	IRWIN 30	SLP	SA/CR	FBG	KL	IB	30	UNIV	10	2	10000	5	4	16800	19100
29	11	IRWIN 30 SHOAL	SLP	SA/CR	FBG	KL	IB	30	UNIV	10	2	10000	5	4	16800	19100
32	6	IRWIN 32 1/2	SLP	SA/CR	FBG	KL	IB	30	UNIV	10		13000	3	11	22400	24900
32	6	IRWIN 32 1/2	SLP	SA/CR	FBG	KL	IB	27D	PISC	10		13000	3	11	22400	24900
32	6	IRWIN 32 1/2	KTH	SA/CR	FBG	KL	IB	30	UNIV	10		13000	3	11	22400	24900
32	6	IRWIN 32 1/2	KTH	SA/CR	FBG	KL	IB	27D	PISC	10		13000	3	11	22500	24900
33		IRWIN 33	SLP	SA/CR	FBG	KC	IB	30	UNIV	11	2	10950	4		19200	21300
33		IRWIN 33	SLP	SA/CR	FBG	KC	IB	27D	PISC	11	2	10950	4		19200	21400
33		IRWIN 33	SLP	SA/CR	FBG	KL	IB	30	UNIV	11	2	10950	5	6	19000	21100
33		IRWIN 33	SLP	SA/CR	FBG	KL	IB	27D	PISC	11	2	10950	5	6	19100	21200
33		IRWIN 33 SHOAL	SLP	SA/CR	FBG	KL	IB	30	UNIV	11	2	10950	3	11	19000	21100
33		IRWIN 33 SHOAL	SLP	SA/CR	FBG	KL	IB	27D	PISC	11	2	10950	3	11	19100	21200
37		IRWIN 37 MK III	SLP	SA/CR	FBG	KL	IB	40D	PERK	11	6	18000	4		32100	35700
37		IRWIN 37 MK III	KTH	SA/CR	FBG	KL	IB	40D	PERK	11	6	18000	4		32100	35700
42	6	IRWIN 42	SLP	SA/CR	FBG	KC	IB	60D	PERK	13	4	29000	4	6	53600	58900
42	6	IRWIN 42	SLP	SA/CR	FBG	KL	IB	60D	PERK	13	4	29000	5	9	53600	58900
42	6	IRWIN 42	KTH	SA/CR	FBG	KC	IB	60D	PERK	13	4	29000	4	6	53700	59100
42	6	IRWIN 42	KTH	SA/CR	FBG	KL	IB	60D	PERK	13	4	29000	5	9	53700	59100
		1974 BOATS														
23		IRWIN 23	SLP	SA/RC	FBG	CB	OB			8		3200	2	5	3600	4150
25	5	IRWIN 25	SLP	SA/RC	FBG	KC	OB			8		5400	2	8	7050	8150
25	5	IRWIN 25	SLP	SA/RC	FBG	KL	OB			8		5400	4		7050	8100
28	5	IRWIN MK III	SLP	SA/CR	FBG	KC	IB	30	UNIV	9		7800	3		12300	13900
28	5	IRWIN MK III	SLP	SA/CR	FBG	KL	IB	30	UNIV	9		7800	4	6	12200	13900
29	11	COMPETITION 30	SLP	SA/RC	FBG	KL	IB	30	UNIV	10	2	10000	5	4	16400	18600
32		IRWIN 32	SLP	SA/CR	FBG	KC	IB	D		9	8	11500	3	6	19400	21500
32		IRWIN 32	SLP	SA/CR	FBG	KL	IB	D		9	8	11500	5		19400	21500
32		IRWIN 32	YWL	SA/CR	FBG	KC	IB	D		9	8	11500	3	6	19400	21500
32		IRWIN 32	YWL	SA/CR	FBG	KL	IB	D		9	8	11500	5		19400	21500
32	6	IRWIN 32 1/2	SLP	SA/CR	FBG	KL	IB	30	UNIV	10		13000	3	11	21800	24200
32	6	IRWIN 32 1/2	SLP	SA/CR	FBG	KL	IB	40D	PERK	10		13000	3	11	21800	24300
33		IRWIN 33	SLP	SA/CR	FBG	KL	IB	30	UNIV	11	2	11500	5	6	19400	21600
33		IRWIN 33	SLP	SA/CR	FBG	KL	IB	40D	PERK	11	2	11500	5	6	19500	21600
37		COMPETITION 37	SLP	SA/RC	FBG	KC	IB	40D	PERK	11	8	15500	4	9	27600	30600
37		COMPETITION 37	SLP	SA/RC	FBG	KL	IB	40D	PERK	11	8	15500	6	3	27600	30600
37		IRWIN 37	SLP	SA/CR	FBG	KC	IB	40D	PERK	11	6	18000	4		31300	34700
45		IRWIN 45	SLP	SA/CR	FBG	KC	IB	40D	PERK	11	6	23000	4	2	51000	56100
45		IRWIN 45	KTH	SA/CR	FBG	KC	IB	40D	PERK	11	6	23000	4	2	51100	56100
		1973 BOATS														
23		IRWIN 23	SLP	SA/RC	FBG	CB	OB			8		3200	2	5	3500	4050
25	4	IRWIN 25	SLP	SA/RC	FBG	KC	OB			8		5400	2	8	6850	7850
28	5	IRWIN 28	SLP	SA/CR	FBG	KC	OB			8		7800	3		11800	13400
28	5	IRWIN 28	SLP	SA/CR	FBG	KC	IB	30	UNIV	9		7800	3		12000	13600
28	5	IRWIN 28	SLP	SA/CR	FBG	KC	IB	25D	VLVO	9		7800	3		12100	13800
29	11	COMPETITION 30	SLP	SA/RC	FBG	KL	IB	30	UNIV	10	2	10000	5	4	16000	18100
32		IRWIN 32	SLP	SA/CR	FBG	KC	IB	30	UNIV	9	8	11500	3	6	19100	21200
32		IRWIN 32	SLP	SA/CR	FBG	KC	IB	25D	VLVO	9	8	11500	3	6	19100	21200
32	6	IRWIN 32 1/2	SLP	SA/CR	FBG	KL	IB	30	UNIV	10		13000	3	11	21300	23700
32	6	IRWIN 32 1/2	SLP	SA/CR	FBG	KL	IB	40D	PERK	10		13000	3	11	21300	23700
37		COMPETITION 37	SLP	SA/RC	FBG	KL	IB	30	UNIV	11	8	15400	6	3	26500	29400
37		COMPETITION 37	SLP	SA/RC	FBG	KL	IB	40D	PERK	11	8	15400	6	3	26800	29700
37		IRWIN 37	SLP	SA/CR	FBG	KL	IB	40D	PERK	11	6	18000	4		30500	33900
45		IRWIN 45	SLP	SA/CR	FBG	KC	IB	40D	PERK	11	6	23000	4	2	49800	54700
45		IRWIN 45	KTH	SA/CR	FBG	KC	IB	40D	PERK	11	6	23000	4	2	49800	54700
		1972 BOATS														
23		IRWIN 23	SLP	SA/RC	FBG	CB	OB			8		3200	2	5	3400	3950
25	4	IRWIN 25	SLP	SA/RC	FBG	KC	OB			8		5400	2	8	6700	7700
25	4	IRWIN 25	SLP	SA/RC	FBG	KL	OB			8		5400	4		6650	7650
28	5	IRWIN 28	SLP	SA/CR	FBG	KC	OB			9		7900	3		11700	13300
28	5	IRWIN 28	SLP	SA/CR	FBG	KC	IB	30	UNIV	9		7900	3		11800	13500
28	5	IRWIN 28	SLP	SA/CR	FBG	KC	IB	25D	VLVO	9		7900	3		12000	13600
28	5	IRWIN 28	SLP	SA/CR	FBG	KL	OB			9		7900	4	6	11700	13300
28	5	IRWIN 28	SLP	SA/CR	FBG	KL	IB	30	UNIV	9		7900	4	6	11800	13400
28	5	IRWIN 28	SLP	SA/CR	FBG	KL	IB	25D	VLVO	9		7900	4	6	12000	13600
32		IRWIN 32	SLP	SA/CR	FBG	KC	IB	30	UNIV	9	8	11500	3	6	18700	20800
32		IRWIN 32	SLP	SA/CR	FBG	KC	IB	25D	VLVO	9	8	11500	3	6	18700	20800
32		IRWIN 32	SLP	SA/CR	FBG	KL	IB	30	UNIV	9	8	11500	5		18700	20800
32		IRWIN 32	SLP	SA/CR	FBG	KL	IB	25D	VLVO	9	8	11500	5		18700	20800
32		IRWIN 32	YWL	SA/CR	FBG	KC	IB	30	UNIV	9	8	11500	3	6	18700	20800
32		IRWIN 32	YWL	SA/CR	FBG	KC	IB	25D	VLVO	9	8	11500	3	6	18700	20800
32		IRWIN 32	YWL	SA/CR	FBG	KL	IB	30	UNIV	9	8	11500	5		18700	20800
32		IRWIN 32	YWL	SA/CR	FBG	KL	IB	25D	VLVO	9	8	11500	5		18700	20800
32	6	IRWIN 32 1/2	SLP	SA/CR	FBG	KL	IB	30	UNIV	10		13000	3	11	20800	23100
32	6	IRWIN 32 1/2	SLP	SA/CR	FBG	KL	IB	40D	PERK	10		13000	3	11	20800	23200
37		IRWIN 37	SLP	SA/CR	FBG	KL	IB	40D	PERK	11	6	18000	4		29800	33100
40	2	IRWIN 38	SLP	SA/CR	FBG	KC	IB	30	UNIV	10	6	15400	3	9	27100	30100
40	2	IRWIN 38	SLP	SA/CR	FBG	KC	IB	40D	PERK	10	6	15400	3	9	27400	30400
40	2	IRWIN 38	SLP	SA/CR	FBG	KL	IB	30	UNIV	10	6	15400	5	9	27100	30100
40	2	IRWIN 38	SLP	SA/CR	FBG	KL	IB	40D	PERK	10	6	15400	5	9	27400	30400
45	6	IRWIN 43	SLP	SA/CR	FBG	KC	IB	40D	PERK	11	6	22500	4	2	47800	52600
45	6	IRWIN 43	SLP	SA/CR	FBG	KL	IB	40D	PERK	11	6	22500	6	6	47800	52600
45	6	IRWIN 43	KTH	SA/CR	FBG	KC	IB	40D	PERK	11	6	22500	4	2	47900	52600
45	6	IRWIN 43	KTH	SA/CR	FBG	KL	IB	40D	PERK	11	6	22500	6	6	47900	52600

CONTINUED ON NEXT PAGE

LOA FT IN	NAME AND/OR MODEL	TOP/RIG	BOAT TYPE	MTL	TP	TP	# HP	MFG	BEAM FT IN	WGT LBS	DRAFT FT IN	RETAIL LOW	RETAIL HIGH
1971 BOATS													
21	IRWIN 21	SLP	SA/RC	FBG	KL				7		2 6	1950	2350
23	IRWIN 23	SLP	SA/RC	FBG	CB	OB			8	3200	2 5	3350	3900
25 3	IRWIN 25	SLP	SA/RC	FBG	KL	OB			8	5400		6500	7450
25 4	IRWIN 25	SLP	SA/RC	FBG	KC	OB			8	5400	2 8	6550	7550
28 4	IRWIN 28	SLP	SA/RC	FBG	KL	OB			9	7800	4 6	11300	12800
28 5	IRWIN 28	SLP	SA/CR	FBG	KC	OB			9	7900	3	11500	13000
28 5	IRWIN 28	SLP	SA/RC	FBG	KC	IB	30	UNIV	9	7900	3	11600	13200
32	IRWIN 32	SLP	SA/CR	FBG	KC	IB	30	UNIV	9 8	11500	3 6	18300	20400
32	IRWIN 32	SLP	SA/RC	FBG	KL	IB			9 8	11500	5	18300	20300
35 6	IRWIN 36	KTH	SA/RC	FBG	KL				10 3		4	17300	19700
37	IRWIN 37	SLP	SA/CR	FBG	KL	IB	40D	WEST	11 6	18000	3 11	29400	32600
40 2	IRWIN 38	YWL	SA/CR	FBG	KC	IB	30	UNIV	10 6	22995	3 9	38700	43100
40 2	IRWIN 38	SLP	SA/RC	FBG	KL	IB			10 6	20000	5 9	32600	36200
45 6	IRWIN 43	YWL	SA/RC	FBG	KL	IB	50	UNIV	11 6	22500	4 2	43300	48100
45 6	IRWIN 43	SLP	SA/RC	FBG	KL	IB			11 6		6 6	**	**
1970 BOATS													
23	IRWIN 23	SLP	SA/RC	FBG	CB	OB			8	3200	2 5	3250	3800
25 4	IRWIN 25	SLP	SA/RC	FBG	KC	OB			8	5000	2 8	5950	6800
27 1	IRWIN 27	SLP	SA/RC	FBG	KC	OB			8	6600	2 8	8900	10100
28 5	IRWIN 28	SLP	SA/RC	FBG	KC	IB	30	UNIV	8 11	7800	3	11300	12800
31 1	IRWIN 31	SLP	SA/RC	FBG	KC	IB	30		9 7	9600	3 4	14600	16600
32	IRWIN 32	SLP	SA/CR	FBG	KC	IB	30	UNIV	9 8	11700	3 6	18300	20300
40 2	IRWIN 38	YWL	SA/CR	FBG	KC	IB	30	UNIV	10 6	15400	3 9	26000	28900
45 6	IRWIN 43	SLP	SA/CR	FBG	KC	IB	50	UNIV	11 6	22500	4 2	42500	47300
45 6	IRWIN 43	SLP	SA/CR	FBG	KC	IB	50	UNIV	11 6	22500	4 2	42500	47300
1969 BOATS													
23	IRWIN 23	SLP	SA/RC	FBG	CB	OB			8	3200	2 5	3200	3750
24	IRWIN 24	SLP	SA/RC	FBG	KL	OB			8	3000	3 6	3300	3850
25 3	IRWIN 25	SLP	SA/RC	FBG	KC	OB			8	5000	2 8	5800	6700
27 1	IRWIN 27	SLP	SA/RC	FBG	KC	OB			8 8	6600	2 8	8650	9950
27 1	IRWIN 27	SLP	SAIL	FBG	KC				8 8	6600	2 8	8950	10100
29 3	IRWIN 29	SLP	SA/RC	FBG	KC				9 3	7800	3	9500	10800
31 1	IRWIN 31	SLP	SA/CR	FBG	KC	IB	30	UNIV	9 7	9600	3 4	14400	16400
37 9	IRWIN 38	YWL	SA/CR	FBG	KC	IB	30	UNIV	10 6	15400	3 9	25200	28000
1968 BOATS													
24	IRWIN 24	SLP	SA/RC	FBG	KL	OB			8	3000	3 6	3250	3800
27 1	IRWIN 27	SLP	SA/RC	FBG	KC	OB			8 8	6600	2 8	8550	9800
27 1	IRWIN 27	SLP	SA/RC	FBG	KC	IB	30	UNIV	8 8	6600	2 8	8800	10000
31 1	IRWIN 31	SLP	SA/CR	FBG	KC	IB	30	UNIV	9 7	9600	3 4	14200	16200
37 9	IRWIN 38	SLP	SA/CR	FBG		IB	30	UNIV	10 6	15400	3 9	24900	27600
1967 BOATS													
24	IRWIN 24	SLP	SA/CR	FBG	KL	OB			8	3000	3 6	3200	3750
27 1	IRWIN 27	SLP	SA/RC	FBG	CB	OB			8 8	6600		8400	9650
27 1	IRWIN 27	SLP	SA/RC	FBG	KL	OB			8 8	6600	2 8	8400	9650
31 1	IRWIN 31	SLP	SA/CR	FBG	CB	IB	30		9 8	9600		14000	15900
31 1	IRWIN 31	SLP	SA/RC	FBG	KL	IB	30		9 8	9600	3 3	14000	15900
1966 BOATS													
24	IRWIN 24	SLP	SA/CR	FBG	KL				8	3000	3 6	3200	3700
26 11	IRWIN 27	SLP	SA/CR	FBG	KC				8	6600	2 10	7200	8300
31 1	IRWIN 31	SLP	SA/CR	FBG	KL	IB	30		9 8	9600	2 3	13900	15800
32 1	WHISPER	SLP	SA/CR	FBG	TM	IB	30		18 9		1 8	15500	17600
37	IRWIN 37	SLP	SA/CR	FBG	KC	IB	30		10 10	18000	3 11	27000	30000

ISLAND CREEK BOAT SERVICE
COAST GUARD MFG ID- GSA

Call 1-800-327-6929 for BUC Personalized Evaluation Service
Or, for 1982 to 1988 boats, sign onto www.BUCValuPro.com

ISLAND FIBERGLASS
COAST GUARD MFG ID- ZIF

Call 1-800-327-6929 for BUC Personalized Evaluation Service
Or, for 1982 to 1983 boats, sign onto www.BUCValuPro.com

ISLAND HOPPER
DE LEON SPRINGS FL 3213 COAST GUARD MFG ID- AXA See inside cover to adjust price for area
FORMERLY AQUA MARINE

For more recent years, see the BUC Used Boat Price Guide, Volume 1 or Volume 2

LOA FT IN	NAME AND/OR MODEL	TOP/RIG	BOAT TYPE	MTL	TP	TP	# HP	MFG	BEAM FT IN	WGT LBS	DRAFT FT IN	RETAIL LOW	RETAIL HIGH
1979 BOATS													
30	ISLAND-HOPPER 30	TT	CTRCN	FBG	SV	IB	80D	VLVO	12 4	6000		21800	24300
30	ISLAND-HOPPER 30	ST	CUD	FBG	SV	IB	80D	VLVO	12 4	6000	2 6	20700	23000
30	ISLAND-HOPPER 30	OP	FSH	FBG	SV	IB	80D	VLVO	12 4	6000	2	20700	23000

ISLAND MAID
Call 1-800-327-6929 for BUC Personalized Evaluation Service
Or, for 1969 boats, sign onto www.BUCValuPro.com

ISLAND PACKET YACHTS
LARGO FL 34641 COAST GUARD MFG ID- TDL See inside cover to adjust price for area
FORMERLY TRADITIONAL

For more recent years, see the BUC Used Boat Price Guide, Volume 1 or Volume 2

LOA FT IN	NAME AND/OR MODEL	TOP/RIG	BOAT TYPE	MTL	TP	TP	# HP	MFG	BEAM FT IN	WGT LBS	DRAFT FT IN	RETAIL LOW	RETAIL HIGH
1983 BOATS													
30	ISLAND PACKET 26MKII	CUT	SA/CR	FBG	KC	IB	15D	YAN	10 6	8000	3 8	30100	33400
30	ISLAND PACKET 26MKII	CUT	SA/CR	FBG	KL	IB	15D	YAN	10 6	8000	3 8	30100	33400
1982 BOATS													
21	LIGHTFOOT CAT/KTH	KTH	SAIL	FBG	CB	OB			6	700	1	3600	4200
30	ISLAND PACKET 26MKII	CUT	SA/CR	FBG	KC	IB	15D	YAN	10 6	8000	3 8	28800	32000
30	ISLAND PACKET 26MKII	CUT	SA/CR	FBG	KL	IB	15D	YAN	10 6	8000	3 8	27200	30200
1981 BOATS													
21	LIGHTFOOT CAT/KTH	KTH	SAIL	FBG	CB	OB			6	1000	1	3800	4400
30	ISLAND PACKET 26	CUT	SA/CR	FBG	KC	IB	15D	YAN	10 6	8000	2 4	26300	29200
1980 BOATS													
21	LIGHTFOOT CAT/KTH	KTH	SAIL	FBG	CB	OB			6	750	1	3250	3800
30	ISLAND PACKET 26	CUT	SA/CR	FBG	KC	IB	12D	YAN	10 6	8000	2 4	24900	27700
1979 BOATS													
21	LIGHTFOOT CAT/KTH	KTH	SAIL	FBG	CB	OB			6	750	1	3100	3600

ISLAND QUEEN INC
COAST GUARD MFG ID- XLE

Call 1-800-327-6929 for BUC Personalized Evaluation Service
Or, for 1969 to 1970 boats, sign onto www.BUCValuPro.com

ISLANDER CRAFT CORP
ST PETERSBURG FL 33714 See inside cover to adjust price for area

LOA FT IN	NAME AND/OR MODEL	TOP/RIG	BOAT TYPE	MTL	TP	TP	# HP	MFG	BEAM FT IN	WGT LBS	DRAFT FT IN	RETAIL LOW	RETAIL HIGH
1967 BOATS													
16 4	ISLANDER 17			FBG	TM	IO	120		5 9			2500	2900
16 6	ISLANDER V-17	UTL		FBG		OB			5 9			1900	2250
17 9	ISLANDER V-18	UTL	UTL	FBG		IO	400		7			7200	8300
18 7	ISLANDER 19			FBG	TM	IO	150		7 2			4150	4800
19 6	ISLANDER 20			FBG		IO	150		7 8			4700	5450
19 6	ISLANDER TRIMARAN 19			FBG	TM	IO			7 2			2450	2850
22 4	ISLANDER V-22	UTL		FBG		IO	400		8			10100	11500
22 4	ISLANDER V-22	HT	UTL	FBG		IO	400		8			10100	11500
23 9	ISLANDER V-24			FBG		IO	300		8			10200	11600
26	ISLANDER V-26			FBG		IO	300		8			14300	16300

ISLANDER YACHTS
IRVINE CA 92714 COAST GUARD MFG ID- XLY See inside cover to adjust price for area

For more recent years, see the BUC Used Boat Price Guide, Volume 1 or Volume 2

LOA FT IN	NAME AND/OR MODEL	TOP/RIG	BOAT TYPE	MTL	TP	TP	# HP	MFG	BEAM FT IN	WGT LBS	DRAFT FT IN	RETAIL LOW	RETAIL HIGH
1983 BOATS													
27 11	BAHAMA 28	SLP	SA/RC	FBG	KL	IB	15D	YAN	9 11	7000	5	18900	21000
29 11	BAHAMA 30	SLP	SA/RC	FBG	KL	SD	15D	VLVO	10	8230	5	23100	25400
29 11	BAHAMA 30 SHOAL	SLP	SA/RC	FBG	KL	SD	15D	VLVO	10	8322	4	22300	24800
35 9	FREEPORT 36	SLP	SA/RC	FBG	KL	IB	42D	PATH	12	17000	5 3	45600	50100
36 1	ISLANDER 36	SLP	SA/RC	FBG	KL	IB	42D	PATH	11 2	13450	6	36900	41000
36 1	ISLANDER 36 SHOAL	SLP	SA/RC	FBG	KL	IB	42D	PATH	11 2	13600	4	37300	41400
39 7	ISLANDER 40	SLP	SA/CR	FBG	KL	IB	42D	PATH	11 10	17000	7 2	52400	57600
39 7	ISLANDER 40 SHOAL	SLP	SA/CR	FBG	KL	IB	42D	PATH	11 10	17000	5 1	52400	57600
41	FREEPORT 41	KTH	SA/CR	FBG	KL	IB	85D	PATH	13 3	22000	5	66700	73300

ISLANDER YACHTS -CONTINUED See inside cover to adjust price for area

LOA FT	LOA IN	NAME AND/ OR MODEL	TOP/ RIG	BOAT TYPE	-HULL- MTL	-HULL- TP	ENGINE TP	ENGINE # HP	ENGINE MFG	BEAM FT	BEAM IN	WGT LBS	DRAFT FT	DRAFT IN	RETAIL LOW	RETAIL HIGH
		1983 BOATS														
47	6	ISLANDER 48	SLP	SA/CR	FBG	KL	IB	82D	PATH	13	10	29125	5	11	103500	113500
47	6	ISLANDER 48	CUT	SA/CR	FBG	KL	IB	82D	PATH	13	10	29125	5	11	103500	113500
		1982 BOATS														
27	11	BAHAMA 28	SLP	SA/RC	FBG	KL	IB	15D	YAN	9	11	7000	5		17500	19900
29	11	BAHAMA 30	SLP	SA/RC	FBG	KL	IB	13D	VLVO	10		8230	5		20900	23200
35	9	FREEPORT 36	SLP	SA/RC	FBG	KL	IB	42D	PATH	12		17000	5	3	42700	47500
35	9	FREEPORT 36 CTR CPT	SLP	SA/CR	FBG	KL	IB	42D	PATH	12		17000	5	3	42700	47500
36	1	ISLANDER 36	SLP	SA/RC	FBG	KL	IB	42D	PATH	11	2	13450	6		35000	38900
39	7	ISLANDER 40	SLP	SA/RC	FBG	KL	IB	42D	PATH	11	10	17000	7	2	49700	54600
39	7	ISLANDER 40-R	SLP	SA/OD	FBG	KL	IB	42D	PATH	11	10	16000	7	2	47800	52500
41		FREEPORT 41	KTH	SA/CR	FBG	KL	IB	85D	PATH	13	3	22000	5		63200	69500
47	6	ISLANDER 48	SLP	SA/RC	FBG	KL	IB	85D	PATH	13	10	29125	5	11	98000	107500
		1981 BOATS														
27		BAHAMA 28	SLP	SA/CR	FBG	KL	IB	15D	YAN	9	11	7000	5		16500	18800
29	11	BAHAMA 30	SLP	SA/CR	FBG	KL	IB	13D	VLVO	10		8230	5		19800	22000
29	11	BAHAMA 30 SHOAL	SLP	SA/CR	FBG	KL	IB	13D	VLVO	10		8322	4		20000	22300
35	9	FREEPORT 36	SLP	SA/CR	FBG	KL	IB	42D	PATH	12		17000	5	3	40500	45000
36	1	ISLANDER 36	SLP	SA/CR	FBG	KL	IB	42D	PATH	11	2	13450	6		33200	36900
36	1	ISLANDER 36 SHOAL	SLP	SA/CR	FBG	KL	IB	42D	PATH	11	2	13600	4	9	33500	37300
39	7	ISLANDER 40	SLP	SA/CR	FBG	KL	IB	42D	PATH	11	10	17000	7	2	47300	52000
39	7	ISLANDER 40 SHOAL	SLP	SA/CR	FBG	KL	IB	42D	PATH	11	10	17000	5	1	47300	52000
41		FREEPORT 41	SLP	SA/CR	FBG	KL	IB	85D	PATH	13	2	22000	5		59900	65800
		1980 BOATS														
29	11	BAHAMA 30	SLP	SA/CR	FBG	KL	IB	13D	VLVO	10		8230	5		19100	21200
32		ISLANDER 32	SLP	SA/CR	FBG	KL	IB	22D-	30D	11	1	10500	5	4	23800	26500
32		ISLANDER 32 SHOAL	SLP	SA/CR	FBG	KL	IB	22D-	30D	11	1	10500	4		23800	26500
35	9	FREEPORT 36	SLP	SA/CR	FBG	KL	IB	50D	PERK	12		17000	5	3	38900	43200
35	9	FREEPORT 36	SLP	SA/CR	FBG	KL	IB	100D	CHRY	12		17000	5	3	39300	43600
36	1	ISLANDER 36	SLP	SA/CR	FBG	KL	IB	22D	WEST	11	2	13450	6		31800	35300
36	1	ISLANDER 36	SLP	SA/CR	FBG	KL	IB	30D	UNIV	11	2	13450	6		31900	35400
36	1	ISLANDER 36 SHOAL	SLP	SA/CR	FBG	KL	IB	22D	WEST	11	2	13600	4	9	32100	35700
36	1	ISLANDER 36 SHOAL	SLP	SA/CR	FBG	KL	IB	30D	UNIV	11	2	13600	4	9	32200	35700
39	7	ISLANDER 40	SLP	SA/CR	FBG	KL	IB	42D	PATH	11	10	17000	7	3	45500	50000
41		FREEPORT 41	SLP	SA/CR	FBG	KL	IB	100D	CHRY	13	2	22000	5	3	57800	63500
		1979 BOATS														
27	11	ISLANDER 28	SLP	SA/CR	FBG	KL	IB	13D-	30D	9	11	7000	5		15400	17800
27	11	ISLANDER 28 SHOAL	SLP	SA/CR	FBG	KL	IB	13D-	30D	9	11	7000	4		15400	17800
29	11	BAHAMA 30	SLP	SA/CR	FBG	KL	IB	13D-	30D	10		8230	5		18700	20900
32		ISLANDER 32	SLP	SA/CR	FBG	KL	IB	22D-	30D	11	1	10500	5	4	23100	25600
32		ISLANDER 32 SHOAL	SLP	SA/CR	FBG	KL	IB	22D-	30D	11	1	10500	4		23100	25600
35	9	FREEPORT 36	SLP	SA/CR	FBG	KL	IB	36D	PERK	12		17000	5	3	37600	41700
36	1	ISLANDER 36	SLP	SA/CR	FBG	KL	IB	22D	WEST	11	2	13450	6		30800	34200
36	1	ISLANDER 36	SLP	SA/CR	FBG	KL	IB	30D	UNIV	11	2	13450	6		30900	34300
36	1	ISLANDER 36 SHOAL	SLP	SA/CR	FBG	KL	IB	22D	WEST	11	2	13600	4	9	31100	34600
36	1	ISLANDER 36 SHOAL	SLP	SA/CR	FBG	KL	IB	30D	UNIV	11	2	13600	4	9	31200	34600
39	7	ISLANDER PI40	SLP	SA/CR	FBG	KL	IB	42D	PATH	11	10	15674	7	3	41200	45700
41		FREEPORT 41	SLP	SA/CR	FBG	KL	IB	100D	CHRY	13	2	22000	5	3	56000	61500
		1978 BOATS														
25	11	BAHAMA 26	SLP	SA/CR	FBG	KL	IB	D		10		5500	4		11500	13100
27	11	ISLANDER 28	SLP	SA/CR	FBG	KL	IB	15D	OMC	9	11	7000	5		15000	17100
27	11	ISLANDER 28 SHOAL	SLP	SA/CR	FBG	KL	IB	15D	OMC	9	11	7000	4		15000	17100
32		ISLANDER 32	SLP	SA/CR	FBG	KL	VD		UNIV	11	1	10500	5	4	22400	24900
32		ISLANDER 32 SHOAL	SLP	SA/CR	FBG	KL	VD		UNIV	11	1	10500	4		22400	24900
35	9	FREEPORT 36	SLP	SA/CR	FBG	KL	VD	50D	PERK	12		17000	5	3	36600	40600
36	1	ISLANDER 36	SLP	SA/CR	FBG	KL	VD		UNIV	11	2	13450	6		29600	32900
36	1	ISLANDER 36 SHOAL	SLP	SA/CR	FBG	KL	VD		UNIV	11	2	13600	4	9	29900	33200
41		FREEPORT 41	KTH	SA/CR	FBG	KL	VD	70D	PERK	13	2	22000	5		53900	59200
		1977 BOATS														
25	11	ISLANDER 26	SLP	SA/CR	FBG	KL	IB	D		10		4760	3	11	9750	11100
27	11	ISLANDER 28	SLP	SA/CR	FBG	KL	IB	30	UNIV	9	11	7000	5		14400	16400
27	11	ISLANDER 28	SLP	SA/CR	FBG	KL	IB	10D	VLVO	9	11	7000	5		14600	16500
27	11	ISLANDER 28 SHOAL	SLP	SA/CR	FBG	KL	IB	30	UNIV	9	11	7000	4		14400	16400
27	11	ISLANDER 28 SHOAL	SLP	SA/CR	FBG	KL	IB	10D	VLVO	9	11	7000	4		14600	16500
32		ISLANDER 32	SLP	SAIL	FBG	KL	IB	30	UNIV	11	1	10500	5	4	21800	24200
32		ISLANDER 32	SLP	SAIL	FBG	KL	IB	D		11	1	10500	5	4	21800	24200
32		ISLANDER 32 SHOAL	SLP	SAIL	FBG	KL	IB	30	UNIV	11	1	10500	4		21800	24200
32		ISLANDER 32 SHOAL	SLP	SAIL	FBG	KL	IB	D		11	1	10500	4		21800	24200
36	1	ISLANDER 36	SLP	SAIL	FBG	KL	IB	30	UNIV	11	2	13450	6		28800	32000
36	1	ISLANDER 36	SLP	SAIL	FBG	KL	IB	D		11	2	13450	6		29100	32400
36	1	ISLANDER 36 SHOAL	SLP	SAIL	FBG	KL	IB	30	UNIV	11	2	13600	4	9	29100	32300
36	1	ISLANDER 36 SHOAL	SLP	SAIL	FBG	KL	IB	D		11	2	13600	4	9	29400	32700
41		FREEPORT 41	KTH	SA/CR	FBG	KL	IB	75D	CHRY	13	2	22000	5		52800	58000
41		FREEPORT 41	KTH	SA/CR	FBG	KL	IB	100D	CHRY	13	2	22000	5		52900	58200
		1976 BOATS														
27	11	ISLANDER 28	SLP	SAIL	FBG	KL	IB	30	UNIV	9	11	7000	5		14100	16000
27	11	ISLANDER 28	SLP	SAIL	FBG	KL	IB	10D	VLVO	9	11	7000	5		14200	16100
27	11	ISLANDER 28 SHOAL	SLP	SAIL	FBG	KL	IB	30	UNIV	9	11	7000	4		14100	16000
27	11	ISLANDER 28 SHOAL	SLP	SAIL	FBG	KL	IB	10D	VLVO	9	11	7000	4		14200	16100
30		ISLANDER 30	SLP	SAIL	FBG	KL	IB	30	UNIV	10		8600	5		17500	19900
30		ISLANDER 30	SLP	SAIL	FBG	KL	IB	10D	VLVO	10		8600	5		17600	20000
36	1	ISLANDER 36	SLP	SAIL	FBG	KL	IB	30	UNIV	11	2	13450	6		28100	31200
36	1	ISLANDER 36	SLP	SAIL	FBG	KL	IB	D		11	2	13450	6		28400	31600
36	1	ISLANDER 36 SHOAL	SLP	SAIL	FBG	KL	IB	30	UNIV	11	2	13600	4	9	28400	31500
36	1	ISLANDER 36 SHOAL	SLP	SAIL	FBG	KL	IB	D		11	2	13600	4	9	28700	31900
41		FREEPORT 41	KTH	MS	FBG	KL	IB	70D	CHRY	13	2	22000	5		51400	56500
41		FREEPORT 41	KTH	MS	FBG	KL	IB	100D	CHRY	13	2	22000	5		51600	56700
		1975 BOATS														
30		ISLANDER 30	SLP	SAIL	FBG	KL	IB	10D-	25D	10		8600	5		17200	19600
36		ISLANDER 36	SLP	SAIL	FBG	KL	IB	25	UNIV	11	2	13000	4	11	26600	29500
36		ISLANDER 36	SLP	SAIL	FBG	KL	IB	15D	PERK	11	2	13000	4	11	26700	29700
41		FREEPORT 41	KTH	MS	FBG	KL	IB	70D	CHRY	13	2	22000	5		50300	55200
41		FREEPORT 41	KTH	MS	FBG	KL	IB	100D	CHRY	13	2	22000	5		50500	55500
		1974 BOATS														
30		ISLANDER 30 MK II	SLP	SAIL	FBG	KL	IB	22D	PALM	10		8600	5		16900	19200
36	1	ISLANDER 36	SLP	SAIL	FBG	KL	IB	22D	PALM	11	2	13000	6	11	26300	29300
39	11	ISLANDER 40	KTH	MS	FBG	KL	IB	100D	CHRY	13	2	22000	4	9	47700	52500
41	2	ISLANDER 41	SLP	SAIL	FBG	KL	IB	47D	PERK	13		21800	6	6	48700	53500
		1973 BOATS														
30		ISLANDER 30 MK II	SLP	SAIL	FBG	KL	IB	22D	PALM	10		8600	5		16600	18900
36	1	ISLANDER 36	SLP	SAIL	FBG	KL	IB	22D	PALM	11	2	13000	6	11	25900	28700
39	11	ISLANDER 40	KTH	MS	FBG	KL	IB	100D	CHRY	13	2	22000	4	9	47100	51800
41	2	ISLANDER 41	SLP	MS	FBG	KL	IB	47D	PERK	13		21800	6	6	47800	52500
		1972 BOATS														
30		ISLANDER 30 MK II	SLP	SAIL	FBG	KL	IB	30	PALM	10		8600	5		16100	18300
36	1	ISLANDER 36	SLP	SAIL	FBG	KL	IB	30	PALM	11	2	13000	6	1	25100	27900
37	11	ISLANDER 38	KTH	MS	FBG	KL	IB	85		13	2	25800	5		47200	51900
39	11	ISLANDER 40	KTH	MS	FBG	KL	IB	85D	PERK	13		21000	4	8	43800	48600
		1971 BOATS														
22	11	ISLANDER 23	SLP	SAIL	FBG	CB	OB			7	8	2000	1	9	3500	4050
24		BAHAMA 24	SLP	SA/RC	FBG	KL	OB			7	10	4200	3	10	6500	7500
25	11	EXCALIBUR 26	SLP	SA/RC	FBG	KL	OB			7	10	3770	4	8	6350	7300
30		ISLANDER 30 MK II	SLP	SAIL	FBG	KL	IB	30	UNIV	10		8600	5		15700	17900
32	4	ISLANDER 32	SLP	SA/RC	FBG	KL	IB			9	6	10500	5	6	19100	21200
35		ISLANDER 35	SLP	SA/RC	FBG	KL	IB			11	2	10500	5	11	19500	21700
36	1	ISLANDER 36	SLP	SAIL	FBG	KL	IB	30	UNIV	11	2	13000	6		24400	27100
36	6	ISLANDER 37	SLP	MS	FBG	KL	IB	50D	PERK	10	10	14900	5	11	28200	31400
36	9	ISLANDER 37	SLP	SAIL	FBG	KL	IB	30	UNIV	10	10	14000	5	8	26600	29600
43	11	ISLANDER 44	SLP	SA/RC	FBG	KL	IB	D		11		22500	5	10	53000	58200
54	8	ISLANDER 55	SLP	SA/RC	FBG	KL	IB	D		14		41000	5	9	123500	136000
		1970 BOATS														
22	11	ISLANDER 23	SLP	SAIL	FBG	SK	OB			7	8	1700	4	3	3100	3650
24		BAHAMA 24	SLP	SAIL	FBG	KL	OB			7	10	4200	3	5	6350	7300
25	11	EXCALIBUR 26	SLP	SAIL	FBG	KL	OB			7	9	3770	4	8	6200	7100
26	8	ISLANDER 27	SLP	SAIL	FBG	KL	OB			8		4100	4		6850	7850
26	8	ISLANDER 27	SLP	SAIL	FBG	KL	IB			8		4100	4		7050	8100
29	1	ISLANDER 29	SLP	SAIL	FBG	KL	IB	30	UNIV	8	11	7800	3	8	13900	15800
29	1	ISLANDER 30	SLP	SAIL	FBG	KL	OB			8	11	7750	4		13600	15500
29	1	ISLANDER 30	SLP	SAIL	FBG	KL	IB	30	UNIV	8	11	7750	4		13800	15600
32	7	ISLANDER 33	SLP	SAIL	FBG	KL	IB	30	UNIV	10	2	10000	4	6	17600	20000
33	9	ISLANDER 34	SLP	SAIL	FBG	KL	IB	30	UNIV	10		10400	4	6	18700	20800
36	6	ISLANDER 37	SLP	MS	FBG	KL	IB	40D	PERK	10	10	14000	5	5	26000	28900
36	6	ISLANDER 37	SLP	SAIL	FBG	KL	IB	30	UNIV	10	10	14000	5	5	25800	28600
36	6	ISLANDER 37	SLP	SAIL	FBG	KL	IB	40D	PERK	10	10	14000	5	5	26100	28900
43	11	ISLANDER 44	SLP	SAIL	FBG	KL	IB	40D	PERK	11		22500	5	10	51400	56500
54	8	ISLANDER 55	SLP	SAIL	FBG	KL	IB	80D	PERK	14		41000	5	9	120000	132000
		1969 BOATS														
20	10	ISLANDER 21	SLP	SAIL	FBG	KL	OB			7		1950	3	4	3000	3500
22	11	ISLANDER 23	SLP	SAIL	FBG	SK	OB			7	8	1700	4	3	3050	3550
24		BAHAMA 24	SLP	SAIL	FBG	KL	OB			7	10	4200	3	5	6200	7150
25	11	EXCALIBUR 26	SLP	SAIL	FBG	KL	OB			7	9	3770	4	8	6050	6950
27		ISLANDER 27	SLP	SAIL	FBG	KL	IB	30	UNIV	8		4100	4		6950	8000
29	1	ISLANDER 29	SLP	SAIL	FBG	KL	IB	30	UNIV	8	11	7800	3	8	13600	15400
29	1	ISLANDER 30	SLP	SAIL	FBG	KL	IB	30	UNIV	8	11	7750	4		13500	15300
32	7	ISLANDER 33	SLP	SAIL	FBG	KL	IB	30	UNIV	10	2	10000	4	6	17200	19500
33	9	ISLANDER 34	SLP	SAIL	FBG	KL	IB	30	UNIV	10		10400	4	6	18300	20400
36	6	ISLANDER 37	SLP	SAIL	FBG	KL	IB	40D	PERK	10	10	14000	5	5	25500	28300
43	11	ISLANDER 44	SLP	SAIL	FBG	KL	IB	40D	PERK	11		22500	5	10	50300	55300
54	8	ISLANDER 55	SLP	SAIL	FBG	KL	IB	80D	PERK	14		41000	5	9	117500	129000
		1968 BOATS														
20	10	ISLANDER 21	SLP	SAIL	FBG	KL	OB			7		1950			2950	3400
22	11	ISLANDER 23	SLP	SAIL	FBG		OB			7	8				4550	5250
24		BAHAMA 24	SLP	SAIL	FBG	KL	OB			7	10	3200	3	5	4800	5500
24		BAHAMA 24	SLP	SAIL	FBG	KL	IB	8		7	10	3500	3	5	5400	6200

 CONTINUED ON NEXT PAGE

ISLANDER YACHTS — CONTINUED

LOA FT IN	NAME AND/ OR MODEL	TOP/ RIG	BOAT TYPE	HULL MTL	HULL TP	ENG TP	ENG #	ENG HP	ENG MFG	BEAM FT IN	WGT LBS	DRAFT FT IN	RETAIL LOW	RETAIL HIGH
1968 BOATS														
25 11	EXCALIBUR 26	SLP	SAIL	FBG	KL	OB				7	4000	4 8	6250	7200
29 11	ISLANDER 29	SLP	SAIL	FBG	KL	IB		30		8 11	8100	3 8	13800	15700
30	ISLANDER 30	SLP	SAIL	FBG	KL	OB				8 11	8200	3 8	13900	15800
30	ISLANDER 30	SLP	SAIL	FBG	KL	IB		30		8 11	8500	3 8	14500	16500
32 6	ISLANDER 32	SLP	SAIL	FBG	KL	IB		30		10	9750	4 6	16400	18600
32 7	ISLANDER 33	SLP	SAIL	FBG	KL	IB		30		10	10000	4 6	16800	19100
33 10	ISLANDER 34	SLP	SAIL	FBG	KL	IB		30		10 2	10800	4 6	18600	20700
33 10	ISLANDER 34	SLP	SAIL	FBG	KL	IB		D		10 2	10800	4 6	18700	20800
36 6	ISLANDER 37	SLP	SAIL	FBG	KL	IB		30		10 10	14000	5 5	24700	27400
36 6	ISLANDER 37	SLP	SAIL	FBG	KL	IB		D		10 10	14000	5 5	25000	27800
43 10	ISLANDER 44	SLP	SAIL	FBG	KL	IB		72		11	19000	5 10	44500	49400
43 10	ISLANDER 44	SLP	SAIL	FBG	KL	IB		50D		11	19000	5 10	45500	50100
1967 BOATS														
20 10	ISLANDER 21	SLP	SAIL	FBG		OB				7	1950		2900	3350
24	BAHAMA 24	SLP	SAIL	FBG		IB				7 10	3200	3 5	4350	5000
24	BAHAMA 24	SLP	SAIL	FBG		IB		30		7 10	3500	3 5	5400	6250
24	ISLANDER 24	SLP	SAIL	FBG		OB				7 10			5500	6300
25 11	EXCALIBUR 26	SLP	SAIL	FBG		OB				7 9	4000	4 8	6150	7050
29 2	ISLANDER 29	SLP	SAIL	FBG		IB				8 11	8100	3 8	13600	15400
30	ISLANDER 30	SLP	SAIL	FBG		OB				8 11	8200	3 8	13600	15500
30	ISLANDER 30	SLP	SAIL	FBG		IB		30		8 11	8500	3 8	14200	16200
32 6	ISLANDER 32	SLP	SAIL	FBG		IB		30		10	9750	4 6	16100	18300
32 7	ISLANDER 33	SLP	SAIL	FBG		IB		30		10	10000	4 6	16500	18800
33 9	ISLANDER 34	SLP	SAIL	FBG		IB		30		10 2	10800	4 6	18300	20300
33 9	ISLANDER 34	SLP	SAIL	FBG		IB		D		10 2	10800	4 6	18400	20400
36 6	ISLANDER 37	SLP	SAIL	FBG		IB				10 10	14000	5 5	24200	26900
36 6	ISLANDER 37	SLP	SAIL	FBG		IB		30D		10 10	14000	5 5	24500	27300
43 10	ISLANDER 44	SLP	SAIL	FBG		IB		72		11	19000	5 10	43600	48500
43 10	ISLANDER 44	SLP	SAIL	FBG		IB		50D		11	19000	5 10	44200	49100
1966 BOATS														
20 10	ISLANDER 21	SLP	SAIL	FBG		OB				7	1950		2850	3300
24	BAHAMA 24	SLP	SAIL	FBG		OB				7 10	3200	3 5	4250	4950
24	ISLANDER 24	SLP	SAIL	FBG		OB				7 10			5400	6200
25 11	EXCALIBUR 26	SLP	SAIL	FBG		OB				7 9	4000	4 8	6050	6950
29 2	ISLANDER 29	SLP	SAIL	FBG		IB		30		8 11	8100	3 8	13300	15200
32 6	ISLANDER 32	SLP	SAIL	FBG		IB		30		10	9750	4 6	15800	18000
32 7	ISLANDER 33	SLP	SAIL	FBG		IB		30		10	10000	4 6	16200	18400
36 6	ISLANDER 37	SLP	SAIL	FBG		IB		30		10 10	14000	5 5	23800	26500
43 10	ISLANDER 44	SLP	SAIL	FBG		IB		72		11	19000	5 10	42900	47700
1965 BOATS														
20 10	ISLANDER 21	SLP	SAIL	FBG		OB				7	1950		2800	3250
24	BAHAMA 24	SLP	SAIL	FBG		OB				7 10	3200	3 5	4200	4900
24	BAHAMA 24	SLP	SAIL	FBG		IB		8		7 10	3500	3 5	5150	5900
24	ISLANDER 24	SLP	SAIL	FBG		OB				7 10			5300	6050
25 11	EXCALIBUR 26	SLP	SAIL	FBG		OB				7 9	4000	4 8	5950	6850
29 1	ISLANDER 29	SLP	SAIL	FBG		IB		30		8 11	8100	3 8	13100	14900
32 6	ISLANDER 32	SLP	SAIL	FBG		IB		30		10	9750	4 6	15600	17700
32 7	ISLANDER 33	SLP	SAIL	FBG		IB		30		10	10000	4 6	16000	18200
43 10	ISLANDER 44	SLP	SAIL	FBG		IB		72		11	19000	5 10	42300	47000
1964 BOATS														
24	BAHAMA 24	SLP	SAIL	FBG		OB				7 10	3200	3 5	3950	4600
24	ISLANDER 24	SLP	SAIL	FBG		OB				7 10			5450	6250
32 6	ISLANDER 32	SLP	SAIL	FBG		IB		30		10	9750	4 6	15400	17500
32 7	ISLANDER 33	SLP	SAIL	FBG		IB		30		10	10000	4 6	15800	17900
1963 BOATS														
24	BAHAMA 24	SLP	SAIL	FBG		OB				7 10	3200	3 5	3900	4550
24	ISLANDER 24	SLP	SAIL	FBG		OB				7 10			5350	6150
32 6	ISLANDER 32	SLP	SAIL	FBG		IB		30		10	9750	4 6	15200	17300

DAN ISREAL

Call 1-800-327-6929 for BUC Personalized Evaluation Service
Or, for 1970 to 1973 boats, sign onto www.BUCValuPro.com

ITALCRAFT

ROME ITALY 00197   See inside cover to adjust price for area

LOA FT IN	NAME AND/ OR MODEL	TOP/ RIG	BOAT TYPE	HULL MTL	HULL TP	ENG TP	ENG HP	ENG MFG	BEAM FT IN	WGT LBS	DRAFT FT IN	RETAIL LOW	RETAIL HIGH
1977 BOATS													
27 9	MINI-DRAGO	OP	OFF	WD	DV	IB	T135D	FIAT	5 8	5000	1 7	20500	22800
36	AERMAR	OP	CR	FBG	DV	IB	T240D	CUM	12 8	16900	2 6	72400	79600
36	AERMAR	OP	CR	FBG	DV	IB	T240D	FIAT	12 8	16500	2 4	71700	78800
36	AERMAR	OP	CR	FBG	DV	IB	T275D	VLVO	12 8	17100	2 6	73700	80900
36	AERMAR FB	FB	CR	FBG	DV	IB	T240D	FIAT	12 8	18300	2 7	76400	84000
42 8	DRAGO	OP	OFF	WD	DV	IB	T370D	CUM	8 8	14980	2 5	130500	143500
44	ESPADA X	FB	MY	FBG	DV	IB	T275D	VLVO	13 2	27500	3 5	123000	135000
50 10	M 74	HT	MY	FBG	DV	IB	T370D	CUM	13 1	28750	2 8	165000	181500
50 10	M 74	HT	MY	FBG	DV	IB	T500D	GM	13 1	29900	2 8	195500	214500
50 10	M 74	OP	SPTCR	FBG	DV	IB	T370D	CUM	13 1	28750	2 8	151000	165500
50 10	M 74	OP	SPTCR	FBG	DV	IB	T500D	GM	13 1	29900	2 8	177500	195000
52 6	BLUE-MARLIN X	FB	TCMY	FBG	DV	IB	T400D	CUM	14 1	42900	3 8	197500	217000
1976 BOATS													
27 9	MINI-DRAGO	OP	OFF	WD	DV	IB	T135D	FIAT	5 8	5000	1	19800	22000
36	AERMAR	OP	CR	FBG	DV	IB	T240D	FIAT	12 8	16900	2 6	69400	76300
36	AERMAR	OP	CR	FBG	DV	IB	T240D	FIAT	12 8	16500	2 4	68700	75500
36	AERMAR	OP	CR	FBG	DV	IB	T275D	VLVO	12 8	17100	2 6	70600	77600
36	AERMAR FB	FB	CR	FBG	DV	IB	T240D	FIAT	12 8	18300	2 7	73300	80500
42 8	DRAGO	OP	OFF	WD	DV	IB	T370D	CUM	8 8	14980	2 5	125000	137500
44	ESPADA X	FB	MY	FBG	DV	IB	T275D	VLVO	13 2	27500	3 5	117500	129500
50 10	M 74	HT	MY	FBG	DV	IB	T370D	CUM	13 1	28750	2 8	158500	174000
50 10	M 74	HT	MY	FBG	DV	IB	T500D	GM	13 1	29900	2 8	187500	206000
50 10	M 74	OP	SPTCR	FBG	DV	IB	T370D	CUM	13 1	28750	2 8	144500	159000
50 10	M 74	OP	SPTCR	FBG	DV	IB	T500D	GM	13 1	29900	2 8	170000	187000
52 6	BLUE-MARLIN X	FB	TCMY	FBG	DV	IB	T400D	CUM	14 1	42900	3 8	189500	208000
1975 BOATS													
27 9	MINI-DRAGO	OP	OFF	WD	DV	IB	T135D	FIAT	5 8	5000	2	19200	21300
42 8	DRAGO	OP	OFF	WD	DV	IB	T350D	CUM	8 8	14980	3	118500	130500
44	ESPADA W	FB	MY	FBG	DV	IB	T275D	VLVO	13 2	27500	3 2	114500	122500
50 10	M 74	HT	MY	FBG	DV	IB	T370D	CUM	13 1	28750	2 8	152000	167000
50 10	M 74	HT	MY	FBG	DV	IB	T500D	CUM	13 1	29900	2 8	180000	198000
50 10	M 74	OP	SPTCR	FBG	DV	IB	T370D	CUM	13 1	28750	2 8	139000	152500
52 6	BLUE-MARLIN X	FB	TCMY	FBG	DV	IB	T400D	CUM	14 1	42900	3 8	181500	199500
1974 BOATS													
27 9	MINI-DRAGO	OP	OFF	FBG	DV	IB	T120D	FIAT	5 8	4580	2	16800	19100
42 8	DRAGO	OP	OFF	FBG	DV	IB	T350D	CUM	8 8	12350	3	99300	109300
44	ESPADA X	FB	MY	FBG	DV	IB	T275D	VLVO	13 2	23000	3 2	99200	109000
52 6	BLUE-MARLIN	FB	TCMY	FBG	DV	IB	T370D	CUM	14 1	32000	3 8	150500	165500

E W IVES CO

Call 1-800-327-6929 for BUC Personalized Evaluation Service
Or, for 1967 to 1968 boats, sign onto www.BUCValuPro.com

J & J NASH IND LTD

COAST GUARD MFG ID- ZJN

Call 1-800-327-6929 for BUC Personalized Evaluation Service
Or, for 1976 to 1986 boats, sign onto www.BUCValuPro.com

J BOATS INC

TPI INC
NEWPORT RI 02840   COAST GUARD MFG ID- PCX   See inside cover to adjust price for area

For more recent years, see the BUC Used Boat Price Guide, Volume 1 or Volume 2

LOA FT IN	NAME AND/ OR MODEL	TOP/ RIG	BOAT TYPE	HULL MTL	HULL TP	ENG TP	ENG HP	ENG MFG	BEAM FT IN	WGT LBS	DRAFT FT IN	RETAIL LOW	RETAIL HIGH
1983 BOATS													
24	J/24	SLP	SA/OD	F/S	KL	OB			8 11	2700	4	7300	8350
29 6	J/29	SLP	SA/OD	F/S	KL	OB			11	6000	5 7	20900	23300
29 6	J/29	SLP	SA/OD	F/S	KL	IB	8		11	6000	5 7	21100	23400
29 11	J/30	SLP	SA/OD	F/S	KL	IB	15D	YAN	11 3	7000	5 3	25200	28000
36	J/36	SLP	SA/OD	F/S	KL	IB	23D	YAN	11 10	10700	6 7	41400	46000
1982 BOATS													
24	J/24	SLP	SA/OD	F/S	KL	OB			8 11	2700	4	6850	7850
29 11	J/30	SLP	SA/OD	F/S	KL	IB	15D	YAN	11 3	7000	5 3	23600	26200
36	J/36	SLP	SA/OD	F/S	KL	IB	23D	YAN	11 10	10700	6 7	38700	43100
1981 BOATS													
24	J/24	SLP	SA/OD	F/S	KL	OB			8 11	2700	4	6400	7350
29 10	J/30	SLP	SA/OD	F/S	KL	IB	D		11	6700	5 3	21100	23400
35 10	J/36	SLP	SA/OD	F/S	KL	IB	D		11 5	9700	6 7	32900	36500
1980 BOATS													
24	J/24	SLP	SA/OD	F/S	KL	OB			8 11	2700	4	6050	7000
29 11	J/30	SLP	SA/OD	F/S	KL	IB	D		11 2	6700	5 3	20100	22300
1979 BOATS													
24	J/24	SLP	SA/OD	F/S	KL	OB			8 11	2700	4	5800	6650
29 11	J/30	SLP	SA/OD	F/S	KL	IB	15D	YAN	11 3	6700	5 3	19200	21300

LOA FT IN	NAME AND/ OR MODEL	TOP/ RIG	BOAT TYPE	-HULL- MTL TP TP	----ENGINE--- # HP MFG	BEAM FT IN	WGT LBS	DRAFT FT IN	RETAIL LOW	RETAIL HIGH
				1978 BOATS						
24	J/24	SLP	SA/OD	F/S KL OB		8 11	2600	4	5400	6200

J BOATS WEST
FORMERLY PERFORMANCE SAILCRAFT

Call 1-800-327-6929 for BUC Personalized Evaluation Service
Or, for 1983 boats, sign onto www.BUCValuPro.com

J C CUSTOM BOATS INC
HOLLIS NH 03049 COAST GUARD MFG ID- JCA See inside cover to adjust price for area
FORMERLY J C BOAT WORKS

For more recent years, see the BUC Used Boat Price Guide, Volume 1 or Volume 2

LOA FT IN	NAME AND/ OR MODEL	TOP/ RIG	BOAT TYPE	-HULL- MTL TP TP	----ENGINE--- # HP MFG	BEAM FT IN	WGT LBS	DRAFT FT IN	RETAIL LOW	RETAIL HIGH
				1979 BOATS						
31 4	CASCO BAY 31	FB	CR	F/S DS IB	150	11 2	11370	3	25400	28200
31 4	CASCO-BAY 31	HT	FSH	F/S SV IB	350	11 2	6000	3 2	20300	22500
31 4	CASCO-BAY 31	HT	FSH	F/S SV IB	280D	11 2	6000	3 2	22600	25100
31 4	CHESAPEAKE 31	HT	FSH	F/S SV IB	350	11 2	6000	3 2	20300	22500
31 4	CHESAPEAKE 31	HT	FSH	F/S SV IB	280D	11 2	6000	3 2	22600	25100
31 4	PROVINCETOWN 31	ST	SF	F/S SV IB	310	11 2	6000	3 2	19800	22000
31 4	PROVINCETOWN 31	ST	SF	F/S SV IB	250D	11 2	6000	3 2	21800	24300
40	OFFSHORE 40	HT	OFF	F/S SV IB	450	13 10	10000	4 6	37800	42000
40	OFFSHORE 40	HT	OFF	F/S SV IB	D	13 10	10000	4 6	**	**

J C L MARINE LTD
MOONRAKER COAST GUARD MFG ID- MRG

DIST MOONRAKER EAST INC

Call 1-800-327-6929 for BUC Personalized Evaluation Service
Or, for 1974 to 1981 boats, sign onto www.BUCValuPro.com

J G MEAKES

Call 1-800-327-6929 for BUC Personalized Evaluation Service
Or, for 1977 to 1979 boats, sign onto www.BUCValuPro.com

J T C MOLDS INC
COAST GUARD MFG ID- RYT

Call 1-800-327-6929 for BUC Personalized Evaluation Service
Or, for 1981 boats, sign onto www.BUCValuPro.com

JACOBS & HUSBY MARINE DESIGN

Call 1-800-327-6929 for BUC Personalized Evaluation Service
Or, for 1980 to 1981 boats, sign onto www.BUCValuPro.com

JAEGER YACHTS
COAST GUARD MFG ID- ZJY

Call 1-800-327-6929 for BUC Personalized Evaluation Service
Or, for 1983 to 1984 boats, sign onto www.BUCValuPro.com

JAGUAR YACHTS LTD
DIV OF RUSSELL MARINE LTD See inside cover to adjust price for area
ESSEX ENGLAND

JAGUAR YACHTS USA
PUNTAGORDA FL 33950

For more recent years, see the BUC Used Boat Price Guide, Volume 1 or Volume 2

LOA FT IN	NAME AND/ OR MODEL	TOP/ RIG	BOAT TYPE	-HULL- MTL TP TP	----ENGINE--- # HP MFG	BEAM FT IN	WGT LBS	DRAFT FT IN	RETAIL LOW	RETAIL HIGH
				1983 BOATS						
21 6	JAGUAR 21 C/R	SLP	SA/CR	FBG KL SD		8	2550	10	6200	7150
28	JAGUAR 28	SLP	SA/CR	FBG KL SD	8D- 17D	9 1	6600	4 9	17100	19600
28	JAGUAR 28	SLP	SA/CR	FBG TK SD	8D- 17D	9 1	6600	3 11	17100	19600
28	JAGUAR 28 SHOAL	SLP	SA/CR	FBG KL SD	8D- 17D	9 1	6600	3 11	17100	19600
				1982 BOATS						
28	JAGUAR 28	SLP	SA/CR	FBG KL IB	8D- 18D	9 1	6600	4 9	16100	18400
28	JAGUAR 28 SHOAL	SLP	SA/CR	FBG KL IB	8D- 18D	9 1	6600	3 11	16100	18400
				1980 BOATS						
21 5	JAGUAR 21	SLP	SA/RC	FBG CB OB		8 3	1984	10	4050	4700
21 10	JAGUAR 22	SLP	SA/CR	FBG KL OB		7 8	2000	3 6	4100	4800
21 10	JAGUAR 22	SLP	SA/CR	FBG KL SD	8D VLVO	7 8	2000	3 6	5300	6100
21 10	JAGUAR 22	SLP	SA/CR	FBG SK OB		7 8	2000	1 8	4100	4800
21 10	JAGUAR 22	SLP	SA/CR	FBG SK SD	8D VLVO	7 8	2000	1 8	5300	6100
23	JAGUAR 23	SLP	SA/CR	FBG KL OB		8 3	2920	4 6	5500	6350
23	JAGUAR 23	SLP	SA/CR	FBG KL SD	8D VLVO	8 3	2920	4 6	6450	7450
23	JAGUAR 23	SLP	SA/CR	FBG TK OB		8 3	2920	3 3	5500	6350
23	JAGUAR 23	SLP	SA/CR	FBG TK SD	8D VLVO	8 3	2920	3 3	6450	7450
25	JAGUAR 25	SLP	SA/CR	FBG KC OB		8	3950	2	7750	8900
25	JAGUAR 25	SLP	SA/CR	FBG KC SD	8D VLVO	8	3950	2	8400	9650
25	JAGUAR 25	SLP	SA/CR	FBG KL OB		8	3950	3 9	7750	8900
25	JAGUAR 25	SLP	SA/CR	FBG KL SD	8D VLVO	8	3950	3 9	8400	9650
25	JAGUAR 25	SLP	SA/CR	FBG TK OB		8	3950	3 6	7750	8900
25	JAGUAR 25	SLP	SA/CR	FBG TK SD	8D VLVO	8	3950	3 6	8400	9650
26 10	JAGUAR 27	SLP	SA/CR	FBG KL OB		8 11	5600	4 8	11600	13200
26 10	JAGUAR 27	SLP	SA/CR	FBG KL IB	8D- 13D	8 11	5600	4 8	12100	13800
26 10	JAGUAR 27	SLP	SA/CR	FBG TK OB		8 11	5600	3 11	11600	13200
26 10	JAGUAR 27	SLP	SA/CR	FBG TK IB	8D- 13D	8 11	5600	3 11	12100	13800
28	JAGUAR 28	SLP	SA/CR	FBG KL OB		9 1	5900	4 9	12500	14200
28	JAGUAR 28	SLP	SA/CR	FBG KL IB	13D VLVO	9 1	5900	4 9	13000	14700
28	JAGUAR 28	SLP	SA/CR	FBG TK OB		9 1	5900	3 6	12500	14200
28	JAGUAR 28	SLP	SA/CR	FBG TK IB	13D VLVO	9 1	5900	3 6	13000	14700
29 11	JAGUAR 30	SLP	SA/CR	FBG KL IB	23D VLVO	10 10	10200	5 3	23000	25600
36 6	SENATOR 37	TRWL	FBG	DS IB	T120D LEHM	13 2	23000	3 9	81100	89200

JAMESTOWNER HOUSEBOATS
DIV MEDARIS MARINE INC COAST GUARD MFG ID- MWC

Call 1-800-327-6929 for BUC Personalized Evaluation Service
Or, for 1981 to 1998 boats, sign onto www.BUCValuPro.com

JAN-DAL BOAT CO

Call 1-800-327-6929 for BUC Personalized Evaluation Service
Or, for 1960 boats, sign onto www.BUCValuPro.com

JARMADA MARINE SERVICES INC
JAMES A RYDER CO COAST GUARD MFG ID- HDA

Call 1-800-327-6929 for BUC Personalized Evaluation Service
Or, for 1983 to 1984 boats, sign onto www.BUCValuPro.com

JAY BEE BOATS
JAY BEE ENTERPRISES INC COAST GUARD MFG ID- JBE

Call 1-800-327-6929 for BUC Personalized Evaluation Service
Or, for 1976 to 1987 boats, sign onto www.BUCValuPro.com

JEANNEAU
DIV OF GROUPE BENETEAU See inside cover to adjust price for area
ANNAPOLIS MD 21403 COAST GUARD MFG ID- IRI

For more recent years, see the BUC Used Boat Price Guide, Volume 1 or Volume 2

LOA FT IN	NAME AND/ OR MODEL	TOP/ RIG	BOAT TYPE	-HULL- MTL TP TP	----ENGINE--- # HP MFG	BEAM FT IN	WGT LBS	DRAFT FT IN	RETAIL LOW	RETAIL HIGH
				1981 BOATS						
27	AQUILA	SLP	SA/RC	FBG KL IB	10		5200	4 4	11600	13200
31	SYMPHONIE	SLP	SA/RC	FBG KL IB	D 11		8200	4 11	19700	21900
34	MELODY	SLP	SA/RC	FBG KL IB	11		13200	5 10	30900	34300
38	GIN-FIZZ	SLP	SA/RC	FBG KL IB	D 12		15400	5 11	37700	41900
38	GIN-FIZZ	KTH	SA/RC	FBG KL IB	D 12		15400	5 11	37700	41900

LOA FT IN	NAME AND/ OR MODEL	TOP/ RIG	BOAT TYPE	-HULL- MTL TP	TP	----ENGINE--- # HP MFG	BEAM FT IN	WGT LBS	DRAFT FT IN	RETAIL LOW	RETAIL HIGH
				1980 BOATS							
27 3	AQUILA	SLP	SA/CR	FBG KL	OB		9 10	5720		12300	13900
27 3	AQUILA	SLP	SA/CR	FBG KL	IB		9 10	5720	5 6	12800	14500
27 3	AQUILA SHOAL	SLP	SA/CR	FBG KL	OB	12D YAN	9 10	5720	4 4	12300	13900
27 3	AQUILA SHOAL	SLP	SA/CR	FBG KL	IB	12D YAN	9 10	5720	4 4	12800	14500
31	SYMPHONIE	SLP	SA/CR	FBG KL	IB	D	11	8200	4 11	19100	21200
33 9	MELODY	SLP	SA/CR	FBG KL	IB	27D YAN	11 1	13200	5 6	29500	32800
37 6	GIN-FIZZ	SLP	SA/CR	FBG KL	IB	37D PERK	12 4	15400	5 11	35300	39200
37 6	GIN-FIZZ	KTH	SA/CR	FBG KL	IB	37D PERK	12 4	15400	5 11	35300	39200
				1979 BOATS							
27 3	AQUILA	SLP	SA/CR	FBG KL	OB		9 10	5200	5 6	10700	12200
31	SYMPHONIE	SLP	SA/CR	FBG KL	IB	D	10 9	8200	4 11	18300	20400
33 9	MELODY	SLP	SA/CR	FBG KL	IB	27D YAN	11 1	13200	5 10	28400	31500
37 6	GIN-FIZZ	SLP	SA/RC	FBG KL	IB	40D PERK	12 4	15400	5 11	33900	37700
				1978 BOATS							
27 3	AQUILA	SLP	SA/CR	FBG KL	OB		9 10	5200	5 6	10300	11700
27 3	AQUILA SCHOAL	SLP	SA/CR	FBG KL	OB		9 10	5200	4 4	10300	11700
29 6	BRIN-DE-FOLIE	SLP	SAIL	FBG KL	IB	D	9 10	5000	4 6	10600	12000
33 8	MELODY	SLP	SA/CR	FBG KL	IB	37D PERK	11 2	13200	5 10	27300	30400
37 6	GIN-FIZZ	SLP	SA/CR	FBG KL	IB	40D PERK	12 4	15400	6 2	32700	36300
				1977 BOATS							
16 1	SEA-BIRD	OP	RNBT	FBG TR	OB		6 7			2100	2500
17 1	MUSTANG	OP	RNBT	FBG SV	IO		6 7			**	**
17 1	PALAOS	OP	CUD	FBG SV	IO		6 7			**	**
17 2	ARCACHONNAIS	SLP	SAIL	FBG KL			7 7			2200	2550
19 8	FLIRT	SLP	SAIL	FBG KC			7 7	1764	2	3000	3500
19 8	FLIRT	SLP	SAIL	FBG KL			7 7	1764	3 3	3000	3500
20 8	CAPTAIN	SLP	SAIL	FBG KL			8 2			3600	4150
20 8	CAPTAIN-CLIPPER	HT	PH	FBG DV	IB		8 2			**	**
20 8	EUROPA-JUNIOR	OP	RNBT	FBG DV	IO		7 5			**	**
21 8	LAMPARO	HT	EXP	FBG DV	IB		7 6		2 3	**	**
21 8	LOVE-LOVE	SLP	SAIL	FBG KL			8	2646	3 3	4150	4800
23	EUROPA 700	OP	CR	FBG DV	IO	T	8 2			**	**
24 7	ISLANDER	HT	PH	FBG DV	IB		9 2		2 3	**	**
24 11	SANGRIA	SLP	SAIL	FBG KL			8 10	3748	4	6300	7250
26 3	EXCELLENCE	HT	EXP	FBG DV	IO	T	9 4			**	**
26 3	EXCELLENCE	FB	SDN	FBG DV	IO	T	9 4			**	**
27 1	POKER	SLP	SAIL	FBG KL			9 4	4850		8500	9800
29 6	BRIN-DE-FOLIE	SLP	SAIL	FBG KL	IB	D	9 10	5600	4 9	11400	13000
29 6	BRIN-DE-FOLIE GTE	SLP	SAIL	FBG KL	IB	D	9 10	5600	5 5	11400	13000
29 6	IMPERATOR	FB	SDN	FBG DV	IB	T	9 9			**	**
33 8	MELODY	SLP	SAIL	FBG KL	IB		11 1	13440	6 3	26900	29900
37 5	AMERICA	FB	SDN	FBG DV	IB	D	12 4			**	**
37 6	GIN-FIZZ	SLP	SAIL	FBG KL	IB	D	12 4	15400	6 2	31700	35300
37 6	GIN-FIZZ	KTH	SAIL	FBG KL	IB	D	12 4	15400	6 2	31700	35300
				1976 BOATS							
37 6	GIN-FIZZ	SLP	SAIL	FBG KL	IB	30D PERK	12 4	15400	6 2	30500	33900

JEFFERSON YACHTS INC
JEFFERSONVILLE IN 47130

See inside cover to adjust price for area

For more recent years, see the BUC Used Boat Price Guide, Volume 1 or Volume 2

LOA FT IN	NAME AND/ OR MODEL	TOP/ RIG	BOAT TYPE	-HULL- MTL TP	TP	----ENGINE--- # HP MFG	BEAM FT IN	WGT LBS	DRAFT FT IN	RETAIL LOW	RETAIL HIGH
				1983 BOATS							
36 6	JEFFERSON 37 CNV	FB	SDN	FBG DV	IB	200D CHRY 13		16500	3 11	54200	59600
	IB 200D PERK 54700	60100,	IB	240D PERK		55500 61000, IB T330 CHRY				53300	58500
	IB T200D CHRY 59100	64900,	IB	T200D PERK		60100 66000, IB T240D PERK				61800	67900

JEFFRIES BOATS
VENICE CA

See inside cover to adjust price for area

LOA FT IN	NAME AND/ OR MODEL	TOP/ RIG	BOAT TYPE	-HULL- MTL TP	TP	----ENGINE--- # HP MFG	BEAM FT IN	WGT LBS	DRAFT FT IN	RETAIL LOW	RETAIL HIGH
				1965 BOATS							
22 8			EXP	WD	IB	95	8		1 10	5400	6200
22 8			UTL	WD	IB	95	8		1 10	4100	4800
24	MARLIN SPECIAL		EXP	WD	IB	185	9			5900	6750
25 6	TRILOGY I	SLP	SAIL	FBG	TM		15		11	9500	10800
27	MARLIN	FB	EXP	WD	IB	185	10 6		2	9300	10600
30			EXP	WD	IB	275	12		2 8	15300	17300
32	SPORTSMAN	FB	EXP	FBG	IB	275	12 6		2 8	19900	22100
				1961 BOATS							
27	MARLIN		SF	PLY	IB	177	11		2 5	7800	8950
30	CUSTOM EXP		EXP	PLY	IB	225	12		2 9	13200	15000
30	MARLIN SPEC		SF	PLY	IB	225	12		2 9	11400	13000
33	MARLIN CUSTOM		SF	WD	IB	354	13		3	16300	18600
36	MARLIN CUST		SF	PLY	IB	225	14		3	27200	30200
36	MARLIN SPEC		SF	PLY	IB	225	14		3	27200	30200
42	DEL-REY SALON		SF	PLY	IB	354	15 9		3 4	40000	44500
46	AVALON SALON		DC	WD	IB	450	16		3 4	51300	56300
65	PRESIDENT		SF	WD	IB	450	16		3 7	60400	66400
							18		4 5	**	**
				1959 BOATS							
27	MARLIN		SF	PLY	IB	T225	11			9050	10300
30	MARLIN CUST		SF	PLY	IB	T225	12			12200	13900
36	MARLIN CUST		SF	PLY	IB	T225	14			27200	30200
42	CUSTOM		SF	PLY	IB	T225	16			26900	29900
48	CUSTOM		SF	PLY	IB	T	18			**	**

JEM-CRAFT
SOUTHWIND BOATS   COAST GUARD MFG ID- JNC

Call 1-800-327-6929 for BUC Personalized Evaluation Service
Or, for 1978 to 1980 boats, sign onto www.BUCValuPro.com

JERSEY YACHTS
LUMBERTON NJ 08048   COAST GUARD MFG ID- NJB See inside cover to adjust price for area
FORMERLY JERSEY BOATS INC

For more recent years, see the BUC Used Boat Price Guide, Volume 1 or Volume 2

LOA FT IN	NAME AND/ OR MODEL	TOP/ RIG	BOAT TYPE	-HULL- MTL TP	TP	----ENGINE--- # HP MFG	BEAM FT IN	WGT LBS	DRAFT FT IN	RETAIL LOW	RETAIL HIGH
				1983 BOATS							
40	DAWN PLAN A	FB	SDN	FBG SV	IB	T235D VLVO 14	6 26000		3 5	90400	99300
40	DAWN PLAN B	FB	SDN	FBG SV	IB	T235D VLVO 14	6 26000		3 5	94500	103000
40	DAWN PLAN C	FB	SDN	FBG SV	IB	T235D VLVO 14	6 26000		3 5	97400	107000
40	EXECUTIVE PLAN A	FB	SDNSF	FBG SV	IB	T350 CRUS 14	6 30000		3 9	95400	105000
	IB T210D CAT 106000	116500,	IB	T300D CAT		109000 120000, IB T310D J&T				109500	120500
40	EXECUTIVE PLAN B	FB	SDNSF	FBG SV	IB	T350 CRUS 14	6 30000		3 9	100500	110000
	IB T210D CAT 110000	121000,	IB	T300D CAT		113000 124500, IB T310D J&T				113500	124500
	IB T410D J&T 118500	130500									
40	EXECUTIVE PLAN C	FB	SDNSF	FBG SV	IB	T350 CRUS 14	6 30000		3 9	103500	114000
	IB T210D CAT 108000	118500,	IB	T300D CAT		116000 127500, IB T310D J&T				111500	122500
	IB T410D J&T 121500	133500									
44	DEVIL PLAN A	FB	SDNSF	FBG SV	IB	T210D CAT 14	6 34800		3 10	107500	118000
	IB T300D CAT 118000	130000,	IB	T310D J&T		118500 130500, IB T410D J&T				133000	146000
44	DEVIL PLAN B	FB	SDNSF	FBG SV	IB	T210D CAT 14	6 34800		3 10	111500	122500
	IB T300D CAT 122000	134500,	IB	T310D J&T		122500 134500, IB T410D J&T				137000	150500
44	DEVIL PLAN C	FB	SDNSF	FBG SV	IB	T210D CAT 14	6 34800		3 10	113500	125000
	IB T300D CAT 124500	137000,	IB	T310D J&T		125000 137500, IB T420D J&T				136000	149500
47 10	JERSEY 48	FB	YTFS	FBG SV	IB	T410D J&T 14	9 40200		3 10	134000	147000
47 10	MAKAIRA 48	FB	YTFS	FBG SV	IB	T300D CAT 14	9 40200		3 10	128500	141500
				1982 BOATS							
40	EXECUTIVE PLAN A	FB	SDNSF	FBG SV	IB	T350 CRUS 14	6 30000		3 9	91000	100000
	IB T150D CAT 99000	109000,	IB	T200D CAT		99400 109000, IB T300D J&T				103500	114000
	IB T410D J&T 109500	120500									
40	EXECUTIVE PLAN B	FB	SDNSF	FBG SV	IB	T350 CRUS 14	6 30000		3 9	95700	105000
	IB T150D CAT 103000	113000,	IB	T200D CAT		103000 113500, IB T300D J&T				108000	118000
	IB T410D J&T 113000	124500									
40	EXECUTIVE PLAN C	FB	SDNSF	FBG SV	IB	T350 CRUS 14	6 30000		3 9	98900	108500
	IB T150D CAT 101000	111000,	IB	T200D CAT		105500 116000, IB T300D J&T				106000	116500
	IB T410D J&T 116000	127000									
44	DEVIL PLAN A	FB	SDNSF	FBG SV	IB	T150D CAT 14	6 34800		3 10	99700	109500
	IB T200D CAT 103500	113500,	IB	T300D J&T		113500 124500, IB T410D J&T				127000	139500
44	DEVIL PLAN B	FB	SDNSF	FBG SV	IB	T150D CAT 14	6 34800		3 10	103000	113500
	IB T200D CAT 107000	117500,	IB	T300D J&T		117500 129000, IB T410D J&T				131000	144000
44	DEVIL PLAN C	FB	SDNSF	FBG SV	IB	T	14 6			**	**

LOA FT	LOA IN	NAME AND/ OR MODEL	TOP/ RIG	BOAT TYPE	-HULL- MTL	-HULL- TP	ENGINE TP	ENGINE # HP	ENGINE MFG	BEAM FT	BEAM IN	WGT LBS	DRAFT FT	DRAFT IN	RETAIL LOW	RETAIL HIGH
		1982 BOATS														
44		DEVIL PLAN C	FB	SDNSF	FBG	SV	IB	T150D	CAT	14	6		3	10	101500	111500
		IB T200D CAT 105000 115500, IB T300D J&T 115000 126500, IB T410D J&T													128500	141500
47	10	JERSEY 48	FB	YTFS	FBG	SV	IB	T300D	CAT	14	9	40200	3	10	120000	132000
47	10	JERSEY 48	FB	YTFS	FBG	SV	IB	T410D	J&T	14	9	40200	3	10	128000	141000
		1981 BOATS														
35	6	EXECUTIVE PLAN A	FB	SDNSF	FBG	SV	IB	T300D	CAT	14	6	26500	3	9	64800	71300
35	6	EXECUTIVE PLAN A	FB	SDNSF	FBG	SV	IB	T410D	J&T	14	6	26500	3	9	68900	75700
35	6	EXECUTIVE PLAN B	FB	SDNSF	FBG	SV	IB	T300D	CAT	14	6	26500	3	9	67200	73900
35	6	EXECUTIVE PLAN B	FB	SDNSF	FBG	SV	IB	T410D	J&T	14	6	26500	3	9	71200	78300
40		EXECUTIVE PLAN A	FB	SDNSF	FBG	SV	IB	T350	CRUS	14	6	30000	3	9	88400	97100
40		EXECUTIVE PLAN A	FB	SDNSF	FBG	SV	IB	T210D	CAT	14	6	30000	3	9	96300	106000
40		EXECUTIVE PLAN A	FB	SDNSF	FBG	SV	IB	T310D	J&T	14	6	30000	3	9	99500	109500
40		EXECUTIVE PLAN B	FB	SDNSF	FBG	SV	IB	T350	CRUS	14	6	30000	3	9	92900	102000
40		EXECUTIVE PLAN B	FB	SDNSF	FBG	SV	IB	T210D	CAT	14	6	30000	3	9	100000	110000
40		EXECUTIVE PLAN B	FB	SDNSF	FBG	SV	IB	T310D	J&T	14	6	30000	3	9	103000	113500
44		DEVIL PLAN A	FB	SDNSF	FBG	SV	IB	T350	CRUS	14	6	34800	3	10	98800	108500
		IB T210D CAT 99300 109000, IB T300D CAT 109000 119500, IB T310D J&T													109500	120000
		IB T410D J&T 121000 133000														
44		DEVIL PLAN B	FB	SDNSF	FBG	SV	IB	T350	CRUS	14	6	34800	3	10	103500	113500
		IB T210D CAT 102500 113000, IB T300D CAT 112500 124000, IB T310D J&T													113000	124000
		IB T410D J&T 124500 137000														
47	10	JERSEY 48	FB	YTFS	FBG	SV	IB	T410D	J&T	14	9	40200	3	10	122000	134000
48		JERSEY 48	FB	YTFS	FBG	SV	IB	T300D	CAT	14	9	40200	3	10	114500	126000
48		JERSEY 48	FB	YTFS	FBG	SV	IB	T310D	J&T	14	9	40200	3	10	114000	125500
		1980 BOATS														
40		EXECUTIVE PLAN A	FB	SDNSF	FBG	SV	IB	T350	CRUS	14	6	30000	3	9	84300	92700
40		EXECUTIVE PLAN A	FB	SDNSF	FBG	SV	IB	T210D	CAT	14	6	30000	3	9	91900	101000
40		EXECUTIVE PLAN A	FB	SDNSF	FBG	SV	IB	T310D	J&T	14	6	30000	3	9	95000	104500
40		EXECUTIVE PLAN B	FB	SDNSF	FBG	SV	IB	T350	CRUS	14	6	30000	3	9	88700	97400
40		EXECUTIVE PLAN B	FB	SDNSF	FBG	SV	IB	T210D	CAT	14	6	30000	3	9	95500	105000
40		EXECUTIVE PLAN B	FB	SDNSF	FBG	SV	IB	T310D	J&T	14	6	30000	3	9	98400	108000
47	10	JERSEY 48	FB	YTFS	FBG	SV	IB	T410D	J&T	14	9	40200	3	10	116500	128000
		1979 BOATS														
40		EXECUTIVE PLAN A	FB	SDNSF	FBG	SV	IB	T350	CRUS	14	6	30000	3	9	80600	88600
40		EXECUTIVE PLAN A	FB	SDNSF	FBG	SV	IB	T310D	J&T	14	6	30000	3	9	90700	99700
40		EXECUTIVE PLAN B	FB	SDNSF	FBG	SV	IB	T350	CRUS	14	6	30000	3	9	84600	93000
40		EXECUTIVE PLAN B	FB	SDNSF	FBG	SV	IB	T310D	J&T	14	6	30000	3	9	94000	103500
47	10	JERSEY 48	FB	YTFS	FBG	SV	IB	T410D	J&T	14	9	40200	3	10	111000	122000
		1978 BOATS														
30	7	JERSEY 31	FB	EXP	FBG	SV	IB	T350		11	7	8000	2	4	19600	21800
40		EXECUTIVE	FB	SDNSF	FBG	SV	IB	T330	CHRY	14	6	30000	3	9	77900	85600
		IB T350 CRUS 79000 86900, IB T210D CAT 85600 94100, IB T310D J&T													88300	97100
40		LEADER	FB	SF	FBG	SV	IB	T350		14	6				69100	75900
47	10	JERSEY 48	FB	YTFS	FBG	SV	IB	T380D	J&T	14	9	40200	3	10	103500	114000
		1977 BOATS														
30	7	JERSEY 31	FB	SF	FBG	SV	IB	T225	CHRY	11	7	11200	2	4	19300	21400
40		EXECUTIVE	FB	SDNSF	FBG	SV	IB	T330	CHRY	14	6	30000	3	9	74600	82000
40		EXECUTIVE	FB	SDNSF	FBG	SV	IB	T220D	CAT	14	6	30000	3	9	82300	90500
40		EXECUTIVE	FB	SDNSF	FBG	SV	IB	T320D	GM	14	6	30000	3	9	84600	93000
40		LEADER	FB	SF	FBG	SV	IB	T330	CHRY	14	6	27600	3	9	69400	76200
40		LEADER	FB	SF	FBG	SV	IB	T220D	CAT	14	6	27600	3	9	77000	84600
40		LEADER	FB	SF	FBG	SV	IB	T320D	GM	14	6	27600	3	9	79300	87200
		1976 BOATS														
30	7	JERSEY 31	FB	EXP	FBG	SV	IB	250	CHRY	11	7	10900	2	4	16200	18400
30	7	JERSEY 31	FB	EXP	FBG	SV	IB	T225	CHRY	11	7	10900	2	4	17600	20000
30	7	JERSEY 31	FB	EXP	FBG	SV	IB	T140D	GM	11	7	10900	2	4	22500	25000
30	7	JERSEY 31	FB	SDN	FBG	SV	IB	250	CHRY	11	7	10900	2	4	17400	19800
30	7	JERSEY 31	FB	SDN	FBG	SV	IB	T225	CHRY	11	7	10900	2	4	19500	21700
30	7	JERSEY 31	FB	SDN	FBG	SV	IB	T140D	GM	11	7	10900	2	4	25200	28000
30	7	JERSEY 31	FB	SF	FBG	SV	IB	250	CHRY	11	7	10200	2	4	16100	18300
30	7	JERSEY 31	FB	SF	FBG	SV	IB	T225	CHRY	11	7	10900	2	4	18400	20400
30	7	JERSEY 31	FB	SF	FBG	SV	IB	T140D	GM	11	7	10900	2	4	23000	25500
40		EXECUTIVE	FB	SDNSF	FBG	SV	IB	T330	CHRY	14	6	30000	3	9	71600	78700
40		EXECUTIVE	FB	SDNSF	FBG	SV	IB	T210D	CAT	14	6	30000	3	9	78600	86400
40		EXECUTIVE	FB	SDNSF	FBG	SV	IB	T310D	GM	14	6	30000	3	9	80700	88700
40		LEADER	FB	SF	FBG	SV	IB	T330	CHRY	14	6	27600	3	9	66500	73100
40		LEADER	FB	SF	FBG	SV	IB	T210D	CAT	14	6	27600	3	9	73500	80800
40		LEADER	FB	SF	FBG	SV	IB	T310D	GM	14	6	27600	3	9	75700	83200
		1975 BOATS														
30	7	JERSEY 31	FB	EXP	FBG	DV	IO	250	CHRY	11	7	9600	2	3	17400	19700
30	7	JERSEY 31	FB	EXP	FBG	DV	IO	T225	CHRY	11	7	9600	2	3	19200	21300
30	7	JERSEY 31	FB	EXP	FBG	DV	IO	T140D	GM	11	7	9600	2	3	21700	24100
30	7	JERSEY 31	FB	SDN	FBG	DV	IO	250	CHRY	11	7	9600	2	3	16800	19100
30	7	JERSEY 31	FB	SDN	FBG	DV	IO	T225	CHRY	11	7	9600	2	3	19100	21200
30	7	JERSEY 31	FB	SDN	FBG	DV	IO	T140D	GM	11	7	9600	2	3	22200	24600
30	7	JERSEY 31	FB	SF	FBG	DV	IO	250	CHRY	11	7	9600	2	3	16700	19000
30	7	JERSEY 31	FB	SF	FBG	DV	IO	T225	CHRY	11	7	9600	2	3	18600	20700
30	7	JERSEY 31	FB	SF	FBG	DV	IO	T140D	GM	11	7	9600	2	3	22900	25500
40		JERSEY 40	FB	SDNSF	FBG	DV	IO	T330	CHRY	14	6	24500	3	9	70100	77000
40		JERSEY 40	FB	SDNSF	FBG	DV	IO	T225D	CAT	14	6	24500	3	9	75500	83000
40		JERSEY 40	FB	SDNSF	FBG	DV	IO	T255D	GM	14	6	24500	3	9	75100	82500
		1974 BOATS														
30	7		FB	EXP	FBG		IB	225	CHRY	11	7	10400	2	4	14500	16500
30	7		FB	EXP	FBG		IB	T225	CHRY	11	7	11400	2	4	16400	18700
30	7		FB	EXP	FBG		IB	T160D	GM	11	7	12300	2	4	23400	26000
30	7		FB	SDN	FBG		IB	225	CHRY	11	7	10700	2	4	15700	17900
30	7		FB	SDN	FBG		IB	T225	CHRY	11	7	11700	2	4	18500	20500
30	7		FB	SDN	FBG		IB	T160D	GM	11	7	12600	2	4	26300	29200
30	7		FB	SF	FBG		IB	225	CHRY	11	7	10000	2	4	14500	16500
30	7		FB	SF	FBG		IB	T225	CHRY	11	7	11000	2	4	16600	18900
30	7		FB	SF	FBG		IB	T160D	GM	11	7	11900	2	4	23300	25900
40			FB	SDNSF	FBG		IB	T210D	CAT	14	6	26800	3	9	66400	72900
40			FB	SDNSF	FBG		IB	T310D	GM	14	6	27400	3	9	69500	76400
40		CHARTER FISHERMAN	FB		FBG		IB	T210D	CAT	14	6	24300	3	9	61600	67700
40		CHARTER FISHERMAN	FB		FBG		IB	T310D	GM	14	6	25500	3	9	66000	72500
		1973 BOATS														
30	7	JERSEY		EXP	FBG		IB	T225	CHRY	11	7	11200	2	7	15700	17800
30	7	JERSEY		EXP	FBG		IB	T140D	GM	11	7	12400	2	8	22500	24900
30	7	JERSEY		SDN	FBG		IB	T225	CHRY	11	7	11400	2	7	17300	19600
30	7	JERSEY		SDN	FBG		IB	T140D	GM	11	7	12600	2	9	25000	27800
30	7	JERSEY		SF	FBG		IB	T225	CHRY	11	7	10800	2	6	15500	17600
30	7	JERSEY		SF	FBG		IB	T140D	GM	11	7	12000	2	8	21900	24300
39	11	JERSEY SPORT		SDN	FBG		IB	T310D	GM	14	6	30000	3	2	71700	78800
		1972 BOATS														
30	7			EXP	FBG		IB	225-330		11	7	10200	2	4	13300	15900
30	7			EXP	FBG		IB	T220-T250		11	7	10200	2	4	14600	16900
30	7			EXP	FBG		IB	T101D-T140D		11	7	10200	2	4	18500	21300
30	7		FB	EXP	FBG		IB	225-330		11	7		2	4	13300	15800
30	7		FB	EXP	FBG		IB	T220-T250		11	7		2	4	14600	16900
30	7		FB	EXP	FBG		IB	T101D-T140D		11	7		2	4	21900	25100
30	7			SDN	FBG		IB	225-330		11	7	10200	2	4	14300	17300
30	7			SDN	FBG		IB	T220-T250		11	7	10200	2	4	16100	18700
30	7			SDN	FBG		IB	T101D-T140D		11	7	10200	2	4	20400	24100
30	7		FB	SDN	FBG		IB	225-330		11	7		2	4	13000	15700
30	7		FB	SDN	FBG		IB	T220-T250		11	7		2	4	14600	17000
30	7		FB	SDN	FBG		IB	T101D-T140D		11	7		2	4	21200	24800
30	7	JERSEY		SF	FBG		IB	225-330		11	7	10200	2	4	13300	15900
30	7	JERSEY		SF	FBG		IB	T220-T250		11	7	10200	2	4	14600	16900
30	7	JERSEY		SF	FBG		IB	T101D-T140D		11	7	10200	2	4	18500	21300
30	7	JERSEY	FB	SF	FBG		IB	225-330		11	7		2	4	11500	13600
30	7	JERSEY	FB	SF	FBG		IB	T220-T250		11	7		2	4	12600	14500
30	7	JERSEY	FB	SF	FBG		IB	T101D-T140D		11	7		2	4	16500	19500
		1971 BOATS														
30	7	JERSEY		EXP	FBG		IB	225	CHRY	11	7		2	4	12800	14500
30	7	JERSEY		EXP	FBG		IB	T225	CHRY	11	7		2	4	14100	16000
30	7	JERSEY		SDN	FBG		IB	225	CHRY	11	7		2	4	12500	14300
30	7	JERSEY		SDN	FBG		IB	T225	CHRY	11	7		2	4	14100	16000
30	7	JERSEY		SF	FBG		IB	225	CHRY	11	7		2	4	10800	12300
30	7	JERSEY		SF	FBG		IB	T225	CHRY	11	7		2	4	11900	13500
30	7	JERSEY 31		EXP	FBG	SV	IB	225		11	7		2	4	12800	14500
30	7	JERSEY 31		EXP	FBG	SV	IB	T212	PALM	11	7	11000	2	4	14300	16300
30	7	JERSEY 31		SDN	FBG	SV	IB	225		11	7		2	4	12600	14300
30	7	JERSEY 31		SDN	FBG	SV	IB	T212	PALM	11	7	11500	2	4	15800	18000
30	7	JERSEY 31		SF	FBG	SV	IB	225		11	7		2	4	10800	12300
30	7	JERSEY 31		SF	FBG	SV	IB	T212	PALM	11	7	10200	2	4	14000	15900
30	7	JERSEY 31		SF	FBG	SV	IB	T101D	GM	11	7	11100	2	4	19200	21300
40		JERSEY 40		DC	FBG	SV	IB	T300		14	2		2	11	55800	61300
40		JERSEY 40		SF	FBG	SV	IB	T300	CHRY	14	2	21000	3		43800	48700
40		JERSEY 40		SF	FBG	SV	IB	T280D	GM	14	2	23000	3		54400	59800
		1970 BOATS														
30	7		FB	SDN	FBG		IB	225-260		11	7	11400	2	4	13700	16000
30	7		FB	SDN	FBG		IB	T225	CHRY	11	7	13200	2	4	16000	18100
30	7		FB	SDN	FBG		IB	T101D	GM	11	7	14300	2	4	24300	27000
30	7	JERSEY 31	HT	EXP	FBG	SV	IB	225-260		11	7	10600	2	4	12500	14500
30	7	JERSEY 31	HT	EXP	FBG	SV	IB	T225	CHRY	11	7	12400	2	4	14500	16500
30	7	JERSEY 31	HT	EXP	FBG	SV	IB	T101D	GM	11	7	13500	2	4	21900	24400

JERSEY YACHTS — continued

LOA FT IN	NAME AND/OR MODEL	TOP/RIG	BOAT TYPE	HULL MTL TP	ENGINE TP #HP MFG	BEAM FT IN	WGT LBS	DRAFT FT IN	RETAIL LOW	RETAIL HIGH
1970 BOATS										
30 7	JERSEY 31	FB	EXP	FBG SV	IB 225-260	11 7	11200	2 4	12800	14800
30 7	JERSEY 31	FB	EXP	FBG SV	IB T225 CHRY	11 7	13000	2 4	14700	16700
30 7	JERSEY 31		EXP	FBG SV	IB T101D GM	11 7	14100	2 4	22800	25300
30 7	JERSEY 31		SDN	FBG SV	IB 225-260	11 7	10800	2 4	13500	15700
30 7	JERSEY 31		SDN	FBG SV	IB T225 CHRY	11 7	12600	2 4	15700	17900
30 7	JERSEY 31		SDN	FBG SV	IB T101D GM	11 7	13700	2 4	23600	26200
30 7	JERSEY 31	FB	SF	FBG SV	IB 225-260	11 7	10100	2 4	12400	14400
30 7	JERSEY 31	FB	SF	FBG SV	IB T225 CHRY	11 7	11200	2 4	14100	16000
30 7	JERSEY 31	FB	SF	FBG SV	IB T101D GM	11 7	12300	2 4	20600	22800
1969 BOATS										
30 7	JERSEY 31	FB	CNV	FBG	IB 210 CHRY	11 7	11000	2 4	13000	14700
30 7	JERSEY 31	FB	CNV	FBG	IB T210 CHRY	11 7	12200	2 4	15000	17000
30 7	JERSEY 31	HT	EXP	FBG	IB 210 CHRY	11 7	10700	2 4	12000	13700
30 7	JERSEY 31	HT	EXP	FBG	IB 160D PERK	11 7	11000	2 4	18100	20200
30 7	JERSEY 31	HT	EXP	FBG	IB T210 CHRY	11 7	11700	2 4	13500	15300
30 7	JERSEY 31	FB	EXP	FBG	IB 210 CHRY	11 7	11000	2 4	12100	13800
30 7	JERSEY 31	FB	EXP	FBG	IB T210 CHRY	11 7	12100	2 4	13700	15600
30 7	JERSEY 31		FSH	FBG	IB 210 CHRY	11 7	10200	2 4	11900	13500
30 7	JERSEY 31		FSH	FBG	IB 160D PERK	11 7	10500	2 4	17100	19400
30 7	JERSEY 31		FSH	FBG	IB T210 CHRY	11 7	11200	2 4	13400	15200
30 7	JERSEY 31		SDN	FBG	IB 210 CHRY	11 7	10800	2 4	12800	14600
30 7	JERSEY 31		SDN	FBG	IB 160D PERK	11 7	11000	2 4	19200	21300
30 7	JERSEY 31		SDN	FBG	IB T210 CHRY	11 7	11800	2 4	14700	16700
1966 BOATS										
28 2	CUSTOM		SF	WD	IB 185-225	10		2	6850	8050
28 2	SPORT CUSTOM	FB	SDN	WD	IB 185-225	10		2	7600	9000
33 4	JERSEY 33		SPTCR	WD	IB T185	12 2		2 6	12700	14400
1965 BOATS										
27 5	4 SLEEPER	FB	SF	WD	IB 195-238				5550	6600
27 5	6 SLEEPER		EXP	WD	IB 195-238				5700	6750
27 5	6 SLEEPER	FB	EXP	WD	IB 195-238				5700	6750
27 5	6 SLEEPER		SDN	WD	IB 195-238				7150	8450
27 5	6 SLEEPER	FB	SDN	WD	IB 195-238				7150	8450

JERSEY YORK MARINE

Call 1-800-327-6929 for BUC Personalized Evaluation Service
Or, for 1966 boats, sign onto www.BUCValuPro.com

JET SET MARINE
COAST GUARD MFG ID- FUF
FORMERLY OFFSHORE UNLIMITED

Call 1-800-327-6929 for BUC Personalized Evaluation Service
Or, for 1983 to 1987 boats, sign onto www.BUCValuPro.com

MORTON JOHNSON & CO
BAY HEAD NJ   See inside cover to adjust price for area

LOA FT IN	NAME AND/OR MODEL	TOP/RIG	BOAT TYPE	HULL MTL TP	ENGINE TP #HP MFG	BEAM FT IN	WGT LBS	DRAFT FT IN	RETAIL LOW	RETAIL HIGH
1969 BOATS										
19	LIGHTNING	SLP	SA/OD	WD CB		6 6	700	5	1800	2150
1953 BOATS										
27		HT	SF	WD	IB T CHRY				**	**
31 6		OP	EXP	MHG RB	IB T CHRY				**	**
31 6		HT	SDN	MHG RB	IB T CHRY				**	**
31 6		FB	SF	MHG RB	IB T CHRY				**	**
33		HT	SF	WD	IB T CHRY				**	**
33		HT	SF	WD	IB T NORD				**	**
36		OP	EXP	MHG RB	IB T CHRY				**	**
36		HT	SDN	MHG RB	IB T CHRY				**	**
36		FB	SF	MHG RB	IB T				**	**
1952 BOATS										
32		OP	EXP	WD	IB T	10		2 11	**	**
33		HT	SF	WD	IB T CHRY				**	**
33		HT	SF	WD	IB T NORD				**	**
1950 BOATS										
22			UTL	WD	IB				**	**
26		SLP	SAIL	WD KL	IB				10000	11400
26			SF	WD	IB				**	**
32		HT	CR	WD	IB T104 CHRY	10		2 2	9500	10800
35			SF	WD	IB				**	**

FOREST E JOHNSON & SON INC
PROWLER
MIAMI FL 33136   COAST GUARD MFG ID- FEJ   See inside cover to adjust price for area

LOA FT IN	NAME AND/OR MODEL	TOP/RIG	BOAT TYPE	HULL MTL TP	ENGINE TP #HP MFG	BEAM FT IN	WGT LBS	DRAFT FT IN	RETAIL LOW	RETAIL HIGH
1977 BOATS										
22 9	PROWLER CONVERTIBLE		CUD	FBG SV	IB 233	8	3700	2 4	12900	14600
22 9	PROWLER CONVERTIBLE		CUD	FBG SV	IB D	8	3700	2 4	**	**
22 9	PROWLER OPEN FISH		OPFSH	FBG SV	IB 233	8	3400	2 4	12500	14300
22 9	PROWLER OPEN FISH		OPFSH	FBG SV	IB D	8	3400	2 4	**	**
31 10	ROWLER		CR	FBG SV	IB D	11		2 8	**	**
31 10	PROWLER		CR	FBG SV	IB 233	11		2 8	38100	42300
31 10	PROWLER PRO FISH		OPFSH	FBG SV	IB 233	11		2 8	45900	50400
1976 BOATS										
22 9	PROWLER CONVERTIBLE	OP	CUD	FBG SV	IB 233-350	8	3700	2 1	12400	14800
22 9	PROWLER CONVERTIBLE	OP	CUD	FBG SV	IB 160D-225D	8	3700	2 1	19500	23100
22 9	PROWLER OPEN FISH	OP	OPFSH	FBG SV	IB 233-350	8	3400	2 1	12100	14400
22 9	PROWLER OPEN FISH	OP	OPFSH	FBG SV	IB 160D-225D	8	3400	2 1	19400	23000
31 10	PROWLER CONVERTIBLE	ST	CUD	FBG SV	IB T233-T350	11	6800	2 4	38800	47200
31 10	PROWLER CONVERTIBLE	ST	CUD	FBG SV	IBT160D-T210D	11	6800	2 4	43200	51900
31 10	PROWLER FLYBRIDGE CR	FB	CR	FBG SV	IB T233-T350	11	8300	2 8	41000	49100
31 10	PROWLER FLYBRIDGE CR	FB	CR	FBG SV	IBT160D-T210D	11	8300	2 8	51600	59900
31 10	PROWLER SPORT FISH	FB	SF	FBG SV	IB T233-T350	11	8000	2 4	40400	47100
31 10	PROWLER SPORT FISH	FB	SF	FBG SV	IBT160D-T210D	11	8000	2 7	51300	60300
31 10	PROWLER TUNA FISH	TT	SF	FBG SV	IB T233-T350	11	6900	2 4	36900	44800
31 10	PROWLER TUNA FISH	TT	SF	FBG SV	IBT160D-T210D	11	6900	2 4	44600	52800
1975 BOATS										
22 9	PROWLER	OP	OPFSH	FBG SV	IB 233-350	8	3400	2 1	11700	14000
22 9	PROWLER	OP	OPFSH	FBG SV	IB 140D REN	8	3400	2 1	17100	19400
22 9	PROWLER	OP	OPFSH	FBG SV	IB 225D CAT	8	3400	2 1	20000	22200
22 9	PROWLER CONVERTIBLE	OP	UTL	FBG SV	IB 233-350	8	3700	2 1	12100	14400
22 9	PROWLER CONVERTIBLE	OP	UTL	FBG SV	IB 140D REN	8	3700	2 1	17500	19800
22 9	PROWLER CONVERTIBLE	OP	UTL	FBG SV	IB 225D CAT	8	3700	2 1	20300	22600
31 10	PROWLER	OP	CNV	FBG SV	IB T233-T350	11	6800	2 4	42500	48200
31 10	PROWLER	OP	CNV	FBG SV	IB T140D REN	11	6800	2 4	50800	55800
31 10	PROWLER	OP	CNV	FBG SV	IB T225D CAT	11	6800	2 4	58300	63900
31 10	PROWLER	HT	SDN	FBG SV	IB T233-T350	11	7600	2 4	44200	50700
31 10	PROWLER	HT	SDN	FBG SV	IBT140D-T225D	11	7600	2 5	52900	65900
31 10	PROWLER	FB	SDNSF	FBG SV	IB T140-T233	11	8300	2 8	38100	45600
31 10	PROWLER	FB	SDNSF	FBG SV	IB T350 MRCR	11	8300	2 8	44600	49600
31 10	PROWLER	FB	SDNSF	FBG SV	IB T225D CAT	11	8300	2 8	53500	58800
31 10	PROWLER	FB	SF	FBG SV	IB T233-T350	11	8000	2 8	48300	45300
31 10	PROWLER PRO FISH	FB OP	UTL	FBG SV	IB T225D CAT	11	6200	2 9	42300	47000

    IB T233-T350 40300 48500, IB T140D REN 44900 49900, IB T225D CAT 52100 57200

LOA FT IN	NAME AND/OR MODEL	TOP/RIG	BOAT TYPE	HULL MTL TP	ENGINE TP #HP MFG	BEAM FT IN	WGT LBS	DRAFT FT IN	RETAIL LOW	RETAIL HIGH
31 10	PROWLER PRO FISH HHT	HT	UTL	FBG SV	IB 225D CAT	11	6200	2 9	42300	47000

    IB T233-T350 40200 48200, IB T140D REN 44900 49900, IB T225D CAT 52100 57200

LOA FT IN	NAME AND/OR MODEL	TOP/RIG	BOAT TYPE	HULL MTL TP	ENGINE TP #HP MFG	BEAM FT IN	WGT LBS	DRAFT FT IN	RETAIL LOW	RETAIL HIGH
31 10	PROWLER TUNA FISH	TT	FSH	FBG SV	IB T140-T233	11	6900	2 4	34300	41500
31 10	PROWLER TUNA FISH	TT	FSH	FBG SV	IB T350 MRCR	11	6900	2 4	40900	45400
31 10	PROWLER TUNA FISH	TT	FSH	FBG SV	IB T225D CAT	11	6900	2 4	47200	51900
1974 BOATS										
23	PROWLER		CNV	FBG	IB 225-330	8	4300	2 2	12600	14800
23	PROWLER		CNV	FBG	IB 160D-225D	8	4300	2 2	19500	22200
23	PROWLER	OP	FSH	FBG	IB 225-330	8	4000	2 2	12500	15000
23	PROWLER	OP	FSH	FBG	IB 160D-225D	8	4000	2 2	20000	23600
31 10	PROWLER	HT		FBG	IB T225	11	8400	2 5	34500	38400
31 10	PROWLER	HT		FBG	IB T160D	11	8400	2 5	47100	51800
31 10	PROWLER		CNV	FBG	IB T225	11	7600	2 4	41400	46100
31 10	PROWLER		CNV	FBG	IBT160D-T225D	11	7600	2 4	52400	63200
31 10	PROWLER	FB	EXP	FBG	IB T225	11	9100	2 8	42400	49000
31 10	PROWLER	FB	EXP	FBG	IB T160D	11	8800	2 8	54400	57600
31 10	PROWLER		SF	FBG	IB T225	11	8800	2 7	42400	46900
31 10	PROWLER		SF	FBG	IB T160D	11	8800	2 7	46700	51300
31 10	PROWLER PRO FISH		FSH	FBG	IB 225D CAT		6400	2 10	36100	39400
31 10	PROWLER PRO FISH		FSH	FBG	IB T225		6400	2 10	35400	39400
31 10	PROWLER PRO FISH		FSH	FBG	IB 160D PERK		6400	2 10	40100	44200
31 10	PROWLER PRO FISH		FSH	FBG	IB 225D CAT		6400	2 10	35200	40200
31 10	PROWLER PRO FISH	HT	FSH	FBG	IB T225		6400	2 10	35500	39400
31 10	PROWLER PRO FISH	HT	FSH	FBG	IBT160D-T225D		6400	2 10	39800	44900
31 10	PROWLER TUNA FISH	TT	FSH	FBG	IB T225	11	7600	2 8	35800	39700
31 10	PROWLER TUNA FISH	TT	FSH	FBG	IB T160D	11	7600	2 8	42000	46700

LOA FT IN	NAME AND/ OR MODEL	TOP/ RIG	BOAT TYPE	-HULL- MTL TP	----ENGINE--- TP # HP	MFG	BEAM FT IN	WGT LBS	DRAFT FT IN	RETAIL LOW	RETAIL HIGH
					1973 BOATS						
31 6	PROWLER	HT		FBG	IO T225	MRCR	11	7500	2 4	41500	46100
31 6	PROWLER	HT		FBG	IOT160D-T225D		11	8500	2 4	52100	63000
31 6	PROWLER		CNV	FBG	IO T225	MRCR	11	7000	2 4	46200	50700
31 6	PROWLER		CNV	FBG	IOT160D-T225D		11	8000	2 4	63700	79600
31 6	PROWLER	FB	EXP	FBG	IO T225	MRCR	11	8000	2 4	45600	50100
31 6	PROWLER	FB	EXP	FBG	IOT160D-T225D		11	9000	2 4	52900	63600
31 6	PROWLER		SF	FBG	IO T225	MRCR	11	8000	2 4	44200	49100
31 6	PROWLER		SF	FBG	IOT160D-T225D		11	9000	2 4	56600	68600
31 6	PROWLER PRO FISH		FSH	FBG	IO 225D	CAT	11	7000	2 4	46800	51400
31 6	PROWLER PRO FISH	HT	FSH	FBG	IO 225D	CAT	11	7500	2 4	48100	52900
31 6	PROWLER TUNA FISH		FSH	FBG	IO T225	MRCR	11	8500	2 4	42600	47300
31 6	PROWLER TUNA FISH		FSH	FBG	IO T160D	PERK	11	9500	2 4	57000	62600
31 6	PROWLER TUNA FISH		FSH	FBG	IO T225D	CAT	11	10000	2 4	69800	76800
					1971 BOATS						
31 6	PROWLER	OP		FBG SV	IB D		11	12000	1 10	**	**
31 6	PROWLER	OP		FBG SV	IB T225	MRCR	11	12000	1 10	38400	42700
31 6	PROWLER	FB	SDN	FBG SV	IB D		11	14000	1 10	**	**
31 6	PROWLER	FB	SDN	FBG SV	IB T225	MRCR	11	14000	1 10	44800	49800
31 6	PROWLER	SF		FBG SV	IB D		11	14000	1 10	**	**
31 6	PROWLER	SF		FBG SV	IB T225	MRCR	11	14000	1 10	40600	45100
					1970 BOATS						
23	PROWLER			FBG SV	IB 100	8				9800	11100
31 6	PROWLER			FBG SV	IB 100	11				27100	30100
					1968 BOATS						
23	PROWLER			FBG	IB T210	CHRY				10500	12000
					1964 BOATS						
19	PROWLER				IB 450	FORD				**	**
31	PROWLER				IB T310					24600	27400
					1956 BOATS						
22	PROWLER		CR	WD	IB 110					6750	7750
22	PROWLER		CR	WD	IB T110					7350	8450
24	PROWLER		CR	WD	IB 130					7700	8850
24	PROWLER		CR	WD	IB T110					8200	9400
26	PROWLER		CR	WD	IB 130					11200	12800
26	PROWLER		CR	WD	IB T110					12200	13900
30	PROWLER		CR	WD	IB T130					17100	19500
32	PROWLER		CR	WD	IB T130					20600	22800
					1954 BOATS						
30	PROWLER	FB	SF	WD	IB T145	12				18800	20900
					1953 BOATS						
22	PROWLER	OP	EXP	WD	IB					**	**
24	PROWLER	OP	UTL	WD	IB T145	UNIV 10				8350	9600
26	PROWLER	OP	EXP	WD	IB					**	**
30	PROWLER	OP	EXP	WD	IB T130					18200	20200
					1952 BOATS						
22	PROWLER	OP	EXP	WD	IB					**	**
24	PROWLER	OP	EXP	WD	IB					**	**
26	PROWLER	OP	EXP	WD	IB					**	**
30	PROWLER	OP	EXP	WD	IB					**	**
					1950 BOATS						
26	PROWLER	HT	EXP	WD	IB T	SCRI				**	**
					1949 BOATS						
22	PROWLER	OP	CR	WD	IB	8 6				**	**
24	PROWLER	OP	CR	WD	IB	9 6				**	**
26	PROWLER	OP	CR	WD	IB T125	10				12100	13700
					1946 BOATS						
22	PROWLER	OP	CUD	WD	IB					**	**

JOHNSON & STAPLES

Call 1-800-327-6929 for BUC Personalized Evaluation Service
Or, for 1931 to 1932 boats, sign onto www.BUCValuPro.com

JOHNSON BASS-HAWK INC
COAST GUARD MFG ID- BHF

Call 1-800-327-6929 for BUC Personalized Evaluation Service
Or, for 1980 to 1981 boats, sign onto www.BUCValuPro.com

HUBERT S JOHNSON BOAT MFG INC
BAY HEAD NJ   COAST GUARD MFG ID- HJN See inside cover to adjust price for area

LOA FT IN	NAME AND/ OR MODEL	TOP/ RIG	BOAT TYPE	-HULL- MTL TP	----ENGINE--- TP # HP	MFG	BEAM FT IN	WGT LBS	DRAFT FT IN	RETAIL LOW	RETAIL HIGH
					1968 BOATS						
24 5	BLACK-JACK	OP		WD	IB 210	CHRY 9		4800	2	7650	8800
28	SPORTSMAN 28		SF	WD	IB 195	CHRY 10		7800	2 6	12400	14100
31 5	FISHERMAN 31		SF	WD	IB T210	CHRY 11 6 11500			2 6	22300	24700
33 5	FISHERMAN 33		SF	WD	IB T290	CHRY 11 8 13500			2 8	27800	30900
					1967 BOATS						
24 5	BLACK-JACK 24		MHG		IB 210	9			2	7350	8450
28	SPORTSMAN 28		MHG		IB 210	10			2 6	12200	13900
31 5	FISHERMAN 31	FSH	MHG		IB	11 6			2 6	**	**
33 5	SPORT FISH 33	SF	MHG		IB	11 8			2 8	**	**
					1966 BOATS						
24 5	BLACK-JACK DELUXE		FSH	WD	IB 225	9			2	7550	8700
28		HT	SF	WD	IB T195	10 4			2 6	12900	14600
31 5		HT	SF	WD	IB T225	11 6			2 6	17300	19600
					1965 BOATS						
24 5	BLACK-JACK		FSH	WD	IB 220					7300	8350
24 5	BLACK-JACK DELUXE			WD	IB 220					6900	7900
28	SPORT SKIFF	HT		WD	IB 238					11700	13200
28	SPORT SKIFF	HT		WD	IB T195					12700	14500
28	SPORT SKIFF	FB		WD	IB 235					11600	13200
28	SPORT SKIFF	FB		WD	IB T195					12700	14500
31 5		HT	SF	WD	IB					15300	17400
31 5		HT	SF	WD	IB T225					16700	19000
					1964 BOATS						
24 5	BLACK-JACK DLX			WD	IB 210					6650	7600
					1963 BOATS						
24	BLACK-JACK SEA SKIFF			WD	IB 210					6300	7200
					1962 BOATS						
24	BLACK-JACK SEA SKIFF			WD	IB 210					6050	6950
31 5		HT	FSH	WD	IB 225					13900	15800
					1961 BOATS						
24	BLACK-JACK SEA SKIFF			WD	IB 125-185	9 1			2	5850	6850
31 5		HT	FSH	WD	IB 225					13600	15400
					1960 BOATS						
24	BLACK-JACK SEA SKIFF			L/P	IB 125	9 1			2	5650	6500
24	BLACK-JACK SEA SKIFF			WD	IB 125					5700	6550
24	BLACK-JACK SEA SKIFF			L/P	IB 185	9 1			2	5800	6650
24	BLACK-JACK SEA SKIFF			WD	IB 185					5850	6700
					1959 BOATS						
24	BLACK-JACK SEA SKIFF			P/M	IB 125	9 1				5650	6500
24	BLACK-JACK SEA SKIFF			WD	IB 185					5700	6550
36	SPORT SKIFF			WD	IB T185					29000	32200
					1958 BOATS						
24	BLACK-JACK SEA SKIFF			WD	IB 125					5550	6350
					1955 BOATS						
24			SF	WD	IB 125					5100	5850
30	SPORT SKIFF			WD	IB T125					11500	13100
					1954 BOATS						
24	SPORTSMAN	OP	EXP	MHG	IB					**	**
26	SPORT SKIFF	OP	EXP	MHG	IB T					**	**
26	SPORT SKIFF	OP	EXP	MHG	IB					**	**
28	SHELTER SKIFF		EXP	MHG	IB					**	**
28	SHELTER SKIFF		EXP	MHG	IB T					**	**
30	SEABALLER			MHG	IB T					**	**
33			SF	MHG	IB T					**	**
33	SEDAN SKIFF		SDN	MHG	IB T					**	**
35			EXP	MHG	IB T					**	**
37			SF	MHG	IB T					**	**
42			SF	MHG	IB T					**	**
					1953 BOATS						
24	SPORTSMAN SEA SKIFF		EXP	WD	IB					**	**
28	SHELTER SKIFF		CR	WD	IB 145					8600	9850
33			SDN	WD	IB T177					17100	19400
					1952 BOATS						
24	SPORTSMAN	OP	CUD	WD	IB 104	CHRY				5050	5750
33			SDN	WD	IB 104	CHRY				15300	17400
					1951 BOATS						
24	SEA-SKIFF			WD	IB 125					5000	5750
30	SPORT SKIFF			WD	IB T125					11000	12500
					1950 BOATS						
24	SEA-SKIFF			WD	IB 125					5000	5700
28	ECONOMY SKIFF	OP	CUD	WD	IB 135	CHRY				8100	9300
28	SKIFF		CR	WD	IB 135	CHRY				8200	9450
35			SF	WD	IB T225					18300	20400
					1949 BOATS						
27	SEA-SKIFF		SDN	WD	IB					**	**
33	SEA-SKIFF	HT	FSH	WD	IB T	PACK				**	**
35			SF	WD	IB T200					17600	20000

HUBERT S JOHNSON BOAT MFG INC -CONTINUED

See inside cover to adjust price for area

LOA FT IN	NAME AND/OR MODEL	TOP/RIG	BOAT TYPE	HULL MTL	HULL TP	ENG TP	ENG HP	ENG MFG	BEAM FT IN	WGT LBS	DRAFT FT IN	RETAIL LOW	RETAIL HIGH
1948 BOATS													
35			CR	WD		IB	T150					18800	20900
1947 BOATS													
35		FB	SF	WD		IB	T125					16700	19000
46		FB	SPTCR	WD		IB	T225					26500	29500
1946 BOATS													
36			SF	WD		IB	T215					22800	25400
1942 BOATS													
35			SF	WD		IB	T135					16200	18400
1941 BOATS													
20			SF	MHG		IB						**	**
20	SPORTSMAN SKIFF		FSH	MHG		IB						**	**
24			SF	MHG		IB						**	**
24	SPORTSMAN SKIFF		FSH	MHG		IB						**	**
29	DAY CRUISER		CR	MHG		IB						**	**
29	DELUXE SPORT SKIFF		FSH	MHG		IB						**	**
32			CR	MHG		IB						**	**
32	DAY CRUISER		CR	MHG		IB						**	**
32	DELUXE SPORT SKIFF		FSH	MHG		IB						**	**
32	DELUXE SPORT SKIFF	OP	SF	MHG		IB						**	**
32	SPORT SKIFF	HT	SPTCR	MHG		IB						**	**
36			CR	MHG		IB						**	**
36		OP	SF	MHG		IB						**	**
39		SLP	SAIL	MHG		IB						65400	71900
39		SLP	SAIL	MHG	KC	IB			10 6		4	65400	71900
43		SLP	SAIL	MHG		IB						90200	99100
1940 BOATS													
32			EXP	WD		IB	T115					13500	15300
1939 BOATS													
20	SPORTSMAN SKIFF	OP	FSH	WD		IB		CHRY				**	**
24	SPORTSMAN SKIFF	OP	FSH	WD		IB		CHRY				**	**
33	6 SKIFF	OP		WD		IB	T135	CHRY				14100	16100
39		HT	DC	WD		IB						**	**
44		HT	DC	WD		IB						**	**
1937 BOATS													
18			UTL	WD		IB						**	**
20	SKIFF	OP		WD		IB	90					2200	2550
24		OP		WD		IB						**	**
25	CONVERTIBLE SKIFF			WD		IB	115					4650	5350
28	SEA SKIFF			WD		IB	T					**	**
32		HT	CR	WD		IB						**	**
38			SF	WD		IB						**	**
1931 BOATS													
33	COMMUTING SEA SKIFF	OP	CR	WD		IB	200	KERM				14000	15900
1928 BOATS													
34 6				WD		IB	155	PALM				**	**
1926 BOATS													
42				WD		IB	160	CHRY				**	**

JOHNSON BOAT WORKS INC

WHITE BEAR LAKE MN 5511 COAST GUARD MFG ID- JBW See inside cover to adjust price for area

For more recent years, see the BUC Used Boat Price Guide, Volume 1 or Volume 2

LOA FT IN	NAME AND/OR MODEL	TOP/RIG	BOAT TYPE	HULL MTL	HULL TP	ENG TP	BEAM FT IN	WGT LBS	DRAFT FT IN	RETAIL LOW	RETAIL HIGH
1983 BOATS											
16	JOHNSON DAYSAILER 16	SLP	SAIL	FBG	CB		6 1			2900	3350
16	JOHNSON J-SCOW	CAT	SA/OD	FBG	BB		5 8	420		2750	3200
16	JOHNSON M-16 SCOW	SLP	SA/OD	FBG	BB		5 8	440		2900	3350
16	JOHNSON MC SCOW	CAT	SA/OD	FBG	BB		5 8			3050	3550
16	JOHNSON X-BOAT	SLP	SA/OD	FBG	CB		6 1	500		3000	3500
19	JOHNSON DAYSAILER 19	SLP	SAIL	FBG	CB		6 1			3500	4100
20	JOHNSON C-SCOW	CAT	SA/OD	FBG	BB		6 10	650		4050	4700
20	JOHNSON M-20 SCOW	SLP	SA/OD	FBG	BB		5 10			5300	6100
28	JOHNSON E-SCOW	SLP	SA/OD	FBG	BB		6 9	965	3 9	7800	8950
1982 BOATS											
16	JOHNSON DAYSAILER 16	SLP	SAIL	FBG	CB		6 1			2750	3200
16	JOHNSON J-SCOW	CAT	SA/OD	FBG	BB		5 8	420		2600	3050
16	JOHNSON M-16 SCOW	SLP	SA/OD	FBG	BB		5 8	440		2750	3200
16	JOHNSON MC SCOW	CAT	SA/OD	FBG	BB		5 8			2900	3350
16	JOHNSON X-BOAT	SLP	SA/OD	FBG	CB		6 1	500		2850	3350
19	JOHNSON DAYSAILER 19	SLP	SAIL	FBG	CB		6 1			3350	3850
20	JOHNSON C-SCOW	CAT	SA/OD	FBG	BB		6 10	650		3850	4500
20	JOHNSON M-20 SCOW	SLP	SA/OD	FBG	BB		5 10			5000	5750
28	JOHNSON E-SCOW	SLP	SA/OD	FBG	BB		6 9	965	3 9	7400	8550
1981 BOATS											
16	JOHNSON J-SCOW	CAT	SA/OD	FBG	BB		5 8	420		2600	3050
16	JOHNSON M-16 SCOW	SLP	SA/OD	FBG	BB		5 8	440		2600	3050
16	JOHNSON X-BOAT	SLP	SA/OD	FBG	CB		6 1	500		2800	3250
20	JOHNSON C-SCOW	CAT	SA/OD	FBG	BB		6 10	650		3700	4300
20	JOHNSON M-20 SCOW	SLP	SA/OD	FBG	BB		5 10			4750	5500
28	JOHNSON E-SCOW	SLP	SA/OD	FBG	BB		6 9	965	3 9	7050	8150
1980 BOATS											
16	J-SCOW	CAT	SA/OD	FBG	BB		5 8	420	6	2500	2900
1979 BOATS											
16	J-SCOW	CAT	SA/OD	FBG	BB		5 8	420		2450	2850
16	M-16 SCOW	SLP	SA/OD	FBG	BB		5 8	440		2450	2850
16	X-SCOW	SLP	SA/RC	FBG	BB		6 1	500		2550	2950
19	CLASS Y BOAT	SLP	SA/RC	FBG	CB		6 7	600		3100	3650
20	C-SCOW	CAT	SA/OD	FBG	BB		6 10	650		3400	3950
28	E-SCOW	SLP	SA/OD	FBG	BB		6 9	965		6500	7450
1978 BOATS											
16	J-SCOW	CAT	SA/RC	FBG	LB		6 1	420	3	2350	2750
16	X-SCOW	SLP	SA/RC	FBG	BB		6 1	500	6 1	2500	2900
19	CLASS Y	SLP	SA/RC	FBG	CB		6 7	600		3000	3500
20	C-SCOW	CAT	SA/OD	FBG	BB		6 10	650	3 3	3350	3850
28	E-SCOW	SLP	SA/OD	FBG	BB		6 9	965	3 9	6300	7250
1976 BOATS											
16	M-16 SCOW	SLP	SA/OD	F/S	BB		5 9	440	6	2150	2500
16	X-SCOW	SLP	SA/OD	FBG	BB		5 3	500	6	2300	2700
20	C-SCOW	CAT	SA/OD	FBG	BB		7	650	6	3100	3600
20	C-SCOW	SLP	SA/OD	FBG	BB		7	650	6	3100	3600
28	E-SCOW	SLP	SA/OD	FBG	BB		6 9	965	6	5850	6700
28	E-SCOW	SLP	SA/OD	P/C	BB		6 9	965	6	5850	6700
38	A-SCOW	SLP	SA/OD	P/C	BB		8 6	1850	8	3350	3900
1975 BOATS											
16	J-BOAT		SAIL	FBG	CB		6 4	400	6	1950	2350
16	K-BOAT		SAIL	FBG	CB		6 1	500	6	2250	2600
16	M-16 SCOW	SLP	SA/OD	F/S	BB		5 9	440	2	2050	2450
16	X-SCOW	SLP	SA/OD	FBG	BB		6 3	500	2	2250	2600
16	X-SCOW	SLP	SA/OD	WD	BB		6 3	500	2	2250	2600
19	Y-BOAT		SAIL	FBG	CB		7	600	6	2750	3200
20	C-SCOW	CAT	SA/OD	F/S	BB		7	650	6	3000	3450
20	C-SCOW	CAT	SA/OD	F/S	BB		7	650	6	3000	3450
28	E-SCOW	SLP	SA/OD	P/C	BB		6 9	965	6	5700	6550
28	E-SCOW	SLP	SA/OD	P/C	BB		6 9	965	6	5700	6550
38	A-SCOW	SLP	SA/OD	P/C	BB		8 6	1850	8	3300	3850
1974 BOATS											
16	M-16 SCOW	SLP	SA/OD	FBG	BB	OB	5 9	440	6	2000	2350
16	X-SCOW	SLP	SA/OD	FBG	BB	OB	5 3	500	6	2150	2500
19	CLASS Y		SAIL	FBG		OB	6 7	600	6	2650	3100
20	C-SCOW	CAT	SA/OD	FBG	BB	OB	6 10	650	6	2900	3350
20	C-SCOW	CAT	SA/OD	FBG	BB	OB	6 10	650	6	2900	3350
20	D-SCOW		SAIL	FBG		OB	6 10			2850	3300
20	D-SCOW		SAIL	WD		OB	6 10			2850	3300
28	E-SCOW	SLP	SA/OD	WD	BB	OB	6 10	965	6	3550	4100
38	A-SCOW	SLP	SA/OD	FBG	BB	OB	8 6	1850	3	5450	6250
1973 BOATS											
16	CLASS N		SAIL	FBG		OB				1900	2300
16	M-16 SCOW	SLP	SA/OD	F/S	BB	OB	5 9	440	6	1950	2300
16	X-SCOW	SLP	SA/OD	FBG	BB	OB	6 3			1900	2300
16	X-SCOW	SLP	SA/OD	WD	BB	OB	6 3			1900	2300
19	CLASS Y		SAIL	FBG		OB	6 7			1900	2300
20	C-SCOW	CAT	SA/OD	FBG	BB	OB	6 8			2450	2850
20	C-SCOW	CAT	SA/OD	FBG	BB	OB	6 8			2850	3350
20	D-SCOW		SAIL	WD		OB	6 8			2850	3350
28	E-SCOW	SLP	SA/OD	WD	BB	OB				3500	4050
38	A-SCOW	SLP	SA/OD	P/C	BB		8 6	1850	8	3100	3600
1972 BOATS											
16	CLASS X SCOW	SLP	SA/OD	FBG	CB		6			2000	2400
18	ARROW	SLP	SA/OD	FBG	CB	OB	6 4	1100	1 2	3050	3550
18	ARROW	SLP	SA/OD	WD	CB	OB	6 4	1100	1 2	3050	3550
20	CLASS C SCOW	CAT	SA/OD	FBG	BB		6 6	650	2	2800	3250
20	CLASS C SCOW	SLP	SA/OD	FBG	BB		6 6			3350	3850
28	CLASS E SCOW	SLP	SA/OD	FBG	BB		6 8	965	3	5200	6000
38	CLASS A SCOW	SLP	SA/OD	P/C	BB		8 6	1850	3	3000	3350
1970 BOATS											
16	X CLASS SCOW	SLP	SA/OD		BB		6	500	3	1900	2300
18	ARROW	SLP	SA/OD		BB		6 4	1100	1 2	2950	3400
18	ARROW	SLP	SA/OD	WD	CB		6 4	1100	1 2	2950	3400
20	C CLASS SCOW	CAT	SA/OD		BB		6 6	650	3	2650	3100
20	D CLASS SCOW	SLP	SA/OD		BB		6 6			3150	3650
28	E CLASS SCOW	SLP	SA/OD		BB		6 6	965	3	4950	5700
38	A CLASS SCOW	SLP	SA/OD		BB		8 6	1850	3	2900	3350

LOA FT IN	NAME AND/ OR MODEL	TOP/ RIG	BOAT TYPE	HULL MTL	HULL TP	ENGINE TP	#	HP	MFG	BEAM FT IN	WGT LBS	DRAFT FT IN	RETAIL LOW	RETAIL HIGH
1968 BOATS														
16	CLASS X SCOW	SLP	SA/OD	FBG	CB					6	500	2	1850	2200
20	CLASS C SCOW	CAT	SA/OD	FBG	BB					6 6	650	3	2550	2950
20	CLASS D SCOW	SLP	SA/OD	FBG	BB					6 6	650	3	2500	2900
28	CLASS E SCOW	SLP	SA/OD	FBG	BB					6 8	965	3	4700	5400
1967 BOATS														
20	C-SCOW	CAT	SA/OD	FBG	BB					6 6	650	6	2500	2900
20	C-SCOW	CAT	SA/OD	WD	BB					6 6	650	6	2500	2900
28	E-SCOW	SLP	SA/OD	FBG	BB					6 9	965	9	4650	5350
28	E-SCOW	SLP	SA/OD	WD	BB					6 9	965	9	4650	5350
38	A-SCOW	SLP	SA/OD	WD	BB					8 6	1850	11	2800	3250
1966 BOATS														
16	X-SCOW	SLP	SA/OD	FBG	BB					6 1	500	5	1800	2150
19	Y CLASS	SLP	SA/OD	FBG	CB					6 7			2850	3300
20	C-SCOW	CAT	3A/OD	WD	BB					6 6	650	6	2500	2900
28	E-SCOW	SLP	SA/OD	WD	BB					6 9	965	9	4580	6250
38	A-SCOW	SLP	SA/OD	WD	BB					8 6	1850	11	2750	3200
1965 BOATS														
19	Y CLASS	SLP	SA/OD	FBG	CB					6 7			2800	3250
1961 BOATS														
20	C-SCOW	CAT	SAIL	WD	BB					6 6		6	2500	2900
20	G-SCOW	SLP	SAIL	WD	BB					6 6		6	2450	2850
28	E-SCOW	SLP	SAIL	WD	BB					6 9		6	7250	8350
38	A-SCOW	SLP	SAIL	WD	BB					8 6		8	19700	21900
1959 BOATS														
20	C-SCOW		SA/OD	P/C	BB					6 6			2800	3250
20	D-SCOW		SA/OD	P/C	BB					6 6			2800	3250
28	E-SCOW		SA/OD	P/C	BB					6 8			11500	13000
38	A-SCOW		SA/OD	P/C	BB					8 6			24900	27700

JOHNSON BOATS
DIV OUTBOARD MARINE CORP
WAUKEGAN IL 60085

See inside cover to adjust price for area

LOA FT IN	NAME AND/ OR MODEL	TOP/ RIG	BOAT TYPE	HULL MTL	HULL TP	ENGINE TP	#	HP	MFG	BEAM FT IN	WGT LBS	DRAFT FT IN	RETAIL LOW	RETAIL HIGH
1970 BOATS														
16 2	FRONT-RUNNER		RNBT	FBG	TR	IO		155	OMC	7 1	1925	1 11	3050	3550
16 2	REVELER		RNBT	FBG	TR	IO		155	OMC	7 1	1950	2 7	3050	3550
16 2	SEASPORT		RNBT	FBG	TR	IO		155	OMC	7 1	1950	2 7	3100	3650
19 1	SURFER		RNBT	FBG	TR	IO		210	OMC	7 4	2450	2 3	4300	5000
19 1	TIDE-RIDER		RNBT	FBG	TR	IO		120	OMC	7 4	2050	2 2	3800	4450
19 1	TRADEWIND		RNBT	FBG	TR	IO		210	OMC	7 4	2450	2 3	4200	4900
1969 BOATS														
16 2	REVELER	OP	RNBT	FBG	TR	IO		155	OMC	7 1	1950	2 7	3200	3700
16 2	SEAPORT	OP	RNBT	FBG	TR	IO		120-155		7 1	1875	2 7	3150	3750
19 1	191	OP	RNBT	FBG	TR	IO		120	CHEV	7 4	1950	2 6	3900	4550
19 1	SURFER	OP	RNBT	FBG	TR	IO		210	CHEV	7 4	2300	2 8	4350	5000
1968 BOATS														
16 3	REVELER 120	OP	RNBT	FBG	TR	IO		120	CHEV	7 1	1850	2 7	3250	3750
16 3	REVELER 155	OP	RNBT	FBG	TR	IO		155		7 1	1950	2 7	3350	3900
16 3	SEASPORT 11 120 W/T	OP	RNBT	FBG	TR	IO		120	CHEV	7 1	1875	2 7	3250	3800
16 3	SEASPORT 155 W/T	OP	RNBT	FBG	TR	IO		155		7 1	1975	2 7	3350	3900
19 1	SURFER	OP	RNBT	FBG	TR	IO		210	CHEV	7 4	2300	2 7	4500	5150
1967 BOATS														
16 2	REVELER		RNBT	FBG	TR	IO		120-155		7 1	1750	10	3250	3900
19 1	SURFER		RNBT	FBG	TR	IO		200		7 4	2300	1	4600	5300
1966 BOATS														
16	REVELER		RNBT	FBG	SV	IO		120-150		7 2		2 3	3500	4050
17	DELUXE			FBG		IO		120-150					3600	4200
17	SEASPORT		RNBT	FBG	TR	IO		120-150		7 4		2	3750	4400
17 3			RNBT	FBG	SV	OB				7 4	1050		2900	3350
19	SURFER		RNBT	FBG	SV	IO		150-200		7 4		2 4	4650	5400
1965 BOATS														
17 3			RNBT	FBG		OB							2900	3400
17 3	DELUXE		RNBT	FBG		IO		88-150					4100	4800
17 3	SEASPORT		RNBT	FBG		IO		88-150					3750	4450
1964 BOATS														
17 3			RNBT	FBG		OB							2950	3400
17 3	CUSTOM		RNBT	FBG		IO		88-110					3950	4600
17 3	DELUXE		RNBT	FBG		IO		88-150					4450	5100
17 3	DUAL		RNBT	FBG		IO	T	88					5150	5900
17 3	SEASPORT		RNBT	FBG		IO		88-150					3900	4550
1963 BOATS														
17 2	CUSTOM			FBG		IO		88					4050	4700
17 2	DELUXE			FBG		IO		88					4550	5250
17 2	DUAL DELUXE			FBG		IO	T	88					5150	5900
17 2	OMC			FBG		IO		88					3650	4250
17 2	SEASPORT			FBG		IO		88					3850	4500
1962 BOATS														
17	OMC 17			FBG		IO		80					4100	4800
17	OMC 17 DELUXE			FBG		IO		80					4100	4800

JOHNSON BROTHERS BOAT WORKS
POINT PLEASANT NJ   COAST GUARD MFG ID- JBR See inside cover to adjust price for area

LOA FT IN	NAME AND/ OR MODEL	TOP/ RIG	BOAT TYPE	HULL MTL	HULL TP	ENGINE TP	#	HP	MFG	BEAM FT IN	WGT LBS	DRAFT FT IN	RETAIL LOW	RETAIL HIGH
1965 BOATS														
28		HT	CR	L/P		IB		225		9 6		2 4	7600	8750
28	TRUNK CABIN		CUD	L/P		IB		225		9 6		2 4	7450	8550
31 4			CBNCR	L/P		IB		T450		11 2		2 6	15500	17600
1963 BOATS														
28		HT		WD		IB		215					7000	8050
31 4			CBNCR	WD		IB		T215					13900	15800
38 5			SPTCR	WD		IB		T280					24700	27400
1961 BOATS														
20 4	TIDE-RUNNER		RNBT	MHG		IB		10		7		1 8	1800	2100
26	TIDE-MASTER TRUNK CA		CR	MHG		IB		25		9 6		2 6	5100	5850
26	TIDE-WINNER SKIFF		CR	MHG		IB		25		9 6		2 6	4400	5050
1960 BOATS														
20 4	CUSTOM SKIFF			L/P		IB		70		7		1	1700	2000
20 4	CUSTOM SKIFF DLX			L/P		IB		110		7		1	1800	2100
26	CUSTOM			WD		IB		25					4250	4950
26	CUSTOM HARDTOP	HT		L/P		IB		125		9 6		2	4550	5250
26	TRUNK CABIN		CR	WD		IB		25		9 6		2	5000	5750
26	TRUNK CABIN		CR	L/P		IB		125		9 6		2	5200	5950
1959 BOATS														
21 1	SEA-SKIFF			L/P		IB		99		6 11			2050	2400
1958 BOATS														
38		FB	SF			IB		T215					27600	30700
1956 BOATS														
33		FB	SDN	WD		IB		T135	CHRY				12000	13600
1950 BOATS														
36		FB	SF			IB		T115					17200	19600

JOEL J JOHNSON YACHT BUILDER

Call 1-800-327-6929 for BUC Personalized Evaluation Service
Or, for 1960 boats, sign onto www.BUCValuPro.com

JOMAR-CRAFT LTD

Call 1-800-327-6929 for BUC Personalized Evaluation Service
Or, for 1979 boats, sign onto www.BUCValuPro.com

JUTAHELA OY

Call 1-800-327-6929 for BUC Personalized Evaluation Service
Or, for 1980 to 1982 boats, sign onto www.BUCValuPro.com

K M S MARINE
FLAIR MARKETING   COAST GUARD MFG ID- KMS

Call 1-800-327-6929 for BUC Personalized Evaluation Service
Or, for 1976 to 1977 boats, sign onto www.BUCValuPro.com

KACHINA BOATS
COAST GUARD MFG ID- KBT

Call 1-800-327-6929 for BUC Personalized Evaluation Service
Or, for 1973 to 2008 boats, sign onto www.BUCValuPro.com

KADEY-KROGEN YACHTS INC
STUART FL 34994   COAST GUARD MFG ID- CBK See inside cover to adjust price for area

For more recent years, see the BUC Used Boat Price Guide, Volume 1 or Volume 2

LOA FT IN	NAME AND/ OR MODEL	TOP/ RIG	BOAT TYPE	-HULL- MTL TP	TP	----ENGINE--- # HP MFG	BEAM FT IN	WGT LBS	DRAFT FT IN	RETAIL LOW	RETAIL HIGH
--- 1982 BOATS ---
38 2	KROGEN 38	CUT	SA/CR	FBG CB	IB	D	12 8	21700		80100	88000
38 2	KROGEN 38	CUT	SA/CR	FBG KL	IB	D	12 8	21700	6 6	80100	88000
42 4	KROGEN 42	FB	TRWL	FBG DS	IB	120D	15	39500		164000	180000
--- 1981 BOATS ---
38 2	KROGEN 38	CUT	SA/CR	FBG CB	IB	D	12 8	21700		75900	83400
38 2	KROGEN 38	CUT	SA/CR	FBG KL	IB	D	12 8	21700	6 6	75900	83400
42 4	KROGEN 42	FB	TRWL	FBG DS	IB	120D	15	39500		156000	171500
--- 1980 BOATS ---
38	KROGEN 38	CUT	SA/CR	FBG CB	IB	D	12 8	21300		71700	78800
38	KROGEN 38	CUT	SA/CR	FBG KL	IB	D	12 8	21300	6 6	71700	78800
42 4	KROGEN 42	FB	TRWL	FBG DS	IB	120D	15	39500		149000	163500

JOHN KAISER ASSOC INC
WILMINGTON DE 19807-098 COAST GUARD MFG ID- JRK See inside cover to adjust price for area

For more recent years, see the BUC Used Boat Price Guide, Volume 1 or Volume 2

LOA FT IN	NAME AND/ OR MODEL	TOP/ RIG	BOAT TYPE	-HULL- MTL TP	TP	----ENGINE--- # HP MFG	BEAM FT IN	WGT LBS	DRAFT FT IN	RETAIL LOW	RETAIL HIGH
--- 1983 BOATS ---
39	GALE-FORCE	CUT	SA/CR	FBG KL	IB	D	10 6	20200	5 6	97200	107000
39	GALE-FORCE	KTH	SA/CR	FBG KL	IB	D	10 6	20000	5 2	96500	106000
45	GALE-FORCE	KTH	SA/CR	FBG KL	IB	D	12	31000	5	157500	173000
--- 1982 BOATS ---
39	GALE-FORCE 9 TON	CUT	SA/CR	FBG KL	IB	D	10 6	18000	5 2	83900	92200
39	GALE-FORCE 9 TON	KTH	SA/CR	FBG KL	IB	D	10 6	18000	5 2	83900	92200
45	GALE-FORCE 45	KTH	SA/CR	FBG KC	IB	D	12	29000	5	143500	157500
--- 1981 BOATS ---
39	GALE-FORCE	CUT	SA/CR	FBG KL	IB	D	10 6	18000	5 2	78900	86800
39	GALE-FORCE	KTH	SA/CR	FBG KL	IB	D	10 6	18000	5 2	79000	86800
46	CHRISTINA	KTH	SA/CR	FBG KL	IB	D	12	29000	5	141000	155000
--- 1980 BOATS ---
39	GALE-FORCE 39	CUT	SA/CR	FBG KL	IB	D	10 6	18000	5 2	75400	82900
39	GALE-FORCE 39	KTH	SA/CR	FBG KL	IB	D	10 6	18000	5 2	75400	82900
46	CHRISTINA II	KTH	SA/CR	FBG KL	IB	D	12	29000	5	135000	148000
--- 1979 BOATS ---
33 6	GALE-FORCE	CUT	SA/CR	FBG KL	IB	D	10 6	18000	5 2	66100	72700
33 6	GALE-FORCE	KTH	SA/CR	FBG KL	IB	D	10 6	18000	5 2	66100	72700
43 6	CHRISTINA	KTH	SA/CR	FBG KL	IB	D	12	27000	4 10	112000	123500
--- 1978 BOATS ---
17	SWEET-SEVENTEEN	SLP	SA/OD	FBG KL			5			2300	2700
33 6	GALE-FORCE 33	CUT	SA/CR	FBG KL	IB	D	10 6	18000	5 2	63800	70100
43 6	CHRISTINA KETCH	KTH	SA/CR	FBG KL	IB	D	12	32000	5 6	118500	130000
--- 1977 BOATS ---
33 6	GALE-FORCE	CUT	SA/CR	FBG KL	IB	25D WEST	10 6	18000	5 2	61600	67700
43	CHRISTINA	KTH	SA/CR	FBG KC	IB	77D	12 2	29000	4 6	107000	117500
--- 1976 BOATS ---
33 6	GALE-FORCE	CUT	SA/CR	FBG KL	IB	25D	10 6	17800	5	59000	64800
43	CHRISTINA	KTH	SA/CR	FBG KC	IB	77D	12 2	31000	4 6	107500	118000
43	CHRISTINA	KTH	SA/CR	FBG KC	IB	77D	12 2	31000	4 6	107500	118000
--- 1975 BOATS ---
29	SALTWIND	SLP	SA/CR	FBG KC	IB	25D	10	10500	2 5	34000	37700
33 6	GALE-FORCE	CUT	SA/CR	FBG KL	IB	40D	10 6	17000	5	55000	60400
43	CHRISTINA	KTH	MS	FBG KC	IB	90D	12 2	26000	5	94900	104500
43	CHRISTINA	KTH	SA/CR	FBG KC	IB	77D	12 2	25000	4 6	92700	102000
--- 1974 BOATS ---
25 6	K-26 MARK II	SLP	SA/CR	FBG KL	IB	5D	7 10	7000	4	19500	21600
25 6	VIATOR	SLP	SA/CR	FBG KL	IB	D	7 10		3 10	14800	16800
29	SALTWIND	SLP	SA/CR	FBG KC	IB	25D	10	10500	2 5	33100	36700
33 6	GALE-FORCE	CUT	SA/CR	FBG KL	IB	40D	10 6	17000	4 10	53500	58800
38	KAISER	KTH	SA/CR	FBG KL	IB	40D	10 6	19500	5	63400	69700
43	CHRISTINA	KTH	MS	FBG KC	IB	90D	12 2	24000	4 5	92400	101500
43	CHRISTINA	KTH	SA/CR	FBG KC	IB	77D	12 2	25000	4 4	90300	99200
--- 1973 BOATS ---
25 6	KAISER-VIATOR	SLP	SA/CR	FBG KL	IB	D	7 7		3 10	14400	16300
27 8	KAISER 26	SLP	SA/CR	FBG KL	IB	D	7 10		4	20700	23000
33 6	KAISER	CUT	SA/CR	FBG KL	IB	D	9 10		4 7	60700	66700
38	KAISER	KTH	SA/CR	FBG KL	IB	D	10 4		5	59400	65300
--- 1972 BOATS ---
26	KAISER 26	SLP	SA/CR	FBG KL	IB	D	9 8		4 6	13800	15700
32	KAISER	CUT	SA/CR	FBG KL	IB	D	9 8		4 6	37800	42000
39	KAISER TRWL		MS	FBG KL	IB	D	13 6		4 6	60400	66400
44	KAISER	KTH	SA/CR	FBG KL	IB	D	10 4		3 6	98200	108000
--- 1971 BOATS ---
25 10	KAISER 26	SLP	SA/CR	FBG KL			7 10	6200	4	14400	16400
44	KAISER	KTH	SA/CR	FBG KL	IB	D	10 4	19600	4 11	77500	85100
--- 1969 BOATS ---
25 10	KAISER 26	SLP	SA/CR	FBG KL			7 10	6200	4	13900	15800
37 10	KAISER 38	CUT	SA/CR	FBG KL	IB	D	10 2	19000	4 10	55900	61400
37 10	KAISER 38	KTH	SA/CR	FBG KL	IB	D	10 2	19000	4 10	55900	61400
--- 1968 BOATS ---
25 10	KAISER	SLP	SA/CR	FBG KL	IB	25	7 10	6200	4	15100	17100
37 10	KAISER 38	CUT	SA/CR	FBG KL	IB	40D	10 2	19000	4 9	55200	60600
37 10	KAISER 38	KTH	SA/CR	FBG KL	IB	40D	10 2	19000	4 9	55200	60600
--- 1967 BOATS ---
26	K-26	SLP	SA/CR	FBG KL	IB		8		4	12700	14500
38	K-38	SLP	SA/CR	FBG KL	IB		10 2		4 9	50500	55500
--- 1966 BOATS ---
25 4	EVENING-STAR	SLP	SA/CR	FBG KL			8		3 8	6300	7250
25 4	SUMMER-BREEZE	SLP	SA/CR	FBG KL			8		3 8	9800	11100
36 4	ADVENTURER 36	KTH	SA/CR	FBG KL	IB	20D	10		4 8	43400	48300
37 10	KAISER 38	KTH	SA/CR	FBG KL	IB	30D	10 2		4 9	52800	58000
--- 1965 BOATS ---
25 4	EVENING STAR	SLP	SAIL	FBG KL			8		3 8	6350	7300
25 4	SUMMER-BREEZE	SLP	SAIL	FBG KL			8		3 8	9650	11000
36 4	ADVENTURE 36	KTH	SAIL	FBG KL			10		4 8	30300	33600

R J KAISER CO
RAVEAU-YANKEE

Call 1-800-327-6929 for BUC Personalized Evaluation Service
Or, for 1959 boats, sign onto www.BUCValuPro.com

KANTER YACHTS
ST THOMAS ONTARIO CANADA   See inside cover to adjust price for area

For more recent years, see the BUC Used Boat Price Guide, Volume 1 or Volume 2

LOA FT IN	NAME AND/ OR MODEL	TOP/ RIG	BOAT TYPE	-HULL- MTL TP	TP	----ENGINE--- # HP MFG	BEAM FT IN	WGT LBS	DRAFT FT IN	RETAIL LOW	RETAIL HIGH
--- 1982 BOATS ---
44 6	ATLANTIC 45	CUT	SA/CR	STL KL	IB	60D LEHM	13 9	36000	6	133000	146500
44 6	ATLANTIC 45	KTH	SA/CR	STL KL	IB	60D LEHM	13 9	36000	6	133500	146500

KAUFFMAN BOAT BUILDERS
COAST GUARD MFG ID- KBB

Call 1-800-327-6929 for BUC Personalized Evaluation Service
Or, for 1966 to 1971 boats, sign onto www.BUCValuPro.com

KAVALK BOATS LTD
COAST GUARD MFG ID- ZKV

Call 1-800-327-6929 for BUC Personalized Evaluation Service
Or, for 1983 to 1991 boats, sign onto www.BUCValuPro.com

KELLER KRAFT INC

Call 1-800-327-6929 for BUC Personalized Evaluation Service
Or, for 1960 boats, sign onto www.BUCValuPro.com

KELLS CORPORATION
TIVERTON RI 02878   COAST GUARD MFG ID- KEL See inside cover to adjust price for area

LOA FT IN	NAME AND/ OR MODEL	TOP/ RIG	BOAT TYPE	-HULL- MTL TP	TP	----ENGINE--- # HP MFG	BEAM FT IN	WGT LBS	DRAFT FT IN	RETAIL LOW	RETAIL HIGH
--- 1979 BOATS ---
20 2	BRENTON REEF FISHER		FSH	FBG SV	OB		8	1900	1	5450	6250
21 6	HILINER GYPSY		CR	FBG SV	IB	225	8	2810		5250	6050
21 9	KELLS	SLP	SAIL	FBG KL	OB		7 1	1675	1 6	1800	2100
22 7	COASTER	SLP	SAIL	FBG KL	OB		7 10	2350	2 4	2300	2650
22 7	KELLS	SLP	SAIL	FBG CB	OB		7 9	1980	11	2000	2400
27 7	KELLS	SLP	SAIL	FBG KL	IB	12D	9 2	8300	4 7	9700	11000

96th ed. - Vol. III   CONTINUED ON NEXT PAGE   339

LOA FT IN	NAME AND/ OR MODEL	TOP/ RIG	BOAT TYPE	-HULL- MTL TP	TP	----ENGINE--- # HP MFG	BEAM FT IN	WGT LBS	DRAFT FT IN	RETAIL LOW	RETAIL HIGH
				---- 1978 BOATS							
22 7	KELLS	SLP	SAIL	FBG KC	OB		7 9	1980	1 6	1950	2300
24 10	KELLS 25	SLP	SA/CR	FBG KL	OB		7 9	4400	2 10	4100	4800
27 7	OUTRIDER	SLP	SAIL	FBG KL	IB	12D YAN	9 2	8200	4 7	9300	10600
				---- 1977 BOATS							
22 7	KELLS	SLP	SAIL	FBG KC	OB		7 9	1980	11	1900	2250
27 7	OUTRIDER	SLP	SAIL	FBG KL	IB	8D- 12D	9 2	6800	4 7	7250	8400
				---- 1976 BOATS							
22 7	KELLS 23	SLP	SAIL	FBG CB	OB		7 9	1980	11	1800	2150
27 7	OUTRIDER	SLP	SAIL	FBG KL	IB	8D	9 2	6800	4 7	7050	8100
				---- 1975 BOATS							
22 7	KELLS 23	SLP	SAIL	FBG CB	OB		7 9	2000	7 7	1800	2100
				---- 1974 BOATS							
22 7	KELLS 23	SLP	SAIL	FBG CB	OB		7 7	2000	11	1750	2050
				---- 1973 BOATS							
22 7	KELLS 23	SLP	SAIL	FBG CB	OB		7 9	2000	4 6	1700	2000

JACK KELLY YACHT SALES INC
SAN DIEGO CA 92106   COAST GUARD MFG ID- JKY See inside cover to adjust price for area

For more recent years, see the BUC Used Boat Price Guide, Volume 1 or Volume 2

LOA FT IN	NAME AND/ OR MODEL	TOP/ RIG	BOAT TYPE	-HULL- MTL TP	TP	----ENGINE--- # HP MFG	BEAM FT IN	WGT LBS	DRAFT FT IN	RETAIL LOW	RETAIL HIGH
				---- 1983 BOATS							
46 3	KELLY/PETERSON 46	CUT	SA/CR	F/S	IB	82D PATH	13 4	33300	6 8	140500	154500
				---- 1982 BOATS							
43 10	PETERSON 44	CUT	SA/CR	F/S KL	IB	60D PERK	12 11	30000	6 4	114000	125500
46 2	KELLY/PETERSON 46	CUT	SA/CR	F/S KL	IB	80D PATH	13 4	33300	6 8	132500	145500
46 2	KELLY/PETERSON 46	CUT	SA/CR	F/S KL	IB	85D PATH	13 5	33240	6 5	132500	145500
55	PETERSON 55	KTH	SA/CR	FBG KL	IB	D	15	45000	7	236000	259500
				---- 1981 BOATS							
39	CAVALIER 39	SLP	SA/CR	FBG KL	IB	D	11 4	18000	6	65600	72100
43 10	PETERSON 44	CUT	SA/CR	F/S KL	IB	60D PERK	12 11	30000	6 4	108000	119000
43 10	PETERSON 44	CUT	SA/CR	F/S KL	IB	60D WEST	12 11	30000	6 4	109000	119500
				---- 1980 BOATS							
43 10	PETERSON 44	CUT	SA/CR	F/S KL	IB	60D PERK	12 11	30000	6 4	104000	114500
43 10	PETERSON 44	CUT	SA/CR	F/S KL	IB	60D WEST	12 11	30000	6 4	105000	115000
				---- 1979 BOATS							
43 10	PETERSON 44	CUT	SA/CR	FBG KL	IB	60D	12 11	30000	6 4	101500	111500
				---- 1978 BOATS							
43 10	PETERSON 44	CUT	SA/CR	FBG KL	IB	62D WEST	12 11	30000	6 4	98600	108500

KELT MARINE INC
56000 VANNES FRANCE   See inside cover to adjust price for area

For more recent years, see the BUC Used Boat Price Guide, Volume 1 or Volume 2

LOA FT IN	NAME AND/ OR MODEL	TOP/ RIG	BOAT TYPE	-HULL- MTL TP	TP	----ENGINE--- # HP MFG	BEAM FT IN	WGT LBS	DRAFT FT IN	RETAIL LOW	RETAIL HIGH
				---- 1982 BOATS							
24 11	KELT 7.60	SLP	SA/RC	KL	OB		9 5	4189	4 3	8650	9900
24 11	KELT 7.60	SLP	SA/RC	KL	IB	8D YAN	9 5	4189	4 3	9400	10700

KENDALL YACHT CORP
Call 1-800-327-6929 for BUC Personalized Evaluation Service
Or, for 1971 boats, sign onto www.BUCValuPro.com

KENNEBEC YACHT BLDG CO
Call 1-800-327-6929 for BUC Personalized Evaluation Service
Or, for 1928 to 1966 boats, sign onto www.BUCValuPro.com

KENNEDY INC
COAST GUARD MFG ID- KDI

Call 1-800-327-6929 for BUC Personalized Evaluation Service
Or, for 1969 to 1998 boats, sign onto www.BUCValuPro.com

KENNEDY INT'L BOATS LTD
Call 1-800-327-6929 for BUC Personalized Evaluation Service
Or, for 1973 boats, sign onto www.BUCValuPro.com

KENNER MFG CO INC
SPRINGFIELD MO 65803   COAST GUARD MFG ID- KEN See inside cover to adjust price for area

For more recent years, see the BUC Used Boat Price Guide, Volume 1 or Volume 2

LOA FT IN	NAME AND/ OR MODEL	TOP/ RIG	BOAT TYPE	-HULL- MTL TP	TP	----ENGINE--- # HP MFG	BEAM FT IN	WGT LBS	DRAFT FT IN	RETAIL LOW	RETAIL HIGH
				---- 1983 BOATS							
28	TRAILER HOUSEBOAT		HB	FBG	OB		8	4500	1	**	**
32	CRUISING HOUSEBOAT		HB	FBG	IO		12	9000	1 4	29300	32500
47	CRUISING HOUSEBOAT	HT	HB	FBG	IB		12 10	14000	2 10	31900	35400
47	SKIPJACK 35	HT	SA/CR	FBG KC	IB	30D	11 10	14000	2 5	61300	67400
55	CRUISING HOUSEBOAT	HT	HB	FBG	IB		14	28000	2 10	58900	64800
				---- 1982 BOATS							
47	SKIPJACK 35	KTH	SA/CR	FBG KC	IB	30D UNIV	11 10	14000	2 5	57700	63400
				---- 1981 BOATS							
35	SKIPJACK 35	KTH	SA/CR	FBG CB	IB	30D UNIV	12	12000	2 6	24500	27200
				---- 1979 BOATS							
35 8	SKIPJACK	KTH	SA/CR	FBG KC	IB	26D WEST	12	12000	2 8	22800	25300
				---- 1978 BOATS							
35 8	SKIPJACK	KTH	SA/CR	FBG KC	IB	26D WEST	12	12000	2 8	21800	24200
				---- 1977 BOATS							
35	PRIVATEER	KTH	SAIL	FBG KL	IB	30 UNIV	10 8	16000	5	26400	29300
35	SKIPJACK	KTH	SA/CR	FBG CB	IB	30 UNIV	11 10	12000	2 6	20300	22500
				---- 1976 BOATS							
35	PRIVATEER 35	KTH	SAIL	FBG KL	IB	30 UNIV	10 8	16000	5	25400	28300
35	SKIPJACK 35	KTH	SAIL	FBG KC	IB	30 UNIV	11 10	12000	2 6	19700	21800
				---- 1975 BOATS							
35	PRIVATEER	KTH	SA/CR	FBG KL	IB	30 UNIV	10 8	16000	5	24600	27400
35	SKIPJACK	KTH	SA/CR	FBG KC	IB	30 UNIV	11 10	12000	2 6	19000	21100
				---- 1974 BOATS							
35	PRIVATEER	KTH	SA/CR	FBG KL	IB	30 UNIV	10 8	16000	5	23800	26500
35	SKIPJACK	KTH	SA/CR	FBG KC	IB	30 UNIV	11 8	12000	2 6	18400	20500
				---- 1971 BOATS							
18 10	BARRACUDA EXPRESS		RNBT	FBG	OB		7 2	875	8	2450	2850
18 10	BARRACUDA II		RNBT	FBG	OB		7 2	855	8	2250	2600
18 10	BARRACUDA III		RNBT	FBG	OB		7 2	865	8	2250	2600
18 10	MARLIN EXPRESS		RNBT	FBG	OB		7 2	900	8	2350	2750
18 10	MARLIN II		RNBT	FBG	OB		7 2	875	8	2150	2500
18 10	MARLIN III		RNBT	FBG	OB		7 2	885	8	2300	2700
23 7	KITTIWAKE	SLP	SAIL	FBG	OB		7 5	3700	2 10	4050	4750
31 3	PRIVATEER 26	CUT	SAIL	FBG	OB		8	6500	3 6	8250	9500
31 3	PRIVATEER 26	CUT	SAIL	FBG	IB	18 UNIV	8		3 6	12000	13700
31 3	PRIVATEER 26	CUT	SAIL	FBG	IB	7D VLVO	8		3 6	13800	15700
35	PRIVATEER 35	KTH	SAIL	FBG	IB	30 UNIV	10 8	16000	5	22000	24500
35	PRIVATEER 35	KTH	SAIL	FBG	IB	36 PERK	10 8	16000	5	22000	24500
35	RUM-RUNNER	HT	CBNCR	FBG	IO	T155	11 7	8500	5	15400	17500
35	SKIPJACK 35	KTH	SAIL	FBG	IB	30 UNIV	11 8	12000	2 6	16500	18700
35	SUWANEE 35	HT	HB	FBG	IO	T120	11 7	9000	1	27200	30200
35	SUWANEE 35	HT	HB	FBG	SV IO	155	11 7		1 2	24600	27300
47	SUWANEE 47 AFT DECK	HT	HB	FBG	IO	T155	12	15000	1	30500	33900
47	SUWANEE 47 TRI CABIN	HT	HB	FBG	IO	T155	12	15000	1	33500	37200
62	SUWANEE 62	HT	HB	FBG	IO	T210	15 6	30000	6 1	52600	57800
62	SUWANEE 62	HT	HB	FBG	IO	T225	15 6		1	56100	61600
				---- 1970 BOATS							
18 10	BARRACUDA EXPRESS		RNBT	FBG	OB		7 2	875	8	2450	2850
18 10	BARRACUDA II		RNBT	FBG	OB		7 2	855	8	2250	2600
18 10	BARRACUDA III		RNBT	FBG	OB		7 2	865	8	2300	2700
18 10	MARLIN EXPRESS		RNBT	FBG	OB		7 2	900	8	2350	2750
18 10	MARLIN II		RNBT	FBG	OB		7 2	875	8	2200	2550
18 10	MARLIN III		RNBT	FBG	OB		7 2	885	8	2350	2700
23 7	KITTIWAKE	SLP	SAIL	FBG KL	OB		7 5	3700	2 10	4000	4650
31 3	PRIVATEER	KTH	SA/CR	FBG KL			8	6140	3 6	8000	9200
31 3	PRIVATEER 26	CUT	SAIL	FBG KL			8	6500	3 6	8500	9700
35	PRIVATEER 35	KTH	SAIL	FBG	IB	18 UNIV	10 8	16000	5	21500	23900
35	SKIPJACK 35	KTH	SAIL	FBG CB	IB	30 UNIV	11 8	12000	2 6	16200	18400
35	SUWANEE 35	HT	HB	FBG	SV IO	T120	11 7	9000	1	25700	28600
41 7	GILLMER 35	KTH	SA/CR	FBG KL		30	10 6	16650	5	27800	30900
47	SUWANEE 47 AFT DECK	HT	HB	FBG	SV IO	T155 OMC	12	15000	1	29000	32300
47	SUWANEE 47 TRI CABIN	HT	HB	FBG	SV IO	T155 OMC	12	15000	1	31700	35200
62	SUWANEE 62	HT	HB	FBG	IO	T210 OMC	15 6	30000	1	50000	54900

KENNER MFG CO INC   -CONTINUED

See inside cover to adjust price for area

LOA FT IN	NAME AND/OR MODEL	TOP/RIG	BOAT TYPE	HULL MTL	HULL TP	ENG TP	ENG #	ENG HP	ENG MFG	BEAM FT IN	WGT LBS	DRAFT FT IN	RETAIL LOW	RETAIL HIGH
1969 BOATS														
18 11	BARRACUDA EXPRESS		RNBT	FBG	RB	OB				7	900	9	2400	2800
18 11	BARRACUDA II		RNBT	FBG	RB	OB				7	850	9	2300	2650
18 11	BARRACUDA III		RNBT	FBG	RB	OB				7	875	9	2350	2750
23 7	KITTIWAKE	SLP	SAIL	FBG	KL	OB				7 6	3700	2 11	3950	4550
28	ROZINANTE	KTH	SA/OD	FBG	KL	OB				6 4	6500	3 9	7650	8800
31 3	PRIVATEER	CUT	SAIL	FBG	KL	OB				8	6140	3 6	7450	8600
31 3	PRIVATEER	KTH	SAIL	FBG	KL	OB				8	6140	3 6	7450	8600
35	SKIPJACK 35	KTH	SAIL	FBG	KC	IB		30	UNIV	11 8	12000	2 6	16000	18100
41 7	GILLMER 35	KTH	SA/CR	FBG	KL					10 6	16650	4 6	27300	30300
47	SUWANEE 47	HT	HB	FBG	SV	IO		T155		12	12000	2 9	24900	27700
47	SUWANEE 47 TRI CABIN	HT	HB	FBG	SV	IO		T155		12	12000	2 9	27200	30200
62	SUWANEE 62	HT	HB	FBG	SV	IO		T200		15 6	30000	1 2	50200	55100
1968 BOATS														
19	BARRACUDA EXP		RNBT	FBG		OB				7	900	9	2450	2800
19	BARRACUDA II	OP	RNBT	FBG		OB				7	850	9	2350	2700
19	BARRACUDA III	OP	RNBT	FBG		OB				7	875	9	2400	2800
19 8	MARLIN EXPRESS		RNBT	FBG		OB				7 10			2600	3000
19 8	MARLIN II SKI BARGE		RNBT	FBG		OB				7 10			2150	2500
19 8	MARLIN III SKI BARGE		RNBT	FBG		OB				7 10			2250	2600
23 7	KITTIWAKE	SLP	SAIL	FBG	KL	OB				7 6	3700	2 11	3900	4500
24	VIKING	OP	CTRCN	FBG		OB				7 11	1800	10	4800	5500
24	VIKING	OP	CTRCN	FBG		IO		120-155		7 11	1800	10	2700	3150
24	VIKING	OP	CUD	FBG		IO		120-155		7 11	1800	10	2550	3000
24	VIKING EXPRESS	OP	EXP	FBG		OB				7 11	1800	10	4800	5550
24	VIKING EXPRESS	OP	EXP	FBG		IO		120-155		7 11	1800	10	2550	3000
28	ROZINANTE	KTH	SA/OD	FBG	KL	OB				6 4	6550	3 9	7650	8800
31 3	PRIVATEER	CUT	SAIL	FBG	KL	OB				8	6140	3 6	7450	8550
31 3	PRIVATEER	KTH	SAIL	FBG	KL	OB				8	6140	3 6	7450	8550
35	SKIPJACK 35	KTH	SAIL	FBG	KL	IB		30		11 8	12000	2 6	14600	16600
47	SUWANEE 47	HT	HB	FBG	DV	IO		200		12	12000	2 9	25300	28100
47	SUWANEE 47	HT	HB	FBG	DV	IO		T150		12	12000	2 9	27100	30100
1967 BOATS														
19 8	MARLIN EXPRESS		RNBT	FBG		OB							2450	2850
19 8	MARLIN II		RNBT	FBG		OB				7 10	825		2350	2700
19 8	MARLIN III		RNBT	FBG		OB							2200	2550
23 7	KITTIWAKE	SLP	SAIL	FBG	KL	OB				7 6	3700	2 11	3850	4450
24	VIKING	OP	CTRCN	FBG		IO		110-150					3050	3550
24	VIKING EXPRESS	OP	EXP	FBG		IO		110-150		8	2250	10	2800	3300
28	PRIVATEER	CUT	SAIL	FBG		OB					6140		7050	8100
28	ROZINANTE	KTH	SAIL	FBG		OB					6140		7050	8100
28	ROZINANTE	KTH	SA/OD	FBG		OB				6 4	6650	3 9	7650	8800
31 3	PRIVATEER	CUT	SA/CR	FBG	KL					8		3 6	10300	11600
31 3	PRIVATEER	KTH	SA/CR	FBG	KL					8		3 6	10300	11600
47	TRADEWINDS 47	HT	HB	FBG		OB						10	**	**
47	TRADEWINDS 47	HT	HB	FBG		IO		200			12000	10	**	**
47	TRADEWINDS 47	HT	HB	FBG		IO		T120				10	**	**
1966 BOATS														
19 8	MARLIN EXPRESS		RNBT	FBG		OB							2450	2850
19 8	MARLIN II		RNBT	FBG		OB				7 10	825		2350	2750
19 8	MARLIN III		RNBT	FBG		OB							2200	2550
24	SKI-BARGE-VIKING		UTL	FBG		IO		150		7 11		10	4050	4700
1965 BOATS														
19 8	BEACHCOMBER	OP	RNBT	FBG		OB							2400	2750
19 8	MARLIN		RNBT	FBG		OB							2150	2500
19 8	MARLIN II		RNBT	FBG		OB							2350	2700
19 8	MARLIN III		RNBT	FBG		OB							2550	3000
1964 BOATS														
19 8	SKI-BARGE 20	OP	SKI	FBG		OB							2350	2700
1961 BOATS														
17 5	DARDANELLA		CR	FBG		OB				6 11	800		2200	2550
1959 BOATS														
25	HOUSEBOAT	HT	HB	F/W		OB				8	5500		**	**
33	HOUSEBOAT	HT	HB	F/W		OB				10	18000		30900	34400
36	CLIPPER	HT	HB	F/W		OB				12	11000		21100	23400

KETTENBURG MARINE INC

DIV OF WHITTAKER CORP
SAN DIEGO CA 92106   COAST GUARD MFG ID- KET   See inside cover to adjust price for area

LOA FT IN	NAME AND/OR MODEL	TOP/RIG	BOAT TYPE	HULL MTL	HULL TP	ENG TP	ENG #	ENG HP	ENG MFG	BEAM FT IN	WGT LBS	DRAFT FT IN	RETAIL LOW	RETAIL HIGH
1971 BOATS														
41	K-41	SLP	SAIL	FBG	KL	IB		30		10 4	15000	5 6	35800	39800
1970 BOATS														
31 10	PACIFIC-CLASS	SLP	SA/OD	MHG	KL					6 8		4 6	9950	11300
41	K-41	SLP	SAIL	FBG	KL	IB		30		10 4	15000	5 6	34900	38800
50	K-50	SLP	SAIL	AL	KL	IB		75		13		7 8	84600	92900
1969 BOATS														
26 1	PACIFIC-INTER-CLUB	SLP	SAIL	WD	KL					6		4	6100	7000
31 10	PACIFIC-CLASS	SLP	SA/OD	MHG	KL					6 8		4 6	9750	11100
41	K-41	SLP	SA/CR	FBG	KL					10 4		5 6	33800	37500
41	K-41	SLP	SAIL	FBG	KL	IB		30		10 4	15000	5 6	34200	38000
43	K-43	SLP	SAIL	AL	KL	IB		45		11	19000	6 2	44300	49200
43	K-43	SLP	SAIL	WD	KL	IB		45		11	19000	6 2	44300	49200
46	K-46	SLP	SAIL	AL	KL	IB		50		11 6		6 6	62700	68900
46	K-46	SLP	SAIL	WD	KL	IB		50		11 6		6 6	62700	68900
50	K-50	SLP	SAIL	WD	KL	IB		75		13		7 8	82500	90600
1968 BOATS														
32	PACIFIC-CLASS	SLP	SAIL	MHG	KL					6 8		4 6	**	**
41	K-41	SLP	SAIL	FBG	KL	IB		30		10 4	15000	5 6	33500	37200
1967 BOATS														
26 1	PACIFIC-INTERCLUB	SLP	SA/OD	P/M	KL					6		4	5100	5850
32	PC	SLP	SA/OD	P/M	KL					6 8		4 6	**	**
41	K-41	SLP	SAIL	FBG	KL	IB		30		10 4	15000	5 6	32900	36500
43	K-43	SLP	SA/CR	AL	KL	IB		45		11		6	43900	47700
43	K-43	SLP	SA/CR	WD	KL	IB		70		11	20000	6	43900	48700
50	K-50	SLP	SA/CR	WD	KL	IB		110		13		7	81700	89800
1966 BOATS														
26 1	PACIFIC-INTER-CLUB	SLP	SA/OD	WD	KL					6		4		5750
41	K-41	SLP	SA/RC	FBG	KL	IB		25		10 4		5 6	32300	35900
43	K-43	SLP	SA/RC	AL	KL	IB		45		11		6	42300	47000
43	K-43	SLP	SA/RC	WD	KL	IB		45		11		6	42300	47000
50	K-50	SLP	SA/RC	WD	KL	IB		110		13		7	**	**
1965 BOATS														
26 1	PACIFIC-INTER-CLUB	SLP	SAIL	WD	KL					6		4	4950	5650
43	K-43	SLP	SAIL	WD		IB				11		6 2	41600	46300
50	K-50	SLP	SAIL	WD		IB				13		6 10	79000	86800
1963 BOATS														
39 11	K-40	SLP	SAIL	WD		OB							29000	32300
1962 BOATS														
39 11	K-40	SLP	SAIL	WD		OB							28800	32000
1961 BOATS														
32	PC	SLP	SA/CR	P/M	KL	OB				6 8		4 6	11800	13400
1958 BOATS														
46 4	PCC	SLP	SA/CR	P/M	KL	IB				9 6		6	56500	62100
1952 BOATS														
38		SLP	SAIL	WD		IB							29700	33000
42		FB	MY	WD		IB	T		CHRY	13 4		3	**	**

KEY WEST'R YACHTS INC

COAST GUARD MFG ID- KWT

Call 1-800-327-6929 for BUC Personalized Evaluation Service
Or, for 1979 to 1980 boats, sign onto www.BUCValuPro.com

KING CABIN

Call 1-800-327-6929 for BUC Personalized Evaluation Service
Or, for 1939 boats, sign onto www.BUCValuPro.com

KINGS CRAFT INC

FLORENCE AL 35630   COAST GUARD MFG ID- KCR See inside cover to adjust price for area

For more recent years, see the BUC Used Boat Price Guide, Volume 1 or Volume 2

LOA FT IN	NAME AND/OR MODEL	TOP/RIG	BOAT TYPE	HULL MTL	HULL TP	ENG TP	ENG #	ENG HP	ENG MFG	BEAM FT IN	WGT LBS	DRAFT FT IN	RETAIL LOW	RETAIL HIGH
1982 BOATS														
35	KINGS-CRAFT	HT	HB	AL	SV	VD		225		12	8000	2 6	22600	25100
35	KINGS-CRAFT	FB	HB	AL	SV	VD		225		12	8300	2 6	23200	25800
40	KINGS-CRAFT	HT	HB	AL	SV	VD		225		15	11500	2 7	26500	29400
40	KINGS-CRAFT	FB	HB	AL	SV	VD		225		15	11500	2 7	27000	27800
40	KINGS-CRAFT FD	HT	HB	AL	SV	VD		225		15	11200	2 7	29000	29400
40	KINGS-CRAFT FD	FB	HB	AL	SV	VD		225		15	11500	2 7	29000	32200
44	KINGS-CRAFT	HT	HB	AL	SV	VD		T225		15	14000	2 8	33100	36800
44	KINGS-CRAFT	FB	HB	AL	SV	VD		T225		15	14000	2 8	33100	36800
47	KINGS-CRAFT	HT	HB	AL	SV	VD		T225		15	15000	2 8	35000	38900
47	KINGS-CRAFT	FB	HB	AL	SV	VD		T225		15	15300	2 8	35400	39400
48	KINGS-CRAFT FD	HT	HB	AL	SV	VD		T225		15	16000	2 8	37000	41200
48	KINGS-CRAFT FD	FB	HB	AL	SV	VD		T225		15	16300	2 8	37400	41600

KINGS CRAFT INC -CONTINUED See inside cover to adjust price for area

LOA FT	LOA IN	NAME AND/ OR MODEL	TOP/ RIG	BOAT TYPE	HULL MTL	HULL TP	ENGINE TP	ENGINE # HP	ENGINE MFG	BEAM FT	BEAM IN	WGT LBS	DRAFT FT	DRAFT IN	RETAIL LOW	RETAIL HIGH
		1982 BOATS														
55		KINGS-CRAFT	HT	HB	AL	SV	VD	T225		15		18500	2	10	50700	55700
55		KINGS-CRAFT	FB	HB	AL	SV	VD	T225		15		18500	2	10	50700	55700
		1980 BOATS														
35		KINGS-CRAFT	HT	HB	AL	SV	VD	225		12		8000	2	6	21900	24300
35		KINGS-CRAFT	FB	HB	AL	SV	VD	225		12		8000	2	6	21900	24300
40		KINGS-CRAFT	HT	HB	AL	SV	VD	225		15					25700	28500
40		KINGS-CRAFT	HT	HB	AL	SV	VD	225		12		10500	2	7	24400	27200
40		KINGS-CRAFT	FB	HB	AL	SV	VD	225		15					25600	28400
40		KINGS-CRAFT	FB	HB	AL	SV	VD	225		12		10500	2	7	24400	27200
40		KINGS-CRAFT FD	HT	HB	AL	SV	VD	225		15					24700	27400
40		KINGS-CRAFT FD	FB	HB	AL	SV	VD	225		15					24700	27500
44		KINGS-CRAFT	HT	HB	AL	SV	VD	T225		15		14000	2	8	32000	35600
44		KINGS-CRAFT	FB	HB	AL	SV	VD	T225		15		14000	2	8	32000	35600
47		KINGS-CRAFT	HT	HB	AL	SV	VD	T225		15					34100	37900
47		KINGS-CRAFT	FB	HB	AL	SV	VD	T225		15					34100	37900
48		KINGS-CRAFT FD	HT	HB	AL	SV	VD	T225		15					36000	40000
48		KINGS-CRAFT FD	FB	HB	AL	SV	VD	T225		15					36000	40000
55		KINGS-CRAFT	HT	HB	AL	SV	VD	T225		15		18500	2	10	49100	54000
55		KINGS-CRAFT	FB	HB	AL	SV	VD	T225		15		18500	2	10	49100	54000
		1978 BOATS														
35		KINGS-CRAFT	HT	HB	AL	SV	IB	225		12					21400	23800
38		KINGS-CRAFT	HT	HB	AL	SV	IO	233		13	6				29500	32700
40		KINGS-CRAFT	HT	HB	AL	SV	IB	250		12					24300	27000
44		KINGS-CRAFT	HT	HB	AL	SV	IB	250		15					29000	32200
47		KINGS-CRAFT	HT	HB	AL	SV	IB	250		15		14000	2	8	29600	32900
55		KINGS-CRAFT	HT	HB	AL	SV	IB	250		15		18000	2	8	44700	49700
65		KINGS-CRAFT	HT	HB	AL	SV	IB	T450D		19		70000	3	6	90800	99700
75		KINGS-CRAFT	HT	HB	AL	SV	IB	T400D		22		95000	4	5	**	**
		1977 BOATS														
35		KINGS-CRAFT 35	HT	HB	AL	DV	IB	T225		12					23300	25900
38		KINGS-CRAFT 38	HT	HB	AL	DV	OB			13	6				20300	22600
38		KINGS-CRAFT 38	HT	HB	STL	DV	OB			13	6				17600	20000
39	6	SANDPIPER 40	HT	HB	AL	SV	IO	233	MRCR	13	6	10000	2	6	22900	25400
40		KINGS-CRAFT 40	HT	HB	AL	DV	IB	T250		12					27300	30300
44		KINGS-CRAFT 44	HT	HB	AL	DV	IB	T250		15			3	4	32200	35800
47		KINGS-CRAFT 47	HT	HB	AL	SV	VD	T250	CC	15		14000	2	8	31200	34700
50		SANDPIPER 50	HT	HB	AL	SV	IO	233	MRCR	13	6	14000	2	6	32800	36500
55		KINGS-CRAFT 55	HT	HB	AL	SV	VD	T250	CC	15		18000	2	8	47100	51700
65		KINGS-CRAFT 65	HT	HB	AL	DV	IB	T185D		18	6	72000	3	6	78100	85800
65		KINGS-CRAFT 65	HT	HB	AL	DV	IB	T374D	CUM	18	6	72000	3	6	87200	95800
75		SALON CRUISER	HT	HB	AL	SV	VD	T390D	GM	22		99000	4	5	**	**
		1976 BOATS														
35		KINGS-CRAFT	HT	HB	AL	DV	IB	225		12			3	2	21000	23300
35		KINGS-CRAFT	HT	HB	AL	DV	IB	T225		12			3	2	23100	25600
36		KINGS-CRAFT		CR	AL	DV	IB	T225		13					28300	31500
36		KINGS-CRAFT		SF	AL	DV	IB	T225		13					30400	33800
40		KINGS-CRAFT	HT	HB	AL	DV	IB	225		12			3	4	24700	27500
40		KINGS-CRAFT	HT	HB	AL	DV	IB	T225		12			3	4	26800	29800
44		KINGS-CRAFT	HT	HB	AL	DV	IB	225		15			3	4	29600	32900
44		KINGS-CRAFT	HT	HB	AL	DV	IB	T225		15			3	4	31700	35200
55		KINGS-CRAFT	HT	HB	AL	DV	IB	225		15			3	6	44400	49300
55		KINGS-CRAFT	HT	HB	AL	DV	IB	T225		15					47100	51700
75		KINGS-CRAFT	HT	MY	AL	DV	IB	T325D		18					**	**
		1975 BOATS														
35		KINGS-CRAFT	HT	HB	AL	DV	IB	T225		9			2	6	22800	25400
36		KINGS-CRAFT		DC	AL	DV	IB	T225		13					30800	34300
36		KINGS-CRAFT		SDN	AL	DV	IB	T225		13					29800	33200
36		KINGS-CRAFT		SF	AL	DV	IB	T225		13					29200	32400
40		KINGS-CRAFT	HT	HB	AL	DV	IB	T225		9			2	7	26600	29500
44		KINGS-CRAFT	HT	HB	AL	DV	IB	T225		15			2	8	31400	34900
55		KINGS-CRAFT	HT	HB	AL	DV	IB	T225		15			2	10	46600	51200
		1974 BOATS														
35		KINGS-CRAFT	HT	HB	AL		IB	225	CHRY	12		8000	2	6	20300	22600
		IB 225 MRCR 20400 22700, IB T225 CHRY 23800 26500, IB T225 MRCR 24000 26700														
35		KINGS-CRAFT	FB	HB	AL		IB	225	CHRY	12			2	6	20400	22700
		IB 225 MRCR 20500 22800, IB T225 CHRY 22400 24900, IB T225 MRCR 22600 25100														
36				DC	AL		IB	T225	CHRY	13		10400	2	6	23200	25700
36				DC	AL		IB	T225	MRCR	13		10400	2	6	23200	25800
36				SDN	AL		IB	T225	CHRY	13		10100	2	6	23500	26100
36				SDN	AL		IB	T225	MRCR	13		10100	2	6	23600	26200
36			FB	SDN	AL		IB	T225	CHRY	13			2	6	28700	31900
36			FB	SDN	AL		IB	T225	MRCR	13			2	6	28700	31900
36			FB	SF	AL		IB	T225	CHRY	13		10300	2	6	21600	24000
36			FB	SF	AL		IB	T225	MRCR	13		10300	2	6	21700	24100
40		KINGS-CRAFT	HT	HB	AL		IB	225	CHRY	12		10500	2	7	23400	26100
		IB 225 MRCR 23600 26200, IB T225 CHRY 26700 29700, IB T225 MRCR 26900 29900														
40		KINGS-CRAFT	FB	HB	AL		IB	225	CHRY	12			2	7	24100	26800
		IB 225 MRCR 24300 26900, IB T225 CHRY 26100 29000, IB T225 MRCR 26300 29200														
44		KINGS-CRAFT	HT	HB	AL		IB	T225	CHRY	15		14000	2	8	30900	34300
44		KINGS-CRAFT	HT	HB	AL		IB	T225	MRCR	15		14000	2	8	31100	34500
44		KINGS-CRAFT	FB	HB	AL		IB	T225	CHRY	15			2	8	30900	34300
44		KINGS-CRAFT	FB	HB	AL		IB	T225	MRCR	15			2	8	31100	34500
55		KINGS-CRAFT	HT	HB	AL		IB	T225	CHRY	15		18500	2	10	45700	50200
55		KINGS-CRAFT	HT	HB	AL		IB	T225	MRCR	15		18500	2	10	45900	50400
55		KINGS-CRAFT	FB	HB	AL		IB	T225	CHRY	15			2	10	45800	50300
55		KINGS-CRAFT	FB	HB	AL		IB	T225	MRCR	15			2	10	46000	50500
75		KINGS-CRAFT	FB	HB	AL		IB	T325	MRCR	18					**	**
75		KINGS-CRAFT	FB	HB	AL		IB	T330	CHRY	18					**	**
		1973 BOATS														
35		KINGS-CRAFT	HT	HB	AL		IO	T225	CHRY	12		8800	2	6	24600	27300
35		KINGS-CRAFT	HT	HB	AL		IB	T225	CHRY	12		8800	2	6	23600	26200
35		KINGS-CRAFT	HT	HB	AL		IB	T225	MRCR	12		8800	2	6	23800	26500
35		KINGS-CRAFT	FB	HB	AL		IO	T225	CHRY	12			2	6	23100	25700
35		KINGS-CRAFT	FB	HB	AL		IB	T225	CHRY	12			2	6	22200	24700
35		KINGS-CRAFT	FB	HB	AL		IB	T225	MRCR	12			2	6	22400	24900
36				DC	AL		IO	T225	CHRY	12		10400	2	2	31600	35200
36				DC	AL		IB	T225	CHRY	12		10400	2	2	24100	26700
36				DC	AL		IB	T225	MRCR	12		10400	2	2	24100	26800
36				SDN	AL		IO	T225	CHRY	12		10100	2	1	23900	26600
36				SDN	AL		IB	T225	CHRY	12		10100	2	1	23800	26500
36				SDN	AL		IB	T225	MRCR	12		10100	2	1	23900	26600
36			FB	SDN	AL		IO	T225	CHRY	12			2	1	28900	32100
36			FB	SDN	AL		IB	T225	CHRY	12			2	1	28800	32000
36			FB	SDN	AL		IB	T225	MRCR	12			2	1	28900	32100
36				SF	AL		IO	T225	CHRY	12		10300	2	1	29300	32600
36				SF	AL		IB	T225	CHRY	12		10300	2	1	22300	24800
36				SF	AL		IB	T225	MRCR	12		10300	2	1	22400	24900
36			FB	SF	AL		IO	T225	CHRY	12			2	1	36800	40800
36			FB	SF	AL		IB	T225	CHRY	12			2	1	28700	31800
36			FB	SF	AL		IB	T225	MRCR	12			2	1	28700	31900
40		KINGS-CRAFT	HT	HB	AL		IO	T225	CHRY	12		11300	2	7	27200	30200
40		KINGS-CRAFT	HT	HB	AL		IB	T225	CHRY	12		11300	2	7	26500	29400
40		KINGS-CRAFT	HT	HB	AL		IB	T225	MRCR	12		11300	2	7	26700	29700
40		KINGS-CRAFT	FB	HB	AL		IO	T225	CHRY	12			2	7	26600	29500
40		KINGS-CRAFT	FB	HB	AL		IB	T225	CHRY	12			2	7	25800	28700
40		KINGS-CRAFT	FB	HB	AL		IB	T225	MRCR	12			2	7	26100	29000
44		KINGS-CRAFT	HT	HB	AL		IO	T225	CHRY	15		14000	2	8	32200	35800
44		KINGS-CRAFT	HT	HB	AL		IB	T225	CHRY	15		14000	2	8	30600	34000
44		KINGS-CRAFT	HT	HB	AL		IB	T225	MRCR	15		14000	2	8	30800	34200
44		KINGS-CRAFT	FB	HB	AL		IO	T225	CHRY	15			2	8	32200	35800
44		KINGS-CRAFT	FB	HB	AL		IB	T225	CHRY	15			2	8	30600	34000
44		KINGS-CRAFT	FB	HB	AL		IB	T225	MRCR	15			2	8	30800	34200
55		KINGS-CRAFT	HT	HB	AL		IO	T225	CHRY	15		18500	2	10	46500	51100
55		KINGS-CRAFT	HT	HB	AL		IB	T225	CHRY	15		18500	2	10	44700	49700
55		KINGS-CRAFT	HT	HB	AL		IB	T225	MRCR	15		18500	2	10	44900	49900
55		KINGS-CRAFT	FB	HB	AL		IO	T225	CHRY	15			2	10	46500	51100
55		KINGS-CRAFT	FB	HB	AL		IB	T225	CHRY	15			2	10	44700	49700
55		KINGS-CRAFT	FB	HB	AL		IB	T225	MRCR	15			2	10	44900	49900
		1972 BOATS														
35		KINGS-CRAFT	HT	HB	AL		IB	215	MRCR	12		8000	2	6	20100	22300
		IB 225 CHRY 20000 22200, IB T215 MRCR 23600 26200, IB T225 CHRY 23400 26000														
35		KINGS-CRAFT	FB	HB	AL		IB	215	MRCR	12			2	6	20200	22400
		IB 225 CHRY 20100 22300, IB T215 MRCR 22200 24700, IB T225 CHRY 22000 24500														
36				DC	AL		IB	T215	MRCR	12		10400	2	2	23200	25800
36				DC	AL		IB	T225	CHRY	12		10400	2	2	23200	25700
36			FB	DC	AL		IB	T215	MRCR	12			2	2	28700	31900
36			FB	DC	AL		IB	T225	CHRY	12			2	2	28700	31900
36				SDN	AL		IB	T215	MRCR	12		10100	2	1	22900	25500
36				SDN	AL		IB	T225	CHRY	12		10100	2	1	23000	25500
36			FB	SDN	AL		IB	T215	MRCR	12			2	1	27700	30800
36			FB	SDN	AL		IB	T225	MRCR	12			2	1	27800	30900
36				SF	AL		IB	T215	MRCR	12		10300	2	1	21500	23900
36				SF	AL		IB	T225	CHRY	12		10300	2	1	21500	23900
36			FB	SF	AL		IB	T215	MRCR	12			2	1	27600	30700
36			FB	SF	AL		IB	T225	CHRY	12			2	1	27600	30700

 CONTINUED ON NEXT PAGE

LOA FT IN	NAME AND/OR MODEL	TOP/RIG	BOAT TYPE	HULL MTL	HULL TP	ENG TP	HP	MFG	BEAM FT IN	WGT LBS	DRAFT FT IN	RETAIL LOW	RETAIL HIGH
1972 BOATS													
40	KINGS-CRAFT	HT	HB	AL		IB	215	MRCR	12	10500	2 7	23100	25700
						IB	225	CHRY				23000	25600
						IB	T215	MRCR				26400	29400
						IB	T225	CHRY				26200	29200
40	KINGS-CRAFT	FB	HB	AL		IB	215	MRCR	12		2 7	23800	26500
						IB	225	CHRY				23700	26400
						IB	T215	MRCR				25800	28700
						IB	T225	CHRY				25600	28500
44	KINGS-CRAFT	HT	HB	AL		IB	T215	MRCR	15	14000	2 8	30500	33900
44	KINGS-CRAFT	HT	HB	AL		IB	T225	CHRY	15	14000	2 8	30300	33700
44	KINGS-CRAFT	FB	HB	AL		IB	T215	MRCR	15		2 8	30500	33900
44	KINGS-CRAFT	FB	HB	AL		IB	T225	CHRY	15		2 8	30300	33700
55	KINGS-CRAFT	HT	HB	AL		IB	T215	MRCR	15	18500	2 10	44400	49300
55	KINGS-CRAFT	HT	HB	AL		IB	T225	CHRY	15	18500	2 10	44200	49100
55	KINGS-CRAFT	FB	HB	AL		IB	T215	MRCR	15		2 10	44400	49300
55	KINGS-CRAFT	FB	HB	AL		IB	T225	CHRY	15		2 10	44200	49100
1971 BOATS													
35	KINGS-CRAFT	HT	HB	AL		IO	225	CHRY	12	8000	2 6	20300	22500
35	KINGS-CRAFT	HT	HB	AL		IO	225	CHRY	12	8800	2 6	24200	26900
35	KINGS-CRAFT	FB	HB	AL		IO	225	CHRY	12		2 6	20400	22700
35	KINGS-CRAFT	FB	HB	AL		IO	225	CHRY	12		2 6	22800	25300
40	KINGS-CRAFT	HT	HB	AL		IO	225	CHRY	12	10500	2 7	23100	25700
40	KINGS-CRAFT	HT	HB	AL		IO	225	CHRY	12	11300	2 7	26700	29700
40	KINGS-CRAFT	FB	HB	AL		IO	225	CHRY	12		2 7	23800	26400
40	KINGS-CRAFT	FB	HB	AL		IO	225	CHRY	12		2 7	26100	29000
44	KINGS-CRAFT	HT	HB	AL		IO	T225	CHRY	15	14000	2 8	31600	35100
44	KINGS-CRAFT	FB	HB	AL		IO	T225	CHRY	15		2 8	31700	35200
55	KINGS-CRAFT	HT	HB	AL		IO	T225	CHRY	15	18500	2 10	45800	50300
55	KINGS-CRAFT	FB	HB	AL		IO	T225	CHRY	15	18500	2 10	45800	50300
1970 BOATS													
34	KINGS-CRAFT 34	HT	HB	AL		IO	210		12	7000	2	18200	20200
34	KINGS-CRAFT 34	HT	HB	AL		IB	225		12	7000	2 4	17500	19900
44	KINGS-CRAFT 44	HT	HB	AL		IO	T225		15	14000	2 5	31400	34900
44	KINGS-CRAFT 44	HT	HB	AL		IB	T225		15	14000	2 5	30000	33300

KLAMATH BOAT CO INC
COAST GUARD MFG ID- KLO
FORMERLY TRAILORBOAT CO

Call 1-800-327-6929 for BUC Personalized Evaluation Service
Or, for 1960 to 2008 boats, sign onto www.BUCValuPro.com

KLAUS BAESS

Call 1-800-327-6929 for BUC Personalized Evaluation Service
Or, for 1966 to 1967 boats, sign onto www.BUCValuPro.com

KLOPSTOCK & SAMSON

Call 1-800-327-6929 for BUC Personalized Evaluation Service
Or, for 1961 boats, sign onto www.BUCValuPro.com

KNOX MARINE EXCHANGE

Call 1-800-327-6929 for BUC Personalized Evaluation Service
Or, for 1965 to 1968 boats, sign onto www.BUCValuPro.com

THOMAS KNUTSON SHIPBLDNG CORP
HALESITE NY 11743   See inside cover to adjust price for area

LOA FT IN	NAME AND/OR MODEL	TOP/RIG	BOAT TYPE	HULL MTL	HULL TP	ENG TP	HP	MFG	BEAM FT IN	WGT LBS	DRAFT FT IN	RETAIL LOW	RETAIL HIGH
1967 BOATS													
35	KNUTSON 35	SLP	SA/CR	WD	KL	IB			9 10		4 10	27200	30200
35	KNUTSON 35	YWL	SA/CR	WD	KL	IB			9 10		4 10	27200	30200
1960 BOATS													
35	K-35	SLP	SA/CR	P/M	KL	OB			9 10		5	24000	26700
35	K-35 MASTHEAD	YWL	SA/CR	P/M	KL	OB			9 10		5	24000	26700
37	K-37	SLP	SA/CR	P/M	KL	OB			8 4		5 3	22000	24500
1959 BOATS													
35	K-35	SLP	SAIL	KL								24100	26800
35	K-35	YWL	SAIL	KL								24100	26800
37	K-37	SLP	SAIL	P/M	KL	OB			8 4		5 3	22100	24600

KOCKUMS SHIPYARD INC

Call 1-800-327-6929 for BUC Personalized Evaluation Service
Or, for 1969 boats, sign onto www.BUCValuPro.com

KOFFLER BOATS INC
COAST GUARD MFG ID- BKA

Call 1-800-327-6929 for BUC Personalized Evaluation Service
Or, for 1983 to 2000 boats, sign onto www.BUCValuPro.com

KOMA BOATS
CHAS CHAPMAN CO LTD   COAST GUARD MFG ID- ZKO

Call 1-800-327-6929 for BUC Personalized Evaluation Service
Or, for 1968 to 1979 boats, sign onto www.BUCValuPro.com

KONA BOATS INC

Call 1-800-327-6929 for BUC Personalized Evaluation Service
Or, for 1974 to 1979 boats, sign onto www.BUCValuPro.com

KORALLE SAILBOAT CO
COAST GUARD MFG ID- KRL

Call 1-800-327-6929 for BUC Personalized Evaluation Service
Or, for 1969 to 1974 boats, sign onto www.BUCValuPro.com

KULAS CUST SEA SKIFFS INC
COAST GUARD MFG ID- KCS

Call 1-800-327-6929 for BUC Personalized Evaluation Service
Or, for 1958 to 1973 boats, sign onto www.BUCValuPro.com

L B I INC
COAST GUARD MFG ID- LBK

Call 1-800-327-6929 for BUC Personalized Evaluation Service
Or, for 1975 to 1987 boats, sign onto www.BUCValuPro.com

L M GLASFIBER A/S
LUNDERSKOV DENMARK   See inside cover to adjust price for area

LOA FT IN	NAME AND/OR MODEL	TOP/RIG	BOAT TYPE	HULL MTL	HULL TP	ENG TP	HP	MFG	BEAM FT IN	WGT LBS	DRAFT FT IN	RETAIL LOW	RETAIL HIGH
1976 BOATS													
22	LM22	SLP	SAIL	F/S	KL	OB			8 11	3000	4 4	5850	6700
24	LM24	SLP	MS	FBG	KL	IB	25D	VLVO	8	4800	4 3	11000	12500
27	LM27	SLP	MS	FBG	KL	IB	36D	VLVO	9 2	8000	3 1	20700	23000
29	LM29 PH	HT	FSH	FBG	DS	IB	80D	FORD	10	13000	3 8	28600	31800

LA FITTE YACHTS INC
ANNAPOLIS MD 21403   COAST GUARD MFG ID- PKE See inside cover to adjust price for area

LA FITTE YACHTS INC
NEWPORTBCH CA 92663

FORMERLY PACIFIC FAR EAST INDUSTRIES

For more recent years, see the BUC Used Boat Price Guide, Volume 1 or Volume 2

LOA FT IN	NAME AND/OR MODEL	TOP/RIG	BOAT TYPE	HULL MTL	HULL TP	ENG TP	HP	MFG	BEAM FT IN	WGT LBS	DRAFT FT IN	RETAIL LOW	RETAIL HIGH
1983 BOATS													
44 4	LAFITTE 44	CUT	SA/RC	FBG	KL	IB	60D	PERK	12 8	28000	6 4	109500	120500
1982 BOATS													
44 4	LAFITTE 44	CUT	SA/RC	FBG	KL	IB	62D	PEUG	12 8	28000	6 4	113500	114000
66	LAFITTE 66	KTH	SA/CR	FBG	KL	IB	135D	PERK	16 4	67000	6 9	353000	388000

LA FITTE YACHTS INC   -CONTINUED   See inside cover to adjust price for area

LOA FT IN	NAME AND/ OR MODEL	TOP/ RIG	BOAT TYPE	-HULL- MTL TP TP	----ENGINE--- # HP MFG	BEAM FT IN	WGT LBS	DRAFT FT IN	RETAIL LOW	RETAIL HIGH
				--- 1981 BOATS ---						
44 4	LAFITTE 44	CUT	SA/CR	FBG KL IB	62D PEUG	12 8	28000	6 4	97600	107000
44 4	LAFITTE 44	CUT	SA/RC	FBG KL IB	60D PERK	12 8	28000	6 4	97200	107000
				--- 1980 BOATS ---						
44 4	LAFITTE 44	CUT	SA/CR	F/S KL IB	60D WEST	12 8	28000	6 4	93400	102500
44 4	LAFITTE 44	CUT	SA/CR	FBG KL IB	60D WEST	12 8	28000	6 4	93400	102500
44 4	LAFITTE 44	CUT	SA/CR	FBG KL IB	62D PEUG	12 8	28000	6 4	93200	102500
44 4	LAFITTE 44	CUT	SA/RC	FBG KL IB	62D PEUG	12 8	28000	6 4	93200	102500
				--- 1979 BOATS ---						
44 4	LAFITTE 44	SLP	SA/CR	F/S KL IB	60D WEST	12 8	28000	6 4	89800	98700
44 4	LAFITTE 44	CUT	SA/CR	FBG KL IB	60D PISC	12 8	28000	6 4	89600	98400
44 4	LAFITTE 44	CUT	SA/CR	F/S KL IB	60D WEST	12 8	28000	6 4	89800	98600
44 4	LAFITTE 44 SHOAL	SLP	SA/CR	F/S KL IB	60D WEST	12 8	28000	5 6	89800	98700
44 4	LAFITTE 44 SHOAL	CUT	SA/CR	F/S KL IB	60D WEST	12 8	28000	5 6	89800	98600
				--- 1978 BOATS ---						
44 4	LAFITTE 44	SLP	SA/CR	FBG KL IB	60D PISC	12 8	31700		91800	101000

LA JOLLA BOATS

Call 1-800-327-6929 for BUC Personalized Evaluation Service
Or, for 1979 boats, sign onto www.BUCValuPro.com

LACE YACHTS
FT LAUDERDALE FL 33315   See inside cover to adjust price for area
FORMERLY REX LACE

For more recent years, see the BUC Used Boat Price Guide, Volume 1 or Volume 2

LOA FT IN	NAME AND/ OR MODEL	TOP/ RIG	BOAT TYPE	-HULL- MTL TP TP	----ENGINE--- # HP MFG	BEAM FT IN	WGT LBS	DRAFT FT IN	RETAIL LOW	RETAIL HIGH
				--- 1983 BOATS ---						
44	MIDNIGHT-LACE 44	HT	EXP	F/S SV IB	T210D REN	11	15400	2 10	92500	101550
44	MIDNIGHT-LACE 44	FB	EXP	F/S SV IB	T210D REN	11	15400	2 10	92100	101100
52 6	MIDNIGHT-LACE 52	HT	EXP	F/S SV IB	T240D REN	13 2	19850	3	152000	167000
52 6	MIDNIGHT-LACE 52	FB	EXP	F/S SV IB	T240D REN	13 2	19850	3	150500	165000
				--- 1982 BOATS ---						
44	MIDNIGHT-LACE 44		EXP	FBG DS IB	T210D REN	11	15400	2 10	89300	98100
44	MIDNIGHT-LACE 44	SF	EXP	FBG DS IB	T240D	11	15400		113000	124500
52	MIDNIGHT-LACE 52		EXP	FBG DS IB	T240D REN	13	19850	3	144500	158500
52	MIDNIGHT-LACE 52		EXP	FBG DS IB	T260D	13	19850		148500	163000
				--- 1981 BOATS ---						
44	MIDNIGHT-LACE 44	HT	EXP	F/S SV IB	T210D REN	11	15400	2 10	84100	92400
44	MIDNIGHT-LACE 44	FB	EXP	F/S DS IB	T210D	11	15400		85300	93700
44	MIDNIGHT-LACE 44	SF	EXP	FBG DS IB	T240D	11			148000	162500
52 6	MIDNIGHT-LACE 52	HT	EXP	F/S DS IB	T260D	13	19850		148000	162500
52 6	MIDNIGHT-LACE 52	HT	EXP	F/S SV IB	T240D REN	13 2	19850	3	138000	151500
52 6	MIDNIGHT-LACE 52	FB	EXP	F/S SV IB	T240D REN	13 2	19850	3	136500	150000
				--- 1980 BOATS ---						
44	MIDNIGHT-LACE	HT	EXP	FBG DS IB	T210D	11	17000		86600	95100
44	MIDNIGHT-LACE	HT	EXP	FBG DS IB	T240D	11	17000		88700	97500
44	MIDNIGHT-LACE	HT	EXP	FBG RB IB	T210D	11	17000		85700	94200
44	MIDNIGHT-LACE	HT	EXP	FBG DS IB	T300D	11	17000		92000	101000
44	MIDNIGHT-LACE	SF	EXP	FBG DS IB	T240D	11	17000		73700	81000
44	MIDNIGHT-LACE	SF	EXP	FBG DS IB	T340	11	17000		82700	90900
52	MIDNIGHT-LACE	MY	EXP	FBG DS IB	T260	13	25000		143000	157500
52	MIDNIGHT-LACE	MY	EXP	FBG DS IB	T425	13	25000		156500	172000
52	MIDNIGHT-LACE	MY	EXP	FBG DS IB	T280D	13	26200		141500	155500
52	MIDNIGHT-LACE	HT	MY	FBG RB IB	T300D	13	21000		138000	152000
52	MIDNIGHT-LACE	SF	EXP	FBG DS IB	T280D	13	24900		141500	155500
52	VENETIAN-LACE	HT	MY	FBG RB IB	T210D	13	25000		139500	153500
52	VENETIAN-LACE	HT	MY	FBG RB IB	T300D	13	25000		154500	169500

TOM LACK CATAMARANS LTD
DORSET ENGLAND   COAST GUARD MFG ID- TLC See inside cover to adjust price for area

For more recent years, see the BUC Used Boat Price Guide, Volume 1 or Volume 2

LOA FT IN	NAME AND/ OR MODEL	TOP/ RIG	BOAT TYPE	-HULL- MTL TP TP	----ENGINE--- # HP MFG	BEAM FT IN	WGT LBS	DRAFT FT IN	RETAIL LOW	RETAIL HIGH
				--- 1983 BOATS ---						
27	CATALAC 8M	SLP	SAIL	FBG CT OB		13 10	4850	2 1	30100	33500
30	CATALAC 9M MKII	SLP	SAIL	FBG CT OB		13 10	7720	2 4	47500	52200
30	CATALAC 9M MKII	SLP	SAIL	FBG CT IB	T 8D YAN	13 10	7720	2 4	47600	52300
40 10	CATALAC 12M	SLP	SAIL	FBG CT IB	T 30D YAN	17 3	15680	3 3	127500	140000
				--- 1982 BOATS ---						
27	CATALAC 8M	SLP	SAIL	FBG CT OB		13 10	4850	2 1	28500	31700
30	CATALAC 9M MKII	SLP	SAIL	FBG CT OB		13 10	7720	2 4	44200	49200
30	CATALAC 9M MKII	SLP	SAIL	FBG CT IB	T 12 RCA	13 10	7720	2 4	44200	49200
30	CATALAC 9M MKII	SLP	SAIL	FBG CT IB	T 8D REN	13 10	7720	2 4	44300	49200
				--- 1981 BOATS ---						
27	CATALAC 8M	SLP	SAIL	FBG CT OB		13 10	4850	2 1	27000	30000
30	CATALAC 9M MKII	SLP	SAIL	FBG CT OB		13 10	7720	2 4	41600	46300
30	CATALAC 9M MKII	SLP	SAIL	FBG CT IB	T 12 RCA	13 10	7720	2 4	41600	46300
30	CATALAC 9M MKII	SLP	SAIL	FBG CT IB	T 8D REN	13 10	7720	2 4	41600	46300
				--- 1980 BOATS ---						
27	CATALAC 8M	SLP	SAIL	FBG CT OB		13 10	4850	2 1	25800	28600
30	CATALAC 9M MKII	SLP	SAIL	FBG CT OB		13 10	7720	2 4	39800	44200
30	CATALAC 9M MKII	SLP	SAIL	FBG CT IB	T 12 RCA	13 10	7720	2 4	39800	44200
30	CATALAC 9M MKII	SLP	SAIL	FBG CT IB	T 8D REN	13 10	7720	2 4	39800	44200
				--- 1979 BOATS ---						
27	CATALAC 8M	SLP	SAIL	FBG CT OB		13 10	5600	2	25700	28600
30	CATALAC 9M MKII	SLP	SAIL	FBG CT OB		13 10	6720	2 4	36800	40900
30	CATALAC 9M MKII	SLP	SAIL	FBG CT IB	T 12 RCA	13 10	6720	2 4	36800	40900
30	CATALAC 9M MKII	SLP	SAIL	FBG CT IB	T 8D REN	13 10	6720	2 4	36800	40900
				--- 1978 BOATS ---						
26 3	CATALAC 8M	SLP	SAIL	FBG CT OB		13 2	6283	2	23600	26200
29 7	CATALAC 9M	SLP	SAIL	FBG CT OB		13 10	6614	2 6	34000	37800

LAGUNA YACHTS INC
STANTON CA 90680   COAST GUARD MFG ID- LAY See inside cover to adjust price for area

For more recent years, see the BUC Used Boat Price Guide, Volume 1 or Volume 2

LOA FT IN	NAME AND/ OR MODEL	TOP/ RIG	BOAT TYPE	-HULL- MTL TP TP	----ENGINE--- # HP MFG	BEAM FT IN	WGT LBS	DRAFT FT IN	RETAIL LOW	RETAIL HIGH
				--- 1983 BOATS ---						
16	LAGUNA 16	SLP	SAIL	FBG KL OB		7 5	1000	2 5	1750	2050
18	LAGUNA 18 RC	SLP	SAIL	FBG SK OB		8	1500	4 6	2300	2650
18	LAGUNA 18 SC	SLP	SAIL	FBG SK OB		8	1500	2 3	2250	2600
18	LAGUNA DAYSAILER-R	SLP	SAIL	FBG KL OB		8	1200	4 6	2000	2350
18	LAGUNA DAYSAILER-S	SLP	SAIL	FBG KL OB		8	1200	1	1950	2300
18	WINDROSE 5.5R	SLP	SAIL	FBG KL OB		8	1500	2 3	2300	2650
18	WINDROSE 5.5S	SLP	SAIL	FBG KL OB		8	1500	2 3	2250	2600
18	WINDROSE DAYSAILER R	SLP	SAIL	FBG KL OB		8	1200	1	1950	2300
18	WINDROSE DAYSAILER S	SLP	SAIL	FBG SK OB		8	1260	3	2000	2400
21 7	LAGUNA 22 RF	SLP	SAIL	FBG KL OB		8	1980	1 3	3050	3550
21 7	LAGUNA 22 RS	SLP	SAIL	FBG KL OB		8	1980	1 3	3050	3550
21 7	LAGUNA 22 SF	SLP	SAIL	FBG KL OB		8	2280	2 11	3250	3750
21 7	LUGUNA 22 SR	SLP	SAIL	FBG KL OB		8	2280	2 11	3250	3750
21 7	WINDROSE 22R	SLP	SAIL	FBG KL OB		8	1980	1 3	2700	3100
21 7	WINDROSE 22S	SLP	SAIL	FBG KL OB		8	2280	2 11	3100	3600
23 7	LAGUNA 24	SLP	SAIL	FBG KL OB		8 4	2600	2 11	3850	4500
25 9	LAGUNA 26	SLP	SA/CR	FBG KL OB		8 4	3900	3 1	6000	6850
25 9	WINDROSE 26	SLP	SA/CR	FBG KL OB		8 4	3900	3 1	6000	6850
29 11	LAGUNA 30	SLP	SA/CR	FBG KL OB		10 10	8700	6	14800	16800
				--- 1982 BOATS ---						
18 5	WINDROSE 5.5	SLP	SAIL	FBG KL OB		8	1500	2 3	2100	2450
18 5	WINDROSE 18	SLP	SAIL	FBG SK OB		8	1540	4 6	2150	2550
20 3	WINDROSE 20	SLP	SAIL	FBG KL OB		7 6	1650	1	2350	2750
21 7	WINDROSE 22 MK II	SLP	SAIL	FBG KL OB		8	1980	1 3	3200	3700
21 7	WINDROSE 225 MK II	SLP	SAIL	FBG KL OB		8	1980		2900	3350
24 8	WINDROSE 25	SLP	SA/CR	FBG KL OB		7 10	2500	1 6	3750	4350
25 9	LAGUNA 26	SLP	SA/CR	FBG KL OB		8 4	3600	3 1	5250	6000
				--- 1981 BOATS ---						
18 5	WINDROSE 5.5	SLP	SAIL	FBG KL OB		8	1500	2 3	1950	2300
18 5	WINDROSE 18	SLP	SAIL	FBG SK OB		8	1540	4 6	2000	2400
20 3	WINDROSE 20	SLP	SAIL	FBG KL OB		7 6	1650	1	2250	2600
21 7	WINDROSE 22 MK II	SLP	SAIL	FBG KL OB		8	1980	1 3	2600	3000
24 8	WINDROSE 25	SLP	SAIL	FBG KL OB		7 10	2400	1 6	3350	3850
24 8	WINDROSE 25	SLP	SAIL	FBG KL OB		7 10	2500	1 6	3500	4100
				--- 1980 BOATS ---						
18 5	WINDROSE 18	SLP	SA/RC	FBG SK OB		7	1500	4 6	1900	2250
20 3	WINDROSE 20	SLP	SA/RC	FBG KL OB		7 6	1650	1	2100	2500
21 7	WINDROSE 22-MKI	SLP	SA/RC	FBG KL OB		8	1980	1	2450	2850
24 7	WINDROSE 24	SLP	SA/RC	FBG KL OB		7 10	2400	6 4	3200	3700
24 8	WINDROSE 25	SLP	SA/RC	FBG KL OB		7 10	2500	6 4	3350	3900
				--- 1979 BOATS ---						
18 5	WINDROSE 18	SLP	SAIL	FBG SK OB		7	1540	1	1850	2200
20 3	WINDROSE	SLP	SA/OD	FBG KL OB		7 6	1500	1	2000	2400
21 7	WINDROSE 22	SLP	SAIL	FBG SK OB		8	1980	1 3	2350	2750
21 7	WINDROSE 22 MK II	SLP	SAIL	FBG SK OB		8	1980	1 3	2400	2800

CONTINUED ON NEXT PAGE   96th ed. - Vol. III

LOA FT	IN	NAME AND/ OR MODEL	TOP/ RIG	BOAT TYPE	HULL MTL	TP	ENGINE TP	#	HP	MFG	BEAM FT	IN	WGT LBS	DRAFT FT	IN	RETAIL LOW	RETAIL HIGH
---				1979 BOATS													
24	4	WINDROSE 24	SLP	SAIL	FBG	SK	OB				7	10	2400	1	6	3050	3550
24	8	WINDROSE 25	SLP	SAIL	FBG	SK	OB				7	10	2500	1	6	3250	3750
---				1978 BOATS													
18	5	WINDROSE 18	SLP	SA/RC	FBG	SK	OB				7		1500	1		1750	2050
20	3	WINDROSE	SLP	SA/OD	FBG	SK	OB				7	6	1650			1950	2300
21	7	WINDROSE 22	SLP	SA/RC	FBG	SK	OB				8		1980	1	5	2300	2700
24		WINDROSE 24	SLP	SA/RC	FBG	SK	OB				7	10	2400	1	6	2950	3450
24	8	WINDROSE 25	SLP	SA/RC	FBG	SK	OB				7	10	2500			3100	3600
---				1977 BOATS													
18	5	WINDROSE	SLP	SAIL	FBG	SK	OB				7		1500	1		1700	2000
21	7	WINDROSE	SLP	SAIL	FBG	SK	OB				8		1980	1	5	2250	2600
24		WINDROSE	SLP	SAIL	FBG	SK	OB				7	10	2400	1	6	2850	3300
---				1976 BOATS													
24		WINDROSE	SLP	SAIL	FBG	SK	OB				7	10	2400	1	6	2750	3200
---				1975 BOATS													
24		WINDROSE	SLP	SAIL	FBG	SK	OB				7	10	2400	1	6	2700	3100

LAHAINA CATAMARAN CORP

Call 1-800-327-6929 for BUC Personalized Evaluation Service
Or, for 1978 boats, sign onto www.BUCValuPro.com

LAKE CHARLES YACHT SALES

Call 1-800-327-6929 for BUC Personalized Evaluation Service
Or, for 1970 boats, sign onto www.BUCValuPro.com

LAKER

Call 1-800-327-6929 for BUC Personalized Evaluation Service
Or, for 1906 boats, sign onto www.BUCValuPro.com

LAMINATED PRODUCTS INC
GOODLETTSVILLE TN 37072 COAST GUARD MFG ID- LMG See inside cover to adjust price for area

LOA FT	IN	NAME AND/ OR MODEL	TOP/ RIG	BOAT TYPE	HULL MTL	TP	ENGINE TP	#	HP	MFG	BEAM FT	IN	WGT LBS	DRAFT FT	IN	RETAIL LOW	RETAIL HIGH
---				1981 BOATS													
37		CARLCRAFT	HT	HB	FBG	SV	IB		220		12					30900	34300
45		CARLCRAFT	HT	HB	FBG	SV	IB		T270		14					37000	41100
57		CARLCRAFT	HT	HB	FBG	SV	IB		T350		14					61100	67200
---				1980 BOATS													
37		CARLCRAFT	HT	HB	FBG	SV	IB		220		12					30400	33800
45		CARLCRAFT	HT	HB	FBG	SV	IB		270		14					34000	37800
57		CARLCRAFT	HT	HB	FBG	SV	IB		350		14					57400	63100
---				1979 BOATS													
37		CARLCRAFT 37	HT	HB	FBG	SV	IO		220		12					29400	32700
43		CARLCRAFT 43	HT	HB	FBG	SV	IO		220		12					26100	29000
43		CARLCRAFT 43	HT	HB	FBG	SV	IO		T220		12					28200	31400
57		CARLCRAFT 57	HT	HB	FBG	SV	IO		T350		14					67200	73800
---				1978 BOATS													
37		CARLCRAFT 37	HT	HB	FBG	SV	VD		220	CRUS	12			1	7	30300	33700
		VD 220 PALM	30000	33400,	IO		228		MRCR		29100	32300,	VD	270	CRUS	30500	33900
		VD 270 PALM	30200	33500,	IO		330		MRCR		31100	34600,	VD	T220	CRUS	32600	36200
		VD T220 PALM	32000	35600,	IO		T228		MRCR		31400	34800,	VD	T270	CRUS	32900	36600
		VD T270 PALM	32300	35900													
37		CARLCRAFT 37	FB	HB	FBG	SV	VD		220	CRUS	12			1	7	30300	33700
		VD 220 PALM	30000	33400,	IO		228		MRCR		29100	32300,	VD	270	CRUS	30500	33900
		VD 270 PALM	30200	33500,	IO		330		MRCR		31100	34600,	VD	T220	CRUS	32600	36200
		VD T220 PALM	32000	35600,	IO		T228		MRCR		31400	34800,	VD	T270	CRUS	32900	36600
		VD T270 PALM	32300	35900													
43		CARLCRAFT 43	HT	HB	FBG	SV	IO		330	MRCR	12		14000	1	7	27800	30800
		VD T220 CRUS	27500	30600,	VD		T220		PALM		27000	30000,	IO	T228	MRCR	28000	31100
		VD T270 CRUS	27800	30900,	VD		T270		PALM		27300	30300					
43		CARLCRAFT 43	FB	HB	FBG	SV	IO		330	MRCR	12		14000	1	7	27800	30800
		VD T220 CRUS	27500	30600,	VD		T220		PALM		27000	30000,	IO	T228	MRCR	28000	31100
		VD T270 CRUS	27800	30900,	VD		T270		PALM		27300	30300					
57		CARLCRAFT 57	HT	HB	FBG	SV	VD		T350	CRUS						59300	65100
57		CARLCRAFT 57	HT	HB	FBG	SV	VD		T350	PALM						58400	64200
57		CARLCRAFT 57	FB	HB	FBG	SV	VD		T350	CRUS						59300	65100
57		CARLCRAFT 57	FB	HB	FBG	SV	VD		T350	PALM						58400	64200

LAMINEX IND OF CANADA LTD

Call 1-800-327-6929 for BUC Personalized Evaluation Service
Or, for 1983 to 1984 boats, sign onto www.BUCValuPro.com

LANAVERRE JEAN MORIN BOAT DIV
TRANS ATLANTIC TRADE CO COAST GUARD MFG ID- LNV

L LANAVERRE CONST NAUTIQUES

Call 1-800-327-6929 for BUC Personalized Evaluation Service
Or, for 1967 to 1979 boats, sign onto www.BUCValuPro.com

LANCER YACHT CORP
IRVINE CA 92714   COAST GUARD MFG ID- LYP See inside cover to adjust price for area
                    SEE ALSO WILLARD COMPANY INC

For more recent years, see the BUC Used Boat Price Guide, Volume 1 or Volume 2

LOA FT	IN	NAME AND/ OR MODEL	TOP/ RIG	BOAT TYPE	HULL MTL	TP	ENGINE TP	#	HP	MFG	BEAM FT	IN	WGT LBS	DRAFT FT	IN	RETAIL LOW	RETAIL HIGH
---				1983 BOATS													
24	8	LANCER 25	SLP	SAIL	FBG	KL	OB				8		3600	3		5400	6200
24	8	LANCER 25 MKV	SLP	SAIL	FBG	KL	OB				8		3600	3		5400	6200
24	8	LANCER 25 MKV	SLP	SAIL	FBG	KL	SE		115	OMC	8		3600	3		6100	7000
27	8	LANCER 28	SLP	SAIL	FBG	KL	OB				8		5200	3		9400	10700
27	8	LANCER 28 MKV	SLP	SAIL	FBG	KL	SE		115	OMC	8		5200	3		9750	11100
27	8	LANCER 28 MKV	SLP	SAIL	FBG	KL	IB		8D	YAN	8		5200	3		9700	11000
27	8	LANCER 28T MKV	SLP	SAIL	FBG	KL	OB				8		5200	3		9400	10700
28	8	LANCER 29	SLP	SAIL	FBG	KL	IB		15D	YAN	10		7800	5	2	16300	18500
28	8	LANCER 29 MKII	SLP	SAIL	FBG	KL	IB				10		7800	5	2	14400	16400
28	8	LANCER 29 MKIII	SLP	SAIL	FBG	KL	SE		115	OMC	10		7800	5	2	14800	16800
28	8	LANCER 29 MKIII	SLP	SAIL	FBG	KL	IB		8D-	15D	10		7800	5	2	14700	16800
28	8	LANCER 29 MKIIISHOAL	SLP	SAIL	FBG	KL	IB				10		7800	4	2	15400	17400
28	8	LANCER 29 MKIIISHOAL	SLP	SAIL	FBG	KL	SE		115	OMC	10		7800	4	2	15600	17800
28	8	LANCER 29 MKIIISHOAL	SLP	SAIL	FBG	KL	IB		8D-	15D	10		7800	4	2	15600	17700
29	6	LANCER 30	SLP	SAIL	FBG	KL	IB		15D	YAN	10		8200	5	2	17000	19300
29	6	LANCER 30 MKV	SLP	SAIL	FBG	KL	OB				10		8200	5	2	15700	17800
29	6	LANCER 30 MKV	SLP	SAIL	FBG	KL	SE		115	OMC	10		8200	5	2	16000	18100
29	6	LANCER 30 MKV	SLP	SAIL	FBG	KL	IB		8D-	12D	10		8200	5	2	15900	18100
29	6	LANCER 30 MKV SHOAL	SLP	SAIL	FBG	KL	OB				10		8200	4	2	16600	18900
29	6	LANCER 30 MKV SHOAL	SLP	SAIL	FBG	KL	SE		115	OMC	10		8200	4	2	16800	19100
29	6	LANCER 30 MKV SHOAL	SLP	SAIL	FBG	KL	IB		8D-	15D	10		8200	4	2	16800	19100
36	2	LANCER 36	SLP	SAIL	FBG	KL	OB				11	9	10500	6	2	24600	27300
		IB 115 OMC	25100	27900,	IB		15D		YAN		25200	28000,	IB	20D	YAN	28300	31400
		IB 30D YAN	25400	28200													
36	2	LANCER 36 SHOAL	SLP	SAIL	FBG	KL	OB				11	9	10500	4	11	25800	28600
		IB 115 OMC	26300	29200,	IB		15D		YAN		26300	29200,	IB	20D	YAN	23300	25900
		IB 30D YAN	26400	29400													
37		LANCER 37	SLP	SAIL	FBG	KL	IB				12		15000	6	3	36600	40600
37	7	LANCER 38	SLP	SAIL	FBG	KL	IB				12		15000	6	3	37700	41900
39		LANCER 39	SLP	MS	FBG	KL	IB				12		16000	6	3	43400	48200
39	6	LANCER 40 AC	SLP	SAIL	FBG	KL	IB				12		15500	6	3	42300	47000
		SD 23D VLVO	42800	47600,	SD		35D		VLVO		45700	50300,	SD	61D	VLVO	43400	48300
39	6	LANCER 40 AC SHOAL	SLP	SAIL	FBG	KL	IB				12		15500	4	11	43400	48200
		IB VLVO	43400	48200,	SD		23D		VLVO		43800	48700,	SD	35D	VLVO	42200	46800
		SD 61D VLVO	44500	49400													
39	6	LANCER 40 MC	SLP	SAIL	FBG	KL	IB				12		15500	6	3	44800	49800
		SD 23D VLVO	45600	50100,	SD		35D		VLVO		47500	52300,	SD	61D	VLVO	46200	50800
39	6	LANCER 40 MC SHOAL	SLP	SAIL	FBG	KL	IB				12		15500	4	11	46000	51000
		SD 23D VLVO	46700	51300,	SD		35D		VLVO		44400	49300,	SD	61D	VLVO	47300	52000
39	6	LANCER 40 MS	SLP	MS	FBG	KL	IB				12		16000	6	3	44400	49400
		IB 62D PERK	45800	50400,	IB		85D		PERK		45000	50000,	IB	T50D	PERK	47000	51600
		IB T 62D PERK	47200	51900,	IB		T85D		PERK		47300	52000					

```
     LOA  NAME AND/             TOP/ BOAT  -HULL-  ----ENGINE---  BEAM    WGT  DRAFT  RETAIL RETAIL
    FT IN  OR MODEL             RIG  TYPE  MTL TP TP # HP  MFG   FT IN   LBS  FT IN   LOW   HIGH
   -------------------- 1983 BOATS -------------------------------------------------------------
    39  6 LANCER 40 MS SHOAL    SLP MS     FBG KL IB         12          16000 4 11  46000  50600
        IB   62D PERK  46800    51400, IB   85D PERK  46400  51000, IB T 50D PERK  47800  52600
        IB T 62D PERK  47800    52600, IB T 85D PERK  47900  52700

    42  7 LANCER 42             SLP SAIL   FBG KL OB         13  9 21000  6      61100  67100
    42  7 LANCER 43             SLP SAIL   FBG KL IB         13  9 23000  6      65000  71400
    44  7 LANCER 45                 MY     FBG DV IB T200D PERK 13 9 20000 3  9   60800  66800
    44  7 LANCER 45             HT  MY     FBG DV IB  135D PERK 13 9 20000 3  9   59500  65400
        IB  200D PERK  60500    66500, IB T 85D PERK  61100  67200, IB T135D PERK  53200  58500
        IB T240D PERK  65500    71900, IB T300D CAT   71600  78600

    44  7 LANCER 45             FB  MY     FBG DV IB         13  9 20000  4 11    **     **
        IB  135D PERK  59200    65100, IB  200D PERK  60200  66100, IB T 85D PERK  60800  66800
        IB T135D PERK  53000    58300, IB T200D PERK  61000  67000, IB T240D PERK  65200  71600
        IB T300D CAT   71200    78200

    44  7 LANCER 45 AC          SLP SAIL   FBG KL IB   62D PERK 13 9 24000  6     70200  77200
        IB   85D PERK  73600    80900, IB  135D PERK  71100  78100, IB  200D PERK  71600  78700
        IB T 50D PERK  72800    80000

    44  7 LANCER 45 AC SHOAL    SLP SAIL   FBG KL IB   62D PERK 13 9 24000  4 11  72900  80100
        IB   85D PERK  70200    77100, IB  135D PERK  73600  80800, IB  200D PERK  74100  81400
        IB T 50D PERK  75300    82700

    44  7 LANCER 45 FLYBRIDGE   SLP MS     FBG KL IB         13  9 24000  6      67800  74600
    44  7 LANCER 45 MC          SLP MS     FBG KL IB         13  9 24000  6      70800  77800
    44  7 LANCER 45 MC          SLP SAIL   FBG KL IB   62D PERK 13 9 24000  6     73000  80200
        IB   85D PERK  76200    83700, IB  135D PERK  73700  81000, IB  200D PERK  74300  81600

    44  7 LANCER 45 MC SHOAL    SLP MS     FBG KL IB         13  9 24000  4 11   73500  80800
    44  7 LANCER 45 MC SHOAL    SLP SAIL   FBG KL IB   62D PERK 13 9 24000  4 11  75600  83100
        IB   85D PERK  72700    79900, IB  135D PERK  76200  83700, IB  200D PERK  76800  84400

    44  7 LANCER 45 MS          SLP MS     FBG KL IB         13  9 24000  6      73800  81100
        IB   85D PERK  73200    80400, IB  135D PERK  72500  79600, IB  200D PERK  73000  80200
        IB T 50D PERK  72900    80100, IB T 62D PERK  73200  80400, IB T 85D PERK  77300  84900
        IB T135D PERK  74700    82100, IB T200D PERK  75800  83300

    44  7 LANCER 45 MS SHOAL    SLP MS     FBG KL IB         13  9 24000  4 11   76500  84100
        IB   85D PERK  73200    80400, IB  135D PERK  74800  82200, IB  200D PERK  75400  82800
        IB T 50D PERK  75200    82700, IB T 62D PERK  75400  82900, IB T 85D PERK  72300  79500
        IB T135D PERK  76800    84400, IB T200D PERK  77900  85600

    44  7 LANCER 45 SHOAL       SLP MS     FBG KL IB         13  9 24000  4 11   70600  77600
    65  4 LANCER 65             SLP MS     FBG KL IB         17 10 55000  6 11  202500 223000
        IB  135D PERK 124000   136500, IB  200D PERK 200000 219500, IB  240D PERK 200500 220000
        IB  350D PERK 201500   221500, IB T135D PERK 201500 221500, IB T200D PERK 203500 223000
        IB T240D PERK 203500   223500, IB T350D PERK 206000 226000

    65  4 LANCER 65 FB          SLP MS     FBG KL IB  130D PERK 17 11 55000  6 11 205000 225500
        IB  200D PERK 208000   229000, IB  240D PERK 208500 229000, IB  350D PERK 209500 230000
        IB T135D PERK 209500   230000, IB T200D PERK 210500 231500, IB T240D PERK 211500 232000
        IB T350D PERK 213000   234500

    65  4 LANCER 65 FB SHOAL    SLP MS     FBG KL IB  135D PERK 17 11 55000  5  8 209500 230000
        IB  200D PERK 211500   232500, IB  240D PERK 212000 233000, IB  350D PERK 212500 234000
        IB T135D PERK 213000   234000, IB T200D PERK 213500 235000, IB T240D PERK 214500 235500
        IB T350D PERK 216500   238000

    65  4 LANCER 65 SHOAL       SLP MS     FBG KL IB         17 10 55000  5  8 206500 227000
        IB  135D PERK 201000   221000, IB  200D PERK 203500 223500, IB  240D PERK 203500 223500
        IB  350D PERK 205000   225000, IB T135D PERK 205000 225000, IB T200D PERK 206000 226500
        IB T240D PERK 206500   227000, IB T350D PERK 209000 229500
   -------------------- 1982 BOATS -------------------------------------------------------------
    24  8 LANCER 25 MKV         SLP SAIL   FBG KL OB          8       3600  3       5100   5850
    27  8 LANCER 28T MKV        SLP SAIL   FBG KL OB          8       5200  3       8850  10100
    28  8 LANCER 29 MKII        SLP SAIL   FBG KL OB         10       7800  5  2   14000  15900
    29  6 LANCER 30 MKV         SLP SAIL   FBG KL OB         10       8200  5  2   15200  17300
    36  2 LANCER 36             SLP SAIL   FBG KL OB         11  9 10500  6  2   23700  26300
    37    LANCER 37             SLP SAIL   FBG KL IB         12      15000  6  3   34400  38200
    37  7 LANCER 38             SLP SAIL   FBG KL IB         12      15000  6  3   35500  39400
    39    LANCER 39             SLP MS     FBG KL IB         12      16000  6  3   40800  45300
    42  7 LANCER 42             SLP SAIL   FBG KL OB         13  9 21000  6      57400  63100
    42  7 LANCER 43             SLP SAIL   FBG KL IB         13  9 23000  6      61200  67200
    44  2 LANCER 44 FLYBRIDGE   SLP MS     FBG KL IB         13  9 23000  6      64700  71100
    44  7 LANCER 45             FB  MY     FBG DV IB         13  9 20000  3  9     **     **

    65  4 LANCER 65             SLP MS     FBG KL IB         17 10 55000  6 11  192500 211500
   -------------------- 1981 BOATS -------------------------------------------------------------
    24  8 LANCER 25 MKV         SLP SAIL   FBG KL OB          8       3600  3       4800   5500
    24  8 LANCER 25 MKV         SLP SAIL   FBG KL SD  15  OMC   8       3695  3       5150   5900
    27  8 LANCER 28T MKV        SLP SAIL   FBG KL OB          8       5200  3       8250   9450
    27  8 LANCER 28T MKV        SLP SAIL   FBG KL SD  15  OMC   8       5295  3       8500   9800
    27  8 LANCER 28T MKV        SLP SAIL   FBG KL SD      6D REN   8    5295  3       8650   9950
    28  8 LANCER 29 MKII        SLP SAIL   FBG KL OB         10       7800  5  2   12900  14600
    28  8 LANCER 29 MKII        SLP SAIL   FBG KL SD  15  OMC  10       7800  5  2   13000  14800
    28  8 LANCER 29 MKII        SLP SAIL   FBG KL SD  8D- 15D  10      7800  5  2   13100  15000
    28  8 LANCER 29 MKIII SHL   SLP SAIL   FBG KL OB         10       7800  4  2   13500  15300
    28  8 LANCER 29 MKIII SHL   SLP SAIL   FBG KL SD  15  OMC  10      7800  4  2   13600  15400
    28  8 LANCER 29 MKIII SHL   SLP SAIL   FBG KL SD   8D YAN  10      7800  4  2   13700  15500
    28  8 LANCER 29 MKIII SHOA  SLP SAIL   FBG KL IB  12D- 15D  10     7800  4  2   13700  15600

    29  6 LANCER 30 MKV         SLP SAIL   FBG KL OB         10       8200  5  2   14000  15900
    29  6 LANCER 30 MKV         SLP SAIL   FBG KL SD  15  OMC  10      8200  5  2   14100  16000
    29  6 LANCER 30 MKV         SLP SAIL   FBG KL SD  8D- 15D  10     8200  5  2   14200  16200
    29  6 LANCER 30 MKV SHOAL   SLP SAIL   FBG KL OB         10       8200  4  2   14600  16600
    29  6 LANCER 30 MKV SHOAL   SLP SAIL   FBG KL SD  15  OMC  10      8200  4  2   14700  16700
    29  6 LANCER 30 MKV SHOAL   SLP SAIL   FBG KL SD  8D- 15D  10     8200  4  2   14700  16800
    36  2 LANCER 36             SLP SA/CR  FBG KL OB         11  9 10500  4  2   21900  24300
        SD   15  OMC   22300    24800, IB  15D YAN  23100  25700, IB   22D YAN   23400  26000
        IB   33D YAN   23800    26400

    36  2 LANCER 36             SLP SAIL   FBG KL OB         11  9  8600  6  2   18200  20300
        SD   15  OMC   18600    20700, IB  15D YAN  19600  21800, IB   22D YAN   19900  22100
        IB   33D YAN   20000    22200

    36  2 LANCER 36 SHOAL       SLP SA/CR  FBG KL OB         11  9 10500  4 11   22700  25200
        SD   15  OMC   23000    25600, IB  15D YAN  23800  26500, IB   22D YAN   24100  26800
        IB   33D YAN   24500    27200

    36  2 LANCER 36 SHOAL       SLP SAIL   FBG KL OB         11  9  8600  4 11   18900  21000
        SD   15  OMC   19100    21200, IB  15D YAN  19600  21800, IB   22D YAN   19900  22100
        IB   33D YAN   20600    22900

    42  7 LANCER 42             SLP SAIL   FBG KL OB         13  9 21000  6      53200  58500
        IB   62D PERK  55700    61200, IB   85D PERK  56200  61800, IB  130D PERK  57200  62900
        IB  200D PERK  57800    63500, IB T 50D PERK  57400  63100

    42  7 LANCER 42 SHOAL       SLP SAIL   FBG KL OB         13  9 21000  4 11   54800  60300
        IB   62D PERK  57300    63000, IB   85D PERK  57800  63500, IB  130D PERK  58700  64500
        IB  200D PERK  59300    65200, IB T 50D PERK  58900  64700

    44  2 LANCER 44             SLP MS     FBG KL OB         13  9 23000  6      61400  67500
        IB   85D PERK  69000    69200, IB  130D PERK  63600  69700, IB  200D PERK  77300  85000
        IB T 50D PERK  63900    70300, IB T 62D PERK  64700  71100, IB T 85D PERK  65700  72200
        IB T130D PERK  67200    73900, IB T200D PERK  68900  75700

    44  2 LANCER 44 FLYBRIDGE   SLP MS     FBG KL OB         13  9 23000  6      60800  66800
        IB   85D PERK  69000    69200, IB  130D PERK  64400  70800, IB  200D PERK  65300  71700
        IB T 50D PERK  64700    71100, IB T 62D PERK  65500  72000, IB T 85D PERK  66400  73000
        IB T130D PERK  68000    74700, IB T200D PERK  69700  76600

    44  2 LANCER 44 SHOAL       SLP MS     FBG KL OB         13  9 23000  4 11   61400  66800
        IB   85D PERK  64500    70900, IB  130D PERK  65200  71600, IB  200D PERK  65300  71700
        IB T 50D PERK  65500    72000, IB T 62D PERK  66300  72800, IB T 85D PERK  67200  73800
        IB T130D PERK  68700    75500, IB T200D PERK  70400  77400

    44  7 LANCER 45             HT  MY     FBG SV IB  130D PERK 13 9 21330  3  9   50500  60500
        IB  200D PERK  56300    61900, IB T 85D PERK  57600  63300, IB T130D PERK  51100  56200
        IB T200D PERK  59100    65000

    44  7 LANCER 45             FB  MY     FBG SV IB  130D PERK 13 9 21330  3  9   54800  60200
        IB  200D PERK  56100    61500, IB T 85D PERK  57400  63000, IB T130D PERK  51000  56000
        IB T200D PERK  58900    64700
   -------------------- 1980 BOATS -------------------------------------------------------------
    24  8 LANCER 25             SLP SAIL   FBG KL OB          8       3600  3       4600   5300
    27  8 LANCER 28             SLP SAIL   FBG KL OB          8       5200  3       7850   9050
    27  8 LANCER 28             SLP SAIL   FBG KL SD  15  OMC   8       5200  3       8100   9300
    27  8 LANCER 28             SLP SAIL   FBG KL SD      7D REN   8    5200  3       8100   9300
    28  8 LANCER 29             SLP SAIL   FBG KL OB         10       7800  5  2   12300  14000
    28  8 LANCER 29             SLP SAIL   FBG KL SD  15  OMC  10      7800  5  2   12400  14100
    28  8 LANCER 29             SLP SAIL   FBG KL SD  8D- 15D  10     7800  5  2   12500  14300
    28  8 LANCER 29 SHOAL       SLP SAIL   FBG KL OB         10       7800  4  2   12900  14600
    28  8 LANCER 29 SHOAL       SLP SAIL   FBG KL SD  15  OMC  10      7800  4  2   13000  14700
    28  8 LANCER 29 SHOAL       SLP SAIL   FBG KL SD  8D- 15D  10     7800  4  2   13100  14900
    29  6 LANCER 30             SLP SAIL   FBG KL OB         10       8200  5  2   13400  15200
```

LANCER YACHT CORP   -CONTINUED   See inside cover to adjust price for area

LOA FT IN	NAME AND/ OR MODEL	TOP/ RIG	BOAT TYPE	-HULL- MTL TP TP	----ENGINE--- # HP MFG	BEAM FT IN	WGT LBS	DRAFT FT IN	RETAIL LOW	RETAIL HIGH
---	---	---	--- 1980 BOATS	---	---	---	---	---	---	---
29 6	LANCER 30	SLP SAIL		FBG KL SD	15 OMC 10		8200	5 2	13500	15300
29 6	LANCER 30	SLP SAIL		FBG KL IB	8D- 15D 10		8200	5 2	13600	15500
29 6	LANCER 30 SHOAL	SLP SAIL		FBG KL OB	10		8200	4 2	13900	15800
29 6	LANCER 30 SHOAL	SLP SAIL		FBG KL SD	15 OMC 10		8200	4 2	14000	15900
29 6	LANCER 30 SHOAL	SLP SAIL		FBG KL IB	8D- 15D 10		8200	4 2	14100	16000
36 2	LANCER 36 CR	SLP SA/CR		FBG KL SD	15 OMC 11	9 10500	6 2	21100	23400
IB 15D YAN 21400		23800, IB		22D YAN	21500 23800, IB	33D YAN		21600	24000
36 2	LANCER 36 CR SHOAL	SLP SA/CR		FBG KL SD	15 OMC 11	9 10500	4 11	21800	24300
IB 15D YAN 22100		24500, IB		22D YAN	22200 24600, IB	33D YAN		22300	24700
36 2	LANCER 36 STD	SLP SAIL		FBG KL SD	15 OMC 11	9 8600	6 2	17200	19600
IB 15D YAN 17500		19900, IB		22D YAN	18000 20000, IB	33D YAN		18100	20100
36 2	LANCER 36 STD SHOAL	SLP SAIL		FBG KL SD	15 OMC 11	9 8600	4 11	18200	20200
IB 15D YAN 18500		20600, IB		22D YAN	18600 20600, IB	33D YAN		18700	20700
42 7	LANCER 42	SLP SAIL		FBG KL IB		13 9		6	54900	60400
44 2	LANCER 44	SLP MS		FBG KL IB	85D PERK 13	9 22000	6	57400	63100
IB 130D PERK 57800		63600, IB		200D PERK	58300 64100, IB T 50D PERK			58200	64000
IB T 62D PERK 58500		64200, IB T 85D PERK			58900 64700, IB T130D PERK			59600	65500
IB T200D PERK 60600		66600								
44 2	LANCER 44 SHOAL	SLP MS		FBG KL IB	85D PERK 13	9 22000	4 11	58900	64800
IB 130D PERK 59200		65100, IB		200D PERK	59800 65700, IB T 50D PERK			59600	65500
IB T 62D PERK 59900		65800, IB T 85D PERK			60300 66300, IB T130D PERK			61000	67000
IB T200D PERK 62000		68100								
44 7	LANCER 45	MY		FBG SV IB	D	13 9		3 9	**	**
---	---	---	--- 1979 BOATS	---	---	---	---	---	---	---
24 8	LANCER 25	SLP SAIL		FBG KL OB	8		3600	3	4400	5100
27 8	LANCER 28	SLP SAIL		FBG KL OB	8		5200	3	7550	8700
27 8	LANCER 28	SLP SAIL		FBG KL SD	15 OMC 8		5200	3	7700	8850
28 8	LANCER 29	SLP SAIL		FBG KL OB	10		7800	5 2	11800	13500
28 8	LANCER 29	SLP SAIL		FBG KL SD	15 OMC 10		7800	5 2	12000	13600
28 8	LANCER 29	SLP SAIL		FBG KL IB	8D- 15D 10		7800	5 2	12100	13800
28 8	LANCER 29 SHOAL	SLP SAIL		FBG KL OB	10		7800	4 2	12400	14000
28 8	LANCER 29 SHOAL	SLP SAIL		FBG KL SD	15 OMC 10		7800	4 2	12400	14100
28 8	LANCER 29 SHOAL	SLP SAIL		FBG KL IB	8D- 15D 10		7800	4 2	12500	14300
29 6	LANCER 30	SLP SAIL		FBG KL OB	10		8200	5 2	12900	14600
29 6	LANCER 30	SLP SAIL		FBG KL SD	15 OMC 10		8200	5 2	13000	14800
29 6	LANCER 30	SLP SAIL		FBG KL IB	8D- 15D 10		8200	5 2	13100	14900
29 6	LANCER 30 SHOAL	SLP SAIL		FBG KL OB	10		8200	4 2	13400	15200
29 6	LANCER 30 SHOAL	SLP SAIL		FBG KL SD	15 OMC 10		8200	4 2	13400	15300
29 6	LANCER 30 SHOAL	SLP SAIL		FBG KL IB	8D- 15D 10		8200	4 2	13500	15400
36 2	LANCER 36 CR	SLP SA/CR		FBG KL OB	11	9 10500	6 2	20500	22700
SD 15 OMC 20400		22700, IB		15 YAN	20600 22900, IB	22D YAN		20700	23000
IB 33D YAN 20800		23200								
36 2	LANCER 36 CR SHOAL	SLP SA/CR		FBG KL OB	11	9 10500	4 11	20900	23200
IB 15D YAN 20900		23200, IB		22D YAN	21200 23600, IB	33D YAN		21300	23700
36 2	LANCER 36 SHOAL	SLP SAIL		FBG KL OB	11	9 8600	4 11	16700	18900
SD 15 OMC 17100		19400, IB		15D YAN	17300 19700, IB	22D YAN		17400	19800
IB 33D YAN 17500		19900								
36 2	LANCER 36 STD	SLP SAIL		FBG KL SD	15 OMC 11	9 8600	6 2	16600	18900
IB 15D YAN 16900		19200, IB		22D YAN	17000 19300, IB	33D YAN		17100	19400
43 7	LANCER 44	SLP MS		FBG KL		13	8 22000	5 11	53200	58400
---	---	---	--- 1978 BOATS	---	---	---	---	---	---	---
24 8	LANCER 25	SLP SAIL		FBG KL OB	8		3600	2 10	4200	4900
27 8	LANCER 28	SLP SAIL		FBG KL OB	8		5200	2 10	7300	8400
29 6	LANCER 30	SLP SAIL		FBG KL OB	10		8000	5 2	12300	14000
29 6	LANCER 30	SLP SAIL		FBG KL SD	15 OMC 10		8000	5 2	12400	14100
29 6	LANCER 30	SLP SAIL		FBG KL IB	8D- 12D 10		8000	5 2	12500	14200
36 2	LANCER 36	SLP SAIL		FBG KL OB	11		10500	5 11	19700	21900
IB 12D YAN 20100		22400, IB		14D YAN	20100 22400, IB	22D YAN		20200	22500
---	---	---	--- 1977 BOATS	---	---	---	---	---	---	---
23 6	LANCER 23	SLP SAIL		FBG KL EL	8		2700	2 4	**	**
23 6	LANCER 23	SLP SAIL		FBG KL OB	8		2700	2 4	3000	3450
23 6	LANCER 23	SLP SAIL		FBG KL IB	10 BALD 8		2700	2 4	3200	3700
24 8	LANCER 25	SLP SAIL		FBG KL EL	8		3400	2 4	**	**
24 8	LANCER 25	SLP SAIL		FBG KL OB	8		3400	2 4	3850	4500
24 8	LANCER 25	SLP SAIL		FBG KL IB	10 BALD 8		3400	2 4	4050	4700
27 8	LANCER 28	SLP SAIL		FBG KL IB	10 BALD 8		4700	2 10	6350	7300
27 8	LANCER 28	SLP SAIL		FBG KL IB	10 BALD 8		4700	2 10	6450	7450
27 8	LANCER 28	SLP SAIL		FBG KL IB	8D PETT 8		4700	2 10	6600	7600
29 6	LANCER 30	SLP SAIL		FBG KL IB	7D PETT 9 10		6300	4 6	9450	10700
---	---	---	--- 1976 BOATS	---	---	---	---	---	---	---
23 6	WILLARD 23	SLP SAIL		FBG KL OB	8		2700	2 4	2900	3350
24 8	WILLARD 25	SLP SAIL		FBG KL OB	8		3400	2 4	3750	4350
24 8	WILLARD 25	SLP SAIL		FBG KL IB	10 BALD 8		3400	2 4	3950	4550
27 8	WILLARD 28	SLP SAIL		FBG KL IB	8		4700	2 10	6150	7100
27 8	WILLARD 28	SLP SAIL		FBG KL IB	10 BALD 8		4700	2 10	6250	7200
27 8	WILLARD 28	SLP SAIL		FBG KL IB	8D PETT 8		4700	2 10	6400	7350
29 5	WILLARD 30	SLP SAIL		FBG KL IB	D	9 8	6300	4 5	9250	10500
---	---	---	--- 1975 BOATS	---	---	---	---	---	---	---
24 8	LANCER 25	SLP SAIL		FBG KL OB	8		3400	2 4	3650	4250

LANCRAFT
COAST GUARD MFG ID- LCM

Call 1-800-327-6929 for BUC Personalized Evaluation Service
Or, for 1972 to 1973 boats, sign onto www.BUCValuPro.com

LAND & SEA INT'L
DIV CALIFORNIA LAND & SEA INC   See inside cover to adjust price for area
SANTA CLARA CA 95054   COAST GUARD MFG ID- LND

LOA FT IN	NAME AND/ OR MODEL	TOP/ RIG	BOAT TYPE	-HULL- MTL TP TP	----ENGINE--- # HP MFG	BEAM FT IN	WGT LBS	DRAFT FT IN	RETAIL LOW	RETAIL HIGH
---	---	---	--- 1979 BOATS	---	---	---	---	---	---	---
28	TRAIL-A-CRUISER	HT	CBNCR	F/S TR IO	225 CHRY 8		7000	1 2	20800	23100
28	TRAIL-A-CRUISER	HT	CBNCR	F/S TR IO	225-240	8		7000	1 2	20800	23400
28	TRAIL-A-CRUISER	FB	CBNCR	F/S TR IO	T140 VLVO 8		7000	1 2	22300	24700
---	---	---	--- 1978 BOATS	---	---	---	---	---	---	---
28	TRAIL-A-CRUISER	HT	CBNCR	F/S TR IO	240-260	8		7500	1 6	21800	24700
28	TRAIL-A-CRUISER	HT	CBNCR	F/S TR IO	T170 VLVO 8		7500	1 6	23600	26200
28	TRAIL-A-CRUISER	FB	CBNCR	F/S TR IO	240-260	8		7500	1 6	21800	24700
28	TRAIL-A-CRUISER	FB	CBNCR	F/S TR IO	T170 VLVO 8		7500	1 6	23600	26200
---	---	---	--- 1977 BOATS	---	---	---	---	---	---	---
28	TRAIL-A-CRUISER	HT	CBNCR	F/S TR IO	225-250	8		6000	1 2	20300	23000
28	TRAIL-A-CRUISER	HT	CBNCR	F/S TR IO	T170 VLVO 8		7500	1 2	23900	26600
28	TRAIL-A-CRUISER	FB	CBNCR	F/S TR IO	225-250	8		6000	1 2	20300	23000
28	TRAIL-A-CRUISER	FB	CBNCR	F/S TR IO	T170 VLVO 8		7500	1 6	23900	26600
---	---	---	--- 1976 BOATS	---	---	---	---	---	---	---
28	TRAIL-A-CRUISER I	HT	CBNCR	FBG TR IO	225 CHRY 8		7000	1 2	21800	24200
28	TRAIL-A-CRUISER II	HT	CBNCR	FBG TR IO	225 CHRY 8		7000	1 2	21800	24200
28	TRAIL-A-CRUISER III	HT	CBNCR	FBG TR IO	T170 VLVO 8		7000	1 2	23700	26300
28	TRAIL-A-CRUISER III	FB	CBNCR	FBG TR IO	T170 VLVO 8		7000	1 2	23700	26300
---	---	---	--- 1975 BOATS	---	---	---	---	---	---	---
28	TRAIL-A-CRUISER	HT	CBNCR	FBG TR IO	170 CHRY	6000	1 2	20700	23000
28	TRAIL-A-CRUISER	HT	CBNCR	FBG TR IO	T170 CHRY	6000	1 2	23700	26300
38	TRAIL-A-CRUISER	FB	CBNCR	FBG TR IO	225 CHRY	6000	1 2	44200	49100
38	TRAIL-A-CRUISER	FB	CBNCR	FBG TR IO	T250 CHRY	6000	1 2	46800	51400
---	---	---	--- 1974 BOATS	---	---	---	---	---	---	---
28	TRAIL-A-CRUISER	FB	CBNCR	FBG TR IO	270 CHRY	5900	1 2	22700	25200
28	TRAIL-A-CRUISER	FB	CBNCR	FBG TR IO	T170 CHRY	6200	1 3	23600	26200
---	---	---	--- 1973 BOATS	---	---	---	---	---	---	---
28	LAND-N-SEA	HB		FBG	IO 200-270	8		5200	1 2	**	**
28	LAND-N-SEA	HB		FBG	IO 105D CHRY	8		5200	1 2	**	**
28	LAND-N-SEA	HB		FBG	IO T130-T170	8		5200	1 2	**	**
28	LAND-N-SEA	FB	HB	FBG	IO 200-270	8			1 2	**	**
28	LAND-N-SEA	FB	HB	FBG	IO 105D CHRY	8			1 2	**	**
28	LAND-N-SEA	FB	HB	FBG	IO T130-T170	8			1 2	**	**
28	MATADOR 28	CR		FBG	OB	8		3900		16000	18100
---	---	---	--- 1972 BOATS	---	---	---	---	---	---	---
28	LAND-N-SEA	HB		FBG	IO 200-225	8		5200	1 2	**	**
28	LAND-N-SEA	HB		FBG	IO 215 OMC	8			1 2	**	**
28	LAND-N-SEA	HT	HB	FBG	IO T170	8			1 2	**	**
28	LAND-N-SEA	HT	HB	FBG	IO 200D	8			1 2	**	**
28	LAND-N-SEA	FB	HB	FBG	IO 200-225	8			1 2	**	**
28	LAND-N-SEA	FB	HB	FBG	IO T170-T215	8			1 2	**	**
28	LAND-N-SEA	FB	HB	FBG	IO T200D	8			1 2	**	**

LAND N' SEA WEST

Call 1-800-327-6929 for BUC Personalized Evaluation Service
Or, for 1980 to 1986 boats, sign onto www.BUCValuPro.com

LANDAU BOATS INC
LEBANON MO 65536   COAST GUARD MFG ID- LBO See inside cover to adjust price for area
                          FORMERLY LANDAU MANUFACTURING CO

For more recent years, see the BUC Used Boat Price Guide, Volume 1 or Volume 2

LOA FT IN	NAME AND/ OR MODEL	TOP/ RIG	BOAT TYPE	-HULL- MTL TP	----ENGINE--- TP # HP MFG	BEAM FT IN	WGT LBS	DRAFT FT IN	RETAIL LOW	RETAIL HIGH
--- 1979 BOATS ---
16	1675 VPB	OP	BASS	AL DV	OB	6 3	650		1800	2100
16	CHEROKEE	OP	RNBT	AL DV	OB	6 4	755		2100	2500

THE LANDING SCHOOL
KENNEBNKPRT ME 04046   COAST GUARD MFG ID- LKS See inside cover to adjust price for area
                          ALSO LANDING SCHOOL OF BOAT BLDG

For more recent years, see the BUC Used Boat Price Guide, Volume 1 or Volume 2

LOA FT IN	NAME AND/ OR MODEL	TOP/ RIG	BOAT TYPE	-HULL- MTL TP	----ENGINE--- TP # HP MFG	BEAM FT IN	WGT LBS	DRAFT FT IN	RETAIL LOW	RETAIL HIGH
--- 1983 BOATS ---
16	CATBOAT	CAT	SAIL	CDR CB		7 6	2500	2 2	7200	8300
17	SWAMPSCOTT-DORY	GAF	SAIL	WD CB		4 3	250	6	2300	2650
17 8	CONCORDIA SLOOP	GAF	SAIL	WD CB		5 6	1200	1 6	4700	5400
18 1	O-BOAT	SLP	SAIL	WD CB		6 8	1200	1 6	4700	5400
18 8	BUZZARDS-BAY SLOOP	GAF	SAIL	WD KC		6	2000	2 6	6200	7100
--- 1982 BOATS ---
16	CATBOAT	SLP	SAIL	CDR CB		7 6	2500	2 2	6800	7800
18 1	O-BOAT	SLP	SAIL	WD CB		6 8	800	1 2	3600	4200
18 8	BUZZARDS-BAY SLOOP	GAF	SAIL	WD KC		6	1600	1 10	5150	5900

LANG YACHTS
ROCKLAND ME 04841   COAST GUARD MFG ID- LAN See inside cover to adjust price for area

LOA FT IN	NAME AND/ OR MODEL	TOP/ RIG	BOAT TYPE	-HULL- MTL TP	----ENGINE--- TP # HP MFG	BEAM FT IN	WGT LBS	DRAFT FT IN	RETAIL LOW	RETAIL HIGH
--- 1971 BOATS ---
27 3	LANG		FB	SDN	FBG	IB 250-325	11 2	8100	2 8	12600	15200
27 3	LANG		FB	SDN	FBG	IB 155D PALM	11 2	9000	2 8	20300	22600
31 1	LANG		FB	SDN	FBG	IB T277 SEA	12 2	14400	3 1	24700	27400
31 3	LANG		FB	SDN	FBG	IBT155D-T220D	12 2	16000	3 1	37800	44700
31 3	LANG		FB	SDN	FBG	IB T370D CUM	12 2	17200	3 1	47600	52400
31 3	LANG		FB	SDN	FBG	IB T155D PALM	13 8	19400	3 4	37400	41600
37 3	LANG		FB	SDN	FBG	IB 19400	13 8				
	IB T220D CRUS 39000	43300, IB T310D GM		43100	47800, IB T370D CUM				44200	49200
64 11 650			MY	FBG	IB T523D GM	22	85000	4	227500	250000
--- 1969 BOATS ---
27 3	LANG 280		SF	FBG	IB 210	11 2	8100	2 8	10800	12200
27 3	LANG 280S		FB	SDN	FBG	IB 210	11 2	8100	2 8	11400	13000
31 3	LANG 330		SF	FBG	IB 210	12 2	14400	3 1	19300	21400
31 3	LANG 330S		FB	SDN	FBG	IB 210	12 2	14400	3 1	20000	22200
37 3	LANG 400		FB	CNV	FBG	IB T210	13 8	19400	3 4	30500	33900

LANPHERE & SON MARINE
WESTPORT WA 98595   See inside cover to adjust price for area

LOA FT IN	NAME AND/ OR MODEL	TOP/ RIG	BOAT TYPE	-HULL- MTL TP	----ENGINE--- TP # HP MFG	BEAM FT IN	WGT LBS	DRAFT FT IN	RETAIL LOW	RETAIL HIGH
--- 1982 BOATS ---
64 10 JJ 65		SF	FBG DV	IB T650D		19 3	75000		332500	365500
74 10 JJ 75		SF	FBG DV	IB T650D		19 3	85000		**	**

LANTANA BOATYARD INC
LANTANA FL 33462   COAST GUARD MFG ID- LBY See inside cover to adjust price for area

LOA FT IN	NAME AND/ OR MODEL	TOP/ RIG	BOAT TYPE	-HULL- MTL TP	----ENGINE--- TP # HP MFG	BEAM FT IN	WGT LBS	DRAFT FT IN	RETAIL LOW	RETAIL HIGH
--- 1973 BOATS ---
65	LANTANA		MY	AL SV	IB T525D	22			261000	287000
72	LANTANA		MY	AL SV	IB T525D	18			**	**
--- 1970 BOATS ---
72	SEMI-CUSTOM 72		MY	AL SV	IB T525D GM	18		4 9	**	**
--- 1969 BOATS ---
16	REBEL		SLP	SAIL	FBG CB		6 6	700		2150	2550
65 3	RESOLUTE		MY	FBG SV	IB T336D	17		4 9	195000	214000
68 10	RANGER		MY	AL SV	IB T215D	19		4 5	224500	246500
69 9	AMERICA		MY	AL SV	IB T478D	17 9		4 6	239500	263000
72	COLUMBIA		MY	AL SV	IB T336	17 3		4 6	**	**
--- 1968 BOATS ---
16	REBEL		SLP	SA/OD	FBG CB		6 6	700	7	2100	2500
17	AZTEC		RNBT	FBG	OB		7	1250		1950	2350
17	SPORTCRAFT		RNBT	FBG	OB		7	1200		1900	2250
17	HYDRODIVE		RNBT	FBG	OB		7	1100		1750	2100
18 3	FIBERCRAFT		RNBT	FBG	OB		7 5	1400		2250	2650
20	ALIM V-20		RNBT	FBG	OB		8	1600		2850	3350
23 3	FORMULA		RNBT	FBG	OB		8	1800		3550	4100
64	RESOLUTE		SF	FBG	IB T225	17		4 6	**	**
64	RESOLUTE		SF	FBG	IB T478	17		4 6	**	**
65	RESOLUTE		CR	FBG	IB T225	17		4 6	175500	192500
65	RESOLUTE		CR	FBG	IB T478	17		4 6	177500	195000
68 9	RANGER		MY	AL	IB T225	19		4 6	196000	215500
72	COLUMBIA		MY	AL	IB T478	17		4 6	**	**

LARSEN MARINA

Call 1-800-327-6929 for BUC Personalized Evaluation Service
Or, for 1961 boats, sign onto www.BUCValuPro.com

LARSHIP INC
COAST GUARD MFG ID- LSH

Call 1-800-327-6929 for BUC Personalized Evaluation Service
Or, for 1974 to 1976 boats, sign onto www.BUCValuPro.com

LARSON BOATS
DIV OF GENMAR INDUSTRIES   See inside cover to adjust price for area
LITTLE FALLS MN 56345   COAST GUARD MFG ID- LAR
                          FORMERLY LUND AMERICAN

For more recent years, see the BUC Used Boat Price Guide, Volume 1 or Volume 2

LOA FT IN	NAME AND/ OR MODEL	TOP/ RIG	BOAT TYPE	-HULL- MTL TP	----ENGINE--- TP # HP MFG	BEAM FT IN	WGT LBS	DRAFT FT IN	RETAIL LOW	RETAIL HIGH
--- 1983 BOATS ---
16 2	ALL-AMERICAN 5000B/R	OP	RNBT	FBG SV	OB	6 8	1000		1750	2050
16 2	ALL-AMERICAN 5000B/R	ST	RNBT	FBG SV	OB	6 8	1700		1950	2300
16 2	ALL-AMERICAN 5000B/R	ST	RNBT	FBG SV	IO 120 MRCR	6 8	1700		1900	2250
16 2	ALL-AMERICAN 5000B/R	ST	RNBT	FBG SV	IO 120 OMC	6 8	1700		2050	2450
17 2	CITATION 5500	OP	RNBT	FBG SV	OB	6 11	1100		1950	2300
17 2	CITATION 5500	ST	RNBT	FBG SV	OB	6 11	1850		2250	2750
17 2	CITATION 5500 B/R	OP	RNBT	FBG SV	OB	6 11	1150		2000	2400
17 2	CITATION 5500 B/R	ST	RNBT	FBG SV	IO 120-188	6 11	1900		2500	2800
17 2	CITATION 5500 SE	OP	RNBT	FBG SV	IO 120-188	6 11	1900		2250	2800
19 5	FARALLON 6500	OP	RNBT	FBG DV	IO 170-200	7 8	2600		3300	4000
19 5	FARALLON 6500	OP	RNBT	FBG DV	IO 225-260	7 8	2600		3550	4300
19 5	FARALLON 6500 B/R	ST	RNBT	FBG DV	IO 170-230	7 8	2600		3150	3950
19 5	FARALLON 6500 B/R	ST	RNBT	FBG DV	IO 260 MRCR	7 8	3050		3450	3950
19 5	FARALLON 6500 B/R	ST	RNBT	FBG DV	IO 260	7 8	3060		3650	4250
19 5	NANTUCKET EXP 6500	ST	RNBT	FBG DV	IO 170-230	7 8	2800		3450	4300
19 5	NANTUCKET EXP 6500	CUD	RNBT	FBG DV	IO 260	7 8	2800		3400	4450
21 3	DELTA-SPORT 7000	ST	SPTCR	FBG DV	IO 170-260	8	2900		4400	5350
22	NANTUCKET 7500	OP	EXP	FBG DV	IO 170-230	7 11	3500		5100	6200
22	NANTUCKET 7500	OP	EXP	FBG DV	IO 260	7 11	3500		5350	6400
23 2	ADMIRAL DAY 8000	ST	CR	FBG DV	IO 175-260	8	3000		5100	6000
--- 1982 BOATS ---
16 1	ALL AMER CHAL 5000BR	ST	RNBT	FBG	IO 120	6 8	1618		1850	2200
16 1	WILDFIRE 5000	OP	RNBT	FBG SV	IO 120	6 3			1950	2300
16 2	ALL-AMERICAN 5000	ST	RNBT	FBG SV	IO 120 MRCR	6 9	1775		1950	2300
16 2	ALL-AMERICAN 5000	ST	RNBT	FBG SV	IO 120 OMC	6 9	1775		1900	2250
16 2	ALL-AMERICAN 5000	ST	RNBT	FBG SV	IO 120-185	6 9	1775		2050	2450
16 2	ALL-AMERICAN 5000	OP	RNBT	FBG SV	OB	6 9	1030		1750	2050
16 2	ALL-AMERICAN 5000B/R	ST	RNBT	FBG SV	IO 120 MRCR	6 9	1765		1950	2300
16 2	ALL-AMERICAN 5000B/R	ST	RNBT	FBG SV	IO 120 OMC	6 9	1768		1900	2300
16 2	ALL-AMERICAN 5000B/R	ST	RNBT	FBG SV	IO 120-185	6 9	1768		2050	2450
17 2	CITATION 5500	OP	RNBT	FBG SV	OB	6 11	1148		1950	2350

LOA FT	LOA IN	NAME AND/ OR MODEL	TOP/ RIG	BOAT TYPE	-HULL- MTL	-HULL- TP	TP	ENGINE # HP	ENGINE MFG	BEAM FT	BEAM IN	WGT LBS	DRAFT FT IN	RETAIL LOW	RETAIL HIGH
		1982 BOATS													
17	2	CITATION 5500	ST	RNBT	FBG	SV	IO	120-200		6	11	1939		2250	2800
17	2	CITATION 5500 B/R	OP	RNBT	FBG	SV	OB			6	11	1220		2050	2450
17	2	CITATION 5500 B/R	ST	RNBT	FBG	SV	IO	120-198		6	11	1890		2200	2700
17	2	CITATION 5500 B/R	ST	RNBT	FBG	SV	IO	200		6	11	1890		2250	2750
17	2	CITATION 5500 SPORT	OP	RNBT	FBG	DV	IO	120-200		6	11	1950		2250	2800
17	2	CITATION CHAL 5500BR	OP	RNBT	FBG	DV	OB			6	11	1120		1900	2300
17	2	CITATION CHAL 5500BR	ST	RNBT	FBG	DV	IO	140	MRCR	6	11	1790		2150	2500
17	2	CITATION CHAL 5500BR	ST	RNBT	FBG	DV	IO	470	MRCR	6	11	1790		5300	6100
17	2	MANTA 5500	OP	RNBT	FBG	TR	OB			6	10	1100		1900	2250
17	2	MANTA 5500	ST	RNBT	FBG	TR	IO	120-185		6	10	1860		2200	2700
18	3	ALL-AMERICAN 5500	OP	RNBT	FBG	SV	OB			7	2	1275		2250	2600
18	3	ALL-AMERICAN 5500	ST	RNBT	FBG	SV	IO	140-200		7	2	2145		2500	3150
18	3	ALL-AMERICAN 5500	ST	RNBT	FBG	SV	IO	225-260		7	2	2145		2750	3200
18	3	ALL-AMERICAN 5500B/R	OP	RNBT	FBG	SV	OB			7	2	1360		2350	2750
18	3	ALL-AMERICAN 5500B/R	ST	RNBT	FBG	SV	IO	140-200		7	2	2145		2500	3150
18	3	ALL-AMERICAN 5500B/R	ST	RNBT	FBG	SV	IO	225-260		7	2	2145		2750	3200
19	1	MANTA 6000	OP	RNBT	FBG	TR	OB			7	6	1440		2500	2900
19	1	MANTA 6000	OP	RNBT	FBG	TR	IO	170		7	6			2800	3300
21	2	COMMANDER EXP 7000	HT	EXP	FBG	DV	IO	198		7	6			4400	5050
21	3	DELTA DAY 7000	ST	CR	FBG	DV	IO	198-260		8		2840		4250	5150
21	3	DELTA-SPORT 7000	ST	SPTCR	FBG	DV	IO	170-260		8		2840		4200	5200
23	2	ADMIRAL DAY 8000	ST	CR	FBG	DV	IO	185-260		8		3315		5150	6200
24	7	DELTA SPORT CR 8500	ST	SPTCR	FBG	DV	IO	198-260		7	11			8350	9600
24	7	DELTA SPORT CR 8500	ST	SPTCR	FBG	DV	IO	T185	MRCR	8		4353		7600	8750
		1981 BOATS													
16	1	WILDFIRE 5000	OP	RNBT	FBG	SV	IO	170-198		6	6	1575		1800	2150
16	1	WILDFIRE 5000	OP	RNBT	FBG	SV	IO	200	OMC	6	6	1575		1800	2100
16	1	WILDFIRE 5000	OP	RNBT	FBG	SV	IO	200	VLVO	6	6	1575		1950	2300
16	2	ALL-AMERICAN 5000	ST	RNBT	FBG	SV	IO	120	MRCR	6	9	1775		1900	2250
16	2	ALL-AMERICAN 5000	ST	RNBT	FBG	SV	IO	120	OMC	6	9	1775		1900	2250
16	2	ALL-AMERICAN 5000	ST	RNBT	FBG	SV	IO	120-200		6	9	1775		2050	2500
16	2	ALL-AMERICAN 5000B/R	ST	RNBT	FBG	SV	OB			6	9	1030		1700	2000
16	2	ALL-AMERICAN 5000B/R	ST	RNBT	FBG	SV	IO	120	MRCR	6	9	1765		1900	2250
16	2	ALL-AMERICAN 5000B/R	ST	RNBT	FBG	SV	IO	120	OMC	6	9	1768		1900	2250
16	2	ALL-AMERICAN 5000B/R	ST	RNBT	FBG	SV	IO	120-200		6	9	1768		2050	2500
17	2	CITATION 5500	ST	RNBT	FBG	SV	OB			6	11	1148		1900	2250
17	2	CITATION 5500	ST	RNBT	FBG	SV	IO	120-200		6	11	1939		2200	2750
17	2	CITATION 5500 B/R	ST	RNBT	FBG	SV	OB			6	11	1220		2000	2400
17	2	CITATION 5500 B/R	ST	RNBT	FBG	SV	IO	120-198		6	11	1890		2150	2700
17	2	CITATION 5500 B/R	ST	RNBT	FBG	SV	IO	200		6	11	1890		2200	2700
17	2	MANTA 5500	ST	RNBT	FBG	TR	OB			6	10	1100		1850	2200
17	2	MANTA 5500	ST	RNBT	FBG	TR	IO	120	MRCR	6	10	1860		2100	2500
17	2	MANTA 5500	ST	RNBT	FBG	TR	IO	120	OMC	6	10	1860		2050	2450
17	2	MANTA 5500	ST	RNBT	FBG	TR	IO	120-200		6	10	1860		2250	2700
18	3	ALL-AMERICAN 5500	ST	RNBT	FBG	SV	OB			7	2	1275		2200	2550
18	3	ALL-AMERICAN 5500	ST	RNBT	FBG	SV	IO	140-198		6	10	2145		2400	2950
18	3	ALL-AMERICAN 5500	ST	RNBT	FBG	SV	IO	200		7	2	2145		2550	3050
18	3	ALL-AMERICAN 5500	ST	RNBT	FBG	SV	IO	225-260		7	2	2145		2700	3150
18	3	ALL-AMERICAN 5500B/R	ST	RNBT	FBG	SV	OB			7	2	1360		2300	2700
18	3	ALL-AMERICAN 5500B/R	ST	RNBT	FBG	SV	IO	140-200		7	2	2145		2500	3050
18	3	ALL-AMERICAN 5500B/R	ST	RNBT	FBG	SV	IO	225-260		7	2	2145		2700	3150
19	1	MANTA 6000	ST	RNBT	FBG	TR	OB			7	7	1440		2450	2850
19	1	MANTA 6000	ST	RNBT	FBG	TR	IO	165-200		7	7	2310		2800	3450
19	1	MANTA 6000	ST	RNBT	FBG	TR	IO	225-260		7	7	2310		3050	3500
21	2	COMMANDER EXP 7000	HT	EXP	FBG	DV	IO	170-260		7	10	3570		4750	5750
21	3	DELTA-SPORT 7000	ST	SPTCR	FBG	DV	IO	140-260		8		2840		4100	5100
23	2	ADMIRAL DAY 8000	ST	CR	FBG	DV	IO	185-260		8		3315		5100	6100
23	2	ADMIRAL DAY 8000	ST	CR	FBG	DV	IO	T120-T170		8		3315		5700	6900
23	2	ADMIRAL DUAL 8000	FB	EXP	FBG	DV	IO	198-260		8		3936		5750	6850
24	7	DELTA SPORT CR 8500	ST	SPTCR	FBG	DV	IO	185-260		8		4353		6600	7950
24	7	DELTA SPORT CR 8500	ST	SPTCR	FBG	DV	IO	T120-T185		8		4353		7250	8600
		1980 BOATS													
16	1	WILDFIRE 5000	OP	RNBT	FBG	SV	IO	170-198		6	6	1575		1750	2150
16	1	WILDFIRE 5000	OP	RNBT	FBG	SV	IO	200	OMC	6	6	1575		1750	2100
16	1	WILDFIRE 5000	OP	RNBT	FBG	SV	IO	200	VLVO	6	6	1575		1950	2300
16	2	ALL-AMERICAN 5000	ST	RNBT	FBG	SV	IO	120	MRCR	6	9	1765		1850	2200
16	2	ALL-AMERICAN 5000	ST	RNBT	FBG	SV	IO	120	OMC	6	9	1765		1850	2200
16	2	ALL-AMERICAN 5000	ST	RNBT	FBG	SV	IO	120-200		6	9	1765		1950	2450
16	2	ALL-AMERICAN 5000B/R	ST	RNBT	FBG	SV	IO	120	MRCR	6	9	1765		1950	2300
16	2	ALL-AMERICAN 5000B/R	ST	RNBT	FBG	SV	IO	120	OMC	6	9	1765		1900	2250
16	2	ALL-AMERICAN 5000B/R	ST	RNBT	FBG	SV	IO	120-200		6	9	1765		2050	2500
16	4	MANTA 5000		RNBT	FBG	SV	OB			6	6	1355		2150	2500
17	2	CITATION 5500	ST	RNBT	FBG	SV	OB			6	11	1148		1850	2200
17	2	CITATION 5500	ST	RNBT	FBG	SV	IO	120-200		6	11	1939		2200	2700
17	2	CITATION 5500 B/R	ST	RNBT	FBG	SV	OB			6	11	1220		1950	2350
17	2	CITATION 5500 B/R	ST	RNBT	FBG	SV	IO	120-198		6	11	1890		2150	2650
17	2	CITATION 5500 B/R	ST	RNBT	FBG	SV	IO	200		6	11	1890		2200	2700
17	2	MANTA 5500	ST	RNBT	FBG	TR	OB			6	10	1100		1800	2150
17	2	MANTA 5500	ST	RNBT	FBG	TR	IO	120	MRCR	6	10	1860		2050	2450
17	2	MANTA 5500	ST	RNBT	FBG	TR	IO	120	OMC	6	10	1860		2050	2450
17	2	MANTA 5500	ST	RNBT	FBG	TR	IO	120-200		6	10	1860		2250	2700
18	3	ALL-AMERICAN 5500	ST	RNBT	FBG	SV	OB			7	2	1275		2100	2500
18	3	ALL-AMERICAN 5500	ST	RNBT	FBG	SV	IO	140-198		6	10	2145		2400	2900
18	3	ALL-AMERICAN 5500	ST	RNBT	FBG	SV	IO	200		7	2	2145		2500	3050
18	3	ALL-AMERICAN 5500	ST	RNBT	FBG	SV	IO	225-260		7	2	2145		2700	3150
18	3	ALL-AMERICAN 5500B/R	ST	RNBT	FBG	SV	OB			7	2	1360		2250	2600
18	3	ALL-AMERICAN 5500B/R	ST	RNBT	FBG	SV	IO	140-198		7	2	1360		2100	2550
18	3	ALL-AMERICAN 5500B/R	ST	RNBT	FBG	SV	IO	200	OMC	7	2	1360		2100	2500
18	3	ALL-AMERICAN 5500B/R	ST	RNBT	FBG	SV	IO	200-260		7	2	1360		2300	2750
19	1	MANTA 6000	ST	RNBT	FBG	TR	OB			7	7	1440		2400	2800
19	1	MANTA 6000	ST	RNBT	FBG	TR	IO	165-200		7	7	2310		2750	3400
19	1	MANTA 6000	ST	RNBT	FBG	TR	IO	225-260		7	7	2310		3000	3500
21	2	COMMANDER EXP 7000	HT	EXP	FBG	DV	IO	170-260		7	10	3570		4700	5700
21	3	DELTA-SPORT 7000	ST	SPTCR	FBG	DV	IO	140-260		8		2840		4050	5050
21	3	DELTA-SPORT 7000	HT	SPTCR	FBG	DV	IO	140-260		8		3090		4300	5300
23	2	ADMIRAL DAY 8000	ST	CR	FBG	DV	IO	198-260		8		3315		5050	6050
23	2	ADMIRAL DAY 8000	ST	CR	FBG	DV	IO	T120-T170		8		3315		5650	6850
25	10	FLEETMASTER 9000	HT	EXP	FBG	DV	IO	198-260		8		5520		8200	9800
25	10	FLEETMASTER 9000	HT	EXP	FBG	DV	IO	T120-T170		8		5520		8850	10500
		1979 BOATS													
16	1	WILDFIRE 5000	OP	RNBT	FBG	SV	IO	170-198		6	3	1650		1750	2150
16	1	WILDFIRE 5000	OP	RNBT	FBG	SV	IO	200	OMC	6	3	1650		1800	2100
16	1	WILDFIRE 5000	OP	RNBT	FBG	SV	IO	200	VLVO	6	3	1650		1950	2300
16	2	ALL-AMERICAN 5000	ST	RNBT	FBG	SV	OB			6	5	1240		1900	2300
16	2	ALL-AMERICAN 5000	ST	RNBT	FBG	SV	IO	140	MRCR	6	5	1733		1850	2200
16	2	ALL-AMERICAN 5000	ST	RNBT	FBG	SV	IO	140	OMC	6	5	1733		1800	2150
16	2	ALL-AMERICAN 5000	ST	RNBT	FBG	SV	IO	140-200		6	5	1733		1950	2400
16	5	MANTA 5000	ST	RNBT	FBG	TR	OB			6	6	1355		2050	2450
16	5	MANTA 5000	ST	RNBT	FBG	TR	IO	140	MRCR	6	6	1980		2000	2400
16	5	MANTA 5000	ST	RNBT	FBG	TR	IO	140	OMC	6	6	1980		2000	2350
16	5	MANTA 5000	ST	RNBT	FBG	TR	IO	140-200		6	6	1980		2150	2600
17	2	MANTA 5500	ST	RNBT	FBG	TR	OB			6	9	1290		2000	2400
17	2	MANTA 5500	ST	RNBT	FBG	TR	IO	140-200		6	9	2248		2300	2900
18	3	ALL-AMERICAN 5500	ST	RNBT	FBG	SV	OB			6	10	1600		2500	2900
18	3	ALL-AMERICAN 5500	ST	RNBT	FBG	SV	IO	170-200		6	10	2400		2550	3150
18	3	ALL-AMERICAN 5500	ST	RNBT	FBG	SV	IO	225-260		6	10	2400		2800	3250
19	1	MANTA 6000	ST	RNBT	FBG	TR	OB			7	6	1705		2600	3000
19	1	MANTA 6000	ST	RNBT	FBG	TR	IO	170-200		7	6	2660		2950	3650
19	1	MANTA 6000	ST	RNBT	FBG	TR	IO	225-260		7	6	2660		3200	3700
21	2	COMMANDER DAY 7000	ST	CR	FBG	DV	IO	198-260		8		2845		4100	5050
21	2	COMMANDER EXP 7000	ST	EXP	FBG	DV	IO	198-260		8		3185		4450	5400
21	2	COMMANDER EXP 7000	HT	EXP	FBG	DV	IO	198-260		8		3185		4450	5400
21	5	COMMANDER CUDDY 7000	ST	CUD	FBG	DV	IO	198-260		8		3010		4350	5250
23	2	ADMIRAL CUDDY 8000	ST	CUD	FBG	DV	IO	198-260		7	10	4350		6100	7300
23	2	ADMIRAL DAY 8000	ST	CR	FBG	DV	IO	198-260		7	10	3315		5000	6000
25	10	FLEETMASTER 9000	HT	EXP	FBG	DV	IO	198-260		7	10	5519		8150	9750
25	10	FLEETMASTER 9000	HT	EXP	FBG	DV	IO	T140-T170		7	10	5519		8900	10400
		1978 BOATS													
16	1	WILDFIRE	OP	RNBT	FBG	SV	IO	120		6	6	1650		1800	2150
		IO 140 MRCR 1800 2150, IO 140 OMC 1800 2100, IO 140-228												1900	2300
16	2	ALL-AMERICAN 160	ST	RNBT	FBG	SV	OB			6	9	1240		1900	2250
16	2	ALL-AMERICAN 160	ST	RNBT	FBG	SV	IO	120		6	9	1733		1900	2250
		IO 140 MRCR 1900 2250, IO 140 OMC 1850 2200, IO 140-170												2000	2400
16	5	FORCE 16 B/R	ST	RNBT	FBG	*	OB			6	7	1355		2050	2400
16	5	FORCE 16 B/R	ST	RNBT	FBG	*	IO	120		6	7	1600		1800	2150
		IO 140 MRCR 1800 2150, IO 140 OMC 1800 2150, IO 140-185												1950	2300
17	2	MANTA 175	ST	RNBT	FBG	TR	OB			6	11	1290		1950	2350
17	2	MANTA 175	ST	RNBT	FBG	TR	IO	120-185		6	11	2248		2350	2850
17	3	ALL-AMERICAN 170	ST	RNBT	FBG	SV	OB			7	2	1105		1750	2050
17	3	ALL-AMERICAN 170	ST	RNBT	FBG	SV	IO	140-200		7	2	1968		2250	2800
17	3	ALL-AMERICAN 170	ST	RNBT	FBG	SV	IO	225		7	2	1968		2350	2900
18		ALL-AMERICAN 186	ST	RNBT	FBG	SV	OB			6	10	1335		2050	2450
18		ALL-AMERICAN 186	ST	RNBT	FBG	SV	IO	140-198		6	11	2260		2450	3000

CONTINUED ON NEXT PAGE

LOA FT	IN	NAME AND/ OR MODEL	TOP/ RIG	BOAT TYPE	-HULL- MTL	TP	----ENGINE--- TP	# HP	MFG	BEAM FT	IN	WGT LBS	DRAFT FT	IN	RETAIL LOW	RETAIL HIGH
		1978 BOATS														
18		ALL-AMERICAN 186	ST	RNBT	FBG	SV	IO	200-250		6	11	2260			2650	3150
18	1	SEAFAIR SEDAN 180	ST	CAMPR	FBG	SV	OB			7	4	1400			2150	2500
18	1	SEAFAIR SEDAN 180	ST	CAMPR	FBG	SV	IO	140-185		7	4	2300			2650	3200
18	3	CHARGER	ST	RNBT	FBG	*	OB			7	2	1600			2450	2850
18	3	CHARGER	ST	RNBT	FBG	*	IO	140-200		7	2	2400			2600	3250
18	3	CHARGER	ST	RNBT	FBG	*	IO	225-250		7	2	2400			2700	3350
19	1	MANTA 195	ST	RNBT	FBG	TR	OB			7	7	1705			2550	2950
19	1	MANTA 195	ST	RNBT	FBG	TR	IO	140-200		7	7	2660			3000	3700
19	1	MANTA 195	ST	RNBT	FBG	TR	IO	225-250		7	7	2660			3050	3750
21	2	COMMANDER 21	ST	EXP	FBG	DV	IO	185-250		7	10	3185			4400	5350
21	2	COMMANDER 21	HT	EXP	FBG	DV	IO	185-250		8					4400	5350
21	2	COMMANDER DAY 21	ST	CR	FBG	DV	IO	165-250		7	10	2845			4050	5000
21	5	BARON 21	ST	CUD	FBG	DV	IO	165-250		8		3010			4300	5300
23	2	ADMIRAL 23	ST	CUD	FBG	DV	IO	140-225		8		4350			6150	7400
23	2	ADMIRAL 23	ST	CUD	FBG	DV	IO	T170-T250		8		4350			6850	8300
23	2	ADMIRAL 23	HT	EXP	FBG	DV	IO	140-225		8		4729			6550	7850
23	2	ADMIRAL 23	HT	EXP	FBG	DV	IO	T170-T250		8		4729			7300	8800
23	2	COMMAND BRIDGE 23	FB	CR	FBG	DV	IO	140-198		8					5700	6700
23	2	COMMAND BRIDGE 23	FB	CR	FBG	DV	IO	T170-T250		8					6400	7950
23	2	COMMODORE DAY 23	ST	CUD	FBG	DV	IO	140-198		8		3315			5050	5950
23	2	COMMODORE DAY 23	ST	CUD	FBG	DV	IO	T170-T200		8		3315			5750	7050
23	2	COMMODORE DAY 23	ST	CUD	FBG	DV	IO	T225-T250		8		3315			5850	7200
25	10	COMMAND BRIDGE 26	FB	CR	FBG	DV	IO	198	MRCR	8					8050	9250
25	10	FLEETMASTER 26	HT	EXP	FBG	DV	IO	140-240		8		5519			7950	9750
25	10	FLEETMASTER 26	HT	EXP	FBG	DV	IO	T170-T250		8		5519			9250	11300
		1977 BOATS														
16	1	SHARK 165	ST	RNBT	FBG	TR	OB			6		1330			1950	2350
16	1	SHARK 165	ST	RNBT	FBG	TR	IO	120		6					1900	2250
16	1	SHARK 165	ST	RNBT	FBG	TR	IO	130-140		6					2000	2400
16	2	ALL-AMERICAN 160	ST	RNBT	FBG	SV	OB			6	5	1240			1850	2200
16	2	ALL-AMERICAN 160	ST	RNBT	FBG	SV	IO	120		6	5				1950	2350
16	2	ALL-AMERICAN 160	ST	RNBT	FBG	SV	IO	130-170		6	5				2100	2500
16	5	FORCE 16 B/R	ST	RNBT	FBG	*	IO	120		6	6				2000	2400
16	5	FORCE 16 B/R	ST	RNBT	FBG	*	IO	130-175		6	6				2200	2550
17	2	MANTA 175	ST	RNBT	FBG	TR	OB			6	9	1290			1950	2300
17	2	MANTA 175	ST	RNBT	FBG	TR	IO	120-170		6	9				2200	2700
17	4	ALL-AMERICAN 170	ST	RNBT	FBG	SV	OB			6	6	1105			1700	2050
17	4	ALL-AMERICAN 170	ST	RNBT	FBG	SV	IO	130-225		6	6				2300	2750
17	4	VOLERO 172	ST	RNBT	FBG	DV	IO	140-200		6	7				2200	2700
17	4	VOLERO 172	ST	RNBT	FBG	DV	IO	225-233		6	7				2250	2800
17	4	VOLERO 172	ST	RNBT	FBG	DV	JT	245-320		6	7				2650	3100
18		ALL-AMERICAN 186	ST	RNBT	FBG	SV	OB			6	9	1335			2050	2400
18		ALL-AMERICAN 186	ST	RNBT	FBG	SV	IO	130-235		6	9				2600	3150
19	1	MANTA 195	ST	RNBT	FBG	TR	OB			7	6	1705			2500	2900
19	1	MANTA 195	ST	RNBT	FBG	TR	IO	140-170		7	6				2800	3450
19	1	MANTA 195	ST	RNBT	FBG	TR	IO	225-280		7	6				3050	3650
21	2	COMMANDER 21	ST	EXP	FBG	DV	IO	175-233		7	6				4250	5300
21	2	COMMANDER 21	HT	EXP	FBG	DV	IO	175-233		7	6				4250	5300
21	2	COMMANDER DAY 21	ST	CR	FBG	DV	IO	165-233		7	6				4300	5300
21	5	BARON 21	ST	CUD	FBG	DV	IO	165-233		8					4500	5450
23	2	ADMIRAL 23	HT	EXP	FBG	DV	IO	188-233		7	10				5800	6950
23	2	ADMIRAL 23	HT	EXP	FBG	DV	IO	T130-T140		7	10				6750	7750
23	2	ADMIRAL 23	ST	OVNTR	FBG	DV	IO	188-233		7	10				5800	6950
23	2	ADMIRAL 23	ST	OVNTR	FBG	DV	IO	T130-T140		7	10				6750	7750
23	2	COMMODORE DAY 23	ST	CUD	FBG	DV	IO	188-233		7	10				6050	7250
23	2	COMMODORE DAY 23	ST	CUD	FBG	DV	IO	T130-T140		7	10				7000	8050
		1976 BOATS														
16		FORCE 16 B/R	ST	RNBT	FBG	*	IO	120-140							2150	2700
16	1	SHARK 165	ST	RNBT	FBG	TR	OB			6	5	1330			1950	2300
16	1	SHARK 165	ST	RNBT	FBG	TR	IO	120-140		6	5	2090			2150	2650
16	2	ALL-AMERICAN 160	ST	RNBT	FBG	SV	OB			6	9	1240			1850	2200
16	2	ALL-AMERICAN 160	ST	RNBT	FBG	TR	IO	120		6	9	1755			2000	2350
16	2	ALL-AMERICAN 160	ST	RNBT	FBG	TR	IO	130-140		6	9	1755			2150	2500
17	2	MANTA 175	ST	RNBT	FBG	TR	OB			6	10	1290			1900	2300
17	2	MANTA 175	ST	RNBT	FBG	TR	IO	120-165		6	10	2260			2450	3000
17	3	ALL-AMERICAN 170	ST	RNBT	FBG	SV	OB			7	2	1105			1700	2000
17	3	ALL-AMERICAN 170	ST	RNBT	FBG	TR	IO	130-230		7	2	1990			2500	3050
17	4	VOLERO 172	ST	RNBT	FBG	DV	IO	140-190		6	9	2307			2450	3050
17	4	VOLERO 172	ST	RNBT	FBG	DV	IO	200-233		6	9	2307			2650	3200
18		ALL-AMERICAN 186	ST	RNBT	FBG	SV	OB			6	11	1335			2000	2400
18		ALL-AMERICAN 186	ST	RNBT	FBG	SV	IO	130-225		6	11	2282			2700	3200
19	1	MANTA 195	ST	RNBT	FBG	TR	OB			7	7	1705			2500	2900
19	1	MANTA 195	ST	RNBT	FBG	TR	IO	140-225		7	7	2680			3150	3850
19	1	MANTA 195	ST	RNBT	FBG	TR	IO	230-233		7	7	2680			3400	3950
21	2	COMMANDER 21	ST	EXP	FBG	DV	IO	175-233		7	10	3640			5000	6100
21	3	COMMANDER DAY 21	ST	CR	FBG	SV	IO	165-233		7	10	2845			4250	5300
21	5	BARON 21	ST	CUD	FBG	DV	IO	165-233		8		3005			4550	5500
23	2	ADMIRAL 23	ST	CUD	FBG	DV	IO	188-233		8		4350			6450	7700
23	2	ADMIRAL 23	ST	CUD	FBG	DV	IO	T140		8		4350			7100	8150
23	2	ADMIRAL 23	ST	EXP	FBG	DV	IO	188-233		8		4729			6900	8200
23	2	ADMIRAL 23	ST	EXP	FBG	DV	IO	T140		8		4729			7550	8700
23	2	COMMODORE DAY 23	ST	CUD	FBG	DV	IO	188-233		8		3315			5300	6400
23	2	COMMODORE DAY 23	ST	CUD	FBG	DV	IO	T140		8		3315			5950	6850
		1975 BOATS														
16	1	SHARK 1650	OP	RNBT	FBG	TR	IO	120		6	5	1896			2050	2450
16	1	SHARK 1650	OP	RNBT	FBG	TR	IO	130-140		6	5	1896			2250	2600
16	2	ALL-AMERICAN 160	OP	RNBT	FBG	SV	OB			6	9	1236			1800	2150
16	2	ALL-AMERICAN 160	OP	RNBT	FBG	SV	IO	120-140				1806			2200	2700
16	4	SHARK 1700	OP	RNBT	FBG	TR	OB			7	5	1476			2100	2500
16	4	SHARK 1700	OP	RNBT	FBG	TR	IO	120		7	5	1476			2000	2400
16	4	SHARK 1700	OP	RNBT	FBG	TR	IO	130-170		7	5	1476			2200	2600
17	2	MANTA 175	OP	RNBT	FBG	TR	IO	120-188		6	10	2004			2350	2950
17	4	VOLERO SPORT 187	OP	RNBT	FBG	DV	IO	140-190		6	7	2131			2400	3000
17	4	VOLERO SPORT 187	OP	RNBT	FBG	DV	IO	200-233		6	7	2131			2600	3100
18		ALL-AMERICAN 186	OP	RNBT	FBG	SV	OB			6	11	1272			1900	2300
18		ALL-AMERICAN 186	OP	RNBT	FBG	SV	IO	120-190		6	11	1998			2500	3100
18		ALL-AMERICAN 186	OP	RNBT	FBG	SV	IO	200-233		6	11	1998			2700	3200
18		ALL-AMERICAN B/R 186	OP	RNBT	FBG	SV	OB			6	11	1375			2050	2400
18		ALL-AMERICAN B/R 186	OP	RNBT	FBG	SV	IO	120-190		6	11	1945			2450	3050
18		ALL-AMERICAN B/R 186	OP	RNBT	FBG	SV	IO	200-233		6	11	1945			2650	3150
18	1	SHARK 1800	OP	RNBT	FBG	TR	OB			6	10	1430			2100	2500
18	1	SHARK 1800	OP	RNBT	FBG	TR	IO	120-190		6	10	2034			2500	3100
19	2	MANTA 195	OP	RNBT	FBG	TR	OB			7	7	1516			2300	2700
19	2	MANTA 195	OP	RNBT	FBG	TR	IO	120-200		7	7	2470			3100	3850
19	2	MANTA 195	OP	RNBT	FBG	TR	IO	225-233		7	7	2470			3200	3900
21	2	COMMANDER EXPRESS 21	HT	CR	FBG	DV	IO	165-233		7	9	3640			5150	6250
21	2	COMMANDER RUNABOUT	ST	SPTCR	FBG	DV	IO	165-233		7	10	2845			4400	5400
21	5	BARON	ST	CUD	FBG	DV	IO	165-233		8		3005			4700	5700
23	2	COMMODORE CUDDY CR	ST	CUD	FBG	DV	IO	188-233		8		4350			6650	7950
23	2	COMMODORE CUDDY CR	ST	CUD	FBG	DV	IO	T140		8		4350			7350	8450
23	2	COMMODORE EXPRESS	HT	CR	FBG	DV	IO			8		4729			**	**
23	2	COMMODORE RUNABOUT	ST	SPTCR	FBG	DV	IO	165-233		8		3315			5450	6600
23	2	COMMODORE RUNABOUT	ST	SPTCR	FBG	DV	IO	T140		8		3315			6150	7050
		1974 BOATS														
16	3	ALL-AMERICAN 160			FBG		IO	120-140		6	9	1651			1900	2300
16	3	ALL-AMERICAN SP 160			FBG		IO	120-140		6	9	1651			2000	2400
16	3	SHARK 1650		RNBT	FBG		IO	120-140		6	3	1644			1950	2300
16	3	SHARK SPEC 1650		RNBT	FBG		IO	120-140		6	3	1644			2000	2450
16	4	SHARK 1700		RNBT	FBG		OB			7	5	1279			1850	2200
16	4	SHARK 1700		RNBT	FBG		IO	120-170		7	5	1911			2400	2900
17	2	VOLERO SPORT 187	ST	CR	FBG		IO	140-170		6	11	1993			2500	3000
17	2	VOLERO SPORT 187	ST	CR	FBG		IO	188	MRCR	6	11	2421			2800	3250
18		ALL-AMERICAN 186 B/R	ST	RNBT	FBG		OB			7	1	1101			1700	2000
18		ALL-AMERICAN 186 B/R	ST	RNBT	FBG		IO	120-170		7	1	1824			2500	3050
18		ALL-AMERICAN 186 B/R	ST	RNBT	FBG		IO	188	MRCR	7	1	2274			2800	3300
18		ALL-AMERICAN 186-CB	ST	RNBT	FBG		OB			7	1	1229			1850	2200
18		ALL-AMERICAN 186-CB	ST	RNBT	FBG		IO	120-170		7	1	1804			2500	3000
18		ALL-AMERICAN 186-CB	ST	RNBT	FBG		IO	188	MRCR	7	1	2254			2800	3250
18	2	SHARK 1800	ST	RNBT	FBG		OB			6	10	1398			2050	2450
18	2	SHARK 1800	ST	RNBT	FBG		IO	140-170		6	10	2124			2650	3200
18	2	SHARK 1800	ST	RNBT	FBG		IO	188	MRCR	6	10	2552			2950	3450
18	3	SHARK 1900		RNBT	FBG		OB			7	5	1338			2000	2350
18	3	SHARK 1900		RNBT	FBG		IO	140-170		7	5	2040			2750	3300
18	3	SHARK 1900		RNBT	FBG		IO	188	MRCR	7	5	2468			3050	3550
20		COMMANDANT			FBG		IO	165-170		7	4	2324			3450	4050
20		COMMANDANT			FBG		IO	188	MRCR	7	4	2634			3750	4350
21	3	COMMANDER		CR	FBG		IO	188-225		8		3100			4900	5800
21	3	COMMANDER		EXP	FBG		IO	188-225		8		3200			5000	5900
21	5	BARON			FBG		IO	165-188		8		2465			4100	5050
23	3	COMMODORE		CUD	FBG		IO	188-225		8		3475			5850	6900
23	3	COMMODORE		CUD	FBG		IO	T140		8		3644			6750	7750
23	3	COMMODORE		RNBT	FBG		IO	188-225		8		3475			5500	6500
23	3	COMMODORE		RNBT	FBG		IO	T140		8		3644			6350	7300
		1973 BOATS														
16	1	SHARK 1600	ST	RNBT	FBG		IO	120-140		6	3	1725			2050	2500
16	3	SHARK 1650		RNBT	FBG		IO	120-140		6	3	1783			2200	2550

CONTINUED ON NEXT PAGE

LARSON BOATS   -CONTINUED   See inside cover to adjust price for area

LOA FT IN	NAME AND/ OR MODEL	TOP/ RIG	BOAT TYPE	-HULL- MTL TP	----ENGINE--- TP # HP MFG	BEAM FT IN	WGT LBS	DRAFT FT IN	RETAIL LOW	RETAIL HIGH
					---- 1973 BOATS ----					
16 4	SHARK 1700		RNBT	FBG	IO 120-165	7 5	1905		2450	2950
16 9	ALL-AMERICAN 176	ST	RNBT	FBG	IO 120-140	6 5	1725		2250	2600
17 2	VOLERO SPORT 187	ST	CR	FBG	IO 140-170	6 11	1835		2450	3000
17 2	VOLERO SPORT 187	ST	CR	FBG	IO 188 MRCR	6 11	2105		2700	3100
18	ALL-AMERICAN 186	ST	RNBT	FBG	OB	7 1	1135		1700	2050
18	ALL-AMERICAN 186	ST	RNBT	FBG	IO 120-170	7 1	1555		2450	2950
18	ALL-AMERICAN 186	ST	RNBT	FBG	IO 188 MRCR	7 1	1825		2650	3050
18 2	SHARK 1800	ST	RNBT	FBG	OB	6 10	1402		2050	2400
18 2	SHARK 1800	ST	RNBT	FBG	IO 140-188	6 10	1910		2600	3250
18 3	ALL-AMERICAN 186	ST	RNBT	FBG	IO 120-170	7 2	1875		2700	3250
18 3	ALL-AMERICAN 186	ST	RNBT	FBG	IO 188 MRCR	7 2	2145		2900	3350
18 3	SHARK 1900		RNBT	FBG	OB	7 5	1350		2000	2350
18 3	SHARK 1900		RNBT	FBG	IO 140-188	7 5	1870		2750	3400
20	COMMANDANT			FBG	IO 140-188	7 4	2021		3350	4150
20	CONSORT			FBG	IO 165-188	7 4	2213		3300	4200
21 5	BARON			FBG	IO 165-188	8	2865		4600	5450
21 5	BARON			FBG	IO 225	8	3235		5050	5800
					---- 1972 BOATS ----					
16 3	SHARK 1600	ST	RNBT	FBG	IO 120-140	6 3	1671		2200	2700
16 4	SHARK 165	ST	RNBT	FBG	IO 120-155	7 5	1905		2550	3100
16 9	ALL-AMERICAN 176	ST	RNBT	FBG	IO 120-140	6 5	1725		2300	2850
17 2	VOLERO SPORT 187	ST	CR	FBG	IO 120-225	6 11	1825		2550	3150
18	ALL-AMERICAN 186	ST	RNBT	FBG	IO 120-225	7 1	1835		2650	3300
18 2	SHARK 1800	ST	RNBT	FBG	OB	6 9	1402		2000	2400
18 3	ALL-AMERICAN 186	ST	RNBT	FBG	IO 120-225	6 9	2167		2850	3500
18 3	ALL-AMERICAN 186	ST	RNBT	FBG	OB	6 4	1155		1750	2050
18 3	SHARK 1850		RNBT	FBG	IO 120-225	7 2	1875		2750	3400
18 3	SHARK 1850		RNBT	FBG	OB	7 5	1500		2200	2550
20	CAVALIER	ST	CR	FBG	IO 120-225	7 5	2265		3100	3800
					IO 140-225	7 4	2235		3800	4650
21 5	VOLERO SPORT 217	ST	CR	FBG	IO 140-225	8	2750		4850	5800
					---- 1971 BOATS ----					
16	M-SCOW	SLP	SA/OD	FBG BB		5 8	440	2	1750	2100
16 3	SHARK 1600	ST	RNBT	FBG	IO 120-140	6 2	1671		2200	2700
16 4	SHARK 165	ST	RNBT	FBG	IO 120-140	7 5	1905		2600	3050
16 9	ALL-AMERICAN 176	ST	RNBT	FBG	IO 120-140	6 5	1725		2350	2900
17 2	VOLERO 187	ST	RNBT	FBG	IO 120-215	6 11	1825		2600	3150
18	ALL-AMERICAN 186	ST	RNBT	FBG	OB	7 2	1130		1700	2050
18 3	ALL-AMERICAN 186	ST	RNBT	FBG	IO 120	7 2	1850		2850	3300
18 3	ALL-AMERICAN 186	ST	RNBT	FBG	IO 140-215	7 2			3150	3700
18 3	ALL-AMERICAN 186 W/T		RNBT	FBG SV	OB	7 2	1130		1700	2050
18 3	SHARK 185	ST	RNBT	FBG	OB	7 5	1470		2100	2500
18 3	SHARK 185	ST	RNBT	FBG	IO 120-215	7 5	2190		3150	3800
18 3	SHARK 195	ST	CAMPR	FBG	OB	7 5	1500		2100	2500
18 3	SHARK 195	ST	CAMPR	FBG	IO 120-215	7 5	2200		3200	3900
18 3	SHARK 195 CAMPER W/T		CAMPR	FBG TR	OB	7 5	1500		2100	2500
18 3	SHARK 195 CAMPER W/T		CAMPR	FBG TR	IO 120	7 5			3250	3800
18 3	SHARK DAY CRUISER WT		CR	FBG TR	OB	7 5	1150		1700	2050
18 3	SHARK DAY CRUISER WT		CR	FBG TR	IO 120	7 5			3250	3800
21 3	CRUISER HOME		SDN	FBG TR	IO 155	8			5400	6200
21 5	VOLERO 217	ST	CR	FBG	IO 140-165	8	2750		5000	6250
21 5	VOLERO 217	ST	CR	FBG	IO 215 OMC	8			5500	6350
23 2	RAIDER	HT	CR	FBG	IO 155-215	8	4000		7050	8100
					---- 1970 BOATS ----					
16	REGATTA	SLP	SA/OD	FBG LB	OB	5 8	450		1750	2100
16 4	SHARK 165	ST	RNBT	FBG TR	IO 120	7 3	1905		2650	3100
16 9	ALL-AMERICAN 166	ST	RNBT	FBG SV	IO 120	6 5	1700		2400	2800
16 9	ALL-AMERICAN 176 DLX	ST	RNBT	FBG SV	IO 120	6 5	1725		2450	2850
17 2	VOLERO 187	ST	RNBT	FBG DV	IO 120-215	6 11	1760		2650	3200
17 11	ALL-AMERICAN 186 DLX	ST	RNBT	FBG SV	OB	7 2	1130		1700	2000
18 3	ALL-AMERICAN 186	ST	RNBT	FBG SV	IO 120-215	7 2	1850		2950	3550
18 3	SHARK 185	ST	RNBT	FBG TR	OB	7 6	1470		2100	2500
18 3	SHARK 185	ST	RNBT	FBG TR	IO 120-215	7 6	2190		3250	3900
18 3	SHARK 195	ST	CAMPR	FBG TR	OB	7 6	1500		2100	2500
18 3	SHARK 195	ST	CAMPR	FBG TR	IO 120-215	7 6	2200		3350	4000
19 2	VOLERO 197	ST	CR	FBG DV	IO 120-215	7 8	2520		3850	4600
21 3	CRUISER HOME	HT	FH	FBG TR	IO 155-215	7 5	2900		**	**
21 5	VOLERO 217	ST	CR	FBG DV	IO 120-215	8	2750		5200	6100
23 2	RAIDER	HT	CR	FBG DV	IO 155-215	8	4200		7550	8850
					---- 1969 BOATS ----					
16	M-SCOW	SLP	SA/OD		BB	5 8	440	2	1700	2050
16	REGATTA	SLP	SAIL	FBG CB	OB	5 8	450		1700	2050
16 4	SHARK 165	ST	RNBT	FBG TR	IO 120 MRCR	7 6	1730		2700	3150
16 11	ALL-AMERICAN 166	ST	RNBT	FBG SV	IO 120 MRCR	6 5	1560		2450	2850
16 11	LARSON 16	OP	RNBT	FBG SV	IO 120 MRCR	6 5	1540		2400	2800
17 5	VOLERO 177	ST	RNBT	FBG DV	IO 120 MRCR	6 11	1720		2750	3200
17 5	VOLERO 177 DLX	ST	RNBT	FBG	IO 120 MRCR	6 11	1725		2750	3200
18 4	SHARK 185	ST	RNBT	FBG TR OB		7 6	1370		2000	2350
18 4	SHARK 185	ST	RNBT	FBG TR	IO 120 MRCR	7 6	2130		3350	3900
18 6	ALL-AMERICAN 186	ST	RNBT	FBG SV	IO 120 MRCR	7 3	1730		3050	3550
19 6	VOLERO 197	ST	CR	FBG DV	IO 120 MRCR	7 8	2420		3950	4600
21 6	VOLERO 217	ST	CR	FBG DV	IO 120 MRCR	8 3	2588		5300	6100
					---- 1968 BOATS ----					
16 4	ALL-AMERICAN 166	ST	RNBT	FBG	IO 120	6 5	1350	3 11	2300	2650
16 4	SHARK 165	ST	RNBT	FBG TR	IO 120	7 6	1880	3	2900	3350
17 3	VOLERO 177	ST	RNBT	FBG	IO 120	6 11	1350	3	2550	3100
17 3	VOLERO 177	ST	RNBT	FBG DV	IO 210	6 11	1578	3	2800	3250
17 11	ALL-AMERICAN 186	ST	RNBT	FBG DV	IO 120-200	7 3	2765	3 11	3800	4550
17 11	ALL-AMERICAN 186	ST	RNBT	FBG DV	IO 210	7 3	2993	3 11	4100	4750
19 6	VOLERO 197	ST	CR	FBG DV	IO 120-200	7 8	2250	4 8	3950	4750
19 6	VOLERO 197	ST	CR	FBG DV	IO 210	7 8	2478	4 8	4250	4950
21 6	VOLERO 217	ST	CR	FBG DV	IO 120-210	8 3	3070	5	6000	7350
					---- 1967 BOATS ----					
16	REGATTA 165	SLP	SAIL	FBG	OB		440		1700	2050
16 11	ALL-AMERICAN 166	ST	RNBT	FBG	IO 120		1350		2650	3100
17 5	VOLERO 177	ST	RNBT	FBG	IO 120-200		1350		2800	3300
18 6	ALL-AMERICAN 186	ST	RNBT	FBG	IO 120-200		1500		3350	3950
21 6	VOLERO 217	ST	CR	FBG	IO 120-200		2000		5150	6050
					---- 1966 BOATS ----					
16	REGATTA 162 SCOW	SLP	SAIL	FBG BB	OB	5 8			1950	2300
16	REGATTA 165 SCOW	SLP	SAIL	FBG BB	OB	5 8			2100	2500
16 5	VOLERO 167	ST	RNBT	FBG	IO 110-120	6 7			2900	3350
16 8	ALL-AMERICAN 176	ST	RNBT	FBG SV	IO 110-120	6 5			2950	3450
16 11	ALL-AMERICAN 176	ST	RNBT	FBG SV	IO 110-120	6 5			2850	3300
16 11	MEDALLION 166	ST	RNBT	FBG	IO 110-120	6 5			3050	3550
18 2	VOLERO 187	ST	RNBT	FBG DV	IO 110-150	7 5			3750	4350
					---- 1965 BOATS ----					
16 4	VOLERO 167 COMBOARD	ST	RNBT	FBG	IO 110-120				3150	3650
16 7	ALL-AMERICAN 176	ST	RNBT	FBG	IO 120				3200	3700
16 7	ALL-AMERICAN 176	ST	RNBT	WD	IO 120				3200	3700
18	VOLERO 187 COMBOARD	ST	RNBT	FBG	IO 110-150				3950	4650
					---- 1963 BOATS ----					
16	ALL-AMERICAN DELUXE			FBG	IO 80				3300	3800
17	TAHATI			FBG	IO 110				3350	3900
18	CARIBE DELUXE		CR	FBG	OB				2200	2600
18	CARIBE DELUXE		UTL	FBG	IO 110				4400	5050
18	SEA-WOLFE			FBG	OB				2050	2450
18	SEA-WOLFE DELUXE			FBG	OB				2200	2600
18	SEA-WOLFE DELUXE			FBG	IO 110				4100	4800
					---- 1962 BOATS ----					
16 7	ALL-AMERICAN				IO 80-100				3350	3900
18 3	SEA-WOLFE				OB				2250	2600
18 3	SEA-WOLFE				IO 80-100				4350	5050
18 3	TRADEWIND				OB				2250	2600
18 3	TRADEWIND				IO				2250	2600
19 2	SURFMASTER				OB				2300	2650
19 2	SURFMASTER				OB				**	**
					---- 1961 BOATS ----					
17 10	SEA-LION 185		RNBT	FBG	OB	6 10			2250	2600
17 10	SEA-LION 188		CR	FBG	OB	6 10			2200	2550
19 2	SURFMASTER 195		RNBT	FBG	OB	7 1			2350	2700
19 2	SURFMASTER 198		CR	FBG	OB	7 1			2300	2700
					---- 1960 BOATS ----					
18	SEA-LION		RNBT		OB				2250	2600
18	SEA-LION		RNBT		OB				2300	2650
19	SURFMASTER		CR		OB				2300	2660
19	SURFMASTER		RNBT		OB				2300	2700
25	CRUISEMASTER		CR		OB				7350	8450
					---- 1959 BOATS ----					
18				WD	OB		1260		**	**
25	CRUISEMASTER		CBNCR	FBG	OB	8			9350	10600
					---- 1954 BOATS ----					
28				WD	IB 18				**	**

LARSON TRADE U-S-A

Call 1-800-327-6929 for BUC Personalized Evaluation Service
Or, for 1969 to 1971 boats, sign onto www.BUCValuPro.com

LASCO MARINE

Call 1-800-327-6929 for BUC Personalized Evaluation Service
Or, for 1965 to 1967 boats, sign onto www.BUCValuPro.com

LASER BOATS OF TEXAS
COAST GUARD MFG ID- CJM

Call 1-800-327-6929 for BUC Personalized Evaluation Service
Or, for 1980 to 2004 boats, sign onto www.BUCValuPro.com

LASER INTERNATIONAL
HAWKESBURY ONTARIO CANA COAST GUARD MFG ID- PSL See inside cover to adjust price for area
FORMERLY PERFORMANCE SAILCRAFT INC

For more recent years, see the BUC Used Boat Price Guide, Volume 1 or Volume 2

LOA FT IN	NAME AND/ OR MODEL	TOP/ RIG	BOAT TYPE	-HULL- MTL TP	----ENGINE--- TP # HP MFG	BEAM FT IN	WGT LBS	DRAFT FT IN	RETAIL LOW	RETAIL HIGH
				---- 1975 BOATS ----						
22 9	STAR	SLP	SA/OD	FBG KL		5 8	1480	3 6	4600	5250

LATITUDE 33 INC

Call 1-800-327-6929 for BUC Personalized Evaluation Service
Or, for 1982 boats, sign onto www.BUCValuPro.com

LAVRO INC
COAST GUARD MFG ID- LAJ

Call 1-800-327-6929 for BUC Personalized Evaluation Service
Or, for 1978 boats, sign onto www.BUCValuPro.com

GEORGE LAWLEY & SON

See inside cover to adjust price for area

LOA FT IN	NAME AND/ OR MODEL	TOP/ RIG	BOAT TYPE	-HULL- MTL TP	----ENGINE--- TP # HP MFG	BEAM FT IN	WGT LBS	DRAFT FT IN	RETAIL LOW	RETAIL HIGH
				---- 1931 BOATS ----						
42		HT	CR	MHG	IB 175 STER 10 3		2 11	167500	184000	
				---- 1908 BOATS ----						
39 3			LNCH		IB 225	5 4			**	**

LAWRENCE STEEL YACHT CO INC

Call 1-800-327-6929 for BUC Personalized Evaluation Service
Or, for 1959 to 1966 boats, sign onto www.BUCValuPro.com

LAWRENCE YACHT CO
COAST GUARD MFG ID- LYX

Call 1-800-327-6929 for BUC Personalized Evaluation Service
Or, for 1979 boats, sign onto www.BUCValuPro.com

LAZY DAYS MFG CO INC
BUFORD GA 30518   COAST GUARD MFG ID- LDM See inside cover to adjust price for area

For more recent years, see the BUC Used Boat Price Guide, Volume 1 or Volume 2

LOA FT IN	NAME AND/ OR MODEL	TOP/ RIG	BOAT TYPE	-HULL- MTL TP	----ENGINE--- TP # HP MFG	BEAM FT IN	WGT LBS	DRAFT FT IN	RETAIL LOW	RETAIL HIGH
				---- 1983 BOATS ----						
50	2 SPORTSMAN	HT	HB	AL	TR IO T200 VLVO 14	6		3	65600	72100
50	2 SPORTSMAN	FB	HB	AL	TR IO T200 VLVO 14	6		3	65600	72100
	VD T200 CRUS 64400	70700, IO T225 VLVO 66200 72800, IO T260 VLVO 67700 74400								
	IO T290 VLVO 69700	76600, IO T330 MRCR 71100 78200, IO T130D VLVO 71800 78900								
	IO T165D VLVO 73100	80300, VD T165D VLVO 73100 80300								
52	HIGH BOW SPORTSMAN	HT	HB	AL	TR IO T200 VLVO 14	6		3	66300	72800
	VD T200 CRUS 65100	71500, IO T225 VLVO 66900 73500, IO T260 VLVO 68200 75000								
	IO T290 VLVO 70200	77100, IO T330 MRCR 71600 78600, IO T130D VLVO 71800 78900								
	IO T165D VLVO 73200	80500, VD T165D VLVO 73100 80300								
52	HIGH BOW SPORTSMAN	FB	HB	AL	TR IO T200 VLVO 14	6		3	66300	72900
	VD T200 CRUS 65200	71600, IO T225 VLVO 66800 73500, IO T260 VLVO 68300 75100								
	IO T290 VLVO 70300	77200, IO T330 MRCR 71600 78700, IO T130D VLVO 72900 80100								
	IO T165D VLVO 74400	81700, VD T165D VLVO 73400 80700								
57	SPORTSMAN	HT	HB	AL	TR IO T200 VLVO 14	6		3	75600	83100
	VD T200 CRUS 74400	81800, IO T225 VLVO 76200 83700, IO T260 VLVO 77600 85200								
	IO T290 VLVO 79500	87400, IO T330 MRCR 80900 88900, IO T130D VLVO 73700 81000								
	IO T165D VLVO 75200	82700, VD T165D VLVO 74200 81500								
57	SPORTSMAN	FB	HB	AL	TR IO T200 VLVO 14	6		3	75600	83100
	VD T200 CRUS 74400	81800, IO T225 VLVO 76200 83700, IO T260 VLVO 77600 85200								
	IO T290 VLVO 79500	87400, IO T330 MRCR 80900 88900, IO T130D VLVO 74100 81500								
	IO T165D VLVO 75700	83200, VD T165D VLVO 74200 81500								
59	HIGH BOW SPORTSMAN	HT	HB	AL	TR IO T200 VLVO 14	6		3	75600	83000
	VD T200 CRUS 74400	81700, IO T225 VLVO 76100 83700, IO T260 VLVO 77500 85200								
	IO T290 VLVO 79500	87300, IO T330 MRCR 80900 88900, IO T130D VLVO 77600 85300								
	IO T165D VLVO 79600	87500, VD T165D VLVO 78600 86300								
59	HIGH BOW SPORTSMAN	FB	HB	AL	TR IO T200 VLVO 14	6		3	75800	83300
	VD T200 CRUS 74600	81900, IO T225 VLVO 76400 83900, IO T260 VLVO 77700 85400								
	IO T290 VLVO 79500	87400, IO T330 MRCR 81200 89200, IO T130D VLVO 78200 86000								
	IO T165D VLVO 79600	87500, VD T165D VLVO 78700 86500								
62	2 CUSTOM	HT	HB	AL	SV IO T200 VLVO 14	6		3	91900	101000
	VD T200 CRUS 77200	84800, IO T225 VLVO 92600 102000, IO T260 VLVO 93900 103000								
	IO T290 VLVO 96700	106500, IO T330 MRCR 98500 108000, VD T330 MRCR 88900 97600								
	IO T130D VLVO **	** , IO T165D VLVO ** ** , VD T165D VLVO ** **								
	VD T310D J&T **	**								
62	2 CUSTOM	FB	HB	AL	SV IO T200 VLVO 14	6		3	91900	101000
	VD T200 CRUS 77600	85300, IO T225 VLVO 92600 102000, IO T260 VLVO 94100 103500								
	IO T290 VLVO 96700	106500, IO T330 MRCR 98500 108000, VD T330 MRCR 88900 97700								
	IO T130D VLVO **	** , IO T165D VLVO ** ** , VD T165D VLVO ** **								
	VD T310D J&T **	**								
62	2 MOTOR YACHT	HT	HB	AL	SV VD T200 CRUS 14	6		4	98000	107500
62	2 MOTOR YACHT	HT	HB	AL	SV IO T165D VLVO 14	6		4	**	**
62	2 MOTOR YACHT	HT	HB	AL	SV IO T200 VLVO 14	6		4	**	**
62	2 MOTOR YACHT	FB	HB	AL	SV VD T200 CRUS 14	6		4	97600	107000
62	2 MOTOR YACHT	FB	HB	AL	SV IO T165D VLVO 14	6		4	**	**
62	2 MOTOR YACHT	FB	HB	AL	SV IO T200 VLVO 14	6		4	**	**
62	2 MOTOR YACHT	HT	MY	AL	SV IO T200 VLVO 14	6		4	92400	101500
	IO T225 VLVO 92500	101500, IO T260 VLVO 92700 102000, IO T290 VLVO 92900 102000								
	IO T330 MRCR 96400	106000, VD T330 MRCR 128000 140500, IO T130D VLVO 68700 75500								
	VD T310D J&T 96600	106000								
62	2 MOTOR YACHT	FB	MY	AL	SV IO T200 VLVO 14	6		3	92400	101500
	IO T225 VLVO 92500	101500, IO T260 VLVO 92700 102000, IO T290 VLVO 92900 102000								
	IO T330 MRCR 96400	106000, VD T330 MRCR 128000 140500, IO T130D VLVO 68700 75500								
	VD T310D J&T 96600	106000								
				---- 1982 BOATS ----						
50	2 SPORTSMAN	HT	HB	AL	TR IO T200 VLVO 14	6		3	64500	70900
	IO T225 VLVO 65100	71500, IO T260 VLVO 66500 73100, IO T290 VLVO 68500 75300								
	IO T330 MRCR 69900	76800, IO T130D VLVO 70500 77500								
50	2 SPORTSMAN	FB	HB	AL	TR IO T200 VLVO 14	6		3	64500	70900
	IO T225 VLVO 65100	71500, IO T260 VLVO 66500 73100, IO T290 VLVO 68500 75300								
	IO T330 MRCR 69900	76800, IO T130D VLVO 70500 77500								
52	HIGH BOW SPORTSMAN	HT	HB	AL	TR IO T200 VLVO 14	6		3	65500	72000
	IO T225 VLVO 66100	72700, IO T260 VLVO 67500 74200, IO T290 VLVO 69300 76100								
	IO T330 MRCR 70600	77600, IO T130D VLVO 70800 77800								
52	HIGH BOW SPORTSMAN	FB	HB	AL	TR IO T200 VLVO 14	6		3	65600	72100
	IO T225 VLVO 66100	72700, IO T260 VLVO 67500 74200, IO T290 VLVO 69300 76100								
	IO T330 MRCR 70700	77700, IO T130D VLVO 71600 78700								
57	SPORTSMAN	HT	HB	AL	TR IO T200 VLVO 14	6		3	74400	81800
	IO T225 VLVO 75000	82400, IO T260 VLVO 76300 83800, IO T290 VLVO 78200 85900								
	IO T330 MRCR 79600	87500, IO T130D VLVO 72700 79900								
57	SPORTSMAN	FB	HB	AL	TR IO T200 VLVO 14	6		3	74600	82000
	IO T225 VLVO 75100	82600, IO T260 VLVO 76300 83800, IO T290 VLVO 78400 86200								
	IO T330 MRCR 79800	87700, IO T130D VLVO 73100 80400								
59	HIGH BOW SPORTSMAN	HT	HB	AL	TR IO T200 VLVO 14	6		3	74500	81900
	IO T225 VLVO 75100	82500, IO T260 VLVO 76500 84000, IO T290 VLVO 78400 86100								

```
LOA  NAME AND/                TOP/ BOAT  -HULL-  ----ENGINE--- BEAM  WGT  DRAFT RETAIL RETAIL
FT IN  OR MODEL               RIG  TYPE  MTL TP TP # HP  MFG   FT IN  LBS FT IN  LOW    HIGH
--------------------- 1982 BOATS -------------------------------------------------------------
59   HIGH BOW SPORTSMAN       HT  HB  AL  TR IO T330  MRCR 14  6      3     79800  87600
59   HIGH BOW SPORTSMAN       HT  HB  AL  TR IO T130D VLVO 14  6      3     76500  84100
59   HIGH BOW SPORTSMAN       FB  HB  AL  TR IO T200  VLVO 14  6      3     74600  82000
     IO T225  VLVO  75400  82900, IO T260  VLVO  76700  84300, IO T290  VLVO  78600  86300
     IO T330  MRCR  79900  87800, IO T130D VLVO  77200  84800

62   2 CUSTOM                 HT  HB  AL  SV IO T200  VLVO 14  6      3     90700  99700
     IO T225  VLVO  91300 100500, IO T260  VLVO  92900 102000, IO T290  VLVO  95000 104500
     IO T330  MRCR  96600 106000, VD T330  MRCR  87200  95900, IO T130D VLVO   **     **
     VD T310D GM     **     **

62   2 CUSTOM                 FB  HB  AL  SV IO T200  VLVO 14  6      3     90700  99700
     IO T225  VLVO  91300 100500, IO T260  VLVO  92900 102000, IO T290  VLVO  95000 104500
     IO T330  MRCR  96600 106000, VD T330  MRCR  87100  95800, IO T130D VLVO   **     **
     VD T310D GM     **     **

62   2 MOTOR YACHT            HT  MY  AL  SV IO T200  VLVO 14  6      3     89000  97800
     IO T225  VLVO  89100  97900, IO T260  VLVO  89300  98100, IO T290  VLVO  89600  98400
     IO T330  MRCR  93600 103000, VD T330  MRCR 122500 135000, IO T130D VLVO  66100  72600
     VD T310D GM   91300 100500

62   2 MOTOR YACHT            FB  MY  AL  SV IO T200  VLVO 14  6      3     89000  97800
     IO T225  VLVO  89100  97900, IO T260  VLVO  89300  98100, IO T290  VLVO  89600  98400
     IO T330  MRCR  93600 103000, VD T330  MRCR 122500 135000, IO T130D VLVO  66100  72600
     VD T310D GM   91300 100500
--------------------- 1981 BOATS -------------------------------------------------------------
50   2 SPORTSMAN              HT  HB  AL  TR IO T200  VLVO 14  6      3     63500  69700
     IO T225  VLVO  64000  70400, IO T260  VLVO  65400  71900, IO T290  VLVO  67400  74100
     IO T330  MRCR  68800  75600, IO T130D VLVO  69400  76300

50   2 SPORTSMAN              FB  HB  AL  TR IO T200  VLVO 14  6      3     63500  69700
     IO T225  VLVO  64000  70400, IO T260  VLVO  65400  71900, IO T290  VLVO  67400  74100
     IO T330  MRCR  68800  75600, IO T130D VLVO  69400  76300

52   HIGH BOW SPORTSMAN       HT  HB  AL  TR IO T200  VLVO 14  6      3     64100  70400
     IO T225  VLVO  64600  71000, IO T260  VLVO  66000  72500, IO T290  VLVO  67800  74500
     IO T330  MRCR  69200  76000, IO T130D VLVO  69300  76100

52   HIGH BOW SPORTSMAN       FB  HB  AL  TR IO T200  VLVO 14  6      3     64100  70400
     IO T225  VLVO  64600  71000, IO T260  VLVO  66000  72500, IO T290  VLVO  67800  74500
     IO T330  MRCR  69200  76000, IO T130D VLVO  69600  76500

57   SPORTSMAN                HT  HB  AL  TR IO T200  VLVO 14  6      3     73100  80300
     IO T225  VLVO  73700  80900, IO T260  VLVO  75000  82400, IO T290  VLVO  76900  84500
     IO T330  MRCR  78200  86000, IO T130D VLVO  70300  77200

57   SPORTSMAN                FB  HB  AL  TR IO T200  VLVO 14  6      3     73100  80300
     IO T225  VLVO  73700  80900, IO T260  VLVO  75000  82400, IO T290  VLVO  76900  84500
     IO T330  MRCR  78200  86000, IO T130D VLVO  70500  77500

59   HIGH BOW SPORTSMAN       HT  HB  AL  TR IO T200  VLVO 14  6      3     73100  80300
     IO T225  VLVO  73600  80900, IO T260  VLVO  75000  82400, IO T290  VLVO  76900  84500
     IO T330  MRCR  78200  86000, IO T130D VLVO  74500  81800

59   HIGH BOW SPORTSMAN       FB  HB  AL  TR IO T200  VLVO 14  6      3     73100  80300
     IO T225  VLVO  73600  80900, IO T260  VLVO  75000  82400, IO T290  VLVO  76900  84500
     IO T330  MRCR  78200  86000, IO T130D VLVO  74500  81800

62   2 CUSTOM                 HT  HB  AL  SV IO T200  VLVO 14  6      3     86900  95500
     IO T225  VLVO  87300  95900, IO T260  VLVO  89500  98300, IO T290  VLVO  92800 102000
     IO T330  MERV  94500 104000, IO T130D VLVO   **     **,  VD T282D GM     **     **

62   2 CUSTOM                 FB  HB  AL  SV IO T200  VLVO 14  6      3     87300  95900
     IO T225  VLVO  88300  97000, IO T260  VLVO  89300  98200, IO T290  VLVO  92600 102000
     IO T330  MERV  94500 104000, IO T130D VLVO   **     **,  VD T282D GM     **     **

62   2 MOTOR YACHT            HT  MY  AL  SV IO T200  VLVO 14  6      3     86300  94800
     IO T225  VLVO  86400  94900, IO T260  VLVO  86600  95000, IO T290  VLVO  86800  95400
     IO T330  MRCR  91600 100500, IO T130D VLVO  64000  70300, VD T282D GM   86800  95300

62   2 MOTOR YACHT            FB  MY  AL  SV IO T200  VLVO 14  6      3     86300  94800
     IO T225  VLVO  86400  94900, IO T260  VLVO  86600  95100, IO T290  VLVO  86800  95400
     IO T330  MRCR  91600 100500, IO T130D VLVO  64000  70300, VD T282D GM   86800  95300
--------------------- 1980 BOATS -------------------------------------------------------------
50   SPORTSMAN                HT  HB  AL  TR IO T200  VLVO 14  6      3     62400  68600
50   SPORTSMAN                HT  HB  AL  TR IO T228  MRCR 14  6      3     61700  67800
50   SPORTSMAN                HT  HB  AL  TR IO T330  MRCR 14  6      3     67600  74300
50   SPORTSMAN                FB  HB  AL  TR IO T200  VLVO 14  6      3     62400  68600
50   SPORTSMAN                FB  HB  AL  TR IO T228  MRCR 14  6      3     61700  67800
50   SPORTSMAN                FB  HB  AL  TR IO T330  MRCR 14  6      3     67600  74300
52   HIGH BOW SPORTSMAN       HT  HB  AL  TR IO T200  VLVO 14  6      3  6  63100  69400
52   HIGH BOW SPORTSMAN       HT  HB  AL  TR IO T228  MRCR 14  6      3  6  62400  68600
52   HIGH BOW SPORTSMAN       HT  HB  AL  TR IO T330  MRCR 14  6      3     68200  74900
52   HIGH BOW SPORTSMAN       FB  HB  AL  TR IO T200  VLVO 14  6      3  6  63100  69400
52   HIGH BOW SPORTSMAN       FB  HB  AL  TR IO T228  MRCR 14  6      3  6  62400  68600
52   HIGH BOW SPORTSMAN       FB  HB  AL  TR IO T330  MRCR 14  6      3     68200  74900

57   SPORTSMAN                HT  HB  AL  TR IO T200  VLVO 14  6      3     72000  79200
57   SPORTSMAN                HT  HB  AL  TR IO T228  MRCR 14  6      3     71300  78400
57   SPORTSMAN                HT  HB  AL  TR IO T330  MRCR 14  6      3     77100  84700
57   SPORTSMAN                FB  HB  AL  TR IO T200  VLVO 14  6      3     72000  79200
57   SPORTSMAN                FB  HB  AL  TR IO T228  MRCR 14  6      3     71300  78400
57   SPORTSMAN                FB  HB  AL  TR IO T330  MRCR 14  6      3     77100  84700
59   HIGH BOW SPORTSMAN       HT  HB  AL  TR IO T200  VLVO 14  6      3     72000  79100
59   HIGH BOW SPORTSMAN       HT  HB  AL  TR IO T228  MRCR 14  6      3     71300  78400
59   HIGH BOW SPORTSMAN       HT  HB  AL  TR IO T330  MRCR 14  6      3     77000  84700
59   HIGH BOW SPORTSMAN       FB  HB  AL  TR IO T200  VLVO 14  6      3     72000  79100
59   HIGH BOW SPORTSMAN       FB  HB  AL  TR IO T228  MRCR 14  6      3     71300  78400
59   HIGH BOW SPORTSMAN       FB  HB  AL  TR IO T330  MRCR 14  6      3     77000  84700

62   CUSTOM                   HT  HB  AL  SV IO T330  MRCR 14  6      3  6  92700 102000
62   CUSTOM                   HT  HB  AL  SV VD T330  MRCR 14  6      3  6  83500  91800
62   CUSTOM                   HT  HB  AL  SV VD T282D GM   14  6      3  6   **     **
62   CUSTOM                   FB  HB  AL  SV IO T330  MRCR 14  6      3  6  92700 102000
62   CUSTOM                   FB  HB  AL  SV VD T330  MRCR 14  6      3  6  83500  91800
62   CUSTOM                   FB  HB  AL  SV VD T282D GM   14  6      3  6   **     **
62   MOTOR YACHT              HT  MY  AL  SV IO T330  MRCR 14  6      3  6  90300  99200
62   MOTOR YACHT              HT  MY  AL  SV VD T330  MRCR 14  6      3  6 111500 122500
62   MOTOR YACHT              HT  MY  AL  SV VD T282D GM   14  6      3  6  82200  90300
62   MOTOR YACHT              FB  MY  AL  SV IO T330  MRCR 14  6      3  6  90300  99200
62   MOTOR YACHT              FB  MY  AL  SV VD T330  MRCR 14  6      3  6 111500 122500
62   MOTOR YACHT              FB  MY  AL  SV VD T282D GM   14  6      3  6  82200  90300
--------------------- 1979 BOATS -------------------------------------------------------------
50   SPORTSMAN                HT  HB  AL  TR IO T228  MRCR 14  6      3     60800  66800
50   SPORTSMAN                HT  HB  AL  TR IO T330  MRCR 14  6      3     66700  73300
50   SPORTSMAN                FB  HB  AL  TR IO T228  MRCR 14  6      3     60800  66800
50   SPORTSMAN                FB  HB  AL  TR IO T330  MRCR 14  6      3     66700  73300
52   HIGH BOW SPORTSMAN       HT  HB  AL  TR IO T228  MRCR 14  6      3     61600  67700
52   HIGH BOW SPORTSMAN       HT  HB  AL  TR IO T330  MRCR 14  6      3     67200  73900
52   HIGH BOW SPORTSMAN       FB  HB  AL  TR IO T228  MRCR 14  6      3     61600  67700
52   HIGH BOW SPORTSMAN       FB  HB  AL  TR IO T330  MRCR 14  6      3     67200  73900
57   SPORTSMAN                HT  HB  AL  TR IO T228  MRCR 14  6      3     70400  77300
57   SPORTSMAN                HT  HB  AL  TR IO T330  MRCR 14  6      3     76000  83500
57   SPORTSMAN                FB  HB  AL  TR IO T228  MRCR 14  6      3     70400  77300
57   SPORTSMAN                FB  HB  AL  TR IO T330  MRCR 14  6      3     76000  83500

59   HIGH BOW SPORTSMAN       HT  HB  AL  TR IO T228  MRCR 14  6      3     70300  77300
59   HIGH BOW SPORTSMAN       HT  HB  AL  TR IO T330  MRCR 14  6      3     76000  83500
59   HIGH BOW SPORTSMAN       FB  HB  AL  TR IO T228  MRCR 14  6      3     70300  77300
59   HIGH BOW SPORTSMAN       FB  HB  AL  TR IO T330  MRCR 14  6      3     76000  83500
62   CUSTOM                   HT  HB  AL  SV IO T330  MRCR 14  6      3  6  91100 100000
62   CUSTOM                   HT  HB  AL  SV VD T330  MRCR 14  6      3  6  81300  89300
62   CUSTOM                   HT  HB  AL  SV VD T282D GM   14  6      3  6   **     **
62   CUSTOM                   FB  HB  AL  SV IO T330  MRCR 14  6      3  6  90800  99800
62   CUSTOM                   FB  HB  AL  SV VD T330  MRCR 14  6      3  6  81900  90000
62   CUSTOM                   FB  HB  AL  SV VD T282D GM   14  6      3  6   **     **
62   MOTOR YACHT              HT  MY  AL  SV IO T330  MRCR 14  6      3  6  89900  98800
62   MOTOR YACHT              HT  MY  AL  SV VD T330  MRCR 14  6      3  6 107400 117500

62   MOTOR YACHT              HT  MY  AL  SV VD T282D GM   14  6      3  6  78700  86500
62   MOTOR YACHT              FB  MY  AL  SV IO T330  MRCR 14  6      3  6  89900  98800
62   MOTOR YACHT              FB  MY  AL  SV VD T330  MRCR 14  6      3  6 107400 117500
62   MOTOR YACHT              FB  MY  AL  SV VD T282D GM   14  6      3  6  78700  86500
--------------------- 1978 BOATS -------------------------------------------------------------
50   2 SPORTSMAN              HT  HB  AL  TR IO T228  MRCR 14  6      2  8  58800  64600
50   2 SPORTSMAN              HT  HB  AL  TR IO T330  MRCR 14  6      2  8  64600  70900
50   2 SPORTSMAN              FB  HB  AL  TR IO T228  MRCR 14  6      2  8  58900  64700
50   2 SPORTSMAN              FB  HB  AL  TR IO T330  MRCR 14  6      2  8  64700  71100
50   2 SPORTSMAN ONE LEVEL    HT  HB  AL  TR IO T228  MRCR 14  6      2  8  61600  67700
50   2 SPORTSMAN ONE LEVEL    HT  HB  AL  TR IO T330  MRCR 14  6      2  8  67300  74000
50   2 SPORTSMAN ONE LEVEL    FB  HB  AL  TR IO T228  MRCR 14  6      2  8  61400  67500
50   2 SPORTSMAN ONE LEVEL    FB  HB  AL  TR IO T330  MRCR 14  6      2  8  67300  74000
52   HIGH BOW SPORTSMAN       HT  HB  AL  TR IO T228  MRCR 14  6      2  8  60800  66800
```

LOA FT	IN	NAME AND/ OR MODEL	TOP/ RIG	BOAT TYPE	-HULL- MTL	TP	----ENGINE--- TP	# HP	MFG	BEAM FT	IN	WGT LBS	DRAFT FT	IN	RETAIL LOW	RETAIL HIGH
		1978 BOATS														
52		HIGH BOW SPORTSMAN	HT	HB	AL	TR	IO	T330	MRCR	14	6		2	8	66400	72900
52		HIGH BOW SPORTSMAN	FB	HB	AL	TR	IO	T228	MRCR	14	6		2	8	60800	66800
52		HIGH BOW SPORTSMAN	FB	HB	AL	TR	IO	T330	MRCR	14	6		2	8	66400	72900
57		SPORTSMAN	HT	HB	AL	TR	IO	T228	MRCR	14	6		2	8	67900	74600
57		SPORTSMAN	HT	HB	AL	TR	IO	T330	MRCR	14	6		2	8	73400	80700
57		SPORTSMAN	FB	HB	AL	TR	IO	T228	MRCR	14	6		2	8	67900	74700
57		SPORTSMAN	FB	HB	AL	TR	IO	T330	MRCR	14	6		2	8	73500	80800
57		SPORTSMAN ONE LEVEL	HT	HB	AL	TR	IO	T228	MRCR	14	6		2	8	71100	78100
57		SPORTSMAN ONE LEVEL	HT	HB	AL	TR	IO	T330	MRCR	14	6		2	8	76700	84300
57		SPORTSMAN ONE LEVEL	FB	HB	AL	TR	IO	T228	MRCR	14	6		2	8	71000	78000
57		SPORTSMAN ONE LEVEL	FB	HB	AL	TR	IO	T330	MRCR	14	6		2	8	76600	84200
59		HIGH BOW ONE LEVEL	HT	HB	AL	TR	IO	T228	MRCR	14	6		2	8	71000	78000
59		HIGH BOW ONE LEVEL	HT	HB	AL	TR	IO	T330	MRCR	14	6		2	8	76600	84200
59		HIGH BOW ONE LEVEL	FB	HB	AL	TR	IO	T228	MRCR	14	6		2	8	70900	77900
59		HIGH BOW ONE LEVEL	FB	HB	AL	TR	IO	T330	MRCR	14	6		2	8	76500	84100
59		HIGH BOW SPORTSMAN	HT	HB	AL	TR	IO	T228	MRCR	14	6		2	8	67900	74600
59		HIGH BOW SPORTSMAN	HT	HB	AL	TR	IO	T330	MRCR	14	6		2	8	73500	80700
59		HIGH BOW SPORTSMAN	FB	HB	AL	TR	IO	T228	MRCR	14	6		2	8	68000	74700
59		HIGH BOW SPORTSMAN	FB	HB	AL	TR	IO	T330	MRCR	14	6		2	8	73500	80800
62		CUSTOM	HT	HB	AL	SV	IO	T228	MRCR	14	6		3		79000	86800
		IO T330 MRCR 87200 95800, VD T330 MRCR 78100 85800, VD T282D GM													**	**
62		CUSTOM	FB	HB	AL	SV	IO	T228	MRCR	14	6		3		79200	87000
		IO T330 MRCR 87700 96400, VD T330 MRCR 78600 86300, VD T282D GM													**	**
62		CUSTOM ONE LEVEL	HT	HB	AL	SV	IO	T228	MRCR	14	6		3		82200	90400
		IO T330 MRCR 90900 99900, VD T330 MRCR 81000 89100, VD T282D GM													**	**
62		CUSTOM ONE LEVEL	FB	HB	AL	SV	IO	T228	MRCR	14	6		3		82100	90300
		IO T330 MRCR 90600 99600, VD T330 MRCR 80900 88900, VD T282D GM													**	**
62		MOTOR YACHT	HT	MY	AL	SV	VD	T330	MRCR	14	6		3		102500	112500
62		MOTOR YACHT	HT	MY	AL	SV	VD	T282D	GM	14	6		3		75300	82800
62		MOTOR YACHT	FB	MY	AL	SV	VD	T330	MRCR	14	6		3		102500	112500
62		MOTOR YACHT	FB	MY	AL	SV	VD	T282D	GM	14	6		3		75300	82800
		1977 BOATS														
50		SPORTSMAN	HT	HB	AL	TR	IO	T255	MRCR	14	6		2	8	60200	66100
50		SPORTSMAN	FB	HB	AL	TR	IO	T255	MRCR	14	6		2	8	60200	66100
52		HIGH BOW SPORTSMAN	HT	HB	AL	TR	IO	T255	MRCR	14	6		2	8	60900	66900
52		HIGH BOW SPORTSMAN	FB	HB	AL	TR	IO	T255	MRCR	14	6		2	8	60900	66900
56		SPORTSMAN	HT	HB	AL	TR	IO	T255	MRCR	14	6		2	8	61900	68100
56		SPORTSMAN	FB	HB	AL	TR	IO	T255	MRCR	14	6		2	8	62100	68200
56		SPORTSMAN ONE LEVEL	HT	HB	AL	TR	IO	T255	MRCR	14	6		2	8	65000	71400
56		SPORTSMAN ONE LEVEL	FB	HB	AL	TR	IO	T255	MRCR	14	6		2	8	64900	71300
58		HIGH BOW ONE LEVEL	HT	HB	AL	TR	IO	T255	MRCR	14	6		2	8	68700	75500
58		HIGH BOW ONE LEVEL	FB	HB	AL	TR	IO	T255	MRCR	14	6		2	8	68600	75400
58		HIGH BOW SPORTSMAN	HT	HB	AL	TR	IO	T255	MRCR	14	6		2	8	65600	72100
58		HIGH BOW SPORTSMAN	FB	HB	AL	TR	IO	T255	MRCR	14	6		2	8	65800	72300
62		CUSTOM	HT	HB	AL	DV	IO	T255	MRCR	14	6		3		81900	90000
62		CUSTOM	HT	HB	AL	DV	VD	T330	MRCR	14	6		3		78600	86400
62		CUSTOM	HT	HB	AL	DV	VD	T282D	GM	14	6		3		**	**
62		CUSTOM	FB	HB	AL	DV	IO	T255	MRCR	14	6		3		82000	90100
62		CUSTOM	FB	HB	AL	DV	VD	T330	MRCR	14	6		3		78900	86700
62		CUSTOM	FB	HB	AL	DV	VD	T282D	GM	14	6		3		**	**
62		CUSTOM ONE LEVEL	HT	HB	AL	DV	IO	T255	MRCR	14	6		3		84700	93100
62		CUSTOM ONE LEVEL	HT	HB	AL	DV	VD	T330	MRCR	14	6		3		82000	90100
62		CUSTOM ONE LEVEL	HT	HB	AL	DV	VD	T282D	GM	14	6		3		**	**
62		CUSTOM ONE LEVEL	FB	HB	AL	DV	IO	T255	MRCR	14	6		3		84600	93000
62		CUSTOM ONE LEVEL	FB	HB	AL	DV	VD	T330	MRCR	14	6		3		82100	90200
62		CUSTOM ONE LEVEL	FB	HB	AL	DV	VD	T282D	GM	14	6		3		**	**
62		MOTOR YACHT	HT	MY	AL	DV	VD	T330	MRCR	14	6		3		97900	107500
62		MOTOR YACHT	HT	MY	AL	DV	VD	T282D	GM	14	6		3		72200	79300
62		MOTOR YACHT	FB	MY	AL	DV	VD	T330	MRCR	14	6		3		97900	107500
62		MOTOR YACHT	FB	MY	AL	DV	VD	T282D	GM	14	6		3		72200	79300
		1976 BOATS														
50		SPORTSMAN	HT	HB	AL	SV	IO	T225	MRCR	14	6		2	8	58500	64300
50		SPORTSMAN	HT	HB	AL	SV	IO	T255	MRCR	14	6		2	8	59400	65300
50		SPORTSMAN	FB	HB	AL	SV	IO	T225	MRCR	14	6		2	8	58600	64400
50		SPORTSMAN	FB	HB	AL	SV	IO	T255	MRCR	14	6		2	8	59500	65300
52		HIGH BOW SPORTSMAN	HT	HB	AL	SV	IO	T225	MRCR	14	6		2	8	59400	65200
52		HIGH BOW SPORTSMAN	HT	HB	AL	SV	IO	T255	MRCR	14	6		2	8	60200	66200
52		HIGH BOW SPORTSMAN	FB	HB	AL	SV	IO	T225	MRCR	14	6		2	8	59400	65200
52		HIGH BOW SPORTSMAN	FB	HB	AL	SV	IO	T255	MRCR	14	6		2	8	60200	66200
56		SPORTSMAN	HT	HB	AL	SV	IO	T225	MRCR	14	6		2	8	61900	68000
56		SPORTSMAN	HT	HB	AL	SV	IO	T255	MRCR	14	6		2	8	62800	69000
56		SPORTSMAN	FB	HB	AL	SV	IO	T225	MRCR	14	6		2	8	61900	68000
56		SPORTSMAN	FB	HB	AL	SV	IO	T255	MRCR	14	6		2	8	62800	69000
58		HIGH BOW SPORTSMAN	HT	HB	AL	SV	IO	T225	MRCR	14	6		2	8	65600	72100
58		HIGH BOW SPORTSMAN	HT	HB	AL	SV	IO	T255	MRCR	14	6		2	8	66400	73000
58		HIGH BOW SPORTSMAN	FB	HB	AL	SV	IO	T225	MRCR	14	6		2	8	65600	72100
58		HIGH BOW SPORTSMAN	FB	HB	AL	SV	IO	T255	MRCR	14	6		2	8	66400	73000
62		CUSTOM	HT	HB	AL	SV	IO	T255	MRCR	14	6		2	10	79300	87200
62		CUSTOM	HT	HB	AL	SV	VD	T350	MRCR	14	6		2	10	76700	84300
62		CUSTOM	HT	HB	AL	SV	VD	T282D	GM	14	6		2	10	**	**
62		CUSTOM	FB	HB	AL	SV	IO	T255	MRCR	14	6		2	8	79400	87200
62		CUSTOM	FB	HB	AL	SV	VD	T350	MRCR	14	6		2	10	76800	84400
62		CUSTOM	FB	HB	AL	SV	VD	T282D	GM	14	6		2	10	**	**
62		MOTOR YACHT	HT	MY	AL	SV	VD	T350	MRCR	14	6		2	10	94000	103500
62		MOTOR YACHT	HT	MY	AL	SV	VD	T282D	GM	14	6		2	10	69100	76000
62		MOTOR YACHT	FB	MY	AL	SV	VD	T350	MRCR	14	6		2	10	94000	103500
62		MOTOR YACHT	FB	MY	AL	SV	VD	T282D	GM	14	6		2	10	69100	76000
		1975 BOATS														
50	2	SPORTSMAN	HT	HB	AL	SV	IO	T225	MRCR	14	6		2	8	58000	63700
50	2	SPORTSMAN	HT	HB	AL	SV	IO	T255	MRCR	14	6		2	8	58800	64700
50	2	SPORTSMAN	FB	HB	AL	SV	IO	T225	MRCR	14	6		2	8	58100	63800
50	2	SPORTSMAN	FB	HB	AL	SV	IO	T255	MRCR	14	6		2	8	59000	64800
56	2	SPORTSMAN	HT	HB	AL	SV	IO	T225	MRCR	14	6		2	8	61400	67500
56	2	SPORTSMAN	HT	HB	AL	SV	IO	T255	MRCR	14	6		2	8	62300	68400
56	2	SPORTSMAN	FB	HB	AL	SV	IO	T225	MRCR	14	6		2	8	61400	67500
56	2	SPORTSMAN	FB	HB	AL	SV	IO	T255	MRCR	14	6		2	8	62300	68400
62	2	CUSTOM	HT	HB	AL	SV	IO	T255	MRCR	14	6		2	10	78500	86300
62	2	CUSTOM	HT	HB	AL	SV	VD	T350	MRCR	14	6		2	10	75900	83400
62	2	CUSTOM	HT	HB	AL	SV	VD	T282D	GM	14	6		2	10	**	**
62	2	CUSTOM	FB	HB	AL	SV	IO	T255	MRCR	14	6		2	10	78500	86300
62	2	CUSTOM	FB	HB	AL	SV	VD	T350	MRCR	14	6		2	10	75900	83400
62	2	CUSTOM	FB	HB	AL	SV	VD	T282D	GM	14	6		2	10	**	**
62	2	MOTOR YACHT	HT	HB	AL	SV	VD	T350	MRCR	14	6	32000	2	10	72900	80100
62	2	MOTOR YACHT	HT	HB	AL	SV	VD	T282D	GM	14	6	32000	2	10	87500	96200
62	2	MOTOR YACHT	FB	HB	AL	SV	VD	T350	MRCR	14	6	32000			72900	80100
62	2	MOTOR YACHT	FB	HB	AL	SV	VD	T282D	GM	14	6	32000			87500	96200
		1974 BOATS														
50	2	SPORTSMAN	HT	HB	AL		IO	T225	MRCR	14	6		2	6	57600	63300
50	2	SPORTSMAN	HT	HB	AL		IO	T255	MRCR	14	6		2	6	58500	64300
55	6	CUSTOM	HT	HB	AL		IO	T225	MRCR	14	6		2	10	60400	66400
		IO T255 MRCR 61200 67300, IO T325 MRCR 65400 71800, IO T282D GM													84200	92500
56	2	SPORTSMAN	HT	HB	AL		IO	T225	MRCR	14	6		2	6	60800	66800
56	2	SPORTSMAN	HT	HB	AL		IO	T255	MRCR	14	6		2	6	61700	67800
61		CUSTOM	HT	HB	AL		IO	T255	MRCR	14	6		2	10	76200	83800
61		CUSTOM	HT	HB	AL		IO	T325	MRCR	14	6		2	10	81000	89000
61		CUSTOM	HT	HB	AL		IO	T282D	GM	14	6		2	10	**	**
62			HT	HB	AL		IO	T325	MRCR	14	6		2	10	84800	93200
62			HT	HB	AL		IO	T282D	GM	14	6		2	10	**	**
		1973 BOATS														
50	2	SPORTSMAN	HT	HB	AL		IO	T225	MRCR	14	6		1		57100	62700
50	2	SPORTSMAN	HT	HB	AL		IO	T255	MRCR	14	6		1		58000	63700
50	2	SPORTSMAN	HT	HB	AL		IO	T325	MRCR	14	6		1		62200	68400
50	2	SPORTSMAN	FB	HB	AL		IO	T225	MRCR	14	6		1		57100	62700
50	2	SPORTSMAN	FB	HB	AL		IO	T255	MRCR	14	6		1		58000	63700
50	2	SPORTSMAN	FB	HB	AL		IO	T325	MRCR	14	6		1		62200	68400
55	6	CUSTOM	HT	HB	AL		IO	T325	MRCR	14	6				64800	71200
55	6	CUSTOM	HT	HB	AL		VD	T282D	GM	14	6				83300	91500
55	6	CUSTOM	FB	HB	AL		IO	T325	MRCR	14	6		1	4	64800	71200
55	6	CUSTOM	FB	HB	AL		VD	T282D	GM	14	6		1	4	83300	91500
56	2	SPORTSMAN	HT	HB	AL		IO	T225	MRCR	14	6		1		60300	66300
56	2	SPORTSMAN	HT	HB	AL		IO	T255	MRCR	14	6		1		61100	67200
56	2	SPORTSMAN	HT	HB	AL		IO	T325	MRCR	14	6		1		65200	71700
56	2	SPORTSMAN	FB	HB	AL		IO	T225	MRCR	14	6		1		60300	66300
56	2	SPORTSMAN	FB	HB	AL		IO	T255	MRCR	14	6		1		61100	67200
56	2	SPORTSMAN	FB	HB	AL		IO	T325	MRCR	14	6		1		65200	71700
61			FB	HB	AL		VD	T325	MRCR	14	6		1	4	81100	89100
61			FB	HB	AL		VD	T282D	GM	14	6		1	4	**	**
61		CUSTOM	FB	HB	AL		IO	T325	MRCR	14	6		1	4	80000	87900
61		CUSTOM	FB	HB	AL		VD	T325	MRCR	14	6		1	4	63700	70000
61		CUSTOM	FB	HB	AL		VD	T282D	GM	14	6		1	4	**	**
		1972 BOATS														
50	2	SPORTSMAN	HT	HB	AL		IO	325	MRCR	14	6		2	2	56200	61700
		IO T165 MRCR 55900 61400, IO T215 MRCR 56400 62000, IO T270 MRCR													58100	63800
		IO T325 MRCR 61700 67800														

CONTINUED ON NEXT PAGE

```
LOA   NAME AND/          TOP/ BOAT  -HULL-  ----ENGINE--- BEAM   WGT   DRAFT RETAIL RETAIL
FT IN OR MODEL           RIG  TYPE  MTL TP TP # HP  MFG  FT IN  LBS   FT IN  LOW    HIGH
------------------------ 1972 BOATS -------------------------------------------------------
55  8 CUSTOM                    AL      IO T215      14 6       2 8  50500  55500
55  8 CUSTOM             HT HB   AL      IO T325 MRCR 14 6       2 8  64400  70700
      IB T330 CHRY 59700 65600, IB T160D PERK 78200 85900, IB T282D GM  82300  90400

56  2 SPORTSMAN          HT HB   AL      IO T165 MRCR 14 6       2 4  59100  64900
      IO T215 MRCR 59600 65500, IO T270 MRCR 61200 67300, IO T325 MRCR   64700  71100

61    CUSTOM                    AL      IO T270      14 6       2 8   **     **
61    CUSTOM             HT HB   AL      IO T325 MRCR 14 6       2 8  79300  87100
61    CUSTOM             HT HB   AL      IB T330 CHRY 14 6       2 8  71400  78500
61    CUSTOM             HT HB   AL      IB T282D GM  14 6       2 8   **     **
------------------------ 1971 BOATS -------------------------------------------------------
50  2 SPORTSMAN          HT HB   AL      IO  325 MRCR 14 6       2 2  55700  61300
      IO T165 MRCR 55400 60900, IO T215 MRCR 56000 61500, IO T270 MRCR   57600  63300
      IO T325 MRCR 61200 67300

53  2 CUSTOM             HT HB   AL      IO T325 MRCR 14 6       2 8  58300  64100
53  2 CUSTOM             HT HB   AL   SV IO T215      14 6       2 8  53300  58500
53  2 CUSTOM             HT HB   AL   SV IO T270      14 6       2 8  54900  60300
55  8 SPORTSMAN          HT HB   AL      IO T215 MRCR 14 6       2 4  58800  64700
55  8 SPORTSMAN          HT HB   AL      IO T270 MRCR 14 6       2 4  60400  66400
55  8 SPORTSMAN          HT HB   AL      IO T325 MRCR 14 6       2 4  63900  70200
58  8 CUSTOM             HT HB   AL      IO T325 MRCR 14 6       2 8  69500  76400
58  8 CUSTOM             HT HB   AL   SV IO T270      14 6       2 8  66000  72600
------------------------ 1970 BOATS -------------------------------------------------------
45    SPORTSMAN          HT HB   AL   TR IO T165 MRCR 12 6       2    40800  45400
      IO T215 MRCR 41400 46000, IO T270 MRCR 43000 47800, IO T325 MRCR   47200  51800

50    SPORTSMAN          HT HB   AL   TR IO T165 MRCR 12 6       2 1  54900  60300
      IO T215 MRCR 55500 60900, IO T270 MRCR 57100 62800, IO T325 MRCR   60700  66700
      IO T390 MRCR 68200 74900

52  4 CUSTOM             HT HB   AL      IO T250      10         2 4  57300  62900
56  2 CUSTOM             HT HB   AL   SV IO T270 MRCR 13 6       2 5  60300  66300
      IB T300 CC 58700 64500, IB T300 CHRY 58400 64100, IO T325 MRCR   63700  70000
      IB T283D GM 79500 87400

61  3 CUSTOM             HT HB   AL   SV IB T300 CHRY 13 6       2 6  67400  74100
61  3 CUSTOM             HT HB   AL   SV IB T325 MRCR 13 6       2 6  75400  82800
61  3 CUSTOM             HT HB   AL   SV IB T283D GM  13 6       2 6   **     **
------------------------ 1969 BOATS -------------------------------------------------------
38    SPORTSMAN          HT HB   AL      IO  160       9 6       2    36200  40300
45    SPORTSMAN          HT HB   AL   TM IO T160 MRCR 12 6       2    40500  45000
      IO T225 MRCR 41300 45900, IO T250 MRCR 42000 46600, IO T325 MRCR   46800  51500

50    SPORTSMAN          HT HB   AL   TM IO  225 MRCR 12 6       2 1  52400  57500
      IO  250 MRCR 52700 57900, IO  325 MRCR 54800 60300, IO T160 MRCR   54500  59900
      IO T225 MRCR 55300 60700, IO T250 MRCR 56000 61500, IO T325 MRCR   60200  66200

52  4 CUSTOM             HT HB   AL   SV IO  325 MRCR 13 6       2 4  55800  61300
      IO T225 MRCR 56200 61800, IO T250 MRCR 56900 62500, IO T325 MRCR   61000  67000
      IB T283D GM 69000 75800

56  2 CUSTOM             HT HB   AL   SV IO T250 MRCR 13 6       2 5  59200  65000
      IB T300 CC 58300 64000, IO T325 MRCR 63300 69600, IB T283D GM     78800  86600

61  3 CUSTOM             HT HB   AL      IB T400 HOLM 13 6       2 6  72800  80000
61  3 CUSTOM             HT HB   AL      IB T283D GM  13 6       2 6   **     **
61  3 CUSTOM             HT HB   AL   SV IO T325 MRCR 13 6       2 6  74800  82200
------------------------ 1968 BOATS -------------------------------------------------------
43    SPORTSMAN          HT HB   AL   TR IO  160      12 6  8320   10 21100  23500
      IO  200 21300 23700, IO  225      21500 23900, IO  225 MRCR 10    21500  23900
      IO T160 23600 26200

48    SPORTSMAN          HT HB   AL   TR IO  160      12 6  9220   10 26300  29300
      IO  200 26500 29500, IO  225      26700 29700, IO  225 MRCR 10    26700  29700
      IO T160 28900 32100

50    CUSTOM             HT HB   AL DV IB T210     13 4 14511   10 42000  46700
50    CUSTOM             HT HB   AL DV IB T225     13 4 14511   10 43200  48000
50    CUSTOM             HT HB   AL DV IB T300     13 4 14511   10 42900  47700
54    CUSTOM             HT HB   AL DV IB T210     13 4 17805   10 48200  53000
54    CUSTOM             HT HB   AL DV IB T225     13 4 17805   10 49200  54000
54    CUSTOM             HT HB   AL DV IB T300     13 4 17805   10 49100  53900
57    CUSTOM             HT HB   AL DV IB T210     13 4 20014   10 52800  58000
57    CUSTOM             HT HB   AL DV IB T225     13 4 20014   10 53700  59000
57    CUSTOM             HT HB   AL DV IB T300     13 4 20014   10 53600  58900
------------------------ 1967 BOATS -------------------------------------------------------
38    SPORTSMAN          HT HB   AL                9 6        1 8  24200  26900
43    SPORTSMAN          HT HB   AL               10          2 2  32600  36200
43    SPORTSMAN          HT HB   AL                9 6        2 2  32600  36200
50    CUSTOM             HT HB   AL               10          2 4  38700  43000
54    CUSTOM             HT HB   AL               10          2 6  48700  53500
57    CUSTOM             HT HB   AL               10          2 6  54200  59600
------------------------ 1966 BOATS -------------------------------------------------------
38    SPORTSMAN          HT HB   STL     IO T150      12 6      2 6  37300  41500
43    CUSTOM             HT HB   AL      IO T225      12 6      2 6  40200  44600
50    CUSTOM             HT HB   AL      IO T310      13 4      2 8  58000  63700
54    CUSTOM             HT HB   AL      IO T310      13 4      2 8  63800  70100
```

A LE COMTE COMPANY INC

For more recent years, see the BUC Used Boat Price Guide, Volume 1 or Volume 2

```
LOA   NAME AND/          TOP/ BOAT  -HULL-  ----ENGINE--- BEAM   WGT   DRAFT RETAIL RETAIL
FT IN OR MODEL           RIG  TYPE  MTL TP TP # HP  MFG  FT IN  LBS   FT IN  LOW    HIGH
------------------------ 1983 BOATS -------------------------------------------------------
45 10 A-L-C 46           SLP SA/CR FBG KL IB  40D WEST 12 3 25000  6 9 140500 154000
45 10 A-L-C 46           KTH SA/CR FBG KL IB  40D WEST 12 3 25000  6 9 144500 159000
45 10 A-L-C 46 TALL RIG  KTH SA/CR FBG KL IB  40D WEST 12 3 25000  5 6 145500 159500
------------------------ 1982 BOATS -------------------------------------------------------
45 10 A-L-C 46           SLP SA/CR FBG KL IB  40D WEST 12 3 25000  6 9 133000 146000
45 10 A-L-C 46           KTH SA/CR FBG KL IB  40D WEST 12 3 25000  6 9 137000 150500
------------------------ 1981 BOATS -------------------------------------------------------
45 10 A-L-C 46           SLP SA/CR FBG KL IB  40D WEST 12 3 25000  6 9 126000 138500
45 10 A-L-C 46           KTH SA/CR FBG KL IB  40D WEST 12 3 25000  6 9 129500 142500
------------------------ 1980 BOATS -------------------------------------------------------
45 10 A-L-C 46           SLP SA/CR FBG KL IB  40D WEST 12 3 25000  6 9 120000 131500
45 10 A-L-C 46           KTH SA/CR FBG KL IB  40D WEST 12 3 25000  6 9 123500 135500
------------------------ 1978 BOATS -------------------------------------------------------
34  7 A-L-C 35             SLP SA/CR F/S KL IB  13D VLVO 10    12000  5 6  36500  40500
39  7 A-L-C 40             SLP SA/CR FBG KL IB  35D VLVO 11 8 16000  5 9  62700  68900
39  7 A-L-C 40             KTH SA/CR FBG KL IB  35D VLVO 11 8 16000  5 9  62700  68900
44 10 FASTNET 45 TRUNK CBN SLP SA/CR FBG KL IB  45D REN  12 3 24000  6 9 103500 114000
44 10 FASTNET 45 TRUNK CBN YWL SA/CR FBG KL IB  45D REN  12 3 24000  6 9 103500 114000
45  7 A-L-C 46             SLP SA/CR FBG KL IB  45D REN  12 3 25000  6 9 109000 119500
45  7 A-L-C 46             KTH SA/CR FBG KL IB  45D REN  12 3 25000  6 9 112500 123500
45  7 A-L-C 46 SHOAL       SLP SA/CR FBG KL IB  45D REN  12 3 25000  6 9 109000 119500
45  7 A-L-C 46 SHOAL       KTH SA/CR FBG KL IB  45D REN  12 3 25000  6 9 112500 123500
45  7 FASTNET 45 FLUSH DCK SLP SA/CR FBG KL IB  45D REN  12 3 24000  6 9 107000 117500
45  7 FASTNET 45 FLUSH DCK YWL SA/CR FBG KL IB  45D REN  12 3 24000  6 9 107000 117500
------------------------ 1977 BOATS -------------------------------------------------------
34  7 A-L-C            SLP SAIL  F/S KL IB  13D VLVO      12000  5 6  35300  39200
39  7 A-L-C            SLP SAIL  FBG KL IB  35D VLVO 11 8 15400  5 9  58900  64800
39  7 A-L-C            KTH SAIL  FBG KL IB  35D VLVO 11 8 15400  5 9  58900  64800
45    FASTNET 45       SLP SAIL  FBG KL IB  45D REN      23000      9  98400 108000
45    FASTNET 45       YWL SAIL  FBG KL IB  45D REN   12 3 23000  6 9  98400 108000
45 10 A-L-C            SLP SAIL  F/S KL IB  45D REN   12 3 25000  6 9 105500 116000
45 10 A-L-C            KTH SAIL  F/S KL IB  45D REN   12 3 25000  6 9 109500 120000
------------------------ 1976 BOATS -------------------------------------------------------
34  7 A-L-C            SLP SAIL  F/S KL IB  10D VLVO      12000  5 6  34100  37900
38    NORTHEAST        SLP SAIL  FBG KL IB  37D WEST 10 11 16000  5 6  53500  58800
39  7 A-L-C            SLP SAIL  FBG KL VD  37D WEST 11 8 15400  5 9  57300  62900
39  7 A-L-C            KTH SAIL  FBG KL VD  37D WEST 11 8 15400  5 9  57300  62900
45    FASTNET 45       SLP SAIL  FBG KL IB  37D WEST 12 3 24000  6 9  96800 106500
45    FASTNET 45       YWL SAIL  FBG KL IB  37D WEST 12 3 24000  6 9  96800 106500
45 10 A-L-C            SLP SAIL  F/S KL IB  37D WEST 12 3 25000  6 9 102000 112000
45 10 A-L-C            KTH SAIL  F/S KL IB  37D WEST 12 3 25000  6 9 105500 116000
------------------------ 1975 BOATS -------------------------------------------------------
34  7 A-L-C            SLP SAIL  F/S KL IB  10D VLVO      12000  5 6  33100  36500
38  3 NORTHEAST        SLP SAIL  FBG KL IB  37D WEST 10 11 16000  5 6  52000  57100
38  3 NORTHEAST        YWL SAIL  FBG KL IB  37D WEST 10 11 16000  5 6  52000  57100
38  3 NORTHEAST        KTH SAIL  FBG KL IB  37D WEST 10 11 16000  5 6  52000  57100
39  7 A-L-C            SLP SAIL  FBG KL VD  37D WEST 11 8 15400  5 9  55600  61100
39  7 A-L-C            KTH SAIL  FBG KL VD  37D WEST 11 8 15400  5 9  55600  61100
45    FASTNET 45       SLP SAIL  FBG KL IB  37D WEST 12 3 24000  6 9  93500 103000
45    FASTNET 45       YWL SAIL  FBG KL IB  37D WEST 12 3 24000  6 9  93500 103000
45 10 A-L-C            SLP SAIL  F/S KL IB  37D WEST 12 3 25000  6 9  98400 108000
45 10 A-L-C            KTH SAIL  F/S KL IB  37D WEST 12 3 25000  6 9 102500 112000
51 10 OCEAN            SLP SA/CR FBG KL IB  65D      13 6 36000  7   148000 162500
------------------------ 1974 BOATS -------------------------------------------------------
34  7 A-L-C            SLP SAIL  F/S KL IB  10D VLVO      12000  5 6  32300  35800
38    NORTHEAST        SLP SAIL  FBG KL IB  37D WEST 10 11 16000  5 6  50600  55500
39  7 A-L-C            SLP SAIL  F/S KL VD  37D WEST 11 8 15400  5 9  54100  59500
```

LOA FT IN	NAME AND/ OR MODEL	TOP/ RIG	BOAT TYPE	HULL MTL	TP	ENG TP	# HP	MFG	BEAM FT IN	WGT LBS	DRAFT FT IN	RETAIL LOW	RETAIL HIGH
1974 BOATS													
39 7	A-L-C	SLP	SAIL	FBG	KL	VD	37D	WEST	11 8	15400	5 9	54100	59500
45 10	A-L-C	SLP	SAIL	F/S	KL	IB	37D	WEST	12 3	25000	6 9	95200	104500
45 10	A-L-C	KTH	SAIL	F/S	KL	IB	37D	WEST	12 3	25000	6 9	98800	108500
51 10	OCEAN	SLP	SA/CR	FBG	KL	IB	65D		13 6	36000	7	143000	157500
1973 BOATS													
34 7	A-L-C	SLP	SAIL	F/S	KL	IB	25D		10	12000	5 6	31600	35100
38 3	NORTHEAST	SLP	SAIL	FBG	KL	IB	37D		10 11	16000	5 4	49200	54100
39 7	A-L-C	SLP	SAIL	F/S	KL	VD	37D		11 8	15400	5 9	52600	57800
45 7	FASTNET 45	SLP	SAIL	FBG	KL	IB	37D		12 3	23000	6 9	86000	94500
45 10	A-L-C	SLP	SAIL	F/S	KL	IB	37D		12 3	25000	6 9	92200	101500
45 10	A-L-C	KTH	SAIL	F/S	KL	IB	37D		12 3	25000	6 9	95800	105500
51 10	OCEAN	SLP	SA/RC	FBG	KL	IB	87D		13 6	36000	7	139500	153000
51 10	OCEAN	YWL	SA/RC	FBG	KL	IB	87D		13 6	36000	7	139500	153000
1972 BOATS													
34 6	A-L-C 35 FLUSH DECK	SLP	SA/CR	FBG	KL	IB	31		10	12000	5 6	30600	34000
34 6	A-L-C 35 TRUNK CBN	SLP	SA/CR	FBG	KL	IB	31		10	12000	5 6	30600	34000
38 3	NORTHEAST 38	SLP	SA/CR	FBG	KL	IB	31		10 11	16000	5 4	47600	52300
39 7	A-L-C 40	SLP	SA/CR	FBG	KL	IB	46D		11 8	15400	5 9	51600	56700
44 10	FASTNET 45 TRNK CBN	SLP	SA/CR	FBG	KL	IB	46D		12 3	24000	6 9	85000	93400
45 7	FASTNET 45 FD	SLP	SA/CR	FBG	KL	IB	46D		12 3	24000	6 9	87400	96100
51 10	OCEAN CRUISER	SLP	SA/CR	FBG	KL	IB	72D		13 6	36000	7	135000	148500
1971 BOATS													
34 7	A-L-C	SLP	SA/RC	FBG	KL	IB			10		5 6	30000	33400
38 3	NORTHEAST	SLP	SA/RC	FBG	KL	IB			10 11		5 4	30600	34000
38 3	NORTHEAST	YWL	SA/RC	FBG	KL	IB			10 11		5 4	30600	34000
44 10	FASTNET 45	SLP	SA/RC	FBG	KL	IB	D		12 3		6 9	84600	93000
44 10	FASTNET 45	YWL	SA/RC	FBG	KL	IB	D		12 3		6 9	84600	93000
45 7	FASTNET 46	SLP	SA/RC	FBG	KL				12 3	24800	6 9	84800	93200
45 7	FASTNET 46	YWL	SA/RC	FBG	KL				12 3	24800	6 9	84800	93200
51 10	OCEAN	SLP	SA/RC	FBG	KL	IB	D		13 6		7	128500	141500
51 10	OCEAN	YWL	SA/RC	FBG	KL	IB	D		13 6		7	128500	141500
51 10	OCEAN	KTH	SA/RC	FBG	KL	IB	D		13 6		7	132500	145500
1970 BOATS													
33 3	MEDALIST MARK I	SLP	SA/RC	FBG	KL	IB			10		5 2	22400	24900
33 3	MEDALIST MARK II	SLP	SA/RC	FBG	KL	IB			10		5 2	22400	24900
33 3	MEDALIST MARK III	SLP	SA/RC	FBG	KL	IB			10		5 2	22400	24900
34 6	A-L-C	SLP	SA/CR	FBG	KL	IB	30		10		5 2	29400	32700
38 2	NORTHEAST MARK I	SLP	SA/CR	FBG	KL	IB	30		10 11	17000	5 4	47800	52500
38 2	NORTHEAST MARK I	YWL	SA/CR	FBG	KL	IB	30		10 11	17000	5 4	47800	52500
38 2	NORTHEAST MARK II	SLP	SA/CR	FBG	KL	IB	30		10 11	17000	5 4	47800	52500
38 2	NORTHEAST MARK II	YWL	SA/CR	FBG	KL	IB	30		10 11	17000	5 4	47800	52500
38 2	NORTHEAST MARK III	SLP	SA/CR	FBG	KL	IB	30		10 11	17000	5 4	47800	52500
38 2	NORTHEAST MARK III	YWL	SA/CR	FBG	KL	IB	30		10 11	17000	5 4	47800	52500
45	FASTNET 45	SLP	SA/CR	FBG	KL	IB	37		12 3	24800	6 9	81700	89800
45	FASTNET 45	YWL	SA/CR	FBG	KL	IB	37		12 3	24800	6 9	81600	89700
51 10	OCEAN	SLP	SA/RC	FBG	KL	IB	87		13 6	37000	7	128500	141000
51 10	OCEAN	YWL	SA/RC	FBG	KL	IB	87		13 6	37000	7	128500	141500
1969 BOATS													
33 3	MEDALIST MARK I	SLP	SA/CR	FBG	KL	IB	30		10	11700	5 2	27300	30300
33 3	MEDALIST MARK II	SLP	SA/CR	FBG	KL	IB	30		10	11700	5 2	27300	30300
33 3	MEDALIST MARK III	SLP	SA/CR	FBG	KL	IB	30		10	11700	5 2	27300	30300
38 3	NORTH-EAST 38 MARK I	SLP	SA/CR	FBG	KL	IB	30		10 11	17000	5 4	47300	52000
38 3	NORTH-EAST 38 MARK I	YWL	SA/CR	FBG	KL	IB	30		10 11	17000	5 4	47300	52000
38 3	NORTH-EAST 38 MARKII	SLP	SA/CR	FBG	KL	IB	30		10 11	17000	5 4	47300	52000
38 3	NORTH-EAST 38 MARKII	YWL	SA/CR	FBG	KL	IB	30		10 11	17000	5 4	47300	52000
38 3	NORTH-EAST 38 MK III	SLP	SA/CR	FBG	KL	IB	30		10 11	17000	5 4	47300	52000
38 3	NORTH-EAST 38 MK III	YWL	SA/CR	FBG	KL	IB	30		10 11	17000	5 4	47300	52000
45	FASTNET 45	SLP	SA/CR	FBG	KL	IB	37D		12 3	24800	6 9	80800	88800
45	FASTNET 45	YWL	SA/CR	FBG	KL	IB	37D		12 3	24800	6 9	80800	88800
51 10	OCEAN	SLP	SA/RC	FBG	KL	IB	87D		13 6	37000	7	127000	139500
51 10	OCEAN	YWL	SA/RC	FBG	KL	IB	87D		13 6	37000	7	127000	140000
1968 BOATS													
33 3	MEDALIST MARK I	SLP	SAIL	FBG	KL	IB	30		10	12500	5 2	28700	31900
33 3	MEDALIST MARK II	SLP	SAIL	FBG	KL	IB	30		10	12500	5 2	28700	31900
33 3	MEDALIST MARK III	SLP	SAIL	FBG	KL	IB	30		10	12500	5 2	28700	31900
38 2	NORTHEAST MARK I	SLP	SAIL	FBG	KL	IB	30		10 11	16500	5 4	44900	49900
38 2	NORTHEAST MARK II	SLP	SAIL	FBG	KL	IB	30		10 11	16500	5 4	44900	49900
38 2	NORTHEAST MARK III	SLP	SAIL	FBG	KL	IB	30		10 11	16500	5 4	44900	49900
45	FASTNET	SLP	SAIL	FBG	KL	IB	46D		12 3	23000	6 9	80400	88400
51 10	OCEAN	SLP	SA/RC	FBG	KL	IB	87D		13 6	38000	7	133000	146000
1967 BOATS													
33	MEDALIST MARK I	SLP	SA/CR	FBG	KL	IB	30		10	12500	5 3	28200	31400
33	MEDALIST MARK III	SLP	SA/CR	FBG	KL	IB	30		10	12500	5 3	28200	31400
33 3	MEDALIST MARK II	SLP	SA/CR	FBG	KL	IB	30		10			23300	25900
38 2	NORTHEAST MARK I	SLP	SA/CR	FBG	KL	IB	30		10 11	16500	5 4	44400	49300
38 2	NORTHEAST MARK II	SLP	SA/CR	FBG	KL	IB	30		10 11	16500	5 4	44400	49300
38 2	NORTHEAST MARK III	SLP	SA/CR	FBG	KL	IB	30		10 11	16500	5 4	44400	49300
45	FASTNET	SLP	SA/CR	FBG	KL	IB	30		12	23000	6 6	78200	85900
51 10	OCEAN	SLP	SA/RC	FBG	KL	IB	87D		13 6	38000	7	131000	143500
1966 BOATS													
32 8	MEDALIST	SLP	SAIL	FBG	KL	IB	30		10		5 4	22800	25300
37 8	NORTHEAST	SLP	SAIL	FBG	KL	IB	30		10 10		5 4	42300	47100
51 10	OCEAN	SLP	SA/RC	FBG	KL	IB	87D		13 6		7	124000	136500
1965 BOATS													
32 8	MEDALIST		SAIL	FBG		IB	30					22600	25100
33	MARK II	SLP	SAIL	FBG	KL	IB			10		5 3	22800	25300
37 8	NORTHEAST		SAIL	FBG		IB	30					41900	46600
51 7	OCEAN	SLP	SA/RC	FBG	KL	IB			13 6		7	**	**
1964 BOATS													
32 8	MEDALIST		SAIL	FBG		IB	30					22500	25000
37 8	NORTHEAST		SAIL	FBG		IB	30					41500	46100
1963 BOATS													
32 8	MEDALIST		SAIL	FBG		IB	30					22400	24900
37 8	NORTHEAST		SAIL	FBG		IB	30					41300	45800
1962 BOATS													
32 8	MEDALIST		SAIL	FBG		IB	30					22400	24800
37 8	NORTHEAST		SAIL	FBG		IB	30					41100	45600
1961 BOATS													
35 10	ZEPHYR	YWL	SA/CR	FBG	CB	OB			10 4		3 6	25200	28000
38		SLP	SA/CR	FBG	KL	OB			10 10		5 4	20300	22500
38		YWL	SA/CR	FBG	KL	OB			10 10		5 4	20300	22500
38 6	CHALLENGER	YWL	SA/CR	FBG	KL	OB			11		4	42600	47300
42 3	NORDFARER	YWL	SA/CR	P/M	KL	OB			11 2		6	70300	77300
47 1	CRUISER	CR		FBG		IB			14		3 2	**	**
55	CRUISER	CR		STL		IB			14 8		3 9	**	**
65	CRUISER	CR		FBG		IB			15 4		4 3	**	**
66 8	CRUISER	CR		FBG		IB			16 4		4 3	**	**
1960 BOATS													
35 10	ZEPHYR	YWL	SA/CR	FBG	KC	OB			10 4			25300	28100
38 6	CHALLENGER	YWL	SA/CR	FBG	KC	OB			11			42700	47400
42 3	NORDFARER	YWL	SA/CR	P/M		OB			11 2		6	70400	77400
47 1	CRUISER	MY		FBG		IB			14		3 2	**	**
55	CRUISER	MY		STL		IB			14 8		3 9	**	**
65	CRUISER	MY		STL		IB			15 4		4 3	**	**
66 8	CRUISER	MY		FBG		IB			16 4		4 3	**	**
1959 BOATS													
33 3	MALABAR-SR	SLP	SA/CR	P/M	KL	OB			9 9		5	24100	26800
42	NORDFARER		SA/CR	P/M	KL	OB			11 1		6	70000	76900
55	FLUSHDECK	CR		STL		IB	470		15			38100	42400
65	FLUSHDECK	CR		STL		IB	470		16			73500	80800

LEISURE CRAFT
WESTATES TRUCK EQUIPMENT CORP
MENLO PARK CA 94025   See inside cover to adjust price for area

LOA FT IN	NAME AND/ OR MODEL	TOP/ RIG	BOAT TYPE	HULL MTL	TP	ENG TP	# HP	MFG	BEAM FT IN	WGT LBS	DRAFT FT IN	RETAIL LOW	RETAIL HIGH
1973 BOATS													
35	CAPTAIN		AL			OB	12			9000	1 6	18600	20700
42	PRESIDENT		AL			OB	12			10500	1 6	**	**
44	IMPERIAL		AL			OB	14			12000	1 6	**	**

LEISURE INDUSTRIES INC

Call 1-800-327-6929 for BUC Personalized Evaluation Service
Or, for 1969 to 1970 boats, sign onto www.BUCValuPro.com

LENMAN INDUSTRIES INC
COAST GUARD MFG ID- LNM

Call 1-800-327-6929 for BUC Personalized Evaluation Service
Or, for 1973 to 1978 boats, sign onto www.BUCValuPro.com

LEWIS MARINE CO

Call 1-800-327-6929 for BUC Personalized Evaluation Service
Or, for 1966 to 1967 boats, sign onto www.BUCValuPro.com

LIBERTY YACHT CORPORATION
LELAND NC 28451   COAST GUARD MFG ID- LYH See inside cover to adjust price for area

For more recent years, see the BUC Used Boat Price Guide, Volume 1 or Volume 2

LOA FT IN	NAME AND/ OR MODEL	TOP/ RIG	BOAT TYPE	-HULL- MTL TP	---- TP	ENGINE--- # HP	MFG	BEAM FT IN	WGT LBS	DRAFT FT IN	RETAIL LOW	RETAIL HIGH
------- 1983 BOATS -------
27 9	PIED-PIPER 28	SLP	SAIL	FBG KC	IB	15D	UNIV	8 9	8300	3 3	17400	19800
------- 1982 BOATS -------
27 9	PIED-PIPER 28	SLP	SAIL	FBG KC	IB	15D	YAN	8 9	8300	3 3	16400	18700
------- 1981 BOATS -------
27 9	PIED-PIPER 28	SLP	SAIL	FBG KC	IB	15D	YAN	8 9	8300	3 3	15400	17500
------- 1980 BOATS -------
27 9	PIED-PIPER 28	SLP	SAIL	FBG KC	IB	15D		8 9	8300	3 3	14800	16800
------- 1979 BOATS -------
27 9	PIED-PIPER 28	SLP	SAIL	FBG KC	IB	15D	YAN	8 9	8300	3 3	14200	16100

LIBERTY YACHTS INC
RIVIERA BEACH FL 33404 COAST GUARD MFG ID- LBN See inside cover to adjust price for area

For more recent years, see the BUC Used Boat Price Guide, Volume 1 or Volume 2

LOA FT IN	NAME AND/ OR MODEL	TOP/ RIG	BOAT TYPE	-HULL- MTL TP	---- TP	ENGINE--- # HP	MFG	BEAM FT IN	WGT LBS	DRAFT FT IN	RETAIL LOW	RETAIL HIGH
------- 1983 BOATS -------
28	LIBERTY 28	CUT	SA/CR	FBG KL		15D	VLVO	9 7	12000	4	21300	23600
37 11	LIBERTY 38	CUT	SA/CR	FBG KL	IB	40D		11 6	20000	4 9	50500	55500
------- 1982 BOATS -------
28	LIBERTY 28	CUT	SA/CR	FBG KL	IB	13D	WEST	9 7	12000	4	20000	22200
37 8	LIBERTY 38	CUT	SA/CR	FBG KL		40D		11 6	20000	4 8	46900	51500
------- 1981 BOATS -------
28	LIBERTY 28	CUT	SA/CR	FBG KL	IB	23D	VLVO	9 7	12000	4	19100	21200
------- 1980 BOATS -------
28	LIBERTY 28	CUT	SA/CR	FBG KL	IB	23D	VLVO	9 7	12000	4	18200	20200
33	LIBERTY 28	CUT	SA/CR	FBG KL	IB	D		9 7	12000	4	19200	21400
------- 1979 BOATS -------
28	LIBERTY 28	CUT	SA/CR	FBG KL	IB	23D	VLVO	9 7	12000	4	17100	19500
------- 1978 BOATS -------
28	LIBERTY 28	CUT	SA/CR	FBG KL	IB	23D	VLVO	9 7	12000	4	16500	18800

LIBERTY YACHTS INC
SEATTLE WA 98109   See inside cover to adjust price for area

For more recent years, see the BUC Used Boat Price Guide, Volume 1 or Volume 2

LOA FT IN	NAME AND/ OR MODEL	TOP/ RIG	BOAT TYPE	-HULL- MTL TP	---- TP	ENGINE--- # HP	MFG	BEAM FT IN	WGT LBS	DRAFT FT IN	RETAIL LOW	RETAIL HIGH
------- 1982 BOATS -------
39 5	PASSPORT 40	SLP	SA/CR	FBG KL				12 8	22771	5 9	82900	91100

LIEN HWA INDUSTRIAL CORP
TAIPEI TAIWAN   COAST GUARD MFG ID- LHC See inside cover to adjust price for area

LOA FT IN	NAME AND/ OR MODEL	TOP/ RIG	BOAT TYPE	-HULL- MTL TP	---- TP	ENGINE--- # HP	MFG	BEAM FT IN	WGT LBS	DRAFT FT IN	RETAIL LOW	RETAIL HIGH
------- 1982 BOATS -------
46 2	SEAMASTER 46	CUT MS		FBG KL	IB	85D	PERK	14 3	33000		113500	125000

LIGHTNING BOATS
NORTH AMERICAN PRODUCTS COAST GUARD MFG ID- NAP

Call 1-800-327-6929 for BUC Personalized Evaluation Service
Or, for 1974 to 1976 boats, sign onto www.BUCValuPro.com

M C LINDE

Call 1-800-327-6929 for BUC Personalized Evaluation Service
Or, for 1946 boats, sign onto www.BUCValuPro.com

LINDENBERG YACHTS INC
COCOA FL 32922   COAST GUARD MFG ID- LDB See inside cover to adjust price for area

For more recent years, see the BUC Used Boat Price Guide, Volume 1 or Volume 2

LOA FT IN	NAME AND/ OR MODEL	TOP/ RIG	BOAT TYPE	-HULL- MTL TP	---- TP	ENGINE--- # HP	MFG	BEAM FT IN	WGT LBS	DRAFT FT IN	RETAIL LOW	RETAIL HIGH
------- 1983 BOATS -------
21 6	LINDENBERG 22	SLP	SA/RC	FBG DB	OB			8	1800	9	4050	4700
24	LINDENBERG 24	SLP	SA/RC	FBG KL	OB			9	2750	4 5	6000	6850
26	LINDENBERG 26	SLP	SA/RC	FBG KL	OB			9 8	5300	4 5	12300	14000
26	LINDENBERG 26	SLP	SA/RC	FBG KL	SD		OMC	9 8	5300	4 5	12700	14400
26	LINDENBERG 26	SLP	SA/RC	FBG KL	IB	D		9 8	5300	4 5	13000	14800
28	LINDENBERG 28	SLP	SA/RC	FBG KL	OB			9 6	4000	5 4	10200	11600
29 11	LINDENBERG 30	SLP	SA/RC	FBG KL	OB			10	7000	5 4	19300	21400
29 11	LINDENBERG 30 FD	SLP	SA/RC	FBG KL	IB	10D	BMW	10	7000	5 4	19500	21700
29 11	LINDENBERG 30 FD	SLP	SA/RC	FBG KL	OB			10	7000	5 4	19300	21400
29 11	LINDENBERG 30 FD	SLP	SA/RC	FBG KL	IB	10D	BMW	10	7000	5 4	19500	21700
------- 1982 BOATS -------
21 6	LINDENBERG 22	SLP	SA/RC	FBG DB	OB			8	1800	9	3800	4450
24	LINDENBERG 24	SLP	SA/RC	FBG KL	OB			9	2750	4 5	5650	6450
26	LINDENBERG 26	SLP	SA/RC	FBG KL	OB			9 8	5300	4 5	11600	13200
26	LINDENBERG 26	SLP	SA/RC	FBG KL	SD		OMC	9 8	5300	4 5	11900	13600
26	LINDENBERG 26	SLP	SA/RC	FBG KL	IB	D		9 8	5300	4 5	12300	13900
29 11	LINDENBERG 30	SLP	SA/RC	FBG KL	OB			10	7000	5 4	18800	20900
29 11	LINDENBERG 30	SLP	SA/RC	FBG KL	IB	10D	BMW	10	7000	5 4	19000	21100
29 11	LINDENBERG 30 FD	SLP	SA/RC	FBG KL	OB			10	7000	5 4	17500	19900
29 11	LINDENBERG 30 FD	SLP	SA/RC	FBG KL	IB	10D	BMW	10	7000	5 4	18100	20100
------- 1981 BOATS -------
21 6	LINDENBERG 22	SLP	SA/RC	FBG DB	OB			8	1800	9	3600	4150
24	LINDENBERG 24	SLP	SA/RC	FBG KL	OB			9	2750	4 5	5300	6100
26	LINDENBERG 26	SLP	SA/RC	FBG KL	OB			9 8	5300	4 5	10900	12400
26	LINDENBERG 26	SLP	SA/RC	FBG KL	SD		OMC	9 8	5300	4 5	11200	12800
26	LINDENBERG 26	SLP	SA/RC	FBG KL	IB	D		9 8	5300	4 5	11500	13100
29 11	LINDENBERG 30	SLP	SA/RC	FBG KL	OB			10	7000	5 4	16900	19200
29 11	LINDENBERG 30	SLP	SA/RC	FBG KL	IB	12D	BMW	10	7000	5 4	17100	19400
29 11	LINDENBERG 30 FD	SLP	SA/RC	FBG KL	OB			10	7000	5 4	16900	19200
29 11	LINDENBERG 30 FD	SLP	SA/RC	FBG KL	IB	12D	BMW	10	7000	5 4	17100	19400
------- 1980 BOATS -------
21 6	LINDENBERG 22	SLP	SA/RC	FBG DB	OB			8	1800	9	3400	4000
26	LINDENBERG 26	SLP	SA/RC	FBG KL	OB			9 8	5300	4 5	10400	11800
26	LINDENBERG 26	SLP	SA/RC	FBG KL	SD		OMC	9 8	5300	4 5	10700	12200
26	LINDENBERG 26	SLP	SA/RC	FBG KL	IB	D		9 8	5300	4 5	11000	12500
29 11	LINDENBERG 30	SLP	SA/RC	FBG KL	OB			10	7000	5 4	16100	18300
29 11	LINDENBERG 30	SLP	SA/RC	FBG KL	IB	12D	BMW	10	7000	5 4	17100	19400
29 11	LINDENBERG 30 FD	SLP	SA/RC	FBG KL	OB			10	7000	5 4	16100	18300
29 11	LINDENBERG 30 FD	SLP	SA/RC	FBG KL	IB	12D	BMW	10	7000	5 4	15500	17700
------- 1979 BOATS -------
21 6	LINDENBERG 22	SLP	SAIL	FBG DB	OB			8	1800	9	3300	3800
26	LINDENBERG 26	SLP	SAIL	FBG KL	OB			9 8	5300	4 5	10800	11400
26	LINDENBERG 26	SLP	SAIL	FBG KL	IB	D		9 8	5300	4 5	10600	12000
------- 1978 BOATS -------
21 6	LINDENBERG 22	SLP	SAIL	FBG DB	OB			8	1800	9	3150	3700
26	LINDENBERG 26	SLP	SAIL	FBG KL	OB			9 8	5300	4 5	9650	11000
26	LINDENBERG 26	SLP	SAIL	FBG KL	SD	15	OMC	9 8	5300	4 5	9900	11200
26	LINDENBERG 26	SLP	SAIL	FBG KL	IB	7D	PETT	9 8	5300	4 5	10100	11500
------- 1977 BOATS -------
26	LINDENBERG 26	SLP	SAIL	FBG KL	OB			9 8	5200	4 6	9200	10400
26	LINDENBERG 26	SLP	SAIL	FBG KL	IB	7D- 8D		9 8	5200	4 6	9650	10900
------- 1976 BOATS -------
26	LINDENBERG 26	SLP	SAIL	FBG KL	OB			9 8	5200	4 6	8900	10100

LINDH BOAT CO

Call 1-800-327-6929 for BUC Personalized Evaluation Service
Or, for 1966 to 1982 boats, sign onto www.BUCValuPro.com

LINDMARK YACHT SALES LTD
DESPLAINES IL 60018   COAST GUARD MFG ID- LDR See inside cover to adjust price for area

For more recent years, see the BUC Used Boat Price Guide, Volume 1 or Volume 2

LOA FT IN	NAME AND/ OR MODEL	TOP/ RIG	BOAT TYPE	-HULL- MTL TP	---- TP	ENGINE--- # HP	MFG	BEAM FT IN	WGT LBS	DRAFT FT IN	RETAIL LOW	RETAIL HIGH
------- 1983 BOATS -------
30	LINDMARK Q30 SDN	FB		TRWL	IB	T 80D	LEHM	11 6	14000	3 6	51500	56600
34 11	LINDMARK G35	FB		TRWL	FBG DS IB	T 120D	LEHM	12	19800	3 6	73700	81000
34 11	LINDMARK G35	FB		TRWL	FBG DS IB	T 80D	LEHM	12	19800	3 6	68700	75500
35 8	LINDMARK SR-36 GC	FB			FBG DS IB	120D	LEHM	13 4	19000	3 3	72600	79800
35 8	LINDMARK SR-36 GC	FB			FBG DS IB	T120D	LEHM	13 4	19000	3 3	80100	88000
35 8	LINDMARK SR-36 SEDAN	FB			FBG DS IB	120D	LEHM	13 4	19000	3 3	72600	79800
35 8	LINDMARK SR-36 SEDAN	FB			FBG DS IB	T120D	LEHM	13 4	19000	3 3	72900	80100

LOA FT IN	NAME AND/ OR MODEL	TOP/ RIG	BOAT TYPE	-HULL- MTL TP	---ENGINE--- TP # HP MFG	BEAM FT IN	WGT LBS	DRAFT FT IN	RETAIL LOW	RETAIL HIGH
1983 BOATS
38 3	LINDMARK G38	FB	TRWL	FBG DS IB	120D LEHM	13 2	22620	4 2	83400	91700
38 3	LINDMARK G38	FB	TRWL	FBG DS IB	T120D LEHM	13 2	22620	4 2	88400	97200
38 3	LINDMARK SR-39 GC	FB		FBG DS IB	120D LEHM	13 8	23000	3 3	86200	94700
38 3	LINDMARK SR-39 GC	FB		FBG DS IB	T120D LEHM	13 8	23000	3 3	90900	99800
38 3	LINDMARK SR-39 SEDAN	FB		FBG DS IB	120D LEHM	13 8	23000	3 3	86200	94700
38 3	LINDMARK SR-39 SEDAN	FB		FBG DS IB	T120D LEHM	13 8	23000	3 3	90900	99800
41	LINDMARK Q41	FB	TRWL	FBG DS IB	120D LEHM	14		4	113000	124500
41	LINDMARK Q41	FB	TRWL	FBG DS IB	T120D LEHM	14	31700	4	122000	134000
44 10	LINDMARK Q45 PH	FB	TRWL	FBG DS IB	T130D PERK	15 10		4 2	129500	142500
44 10	LINDMARK Q45 SDN	FB	TRWL	FBG DS IB	T130D PERK	15	30000	4 2	112000	123000
45 6	LINDMARK Q-46 SUNDK	FB		FBG DS IB	T200D PERK	14 4	30000	4 2	118000	129500
45 6	LINDMARK Q46 SUNDK	FB		FBG DS IB	T145D ISUZ	14 4	30000	4 2	115000	126500
51	LINDMARK SR-51 FD	FD	MY	FBG DS IB	T210D GM	16 8	50000	4 3	163000	179000
51	LINDMARK SR-51 FD	FB	MY	FBG DS IB	T235D VLVO	16 8	50000	4 3	166500	183000
51	LINDMARK SR-51 FD	FB	MY	FBG DS IB	T270D CUM	16 8	50000	4 3	160000	176000
55	LINDMARK SR-55 FD	FB	MY	FBG DS IB	T310D GM	18 7		4 9	193000	212000
55	LINDMARK SR-55 PHS	FB	MY	FBG DS IB	T310D GM	18 7		4 9	176500	194000
60	LINDMARK SR-60	FB	MY	FBG DS IB	T460D GM	19		4 9	273000	300000
65	LINDMARK SR-65	FB	MY	FBG DS IB	T460D GM	19		4 9	387000	425000
1982 BOATS
30	LINDMARK Q30 SDN	FB	TRWL	FBG DS IB	80D LEHM	11 6	14000	3 6	43600	48500
30	LINDMARK Q30 SDN	FB	TRWL	FBG DS IB	T 80D FORD	11 6	14000	3 6	49500	54400
34 11	LINDMARK G35	FB	TRWL	FBG DS IB	120D LEHM	12	19800	3 4	70800	77800
34 11	LINDMARK G35	FB	TRWL	FBG DS IB	T120D LEHM	12	20500	3 4	74500	81800
39 3	LINDMARK G40	FB	TRWL	FBG DS IB	120D LEHM	13 2	22620	4 2	82900	91100
39 3	LINDMARK G40	FB	TRWL	FBG DS IB	T120D LEHM	13 2	22620	4 2	88100	96800
41	LINDMARK Q41	FB	TRWL	FBG DS IB	120D LEHM	14		4	108000	119000
	IB 130D PERK 107000 117500, IB T120D LEHM 116500 128500, IB T130D PERK 115500 127000
42 6	LINDMARK OCEAN 43	FB	DCMY	FBG DS IB	T120D LEHM	14 6	29000	3 8	113000	124500
42 6	LINDMARK OCEAN 43	FB	MY	FBG DS IB	T120D LEHM	14 6	29000	3 8	113500	124500
44 10	LINDMARK Q45 PH	FB	TRWL	FBG DS IB	T120D LEHM	15 10		4 2	123000	135000
44 10	LINDMARK Q45 PH	FB	TRWL	FBG DS IB	T130D PERK	15 10		4	124000	136000
44 10	LINDMARK Q45 SDN	FB	TRWL	FBG DS IB	T120D LEHM	15 10	46500	4 2	140500	154000
44 10	LINDMARK Q45 SDN	FB	TRWL	FBG DS IB	T130D PERK	15 10	46500	4 2	141500	155500
50 3	LINDMARK OCEAN 50 FD	FB	MY	FBG DS IB	T120D LEHM	15 6	48500	4 6	150500	165000
	IB T210D CAT 163500 179500, IB T216D GM 166000 182500, IB T240D VLVO 167500 184000
	IB T270D CUM 172000 189000, IB T295D CUM 176500 193500, IB T310D GM 178500 196500
	IB T400D CUM 191000 210000
50 3	LINDMARK OCEAN 50 PH	HT	MY	FBG DS IB	T120D LEHM	15 6	46500	4 6	140500	154500
	IB T210D CAT 155000 170500, IB T216D GM 158500 174000, IB T240D VLVO 154000 169000
	IB T270D CUM 163000 179000, IB T295D CUM 169000 185500, IB T310D GM 172000 189500
	IB T400D CUM 187000 205500
50 3	LINDMARK OCEAN 50 PH	HT	MY	FBG DS IB	T120D LEHM	15 6	47000	4 6	140000	154500
	IB T210D CAT 154500 169500, IB T216D GM 157500 173000, IB T240D VLVO 160000 175500
	IB T270D CUM 162500 178500, IB T295D CUM 168500 185000, IB T310D GM 171500 188500
	IB T400D CUM 186500 205000
55	LINDMARK SR 55 PH	HT	MY	FBG DS IB	T310D GM	18 7	64900	4 9	204000	224000
59 3	LINDMARK SR-60	FB	MY	FBG DS IB	D GM	19	72000	4 9	**	**
65 6	LINDMARK SR 65	FB	MY	FBG DS IB	T325D GM	19	79400	4 9	345000	379000
1981 BOATS
34 11	GLOUCESTERMAN 34	FB	TRWL	FBG DS IB	120D LEHM	12	19800	3 4	68100	74800
34 11	GLOUCESTERMAN 34	FB	TRWL	FBG DS IB	120D LEHM	12	20500	3 4	71600	78700
38 3	GLOUCESTERMAN 38	FB	TRWL	FBG DS IB	120D LEHM	13 2	22620	4 2	76000	83600
38 3	GLOUCESTERMAN 38	FB	TRWL	FBG DS IB	T120D LEHM	13 2	22620	4 2	80600	88600
41	QUESTAR 41	FB		FBG DS IB	130D PERK	14	30000	4	101500	111500
41	QUESTAR 41	FB		FBG DS IB	T120D LEHM	14	31700	4	111000	121500
44 10	QUESTAR 45 PH	FB		FBG DS IB	T120D LEHM	15 10		4 2	126000	138500
44 10	QUESTAR 45 SEDAN	FB		FBG DS IB	T120D LEHM	15 10		4 2	120500	132500
50 3	QUESTAR 50 AFT	FB	TRWL	FBG DS IB	T120D LEHM	15 6	46500	4 6	148000	163000
50 3	QUESTAROCEAN SO	FB	TRWL	FBG DS IB	T120D LEHM	15 6	46500	4 6	133000	146000
1980 BOATS
34 11	GLOUCESTERMAN 34	FB	TRWL	FBG DS IB	130D PERK	12	19800	3 4	65400	71800
34 11	GLOUCESTERMAN 34	FB	TRWL	FBG DS IB	T120D LEHM	12	20500	3 4	68800	75600
34 11	GLOUCESTERMAN CT34	FB	SV	FBG SV IB	120D	12			60400	66400
34 11	GLOUCESTERMAN CT34	FB	SV	FBG SV IB	160D	12			60100	66000
34 11	GLOUCESTERMAN CT34	FB	SV	FBG SV IB	T160D	12			63700	70000
38 3	GLOUCESTERMAN CT38	FB	SV	FBG SV IB	128D	13 2			73400	80700
38 3	GLOUCESTERMAN CT38	FB	SV	FBG SV IB	185D	13 2			74100	81400
38 4	GLOUCESTERMAN 38	FB		FBG DS IB	130D PERK	13 2	24900	4 2	79600	87500
38 4	GLOUCESTERMAN 38	FB		FBG DS IB	T120D LEHM	13 2	25600	4 2	85100	93600
41	QUESTAR 41	FB		FBG DS IB	130D PERK	14	30000	4	93400	102500
41	QUESTAR 41	FB		FBG DS IB	T120D LEHM	14	31700	4	102000	112000
41	QUESTAR 41 SEDAN	FB		FBG DS IB	130D PERK	14	30000		100500	110500
41	QUESTAR 41 SEDAN	FB		FBG DS IB	T120D LEHM	14	31700		109000	120000
41	QUESTAR 41 TRI-CAB	FB	SV	FBG SV IB	120D	14			98600	108500
41	QUESTAR 41 TRI-CAB	FB	SV	FBG SV IB	185D	14			99700	109500
42	GLOUCESTERMAN CT42PH	HT	TRWL	FBG DS IB	120D	14 7			104000	114000
42	GLOUCESTERMAN PH	HT	TRWL	FBG DS IB	185D PERK	14 7	31800	4 5	101500	111500
42	GLOUCESTERMAN PH	HT	TRWL	FBG DS IB	T120D	14 7	32500	4 5	106500	117000
42	GLOUCESTERMAN SDN	FB	TRWL	FBG DS IB	120D	14 7			102500	112500
42	GLOUCESTERMAN SDN	FB	TRWL	FBG DS IB	185D PERK	14 7	31800	4 5	102500	112500
42	GLOUCESTERMAN SDN	FB	TRWL	FBG DS IB	T120D	14 7	32500	4 5	107000	118000
44 10	QUESTAR PH	FB	TRWL	FBG DS IB	T120D LEHM	14 2	36700	4	121000	133000
50 3	QUESTAR 50 PH	HT	TRWL	FBG SV IB	T120D	15 6			138000	152000
50 3	QUESTAR 50 PH	HT	TRWL	FBG SV IB	T270D	15 6			147000	162000
50 3	QUESTAR 50 PH	HT	TRWL	FBG DS IB	T120D LEHM	15 6	46500	4 6	133500	146500
50 3	QUESTAR PH	FB		FBG DS IB	T120D LEHM	15 6	46500	4 6	132000	145000
1979 BOATS
34 11	GLOUCESTERMAN 34	FB		FBG SV IB	130D PERK	12	19800	3 4	62900	69100
34 11	GLOUCESTERMAN 34	FB		FBG SV IB	T120D LEHM	12	20900	3 4	66300	73600
38 3	GLOUCESTERMAN 38	FB		FBG DS IB	130D PERK	13 2	22600	4 2	70000	76900
38 3	GLOUCESTERMAN 38	FB		FBG DS IB	T120D LEHM	13 2	23700	4 2	76300	83800
41	QUESTAR 41	FB		FBG DS IB	130D PERK	14	30000	4	91800	101000
41	QUESTAR 41	FB		FBG SV IB	T120D LEHM	14	31000	4	99100	109000
42	GLOUCESTERMAN PH	HT		FBG DS IB	185D PERK	14 7	32000	4 5	97600	107500
42	GLOUCESTERMAN PH	HT		FBG DS IB	T120D LEHM	14 7	33600	4 5	104000	114500
42	GLOUCESTERMAN SDN	FB		FBG DS IB	185D PERK	14 7	32000	4 5	98400	108900
42	GLOUCESTERMAN SDN	FB		FBG DS IB	T120D LEHM	14 7	33600	4 5	105000	115500
1978 BOATS
34 11	GLOUCESTERMAN TRICAB	FB		FBG DS IB	120D LEHM	12	19800	3 4	60600	66600
38 3	GLOUCESTERMAN BT-DK	FB		FBG DS IB	130D PERK	13 2	22620	4 2	67500	74200
38 3	GLOUCESTERMAN BT-DK	FB		FBG DS IB	T120D LEHM	13 2	24050	4 2	75000	82400
38 3	GLOUCESTERMAN TRICAB	FB		FBG DS IB	130D PERK	13 2	22620	4 2	65200	71700
38 3	GLOUCESTERMAN TRICAB	FB		FBG DS IB	T120D LEHM	13 2	24050	4 2	72600	79800
41	QUESTAR SEDAN	FB		FBG DS IB	120D LEHM	14	28600	4	83700	92000
41	QUESTAR SEDAN	FB		FBG DS IB	T120D LEHM	14	30000	4	91500	100500
41	QUESTAR TRI-CAB	FB		FBG DS IB	120D LEHM	14	28600	4	83700	92000
41	QUESTAR TRI-CAB	FB		FBG DS IB	T120D LEHM	14	30000	4	91500	100500
42	GLOUCESTERMAN PH	HT		FBG DS IB	120D LEHM	14 7	30600	4 5	88600	97300
42	GLOUCESTERMAN PH	HT		FBG DS IB	T120D LEHM	14 7	32000	4 5	96900	106500
42	GLOUCESTERMAN SEDAN	FB	TRWL	FBG DS IB	120D LEHM	14 7	30600	4 5	88100	96800
42	GLOUCESTERMAN SEDAN	FB	TRWL	FBG DS IB	T120D LEHM	14 7	32000	4 5	95400	105000
1977 BOATS
41 10	QUESTAR	FB	TRWL	FBG DS IB	120D LEHM	14	30000	4	83100	91300
41 10	QUESTAR	FB	TRWL	FBG DS IB	T120D LEHM	14	30000	4	86900	95500
42	GLOUCESTERMAN PH	HT	TRWL	FBG DS IB	T120D LEHM	14	32000	4 5	91900	101000

JOHN LINDSEY

LOA FT IN	NAME AND/ OR MODEL	TOP/ RIG	BOAT TYPE	-HULL- MTL TP	---ENGINE--- TP # HP MFG	BEAM FT IN	WGT LBS	DRAFT FT IN	RETAIL LOW	RETAIL HIGH
1969 BOATS
20 6	NEWPORT 20	SLP	SAIL	FBG KL		7 6		3 4	6050	6950
30	NEWPORT 30	SLP	SAIL	FBG KL IB	UNIV 10 6	10 6	2500	4 9	9800	11100
40 9	NEWPORT 41	SLP	SAIL	FBG KL IB	UNIV 11 3	11 3		6 3	65800	72300
1933 BOATS
22 9			LNCH	IB		6 8			**	**

LINK LEISURE INC
COAST GUARD MFG ID- LLN

Call 1-800-327-6929 for BUC Personalized Evaluation Service
Or, for 1978 boats, sign onto www.BUCValuPro.com

LINSEY YACHT CORP

Call 1-800-327-6929 for BUC Personalized Evaluation Service
Or, for 1975 to 1980 boats, sign onto www.BUCValuPro.com

LITTLE HARBOR CUSTOM YACHTS

PORTSMOUTH RI 02871   COAST GUARD MFG ID- LHB See inside cover to adjust price for area
FORMERLY OCEAN RANGER YACHTS

For more recent years, see the BUC Used Boat Price Guide, Volume 1 or Volume 2

LOA FT IN	NAME AND/ OR MODEL	TOP/ RIG	BOAT TYPE	-HULL- MTL TP TP#	----ENGINE--- HP MFG	BEAM FT IN	WGT LBS	DRAFT FT IN	RETAIL LOW	RETAIL HIGH
				1983 BOATS						
38	LITTLE-HARBOR 38	SLP	SA/RC	FBG KC IB	50D PERK	11 10	20000	4 6	110500	121000
44 3	LITTLE-HARBOR 44 AFT	SLP	SA/RC	FBG KC IB	62D PERK	13 8	30700	5	183500	201500
44 3	LITTLE-HARBOR 44 CTR	SLP	SA/CR	FBG KC IB	62D PERK	13 8	30700	5	183500	201500
50 9	LITTLE-HARBOR 50	SLP	SA/CR	FBG KC IB	85D PERK	15 1	43200	5 6	283500	311500
61 7	LITTLE-HARBOR 62	SLP	SA/CR	FBG KC IB	T135D PERK	16 4	91000	6	837500	920500
74 4	LITTLE-HARBOR 75	SLP	SA/CR	FBG KC IB	T135D PERK	18 5	64T	6 6	**	**
				1982 BOATS						
38	LITTLE-HARBOR	SLP	SA/RC	FBG KC IB	50D PERK	11 10	20600	4 6	105500	116000
38	LITTLE-HARBOR 38	SLP	SA/RC	FBG KC VD	D PERK	11 10	20600	9	105500	116000
50 3	OCEAN 50	FB	MY	FBG SV IB	T200D FORD	15 6	46500	4 6	225500	248000
50 3	OCEAN 50	HT	PH	FBG DS IB	T120D LEHM	15 6	46500	4 6	224500	246500
50 3	OCEAN 50	FB	TRWL	FBG DS IB	T120D LEHM	15 6	46500	4 6	216000	237500

IB T210D CAT 225500 247500, IB T216D GM 223000 245000, IB T240D VLVO 224000 246500
IB T270D CUM 229500 252000, IB T295D CUM 232000 255000, IB T310D GM 233500 256500
IB T400D CUM 245500 270000

LOA FT IN	NAME AND/ OR MODEL	TOP/ RIG	BOAT TYPE	-HULL- MTL TP TP#	----ENGINE--- HP MFG	BEAM FT IN	WGT LBS	DRAFT FT IN	RETAIL LOW	RETAIL HIGH
50 3	OCEAN 500	FB	TRWL	FBG SV IB	T120D LEHM	15 6	46500	4 6	216000	237500
62	LITTLE-HARBOR 62	SLP	SA/CR	FBG KC IB	T130D PERK	16 4	88000	13 9	765500	841500
62 7	LITTLE-HARBOR	SLP	SA/CR	FBG KC IB	T130D PERK	16 4	88000	5 11	780000	857000
75	LITTLE-HARBOR 75	SLP	SA/CR	FBG KC IB	T165D PERK	18 5	59T	13 9	**	**
				1981 BOATS						
35 9	OCEAN-RANGER	FB	TRWL	FBG DS IB	T120D LEHM	13 10	19091	3 3	108500	119000
38	LITTLE-HARBOR	SLP	SA/RC	FBG KC IB	50D PERK	11 10	20600	3 3	98900	108500
38 3	OCEAN-RANGER	FB	TRWL	FBG DS IB	T120D LEHM	13 8	23000	3 3	129500	142500
50 3	OCEAN-RANGER	HT	PH	FBG DS IB	T120D LEHM	15 6	46500	4 6	214500	235500
50 3	OCEAN-RANGER	FB	TRWL	FBG DS IB	T120D LEHM	15 6	46500	4 6	206000	226500

IB T210D CAT 215000 236500, IB T216D GM 213000 234000, IB T240D VLVO 214000 235000
IB T270D CUM 219000 240500, IB T295D CUM 221500 243500, IB T310D GM 222500 244500
IB T400D CUM 234500 257500

LOA FT IN	NAME AND/ OR MODEL	TOP/ RIG	BOAT TYPE	-HULL- MTL TP TP#	----ENGINE--- HP MFG	BEAM FT IN	WGT LBS	DRAFT FT IN	RETAIL LOW	RETAIL HIGH
59 3	OCEAN-RANGER	FB	TRWL	FBG DS IB	T325D GM	19	72000	4 9	350500	385000
61 7	LITTLE-HARBOR	SLP	SA/CR	FBG KC IB	T130D PERK	16 4	88000	5 11	707500	777500
				1976 BOATS						
39 10	LITTLE-HARBOR 39	SLP	SA/CR	FBG KL IB	D	12	19400	7 3	83100	91400

LIVINGSTON BOAT SHIP

Call 1-800-327-6929 for BUC Personalized Evaluation Service
Or, for 1966 to 1970 boats, sign onto www.BUCValuPro.com

LOFLAND INDUSTRIES INC

Call 1-800-327-6929 for BUC Personalized Evaluation Service
Or, for 1961 to 1973 boats, sign onto www.BUCValuPro.com

JOHN LOGAN

Call 1-800-327-6929 for BUC Personalized Evaluation Service
Or, for 1969 boats, sign onto www.BUCValuPro.com

LOHI OY
COAST GUARD MFG ID- LHY

Call 1-800-327-6929 for BUC Personalized Evaluation Service
Or, for 1975 boats, sign onto www.BUCValuPro.com

LONE STAR BOAT CO
GRAND PRAIRIE TX 75050   See inside cover to adjust price for area

LOA FT IN	NAME AND/ OR MODEL	TOP/ RIG	BOAT TYPE	-HULL- MTL TP TP#	----ENGINE--- HP MFG	BEAM FT IN	WGT LBS	DRAFT FT IN	RETAIL LOW	RETAIL HIGH
				1965 BOATS						
16 4	MAYPORT	RNBT		OB		6 3	555		2450	2900
16 8	FLEETWOOD	RNBT		OB		6 7			3350	3850
18	CHEASAPEAK	CR		OB		7 4	830		3800	4450
22 3	SOUTHWIND	SKI		OB		8			5450	6250
				1960 BOATS						
16	BERMUDA	RNBT	FBG SV	OB		6 3	660		2900	3350
16 8	VACATIONER	CR	FBG SV	OB		6 6	750		3350	3900
17 9	BAR-HARBOR	CR	FBG SV	OB		7	1030		4700	5400
17 9	BEL-ISLE	CR	FBG SV	OB		7	860		4000	4600
18	EL-DORADO	CR	AL SV	OB		7 1	800		3800	4400
21	CRUISE-MASTER	CR	AL SV	OB		7 5	1100		6000	6900
23 2	CRUISE-LINER	CR	AL SV	OB		8	1100		5900	6750

LONG ISLAND SAILING CENTER

Call 1-800-327-6929 for BUC Personalized Evaluation Service
Or, for 1965 to 1968 boats, sign onto www.BUCValuPro.com

LONG ISLAND YACHT SALES

Call 1-800-327-6929 for BUC Personalized Evaluation Service
Or, for 1960 to 1961 boats, sign onto www.BUCValuPro.com

LOREQUIN MARINE INC
COAST GUARD MFG ID- LMK

Call 1-800-327-6929 for BUC Personalized Evaluation Service
Or, for 1978 to 1981 boats, sign onto www.BUCValuPro.com

W R LOUGHLIN

Call 1-800-327-6929 for BUC Personalized Evaluation Service
Or, for 1965 to 1967 boats, sign onto www.BUCValuPro.com

LOVFALD MARINE
COAST GUARD MFG ID- LVF

Call 1-800-327-6929 for BUC Personalized Evaluation Service
Or, for 1978 to 1987 boats, sign onto www.BUCValuPro.com

PERT LOWELL CO INC
COAST GUARD MFG ID- PLO

Call 1-800-327-6929 for BUC Personalized Evaluation Service
Or, for 1959 to 2008 boats, sign onto www.BUCValuPro.com

LOWELL'S BOAT SHOP INC
COAST GUARD MFG ID- LMR

Call 1-800-327-6929 for BUC Personalized Evaluation Service
Or, for 1965 to 1987 boats, sign onto www.BUCValuPro.com

LOZIER

Call 1-800-327-6929 for BUC Personalized Evaluation Service
Or, for 1905 to 1910 boats, sign onto www.BUCValuPro.com

NILS LUCANDER

Call 1-800-327-6929 for BUC Personalized Evaluation Service
Or, for 1967 boats, sign onto www.BUCValuPro.com

LUCKY BOATS MFG
COAST GUARD MFG ID- LBM

Call 1-800-327-6929 for BUC Personalized Evaluation Service
Or, for 1976 boats, sign onto www.BUCValuPro.com

LUCRAFT BOATS
DIV OF LABRAY CORP   COAST GUARD MFG ID- LBL

Call 1-800-327-6929 for BUC Personalized Evaluation Service
Or, for 1978 to 1980 boats, sign onto www.BUCValuPro.com

LUDERS MARINE CONST CO
STAMFORD CT   See inside cover to adjust price for area

LOA FT IN	NAME AND/ OR MODEL	TOP/ RIG	BOAT TYPE	-HULL- MTL TP	TP	ENGINE # HP	MFG	BEAM FT IN	WGT LBS	DRAFT FT IN	RETAIL LOW	RETAIL HIGH
--------- 1963 BOATS ---------
26		SLP	SAIL	WD	OB						8350	9600
40	LUDERS		SAIL	WD	OB						39600	44000
--------- 1962 BOATS ---------
40	LUDERS		SAIL	WD	OB						39300	43700
--------- 1961 BOATS ---------
26	L-16	SLP	SA/OD	WD	KL			5 9		4	6650	7650
31	VIKING	SLP	SA/CR	PLY KL	OB			8 10		4 3	18900	21000
40	L-27	SLP	SA/CR	PLY KL	IB	D		9 10		5 5	53100	58300
--------- 1960 BOATS ---------
26 4	L-16	SLP	SA/OD	FBG KL				5 9		4	6750	7750
31	VIKING	SLP	SA/CR	PLY KL	OB			8 10		4 3	18900	21000
40	L-27	SLP	SA/CR	PLY KL	IB	D		9 10		5 5	53100	58400
--------- 1959 BOATS ---------
26 6	L-16	SLP	SAIL	FBG KL				5 9		4	8450	9750
31 5	VIKING	SLP	SAIL	PLY KL				8 10		4 3	15700	17800
38 3	L-24		SAIL	PLY KL				6 3		4 10	20500	22800
40	L-27	SLP	SAIL	PLY KL				9 10		5 5	39900	44300
44		YWL	SAIL	WD	IB	40D	PERK				66700	73300
--------- 1950 BOATS ---------
23 9		SLP	SA/RC	WD	KC			6		3 3	5400	6200
23 9		SLP	SA/RC	WD	KL			6		3 3	5400	6200
--------- 1946 BOATS ---------
24	LITTLE-GULFER	HT	CR	PLY	IB			8 1		2 8	**	**
26		SLP	SAIL	PLY				5 9		4	9550	10800
35	GULFER	HT	CR	PLY	IB			10 6		3 6	**	**
40		HT	CR	PLY	IB			11 6		4	**	**
--------- 1939 BOATS ---------
26	FISHERS-ISLAND	SLP	SAIL	WD	KL			5 8		4	11600	13200
--------- 1937 BOATS ---------
26		SLP	SAIL	MHG KL				5 9		4	12300	14000
--------- 1931 BOATS ---------
16	RED-WING	SLP	SA/OD	WD	KL						2500	2900
45	LUDERSHIP COMMUTER	HT	MY	MHG	SV	IB T	STER				**	**

LUGER BOATS INC
ST JOSEPH MO 64502   COAST GUARD MFG ID- LUG See inside cover to adjust price for area
FORMERLY LUGER INDUSTRIES

For more recent years, see the BUC Used Boat Price Guide, Volume 1 or Volume 2

LOA FT IN	NAME AND/ OR MODEL	TOP/ RIG	BOAT TYPE	-HULL- MTL TP	TP	ENGINE # HP	MFG	BEAM FT IN	WGT LBS	DRAFT FT IN	RETAIL LOW	RETAIL HIGH
--------- 1983 BOATS ---------
20	SOUTHWIND	SLP	SA/CR	FBG SK	OB			7	1850	4	2250	2650
25 6	PILOTHOUSE	OP	PH	FBG RB	OB			8	1800	2	7800	8950
25 6	SPORT FISHERMAN	OP	CTRCN	FBG RB	OB			8	1700	2	7650	8750
25 7	TRADEWINDS	SLP	SA/CR	FBG SK	OB			8	2600	4	3700	4300
26 11	FAIRWINDS 2702	SLP	SA/CR	FBG SK	OB			8	2800	4 8	4050	4700
29 11	ADVENTURER	SLP	MS	FBG KC	IB	D		8	8500	3	12700	14400
29 11	ADVENTURER	KTH	MS	FBG KC	IB	D		8	8500	3	12700	14400
29 11	VOYAGER	SLP	SA/CR	FBG KC	OB			8	8000	3	11800	13400
29 11	VOYAGER	KTH	SA/CR	FBG KC	OB			8	8500	3	12500	14200
--------- 1982 BOATS ---------
20	SOUTHWIND	SLP	SA/CR	FBG SK	OB			7	1850	8	2100	2500
25 6	PILOTHOUSE	OP	PH	FBG RB	OB			8	1800	1 1	7650	8750
25 6	SPORT FISHERMAN	OP	CTRCN	FBG RB	OB			8	1700	1 1	7500	8600
25 7	TRADEWINDS	SLP	SA/CR	FBG SK	OB			8	2600	2 2	3500	4050
26 11	FAIRWINDS 2702	SLP	SA/CR	FBG SK	OB			8	2800	2 3	3800	4400
29 11	ADVENTURER	SLP	MS	FBG KC	IB	20D		8	8500	3	12000	13600
29 11	ADVENTURER	KTH	MS	FBG KC	IB	20D		8	8500	3	12000	13600
29 11	VOYAGER	SLP	SA/CR	FBG KC	OB			8	8000	3	11100	12600
29 11	VOYAGER	KTH	SA/CR	FBG KC	OB			8	8500	3	11800	13400
--------- 1981 BOATS ---------
20	SOUTHWIND	SLP	SA/CR	FBG SK	OB			7	1850	8	1950	2350
25 6	PILOTHOUSE	OP	PH	FBG RB	OB			8	1800	1 1	7500	8600
25 6	SPORT FISHERMAN	OP	CTRCN	FBG RB	OB			8	1700	1 1	7350	8450
25 7	TRADEWINDS	SLP	SA/CR	FBG SK	OB			8	2600	2 2	3300	3800
26 11	FAIRWINDS 2702	SLP	SA/CR	FBG SK	OB			8	2800	2 3	3550	4150
29 11	VOYAGER	SLP	SA/CR	FBG KC	OB			8	8000	3	10400	11800
29 11	VOYAGER	KTH	SA/CR	FBG KC	OB			8	8500	3	11100	12600
--------- 1980 BOATS ---------
20	SOUTHWIND	SLP	SA/CR	FBG CB	OB			7	1850	8	1900	2250
20	SOUTHWIND	SLP	SA/CR	FBG SK	OB			7	1850	8	1900	2250
21	WESTWIND 21	SLP	SA/CR	FBG CB	IB			7			2450	2850
25 6	SPORT FISHERMAN 2661	OP	CTRCN	FBG RB	OB			8	1700	1 1	7200	8300
25 7	TRADEWINDS	SLP	SA/CR	FBG SK	OB			8	2600	2 2	3150	3650
25 7	WINDWARD	SLP	SAIL	FBG SK	OB			8	2400	2 2	2950	3450
26 11	FAIRWINDS 2702	SLP	SA/CR	FBG SK	OB			8	2800	2 3	3400	3950
29 9	VAGABOND 3051	HT	MY	FBG DS	IB	50D		8	8500	3	17100	19400
29 11	VOYAGER	SLP	SA/CR	FBG KC	OB			8	8000	3	9950	11300
29 11	VOYAGER	KTH	SA/CR	FBG KC	OB			8	8500	3	10600	12000
--------- 1979 BOATS ---------
20	SOUTHWIND	SLP	SA/CR	FBG SK	OB			7	1850		1800	2150
25 7	TRADEWINDS	SLP	SA/CR	FBG SK	OB			7 11	2600		3000	3500
30	VOYAGER	SLP	SA/CR	FBG KC	OB			8	6800		8050	9250
30	VOYAGER	KTH	SA/CR	FBG KC	OB			8	6800		8050	9250
--------- 1978 BOATS ---------
21	SOUTHWIND 21 KIT	SLP	SA/CR	FBG KL	OB			7			1800	2150
21	WINDWARD 21 KIT	SLP	SA/CR	FBG KL	OB			7			1800	2150
24	MONTE-CARLO KIT		CR	FBG DV	IO			8			**	**
25 7	TRADEWINDS 26 KIT	SLP	SA/CR	FBG KL	OB			8			2900	3350
--------- 1971 BOATS ---------
17	MALIBU		CR	FBG DV	IO			6 8			**	**
17	MONACO W/T	RNBT		FBG DV	IO			6 8			**	**
17	MONTEREY W/T	RNBT		FBG DV	IO	130		6 8		2 6	2500	2900
20	COMMODORE		CR	FBG DV	IO	200		7 10			4150	4800
20	ISLANDER		CR	FBG DV	IO	200		7 10			4050	4700
22	CARIBBEAN		CR	FBG DV	IO	250		7 11			6050	6950
22	NEWPORT		SF	FBG DV	IO	225		7 11			6850	7850
24	CORONADO		CR	FBG DV	IO	300		7 11		3	7750	8900
24	MONTE-CARLO		CR	FBG DV	IO	250		7 11		2 6	7350	8450
32	CORONADO EXPRESS	EXP		FBG DV	IO	250		10 5		2 6	23100	25600
--------- 1966 BOATS ---------
22	CARIBBEAN		CR	FBG DV	OB			7 11			6900	7950

LUHRS CORPORATION
ST AUGUSTINE FL 32086   COAST GUARD MFG ID- LHR See inside cover to adjust price for area

For more recent years, see the BUC Used Boat Price Guide, Volume 1 or Volume 2

LOA FT IN	NAME AND/ OR MODEL	TOP/ RIG	BOAT TYPE	-HULL- MTL TP	TP	ENGINE # HP	MFG	BEAM FT IN	WGT LBS	DRAFT FT IN	RETAIL LOW	RETAIL HIGH
--------- 1979 BOATS ---------
25	250	OP	FSH	FBG SV	IB	225-250		9 4			11300	13000
25	250	FB	SF	FBG SV	IB	225-250		9 4			9500	10900
28	280	OP	CR	FBG SV	IB	T225		11 2			15900	18100
28	280	FB	SDN	FBG SV	IB	T225		11 2			18500	20500
32	320	OP	CR	FBG SV	IB	T225-T250		12 7			27100	30700
37 8	380	OP	CR	FBG SV	IB	T330		12 9			55200	60600
--------- 1978 BOATS ---------
25	SPORTFISHERMAN	FB	SF	FBG SV	IB	225-250		9 4	6000		11700	13400
25	SPORTSMAN	OP	UTL	FBG SV	IB	225-250		9 4			7100	8300
28	FLYBRIDGE CRUISER	FB	SDN	FBG SV	IB	225-250		11 2	9000		19000	21500
28	FLYBRIDGE CRUISER	FB	SDN	FBG SV	IB	160D-200D		11 2	9000		26900	30700
28	FLYBRIDGE CRUISER	FB	SDN	FBG SV	IB	T225	CHRY	11 2	9000		21400	23800
32	FLYBRIDGE CRUISER	FB	SDN	FBG SV	IB	T225	CHRY	12 7	9000		28400	31600
32	FLYBRIDGE CRUISER	FB	SDN	FBG SV	IB	T250	CHRY	12 7	12000		33700	37400
32	FLYBRIDGE CRUISER	FB	SDN	FBG SV	IB	IBT160D-T200D		12 7	12000		42100	49000
38	FLYBRIDGE CRUISER	FB	SDN	FBG SV	IB	T225		13 7	21000		**	**
--------- 1977 BOATS ---------
25	SPORTFISHERMAN	FB	SF	FBG SV	IB	225-250		9 4	6000	2 8	11300	12900
25	SPORTFISHERMAN	FB	SF	FBG SV	IB	200D CHRY		9 4	6000	2 8	16000	18100
25	SPORTSMAN	OP	UTL	FBG SV	IB	225-250		9 4	5800	2 5	6900	7900
25	SPORTSMAN	OP	UTL	FBG SV	IB	200D CHRY		9 4	5800	2 5	15600	17700
28	FLYBRIDGE CRUISER	FB	SDN	FBG SV	IB	225-250		11 2	9000	2 9	17800	20800
28	FLYBRIDGE CRUISER	FB	SDN	FBG SV	IB	160D-200D		11 2	10000	2 10	28100	32200
28	FLYBRIDGE CRUISER	FB	SDN	FBG SV	IB	T225	CHRY	11 2	9000	2 10	21500	23900
32	FLYBRIDGE CRUISER	FB	SDN	FBG SV	IB	T225	CHRY	12 7	12000		31700	35900
32	FLYBRIDGE CRUISER	FB	SDN	FBG SV	IB	IBT160D-T200D		12 7	14600		44600	51500
--------- 1976 BOATS ---------
25	FLYBRIDGE CRUISER	FB	SDN	FBG SV	IB	215-250		9 4	6200		11300	13200
25	SPORTFISHERMAN	FB	SF	FBG SV	IB	215-250		9 4	6000		10500	12100
25	SPORTSMAN	OP	UTL	FBG SV	IB	215-250		9 4	5000		9450	10900
28	280 FLYBRIDGE CR	FB	SDN	FBG SV	IB	215-250		11 2	9000		16800	19500
28	280 FLYBRIDGE CR	FB	SDN	FBG SV	IB	T215-T225		11 2	10000		20600	23000

LOA FT	LOA IN	NAME AND/ OR MODEL	TOP/ RIG	BOAT TYPE	-HULL- MTL	-HULL- TP	ENGINE TP	ENGINE # HP	ENGINE MFG	BEAM FT	BEAM IN	WGT LBS	DRAFT FT	DRAFT IN	RETAIL LOW	RETAIL HIGH
		1976 BOATS														
28		EXPRESS CRUISER	OP	EXP	FBG	SV	IB	215-250		11	2	7500			14700	17000
28		EXPRESS CRUISER	OP	EXP	FBG	SV	IB	T215-T225		11	2	9000			18300	20400
28		EXPRESS CRUISER	HT	EXP	FBG	SV	IB	215-250		11	2	7500			14700	17000
28		EXPRESS CRUISER	HT	EXP	FBG	SV	IB	T215-T225		11	2	9000			18300	20400
32		320 FLYBRIDGE CR	FB	SDN	FBG	SV	IB	T225-T250		12	7	10000			26400	29900
32		320 FLYBRIDGE CR	FB	SDN	FBG	SV	IB	T160D	PERK	12	7	11000			37700	41900
32	6	CONVERTIBLE SEDAN	FB	SDN	FBG	SV	IB	T215-T250		12	6	12500			31300	35600
32	6	SPORTFISHERMAN	FB	SF	FBG	SV	IB	T215-T250		12	6	9700			22900	26100
32	6	SPORTFISHERMAN	FB	SF	FBG	SV	IB	T160D	PERK	12	6	10700			33600	37400
		1975 BOATS														
25		250	FB	SF	FBG	SV	IB	215-250		9	4				8550	9800
25		MARLBORO	HT	EXP	FBG	SV	IB	215	WAUK	9	4				9050	10300
25		MARLBORO	FB	SDN	FBG	SV	IB	215	WAUK	9	4				10400	11800
25		MARLBORO	FB	SF	FBG	SV	IB	215	WAUK	9	4				7400	8550
28		280	FB	SDN	FBG	SV	IB	225-250		11	2				15100	17500
28		280	FB	SDN	FBG	SV	IB	T185	WAUK	11	2				16800	19000
28		280	FB	SDN	FBG	SV	IB	T105D	CHRY	11	2				24500	27200
28		MARLBORO	FB	SDN	FBG	SV	IB	215-250							14800	17200
28		MARLBORO	FB	SDN	FBG	SV	IB	160D	PERK						22500	25000
28		MARLBORO	FB	SDN	FBG	SV	IB	T185	WAUK						16600	18800
32	6	320	FB	SDN	FBG	SV	IB	T225-T250		12	6				27600	31200
32	6	320	FB	SDN	FBG	SV	IB	T160D	PERK	12	6				36300	40400
32	6	MARLBORO	FB	SDN	FBG	SV	IB	T215-T250		12	6				25800	28700
32	6	MARLBORO	FB	SDN	FBG	SV	IB	T160D	PERK	12	6				32700	36300
32	6	MARLBORO	FB	SF	FBG	SV	IB	T215-T250		12	6				22200	25200
32	6	MARLBORO	FB	SF	FBG	SV	IB	T160D	PERK	12	6				34700	38500
35	2	OFFSHORE 360	FB	OFF	FBG	SV	IB	T225		12	9		3		35900	39800
35	2	OFFSHORE 360	FB	OFF	FBG	SV	IB	T330		12	9		3		37100	41200
		1974 BOATS														
25		MARLBORO	FB	SDN	FBG	SV	IB	215	WAUK	9	4		2	9	10000	11400
25		MARLBORO	FB	SF	FBG	SV	IB	215	WAUK	9	4		2	9	7650	8800
25		MARLBORO SHELTER CBN	HT	EXP	FBG	SV	IB	215	WAUK	9	4		2	9	8600	9900
25		SUPER 250 FBG FB	FB	SF	FBG	SV	IB	225-250		9	4		2	9	7650	8900
28		MARLBORO	FB	SDN	FBG	SV	IB	215-250		11	2		2	9	14400	16800
28		MARLBORO	FB	SDN	FBG	SV	IB	160D	PERK	11	2		2	9	22100	24600
28		MARLBORO	FB	SDN	FBG	SV	IB	T155	WAUK	11	2		2	9	15600	17700
28		SUPER 280 FBG FB	FB	SDN	FBG	SV	IB	225-330		11	4				14600	17700
		IB 160D PERK 22100 24600, IB T155-T185 15600 18300, IB T100D CHRY													23600	26200
32	6	MARLBORO	FB	SDN	FBG	SV	IB	T215-T225		12	6		3		24800	27800
32	6	MARLBORO	FB	SDN	FBG	SV	IB	T160D	PERK	12	6		3		33500	37300
32	6	SUPER 320 FBG FB	FB	SDN	FBG	SV	IB	330	CHRY	12	7		3		23700	26400
		IB 185D PERK 30400 33800, IB T225-T250 25000 28400, IB T160D PERK													33600	37300
35	2	OFFSHORE 360	FB	OFF	FBG	SV	IB	T225	CHRY	12	10				34300	38200
		IB T250 CHRY 34600 38400, IB T330 CHRY 35500 39500, IB T185D PERK													47200	51900
41			FB	SDN	FBG	SV	IB	T330	CHRY	14	3		3	8	57000	62700
41			FB	SDN	FBG	SV	IB	T185D	PERK	14	3		3	8	73000	80200
41			FB	SDN	FBG	SV	IB	T225D	CAT	14	3		3	8	74500	81900
		1973 BOATS														
25		MARLBORO	FB	SDN	FBG	SV	IB	225	CHRY	9	4		2	5	9650	11000
25		MARLBORO	FB	SF	FBG	SV	IB	225	CHRY	9	4		2	5	6450	7400
25		MARLBORO SHELTER CBN	HT	EXP	FBG	SV	IB	225	CHRY	9	4		2	5	8250	9500
25		SUPER 250 FBG FB	OP	SF	FBG	SV	IB	225	CHRY	9	4		2	5	7350	8450
25		SUPER 250 FBG FB	FB	SF	FBG	SV	IB	225-250		9	4		2	5	8300	9550
28		4-6 SLEEPER	FB	SDN	FBG	SV	IB	225-330		11	2		2	9	14000	17000
28		4-6 SLEEPER	FB	SDN	FBG	SV	IB	160D	PERK	11	2		2	9	21500	23900
28		4-6 SLEEPER	FB	SDN	FBG	SV	IB	T155	WAUK	11	2		2	9	15000	17000
28		4-6 SLPR SUPER 280	FB	SDN	FBG	SV	IB	225-330		11	4		2	9	14000	17000
28		4-6 SLPR SUPER 280	FB	SDN	FBG	SV	IB	160D	PERK	11	4		2	9	21600	24000
28		4-6 SLPR SUPER 280	FB	SDN	FBG	SV	IB	T155	WAUK	11	4		2	9	15000	17000
32	6	MARLBORO	FB	SDN	FBG	SV	IB	330	CHRY	12	6		3		21100	23500
32	6	MARLBORO	FB	SDN	FBG	SV	IB	T225	CHRY	12	6		3		22400	24900
32	6	MARLBORO	FB	SDN	FBG	SV	IB	T160D	PERK	12	6		3		31000	34400
32	6	SUPER 320 FBG FB	FB	SDN	FBG	SV	IB	330	CHRY	12	6		3		24500	27200
32	6	SUPER 320 FBG FB	FB	SDN	FBG	SV	IB	T225-T250		12	6		3		25800	28600
32	6	SUPER 320 FBG FB	FB	SDN	FBG	SV	IB	T160D	PERK	12	6		3		34400	38200
35		OFFSHORE 360	FB	OFF	FBG	SV	IB	T225	CHRY	12	9		3		32700	36300
		IB T250 CHRY 32900 36600, IB T330 CHRY 33800 37600, IB T185D PERK													45600	50100
38	9		FB	SDNSF	FBG	SV	IB	T330		14	3		3	6	49800	54700
44			FB	SDNSF	FBG	SV	IB	T330		13	11		3	6	**	**
		1972 BOATS														
25			FB	SDN	FBG	SV	IB	225	CHRY	9	4				9300	10600
25			FB	SF	FBG	SV	IB	225	CHRY	9	4				7100	8150
25		SHELTER CABIN	HT	CR	FBG	SV	IB	225	CHRY	9	4				7900	9100
25		SPORTSMAN	OP	UTL	FBG	SV	IB	225	CHRY	9	4				5600	6450
25	2	SUPER 250 FBG FB	FB	SF	FBG	SV	IB	225	CHRY	9	4		2	9	7150	8250
27	10		FB	SF	FBG	SV	IB	225	CHRY	11	4		2	9	11700	13300
27	10		FB	SF	FBG	SV	IB	160D	PERK	11	4		2	9	16600	18900
27	10	4 SLEEPER	FB	SDN	FBG	SV	IB	225	CHRY	11	4		2	9	11900	13500
27	10	4 SLEEPER	FB	SDN	FBG	SV	IB	160D	PERK	11	4		2	9	19600	21700
27	10	SUPER 280 FBG FB	FB	SDN	FBG	SV	IB	225	CHRY	11	4		2	9	14100	16000
27	10	SUPER 280 FBG FB	FB	SDN	FBG	SV	IB	160D	PERK	11	4		2	9	21300	23700
27	10	SUPER 280 FBG FB	FB	SDN	FBG	SV	IB	T225	CHRY	11	4		2	9	14900	16900
32	2		FB	SDN	FBG	SV	IB	330	CHRY	12	6		3		19300	21400
		IB 185D PERK 26200 29100, IB T225 CHRY 20600 22900, IB T160D PERK													29200	32500
32	2		FB	SF	FBG	SV	IB	330	CHRY	12	6		3		18600	20700
		IB 185D PERK 31300 34800, IB T225 CHRY 19300 21400, IBT160D-T185D													31400	35500
32	2	CONVERTIBLE	HT	SDN	FBG	SV	IB	330	CHRY	12	6		3		21500	23800
32	2	CONVERTIBLE	HT	SDN	FBG	SV	IB	T225	CHRY	12	6		3		22700	25200
32	2	SUPER 320 FBG FB	FB	SDN	FBG	SV	IB	330	CHRY	12	6		3		23600	26200
		IB 185D PERK 30700 34100, IB T225 CHRY 24800 27500, IB T160D PERK													33600	37300
38	9		FB	SDN	FBG	SV	IB	T330	CHRY	14	3		3	6	47800	52500
38	9		FB	SDN	FBG	SV	IB	T185D	PERK	14	3		3	6	53600	58900
44			FB	SDN	FBG	SV	IB	T330	CHRY	13	11		3	6	49400	54300
44			FB	SDN	FBG	SV	IB	T185D	PERK	13	11		3	6	52500	57700
44			FB	SF	FBG	SV	IB	T330	CHRY	13	11		3	6	48900	53700
44			FB	SF	FBG	SV	IB	T185D	PERK	13	11		3	6	64900	71300
		1971 BOATS														
25			FB	SDN	FBG	SV	IB	225	CHRY	9	4		2	5	8950	10200
25			FB	SF	FBG	SV	IB	225	CHRY	9	4		2	5	5950	6850
25		SHELTER CABIN	HT	CR	FBG	SV	IB	225	CHRY	9	4		2	5	7600	8750
25		SPORTSMAN	OP	UTL	FBG	SV	IB	225	CHRY	9	4		2	5	5400	6200
25		SUPER 250 FBG FB	FB	SF	FBG	SV	IB	225	CHRY	9	4		2	5	7700	8850
28			FB	SF	FBG	SV	IB	225	CHRY	11	2		2	9	11600	13200
28			FB	SF	FBG	SV	IB	160D	PERK	11	2		2	9	16600	18900
28		4 SLEEPER	FB	SDN	FBG	SV	IB	225	CHRY	11	2		2	9	12200	13800
28		4 SLEEPER	FB	SDN	FBG	SV	IB	160D	PERK	11	2		2	9	19900	22100
28		6 SLEEPER	FB	SDN	FBG	SV	IB	225	CHRY	11	2		2	9	12200	13800
28		6 SLEEPER	FB	SDN	FBG	SV	IB	160D	PERK	11	2		2	9	19900	22100
28		SUPER 280 FBG FB	FB	SDN	FBG	SV	IB	225	CHRY	11	2		2	9	14400	16400
28		SUPER 280 FBG FB	FB	SDN	FBG	SV	IB	160D	PERK	11	2		2	9	21700	24100
28		SUPER 280 FBG FB	FB	SDN	FBG	SV	IB	T225	CHRY	11	2	11500	2	9	18400	20400
32	6		FB	SDN	FBG	SV	IB	330	CHRY	12	6		3		21100	23400
		IB 185D PERK 28200 31300, IB T225 CHRY 22300 24700, IB T160D PERK													31100	34600
32	6		FB	SF	FBG	SV	IB	330	CHRY	12	6		3		18500	20500
		IB 185D PERK 31000 34500, IB T225 CHRY 19100 21200, IB T160D PERK													31200	34700
32	6	SUPER 320 FBG FB	FB	SDN	FBG	SV	IB	330	CHRY	12	8		3		21100	23500
		IB 185D PERK 28200 31300, IB T225 CHRY 22300 24800, IB T160D PERK													31100	34600
38	6		FB	SDN	FBG	SV	IB	T330D	CHRY	13	11		3	6	55200	60700
44			FB	SDN	FBG	SV	IB	T330D	CHRY	13	11		3	6	55800	61300
44			FB	SF	FBG	SV	IB	T330D	CHRY	13	11		3	6	74300	81600
		1970 BOATS														
25			FB	SDN	FBG	SV	IB	225	CHRY	9	4		2	4	8550	9800
25			FB	SF	FBG	SV	IO	160	MRCR	9	4		2	4	12300	14000
25			FB	SF	FBG	SV	IB	225	CHRY	9	4		2	4	5750	6600
25			OP	UTL	FBG	SV	IO	160	MRCR	9	4		2	4	8900	10100
25			OP	UTL	FBG	SV	IB	225	CHRY	9	4		2	4	5200	5950
25		SHELTER CABIN	HT	CR	FBG	SV	IO	160	MRCR	9	4		2	4	12100	13700
25		SHELTER CABIN	HT	CR	FBG	SV	IB	225	CHRY	9	4		2	4	7300	8400
25		SHELTER CABIN 250	HT	CR	FBG	SV	IB	225	CHRY	9	4		2	4	7300	8400
25		SUPER 250 FBG FB	FB	SF	FBG	SV	IB	225	CHRY	9	4		2	4	7400	8500
28			FB	SDN	FBG	SV	IB	225	CHRY	11	2		3		11800	13400
28			FB	SDN	FBG	SV	IB	160D	PERK	11	2		3		20000	22300
28			FB	SF	FBG	SV	IB	225	CHRY	11	2		3		11200	12700
28		6 SLEEPER	FB	SDN	FBG	SV	IB	225	CHRY	11	2		3		11800	13400
28		6 SLEEPER	FB	SDN	FBG	SV	IB	160D	PERK	11	2		3		20000	22300
28		SUPER 280	FB	SDN	FBG	SV	IB	250-300		11	2		3		12700	14900
28		SUPER 280	FB	SDN	FBG	SV	IB	160D	PERK	11	2		3		20000	22300
28		SUPER 280 FBG FB	FB	SDN	FBG	SV	IB	225	CHRY	11	2		3		13700	15600
32	6		FB	SDN	FBG	SV	IB	300	CHRY	12	4		3		20000	22200
32	6		FB	SDN	FBG	SV	IB	160D	PERK	12	4				27100	30100
32	6		FB	SF	FBG	SV	IB	300	CHRY	12	4		3		17200	19500

CONTINUED ON NEXT PAGE

LUHRS CORPORATION -CONTINUED See inside cover to adjust price for area

LOA FT	LOA IN	NAME AND/ OR MODEL	TOP/ RIG	BOAT TYPE	-HULL- MTL	-HULL- TP	ENGINE TP	ENGINE # HP	ENGINE MFG	BEAM FT	BEAM IN	WGT LBS	DRAFT FT	DRAFT IN	RETAIL LOW	RETAIL HIGH
		1970 BOATS														
32	6	SUPER 320	FB	SDN	FBG	SV	IB	325		12	4		3		20300	22500
		IB 160D PERK 27100 30100, IB T215-T225 21300 23800, IB T160D PERK													30400	33800
32	6	SUPER 320 FBG FB	FB	SDN	FBG	SV	IB	300	CHRY	12	4		3		20000	22200
		1969 BOATS														
25			OP	CR	FBG	SV	IB	225	CHRY	9	4		2	5	7050	8100
25			HT	CR	FBG	SV	IB	225	CHRY	9	4		2	5	7050	8100
25			FB	SDN	FBG	SV	IB	225	CHRY	9	4		2	5	8200	9450
25			FB	SF	FBG	SV	IB	225	CHRY	9	4		2	5	6300	7250
26			FB	SF	MHG	RB	IB	225	CHRY	10	4		3		8300	9500
26		SHELTER	HT	CR	MHG	RB	IB	225	CHRY	10	4		3		8800	10000
28			FB	SDN	MHG		IB	225	CHRY	11	4		3		12000	13600
28			FB	SDN	FBG	SV	IB	225	CHRY	11	2		3		12000	13600
28			FB	SF	FBG	SV	IB	225	CHRY	11	2		3		10800	12200
30			FB	SF	MHG	RB	IB	225	CHRY	11	4		3		16700	19000
30		SHELTER	HT	CR	MHG	RB	IB	225	CHRY	11	4		3		18000	20000
32			FB	SDN	MHG	RB	IB	225	CHRY	11	4		3		17400	19700
32	6		HT	DC	FBG	SV	IB	T225	CHRY	12	4		3		20100	22300
32	6		FB	DC	FBG	SV	IB	T225	CHRY	12	4		3		20100	22300
32	6		FB	SDN	FBG	SV	IB	300	CHRY	12	4		3		19300	21400
		IB 160D PERK 26500 29400, IB T225 CHRY 20600 22900, IB T160D PERK													29800	33100
32	6		FB	SF	FBG	SV	IB	300	CHRY	12	4		3		16500	18800
		IB 160D PERK 30000 33400, IB T225 CHRY 17500 19800, IB T160D PERK													29900	33200
32	6	WORKBOAT			FBG	SV	IB	300	CHRY	12	4		3		16500	18800
		IB 160D PERK 23000 25600, IB T225 CHRY 17500 19800, IB T160D PERK													24600	27300
		1968 BOATS														
25			OP	CR	FBG		IB	210-235		9	4		2	5	6800	7850
25			FB	SF	FBG	SV	IB	210-290		9	4		2	5	6100	7250
25		SHELTER CBN SPORT	HT	CR	FBG	SV	IB	210-290		9	4		2	5	6800	8050
26			FB	CR	MHG		IB	210-290		10	4		3		8350	10000
26		SHELTER CABIN	HT	CR	MHG		IB	210-290		10	4		3		8350	10000
27	9		FB	SDN	FBG	SV	IB	210-290		11	2		2	9	11000	13100
27	9		FB	SDN	FBG	SV	IB	T210	GRAY	11	2		2	9	12600	14300
27	9		FB	SF	FBG		IB	290		11	2		2	9	10300	11700
27	9		FB	SF	FBG	SV	IB	210-235		11	2		2	9	9850	11400
27	9		FB	SF	FBG	SV	IB	T210	GRAY	11	2		2	9	11100	12600
28			FB	SDN	MHG		IB	235		11			3		11600	13200
28			FB	SDN	MHG		IB	T210	GRAY	11			3		13100	14900
28			FB	SDNSF	MHG		IB	210	GRAY	11			3		9250	10500
30			FB	CR	MHG		IB	210-290		11			3		16900	19300
30			FB	CR	MHG		IB	T210	GRAY	11			3		18100	20100
30		SHELTER CABIN	HT	CR	MHG		IB	210-290		11			3		16900	19300
30		SHELTER CABIN	HT	CR	MHG		IB	T210	GRAY	11			3		18100	20100
32			FB	SDN	MHG		IB	210-290		11			3		16500	19700
32			FB	SDN	MHG		IB	T210	GRAY	11			3		18900	21000
32	6		FB	SDN	FBG	SV	IB	290		12	4		2	10	18700	20700
		IB 160D PERK 26000 28900, IB T210 GRAY 19600 21800, IB T160D PERK													29200	32500
32	6		FB	SF	FBG	SV	IB	290		12	4		2	10	15900	18000
		IB 160D PERK 29500 32700, IB T210 GRAY 16700 18900, IB T160D PERK													29300	32600
		1967 BOATS														
24			FB	CR	MHG		IB	150-238		10		3500	2	6	4900	5750
24		SHELTER CABIN	HT	CR	MHG		IB	150-238		10		3500	2	6	4900	5750
25			FB	CR	FBG	SV	IB	210	GRAY	10	4	3800	3		5650	6500
25		SHELTER CABIN	HT	CR	FBG	SV	IB	210	GRAY	10	4	3800	3		5650	6500
25	9			RNBT	FBG	SV	IO	200	GRAY	10	4	3800	3		11400	12900
26			FB	CR	MHG		IB	185-280		10	4	3800	3		6000	7400
26		SHELTER CABIN	HT	CR	MHG		IB	185-280		10	4	3800	3		6000	7400
28			FB	SDN	MHG		IB	238	GRAY	11		6300	3		10600	12000
28			FB	SDN	MHG		IB	T185-T238		11		6300	3		11700	13700
29			FB	SDN	FBG	SV	IB	238	GRAY	10	11	7000	2	5	11900	13500
29			FB	SDN	FBG	SV	IB	160D	PERK	10	11	7000	2	5	17200	19600
29			FB	SDN	FBG	SV	IB	T238	GRAY	10	11	7000	2	5	13700	15600
29			FB	SF	FBG	SV	IB	238	GRAY	10	11	7000	2	5	10900	12400
29			FB	SF	FBG	SV	IB	160D	PERK	10	11	7000	2	5	15000	17000
29			FB	SF	FBG	SV	IB	T238	GRAY	10	11	7000	2	5	12400	14000
30			FB	CR	MHG		IB	185-280		11		5500	3		10300	12600
30			FB	CR	MHG		IB	160D	PERK	11		5500	3		13100	14800
30			FB	CR	MHG		IB	T185-T238		11		5500	3		11800	14100
30		SHELTER CABIN	HT	CR	MHG		IB	185-280		11		5500	3		10300	12600
30		SHELTER CABIN	HT	CR	MHG		IB	160D	PERK	11		5500	3		13100	14800
30		SHELTER CABIN	HT	CR	MHG		IB	T185-T238		11		5500	3		11800	14100
32			FB	CR	MHG		IB	238-280		11		5800	3		14100	16500
32			FB	CR	MHG		IB	160D	PERK	11		5800	3		16500	18800
32			FB	CR	MHG		IB	T185-T238		11		5800	3		15300	18200
32			FB	SDN	MHG		IB	238-280		11		5800	3		15700	18400
32			FB	SDN	MHG		IB	160D	PERK	11		5800	3		20100	22300
32			FB	SDN	MHG		IB	T185-T238		11		5800	3		17200	19700
32		SHELTER CABIN	HT	CR	MHG		IB	238-280		11		5800	3		14100	16500
32		SHELTER CABIN	HT	CR	MHG		IB	160D	PERK	11		5800	3		16500	18800
32		SHELTER CABIN	HT	CR	MHG		IB	T185-T238		11		5800	3		15300	18200
32	6		FB	SDN	FBG	SV	IB	290	GRAY						18000	20000
		IB 160D PERK 25600 28400, IB T210 GRAY 19200 21300, IB T160D PERK													28700	31900
32	6		FB	SF	FBG	SV	IB	290	GRAY						15400	17400
		IB 160D PERK 28700 31900, IB T210 GRAY 16100 18300, IB T160D PERK													28600	31700
		1966 BOATS														
24			OP	CR	MHG		IB	150-280		10		3500	2	6	4750	5600
24			FB	CR	MHG		IB	150-280		10		3500	2	6	4750	5600
24		SHELTER	HT	CR	MHG		IB	150-280		10		3500	2	6	4750	5600
26			FB	CR	MHG		IB	185-280		10	4	3800	3		5800	7150
26		SHELTER	HT	CR	MHG		IB	185-280		10	4	3800	3		5800	7150
28			FB	CR	MHG		IB	185-280		11			3		9400	11200
28			FB	CR	MHG		IB	T185-T238		11			3		10500	12400
28			FB	SDN	MHG		IB	238	GRAY	11		6300	3		10200	11600
28			FB	SDN	MHG		IB	T185-T238		11		6300	3		11300	13200
28		SHELTER	HT	CR	MHG		IB	185-280		11			3		9400	11200
28		SHELTER	HT	CR	MHG		IB	T185-T238		11			3		10500	12400
29			FB	SDN	FBG	SV	IB	238	GRAY	10	11	7000	2	5	11500	13000
29			FB	SDN	FBG	SV	IB	T238	GRAY	10	11	7000	2	5	13200	15000
29			FB	SF	FBG	SV	IB	238	GRAY	10	11	7000	2	5	10500	11900
29			FB	SF	FBG	SV	IB	T238	GRAY	10	11	7000	2	5	11900	13500
30			FB	CR	MHG		IB	185-280		11		5500	3		9950	12100
30			FB	CR	MHG		IB	T185-T238		11		5500	3		11300	13600
30			FB	FD	MHG		IB	130D-160D		11		5500	3		12800	15300
30		SHELTER	HT	CR	MHG		IB	185-280		11		5500	3		9950	12100
30		SHELTER	HT	CR	MHG		IB	T185-T238		11		5500	3		11300	13600
30		SHELTER	HT	FD	MHG		IB	130D-160D		11		5500	3		12800	15300
32			FB		WD		IB	T185							14400	16400
32			FB	CR	MHG		IB	238-280		11		5500	3		13600	15900
32			FB	CR	MHG		IB	T220-T238		11		5800	3		15200	17600
32			FB	FD	MHG		IB	130D-160D		11		5800	3		16600	19700
32			FB	SDN	MHG		IB	238-280		11		5800	3		15100	17700
32			FB	SDN	MHG		IB	160D	PERK	11		5800	3		19700	21900
32			FB	SDN	MHG		IB	T185-T238		11		5800	3		16600	19000
32		SHELTER	HT	CR	MHG		IB	238-280		11		5800	3		13600	15900
32		SHELTER	HT	CR	MHG		IB	130D		11		5800	3		15600	17700
32		SHELTER	HT	CR	MHG		IB	T185-T238		11		5800	3		14700	17600
32		SHELTER	HT	FD	MHG		IB	130D-160D		11		5800	3		16600	19700
		1965 BOATS														
24			OP	CR	MHG		IB	150-280		9			1	6	4950	5900
24			FB	CR	MHG		IB	150-280		9			1	6	5000	5900
24		SHELTER	HT	CR	MHG		IB	150-280		9			1	6	4950	5900
26			FB	CR	WD		IB	175	GRAY	10	4		3		7350	8450
26			FB	CR	MHG		IB	195-280		10	4		3		7450	8900
26			FB	SDN	MHG		IB	225	GRAY	10	4		3		8950	10200
26		SHELTER	HT	CR	MHG		IB	150-280		10	4		3		7250	8900
28			FB	CR	MHG		IB	175-280		10			3		8850	10700
28			FB	CR	MHG		IB	T175-T225		10			3		9850	11700
28			FB	SDN	MHG		IB	225-238		10		6300	3		9550	11000
28			FB	SDN	MHG		IB	T175-T225		10		6300	3		10600	12500
28		SHELTER	HT	CR	MHG		IB	175-280		10			3		8850	10700
28		SHELTER	HT	CR	MHG		IB	T175-T225		10			3		9850	11700
29		ALURA	OP	EXP	FBG		IB	238-280		10	11	7500	2	5	10400	12100
29		ALURA	OP	EXP	FBG		IB	T195	GRAY	10	11	7500	2	5	11300	12900
29		ALURA	HT	EXP	FBG		IB	238-280		10	11	7500	2	5	10400	12100
29		ALURA	HT	EXP	FBG		IB	T195	GRAY	10	11	7500	2	5	11300	12900
29		ALURA	FB	SF	FBG		IB	238-280		10	11	7500	2	5	10000	11700
29		ALURA	FB	SF	FBG		IB	T195	GRAY	10	11	7500	2	5	11000	12500
29		ALURA DLX	FB	SF	FBG		IB	238-280		10	11	7500	2	5	10700	12500
29		ALURA DLX	FB	SF	FBG		IB	T195	GRAY	10	11	7500	2	5	11600	13200
30			FB	CR	MHG		IB	175-280		10			3		14900	17100
30			FB	CR	MHG		IB	130D-160D		10			3		30100	33400

CONTINUED ON NEXT PAGE

LOA FT	LOA IN	NAME AND/ OR MODEL	TOP/ RIG	BOAT TYPE	HULL MTL	HULL TP	ENGINE TP	# HP	MFG	BEAM FT	BEAM IN	WGT LBS	DRAFT FT	DRAFT IN	RETAIL LOW	RETAIL HIGH
		1965 BOATS														
30			FB	CR	MHG		IB	T175-T225		10			3		15400	17900
30			FB	FD	MHG		IB	130D-160D		10			3		31600	35100
30		SHELTER	HT	CR	MHG		IB	175-280		10			3		14900	17100
30		SHELTER	HT	CR	MHG		IB	130D-160D		10			3		30100	33400
30		SHELTER	HT	CR	MHG		IB	T175-T225		10			3		15400	17900
30		SHELTER	HT	FD	MHG		IB	130D-160D		10			3		31600	35100
32			FB	CR	MHG		IB	210-280		10	6		3		13700	16100
32			FB	CR	MHG		IB	130D-160D		10	6		3		22200	24700
32			FB	CR	MHG		IB	T175-T225		10	6		3		14600	17200
32			FB	FD	MHG		IB	130D-160D		10	6		3		23700	26300
32			FB	SDN	MHG		IB	210-280		10	6		3		14700	17400
32			FB	SDN	MHG		IB	T175-T225		10	6		3		15900	18900
32		SHELTER	HT	CR	MHG		IB	210-280		10	6		3		13700	16100
32		SHELTER	HT	CR	MHG		IB	130D-160D		10	6		3		22200	24700
32		SHELTER	HT	CR	MHG		IB	T175-T225		10	6		3		14600	17200
32		SHELTER	HT	FD	MHG		IB	130D-160D		10	6		3		23700	26300
		1964 BOATS														
24			OP	CR	MHG		IB	122-280		9			1	6	4750	5700
24			HT	CR	MHG		IB	122-150		9			1	6	5050	5900
24			FB	CR	MHG		IB	175-280		9			1	6	4850	5700
24		SHELTER	HT	CR	MHG		IB	122-150		9			1	6	4450	5200
24		SHELTER	HT	CR	MHG		IB	175-280		9			1	6	4850	5700
26			FB	CR	MHG		IB	175-280							6950	8400
26		SHELTER	HT	CR	MHG		IB	150-280							6850	8400
28			FB	CR	MHG		IB	175-280		10			3		8450	10300
28			FB	CR	MHG		IB	T175-T225		10			3		9500	11300
28			FB	SDN	MHG		IB	225-238		10			3		9800	11200
28			FB	SDN	MHG		IB	T175-T225		10			3		10700	12800
30			FB	CR	MHG		IB	175-280		10			3		14400	16400
30			FB	CR	MHG		IB	T175-T225		10			3		14800	17200
30		SHELTER	HT	CR	MHG		IB	175-280		10			3		14400	16400
30		SHELTER	HT	CR	MHG		IB	T175-T225		10			3		14800	17200
32			FB	CR	MHG		IB	210-280		10	6	11477	3		13800	15700
32			FB	CR	MHG		IB	T175-T225		10	6		3		14100	16600
32			FB	SDN	MHG		IB	210-280		10	6		3		14100	16800
32			FB	SDN	MHG		IB	T175-T225		10	6		3		15300	18200
32		SHELTER	HT	CR	MHG		IB	210-280		10	6		3		13200	15500
32		SHELTER	HT	CR	MHG		IB	T175-T225		10	6		3		14100	16600
		1963 BOATS														
24			FB	CR	MHG		IB	109-225		9			1	6	4550	5400
24		SHELTER CABIN		CR	WD		IB	225							4600	5300
24		SHELTER CABIN	HT	CR	MHG		IB	109-195		9			1	6	4550	5400
24		SKIFF	OP	CR	MHG		IB	109-225		9			1	6	4550	5400
26			FB	CR	MHG		IB	138-225							6550	7900
26		SHELTER CABIN	HT	CR	MHG		IB	138-225							6550	7900
28			FB	CR	MHG		IB	138-225		10			3		7900	9650
28			FB	SDN	MHG		IB	225	GRAY	10			3		9450	10700
28			FB	SDN	MHG		IB	T138-T195		10			3		9900	12000
28			FB	SDN	MHG		IB	T225	GRAY	10			3		10900	12400
28		SHELTER CABIN	HT	CR	MHG		IB	138-225		10			3		7900	9650
30			FB	CR	MHG		IB	138-225		10			3		13900	15800
30			FB	CR	MHG		IB	T138-T225		10			3		14000	16600
30		SHELTER CABIN	HT	CR	MHG		IB	138-225		10			3		13900	15800
30		SHELTER CABIN	HT	CR	MHG		IB	T138-T225		10			3		14000	16600
32			FB	CR	MHG		IB	225	GRAY	10	6		3		12900	14600
32			FB	CR	MHG		IB	T138-T225		10	6		3		13200	16000
32			FB	SDN	MHG		IB	225	GRAY	10	6		3		13800	15700
32			FB	SDN	MHG		IB	T138-T225		10	6		3		14200	17600
32		SHELTER CABIN	HT	CR	MHG		IB	225	GRAY	10	6		3		12900	14600
32		SHELTER CABIN	HT	CR	MHG		IB	T138-T225		10	6		3		13200	16000
		1962 BOATS														
24			FB	CR	MHG		IB	109-225		9			1	6	4450	5350
24		SHELTER CABIN	HT	CR	MHG		IB	109-225		9			1	6	4450	5350
24		SKIFF	OP	CR	MHG		IB	85-225		9			1	6	4400	5350
27			FB	CR	MHG		IB	125-225		9	6		2		6850	8450
27			FB	CR	MHG		IB	T109-T135		9	6		2		7400	8800
27		SHELTER CABIN	HT	CR	MHG		IB	125-225		9	6		2		6850	8450
27		SHELTER CABIN	HT	CR	MHG		IB	T109-T135		9	6		2		7400	8800
30			FB	CR	MHG		IB	125-225		10			3		13500	15400
30			FB	CR	MHG		IB	T135	GRAY	10			3		13700	15500
30		SHELTER CABIN	HT	CR	MHG		IB	125-225		10			3		13600	15400
30		SHELTER CABIN	HT	CR	MHG		IB	T135	GRAY	10			3		13700	15500
31			FB	SDN	MHG		IB	215	GRAY	10	4		3		14300	16200
		1961 BOATS														
23	6		OP	CR	MHG		IB	85-225		8			2		4000	4950
23	6	SHELTER CABIN	HT	CR	MHG		IB	109-225		8			2		4100	4950
27			FB	CR	MHG		IB	125-225		9	6		2		6750	8300
27			FB	CR	MHG		IB	T109-T135		9	6		2		7250	8650
27		SHELTER CABIN	HT	CR	MHG		IB	125-188		9	6		2		6150	7450
27		SHELTER CABIN	HT	CR	MHG		IB	T109-T135		9	6		2		7250	8350
27		TRUNK CABIN	HT	CR	MHG		IB	125-225		9	6		2		7300	8800
27		TRUNK CABIN	HT	CR	MHG		IB	T135	GRAY	9	6		2		8000	9200
30			FB	CR	MHG		IB	125-225		10			2		13300	15100
30			FB	CR	MHG		IB	T135	GRAY	10			2		13400	15200
30		SHELTER CABIN	HT	CR	MHG		IB	125-225		10			2		13300	15100
30		SHELTER CABIN	HT	CR	MHG		IB	T135	GRAY	10			2		13400	15200
		1960 BOATS														
23		SHELTER CABIN	HT	CR	MHG		IB	109							3600	4150
23		SKIFF	OP	CR	MHG		IB	109							3600	4150
25		SHELTER CABIN	HT	CR	MHG		IB	135							5050	5800
25		SKIFF	OP	CR	MHG		IB	135							5050	5800
28			FB	CR	MHG		IB	135							7400	8500
28		SHELTER CABIN	HT	CR	MHG		IB	135							7400	8500
30			FB	CR	MHG		IB	188							13300	15100
30			FB	CR	MHG		IB	T188							13700	15600
		1959 BOATS														
23		SEA-SKIFF SHEL ISLND		CR	MHG		IB	109		8					3550	4100
27		SEA-SKIFF		CR	MHG		IB	109		9	2				6400	7350
27		SEA-SKIFF	FB	CR	MHG		IB	125		9	2				6450	7400
31		SEA-SKIFF		CR	MHG		IB	125							13300	15100
		1958 BOATS														
23		SEA-SKIFF		CR	MHG		IB	109							3450	4000
27		SEA-SKIFF		CR	MHG		IB	109-185							6300	7650
		1957 BOATS														
23		SEA-SKIFF		CR	MHG		IB	109							3400	3950
27		SEA-SKIFF		CR	MHG		IB	109							6200	7100
		1956 BOATS														
22		SEA-SKIFF		CR	MHG		IB	95							3050	3550
24		SEA-SKIFF		CR	MHG		IB	125							3900	4500
		1955 BOATS														
21		SEA-SKIFF		CR	MHG		IB	95							2500	2900
26		SEA-SKIFF		CR	MHG		IB								**	**
		1954 BOATS														
21		SEA-SKIFF		CR	MHG		IB	60							2400	2800
		1953 BOATS														
21		SEA-SKIFF		CR	MHG		IB	60							2350	2750

LUND BOAT COMPANY

DIV OF GENMAR INDUSTRIES INC
N Y MILLS MN 56567
COAST GUARD MFG ID- LUN
FORMERLY LUND AMERICAN INC

See inside cover to adjust price for area

For more recent years, see the BUC Used Boat Price Guide, Volume 1 or Volume 2

LOA FT	LOA IN	NAME AND/ OR MODEL	TOP/ RIG	BOAT TYPE	HULL MTL	HULL TP	ENGINE TP	# HP	MFG	BEAM FT	BEAM IN	WGT LBS	DRAFT FT	DRAFT IN	RETAIL LOW	RETAIL HIGH
		1982 BOATS														
16	1	MIRADO B/R	OP	RNBT	FBG	DV	OB			7	1	1065			3050	3500
16	1	MIRADO FD SPORT	OP	RNBT	FBG	DV	OB			7	1	890			2600	3050
16	1	MIRADO FULL DECK	OP	RNBT	FBG	DV	OB			7	1	890			2550	3000
16	1	MIRADO SPORT B/R	OP	RNBT	FBG	DV	OB			7	1	1065			3100	3600
16	1	MR-PIKE 16	OP	FSH	AL	SV	OB			6		595			1750	2050
16	1	S/L 1600		RNBT	FBG	DV	IO	120		7	1				2700	3150
16	2	PREMIER I	OP	FSH	FBG	SV	OB			6	5	940			2750	3200
16	2	PREMIER II	OP	FSH	FBG	SV	OB			6	5	940			2700	3150
16	3	SUPER-PIKE XRF 4.9	OP	BASS	AL	DV	OB			6	7	830			2450	2850
16	3	XRV 4.9 B/R		RNBT	AL	DV	IO	120		6	7				2650	3050
16	3	XRV 4.9 B/R	OP	RNBT	AL	DV	OB			6	7	910			2650	3100
16	3	XRV 4.9 SPORT	OP	RNBT	AL	DV	OB			6	7	910			2650	3100
17	2	SIRIUS 17	OP	RNBT	FBG	DV	OB			6	10	1145			3350	3900
17	2	SIRIUS 17	OP	RNBT	FBG	DV	IO	140	MRCR	6	10	1975			3000	3500
17	2	SIRIUS 17	ST	RNBT	FBG	DV	IO	140-170		6	10	1975			2950	3500
17	4	TYEE 5.3	ST	FSH	AL	SV	OB			6	10	950			2850	3350
17	11	XRV 5.5	OP	RNBT	AL	DV	OB			7	4	1017			3100	3600
18		MR-PIKE 18	OP	FSH	AL	SV	OB			5	10	695			2250	2600
18		MR-PIKE 18 LTD	OP	FSH	AL	SV	OB			6	3	745			2350	2750
18		PIKE 18 DELUXE	OP	FSH	AL	SV	OB			6		590			1900	2250
19		ROYALE 19	OP	RNBT	FBG	DV	OB			7	1	1375			4100	4750
19	6	SIRIUS 19		RNBT	FBG	DV	IO	200		7	9				4650	5350
20		TYEE		RNBT	AL	DV	IO	170		7	4				4550	5200

CONTINUED ON NEXT PAGE

LUND BOAT COMPANY   -CONTINUED   See inside cover to adjust price for area

LOA FT IN	NAME AND/ OR MODEL	TOP/ RIG	BOAT TYPE	-HULL- MTL TP TP	----ENGINE--- # HP MFG	BEAM FT IN	WGT LBS	DRAFT FT IN	RETAIL LOW	RETAIL HIGH

--------------------- 1981 BOATS ---------------------

LOA FT IN	NAME AND/ OR MODEL	TOP/ RIG	BOAT TYPE	HULL MTL TP TP	ENGINE # HP MFG	BEAM FT IN	WGT LBS	RETAIL LOW	RETAIL HIGH
16 1	MIRADO B/R	OP	RNBT	FBG DV OB		7 1	1065	3050	3500
16 1	MIRADO FULL DECK	OP	RNBT	FBG DV OB		7 1	890	2550	2950
16 1	MIRADO SPORT B/R	OP	RNBT	FBG DV OB		7 1	1065	3000	3450
16 1	MR-PIKE 16	OP	FSH	AL SV OB		6	595	1700	2050
16 1	S/L 1600	OP	RNBT	FBG DV OB		7 1	980	2800	3250
16 1	S/L 1600	OP	RNBT	FBG DV IO 140-185		7 1	1815	2700	3200
16 3	XRV 4.9 B/R	OP	RNBT	AL DV OB		6 7	910	2600	3050
16 3	XRV 4.9 B/R	OP	RNBT	AL DV IO 120-140		6 7	1720	2550	2950
17 2	SIRIUS 17	OP	RNBT	FBG DV OB		6 10	1145	3300	3800
17 2	SIRIUS 17	ST	RNBT	FBG DV IO 120-170		6 10	1975	2950	3450
18	MR-PIKE 18	OP	FSH	AL SV OB		5 10	695	2200	2550
18	MR-PIKE 18 LTD	OP	FSH	AL SV OB		6 3	745	2350	2700
18	PIKE 18 DELUXE	OP	FSH	AL SV OB		6	590	1850	2200
19	ROYALE 19	OP	RNBT	FBG DV OB		7 1	1375	4000	4700
19 6	SIRIUS 19	ST	RNBT	FBG DV IO 170-260		7 9	2610	4150	5150
20	TYEE		RNBT	AL DV IO 170		7 4		4450	5150
20	TYEE 5.3	ST	RNBT	FBG DV OB		7 4	1220	3450	4050

--------------------- 1980 BOATS ---------------------

16	PRO-ANGLER	OP	FSH	AL SV OB		6 1	637	1800	2150
16	S/L 1600	OP		FBG TR OB		7	980	3250	3200
16 1	MR-PIKE 16	OP	FSH	AL SV OB		6	616	1750	2050
17	SIRIUS 17	OP		FBG TR OB		6 8		2600	3000
17	SIRIUS 17	OP		FBG TR IO		6 8		**	**
17 4	VFR-17	ST	RNBT	AL DV OB		6 11	940	2750	3200
17 4	VFR-17	ST	RNBT	AL DV IO 140		6 11	1880	2900	3350
18	MR-PIKE 18 DELUXE	OP	FSH	AL SV OB		5 10	775	2400	2750
18	MR-PIKE 18 LTD	OP	FSH	AL SV OB		6 3	760	2350	2700
18	PIKE 18	OP	FSH	AL SV OB		6	540	1700	2000
19	ROYALE 19	OP		FBG TR OB		7 2	1400	4000	4700
20	SIRIUS 19	OP		FBG TR IO		7 9		**	**
20	TYEE	ST	RNBT	AL DV OB		7 4	1220	3400	4000
20	TYEE	ST	RNBT	AL DV IO 165-200		7 4	2080	3600	4250

--------------------- 1979 BOATS ---------------------

16 1	MR-PIKE 16	OP	FSH	AL SV OB		5 5	605	1700	2000
17 4	VFR-17	OP	RNBT	AL DV OB		6 11	940	2750	3150
17 4	VFR-17	OP	RNBT	AL DV IO 140		6 11	1880	2900	3350
18	MR-PIKE 18	OP	FSH	AL SV OB		6 3	810	2450	2850
18	MR-PIKE 18 LTD	OP	FSH	AL SV OB		6 3	760	2350	2700
20	TYEE	ST	RNBT	AL DV OB		7 4	1220	3400	3950
20	TYEE	ST	RNBT	AL DV IO 198-200		7 4	2080	3650	4250

--------------------- 1978 BOATS ---------------------

17 5	VFR-17	ST	RNBT	AL DV OB		7 1	970	2800	3250
17 5	VFR-17	ST	RNBT	AL DV IO 140		7 1	1905	3000	3500
18	PIKE 18 DELUXE	OP	FSH	AL DV OB		5 10	675	2050	2400
18	PRO-PIKER 18	OP	FSH	AL DV OB		5 10	830	2500	2900
20	TYEE	ST	RNBT	AL DV OB		7 4	1220	3350	3900
20	TYEE	ST	RNBT	AL DV IO 165-185		7 4	2080	3650	4250

--------------------- 1977 BOATS ---------------------

17 5	VFR-17 DECK	ST	RNBT	AL DV OB		7 1	915	2600	3050
17 5	VFR-17 DECK	ST	RNBT	AL DV IO 140		7 1	1903	3050	3550
18	PIKE BOAT DELUXE	OP	FSH	AL SV OB		5 10	643	1950	2300
20	TYEE OFFSHORE	ST	OFF	AL DV OB		7 4	1220	3300	3850
20	TYEE OFFSHORE	ST	OFF	AL DV IO 165-190		7 4	2080	3850	4450

--------------------- 1976 BOATS ---------------------

18	PIKE BOAT DELUXE 18	OP	FSH	AL DV OB		5 10	643	1900	2300
18	VFR-17	OP	RNBT	AL DV OB		6 6	822	2400	2800
18	VFR-17	ST	RNBT	AL DV IO 120-140		6 6	1590	2850	3350
20	TYEE CUDDY	HT	CUD	AL DV IO 140-165		7 4	2430	4200	4900
20	TYEE OFFSHORE	ST	OFF	AL DV OB		7 4	1220	3300	3850
20	TYEE OFFSHORE	ST	OFF	AL DV IO 140-165		7 4	1950	3800	4450

--------------------- 1975 BOATS ---------------------

17 5	VER-17	OP	RNBT	AL SV OB		6 6	822	2350	2750
17 5	VER-17	OP	RNBT	AL SV IO 120-140		6 6	1590	2850	3300
20	TYEE	OP	CUD	AL SV IO 140-165		7 4	2430	4400	5100
20	TYEE	OP	OFF	AL DV OB		7 4	1220	3300	3800
20	TYEE	OP	OFF	AL SV IO 140-165		7 4	1950	3950	4600

--------------------- 1974 BOATS ---------------------

17 5	VFR-17 FISH-N-SKI	ST	RNBT	AL OB		6 6	822	2350	2750
17 5	VFR-17 FISH-N-SKI	ST	RNBT	AL IO 120-140		6 6	1590	2950	3400
20	TYEE OFFSHORE	OP	RNBT	AL OB		7 4	1220	3250	3800
20	TYEE OFFSHORE	ST	OFF	AL IO 140-165		7 4	1950	4100	4750

--------------------- 1973 BOATS ---------------------

17 5	VFR-17 FISH-N-SKI	OP	RNBT	AL OB		6 6	822	2350	2750
17 5	VFR-17 FISH-N-SKI	OP	RNBT	AL IO 120-140		6 6	1590	3050	3550
20	TYEE OFFSHORE	OP	OFF	AL OB		7 4	1220	3250	3800
20	TYEE OFFSHORE	OP	OFF	AL IO 140-165		7 4	1950	4200	4900

--------------------- 1972 BOATS ---------------------

17 5	VFR-17 FISH-N-SKI	ST	RNBT	AL OB		6 6	822	2350	2700
17 5	VFR-17 FISH-N-SKI	ST	RNBT	AL IO 120 MRCR		6 6		3650	4250
20	TYEE OFFSHORE	OP	OFF	AL OB		7 4	1220	3250	3800
20	TYEE OFFSHORE	OP	OFF	AL IO 120-140		7 4	1950	4400	5050

--------------------- 1971 BOATS ---------------------

17 5	VFR-17 FISH-N-SKI	ST	RNBT	AL IO		6 6	850	2400	2800
17 5	VFR-17 FISH-N-SKI	ST	RNBT	AL IO 90-120		6 6	1390	3100	3600
18	TYEE 18		RNBT	AL		6 10	851	2450	2850

--------------------- 1970 BOATS ---------------------

17 1	VFR-17 FISH-N-SKI	ST	RNBT	AL OB		6 6	680	1900	2300
18	TYEE 18 K-18		RNBT	AL OB		6 10	851	2450	2850
19 3	K-19		RNBT	AL OB		6 9	912	2750	3200
19 3	NEW-YORKER K-19		RNBT	AL SV OB		6 9	912	2750	3200

--------------------- 1969 BOATS ---------------------

17 3	FISH-N-SKI FR-17	OP	RNBT	AL SV OB		6 6	680	1950	2300
18	TYEE 18	OP	RNBT	AL SV OB		6 10	851	2500	2900
19	K-19			AL IO		6 10	1530	3800	4450
19	NEW YORKER K-19			AL SV OB	120	6 10	840	2550	2950

--------------------- 1968 BOATS ---------------------

17 1	FISH-N-SKI FR-17	OP	RNBT	AL IO		6 5	680	1950	2300
18	HOLIDAY K-18	OP	CR	AL IO 120		6 10	1530	3800	4450
18	NEW-YORKER K-20	EXP		AL SV OB 120		6 10	930	2700	3150
19 8	NEW-YORKER		CR	AL IO 120		6 10	1600	4500	5150

--------------------- 1967 BOATS ---------------------

18 1	HOLIDAY K-18	OP	RNBT	AL OB		6 10	840	2500	2900
18 1	HOLIDAY K-18	OP	RNBT	AL IO 120		6 10	1530	3950	4550
19 9	NEW-YORKER K-20	OP	RNBT	AL OB		6 10	930	2850	3300
19 9	NEW-YORKER K-20	OP	RNBT	AL IO 120		6 10	1600	4500	5200

--------------------- 1965 BOATS ---------------------

16	FISH-N-SKI FR-16		RNBT	AL OB				2550	2950
17 8	LAKER K-18		RNBT	AL OB				3800	4400
20	NEW-YORKER K-20		RNBT	AL OB				4500	5200

--------------------- 1964 BOATS ---------------------

16 1	BIG-LAKES S-16	OP	FSH	AL OB				1700	2050
17 8	LAKER K-18	OP	RNBT	AL OB				3850	4450
20	NEW-YORKER K-20	OP	RNBT	AL OB				4550	5250

--------------------- 1963 BOATS ---------------------

16 1	BIG-LAKES S-16	OP	FSH	AL OB				1700	2050
16 10	WATER-KING K-17		RNBT	AL OB				3100	3600
19	AQUACRUISER K-19			AL OB				3000	3500

--------------------- 1961 BOATS ---------------------

| 16 8 | WATER-KING K-17 | | RNBT | AL OB | | 6 2 | 575 | 1700 | 2050 |
| 18 8 | LOUNGER K-19 | | RNBT | AL OB | | 7 10 | 625 | 2050 | 2400 |

--------------------- 1960 BOATS ---------------------

| 17 | WATER-KING | | RNBT | AL RB OB | | 6 2 | 565 | 1750 | 2050 |
| 19 | LAKE-LOUNGER | | RNBT | AL RB OB | | 6 10 | 700 | 2300 | 2700 |

GEORGE LUZIER BOATBUILDER INC

Call 1-800-327-6929 for BUC Personalized Evaluation Service
Or, for 1965 to 1971 boats, sign onto www.BUCValuPro.com

LYDIA YACHTS INC
FT LAUDERDALE FL 33334   See inside cover to adjust price for area

LOA FT IN	NAME AND/ OR MODEL	TOP/ RIG	BOAT TYPE	-HULL- MTL TP TP	----ENGINE--- # HP MFG	BEAM FT IN	WGT LBS	DRAFT FT IN	RETAIL LOW	RETAIL HIGH

--------------------- 1970 BOATS ---------------------

53			YTFS	F/W IB 500	16				183000	201000
53	FISHING-YACHT		YTFS	F/W IB 500	16				183000	201000
60			MY	F/W IB 500	18				227500	250000

M F G

Call 1-800-327-6929 for BUC Personalized Evaluation Service
Or, for 1967 to 1971 boats, sign onto www.BUCValuPro.com

FRANS MAAS B V
BRESKENS HOLLAND

STANDFAST YACHTS U S A INC
SOLOMONS MD 20688

See inside cover to adjust price for area

LOA FT IN	NAME AND/ OR MODEL	TOP/ RIG	BOAT TYPE	-HULL- MTL TP	----ENGINE--- TP # HP MFG	BEAM FT IN	WGT LBS	DRAFT FT IN	RETAIL LOW	RETAIL HIGH
------------------------- 1981 BOATS -------------------------
24 8	CONTEST 25	SLP	SA/RC	FBG KL	IB D	8 3	5160	4 1	14000	15900
26 11	STANDFAST 27	SLP	SA/RC	FBG KL	IB D	8 10	5071	4 11	15300	17400
27 11	CONTEST 28	SLP	SA/RC	FBG KL	IB D	9 4	6570	4 7	20700	23000
30	CONTEST 30AC	SLP	SA/RC	FBG KL	IB D	10 3	9100	4 9	29400	32600
31 2	CONTEST 31	SLP	SA/RC	FBG KL	IB D	10 4	11157	4 9	36900	41000
31 10	CONTEST 32	KTH	SA/RC	FBG KL	IB D	10 11	14300	4 3	48000	52700
32 10	STANDFAST 33	SLP	SA/RC	FBG KL	IB D	10 7	10143	5 9	33700	37500
34	CONTEST 34	SLP	SA/RC	FBG KL	IB D	11 2	16315	5 9	53000	58200
36	CONTEST 36	KTH	SA/RC	FBG KL	IB D	11 2	17957	4 11	58900	64800
37 3	CONTEST 38	KTH	SA/RC	FBG KL	IB D	12	21819	5 5	70100	77100
39 9	CONTEST 40	KTH	SA/RC	FBG KL	IB D	12 8	25297	5 11	84400	92800
40	STANDFAST 40	SLP	SA/RC	FBG KL	IB D	13 5	22000	6 10	73500	80800
40	STANDFAST 40P	SLP	SA/RC	FBG KL	IB D	13 1	22050	6 6	73600	80900
42 7	CONTEST 42	KTH	SA/RC	FBG KL	IB D	13 1	27403	6 1	92700	102000
47	STANDFAST 47	KTH	SA/CR	FBG KL	IB D	14 5	37400	6 8	119500	131500
48 3	CONTEST 48	KTH	SA/RC	FBG KL	IB D	14 2	36000	5 9	122000	134000
------------------------- 1980 BOATS -------------------------
26 11	STANDFAST 27	SLP	SA/CR	F/S KL	IB 7D REN	8 10	5071	4 11	14500	16500
29 9	STANDFAST 30	SLP	SA/CR	F/S KL	IB 10D VLVO	9 8	8360	5 6	25600	28400
32 10	STANDFAST 33	SLP	SA/CR	F/S KL	IB 20D BUKH	10 7	10143	5 11	32000	35600
40 2	STANDFAST 40	SLP	SA/CR	F/S KL	IB 45D PEUG	13 3	22050	6 9	64200	70600
40 2	STANDFAST 40P	SLP	SA/CR	F/S KL	IB 45D PEUG	13 3	22050	6 9	76100	83600
46 11	STANDFAST 47	SLP	SA/CR	F/S KL	IB 75D VLVO	14 3	39690	6 7	111500	122500

MAC GREGORS OF FALMOUTH
BARTENDER

Call 1-800-327-6929 for BUC Personalized Evaluation Service
Or, for 1965 boats, sign onto www.BUCValuPro.com

MAC KENZIE CUTTYHUNK BOAT CO
HYANNIS MA 02601   COAST GUARD MFG ID- MCT See inside cover to adjust price for area

LOA FT IN	NAME AND/ OR MODEL	TOP/ RIG	BOAT TYPE	-HULL- MTL TP	----ENGINE--- TP # HP MFG	BEAM FT IN	WGT LBS	DRAFT FT IN	RETAIL LOW	RETAIL HIGH
------------------------- 1974 BOATS -------------------------
23 2	BASS BOAT	OP	BASS	F/W SV	IB 190	8 4		1 10	7050	8100
26 3	BASS BOAT	OP	BASS	F/W SV	IB 250-300	9		2	9700	11300
30	BASS BOAT	OP	BASS	F/W SV	IB 250	11		2 8	16000	18200
30	BASS BOAT	OP	BASS	F/W SV	IB D	11		2 8	**	**
39	SPORT FISHERMAN	SF		F/W SV	IB D	12		3	**	**
39	SPORT FISHERMAN	SF		F/W SV	IB T320	12		3	51800	56900
------------------------- 1973 BOATS -------------------------
23 2	BASS BOAT	OP	BASS	MHG SV	IB 225	8 4	4300	1 10	6600	7600
26 3	BASS BOAT	OP	BASS	MHG SV	IB 250	9	5500	2	9450	10800
30	BASS BOAT	OP	BASS	MHG SV	IB 250	11	8000	2 8	15600	17800
------------------------- 1972 BOATS -------------------------
23		OP	BASS	WD SV	IB 225	8 4			6500	7450
26		OP	BASS	WD SV	IB 250	9			8900	10100
30		OP	BASS	WD SV	IB 250	11			14800	16800
------------------------- 1971 BOATS -------------------------
23 2	BASS BOAT	OP	BASS	WD SV	IB PALM	8 4	4600	1 10	**	**
26 3	BASS BOAT	OP	BASS	WD SV	IB PALM	9	5000	2	**	**
30	BASS BOAT	OP	BASS	WD SV	IB PALM	11	6500	2 8	**	**
34	CRUISER	CR		FBG DS	IB D FORD	11 4	9000	2	**	**
34	LOBSTER BOAT	FSH		FBG DS	IB D FORD	11 4	9000	2	**	**
------------------------- 1970 BOATS -------------------------
23 2		OP	BASS	WD SV	IB PALM	8 4	4600	1 10	**	**
26 3		OP	BASS	WD SV	IB PALM	9	5000	2	**	**
30		OP	BASS	WD SV	IB PALM	11	6500	2 8	**	**
34		CR		FBG RB	IB FORD	11 4	9000	2	**	**
34	LOBSTER BOAT	FSH		FBG RB	IB FORD	11 4	9000	2	**	**
------------------------- 1969 BOATS -------------------------
23 2			BASS	MHG	IB 195 PALM	8 4	4300	1 10	5650	6500
26 3			BASS	MHG	IB 225-265	9	5500	2	7950	9350
26 3			BASS	MHG	IB 160D PERK	9	5500		11600	13200
30			BASS	MHG	IB 265 PALM	11	8000	2 8	13500	15400
30			BASS	MHG	IB 185D CUM	11	8000	2 8	18500	20600
30			BASS	MHG	IB T195 PALM	11	8000	2 8	14400	16400
------------------------- 1968 BOATS -------------------------
26 3			BASS	MHG	IB 225-265	9	5500	2	7650	9000
26 3			BASS	MHG	IB 160D	9	5500		11200	12700
30			BASS	MHG	IB 265	11	8000	2 8	13000	14800
30			BASS	MHG	IB 185D	11	8000	2 8	18200	20200
30			BASS	MHG	IB T195	11	8000	2 8	13900	15800
------------------------- 1967 BOATS -------------------------
23 2	CUTTYHUNK		BASS	WD	IB 125		4200		5000	5750
26 3	CUTTYHUNK		BASS	WD	IB 185-280		5500		7250	8800
26 3	CUTTYHUNK		BASS	WD	IB 130D		5500		10600	12000
------------------------- 1966 BOATS -------------------------
23 2	CUTTYHUNK		BASS	WD	IB 138	8 4		1 10	5100	5850
26 3	CUTTYHUNK		BASS	WD	IB 220-280	9		2	7000	8300
26 3	CUTTYHUNK		BASS	WD	IB 130D	9		2	10300	11800
------------------------- 1965 BOATS -------------------------
23 2	CUTTYHUNK		BASS	WD	IB 138				4900	5650
26 3	CUTTYHUNK		BASS	WD	IB 225				6800	7800
------------------------- 1964 BOATS -------------------------
23 2	CUTTYHUNK		BASS	WD	IB 138				4750	5450
26 3	CUTTYHUNK		BASS	WD	IB 225				6550	7550
------------------------- 1963 BOATS -------------------------
26 3	CUTTYHUNK		BASS	WD	IB 225				6300	7250
------------------------- 1962 BOATS -------------------------
26 3	CUTTYHUNK		BASS	WD	IB 170-230				5950	7100
------------------------- 1961 BOATS -------------------------
26 3	CUTTYHUNK		BASS	WD	IB 140	9		2	5650	6500

MACGREGOR YACHT CORP
COSTA MESA CA 92627   COAST GUARD MFG ID- MAC See inside cover to adjust price for area

For more recent years, see the BUC Used Boat Price Guide, Volume 1 or Volume 2

LOA FT IN	NAME AND/ OR MODEL	TOP/ RIG	BOAT TYPE	-HULL- MTL TP	----ENGINE--- TP # HP MFG	BEAM FT IN	WGT LBS	DRAFT FT IN	RETAIL LOW	RETAIL HIGH
------------------------- 1983 BOATS -------------------------
21	MAC-GREGOR 21	SLP	SA/CR	FBG SK	OB	6 10	1175	1	2550	2950
22	MAC-GREGOR 22	SLP	SA/CR	FBG SK	OB	7 4	1800	1	3150	3650
22 7	MAC-GREGOR 23	SLP	SA/CR	FBG SK	OB	7 2	2000	1 6	3350	3900
24 11	MAC-GREGOR 25	SLP	SA/CR	FBG SK	OB	5 8	2100	1 10	3800	4450
35 6	MAC-GREGOR CAT	CAT	SA/RC	FBG CT	OB	18	3000	8	27100	30100
------------------------- 1982 BOATS -------------------------
21	VENTURE 21	SLP	SA/CR	FBG SK	OB	6 10	1175	1	2400	2750
22	VENTURE 22	SLP	SA/CR	FBG SK	OB	7 4	1800	1	2950	3450
22 7	VENTURE 23	SLP	SA/CR	FBG SK	OB	7 2	2000	1 6	3150	3700
24 11	MAC-GREGOR 25	SLP	SA/CR	FBG SK	OB	5 8	2100	1 10	3550	4150
35 6	MAC-GREGOR CAT	CAT	SA/RC	FBG CT	OB	18	3000	8	25500	28400
------------------------- 1981 BOATS -------------------------
21	VENTURE 21	SLP	SA/CR	FBG SK	OB	6 10	1175	1	2250	2650
22	VENTURE 22	SLP	SA/CR	FBG SK	OB	7 4	1800	1	2800	3250
22 7	VENTURE 23	SLP	SA/CR	FBG SK	OB	7 2	2000	1 6	3000	3450
24 11	MAC-GREGOR 25	SLP	SA/CR	FBG SK	OB	5 8	2100	1 10	3350	3900
35 6	MAC-GREGOR CAT	CAT	SA/RC	FBG CT	OB	18	3000	8	24000	26700
------------------------- 1980 BOATS -------------------------
21	VENTURE 21	SLP	SA/CR	FBG SK	OB	6 10	1175	1	2150	2500
22	VENTURE 22	SLP	SA/CR	FBG SK	OB	7 4	1800	1	2650	3100
22 7	VENTURE 23	SLP	SA/CR	FBG SK	OB	7 2	2000	1 6	2850	3300
25	MAC-GREGOR 25	SLP	SA/CR	FBG SK	OB	7 11	2000	1 6	3350	3900
35 6	MAC-GREGOR CAT	CAT	SA/RC	FBG CT	OB	18	3000	8	23000	25500
------------------------- 1979 BOATS -------------------------
21	VENTURE 21	SLP	SA/CR	FBG SK	OB		1500	1	2350	2700
22	VENTURE 22	SLP	SA/CR	FBG SK	OB	7 6	1900	1	2650	3050
22 7	VENTURE-OF-NEWPORT	SLP	SA/CR	FBG SK	OB	7 2	2000	1	2750	3200
23	VENTURE 23	SLP	SA/CR	FBG SK	OB	7 5	2000	1 6	2750	3200
24 11	VENTURE 25	SLP	SA/CR	FBG SK	OB	7 11	2300	1 6	3300	3800
35 6	MAC-GREGOR CAT	CAT	SA/RC	FBG CT	OB	18 6	3800	2	23500	26100
------------------------- 1978 BOATS -------------------------
21	VENTURE 21	SLP	SA/RC	FBG SK	OB	6 10	1500	1	2250	2600
22	VENTURE 222	SLP	SA/CR	FBG SK	OB	7 4	2000	1	2600	3050
22 7	VENTURE-OF-NEWPORT	SLP	SA/CR	FBG SK	OB	7 2	2000	1	2650	3050
24 11	VENTURE 25	SLP	SA/CR	FBG SK	OB	7 11	2300	1 6	3150	3700
35 6	MAC-GREGOR CAT	CAT	SA/RC	FBG CT	OB	18	3800	2	22700	25200
------------------------- 1977 BOATS -------------------------
21	VENTURE 21	SLP	SA/CR	FBG SK	OB	6 10	1500	1	2150	2500
22	VENTURE 22	SLP	SA/CR	FBG SK	OB	7 4	2000	1	2550	2950
23	VENTURE 23	SLP	SA/CR	FBG SK	OB	7 2	2000	1	2550	3000
25	VENTURE 25	SLP	SA/CR	FBG SK	OB	7 11	2300	1 6	3100	3600
36	MAC-GREGOR CAT	CAT	SA/RC	FBG CT	OB	18	4200	2	24700	27400

LOA FT IN	NAME AND/ OR MODEL	TOP/ RIG	BOAT TYPE	-HULL- MTL TP TP	----ENGINE--- # HP MFG	BEAM FT IN	WGT LBS	DRAFT FT IN	RETAIL LOW	RETAIL HIGH
	------------------ 1976 BOATS ------------------									
21	VENTURE 21	SLP	SAIL	FBG SK OB		6 10	1500	1	2050	2450
22	VENTURE 222	SLP	SAIL	FBG SK OB		7 4	2400		2750	3200
22 7	VENTURE-OF-NEWPORT	SLP	SAIL	FBG SK OB		7 2	2400	1 6	2750	3200
24 11	VENTURE 25	SLP	SAIL	FBG SK OB		7 11	2300	1 6	2950	3450
36	MAC-GREGOR 36	CAT	SA/RC	FBG CT OB		17 10	4200	2	23800	26500
	------------------ 1975 BOATS ------------------									
21	VENTURE 21	SLP	SAIL	FBG SK OB		6 10	1500	5 6	2000	2350
22	VENTURE 2-22	SLP	SAIL	FBG SK OB		7 4	1800	1	2250	2650
22	VENTURE 22	SLP	SAIL	FBG SK OB		7 4	2000	4 6	2400	2750
22 7	VENTURE OF NEWPORT	CUT	SAIL	FBG SK OB		7 2	2000	5 6	2400	2800
24 11	VENTURE 25	SLP	SAIL	FBG SK OB		7 11	2300	5	2900	3350
36	MAC-GREGOR 36	CAT	SA/RC	FBG CT OB		18 6	4000	9	23000	25500
	------------------ 1974 BOATS ------------------									
21	VENTURE 21	SLP	SA/CR	FBG SK OB		6 10	1500	1	1950	2300
22	VENTURE 2 22	SLP	SA/CR	FBG SK OB		7 4	1800	1	2200	2550
22 7	VENTURE-OF-NEWPORT	CUT	SA/CR	FBG SK OB		7 4	2000	1 6	2350	2700
24 11	VENTURE 25	SLP	SA/CR	FBG SK OB		7 11	2300	1 6	2800	3250
	------------------ 1973 BOATS ------------------									
21	VENTURE 21	SLP	SAIL	FBG SK OB		6 10	1200	5 6	1700	2050
22	VENTURE 2-22	SLP	SAIL	FBG SK OB		7 4	1800	4 6	2150	2500
22	VENTURE 22	SLP	SAIL	FBG SK OB		7 4	1700	4 6	2050	2450
23	VENTURE-OF-NEWPORT	SLP	SAIL	FBG SK OB		7 11	2600	5	2700	3150
24 7	VENTURE 2-24	SLP	SAIL	FBG SK OB		7 11	2100	5	2550	3000
24 7	VENTURE 24	SLP	SAIL	FBG SK OB		7 11	2100	5	2500	2900
	------------------ 1972 BOATS ------------------									
22	VENTURE 2-22	SLP	SAIL	FBG SK OB		7 4	1800	4 6	2050	2450
22	VENTURE 22	SLP	SAIL	FBG SK OB		7 4	1700	4 6	2000	2400
24	VENTURE 2-24	SLP	SAIL	FBG SK OB		7 11	2100	5	2500	2900
24 7	VENTURE 24	SLP	SAIL	FBG SK OB		7 11	2100	5	2400	2800
	------------------ 1971 BOATS ------------------									
22	VENTURE 2-22	SLP	SAIL	FBG SK OB		7 4	1800	6 6	2000	2400
22	VENTURE 22	SLP	SAIL	FBG SK OB		7 4	1600	4 6	1900	2250
24	VENTURE 24	SLP	SAIL	FBG SK OB		7 11	2000	4 6	2350	2750
	------------------ 1970 BOATS ------------------									
22	VENTURE 22	SLP	SAIL	FBG SK		7 3	1600		1850	2200
24 7	VENTURE 24	SLP	SAIL	FBG SK OB		7 11	1900	1 6	2250	2650
	------------------ 1969 BOATS ------------------									
24 7	VENTURE 24	SLP	SAIL	FBG SK OB		7 11	2000	4 6	2300	2650

MACKIE BOATS
INDUST PLASTICS LOUISBU COAST GUARD MFG ID- NPL

Call 1-800-327-6929 for BUC Personalized Evaluation Service
Or, for 1976 to 1979 boats, sign onto www.BUCValuPro.com

HARRY MACKLOWE YT IMPORTS
DOUG PETERSON DESIGNS   COAST GUARD MFG ID- HRP

Call 1-800-327-6929 for BUC Personalized Evaluation Service
Or, for 1978 boats, sign onto www.BUCValuPro.com

MACWESTER MARINE CO LTD
COAST GUARD MFG ID- MWS

Call 1-800-327-6929 for BUC Personalized Evaluation Service
Or, for 1980 boats, sign onto www.BUCValuPro.com

MAGELLAN YACHTS LTD

Call 1-800-327-6929 for BUC Personalized Evaluation Service
Or, for 1981 to 1982 boats, sign onto www.BUCValuPro.com

MAGIC MARINE
COAST GUARD MFG ID- MGX

Call 1-800-327-6929 for BUC Personalized Evaluation Service
Or, for 1973 boats, sign onto www.BUCValuPro.com

MAGNUM MARINE CORPORATION
N MIAMI BEACH FL 33180   COAST GUARD MFG ID- MAG See inside cover to adjust price for area

For more recent years, see the BUC Used Boat Price Guide, Volume 1 or Volume 2

LOA FT IN	NAME AND/ OR MODEL	TOP/ RIG	BOAT TYPE	-HULL- MTL TP TP	----ENGINE--- # HP MFG	BEAM FT IN	WGT LBS	DRAFT FT IN	RETAIL LOW	RETAIL HIGH
	------------------ 1983 BOATS ------------------									
27	SEDAN	OP	CR	FBG DV IO	T330 MRCR	7 10	5600	2 5	18100	20100
27	SPORT	OP	RNBT	FBG DV IO	T260 MRCR	7 10	5200	2 4	14200	16100
27 4	STARFIRE	OP	SPTCR	FBG DV IO	T260-T330	7 10	5200	2 4	16000	20000
27 4	STARFIRE	OP	SPTCR	FBG DV IO	T450 BPM	7 10	5200	2 4	22700	25200
27 6	MALTESE	OP	RNBT	FBG DV IO	T330 MRCR	7 11	5200	2 4	16300	18600
27 6	MALTESE	OP	RNBT	FBG DV IO	T450 MRCR	7 11	5200	2 4	20100	22400
38	FLYBRIDGE CRUISER	FB	SDN	FBG DV IO	T330 MRCR 12	3 19000		3 4	65500	72000
	IB T375 BPM 106500 117000,		IB T450 BPM	110500 121500,	IB T620 BPM				122500	134500
	IB T300D GM 122500 135000,		IB T500D GM	144000 158500						
38	FLYBRIDGE FISHERMAN	FB	SDNSF	FBG DV IO	T330 MRCR 12	3 19000		3 4	84900	93300
	IB T375 BPM 105500 116000,		IB T450 BPM	109500 120500,	IB T620 BPM				121500	133500
	IB T300D GM 121500 134000,		IB T500D GM	143000 157000						
38	HARDTOP	HT	SPTCR	FBG DV IO	T330 MRCR 12	3		3 4	38500	42800
	IB T375 BPM 61600		67000, IB T450 BPM	65000 72200,	IB T620 BPM				77400	85100
	IB T300D GM 76200		83700, IB T500D GM	97600 107500						
38	HARDTOP CRUISER	HT	SDN	FBG DV IO	T330 MRCR 12	3		3 4	39100	43500
	IB T375 BPM 61500		67600, IB T450 BPM	65500 71900,	IB T620 BPM				77100	84700
	IB T300D GM 77000		84600, IB T500D GM	97400 107000						
38	SPORT	OP	SPTCR	FBG DV IO	T330 MRCR 12	3 16500		3 4	59400	65300
	IB T375 BPM 96000 105500,		IB T450 BPM	100000 110000,	IB T620 BPM				112500	123000
	IB T300D GM 111500 122500,		IB T500D GM	132500 146000						
40	FLYBRIDGE CRUISER	FB	SPTCR	FBG DV IB	T700 BPM	12 3	5000	2 4	115500	126500
40	HARDTOP	HT	SPTCR	FBG DV IB	T330 MRCR 12	3	5000	2 4	115500	126500
40	HARDTOP	HT	SPTCR	FBG DV IB	T500D S&S	12 3	5000	2 4	116500	128500
40	SPORT	OP	SPTCR	FBG DV IB	T330 MRCR 12	3	5000	3 4	35700	39600
40	SPORT	OP	SPTCR	FBG DV IB	T700 BPM	12 3	5000	3 4	115500	126500
40	SPORT	OP	SPTCR	FBG DV IB	T500D S&S	12 3	5000	3 4	116500	128500
52 11	FLYBRIDGE CRUISER	FB	CR	FBG DV IB	T120D GM	15 9	44000	5	180500	198000
	IB T200D GM 212000 233000,		IB T640D GM	305000 335000,	IB T12CD GM				422000	464000
52 11	HARDTOP	HT	SPTCR	FBG DV IB	T330 MRCR 15	9 44000		5	160000	175500
	IB T120D GM 158500 174500,		IB T200D GM	184000 202500,	IB T640D GM				320500	352500
	IB T12CD GM 471500 518000)									
52 11	SPORT	OP	SPTCR	FBG DV IB	T120D GM	15 9	44000	5	156000	171500
	IB T200D GM 170500 187500,		IB T640D GM	310000 341000,	IB T12CD GM				438500	481500
63	HARDTOP	HT	MY	FBG DV IB	T13CD GM	17			608500	669000
63	SPORT	OP	CR	FBG DV IB	T13CD GM	17			602500	662000
63	SPORT CONVERTIBLE	OP	CR	FBG DV IB	T13CD GM	17			602500	662000
	------------------ 1982 BOATS ------------------									
27	SEDAN	OP	CR	FBG DV IO	T330 MRCR	7 10	5600	2 5	17300	19700
27	SPORT	OP	RNBT	FBG DV IO	T260 MRCR	7 10	5200	2 4	13700	15600
27 4	STARFIRE	OP	SPTCR	FBG DV IO	T260-T330	7 10	5000	2 4	15500	19200
27 4	STARFIRE	OP	SPTCR	FBG DV IO	T450 BPM	7 10	5000	2 4	21300	23700
27 6	MALTESE	OP	RNBT	FBG DV IO	T450 MRCR	7 11	5200	2 4	16000	18200
27 6	MALTESE	OP	RNBT	FBG DV IO	T450 MRCR	7 11	5200	2 4	19700	21900
38	FLYBRIDGE CRUISER	FB	SDN	FBG DV IO	T330 MRCR 12	3 19000		3 4	99500	109500
	IB T375 BPM 101500 111500,		IB T450 BPM	105500 116000,	IB T620 BPM				117000	128500
	IB T300D GM 117000 128500,		IB T500D GM	137500 151000						
38	FLYBRIDGE FISHERMAN	FB	SDNSF	FBG DV IB	T330 MRCR 12	3 19000		3 4	98800	108500
	IB T375 BPM 101000 111000,		IB T450 BPM	104500 115000,	IB T620 BPM				116000	127500
	IB T300D GM 116000 127500,		IB T500D GM	136500 150000						
38	HARDTOP	HT	SPTCR	FBG DV IB	T330 MRCR 12	3		3 4	56700	62300
	IB T375 BPM 58700		64500, IB T450 BPM	62700 68900,	IB T620 BPM				73900	81200
	IB T300D GM 72700		79900, IB T500D GM	93200 102500						
38	HARDTOP CRUISER	HT	SDN	FBG DV IB	T330 MRCR 12	3		3 4	56900	62500
	IB T375 BPM 58800		64600, IB T450 BPM	62500 68700,	IB T620 BPM				73600	80900
	IB T300D GM 73400		80700, IB T500D GM	92900 102000						
38	SPORT	OP	SPTCR	FBG DV IB	T330 MRCR 12	3 16500		3 4	89700	98500
	IB T375 BPM 91700 100500,		IB T450 BPM	95600 105000,	IB T620 BPM				107000	117500
	IB T300D GM 106500 117000,		IB T500D GM	126500 139000						
40	FLYBRIDGE CRUISER	FB	SPTCR	FBG DV IB	T330 MRCR 12	3	5000	2 4	51900	57000
40	FLYBRIDGE CRUISER	FB	SPTCR	FBG DV IB	T700 BPM	12 3	5000	2 4	110500	121000

```
  LOA    NAME AND/            TOP/ BOAT  -HULL-  ----ENGINE--- BEAM   WGT  DRAFT RETAIL RETAIL
  FT IN  OR MODEL             RIG  TYPE  MTL TP TP # HP  MFG   FT IN  LBS  FT IN  LOW    HIGH
---------------------------- 1982 BOATS ---------------------------------------------------------
  40   HARDTOP               HT   SPTCR FBG DV IB T330  MRCR 12  3  5000  2  4  51800  56900
  40   HARDTOP               HT   SPTCR FBG DV IB T700  BPM  12  3  5000  2  4 110000 121000
  40   HARDTOP               HT   SPTCR FBG DV IB T500D S&S  12  3  5000  2  4 111500 122500
  40   SPORT                 OP   SPTCR FBG DV IB T330  MRCR 12  3  5000  2  4  51800  56900
  40   SPORT                 OP   SPTCR FBG DV IB T700  BPM  12  3  5000  2  4 110000 121000
  40   SPORT                 OP   SPTCR FBG DV IB T500D S&S  12  3  5000  2  4 111500 122500
  44 7 FLYBRIDGE CRUISER     FB   OFF   FBG DV IB T330  MRCR 13  8                85400  93900
       IB T620  BPM  109500 120500, IB T700  BPM  116000 127500, IB T500D S&S  165500 182000
       IB T570D GM  179500 197500, IB T640D S&S  189500 208500

  44 7 HARDTOP               HT   OFF   FBG DV IB T570D      13  8               182000 200000
  44 7 SPORT                 OP   OFF   FBG DV IB T570D      13  8               171000 188000
  52 11 FLYBRIDGE CRUISER    FB   CR    FBG DV IB T120D GM   15  9 44000  4  4  172000 189000
       IB T200D GM  202500 222500, IB T640D GM   292500 321500, IB T12CD GM  402500 442500

  52 11 HARDTOP              HT   SPTCR FBG DV IB T330  MRCR 15  9 44000  4  4  218500 240000
       IB T120D GM  152000 167000, IB T200D GM  175500 193000, IB T640D GM  307500 337500
       IB T12CD GM  450000 494500

  52 11 SPORT                OP   SPTCR FBG DV IB T120D GM   15  9 44000  4  4  149500 164500
       IB T200D GM  163000 179000, IB T640D GM   296500 326000, IB T12CD GM  418500 459500
---------------------------- 1981 BOATS ---------------------------------------------------------
  27   SEDAN                 OP   CR    FBG DV IO T330  MRCR  7 10  5600  2  5  17000  19300
  27 4 SPORT                 OP   RNBT  FBG DV IO T260  MRCR  7 10  5000  2  4  13500  15300
  27 4 STARFIRE              OP   SPTCR FBG DV IO T330  MRCR  7 10  5000  2  4  16600  18900
  27 4 STARFIRE              OP   SPTCR FBG DV IO T450  BPM   7 10  5000  2  2  20200  22500
  27 6 MALTESE               OP   RNBT  FBG DV IO T330  MRCR  7 11  5200  2  4  15700  17900
  27 6 MALTESE               OP   RNBT  FBG DV IO T450  MRCR  7 11  5200  2  4  19400  21500
  38   BIMINI SPORT FISH     TT   SF    FBG DV IB T330  MRCR 12  3 16500  3  4  85400  93800
       IB T375  BPM  87200  95900, IB T450  BPM   91000  99900, IB T620  BPM  102000 112000
       IB T300D GM  101000 111000, IB T500D GM  120500 132500

  38   FLYBRIDGE CRUISER     FB   SDN   FBG DV IB T330  MRCR 12  3 19000  3  4  94800 104000
       IB T375  BPM  96700 106500, IB T450  BPM  100500 110500, IB T620  BPM  111500 122500
       IB T300D GM  111500 122500, IB T500D GM  131000 144000

  38   FLYBRIDGE FISHERMAN   FB   SDNSF FBG DV IB T330  MRCR 12  3 19000  3  4  94200 103500
       IB T375  BPM  96000 105500, IB T450  BPM   99700 109500, IB T620  BPM  110500 121500
       IB T300D GM  110500 121500, IB T500D GM  130000 143000

  38   HARDTOP               HT   SPTCR FBG DV IB T330  MRCR 12  3               54000  59400
       IB T375  BPM  56000  61500, IB T450  BPM   59700  65600, IB T620  BPM   70400  77300
       IB T300D GM  69300  76100, IB T500D GM   88800  97600

  38   HARDTOP CRUISER       HT   SDN   FBG DV IB T330  MRCR 12  3               54300  59600
       IB T375  BPM  56000  61500, IB T450  BPM   59600  65500, IB T620  BPM   70100  77100
       IB T300D GM  70000  76900, IB T500D GM   88500  97300

  38   SPORT                 OP   SPTCR FBG DV IB T330  MRCR 12  3 16500  3  4  85400  93900
       IB T375  BPM  87300  96000, IB T450  BPM   91000 100000, IB T620  BPM  102000 112000
       IB T300D GM  101500 111500, IB T500D GM  120500 132500

  44 7 FLYBRIDGE CRUISER     FB   OFF   FBG DV IB T620  BPM  13  8               104500 115000
  44 7 FLYBRIDGE CRUISER     FB   OFF   FBG DV IB T570D GM   13  8               171000 188000
  44 7 FLYBRIDGE CRUISER     FB   OFF   FBG DV IB T640D S&S  13  8               180500 198500
  44 7 HARDTOP               HT   OFF   FBG DV IB T620  BPM  13  8               104500 115000
  44 7 HARDTOP               HT   OFF   FBG DV IB T570D GM   13  8               173500 190500
  44 7 SPORT                 OP   OFF   FBG DV IB T640D S&S  13  8               183500 201500
  44 7 SPORT                 OP   OFF   FBG DV IB T620  BPM  13  8               101000 111000
  44 7 SPORT                 OP   OFF   FBG DV IB T570D GM   13  8               163000 179000
  44 7 SPORT                 OP   OFF   FBG DV IB T640D S&S  13  8               171500 188500
  52 11 FLYBRIDGE CRUISER    FB   CR    FBG DV IB T640D GM   15  9 44000  4  4  279000 307000
  52 11 FLYBRIDGE CRUISER    FB   CR    FBG DV IB T12CD GM   15  9 44000  4  4  383500 421500

  52 11 HARDTOP              HT   SPTCR FBG DV IB T640D GM   15  9 44000  4  4  293500 322500
  52 11 HARDTOP              HT   SPTCR FBG DV IB T12CD GM   15  9 44000  4  4  428500 471000
  52 11 SPORT                OP   SPTCR FBG DV IB T640D GM   15  9 44000  4  4  303500 334000
  52 11 SPORT                OP   SPTCR FBG DV IB T12CD GM   15  9 44000  4  4  398500 438000
---------------------------- 1980 BOATS ---------------------------------------------------------
  27   SEDAN                 OP   CR    FBG DV IO T330  MRCR  7 10  5600  2  5  16900  19200
  27   SPORT                 OP   RNBT  FBG DV IO T260  MRCR  7 10  5000  2  4  13400  15200
  27 4 STARFIRE              OP   SPTCR FBG DV IO T330  MRCR  7 10  5000  2  4  16500  18700
  27 6 MALTESE               OP   RNBT  FBG DV IO T330  MRCR  7 11  5200  2  4  15200  17300
  27 6 MALTESE               OP   RNBT  FBG DV IO T450  MRCR  7 11  5200  2  4  19200  21700
  38   BIMINI SPORT FISH     TT   SF    FBG DV IB T330  MRCR 12  3 16500  3  4  81400  89500
       IB T375  BPM  83200  91400, IB T620  BPM   97100 106500, IB T300D GM   96600 106000
       IB T600D GM  126000 138500

  38   FLYBRIDGE CRUISER     FB   SDN   FBG DV IB T330  MRCR 12  3 19000  3  4  90400  99300
       IB T375  BPM  92200 101500, IB T620  BPM  106000 117000, IB T300D GM  106500 117000
       IB T600D GM  136000 149500

  38   FLYBRIDGE FISHERMAN   FB   SDNSF FBG DV IB T330  MRCR 12  3 19000  3  4  89800  98700
       IB T375  BPM  91600 100500, IB T620  BPM  105500 116000, IB T300D GM  105500 116000
       IB T600D GM  135000 148000

  38   HARDTOP               HT   SPTCR FBG DV IB T330  MRCR 12  3               51500  56600
       IB T375  BPM  53400  58700, IB T620  BPM   67100  73800, IB T300D GM   66100  72600
       IB T600D GM  95300 104500

  38   HARDTOP CRUISER       HT   SDN   FBG DV IB T330  MRCR 12  3               51800  56900
       IB T375  BPM  53500  58800, IB T620  BPM   66900  73500, IB T300D GM   66700  73300
       IB T600D GM  95000 104500

  38   SPORT                 OP   SPTCR FBG DV IB T330  MRCR 12  3 16500  3  4  81500  89600
       IB T375  BPM  83300  91500, IB T620  BPM   97200 107000, IB T300D GM   96600 106000
       IB T600D GM  126000 138500

  44 7 FLYBRIDGE CRUISER     FB   SDN   FBG DV IB T500D      13  8               150500 165000
  44 7 HARDTOP               HT   SPTCR FBG DV IB T500D      13  8               168000 184500
  44 7 SPORT                 OP   SPTCR FBG DV IB T500D      13  8               161500 177500
  52 11 FLYBRIDGE CRUISER    FB   CR    FBG DV IB T570       15  9               199000 219000
  52 11 FLYBRIDGE CRUISER    FB   CR    FBG DV IB T   D GM   15  9 44000  4  4     **     **
  52 11 FLYBRIDGE CRUISER    FB   CR    FBG DV IB T640D GM   15  9 44000  4  4  266500 293000
  52 11 HARDTOP              HT   SPTCR FBG DV IB T   D GM   15  9 44000  4  4     **     **
  52 11 HARDTOP              HT   SPTCR FBG DV IB T640D GM   15  9 44000  4  4  280500 308000
  52 11 HARDTOP              HT   SPTCR FBG DV IB T570       15  9                  **     **
  52 11 SPORT                OP   SPTCR FBG DV IB T   D GM   15  9 44000  4  4     **     **
  52 11 SPORT                OP   SPTCR FBG DV IB T640D GM   15  9 44000  4  4  270000 297000
---------------------------- 1979 BOATS ---------------------------------------------------------
  27   MALTESE               OP   RNBT  FBG DV IO T330  MRCR  7 10  5200  2  4  15000  17100
  27   SEDAN                 OP   CR    FBG DV IO T330  MRCR  7 10  5600  2  5  16900  19200
  27   SPORT                 OP   RNBT  FBG DV IO T260  MRCR  7 10  5000  2  4  13300  15200
  27   STARFIRE              OP   SPTCR FBG DV IO T330  MRCR  7 10                16700  19000
  27   STARFIRE              OP   SPTCR FBG DV IO T450  BPM   7 10                20500  22000
  38   BIMINI SPORT FISH     TT   SF    FBG DV IB T330  MRCR 12  3 16500  3  4  77800  85500
       IB T375  BPM  79500  87300, IB T620  BPM   92800 102000, IB T300D GM  101500 111500
       IB T600D GM  120000 132000

  38   FLYBRIDGE CRUISER     FB   SDN   FBG DV IB T330  MRCR 12  3 19000  3  4  86300  94900
       IB T375  BPM  88100  96800, IB T620  BPM  101500 111500, IB T300D GM  101500 111500
       IB T600D GM  130000 143000

  38   FLYBRIDGE FISHERMAN   FB   SDNSF FBG DV IB T330  MRCR 12  3 19000  3  4  85800  94200
       IB T375  BPM  87500  96500, IB T620  BPM  100500 110500, IB T300D GM  101000 111000
       IB T600D GM  129000 141500

  38   HARDTOP               HT   SPTCR FBG DV IB T330  MRCR 12  3               49200  54100
       IB T375  BPM  51000  56000, IB T620  BPM   64100  70500, IB T300D GM   63100  69400
       IB T600D GM  91000 100000

  38   HARDTOP CRUISER       HT   SDN   FBG DV IB T330  MRCR 12  3               49300  54400
       IB T375  BPM  51100  56200, IB T620  BPM   63900  70200, IB T300D GM   63800  70100
       IB T600D GM  90700  99700

  38   KEVLAR SPECIAL        CR   KEV   DV IB T620  BPM  12  3               3  4  64100  70500
  38   SPORT                 OP   SPTCR FBG DV IB T330  MRCR 12  3 16500  3  4  77800  85500
       IB T375  BPM  79600  87400, IB T620  BPM   92900 102000, IB T300D GM   92300 101500
       IB T600D GM  120500 132000

  52 11 FLYBRIDGE CRUISER    FB   CR    FBG DV IB T   D GM   15  9               4  4     **     **
  52 11 FLYBRIDGE CRUISER    FB   CR    FBG DV IB T570D GM   15  9               4  4  192000 211000
  52 11 HARDTOP              HT   SPTCR FBG DV IB T   D GM   15  9               4  4     **     **
  52 11 HARDTOP              HT   SPTCR FBG DV IB T570D GM   15  9               4  4  251000 276000
  52 11 SPORT                OP   SPTCR FBG DV IB T   D GM   15  9 44000  4  4     **     **
  52 11 SPORT                OP   SPTCR FBG DV IB T570D GM   15  9 44000  4  4  244000 268000
---------------------------- 1978 BOATS ---------------------------------------------------------
  27 4 SEDAN                 OP   CR    FBG DV IO 300-330     7 11        2  5  13900  15800
  27 4 SEDAN                 OP   CR    FBG DV IO T165        7 11        2  5  14300  16200
  27 4 SEDAN                 OP   CR    FBG DV IO T280-T330   7 11        2  5  14300  16200
  27 4 SPORT                 OP   RNBT  FBG DV IO 300-330     7 11        2  4  12900  15000
  27 4 SPORT                 OP   RNBT  FBG DV IO T280-T330   7 11        2  4  14700  17900
  27 6 MALTESE               OP   RNBT  FBG DV IO 300-330     7 11        2  4  12900  14700
  27 6 MALTESE               OP   RNBT  FBG DV IO T280-T330   7 11        2  4  14900  18100
```

LOA FT	LOA IN	NAME AND/ OR MODEL	TOP/ RIG	BOAT TYPE	-HULL- MTL	-HULL- TP	TP	ENGINE # HP	ENGINE MFG	BEAM FT	BEAM IN	WGT LBS	DRAFT FT	DRAFT IN	RETAIL LOW	RETAIL HIGH
		1978 BOATS														
38		BIMINI SPORT FISH	TT	SF	FBG	DV	IB	T350	MRCR	12	3	16500	3	4	74900	82300
		IB T375 CHRY 47800 52500, IB T730 BPM 65800 72300, IB T300D GM													59700	65600
		IB T350D IF 63100 69400, IB T500D GM 76500 84100														
38		FLYBRIDGE CRUISER	FB	SDN	FBG	DV	IB	T350	MRCR	12	3		3	4	47800	52600
		IB T375 CHRY 48300 53000, IB T730 BPM 66300 72800, IB T300D GM													61000	67000
		IB T350D IF 64200 70600, IB T500D GM 77200 84800														
38		FLYBRIDGE FISHERMAN	FB	SDNSF	FBG	DV	IB	T350	MRCR	12	3	19000	3	4	82500	90700
		IB T375 CHRY 48600 53400, IB T730 BPM 66800 73400, IB T300D GM													99800	109500
		IB T350D IF 64300 70700, IB T500D GM 77800 85500														
38		HARDTOP	HT	SPTCR	FBG	DV	IB	T350	MRCR	12	3	18000	3	4	79900	87800
		IB T375 CHRY 48100 52900, IB T620 BPM 61300 67400, IB T300D GM													96700	106500
		IB T350D IF 63900 70200, IB T500D GM 77400 85000														
38		HARDTOP CRUISER	HT	SDN	FBG	DV	IB	T350	MRCR	12	3		3	4	47800	52600
		IB T375 CHRY 48200 53000, IB T730 BPM 66200 72800, IB T300D GM													61000	67000
		IB T350D IF 64200 70600, IB T500D GM 77200 84800														
38		SPORT	OP	SPTCR	FBG	DV	IB	T350	MRCR	12	3	17000	3	4	76600	84200
		IB T375 CHRY 48100 52900, IB T620 BPM 61300 67400, IB T300D GM													93200	102500
		IB T350D IF 63700 70000, IB T500D GM 77200 84800														
52	11	MALTESE FB CRUISER	FB	CR	FBG	DV	IB	T D	GM	15	9		4	4	**	**
52	11	MALTESE FB CRUISER	FB	CR	FBG	DV	IB	T570D	GM	15	9	47000	4	4	221000	243000
52	11	MALTESE HARDTOP	HT	SPTCR	FBG	DV	IB	T D	GM	15	9		4	4	**	**
52	11	MALTESE HARDTOP	HT	SPTCR	FBG	DV	IB	T570D	GM	15	9	45000	4	4	232000	254500
52	11	MALTESE SPORT	OP	SPTCR	FBG	DV	IB	T D	GM	15	9		4	4	**	**
52	11	MALTESE SPORT	OP	SPTCR	FBG	DV	IB	T570D	GM	15	9	44000	4	4	217000	238500
		1977 BOATS														
27	4	SEDAN 27	OP	CR	FBG	DV	IO	T165	MRCR	7	10	5400	1	7	14300	16200
27	4	SEDAN 27	OP	CR	FBG	DV	IO	T280-T300		7	10	5400	1	7	16200	19000
27	4	SPORT 27	OP	RACE	FBG	DV	IO	T280-T300		7	10	4800	1	6	14200	16600
27	6	MALTESE 28	OP	RACE	FBG	DV	IO	T280-T300		7	11	5200	1	6	14900	17300
38		BIMINI SPORT FISH 38	TT	SF	FBG	DV	IB	T350	MRCR	12	3	16500	2	4	71700	78800
		IB T375 CHRY 72200 79300, IB T300D GM 84500 92900, IB T350D IF													87800	96500
38		HARDTOP 38	HT	SPTCR	FBG	DV	IB	T350	MRCR	12	3	17500	2	4	75000	82400
		IB T375 CHRY 75400 82800, IB T300D GM 87900 96600, IB T350D IF													91200	100000
38		HARDTOP CRUISER 38	HT	CR	FBG	DV	IB	T350	MRCR	12	3	17500	2	4	74900	82400
		IB T375 CHRY 75400 82800, IB T300D GM 87800 96400, IB T350D IF													91100	100000
38		SEDAN 38	FB	SDN	FBG	DV	IB	T350	MRCR	12	3	19000	2	4	79600	87500
		IB T375 CHRY 80000 87900, IB T300D GM 93100 102500, IB T350D IF													96400	106000
38		SEDAN SPORT FISH 38	FB	SDNSF	FBG	DV	IB	T350	MRCR	12	3	19000	2	4	79000	86800
		IB T375 CHRY 79400 87300, IB T300D GM 92400 101500, IB T350D IF													95700	105000
38		SPORT 38	OP	SPTCR	FBG	DV	IB	T350	MRCR	12	3	16500	2	4	71800	78900
		IB T375 CHRY 72200 79400, IB T300D GM 84500 92900, IB T350D IF													87800	96500
52	6	FLYBRIDGE FISH	FB	YTFS	FBG	DV	IB	T570D	GM	16		35000	4	4	154500	169500
52	6	FLYBRIDGE FISH I	FB	YTFS	FBG	DV	IB	T570D	GM	16		35000	4	4	219000	241000
52	6	FLYBRIDGE FISH II	FB	YTFS	FBG	DV	IB	T570D	GM	16		35000	4	4	207000	227500
52	6	FLYBRIDGE FISH III	FB	YTFS	FBG	DV	IB	T570D	GM	16		35000	4	4	213500	234500
52	6	HARDTOP 53	HT	SPTCR	FBG	DV	IB	T570D	GM	16		34000	4	4	147000	161500
52	6	HARDTOP I 53	HT	SPTCR	FBG	DV	IB	T570D	GM	16		34000	4	4	215000	236500
52	6	HARDTOP II 53	HT	SPTCR	FBG	DV	IB	T570D	GM	16		34000	4	4	202500	222500
52	6	HARDTOP III 53	HT	SPTCR	FBG	DV	IB	T570D	GM	16		34000	4	4	209000	230000
52	6	SPORT 53	OP	SPTCR	FBG	DV	IB	T570D	GM	16		30000	4	4	136000	149500
52	6	SPORT I 53	OP	SPTCR	FBG	DV	IB	T570D	GM	16		30000	4	4	204000	224000
52	6	SPORT II 53	OP	SPTCR	FBG	DV	IB	T570D	GM	16		30000	4	4	191500	210500
52	6	SPORT III 53	OP	SPTCR	FBG	DV	IB	T570D	GM	16		30000	4	4	198000	217500
		1976 BOATS														
25	4	SPORT 25	OP	RNBT	FBG	DV	IO	280-300		8			1	4	9800	11400
25	4	SPORT 25	OP	RNBT	FBG	DV	IO	T170		8			1	4	10300	11800
27	4	SEDAN 27	OP	SDN	FBG	DV	IO	T165-T300		7	10	5400	1	7	16300	19800
27	4	SPORT 27	OP	RNBT	FBG	DV	IO	T250-T300		7	10	4800	1	6	14000	17100
27	6	MALTESE 28	OP	RNBT	FBG	DV	IO	T250-T300		7	11	5200	1	6	14700	17800
38		BIMINI SPORT FISH	FB	SF	FBG	DV	IB	T350	MRCR	12	3	19000	2	4	76000	83500
		IB T375 CHRY 76400 84000, IB T240D CUM 85100 93500, IB T300D S&S													87700	96400
		IB T320D GM 89800 98700														
38		SEDAN SPORT FISH	FB	SDNSF	FBG	DV	IB	T350	MRCR	12	3	20000	2	4	78700	86500
		IB T375 CHRY 79100 86900, IB T240D CUM 88100 96800, IB T300D S&S													90700	99700
		IB T320D GM 92800 102000														
38		SEDAN SPORTCRUISER	FB	SPTCR	FBG	DV	IB	T350	MRCR	12	3	21000	2	4	82300	90400
		IB T375 CHRY 82700 90800, IB T240D CUM 92000 101000, IB T300D S&S													94600	104000
		IB T320D GM 96700 106500														
38		SPORT 38	OP	SPTCR	FBG	DV	IB	T350	MRCR	12	3	17000	2	4	70300	77300
		IB T375 CHRY 70700 77700, IB T240D CUM 79000 86800, IB T300D S&S													81700	89700
		IB T320D GM 83800 92100														
		1975 BOATS														
25	4	SPORT 25	OP	RNBT	FBG	DV	IO	188-290		8			1	4	9400	11600
25	4	SPORT 25	OP	RNBT	FBG	DV	IO	300		8			1	4	10400	11800
25	4	SPORT 25	OP	RNBT	FBG	DV	IO	T165-T220		8			1	4	10700	12700
27	4	SEDAN 27	OP	SDN	FBG	DV	IO	T165-T300		7	10	5400	1	7	16800	20500
27	4	SPORT 27	OP	RNBT	FBG	DV	IO	T215-T280		7	10	4800	1	6	13900	17200
27	4	SPORT 27	OP	RNBT	FBG	DV	IO	T300		7	10	4800	1	6	15500	17700
27	6	MALTESE 28	OP	RNBT	FBG	DV	IO	T215-T280		7	11	5200	1	6	14600	17900
27	6	MALTESE 28	OP	RNBT	FBG	DV	IO	T300		7	11	5200	1	6	16100	18300
35	2	MAGNUM 35	FB	SF	FBG	DV	IB	T325		12	3	14000	3		49400	54300
35	2	MAGNUM 35 BIMINI SPT		SF	FBG	DV	IB	T325		12	3	14000	3		49300	54100
38		BIMINI SPORT FISH	FB	SF	FBG	DV	IO	T350	MRCR	12	3	19000	2	4	87300	95900
38		BIMINI SPORT FISH	FB	SF	FBG	DV	IO	T375	CHRY	12	3	19000	2	4	89700	98600
38		BIMINI SPORT FISH	FB	SF	FBG	DV	IO	T320D	GM	12	3	19000	2	4	99700	109500
38		SEDAN SPORT CRUISER	FB	SPTCR	FBG	DV	IO	T350	MRCR	12	3	20000	2	4	71600	78700
38		SEDAN SPORT CRUISER	FB	SPTCR	FBG	DV	IO	T375	CHRY	12	3	20000	2	4	73500	80800
38		SEDAN SPORT CRUISER	FB	SPTCR	FBG	DV	IO	T320D	GM	12	3	20000	2	4	89400	98200
38		SEDAN-SPORT FISH	FB	SDNSF	FBG	DV	IO	T350	MRCR	12	3	20000	2	4	89700	98500
38		SEDAN-SPORT FISH	FB	SDNSF	FBG	DV	IO	T375	CHRY	12	3	20000	2	4	92100	101000
38		SEDAN-SPORT FISH	FB	SDNSF	FBG	DV	IO	T320D	GM	12	3	20000	2	4	102500	112500
38		STANDARD 38	OP		FBG	DV	IO	T350	MRCR	12	3		2	4	42200	46900
38		STANDARD 38	OP		FBG	DV	IO	T375	CHRY	12	3		2	4	44100	49000
38		STANDARD 38	OP		FBG	DV	IO	T320D	GM	12	3		2	4	55000	60500
		1974 BOATS														
25	4	MAGNUM 25 SPORT			FBG		IO	188-300		8		5500	2	2	12700	15600
25	4	MAGNUM 25 SPORT			FBG		IO	320	CC	8		5500	2	2	14100	16000
25	4	MAGNUM 25 SPORT			FBG		IO	T165-T220		8		5500	2	5	14100	16700
27	4	MAGNUM 27		SDN	FBG		IO	T165-T320		7	10	5400	2	5	17400	21300
27	4	MAGNUM 27 SPORT			FBG		IO	T235-T300		7	10	5250	2	5	17500	21400
27	4	MAGNUM 27 SPORT			FBG		IO	T320	CC	7	10	5250	2	5	19900	22100
27	8	MALTESE 28	OP	RNBT	FBG	DV	IO	T300		8		5200	1	8	16900	19200
27	8	MALTESE 28	OP	RNBT	FBG	DV	IO	T400		8		5200	1	8	20100	22300
35	2	MAGNUM		SDN	FBG		IO	T325	MRCR	12	3	14000	3		57400	63100
35	2	MAGNUM		SDN	FBG		IO	T375	CHRY	12	3	14000	3		59600	65500
35	2	MAGNUM		SDN	FBG		IO	T320D	GM	12	3	14000	3		68600	75300
35	2	MAGNUM 35	FB	SDN	FBG		IO	T325	MRCR	12	3	14000	3		57600	63200
35	2	MAGNUM 35	FB	SDN	FBG		IO	T375	CHRY	12	3	14000	3		59800	65700
35	2	MAGNUM 35	FB	SDN	FBG		IO	T320D	GM	12	3	14000	3		68800	75600
35	2	MAGNUM 35 BIMINI SPT			FBG		IO	T325	MRCR	12	3	14000	3		63200	69500
35	2	MAGNUM 35 BIMINI SPT			FBG		IO	T375	CHRY	12	3	14000	3		65800	72300
35	2	MAGNUM 35 BIMINI SPT			FBG		IO	T320D	GM	12	3	14000	3		77500	85200
35	2	MAGNUM 35 STD			FBG		IO	T325	MRCR	12	3	14000	3		58600	64400
35	2	MAGNUM 35 STD			FBG		IO	T375	CHRY	12	3	14000	3		60700	66700
35	2	MAGNUM 35 STD			FBG		IO	T320D	GM	12	3	14000	3		72600	79700
		1973 BOATS														
25	4	SPORT 25	OP	CUD	FBG	DV	IO	188-300		8		5100	1	4	12500	15400
25	4	SPORT 25	OP	CUD	FBG	DV	IO	320	CC	8		5100	1	4	13900	15800
25	4	SPORT 25	OP	CUD	FBG	DV	IO	T165-T220		8		5100	1	4	13900	16500
27	4		OP	SDN	FBG	DV	IO	T165-T320		7	10	5400	1	7	18400	22000
27	4	SPORT 27	OP	RNBT	FBG	DV	IO	T235-T300		7	10	4800	1	6	15200	18900
27	4	SPORT 27	OP	RNBT	FBG	DV	IO	T320	CC	7	10	4800	1	6	17100	19500
35	2		FB	SDN	FBG	DV	VD	T325	MRCR	12	3	18000	2	4	53400	58700
35	2		FB	SDN	FBG	DV	VD	T375	CHRY	12	3	18000	2	4	54500	59900
35	2		FB	SDN	FBG	DV	VD	T320D	GM	12	3	18000	2	4	73800	81100
35	2		FB	SDNSF	FBG	DV	VD	T325	MRCR	12	3	17000	2	4	50300	55200
35	2		FB	SDNSF	FBG	DV	VD	T375	CHRY	12	3	17000	2	4	51200	56300
35	2		FB	SDNSF	FBG	DV	VD	T320D	GM	12	3	17000	2	4	69000	75800
35	2	BIMINI	FB	SF	FBG	DV	VD	T325	MRCR	12	3	16000	2		48900	53700
35	2	BIMINI	FB	SF	FBG	DV	VD	T375	CHRY	12	3	16000	2		49800	54700
35	2	BIMINI	FB	SF	FBG	DV	VD	T320D	GM	12	3	16000	2		66900	73500
35	2	SPORT 35	OP	SPTCR	FBG	DV	VD	T325	MRCR	12	3	14000	2		46300	50900
35	2	SPORT 35	OP	SPTCR	FBG	DV	VD	T375	CHRY	12	3	14000	2		47200	51900
35	2	SPORT 35	OP	SPTCR	FBG	DV	VD	T320D	GM	12	3	14000	2		62000	68100

 CONTINUED ON NEXT PAGE

LOA FT IN	NAME AND/ OR MODEL	TOP/ RIG	BOAT TYPE	-HULL- MTL TP	----ENGINE--- TP # HP MFG	BEAM FT IN	WGT LBS	DRAFT FT IN	RETAIL LOW	RETAIL HIGH
					1972 BOATS					
25 4	MAGNUM	RNBT	FBG	IO	325 MRCR	8	4500		12400	14100
27 4	MAGNUM	SDN	FBG	IO	T235-T290	7 10	5400		19400	22100
27 4	MAGNUM SPORTS		FBG	IO	T165-T235	7 10	4800		16800	20600
27 4	MAGNUM SPORTS		FBG	IO	T290	7 10	4800		19700	21900
35 2		FB SDN	FBG	IB	T325 MRCR	12 3	18000		51300	56400
35 2		FB SDN	FBG	IB	T375	12 3	18000		52400	57600
35 2		FB SDNSF	FBG	IB	T325 MRCR	12 3	17000		48200	53000
35 2		FB SDNSF	FBG	IB	T375	12 3	17000		49300	54200
35 2	MAGNUM	SF	FBG	IB	T375 MRCR	12 3	16000		47100	51700
35 2	MAGNUM	SF	FBG	IB	T325	12 3	16000		47900	52700
35 2	MAGNUM SPORTS		FBG	IB	T325 MRCR	12 3	14000		44600	49600
35 2	MAGNUM SPORTS		FBG	IB	T375	12 3	14000		46200	50800
					1971 BOATS					
16	MAGNUM-MARAUDER		FBG	SV OB		6 8	725		3350	3900
16 6	MAGNUM-MISSILE		FBG	SV OB		7 1	700	1	3300	3850
27 4	MAGNUM	SDN	FBG	IO	T235 HOLM	7 10	5400		20000	22200
27 4	MAGNUM	SDN	FBG	SV IO	T165 MRCR	7 10	5400	1 7	19400	21600
27 4	MAGNUM SPORTS		FBG	IO	T235 HOLM	7 10	4800		19000	21100
35 2		FB SDN	FBG	IB	T325 MRCR	12 3	18000		49400	54200
35 2		FB SDNSF	FBG	IB	T325 MRCR	12 3	17000		46700	51300
35 2		FB SDNSF	FBG	DV IB	T375D CHRY	12 3		3	64100	70400
35 2		SF	FBG	IB	T325 MRCR	12 3	16000		44800	49800
35 2	MAGNUM SPORTS		FBG	IB	T325 MRCR	12 3	14000		42900	47700
					1970 BOATS					
16	MAGNUM-MARAUDER		FBG	SV OB		6 8	725		3350	3900
16 6	MAGNUM-MISSILE		FBG	SV OB		7 1	700	1	3300	3850
27 4	MAGNUM 27	CR	FBG	SV IO	T160-T235	7 10	5400	1 7	18100	21600
27 4	MAGNUM 27	CR	FBG	SV IO	T290 HOLM	7 10	5400	1 7	20800	23100
27 4	MAGNUM 27 SPORT		FBG	IO	T160-T235	7 10	4800	1 6	18200	21700
27 4	MAGNUM 27 SPORT		FBG	SV IO	T290 HOLM	7 10	4800	1 6	21000	23300
35 2	MAGNUM 35	FB SF	FBG	IB	T325 DAY	12 3		3	35700	39700
	IB T325 MRCR 35700	39700,	IB T390 MRCR	36900	41000,	IB T425 DAY			37700	41800
	IB T440D BARR 64900	71300,	IB T500D DAY	67900	74600,	IB T600D DAY			73700	81000
35 2	MAGNUM 35 SPORT	EXP	FBG	SV IB	T325 DAY	12	3 14000	3	41000	45600
	IB T325 MRCR 41000	45500,	IB T390 MRCR	42300	47000,	IB T425 DAY			41300	45900
	IB T440D BARR 70200	77100,	IB T500D DAY	73600	80900,	IB T600D DAY			80300	88200
					1969 BOATS					
16	MAGNUM-MARAUDER 16	SKI	FBG	SV OB		6 8	725	1	3350	3900
16 6	MAGNUM-MISSILE 16	SKI	FBG	SV OB		7	800	1	3750	4350
27 4	MAGNUM 27	CBNCR	FBG	SV IO	T160 MRCR	7 10	5400	1 8	22200	24700
27 4	MAGNUM 27	SPTCR	FBG	SV IO	T160 MRCR	7 10	4800	1 6	17500	19900
35 2	MAGNUM 35	CR	FBG	IB	T425	12 3		2 6	37900	42100
					1968 BOATS					
35 2		FB SF	FBG	IB	T320	12	3 14000	3	37200	41400
	IB T325 37300	41500,	IB T400		38800	43100,	IB T425		39300	43700
	IB T235D 56200	61700								
35 2		TT SF	FBG	IB	T320	12	3 14000	3	37500	41700
	IB T325 37600	41800,	IB T400		39000	43400,	IB T425		39600	44000
	IB T235D 56300	61900								
35 2	MALTESE	SPTCR	FBG	IB	T320	12	3 13000	3	36800	40900
	IB T325 36900	41000,	IB T400		38400	42600,	IB T425		38900	43300
	IB T235D 53600	58900								
					1967 BOATS					
35 2	MAGNUM 35	FB	SPTCR FBG	DV IB	T320	12 3			30300	33600
35 2	MAGNUM 35	FB	SPTCR FBG	DV IB	T600	12 3			36700	40800

MAINE SHIPBUILDING CORP

Call 1-800-327-6929 for BUC Personalized Evaluation Service
Or, for 1971 boats, sign onto www.BUCValuPro.com

MAINSHIP CORPORATION

For more recent years, see the BUC Used Boat Price Guide, Volume 1 or Volume 2

LOA FT IN	NAME AND/ OR MODEL	TOP/ RIG	BOAT TYPE	-HULL- MTL TP	----ENGINE--- TP # HP MFG	BEAM FT IN	WGT LBS	DRAFT FT IN	RETAIL LOW	RETAIL HIGH
					1983 BOATS					
30	MAINSHIP 30	FB	TRWL	FBG DS	IB 165 CRUS	10 3	9200	2 3	20300	22600
34	MAINSHIP 34 III	FB	TRWL	FBG DS	IB 165D-200D	11 11	14000	2 10	51200	57300
40	MAINSHIP 40	FB	TRWL	FBG DS	IB T165D PERK	14	23400	3 4	81000	89000
40	MAINSHIP 40	FB	TRWL	FBG DS	IB T200D PERK	14	23400	3 4	82200	90300
					1982 BOATS					
30	MAINSHIP 30	FB	TRWL	FBG DS	IB 165 CRUS	10 3	9200	2 3	19500	21600
30	MAINSHIP 30	FB	TRWL	FBG DS	IB 124D VLVO	10 3	9200	2 3	25900	28800
34	MAINSHIP 34	FB	TRWL	FBG DS	IB 165D-200D	11 11	14000	2 10	49200	57600
34	MAINSHIP II	FB	TRWL	FBG DS	IB 200D PERK	11 11	14000	2 10	47800	52500
40	MAINSHIP 40	FB	TRWL	FBG DS	IB T165D PERK	14	23400	3 4	77200	84900
40	MAINSHIP 40	FB	TRWL	FBG DS	IB T200D PERK	14	23400	3 4	78400	86200
					1981 BOATS					
30	MAINSHIP 30	FB	TRWL	FBG DS	IB D	10 3	9200	2 3	**	**
34	MAINSHIP 34	FB	TRWL	FBG DS	IB 165D-200D	11 11	14000	2 10	47600	55400
34	MAINSHIP II	FB	TRWL	FBG DS	IB 200D PERK	11 11	14000	2 10	46200	50700
40	MAINSHIP	FB	TRWL	FBG DS	IB T165D PERK	14	23400	3 4	73600	80900
40	MAINSHIP	FB	TRWL	FBG DS	IB T200D PERK	14	23400	3 4	74700	82100
					1980 BOATS					
34	MAINSHIP	FB	TRWL	FBG DS	IB 160D PERK	11 11	14000	2 10	45600	50200
34	MAINSHIP II	FB	TRWL	FBG DS	IB 200D PERK	11 11	14000	2 10	46600	51200
40	MAINSHIP	FB	TRWL	FBG DS	IB T D	14	23400	3 4	**	**
					1979 BOATS					
34	MAINSHIP	FB	TRWL	FBG SV	IB 160D PERK	11 11	14000	2 10	44400	49300
34	MAINSHIP II	FB	TRWL	FBG SV	IB 160D PERK	11 11	14000	2 10	42500	47300
					1978 BOATS					
34	MAINSHIP DKHS	FB	TRWL	FBG DS	IB 160D-200D	11 11	14000	2 10	41800	47300

MAKAI INDUSTRIES INC

Call 1-800-327-6929 for BUC Personalized Evaluation Service
Or, for 1977 boats, sign onto www.BUCValuPro.com

MAKO BOATS

For more recent years, see the BUC Used Boat Price Guide, Volume 1 or Volume 2

LOA FT IN	NAME AND/ OR MODEL	TOP/ RIG	BOAT TYPE	-HULL- MTL TP	----ENGINE--- TP # HP MFG	BEAM FT IN	WGT LBS	DRAFT FT IN	RETAIL LOW	RETAIL HIGH
					1983 BOATS					
17	MAKO 171 ANGLER	OP	CTRCN	FBG SV	OB	7 2	1200	7	3000	3500
17	MAKO 172 STANDARD	OP	CTRCN	FBG SV	OB	7 2	1200	7	3000	3450
20	MAKO 20B	OP	CTRCN	FBG DV	OB	8	1775	9	4850	5550
21 3	MAKO 21	OP	CTRCN	FBG DV	OB	8	2100	1	5850	6750
22	MAKO 224	OP	CTRCN	FBG DV	OB	8	2300	1	6700	7700
22 7	MAKO 228	OP	CUD	FBG DV	OB	8	2300	1 1	6750	7750
23	MAKO 235	OP	CTRCN	FBG DV	OB	8	2300		6800	7800
23	MAKO 236	OP	CTRCN	T390	IB 250-260	8	3800	2	11400	13500
23	MAKO 236	OP	CTRCN	FBG DV	IB 140D VLVO	8	4200	2	16300	18600
23	MAKO 236	OP	CTRCN	FBG DV	IB 165D-200D	8	4200	2	18600	21300
23	MAKO 238	OP	CBNCR	FBG DV	OB	8	2500	1 2	7300	8350
25 6	MAKO 254	OP	CTRCN	FBG DV	OB	8	3000	1 2	10200	11600
25 7	MAKO 258	OP	CUD	FBG DV	OB	8	3200	1 6	10700	12200
					1982 BOATS					
17	MAKO 171 ANGLER	OP	CTRCN	FBG SV	OB	7 2	1200	7	2950	3450
17	MAKO 172 STANDARD	OP	CTRCN	FBG SV	OB	7 2	1200	7	2900	3400
18 2	MAKO 18	OP	OPFSH	FBG DV	OB	6 7	1150	6	2850	3300
20	MAKO 20B	OP	CTRCN	FBG DV	OB	8	1775	9	4750	5450
21 3	MAKO 21	OP	CTRCN	FBG DV	OB	8	2100	1	5750	6650
22	MAKO 224	OP	CTRCN	FBG DV	OB	8	2300	1	6550	7550
22 7	MAKO 228	OP	CUD	FBG DV	OB	8	2300	1 1	6600	7600
23	MAKO 235	OP	CTRCN	FBG DV	OB	8	2300	1	6650	7650
23	MAKO 236	OP	CTRCN	T390	IB 250-260	8	3800	2	10900	12900
23	MAKO 236	OP	CTRCN	FBG DV	IB 140D VLVO	8	4200	2	15700	17800
23	MAKO 236	OP	CTRCN	FBG DV	IB 160D-200D	8	4200	2	17400	20700
23	MAKO 238	OP	CBNCR	FBG DV	OB	8	2500	1 2	7150	8200
25 6	MAKO 254	OP	CTRCN	FBG DV	OB	8	3000	1 2	10100	11400
25 7	MAKO 258	OP	CUD	FBG DV	OB	8	3200	1 6	10500	12000
					1981 BOATS					
17	MAKO 17 ANGLER	OP	CTRCN	FBG SV	OB	7 2	1200	7	2950	3400
17	MAKO 17 STANDARD	OP	CTRCN	FBG SV	OB	7 2	1200	7	2850	3300
18 2	MAKO 18	OP	OPFSH	FBG DV	OB	6 7	1150	6	2850	3300
18 7	MAKO 19B	OP	FSH	FBG DV	OB	8	1525		3600	4200
20	MAKO 20	OP	CTRCN	FBG DV	OB	8	1775	9	4700	5400
21 3	MAKO 21	OP	CTRCN	FBG DV	OB	8	2100	1	5700	6550

MAKO BOATS — CONTINUED

See inside cover to adjust price for area

LOA	Name/Model	Top/Rig	Type	Hull Mtl	Hull Tp	Eng Tp	#HP	Eng Mfg	Beam	Wgt	Draft	Retail Low	Retail High
	1981 BOATS												
22 7	MAKO 224	OP	CTRCN	FBG	DV	OB			8	2200	1 1	6250	7200
22 7	MAKO 228	OP	CUD	FBG	DV	OB			8	2400	1 1	6700	7700
23	MAKO 23	OP	CTRCN	FBG	DV	OB			8	2300	1	6550	7550
23	MAKO 23	OP	CTRCN	FBG	DV	IB			8	3800	2	**	**
23	MAKO 23	OP	CTRCN	FBG	DV	IB	D		8	4000	2	**	**
23	MAKO 235		FSH	FBG	SV	OB			8	2300		6550	7550
23	MAKO 236		FSH	FBG	SV	IB	225		8			10400	11800
23	MAKO 238	OP	CBNCR	FBG	DV	OB			8	2500	1 2	7050	8100
25 6	MAKO 25	OP	CTRCN	FBG	DV	OB			8	3000	1 2	9900	11300
25 6	MAKO 258	OP	CUD	FBG	DV	OB			8	2700	1 2	9550	10800
	1980 BOATS												
17	MAKO 17 ANGLER	OP	CTRCN	FBG	SV	OB			7 2	1200	7	2850	3300
17	MAKO 17 STANDARD	OP	CTRCN	FBG	SV	OB			7 2	1200	7	2850	3300
18 2	MAKO 18	OP	OPFSH	FBG	SV	OB			6 7	1150	6	2850	3300
18 7	MAKO 19	OP	CTRCN	FBG	SV	OB			8	1525	8	3550	4150
20	MAKO 20	OP	CTRCN	FBG	SV	OB			8	1775	9	4650	5350
21	MAKO 21	OP	CTRCN	FBG	DV	OB			8	2100	1	5550	6350
22 6	MAKO 224	OP	CTRCN	FBG	DV	OB			8	2200	1 2	6150	7050
22 6	MAKO 228	OP	CUD	FBG	DV	OB			8	2300	1 2	6400	7350
23	MAKO 23	OP	CTRCN	FBG	DV	OB			8	2500	10	6950	7950
23	MAKO 23	OP	CTRCN	FBG	DV	IB			8	3800	2	**	**
23	MAKO 23	OP	CTRCN	FBG	DV	IB	D		8	4000	2	**	**
23	MAKO 23	OP	CTRCN	FBG	SV	IB	225		8			9700	11000
23	MAKO 23	OP	CTRCN	FBG	SV	IB	126D		8			12900	14700
23	MAKO 238	OP	CBNCR	FBG	DV	OB			8	2500	1 2	6950	7950
25 6	MAKO 25	OP	CTRCN	FBG	DV	OB			8	2700	1 2	9400	10700
	1979 BOATS												
17	MAKO 17 ANGLER	OP	CTRCN	FBG	SV	OB				1200	7	2850	3300
17	MAKO 17 STANDARD	OP	CTRCN	FBG	SV	OB				1200	7	2750	3200
18 7	MAKO 19	OP	CTRCN	FBG	SV	OB			8	1525	8	3500	4100
20	MAKO 20	OP	CTRCN	FBG	SV	OB			8	1775	9	4600	5300
21 3	MAKO 21	OP	CTRCN	FBG	DV	OB			8	2100	1	5550	6350
23	MAKO 235	OP	CTRCN	FBG	SV	OB			8	2300	1	6400	7350
23	MAKO 236 INBOARD	OP	CTRCN	FBG	SV	IB		OMC	8	3800	2	**	**
	IB 225-255 9550 11000, IB 126D-130D 13400 15900, IB 160D PERK 15100 17100												
23	MAKO 238 CABIN	OP	CBNCR	FBG	DV	OB			8	2500	1	6850	7900
25 6	MAKO 25	OP	CTRCN	FBG	DV	OB			8	2700	1 2	9300	10600
	1978 BOATS												
17	MAKO 17 ANGLER	OP	CTRCN	FBG	SV	OB			7 2	1200	7	2750	3200
17	MAKO 17 STANDARD	OP	CTRCN	FBG	SV	OB			7 2	1200	7	2750	3200
18 7	MAKO 19	OP	CTRCN	FBG	SV	OB			8	1525	8	3450	4000
20	MAKO 20	OP	CTRCN	FBG	SV	OB			8	1775	9	4550	5250
21 3	MAKO 21	OP	CTRCN	FBG	DV	OB			8	2100	1	5500	6300
21 9	MAKO 22	OP	CTRCN	FBG	SV	OB			8	2000	10	5400	6200
23	MAKO 23	OP	CTRCN	FBG	SV	OB			8	2300	10	6350	7300
23	MAKO 23	OP	CTRCN	FBG	SV	IB	225-260		8	3600	1 10	8850	10500
25 6	MAKO 25	OP	CTRCN	FBG	DV	OB			8	2700	1 2	9200	10500
26	MAKO 26	OP	CTRCN	FBG	SV	IB	T225-T255		9 6	6500	1 10	18400	20900
26	MAKO 26	TT	CTRCN	FBG	SV	IB	T225-T255		9 6	6500	1 10	18400	20900
	1977 BOATS												
17	MAKO 17	OP	OPFSH	FBG	SV	OB			7 2	1200	7	2750	3200
17	MAKO 17 ANGLER	OP	OPFSH	FBG	SV	OB			7 2	1200	7	2750	3200
18 7	MAKO 19B	OP	OPFSH	FBG	SV	OB			8	1525	8	3450	4000
20	MAKO 20	OP	OPFSH	FBG	SV	OB			8	1775	9	4500	5200
21 9	MAKO 22B	OP	OPFSH	FBG	SV	OB			8	1950	10	5250	6050
23	MAKO 23	OP	OPFSH	FBG	SV	OB			8	2300	10	6700	7250
23	MAKO 23 CABIN	OP	OPFSH	FBG	SV	IO	188-235		8	3800	1	9500	11000
23	MAKO 23 CABIN	OP	OPFSH	FBG	SV	IO	T120-T140		8	3800	1	10600	12100
23	MAKO 23 IB	OP	OPFSH	FBG	SV	IB	225-260		8	3600	1 10	8400	10100
23	MAKO 23 OPEN	OP	OPFSH	FBG	SV	IO	188-235		8	3650	1	9300	10700
23	MAKO 23 OPEN	OP	OPFSH	FBG	SV	IO	T120-T140		8	3650	1	10300	11800
25 6	MAKO 25	OP	OPFSH	FBG	DV	OB			8	2900	1 2	9350	10600
26	MAKO 26	OP	OPFSH	FBG	SV	IB	T225-T255		9 6	6500	1 10	17000	19700
26	MAKO 26	TT	OPFSH	FBG	SV	IB	T225-T255		9 6	6500	1 10	17000	19700
	1976 BOATS												
17	MAKO 17	OP	FSH	FBG	SV	OB			7 2	1200	7	2750	3150
17	MAKO 17 ANGLER	OP	FSH	FBG	SV	OB			7 2	1200	7	2750	3150
18 7	MAKO 19	OP	FSH	FBG	SV	OB			8	1525	8	3400	4000
20	MAKO 20	OP	FSH	FBG	SV	OB			8	1775	9	4500	5150
21 9	MAKO 22B	OP	FSH	FBG	SV	OB			8	1950	10	5200	6000
23	MAKO 23	OP	OPFSH	FBG	SV	OB			8	2300	10	6250	7200
23	MAKO 23	OP	OPFSH	FBG	SV	IB	225-260		8	3600	1 10	8050	9800
23	MAKO 23 CABIN	OP	OPFSH	FBG	SV	IO	188-225		8	3800	1	9750	11200
23	MAKO 23 CABIN	OP	OPFSH	FBG	SV	IO	T120-T140		8	3800	1	10900	12400
23	MAKO 23 OPEN	OP	OPFSH	FBG	SV	IO	188-225		8	3650	1	9500	10900
23	MAKO 23 OPEN	OP	OPFSH	FBG	SV	IO	T120-T140		8	3650	1	10600	12100
26	MAKO 26	OP	OPFSH	FBG	SV	IB	T225-T255		9 6	6500	1 10	16300	18800
26	MAKO 26	TT	OPFSH	FBG	SV	IB	T225-T255		9 6	6500	1 10	16300	18900
	1975 BOATS												
17	MAKO 17 ANGLER	OP	OPFSH	FBG	SV	OB			7 2	1200	7	2700	3150
17	MAKO 17 STANDARD	OP	OPFSH	FBG	SV	OB			7 2	1200	7	2700	3150
18 7	MAKO 19	OP	OPFSH	FBG	SV	OB			8	1525	8	3400	3950
20	MAKO 20	OP	OPFSH	FBG	SV	OB			8	1775	8	4450	5100
21 9	MAKO 22	OP	OPFSH	FBG	SV	OB			8	1950	10	5200	5950
23	MAKO 23 I/O CABIN	OP	OPFSH	FBG	SV	IO	188-225		8	3800	1	10100	11600
23	MAKO 23 I/O CABIN	OP	OPFSH	FBG	SV	IO	T120-T140		8	4400	1	12400	14100
23	MAKO 23 I/O OPEN	OP	OPFSH	FBG	SV	IO	188-225		8	3650	1	9800	11200
23	MAKO 23 I/O OPEN	OP	OPFSH	FBG	SV	IO	T120-T140		8	4250	1	12100	13800
23	MAKO 23 INBOARD	OP	OPFSH	FBG	SV	IB	225-260		8	3600	1	7750	9300
23	MAKO 23 OUTBOARD	OP	OPFSH	FBG	SV	OB			8	2300	10	6200	7150
26	MAKO 26 INBOARD	OP	OPFSH	FBG	SV	IB	T225-T255		9 6	7000	1 10	16400	19000
26	MAKO 26 INBOARD	TT	OPFSH	FBG	SV	IB	T225-T255		9 6	7000	1 10	16400	19000
	1974 BOATS												
17	MAKO ANGLER			FBG		OB			7 2	1100	7	2500	2900
17	MAKO STD			FBG		OB			7 2	1100	7	2500	2900
18 7	MAKO 19			FBG		OB			8	1450	8	3250	3800
20	MAKO 20			FBG		OB			8	1600	9	4050	4750
21 9	MAKO 22			FBG		OB			8	1850	10	4950	5700
23	MAKO 23			FBG		OB			8	2550	10	6750	7750
23	MAKO 23	OP		FBG		IO	155-225		8	3650	1	9100	10500
23	MAKO 23	OP		FBG		IO	T120-T140		8	3650	1	10200	11600
23	MAKO 23		CBNCR	FBG		IO	155-225		8	3800	1	11000	12700
23	MAKO 23		CBNCR	FBG		IO	T120-T140		8	3800	1	12400	14100
26	MAKO 26	OP	OPFSH	FBG	SV	IB	T200	MRCR	9 6	5800	2	13900	15800
26	MAKO 26	TT	OPFSH	FBG	SV	IB	T225	MRCR	9 6	5800	2	14100	16100
	1973 BOATS												
17	MAKO ANGLER			FBG		OB			7 2	1100	7	2500	2900
17	MAKO STD			FBG		OB			7 2	1100	7	2500	2900
18 7	MAKO 19			FBG		OB			8	1450	8	3250	3800
20	MAKO 20			FBG		OB			8	1600	9	4050	4700
21 9	MAKO 22			FBG		OB			8	1850	10	4950	5700
23	MAKO 23			FBG		IO	155-225		8	3650	1	9400	10800
23	MAKO 23	OP		FBG		IO	155-225		8	3650	1	10500	12000
23	MAKO 23		CBNCR	FBG		IO	T120-T140		8	3800	1	11300	13100
23	MAKO 23		CBNCR	FBG		IO	T120-T140		8	3800	1	12800	14500
26	MAKO 26			FBG		IB	T200	MRCR	9 6	5800	2	13600	15500
	1972 BOATS												
17	MAKO ANGLER			FBG		OB			7 2	1100	7	2500	2900
17	MAKO STANDARD			FBG		OB			7 2	1100	7	2500	2900
18 7	MAKO 19			FBG		OB			8	1400	8	3200	3700
21 9	MAKO 22			FBG		OB			8	1800	10	4850	5550
23	MAKO 23			FBG		IO	155-225		8	3650	1	9650	11200
23	MAKO 23	OP		FBG		IO	T120-T140		8	3650	1	10900	12400
23	MAKO 23		CBNCR	FBG		IO	155-225		8	3800	1	11700	13600
23	MAKO 23		CBNCR	FBG		IO	T120-T140		8	3800	1	12200	13600
26	MAKO 26			FBG		IB	T200	MRCR	9 6	5800	2	13100	14900
	1971 BOATS												
16 6	ANGLER	RNBT		FBG	RB	OB			7 3	1200		2650	3100
16 6	SEA-SPORT	RNBT		FBG	RB	OB			7 3	1200		2650	3100
17	MAKO 17			FBG		OB			7 2	1050	7	2400	2800
18 7	MAKO 19			FBG		OB			8	1400	8	3200	3700
21 9	MAKO 22			FBG		OB			8	1800	10	4850	5550
	1970 BOATS												
17	MAKO 17			FBG	SV	OB			7 2	1140	7	2600	3000
18 7	MAKO 19			FBG	SV	OB			8	1350	8	3100	3600
21 9	MAKO 22			FBG	SV	OB			8	1800	10	4850	5550
	1969 BOATS												
18 8	MAKO 19		FSH	FBG	SV	OB			8	1400	8	3200	3700

MANATEE BOATS INC

PALMETTO FL 33561   COAST GUARD MFG ID- MNT   See inside cover to adjust price for area
FORMERLY MANATEE MARINE PROD INC

For more recent years, see the BUC Used Boat Price Guide, Volume 1 or Volume 2

LOA	Name/Model	Top/Rig	Type	Hull Mtl	Hull Tp	Eng Tp	#HP	Eng Mfg	Beam	Wgt	Draft	Retail Low	Retail High
	1983 BOATS												
18 2	19 VBR	ST	RNBT	FBG	DV	IO	120-228		7 4	2225		2700	3300
21	22 VC	ST	CUD	FBG	DV	OB			8	2800		2600	3050

```
     LOA  NAME AND/        TOP/ BOAT -HULL- ----ENGINE---  BEAM   WGT  DRAFT RETAIL RETAIL
     FT IN OR MODEL        RIG  TYPE MTL TP TP # HP  MFG    FT IN  LBS  FT IN  LOW   HIGH
--------------------- 1983 BOATS ---------------------------------------------------------
21   22 VC               ST  CUD  FBG DV IO 170-260       8     3600         4650  5550
23 7 24 VC               ST  CUD  FBG DV IO 170-260       8     4050         5750  6900
--------------------- 1982 BOATS ---------------------------------------------------------
18 2 19 V                ST  RNBT FBG DV IO 120-228     7 4     2150         2600  3150
18 2 19 VBR              ST  RNBT FBG DV IO 120-228     7 4     2225         2650  3200
18 2 19 VC               ST  CUD  FBG DV IO 120-228     7 4     2310         2750  3350
20 7 21 VBR              ST  RNBT FBG DV IO 120-260     7 4     2450         3150  3900
20 7 21 VC               ST  CUD  FBG DV IO 120-260     7 4     2500         3300  4150
20 7 21 VJ               ST  RNBT FBG DV IO 120-260     7 4     2320         3050  3850
21   22 VC               ST  CUD  FBG DV OB             8       2800         2550  2950
21   22 VC               ST  CUD  FBG DV IO 170-260     8       3600         4550  5450
23 7 24 VC               ST  CUD  FBG DV IO 170-260     8       4050         5650  6750
--------------------- 1981 BOATS ---------------------------------------------------------
18 2 19 V                ST  RNBT FBG DV IO 120-198     7 4     2150         2550  3050
18 2 19 VBR              ST  RNBT FBG DV IO 120-198     7 4     2225         2600  3100
18 2 19 VC               ST  CUD  FBG DV IO 120-198     7 4     2310         2700  3200
20 7 21 VBR              ST  RNBT FBG DV IO 120-260     7 4     2450         3100  3850
20 7 21 VC               ST  CUD  FBG DV IO 120-260     7 4     2500         3250  4050
20 7 21 VJ               ST  RNBT FBG DV IO 120-260     7 4     2320         3000  3750
21   22 VC               ST  CUD  FBG DV OB             8       2800         2550  2950
21   22 VC               ST  CUD  FBG DV IO 165-260     8       3600         4450  5400
21   22 VF               ST  FSH  FBG DV IO 170         8                    4700  5400
21   MANATEE 21VF             FSH  FBG DV OB             8       3290         2700  3150
23 7 24 VC               ST  CUD  FBG DV IO 165-260     8       4050         5550  6600
--------------------- 1980 BOATS ---------------------------------------------------------
18 2 19 V                ST  RNBT FBG DV IO 120-230     7 4     2150         2550  3050
18 2 19 VBR              ST  RNBT FBG DV IO 120-230     7 4     2225         2550  3100
18 2 19 VC               ST  CUD  FBG DV IO 120-230     7 4     2310         2700  3250
20 7 21 VBR              ST  RNBT FBG DV IO 120-260     7 4     2450         3050  3800
20 7 21 VC               ST  CUD  FBG DV IO 120-260     7 4     2500         3250  4050
20 7 21 VJ               ST  RNBT FBG DV IO 120-260     7 4     2320         3000  3750
21   22 VC               ST  CUD  FBG DV IO 165-260     8       3600         4400  5350
21   22 VF               OP  FSH  FBG DV OB             8       2350         2250  2650
21   22 VF               OP  FSH  FBG DV IO 140-260     8       3340         4400  5350
23 7 24 VC               ST  CUD  FBG DV IO 165-260     8       4050         5500  6550
--------------------- 1979 BOATS ---------------------------------------------------------
18 2 19 V                ST  RNBT FBG DV IO     MRCR   7 4                     **    **
18 2 19 V                ST  RNBT FBG DV IO     OMC    7 4                     **    **
18 2 19 VBR              ST  RNBT FBG DV IO     MRCR   7 4                     **    **
18 2 19 VBR              ST  RNBT FBG DV IO     OMC    7 4                     **    **
18 2 19 VC               ST  CUD  FBG DV IO     MRCR   7 4                     **    **
18 2 19 VC               ST  CUD  FBG DV IO     OMC    7 4                     **    **
20 7 21 VBR              ST  RNBT FBG DV IO     MRCR   7 4                     **    **
20 7 21 VBR              ST  RNBT FBG DV IO     OMC    7 4                     **    **
20 7 21 VC               ST  CUD  FBG DV IO     MRCR   7 4                     **    **
21   22 VC               ST  CUD  FBG DV IO 250 OMC    7 4                   4600  5250
23 7 24 VC               ST  CUD  FBG DV IO     MRCR   8       3890            **    **
23 7 24 VC               ST  CUD  FBG DV IO     OMC    8       3890            **    **
--------------------- 1978 BOATS ---------------------------------------------------------
17 6 MARK III                RNBT FBG TR IO 140-190    7 4                   2450  2850
18 2 1900 W/T                RNBT FBG DV IO 140-190    7 4                   2600  3050
18 2 CRUISER I               CR   FBG    IO 140-190    7 4                   2650  3150
20 7 2100 W/T                RNBT FBG    IO 140-240    7 4                   3950  4750
20 11 CRUISER II             CR   FBG DV OB 165-240    7 4     2150         2000  2400
20 11 CRUISER II             CR   FBG DV IO            8                    4400  5250
23 7 CRUISER III         OP  CUD  FBG DV IO            8                      **    **
--------------------- 1977 BOATS ---------------------------------------------------------
18 2 1900 VBR            OP  RNBT FBG DV IO 140-188    7 4                   2650  3100
20   2000V               OP  CUD  FBG DV OB            7 6     1855         1700  2050
21   CRUISER II          ST  CUD  FBG DV OB            8                    1700  2000
21   CRUISER II          ST  CUD  FBG DV IO 165        8       3155         4100  4750
--------------------- 1976 BOATS ---------------------------------------------------------
16 4 MANATEE MARK II         RNBT FBG TR IO 120-140    6 7                   2000  2400
18 2 CRUISER I-V             RNBT FBG DV IO 140-165    7 4                   2750  3250
18 2 MANATEE 1900-V          RNBT FBG SV IO 140-165    7 4                   2700  3150
18 2 MANATEE 1900-V          UTL  FBG SV IO 140-165    7 4                   3300  3400
20 7 MANATEE 2100            RNBT FBG    IO 165-188    7 4                   4100  4800
20 11 CRUISER II-V           CR   FBG    OB            8       2150         2000  2350
20 11 CRUISER II-V           CR   FBG    IO 165-188    8                    4600  5350
--------------------- 1975 BOATS ---------------------------------------------------------
17 5 MARK-III             ST  CR   FBG TR IO 120-140                        2700  3100
18 2 CRUISER I            OP  CR   FBG DV IO 120-140   7 4                   2850  3350
20 11 CRUISER II          OP  CR   FBG DV OB           8       2150         1950  2350
20 11 CRUISER II          OP  CR   FBG    IO 140-165   8                    4700  5450
--------------------- 1974 BOATS ---------------------------------------------------------
17 5 MANATEE MARK III     ST  RNBT FBG TR IO 120-140          1700  2  4    2400  2750
18 2 MANATEE 1900 V            FBG    IO 140-145       7 4     1700  2  9    2500  2900
18 2 MANATEE 1900 V       ST  RNBT FBG DV IO 120  MRCR 7 4     1700  2  9    2550  3000
18 2 MANATEE I            CR   FBG    IO 120-145       7 4     1900  2  9    2550  3200
18 5 MANATEE 1950 T           RNBT FBG TR IO 140-165   7 5                   2950  3450
20 11 MANATEE II          CR   FBG    IO 140-165       8       2000  2 11    3550  4250
--------------------- 1973 BOATS ---------------------------------------------------------
16 11 MANATEE 1750            RNBT FBG TR IO 125       6  2                  2550  2950
17   MANATEE 1850             RNBT FBG DV IO 125       6 10                  2700  3150
17   MANATEE 1850 L           RNBT FBG SV IO 125       6 10                  2650  3100
18 5 MANATEE 1950 T           RNBT FBG TR IO 140       7  5    1500         2650  3050
20 11 CRUISER II             CR   FBG DV OB            8       2150         1950  2300
20 11 CRUISER II             CR   FBG DV IO 165        8                    5050  5800
```

MANDELLA BOATS
LOUIS H BRUMMETT INC   COAST GUARD MFG ID- MAN

Call 1-800-327-6929 for BUC Personalized Evaluation Service
Or, for 1965 to 1980 boats, sign onto www.BUCValuPro.com

ERICK J MANNERS

Call 1-800-327-6929 for BUC Personalized Evaluation Service
Or, for 1973 to 1974 boats, sign onto www.BUCValuPro.com

MANSON BOAT WORKS INC
SALISBURY MA 01950   COAST GUARD MFG ID- MBN See inside cover to adjust price for area

For more recent years, see the BUC Used Boat Price Guide, Volume 1 or Volume 2

```
     LOA  NAME AND/      TOP/  BOAT -HULL- ----ENGINE---  BEAM    WGT   DRAFT RETAIL RETAIL
     FT IN OR MODEL      RIG   TYPE MTL TP TP # HP  MFG    FT IN   LBS   FT IN  LOW   HIGH
--------------------- 1983 BOATS -----------------------------------------------------------
34          HT SDN   WD      IB T225  12  1              24800  27500
34          FB SDNSF WD      IB T225  12  1              25000  27800
34             TRWL  WD      IB T225  12  1              24400  27100
41          MY SDN   WD      IB T330  14  2              51400  56500
41          HT SDN   WD      IB T330  14  2              51600  56700
41          FB SDNSF WD      IB T330  14  2              52100  57300
41             TRWL  WD      IB T330  14  2              56900  56900
45          MY SDN   WD      IB T330  15 10              67900  74600
45          HT SDN   WD      IB T330  15 10              60600  66600
45          FB SDNSF WD      IB T330  15 10              63800  70100
45             TRWL  WD      IB T330  15 10              65100  71500
50          MY       WD      IB T330  15 10              93600 103000
50          HT MYDKH WD      IB T350  15 10              98600 108500
50          FB SDNSF WD      IB T310  15 10              91800 101000
--------------------- 1980 BOATS -----------------------------------------------------------
34   MANSON         SF   WD  SV IB T225  12  1           21000  23400
41   MANSON         CR   WD  SV IB T330  14  2           46000  50600
41   MANSON         MY   WD  SV IB T330  14  2           44500  49400
45   MANSON         MY   WD  SV IB T210  15 11           57600  63300
45   MANSON         SF   WD  SV IB T210  15 11           53400  58700
50   MANSON         MY   WD  SV IB T330  15 11           81600  89600
50   MANSON         SF   WD  SV IB T330  15 11           81400  89500
--------------------- 1979 BOATS -----------------------------------------------------------
34   CONVERTIBLE SEDAN   FB  SDN  WD  RB IB  200D CHRY 12 1 14750 2 9  27200 30300
34   CONVERTIBLE SEDAN   FB  SDN  WD  RB IB T225-T270 12 1 14750 2 9  22900 26100
34   CONVERTIBLE SEDAN   FB  SDN  WD  RB IBT160D-T210D 12 1 14750 2 9  29100 33700
34   SPORT FISHERMAN     FB  SF   WD  RB IB  200D CHRY 12 1 14750 2 9  26400 29300
34   SPORT FISHERMAN     FB  SF   WD  RB IB T225-T270 12 1 14750 2 9  21900 24800
34   SPORT FISHERMAN     FB  SF   WD  RB IBT160D-T210D 12 1 14750 2 9  28200 32400
34   SPORT FISHERMAN     F+T SF   WD  RB IB  200D CHRY 12 1 14750 2 9  26500 29400
34   SPORT FISHERMAN     F+T SF   WD  RB IB T225-T270 12 1 14750 2 9  21900 24900
34   SPORT FISHERMAN     F+T SF   WD  RB IBT160D-T210D 12 1 14750 2 9  28300 32500
41   CONVERTIBLE SEDAN   FB  SDN  WD  RB IB T330  CHRY 14 2 25150 3    43800 48600
          IB T350  CRUS 44500,  IB T197D CUM  48600,  IB T210D CAT        50000  54900
          IB T216D GM  49200    54100,  IB T310D GM   51600  56700
41   MOTOR YACHT         HT  MY   WD  RB IB T330  CHRY 14 2 23850 3    42600 47300
          IB T350  CRUS 43400   48200,  IB T210D CAT 49100 53900, IB T220D GM 48400 53200
          IB T247D PERK 50100   55000
41   SPORT FISHERMAN     FB  SF   WD  RB IB T330  CHRY 14 2 25150 3    43900 48800
          IB T350  CRUS 44600   49600,  IB T197D CUM 48800 53600, IB T210D CAT 50200 55100
```

MANSON BOAT WORKS INC -CONTINUED See inside cover to adjust price for area

LOA FT	IN	NAME AND/ OR MODEL	TOP/ RIG	BOAT TYPE	-HULL- MTL	TP	TP	----ENGINE--- # HP	MFG	BEAM FT	IN	WGT LBS	DRAFT FT	IN	RETAIL LOW	RETAIL HIGH
		1979 BOATS														
41		SPORT FISHERMAN	FB	SF	WD	RB	IB	T216D	GM	14	2	25150	3		49400	54300
41		SPORT FISHERMAN	FB	SF	WD	RB	IB	T310D	GM	14	2	25150	3		52000	57200
41		SPORT FISHERMAN	F+T	SF	WD	RB	IB	T330	CHRY	14	2	25150	3		43900	48800
		IB T350 CRUS 44600 49600, IB T197D CUM 49100 53900, IB T210D CAT													50400	55400
		IB T216D GM 49700 54600, IB T310D GM 52200 57400														
45		CONVERTIBLE SEDAN	FB	SDN	WD	RB	IB	T330	CHRY	15	10	25000	3	5	50400	55400
		IB T210D CAT 54600 60000, IB T216D GM 54000 59400, IB T310D GM													56800	62400
		IB T410D GM 60400 66400														
45		LONG RANGE CRUISER	HT	CR	WD	RB	IB	T210D	CAT	15	10	28100	3	5	59200	65000
45		LONG RANGE CRUISER	HT	CR	WD	RB	IB	T310D	GM	15	10	28100	3	5	61300	67300
45		LONG RANGE CRUISER	FB	CR	WD	RB	IB	T210D	CAT	15	10	28100	3	5	59100	64900
45		LONG RANGE CRUISER	FB	CR	WD	RB	IB	T310D	GM	15	10	28100	3	5	61100	67200
45		MOTOR YACHT	HT	MY	WD	RB	IB	T330	CHRY	15	10	28100	3	5	56700	62300
45		MOTOR YACHT	HT	MY	WD	RB	IB	T310D	GM	15	10	28100	3	5	63300	69600
45		MOTOR YACHT	HT	MY	WD	RB	IB	T410D	GM	15	10	28100	3	5	67100	73700
45		MOTOR YACHT	FB	MY	WD	RB	IB	T330	CHRY	15	10	28100	3	5	56500	62100
45		MOTOR YACHT	FB	MY	WD	RB	IB	T310D	GM	15	10	28100	3	5	63200	69400
45		MOTOR YACHT	FB	MY	WD	RB	IB	T410D	GM	15	10	28100	3	5	66900	73500
45		SPORT FISHERMAN	FB	SF	WD	RB	IB	T330	CHRY	15	10	25000	3	5	52600	57800
		IB T210D CAT 57000 62600, IB T216D GM 56300 61900, IB T310D GM													59200	65000
		IB T410D GM 63400 69600														
45		SPORT FISHERMAN	F+T	SF	WD	RB	IB	T330	CHRY	15	10	25000	3	5	52600	57800
		IB T210D CAT 57000 62600, IB T216D GM 56300 61900, IB T310D GM													59100	65000
		IB T410D GM 63000 69200														
50		DECKHS MOTOR YACHT	HT	MYDKH	WD	RB	IB	T330	CHRY	15	10	39400	3	6	81100	89100
50		DECKHS MOTOR YACHT	HT	MYDKH	WD	RB	IB	T310D	GM	15	10	39400	3	6	84700	93000
50		DECKHS MOTOR YACHT	HT	MYDKH	WD	RB	IB	T410D	GM	15	10	39400	3	6	89600	98500
50		DECKHS MOTOR YACHT	FB	MYDKH	WD	RB	IB	T330	CHRY	15	10	39400	3	6	80700	88600
50		DECKHS MOTOR YACHT	FB	MYDKH	WD	RB	IB	T310D	GM	15	10	39400	3	6	84200	92600
50		DECKHS MOTOR YACHT	FB	MYDKH	WD	RB	IB	T410D	GM	15	10	39400	3	6	89200	98000
50		LONG RANGE CRUISER	HT	CR	WD	RB	IB	T330	CHRY	15	10	39400	3	6	73000	80200
50		LONG RANGE CRUISER	HT	CR	WD	RB	IB	T310D	GM	15	10	39400	3	6	76400	83900
50		LONG RANGE CRUISER	HT	CR	WD	RB	IB	T410D	GM	15	10	39400	3	6	81000	89000
50		LONG RANGE CRUISER	FB	CR	WD	RB	IB	T330	CHRY	15	10	39400	3	6	72600	79800
50		LONG RANGE CRUISER	FB	CR	WD	RB	IB	T310D	GM	15	10	39400	3	6	76000	83500
50		LONG RANGE CRUISER	FB	CR	WD	RB	IB	T410D	GM	15	10	39400	3	6	80600	88500
50		MOTOR YACHT	HT	MY	WD	RB	IB	T330	CHRY	15	10	39400	3	6	77600	85300
50		MOTOR YACHT	HT	MY	WD	RB	IB	T310D	GM	15	10	39400	3	6	81000	89000
50		MOTOR YACHT	HT	MY	WD	RB	IB	T410D	GM	15	10	39400	3	6	85900	94400
50		MOTOR YACHT	FB	MY	WD	RB	IB	T330	CHRY	15	10	39400	3	6	77200	84900
50		MOTOR YACHT	FB	MY	WD	RB	IB	T310D	GM	15	10	39400	3	6	80600	88600
50		MOTOR YACHT	FB	MY	WD	RB	IB	T410D	GM	15	10	39400	3	6	85400	93900
50		SPORT FISHERMAN	FB	SF	WD	RB	IB	T330	CHRY	15	10	39400	3	6	77100	84700
		IB T310D GM 80500 88400, IB T400D CUM 85100 93500, IB T410D GM													85500	94000
		IB T435D GM 87000 95600														
50		SPORT FISHERMAN	F+T	SF	WD	RB	IB	T330	CHRY	15	10	39400	3	6	76800	84400
		IB T310D GM 80100 88100, IB T400D CUM 84600 93000, IB T410D GM													85000	93400
		IB T435D GM 86400 94900														
		1978 BOATS														
34		CONVERTIBLE SEDAN		SDN	WD	RB	IB	T225	CHRY	12	1				20000	22200
34		EXPRESS		EXP	WD	RB	IB	T225	CHRY	12	1				21300	23700
41		MOTOR YACHT		MY	WD	RB	IB	T330	CHRY	14	2				40800	45300
41		SEDAN SPORT FISH		SDNSF	WD	RB	IB	T330	CHRY	14	2				41100	45700
45		LONG RANGE CRUISER		CR	WD	RB	IB	T210D	CAT	15	11				56400	62000
45		MOTOR YACHT		MY	WD	RB	IB	T330	CHRY	15	11				54000	59300
45		SEDAN SPORT FISH		SDNSF	WD	RB	IB	T330	CHRY	15	11				50600	55600
50		MOTOR YACHT		MY	WD	RB	IB	T330	CHRY	15	11				72100	79200
50		SALON MOTOR YACHT		MY	WD	RB	IB	T330	CHRY	15	11				75800	83300
50		SPORT FISHERMAN		SF	WD	RB	IB	T330	CHRY	15	11				73800	81100
		1977 BOATS														
34		CONVERTIBLE SEDAN		SDN	WD	RB	IB	T225	CHRY	12	1				19200	21400
34		EXPRESS		EXP	WD	RB	IB	T225	CHRY	12	1				20400	22700
34		SPORT FISHERMAN		SF	WD	RB	IB	T225	CHRY	12	1				18500	20600
41		MOTOR YACHT		MY	WD	RB	IB	T330	CHRY	14	2				39100	43400
41		SEDAN SPORT FSH		SDNSF	WD	RB	IB	T330	CHRY	14	2				39500	43900
45		CONVERTIBLE SEDAN		SDN	WD	RB	IB	T330	CHRY	15	10				46000	50600
45		MOTOR YACHT		MY	WD	RB	IB	T330	CHRY	15	10				51800	56900
45		SEDAN SPORT FSH		SDNSF	WD	RB	IB	T330	CHRY	15	10				48600	53400
50		MOTOR YACHT		MY	WD	RB	IB	T330	CHRY	15	10				70900	77900
50		SEDAN SPORT FSH		SDNSF	WD	RB	IB	T330	CHRY	15	10				69700	76600
60		MOTOR YACHT		MY	WD	RB	IB	T350D	GM	16	11				114000	125500
60		SPORT FISHERMAN		YTFS	WD	RB	IB	T350D	GM	16	11				114000	125500
		1976 BOATS														
34		CONVERTIBLE SEDAN	FB	SDN	FBG	RB	IB	220D	CRUS	12	1	14750	2	9	24500	27200
34		CONVERTIBLE SEDAN	FB	SDN	MHG	RB	IB	220D	CRUS	12	1	14750	2	9	24500	27200
34		CONVERTIBLE SEDAN	FB	SDN	FBG	RB	IB	T225	CHRY	12	1	14750	2	9	20200	22500
34		CONVERTIBLE SEDAN	FB	SDN	MHG	RB	IB	T225	CHRY	12	1	14750	2	9	20200	22500
34		CONVERTIBLE SEDAN	FB	SDN	FBG	RB	IB	T250	CHRY	12	1	14750	2	9	20500	22700
34		CONVERTIBLE SEDAN	FB	SDN	MHG	RB	IB	T250	CHRY	12	1	14750	2	9	20500	22700
34		CONVERTIBLE SEDAN	FB	SDN	FBG	RB	IB	T270	CRUS	12	1	14750	2	9	20700	23000
34		CONVERTIBLE SEDAN	FB	SDN	MHG	RB	IB	T270	CRUS	12	1	14750	2	9	20700	23000
34		CONVERTIBLE SEDAN	FB	SDN	FBG	RB	IB	T170D	CRUS	12	1	14750	2	9	26000	28900
34		CONVERTIBLE SEDAN	FB	SDN	MHG	RB	IB	T170D	CRUS	12	1	14750	2	9	26000	28900
34		CONVERTIBLE SEDAN	FB	SDN	FBG	RB	IB	T185D	PERK	12	1	14750	2	9	26500	29400
34		CONVERTIBLE SEDAN	FB	SDN	MHG	RB	IB	T185D	PERK	12	1	14750	2	9	26500	29400
34		CONVERTIBLE SEDAN	FB	SDN	FBG	RB	IB	T210D	CUM	12	1	14750	2	9	26800	29800
34		CONVERTIBLE SEDAN	FB	SDN	MHG	RB	IB	T210D	CUM	12	1	14750	2	9	26800	29800
34		CONVERTIBLE SEDAN	FB	SDN	FBG	RB	IB	T220D	CRUS	12	1	14750	2	9	27100	30100
34		CONVERTIBLE SEDAN	FB	SDN	MHG	RB	IB	T220D	CRUS	12	1	14750	2	9	27100	30100
34		EXPRESS	FB	EXP	FBG	RB	IB	T225	CHRY	12	1	14750	2	9	19700	21900
34		EXPRESS	FB	EXP	MHG	RB	IB	T225	CHRY	12	1	14750	2	9	19700	21900
34		EXPRESS	FB	EXP	FBG	RB	IB	T140D	GM	12	1	14750	2	9	25200	28000
34		EXPRESS	FB	EXP	MHG	RB	IB	T140D	GM	12	1	14750	2	9	25200	28000
34		EXPRESS	FB	EXP	FBG	RB	IB	T160D	PERK	12	1	14750	2	9	26000	28900
34		EXPRESS	FB	EXP	MHG	RB	IB	T160D	PERK	12	1	14750	2	9	26000	28900
34		SPORT SEDAN FSH	FB	SDNSF	FBG	RB	IB	220D	CRUS	12	1	14750	2	9	23400	26100
34		SPORT SEDAN FSH	FB	SDNSF	MHG	RB	IB	220D	CRUS	12	1	14750	2	9	23400	26100
34		SPORT SEDAN FSH	FB	SDNSF	FBG	RB	IB	T225	CHRY	12	1	14750	2	9	19300	21500
34		SPORT SEDAN FSH	FB	SDNSF	MHG	RB	IB	T225	CHRY	12	1	14750	2	9	19300	21500
34		SPORT SEDAN FSH	FB	SDNSF	FBG	RB	IB	T250	CHRY	12	1	14750	2	9	19500	21700
34		SPORT SEDAN FSH	FB	SDNSF	MHG	RB	IB	T250	CHRY	12	1	14750	2	9	19500	21700
34		SPORT SEDAN FSH	FB	SDNSF	FBG	RB	IB	T270	CRUS	12	1	14750	2	9	19700	21900
34		SPORT SEDAN FSH	FB	SDNSF	MHG	RB	IB	T270	CRUS	12	1	14750	2	9	19700	21900
34		SPORT SEDAN FSH	FB	SDNSF	FBG	RB	IB	T170D	CRUS	12	1	14750	2	9	24700	27400
34		SPORT SEDAN FSH	FB	SDNSF	MHG	RB	IB	T170D	CRUS	12	1	14750	2	9	24600	27400
34		SPORT SEDAN FSH	FB	SDNSF	FBG	RB	IB	T185D	PERK	12	1	14750	2	9	25300	28100
34		SPORT SEDAN FSH	FB	SDNSF	MHG	RB	IB	T185D	PERK	12	1	14750	2	9	25300	28100
34		SPORT SEDAN FSH	FB	SDNSF	FBG	RB	IB	T210D	CUM	12	1	14750	2	9	25200	28000
34		SPORT SEDAN FSH	FB	SDNSF	MHG	RB	IB	T210D	CUM	12	1	14750	2	9	25200	28000
34		SPORT SEDAN FSH	FB	SDNSF	FBG	RB	IB	T220D	CRUS	12	1	14750	2	9	25500	28300
34		SPORT SEDAN FSH	FB	SDNSF	MHG	RB	IB	T220D	CRUS	12	1	14750	2	9	25500	28300
41		CONVERTIBLE SEDAN	FB	SDN	FBG	RB	IB	T330	CHRY	14	2	25150	3		38600	42800
41		CONVERTIBLE SEDAN	FB	SDN	MHG	RB	IB	T330	CHRY	14	2	25150	3		38600	42800
41		CONVERTIBLE SEDAN	FB	SDN	FBG	RB	IB	T350	CRUS	14	2	25150	3		39200	43500
41		CONVERTIBLE SEDAN	FB	SDN	MHG	RB	IB	T350	CRUS	14	2	25150	3		39200	43500
41		CONVERTIBLE SEDAN	FB	SDN	FBG	RB	IB	T210D	CAT	14	2	25150	3		43700	48500
41		CONVERTIBLE SEDAN	FB	SDN	MHG	RB	IB	T210D	CAT	14	2	25150	3		43700	48500
41		CONVERTIBLE SEDAN	FB	SDN	FBG	RB	IB	T210D	CUM	14	2	25150	3		42700	47500
41		CONVERTIBLE SEDAN	FB	SDN	MHG	RB	IB	T210D	CUM	14	2	25150	3		42700	47500
41		CONVERTIBLE SEDAN	FB	SDN	FBG	RB	IB	T220D	GM	14	2	25150	3		43100	47900
41		CONVERTIBLE SEDAN	FB	SDN	MHG	RB	IB	T220D	GM	14	2	25150	3		43100	47900
41		CONVERTIBLE SEDAN	FB	SDN	FBG	RB	IB	T310D	GM	14	2	25150	3		45000	50000
41		CONVERTIBLE SEDAN	FB	SDN	MHG	RB	IB	T310D	GM	14	2	25150	3		45000	50000
41		MOTOR YACHT	HT	MY	FBG	RB	IB	T330	CHRY	14	2	23850	3	3	37300	41500
41		MOTOR YACHT	HT	MY	MHG	RB	IB	T330	CHRY	14	2	23850	3	3	37300	41500
41		MOTOR YACHT	HT	MY	FBG	RB	IB	T350	CRUS	14	2	23850	3	3	38200	42500
41		MOTOR YACHT	HT	MY	MHG	RB	IB	T350	CRUS	14	2	23850	3	3	38200	42500
41		MOTOR YACHT	HT	MY	FBG	RB	IB	T210D	CAT	14	2	23850	3	3	42900	47700
41		MOTOR YACHT	HT	MY	MHG	RB	IB	T210D	CAT	14	2	23850	3	3	42900	47700
41		MOTOR YACHT	HT	MY	FBG	RB	IB	T210D	CUM	14	2	23850	3	3	42000	46600
41		MOTOR YACHT	HT	MY	MHG	RB	IB	T210D	CUM	14	2	23850	3	3	42000	46600
41		MOTOR YACHT	HT	MY	FBG	RB	IB	T220D	GM	14	2	23850	3	3	42300	47000
41		MOTOR YACHT	HT	MY	MHG	RB	IB	T220D	GM	14	2	23850	3	3	42300	47000
41		MOTOR YACHT	HT	MY	FBG	RB	IB	T310D	GM	14	2	23850	3	3	44300	49200
41		MOTOR YACHT	HT	MY	MHG	RB	IB	T310D	GM	14	2	23850	3	3	44300	49200
41		MOTOR YACHT	FB	MY	FBG	RB	IB	T330	CHRY	14	2	23850	3	3	37400	41500
41		MOTOR YACHT	FB	MY	MHG	RB	IB	T330	CHRY	14	2	23850	3	3	37400	41500
41		MOTOR YACHT	FB	MY	FBG	RB	IB	T350	CRUS	14	2	23850	3	3	38300	42500
41		MOTOR YACHT	FB	MY	MHG	RB	IB	T350	CRUS	14	2	23850	3	3	38300	42500
41		MOTOR YACHT	FB	MY	FBG	RB	IB	T210D	CAT	14	2	23850	3	3	43000	47800
41		MOTOR YACHT	FB	MY	MHG	RB	IB	T210D	CAT	14	2	23850	3	3	43000	47800
41		MOTOR YACHT	FB	MY	FBG	RB	IB	T210D	CUM	14	2	23850	3	3	42100	46700
41		MOTOR YACHT	FB	MY	MHG	RB	IB	T210D	CUM	14	2	23850	3	3	42100	46700
41		MOTOR YACHT	FB	MY	FBG	RB	IB	T220D	GM	14	2	23850	3	3	42400	47200

 CONTINUED ON NEXT PAGE

LOA FT IN	NAME AND/ OR MODEL	TOP/ RIG	BOAT TYPE	-HULL- MTL	TP	TP	----ENGINE--- # HP	MFG	BEAM FT IN	WGT LBS	DRAFT FT IN	RETAIL LOW	RETAIL HIGH
	1976 BOATS												
41	MOTOR YACHT	FB	MY	MHG	RB	IB	T220D	GM	14 2	23850	3 3	42400	47200
41	MOTOR YACHT	FB	MY	FBG	RB	IB	T310D	GM	14 2	23850	3 3	44400	49300
41	MOTOR YACHT	FB	MY	MHG	RB	IB	T310D	GM	14 2	23850	3 3	44400	49300
41	SEDAN SPORT FSH	FB	SDNSF	FBG	RB	IB	T330	CHRY	14 2	25150	3	38300	42600
41	SEDAN SPORT FSH	FB	SDNSF	MHG	RB	IB	T330	CHRY	14 2	25150	3	38300	42600
41	SEDAN SPORT FSH	FB	SDNSF	FBG	RB	IB	T350	CRUS	14 2	25150	3	39100	43400
41	SEDAN SPORT FSH	FB	SDNSF	MHG	RB	IB	T350	CRUS	14 2	25150	3	39100	43400
41	SEDAN SPORT FSH	FB	SDNSF	FBG	RB	IB	T210D	CAT	14 2	25150	3	43300	48200
41	SEDAN SPORT FSH	FB	SDNSF	MHG	RB	IB	T210D	CAT	14 2	25150	3	43300	48200
41	SEDAN SPORT FSH	FB	SDNSF	FBG	RB	IB	T210D	CUM	14 2	25150	3	42400	47100
41	SEDAN SPORT FSH	FB	SDNSF	MHG	RB	IB	T210D	CUM	14 2	25150	3	42400	47100
41	SEDAN SPORT FSH	FB	SDNSF	FBG	RB	IB	T220D	GM	14 2	25150	3	42800	47600
41	SEDAN SPORT FSH	FB	SDNSF	MHG	RB	IB	T220D	GM	14 2	25150	3	42800	47600
41	SEDAN SPORT FSH	FB	SDNSF	FBG	RB	IB	T310D	GM	14 2	25150	3	44900	49800
41	SEDAN SPORT FSH	FB	SDNSF	MHG	RB	IB	T310D	GM	14 2	25150	3	44900	49800
45	CONVERTIBLE SEDAN	FB	SDN	FBG	RB	IB	T330	CHRY	15 11	25000	3 5	43900	48700
45	CONVERTIBLE SEDAN	FB	SDN	MHG	RB	IB	T330	CHRY	15 11	25000	3 5	43900	48700
45	CONVERTIBLE SEDAN	FB	SDN	FBG	RB	IB	T210D	CAT	15 11	25000	3 5	48100	52800
45	CONVERTIBLE SEDAN	FB	SDN	MHG	RB	IB	T210D	CAT	15 11	25000	3 5	48100	52800
45	CONVERTIBLE SEDAN	FB	SDN	FBG	RB	IB	T220D	GM	15 11	25000	3 5	47600	52300
45	CONVERTIBLE SEDAN	FB	SDN	MHG	RB	IB	T220D	GM	15 11	25000	3 5	47600	52300
45	CONVERTIBLE SEDAN	FB	SDN	FBG	RB	IB	T310D	GM	15 11	25000	3 5	50000	54900
45	CONVERTIBLE SEDAN	FB	SDN	MHG	RB	IB	T310D	GM	15 11	25000	3 5	50000	54900
45	CONVERTIBLE SEDAN	FB	SDN	FBG	RB	IB	T435D	GM	15 11	25000	3 5	54100	59400
45	CONVERTIBLE SEDAN	FB	SDN	MHG	RB	IB	T435D	GM	15 11	25000	3 5	54100	59400
45	PROMENADE	HT	MY	FBG	RB	IB	T330	CHRY	15 11	28100	3 5	49900	54800
45	PROMENADE	HT	MY	MHG	RB	IB	T330	CHRY	15 11	28100	3 5	49900	54800
45	PROMENADE	HT	MY	FBG	RB	IB	T310D	GM	15 11	28100	3 5	55800	61300
45	PROMENADE	HT	MY	MHG	RB	IB	T310D	GM	15 11	28100	3 5	55800	61300
45	PROMENADE	HT	MY	FBG	RB	IB	T320D	CUM	15 11	28100	3 5	55800	61400
45	PROMENADE	HT	MY	MHG	RB	IB	T320D	CUM	15 11	28100	3 5	55800	61400
45	PROMENADE	FB	MY	FBG	RB	IB	T330	CHRY	15 11	28100	3 5	49700	54700
45	PROMENADE	FB	MY	MHG	RB	IB	T330	CHRY	15 11	28100	3 5	49700	54700
45	PROMENADE	FB	MY	FBG	RB	IB	T310D	GM	15 11	28100	3 5	55600	61100
45	PROMENADE	FB	MY	MHG	RB	IB	T310D	GM	15 11	28100	3 5	55600	61100
45	PROMENADE	FB	MY	FBG	RB	IB	T320D	CUM	15 11	28100	3 5	55700	61200
45	PROMENADE	FB	MY	MHG	RB	IB	T320D	CUM	15 11	28100	3 5	55700	61200
45	SEDAN SPORT FSH	FB	SDNSF	FBG	RB	IB	T330	CHRY	15 11	25000	3 5	45600	50100
45	SEDAN SPORT FSH	FB	SDNSF	MHG	RB	IB	T330	CHRY	15 11	25000	3 5	45600	50100
45	SEDAN SPORT FSH	FB	SDNSF	FBG	RB	IB	T210D	CAT	15 11	25000	3 5	49400	54200
45	SEDAN SPORT FSH	FB	SDNSF	MHG	RB	IB	T210D	CAT	15 11	25000	3 5	49400	54200
45	SEDAN SPORT FSH	FB	SDNSF	FBG	RB	IB	T220D	GM	15 11	25000	3 5	48900	53700
45	SEDAN SPORT FSH	FB	SDNSF	MHG	RB	IB	T220D	GM	15 11	25000	3 5	48900	53700
45	SEDAN SPORT FSH	FB	SDNSF	FBG	RB	IB	T310D	GM	15 11	25000	3 5	51300	56300
45	SEDAN SPORT FSH	FB	SDNSF	MHG	RB	IB	T310D	GM	15 11	25000	3 5	51300	56300
45	SEDAN SPORT FSH	FB	SDNSF	FBG	RB	IB	T435D	GM	15 11	25000	3 5	56000	61500
45	SEDAN SPORT FSH	FB	SDNSF	MHG	RB	IB	T435D	GM	15 11	25000	3 5	56000	61500
50	DECKHS MOTOR YACHT	HT	MYDKH	FBG	RB	IB	T330	CHRY	15 11	39400	3 6	71400	78400
50	DECKHS MOTOR YACHT	HT	MYDKH	MHG	RB	IB	T330	CHRY	15 11	39400	3 6	71300	78400
50	DECKHS MOTOR YACHT	HT	MYDKH	FBG	RB	IB	T310D	GM	15 11	39400	3 6	74500	81900
50	DECKHS MOTOR YACHT	HT	MYDKH	MHG	RB	IB	T310D	GM	15 11	39400	3 6	74500	81900
50	DECKHS MOTOR YACHT	HT	MYDKH	FBG	RB	IB	T350D	GM	15 11	39400	3 6	76200	83700
50	DECKHS MOTOR YACHT	HT	MYDKH	MHG	RB	IB	T350D	GM	15 11	39400	3 6	76200	83700
50	DECKHS MOTOR YACHT	FB	MYDKH	FBG	RB	IB	T330	CHRY	15 11	39400	3 6	71000	78000
50	DECKHS MOTOR YACHT	FB	MYDKH	MHG	RB	IB	T330	CHRY	15 11	39400	3 6	71000	78000
50	DECKHS MOTOR YACHT	FB	MYDKH	FBG	RB	IB	T310D	GM	15 11	39400	3 6	74200	81500
50	DECKHS MOTOR YACHT	FB	MYDKH	MHG	RB	IB	T310D	GM	15 11	39400	3 6	74100	81500
50	DECKHS MOTOR YACHT	FB	MYDKH	FBG	RB	IB	T350D	GM	15 11	39400	3 6	75800	83300
50	DECKHS MOTOR YACHT	FB	MYDKH	MHG	RB	IB	T350D	GM	15 11	39400	3 6	75800	83300
50	MOTOR YACHT	FB	MY	FBG	RB	IB	T330	CHRY	15 11	39400	3 6	68000	74700
50	MOTOR YACHT	FB	MY	MHG	RB	IB	T330	CHRY	15 11	39400	3 6	68000	74700
50	MOTOR YACHT	FB	MY	FBG	RB	IB	T310D	GM	15 11	39400	3 6	71000	78000
50	MOTOR YACHT	FB	MY	MHG	RB	IB	T310D	GM	15 11	39400	3 6	70900	78000
50	MOTOR YACHT	FB	MY	FBG	RB	IB	T350D	GM	15 11	39400	3 6	72600	79800
50	MOTOR YACHT	FB	MY	MHG	RB	IB	T350D	GM	15 11	39400	3 6	72600	79700
50	SEDAN SPORT FSH	FB	SDNSF	FBG	RB	IB	T330	CHRY	15 11	39400	3 6	66900	73500
50	SEDAN SPORT FSH	FB	SDNSF	MHG	RB	IB	T330	CHRY	15 11	39400	3 6	66800	73500
50	SEDAN SPORT FSH	FB	SDNSF	FBG	RB	IB	T310D	GM	15 11	39400	3 6	69800	76700
50	SEDAN SPORT FSH	FB	SDNSF	MHG	RB	IB	T310D	GM	15 11	39400	3 6	69800	76700
50	SEDAN SPORT FSH	FB	SDNSF	FBG	RB	IB	T350D	GM	15 11	39400	3 6	71400	78500
50	SEDAN SPORT FSH	FB	SDNSF	MHG	RB	IB	T350D	GM	15 11	39400	3 6	71400	78500
50	SEDAN SPORT FSH	FB	SDNSF	FBG	RB	IB	T435D	GM	15 11	39400	3 6	75400	82800
50	SEDAN SPORT FSH	FB	SDNSF	MHG	RB	IB	T435D	GM	15 11	39400	3 6	75400	82800
60	DELUXE MOTOR YACHT	HT	MY	FBG	RB	IB	T350D	GM	17	51200	3 9	103000	113000
60	DELUXE MOTOR YACHT	HT	MY	MHG	RB	IB	T350D	GM	17	51200	3 9	103000	113000
60	DELUXE MOTOR YACHT	HT	MY	FBG	RB	IB	T530D	GM	17	51200	3 9	113000	124000
60	DELUXE MOTOR YACHT	HT	MY	MHG	RB	IB	T530D	GM	17	51200	3 9	113000	124000
60	DELUXE MOTOR YACHT	FB	MY	FBG	RB	IB	T350D	GM	17	51200	3 9	103000	113000
60	DELUXE MOTOR YACHT	FB	MY	MHG	RB	IB	T350D	GM	17	51200	3 9	103000	113000
60	DELUXE MOTOR YACHT	FB	MY	FBG	RB	IB	T530D	GM	17	51200	3 9	113000	124000
60	DELUXE MOTOR YACHT	FB	MY	MHG	RB	IB	T530D	GM	17	51200	3 9	113000	124000
60	MOTOR YACHT FSH	HT	YTFS	FBG	RB	IB	T350D	GM	17	51200	3 9	101000	111000
60	MOTOR YACHT FSH	HT	YTFS	MHG	RB	IB	T350D	GM	17	51200	3 9	101000	111000
60	MOTOR YACHT FSH	HT	YTFS	FBG	RB	IB	T530D	GM	17	51200	3 9	110500	121500
60	MOTOR YACHT FSH	HT	YTFS	MHG	RB	IB	T530D	GM	17	51200	3 9	110500	121500
60	MOTOR YACHT FSH	FB	YTFS	FBG	RB	IB	T350D	GM	17	51200	3 9	101000	111000
60	MOTOR YACHT FSH	FB	YTFS	MHG	RB	IB	T350D	GM	17	51200	3 9	101000	111000
60	MOTOR YACHT FSH	FB	YTFS	FBG	RB	IB	T530D	GM	17	51200	3 9	110500	121500
60	MOTOR YACHT FSH	FB	YTFS	MHG	RB	IB	T530D	GM	17	51200	3 9	110500	121500
	1975 BOATS												
34	MANSON	FB	EXP	FBG	RB	IB	T225	CHRY	12 1	14750	2 11	18900	21000
34	MANSON	FB	EXP	MHG	RB	IB	T225	CHRY	12 1	14750	2 11	18900	21000
34	MANSON	FB	EXP	FBG	RB	IB	T160D	PERK	12 1	14750	2 11	25100	27800
34	MANSON	FB	EXP	MHG	RB	IB	T160D	PERK	12 1	14750	2 11	25100	27800
34	MANSON	FB	SDNSF	FBG	RB	IB	T250	CHRY	12 1	14750	2 11	18700	20800
34	MANSON	FB	SDNSF	MHG	RB	IB	T250	CHRY	12 1	14750	2 11	18700	20800
34	MANSON	FB	SDNSF	FBG	RB	IB	T220D	CRUS	12 1	14750	2 11	24600	27300
34	MANSON	FB	SDNSF	MHG	RB	IB	T220D	CRUS	12 1	14750	2 11	24600	27300
34	MANSON CONV	FB	SDN	FBG	RB	IB	220D	CRUS	12 1	14750	2 11	23700	26300
34	MANSON CONV	FB	SDN	MHG	RB	IB	220D	CRUS	12 1	14750	2 11	23700	26300
34	MANSON CONV	FB	SDN	FBG	RB	IB	T225	CHRY	12 1	14750	2 11	19500	21600
34	MANSON CONV	FB	SDN	MHG	RB	IB	T225	CHRY	12 1	14750	2 11	19500	21600
34	MANSON CONV	FB	SDN	FBG	RB	IB	T170D	CRUS	12 1	14750	2 11	25100	27900
34	MANSON CONV	FB	SDN	MHG	RB	IB	T170D	CRUS	12 1	14750	2 11	25100	27900
41	MANSON	FB	MY	FBG	RB	IB	T330	CHRY	14 2	25150	3 3	37500	41600
41	MANSON	FB	MY	MHG	RB	IB	T330	CHRY	14 2	25150	3 3	37500	41600
41	MANSON	FB	MY	FBG	RB	IB	T350	CRUS	14 2	25250	3 3	38500	42700
41	MANSON	FB	MY	MHG	RB	IB	T350	CRUS	14 2	25250	3 3	38500	42700
41	MANSON	FB	MY	FBG	RB	IB	T210D	CAT	14 2	25250	3 3	43000	47800
41	MANSON	FB	MY	MHG	RB	IB	T210D	CAT	14 2	25250	3 3	43000	47800
41	MANSON	FB	MY	FBG	RB	IB	T310D	GM	14 2	25250	3 3	44400	49300
41	MANSON	FB	MY	MHG	RB	IB	T310D	GM	14 2	25250	3 3	44400	49300
41	MANSON	FB	SDNSF	FBG	RB	IB	T330	CHRY	14 2	23850	3	35400	39300
41	MANSON	FB	SDNSF	MHG	RB	IB	T330	CHRY	14 2	23850	3	35400	39300
41	MANSON	FB	SDNSF	FBG	RB	IB	T310D	GM	14 2	23850	3	41800	46500
41	MANSON	FB	SDNSF	MHG	RB	IB	T310D	GM	14 2	23850	3	41800	46500
41	MANSON CONV	FB	SDN	FBG	RB	IB	T210D	CAT	14 2	23850	3	40600	45100
41	MANSON CONV	FB	SDN	MHG	RB	IB	T210D	CAT	14 2	23850	3	40600	45100
45	MANSON	FB	MY	FBG	RB	IB	T330	CHRY	15 11	28100	3 5	47800	52500
45	MANSON	FB	MY	MHG	RB	IB	T330	CHRY	15 11	28100	3 5	47800	52500
45	MANSON	FB	MY	FBG	RB	IB	T310D	GM	15 11	28100	3 5	53400	58700
45	MANSON	FB	MY	MHG	RB	IB	T310D	GM	15 11	28100	3 5	53400	58700
45	MANSON	FB	MY	FBG	RB	IB	T320D	CUM	15 11	28100	3 5	53500	58800
45	MANSON	FB	MY	MHG	RB	IB	T320D	CUM	15 11	28100	3 5	53500	58800
45	MANSON	FB	SDNSF	FBG	RB	IB	T330	CHRY	15 11	27000	3 5	45000	50000
45	MANSON	FB	SDNSF	MHG	RB	IB	T330	CHRY	15 11	27000	3 5	45000	50000
45	MANSON CONV	FB	SDN	FBG	RB	IB	T310D	GM	15 11	27000	3 5	50200	55100
45	MANSON CONV	FB	SDN	MHG	RB	IB	T310D	GM	15 11	27000	3 5	50200	55100
45	MANSON CONV	FB	SDN	FBG	RB	IB	T435D	GM	15 11	27000	3 5	54100	59500
45	MANSON CONV	FB	SDN	MHG	RB	IB	T435D	GM	15 11	27000	3 5	54100	59500
50	MANSON	FB	MY	FBG	RB	IB	T330	CHRY	15 11	39400	3 6	65300	71700
50	MANSON	FB	MY	MHG	RB	IB	T330	CHRY	15 11	39400	3 6	65300	71700
50	MANSON	FB	MY	FBG	RB	IB	T310D	GM	15 11	39400	3 6	68100	74900
50	MANSON	FB	MY	MHG	RB	IB	T310D	GM	15 11	39400	3 6	68100	74900
50	MANSON	FB	MY	FBG	RB	IB	T350D	GM	15 11	39400	3 6	69700	76600
50	MANSON	FB	MY	MHG	RB	IB	T350D	GM	15 11	39400	3 6	69700	76600
50	MANSON	FB	SDNSF	FBG	RB	IB	T330	CHRY	15 11	27900	3 5	58200	64000
50	MANSON	FB	SDNSF	MHG	RB	IB	T330	CHRY	15 11	27900	3 5	58200	64000
50	MANSON	FB	SDNSF	FBG	RB	IB	T310D	GM	15 11	27900	3 5	60200	66200
50	MANSON	FB	SDNSF	MHG	RB	IB	T310D	GM	15 11	27900	3 5	60200	66200
50	MANSON	FB	SDNSF	FBG	RB	IB	T350D	GM	15 11	27900	3 5	61800	68000
50	MANSON	FB	SDNSF	MHG	RB	IB	T350D	GM	15 11	27900	3 5	61800	68000
50	MANSON	FB	SDNSF	FBG	RB	IB	T435D	GM	15 11	27900	3 5	65900	72400
50	MANSON	FB	SDNSF	MHG	RB	IB	T435D	GM	15 11	27900	3 5	65900	72400
50	MANSON PRMDK	FB	MY	FBG	RB	IB	T330	CHRY	15 11	39500	3 6	65300	71800

 CONTINUED ON NEXT PAGE

```
LOA   NAME AND/           TOP/ BOAT -HULL-  ----ENGINE---  BEAM   WGT  DRAFT RETAIL RETAIL
FT IN OR MODEL            RIG  TYPE MTL TP  TP  #  HP  MFG  FT IN  LBS  FT IN  LOW    HIGH
--------------------- 1975 BOATS -----------------------------------------------------------
50  MANSON PRMDK         FB  MY   MHG RB  IB T330  CHRY 15 11 39500  3  6  65300  71800
50  MANSON PRMDK         FB  MY   FBG RB  IB T310D GM   15 11 39500  3  6  68200  74900
50  MANSON PRMDK         FB  MY   MHG RB  IB T310D GM   15 11 39500  3  6  68200  74900
50  MANSON PRMDK         FB  MY   FBG RB  IB T350D GM   15 11 39500  3  6  69700  76600
50  MANSON PRMDK         FB  MY   MHG RB  IB T350D GM   15 11 39500  3  6  69700  76600
60  MANSON               FB  MY   FBG RB  IB T350D GM   17    51200  3  9  98600 108500
60  MANSON               FB  MY   MHG RB  IB T350D GM   17    51200  3  9  98500 108500
60  MANSON               FB  YTFS FBG RB  IB T530D GM   17    51200  3  9 106000 116500
60  MANSON               FB  YTFS MHG RB  IB T530D GM   17    51200  3  9 106000 116500
--------------------- 1974 BOATS -----------------------------------------------------------
34              EXP  MHG      IB T225      CHRY 12  1 14150  2  9  17300  19700
34              EXP  MHG      IBT140D-T160D     12  1 14150  2  9  22600  26000
34              SDN  MHG      IB  220D     CRUS 12  1 14150  2  9  22400  24900
34              SDN  MHG      IB T225-T250      12  1 14150  2  9  18500  20800
34              SDN  MHG      IBT140D-T220D     12  1 14150  2  9  23300  27700
34              SDNSF MHG     IB  220D     CRUS 12  1 14150  2  9  21300  23700
34              SDNSF MHG     IB T225-T250      12  1 14150  2  9  17200  19700
34              SDNSF MHG     IBT140D-T220D     12  1 14150  2  9  21900  25700
41              EXP  MHG      IB T330      CHRY 14  2 23150  3  3  34000  37800
41              EXP  MHG      IB T210D     CUM  14  2 23150  3  3  38600  42800
41              EXP  MHG      IB T220D     CRUS 14  2 23150  3  3  38900  43200

41              SDN  MHG      IB T330  CHRY 14  2 23150  3  3  33200  36900
   IB T220D GM  37200 41300, IB T225D CAT  38200 42500, IB T240D CUM  37400 41600
   IB T310D GM  39300 43700

41              SDNSF MHG     IB T330  CHRY 14  2 23150  3  3  32900  36600
   IB T220D GM  36800 40900, IB T225D CAT  37900 42100, IB T240D CUM  37100 41200
   IB T310D GM  39200 43500

41  PROMENADE DECK DLX   MY  MHG      IB T330  CHRY 14  1 23850  3  3  34700  38600
   IB T185D PERK 39300 43600, IB T220D GM   39200 43600, IB T225D CAT  40100 44500
   IB T310D GM  41600 46200

45              SDN  MHG      IB T330  CHRY 15 11 25600  3  6  41500  46100
   IB T220D CRUS 43900 48800, IB T220D GM   43900 48800, IB T225D CAT  44600 49600
   IB T310D GM  46500 51100

45              SDNSF MHG     IB T330  CHRY 15 11 25600  3  6  42200  46900
   IB T220D CRUS 45600 50100, IB T220D GM   45600 50100, IB T225D CAT  46300 50900
   IB T310D GM  47700 52400

45  PROMENADE DECK DLX   MY  MHG      IB T330  CHRY 15 11 28100  3  6  45800  50400
   IB T220D GM  49100 53900, IB T300D CUM   50800 55800, IB T310D GM   51300 56300

50              SDNSF MHG     IB T330  CHRY 15 11 26900  3  5  55300  60900
   IB T310D GM  57300 62900, IB T350D GM   58800 64600, IB T370D CUM   59700 65600

50  DELUXE               MY  MHG      IB T330  CHRY 15 11 39500  3  6  65200  71600
50  DELUXE               MY  MHG      IB T240D CUM  15 11 39500  3  6  63300  69600
50  DELUXE               MY  MHG      IB T310D GM   15 11 39500  3  6  67600  74200
50  PROMENADE DECK DLX   MY  MHG      IB T330  CHRY 15 11 39500  3  6  60400  66400
50  PROMENADE DECK DLX   MY  MHG      IB T220D GM   15 11 39500  3  6  62600  68800
50  PROMENADE DECK DLX   MY  MHG      IB T310D GM   15 11 39500  3  6  63500  69800
60  DELUXE               FSH MHG      IB T350D GM   16    51200  3  9  96400 106000
60  DELUXE               FSH MHG      IB T530D GM   16    51200  3  9 101500 111500
60  DELUXE               MY  MHG      IB T350D GM   16    51200  3  9  99010  99000
60  DELUXE               MY  MHG      IB T530D GM   16    51200  3  9  99300 109000
--------------------- 1973 BOATS -----------------------------------------------------------
34              EXP  MHG      IB T225      CHRY 12  1 14150  2  9  16800  19100
34              EXP  MHG      IBT140D-T160D     12  1 14150  2  9  22000  25200
34              SDN  MHG      IB  160D     PERK 12  1 14150  2  9  21400  23700
34              SDN  MHG      IB T225-T250      12  1 14150  2  9  17400  20000
34              SDN  MHG      IBT130D-T160D     12  1 14150  2  9  22600  25700
34              SDNSF MHG     IB  160D     PERK 12  1 14150  2  9  21100  23400
34              SDNSF MHG     IB T225-T250      12  1 14150  2  9  16600  19100
34              SDNSF MHG     IBT130D-T160D     12  1 14150  2  9  21400  24300
41              EXP  MHG      IB T330      CHRY 14  2 23150  3  3  32700  36400
41              EXP  MHG      IB T160D     PERK 14  2 23150  3  3  36800  40900
41              EXP  MHG      IB T210D     CUM  14  2 23150  3  3  36800  40900

41              SDN  MHG      IB T330  CHRY 14  2 23150  3  3  32000  35600
   IB T160D PERK 35400 39300, IB T185D PERK  35800 39800, IB T216D GM   35700 39700
   IB T225D CAT  36600 40600, IB T283D GM   37000 41100

41              SDNSF MHG     IB T330  CHRY 14  2 23150  3  3  31700  35200
   IB T160D PERK 35000 38900, IB T185D PERK  35400 39400, IB T216D GM   35400 39300
   IB T225D CAT  36200 40200, IB T283D GM   36800 40900

41  PROMENADE DECK DLX   MY  MHG      IB T300  CHRY 14  1 23850  3  3  33100  36800
   IB T160D PERK 37000 41100, IB T185D PERK  37800 42000, IB T216D GM   37700 41900
   IB T283D GM  39100 43400

45              SDN  MHG      IB T330  CHRY 14  8 25600  3  5  39900  44300
   IB T185D PERK 42700 47400, IB T216D GM   42700 47500, IB T225D CAT  43300 48100
   IB T283D GM  44000 48900

45              SDNSF MHG     IB T330  CHRY 14  8 25600  3  5  41300  45900
   IB T185D PERK 43600 48400, IB T216D GM   43600 48400, IB T225D CAT  44400 49400
   IB T283D GM  45600 50100

45  PROMENADE DECK DLX   MY  MHG      IB T330  CHRY 14  8 28100  3  5  44000  48900
   IB T216D GM  47500 52200, IB T283D GM   49100 53900, IB T300D CUM   49400 54300

50              SDNSF MHG     IB T330  CHRY 15 11 26900  3  5  53300  58600
   IB T185D PERK 51800 56900, IB T283D GM   54200 59500, IB T350D GM   56600 62200
   IB T370D CUM  57400 63100

50  DELUXE               MY  MHG      IB T330  CHRY 15 11 39400  3  6  62100  68200
50  DELUXE               MY  MHG      IB T185D PERK 15 11 39400  3  6  59900  65800
50  DELUXE               MY  MHG      IB T283D GM   15 11 39400  3  6  63500  69700
50  PROMENADE DECK DLX   MY  MHG      IB T330  CHRY 15 11 39400  3  6  58700  64500
50  PROMENADE DECK DLX   MY  MHG      IB T216D GM   15 11 39400  3  6  60100  66000
50  PROMENADE DECK DLX   MY  MHG      IB T283D GM   15 11 39400  3  6  60800  66800
60              YTFS MHG      IB T350D GM   16    51200  3  9  84800  93100
60              YTFS MHG      IB T530D GM   16    51200  3  9  93400 102500
60  DELUXE               MY  MHG      IB T350D GM   16    51200  3  9  86400  95000
60  DELUXE               MY  MHG      IB T530D GM   16    51200  3  9  95200 104500
--------------------- 1972 BOATS -----------------------------------------------------------
34              EXP  MHG      IB T225      CHRY 12  1 14150  2  9  16200  18400
34              EXP  MHG      IBT140D-T160D     12  1 14150  2  9  21300  24400
34              SDN  MHG      IB  160D     PERK 12  1 14150  2  9  20800  23100
34              SDN  MHG      IB T225-T250      12  1 14150  2  9  16800  19300
34              SDN  MHG      IBT130D-T160D     12  1 14150  2  9  22000  25000
34              SDNSF MHG     IB  160D     PERK 12  1 14150  2  9  20500  22800
34              SDNSF MHG     IB T225-T250      12  1 14150  2  9  16200  18600
34              SDNSF MHG     IBT130D-T160D     12  1 14150  2  9  20800  23600
41              EXP  MHG      IB T330      CHRY 14  2 23150  3  3  31500  35000
41              EXP  MHG      IB T160D     PERK 14  2 23150  3  3  35400  39400
41              EXP  MHG      IB T185D     CUM  14  2 23150  3  3  35100  39000

41              SDNSF MHG     IB T330  CHRY 14  2 23150  3  3  30500  33900
   IB T160D PERK 33700 37400, IB T185D PERK  34100 37900, IB T216D GM   34100 37800
   IB T283D GM  35400 39400

41  DELUXE               SDN MHG      IB T330  CHRY 14  2 23150  3  3  30800  34200
41  DELUXE               SDN MHG      IB T160D PERK 14  2 23150  3  3  33300  37000
41  DELUXE               SDN MHG      IB T185D PERK 14  2 23150  3  3  34500  38300
41  PROMENADE DECK DLX   MY  MHG      IB T330  CHRY 14  1 23850  3  3  32200  35800
   IB T160D PERK 35700 39600, IB T185D PERK  36100 40100, IB T216D GM   36000 40000
   IB T283D GM  37400 41600

45              SDNSF MHG     IB T330  CHRY 14  8 25600  3  5  39400  43800
45              SDNSF MHG     IB T216D GM   14  8 25600  3  5  43400  46900
45              SDNSF MHG     IB T283D GM   14  8 25600  3  5  43400  48200
45  DELUXE               SDN MHG      IB T330  CHRY 14  8 25600  3  5  38400  42700
45  DELUXE               SDN MHG      IB T185D PERK 14  8 25600  3  5  41500  46100
45  DELUXE               SDN MHG      IB T216D GM   14  8 25600  3  5  41500  46100
45  PROMENADE DECK DLX   MY  MHG      IB T330  CHRY 14  8 28100  3  5  42600  47400
   IB T216D GM  45800 50300, IB T283D GM   47300 52000, IB T300D CUM   47600 52300

50              FB  SDNSF MHG  IB T185D PERK 14  8 26900  3  5  49900  54800
   IB T283D GM  52200 57300, IB T350D GM   54500 59900, IB T370D CUM   55300 60800

50  DELUXE               MY  MHG      IB T330  CHRY 14  8 39400  3  6  59300  65100
50  DELUXE               MY  MHG      IB T185D PERK 14  8 39400  3  6  57100  63400
50  DELUXE               MY  MHG      IB T283D GM   14  8 39400  3  6  61700  67800
50  PROMENADE DECK DLX   MY  MHG      IB T330  CHRY 14  8 39400  3  6  56700  62800
50  PROMENADE DECK DLX   MY  MHG      IB T216D GM   14  8 39400  3  6  57900  63600
50  PROMENADE DECK DLX   MY  MHG      IB T283D GM   14  8 39400  3  6  58100  63900
60              YTFS MHG      IB T350D GM   16    51200  3  9  81300  89400
60              YTFS MHG      IB T530D GM   16    51200  3  9  89700  98500
60  DELUXE               MY  MHG      IB T350D GM   16    51200  3  9  82900  91100
60  DELUXE               MY  MHG      IB T530D GM   16    51200  3  9  91400 100500
```

```
 LOA  NAME AND/       TOP/ BOAT  -HULL- ----ENGINE---  BEAM   WGT  DRAFT RETAIL RETAIL
 FT IN  OR MODEL       RIG TYPE  MTL TP TP # HP   MFG  FT IN   LBS  FT IN  LOW   HIGH
---------------------- 1971 BOATS ------------------------------------------------------
 34                        EXP  MHG      IB T225-T250 12 1 14150 2 9 15600 17800
 34                        EXP  MHG      IBT140D-T160D 12 1 14150 2 9 20700 23700
 34                        SDN  MHG      IB  160D PERK 12 1 14150 2 9 20300 22600
 34                        SDN  MHG      IB T225-T250 12 1 14150 2 9 16200 18600
 34                        SDN  MHG      IBT140D-T160D 12 1 14150 2 9 21500 24400
 34                        SDN  MHG DS   IB T140D GM   12 1       2 9 20900 23200
 34                        SDNSF MHG     IB  160D PERK 12 1 14150 2 9 20000 22200
 34                        SDNSF MHG     IB T225-T250 12 1 14150 2 9 15400 17700
 34                        SDNSF MHG     IBT140D-T160D 12 1 14150 2 9 20200 23000
 41                        EXP  MHG      IB T330  CHRY 14 2 23150 3 3 30400 33800
 41                        EXP  MHG      IB T160D PERK 14 2 23150 3 3 34200 38000
 41                        EXP  MHG      IB T185D CUM  14 2 23150 3 3 33800 37600

 41                        EXP  MHG DS   IB T300  CHRY 14 2       3 3 31400 34900
 41                        SDNSF MHG     IB T330  CHRY 14 2 23150 3 3 29500 32700
      IB T160D PERK 32500 36100, IB T185D PERK 32900 36600, IB T216D GM 32900 36500
      IB T283D GM   34200 38000

 41  DELUXE                SDNSF MHG DS  IB T300 CHRY 14 2       3 3 30800 34200
 41  DELUXE                SDN  MHG      IB T330  CHRY 14 2 23150 3 3 29700 33000
 41  DELUXE                SDN  MHG      IB T160D PERK 14 2 23150 3 3 32900 36600
 41  DELUXE                SDN  MHG      IB T185D PERK 14 2 23150 3 3 33300 37000
 41  DELUXE                SDN  MHG DS   IB T300 CHRY 14 2       3 3 30500 33900
 41  PROMENADE DECK DLX    MY   MHG      IB T330  CHRY 14 1 23850 3 3 31100 34600
      IB T160D PERK 34400 38200, IB T185D PERK 34800 38700, IB T216D GM 34700 38600
      IB T283D GM   36100 40100

 41  PROMENADE DECK DLX    MY   MHG DS   IB T300 CHRY 14 2       3 3 30700 34100
 45                        SDNSF MHG     IB T330  CHRY 14 8 25600 3 5 38000 42300
 45                        SDNSF MHG     IB T216D GM  14 8 25600 3 5 40700 45200
 45                        SDNSF MHG     IB T283D GM  14 8 25600 3 5 42100 46800
 45                        SDNSF MHG DS  IB T300 CHRY 14 9       3 5 38100 42400
 45  DELUXE                SDN  MHG      IB T330  CHRY 14 8 25600 3 5 36700 40800
 45  DELUXE                SDN  MHG      IB T185D PERK 14 8 25600 3 5 39600 44000
 45  DELUXE                SDN  MHG      IB T216D GM  14 8 25600 3 5 39700 44100
 45  DELUXE                SDN  MHG DS   IB T300 CHRY 14 9       3 5 35800 39800
 45  PROMENADE DECK DLX    MY   MHG      IB T330  CHRY 14 8 28100 3 5 41500 46100
      IB T216D GM   43700 48500, IB T283D GM 45600 50100, IB T300D CUM 45900 50400

 45  PROMENADE DECK DLX    MY   MHG DS   IB T300 CHRY 14 9       3 5 40800 45300
 50                        SDNSF MHG     IB T185D PERK 14 8 26900 3 5 48100 52900
      IB T283D GM   50300 55300, IB T350D GM 52600 57700, IB T370D CUM 53300 58600

 50  DELUXE                MY   MHG      IB T330  CHRY 14 8 39400 3 6 57200 62900
 50  DELUXE                MY   MHG      IB T185D PERK 14 8 39400 3 6 55700 61200
 50  DELUXE                MY   MHG      IB T283D GM  14 8 39400 3 6 59500 65400
 50  PROMENADE DECK DLX    MY   MHG      IB T330  CHRY 14 8 39400 3 6 55100 60500
 50  PROMENADE DECK DLX    MY   MHG      IB T216D GM  14 8 39400 3 6 55800 61400
 50  PROMENADE DECK DLX    MY   MHG      IB T283D GM  14 8 39400 3 6 56000 61500
 60                        YTFS MHG      IB T350D GM  16   51200 3 9 78100 85800
 60                        YTFS MHG      IB T530D GM  16   51200 3 9 86100 94600
 60  DELUXE                MY   MHG      IB T350D GM  16   51200 3 9 79600 87500
 60  DELUXE                MY   MHG      IB T530D GM  16   51200 3 9 87700 96400
---------------------- 1970 BOATS ------------------------------------------------------
 34                        EXP  MHG RB  IB T225-T260 12 1 14150 2 9 15000 17200
 34                        EXP  MHG RB  IBT140D-T160D 12 1 14150 2 9 20200 23100
 34                        SDN  MHG RB  IB  160D PERK 12 1 14150 2 9 19800 22000
 34                        SDN  MHG RB  IB T225-T260 12 1 14150 2 9 15600 18000
 34                        SDN  MHG RB  IBT140D-T160D 12 1 14150 2 9 21000 23900
 34                        SDNSF MHG RB IB  160D PERK 12 1 14150 2 9 19600 21800
 34                        SDNSF MHG RB IB T225-T260 12 1 14150 2 9 14800 17100
 34                        SDNSF MHG RB IBT140D-T160D 12 1 14150 2 9 19800 22400
 41                        EXP  MHG RB  IB T300  CHRY 14 2 23150 3 3 29200 32400
 41                        EXP  MHG RB  IB T160D PERK 14 2 23150 3 3 33000 36700
 41                        EXP  MHG RB  IB T185D CUM  14 2 23150 3 3 32700 36300

 41                        SDNSF MHG RB IB T300 CHRY 14 2 23150 3 3 28100 31300
      IB T160D PERK 31400 34900, IB T185D CUM 31100 34600, IB T215D GM 31700 35300
      IB T283D GM   33000 36700

 41  DELUXE                SDN  MHG RB  IB T300  CHRY 14 2 23150 3 3 28500 31700
 41  DELUXE                SDN  MHG RB  IB T185D CUM  14 2 23150 3 3 31500 35000
 41  DELUXE                SDN  MHG RB  IB T185D PERK 14 2 23150 3 3 32200 35800
 41  PROMENADE DECK DLX    MY   MHG RB  IB T300  CHRY 14 1 23850 3 3 29800 33100
      IB T160D PERK 33200 36900, IB T185D CUM 32900 36600, IB T215D GM 33600 37300
      IB T283D GM   34900 38700

 45                        SDNSF MHG RB IB T300  CHRY 14 8 25600 3 5 36000 40100
 45                        SDNSF MHG RB IB T215D GM  14 8 25600 3 5 39300 43700
 45                        SDNSF MHG RB IB T283D GM  14 8 25600 3 5 40600 45200
 45  DELUXE                SDN  MHG RB  IB T300  CHRY 14 8 25600 3 5 35100 39000
 45  DELUXE                SDN  MHG RB  IB T185D CUM  14 8 25600 3 5 37700 41800
 45  DELUXE                SDN  MHG RB  IB T215D GM  14 8 25600 3 5 38300 42600
 45  PROMENADE DECK DLX    MY   MHG RB  IB T300  CHRY 14 8 28100 3 5 39400 43700
      IB T215D GM   42400 47100, IB T283D GM 43600 48400, IB T300D CUM 43800 48700

 50                        SDNSF MHG RB IB T215D GM  14 8 36900 3 5 51700 56900
      IB T283D GM   53600 58900, IB T320D GM 54700 60100, IB T370D CUM 56500 62100

 50  DELUXE                MY   MHG RB  IB T215D GM  14 8 39400 3 6 55700 61200
 50  DELUXE                MY   MHG RB  IB T283D GM  14 8 39400 3 6 57500 63200
 50  PROMENADE DECK DLX    MY   MHG RB  IB T215D GM  14 8 39400 3 6 52100 57200
 50  PROMENADE DECK DLX    MY   MHG RB  IB T283D GM  14 8 39400 3 6 54100 59500
 60                        YTFS MHG RB  IB T320D GM  16   51200 3 9 73900 81200
 60                        YTFS MHG RB  IB T478D GM  16   51200 3 9 80300 88200
 60  DELUXE                MY   MHG RB  IB T320D GM  16   51200 3 9 75300 82800
 60  DELUXE                MY   MHG RB  IB T478D GM  16   51200 3 9 81800 89900
---------------------- 1969 BOATS ------------------------------------------------------
 34                        EXP  MHG RB  IB  300  CHRY 12 1 14050 2 9 13600 15500
 34                        EXP  MHG RB  IB T210  CHRY 12 1 14050 2 9 14100 16000
 34                        EXP  MHG RB  IB T140D GM  12 1 14050 2 9 19600 21800
 34                        SDN  MHG RB  IB  140D GM  12 1 14050 2 9 19200 21400
 34                        SDN  MHG RB  IB T210-T260 12 1 14050 2 9 14100 17300
 34                        SDN  MHG RB  IB T140D GM  12 1 14050 2 9 20500 22700
 34                        SDNSF MHG RB IB T210-T260 12 1 14050 2 9 14000 16200
 34                        SDNSF MHG RB IBT140D-T220D 12 1 14050 2 9 19300 22500
 41                        EXP  MHG RB  IB T300  CHRY 14 2 22150 3 3 27300 30300
 41                        EXP  MHG RB  IB T140D GM  14 2 22150 3 3 30100 33500
 41                        EXP  MHG RB  IB T220D CRUS 14 2 22150 3 3 31200 34700

 41                        SDNSF MHG RB IB T300 CHRY 14 2 22150 3 3 26300 29200
      IB T140D GM   28600 31800, IB T215D GM 29700 33000, IB T220D CRUS 29800 33100
      IB T283D GM   31000 34500

 41  DELUXE                SDN  MHG RB  IB T300  CHRY 14 2 22150 3 3 26700 29700
 41  DELUXE                SDN  MHG RB  IB T140D GM  14 2 22150 3 3 29000 32300
 41  DELUXE                SDN  MHG RB  IB T220D CRUS 14 2 22150 3 3 30100 33500
 41  PROMENADE DECK DLX    MY   MHG RB  IB T300  CHRY 14 1 23850 3 3 28800 32000
      IB T140D GM   31300 34800, IB T215D GM 32400 36100, IB T283D GM 33700 37500

 45                        SDNSF MHG RB IB T300  CHRY 14 8 25600 3 5 34800 38700
 45                        SDNSF MHG RB IB T215D GM  14 8 25600 3 5 38000 42200
 45                        SDNSF MHG RB IB T283D GM  14 8 25600 3 5 39300 43600
 45  DELUXE                SDN  MHG RB  IB T300  CHRY 14 8 25600 3 5 34000 37700
 45  DELUXE                SDN  MHG RB  IB T215D GM  14 8 25600 3 5 36700 40800
 45  DELUXE                SDN  MHG RB  IB T220D CRUS 14 8 25600 3 5 36600 40900
 45  PROMENADE DECK DLX    MY   MHG RB  IB T300  CHRY 14 8 28100 3 5 38100 42300
 45  PROMENADE DECK DLX    MY   MHG RB  IB T215D GM  14 8 28100 3 5 41400 45900
 45  PROMENADE DECK DLX    MY   MHG RB  IB T283D GM  14 8 28100 3 5 42300 47100
 50                        SDNSF MHG RB IB T283D GM  14 8 36900 3 5 50000 55000
 50                        SDNSF MHG RB IB T283D GM  14 8 36900 3 5 51800 56900
 50                        SDNSF MHG RB IB T320D GM  14 8 36900 3 5 52900 58100

 50  DELUXE                MY   MHG RB  IB T215D GM  14 8 39400 3 6 54000 59400
 50  DELUXE                MY   MHG RB  IB T283D GM  14 8 39400 3 6 55800 61400
 50  PROMENADE DECK DLX    MY   MHG RB  IB T215D GM  14 8 39400 3 6 50100 55100
 50  PROMENADE DECK DLX    MY   MHG RB  IB T283D GM  14 8 39400 3 6 52100 57200
 60                        YTFS MHG RB  IB T320D GM  16   51200 3 9 71000 78000
 60                        YTFS MHG RB  IB T478D GM  16   51200 3 9 77200 84800
 60  DELUXE                MY   MHG RB  IB T320D GM  16   51200 3 9 72400 79500
 60  DELUXE                MY   MHG RB  IB T478D GM  16   51200 3 9 78700 86400
---------------------- 1968 BOATS ------------------------------------------------------
 34                        SF   MHG     IB T210-T250 12 2 14050 2 9 13500 15600
 34                        SF   MHG     IB T140D     12 2 14050 2 9 18800 20900
 34                    FB  SF   MHG     IB T210-T250 12 2       2 9 12300 14200
 34                    FB  SF   MHG     IB T140D     12 2       2 9 14200 16100
 34  DELUXE                EXP  MHG     IB  290  CHRY 12 2 14050 2 9 13100 14900
 34  DELUXE                EXP  MHG     IB T210  CHRY 12 2 14050 2 9 13500 15400
 34  DELUXE                EXP  MHG     IB T140D     12 2 14050 2 9 19100 21200
 34  DELUXE            FB  EXP  MHG     IB  290  CHRY 12 2       2 9 13400 15200
 34  DELUXE            FB  EXP  MHG     IB T140D     12 2       2 9 13900 15800
 34  DELUXE            FB  EXP  MHG     IB T140D     12 2       2 9 20400 22700
 34  DELUXE                SDN  MHG     IB T210-T250 12 2 14050 2 9 14100 16600
 34  DELUXE                SDN  MHG     IB T140D     12 2 14050 2 9 20000 22200

 34  DELUXE            FB  SDN  MHG     IB T210-T250 12 2       2 9 13000 15100
```

LOA FT IN	NAME AND/ OR MODEL	TOP/ RIG	BOAT TYPE	-HULL- MTL	TP	ENGINE TP	# HP	MFG	BEAM FT	BEAM IN	WGT LBS	DRAFT FT	DRAFT IN	RETAIL LOW	RETAIL HIGH
1968 BOATS															
34	DELUXE	FB	SDN	MHG		IB	T140D		12	2		2	9	19600	21800
41			SF	MHG		IB	T290	CHRY	14	2	22150	3	3	25500	28400
41			SF	MHG		IB	T140D		14	2	22150	3	3	28000	31200
41			SF	MHG		IB	T210D		14	2	22150	3	3	29000	32200
41		FB	SF	MHG		IB	T290	CHRY	14	2		3	3	28200	31400
41		FB	SF	MHG		IB	T140D		14	2		3	3	30900	34400
41		FB	SF	MHG		IB	T210D		14	2		3	3	31900	35400
41	DELUXE		EXP	MHG		IB	T290		14	2	22150	3	3	26400	29300
41	DELUXE		EXP	MHG		IB	T140D		14	2	22150	3	3	29200	32400
41	DELUXE	FB	EXP	MHG		IB	T290		14	2		3	3	28500	31700
41	DELUXE	FB	EXP	MHG		IB	T136D		14	2		3	3	31700	35200
41	DELUXE		SDN	MHG		IB	T290		14	2	22150	3	3	25800	28700
41	DELUXE		SDN	MHG		IB	T140D		14	2	22150	3	3	28100	31200
41	DELUXE	FB	SDN	MHG		IB	T290		14	2		3	3	27700	30700
41	DELUXE	FB	SDN	MHG		IB	T136D		14	2		3	3	30500	33900
41	PROMENADE DECK DLX		MY	MHG		IB	T290		14	2	28850	3	3	32300	35900
41	PROMENADE DECK DLX		MY	MHG		IB	T140D		14	2	28850	3	3	35200	39100
41	PROMENADE DECK DLX		MY	MHG		IB	T210D		14	2	28850	3	3	35900	39900
45			SF	MHG		IB	T290	CHRY	14	9	25600	3	5	34100	37900
45			SF	MHG		IB	T210D		14	9	25600	3	5	36800	40900
45			SF	MHG		IB	T275D		14	9	25600	3	5	38400	42700
45		FB	SF	MHG		IB	T290	CHRY	14	9		3	5	33800	37600
45		FB	SF	MHG		IB	T210D		14	9		3	5	36500	40600
45		FB	SF	MHG		IB	T275D		14	9		3	5	38100	42300
45	DELUXE		SDN	MHG		IB	T290	CHRY	14	9	25600	3	5	32700	36400
45	DELUXE		SDN	MHG		IB	T210D		14	9	25600	3	5	35400	39300
45	DELUXE	FB	SDN	MHG		IB	T290		14	9		3	5	32400	36000
45	DELUXE	FB	SDN	MHG		IB	T210D		14	9		3	5	35000	38900
45	PROMENADE DECK DLX		DCMY	MHG		IB	T290	CHRY	14	9	28100	3	5	35700	39700
45	PROMENADE DECK DLX		DCMY	MHG		IB	T210D		14	9	28100	3	5	38800	43100
45	PROMENADE DECK DLX		MY	MHG		IB	T290	CHRY	14	9	28100	3	5	36300	40400
45	PROMENADE DECK DLX		MY	MHG		IB	T210D		14	9	28100	3	5	39500	43900
50			SDNSF	MHG		IB	T210D		14	9	37250	3	5	49000	53900
50			SDNSF	MHG		IB	T275D		14	9	37250	3	5	50700	55700
50			SDNSF	MHG		IB	T321D		14	9	37250	3	5	52100	57200
50		FB	SDNSF	MHG		IB	T210D		14	9		3	5	50000	54900
50		FB	SDNSF	MHG		IB	T275D		14	9		3	5	51700	56800
50		FB	SDNSF	MHG		IB	T321D		14	9		3	5	53000	58300
50	DELUXE		DCCPT	MHG		IB	T325		14	9	37250	3	5	48800	53600
50	DELUXE		DCCPT	MHG		IB	T210D		14	9	37250	3	5	48300	53100
50	DELUXE		DCCPT	MHG		IB	T275D		14	9	37250	3	5	50000	54900
50	DELUXE		MY	MHG		IB	T325		14	9	37250	3	5	50300	55300
50	DELUXE		MY	MHG		IB	T210D		14	9	37250	3	5	49900	54800
50	DELUXE		MY	MHG		IB	T275D		14	9	37250	3	5	51600	56700
50	DELUXE	FB	MY	MHG		IB	T325		14	9		3	5	51100	56200
50	DELUXE	FB	MY	MHG		IB	T210D		14	9		3	5	50900	55900
50	DELUXE	FB	MY	MHG		IB	T275D		14	9		3	5	52500	57700
60	DELUXE		MY	MHG		IB	T321D		16	6		3	10	78700	86500
60	DELUXE		MY	MHG		IB	T365D		16	6		3	10	80400	88300
60	DELUXE	FB	MY	MHG		IB	T321D		16	6		3	10	78700	86500
60	DELUXE	FB	MY	MHG		IB	T365D		16	6		3	10	80400	88300
65	DELUXE		MY	MHG		IB	T321D		16	6		3	10	110500	121500
65	DELUXE		MY	MHG		IB	T365D		16	6		3	5	111500	122500
65	DELUXE	FB	MY	MHG		IB	T321D		16	6		3	10	110500	121500
65	DELUXE	FB	MY	MHG		IB	T365D		16	6		3	10	111500	122500
1967 BOATS															
34			SF	MHG		IB	T210-T215		12	1	14050	2	9	13000	14800
34			SF	MHG		IB	T136D		12	1	14050	2	9	18500	20500
34		FB	SF	MHG		IB	T210-T215		12	1		2	9	11900	13600
34		FB	SF	MHG		IB	T136D		12	1		2	9	17400	19800
34	DELUXE		EXP	MHG		IB	290		12	1	14050	2	9	12600	14300
34	DELUXE		EXP	MHG		IB	136D		12	1	14050	2	9	18700	20700
34	DELUXE		EXP	MHG		IB	T215		12	1	14050	2	9	13100	14900
34	DELUXE	FB	EXP	MHG		IB	290		12	1		2	9	12900	14700
34	DELUXE	FB	EXP	MHG		IB	136D		12	1		2	9	20200	22500
34	DELUXE	FB	EXP	MHG		IB	T210-T215		12	1		2	9	13400	15300
34	DELUXE		SDN	MHG		IB	290		12	1	14050	2	9	13000	14800
	IB 136D 18500 20600, IB T210-T215 13600 15500, IB T136D													19600	21800
34	DELUXE	FB	SDN	MHG		IB	290		12	1		2	9	12000	13700
	IB 136D 18200 20300, IB T210-T215 12600 14300, IB T136D													19200	21300
41			SF	MHG		IB	T290		14	2	22150	3	3	24800	27600
41			SF	MHG		IB	T136D		14	2	22150	3	3	27100	30100
41			SF	MHG		IB	T210D		14	2	22150	3	3	28100	31200
41		FB	SF	MHG		IB	T290		14	2		3	3	27500	30500
41		FB	SF	MHG		IB	T136D		14	2		3	3	29900	33200
41		FB	SF	MHG		IB	T210D		14	2		3	3	30900	34300
41	DELUXE		DC	MHG		IB	T290		14	2	23350	3	3	26200	29100
41	DELUXE		DC	MHG		IB	T136D		14	2	23350	3	3	28700	31900
41	DELUXE		EXP	MHG		IB	T290		14	2	22150	3	3	25600	28400
41	DELUXE		EXP	MHG		IB	T136D		14	2	22150	3	3	28200	31400
41	DELUXE	FB	EXP	MHG		IB	T290		14	2		3	3	27700	30700
41	DELUXE	FB	EXP	MHG		IB	T136D		14	2		3	3	30700	34100
41	DELUXE		SDN	MHG		IB	T290		14	2	22150	3	3	25100	27800
41	DELUXE		SDN	MHG		IB	T136D		14	2	22150	3	3	27200	30200
41	DELUXE	FB	SDN	MHG		IB	T290		14	2		3	3	26800	29800
41	DELUXE	FB	SDN	MHG		IB	T136D		14	2		3	3	29600	32900
41	PROMENADE DECK DLX		MY	MHG		IB	T290		14	2	28850	3	3	31300	34800
41	PROMENADE DECK DLX		MY	MHG		IB	T136D		14	2	28850	3	3	34100	37900
41	PROMENADE DECK DLX		MY	MHG		IB	T210D		14	2	28850	3	3	34800	38700
45			SF	MHG		IB	T290		14	9	25600	3	5	33100	36800
45			SF	MHG		IB	T210D		14	9	25600	3	5	35700	39700
45			SF	MHG		IB	T275D		14	9	25600	3	5	36900	40900
45		FB	SF	MHG		IB	T290		14	9		3	5	32800	36500
45		FB	SF	MHG		IB	T210D		14	9		3	5	35400	39300
45		FB	SF	MHG		IB	T275D		14	9		3	5	36500	40600
45	DELUXE		DC	MHG		IB	T290		14	9		3	5	33400	37100
45	DELUXE		DC	MHG		IB	T210D		14	9		3	5	36000	40000
45	DELUXE		SDN	MHG		IB	T290		14	9	25600	3	5	31800	35300
45	DELUXE		SDN	MHG		IB	T210D		14	9	25600	3	5	34300	38100
45	DELUXE	FB	SDN	MHG		IB	T290		14	9		3	5	31400	34900
45	DELUXE	FB	SDN	MHG		IB	T210D		14	9		3	5	33900	37700
45	PROMENADE DECK DLX		MY	MHG		IB	T290		14	9	28100	3	5	34700	38500
45	PROMENADE DECK DLX		MY	MHG		IB	T210D		14	9	28100	3	5	38800	43100
50			SDNSF	MHG		IB	T210D		14	9	37250	3	5	47500	52200
50			SDNSF	MHG		IB	T275D		14	9	37250	3	5	49100	54000
50			SDNSF	MHG		IB	T321D		14	9	37250	3	5	50400	55400
50		FB	SDNSF	MHG		IB	T210D		14	9		3	5	48400	53200
50		FB	SDNSF	MHG		IB	T275D		14	9		3	5	50100	55000
50		FB	SDNSF	MHG		IB	T321D		14	9		3	5	51400	56500
50	DELUXE		MY	MHG		IB	T290		14	9	37250	3	5	47900	52600
50	DELUXE		MY	MHG		IB	T210D		14	9	37250	3	5	47900	52600
50	DELUXE		MY	MHG		IB	T275D		14	9	37250	3	5	49500	54400
50	DELUXE	FB	MY	MHG		IB	T290		14	9		3	5	49300	54100
50	DELUXE	FB	MY	MHG		IB	T210D		14	9		3	5	49300	54200
50	DELUXE	FB	MY	MHG		IB	T275D		14	9		3	5	50900	56000
60	DELUXE		MY	MHG		IB	T D	GM	16	11		4	4	**	**
60	DELUXE		MY	MHG		IB	T210D		16	11		4	4	73700	81000
60	DELUXE		MY	MHG		IB	T275D		16	11		4	4	75600	83000
60	DELUXE	FB	MY	MHG		IB	T D	GM	16	11		4	4	**	**
60	DELUXE	FB	MY	MHG		IB	T210D		16	11		4	4	73700	81000
60	DELUXE	FB	MY	MHG		IB	T275D		16	11		4	4	75600	83000
65	DELUXE		MY	MHG		IB	T D	GM	16	11		4	4	**	**
65	DELUXE		MY	MHG		IB	T210D		16	11		4	4	107500	118000
65	DELUXE		MY	MHG		IB	T275D		16	11		4	4	108000	118500
65	DELUXE	FB	MY	MHG		IB	T D	GM	16	11		4	4	**	**
65	DELUXE	FB	MY	MHG		IB	T210D		16	11		4	4	107500	118000
65	DELUXE	FB	MY	MHG		IB	T275D		16	11		4	4	108000	118500
1966 BOATS															
34			SF	WD		IB	T210-T215							11500	13100
34			SF	WD		IB	T130D							17000	19300
34	DELUXE		EXP	WD		IB	290		11			2	6	12900	14600
34	DELUXE		EXP	WD		IB	130D		11			2	6	20100	22400
34	DELUXE		EXP	WD		IB	T210-T215		11			2	6	13300	15200
34	DELUXE		SDN	WD		IB	290		11			2	6	11800	13400
	IB 130D 18200 20200, IB T210-T215 12400 14100, IB T130D													19000	21100
41			SF	WD		IB	T290		14	2		3	3	26600	29500
41			SF	WD		IB	T130D		14	2		3	3	28900	32100
41			SF	WD		IB	T216D		14	2		3	3	30000	33300
41	DELUXE		DC	WD		IB	T290							26600	29500
41	DELUXE		DC	WD		IB	T130D							29100	32400
41	DELUXE		EXP	WD		IB	T290							26700	29700
41	DELUXE		EXP	WD		IB	T130D							29600	32900
41	DELUXE		SDN	WD		IB	T290							25900	28800
41	DELUXE		SDN	WD		IB	T130D							28500	31700
41	PROMENADE DECK DLX		MY	WD		IB	T290		14	1		3	3	26200	29100

 CONTINUED ON NEXT PAGE

MANSON BOAT WORKS INC -CONTINUED   See inside cover to adjust price for area

LOA FT IN	NAME AND/ OR MODEL	TOP/ RIG	BOAT TYPE	HULL MTL TP	ENGINE TP	ENGINE # HP	ENGINE MFG	BEAM FT IN	WGT LBS	DRAFT FT IN	RETAIL LOW	RETAIL HIGH
1966 BOATS												
41	PROMENADE DECK DLX		MY	WD	IB	T130D		14 1		3 3	28400	31600
41	PROMENADE DECK DLX		MY	WD	IB	T216D		14 1		3 3	29600	32900
45			SF	WD	IB	T290					31600	35100
45			SF	WD	IB	T216D					34100	37900
45			SF	WD	IB	T283D					35300	39200
45	DELUXE		DC	WD	IB	T290					32200	35700
45	DELUXE		DC	WD	IB	T216D					34800	38600
45	DELUXE		SDN	WD	IB	T290					30200	33500
45	DELUXE		SDN	WD	IB	T216D					32700	36300
45	PROMENADE DECK DLX		MY	WD	IB	T290					34000	37700
45	PROMENADE DECK DLX		MY	WD	IB	T216D					36600	40700
50			SDNSF	WD	IB	T216D					47100	51800
50			SDNSF	WD	IB	T283D					48800	53600
50			SDNSF	WD	IB	T350D					50700	55700
50	DELUXE		MY	WD	IB	T290		14 9		3 5	47800	52500
50	DELUXE		MY	WD	IB	T216D		14 9		3 5	48000	52700
50	DELUXE		MY	WD	IB	T283D		14 9		3 5	49600	54500
60	DELUXE		MY	WD	IB	T170D					69300	76200
60	DELUXE		MY	WD	IB	T283D					72200	79400
60	DELUXE		MY	WD	IB	T350D					74400	81800
65	DELUXE		MY	WD	IB	T170D					109000	120000
65	DELUXE		MY	WD	IB	T283D					110500	121500
65	DELUXE		MY	WD	IB	T350D					111500	122500
1965 BOATS												
34	DELUXE		SDN	WD	IB	T210					11700	13300
39		FB	SF	WD	IB	T130D					23800	26500
41	PROMENADE DECK DLX		MY	WD	IB	T280					25100	27900
41	PROMENADE DECK DLX		MY	WD	IB	T130D					27400	30500
45	PROMENADE DECK DLX		MY	WD	IB	T280					32900	36600
50	DELUXE		MY	WD	IB	T195D					46200	50700
1964 BOATS												
33			SF	WD	IB	T195-T215					9900	11300
33			SF	WD	IB	T120D					15400	17500
33	DELUXE		EXP	WD	IB	195-215					10600	12000
33	DELUXE		EXP	WD	IB	120D					18800	20800
33	DELUXE		EXP	WD	IB	T195-T215					11100	12700
33	DELUXE		SDN	WD	IB	195-215					9550	11000
33	DELUXE		SDN	WD	IB	120D					16500	18700
33	DELUXE		SDN	WD	IB	T195-T215					10300	11800
33	DELUXE		SDN	WD	IB	T120D					16900	19200
39			SF	WD	IB	T210					18500	20600
39			SF	WD	IB	T280					18700	20700
39			SF	WD	IB	T120D					23100	25600
39	DELUXE		EXP	WD	IB	T210					19400	21500
39	DELUXE		EXP	WD	IB	T280					19500	21700
39	DELUXE		EXP	WD	IB	T120D					22900	25400
39	DELUXE		SDN	WD	IB	T210					18700	20800
39	DELUXE		SDN	WD	IB	T280					18900	21000
39	DELUXE		SDN	WD	IB	T120D					23700	26300
41	DELUXE		DC	WD	IB	T280					25100	27900
41	DELUXE		DC	WD	IB	T120D					27700	30700
41	PROMENADE DECK DLX		MY	WD	IB	T280					24400	27100
41	PROMENADE DECK DLX		MY	WD	IB	T120D					26600	29500
44			SF	WD	IB	T280					27700	30700
44			SF	WD	IB	T181D					29900	33200
44	DELUXE		DC	WD	IB	T280					28500	31600
44	DELUXE		DC	WD	IB	T181D					30800	34200
44	DELUXE		SDN	WD	IB	T280					26600	29600
44	DELUXE		SDN	WD	IB	T181D					28900	32100
44	PROMENADE DECK DLX		MY	WD	IB	T280					30100	33400
44	PROMENADE DECK DLX		MY	WD	IB	T181D					32400	36000
1963 BOATS												
33			SF	WD	IB	T195-T215					9550	10900
33			SF	WD	IB	T120D					15200	17200
33	DELUXE		EXP	WD	IB	195-215					10200	11600
33	DELUXE		EXP	WD	IB	120D					18500	20600
33	DELUXE		EXP	WD	IB	T195-T215					10700	12200
33	DELUXE		SDN	WD	IB	195-215					9250	10600
33	DELUXE		SDN	WD	IB	120D					16400	18700
33	DELUXE		SDN	WD	IB	T195-T215					9900	11400
39			SF	WD	IB	T210					18100	20100
39			SF	WD	IB	T280					18300	20300
39			SF	WD	IB	T120D					22500	25000
39	DELUXE		EXP	WD	IB	T210					18900	21000
39	DELUXE		EXP	WD	IB	T280					19000	21100
39	DELUXE		EXP	WD	IB	T120D					22300	24800
39	DELUXE		SDN	WD	IB	T210					18300	20300
39	DELUXE		SDN	WD	IB	T280					18400	20400
39	DELUXE		SDN	WD	IB	T120D					23100	25700
40	DELUXE		DC	WD	IB	T210					23800	26400
40	DELUXE		DC	WD	IB	T280					23900	26600
40	DELUXE		DC	WD	IB	T120D					26300	29300
44			SF	WD	IB	T280					27000	30000
44			SF	WD	IB	T181D					29100	32400
44	DELUXE		DC	WD	IB	T280					27700	30800
44	DELUXE		DC	WD	IB	T181D					30000	33300
44	DELUXE		EXP	WD	IB	T280					27600	30600
44	DELUXE		EXP	WD	IB	T181D					29900	33200
44	DELUXE		SDN	WD	IB	T280					25900	28800
44	DELUXE		SDN	WD	IB	T181D					28100	31200
44	PROMENADE DECK DLX		MY	WD	IB	T280					29300	32500
44	PROMENADE DECK DLX		MY	WD	IB	T181D					31600	35100
50	DELUXE		MY	WD	IB	T280					43500	48300
50	DELUXE		MY	WD	IB	T165D					42900	47700
50	DELUXE		MY	WD	IB	T181D					43200	48000
1962 BOATS												
32	DELUXE		EXP	WD	IB	195-225					7750	9000
32	DELUXE		EXP	WD	IB	120D					13100	14900
32	DELUXE		EXP	WD	IB	T195-T225					8400	9850
32	DELUXE		SDN	WD	IB	195-225					7500	8800
32	DELUXE		SDN	WD	IB	120D					12900	14600
32	DELUXE		SDN	WD	IB	T195-T225					8300	9750
38	DELUXE	FB	DC	WD	IB	T210					17600	20000
38	DELUXE	FB	DC	WD	IB	T280					18100	20100
38	DELUXE	FB	DC	WD	IB	T120D					21500	23900
38	DELUXE		EXP	WD	IB	T210					16400	18700
38	DELUXE		EXP	WD	IB	T280					16600	18800
38	DELUXE		EXP	WD	IB	T120D					23500	26100
38	DELUXE		SDN	WD	IB	T210					20000	22200
38	DELUXE		SDN	WD	IB	T280					20100	22300
38	DELUXE		SDN	WD	IB	T120D					22200	24600
43	DELUXE	FB	DC	WD	IB	T210					26800	29700
43	DELUXE	FB	DC	WD	IB	T280					27100	30100
43	DELUXE	FB	DC	WD	IB	T181D					30000	33300
43	DELUXE		EXP	WD	IB	T210					24600	27300
43	DELUXE		EXP	WD	IB	T280					24900	27700
43	DELUXE		EXP	WD	IB	T181D					31200	34700
43	DELUXE		SDN	WD	IB	T210					22200	24700
43	DELUXE		SDN	WD	IB	T280					22500	25000
43	DELUXE		SDN	WD	IB	T181D					25600	28500
43	PROMENADE DECK DLX		MY	WD	IB	T210					28700	31900
43	PROMENADE DECK DLX		MY	WD	IB	T280					29100	32300
43	PROMENADE DECK DLX		MY	WD	IB	T181D					32000	35600
1961 BOATS												
32	MANSON		EXP	P/M	IB	125		11		2 6	7350	8450
32	MANSON		SDN	P/M	IB	125		11		2 6	6850	7900
38	MANSON		DC	P/M	IB	354		12 8		3 3	18200	20300
38	MANSON		EXP	P/M	IB	354		12 8		3 3	15100	17200
38	MANSON		SDN	P/M	IB	354		12 8		3 3	19800	22000
44	MANSON		DC	P/M	IB	354		13		3 6	26800	29800
44	MANSON		EXP	P/M	IB	354		13		3 6	26400	29300
44	MANSON		SDN	P/M	IB	354		13		3 6	24800	27500
1960 BOATS												
32	EXPRESS		EXP	P/M	IB	T450		10 8		2 11	9500	10800
32	SEDAN		SDN	P/M	IB	T450		10 8		2 11	9150	10400
38	EXPRESS		EXP	P/M	IB	550		12 6		3 4	16000	18100
38	SEDAN		SDN	P/M	IB	550		12 6		3 4	20500	22800
44	DOUBLE CABIN		DC	P/M	IB			13		3 6	**	**
44	EXPRESS		EXP	P/M	IB	550		13		3 6	27100	30100
44	EXPRESS		SDN	P/M	IB			13		3 6	**	**
1959 BOATS												
32	MERRIMAC		CR	P/M	IB	275		10 8			6500	7450
38	MERRIMAC		CR	P/M	IB	275		12 6			14100	16100
44	MERRIMAC		CR	P/M	IB	275					23800	26400

MANTA RACING INC
COAST GUARD MFG ID- MNN
FORMERLY MANTA MARINE INC

Call 1-800-327-6929 for BUC Personalized Evaluation Service
Or, for 1976 to 2000 boats, sign onto www.BUCValuPro.com

MANTRA MARINE INC
COAST GUARD MFG ID- MMJ

Call 1-800-327-6929 for BUC Personalized Evaluation Service
Or, for 1977 to 1978 boats, sign onto www.BUCValuPro.com

MANUFACTURAS MISTRAL S/A

GOODWIN YACHT-US AGENTS

Call 1-800-327-6929 for BUC Personalized Evaluation Service
Or, for 1976 to 1978 boats, sign onto www.BUCValuPro.com

MARAUDER MARINE
AUTOCOAST COMPANY
COSTA MESA CA 92627

See inside cover to adjust price for area

LOA FT IN	NAME AND/ OR MODEL	TOP/ RIG	BOAT TYPE	-HULL- MTL TP	----ENGINE--- TP # HP	MFG	BEAM FT IN	WGT LBS	DRAFT FT IN	RETAIL LOW	RETAIL HIGH
---	---	1974	BOATS	---							
22 1	SUPER SPORT		FBG	FBG	IO 165	MRCR	7 8	3500	1 10	5650	6450
24 4		HT	FBG	FBG	IO 255	MRCR	7 11	4750	1 10	8450	9700
24 4		HT	FBG	FBG	IO T275-T275		7 11	4750	1 10	9200	11400
24 4		FB	FBG	FBG	IO 255	MRCR	7 11	5500	1 10	9550	10800
24 4		FB	FBG	FBG	IO T165-T275		7 11	5500	1 10	10200	12600
24 4		FB CR	FBG	FBG	IO 255	MRCR	7 11	5000	1 10	9250	10500
24 4		FB CR	FBG	FBG	IO T165-T188		7 11	5000	1 10	9850	11300
24 4	OUT-BACK		FBG	FBG	IO 255	MRCR	7 11	5500	1 10	9550	10800
24 4	OUT-BACK		FBG	FBG	IO T165-T275		7 11	5500	1 10	10200	12600
24 4	SUPER SPORT		FBG	FBG	IO 255	MRCR	7 11	4500	1 10	8100	9350
24 4	SUPER SPORT		FBG	FBG	IO T165-T275		7 11	4500	1 10	8850	11000
28 4		FB	FBG	FBG	IO T165-T215		7 11	6500	1 10	15400	18400
28 4		FB	FBG	FBG	IB T225	CHRY	7 11	6500	1 10	12500	14300
28 4		FB	FBG	FBG	IO T235-T275		7 11	6500	1 10	16500	19600
---	---	1973	BOATS	---							
22 1	SUPER-SPORT 22		RNBT	FBG DV	IO 165		7 8	3500	1 10	5800	6650
24 4	FLYBRIDGE	FB	CR	FBG DV	IO T165		7 11	5000	1 10	10200	11600
24 4	SUPER-SPORT		SF	FBG DV	IO T165		7 11	5000	1 10	11500	13100
---	---	1971	BOATS	---							
24 4		HT	EXP	FBG DV	IO 460		7 11		1 3	14300	16200
24 4		HT	EXP	FBG DV	IO 750		7 11		1 3	19800	22000
24 4		HT	EXP	FBG DV	IO T165		7 11		1 3	10900	12300
24 4		FB	EXP	FBG DV	IO 460		7 11		1 3	14300	16200
24 4		FB	EXP	FBG DV	IO 750		7 11		1 3	19800	22000
24 4		FB	EXP	FBG DV	IO T165		7 11		1 3	10900	12300
24 4		HT	SF	FBG DV	IO 460		7 11		1 3	16100	18300
24 4		HT	SF	FBG DV	IO 750		7 11		1 3	22500	25000
24 4		HT	SF	FBG DV	IO T165		7 11		1 3	12300	14000
24 4		FB	SF	FBG DV	IO 460		7 11		1 3	16300	18600
24 4		FB	SF	FBG DV	IO 750		7 11		1 3	22900	25400
24 4		FB	SF	FBG DV	IO T165		7 11		1 3	12500	14200
---	---	1970	BOATS	---							
24 4	MARAUDER	FB	SF	FBG DV	IO 300		7 11		1 3	12500	14200
24 4	OUT-BACK		SF	FBG DV	IO 300		7 11		1 3	12400	14100

MARBLEHEAD BOAT YARD
COAST GUARD MFG ID- MBL

Call 1-800-327-6929 for BUC Personalized Evaluation Service
Or, for 1933 to 1985 boats, sign onto www.BUCValuPro.com

MARI-MAR INDUSTRIES INC
KELLER KRAFT

Call 1-800-327-6929 for BUC Personalized Evaluation Service
Or, for 1959 to 1966 boats, sign onto www.BUCValuPro.com

MARIEHOLMS PLAST AB
HILLERSTORP SWEDEN   COAST GUARD MFG ID- MHM See inside cover to adjust price for area

ATKINS YACHT SALES
ANNAPOLIS MD 21403

For more recent years, see the BUC Used Boat Price Guide, Volume 1 or Volume 2

LOA FT IN	NAME AND/ OR MODEL	TOP/ RIG	BOAT TYPE	-HULL- MTL TP	----ENGINE--- TP # HP	MFG	BEAM FT IN	WGT LBS	DRAFT FT IN	RETAIL LOW	RETAIL HIGH
---	---	1982	BOATS	---							
20	MARIEHOLM MS-20	SLP	SA/CR FBG	KL IB	8D	VLVO	7 5	2400	3	6100	7000
20 3	MARIEHOLM MS-20	SLP	SA/CR FBG	KL IB	8D	VLVO	7 5	2800	3 1	6600	7550
25 9	INTERNATL-FOLKBOAT	SLP	SA/OD FBG	KL OB			7 5	4300	4	9750	11100
25 9	INTERNATL-FOLKBOAT	SLP	SA/OD FBG	KL IB	8D	VLVO	7 5		4	11500	13100
25 10	INTERNATL-FOLKBOAT	SLP	SA/OD FBG	KL OB			7 4	5000	3 11	11400	12900
26	MARIEHOLM 26	SLP	SA/CR FBG	KL IB	8D	VLVO	7 5	5500	4	13200	15000
26 2	MARIEHOLM 26	SLP	SA/CR FBG	KL IB	8D	VLVO	7 5	5500	4	13300	15100
---	---	1981	BOATS	---							
20	MARIEHOLM MS-20	SLP	SA/CR FBG	KL IB	8D	VLVO	7 4	2450	3	5850	6750
25 9	INT'L-FOLKBOAT	SLP	SA/OD FBG	KL OB			7 5	4800	3 11	10300	11800
25 9	INT'L-FOLKBOAT	SLP	SA/OD FBG	KL IB	8D	VLVO	7 5		3 11	10900	12400
26	MARIEHOLM 26	SLP	SA/CR FBG	KL IB	8D	VLVO	7 5	5500	4	12600	14300
---	---	1978	BOATS	---							
20	MARIEHOLM AC20	SLP	SA/CR FBG	KL IB	10D		7 4	2450	3	5300	6100
20	MARIEHOLM MS20	SLP	SA/CR FBG	KL IB	10D		7 4	2450	3	5300	6100
20	MARIEHOLM S20	SLP	SA/CR FBG	KL OB			7 4	2450	3	3950	4600
25 9	INTERNATL-FOLKBOAT	SLP	SA/OD FBG	KL OB			7 5	4800	3 11	9350	10600
25 9	INTERNATL-FOLKBOAT	SLP	SA/OD FBG	KL IB	8D	VLVO	7 5	4800	3 11	9900	11200
26 3	MARIEHOLM 26	SLP	SA/CR FBG	KL IB	8D	VLVO	7 7	5000	4	10500	11900
28	MARIEHOLM 28	SLP	SA/CR FBG	KL IB	7D		9 4	7716	4 11	17200	19600
31 4	MARIEHOLM 32E	SLP	SA/CR FBG	KL IB	25D	VLVO	9 10	9000	5 1	21800	24200
---	---	1977	BOATS	---							
20	MARIEHOLM AC20	SLP	SAIL FBG	KL IB	10D	VLVO	7 4	2450	3	5350	6100
20	MARIEHOLM MS20	SLP	SAIL FBG	KL IB	10D	VLVO	7 4	2450	3	5100	5850
20	MARIEHOLM S20	SLP	SAIL FBG	KL OB			7 4	2450	3	3850	4500
25 9	INTERNATL-FOLKBOAT	SLP	SA/OD FBG	KL OB			7 4	4300	3 11	8100	9300
25 9	INTERNATL-FOLKBOAT	SLP	SA/OD FBG	KL IB	10D	VLVO	7 5	4300	3 11	8650	9950
31 4	MARIEHOLM 32E	SLP	SA/CR FBG	KL IB	D		9 10	9000	5 1	21200	23600
---	---	1976	BOATS	---							
20	MARIEHOLM AC20	SLP	SAIL FBG	KL IB	10D	VLVO	7 4	2500	3	5300	6050
20	MARIEHOLM MS20	SLP	SAIL FBG	KL IB	10D	VLVO	7 4	2500	3	4950	5700
20	MARIEHOLM S20	SLP	SAIL FBG	KL OB			7 4	2500	3	3800	4450
25 9	INTERNATL-FOLKBOAT	SLP	SA/OD FBG	KL OB			7 4	5000	3 11	9250	10500
25 9	INTERNATL-FOLKBOAT	SLP	SA/OD FBG	KL IB	10D	VLVO	7 5	5000	3 11	9750	11100
31 4	MARIEHOLM 32	SLP	SAIL FBG	KL IB	25D	VLVO	9 10	8000	5 1	18300	20400
31 4	MARIEHOLM M32E	SLP	SAIL FBG	KL IB	25D	VLVO	9 10	8000	5 1	18900	21000
---	---	1975	BOATS	---							
20	MARIEHOLM MS20	SLP	SAIL FBG	KL IB	12D	VLVO	7 4	2500	3	5050	5800
25 9	INTERNATL-FOLKBOAT	SLP	SA/OD FBG	KL OB			7 5	5000	3 11	9050	10300
25 9	INTERNATL-FOLKBOAT	SLP	SA/OD FBG	KL IB	12D	VLVO	7 5	5000	3 11	9550	10900
31 4	MARIEHOLM 32	SLP	SAIL FBG	KL IB	25D	VLVO	9 10	8000	5 1	18200	20200

MARIN YACHT SALES
SAN RAFAEL CA 94901   COAST GUARD MFG ID- MYA See inside cover to adjust price for area

For more recent years, see the BUC Used Boat Price Guide, Volume 1 or Volume 2

LOA FT IN	NAME AND/ OR MODEL	TOP/ RIG	BOAT TYPE	-HULL- MTL TP	----ENGINE--- TP # HP	MFG	BEAM FT IN	WGT LBS	DRAFT FT IN	RETAIL LOW	RETAIL HIGH
---	---	1977	BOATS	---							
39 4	BLUEWATER AFT CAB		TRWL	FBG DS	IB 120D		13		4 3	47600	52300
39 4	BLUEWATER AFT CAB		TRWL	FBG DS	IB T120D		13		4 3	50200	55200
39 4	BLUEWATER PILOTHOUSE		TRWL	FBG DS	IB 120D		13		4 3	47600	52300
39 4	BLUEWATER PILOTHOUSE		TRWL	FBG DS	IB T120D		13		4 3	50200	55200
46 7	VAGABOND	KTH	SA/CR FBG	KL IB	D		13 5	40000	5 3	74200	81500
46 7	VAGABOND PILOTHOUSE	KTH	SA/CR FBG	KL IB	D		13 5	40000	5 3	80700	88700

MARINE CONCEPTS
TARPON SPRINGS FL 34689 COAST GUARD MFG ID- MHC See inside cover to adjust price for area

For more recent years, see the BUC Used Boat Price Guide, Volume 1 or Volume 2

LOA FT IN	NAME AND/ OR MODEL	TOP/ RIG	BOAT TYPE	-HULL- MTL TP	ENGINE TP # HP MFG	BEAM FT IN	WGT LBS	DRAFT FT IN	RETAIL LOW	RETAIL HIGH
1983 BOATS										
21	SEA-PEARL 21	KTH	SAIL	FBG LB		5 6	550	6	3900	4500
23	ROB-ROY 23	YWL	SA/CR	F/S CB		6 10	1800	1 6	6600	7600
1982 BOATS										
21	SEA-PEARL 21	CAT	SAIL	FBG LB OB		5 6	550		3700	4300

MARINE CONSTRUCTION LTD
MARCON YACHTS   COAST GUARD MFG ID- MDF

Call 1-800-327-6929 for BUC Personalized Evaluation Service
Or, for 1972 to 1979 boats, sign onto www.BUCValuPro.com

MARINE CRAFTS INT'L
COAST GUARD MFG ID- MCX

Call 1-800-327-6929 for BUC Personalized Evaluation Service
Or, for 1974 boats, sign onto www.BUCValuPro.com

MARINE FIBERGLASS&PLASTIC INC
COAST GUARD MFG ID- MPF

Call 1-800-327-6929 for BUC Personalized Evaluation Service
Or, for 1960 to 1965 boats, sign onto www.BUCValuPro.com

MARINE GROUP INC
DIV OF TRACKER MARINE   COAST GUARD MFG ID- MGI

Call 1-800-327-6929 for BUC Personalized Evaluation Service
Or, for 1977 to 1988 boats, sign onto www.BUCValuPro.com

MARINE IMPORTS CO OF AMER
NEW HAVEN CT 06501   COAST GUARD MFG ID- MRP See inside cover to adjust price for area

LOA FT IN	NAME AND/ OR MODEL	TOP/ RIG	BOAT TYPE	-HULL- MTL TP	ENGINE TP # HP MFG	BEAM FT IN	WGT LBS	DRAFT FT IN	RETAIL LOW	RETAIL HIGH
1972 BOATS										
22 9	HALCYON	SLP	SA/CR	FBG KL IB		7 6		2 5	4800	5500
26 3	OFFSHORE	SLP	SA/CR	FBG KL IB		7 10		4 2	10300	11700
27	HALCYON	SLP	SA/CR	FBG KL IB		7 8		4	9750	11100
29	TRINTELLA I	SLP	SA/CR	FBG KL IB	D	8 3		4 3	14400	16400
31 8	NANTUCKET-CLIPPER	SLP	SA/CR	FBG KL IB	D	9 1		4 2	24400	27200
35 3	TRINTELLA III	SLP	SA/CR	FBG KL IB	D	10 6		4 7	27800	30900
1971 BOATS										
20 9	LEAP 21	SLP	SA/CR	FBG KL		8	2700	3 4	3600	4150
23	HALCYON 23	SLP	SAIL	FBG	IB	7 ALBN	7 6	3100	2 3	4650	5350
26 8	OFFSHORE		SAIL	FBG	IB	7 ALBN	8	4500	4 2	7600	8750
27	HALCYON 27	SLP	SAIL	FBG	IB	10 ALBN	7 8	6000	4	10400	11800
29	TRINTELLA I	SLP	SA/CR	FBG KL IB	D	8 3		4 3	14100	16000
31 6	NANTUCKET CLIPPER 30		SAIL	FBG	IB	10 SABB	8	8250	4 2	16000	18200
35 3	TRINTELLA III	SLP	SA/CR	FBG KL IB	40D	10 6	15000	4 7	27300	30300
35 3	TRINTELLA III	YWL	SA/CR	FBG KL IB	40D	10 6	15000	4 7	27300	30300
1970 BOATS										
22 9	HALCYON 23	SLP	SAIL	FBG KL IB	5 VLVO	7 6	3000	2 3	4350	5050
26 2	OFFSHORE 26	SLP	SAIL	FBG KL IB	D	7 10		4	9000	10300
26 8	HALCYON 27	SLP	SAIL	FBG KL IB	10 VLVO	7 8	6000	4	10000	11400
29	TRINTELLA I	SLP	SAIL	FBG KL IB		8 3	8750	4 3	15900	18100
1969 BOATS										
22 9	HALCYON 23	SLP	SA/CR	FBG KL IB	5	7 6	3100	2 3	4400	5050
26 3	HALCYON 27	SLP	SA/CR	FBG KL IB	8	7 8	6000	4	9700	11000

MARINE PERFORMANCE
COAST GUARD MFG ID- MPP

Call 1-800-327-6929 for BUC Personalized Evaluation Service
Or, for 1980 to 1999 boats, sign onto www.BUCValuPro.com

MARINE PROJECTS (PLYMOUTH) LTD
PLYMOUTH DEVON ENGLAND PL1 3QG   See inside cover to adjust price for area

EASTERN YACHT SALES
HINGHAM MA 02043

For more recent years, see the BUC Used Boat Price Guide, Volume 1 or Volume 2

LOA FT IN	NAME AND/ OR MODEL	TOP/ RIG	BOAT TYPE	-HULL- MTL TP	ENGINE TP # HP MFG	BEAM FT IN	WGT LBS	DRAFT FT IN	RETAIL LOW	RETAIL HIGH
1983 BOATS										
30	PRINCESS 30DS	HT	CR	FBG DV IO	T200 VLVO				24100	26800
30	PRINCESS 30S	HT	CR	FBG DV IO	T200 VLVO				22600	25200
30	PRINCESS 30S	HT	CR	FBG DV IO	T130D VLVO				26100	29000
32 6	SIGMA 33	SLP	SA/RC	FBG KL IB	D	10 6	9200	5 9	35600	39600
32 6	SIGMA 3300D	SLP	SA/OD	FBG		10 6		5 9	22600	25100
32 6	SIGMA 33C	SLP	SA/CR	FBG KL IB	D	10 6	9500	4 10	36800	40900
33	PRINCESS 33	HT	CR	FBG DV IB	T158D VLVO				55600	61100
33	PRINCESS 33	HT	CR	FBG DV IO	T165D VLVO				41200	45800
33	PRINCESS 33	FB	CR	FBG DV IB	T158D VLVO				55600	61100
33	PRINCESS 33	FB	CR	FBG DV IO	T165D VLVO				41200	45800
36	SIGMA 36	SLP	SA/RC	FBG KL IB	D	11 6	12300	6 1	47900	52700
36	SIGMA 36C	SLP	SA/CR	FBG KL IB	D	11 6	12500	5 1	48700	53500
38 1	PRINCESS 38	FB	SDN	FBG DV IO	T188D FORD	13	16400	3	49800	54700
38 1	PRINCESS 38	FB	SDN	FBG DV IO	T235D VLVO	13	16400	3	73900	81200
41	PRINCESS 412	FB	MY	FBG DV IO	T235D VLVO				98100	108000
41	PRINCESS 414	FB	MY	FBG DV IB	T235D VLVO				101500	111500
41 9	SIGMA 41	SLP	SA/RC	FBG KL IB	D	12 10	18000	6 10	78600	86400
45	PRINCESS 45	FB	MY	FBG DV IO	T286D VLVO				120500	132500
1976 BOATS										
25 2	PRINCESS 25	HT	CR	FBG DV IO	130 VLVO	9 2	4350	1 6	11100	12600
31 10	PROJECT 31		CR	FBG SV IO	T 75-T130	9 10		2 9	25000	29300
32 3	PRINCESS 32	HT	CR	FBG DV IO	106D VLVO	10	9036	1 9	29800	33100
33	PRINCESS 33	HT	CR	FBG DV IB	T 80D MAID	11 3	11170	3	39600	44000
37 1	PRINCESS 37	FB	CR	FBG DV IB	T180D MAID	13	15428	3	48400	53200
1975 BOATS										
25 2	PRINCESS 25	HT	EXP	FBG DV IO	130	9 2	4350	1 6	11100	12600
25 2	PRINCESS 25	HT	EXP	FBG DV IO	T130	9 2	4350	1 6	12400	14400
32 3	PRINCESS 32	HT	CR	FBG SV IB	T 75-T106	10	9036	1 9	23300	26700
37 1	PRINCESS 37	FB	EXP	FBG DV IB	T120	13	15428	3	40100	44500
37 1	PRINCESS 37	FB	EXP	FBG DV IB	T180	13	15428	3	40800	45400
1974 BOATS										
25 2	PRINCESS 25	HT	CR	FBG DV IO	130	8 9	4350	3	13100	13000
25 2	PRINCESS 25	HT	CR	FBG DV IO	T130	8 9	4350	3	13100	14800
32 3	PRINCESS 32	HT	CR	FBG SV IB	T 75-T106	9 7	9036	3	28000	32100
33	PRINCESS 33	HT	CR	FBG DV IB	T120-T180	11 6	11170	3	30000	34700
37 1	PRINCESS 37	FB	EXP	FBG DV IB	T180	13	15428	3	39300	43600
37 1	PRINCESS 37	FB	EXP	FBG DV IB	T220	13	15428	3	39500	43900
1973 BOATS										
24	PRINCESS 25		CR	FBG DV IO	130	9		1 6	11000	12500
25 2	PRINCESS 25	HT	CR	FBG DV IO	130	9 2	4350	1 6	11900	13500
32 3	PRINCESS 32	HT	CR	FBG DV IO	106D	10	9036	1 9	32900	36600
33	PRINCESS 33	HT	CR	FBG DV IB	T180D	11 3	11170	3	38700	43000
37 1	PRINCESS 37	FB	EXP	FBG DV IB	T180D	13	15428	3	42800	47500
1972 BOATS										
24 10	PILGRIM		EXP	FBG DV IO	115	9		1 10	13000	14800
24 10	PILGRIM		EXP	FBG DV IO	130	9		1 10	14700	16700
31 8	PROJECT		CR	FBG SV IO	130	9 8		2 3	27700	30800
31 8	PROJECT		CR	FBG SV IO	130	9 8		2 3	29300	32600
31 8	PROJECT		CR	FBG SV IO	T75D-T106D	9 8		2 3	36400	40400
32	PRINCESS		CR	FBG SV IO	130	10		2 9	29100	32300
	PRINCESS	VD T 48-T155	20200	24200, IO T170	31800	35300, IO T 75D			37200	41400
		VD T75D-T100D	30200	33600, IO T106D	36900	41000				
1971 BOATS										
25	PILGRIM 25		CR	FBG DV IO	130	9 2		1 6	13700	15500
25	PILGRIM 25		CR	FBG DV IO	T130	9 2		1 6	15400	17500
32	PRINCESS 32		CR	FBG SV IO	130	10		2 9	**	**
32	PRINCESS 32		CR	FBG SV IO	T 96-T130	10		2 9	30600	35200

MARINE TECHNICAL SERVS

Call 1-800-327-6929 for BUC Personalized Evaluation Service
Or, for 1979 to 1982 boats, sign onto www.BUCValuPro.com

MARINE TRADING INTERNATIONAL

TOMS RIVER NJ 08754 See inside cover to adjust price for area

For more recent years, see the BUC Used Boat Price Guide, Volume 1 or Volume 2

LOA FT	LOA IN	NAME AND/ OR MODEL	TOP/ RIG	BOAT TYPE	-HULL- MTL	-HULL- TP	ENGINE TP	ENGINE # HP	ENGINE MFG	BEAM FT	BEAM IN	WGT LBS	DRAFT FT	DRAFT IN	RETAIL LOW	RETAIL HIGH
		1983 BOATS														
31	4	MARINE-TRADER SDN	FB	TRWL	FBG	DS	IB	80D	LEHM	11	4		3	6	30700	34200
33	6	MARINE-TRADER DC	FB	TRWL	FBG	DS	IB	120D	LEHM	11	9		3	6	54200	59600
33	6	MARINE-TRADER DC	FB	TRWL	FBG	DS	IB	T 65D		11	9		3	6	54800	60200
33	6	MARINE-TRADER PH	FB	TRWL	FBG	DS	IB	120D	LEHM	11	9		3	6	54200	59600
33	6	MARINE-TRADER SDN	FB	TRWL	FBG	DS	IB	120D	LEHM	11	9		3	6	54200	59600
33	6	MARINE-TRADER SDN	FB	TRWL	FBG	DS	IB	T 65D		11	9		3	6	54800	60200
36		MARINE-TRADER DC	FB	TRWL	FBG	DS	IB	120D	LEHM	12	2		3	6	60300	66200
36		MARINE-TRADER DC	FB	TRWL	FBG	DS	IB	T 65D		12	2		3	6	61400	67400
36		MARINE-TRADER SDN	FB	TRWL	FBG	DS	IB	120D	LEHM	12	2		3	6	60300	66200
36		MARINE-TRADER SDN	FB	TRWL	FBG	DS	IB	T 65D		12	2		3	6	61400	67400
37	4	ISLAND-TRADER	KTH	SA/CR	FBG	KL	IB	D		12		26400	4	6	59300	65200
38		MARINE-TRADER DC	FB	TRWL	FBG	DS	IB	120D	LEHM	12	10		4		70100	77000
38		MARINE-TRADER DC	FB	TRWL	FBG	DS	IB	T 80D	LEHM	12	10		4		72700	79900
39	4	MARINE-TRADER DC SDK	FB	TRWL	FBG	DS	IB	120D	LEHM	12	11		4		84600	93000
39	8	MARINE-TRADER DC	FB	TRWL	FBG	DS	IB	120D	LEHM	13	8		4		86500	95000
39	8	MARINE-TRADER DC	FB	TRWL	FBG	DS	IB	T120D	LEHM	13	8		4		90600	99600
39	8	MARINE-TRADER SDN	FB	TRWL	FBG	DS	IB	120D	LEHM	13	8		4		86500	95000
39	8	MARINE-TRADER SDN	FB	TRWL	FBG	DS	IB	T120D	LEHM	13	8		4		90600	99600
39	9	ISLAND-TRADER	SLP	MS	FBG	KL	IB	120D	LEHM	13	4	34400	4	9	74700	82000
40	3	ISLAND-TRADER AFTCPT	KTH	SA/CR	FBG	KL	IB	D		12		29000	6		65300	71800
40	3	ISLAND-TRADER CTRCPT	KTH	SA/CR	FBG	KL	IB	D		12		29000	6		68400	75200
43	6	MARINE-TRADER	FB	TRWL	FBG	DS	IB	T120D	LEHM	14	4		4	2	123000	135000
43	6	MARINE-TRADER 2 STRM	FB	TRWL	FBG	DS	IB	120D	LEHM	14	4		4	2	114500	125500
43	6	MARINE-TRADER 2 STRM	FB	TRWL	FBG	DS	IB	T120D	LEHM	14	4		4	2	118000	130000
43	6	MARINE-TRADER 3 STRM	FB	TRWL	FBG	DS	IB	120D	LEHM	14	4		4	2	114500	125500
43	6	MARINE-TRADER 3 STRM	FB	TRWL	FBG	DS	IB	T120D	LEHM	14	4		4	2	118000	130000
43	6	MARINE-TRADER MK II	FB	TRWL	FBG	DS	IB	120D	LEHM	14	4		4	2	114500	125500
43	6	MARINE-TRADER MK II	FB	TRWL	FBG	DS	IB	T120D	LEHM	14	4		4	2	118000	130000
43	6	MARINE-TRADER SUNDCK	FB	TRWL	FBG	DS	IB	120D	LEHM	14	4		4	2	119500	131000
44	10	ISLAND-TRADER	KTH	SA/CR	FBG	KL	IB	D		13	6	31600	5	2	78200	86000
44	10	ISLAND-TRADER CHARTR	KTH	SA/CR	FBG	KL	IB	D		13	6	31600	5	2	80500	88400
45	6	ISLAND-TRADER	KTH	MS	FBG	KL	IB	120D	LEHM	15	2	48363	5	6	98900	108500
48	6	MARINE-TRADER PH	FB	TRWL	FBG	DS	IB	T120D	LEHM	15			4	6	151500	166500
48	6	MARINE-TRADER PH	FB	TRWL	FBG	DS	IB	T165D	PERK	15			4	6	154000	169000
48	6	MARINE-TRADER PH SDK	FB	TRWL	FBG	DS	IB	T120D	LEHM	15			4	6	133000	146000
48	6	MARINE-TRADER PH SDK	FB	TRWL	FBG	DS	IB	T160D	LEHM	15			4	6	134500	148000
50		MARINE-TRADER MY	FB	TRWL	FBG	DS	IB	T120D	LEHM	15	5	47500	4	6	149500	164500
50		MARINE-TRADER MY	FB	TRWL	FBG	DS	IB	T165D	PERK	15	5	47500	4	6	155000	170500
50	10	ISLAND-TRADER CTRCPT	KTH	SA/CR	FBG	KL	IB	120D	LEHM	14	1	52000	6	2	119500	131500
50	10	ISLAND-TRADER PH	KTH	SA/CR	FBG	KL	IB	120D	LEHM	14	1	52000	6	2	115500	126500
56	1	MARINE-TRADER MY	FB	TRWL	FBG	DS	IB	T160D	PERK	17	1		4	4	131000	144000
		1982 BOATS														
31	4	MARINE-TRADER SDN	FB	TRWL	FBG	DS	IB	80D	LEHM	11	4		3	6	29500	32800
33	6	MARINE-TRADER DC	FB	TRWL	FBG	DS	IB	120D	LEHM	11	9		3	6	52100	57200
33	6	MARINE-TRADER DC	FB	TRWL	FBG	DS	IB	T 65D	LEHM	11	9		3	6	52700	57900
33	6	MARINE-TRADER PH	FB	TRWL	FBG	DS	IB	120D	LEHM	11	9		3	6	52100	57200
33	6	MARINE-TRADER SDN	FB	TRWL	FBG	DS	IB	120D	LEHM	11	9		3	6	52100	57200
33	6	MARINE-TRADER SDN	FB	TRWL	FBG	DS	IB	T 65D	LEHM	11	9		3	6	52700	57900
36		MARINE-TRADER DC	FB	TRWL	FBG	DS	IB	120D	LEHM	12	2		3	6	57500	63200
36		MARINE-TRADER DC	FB	TRWL	FBG	DS	IB	T 65D	LEHM	12	2		3	6	58600	64400
36		MARINE-TRADER SDN	FB	TRWL	FBG	DS	IB	120D	LEHM	12	2		3	6	57500	63200
36		MARINE-TRADER SDN	FB	TRWL	FBG	DS	IB	T 65D	LEHM	12	2		3	6	58600	64400
37	4	ISLAND-TRADER	KTH	SA/CR	FBG	KL	IB	D		12		26400	4	6	55800	61300
38		MARINE-TRADER DC	FB	TRWL	FBG	DS	IB	120D	LEHM	12	10		4		66900	73500
38		MARINE-TRADER DC	FB	TRWL	FBG	DS	IB	T 80D	LEHM	12	10		4		69400	76200
39	8	MARINE-TRADER DC	FB	TRWL	FBG	DS	IB	120D	LEHM	13	8		4		82500	90700
39	8	MARINE-TRADER DC	FB	TRWL	FBG	DS	IB	T120D	LEHM	13	8		4		86500	95000
39	8	MARINE-TRADER SDN	FB	TRWL	FBG	DS	IB	120D	LEHM	13	8		4		82500	90700
39	8	MARINE-TRADER SDN	FB	TRWL	FBG	DS	IB	T120D	LEHM	13	8		4		86500	95000
39	9	ISLAND-TRADER	SLP	MS	FBG	KL	IB	120D	LEHM	13	4	34400	4	9	70300	77200
40	3	ISLAND-TRADER AFTCPT	KTH	SA/CR	FBG	KL	IB	D		12		29000	6		61400	67500
40	3	ISLAND-TRADER CTRCPT	KTH	SA/CR	FBG	KL	IB	D		12		29000	6		64300	70700
43	6	MARINE-TRADER 2 STRM	FB	TRWL	FBG	DS	IB	120D	LEHM	14	4		4	2	110500	121500
43	6	MARINE-TRADER 2 STRM	FB	TRWL	FBG	DS	IB	T120D	LEHM	14	4		4	2	114000	125000
43	6	MARINE-TRADER 3 STRM	FB	TRWL	FBG	DS	IB	120D	LEHM	14	4		4	2	110500	121500
43	6	MARINE-TRADER 3 STRM	FB	TRWL	FBG	DS	IB	T120D	LEHM	14	4		4	2	114000	125000
43	6	MARINE-TRADER MK II	FB	TRWL	FBG	DS	IB	120D	LEHM	14	4		4	2	110500	121500
43	6	MARINE-TRADER MK II	FB	TRWL	FBG	DS	IB	T120D	LEHM	14	4		4	2	114000	125000
44	10	ISLAND-TRADER	KTH	SA/CR	FBG	KL	IB	D		13	6	31600	5	2	73600	80900
44	10	ISLAND-TRADER CHARTR	KTH	SA/CR	FBG	KL	IB	D		13	6	31600	5	2	75700	83200
45	6	ISLAND-TRADER	KTH	MS	FBG	KL	IB	120D	LEHM	15	2	48363	5	6	93200	102500
48	6	MARINE-TRADER PH	FB	TRWL	FBG	DS	IB	T120D	LEHM	15			4	6	144500	159000
48	6	MARINE-TRADER PH	FB	TRWL	FBG	DS	IB	T160D	PERK	15			4	6	146500	161000
50		MARINE-TRADER MY	FB	TRWL	FBG	DS	IB	T120D	LEHM	15	5	47500	4	6	143000	157000
50		MARINE-TRADER MY	FB	TRWL	FBG	DS	IB	T160D	PERK	15	5	47500	4	6	147500	162000
50	10	ISLAND-TRADER CTRCPT	KTH	SA/CR	FBG	KL	IB	120D	LEHM	14	1	52000	6	2	113000	124000
50	10	ISLAND-TRADER PH	KTH	SA/CR	FBG	KL	IB	120D	LEHM	14	1	52000	6	2	109000	120000
		1981 BOATS														
31	4	MARINE-TRADER SDN	FB	TRWL	FBG	DS	IB	80D	LEHM	11	4		3	6	28400	31500
33	6	MARINE-TRADER DC	FB	TRWL	FBG	DS	IB	120D	LEHM	11	9		3	6	50100	55000
33	6	MARINE-TRADER DC	FB	TRWL	FBG	DS	IB	T 80D	LEHM	11	9		3	6	51100	56200
33	6	MARINE-TRADER PH	FB	TRWL	FBG	DS	IB	120D	LEHM	11	9		3	6	50100	55000
33	6	MARINE-TRADER SDN	FB	TRWL	FBG	DS	IB	120D	LEHM	11	9		3	6	50100	55000
36		MARINE-TRADER DC	FB	TRWL	FBG	DS	IB	120D	LEHM	12	2		3	6	54800	60200
36		MARINE-TRADER DC	FB	TRWL	FBG	DS	IB	T 80D	LEHM	12	2		3	6	55700	61200
36		MARINE-TRADER SDN	FB	TRWL	FBG	DS	IB	120D	LEHM	12	2		3	6	54800	60200
36	6	MARINE-TRADER DC	FB	TRWL	FBG	DS	IB	120D	LEHM	12	2		3	6	56600	62200
36	6	MARINE-TRADER DC	FB	TRWL	FBG	DS	IB	T 80D	LEHM	12	2		3	6	58000	63800
36	6	MARINE-TRADER SDN	FB	TRWL	FBG	DS	IB	120D	LEHM	12	2		3	6	56600	62200
37	4	ISLAND-TRADER	KTH	SA/CR	FBG	KL	IB	D		12		26400	4	6	52500	57700
37	4	ISLAND-TRADER	KTH	SA/CR	FBG	KL	IB	35D	VLVO	12		26400	4	6	52300	57500
38		MARINE-TRADER DC	FB	TRWL	FBG	DS	IB	120D	LEHM	12	10		4		63700	70000
38		MARINE-TRADER DC	FB	TRWL	FBG	DS	IB	T 80D	LEHM	12	10		4		66100	72600
39	8	MARINE-TRADER DC	FB	TRWL	FBG	DS	IB	120D	LEHM	13	8		4		78600	86400
39	8	MARINE-TRADER DC	FB	TRWL	FBG	DS	IB	T120D	LEHM	13	8		4		82400	90500
39	8	MARINE-TRADER SDN	FB	TRWL	FBG	DS	IB	120D	LEHM	13	8		4		78600	86400
39	8	MARINE-TRADER SDN	FB	TRWL	FBG	DS	IB	T120D	LEHM	13	8		4		82400	90500
39	9	ISLAND-TRADER TRAWLR	SLP	MS	FBG	KL	IB	120D	LEHM	13	4	34400	4	9	66100	72700
40	3	ISLAND-TRADER AFTCPT	KTH	SA/CR	FBG	KL	IB	D		12		29000	6		57600	63300
40	3	ISLAND-TRADER CTRCPT	KTH	SA/CR	FBG	KL	IB	D		12		29000	6		60700	66700
40	3	ISLAND-TRADER CTRCPT	KTH	SA/CR	FBG	KL	IB	46D	LEHM	12		29000	6		59000	64800
43	6	MARINE-TRADER	FB	TRWL	FBG	DS	IB	120D	LEHM	14	4		4	2	101500	111500
43	6	MARINE-TRADER	FB	TRWL	FBG	DS	IB	T120D	LEHM	14	4		4	2	103500	113500
43	6	MARINE-TRADER 2 STRM	FB	TRWL	FBG	DS	IB	120D	LEHM	14	4		4	2	106000	116500
43	6	MARINE-TRADER 2 STRM	FB	TRWL	FBG	DS	IB	T120D	LEHM	14	4		4	2	110000	120500
43	6	MARINE-TRADER 3 STRM	FB	TRWL	FBG	DS	IB	120D	LEHM	14	4		4	2	106000	116500
43	6	MARINE-TRADER 3 STRM	FB	TRWL	FBG	DS	IB	T120D	LEHM	14	4		4	2	110000	120500
43	6	MARINE-TRADER MK II	FB	TRWL	FBG	DS	IB	120D	LEHM	14	4		4	2	106000	116500
43	6	MARINE-TRADER MK II	FB	TRWL	FBG	DS	IB	T120D	LEHM	14	4		4	2	110000	120500
43	6	MARINE-TRADER SDN	FB	TRWL	FBG	DS	IB	120D	LEHM	14	4		4	2	106000	116500
43	6	MARINE-TRADER SDN	FB	TRWL	FBG	DS	IB	T120D	LEHM	14	4		4	2	110000	120500
44	10	ISLAND-TRADER	KTH	SA/CR	FBG	KL	IB	D		13	6	31600	5	2	69200	76000
44	10	ISLAND-TRADER CHARTR	KTH	SA/CR	FBG	KL	IB	D		13	6	31600	5	2	71300	78300
44	10	ISLAND-TRADER CHARTR	KTH	SA/CR	FBG	KL	IB	65D	LEHM	13	6	31600	5	2	70100	77100
44	10	ISLAND-TRADER CTRCPT	KTH	SA/CR	FBG	KL	IB	80D	LEHM	13	6	31600	5	2	70300	77300
45	6	ISLAND-TRADER MS	KTH	SA/CR	FBG	KL	IB	120D	LEHM	15	2	48400	5	6	87800	96500
45	6	ISLAND-TRADER TRAWLR	KTH	MS	FBG	KL	IB	120D	LEHM	15	2	48363	5	6	87800	96500
48	6	MARINE-TRADER PH	FB	TRWL	FBG	DS	IB	T120D	LEHM	15			4	6	137500	151500
48	6	MARINE-TRADER PH	FB	TRWL	FBG	DS	IB	T160D	PERK	15			4	6	139500	153500
50		MARINE-TRADER MY	FB	TRWL	FBG	DS	IB	T120D	LEHM	15	5		4	6	142000	156000
50		MARINE-TRADER MY	FB	TRWL	FBG	DS	IB	T160D	PERK	15	5	47500	4	6	140500	154500
50	8	MARINE-TRADER MY	FB	TRWL	FBG	DS	IB	T120D	LEHM	15			4	6	144500	158500
50	8	MARINE-TRADER MY	FB	TRWL	FBG	DS	IB	T160D	PERK	15			4	6	147000	161500
50	10	ISLAND-TRADER CTRCPT	KTH	SA/CR	FBG	KL	IB	120D	LEHM	14	1	52000	6	2	106500	117000
50	10	ISLAND-TRADER PH	KTH	SA/CR	FBG	KL	IB	120D	LEHM	14	1	52000	6	2	104000	114500
		1980 BOATS														
28	6	ISLAND-TRADER	SLP	SA/CR	FBG	KL	IB	D		9	10	9750	4		19000	21100
29		ISLAND-TRADER	CUT	SA/CR	FBG	KL	IB	20D	YAN	9	10	9725	4		19200	21300
31	4	MARINE-TRADER SDN	FB	TRWL	FBG	DS	IB	80D	LEHM	11	4		3	6	27300	30300
33	6	MARINE-TRADER DC	FB	TRWL	FBG	DS	IB	120D	LEHM	11	9		3	6	48300	53100
33	6	MARINE-TRADER DC	FB	TRWL	FBG	DS	IB	T 80D	LEHM	11	9		3	6	49200	54100
33	6	MARINE-TRADER PH	FB	TRWL	FBG	DS	IB	120D	LEHM	11	9		3	6	48300	53100
33	6	MARINE-TRADER SDN	FB	TRWL	FBG	DS	IB	120D	LEHM	11	9		3	6	48300	53100
36		MARINE-TRADER DC	FB	TRWL	FBG	DS	IB	120D	LEHM	12	2		3	6	52300	57400
36		MARINE-TRADER DC	FB	TRWL	FBG	DS	IB	T 80D	LEHM	12	2		3	6	53100	58400
36		MARINE-TRADER SDN	FB	TRWL	FBG	DS	IB	120D	LEHM	12	2		3	6	52300	57400
37	4	ISLAND-TRADER	KTH	SA/CR	FBG	KL	IB	35D	VLVO	12		26400	4	6	50000	54900
38		MARINE-TRADER DC	FB	TRWL	FBG	DS	IB	120D	LEHM	12	10		4		60800	66800
38		MARINE-TRADER DC	FB	TRWL	FBG	DS	IB	T 80D	LEHM	12	10		4		63000	69300
39	8	MARINE-TRADER DC	FB	TRWL	FBG	DS	IB	120D	LEHM	13	8		4		75000	82400
39	8	MARINE-TRADER DC	FB	TRWL	FBG	DS	IB	T120D	LEHM	13	8		4		78600	86400

 CONTINUED ON NEXT PAGE

LOA FT	LOA IN	NAME AND/ OR MODEL	TOP/ RIG	BOAT TYPE	-HULL- MTL	-HULL- TP	ENGINE TP	ENGINE # HP	ENGINE MFG	BEAM FT	BEAM IN	WGT LBS	DRAFT FT	DRAFT IN	RETAIL LOW	RETAIL HIGH
		1980 BOATS														
39	8	MARINE-TRADER SDN	FB	TRWL	FBG	DS	IB	120D	LEHM	13	8		4		75000	82400
39	8	MARINE-TRADER SDN	FB	TRWL	FBG	DS	IB	T120D	LEHM	13	8		4		78600	86400
40	3	ISLAND-TRADER AFTCPT	KTH	SA/CR	FBG	KL	IB	46D	LEHM	12		29000	6		55200	60700
40	3	ISLAND-TRADER CTRCPT	KTH	SA/CR	FBG	KL	IB	46D	LEHM	12		29000	6		57400	63100
43	6	MARINE TRADER STRM	FB	TRWL	FBG	DS	IB	120D	LEHM	14	4		4	2	100500	110000
43	6	MARINE-TRADER 2 STRM	FB	TRWL	FBG	DS	IB	T120D	LEHM	14	4		4	2	101500	111500
43	6	MARINE-TRADER 3 STRM	FB	TRWL	FBG	DS	IB	120D	LEHM	14	4		4	2	100500	110000
43	6	MARINE-TRADER MK II	FB	TRWL	FBG	DS	IB	120D	LEHM	14	4		4	2	100500	110000
43	6	MARINE-TRADER MK II	FB	TRWL	FBG	DS	IB	T120D	LEHM	14	4		4	2	101500	111500
43	6	MARINE-TRADER SEDAN	FB	TRWL	FBG	DS	IB	120D	LEHM	14	4		4	2	100500	110000
43	6	MARINE-TRADER SEDAN	FB	TRWL	FBG	DS	IB	T120D	LEHM	14	4		4	2	109000	120000
43	6	MARINE-TRADER STRM	FB	TRWL	FBG	DS	IB	T120D	LEHM	14	4		4	2	101500	111500
44	10	ISLAND-TRADER CHARTR	KTH	SA/CR	FBG	KL	IB	65D	LEHM	13	6	31600	5	2	67000	73600
44	10	ISLAND-TRADER CTRCPT	KTH	SA/CR	FBG	KL	IB	80D	LEHM	13	6	31600	5	2	67200	73800
45	6	ISLAND-TRADER MS	KTH	SA/CR	FBG	KL	IB	120D	LEHM	15	2	48360	5	6	83800	92100
48	6	MARINE-TRADER PH	FB	TRWL	FBG	DS	IB	T120D	LEHM	15			4	6	131500	144500
48	6	MARINE-TRADER PH	FB	TRWL	FBG	DS	IB	T150D	LEHM	15			4	6	133000	146000
48	6	MARINE-TRADER PH	FB	TRWL	FBG	DS	IB	T160D	PERK	15			4	6	133500	146500
50	8	MARINE-TRADER MY	FB	TRWL	FBG	DS	IB	T120D	LEHM	15		46000	4	6	121000	133000
50	8	MARINE-TRADER MY	FB	TRWL	FBG	DS	IB	T160D	PERK	15		46000	4	6	126000	138500
50	10	ISLAND-TRADER CTRCPT	KTH	SA/CR	FBG	KL	IB	120D	LEHM	14	1	52000	6	2	101500	111500
50	10	ISLAND-TRADER PH	KTH	SA/CR	FBG	KL	IB	120D	LEHM	14	1	52000	6	2	99200	109000
		1979 BOATS														
28	6	ISLAND-TRADER	CUT	SA/CR	FBG	KL	IB	80D	PISC	9	10	9750	4		18800	20800
31	4	MARINE-TRADER SDN	FB	TRWL	FBG	DS	IB	80D	LEHM	11	4		3	6	26300	29200
33	6	MARINE-TRADER DC	FB	TRWL	FBG	DS	IB	120D	LEHM	11	9		3	6	46500	51100
33	6	MARINE-TRADER DC	FB	TRWL	FBG	DS	IB	T 80D	LEHM	11	9		3	6	47500	52200
33	6	MARINE-TRADER PH	FB	TRWL	FBG	DS	IB	120D	LEHM	11	9		3	6	46500	51100
33	6	MARINE-TRADER SDN	FB	TRWL	FBG	DS	IB	120D	LEHM	11	9		3	6	46500	51100
36		MARINE-TRADER DC	FB	TRWL	FBG	DS	IB	120D	LEHM	12	2		3	6	49900	54900
36		MARINE-TRADER DC	FB	TRWL	FBG	DS	IB	T 80D	LEHM	12	2		3	6	50800	55800
36		MARINE-TRADER SDN	FB	TRWL	FBG	DS	IB	120D	LEHM	12	2		3	6	49900	54900
37		MARINE-TRADER DC	FB	TRWL	FBG	DS	IB	120D	LEHM	12	8		4	6	52300	57500
37		MARINE-TRADER DC	FB	TRWL	FBG	DS	IB	T 80D	LEHM	12	8		4	6	54000	59300
37	4	ISLAND-TRADER	KTH	SA/CR	FBG	KL	IB	35D	VLVO	11	10	18600	4	7	36100	40100
39	8	MARINE-TRADER DC	FB	TRWL	FBG	DS	IB	120D	LEHM	13	8		4		71600	78700
39	8	MARINE-TRADER DC	FB	TRWL	FBG	DS	IB	T120D	LEHM	13	8		4		75100	82500
39	8	MARINE-TRADER SDN	FB	TRWL	FBG	DS	IB	120D	LEHM	13	8		4		71600	78700
39	8	MARINE-TRADER SDN	FB	TRWL	FBG	DS	IB	T120D	LEHM	13	8		4		75100	82500
40	3	ISLAND-TRADER AFTCPT	KTH	SA/CR	FBG	KL	IB	50D	PERK	12	2	29000	6		51400	56400
40	3	ISLAND-TRADER CTRCPT	KTH	SA/CR	FBG	KL	IB	50D	PERK	12	2	29000	6		56500	62100
43	6	MARINE-TRADER DC	FB	TRWL	FBG	DS	IB	120D	LEHM	14	4		4	2	95800	105500
43	6	MARINE-TRADER DC	FB	TRWL	FBG	DS	IB	T120D	LEHM	14	4		4	2	98800	108500
44	10	ISLAND-TRADER CTRCPT	KTH	SA/CR	FBG	KL	IB	65D	PISC	13	6	31600	5	2	64400	70800
45	6	ISLAND-TRADER	KTH	MS	FBG	KL	IB	120D	LEHM	15	2	48363	5	6	80500	88500
48	6	MARINE-TRADER PH	FB	TRWL	FBG	DS	IB	T120D	LEHM	15			4	6	125500	138000
48	6	MARINE-TRADER PH	FB	TRWL	FBG	DS	IB	T150D	LEHM	15			4	6	127000	139500
50		MARINE-TRADER MY	FB	TRWL	FBG	DS	IB	T120D	LEHM	15			4	6	129000	142000
50		MARINE-TRADER MY	FB	TRWL	FBG	DS	IB	T150D	LEHM	15			4	6	131000	144000
50	10	ISLAND-TRADER CTRCPT	KTH	SA/CR	FBG	KL	IB	120D	LEHM	14	1	52000	6	2	97300	107000
50	10	ISLAND-TRADER PH	KTH	SA/CR	FBG	KL	IB	120D	LEHM	14	1	52000	6	2	94800	104000
		1978 BOATS														
29		ISLAND-TRADER	CUT	SA/CR	FBG	KL				9	10	9725	4		15500	17600
31	4	MARINE-TRADER SDN	FB	TRWL	FBG	DS	IB	120D	LEHM	11	4		3	6	29500	32800
33	6	MARINE-TRADER DC	FB	TRWL	FBG	DS	IB	120D-160D		11	9		3	6	44400	49800
33	6	MARINE-TRADER DC	FB	TRWL	FBG	DS	IB	T 80D	LEHM	11	9		3	6	45800	50300
33	6	MARINE-TRADER PH	FB	TRWL	FBG	DS	IB	120D-160D		11	9		3	6	44400	49800
33	6	MARINE-TRADER SDN	FB	TRWL	FBG	DS	IB	120D-160D		11	9		3	6	44400	49800
36		MARINE-TRADER DC	FB	TRWL	FBG	DS	IB	120D	LEHM	12	2		3	6	48000	52700
36		MARINE-TRADER DC	FB	TRWL	FBG	DS	IB	240D		12	2		3	6	48400	53200
36		MARINE-TRADER DC	FB	TRWL	FBG	DS	IB	T 80D	LEHM	12	2		3	6	48500	53300
36		MARINE-TRADER SDN	FB	TRWL	FBG	DS	IB	120D	LEHM	12	2		3	6	48000	52700
36		MARINE-TRADER SDN	FB	TRWL	FBG	DS	IB	240D		12	2		3	6	48400	53200
37		ISLAND-TRADER	KTH	SA/CR	FBG	KL	IB	35D	VLVO	11	10	18600	4	7	34600	38400
39	8	MARINE-TRADER DC	FB	TRWL	FBG	DS	IB	120D	LEHM	13	8		4		68500	75300
39	8	MARINE-TRADER DC	FB	TRWL	FBG	DS	IB	240D		13	8		4		69900	76800
39	8	MARINE-TRADER DC	FB	TRWL	FBG	DS	IB	T120D	LEHM	13	8		4		71800	78900
39	8	MARINE-TRADER SDN	FB	TRWL	FBG	DS	IB	120D	LEHM	13	8		4		68500	75300
39	8	MARINE-TRADER SDN	FB	TRWL	FBG	DS	IB	240D		13	8		4		69900	76800
40	3	ISLAND-TRADER	KTH	SA/CR	FBG	KL	IB	50D	PERK	12	2	28000	6		50800	55900
40	3	ISLAND-TRADER	KTH	SA/CR	FBG	KL	IB	80D		12	2	28000	6		51400	56500
40	3	ISLAND-TRADER CTR	KTH	SA/CR	FBG	KL	IB	50D	PERK	12	2	29000	6		52000	57200
40	3	ISLAND-TRADER CTR	KTH	SA/CR	FBG	KL	IB	80D		12	2	29000	6		52500	57700
43	6	MARINE-TRADER TC	FB	TRWL	FBG	DS	IB	120D	LEHM	14	4		4	2	91600	100500
43	6	MARINE-TRADER TC	FB	TRWL	FBG	DS	IB	240D		14	4		4	2	93500	102500
43	6	MARINE-TRADER TC	FB	TRWL	FBG	DS	IB	T120D	LEHM	14	4		4	2	94500	104000
48	6	MARINE-TRADER MY	FB	TRWL	FBG	DS	IB	120D		15			4	6	123500	136000
48	6	MARINE-TRADER MY	FB	TRWL	FBG	DS	IB	240D		15			4	6	126500	139000
48	6	MARINE-TRADER MY	FB	TRWL	FBG	DS	IB	T120D	LEHM	15			4	6	127500	140000
50	10	ISLAND-TRADER CTR	KTH	SA/CR	FBG	KL	IB	120D	LEHM	14	1	52000	6	2	92700	102000
50	10	ISLAND-TRADER PH	KTH	SA/CR	FBG	KL	IB	120D	LEHM	14	1	52000	6	2	91800	101000
		1977 BOATS														
28	6	ISLAND-TRADER	CUT	SA/CR	FBG	KL	IB	D		9	10	9725	4		16800	19100
33	6	MARINE-TRADER DC	FB	TRWL	FBG	DS	IB	120D	FORD	11	9		3	6	42800	47500
33	6	MARINE-TRADER DC	FB	TRWL	FBG	DS	IB	T 80D	FORD	11	9	19600	3	6	53800	59100
33	6	MARINE-TRADER PH	HT	TRWL	FBG	DS	IB	120D	FORD	11	9	19600	3	6	53700	59000
33	6	MARINE-TRADER PH	FB	TRWL	FBG	DS	IB	120D	FORD	11	9	19600	3	6	53700	59000
33	6	MARINE-TRADER SDN	FB	TRWL	FBG	DS	IB	120D	FORD	11	9	19600	3	6	53700	59000
35	6	MARINE-TRADER DC	FB	TRWL	FBG	DS	IB	120D	FORD	12	2		3	6	56700	62300
35	6	MARINE-TRADER DC	FB	TRWL	FBG	DS	IB	T120D	FORD	12	2		3	6	58200	64000
35	6	MARINE-TRADER SDN	FB	TRWL	FBG	DS	IB	120D	FORD	12	2		3	6	56700	62300
37		ISLAND-TRADER	KTH	SA/CR	FBG	KL	IB	D	VLVO	11	10	18600	4	7	33500	37200
40		MARINE-TRADER DC	FB	TRWL	FBG	DS	IB	120D	FORD	13	8		4		66500	73100
40		MARINE-TRADER DC	FB	TRWL	FBG	DS	IB	T120D	FORD	13	8		4		69700	76600
40		MARINE-TRADER SDN	FB	TRWL	FBG	DS	IB	120D	FORD	13	8		4		66500	73100
40		MARINE-TRADER SDN	FB	TRWL	FBG	DS	IB	T120D	FORD	13	8		4		69700	76600
40	11	ISLAND-TRADER AFT	KTH	SA/CR	FBG	KL	IB	50D	VLVO	12	2	28000	6		50000	54900
44		MARINE-TRADER TRICAB		TRWL	FBG	DS	IB	120D		14	4		4	2	82400	90600
44		MARINE-TRADER TRICAB		TRWL	FBG	DS	IB	240D		14	4		4	2	84100	92400
47	11	MARINE-TRADER	HT	MY	FBG	DS	IB	T120D	FORD	15			4	6	89100	97900
50	10	ISLAND-TRADER CPT	KTH	SA/CR	FBG	KL	IB	120D	VLVO	14	1	52000	6	2	89300	98100
50	10	ISLAND-TRADER PH	KTH	SA/CR	FBG	KL	IB	120D	VLVO	14	1	52000	6	2	88400	97100
		1976 BOATS														
28	6	ISLAND-TRADER 29	CUT	SA/CR	FBG	KL	IB	12D	YAN	9	10	9750	4		16300	18500
33	6	MARINE-TRADER DC	FB	TRWL	FBG	DS	IB	120D	LEHM	11	9	19600	3	6	51700	56900
33	6	MARINE-TRADER DC	FB	TRWL	FBG	DS	IB	T 80D	LEHM	11	9	19600	3	6	51800	57000
33	6	MARINE-TRADER PH	HT	TRWL	FBG	DS	IB	120D	LEHM	11	9	19600	3	6	51700	56800
33	6	MARINE-TRADER PH	FB	TRWL	FBG	DS	IB	120D	LEHM	11	9	19600	3	6	51700	56900
33	6	MARINE-TRADER SDN	FB	TRWL	FBG	DS	IB	120D	LEHM	11	9	19600	3	6	51700	56900
33	6	MARINE-TRADER SDN	FB	TRWL	FBG	DS	IB	T 80D	LEHM	11	9	19600	3	6	51800	57000
35	6	MARINE-TRADER DC	FB	TRWL	FBG	DS	IB	120D	LEHM	12	2	21000	3	6	58300	64100
35	6	MARINE-TRADER DC	FB	TRWL	FBG	DS	IB	T120D	LEHM	12	2	21000	3	6	59900	65800
35	6	MARINE-TRADER SDN	FB	TRWL	FBG	DS	IB	120D	LEHM	12	2	21000	3	6	58300	64100
36	6	ISLAND-TRADER	KTH	SA/CR	FBG	KL	IB	50D	VLVO	11	10	18600	4	6	32200	35800
40		MARINE-TRADER DC	FB	TRWL	FBG	DS	IB	120D	LEHM	13	8	28000	4		64400	70800
40		MARINE-TRADER DC	FB	TRWL	FBG	DS	IB	T120D	LEHM	13	8	28000	4		67500	74200
40	11	ISLAND-TRADER	KTH	SA/CR	FBG	KL	IB	50D	PERK	12	2	28000	6		48200	52900
47	6	MARINE-TRADER MY	FB	TRWL	FBG	DS	IB	120D	LEHM	15		44000	4	6	111500	122500
47	6	MARINE-TRADER MY	FB	TRWL	FBG	DS	IB	T256D	LEHM	15		46000	4	7	122500	134500
50	10	ISLAND-TRADER CTR	KTH	SA/CR	FBG	KL	IB	85D	PERK	14	1	52000	6	2	86700	95300
50	10	ISLAND-TRADER PH	KTH	SA/CR	FBG	KL	IB	85D	PERK	14	1	52000	6	2	85800	94300
		1975 BOATS														
33	6	MARINE-TRADER DC	FB	TRWL	FBG	DS	IB	120D	FORD	11	9		3	6	39900	44300
33	6	MARINE-TRADER PH	HT	TRWL	FBG	DS	IB	120D	FORD	11	9		3	6	39900	44300
33	6	MARINE-TRADER PH	FB	TRWL	FBG	DS	IB	120D	FORD	11	9		3	6	39900	44300
33	6	MARINE-TRADER SDN	HT	TRWL	FBG	DS	IB	120D	FORD	11	9		3	6	39900	44300
34	11	ISLAND-TRADER	SLP	SA/CR	FBG	KL	IB	120D	FORD	11	3	12041	4	5	21000	23300
34	11	ISLAND-TRADER	KTH	SA/CR	FBG	KL	IB	120D	FORD	11	3	12041	4	5	21000	23300
35	6	MARINE-TRADER DC	FB	TRWL	FBG	DS	IB	120D	FORD	12	2		3	6	52900	58100
40		MARINE-TRADER DC	FB	TRWL	FBG	DS	IB	120D	FORD	13	8		4		61300	67300
40	11	ISLAND-TRADER	KTH	SA/CR	FBG	KL	IB	50D	FORD	12	2	28000	6		46100	50700
40	11	ISLAND-TRADER AFTCBN	KTH	SA/CR	FBG	KL	IB	50D	FORD	12	2	28000	6		48100	52900
40	11	ISLAND-TRADER PH	KTH	SAIL	FBG	KL	IB	50D	FORD	12	2	28000	6		47200	51900
45		MARINE-TRADER		TRWL	FBG	DS	IB	T160D		15					76100	83600
50	10	ISLAND-TRADER	KTH	SA/CR	FBG	KL	IB	85D	FORD	16	2	52000	6	2	83700	92000
		1974 BOATS														
33	6	DOUBLE CABIN	FB	TRWL	FBG	DS	IB	120D	FORD	11	9	19600	3	4	48700	53500
33	6	OFFSHORE SDN	FB	TRWL	FBG	DS	IB	120D	FORD	11	9	19600	3	4	48700	53500
33	6	PILOTHOUSE	HT	TRWL	FBG	DS	IB	120D	FORD	11	9	19600	3	4	48700	53500
35	6	MARINE-TRADER	FB	TRWL	FBG	DS	IB	120D	FORD	12	2	21000	3	6	54900	60300
40	11	ISLAND-TRADER	KTH	SA/CR	FBG	KL	IB	50D	PERK	12	2	28000	6		45800	50300
45		MARINE-TRADER		TRWL	FBG	DS	IB	T160D		15					73100	80400
50	10	ISLAND-TRADER	KTH	SA/CR	FBG	KL	IB	D		14	1	52000	6	2	81300	89300
		1973 BOATS														
33	6	DOUBLE CABIN	FB	TRWL	FBG	DS	IB	120D	FORD	11	9		3	4	37700	41900
33	6	OFFSHORE SDN	FB	TRWL	FBG	DS	IB	120D	FORD	11	9	19600	3	4	47600	52400
33	6	PILOTHOUSE	FB	TRWL	FBG	DS	IB	120D	FORD	11	9		3	4	37700	41900
40	11	ISLAND-TRADER	KTH	SA/CR	FBG	KL	IB	50D	PERK	12	2	28000	6		44200	49100

CONTINUED ON NEXT PAGE

LOA FT IN	NAME AND/ OR MODEL	TOP/ RIG	BOAT TYPE	-HULL- MTL TP	----ENGINE--- TP # HP MFG	BEAM FT IN	WGT LBS	DRAFT FT IN	RETAIL LOW	RETAIL HIGH
					1973 BOATS					
45	MARINE-TRADER	FB	TRWL	FBG DS IB	D 15				**	**
50 10	ISLAND-TRADER	KTH	SA/CR	FBG KL IB	D 14 1 52000		6 2	79000	86800

MARINER BOAT CO
MARINE CITY MI   See inside cover to adjust price for area

LOA FT IN	NAME AND/ OR MODEL	TOP/ RIG	BOAT TYPE	-HULL- MTL TP	----ENGINE--- TP # HP MFG	BEAM FT IN	WGT LBS	DRAFT FT IN	RETAIL LOW	RETAIL HIGH
					1965 BOATS					
18	SPORT	RNBT	WD	IB 170		7 6		1 6	1950	2300
20		UTL	WD	IB 215		7 9		1 9	2600	3050
22		UTL	WD	IB 215		7 10		1 10	2700	3150
					1959 BOATS					
19 6	SPORTSMAN	UTL	P/M	IB 290		6 9			1950	2300

MARINER INDUSTRIES
LONG BEACH CA 90813   See inside cover to adjust price for area
       FOR MORE RECENT YEARS SEE IMPERIAL YACHT CO WEST

LOA FT IN	NAME AND/ OR MODEL	TOP/ RIG	BOAT TYPE	-HULL- MTL TP	----ENGINE--- TP # HP MFG	BEAM FT IN	WGT LBS	DRAFT FT IN	RETAIL LOW	RETAIL HIGH
					1982 BOATS					
31 11	MARINER 32	KTH	SA/CR	FBG KL IB	D	9 9	12400	3 8	31300	34800
35 10	MARINER 36	CUT	SA/CR	FBG KL IB	D	11	21000	5	53600	58900
35 10	MARINER 36	KTH	SA/CR	FBG KL IB	D	11	21000	5	53600	58900
36	MARINER 36	MY		FBG DS IB	T120D	12 5			62700	68900
40 4	MARINER 40	KTH	SA/CR	FBG KL IB	D	11 5	26500	5 8	73300	80500
47 11	MARINER 48	KTH	SA/CR	FBG KL IB	D	13 6	36000	6 5	113500	124500
50	MARINER 50	CUT	MS	FBG KL IB	D	15	36000	4 6	122000	134500
					1980 BOATS					
31 11	MARINER 32	KTH	SA/CR	FBG KL IB	D	9 9	12400	3 8	48200	31300
35 10	MARINER 36	CUT	SA/CR	FBG KL IB	D	11	21000	5	48200	52900
35 10	MARINER 36	KTH	SA/CR	FBG KL IB	D	11	21000	5	48200	52900
36	MARINER 36	MY		FBG DS IB	T120D	12 5			58100	63900
40 4	MARINER 40	KTH	SA/CR	FBG KL IB	D	11 5	26500	5 8	65800	72400
41 8	MARINER 42	CUT	SA/CR	FBG KL IB	D	12 10	28500	5 6	71500	78600
47 11	MARINER 48	KTH	SA/CR	FBG KL IB	D	13 6	36000	6 5	102000	112000
50	MARINER 50	CUT	SA/CR	FBG KL IB	D	15	36000	4 6	112000	123000
					1979 BOATS					
31 10	MARINER 32	KTH	SA/CR	FBG KL IB	50D PERK	9 9	12400	3 8	27100	30100
35 10	MARINER 36	CUT	SA/CR	FBG KL IB	40D PISC	11	21000	5	46500	51100
35 10	MARINER 36	KTH	SA/CR	FBG KL IB	50D PERK	11	21000	5	46400	51000
36	MARINER 36	MY		FBG IB	130D PERK	12 4	16200	2 10	54300	59700
36	MARINER 36	MY		FBG IB	T130D PERK	12 4	16200	2 10	56700	62300
40 4	MARINER 40	KTH	SA/CR	FBG KL IB	50D PERK	11 5	26500	5 8	62900	69200
41 8	MARINER 42	CUT	SA/CR	FBG KL IB	50D PERK	12 10	28500	5 6	68300	75000
47 11	MARINER 48	KTH	SA/CR	FBG KL IB	75D PERK	13 6	36000	6 5	97600	107500
50	MARINER 50	SLP	MS	FBG KL IB	185D PERK	15	40000	4 6	111000	122000
50	MARINER 50	SLP	MS	FBG KL IB	T185D PERK	15	40000	4 6	113500	124500

THE MARINER YACHT CO INC
E ROCHESTER NH 03867   COAST GUARD MFG ID- MYN See inside cover to adjust price for area

LOA FT IN	NAME AND/ OR MODEL	TOP/ RIG	BOAT TYPE	-HULL- MTL TP	----ENGINE--- TP # HP MFG	BEAM FT IN	WGT LBS	DRAFT FT IN	RETAIL LOW	RETAIL HIGH
					1983 BOATS					
28 2	MARINER 28	SLP	SA/CR	FBG KL IB	12D UNIV	9 5	7450	4 5	17400	19800
28 2	MARINER 28 SHOAL	SLP	SA/CR	FBG KL IB	12D UNIV	9 5	7450	3 6	18200	20200
36	MARINER 36	SLP	SA/CR	FBG KL IB	36D UNIV	11	17000	5	43000	47800
36	MARINER 36	KTH	SA/CR	FBG KL IB	50D UNIV	11 6	17250	5	43700	48600
38	MARINER 38 PH	SLP	SA/CR	FBG KL IB	50D UNIV	11 6	18000	5	46700	51300
38	MARINER 38 PH	KTH	SA/CR	FBG KL IB	50D UNIV	11 6	18250	5	48900	53700
38	MARINER 38 TRNK CBN	SLP	SA/CR	FBG KL IB	50D UNIV	11 6	18000	5	50200	55200
38 9	MARINER 39	SLP	SAIL	FBG KL IB	50D UNIV	11 8	18000	5 6	49900	54900
					1982 BOATS					
28 2	MARINER 28	SLP	SA/CR	FBG KL IB	12D UNIV	9 5	7450	4 5	16600	18700
28 2	MARINER 28 SHOAL	SLP	SA/CR	FBG KL IB	12D UNIV	9 5	7450	3 6	16600	18900
36	MARINER 36	SLP	SA/CR	FBG KL IB	32D UNIV	11 6	17000	5	40500	44900
36	MARINER 36	KTH	SA/CR	FBG KL IB	32D UNIV	11 6	17250	5	41000	45500
37 8	MARINER 38 PH	SLP	SA/CR	FBG KL IB	32D UNIV	11 7	18000	5	44700	49700
37 8	MARINER 38 PH	KTH	SA/CR	FBG KL IB	32D UNIV	11 7	18250	5	45700	50200
37 8	MARINER 38 TRNK CBN	SLP	SA/CR	FBG KL IB	32D UNIV	11 7	18000	5	44100	49000
37 8	MARINER 38 TRNK CBN	KTH	SA/CR	FBG KL IB	32D UNIV	11 7	18250	5	44700	49600
38 9	MARINER 39	KTH	SA/CR	FBG KL IB	32D UNIV	11 8	18250	5 6	47400	52100
38 9	MARINER 39	SLP	SAIL	FBG KL IB	32D UNIV	11 8	18000	5 6	47000	51600
47	MARINER 47	KTH	SA/CR	FBG KL IB	75D PERK	13 10	32000	6	90600	99500
					1981 BOATS					
28 2	MARINER 28	SLP	SA/CR	FBG KL IB	12D UNIV	9 5	7450	4 5	15500	17600
28 2	MARINER 28 SHOAL	SLP	SA/CR	FBG KL IB	12D UNIV	9 5	7450	3 6	15600	17700
36	MARINER 36	SLP	SA/CR	FBG KL IB	36D UNIV	11 6	17000	5	38100	42300
36	MARINER 36	KTH	SA/CR	FBG KL IB	36D UNIV	11 6	17250	5	38600	42900
38	MARINER 38 PH	SLP	SA/CR	FBG KL IB	50D PERK	11 6	18000	5	44100	49000
38	MARINER 38 PH	KTH	SA/CR	FBG KL IB	50D PERK	11 6	18250	5	42700	47500
38	MARINER 38 TRNK CBN	SLP	SA/CR	FBG KL IB	50D PERK	11 6	18000	5	40400	44900
38 9	MARINER 39	SLP	SAIL	FBG KL IB	50D PERK	11 8	18000	5 6	43600	48500
42	MARINER COMMERCIAL	FSH		FBG IB	174	14			**	**
47	MARINER 47	KTH	SA/CR	FBG KL IB	75D WEST	13 10	32000	6	85700	94200
					1980 BOATS					
28 2	MARINER 28	SLP	SA/CR	FBG KL IB	12D UNIV	9 5	7450	4 5	14800	16800
28 2	MARINER 28 SHOAL	SLP	SA/CR	FBG KL IB	12D UNIV	9 5	7450	3 6	14900	16900
36	MARINER 36	SLP	SA/CR	FBG KL IB	36D UNIV	11 6	17000	5	36400	40400
36	MARINER 36	KTH	SA/CR	FBG KL IB	36D UNIV	11 6	17250	5	36800	40900
38	MARINER 38 PH	SLP	SA/CR	FBG KL IB	36D PERK	11 6	18000	5	40200	44700
38	MARINER 38 PH	KTH	SA/CR	FBG KL IB	50D PERK	11 6	18250	5	40800	45300
38	MARINER 38 TRNK CBN	SLP	SA/CR	FBG KL IB	50D PERK	11 6	18000	5	40400	44900
38 9	MARINER 39	SLP	SAIL	FBG KL IB	50D PERK	11 8	18000	5 6	41700	46300
47	MARINER 47	KTH	SA/CR	FBG KL IB	75 WEST	13 10	32000	6	80700	88700
					1979 BOATS					
28 2	MARINER 28	SLP	SA/CR	FBG KL IB	15D YAN	9 5	7450	4 5	14200	16400
28 2	MARINER 28 SHOAL	SLP	SA/CR	FBG KL IB	15D YAN	9 5	7450	3 6	14400	16400
36	MARINER 36	SLP	SA/CR	FBG KL IB	33D YAN	11 6	16000	5	33200	36900
36	MARINER 36	KTH	SA/CR	FBG KL IB	50D PERK	11 6	16000	5	33100	36800
					1978 BOATS					
28 2	MARINER 28	SLP	SA/CR	FBG KL IB	12D YAN	9 5	7850	4 5	14500	16500

MARINER YACHTS
NEWPORT BEACH CA 92663   See inside cover to adjust price for area

LOA FT IN	NAME AND/ OR MODEL	TOP/ RIG	BOAT TYPE	-HULL- MTL TP	----ENGINE--- TP # HP MFG	BEAM FT IN	WGT LBS	DRAFT FT IN	RETAIL LOW	RETAIL HIGH
					1971 BOATS					
30 9	MARINER 31	KTH	SA/CR	FBG KL IB	D	9 9		3 9	20200	22500
32	CENTURION 32	SLP	SA/RC	FBG KL IB	D	9 10		5 10	16200	18400
32	MARINER 32	KTH	SA/CR	FBG KL IB	D	9 9		3 9	24500	27200
33	BIANCA 33	KTH	MS	FBG KL IB	D	11		4 5	26700	29600
40 4	MARINER 40	KTH	SA/CR	FBG KL IB	D	11 5		6	46700	51300

MARINUS BOATS INC
BAJA   COAST GUARD MFG ID- MAB

Call 1-800-327-6929 for BUC Personalized Evaluation Service
Or, for 1970 to 1979 boats, sign onto www.BUCValuPro.com

MARITIME INDUSTRIES INC
COAST GUARD MFG ID- MIE

Call 1-800-327-6929 for BUC Personalized Evaluation Service
Or, for 1970 to 1985 boats, sign onto www.BUCValuPro.com

MARITIME MFGS INC
CONCORDE   See inside cover to adjust price for area
BALTIMORE MD 21222   COAST GUARD MFG ID- MMV
       FOR OLDER MODELS SEE OWENS YACHT DIVISION   NCORDES

LOA FT IN	NAME AND/ OR MODEL	TOP/ RIG	BOAT TYPE	-HULL- MTL TP	----ENGINE--- TP # HP MFG	BEAM FT IN	WGT LBS	DRAFT FT IN	RETAIL LOW	RETAIL HIGH
					1979 BOATS					
30	SPORT FISHERMAN	FB	SF	FBG DV IB	T225	11 2	10000	2 6	19700	21900
31	SEDAN CRUISER		SDN	FBG DV IB	T225	12	12000	2 6	24500	27300
33 4	SPORT FISHERMAN	FB	SF	FBG DV IB	T250	12	15000	2 6	29600	32900
35	SEDAN CRUISER	FB	SDN	FBG DV IB	T250	12 2	17300	3	37000	41100
41	MOTOR YACHT	FB	MY	FBG DV IB	T330	13 5	23500	3 2	63300	69500
41	SEDAN CRUISER		SDN	FBG DV IB	T330	13 5	23500	3 2	62700	68900
46 11	MOTOR YACHT		MY	FBG DV IB	T350D GM	16	44000	4 1	105000	115500
54	MOTOR YACHT		MY	FBG DV IB	T350D GM	16	60000	4 1	163500	179500
54	YACHT FISHERMAN	FB	YTFS	FBG DV IB	T350D GM	16	50000	4 1	136500	150000
					1978 BOATS					
30	SPORT FISHERMAN	FB	SF	FBG DV IB	T220-T225	11 2	10000	2 6	19100	21200
31	SEDAN CRUISER	HT	SDN	FBG DV IB	T220-T270	12	12000	2 6	23500	27100

```
LOA  NAME AND/           TOP/ BOAT -HULL- ----ENGINE--- BEAM  WGT  DRAFT RETAIL RETAIL
FT IN OR MODEL           RIG  TYPE MTL TP TP # HP  MFG  FT IN LBS  FT IN  LOW   HIGH
-------------------- 1978 BOATS ----------------------------------------------------
31   SEDAN CRUISER       HT   SDN  FBG DV IB T   D CRUS 12  13300  2  6    **     **
31   SEDAN CRUISER       FB   SDN  FBG DV IB T220-T270 12  12000  2  6  23500  27100
31   SEDAN CRUISER       FB   SDN  FBG DV IB T   D      12  13300  2  6    **     **
33 4 SPORT FISHERMAN     FB   SF   FBG DV IB T250-T350 12  15000  2  6  28400  33100
33 4 SPORT FISHERMAN     FB   SF   FBG DV IB T   D      12  17000  2  6    **     **
35   SEDAN CRUISER       FB   SDN  FBG DV IB T250  CHRY 12  2 17300 3    35400  39300
     IB T270  CRUS 35800 39800, IB T330  CHRY 36600 40700, IB T350  CRUS 37100 41300
     IB T     D     **    **

41   DOUBLE CABIN MY     FB   DCMY FBG DV IB T330  CHRY 13  5 23500 3  2 60700  66700
     IB T350  CRUS 61800 67900, IB T257D GM   73500 80800, IB T325D GM   76800 84400

46 11 MOTOR YACHT        HT   MY   FBG DV IB T425D GM   16  44000  4  1 107500 118500
46 11 MOTOR YACHT        FB   MY   FBG DV IB T425D GM   16  44000  4  1 107000 117500
54    MOTOR YACHT        HT   MY   FBG DV IB T425D GM   16  60000  4  1 171500 188500
54    MOTOR YACHT        FB   MY   FBG DV IB T425D GM   16  60000  4  1 168000 184500
54    YACHT FISHERMAN    FB   YTFS FBG DV IB T425D GM   16  50000  4  1 143000 157000
-------------------- 1977 BOATS ----------------------------------------------------
30    FISHERMAN          FB   SF   FBG DV IB T225    11  2  9500   2  6  18000  20000
31    SEDAN              FB   SDN  FBG DV IB T225    12    11300  2  6  22300  24800
33 4  FISHERMAN          FB   SF   FBG DV IB T225    12    15000  2  6  26900  29900
35    SEDAN              FB   SDN  FBG DV IB T250    12  2 17300 3    34000  37800
41    DOUBLE CABIN       FB   DCMY FBG DV IB T330    13  5 23500 3  2 57100  62800
46 11 MOTOR YACHT        FB   MY   FBG DV IB T400D   16    44000  4  1 100500 110500
54    MOTOR YACHT        FB   MY   FBG DV IB T400D   16    60000    4  1 157500 173000
54    YACHT FISHERMAN    FB   YTFS FBG DV IB T400D   16    50000  4  1 133000 146000
-------------------- 1976 BOATS ----------------------------------------------------
30    SPORT CRUISER      FB   SPTCR FBG DV IB T225-T233 11  2 10000  2  6  17200  19700
31    SEDAN              HT   SDN  FBG DV IB T225-T255 12    12000  2  6  21700  24700
31    SEDAN              FB   SDN  FBG DV IB T225-T255 12    12000  2  6  21700  24700
33 4  SPORT FISHERMAN    FB   SF   FBG DV IB T250-T350 12    15000  2  6  26100  30400
33 4  SPORT FISHERMAN    FB   SF   FBG DV IB T210D CAT 12    15000  2  6  34200  38000
35    SEDAN              FB   SDN  FBG DV IB T250  CHRY 12  2 17300 3    32600  36200
      IB T255  MRCR 32700 36300, IB T330  CHRY 33700 37500, IB T350  MRCR 34100 37900
      IB T    D     **    **

41    DOUBLE CABIN FB    FB   DC   FBG DV IB T330  CHRY 13  5 24000  3  2 56300  61900
      IB T350  MRCR 56900 62600, IB T240D CUM  61500 67600, IB T265D GM   62800 69000

46 11 DOUBLE CABIN MY    HT   MY   FBG DV IB T400D CUM  16    44000  4  1 98700 108500
46 11 DOUBLE CABIN MY    HT   MY   FBG DV IB T435D GM   16    44000  4  1 101500 111500
46 11 DOUBLE CABIN MY    FB   MY   FBG DV IB T400D CUM  16    44000  4  1 97900 107500
46 11 DOUBLE CABIN MY    FB   MY   FBG DV IB T435D GM   16    44000  4  1 100500 110500
54    MOTOR YACHT        HT   MY   FBG DV IB T400D CUM  16    60000  4  1 154500 169500
54    MOTOR YACHT        HT   MY   FBG DV IB T435D GM   16    60000  4  1 158500 174500
54    MOTOR YACHT        FB   MY   FBG DV IB T400D CUM  16    60000  4  1 151000 166000
54    MOTOR YACHT        FB   MY   FBG DV IB T435D GM   16    60000  4  1 155500 171000
54    YACHT FISHERMAN    FB   YTFS FBG DV IB T400D CUM  16    60000  4  1 150500 165500
54    YACHT FISHERMAN    FB   YTFS FBG DV IB T435D GM   16    60000  4  1 154500 170000
-------------------- 1975 BOATS ----------------------------------------------------
30    CONCORDE           SPTCR FBG SV IB T233      11  2     2  6  15100  17100
31    CONCORDE           EXP   FBG SV IB T233      12        2  6  19100  21200
31    CONCORDE           SDN   FBG SV IB T233      12        2  6  19800  21000
33 4  CONCORDE           SF    FBG SV IB T255      12        2  6  21400  23800
35    CONCORDE           EXP   FBG SV IB T255      12  2     3    30200  33600
35    CONCORDE           SDN   FBG SV IB T255      12  2     3    29000  32200
41    CONCORDE           DCMY  FBG SV IB T350      13  5     3  2 54200  59500
46 9  CONCORDE           SF    FBG SV IB T400D     15  9     3  2 95300 105000
46 11 CONCORDE           MY    FBG SV IB T400D     16        4  1 93700 103000
54    CONCORDE           MY    FBG SV IB T400D     16        4  1 119000 130500
54    CONCORDE           YTFS  FBG SV IB T400D     16        4  1 120000 132000
-------------------- 1974 BOATS ----------------------------------------------------
27    CONCORDE           EXP   FBG   IB T225-T255 10  6  8100  2  4 11000  12700
27    CONCORDE           HT EXP FBG  IB T225-T255 10  6  8100  2  4 11000  12700
27    CONCORDE           FB SF  FBG  IB T225-T255 10  6  8200  2  4 11100  12800
27    CONCORDE XL        FBG        IB T225-T255 10  6  7400  2  4 10600  11800
27    CONCORDE XL HT     FBG        IB T225-T255 10  6  7400  2  4 10800  12500
30    CONCORDE           FB SF  FBG  IB T225-T255 11  2  8200  2  4 12800  14900
30    CONCORDE           FB SF  FBG  IB T185D PERK 11 2  8400  2  6 17500  19900
31    CONCORDE           HT EXP FBG  IB T225-T255 12    11000  2  6 18200  20600
31    CONCORDE           HT EXP FBG  IBT185D-225D 12    13000  2  6 26500  30500
31    CONCORDE           FB EXP FBG  IB T225-T255 12    11000  2  6 18200  20600
31    CONCORDE           FB EXP FBG  IBT185D-225D 12    13000  2  6 26500  30500
31    CONCORDE           HT SDN FBG  IB T225-T255 12    11300  2  6 19800  22500
31    CONCORDE           HT SDN FBG  IBT185D-225D 12    13300  2  6 29800  34500
31    CONCORDE           FB SDN FBG  IB T225-T255 12    11300  2  6 19800  22500
31    CONCORDE           FB SDN FBG  IBT185D-225D 12    13300  2  6 29800  34500
33 4  CONCORDE           FB SF  FBG  IB T255-T350 12    15000  2  6 24200  28100
33 4  CONCORDE           FB SF  FBG  IBT185D-225D 12    17000  2  6 34800  39900
35    CONCORDE           EXP   FBG   IB T255  MRCR 12  2 17000 3   29000  32200
      IB T350  MRCR 30000 33400, IB T185D PERK 37500 41700, IB T225D CAT  38400 42700

35    CONCORDE           FB SDN FBG  IB T255  MRCR 12  2 17300 3   30200  33500
      IB T350  MRCR 31400 34900, IB T185D PERK 41500 46100, IB T225D CAT  36400 47300

41    CONCORDE           FB DC  FBG  IB T350  MRCR 13  5 23500 3  2 52100  57300
      IB T185D PERK 60500 66400, IB T225D CAT  62000 68100, IB T310D GM   64400 70800

46 9  CONCORDE           FB SF  FBG  IB T310D GM   15  9 41500  4  1 83400  91700
46 9  CONCORDE           FB SF  FBG  IB T350D GM   15  9 41500  4  1 87400  96000
46 9  CONCORDE           FB SF  FBG  IB T435D GM   15  9 41500  4  1 95300 105000
46 11 CONCORDE           MY    FBG   IB T310D GM   16    44000  4  1 83600  91900
46 11 CONCORDE           MY    FBG   IB T350D GM   16    44000  4  1 87500  95100
46 11 CONCORDE           MY    FBG   IB T435D GM   16    44000  4  1 92600 102000
54    CONCORDE           YTFS  FBG   IB T350D GM   16    50000  4  1 115500 127000
54    CONCORDE           YTFS  FBG   IB T435D GM   16    50000  4  1 127500 140000
-------------------- 1973 BOATS ----------------------------------------------------
27    CONCORDE           HT EXP FBG  IB 225      10  6  8100  2  4  9550  10900
27    CONCORDE           FB SF  FBG  IB 225      10  6  8200  2  4  9650  11000
31    CONCORDE           HT EXP FBG  IB T250     12    11000  2  6 17400  19800
31    CONCORDE           FB EXP FBG  IB T250     12    11000  2  6 17400  19800
31    CONCORDE           HT SDN FBG  IB T250     12    11300  2  6 19400  21500
31    CONCORDE           FB SDN FBG  IB T250     12    11300  2  6 19400  21500
33 4  CONCORDE           FB SF  FBG  IB T330     12    15000  2  6 23200  25800
35    CONCORDE           HT EXP FBG  IB T330     12  2 17000 3   28600  31800
35    CONCORDE           FB SDN FBG  IB T330     12  2 17300 3   29900  33300
41    CONCORDE           FB DC  FBG  IB T   D    13  5 23500 3  2 49700  54600
46 9  CONCORDE           FB SF  FBG  IB T   D    15  9 41500  4  1    **     **
46 11 CONCORDE           HT MY  FBG  IB T325D    16    44000  4  1 82600  90800

46 11 CONCORDE           FB MY  FBG  IB T325D    16    44000  4  1 82000  90100
54    CONCORDE           FB YTFS FBG IB T   D    16    50000  4  1    **     **
-------------------- 1972 BOATS ----------------------------------------------------
27                       SF    FBG   IB 215-325  10  6  7100  2  4  8400  10200
27                       SF    FBG   IB T215  MRCR 10  6 8200  2  4 10200  11600
27    XL 27              FBG         IB 215-325  10  6  6300  2  4  7800   9550
27    XL 27              FBG         IB T215-T250 10 6  7400  2  4  9650  11200
30                       SF    FBG   IB T215-T270 11 2  9200  2  4 12100  14300
31                       EXP   FBG   IB T215-T250 12   11000  2  6 16400  19300
31                       EXP   FBG   IB T215-T270 12   13000  2  6 26000  28900
31                       FB EXP FBG  IB T225D CAT 12          2  6 27500  30500
31                       FB SDN FBG  IB T215-T250 12   11300  2  6 18300  20900
31                       SDN   FBG   IB T225D CAT 12   13300  2  6 29500  32700

33 4                     SF    FBG   IB T250-T325 12   15000  2  6 22300  25700
33 4                     SF    FBG   IB T225D CAT 12   17000  2  6 33200  36900
35                       SF    FBG   IB T270  MRCR 12  2 17000 3   29400  29900
      IB T325  MRCR 27500 30500, IB T216D GM   37800 42000, IB T225D CAT  38200 42500

35                       SDNSF FBG   IB T270  MRCR 12  2 17000 3   26900  29900
      IB T325  MRCR 27400 30500, IB T216D GM   37600 41800, IB T225D CAT  38200 42400

39                       SPTCR FBG   IB T325  MRCR 13  4 20000 3  2 38800  43100
      IB T390  MRCR 39700 44100, IB T283D GM   49800 54700, IB T310D GM   50600 55600

41                       FB DC  FBG  IB T325  MRCR 13  5 23500 3  2 48000  52700
41                       FB DC  FBG  IB T225D CAT 13  5 26500 3   57600  63300
41                       FB DC  FBG  IB T310D GM  13  5 26500 3   65900  65800
46 9                     FB SF  FBG  IB T290D GM  15  9 41500  4  1 81800  89900
46 9                     FB SF  FBG  IB T350D GM  15  9 41500  4  1 81800  89900
46 11                    MY    FBG   IB T290D GM  16    44000  4  1 81000  89000
46 11                    MY    FBG   IB T350D GM  16    44000  4  1 81000  89000
46 11                    FB MY  FBG  IB T290D GM  16          4  1 77200  84800
46 11                    FB MY  FBG  IB T350D GM  16          4  1 81400  89500
-------------------- 1971 BOATS ----------------------------------------------------
27                       EXP   FBG   IB 215-325  10  6       2  4 14400  16400
27                       EXP   FBG   IB 225D CAT 10  6  8500  2  4 14400  16400
27                       EXP   FBG   IB T215-T250 10 6  8100  2  4 11300  13100
27                       HT EXP FBG  IB 215-325  10  6       2  4 10900  12600
27                       HT EXP FBG  IB 225D CAT 10  6       2  4 10800  12300
27                       HT EXP FBG  IB T215-T250 10 6       2  4  9750  11300
27                       SF    FBG   IB 215-325  10  6  7100  2  4  8050   9800
27                       SF    FBG   IB 225D CAT 10  6  8500  2  4 14600  16500
27                       SF    FBG   IB T215-T250 10 6  8200  2  4  9800  11400
```

MARITIME MFGS INC — CONTINUED

LOA FT IN	NAME AND/ OR MODEL	TOP/ RIG	BOAT TYPE	HULL MTL	HULL TP	ENGINE TP	#	HP	MFG	BEAM FT IN	WGT LBS	DRAFT FT IN	RETAIL LOW	RETAIL HIGH
1971 BOATS														
30		SF	FBG	IB		225D		CAT		11 2	10700	2 6	19200	21400
30		SF	FBG	IB		T215-T270				11 2	9200	2 6	11700	13800
31		EXP	FBG	IB		T215-T250				12	11000	2 6	15700	18300
31		EXP	FBG	IB		T225D		CAT		12	13000	2 6	25400	28200
31		FB EXP	FBG	IB		T215-T250				12		2 6	15800	18400
31		FB EXP	FBG	IB		T225D		CAT		12		2 6	26800	29800
31		SDN	FBG	IB		T215-T250				12	11300	2 6	17200	20200
31		SDN	FBG	IB		T225D		CAT		12	13300	2 6	28800	32000
31		FB SDN	FBG	IB		T215-T250				12		2 6	15600	18200
31		FB SDN	FBG	IB		T225D		CAT		12		2 6	27200	30200
33 4		SF	FBG	IB		T250-T325				12	15000	2 6	21500	24700
33 4		SF	FBG	IB		T225D		CAT		12	17000	2 6	32400	36000
35		EXP	FBG	IB		T270		MRCR		12 2	17000	3	25900	28800

IB T325 MRCR 26400 29400, IB T216D GM 36900 41000, IB T225D CAT 37300 41500

LOA FT IN	NAME	TOP/RIG	BOAT	HULL		ENGINE	#	HP	MFG	BEAM	WGT	DRAFT	LOW	HIGH
35		SDNSF	FBG	IB		T270		MRCR		12 2	17000	3	25900	28700

IB T325 MRCR 26400 29300, IB T216D GM 36700 40800, IB T225D CAT 37300 41400

| 39 | | FB DC | FBG | IB | | T325 | | MRCR | | 13 4 | 22000 | 3 2 | 40300 | 44800 |

IB T390 MRCR 41200 45700, IB T216D GM 49600 54500, IB T283D GM 51100 56200
IB T310D GM 51900 57000

| 39 | | SPTCR | FBG | IB | | T325 | | MRCR | | 13 4 | 20000 | 3 2 | 37500 | 41600 |

IB T390 MRCR 38400 42600, IB T216D GM 46800 51400, IB T283D GM 48100 52900
IB T310D GM 48900 53700

46 9		FB SF	FBG	IB		T390		MRCR		15 9	41500	4 1	72400	79600
46 9		FB SF	FBG	IB		T290D		GM		15 9	41500	4 1	73600	80800
46 9		FB SF	FBG	IB		T350D		GM		15 9	41500	4 1	79000	86900
46 11		MY	FBG	IB		T390		MRCR		16		4 1	66300	72800
46 11		MY	FBG	IB		T290D		GM		16	44000	4 1	74200	81500
46 11		MY	FBG	IB		T350D		GM		16	44000	4 1	78200	86000
46 11		FB MY	FBG	IB		T390		MRCR		16		4 1	66500	73100
1970 BOATS														
27 1		EXP	FBG	IB		215-250				10 5	6100	2 4	7100	8350
27 1		EXP	FBG	IB		T215-T250				10 5	6100	2 4	8100	9550
27 1		SF	FBG	IB		215-250				10 5	7080	2 2	7750	9100
27 1		SF	FBG	IB		T215-T250				10 5	7080	2 2	8700	10200
27 1 DAY BOAT			FBG	IB		215-325				10 5	6200	2 4	7200	8800
31		EXP	FBG	IB		T215-T250				12	9500	2 6	14700	17100
31		EXP	FBG	IB		T185D		CUM		12	9500	2 6	21100	23500
31		SDN	FBG	IB		T215-T325				12	9900	2 6	16200	20000
31		SDN	FBG	IB		T185D		CUM		12	9900	2 6	23500	26100
33 4		SF	FBG	IB		T250-T325				12	16000	2 6	21100	24300
35		EXP	FBG	IB		T325		MRCR		12 3	13800	2 11	26300	26100
35		EXP	FBG	IB		T185D		CUM		12 3		2 11	35000	38900
35		EXP	FBG	IB		T216D		GM		12 3		11	35700	39700
35		SDN	FBG	IB		T325		MRCR		12 3	17400	3	26500	29400
35		SDN	FBG	IB		T185D		CUM		12 6		3	35100	39000
35		SDN	FBG	IB		T216D		GM		12 6		3	35900	39900
40		DC	FBG	IB		T325		MRCR		13 6	21000	3 2	38900	43300

IB T390 MRCR 39800 44200, IB T185D CUM 51000 56100, IB T216D GM 51800 56900
IB T283D GM 53300 58600, IB T300D CUM 53500 58800

| 40 | | FB SDN | FBG | IB | | T325 | | MRCR | | 13 6 | 20500 | 3 2 | 38000 | 42200 |

IB T390 MRCR 38800 43100, IB T185D CUM 49900 54800, IB T216D GM 50600 55700
IB T283D GM 52100 57300, IB T300D CUM 52300 57500

| 40 | | SPTCR | FBG | IB | | T325 | | MRCR | | 13 6 | 20500 | 3 2 | 38400 | 42700 |

IB T390 MRCR 39300 43700, IB T185D CUM 50000 54900, IB T216D GM 50700 55700
IB T283D GM 52200 57400, IB T300D CUM 52400 57600

| 46 9 | | SF | FBG | IB | | T350D | | GM | | 16 | 33000 | 4 1 | 66100 | 72600 |
| 46 9 | | SF | FBG | IB | | T380D | | GM | | 16 | 33000 | 4 1 | 68800 | 75600 |

MARITIME PRODUCTS INC
ALLIANCE OH 44601   See inside cover to adjust price for area

LOA FT IN	NAME AND/ OR MODEL	TOP/ RIG	BOAT TYPE	HULL MTL	HULL TP	ENGINE TP	HP	MFG	BEAM FT IN	WGT LBS	DRAFT FT IN	RETAIL LOW	RETAIL HIGH
1968 BOATS													
17 4		OP	W/T	AL	TR	OB			6 9	950	1 5	2400	2800
17 4	NOVA-SCOTIA	OP	W/T	AL	TR	OB	120-155		6 9	1570	1 5	3300	3900
19 2	LANCER 19			AL		IO	120-160		7 4	1990	2 3	4350	5100
21 1	NEW-BRUNSWICK	CR		AL	TR	OB			7 4	1650	1 9	4600	5300
21 1	NEW-BRUNSWICK	CR		AL	TR	IO	120-185		7 4	2360	1 9	6000	7200
21 1	NEW-BRUNSWICK	OFF		AL	TR	OB			7 4	1590	1 9	4450	5150
21 1	NEW-BRUNSWICK	OFF		AL	TR	IO	120-185		7 4	2310	1 9	5950	7100
21 1	NEW-BRUNSWICK OS	W/T		AL	TR	OB			7 4	1590	1 9	4450	5150
21 1	NEW-BRUNSWICK OS	W/T		AL	TR	IO	120-185		7 4	2340	1 9	6050	7250
1967 BOATS													
17 2		UTL		AL		OB			6 9	950		2300	2700
17 2	NOVA-SCOTIA W/T	RNBT		AL	TR	OB			6 9	950		2300	2700
17 2	NOVA-SCOTIA W/T	RNBT		AL	TR	IO	110-120		6 9		1 3	3500	4050
17 2	SANDPIPER			AL		OB			6 9	950		2400	2800
18 3	PRINCE-EDWARD	RNBT		AL	DV	OB			6 9	1000	1 3	2600	3050
18 3	PRINCE-EDWARD	RNBT		AL	DV	IO	110-200		6 9		1 3	3750	4500
21 1		UTL		AL		OB			7 4	1400		3400	3950
21 1	CONTINENTAL	EXP		AL	TR	IO	120-160		7 4		1 3	6300	7250
21 1	NEW-BRUNSWICK	CR		AL	TR	IO	110-160		7 4		1 3	6300	7300
21 1	NEW-BRUNSWICK	OFF		AL	TR	IO	110-160		7 4		1 3	6250	7250
21 1	NEW-BRUNSWICK OS	W/T		AL	TR	IO	110-160		7 4		1 3	6400	7350
1966 BOATS													
17 2	NOVA-SCOTIA STANDARD	RNBT		AL	TR	OB			6 8	850		2100	2500
17 2	NOVA-SCOTIA STANDARD	RNBT		AL	TR	IO	60-120		6 8			3500	4100
17 2	NOVA-SCOTIA W/T	RNBT		AL	TR	OB			6 8	850		2300	2700
17 2	NOVA-SCOTIA W/T	RNBT		AL	TR	IO	60-120		6 8			3650	4250
18 3	PRINCE-EDWARD	RNBT		AL	DV	OB			6 8	700		1900	2250
18 3	PRINCE-EDWARD	RNBT		AL	DV	IO	110-150		6 8			3850	4500
21 1	NEW-BRUNSWICK	CR		AL	TR	IO	110-150		7 6			6600	7600
21 1	NEW-BRUNSWICK	OFF		AL	TR	IO	110-150		7 6			6500	7500
1965 BOATS													
17 2		W/T		AL		OB						2400	2800
17 2		W/T		AL		OB	110-120					3600	4150
17 2	STANDARD			AL		OB						2400	2800
20 6		CR		AL		OB						4550	5250
20 6		CR		AL		IO	110-150					6550	7550
1964 BOATS													
17 4		RNBT		AL		OB						2300	2700

MARITIMER LTD
COAST GUARD MFG ID- MTV
FORMERLY RAJ YACHT INC

Call 1-800-327-6929 for BUC Personalized Evaluation Service
Or, for 1978 to 1980 boats, sign onto www.BUCValuPro.com

MARK LINDSAY BOAT BUILDERS
EAST BOSTON MA 02128-2800   See inside cover to adjust price for area
FORMERLY MARK LINDSAY BOATBUILDERS LTD

For more recent years, see the BUC Used Boat Price Guide, Volume 1 or Volume 2

LOA FT IN	NAME AND/ OR MODEL	TOP/ RIG	BOAT TYPE	HULL MTL	HULL TP	ENGINE TP	#	HP	MFG	BEAM FT IN	WGT LBS	DRAFT FT IN	RETAIL LOW	RETAIL HIGH
1983 BOATS														
19 10	FLYING-DUTCHMAN	SLP	SA/OD	CB						5 8	365	8	2150	2500
20	TORNADO	SLP	SA/OD	CT						10	300	8	1850	2250

MARK MARINE INC
COAST GUARD MFG ID- MXK

Call 1-800-327-6929 for BUC Personalized Evaluation Service
Or, for 1980 to 1982 boats, sign onto www.BUCValuPro.com

MARK O'CUSTOM BOATS
COLOGNE NJ 08213   COAST GUARD MFG ID- MKU See inside cover to adjust price for area

For more recent years, see the BUC Used Boat Price Guide, Volume 1 or Volume 2

LOA FT IN	NAME AND/ OR MODEL	TOP/ RIG	BOAT TYPE	HULL MTL	HULL TP	ENGINE TP	#	HP	MFG	BEAM FT IN	WGT LBS	DRAFT FT IN	RETAIL LOW	RETAIL HIGH
1982 BOATS														
24	ATLANTIC-CITY	CAT	SA/CR	FBG	KC	IB		10D	BMW	11	8000	2	17400	19700
1978 BOATS														
18 7	MARK-O 19	OP	CTRCN	FBG	SV	IO				6 10	1100	9	**	**

MARK TWAIN MARINE IND INC

BOCA RATON FL 33487-160 COAST GUARD MFG ID- MTM See inside cover to adjust price for area

For more recent years, see the BUC Used Boat Price Guide, Volume 1 or Volume 2

LOA FT	LOA IN	NAME AND/ OR MODEL	TOP/ RIG	BOAT TYPE	-HULL- MTL	-HULL- TP	ENGINE TP	ENGINE # HP	ENGINE MFG	BEAM FT	BEAM IN	WGT LBS	DRAFT FT	DRAFT IN	RETAIL LOW	RETAIL HIGH
		1983 BOATS														
17	1	169BR	OP	RNBT	FBG	DV	OB			7	2	1650			4150	4800
17	1	169BR	OP	RNBT	FBG	DV	SE	115	OMC	7	2	2050			4750	5450
17	1	169BR	OP	RNBT	FBG	DV	IO	120-188		7	2	2250			2050	2500
17	1	169S	OP	RNBT	FBG	DV	OB			7	2	1600			4050	4700
17	1	169S	OP	RNBT	FBG	DV	SE	115	OMC	7	2	2050			4850	5550
17	1	169S	OP	RNBT	FBG	DV	IO	120-188		7	2	2350			2150	2550
17	3	175BR	OP	RNBT	FBG	DV	OB			7		1400			3650	4250
17	3	175BR	OP	RNBT	FBG	DV	IO	120-230		7		2100			1950	2450
18	8	186BR	OP	RNBT	FBG	DV	OB			7	10	1850			4650	5350
18	8	186BR	OP	RNBT	FBG	DV	IO	120-230		7	10	2500			2500	3050
18	8	186BR	OP	RNBT	FBG	DV	IO	260		7	10	2500			2700	3150
18	8	186S	OP	RNBT	FBG	DV	OB			7	10	1800			4550	5250
18	8	186S	OP	RNBT	FBG	DV	IO	120-230		7	10	2600			2600	3100
18	8	186S	OP	RNBT	FBG	DV	IO	260		7	10	2600			2750	3200
18	8	190XL	OP	CUD	FBG	DV	IO	140-260		7	10	2800			2800	3450
19	9	169BR	OP	RNBT	FBG	DV	IO	120	MRCR	7	2	2250			2400	2800
21		210SD	OP	CUD	FBG	DV	IO	205	OMC	7	10	3650			4100	4800
21		210SF	OP	CUD	FBG	DV	OB			7	10	2650			7400	8500
21		210SF	OP	CUD	FBG	DV	IO	140-260		7	10	3500			3950	4800
21		210XL	OP	CUD	FBG	DV	IO	140-260		7	10	3700			4100	5050
21		ESCAPE 210	OP	OVNTR	FBG	DV	IO	170-260		8		4300			4700	5650
24	1	240XL	OP	OVNTR	FBG	DV	IO	198-260		8		4100			5350	6400
25	1	COSTA-BRAVA 250	OP	OVNTR	FBG	DV	IO	260		8		5150			6900	7900
25	1	COSTA-BRAVA 250	OP	OVNTR	FBG	DV	IO	T140-T200		8		5150			7200	8600
		1982 BOATS														
16		16V		RNBT	FBG	DV	IO	140		7	2				1750	2050
16	3	162T		RNBT	FBG	TR	IO	120		6	9				1700	2050
17	1	169BR	OP	RNBT	FBG	DV	OB			7	4	1650			4050	4700
17	1	169BR	OP	RNBT	FBG	DV	IO	120-185		7	4	2250			2050	2450
17	1	169S	OP	RNBT	FBG	DV	OB			7	4	1600			3950	4600
17	1	169S	OP	RNBT	FBG	DV	IO	120-185		7	4	2350			2100	2500
17	3	175BR	OP	RNBT	FBG	DV	OB			7		1400			3600	4200
17	3	175BR	OP	RNBT	FBG	DV	IO	120-230		7		2100			1950	2400
18	8	186BR	OP	RNBT	FBG	DV	OB			7	10	1850			4550	5250
18	8	186BR	OP	RNBT	FBG	DV	IO	120-230		7	10	2500			2450	3000
18	8	186BR	OP	RNBT	FBG	DV	IO	260		7	10	2500			2650	3100
18	8	186S	OP	RNBT	FBG	DV	OB			7	10	1800			4500	5150
18	8	186S	OP	RNBT	FBG	DV	IO	120-230		7	10	2600			2500	3050
18	8	186S	OP	RNBT	FBG	DV	IO	260		7	10	2600			2700	3150
19	8	195BR	OP	RNBT	FBG	DV	OB			7	10	1560			4250	4950
19	8	195BR	OP	RNBT	FBG	DV	IO	140-260		7	10	2700			2700	3350
21		210SD	OP	CUD	FBG	DV	IO	205	OMC	7	11	3650			4050	4700
21		210SF	OP	CUD	FBG	DV	OB			7	11	2650			7250	8350
21		210SF	OP	CUD	FBG	DV	IO	140-260		7	11	3500			3900	4750
21		210XL	OP	CUD	FBG	DV	IO	140-260		7	11	3700			4050	4950
21		ESCAPE 210	HT	OVNTR	FBG	DV	IO	200-260		7	11	4300			4600	5500
24	1	240XL	OP	OVNTR	FBG	DV	IO	198-260		8		4100			5250	6250
		1981 BOATS														
16		160VBR		RNBT	FBG	DV	OB			7	2	1250			3200	3700
16		16V		RNBT	FBG	DV	IO	140		7	2				1700	2050
17	1	170VBR		RNBT	FBG	DV	OB			7		1250			3250	3750
17	3	175V		RNBT	FBG	DV	IO	165		7	2				2000	2400
17	3	175V W/T		RNBT	FBG	DV	IO	165		7	2				2000	2400
19	8	195V		RNBT	FBG	DV	IO	175		7	10				2700	3150
21		210V		CUD	FBG	DV	IO			7	10				**	**
24	1	240V		CUD	FBG	DV	IO	228		8					5150	5900
		1980 BOATS														
16		160V		RNBT	FBG	DV	OB			7	2	1250			3150	3650
16		160V	OP	RNBT	FBG	DV	IO	140		7	2				1700	2000
16		160VBR		RNBT	FBG	DV	OB			7	2	1250			3150	3650
17	1	170VBR		RNBT	FBG	DV	OB			7		1250			3200	3700
17	3	180V	OP	RNBT	FBG	DV	IO	165-190		7	2				2000	2400
17	3	180VBR	OP	RNBT	FBG	DV	IO	165-233		7	2				2000	2500
18		175V	OP	RNBT	FBG	DV	IO	165		7	2				2050	2450
19	8	200V	OP	RNBT	FBG	DV	IO	175-233		7	10				2650	3200
20		195V	OP	RNBT	FBG	DV	IO	198		7	10				2950	3450
20		210V		CR	FBG	DV	IO	198		7	7				3050	3550
21	9	220		CR	FBG	DV	IO	198-260		8					3950	4800
23	10	240V		CUD	FBG	DV	IO	228-260		8					5050	5900
23	10	240V		CUD	FBG	DV	IO	140D		8					6900	7900
		1979 BOATS														
16		160VBR	ST	RNBT	FBG	DV	OB			7	2	1250			3100	3600
16		160VBR	ST	RNBT	FBG	DV	IO	120-170		7	2	2280			1850	2250
16	3	162T	ST	RNBT	FBG	TR	OB			6	9	1250			3100	3600
16	3	162T	ST	RNBT	FBG	TR	IO	120-170		6	9	2010			1700	2050
17	1	170VBR	ST	RNBT	FBG	DV	OB			7		1200			3050	3550
17	2	170T	ST	RNBT	FBG	TR	OB			7	2	1300			3250	3800
17	3	180VBR	ST	RNBT	FBG	DV	IO	140-230		7	2	2450			2050	2550
17	5	180T	ST	RNBT	FBG	TR	IO	140-230		7	2	2400			2150	2650
17	5	180V	ST	RNBT	FBG	DV	IO	140-230		7	2	2400			2000	2500
19	8	200V	ST	RNBT	FBG	DV	IO	185-250		7	10	2770			2650	3200
19	8	200V	ST	RNBT	FBG	DV	IO	260		7	10	2770			2850	3300
19	8	200VBR	ST	RNBT	FBG	DV	IO	185-260		7	10	2770			2700	3400
19	8	200VCC	ST	CUD	FBG	DV	IO	185-260		7	10	3000			2950	3600
21	9	220VCC	ST	CAMPR	FBG	DV	IO	185-260		8		3440			3950	4800
22	1	225	OP	FSH	FBG	DV	OB			7	10	2330			6800	7800
24	1	AQUARIUS 240VCC		CAMPR	FBG	DV	IO	198-260		8		4050			5050	6000
24	1	AQUARIUS 240VCC		CAMPR	FBG	DV	IO	T170	MRCR	8		4050			5650	6450
24	1	CASINO SUPER 240VCC		CR	FBG	DV	IO	198-260		8		4050			5050	6000
24	1	CASINO SUPER 240VCC		CR	FBG	DV	IO	T170	MRCR	8		4050			5650	6450
24	1	PISCES 240VCC		FSH	FBG	DV	IO	198-260		8		4050			5350	6350
24	1	PISCES 240VCC		FSH	FBG	DV	IO	T170	MRCR	8		4050			5950	6850
		1978 BOATS														
16	3	162T DELUXE	ST	RNBT	FBG	TR	IO	120-170		6	9	2000			1700	2050
16	3	162TBR	ST	RNBT	FBG	TR	OB			6	9	1100			2750	3200
17	1	170VBR	ST	RNBT	FBG	DV	OB			7		1150			2900	3350
17	3	180VBR	ST	RNBT	FBG	DV	IO	140-240		7	2	2300			2000	2500
17	5	180T	ST	RNBT	FBG	TR	IO	120-198		7	2	2400			2100	2600
17	5	180T	ST	RNBT	FBG	TR	IO	225-240		7	2	2400			2250	2650
17	5	180V	ST	RNBT	FBG	DV	IO	140-228		7	2	2400			2050	2500
17	5	180V	ST	RNBT	FBG	DV	IO	240	OMC	7	2	2400			2250	2600
19	8	200V	ST	CUD	FBG	DV	IO	165-260		7	10	3000			2950	3650
19	8	200VBR	ST	RNBT	FBG	DV	IO	185-260		7	10	2550			2600	3200
20	1	200T	ST	RNBT	FBG	TR	IO	185-260		8		2850			3100	3800
21	9	220V	ST	CUD	FBG	DV	IO	185-260		8		3440			3950	4850
		1977 BOATS														
16	3	162T	ST	RNBT	FBG	TR	OB			6	9	1190		10	2900	3400
16	3	162T	ST	RNBT	FBG	TR	IO	120-165		6	9	2000	1	2	1750	2100
17		BASSBOAT 175	OP	BASS	FBG	TR	OB			6	2				3450	4050
17	1	170VBR	ST	RNBT	FBG	DV	OB			7		1150		11	2850	3350
17	2	170T	ST	RNBT	FBG	TR	OB			7	2	1300		11	3200	3700
17	3	180V	ST	RNBT	FBG	DV	IO	165-190		7		2300	1	3	2050	2450
17	3	180VBR	ST	RNBT	FBG	DV	IO	140-233		7		2300	1	3	2000	2550
17	5	180T	ST	RNBT	FBG	TR	IO	140-190		7	2	2400	1	3	2150	2550
19	8	200V	ST	RNBT	FBG	DV	IO	188-233		7	10	2800	1	5	2800	3350
19	8	200VBR	ST	RNBT	FBG	DV	IO	188-233		7	10	2850	1	5	2800	3350
20		200T	ST	RNBT	FBG	TR	IO	188-233		8		2850	1	5	3150	3750
20		210V		CR	FBG	DV	IO	188		7	7				3150	3650
21	9	220V	ST	CUD	FBG	DV	IO	188-233		8		3440	1	7	4050	4800
		1976 BOATS														
16	3	162T	ST	RNBT	FBG	TR	OB			6	9	1150			2800	3250
16	3	162T CUSTOM	ST	RNBT	FBG	TR	IO	120-140		6	9	2000			1750	2100
16	3	162T DELUXE	ST	RNBT	FBG	TR	IO	120-140		6	9	2000			1900	2250
17	1	170V BOWRIDER	ST	RNBT	FBG	DV	OB			7		1150			2850	3300
17	2	170T	ST	RNBT	FBG	TR	OB			7	2	1200			2950	3450
17	3	180V	ST	RNBT	FBG	DV	IO	165-190		7	2	2200			2050	2500
17	3	180V BOWRIDER	ST	RNBT	FBG	DV	IO	165-235		7	2	2300			2150	2650
17	3	BASS BOAT DELUXE		BASS	FBG	TR	OB			6	6	875			2300	2650
17	5	180T	ST	RNBT	FBG	TR	IO	140-190		7	2	2400			2200	2600
19	2	CRUIS/AIRE 210V	ST	CUD	FBG	DV	IO	140-235		7	7	3100			3000	3600
19	8	200V	ST	RNBT	FBG	DV	IO	175-235		7	10	2500			2600	3150
19	8	200V BOWRIDER	ST	RNBT	FBG	DV	IO	175-235		7	10	2500			2750	3300
19	8	200V FISHERMAN	OP	FSH	FBG	DV	OB			7	10	1100			2950	3450
20	1	200T	ST	RNBT	FBG	DV	IO	175-235		8		2850			3200	3850
23	7	CRUIS/AIRE 240V	HT	CR	FBG	DV	IO	233		8		3550			4800	5500
		1975 BOATS														
16	3	162T	ST	RNBT	FBG	TR	OB			6	9	1100			2650	3100
16	3	162T	ST	RNBT	FBG	TR	IO	120-165		6	9	2000			1850	2200
17	1	170V	ST	RNBT	FBG	DV	OB			7		1150			2750	3200
17	1	170VBR	ST	RNBT	FBG	DV	OB			7		1150			2900	3400
17	2	170T	ST	RNBT	FBG	TR	OB			7	2	1200			2950	3400
17	3	180V	ST	RNBT	FBG	DV	IO	120-188				2400			2150	2600
17	3	180V	ST	RNBT	FBG	DV	JT	290	OMC			2400			2350	2750
17	3	180VBR	ST	RNBT	FBG	DV	IO	120-188				2400			2350	2750
17	5	180T	ST	RNBT	FBG	TR	IO	120-188		7	2	2400			2300	2700
17	5	180T	ST	RNBT	FBG	TR	JT	290	OMC	7	2	2400			2400	2800

CONTINUED ON NEXT PAGE

LOA FT IN	NAME AND/ OR MODEL	TOP/ RIG	BOAT TYPE	HULL MTL TP	ENG TP	# HP	MFG	BEAM FT IN	WGT LBS	DRAFT FT IN	RETAIL LOW	RETAIL HIGH
	1975 BOATS											
19 2	210VCRSR	ST	CR	FBG DV	IO	120-188		7 7	3100		3100	3650
19 8	200V	ST	RNBT	FBG DV	IO	165-188			2500		2750	3200
19 8	200V	ST	RNBT	FBG DV	JT	290	OMC		2500		2800	3300
19 8	200VBR	ST	RNBT	FBG DV	IO	170-190			2500		2750	3300
20 1	200T	ST	RNBT	FBG TR	IO	165-188			2850		3300	3850
20 1	200T	ST	RNBT	FBG TR	JT	290	OMC		2850		3300	3850
	1974 BOATS											
16 2	MARK 162T			FBG	IO	120-165		6 11	1940	6	1800	2250
17 1	MARK 170T			FBG	IO			7 2	1325	5	3150	3650
17 1	MARK 170V			FBG	OB			7	1225		2950	3400
17 3	MARK 180V W/T		RNBT	FBG	IO	165-188		7	2300	1 3	2300	2650
17 5	MARK 180T			FBG	IO	120-188		7 2	2130	6	2100	2600
17 5	MARK 180T			FBG	JT	455	HARD	7 2	2400	6	2250	2600
17 5	MARK 180V		B/R	FDG	IO	165-188		7	2180	6	2100	2550
19 2	MARK 210V B/R		CR	FBG	IO	165-188		7 7	3100		3200	3750
19 8	MARK 200V			FBG	IO	165-188		8	2385	7	2800	3300
19 8	MARK 200V			FBG	JT	455	HARD	8	2500	7	2700	3100
20	MARK 210V		CR	FBG	IO	165-188		8	3150	7	3800	4450
20	MARK 210V		CR	FBG	JT	455	HARD	8	3225	7	3400	3950
20 1	MARK 200T			FBG	IO	165-188		8	2835	7	3400	4000
20 1	MARK 200T			FBG	JT	455	HARD	8	2900	7	3200	3700
	1973 BOATS											
16 1	MARK 160V			FBG	OB			6 6	950		2300	2700
16 1	MARK 160V			FBG	IO	120-140		6 6	1760		1700	2000
16 2	MARK 162T			FBG	IO	120-165		6 6	1960		1900	2300
17 8	MARK 180T			FBG	OB			7 2	1325		3150	3700
17 8	MARK 180T			FBG	IO	120-188		7 2	2130		2250	2700
17 8	MARK 180T			FBG	JT	455	OLDS	7 2	2280		2050	2450
17 9	MARK 180V			FBG	OB			7 3	1225		3000	3450
17 9	MARK 180V			FBG	IO	120-188		7 3	2180		2300	2750
17 9	MARK 180V			FBG	JT	455	OLDS	7 3	2330		2150	2500
19 10	MARK 200V			FBG	IO	165-188		7 10	2385		2850	3350
19 10	MARK 200V			FBG	JT	455	OLDS	7 10	2535		2600	3000
20 1	MARK 200T			FBG	IO	165-188		8	2835		3500	4100
20 1	MARK 200T			FBG	JT	455	OLDS	8	2985		3100	3650
	1972 BOATS											
16 1	MARK 160V V-SONIC			FBG	OB			6 6	950		2300	2650
16 1	MARK 160V V-SONIC			FBG	IO	120-140		6 6	1760		1750	2100
17 8	MARK 180T			FBG TR	OB			7 2	1325		3150	3650
17 8	MARK 180T			FBG TR	IO	120-188		7 2	2130		2350	2700
17 9	MARK 180V V-SONIC			FBG	OB			7 3	1225		3000	3450
17 9	MARK 180V V-SONIC			FBG	IO	120-188		7 3	2180		2350	2800
19 7	MARK 200T			FBG TR	IO	165-215		8	2682		3150	3750
19 10	MARK 200V V-SONIC			FBG	IO	165-215		7 10	2385		2950	3500
	1971 BOATS											
16 1	MARK 16 V-SONIC			FBG	OB			6 6	950		2300	2650
16 1	MARK 16 V-SONIC			FBG	IO	120-140		6 6	1760		1800	2150
17 8	MARK 18			FBG TR	OB			7 2	1325		3150	3650
17 8	MARK 18			FBG TR	IO	120-165		7 2			2450	2900
17 9	MARK 18 V-SONIC			FBG	OB			7 3	1225		2950	3450
17 9	MARK 18 V-SONIC			FBG	IO	120-165		7 3			2500	2900
19 7	MARK 20			FBG TR	IO	165	MRCR	8	2682		3250	3800
19 7	MARK 20			FBG TR	IO	T165	MRCR	8	2682		3900	4500
19 10	MARK 20 V-SONIC			FBG	IO	165	MRCR	7 10	2385		3050	3550
19 10	MARK 20 V-SONIC EXEC			FBG	IO	T165	MRCR	7 10	2485		3750	4350
23 9	MARK 24		OFF	FBG	IO	165-215		8	3600		5600	6550
23 9	MARK 24		OFF	FBG	IO	T120-T140		8	3600		6300	7250
23 9	MARK 24 V-SONIC	HT		FBG	IO	165-215		8	3600		5350	6200
23 9	MARK 24 V-SONIC	HT		FBG	IO	T120-T140		8	3600		6000	6900
	1969 BOATS											
16 1	MARK 16 V-SONIC	SKI		FBG	OB			6 6	1930		4250	4950
16 1	MARK 16 V-SONIC	SKI		FBG	IO	160	MRCR	6 6	1930		2000	2400
17 8	MARK 18 V-SONIC	RNBT		FBG	OB			7 3	1325		3200	3700
17 9	MARK 18 V-SONIC	RNBT		FBG	IO	120	MRCR	7 3	2090		2650	3050
19 10	MARK 20 V-SONIC	CR		FBG	IO	120	MRCR	8	2682		3700	4300
	1968 BOATS											
16 4	MARK 16	RNBT		FBG DV	IO	120-160		6 4			2250	2650
17 9	MARK 18	RNBT		FBG DV	OB			7 3	800		2100	2450
17 9	MARK 18	RNBT		FBG DV	IO	120-225		7 3			2800	3400
19 10	MARK 20	RNBT		FBG DV	IO	120-225		7 10			3650	4400
	1966 BOATS											
17 6	MARK 18	RNBT		FBG	OB			7 3			3450	4000
19 9	MARK 20 CUSTOM DLX	RNBT		FBG	IO	110		6 11			3650	4200

MARKOS YACHTS LTD
COAST GUARD MFG ID- ZMJ

Call 1-800-327-6929 for BUC Personalized Evaluation Service
Or, for 1978 to 1983 boats, sign onto www.BUCValuPro.com

MARLIN BOAT COMPANY
COAST GUARD MFG ID- MBD

Call 1-800-327-6929 for BUC Personalized Evaluation Service
Or, for 1982 to 1998 boats, sign onto www.BUCValuPro.com

MARLIN BOAT WORKS INC
SEE GRADY-WHITE BOATS INC

Call 1-800-327-6929 for BUC Personalized Evaluation Service
Or, for 1965 to 1967 boats, sign onto www.BUCValuPro.com

MARLIN BOATS INC
WHITE CITY OR 97503   COAST GUARD MFG ID- EKW See inside cover to adjust price for area

For more recent years, see the BUC Used Boat Price Guide, Volume 1 or Volume 2

LOA FT IN	NAME AND/ OR MODEL	TOP/ RIG	BOAT TYPE	HULL MTL TP	ENG TP	# HP	MFG	BEAM FT IN	WGT LBS	DRAFT FT IN	RETAIL LOW	RETAIL HIGH
	1983 BOATS											
16 2	SATELLITE	ST	RNBT	F/W DV	OB			6 7	1060		2500	2900
16 2	SATELLITE	ST	RNBT	F/W DV	IO	120-170		6 7	1840		2750	3250
16 2	SATELLITE B/R	ST	RNBT	F/W DV	IO			6 7	1060		2550	3000
16 2	SATELLITE B/R	ST	RNBT	F/W DV	IO			6 7	1840		**	**
16 3	VENUS B/R	ST	RNBT	F/W TR	OB			6 5	790		1900	2250
16 3	VENUS B/R	ST	RNBT	F/W TR	IO	120-170		6 5	1750		2700	3150
16 5	AURORA	OP	SKI	F/W SV	OB			7 1	740		1750	2050
16 5	AURORA	OP	SKI	F/W SV	IO	140-170		7 1	1600		2550	3000
16 7	170	ST	RNBT	F/W DV	OB			7	1060		2550	3000
16 7	CHALLENGER	ST	RNBT	F/W DV	IO	140-170		7	1830		2950	3450
16 7	CHALLENGER	ST	RNBT	F/W DV	JT	350		7	1830		4400	5050
17 6	MERCURY	ST	RNBT	F/W DV	OB			7 2	1270		3050	3550
17 6	MERCURY	ST	RNBT	F/W DV	IO	120-230		7 2	2120		3350	4100
17 6	MERCURY	ST	RNBT	F/W DV	IO	260		7 2	2120		3700	4300
17 6	MERCURY B/R	ST	RNBT	F/W DV	IO			7 2	2120		**	**
17 8	JUPITER	OP	RNBT	F/W TR	IO	170-230		7	1425		2900	3500
17 8	JUPITER	OP	RNBT	F/W TR	IO	260		7	1425		3200	3700
17 11	TIGERSHARK	OP	SKI	F/W SV	OB			7 2	900		2300	2650
17 11	TIGERSHARK	OP	SKI	F/W SV	JT	350-460		7 2	1800		4800	5500
18	BARRACUDA	OP	RNBT	F/W SV	JT	260-330		6 7	850		4250	4950
18	CAPRI	ST	CBNCR	F/W SV	IO	120-170		6 8	1490		3450	4000
18	CAPRI	ST	CBNCR	F/W SV	IO	120-170		6 8	2270		3650	4250
18	RENEGADE	OP	RNBT	F/W TH	JT	260-330		6 3	550		4350	5000
18 6	ISLANDER	ST	RNBT	F/W DV	IO	140-230		8	2350		4000	4850
18 6	ISLANDER	ST	RNBT	F/W DV	IO	260		8	2350		4400	5050
18 6	ISLANDER B/R	ST	RNBT	F/W DV	IO			8	2350		**	**
19 2	SPORTFISHER	HT	CBNCR	F/W DV	IO	140-260		8	2890		5000	6150
20 2	ARIES B/R	OP	SKI	F/W SV	OB			8 8	1100		3100	3600
20 2	ARIES B/R	OP	SKI	F/W SV	IO	170-260		8 8	2000		4200	5250
20 2	ARIES B/R	OP	SKI	F/W SV	JT	350-460		8 8	2000		6250	7200
20 2	LUNAR	OP	SKI	F/W SV	OB			8 8	1100		3100	3600
20 2	LUNAR	OP	SKI	F/W SV	IO	170-260		8 8	2000		4200	5250
20 2	LUNAR	OP	SKI	F/W SV	JT	350-460		8 8	2000		6250	7200
20 4	LIBRA	OP	SKI	F/W DV	IO	198	MRCR	8 8	1100		4100	4750

    JT 200 OMC   6000   6900, IO 228-260   4150 5050, JT 350-460   6050 6950

LOA FT IN	NAME AND/ OR MODEL	TOP/ RIG	BOAT TYPE	HULL MTL TP	ENG TP	# HP	MFG	BEAM FT IN	WGT LBS	DRAFT FT IN	RETAIL LOW	RETAIL HIGH
22	MARIAH	ST	CR	F/W DV	IO	198-260		8	3550		6450	7700
24	ESCORT	OP	CUD	F/W DV	IO	198-260		7 11	3300		6800	8100
24	ESCORT	OP	CUD	F/W DV	IO	T120-T170		7 11	3300		7550	8800
24	ESCORT	HT	SDN	F/W DV	IO	198-260		7 11	4000		7800	9250
24	ESCORT	HT	SDN	F/W DV	IO	T120-T170		7 11	4000		8550	9900
24	ESCORT	FB	SDN	F/W DV	IO	198-260		7 11	4400		8350	9900
24	ESCORT	FB	SDN	F/W DV	IO	T120-T170		7 11	4400		9250	10600
26	EMPEROR	ST	OVNTR	F/W DV	IO	260		8	3800		9200	10500
	1982 BOATS											
16 2	SATELLITE	ST	RNBT	F/W DV	OB			6 7	1060		2450	2850
16 2	SATELLITE	ST	RNBT	F/W DV	IO		OMC	6 7	1840		**	**

LOA FT	LOA IN	NAME AND/ OR MODEL	TOP/ RIG	BOAT TYPE	HULL MTL	HULL TP	ENGINE TP	ENGINE # HP	ENGINE MFG	BEAM FT	BEAM IN	WGT LBS	DRAFT FT	DRAFT IN	RETAIL LOW	RETAIL HIGH
		1982 BOATS														
16	2	SATELLITE	ST	RNBT	F/W	DV	IO	120-140		6	7	1840			2750	3200
16	2	SATELLITE B/R	ST	RNBT	F/W	DV	OB			6	7	1060			2500	2900
16	2	SATELLITE B/R	ST	RNBT	F/W	DV	IO		OMC	6	7	1840			**	**
16	2	SATELLITE B/R	ST	RNBT	F/W	DV	IO	120-140		6	7	1840			2800	3250
16	3	VENUS B/R	ST	RNBT	F/W	TR	OB			6	5	790			1850	2200
16	3	VENUS B/R	ST	RNBT	F/W	TR	IO		OMC	6	5	1750			**	**
16	3	VENUS B/R	ST	RNBT	F/W	TR	IO	120-185		6	5	1750			2600	3100
16	5	AURORA	OP	RNBT	F/W	SV	OB			7	1	740			1700	2000
16	5	AURORA	OP	RNBT	F/W	SV	IO		OMC	7	1	1600			**	**
16	5	AURORA	OP	RNBT	F/W	SV	IO	140		7	1	1600			2700	3100
16	5	AURORA B/R	OP	RNBT	F/W	SV	OB			7	1	740			1750	2100
17	6	MERCURY	OP	RNBT	F/W	DV	OB			7	2	1270			2950	3450
17	6	MERCURY	OP	RNBT	F/W	DV	IO		OMC	7	2	2120			**	**
17	6	MERCURY	OP	RNBT	F/W	DV	IO	120-230		7	2	2120			3350	4000
17	6	MERCURY	OP	RNBT	F/W	DV	IO	260		7	2	2120			3700	4300
17	6	MERCURY B/R	OP	RNBT	F/W	DV	IO			7	2	2120			**	**
		IO OMC ** ** , IO 120-230 3400 4000, IO 260													3750	4350
17	11	TIGERSHARK	OP	RNBT	F/W	SV	OB			7	2	900			2250	2650
17	11	TIGERSHARK	OP	RNBT	F/W	SV	JT	350-460		7	2	1800			4800	5500
18		CAPRI	ST	RNBT	F/W	SV	OB			6	8	1490			3400	3950
18		CAPRI	ST	RNBT	F/W	SV	IO		OMC	6	8	2270			**	**
18		CAPRI	ST	RNBT	F/W	SV	IO	120-185		6	8	2270			3350	3950
18		JUPITER	OP	RNBT	F/W	SV	IO	260	MRCR	6	8	2270			3700	4250
18		JUPITER	OP	RNBT	F/W	TR	IO		OMC	6	8	2270			**	**
18		JUPITER	OP	RNBT	F/W	TR	IO	170-260		6	8	2270			3400	4200
18	6	ISLANDER	ST	CUD	F/W	DV	IO		OMC	8		2350			**	**
18	6	ISLANDER	ST	CUD	F/W	DV	IO	140-230		8		2350			4050	4900
18	6	ISLANDER	ST	CUD	F/W	DV	IO	260		8		2350			4400	5100
18	6	ISLANDER B/R	ST	RNBT	F/W	DV	IO			8		2350			**	**
		IO OMC ** ** , IO 140-230 3950 4750, IO 260													4250	4900
19		SPORTFISHER	OP	CR	F/W	DV	IO		OMC	7	8	2730			**	**
19		SPORTFISHER	OP	CR	F/W	DV	IO	140-260		7	8	2730			4400	5450
20	2	ARIES B/R	OP	SKI	F/W	SV	OB			8	8	1100			3000	3500
20	2	ARIES B/R	OP	SKI	F/W	SV	IO	170-230		8	8	2000			4100	4900
20	2	ARIES B/R	OP	SKI	F/W	SV	IO	260		8	8	2000			4550	5250
20	2	ARIES B/R	OP	SKI	F/W	SV	JT	350-460		8	8	2000			6000	6900
20	2	LUNAR	OP	SKI	F/W	SV	OB			8	8	1100			3000	3500
20	2	LUNAR	OP	SKI	F/W	SV	IO	170-230		8	8	2000			4100	4900
20	2	LUNAR	OP	SKI	F/W	SV	IO	260		8	8	2000			4550	5250
20	2	LUNAR	OP	SKI	F/W	SV	JT	350-460		8	8	2000			6000	6900
20	4	LIBRA	OP	CUD	F/W	DV	IO	170-198		7	7	2300			4250	5000
		JT 200 OMC 5800 6700, IO 228-260 4450 5300, JT 350-460													5850	6750
22		MARIAH	OP	CR	F/W	DV	IO	198-260		8		3550			6300	7500
24		ESCORT	OP	CUD	F/W	DV	IO	198-260		7	11	3300			6650	7900
24		ESCORT	OP	CUD	F/W	DV	IO	T120-T185		7	11	3300			7400	8600
24		ESCORT	HT	SDN	F/W	DV	IO	198-260		7	11	4000			7600	9000
24		ESCORT	HT	SDN	F/W	DV	IO	T120-T185		7	11	4000			8350	9750
24		ESCORT	FB	SDN	F/W	DV	IO	198-260		7	11	4400			8200	9700
24		ESCORT	FB	SDN	F/W	DV	IO	T120-T185		7	11	4400			9050	10400
		1981 BOATS														
16	2	SATELLITE	ST	RNBT	F/W	DV	OB			6	7				2100	2500
16	2	SATELLITE	ST	RNBT	F/W	DV	IO			6	7	1840			**	**
16	2	SATELLITE B/R	ST	RNBT	F/W	DV	OB			6	7	750			1700	2000
16	2	SATELLITE B/R	ST	RNBT	F/W	DV	IO			6	7	1840			**	**
16	3	VENUS B/R	ST	RNBT	F/W	TR	OB			6	5	790			1800	2100
16	3	VENUS B/R	ST	RNBT	F/W	TR	IO			6	5	1750			**	**
16	5	AURORA	OP	RNBT	F/W	SV	JT			7	1	1600			**	**
16	5	AURORA	OP	RNBT	F/W	SV	IO			7	1	1600			**	**
16	5	AURORA B/R	OP	RNBT	F/W	SV	OB			7	1	740			1700	2050
17	6	MERCURY	OP	RNBT	F/W	DV	OB			7	2	980			2350	2700
17	6	MERCURY	OP	RNBT	F/W	DV	IO			7	2	2120			**	**
17	6	MERCURY B/R	OP	RNBT	F/W	DV	IO			7	2	2120			**	**
17	10	LEO	OP	SKI	F/W	SV	IO			7	3	1850			**	**
17	11	TIGERSHARK	OP	RNBT	F/W	SV	OB			7	2	900			2200	2550
17	11	TIGERSHARK	OP	RNBT	F/W	SV	JT			7	2	1800			**	**
18		CAPRI	ST	RNBT	F/W	SV	OB			6	8	1300			3000	3500
18		CAPRI	ST	RNBT	F/W	SV	IO			6	8	2270			**	**
18	6	ISLANDER	ST	CUD	F/W	DV	IO			8		2700			**	**
18	6	ISLANDER B/R	ST	RNBT	F/W	DV	IO			8		2700			**	**
19	2	SPORTFISHER	OP	CR	F/W	DV	IO			7	8	2890			**	**
20	2	ARIES B/R		RNBT	F/W	SV	OB			8	8	1100			2950	3400
20	2	ARIES B/R		RNBT	F/W	SV	JT			8	8	2000			**	**
20	2	ARIES B/R		RNBT	F/W	SV	IO			8	8	2000			**	**
20	2	LUNAR	OP	RNBT	F/W	SV	OB			8	8	1100			2950	3400
20	2	LUNAR	OP	RNBT	F/W	SV	JT			8	8	2000			**	**
20	4	LIBRA	OP	CUD	F/W	DV	IO			7	7	2300			**	**
22		MARIAH	OP	CR	F/W	DV	IO			8		3550			**	**
24		ESCORT	HT	SDN	F/W	DV	IO			7	11	4000			**	**
24		ESCORT	FB	SDN	F/W	DV	IO			7	11	4400			**	**

MARLINEER MARINE INC

POMONA CA 91767 See inside cover to adjust price for area

LOA FT	LOA IN	NAME AND/ OR MODEL	TOP/ RIG	BOAT TYPE	HULL MTL	HULL TP	ENGINE TP	ENGINE # HP	ENGINE MFG	BEAM FT	BEAM IN	WGT LBS	DRAFT FT	DRAFT IN	RETAIL LOW	RETAIL HIGH
		1967 BOATS														
60		MARLINEER	FB	MY	P/C	DV	IB	450D	CAT						197500	217000

MARLOWE YACHT CORP

Call 1-800-327-6929 for BUC Personalized Evaluation Service
Or, for 1970 to 1972 boats, sign onto www.BUCValuPro.com

MARQUIS BOATS INC

HARTSVILLE SC 29550 COAST GUARD MFG ID- MRB See inside cover to adjust price for area

LOA FT	LOA IN	NAME AND/ OR MODEL	TOP/ RIG	BOAT TYPE	HULL MTL	HULL TP	ENGINE TP	ENGINE # HP	ENGINE MFG	BEAM FT	BEAM IN	WGT LBS	DRAFT FT	DRAFT IN	RETAIL LOW	RETAIL HIGH
		1983 BOATS														
16	6	SPRINT		RNBT	FBG		OB			7	1	1250			2450	2850
17	1	DAYTONA		RNBT	FBG		IO	125		7	1				1750	2050
17	3	CATALINA		RNBT	FBG		OB			7	6	1500			2850	3300
17	3	CATALINA		RNBT	FBG		IO	125		7	6				1850	2200
18	11	CAPRI		RNBT	FBG		IO	125		7	6				2350	2750
18	11	CARIBBEAN		CR	FBG		OB			7	6	1700			3250	3800
18	11	CARIBBEAN		CR	FBG		IO	125		7	6				2400	2750
18	11	FREEPORT		RNBT	FBG		OB			7	6	1600			3100	3650
18	11	FREEPORT		RNBT	FBG		IO	125		7	6				2350	2750
18	11	STRIPER		FSH	FBG		OB			7	6	1700			3250	3800
20	9	MARLIN		CR	FBG		IO	125		7	9				3100	3600
		1980 BOATS														
17	6	CATALINA 17		RNBT	FBG	SV	IO	140		7	6				1850	2200
17	6	CATALINA 17		RNBT	FBG	SV	IO	260		7	6				2050	2450
18	11	CARIBBEAN 19		CUD	FBG	SV	IO	165		7	6				2300	2700
18	11	CARIBBEAN 19		CUD	FBG	SV	IO	260		7	6				2500	2900
18	11	FREEPORT 19		RNBT	FBG	SV	IO	170-260		7	6				2250	2800
20	9	GULFSTREAM 20		CUD	FBG	SV	IO	200-260		8					3300	4050
22	7	DOLPHIN 22		CUD	FBG	SV	IO	198-260		8					4050	4900
		1979 BOATS														
16	6	RIVIERA	ST	RNBT	FBG	TR	OB			7	1	1250			2350	2700
17	6	CATALINA	ST	RNBT	FBG	DV	OB			7	6	1600			2850	3300
17	6	CATALINA	ST	RNBT	FBG	DV	IO	120-230		7	6				1850	2300
18	11	CARIBBEAN	ST	CUD	FBG	DV	IO	120-230		7	6				2300	2750
18	11	CARIBBEAN	ST	CUD	FBG	DV	IO	260		7	6				2500	2900
18	11	FREEPORT	ST	RNBT	FBG	DV	OB			7	6	1700			3050	3550
18	11	FREEPORT	ST	RNBT	FBG	DV	IO	120-230		7	6				2250	2700
18	11	FREEPORT	ST	RNBT	FBG	DV	IO	260		7	6				2400	2800
20	9	GULFSTREAM	ST	RNBT	FBG	DV	IO	200-260		8					2750	3400
22	7	DOLPHIN	ST	CUD	FBG	DV	IO	170-260		8					3600	4400
22	7	DOLPHIN	ST	CUD	FBG	DV	IO	330	MRCR	8					4350	5000
22	7	MARK VII	ST	CUD	FBG	DV	IO	170-260		8					4450	5350
22	7	MARK VII	ST	CUD	FBG	DV	IO	330	MRCR	8					5100	5850
		1978 BOATS														
16	9	STING-RAY V170	ST	RNBT	FBG	DV	OB			6	11	1150			2150	2500
16	9	STING-RAY V175	ST	RNBT	FBG	DV	OB			6	11	1200			2250	2600
17	6	BARRACUDA 180T	ST	RNBT	FBG	TR	IO	120-225		7		1350			1800	2200
17	6	BARRACUDA 180T	ST	RNBT	FBG	TR	IO	228-240		7		1350			1900	2250
17	6	BARRACUDA 180T	ST	RNBT	FBG	TR	IO	260	MRCR	7		1350			2000	2350
18	11	CARIBBEAN V190	ST	RNBT	FBG	DV	OB			7	6	1650			3000	3450
18	11	CARIBBEAN V190	ST	RNBT	FBG	DV	IO	120-240		7	6	1650			2250	2750
18	11	CARIBBEAN V190	ST	RNBT	FBG	DV	IO	260	MRCR	7	6	1650			2400	2800
18	11	FREEPORT V195	ST	RNBT	FBG	DV	OB			7	6	1700			3050	3550
18	11	FREEPORT V195	ST	RNBT	FBG	DV	IO	120-240		7	6	1700			2250	2700
18	11	FREEPORT V195	ST	RNBT	FBG	DV	IO	260	MRCR	7	6	1700			2450	2850

 CONTINUED ON NEXT PAGE

LOA FT	LOA IN	NAME AND/ OR MODEL	TOP/ RIG	BOAT TYPE	HULL MTL	HULL TP	ENGINE TP	ENGINE # HP	ENGINE MFG	BEAM FT	BEAM IN	WGT LBS	DRAFT FT	DRAFT IN	RETAIL LOW	RETAIL HIGH
		1978 BOATS														
20	9	GULFSTREAM V21C	ST	RNBT	FBG	DV	OB			7	6	2000			3950	4600
20	9	GULFSTREAM V21C	ST	RNBT	FBG	DV	IO	120-240		7	6	2000			2650	3200
20	9	GULFSTREAM V21C	ST	RNBT	FBG	DV	IO	260	MRCR	7	6	2000			2850	3300
20	9	WAHOO V22C	ST	CUD	FBG	DV	IO	165-260		8		2700			3300	4050
22	7	DOLPHIN V23C	ST	CUD	FBG	DV	IO	170-260		8		3200			4050	4900
24	3	MARK VII V25C	ST	CR	FBG	DV	IO	170-260		8		4500			5650	6750
		1977 BOATS														
16	9	STING-RAY V170	ST	RNBT	FBG	DV	OB			6	11	1150			2000	2350
16	9	STING-RAY V175	ST	RNBT	FBG	DV	OB			6	11	1150			2250	2600
17	6	BARRACUDA 180T	ST	RNBT	FBG	TR	IO	120-198		7					1800	2200
17	6	BARRACUDA 180T	ST	RNBT	FBG	TR	IO	228-250		7					1900	2350
18	11	CARIBBEAN V190	ST	RNBT	FBG	DV	OB			7	6	1650			2800	3300
18	11	CARIBBEAN V190	ST	RNBT	FBG	DV	IO	120-250		7	6				2250	2800
18	11	FREEPORT V195	ST	RNBT	FBG	DV	OB			7	6	1650			3100	3600
18	11	FREEPORT V198	ST	RNBT	FBG	DV	IO	120-250		7	6				2350	2900
20	9	GULFSTREAM V21C	ST	RNBT	FBG	DV	OB			7	6	2000			3950	4550
20	9	GULFSTREAM V21C	ST	RNBT	FBG	DV	IO	120-250		7	6				2700	3300
20	9	WAHOO V22C	ST	CUD	FBG	DV	IO	165-250		8					3350	4100
		1976 BOATS														
16	8	STING-RAY SS-CIV-17	ST	RNBT	FBG	DV	OB			6	11	1100	3	7	2000	2350
16	9	RIVIERA 170T	ST	RNBT	FBG	TR	OB			6	7	1150	3	4	2050	2450
16	11	CHESAPEAKE 1750	ST	RNBT	FBG	DV	OB			7		1000			1850	2200
17	1	MARK-VII 007	OP	RACE	FBG	SV	OB			7	5	1000	3		1800	2150
17	1	MARK-VII 007	OP	RACE	FBG	SV	IO	233-235		7	5	1000	3		1750	2100
17	1	MARK-VII 007	OP	RACE	FBG	SV	JT	325-580		7	5	1000	3		1950	2350
17	2	NEWPORT 1700R	ST	RNBT	FBG	DV	OB			7		1150	3	10	2100	2500
17	2	NEWPORT 1700R	ST	RNBT	FBG	DV	IO	120-165		7		1150	3	10	1750	2100
17	6	BARRACUDA SS-CIT-18	ST	RNBT	FBG	TR	OB			7		1350	3	6	2450	2850
17	6	BARRACUDA SS-CIT-18	ST	RNBT	FBG	TR	IO	120-190		7		1350	3	6	1850	2250
17	9	BISCAYNE 180T	ST	RNBT	FBG	TR	OB			7	3	1300	3	10	2400	2750
17	9	BISCAYNE 180T	ST	RNBT	FBG	TR	IO	120-190		7	3	1300	3	10	1900	2350
17	9	BISCAYNE 180T	ST	RNBT	FBG	TR	IO	233-235		7	3	1300	3	10	2050	2450
18	4	CHIMERA SS-CIV-19	ST	RNBT	FBG	DV	OB			7	6	1700	4	4	2900	3400
18	4	CHIMERA SS-CIV-19	ST	RNBT	FBG	DV	IO	120-235		7	6	1700	4	4	2250	2750
18	11	CARIBBEAN	ST	RNBT	FBG	DV	IO	120	OMC	7	6	1550	4		2300	2650
18	11	CARIBBEAN 1900R	ST	RNBT	FBG	DV	OB			7	6	1550	4		2800	3250
18	11	CARIBBEAN 1900R	ST	RNBT	FBG	DV	IO	120-235		7	6	1550	4		2300	2800
18	11	CARIBBEAN 1900R	ST	RNBT	FBG	DV	IO	280	MRCR	7	6	1550	4		2600	3000
18	11	FREEPORT 1950 BR	ST	RNBT	FBG	DV	OB			7	6	1650	4		2950	3400
18	11	FREEPORT 1950 BR	ST	RNBT	FBG	DV	IO	120-235		7	6	1650	4		2350	2800
18	11	FREEPORT 1950 BR	ST	RNBT	FBG	DV	IO	280	MRCR	7	6	1650	4		2600	3050
19	3	GULFSTREAM 2000		SF	FBG	DV	OB			8		1750	3	5	3100	3600
20	6	DOLPHIN 2100R	ST	RNBT	FBG	DV	IO	120-235		7	6	1800	4	6	2600	3200
20	6	DOLPHIN 2100R	ST	RNBT	FBG	DV	IO	280	MRCR	7	6	1800	4	6	2950	3400
20	9	WAHOO SS-CIV-22	ST	CUD	FBG	DV	IO	165-235		7	11	2700	4	9	3400	4100
20	9	WAHOO SS-CIV-22	ST	CUD	FBG	DV	IO	280	MRCR	7	11	2700	4	9	3750	4350
		1975 BOATS														
16	11	RIVIERA 170T	ST	RNBT	FBG	TR	OB			6	7	1100			2000	2350
16	11	RIVIERA 170TDB	ST	RNBT	FBG	TR	OB			6	7	1125			2050	2400
17	1	MARK-VII 007	OP	RNBT	FBG	DV	OB			7	5	1000			1850	2200
17	1	MARK-VII 007	OP	RNBT	FBG	DV	IO	140-188		7	5	1000			1800	2200
17	1	MARK-VII 007	OP	RNBT	FBG	DV	JT	390	BERK	7	5	1000			2000	2350
17	1	NEWPORT 1700R	ST	RNBT	FBG	SV	OB			7	3	1100			2000	2400
17	1	NEWPORT 1700R	ST	RNBT	FBG	SV	IO	120-188		7	3	1100			1800	2200
17	1	NEWPORT 1700R	ST	RNBT	FBG	SV	JT	390	BERK	7	3	1100			2000	2350
17	9	BISCAYNE 180T	ST	RNBT	FBG	TR	OB			7	3	1250			2300	2700
17	9	BISCAYNE 180T	ST	RNBT	FBG	TR	IO	120-188		7	3	1250			1950	2400
17	9	BISCAYNE 180T	ST	RNBT	FBG	TR	JT	390	BERK	7	3	1250			2200	2550
17	9	BISCAYNE 180TDB	ST	RNBT	FBG	TR	OB			7	3	1275			2350	2700
17	9	BISCAYNE 180TDB	ST	RNBT	FBG	TR	IO	120-188		7	3	1275			2000	2400
17	9	BISCAYNE 180TDB	ST	RNBT	FBG	TR	JT	390	BERK	7	3	1275			2200	2550
18	9	CARIBBEAN 1900R	ST	RNBT	FBG	SV	OB			7	3	1250			2350	2750
18	9	CARIBBEAN 1900R	ST	RNBT	FBG	SV	IO	120-188		7	3	1250			2200	2600
18	9	CARIBBEAN 1900R	ST	RNBT	FBG	SV	JT	390	BERK	7	3	1250			2350	2700
20	6	DOLPHIN 2100R	ST	RNBT	FBG	SV	IO	120-188		7	5	1700			2650	3150
20	6	DOLPHIN 2100R	ST	RNBT	FBG	SV	JT	390	BERK	7	5	1700			2750	3200
		1974 BOATS														
16	8	RIVIERA 170T			FBG		OB			6	7	1100			1950	2350
16	8	RIVIERA 170T DB			FBG		OB			6	7	1125			2000	2400
16	8	RIVIERA 170T DB			FBG		IO	120-140		6	7	1890			1950	2350
17	1	MARK VII 007			FBG		OB			7	5	1000			1850	2200
17	1	MARK VII 007			FBG		IO	140-165		7	5	1850			2200	2600
17	1	MARK VII 007			FBG		IO	188	MRCR	7	5	2150			2400	2800
17	1	MARK VII 007			FBG		JT	255-390		7	5	2150			2350	2750
17	1	NEWPORT 1700R			FBG		OB			6	11	1100			2000	2350
17	1	NEWPORT 1700R			FBG		IO	120-165		6	11	1950			2150	2550
17	1	NEWPORT 1700R			FBG		IO	188	MRCR	6	11	2250			2350	2750
17	1	NEWPORT 1700R			FBG		JT	255-390		6	11	2250			2300	2650
17	9	BISCAYNE 180T			FBG		OB			7	3	1250			2300	2700
17	9	BISCAYNE 180T DB			FBG		OB			7	3	1275			2300	2700
17	9	BISCAYNE 180T DB			FBG		IO	120-188		7	3	2000			2350	2900
17	9	BISCAYNE 180T DB			FBG		JT	390	BERK	7	3	2300			2450	2850
18	9	CARIBBEAN 1900R			FBG		OB			7	3	1250			2350	2750
18	9	CARIBBEAN 1900R			FBG		IO	120-188		7	3	2100			2550	3050
18	9	CARIBBEAN 1900R			FBG		JT	255-390		7	3	2200			2500	3100
20	6	DOLPHIN 2100R			FBG		IO	120-188		7	6	2500			3150	3900
20	6	DOLPHIN 2100R			FBG		JT	255-390		7	6	2700			3100	3600
		1972 BOATS														
16	8	RIVIERA 170		RNBT	FBG		OB			6	7	1100		8	1950	2350
16	8	RIVIERA 170		RNBT	FBG		IO	120-165		6	7			8	1800	2150
17	9	BISCAYNE 180	ST	RNBT	FBG		OB			7	2	1250		7	2300	2650
17	9	BISCAYNE 180	ST	RNBT	FBG		IO	120-188		7	2			7	2250	2650
18	8	CARIBBEAN 1900		RNBT	FBG		OB			7	2	1200		8	2300	2650
18	8	CARIBBEAN 1900		RNBT	FBG		IO	120-215		7	2			8	2500	3050
20	5	CLASSIC 2100		CR	FBG		OB			7	6	1900	1		3650	4200
20	5	CLASSIC 2100		CR	FBG		IO	140-215		7	6		1		3050	3650

MARRIOTS COVE YACHT BLDR

Call 1-800-327-6929 for BUC Personalized Evaluation Service
Or, for 1965 to 1967 boats, sign onto www.BUCValuPro.com

MARSCOT PLASTICS

Call 1-800-327-6929 for BUC Personalized Evaluation Service
Or, for 1960 boats, sign onto www.BUCValuPro.com

MARSHALL BOAT CO

TUSTIN CA 92680 COAST GUARD MFG ID- JCM See inside cover to adjust price for area

LOA FT	LOA IN	NAME AND/ OR MODEL	TOP/ RIG	BOAT TYPE	HULL MTL	HULL TP	ENGINE TP	ENGINE # HP	ENGINE MFG	BEAM FT	BEAM IN	WGT LBS	DRAFT FT	DRAFT IN	RETAIL LOW	RETAIL HIGH
		1982 BOATS														
29	6	CALIFORNIAN 30	FB	OFF	FBG	SV	IB	130D	PERK	10	3	9200	2	2	28300	31500
34	4	CALIFORNIAN 34	FB	OFF	FBG	SV	IB	130D-210D		12	4	18000	3	2	58100	63800
34	4	CALIFORNIAN 34	FB	OFF	FBG	SV	IB	T85D-T200D		12	4	18000	3	2	58000	63700
35	8	CALIFORNIAN 36	FB	MY	FBG	SV	IB	130D	PERK	13		25000	3	6	76900	84500
35	8	CALIFORNIAN 36	FB	MY	FBG	SV	IB	T200D	PERK	13		25000	3	6	79500	87400
35	8	CALIFORNIAN 36	FB	MY	FBG	SV	IB	T210D	CAT	13		25000	3	6	79900	87800
37	9	CALIFORNIAN 38	FB	OFF	FBG	SV	IB	T155D	CAT	14	8	28000	4		83300	91500
38	10	CALIFORNIAN 38	FB	MY	FBG	SV	IB	210D	CAT	13	8	29000	3	4	89200	98000
		IB T200D PERK 95000 104500, IB T210D CAT 95300 105000, IB T300D													97600	107000
41	8	CALIFORNIAN 42	FB	MY	FBG	SV	IB	T210D	CAT	13	8	31000	3	4	104500	114500
41	8	CALIFORNIAN 42	FB	MY	FBG	SV	IB	T300D		13	8	31000	3	4	109000	120000
46		CALIFORNIAN 46	FB	MY	FBG	SV	IB	T210D	CAT	14	8	40000	4	6	116500	128000
46		CALIFORNIAN 46	FB	MY	FBG	SV	IB	T300D		14	8	40000	4	6	127000	140000
50		CALIFORNIAN 50	FB	MY	FBG	SV	IB	210D	CAT	14	8	42000			105500	116000
50		CALIFORNIAN 50	FB	MY	FBG	SV	IB	T300D		14	8	42000			123500	135500
52		CALIFORNIAN 52	FB	MY	FBG	SV	IB	T300D				46000			128500	141000
		1981 BOATS														
29	6	CALIFORNIAN 30	FB	OFF	FBG	SV	IB	135D-200D		10	3	9200	2	2	27200	30200
34	4	CALIFORNIAN 34	FB	OFF	FBG	SV	IB	T85D-T200D		12	4	18000	3	2	55700	61200
35	8	CALIFORNIAN 36	FB	MY	FBG	SV	IB	T130D	PERK	13		25000	3	6	74300	81600
35	8	CALIFORNIAN 36	FB	MY	FBG	SV	IB	T200D	PERK	13		25000	3	6	76500	84000
35	8	CALIFORNIAN 36	FB	MY	FBG	SV	IB	T210D	CAT	13		25000	3	6	76800	84400
37	9	CALIFORNIAN 38	FB	OFF	FBG	SV	IB	T155D	FORD	14	8	28000	4		78200	86000
38	10	CALIFORNIAN 38	FB	MY	FBG	SV	IB	T200D	PERK	13	8	29000	3	4	90500	99500
41	8	CALIFORNIAN 42	FB	MY	FBG	SV	IB	T210D	CAT	13	8	31000	3	4	99400	109000
46		CALIFORNIAN 46	FB	MY	FBG	SV	IB	T250D		14	8	40000	4	6	115500	127000
50		CALIFORNIAN 50	FB	MY	FBG	SV	IB			14	8	42000			**	**
52		CALIFORNIAN 52	FB	MY	FBG	SV	IB					46000			**	**
		1980 BOATS														
29	6	CALIFORNIAN 30	FB	OFF	FBG	SV	IB	135D-200D		10	3	9200	2	2	26100	29000
34	4	CALIFORNIAN 34	FB	OFF	FBG	SV	IB	T85D-T200D		12	4	18000	3	2	53600	58900
35	8	CALIFORNIAN 36	FB	MY	FBG	SV	IB	T130D	PERK	13		25000	3	6	71400	78500
35	8	CALIFORNIAN 36	FB	MY	FBG	SV	IB	T200D	PERK	13		25000	3	6	73500	80800
35	8	CALIFORNIAN 36	FB	MY	FBG	SV	IB	T210D	CAT	13		25000	3	6	73900	81200
37	9	CALIFORNIAN 38	FB	OFF	FBG	SV	IB	T155D	FORD	14	8	28000	4		74600	82000

CONTINUED ON NEXT PAGE

MARSHALL BOAT CO — CONTINUED

LOA FT IN	NAME AND/ OR MODEL	TOP/ RIG	BOAT TYPE	-HULL- MTL TP	TP	ENGINE #	HP	MFG	BEAM FT IN	WGT LBS	DRAFT FT IN	RETAIL LOW	RETAIL HIGH
1980 BOATS
38 10	CALIFORNIAN 38	FB	MY	FBG SV	IB		T200D	PERK	13 8	29000	3 4	86300	94900
41 8	CALIFORNIAN 42	FB	MY	FBG SV	IB		T210D	CAT	13 8	31000	3 4	94800	104000
46	CALIFORNIAN 46	FB	MY	FBG SV	IB		T250D		14 8	40000	4 6	110000	121000
1979 BOATS
29 6	CALIFORNIAN 30	FB	OFF	FBG SV	IB		130D-185D		10 3	9200	1 10	25200	28000
34 4	CALIFORNIAN 34	FB	OFF	FBG SV	IB		T85D-T185D		12 4	18000	3 2	51600	56700
35 8	CALIFORNIAN 36	FB	OFF	FBG SV	IB		T185D	PERK	13	27000	3 6	73000	80200
38 10	CALIFORNIAN 38	FB	OFF	FBG SV	IB		T185D	PERK	13 8	29000	3 4	81900	90000
41 8	CALIFORNIAN 42	FB	OFF	FBG SV	IB		T185D	PERK	13 8	31000	3 4	90900	99900
41 8	CALIFORNIAN 42	FB	OFF	FBG SV	IB		T210D	CAT	13 8	31000	3 4	91900	101000
1975 BOATS
38	DOUBLE CABIN		OFF	FBG SV	IB		T185D		13 8		3 4	63300	69600
38	DOUBLE CABIN		OFF	FBG SV	IB		T250D		13 8		3 4	64800	71200
42	DOUBLE CABIN		OFF	FBG SV	IB		T185D		13 8		3 4	67500	74200
42	DOUBLE CABIN		OFF	FBG SV	IB		T250D		13 8		3 4	69800	76700
1974 BOATS
29			SF	FBG SV	IB		T100D		10 2		2	20800	23100
29			SF	FBG SV	IB		T225D		10 2		2	24400	27100
38		FB	SF	FBG SV	IB		T240D		13 10		3 2	61300	67400
38	OFFSHORE		OFF	FBG SV	IB		T185D		13 10		3 2	60500	66500
38	OFFSHORE		OFF	FBG SV	IB		T240D		13 10		3 2	61700	67800
42	OFFSHORE		OFF	FBG SV	IB		T240D		13 10		3 3	66400	73000
1972 BOATS
19	MUSTANG		RNBT	FBG	IO		160		6 8		8	3550	4100
19	MUSTANG		RNBT	FBG	IO		300		6 8		8	4100	4800
22	MARSHALL 22	CAT	SA/CR	FBG CB	IB		22		10 2	5660	2	10300	11700
28 8	CALIFORNIAN			FBG	IB		450		10 2		1 6	14100	16000
28 8	CALIFORNIAN			FBG	IB		700		10 2		1 6	15900	18000
36 6	CALIFORNIAN			FBG	IB		320		13 8		3 2	26900	29900

MARSHALL MARINE CORP
S DARTMOUTH MA 02748   COAST GUARD MFG ID- MMC See inside cover to adjust price for area

For more recent years, see the BUC Used Boat Price Guide, Volume 1 or Volume 2

LOA FT IN	NAME AND/ OR MODEL	TOP/ RIG	BOAT TYPE	-HULL- MTL TP	TP	ENGINE #	HP	MFG	BEAM FT IN	WGT LBS	DRAFT FT IN	RETAIL LOW	RETAIL HIGH
1983 BOATS
18 2	SANDERLING	CAT	SA/OD	FBG CB	OB				8 6	2200	1 7	8950	10200
18 2	SANDERLING	CAT	SA/OD	FBG CB	IB	7D	YAN		8 6	2200	1 7	12900	14700
22 2	MARSHALL 22	CAT	SA/CR	FBG CB	IB	22D	YAN		10 2	5660	2	20400	22600
22 2	MARSHALL 22	SLP	SA/CR	FBG CB	IB	22D	YAN		10 2	5660	2	20400	22600
1982 BOATS
18 2	SANDERLING	CAT	SA/OD	FBG CB	OB				8 6	2200	1 7	8400	9650
18 2	SANDERLING	CAT	SA/OD	FBG CB	IB	7D	WEST		8 6	2200	1 7	12300	14000
22 2	MARSHALL 22	CAT	SA/CR	FBG CB	IB	22D	YAN		10 2	5660	2	19300	21400
22 2	MARSHALL 22	SLP	SA/CR	FBG CB	IB	22D	YAN		10 2	5660	2	19300	21400
26 6	MARSHALL 26	CAT	SA/CR	FBG CB	IB	D			11 9	10000	2 6	39800	44200
1981 BOATS
18 2	SANDERLING	CAT	SA/OD	FBG CB	OB				8 6	2200	1 7	7950	9150
22 2	MARSHALL 22	CAT	SA/CR	FBG CB	IB	16D-25D			10 2	5660	2	18200	20700
22 2	MARSHALL 22	SLP	SA/CR	FBG CB	IB	16D-25D			10 2	5660	2	18200	20700
1980 BOATS
18 2	SANDERLING	CAT	SA/OD	FBG CB	OB				8 6	2200	1 7	7650	8800
18 2	SANDERLING	CAT	SA/OD	FBG CB	IB	7D	WEST		8 6	2200	1 7	11200	12700
22 2	MARSHALL 22	CAT	SA/CR	FBG CB	IB	15D-25D			10 2	5660	2	17100	19900
22 2	MARSHALL 22	SLP	SA/CR	FBG CB	IB	15D-25D			10 2	5660	2	17100	19900
26 6	MARSHALL 26	CAT	SA/CR	FBG CB	IB	30D	WEST		11 9	10000	2 6	36500	40500
26 6	MARSHALL 26	SLP	SA/CR	FBG CB	IB	30D	WEST		11 9	10000	2 6	36500	40500
1979 BOATS
18 2	SANDERLING	CAT	SA/OD	FBG CB	OB				8 6	2200	1 7	7400	8550
22 2	MARSHALL 22	CAT	SA/CR	FBG CB	IB	15D-25D			10 2	5660	2	16600	19200
22 2	MARSHALL 22	SLP	SA/CR	FBG CB	IB	15D-25D			10 2	5660	2	16600	19200
26 6	MARSHALL 26	CAT	SA/CR	FBG CB	IB	30D	WEST		11 9	10000	3	35300	39200
26 6	MARSHALL 26	SLP	SA/CR	FBG CB	IB	30D	WEST		11 9	10000	3	35300	39200
1978 BOATS
18 2	SANDERLING	CAT	SA/OD	FBG CB	OB				8 6	2300	1 7	7400	8500
22 2	MARSHALL 22	SLP	SA/CR	FBG CB	IB				10 2	5660	2	16100	18300
22 2	MARSHALL 22	CAT	SAIL	FBG CB	IB	27D			10 2	5660	2	16300	18500
26 6	MARSHALL 26	CAT	SAIL	FBG CB	IB	30D			11 9	10000	2 6	34100	37900
1977 BOATS
18 3	SANDERLING	CAT	SA/OD	FBG CB	OB				8 6	2300	1 7	7200	8300
22 2	MARSHALL 22	CAT	SAIL	FBG CB	IB	25D	PALM		10 2	5600	2 1	15600	17800
26 6	MARSHALL 26	CAT	SAIL	FBG CB	IB	30D	WEST		11 9	10000	2 6	33300	37000
1976 BOATS
18 2	SANDERLING	CAT	SA/OD	FBG CB	OB				8 6	2300	1 7	7050	8100
22 2	MARSHALL 22	CAT	SAIL	FBG CB	IB	27D			10 2	5660	2	15500	17600
1975 BOATS
22 2	MARSHALL 22	CAT	SAIL	FBG CB	IB	22D			10 2	5660	2	15000	17000
1974 BOATS
18 2	SANDERLING	CAT	SA/OD	FBG CB	OB				8 6	2200	1 7	6550	7550
22 2	MARSHALL 22	CAT	SAIL	FBG CB	IB	27D	PALM		10 2	5660	2	14800	16800
1973 BOATS
18 2	SANDERLING	CAT	SA/OD	FBG CB	OB				8 6	2200	1 7	6450	7400
22 2	MARSHALL 22	CAT	SAIL	FBG CB	IB	22D	PALM		10 2	5660	2	14400	16400
1972 BOATS
18	SANDERLING	CAT	SA/OD	FBG CB					8 6	2200		6300	7250
1971 BOATS
18 3	SANDERLING	CAT	SAIL	FBG CB					8 6	2200	1 7	6150	7050
22 2	MARSHALL 22	CAT	SA/CR	FBG CB	IB	22			10 2	5500	2 1	12600	14300
1970 BOATS
18 3	SANDERLING	CAT	SAIL	FBG CB					8 6	2200	1 7	6000	6900
22 2	MARSHALL 22	CAT	SAIL	FBG CB	IB	22			10 2	5500	2 1	12300	14000
1969 BOATS
18 3	SANDERLING	CAT	SAIL	FBG CB					8 6	2200	1 7	5850	6750
22 2	MARSHALL	CAT	SA/CR	FBG CB					10 2	5500	2	12000	13700
1968 BOATS
18 3	SANDERLING	CAT	SAIL	FBG CB					8 6	2200	1 7	5750	6600
22 2	MARSHALL 22	CAT	SA/CR	FBG CB					10 2	5500	2 1	11300	12800
1966 BOATS
18 2	SANDERLING	CAT	SAIL	FBG CB					8 6	2200	1 9	5550	6350
22 2	MARSHALL 22	CAT	SA/CR	FBG CB	IB	30			10 2	5660	2 1	11800	13400
1965 BOATS
18 2	SANDERLING	CAT	SAIL	FBG CB	OB				8 6	2200	1 7	5450	6250
22 2	MARSHALL 22	CAT	SAIL	FBG CB	IB	25			10 6	5660	2	11600	13100

MARSHALL'S BOAT SHOP

Call 1-800-327-6929 for BUC Personalized Evaluation Service
Or, for 1966 to 1971 boats, sign onto www.BUCValuPro.com

MARTHAS VINEYARD SHIPYD INC
VINEYARD HVN MA 02568   COAST GUARD MFG ID- MVS See inside cover to adjust price for area

For more recent years, see the BUC Used Boat Price Guide, Volume 1 or Volume 2

LOA FT IN	NAME AND/ OR MODEL	TOP/ RIG	BOAT TYPE	-HULL- MTL TP	TP	ENGINE #	HP	MFG	BEAM FT IN	WGT LBS	DRAFT FT IN	RETAIL LOW	RETAIL HIGH
1983 BOATS
29 7	VINEYARD-VIXEN	SLP	SA/CR	FBG KL	SD	15D	VLVO		8 6	8600	4 6	38200	42500
34 4	VIXEN 34	SLP	SA/CR	FBG KL	IB	42D	PATH		10 6	12500	5 2	58000	63700
1982 BOATS
29 7	VINEYARD-VIXEN	SLP	SA/CR	FBG KL	IB	13D	VLVO		8 6	8600	4 6	36200	40200
34 4	VIXEN 34	SLP	SA/CR	FBG KL	IB	42D	PATH		10 6	12500	5 2	50900	60400
1981 BOATS
29 7	VINEYARD-VIXEN	SLP	SA/CR	FBG KL	IB	15D	VLVO		8 6	8600	4 6	34300	38100
34 4	VIXEN 34	SLP	SA/CR	FBG KL	IB	42D	PATH		10 6	12500	5 2	52300	57500
1980 BOATS
29 7	VINEYARD-VIXEN	SLP	SA/CR	FBG KL	IB	15D	VLVO		8 6	8600	4 6	32700	36300
34 4	VIXEN 34	SLP	SA/CR	FBG KL	IB	30D	WEST		10 6	12500	5 2	49900	54800
1979 BOATS
29 7	VINEYARD-VIXEN	SLP	SA/CR	FBG KL	IB	15D	VLVO		8 6	8600	4 6	31300	34800
34 4	VIXEN 34	SLP	SA/CR	FBG KL	IB	23D	VLVO		10 6	12500	5 2	47700	52400
1978 BOATS
29 7	VINEYARD-VIXEN	SLP	SA/CR	FBG KL	IB	15D	VLVO		8 6	8600	4 6	30000	33400
34 4	VIXEN 34	SLP	SA/CR	FBG KL	IB	20D	WEST		10 6	12500	5 2	46000	50500
1977 BOATS
29 7	VINEYARD-VIXEN	SLP	SAIL	FBG KL	IB	15D	VLVO		8 6	8500	4	28500	31700
1975 BOATS
29 7	VINEYARD-VIXEN	SLP	SAIL	FBG KL	IB	15D	VLVO		8 6	8500	4	26600	29600
29 7	VINEYARD-VIXEN	YWL	SAIL	FBG KL	IB	15D	WEST		8 6	8500	4	26600	29600
1974 BOATS
21	VINEYARD 21	SLP	SA/OD	FBG KL					5 6	2200	4	5050	5850
29 7	VINEYARD VIXEN	SLP	SA/OD	FBG KL	IB	15D	VLVO		8 6	7800	4 6	23700	26300
29 7	VINEYARD VIXEN	YWL	SAIL	FBG KL	IB	15D	WEST		8 6	7800	4 6	23700	26300
1973 BOATS
21	VINEYARD 21	SLP	SA/OD	FBG KL					5 6	2200	4	4900	5650
1972 BOATS
21	VINEYARD 21	SLP	SA/OD	FBG KL					5 6	2200	4	4850	5550
1971 BOATS
21	VINEYARD 21	SLP	SA/OD	FBG KL					5 6	2200	4	4700	5400

MARTHAS VINEYARD SHIPYD INC   -CONTINUED

See inside cover to adjust price for area

LOA FT IN	NAME AND/ OR MODEL	TOP/ RIG	BOAT TYPE	MTL	-HULL- TP TP	ENGINE # HP	MFG	BEAM FT IN	WGT LBS	DRAFT FT IN	RETAIL LOW	RETAIL HIGH
1970 BOATS												
21	VINEYARD 21	SLP	SA/OD	KL				5 6	2200	4	4600	5300
1969 BOATS												
21	VINEYARD 21	SLP	SA/OD	FBG KL				5 6	2200	4	4550	5200
1968 BOATS												
21	VINEYARD 21	SLP	SA/OD	FBG KL				5 6	2200	4	4400	5100
1967 BOATS												
21	VINEYARD 21	SLP	SA/OD	FBG KL				5 6	2200	4	4350	5000
21	VINEYARD-HAVEN 15	SLP	SA/RC	FBG KL				5 6	2200	4	4350	5000
1966 BOATS												
21	VINEYARD-HAVEN 15	SLP	SA/OD	FBG KL				5 6	2200	4	4300	4950

MARTINI MARINE INC
COAST GUARD MFG ID- MPB

Call 1-800-327-6929 for BUC Personalized Evaluation Service
Or, for 1976 to 1981 boats, sign onto www.BUCValuPro.com

MASON BOATS LTD
COAST GUARD MFG ID- MAS

Call 1-800-327-6929 for BUC Personalized Evaluation Service
Or, for 1964 to 1988 boats, sign onto www.BUCValuPro.com

MASTER FABRICATORS
REDDING CA 96001   COAST GUARD MFG ID- HLR See inside cover to adjust price for area

MASTER FABRICATORS
RUSSELLVLE AR 72801

For more recent years, see the BUC Used Boat Price Guide, Volume 1 or Volume 2

LOA FT IN	NAME AND/ OR MODEL	TOP/ RIG	BOAT TYPE	MTL	-HULL- TP TP	ENGINE # HP	MFG	BEAM FT IN	WGT LBS	DRAFT FT IN	RETAIL LOW	RETAIL HIGH
1983 BOATS												
37	MASTER FABRICATORS	HT	HB	STL	PN IO	140	OMC	14	12800	2 6	14600	16600
42	MASTER FABRICATORS	HT	HB	STL	PN IO	140	OMC	14	15000	2 6	15000	17000
47	MASTER FABRICATORS	HT	HB	STL	PN IO	140	OMC	14	17000	2 6	17100	19500
50	MASTER FABRICATORS	HT	HB	STL	PN IO	140	OMC	14	18400	2 6	19300	21400
52	MASTER FABRICATORS	HT	HB	STL	PN IO	140	OMC	14	26000	2 6	25600	28500

MASTER MARINERS CORP
NEWPORT BEACH CA 92663   See inside cover to adjust price for area

For more recent years, see the BUC Used Boat Price Guide, Volume 1 or Volume 2

LOA FT IN	NAME AND/ OR MODEL	TOP/ RIG	BOAT TYPE	MTL	-HULL- TP TP	ENGINE # HP	MFG	BEAM FT IN	WGT LBS	DRAFT FT IN	RETAIL LOW	RETAIL HIGH
1967 BOATS												
31	HERRESHOFF 31	KTH	SA/CR	P/M	KL IB			9 6		4	17300	19700
32	GULF 32	SLP	SA/CR	FBG	KL IB			10		5 2	12000	13600
34 6	MARINER 35	KTH	SA/CR	MHG	KL IB			10 3		5	26500	29400
39 11	S&S 40	SLP	SA/CR	P/M	KL IB			10 1		6 2	34000	37700
40	CAPE-SAN-LUCAS	SLP	SA/CR	FBG	KL IB			11		6	36700	40800
40	GULF 40	SLP	SA/CR	FBG	KL IB			11		6	31600	35100
40	MARINER 40	KTH	SA/CR	MHG	KL IB			11 6		6	34200	38000
47	VICTOR 47		CR	STL	IB	235		15		6	49400	54200
57	VICTORIOUS		CR	STL	IB	235		18		6	90900	99800
67	DAUNTLESS		CR	STL	IB	T700		21		4 4	**	**
68	DEFIANCE		CR	STL	IB	230		20		7 7	**	**
68	RELIANCE		CR	STL	IB	230		20		7 7	**	**

MASTER MOLDERS INC
KINGFISHER BOATS   COAST GUARD MFG ID- KNG

Call 1-800-327-6929 for BUC Personalized Evaluation Service
Or, for 1969 to 1993 boats, sign onto www.BUCValuPro.com

MASTERCRAFT BOAT CO INC
VONORE TN 37885   COAST GUARD MFG ID- MBC See inside cover to adjust price for area

For more recent years, see the BUC Used Boat Price Guide, Volume 1 or Volume 2

LOA FT IN	NAME AND/ OR MODEL	TOP/ RIG	BOAT TYPE	MTL	-HULL- TP TP	ENGINE # HP	MFG	BEAM FT IN	WGT LBS	DRAFT FT IN	RETAIL LOW	RETAIL HIGH
1983 BOATS												
19	TOURNAMENT-SKIER DLX OP	SKI	FBG	SV	IB	250		6 9	2200	1 7	5600	6450
1982 BOATS												
19	MASTERCRAFT 19	RNBT	FBG	SV	IB	190		6 9			6050	6950
19	POWERSLOT 19	SKI	FBG	SV	IB	240		6 9			5900	6800
19	SUPERSLOT 19	SKI	FBG	SV	IB	425		6 9			7250	8350
19	TOURNAMENT-SKIER DLX OP	SKI	FBG	SV	IB	255-280		6 9	2200	1 7	5350	6250
19	TOURNAMENT-SKIER DLX OP	SKI	FBG	SV	IB	350	CHEV	6 9	2200	1 7	5850	6750
20 2	MASTERCRAFT 20	RNBT	FBG	SV	IO	255		6 9	2200	2 1	4900	5650
1981 BOATS												
19	MASTERCRAFT 19	RNBT	FBG	SV	IB	190		6 9			5800	6650
19	POWERSLOT 19	SKI	FBG	SV	IB	240		6 9			5650	6500
19	TOURNAMENT-SKIER DLX OP	SKI	FBG	SV	IB	255	PCM	6 9	2200	1 7	5300	6100
19	TOURNAMENT-SKIER STD OP	SKI	FBG	SV	IB	255	PCM	6 9	2200	1 7	4950	5700
20 2	MASTERCRAFT 20	RNBT	FBG	SV	IO	255		6 9			5300	6100
1980 BOATS												
19	TOURNAMENT-SKIER	OP	SKI	FBG	SV	IB	210	PCM	6 9	2200	1 7	4850	5600
19	TOURNAMENT-SKIER	OP	SKI	FBG	SV	IB	220-255		6 9			5400	6300
20	TOURNAMENT-SKIER	OP	SKI	FBG	SV	OB			6 9			1900	2300
20	TOURNAMENT-SKIER	OP	SKI	FBG	SV	IO	233-260		6 9	2400	1 7	4700	5850
1979 BOATS												
19	TOURNAMENT SKIER	OP	SKI	FBG	SV	IB	240	PCM	6 9	2000	1 7	4500	5200
20 2	TOURNAMENT SKIER	OP	SKI	FBG	SV	IO	240	PCM	6 9	2200	2 1	4600	5300
1978 BOATS												
19	MASTER-CRAFT	OP	SKI	FBG	SV	IB	220-240		6 9	2000	1 7	4250	5000
1977 BOATS												
19	TOURNAMENT SKI BOAT	OP	SKI	F/S	SV	IB	220-255		6 9	2000	10	4100	4800
1976 BOATS												
17 10	TOURNAMENT SKI BOAT	OP	SKI	FBG	SV	IB	220-255		6 9	1950	10	3600	4200
1975 BOATS												
18	TOURNAMENT SKI BOAT	OP	SKI	FBG	SV	IB	220-250		6 10	1900	1 6	3450	4050

MASTERCRAFTERS CAJUN BOATS
WEST MONROE LA 71291-52 COAST GUARD MFG ID- MBV See inside cover to adjust price for area
FORMERLY MASTERCRAFTERS CORP

For more recent years, see the BUC Used Boat Price Guide, Volume 1 or Volume 2

LOA FT IN	NAME AND/ OR MODEL	TOP/ RIG	BOAT TYPE	MTL	-HULL- TP TP	ENGINE # HP	MFG	BEAM FT IN	WGT LBS	DRAFT FT IN	RETAIL LOW	RETAIL HIGH
1983 BOATS												
20 1	GRANDE-BATEAU	OP	BASS	FBG	DV	OB			7 2	1200		1700	2050

MATLACK YACHT BLDRS INC
COAST GUARD MFG ID- MYB

Call 1-800-327-6929 for BUC Personalized Evaluation Service
Or, for 1973 to 1979 boats, sign onto www.BUCValuPro.com

MATT BOAT CO

Call 1-800-327-6929 for BUC Personalized Evaluation Service
Or, for 1966 to 1976 boats, sign onto www.BUCValuPro.com

F C MATTESON

Call 1-800-327-6929 for BUC Personalized Evaluation Service
Or, for 1967 boats, sign onto www.BUCValuPro.com

THE MATTHEWS CO
PT CLINTON OH 43452   COAST GUARD MFG ID- MAT See inside cover to adjust price for area

LOA FT IN	NAME AND/ OR MODEL	TOP/ RIG	BOAT TYPE	MTL	-HULL- TP TP	ENGINE # HP	MFG	BEAM FT IN	WGT LBS	DRAFT FT IN	RETAIL LOW	RETAIL HIGH
1975 BOATS												
46	FLUSH DECK	FB	DC	FBG	RB	IB	T275D	VLVO	14 10	34000	3 6	90800	99800
46	SPORT FISH	FB	SF	FBG	RB	IB	T275D	VLVO	14 10	34000	3 6	89300	98100
IB 730D GM	91900 101000, IB T320D GM					93300 102500, IB T400D CUM					101500 111500
56	FLUSH DECK	HT	FD	FBG	RB	IB	T400D	CUM	16	63000	4 3	204500	225000
56	FLUSH DECK	HT	FD	FBG	RB	IB	T435D	GM	16	63000	4 3	209000	230000

LOA FT	IN	NAME AND/ OR MODEL	TOP/ RIG	BOAT TYPE	-HULL- MTL	TP	ENGINE TP	# HP	MFG	BEAM FT	IN	WGT LBS	DRAFT FT	IN	RETAIL LOW	RETAIL HIGH
		1975 BOATS														
56		OFFSHORE	FB	OFF	FBG	RB	IB	T400D	CUM	16		63000	4	3	199000	219000
56		OFFSHORE	FB	OFF	FBG	RB	IB	T435D	GM	16		63000	4	3	202000	222000
56		SPORT FISH	FB	SF	FBG	RB	IB	T400D	CUM	16		60000	4	1	196000	215000
56		SPORT FISH	FB	SF	FBG	RB	IB	T435D	GM	16		60000	4	1	202000	221500
56		VOYAGEUR	FB	MY	FBG	RB	IB	T400D	CUM	16		67000	4	4	209500	230000
56		VOYAGEUR	FB	MY	FBG	RB	IB	T435D	GM	16		67000	4	4	213500	234500
65	3	FISHERMAN	FB	SF	FBG	SV	IB	T525D		17		75000	4	9	320000	351500
65	3	VOYAGEUR III	FB	MY	FBG	SV	IB	T525D		17		75000	4	9	341000	375000
		1974 BOATS														
46			FB	DCFD	FBG		IB	T275D	VLVO	14	10	34000	3	6	86800	95300
		IB T300D GM 89400 98200, IB T320D CUM 90900 99900, IB T400D CUM 98000 107500														
46			HT	SDN	FBG		IB	T275D	VLVO	14	10	34000	3	6	94500	104000
		IB T300D GM 96200 105500, IB T320D CUM 97100 106500, IB T400D CUM 101000 111000														
46			FB	SF	FBG		IB	T275D	VLVO	14	10	34000	3	6	85600	94100
		IB T300D GM 88100 96800, IB T320D CUM 89300 98100, IB T400D CUM 96600 106000														
56			FB	SF	FBG		IB	T350D	GM	16		58000	4	1	172500	190000
56			FB	SF	FBG		IB	T400D	CUM	16		58000	4	1	182000	200000
56			FB	SF	FBG		IB	T435D	GM	16		58000	4	1	188500	207000
56			HT	TCMY	FBG		IB	T350D	GM	16		62000	4	3	193000	212500
56			HT	TCMY	FBG		IB	T400D	CUM	16		62000	4	3	203500	223500
56			HT	TCMY	FBG		IB	T435D	GM	16		62000	4	3	209000	229500
56		OFFSHORE	FB	OFF	FBG		IB	T350D	GM	16		62000	4	3	179000	196500
56		OFFSHORE	FB	OFF	FBG		IB	T400D	CUM	16		62000	4	3	189500	208500
56		OFFSHORE	FB	OFF	FBG		IB	T435D	GM	16		62000	4	3	192500	211500
56		VOYAGEUR	HT	MY	FBG		IB	T350D	GM	16		66000	4	3	191000	210000
56		VOYAGEUR	HT	MY	FBG		IB	T400D	CUM	16		66000	4	3	202000	222000
56		VOYAGEUR	HT	MY	FBG		IB	T435D	GM	16		66000	4	3	205500	225500
65	3	VOYAGEUR III	FB	MY	FBG		IB	T478D	GM	17		75000	4	9	325500	357500
65	3	VOYAGEUR III	FB	MY	FBG		IB	T525D		17		75000	4	9	328000	360500
		1973 BOATS														
45	10		HT	DCFD	FBG		IB	T275D	VLVO	14	10	34000	3	6	83800	92100
		IB T300D CUM 86200 94800, IB T300D GM 86400 94900, IB T320D CUM 87900 96600														
		IB T370D CUM 92200 101500														
45	10		FB	DCFD	FBG		IB	T275D	VLVO	14	10	34000	3	6	83300	91600
		IB T300D CUM 85700 94200, IB T300D GM 85900 94400, IB T320D CUM 87400 96000														
		IB T370D CUM 91600 100500														
45	10		HT	SDN	FBG		IB	T300D	CUM	14	10	34000	3	6	92000	101000
		IB T300D GM 92100 101000, IB T320D CUM 92900 102000, IB T370D CUM 95300 104500														
45	10		FB	SDN	FBG		IB	T300D	CUM	14	10	34000	3	6	91300	100500
		IB T300D GM 91400 100500, IB T320D CUM 92300 101500, IB T370D CUM 94600 104000														
45	10		FB	SF	FBG		IB	T300D	CUM	14	10	34000	3	6	84200	92500
		IB T300D GM 84400 92800, IB T320D CUM 85600 94100, IB T370D CUM 90000 98900														
56			HT	SF	FBG		IB	T350D	GM	16		62000	4	1	181000	198500
56			HT	SF	FBG		IB	T380D	CUM	16		62000	4	1	187500	206000
56			HT	TCMY	FBG		IB	T350D	GM	16		62000	4	3	186000	204500
56			HT	TCMY	FBG		IB	T380D	CUM	16		62000	4	3	192000	211000
56		OFFSHORE	FB	OFF	FBG		IB	T350D	GM	16		62000	4	3	172000	189000
56		OFFSHORE	FB	OFF	FBG		IB	T380D	CUM	16		62000	4	3	179000	197000
56		OFFSHORE	FB	OFF	FBG		IB	T435D	GM	16		62000	4	3	185500	203500
56		VOYAGEUR	HT	MY	FBG		IB	T350D	GM	16		66000	4	3	184000	202000
56		VOYAGEUR	HT	MY	FBG		IB	T380D	CUM	16		66000	4	3	191000	210000
56		VOYAGEUR	HT	MY	FBG		IB	T435D	GM	16		66000	4	3	197500	217000
65	3	VOYAGEUR III	FB	MY	FBG		IB	T478D	GM	16		65000	4	9	273000	300000
		1972 BOATS														
45	9		HT	DC	FBG		IB	T283D	GM	14	10	35000	3	7	83400	91700
		IB T300D CUM 84600 93000, IB T300D GM 84800 93100, IB T320D CUM 86300 94800														
		IB T370D CUM 90500 99400														
45	9		FB	DC	FBG		IB	T283D	GM	14	10	35000	3	7	83000	91200
		IB T300D CUM 84100 92500, IB T300D GM 84300 92600, IB T320D CUM 85700 94200														
		IB T370D CUM 89900 98800														
45	9		HT	SDN	FBG		IB	T283D	GM	14	10	35000	3	7	89500	98400
		IB T300D CUM 90200 99100, IB T300D GM 90300 99200, IB T320D CUM 91100 100000														
		IB T370D CUM 93400 102500														
45	9		FB	SDN	FBG		IB	T283D	GM	14	10	35000	3	7	88900	97700
		IB T300D CUM 89600 98500, IB T300D GM 89700 98600, IB T320D CUM 90500 99500														
		IB T370D CUM 92700 102000														
45	9		FB	SF	FBG		IB	T283D	GM	14	10	34000	3	7	80200	88100
		IB T300D CUM 81000 89000, IB T300D GM 81200 89300, IB T370D CUM 86700 95200														
45	9	MYSTIC	FB	MY	FBG		IB	T300D	CUM	14	10	25000	3	7	74200	81600
45	9	MYSTIC	FB	MY	FBG		IB	T300D	GM	14	10	25000	3	7	74400	81700
45	9	MYSTIC	FB	MY	FBG		IB	T320D	CUM	14	10	25000	3	7	76200	83800
56			FB	SF	FBG		IB	T350D	GM	16		58000	4	1	160500	176000
56			FB	SF	FBG		IB	T380D	CUM	16		58000	4	1	166000	182000
56			FB	SF	FBG		IB	T400D	GM	16		58000	4	1	169000	186000
56			HT	TCMY	FBG		IB	T350D	GM	16		62000	4	3	179500	197000
56			HT	TCMY	FBG		IB	T380D	CUM	16		62000	4	3	185500	203500
56			HT	TCMY	FBG		IB	T400D	GM	16		62000	4	3	188000	206500
56		OFFSHORE	FB	OFF	FBG		IB	T350D	GM	16		62000	4	3	166000	182000
56		OFFSHORE	FB	OFF	FBG		IB	T380D	CUM	16		62000	4	3	172500	190000
56		OFFSHORE	FB	OFF	FBG		IB	T400D	GM	16		62000	4	3	173000	190500
56		VOYAGEUR	HT	MY	FBG		IB	T350D	GM	16		66000	4	3	177500	195000
56		VOYAGEUR	HT	MY	FBG		IB	T380D	CUM	16		66000	4	3	184000	202500
56		VOYAGEUR	HT	MY	FBG		IB	T400D	GM	16		66000	4	3	185000	203500
56		VOYAGEUR	FB	MY	FBG		IB	T350D	GM	16		66000	4	3	175500	192500
56		VOYAGEUR	FB	MY	FBG		IB	T380D	GM	16		66000	4	3	180000	197500
56		VOYAGEUR	FB	MY	FBG		IB	T400D	GM	16		66000	4	3	183000	201000
65	3	VOYAGEUR III	FB	MY	FBG		IB	T478D	GM	16		65000	4	9	263000	289000
		1971 BOATS														
45	7		HT	DCFD	FBG		IB	T335		14	10		3	4	67100	73700
		IB T283D GM 82000 90100, IB T300D CUM 83200 91400, IB T370D CUM 88800 97600														
45	7		HT	SDN	FBG		IB	T335		14	10		3	4	63000	69300
		IB T283D GM 77800 85500, IB T300D CUM 78500 86300, IB T370D CUM 81700 89800														
45	7		FB	SF	FBG		IB	T335		14	10		3	4	66600	73200
		IB T283D GM 72400 79600, IB T300D CUM 73200 80400, IB T370D CUM 78600 86300														
45	7	COCKPIT		DC	FBG		IB	T335		14	10		3	4	66600	73200
45	7	MYSTIC	FB	MY	FBG		IB	T130D	PERK	14	10	33000	3	4	81000	89000
45	7	MYSTIC	FB	MY	FBG		IB	T283D	GM	14	10	33000	3	4	81700	89800
45	7	MYSTIC	FB	MY	FBG		IB	T300D	CUM	14	10	33000	3	4	83200	91400
53	10		HT	DCFD	WD		IB	T350D	GM	15	3	52000	3	8	138000	151500
53	10		HT	DCFD	WD		IB	T360D	CAT	15	3	52000	3	8	139500	153500
53	10		HT	DCFD	WD		IB	T370D	CUM	15	3	52000	3	8	141500	155000
53	10		FB	SF	WD		IB	T350D	GM	15	3	48000	3	8	126000	138500
53	10		FB	SF	WD		IB	T360D	CAT	15	3	48000	3	8	127500	140000
53	10		FB	SF	WD		IB	T370D	CUM	15	3	48000	3	8	129500	142000
56				DC	FBG	DS	IB	T350D	GM	16		55000	3	8	142500	156500
56			HT	DCFD	FBG		IB	T425D	GM	16		58000			168500	185000
56		OFFSHORE		OFF	FBG	DS	IB	T350D	GM	16		53000	3	8	140500	154500
56		VOYAGEUR	HT	MY	FBG		IB	T425D	GM	16		62000			174500	192000
56		VOYAGEUR II		MY	FBG		IB	T350		16			3	8	132000	145000
60				SF	WD	DS	IB	T350D	GM	16	3	58000	3	8	171500	188500
60		SALON		DC	WD	DS	IB	T350D	GM	16	3	62000	3	8	192000	211000
60		VOYAGEUR I	HT	MY	WD		IB	T350D	GM	16	3	60000	3	8	186500	205000
		IB T360D CAT 187500 206000, IB T370D CUM 193000 212000, IB T425D GM 202500 222500														
60	8	VOYAGEUR II		MY	WD		IB	T425D	GM	16	4	68000	3	10	231000	253500
60	8	VOYAGEUR II		MY	WD	DS	IB	T400D	GM	16	4	68000	3	10	225500	248000
60	8	VOYAGEUR II	FB	MY	WD		IB	T425D	GM	16	4	68000	3	10	231500	254000
65	3	VOYAGEUR III		MY	FBG		IB	T478D	GM	16		65000	3	8	254000	279000
65	3	VOYAGEUR III	FB	MY	FBG		IB	T478D	GM	16		65000	3	8	254000	279000
		1970 BOATS														
45	4		HT	DCFD	WD	RB	IB	T283D	GM	14		36000	3	4	84500	92900
45	4		HT	DCFD	WD	RB	IB	T300D	CUM	14		36000	3	4	85800	94200
45	4		HT	SDN	WD	RB	IB	T283D	GM	14		30000	3	4	75700	83200
45	4		HT	SDN	WD	RB	IB	T300D	CUM	14		30000	3	4	76300	83900
45	4		FB	SF	WD	RB	IB	T300	CHRY	14		30000	3	4	62800	69000
45	4		FB	SF	WD	RB	IB	T283D	GM	14		30000	3	4	70000	76900
45	4		FB	SF	WD	RB	IB	T370D	CUM	14		30000	3	4	76700	84300
45	4	FLUSH DECK		DC	FBG		IB	T283D		14	10		3	5	71400	78500
45	4	FLUSH DECK		TCMY	FBG		IB	T283D		14	10		3	5	79900	87800
45	4	VOYAGER II	FB	SDN	WD		IB	T283D	GM	14		30000	3	4	74500	81900
45	4	VOYAGER II	FB	SDN	WD		IB	T300D	CUM	14		30000	3	4	75200	82600
45	7		HT	DC	FBG	RB	IB	T283D	GM	14	10	35000	3	5	78300	86100
45	7		HT	DC	FBG	RB	IB	T300D	CUM	14	10	35000	3	5	79600	87400
45	7		HT	SDN	FBG	RB	IB	T300	CHRY	14	10	30000	3	5	69100	76000
45	7		HT	SDN	FBG	RB	IB	T283D	GM	14	10	30000	3	5	76000	83500

CONTINUED ON NEXT PAGE

LOA FT	LOA IN	NAME AND/ OR MODEL	TOP/ RIG	BOAT TYPE	-HULL- MTL	-HULL- TP	ENGINE TP	ENGINE # HP	ENGINE MFG	BEAM FT	BEAM IN	WGT LBS	DRAFT FT	DRAFT IN	RETAIL LOW	RETAIL HIGH
1970 BOATS																
45	7		HT	SDN	FBG	RB	IB	T300D	CUM	14	10	30000	3	5	76700	84200
45	7		FB	SF	FBG	RB	IB	T300	CHRY	14	10	30000	3	5	63200	69400
45	7		FB	SF	FBG	RB	IB	T283D	GM	14	10	30000	3	5	70100	77100
45	7		FB	SF	FBG	RB	IB	T300D	CUM	14	10	30000	3	5	70900	77900
53	10		HT	DCFD	WD	RB	IB	T350D	GM	15	3	52000	3	8	134000	147500
53	10		HT	DCFD	WD	RB	IB	T370D	CUM	15	3	52000	3	8	137000	150500
53	10	MARAUDER	FB	SF	WD	RB	IB	T350D	GM	15	3	48000	3	8	117000	129000
53	10	MARAUDER	FB	SF	WD	RB	IB	T370D	CUM	15	3	48000	3	8	120500	132500
60			HT	DCFD	WD	RB	IB	T350D	GM	16	3	60000	3	8	182000	200000
60			HT	DCFD	WD	RB	IB	T370D	CUM	16	3	60000	3	8	188000	206500
60		VOYAGER II	FB	MY	WD		IB	T400D	GM	16	3	62000	4	8	195500	214500
60	4	VOYAGEUR II		MY	WD	RB	IB	T400D	GM	16	3	62000	4	8	196000	215500
1969 BOATS																
45	4		HT	DCFD	WD	RB	IB	T300	CHRY	14		32000	3	4	66900	73500
45	4		HT	DCFD	WD	RB	IB	T283D	GM	14		32000	3	4	75600	83000
45	4		HT	DCFD	WD	RB	IB	T300D	CUM	14		32000	3	4	76900	84500
45	4		HT	SDN	WD	RB	IB	T300	CHRY	14		28000	3	4	63900	70300
45	4		HT	SDN	WD	RB	IB	T283D	GM	14		30000	3	4	73300	80500
45	4		HT	SDN	WD	RB	IB	T300D	CUM	14		30000	3	4	73900	81200
45	4		FB	SDN	WD		IB	T300	CHRY	14		28000	3	4	63000	69200
45	4		FB	SDN	WD		IB	T283D	GM	14		30000	3	4	72200	79300
45	4		FB	SDN	WD		IB	T300D	CUM	14		30000	3	4	72800	80000
45	4		FB	SF	WD	RB	IB	T300	CHRY	14		28000	3	4	58700	64500
45	4		FB	SF	WD	RB	IB	T283D	GM	14		30000	3	4	67700	74400
45	4		FB	SF	WD	RB	IB	T370D	CUM	14		30000	3	4	74300	81600
45	4		HT	TCMY	WD	RB	IB	T300	CHRY	14		32000	3	4	74400	81800
45	4		HT	TCMY	WD	RB	IB	T283D	GM	14		32000	3	4	84300	92700
45	4		HT	TCMY	WD	RB	IB	T300D	CUM	14		32000	3	4	85900	94400
53	10		HT	DCFD	WD		IB	T370D	CUM	15	3	48000	3	8	123000	135000
53	10		HT	DCFD	WD	RB	IB	T350D	GM	15	3	48000	3	8	120500	132500
53	10	DOUBLE SALON	HT	MY	WD		IB	T350D	GM	15	3	48000	3	8	118000	129500
53	10	DOUBLE SALON	HT	MY	WD		IB	T370D	CUM	15	3	48000	3	8	121000	133000
53	10	MARAUDER	FB	SF	WD	RB	IB	T350D	GM	15	3	48000	3	8	113500	124500
53	10	MARAUDER	FB	SF	WD	RB	IB	T370D	CUM	15	3	48000	3	8	116500	128000
60			HT	DCFD	WD		IB	T370D	CUM	16	3	56000	3	8	169000	185500
60				SF	WD		IB	T350D	GM	16	3	56000	3	1	157500	173000
60			HT	TCMY	WD		IB	T350D	GM	16	3	56000	3	8	167000	183500
60			HT	TCMY	WD		IB	T370D	CUM	16	3	56000	3	8	172500	189500
60		DOUBLE SALON	HT	MY	WD		IB	T350D	GM	16	3	56000	3	8	161500	177500
60		DOUBLE SALON	HT	MY	WD		IB	T370D	CUM	16	3	56000	3	8	167000	184000
60		VOYAGER	HT	DCFD	WD		IB	T350D	GM	16	3	56000	3	8	163500	179500
1968 BOATS																
45	4		HT	SDN	WD		IB	T250	CHRY	14		26000	3	3	57200	62800
		IB T290 CHRY 58700 64500, IB T283D GM 65900 72500, IB T300D CUM													66600	73200
45	4		FB	SDN	WD		IB	T250	CHRY	14		26000	3	3	56800	62400
		IB T290 CHRY 58300 64100, IB T283D GM 65500 72000, IB T300D CUM													66200	72700
45	4		FB	SF	WD		IB	T250	CHRY	14		26000	3	3	54000	59300
		IB T290 CHRY 54600 60000, IB T283D GM 61800 67900, IB T300D CUM													62500	68700
		IB T370D CUM 67900 74600														
45	4		FB	TCMY	WD		IB	T250	CHRY	14		30000	3	3	63600	69900
		IB T290 CHRY 67100 73700, IB T283D GM 77300 85000, IB T300D CUM													78800	86600
45	4	FLUSH OR COCKPIT	FB	DC	WD		IB	T250	CHRY	14		30000	3	3	58700	64500
		IB T290 CHRY 60600 66600, IB T283D GM 69400 76200, IB T300D CUM													70600	77600
53	10		HT	TCMY	WD		IB	T350D	GM	15	3	48000	3	8	126000	138500
53	10		HT	TCMY	WD		IB	T370D	CUM	15	3	48000	3	8	129500	142000
53	10	FLUSH OR COCKPIT	HT	DC	WD		IB	T350D	GM	15	3	48000	3	8	116500	128000
53	10	FLUSH OR COCKPIT	HT	DC	WD		IB	T370D	CUM	15	3	48000	3	8	119500	131000
60			FB	SF	WD		IB	T350D	GM	16	3	52000	3	8	148000	162500
60			FB	SF	WD		IB	T370D		16	3	52000	3	8	154000	169000
60			HT	TCMY	WD		IB	T350D		16	3	52000	3	8	156000	171500
60			HT	TCMY	WD		IB	T370D		16	3	52000	3	8	158000	174000
60		FLUSH OR COCKPIT	HT	DC	WD		IB	T350D		16	3	52000	3	8	153000	168500
60		FLUSH OR COCKPIT	HT	DC	WD		IB	T370D		16	3	52000	3	8	155500	170500
1967 BOATS																
45	4		HT	SDN	WD		IB	T250	CHRY	14		26000	3	3	55500	61000
		IB T290 CHRY 57000 62600, IB T215D CUM 60300 66300, IB T216D GM													60500	66400
		IB T283D GM 63500 69700, IB T300D CUM 64100 70400														
45	4		FB	SDN	WD		IB	T250	CHRY	14		26000	3	3	55200	60600
		IB T290 CHRY 56600 62200, IB T215D CUM 60000 65900, IB T216D GM													60100	66000
		IB T283D GM 63100 69300, IB T300D CUM 63700 70000														
45	4	MARAUDER	FB	SF	WD		IB	T250	CHRY	14		23700	3	3	50100	55100
		IB T290 CHRY 50600 55600, IB T215D CUM 54400 59800, IB T216D GM													54600	60000
		IB T283D GM 56600 62200, IB T300D CUM 56900 62600														
45	4	WANDERER	FB	DC	WD		IB	T250	CHRY	14		26000	3	3	52600	57800
		IB T290 CHRY 54200 59600, IB T215D CUM 57500 63200, IB T216D GM													57700	63400
		IB T283D GM 62300 68500, IB T300D CUM 63600 69900														
45	4	WANDERER	FB	TCMY	WD		IB	T250	CHRY	14		26000	3	3	56100	61700
		IB T290 CHRY 59600 65500, IB T215D CUM 62500 68600, IB T216D GM													62600	68800
		IB T283D GM 69500 76300, IB T300D CUM 71000 78000														
53	10			FD	WD		IB	T350D	GM	15	3	39000	3	8	109000	119500
53	10			FD	WD		IB	T370D	CUM	15	3	39000	3	8	111500	123000
53	10			FD	WD		IB	T370D	GM	15	3	39000	3	8	111500	122500
53	10	COCKPIT		DCCPT	WD		IB	T350D	GM	15	3	39000	3	8	92600	102000
53	10	COCKPIT		DCCPT	WD		IB	T370D	CUM	15	3	39000	3	8	95500	105000
53	10	FLUSH DECK		TCMY	WD		IB	T350D	GM	15	3	39000	3	8	101500	111500
53	10	MARAUDER	FB	SF	WD		IB	T350D	GM	15	3	39000	3	8	94200	103500
53	10	MARAUDER	FB	SF	WD		IB	T370D	CUM	15	3	39000	3	8	97200	107000
60		VOYAGEUR		TCMY	WD		IB	T350D	GM	16	3	50000	3	8	144500	159000
60		VOYAGEUR		TCMY	WD		IB	T370D	CUM	16	3	50000	3	8	148000	162500
1966 BOATS																
44	8	CONVERTIBLE	HT	SDN	WD		IB	T250		14		28000	3	3	55100	60500
		IB T290 56300 61900, IB T215D 59900 65800, IB T215D CUM													59800	65700
		IB T280D 62500 68600, IB T300D 63300 69500														
44	8	CONVERTIBLE	FB	SDN	WD		IB	T250		14		28000	3	3	54800	60200
		IB T290 56000 61600, IB T215D 59600 65500, IB T215D CUM													59500	65400
		IB T280D 62100 68300, IB T300D 62900 69100														
44	8	MARAUDER	FB	SF	WD		IB	T250		14		28000	3	3	50700	55700
		IB T290 51200 56300, IB T215D 55400 60900, IB T215D CUM													55200	60700
		IB T280D 57300 63000, IB T300D 58000 63700, IB T370D													61100	67200
44	8	WANDERER	FB	DC	WD		IB	T250		14		28000	3	3	52200	57300
		IB T290 54100 59500, IB T215D 57500 63200, IB T215D CUM													57400	63100
		IB T280D 62000 68100, IB T300D 63400 69700														
44	8	WANDERER	FB	TCMY	WD		IB	T250		14		28000	3	3	56200	61700
		IB T290 59200 65100, IB T215D 62500 68600, IB T215D CUM													62400	68500
		IB T280D 68100 74900, IB T300D 69800 76700														
53	10		HT	FD	WD		IB	T300D		15	3	39000	3	8	101000	111000
53	10		HT	FD	WD		IB	T350D		15	3	39000	3	8	108500	119000
53	10	FLUSH DECK	HT	TCMY	WD		IB	T300D		15	3	39000	3	8	95000	104500
53	10	FLUSH DECK	HT	TCMY	WD		IB	T350D		15	3	39000	3	8	101500	111500
53	10	MARAUDER	FB	SF	WD		IB	T300D		15	3	39000	3	8	90700	99700
53	10	MARAUDER	FB	SF	WD		IB	T350D		15	3	39000	3	8	94900	104500
60		VOYAGEUR	HT	DC	WD		IB	T370D		16	3	50000	3	8	143500	157500
60		VOYAGEUR	HT	TCMY	WD		IB	T350D		16	3	50000	3	8	144000	158000
1965 BOATS																
36	3			EXP	WD		IB	T130		12	7		3		24900	27700
43	3		HT	DCCPT	WD		IB	T190	CHRY	13		26000	3	4	45600	50100
		IB T250 CHRY 47900 52600, IB T280 CHRY 49600 54500, IB T280 GRAY													49600	54600
		IB T290 CHRY 50200 55100, IB T200D CAT 52800 58000, IB T215D CUM													52900	58200
		IB T215D GM 53100 58300														
43	3		HT	DCFD	WD		IB	T190	CHRY	13		26000	3	4	51400	56500
		IB T250 CHRY 54600 60000, IB T280 CHRY 56100 61700, IB T280 GRAY													56200	61700
		IB T290 CHRY 56600 62200, IB T200D CAT 59800 65700, IB T215D CUM													60100	66000
		IB T215D GM 60200 66200														
43	3	CONVERTIBLE	HT	SDN	WD		IB	T190	CHRY	13		26000	3	4	52300	57500
		IB T250 CHRY 53800 59200, IB T280 CHRY 54600 60000, IB T280 GRAY													54600	60000
		IB T290 CHRY 54800 60200, IB T200D CAT 58900 64700, IB T215D CUM													59100	64900
		IB T215D GM 58500 64300														
43	3	CONVERTIBLE	FB	SDN	WD		IB	T190	CHRY	13		26000	3	4	52000	57100
		IB T250 CHRY 53400 58700, IB T280 CHRY 54200 59500, IB T280 GRAY													54200	59600
		IB T290 CHRY 54400 59800, IB T200D CAT 58500 64300, IB T215D CUM													58600	64400
		IB T215D GM 58100 63900														
43	3	DELUXE	HT	SDN	WD		IB	T190	CHRY	13		26000	3	4	52300	57500

CONTINUED ON NEXT PAGE

```
THE MATTHEWS CO              -CONTINUED      See inside cover to adjust price for area
 LOA NAME AND/           TOP/ BOAT  -HULL- ----ENGINE--- BEAM     WGT  DRAFT  RETAIL RETAIL
 FT IN  OR MODEL         RIG  TYPE  MTL TP TP # HP  MFG  FT IN   LBS   FT IN   LOW   HIGH
 ------------------- 1965 BOATS --------------------------------------------------------
 43 3 DELUXE            HT  SDN    WD      IB T250  CHRY 13     26000  3  4   53800  59200
    IB T280   CHRY 54600  60000, IB T280 GRAY 54600  60000, IB T290  CHRY   54800  60200
    IB T200D CAT  58900  64700, IB T215D CUM  59100  64900, IB T215D GM     58500  64300

 43 3 DELUXE            FB  SDN    WD      IB T190  CHRY 13     26000  3  4   52400  57600
    IB T250   CHRY 53900  59200, IB T280 CHRY 54600  60000, IB T280  GRAY   54700  60100
    IB T290   CHRY 54800  60300, IB T200D CAT  58900  64700, IB T215D CUM   59100  64900
    IB T215D  GM   58500  64300

 43 3 MARTINIQUE        HT  EXP    WD      IB T190  CHRY 13     26000  3  4   51700  56800
    IB T250   CHRY 53200  58400, IB T280 CHRY 53900  59200, IB T280  GRAY   54000  59300
    IB T290   CHRY 54100  59500, IB T200D CAT  58100  63900, IB T215D GM    58100  63900

 43 3 MARTINIQUE        FB  EXP    WD      IB T190  CHRY 13     26000  3  4   51600  56700
    IB T250   CHRY 53000  58300, IB T280 CHRY 53700  59000, IB T280  GRAY   53800  59100
    IB T290   CHRY 53900  59300, IB T200D CAT  57900  63700, IB T215D CUM   57800  63500
    IB T215D  GM   57900  63700

 53 10                  HT  MY     WD      IB T215D GM   15   3 39000  3  8   78200  85900
    IB T280D  CAT  84200  92600, IB T280D GM   82500  90700, IB T300D CUM   85100  93500

 53 10                  FB  MY     WD      IB T215D GM   15   3 39000  3  8   78000  85700
 59 10 VOYAGEUR         HT  MY     WD      IB T280D GM   16   3 50000  3  8  107500 118000
 59 10 VOYAGEUR         HT  MY     WD      IB T300D CUM  16   3 50000  3  8  110000 121000
 59 10 VOYAGEUR         HT  MY     WD      IB T320D GM   16   3 50000  3  8  110500 121500
 ------------------- 1964 BOATS --------------------------------------------------------
 36 3                   HT  EXP    WD  RB IB T190  CHRY       18500  3        31800  35400
 36 3                   HT  EXP    WD  RB IB T220  CHRY 12  7 18500  3        31300  34800
 36 3                   HT  EXP    WD  RB IB T130D GM   12  7 18500  3        34700  38500
 36 3                   FB  EXP    WD  RB IB T190  CHRY 12  7 18500  3        31100  34500
 36 3                   FB  EXP    WD  RB IB T220  GRAY 12  7 18500  3        31300  34800
 36 3                   FB  EXP    WD  RB IB T130D GM   12  7 18500  3        34700  38500
 36 3                   HT  SDN    WD      IB T190  CHRY 12  7 18500  3        31600  35100
 36 3                   HT  SDN    WD  RB IB T220  GRAY 12  7 18500  3        31900  35400
 36 3                   HT  SDN    WD  RB IB T130D GM   12  7 18500  3        35200  39100
 36 3                   FB  SDN    WD      IB T190  CHRY 12  7 18500  3        31600  35100
 36 3                   FB  SDN    WD  RB IB T220  GRAY 12  7 18500  3        31900  35400
 36 3                   FB  SDN    WD  RB IB T130D GM   12  7 18500  3        35200  39100

 43 3                   FB  DC     WD      IB  190  CHRY 13     25000  3  4   42300  47000
    IB  225   CHRY 42400  47200, IB T190  CHRY 48500  53300, IB T225  GRAY   50500  55500
    IB T250        51800  56900, IB T250 CHRY 51700  56800, IB T260  GRAY   52200  57400
    IB T275   INT  53000  58200, IB T280 CHRY 53200  58400, IB T280  GRAY   53200  58500
    IB T185D       55100  60600

 43 3                   HT  SF     WD      IB  190  CHRY 13        3  4        43200  48000
    IB  225   CHRY 43300  48200, IB T190  CHRY 41700  46300, IB T225  GRAY   47100  51700
    IB T250   CHRY 48100  52800, IB T250 RR   48200  52900, IB T260  CHRY   48400  53200
    IB T275   INT  49300  54100, IB T280 CHRY 49500  54400, IB T280  GRAY   49500  54400
    IB T185D  GM   52600  57800

 43 3                   FB  SF     WD      IB  190  CHRY 13        3  4        43200  48000
    IB  225   CHRY 43300  48200, IB T190  CHRY 45900  50400, IB T225  GRAY   47000  51600
    IB T250   CHRY 48000  52700, IB T250 RR   48100  52800, IB T260  CHRY   48300  53100
    IB T275   INT  49100  54000, IB T280 CHRY 49300  54200, IB T280  GRAY   49400  54300
    IB T185D  GM   52600  57800

 43 3 CONVERTIBLE       HT  SDN    WD      IB  190  CHRY 13     23000  3  4   43500  48300
    IB  225   CHRY 44100  49000, IB T190  GRAY 47500  52200, IB T225  GRAY   48200  52900
    IB T250   CHRY 48700  53600, IB T250 RR   48800  53600, IB T260  CHRY   49000  53800
    IB T275   INT  49400  54300, IB T280 CHRY 49500  54400, IB T280  GRAY   49500  54400
    IB T185D  GM   52400  57600

 43 3 CONVERTIBLE       FB  SDN    WD      IB  190  CHRY 13     23000  3  4   43300  48100
    IB  225   CHRY 44000  48900, IB T190  CHRY 47300  52000, IB T225  GRAY   48000  52800
    IB T250   CHRY 48600  53400, IB T250 RR   48600  53400, IB T260  CHRY   48800  53600
    IB T275   INT  49200  54100, IB T280 CHRY 49300  54200, IB T280  GRAY   49400  54200
    IB T185D       52300  57400

 43 3 DELUXE            HT  SDN    WD      IB  190  CHRY 13     22000  3  4   42200  46900
    IB  225   CHRY 42800  47600, IB T190  CHRY 46200  50800, IB T225  GRAY   47200  51900
    IB T250   CHRY 47800  52500, IB T250 RR   47900  52600, IB T260  CHRY   47800  52500
    IB T275   INT  48300  53000, IB T280 CHRY 48300  53100, IB T280  GRAY   48400  53200
    IB T185D  GM   51200  56300

 43 3 DELUXE            FB  SDN    WD      IB  190  CHRY 13     22000  3  4   42100  46700
    IB  225   CHRY 42700  47500, IB T190  CHRY 46100  50600, IB T225  GRAY   47100  51700
    IB T250   CHRY 47600  52300, IB T250 GRAY 47700  52400, IB T260  CHRY   47900  52600
    IB T275   INT  48100  52800, IB T280 CHRY 48100  52900, IB T280  GRAY   48200  53000
    IB T185D  GM   51000  56100

 43 3 MARTINIQUE        HT  EXP    WD      IB  190  CHRY 13     22000  3  4   41700  46400
    IB  225   CHRY 42400  47100, IB T190  CHRY 45600  50200, IB T225  GRAY   46600  51200
    IB T250   CHRY 47200  51900, IB T250 RR   47300  51900, IB T260  CHRY   47400  52100
    IB T275   INT  47900  52600, IB T280 CHRY 47900  52700, IB T280  GRAY   47700  52500
    IB T185D  GM   50600  55600

 43 3 MARTINIQUE        FB  EXP    WD      IB  190  CHRY 13     22000  3  4   41600  46300
    IB  225   CHRY 42200  46900, IB T190  CHRY 45400  50000, IB T225  GRAY   46500  51100
    IB T250   CHRY 47000  51700, IB T250 RR   47100  51800, IB T260  CHRY   47300  51900
    IB T275   INT  47700  52400, IB T280 CHRY 47800  52500, IB T280  GRAY   47800  52600
    IB T185D  GM   50400  55400

 52 5                   FB  CR     WD      IB T275  INT  14   3 33000  3  6   74700  82100
    IB T280   CHRY 75000  82400, IB T180D CAT  68700  75500, IB T185D GM     67900  74600
    IB T235D  GM   71800  78900, IB T275D GM   76200  83700, IB T300D CUM   79100  87000

 52 5                   FB  EXP    WD      IB T275  INT  14   3 33000  3  6   84100  92500
    IB T280   CHRY 84800  93200, IB T180D CAT  74300  81600, IB T185D GM     74300  81600
    IB T235D  GM   81600  89200, IB T275D GM   87400  96000, IB T300D CUM   90800  99700
 ------------------- 1963 BOATS --------------------------------------------------------
 42 4                   FB  DC     WD      IB  190  CHRY 13     25000  3  4   40800  45300
    IB  225   CHRY 40900  45400, IB  151D GM   50100  55100, IB T190  CHRY   47500  52200
    IB T225   CHRY 48600  53400, IB T225 GRAY 48600  53500, IB T260  CHRY   49800  54700
    IB T275   INT  50400  55400, IB T275 UNIV 50400  55400, IB T280  CHRY   50500  55500
    IB T280   GRAY 50600  55600, IB T151D GM  56300  36.39, IB T185D GM     53100  58300

 42 4                   SF     WD      IB  151D                       3        42800  47600
 42 4                   HT  SF     WD      IB  190  CHRY 13     23000  3  4   48300  53100
    IB  225   CHRY 36700  40800, IB T190  CHRY 39900  44400, IB T225  CHRY   41500  46100
    IB T225   GRAY 41500  46200, IB T260  CHRY 43100  47900, IB T275  INT    43900  48800
    IB T275   UNIV 43900  48800, IB T280  CHRY 44000  48900, IB T280  GRAY   44100  49000
    IB T151D  GM   43800  48700, IB T185D GM  46100  50700

 42 4                   FB  SDN    WD      IB  190  CHRY 13     23000  3  4   48300  53100
    IB  225   CHRY 36700  40800, IB  151D GM  98400 108000, IB T190  CHRY   39900  44300
    IB T225   CHRY 41400  46000, IB T225 GRAY 41500  46100, IB T260  CHRY   43000  47800
    IB T275   INT  43800  48700, IB T275 UNIV 43800  48700, IB T280  CHRY   44000  48800
    IB T280   GRAY 44000  48900, IB T151D GM  43800  48700, IB T185D GM     46100  50600

 42 4 CONVERTIBLE       HT  SDN    WD      IB  190  CHRY 13     23000  3  4   42600  47300
    IB  225   CHRY 43100  47800, IB  151D GM  45800  50300, IB T190  CHRY   45800  50300
    IB T225   CHRY 46400  51000, IB T225 GRAY 46500  51100, IB T260  CHRY   47100  51700
    IB T275   INT  47400  52100, IB T275 UNIV 47500  52100, IB T280  CHRY   47500  52200
    IB T280   GRAY 47500  52200, IB T151D GM  52000  57200, IB T185D GM     50400  55400

 42 4 CONVERTIBLE       FB  SDN    WD      IB  190  CHRY 13     23000  3  4   42700  47400
    IB  225   CHRY 43100  47800, IB  151D GM  45800  50400, IB T190  CHRY   45900  50400
    IB T225   CHRY 47100  51700, IB T225 GRAY 46600  50500, IB T260  CHRY   47200  51800
    IB T275   INT  47400  52100, IB T275 UNIV 47600  52300, IB T280  CHRY   47400  52100
    IB T280   GRAY 47700  52400, IB T151D GM  51900  57100, IB T185D GM     50500  55400

 42 4 DELUXE            HT  SDN    WD      IB  190  CHRY 13     23000  3  4   42600  47300
    IB  225   CHRY 43100  47800, IB  151D GM  45800  50400, IB T190  CHRY   45800  50300
    IB T225   CHRY 46400  51000, IB T225 GRAY 46500  51100, IB T260  CHRY   47100  51700
    IB T275   INT  47400  52100, IB T275 UNIV 47600  52300, IB T280  CHRY   47100  51700
    IB T280   GRAY 47500  52200, IB T151D GM  49400  54200, IB T185D GM     50400  55400

 42 4 DELUXE            FB  SDN    WD      IB  190  CHRY 13     23000  3  4   42300  47100
    IB  225   CHRY 42800  47500, IB  151D GM  45600  50100, IB T190  CHRY   45600  50100
    IB T225   CHRY 46700  51400, IB T225 GRAY 46200  50500, IB T260  CHRY   47100  51800
    IB T275   INT  47100  51800, IB T275 UNIV 47200  51900, IB T280  CHRY   47100  51800
    IB T280   GRAY 47300  52000, IB T151D GM  49200  54100, IB T185D GM     50100  55100

 42 4 MARTINIQUE        HT  EXP    WD      IB  190  CHRY 13     23000  3  4   42300  47000
    IB  225   CHRY 42700  47500, IB  151D GM  45400  49900, IB T190  CHRY   44800  49400
    IB T225   CHRY 46000  50700, IB T225 GRAY 46100  50800, IB T260  CHRY   46700  51300
    IB T275   INT  47000  51700, IB T275 UNIV 46100  50800, IB T280  CHRY   47000  51700
    IB T280   GRAY 47100  51800, IB T151D GM  48900  53800, IB T185D GM     50000  55000

 42 4 MARTINIQUE        FB  EXP    WD      IB  190  CHRY 13     23000  3  4   42400  46900
    IB  225   CHRY 42700  47400, IB  151D GM  45400  49800, IB T190  CHRY   44800  49400
    IB T225   CHRY 45900  50500, IB T225 GRAY 46000  50600, IB T260  CHRY   46600  51200
    IB T275   INT  46900  51500, IB T275 UNIV 46900  51500, IB T280  CHRY   46900  51600
    IB T280   GRAY 47000  51600, IB T151D GM  48800  53700, IB T185D GM     49900  54800
```

```
LOA  NAME AND/        TOP/ BOAT  -HULL-  ----ENGINE---  BEAM  WGT  DRAFT  RETAIL RETAIL
FT IN  OR MODEL       RIG  TYPE  MTL TP TP # HP  MFG  FT IN  LBS  FT IN  LOW    HIGH
------------------- 1963 BOATS -------------------------------------------------------
51  7                  FB   CR   WD      IB T275 INT 14 3 33000  3  6  62000  68200
    IB T280  CHRY 62300 68500, IB T151D GM   56000 61600, IB T185D GM   57500  63200
    IB T235D GM   60800 66900
51  7                  FB   SDN  WD      IB T275 INT 14 3 33000  3  6  70800  77800
    IB T280  CHRY 71300 78400, IB T151D GM   60300 66300, IB T185D GM   64200  70500
    IB T235D GM   69900 76900
------------------- 1962 BOATS -------------------------------------------------------
42  4                  FB   DC   WD      IB  190 CHRY 13        3  4  40400  44900
    IB  225  CHRY 40400 44900, IB  151D GM   47700 52400, IB T190  UNIV 46800  51400
    IB T225  CHRY 47900 52600, IB T260  CHRY 49100 54000, IB T275  UNIV 49700  54600
    IB T151D GM   49900 54800, IB T185D GM   51000 56000
42  4                  HT   SF   WD      TB  190 CHRY 13        3  4  26600  29600
    IB  225  CHRY 26800 29800, IB  151D GM   42600 47300, IB T190  CHRY 26700  29700
    IB T225  CHRY 28500 31700, IB T260  CHRY 29400 32700, IB T275  UNIV 29800  33100
    IB T151D GM   47600 52300, IB T185D GM   49200 54100
42  4                  FB   SF   WD      IB  190 CHRY 13        3  4  26700  29600
    IB  225  CHRY 26900 29800, IB  151D GM   42700 47400, IB T190  CHRY 26700  29600
    IB T225  CHRY 28500 31700, IB T260  CHRY 29500 32700, IB T275  UNIV 29800  33200
    IB T151D GM   47500 52200, IB T185D GM   49100 54000
42  4 CONVERTIBLE       HT   SDN  WD      IB  190 CHRY 13        3  4  44400  49300
    IB  225  CHRY 44600 49600, IB  151D GM   49000 53900, IB T190  CHRY 47000  51700
    IB T225  CHRY 47600 52400, IB T260  CHRY 48100 52900, IB T275  UNIV 48600  53400
    IB T151D GM   52200 57400, IB T185D GM   53100 58300
42  4 CONVERTIBLE       FB   SDN  WD      IB  190 CHRY 13        3  4  44600  49500
    IB  225  CHRY 44800 49800, IB  151D GM   49200 54100, IB T190  CHRY 47200  51900
    IB T225  CHRY 47800 52500, IB T260  CHRY 48300 53100, IB T275  UNIV 49000  53800
    IB T151D GM   52400 57600, IB T185D GM   53200 58500
42  4 DELUXE            HT   SDN  WD      IB  190 CHRY 13        3  4  44400  49300
    IB  225  CHRY 44600 49600, IB  151D GM   49000 53900, IB T190  CHRY 47000  51700
    IB T225  CHRY 47600 52400, IB T260  CHRY 48100 52900, IB T275  UNIV 48600  53400
    IB T151D GM   52200 57400, IB T185D GM   53100 58300
42  4 DELUXE            FB   SDN  WD      IB  190 CHRY 13        3  4  44200  49100
    IB  225  CHRY 44500 49400, IB  151D GM   48900 53800, IB T190  CHRY 46800  51500
    IB T225  CHRY 47500 52200, IB T260  CHRY 47900 52700, IB T275  UNIV 48100  52800
    IB T151D GM   52100 57200, IB T185D GM   52900 58100
42  4 MARTINIQUE        HT   EXP  WD      IB  190 CHRY 13        3  4  30800  34300
    IB  225  CHRY 31000 34500, IB  151D GM   35700 39700, IB T190  CHRY 32600  36300
    IB T225  CHRY 33100 36700, IB T260  CHRY 33600 37300, IB T275  UNIV 33900  37700
    IB T151D GM   39100 43400, IB T185D GM   39900 44300
42  4 MARTINIQUE        FB   EXP  WD      IB  190 CHRY 13        3  4  30900  34300
    IB  225  CHRY 31000 34500, IB  151D GM   35800 39800, IB T190  CHRY 32600  36300
    IB T225  CHRY 33100 36800, IB T260  CHRY 33600 37300, IB T275  UNIV 33900  37700
    IB T151D GM   39100 43500, IB T185D GM   39900 44300
52                     FB   CR   WD      IB T275 INT              67700  74400
    IB T280  CHRY 67800 74500, IB T151D GM   63500 69800, IB T185D GM   64900  71300
    IB T235D GM   67200 73900
52  CONVERTIBLE        FB   SDN  WD      IB T275 INT 13        3  4   **     **
    IB T280  CHRY  **    **  , IB T151D GM   72700 79900, IB T185D GM   74100  81400
    IB T235D GM   76400 83900
------------------- 1961 BOATS -------------------------------------------------------
42  4                  FB   DC   WD      IB  190 CHRY 13        3  4  39500  43900
    IB  151D GM   46700 51300, IB T190  CHRY 45800 50300, IB T275  INT  48700  53500
    IB T151D GM   48800 53700
42  4                  HT   SF   WD      IB  190 CHRY 13        3  4  26000  28900
42  4 CONVERTIBLE       HT   SDN  WD      IB  190 CHRY 13        3  4  43500  48300
    IB  151D GM   48100 52900, IB T190  CHRY 46200 50700, IB T275  INT  47900  52700
    IB T151D GM   51200 56300
42  4 CONVERTIBLE       FB   SDN  WD      IB  190 CHRY 13        3  4  43600  48400
    IB  151D GM   48200 52900, IB T190  CHRY 46200 50800, IB T275  INT  47800  52600
    IB T151D GM   51200 56300
42  4 CONVERTIBLE       HT   SF   WD      IB  151D GM  13        3  4  41700  46300
    IB T190  CHRY 26100 29000, IB T275  INT 29100 32400, IB T151D GM   46500  51100
42  4 CONVERTIBLE       FB   SF   WD      IB  190 CHRY 13        3  4  26100  29000
    IB  151D GM   41700 46300, IB T190  CHRY 26100 29000, IB T275  INT  29200  32400
    IB T151D GM   46500 51100
42  4 DELUXE            HT   SDN  WD      IB  190 CHRY 13        3  4  43500  48300
    IB  151D GM   47800 52500, IB T190  CHRY 45800 50300, IB T275  INT  47500  52200
    IB T151D GM   50900 55900
42  4 DELUXE            FB   SDN  WD      IB  190 CHRY 13        3  4  43300  48200
    IB  151D GM   47800 52500, IB T190  CHRY 45800 50400, IB T275  INT  47600  52300
    IB T151D GM   50900 55900
42  4 MARTINIQUE        HT   EXP  WD      IB  190 CHRY 13        3  4  30100  33500
    IB  151D GM   34900 38800, IB T190  CHRY 31900 35500, IB T275  INT  33200  36900
    IB T151D GM   38300 42500
42  4 MARTINIQUE        FB   EXP  WD      IB  190 CHRY 13        3  4  30200  33500
    IB  151D GM   35000 38900, IB T190  CHRY 31900 35500, IB T275  INT  33200  36900
    IB T151D GM   38300 42600
52                     FB   CR   WD      IB T260  CHRY            65400  71900
52                     FB   CR   WD      IB T235D GM              65400  71900
52  MARTINIQUE         FB   CR   WD      IB T275  INT 13          65800  72300
52  MARTINIQUE         FB   CR   WD      IB T151D GM  13        3  4  61700  67800
52  MARTINIQUE         FB   CR   WD      IB T185D GM  13        3  4  63100  69300
------------------- 1960 BOATS -------------------------------------------------------
42                     FB   DC   WD      IB T225                  41000  45500
42                          SDN  WD      IB T225                  44200  49100
42                          SF   WD      IB T225                  26800  29700
42  DELUXE                  SDN  WD      IB T225                  44200  49100
42  MARTINIQUE              EXP  WD      IB T225                  31800  35400
52                     FB   CR   WD      IB T225                  64000  70400
52                     FB   CR   WD      IB T270D                 66600  73200
------------------- 1959 BOATS -------------------------------------------------------
42                     FB   DC   WD      IB T225                  40200  44600
42  DELUXE                  SDN  WD      IB T225                  43300  48200
42  MARTINIQUE              EXP  WD      IB T225                  31200  34700
42  SPEAR-FISH             OP   FSH  WD      IB T225                    **     **
------------------- 1958 BOATS -------------------------------------------------------
42                     FB   DC   WD      IB T225                  39500  43900
42                          SDN  WD      IB T225                  42600  47300
42                          SF   WD      IB T225                  25800  28700
42  DELUXE                  SDN  WD      IB T225                  42600  47300
42  MARTINIQUE              EXP  WD      IB T225                  30700  34100
------------------- 1957 BOATS -------------------------------------------------------
42                     FB   DC   WD      IB T225                  38900  43200
42                     FB   SDN  WD      IB T225                  42000  46600
42                          SF   WD      IB T225                  25400  28200
42  DELUXE                  SDN  WD      IB T225                  41900  46600
------------------- 1956 BOATS -------------------------------------------------------
42                     FB   DC   WD      IB T225                  38300  42500
42                     FB   SDN  WD      IB T225                  41300  45900
42                          SF   WD      IB T225                  25000  27800
42  DELUXE                  SDN  WD      IB T225                  41300  45900
------------------- 1955 BOATS -------------------------------------------------------
39                          SDN  WD      IB T170D                 37400  41500
42                     FB   DC   WD      IB T200                  37100  41200
42                     FB   SDN  WD      IB T200                  40400  44900
42  DELUXE                  SDN  WD      IB T200                  40400  44800
------------------- 1954 BOATS -------------------------------------------------------
42                     FB   DC   WD      IB T200                  36600  40700
42                          SDN  WD      IB T200                  39900  44300
42                          SDN  WD      IB T200                  39900  44300
------------------- 1953 BOATS -------------------------------------------------------
42                     FB   DC   WD      IB T200                  36300  40300
42                          SDN  WD      IB T200                  39400  43800
42                     FB   SDN  WD      IB T200                  39400  43800
------------------- 1952 BOATS -------------------------------------------------------
42                     FB   DC   WD      IB T145                  34300  38200
42                          SDN  WD      IB T145                  38100  42300
42                          SF   WD      IB T145                  19800  22000
------------------- 1951 BOATS -------------------------------------------------------
32                          SDN  WD      IB T165                  12100  13800
40                          SDN  WD      IB T165                  35500  39500
40                     FB   SDN  WD      IB T165                  35500  39500
45                     FB   DC   WD      IB T165                  38900  43200
```

      CONTINUED ON NEXT PAGE   96th ed. - Vol. III

LOA FT IN	NAME AND/ OR MODEL	TOP/ RIG	BOAT TYPE	-HULL- MTL TP	TP	----ENGINE--- # HP	MFG	BEAM FT IN	WGT LBS	DRAFT FT IN	RETAIL LOW	RETAIL HIGH
						1950 BOATS						
32	PLAYBOAT	HT	CR	WD	RB	IB 104	CHRY				9850	11200
40			SDN	WD		IB T177					35300	39200
40		FB	SDN	WD		IB T177					35300	39300
45		FB	DC	WD		IB T177					38700	43000
						1949 BOATS						
40			SF	WD		IB T200					32900	36600
40			SF	WD		IB T225	GRAY				33000	36600
40	DELUXE	FB	SDN	WD		IB T225					35200	39200
						1948 BOATS						
40			SDN	WD		IB T145					34800	38700
40		FB	SF	WD		IB T145					32600	36200
						1947 BOATS						
40			SDN	WD		IB T145					34700	38600
40		FB	SF	WD		IB T145					32500	36100
						1946 BOATS						
40			SDN	WD		IB T145					34700	38600
40		FB	SF	WD		IB T145					32500	36100
						1942 BOATS						
46		FB	SDN	WD		IB T127					38400	42600
						1941 BOATS						
34		HT	SDN	WD		IB					**	**
34		OP	SPTCR	WD		IB					**	**
38	5 BERTH		SDN	WD		IB T145					31400	34800
46		HT	DC	WD		IB					**	**
46		HT	DC	WD		IB T140	CHRY				38900	43200
50		HT	CR	WD		IB					**	**
50	SPORT	HT	SDN	WD		IB					**	**
						1940 BOATS						
29			SDN	WD		IB 130					8850	10100
51		FB	DC	WD		IB T200					**	**
51			SF	WD		IB T200					54300	59700
						1939 BOATS						
34		HT	SDN	WD		IB	KERM				**	**
38		HT	DC	WD		IB					**	**
38			SDN	WD		IB T145					31800	35400
38		HT	TCMY	WD		IB					**	**
46		HT	DC	WD		IB					**	**
46		HT	SDN	WD		IB					**	**
50		HT	MY	WD		IB					**	**
50		HT	SDN	WD		IB					**	**
						1938 BOATS						
38				WD		IB 260	KERM				**	**
40			SDN	WD		IB T145					36100	40100
46				WD		IB T185	CC				**	**
						1937 BOATS						
38			EXP	WD		IB T105					26200	29100
38	DELUXE	HT	SDN	WD		IB					**	**
38 10				WD		IB T105D	GM				**	**
40			SDN	WD		IB T115					36200	40200
46			SDN	WD		IB T200					40500	45000
						1936 BOATS						
25		SLP	SAIL	WD		IB	GRAY	8 6		2 8	11400	12900
38		HT	DC	WD		IB T180	STER				29400	32600
38		HT	SDN	WD		IB T180	STER				33100	36800
38			SPTCR	WD		IB T180	STER				24200	26900
46		FB	SDN	WD		IB T200					41400	46000
						1933 BOATS						
38				WD		IB 150	PACK				**	**
46		FB	DC	WD		IB T200					45600	50100
						1932 BOATS						
38		HT	DC	WD		IB	KERM				**	**
38		HT	DC	WD		IB 100D	LEHM				34600	38400
						1931 BOATS						
38		HT	CR	WD		IB 150	KERM				27700	30800
38		HT	SPTCR	WD		IB 175	KERM				25400	28200
46		HT	DC	WD		IB					**	**
						1930 BOATS						
40			SDN	WD		IB T115					40600	45200
						1929 BOATS						
38			SDN	WD		IB 125					36400	40500
39				WD		IB 150	PACK				**	**
						1927 BOATS						
28				WD		IB 115-140					**	**
						1926 BOATS						
38				WD		IB	FORD				**	**
						1923 BOATS						
38		HT	DC	WD		IB					**	**
						1905 BOATS						
25	LAUNCH W/SURREY	ST	LNCH	WD	DV	IB 3		5 6	1200	8	6850	7900

MATTIE RIVER YACHTS
M OF LA CROSSE LTD   COAST GUARD MFG ID- MLG

Call 1-800-327-6929 for BUC Personalized Evaluation Service
Or, for 1978 boats, sign onto www.BUCValuPro.com

MAURELL PRODUCTS INC
OWOSSO MI 48867   COAST GUARD MFG ID- MAU See inside cover to adjust price for area

For more recent years, see the BUC Used Boat Price Guide, Volume 1 or Volume 2

LOA FT IN	NAME AND/ OR MODEL	TOP/ RIG	BOAT TYPE	-HULL- MTL	TP	----ENGINE--- # HP	MFG	BEAM FT IN	WGT LBS	DRAFT FT IN	RETAIL LOW	RETAIL HIGH
						1982 BOATS						
35	3510	HT	HB	AL	PN	OB		10	7200		12200	13900
35	3514	HT	HB	AL	PN	OB		12 9	7600		12900	14600
						1981 BOATS						
35	3510	HT	HB	AL	PN	OB		10	7200		12000	13700
35	3514	HT	HB	AL	PN	OB		12 9	7600		12700	14400
						1980 BOATS						
35	3508	HT	HB	AL	PN	OB		8	4700		7200	8300
35	3510	HT	HB	AL	PN	OB		10	7200		11800	13500
35	3514	HT	HB	AL	PN	OB		12 9	7600		12500	14200
						1976 BOATS						
35	3508	HT	HB	AL	PN	OB		8	4700		6850	7850
35	3510	HT	HB	AL	PN	OB		10	7200		11300	12800
35	3514 A	HT	HB	AL	PN	OB		12 9			10200	11600
35	3514 B	HT	HB	AL	PN	OB		12 9			11400	13000
43	4315	HT	HB	AL	PN	OB		14 9	9500		10100	11500

MAY CRAFT MFG CO INC
MAYS LANDING NJ   See inside cover to adjust price for area

LOA FT IN	NAME AND/ OR MODEL	TOP/ RIG	BOAT TYPE	-HULL- MTL	TP	----ENGINE--- # HP	MFG	BEAM FT IN	WGT LBS	DRAFT FT IN	RETAIL LOW	RETAIL HIGH
						1964 BOATS						
23 2		HT		WD		IB 215					22700	25200
23 2			UTL	WD		IB 215					21200	23500
26		HT		WD		IB 225					35500	39500
26			EXP	WD		IB 225					36300	40400
26			SF	WD		IB 225					38000	42300
30		HT	CR	WD		IB 225					59500	65300
30		HT	CR	WD		IB T225					66500	73100
30			EXP	WD		IB 225					66800	73500
30			EXP	WD		IB T225					74600	82000
30			OVNTR	WD		IB 225					58400	64200
30			OVNTR	WD		IB T225					65600	72100
30			RNBT	WD		IB 225					53400	58700
30			RNBT	WD		IB T225					60700	66700
30			SDN	WD		IB 225					63300	69600
30			SDN	WD		IB T225					73200	80400
30			SF	WD		IB 225					58100	63800
30			SF	WD		IB T225					64400	70800
30			SPTCR	WD		IB 225					65400	71900
30			SPTCR	WD		IB T225					72100	79200
30	HOME AFLOAT		SPTCR	WD		IB 225					66900	73500
30	HOME AFLOAT		SPTCR	WD		IB T225					73400	80700
30	HOME-AFLOAT		SPTCR	WD		IB 225					61400	67400
30	HOME-AFLOAT		SPTCR	WD		IB T225					67100	73700
30	SOUTHERN	HT		WD		IB 225					57700	63400
30	SOUTHERN	HT		WD		IB T225					64000	70400
30	SOUTHERN		CR	WD		IB 225					59500	65300
30	SOUTHERN		CR	WD		IB T225					66500	73100
30	SOUTHERN		SPTCR	WD		IB 225					59800	65700
30	SOUTHERN		SPTCR	WD		IB T225					67200	73900
32		HT	CR	WD		IB T225					83700	92300
32			EXP	WD		IB T225					95500	105000
32			OVNTR	WD		IB T225					85600	94000
32			SDN	WD		IB T225					94300	103500
32			SF	WD		IB T225					70800	77800
32			SF	WD		IB T225					77800	85500

LOA FT IN	NAME AND/ OR MODEL	TOP/ RIG	BOAT TYPE	-HULL- MTL TP	----ENGINE--- TP # HP MFG	BEAM FT IN	WGT LBS	DRAFT FT IN	RETAIL LOW	RETAIL HIGH
			1964 BOATS							
32			SPTCR	WD	IB T225				82100	90300
32	HOME AFLOAT		SPTCR WD		IB T225				86400	95000
32	HOME-AFLOAT		SPTCR WD		IB T225				80200	88100
32	SOUTHERN		CR	WD	IB T225				83700	92000
32	SOUTHERN		SPTCR WD		IB T225				80300	88200
32	SOUTHERN-CROSS	HT		WD	IB T225				77300	84900
36			EXP	WD	IB T225				142000	156000
36			SDN	WD	IB T225				153500	168500
36	AFTER CABIN			WD	IB T225				157500	173000
			1963 BOATS							
23		HT		WD	IB 215				21700	24100
23			UTL	WD	IB 215				20300	22500
26			EXP	WD	IB 225				35000	38900
26		FB	SF	WD	IB 225				36700	40800
26		HT	3PTCR	WD	IB 225				35000	38900
30		HT	CR	WD	IB 225				57400	63000
30			EXP	WD	IB 225				64500	70900
30			OVNTR	WD	IB 225				56400	62000
30			RNBT	WD	IB 225				51500	56600
30			SDN	WD	IB 225				61100	67100
30			SF	WD	IB 225				56000	61600
30		FB	SF	WD	IB 225				56000	61600
30	HOME-AFLOAT		SPTCR	WD	IB 225				61100	67200
30	SOUTHERN		CR	WD	IB 225				57400	63000
36			EXP	WD	IB T225				138500	152000
36			SDN	WD	IB T225				150000	164500
36		FB	SF	WD	IB T225				143000	157500
36	CUSTOM		SF	WD	IB T225				143000	157500
			1962 BOATS							
23 2		HT		WD	IB 110				20400	22600
23 2			CR	WD	IB 110				22000	24400
23 2			UTL	WD	IB 110				19000	21100
26		HT		WD	IB 110				39500	33900
26			CR	WD	IB 110				35000	38900
26		FB	EXP	WD	IB 110				31300	34800
26			UTL	WD	IB 110				28100	31200
26	DK LAPSTRAKE		CR	WD	IB 110				35000	38900
26	LAPSTRAKE	HT		WD	IB 110				30500	33900
26	LAPSTRAKE		CR	WD	IB 110				35000	38900
26	LAPSTRAKE		UTL	WD	IB 110				28100	31200
30		HT	CR	WD	IB 195				55000	60500
30			EXP	WD	IB 195				61900	68000
30			SDN	WD	IB 195				58200	64000
30			SF	WD	IB 195				53800	59200
30			SPTCR	WD	IB 195				58800	64600
30			UTL	WD	IB 195				64700	71100
			1961 BOATS							
23 3	CRUISER		CR	PLY	IB 110	8 6		1 8	21600	24000
23 3	SEMI-ENCLOSED			PLY	IB 110	8 6		1 8	20100	22300
23 3	UTL		UTL	PLY	IB 110	8 6		1 8	18900	21000
25	CUSTOM		EXP	PLY	IB 195	8 6		1 10	30100	33500
25	SEMI-ENCLOSED			PLY	IB 110	8 6		1 10	26800	29800
25	SPORT FISH		SF	PLY	IB 110	8 6		1 10	25000	27800
25	UTL		UTL	PLY	IB 110	8 6		1 10	19100	21200
28	EXPRESS CR		EXP	P/C	IB 125	9 9		2 2	43200	48000
28	SPORT FISH		SF	P/C	IB 125	9 9		2 2	42500	47200
			1960 BOATS							
23	SPORTSTER			WD	IB 110-177				19400	22500
25	CUSTOM		EXP	WD	IB 110				27900	31100
			1959 BOATS							
23	SPORTSTER			WD	IB 110				19100	21200
25	SPORTSTER			WD	IB 110				25900	28800
			1958 BOATS							
23	SPORTSTER			WD	IB 110				18900	21000
25	SPORTSTER			WD	IB 110				25400	28200
			1957 BOATS							
23	SPORTSTER			WD	IB 110				18600	20700
25	SPORTSTER			WD	IB 110				25000	27800
			1956 BOATS							
23	SPORTSTER			WD	IB 90				18000	20000
25	SPORTSTER			WD	IB 85				24000	26600

MAYHEW & STRUTT
COAST GUARD MFG ID- MHS

Call 1-800-327-6929 for BUC Personalized Evaluation Service
Or, for 1968 boats, sign onto www.BUCValuPro.com

J M MC CLINTOCK & CO
COAST GUARD MFG ID- JMM

Call 1-800-327-6929 for BUC Personalized Evaluation Service
Or, for 1968 to 1979 boats, sign onto www.BUCValuPro.com

MC CONNELL MARINE LTD
GEORGIAN BAY SHOAL BOATS   See inside cover to adjust price for area
NOBEL ONTARIO CANADA

LOA FT IN	NAME AND/ OR MODEL	TOP/ RIG	BOAT TYPE	-HULL- MTL TP	----ENGINE--- TP # HP MFG	BEAM FT IN	WGT LBS	DRAFT FT IN	RETAIL LOW	RETAIL HIGH
			1983 BOATS							
21	SKIPJACK 21	SLP	SA/OD	AL CB		8 6	1200		3400	3950
21	SKIPJACK 21	SLP	SA/OD	STL CB		8 6	1900		4200	4850
			1982 BOATS							
21	SKIPJACK 21	SLP	SA/CR	AL CB IB	D	8 6	1200		4550	5250
21	SKIPJACK 21	SLP	SA/CR	STL CB IB	D	8 6	1900		5350	6150
22		SLP	SA/CR	AL CB IB	D	8 6	2000		5450	6250
22		SLP	SA/CR	STL CB IB	D	8 6	2600		6250	7150
26 6		SLP	SA/CR	AL KL IB	D	8 7	6400	3 6	15300	17400
26 6		SLP	SA/CR	STL KL IB	D	8 7	6400	3 6	15300	17400
35		CUT	SA/CR	AL KL IB	D	10 5	15300	5	40100	44600
35		CUT	SA/CR	STL KL IB	D	10 5	15300	5	40100	44600
35 4		CUT	SA/CR	AL KL IB	D	10 9	17800	5	46600	51200
35 4		CUT	SA/CR	STL KL IB	D	10 9	17800	5	46600	51200
40 11		CUT	SA/CR	AL KL IB	D	12 2	23500	6 3	63600	69900
40 11		CUT	SA/CR	STL KL IB	D	12 2	23500	6 3	63600	69900
40 11		KTH	SA/CR	AL KL IB	D	12 2	23500	6 3	67800	74500
40 11		KTH	SA/CR	STL KL IB	D	12 2	23500	6 3	67800	74500
42		CUT	SA/CR	AL KL IB	D	12 5	24800	5 9	67400	74100
42		CUT	SA/CR	STL KL IB	D	12 5	24800	5 9	67400	74100
42		KTH	SA/CR	AL KL IB	D	12 5	24800	5 9	72100	79200
42		KTH	SA/CR	STL KL IB	D	12 5	24800	5 9	72100	79200
47 6		KTH	SA/CR	AL KL IB	D	14 2	39160	5 6	101500	111500
47 6		KTH	SA/CR	AL KL IB	D	14 2	39160	5 6	103500	113500
			1981 BOATS							
18	MC-CONNELL 18	SLP	SA/OD			7 6			2000	2350
18	SKIFF 18	SLP	SAIL	AL CB		7 6			2700	3150
18	SKIFF 18	SLP	SAIL	STL CB		7 6			2700	3150
18	UTILITY		UTL	AL	IO 160	8 6			3750	4350
18	UTILITY		UTL	STL	IO 160	8 6			3750	4350
21	SKIPJACK 21	SLP	SA/CR	AL CB IB	D	8 6			4750	5450
21	SKIPJACK 21	SLP	SA/CR	STL CB IB	D	8 6			4750	5450
21	SKIPJACK 21	SLP	SA/OD	CB IB	D	8 6			4700	5400
22		SLP	SA/CR	AL CB IB	D	8 6			5600	6450
22		SLP	SA/CR	STL CB IB	D	8 6			5600	6450
23	UTILITY		UTL	AL	IO 160	8 6			6500	7500
23	UTILITY		UTL	STL	IO 160	8 6			6500	7500
26 6		SLP	SA/CR	AL KL IB	D	8 7		3 6	14700	16700
26 6		SLP	SA/CR	STL KL IB	D	8 7		3 6	14700	16700
27		SF		AL	DV IO 235	9 8			13800	15700
28	CRUISER		EXP	AL	DV IO 210	9 10			14800	16800
28	CRUISER		EXP	STL	DV IO 210	9 10			14800	16800
28	CRUISER		EXP	AL	DV IB 210	9 10			17400	19800
28	CRUISER		EXP	STL	DV IB 210	9 10			17400	19800
35		CUT	SA/CR	AL KL IB	D	10 5		5	41100	45700
35		CUT	SA/CR	STL KL IB	D	10 5		5	41100	45700
35 4		CUT	SA/CR	AL KL IB	D	10 9		5	41200	45700
35 4		CUT	SA/CR	STL KL IB	D	10 9		5	41200	45700
40 11		CUT	SA/CR	STL KL IB	D	12 2		6 3	60700	66700
40 11		CUT	SA/CR	STL KL IB	D	12 2		6 3	64600	70900
40 11		KTH	SA/CR	STL KL IB	D	12 2		6 3	64600	70900
42		CUT	SA/CR	STL KL IB	D	12 5		5 9	59900	65800
42		CUT	SA/CR	AL KL IB	D	12 5		5 9	59900	65800
42		KTH	SA/CR	AL KL IB	D	12 5		5 9	63800	70100
42		KTH	SA/CR	AL KL IB	D	12 5		5 9	63800	70100
47 6		KTH	SA/CR	AL KL IB	D	14 2		5 9	99000	109000
47 6		KTH	SA/CR	AL KL IB	D	14 2		5 6	99000	109000

LOA FT IN	NAME AND/ OR MODEL	TOP/ RIG	BOAT TYPE	-HULL- MTL TP	----ENGINE--- TP # HP MFG	BEAM FT IN	WGT LBS	DRAFT FT IN	RETAIL LOW	RETAIL HIGH
					1979 BOATS					
17 9	SKIFF 18	SLP	SAIL	AL CB	IB D	6 9	1300	3 1	4650	5350
17 9	SKIFF 18	SLP	SAIL	STL CB	IB D	6 9	1300	3 1	4650	5350
21 1	SKIPJACK 21	SLP	SAIL	AL CB	IB D	8	1400	5 2	4150	4850
32	TAHITIANA	KTH	SA/CR	STL KL	IB D	10	18194	4 3	41500	46100
33 1	SNUG-HAVEN 33	SLP	SA/CR	AL KL	IB D	10 10	13700	5 1	32100	35700
33 1	SNUG-HAVEN 33	SLP	SA/CR	STL KL	IB D	10 10		5 1	32300	35900
33 4	SAUGEEN-WITCH 33	KTH	SA/CR	STL KL	IB D	9 10	14000	3 9	32600	36300
36 4	PINKY 36	SCH	SA/CR	AL KL	IB D	10 9	22000	3 7	49300	54200
36 4	PINKY 36	SCH	SA/CR	STL KL	IB D	10 9	22000	3 7	49300	54200
42	GAZELLE 42	SCH	SA/CR	AL KL	IB D	11 4	18000	3 10	50100	55100
42	GAZELLE 42	SCH	SA/CR	STL KL	IB D	11 4	18000	3 10	50100	55100
42	GAZELLE 42 JUNK	LAT	SA/CR	AL KL	IB D	11 4	18000	3 10	50400	55400
42	GAZELLE 42 JUNK	LAT	SA/CR	STL KL	IB D	11 4	18000	3 10	50400	55400

MC CULLY MARINE
COAST GUARD MFG ID- RLP

Call 1-800-327-6929 for BUC Personalized Evaluation Service
Or, for 1977 to 1978 boats, sign onto www.BUCValuPro.com

MC GLASSON MARINE
FOR MORE RECENT YEARS SEE ISLANDER YACHTS

Call 1-800-327-6929 for BUC Personalized Evaluation Service
Or, for 1959 to 1962 boats, sign onto www.BUCValuPro.com

MC GRUER & CLARK LTD
COAST GUARD MFG ID- VMG

Call 1-800-327-6929 for BUC Personalized Evaluation Service
Or, for 1966 to 1975 boats, sign onto www.BUCValuPro.com

MC KENZIE BOAT MFG CO
CHEROKEE   COAST GUARD MFG ID- MBM

Call 1-800-327-6929 for BUC Personalized Evaluation Service
Or, for 1968 to 1977 boats, sign onto www.BUCValuPro.com

MC LAUGHLIN BOAT WORKS
COAST GUARD MFG ID- MGH

Call 1-800-327-6929 for BUC Personalized Evaluation Service
Or, for 1983 to 2002 boats, sign onto www.BUCValuPro.com

DAMIAN MC LAUGHLIN JR CO
COAST GUARD MFG ID- DAM

Call 1-800-327-6929 for BUC Personalized Evaluation Service
Or, for 1977 to 1985 boats, sign onto www.BUCValuPro.com

MC NICHOLS BOAT SALES
SHEARWATER

Call 1-800-327-6929 for BUC Personalized Evaluation Service
Or, for 1961 to 1970 boats, sign onto www.BUCValuPro.com

MC VAY YACHTS
SINCLAIR IND INC   See inside cover to adjust price for area
KITCHENER ONTARIO CANAD COAST GUARD MFG ID- MCF

LOA FT IN	NAME AND/ OR MODEL	TOP/ RIG	BOAT TYPE	-HULL- MTL TP	----ENGINE--- TP # HP MFG	BEAM FT IN	WGT LBS	DRAFT FT IN	RETAIL LOW	RETAIL HIGH
					1983 BOATS					
18 4	MINUET	SLP	SA/OD	FBG KL		5 5	1000	2 11	2900	3400
23 6	BLUENOSE	SLP	SA/OD	FBG KL		6 2	2000	3 6	4800	5500
					1982 BOATS					
23 6	BLUENOSE 24	SLP	SAIL	FBG CB		6 2	2000	1	4550	5250
23 6	BLUENOSE 24	SLP	SAIL	FBG KL		6 2	2000	3 6	4550	5250
26	MICMAC 26	SLP	SA/CR	FBG KL		7 2	5000	3 8	10000	11400
32	MC-VAY 32	SLP	SA/CR	FBG KL		9 5	10500	4 10	**	**
					1981 BOATS					
18 4	MINUET	SLP	SA/OD	FBG KL		5 5		2 11	2650	3050
23 6	BLUENOSE 24	SLP	SAIL	FBG KL		6 2	2000	3 6	4300	5000
26	MICMAC 26	SLP	SA/CR	FBG KL		7 2	5000	3 8	9600	10900
					1980 BOATS					
18 4	MINUET	SLP	SA/OD	FBG KL		5 5		2 11	2500	2900
23 6	BLUENOSE	SLP	SAIL	FBG CB		6 2	2000		4100	4750
23 6	BLUENOSE	SLP	SAIL	FBG KL		6 2	2000	3 6	4100	4750
26	MICMAC	SLP	SA/CR	FBG KL		7 2	5000	3 8	9150	10400
					1979 BOATS					
18 4	MINUET	SLP	SAIL	FBG KC	OB	5 5	1000	1	2400	2800
18 4	MINUET	SLP	SAIL	FBG KC	OB	5 5	1000	2 11	2400	2800
23 6	BLUENOSE	SLP	SAIL	FBG KL	OB	6 2	2000	1	3900	4550
23 6	BLUENOSE	SLP	SAIL	FBG KL	OB	6 2	2000	3 6	3900	4550
26	MICMAC	SLP	SA/CR	FBG KL		7 2	5000	3 8	8700	10000
					1978 BOATS					
18 4	MINUET	SLP	SAIL	FBG CB	OB	5 5	1000	1	2350	2700
18 4	MINUET	SLP	SAIL	FBG KL	OB	5 5	1000	2 11	2350	2700
23 6	BLUENOSE	SLP	SAIL	FBG CB	OB	6 2		1	3750	4400
23 6	BLUENOSE	SLP	SAIL	FBG KL	OB	6 2		3 6	3750	4400
26	MICMAC	SLP	SAIL	FBG KL		7 2		3 8	8350	9600
					1977 BOATS					
18 4	MINUET	SLP	SAIL	FBG KL	OB	5 5	1000	2 11	2250	2600
23 6	BLUENOSE	SLP	SAIL	FBG KL	OB	6 2	2000	3 6	3600	4200
					1976 BOATS					
18 4	MINUET	SLP	SAIL	FBG KL		5 5	1000	2 11	2200	2550
23 6	BLUENOSE	SLP	SAIL	FBG KL		6 2		3 6	3550	4100
					1974 BOATS					
18 4	MINUET	SLP	SAIL	FBG KL	OB	5 5	1000	2 11	2000	2400
21	MINI-CRUISER	SLP	SA/CR	FBG KL		7 4	1800	1 8	2850	3350
23 6	BLUENOSE	SLP	SAIL	FBG KL		6 2	2100	3 6	3400	3950
26	MICMAC	SLP	SAIL	FBG KL		7 2	5000	3 8	7250	8350
26	MICMAC	SCH	SA/CR	FBG KL		7 2	5000	3 8	7250	8350
					1973 BOATS					
18 4	MINUET	SLP	SAIL	FBG KL	OB	5 5	1000	2 11	1950	2300
23 6	BLUENOSE	SLP	SAIL	FBG KL	OB	6 2	2100	3 6	3300	3850
26	MICMAC	SLP	SAIL	FBG KL	OB	7 2	4500	3 8	6900	7950
26	MICMAC	SCH	SAIL	FBG KL	IB 5D WEST	7 2	5000	3 8	8100	9300
					1972 BOATS					
18 4	MINUET		SAIL	FBG	OB	5 5	1000	2 11	1900	2250
23 6	BLUENOSE		SAIL	FBG	OB	6 2	2100	3 6	3250	3750
26	MICMAC		SAIL	FBG	OB	7 2	4500	3 8	6750	7800
					1971 BOATS					
18 4	MINUET		SAIL	FBG	OB	5 5	1000	2 11	1850	2200
23 6	BLUENOSE		SAIL	FBG	OB	6 2	2100	3 6	3200	3700
26	MICMAC		SAIL	FBG	OB	7 2	4500	3 8	6600	7600
					1970 BOATS					
18 4	MINUET	SLP	SA/OD	FBG KL	OB	5 5	1000	2 11	1800	2150
23 6	BLUENOSE	SLP	SAIL	FBG KL	OB	6 2	2100	3 6	3150	3650
26	MICMAC	SLP	SAIL	FBG KL	OB	7 2	4500	3 8	6450	7450
					1969 BOATS					
18	MINUETE	SLP	SA/OD	FBG KL		5 5	1100	3	1850	2200
23 6	BLUENOSE	SLP	SA/OD	FBG KL		6 2	2100	3 6	3050	3550
26	MICMAC	SLP	SA/OD	FBG KL	IB 9	7 2	4500	3 8	6500	7500
					1968 BOATS					
23 6	BLUENOSE	SLP	SA/OD	FBG KL	OB	6 2	2100	3 6	2950	3400
26	MICMAC	SLP	SA/OD	FBG KL	OB	7 4	4600	3 8	6300	7250
					1967 BOATS					
23 6	BLUENOSE	SLP	SA/CR	FBG KL		6 2	2100	3 6	2900	3350
					1966 BOATS					
23 6	BLUENOSE	SLP	SA/OD	FBG KL		6 2	2100	3 6	2850	3300

MCKEE CRAFT
MC KEE CRAFT   See inside cover to adjust price for area
FAIRMONT NC 28340
COAST GUARD MFG ID- MKC
FORMERLY LANNESS K MCKEE & CO

For more recent years, see the BUC Used Boat Price Guide, Volume 1 or Volume 2

LOA FT IN	NAME AND/ OR MODEL	TOP/ RIG	BOAT TYPE	-HULL- MTL TP	----ENGINE--- TP # HP MFG	BEAM FT IN	WGT LBS	DRAFT FT IN	RETAIL LOW	RETAIL HIGH
					1983 BOATS					
16	CAPE-FEAR	OP	RNBT	FBG TR	OB	6 6	1170		1900	2250
16	WACCAMAW	OP	RNBT	FBG TR	OB	6 6	1170		1950	2350
17 4	OFFSHOREMAN	OP	RNBT	FBG TR	OB	7 4	1480		2150	2500
17 4	SOUTHPORTER	OP	RNBT	FBG TR	OB	7 4	1480		2250	2650

MCKEE CRAFT -CONTINUED
See inside cover to adjust price for area

LOA FT IN	NAME AND/ OR MODEL	TOP/ RIG	BOAT TYPE	-HULL- MTL TP	TP	# HP	MFG	BEAM FT IN	WGT LBS	DRAFT FT IN	RETAIL LOW	RETAIL HIGH
--- 1983 BOATS ---												
20	BREAKERS	OP	RNBT	FBG TR	OB			7	1705		3350	3850
20	OFFSHOREMAN	OP	RNBT	FBG TR	OB			7	1705		3200	3700
--- 1982 BOATS ---												
16	CAPE-FEAR	OP	RNBT	FBG TR	OB			6 6	1170		1850	2200
16	WACCAMAW	OP	RNBT	FBG TR	OB			6 6	1170		1900	2250
17 4	OFFSHOREMAN	OP	RNBT	FBG TR	OB			7 4	1480		2050	2450
17 4	SOUTHPORTER	OP	RNBT	FBG TR	OB			7 4	1480		2150	2550
20	BREAKERS	OP	RNBT	FBG TR	OB			7	1705		3250	3750
20	OFFSHOREMAN	OP	RNBT	FBG TR	OB			7	1705		3100	3600
--- 1981 BOATS ---												
16	CAPE-FEAR	OP	RNBT	FBG TR	OB			6 6	1170		1800	2150
16	WACCAMAW	OP	RNBT	FBG TR	OB			6 6	1170		1850	2150
17 4	OFFSHOREMAN	OP	RNBT	FBG TR	OB			7 4	1480		2000	2400
17 4	SOUTHPORTER	OP	RNDT	FBC TR	OB			7 4	1480		2100	2450
20	BREAKERS	OP	RNBT	FBG TR	OB			7	1800		3300	3800
20	OFFSHOREMAN	OP	RNBT	FBG TR	OB			7	1800		3150	3650
--- 1980 BOATS ---												
16	CAPE-FEAR	OP	RNBT	FBG TR	OB			6 6	1170		1750	2100
16	WACCAMAW	OP	RNBT	FBG TR	OB			6 6	1170		1800	2150
17 4	OFFSHOREMAN	OP	RNBT	FBG TR	OB			7 4	1480		1950	2350
17 4	SOUTHPORTER	OP	RNBT	FBG TR	OB			7 4	1480		2050	2400
20	BREAKERS	OP	RNBT	FBG TR	OB			7	1800		3200	3750
20	OFFSHOREMAN	OP	RNBT	FBG TR	OB			7	1800		3100	3600
--- 1979 BOATS ---												
16	CAPE-FEAR	OP	RNBT	FBG TR	OB			6 6	1170		1700	2050
16	WACCAMAW	OP	RNBT	FBG TR	OB			6 6	1170		1750	2100
17	OFFSHOREMAN	OP	RNBT	FBG TR	OB			7 4	1480		1900	2300
17	SOUTHPORTER	OP	RNBT	FBG TR	OB			7 4	1480		1950	2350
20	BREAKERS	OP	RNBT	FBG TR	OB			7	1800		3150	3650
20	OFFSHOREMAN	OP	RNBT	FBG TR	OB			7	1800		3000	3500
--- 1978 BOATS ---												
17	OFFSHOREMAN	OP	RNBT	FBG TR	OB			7 4	1480	11	1850	2250
17	SOUTHPORTER	OP	RNBT	FBG TR	OB			7 4	1480	11	1950	2300
20	BREAKERS	OP	RNBT	FBG TR	OB			7	1800	1 2	3100	3600
20	OFFSHOREMAN	OP	RNBT	FBG TR	OB			7	1800	1 2	2950	3450
--- 1977 BOATS ---												
17 4	OFFSHOREMAN	OP	OPFSH	F/S TR	OB			7 4	1480		1750	2050
17 4	SOUTHPORTER	OP	RNBT	F/S TR	OB			7 4	1450		1800	2150
17 4	SOUTHPORTER	OP	RNBT	F/S TR	IO	140		7 4	2080		3400	3950
20	BARE HULL	OP	UTL	F/S TR	OB			7	1600		2500	2900
20	BREAKERS	OP	RNBT	F/S TR	OB			7	1850		3050	3550
20	BREAKERS	OP	RNBT	F/S TR	IO	140		7	2480		4600	5300
20	CAPE-FEAR	OP	OPFSH	F/S TR	OB			7	1850		3050	3550
--- 1976 BOATS ---												
17 4	SOUTHPORTER	OP	OFF	FBG TR	IO	140		7 4	1250		2900	3400
20	BREAKERS	OP	OFF	FBG TR	OB			7	1920		3050	3550
20	BREAKERS	OP	OFF	FBG TR	IO	140		7			4950	5700
20	CAPE-FEAR	OP	OFF	FBG TR	OB			7	1850		3000	3400
--- 1975 BOATS ---												
17 4	SOUTHPORTER I/O		UTL	FBG TR	IO	140	OMC	7 4	2150		3900	4550
17 4	SOUTHPORTER I/O	OP	UTL	FBG TR	IO	140	MRCR	7 4	2150		3950	4600
20	BARE-HULL	OP	UTL	FBG TR	OB			7	1300		2000	2350
20	BREAKERS	OP	UTL	FBG TR	OB			7	1800		2650	3050
20	BREAKERS I/O		UTL	FBG TR	IO	140	OMC	7	2500		5300	6100
20	BREAKERS I/O	OP	UTL	FBG TR	IO	140	MRCR	7	2500		5350	6150
20	CAPE-FEAR	OP	UTL	FBG TR	OB			7	1700		2500	2950
--- 1974 BOATS ---												
17 4	SOUTHPORTER			FBG	IO	140	OMC	7 4	1840	11	3350	3900
17 4	SOUTHPORTER	OP	UTL	FBG	IO	140	MRCR	7 4	1840	11	3750	4400
20	BARE HULL	OP	UTL	FBG	OB			7	1600	11	2400	2800
20	BREAKERS			FBG	IO	140	OMC	7	2575	1	5000	5750
20	BREAKERS	OP	UTL	FBG	IO			7	1920	11	2700	3150
20	BREAKERS	OP	UTL	FBG	IO	140	MRCR	7	2575	1 11	5600	6450
20	CAPE-FEAR	OP	UTL	FBG	OB			7	1850	11	2650	3150
--- 1973 BOATS ---												
17 4	CF-17-L CUS			FBG	IO	120	OMC	7 4	1895	11	3500	4100
17 4	CF-17-L CUS		FSH	FBG	IO	140	OMC	7 4	1800	11	3900	4550
17 4	CF-17-L CUS	OP	FSH	FBG	IO	140	MRCR	7 4	1800	11	3900	4550
17 4	CF-17-L CUS	OP	UTL	FBG	IO	120	MRCR	7 4	1895	11	3950	4600
17 4	DF-17-L DLX			FBG	IO	120	OMC	7 4	1800	11	3450	4000
17 4	DF-17-L DLX		FSH	FBG	IO	140	OMC	7 4	1800	11	3800	4450
17 4	DF-17-L DLX	OP	FSH	FBG	IO	120-140		7 4	1800	11	3800	4500
17 4	F-17-L		FSH	FBG	IO	120-140		7 4	1800	11	3800	4450
17 4	F-17-L	OP	FSH	FBG	IO	120	MRCR	7 4	1800	11	3850	4450
20	B-H BARE HULL	OP	UTL	FBG	OB			7	1600	11	2400	2800
20	CAPE-FEAR CF-20	OP	UTL	FBG	OB			7	2000	11	2700	3150
20	MCS-20			FBG	IO	120-140		7	2700	1	5300	6450
20	MCS-20	OP	UTL	FBG	OB			7	2000	11	2850	3350
20	MCS-20	OP	UTL	FBG	IO	120	MRCR	7	2700	1 11	5950	6850
20	S-20 STD	OP	UTL	FBG	IO			7	1700	11	2500	2900
--- 1972 BOATS ---												
20	B-H BARE HULL			FBG	OB			7	1600		2100	2500
20	CAPE-FEAR CF-20			FBG	OB			7	1600		2900	3350
20	CAPE-FEAR CF-20			FBG	IO	120-165		7			5200	6000
20	MC-KEE-CRAFT MCS-20			FBG	OB			7	1600		2850	3300
20	MC-KEE-CRAFT MCS-20			FBG	IO	120-165		7			5150	5950
20	S-20 STD			FBG	OB			7	1600		2700	3150
20	S-20 STD			FBG	IO	120-165		7			5000	5800

MEDITERRANEAN YACHTS
CASSOPOLIS MI 49031-938 COAST GUARD MFG ID- WHI See inside cover to adjust price for area
FORMERLY INTERNATIONAL OFFSHORE MARINE

For more recent years, see the BUC Used Boat Price Guide, Volume 1 or Volume 2

LOA FT IN	NAME AND/ OR MODEL	TOP/ RIG	BOAT TYPE	-HULL- MTL TP	TP	# HP	MFG	BEAM FT IN	WGT LBS	DRAFT FT IN	RETAIL LOW	RETAIL HIGH
--- 1979 BOATS ---												
47 4	CUSTOM	FB	TRWL	FBG DS	IB	T	D	15 4		4	**	**
60	CUSTOM	FB	MY	FBG SV	IB	T	D	17 6			**	**
65	CUSTOM	FB	MY	FBG SV	IB	T	D	18			**	**
--- 1978 BOATS ---												
47 4	CUSTOM	FB	TRWL	FBG DS	IB	T210D		15 4	40186	4	94200	103500
47 4	CUSTOM	FB	TRWL	FBG DS	IB	T250D		15 4	40186	4	95500	105000

MEIJER YACHTS

SAILSPIRIT

Call 1-800-327-6929 for BUC Personalized Evaluation Service
Or, for 1982 to 1984 boats, sign onto www.BUCValuPro.com

MEL-HART PRODUCTS INC
BARETTA & SUCCESS BOATS See inside cover to adjust price for area
CONWAY 32 AR 72032 COAST GUARD MFG ID- MHP

For more recent years, see the BUC Used Boat Price Guide, Volume 1 or Volume 2

LOA FT IN	NAME AND/ OR MODEL	TOP/ RIG	BOAT TYPE	-HULL- MTL TP	TP	# HP	MFG	BEAM FT IN	WGT LBS	DRAFT FT IN	RETAIL LOW	RETAIL HIGH
--- 1983 BOATS ---												
16 2	LEGEND 162 B/R	OP	RNBT	FBG DV	OB			6 11			1750	2100
16 4	ADVANTAGE 164 B/R	OP	RNBT	FBG DV	OB			6 4			1750	2100
18 3	ADVANTAGE 183 B/R	OP	RNBT	FBG DV	OB			7 2			2200	2550
18 9	BARETTA 191 CC	ST	CUD	FBG DV	IO	120-230		7 7			1700	2150
18 9	SUCCESS 191	ST	OVNTR	FBG DV	IO	198-230		7 7			1700	2050
18 9	SUCCESS 191 CC	ST	CUD	FBG DV	IO	120-200		7 7			1800	2200
18 9	SUCCESS 191 CC	ST	CUD	FBG DV	IO	228-230		7 7			1900	2250
20 4	BARETTA 204 B/R	ST	RNBT	FBG DV	IO	170-260		8			2250	2800
20 4	BARETTA 204 CC	ST	CUD	FBG DV	IO	170-260		8			2500	3100
20 4	SUCCESS 204 B/R	ST	RNBT	FBG DV	IO	170-260		8			2350	2900
20 4	SUCCESS 204 CC	ST	CUD	FBG DV	IO	170-260		8			2600	3150
--- 1982 BOATS ---												
16 2	ADVANTAGE B/R	OP	RNBT	FBG DV	OB			6 11			1750	2050
16 4	ADVANTAGE B/R	OP	RNBT	FBG DV	OB			6 4	1095		1750	2000
18 3	ADVANTAGE B/R	OP	RNBT	FBG DV	OB			7 2			2150	2500
20 4	BARETTA 204 B/R	OP	RNBT	FBG DV	IO	170-260		8			2250	2750
20 4	BARETTA 204 C/C	OP	CUD	FBG DV	IO	170-260		8			2500	3050

MELEN MARINE LTD
COAST GUARD MFG ID- MML

Call 1-800-327-6929 for BUC Personalized Evaluation Service
Or, for 1974 to 1977 boats, sign onto www.BUCValuPro.com

MELGES BOAT WORKS INC

ZENDA WI 53195   COAST GUARD MFG ID- MEB See inside cover to adjust price for area

For more recent years, see the BUC Used Boat Price Guide, Volume 1 or Volume 2

LOA FT IN	NAME AND/ OR MODEL	TOP/ RIG	BOAT TYPE	-HULL- MTL TP	----ENGINE--- TP # HP MFG	BEAM FT IN	WGT LBS	DRAFT FT IN	RETAIL LOW	RETAIL HIGH
--- 1983 BOATS ---
16	M-16-SCOW	SLP	SA/OD	FBG BB		5 8	440	3	3100	3650
16	M-C-SCOW	CAT	SA/OD	FBG BB		5 8	420	6	2450	2850
16	X-SCOW	SLP	SA/OD	FBG BB		6	500	2	2350	2700
20	C-SCOW	CAT	SA/OD	FBG BB		6 6	650	3 9	4550	5250
20	M-20-SCOW	SLP	SA/OD	FBG BB		5 8	595	3 9	4450	5100
28	E-SCOW	SLP	SA/OD	FBG BB		6 9	650	6	8450	9700
38	A-SCOW	SLP	SA/OD	FBG BB		8 6	1850	6 4	2400	2800
--- 1981 BOATS ---
16	M-16-SCOW	SLP	SA/OD	FBG BB OB		5 8	440	3	2750	3200
16	M-C-SCOW	CAT	SA/OD	FBG BB OB		5 8	420	6	2200	2550
16	X-SCOW	SLP	SA/OD	FBG BB OB		6	500	2	2000	2400
20	C-SCOW	CAT	SA/OD	FBG BB OB		6 6	650	3	3950	4600
20	M-20-SCOW	SLP	SA/OD	FBG BB OB		5 8	595		3850	4450
28	E-SCOW	SLP	SA/OD	FBG BB OB		6 9	965	6	5100	5850
38	A-SCOW	SLP	SA/OD	FBG BB OB		8 6	1850	5	3500	4050
--- 1980 BOATS ---
16	M-16-SCOW	SLP	SA/OD	FBG BB OB		5 8	440	3	2600	3050
16	M-16-SCOW	SLP	SA/OD	WD BB OB		5 8	420	3	2550	2950
16	MC-SCOW	CAT	SA/OD	FBG BB OB		5 8	500	6	2300	2650
16	X-SCOW	SLP	SA/OD	FBG CB OB		6	500	2	1900	2300
20	C-SCOW	CAT	SA/OD	FBG BB OB		6 6	650	3	3750	4350
20	C-SCOW	CAT	SA/OD	WD BB OB		6 6	650	3	3750	4350
20	M-20-SCOW	SLP	SA/OD	FBG BB OB		5 8	595	6	3650	4250
28	E-SCOW	SLP	SA/OD	FBG BB OB		6 9	965	6	4850	5600
28	E-SCOW	SLP	SA/OD	WD BB OB		6 9	965	6	4850	5600
38	A-SCOW	SLP	SA/OD	FBG BB OB		8 6	1850	5	3150	3650
--- 1979 BOATS ---
16	M-16 SCOW	SLP	SA/OD	FBG BB OB		5 8	440	6	2500	2900
16	M-16 SCOW	SLP	SA/OD	WD BB OB		5 8	440	6	2500	2900
16	MC SCOW	CAT	SA/OD	FBG BB OB		5 8	420	6	1950	2300
16	X-SCOW	SLP	SA/OD	FBG BB OB		6	500	2	1850	2200
20	C-SCOW	SLP	SA/OD	FBG BB OB		6 6	650	3	3600	4300
20	C-SCOW	CAT	SA/OD	WD BB OB		6 6	650	3	3600	4200
20	M-20 SCOW	SLP	SA/OD	FBG BB OB		5 8	595	6	3500	4050
28	E-SCOW	SLP	SA/OD	FBG BB OB		6 9	965	6	4700	5400
28	E-SCOW	SLP	SA/OD	WD BB OB		6 9	965	6	4700	5400
38	A-SCOW	SLP	SA/OD	FBG BB OB		8 6	1850	6	3000	3450
--- 1978 BOATS ---
16	M C	CAT	SA/RC	FBG DB OB		5 8	440	3	1900	2300
16	M-16 SCOW	SLP	SA/OD	FBG BB OB		5 8	440	3	2400	2800
16	X-SCOW	SLP	SA/OD	FBG BB OB		6 1	500	2 9	1750	2100
20	C-SCOW	CAT	SA/OD	FBG BB OB		6 6	650	3	3450	4000
20	C-SCOW	CAT	SA/OD	WD BB OB		6 6	650	3	3400	3950
20	M-20 SCOW	SLP	SA/OD	FBG BB OB		5 6	595	3	3350	3900
28	E-SCOW	SLP	SA/OD	FBG BB OB		6 9	965	4	4500	5150
28	E-SCOW	SLP	SA/OD	WD BB OB		6 9		4	4500	5150
--- 1977 BOATS ---
16	M-16 SCOW	SLP	SA/OD	FBG BB OB		5 8	440	3	2350	2700
16	M-16 SCOW	SLP	SA/OD	WD BB OB		5 8	440	3	2350	2700
16	MC SCOW	CAT	SA/OD	FBG BB OB		5 8	420	3	1800	2150
20	C-SCOW	CAT	SA/OD	FBG BB OB		6 6	650	3	3300	3850
20	C-SCOW	CAT	SA/OD	WD BB OB		6 6	650	3	3300	3850
20	M-20 SCOW	SLP	SA/OD	FBG BB OB		5 8	595	3 6	3250	3750
28	E-SCOW	SLP	SA/OD	FBG BB OB		6 8	965	3	4300	4950
28	E-SCOW	SLP	SA/OD	WD BB OB		6 8	965	3	4300	4950
--- 1976 BOATS ---
16	M-16 SCOW	SLP	SA/OD	FBG BB OB		5 8		6	2250	2650
16	MC SCOW	CAT	SA/OD	FBG BB OB		5 8	420	6	1750	2050
20	C-SCOW	CAT	SA/OD	FBG BB OB		6 6	650	6	3200	3750
20	C-SCOW	CAT	SA/OD	WD BB OB		6 6	650	6	3200	3750
20	M-20 SCOW	SLP	SA/OD	FBG BB OB		6 6		6	3150	3700
28	E-SCOW	SLP	SA/OD	FBG BB OB		6 8	965	6	4150	4800
28	E-SCOW	SLP	SA/OD	WD BB OB		6 8	965	6	4150	4800
--- 1975 BOATS ---
16	M-16 SCOW	SLP	SA/OD	FBG BB OB		5 8	440	2	2200	2550
16	M-16 SCOW	SLP	SA/OD	WD BB OB		5 8	440	2	2200	2550
20	C-SCOW	CAT	SA/OD	FBG BB OB		6 6	650	3	3100	3600
20	C-SCOW	CAT	SA/OD	WD BB OB		6 6	650	3	3100	3600
20	M-20 SCOW	SLP	SA/OD	FBG BB OB		5 8		4	3050	3550
28	E-SCOW	SLP	SA/OD	FBG BB OB		6 8	965	3	4000	4650
28	E-SCOW	SLP	SA/OD	WD BB OB		6 8	965	3	4000	4650
--- 1974 BOATS ---
16	M-16 SCOW	SLP	SA/OD	FBG BB OB		5 8	440	3	2050	2450
16	M-16 SCOW	SLP	SA/OD	WD BB OB		5 8	440	3	2050	2450
20	C-SCOW	CAT	SA/OD	FBG BB OB		6 6	650	3 5	3000	3500
20	M-20 SCOW	SLP	SA/OD	FBG BB OB		5 9	595	3 6	2950	3400
28	E-SCOW	SLP	SA/OD	WD BB OB		6 5	965	4	3900	4500
--- 1973 BOATS ---
16	M-16 SCOW	SLP	SA/OD	FBG BB OB		5 8	440		2000	2400
16	M-16 SCOW	SLP	SA/OD	WD BB OB		5 8	440		2000	2400
20	C-SCOW	CAT	SA/OD	FBG BB OB		6 6	650		2950	3450
20	C-SCOW	CAT	SA/OD	WD BB OB		6 6	650		2950	3450
20	M-20 SCOW	SLP	SA/OD	FBG BB OB		5 8	595		2850	3350
28	E-SCOW	SLP	SA/OD	WD BB OB		6 8	965		3800	4400
--- 1972 BOATS ---
16	CLASS M SCOW	SLP	SA/OD	FBG BB		5 8	440	2	2000	2350
16	CLASS M SCOW	SLP	SA/OD	WD BB		5 8	440	2	2000	2350
20	CLASS C SCOW	CAT	SA/OD	FBG BB		6 6	650	3	2900	3350
20	CLASS C SCOW	CAT	SA/OD	WD BB		6 6	650	3	2900	3350
20	CLASS M-20 SCOW	SLP	SA/OD	FBG BB		5 8		4	2850	3300
28	CLASS E SCOW	SLP	SA/OD	FBG BB		6 8	965	3	5750	6600
28	CLASS E SCOW	SLP	SA/OD	WD BB		6 8	965	3	5750	6600
--- 1971 BOATS ---
16	SCOW M-16	SAIL		FBG OB		5 8	440	2	1950	2300
20	C-SCOW	CAT	SA/OD	FBG BB OB		6 6	650	3 6	2850	3300
20	M-20 SCOW	SLP	SA/OD	FBG BB OB		5 8	595	3	2750	3200
28	E-SCOW	SLP	SA/OD	WD BB OB		6 8	965	4	3650	4250
--- 1969 BOATS ---
16	M-16 SCOW	SLP	SA/OD	FBG BB		5 8	440	2	1900	2250
20	C-SCOW	CAT	SA/OD	WD BB OB		6 6	650	3	2750	3200
20	M20-SCOW	SLP	SA/OD	FBG BB		6 6	600	4	2700	3150
28	E-SCOW	SLP	SA/OD	WD BB		6 8	965	3	5450	6300
--- 1968 BOATS ---
16	M-16 SCOW	SLP	SA/OD	FBG BB		5 6	440	3	1850	2250
20	CLASS C SCOW	CAT	SA/OD	FBG BB		6 8	650	6	2750	3200
20	CLASS D SCOW	SLP	SA/OD	FBG BB		6 6		3	2700	3100
20	M-20 SCOW	SLP	SA/OD	FBG BB		5 8	600	3	2650	3100
28	CLASS E SCOW	SLP	SA/OD	WD BB		6 9	965	8	5400	6250
--- 1967 BOATS ---
16	M-16 SCOW	SLP	SA/OD	FBG		5 6	440	6	1850	2200
16	M-16 SCOW	SLP	SA/OD	WD		5 6	440	6	1850	2200
16	M-16 SCOW	SLP	SA/OD	FBG BB		5 8	440	6	1850	2200
16	M-16 SCOW	SLP	SA/OD	WD BB		5 8	440	6	1850	2200
16	MC SCOW	CAT	SA/OD	FBG BB		5 8		6	1850	2250
20	C-SCOW	CAT	SA/OD	FBG BB		6 6	650	6	2700	3150
20	C-SCOW	CAT	SA/OD	WD BB		6 6	650	6	2700	3150
20	M-20 SCOW	SLP	SA/OD	FBG BB		5 8		6	2650	3100
28	E-SCOW	SLP	SA/OD	FBG BB		6 9	965	6	5400	6200
28	E-SCOW	SLP	SA/OD	WD BB		6 9	965	6	5400	6200
--- 1966 BOATS ---
16	M-16 SCOW	SLP	SA/OD	FBG BB		5 8	440	5	1850	2200
20	C-SCOW	CAT	SA/OD	FBG BB		5 8		6	2700	3150
20	M-20 SCOW	SLP	SA/OD	FBG BB		5 8	600	6	2650	3050
28	E-SCOW	SLP	SA/OD	FBG BB		5 7	965	5	5350	6150
--- 1965 BOATS ---
16	X-SCOW	SLP	SA/OD	PLY CB		6 1			1850	2200
20	C-SCOW	CAT	SA/OD	FBG BB		6 6	650	6	2700	3100
20	D-SCOW	SLP	SA/OD	FBG BB		6 9			2650	3100
20	M-20 SCOW	SLP	SA/OD	FBG BB		5 8	600	6	2650	3050
28	E-SCOW	SLP	SA/OD	FBG BB		6 7	965	5	5350	6150
--- 1959 BOATS ---
16	M-16-SCOW	SLP	SA/OD	P/C BB		5 6	440	5	1900	2250
20	C-SCOW	CAT	SA/OD	P/C BB		6 8	650	6	2750	3200
20	D-SCOW	SLP	SA/OD	P/C BB				5	2750	3200
28	E-SCOW	SLP	SA/OD	P/C BB		6 8	965	5	5500	6300

MENGER BOATWORKS INC

OYSTER BAY NY 11771-151 COAST GUARD MFG ID- MEN See inside cover to adjust price for area
FORMERLY MENGER ENTERPRISES INC

For more recent years, see the BUC Used Boat Price Guide, Volume 1 or Volume 2

LOA FT IN	NAME AND/ OR MODEL	TOP/ RIG	BOAT TYPE	-HULL- MTL TP	----ENGINE--- TP # HP MFG	BEAM FT IN	WGT LBS	DRAFT FT IN	RETAIL LOW	RETAIL HIGH
--- 1983 BOATS ---
17	MENGER CAT	CAT	SA/CR	FBG CB OB		8	2200	1 8	5450	6250
17	MENGER CAT	CAT	SA/CR	FBG CB IB	8D	8	2200	1 8	8150	9350
22 6	OYSTERMAN 23	SLP	SA/CR	FBG CB OB		8	2800	1 8	6250	7200
22 6	OYSTERMAN 23	SLP	SA/CR	FBG CB IB	8D	8	2800	1 8	7500	8650
22 6	OYSTERMAN 23	KTH	SA/CR	FBG CB OB		8	2800	1 8	6250	7200
22 6	OYSTERMAN 23	KTH	SA/CR	FBG CB IB	8D	8	2800	1 8	7500	8650

MENGER BOATWORKS INC   -CONTINUED   See inside cover to adjust price for area

LOA FT IN	NAME AND/ OR MODEL	TOP/ RIG	BOAT TYPE	-HULL- MTL TP	----ENGINE--- TP # HP MFG	BEAM FT IN	WGT LBS	DRAFT FT IN	RETAIL LOW	RETAIL HIGH
--- 1982 BOATS ---										
16 7	MENGER CAT	CAT	SA/CR	FBG CB	OB 8		2200	1 8	5150	5950
22 6	OYSTERMAN 23	SLP	SA/CR	FBG CB	OB 8		2800	1 8	5900	6750
22 6	OYSTERMAN 23	SLP	SA/CR	FBG CB	OB 8D 8		2800	1 8	7050	8150
22 6	OYSTERMAN 23	KTH	SA/CR	FBG CB	OB 8		2800	1 8	5900	6750
22 6	OYSTERMAN 23	KTH	SA/CR	FBG CB	IB 8D 8		2800	1 8	7050	8150
41 6	ARIEL	SLP	SA/CR	FBG CT	OB 18	10	12500	2 6	71900	79000
--- 1981 BOATS ---										
17	SOUTH-BAY CAT	CAT	SA/CR	FBG CB	OB 8		2200	1 8	4800	5550
22 6	OYSTERMAN 23	SLP	SA/CR	FBG CB	OB 8		2800	1 8	5550	6350
22 6	OYSTERMAN 23	SLP	SA/CR	FBG CB	OB 8D 8		2800	1 8	6650	7650
22 6	OYSTERMAN 23	KTH	SA/CR	FBG CB	OB 8		2800	1 8	5550	6350
22 6	OYSTERMAN 23	KTH	SA/CR	FBG CB	IB 8D 8		2800	1 8	6650	7650
41 6	ARIEL	SLP	SA/CR	FBG CT	OB 18	10	12500	2 6	67600	74300
--- 1980 BOATS ---										
22 6	OYSTERMAN 23	SLP	SA/CR	FBG CB	OB 8		2800	1 8	5300	6100
22 6	OYSTERMAN 23	SLP	SA/CR	FBG CB	IB 8D 8		2800	1 8	6350	7300
22 6	OYSTERMAN 23	KTH	SA/CR	FBG CB	OB 8		2800	1 8	5300	6100
22 6	OYSTERMAN 23	KTH	SA/CR	FBG CB	IB 8D 8		2800	1 8	6350	7300
--- 1979 BOATS ---										
23	OYSTERMAN 23	SLP	SA/CR	FBG CB	OB 8		2600	1 8	4850	5600
23	OYSTERMAN 23	SLP	SA/CR	FBG CB	IB 8D 8		2600	1 8	5800	6650
23	OYSTERMAN 23	KTH	SA/CR	FBG CB	OB 8		2600	1 8	4850	5600
23	OYSTERMAN 23	KTH	SA/CR	FBG CB	IB 8D 8		2600	1 8	5800	6650
--- 1978 BOATS ---										
23	OYSTERMAN 23	SLP	SA/CR	FBG CB	OB 8		2600	1 8	4700	5400
23	OYSTERMAN 23	KTH	SA/CR	FBG CB	OB 8		2600	1 8	4700	5400
--- 1977 BOATS ---										
22	OYSTERMAN 22	SLP	SA/CR	FBG CB	OB 8		2200	1 8	4000	4650
22	OYSTERMAN 22	KTH	SA/CR	FBG CB	OB 8		2200	1 8	4000	4650
23	OYSTERMAN 23	SLP	SA/CR	FBG CB	OB 8		2100	1 8	3950	4550
23	OYSTERMAN 23	KTH	SA/CR	FBG CB	OB 8		2100	1 8	3950	4550

MERCATOR INDUSTRIES INC
KENT WA 98031   COAST GUARD MFG ID- PMT See inside cover to adjust price for area

LOA FT IN	NAME AND/ OR MODEL	TOP/ RIG	BOAT TYPE	-HULL- MTL TP	----ENGINE--- TP # HP MFG	BEAM FT IN	WGT LBS	DRAFT FT IN	RETAIL LOW	RETAIL HIGH
--- 1979 BOATS ---										
30	MERCATOR	SLP	SAIL	FBG KL	IB 22D VLVO	8 10	11600	5	20900	23200
--- 1978 BOATS ---										
30	MERCATOR	SLP	SAIL	FBG KL	IB D	8 10	11600	5	20100	22400
--- 1977 BOATS ---										
30	MERCATOR	SLP	SAIL	FBG KL	IB D	8 10	11600	5	19400	21600
--- 1976 BOATS ---										
30	MERCATOR	SLP	SAIL	FBG KL	IB D	8 10	11600	5	19100	21200
--- 1975 BOATS ---										
30	MERCATOR	SLP	SAIL	FBG KL	IB D	8 10	11600	5	18500	20600

MERCER REINFORCED PLASTICS CO
FOR NEWER MODELS SEE CAPE COD SHIPBUILDING

Call 1-800-327-6929 for BUC Personalized Evaluation Service
Or, for 1960 to 1963 boats, sign onto www.BUCValuPro.com

MERIDIAN NORTH YACHTS

Call 1-800-327-6929 for BUC Personalized Evaluation Service
Or, for 1978 boats, sign onto www.BUCValuPro.com

MERIDIAN YACHT
DIV OF WHITTAKER CORP   See inside cover to adjust price for area
LANCASTER PA 17604

LOA FT IN	NAME AND/ OR MODEL	TOP/ RIG	BOAT TYPE	-HULL- MTL TP	----ENGINE--- TP # HP MFG	BEAM FT IN	WGT LBS	DRAFT FT IN	RETAIL LOW	RETAIL HIGH
--- 1976 BOATS ---										
47 11	MERIDIAN 48	HT	TRWL	FBG DS	IB T185D PERK	14	38000	3 4	118000	129500
47 11	MERIDIAN 48	FB	TRWL	FBG DS	IB T185D PERK	14	38000	3 4	117000	128500
47 11	MERIDIAN 48	FB	TRWL	FBG DS	IB T210D GM	14	38000	3 4	117000	128500
--- 1975 BOATS ---										
47 11	MERIDIAN 48	HT	TRWL	FBG DS	IB T185D PERK	14	39000	3 4	114000	125500
47 11	MERIDIAN 48	FB	TRWL	FBG DS	IB T185D PERK	14	39000	3 4	113500	124500
--- 1974 BOATS ---										
47 11	MERIDIAN	HT	TRWL	FBG DS	IB T185D PERK	14	38000	3 4	108500	119500

MERIT MARINE
PACOIMA CA 91331   See inside cover to adjust price for area

For more recent years, see the BUC Used Boat Price Guide, Volume 1 or Volume 2

LOA FT IN	NAME AND/ OR MODEL	TOP/ RIG	BOAT TYPE	-HULL- MTL TP	----ENGINE--- TP # HP MFG	BEAM FT IN	WGT LBS	DRAFT FT IN	RETAIL LOW	RETAIL HIGH
--- 1983 BOATS ---										
22	MERIT 22	SLP	SA/RC	F/S KL	OB 8		2000	4	3150	3650
25	MERIT 25	SLP	SA/RC	F/S KL	OB 8		3000	4	4850	5550
--- 1982 BOATS ---										
25	MERIT 25	SLP	SA/RC	F/S KL	IB D 8		2900	4	4900	5650

MERRITT BOAT & ENG WORKS
POMPANO BEACH FL 33062   COAST GUARD MFG ID- MBN See inside cover to adjust price for area

For more recent years, see the BUC Used Boat Price Guide, Volume 1 or Volume 2

LOA FT IN	NAME AND/ OR MODEL	TOP/ RIG	BOAT TYPE	-HULL- MTL TP	----ENGINE--- TP # HP MFG	BEAM FT IN	WGT LBS	DRAFT FT IN	RETAIL LOW	RETAIL HIGH
--- 1976 BOATS ---										
43	MERRITT	TT	SF	FBG DV	IB T400D CUM	13 2	18000	2 4	192500	211500

METALMAST MARINE INC
PUTNAM CT 06260   COAST GUARD MFG ID- MET See inside cover to adjust price for area

For more recent years, see the BUC Used Boat Price Guide, Volume 1 or Volume 2

LOA FT IN	NAME AND/ OR MODEL	TOP/ RIG	BOAT TYPE	-HULL- MTL TP	----ENGINE--- TP # HP MFG	BEAM FT IN	WGT LBS	DRAFT FT IN	RETAIL LOW	RETAIL HIGH
--- 1983 BOATS ---										
29 11	METALMAST 30	SLP	SA/CR	FBG KL	IB 8D YAN	10 2	7100	5 4	20600	22900
35 6	METALMAST 36	SLP	SA/CR	FBG KL	IB 15D YAN	11 2	13000	6 4	38600	42900
--- 1982 BOATS ---										
29 11	METALMAST 30	SLP	SA/CR	FBG KL	IB 8D YAN	10 2	7100	5 4	19400	21600
35 6	METALMAST 36	SLP	SA/CR	FBG KL	IB 20D YAN	11 2	13000	6 4	36400	40400
--- 1981 BOATS ---										
29 11	METALMAST 30	SLP	SA/CR	FBG KL	IB 8D YAN	10 2	7100	5 4	18500	20500
35 6	METALMAST 36	SLP	SA/CR	FBG KL	IB 20D YAN	11 2	13000	6 4	34300	38100
--- 1980 BOATS ---										
29 11	METALMAST 30	SLP	SA/CR	FBG KL	IB 8D YAN	10 2	7100	5 4	17200	19600
35 6	METALMAST 36	SLP	SA/CR	FBG KL	IB 20D YAN	11 2	13000	6 4	32700	36400
--- 1979 BOATS ---										
29 10	METALMAST 30	SLP	SA/CR	FBG KL	IB 8D YAN	10 2	6400	5 1	14900	16900
35 6	METALMAST 36	SLP	SA/CR	FBG KL	IB 20D YAN	11 2	13000	6 2	31400	34900
--- 1978 BOATS ---										
29 10	METALMAST 30	SLP	SA/CR	FBG KL	IB 8D YAN	10 2	6400	5 6	14400	16300
35 6	METALMAST 36	SLP	SA/CR	FBG KL	IB 15D YAN	11 2	13000	6 2	30200	33600
--- 1977 BOATS ---										
35 6	ONE-TONNER	SLP	SA/CR	FBG KL	IB 12D YAN	11 2	13000	6 3	29200	32400
39	BLOCK-ISLAND	SLP	SA/CR	FBG KC	IB 40D YAN	11 8	18500	4	43800	48600
--- 1976 BOATS ---										
31 5	GALAXY	SLP	SAIL	FBG KL	IB 10D	10 2	9000	5 2	19500	21700
35 6	COMPETITION-ONE-TON	SLP	SA/CR	FBG KL	IB 10D YAN	11 2	13000	6 2	28400	31500
40 8	BLOCK-ISLAND	SLP	SA/CR	FBG KC	IB 40D PERK	11 8	18000	4	44300	49200
40 8	BLOCK-ISLAND	YWL	SA/CR	FBG KC	IB 40D PERK	11 8	18000	4	44300	49200
--- 1975 BOATS ---										
31 5	GALAXY	SLP	SAIL	FBG KL	IB 10D- 16D	10 2	9600	5	20200	22400
40 8	BLOCK-ISLAND	SLP	SAIL	FBG KC	IB 35D PERK	11 8	18100	4	43100	47900
40 8	BLOCK-ISLAND	YWL	SAIL	FBG KC	IB 35D PERK	11 8	18100	4	43100	47900
--- 1974 BOATS ---										
25 8	BLOCK-ISLAND	SLP	SAIL	FBG KL	IB D	16 7		4	9600	10900
29 11	GALAXY	SLP	SA/CR	FBG KL	IB D	10		4	13800	15700
31 5	GALAXY	SLP	SA/CR	FBG KL	IB D	10 2	9600	5	19700	21900
40 8	BLOCK-ISLAND	SLP	SA/CR	FBG KC	IB D	11 8	18100	4	42300	47000
--- 1973 BOATS ---										
25 8	BLOCK-ISLAND	SLP	SAIL	FBG KL	IB 10D	16 7		4 6	9450	10700
31 5	GALAXY	SLP	SA/CR	FBG KL	IB 10D	10 2	9600	5	19200	21300
40 8	BLOCK-ISLAND	SLP	SA/CR	FBG KL	IB 35D	11 8	18100	4	41100	45700
40 8	BLOCK-ISLAND	YWL	SA/CR	FBG KC	IB 35D	11 8	18100	4	41100	45700

METRO MARINE
Call 1-800-327-6929 for BUC Personalized Evaluation Service
Or, for 1965 to 1972 boats, sign onto www.BUCValuPro.com

MIAMI BEACH YACHT CORP
Call 1-800-327-6929 for BUC Personalized Evaluation Service
Or, for 1959 to 1961 boats, sign onto www.BUCValuPro.com

MID-AMERICA YACHTING SALES
Call 1-800-327-6929 for BUC Personalized Evaluation Service
Or, for 1965 to 1967 boats, sign onto www.BUCValuPro.com

MID-WEST HYDROFIN CO
Call 1-800-327-6929 for BUC Personalized Evaluation Service
Or, for 1960 to 1973 boats, sign onto www.BUCValuPro.com

MIDGET YACHTS INC
Call 1-800-327-6929 for BUC Personalized Evaluation Service
Or, for 1961 boats, sign onto www.BUCValuPro.com

MIDNIGHT EXPRESS
OPA LOCKA FL 33054   See inside cover to adjust price for area
FOR MORE RECENT YEARS SEE GOLDEN WAVE SHIPYARD

For more recent years, see the BUC Used Boat Price Guide, Volume 1 or Volume 2

LOA FT IN	NAME AND/ OR MODEL	TOP/ RIG	BOAT TYPE	HULL MTL TP	TP	ENGINE # HP	MFG	BEAM FT IN	WGT LBS	DRAFT FT IN	RETAIL LOW	RETAIL HIGH
--- 1982 BOATS ---
30	OPEN FISHERMAN	OP	OPFSH	FBG DV	IO	T200	MRCR	8	4500	2 6	22200	24700
32	MIDNIGHT-EXPRESS 32	OP	SPTCR	FBG DV	IO	T330-T400	8		6500	1	31500	36700
32	RACE BOAT 32	HT	EXP	FBG DV	IO	T500	MRCR	8	5500	2 6	37400	41600
37	MIDNIGHT-EXPRESS 37	OP	SPTCR	FBG DV	IO	T370	MRCR	9 6	8500	1 6	44800	49800
37	MIDNIGHT-EXPRESS 37	OP	SPTCR	FBG DV	IO	T400	MRCR	9 6	8500	1 6	47300	52000
37	MIDNIGHT-EXPRESS 37	OP	SPTCR	FBG DV	IO	T300D	CAT	9 6	8500	1 6	57500	63200
37	OPEN FISHERMAN 37	OP	OPFSH	FBG DV	IO	R200	MRCR	9 6	4850	2 6	40700	45200

MIDSHIP YACHTS
COAST GUARD MFG ID- MDS

Call 1-800-327-6929 for BUC Personalized Evaluation Service
Or, for 1972 to 1974 boats, sign onto www.BUCValuPro.com

MIDWESTERN INDUST CORP
HYDRODYNE BOATS

Call 1-800-327-6929 for BUC Personalized Evaluation Service
Or, for 1961 to 1972 boats, sign onto www.BUCValuPro.com

MILLAR MARINE
COAST GUARD MFG ID- RNN

Call 1-800-327-6929 for BUC Personalized Evaluation Service
Or, for 1983 to 1984 boats, sign onto www.BUCValuPro.com

MILLER CATAMARAN INC
COAST GUARD MFG ID- YDS

Call 1-800-327-6929 for BUC Personalized Evaluation Service
Or, for 1979 to 1994 boats, sign onto www.BUCValuPro.com

MILLER MARINE CONST
COAST GUARD MFG ID- MMR

Call 1-800-327-6929 for BUC Personalized Evaluation Service
Or, for 1979 boats, sign onto www.BUCValuPro.com

MINETT SHIELDS
Call 1-800-327-6929 for BUC Personalized Evaluation Service
Or, for 1910 to 1955 boats, sign onto www.BUCValuPro.com

MIRAGE BOAT CORP
OPA LOCKA FL 33054   COAST GUARD MFG ID- CDB See inside cover to adjust price for area
FORMERLY CORMED MARINE INC

LOA FT IN	NAME AND/ OR MODEL	TOP/ RIG	BOAT TYPE	HULL MTL TP	TP	ENGINE # HP	MFG	BEAM FT IN	WGT LBS	DRAFT FT IN	RETAIL LOW	RETAIL HIGH
--- 1983 BOATS ---
29	OPEN FISHERMAN	OP	OPFSH	FBG DV	IO	280	MRCR	8	4500	2 1	17500	19900
29	SPORT	OP	SPTCR	FBG DV	IO	T280	MRCR	8	5200	2 3	21200	23600
36	MIRAGE 36	OP	SPTCR	FBG DV	IO			8 6	7500	2 3	**	**
--- 1978 BOATS ---
29	MIRAGE 9 METER SS	OP	RACE	FBG DV	IO	T165-T188	8		5200	2 3	13900	16200
29	MIRAGE 9 METER SS	OP	RACE	FBG DV	IO	T300-T330	8		5200	2 3	16000	18900
29	MIRAGE 9 METER SS	OP	RACE	FBG DV	IO	T395	MRCR	8	5200	2 3	18600	20600
29	OPEN FISHERMAN	OP	OPFSH	FBG DV	IO	330	MRCR	8	4500	2 1	16900	19200
29	OPEN FISHERMAN	OP	OPFSH	FBG DV	IO	T165-T170	8		4500	2 1	17000	19400

MIRAGE MANUFACTURING CO
GAINESVILLE FL 32609   COAST GUARD MFG ID- MGY See inside cover to adjust price for area

For more recent years, see the BUC Used Boat Price Guide, Volume 1 or Volume 2

LOA FT IN	NAME AND/ OR MODEL	TOP/ RIG	BOAT TYPE	HULL MTL TP	TP	ENGINE # HP	MFG	BEAM FT IN	WGT LBS	DRAFT FT IN	RETAIL LOW	RETAIL HIGH
--- 1983 BOATS ---
20	MIRAGE 5.5	SLP	SA/RC	FBG CB	OB			7 11	1200	1 4	2800	3250
23 6	MIRAGE 236	SLP	SA/RC	FBG DB	OB			9	2950	4 6	5450	6300
27 5	MIRAGE 28	SLP	SA/RC	FBG KL	IB	8D	YAN	9	5580	5	13500	15400
--- 1982 BOATS ---
20	MIRAGE 5.5	SLP	SA/RC	FBG CB	OB			7 11	1200	1 4	2650	3050
23 6	MIRAGE 236	SLP	SA/RC	FBG DB	OB			9	2950	1 4	5150	5950
27 5	MIRAGE 28	SLP	SA/RC	FBG KL	IB	8D	YAN	9 2	5580		12800	14500
--- 1981 BOATS ---
20	MIRAGE 5.5	SLP	SA/RC	FBG CB	OB			7 11	1200	1 4	2500	2900
23 6	MIRAGE 236	SLP	SA/RC	FBG DB	OB			9	2950	1 4	4900	5650
27 5	MIRAGE 28	SLP	SA/RC	FBG KL	OB			9 2	5580		11700	13200
--- 1980 BOATS ---
20	MIRAGE 5.5	SLP	SA/RC	FBG CB	OB			7 11	1200	1 4	2400	2800
23 6	MIRAGE 236	SLP	SA/RC	FBG DB	OB			9	2950	1 4	4700	5400
--- 1979 BOATS ---
20	MIRAGE 5.5	SLP	SA/RC	FBG CB	OB			7 11	1200	1 4	2300	2650
23 6	MIRAGE 236	SLP	SA/RC	FBG DB	OB			9 2	2750	2	4200	4900
--- 1978 BOATS ---
20	MIRAGE 5.5	SLP	SA/RC	FBG CB	OB			7 11	1200	1 4	2200	2550

MIRROCRAFT BOATS
NORTHPORT CORP OF ST CLAIR
GILLETT WI 54124   COAST GUARD MFG ID- MRR See inside cover to adjust price for area
FORMERLY NORTHPORT INC

For more recent years, see the BUC Used Boat Price Guide, Volume 1 or Volume 2

LOA FT IN	NAME AND/ OR MODEL	TOP/ RIG	BOAT TYPE	HULL MTL TP	TP	ENGINE # HP	MFG	BEAM FT IN	WGT LBS	DRAFT FT IN	RETAIL LOW	RETAIL HIGH
--- 1977 BOATS ---
18 11	ALBACORE	OP	UTL	FBG	OB			7 5	1600		1800	2100
19 2	F-4628	ST	RNBT	AL	DV IO	120-175		7 8	1900		2850	3350
21 2	F-4621	ST	CUD	AL	DV IO	140-175		7 8	2800		4400	5100
21 2	F-4621-58	ST	CAMPR	AL	DV IO	140-175		7 8	2950		4550	5250
--- 1976 BOATS ---
18 11	ALBACORE 192	OP	UTL	FBG DV	OB			7 6	1600		1800	2100
19 2	MARINER F-4629	ST	B/R	AL	SV OB			7 8	2250		3050	3550
19 2	MARINER T-4628	ST	RNBT	AL	SV OB			7 8	1800		2200	2550
19 2	MARINER T-4628	ST	RNBT	AL	SV IO	120-165		7 8	2150		3050	3600
21 2	MARINER F-4621	ST	CUD	AL	SV IO	120-165		8	2700		4550	5250
21 2	MARINER F-4621-58	ST	CAMPR	AL	SV IO	120-165		8	2700		4550	5250
--- 1975 BOATS ---
21 2	MARINER EXPRESS 2100	ST	CUD	AL	SV IO	120-165		8	2700		4700	5400

LOA FT IN	NAME AND/ OR MODEL	TOP/ RIG	BOAT TYPE	-HULL- MTL TP	TP	----ENGINE--- # HP	MFG	BEAM FT IN	WGT LBS	DRAFT FT IN	RETAIL LOW	RETAIL HIGH
--- 1973 BOATS ---
16	EXPLORER F-4616			FBG	IO	120-140		6 5	1650		2050	2500

MISHEY BOATS & MOTORS

Call 1-800-327-6929 for BUC Personalized Evaluation Service
Or, for 1961 to 1968 boats, sign onto www.BUCValuPro.com

MISTRAL SAILBOAT INC
MISTAL INC   COAST GUARD MFG ID- ZMI

Call 1-800-327-6929 for BUC Personalized Evaluation Service
Or, for 1977 to 1986 boats, sign onto www.BUCValuPro.com

FREDERICK MITCHELL & SONS LTD
DORSET ENGLAND   See inside cover to adjust price for area

LOA FT IN	NAME AND/ OR MODEL	TOP/ RIG	BOAT TYPE	-HULL- MTL TP	TP	----ENGINE--- # HP	MFG	BEAM FT IN	WGT LBS	DRAFT FT IN	RETAIL LOW	RETAIL HIGH
--- 1983 BOATS ---
21	PARKSTONE-BAY	OP	CBNCR	FBG DV	IB	10D	SAAB	7 3	2500	1 10	6150	7050
21	PARKSTONE-BAY	OP	FSH	FBG DS	IB	42D	BENZ	7 3	2800	1 10	7750	8900
21	PARKSTONE-BAY	OP	FSH	FBG DS	IB	10D- 42D		7 3	2800	1 10	6750	8250
21	PARKSTONE-BAY	OP	LNCH	FBG DS	IB	42D	BENZ	7 3	2500	1 10	10000	11300
21	PARKSTONE-BAY	OP	LNCH	FBG DV	IB	10D- 18D		7 3	3360	1 10	9000	10600
21	PARKSTONE-BAY	OP	LNCH	FBG DV	IB	42D	BENZ	7 3	3360	1 10	10000	11300
28	PARKSTONE-BAY 28	HT	CBNCR	FBG DS	IB	T 42D	BENZ	10	7840	2 6	22900	25500
28	PARKSTONE-BAY 28	HT	FSH	FBG DS	IB	80D-120D		10	7000	2 6	19600	22500
32 6	BARBARY CLASS	KTH	MS	FBG KL	IB	42D	BENZ	10 4	14000	4 9	43600	48500
33	TRADEWIND 33	SLP	SA/CR	FBG KL	IB	20D- 42D		10 6	17900	5 6	55500	61000
35	TRADEWIND 35	CUT	SA/CR	FBG KL	IB	36D	BUKH	10 6	17400	5 6	55100	60500
38 9	TRADEWIND 39	SLP	SA/CR	FBG KL	IB	36D	BUKH	11 6	21200	5 6	71800	78900
--- 1982 BOATS ---
39 6	ATLANTIC CLASS	KTH	MS	FBG KL	IB	68D	BENZ	11 6	19200	5 3	69800	76700
21	PARKSTONE-BAY	OP	CBNCR	FBG DV	IB	10D- 18D		7 3	2500	1 10	5900	7050
21	PARKSTONE-BAY	OP	CBNCR	FBG DV	IB	42D	BENZ	7 3	2500	1 10	6600	7600
21	PARKSTONE-BAY	OP	FSH	FBG DS	IB	42D	BENZ	7 3	2800	1 10	7450	8550
21	PARKSTONE-BAY	OP	FSH	FBG DV	IB	10D- 42D		7 3	2800	1 10	6500	7900
21	PARKSTONE-BAY	OP	LNCH	FBG DS	IB	42D	BENZ	7 3	2500	1 10	9700	11000
21	PARKSTONE-BAY	OP	LNCH	FBG DV	IB	10D- 18D		7 3	3360	1 10	8550	10200
21	PARKSTONE-BAY	OP	LNCH	FBG DV	IB	42D	BENZ	7 3	3360	1 10	9700	11000
28	PARKSTONE-BAY 28	HT	CBNCR	FBG DS	IB	T 42D	BENZ	10	7840	2 6	22000	24500
28	PARKSTONE-BAY 28	HT	FSH	FBG DS	IB	80D-120D		10	7000	2 6	18800	22000
32 6	BARBARY CLASS	KTH	MS	FBG KL	IB	42D	BENZ	10 4	14000	4 9	41000	45600
33	TRADEWIND 33	SLP	SA/CR	FBG KL	IB	20D- 42D		10 6	17900	5 6	52200	57400
35	TRADEWIND 35	CUT	SA/CR	FBG KL	IB	363D	BUKH	10 6	17400	5 6	53900	59300
--- 1981 BOATS ---
38 9	TRADEWIND 39	SLP	SA/CR	FBG KL	IB	36D	BUKH	11 6	21200	5 6	67500	74200
39 6	ATLANTIC CLASS	KTH	MS	FBG KL	IB	68D	BENZ	11 6	19200	5 3	65600	72100
21	PARKSTONE-BAY	OP	CBNCR	FBG DV	IB	10D- 18D		7 3	2500	1 10	5650	6800
21	PARKSTONE-BAY	OP	CBNCR	FBG DV	IB	42D	BENZ	7 3	3360	1 10	7350	8450
21	PARKSTONE-BAY	OP	FSH	FBG DS	IB	42D	BENZ	7 3	2800	1 10	7150	8200
21	PARKSTONE-BAY	OP	FSH	FBG DV	IB	10D- 18D		7 3	2500	1 10	5950	7100
21	PARKSTONE-BAY	OP	FSH	FBG DV	IB	42D	BENZ	7 3	2500	1 10	6650	7650
21	PARKSTONE-BAY	OP	LNCH	FBG DS	IB	42D	BENZ	7 3	2500	1 10	9300	10600
21	PARKSTONE-BAY	OP	LNCH	FBG DV	IB	10D- 18D		7 3	3360	1 10	8200	9800
28	PARKSTONE-BAY 28	HT	CBNCR	FBG DS	IB	T 42D	BENZ	10	7840	2 6	21600	24000
28	PARKSTONE-BAY 28	HT	FSH	FBG DS	IB	80D-120D		10	7000	2 6	18100	21100
32 6	BARBARY CLASS	KTH	MS	FBG KL	IB	42D	BENZ	10 4	14000	4 9	38600	42900
33	TRADEWIND 33	SLP	SA/CR	FBG KL	IB	20D	BUKH	10 6	17900	5 6	49100	54000
38 9	TRADEWIND 39	SLP	SA/CR	FBG KL	IB	36D	BUKH	11 6	21200	5 6	63500	69800
--- 1980 BOATS ---
21	PARKSTONE-BAY		CBNCR	FBG DS	IB	42D	BENZ	7 3	3360	1 10	7250	8300
21	PARKSTONE-BAY		FSH	FBG DS	IB	42D	BENZ	7 3	2800	1 10	6900	7950
21	PARKSTONE-BAY		LNCH	FBG DS	IB	42D	BENZ	7 3	2500	1 10	8950	10200
28	PARKSTONE-BAY 28	HT	FSH	FBG DS	IB	T 42D	BENZ	10	7840	2 6	20700	23100
28	PARKSTONE-BAY 28	HT	FSH	FBG DS	IB	60D	BENZ	10	7000	2 6	16900	19100
32 6	BARBARY CLASS	KTH	MS	FBG KL	IB	42D	BENZ	10 4	15650	4 9	41000	45600
33	TRADEWIND 33	SLP	SA/CR	FBG KL	IB	42D	BENZ	10 6	17900	5 6	47200	51900

MITCHELL & STEVENS

Call 1-800-327-6929 for BUC Personalized Evaluation Service
Or, for 1959 boats, sign onto www.BUCValuPro.com

MOBJACK SALES CORP

Call 1-800-327-6929 for BUC Personalized Evaluation Service
Or, for 1965 to 1999 boats, sign onto www.BUCValuPro.com

MODERN MARINE MFG INC
RICHLAND MO 65556   COAST GUARD MFG ID- MDR See inside cover to adjust price for area

LOA FT IN	NAME AND/ OR MODEL	TOP/ RIG	BOAT TYPE	-HULL- MTL TP	TP	----ENGINE--- # HP	MFG	BEAM FT IN	WGT LBS	DRAFT FT IN	RETAIL LOW	RETAIL HIGH
--- 1982 BOATS ---
51 10	GOLDCOAST 52		MY	FBG SV	IB	T250		12 2	30000	3 2	81300	89300
--- 1981 BOATS ---
51 10	COASTAL 52	FB	MY	FBG SV	IB	T210D		12 2	30000	3 2	73700	81000
51 10	GOLDCOAST 52		CR	FBG SV	IB	T250		12 2	30000	3 2	73000	80200
--- 1980 BOATS ---
50	GOLDCOAST 50	FB	MY	FBG SV VD	IB	T250	CHRY	12	30000	3 2	70100	77000
	VD T250 OMC	70500	77500, VD T300 CHRY		70700	77700, VD T330	MRCR		71900		79000	
	VD T330 OMC	71700	78800, VD T200D PERK		70100	77100, VD T210D CAT			70600		77600	
	VD T215D CUM	69000	76900, VD T220D GM		70000	77000, VD T260D CAT			72700		79900	
	VD T300D GM	73400	80700									
51 10	GOLDCOAST 52	FB	MY	FBG SV VD	IB	T250	CHRY	12 2	30000	3 2	72400	79500
	VD T250 OMC	72700	79800, VD T300 CHRY		73500	80700, VD T330	MRCR		76000		83500	
	VD T330 OMC	75400	82900, VD T200D PERK		69100	76000, VD T210D CAT			69800		76700	
	VD T215D CUM	69400	76200, VD T220D GM		69200	76100, VD T260D CAT			73000		80300	
	VD T300D GM	76500	84100									
--- 1979 BOATS ---
50	GOLDCOAST 50	HT	MY	FBG SV VD	IB	T250	CHRY	12	30000	3 2	67200	73900
	VD T330 OMC	68800	75600, VD T350 CHRY		68700	75500, VD T350	MRCR		69300		76200	
	VD T200D CHRY	66700	73300, VD T210D CAT		67700	74400, VD T220D GM			67200		73800	
	VD T300D GM	70500	77400									
50	GOLDCOAST 50	FB	MY	FBG SV VD	IB	T250	CHRY	12	30000	3 2	66900	73500
	VD T330 OMC	68400	75200, VD T350 CHRY		68300	75000, VD T350	MRCR		69000		75800	
	VD T200D CHRY	66400	72900, VD T210D CAT		67400	74400, VD T220D GM			66800		73400	
	VD T300D GM	70100	77000, VD T350D CAT		73700	80900						
52	GOLDCOAST 52	FB	MY	FBG SV VD	IB	T250	CHRY	12	30000	3 2	75100	82500
	VD T330 OMC	76800	84400, VD T330 OMC		77100	84700, VD T350	CHRY		78100		85800	
	VD T350 MRCR	78900	86800, VD T200D CHRY		71000	78000, VD T210D CAT			72100		79200	
	VD T220D GM	71400	78400, VD T300D GM		77200	84800, VD T350D CAT			83300		91500	
--- 1978 BOATS ---
50	GOLDCOAST 50	HT	MY	FBG SV VD	IB	T250	CHRY	12	25000	3 2	61200	67200
	VD T330 CHRY	62200	68400, VD T350 MRCR		63200	69500, VD T350	OMC		63100		69300	
	VD T D CAT	**	** , VD T D GM		**	** , VD T200D	CHRY		59300		65200	
	VD T200D CHRY	60200	66200									
50	GOLDCOAST 50	FB	MY	FBG SV VD	IB	T250	CHRY	12	25000	3 2	60900	66900
	VD T330 CHRY	61900	68000, VD T350 MRCR		62900	69100, VD T350	OMC		62800		69000	
	VD T D CAT	**	** , VD T D GM		**	** , VD T192D	VLVO		59000		64800	
	VD T200D CHRY	59900	65800									
50 1	GOLDCOAST 50	FB	MY	FBG DV	IB	T250		12	25000	3 2	61700	67800
50 1	GOLDCOAST 50	FB	MY	FBG DV	IB	T350		12	25000	3 2	63100	69400
--- 1977 BOATS ---
50 1	GOLDCOAST 50	FB	MY	FBG SV	IB	T250	CHRY	12	24500	3 2	58300	64000
--- 1976 BOATS ---
50	WHITCRAFT 50		MY	FBG DV	IB	T250		12			58600	64400

MODERN PLASTICS
DIV OF HOLIDAY INNS INC COAST GUARD MFG ID- MDP

Call 1-800-327-6929 for BUC Personalized Evaluation Service
Or, for 1971 boats, sign onto www.BUCValuPro.com

MODERNETTE MARINE CORP

Call 1-800-327-6929 for BUC Personalized Evaluation Service
Or, for 1960 to 1961 boats, sign onto www.BUCValuPro.com

MOLDED FIBER GLASS BOAT CO

M F G
UNION CITY PA 16438 COAST GUARD MFG ID- MFG

See inside cover to adjust price for area

LOA FT	LOA IN	NAME AND/ OR MODEL	TOP/ RIG	BOAT TYPE	-HULL- MTL	-HULL- TP	ENGINE TP	ENGINE # HP	ENGINE MFG	BEAM FT	BEAM IN	WGT LBS	DRAFT FT	DRAFT IN	RETAIL LOW	RETAIL HIGH
		1981 BOATS														
16		GYPSY-STAR 16		RNBT	FBG	TR	OB			6	11	1100			2750	3200
16	11	CAPRICE 15		RNBT	FBG	DV	OB			6	5	1100			2800	3250
17	4	GYPSY-STAR 17		RNBT	FBG	TR	OB			7	2	1250			3150	3650
17	4	GYPSY-STAR 17		RNBT	FBG	TR	IO	120		7	2				1850	2200
18	10	CAPRICE 19		RNBT	FBG	DV	OB			7	6	1560			3850	4500
18	10	CAPRICE 19 THRIFT		RNBT	FBG	DV	OB			7	6	1450			3650	4250
18	10	CAPRICE 19 W/T		RNBT	FBG	DV	OB			7	6	1560			3850	4500
18	10	CAPRICE 19 W/T		RNBT	FBG	DV	IO	170		7	6				2250	2600
19	2	MFG 19	SLP	SAIL	FBG	KL				7					5100	5900
20	4	MORRISON 20		CR	FBG	DV	OB			7	6	2000			5500	6350
20	4	MORRISON 20		CR	FBG	DV	IO	185		7	6				3600	4150
22	3	MORRISON 22		CR	FBG	DV	IO	228		8					4650	5350
22	3	MORRISON-ELITE 22		CR	FBG	DV	IO	228		8					4650	5350
24	10	MORRISON 25		CR	FBG	DV	IO	228		8					6800	7850
		1980 BOATS														
16		CAMELOT 16	ST	RNBT	FBG	TR	OB			6	11	1100			2700	3150
16		CAMELOT 16	ST	RNBT	FBG	TR	IO	120-140		6	11	1800			1750	2100
16		GYPSY-STAR 16		RNBT	FBG	TR	OB			6	11	1100			2700	3150
16	11	CAPRICE 17		RNBT	FBG	DV	OB			6	5	1100			2750	3200
16	11	TARTAN 17	ST	RNBT	FBG	DV	OB			6	5	1100			2750	3200
16	11	TARTAN 17	ST	RNBT	FBG	DV	IO	120-140		6	5	1800			1800	2150
17	4	GYPSY-STAR 17		RNBT	FBG	TR	OB			7	2	1250			3100	3600
17	4	GYPSY-STAR 17		RNBT	FBG	TR	IO	120-170		7	2				1800	2200
17	4	ROYAL 1700	ST	RNBT	FBG	TR	OB			7	2	1250			3100	3600
17	4	ROYAL 1700	ST	RNBT	FBG	TR	IO	120		7	2	2050			1900	2250
17	4	ROYAL 1700	ST	RNBT	FBG	TR	IO	140-230		7	2	2050			2000	2450
17	4	ROYAL-ELITE 1700 BBB	ST	RNBT	FBG	TR	IO	140-230		7	2	2050			2250	2650
17	4	ROYAL-ELITE 1700 MBJ	ST	RNBT	FBG	TR	IO	140-230		7	2	2050			2100	2550
17	4	ROYAL-ELITE SPEC ANN	ST	RNBT	FBG	TR	IO	120-230		7	2	2050			2350	2750
18	10	CAPRICE 19		RNBT	FBG	DV	OB			7	6	1560			3800	4450
18	10	CAPRICE 19		RNBT	FBG	DV	IO	170-200		7	6				2250	2650
18	10	CAPRICE 19 B/R		RNBT	FBG	DV	OB			7	6	1560			3800	4450
18	10	CAPRICE 19 B/R		RNBT	FBG	DV	IO	170-200		7	6				2250	2650
18	10	CAPRICE 19 THRIFT		RNBT	FBG	DV	OB			7	6	1450			3600	4200
18	10	CORONET 19	ST	RNBT	FBG	DV	OB			7	6	1560			3900	4500
18	10	CORONET 19	ST	RNBT	FBG	DV	IO	170-260		7	6	2260			2300	2850
18	10	CORONET SPORTSMAN 19	ST	RNBT	FBG	DV	OB			7	6	1560			3400	3950
18	10	EMPEROR 1900	ST	RNBT	FBG	DV	OB			7	6	1560			4150	4850
18	10	EMPEROR 1900	ST	RNBT	FBG	DV	IO	170-230		7	6	2260			2400	2900
18	10	EMPEROR 1900	ST	RNBT	FBG	DV	IO	260		7	6	2260			2600	3000
18	10	EMPEROR-ELITE B/R	ST	RNBT	FBG	DV	IO	170-260		7	6	2260			2600	3250
18	10	EMPEROR-ELITE B/R SA	ST	RNBT	FBG	DV	IO	170-260		7	6	2260			2700	3350
19	2	MFG 19	SLP	SAIL	FBG	KL				7		1600			4900	5600
20	4	BARON 2000	ST	CUD	FBG	DV	OB			7	6	2000			5100	5900
20	4	BARON FAMILY 2000	ST	CUD	FBG	DV	IO	228-260		7	6	3050			3450	4200
20	4	BARON SPORTSMAN 2000	ST	CUD	FBG	DV	OB			7	6	2000			5750	6600
20	4	BARON SPORTSMAN 2000	ST	CUD	FBG	DV	IO	228-260		7	6	3050			3700	4450
20	4	BARON-ELITE 2000	ST	CUD	FBG	DV	IO	228-260		7	6	3050			3700	4450
20	4	MORRISON 20		CR	FBG	DV	OB			7	6	2000			5450	6250
20	4	MORRISON 20		CR	FBG	DV	IO	185-230		7	6				3550	4250
22	3	DUKE FAMILY 2200	ST	CUD	FBG	DV	IO	228-260		8		3500			4450	5250
22	3	DUKE FAMILY 2200	ST	CUD	FBG	DV	IO	T228-T260		8		3500			5150	6200
22	3	DUKE-ELITE 2200	ST	CUD	FBG	DV	IO	228-260		8		3500			4700	5550
22	3	DUKE-ELITE 2200	ST	CUD	FBG	DV	IO	T228-T260		8		3500			5400	6500
22	3	MORRISON 22		CR	FBG	DV	IO	228-260		8					4600	5400
22	3	MORRISON-ELITE 22		CR	FBG	DV	IO	228-260		8					4600	5400
24	10	EDWARDIAN 2500	ST	CUD	FBG	DV	IO	260-330		8		5000			6900	8550
24	10	EDWARDIAN 2500	ST	CUD	FBG	DV	IO	T228-T260		8		5000			7650	9150
24	10	EDWARDIAN-ELITE 2500	ST	CUD	FBG	DV	IO	260-330		8		5000			6900	8550
24	10	EDWARDIAN-ELITE 2500	ST	CUD	FBG	DV	IO	T228-T260		8		5000			7650	9150
24	10	MORRISON 25		CR	FBG	DV	IO	228		8					6750	7750
24	10	MORRISON 25		CR	FBG	DV	IO	T170		8					7350	8450
		1979 BOATS														
16		GYPSY-STAR 16	ST	RNBT	FBG	TR	OB			6	11	1100			2650	3100
16	11	CAPRICE 17 B/R	ST	RNBT	FBG	DV	OB			6	5	1100			2700	3150
17	4	GYPSY-STAR 17	ST	RNBT	FBG	TR	OB			7	2	1250			3050	3550
17	4	GYPSY-STAR 17	ST	RNBT	FBG	TR	IO	120-170		7	2				1800	2200
18	10	CAPRICE 19 B/R	ST	RNBT	FBG	DV	OB			7	6	1560			3850	4500
18	10	CAPRICE 19 B/R	ST	RNBT	FBG	DV	IO	170-200		7	6				2250	2650
18	10	CAPRICE 19 THRIFT	OP	RNBT	FBG	DV	OB			7	6	1560			3750	4350
18	10	ROYAL-CAPRICE 19	ST	RNBT	FBG	DV	OB			7	6	1560			3650	4250
18	10	ROYAL-CAPRICE 19	ST	RNBT	FBG	DV	IO	170-200		7	6				2200	2600
20	4	MORRISON 20	OP	CR	FBG	DV	OB			7	6	2000			5350	6150
20	4	MORRISON 20	OP	CR	FBG	DV	IO	185-230		7	6				3500	4200
20	10	ROYAL-GYPSY 21 E/Z	ST	CR	FBG	TR	IO	170-200		7	11	3000			3700	4350
22	3	MORRISON 22	ST	CUD	FBG	DV	IO	228-260		8		3500			4600	5400
22	3	MORRISON-ELITE 22	ST	SPTCR	FBG	DV	IO	228-260		8		3500			4600	5400
22	3	MORRISON-ELITE 22	ST	SPTCR	FBG	DV	IO	T140		8		3500			5050	5800
24	10	MORRISON 25	ST	CR	FBG	DV	IO	260		8		5000			6900	7950
24	10	MORRISON 25	ST	CR	FBG	DV	IO	T140-T170		8		5000			7250	8450
		1978 BOATS														
16		GYPSY-STAR 16	ST	RNBT	FBG	TR	OB			6	11	1100			2650	3050
16	11	CAPRICE 17 B/R	ST	RNBT	FBG	DV	OB			6	5	1100			2700	3100
17	4	GYPSY-STAR 17	ST	RNBT	FBG	TR	OB			7	2	1250			3000	3500
17	4	GYPSY-STAR 17	ST	RNBT	FBG	TR	IO	120-170		7	2				1850	2200
18	10	CAPRICE 19 THRIFT	OP	RNBT	FBG	DV	OB			7	6	1560			3700	4300
18	10	ROYAL-CAPRICE	ST	RNBT	FBG	DV	IO	120		7	6				2250	2600
18	10	ROYAL-CAPRICE 19	ST	RNBT	FBG	DV	OB			7	6	1560			3600	4200
18	10	ROYAL-CAPRICE 19	ST	RNBT	FBG	DV	IO	140-198		7	6				2200	2600
18	10	ROYAL-CAPRICE 19 B/R	ST	RNBT	FBG	DV	OB			7	6	1560			3800	4450
18	10	ROYAL-CAPRICE 19 B/R	ST	RNBT	FBG	DV	IO	140-198		7	6				2250	2700
18	10	ROYAL-CAPRICE B/R	ST	RNBT	FBG	DV	IO	120		7	6				2250	2600
20	4	MORRISON 20	ST	CUD	FBG	DV	IO	120-228		7	6				3550	4200
20	10	GYPSY 21 E-Z	ST	CR	FBG	TR	IO	170-198		7	11	3000			3750	4400
20	11	GYPSY 21 E-Z	ST	CR	FBG	TR	IO	235		7	11	3000			3850	4500
22	3	MORRISON 22	ST	CUD	FBG	DV	IO	185-240		8		3500			4500	5350
24	10	MORRISON 25	ST	CR	FBG	DV	IO	228-260		8		5000			6800	8000
24	10	MORRISON 25	ST	CR	FBG	DV	IO	T140-T170		8		5000			7300	8500
		1977 BOATS														
16		GYPSY-STAR 16	ST	RNBT	FBG	DV	OB			6	11	1100			2600	3050
16	2	GYPSY 16 THRIFT	OP	RNBT	FBG	TR	OB			6	9	950			2300	2700
16	11	ROYAL-CAPRICE 17 B/R	ST	RNBT	FBG	DV	OB			6	5	1100			2650	3100
17		SUPER-BASS 17	OP	BASS	FBG	TR	OB			6	3	900			2250	2600
17	3	ROYAL-GYPSY 17	ST	RNBT	FBG	TR	OB			7	2	1260			3000	3500
17	3	ROYAL-GYPSY 17	ST	RNBT	FBG	TR	IO	120-165		7	2	1260			1750	2100
17	4	GYPSY-STAR 17	ST	RNBT	FBG	DV	OB			7	2	1250			3000	3450
17	4	GYPSY-STAR 17	ST	RNBT	FBG	DV	IO	120	MRCR	7	2	1250			1750	2100
		IO 120 OMC 1750 2100, IB 120 1700 2000, IO 140-165													1800	2150
18	10	CAPRICE 19 THRIFT	OP	RNBT	FBG	DV	OB			7	6	1560			3650	4250
18	10	CAPRICE 19 THRIFT	OP	RNBT	FBG	DV	IO	140		7	6	1560			2250	2600
18	10	CAPRICE CABIN	OP	CUD	FBG	DV	OB			7	6	1700			3900	4500
18	10	CAPRICE CABIN	OP	CUD	FBG	DV	IO	140		7	6	1700			2350	2700
18	10	ROYAL-CAPRICE 19	ST	RNBT	FBG	DV	OB			7	6	1560			3600	4200
18	10	ROYAL-CAPRICE 19	ST	RNBT	FBG	DV	IO	140-190		7	6	1560			2200	2600
18	10	ROYAL-CAPRICE 19 B/R	ST	RNBT	FBG	DV	OB			7	6	1560			3700	4300
18	10	ROYAL-CAPRICE 19 B/R	ST	RNBT	FBG	DV	IO	140-190		7	6	1560			2250	2650
19	2	ROYAL-GYPSY 19	ST	RNBT	FBG	TR	IO	140-190		7	8	1450			2300	2700
20	10	ROYAL-GYPSY 21	ST	CUD	FBG	TR	IO	165-190		7	11	3000			3800	4450
22	3	MORRISON 22	ST	CR	FBG	DV	IO	188	MRCR	8		3500			4600	5300
22	3	MORRISON 22	ST	CR	FBG	DV	IB	188		8		3500			4500	5200
22	3	MORRISON 22	ST	CR	FBG	DV	IO	190-235		8		3500			4600	5400
24	10	MORRISON 25	ST	CR	FBG	DV	IO	233-235		8		5000			6950	7950
		1976 BOATS														
16	2	GYPSY 16 THRIFT	OP	RNBT	FBG	TR	OB			6	9	950			2300	2650
16	2	ROYAL-GYPSY 16	ST	RNBT	FBG	TR	OB			6	9	950			2300	2650
16	11	ROYAL-CAPRICE 17	ST	RNBT	FBG	DV	OB			6	5	1100			2550	2950
16	11	ROYAL-CAPRICE B/R 17	ST	RNBT	FBG	DV	OB			6	5	1100			2700	3150
17		SUPER-BASS 17	OP	BASS	FBG	TR	OB			6	3	900			2250	2600
17	3	ROYAL-GYPSY 17	ST	RNBT	FBG	TR	OB			7	2	1260			2950	3450
17	3	ROYAL-GYPSY 17	ST	RNBT	FBG	TR	IO	120-165		7	2	1260			1800	2150
17	4	GYPSY-STAR 17	ST	RNBT	FBG	TR	OB			7	2	1250			2950	3450
17	4	GYPSY-STAR 17	ST	RNBT	FBG	TR	IO	120-188		7	2	1250			1800	2200
18	10	CABIN-CAPRICE 19	ST	CUD	FBG	DV	OB			7	6	1700			3850	4450
18	10	CABIN-CAPRICE 19	ST	CUD	FBG	DV	IO	120-190		7	6	1700			2350	2800
18	10	CAPRICE 19 THRIFT	OP	RNBT	FBG	DV	OB			7	6	1560			3650	4200
18	10	CAPRICE 19 THRIFT	OP	RNBT	FBG	DV	IO	120-140		7	6	1560			2300	2650
18	10	FISHIN-CAPRICE II 19	OP	FSH	FBG	DV	OB			7	6	1560			3600	4200
18	10	ROYAL-CAPRICE 19	ST	RNBT	FBG	DV	OB			7	6	1560			3650	4200

CONTINUED ON NEXT PAGE

LOA FT	LOA IN	NAME AND/ OR MODEL	TOP/ RIG	BOAT TYPE	-HULL- MTL	-HULL- TP	ENGINE TP	ENGINE # HP	ENGINE MFG	BEAM FT	BEAM IN	WGT LBS	DRAFT FT	DRAFT IN	RETAIL LOW	RETAIL HIGH
		1976 BOATS														
18	10	ROYAL-CAPRICE 19	ST	RNBT	FBG	DV	IO	120-190		7	6	1560			2300	2700
18	10	ROYAL-CAPRICE B/R 19	ST	RNBT	FBG	DV	OB			7	6	1560			3650	4200
18	10	ROYAL-CAPRICE B/R 19	ST	RNBT	FBG	DV	IO	120-190		7	6	1560			2300	2700
19	2	ROYAL-GYPSY 19	ST	RNBT	FBG	TR	OB			7	8	1450			3500	4050
19	2	ROYAL-GYPSY 19	ST	RNBT	FBG	TR	IO	120-190		7	8	1450			2350	2750
20	10	ROYAL-GYPSY 21 E/Z	OP	CR	FBG	TR	IO	165-190		7	11	3000			3900	4550
25		MORRISON 25	OP	CR	FBG	DV	IO								**	**
		1975 BOATS														
16	2	GYPSY 16 SUPER	ST	RNBT	FBG	TR	IO	140	OMC	6	9	1100			1700	2000
16	2	SUPER-GYPSY SUPER	ST	RNBT	FBG	TR	OB			6	9	1100			2900	3400
16	2	SUPER-GYPSY THRIFT	ST	RNBT	FBG	TR	OB			6	9	1100			2250	2600
16	11	CAPRICE 17	ST	RNBT	FBG	DV	OB			6	5	1100			2600	3050
17	4	GYPSY 17 ROYAL	ST	RNBT	FBG	TR	OB			7	2	1375			3200	3750
17	4	GYPSY 17 ROYAL	ST	RNBT	FBG	TR	IO	120-165		7	2	1375			1950	2350
17	4	GYPSY 17 SUPER	ST	RNBT	FBG	TR	OB			7	2	1375			3100	3600
17	4	GYPSY 17 SUPER	ST	RNBT	FBG	TR	IO	120-165		7	2	1375			1900	2300
18	10	CAPRICE 19 ROYAL	ST	RNBT	FBG	DV	OB			7	6	1540			3900	4550
18	10	CAPRICE 19 ROYAL	ST	RNBT	FBG	DV	IO	120-225				1540			2350	2850
18	10	CAPRICE 19 SPT ROYAL	ST	RNBT	FBG	DV	IO	120-225		7	6	1540			2350	2900
18	10	CAPRICE 19 SPT SUPER	ST	RNBT	FBG	DV	IO	120-225		7	6	1540			2350	2900
18	10	CAPRICE 19 SPT THRFT	ST	RNBT	FBG	DV	IO	140-165		7	6	1540			2200	2600
18	10	CAPRICE 19 SUPER	ST	RNBT	FBG	DV	OB			7	6	1540			3850	4450
18	10	CAPRICE 19 SUPER	ST	RNBT	FBG	DV	IO	120-225				1540			2350	2750
18	10	CAPRICE 19 THRIFT	ST	RNBT	FBG	DV	OB			7	6	1540			2950	3450
18	10	CAPRICE 19 THRIFT	ST	RNBT	FBG	DV	IO	140-165		7	6	1540			2200	2600
18	10	FISHIN-CAPRICE II 19	OP	FSH	FBG	DV	OB			7	6	1500			3500	4050
19	2	GYPSY 19 ROYAL	ST	RNBT	FBG	TR	OB			7	8	1560			3700	4300
19	2	GYPSY 19 ROYAL	ST	RNBT	FBG	TR	IO	120-140				1560			2400	2800
		IO 165 MRCR 2400 2800, IB 165 OMC 2300 2650, IO 188-225													2450	2850
19	2	GYPSY 19 SUPER	ST	RNBT	FBG	TR	OB			7	8	1560			3650	4200
19	2	GYPSY 19 SUPER	ST	RNBT	FBG	TR	IO	120-225		7	8	1560			2450	2900
20	11	GYPSY 21 E-Z	OP	CR	FBG	TR	IO	165-225		7	11	2800			3900	4600
		1974 BOATS														
16	2	GYPSY 16 SUPER	ST	RNBT	FBG		OB			6	9	1100			2550	2950
16	2	GYPSY 16 SUPER	ST	RNBT	FBG		IO	120-140		6	9	1725			1950	2300
16	11	CAPRICE 17 SUPER	ST	RNBT	FBG		OB			6	5	1100			2600	3000
16	11	CAPRICE 17 SUPER	ST	RNBT	FBG		IO	120-165		6	5	1700			1950	2350
17	3	FISHIN-GYPSY SUPER	OP	FSH	FBG		OB			7	2	1325			3000	3500
17	3	GYPSY 17 STD	OP	RNBT	FBG		OB			7	2	1325			3050	3550
17	3	GYPSY 17 SUPER	ST	RNBT	FBG		OB			7	2	1325			3050	3550
17	3	GYPSY 17 SUPER	ST	RNBT	FBG		IO	120-165		7	2	1950			2300	2700
18	3	CAPRICE 18 SUPER	OP	RNBT	FBG		JT	245	OMC	7	4	2055			2500	2900
18	10	CAPRICE 19	OP	RNBT	FBG		OB			7	6	1200			2950	3400
18	10	CAPRICE 19 SPT	ST	RNBT	FBG		OB			7	6	1200			2950	3400
18	10	CAPRICE 19 SPT	ST	RNBT	FBG		IO	120-188		7	6	2155			2700	3200
18	10	CAPRICE 19 SUPER	ST	RNBT	FBG		OB			7	6	1200			2950	3400
18	10	CAPRICE 19 SUPER	ST	RNBT	FBG		IO	120-188		7	6	2155			2700	3200
20	10	CAPRICE 21	OP	CR	FBG		OB			7	11	3590			7000	8050
20	10	CAPRICE 21	OP	CR	FBG		IO	165-225		7	11	3590			4700	5500
20	10	GYPSY 21 E-Z	OP	CR	FBG		IO	165-225		7	11	2800			4000	4700
		1973 BOATS														
16	2	GYPSY 16 STD	OP	RNBT	FBG		OB			6	9	1100			2550	2950
16	2	GYPSY 16 SUPER	ST	RNBT	FBG		OB			6	9	1100			2550	2950
16	2	GYPSY 16 SUPER	ST	RNBT	FBG		IO	120-140		6	9	1600			1900	2300
16	3	SUPER-CAPRICE 16		RNBT	FBG		OB			6	5	900			2100	2500
17	3	GYPSY 17 STD	OP	RNBT	FBG		OB			7	2	1325			3050	3500
17	3	GYPSY 17 SUPER	ST	RNBT	FBG		OB			7	2	1325			3050	3500
17	3	GYPSY 17 SUPER	ST	RNBT	FBG		IO	120-165		7	2	1950			2350	2750
18	3	FISHIN-CAPRICE	OP	FSH	FBG		OB			7	5	1100			2650	3100
18	3	SUPER-CAPRICE 18		RNBT	FBG		OB			7	5	1240			2950	3450
18	3	SUPER-CAPRICE 18		RNBT	FBG		IO	120-165		7	5	2055			2650	3050
18	3	SUPER-CAPRICE 18		RNBT	FBG		JT	245	OMC	7	5	2055			2400	2800
20	10	GYPSY 21 E-Z	OP	CR	FBG		IO	165-225		7	11	2800			4100	4850
20	11	CAPRICE 21	OP	CR	FBG		OB			7	11	2500			6100	7000
20	11	CAPRICE 21	OP	CR	FBG		IO	165-225		7	11	3590			4900	5700
		1972 BOATS														
16	3	SPRINT		RNBT	FBG		OB			6	5	900	3	4	2100	2500
17	3	GYPSY 17	OP	RNBT	FBG		OB			7	2	1325	3	7	3000	3500
17	3	GYPSY 17	OP	RNBT	FBG		IO	120-165		7	2	1950	3	7	2450	2850
18	3	CAPRICE	OP	RNBT	FBG		OB			7	5	1240	3	10	2950	3400
18	3	CAPRICE	OP	RNBT	FBG		IO	120-165		7	5	2055	3	10	2700	3200
18	3	FISHIN-CAPRICE	OP	FSH	FBG		OB			7	5	1100	3	10	2650	3100
20	10	GYPSY 21 E-Z	OP	CR	FBG		IO	155-188		7	11	2800	4	4	4200	5000
		1971 BOATS														
16	3	SPRINT		RNBT	FBG		OB			6	5	900	3	4	2100	2500
17	3	GYPSY 17	OP	RNBT	FBG		OB			7	2	1325	3	7	3000	3500
17	3	GYPSY 17	OP	RNBT	FBG		IO	120-165		7	2	1950	3	7	2550	2950
18	3	CAPRICE	OP	RNBT	FBG		OB			7	5	1240	3	10	2950	3400
18	3	CAPRICE	OP	RNBT	FBG		IO	120-165		7	5	2055	3	10	2800	3300
18	3	FISHIN-CAPRICE	OP	FSH	FBG		OB			7	5	1090	3	10	2650	3050
		1970 BOATS														
16	3	SPRINT		RNBT	FBG	DV	IO	120	MRCR	6	5	1485			2000	2400
16	3	SPRINT		RNBT	FBG	SV	OB			6	5	845			1950	2350
16	7	EDINBORO	OP	RNBT	FBG	DV	OB			6	7	945			2250	2650
17	3	GYPSY 17	OP	RNBT	FBG	TR	OB			7	2	1325			3000	3500
17	3	GYPSY 17	OP	RNBT	FBG	TR	IO	160	MRCR	7	2	1950			2650	3050
18	3	CAPRICE	OP	RNBT	FBG	DV	IO	160	MRCR	7	5	1890			2800	3250
18	3	CAPRICE	OP	RNBT	FBG	SV	OB			7	5	1240			2950	3400
		1969 BOATS														
16	2	SPRINT 170 DLX	ST	RNBT	FBG	DV	OB			6	5				2450	2850
16	2	SPRINT 170 DLX	ST	RNBT	FBG	DV	IO	120	MRCR	6	5	1600			2200	2550
16	2	SPRINT 170 STD	OP	RNBT	FBG	DV	OB			6	5	900			2100	2500
16	2	SPRINT 170 STD	OP	RNBT	FBG	DV	IO	120		6	5				1850	2200
16	7	EDINBORO 179	OP	RNBT	FBG	DV	OB			6	7	945			2250	2650
17	10	CONVAIR 198	OP	RNBT	FBG	TR	OB			6	9	1460			3300	3850
17	10	CONVAIR 198	OP	RNBT	FBG	TR	IO	160	MRCR	6	9	1170			2350	2700
18	3	CAPRICE 197	OP	EXP	FBG	DV	OB			7	5	1500			3350	3900
18	3	CAPRICE 197	OP	EXP	FBG	DV	IO	160	MRCR	7	5	1890			2950	3450
18	3	CAPRICE 197	ST	EXP	FBG	DV	IO	160	MRCR	7	5	2000			3050	3550
21	1	CAROUSEL 269	OP	CR	FBG	TR	IO	210	MRCR	7	7	2475			4500	5150
		1968 BOATS														
16	6	EDINBORO SPECIAL	OP	RNBT	FBG		OB			6	6	720			1700	2050
16	7	CHEVRON B/R	OP	RNBT	FBG	TR	OB			6	2	870			2050	2450
16	7	CHEVRON B/R	OP	RNBT	FBG	TR	IO	120-160		6	2				2200	2600
17	9	CONVAIR B/R	OP	RNBT	FBG	TR	OB			6	9	1450			3300	3800
17	9	CONVAIR B/R	OP	RNBT	FBG	TR	IO	120-160		6	9	1850			2700	3150
18	3	CAPRICE	OP	RNBT	FBG		IO	120-225							2650	3200
21	1	CAROUSEL	OP	CR	FBG	TR	IO	120-210		7	7	2200			4250	5050
		1967 BOATS														
16	1	BEACHCOMBER CUSTOM	OP	RNBT	FBG		OB			6		700			1800	2100
16	6	EDINBORO CUSTOM	OP	RNBT	FBG		OB			6	6	720			1700	2050
16	7	CHEVRON		RNBT	FBG		OB								2750	3200
16	7	CHEVRON		RNBT	FBG		IO	120							2400	2800
17	9	CONVAIR		RNBT	FBG		IO	120-160		6	9				2600	3000
17	9	CONVAIR		RNBT	FBG	TR	OB			6	9	1450			3300	3800
18	10	SEACRUISER	OP	CR	FBG		OB			7	1	1300			3100	3600
18	10	SEACRUISER	OP	CR	FBG		IO	120		7	1				3050	3550
18	10	SEAWAY CUSTOM	OP	RNBT	FBG		OB			7	1	1140			2800	3250
21	1	CAROUSEL	OP	CR	FBG		IO	120-200		7	7				5150	5950
		1966 BOATS														
16	3	CONSTELLATION	OP	RNBT	AL		IO	60		6	2				2050	2400
16	6	EDINBORO CUSTOM	OP	RNBT	FBG		OB			6	5	720			1750	2050
17	1	PLANET	OP	RNBT	AL	DV	OB			6	10	850			2050	2450
17	1	PLANET	OP	RNBT	AL	DV	IO	110-120		6	10				2550	2950
17	9	ERIE CUSTOM	OP	RNBT	FBG		OB			7	1	1170			2800	3250
17	9	ERIE CUSTOM	OP	RNBT	FBG		IO	110-150		7	1				2750	3200
18	10	SEACRUISER	OP	CR	FBG		OB			7	1				3550	4150
18	10	SEACRUISER	OP	CR	FBG		IO	110-120		7	1				3150	3650
18	10	SEAWAY CUSTOM	OP	RNBT	FBG		OB			7	1	1140			2800	3300
18	10	SEAWAY CUSTOM	OP	RNBT	FBG		IO	110-120		7	1				3050	3550
19		NORTH-STAR	OP	RNBT	AL	DV	OB			7	4	1060			2650	3100
19		NORTH-STAR	OP	RNBT	AL	DV	IO	110-150		7	4				3150	3700
19		SOUTHERN-CROSS	OP	CR	AL		OB			7	4	1300			3150	3650
19		SOUTHERN-CROSS	OP	CR	AL		IO	120-150		7	4				3250	3800
21	1	CAROUSEL	OP	CR	FBG	TR	IO	120-200							5400	6250
		1965 BOATS														
16		SEA-FISHER	OP	RNBT	AL		OB								2500	2900
16	4	CONSTELLATION	OP	RNBT	AL		OB								2500	2900
16	6	EDINBORO	OP	RNBT	FBG		OB								2500	2900
16	6	EDINBORO	HT	RNBT	FBG		OB								2750	3200
16	6	EDINBORO CUSTOM	OP	RNBT	FBG		OB								3050	3550
17	10	ERIE CUSTOM	OP	RNBT	FBG		OB								2850	3300
17	10	ERIE CUSTOM	OP	RNBT	FBG		IO	120							2800	3250
18	10	SEACRUISER	OP	CR	FBG		OB								3550	4150
18	10	SEACRUISER	OP	CR	FBG		IO	110-120							3400	4150
18	10	SEAWAY	OP	RNBT	FBG		OB								3400	3950
18	10	SEAWAY	OP	RNBT	FBG		IO	110							3150	3650
18	10	SEAWAY	OP	RNBT	FBG		IO	110-120							3450	4000
18	10	SEAWAY CUSTOM	OP	RNBT	FBG		OB								3700	4350
18	10	SEAWAY CUSTOM	OP	RNBT	FBG		IO	110							3300	3850

CONTINUED ON NEXT PAGE

LOA FT	LOA IN	NAME AND/ OR MODEL	TOP/ RIG	BOAT TYPE	HULL MTL	HULL TP	ENGINE TP	ENGINE # HP	ENGINE MFG	BEAM FT	BEAM IN	WGT LBS	DRAFT FT	DRAFT IN	RETAIL LOW	RETAIL HIGH
		1965 BOATS														
18	10	SEAWAY CUSTOM	OP	RNBT	FBG		IO	110-120							3600	4200
		1964 BOATS														
16	6	EDINBORO CUSTOM	OP	RNBT	FBG		OB								2750	3200
16	6	EDINBORO CUSTOM	HT	RNBT	FBG		OB								2750	3200
18	10	SEAWAY CUSTOM	OP	RNBT	FBG		OB								3550	4150
18	10	SEAWAY CUSTOM	OP	RNBT	FBG		IO	110							3400	3950
18	10	SEAWAY CUSTOM	HT	RNBT	FBG		OB								3550	4150
		1963 BOATS														
16	6	EDINBORO CUSTOM	OP	RNBT	FBG		OB								2800	3250
16	6	EDINBORO CUSTOM	HT	RNBT	FBG		OB								2800	3250
18	10	SEAWAY CUSTOM	OP	RNBT	FBG		OB								3600	4150
18	10	SEAWAY CUSTOM	OP	RNBT	FBG		IO	100-110							3500	4100
18	10	SEAWAY CUSTOM	HT	RNBT	FBG		OB								3600	4150
		1962 BOATS														
16	6	EDINBORO	OP	RNBT	FBG		OB								2800	3250
18	10	SEAWAY	OP	RNBT	FBG		OB								3600	4150
18	10	SEAWAY	OP	RNBT	FBG		IO	80-100							3650	4250
		1961 BOATS														
16	6	EDINBORO		RNBT	FBG		OB			6	8	750			1800	2150
16	6	NORTHEAST	HT	RNBT	FBG		OB			6	8	750			1800	2150
18	10	SEAWAY		RNBT	FBG		OB			7	1	1000			2600	3000
18	10	SEAWAY RUNAWAY	HT	RNBT	FBG		OB			7	1	1000			2600	3000
19	8	SEAWAY		CR	FBG		OB			7	4	1500			3650	4250
		1960 BOATS														
16		ALBION		RNBT	FBG		OB								2500	2900
16		EDINBORO		RNBT	FBG		OB								2500	2900
16		NORTHEAST	HT	RNBT	FBG		OB								2500	2900
19		SEAWAY	FB	EXP	FBG		OB								3600	4200
19		SEAWAY		RNBT	FBG		OB								3650	4200
19		SEAWAY	HT	RNBT	FBG		OB								3650	4200
		1959 BOATS														
16		EDINBORO		RNBT	FBG		OB								2500	2900
		1957 BOATS														
17				RNBT	FBG		OB								2850	3300

MOLDED PRODUCTS INC

Call 1-800-327-6929 for BUC Personalized Evaluation Service
Or, for 1959 to 1962 boats, sign onto www.BUCValuPro.com

MOLLYS COVE BOAT WORKS

Call 1-800-327-6929 for BUC Personalized Evaluation Service
Or, for 1982 to 1985 boats, sign onto www.BUCValuPro.com

MONARK MARINE

TOPEKA IN 46571 COAST GUARD MFG ID- MAK See inside cover to adjust price for area
FORMERLY MONARK BOAT CO

For more recent years, see the BUC Used Boat Price Guide, Volume 1 or Volume 2

LOA FT	LOA IN	NAME AND/ OR MODEL	TOP/ RIG	BOAT TYPE	HULL MTL	HULL TP	ENGINE TP	ENGINE # HP	ENGINE MFG	BEAM FT	BEAM IN	WGT LBS	DRAFT FT	DRAFT IN	RETAIL LOW	RETAIL HIGH
		1983 BOATS														
16	7	S1-O/B	OP	RNBT	FBG		OB			7		1150			1700	2050
16	7	SPORTBOAT S1 I-O	OP	RNBT	FBG	SV	IO	140		7		1900			2000	2400
17	2	MC-FAST 150	OP	FSH	FBG	FL	OB			7		1275			1850	2200
17	2	MC-FAST 150 I-O	OP	SF	FBG	FL	IO	170		7		1850			2400	2800
17	2	MC-FAST V-172 I-O	OP	FSH	FBG	FL	IO	170		7	1	1750			2100	2500
		1982 BOATS														
16	7	SPORTBOAT SI	OP	RNBT	FBG	SV	IO	140		7		1900			1950	2350
17	2	MC-FAST 150	OP	FSH	FBG	FL	OB			7		1275			1800	2150
17	2	MC-FAST 150 I-O	OP	SF	FBG	FL	IO	170		7		1850			2350	2700
17	3	LITTLE-GIANT 17		UTL	AL	TR	IO	140		7	3				2300	2650
17	3	LITTLE-GIANT 17	OP	UTL	AL	TR	OB			7	3	1400			1800	2150
17	3	MONARK 17		UTL	AL	TR	IO	140		7	3				2300	2650
19		LITTLE-GIANT 19		UTL	AL	TR	IO	165		7	6				2500	2900
19		LITTLE-GIANT 19	OP	UTL	AL	TR	OB			7	6	1600			2000	2400
19		MONARK 19		UTL	AL	TR	IO	165		7	6				2500	2900
19		MONARK 19	OP	UTL	AL	TR	OB			7	6	1450			1850	2200
20	3	2008		UTL	AL	TR	IO	165		8					3800	4450
20	6	LITTLE-GIANT 21		UTL	AL	TR	OB			7	9	2000			2650	3100
20	6	MONARK 21		UTL	AL	TR	OB			7	9	1850			2500	2950
21		LITTLE-GIANT 21		UTL	AL	TR	IO	165		7	9				3850	4450
21		MONARK 21		UTL	AL	TR	IO	165		7	9				3850	4450
21	4	WORKBOAT 21V		UTL	AL	DV	OB			8		2600			3550	4150
21	4	WORKBOAT 21V		UTL	AL	DV	IO	228		8					4050	4750
23		2308C		UTL	AL	TR	IO	T165		8					5550	6350
24	8	2408J		FD	AL	SV	IO			8	8				**	**
26	8	2609J		FD	AL	SV	IO			9	8				**	**
28	8	2810V		FD	AL	DV	IO			10	8				**	**
32	8	3211V		FD	AL	DV	IO			11	5				**	**
36	8	3612V		FD	AL	DV	IO			12	8				**	**
40	4	4014V		FD	AL	DV	IO			14					**	**
		1981 BOATS														
16	7	SPORTBOAT SI	OP	RNBT	FBG	SV	IO	140		7		1900			1900	2300
17	2	MC-FAST 150	OP	FSH	FBG	FL	OB			7		1275			1700	2050
17	2	MC-FAST 150 I-O	OP	SF	FBG	FL	IO	140		7		1850			2250	2650
17	2	MCFAST 150	OP	BASS	FBG	SV	OB			7		1275			1800	2150
17	2	MCFAST 150	OP	BASS	FBG	SV	IO	140		7		1850			2000	2400
17	3	LITTLE-GIANT 17		UTL	AL	TR	IO	140		7	3				2250	2600
17	3	MONARK 17		UTL	AL	TR	IO	140		7	3				2250	2600
20	3	2008		UTL	AL	TR	IO			8					**	**
21	4	MONARK 21		UTL	AL	DV	IO	200		8					3900	4550
23		2308C		UTL	AL	TR	IO			8					**	**
24	8	2408J		FD	AL	SV	IO			8	8				**	**
26	8	2609J		FD	AL	SV	IO			9	8				**	**
28	8	2810V		FD	AL	DV	IO			10	8				**	**
32	8	3211V		FD	AL	DV	IO			11	5				**	**
36	8	3612V		FD	AL	DV	IO			12	8				**	**
		1980 BOATS														
17		LITTLE-GIANT		UTL	AL	TR	IB	125		7	3	1400			2000	2350
17		MC-FAST 150	OP	BASS	FBG	TR	OB			6	11	1275			1700	2050
17		MC-FAST 150	OP	BASS	FBG	TR	IB	150		6	11	1275			1800	2150
17		MC-FAST 150	OP	BASS	FBG	TR	IO	170		6	11	2200			2200	2550
17		ROUSTABOUT		UTL	AL	TR	IB	125		7	3	1250			1900	2250
17	3	LITTLE-GIANT 17		UTL	AL	TR	IO	140		7	3				2200	2550
17	3	MONARK 17		UTL	AL	TR	IO	140		7	3				2200	2550
19		LITTLE-GIANT		UTL	AL	TR	IB	160		7	6	1600			2650	3100
19		ROUSTABOUT		UTL	AL	TR	IB	160		7	6	1450			2600	3000
20	3	WORKBOAT 2008		UTL	AL	TR	IO			8					**	**
21		LITTLE-GIANT		UTL	AL	TR	IB	190		7	9	2000			3750	4350
21		ROUSTABOUT		UTL	AL	TR	IB	190		7	9	1850			3650	4250
21	4	WORKBOAT 21V		UTL	AL	DV	IO	200		8					3850	4450
23		WORKBOAT 2308C		UTL	AL	TR	IO			8					**	**
24	8	WORKBOAT 2408		FD	AL	DV	IB	125D		8	8	6200			12700	14500
24	8	WORKBOAT 2408J		FD	AL	TR	IO			8	8				**	**
26	8	WORKBOAT 2609		FD	AL	DV	IB	175D		9	8	7300			16200	18400
26	8	WORKBOAT 2609J		FD	AL	TR	IO			9	8				**	**
28	8	WORKBOAT 2810V		FD	AL	DV	IO			10	8				**	**
28	8	WORKBOAT 2810V		FD	AL	DV	IB	T125D		10	8	9600			23400	26000
30		3012		UTL	AL	FL	IO	165		12					15600	17700
30		WORKBOAT 3010V		FD	AL	DV	IB			10					**	**
32	8	WORKBOAT 3211V		FD	AL	DV	IO			11	5				**	**
32	8	WORKBOAT 3211V		FD	AL	DV	IB	T175D		11	5	12000			36100	40100
35		3512		UTL	AL	FL	IO	228		12					20600	22900
36	8	WORKBOAT 3612V		FD	AL	DV	IO			12	8				**	**
36	8	WORKBOAT 3612V		FD	AL	DV	IB	T203D		12	8	15000			42500	47200
40	4	WORKBOAT 4014V		FD	AL	DV	IB	T272D		14		18000			56800	62500
		1979 BOATS														
17	2	MC-FAST 150 4649	OP	BASS	FBG	SV	OB			7		1275			1700	2000
17	3	LITTLE-GIANT	HT	UTL	AL	TR	IO	140		7	3	2000			2300	2700
17	3	ROUSTABOUT	OP	UTL	AL	TR	IO	140		7	3	1850			2250	2600
19		ROUSTABOUT	OP	UTL	AL	TR	IO	165		7	3	1850			2500	2900
19		ROUSTABOUT	HT	UTL	AL	TR	IO	165		7	3	2000			2550	3000
20	3	WORKBOAT 2008	HT	UTL	AL	TR	IO	165		8		2000			3300	3850
20	6	LITTLE-GIANT	HT	UTL	AL	TR	OB			7	9	1600			2050	2400
20	6	LITTLE-GIANT	HT	UTL	AL	TR	IO	165		7	9	2400			3550	4150
20	6	ROUSTABOUT	OP	UTL	AL	TR	OB			7	9	1450			1850	2200
20	6	ROUSTABOUT	OP	UTL	AL	TR	IO	165		7	9	2250			3450	4000
21	4	WORKBOAT 21V	OP	UTL	AL	DV	OB			8		2600			3250	3750
21	4	WORKBOAT 21V	OP	UTL	AL	DV	IO	228		8		3500			4800	5500
23		WORKBOAT 2308C	HT	UTL	AL	TR	OB			8					4000	4650
23		WORKBOAT 2308C	HT	UTL	AL	TR	IO	T165		8					5250	6050
24	8	WORKBOAT 2408J	HT	FD	AL	SV	IB	T		8	8	6200			**	**
24	8	WORKBOAT 2408V	HT	FD	AL	SV	IB	T		8	8	6200			**	**
26	8	WORKBOAT 2609J	HT	FD	AL	SV	IB	T		9	8	7300			**	**
26	8	WORKBOAT 2609V	HT	FD	AL	DV	IB	T		9	8	7300			**	**

 CONTINUED ON NEXT PAGE

LOA FT	IN	NAME AND/ OR MODEL	TOP/ RIG	BOAT TYPE	-HULL- MTL	TP	ENGINE TP	# HP	MFG	BEAM FT	IN	WGT LBS	DRAFT FT	IN	RETAIL LOW	RETAIL HIGH
		1979 BOATS														
28	8	WORKBOAT 2810V	HT	FD	AL	DV	IB	T		10	8	9600			**	**
32	8	WORKBOAT 3211V	HT	FD	AL	DV	IB	T		11	5	12000			**	**
36	8	WORKBOAT 3612V	HT	FD	AL	DV	IB	T		12	8	15000			**	**
40	4	WORKBOAT 4014V	HT	FDPH	AL	DV	IB	T		14		18000			**	**
		1978 BOATS														
17	3	LITTLE-GIANT	HT	UTL	AL	TR	IO	140		7	3	2000			2300	2700
17	3	ROUSTABOUT	OP	UTL	AL	TR	IO	140		7	3	1850			2200	2600
19		LITTLE-GIANT	HT	UTL	AL	TR	OB			7	6	1600			1800	2100
19		LITTLE-GIANT	HT	UTL	AL	TR	IO	165		7	6	2400			2850	3300
19		ROUSTABOUT	OP	UTL	AL	TR	IO	165		7	6	2250			2750	3200
20	3	WORKBOAT 2008	HT	UTL	AL	TR	IO	165		8					3550	4150
20	6	LITTLE-GIANT	HT	UTL	AL	TR	OB			7	9	2000			2500	2900
20	6	LITTLE-GIANT	HT	UTL	AL	TR	IO	165		7	9	2800			3850	4450
20	6	ROUSTABOUT	OP	UTL	AL	TR	OB			7	9	1850			2350	2700
20	6	ROUSTABOUT	OP	UTL	AL	TR	IO	165		7	9	2650			3750	4350
21	4	21V	OP	UTL	AL	DV	OB			8		2600			3150	3650
21	4	21V	OP	UTL	AL	DV	IO	228		8		3500			4800	5500
23		2308C	HT	UTL	AL	TR	OB			8					3900	4550
23		2308C	HT	UTL	AL	TR	IO	T165		8					5250	6050
24	8	WORKBOAT 2408J	HT	FD	AL	SV	IB	T D		8	8	6200			**	**
24	8	WORKBOAT 2408V	HT	FD	AL	DV	IB	T D		8	8	6200			**	**
26	8	WORKBOAT 2609J	HT	FD	AL	DV	IB	T D		9	8	7300			**	**
26	8	WORKBOAT 2609J	HT	FD	AL	SV	IB	T D		9	8	7300			**	**
28	8	WORKBOAT 2810V	HT	FD	AL	DV	IB	T D		10	8	9600			**	**
32	8	3211-V WORKBOAT	HT	FD	AL	DV	IB	T D		11	5	12000			**	**
36	8	3612-V WORKBOAT	HT	FD	AL	DV	IB	T D		12	8	15000			**	**
40	4	4014-V WORKBOAT	HT	FDPH	AL	DV	IB	T D		14		18000			**	**
		1974 BOATS														
16	4	SUPER-PRO	OP	BASS	FBG		IO	140	MRCR	5	8	1613	2	8	1700	2050
17		4761	OP	UTL	AL		IO	140	MRCR						2200	2550
17		LITTLE-GIANT 4776	HT	UTL	AL		IO	140							2200	2550
18	2	MARAUDER 4648	OP	BASS	FBG		OB			5	11	1408	2	10	1800	2150
18	2	MARAUDER 4650	OP	BASS	FBG		IO	140		5	11	2113	2	10	2300	2650
18	2	MARAUDER 4650	OP	BASS	FBG		JT	245	OMC	5	11	2113	2	10	2200	2550
19		4766	OP	UTL	AL		IO	140-165							2650	3100
21		4770	OP	UTL	AL		OB								2700	3150
21		4771	OP	UTL	AL		IO	140-165							4100	4750
21		LITTLE-GIANT 4780	HT	UTL	AL		OB								2700	3150
21		LITTLE-GIANT 4781	HT	UTL	AL		IO	165							4100	4750
		1973 BOATS														
16	4	MJ			FBG		OB			5	8	1620			1900	2250
17		4761	OP	UTL	AL		IO	120-140							2250	2650
17	4	STINGER 4711	OP	RNBT	AL		IO			6	9	1705			**	**
19		4766	OP	UTL	AL		IO	120-140							2750	3200
19		4766	OP	UTL	FBG		IO	165	MRCR						2750	3200
19	1	DOLPHIN 4716	OP	RNBT	AL		IO			6	11	1935			**	**
21		4770	OP	UTL	AL		OB								2650	3100
21		4771	OP	UTL	AL		IO	120-165							4200	4900
21		LITTLE-GIANT 4781	HT	UTL	AL		OB								2650	3100
21	1	MARLIN 4720	OP	RNBT	AL		OB			7	4	1692			2550	3000
21	1	MARLIN 4721	OP	RNBT	AL		IO			7	4	2564			**	**
53		EMPRESS 53	HT	HB	AL	TR	IB	T270							36600	40700
53		EXECUTIVE 53	HT	HB	AL	TR	IB	T270							37500	41700
		1972 BOATS														
17	4	STINGER	OP	RNBT	AL		IO	120-140		6	9	1500	1		2000	2400
17	5	1700	OP	UTL	AL		IO	120-140		7		1500	1		2300	2700
19	1	DOLPHIN	OP	RNBT	AL		IO	120-165		6	11	1625	1		2400	2800
19	4	1900		UTL	AL		IO	120-165		7	3	1625	1		2800	3250
21	1	MARLIN	OP	RNBT	AL		OB					1692		9	2600	3000
21	1	MARLIN	OP	RNBT	AL		IO	120-165		7	4	2300	1		3550	4150
21	1	SKIPJACK		RNBT	AL		OB			7	4	1875			2800	3250
21	3	2100	OP	UTL	AL		OB			7	8	1692		9	2200	2550
21	3	2100	OP	UTL	AL		IO	120-165		7	8	2300	1		4100	4750
21	3	LITTLE-GIANT 2100	HT	UTL	AL		OB			7	8	2100		9	2650	3050
53		EMPRESS	HT	HB	AL	TR	IO	T270		10			3		38700	43000
53		EXECUTIVE	HT	HB	AL	TR	IO	T270		10			3		39600	44000
		1971 BOATS														
28		PH-1028	HT	HB	AL	PN	OB			10		4000	1		**	**
36		PH-1036	HT	HB	AL	PN	OB			10		6000	1	2	9550	10900
53		EMPRESS CH-53	HT	HB	AL	SV	IO	T		13		14500	1	10	30700	34100
53		EXECUTIVE CH-53	HT	HB	AL	SV	IO	T		13		15000	2		31200	34700
		1970 BOATS														
17	4	STINGER		RNBT	AL	TR	IO	120		6	9		2		2450	2850
19	1	DOLPHIN	OP	RNBT	AL	TR	IO	120-165		6	11		2		2500	2900
21	1	MARLIN	OP	RNBT	AL	TR	OB			7	4	1692			2600	3050
21	1	MARLIN	OP	RNBT	AL	TR	IO	120-165		7	4		2		3850	4500
21	1	SKIPJACK	OP	CUD	AL	TR	OB			7	4	1875	2		2850	3300
21	1	SKIPJACK	OP	CUD	AL	TR	IO	120-165		7	4	1875	2		3600	4250
28		PH-1028	HT	HB	AL	PN	OB			10		4000	1		**	**
28		V-I-P	HT	HB	AL	PN	OB			10		5000	1		**	**
36		AMBASSADOR	HT	HB	AL	PN	OB			10		7500	1		11700	13300
36		PH-1036	HT	HB	AL	PN	OB			10		6000	1	2	9500	10800
43		CH-1353	HT	HB	AL	TR	IO	T250		10			3		22500	25000
43		PH-1343	HT	HB	AL	TR	IO	225		10			2	6	20900	23200
53		EMPRESS CH-53	HT	HB	AL	SV	IO			13		14500	1	10	28500	31700
53		EXECUTIVE CH-53	HT	HB	AL	SV	IO			13		15000	2		29100	32300
		1969 BOATS														
19	4	1920		UTL	AL	TR	IB	T160		8					2000	2400
21	4	2122		UTL	AL	TR	IB	T160		8					2950	3400
25	4	2526		UTL	AL	TR	IB	T D		10					**	**
28		1028-PH	HT	HB	AL	PN	OB			10		4500		11	**	**
36		1036-PH	HT	HB	AL	PN	OB			10		7500	1	2	11600	13200
40		1340	HT	HB	AL	TR	IB	160	MRCR	13		17400	1	3	21700	24100
		IB 210 CHRY 21500 23900, IB 225 MRCR 21700 24100, IB T160 MRCR													22800	25400
		IB T210 CHRY 22900 25400, IB T225 MRCR 23000 25500														
50		1350	HT	HB	AL	TR	IB	210	CHRY	13		19400	1	3	23800	26400
50		1350	HT	HB	AL	TR	IB	225	MRCR	13		19500	1	3	23900	26600
50		1350	HT	HB	AL	TR	IB	T210	CHRY	13		20800	1	3	25800	28600
60		1360	HT	HB	AL	TR	IB	290		13		22000	1	3	30500	33900
60		1360	HT	HB	AL	TR	IB	T225	MRCR	13		23600	1	3	32500	36100
60		1360	HT	HB	AL	TR	IB	T290		13		23900	1	3	33000	36600
		1968 BOATS														
28		1028-PH	HT	HB	AL	PN	OB			10		4500		11	**	**
34		PH-1034		HB	AL	PN	OB			10		6000	1	2	9050	10300
36		1036-PH	HT	HB	AL	PN	OB			10		7500	1	2	11600	13100
36		CH-1336		HB	AL	CT	IO			13		10000	1		15900	18000
40		1340	HT	HB	AL	TR	IO	160		13		17400	1	3	21500	23900
		IO 210 21700 24100, IO 225 21500 23900, IO 290													22300	24800
		IO T160 22700 25300, IO T210 22900 25500, IO T225													23000	25600
		IO T290 24700 27400														
44		CH-1344		HB	AL	CT	IO	T		13		14000	1		21100	23500
50		1350	HT	HB	AL	TR	IO	210		13		19400	1	3	25000	27800
		IO 225 25200 27900, IO 290 25900 28800, IO T210													27300	30400
		IO T225 27600 30600, IO T290 29200 32400														
54		CH-1354		HB	AL	CT	IO	T		13		19000	1		35900	39900
60		1360	HT	HB	AL	TR	IO	290		13		22000	1	3	32500	36100
60		1360	HT	HB	AL	TR	IO	T225		13		23600	1	3	34300	38100
60		1360	HT	HB	AL	TR	IO	T290		13		23900	1	3	35800	39800
		1967 BOATS														
36		CH-1336	HT	HB	AL	TR	OB			10			1		14200	16100
44		CH-1344	HT	HB	AL	TR	OB			10			1		18700	20800
54		CH-1354	HT	HB	AL	TR	OB			10			1		33500	37200
		1966 BOATS														
25		GULF-STREAM C			AL	TR	IB	120		8			3		3300	3850
25		RIVER-BELLE	HT	HB	AL					8			2	6	**	**
26		GULF-STREAM		SF	AL	DV	IB	150		8			3	4	4900	5650
36		RIVER-BELLE	HT	HB	AL					13			2	10	14100	16000
44		RIVER-BELLE	HT	HB	AL					13			3		18600	20700
52		RIVER-BELLE	HT	HB	AL					14			3		30400	33800
		1965 BOATS														
20		2048	OP	JON	AL		OB								2300	2700
20		2052	OP	JON	AL		OB								2950	3450
		1964 BOATS														
20		2048	OP	JON	AL		OB								2300	2700
20		2052	OP	JON	AL		OB								3000	3500
		1963 BOATS														
20		2052	OP	JON	AL		OB								2550	2950

MONK COAST GUARD MFG ID- MKD

See inside cover to adjust price for area

LOA FT	IN	NAME AND/ OR MODEL	TOP/ RIG	BOAT TYPE	-HULL- MTL	TP	ENGINE TP	# HP	MFG	BEAM FT	IN	WGT LBS	DRAFT FT	IN	RETAIL LOW	RETAIL HIGH
		1972 BOATS														
45			FB	DC	WD		IB	200D	GM						73000	80200
		1971 BOATS														
35	9			TRWL	WD	DS	IB	85D	PERK						45800	50400
		1953 BOATS														
68		AMSTERDAM HOLLAND	FB	MY	STL		IB	T D	GM	16			5	6	**	**

 CONTINUED ON NEXT PAGE

MONK DESIGN BOATS   -CONTINUED   See inside cover to adjust price for area

LOA FT IN	NAME AND/ OR MODEL	TOP/ RIG	BOAT TYPE	-HULL- MTL TP	----ENGINE--- TP # HP MFG	BEAM FT IN	WGT LBS	DRAFT FT IN	RETAIL LOW	RETAIL HIGH
--- 1940 BOATS ---
35		FB	DC	WD	IB 250 CHRY				16300	18600
--- 1939 BOATS ---
52		HT	CR	WD	IB 180D CAT				40700	45300
--- 1938 BOATS ---
38		FB	DC	WD	IB 125 CHRY				26900	29900

MONTEREY YACHTS
STUART FL 33494   See inside cover to adjust price for area

LOA FT IN	NAME AND/ OR MODEL	TOP/ RIG	BOAT TYPE	-HULL- MTL TP	----ENGINE--- TP # HP MFG	BEAM FT IN	WGT LBS	DRAFT FT IN	RETAIL LOW	RETAIL HIGH
--- 1980 BOATS ---
53 8	MONTEREY	TT	SF	FBG SV	IB T340D CUM	15	30000	3 4	244000	268000

MONTGOMERY MARINE PROD
COSTA MESA CA 92627   COAST GUARD MFG ID- MMP See inside cover to adjust price for area

For more recent years, see the BUC Used Boat Price Guide, Volume 1 or Volume 2

LOA FT IN	NAME AND/ OR MODEL	TOP/ RIG	BOAT TYPE	-HULL- MTL TP	----ENGINE--- TP # HP MFG	BEAM FT IN	WGT LBS	DRAFT FT IN	RETAIL LOW	RETAIL HIGH
--- 1981 BOATS ---
17 2	MONTGOMERY 17	SLP	SAIL	FBG KC		7 4	1550	1 9	5600	6400
23	MONTGOMERY 23	SLP	SAIL	FBG KC OB		8	3600	2 5	12000	13600
--- 1980 BOATS ---
17 1	MONTGOMERY 17	SLP	SAIL	FBG KC		7 4	1500	1 9	5200	6000
23	MONTGOMERY 23	SLP	SAIL	FBG KC IB	D	8	3600	2 5	13100	14800
--- 1979 BOATS ---
17 2	MONTGOMERY 17	SLP	SAIL	FBG KC		7 4	1600	1 9	5200	6000
23	MONTGOMERY 23	SLP	SAIL	FBG KC IB	D	8	3600	2 5	12500	14300
--- 1978 BOATS ---
17 2	MONTGOMERY 17	SLP	SA/CR	FBG KC		7 4	1600	1 9	5000	5750
23	MONTGOMERY 23	SLP	SA/CR	FBG KC IB	D	8	3600	2 5	12100	13700
--- 1976 BOATS ---
17 1	MONTGOMERY 17	SLP	SA/CR	FBG KC		7 4	1400	3 6	4350	5000
17 1	MONTGOMERY 17	SLP	SA/CR	FBG KL		7 4	1400	3 6	4350	5000
--- 1975 BOATS ---
17 1	MONTGOMERY	SLP	SAIL	FBG KC		7 4	1400	3 6	4200	4850
17 1	MONTGOMERY	SLP	SAIL	FBG KL		7 4	1400	3 6	4200	4850
--- 1974 BOATS ---
17 1	MONTGOMERY 17	SLP	SA/RC	FBG KC		7 2	1400	3 5	4050	4700

MONTGOMERY WARD
SEA KING   COAST GUARD MFG ID- MGW

Call 1-800-327-6929 for BUC Personalized Evaluation Service
Or, for 1963 to 1980 boats, sign onto www.BUCValuPro.com

MONZA MARINE INC
COAST GUARD MFG ID- MXU
FORMERLY MONZA MARINE CORP

Call 1-800-327-6929 for BUC Personalized Evaluation Service
Or, for 1970 to 2008 boats, sign onto www.BUCValuPro.com

A H MOODY & SON LTD
S HAMPTON HANTS ENGLAND   See inside cover to adjust price for area

IMPEX ENTERPRISES LTD
READING PA 19603

For more recent years, see the BUC Used Boat Price Guide, Volume 1 or Volume 2

LOA FT IN	NAME AND/ OR MODEL	TOP/ RIG	BOAT TYPE	-HULL- MTL TP	----ENGINE--- TP # HP MFG	BEAM FT IN	WGT LBS	DRAFT FT IN	RETAIL LOW	RETAIL HIGH
--- 1983 BOATS ---
27 8	MOODY 27 BILGE KEEL	SLP	SA/CR	FBG TK IB	17D VLVO	9 8	5750	3 5	19100	21200
27 8	MOODY 27 FIN KEEL	SLP	SA/CR	FBG KL IB	17D VLVO	9 8	5750	4 8	18700	20800
28 6	MOODY 29 BILGE KL	SLP	SA/CR	FBG TK IB	20D BUKH	10 6	7300	3 6	24800	27500
28 6	MOODY 29 FIN KL	SLP	SA/CR	FBG KL IB	20D BUKH	10 6	7300	4 6	24200	26800
33	MOODY 33 BILGE KL	SLP	SA/CR	FBG TK IB	35D THOR	11 5	9380	3 5	32800	36400
33	MOODY 33 FIN KL	SLP	SA/CR	FBG KL IB	35D THOR	11 5	9380	4 5	32100	35700
33 5	MOODY 34 BILGE	SLP	SA/CR	FBG TK IB	35D THOR	11 7	11200	3	38600	42800
33 5	MOODY 34 FIN	SLP	SA/CR	FBG KL IB	35D THOR	11 7	11200	3 9	38600	42800
39 6	MOODY 40	SLP	SA/CR	FBG KL IB	47D THOR	13 4	18150	5 6	66100	72700
41	MOODY 41	SLP	SA/CR	FBG KL IB	48D THOR	13 2	20600		75900	83400
41	MOODY 41	SLP	SA/CR	FBG SK IB	48D THOR	13 2	20600		75900	83400
41 10	MOODY 42 AFT CPT	KTH	MS	FBG KL IB	72D PERK	13 4	24200	5 6	86100	94700
41 10	MOODY 42 CTR CPT	KTH	MS	FBG KL IB	72D PERK	13 4	24200	5 6	86100	94700
44	MOODY-GRENADIER 134	KTH	SA/CR	FBG KL IB	72D PERK	13 6	29000	6 3	103000	113000
51 9	MOODY 52	KTH	MS	FBG KL IB	109D PERK	14 2	38260	6 9	188500	207000
63	MOODY 63	KTH	MS	FBG KL IB	160D PERK	16 5	71000	8	476500	523500
--- 1982 BOATS ---
29	MOODY 29	SLP	SA/RC	FBG KL IB	D	10 2	8100	4 5	25800	28600
33	MOODY 33 AFT CPT	SLP	SA/CR	FBG KL IB	D	11 5	10525	4 6	34200	38000
33	MOODY 33 CTR CPT	SLP	SA/CR	FBG KL IB	D	11 5	10525	4 6	34200	38000
36	MOODY 36	SLP	SA/CR	FBG KL IB	40D LEYL	12 4	14700	5	47800	52500
39 6	MOODY 40	SLP	SA/CR	FBG KL IB	D	13 4	18150	5 6	62200	68300
41 9	MOODY 42 AFT CPT	KTH	MS	FBG KL IB	D	13 4	24200	5 6	81000	89000
41 9	MOODY 42 CTR CPT	KTH	MS	FBG KL IB	D	13 4	24200	5 6	81000	89000
44	MOODY 44	SLP	SA/CR	FBG KL IB	D	13 7	29000	6 3	97100	106500
52	MOODY 52	KTH	MS	FBG KL IB	D	14 2	39000	6 9	181500	199500
63	MOODY 63/66	KTH	MS	FBG KL IB	D	16 5	72000	8	457000	502500
--- 1981 BOATS ---
28 6	MOODY 29 BILGE KL	SLP	SA/CR	FBG TK IB	20D BUKH	10 6	7300	3 6	22000	24400
28 6	MOODY 29 FIN KL	SLP	SA/CR	FBG KL IB	20D BUKH	10 6	7300	4 6	21300	23700
33	MOODY 33 BILGE KL	SLP	SA/CR	FBG TK IB	35D THOR	11 5	9380	3 5	29100	32300
33	MOODY 33 FIN KL	SLP	SA/CR	FBG KL IB	35D THOR	11 5	9380	4 5	28400	31500
33	MOODY 33 S BILGE KL	SLP	SA/CR	FBG TK IB	20D BUKH	11 5	9380	3 5	29000	32200
33	MOODY 33 S FIN KL	SLP	SA/CR	FBG KL IB	20D BUKH	11 5	9380	4 5	28400	31500
36	MOODY 36	SLP	MS	FBG KL IB	35D THOR	12 4	14700	5	44400	49300
36	MOODY 36 DS	SLP	MS	FBG KL IB	61D VLVO	12 4	14700	5	44700	49600
37 10	MOODY 379	SLP	SA/RC	FBG KL IB	36D BUKH	12 4	14000	6 6	44500	49600
39 6	MOODY 40	SLP	SA/CR	FBG KL IB	47D THOR	13 4	18150	5 6	58500	64300
41 10	MOODY 42 AFT CPT	KTH	MS	FBG KL IB	62D PERK	13 4	24200	5 6	76100	83600
41 10	MOODY 42 CTR CPT	KTH	MS	FBG KL IB	62D PERK	13 4	24200	5 6	76100	83600
44	MOODY-GRENADIER 134	KTH	SA/CR	FBG KL IB	62D PERK	13 6	29000	6 3	90800	99800
51 9	MOODY 52	KTH	MS	FBG KL IB	109D PERK	14 2	38260	6 9	168000	185000
63	MOODY 63	KTH	MS	FBG KL IB	140D PERK	16 5	71000	8	427000	469000
--- 1980 BOATS ---
28 6	MOODY 29	SLP	SA/CR	FBG TK IB	20D BUKH	10 6	7300	4 6	20700	23000
33	MOODY 33	SLP	SA/CR	FBG TK IB	35D THOR	11 5	9380	3 5	28000	31100
33	MOODY 33 CTR CPT	SLP	SA/CR	FBG KL IB	35D THOR	11 5	9380	4 5	26900	29900
33	MOODY 33 S	SLP	SA/CR	FBG KL IB	20D BUKH	11 5	9380	4 5	27400	30500
36	MOODY 36	SLP	MS	FBG KL IB	62D VLVO	12 4	14700	5	42700	47400
36	MOODY 36	SLP	MS	FBG KL IB	35D THOR	12 4	14700	5	42400	47100
37 10	MOODY 379	SLP	SA/RC	FBG KL IB	36D BUKH	12 4	14000	6 6	42400	47100
39 6	MOODY 40	SLP	SA/CR	FBG KL IB	47D THOR	13 4	18150	5 6	55900	61400
42	MOODY 42 AFT CPT	KTH	MS	FBG KL IB	65D PERK	13 4	24200	5 6	71100	78100
42	MOODY 42 CTR CPT	KTH	MS	FBG KL IB	65D PERK	13 4	24200	5 6	75200	82600
44	MOODY-GRENADIER 134	KTH	SA/CR	FBG KL IB	62D PERK	13 6	29000	6 3	86800	95400
51 9	MOODY-CARBINER 52	KTH	MS	FBG KL IB	109D PERK	14 2	38260	6 9	160500	176000
63	MOODY-CARBINEER 63	KTH	MS	FBG KL IB	140D PERK	16 5	71000	8	407000	447500
--- 1979 BOATS ---
30	MOODY 30	SLP	SA/CR	FBG KL IB	D	10	8100	4	22600	25100
33	MOODY 33	SLP	SA/CR	FBG KL IB	D	11 5	10525	4 6	29500	32700
36	MOODY 36	SLP	SA/CR	FBG KL IB	D	12 4	14700	5	40800	45300
38 6	MOODY 39	SLP	SA/CR	FBG KL IB	D	13 4	18150	5 6	53700	56900
41 9	MOODY 42	SLP	SA/CR	FBG KL IB	D	13 2	24200	5 6	70000	76900
44	MOODY 44	SLP	SA/CR	FBG KL IB	D	13 7	22000	6	72800	80000
46 6	MOODY 46	SLP	SA/CR	FBG KL IB	D	14 2	22000	6	88500	97200
51 9	MOODY 52	KTH	SA/CR	FBG KL IB	D	14 2	38260	7	154000	169500
63	MOODY 63	KTH	SA/CR	FBG KL IB	D	16 5	71000	8	391000	430000
--- 1978 BOATS ---
30	MOODY 30	SLP	SA/CR	FBG KL IB	23D	10	8100	4	21800	24200
33	MOODY 33	SLP	SA/CR	FBG KL IB	38D	11 5	10525	4 6	28100	31700
36	MOODY 36	SLP	SA/CR	FBG KL IB	38D	12 4	14700	5	39300	43700
38 6	MOODY 39	SLP	SA/CR	FBG KL IB	38D	13 4	18150	5 6	49700	54700
41 9	MOODY 42	KTH	SA/CR	FBG KL IB	72D	13 2	24200	5 6	64700	71100
41 9	MOODY 42 CTR CPT	KTH	SA/CR	FBG KL IB	72D	13 2	24200	5 6	67700	74300
44	MOODY 44	SLP	SA/CR	FBG KL IB	42D	12	22000	6	69700	76900
46 6	MOODY 46	SLP	SA/CR	FBG KL IB	85D	14 2	22000	6	77400	85000
51 9	MOODY 52	KTH	SA/CR	FBG KL IB	120D	14 2	40000	7	150000	165000
63	MOODY 63	KTH	SA/CR	FBG KL IB	160D	16 5	71000	8	376000	413000
--- 1977 BOATS ---
30	MOODY 30	SLP	SA/CR	FBG KL IB	25D	10 1	8100	4 8	21000	23400
33	MOODY 33	SLP	SA/CR	FBG KL IB	38D	11 5	10525	4 7	27500	30600
38 6	MOODY 39	SLP	SA/CR	FBG KL IB	38D	13	18150	5 5	48100	52900

LOA FT IN	NAME AND/ OR MODEL	TOP/ RIG	BOAT TYPE	-HULL- MTL TP	----ENGINE--- TP # HP MFG	BEAM FT IN	WGT LBS	DRAFT FT IN	RETAIL LOW	RETAIL HIGH
					1977 BOATS					
41 9	MOODY 42	KTH	MS	FBG KL	IB D	13 4	20500	5 6	59000	64800
44	MOODY 44	SLP	SA/CR	FBG KL	IB 40D	12 7	22000	6 6	67600	74200
44	MOODY 44	KTH	SA/CR	FBG KL	IB 40D	12 7	22000	6 6	67600	74300
46 6	CABINEER 46	KTH	SA/CR	FBG KL	IB 85D	12	26000	6	82700	90900
52	MOODY 52	KTH	SA/CR	FBG KL	IB 96D	14 2	40000	6 9	147000	161500
63	MOODY 63	KTH	SA/CR	FBG KL	IB 140D	16 5	71000	8	361500	397000
					1976 BOATS					
30	MOODY 30	SLP	SA/CR	FBG KL	IB D	10 1	8100	4 8	20400	22600
33	MOODY 33	SLP	SA/CR	FBG KL	IB D	11 6	10525	4 5	26600	29600
38 6	MOODY 39	SLP	SA/CR	FBG KL	IB D	13 4	18150	5 6	46900	51600
44	MOODY 44	KTH	SA/CR	FBG KL	IB D	12 7	22000	6 6	65700	72200
46 6	CABINEER 46	KTH	SA/CR	FBG KL	IB D	12 2	26000	6	79800	87700
63	MOODY 63	KTH	SA/CR	FBG KL	IB D	16 5	71000	8	349000	383500

MOONEY MARINE INC
COAST GUARD MFG ID- MYH
FORMERLY MOONEY BROS BOATBUILDING

Call 1-800-327-6929 for BUC Personalized Evaluation Service
Or, for 1980 to 1985 boats, sign onto www.BUCValuPro.com

MOORE SAILBOATS
COAST GUARD MFG ID- MSS

Call 1-800-327-6929 for BUC Personalized Evaluation Service
Or, for 1981 to 2008 boats, sign onto www.BUCValuPro.com

MOORMAN MFG INC
M M I   COAST GUARD MFG ID- MRM

Call 1-800-327-6929 for BUC Personalized Evaluation Service
Or, for 1969 to 1980 boats, sign onto www.BUCValuPro.com

MORAVIA INDUSTRIES INC
COAST GUARD MFG ID- MVR

Call 1-800-327-6929 for BUC Personalized Evaluation Service
Or, for 1978 to 1979 boats, sign onto www.BUCValuPro.com

MORETTES LTD
COAST GUARD MFG ID- ZMT

Call 1-800-327-6929 for BUC Personalized Evaluation Service
Or, for 1979 to 1985 boats, sign onto www.BUCValuPro.com

MORGAN MARINE
BY CATALINA YACHTS
WOODLAND HILLS CA 91367 COAST GUARD MFG ID- MRY   See inside cover to adjust price for area

For more recent years, see the BUC Used Boat Price Guide, Volume 1 or Volume 2

LOA FT IN	NAME AND/ OR MODEL	TOP/ RIG	BOAT TYPE	-HULL- MTL TP	----ENGINE--- TP # HP MFG	BEAM FT IN	WGT LBS	DRAFT FT IN	RETAIL LOW	RETAIL HIGH
					1983 BOATS					
31 11	MORGAN 323	SLP	SA/CR	FBG KL	IB 23D YAN	11 6	11000	4	23500	26100
36	MORGAN 36	SLP	SA/RC	FBG KC	IB 21D UNIV	11 10	11000	4 6	26600	29500
36	MORGAN 36	SLP	SA/CR	FBG KL	IB 21D UNIV	11 10	11000	4 6	26600	29500
38 4	MORGAN 384	SLP	SA/RC	FBG KL	IB 50D PERK	12	18000	5	46200	50800
41 3	OUT-ISLAND 416	KTH	SA/CR	FBG KL	IB 62D PERK	13 10	27000	4 2	69200	76100
45	MORGAN 45	SLP	SA/CR	FBG KC	IB 50D PATH	13 5	22500	5	73700	81000
45	MORGAN 45	SLP	SA/CR	FBG KL	IB 50D PATH	13 5	22500	7 11	73700	81000
45	MORGAN 45	SLP	SA/RC	FBG KC	IB 50D PATH	13 5	21000	5	71400	78500
45	MORGAN 45	SLP	SA/RC	FBG KL	IB 50D PATH	13 5	21000	7 11	71400	78500
60 1	MORGAN 60	SCH	SA/CR	FBG KL	IB 135D PERK	15 8	60000	13	245000	269000
					1982 BOATS					
31 11	MORGAN 32	SLP	SA/CR	FBG KL	IB 15D YAN	11 6	11000	4	22300	24700
38 4	MORGAN 38	SLP	SA/CR	FBG KL	IB 50D PERK	12	18000	5	43300	48100
38 4	MORGAN 38	SLP	SA/RC	FBG KL	IB 50D PERK	12	18000	6	43300	48100
41 3	OUT-ISLAND 41	KTH	SA/CR	FBG KL	IB 62D PERK	13 10	27000	4 2	62200	68300
46 6	MORGAN 46	SLP	SA/CR	FBG KL	IB 62D PERK	13 6	30000	5 3	85100	93500
46 6	MORGAN 46	KTH	SA/CR	FBG KL	IB 62D PERK	13 6	30000	5 3	85100	93500
59 11	MORGAN 60	SCH	SA/CR	FBG KL	IB 130D PERK	15 10	60000	6 10	231500	254500
59 11	MORGAN 60 SHOAL	SCH	SA/CR	FBG KL	IB 130D PERK	15 10	60000	6 10	231500	254500
					1981 BOATS					
31 11	MORGAN 32	SLP	SA/CR	FBG KL	IB 20D YAN	11 6	11000	5 6	21100	23400
31 11	MORGAN 32 SHOAL	SLP	SA/CR	FBG KL	IB 20D YAN	11 6	11000	4	21100	23400
33	OUT-ISLAND 335	SLP	SA/CR	FBG KL	IB D	11 10	14500	3 11	28200	31300
38 4	MORGAN 38	SLP	SA/CR	FBG KL	IB 50D PERK	12	17000	5	39300	43600
38 4	MORGAN 38 SHOAL	SLP	SA/CR	FBG KL	IB 50D PERK	12	17000	5	39300	43600
41 3	OUT-ISLAND 41	SLP	SA/CR	FBG KL	IB 62D PERK	13 10	27000	4 2	62200	68300
41 3	OUT-ISLAND 41	KTH	SA/CR	FBG KL	IB 62D PERK	13 10	27000	4 2	62200	68300
46 6	MORGAN 46	SLP	SA/CR	FBG KL	IB 62D PERK	13 6	30000	6	80700	88600
46 6	MORGAN 46	KTH	SA/CR	FBG KL	IB 62D PERK	13 6	30000	6	80700	88600
46 6	MORGAN 46 SHOAL	SLP	SA/CR	FBG KL	IB 62D PERK	13 6	30000	5 3	80700	88600
46 6	MORGAN 46 SHOAL	KTH	SA/CR	FBG KL	IB 62D PERK	13 6	30000	5 3	80700	88600
51 6	OUT-ISLAND 51	KTH	SA/CR	FBG KL	IB 85D PERK	15	46000	5 6	119500	131000
					1980 BOATS					
31 11	MORGAN 32	SLP	SA/CR	FBG KL	IB 20D YAN	11 6	11000	5 6	20200	22500
31 11	MORGAN 32 SHOAL	SLP	SA/CR	FBG KL	IB 20D YAN	11 6	11000	4	20400	22600
33	OUT-ISLAND 33	SLP	MS	FBG KL	IB 50D PERK	11 10	15500	3 11	28900	32100
38 4	MORGAN 38	SLP	SA/RC	FBG KL	IB 50D PERK	12	17000	5	37800	42000
38 4	MORGAN 38 SHOAL	SLP	SA/CR	FBG KL	IB 50D PERK	12	17000	5	37800	42000
41 3	OUT-ISLAND 41	SLP	SA/CR	FBG KL	IB 62D PERK	13 10	27000	4 2	59800	65700
41 3	OUT-ISLAND 41	KTH	SA/CR	FBG KL	IB 62D PERK	13 10	27000	4 2	59800	65700
46 6	MORGAN 46	SLP	SA/CR	FBG KL	IB 65D PERK	13 6	30000	6	77600	85300
46 6	MORGAN 46	KTH	SA/CR	FBG KL	IB 65D PERK	13 6	30000	6	77700	85400
46 6	MORGAN 46 SHOAL	SLP	SA/CR	FBG KL	IB 65D PERK	13 6	30000	5 3	77600	85300
46 6	MORGAN 46 SHOAL	KTH	SA/CR	FBG KL	IB 65D PERK	13 6	30000	5 3	77600	85300
51 6	OUT-ISLAND 462	KTH	SA/CR	FBG KL	IB 85D PERK	15	46000	5 6	115000	126000
51 6	OUT-ISLAND 51	KTH	SA/CR	FBG KL	IB D	15		5 6	113000	124000
					1979 BOATS					
29 10	OUT-ISLAND 30	SLP	SA/CR	FBG KL	IB D	9 2	9500	3 4	15100	17100
31 11	MORGAN 32	SLP	SA/CR	FBG KL	IB 20D YAN	11 6	10000	5 6	18100	20100
31 11	MORGAN 32 SHOAL	SLP	SA/CR	FBG KL	IB 20D YAN	11 6	10000	4	18100	20100
33	OUT-ISLAND 33	SLP	SA/CR	FBG KL	IB 50D PERK	11 10	14500	3 11	26300	29200
38 4	MORGAN 38	SLP	SA/RC	FBG KL	IB 33D YAN	12	17000	4	36700	40800
38 4	MORGAN 38 SHOAL	SLP	SA/CR	FBG KL	IB 33D YAN	12	17000	5	36700	40800
41 3	OUT-ISLAND 41	SLP	SA/CR	FBG KL	IB 62D PERK	13 10	27000	4 2	58000	63700
41 3	OUT-ISLAND 41	KTH	SA/CR	FBG KL	IB 62D PERK	13 10	27000	4 2	58000	63700
45	MORGAN 45	SLP	SA/CR	FBG KL	IB 62D PERK	13 6	30000	5 6	70500	77400
46	OUT-ISLAND 462	SLP							68300	75000
46	OUT-ISLAND 462	SLP							68300	75000
					1978 BOATS					
29 10	OUT-ISLAND 30	SLP	SA/CR	FBG KL	IB 30 UNIV	9 2	9500	3 4	14600	16600
29 10	OUT-ISLAND 30	SLP	SA/CR	FBG KL	IB D	9 2	9500	3 4	14600	16600
33	OUT-ISLAND 33	SLP	SA/CR	FBG KL	IB 50D PERK	11 10	14500	5	25500	28300
36 6	OUT-ISLAND 37 MK II	KTH	SA/CR	FBG KL	IB 50D PERK	11	18000	4	34100	37900
36 6	OUT-ISLAND 37 MK II	SLP	SA/CR	FBG KL	IB 50D PERK	11	18000	4	34100	37900
38 4	MORGAN 38	SLP	SA/RC	FBG KL	IB 33D YAN	12	17000	5	35600	39600
41 3	OUT-ISLAND 41	SLP	SA/CR	FBG KL	IB 62D PERK	13 10	27000	4 2	56200	61700
41 3	OUT-ISLAND 41	KTH	SA/CR	FBG KL	IB 62D PERK	13 10	27000	4 2	56200	61700
45	MORGAN 45	SLP	SA/CR	FBG KL	IB 62D PERK	13 6	30000	5 6	68400	75200
49 7	OUT-ISLAND 49	KTH	SA/CR	FBG KL	IB 85D PERK	15	43000	5 3	96100	105500
49 7	OUT-ISLAND 49	KTH	SA/CR	FBG KL	IB 115D PERK	15	43000	5 3	96200	106000
51 6	OUT-ISLAND 51	KTH	SA/CR	FBG KC	IB 85D PERK	15	48000	5 6	109000	120000
51 6	OUT-ISLAND 51	KTH	SA/CR	FBG KC	IB 115D PERK	15	48000	5 6	109500	120000
					1977 BOATS					
29 10	OUT-ISLAND 30	SLP	SA/CR	FBG KL	IB 30 UNIV	9 2	9500	3 4	14200	16100
29 10	OUT-ISLAND 30	SLP	SA/CR	FBG KL	IB 20D	9 2	9500	3 4	14300	16200
33	OUT-ISLAND 33	SLP	SA/CR	FBG KL	IB 50D PERK	11 10	14500	5	24800	27600
36 6	OUT-ISLAND 37 MK II	KTH	SA/CR	FBG KL	IB 50D PERK	11	18000	4	33600	37300
36 6	OUT-ISLAND 37 MK II	KTH	SA/CR	FBG KL	IB 50D PERK	11	18000	4	33600	37300
36 6	OUT-ISLAND 371	KTH	SA/CR	FBG KL	IB 50D PERK	11	18000	4	33600	37300
36 6	OUT-ISLAND 371	SLP	SA/CR	FBG KL	IB 50D PERK	11	18000	4	33600	37300
41 3	OUT-ISLAND 41	SLP	SA/CR	FBG KL	IB 50D PERK	13 10	27000	4 2	54700	60100
41 3	OUT-ISLAND 41	KTH	SA/CR	FBG KL	IB 50D PERK	13 10	27000	4 2	54700	60100
41 3	OUT-ISLAND 41	SLP	SA/CR	FBG KL	IB 62D PERK	13 10	27000	4 2	54700	60100
41 3	OUT-ISLAND 41	KTH	SA/CR	FBG KL	IB 62D PERK	13 10	27000	4 2	54700	60100
49 7	OUT-ISLAND 49	KTH	SA/CR	FBG F/S	IB 85D PERK	15	43000	5 3	93500	102500
51 6	OUT-ISLAND 51	KTH	SA/CR	FBG F/S	IB 85D PERK	15	48000	5 6	106000	116500
51 6	OUT-ISLAND 51	KTH	SA/CR	FBG KC	IB 115D WEST	15	48000	5 6	107000	117500
					1976 BOATS					
22 6	MORGAN 22	SLP	SA/RC	FBG KC	OB	8	3500	1 10	3350	3900
25	MORGAN 25	SLP	SA/RC	FBG KL	IB D	8	5000	2 9	4800	5600
25	MORGAN 25	SLP	SA/RC	FBG KL	IB D	8	5000	2 9	5150	5500
27 6	MORGAN 27	SLP	SA/RC	FBG KL	IB D	9 10	7000	4 6	8700	10000

LOA FT	LOA IN	NAME AND/ OR MODEL	TOP/ RIG	BOAT TYPE	-HULL- MTL	-HULL- TP	ENGINE TP	ENGINE # HP	ENGINE MFG	BEAM FT	BEAM IN	WGT LBS	DRAFT FT	DRAFT IN	RETAIL LOW	RETAIL HIGH
		1976 BOATS														
28	5	OUT-ISLAND 28	SLP	SA/CR	FBG	KL	IB	30	UNIV	9	3	8000	3	6	10600	12000
28	5	OUT-ISLAND 28	SLP	SA/CR	FBG	KL	IB	D		9	3	8000	3	6	10700	12100
29	11	MORGAN 30	SLP	SA/RC	FBG	KC	IB	D		9	3	10000	3	6	14700	16700
33		OUT-ISLAND 33	SLP	SA/CR	FBG	KL	IB	50D	PERK	11	10	14500	3	11	24200	26900
35	10	OUT-ISLAND 36	SLP	SA/CR	FBG	KL	IB	D		11	5	16000	3	9	28600	31800
35	10	OUT-ISLAND 36	KTH	SA/CR	FBG	KL	IB	D		11	5	16000	3	9	28600	31800
36	6	OUT-ISLAND 37	SLP	SA/CR	FBG	KL	IB	50D		11		18000	4		32500	36100
36	6	OUT-ISLAND 37	KTH	SA/CR	FBG	KL	IB	50D		11		18000	4		32500	36100
41	3	OUT-ISLAND 41	SLP	SA/CR	FBG	KC	IB	D		13	10	27000	4	2	53800	59100
41	3	OUT-ISLAND 41	SLP	SA/CR	FBG	KL	IB	D		13	10	27000	4	2	53800	59100
41	3	OUT-ISLAND 41	KTH	SA/CR	FBG	KC	IB	D		13	10	27000	4	2	53800	59100
41	3	OUT-ISLAND 41	KTH	SA/CR	FBG	KL	IB	D		13	10	27000	4	2	53800	59100
49	7	OUT-ISLAND 49	KTH	SA/CR	F/S	KL	IB	85D	PERK	15		43000	5	3	91200	100000
51	6	OUT-ISLAND 51	KTH	SA/CR	F/S	KC	IB	85D	PERK	15		48000	5		103500	114000
51	6	OUT-ISLAND 51	KTH	SA/CR	F/S	KC	IB	115D	WEST	15		48000	5		104500	114500
		1975 BOATS														
22	6	MORGAN 22	SLP	SA/RC	FBG	KC	IB	D		8		3500	1	10	3200	3750
25		CLASSIC 250	SLP	SA/CR	FBG	KC	OB			8		5000	2	9	4700	5400
25		CLASSIC 250	SLP	SA/CR	FBG	KC	IB	D		8		5000	2	9	5000	5750
27	6	MORGAN 27	SLP	SA/RC	FBG	KL	OB			9	10	7000	4	6	8250	9500
27	6	MORGAN 27	SLP	SA/RC	FBG	KL	IB	30	UNIV	9	10	7000	4	6	8350	9600
28	5	OUT-ISLAND 28	SLP	SA/CR	FBG	KL	IB	18	UNIV	9	3	8000	3	6	10300	11700
28	5	OUT-ISLAND 28	SLP	SA/CR	FBG	KL	IB	D		9	3	8000	3	6	10400	11900
29	11	CLASSIC 300	SLP	SA/CR	FBG	KC	IB	30	UNIV	9	3	10000	3	6	14300	16300
29	11	CLASSIC 300	SLP	SA/CR	FBG	KC	IB	D		9	3	10000	3	6	14400	16400
32	9	MORGAN 33T	SLP	SA/RC	FBG	KL	IB	20D		10	7	9800	5	6	15900	18100
33		OUT-ISLAND 33	SLP	SA/CR	FBG	KL	IB	D		11	10	14500	3	11	23700	26300
35	9	MORGAN 36T	SLP	SA/RC	FBG	KL	VD	30	UNIV	11	9	14000	6	3	24500	27200
35	9	MORGAN 36T	SLP	SA/RC	FBG	KL	VD	50D	PERK	11	9	14000	6	3	24700	27500
35	10	OUT-ISLAND 36	SLP	SA/CR	FBG	KL	IB	50D	PERK	11	5	16000	3	9	27900	31000
35	10	OUT-ISLAND 36	KTH	SA/CR	FBG	KL	IB	50D	PERK	11	5	16000	3	9	27900	31000
41	3	OUT-ISLAND 41-3	KTH	SA/CR	FBG	KL	IB	50D	PERK	13	10	24000	4	2	47900	52700
41	3	OUT-ISLAND 41-4	KTH	SA/CR	FBG	KL	IB	50D	PERK	13	10	24000	4	2	49100	53900
51	6	OUT-ISLAND 51	KTH	SA/CR	FBG	KC	IB	50D	PERK	15		41000	5		97000	106500
51	6	OUT-ISLAND 51	KTH	SA/CR	FBG	KC	IB	115D	WEST	15		41000	5		98100	108000
		1974 BOATS														
22	6	MORGAN 22	SLP	SA/RC	FBG	KC	OB			8		3500	1	10	2650	3100
27	6	MORGAN 27	SLP	SA/RC	FBG	KL	OB			9	10	7000	4	6	8050	9250
27	6	MORGAN 27	SLP	SA/RC	FBG	KL	IB	30	UNIV	9	10	7000	4	6	8200	9400
28	5	OUT-ISLAND 28	SLP	SA/CR	FBG	KL	IB	30	UNIV	9	3	8000	3	6	10100	11500
28	5	OUT-ISLAND 28	SLP	SA/CR	FBG	KL	IB	15D	WEST	9	3	8000	3	6	10200	11600
29	11	MORGAN 30/2	SLP	SA/RC	FBG	KL	IB	30	UNIV	11	4	10000	5	3	14000	15900
29	11	MORGAN 30/2	SLP	SA/RC	FBG	KL	IB	15D	WEST	11	4	10000	5	3	14100	16000
33		MORGAN 33 3/4 TON	SLP	SA/CR	FBG	KL	IB	D		10	6	9800	5	6	15700	17800
33		OUT-ISLAND 33	SLP	SA/CR	FBG	KL	IB	30	UNIV	11	10	14500	3	11	23100	25700
33		OUT-ISLAND 33	SLP	SA/CR	FBG	KL	IB	37D	WEST	11	10	14500	3	11	23200	25800
35	9	MORGAN 36 1-TON	SLP	SA/RC	FBG	KL	IB	30	UNIV	11	9	14000	6	3	24000	26600
35	9	MORGAN 36 1-TON	SLP	SA/RC	FBG	KL	IB	37D	WEST	11	9	14000	6	3	24300	27000
35	10	OUT-ISLAND 36	SLP	SA/CR	FBG	KC	IB	30	UNIV	11	5	16000	3	9	27100	30100
35	10	OUT-ISLAND 36	SLP	SA/CR	FBG	KL	IB	30	UNIV	11	5	16000	3	9	27100	30100
35	10	OUT-ISLAND 36	KTH	SA/CR	FBG	KC	IB	30	UNIV	11	5	16000	3	9	27100	30100
35	10	OUT-ISLAND 36	KTH	SA/CR	FBG	KL	IB	30	UNIV	11	5	16000	3	9	27100	30100
41	3	OUT-ISLAND 41	SLP	SA/CR	FBG	KL	IB	37D	WEST	13	10	24000	4	2	47700	52400
41	3	OUT-ISLAND 41	KTH	SA/CR	FBG	KL	IB	37D	WEST	13	10	24000	4	2	47700	52400
		1973 BOATS														
22	6	MORGAN 22	SLP	SA/RC	FBG	KC	OB			8		3500	1	10	2600	3050
27	6	MORGAN 27	SLP	SA/RC	FBG	KL	OB			9	10	7000	4	6	7900	9100
27	6	MORGAN 27	SLP	SA/RC	FBG	KL	IB	30	UNIV	9	10		4	6	6350	7250
28	5	OUT-ISLAND 28	SLP	SA/CR	FBG	KL	IB	30	UNIV	9	3	8000	3	6	9950	11300
28	5	OUT-ISLAND 28	SLP	SA/CR	FBG	KL	IB	15D	WEST	9	3	8000	3	6	10000	11400
29	11	MORGAN 30/2	SLP	SA/RC	FBG	KL	IB	30	UNIV	11	4	10000	5	3	13800	15600
29	11	MORGAN 30/2	SLP	SA/RC	FBG	KL	IB	15D	WEST	11	4	10000	5	3	13800	15700
33		OUT-ISLAND 33	SLP	SA/CR	FBG	KL	IB	30	UNIV	11	10	14500	3	11	22700	25200
33		OUT-ISLAND 33	SLP	SA/CR	FBG	KL	IB	37D	WEST	11	10	14500	3	11	22800	25300
35		MORGAN 35	SLP	SA/RC	FBG	KC	IB	30D		10	9	11900	4	3	19900	22100
35	9	MORGAN 36 1-TON	SLP	SA/RC	FBG	KL	IB	30	UNIV	11	9	14000	6	3	23500	26100
35	9	MORGAN 36 1-TON	SLP	SA/RC	FBG	KL	IB	37D	WEST	11	9	14000	6	3	23900	26500
35	10	OUT-ISLAND 36	SLP	SA/CR	FBG	KC	IB	30	UNIV	11	5	16000	3	9	26600	29500
35	10	OUT-ISLAND 36	SLP	SA/CR	FBG	KL	IB	30	UNIV	11	5	14000	3	9	23600	26200
35	10	OUT-ISLAND 36	KTH	SA/CR	FBG	KC	IB	30	UNIV	11	5	16000	3	9	26600	29500
35	10	OUT-ISLAND 36	KTH	SA/CR	FBG	KL	IB	30	UNIV	11	5	14000	3	9	23600	26200
40		MORGAN 40	SLP	MS	FBG	KL	IB	37D		11	3	21500	4	3	41700	46300
40		MORGAN 40	KTH	SA/CR	FBG	KL	IB	65D		11	3	21000	4	2	41400	46000
41	3	OUT-ISLAND 41	SLP	SA/CR	FBG	KL	IB	37D	WEST	13	10	24000	4	2	47100	51700
41	3	OUT-ISLAND 41	KTH	SA/CR	FBG	KL	IB	37D	WEST	13	10	24000	4	2	47100	51700
42		MORGAN 42 MARK II	SLP	SA/RC	FBG	KL	IB	30D		11	6	18500	6		40900	45400
42		MORGAN 42 MARK II	YWL	SA/RC	FBG	KL	IB	30D		11	6	18500	6		40900	45400
54		MORGAN 54	SLP	SA/RC	FBG	KC	IB	60D		12	6	38000	5	8	105500	116000
54		MORGAN 54	SLP	SA/RC	FBG	KL	IB	60D		12	6	36000	7	8	105000	115000
		1972 BOATS														
22	6	MORGAN 22	SLP	SA/RC	FBG	KC	OB			8		3500	1	10	2550	2950
25		MORGAN 25	SLP	SA/RC	FBG	KC	OB			8		5000	2	9	4400	5050
25		MORGAN 25	SLP	SA/RC	FBG	KC	IB	30	UNIV	8		5000	2	9	4550	5250
27	6	MORGAN 27	SLP	SA/RC	FBG	KL	OB			9	10	7000	4	6	7750	8900
27	6	MORGAN 27	SLP	SA/RC	FBG	KL	IB	30	UNIV	9	10	7000	4	6	7850	9050
27	10	MORGAN 28	SLP	SA/RC	FBG	KC	IB	30	UNIV	9		7600	3		8900	10100
29	11	MORGAN 30	SLP	SA/RC	FBG	KC	IB	30	UNIV	9	3	10000	3	8	13500	15300
29	11	MORGAN 30/2	SLP	SA/RC	FBG	KL	IB	30	UNIV	11	4	9500	5	3	12800	14500
32	6	MORGAN 33	SLP	SA/RC	FBG	KL	IB	30	UNIV	9	4	11000	5		16700	19000
34		MORGAN 34	SLP	SA/CR	FBG	KC	IB	30		10		12500	3	3	19700	21900
35		MORGAN 35	SLP	SA/RC	FBG	KC	IB	30	UNIV	10	9	11900	4	3	19300	21400
35		MORGAN 35	SLP	SA/RC	FBG	KC	IB	37D	WEST	10	9	11900	4	3	19600	21700
37	8	MORGAN 38	SLP	SA/CR	FBG	KC	IB	30		11		16000	3	9	28200	31300
40	2	MORGAN 40	SLP	MS	FBG	KL	IB	65	UNIV	11	3	21500	4	3	40500	45000
40	2	MORGAN 40	SLP	MS	FBG	KL	IB	37D	WEST	11	3	21500	4	3	41100	45700
40	2	MORGAN 40	KTH	SA/CR	FBG	KL	IB	65	UNIV	11	3	21000	4	2	39900	44300
40	2	MORGAN 40	KTH	SA/CR	FBG	KL	IB	37D	WEST	11	3	21000	4	2	40500	45000
41		MORGAN 41	SLP	SA/CR	FBG	KC	IB	30	UNIV	11	3	19500	4	2	39000	43300
41		MORGAN 41	SLP	SA/CR	FBG	KC	IB	37D	WEST	11	3	19500	4	2	39700	44100
41		MORGAN 41	YWL	SAIL	FBG	KC	IB	30	UNIV	11	3	19500	4	2	39000	43300
41		MORGAN 41	YWL	SAIL	FBG	KC	IB	37D	WEST	11	3	19500	4	2	39700	44100
41	3	OUT-ISLAND 41	SLP	SA/CR	FBG	KL	IB	60D	PERK	13	10	24000	4	2	46000	50500
41	3	OUT-ISLAND 41	SLP	SA/CR	FBG	KL	IB	60D	WEST	13	10	24000	4	2	46400	50900
41	3	OUT-ISLAND 41	KTH	SA/CR	FBG	KL	IB	60D	PERK	13	10	24000	4	2	46000	50500
41	3	OUT-ISLAND 41	KTH	SA/CR	FBG	KL	IB	60D	WEST	13	10	24000	4	2	46400	50900
42		MORGAN 42 MARK II	SLP	SA/RC	FBG	KL	IB	30	UNIV	11	6	18500	6		39500	43800
42		MORGAN 42 MARK II	SLP	SA/RC	FBG	KL	IB	37D	WEST	11	6	18500	6		40200	44600
42		MORGAN 42 MARK II	YWL	SA/RC	FBG	KL	IB	37D	WEST	11	6	18500	6		40200	44600
42		MORGAN 42 MARK II	YWL	SAIL	FBG	KL	IB	30	UNIV	11	6	18500	6		39500	43800
46		OUT-ISLAND 46	SLP	SA/CR	FBG	KL	IB								59500	65300
53	6	MORGAN 54	SLP	SA/RC	FBG	KC	IB	60D	PERK	12	6	38000	5	8	100000	110000
53	6	MORGAN 54	SLP	SA/RC	FBG	KC	IB	60D	WEST	12	6	38000	5	8	100500	110500
53	6	MORGAN 54	SLP	SA/RC	FBG	KL	IB	60D	PERK	12	6	36000	7	8	99200	109000
53	6	MORGAN 54	SLP	SA/RC	FBG	KL	IB	60D	WEST	12	6	36000	7	8	99600	109500
53	6	MORGAN 54	YWL	SAIL	FBG	KC	IB	60D	PERK	12	6	38000	5	8	100000	110000
53	6	MORGAN 54	YWL	SAIL	FBG	KL	IB	60D	PERK	12	6	36000	7	8	99300	109000
		1971 BOATS														
22	6	MORGAN 22	SLP	SA/RC	FBG	KC	OB			8		3500	1	10	2500	2900
25		MORGAN 25	SLP	SA/RC	FBG	KC	OB			8		5000	2	9	4250	4950
25		MORGAN 25	SLP	SA/RC	FBG	KC	IB	22- 30		8		5000	2	9	4450	5150
27	10	MORGAN 28	SLP	SA/RC	FBG	KC	IB	30	UNIV	9		7600	3		8600	9850
29	11	MORGAN 30	SLP	SA/RC	FBG	KC	IB	30	UNIV	9	3	10000	3	8	13100	14900
32	6	MORGAN 33	SLP	SA/RC	FBG	KL	IB	30	UNIV	9	4	11000	5		16300	18500
34		MORGAN 34 CUSTOM	SLP	SA/RC	FBG	KC	IB	30	UNIV	10		12500	3	3	19200	21300
34		MORGAN 34 CUSTOM	SLP	SA/RC	FBG	KC	IB	60D	WEST	10		12500	3	3	19400	21600
34		MORGAN 34 CUSTOM	YWL	SA/RC	FBG	KC	IB	30	UNIV	10		12500	3	3	19200	21300
34		MORGAN 34 CUSTOM	YWL	SA/RC	FBG	KC	IB	60D	WEST	10		12500	3	3	19400	21600
35		MORGAN 35	SLP	SA/RC	FBG	KC	IB	30	UNIV	10	9	11900	4	3	19000	21100
35		MORGAN 35	SLP	SA/RC	FBG	KC	IB	60D	WEST	10	9	11900	4	3	19200	21300
37	8	MORGAN 38	SLP	SA/RC	FBG	KC	IB	30	UNIV	11		16000	3	9	27400	30500
37	8	MORGAN 38	SLP	SA/RC	FBG	KC	IB	60D	WEST	11		16000	3	9	28100	31300
40	2	MORGAN 40	SLP	MS	FBG	KL	IB	70	UNIV	11	3	19500	4	2	37000	41100
40	2	MORGAN 40	KTH	SA/CR	FBG	KL	IB	70	UNIV	11	3	21000	4	2	38900	43200
40	2	MORGAN 40	KTH	SA/CR	FBG	KL	IB	60D	WEST	11	3	21000	4	2	39700	44100
41		MORGAN 41	SLP	SA/CR	FBG	KC	IB	70	UNIV	11	3	19500	4	2	38100	42400
41		MORGAN 41	SLP	SA/CR	FBG	KC	IB	60D	WEST	11	3	19500	4	2	38900	43300
41		MORGAN 41	YWL	SA/CR	FBG	KC	IB	70	UNIV	11	3	19500	4	2	38100	42400
41		MORGAN 41	YWL	SA/CR	FBG	KC	IB	60D	WEST	11	3	19500	4	2	38900	43300
42		MORGAN 42 MARK II	SLP	SA/RC	FBG	KC	IB	70	UNIV	11	6	18500	6		38600	42900
42		MORGAN 42 MARK II	SLP	SA/RC	FBG	KC	IB	60D	WEST	11	6	18500	6		39400	43800
54		MORGAN 54	SLP	SA/RC	FBG	KC	IB	60D	WEST	12	6	38000	5	8	101500	111500
54		MORGAN 54	SLP	SA/RC	FBG	KL	IB	60D	WEST	12	6	36000	7	8	100500	110500
54		MORGAN 54	YWL	SA/RC	FBG	KC	IB	60D	WEST	12	6	38000	5	8	101500	111500
54		MORGAN 54	YWL	SAIL	FBG	KL	IB	60D	WEST	12	6	36000	7	8	100500	110500
56		MORGAN 56		OFF	FBG		IB	280		18	3		4	2	**	**
56		MORGAN 56		OFF	FBG		IB	320		18	3		4	2	**	**

 CONTINUED ON NEXT PAGE

LOA FT IN	NAME AND/ OR MODEL	TOP/ RIG	BOAT TYPE	-HULL- MTL TP	----ENGINE--- TP # HP MFG	BEAM FT IN	WGT LBS	DRAFT FT IN	RETAIL LOW	RETAIL HIGH
					1970 BOATS					
22 6	MORGAN 22	SLP	SA/RC	FBG KC	OB	8	2700	1 10	1950	2300
24 11	MORGAN 24	SLP	SA/CR	FBG KC	IB	8	4900	2 9	4200	4850
26	MORGAN 26	SLP	SA/RC	FBG KC	OB	8 9	5000	3 2	4550	5250
26	MORGAN 26	SLP	SA/RC	FBG KL	OB	8 9	5000	4 4	4550	5250
28	MORGAN 28	SLP	SA/RC	FBG KC	IB	22 PALM	9	7600	3	8450	9700
28	MORGAN 28	SLP	SAIL	FBG KC	IB	30 UNIV	9	7600	3	8450	9750
29 11	MORGAN 30	SLP	SA/RC	FBG KC	IB	22 PALM	9 3	10500	3 6	13500	15300
29 11	MORGAN 30	SLP	SAIL	FBG KC	IB	30 UNIV	9 3	10500	3 6	13500	15300
32 6	MORGAN 33	SLP	SA/RC	FBG KL	IB	22 PALM	9 4	11000	5	15900	18000
32 6	MORGAN 33	SLP	SAIL	FBG KL	IB	30 UNIV	9 4	11000	5	15900	18000
34	MORGAN 34	SLP	SA/CR	FBG KC	IB	30	10	12500	3 3	18900	21000
35	MORGAN 35	SLP	SA/RC	FBG KC	IB	30 UNIV	10 6	11900	3 9	18600	20600
37 8	MORGAN 38	SLP	SA/RC	FBG KC	ID	30 UNIV	11	16000	3 9	26800	29800
37 8	MORGAN 38	YWL	SAIL	FBG KC	IB	30 UNIV	11	16000	3 9	26800	29800
40 2	MORGAN 40	KTH	SA/CR	FBG KL	IB	70 UNIV	11 3	22000	4 2	39200	43500
41	MORGAN 41	SLP	SA/CR	FBG KC	IB	30 UNIV	11 3	19500	4 2	37100	41200
42	MORGAN 42	SLP	SA/RC	FBG KL	IB	30 UNIV	11 6	18000	6	36900	41000
45 8	MORGAN 45	SLP	SA/CR	FBG KL	IB	40	11	25000	6 1	53400	58700
54	MARAUDER	SLP	SA/RC	FBG KC	IB	37D WEST	12 6	38000	5 8	98500	108800
54	MARAUDER	SLP	SA/RC	FBG KL	IB	37D WEST	12 6	36000	7 8	97600	107500
54	MARAUDER	YWL	SAIL	FBG KC	IB	37D WEST	12 6	38000	5 8	98500	108500
54	MARAUDER	YWL	SAIL	FBG KL	IB	37D WEST	12 6	36000	7 8	97700	107500
56	OFFSHORE	FB	TRWL	FBG	IB	T160D PERK	18 3	42500	4 2	52600	57800
					1969 BOATS					
18 4	MORGAN-BUCCANEER	RNBT		FBG TR	OB	7 4	1250			3400	3950
19 7	MORGAN-BUCCANEER	RNBT		FBG DV	IO	120	7 8		2 5	4950	5700
22 6	MORGAN 22	SLP	SAIL	FBG KC	OB	8	2700	1 10	1900	2250
24 11	MORGAN 24	SLP	SAIL	FBG KC	OB	8	4900	2 9	3900	4550
28	MORGAN 28	SLP	SAIL	FBG KC	IB	30 UNIV	8 6	7000	3	7600	8750
29 11	MORGAN 30	SLP	SAIL	FBG KC	OB	9	11000	3 6	13800	15700
33	MORGAN 33	SLP	SAIL	FBG KL	IB	30 UNIV	9 4	10800	4	15400	17500
34	MORGAN 34	SLP	SAIL	FBG KC	IB	30 UNIV	10	12500	3 3	18500	20600
34 6	MORGAN 34	YWL	SAIL	FBG KC	IB	30 UNIV	10	12500	3 3	18700	20800
37 6	MORGAN 37	SLP	SAIL	FBG KC	IB	30 UNIV	11	15500	3 9	25300	28100
37 6	MORGAN 37	YWL	SAIL	FBG KC	IB	30 UNIV	11	15500	3 9	25300	28100
41	MORGAN 41	SLP	SAIL	FBG KC	IB	30 UNIV	11 3	19000	4 2	35600	39600
41	MORGAN 41	YWL	SAIL	FBG KC	IB	30 UNIV	11 3	19000	4 2	35600	39600
45 8	MORGAN 45	SLP	SAIL	FBG KL	IB	70 UNIV	11	25000	6 1	52300	57500
45 8	MORGAN 45	YWL	SAIL	FBG KL	IB	70 UNIV	11	25000	6 1	52300	57500
					1968 BOATS					
24 11	MORGAN 24	SLP	SAIL	FBG KC	OB	8	4900	2 9	3800	4450
34	MORGAN 34	SLP	SAIL	FBG KC	IB	30 UNIV	10	12500	3 3	18100	20100
41	MORGAN 41	SLP	SAIL	FBG KC	IB	30 UNIV	11 3	19000	4 2	34900	38800
45 8	MORGAN 45	SLP	SAIL	FBG KL	IB	30D WEST	11	25000	6 1	51700	56800
					1967 BOATS					
24 11	MORGAN 24	SLP	SAIL	FBG KC	OB	8	5000	2 9	3800	4450
30	MORGAN 30	SLP	SA/CR	FBG KL	IB	30	9 3		4 6	7200	8300
34	MORGAN 34	SLP	SAIL	FBG KC	IB	30 UNIV	10	12500	3 3	17400	19800
45 8	MORGAN 45	SLP	SAIL	FBG KL	IB	30D WEST	11	25000	6 1	50700	55700
					1966 BOATS					
24	RACING DAYSAILER	SLP	SA/RC	FBG KL		7		3 10	1950	2350
24 6	MORGAN 24	SLP	SAIL	FBG KC	OB	8	4900	2 9	3500	4100
34	MORGAN 34	SLP	SAIL	FBG KC	IB	30 UNIV	10	12500	3 3	17100	19400
34	MORGAN 34	SLP	SAIL	FBG KC	IB	30D WEST	10	12500	3 3	17200	19600
42	MORGAN 42	YWL	SA/CR	FBG KC	IB	30	11 3		4 3	36800	40900
					1965 BOATS					
24	PIONEER	SLP	SAIL	FBG KL		6 11		3 10	2400	2800
24 6	MORGAN 24	SLP	SAIL	FBG KL	OB	8 6		3 10	3600	4200
35 6	MORGAN 36	SLP	SAIL	FBG KC	IB	30	10 6		3 9	15100	17200
42	MORGAN 42	YWL	SAIL	FBG KC	IB	30	11 2		4 3	36300	40300
					1963 BOATS					
28 6	TIGER-CUB	YWL	SA/RC	FBG		OB				3250	3750
					1962 BOATS					
28 6	TIGER-CUB	YWL	SA/RC	FBG		OB				3200	3750

MORGANCRAFT BOAT CO
COAST GUARD MFG ID- MGC

Call 1-800-327-6929 for BUC Personalized Evaluation Service
Or, for 1967 to 1973 boats, sign onto www.BUCValuPro.com

MORRIS BOAT WORKS

Call 1-800-327-6929 for BUC Personalized Evaluation Service
Or, for 1966 to 1969 boats, sign onto www.BUCValuPro.com

MORRIS YACHTS
BASS HARBOR ME 04653-03 COAST GUARD MFG ID- TMY See inside cover to adjust price for area

For more recent years, see the BUC Used Boat Price Guide, Volume 1 or Volume 2

LOA FT IN	NAME AND/ OR MODEL	TOP/ RIG	BOAT TYPE	-HULL- MTL TP	----ENGINE--- TP # HP MFG	BEAM FT IN	WGT LBS	DRAFT FT IN	RETAIL LOW	RETAIL HIGH
					1983 BOATS					
26	FRANCES 26	SLP	SAIL	FBG KL	SD	8D VLVO	8	6800	3 10	36300	40300
26	FRANCES 26	CUT	SAIL	FBG KL	SD	8D VLVO	8	6800	3 10	36300	40300
26	FRANCES 26	CUT	SAIL	FBG KL	IB	10D BMW	8	6800	3 10	36300	40400
29 5	ANNIE	SLP	SA/CR	FBG KL	SD	13D WEST	9 6	11027	4 6	67600	74300
29 5	ANNIE	SLP	SAIL	FBG KL	SD	15D VLVO	9 4	11027	4 6	67600	74200
29 8	LEIGH 30	SLP	SA/CR	FBG KL	SD	13D WEST	9 7	9100	4 7	55600	61100
29 8	LEIGH 30	CUT	SAIL	FBG KL	SD	13D WEST	9 7	9100	4 7	55600	61100
29 8	LEIGH 30	CUT	SAIL	FBG KL	SD	15D VLVO	9 2	9100	4 7	55600	61100
					1982 BOATS					
26	FRANCES 26	SLP	SAIL	FBG KL	IB	8D VLVO	8	6800	3 10	34100	37900
26	FRANCES 26	CUT	SAIL	FBG KL	IB	8D VLVO	8	6800	3 10	34100	37900
29 5	ANNIE	SLP	SA/CR	FBG KL	IB	13D WEST	9 6	11027	4 6	63600	69800
29 5	ANNIE	SLP	SAIL	FBG KL	IB	15D VLVO	9 4	11027	4 6	63500	69800
29 8	LEIGH 30	SLP	SA/CR	FBG KL	IB	13D WEST	9 2	9100	4 7	52300	57500
29 8	LEIGH 30	CUT	SAIL	FBG KL	IB	13D	9 2	9100	4 7	52300	57500
					1981 BOATS					
26	FRANCES 26	SLP	SAIL	FBG KL	IB	8D	8 2	6800	3 10	32100	35700
26	FRANCES 26	CUT	SAIL	FBG KL	IB	8D	8 2	6800	3 10	32100	35700
29 2	ANNIE	SLP	SAIL	FBG KL	IB	13D- 15D	9 4	10800	4 6	58200	64000
29 8	LEIGH 30	SLP	SA/CR	FBG KL	IB	13D- 15D	9 2	9100	4 7	49200	54100
29 8	LEIGH 30	CUT	SAIL	FBG KL	IB	13D- 15D	9 7	9100	4 7	49200	54100
					1980 BOATS					
26	FRANCES 26	SLP	SA/CR	FBG KL	IB	D	8 3	6800	3 10	30900	34300
26	FRANCES 26	CUT	SAIL	FBG KL	IB	D	8 2	6800	3 10	30900	34300
26	FRANCES 26	SLP	SAIL	FBG KL	IB	8D VLVO	8 2	6800	3 10	30600	34100
26	FRANCES 26	CUT	SAIL	FBG KL	IB	8D VLVO	8 2	6800	3 10	30600	34100
29 2	ANNIE	SLP	SAIL	FBG KL	IB	15D VLVO	9 4	10800	4 6	55100	61100
29 8	LEIGH 29	SLP	SA/CR	FBG KL	IB	D	9 7	9100	4 7	47300	52000
29 8	LEIGH 30	SLP	SA/CR	FBG KL	IB	D	9 7	9100	4 7	47300	52000
29 8	LEIGH 30	SLP	SAIL	FBG KL	IB	15D VLVO	9 2	9100	4 7	47200	51900
29 8	LEIGH 30	CUT	SAIL	FBG KL	IB	15D VLVO	9 2	9100	4 7	47200	51900

SAM L MORSE CO
COSTA MESA CA 92627   COAST GUARD MFG ID- SFJ See inside cover to adjust price for area

For more recent years, see the BUC Used Boat Price Guide, Volume 1 or Volume 2

LOA FT IN	NAME AND/ OR MODEL	TOP/ RIG	BOAT TYPE	-HULL- MTL TP	----ENGINE--- TP # HP MFG	BEAM FT IN	WGT LBS	DRAFT FT IN	RETAIL LOW	RETAIL HIGH
					1983 BOATS					
22	FALMOUTH CUTTER	CUT	SA/CR	FBG KL	IB	8D YAN	8	7400	3 6	32400	36000
28 1	BRISTOL-CHANNEL	CUT	SA/CR	FBG KL	IB	15D VLVO	10 1	14000	4 10	68900	75700
					1982 BOATS					
22	GALMOUTH	CUT	SA/CR	FBG KL	IB	7D YAN	8	7400	3 6	30900	34300
28 1	BRISTOL-CHANNEL	CUT	SA/CR	FBG KL	IB	13D VLVO	10 1	14000	4 10	65500	71900
					1981 BOATS					
22	FALMOUTH 22	CUT	SA/CR	FBG KL	IB	7D BMW	8	7400	3 6	29400	32600
28 1	BRISTOL-CHANNEL	CUT	SA/CR	FBG KL	IB	13D VLVO	10 1	14000	4 10	62300	68200
					1980 BOATS					
28 1	BRISTOL-CHANNEL	CUT	SA/CR	FBG KL	IB	13D VLVO	10 1	12300	4 10	51800	56900
30 6	FALMOUTH	CUT	SA/CR	FBG KL	IB	7D BMW	9 4	7400	3 10	28400	31600
37 6	BRISTOL-CHANNEL 37	CUT	SA/CR	FBG KL	IB	D	10 1	14000	4 10	53800	59100
37 9	BRISTOL-CHANNEL	CUT	SA/CR	FBG KL	IB	13D VLVO	10 1	14000	4 10	54000	59300

MORTON & HERSLOFF INC
COAST GUARD MFG ID- MHF

Call 1-800-327-6929 for BUC Personalized Evaluation Service
Or, for 1976 to 1980 boats, sign onto www.BUCValuPro.com

MOUNT DESERT YACHT YARDS INC

MOUNT DESERT ME   COAST GUARD MFG ID- MDY See inside cover to adjust price for area

LOA FT IN	NAME AND/ OR MODEL	TOP/ RIG	BOAT TYPE	HULL MTL	HULL TP	ENG TP	ENG #	ENG HP	ENG MFG	BEAM FT IN	WGT LBS	DRAFT FT IN	RETAIL LOW	RETAIL HIGH
1971 BOATS														
25 5	AMPHIBI-CON	SLP	SA/CR	FBG	KC					7 9	4400	2 5	8100	9350
25 5	AMPHIBI-CON	SLP	SA/CR	WD	KC					7 9	4400	2 5	8100	9350
25 6	AMPHIBI-CON	SLP	SA/OD	FBG	KC					7 9	4400	2 4	8150	9350
27 8	MOUNT-DESERT C/27	SLP	SA/CR	FBG	KC					7 11	4600	2 10	9100	10400
27 8	MOUNT-DESERT C/27	SLP	SA/CR	WD	KC					7 11	4600	2 10	9100	10400
28 5	CONTROVERSY 28	SLP	SA/CR	WD	KC					8 6	6000	3 4	11900	13600
37 1	CONTROVERSY 36	YWL	SA/CR	WD	KL					10 1	13000	5 6	32900	36500
1970 BOATS														
25 5	AMPHIBI-CON	SLP	SA/CR	FBG	KC					7 9	4400	2 5	7950	9150
25 5	AMPHIBI-CON	SLP	SA/CR	WD	KC					7 9	4400	2 5	7950	9150
27 8	MOUNT-DESERT C/27	SLP	SA/CR	FBG	KC					7 11	4600	2 10	8950	10200
27 8	MOUNT-DESERT C/27	SLP	SA/CR	WD	KC					7 11	4600	2 10	8950	10200
28 5	CONTROVERSY 28	SLP	SA/CR	WD	KC					8 6	6000	3 4	11700	13300
37 1	CONTROVERSY 36	YWL	SA/CR	WD	KL					10 1	13000	5 6	32300	35900
1969 BOATS														
25 5	AMPHIBI-CON	SLP	SA/CR	FBG	KC					7 9	4400	2 5	7850	9000
25 5	AMPHIBI-CON	SLP	SA/CR	WD	KC					7 9	4400	2 5	7850	9000
27 8	MOUNT-DESERT C27	SLP	SA/CR	FBG	KC					7 11	4600	2 10	8800	10000
27 8	MOUNT-DESERT C27	SLP	SA/CR	WD	KC					7 11	4600	2 10	8800	10000
28 5	CONTROVERSY 28	SLP	SA/CR	WD	KC					8 6	6000	3 4	11500	13100
37 1	CONTROVERSY 36	YWL	SA/CR	WD	KL					10 1	13000	5 6	31800	35300
1968 BOATS														
25 6	AMPHIBI-CON	SLP	SA/CR	FBG	KC					7 9	4400	2 4	7750	8900
25 6	AMPHIBI-CON	SLP	SA/CR	WD	KC					7 9	4400	2 4	7750	8900
27 8	MOUNT-DESERT 27	SLP	SAIL	FBG	KC					7 11	4600	2 11	8600	9850
27 8	MOUNT-DESERT 27	SLP	SAIL	WD	KC	OB				7 11	4600	2 11	9400	10700
27 8	MOUNT-DESERT 27	SLP	SAIL	WD	KC	IB				7 11	4600	2 11	9550	10900
28 5	CONTROVERSY 28	SLP	SAIL	WD	KC	IB				8 6	6000	3 4	12700	14400
37 1	CONTROVERSY 36	YWL	SAIL	WD	KL	IB				10 1	13000	5 6	30900	34400
1967 BOATS														
25 5	AMPHIBI-CON	SLP	SA/CR	WD	KC					7 9			7650	8800
25 7	AMPHIBI-CON	SLP	SA/OD	FBG	KC					7 9	4400	2 4	7700	8850
25 7	AMPHIBI-CON	SLP	SA/OD	WD	KC					7 9	4400	2 4	7700	8850
27 8	MOUNT-DESERT	SLP	SA/CR	FBG	CB	OB				7 11			10400	11800
27 8	MOUNT-DESERT	SLP	SA/CR	FBG	CB	IB				7 11			10400	11800
27 8	MOUNT-DESERT	SLP	SA/CR	FBG	KL	OB				7 11		2 11	10400	11800
27 8	MOUNT-DESERT	SLP	SA/CR	FBG	KL	IB				7 11		2 11	10900	12400
27 8	MOUNT-DESERT C/27	SLP	SA/CR	WD	CB	OB				7 11			10400	11800
27 8	MOUNT-DESERT C/27	SLP	SA/CR	WD	CB	IB				7 11			10900	12400
27 8	MOUNT-DESERT C/27	SLP	SA/CR	WD	KL	OB				7 11		2 11	10400	11800
27 8	MOUNT-DESERT C/27	SLP	SA/CR	WD	KL	IB				7 11		2 11	10900	12400
28 5	CONTROVERSY 28	SLP	SA/CR	WD	CB	OB				8 6		3 4	10600	12100
28 5	CONTROVERSY 28	SLP	SA/CR	WD	KL	OB				8 6		3 4	10600	12100
37 1	CONTROVERSY 36	YWL	SA/CR	WD	KL	OB				10 1		5 6	30300	33600
1966 BOATS														
24	AMPHIBI-ETTE	SLP	SA/CR	WD						7 9		2 4	7250	8350
25 5	AMPHIBI-CON	SLP	SA/OD	FBG	KC					7 9	4400	2 5	7550	8700
25 5	AMPHIBI-CON	SLP	SA/CR	WD	KC					7 9	4400	2 5	8100	9350
25 11	CONTROVERSY 26	SLP	SA/CR	WD	KC	OB				8 3		2 6	8100	9350
27 8	CONTROVERSY 27	SLP	SA/CR	WD	KC	OB				7 11		2 10	10300	11700
28 5	CONTROVERSY 28	SLP	SA/CR	WD	KC	OB				8 6	6000	3 4	12300	13900
37 1	CONTROVERSY 36	YWL	SA/CR	WD	KL	OB				10 1	13000	5 6	30000	33300
1965 BOATS														
25 5	AMPHIBI-CON	SLP	SAIL	FBG	KC	IB				7 9		2 5	7950	9150
27 8	CONTROVERSY 27	SLP	SAIL	WD	KC					7 11		2 10	9350	10600
1963 BOATS														
24	AMPHIBI-ETTE		SAIL	WD		OB							7150	8200
25 5	AMPHIBI-CON	SLP	SAIL	WD		OB							7800	8950
27 8	MOUNT-DESERT		SAIL	FBG		OB							10100	11500
27 8	MOUNT-DESERT		SAIL	WD		OB							10100	11500
28 5	CONTROVERSY 28		SAIL	WD		OB							10300	11800
37 1	CONTROVERSY 36		SAIL	WD		OB							29500	32800
1962 BOATS														
24	AMPHIBI-ETTE		SAIL	WD		OB							7150	8200
25 5	AMPHIBI-CON	SLP	SAIL	WD		OB							7750	8950
27 6	CONTROVERSY 27	SLP	SAIL	FBG		OB							10000	11400
27 6	CONTROVERSY 27	SLP	SAIL	WD		OB							10000	11400
28 5	CONTROVERSY 28	SLP	SAIL	WD		OB							10300	11700
37 1	CONTROVERSY	SLP	SAIL	WD		OB							29500	32700
1961 BOATS														
25 5	AMPHIBI-CON	SLP	SAIL	WD		OB							7750	8950
27 6	CONTROVERSY 27	SLP	SA/CR	FBG	KC	OB				7 11		2 10	10000	11400
27 6	CONTROVERSY 27	SLP	SA/CR	WD	KC	OB				7 11		2 10	10000	11400
28 5	CONTROVERSY	SLP	SA/CR	WD	KL	OB				8 6		3 4	10300	11700
37 2	CONTROVERSY	SLP	SA/CR	WD	KL	OB				10 1		5 4	29600	32800
37 2	CONTROVERSY	YWL	SA/CR	WD	KL	OB				10 1		5 4	29600	32800
1960 BOATS														
24	AMPHIBI-ETTE	SLP	SA/OD	CDR						7 9			7150	8250
24	AMPHIBI-ETTE	SLP	SA/OD	PLY						7 9			7150	8250
25 6	AMPHIBI-CON	SLP	SA/OD	CDR	KC					7 9		2 4	7450	8550
28 5	CONTROVERSY 28	SLP	SA/CR	CDR	CB	OB				8 6			10400	11800
28 5	CONTROVERSY 28	SLP	SA/CR	CDR	KL	OB				8 6		3 4	10400	11800
37 2	CONTROVERSY 36	CUT	SA/CR	CDR	KL	OB				10 1		5 4	29600	32900
37 2	CONTROVERSY 36	YWL	SA/CR	CDR	KL	OB				10 1		5 4	29600	32900
1959 BOATS														
24	AMPHIBI-ETTE	SLP	SAIL	PLY	KC					7 9			7150	8250
25 5	AMPHIBI-CON	SLP	SAIL	WD	KC					7 9			7450	8600
26	CONTROVERSY	SLP	SA/CR	CDR	KC					8 3			7600	8750
28 5	CONTROVERSY	SLP	SA/CR	CDR	KC					8 6			9450	10800
37 1	CONTROVERSY	SLP	SA/CR	WD	KL					10 1			30400	33800
1955 BOATS														
26	CONTROVERSY		SAIL	WD		IB		25	UNIV				10300	11700
1953 BOATS														
23	MERMAID	SLP	SAIL	WD	KL								5450	6250
26		SLP	SAIL	WD	KC					8 3		2 6	8050	9250
30		SLP	SAIL	WD	KL							5 3	12700	14400
37		YWL	SAIL	WD	KL								32100	35700
1951 BOATS														
31	CONTROVERSY		SAIL	WD		IB		16	GRAY				22500	25000
1949 BOATS														
23	MERMAID	SLP	SAIL	WD	KL								5800	6700
1946 BOATS														
35 2	MAINE-COAST	SLP	SAIL	WD	KL	IB				8	10000	5	27100	30100

MUELLER BOAT COMPANY
COAST GUARD MFG ID- JWM

Call 1-800-327-6929 for BUC Personalized Evaluation Service
Or, for 1970 to 1985 boats, sign onto www.BUCValuPro.com

MULTIHULL CRAFT
COAST GUARD MFG ID- MLT

Call 1-800-327-6929 for BUC Personalized Evaluation Service
Or, for 1967 boats, sign onto www.BUCValuPro.com

THE MULTIHULL EXPERIENCE INC
COAST GUARD MFG ID- MWR

Call 1-800-327-6929 for BUC Personalized Evaluation Service
Or, for 1980 to 1982 boats, sign onto www.BUCValuPro.com

MULTIHULL INDUSTRIES

Call 1-800-327-6929 for BUC Personalized Evaluation Service
Or, for 1967 boats, sign onto www.BUCValuPro.com

MURPHY BOAT WORKS
COAST GUARD MFG ID- MOF

Call 1-800-327-6929 for BUC Personalized Evaluation Service
Or, for 1983 to 1989 boats, sign onto www.BUCValuPro.com

MURRAY BOATS
COAST GUARD MFG ID- ZDZ

Call 1-800-327-6929 for BUC Personalized Evaluation Service
Or, for 1983 to 1985 boats, sign onto www.BUCValuPro.com

MUSTANG BOAT COMPANY
COAST GUARD MFG ID- MNG

Call 1-800-327-6929 for BUC Personalized Evaluation Service
Or, for 1966 to 1993 boats, sign onto www.BUCValuPro.com

MYSTIC YACHT DESIGN INC

Call 1-800-327-6929 for BUC Personalized Evaluation Service
Or, for 1977 boats, sign onto www.BUCValuPro.com

NACRA

NORTH AMERICAN CAT RACING ASC   See inside cover to adjust price for area
PERFORMANCE CATAMARANS INC
SANTA ANA CA 92705   COAST GUARD MFG ID- NAC

For more recent years, see the BUC Used Boat Price Guide, Volume 1 or Volume 2

LOA FT IN	NAME AND/ OR MODEL	TOP/ RIG	BOAT TYPE	-HULL- MTL TP	----ENGINE--- TP # HP MFG	BEAM FT IN	WGT LBS	DRAFT FT IN	RETAIL LOW	RETAIL HIGH
			--- 1983 BOATS							
16 8	INTERNATIONAL 5.0	SLP	SA/OD FBG CT		8		335	8	3100	3600
17	INTERNATIONAL 5.2	SLP	SA/OD FBG CT		8		350	4	3250	3800
18	INTERNATIONAL 5.5	CAT	SA/OD FBG CT		11		330	4	3750	3800
19	INTERNATIONAL 5.8	SLP	SA/OD FBG CT		8		410	6	4050	4700
			--- 1982 BOATS							
18	INTERNATIONAL 5.5	SLP	SA/OD FBG CT		11		325	6	3050	3550
18 3	SOL-CAT 18	SLP	SA/OD FBG CT		7 11		400	4	3600	4200
36	ROLAND 36	SLP	SA/RC FBG CT		20				56800	62400
			--- 1981 BOATS							
17	INTERNATIONAL 5.2	SLP	SA/OD FBG CT		8		350	4	2950	3400
18	INTERNATIONAL 5.5	SLP	SA/OD FBG CT		11		330	4	2950	3450
18 3	SOL-CAT 18	SLP	SA/OD FBG CT		7 11		330	4	3000	3500
			--- 1980 BOATS							
17	INTERNATIONAL 5.2	SLP	SA/OD FBG CT		7 11		350	4	2800	3300
18 3	SOL-CAT 18	SLP	SA/OD FBG CT		7 11		350	4	2950	3450
			--- 1979 BOATS							
17	INTERNATIONAL 5.2	SLP	SA/OD FBG CT		8		350	6	2700	3150
17	NACRA 18 SQ METER	CAT	SA/OD FBG CT		10			6	2600	3050
18	ALPHA-CAT	SLP	SA/OD FBG CT		10		380	6	2950	3450
			--- 1978 BOATS							
17	INTERNATIONAL 5.2	SLP	SA/OD FBG CT		8		350		2600	3000
17	NACRA 18 SQ METER	CAT	SA/OD FBG CT		10		350	6	2550	3000
18	ALPHA-CAT	SLP	SA/OD FBG CT		10		380	6	2850	3350
			--- 1977 BOATS							
17	5.2	SLP	SA/OD FBG CT		8		350	6	2500	2900
17	CENTARI 18 SQ METER	CAT	SA/OD FBG CT		10		350	6	2500	2950
18	ALPHA-CAT	SLP	SA/OD FBG CT		10		395	6	2900	3350
			--- 1976 BOATS							
17	5.2	SLP	SA/OD FBG CT		8		325	6	2350	2700
18	ALPHA-CAT	SLP	SA/OD FBG CT		10		385	6	2750	3200

N V FIBOCON

Call 1-800-327-6929 for BUC Personalized Evaluation Service
Or, for 1965 to 1967 boats, sign onto www.BUCValuPro.com

NADEN INDUSTRIES
COAST GUARD MFG ID- NAD

Call 1-800-327-6929 for BUC Personalized Evaluation Service
Or, for 1959 to 1973 boats, sign onto www.BUCValuPro.com

NARWHAL MARINE LTD

Call 1-800-327-6929 for BUC Personalized Evaluation Service
Or, for 1969 boats, sign onto www.BUCValuPro.com

NATIONAL BOAT CORP
COAST GUARD MFG ID- NBC

Call 1-800-327-6929 for BUC Personalized Evaluation Service
Or, for 1973 to 1974 boats, sign onto www.BUCValuPro.com

NATIONAL BOAT WORKS

Call 1-800-327-6929 for BUC Personalized Evaluation Service
Or, for 1970 boats, sign onto www.BUCValuPro.com

NATIONAL SAIL SHOP

Call 1-800-327-6929 for BUC Personalized Evaluation Service
Or, for 1966 to 1968 boats, sign onto www.BUCValuPro.com

NAUGUS FIBERGLASS IND

Call 1-800-327-6929 for BUC Personalized Evaluation Service
Or, for 1966 boats, sign onto www.BUCValuPro.com

NAUSET MARINE INC
ORLEANS MA 02653   COAST GUARD MFG ID- ACJ See inside cover to adjust price for area

For more recent years, see the BUC Used Boat Price Guide, Volume 1 or Volume 2

LOA FT IN	NAME AND/ OR MODEL	TOP/ RIG	BOAT TYPE	-HULL- MTL TP	----ENGINE--- TP # HP MFG	BEAM FT IN	WGT LBS	DRAFT FT IN	RETAIL LOW	RETAIL HIGH
			--- 1983 BOATS							
18	SEA-OTTER	OP	CTRCN FBG SV IO	120 MRCR	7 10	1800	1	4700	5400	
18 2	NAUSET AMERICA II	GAF	SA/CR FBG CB OB		8	2500	1 10	6100	7050	
18 2	NAUSET AMERICA II	GAF	SA/CR FBG CB SD	OMC	8	2500	1 10	6850	7850	
18 2	NAUSET AMERICA II	GAF	SA/CR FBG CB IB	7D YAN	8	2500	1 10	8600	9900	
18 2	NAUSET BAY FISH	OP	FSH FBG DS IB	15D YAN	8	2100	1 10	7250	8350	
18 2	NAUSET BAY FISH	OP	FSH FBG DS IB	35D- 45D	8	2100	1 10	7900	9350	
18 2	NAUSET HBR PILOT	HT	PH FBG DS IB	15D- 35D	8	2200	1 10	7400	9250	
18 2	NAUSET HBR PILOT	HT	PH FBG DS IB	45D BMW	8	2200	1 10	8300	9550	
20 2	NAUSET 20	OP	CUD FBG SV OB		8	2200	1	6450	7450	
24	DOWNEASTER	GAF	SA/OD FBG CB OB		8	2500	1 10	7450	8600	
24	NAUSET 24	ST	CUD FBG SV OB		9 6	4000	2	12400	14100	
24	NAUSET 24	ST	CUD FBG SV IO	120 MRCR	9 6	4000	2	11300	12800	
24	NAUSET 24	ST	CUD FBG SV IB	170 MRCR	9 6	400	2	15300	17400	
24	NAUSET 24	ST	CUD FBG SV IB	124D VLVO	9 6	4000	2	18600	20700	
24	NAUSET 24	HT	CUD FBG SV IB	170 MRCR	9 6	4200	2	16400	16400	
27 6	NAUSET 27	HT	CBNCR FBG DS IB	230 MRCR	9 10	7000	3	28100	31200	
27 6	NAUSET 27	HT	CBNCR FBG DS IB	124D VLVO	9 10	7000	3	35100	39000	
27 6	NAUSET 27	FB	CBNCR FBG DS IB	230-260	11 8	7300	3 6	29400	33400	
27 6	NAUSET 27	ST	FSH FBG DS IB	170 MRCR	9 10	7000	3	23500	26100	
			--- 1980 BOATS							
21	NAUSET 21CC		CTRCN FBG DS IB	120	7 4	2000		6000	6850	
21	NAUSET 21CC		CTRCN FBG DS IB	50D	7 4	2000		8900	10100	
27	NAUSET 27 COMMERCIAL		FSH FBG DS IB	198	9 10	6500		19700	21800	
27	NAUSET 27 COMMERCIAL		FSH FBG DS IB	130D	9 10	6500		24500	27200	
27	NAUSET 27 FAMILY FSH		FSH FBG DS IB	170	9 10	6000		18600	20700	
27	NAUSET 27 FAMILY FSH		FSH FBG DS IB	85D	9 10	6000		21000	23300	
27	NAUSET 27CC		CTRCN FBG DS IB	170	9 10	5000		16500	18700	
27	NAUSET 27CC		CTRCN FBG DS IB	85D	9 10	5000		16900	19200	
27	NAUSET 27SF		SF FBG DS IB	198	9 10	6500		19600	21800	
27	NAUSET 27SF		SF FBG DS IB	130D	9 10	6500		24500	27200	
			--- 1979 BOATS							
21	NAUSET	OP	CTRCN FBG DS OB		7 4	1100		3600	4200	
21	NAUSET	OP	CTRCN FBG DS IB	120	7 4	2000		5750	6600	
21	NAUSET	OP	CTRCN FBG DS IB	50D- 80D	7 4	2000		9050	10400	
27 6	NAUSET	HT	FSH FBG DS IB	198-330	9 10		3	24500	28700	
27 6	NAUSET	HT	FSH FBG DS IB	85D-160D	9 10		3	23100	28400	
27 6	NAUSET	HT	FSH FBG DS IB	185D-220D	9 10		3	26300	30400	

NAUTA CRAFT INC
NAUTA-LINE HOUSEBOATS   See inside cover to adjust price for area
LEXINGTON AL 35648   COAST GUARD MFG ID- NTA

LOA FT IN	NAME AND/ OR MODEL	TOP/ RIG	BOAT TYPE	-HULL- MTL TP	----ENGINE--- TP # HP MFG	BEAM FT IN	WGT LBS	DRAFT FT IN	RETAIL LOW	RETAIL HIGH
			--- 1980 BOATS							
43	NAUTA-LINE	HT	HB FBG SV VD	T255 PCM	14	22000	2 5	29800	33100	
	VD T270 CRUS 30300		33700, VD T350	CRUS 31600	35100, VD T355	PCM		31100	34500	
43	NAUTA-LINE	FB	HB FBG SV VD	T255 PCM	14	22000	2 5	29800	33100	
	VD T270 CRUS 30300		33700, VD T350	CRUS 31600	35100, VD T355	PCM		31100	34500	
48	NAUTA-LINE	FB	HB FBG SV VD	T350 CRUS	14	25000	2 6	37900	42100	
48	NAUTA-LINE	FB	HB FBG SV VD	T350 INT	14	25000	2 6	37300	41400	
48	NAUTA-LINE	FB	HB FBG SV VD	T355 PCM	14	25000	2 6	37400	41500	
			--- 1979 BOATS							
43	NAUTA-LINE	HT	HB FBG SV VD	T255 PCM	14	22000	2 5	29300	32500	
	VD T270 CRUS 29800		33100, VD T350	CRUS 31100	34500, VD T355	PCM		30600	34000	

```
LOA  NAME AND/        TOP/ BOAT -HULL-  ----ENGINE--- BEAM   WGT  DRAFT RETAIL RETAIL
FT IN  OR MODEL        RIG TYPE MTL TP TP # HP  MFG  FT IN  LBS  FT IN  LOW   HIGH
-------------------- 1979 BOATS -------------------------------------------------
43  NAUTA-LINE          FB  HB  FBG SV VD T255  PCM  14     22000  2  5 29300 32500
    VD T270 CRUS 29800 33100, VD T350 CRUS 31100 34500, VD T355 PCM 30600 34000

48  NAUTA-LINE          FB  HB  FBG SV VD T350  CRUS 14     25000  2  6 37400 41600
48  NAUTA-LINE          FB  HB  FBG SV VD T350  INT  14     25000  2  6 36800 40900
48  NAUTA-LINE          FB  HB  FBG SV VD T355  PCM  14     25000  2  6 36900 41000
-------------------- 1978 BOATS -------------------------------------------------
43  NAUTA-LINE          FB  HB  FBG SV IB T255       13 11 17000  1 10 25200 28000
-------------------- 1977 BOATS -------------------------------------------------
43  NAUTA-LINE          FB  HB  FBG SV VD T215  PCM  13  6 17000  1 10 24800 27600
    VD T250 CC   25000 27700, VD T255 MRCR  25000 27800, VD T255 PCM 25000 27800
    VD T270 PALM 25100 27900, VD T330 CHRY  25600 28400
-------------------- 1976 BOATS -------------------------------------------------
38  NAUTA-LINE          HT  HB  FBG SV IO  255   MRCR 11 10 15000  1  9 23900 26600
38  NAUTA-LINE          HT  HB  FBG SV VD T225   MRCR 11 10 15000  1  9 26100 29000
38  NAUTA-LINE          HT  HB  FBG SV VD T230   OMC  11 10 15000  1  9 26900 29900
38  NAUTA-LINE          FB  HB  FBG SV VD T225   MRCR 11 10 15000  1  9 26100 29000
38  NAUTA-LINE          FB  HB  FBG SV VD T230   OMC  11 10 15000  1  9 26900 29900
43  NAUTA-LINE          HT  HB  FBG SV VD T225   MRCR 14    17000  1 10 24600 27300
    VD T230 OMC  25300 28100, IO T255 MRCR  25800 28600, VD T260 OMC 25500 28300

43  NAUTA-LINE          FB  HB  FBG SV VD T225   MRCR 14    17000  1 10 24600 27300
    VD T230 OMC  25300 28100, IO T255 MRCR  25800 28600, VD T260 OMC 25500 28300

48  NAUTA-LINE          HT  HB  FBG SV VD T255   MRCR 13 11 21000  2  8 31900 35400
48  NAUTA-LINE          HT  HB  FBG SV VD T260   OMC  13 11 21000  2  8 32700 36300
48  NAUTA-LINE          HT  HB  FBG SV VD T350   MRCR 13 11 21000  2  8 33100 36800
48  NAUTA-LINE          FB  HB  FBG SV VD T255   MRCR 13 11 21000  2  8 31900 35400
48  NAUTA-LINE          FB  HB  FBG SV VD T260   OMC  13 11 21000  2  8 32700 36300
48  NAUTA-LINE          FB  HB  FBG SV VD T350   MRCR 13 11 21000  2  8 33100 36800
-------------------- 1975 BOATS -------------------------------------------------
38  NAUTA-LINE          HT  HB  FBG SV IO T225   MRCR 11 10 15000  1  9 23400 26000
    IO T225 MRCR 25200 28000, VD T225 MRCR  25800 28600, VD T230 OMC 26600 29600

38  NAUTA-LINE          FB  HB  FBG SV IO T225   MRCR       15000        25200 28000
38  NAUTA-LINE          FB  HB  FBG SV IO T225   MRCR       15000        25800 28600
38  NAUTA-LINE          FB  HB  FBG SV IO T230   OMC        15000        26600 29600
43  NAUTA-LINE          HT  HB  FBG SV IO T225   MRCR 14    17000  1 10 25000 27800
    VD T225 MRCR 24300 27000, VD T230 OMC   25000 27800, IO T255 MRCR 25500 28300
    VD T255 MRCR 24400 27100, VD T260 OMC   25200 27900

43  NAUTA-LINE          FB  HB  FBG SV IO T225   MRCR 14    17000  1 10 25000 27800
    VD T225 MRCR 24300 27000, VD T230 OMC   25000 27800, IO T255 MRCR 25500 28300
    VD T255 MRCR 24400 27100, VD T260 OMC   25200 27900

48  NAUTA-LINE          HT  HB  FBG SV VD T225   MRCR 13 11 21000  2  8 31400 34900
48  NAUTA-LINE          HT  HB  FBG SV VD T260   OMC  13 11 21000  2  8 32400 36000
48  NAUTA-LINE          HT  HB  FBG SV VD T350   MRCR 13 11 21000  2  8 32700 36400
48  NAUTA-LINE          FB  HB  FBG SV VD T255   MRCR 13 11 21000  2  8 31500 35000
48  NAUTA-LINE          FB  HB  FBG SV VD T260   OMC  13 11 21000  2  8 32400 36000
48  NAUTA-LINE          FB  HB  FBG SV VD T350   MRCR 13 11 21000  2  8 32700 36400
-------------------- 1974 BOATS -------------------------------------------------
34  NAUTA-LINE          HT  HB  FBG    IO 215-255     11 10 14000  1  9 25900 29200
34  NAUTA-LINE          HT  HB  FBG    IO T225        11 10 15000  1  9 28600 31800
34  NAUTA-LINE          FB  HB  FBG    IO 215-255     11 10 14300  1  9 26200 30400
34  NAUTA-LINE          FB  HB  FBG    IO T225-T255   11 10 15300  1  9 28900 32700
43  NAUTA-LINE          HT  HB  FBG    IO T215  WAUK  13 11 18500  1 10 27100 30100
    IO T225 CHRY 27200 30300, IO T225 MRCR  27200 30000, VD T225 CHRY 26300 29200
    VD T225 MRCR 26500 29400, IO T255 WAUK  27800 30800, IO T255 MRCR 27800 30800
    VD T255 MRCR 26600 29600

43  NAUTA-LINE          FB  HB  FBG    IO T215  WAUK  13 11 18800  1 10 27300 30400
    IO T225 CHRY 27500 30500, IO T225 MRCR  27500 30000, VD T225 CHRY 26500 29500
    VD T225 MRCR 26700 29700, IO T255 WAUK  28000 31100, IO T255 MRCR 28000 31100
    VD T255 MRCR 26800 29800

48  NAUTA-LINE          HT  HB  FBG    VD T255  MRCR  13 11 20500  2    30900 34400
    VD T355 WAUK 30900 34400, VD T325 MRCR  31700 35200, VD T330 CHRY 31500 35000
    VD T355 WAUK 32200 35800

48  NAUTA-LINE          FB  HB  FBG    VD T255  MRCR  13 11 20800  2    31100 34600
    VD T255 WAUK 31100 34600, VD T325 MRCR  31900 35400, VD T330 CHRY 31700 35200
    VD T355 WAUK 32400 36000
-------------------- 1973 BOATS -------------------------------------------------
34  NAUTA-LINE          HT  HB  FBG    IO 215-255     11 10 14000  1  9 25700 28900
34  NAUTA-LINE          HT  HB  FBG    IO T170-T255   11 10 15000  1  9 28600 32100
34  NAUTA-LINE          FB  HB  FBG    IO 215-225     11 10 14300  1  9 26000 28900
34  NAUTA-LINE          FB  HB  FBG    IO T170-T255   11 10 15300  1  9 28900 32400
43  NAUTA-LINE          HT  HB  FBG    IO T215  WAUK  13 11 18500  1 10 26800 29800
    VD T215 WAUK 26200 29100, IO T225 CHRY  27000 30000, IO T225 MRCR 27000 30000
    VD T225 CHRY 26000 28900, VD T225 MRCR  26200 29100, IO T255 MRCR 27500 30500
    IO T255 WAUK 27500 30500, VD T255 WAUK  26300 29300

43  NAUTA-LINE          FB  HB  FBG    IO T215  WAUK  13 11 18800  1 10 27100 30100
    VD T215 WAUK 26400 29300, IO T225 CHRY  27200 30200, IO T225 MRCR 27200 30000
    VD T225 MRCR 26400 29400, IO T255 MRCR  27700 30800, IO T255 WAUK 27700 30800
    VD T255 MRCR 26500 29500

48  NAUTA-LINE          HT  HB  FBG    VD T255  WAUK  13 11 20500  2    30600 34000
48  NAUTA-LINE          HT  HB  FBG    VD T325  MRCR  13 11 20500  2    31400 34900
48  NAUTA-LINE          HT  HB  FBG    VD T330  CHRY  13 11 20500  2    31200 34700
48  NAUTA-LINE          FB  HB  FBG    VD T255  WAUK  13 11 20800  2    30800 34300
48  NAUTA-LINE          FB  HB  FBG    VD T325  MRCR  13 11 20800  2    31600 35100
48  NAUTA-LINE          FB  HB  FBG    VD T330  CHRY  13 11 20800  2    31400 34900
-------------------- 1972 BOATS -------------------------------------------------
28 9 NAUTA-LINE         HT  HB  FBG    IO 170-225     11 10  7000  1  5   **    **
34  NAUTA-LINE          HT  HB  FBG    IO 215-270     11 10 12000  1  9 23400 26600
34  NAUTA-LINE          HT  HB  FBG    IO 160D  PERK  11 10 12000  1  9 27500 30600
34  NAUTA-LINE          HT  HB  FBG    IO T170  VLVO  11 10 12000  1  9 25600 28400
34  NAUTA-LINE          FB  HB  FBG    IO 215-270     11 10 12000  1  9 23400 26600
34  NAUTA-LINE          FB  HB  FBG    IO 160D  PERK  11 10 12000  1  9 26900 30100
34  NAUTA-LINE          FB  HB  FBG    IO T170  VLVO  11 10 12000  1  9 25600 28400
43  NAUTA-LINE          HT  HB  FBG    IO T215  MRCR  13 11 18000  1 10 26200 29100
    VD T215 MRCR 25600 28400, IO T225 CHRY  26300 29400, IO T255 CHRY 25400 28300
    IO T270 MRCR 27200 30200, IO T160D PERK 31900 35400

43  NAUTA-LINE          FB  HB  FBG    IO T215  MRCR  13 11 18000  1 10 26200 29100
    VD T215 MRCR 25600 28400, IO T225 CHRY  26300 29300, VD T225 CHRY 25400 28300
    IO T270 MRCR 27200 30200, IO T160D PERK 31900 35400
-------------------- 1971 BOATS -------------------------------------------------
28 9 NAUTA-LINE         HT  HB  FBG    IO 170-225     11 10  7000  1  5   **    **
28 9 NAUTA-LINE         HT  HB  FBG    IO T130  VLVO  11 10  7000  1  5   **    **
34  NAUTA-LINE          HT  HB  FBG    IO 215-270     11 10 12000  1  9 23200 26400
34  NAUTA-LINE          HT  HB  FBG    IO T170-T225   11 10 12000  1  9 24600 28200
43  NAUTA-LINE          HT  HB  FBG    IO T215  MRCR  14    18000  1 10 26000 28900
    IO T225 CHRY 26100 29000, IB T225 CHRY  25000 27800, IO T270 MRCR 27000 29900
    IB T160D PERK 31200 34600

43  NAUTA-LINE          FB  HB  FBG    IO T215  MRCR  14    18000  1 10 26000 28900
    IO T225 CHRY 26100 29000, IB T225 CHRY  25000 27800, IO T270 MRCR 27000 29900
    IB T160D PERK 31200 34600
-------------------- 1970 BOATS -------------------------------------------------
28 9 NAUTA-LINE         HT  HB  FBG SV IO 130        11 11  9500  1  8   **    **
34  NAUTA-LINE          HT  HB  FBG SV IB 225   CHRY 12    10500  1  3 20500 22800
43  NAUTA-LINE          HT  HB  FBG SV IB T225  CHRY 14    14000  2  9 20600 22800
-------------------- 1969 BOATS -------------------------------------------------
34  NAUTA-LINE          HT  HB  FBG    IO 225         8 10  8500  1  3 18600 20700
43  NAUTA-LINE          HT  HB  FBG SV IB 225   CHRY 12    10500  1  3 20500 22800
43  NAUTA-LINE          HT  HB  FBG    IO 225   CHRY 12  6 12000  2  9 20300 22600
43  NAUTA-LINE          HT  HB  FBG SV IB T225  CHRY 14    14000  2  9 20400 22700
-------------------- 1968 BOATS -------------------------------------------------
33  NAUTA-LINE          HT  HB  FBG    IO 210          8500       9    18400 20400
43  NAUTA-LINE          HT  HB  FBG    IO 210         12000  2  3 20400 22600
-------------------- 1967 BOATS -------------------------------------------------
32  NAUTA-LINE          HT  HB  FBG    IO 210-260    8 10  8000      9 17300 20200
-------------------- 1966 BOATS -------------------------------------------------
32  NAUTA-LINE          HT  HB  FBG    IO 210   CHRY 11    10000  1  2 20400 22600
```

NAUTICA CORPORATION
COAST GUARD MFG ID- NTC

Call 1-800-327-6929 for BUC Personalized Evaluation Service
Or, for 1959 to 1975 boats, sign onto www.BUCValuPro.com

NAUTICAL BOATS LTD

VIRGINIA BEACH VA COAST GUARD MFG ID- NBW See inside cover to adjust price for area

LOA FT	LOA IN	NAME AND/ OR MODEL	TOP/ RIG	BOAT TYPE	HULL MTL	HULL TP	ENGINE TP	#	HP	MFG	BEAM FT	BEAM IN	WGT LBS	DRAFT FT	DRAFT IN	RETAIL LOW	RETAIL HIGH
		1974 BOATS															
17		KIT-KAT CT-12	SLP	SAIL	FBG	CB					7	11	250			1850	2200
20	6	GLOUCESTER	OP	FSH	FBG		OB				8		1800		10	3250	3800
		1973 BOATS															
16	6	INTERNATIONAL-505	SLP	SA/OD	FBG	CB	OB				6		280	3	9	1850	2200
20	6	GLOUCESTER		FSH	FBG		OB				8		1800		10	3250	3750
		1972 BOATS															
16	6	INTERNATIONAL-505	SLP	SA/OD	FBG	CB	OB				6		280			1800	2150
17		MOBJACK	SLP	SA/OD	FBG	CB					6	6	400		9	2200	2550
20	6	GLOUCESTER		FSH	FBG		OB				8		1800		10	3250	3750
		1971 BOATS															
16	6	INTERNATIONAL-505	SLP	SA/OD	FBG	CB	OB				6		280			1750	2100
20	7	GLOUCESTER	OP	FSH	FBG	SV	OB				8		1600		8	2950	3450

NAUTICAL DEVELOPMENT CORP

LARGO FL 33541 COAST GUARD MFG ID- NDV See inside cover to adjust price for area

For more recent years, see the BUC Used Boat Price Guide, Volume 1 or Volume 2

LOA FT	LOA IN	NAME AND/ OR MODEL	TOP/ RIG	BOAT TYPE	HULL MTL	HULL TP	ENGINE TP	#	HP	MFG	BEAM FT	BEAM IN	WGT LBS	DRAFT FT	DRAFT IN	RETAIL LOW	RETAIL HIGH
		1983 BOATS															
55	9	NAUTICAL 56	KTH	SA/CR	FBG	KL	IB		120D	LEHM	15	7	50000	5	6	228500	251500
59	6	NAUTICAL 60	KTH	SA/CR	FBG	KL	IB		120D	LEHM	15	7	52000	5	6	284500	312500
61	9	NAUTICAL 62	KTH	SA/CR	FBG	KL	IB		120D	LEHM	15	7	63000	5	10	327000	359000
		1982 BOATS															
39		NAUTICAL 39	SLP	SA/CR	FBG	KL	IB		50D	UNIV	12		22500	5	4	74800	82200
55	9	NAUTICAL 56	KTH	SA/CR	FBG	KL	IB		120D	LEHM	15	7	50000	5	6	217000	238500
59	6	NAUTICAL 60	KTH	SA/CR	FBG	KL	IB		120D	LEHM	15	7	52000	5	6	269500	296000
		1981 BOATS															
38	9	CORTEZ 39	KTH	SA/CR	FBG	KL	IB		D		12		22000	5	4	69100	75900
55	9	CUSTOM 56	KTH	SA/CR	FBG	KL	IB		D		15	9	50000	5	6	205500	226000
		1980 BOATS															
55	9	STEVENS 56	KTH	SA/CR	FBG	KL	IB		D		15	7	50000	5	6	197500	217000

NAUTICAT YACHTS

RIIHIKOSKI FINLAND FIN- COAST GUARD MFG ID- SLT See inside cover to adjust price for area
ALSO SILTALA YACHTS

For more recent years, see the BUC Used Boat Price Guide, Volume 1 or Volume 2

LOA FT	LOA IN	NAME AND/ OR MODEL	TOP/ RIG	BOAT TYPE	HULL MTL	HULL TP	ENGINE TP	#	HP	MFG	BEAM FT	BEAM IN	WGT LBS	DRAFT FT	DRAFT IN	RETAIL LOW	RETAIL HIGH
		1983 BOATS															
33		NAUTICAT 33	KTH	SAIL	FBG	KL	IB		80D	FORD	10	8	15200	5	8	65500	72000
38		NAUTICAT 38	KTH	SAIL	FBG	KL	IB		80D	FORD	11	2	24000	5	11	104500	115000
44		NAUTICAT 44	KTH	SAIL	FBG	KL	IB		120D	FORD	12	1	39700	6		170500	187500
52		NAUTICAT 52	KTH	SAIL	FBG	KL	IB		120D	FORD	15		54000	7	2	262500	288500
52		NAUTICAT 52	KTH	SAIL	FBG	KL	IB	T	80D	FORD	15		54000	7	2	265500	291500
		1982 BOATS															
33	1	NAUTICAT 33	KTH	MS	FBG	KL	IB		D		10	8	16500	4	1	66900	73500
37	5	NAUTICAT 38	KTH	MS	FBG	KL	IB		D		11	1	24200	5	10	97900	107500
43	7	NAUTICAT 44	SCH	MS	FBG	KL	IB		D		12	1	39600	6		158500	174500
43	7	NAUTICAT 44	KTH	MS	FBG	KL	IB		D		12	1	39600	6		158500	174500
51	3	NAUTICAT 52	KTH	MS	FBG	KL	IB	T	D		15	1	52000	7	3	241000	265000
		1981 BOATS															
33	1	NAUTICAT 33	KTH	MS	FBG	KL	IB		D		10	8	15000	4	1	58000	63700
37	5	NAUTICAT 38	KTH	MS	FBG	KL	IB		D		11	1	22000	5	10	86000	94500
43	7	NAUTICAT 44	SCH	MS	FBG	KL	IB		D		12	1	36000	6		143000	157000
43	7	NAUTICAT 44	KTH	MS	FBG	KL	IB		D		12	1	36000	6		143000	157000
43	7	NAUTICAT 44	SCH	SA/CR	FBG	KL	IB		D		12	1	39600	6		150500	165500
		1980 BOATS															
32	10	NAUTI-CAT 33	KTH	SA/CR	FBG	KL	IB		D		10	8	14000	4	1	52200	57300
37	9	NAUTI-CAT 38	KTH	SA/CR	FBG	KL	IB		D		11	3	24200	5	3	90000	98900
43	7	NAUTI-CAT 44	SCH	SA/CR	FBG	KL	IB		D		12	1	29600	6		124000	136000
43	7	NAUTI-CAT 44	KTH	SA/CR	FBG	KL	IB		D		12	1	29600	6		124000	136000
		1979 BOATS															
32	10	NAUTI-CAT 33	KTH	MS	FBG	KL	IB		80D	FORD	10	8	15500		1	55800	61300
37	6	NAUTI-CAT 38	KTH	MS	FBG	KL	IB		80D	FORD	11	3	24000	5	7	86500	95100
43	7	NAUTI-CAT 44	SCH	MS	FBG	KL	IB		120D	FORD	12	1	40000	6		141500	155500
43	7	NAUTI-CAT 44	KTH	MS	FBG	KL	IB		120D	FORD	12	1	40000	6		141500	155500
		1977 BOATS															
33	2	NAUTI-CAT 33	KTH	MS	FBG	KL	IB		80D	FORD	10	9	15500	4	2	52800	58100
37	6	NAUTI-CAT 38	KTH	MS	FBG	KL	IB		80D	FORD	11	2	24000	5	3	81800	89900
43	8	NAUTI-CAT 44	KTH	MS	FBG	KL	IB		115D	FORD	12	2	30000	5	3	115500	127000
		1976 BOATS															
33		NAUTI-CAT	KTH	MS	FBG	KL	IB		80D	FORD	10	6	16000	4	6	53100	58300
38		NAUTI-CAT	KTH	MS	FBG	KL	IB		80D	PERK	11	2	22500	5	2	76500	84100
44		NAUTI-CAT	KTH	MS	FBG	KL	IB		106D	VLVO	12	2	40000	5	2	132000	145000

NAUTILUS BOAT WORKS

Call 1-800-327-6929 for BUC Personalized Evaluation Service
Or, for 1959 boats, sign onto www.BUCValuPro.com

NAUTOR AB

PIETARSAARI FINLAND FIN COAST GUARD MFG ID- NAJ See inside cover to adjust price for area

NAUTOR AB
PIETARSAARI FINDLAND 68601

For more recent years, see the BUC Used Boat Price Guide, Volume 1 or Volume 2

LOA FT	LOA IN	NAME AND/ OR MODEL	TOP/ RIG	BOAT TYPE	HULL MTL	HULL TP	ENGINE TP	#	HP	MFG	BEAM FT	BEAM IN	WGT LBS	DRAFT FT	DRAFT IN	RETAIL LOW	RETAIL HIGH
		1983 BOATS															
36	8	SWAN 371	SLP	SA/RC	FBG	KL	IB		20D	BUKH	11	3	13700	6	6	82800	91000
39	10	SWAN 391	SLP	SA/CR	FBG	KL	IB		50D	PERK	12	5	18000	7	2	118000	130000
41	10	SWAN 42	SLP	SA/RC	FBG	KL	IB		40D	PERK	13		22000	7	9	144000	158000
47	1	SWAN 46	SLP	SA/RC	FBG	KC	IB		D		14	4		9	5	213000	234000
47	9	SWAN 47	SLP	SA/RC	FBG	KC	SD		61D	VLVO	13	9	34100	5	9	225000	247500
51	3	SWAN 51	SLP	SA/RC	FBG	KC	IB		85D	PERK	14	7	39600			281000	308500
57	5	SWAN 57	SLP	SA/RC	FBG	KL	IB		73D	PERK	15	9	47600	9	1	449000	493500
64	6	SWAN 65	SLP	SA/RC	FBG	KL	IB		124D	VLVO	16	4	70000	9	6	630500	693000
65	6	SWAN 651	KTH	SA/RC	FBG	KC	IB		135D	PERK	17	5	75000	11	5	683000	750500
76	3	SWAN 76	KTH	SA/RC	FBG	KC	IB		200D	BENZ	19		50T	7		**	**
		1982 BOATS															
36	8	SWAN 371	SLP	SA/RC	FBG	KL	IB		D		11	3	13700	6	6	78600	86400
36	8	SWAN 371	SLP	SA/RC	FBG	KL	IB		20D	BUKH	11	3	13700	6	6	78500	86300
39	1	NAUTOR 39	KTH	SA/CR	FBG	KL	IB		D		12	9	22000	5	4	125000	137500
39	4	SWAN 39	SLP	SA/RC	FBG	KL	IB		D		12	6	17600	7	4	107500	118500
39	9	SWAN 391	SLP	SA/CR	FBG	KL	IB		D		12	5	18000	7	2	112000	123000
39	10	SWAN 391	SLP	SA/CR	FBG	KL	IB		40D		12	5	18000	7	2	112500	123500
41	9	SWAN 42	SLP	SA/CR	FBG	KL	IB		D		13		20900	7	9	132500	146000
41	10	SWAN 42	SLP	SA/RC	FBG	KL	IB		40D	PERK	13		22000	7	9	136000	149500
42	9	NAUTOR 43	KTH	SA/CR	FBG	KL	IB		D		13	9	32500	5	9	177500	195000
44	5	SWAN 441	SLP	SA/RC	FBG	KL	IB		D		13	5	24000	8		160500	176000
44	5	SWAN 441	SLP	SA/RC	FBG	KL	IB		40D	PERK	13	5	24000	8		159000	174500
47	9	NYYC 48	SLP	SA/RC	FBG	CB	IB		D		13	9	33400			212000	233000
47	9	SWAN 47	SLP	SA/RC	FBG	KC	IB		61D	VLVO	13	9	34100	5	9	213500	234500
47	9	SWAN 47	SLP	SA/RC	FBG	KL	IB		D		13	9	32400	7	9	209500	230500
47	9	SWAN 47	SLP	SA/RC	FBG	KL	IB		61D	VLVO	13	9	32400	7	9	209500	230000
49	9	NAUTOR 50	KTH	SA/CR	FBG	KL	IB		D		15		51000	5	7	268000	294500
51		SWAN 51	SLP	SA/CR	FBG	KL	IB		D		14	5	38600	8	9	262000	287500
51	3	SWAN 51	SLP	SA/RC	FBG	KC	IB		73D		14	7	39600			266500	293000
51	3	SWAN 51	SLP	SA/RC	FBG	KL	IB		73D		14	7	39600	8	9	266500	293000
57	5	SWAN 57	SLP	SA/RC	FBG	KC	IB		D		15	9	47600	9	1	428000	470000
57	5	SWAN 57	SLP	SA/RC	FBG	KC	IB		73D	PERK	15	9	51500	6	4	439000	482500
57	5	SWAN 57	SLP	SA/RC	FBG	KL	IB		73D	PERK	15	9	47600	9	1	425500	467500
57	5	SWAN 57	KTH	SA/RC	FBG	KC	IB		D		15	9	47600	9	1	428000	470000
57	5	SWAN 57	KTH	SA/RC	FBG	KC	IB		73D	PERK	15	9	51500	6	4	439000	482500
57	5	SWAN 57	KTH	SA/RC	FBG	KL	IB		73D	PERK	15	9	47600	9	1	425500	467500
64	6	SWAN 65	KTH	SA/RC	FBG	KL	IB		D		16	4	70000	9	6	598000	657500
65	5	SWAN 651	SLP	SA/CR	FBG	KL	IB		D		17	4	75000	11	5	648500	713000
65	5	SWAN 651	KTH	SA/CR	FBG	KL	IB		D		17	4	75000	11	5	648500	713000
65	6	SWAN 651		SA/RC	FBG	KC	IB		115D		17	5	75000	11	5	648000	712000
65	6	SWAN 651	SLP	SA/RC	FBG	KC	IB		115D		17	5	75000	11	5	648000	712000
65	6	SWAN 651	SLP	SA/RC	FBG	KL	IB		115D		17	5	75000	11	5	648000	712000
65	6	SWAN 651	KTH	SA/RC	FBG	KC	IB		115D		17	5	75000	11	5	648000	712000
65	6	SWAN 651	KTH	SA/RC	FBG	KL	IB		115D		17	5	75000	11	5	648000	712000
76	3	SWAN 76	SLP	SA/RC	FBG	KC	IB		D		19		50T	15	5	**	**
76	3	SWAN 76	SLP	SA/RC	FBG	KC	IB		200D	BENZ	19		50T	7		**	**
76	3	SWAN 76	SLP	SA/RC	FBG	KL	IB		200D	BENZ	19		50T	12		**	**
76	3	SWAN 76	KTH	SA/RC	FBG	KC	IB		D		19		50T			**	**
76	3	SWAN 76	KTH	SA/RC	FBG	KC	IB		D		19		50T	15	5	**	**
76	3	SWAN 76	KTH	SA/RC	FBG	KC	IB		200D	BENZ	19		50T	7		**	**
76	3	SWAN 76	KTH	SA/RC	FBG	KL	IB		200D	BENZ	19		50T	12		**	**

CONTINUED ON NEXT PAGE

LOA FT	LOA IN	NAME AND/ OR MODEL	TOP/ RIG	BOAT TYPE	HULL MTL	HULL TP	ENGINE TP	# HP	MFG	BEAM FT	BEAM IN	WGT LBS	DRAFT FT	DRAFT IN	RETAIL LOW	RETAIL HIGH
1981 BOATS																
36	8	SWAN 371	SLP	SA/RC	FBG	KL	IB	D		11	3	13700	6	6	74500	81900
39	1	NAUTOR 39	KTH	SA/CR	FBG	KL	IB	D		12	9	22000	5	4	118500	130500
41	9	SWAN 42	SLP	SA/CR	FBG	KL	IB	D		13		20900	7	9	126000	138000
42	9	NAUTOR 43	KTH	SA/CR	FBG	KL	IB	D		13	9	32500	5	9	168000	185000
44	5	SWAN 441	SLP	SA/RC	FBG	KL	IB	D		13	5	24000	8		152000	167000
47	9	N-Y-Y-C 48	SLP	SA/RC	FBG	KC	IB	D		13	9	33400			201000	221000
47	9	SWAN 47	SLP	SA/RC	FBG	KL	IB	D		13	9	32400	7	9	198500	218500
49	9	NAUTOR 50	KTH	SA/CR	FBG	KL	IB	D		15		51000	5	7	254000	279000
51		SWAN 51	SLP	SA/CR	FBG	KL	IB	D		14	5	38600	8	9	248000	272500
57	5	SWAN 57	SLP	SA/RC	FBG	KC	IB	D		15	9	47600	9	1	405500	445500
57	5	SWAN 57	KTH	SA/RC	FBG	KC	IB	D		15	9	47600	9	1	405500	445500
64	6	SWAN 65	KTH	SA/RC	FBG	KL	IB	D		16	4	70000	9	6	567000	623000
76	3	SWAN 76	SLP	SA/RC	FBG	KC	IB	D		19		50T	15	5	**	**
76	3	SWAN 76	KTH	SA/RC	FBG	KC	IB	D		19		50T	15	5	**	**
1980 BOATS																
36	8	SWAN 371	SLP	SA/RC	FBG	KL	IB	D		11	3	13700	6	6	71700	78800
39	1	NAUTOR 39	KTH	SA/CR	FBG	KL	IB	D		12	9	22000	5	4	114000	125500
39	4	SWAN 39	SLP	SA/RC	FBG	KL	IB	D		12	6	17600	7	4	98200	108000
42	9	NAUTOR 43	KTH	SA/CR	FBG	KL	IB	D		13	9	32500	5	9	162000	178000
44	5	SWAN 441	SLP	SA/RC	FBG	KL	IB	D		13	5	24000	8		146000	160500
47	9	NYYC 48	SLP	SA/RC	FBG	CB	IB	D		13	9	33400			193500	212500
47	9	SWAN 47	SLP	SA/RC	FBG	KL	IB	D		13	9	32400	7	9	191000	210000
49	9	NAUTOR 50	KTH	SA/CR	FBG	KL	IB	D		15		51000	5	7	244500	268500
57	5	SWAN 57	SLP	SA/RC	FBG	KC	IB	D		15	9	47600			390000	429000
57	5	SWAN 57	SLP	SA/RC	FBG	KC	IB	D		15	9	47600	9	1	390000	429000
57	5	SWAN 57	KTH	SA/RC	FBG	KC	IB	D		15	9	47600			390000	429000
57	5	SWAN 57	KTH	SA/RC	FBG	KC	IB	D		15	9	47600	9	1	390000	429000
64	6	SWAN 65	KTH	SA/RC	FBG	KL	IB	D		16	4	70000	9	6	545500	599500
76	3	SWAN 76	SLP	SA/RC	FBG	KC	IB	D		19		50T			**	**
76	3	SWAN 76	SLP	SA/RC	FBG	KC	IB	D		19		50T	15	5	**	**
76	3	SWAN 76	KTH	SA/RC	FBG	KC	IB	D		19		50T			**	**
76	3	SWAN 76	KTH	SA/RC	FBG	KC	IB	D		19		50T	15	5	**	**
1979 BOATS																
38	3	SWAN 38	SLP	SA/CR	FBG	KL	IB	D		11	7	18250	6	6	93100	102500
39	1	NAUTOR 39	KTH	SA/CR	FBG	KL	IB	D		12	9	22000	5	4	110500	121500
39	4	SWAN 39	SLP	SA/CR	FBG	KL	IB	D		12	6	17600	7	4	95100	104500
41		SWAN 411	SLP	SA/CR	FBG	KL	IB	D		12		22000	7		118000	129500
42	9	NAUTOR 43	KTH	SA/CR	FBG	KL	IB	D		13	9	32500	5	9	156500	172000
43	3	SWAN 431	SLP	SA/CR	FBG	KL	IB	D		13	5	27500	7	3	109000	119500
44	5	SWAN 441	SLP	SA/CR	FBG	KL	IB	D		13	5	24000	8		141500	155500
47	9	N-Y-Y-C 48	SLP	SA/CR	FBG	KC	IB	D		13	9	33400	9	1	187500	206000
47	9	SWAN 47	SLP	SA/CR	FBG	KL	IB	D		13	9	32400	7	9	185500	203500
49	9	NAUTOR 50	KTH	SA/CR	FBG	KL	IB	D		15		51000	5	7	237000	260500
57	5	SWAN 57	SLP	SA/CR	FBG	KL	IB	D		15	9	47600	9	1	378000	415500
57	5	SWAN 57	KTH	SA/CR	FBG	KL	IB	D		15	9	47600	9	1	378000	415500
64	6	SWAN 65	KTH	SA/CR	FBG	KL	IB	D		16	4	70000	9	6	528500	581000
1978 BOATS																
38		SWAN 38	SLP	SAIL	FBG	KL	IB	20D	BUKH	11	7	16120	6	4	80900	88900
39	3	NAUTOR 39	SLP	MS	FBG	KL	IB	73D	PERK	13	2	29400	5	7	132000	145500
40	8	SWAN 411	SLP	SAIL	FBG	KL	IB	47D	PERK	11	10	23000	7	2	116000	127500
42	8	NAUTOR 43	KTH	MS	FBG	KL	IB	84D	PERK	13	9	32500	5	11	151500	166500
43	3	SWAN 431	SLP	SAIL	FBG	KL	IB	47D	PERK	13	4	27500	7	4	105000	115000
47	9	SWAN 47	SLP	SAIL	FBG	KL	IB	61D	VLVO	13	8	32400	7	8	179500	197500
49	7	NAUTOR 50	KTH	MS	FBG	KL	IB	115D	PERK	15	1	51500	5	8	228500	251000
57	5	SWAN 57	SLP	SAIL	FBG	KL	IB	73D	PERK	15	9	47000	9	2	363500	399500
57	5	SWAN 57	KTH	SAIL	FBG	KL	IB	73D	PERK	15	9	47000	9	2	363500	399500
64	7	SWAN 65	SLP	SAIL	FBG	KL	IB	106D	VLVO	16	4	57400	9	2	432500	475500
64	7	SWAN 65	KTH	SAIL	FBG	KL	IB	106D	VLVO	16	4	57400	9	2	432500	475500
1977 BOATS																
38		SWAN	SLP	SA/CR	FBG	KL	IB	20D	BUKH	11	7	16120	6	4	78700	86500
41		SWAN	SLP	SA/CR	FBG	KL	IB	36D	PERK	11	9	17750	6	5	96400	106000
43		NAUTOR	KTH	MS	FBG	KL	IB	89D	VLVO	13	8	28000	5	7	103500	113500
43	1	SWAN	SLP	SA/CR	FBG	KL	IB	47D	PERK	13	4	27500	7	4	101500	111500
47		SWAN	SLP	SA/CR	FBG	KL	IB	61D	VLVO	13	8	32400	7	8	170000	187000
65		SWAN	SLP	SA/CR	FBG	KL	IB	106D	VLVO	16	4	57400	9	3	421000	462500
65		SWAN	KTH	SA/CR	FBG	KL	IB	106D	VLVO	16	4	57400	9	3	421000	462500
76		SWAN	KTH	SA/CR	FBG	KL	IB	237D		18	5	52T	12		**	**
1976 BOATS																
38	3	SWAN 38	SLP	SA/CR	FBG	KL	IB	20D	BUKH	11	7	16120	6	4	77600	85300
41		SWAN 41	SLP	SA/CR	FBG	KL	IB	36D	PERK	11	9	17750	6	5	94100	103500
44		SWAN 44	SLP	SA/CR	FBG	KL	IB	36D	PERK	12	6	26000	7	2	132500	145500
47	9	SWAN 47	SLP	SA/CR	FBG	KL	IB	61D	VLVO	13	8	32400	8		170500	187500
49	7	NAUTOR 50	YWL	MS	FBG	KL	IB	115D	PERK	15	1	51000	5	7	216500	238000
49	7	NAUTOR 50	KTH	MS	FBG	KL	IB	115D	PERK	15	1	51000	5	7	216500	238000
64	8	SWAN 65	KTH	SA/CR	FBG	KL	IB	106D	VLVO	16	4	70000	9	3	487500	536000
65	1	SWAN 65	SLP	SA/CR	FBG	KL	IB	106D	VLVO	16	4	70000	9	3	490500	539000
1975 BOATS																
38		SWAN 38	SLP	SAIL	FBG	KL	IB	20D	BUKH	11	7	16120	6	4	75100	82500
41		SWAN 41	SLP	SAIL	FBG	KL	IB	37D	PERK	11	9	17750	6	5	92000	101000
44		SWAN 44	SLP	SAIL	FBG	KL	IB	37D	PERK	12	6	26000	7	2	129500	142500
48		SWAN 48	SLP	SAIL	FBG	KL	IB	75D	VLVO	13	7	30000	7	9	164000	180000
64	8	SWAN 65	KTH	SAIL	FBG	KL	IB	106D	VLVO	16	4	49600	5	7	359500	395000
65	1	SWAN 65	SLP	SAIL	FBG	KL	IB	106D	VLVO	16	4	49600			356000	391000
1974 BOATS																
38		SWAN 38	SLP	SAIL	FBG	KL	IB	20D	BUKH	11	7	16120	6	4	73600	80900
41		SWAN 41	SLP	SAIL	FBG	KL	IB	37D	PERK	11	9	17500	6	5	89400	98200
44		SWAN 44	SLP	SAIL	FBG	KL	IB	37D	PERK	12	5	23800	7	7	121500	133000
48		SWAN 48	SLP	SAIL	FBG	KL	IB	36D	VLVO	13	8	30000	7	9	159500	175500
64	11	SWAN 65	SLP	SAIL	FBG	KL	IB	106D	VLVO	16	4	57400	9	3	393500	432500
1969 BOATS																
36		SWAN 36	SLP	SAIL	FBG	KL	IB	D		9	8	14250	6		55700	61200
43		SWAN 43	SLP	SAIL	FBG	KL	IB			11	8	19800	6	11	69900	76800

NAVY

Call 1-800-327-6929 for BUC Personalized Evaluation Service
Or, for 1938 boats, sign onto www.BUCValuPro.com

NELSON BOAT

NELSON CORP

Call 1-800-327-6929 for BUC Personalized Evaluation Service
Or, for 1967 boats, sign onto www.BUCValuPro.com

NELSON/MAREK YACHT DESIGN

SAN DIEGO CA 92106

See inside cover to adjust price for area

LOA FT	LOA IN	NAME AND/ OR MODEL	TOP/ RIG	BOAT TYPE	HULL MTL	HULL TP	ENGINE TP	# HP	MFG	BEAM FT	BEAM IN	WGT LBS	DRAFT FT	DRAFT IN	RETAIL LOW	RETAIL HIGH
1982 BOATS																
29	1	NELSON/MAREK 29-1/2T	SLP	SA/RC	FBG	KL	IB	D		10		5810	5	6	14200	16200
36		NELSON/MAREK 36	SLP	SA/RC	FBG	KL	IB	D		11	9	10800	6	8	24000	26700
36		NELSON/MAREK 36	SLP	SA/RC	WD	KL	IB	D		11	9		6	8	24000	26700
39		NELSON/MAREK 39	SLP	SA/CR	FBG	KL	IB	D		12	7	13730	7	1	30000	33300
41		NELSON/MAREK 41	SLP	SA/RC	AL	KL	IB	D		12			7	4	33500	37200
41		NELSON/MAREK 41	SLP	SA/RC	FBG	KL	IB	D		12		15300	7	4	35100	39000
41		NELSON/MAREK 41	SLP	SA/RC	WD	KL	IB	D		12			7	4	33500	37200
44		NELSON/MAREK 44	SLP	SA/RC	AL	KL	IB	D		13	3		7	9	48400	53200
44		NELSON/MAREK 44	SLP	SA/RC	FBG	KL	IB	D		13	3	19000	7	9	49100	53900
44		NELSON/MAREK 44	SLP	SA/RC	WD	KL	IB	D		13	3		7	9	48400	53200
47		NELSON/MAREK 47	SLP	SA/RC	FBG	KL	IB	D		13	10	24000	8	3	67500	74200
1981 BOATS																
29	1	NELSON/MAREK 29-1/2T	SLP	SA/RC	FBG	KL	IB	D		10		5810	5	6	13300	15200
36		NELSON/MAREK 36	SLP	SA/RC	FBG	KL	IB	D		11	9	10800	6	8	22500	25000
36		NELSON/MAREK 36	SLP	SA/RC	WD	KL	IB	D		11	9		6	8	22500	25000
38	11	NELSON/MAREK 38	SLP	SA/RC	FBG	KL	IB	D		12		16410	6	6	32500	36100
40	9	NELSON/MAREK 41	SLP	SA/RC	AL	KL	IB	D		12	7		7	4	31200	34600
40	9	NELSON/MAREK 41	SLP	SA/RC	FBG	KL	IB	D		12	7	14000	7	4	30800	34200
40	9	NELSON/MAREK 41	SLP	SA/RC	WD	KL	IB	D		12	7		7	4	31200	34600
44		NELSON/MAREK 44	SLP	SA/RC	AL	KL	IB	D		13	4		7	9	45700	50200
44		NELSON/MAREK 44	SLP	SA/RC	FBG	KL	IB	D		13	4	18000	7	9	44600	49500
44		NELSON/MAREK 44	SLP	SA/RC	WD	KL	IB	D		13	4		7	9	45700	50200
1980 BOATS																
25		N/M 25-1/4T	SLP	SA/RC	WD	KL	IB	D		9	1	3000	5		6250	7150
29	1	N/M 29-1/2T	SLP	SA/RC	FBG	KL	IB	D		10		5810	5	6	12700	14400
32		N/M 32	SLP	SA/RC	FBG	KL	IB	D		10	9	7200	5	11	16200	18400
37		N/M 37	SLP	SA/RC	FBG	KL	IB	D		11	10	12000	6	7	23300	25900
37		N/M 37	SLP	SA/RC	WD	KL	IB	D		11	10	12000	6	7	23300	25900
38	11	N/M 38	SLP	SA/RC	FBG	KL	IB	D		12		16410	6	6	30800	34200
40	9	N/M 41	SLP	SA/RC	AL	KL	IB	D		12	7	14000	7	4	29200	32400
40	9	N/M 41	SLP	SA/RC	FBG	KL	IB	D		12	7	14000	7	4	29200	32400
40	9	N/M 41	SLP	SA/RC	WD	KL	IB	D		12	7	14000	7	4	29200	32400
54		N/M 54	CUT	SA/CR	FBG	KC	IB	D		15	6	50000	9	10	115000	126000
54		N/M 54	CUT	SA/CR	STL	KC	IB	D		15	6	50000	9	10	115000	126000
54		N/M 54	KTH	SA/CR	FBG	KC	IB	D		15	6	50000	9	10	115000	126000
54		N/M 54	KTH	SA/CR	STL	KC	IB	D		15	6	50000	9	10	115000	126000

NEPTUNE BOOTE
LAGE LIPPE GERMANY

See inside cover to adjust price for area

LOA FT IN	NAME AND/ OR MODEL	TOP/ RIG	BOAT TYPE	-HULL- MTL TP	TP #	--ENGINE--- HP MFG	BEAM FT IN	WGT LBS	DRAFT FT IN	RETAIL LOW	RETAIL HIGH
					1978 BOATS						
24 7	NEPTUNE 25	SLP	SA/OD FBG CB	IB	8D		8 3	2755	2 2	3850	4450
26 9	NEPTUNE 27	SLP	SA/CR FBG CB	OB			8 3	3640	2 2	5000	5750
26 9	NEPTUNE 27	SLP	SA/CR FBG CB	IB	D		8 3	3640	2 2	5250	6000
26 9	NEPTUNE 27	SLP	SA/CR FBG KL	OB			8 3	3640	4 1	5000	5700
26 9	NEPTUNE 27	SLP	SA/CR FBG KL	IB	D		8 3	3640	4 1	5200	6000
31	NEPTUNE 31	SLP	SA/CR FBG KL	IB	20D	WEST	10 4	10000	5 3	15400	17500

NEPTUNUS SHIPYARD BV
VERRDAM 1NL 5308 HOLLAND

See inside cover to adjust price for area

LOA FT IN	NAME AND/ OR MODEL		TOP/ RIG	BOAT TYPE	-HULL- MTL TP	TP #	--ENGINE--- HP MFG	BEAM FT IN	WGT LBS	DRAFT FT IN	RETAIL LOW	RETAIL HIGH
						1983 BOATS						
35 6	NEPTUNUS 106		HT	MY	FBG SV	IB	85D VLVO	12	17650	3 1	53800	59100
	IB 124D VLVO	56300	61800,	IB	158D VLVO	55700	61200, IB	235D VLVO			56200	61800
	IB T 85D VLVO	56500	62000,	IB	T124D VLVO	57300	62900, IB	T158D VLVO			58300	64100
	IB T235D VLVO	61000	67100									
35 6	NEPTUNUS 106		FB	MY	FBG SV	IB	85D VLVO	12	17650	3 1	53800	59100
	IB 124D VLVO	56300	61800,	IB	158D VLVO	55700	61200, IB	235D VLVO			56200	61800
	IB T 85D VLVO	56500	62000,	IB	T124D VLVO	57300	62900, IB	T158D VLVO			58300	64100
	IB T235D VLVO	61000	67100									
38 8	NEPTUNUS 118AK		HT	MY	FBG SV	IB	T124D VLVO	12 8	19850	3 7	68300	75100
38 8	NEPTUNUS 118AK		HT	MY	FBG SV	IB	T158D VLVO	12 8	19850	3 7	69200	76000
38 8	NEPTUNUS 118AK		HT	MY	FBG SV	IB	T235D VLVO	12 8	19850	3 7	71400	78400
38 8	NEPTUNUS 118AK		FB	MY	FBG SV	IB	T124D VLVO	12 8	19850	3 7	68300	75100
38 8	NEPTUNUS 118AK		FB	MY	FBG SV	IB	T158D VLVO	12 8	19850	3 7	69200	76000
38 8	NEPTUNUS 118AK		FB	MY	FBG SV	IB	T235D VLVO	12 8	19850	3 7	71400	78400
38 8	NEPTUNUS 118FM		FB	YTFS	FBG SV	IB	T124D VLVO	12 8	17560	3 7	62700	68800
38 8	NEPTUNUS 118FM		FB	YTFS	FBG SV	IB	T158D VLVO	12 8	17560	3 7	63500	69800
38 8	NEPTUNUS 118FM		FB	YTFS	FBG SV	IB	T235D VLVO	12 8	17560	3 7	65800	72300
43	NEPTUNUS 131		FB	MY	FBG SV	IB	T235D VLVO	13 2	24250	3 11	92200	101500

NEREIA YACHTS
COAST GUARD MFG ID- KAT

Call 1-800-327-6929 for BUC Personalized Evaluation Service
Or, for 1979 to 1988 boats, sign onto www.BUCValuPro.com

NETHERLANDS INT'L YACHTS

Call 1-800-327-6929 for BUC Personalized Evaluation Service
Or, for 1982 boats, sign onto www.BUCValuPro.com

HENRY B NEVINS

See inside cover to adjust price for area

LOA FT IN	NAME AND/ OR MODEL	TOP/ RIG	BOAT TYPE	-HULL- MTL TP	TP #	--ENGINE--- HP MFG	BEAM FT IN	WGT LBS	DRAFT FT IN	RETAIL LOW	RETAIL HIGH
					1924 BOATS						
30				IB	240					**	**

NEW BOMBAY TRADING CO
BOMBAY YACHTS
CLEARWATER FL 33520   COAST GUARD MFG ID- NBT

See inside cover to adjust price for area

LOA FT IN	NAME AND/ OR MODEL	TOP/ RIG	BOAT TYPE	-HULL- MTL TP	TP #	--ENGINE--- HP MFG	BEAM FT IN	WGT LBS	DRAFT FT IN	RETAIL LOW	RETAIL HIGH
					1979 BOATS						
25 7	DAWSON 26	SLP	SA/CR FBG SK	IB	8D	YAN	8	4700	1 8	6800	7800
25 7	DAWSON 26	KTH	SA/CR FBG SK	IB	8D	YAN	8	4700	1 8	6800	7800
26	BOMBAY EXPRESS	SLP	SA/CR FBG KC	IB	8D	YAN	10 6	7500	2 4	11200	12700
31	BOMBAY CLIPPER	SLP	SA/CR FBG KL	IB	15D-	30D YAN	11	10250	3 5	18500	20600
31	BOMBAY PILOT	SLP	MS	FBG KL	IB	15D-	30D YAN	11	11000	3 6	19600	21800
42 9	BOMBAY TRAWLER	HT	TRWL	FBG DS	IB	130D	PERK 12	9	35000	4	103000	113500
45 4	BOMBAY EXPLORER	SLP	SA/CR FBG KC	IB	45D	PERK 13	1	28600	4 10	49900	54800
45 4	BOMBAY EXPLORER	SLP	SA/CR FBG KC	IB	62D	PERK 13	1	28600	4 10	50000	55000
45 4	BOMBAY EXPLORER	SLP	SA/CR FBG KL	IB	45D	PERK 13	1	28600	6 10	49900	54800
45 4	BOMBAY EXPLORER	SLP	SA/CR FBG KL	IB	62D	PERK 13	1	28600	6 10	50000	55000
45 4	BOMBAY EXPLORER SHL	SLP	SA/CR FBG KL	IB	45D	PERK 13	1	28600	4 10	49300	54200
45 4	BOMBAY EXPLORER SHL	SLP	SA/CR FBG KL	IB	62D	PERK 13	1	28600	4 10	49400	54300
					1978 BOATS						
25 7	DAWSON 26	SLP	SA/CR FBG SK	IB	8D	YAN	8	4700	1 8	6550	7500
25 7	DAWSON 26	KTH	SA/CR FBG SK	IB	8D	YAN	8	4700	1 8	6550	7500
26	BOMBAY EXPRESS	SLP	SA/CR FBG KC	IB	15D	YAN	10 6	7500	2 4	10900	12300
31	BOMBAY CLIPPER	SLP	SA/CR FBG KL	IB	15D	YAN	11	10000	3 5	17000	19300
31	BOMBAY PILOT	SLP	MS	FBG KL	IB	15D	YAN	11	10500	3 6	17400	19800
42 9	BOMBAY TRAWLER	HT	TRWL	FBG DS	IB	130D	PERK 12	9	35000	4	98600	108500
44 5	BOMBAY EXPLORER	SLP	SA/CR FBG KL	IB	62D	PERK 13	1	28600	6 10	47200	51900
					1977 BOATS						
31	BOMBAY CLIPPER	SLP	SA/CR FBG KL	IB	12D	YAN	11	10000	3 5	16400	18700
31	MOTOR SAILER	SLP	MS	FBG KL	IB	25D	VLVO 11		10250	3 6	16900	19200
42 9	BOMBAY TRAWLER	HT	TRWL	FBG DS	IB	130D	PERK 12	9	35000	4	94400	104000
					1976 BOATS						
31	BOMBAY CLIPPER	SLP	SA/CR FBG KL	IB	30	UNIV	11	10000	3 5	15900	18000
31	BOMBAY CLIPPER	SLP	SA/CR FBG KL	IB	12D	YAN	11	10000	3 5	15900	18100
31	MOTOR SAILER	SLP	MS	FBG KL	IB	30	UNIV	11	10250	3 6	16300	18500
31	MOTOR SAILER	SLP	MS	FBG KL	IB	22D	YAN	11	10250	3 6	16300	18600
50	SCHOONER	SCH	SA/CR FBG KL	IB	85D	PERK 13	6	38000	4 10	59500	65400
					1975 BOATS						
31	BOMBAY CLIPPER	SLP	SA/CR FBG KL	IB	30	UNIV	11	9400	3 5	14500	16500

NEW ENGLAND BOAT BLDRS INC
MATTAPOISETT MA 02739   COAST GUARD MFG ID- NEB   See inside cover to adjust price for area

LOA FT IN	NAME AND/ OR MODEL	TOP/ RIG	BOAT TYPE	-HULL- MTL TP	TP #	--ENGINE--- HP MFG	BEAM FT IN	WGT LBS	DRAFT FT IN	RETAIL LOW	RETAIL HIGH
					1979 BOATS						
24 7	MARGARET-D	SLP	SA/CR FBG KL	OB			8	5250	3 4	7200	8250
24 7	MARGARET-D	SLP	SA/CR FBG KL	IB	7D-	10D	8	5250	3 4	7700	8950
24 7	MARGARET-D	KTH	SA/CR FBG KL	OB			8	5250	3 4	7200	8250
24 7	MARGARET-D	KTH	SA/CR FBG KL	IB	7D-	10D	8	5250	3 4	7700	8950
37	MEADOW-LARK	KTH	SA/CR F/S LB	IB	25D	WEST	8	10000	1 8	23000	25600
37	MEADOW-LARK	KTH	SA/CR F/S LB	IB T	13D	VLVO	8	10000	1 8	23400	26000
40	CARTWRIGHT 40	CUT	SA/CR F/S KL	IB	37D	WEST	11 3	23500	5 10	51400	56500
					1978 BOATS						
24 7	MARGARET-D	SLP	SAIL	FBG KL	OB		8	5200	3 4	6850	7900
24 7	MARGARET-D	SLP	SAIL	FBG KL	IB	10	UNIV	8	5200	3 4	7050	8150
24 7	MARGARET-D	SLP	SAIL	FBG KL	IB	7D	WEST	8	5200	3 4	7350	8450
24 7	MARGARET-D	KTH	SAIL	FBG KL	OB		8	5200	3 4	6850	7900
24 7	MARGARET-D	KTH	SAIL	FBG KL	IB	10	UNIV	8	5200	3 4	7050	8150
24 7	MARGARET-D	KTH	SAIL	FBG KL	IB	7D	WEST	8	5200	3 4	7350	8450
37	MEADOW-LARK	KTH	SAIL	F/S LB	IB	24D	FARY	8 2	10200	1 8	22500	25000
37	MEADOW-LARK	KTH	SAIL	F/S LB	IB	25D	WEST	8 2	10200	1 8	22500	25100
40	CARTWRIGHT 40	CUT	SAIL	F/S KL	IB	37D	WEST	11 3	23500	5 10	49400	54300
					1977 BOATS						
24 7	MARGARET-D	SLP	SAIL	FBG KL	OB		8	5200	3 4	6600	7600
24 7	MARGARET-D	SLP	SAIL	FBG KL	IB	10	UNIV	8	5200	3 4	6850	7850
24 7	MARGARET-D	SLP	SAIL	FBG KL	IB	5D	WEST	8	5400	3 7	7350	8450
24 7	MARGARET-D	KTH	SAIL	FBG KL	OB		8	5200	3 4	6600	7600
24 7	MARGARET-D	KTH	SAIL	FBG KL	IB	10	UNIV	8	5200	3 4	6850	7850
24 7	MARGARET-D	KTH	SAIL	FBG KL	IB	5D	WEST	8	5400	3 7	7350	8450
37	MEADOW-LARK	KTH	SAIL	F/S CB	IB	30	UNIV	8	10200		21400	23800
37	MEADOW-LARK	KTH	SAIL	F/S CB	IB	25D	WEST	8	10200		22000	24500
37	MEADOW-LARK	KTH	SAIL	F/S CB	IB T	12D	FARY	8	10200		21400	23900
37	MEADOW-LARK	KTH	SAIL	F/S LB	IB	30	UNIV	8	10200	1 8	21400	23800
37	MEADOW-LARK	KTH	SAIL	F/S LB	IB	25D	WEST	8	10200	1 8	22000	24500
37	MEADOW-LARK	KTH	SAIL	F/S LB	IB T	12D	FARY	8	10200	1 8	21400	24000
40	CARTWRIGHT 40	CUT	SAIL	F/S KL	IB	37D	WEST	11 3	23500	5 10	47700	52400

NEW HAMPSHIRE BOAT BLDRS INC
COAST GUARD MFG ID- JCA
FORMERLY J C BOAT WORKSINC

Call 1-800-327-6929 for BUC Personalized Evaluation Service
Or, for 1982 to 1983 boats, sign onto www.BUCValuPro.com

NEW JAPAN MARINE CO LTD
COAST GUARD MFG ID- NJM

Call 1-800-327-6929 for BUC Personalized Evaluation Service
Or, for 1967 to 1979 boats, sign onto www.BUCValuPro.com

NEW ORLEANS MARINE INC

NEW OLEANS LA 70115 .... See inside cover to adjust price for area

For more recent years, see the BUC Used Boat Price Guide, Volume 1 or Volume 2

LOA FT IN	NAME AND/ OR MODEL	TOP/ RIG	BOAT TYPE	-HULL- MTL TP	----ENGINE--- TP # HP MFG	BEAM FT IN	WGT LBS	DRAFT FT IN	RETAIL LOW	RETAIL HIGH
			----- 1982 BOATS -----							
37 11	FRERS 38	SLP	SA/RC	FBG KL	IB D	12 4	13000	6 6	27900	31000
42 6	PETERSON 43	SLP	SA/RC	FBG KL	IB D	13 4	17500	7 5	44100	49000
			----- 1981 BOATS -----							
42 6	PETERSON 43	SLP	SA/RC	FBG KL	IB D	13 4	17500	7 5	41500	46100

NEW YORK WELDING WORKS
BARTOLD'S BOATS

Call 1-800-327-6929 for BUC Personalized Evaluation Service
Or, for 1959 to 1961 boats, sign onto www.BUCValuPro.com

NEW ZEALAND OVERSEAS YACHTS
COAST GUARD MFG ID- NZY

Call 1-800-327-6929 for BUC Personalized Evaluation Service
Or, for 1983 boats, sign onto www.BUCValuPro.com

NEWBRIDGE BOATS LTD
COAST GUARD MFG ID- NBL

INTERNATIONAL YACHT AGY LTD

Call 1-800-327-6929 for BUC Personalized Evaluation Service
Or, for 1975 to 1982 boats, sign onto www.BUCValuPro.com

RICHARD C NEWICK
COAST GUARD MFG ID- RCN

Call 1-800-327-6929 for BUC Personalized Evaluation Service
Or, for 1977 to 1980 boats, sign onto www.BUCValuPro.com

NEWMAN FINE BOATS INC
VELVET FLEET .... COAST GUARD MFG ID- NEW

Call 1-800-327-6929 for BUC Personalized Evaluation Service
Or, for 1968 to 1984 boats, sign onto www.BUCValuPro.com

JARVIS NEWMAN MARINE BROKERS

NE HARBOR ME 04662-0331 COAST GUARD MFG ID- JNY See inside cover to adjust price for area

For more recent years, see the BUC Used Boat Price Guide, Volume 1 or Volume 2

LOA FT IN	NAME AND/ OR MODEL	TOP/ RIG	BOAT TYPE	-HULL- MTL TP	----ENGINE--- TP # HP MFG	BEAM FT IN	WGT LBS	DRAFT FT IN	RETAIL LOW	RETAIL HIGH
			----- 1983 BOATS -----							
25	FRIENDSHIP SLP	GAF	SA/CR	FBG KL	SD 8D VLVO	8 8	7000	4 3	14800	16800
31	FRIENDSHIP SLP	GAF	SA/CR	FBG KL	IB 40D	11	17500	5	45500	50000
32 2	NEWMAN 32	HT	MYDKH	FBG DS	IB 160D	11	13000	3 6	82900	91100
36	NEWMAN 36	HT	MYDKH	FBG DS	IB 210D	11	14000	3 5	108000	118500
38	NEWMAN 38	HT	MYDKH	FBG DS	IB 350D	13 5	22000	4 5	150500	165000
46 2	NEWMAN 46	HT	MYDKH	FBG DS	IB 450D	15 4	30000	4 6	200500	220000
			----- 1982 BOATS -----							
25	FRIENDSHIP SLP	GAF	SA/CR	FBG KL	IB 12D VLVO	8 8		4 3	14100	16000
31	FRIENDSHIP SLP	GAF	SA/CR	FBG KL	IB 40D	11		5	42700	47400
32 2	NEWMAN 32	HT	MYDKH	FBG RB	IB 160D	11		3 6	81900	89900
36	NEWMAN 36	HT	MYDKH	FBG RB	IB 210D	11		3 5	110500	121500
38	NEWMAN 38	HT	MYDKH	FBG RB	IB 350D	13 5		4 5	143500	157500
46 2	NEWMAN 46	HT	MYDKH	FBG RB	IB 450D	15 4		4 6	192000	211000
			----- 1980 BOATS -----							
32	NEWMAN LOBSTER		FSH	FBG DS	IB	11	14000		**	**
32	NEWMAN PLEASURE		CR	FBG DS	IB	11	14000		**	**
36	NEWMAN LOBSTER		FSH	FBG DS	IB	11 4	15000		**	**
36	NEWMAN PLEASURE		CR	FBG DS	IB	11 4	15000		**	**
38	NEWMAN LOBSTER		FSH	FBG DS	IB	13 4	22000		**	**
38	NEWMAN PLEASURE		CR	FBG DS	IB	13 4	22000		**	**
46	NEWMAN LOBSTER		FSH	FBG DS	IB	15	34000		**	**
46	NEWMAN PLEASURE		CR	FBG DS	IB	15	34000		**	**
			----- 1978 BOATS -----							
25	PEMAQUID	GAF	SA/CR	FBG KL	IB 10D	8 8	7000	4	11700	13300
25	PEMAQUID	SLP	SA/CR	FBG KL	IB 10D	8 8	7000	4	11700	13300
31	DICTATOR	GAF	SA/CR	FBG KL	IB 25D	10 10	17000	5	34300	38100
31	DICTATOR	SLP	SA/CR	FBG KL	IB 25D	10 10	17000	5	34300	38100
31	DICTATOR	SCH	SA/CR	FBG KL	IB 25D	10 10	17000	5	34300	38100
32	NEWMAN LOBSTER		FSH	FBG DS	IB 250	11	14000	3 6	47100	51800
32	NEWMAN LOBSTER		FSH	FBG DS	IB 250D	11	14000	3 6	63600	69900
32	NEWMAN PLEASURE		CR	FBG DS	IB 250	11	14000	3 6	47100	51800
32	NEWMAN PLEASURE		CR	FBG DS	IB 250D	11	14000	3 6	63500	69800
36	NEWMAN LOBSTER		FSH	FBG DS	IB 250	11 4	15000	3 6	74500	81900
36	NEWMAN LOBSTER		FSH	FBG DS	IB 250D	11 4	15000	3 6	83600	91900
36	NEWMAN PLEASURE		CR	FBG DS	IB 250	11 4	15000	3 6	74600	82000
36	NEWMAN PLEASURE		CR	FBG DS	IB 250D	11 4	15000	3 6	83700	92000
46	NEWMAN LOBSTER		FSH	FBG DS	IB 350D	15	34000		209500	230000
46	NEWMAN PLEASURE		CR	FBG DS	IB 350D	15	34000		212500	233500
			----- 1977 BOATS -----							
25	PEMAQUID FRIENDSHIP	SLP	SAIL	FBG KL	IB D	8 8	7000	4	11300	12900
25	PEMAQUID FRIENDSHIP	YWL	SAIL	FBG KL	IB D	8 8	7000	4	11300	12900
25	PEMAQUID GAFF	SLP	SA/CR	FBG KL	IB 10D	8 8	7000	4	11200	12800
25	SURF-HUNTER	OP	CR	FBG DV	IO 250	9 2	5000	1 6	16400	18700
31	DICTATOR GAFF	SLP	SA/CR	FBG KL	IB 25D	10 10	17000	5	32900	36500
31	DICTATOR GAFF	SCH	SA/CR	FBG KL	IB 25D	10 10	17000	5	32900	36500
32	NEWMAN LOBSTER		SF	FBG	IB 250	11	14000	3 6	44700	49700
32	NEWMAN LOBSTER		SF	FBG	IB 250D	11	14000	3 6	61200	67200
32	NEWMAN PLEASURE		CR	FBG	IB 250	11	14000	3 6	44700	49700
32	NEWMAN PLEASURE		CR	FBG	IB 250D	11	14000	3 6	61200	67200
36	NEWMAN LOBSTER		SF	FBG	IB 250	11 4	15000	3 6	71400	78500
36	NEWMAN LOBSTER		SF	FBG	IB 250D	11 4	15000	3 6	80100	88000
36	NEWMAN PLEASURE		CR	FBG	IB 250	11 4	15000	3 6	71400	78500
36	NEWMAN PLEASURE		CR	FBG	IB 250D	11 4	15000	3 6	80200	88100
			----- 1976 BOATS -----							
25	PEMAQUID DAYSAILOR	SLP	SAIL	FBG KL	IB D	8	7000	4	10900	12400
25	PEMAQUID DAYSAILOR	YWL	SAIL	FBG KL	IB D	8	7000	4	10900	12400
25	PEMAQUID GAFF	SLP	SA/CR	FBG KL	IB 10D	8 8	7000	4	10800	12300
25	SURF-HUNTER	OP	CR	FBG DV	IO 250	9 2	5000	1 6	16900	19100
31	DICTATOR GAFF	SLP	SA/CR	FBG KL	IB 25D	10 10	17000	5	31600	35100
31	DICTATOR GAFF	SCH	SA/CR	FBG KL	IB 25D	10 10	17000	5	31600	35100
32	NEWMAN		CR	FBG SV	IB 250	11	14000		42900	47700
32	NEWMAN		CR	FBG SV	IB 250D	11	14000		59000	64800
36	NEWMAN		CR	FBG SV	IB 250	11 4	15000		68500	75300
36	NEWMAN		CR	FBG SV	IB 250D	11 4	15000		76900	84500
36	NEWMAN LOBSTER		SF	FBG SV	IB 250D	11 4	15000		76800	84400
			----- 1975 BOATS -----							
25	PEMAQUID GAFF	SLP	SA/CR	FBG KL	IB 10D	8 8	7000	4	10500	11900
25	SURF-HUNTER	OP	CR	FBG DV	IO 250	9 2	5000	1 6	14700	16700
31	DICTATOR GAFF	SLP	SA/CR	FBG KL	IB 25D	10 9	17000	5	30500	33800
32	NEWMAN		CR	FBG SV	IB 250	11	14000		41200	45800
32	NEWMAN		CR	FBG SV	IB 250D	11	14000		57200	62800
36	NEWMAN		CR	FBG SV	IB 250	11 4	15000		65800	72300
36	NEWMAN		CR	FBG SV	IB 250D	11 4	15000		73800	81100
36	NEWMAN-LOBSTER		SF	FBG SV	IB 250	11 4	15000		65800	72300
36	NEWMAN-LOBSTER		SF	FBG SV	IB 250D	11 4	15000		73700	81000
			----- 1974 BOATS -----							
25	FRIENDSHIP	SLP	SA/CR	FBG KL	IB D	8 8	7000	4	10200	11600
25	SURF-HUNTER		CR	FBG	OB	9 2	5000	1 6	18700	20800
30 10	FRIENDSHIP	SLP	SAIL	FBG	IB 25D WEST	11	17500	5	30300	33600
36			EXP	FBG	IB	11	14000	3 4	**	**
36		FB	EXP	FBG	IB	11	16200	3 6	**	**

NEWPORT BOATS

DIV OF BROWNING
GLOUCESTER VA 23061 .... See inside cover to adjust price for area
COAST GUARD MFG ID- NPT
FOR MORE RECENT MODELS SEE LOCKLEY MFG CO INC

LOA FT IN	NAME AND/ OR MODEL	TOP/ RIG	BOAT TYPE	-HULL- MTL TP	----ENGINE--- TP # HP MFG	BEAM FT IN	WGT LBS	DRAFT FT IN	RETAIL LOW	RETAIL HIGH
			----- 1977 BOATS -----							
21 2	NEWPORT 212	SLP	SA/CR	FBG SK	OB	7 8	2000	9	2600	3050
			----- 1976 BOATS -----							
21 2	NEWPORT 212	SLP	SAIL	FBG CB	OB	7 8	1500	9	2200	2550
			----- 1975 BOATS -----							
21 2	NEWPORT 212	SLP	SAIL	FBG CB	OB	7 8	1500	5	2100	2500

LOA FT IN	NAME AND/ OR MODEL	TOP/ RIG	BOAT TYPE	HULL MTL TP	TP #	ENGINE HP	MFG	BEAM FT IN	WGT LBS	DRAFT FT IN	RETAIL LOW	RETAIL HIGH
										1974 BOATS		
21 2	NEWPORT 212	SLP	SAIL	FBG CB	OB			7 8	1500	11	2050	2400
										1973 BOATS		
20 6	NEWPORT	SLP	SA/OD	FBG CB	OB			6 8	1200	11	1750	2050
										1967 BOATS		
22 7	NOMAD		SAIL	FBG	OB			7 6	1950	11	2200	2600
										1966 BOATS		
22 7	NOMAD	SLP	SAIL	FBG	OB			7 6			3050	3550

NEWPORTER INC
NEWPORT BEACH CA

See inside cover to adjust price for area

LOA FT IN	NAME AND/ OR MODEL	TOP/ RIG	BOAT TYPE	HULL MTL TP	TP #	ENGINE HP	MFG	BEAM FT IN	WGT LBS	DRAFT FT IN	RETAIL LOW	RETAIL HIGH
										1960 BOATS		
40	NEWPORTER	SLP	SA/CR	PLY KL	OB			13		6	38000	42200
40	NEWPORTER	KTH	SA/CR	PLY KL	OB			13		6	30000	42200
										1959 BOATS		
40	NEWPORTER	SLP	SA/CR	F/W KL				13		6	38200	42400
40	NEWPORTER	KTH	SA/CR	F/W KL				13		6	38200	42400

NEWPORTER YACHTS INC

Call 1-800-327-6929 for BUC Personalized Evaluation Service
Or, for 1968 to 1970 boats, sign onto www.BUCValuPro.com

NEXUS MARINE CORPORATION
EVERETT WA 98201   COAST GUARD MFG ID- RAK See inside cover to adjust price for area
                      ALSO NEXUS MARINE CONST

For more recent years, see the BUC Used Boat Price Guide, Volume 1 or Volume 2

LOA FT IN	NAME AND/ OR MODEL	TOP/ RIG	BOAT TYPE	HULL MTL TP	TP #	ENGINE HP	MFG	BEAM FT IN	WGT LBS	DRAFT FT IN	RETAIL LOW	RETAIL HIGH
										1983 BOATS		
22	ALASKAN SKIFF	OP	UTL	WD FL	OB		8		875	1 6	1800	2150
28	CARGO SKIFF	OP	UTL	WD FL	OB		10		1500		12800	14500
										1981 BOATS		
22	SET-NET	OP	DGY	PLY FL	OB		8				2100	2500
28	CARGO	OP	DGY	PLY FL	OB		10				12300	14000
33 6		CUT	SA/CR	WD	KL		10 9	15600		5 4	44100	49000

NIAGARA NAUTIC INC
NIAGARA LAKE ONTARIO CA COAST GUARD MFG ID- ZNN See inside cover to adjust price for area

For more recent years, see the BUC Used Boat Price Guide, Volume 1 or Volume 2

LOA FT IN	NAME AND/ OR MODEL	TOP/ RIG	BOAT TYPE	HULL MTL TP	TP #	ENGINE HP	MFG	BEAM FT IN	WGT LBS	DRAFT FT IN	RETAIL LOW	RETAIL HIGH
										1983 BOATS		
36 9	NAUTILUS 36	SLP	SA/CR	FBG KL	IB	D		11 6	14500	4 9	61400	67500
39 9	NAUTILUS 40	SLP	SA/CR	FBG KL	IB	D		11 10	17500	5 9	81300	89300
										1982 BOATS		
36 9	NAUTILUS 36	SLP	SA/CR	FBG KL	IB	36D	PERK	11 6	14500	4 9	57600	63300
39 9	NAUTILUS 40	SLP	SA/CR	F/S KL	IB	36D	PERK	11 10	17300	5 9	75300	82700
										1981 BOATS		
36 9	NAUTILUS 36	SLP	SA/CR	FBG KL	IB	36D	PERK	11 6	14500	4 9	54100	59500
39 9	NAUTILUS 40	SLP	SA/CR	F/S KL	IB	36D	PERK	11 10	17300	5 9	70800	77800
										1980 BOATS		
36 9	NAUTILUS 36	SLP	SA/CR	FBG KL	SD	24D	VLVO	11 6	14500	4 9	51800	56900
IB 28D WEST 51900 57100, IB 35D PERK 51700 56800, IB 35D VLVO 51900 57100												
										1979 BOATS		
36 9	NAUTILUS 36	SLP	SA/CR	FBG KL	SD	24D	VLVO	11 6	14500	4 9	49800	54700
36 9	NAUTILUS 36	SLP	SA/CR	FBG KL	SD	25D	WEST	11 6	14500	4 9	49900	54800
36 9	NAUTILUS 36	SLP	SA/CR	FBG KL	SD	35D	VLVO	11 6	14500	4 9	49900	54900
										1978 BOATS		
36 9	NAUTILUS 36	SLP	SA/CR	FBG KL	IB	25D	WEST	11 6	14500		48100	52800
40 11	AURORA 40	SLP	SA/CR	FBG CB	IB	D		12 6	22500		78700	86500

NICHOLS BOAT WORKS

Call 1-800-327-6929 for BUC Personalized Evaluation Service
Or, for 1960 to 1961 boats, sign onto www.BUCValuPro.com

NIMPHIUS BOAT CO
NESHKORO WI 54960

See inside cover to adjust price for area

LOA FT IN	NAME AND/ OR MODEL	TOP/ RIG	BOAT TYPE	HULL MTL TP	TP #	ENGINE HP	MFG	BEAM FT IN	WGT LBS	DRAFT FT IN	RETAIL LOW	RETAIL HIGH
										1969 BOATS		
27		CAT	SA/CR	P/C KC	IB	D		12 2		2 6	11200	12800
										1968 BOATS		
40		SLP	SAIL	F/W TM		24				2 10	46000	50600
										1967 BOATS		
18	ARROW	SLP	SA/OD	MHG CB		6 4	1100	1 2			2700	3150
18	N-18	SLP	SAIL	P/M CB		6 4			10		2700	3150
18	N-18	SLP	SAIL	P/M KL		6 4		3			2700	3150
										1966 BOATS		
18	N-18	SLP	SAIL	P/M CB		6 4			10		2650	3100
18	N-18	SLP	SAIL	P/M KL		6 4		3			2650	3100
										1965 BOATS		
18	ARROW	SLP	SA/OD	WD CB		6 4		1 2			2650	3100
18	N-18	SLP	SAIL	MHG CB		6 4			10		2650	3100
18	N-18	SLP	SAIL	MHG KL		6 4		3			2650	3100
29 2	DRAGON	SLP	SA/OD	WD KL		6 4	3747	3 10			6100	7000
40		SLP	SAIL	F/W TM		24				2 9	44300	49200
										1961 BOATS		
18	NIMPHIUS N-18	SLP	SAIL	MHG KL		6 4		3			2600	3050
21 9	ARROW	SLP	SA/OD	MHG KL		6 4		2 4			3200	3750

NOR'WEST YACHTS INC
ALAMEDA CA 94501   COAST GUARD MFG ID- WCF See inside cover to adjust price for area

LOA FT IN	NAME AND/ OR MODEL	TOP/ RIG	BOAT TYPE	HULL MTL TP	TP #	ENGINE HP	MFG	BEAM FT IN	WGT LBS	DRAFT FT IN	RETAIL LOW	RETAIL HIGH
										1982 BOATS		
33 6	NOR'WEST 33	SLP	SA/CR	FBG KL	IB	21D	WEST	10	11500	4 9	35100	39000
										1981 BOATS		
29 6	NOR'WEST 29	SLP	SA/CR	FBG KL	IB	D		9 5	9000	4 5	25400	28300
33 6	NOR'WEST 33	SLP	SA/CR	FBG KL	IB	21D	WEST	10	12000	4 9	34400	38200
										1980 BOATS		
33 6	NOR'WEST 33	SLP	SA/CR	FBG KL	IB	20D	YAN	10	12000	4 9	32800	36500

NORD YACHTS
DIV OF RECREATIONAL EQU COAST GUARD MFG ID- NRD
SEE ALSO OY FISKARS A/B

Call 1-800-327-6929 for BUC Personalized Evaluation Service
Or, for 1980 to 1986 boats, sign onto www.BUCValuPro.com

NORDBORG

Call 1-800-327-6929 for BUC Personalized Evaluation Service
Or, for 1906 to 1965 boats, sign onto www.BUCValuPro.com

NORDIC BOATS INC
LAKE HAVASU CITY AZ 864 COAST GUARD MFG ID- NDC See inside cover to adjust price for area

For more recent years, see the BUC Used Boat Price Guide, Volume 1 or Volume 2

LOA FT IN	NAME AND/ OR MODEL	TOP/ RIG	BOAT TYPE	HULL MTL TP	TP #	ENGINE HP	MFG	BEAM FT IN	WGT LBS	DRAFT FT IN	RETAIL LOW	RETAIL HIGH
										1976 BOATS		
18	THOR	OP	SKI	FBG SV	JT	6 7					**	**
18 3	SCANDIA	OP	SKI	FBG SV	JT						**	**
18 3	SCANDIA	OP	SKI	FBG SV	IB						**	**
21	VIKING CRUISER	OP	SKI	FBG SV	JT	8					**	**
21	VIKING CRUISER	OP	SKI	FBG SV	IB	8					**	**

NORDIC YACHTS INC
BELLINGHAM WA 98227   COAST GUARD MFG ID- NYA See inside cover to adjust price for area

For more recent years, see the BUC Used Boat Price Guide, Volume 1 or Volume 2

LOA FT IN	NAME AND/ OR MODEL	TOP/ RIG	BOAT TYPE	-HULL- MTL TP	TP	#	----ENGINE--- HP	MFG	BEAM FT IN	WGT LBS	DRAFT FT IN	RETAIL LOW	RETAIL HIGH
---	--- 1983 BOATS	---	---	---	---	---	---	---	---	---	---	---	---
39 9	NORDIC 40	SLP	SA/CR	FBG KL	VD		32D	UNIV	12 5	18000	6 6	79800	87700
39 9	NORDIC 40 SHOAL	SLP	SA/CR	FBG KL	VD		32D	UNIV	12 5	18000	5 2	81200	89300
43 10	NORDIC 44	SLP	SA/CR	FBG KL	VD		44D	UNIV	12 11	24000	7	113000	124500
43 10	NORDIC 44 SHOAL	SLP	SA/CR	FBG KL	VD		44D	UNIV	12 11	24000	5 11	115500	126500
---	--- 1982 BOATS	---	---	---	---	---	---	---	---	---	---	---	---
39 9	NORDIC 40	SLP	SA/CR	FBG KL	VD		32D	UNIV	12 5	18000	6 6	75600	83100
39 9	NORDIC 40 SHOAL	SLP	SA/CR	FBG KL	VD		32D	UNIV	12 5	18000	5 2	77000	84600
43 10	NORDIC 44	SLP	SA/CR	FBG KL	VD		44D	UNIV	12 11	24000	7	107500	118000
43 10	NORDIC 44 SHOAL	SLP	SA/CR	FBG KL	VD		44D	UNIV	12 11	24000	5 11	109000	120000
---	--- 1981 BOATS	---	---	---	---	---	---	---	---	---	---	---	---
39 9	NORDIC 40	SLP	SA/CR	FBG KL	VD		32D	UNIV	12 5	18000	6 6	71700	78800
39 9	NORDIC 40 SHOAL	SLP	SA/CR	FBG KL	VD		32D	UNIV	12 5	18000	5 2	73000	80200
43 10	NORDIC 44	SLP	SA/CR	FBG KL	VD		44D	UNIV	12 11	24000	7	101500	111500
43 10	NORDIC 44 SHOAL	SLP	SA/CR	FBG KL	VD		44D	UNIV	12 11	24000	5 11	103500	114000
---	--- 1980 BOATS	---	---	---	---	---	---	---	---	---	---	---	---
43 10	NORDIC 44	SLP	SA/CR	FBG KL	VD		41D	WEST	12 11	24000	7	98800	108500
43 10	NORDIC 44	CUT	SA/CR	FBG KL	VD		41D	WEST	12 11	24000	7	98800	108500

NORDSWED LTD

Call 1-800-327-6929 for BUC Personalized Evaluation Service
Or, for 1966 boats, sign onto www.BUCValuPro.com

NORGE BOATS INC
MOBACO MARINE

Call 1-800-327-6929 for BUC Personalized Evaluation Service
Or, for 1959 to 1960 boats, sign onto www.BUCValuPro.com

NORSE NAUTIC

Call 1-800-327-6929 for BUC Personalized Evaluation Service
Or, for 1980 to 1981 boats, sign onto www.BUCValuPro.com

NORSEMAN BOAT CO
BELLINGHAM WA   See inside cover to adjust price for area

LOA FT IN	NAME AND/ OR MODEL	TOP/ RIG	BOAT TYPE	-HULL- MTL TP	TP	#	----ENGINE--- HP	MFG	BEAM FT IN	WGT LBS	DRAFT FT IN	RETAIL LOW	RETAIL HIGH
---	--- 1961 BOATS	---	---	---	---	---	---	---	---	---	---	---	---
18 2	ADVENTURER	FSH	PLY		OB				7 3			3100	3600
18 5	VENTURE	CBNCR	PLY		OB				7 7			3750	4400
20 1	VALOR	EXP	PLY		OB				7 1			5700	6550
23 10	VACATIONER	CBNCR	PLY		OB				8 7			7600	8750
27 5	VOYAGER	CBNCR	PLY		OB			10				16500	18700

NORSEMAN SHIPBLDG CORP
MIAMI FL 33136   COAST GUARD MFG ID- NSM See inside cover to adjust price for area

For more recent years, see the BUC Used Boat Price Guide, Volume 1 or Volume 2

LOA FT IN	NAME AND/ OR MODEL	TOP/ RIG	BOAT TYPE	-HULL- MTL TP	TP	#	----ENGINE--- HP	MFG	BEAM FT IN	WGT LBS	DRAFT FT IN	RETAIL LOW	RETAIL HIGH
---	--- 1983 BOATS	---	---	---	---	---	---	---	---	---	---	---	---
52		FB	SF	FBG SV	IB		T630D	S&S	16 6	52000	4 3	225500	247500
62		TT	SF	FBG DV	IB		T570D	GM	19 4	80000	4 6	323000	355000
---	--- 1980 BOATS	---	---	---	---	---	---	---	---	---	---	---	---
52	NORSEMAN	FB	SF	FBG DV	IB		T450D		16	44000		154000	169500
62	NORSEMAN	FB	SF	FBG DV	IB		T650D		19 6	88000		305000	335000
---	--- 1979 BOATS	---	---	---	---	---	---	---	---	---	---	---	---
52	NORSEMAN	FB	SF	FBG DV	IB		T240D		16	44000		127500	140000
62	NORSEMAN	FB	SF	FBG DV	IB		T650D		19 6	88000		291000	319500
---	--- 1978 BOATS	---	---	---	---	---	---	---	---	---	---	---	---
26	NORSEMAN	FB	SF	FBG DV	IO		T165		8	5600	2 2	11600	13100
26	NORSEMAN	FB	SF	FBG DV	IO		T330		8	5600	2 2	14000	15900
36	NORSEMAN	FB	SF	FBG DV	IB		T225D		14	18000		57900	63600
52	NORSEMAN	FB	SF	FBG DV	IB		T450D		16	32000		128000	141000
62	NORSEMAN	FB	MY	FBG DV	IB		T525D		19 6	50T		312000	343000
62	NORSEMAN	FB	SF	FBG DV	IB		T525D		19 6	50T		298500	328000
---	--- 1977 BOATS	---	---	---	---	---	---	---	---	---	---	---	---
26	NORSEMAN	ST	CR	FBG DV	IO		T165		8	5600	2 2	10000	11400
26	NORSEMAN	ST	CR	FBG DV	IO		T280		8	5600	2 2	11200	12800
54	NORSEMAN	FB	SF	MHG DV	IB		T450D		16 6	64000	3 6	172500	190000
---	--- 1976 BOATS	---	---	---	---	---	---	---	---	---	---	---	---
26	NORSEMAN	ST	CR	FBG DV	IB		225D		8	5600	2 2	12400	14100
26	NORSEMAN	ST	CR	FBG DV	IO		T280	MRCR	8	5600	2 2	11500	13100
54	NORSEMAN	FB	SF	MHG DV	IB		T450D	CUM	16 6	64000	3 6	165500	182000
---	--- 1975 BOATS	---	---	---	---	---	---	---	---	---	---	---	---
46	NORSEMAN	FB	SF	WD	DV	IB	T370D		15 6		3 6	91200	101000
46	NORSEMAN	FB	SF	WD	DV	IB	T400D		15 6		3 6	92800	102000
53	NORSEMAN	FB	SF	WD	DV	IB	T370D		16 6		3 6	118000	130000
53	NORSEMAN	FB	SF	WD	DV	IB	T400D		16 6		3 6	121000	133000
55	NORSEMAN	FB	SF	WD	DV	IB	T370D		16 6		3 6	123000	135000
55	NORSEMAN	FB	SF	WD	DV	IB	T450D		16 6		3 6	129500	142500
58	NORSEMAN	FB	SF	WD	DV	IB	T370D		17		3 6	142500	157000
58	NORSEMAN	FB	SF	WD	DV	IB	T450D		17		3 6	150500	165000
60	NORSEMAN	FB	SF	WD	DV	IB	T370D		17		3 6	164500	180500
60	NORSEMAN	FB	SF	WD	DV	IB	T450D		17		3 6	170500	187500
65	NORSEMAN	FB	SF	WD	DV	IB	T370D		17 6		4	223000	245000
65	NORSEMAN	FB	SF	WD	DV	IB	T500D		17 6		4	229000	251500
---	--- 1972 BOATS	---	---	---	---	---	---	---	---	---	---	---	---
53	NORSEMAN	FB	SF	WD	DV	IB	T370D		16		3 6	105000	115500
---	--- 1970 BOATS	---	---	---	---	---	---	---	---	---	---	---	---
47	NORSEMAN	FB	SF	WD		IB	T D					**	**
53	NORSEMAN	FB	SF	WD		IB	T370D	CUM	16 6		3 6	95200	104500
---	--- 1969 BOATS	---	---	---	---	---	---	---	---	---	---	---	---
48	NORSEMAN	FB	SF	WD		IB	T370D	CUM				80900	88900

NORTH AMERICAN BOAT CORP
FORT LAUDERDALE FL   COAST GUARD MFG ID- NAB See inside cover to adjust price for area

LOA FT IN	NAME AND/ OR MODEL	TOP/ RIG	BOAT TYPE	-HULL- MTL TP	TP	#	----ENGINE--- HP	MFG	BEAM FT IN	WGT LBS	DRAFT FT IN	RETAIL LOW	RETAIL HIGH
---	--- 1983 BOATS	---	---	---	---	---	---	---	---	---	---	---	---
24	W-24	ST	WKNDR	FBG SV	IO		165-260		8	3780	2 2	5450	6500
---	--- 1981 BOATS	---	---	---	---	---	---	---	---	---	---	---	---
20 4	C-20		FSH	FBG SV	OB			7 6	1925			3900	4550
22	C-22		FSH	FBG SV	OB			7	2200			4750	5450
22	C-22 FSH		CTRCN	FBG SV	IO		165	8				4400	5100
22	C-22 FSH		CTRCN	FBG SV	IB		225	8				4900	5650
22	CF-22		FSH	FBG SV	OB			8	2500			5200	6000
22	CF-22 FSH		CUD	FBG SV	IO		165	8				4350	5000
22	SX-22		RNBT	FBG SV	OB			8	2500			5200	6000
22	SX-22		RNBT	FBG SV	IO		165	8				3650	4250
24	W-24	ST	WKNDR	FBG SV	IO		165-260	8	3780	2 2		5250	6250
26	C-26		FSH	FBG SV	OB			8	3525			8900	10100
26	C-26 FSH		CTRCN	FBG SV	IO		228	8				7300	8400
26	C-26 FSH		CTRCN	FBG SV	IB		255	8				8250	9400
26	CF-26		FSH	FBG SV	OB			8	3950			9200	10400
26	SX-26		CR	FBG SV	OB			8	4250			9350	10700
26	SX-26 CR		SPTCR	FBG SV	IO		228	8				7350	8450
---	--- 1980 BOATS	---	---	---	---	---	---	---	---	---	---	---	---
20	SX-20		RNBT	FBG SV	OB		165	7 6	3100			3350	3900
20 4	C-20		OP	CTRCN	FBG SV	OB		7 6	1925	10		3850	4500
22	C-22		OP	CTRCN	FBG SV	OB		8	2200	10		4700	5350
22	C-22 FSH		OP	CTRCN	FBG SV	IO	165-200	8	3160	10		4400	5100
	IB 225	4700	5400, IO	228	MRCR	4500	5150, IB	228	MRCR	4700	5400
	IO 230	OMC	4450	5100, IB	255	MRCR	4750	5450, IO	260		4600	5300
	IB 305-350	5050	6050
22	CF-22 FSH		OP	CUD	FBG SV	OB		8	2500	10		5150	5900
22	CF-22 FSH		OP	CUD	FBG SV	IO	165-200	8	3360	10		4250	5000
	IO 228	MRCR	4400	5100, IO	228	MRCR	4900	5650, IO	230	OMC	4400	5050
	IB 255	MRCR	4950	5650, IO	260		4550	5200, IB	305-350	OMC	5250	6250
22	SX-22		OP	RNBT	FBG SV	OB		8	2500	10		5150	5900
22	SX-22		OP	RNBT	FBG SV	IO	165-200	8	3360	10		4250	4750
	IO 228	MRCR	4150	4800, IO	228	MRCR	4950	5700, IO	230	OMC	4100	4800
	IB 255	MRCR	5000	5700, IO	260		4250	4950, IB	305-350	OMC	5300	6300
24	W-24		ST	WKNDR	FBG SV	IO	165-260	8	3780	2 2		6200	6200
26	C-26		OP	CTRCN	FBG SV	OB		8	3475	2 2		8650	9950
26	C-26		OP	CTRCN	FBG SV	IO	228-230	8	4375	2 8		8050	9050
	IB 255	MRCR	7600	8750, IO	260		7200	8250, IB	350	OMC	8300	9550
	IO T165	MRCR	8150	9350, IO	T170	MRCR	8200	9400, IB	T170-T225		8850	10500

LOA FT	IN	NAME AND/ OR MODEL	TOP/ RIG	BOAT TYPE	-HULL- MTL	TP	ENGINE TP	# HP	MFG	BEAM FT	IN	WGT LBS	DRAFT FT	IN	RETAIL LOW	RETAIL HIGH
		1980 BOATS														
26		C-26	OP	CTRCN	FBG	SV	IO	T228-T260		8		4875	2	8	8650	10300
26		C-26	OP	CTRCN	FBG	SV	IB	T350	OMC	8		4845	2	6	10400	11800
26		C-26	TT	CTRCN	FBG	SV	OB			8		3475	2		8650	9950
26		C-26	TT	CTRCN	FBG	SV	IO	228-230		8		4375	2	8	7000	8050
		IB 255 MRCR 7600 8750, IO 260 7200 8250, IB 350 OMC													8300	9550
		IO T165 MRCR 8150 9350, IO T170 MRCR 8200 9400, IB T170-T225													8850	10500
		IO T228-T260 8650 10300, IB T350 OMC 10400 11800														
26		CF-26 FSH	OP	CUD	FBG	SV	OB			8		3625	2		8850	10100
26		CF-26 FSH	OP	CUD	FBG	SV	IO	228-230		8		4525	2	8	6750	7750
		IB 255 MRCR 7750 8900, IO 260 6950 7950, IB 350 OMC													8450	9700
		IO T165 MRCR 7850 9000, IO T170 MRCR 7900 9050, IB T170-T225													9000	10700
		IO T228-T230 8300 9550, IB T250 OMC 9800 11100, IO T260													8650	9950
26		CF-26 FSH	TT	CUD	FBG	SV	OD			8		3625	2		8850	10100
26		CF-26 FSH	TT	CUD	FBG	SV	IO	228-230		8		4525	2	8	6750	7750
		IB 255 MRCR 7750 8900, IO 260 6950 7950, IB 350 OMC													8450	9700
		IO T165 MRCR 7850 9000, IO T170 MRCR 7900 9050, IB T170-T225													9000	10700
		IO T228-T260 8300 9950, IB T350 OMC 10600 12000														
26		FBSF			FBG	SV	IO			8		7000			**	**
26		SX-26	ST	SPTCR	FBG	SV	OB			8		4000	2		9100	10400
26		SX-26	ST	SPTCR	FBG	SV	IO	228-230		8		4900	2	8	7050	8100
		IB 255 MRCR 8100 9300, IO 260 7250 8350, IB 350 OMC													8900	10100
		IO T165 MRCR 8150 9400, IO T170 MRCR 8200 9400, IB T170-T225													9350	11000
		IO T228-T260 8650 10300, IB T350 OMC 11000 12500														
		1979 BOATS														
20	4	C-20	OP	CTRCN	FBG	SV	OB			7	6	1925		10	3800	4400
22		C-22 FSH	OP	CTRCN	FBG	SV	OB			8		2200		10	4650	5350
22		C-22 FSH	OP	CTRCN	FBG	SV	IO	165-260		8		3160		10	4400	5300
22		CF-22 FSH	OP	CUD	FBG	SV	OB			8		2500		10	5050	5850
22		CF-22 FSH	OP	CUD	FBG	SV	IO	165-260		8		3360		10	4250	5200
22		SX-22	OP	RNBT	FBG	SV	OB			8		2500		10	5050	5850
22		SX-22	OP	RNBT	FBG	SV	IO	165-260		8		3360		10	4050	4950
		1978 BOATS														
17	2	DRIFTER C-17	OP	CTRCN	FBG	SV	OB			6	9	1490	1		2700	3100
17	2	SANIBEL S-17	ST	RNBT	FBG	SV	OB			6	9	1410	1		2600	3000
17	2	SANIBEL S-17	ST	RNBT	FBG	SV	IO	120-140		6	9	2170	1		2050	2450
19		FISHERMAN C-19	OP	CTRCN	FBG	SV	OB			8		1525		10	2850	3350
19		SUNCHASER S-19	ST	RNBT	FBG	SV	OB			7	2	1740			3150	3650
19		SUNCHASER S-19	ST	RNBT	FBG	SV	IO	120-240		7	2	2380	2	4	2500	3000
21	10	HERITAGE SS-22	ST	CUD	FBG	SV	OB			7	11	2365	1	1	4800	5500
21	10	HERITAGE SS-22	ST	CUD	FBG	SV	IO	140-240		7	11	3310	1	1	4200	5000
21	10	HERITAGE SS-22	ST	CUD	FBG	SV	IO	T120-T140		7	11	3310	1	1	4800	5550
21	10	HERITAGE SS-22	HT	CUD	FBG	SV	OB			7	11	2365	1	1	4800	5500
21	10	HERITAGE SS-22	HT	CUD	FBG	SV	IO	140-240		7	11	3310	1	1	4200	5000
21	10	HERITAGE SS-22	HT	CUD	FBG	SV	IO	T120-T140		7	11	3310	1	1	4800	5550
21	10	OFFSHORE S-22	ST	RNBT	FBG	SV	OB			7	11	2100	1	1	4400	5050
21	10	OFFSHORE S-22	ST	RNBT	FBG	SV	IO	140-240		7	11	3050	1	1	3750	4500
21	10	OFFSHORE S-22	ST	RNBT	FBG	SV	IO	T120-T140		7	11	3050	1	1	4400	5050
21	10	OFFSHORE S-22	HT	RNBT	FBG	SV	OB			7	11	2100	1	1	4400	5050
21	10	OFFSHORE S-22	HT	RNBT	FBG	SV	IO	140-240		7	11	3050	1	1	3750	4500
21	10	OFFSHORE S-22	HT	RNBT	FBG	SV	IO	T120-T140		7	11	3050	1	1	4400	5050
22		MARINER C-22	OP	OPFSH	FBG	SV	OB			8		2200		10	4600	5250
22		MARINER C-22	OP	OPFSH	FBG	SV	IO	140-240		8		3160		10	4400	5200
23		TEMPTRESS S-23		CR	FBG	DV	IO	225-240		8			2	11	4450	5150
23		TEMPTRESS S-23		CR	FBG	DV	IO	T120-T170		8			2	11	4950	5700
24		PRIVATEER SD-24	ST	WKNDR	FBG	SV	IO	185-225		8		3780	2	2	5200	6050
		IO 228 MRCR 5300 6100, IB 228 MRCR 5500 6350, IO 240 OMC													5350	6100
		IB 305 OMC 5800 6700, IO T120-T170 5800 6750														
24		PRIVATEER SD-24	HT	WKNDR	FBG	SV	IO	185-225		8		3780	2	2	5200	6050
		IO 228 MRCR 5300 6100, IB 228 MRCR 5500 6350, IO 240 OMC													5350	6100
		IB 305 OMC 5800 6700, IO T120-T170 5800 6750														
26		SWORDFISHER C-26		CR	FBG	DV	OB			8		3250	2	9	8300	9550
26		SWORDFISHER C-26		CR	FBG	DV	IO	225-240		8		4500	2	9	6700	7800
26		SWORDFISHER C-26		CR	FBG	DV	IO	T120-T198		8		4500	2	9	7150	8850
		1977 BOATS														
17		S-17	OP	RNBT	FBG	SV	OB			6	11	1400			2550	2950
18		BOSS S-18	OP	SKI	FBG	SV	IO	165-235		7	5	2300			2350	2800
19		FISHERMAN C-19I	OP	FSH	FBG	SV	OB			7	11	1525			2700	3150
19		FISHERMAN C-19II	OP	FSH	FBG	SV	OB			7	11	1525			3000	3500
19		SUNCHASER S-19	ST	RNBT	FBG	SV	OB			7	2	2200			3550	4100
19		SUNCHASER S-19	ST	RNBT	FBG	SV	IO	120-235		7	2	2200			2400	2950
19		SUNCHASER S-19	HT	RNBT	FBG	SV	OB			7	2	2200			3550	4100
19		SUNCHASER S-19	HT	RNBT	FBG	SV	IO	120-235		7	2	2200			2400	2950
22		HERITAGE SS-22	ST	CUD	FBG	SV	OB			8		3450			6050	6950
22		HERITAGE SS-22	ST	CUD	FBG	SV	IO	165-235		8		3450			4500	5300
22		HERITAGE SS-22	ST	CUD	FBG	SV	JT	245	OMC	8		3450			4800	5500
22		HERITAGE SS-22	ST	CUD	FBG	SV	IO	T120-T140		8		3450			5100	5850
22		HERITAGE SS-22	HT	CUD	FBG	SV	OB			8		3450			6050	6950
22		HERITAGE SS-22	HT	CUD	FBG	SV	IO	165-235		8		3450			4500	5300
22		HERITAGE SS-22	HT	CUD	FBG	SV	JT	245	OMC	8		3450			4800	5500
22		HERITAGE SS-22	HT	CUD	FBG	SV	IO	T120-T140		8		3450			5100	5850
22		OFFSHORE S-22	ST	RNBT	FBG	SV	OB			8		2100			4350	5050
22		OFFSHORE S-22	ST	RNBT	FBG	SV	IO	165-235		8		2100			3250	3900
22		OFFSHORE S-22	ST	RNBT	FBG	SV	JT	245	OMC	8		2100			3800	4400
22		OFFSHORE S-22	ST	RNBT	FBG	SV	IO	T120-T140		8		2100			3800	4450
22		OFFSHORE S-22	HT	RNBT	FBG	SV	OB			8		2100			4350	5050
22		OFFSHORE S-22	HT	RNBT	FBG	SV	IO	165-235		8		2100			3250	3900
22		OFFSHORE S-22	HT	RNBT	FBG	SV	JT	245	OMC	8		2100			3800	4400
22		OFFSHORE S-22	HT	RNBT	FBG	SV	IO	T120-T140		8		2100			3800	4450
24		PRIVATEER SD-24	ST	CUD	FBG	SV	IO	188-190		8		3850			5400	6200
		IB 230 OMC 5450 6250, IO 233 MRCR 5500 6300, IB 233 MRCR													5300	6100
		IO 235 OMC 5450 6300, IO T140-T165 6000 6900														
		1976 BOATS														
19		FISHERMAN C-19	OP	FSH	FBG	SV	OB			7	11	1525	1	2	2800	3250
19	2	SUNCHASER S-19	ST	RNBT	FBG	DV	OB			7	2	1600	2	4	2950	3450
19	2	SUNCHASER S-19	ST	RNBT	FBG	DV	IO	120-225		7	2	2200	2	4	2500	3000
22		HERITAGE SS-22	ST	CR	FBG	SV	OB			8		2350	2	4	4700	5400
22		HERITAGE SS-22	ST	CR	FBG	SV	IO	165-235		8		3450	2	4	4600	5400
22		HERITAGE SS-22	ST	CR	FBG	SV	JT	245	OMC	8		3450	2	4	4650	5300
22		HERITAGE SS-22	ST	CR	FBG	SV	IO	T120-T140		8		3450	2	4	5200	6000
22		OFFSHORE S-22	ST	RNBT	FBG	SV	OB			8		2100	2	4	4300	5000
22		OFFSHORE S-22	ST	RNBT	FBG	SV	IO	165-235		8		3200	2	4	4100	4900
22		OFFSHORE S-22	ST	RNBT	FBG	SV	JT	245	OMC	8		3200	2	4	4450	5150
22		OFFSHORE S-22	ST	RNBT	FBG	SV	IO	T120-T140		8		3200	2	4	4700	5450
24		PRIVATEER	ST	CUD	FBG	SV	IB	233-260		8		3850	1	4	5100	5900
		1975 BOATS														
19		FISHERMAN C19	OP	FSH	FBG	SV	OB			7	11	1325	1		2550	2950
19	2	SUNCHASER S19	ST	CR	FBG	DV	OB			7	2	1600	2	4	2900	3400
19	2	SUNCHASER S19	ST	CR	FBG	DV	IO	120-225		7	2	2200	2	4	2650	3200
22		HERITAGE S22	ST	CR	FBG	SV	IO	165-233		8		3450	2	4	4750	5600
		JT 245 OMC 4450 5100, IO 106D VLVO 5800 6650, IO T120-T140													5400	6200
22		OFFSHORE S-22	ST	CR	FBG	SV	OB			8		2100	2	4	4250	4950
22		OFFSHORE S-22	ST	CR	FBG	SV	IO	165-233		8		3200	2	4	4550	5350
		JT 245 OMC 4200 4900, IO 106D VLVO 5550 6400, IO T120-T140													5150	5950
24		PRIVATEER SD24	ST	CR	FBG	TH	IB	225	MRCR	8		3850	1	6	4900	5600
26		DIPLOMAT S26	ST	CR	FBG	DV	IO	225	OMC	8		6000			8650	9950
26		DIPLOMAT S26	ST	CR	FBG	DV	IO	T120-T170		8		6000			9200	11000
26		DIPLOMAT S26	ST	CR	FBG	DV	IO	T106D	VLVO	8		6000			11500	13000
		1974 BOATS														
19		C-19		FSH	FBG		OB			7	11	1325	1		2500	2900
19	2	SUNCHASER S-19		CR	FBG		OB			7	2				3100	3650
19	2	SUNCHASER S-19		CR	FBG		IO	120-225		7	2	2200	2	5	2750	3300
22		S-22 OFFSHORE		OFF	FBG		OB			8		2100			4250	4900
22		S-22 OFFSHORE		OFF	FBG		IO	165-225		8		3200	2	5	4700	5450
		JT 245 OMC 4050 4700, IO 245 OMC 4800 5500, IO 106D VLVO													5750	6600
		IO T120-T140 5300 6150														
24		PRIVATEER SD-24		CR	FBG		JT	225	MRCR	8		3850	1	4	5050	5800
24		PRIVATEER SD-24		CR	FBG		IB	255	MRCR	8		3850	1	4	4700	5400
26		DIPLOMAT S-26		CR	FBG		IO	225	OMC	8		6000			9050	10300
26		DIPLOMAT S-26		CR	FBG		IO	T120-T170		8		6000			9450	11400
26		DIPLOMAT S-26		CR	FBG		IO	T106D	VLVO	8		6000			11800	13500
26		DIPLOMAT S-26		RNBT	FBG		IO	T140	OMC	8		6000			8900	10100
		1973 BOATS														
18		BOSS	OP	SKI	FBG	SV	IO	165		7	5	2300			2600	3050
19	2	SUNCHASER S-19		CR	FBG		OB			7	2		2	5	3100	3600
19	2	SUNCHASER S-19		CR	FBG		IO	120-225		7	2	2200	2	5	2850	3450
19	2	SUNCHASER S-19	HT	CR	FBG		OB			7	2		2	5	3100	3600
19	2	SUNCHASER S-19	HT	CR	FBG		IO	120-225		7	2		2	5	2900	3450
22		S-22 OFFSHORE		OFF	FBG		OB			8			2	5	4750	5450
22		S-22 OFFSHORE		OFF	FBG		IO	165-225		8		3200	2	5	4800	5600
		JT 245 OMC 3800 4450, IO 245 OMC 4850 5600, IO 106D VLVO													**	**
		IO T120-T140 5400 6550														
24		PRIVATEER SD-24		CR	FBG		TD	225-255		8		3850	1	4	4550	5250
26		DIPLOMAT S-26		CR	FBG		IO	225	OMC	8		6000			9350	10600

 CONTINUED ON NEXT PAGE

LOA FT	LOA IN	NAME AND/ OR MODEL	TOP/ RIG	BOAT TYPE	HULL MTL	HULL TP	ENGINE TP	ENGINE # HP	ENGINE MFG	BEAM FT	BEAM IN	WGT LBS	DRAFT FT	DRAFT IN	RETAIL LOW	RETAIL HIGH
		1973 BOATS														
26		DIPLOMAT S-26		CR	FBG		IO	T120-T170		8		6000			9750	11700
26		DIPLOMAT S-26		CR	FBG		IO	T106D	VLVO	8		6000			12200	13900
		1972 BOATS														
18		BOSS 1 S-18			FBG		IO	165-225		7	5	2050	2		2600	3200
18		BOSS 1 S-18			FBG		IO	245	OMC	7	5	2200	2		2800	3250
18		BOSS 2 S-18			FBG		IO	165-245		7	5	2200	2		2700	3350
19	2	SUNCHASER S-19			FBG		IO	120-188		7	2	2200	2	5	2800	3450
19	2	SUNCHASER S-19			FBG		IO	225	OMC	7	2	2400	2	5	3000	3500
22		S-22 OFFSHORE		OFF	FBG		OB			8		2100	2	3	4200	4900
22		S-22 OFFSHORE		OFF	FBG		IO	140-225		8		3200	2	3	4950	5900
22		S-22 OFFSHORE		OFF	FBG		IO	106D	VLVO	8		3200	2	3	6100	7050
22		S-22 OFFSHORE		OFF	FBG		IO	T100-T140		8		3200	2	3	5600	6900
26		DIPLOMAT S-26			FBG		IO	225	OMC	8		6000	2	5	9750	11100
26		DIPLOMAT S-26			FBG		IO	T120-T140		8		6000	2	5	10200	11900
		1971 BOATS														
18		BOSS 1 S-18			FBG		IO	165-235		7	5	2050	2		2650	3200
18		BOSS 2 S-18			FBG		IO	165-235		7	5	2300	2		2850	3400
19		SUNCHASER S-19			FBG		IO	120-215		7	2	2200	2	3	2850	3400
22		S-22 OFFSHORE		OFF	FBG		OB			8		1600	2	3	3350	3900
22		S-22 OFFSHORE		OFF	FBG		IO	140-235		8		3200	2	3	5150	6050
22		S-22 OFFSHORE		OFF	FBG		IO	106D	VLVO	8		3200	2	3	6350	7250
22		S-22 OFFSHORE		OFF	FBG		IO	T 90-T140		8		3200	2	3	5800	6750
25	11	DIPLOMAT S-26			FBG		IO	165-215		8		6000	2	4	9650	11300
25	11	DIPLOMAT S-26			FBG		IO	106D	VLVO	8		6000	2	4	11300	12800
25	11	DIPLOMAT S-26			FBG		IO	T120-T140		8		6000	2	4	10500	12100
		1970 BOATS														
18		BOSS 1 S-18		RNBT	FBG	SV	IO	165-215		7	5	2450	2		3000	3600
18		BOSS 1 S-18		RNBT	FBG	SV	JT	290	HOLM	7	5	2350	1	2	2200	2550
18		BOSS 1 S-18		RNBT	FBG	SV	IO	290	HOLM	7	5	2450	2		3450	4000
18		BOSS 2 S-18		RNBT	FBG	SV	IO	165-215		7	5	2450	2		3200	3800
18		BOSS 2 S-18		RNBT	FBG	SV	JT	290	HOLM	7	5	2350	1	2	2300	2650
18		BOSS 2 S-18		RNBT	FBG	SV	IO	290	HOLM	7	5	2450	2		3600	4200
19	1	SUNCHASER S-19		CR	FBG	SV	IO	120-165		7	2	2350	2	3	3250	3850
22		S-22 OFFSHORE		OFF	FBG	SV	OB			8		1600	1	11	3350	3900
22		S-22 OFFSHORE		OFF	FBG	SV	IO	140-215		8		2800	2	3	4900	5950
22		S-22 OFFSHORE		OFF	FBG	SV	JT	290	HOLM	8		3200	1	4	3450	4000
22		S-22 OFFSHORE		OFF	FBG	SV	IO	T 90-T140		8		3600	2	3	6450	7500
26		DIPLOMAT S-26		EXP	FBG	SV	IO	210-215		8	6	4500	2	4	8550	9850
26		DIPLOMAT S-26		EXP	FBG	SV	IO	T120-T155		8	6	5000	2	4	9750	11400
		1969 BOATS														
18		BOSS S-18		SKI	FBG	DV	IO	155-225		7	5	2050	1	10	2750	3450
19	2	SUNCHASER S-19		CR	FBG	DV	IO	120-160		7	2	2400	2		3400	4150
22		S-22 OFFSHORE		OFF	FBG	DV	OB			8		2500	2	4	4850	5550
22		S-22 OFFSHORE		OFF	FBG	DV	IO	140-225		8		3200	2	4	5500	6650
22		S-22 OFFSHORE		OFF	FBG	DV	IO	T120-T140		8		3500	2	4	6600	8000
22		S-22 OFFSHORE		OFF	FBG	SV	IB	250	MRCR	8			2	3	3000	3500
25	5	DIPLOMAT S-26		CBNCR	FBG	DV	IO	T120	MRCR	8		4200	2	6	10500	11900
		1968 BOATS														
18		BOSS S-18	OP	RNBT	FBG	DV	IO	155-225		7	6	2175	2	2	3100	3800
19	2	SUNCHASER S-19	OP	CR	FBG	DV	IO	110-160		7	2	2250	2	4	3550	4150
22		S-22 OFFSHORE		OFF	FBG	DV	OB			8			1	8	4750	5450
22		S-22 OFFSHORE		OFF	FBG	DV	IO	110-225		8		3000	1	8	5600	6450
22		S-22 OFFSHORE		OFF	FBG	DV	IO	T 80-T120		8		3000	1	8	6250	7600
		1967 BOATS														
18		BOSS S-18		SKI	FBG		IO	120-225		7	5	2175	2		3050	3700
19	2	SUNCHASER S-19		RNBT	FBG		OB			7	2	1000			2000	2400
19	2	SUNCHASER S-19		RNBT	FBG		IO	110-165		7	2	2250	2	2	3400	4000
19	2	SUNCHASER S-19		RNBT	FBG		IO	60D		7	2	2250	2	2	4400	5100
22		S-22 OFFSHORE		OFF	FBG		OB			8		1400			3000	3500
22		S-22 OFFSHORE		OFF	FBG		IO	110-225		8		3000	2	2	5600	6600
22		S-22 OFFSHORE		OFF	FBG		IO	60D		8		3000	2	2	6850	7850
22		S-22 OFFSHORE		OFF	FBG		IO	T 80-T120		8		3000	2	2	6450	7450
		1966 BOATS														
17	10	S-18		SKI	FBG		IO	110-150		7	6		2	4	3250	3800
18	10	S-19		CR	FBG		OB			7	8	1400			2600	3000
18	10	V S-19		CR	FBG		IO	110-150		7	8		2	4	3700	4350
21	10	S-22		CR	FBG		OB			8		2000	2	4	4050	4700
21	10	S-22		CR	FBG		IO	110-225		8			2	4	5850	6950
21	10	S-22		CR	FBG		IO	310		8			2	4	6700	7700
21	10	S-22		CR	FBG		IO	T 60-T120		8			2	4	6750	7750
		1965 BOATS														
22		S-22			FBG		OB								4800	5500
22		S-22			FBG		IO	110-225							5800	6850
22		S-22			FBG		IO	310							6600	7600
22		S-22			FBG		IO	T 60-T120							6650	7700

NORTH AMERICAN DESIGN ASSN

Call 1-800-327-6929 for BUC Personalized Evaluation Service
Or, for 1980 to 1982 boats, sign onto www.BUCValuPro.com

NORTH AMERICAN ENGINEERING

COAST GUARD MFG ID- NAE

Call 1-800-327-6929 for BUC Personalized Evaluation Service
Or, for 1973 to 1974 boats, sign onto www.BUCValuPro.com

NORTH AMERICAN FIBERGLASS INC

SEA OX BOATS
GREENVILLE NC 27834-904 COAST GUARD MFG ID- XNA

See inside cover to adjust price for area

For more recent years, see the BUC Used Boat Price Guide, Volume 1 or Volume 2

LOA FT	LOA IN	NAME AND/ OR MODEL	TOP/ RIG	BOAT TYPE	HULL MTL	HULL TP	ENGINE TP	ENGINE # HP	ENGINE MFG	BEAM FT	BEAM IN	WGT LBS	DRAFT FT	DRAFT IN	RETAIL LOW	RETAIL HIGH
		1983 BOATS														
16	9	SEA-OX 170	OP	CTRCN	FBG	SV	OB			6		1100		7	2200	2550
16	9	SEA-OX 1700	OP	UTL	FBG	SV	OB			6		950		8	1850	2200
18	9	SEA-OX 1900	OP	FSH	FBG	SV	OB			7	4	1325		6	2650	3100
20	3	SEA-OX 2000	OP	CTRCN	FBG	SV	OB			8		2175		8	4800	5550
20	3	SEA-OX 2000	OP	CTRCN	FBG	SV	IO	170-190		8		1725		9	3900	4850
20	3	SEA-OX 2000	OP	CTRCN	FBG	SV	IO	150D	BMW	8		1725		9	6950	8000
20	3	SEA-OX 200C	OP	CUD	FBG	SV	OB			8		2500		9	5200	6000
20	3	SEA-OX 200C	OP	CUD	FBG	SV	IO	T	OMC	8		2600		9	**	**
22	7	SEA-OX 2300	OP	PH	FBG	SV	OB			8		1875		9	4850	5550
22	7	SEA-OX 2300	OP	PH	FBG	SV	IO	170-190		8		1875		9	4550	5550
22	7	SEA-OX 2300	OP	PH	FBG	SV	IO	150D	BMW	8		1875		9	6650	7650
22	7	SEA-OX 2300	HT	UTL	FBG	SV	OB			8		1875		9	4200	4900
22	7	SEA-OX 2300	HT	UTL	FBG	SV	IO	170-190		8		1875		9	4700	5700
22	7	SEA-OX 2300	HT	UTL	FBG	SV	IO	150D	BMW	8		1875		9	8000	9200
22	9	SEA-OX 230	OP	CTRCN	FBG	SV	OB			8		2350		9	5850	6750
22	9	SEA-OX 230C	OP	CUD	FBG	SV	OB			8		2700		9	6550	7500
22	9	SEA-OX 230C	OP	CUD	FBG	SV	IO		OMC	8		2700		9	**	**
		IO 170-190 5100 6200, IO 150D BMW 7100 8150, IO T OMC													**	**
22	9	SEA-OX 230C	TT	CUD	FBG	SV	OB			8		2700		9	6550	7500
22	9	SEA-OX 230C	TT	CUD	FBG	SV	IO		OMC	8		2700		9	**	**
22	9	SEA-OX 230C	TT	CUD	FBG	SV	IO	170-190		8		2700		9	5100	6200
22	9	SEA-OX 230C	TT	CUD	FBG	SV	IO	150D	BMW	8		2700		9	7100	8150
		1982 BOATS														
16	9	SEA-OX 170	OP	CTRCN	FBG	DV	OB			6		1200		7	2300	2700
16	9	SEA-OX 1700	OP	UTL	FBG	DV	OB			6		950		8	1800	2150
18	9	SEA-OX 1900	OP	UTL	FBG	SV	OB			7	4	1325		6	2400	2800
18	9	SEA-OX 1900 OPENBOW	OP	FSH	FBG	SV	OB			7	4	1350		6	2650	3100
20	3	SEA-OX 200	OP	CTRCN	FBG	DV	OB			8		1950		9	4450	5100
20	3	SEA-OX 2000	OP	UTL	FBG	DV	OB			8		1725		9	3600	4150
20	3	SEA-OX 200C	OP	CUD	FBG	SV	OB			8		2400		9	5000	5750
22	7	SEA-OX 2300	OP	UTL	FBG	DV	OB			8		1875		9	4100	4800
22	9	SEA-OX 230	OP	CTRCN	FBG	DV	OB			8		2150		9	5350	6150
22	9	SEA-OX 230	OP	CTRCN	FBG	SV	IO	170-200		8		2805		9	5400	6500
22	9	SEA-OX 230	OP	CTRCN	FBG	SV	IO	225	VLVO	8		2995		9	5950	6800
22	9	SEA-OX 2300	OP	UTL	FBG	SV	IO	120-225		8				9	5950	7050
22	9	SEA-OX 230C	OP	CUD	FBG	SV	OB			8		2600		9	6250	7150
22	9	SEA-OX 230C	OP	CUD	FBG	SV	IO	170-225		8		3325		9	5650	7050
		1981 BOATS														
16	9	SEA-OX 170	OP	CTRCN	FBG	DV	OB			6		1200		7	2250	2650
16	9	SEA-OX 1700	OP	UTL	FBG	DV	OB			6		950		7	1750	2100
18	9	SEA-OX 1900	OP	UTL	FBG	SV	OB			7	4	1325		6	2350	2750
20	3	SEA-OX 200	OP	CTRCN	FBG	DV	OB			8		1950		9	4350	5000
20	3	SEA-OX 2000	OP	UTL	FBG	DV	OB			8		1650		9	3400	3950
20	3	SEA-OX 200C	OP	CUD	FBG	SV	OB			8		2400		9	4900	5650
22	9	SEA-OX 230	OP	CTRCN	FBG	DV	OB			8		2150		9	5250	6050
22	9	SEA-OX 230	OP	CTRCN	FBG	SV	IO	170-200		8		2805		9	5300	6350
22	9	SEA-OX 2300	OP	UTL	FBG	DV	OB			8		1850		9	4000	4650
22	9	SEA-OX 2300	OP	UTL	FBG	SV	IO	120-225		8				9	5850	6900
22	9	SEA-OX 230C	OP	CUD	FBG	SV	OB			8		2600		9	6100	7050
22	9	SEA-OX 230C	OP	CUD	FBG	SV	IO	170-225		8		3325		9	5550	6900
		1980 BOATS														
16	9	SEA-OX 170	OP	CTRCN	FBG	DV	OB			6		1050		8	1950	2300
16	9	SEA-OX 1700	OP	UTL	FBG	DV	OB			6		950		8	1750	2100

NORTH AMERICAN FIBERGLASS INC -CONTINUED   See inside cover to adjust price for area

LOA FT IN	NAME AND/ OR MODEL	TOP/ RIG	BOAT TYPE	-HULL- MTL	TP	TP	ENGINE #	HP	MFG	BEAM FT IN	WGT LBS	DRAFT FT IN	RETAIL LOW	RETAIL HIGH
---	--- 1980	BOATS	---											
18 9	SEA-OX 1900	OP	UTL	FBG	SV	OB				7 4	1325	6	2350	2700
20 3	SEA-OX 200	OP	CTRCN	FBG	DV	OB				8	1750	9	3950	4600
20 3	SEA-OX 2000	OP	UTL	FBG	DV	OB				8	1650	9	3350	3900
22 7	SEA-OX 230	OP	CTRCN	FBG	DV	OB				8	1980	9	4800	5550
22 7	SEA-OX 230	OP	CTRCN	FBG	SV	IO	170-200			8	2805	9	5200	6200
22 7	SEA-OX 230	OP	CTRCN	FBG	SV	IO	225		VLVO	8	2995	9	5700	6550
22 7	SEA-OX 2300	OP	UTL	FBG	DV	OB				8	1850	9	3950	4600
22 7	SEA-OX 230	OP	UTL	FBG	SV	IO	170-225			8		9	5600	6800
22 7	SEA-OX 230C	OP	CUD	FBG	SV	OB				8	2490	9	5800	6650
22 7	SEA-OX 230C	OP	CUD	FBG	SV	IO	170-225			8	3325	9	5450	6800
---	--- 1979	BOATS	---											
16 9	RIVER-OX 1700	OP	CTRCN	FBG	DV	OB				6	1050	8	1950	2300
16 9	RIVER-OX 1700 COMM	OP	UTL	FBG	DV	OB				6	950	8	1750	2050
18 9	SEA-OX 1900 COMM	OP	UTL	FBG	DV	OB				7 4	1325	6	2350	2700
20 3	SEA-OX 2000	OP	CTRCN	FBG	DV	OB				8	1750	9	3900	4500
20 3	SEA-OX 2000 COMM	OP	UTL	FBG	DV	OB				8	1650	9	3300	3800
22 7	CABIN CAMPER 2300	OP	CTRCN	FBG	DV	OB				8	2030	9	4850	5550
22 7	SEA-OX 2300	OP	CTRCN	FBG	DV	OB				8	1980	9	4750	5450
22 7	SEA-OX 2300 COMM	OP	UTL	FBG	DV	OB				8	1850	9	3900	4500
---	--- 1978	BOATS	---											
16 9	RIVER-OX 1700	OP	FSH	FBG	SV	OB				6	1050	8	1900	2250
16 9	RIVER-OX 1700 COMM	OP	UTL	FBG	SV	OB				6	1050	8	1850	2250
18 9	SEA-OX 1900	OP	FSH	FBG	SV	OB				7 4	1325	6	2500	2900
18 9	SEA-OX 1900 COMM	OP	UTL	FBG	SV	OB				7 4	1325	6	2300	2700
22 7	SEA-OX 2300	OP	FSH	FBG	SV	OB				8	1980	9	4700	5400
22 7	SEA-OX 2300	OP	UTL	FBG	SV	OB				8	1980	9	4100	4750
---	--- 1977	BOATS	---											
18 9	SEA-OX 1900 COMM	OP	OPFSH	FBG	SV	OB				7 4	1300	7	2450	2800

NORTH AMERICAN MARINE
AMERICAN

Call 1-800-327-6929 for BUC Personalized Evaluation Service
Or, for 1959 to 1960 boats, sign onto www.BUCValuPro.com

NORTH CHANNEL YT BLDG CO
JOHN T FREDERICK SALES CO

Call 1-800-327-6929 for BUC Personalized Evaluation Service
Or, for 1977 to 1980 boats, sign onto www.BUCValuPro.com

NORTH COAST MARINE

Call 1-800-327-6929 for BUC Personalized Evaluation Service
Or, for 1978 to 1984 boats, sign onto www.BUCValuPro.com

NORTH COAST YACHTS

Call 1-800-327-6929 for BUC Personalized Evaluation Service
Or, for 1980 to 1982 boats, sign onto www.BUCValuPro.com

NORTH SEA
See inside cover to adjust price for area

LOA FT IN	NAME AND/ OR MODEL	TOP/ RIG	BOAT TYPE	-HULL- MTL	TP	TP	ENGINE #	HP	MFG	BEAM FT IN	WGT LBS	DRAFT FT IN	RETAIL LOW	RETAIL HIGH
---	--- 1979	BOATS	---											
36 10	TRI-CABIN	FB	TRWL			IB	120D		LEHM				73700	81000

NORTH SEA PACIFIC SHIPPING CO

Call 1-800-327-6929 for BUC Personalized Evaluation Service
Or, for 1961 boats, sign onto www.BUCValuPro.com

NORTH STAR YACHTS LTD
HUGHES BOAT WORKS
DIV OF NORTH STAR YACHTS LTD   See inside cover to adjust price for area
HURON PARK ONTARIO CANA COAST GUARD MFG ID- NSX
FOR MORE RECENT YEARS SEE HUGHES COLUMBIA INC

LOA FT IN	NAME AND/ OR MODEL	TOP/ RIG	BOAT TYPE	-HULL- MTL	TP	TP	ENGINE #	HP	MFG	BEAM FT IN	WGT LBS	DRAFT FT IN	RETAIL LOW	RETAIL HIGH
---	--- 1982	BOATS	---											
27 2	COLUMBIA 8.3	SLP	SA/CR	FBG	KL	IB	15D		YAN	9 4	7300	4 4	16000	18200
28 7	COLUMBIA 8.7	SLP	SA/CR	FBG	KL	IB	15D		YAN	10	8500	4 8	19200	21300
31 6	HUGHES 31 S.E.	SLP	SA/RC	FBG	KL	IB	15D		YAN	9 8	9100	5 2	20000	22200
35 2	COLUMBIA 10.7	SLP	SA/CR	FBG	KL	IB	23D		YAN	11 4	13900	5 5	30900	34300
35 6	HUGHES 35 S.E.	SLP	SA/RC	FBG	KL	IB	21D		UNIV	10 4	12000	5 10	27200	30200
35 10	HUGHES-COLUMBIA 36	SLP	SA/CR	FBG	KL	IB	23D		YAN	10 2	15000	4	33600	37300
35 10	HUGHES-COLUMBIA 36	KTH	SA/CR	FBG	KL	IB	23D		YAN	10 2	15000	4	34000	37700
38	HUGHES 38	SLP	SA/RC	FBG	KL	IB	23D		YAN	10 2	14000	5 10	34400	38200
39	COLUMBIA 11-8	SLP	SA/CR	FBG	KL	IB	50D		PERK	12 4	23500	5 10	53800	59100
40	HUGHES 40	SLP	SA/CR	FBG	KL	IB	50D		PERK	13 4	28000	4 9	63100	69300
40	HUGHES 40	KTH	SA/CR	FBG	KL	IB	50D		PERK	13 4	28000	4 9	63500	69800
---	--- 1981	BOATS	---											
26	HUGHES 26	SLP	SA/RC	FBG	KL	IB	D			9		4	10200	11600
31 6	HUGHES 31	SLP	SA/RC	FBG	KL	IB	D			9 6		5 2	19100	21200
35 6	HUGHES 35	SLP	SA/RC	FBG	KL	IB	D			10 4		5 10	27600	30700
35 10	HUGHES 36	SLP	SA/CR	FBG	KL	IB	D			10 2		4 4	31900	35500
38	HUGHES 38	KTH	SA/RC	FBG	KL	IB	D			10 2		4 4	32300	35900
38	HUGHES 38	SLP	SA/RC	FBG	KL	IB	D			10 2		5 10	32600	36200
40	HUGHES 40	KTH	SA/CR	FBG	KL	IB	D			13 4		4 9	58600	64400
---	--- 1980	BOATS	---											
25 11	HUGHES 26	SLP	SA/CR	FBG	KL	SD	14		OMC	9	5000	4	9500	10800
26	HUGHES 26	SLP	SA/CR	FBG	KL	SD		D		9	5000	4	9850	11200
31 6	HUGHES 31	SLP	SA/RC	FBG	KL	SD	14			9 8	9700	4 2	19300	21500
31 6	HUGHES 31	SLP	SA/RC	FBG	KL	IB		D		9 8	9100	5 2	18300	20300
35	HUGHES 35	SLP	SA/RC	FBG	KL	IB	22D		VLVO	10 4	12600	4 10	25600	28400
35	HUGHES 35	SLP	SA/RC	FBG	KL	IB	22D		VLVO	10 4	12000	5 10	24400	27200
35 6	HUGHES 35	SLP	SA/RC	FBG	KL	IB	13D		YAN	10 4	13800	5 10	28200	31300
38	HUGHES 38	SLP	SA/RC	FBG	KL	IB	15D		YAN	10 4	14700	4 10	32500	36100
38	HUGHES 38	SLP	SA/RC	FBG	KL	IB	15D		YAN	10 4	14000	5 10	31200	34700
38	HUGHES 38	SLP	SA/RC	FBG	KL	IB	D			10 2	14000	4 4	31400	34800
38	HUGHES 38	SLP	SA/RC	FBG	KL	IB	23D		VLVO	10 2	14000	5 10	31400	34800
38	HUGHES 38	SLP	SA/RC	FBG	KL	IB	30D		UNIV	10 2	14000	5 10	31400	34900
40	HUGHES 40	KTH	MS	FBG	KL	IB	85D		FORD	13 4	28000	4 9	58200	64000
40	HUGHES 40	KTH	SA/CR	FBG	KL	IB	D			13 4	28000	4 9	58500	64300
---	--- 1979	BOATS	---											
26	HUGHES 26	SLP	SA/CR	FBG	KL	OB				9	5000	4	9000	10200
26	HUGHES 26	SLP	SA/CR	FBG	KL	SD	15		OMC	9	5000	4	9250	10500
26	HUGHES 26	SLP	SA/CR	FBG	KL	SD		D	YAN	9	5000	4	9550	10900
31 8	HUGHES 31	SLP	SA/CR	FBG	KL	SD	15			9 8	8100	4 2	15300	17400
31 8	HUGHES 31	SLP	SA/CR	FBG	KL	IB		D		9 8	8100	4 2	14500	17500
35 6	HUGHES 35	SLP	SA/CR	FBG	KL	VD	20		UNIV	10 4		4 7	22000	24400
	VD 20 UNIV 22000	24400,	SD		23D		VLVO	29400		32600,	SD	23D	VLVO	29400	32600
38	HUGHES 38	SLP	SA/RC	FBG	KL	IB	20D		UNIV	10 2	14000	5 10	30300	33700
38	HUGHES 38	SLP	SA/RC	FBG	KL	IB	23D		VLVO	10 2	14000	5 10	30300	33700
40	HUGHES 40	KTH	SA/CR	FBG	KL	IB	82D		FORD	13 4	24300	4 9	51400	56500
---	--- 1977	BOATS	---											
23 10	NORTH-STAR 727	SLP	SA/CR	FBG	KL	OB				8 4	2700	4 8	4550	5250
23 10	NORTH-STAR 727	SLP	SA/RC	FBG	KL	OB				8 4	2700	4 8	4550	5250
26	NORTH-STAR 26	SLP	SA/CR	FBG	KL	OB				9	4598	4	7750	8900
26	NORTH-STAR 30	SLP	SAIL	FBG	KL	IB	12D		YAN	9	4598	4	8300	9550
30	NORTH-STAR 30	SLP	SAIL	FBG	KL	IB	12D		YAN	9	5200	5 3	9450	10700
35 6	NORTH-STAR 35	SLP	SA/CR	FBG	KL	IB	30		UNIV	10 4		5 10	20800	23100
35 6	NORTH-STAR 35	SLP	SA/CR	FBG	KL	IB	25D		WEST	10 4		5 10	27300	30800
39 7	NORTH-STAR 80/20	KTH	SA/CR	FBG	KL	IB	80D		FORD	13 4	24000	4 9	47500	52100
---	--- 1976	BOATS	---											
23 10	NORTH-STAR 24	SLP	SAIL	FBG	KL	OB				8 3	2700	4 4	4450	5150
26	NORTH-STAR 26	SLP	SAIL	FBG	KL	IB				9	4600	4	7550	8650
26	NORTH-STAR 26	SLP	SAIL	FBG	KL	IB	10		UNIV	9	4598	4	7750	8900
29 11	NORTH-STAR 1000	SLP	SA/CR	FBG	KL	IB		D		9 6	8000	5 3	14200	16200
35 6	NORTH-STAR 1500	SLP	SAIL	FBG	KL	VD	30		UNIV	10 4	11086	5 10	20300	22500
35 6	NORTH-STAR 1500	SLP	SAIL	FBG	KL	IB	20D		WEST	10 4	11086	5 10	20500	22700
39 7	NORTH-STAR 80/20	KTH	SAIL	FBG	KL	IB	80D		FORD	13 4	24000	4 9	44500	50900
---	--- 1975	BOATS	---											
25	NORTH STAR 500	SLP	SAIL	FBG	KL	OB				9	4298	5	6700	7700
25	NORTH STAR 500	SLP	SAIL	FBG	KL	VD	30		UNIV	9	4298	5	7050	8100
25	NORTH STAR 500	SLP	SAIL	FBG	KL	VD	5D		WEST	9	4298	5	7250	8300
26	NORTH STAR 600	SLP	SAIL	FBG	KL	OB				9	4598	4	7350	8500
26	NORTH STAR 600	SLP	SAIL	FBG	KL	VD	30		UNIV	9	4598	4	7650	8800
26	NORTH STAR 600	SLP	SAIL	FBG	KL	VD	7D		WEST	9	4598	4	7850	9050
29 11	NORTH STAR 1000	SLP	SAIL	FBG	KL	IB	30		UNIV	9 6	8000	5 3	13800	15700
35 6	NORTH STAR 1500	SLP	SAIL	FBG	KL	IB	30		UNIV	10 4	11086	5 10	19800	22000
35 6	NORTH STAR 1500	SLP	SAIL	FBG	KL	IB	25D		WEST	10 4	11086	5 10	20000	22300
39 7	NORTH STAR 80/20	KTH	MS	FBG	KL	IB	52D		WEST	13 4	24000	4 9	44800	49700

LOA FT IN	NAME AND/ OR MODEL	TOP/ RIG	BOAT TYPE	-HULL- MTL TP	TP	----ENGINE--- # HP	MFG	BEAM FT IN	WGT LBS	DRAFT FT IN	RETAIL LOW	RETAIL HIGH
------------------------- 1974 BOATS -------------------------
25	500		SAIL	FBG	OB			9	4298	5	6600	7550
25	500		SAIL	FBG	IB	30	UNIV	9	4298	5	6900	7950
25	500		SAIL	FBG	IB	5D	WEST	9	4298	5	7100	8150
25 2	H25		SAIL	FBG	OB		7 6		3500	3 3	5500	6300
26	600		SAIL	FBG	OB			9	4598	4	7250	8300
26	600		SAIL	FBG	IB	30	UNIV	9	4598	4	7500	8650
29 4	H29		SAIL	FBG	OB			8 2	6500	4 4	10800	12300
30	1000		SAIL	FBG	IB	30	UNIV	9 6	8500	5 3	13500	15400
37 10	H38		SAIL	FBG	OB			10 2	12700	6	23900	26600
39 7	80/20		SAIL	FBG	IB	52D	WEST	13 4	24000	4 9	43700	48600
------------------------- 1973 BOATS -------------------------
22	NORTH-STAR 22		SAIL	FBG	OB			7 7	2250	6	3350	3900
25	NORTH-STAR 25		SAIL	FBG	OB			7 6	3500	3 3	5350	6150
25	NORTH-STAR 500		SAIL	FBG	IB	30	UNIV	9	4298	5	6800	7800
37 10	NORTH-STAR 38		SAIL	FBG	IB	30	UNIV	10 2	12700	6	23700	26300
48 2	NORTH-STAR 48		SAIL	FBG	IB	30D	WEST	11 10	32000	6 6	69700	76600
48 2	NORTH-STAR 48	YWL	SAIL	FBG	IB	30D	WEST	11 10	32000	6 6	69700	76600
------------------------- 1972 BOATS -------------------------
22	HUGHES 22		SAIL	FBG	OB			7 7	2200	2	3250	3750
25 2	HUGHES 25		SAIL	FBG	OB			7 6	3500	3 3	5250	6050
29 4	HUGHES 29		SAIL	FBG	IB	30	UNIV	8 2	6700	4 6	10800	12300
37 10	HUGHES 38 MK II		SAIL	FBG	IB	30	UNIV	10 2	12700	6	23200	25700
48 2	HUGHES 48		SAIL	FBG	IB	65	UNIV	11 10	32000	6 6	67800	74500
------------------------- 1971 BOATS -------------------------
25 2	HUGHES 25		SAIL	FBG	OB			7 6	3500	3 3	5150	5900
29 4	HUGHES 29		SAIL	FBG	OB			8 2		4 6	7250	8350
29 4	HUGHES 29		SAIL	FBG	IB	30	UNIV	8 2	6500	4 6	10200	11600
37 10	HUGHES 38 MK II		SAIL	FBG	IB	30	UNIV	10 2	12000	6	21500	23900
48 2	HUGHES 48		SAIL	FBG	IB	65	UNIV	11 10	30000	6 6	64500	70900
------------------------- 1970 BOATS -------------------------
20 3	VOYAGEUR	SLP	SAIL		KC			6 10		9	2750	3200
21	NORTH-STAR 21	SLP	SA/OD	FBG	KL			6 10		3 6	2400	2800
25 2	HUGHES 25	SLP	SA/CR	FBG	KL			7 6	3500	3 7	5000	5750
29 4	HUGHES 29	SLP	SA/CR	FBG	KL	IB	30D	8 2	6500	4 6	10200	11600
37 10	HUGHES 38	SLP	SA/CR	FBG	KL	IB	30D	10 2	12800	6	22600	25100
------------------------- 1968 BOATS -------------------------
24	HUGHES 24	SLP	SAIL	FBG	KC			7 8		2 8	3750	4350
27	HUGHES 27	SLP	SAIL	FBG	KL			8		3 8	6700	7700
37 8	HUGHES 38	SLP	SAIL	FBG	KL	IB	D	10 2		6	23500	26100

NORTHERN YACHTS INC
COAST GUARD MFG ID- NRY

Call 1-800-327-6929 for BUC Personalized Evaluation Service
Or, for 1974 to 1975 boats, sign onto www.BUCValuPro.com

NORTHSHORE MARINE
COAST GUARD MFG ID- NMK

Call 1-800-327-6929 for BUC Personalized Evaluation Service
Or, for 1978 to 1982 boats, sign onto www.BUCValuPro.com

NORTHSHORE YACHTS LTD
CHICHESTER W SUSSEX UK   COAST GUARD MFG ID- NRS See inside cover to adjust price for area

For more recent years, see the BUC Used Boat Price Guide, Volume 1 or Volume 2

LOA FT IN	NAME AND/ OR MODEL	TOP/ RIG	BOAT TYPE	-HULL- MTL TP	TP	----ENGINE--- # HP	MFG	BEAM FT IN	WGT LBS	DRAFT FT IN	RETAIL LOW	RETAIL HIGH
------------------------- 1979 BOATS -------------------------
23 9	RUM-RUNNER 24	OP	CBNCR	FBG	DV	IO	220	BMW	7 7	2500	1 3	8550	9800
26 9	RUM-RUNNER 27	OP	CBNCR	FBG	DV	IO	T170-T220	8 1	4000	2 6	16100	18700
26 9	RUM-RUNNER 27	OP	CBNCR	FBG	DV	IO	T130D VLVO	8 1	4000	2 6	21900	24300
27 6	SOUTHERLY 28	SLP	SAIL	FBG	CB	IB	20D	YAN	9	8500	2 6	22100	24500
27 6	SOUTHERLY 28	SLP	SAIL	FBG	KL	IB	20D	YAN	9	8500	3 9	22100	24500
32 8	SOUTHERLY 33	SLP	SAIL	FBG	CB	IB	20D	YAN	11 1	12500	2	39100	43400
32 8	SOUTHERLY 33	KTH	SAIL	FBG	CB	IB	20D	YAN	11 1	12500	2	39100	43400
35 8	RANGER 36	HT	EXP	FBG	DV	IO	T210D FORD	12 3		2 10	61100	67100
------------------------- 1978 BOATS -------------------------
27 6	SOUTHERLY 28	SLP	SAIL	FBG	KC	IB	25D	VLVO	9	8500	2 6	21300	23700
------------------------- 1977 BOATS -------------------------
27 6	SOUTHERLY 28	SLP	SAIL	FBG	KC	IB	25D	VLVO	9	8500	2 6	20600	22900
------------------------- 1976 BOATS -------------------------
27 6	SOUTHERLY 28	SLP	SAIL	FBG	KC	IB	25D	VLVO	9	8500	2 6	19900	22200
------------------------- 1972 BOATS -------------------------
27 2	FREEDOM	SLP	SA/CR	FBG	KL	IB	D	9 10		4 5	117500	129000
28 6	KING'S-CRUISER	SLP	SA/CR	FBG	KL	IB	D	8 3		4 11	119000	130500
29 3	FINNCLIPPER	SLP	MS	FBG	KL	IB	D	9 2		3 4	130500	143000
35	FINNCLIPPER	SLP	MS	FBG	KL	IB	D	10 3		3 3	65000	71400
37 3	FINNROSE	SLP	MS	FBG	KL	IB	D	10 11		5 3	44100	49000
42 6	FREEDOM	KTH	SA/CR	FBG	KL	IB	D	13 3		5	94600	104000
50	FREEDOM	KTH	SA/CR	FBG	KL	IB	D	15 3		6 5	123000	135500
------------------------- 1971 BOATS -------------------------
28 6	KING'S-CRUISER	KTH	SA/RC	FBG	KL	IB	D	8 3		4 11	112500	123500
33	COASTER 34		TRWL	FBG	DS	IB	70	11 9		2 10	29500	32700
33 11	SEA-SPIRIT	KTH	SA/CR	WD		IB	D	11 3		4 5	37000	41100
35	FINNCLIPPER	KTH	MS	FBG	KL	IB	D	10 3		3 3	63800	70100
35 6	SEA-WITCH	KTH	SA/CR	FBG	KL	IB	D	11 4		4 6	53000	58200
40	COASTER 40		TRWL	FBG	DS	IB	210	12 5		3 6	72500	79600
50 10	PACIFIC-EAST 50	KTH	SA/CR	FBG	KL	IB	D	12		6	126000	138500

NORTHWEST YACHT CONSTRCTRS
COAST GUARD MFG ID- NYC

Call 1-800-327-6929 for BUC Personalized Evaluation Service
Or, for 1975 to 1979 boats, sign onto www.BUCValuPro.com

NORTHWIND MARINE INC
COAST GUARD MFG ID- NML

Call 1-800-327-6929 for BUC Personalized Evaluation Service
Or, for 1975 to 1977 boats, sign onto www.BUCValuPro.com

NORWALK BOAT WORKS INC
S NORWALK CT   See inside cover to adjust price for area

LOA FT IN	NAME AND/ OR MODEL	TOP/ RIG	BOAT TYPE	-HULL- MTL TP	TP	----ENGINE--- # HP	MFG	BEAM FT IN	WGT LBS	DRAFT FT IN	RETAIL LOW	RETAIL HIGH
------------------------- 1963 BOATS -------------------------
25	NORWALK	SF	WD	IB	145						4450	5100
25	NORWALK FAMILY CR	CR	WD	IB	145						4950	5700
26	NORWALK	SF	WD	IB	145						5650	6500
26	NORWALK FAMILY CR	CR	WD	IB	145						6000	6850
31	NORWALK FAMILY CR	CR	WD	IB	145						10500	11900
37	NORWALK OFFSHORE	OFF	WD	IB	T210						21300	23600
------------------------- 1962 BOATS -------------------------
25	NORWALK DELUXE		WD	IB	110-170						4500	5400
25	NORWALK STANDARD		WD	IB	110-170						4500	5400
31	NORWALK 31		WD	IB	T195						10200	11600
37	NORWALK	FB	SDN	WD	IB	T210						28200	31300
37	NORWALK	FB	SDN	WD	IB	T280						28500	31700
------------------------- 1961 BOATS -------------------------
25	NORWALK FAMILY CR	CR	WD	RB	IB	125-190	8 9		1 10	4700	5600
26	ISLANDER	SF	WD	RB	IB	125-190	8 5		2 1	5300	6350
30	NORWALK FAMILY CR	CR	WD	RB	IB	177	10 8		2 3	8650	9850
30	NORWALK FAMILY CR	CR	WD	RB	IB	T110	10 8		2 3	8950	10100
36	NORWALK OFFSHORE	CR	WD	RB	IB	T275	11 6		3	22300	24800
36	NORWALK OFFSHORE	OFF	WD	RB	IB	T177	11 6		3	17600	20000
------------------------- 1960 BOATS -------------------------
24		CR	WD	IB	177						3850	4500
28		CR	WD	IB	177						7000	8050
34		CR	WD	IB	T135						14900	16900
------------------------- 1959 BOATS -------------------------
24		CR	WD	IB	110						3800	4400
------------------------- 1958 BOATS -------------------------
23		CR	WD	IB	110						3200	3700

NORWAYACHT AMERICAN

Call 1-800-327-6929 for BUC Personalized Evaluation Service
Or, for 1972 to 1978 boats, sign onto www.BUCValuPro.com

NOVA MARINE CORP
HIALEAH GARDENS FL

See inside cover to adjust price for area

```
LOA   NAME AND/       TOP/ BOAT -HULL- ----ENGINE--- BEAM  WGT   DRAFT RETAIL RETAIL
FT IN OR MODEL        RIG  TYPE MTL TP TP # HP MFG   FT IN  LBS  FT IN  LOW   HIGH
------------------- 1969 BOATS --------------------------------------------------
24 9 NOVA 24              CR  FBG    IB 225       8          2 8  5800   6650
24 9 NOVA 24          OP  CR  FBG    IO T160      8          2 8 11500  13100
```

NOVACAL MARINE
DIV OF RUSSELL MARINE U K

RUSSELL MARINE LTD
SEE ALSO JAGUAR YACHTS LTD

Call 1-800-327-6929 for BUC Personalized Evaluation Service
Or, for 1965 to 1978 boats, sign onto www.BUCValuPro.com

NOWAK & WILLIAMS CO
HERRESHOFF
BRISTOL RI 02809

See inside cover to adjust price for area

COAST GUARD MFG ID- NWC
SEE ALSO SQUADRON YACHTS INC

```
LOA   NAME AND/           TOP/ BOAT -HULL- ----ENGINE--- BEAM  WGT   DRAFT RETAIL RETAIL
FT IN OR MODEL            RIG  TYPE MTL TP TP # HP MFG   FT IN  LBS  FT IN  LOW   HIGH
------------------- 1976 BOATS ------------------------------------------------------
18   HERRESHOFF           OP  LNCH FBG DS IB 42        8      2500 1 10  7650   8800
18   SEA-OTTER            OP  RNBT FBG DV IO 130 VLVO 7 10    1800 1     5600   6400
18 2 AMERICA              CAT SAIL FBG CB OB           8      2500 1 10  9050  10300
18 2 HERRESHOFF BAY FISH  OP  FSH  FBG DS IB 42  VLVO  8      2000 1 10  4450   5150
18 2 HERRESHOFF BAY FISH  OP  FSH  FBG DS IB 19D VLVO  8      2000 1 10  6450   7400
18 2 HERRESHOFF BAY FISH  OP  FSH  FBG DS IB 25D WEST  8      2000 1 10  7050   8100
18 2 PILOT                HT  PH   FBG DS IB 42  VLVO  8      2200 1 10  4650   5350
18 2 PILOT                HT  PH   FBG DS IB 19D VLVO  8      2200 1 10  6700   7700
18 2 PILOT                HT  PH   FBG DS IB 25D WEST  8      2200 1 10  7300   8400
18 2 SCOUT                KTH SAIL FBG CB OB           8      2000 1 10  7650   8800
26   EAGLE                SLP SAIL FBG CB OB           8      2700 1 10 12800  14500
------------------- 1975 BOATS ------------------------------------------------------
18   HERRESHOFF AMERICA   CAT SAIL FBG CB              8      2500 1 10  8650   9950
18   HERRESHOFF BAY FISH      FSH  FBG RB IB 42D VLVO  8      2000 1 10  6750   7750
18   HERRESHOFF HARBOR PT          FBG RB IB 42D VLVO  8      2200 1 10  7000   8050
18   HERRESHOFF SCOUT     KTH SAIL FBG CB OB           8      2000 1 10  7400   8500
18   SEA-OTTER                     FBG SV IO 130 VLVO 7 10    1800 1     5600   6450
22   HERRESHOFF EAGLE     SLP SAIL FBG CB              8      2700 1 10 10200  11600
------------------- 1974 BOATS ------------------------------------------------------
18 7 HERRESHOFF AMERICA   CAT SAIL FBG CB              8      2500 1 11  8500   9800
22   HERRESHOFF EAGLE     SLP SAIL FBG CB IB 6D EVIN   8      2700 1 11 12000  13600
------------------- 1973 BOATS ------------------------------------------------------
18 9 HERRESHOFF AMERICA   CAT SAIL FBG CB              8      2500 2 10  8300   9550
```

NUNES BROS

Call 1-800-327-6929 for BUC Personalized Evaluation Service
Or, for 1961 to 1966 boats, sign onto www.BUCValuPro.com

NYE YACHTS
ALLAN NYE SCOTT ENT LTD
BLOOMFIELD ONTARIO CANA   COAST GUARD MFG ID- ZSG

See inside cover to adjust price for area

For more recent years, see the BUC Used Boat Price Guide, Volume 1 or Volume 2

```
LOA   NAME AND/       TOP/ BOAT  -HULL- ----ENGINE--- BEAM  WGT   DRAFT RETAIL RETAIL
FT IN OR MODEL        RIG  TYPE  MTL TP TP # HP MFG   FT IN  LBS  FT IN  LOW   HIGH
------------------- 1983 BOATS ------------------------------------------------------
22   ALBERG 22        SLP SA/CR FBG KL OB        7       3200  3 1  5650   6450
29 3 ALBERG 29        SLP SA/CR FBG KL IB 15D YAN  9 2   9000  4 6 20600  22900
34 1 ALBERG 34        SLP SA/CR FBG    IB 20D YAN 10 1  14000  5 3 31200  34700
34 1 ALBERG PILOT 34  SLP SA/CR FBG    IB 22D YAN 10 1  14000  5 3 31200  34700
------------------- 1982 BOATS ------------------------------------------------------
22   ALBERG 22        SLP SA/CR FBG KL OB        7       3200  3 1  5300   6100
29 3 ALBERG 29        SLP SA/CR FBG KL IB 15D YAN  9 2   9000  4 6 19400  21600
34 1 ALBERG 34        SLP SA/CR FBG    IB 22D YAN 10 1  14000  5 3 29400  32700
------------------- 1981 BOATS ------------------------------------------------------
22   ALBERG 22        SLP SA/CR FBG KL OB        7       3200  3 1  5000   5750
22   ALBERG 22        SLP SA/RC FBG KL OB        7       3200  3 1  5000   5750
29 3 ALBERG 29        SLP SA/CR FBG KL IB 15D YAN  9 2   9000  4 6 18500  20500
29 3 ALBERG 29        SLP SA/RC FBG KL IB  D       9 2   9000  4 6 18500  20500
------------------- 1980 BOATS ------------------------------------------------------
22   ALBERG 22        SLP SA/CR FBG KL OB        7       3200  3 1  4750   5450
29 3 ALBERG 29        SLP SA/CR FBG KL IB 15D YAN  9 2   9000  4 6 17200  19600
------------------- 1979 BOATS ------------------------------------------------------
22   ALBERG 22        SLP SA/CR FBG KL OB        7       3200  3 1  4600   5300
29 2 ALBERG 29        SLP SA/CR FBG KL IB 15D YAN  9 2   9000  4 6 16600  18800
------------------- 1978 BOATS ------------------------------------------------------
22   ALBERG 22        SLP SA/CR FBG KL OB        7       3450  3 1  4700   5400
29 6 ALBERG 29        SLP SA/CR FBG KL IB 15D     9 2    8900  4 6 15800  17900
------------------- 1977 BOATS ------------------------------------------------------
22   ALBERG 22        SLP SA/CR FBG KL OB        7       3200  3 1  4250   4950
------------------- 1976 BOATS ------------------------------------------------------
22   ALBERG 22        SLP SAIL  FBG KL OB        7       3200  3 1  4100   4750
```

O'DAY
PEARSON YACHT CORP
ASSONET MA 02702

See inside cover to adjust price for area

COAST GUARD MFG ID- XDY
formerly LEAR SIEGLER MARINE

For more recent years, see the BUC Used Boat Price Guide, Volume 1 or Volume 2

```
LOA   NAME AND/       TOP/ BOAT  -HULL- ----ENGINE--- BEAM  WGT    DRAFT RETAIL RETAIL
FT IN OR MODEL        RIG  TYPE  MTL TP TP # HP MFG   FT IN  LBS   FT IN  LOW   HIGH
------------------- 1983 BOATS -------------------------------------------------------
19    O'DAY 19        SLP SAIL  FBG CB OB        7  9  1350 1      2650   3100
21 8  O'DAY 22        SLP SA/CR FBG KC OB        7     2100 1  3   3650   4250
21 9  O'DAY 222       SLP SA/CR FBG KC OB        7 11  2200 1  8   3800   4400
22 9  O'DAY 23        SLP SA/CR FBG KC OB        8     3000 2  3   4000   5650
24 10 O'DAY 25        SLP SA/CR FBG KL IB 8D YAN  8    3900 2  3   7500   8650
24 10 O'DAY 25        SLP SA/CR FBG KL IB 8D YAN  8    3850 4  6   7450   8550
28 3  O'DAY 28        SLP SA/CR FBG KL IB 11D UNIV 10 3 7300 3    15200  17300
28 3  O'DAY 28        SLP SA/CR FBG KL IB 11D UNIV 10 4 7300 4  8 15200  17300
29 11 O'DAY 30        SLP SA/RC FBG KC IB 16D UNIV 10 9 10600 3  6 23100  25600
29 11 O'DAY 30        SLP SA/RC FBG KL IB 16D UNIV 10 9 10150 4 11 22100  24500
34    O'DAY 34        SLP SA/CR FBG KL IB 21D UNIV 11 3 11500 5  7 24600  27400
34    O'DAY 34 SHOAL  SLP SA/CR FBG KL IB 21D UNIV 11 3 11500 4  5 24600  27400

37    O'DAY 37        SLP SA/CR FBG KL IB 32D UNIV 11 2 14000 4  9 30600  34000
38 7  O'DAY 39        SLP SA/CR FBG KL IB 44D UNIV 12 8 18000 6  4 39400  43800
38 7  O'DAY 39 SHOAL  SLP SA/CR FBG KL IB 44D UNIV 12 8 18000 4 11 39400  43800
------------------- 1982 BOATS -------------------------------------------------------
19    O'DAY 19        SLP SAIL  FBG CB OB        7  9  1350 1      2500   2900
21 8  O'DAY 22        SLP SA/CR FBG KC OB        7  2  2100 1  3   3450   4000
22 9  O'DAY 23        SLP SA/CR FBG KC OB        7 11  3000 2  3   4650   5350
24 10 O'DAY 25        SLP SA/CR FBG KC OB        8     3900 2  3   6450   7400
24 10 O'DAY 25        SLP SA/CR FBG KL IB         8    3850 4  6   6400   7350
28 3  O'DAY 28        SLP SA/RC FBG KL IB 11D UNIV 10 3 7300 3    14300  16300
28 3  O'DAY 28        SLP SA/RC FBG KL IB 11D UNIV 10 4 7300 4  8 14300  16300
29 11 O'DAY 30        SLP SA/RC FBG KC IB 16D UNIV 10 9 10600 3  6 20700  23100
29 11 O'DAY 30        SLP SA/RC FBG KL IB 16D UNIV 10 9 10150 4 11 20700  23100
34    O'DAY 34        SLP SA/CR FBG KL IB 21D UNIV 11 3 11500 5  7 23200  25800
34    O'DAY 34 SHOAL  SLP SA/CR FBG KL IB 24D UNIV 11 3 11500 4  5 23200  25800
37    O'DAY 37        SLP SA/CR FBG KL IB 32D UNIV 11 2 15000 4  9 30500  33900

38 7  O'DAY 39        SLP SA/CR FBG KL IB 44D UNIV  12 8 18000 4  5 37000  41200
38 7  O'DAY 39        SLP SA/RC FBG KC IB 44D UNIB  12 8 18000 6  4 37000  41100
38 7  O'DAY 39        SLP SA/RC FBG KC IB 44D UNIV  12 8 18000 4  5 37000  41200
38 7  O'DAY 39 DEEP   SLP SA/CR FBG KL IB 44D UNIV  12 8 18000 5  7 37000  41200
38 7  O'DAY 39 SHOAL  SLP SA/CR FBG KL IB 44D UNIV  12 8 18000 4  5 37000  41200
------------------- 1981 BOATS -------------------------------------------------------
19    O'DAY 19        SLP SAIL  FBG CB OB        7  9  1350 1      2350   2750
19 2  RHODES 19       SLP SA/OD FBG CB OB        7        10       2350   2750
21 8  O'DAY 22        SLP SA/CR FBG KC OB        7  2  2100 1  3   3350   3750
22 9  O'DAY 23        SLP SA/CR FBG KC OB        7 11  3000 2  3   4400   5050
24 10 O'DAY 25        SLP SA/CR FBG KC OB        8     3900 2  3   6100   7000
24 10 O'DAY 25        SLP SA/CR FBG KC SD 15 OMC  8    3900 2  4   6350   7300
24 10 O'DAY 25        SLP SA/CR FBG KL SD 15 OMC  8    3850 4  6   6300   7200
28 3  O'DAY 28        SLP SA/CR FBG KC IB 11D UNIV 10 3 7300 3    13300  15100
28 3  O'DAY 28        SLP SA/RC FBG KC IB 11D UNIV 10 3 7300 3    13500  15300
28 3  O'DAY 28        SLP SA/RC FBG KC SD 15 OMC  10 3 7300 3    13500  15300
28 3  O'DAY 28        SLP SA/CR FBG KL IB 11D UNIV 10 3 7300 4  6 13500  15300

29 11 O'DAY 30        SLP SA/RC FBG KC IB 16D UNIV 10 9 10600 3  6 20400  22700
29 11 O'DAY 30        SLP SA/RC FBG KL IB 16D UNIV 10 9 10150 4 11 19500  21700
34    O'DAY 34        SLP SA/CR FBG KL IB 24D UNIV 11 3 11500 4  3 21800  24200
34    O'DAY 34 SHOAL  SLP SA/CR FBG KL IB 24D UNIV 11 3 11500 4  7 21800  24200
37    O'DAY 37        SLP SAIL  FBG KL IB 32D UNIV 11 2 14000 5    27100  30100
```

LOA FT	LOA IN	NAME AND/ OR MODEL	TOP/ RIG	BOAT TYPE	-HULL- MTL	-HULL- TP	ENGINE TP	ENGINE # HP	ENGINE MFG	BEAM FT	BEAM IN	WGT LBS	DRAFT FT	DRAFT IN	RETAIL LOW	RETAIL HIGH
		1980 BOATS														
19		O'DAY 19	SLP	SAIL	FBG	CB	OB			7	9	2040	1		2800	3300
19	2	MARINER 2+2	SLP	SAIL	FBG	CB	OB			7		1966		10	2750	3200
19	2	RHODES 19	SLP	SA/OD	FBG	CB				7				10	2300	2650
19	2	RHODES 19	SLP	SA/OD	FBG	CB	OB			7		1030		10	1950	2350
19	2	RHODES 19	SLP	SA/OD	FBG	CB	OB			7		1355	3	3	2300	2650
21	8	O'DAY 22	SLP	SAIL	FBG	KC	OB			7	2	2623	1	3	3600	4150
22	9	O'DAY 23	SLP	SAIL	FBG	KC	OB			7	11	3725	2	3	4950	5700
22	9	O'DAY 23	SLP	SAIL	FBG	KC	SD	15	OMC	7	11	3725	2	3	5250	6050
24	10	O'DAY 25	SLP	SAIL	FBG	KC	OB			8		4807	2	3	7100	8150
24	10	O'DAY 25	SLP	SAIL	FBG	KC	SD	15	OMC	8		4807	2	3	7350	8450
24	10	O'DAY 25	SLP	SAIL	FBG	KL	OB			8		4762	4	6	7050	8100
24	10	O'DAY 25	SLP	SAIL	FBG	KL	SD	15	OMC	8		4762	4	6	7300	8400
28	3	O'DAY 28	SLP	SAIL	FBG	KC	SD	15	OMC	10	3	7300	3	3	12700	14400
28	3	O'DAY 28	SLP	SAIL	FBG	KC	IB	11D	UNIV	10	3	7300	3	3	12800	14600
28	3	O'DAY 28	SLP	SAIL	FBG	KL	SD	15	OMC	10	3	7300	4	6	12700	14400
28	3	O'DAY 28	SLP	SAIL	FBG	KL	IB	11D	UNIV	10	3	7300	4	6	12800	14600
29	11	O'DAY 30	SLP	SAIL	FBG	KC	IB	16D	UNIV	10	9	10600	3	6	19500	21700
29	11	O'DAY 30	SLP	SAIL	FBG	KL	IB	16D	UNIV	10	9	10150	4	11	18900	20900
37		O'DAY 37	SLP	SAIL	FBG	KL	IB	32D	UNIV	11	2	14000	5		25900	28700
		1979 BOATS														
19		O'DAY 19	SLP	SAIL	FBG	CB	OB			7	6	1350	1		2200	2550
19	2	MARINER 2+2	SLP	SAIL	FBG	CB	OB			7		1966		10	2650	3100
19	2	RHODES 19	SLP	SA/OD	FBG	CB				7		1630		10	2400	2800
19	2	RHODES 19	SLP	SA/OD	FBG	CB				7		1955	3	3	2650	3100
21	8	O'DAY 22	SLP	SAIL	FBG	KC	OB			7	2	2100	1	3	2950	3450
22	9	O'DAY 23	SLP	SAIL	FBG	KC	OB			7	11	3000	2	3	4000	4650
22	9	O'DAY 23	SLP	SAIL	FBG	KC	SD	15	OMC	7	11	3000	2	3	4250	4950
24	10	O'DAY 25	SLP	SAIL	FBG	KC	OB			8		3900	2	3	5600	6400
24	10	O'DAY 25	SLP	SAIL	FBG	KC	SD	15	OMC	8		3900	2	3	5850	6700
24	10	O'DAY 25	SLP	SAIL	FBG	KL	OB			8		3850	4	6	5500	6350
24	10	O'DAY 25	SLP	SAIL	FBG	KL	SD	15	OMC	8		3850	4	6	5750	6650
28	3	O'DAY 28	SLP	SAIL	FBG	KL	SD	15	OMC	10	3	7300	4	6	12200	13900
28	3	O'DAY 28	SLP	SAIL	FBG	KL	IB	D		10	3	7300	4	6	12400	14100
29	11	O'DAY 30	SLP	SAIL	FBG	KC	IB	15D	YAN	10	9	11000	3	6	19500	21600
29	11	O'DAY 30	SLP	SAIL	FBG	KL	IB	15D	YAN	10	9	10500	4	11	18800	20900
37		O'DAY 37	SLP	SAIL	FBG	KL	IB	30D	WEST	11	2	14000	5		24900	27600
37		O'DAY 37	SLP	SAIL	FBG	KL	IB	30D	YAN	11	2	14000	5		24900	27600
		1978 BOATS														
19	2	MARINER 2+2	SLP	SAIL	FBG	CB	OB			7		1305		10	2050	2400
19	2	RHODES 19	SLP	SA/OD	FBG	CB				7		1030		10	1800	2150
19	2	RHODES 19	SLP	SA/OD	FBG	CB				7		1355	3	3	2050	2450
19	7	O'DAY 20	SLP	SAIL	FBG	KC	OB			7		1750	1	2	2400	2800
21	8	O'DAY 22	SLP	SAIL	FBG	KL	OB			7	2	2000	1	11	2800	3250
22	9	O'DAY 23	SLP	SAIL	FBG	KC	OB			7	11	3000	2	3	3850	4450
24	10	O'DAY 25	SLP	SAIL	FBG	KC	OB			8		3900	2	3	5400	6200
24	10	O'DAY 25	SLP	SAIL	FBG	KC	IB	15	OMC	8		3900	2	3	5600	6450
24	10	O'DAY 25	SLP	SAIL	FBG	KL	OB			8		3850	4	6	5300	6100
24	10	O'DAY 25	SLP	SAIL	FBG	KL	IB	15	OMC	8		3850	4	6	5550	6400
27		O'DAY 27	SLP	SAIL	FBG	KL	OB			9		6950	4		10700	12100
27		O'DAY 27	SLP	SAIL	FBG	KL	IB	8D	YAN	9		6950	4		11000	12500
29	11	O'DAY 30	SLP	SAIL	FBG	KC	IB	12D	YAN	10	9	11000	3	6	19000	21100
29	11	O'DAY 30	SLP	SAIL	FBG	KL	IB	12D	YAN	10	9	10500	4	11	18100	20100
31	7	O'DAY 32	SLP	SAIL	FBG	KC	IB	22D	YAN	10	6	11000	3	4	19000	21100
31	7	O'DAY 32	SLP	SAIL	FBG	KL	IB	22D	YAN	10	6	10500	4	6	18100	20100
37		O'DAY 37	SLP	SAIL	FBG	KL	IB	D		10	10	14000	5		23900	26600
		1977 BOATS														
19	2	MARINER 2+2	SLP	SA/CR	FBG	CB	OB			7		1305		10	1950	2350
19	2	RHODES 19	SLP	SA/OD	FBG	CB	OB			7		1030		10	1750	2100
19	2	RHODES 19	SLP	SA/OD	FBG	CB	OB			7		1355	3	3	2000	2400
19	7	O'DAY 20	SLP	SA/CR	FBG	KC	OB			7		1750	1	2	2350	2700
21	8	O'DAY 22	SLP	SA/CR	FBG	KL	OB			7	2	2000	1	11	2700	3150
22	9	O'DAY 23	SLP	SA/CR	FBG	KC	OB			8		2800	2	2	3500	4100
24	10	O'DAY 25	SLP	SA/CR	FBG	KC	OB			8		3600	2	3	4850	5550
24	10	O'DAY 25	SLP	SA/CR	FBG	KC	IB	10	UNIV	8		3600	2	3	5050	5800
24	10	O'DAY 25	SLP	SA/CR	FBG	KC	IB	7D	WEST	8		3600	2	3	5300	6100
24	10	O'DAY 25	SLP	SA/CR	FBG	KL	OB			8		3850	4	6	5150	5900
24	10	O'DAY 25	SLP	SA/CR	FBG	KL	IB	10	UNIV	8		3850	4	6	5350	6150
24	10	O'DAY 25	SLP	SA/CR	FBG	KL	IB	7D	WEST	8		3850	4	6	5600	6450
27		O'DAY 27	SLP	SA/CR	FBG	KL	OB			9		6700	4		9900	11300
27		O'DAY 27	SLP	SA/CR	FBG	KL	IB	10- 30		9		6950	4		10500	12000
27		O'DAY 27	SLP	SA/CR	FBG	KL	IB	7D- 12D		9		6950	4		10600	12200
29	11	O'DAY 30	SLP	SA/CR	FBG	KC	IB	D		10	9		3	4	11600	13200
29	11	O'DAY 30	SLP	SA/CR	FBG	KL	IB	D		10	9		4	9	11600	13200
31	7	O'DAY 32	SLP	SA/CR	FBG	KC	IB	30	UNIV	10	6	11000	3	4	18300	20300
31	7	O'DAY 32	SLP	SA/CR	FBG	KC	IB	25D	WEST	10	6	11000	3	4	18300	20400
31	7	O'DAY 32	SLP	SA/CR	FBG	KL	IB	30	UNIV	10	6	11000	4	6	18300	20300
31	7	O'DAY 32	SLP	SA/CR	FBG	KL	IB	25D	WEST	10	6	11000	4	6	18300	20400
31	7	O'DAY 32	KTH	SA/CR	FBG	KC	IB	30	UNIV	10	6	11000	3	4	18300	20300
31	7	O'DAY 32	KTH	SA/CR	FBG	KC	IB	25D	WEST	10	6	11000	3	4	18300	20400
31	7	O'DAY 32	KTH	SA/CR	FBG	KL	IB	30	UNIV	10	6	11000	4	6	18300	20300
31	7	O'DAY 32	KTH	SA/CR	FBG	KL	IB	25D	WEST	10	6	11000	4	6	18300	20400
		1976 BOATS														
19	2	MARINER 2+2	SLP	SA/OD	FBG	CB				7		1600		10	2150	2500
19	2	RHODES 19	SLP	SA/OD	FBG	CB				7		1030		10	1700	2000
19	2	RHODES 19	SLP	SA/OD	FBG	CB				7		1355	3	3	1950	2300
19	7	O'DAY 20	SLP	SAIL	FBG	KC				7		2300	1	2	2650	3100
21	8	O'DAY 22	SLP	SAIL	FBG	KL				7	2	2000	1	11	2600	3050
24	10	O'DAY 25	SLP	SAIL	FBG	KC	OB			8		4400	2	3	5650	6500
24	10	O'DAY 25	SLP	SAIL	FBG	KC	IB	7D- 25D		8		4400	2	3	6100	7300
24	10	O'DAY 25	SLP	SAIL	FBG	KL	OB			8		3850	2	3	5000	5700
24	10	O'DAY 25	SLP	SAIL	FBG	KL	IB	7D- 25D		8		3850	2	3	5450	6550
27		O'DAY 27	SLP	SAIL	FBG	KL	OB			9		6700	4		9600	10900
27		O'DAY 27	SLP	SAIL	FBG	KL	IB	30	UNIV	9		6950	4		10200	11600
27		O'DAY 27	SLP	SAIL	FBG	KL	IB	7D- 25D		9		6950	4		10300	11900
31	7	O'DAY 32	SLP	SAIL	FBG	KC	IB	30	UNIV	10	6	11000	3	4	17300	19700
31	7	O'DAY 32	SLP	SAIL	FBG	KC	IB	25D	WEST	10	6	11000	3	4	17400	19700
31	7	O'DAY 32	SLP	SAIL	FBG	KL	IB	30	UNIV	10	6	11000	5	1	17300	19700
31	7	O'DAY 32	SLP	SAIL	FBG	KL	IB	25D	WEST	10	6	11000	5	1	17400	19700
31	7	O'DAY 32	KTH	SAIL	FBG	KC	IB	30	UNIV	10	6	11000	3	4	17300	19700
31	7	O'DAY 32	KTH	SAIL	FBG	KC	IB	25D	WEST	10	6	11000	3	4	17400	19700
31	7	O'DAY 32	KTH	SAIL	FBG	KL	IB	30	UNIV	10	6	11000	5	1	17300	19700
31	7	O'DAY 32	KTH	SAIL	FBG	KL	IB	25D	WEST	10	6	11000	5	1	17400	19700
		1975 BOATS														
19	2	MARINER 2+2	SLP	SAIL	FBG	CB	OB			7		1305		10	1850	2200
19	2	RHODES 19	SLP	SA/OD	FBG	CB				7		1355	3	3	1900	2250
19	8	O'DAY 20	SLP	SAIL	FBG	KC				7		1600	1	2	2050	2450
21	8	O'DAY 22	SLP	SAIL	FBG	KL				7	2	1800	1	11	2400	2750
21	11	INTERNATL-TEMPEST	SLP	SA/OD	FBG	KL	OB			6	4	1100	3	7	1900	2250
24	10	O'DAY 25	SLP	SAIL	FBG	KC				8		4400	2	3	5350	6150
27		O'DAY 27	SLP	SAIL	FBG	KL	OB			9		5900	4		8100	9300
27		O'DAY 27	SLP	SAIL	FBG	KL	IB	30	UNIV			6200			8850	10000
27		O'DAY 27	SLP	SAIL	FBG	KL	IB	7D	WEST			6200			8950	10200
31	9	O'DAY 32	SLP	SAIL	FBG	KC	IB	30	UNIV	10	6	10450	3	4	16000	18200
31	9	O'DAY 32	SLP	SAIL	FBG	KC	IB	25D	WEST	10	6	10450	3	4	16000	18200
		1974 BOATS														
19	2	MARINER 2+2	SLP	SAIL	FBG	CB	OB			7		1305		10	1800	2150
19	2	RHODES 19	SLP	SA/OD	FBG	CB	OB			7		1355	3	3	1850	2200
19	8	O'DAY 20	SLP	SAIL	FBG	CB	OB			7		1600	1	2	2000	2400
21	8	O'DAY 22	SLP	SAIL	FBG	KL	OB			7	2	1800	1	11	2300	2700
21	11	INTERNATL-TEMPEST	SLP	SA/OD	FBG	KL	OB			6	4	1100	3	7	1850	2200
23		O'DAY 23 CONV	SLP	SAIL	FBG	CB	OB			7	11	3100	2		3500	4100
27		O'DAY 27	SLP	SAIL	FBG	KL	OB			9		5000	4		6650	7650
		1973 BOATS														
19	2	MARINER 2+2	SLP	SAIL	FBG	CB	OB			7		1305		10	1750	2100
19	2	RHODES 19	SLP	SA/OD	FBG	CB	OB			7		1355	3	3	1800	2100
20	11	YNGLING	SLP	SA/OD	FBG	KL	OB			5	8	1320	3	6	1850	2200
21	8	O'DAY 22	SLP	SAIL	FBG	KL	OB			7	2	1800	1	11	2300	2650
21	11	INTERNATL-TEMPEST	SLP	SA/OD	FBG	KL	OB			6	4	1100	3	7	1800	2150
23		O'DAY 23 FIXED TOP	SLP	SAIL	FBG	KC	OB			7	11	3100	2		3300	3850
23		O'DAY 23 POP TOP	SLP	SAIL	FBG	KC	OB			7	11	3100	2		3550	4150
27		O'DAY 27	SLP	SAIL	FBG	KL	OB			9		5000	4		6500	7450
		1972 BOATS														
19	2	MARINER 2+2	SLP	SAIL	FBG	CB	OB			7		1305		10	1700	2050
19	2	RHODES 19	SLP	SA/OD	FBG	CB	OB			7		1355	3	3	1750	2100
20	11	YNGLING	SLP	SA/OD	FBG	KL	OB			5	8	1320	3	6	1800	2150
21	8	O'DAY 22	SLP	SAIL	FBG	KL	OB			7	2	1800	1	11	2250	2600
21	11	INTERNATL-TEMPEST	SLP	SA/OD	FBG	KL	OB			6	4	1100	3	7	1750	2100
23		O'DAY 23 FIXED TOP	SLP	SAIL	FBG	CB	OB			7	11	3100	2		3250	3750
23		O'DAY 23 POP TOP	SLP	SAIL	FBG	CB	OB			7	11	3100	2		3500	4050
		1971 BOATS														
19	2	MARINER 2+2	SLP	SAIL	FBG	KL	OB			7		1430	3	3	1750	2100
19	2	RHODES 19	SLP	SA/OD	FBG	CB	OB			7		1355	3	3	1700	2050
20	11	YNGLING	SLP	SA/OD	FBG	KL	OB			5	8	1320	3	6	1800	2100
21	11	INTERNATL-TEMPEST	SLP	SA/OD	FBG	KL	OB			6	4	1100	3	7	1750	2050
23		O'DAY 23	SLP	SAIL	FBG	CB	OB			7	11	3100	2		3300	3850
		1970 BOATS														
18	5	HUNT		RNBT	FBG	DV	IO	120-200		7	5	2100	1	2	3750	4500
19	2	MARINER 2+2	SLP	SA/OD	FBG	KL	OB			7		1430	3	3	1750	2050
19	2	RHODES 19	SLP	SA/OD	FBG	KL	OB			7		1355	3	3	1700	2000
20	11	YNGLING	SLP	SA/OD	FBG	KL	OB			5	8	1320	3	6	1750	2100

CONTINUED ON NEXT PAGE

LOA FT IN	NAME AND/ OR MODEL	TOP/ RIG	BOAT TYPE	-HULL- MTL TP	TP	----ENGINE--- # HP MFG	BEAM FT IN	WGT LBS	DRAFT FT IN	RETAIL LOW	RETAIL HIGH
---	---	--- 1970	BOATS	---							
22	INTERNATL-TEMPEST	SLP	SA/OD	FBG KL			6 4	1100	3 7	1700	2050
23 2	TEMPEST	SLP	SA/OD	FBG KL	OB		7 8	3000	3 9	3200	3700
---	---	--- 1969	BOATS	---							
18 5	HUNT 18		RNBT	FBG	IO	50	7 5	2100	2 2	3900	4550
19 2	MARINER 2+2	SLP	SAIL	FBG KL	OB		7	1430	3 3	1700	2050
23 2	TEMPEST	SLP	SAIL	FBG KL	OB		7 8	3000	3 9	3150	3650
26	OUTLAW	SLP	SAIL	FBG KL	OB		8	5050	4 3	5850	6750
26	OUTLAW	SLP	SAIL	FBG KL	IB		8	5050	4 3	6050	6950
---	---	--- 1968	BOATS	---							
23 2	TEMPEST	SLP	SAIL	FBG KL	OB		7 8	3000	3 10	3100	3600
24	DOLPHIN	SLP	SAIL	FBG KC			7 8	4500	2 10	4650	5350
26	OUTLAW	SLP	SAIL	FBG KL	OB		8	5050	4 3	5750	6650
---	---	--- 1967	BOATS	---							
21 11	INTERNATL-TEMPEST	SLP	SA/OD	FBG KL	OB		6 4		3 7	2350	2700
23 2	TEMPEST	SLP	SAIL	FBG KL	OB		7 8	3000	3 9	3050	3550
24 2	DOLPHIN	SLP	SAIL	FDC KC	OB			4500		4650	5350
24 2	DOLPHIN	SLP	SAIL	FBG KC	IB	8- 22		4500		4800	5600
26	OUTLAW	SLP	SAIL	FBG KL	OB		8	5050	4 3	5700	6550
---	---	--- 1966	BOATS	---							
21 11	INTERNATL-TEMPEST	SLP	SA/OD	FBG KL	OB					2350	2700
23 2	TEMPEST	SLP	SAIL	FBG KL	OB					3000	3500
24	DOLPHIN	SLP	SAIL	FBG KC	OB					3150	3650
26	OUTLAW	SLP	SAIL	FBG KL	OB					5350	6150
---	---	--- 1965	BOATS	---							
23 2	TEMPEST	SLP	SAIL	FBG KL	OB					3000	3500
24 2	DOLPHIN	SLP	SA/OD	FBG KC			7 8		5 2	3150	3650
26 3	OUTLAW	SLP	SAIL	FBG KL	OB					5400	6200
---	---	--- 1963	BOATS	---							
24	DOLPHIN	SLP	SAIL	FBG	OB					3100	3600
---	---	--- 1962	BOATS	---							
24	DOLPHIN	SLP	SAIL	FBG	OB					3100	3600
---	---	--- 1961	BOATS	---							
24	DOLPHIN	SLP	SAIL	FBG KL	OB		7 9		2 10	3100	3600
---	---	--- 1960	BOATS	---							
22	MARSCOT 21		CR	FBG	IB	60				2900	3400
22 8	HUNTER 23		RNBT	FBG	IB	150				3350	3900
23	CHRISTINA		CR	MHG	IB	150-260	8 6		2 4	3450	4150
24	DOLPHIN	SLP	SAIL	FBG	OB					3100	3600
26	ATLANTA	SLP	SAIL	WD	OB					5300	6100
26	MARSCOT 26		CR	FBG	IB	75				5450	6250
30 3	SOU'WESTER JR	SLP	SA/CR	FBG KL	OB		8 9		4 7	7900	9050
33	MARSCOT 33		CR	FBG	IB	270				13400	15300
35 6	OHLSON 35	YWL	SAIL	WD	OB					13100	14900
38	ROBB 38	YWL	SAIL	WD	OB					9900	11200
40 9	BERMUDA 40	YWL	SA/CR	FBG	OB		11 9		3 11	21200	23500
---	---	--- 1959	BOATS	---							
26	ATLANTA	SLP	SAIL	F/W CB	OB		7 6		1 1	5300	6100

OCEAN ALEXANDER

81203 KAOHSIUNG TAIWAN   See inside cover to adjust price for area

OCEAN ALEXANDER OF FLORIDA
FT LAUDERDALE FL 33316

FORMERLY ALEXANDER MARINE

For more recent years, see the BUC Used Boat Price Guide, Volume 1 or Volume 2

LOA FT IN	NAME AND/ OR MODEL	TOP/ RIG	BOAT TYPE	-HULL- MTL TP	TP	----ENGINE--- # HP MFG	BEAM FT IN	WGT LBS	DRAFT FT IN	RETAIL LOW	RETAIL HIGH
---	---	--- 1983	BOATS	---							
39 4	OCEAN 40 DC	FB	TRWL	FBG SV	IB	215D CUM	13 4	21000	3 6	82500	90700
IB	270D CUM	83800	92000,	IB T120D LEHM		86700 95200,	IB T200D PERK			92200	101500
39 4	OCEAN 40 S	FB	TRWL	FBG SV	IB	120D LEHM	13 4	19800	3 6	77400	85100
IB	270D CUM	83800	92000,	IB T120D LEHM		86700 95200,	IB T200D PERK			92200	101500
40	OCEAN 40 DC	FB	TRWL	FBG DS	IB	120D LEHM	13 8	29800	4	110000	121000
40	OCEAN 40 DC	FB	TRWL	FBG DS	IB	T120D LEHM	13 8	31600	4	120500	132500
42 6	OCEAN 43 DC	FB	TRWL	FBG SV	IB	T200D GM	14 6	27500	3 6	105000	115500
42 6	OCEAN 43 DC	FB	TRWL	FBG SV	IB	T215D CUM	14 6	29000	3 6	109000	120000
43 8	OCEAN 43 DC	FB	TRWL	FBG DS	IB	T215D CUM	14 6	30000	3 10	112000	123500
43 8	OCEAN 43 DC	FB	TRWL	FBG DS	IB	T270D CUM	14 6	31000	3 10	117000	128500
43 8	OCEAN 43 FD	FB	TRWL	FBG DS	IB	T120D LEHM	14 6	28000	3 10	103000	113000
50 3	OCEAN 50 MY	FB	TRWL	FBG SV	IB	T310D GM	15 6	51000	4 6	152000	167000
50 3	OCEAN 50 MY	FB	TRWL	FBG SV	IB	T320D CUM	15 6	50500	4 6	152500	167500
50 3	OCEAN 50 PH	HT	TRWL	FBG DS	IB	T215D CUM	15 6	43400	4 6	136000	149500
50 3	OCEAN 50 PH	HT	TRWL	FBG DS	IB	T270D CUM	15 6	46000	4 6	142500	156500
50 3	OCEAN 50 PH	HT	TRWL	FBG DS	IB	T320D CUM	15 6	46900	4 6	147500	162000
50 3	OCEAN 50 PH	FB	TRWL	FBG SV	IB	T270D CUM	15 6	46500	4 6	142000	156500
50 3	OCEAN 50 PH	FB	TRWL	FBG DS	IB	T320D CUM	15 6	46500	4 6	146000	160500
59 5	OCEAN 60 MY	FB	MY	F/S SV	IB	T425D CUM	18	58600	4 10	257500	283000
59 5	OCEAN 60 MY	FB	MY	F/S SV	IB	T425D CUM	18	62600	4 10	273500	300500
59 5	OCEAN 60 MY	FB	MY	F/S SV	IB	T550D GM	18	59000	4 10	287000	315500
59 5	OCEAN 60 MY	FB	MY	F/S SV	IB	T550D GM	18	63000	4 10	302500	332000
59 5	OCEAN 60 PH	FB	PH	F/S SV	IB	T425D CUM	18	52000	4 10	246500	270500
59 5	OCEAN 60 PH	FB	PH	F/S SV	IB	T425D CUM	18	56500	4 10	256500	282000
59 5	OCEAN 60 PH	FB	PH	F/S SV	IB	T550D GM	18	53000	4 10	275000	302500
59 5	OCEAN 60 PH	FB	PH	FBG SV	IB	T550D GM	18	56000	4 10	285000	313000
---	---	--- 1982	BOATS	---							
40	OCEAN 40 DC	FB	TRWL	FBG DS	IB	120D LEHM	13 8	29800	4	105000	115500
40	OCEAN 40 DC	FB	TRWL	FBG DS	IB	T120D LEHM	13 8	31600	4	115000	126500
42 6	OCEAN 43 DC	FB	TRWL	FBG DS	IB	T120D LEHM	14	30000	3 10	104500	115000
42 6	OCEAN 43 DC	FB	TRWL	FBG DS	IB	T210D CAT	14	30000	3 10	110000	120000
42 6	OCEAN 43 DC	FB	TRWL	FBG SV	IB	T120D LEHM	14	29000	4	101000	111000
42 6	OCEAN 43 DC	FB	TRWL	FBG SV	IB	T165D PERK	14 6	29000	3 6	103500	114000
42 6	OCEAN 43 DC	FB	TRWL	FBG DS	IB	T270D CUM	14	30800	3 10	112000	123000
50 3	OCEAN 50 FD	FB	MY	FBG SV	IB	T120D LEHM	15	46500	4 6	129500	142500
50 3	OCEAN 50 FD	FB	TRWL	FBG SV	IB	T270D CUM	15	46500	4 6	136500	150000
50 3	OCEAN 50 FD	FB	TRWL	FBG SV	IB	T310D GM	15 6	46500	4 6	139500	153500
50 3	OCEAN 50 PH	HT	TRWL	FBG DS	IB	T210D CAT	15 6	43400	4 6	131000	144000
IB T270D CUM		136500	150000,	IB T310D GM		140000 153500,	IB T320D CUM			136000	149500
50 3	OCEAN 50 PH	HT	TRWL	FBG SV	IB	T120D LEHM	15 6	46500	4 6	128500	141000
50 3	OCEAN 50 PH	HT	TRWL	FBG DS	IB	T165D PERK	15 6	46500	4 6	131500	144500
---	---	--- 1981	BOATS	---							
40	OCEAN 40 DC	FB	TRWL	FBG DS	IB	120D LEHM	13 8	29800	4	99900	110000
40	OCEAN 40 DC	FB	TRWL	FBG DS	IB	T120D LEHM	13 8	31600	4	109500	120500
43 8	OCEAN 43 DC	FB	TRWL	FBG DS	IB	T160D PERK	14	28800	3 10	98600	108500
43 8	OCEAN 43 DC	FB	TRWL	FBG DS	IB	T210D CAT	14 6	30000	3 10	103000	113500
43 8	OCEAN 43 DC	FB	TRWL	FBG DS	IB	T270D CUM	14 6	30800	3 10	106000	116500
50 3	OCEAN 50 PH	HT	TRWL	FBG DS	IB	T120D LEHM	15 6	42000	4 6	118000	130000
IB T160D PERK		121000	133000,	IB T210D CAT		125000 137500,	IB T260D CAT			128500	141500
IB T270D CUM		130000	143000,	IB T310D GM		133500 146500					
---	---	--- 1980	BOATS	---							
40	OCEAN 40 DC	FB	TRWL	FBG DS	IB	120D LEHM	13 8	29800	4	95300	105000
40	OCEAN 40 DC	FB	TRWL	FBG DS	IB	T120D LEHM	13 8	31600	4	104500	115000
43 8	OCEAN 43 DC	FB	TRWL	FBG DS	IB	T160D PERK	14	28800	3 10	94000	103500
43 8	OCEAN 43 DC	FB	TRWL	FBG DS	IB	T210D CAT	14	30000	3 10	98300	108000
43 8	OCEAN 43 DC	FB	TRWL	FBG DS	IB	T270D CUM	14	30800	3 10	101000	111000
50 3	OCEAN 50 PH	FB	TRWL	FBG DS	IB	T120D LEHM	15 6	42000	4 6	113000	124000
IB T160D PERK		115500	127000,	IB T210D CAT		119500 131000,	IB T260D CAT			123000	135000
IB T270D CUM		124000	136500,	IB T310D GM		127500 140000,	IB T340D CUM			131000	144000
---	---	--- 1979	BOATS	---							
50 3	OCEAN 50	HT	TRWL	FBG DS	IB	T120D LEHM	15 6	44500	4 6	110000	121000
50 3	OCEAN 50	HT	TRWL	FBG DS	IB	T270D CUM	15 6	49000	4 6	121500	133000

OCEAN CATAMARANS

FRIDEN ENTERPRISES INC   See inside cover to adjust price for area
MIAMI FL 33174   COAST GUARD MFG ID- XNC

LOA FT IN	NAME AND/ OR MODEL	TOP/ RIG	BOAT TYPE	-HULL- MTL TP	TP	----ENGINE--- # HP MFG	BEAM FT IN	WGT LBS	DRAFT FT IN	RETAIL LOW	RETAIL HIGH
---	---	--- 1979	BOATS	---							
31	QUEST 31	CUT	SA/CR	FBG CT	IB	D	14 3		2 6	12300	14000
37	SNOWGOOSE 37	CUT	SA/CR	FBG CT	IB	D	15 3		2 8	23600	26200
49	QUASAR 49	CUT	SA/CR	FBG CT	IB	T D	19 8		3	73900	81200
---	---	--- 1978	BOATS	---							
27	CATALAC 27	SLP	SA/CR	FBG CT	OB		13 8	3900	2	7800	8950
29 6	CATALAC 30	SLP	SA/CR	FBG CT	IB	24D	13 10	5400	2 6	9800	11200
---	---	--- 1977	BOATS	---							
27	CATALAC 27	SLP	SA/CR	FBG CT	OB		13 8	4500	2	7850	9000
29 6	CATALAC 30	SLP	SA/CR	FBG CT	IB	24D	13 10	6000	2 6	9700	11000
---	---	--- 1976	BOATS	---							
27	CATALAC 27	SLP	SA/CR	FBG CT	OB		13 8	4500	2	7600	8700
27	CATALAC 27	SLP	SA/CR	FBG CT	IB	T 15D RCA	13 8	4500	2	7600	8700
29 6	CATALAC 30	SLP	SA/CR	FBG CT	OB		13 10	6000	2 6	9400	10600
29 6	CATALAC 30	SLP	SA/CR	FBG CT	IB	T 15D RCA	13 10	6000	2 6	9500	10800
35 7	SNOWGOOSE 36	CUT	SAIL	FBG CT	IB	25D VLVO	15	8000	2 9	18300	20400
42	SOLARIS 42	MS		FBG CT		D	17 8			33300	37000
42	SOLARIS 42	CAT	SA/CR	FBG CT	IB	D	17 8			33200	36900
42	SOLARIS 42	SLP	SA/CR	FBG CT	IB	D	17 8			33200	36900

```
OCEAN CATAMARANS          -CONTINUED   See inside cover to adjust price for area
  LOA   NAME AND/            TOP/ BOAT  -HULL- ----ENGINE---  BEAM    WGT  DRAFT RETAIL RETAIL
FT IN   OR MODEL             RIG  TYPE  MTL TP TP # HP  MFG  FT IN    LBS  FT IN  LOW   HIGH
-------------------- 1976 BOATS -------------------------------------------------------------
 42   SOLARIS 42             KTH  SA/CR FBG CT IB     D    17  8            33200 36900
-------------------- 1975 BOATS -------------------------------------------------------------
 41 3 SOLARIS               KTH  SA/CR FBG CT IB          17  9 13000  3 3 29400 32600
-------------------- 1974 BOATS -------------------------------------------------------------
 29 3 CATALAC                    SAIL  FBG CT IB  40  OMC  14          2 3  9050 10300
 30 6 ARISTOCAT                  SAIL  FBG CT IB  40  OMC  14              10600 12000
 36   RANGER                     SAIL  FBG CT IB  25D VLVO 15      9000 2 5 17500 19900
 41 3 SOLARIS                     FBG CT IB T 40D BENZ 17  9 13000  3 3 34100 37900
 41 3 SOLARIS               KTH  SAIL  FBG CT IB     D    17  9 13000  3 3 28900 32200
 45   RANGER 45             CUT  SA/CR FBG CT IB     D    20    15000  2 9 39400 43700
-------------------- 1973 BOATS -------------------------------------------------------------
 29 3 CATALAC               SLP  SAIL  FBG CT IB     D    14          2 3  8150  9350
 30 6 ARISTOCAT             SLP  SAIL  FBG CT IB     D    14          1 5  9250 10500
 36   RANGER 36                  SAIL  FBG CT IB  25D     15          2 7 16700 19000
 36   RANGER 36             CUT  SAIL  FBG CT IB     D    15      9000 2 5 16900 19200
 41   RANGER 41             KTH  SAIL  FBG CT IB     D    17  8      1 11 27200 30200
 41 3 SOLARIS               KTH  SAIL  FBG CT IB     D    17  9 13000  3 3 27900 31000
 45   RANGER 45             CUT  SAIL  FBG CT IB     D    20    15000  2 9 38000 42200
-------------------- 1972 BOATS -------------------------------------------------------------
 31   RANGER 31             SLP  SAIL  FBG CT IB  75-200  12  6     1 10 10500 12000
 34 3 RANGER 34             CUT  SAIL  FBG CT IB  75-200  15  3     2 3  15900 18000
 45   RANGER 45             CUT  SAIL  FBG CT IB  110     20        2 10 40000 44400
 45   RANGER 45             CUT  SAIL  FBG CT IB  250     20        2 10 40100 44600
-------------------- 1971 BOATS -------------------------------------------------------------
 27 3 RANGER 27                  SAIL  FBG CT IB  25  OMC 12  6  4000 1 10  6650  7650
 31   RANGER 31                  SAIL  FBG CT IB  25  OMC 12  6  4500 1 10  8450  9700
 34 3 RANGER 34                  SAIL  FBG CT     15  3  8000  2 3  13200 15000
 34 3 RANGER 34                  SAIL  FBG CT IB  25D     15  3  8000  2 3  13400 15200
 34 3 SNOWGOOSE             CUT  SA/CR FBG KL         15  3      2 3   9550 10900
 45   RANGER 45                  SAIL  FBG CT IB  47D PERK 20    15000  2 9 35100 39000
-------------------- 1970 BOATS -------------------------------------------------------------
 27   RANGER                SLP  SAIL  FBG CT         12  6      1 10  6500  7500
 27 3 RANGER                     CR    FBG CT IO T100 12  6      2 4  19400 21600
 27 3 RANGER                     CR    FBG CT IB T100 12  6      2 4  11200 12700
 27 3 WORKBOAT                   UTL   FBG   OB        12  6          17000 19300
 27 3 WORKBOAT                   UTL   FBG   IO        12  6            **    **
 27 3 WORKBOAT                   UTL   FBG   IB        12  6            **    **
 31   RANGER                     CR    FBG CT IO T150 12  6      2 1  29400 32700
 31   RANGER                     CR    FBG CT IB T150 12  6      2 1  17400 19800
 31   RANGER                SLP  SA/CR FBG CT          12  6     1 10  9450 10800
 45   OCEAN-RANGER          SLP  SA/CR FBG CT          20        2 10 40200 44700
 45   OCEAN-RANGER          SLP  SA/CR FBG CT IB       20        2 10 40200 44700

 45   RANGER                     CR    FBG CT IO T200  16        2 9  71900 79000
 45   RANGER                     CR    FBG CT IB T200  16        2 9  60100 66000
```

OCEAN CRUISING YTS INC
BAR HARBOR ME 04609   COAST GUARD MFG ID- XYG See inside cover to adjust price for area

For more recent years, see the BUC Used Boat Price Guide, Volume 1 or Volume 2

```
  LOA   NAME AND/            TOP/ BOAT  -HULL- ----ENGINE---  BEAM    WGT  DRAFT RETAIL RETAIL
FT IN   OR MODEL             RIG  TYPE  MTL TP TP # HP  MFG  FT IN    LBS  FT IN  LOW   HIGH
-------------------- 1983 BOATS -------------------------------------------------------------
 39 2 OC-39                  SLP  SA/CR FBG KL IB  30D WEST 12  3 18000  6 6  97600 107000
 40 2 OC-40                  SLP  SA/CR FBG KC IB  37D WEST 12  3 20200  4 4 111000 122000
 40 2 OC-40                  SLP  SA/CR FBG KL IB  37D WEST 12  3 20200    111000 122000
 42 3 OC-42 AFT COCKPIT      SLP  SA/CR FBG KC IB  51D     12  4 24800  4 8 136000 149500
 42 3 OC-42 AFT COCKPIT      SLP  SA/CR FBG KL IB  51D     12  4 24800  5 8 129500 142500
 42 3 OC-42 AFT COCKPIT      KTH  SA/CR FBG KC IB  51D     12  4 24800  4 8 136000 149500
 42 3 OC-42 AFT COCKPIT      KTH  SA/CR FBG KL IB  51D     12  4 24800  5 8 130000 149500
 42 3 OC-42 MID COCKPIT      SLP  SA/CR FBG KC IB  51D     12  4 24800  4 8 136000 149500
 42 3 OC-42 MID COCKPIT      SLP  SA/CR FBG KL IB  51D     12  4 24800  5 8 142500 156500
 47 7 OC-48 AFT COCKPIT      SLP  SA/CR FBG KC IB  58D WEST 13  9 34000  4 10 199000 218500
 52   OC-52 AFT-COCKPIT      SLP  SA/CR FBG KC IB  85D     14  8 44000  5 6 264500 290500
 52   OC-52 AFT-COCKPIT      KTH  SA/CR FBG KC IB  85D     14  8 44000  5 6 266000 292500

 52   OC-52 MID COCKPIT      SLP  SA/CR FBG KC IB  85D     14  8 44000  5 6 264500 290500
 52   OC-52 MID COCKPIT      KTH  SA/CR FBG KC IB  85D     14  8 44000  5 6 266000 292500
-------------------- 1982 BOATS -------------------------------------------------------------
 39 2 OC-39                  SLP  SA/CR FBG KC IB  30D WEST 12  3 18000  6 6  91800 101000
 40 2 OC-40                  SLP  SA/CR FBG KC IB  37D WEST 12  3 20200  4 4 104500 115000
 47 7 OC-48                  SLP  SA/CR FBG KC IB  58D WEST 13  9 34000  4 10 187000 205500
 51 11 OC-52                 SLP  SA/CR FBG KC IB  58D WEST 14  9 44000  6 248000 272500
-------------------- 1981 BOATS -------------------------------------------------------------
 39 2 OC-39                  SLP  SA/CR FBG KC IB  30D WEST 12  3 18000  6 6  83600  94900
 40 2 OC-40                  SLP  SA/CR FBG KC IB  37D WEST 12  3 20200  4 4  98300 108000
 47 7 OC-48                  SLP  SA/CR FBG KC IB  58D WEST 13  9 34000  4 10 176000 193500
-------------------- 1980 BOATS -------------------------------------------------------------
 40 2 OC-40                  SLP  SA/CR FBG KC IB  37D WEST 12  3 20200  4 4  93900 103000
-------------------- 1979 BOATS -------------------------------------------------------------
 40 2 OC-40                  SLP  SA/CR FBG KC IB  37D WEST 12  3 20200  4 4  90200  99200
```

OCEAN MASTER MARINE INC
RIVIERA BEACH FL 33404 COAST GUARD MFG ID- OMB See inside cover to adjust price for area

For more recent years, see the BUC Used Boat Price Guide, Volume 1 or Volume 2

```
  LOA   NAME AND/            TOP/ BOAT  -HULL- ----ENGINE---  BEAM    WGT  DRAFT RETAIL RETAIL
FT IN   OR MODEL             RIG  TYPE  MTL TP TP # HP  MFG  FT IN    LBS  FT IN  LOW   HIGH
-------------------- 1981 BOATS -------------------------------------------------------------
 30 7 OCEAN-MASTER 31        TT   SF    FBG SV IO T200-T300 10  3     2 5 28300 33800
-------------------- 1980 BOATS -------------------------------------------------------------
 30 7 OCEAN-MASTER 31        TT   SF    FBG SV IO T200-T300 10  3     2 5 28000 33400
```

OCEAN RANGER YACHTS
MARBLEHEAD MA 01945   See inside cover to adjust price for area
                   SEE LITTLE HARBOR YACHT SALES

```
  LOA   NAME AND/            TOP/ BOAT  -HULL- ----ENGINE---  BEAM    WGT  DRAFT RETAIL RETAIL
FT IN   OR MODEL             RIG  TYPE  MTL TP TP # HP  MFG  FT IN    LBS  FT IN  LOW   HIGH
-------------------- 1980 BOATS -------------------------------------------------------------
 35 9 OCEAN-RANGER           FB   TRWL  FBG DS IB  120D VLVO 13 10 19091  3 3  54000  59400
 35 9 OCEAN-RANGER           FB   TRWL  FBG DS IB T120D LEHM 13 10 19091  3 3  56600  62100
 38 3 HOOD CUSTOM            SLP  SA/RC FBG KC IB  50D PERK 11 10 20600  4 3  47500  52200
 38 3 OCEAN-RANGER           FB   PH    FBG DS IB  120D LEHM 15  3  46500  4 6  66900  73500
 50 3 OCEAN-RANGER           HT   TRWL  FBG DS IB  120D LEHM 15  6  46500  4 6 112500 123500
 50 3 OCEAN-RANGER           FB   TRWL  FBG DS IB  120D LEHM 15  6  46500  4 6 108000 119000
       IB T210D CAT  115000 126500; IB T216D GM  115000 126500; IB T240D VLVO 117000 128500
       IB T270D CUM  119500 131500; IB T295D CUM 121500 133500; IB T310D GM  123000 135000
       IB T400D CUM  130000 143000
 59 3 OCEAN-RANGER           FB   TRWL  FBG DS IB T325D GM  19    72000  4 9 200000 219500
 60 8 HOOD CUSTOM            SLP  SA/CR FBG KC IB T140D PERK 16  4 78000  5 6 278500 306500
 73 6 HOOD CUSTOM            SLP  SA/CR FBG KC IB T165D PERK 18  4  64T  6 6   **     **
```

OCEAN YACHTS INC
COAST GUARD MFG ID- XYX

Call 1-800-327-6929 for BUC Personalized Evaluation Service
Or, for 1977 to 1981 boats, sign onto www.BUCValuPro.com

OCEAN YACHTS INC
EGG HARBOR CITY NJ 0821 COAST GUARD MFG ID- XYU See inside cover to adjust price for area

For more recent years, see the BUC Used Boat Price Guide, Volume 1 or Volume 2

```
  LOA   NAME AND/            TOP/ BOAT  -HULL- ----ENGINE---  BEAM    WGT  DRAFT RETAIL RETAIL
FT IN   OR MODEL             RIG  TYPE  MTL TP TP # HP  MFG  FT IN    LBS  FT IN  LOW   HIGH
-------------------- 1983 BOATS -------------------------------------------------------------
 42   SUN-LINER              FB   CR    FBG SV IB T300D GM  14  4 28000  3 6 100500 110500
 42   SUPER-SPORT            FB   SF    FBG SV IB T300D GM  14  4 30000  3 6 104500 114500
 42   SUPER-SPORT            FB   SF    FBG SV IB T400D GM  14  4 30000  3 6 113500 124500
 46   SUN-LINER              FB   CR    FBG SV IB T450D GM  15  2 40000  3 9 129500 142500
 46   SUN-LINER              FB   CR    FBG SV IB T550D GM  15  2 40000  3 9 139500 153500
 46   SUPER-SPORT            FB   SF    FBG SV IB T450D GM  15  2 40000  3 9 128500 141500
 46   SUPER-SPORT            FB   SF    FBG SV IB T550D GM  15  2 40000  3 9 134500 147500
 50   SUPER-SPORT            FB   SF    FBG SV IB T500D GM  16    50000  4 2 158500 174500
 50   SUPER-SPORT            FB   SF    FBG SV IB T600D GM  16    50000  4 2 170500 187500
 55   SUPER-SPORT            FB   MY    FBG SV IB T600D GM  16  4 62000  4 4 211500 232500
 55   SUPER-SPORT            FB   MY    FBG SV IB T675D S&S 16  4 62000  4 4 221000 243000

 55 8 SUPER-SPORT            FB   SF    FBG SV IB T600D GM  16  4 58000  4 4 210500 231000
 55 8 SUPER-SPORT            FB   SF    FBG SV IB T675D S&S 16  4 58000  4 4 221000 243000
-------------------- 1982 BOATS -------------------------------------------------------------
 42   SUN-LINER              FB   MY    FBG SV IB T300D GM  14  4 28000  3 6 105500 116500
 42   SUPER-SPORT            FB   SF    FBG SV IB T300D GM  14  4 28000  3 6 106500 117500
 42   SUPER-SPORT            FB   SF    FBG SV IB T400D GM  14  4 30000  3 6  99500 109500
 50   SUPER-SPORT            FB   SF    FBG SV IB T500D GM  16    48000  4 2 147500 162000
 50   SUPER-SPORT            FB   SF    FBG SV IB T550D GM  16    48000  4 2 153500 168500
```

OCEAN YACHTS INC   -CONTINUED   See inside cover to adjust price for area

LOA FT IN	NAME AND/ OR MODEL	TOP/ RIG	BOAT TYPE	-HULL- MTL TP TP	----ENGINE--- # HP MFG	BEAM FT IN	WGT LBS	DRAFT FT IN	RETAIL LOW	RETAIL HIGH
--- 1982 BOATS ---										
55 8	SUPER-SPORT	FB	SF	FBG SV IB	T550D GM	16 4	54000	4 4	183500	201500
55 8	SUPER-SPORT	FB	SF	FBG SV IB	T675D GM	16 4	54000	4 4	201500	221500
--- 1981 BOATS ---										
40	40+2	FB	TRWL	FBG DS IB	T160D PERK	14 4	30000	3 6	91100	100000
42	OCEAN 42		SF	FBG SV IB	T250D	14 4	28000			103000
42	SUN-LINER	FB	MY	FBG SV IB	T300D GM	14 4	30000	3 6	98100	108000
42	SUN-LINER	FB	MY	FBG SV IB	T400D GM	14 4	28000	3 6	101500	111500
42	SUPER-SPORT	FB	SF	FBG SV IB	T300D GM	14 4	28000	3 6	90400	99400
42	SUPER-SPORT	FB	SF	FBG SV IB	T400D GM	14 4	30000	3 6	103000	113500
55	SUPER-SPORT	FB	SF	FBG SV IB	T550D GM	16 3	48000	4 4	159000	175000
55	SUPER-SPORT	FB	SF	FBG SV IB	T675D GM	16 3	48000	4 4	176500	194000
--- 1980 BOATS ---										
32	HUSTLER 32		EXP	FBG DV IO	T330				28000	31100
40	TRAWLER YACHT	FB	TRWL	FBG DS IB	T160D PERK	14 4	30000	3 6	86900	95500
42	OCEAN 40+2	FB	TRWL	FBG SV IB	160D	14 4	30000	3 6	82100	90200
42	OCEAN 40+2	FB	TRWL	FBG CV IB	T160D	14 4	30000	3 6	86000	94600
42	OCEAN 42		SF	FBG SV IB	250D	14 4	28000	3 6	74500	81900
42	SUN-LINER	FB	DC	FBG SV IB	T300D GM	14 4	30000	3 6	94100	103500
42	SUN-LINER	FB	DC	FBG SV IB	T410D GM	14 4	30000	3 6	102500	112500
42	SUPER-SPORT	FB	SF	FBG SV IB	T300D GM	14 4	30000	3 6	90500	99400
42	SUPER-SPORT	FB	SF	FBG SV IB	T410D GM	14 4	30000	3 6	99300	109000
--- 1979 BOATS ---										
40	TRAWLER YACHT	FB	TRWL	FBG DS IB	T160D PERK	14 4	30000	3 6	83000	91200
40 2	SUPER-SPORT	FB	SF	FBG SV IB	T410D GM	14 4	30000	3 6	92300	101500
--- 1978 BOATS ---										
40	TRAWLER YACHT	FB	TRWL	FBG DS IB	T160D PERK	14 4	30000	3 6	79400	87200
40 2	SUPER-SPORT	FB	SF	FBG SV IB	T410D GM	14 4	30000	3 6	88300	97000
--- 1977 BOATS ---										
40 2	SUPER-SPORT	FB	SF	FBG SV IB	T410D GM	14 4	30000	3 6	84500	92900

ODYSSEY YACHT SALES

Call 1-800-327-6929 for BUC Personalized Evaluation Service
Or, for 1980 to 1982 boats, sign onto www.BUCValuPro.com

OFFSHORE BOAT CORP
MIAMI FL 33150   See inside cover to adjust price for area

For more recent years, see the BUC Used Boat Price Guide, Volume 1 or Volume 2

LOA FT IN	NAME AND/ OR MODEL	TOP/ RIG	BOAT TYPE	-HULL- MTL TP TP	----ENGINE--- # HP MFG	BEAM FT IN	WGT LBS	DRAFT FT IN	RETAIL LOW	RETAIL HIGH
--- 1982 BOATS ---										
25	WHITEWATER		OP	CTRCN FBG	OB	8	5000	2 8	9600	10900
25	WHITEWATER		OP	CTRCN FBG	IO 250-330	8	5000	2 8	9600	11800
	IO 340-350	11100	12800,	IO 200D-235D	15300 17400,	IO	300D CAT	17400		19800
	IO T170 MRCR	10800	12300							
25	WHITEWATER		TT	CTRCN FBG	OB	8	5000	2 8	9600	10900
25	WHITEWATER		TT	CTRCN FBG	IO 250-330	8	5000	2 8	9600	11800
	IO 340-350	11100	12800,	IO 200D-235D	15300 17400,	IO	300D CAT	17400		19800
	IO T170 MRCR	10800	12300							

OFFSHORE CRUISERS ASSOCIATES

Call 1-800-327-6929 for BUC Personalized Evaluation Service
Or, for 1966 boats, sign onto www.BUCValuPro.com

OFFSHORE THIRTY INC
TITUSVILLE FL 32780   COAST GUARD MFG ID- FFS   See inside cover to adjust price for area

LOA FT IN	NAME AND/ OR MODEL	TOP/ RIG	BOAT TYPE	-HULL- MTL TP TP	----ENGINE--- # HP MFG	BEAM FT IN	WGT LBS	DRAFT FT IN	RETAIL LOW	RETAIL HIGH
--- 1979 BOATS ---										
34			TRWL	FBG RB IB	85D	13	12000		31000	34500
--- 1978 BOATS ---										
33 7		FB	TRWL	FBG RB IB	90D	13	12000		29400	32700
--- 1977 BOATS ---										
28			OP		FBG SV IB	225	10 2			11200	12700
36			SF		FBG SV IB	130D	13			36700	40700

OFFSHORE YACHTS
ALAMEDA CA 94501   See inside cover to adjust price for area

LOA FT IN	NAME AND/ OR MODEL	TOP/ RIG	BOAT TYPE	-HULL- MTL TP TP	----ENGINE--- # HP MFG	BEAM FT IN	WGT LBS	DRAFT FT IN	RETAIL LOW	RETAIL HIGH
--- 1972 BOATS ---										
38	EXPLORER		TRWL	FBG DS IB	160D PERK	13 6		3 8	46800	51400
38	EXPLORER		TRWL	FBG DS IB	280D	13 6		3 8	47600	52300
--- 1971 BOATS ---										
38	EXPLORER		TRWL	FBG DS IB	160D PERK	13 6	23158	3 8	44600	49500
38	EXPLORER		TRWL	FBG DS IB	250D	13 6	23158	3 8	45600	50100
--- 1970 BOATS ---										
33 9	ALBION 33		DC	FBG SV IB	160D PERK	9	17000	3 6	34400	38200
33 9	ALBION 33		DC	FBG SV IB	160D PERK	9	17000	3 6	34800	38600
36	ALBION 36		DC	FBG SV IB	T160D PERK	10 6	19000	3 6	38200	42400
38	EXPLORER 38		DC	FBG SV IB	300D	13 6	24640	3 8	46800	51400
38	EXPLORER 38		DC	FBG SV IB	T160D PERK	13 6	24640	3 8	48600	53400
--- 1969 BOATS ---										
38	EXPLORER 38DC		DC	FBG SV IB	160D PERK	13 6	24640	3 8	43900	48800

OFFSHORE YACHTS INTL LTD
JACK POWLES INTL MARINE LTD
NORFOLK ENGLAND   COAST GUARD MFG ID- FRF   See inside cover to adjust price for area

LOA FT IN	NAME AND/ OR MODEL	TOP/ RIG	BOAT TYPE	-HULL- MTL TP TP	----ENGINE--- # HP MFG	BEAM FT IN	WGT LBS	DRAFT FT IN	RETAIL LOW	RETAIL HIGH
--- 1979 BOATS ---										
31 8	NANTUCKET-CLIPPER	SLP	SA/CR FBG KL IB	13D VLVO	9 1	8240	4 3	20600	22900	
31 8	NANTUCKET-CLIPPER	YWL	SA/CR FBG KL IB	13D VLVO	9 1	8240	4 3	20600	22900	
--- 1978 BOATS ---										
23	HALCYON 23	SLP	SA/CR FBG KL IB	6D- 7D	7 6	3000	2 6	5700	6600	
23	HALCYON 23 FIN KEEL	SLP	SA/CR FBG KL IB	6D- 7D	7 6	3000	3 8	5700	6600	
24 6	OFFSHORE 25 1/4 TON	SLP	SA/RC FBG KL IB	7D PETT	8 2	3450	4 7	6650	7600	
27	HALCYON 27	SLP	SA/CR FBG KL IB	13D	7 8	6720	4	14000	15900	
31 8	NANTUCKET-CLIPPER	SLP	SA/CR FBG KL IB	13D	9 1	8240	4 3	20000	22300	
31 8	NANTUCKET-CLIPPER	YWL	SA/CR FBG KL IB	13D	9 1	8240	4 3	20000	22300	
--- 1977 BOATS ---										
23	HALCYON 23	SLP	SA/CR FBG KL IB	7D WICK	7 6	3000	3 8	5550	6400	
24 6	OFFSHORE 24 1/4 TON	SLP	SA/CR FBG KL IB	7D PETT	8 2	3450	4 7	6400	7350	
27	HALCYON 27	SLP	SA/CR FBG KL IB	10D BUKH	7 8	7250	4	14500	16400	
31 8	NANTUCKET-CLIPPER	YWL	SA/CR FBG KL IB	10D BUKH	9 2	8290	4 3	19400	21500	
34	OFFSHORE 34	SLP	SA/CR FBG KL HD	37D PERK	11	17400	6	37700	41900	
--- 1976 BOATS ---										
27	HALCYON OFFSHORE 27	SLP	SAIL FBG KL IB	7D WEST	7 6	7250	4	13900	15800	
31 8	NANTUCKET-CLIPPER	YWL	SAIL FBG KL IB	10D WEST	9 2	9975	4 3	22200	24600	
34	OFFSHORE 34	SLP	SAIL FBG KL IB	36D- 50D	11	17400	6	36300	40400	
--- 1975 BOATS ---										
23	HALCYON 23	SLP	SA/CR FBG KL IB	D	7 6	3600	3 8	5950	6850	
24 6	OFFSHORE 25	SLP	SA/CR FBG KL IB	D	8 2	3400	4 6	6000	6900	
27	HALCYON 27	SLP	SA/CR FBG KL IB	D	7 9	7250	4	13500	15300	
31 8	NANTUCKET-CLIPPER	YWL	SA/CR FBG KL IB	D	9 2	8500	4 3	18500	20600	
34	OFFSHORE 34	SLP	SA/CR FBG KL IB	D	11	17400	6	35100	39000	

OKAMOTA & SON BOAT WORKS

Call 1-800-327-6929 for BUC Personalized Evaluation Service
Or, for 1961 to 1968 boats, sign onto www.BUCValuPro.com

OLD GREENWICH BOAT CO

Call 1-800-327-6929 for BUC Personalized Evaluation Service
Or, for 1953 to 1972 boats, sign onto www.BUCValuPro.com

OLD TOWN CANOE CO
OLD TOWN ME 04468-0548   COAST GUARD MFG ID- XTC   See inside cover to adjust price for area

For more recent years, see the BUC Used Boat Price Guide, Volume 1 or Volume 2

LOA FT IN	NAME AND/ OR MODEL	TOP/ RIG	BOAT TYPE	-HULL- MTL TP TP	----ENGINE--- # HP MFG	BEAM FT IN	WGT LBS	DRAFT FT IN	RETAIL LOW	RETAIL HIGH
--- 1975 BOATS ---										
16 6	SHRIKE		RNBT	FBG DV IO	120	6 8	1705	1	3800	4400
20	FISHER		FSH	FBG DV IO	120	8	2235	1 3	6000	6900
24 3	ATLANTIS		RNBT	FBG DV IO	165	8	2990	1 2	7850	9000

OLD TOWN CANOE CO   -CONTINUED   See inside cover to adjust price for area

LOA FT	IN	NAME AND/OR MODEL	TOP/RIG	BOAT TYPE	HULL MTL	HULL TP	ENG TP	# HP	MFG	BEAM FT	IN	WGT LBS	DRAFT FT	IN	RETAIL LOW	RETAIL HIGH
		1974 BOATS														
16	6	SHRIKE			FBG		OB			6	8	860	1		2750	3200
16	6	SHRIKE			FBG		IO	120-170		6	8	1705	1		3700	4300
20				FSH	FBG		IO	120-180		8		2235	1	3	6200	7200
20		EAGLE			FBG		IO	170-180		8		2335	1	3	5700	6600
20		GULL			FBG		IO	170-180		8		2560	1	3	5950	6900
24	3	ATLANTIS			FBG		IO	165-225		8		2990	1	2	8350	9850
		1973 BOATS														
16	6	SHRIKE			FBG		OB			6	8	860			2750	3200
16	6	SHRIKE			FBG		IO	120-155		6	8	1550			3600	4400
20				FSH	FBG		IO	120-155		8		2080			6150	7250
20		EAGLE			FBG		IO	120	OMC	8		2180			5650	6500
20		EAGLE			FBG		IO	155	OMC	8		2700			6300	7250
20		GULL			FBG		IO	120-155		8		2500			6050	7250
24	3	ATLANTIS			FBG		IO	120-245		8					10500	11900
24	3	ATLANTIS			FBG		IO	T120	OMC	8					11700	13300
		1972 BOATS														
16	6	SHRIKE			FBG		OB			6	8	860			2750	3200
16	6	SHRIKE			FBG		IO	120-155		6	8	1550			3750	4550
20				FSH	FBG		IO	120-155		8		2080			6350	7500
20		EAGLE			FBG		IO	120	OMC	8		2180			5850	6700
20		GULL			FBG		IO	120-155		8		2500			6250	7500
24	3	ATLANTIS			FBG		IO	120-235		8					10800	12300
24	3	ATLANTIS			FBG		IO	T120	OMC	8					12100	13700
		1971 BOATS														
16	6	SHRIKE			FBG		OB			6	8	860			2750	3200
16	6	SHRIKE			FBG		IO	120-155		6	8	1550			3850	4700
20				FSH	FBG		IO	120-155		8		2080			6600	7750
20		EAGLE			FBG		IO	120	OMC	8		2180			6050	6950
20		GULL			FBG		IO	120-155		8		2500			6450	7750
24	3	ATLANTIS			FBG		IO	120-235		8					11200	12700
24	3	ATLANTIS			FBG		IO	T120	OMC	8					12500	14200
		1970 BOATS														
16	6	DV 1780		RNBT	FBG	DV	OB			6	8	860			2750	3200
16	6	DV 1780		RNBT	FBG	DV	IO	120-155		6	8	1550			4250	5100
20		SEA-EAGLE		FSH	FBG	DV	IO	120-210		8		2080			6800	8350
24	3	ATLANTIS 2560		CR	FBG	DV	IO	155-210		8		2800			9500	11300
24	3	ATLANTIS 2560		CR	FBG	DV	IO	T120	OMC	8		2800			13500	15400
		1969 BOATS														
16	6	DV 1780		RNBT	FBG	DV	OB			6	8	860			2800	3250
16	6	DV 1780		RNBT	FBG	DV	IO	120-155		6	8	1550			4450	5250
24	3	ATLANTIS 2560		CR	FBG	DV	IO	155-210		8		2800			9850	11600
		1968 BOATS														
16	6	DV1780	OP	RNBT	FBG	DV	OB			6	8	860			2800	3250
16	6	DV1780	OP	RNBT	FBG	DV	IO	120-155		6	8	1550			4600	5400
24	3	ATLANTIS 2560	OP	CR	FBG	DV	IO	155-210		8		2800			10200	12000
		1967 BOATS														
16	4	1720		RNBT	L/P		OB			6	5	600			1950	2350
16	6	DV1780		RNBT	FBG		OB			6	8	860			2800	3250
16	6	DV1780		RNBT	FBG		IO	80-120		6	8	1210			4250	5350
16	6	DV1780		RNBT	FBG		IO	155		6	8	1570			4800	5500
17	10	1810		RNBT	L/P		OB			6	11	800			2750	3200
19	2	2040		RNBT	L/P		OB			8		1000			3500	4050
22	8	2400		RNBT	L/P		OB			8		1400			5300	6100
		1966 BOATS														
16	4	LAPSTRAKE		RNBT	WD		OB			6	4	700			2300	2700
16	4	LAPSTRAKE		RNBT	WD		IO	60-90		6	4				5000	5750
16	6	DV 1780		RNBT	FBG		OB			6	8	750			2500	2900
17	10	LAPSTRAKE		RNBT	WD		OB			6	11	800			2750	3200
17	10	LAPSTRAKE		RNBT	WD		IO	110		6	11				6300	7250
19	2	LAPSTRAKE		CR	WD		OB			8		1000			3500	4050
19	2	LAPSTRAKE		CR	WD		IO			8					**	**
22	8	LAPSTRAKE		CR	WD		OB			8		1400			5300	6100
22	8	LAPSTRAKE		CR	WD		IO	120-150		8					12000	13600
		1965 BOATS														
16		KING-SIZE SKIFF			WD		OB								1950	2300
16	4	LAPSTRAKE			WD		OB								1950	2350
16	4	LAPSTRAKE			WD		IO	90							4500	5150
17	10	LAPSTRAKE			WD		OB								3250	3750
17	10	LAPSTRAKE			WD		IO	90-110							5750	6650
20	4	LAPSTRAKE			WD		OB								4350	5000
20	4	LAPSTRAKE			WD		IO	90-165							7700	8900
20	4	LAPSTRAKE			WD		IO	65D							10300	11700
22	8	LAPSTRAKE			WD		OB								6600	7600
22	8	LAPSTRAKE			WD		IO	90-165							10900	12500
22	8	LAPSTRAKE			WD		IO	65D							15000	17000
		1964 BOATS														
16		KING-SIZE SKIFF			WD		OB								2250	2600
16		SKIFF			WD		OB								1700	2000
16	3	LAPSTRAKE 16			WD		OB								1950	2350
17	6	LAPSTRAKE 17-6			WD		OB								3200	3750
19		LAPSTRAKE 19			WD		OB								4350	5000
22	7	LAPSTRAKE 22			WD		IO	80-160							7400	8600
22	7	LAPSTRAKE 22			WD		IO	80-160							11200	12800
		1963 BOATS														
16	3	LAPSTRAKE 16			WD		OB								2000	2350
17	6	LAPSTRAKE 17-6			WD		OB								3200	3750
19		LAPSTRAKE 19			WD		OB								4400	5050
19		LAPSTRAKE 19			WD		IO	100							7650	8800
22	7	LAPSTRAKE 22			WD		OB								6600	7600
22	7	LAPSTRAKE 22			WD		IO	100							11600	13200
		1962 BOATS														
17	6	LAPSTRAKE		RNBT	WD		OB								4200	4900
19		LAPSTRAKE		RNBT	WD		OB								5000	5700
22	2	LAPSTRAKE		RNBT	WD		OB								9550	10900
		1961 BOATS														
17		KINGSIZE	OP	ROW	CVS					4	1	395			**	**
17				RNBT	L/P		OB			6	10	800			2750	3200
17		CRUISETTE		CR	L/P		OB			6	10	850			2850	3300
18	3			CR	L/P		OB			7	9	1300			3450	4000
18	3			RNBT	L/P		OB			7	9	1300			4250	4950
19				RNBT	L/P		OB			8		1000			3550	4100
22	2			RNBT	L/P		OB			8		1500			5650	6500
		1960 BOATS														
17				UTL	WD		OB								2350	2750
18	3			EXP	WD		OB								4050	4700
18	3			UTL	WD		OB								2250	2600
		1959 BOATS														
17		LAPSTRAKE "18"		UTL	L/P		OB			6	10	800			2650	3050
18	3	LAPSTRAKE "20"		UTL	L/P		OB			7	9	1000			3200	3700
		1958 BOATS														
16				CR	WD		OB								2250	2650
16				RNBT	WD		OB								2650	3050
18				CR	WD		OB								3500	4100
18				RNBT	WD		OB								4300	5000
20				CR	WD		OB								5400	6200
		1954 BOATS														
16				RNBT	WD		OB								2650	3100
		1928 BOATS														
16		MOTORBOAT					OB								**	**

OLD WHARF DORY COMPANY
COAST GUARD MFG ID- XWC

Call 1-800-327-6929 for BUC Personalized Evaluation Service
Or, for 1982 to 2002 boats, sign onto www.BUCValuPro.com

OLSEN BOAT WORKS

Call 1-800-327-6929 for BUC Personalized Evaluation Service
Or, for 1960 to 1972 boats, sign onto www.BUCValuPro.com

OLYMPIAN YACHTS

Call 1-800-327-6929 for BUC Personalized Evaluation Service
Or, for 1965 to 1966 boats, sign onto www.BUCValuPro.com

OLYMPIC MOLDED PRODUCTS

Call 1-800-327-6929 for BUC Personalized Evaluation Service
Or, for 1965 to 1971 boats, sign onto www.BUCValuPro.com

OLYMPIC YACHTS LTD
MONTREAL PQ CANADA   COAST GUARD MFG ID- DFN   See inside cover to adjust price for area

LOA FT	IN	NAME AND/OR MODEL	TOP/RIG	BOAT TYPE	HULL MTL	HULL TP	ENG TP	# HP	MFG	BEAM FT	IN	WGT LBS	DRAFT FT	IN	RETAIL LOW	RETAIL HIGH
		1975 BOATS														
22	9	DOLPHIN 23	SLP	SA/OD	FBG	KC	OB			7	3		2		3350	3900
29	7	OLYMPIC 30	SLP	SA/CR	FBG	KC	IB		D	9	11		3		12700	14400
29	7	OLYMPIC 30	SLP	SA/CR	FBG	KL	IB		D	9	11		4	6	12700	14400

OLYMPIC YACHTS LTD   -CONTINUED   See inside cover to adjust price for area

| LOA | NAME AND/ | TOP/ | BOAT | -HULL- | ----ENGINE--- | BEAM | WGT | DRAFT | RETAIL | RETAIL |
FT IN	OR MODEL	RIG	TYPE	MTL TP TP	# HP MFG	FT IN	LBS	FT IN	LOW	HIGH
---	--- 1974 **BOATS**									
22 9	DOLPHIN 23	SLP	SA/OD	FBG KC OB		7 6	2200	2	2650	3100
---	--- 1972 **BOATS**									
23 4	OLYMPIC STAR	SLP	SA/OD	FBG KL		7 5	3850	2 11	4050	4700
---	--- 1971 **BOATS**									
22 9	DOLPHIN 23	SLP	SA/OD	FBG KC OB		7	2000	2 2	2350	2700
23 4	OLYMPIC-STAR	SLP	SA/OD	FBG KL		7 5	3850	2 11	3950	4600
27 9	CORINTHIAN 29	SLP	SA/RC	FBG KL IB		8 8		3 9	6900	7950
30 4	OLYMPIC-PRINCESS	SLP	SA/RC	FBG KL IB	D	9 6		4 2	9400	10700
40	OLYMPIC 40	SLP	SA/RC	FBG KL IB	40D WEST 10 11		20000	5 8	28100	31300
40	OLYMPIC 40	SLP	SA/RC	FBG KL IB	D	10 11		5 8	28100	31200
40	OLYMPIC-QUEEN	KTH	SA/RC	FBG KL IB	D	10 11		5 8	28100	31200
44 1	APOLLO 44	SLP	SA/RC	FBG KL IB	D	11 10		6 7	37000	41100
---	--- 1970 **BOATS**									
23 4	OLYMPIC-STAR	SLP	SA/CR	KL		7 5		2 11	3200	3750
27 9	CORINTHIAN 28	SLP	SA/CR	KL		8 8		3 9	6950	8000
30 4	OLYMPIC-PRINCESS	SLP	SA/CR	KC ID	D	9 6		3	11400	12900
30 4	OLYMPIC-PRINCESS	SLP	SA/CR	KL IB	D	9 6		4 2	11400	12900
30 4	OLYMPIC-PRINCESS	YWL	SA/CR	KC IB	D	9 6		3	11400	12900
30 4	OLYMPIC-PRINCESS	YWL	SA/CR	KL IB	D	9 6		4 2	11400	12900
40	OLYMPIC 40	SLP	SA/CR	KL IB	D	10 11		5 8	27600	30700
40	OLYMPIC-QUEEN	KTH	SA/CR	KC IB	D	10 11		4 8	27600	30700
40	OLYMPIC-QUEEN	KTH	SA/CR	KL IB	D	10 11		5 8	27600	30700
44 1	APOLLO 44	SLP	SA/CR	KL IB	D	11 10		6 7	37900	42100
---	--- 1969 **BOATS**									
21 9	OLYMPIC-SPRINTER	SLP	SA/RC	FBG KL		6 10		3 6	3500	4050
23 4	OLYMPIC-STAR	SLP	SA/RC	FBG KL		7 5	3850	2 11	3800	4450
27 9	OLYMPIC-CORINTHIAN	SLP	SA/RC	FBG KL IB		8 8		3 9	6700	7700
30 4	OLYMPIC-PRINCESS	SLP	SA/RC	FBG KL IB	UNIV	9 6		4 2	6850	7850
30 4	OLYMPIC-PRINCESS	YWL	SA/RC	FBG KL IB		9 6		4 2	6850	7850
40	OLYMPIC-QUEEN	SLP	SA/CR	FBG KL IB		10 10		5 8	22400	24900
40	OLYMPIC-QUEEN	KTH	SA/CR	FBG KL IB		10 10		5 8	22400	24900
---	--- 1968 **BOATS**									
30 3	OLYMPIC-PRINCESS	SLP	SA/RC	FBG KL		9 6		4 1	6450	7450
30 3	OLYMPIC-PRINCESS	YWL	SA/RC	FBG KL		9 6		4 1	6450	7450
40	OLYMPIC-QUEEN	KTH	SA/CR	FBG KL IB	D	10 10		5 6	26800	29800

OLYMPIC YACHTS S A
PIRAEUS GREECE   COAST GUARD MFG ID- PMU See inside cover to adjust price for area

OLYMPIC MARINE S A
MAMARONECK NY

| LOA | NAME AND/ | TOP/ | BOAT | -HULL- | ----ENGINE--- | BEAM | WGT | DRAFT | RETAIL | RETAIL |
FT IN	OR MODEL	RIG	TYPE	MTL TP TP	# HP MFG	FT IN	LBS	FT IN	LOW	HIGH
---	--- 1977 **BOATS**									
38 1	OLYMPIC-ADVENTURE	SLP	SA/CR	FBG KL IB	37D	11 2	17650	4 10	47100	51800
38 1	OLYMPIC-ADVENTURE	KTH	SA/CR	FBG KL IB	37D	11 2	17650	4 10	47200	51800
42 2	OLYMPIC-ADVENTURE	KTH	SA/CR	FBG KL IB	62D	13 2	23750	5 3	66000	72500
44 3	OLYMPIC 44	EXP		FBG DV IB		14 2		2	**	**
47	OLYMPIC 47	KTH	SA/CR	FBG KL IB	62D	14 3	32000	5 11	88200	97000
54 2	OLYMPIC 54	SF		FBG DV IB	275	16 5		6 8	106000	117000
---	--- 1976 **BOATS**									
38 1	OLYMPIC-ADVENTURE	SLP	SA/CR	FBG KL IB	45D	11 2	17650	4 10	45800	50300
42 2	OLYMPIC-ADVENTURE	KTH	SA/CR	FBG KL IB	51D	13 2	23750	5 3	63800	70100
47	OLYMPIC-ADVENTURE	KTH	SA/CR	FBG KL IB	85D	14 3	32000	5 11	85800	94200
---	--- 1975 **BOATS**									
32 5	OLYMPIC 33	SLP	SA/CR	FBG KL IB	D	11	9750	5	23100	25600
37	OLYMPIC 37	SLP	SA/CR	FBG KL IB	D	11 11		6 4	42400	47200
39	OLYMPIC 39	SLP	SA/CR	FBG KL IB	D	12 9		6 9	46200	50800
47	OLYMPIC-ADVENTURE	YWL	SA/CR	FBG KL IB	75D	14 3	32000	5 11	83200	91400
47	OLYMPIC-ADVENTURE	KTH	SA/CR	FBG KL IB	75D	14 3	32000	5 11	83200	91400

OMEGA
FLORIDA BOATS INC   See inside cover to adjust price for area
OJUS INDUSTRIES
MIAMI FL 33163   COAST GUARD MFG ID- FLX

| LOA | NAME AND/ | TOP/ | BOAT | -HULL- | ----ENGINE--- | BEAM | WGT | DRAFT | RETAIL | RETAIL |
FT IN	OR MODEL	RIG	TYPE	MTL TP TP	# HP MFG	FT IN	LBS	FT IN	LOW	HIGH
---	--- 1978 **BOATS**									
25 5	GAMMA	ST	CUD	FBG	IO 190	8			10200	11600
25 5	GAMMA	ST	CUD	FBG	IO T255	8			12600	14400
25 5	GAMMA	HT	CUD	FBG	IO 190	8			10200	11600
25 5	GAMMA	HT	CUD	FBG	IO T255	8			12600	14400
27 9	FLYBRIDGE	FB	CUD	FBG	IO T175-T255	9 9			16700	20500
27 9	SPORT FISHERMAN	HT	SF	FBG	IO T175-T255	9 9			19000	22500
27 9	UTILITY	OP	CUD	FBG	IO 190	9 9			14800	16800
27 9	UTILITY	OP	CUD	FBG	IO T255	9 9			18500	20500
---	--- 1977 **BOATS**									
25 5	GAMMA	ST	CUD	FBG	IO 190	8			10300	11700
25 5	GAMMA	HT	CUD	FBG	IO 190	8			10300	11700
27 9	CUDDY SPORTSMAN	OP	CUD	FBG	IO T	9 9			**	**
27 9	FLYBRIDGE	FB	SF	FBG	IO 235	9 9			19400	21500
27 9	FLYBRIDGE	FB	SF	FBG	IO T175	9 9			20700	23000
27 9	HARDTOP	HT	SF	FBG	IO 235	9 9			17000	19400
27 9	HARDTOP	HT	SF	FBG	IO T	9 9			**	**
27 9	UTILITY	OP	UTL	FBG	IO 235	9 9			16300	18600
---	--- 1976 **BOATS**									
23 3	DISPLACEMENT SKIFF	FSH	FBG	DS IB	60D	8		1 8	11400	13000
23 3	FUNABOUT	RNBT	FBG	SV	IO 165-255	8		2 1	7500	8650
23 3	HARDTOP	HT	RNBT	FBG	SV IO 165-255	8		2 1	7200	8650
23 3	SPORTSMAN	RNBT	FDG	CV	IO 165-255	8		2 1	6950	8650
26	GAMMA	ST	CUD	FBG	IO 188-280				11700	14300
26	GAMMA	HT	CUD	FBG	IO T120-T188				12700	15300
26	GAMMA	HT	CUD	FBG	IO 188-280				11700	14300
26	GAMMA	HT	CUD	FBG	IO T120-T188				12700	15300
27 6	ALPHA	FB	CR	FBG	DV IO T220	10 10		2 9	18400	20400
27 6	ALPHA	EXP		FBG	DV IO T220	10 10		2 9	15900	18100
27 9	CUDDY SPORTSMAN	OP	CUD	FBG	IO 225-280	9 9	6000		14800	17600
27 9	CUDDY SPORTSMAN	OP	CUD	FBG	IO T165-T255	9 9	6000		16300	20100
27 9	FLYBRIDGE	FB	CUD	FBG	IO T165-T255	9 9			16900	20700
27 9	HARDTOP	HT	CUD	FBG	IO 225-280	9 9			15400	18300
27 9	HARDTOP	HT	CUD	FBG	IO T165-T255	9 9			16900	20700
---	--- 1975 **BOATS**									
23 3	FISHERMAN	FSH	FBG	DS	IB IO 45D-100D	8		1 8	10900	13200
23 3	FUNABOUT	CUD	FBG	SV	IO 165-255	8		2 1	7700	9250
23 3	SPORTSMAN	UTL	FBG	SV	IO 165-255	8		2 1	8250	9900
25 5	CONTINENTAL	CUD	FBG	IO 190		8		2 3	13100	12000
25 5	CONTINENTAL	CUD	FBG	IO T255		8		2 3	13100	14900
27 6	EXPRESS	EXP	FBG	DV	IO T215-T255	10 10		2 8	16200	18400
27 9	HARDTOP	HT	CUD	FBG	IO 225	9 9		2 4	15800	18000
27 9	HARDTOP	HT	CUD	FBG	IO T255	9 9		2 4	19200	21400
27 9	SPORT FISHERMAN	FB	SF	FBG	IO 225	9 9		2 4	19900	22100
27 9	SPORT FISHERMAN	FB	SF	FBG	IO T255	9 9		2 4	22600	25100
27 9	SPORTSMAN	CUD	FBG	IO 225		9 9		2 4	16800	19000
27 9	SPORTSMAN	CUD	FBG	IO T255		9 9		2 4	19200	21400
---	--- 1974 **BOATS**									
23 3	FUNABOUT			FBG	IO 165-255	8	3300	2 1	7900	9550
23 3	FUNABOUT	HT		FBG	IO 165-255	8		2 1	8000	9600
23 3	SPORTSMAN		UTL	FBG	IO 165-255	8	3300	2 1	8500	10200
23 3	SPORTSMAN	HT	UTL	FBG	IO 165-255	8		2 1	8500	10200
23 3	SUPERSPORT			FBG	IO 165-255	8	3300	2 1	7400	9050
23 3	SUPERSPORT	HT		FBG	IO 165-255	8		2 1	7350	9050
27 6	ALPHA		SDN	FBG	IO T215	10 10	7500	2 8	21800	24200
27 6	ALPHA	FB	SDN	FBG	IO T215	10 10		2 8	21800	24200

27 9		HT		FBG	IO 215-255	9	7400	2 9	18400	20800

	IO T165 MRCR	20000	22200, IO T165 OMC	19900	22100, IO T165 WAUK	20200	22200
	VD T185 WAUK	16500	18700, IO T170 OMC	20000	22200, IO T185 WAUK	20200	22400
	VD T185 WAUK	16700	19000, IO T188-T190	20200	22500, IO T215 WAUK	20100	22300
	VD T215 WAUK	17100	19500, IO T225	20000	22400, IO T255 COMM	20400	22600
	IO T255 WAUK	20600	22900, VD T255 WAUK	18000	20000

27 9		FB		FBG	IO 215-255	9		2 4	18400	20800

	IO T165 MRCR	20000	22200, IO T165 OMC	19900	22100, IO T165 WAUK	20200	22200
	VD T185 WAUK	16500	18700, IO T170 OMC	20000	22200, IO T185 WAUK	20200	22400
	VD T185 WAUK	16700	19000, IO T188-T190	20200	22500, IO T215 WAUK	20100	22300
	VD T215 WAUK	17100	19500, IO T225	20000	22400, IO T255 COMM	20400	22600
	IO T255 WAUK	20600	22900, VD T255 WAUK	18000	20000

27 9		SDN		FBG	IO 215-255	9		2 4	19100	21900

	IO T165 OMC	20700	22900, IO T165 WAUK	20700	23000, VD T165 WAUK	18400	20400
	VD T185 WAUK	21100	23500, VD T185 WAUK	18800	20900, IO T215 WAUK	21800	24200
	VD T215 WAUK	19300	21500, IO T225 OMC	21900	24400, IO T255 WAUK	22000	24500
	VD T255 WAUK	19800	22000

27 9		FB	SDN	FBG	IO 215-255	9		2 4	19100	21900

	IO T165 OMC	20700	22900, IO T165 WAUK	20700	23000, VD T165 WAUK	18400	20400
	VD T185 WAUK	21100	23500, VD T185 WAUK	18800	20900, IO T215 WAUK	21800	24200
	VD T215 WAUK	19300	21500, IO T225 OMC	21900	24400, IO T255 WAUK	22000	24500
	VD T255 WAUK	19800	22000

```
LOA  NAME AND/           TOP/ BOAT  -HULL- ----ENGINE--- BEAM   WGT  DRAFT RETAIL RETAIL
FT IN OR MODEL           RIG  TYPE  MTL TP TP # HP  MFG  FT IN  LBS  FT IN  LOW   HIGH
-------------------- 1974 BOATS ----------------------------------------------------------
27  9 SPORTSMAN              CUD  FBG   IO 215-255   9  9  6000 2  4  15500 18200
   IO T165 MRCR 17200    19500, IO T165  OMC  17100 19500, IO T165 WAUK  17200 19500
   VD T165 WAUK  14900    17000, IO T170  OMC  17200 19600, IO T185 WAUK  17500 19900
   VD T185 WAUK  15200    17300, IO T188-T190   17600 20000, IO T215 WAUK  18400 20500
   VD T215 WAUK  15700    17800, IO T225        18500 20700, IO T255 COMM  19100 21200
   IO T255 WAUK  19200    21400, VD T255  WAUK  16200 18400
-------------------- 1973 BOATS ----------------------------------------------------------
20    OPEN                  UTL  FBG DV IO  155       8               6700  7700
23  3 FUNABOUT          HT  CUD  FBG   IO 165-255   8     3300 2  1   8200  9850
23  3 FUNABOUT          HT  CUD  FBG   IO 185-255   8     3300 2  1   8250  9850
23  3 SPORTSMAN             UTL  FBG   IO 165-225   8     3300 2  1   8850 10300
23  3 SUPERSPORT            FBG   IO 165-255   8     3300 2  1   7900  9450
26    CRUISER           FB  SDN  FBG DV IB  215     10  6     2  6  14000 15900
27  9                  HT  CUD  FBG   IO 215-255   9  9  6600 2  4  16800 19600
   IO T165 OMC   19900    22100, IO T165  WAUK  19900 22100, IO T165 WAUK  15800 17900
   IO T185 WAUK  20300    22500, VD T185  WAUK  16000 18200, IO T215 WAUK  20400 22600
   VD T215 WAUK  16400    18700, IO T225  OMC  20500 22800
27  9                  FB  CUD  FBG   IO 215-255   9  9  7100 2  4  17500 20400
   IO T165 OMC   20100    22400, IO T165  WAUK  20200 22400, VD T165 WAUK  16300 18500
   IO T185 WAUK  20500    22800, VD T185  WAUK  16600 18800, IO T215 WAUK  21000 23300
   VD T215 WAUK  16900    19200, IO T225  OMC  21100 23500
27  9 FISHERMAN             CUD  FBG   IO 215-255   9  9  6000 2  4  16000 18800
   IO T165 OMC   19100    21200, IO T165  WAUK  19100 21300, VD T165 WAUK  15100 17200
   IO T185 WAUK  19500    21700, VD T185  WAUK  15400 17500, IO T215 WAUK  20000 22200
   VD T255 WAUK  15800    21800, IO T225  OMC  20200 22400, IO T255 WAUK  20400 22700
   VD T255 WAUK  16300    18500
-------------------- 1972 BOATS ----------------------------------------------------------
23  3 OMEGA                 UTL  FBG   IO 155-215   8     3300         9200 10600
23  3 OMEGA CUDDY           RNBT FBG   IO 155-255   8     3300         8100  9750
23  3 OMEGA CUDDY       HT  RNBT FBG   IO 155-225   8                  8100  9500
23  3 OMEGA SUPERSPORT      FBG   IO 155-255   8     3300         8250  9750
27  9 OMEGA CUDDY           FSH  FBG   IO 215-255         6000        18500 21100
   IO T155 OMC   20100    22400, IO T165  WAUK  20200 22400, VD T155 WAUK  14000 16000
   IO T165 WAUK  20000    22200, VD T165  WAUK  14200 16100, IO T185 WAUK  20400 22600
   VD T185 WAUK  14500    16500, IO T188  MRCR  20400 22700, IO T215 WAUK  21000 23300
   VD T215 WAUK  14900    16900, IO T225  OMC  21100 23500
27  9 OMEGA CUDDY       HT  FSH  FBG   IO 215-255   9  9              18400 21100
   IO T155 OMC   20100    22400, IO T155  WAUK  20200 22400, VD T155 WAUK  14000 16000
   IO T165 WAUK  20000    22200, VD T165  WAUK  14200 16100, IO T185 WAUK  20400 22600
   VD T185 WAUK  14500    16500, IO T188  MRCR  20400 22700, IO T215 WAUK  21000 23300
   VD T215 WAUK  14900    16900, IO T225  OMC  21100 23500
27  9 OMEGA CUDDY       FB  FSH  FBG   IO 215-255   9  9              18400 21100
   IO T155 OMC   20100    22400, IO T155  WAUK  20200 22400, VD T155 WAUK  14000 16000
   IO T165 WAUK  20000    22200, VD T165  WAUK  14200 16100, IO T185 WAUK  20400 22600
   VD T185 WAUK  14500    16500, IO T188  MRCR  20400 22700, IO T215 WAUK  21000 23300
   VD T215 WAUK  14900    16900, IO T225  OMC  21100 23500, IO T255 WAUK  21800 24300
   VD T255 WAUK  15400    17500
```

OMNI BY HARRISKAYOT

```
DIV OF HARRISKAYOT INC                          See inside cover to adjust price for area
FORT WAYNE IN 46808    COAST GUARD MFG ID- HAM
                       FORMERLY HARRIS FLOTE-BOTE
```

For more recent years, see the BUC Used Boat Price Guide, Volume 1 or Volume 2

```
LOA  NAME AND/           TOP/ BOAT  -HULL- ----ENGINE--- BEAM   WGT  DRAFT RETAIL RETAIL
FT IN OR MODEL           RIG  TYPE  MTL TP TP # HP  MFG  FT IN  LBS  FT IN  LOW   HIGH
-------------------- 1977 BOATS ----------------------------------------------------------
36    FLOATING-QUEEN     HT  HB    AL  PN OB        10     7300         8700 10000
36    FLOATING-QUEEN     HT  HB    AL  PN IO  140   10     7900        10800 12200
-------------------- 1976 BOATS ----------------------------------------------------------
36    FLOATING-QUEEN 360-A HT HB   AL  PN OB        10     7300         8600  9900
36    FLOATING-QUEEN 360-A HT HB   AL  PN IO  140 OMC 10   7900        10600 12100
-------------------- 1975 BOATS ----------------------------------------------------------
36    FLOATING-QUEEN     HT  HB    AL  PN OB        10     7180         8350  9600
36    FLOATING-QUEEN     HT  HB    AL  PN IO  140 OMC 10   7780        10400 11800
```

ONE DESIGN MARINE INC
COAST GUARD MFG ID- XDM

Call 1-800-327-6929 for BUC Personalized Evaluation Service
Or, for 1970 to 1974 boats, sign onto www.BUCValuPro.com

ONION RIVER BOATWORKS
COAST GUARD MFG ID- NBV

Call 1-800-327-6929 for BUC Personalized Evaluation Service
Or, for 1982 boats, sign onto www.BUCValuPro.com

ONTARIO YACHTS CO LTD

```
BURLINGTON ONTARIO CANA COAST GUARD MFG ID- ZTY See inside cover to adjust price for area
```

For more recent years, see the BUC Used Boat Price Guide, Volume 1 or Volume 2

```
LOA  NAME AND/           TOP/ BOAT  -HULL- ----ENGINE--- BEAM   WGT  DRAFT RETAIL RETAIL
FT IN OR MODEL           RIG  TYPE  MTL TP TP # HP  MFG  FT IN  LBS  FT IN  LOW   HIGH
-------------------- 1983 BOATS ----------------------------------------------------------
19  3 MARK 19             CAT  SAIL  FBG KL OB         7 11  1050 4     3200  3700
30  6 ETCHELLS 22         SLP  SA/OD FBG KL            7     3400 4  6  9800 11100
32    ONTARIO 32          SLP  SA/CR FBG KL IB  15D YAN 11   10000 4  6 30100 33500
32  6 GREAT-LAKES 33      SLP  SA/CR FBG DS IB 124D VLVO 11 6 11000 3 2 56800 62400
33  7 VIKING 34           SLP  SA/RC FBG KL IB  15D YAN  9 10 8807 6   26600 29500
-------------------- 1982 BOATS ----------------------------------------------------------
22  4 GAZELLE 22          SLP  SAIL  FBG KL OB         7     1700 3  9  4200  4900
28  2 VIKING 28           SLP  SA/RC FBG KL IB   7D YAN 8  5 4755 4  6 12700 14400
28  7 ONTARIO 28          SLP  SA/CR FBG KL IB  12D YAN 10   6800 4   18700 20800
30  6 ETCHELLS 22         SLP  SA/OD FBG KL            7     3400 4  6  9300 10600
32    ONTARIO 32          SLP  SA/CR FBG KL IB  15D YAN 11   9800 4  6 27800 30900
32  6 GREAT-LAKES         FB   TRWL  FBG DS IB 120D VLVO 11 6 11000 3 2 54400 59700
33  7 VIKING 33/34        SLP  SA/CR FBG KL IB  15D YAN  9 10 8807 6   25000 27800
-------------------- 1981 BOATS ----------------------------------------------------------
22  4 GAZELLE 22          SLP  SAIL  FBG KL OB         7     1700 3  9  4000  4650
28  2 VIKING 28           SLP  SA/RC FBG KL IB   7D WEST 8 5 4755 4  6 11900 13600
28  7 ONTARIO 28          SLP  SA/CR FBG KL IB  12D YAN 10   6800 4   17200 19600
30  6 ETCHELLS 22         SLP  SA/OD FBG KL            7     3400 4  6  8700 10000
32    ONTARIO 32          SLP  SA/CR FBG KL IB  15D YAN 11   9800 4  6 26100 29100
33  7 VIKING 33/34        SLP  SA/RC FBG KL IB  15D YAN  9 10 8807 6   23600 26200
33  7 VIKING 33/34        SLP  SA/RC FBG KL IB  15D YAN  9 10 8807 6   23600 26200
-------------------- 1980 BOATS ----------------------------------------------------------
22  4 VIKING 22           SLP  SAIL  FBG KL OB         7     1700 3  9  3800  4400
28  2 VIKING 28           SLP  SA/RC FBG KL IB   7D WEST 8 5 4755 4  6 11400 13000
28  7 ONTARIO 28          SLP  SA/CR FBG KL IB  12D YAN 10   6800 4   16500 18700
30  6 ETCHELLS 22         SLP  SA/CR FBG KL            7     3400 4  6  8300  9500
32    ONTARIO 32          SLP  SA/CR FBG KL IB  15D YAN 11   9800 4  6 25000 27700
33  7 VIKING 33/34        SLP  SA/RC FBG KL IB  30D UNIV 9 9 8807 6   22600 25100
33  7 VIKING 33/34        SLP  SA/RC FBG KL IB  30D UNIV 9 9 8807 6   22600 25100
-------------------- 1979 BOATS ----------------------------------------------------------
22  4 VIKING 22           SLP  SAIL  FBG KL OB         7     1700 3  9  3650  4250
28  2 VIKING 28           SLP  SA/RC FBG KL IB   7D WEST 8 5 4755 4  6 11000 12500
28  7 ONTARIO 28          SLP  SA/CR FBG KL IB  12D YAN 10   6800 4   15800 18000
30  6 ETCHELLS 22         SLP  SA/CR FBG KL            7     3400 4  6  7950  9150
32    ONTARIO 32          SLP  SA/CR FBG KL IB  15D YAN 11   9800 4  6 24000 26700
33  7 VIKING 33/34        SLP  SA/RC FBG KL IB  30D UNIV 9 9 8807 6   21700 24100
33  7 VIKING 33/34        SLP  SA/RC FBG KL IB  30D UNIV 9 9 8807 6   21700 24100
-------------------- 1978 BOATS ----------------------------------------------------------
22  4 VIKING 22           SLP  SAIL  FBG KL            7     1700 3  9  3400  4100
28  7 ONTARIO 28          SLP  SA/CR FBG KL IB   D    10    6800 4   15300 17400
30  6 ETCHELLS 22         SLP  SA/CR FBG KL            7     3400 4  6  7600  8800
32    ONTARIO 32          SLP  SA/CR FBG KL IB 15D-20D 11   9800 4  6 23100 25700
33  7 VIKING 33/34        SLP  SA/RC FBG KL IB  30  UNIV 9 10 8800 6  20700 23000
-------------------- 1977 BOATS ----------------------------------------------------------
22  4 VIKING 22           SLP  SAIL  FBG KL OB         7     1700 3  9  3400  3950
30  6 ETCHELLS 22         SLP  SA/CR FBG KL            7     3400 4  6  7400  8500
32    ONTARIO 32          SLP  SA/CR FBG KL IB 12D-20D 11   9500 4  6 21700 24100
33  7 VIKING 33/34        SLP  SA/RC FBG KL IB  30  UNIV 9 10 8807 6  20100 22300
33  7 VIKING 33/34        SLP  SA/RC FBG KL IB  30  UNIV 9 10 8807 6  20100 22300
-------------------- 1976 BOATS ----------------------------------------------------------
22  4 VIKING 22           SLP  SAIL  FBG KL OB         7     1700 3  9  3300  3800
28  4 VIKING 28           SLP  SAIL  FBG KL IB   7D WEST 8 5 4755 4  6  9900 11200
30  6 ETCHELLS 22         SLP  SA/OD FBG KL            7     3400 4  6  7100  8150
32    ONTARIO 32          SLP  SA/CR FBG KL IB 12D- 20D 11  9500 4  6 21000 23300
33  7 VIKING 34           SLP  SAIL  FBG KL IB  30  UNIV 9 10 8800 6  20100 22300
33  7 VIKING 34           SLP  SAIL  FBG KL IB  30  UNIV 9 10 8807 6  20100 22300
-------------------- 1975 BOATS ----------------------------------------------------------
22  4 VIKING              SLP  SAIL  FBG KL OB         7     1700 3  9  3200  3700
28  2 VIKING              SLP  SAIL  FBG KL IB   6D WEST 8 5 4755 4  6  9600 10900
```

LOA FT IN	NAME AND/ OR MODEL	TOP/ RIG	BOAT TYPE	-HULL- MTL TP	----ENGINE--- TP # HP MFG	BEAM FT IN	WGT LBS	DRAFT FT IN	RETAIL LOW	RETAIL HIGH
					1975 BOATS					
30 6	VIKING	SLP	SAIL	FBG KL		7	3400	4 6	6950	7950
32	VIKING	SLP	SAIL	FBG KL	IB 12D ACK	11	9500	4 6	20400	22700
33 7	VIKING	SLP	SAIL	FBG KL	IB 30D UNIV	9 10	8807	6	19000	21100
					1974 BOATS					
22	VIKING 22	SLP	SA/CR	FBG KL	IB D	7	1595	3 9	3800	4450
28 2	VIKING 28	SLP	SA/CR	FBG KL	IB D	8 5	4755	4 6	9400	10700
33 7	VIKING 33	SLP	SA/CR	FBG KL	IB 30D	9 10	8800	5 6	18700	20700
					1973 BOATS					
28 2	VIKING 28	SLP	SAIL	FBG KL	IB 7D	8 5	4755	4 6	9150	10400
30 6	ETCHELLS 22	SLP	SA/OD	FBG KL	OB	7	3400	4 6	6550	7550
33 7	VIKING 33	SLP	SAIL	FBG KL	IB 30D	9 10	8807	6	18200	20300
					1972 BOATS					
22 4	VIKING 22	SLP	SA/OD	FBG KL		7	1595		2850	3350
28 2	VIKING 28	SLP	SAIL	FBG KL	IB 9	8 4	4755	4 6	8650	9950
33 7	VIKING 33	SLP	SAIL	FBG KL	IB 30	9 10	8533	5 6	16800	19100

ORION YACHT ARTIMUS CORP

Call 1-800-327-6929 for BUC Personalized Evaluation Service
Or, for 1978 to 1980 boats, sign onto www.BUCValuPro.com

ORLANDO BOAT CO

LOA FT IN	NAME AND/ OR MODEL	TOP/ RIG	BOAT TYPE	-HULL- MTL TP	----ENGINE--- TP # HP MFG	BEAM FT IN	WGT LBS	DRAFT FT IN	RETAIL LOW	RETAIL HIGH
					1975 BOATS					
16 10	CHALLENGER W/T		RNBT	FBG TR	OB	7	1100		2000	2350
16 10	CHALLENGER W/T		RNBT	FBG TR	IO 140-170	7			2500	2950
18 2	CORONADO W/T		RNBT	FBG	OB	7 6	1235		2300	2700
18 2	CORONADO W/T		RNBT	FBG	IO 140-233	7 6			2950	3650
18 2	CORONADO W/T		RNBT	FBG	IO 260	7 6			3250	3750
20 10	CAPRICE	HT	CR	FBG DV	IO 188-255	8	3160		5450	6550
23 7	CARIBBEAN		CR	FBG SV	IO 188-255	8	4225		7750	9200
					1974 BOATS					
16 10	CHALLENGER DLX			FBG	OB	7	1100		1950	2300
16 10	CHALLENGER DLX			FBG	IO 120-165	7			2450	2900
18	SOMERSET			FBG	OB	7 6	1400		2500	2900
18	SOMERSET			FBG	IO 120-188	7 6			2900	3400
18 2	CORONADO			FBG	OB	7 6	1235		2300	2650
18 2	CORONADO			FBG	IO 120-190	7 6			2950	3450
20 10	CAPRICE			FBG	IO 140-245	8	3160		5300	6300
20 10	RIVIERA			FBG	IO 140-245	8	3150		5250	6300
23 7	CARIBBEAN HOLIDAY	HT		FBG	IO 165-245	8	4225		7600	8900
23 7	CARIBBEAN HOLIDAY	HT		FBG	IO T120-T140	8	4225		8400	9650
23 7	CARIBBEAN HOLIDAY	CR		FBG	IO 165-245	8	4225		8000	9350
23 7	CARIBBEAN HOLIDAY	CR		FBG	IO T120-T140	8	4225		8950	10200
					1973 BOATS					
16 6	KINGSTON	OP	RNBT	FBG TR	IO 140	6 8			2450	2850
16 6	KINGSTON	OP	RNBT	FBG TR	OB	6 8	1030		1850	2200
16 10	CHALLENGER	OP	RNBT	FBG TR	OB	7	1100		1950	2350
16 10	CHALLENGER	OP	RNBT	FBG TR	IO 120	7			2700	3100
18	SOMERSET		CR	FBG SV	OB	7 4	1400		2450	2850
18	SOMERSET		CR	FBG SV	IO 165	7 6			3400	3950
18	YORK V19 B/R	OP	RNBT	FBG SV	OB	7 4	1400		2500	2900
18	YORK V19 B/R	OP	RNBT	FBG SV	IO 165	7 4			3100	3600
20 10	CAPRICE		CR	FBG DV	IO 188	8			5850	6700
20 10	RIVIERA		CR	FBG DV	IO 188	8			5850	6700
23 7	CARIBBEAN		CR	FBG SV	IO 188	8			8200	9450
					1972 BOATS					
16 6	KINGSTON B/R		RNBT	FBG	OB	6 8	1030		1850	2200
16 6	KINGSTON B/R		RNBT	FBG	IO 120-165	6 8			2650	3100
16 6	NASSAU		RNBT	FBG	OB	6 11	1020		1800	2150
16 6	NASSAU		RNBT	FBG	IO 120-140	6 11			2700	3150
18	SOMERSET		CR	FBG	OB	7 4	1400		2450	2850
18	SOMERSET		CR	FBG	IO 120-165	7 4			3400	4000
18	YORK V-19 B/R		RNBT	FBG	OB	7 4	1400		2500	2900
18	YORK V-19 B/R		RNBT	FBG	IO 120-188	7 4			3200	3750
18	YORK V-19 B/R		RNBT	FBG	JT 260 BERK	7 4			2750	3200
18 2	TAHITI B/R		RNBT	FBG TR	OB	6 10	1120		2050	2450
18 2	TAHITI B/R		RNBT	FBG TR	IO 120-188	6 10			3050	3650
20 2	MONTEGO V-20		RNBT	FBG	OB	7 4	1375		2750	3200
20 2	MONTEGO V-20		RNBT	FBG	IO 120-215	7 4			4200	5000
		JT 220 BERK	3500	4100, IO	225 OMC 4350	5000, JT 260-330			3500	4100
20 2	SAN-JUAN V-20		CR	FBG	OB	7 4	1530		3000	3500
20 2	SAN-JUAN V-20		CR	FBG	IO 120-188	7 4			4500	5200
21	GULFSTREAM		CUD	FBG	OB	8	2000		3850	4500
21	GULFSTREAM		CUD	FBG	IO 155-225	8			6000	7050
21	GULFSTREAM		CUD	FBG	IO 280	8			6550	7500
23 7	CARIBBEAN		CUD	FBG	OB	8	3310		6400	7350
23 7	CARIBBEAN		CUD	FBG	IO 155-215	8			7500	8750
		JT 220 BERK	5600	6450, IO	225-245 7600	8850, JT 260 BERK			5600	6450
		IO 280	8000	9200, JT	330 BERK 5600	6450, IO T120-T140			8450	9700
					1971 BOATS					
16 6	KINGSTON		RNBT	FBG TR	OB	6 3	950		1700	2000
16 6	KINGSTON		RNBT	FBG TR	IO 120	6 3			2600	3050
16 6	NASSAU		RNBT	FBG DV	OB	6 11	1020		1800	2150
16 6	NASSAU		RNBT	FBG DV	IO 120	6 11			2750	3200
17 8	BIMINI		FDC	TR	IO 120	7 1			3000	3450
17 8	BIMINI		RNBT	FBG TR	OB	7 1	1160		2100	2500
17 8	TRI-CLIPPER		CR	FBG TR	IO 120	7 6			3500	4100
17 8	TRI-CLIPPER CR		CR	FBG TR	OB	7 4	1400		2450	2850
18	SOMERSET		CR	FBG SV	OB	7 4	1400		2450	2850
18	SOMERSET		CR	FBG SV	IO 120	7 6		1 8	3600	4150
18	YORK		RNBT	FBG SV	OB	7 4	1160		2150	2500
18	YORK		RNBT	FBG SV	IO 120	7 4		1 8	3300	3800
18 2	TAHITI		RNBT	FBG TR	IO 120	6 10		1 8	3200	3700
20	MONTEGO		RNBT	FBG SV	IO 120-160	7 4		2	4300	5000
20 2	SAN-JUAN		CR	FBG SV	IO 120-160	7 4		2	4600	5300
20 2	MONTEGO		RNBT	FBG SV	OB	7 1	1375		2750	3200
20 2	SAN-JUAN		CR	FBG SV	OB	7 1	1530		3000	3500
23 7	CARIBBEAN		CR	FBG SV	IO 160 MRCR	8	3700	2 2	7950	9150
					1970 BOATS					
16 6	KINGSTON			FBG	IO 120 MRCR	6 8			2650	3100
16 6	KINGSTON			FBG TR	OB	6 8	1030		1800	2150
16 6	KINGSTON			FBG TR	IO 120 OMC	6 8			2600	3050
16 6	NASSAU			FBG DV	OB	6 11	1020		1800	2150
16 6	NASSAU			FBG DV	IO	6 11			2700	3150
17 8	BIMINI			FBG TR	OB	7 1	1100		2000	2350
17 8	BIMINI			FBG TR	IO 120-155	7 1			3100	3600
17 8	TRI-CLIPPER		CBNCR	FBG TR	IO 120-155	7 1	1400		2450	2850
17 8	TRI-CLIPPER		CBNCR	FBG TR	IO	7 1			3500	4050
18	SOMERSET		CR	FBG SV	IO 120-160	7 6	1400		2450	2850
18	SOMERSET		CR	FBG SV	IO	7 6			3700	4350
18	YORK		RNBT	FBG SV	OB	7 6	1100		2000	2400
18	YORK		RNBT	FBG SV	IO 120-160	7 6			3450	4050
18 2	TAHITI			FBG SV	OB	6 10	1120		2050	2450
18 2	TAHITI			FBG SV	IO 120-155	6 10			3150	3650
20 2	MONTEGO			FBG SV	OB	7 1	1375		2750	3200
20 2	MONTEGO			FBG SV	IO 120-160	7 1			4250	4950
20 2	SAN-JUAN		CR	FBG DV	OB	7 1	1530		3000	3500
20 2	SAN-JUAN		CR	FBG DV	IO 120-160	7 1			4700	5400
23 7	CARIBBEAN			FBG DV	IO 155-215	8			8600	10100
23 7	CARIBBEAN			FBG DV	IO T120 MRCR	8			9600	10900
					1969 BOATS					
16 6	NASSAU	OP		FBG DV	IO	6 11			1800	2150
16 6	NASSAU	OP		FBG DV	IO 120 OMC	6 11	1620		2750	3200
17 8	BIMINI			FBG TR	IO 120 MRCR	7 1	1100		3200	3700
17 8	BIMINI	OP		FBG TR	OB	7 1			2000	2350
17 8	TRI-CLIPPER		CR	FBG TR	IO	7 1	1400		2450	2850
17 8	TRI-CLIPPER		CR	FBG TR	IO 120 MRCR	7 1	2000		3600	4200
18	SOMERSET		CR	FBG SV	IO	7 6	1400		2450	2850
18	SOMERSET		CR	FBG SV	IO 120 OMC	7 6	1400		3800	4400
18	YORK		RNBT	FBG SV	IO	7 6	1760		3550	4100
18	YORK		RNBT	FBG SV	IO 120 OMC	7 6	1160		2150	2500
20 2	MONTEGO	OP		FBG DV	OB	7 4	1975		4500	5250
20 2	MONTEGO	OP		FBG DV	IO 120-160	7 4			2750	3200
20 2	SAN-JUAN		CR	FBG DV	OB	7 4	1530		3000	3500
20 2	SAN-JUAN		CR	FBG DV	IO 120-155	7 4	2130		4800	5700
23 7	CARIBBEAN		CUD	FBG DV	IO 160-210	8	3310		7850	9300
23 7	CARIBBEAN		CUD	FBG DV	IO T120 MRCR	8	4000		10100	11400
					1968 BOATS					
16 2	DART	OP	RNBT	FBG SV	OB 80	6 5			2850	3350
16 6	NASSAU	OP	RNBT	FBG SV	OB	6 11	1020		1800	2150
16 6	NASSAU	OP	RNBT	FBG SV	IO 120	6 11			3050	3550
17 8	BIMINI	OP	RNBT	FBG TR	OB	7 1	1100		2000	2400
17 8	BIMINI	OP	RNBT	FBG TR	IO 120-160	7 1			3450	4050
17 8	TRI-CLIPPER		CBNCR	FBG TR	IO 120-160	7 1	1400		2450	2850
17 8	TRI-CLIPPER		CBNCR	FBG TR	IO 120-160	7 1			3700	4350

LOA FT	IN	NAME AND/ OR MODEL	TOP/ RIG	BOAT TYPE	-HULL- MTL	TP	TP	----ENGINE--- # HP	MFG	BEAM FT	IN	WGT LBS	DRAFT FT	IN	RETAIL LOW	RETAIL HIGH
		1968 BOATS														
18		SOMERSET		CBNCR	FBG		OB			7	6	1450			2550	2950
18		SOMERSET		CBNCR	FBG		IO	120-160		7	6				3950	4650
18		YORK	OP	RNBT	FBG		OB			7	6	1160			2150	2500
18		YORK	OP	RNBT	FBG		IO	120-160		7	6				3700	4300
20	2	MONTEGO	OP	RNBT	FBG	DV	OB			7	4	1430			2850	3350
20	2	MONTEGO	OP	RNBT	FBG	DV	IO	120-160		7	4				4800	5550
20	2	SAN-JUAN		CBNCR	FBG	DV	OB			7	4	1700			3250	3800
20	2	SAN-JUAN		CBNCR	FBG	DV	IO	120-160		7	4				5350	6200
23	7	CARIBBEAN		CBNCR	FBG	DV	IO	155-160							10900	12300
23	7	CARIBBEAN		CBNCR	FBG	DV	IO	T120-T160							12000	13800
		1967 BOATS														
16	6	NASSAU			FBG		IO	120							3000	3500
16	6	NASSAU		RNBT	FBG	DV	OB			6	11	1020			1800	2150
17	8	BIMINI			FBG		OB								2200	2550
17	8	BIMINI			FBG		IO	120-160							3500	4050
17	8	TRI-CLIPPER		CBNCR	FBG		OB			7	4	1300	2	4	2350	2700
17	8	TRI-CLIPPER		CBNCR	FBG		IO	120-160		7	4		2	4	3950	4600
17	8	TRI-CLIPPER		RNBT	FBG		OB			7	4	1050			1950	2300
17	8	TRI-CLIPPER		RNBT	FBG		IO	120-160		7	4		2	4	3650	4300
18		SOMERSET		CBNCR	FBG		OB			7	4	1300			2350	2750
18		SOMERSET		CBNCR	FBG		IO	120-160		7	4		2	2	4050	4750
18		YORK		RNBT	FBG		OB			7	4	1050			1950	2350
18		YORK		RNBT	FBG		IO	120-160		7	4		2	2	3750	4400
21	5	DREAMBOAT		RNBT	FBG		IO	150							6900	7900
		1966 BOATS														
16		DART			FBG		IO	80				1380			2700	3100
16	6	NASSAU		RNBT	FBG		OB			6	1	1100			1950	2300
16	6	NASSAU		RNBT	FBG		IO	120		6	1	1800			3200	3750
17	8	BIMINI			FBG		OB					1200			2200	2550
18		SOMERSET		CBNCR	FBG		OB			7	4	1600			2700	3150
18		SOMERSET		CBNCR	FBG		IO	120		7	4	2300			4650	5350
18		TRI-CLIPPER		CBNCR	FBG	TR	OB			7	1	1600			2700	3150
18		TRI-CLIPPER		CBNCR	FBG	TR	IO	120		7	1	2300			4550	5250
18		YORK		RNBT	FBG		OB			7	4	1200			2250	2600
18		YORK		RNBT	FBG		IO	120		7	4	2000			4100	4750
23		DREAMBOAT		CBNCR	FBG		OB					4000			6900	7950
23		DREAMBOAT		CBNCR	FBG		IO	T155				5050			14400	16400
		1965 BOATS														
18		TRI-CLIPPER		CUD	FBG		IO	110		7	1				4050	4750
18		TRI-CLIPPER		RNBT	FBG		OB			7	1	1100			2050	2450
18		YORK		CUD	FBG		IO	110		7	3				4150	4800
18		YORK		RNBT	FBG		OB			7	3	1000			1900	2250
		1960 BOATS														
17		RAMBLER		CR	FBG	DV	OB			7	1	950			1750	2100
17		RAMBLER		RNBT	FBG	DV	OB			7	1	950			1750	2100

ORRION MFG INC

HAROLD ENTERPRISES
SACRAMENTO CA 95826 COAST GUARD MFG ID- XRR

See inside cover to adjust price for area

LOA FT	IN	NAME AND/ OR MODEL	TOP/ RIG	BOAT TYPE	-HULL- MTL	TP	TP	----ENGINE--- # HP	MFG	BEAM FT	IN	WGT LBS	DRAFT FT	IN	RETAIL LOW	RETAIL HIGH
		1982 BOATS														
16	9	ALBATROSS 17FR	ST	RNBT	FBG	TR	IO	140-230		7	2	2200			3000	3600
16	9	ALBATROSS 17FR	ST	RNBT	FBG	TR	IO	260		7	2	2200			3300	3850
16	9	EAGLE 17TR	ST	RNBT	FBG	TR	IO	140-230		7	2	2200			3000	3600
16	9	EAGLE 17TR	ST	RNBT	FBG	TR	IO	260		7	2	2200			3350	3900
16	9	EAGLE 17TR	ST	RNBT	FBG	TR	IO	145D	MRCR	7	2	2200			4550	5200
16	9	FALCON 17TB	ST	RNBT	FBG	TR	OB			7	2	1400			2300	2700
17	2	CARDINAL 17CV	ST	RNBT	FBG	SV	IO	140-230		7	5	2200			3100	3750
17	2	CARDINAL 17CV	ST	RNBT	FBG	SV	IO	260		7	5	2200			3450	4000
17	2	CARDINAL 17CV	ST	RNBT	FBG	SV	IO	145D	MRCR	7	5	2200			4650	5350
17	2	SEAHAWK 17VB	ST	RNBT	FBG	SV	IO	140-230		7	5	2200			3150	3750
17	2	SEAHAWK 17VB	ST	RNBT	FBG	SV	IO	260		7	5	2200			3450	4000
17	2	SEAHAWK 17VB	ST	RNBT	FBG	SV	IO	145D	MRCR	7	5	2200			4650	5350
17	2	SWIFT 17VH	ST	RNBT	FBG	SV	OB			7	5	1470			2400	2750
18	2	ORIOLE 19NV	ST	RNBT	FBG	SV	IO	140	MRCR	7	2	2400			3350	3900
18	2	ORIOLE 19NV	ST	RNBT	FBG	SV	IO	140-260		7	2	2900			3700	4300
18	2	ORIOLE 19NV	ST	RNBT	FBG	SV	IO	145D	MRCR	7	2	2400			4950	5700
18	4	RAVEN 19SK	OP	RNBT	FBG	DV	OB			7	1	1150			2000	2400
18	6	FLAMINGO 19FL	ST	RNBT	FBG		IO	140-260		8		2700			3900	4850
21	6	CONDOR 21CR	OP	CBNCR	FBG	DV	IO	140-260		8		4500			8050	9650
21	6	CONDOR 21CR	OP	CBNCR	FBG	DV	IO	145D	MRCR	8		4500			11000	12600
21	6	HAWK 21HK	OP	CUD	FBG	DV	IO	140-260		8		4000			6700	8050
21	6	HAWK 21HK	OP	CUD	FBG	DV	IO	145D	MRCR	8		4000			8700	10000
		1981 BOATS														
16	9	ALBATROSS 17FR	ST	RNBT	FBG	TR	IO	140-230		7	2	2200			2900	3550
16	9	ALBATROSS 17FR	ST	RNBT	FBG	TR	IO	260		7	2	2200			3200	3700
16	9	EAGLE 17TR	ST	RNBT	FBG	TR	IO	140-230		7	2	2200			2900	3550
16	9	EAGLE 17TR	ST	RNBT	FBG	TR	IO	260		7	2	2200			3200	3700
16	9	EAGLE 17TR	ST	RNBT	FBG	TR	IO	145D	MRCR	7	2	2200			4450	5150
16	9	FALCON 17TB	ST	RNBT	FBG	TR	OB			7	2	1400			2250	2650
17	2	CARDINAL 17CV	ST	RNBT	FBG	SV	IO	140-230		7	5	2200			3050	3700
17	2	CARDINAL 17CV	ST	RNBT	FBG	SV	IO	260		7	5	2200			3300	3850
17	2	CARDINAL 17CV	ST	RNBT	FBG	SV	IO	145D	MRCR	7	5	2200			4600	5300
17	2	SEAHAWK 17VB	ST	RNBT	FBG	SV	IO	140-230		7	5	2200			3050	3700
17	2	SEAHAWK 17VB	ST	RNBT	FBG	SV	IO	260		7	5	2200			3300	3850
17	2	SEAHAWK 17VB	ST	RNBT	FBG	SV	IO	145D	MRCR	7	5	2200			4600	5300
17	2	SWIFT 17VH	ST	RNBT	FBG	SV	OB			7	5	1470			2350	2700
18	2	ORIOLE 19NV	ST	RNBT	FBG	SV	IO	140-230		7	2	2400			3300	4000
18	2	ORIOLE 19NV	ST	RNBT	FBG	SV	IO	260		7	2	2400			3550	4150
18	2	ORIOLE 19NV	ST	RNBT	FBG	SV	IO	145D	MRCR	7	2	2400			4900	5600
18	4	RAVEN 19SK	OP	RNBT	FBG	DV	OB			7	1	1150			1950	2350
18	6	FLAMINGO 19FL	ST	RNBT	FBG		IO	140-260		8		2700			3800	4750
21	6	CONDOR 21CR	OP	CBNCR	FBG	DV	IO	140-260		8		4500			7900	9500
21	6	CONDOR 21CR	OP	CBNCR	FBG	DV	IO	145D	MRCR	8		4500			10900	12400
21	6	HAWK 21HK	OP	CUD	FBG	DV	IO	140-260		8		4000			6550	7900
21	6	HAWK 21HK	OP	CUD	FBG	DV	IO	145D	MRCR	8		4000			8550	9850
		1980 BOATS														
16	9	ALBATROSS 17FR	ST	RNBT	FBG	TR	IO	140-230		7	2	2200			2900	3500
16	9	ALBATROSS 17FR	ST	RNBT	FBG	TR	IO	260		7	2	2200			3150	3650
16	9	EAGLE 17TR	ST	RNBT	FBG	TR	IO	140-230		7	2	2200			2900	3500
16	9	EAGLE 17TR	ST	RNBT	FBG	TR	IO	260		7	2	2200			3150	3700
16	9	EAGLE 17TR	ST	RNBT	FBG	TR	IO	145D	MRCR	7	2	2200			4450	5100
16	9	FALCON 17TB	ST	RNBT	FBG	TR	OB			7	2	1400			2250	2600
17	2	CARDINAL 17CV	ST	RNBT	FBG	SV	IO	140-230		7	5	2200			3050	3650
17	2	CARDINAL 17CV	ST	RNBT	FBG	SV	IO	260		7	5	2200			3300	3800
17	2	CARDINAL 17CV	ST	RNBT	FBG	SV	IO	145D	MRCR	7	5	2200			4600	5250
17	2	SEAHAWK 17VB	ST	RNBT	FBG	SV	IO	140-230		7	5	2200			3050	3650
17	2	SEAHAWK 17VB	ST	RNBT	FBG	SV	IO	260		7	5	2200			3300	3850
17	2	SEAHAWK 17VB	ST	RNBT	FBG	SV	IO	145D	MRCR	7	5	2200			4600	5250
17	2	SWIFT 17VH	ST	RNBT	FBG	SV	OB			7	5	1470			2350	2700
18	2	ORIOLE 19NV	ST	RNBT	FBG	SV	IO	140-230		7	2	2400			3250	3950
18	2	ORIOLE 19NV	ST	RNBT	FBG	SV	IO	260		7	2	2400			3550	4100
18	2	ORIOLE 19NV	ST	RNBT	FBG	SV	IO	145D	MRCR	7	2	2400			4850	5550
18	4	RAVEN 19SK	OP	RNBT	FBG	DV	OB			7	1	1150			1950	2300
18	6	FLAMINGO 19FL	ST	RNBT	FBG		IO	140-260		8		2700			3800	4700
21	6	CONDOR 21CR	OP	CBNCR	FBG	DV	IO	140-260		8		4500			7850	9400
21	6	CONDOR 21CR	OP	CBNCR	FBG	DV	IO	145D	MRCR	8		4500			10800	12200
21	6	HAWK 21HK	OP	CUD	FBG	DV	IO	140-260		8		4000			6500	7850
21	6	HAWK 21HK	OP	CUD	FBG	DV	IO	145D	MRCR	8		4000			8500	9750
		1979 BOATS														
16	9	ALBATROSS 17FR	ST	RNBT	FBG	TR	IO	140-250		6	10	2200			2850	3450
16	9	ALBATROSS 17FR	ST	RNBT	FBG	TR	IO	260		6	10	2200			3100	3600
16	9	EAGLE 17TR	ST	RNBT	FBG	TR	IO	140-250		6	10	2200			2850	3500
16	9	EAGLE 17TR	ST	RNBT	FBG	TR	IO	260		6	10	2200			3100	3600
16	9	FALCON 17TB	ST	RNBT	FBG	TR	OB			6	10	1400			2200	2550
17	2	CARDINAL 17CV	ST	RNBT	FBG	SV	IO	140-250		7	5	2200			3050	3700
17	2	CARDINAL 17CV	ST	RNBT	FBG	SV	IO	260		7	5	2200			3250	3800
17	2	SEAHAWK 17VB	ST	RNBT	FBG	SV	IO	140-250		7	5	2200			3050	3700
17	2	SEAHAWK 17VB	ST	RNBT	FBG	SV	IO	260		7	5	2200			3300	3800
17	2	SWIFT 17VH	ST	RNBT	FBG	SV	OB			7	5	1470			2300	2650
18	1	ORIOLE 19NV	ST	RNBT	FBG	SV	IO	140-250		7	2	2300			3150	3900
18	1	ORIOLE 19NV	ST	RNBT	FBG	SV	IO	260		7	2	2300			3450	4000
		1978 BOATS														
16	9	MARK 17F	ST	RNBT	FBG	TR	IO	120-240		7	2	2200			2950	3550
16	9	MARK 17FB	ST	RNBT	FBG	TR	OB			7	2	1350			2050	2450
16	9	MARK 17T	ST	RNBT	FBG	TR	IO	120-240		7	2	2200			2950	3550
16	9	MARK 17TB	ST	RNBT	FBG	TR	OB			7	2	1400			2200	2550
17		MARK 17T	ST	RNBT	FBG	DV	IO	175	OMC	7	2	2200			2950	3400
17		MARK 17V	ST	RNBT	FBG	DV	IO	120-240		7	2	2200			2950	3600
18	2	MARK 19V	ST	RNBT	FBG	DV	IO	120-240		7	2	2300			3200	3900
		1977 BOATS														
16	9	MARK 17F	ST	RNBT	FBG	TR	IO	140-185		7	2				2950	3450
16	9	MARK 17FB	ST	RNBT	FBG	TR	OB			7	2	1400			2100	2500
16	9	MARK 17T	ST	RNBT	FBG	TR	IO	140-185		7	2				2950	3450
16	9	MARK 17TB	ST	RNBT	FBG	TR	OB			7	2	1400			2150	2500
17		MARK 17V	ST	RNBT	FBG	DV	IO	140-185		7	2				3000	3500
18	2	MARK 19V	ST	RNBT	FBG	DV	IO	170-225		7	2				3350	3950

 CONTINUED ON NEXT PAGE

ORRION MFG INC   -CONTINUED   See inside cover to adjust price for area

LOA FT IN	NAME AND/OR MODEL	TOP/RIG	BOAT TYPE	HULL MTL TP TP	ENGINE # HP	ENGINE MFG	BEAM FT IN	WGT LBS	DRAFT FT IN	RETAIL LOW	RETAIL HIGH
				1976 BOATS							
18 9	MARK 17F	ST	RNBT	FBG TR IO	120-200		7 4	2200		3450	4250
18 9	MARK 17FB DELUXE	ST	RNBT	FBG TR OB			7 4	1200		2150	2500
18 9	MARK 17FB STANDARD	ST	RNBT	FBG TR OB			7 4	1200		1800	2100
18 9	MARK 17T	ST	RNBT	FBG TR IO	120-200		7 4	2200		3500	4300
18 9	MARK 17T	ST	RNBT	FBG TR IO	225		7 4	2200		3500	4350
18 9	MARK 17TB	ST	RNBT	FBG TR OB			7 4	1280		2050	2450
19	MARK 18V	ST	RNBT	FBG DV IO	120-170		7 2	1900		3200	3950
19 4	MARK 19V	ST	RNBT	FBG DV IO	120-200		7 2	2200		3500	4350
19 4	MARK 19V	ST	RNBT	FBG DV IO	225		7 2	2200		3600	4450
				1975 BOATS							
18 7	XR 18	OP	SKI	FBG DV JT	455 HARD		6 10	2000		3300	3850
18 9	MARK 17F FRONTRUNNER	OP	RNBT	FBG TR IO	120-165		6 4	2050		3400	4000
	JT 185 3550 4150, IO 185 WAUK 3450 4050, JT 255									3600	4200
18 9	MARK 17FB DELUXE	OP	RNBT	FBG TR OB			7 4			2050	2450
18 9	MARK 17FB STANDARD	OP	RNBT	FBG TR OB			7 4			1850	2200
18 9	MARK 17T BOWRIDER	OP	RNBT	FBG TR IO	120-165		7 4	2050		3400	4000
	JT 185 3550 4150, IO 185 WAUK 3450 4050, JT 255									3600	4200
19	MARK 18V	OP	RNBT	FBG DV IO	120-130		7 4	2050		3450	4250
19 4	MARK 19V	ST	RNBT	FBG DV IO	120-165		7 2	2050		3450	4100
	JT 185 WAUK 4200, IO 185 WAUK 3550 4100, JT 255 WAUK									3650	4250
				1974 BOATS							
18 7	XR 18	OP	SKI	FBG DV JT	390 HARD		6 10	2000		3150	3700
18 9	MARK 17F OR 17T	OP	RNBT	FBG TR IO			7 4			1950	2300
18 9	MARK 17F OR 17T	OP	RNBT	FBG TR IO	120-170		7 4	2050		3550	4350
	JT 185 WAUK 3400 3950, IO 185-225 4250, JT 245 OMC									3450	4050
	IO 245 OMC 3750 4350, JT 255-290									3450	4050
19	MARK 18V	OP	RNBT	FBG DV IO	120-130		7 2	1800		3350	4100
	JT 140 OMC 3150, IO 140-170 3350 4150, JT 185 WAUK									3250	3800
	IO 185-225 3400 4050, JT 245 OMC 3300 3850, IO 245 OMC									3550	4150
	JT 255-290 3300										3850
19 4	MARK 19V	ST	RNBT	FBG DV IO	120-130		7 2	2050		3600	4400
	JT 140 OMC 3350, IO 140-170 3600 4450, JT 185 WAUK									3450	4050
	IO 185-225 3650 4350, JT 245 OMC 3500 4100, IO 245 OMC									3800	4400
	JT 255-290 3500										4150

OSPREY MARINE & ENG CO INC
COAST GUARD MFG ID- XSP

Call 1-800-327-6929 for BUC Personalized Evaluation Service
Or, for 1981 to 1984 boats, sign onto www.BUCValuPro.com

OUACHITA BOATS
RIVER MARINE CORP   COAST GUARD MFG ID- XMR

Call 1-800-327-6929 for BUC Personalized Evaluation Service
Or, for 1966 to 1978 boats, sign onto www.BUCValuPro.com

OUT O'GLOUCESTER ENTERPRISES

Call 1-800-327-6929 for BUC Personalized Evaluation Service
Or, for 1959 to 1961 boats, sign onto www.BUCValuPro.com

OUTER REEF MARINE
PALMETTO FL 33561   COAST GUARD MFG ID- XRJ See inside cover to adjust price for area

For more recent years, see the BUC Used Boat Price Guide, Volume 1 or Volume 2

LOA FT IN	NAME AND/OR MODEL	TOP/RIG	BOAT TYPE	HULL MTL TP TP	ENGINE # HP	ENGINE MFG	BEAM FT IN	WGT LBS	DRAFT FT IN	RETAIL LOW	RETAIL HIGH
				1982 BOATS							
26 6	OUTER-REEF 26	HT	TRWL	FBG DS IB	61D	LEHM	9	7500	2 6	24500	27300
26 6	OUTER-REEF 26	FB	TRWL	FBG DS IB	61D	LEHM	9	7500	2 6	24500	27300
26 6	OUTER-REEF WORKBOAT	HT	UTL	FBG DS IB	61D	LEHM	9	7500	2 6	24200	26900
32	OUTER-REEF WORKBOAT	HT	UTL	FBG DS IB	80D	LEHM	12	12000	3 8	46600	51200
32	OUTER-REEF YACHT	HT	TRWL	FBG DS IB	80D	LEHM	12	14000	3 8	52500	57700
				1981 BOATS							
26 6	OUTER-REEF 26	HT	TRWL	FBG DS IB	61D	LEHM	9	7500	2 6	23600	26200
26 6	OUTER-REEF 26	FB	TRWL	FBG DS IB	61D	LEHM	9	7500	2 6	23600	26200
26 6	OUTER-REEF WORKBOAT	HT	UTL	FBG DS IB	61D- 80D		9	7500	2 6	23300	26100
32	OUTER-REEF WORKBOAT	HT	UTL	FBG DS IB	80D	LEHM	12	12000	3 8	44300	49200
32	OUTER-REEF YACHT	HT	TRWL	FBG DS IB	80D	LEHM	12	14000	3 8	50400	55400
				1980 BOATS							
26 6	OUTER-REEF 26	HT	TRWL	FBG DS IB	62D- 85D		9	7500	2 6	23000	27100
26 6	OUTER-REEF WORKBOAT	HT	UTL	FBG DS IB	62D- 85D		9	7500	2 6	22700	25500
39	OUTER-REEF 39			FBG DS IB	60D		14			82800	91000
39	OUTER-REEF WORKBOAT		TRWL	FBG DS IB	130D		14			84200	92500
				1979 BOATS							
26 6	OUTER-REEF 26	HT	TRWL	FBG DS IB	62D	PERK	9	7500	2 3	22200	24600
26 6	OUTER-REEF WORKBOAT	HT	UTL	FBG DS IB	62D	PERK	9	7500	2 3	21800	24200

OUTLAW MARINE ENTERPRISES INC
COAST GUARD MFG ID- XEC

Call 1-800-327-6929 for BUC Personalized Evaluation Service
Or, for 1981 to 1982 boats, sign onto www.BUCValuPro.com

OVERSEAS PROMOTIONS ASSOC

Call 1-800-327-6929 for BUC Personalized Evaluation Service
Or, for 1965 boats, sign onto www.BUCValuPro.com

OVERSEAS YACHTS INC
MARINA DEL REY CA 90292   See inside cover to adjust price for area

LOA FT IN	NAME AND/OR MODEL	TOP/RIG	BOAT TYPE	HULL MTL TP TP	ENGINE # HP	ENGINE MFG	BEAM FT IN	WGT LBS	DRAFT FT IN	RETAIL LOW	RETAIL HIGH
				1977 BOATS							
33 6	OVERSEAS 33 AFT CBN	FB	TRWL	FBG DS IB	120D	LEHM	11 9	17500	3 2	47000	51700
33 6	OVERSEAS 33 SEDAN	FB	TRWL	FBG DS IB	120D	LEHM	11 9	16500	3	44600	49600
33 6	OVERSEAS 33 SEDAN	FB	TRWL	FBG DS IB	T 85D	LEHM	11 9	16500	3	46300	50900
37 3	OVERSEAS 37	KTH	SA/CR	FBG KL IB	25D	VLVO	11	19500	4 5	45700	50200
38 10	OVERSEAS 39	FB	TRWL	FBG DS IB	120D	LEHM	13 6		3 8	76900	87500
38 10	OVERSEAS 39	FB	TRWL	FBG DS IB	T120D	LEHM	13 6		3 8	83200	91500
38 10	OVERSEAS 39 SUN DECK	FB	TRWL	FBG DS IB	120D	LEHM	13 6		3 8	80700	88700
38 10	OVERSEAS 39 SUN DECK	FB	TRWL	FBG DS IB	T120D	LEHM	13 6		3 8	84400	92800
39 2	OVERSEAS 39	CUT	SA/CR	FBG KL IB	55D	NISS	11 6	23000	5 7	54200	59600
40 11	OVERSEAS 41	KTH	SA/CR	FBG KL IB	50D	PERK	12	28000	6	62600	71600
50 10	OVERSEAS 51	KTH	SA/CR	FBG KL IB	85D	PERK	14	52000	6 2	111000	122000
				1976 BOATS							
33 6	OVERSEAS 33 AFT CBN	FB	TRWL	FBG DS IB	120D	LEHM	11 9	17500	3 2	44800	49800
33 6	OVERSEAS 33 SEDAN	FB	TRWL	FBG DS IB	120D	LEHM	11 9	16500	3	43000	47800
37 3	OVERSEAS 37	KTH	SA/CR	FBG KL IB	20D	VLVO	11	19500	4 5	43700	48500
38 10	OVERSEAS 39	FB	TRWL	FBG DS IB	T120D	LEHM	14	29000	3 10	79300	87200
40 11	OVERSEAS 41	KTH	SA/CR	FBG KL IB	42D	PERK	12	28000	6	63800	69300
50 10	OVERSEAS 51	KTH	SA/CR	FBG KL IB	85D	LEHM	14	52000	6 2	105500	116000
				1967 BOATS							
30	AM S 30	SLP	SA/CR	WD CB			10		2 6	9550	10900

OWENS DIVISION
BRUNSWICK CORPORATION   See inside cover to adjust price for area
WARSAW IN

SEE ALSO OWENS YACHT DIVISION

LOA FT IN	NAME AND/OR MODEL	TOP/RIG	BOAT TYPE	HULL MTL TP TP	ENGINE # HP	ENGINE MFG	BEAM FT IN	WGT LBS	DRAFT FT IN	RETAIL LOW	RETAIL HIGH
				1962 BOATS							
16	BEDFORD			IO	80					3050	3550
17 6	EXETER			IO	80-100					3950	4600
17 6	YORK			IO	80-100					3950	4600
19	BRIGHTON			IO	80-100					5100	5850
19	STAFFORD			IO	80-100					5100	5850
				1959 BOATS							
20	FLEETSHIP	EXP	WD	OB						2350	2700
20	FLEETSHIP	SF	WD	OB						2200	2550
22	FLEETSHIP FAMILY CR	CR	WD	OB						2650	3100

OWENS YACHT DIVISION

BRUNSWICK CORPORATION
BALTIMORE MD 21222

COAST GUARD MFG ID- XNS
FOR OLDER MODELS SEE CONCORDE YACHTS INC

See inside cover to adjust price for area

LOA FT	LOA IN	NAME AND/ OR MODEL	TOP/ RIG	BOAT TYPE	-HULL- MTL	-HULL- TP	ENGINE TP	ENGINE # HP	ENGINE MFG	BEAM FT	BEAM IN	WGT LBS	DRAFT FT	DRAFT IN	RETAIL LOW	RETAIL HIGH
		1970 BOATS														
28	3	BUCCANEER		EXP	PLY	SV	IB	250	MRCR	10	8	6030	2	3	8200	9450
28	3	SULTANA		EXP	PLY	SV	IB	250	MRCR	10	8	6030	2	3	8200	9450
30		EMPRESS		EXP	WD	SV	IB	250	MRCR	10	6	9350	2	4	11800	13400
30		EMPRESS		SDN	WD	SV	IB	250	MRCR	10	6	9850	2	4	12900	14600
33		MARGARITA		SDN	WD	SV	IB	250	MRCR	11		12050	2	3	16200	18400
33		REGENCY		EXP	WD	SV	IB	250	MRCR	11		10300	2	3	16300	18500
37		GRENADA		DC	WD	SV	IB	250	MRCR	13		15400	3	5	24500	27200
42		ARUBA	FB	DC	WD	SV	IB	325	MRCR	13		20350	3	6	34800	38600
42		ARUBA		TCMY	WD	SV	IB	325	MRCR	13		20350	3	6	35700	39600
42		ARUBA AFT WELL		DC	WD	SV	IB	325	MRCR	13		19500	3	6	34000	37800
		1969 BOATS														
27		CONCORDE		EXP	FBG	SV	IB	225	MRCR	10	5	6100	2	4	7150	8200
27		CONCORDE		EXP	FBG	SV	IB	T200	MRCR	10	5	6100	2	4	7950	9150
27		CONCORDE	HT	EXP	FBG	SV	IB	225	MRCR	10	5	6100	2	4	7150	8200
27		CONCORDE	HT	EXP	FBG	SV	IB	T200	MRCR	10	5	6100	2	4	7950	9150
27		CONCORDE		SF	FBG	SV	IB	225	MRCR	10	5	7080	2	2	7800	8950
27		CONCORDE		SF	FBG	SV	IB	T200	MRCR	10	5	7080	2	2	8600	9850
28	4	BUCCANEER FLAGSHIP		EXP	L/P	SV	IB	200	MRCR	10	8	6080	2	3	7700	8900
28	4	BUCCANEER FLAGSHIP	HT	EXP	L/P	SV	IB	200	MRCR	10	8	6080	2	3	7700	8900
28	4	BUCCANEER FLAGSHIP	FB	EXP	L/P	SV	IB	200	MRCR	10	8	6080	2	3	7700	8900
28	4	SULTANA FLAGSHIP		EXP	PLY	SV	IB	200	MRCR	10	8	6080	2	3	7700	8900
28	4	SULTANA FLAGSHIP	HT	EXP	PLY	SV	IB	200	MRCR	10	8	6080	2	3	7700	8900
28	4	SULTANA FLAGSHIP	FB	EXP	PLY	SV	IB	200	MRCR	10	8	6080	2	3	7700	8900
30		EMPRESS FLAGSHIP		EXP	MHG	SV	IB	T225	MRCR	10	6	9350	2	4	12400	14100
30		EMPRESS FLAGSHIP	HT	EXP	MHG	SV	IB	T225	MRCR	10	6	9350	2	4	12400	14100
30		EMPRESS FLAGSHIP	FB	EXP	MHG	SV	IB	T225	MRCR	10	6	9350	2	4	12400	14100
30		EMPRESS FLAGSHIP		SDN	MHG	SV	IB	T225	MRCR	10	6	9900	2	5	13800	15600
30		EMPRESS FLAGSHIP	FB	SDN	MHG	SV	IB	T225	MRCR	10	6	9900	2	5	13800	15600
33		MARGARITA		SDN	MHG	SV	IB	T225	MRCR	11		12050	2	3	16800	19100
33		MARGARITA	FB	SDN	MHG	SV	IB	T225	MRCR	11		12050	2	3	16800	19100
33		REGENCY		EXP	MHG	SV	IB	T225	MRCR	11		10300	2	3	16800	19100
33		REGENCY	HT	EXP	MHG	SV	IB	T225	MRCR	11		10300	2	3	16800	19100
33		REGENCY	FB	EXP	MHG	SV	IB	T225	MRCR	11		10300	2	3	16800	19100
33	4	CONCORDE		SF	FBG	SV	IB	T225-T300		12		16000	2	6	19600	22500
33	4	CONCORDE		SF	FBG	SV	IB	T170D	BARR	12		16000	2	6	28100	31200
35		CONCORDE		EXP	FBG	SV	IB	T300	MRCR	12	6	13800	2	11	21700	24100
35		CONCORDE		EXP	FBG	SV	IB	T170D	BARR	12	6	13800	2	11	28300	31400
35		CONCORDE		EXP	FBG	SV	IB	T216D	GM	12	6	13800	2	11	29200	32400
35		CONCORDE	FB	EXP	FBG	SV	IB	T300	MRCR	12	6	13800	2	11	21700	24100
35		CONCORDE	FB	EXP	FBG	SV	IB	T170D	BARR	12	6	13800	2	11	28300	31400
35		CONCORDE	FB	EXP	FBG	SV	IB	T216D	GM	12	6	13800	2	11	29200	32400
35		CONCORDE		SDN	FBG	SV	IB	T300	MRCR	12	6	17400	3		24600	27300
35		CONCORDE		SDN	FBG	SV	IB	T170D	BARR	12	6	17400	3		33700	37400
35		CONCORDE		SDN	FBG	SV	IB	T216D	GM	12	6	17400	3		34700	38600
35		CONCORDE	FB	SDN	FBG	SV	IB	T300	MRCR	12	6	17400	3		24600	27300
35		CONCORDE	FB	SDN	FBG	SV	IB	T170D	BARR	12	6	17400	3		33700	37400
35		CONCORDE	FB	SDN	FBG	SV	IB	T216D	GM	12	6	17400	3		34700	38600
37		GRENADA	FB	DC	MHG	SV	IB	T225	CHRY	13		15400	2	11	24900	27700
37		GRENADA	FB	DC	MHG	SV	IB	T300	CHRY	13		15400	2	11	24500	27300
37		GRENADA	FB	DC	MHG	SV	IB	T170D	BARR	13		15400	2	11	27100	30100
37		GRENADA HT ON FB	FB	DC	MHG	SV	IB	T225	CHRY	13		15400	2	11	24100	26800
37		GRENADA HT ON FB	FB	DC	MHG	SV	IB	T300	CHRY	13		15400	2	11	25300	28100
37		GRENADA HT ON FB	FB	DC	MHG	SV	IB	T170D	BARR	13		15400	2	11	27800	30800
40		CONCORDE	FB	SDN	FBG	SV	IB	T300	CHRY	13	6	20500			34600	38400
40		CONCORDE	FB	SDN	FBG	SV	IB	T216D	GM	13	6	20500			38600	42900
40		CONCORDE	FB	SDN	FBG	SV	IB	T283D	GM	13	6	20500			40000	44400
42		ARUBA	FB	DCMY	MHG	SV	IB	T300	CHRY	13		22000	2	8	40100	44600
42		ARUBA	FB	DCMY	MHG	SV	IB	T170D	BARR	13		22000	2	8	41300	45800
42		ARUBA	FB	TCMY	MHG	SV	IB	T300	CHRY	13		22000	2	8	40800	45400
42		ARUBA	FB	TCMY	MHG	SV	IB	T170D	BARR	13		22000	2	8	41800	46500
42		ARUBA AFT WELL	FB	DCMY	MHG	SV	IB	T300	CHRY	13		22000	2	11	40300	44700
42		ARUBA AFT WELL	FB	DCMY	MHG	SV	IB	T170D	BARR	13		22000	2	11	41400	46000
42		ARUBA AFT WELL HT+FB	FB	DCMY	MHG	SV	IB	T300	CHRY	13		22000	2	11	41800	46400
42		ARUBA AFT WELL HT+FB	FB	DCMY	MHG	SV	IB	T170D	BARR	13		22000	2	11	42600	47400
42		ARUBA HT ON FB	FB	DCMY	MHG	SV	IB	T300	CHRY	13		22000	2	8	40300	44800
42		ARUBA HT ON FB	FB	DCMY	MHG	SV	IB	T170D	BARR	13		22000	2	8	41400	46000
42		ARUBA HT ON FB	FB	TCMY	MHG	SV	IB	T300	CHRY	13		22000	2	8	43100	47900
42		ARUBA HT ON FB	FB	TCMY	MHG	SV	IB	T170D	BARR	13		22000	2	8	43800	48700
46	8	CONCORDE	FB	MY	FBG	SV	IB	T250D	GM	16		40000	4	1	60400	66400
46	8	CONCORDE	FB	MY	FBG	SV	IB	T283D	GM	16		40000	4	1	61300	67400
46	8	CONCORDE	FB	YTFS	FBG	SV	IB	T283D	GM	16		36000	4	1	56500	62100
46	8	CONCORDE	FB	YTFS	FBG	SV	IB	T350D	GM	16		36000	4	1	61800	67900
		1968 BOATS														
24	7	CONTESSA FLAGSHIP		EXP	PLY		IB	225	FLAG			4900			5100	5850
24	7	CONTESSA FLAGSHIP	HT	EXP	PLY		IB	225	FLAG			5095			5250	6000
26	4	RAIDER FLAGSHIP		EXP	L/P		IB	225	FLAG	10	3	4900	2	3	5850	6700
26	4	RAIDER FLAGSHIP	HT	EXP	L/P		IB	225	FLAG	10	3	5095	2	3	5950	6850
27		CONCORDE		EXP	FBG		IB	225	FLAG	10	5	5500	2	4	6500	7500
27		CONCORDE		EXP	FBG		IB	T185	FLAG	10	5		2	4	7400	8550
27		CONCORDE	HT	EXP	FBG		IB	225	FLAG	10	5	5695	2	4	6600	7600
28	4	BUCCANEER FLAGSHIP			L/P		IB	225	FLAG	10	8	5600	2	4	7350	8400
28	4	BUCCANEER FLAGSHIP	HT		L/P		IB	225	FLAG	10	8	5795	2	4	7400	8550
28	4	BUCCANEER FLAGSHIP	FB		L/P		IB	225	FLAG	10	8	5900	2	4	7450	8600
28	4	SULTANA FLAGSHIP		EXP	PLY		IB	225	FLAG	10	8	5600	2	3	7350	8400
28	4	SULTANA FLAGSHIP	HT	EXP	PLY		IB	225	FLAG	10	8	5795	2	3	7400	8550
28	4	SULTANA FLAGSHIP	FB	EXP	PLY		IB	225	FLAG	10	8	5900	2	3	7450	8600
30		EMPRESS FLAGSHIP		EXP	MHG		IB	T225	FLAG	10	6	9070	2	4	11800	13400
30		EMPRESS FLAGSHIP	HT	EXP	MHG		IB	T225	FLAG	10	6	9265	2	4	11900	13500
30		EMPRESS FLAGSHIP	FB	EXP	MHG		IB	T225	FLAG	10	6	9370	2	4	11900	13600
30		EMPRESS FLAGSHIP		SDN	MHG		IB	T225	FLAG	10	6	9900	2	4	13300	15100
30		EMPRESS FLAGSHIP	FB	SDN	MHG		IB	T225	FLAG	10	6	10005	2	4	13300	15100
33		MARGARITA		SDN	MHG		IB	T225	FLAG	11		9500	2	3	15400	17500
33		MARGARITA	FB	SDN	MHG		IB	T225	FLAG	11		9695	2	3	15500	17600
33		REGENCY		EXP	MHG		IB	T225	FLAG	11		9000	2	3	15800	18000
33		REGENCY	HT	EXP	MHG		IB	T225	FLAG	11		9195	2	3	15900	18100
33		REGENCY	FB	EXP	MHG		IB	T225	FLAG	11		9300	2	3	15900	18100
33	4	CONCORDE		SF	FBG		IB	T225-T320		12		16000	2	6	19100	21800
33	4	CONCORDE		SF	FBG		IB	T160D		12		16000	2	6	27400	30500
35		CONCORDE		EXP	FBG		IB	T320	FLAG	12	6	16500	2	11	22500	25000
35		CONCORDE		EXP	FBG		IB	T160D		12	6	16500	2	11	30400	33800
35		CONCORDE	FB	EXP	FBG		IB	T320	FLAG	12	6	16800	2	11	22600	25200
35		CONCORDE	FB	EXP	FBG		IB	T160D		12	6	16800	2	11	30700	34100
35		CONCORDE		SDN	FBG		IB	T320	FLAG	12	6	17400	2	11	23900	26500
35		CONCORDE		SDN	FBG		IB	T160D		12	6	17400	2	11	32800	36500
35		CONCORDE	FB	SDN	FBG		IB	T320	FLAG	12	6	17700	2	11	24000	26700
35		CONCORDE	FB	SDN	FBG		IB	T160D		12	6	17700	2	11	33200	36800
37		GRENADA	FB	DCMY	MHG		IB	T225	FLAG	13		18195	2	11	27000	30000
37		GRENADA	FB	DCMY	MHG		IB	T320	FLAG	13		18000	2	11	27400	30400
37		GRENADA	FB	DCMY	MHG		IB	T160D		13		18195	2	11	30100	33400
37		GRENADA HT ON FB	FB	DCMY	MHG		IB	T225	FLAG	13		18000	2	11	26800	29700
37		GRENADA HT ON FB	FB	DCMY	MHG		IB	T320	FLAG	13		18195	2	11	27600	30600
37		GRENADA HT ON FB	FB	DCMY	MHG		IB	T160D	FLAG	13		18000	2	11	29800	33200
40		CONCORDE	FB	SDN	FBG		IB	T320	FLAG	13	6	20500	3	3	33700	37500
40		CONCORDE	FB	SDN	FBG		IB	T160D		13	6	20500	3	3	36500	40600
42		ARUBA	FB	DCMY	MHG		IB	T320	FLAG	13		22000	2	8	39000	43300
42		ARUBA	FB	DCMY	MHG		IB	T160D		13		22195	2	8	39600	44000
42		ARUBA	FB	TCMY	MHG		IB	T320	FLAG	13		22000	2	11	40700	45200
42		ARUBA	FB	TCMY	MHG		IB	T160D		13		22000	2	11	40500	45000
42		ARUBA AFT WELL	FB	DCMY	MHG		IB	T320	FLAG	13		22000	2	11	40100	44600
42		ARUBA AFT WELL	FB	DCMY	MHG		IB	T160D		13		22000	2	11	40000	44500
42		ARUBA HT ON FB	FB	DCMY	MHG		IB	T320	FLAG	13		22195	2	11	40600	45100
42		ARUBA HT ON FB	FB	DCMY	MHG		IB	T160D		13		22000	2	11	40100	44600
42		ARUBA HT ON FB	FB	TCMY	MHG		IB	T320	FLAG	13		22195	2	11	42300	46900
42		ARUBA HT ON FB	FB	TCMY	MHG		IB	T160D		13		22195	2	11	41800	46400
		1967 BOATS														
24	7	COMMANDO SEA SKIFF		EXP	L/P		IB	185		8		3910	2	3	4050	4750
24	7	COMMANDO SEA SKIFF	HT	EXP	L/P		IB	185		8		4105	2	3	4200	4900
24	7	CONTESSA FLAGSHIP		EXP	PLY		IB	225				4900			4900	5650
24	7	CONTESSA FLAGSHIP	HT	EXP	PLY		IB	225				5095			5050	5800
24	7	PRINCESS FLAGSHIP		CR	PLY		IB	185		8		3910	2	3	4050	4750
24	7	PRINCESS FLAGSHIP	HT	CR	PLY		IB	185		8		4105	2	3	4200	4900
26	3	CONTESSA		EXP	PLY		IB	185		10	3		2	3	5500	6350
26	3	RAIDER SEA SKIFF		EXP	L/P		IB	225		10	3	4900	2	3	5600	6450
26	3	RAIDER SEA SKIFF	HT	EXP	L/P		IB	225		10	3	5095	2	3	5700	6600
27		MARAUDER FLEETSHIP		EXP	FBG		IB	225		10	5	5500	2	5	6250	7200
27		MARAUDER FLEETSHIP	HT	EXP	FBG		IB	225		10	5	5695	2	5	6400	7350
28	4	BUCCANEER SEA SKIFF		EXP	L/P		IB	225		10	8	5600	2	3	7050	8100
28	4	BUCCANEER SEA SKIFF	HT	EXP	L/P		IB	225		10	8	5795	2	3	7150	8250
28	4	BUCCANEER SEA SKIFF	FB	EXP	L/P		IB	225		10	8	5900	2	3	7200	8300
28	4	SULTANA FLAGSHIP		EXP	PLY		IB	225		10	8	5600	2	3	7050	8100
28	4	SULTANA FLAGSHIP	HT	EXP	PLY		IB	225		10	8	5795	2	3	7150	8250
30					WD		IB	T225	CHRY						**	**

CONTINUED ON NEXT PAGE

LOA FT	LOA IN	NAME AND/ OR MODEL	TOP/ RIG	BOAT TYPE	-HULL- MTL	-HULL- TP	ENGINE TP	ENGINE # HP	ENGINE MFG	BEAM FT	BEAM IN	WGT LBS	DRAFT FT	DRAFT IN	RETAIL LOW	RETAIL HIGH
		1967 BOATS														
30		EMPRESS FLAGSHIP		EXP	P/M		IB	T225		10	6	9070	2	4	11400	12900
30		EMPRESS FLAGSHIP	HT	EXP	P/M		IB	T225		10	6	9265	2	4	11500	13000
30		EMPRESS FLAGSHIP	FB	EXP	P/M		IB	T225		10	6	9370	2	4	11500	13100
30		EMPRESS FLAGSHIP		SDN	P/M		IB	T225		10	6	9900	2	5	12800	14500
30		EMPRESS FLAGSHIP	FB	SDN	P/M		IB	T225		10	6	10005	2	5	12800	14600
33		MARGARITA		SDN	P/M		IB	T225		11		9500	2	3	14900	16900
33		MARGARITA	FB	SDN	P/M		IB	T225		11		9695	2	3	14900	17000
33		REGENCY FLAGSHIP	HT	EXP	P/M		IB	T225		11		9195	2	3	15300	17400
33		REGENCY FLAGSHIP	FB	EXP	P/M		IB	T225		11		9300	2	3	15300	17400
33	4	BRIGANTINE FLEETSHIP		SF	FBG		IB	T225		12		16000	2	6	18400	20400
33	4	BRIGANTINE FLEETSHIP		SF	FBG		IB	T170D		12		16000	2	6	27100	30100
34	6	JAMAICAN	HT	EXP	P/M		IB	T225		12		11695	2	6	18300	20300
34	6	JAMAICAN HT ON FB	FB	EXP	P/M		IB	T225		12		11800	2	6	18300	20400
37		GRENADA	FB	DC	P/M		IB	T225		13		18195	2	11	25900	28800
40		TAHITIAN	FB	DC	P/M		IB	T225		12	2	16500	2	9	29800	33200
42		ARUBA	FB	DC	P/M		IB	T225		13		22000	2	8	35600	39500
42		ARUBA HT ON FB	FB	DC	P/M		IB	T225		13		22195	2	8	36600	40700
42		ARUBA HT ON FB	FB	TCMY	P/M		IB	T225		13		22195	2	11	38000	42200
		1966 BOATS														
19		FLEETSHIP XL-19 CUS		RNBT	FBG		IB	225		7	10		1	7	2000	2400
20	1	FLEETSHIP XL-20 CUS		RNBT	FBG		IO	150		8			1	8	5150	5950
24	8	COMMANDO SEA SKIFF		EXP	L/P		IB	185		8			2	2	4550	5200
24	8	COMMANDO SEA SKIFF	HT	EXP	L/P		IB	185		8			2	2	4550	5200
24	8	PRINCESS FLAGSHIP		EXP	PLY		IB	185		8					4550	5200
24	8	PRINCESS FLAGSHIP	HT	EXP	PLY		IB	185		8					4550	5200
24	8	WILDCAT SEA SKIFF		UTL	L/P		IB	185		8			2	2	4400	5050
24	8	WILDCAT SEA SKIFF	HT	UTL	L/P		IB	185		8			2	2	4400	5050
26	4	CONTESSA FLAGSHIP		EXP	PLY		IB	225		10	3				5500	6300
26	4	CONTESSA FLAGSHIP	HT	EXP	PLY		IB	225		10	3				5500	6300
26	4	RAIDER SEA SKIFF		EXP	L/P		IO	225		10	3				12200	13900
26	4	RAIDER SEA SKIFF		EXP	L/P		IB	225		10	3				5500	6300
26	4	RAIDER SEA SKIFF	HT	EXP	L/P		IO	225		10	3				12200	13900
26	4	RAIDER SEA SKIFF	HT	EXP	L/P		IB	225		10	3				5500	6300
27		MARAUDER FLEETSHIP			FBG		IB	185							6200	7150
28	3	BARONESS		EXP	PLY		IB	225		10	8				6900	7950
28	4	MATADOR SEA SKIFF		EXP	L/P		IB	225		10	8				6950	8000
28	4	MATADOR SEA SKIFF	HT	EXP	L/P		IB	225		10	8				6950	8000
28	4	MATADOR SEA SKIFF	FB	EXP	L/P		IB	225		10	8				6950	8000
28	4	SULTANA FLAGSHIP		EXP	WD		IB	225							6950	7950
28	4	SULTANA FLAGSHIP	HT	EXP	WD		IB	225							6950	7950
28	4	SULTANA FLAGSHIP	FB	EXP	WD		IB	225							6950	7950
30	5	EMPRESS FLAGSHIP		EXP	P/M		IB	T225		10	10		2		11500	13100
30	5	EMPRESS FLAGSHIP	HT	EXP	P/M		IB	T225		10	10		2		11500	13100
30	5	EMPRESS FLAGSHIP	FB	EXP	P/M		IB	T225		10	10		2		11500	13100
33		MARGARITA		SDN	P/M		IB	T225		11			2	3	14600	16600
33		MARGARITA	FB	SDN	P/M		IB	T225		11			2	3	14600	16600
33		REGENCY FLAGSHIP		EXP	P/M		IB	T225		11			2	3	14900	16900
33		REGENCY FLAGSHIP	HT	EXP	P/M		IB	T225		11			2	3	14900	16900
33		REGENCY FLAGSHIP	FB	EXP	P/M		IB	T225		11			2	3	14900	16900
33	4	BRIGANTINE FLEETSHIP		SF	FBG		IB	T225		12			2		14800	16800
34	6	JAMAICAN		EXP	P/M		IB	T225		12			2	6	18700	20800
34	6	JAMAICAN	HT	EXP	P/M		IB	T225		12			2	6	18700	20800
34	6	JAMAICAN	FB	EXP	P/M		IB	T225		12			2	6	18700	20800
37		GRENADA	FB	DC	P/M		IB	T225		12			2	11	26100	29000
37		GRENADA	FB	DC	P/M		IB	T290		12			2	11	26400	29300
37		GRENADA	FB	DC	P/M		IB	T170D		12			2	11	29000	32300
37		MAJORCA SALON		EXP	P/M		IB	T225		12			2	11	24500	27200
37		MAJORCA SALON	HT	EXP	P/M		IB	T225		12			2	11	24500	27200
37		MAJORCA SALON	FB	EXP	P/M		IB	T225		12			2	11	24500	27200
39	9	TAHITIAN	FB	DC	P/M		IB	T225		12	2	16500	2	9	28600	31800
42		ARUBA		TCMY	P/M		IB	T225		13			2	11	35500	39400
42		ARUBA		TCMY	P/M		IB	T290		13			2	11	37300	41500
42		ARUBA		TCMY	P/M		IB	T170D		13			2	11	38700	43000
		1965 BOATS														
19		FLEETSHIP XL-19 CUS		RNBT	FBG		IB	185-225							1950	2300
20	1	FLEETSHIP XL-20 CUS		RNBT	FBG		IO	150							5350	6150
23		FLEETSHIP SL-23		SF	FBG		IO	150							10600	12000
23		FLEETSHIP XL-23 DLX		RNBT	FBG		IO	150							7550	8650
24	7	COMMANDO SEA SKIFF			WD		IB	185							4600	5300
24	7	PRINCESS FLAGSHIP		CR	WD		IO	150							9450	10700
24	7	PRINCESS FLAGSHIP		EXP	WD		IB	185							4350	5000
24	7	SEA-SKIFF		CR	WD		IO	150							8900	10100
24	7	WILDCAT SEA SKIFF			WD		IO	150							9650	11000
24	7	WILDCAT SEA SKIFF			WD		IB	185							3850	4450
26	4	CONTESSA FLAGSHIP		EXP	WD		IB	225							5400	6250
26	4	CONTESSA FLAGSHIP	HT	EXP	WD		IB	225							5400	6250
26	4	RAIDER SEA SKIFF		EXP	WD		IB	225							5100	5900
26	4	RAIDER SEA SKIFF	HT	EXP	WD		IB	225							5100	5900
28	3	BARONESS FLAGSHIP		EXP	WD		IB	225							6850	7900
28	3	BARONESS FLAGSHIP	HT	EXP	WD		IB	225							6850	7900
28	3	BARONESS FLAGSHIP	FB	EXP	WD		IB	225							6650	7650
28	3	MATADOR SEA SKIFF	FB		WD		IB	225							6550	7550
28	3	MATADOR SEA SKIFF		EXP	WD		IB	225							6400	7350
28	3	MATADOR SEA SKIFF	HT	EXP	WD		IB	225							6400	7350
30	5	EMPRESS FLAGSHIP		EXP	WD		IB	T225							11100	12600
30	5	EMPRESS FLAGSHIP	HT	EXP	WD		IB	T225							11100	12600
30	5	EMPRESS FLAGSHIP	FB	EXP	WD		IB	T225							11100	12600
32	3	BONAIRE		SDN	WD		IB	T225							13300	15100
32	3	BONAIRE	FB	SDN	WD		IB	T225							13300	15100
32	3	REGINA FLAGSHIP		EXP	WD		IB	T225							13600	15400
32	3	REGINA FLAGSHIP	HT	EXP	WD		IB	T225							13600	15400
32	3	REGINA FLAGSHIP	FB	EXP	WD		IB	T225							13600	15400
33	4	BRIGANTINE FLEETSHIP		SDN	FBG		IB	T225							14700	16700
33	4	BRIGANTINE FLEETSHIP	FB	SDN	FBG		IB	T225							14700	16700
33	4	BRIGANTINE FLEETSHIP		SF	FBG		IB	T225							14300	16200
33	4	BRIGANTINE FLEETSHIP	FB	SF	FBG		IB	T225							14300	16200
37		GRENADA	FB	DC	WD		IB	T225							24000	26700
37		MAJORCA		EXP	WD		IB	T225							24000	26600
37		MAJORCA	HT	EXP	WD		IB	T225							24000	26600
37		MAJORCA	FB	EXP	WD		IB	T225							24000	26600
39	9	TAHITIAN	FB	DC	WD		IB	T225		12	2	16500	2	9	27900	31000
42		ARUBA		TCMY	WD		IB	T225							31400	34900
		1964 BOATS														
19		SEA-SKIFF XL-19			FBG		IB	185							1700	2050
24	7	COMMANDO SEA SKIFF		EXP	WD		IB	185							4250	4950
24	7	PRINCESS FLAGSHIP		EXP	WD		IB	185							4100	4750
26	4	CONTESSA FLAGSHIP		EXP	WD		IB	185							4850	5550
26	4	RAIDER SEA SKIFF		EXP	WD		IB	185							5050	5850
28	3	BARONESS FLAGSHIP		EXP	WD		IB	225							6300	7250
28	3	MATADOR SEA SKIFF		EXP	WD		IB	225							6500	7500
28	3	MATADOR SEA SKIFF	FB	FSH	WD		IB	225							6400	7350
28	3	MATADOR SEA SKIFF	FB	FSH	WD		IB	T185							7100	8150
30	5	BARBADOS		EXP	WD		IB	T185							11400	13000
30	5	EMPRESS FLAGSHIP		EXP	WD		IB	T185							9400	10700
32	3	BUCCANEER SEA SKIFF		EXP	WD		IB	T225							12400	14000
32	3	REGINA FLAGSHIP		EXP	WD		IB	T225							12100	13800
32	3	TORTIGA		EXP	WD		IB	T225							14800	16900
37					WD		IB	T225	FLAG			16858			**	**
37	1	GALLEON		EXP	WD		IB	T225							23500	26100
39	9	TAHITIAN	FB	DC	WD		IB	T225		12	2	16500	2	9	27200	30200
		1963 BOATS														
24	7	COMMANDO SEA SKIFF		EXP	WD		IB	185							4100	4750
24	7	PRINCESS FLAGSHIP		EXP	WD		IB	185							3950	4550
26	4	CONTESSA FLAGSHIP		EXP	WD		IB	185							4700	5400
26	4	RAIDER SEA SKIFF		EXP	WD		IB	185							4900	5650
28	3	BARONESS FLAGSHIP		EXP	WD		IB	185							5900	6750
28	3	MATADOR SEA SKIFF		EXP	WD		IB	185							6100	7000
28	3	MATADOR SEA SKIFF	FB	FSH	WD		IB	185							6000	6900
28	3	MATADOR SEA SKIFF	FB	FSH	WD		IB	T185							6850	7850
28	3	MATADOR SEA SKIFF		UTL	WD		IB	185							6000	6900
28	3	MATADOR SEA SKIFF		UTL	WD		IB	T185							6850	7850
30	4	BARBADOS 30		EXP	WD		IB	T185							9950	11300
30	5	EMPRESS FLAGSHIP		EXP	WD		IB	T185							9950	11300
30	5	SARACEN SEA SKIFF		EXP	WD		IB	T185							10200	11500
34	7	BRIGANTINE 35		SF	WD		IB	T185							14600	16600
34	7	JAMAICAN 35		EXP	WD		IB	T185							16300	18500
34	7	MARACAIBO 35 SPORT		SDN	WD		IB	T185							16600	18900
39	9	TAHITIAN 40	FB	DC	WD		IB	T185		12	2	16500	2	9	26400	29400
		1962 BOATS														
24	6	MARAUDER			WD		IB	185							3800	4400
24	6	MARQUESSA FLAGSHIP			WD		IB	185							3800	4400
26	7	CORSICAN		EXP	WD		IB	185							5200	5950
26	7	CORSICAN	FB	SPTCR	WD		IB	185							5350	6150
26	7	CORSICAN		UTL	WD		IB	185							5350	6150
26	7	DUCHESS FLAGSHIP		EXP	WD		IB	185							5200	5950
26	7	DUCHESS FLAGSHIP		SDN	WD		IB	185							5700	6550
27					WD		IB	185	CHEV						**	**

 CONTINUED ON NEXT PAGE

LOA FT	IN	NAME AND/ OR MODEL	TOP/ RIG	BOAT TYPE	HULL MTL	TP	ENGINE TP	#	HP	MFG	BEAM FT	IN	WGT LBS	DRAFT FT	IN	RETAIL LOW	RETAIL HIGH
1962 BOATS																	
30	4	BARBADOS			WD		IB		T185							8300	9500
30	4	EMPRESS FLAGSHIP			WD		IB		T185							8300	9500
34	6	BRIGANTINE			WD		IB		T185							14100	16100
34	6	JAMAICAN			WD		IB		T185							14100	16100
40		TAHITIAN	FB	DC	WD		IB		T185		12	2	16500	2	9	26200	29100
1961 BOATS																	
21		FLAGSHIP		EXP	PLY		IB		145		7	10		2		2250	2650
21	4	SEA-SKIFF		EXP	MHG		IB		145		7	10		2		2300	2700
21	4	SEA-SKIFF SEMI ENCL			MHG		IB		145		7	10		2		2250	2600
24	6	FLAGSHIP FAMILY CR		EXP	PLY		IB		185		8			1	11	3800	4450
24	6	FLAGSHIP VACATIONER			PLY		IB		145		8			1	11	3650	4250
24	6	SEA-SKIFF DELUXE		EXP	MHG		IB		185		8			1	11	3800	4450
26	7	FLAGSHIP DELUXE		EXP	PLY		IB		185		9	10		2		5050	5800
26	7	SEA-SKIFF DELUXE		EXP	MHG		IB		185		9	10		2		5050	5800
26	7	SEA-SKIFF SPTSMN DLX	FB		MHG		IB		185		9	10		2		5200	5950
29					P/M		IB		T185		10	5		2	4	7000	8050
35				EXP	P/M		IB		T185		12	1		2	9	16100	18300
40		TAHITIAN	FB	DC	P/M		IB		T185		12	2	16500	2	9	25700	28500
1960 BOATS																	
20		SEA-SKIFF DELUXE		EXP			OB									5750	6600
20		SEA-SKIFF SPORTSMAN					OB									3800	4450
20		SEA-SKIFF SUPER		EXP			OB									5750	6600
21		FLAGSHIP		EXP			IB		145							2250	2600
21		SEA-SKIFF		EXP			IB									4300	5000
21		SEA-SKIFF		EXP			IB		145							2250	2600
21		SEA-SKIFF SEMI ENCL	OP	UTL			IB		145							1800	2150
25		FLAGSHIP FAMILY CR		CR			IB		145							2200	2550
25		FLAGSHIP VACATIONER					IB		185							3450	4000
25		SEA-SKIFF FAMILY CR		CR			IB		185							3650	4250
25		SEA-SKIFF LAPSTRAKE					IB		145							3450	4000
25		SEA-SKIFF VACATIONER					IB		185							3750	4350
27		FLAGSHIP DELUXE		EXP			IB		185							5100	5850
27		SEA-SKIFF		EXP			IB		185							5100	5850
27		SEA-SKIFF SPORTSMAN	FB				IB		185							5200	6000
29			FB				IB		200							6050	7000
29			FB				IB		T200							6950	8000
29		4 SLEEPER		EXP			IB		T200							7000	8050
29		6 SLEEPER		EXP			IB		T200							7000	8050
29		SEA-SKIFF		SF			IB		T200							7000	8050
29		SEA-SKIFF 4 SLEEPER		EXP			IB		T200							7000	8050
29		SEA-SKIFF 6 SLEEPER		EXP			IB		T200							7000	8050
35		PLAN 41		EXP			IB		T200							15900	18000
35		PLAN 42		EXP			IB		T200							15900	18000
1959 BOATS																	
22		SPEEDSHIP DELUXE		CR	WD		IB		150							2650	3050
22		SPEEDSHIP FAMILY CR		CR	WD		IB		60							2450	2850
22		SPEEDSHIP FAMILY CR		CR	WD		IB		150							2650	3050
22	4	CHESAPEAKE SPEEDSHIP		FSH	L/P		IB		150							2600	3000
22	4	SPEEDSHIP DELUXE		CR	PLY		IB		220		8					2900	3400
22	4	SPEEDSHIP FAMILY CR		CR	PLY		IB		220		8					2550	3000
25		SPEEDSHIP DELUXE		CR	WD		IB		220							3450	4000
28	9	FLAGSHIP SUPER CR		CR	WD		IB		T220							6350	7300
28	9	FLAGSHIP		CR	WD		IB		150		10	5				5600	6400
28	9	FLAGSHIP		CR	WD		IB		T150		10	5				6300	7250
28	9	FLAGSHIP	FB	CR	WD		IB		T220		10	5				6800	7800
34	6	FLAGSHIP		CR	WD		IB		T150		12	1				13900	15700
34	6	FLAGSHIP	FB	CR	WD		IB		T220		12	1				14200	16200
35		FLAGSHIP SUPER CR		CR	WD		IB		T220							14900	16900
1958 BOATS																	
16		FLEETSHIP DELUXE		RNBT			OB									2300	2700
16		FLEETSHIP SUPER		RNBT			OB									2300	2700
19		FLEETSHIP DELUXE		RNBT			OB									4500	5200
19		SPEEDSHIP		RNBT	WD		OB									4500	5200
22		FLAGSHIP		EXP	WD		IB		100-220							2450	3050
22		SPEEDSHIP		EXP	WD		OB									6850	7850
27		FLAGSHIP		EXP	WD		IB		200-220							4950	5800
27		FLAGSHIP		EXP	WD		IB		T100							5000	5750
27		FLAGSHIP DELUXE		EXP	WD		IB		T100							5000	5750
31		FLAGSHIP		EXP	WD		IB		200							8900	10100
31		FLAGSHIP		EXP	WD		IB		T136-T200							9250	11100
31		FLAGSHIP		SDN	WD		IB		200							8550	9850
31		FLAGSHIP		SDN	WD		IB		T100							8550	9850
35		FLAGSHIP	FB	SDN	WD		IB		T200							15700	17900
1957 BOATS																	
16				RNBT			OB									2300	2700
16		FLAGSHIP		RNBT			OB									2300	2700
16		SPORT		CR			OB									2000	2350
19				EXP			OB									3600	4150
19				RNBT			OB									4600	5250
19		FLAGSHIP		SPTCR			OB									3200	3700
19		FLAGSHIP		EXP			OB									3600	4150
19		FLAGSHIP		RNBT			OB									4600	5250
19		FLAGSHIP		SPTCR			OB									3200	3700
22				EXP			IB									6950	7950
22				EXP			IB		66							2350	2750
22				UTL			IB		66							1700	2000
22		FLAGSHIP		EXP			IB		100							2400	2800
22		FLAGSHIP		UTL			IB		100							1750	2100
27		411		EXP			IB		100							4500	5200
27		411		EXP			IB		T 66-T100							4650	5650
27		412		EXP			IB		100							4500	5200
27		412		EXP			IB		T 66-T100							4650	5650
27		FLAGSHIP		EXP			IB		T100							4900	5650
31		FLAGSHIP 2 STATERMS		SDN			IB		136							8000	9200
31		FLAGSHIP 2 STATERMS		SDN			IB		T100-T136							8450	10100
31		FLAGSHIP 6 SLEEPER		SDN			IB		T100-T136							8650	10300
35		FLAGSHIP	FB	SDN			IB		T100							14700	16700
35		FLAGSHIP	FB	SDN			IB		T136							15000	17100
1956 BOATS																	
16		FLAGSHIP		RNBT	WD		OB									2350	2750
16		FLAGSHIP DELUXE		RNBT	WD		OB									2350	2750
20		FLAGSHIP		RNBT	WD		OB									5400	6200
20		FLAGSHIP		RNBT	WD		OB		66- 96							1700	2100
20		FLAGSHIP		SPTCR	WD		OB									3500	4050
22	3	FLAGSHIP FAMILY CR		CR	WD		OB		66- 96							6400	7350
22	3	FLAGSHIP FAMILY CR		CR	WD		IB		96							2400	2850
26		FLAGSHIP	FB	SDN	WD		IB		T 66-T 96							4000	4650
26		FLAGSHIP	FB	SDN	WD		IB		96							4200	5250
31		FLAGSHIP STATEROOM		EXP	WD		IB		T 96-T136							8500	10200
31		FLAGSHIP		SDN	WD		IB		T 96-T136							8250	10000
35		FLAGSHIP	FB	SDN	WD		IB		T136							14800	16800
1955 BOATS																	
21		SPEEDSHIP		EXP	WD		IB		66							1850	2250
21		SPEEDSHIP FAMILY CR		CR	WD		OB		66							5900	6800
21		SPEEDSHIP FAMILY CR		CR	WD		IB		66							1900	2300
25		SPEEDSHIP	FB		WD		IB		136							3250	3850
25		SPEEDSHIP SUPER		EXP	WD		IB		136							3200	3750
27		SPEEDSHIP		EXP	WD		IB		136							4550	5200
27		SPEEDSHIP FAMILY CR		CR	WD		IB		136							4450	5150
31		FLAGSHIP 4 BERTH		SDN	WD		IB		T136							8550	9850
31		FLAGSHIP 6 BERTH		SDN	WD		IB		T136							8850	10000
35		FLAGSHIP		SDN	WD		IB		T136							14200	16100
35		FLAGSHIP	FB	SDN	WD		IB		T136							14600	16600
1954 BOATS																	
21		SPEEDSHIP		EXP	WD		IB		66- 96							1850	2250
21		SPEEDSHIP FAMILY CR		CR	WD		OB									6000	6900
21		SPEEDSHIP FAMILY CR		CR	WD		IB		66							1900	2250
25		SPEEDSHIP COMMUTER		CR	WD		IB		136							3350	3900
25		SPEEDSHIP FAMILY CR		CR	WD		IB		136							3050	3550
27		FLAGSHIP		EXP	WD		IB		66							2800	3250
31		FLAGSHIP		EXP	WD		IB		96							4250	4950
31		FLAGSHIP 4 BERTH		SDN	WD		IB		T136							8450	9700
31		FLAGSHIP 6 BERTH		SDN	WD		IB		T136							8600	9900
44		FLAGSHIP	FB	SDN	WD		IB		T136							14400	16300
44		FLAGSHIP		SDN	WD		IB		T185							26300	29200
44		FLAGSHIP		SF	WD		IB		T185							22400	24900
50		FLAGSHIP		CR	WD		IB		T185							35100	39000
1953 BOATS																	
21		SPEEDSHIP		CBNCR	WD		OB									6350	7300
21		SPEEDSHIP		EXP	WD		IB		66							1800	2150
21		SPEEDSHIP DELUXE		EXP	WD		IB		136							1950	2300
21		SPEEDSHIP FAMILY CR		CR	WD		IB		66							1850	2200
25		FLAGSHIP		EXP	WD		IB		136		8	4				3350	3900
31		FLAGSHIP		EXP	WD		IB		136							7950	9150
31		FLAGSHIP		SDN	WD		IB		96							7300	8400
36		FLAGSHIP		EXP	WD		IB		96							15100	17200
40		FLAGSHIP CUTTER			WD		IB		T225							23300	25800
44		FLAGSHIP		FD	WD		IB		T136							29600	32900

LOA FT IN	NAME AND/ OR MODEL	TOP/ RIG	BOAT TYPE	-HULL- MTL TP	TP	----ENGINE--- # HP	MFG	BEAM FT IN	WGT LBS	DRAFT FT IN	RETAIL LOW	RETAIL HIGH
---	---	1952	BOATS	---								
25			EXP	WD	IB	96					3150	3700
30		OP	EXP	MHG	IB	T100-T118					7350	8600
30		HT	SDN	MHG	IB	118	FLAG				6800	7800
31			EXP	WD	IB	T136					8400	9650
31			SDN	WD	IB	96					7200	8300
33			SDN	WD	IB	T 96					9800	11100
42			PD	WD	IB	T150					23200	25800
---	---	1951	BOATS	---								
22	FLAGSHIP		EXP	WD	IB	66					2200	2550
26			FSH	WD	IB	96					3550	4150
26	FLAGSHIP		EXP	WD	IB	96					3500	4100
26	FLAGSHIP FAMILY CR		CR	WD	IB	96					3550	4100
26	SPORTSMAN		UTL	WD	IB	96					3500	4100
33			FSH	WD	IB	136					8850	10100
33	FAMILY CR		SDN	WD	IB	136					9400	10700
33	FAMILY CR		SDN	WD	ID	T136					10100	11500
33	FLAGSHIP		FSH	WD	IB	T136					9150	10400
42			SDN	WD	IB	T130					22200	24600
42	FLAGSHIP	FB	EXP	WD	IB	T150					23100	25700
---	---	1950	BOATS	---								
26			EXP	WD	IB						**	**
26		HT	SDN	WD	IB						**	**
26	SPORTSMAN	ST	UTL	WD	IB	100	FLAG				3500	4050
27			EXP	WD	IB	96					4050	4750
31			EXP	WD	IB	T136					8200	9400
31			SDN	WD	IB	T136					8000	9200
33			EXP	WD	IB	T 96					9950	11300
33			SF	WD	IB	T136					9900	11300
42		FB	DC	WD	IB	T150					23200	25700
---	---	1949	BOATS	---								
26		HT	FSH	PLY DV	IB	45	GRAY				3400	3950
26		HT	SDN	PLY DV	IB	45	GRAY				4200	4850
26		OP	UTL	PLY DV	IB	45	GRAY				3350	3900
26	DAY CRUISER	HT	CR	PLY DV	IB	45	GRAY				3350	3900
27			EXP	WD	IB	96					4050	4700
27			SDN	WD	IB	136					5000	5750
31			EXP	WD	IB	T136					8100	9300
31			SDN	WD	IB	T136					7950	9150
33			EXP	WD	IB	T 96					9850	11200
33	4 BRIGANTINE SF	FB	CR	FBG	IB	T225	FLAG	13 6	20500		13600	15500
40	CONCORDE 40 DC	FB	DC	FBG	IB	T160D	PERK	13 6	20500		26700	29700
42				WD	IB	T115					**	**
42				WD	IB	T125	CHRY				**	**
42		FB	DC	WD	IB	T150					23100	25600
---	---	1948	BOATS	---								
23			SDN	WD	IB	112					2500	2900
27			SDN	WD	IB	100					4950	5700
33			SDN	WD	IB	T115					9600	10900
42		FB	DC	WD	IB	T150					23000	25500
---	---	1947	BOATS	---								
23			EXP	WD	IB	115					2700	3150
27			CR	WD	IB	95					4100	4750
27			SDN	WD	IB	115					5150	5900
31				WD	IB	T130	HERC				**	**
33			EXP	WD	IB	T100					9700	11000
42		FB	DC	WD	IB	T145					22800	25400
---	---	1946	BOATS	---								
27	FLAGSHIP	HT	SDN	WD	IB	90					5200	5950
32	CUSTOM	FB	CR	WD	IB	165					7850	9050
33	FLAGSHIP	HT	DC	WD	IB	90					9450	10700
40		CUT	SAIL	WD	KL					5 8	41300	45900
42		FB	DC	WD	IB	T150					22900	25400
---	---	1941	BOATS	---								
30 6		HT	SDN	WD	IB			10 5			**	**
30 6		HT	SF	WD	IB			10 5			**	**
---	---	1939	BOATS	---								
30		HT	DC	WD	IB			9 8		2 3	**	**
30		HT	SDN	WD	IB			9 8		2 3	**	**
30		OP	SPTCR	WD	IB			9 8		2 3	**	**
---	---	1937	BOATS	---								
30		HT	SDN	MHG RB	IB						**	**
30		HT	SPTCR	MHG RB	IB						**	**
---	---	1932	BOATS	---								
28		HT	CR	WD DV	VD		GRAY	8 8		2 4	**	**

OY FISKARS A/B
TURKU FINLAND   COAST GUARD MFG ID- FKS See inside cover to adjust price for area

DIST E VETTERLEIN INC
ANNAPOLIS MD 21403

For more recent years, see the BUC Used Boat Price Guide, Volume 1 or Volume 2

LOA FT IN	NAME AND/ OR MODEL	TOP/ RIG	BOAT TYPE	-HULL- MTL TP	TP	----ENGINE--- # HP	MFG	BEAM FT IN	WGT LBS	DRAFT FT IN	RETAIL LOW	RETAIL HIGH
---	---	1979	BOATS	---								
29 3	FINNSAILER 29	SLP	MS	FBG KL	IB	49D	PERK	9 2	10340	4 1	31700	35200
29 3	FINNSAILER 29	SLP	SA/CR	FBG KL	IB	D		9 2	10000	3 4	30500	33900
33 2	FINNFIRE 33	SLP	SA/CR	FBG KL	IB	13D	VLVO	10 8	9900	6 1	28900	32200
33 2	FINNFIRE 33	SLP	SA/RC	FBG KL	IB	13D	VLVO	10 8	8360	6 1	24400	27200
33 8	KINGS-CRUISER 33	SLP	SA/CR	FBG KL	IB	D		10 3	9480	5 8	27800	30900
34 2	FINNSAILER 34	SLP	MS	FBG KL	IB	49D	PERK	11 4	13200	5	38600	42900
34 2	FINNSAILER 34	KTH	SA/CR	FBG KL	IB	49D	PERK	11 4	13200	5 2	38600	42900
35	FINNSAILER 35	SLP	SA/CR	FBG KL	IB	D		10 3	15500	4	45700	50200
35 2	FINNSAILER 36	SLP	MS	FBG KL	IB	72D	PERK	10 3	15840	4 1	46800	51500
36	FINNSAILER 36	SLP	SA/CR	FBG KL	IB	D		10 3	16000	4	47800	52500
36	POWLES		CR	FBG	SV	IB	T175D		12 3	15000		51800	56900
37 7	FINNSAILER 38	SLP	SA/CR	FBG KL	IB	D		11 7	20000	5 2	59700	65600
37 7	FINNSAILER 38	KTH	SA/CR	FBG KL	IB	D		11 7	20000	5 3	59700	65600
37 9	FINNSAILER 38	SLP	MS	FBG KL	IB	72D	PERK	11 7	19800	5 3	59600	65400
37 9	FINNSAILER 38	KTH	MS	FBG KL	IB	72D	PERK	11 7	19800	5 3	59600	65400
38	POWLES		CR	FBG	SV	IB	T212D		12 3	18000		67500	74200
38	POWLES 36+2		CR	FBG	SV	IB	T270D		13 2	20000		78600	86400
45	FINNROSE 45	KTH	MS	FBG KL	IB	115D	PERK	14 6	35200	6	119500	131000
45	FINNROSE 45	KTH	SA/CR	FBG KL	IB	D		14 6	35000	6	119000	131000
46	POWLES		CR	FBG	SV	IB	T270D		15	28000		109500	120500
53	POWLES		CR	FBG	SV	IB	T435D		15	40000		168000	184500
---	---	1978	BOATS	---								
29 3	FINNSAILER 29	SLP	MS	FBG KL	IB	50D	PERK	9 2	10000	3 4	29500	32800
33 8	KINGS-CRUISER 33	SLP	SA/CR	FBG KL	IB	D		10 3	9480		26800	29800
35	FINNSAILER 35	SLP	MS	FBG KL	IB	85D	PERK	10 3	15500	4	43700	48600
36	FINNSAILER 36	SLP	MS	FBG KL	IB	85D	PERK	10 3	15000	4	46300	50900
37 7	FINNSAILER 38	SLP	MS	FBG KL	IB	85D	PERK	11 7	20000	5 2	57500	63400
43	TARQUIN		MY	FBG	SV	IB	T280D		15 2			101500	111500
45	FINNROSE 45	KTH	MY	FBG	SV	IB	115D	PERK	14 6	35000	6	114500	126000
46	TARQUIN		MY	FBG	SV	IB	T280D		15 2			120000	131500
---	---	1977	BOATS	---								
28 6	KINGS-CRUISER 29	SLP	SAIL	FBG KL	IB	10D	VLVO	9 3	6615	4 11	18700	20800
29 3	KINGS-CRUISER 29	SLP	SAIL	FBG KL	IB	50D	PERK	9 2	10000	3 4	28500	31700
33 8	KINGS-CRUISER 33	SLP	SAIL	FBG KL	IB	25D	VLVO	10 3	9480	5 8	26000	28800
35	FINNSAILER 35	SLP	MS	FBG KL	IB	75D	PERK	10 3	15500	4	42200	46900
36	FINNSAILER 36	SLP	MS	FBG KL	IB	75D	PERK	10 3	15000	4	44200	49100
37 7	FINNSAILER 38	SLP	MS	FBG KL	IB	75D	PERK	11 7	20000	5 2	55700	61200
37 7	FINNSAILER 38	KTH	MS	FBG KL	IB	75D	PERK	11 7	20000	5 2	55700	61200
45	FINNROSE 45	KTH	MS	FBG KL	IB	115D	PERK	14 6	35000	6	111000	121500
---	---	1976	BOATS	---								
21 8	NORLANDER 22	HT	CR	FBG DV	IB	36D- 42D	VLVO	7 6	2500	2 6	5850	7150
23	NORLANDER 24		CR	FBG DV	IB	36D	VLVO	8		2	9000	10200
26 3	NORLANDER 26		CR	FBG DV	IB	50D	PERK	9 2		2	15000	17000
26 7	NORDIC 26	SLP	MS	FBG DV	IB	25D	VLVO	8 10	7000	2 10	19300	21400
28 6	FINLANDER 28	HT	CR	FBG DV	IB	75D	PERK	9 8		2 10	18200	20200
28 6	KINGS-CRUISER 29	SLP	SAIL	FBG KL	IB	10D	VLVO	9 3	6840	4 11	18700	20800
29 3	KINGS-CRUISER 29	SLP	SAIL	FBG KL	IB	36D- 50D	PERK	9 2		3 4	27700	30900
33 8	KINGS-CRUISER 33	SLP	SAIL	FBG KL	IB	25D	VLVO	10 3	10150	5 2	26900	29900
35	FINNSAILER 35	SLP	MS	FBG KL	IB	70D	PERK	10 3	10150	4	40900	45400
37 7	FINNSAILER 38	SLP	MS	FBG KL	IB	70D	PERK	11 7	19000	5 2	51700	56900
37 7	FINNSAILER 38	KTH	MS	FBG KL	IB	70D	PERK	11 7	19000	5 2	53000	58300
45	FINNROSE 45	KTH	MS	FBG KL	IB	115D	PERK	14 6	35000	6	107000	118000
---	---	1975	BOATS	---								
26 7	NORDIC 26	SLP	MS	FBG KL	IB	36D	VLVO	8 10	5500	2 10	14500	16500
28 6	KINGS-CRUISER 29	SLP	SAIL	FBG KL	IB	10D	VLVO	9 3	6615	4 11	17200	19500
29 3	FINNSAILER 29	SLP	SAIL	FBG KL	IB	49D- 50D	PERK	9 2	10000	3 4	26000	28900
31 10	KINGS-CRUISER 33	SLP	SAIL	FBG KL	IB	25D	VLVO	10 3	10000	5 2	25700	28600
33 8	KINGS-CRUISER 33	SLP	SAIL	FBG KL	IB	25D	VLVO	10 3	13700	5 8	25700	28600
35	FINNSAILER 35	SLP	MS	FBG KL	IB	85D	PERK	10 3	13700	3 8	35500	39500
35	FINNSAILER 35	SLP	MS	FBG KL	IB	85D	PERK	10 3		4	38600	42900
36 6	FINNROSE 37	SLP	MS	FBG KL	IB	49D	PERK	10 11	16000	5 6	41900	46600
38	FINNSAILER 38	KTH	MS	FBG KL	IB	70D	PERK	11 7	19000	5 7	44600	49500
45	FINNROSE 45	KTH	MS	FBG KL	IB	115D	PERK	14 6	35000	6	104000	114500
---	---	1974	BOATS	---								
21 8	NORLANDER 22		CR	FBG	IB	36D	VLVO	7 6	2500	2	5550	6350
23	FINLANDER SEA MAX		CR	FBG	IB	36D	VLVO	8	3500	2 4	7450	8600
25	ROYAL		CR	FBG	IB	75D	VLVO	8 6	4000	2	8350	9600

LOA FT	IN	NAME AND/ OR MODEL	TOP/ RIG	BOAT TYPE	-HULL- MTL	TP	ENGINE TP	# HP	MFG	BEAM FT	IN	WGT LBS	DRAFT FT	IN	RETAIL LOW	RETAIL HIGH
		1974 BOATS														
26	3	NORLANDER 26		CR	FBG		IB	75D	VLVO	9	2	4500	3	3	8950	10200
26	7	NORDIC	SLP	SAIL	FBG		IB	36D	VLVO	8	10	5500	2	10	14200	16100
28	6	FINLANDER		CR	FBG		IB	75D	VLVO	9	4	5250	2	4	10400	11800
28	6	KINGS-CRUISER		SAIL	FBG		IB	10D	VLVO	8	3	6615	4	11	16700	19000
29	3	FINNSAILER		SAIL	FBG		IB	36D	VLVO	9	2	8000	3	4	20700	23100
31	10	KINGS-CRUISER 33	SLP	SAIL	FBG		IB	25D	VLVO	10	3	10150	5	2	25300	28200
34		ROYAL		CR	FBG		IB	T106D	VLVO	10	6	10000	3	1	34000	37800
35		FINNSAILER		SAIL	FBG		IB	85D	PERK	10	3	13700	3	8	34600	38400
37	3	FINNROSE	SLP	SAIL	FBG		IB	49D	PERK	10	11	14000	5	3	37300	41400
42		ROYAL		CR	MHG		IB	T250D	VLVO	13	8	20000	3	3	64900	71300
45		FINNROSE 45		SAIL	FBG		IB	49D	PERK	14	6	32000	6		96100	105500
46	4	NORTHCRUISER 47		MY	FBG		IB	T275		14	8		4	3	89000	97800
46	4	NORTHCRUISER 47		MY	FBG		IB	T350		14	8		4	3	90800	99800
47		ROYAL		CR	MHG		IB	T283D	GM	14	3	30000	4	5	96700	106500
53	2	NORTHCRUISER 53		MY	FBG		IB	T240		14	8		4	3	147000	162000
53	2	NORTHCRUISER 53		MY	FBG		IB	T370		14	8		4	3	149000	164000
		1973 BOATS														
23		FINLANDER SEA MAX			FBG		IB	36D	VLVO	8	6	3500	2	4	7250	8350
25		ROYAL		CR	FBG		IB	75D	VLVO	8	6	4000	2		8100	9350
26	7	NORDIC	SLP	SAIL	FBG		IB	36D	VLVO	8	10	5500	2	10	13800	15700
28	6	FINLANDER		CR	FBG		IB	75D	VLVO	9	4	5250	2	4	10100	11400
28	6	KINGS-CRUISER		SAIL	FBG		IB	10D	VLVO	8	3	6615	4	11	16300	18600
29	3	FINNSAILER		SAIL	FBG		IB	36D	VLVO	9	2	8000	3	4	20200	22500
31	11	LANA	SLP	MS	FBG	KL	IB	D		10	3		4	7	31200	34700
34		ROYAL		CR	FBG		IB	T106D	VLVO	10	6	10000	3	1	32600	36200
35		FINNSAILER		SAIL	FBG		IB	85D	PERK	10	3	13700	3	8	33700	37500
37	3	FINNROSE	SLP	SAIL	FBG		IB	49D	PERK	10	11	14000	5	3	36400	40400
42		ROYAL		CR	MHG		IB	T250D	VLVO	13	8	20000	3	3	62400	68600
45		FINNROSE 45	KTH	SAIL	FBG	KL	IB	115D		14	6	35000	6		99100	109000
47		ROYAL		CR	MHG		IB	T283D	GM	14	3	30000	4	5	93100	102500
		1972 BOATS														
23		NORLANDER		CR	FBG		IB	60D		8		3500	2		7500	8650
26	7	NORDIC	SLP	SAIL	FBG	KL	IB	36D		8	10	5500	2	10	13500	15300
28	5	FINDLANDER 28A		CR	FBG		IB	75D-100D		9	1		2	4	15600	17800
28	5	FINDLANDER 28B		CR	FBG		IB	75D-100D		9	11		2	4	16000	18300
31	11	LAGUNA	SLP	MS	FBG	KL	IB	D		10	3		4	7	30500	33900

OY VATOR AB

Call 1-800-327-6929 for BUC Personalized Evaluation Service
Or, for 1960 to 1969 boats, sign onto www.BUCValuPro.com

OYSTER MARINE LTD

IPSWICH SUFFOLK UNITED KINGDOM

See inside cover to adjust price for area

OYSTER USA
NEWPORT RI 02840

For more recent years, see the BUC Used Boat Price Guide, Volume 1 or Volume 2

LOA FT	IN	NAME AND/ OR MODEL	TOP/ RIG	BOAT TYPE	-HULL- MTL	TP	ENGINE TP	# HP	MFG	BEAM FT	IN	WGT LBS	DRAFT FT	IN	RETAIL LOW	RETAIL HIGH
		1983 BOATS														
34	8	HUSTLER SJ35	SLP	SA/RC	FBG	KL	IB	12D	YAN	11	5	7620	6	3	32400	35900
35	1	OYSTER-MARINER 35	SLP	SA/CR	FBG	KL	SD	23D	VLVO	12		16000	5	3	67200	73800
35	1	OYSTER-MARINER 35	SLP	SA/CR	FBG	KL	IB	40D	PERK	12		16000	5	3	67200	73800
35	1	OYSTER-MARINER 35	KTH	SA/CR	FBG	KL	SD	23D	VLVO	12		16000	5	3	68100	74900
35	1	OYSTER-MARINER 35	KTH	SA/CR	FBG	KL	SD	35D	VLVO	12		16000	5	3	68300	75100
35	1	OYSTER-MARINER 35	KTH	SA/CR	FBG	KL	IB	40D	PERK	12		16000	5	3	68100	74900
35	1	OYSTER-MARINER 35	SLP	SA/RC	FBG	KL	SD	35D	VLVO	12		16000	5	3	67200	73900
39	6	OYSTER 39	KTH	SA/CR	FBG	KL	SD	61D	VLVO	12	10	19500	5	10	100500	110500
39	6	OYSTER 39	KTH	SA/CR	FBG	KL	IB	72D	PERK	12	10	19500	5	10	99900	110000
39	8	OYSTER 41	SLP	SA/RC	FBG	KL	SD	23D	VLVO	13	7	13000	6	10	72000	79100
39	8	OYSTER 41	SLP	SA/RC	FBG	KL	SD	35D	VLVO	13	7	13000	6	10	72400	79500
42		OYSTER 435	SLP	SA/CR	FBG	CB	SD	61D	VLVO	13	8	22600	4	6	113500	125000
42		OYSTER 435	SLP	SA/CR	FBG	KL	SD	61D	VLVO	13	8	22600	6		113500	125000
42	5	OYSTER 43	SLP	SA/RC	FBG	KL	SD	35D	VLVO	14	1	16600	7	6	95800	105500
43	5	OYSTER 435	KTH	SA/CR	FBG	CB	SD	61D	VLVO	13	8	22600	4	6	124500	136500
43	5	OYSTER 435	KTH	SA/CR	FBG	KL	SD	61D	VLVO	13	8	22600	6		124500	136500
46	2	OYSTER 46	KTH	SA/CR	FBG	KL	IB	72D	PERK	14		32000	6	6	159500	175500
		1982 BOATS														
27	4	HUSTLER 27	SLP	SA/RC	FBG	KL	IB	7D	BMW	10		4000	5		12700	14400
28		OYSTER 26	SLP	SA/RC	FBG	KL	SD	8D-	13D	9	10	6350	4	9	20700	23100
30	5	HUSTLER 30	SLP	SA/RC	FBG	KL	SD	8D	VLVO	10	9	6500	5	4	22800	25300
32	4	HUSTLER 32	SLP	SA/RC	FBG	KL	IB	18D	VLVO	11	3	7000	5	10	25500	28400
32	4	HUSTLER 33	SLP	SA/CR	FBG	KL	SD	18D	VLVO	11	3	8000	6		29300	32600
35	1	OYSTER-MARINER 35	SLP	SA/CR	FBG	KL	SD	23D	VLVO	12	5	17115	5	3	67100	73700
35	1	OYSTER-MARINER 35	SLP	SA/CR	FBG	KL	IB	40D	PERK	12	5	17115	5	3	67100	73700
35	1	OYSTER-MARINER 35	KTH	SA/CR	FBG	KL	SD	23D	VLVO	12	5	17115	5	3	68100	74800
35	1	OYSTER-MARINER 35	KTH	SA/CR	FBG	KL	SD	35D	VLVO	12	5	17115	5	3	68200	75000
35	1	OYSTER-MARINER 35	KTH	SA/CR	FBG	KL	IB	40D	PERK	12	5	17115	5	3	68100	74800
35	1	OYSTER-MARINER 35	SLP	SA/RC	FBG	KL	SD	35D	VLVO	12	5	17115	5	3	67200	73800
36		HUSTLER 36	SLP	SA/RC	FBG	KL	SD	23D	VLVO	12	3	8500	6		37000	41100
37		OYSTER 37	SLP	SA/RC	FBG	KL	SD	23D	VLVO	12	1	13800	6	3	60700	66700
37		OYSTER 37	SLP	SA/RC	FBG	KL	SD	35D	VLVO	12	1	13800	6	3	61000	67000
37		OYSTER 37	SLP	SA/RC	FBG	KL	IB	40D	PERK	12	1	13800	6	3	60700	66700
39	6	OYSTER 39	KTH	SA/CR	FBG	KL	IB	61D	VLVO	12	10	19500	5	10	94900	104500
39	8	OYSTER 41	SLP	SA/RC	FBG	KL	SD	23D	VLVO	13	7	13000	6	10	68200	75000
39	8	OYSTER 41	SLP	SA/RC	FBG	KL	SD	35D	VLVO	13	7	13000	6	10	68600	75400
42	5	OYSTER 43	SLP	SA/RC	FBG	KL	IB	35D	VLVO	14	1	16600	7	6	90900	99900
46	2	OYSTER 46	KTH	SA/CR	FBG	KL	IB	72D	PERK	14		32000	6	6	151500	166500
		1981 BOATS														
26	2	OYSTER 26	SLP	SA/RC	FBG	KL	IB	D		9	10	6350	4	9	18300	20300
28		OYSTER 26	SLP	SA/RC	FBG	KL	SD	8D-	13D	9	10	6350	4	9	19500	21700
33	6	OYSTER 34	SLP	SA/RC	FBG	KL	SD	13D	VLVO	10	10	9160	6		32700	36300
35		OYSTER-MARINER 35	SLP	SA/CR	FBG	KL	SD	23D	VLVO	12		16000	5	3	59200	65100
35		OYSTER-MARINER 35	SLP	SA/CR	FBG	KL	IB	40D	PERK	12		16000	5	3	59200	65100
35		OYSTER-MARINER 35	KTH	SA/CR	FBG	KL	SD	23D	VLVO	12		16000	5	3	60100	66000
35		OYSTER-MARINER 35	KTH	SA/CR	FBG	KL	SD	35D	VLVO	12		16000	5	3	60200	66200
35		OYSTER-MARINER 35	KTH	SA/CR	FBG	KL	IB	40D	PERK	12		16000	5	3	60100	66000
35		OYSTER-MARINER 35	SLP	SA/RC	FBG	KL	SD	35D	VLVO	12		16000	5	3	59300	65100
37		OYSTER 37	SLP	SA/RC	FBG	KL	SD	23D	VLVO	12	1	13800	6	3	57400	63100
37		OYSTER 37	SLP	SA/RC	FBG	KL	SD	35D	VLVO	12	1	13800	6	3	57600	63300
37		OYSTER 37	SLP	SA/RC	FBG	KL	IB	40D	PERK	12	1	13800	6	3	57400	63100
39	6	OYSTER 39	KTH	SA/CR	FBG	KL	IB	40D	PERK	12	10	19500	5	10	88800	97600
39	6	OYSTER 39	KTH	SA/CR	FBG	KL	IB	72D	PERK	12	10	19500	5	10	89400	98300
39	8	OYSTER 41	SLP	SA/RC	FBG	KL	SD	23D	VLVO	13	7	13000	6	10	64800	71200
39	8	OYSTER 41	SLP	SA/RC	FBG	KL	SD	35D	VLVO	13	7	13000	6	10	65100	71600
42	5	OYSTER 43	SLP	SA/RC	FBG	KL	IB	36D	VLVO	14	1	16600	7	6	86400	95000
46	2	OYSTER 46	KTH	SA/CR	FBG	KL	IB	72D	PERK	14		32000	6	6	143500	158000
		1980 BOATS														
28		OYSTER 26	SLP	SA/CR	FBG	KL	SD	8D	VLVO	9	10	6350	4	9	18800	20900
33	6	OYSTER 34	SLP	SA/CR	FBG	KL	SD	13D	VLVO	10	10	9160	6		31000	34500
35	1	OYSTER-MARINER 35	SLP	SA/CR	FBG	KL	SD	23D	VLVO	12	5	17116	5	3	59700	65600
35	1	OYSTER-MARINER 35	SLP	SA/CR	FBG	KL	IB	40D	PERK	12	5	17116	5	3	59700	65600
35	1	OYSTER-MARINER 35	KTH	SA/CR	FBG	KL	SD	23D	VLVO	12	5	17116	5	3	60700	66700
35	1	OYSTER-MARINER 35	KTH	SA/CR	FBG	KL	IB	40D	PERK	12	5	17116	5	3	60700	66700
37		OYSTER 37	SLP	SA/CR	FBG	KL	SD	23D	VLVO	12		13800	6	3	54800	60300
37		OYSTER 37	SLP	SA/CR	FBG	KL	IB	40D	PERK	12		13800	6	3	54800	60300
37		OYSTER 37	SLP	SA/RC	FBG	KL	SD	23D	VLVO	12		13800	6	3	54800	60200
39	6	OYSTER 39	KTH	SA/CR	FBG	KL	IB	40D	PERK	12	10	19500	5	10	84700	93100
39	6	OYSTER 39	KTH	SA/CR	FBG	KL	IB	72D	PERK	12	10	19500	5	10	85300	93700
39	8	OYSTER 41	SLP	SA/RC	FBG	KL	SD	23D	VLVO	13	7	13000	6	10	61700	67800
46	2	OYSTER 46	KTH	SA/CR	FBG	KL	IB	72D	PERK	14		32000	6	6	137000	150500
		1979 BOATS														
25	8	OYSTER 25	SLP	SA/RC	FBG	KL	IB	D		8		2569	4	8	7050	8100
26	2	OYSTER 26	SLP	SA/CR	FBG	KL	SD	8D	VLVO	9	10	6350	4	9	16200	18400
30	10	OYSTER 31	SLP	SA/RC	FBG	KL	IB	D		10	7	7750	5	6	23800	26400
33	6	OYSTER 34	SLP	SA/CR	FBG	KL	SD	13D	VLVO	10	10	9160	6		29700	33000
34	4	OYSTER 34	SLP	SA/RC	FBG	KL	IB	D		11		10214	6		34300	38100
35		OYSTER-MARINER 35	KTH	SA/CR	FBG	KL	IB	40D	PERK	12	5	16000	5	3	54800	60200
37		OYSTER 37	SLP	SA/CR	FBG	KL	SD	23D	VLVO	12		13800	6	3	52900	58100
37		OYSTER 37	SLP	SA/RC	FBG	KL	IB	D		12		13000	6	3	50200	55200
39	6	OYSTER 39	KTH	SA/CR	FBG	KL	IB	D		12	10	19500	5	8	81800	89900
39	6	OYSTER 39	KTH	SA/CR	FBG	KL	IB	40D	PERK	12	10	19500	5	10	81200	89200
46	2	OYSTER 46	KTH	SA/CR	FBG	KL	IB	72D	PERK	14		32000	6	6	131000	144000
		1978 BOATS														
30	11	OYSTER 31	SLP	SA/CR	FBG	KL	IB	D		10	2	7632	5	6	22600	25100
34	4	OYSTER 34	SLP	SA/CR	FBG	KL	IB	36D	LEYL	11		10236	6		33300	37000
37		OYSTER 37	SLP	SA/CR	FBG	KL	IB	32D	LEYL	12		13800	6	3	50800	55900

OZARK BOAT WORKS INC

COAST GUARD MFG ID- XBW

Call 1-800-327-6929 for BUC Personalized Evaluation Service
Or, for 1978 to 1993 boats, sign onto www.BUCValuPro.com

P & D BOAT CORP
COAST GUARD MFG ID- PDC

Call 1-800-327-6929 for BUC Personalized Evaluation Service
Or, for 1978 boats, sign onto www.BUCValuPro.com

P & M WORLDWIDE INC

Call 1-800-327-6929 for BUC Personalized Evaluation Service
Or, for 1981 to 1983 boats, sign onto www.BUCValuPro.com

P P I MARINE DIV
PLEASURE PRODUCTS INC   COAST GUARD MFG ID- PPH

Call 1-800-327-6929 for BUC Personalized Evaluation Service
Or, for 1978 to 1980 boats, sign onto www.BUCValuPro.com

P-SQUARED BOAT

Call 1-800-327-6929 for BUC Personalized Evaluation Service
Or, for 1980 boats, sign onto www.BUCValuPro.com

PACEMAKER
DIV OF SEIDELMANN YACHTS
BERLIN NJ 08009   COAST GUARD MFG ID- XFR

See inside cover to adjust price for area

For more recent years, see the BUC Used Boat Price Guide, Volume 1 or Volume 2

LOA FT	LOA IN	NAME AND/ OR MODEL	TOP/ RIG	BOAT TYPE	HULL MTL	HULL TP	ENGINE TP	ENGINE # HP	ENGINE MFG	BEAM FT	BEAM IN	WGT LBS	DRAFT FT	DRAFT IN	RETAIL LOW	RETAIL HIGH
		1983 BOATS														
23	10	SEIDELMANN 24	SLP	SA/RC	FBG	KC	OB			8		3000	1	11	4600	5250
24	2	SEIDELMANN 245	SLP	SA/CR	FBG	KL				8		3000	1	11	4650	5350
24	6	SEIDELMANN 25	SLP	SA/RC	FBG	KL	OB			9	6	4600	4	4	6900	7950
28	5	SEIDELMANN 285	SLP	SA/CR	FBG	KL	OB			10		5400	5	1	9300	10500
29	5	SEIDELMANN 295	SLP	SA/CR	FBG	KC	OB			10	2	7200	3	3	12600	14300
29	5	SEIDELMANN 295	SLP	SA/CR	FBG	KC	IB	12D	YAN	10	2	7400	3	3	13200	15000
29	11	SEIDELMANN 30T	SLP	SA/CR	FBG	KL	IB	15D	YAN	11		8800	5	5	15800	17900
29	11	SEIDELMANN 30T SHOAL	SLP	SA/CR	FBG	KL	IB	15D	YAN	11		8800	4	2	15800	17900
34		SEIDELMANN 34 DEEP	SLP	SA/CR	FBG	KL	IB	23D	YAN	11	10	11000	5	5	19600	21800
34		SEIDELMANN 34 MID	SLP	SA/CR	FBG	KL	IB	23D	YAN	11	10	11000	4	9	19600	21800
34		SEIDELMANN 34 SHOAL	SLP	SA/CR	FBG	KL	IB	23D	YAN	11	10	11000	3	11	19600	21800
36	10	SEIDELMANN 37 DEEP	SLP	SA/CR	FBG	KL	IB	23D	YAN	12		13500	5	11	24800	27600
36	10	SEIDELMANN 37 MID	SLP	SA/CR	FBG	KL	IB	23D	YAN	12		13500	4	11	24800	27600
36	10	SEIDELMANN 37 SHOAL	SLP	SA/CR	FBG	KL	IB	23D	YAN	12		13900	4		25500	28300
		1982 BOATS														
23	10	SEIDELMANN 24	SLP	SA/CR	FBG	KC				8		3000	1	11	4250	4950
24	2	SEIDELMANN 245	SLP	SA/CR	FBG	KL				8		3000	1	11	4400	5050
24	6	SEIDELMANN 25	SLP	SA/CR	FBG	KL	OB			9	6	4600	4	4	6500	7450
24	6	SEIDELMANN 25	SLP	SA/CR	FBG	KL	IB	8D	YAN	9	6	4600	4	4	7050	8100
24	6	SEIDELMANN 25 SHOAL	SLP	SA/CR	FBG	KL	OB			9	6	4600	3	4	6500	7450
24	6	SEIDELMANN 25 SHOAL	SLP	SA/CR	FBG	KL	IB	8D	YAN	9	6	4600	3	4	7050	8100
29	11	SEIDELMANN 299	SLP	SA/CR	FBG	KL	IB	15D	YAN	11		8000	5	5	13500	15300
29	11	SEIDELMANN 299 SHOAL	SLP	SA/CR	FBG	KL	IB	15D	YAN	11		8000	4	2	13500	15300
29	11	SEIDELMANN 30T	SLP	SA/CR	FBG	KL	IB	15D	YAN	11		8800	5	5	14800	16800
29	11	SEIDELMANN 30T SHOAL	SLP	SA/CR	FBG	KL	IB	15D	YAN	11		8800	4	2	14800	16800
34		SEIDELMANN 34 DEEP	SLP	SA/CR	FBG	KL	IB	23D	YAN	11	10	11000	5	5	18600	20700
34		SEIDELMANN 34 MID	SLP	SA/CR	FBG	KL	IB	23D	YAN	11	10	11000	4	9	18600	20700
34		SEIDELMANN 34 SHOAL	SLP	SA/CR	FBG	KL	IB	23D	YAN	11	10	11000	3	11	18600	20700
36	10	SEIDELMANN 37 DEEP	SLP	SA/CR	FBG	KL	IB	23D	YAN	12		13500	5	11	23300	25900
36	10	SEIDELMANN 37 MID	SLP	SA/CR	FBG	KL	IB	23D	YAN	12		13500	4	11	23300	25900
36	10	SEIDELMANN 37 SHOAL	SLP	SA/CR	FBG	KL	IB	23D	YAN	12		13900	4		23900	26600
		1981 BOATS														
23		SONAR	SLP	SA/OD	FBG	KL	OB			7	10	2300	3	10	3200	3700
24	6	SEIDELMANN 25	SLP	SA/CR	FBG	KL	OB			9	6	4600	4	4	6100	7050
24	6	SEIDELMANN 25	SLP	SA/CR	FBG	KL	IB	8D	YAN	9	6	4600	4	4	6650	7650
24	6	SEIDELMANN 25 SHOAL	SLP	SA/CR	FBG	KL	OB			9	6	4600	3	4	6100	7050
24	6	SEIDELMANN 25 SHOAL	SLP	SA/CR	FBG	KL	IB	8D	YAN	9	6	4600	3	4	6650	7650
29	11	SEIDELMANN 299	SLP	SA/CR	FBG	KL	IB	15D	YAN	11		8000	5	5	12700	14400
29	11	SEIDELMANN 299 SHOAL	SLP	SA/CR	FBG	KL	IB	15D	YAN	11		8000	4	2	12700	14400
29	11	SEIDELMANN 30T	SLP	SA/CR	FBG	KL	IB	15D	YAN	11		8800	5	5	13900	15800
29	11	SEIDELMANN 30T SHOAL	SLP	SA/CR	FBG	KL	IB	15D	YAN	11		8800	4	2	13900	15800
36	10	SEIDELMANN 37	SLP	SA/CR	FBG	KL	IB	23D	YAN	12		13000	5	11	21200	23600
36	10	SEIDELMANN 37 SHOAL	SLP	SA/CR	FBG	KL	IB	23D	YAN	12		13000	4	11	21200	23600
47		SEIDELMANN 47	KTH	SA/CR	FBG	KL	IB	D		14		24000	6		52200	57300
		1980 BOATS														
23		SONAR	SLP	SA/OD	FBG	KL	OB			7	10	2100	3	10	2900	3350
24	6	SEIDELMANN 25	SLP	SA/CR	FBG	KL	OB			9	6	4600	4	4	5850	6700
24	6	SEIDELMANN 25	SLP	SA/CR	FBG	KL	IB	8D	YAN	9	6	4600	4	4	6350	7300
24	6	SEIDELMANN 25 SHOAL	SLP	SA/CR	FBG	KL	OB			9	6	4600	3	4	5850	6700
24	6	SEIDELMANN 25 SHOAL	SLP	SA/CR	FBG	KL	IB	8D	YAN	9	6	4600	3	4	6350	7300
29	11	SEIDELMANN 299	SLP	SA/CR	FBG	KL	IB	15D	YAN	11		8000	5	5	11500	13100
29	11	SEIDELMANN 299 SHOAL	SLP	SA/CR	FBG	KL	IB	15D	YAN	11		8000	4	2	11500	13100
29	11	SEIDELMANN 30T	SLP	SA/CR	FBG	KL	IB	15D	YAN	11		8000	5	5	12700	14400
29	11	SEIDELMANN 30T SHOAL	SLP	SA/CR	FBG	KL	IB	15D	YAN	11		8000	4	2	12700	14400
36	10	SEIDELMANN 37	SLP	SA/CR	FBG	KL	IB	24D	UNIV	12		13000	5	11	20300	22500
36	10	SEIDELMANN 37 SHOAL	SLP	SA/CR	FBG	KL	IB	24D	UNIV	12		13000	4	11	20300	22500
		1979 BOATS														
24	6	SEIDELMANN 25	SLP	SA/CR	FBG	KL	OB			9	6	4600	4	4	5600	6450
24	6	SEIDELMANN 25 SHOAL	SLP	SA/CR	FBG	KL	IB	8D	YAN	9	6	4600	3	4	6100	7000
29	11	SEIDELMANN 299	SLP	SA/CR	FBG	KL	IB	15D	YAN	11		8000	5	5	11600	13200
29	11	SEIDELMANN 299 SHOAL	SLP	SA/CR	FBG	KL	IB	15D	YAN	11		8000	4	2	11600	13200
36	10	SEIDELMANN 37	SLP	SA/CR	FBG	KL	IB	24D		12		12000	5	11	18400	20400

PACEMAKER YACHT CO
DIV OF MISSION MARINE
BERLIN NJ 08009   COAST GUARD MFG ID- PAC
SEE ALSO ALGLAS CORP

See inside cover to adjust price for area

LOA FT	LOA IN	NAME AND/ OR MODEL	TOP/ RIG	BOAT TYPE	HULL MTL	HULL TP	ENGINE TP	ENGINE # HP	ENGINE MFG	BEAM FT	BEAM IN	WGT LBS	DRAFT FT	DRAFT IN	RETAIL LOW	RETAIL HIGH
		1980 BOATS														
25	10	EXPRESS CRUISER		EXP	FBG	SV	IB	220	CRUS	9	8	6500	2	2	11700	13200
25	10	EXPRESS CRUISER		EXP	FBG	SV	IB	T125	VLVO	9	8	6500	2	2	12100	13700
25	10	HARDTOP CRUISER	HT	CR	FBG	SV	IB	220	CRUS	9	8	6500	2	2	11700	13200
25	10	HARDTOP CRUISER	HT	CR	FBG	SV	IB	T125	VLVO	9	8	6500	2	2	12100	13700
25	10	SPORT FISHERMAN		SF	FBG	SV	IB	220	CRUS	9	8	6500	2	2	11700	13200
25	10	SPORT FISHERMAN		SF	FBG	SV	IB	T125	VLVO	9	8	6500	2	2	12100	13700
25	10	WAHOO		CTRCN	FBG	SV	IB	220-270		9	10	6400	1	8	11600	13400
25	10	WAHOO		CTRCN	FBG	SV	IB	T125	VLVO	9	10	6400	1	8	12000	13600
26		EXPRESS CRUISER		EXP	FBG	SV	IB	220		9	8	6500			11600	13200
26		FLYBRIDGE CRUISER	FB	SF	FBG	SV	IB	220		9	8	6500			11600	13200
26		HARDTOP CRUISER	HT	CR	FBG	SV	IB	220		9	8	6400			11500	13100
26		WAHOO	OP	OPFSH	FBG	SV	IB	220		9	10	6500			11500	13100
30		FLYBRIDGE CRUISER	FB	SF	FBG	SV	IB	T220		11	6	10500			20800	23200
30		FLYBRIDGE EXP CR	FB	EXP	FBG	SV	IB	T220		11	6	10500			20800	23200
30	8	EXPRESS CRUISER		EXP	FBG	SV	IB	T220	CRUS	11	6	10000	2	6	21600	24000
30	8	EXPRESS CRUISER		EXP	FBG	SV	IB	T124D	VLVO	11	6	10000	2	6	25300	28200
30	8	SPORT FISHERMAN		SF	FBG	SV	IB	T220	CRUS	11	6	10000	2	6	21600	24000
30	8	SPORT FISHERMAN		SF	FBG	SV	IB	T124D	VLVO	11	6	10000	2	6	25300	28200
32		FLYBRIDGE SDN CR	FB	SDN	FBG	SV	IB	T220		12	4	12000			27800	30900
33		SEDAN CRUISER		SDN	FBG	SV	IB	T270	CRUS	13	2	16653	2	5	33100	36800
33		SEDAN CRUISER		SDN	FBG	SV	IB	T235D-T270D		13	2	16653	2	5	46000	52400
33		SPORT FISHERMAN	FB	SF	FBG	SV	IB	T350	CRUS	13	2	16653	2	5	32400	36000
33		SPORT FISHERMAN	FB	SF	FBG	SV	IB	T235D-T270D		13	2	16653	2	5	41900	48000
36		SPORT FISHERMAN		SF	FBG	SV	IB	T350	CRUS	13	3	17100	3		43200	48000
36		SPORT FISHERMAN		SF	FBG	SV	IB	T235D	VLVO	13	3	17100	3		47600	52400
36		SPORT FISHERMAN		SF	FBG	SV	IB	T270D	CAT	13	3	17100	3		50000	55000
38	5	SPORT FISHERMAN		SF	FBG	SV	IB	T350	CRUS	14	5	22400	3	6	56800	62400
		IB T250D CAT 64500 70900, IB T325D GM 66100 72600, IB T435D GM													72000	79100
39	11	MOTOR YACHT		MY	FBG	SV	IB	T350	CRUS	14	1	21200	2	11	59400	65300
39	11	MOTOR YACHT		MY	FBG	SV	IB	T265D	GM	14	1	24000	2	11	72700	79900
46	3	MOTOR YACHT		MY	FBG	SV	IB	T325D	GM	15	3	42000	4		124500	136500
46	3	MOTOR YACHT		MY	FBG	SV	IB	T435D	GM	15	3	41000	4		133500	147000
48	4	SPORT FISHERMAN		SF	FBG	SV	IB	T435D	GM	14	11	40000	3	10	117000	128500
48	4	SPORT FISHERMAN		SF	FBG	SV	IB	T510D	GM	14	11	40000	3	10	125000	137000
57	2	MOTOR YACHT MY57	FB	MY	FBG	DS	IB	T435D	GM	17	2	66300	4	2	194500	213500
62		COCKPIT MY CMY62	FB	YTFS	FBG	DS	IB	T435D	GM	17	2	72000	4	2	228000	251000
62		COCKPIT MY CMY62	FB	YTFS	FBG	DS	IB	T525D	GM	17	2	72000	4	2	243000	267000
62		MOTOR YACHT MY62	FB	MY	FBG	DS	IB	T435D	GM	17	2	73000	4	2	230000	253000
66		MOTOR YACHT MY66	FB	MY	FBG	DS	IB	T675D	GM	17	2	75400	4		292500	321000
		1979 BOATS														
25	10	EXPRESS CRUISER	OP	EXP	FBG	SV	IB	220	CRUS	9	8	6300	2	2	10900	12400
25	10	EXPRESS CRUISER	OP	EXP	FBG	SV	IB	T140	VLVO	9	8	6300	2	2	11500	13100
25	10	FLYBRIDGE CRUISER	FB	SF	FBG	SV	IB	220-270		9	8	6500	2	2	11200	13000
25	10	FLYBRIDGE CRUISER	FB	SF	FBG	SV	IB	T140	VLVO	9	8	6500	2	2	11800	13400
25	10	HARDTOP CRUISER	HT	CR	FBG	SV	IB	220	CRUS	9	8	6400	2	2	11000	12600
25	10	HARDTOP CRUISER	HT	CR	FBG	SV	IB	T140	VLVO	9	8	6400	2	2	11600	13200
25	10	WAHOO	OP	OPFSH	FBG	SV	IB	220-270		9	10	6400	1	8	11000	12700

CONTINUED ON NEXT PAGE

LOA FT	LOA IN	NAME AND/ OR MODEL	TOP/ RIG	BOAT TYPE	-HULL- MTL	-HULL- TP	ENGINE TP	ENGINE # HP	ENGINE MFG	BEAM FT	BEAM IN	WGT LBS	DRAFT FT	DRAFT IN	RETAIL LOW	RETAIL HIGH
		1979 BOATS														
25	10	WAHOO	OP	OPFSH	FBG	SV	IB	124D	VLVO	9	10	6400	1	8	13800	15700
25	10	WAHOO	OP	OPFSH	FBG	SV	IB	T140	VLVO	9	10	6400	1	8	11500	13100
30	7	EXPRESS CRUISER	HT	EXP	FBG	SV	IB	T220	CRUS	11	6	9500	2	6	20400	22600
30	7	EXPRESS CRUISER	HT	EXP	FBG	SV	IB	T124D	VLVO	11	6	9500	2	6	24800	27600
30	7	EXPRESS CRUISER	FB	EXP	FBG	SV	IB	T220	CRUS	11	6	10000	2	6	20600	22900
30	7	EXPRESS CRUISER	FB	EXP	FBG	SV	IB	T124D	VLVO	11	6	10000	2	6	24300	27000
30	7	FLYBRIDGE CRUISER	FB	SF	FBG	SV	IB	T220	CRUS	11	6	9800	2	6	20500	22700
30	7	FLYBRIDGE CRUISER	FB	SF	FBG	SV	IB	T124D	VLVO	11	6	9800	2	6	24000	26700
32	3	SEDAN CRUISER	HT	SDN	FBG	SV	IB	T220-T270		12	4	11000	2	6	26800	30900
32	3	SEDAN CRUISER	HT	SDN	FBG	SV	IB	T235D	VLVO	12	4	11000	2	6	36300	40300
32	3	SEDAN CRUISER	FB	SDN	FBG	SV	IB	T220-T270		12	4	12000	2	6	27100	31300
32	3	SEDAN CRUISER	FB	SDN	FBG	SV	IB	T235D	VLVO	12	4	12000	2	6	37300	41400
33		SEDAN CRUISER		SDN	FBG	SV	IB	T270	CRUS	13	2	16653	2	5	31700	35300
33		SEDAN CRUISER		SDN	FBG	SV	IB	T235D	VLVO	13	2	16653	2	5	43800	48700
33		SPORT FISHERMAN	FB	SF	FBG	SV	IB	T350	CRUS	13	2	16653	2	5	31100	34600
33		SPORT FISHERMAN	FB	SF	FBG	SV	IB	T235D	VLVO	13	2	16653	2	5	40300	44800
36		SPORT FISHERMAN		SF	FBG	SV	IB	T350	CRUS	13	3	17100	3		41300	45900
36		SPORT FISHERMAN		SF	FBG	SV	IB	T235D	VLVO	13	3	17100	3		45500	50000
39	11	MOTOR YACHT	FB	MY	FBG	SV	IB	T350	CRUS	14	1	21200	2	11	56700	62400
39	11	MOTOR YACHT	FB	MY	FBG	SV	IB	T257D	GM	14	1	24000	2	11	69200	76000
39	11	SPORT FISHERMAN		SF	FBG	SV	IB	T350	CRUS	13	10	22500	3		60200	66200
39	11	SPORT FISHERMAN		SF	FBG	SV	IB	T325D	GM	13	10	24200	3		72900	80100
46	3	MOTOR YACHT		MY	FBG	SV	IB	T325D	GM	15	3	41000	4		116500	128000
46	3	MOTOR YACHT		MY	FBG	SV	IB	T425D	GM	15	3	42000	4		129000	141500
48	3	SPORT FISHERMAN		SF	FBG	SV	IB	T D	GM	14	11	40000	3	10	**	**
48	3	SPORT FISHERMAN		SF	FBG	SV	IB	T425D	GM	14	11	40000	3	10	110500	121500
57	2	MOTOR YACHT MY57	FB	MY	FBG	SV	IB	T425D	GM	17	2	66300	4		183500	201500
62		COCKPIT MY CMY62	FB	YTFS	FBG	SV	IB	T425D	GM	17	2	72000	4		216000	237500
62		COCKPIT MY CMY62	FB	YTFS	FBG	SV	IB	T490D	GM	17	2	72000	4		226500	249000
62		MOTOR YACHT MY62	FB	MY	FBG	SV	IB	T425D	GM	17	2	73000	4		218000	239500
66		MOTOR YACHT MY66	FB	MY	FBG	SV	IB	T650D	GM	17	2	73400	4		271000	297500
		1978 BOATS														
25	10	BIMINI SF26	FB	SF	FBG	SV	IB	220	CRUS	9	8	6500	2	2	10700	12200
25	10	CONCEPT SF26	FB	SF	FBG	SV	IB	220	CRUS	9	8	6500	2	2	9100	10300
25	10	EXPRESS BIMINI C26	OP	EXP	FBG	SV	IB	220	CRUS	9	8	6300	2	2	10400	11900
25	10	EXPRESS CONCEPT C26	OP	EXP	FBG	SV	IB	220	CRUS	9	8	6300	2	2	8900	10100
25	10	EXPRESS SUPER C26	OP	EXP	FBG	SV	IB	220	CRUS	9	8	6300	2	2	12100	13800
25	10	HARDTOP CRUISER C26	HT	CR	FBG	SV	IB	220	CRUS	9	8	6400	2	2	10600	12000
25	10	SUPER SF26	FB	SF	FBG	SV	IB	220	CRUS	9	8	6500	2	2	12400	14100
25	10	WAHOO	OP	OPFSH	FBG	SV	IB	220	CRUS	9	10	6400	1	8	10500	11900
25	10	WAHOO	OP	OPFSH	FBG	SV	IB	T155	CHRY	9	10	7200	1	8	12000	13600
25	10	WAHOO	TT	OPFSH	FBG	SV	IB	220	CRUS	9	10	7200	1	8	11500	13000
25	10	WAHOO	TT	OPFSH	FBG	SV	IB	T155	CHRY	9	10	7200	1	8	12000	13600
30	8	BIMINI SF30	FB	SF	FBG	SV	IB	T220	CRUS	11	6	9800	2	6	20000	22200
30	8	CONCEPT SF30	FB	SF	FBG	SV	IB	T220	CRUS	11	6	9800	2	6	17300	19600
30	8	EXPRESS BIMINI C30	HT	EXP	FBG	SV	IB	T220	CRUS	11	6	10000	2	6	20100	22400
30	8	EXPRESS BIMINI C30	FB	EXP	FBG	SV	IB	T220	CRUS	11	6	10000	2	6	20100	22300
30	8	EXPRESS CONCEPT C30	HT	EXP	FBG	SV	IB	T220	CRUS	11	6	10000	2	6	17400	19800
30	8	EXPRESS CONCEPT C30	FB	EXP	FBG	SV	IB	T220	CRUS	11	6	10000	2	6	17600	20000
30	8	EXPRESS SUPER C30	HT	EXP	FBG	SV	IB	T220	CRUS	11	6	10000	2	6	21900	24400
30	8	EXPRESS SUPER C30	FB	EXP	FBG	SV	IB	T220	CRUS	11	6	10000	2	6	21800	24200
30	8	SUPER SF30	FB	SF	FBG	SV	IB	T220	CRUS	11	6	9800	2	6	21800	24300
32	3	SEDAN CRUISER C32	HT	SDN	FBG	SV	IB	T220	CRUS	12	4	12000	2	6	26000	28900
32	3	SEDAN CRUISER C32	FB	SDN	FBG	SV	IB	T220	CRUS	12	4	12000	2	6	26000	28900
36		SPORT FISHERMAN SF36	FB	SF	FBG	SV	IB	T350	CRUS	13	3	17100	3		39500	43900
39	11	MOTOR YACHT MY40	FB	MY	FBG	SV	IB	T350	CRUS	13	11	21200	2	11	54700	60100
39	11	MOTOR YACHT MY40	FB	MY	FBG	SV	IB	T257D	GM	13	11	23000	2	11	64500	70900
39	11	SPORT FISHERMAN SF40	FB	SF	FBG	SV	IB	T350	CRUS	13	10	18500	3		49300	54200
39	11	SPORT FISHERMAN SF40	FB	SF	FBG	SV	IB	T325D	GM	13	10	20098	3		61200	67200
46	3	MOTOR YACHT MY46	FB	MY	FBG	SV	IB	T325D	GM	15	3	41500	4		98800	108500
46	3	MOTOR YACHT MY46	FB	MY	FBG	SV	IB	T425D	GM	15	3	41500	4		106000	116500
48	4	SPORT FISHERMAN SF48	FB	SF	FBG	SV	IB	T425D	GM	14	11	39800	3	10	103500	114000
57	2	MOTOR YACHT MY57	FB	MY	FBG	SV	IB	T425D	GM	17	2		4		140000	154000
62		COCKPIT MY CMY62	FB	YTFS	FBG	SV	IB	T490D	GM	17	2		4		204500	225000
62		MOTOR YACHT MY62	FB	MY	FBG	SV	IB	T425D	GM	17	2		4		198000	217500
66		MOTOR YACHT MY66	FB	MY	FBG	SV	IB	T650D	GM	17	2		4		261500	287500
		1977 BOATS														
25	10	EXPRESS CRUISER C26	OP	EXP	FBG	SV	IB	220-270		9	8	6500	2	2	10300	11900
25	10	HARDTOP CRUISER C26	HT	CR	FBG	SV	IB	220-270		9	8	6500	2	2	10300	11900
25	10	SPORT FISHERMAN SF26	FB	SF	FBG	SV	IB	220-270		9	8	6500	2	2	10300	11900
25	10	WAHOO	OP	OPFSH	FBG	SV	IB	220-270		9	8	6400	1	8	10100	11700
25	10	WAHOO	OP	OPFSH	FBG	SV	IB	350	CRUS	9	8	6800	1	8	11100	12600
25	10	WAHOO	OP	OPFSH	FBG	SV	IB	T155	CHRY	9	8	7200	1	8	11500	13100
25	10	WAHOO	TT	OPFSH	FBG	SV	IB	220-270		9	8	6400	1	8	10100	11700
25	10	WAHOO	TT	OPFSH	FBG	SV	IB	350	CRUS	9	8	6800	1	8	11100	12600
25	10	WAHOO	TT	OPFSH	FBG	SV	IB	T155	CHRY	9	8	7200	1	8	11500	13100
30	8	EXPRESS CRUISER C30	HT	EXP	FBG	SV	IB	220-270		11	6	9100	2	6	16700	19500
30	8	EXPRESS CRUISER C30	HT	EXP	FBG	SV	IB	T220-T270		11	6	10000	2	6	19100	21900
30	8	EXPRESS CRUISER C30	FB	EXP	FBG	SV	IB	220-270		11	6	9100	2	6	16700	19500
30	8	EXPRESS CRUISER C30	FB	EXP	FBG	SV	IB	T220-T270		11	6	9100	2	6	18900	21500
30	8	SF30 4 SLEEPER	FB	SF	FBG	SV	IB	220-270		11	6	9100	2	6	13700	15900
30	8	SF30 4 SLEEPER	FB	SF	FBG	SV	IB	T220-T270		11	6	10000	2	6	18800	21400
30	8	SF30 6 SLEEPER	FB	SF	FBG	SV	IB	220-270		11	6	9100	2	6	14500	16900
30	8	SF30 6 SLEEPER	FB	SF	FBG	SV	IB	T220-T270		11	6	10000	2	6	19600	22500
32	3	SEDAN CRUISER C32	HT	SDN	FBG	SV	IB	T220-T270		12		12200	2	4	25000	28800
32	3	SEDAN CRUISER C32	FB	SDN	FBG	SV	IB	T220-T270		12		12200	2	4	25000	28800
36		SPORT FISHERMAN SF36	FB	SF	FBG	SV	IB	T270	CRUS	13	3	17100	2	9	36700	40800
		IB T330 CHRY 37200 41300, IB T350 CRUS 37800 42000, IB T197D GM													40900	45500
		IB T202D CUM 40900 45400														
39	11	MOTOR YACHT MY40	FB	MY	FBG	SV	IB	T350	CRUS	13	10	21200	2	11	52600	57900
39	11	MOTOR YACHT MY40	FB	MY	FBG	SV	IB	T257D	GM	13	10	23000	2	11	62000	68200
39	11	MOTOR YACHT MY40	FB	MY	FBG	SV	IB	T325D	GM	13	10	23000	2	11	64500	70900
39	11	SPORT FISHERMAN SF40	FB	SF	FBG	SV	IB	T350	CRUS	13	10	18500	2	8	47500	52200
39	11	SPORT FISHERMAN SF40	FB	SF	FBG	SV	IB	T257D	GM	13	10	20098	2	8	56200	61700
39	11	SPORT FISHERMAN SF40	FB	SF	FBG	SV	IB	T325D	GM	13	10	20098	2	8	58600	64400
46	3	MOTOR YACHT MY46	HT	MY	FBG	SV	IB	T325D	GM	15	3	41500	4		93900	103000
46	3	MOTOR YACHT MY46	HT	MY	FBG	SV	IB	T425D	GM	15	3	41500	4		102000	112000
46	3	MOTOR YACHT MY46	FB	MY	FBG	SV	IB	T325D	GM	15	3	41500	4		94700	104000
46	3	MOTOR YACHT MY46	FB	MY	FBG	SV	IB	T425D	GM	15	3	41500	4		101500	111500
48	4	SPORT FISHERMAN SF48	FB	SF	FBG	SV	IB	T325D	GM	14	10	39800	3	8	93700	103000
48	4	SPORT FISHERMAN SF48	FB	SF	FBG	SV	IB	T425D	GM	14	10	39800	3	8	99300	109000
57	2	MOTOR YACHT MY57	HT	MY	FBG	SV	IB	T325D	GM	17	2	66300	4		157000	172500
57	2	MOTOR YACHT MY57	HT	MY	FBG	SV	IB	T425D	GM	17	2	66300	4		172000	189000
57	2	MOTOR YACHT MY57	HT	MY	FBG	SV	IB	T490D	GM	17	2	66300	4		180500	198500
62		MOTOR YACHT MY62	FB	DCMY	FBG	SV	IB	T425D	GM	17	2		4		172000	189000
62		MOTOR YACHT MY62	FB	DCMY	FBG	SV	IB	T490D	GM	17	2		4		176500	194000
62		MOTOR YACHT MY62C	FB	DCCPT	FBG	SV	IB	T425D	GM	17	2		4		170500	187000
62		MOTOR YACHT MY62C	FB	DCCPT	FBG	SV	IB	T490D	GM	17	2		4		175000	192000
66	9	MOTOR YACHT MY66	FB	DCMY	FBG	SV	IB	T490D	GM	17	2		4	1	238000	261500
66	9	MOTOR YACHT MY66	FB	DCMY	FBG	SV	IB	T650D	GM	17	2		4	1	254500	279500
		1976 BOATS														
25	10	EXPRESS CRUISER	OP	EXP	FBG	SV	IB	220-270		9	8	6300	2	2	9650	11200
25	10	HARDTOP CRUISER	HT	CR	FBG	SV	IB	220-270		9	8	6400	2	2	9750	11300
25	10	SPORT FISHERMAN	FB	SF	FBG	SV	IB	220-270		9	8	6500	2	2	9900	11500
28	3	EXPRESS CRUISER	OP	EXP	FBG	SV	IB	220-270		11	2	8200	2	5	12200	14300
28	3	EXPRESS CRUISER	OP	EXP	FBG	SV	IB	T220-T270		11	2	8200	2	5	13700	16100
28	3	SPORT FISHERMAN	FB	SF	FBG	SV	IB	220-270		11	2	8400	2	5	12400	14400
28	3	SPORT FISHERMAN	FB	SF	FBG	SV	IB	T220-T270		11	2	8400	2	5	13800	16200
30	7	EXPRESS CRUISER	HT	EXP	FBG	SV	IB	220-270		11	6	10000	2	6	16400	19000
30	7	EXPRESS CRUISER	HT	EXP	FBG	SV	IB	T220-T270		11	6	10000	2	6	18400	21100
30	7	EXPRESS CRUISER	FB	EXP	FBG	SV	IB	220-270		11	6	10000	2	6	16400	19000
30	7	EXPRESS CRUISER	FB	EXP	FBG	SV	IB	T220-T270		11	6	10000	2	6	18400	21100
30	7	SPORT FISHERMAN-4	FB	SF	FBG	SV	IB	220-270		11	6	9800	2	6	15800	18400
30	7	SPORT FISHERMAN-4	FB	SF	FBG	SV	IB	T220-T270		11	6	9800	2	6	17400	20500
30	7	SPORT FISHERMAN-6	FB	SF	FBG	SV	IB	220-270		11	6	9800	2	6	16700	19500
30	7	SPORT FISHERMAN-6	FB	SF	FBG	SV	IB	T220-T270		11	6	9800	2	6	18800	21300
32	3	SEDAN CRUISER	HT	SDN	FBG	SV	IB	T220-T270		12	4	12000	2	6	24000	27600
32	3	SEDAN CRUISER	HT	SDN	FBG	SV	IB	T160D	PERK	12	4	12000	2	6	30700	34100
32	3	SEDAN CRUISER	FB	SDN	FBG	SV	IB	T220-T270		12	4	12000	2	6	24000	27600
32	3	SEDAN CRUISER	FB	SDN	FBG	SV	IB	T160D	PERK	12	4	12000	2	6	30700	34100
32	3	SPORT FISHERMAN	FB	SF	FBG	SV	IB	T220-T270		12	4	13600	2	6	22800	26100
36		DOUBLE CABIN	FB	DC	FBG	SV	IB	T270	CRUS	13	3	18850	3	2	37200	41300
		IB T330 CHRY 37600 41800, IB T350 CRUS 38200 42500, IB T202D CUM													41700	46300
36		SPORT FISHERMAN	FB	SF	FBG	SV	IB	T270	CRUS	13	3	17100	3		35200	39100
		IB T330 CHRY 35700 39600, IB T350 CRUS 36300 40300, IB T202D CUM													39200	43600
		IB T216D GM 39700 44100														
39	11	MOTOR YACHT	FB	MY	FBG	SV	IB	T330	CHRY	14	1	21200	2	11	48900	53800
		IB T350 CRUS 49900 54800, IB T202D CUM 53700 59000, IB T216D GM													54300	59600
		IB T310D GM 57200 62900														
39	11	SPORT FISHERMAN	FB	SF	FBG	SV	IB	T330	CHRY	13	10	18500	3		44100	49000
		IB T350 CRUS 45600 50100, IB T202D CUM 49100 53900, IB T216D GM													49700	54600
		IB T310D GM 52600 57800														
48	4	SPORT FISHERMAN	FB	SF	FBG	SV	IB	T310D	GM	14	11	39800	3	10	89500	98400
		IB T320D CUM 89800 98700, IB T350D GM 91800 101000, IB T400D CUM													95200	104500

CONTINUED ON NEXT PAGE

```
      LOA  NAME AND/       TOP/ BOAT -HULL- ----ENGINE---  BEAM   WGT  DRAFT RETAIL RETAIL
      FT IN OR MODEL       RIG  TYPE MTL TP TP TP # HP MFG  FT IN  LBS  FT IN LOW    HIGH
--------------------- 1976 BOATS ---------------------
48  4 SPORT FISHERMAN           SF  FBG SV IB T435D GM  14 11 39800  3 10  89200 108000
62  4 COCKPIT YACHT        FB MYCPT FBG SV IB T350D GM  17  2 72000  4    180500 198500
      IB T400D CUM 190500 209000, IB T435D GM 193000 212000, IB T525D GM 205500 226000

62    MOTOR YACHT          FB  MY   FBG SV IB T350D GM  17  2 73000  4    180500 198000
      IB T400D CUM 190500 209500, IB T435D GM 193000 212000, IB T525D GM 205500 225500

--------------------- 1975 BOATS ---------------------
25 10 EXPRESS CRUISER      OP  EXP  FBG SV IB 220-275    9  8  6428  2          9400  10900
25 10 FLYBRIDGE CRUISER    FB  CR   FBG SV IB 220-275    9  8  6428  2          9400  10900
25 10 HARDTOP CRUISER      HT  CR   FBG SV IB 220-275    9  8  6428  2          9400  10900
28  3 EXPRESS CRUISER      HT  EXP  FBG SV IB 220-270   11  2  7379  2  5      11200  13000
28  3 EXPRESS CRUISER      HT  EXP  FBG SV IB 220-270   11  2  8179  2  5      13100  15400
28  3 SPORT FISHERMAN      FB  SF   FBG SV IB 220-270   11  2  7604  2  5      11300  13200
28  3 SPORT FISHERMAN      FB  SF   FBG SV IB T220-T270 11  2  8404  2  5      13300  15600
30  7 EXPRESS CRUISER      HT  EXP  FBG SV IB 220-270   11  6  9100  2  6      15300  17800
30  7 EXPRESS CRUISER      HT  EXP  FBG SV IB T220-T270 11  6 10000  2  6      17300  20300
30  7 EXPRESS CRUISER      FB  EXP  FBG SV IB 220-270   11  6  9100  2  6      15300  17800
30  7 EXPRESS CRUISER      FB  EXP  FBG SV IB T220-T270 11  6 10000  2  6      17300  20300

30  7 SPORT FISHERMAN-4    HT  SF   FBG SV IB 220-270   11  6  8900  2  6      12800  14900
30  7 SPORT FISHERMAN-4    HT  SF   FBG SV IB T220-T270 11  6  9800  2  6      17200  20200
30  7 SPORT FISHERMAN-4    FB  SF   FBG SV IB 220-270   11  6  8900  2  6      13100  15200
30  7 SPORT FISHERMAN-4    FB  SF   FBG SV IB T220-T270 11  6  9800  2  6      17600  20600
30  7 SPORT FISHERMAN-6    FB  SF   FBG SV IB 220-270   11  6  8900  2  6      12600  14600
30  7 SPORT FISHERMAN-6    FB  SF   FBG SV IB T220-T270 11  6  9800  2  6      16800  19800
32  3 CONVERTIBLE          HT  SDN  FBG SV IB 220-270   12    12000  2  4      23000  26500
32  3 CONVERTIBLE          HT  SDN  FBG SV IBT160D-T210D 12   12000  2  4      29700  34900
32  3 CONVERTIBLE          FB  SDN  FBG SV IB T220-T270 12    12000  2  4      23000  26500
32  3 CONVERTIBLE          FB  SDN  FBG SV IBT160D-T210D 12   12000  2  4      29700  34900
32  3 SPORT CRUISER        FB SPTCR FBG SV IB T220-T270 12    13600  2  4      21900  25000
32  3 SPORT CRUISER        FB SPTCR FBG SV IBT160D-T210D 12   13600  2  4      28500  32900

36    DOUBLE CABIN         FB  DC   FBG SV IB T270 CRUS 13  3 18849  2  5      35700  39700
      IB T330 CHRY 36100 40100, IB T350 CRUS 36700 40800, IB T210D CUM 42600 47300

36    SPORT FISHERMAN      HT  SF   FBG SV IB T270 CRUS 13  3 17100  2  3      33800  37600
      IB T330 CHRY 34200 38000, IB T350 CRUS 34800 38700, IB T210D CUM 37800 42000
      IB T216D GM 38100 42300

36    SPORT FISHERMAN      FB  SF   FBG SV IB T270 CRUS 13  3 17100  2  3      33800  37600
      IB T330 CHRY 34200 38000, IB T350 CRUS 34800 38700, IB T210D CUM 37800 42100
      IB T216D GM 38100 42300

39 11 MOTOR YACHT          HT  MY   FBG SV IB T330 CHRY 14  1 21200  2 11      47200  51900
      IB T350 CRUS 47900 52600, IB T210D CUM 55000 60500, IB T216D GM 55400 60900
      IB T290D GM 57600 63200

39 11 MOTOR YACHT          FB  MY   FBG SV IB T330 CHRY 14  1 21200  2 11      47200  51900
      IB T350 CRUS 47900 52600, IB T210D CUM 55000 60500, IB T216D GM 55400 60900
      IB T290D GM 57600 63200

39 11 SPORT FISHERMAN      FB  SF   FBG SV IB T330 CHRY 13 10 18500  2  8      42400  47100
      IB T350 CRUS 43300 48100, IB T210D CUM 50200 55200, IB T216D GM 50600 55600
      IB T290D GM 52700 58000

48  3 SPORT FISHERMAN      FB  SF   FBG SV IB T174D GM  14 10 39800  3  8      81000  89000
      IB T320D CUM 86200 94700, IB T320D GM 86400 94900, IB T370D CUM 89100 98000
      IB T400D CUM 91300 100500, IB T435D GM 94200 103500

62    COCKPIT MY           HT MYCPT FBG SV IB T320D GM  17  2 66500  4        159500 175000
      IB T370D CUM 165500 182000, IB T400D CUM 169000 186000, IB T435D GM 171500 188500
      IB T480D GM 177500 195000

62    COCKPIT MY           FB MYCPT FBG SV IB T320D GM  17  2 66500  4        159500 175000
      IB T370D CUM 165000 181000, IB T400D CUM 168500 185000, IB T435D GM 171000 187500
      IB T480D GM 176500 194000

62    FLUSH DECK MY        HT  FD   FBG SV IB T174D GM  17  2 66500  4        150500 165500
      IB T370D CUM 163500 179500, IB T400D CUM 167000 183500, IB T435D GM 169500 186500
      IB T480D GM 175500 192500

62    FLUSH DECK MY        FB  FD   FBG SV IB T174D GM  17  2 66500  4        150500 165500
      IB T370D CUM 163000 179000, IB T400D CUM 166500 183000, IB T435D GM 168500 185500
      IB T480D GM 174500 191500

--------------------- 1974 BOATS ---------------------
28  3                      OP  EXP  FBG    IB 220-270   11  2  7379  2  5      10700  12500
28  3                      HT  EXP  FBG    IB T220-T270 11  2  8179  2  5      12600  14800
28  3                      HT  EXP  FBG    IB 220-270   11  2  7379  2  5      10700  12500
28  3                      HT  EXP  FBG    IB T220-T270 11  2  8179  2  5      12600  14800
28  3                      FB  SF   FBG    IB 220-270   11  2  7604  2  5      10900  12700
28  3                      FB  SF   FBG    IB T220-T270 11  2  8404  2  5      12700  15000
30  7                      HT  EXP  FBG    IB 220-270   11  6 10000  2  6      14700  17100
30  7                      HT  EXP  FBG    IB T220-T270 11  6 10000  2  6      16600  19500
30  7                      FB  EXP  FBG    IB 220-270   11  6  9100  2  6      14700  17100
30  7                      FB  EXP  FBG    IB T220-T270 11  6 10000  2  6      16600  19500
30  7 4 SLEEPER            HT  SF   FBG    IB 220-270   11  6  8900  2  6      12300  14300
30  7 4 SLEEPER            HT  SF   FBG    IB T220-T270 11  6  9800  2  6      16500  19400

30  7 4 SLEEPER            FB  SF   FBG    IB 220-270   11  6  8900  2  6      12500  14600
30  7 4 SLEEPER            FB  SF   FBG    IB T220-T270 11  6  9800  2  6      16900  19800
30  7 6 SLEEPER            FB  SF   FBG    IB 220-270   11  6  8900  2  6      12100  14100
30  7 6 SLEEPER            FB  SF   FBG    IB T220-T270 11  6  9800  2  6      16100  19000
32  3                      FB SPTCR FBG    IB 210D CUM  12    13600  2  4      26900  29900
32  3                      FB SPTCR FBG    IB T220-T270 12    13600  2  4      21000  24000
32  3                      FB SPTCR FBG    IB T160D PERK 12   13600  2  4      27700  30800
32  3 CONVERTIBLE          HT  SDN  FBG    IB 210D CUM  12    12000  2  4      26900  29900
32  3 CONVERTIBLE          HT  SDN  FBG    IB T220-T270 12    12000  2  4      21000  25400
32  3 CONVERTIBLE          HT  SDN  FBG    IB T160D PERK 12   12000  2  4      28800  32000
32  3 CONVERTIBLE          FB  SDN  FBG    IB 210D CUM  12    12000  2  4      26900  29900
32  3 CONVERTIBLE          FB  SDN  FBG    IB T220-T270 12    12000  2  4      22100  25400

32  3 CONVERTIBLE          FB  SDN  FBG    IB T160D PERK 12   12000  2  4      28800  32000
36                         FB  DC   FBG    IB T270 CRUS 13  3 17100  2  3      32500  36100
      IB T330 CHRY 32900 36600, IB T350 CRUS 33500 37200, IB T210D CUM 36400 40400

36                         HT  SF   FBG    IB T270 CRUS 13  3 17100  2  3      32500  36100
      IB T330 CHRY 32900 36600, IB T350 CRUS 33500 37200, IB T210D CUM 36400 40400
      IB T216D GM 36600 40700

36                         FB  SF   FBG    IB T270 CRUS 13  3 17100  2  3      32500  36100
      IB T330 CHRY 32900 36600, IB T350 CRUS 33500 37200, IB T210D CUM 36400 40400
      IB T216D GM 36600 40700

39 11                      HT  MY   FBG    IB T330 CHRY 14  1 21200  2 11      45000  49900
      IB T350 CRUS 46300 50900, IB T210D CUM 52900 58200, IB T216D GM 53300 58600
      IB T225D CAT 54600 60000, IB T280D GM 55000 60500

39 11                      FB  MY   FBG    IB T330 CHRY 14  1 21200  2 11      45000  49900
      IB T350 CRUS 46300 50900, IB T210D CUM 52900 58200, IB T216D GM 53300 58600
      IB T225D CAT 54600 60000, IB T280D GM 55000 60500

39 11                      FB  SF   FBG    IB T330 CHRY 13 10 18500  2  8      40800  45300
      IB T350 CRUS 41600 46200, IB T210D CUM 48300 53400, IB T216D GM 48700 53500
      IB T225D CAT 50000 54900, IB T280D GM 50400 55400

48  3                      FB  SF   FBG    IB T280D GM  14 10 39800  3  8      81300  89400
      IB T320D CUM 83100 91300, IB T325D GM 83500 91800, IB T370D CUM 86200 94800
      IB T370D GM 86400 94900

62                         FB  FD   FBG    IB T320D CUM 17  2 39800  4        129500 142500
      IB T325D GM 129500 142500, IB T370D GM 131500 144500, IB T480D GM 137000 150500

62                         FB  FD   FBG    IB T320D CUM 17  2 39800  4        129500 142500
      IB T325D GM 129500 142500, IB T370D GM 131500 144500, IB T480D GM 137000 150500

62    COCKPIT              HT MYCPT FBG    IB T320D CUM 17  2 39800  4        131000 144000
      IB T325D GM 131000 144000, IB T370D GM 133000 146000, IB T480D GM 138500 152000

62    COCKPIT              FB MYCPT FBG    IB T320D CUM 17  2 39800  4        131000 144000
      IB T325D GM 131000 144000, IB T370D GM 133000 146000, IB T480D GM 138500 152000

--------------------- 1973 BOATS ---------------------
25  9                      OP  EXP  FBG    IB 220-270    9 10  5200  2 10      7500   8850
25  9                      HT  EXP  FBG    IB 220-270    9 10  5200  2 10      7500   8850
25  9                      HT  SF   FBG    IB 220-270    9 10  5200  2 10      7500   8850
25  9                      FB  SF   FBG    IB 220-270    9 10  5200  2 10      7500   8850
28  4                      OP  EXP  FBG    IB 220-270   10 11  7379  2  5     10300  12100
28  4                      HT  EXP  FBG    IB 220-270   10 11  7379  2  5     11600  13700
28  4                      HT  EXP  FBG    IB T220-T270 10 11  7379  2  5     10300  12100
28  4                      HT  EXP  FBG    IB T220-T270 10 11  7379  2  5     11600  13700
28  4                      FB  SF   FBG    IB T220-T270 10 11  7604  2  5     10500  12200
28  4                      FB  SF   FBG    IB T220-T270 10 11  7604  2  5     11800  13900
30  7                      HT  EXP  FBG    IB 220-270   11  6  9100  2  6     14100  16500
30  7                      HT  EXP  FBG    IB T220-T270 11  6 10000  2  6     16000  18800
```

```
      NAME AND/      TOP/ BOAT  -HULL-  ----ENGINE---   BEAM   WGT  DRAFT  RETAIL RETAIL
LOA   OR MODEL       RIG  TYPE  MTL TP  TP # HP  MFG    FT IN  LBS  FT IN  LOW    HIGH
FT IN
-------------------- 1973 BOATS ----------------------------------------------------------
30  7                FB   EXP   FBG     IB 220-270    11  6  10000  2  6  14500  16900
30  7                FB   EXP   FBG     IB T220-T270  11  6  10000  2  6  16000  18800
30  7 4 SLEEPER   HT SF         FBG     IB 220-270    11  6   8900  2  6  11800  13800
30  7 4 SLEEPER   HT SF         FBG     IB T220-T270  11  6   9800  2  6  15900  18700
30  7 4 SLEEPER      FB   SF    FBG     IB 220-270    11  6   9800  2  6  14700  17100
30  7 4 SLEEPER      FB   SF    FBG     IB T220-T270  11  6   9800  2  6  16200  19100
30  7 6 SLEEPER      FB   SF    FBG     IB 220-270    11  6   9800  2  6  14100  16500
30  7 6 SLEEPER      FB   SF    FBG     IB T220-T270  11  6   9800  2  6  15500  18300
32  3                FB   SPTCR FBG     IB T220-T270  12     13600  2  4  20200  23100
32  3                FB   SPTCR FBG SV  IB 210D  CUM  12     13600  2  4  26200  29100
32  3                FB   SPTCR FBG SV  IB T160D PERK 12     13600  2  4  27000  30000
32  3 CONVERTIBLE  HT SDN        FBG    IB T220-T270  12     12000  2  4  21200  24500

32  3 CONVERTIBLE  HT SDN        FBG SV IB 210D  CUM  12     12000  2  4  26200  29100
32  3 CONVERTIBLE  HT SDN        FBG SV IB T160D PERK 12     12000  2  4  28100  31200
32  3 CONVERTIBLE     FB SDN     FBG    IB T220-T270  12     12000  2  4  21200  24500
32  3 CONVERTIBLE     FB SDN     FBG SV IB 210D  CUM  12     12000  2  4  26200  29100
32  3 CONVERTIBLE     FB SDN     FBG SV IB T160D PERK 12     12000  2  4  28100  31200
35  2 DRIFT-R-CRUZ HT HB         FBG SV IO 220        12     14000  2  6   6450   7400
36                 HT SF         FBG    IB T270  CRUS 13  3  17100  2  3  31300  34800
     IB T330  CHRY 31700 35200, IB T350 CRUS 32300 35800, IB T210D CUM  35000  38900
     IB T216D GM   35300 39200

36                   FB   SF     FBG    IB T270  CRUS 13  3  17100  2  3  31300  34800
     IB T330  CHRY 31700 35200, IB T350 CRUS 32300 35800, IB T210D CUM  35000  38900
     IB T216D GM   35300 39200

37 10                FB   DC     FBG    IB T330  CHRY 13 10 18000  2  9  34700  38500
     IB T350  CRUS 35400 39400, IB T210D CUM 41800 46500, IB T216D GM   42200  46900
     IB T255D GM   43100 47900

37 10                FB   SDNSF  FBG    IB T330  CHRY 13 10 18000  2  9  34700  38500
     IB T350  CRUS 35400 39300, IB T210D CUM 41800 46500, IB T216D GM   42200  46900
     IB T225D CAT  43300 48100, IB T255D GM  43100 47900

39 11              HT MY         FBG    IB T330  CHRY 14  1 21200  2 11  43300  48100
     IB T350  CRUS 44100 49000, IB T210D CUM 51000 56000, IB T216D GM   51300  56400
     IB T225D CAT  52600 57800, IB T255D GM  52300 57500

39 11                FB   MY     FBG    IB T330  CHRY 14  1 23000  2 11  46800  51500
     IB T350  CRUS 47600 52400, IB T210D CUM 51000 56000, IB T216D GM   51300  56400
     IB T225D CAT  52600 57800, IB T255D GM  52300 57500

48  3 6 SLEEPER      FB   SF     FBG    IB T     FORD 14 10 39800  3  8     **     **
     IB T255D GM   77200 84900, IB T350D GM 81300 89400, IB T370D CUM   82300  90400
     IB T400D GM   84400 92700

62    COCKPIT        FB   MYCPT  FBG SV IB T320D      17  2 39800  4     127500 140000
-------------------- 1972 BOATS ----------------------------------------------------------
25  9              HT EXP        FBG    IB 220-270     9 10  5200  2      7200   8500
25  9                FB   EXP    FBG    IB 220-270     9 10  5200  2      7200   8500
25  9              HT SF         FBG    IB 220-270     9 10  5200  2      7200   8500
25  9                FB   SF     FBG    IB 220-270     9 10  5200  2      7200   8500
28  4              OP EXP        FBG    IB 220-270    10 11  7379  2  5   9900  11600
28  4              OP EXP        FBG    IB T220-T270  10 11  7379  2  5  11200  13200
28  4              HT EXP        FBG    IB 220-270    10 11  7379  2  5   9900  11600
28  4              HT EXP        FBG    IB T220-T270  10 11  7379  2  5  11200  13200
28  4                FB   SF     FBG    IB 220-270    10 11  7379  2  5   9900  11600
28  4                FB   SF     FBG    IB T220-T270  10 11  7379  2  5  11200  13200
32  3                     EXP    FBG    IB T220-T270  12     12200  2  4  19100  21700

32  3              OP EXP        FBG    IB 170D-210D  12     12200  2  4  23800  26500
32  3              OP EXP        FBG    IB T160D PERK 12     12200  2  4  24700  27400
32  3                FB   SPTCR  FBG    IB 170D-210D  12     13600  2  4  26000  28800
32  3                FB   SPTCR  FBG    IB T220-T270  12     13600  2  4  19400  22200
32  3                FB   SPTCR  FBG    IB T160D PERK 12     13600  2  4  26300  29300
32  3 CONVERTIBLE  HT SDN        FBG    IB 170D-210D  12     12200  2  4  25200  28600
32  3 CONVERTIBLE  HT SDN        FBG    IB T220-T270  12     12200  2  4  20500  23600
32  3 CONVERTIBLE  HT SDN        FBG    IB T160D PERK 12     12200  2  4  27600  30600
32  3 CONVERTIBLE     FB SDN     FBG    IB 170D-210D  12     12200  2  4  25200  28600
32  3 CONVERTIBLE     FB SDN     FBG    IB T220-T270  12     12200  2  4  20500  23600
32  3 CONVERTIBLE     FB SDN     FBG    IB T160D PERK 12     12200  2  4  27600  30600

35  2 DRIFT-R-CRUZ HT HB         FBG    IO 215   MRCR 12     14000  2  6   6850   7850
     IO 270 MRCR 7000 8050, IO 325 7350 8450, IO T215 MRCR  7400   8500
     IB T215 MRCR 7500 8600, IB T220 CRUS 7600 8750, IB T225 CHRY  7450  8550
     IO T270 MRCR 7700 8850, IB T270 CRUS 7700 8850

35  2 DRIFT-R-CRUZ    FB HB      FBG    IO 215   MRCR 12     14000  2  6   6850   7850
     IO 270 MRCR 7000 8050, IO 325 7350 8450, IO T215 MRCR  7400   8500
     IB T215 MRCR 7500 8600, IB T220 CRUS 7600 8750, IB T225 CHRY  7450  8550
     IO T270 MRCR 7700 8850, IB T270 CRUS 7700 8850

37 10                FB   DC     FBG    IB T320  CRUS 13 10 18500  2  9  34500  38300
     IB T210D CUM 38100 42300, IB T216D GM 38400 42600, IB T255D GM  39300  43600
     IB T283D GM  40000 44500

37 10                FB   SDNSF  FBG    IB T210D CUM  13 10 18000  2  9  37300  41400
     IB T216D GM  37600 41800, IB T255D GM 38500 42800, IB T283D GM  39300  43600

37 10                FB   SF     FBG    IB T320       13 10 18000  2  9  33700  37500
40                 HT MY         FBG    IB T270  CRUS 13 11 21200  2 11  42200  46900
     IB T320  CRUS 42700 47400, IB T210D CUM 49700 54600, IB T216D GM  50000  55000
     IB T255D GM  51000 56000, IB T283D GM  51700 56800

40                   FB   MY     FBG    IB T270       14  1 23000  2 11  45700  50200
     IB T320  CRUS 46100 50600, IB T210D CUM 49700 54600, IB T216D GM  50000  55000
     IB T255D GM  51000 56000, IB T283D GM  51700 56800

41 10              HT MY         MHG    IB T320  CRUS 14  2 24980  3     50400  55400
41 10              HT MY         P/M    IB T210D CUM  14  2 24980  3     53000  58200
     IB T216D GM  53400 58700, IB T255D GM 55200 60700, IB T283D GM  56500  62100

41 10                FB   MY     MHG    IB T320  CRUS 13 10 24980  3     51400  56500
41 10                FB   MY     P/M    IB T210D CUM  13 10 24980  3     53900  59300
     IB T216D GM  54400 59800, IB T255D GM 56200 61700, IB T283D GM  57500  63200

41 10              HT MYDKH      MHG    IB T320  CRUS 13 10 24980  3     52300  57400
41 10              HT MYDKH      P/M    IB T210D CUM  13 10 24980  3     54700  60100
     IB T216D GM  55200 60600, IB T255D GM 57100 62700, IB T283D GM  58400  64200

41 10              HT SF         MHG    IB T320  CRUS 13 10 24680  3     49900  54800
41 10              HT SF         P/M    IB T210D CUM  13 10 24680  3     51700  56800
     IB T216D GM  52200 57300, IB T255D GM 54200 59600, IB T283D GM  55800  61300

41 10                FB   SF     MHG    IB T320  CRUS 13 10 24680  3     49800  54700
41 10                FB   SF     P/M    IB T210D CUM  13 10 24680  3     51600  56700
     IB T216D GM  52100 57300, IB T255D GM 54100 59500, IB T283D GM  55700  61200

46 11              HT MY         MHG    IB T320  CRUS 14 10 39000  3  4  70000  76900
46 11              HT MY         P/M    IB T255D GM   14 10 39000  3  4  74000  81300
46 11              HT MY         P/M    IB T283D GM   14 10 39000  3  4  75400  82800
46 11                FB   MY     MHG    IB T320  CRUS 14 10 39000  3  4  70600  77600
46 11                FB   MY     P/M    IB T255D GM   14 10 39000  3  4  74900  82300
46 11                FB   MY     P/M    IB T283D GM   14 10 39000  3  4  76600  84200
46 11              HT MYDKH      MHG    IB T320  CRUS 14 10 39000  3  4  74900  82300
46 11              HT MYDKH      P/M    IB T255D GM   14 10 39000  3  4  79000  87300
46 11              HT MYDKH      P/M    IB T283D GM   14 10 39000  3  4  80400  88600
46 11              HT SF         MHG    IB T320  CRUS 14 10 38500  3  4  68400  75700
46 11              HT SF         P/M    IB T255D GM   14 10 38500  3  4  72100  79200
46 11              HT SF         P/M    IB T283D GM   14 10 38500  3  4  73300  80500

46 11                FB   SF     P/M    IB T370D CUM  14    38500  3  4  78600  86400
46 11                FB   SF     MHG    IB T320  CRUS 14    38500  3  4  68000  74800
46 11                FB   SF     P/M    IB T255D GM   14    38500  3  4  71700  78800
46 11                FB   SF     P/M    IB T283D GM   14    38500  3  4  72900  80100
48  3                FB   SF     P/M    IB T350  FORD 14 10 39800  3  4  72200  79300
     IB T255D GM  74400 81800, IB T350D GM 78000 86600, IB T370D CUM  80000  87900
     IB T400D GM  82200 90400

55                 HT MY         MHG    IB T350  FORD 16  4 50000  3  6  95800 105500
55                 HT MY         P/M    IB T350D CUM  16  4 50000  3  6  97200 107100
55                 HT MY         P/M    IB T370D CUM  16  4 50000  3  6  99800 109500
55                 HT MY         P/M    IB T525D GM   16  4 50000  3  6 118000 129500
55                   FB   MY     MHG    IB T350  FORD 16  4 50000  3  6  93700 103000
55                   FB   MY     P/M    IB T350D CUM  16  4 50000  3  6  95000 104500
55                   FB   MY     P/M    IB T370D CUM  16  4 50000  3  6  97600 107600
55                   FB   MY     P/M    IB T525D GM   16  4 50000  3  6 116000 126500
55                 HT SF         MHG    IB T350  FORD 16  4 50000  3  6  97100 106800
55                 HT SF         P/M    IB T350D CUM  16  4 50000  3  6  98400 108000
55                   FB   SF     MHG    IB T350  FORD 16  4 50000  3  6  98400 108000
55                   FB   SF     P/M    IB T370D CUM  16  4 50000  3  6 111000 111000
55                   FB   SF     P/M    IB T525D GM   16  4 50000  3  6 119500 131500

55    COCKPIT        FB   MYCPT  MHG    IB T350  FORD 16  4 50000  3  6  99700 109500
55    COCKPIT        FB   MYCPT  P/M    IB T350D CUM  16  4 50000  3  6 101000 111000
```

PACEMAKER YACHT CO   -CONTINUED   See inside cover to adjust price for area

LOA FT IN	NAME AND/ OR MODEL	TOP/ RIG	BOAT TYPE	HULL MTL	TP	ENGINE TP	#	HP MFG	BEAM FT IN	WGT LBS	DRAFT FT IN	RETAIL LOW	RETAIL HIGH
1972 BOATS												
55	COCKPIT	FB	MYCPT	P/M	IB	T370D	CUM	16 4	50000	3 6	104000	114000
55	COCKPIT	FB	MYCPT	P/M	IB	T525D	GM	16 4	50000	3 6	123000	135000
60		HT	MY	MHG	IB	T350	FORD	16 4	58000	3 6	114500	125500
60		HT	MY	P/M	IB	T350D	GM	16 4	58000	3 6	116000	127000
60		HT	MY	P/M	IB	T370D	CUM	16 4	58000	3 6	119500	131500
60		HT	MY	P/M	IB	T525D	GM	16 4	58000	3 6	138000	152000
60		FB	MY	MHG	IB	T350	FORD	16 4	58000	3 6	113000	124000
60		FB	MY	P/M	IB	T350D	GM	16 4	58000	3 6	114500	126000
60		FB	MY	P/M	IB	T370D	CUM	16 4	58000	3 6	118000	130000
60		FB	MY	P/M	IB	T525D	GM	16 4	58000	3 6	136500	150000
60		HT	SF	MHG	IB	T350	FORD	16 4	58000	3 6	110500	121500
60		HT	SF	P/M	IB	T350D	GM	16 4	58000	3 6	114500	125500
60		HT	SF	P/M	IB	T370D	CUM	16 4	58000	3 6	117000	128500
60		HT	SF	P/M	IB	T525D	GM	16 4	58000	3 6	129500	142000
60		FB	SF	MHG	IB	T350	FORD	16 4	58000	3 6	110000	121000
60		FB	SF	P/M	IB	T350D	GM	16 4	58000	3 6	114000	125500
60		FB	SF	P/M	IB	T370D	CUM	16 4	58000	3 6	116500	128000
60		FB	SF	P/M	IB	T525D	GM	16 4	58000	3 6	128000	141000
60	COCKPIT	HT	MYCPT	MHG	IB	T350	FORD	16 4	58000	3 6	118000	130000
60	COCKPIT	HT	MYCPT	P/M	IB	T350D	GM	16 4	58000	3 6	119500	131000
60	COCKPIT	HT	MYCPT	P/M	IB	T370D	CUM	16 4	58000	3 6	123500	135500
60	COCKPIT	HT	MYCPT	P/M	IB	T525D	GM	16 4	58000	3 6	142500	157000
60	COCKPIT	FB	MYCPT	MHG	IB	T350	FORD	16 4	58000	3 6	116500	128500
60	COCKPIT	FB	MYCPT	P/M	IB	T350D	GM	16 4	58000	3 6	118000	130000
60	COCKPIT	FB	MYCPT	P/M	IB	T370D	CUM	16 4	58000	3 6	122000	134000
60	COCKPIT	FB	MYCPT	P/M	IB	T525D	GM	16 4	58000	3 6	141000	155000
65	PLAN G	HT	MY	MHG	IB	T350	FORD	16 7		4	233000	256000
65	PLAN G	HT	MY	P/M	IB	T350D	GM	16 7		4	170000	187000
65	PLAN G	HT	MY	P/M	IB	T370D	CUM	16 7		4	175000	192000
65	PLAN G	HT	MY	P/M	IB	T525D	GM	16 7		4	190000	208500
65	PLAN G	FB	MY	MHG	IB	T350	FORD	16 7		4	233000	256000
65	PLAN G	FB	MY	P/M	IB	T350D	GM	16 7		4	170000	187000
65	PLAN G	FB	MY	P/M	IB	T370D	CUM	16 7		4	175000	192000
65	PLAN G	FB	MY	P/M	IB	T525D	GM	16 7		4	190000	208500
1971 BOATS												
17 5	WARRIOR 700			FBG	SV	OB		6 8	927		1700	2050
17 5	WARRIOR 700			FBG	SV	IO	120	MRCR 6 8		1 6	2550	3000
19 2	WARRIOR 900			FBG	SV	OB		7 4	1152		2250	2600
19 2	WARRIOR 900			FBG	SV	IO	120	MRCR 7 4		1 8	3450	4000
19 2	WARRIOR 900 CABIN	CBNCR		FBG	SV	OB		7 4	1450		2650	3050
19 2	WARRIOR 900 CABIN	CBNCR		FBG	SV	IO	120	MRCR 7 4		1 8	3700	4300
25 7	WARRIOR 2600	SDN		FBG	DS	IB	210	CRUS 9 6	5200	2	7200	8300
28 4		OP	EXP	FBG		IB	210-260	10 11	7379	2 5	9500	11100
28 4		OP	EXP	FBG		IB	T210-T260	10 11	7379	2 5	10700	12600
28 4		HT	EXP	FBG		IB	210-260	10 11	7379	2 5	9500	11100
28 4		HT	EXP	FBG		IB	T210-T260	10 11	7379	2 5	10700	12600
28 4		FB	SF	FBG		IB	210-260	10 11	7604	2 5	9650	11200
28 4		FB	SF	FBG		IB	T210-T260	10 11	7604	2 5	10800	12700
32 8	CONVERTIBLE	SDN		FBG		IB	T210-T260	12	12200	2 4	20100	23100
32 8	CONVERTIBLE	SDN		FBG		IBT160D-T210D	12		12200	2 4	27400	32100
33		FB	DC	FBG		IB	T210-T260	13 2	14500	2 6	20200	23000
33		FB	DC	FBG		IBT170D-T185D	13 2		14500	2 6	27800	31200
35		HT	HB	FBG		IO	215	MRCR 12	14000	2 6	6800	7800

35 2 DRIFT-R-CRUZ — HT HB FBG:
IO 225 CHRY 6800, IO 270 MRCR 6950 8000, IO 325 MRCR 7300 8400
IB T210 CRUS 7550, IO T215 MRCR 7350 8450, IB T215 MRCR 7400 8550
IO T225 CHRY 7350, IB T225 CHRY 7350 8500, IB T260 CRUS 7600 8750
IO T270 MRCR 7650, IO T325 MRCR 8350 9600

| 35 | | FB | HB | FBG | | IO | 215 | MRCR 12 | | 2 6 | 5600 | 6450 |

35 2 DRIFT-R-CRUZ — FB HB FBG:
IO 225 CHRY 5650, IO 270 MRCR 5750 6600, IO 325 MRCR 6100 7000
IB T210 CRUS 6300, IO T215 MRCR 6150 7050, IB T215 MRCR 6200 7100
IO T225 CHRY 6150, IB T225 CHRY 6150 7100, IB T260 CRUS 6350 7300
IO T270 MRCR 6400, IO T325 MRCR 7050 8150

| 37 10 | | FB | DC | FBG | | IB | T320 | CRUS 13 10 | 18500 | 2 9 | 33300 | 37000 |

IB T165D GM 36100 40100, IB T185D CUM 36800 40800, IB T210D CUM 36800 40800
IB T216D GM 37100 41200, IB T265D GM 38200 42400, IB T283D GM 38600 42900

| 37 10 | | HT | SF | FBG | | IB | T320 | CRUS 13 10 | 18000 | 2 9 | 32600 | 36200 |

IB T165D GM 35400 39300, IB T185D CUM 36000 39500, IB T210D CUM 36000 40000
IB T216D GM 36300 40400, IB T265D GM 37400 41600, IB T283D GM 37900 42100

| 37 10 | | FB | SF | FBG | | IB | T320 | CRUS 13 10 | 22400 | 2 9 | 38800 | 43100 |

IB T165D GM 41900 46600, IB T185D CUM 42100 46700, IB T210D CUM 42500 47200
IB T216D GM 42800 47600, IB T265D GM 43900 48800, IB T283D GM 44400 49300

| 39 2 | DRIFT-R-CRUZ | HT | HB | FBG | SV | IO | 225 | 11 11 | 15000 | 2 6 | 6100 | 7000 |
| 41 10 | | HT | MY | P/M | IB | T320 | CRUS 13 10 | 22900 | 3 | 47100 | 51700 |

IB T185D CUM 48000 52800, IB T210D CUM 49100 54000, IB T216D GM 49600 54500
IB T265D GM 51800 56900, IB T283D GM 52700 57900, IB T300D CUM 53200 58500

| 41 10 | | FB | MY | P/M | IB | T320 | CRUS 13 10 | 22900 | 3 | 47000 | 51600 |

IB T185D CUM 48000 52700, IB T210D CUM 49100 53900, IB T216D GM 49500 54400
IB T265D GM 51700 56800, IB T283D GM 52600 57800, IB T300D CUM 53100 58400

| 41 10 | | HT | MYDKH | P/M | IB | T320 | CRUS 13 10 | 22900 | 3 | 47800 | 52500 |

IB T185D CUM 48600 53400, IB T210D CUM 49800 54700, IB T216D GM 50200 55200
IB T265D GM 52600 57800, IB T283D GM 53400 58700, IB T300D CUM 54100 59400

| 41 10 | | FB | SF | P/M | IB | T320 | CRUS 13 10 | 22680 | 3 | 45800 | 50300 |

IB T185D CUM 46100 50600, IB T210D CUM 47300 52000, IB T216D GM 47800 52500
IB T265D GM 50200 55100, IB T283D GM 51100 56200, IB T300D CUM 51900 57000

| 41 10 | | FB | SF | P/M | IB | T320 | CRUS 13 10 | | 3 | 30900 | 34300 |

IB T185D CUM 51000 56100, IB T210D CUM 52200 57400, IB T216D GM 52700 57900
IB T265D GM 55100 60600, IB T283D GM 56000 61600, IB T300D CUM 56700 62300

| 41 10 | COHO | FB | MY | P/M | IB | T320 | CRUS 13 10 | 22700 | 3 | 47900 | 52700 |

IB T185D CUM 48600 53400, IB T210D CUM 49800 54800, IB T216D GM 50300 55300
IB T265D GM 52700 58000, IB T283D GM 53700 59000, IB T300D CUM 54300 59700

| 46 11 | | HT | MY | P/M | IB | T320 | CRUS 14 4 | 39000 | 3 4 | 68600 | 75400 |

IB T265D GM 73300 80600, IB T283D GM 74500 81800, IB T300D CUM 75500 83000

| 46 11 | | HT | MYDKH | P/M | IB | T320 | CRUS 14 4 | 39000 | 3 4 | 72300 | 79400 |

IB T265D GM 77400 85100, IB T283D GM 78700 86500, IB T300D CUM 79900 87800

| 46 11 | | HT | MYDKH | P/M | IB | T320 | CRUS 14 4 | 39000 | 3 4 | 71800 | 78900 |

IB T265D GM 76900 84500, IB T283D GM 78100 85800, IB T300D CUM 79300 87100

| 46 11 | | FB | SF | P/M | IB | 300 | CUM 14 4 | 38500 | 3 4 | 64900 | 71300 |

IB T320 CRUS 66000 72500, IB T265D GM 69900 76800, IB T283D GM 70700 77700
IB T370D CUM 75800 83400

| 46 11 | | FB | SF | P/M | IB | T320 | CRUS 14 4 | 38500 | 3 4 | 65600 | 72100 |

IB T265D GM 69600 76400, IB T283D GM 70300 77300, IB T300D CUM 70900 78000
IB T370D CUM 75300 82800

| 48 3 | | FB | SF | FBG | | IB | T265D | GM 14 10 | 39800 | 3 8 | 72100 | 79300 |

IB T350D GM 76100 83600, IB T370D CUM 77200 84800, IB T380D GM 78000 85700

55		HT	MY	P/M	IB	T350D	GM	16 4		3 6	93700	103000
55		HT	MY	P/M	IB	T370D	CUM	16 4		3 6	94700	104000
55		HT	MY	P/M	IB	T525D	GM	16 4		3 6	102000	112000
55		HT	SF	P/M	IB	T350D	GM	16 4		3 6	95400	105000
55		HT	SF	P/M	IB	T370D	CUM	16 4		3 6	96400	106000
55		FB	SF	P/M	IB	T350D	GM	16 4		3 6	103500	113500
55		FB	SF	P/M	IB	T370D	CUM	16 4		3 6	99500	109500
55	COCKPIT	HT	MYCPT	P/M	IB	T350D	GM	16 4		3 6	100500	110500
55	COCKPIT	HT	MYCPT	P/M	IB	T370D	CUM	16 4		3 6	107500	118000
60	COCKPIT	HT	MYCPT	P/M	IB	T525D	GM	16 4		3 6	114500	126000
60		FB	MY	P/M	IB	T350D	GM	16 4		3 6	115000	129000
60		FB	MY	P/M	IB	T370D	CUM	16 4		3 6	117500	129000
60		FB	MY	P/M	IB	T525D	GM	16 4		3 6	129500	142000
60		FB	SF	P/M	IB	T350D	GM	16 4		3 6	117500	129000
60		FB	SF	P/M	IB	T370D	CUM	16 4		3 6	120000	131500
60		FB	SF	P/M	IB	T525D	GM	16 4		3 6	128500	141500
60	COCKPIT	FB	MYCPT	P/M	IB	T350D	GM	16 4		3 6	111500	122500
60	COCKPIT	FB	MYCPT	P/M	IB	T370D	CUM	16 4		3 6	114000	125500
60	COCKPIT	FB	MYCPT	P/M	IB	T525D	GM	16 4		3 6	126500	139000
64 10	PLAN G	FB	MY	P/M	IB	T350D	GM	16 7		4	163500	179750
64 10	PLAN G	FB	MY	P/M	IB	T370D	CUM	16 7		4	168000	184550
64 10	PLAN G	FB	MY	P/M	IB	T525D	GM	16 7		4	183000	201100
1970 BOATS												
32	CONVERTIBLE	SDN		WD		IB	210-320	11 9	11500	2 4	16200	19600
32	CONVERTIBLE	SDN		WD		IB	170D	CRUS 11 9	11500	2 4	23000	25500
32	CONVERTIBLE	SDN		WD		IB	T210-T260	11 9	11500	2 4	18500	21300
32	DELUXE	EXP		WD		IB	210-320	11 9	11500	2 4	14500	18200
32	DELUXE	EXP		WD		IB	170D	CRUS 11 9	11500	2 4	21400	23800
32	DELUXE	EXP		WD		IB	T210-T260	11 9	11500	2 4	16600	19500
34 7		DC		WD		IB	210-T260	11 10	13900	2 4	22000	25000
34 7		DC		WD		IB	170D	CRUS 11 10	13900	2 4	29300	32500
34 7	CONVERTIBLE	SDN		WD		IB	T210-T260	11 10	13900	2 4	23000	26100

```
LOA  NAME AND/              TOP/ BOAT -HULL- ----ENGINE--- BEAM  WGT  DRAFT RETAIL RETAIL
FT IN  OR MODEL             RIG  TYPE MTL TP TP # HP MFG  FT IN  LBS  FT IN  LOW   HIGH
--------------------- 1970 BOATS --------------------------------------------------------
34  7 CONVERTIBLE           SDN   WD     IB T170D CRUS 11 10 13900  2  6  31300 34700
34  7 DELUXE                EXP   WD     IB T210-T260  11 10 13900  2  6  22000 25000
34  7 TOURNAMENT FISHERMAN  SF    WD     IB T210-T260  11 10 13900  2  6  22000 25000
34  7 TOURNAMENT FISHERMAN  SF    WD     IB T170D CRUS 11 10 13900  2  6  29300 32500
38  1                       DC    WD     IB T210  CRUS 12  8 17700  2  6  32800 36500
       IB T225  CHRY 32600 36200, IB T260  CRUS 33400 37200, IB T320  CRUS 33900 37700
       IB T170D CRUS 36900 41000

38  1                       SDNSF WD     IB T210  CRUS 12  8 17700  2  6  32800 36500
38  1                       SDNSF P/M RB IB T225  CHRY 12  8 17700  2  6  32500 36200
       IB T260  CRUS 33000 36700, IB T320  CRUS 33500 37200, IB T170D CRUS 36500 40500

38  1 CONVERTIBLE           SDN   P/M RB IB T210  CRUS 12  8 17700  2  6  33000 36600
       IB T225  CRUS 33000 36700, IB T260  CRUS 33100 36800, IB T320  CRUS 33600 37400
       IB T170D CRUS 36700 40800

38  1 DELUXE                EXP   P/M RB IB T210  CRUS 12  8 17700  2  6  32800 36500
       IB T225  CHRY 32600 36200, IB T260  CRUS 33000 36700, IB T320  CRUS 33500 37200
       IB T170D CRUS 36500 40500

41 10                       MY    P/M RB IB T320  CRUS 14  2 22980  3     44100 49000
       IB T170D CRUS 44800 49800, IB T185D CUM  45800 50300, IB T216D GM   47300 51900

41 10                       SDNSF P/M RB IB T320  CRUS 14  2 22550  3     43400 48200
       IB T170D CRUS 42800 47600, IB T185D CUM  43400 48300, IB T216D GM   45700 50200

41 10 COHO                  MY    P/M RB IB T320  CRUS 14  2 22550  3     44700 49600
       IB T170D CRUS 45000 50000, IB T185D CUM  46000 50600, IB T216D GM   47700 52400

47                          MY    P/M RB IB T320  CRUS 14  8 38600  3  2  65000 71400
       IB T280D GM   70000 76900, IB T283D GM   70200 77100, IB T300D CUM  71000 78100

47                          SDNSF P/M RB IB T320  CRUS 14  8 37700  3  2  62400 68500
       IB T280D GM   67000 73700, IB T283D GM   67200 73900, IB T300D CUM  68200 74900

55                          SDNSF P/M RB IB T350D GM  16  4 48000  3  6  87300 95900
55                          SDNSF P/M RB IB T370D CUM 16  4 48000  3  6  89800 98700
55                          FB    P/M RB IB T350D GM  16  4 46000  3  6  84500 92900
55                          FB    SDNSF P/M RB IB T370D CUM 16  4 46000  3  6  87200 95800
60                          FB    MY    P/M RB IB T350D GM  16  4 53000  3  6  99700 109500
60                          FB    MY    P/M RB IB T370D CUM 16  4 53000  3  6 102500 112500
60                          FB    MY    P/M RB IB T525D GM  16  4 53000  3  6 118000 130000
60                          YTFS  P/M RB IB T350D GM  16  4 53000  3  6  99100 109000
60                          YTFS  P/M RB IB T370D CUM 16  4 53000  3  6 102000 112000
60                          YTFS  P/M RB IB T525D GM  16  4 53000  3  6 120000 131500
64 10                       FB    MY    P/M RB IB T350D GM  16  4 64500  4    142000 156000
64 10                       FB    MY    P/M RB IB T370D CUM 16  4 64500  4    143500 157500

64 10                       FB    MY    P/M RB IB T525D GM  16  4 64500  4    155500 170500
--------------------- 1969 BOATS --------------------------------------------------------
26  6 PLAN A                SF    P/M RB IB 210-250    9  9  5430  2       6500  7600
26  6 PLAN B                SF    P/M RB IB 210-250    9  9  5430  2       7000  8300
26  6 PLAN C                EXP   P/M RB IB 210-250    9  9  5680  2       6950  8150
26  6 PLAN C                SDNSF P/M RB IB 210-250    9  9  5680  2       6950  8150
29 11                       EXP   P/M RB IB 210-250   10  6  8515  2      10900 12700
29 11                       EXP   P/M RB IB T210  CHRY 10  6  8515  2      12100 13800
29 11 PLAN B                SDNSF P/M RB IB 210-250   10  6  8265  2      10300 11900
29 11 PLAN B                SDNSF P/M RB IB T210  CHRY 10  6  8265  2      11400 13000
32                          EXP   P/M RB IB 210-320   11  9 11500  2  4  14600 17400
32                          EXP   P/M RB IB 170D CRUS 11  9 11500  2  4  20800 23200
32                          EXP   P/M RB IB T210-T250 11  9 11500  2  4  15900 18500

32    CONVERTIBLE           SDN   P/M RB IB 250-320   11  9 11500  2  4  16000 18900
32    CONVERTIBLE           SDN   P/M RB IB 170D CRUS 11  9 11500  2  4  22500 25000
32    CONVERTIBLE           SDN   P/M RB IB T190-T250 11  9 11500  2  4  17100 20400
32    DELUXE                EXP   P/M RB IB 210-320   11  9 11500  2  4  14900 17700
32    DELUXE                EXP   P/M RB IB 170D CRUS 11  9 11500  2  4  21100 23500
32    DELUXE                EXP   P/M RB IB T190-T250 11  9 11500  2  4  15800 18800
32    PLAN B                SDNSF P/M RB IB 210-320   11  9 11200  2  4  14600 17400
32    PLAN B                SDNSF P/M RB IB 170D CRUS 11  9 11200  2  4  20600 22800
32    PLAN B                SDNSF P/M RB IB T210-T250 11  9 11200  2  4  15900 18600
34  7                       DC    P/M RB IB T210-T250 11 10 13900  2  6  21100 23900
34  7                       SF    P/M RB IB T210-T250 11 10 13900  2  6  21800 24600
34  7                       SF    P/M RB IB 170D CRUS 11 10 13900  2  6  29300 32500

34  7 CONVERTIBLE           SDN   P/M RB IB T210-T250 11 10 13900  2  6  22100 25000
34  7 CONVERTIBLE           SDN   P/M RB IB 170D CRUS 11 10 13900  2  6  30600 34000
34  7 DELUXE                EXP   P/M RB IB T210-T250 11 10 13900  2  6  21100 23900
34  7 TOURNAMENT FISHERMAN  SF    P/M RB IB T210-T250 11 10 13900  2  6  20500 23200
34  7 TOURNAMENT FISHERMAN  SF    P/M RB IB 170D CRUS 11 10 13900  2  6  28100 31200
36 11                       DC    P/M RB IB T210  CHRY 12  8 17700  2  7  29800 33100
       IB T250  PACE 30400 33700, IB T320  PACE 30900 34300, IB T170D CRUS 33600 37400

36 11                       EXP   P/M RB IB T210  CHRY 12  8 17700  2  7  29800 33100
       IB T250  PACE 30000 33400, IB T320  PACE 30500 33900, IB T170D CRUS 33300 36900

36 11                       SF    P/M RB IB T210  CHRY 12  8 17700  2  7  33700 37500
36 11                       SF    P/M RB IB T320  PACE 12  8 17700  2  7  34300 38100
36 11                       SF    P/M RB IB T170D CRUS 12  8 17700  2  7  32000 35500
36 11 CONVERTIBLE           SDN   P/M RB IB T210  CHRY 12  8 17700  2  7  30100 33500
       IB T250  PACE 30400 33800, IB T320  PACE 31000 34400, IB T170D CRUS 33800 37600

36 11 DELUXE                EXP   P/M RB IB T210  CHRY 12  8 17700  2  7  29800 33100
       IB T250  PACE 30000 33400, IB T320  PACE 30500 33900, IB T170D CRUS 33300 36900

36 11 DELUXE                SF    P/M RB IB T250  PACE 12  8 17700  2  7  33900 37700
36 11 TOURNAMENT FISHERMAN  SF    P/M RB IB T210  CHRY 12  8 17700  2  7  25800 28700
       IB T250  PACE 26100 29000, IB T320  PACE 26800 29800, IB T170D CRUS 34500 38300

40                          HT    MY    P/M RB IB T210  CHRY 14  2 22700  3     39400 43700
       IB T250  PACE 39600 43900, IB T320  PACE 40000 44400, IB T170D CRUS 43200 48000
       IB T216D GM   44100 49000

40                          SDNSF P/M RB IB T210  CHRY 14  2 21450  3     37500 41700
       IB T250  PACE 37700 41900, IB T320  PACE 38100 42300, IB T170D CRUS 41400 45900
       IB T216D GM   42200 46900

40                          SF    P/M RB IB T210  CHRY 14  2 21450  3     37500 41700
40    COHO                  MY    P/M RB IB T210  CHRY 14  2 22550  3     39100 43500
       IB T250  PACE 39300 43700, IB T320  PACE 39800 44200, IB T170D CRUS 43000 47800
       IB T216D GM   43800 48700

40    DELUXE                SF    P/M RB IB T320  PACE 14  2 21450  3     38100 42300
40    DELUXE                SF    P/M RB IB T170D CRUS 14  2 21450  3     41400 45900
40    DELUXE                SF    P/M RB IB T216D GM  14  2 21450  3     42200 46900
40    PILOTHOUSE            HT    MYDKH P/M RB IB T210  CHRY 14  2 22700  3     38900 43300
       IB T250  PACE 39100 43500, IB T320  PACE 39600 44000, IB T170D CRUS 42900 47600
       IB T216D GM   43700 48600

40    W/EXT PLTHSE          HT    MYDKH P/M RB IB T210  CHRY 14  2 22700  3     39800 44200
       IB T250  PACE 40000 44500, IB T320  PACE 40400 44900, IB T170D CRUS 43700 48500
       IB T216D GM   44500 49400

41 10                       MY    MHG RB IB T250      14  2 22980  3     40400 44900
41 10                       SDNSF MHG RB IB T250      13 10 22550  3     39600 44000
44                          MY    WD  RB IB T320  PACE 14  2 24600  3     43700 48600
44    CONVERTIBLE           SDNSF WD  RB IB T320  PACE 14  2 24600  3     42100 46800
47                          MY    P/M RB IB T320  PACE 14  8 38600  3  2  62600 68800
       IB T283D GM   65800 72300, IB T283D GM   67900 74600, IB T300D CUM  68700 75900

47                          HT    MY    P/M RB IB T320  PACE 14  8 38600  3  2  63200 69400
47                          SDNSF P/M RB IB T210  PACE 14  8 37700  3  2  60100 66100
47                          SDNSF P/M RB IB T283D      14  8 37700  3  2  65000 71400
47                          SDNSF P/M RB IB T320  PACE 14  8 38600  3  2  66000 72700
47    EXTENDED PILOTHOUSE   HT    MYDKH P/M RB IB T320  PACE 14  8 38600  3  2  68500 75300
47    EXTENDED PILOTHOUSE   HT    MYDKH P/M RB IB T283D GM  14  8 38600  3  2  73900 81300
47    EXTENDED PILOTHOUSE   HT    MYDKH P/M RB IB T283D GM  14  8 38600  3  2  73600 80900
47    PILOTHOUSE            HT    MYDKH P/M RB IB T283D      14  8 38600  3  2  64500 70900
47    PILOTHOUSE            HT    MYDKH P/M RB IB T283D GM  14  8 38600  3  2  70900 77900
47    PILOTHOUSE            HT    MYDKH P/M RB IB T283D GM  14  8 38600  3  2  73300 80600
53                          DC    P/M RB IB T350D GM  16  4 47800  3  6  83400 91600
53                          DC    P/M RB IB T370D CUM 16  4 47800  3  6  85500 94000

53                          MY    P/M RB IB T350D GM  16  4 48000  3  6  82000 90100
53                          MY    P/M RB IB T370D CUM 16  4 48000  3  6  84000 92300
53                          FB    SDNSF P/M RB IB T350D GM  16  4 46000  3  6  80800 90300
53                          FB    SDNSF P/M RB IB T370D CUM 16  4 46000  3  6  84400 90800
53    FISHERMAN             DC    P/M RB IB T350D GM  16  4 47600  3  6  83200 91400
53    FISHERMAN             DC    P/M RB IB T370D CUM 16  4 47600  3  6  85300 93700
60                          FB    MY    P/M RB IB T370D CUM 16  4 53000  3  6  96200 105500
60                          FB    MY    P/M RB IB T370D CUM 16  4 53000  3  6  95700 105000
60                          YTFS  P/M RB IB T370D GM  16  4 53000  3  6  98700 108500
60                          YTFS  P/M RB IB T370D CUM 16  4 53000  3  6  98700 108500
--------------------- 1968 BOATS --------------------------------------------------------
26  6 PLAN A                HT    SF    P/M RB IB 210-250    9  9  5430  2       6250  7400
26  6 PLAN B                HT    SF    P/M RB IB 210-250    9  9  5430  2       6750  7950
```

```
LOA  NAME AND/          TOP/ BOAT  -HULL-  ----ENGINE---  BEAM  WGT  DRAFT RETAIL RETAIL
FT IN OR MODEL          RIG  TYPE  MTL TP TP #  HP  MFG   FT IN LBS  FT IN  LOW    HIGH
--------------------- 1968 BOATS -----------------------------------------------------
26  6 PLAN C            HT   EXP   P/M RB IB  210-250   9  9  5680  2      6650   7850
26  6 PLAN C            FB   SDNSF P/M RB IB  210-250   9  9  5680  2      6650   7850
29 11                        EXP   P/M RB IB  210-250  10  6  8515  2     10500  12200
29 11                        EXP   P/M RB IB  T190     10  6  8515  2     11500  13100
29 11 PLAN B                 SDNSF P/M RB IB  210-250  10  6  8265  2      9900  11500
29 11 PLAN B                 SDNSF P/M RB IB  T190     10  6  8265  2     10800  12300
32                           EXP   P/M RB IB  210-320  11  9 11500  2  4  14100  16700
32                           EXP   P/M RB IB  170D CRUS 11 9 11500  2  4  20400  22700
32                           EXP   P/M RB IB  T190-T250 11 9 11500  2  4  15100  17800
32    CONVERTIBLE            SDN   P/M RB IB  210-320  11  9 11500  2  4  15100  18200
32    CONVERTIBLE            SDN   P/M RB IB  170D CRUS 11 9 11500  2  4  22100  24500
32    CONVERTIBLE            SDN   P/M RB IB  T190-T250 11 9 11500  2  4  16400  19600

32    DELUXE                 EXP   P/M RB IB  210-320  11  9 11500  2  4  14300  17000
32    DELUXE                 EXP   P/M RB IB  170D CRUS 11 9 11500  2  4  20700  23000
32    DELUXE                 EXP   P/M RB IB  T190-T250 11 9 11500  2  4  15300  18100
32    PLAN B                 SDNSF P/M RB IB  210-320  11  9 11200  2  4  14100  16800
32    PLAN B                 SDNSF P/M RB IB  170D CRUS 11 9 11200  2  4  20200  22400
32    PLAN B                 SDNSF P/M RB IB  T190-T250 11 9 11200  2  4  15100  17900
34  7                   FB   DC    P/M RB IB  T190-T250 11 10 13900 2  6  20200  23000
34  7                        SF    P/M RB IB  T190-T250 11 10 13900 2  6  20500  23600
34  7                        SF    P/M RB IB  T170D CRUS 11 10 13900 2  6 28800  32000
34  7 CONVERTIBLE            SDN   P/M RB IB  T190-T250 11 10 13900 2  6  21100  24100
34  7 CONVERTIBLE            SDN   P/M RB IB  T170D CRUS 11 10 13900 2  6 30000  33400
34  7 DELUXE                 EXP   P/M RB IB  T210-T250 11 10 13900 2  6  20400  23000

34  7 TOURNAMENT FISHERMAN   SF    P/M RB IB  T190-T250 11 10 13900 2  6  19300  22400
34  7 TOURNAMENT FISHERMAN   SF    P/M RB IB  T170D CRUS 11 10 13900 2  6 27500  30600
36 11                   FB   DC    P/M RB IB  T210 CHRY 12 8 17700 2  7  28900  32100
      IB T250    29400 32700, IB T320      29900 33300, IB T170D CRUS 32600  36200

36 11                        EXP   P/M RB IB  T210 CHRY 12 8 17700 2  7  27500  30500
      IB T250    27700 30800, IB T320 CRUS 28500 31700, IB T170D CRUS 31100  34600

36 11                        SF    P/M RB IB  T210 CHRY 12 8 17700 2  7  28900  32100
      IB T250    29100 32300, IB T320      29600 32900, IB T170D CRUS 32200  35800

36 11 CONVERTIBLE            SDN   P/M RB IB  T210 CHRY 12 8 17700 2  7  29200  32400
      IB T250    29500 32700, IB T320      30000 33400, IB T170D CRUS 32800  36400

36 11 DELUXE                 EXP   P/M RB IB  T210 CHRY 12 8 17700 2  7  30300  33600
      IB T250    30500 33900, IB T320      30900 34300, IB T170D CRUS 33400  37100

36 11 TOURNAMENT FISHERMAN   SF    P/M RB IB  T210 CHRY 12 8 17700 2  7  28900  32100
      IB T250    29100 32300, IB T320      29600 32900, IB T170D CRUS 32200  35800

40                           MY    P/M RB IB  T210 CHRY 14 2 22700 3     38200  42400
      IB T250    38300 42600, IB T320      38800 43100, IB T170D CRUS 41900  46600
      IB T216D GM 42700 47500

40                           SDNSF P/M RB IB  T210 CHRY 14 2 21450 3     36400  40400
      IB T250    36500 40600, IB T320      36900 41000, IB T170D CRUS 40100  44500
      IB T216D GM 40900 45400

40                           SF    P/M RB IB  T210 CHRY 14 2 21450 3     36400  40400
      IB T320 CRUS 37200 41400, IB T170D CRUS 40100 44500, IB T216D GM 40900 45400

40    COHO                   MY    P/M RB IB  T210 CHRY 14 2 22550 3     38000  42200
      IB T250    38100 42400, IB T320      38500 42800, IB T170D CRUS 41700  46300
      IB T216D GM 42500 47200

40    CONV SUN BR            MY    WD     IB  T210 CHRY 14 2 22700 3     38200  42400
      IB T250    38300 42600, IB T320      38800 43100, IB T170D
      IB T216D   42700 47500

40    EXTENDED PILOTHOUSE    HT   MYDKH P/M RB IB  T250      14 2 22700 3  38400  42600
40    EXTENDED PILOTHOUSE    HT   MYDKH P/M RB IB  T320      14 2 22700 3  38800  43100
40    EXTENDED PILOTHOUSE    HT   MYDKH P/M RB IB  T170D CRUS 14 2 22700 3 42000  46600
40    EXTENDED PILOTHOUSE    FB   MYDKH P/M RB IB  T210 CHRY 14 2 22700 3  38200  42400
40    PILOTHOUSE                  MYDKH P/M    IB  T250      14 2 22700 3  38400  42600
40    PILOTHOUSE                  MYDKH P/M RB IB  T216D GM  14 2 22700 3  42800  47500
40    PILOTHOUSE                  MYDKH P/M RB IB  T210 CHRY 14 2 22700 3  38200  42400
40    PILOTHOUSE                  MYDKH P/M RB IB  T320      14 2 22700 3  38800  43100
40    PILOTHOUSE                  MYDKH P/M RB IB  T170D CRUS 14 2 22700 3 42000  46600
40    W/EXT PLTHSE           HT   MY    P/M RB IB  T216D     14 2 22700 3  42800  47500
44                                MY    P/M    IB  T283D GM  14 8 24600 3  48000  52800

44                                MY    P/M RB IB  T320      14 8 24600 3  42200  46900
44                                MY    P/M RB IB  T216D GM  14 8 24600 3  44800  49800
44                                MY    P/M RB IB  T300D CUM 14 8 24600 3  48800  53600
44                                SDNSF P/M RB IB  T320 CHRY 14 8 22600 3  40700  45300
      IB T216D GM 41500 46100, IB T283D GM 46300 50900, IB T300D CUM 47400 52100

44    CONV SUN BRIDGE        FB   MYDKH P/M RB IB  T283D GM  14 8 24600 3  49500  54400
44    CONV SUN BRIDGE        FB   MYDKH P/M RB IB  T320      14 8 24600 3  43700  48600
44    CONV SUN BRIDGE        FB   MYDKH P/M RB IB  T216D GM  14 8 24600 3  46800  51400
44    CONV SUN BRIDGE        FB   MYDKH P/M RB IB  T300D CUM 14 8 24600 3  50500  55500
44    EXTENDED PILOTHOUSE    HT   MYDKH P/M RB IB  T320 CHRY 14 8 24600 3  43900  48800
      IB T216D GM 46900 51500, IB T283D GM 49900 54800, IB T300D CUM 50700 55700

44    PILOTHOUSE                  MYDKH P/M RB IB  T320      14 8 24600 3  43600  48500
      IB T216D GM 46700 51300, IB T283D GM 49600 54500, IB T300D CUM 50300 55300

47                                MY    P/M RB IB  T320      14 8 38600 3 2 60600  66600
47                                MY    P/M RB IB  T283D GM  14 8 38600 3 2 65800  72300
47                                MY    P/M RB IB  T300D CUM 14 8 38600 3 2 65400  71900
47                                SDNSF P/M RB IB  T320      14 8 37700 3 2 58200  63900
47                                SDNSF P/M RB IB  T283D GM  14 8 37700 3 2 63000  69200
47                                SDNSF P/M RB IB  T300D CUM 14 8 37700 3 2 63900  70300
47    CONV SUN BRIDGE        FB   MY    P/M RB IB  T320      14 8 38600 3 2 67800  74500
47    CONV SUN BRIDGE        FB   MY    P/M RB IB  T283D GM  14 8 38600 3 2 60700  66800
47    CONV SUN BRIDGE        FB   MY    P/M RB IB  T300D CUM 14 8 38600 3 2 66700  72500
47    EXTENDED PILOTHOUSE    HT   MYDKH P/M RB IB  T320 CHRY 14 8 38600 3 2 64400  70700
47    EXTENDED PILOTHOUSE    HT   MYDKH P/M RB IB  T283D GM  14 8 38600 3 2 70200  77100
47    EXTENDED PILOTHOUSE    HT   MYDKH P/M RB IB  T300D CUM 14 8 38600 3 2 71200  78200

47    PILOTHOUSE                  MYDKH P/M RB IB  T320 CHRY 14 8 38600 3 2 63800  70100
47    PILOTHOUSE                  MYDKH P/M RB IB  T283D GM  14 8 38600 3 2 69400  76300
47    PILOTHOUSE                  MYDKH P/M RB IB  T300D CUM 14 8 38600 3 2 70400  77300
53                                DC    P/M RB IB  T350D GM  16 4 47800 3 6 80700  88700
53                                DC    P/M RB IB  T370D CUM 16 4 47800 3 6 82700  90900
53                                MY    P/M RB IB  T350D GM  16 4 48000 3 6 79300  87200
53                                MY    P/M RB IB  T370D CUM 16 4 48000 3 6 81300  89400
53                            FB   SDNSF P/M RB IB  T350D GM  16 4 46000 3 6 79600  87500
53                            FB   SDNSF P/M RB IB  T370D CUM 16 4 46000 3 6 81800  89900
53    FISHERMAN                   DC    P/M RB IB  T350D GM  16 4 47600 3 6 80500  88400
53    FISHERMAN                   DC    P/M RB IB  T370D CUM 16 4 47600 3 6 82500  90700

60                            FB   MY    P/M RB IB  T350D GM  16 4 53000 3 6 93000 102000
60                            FB   MY    P/M RB IB  T370D CUM 16 4 53000 3 6 95500 105000
60                                 YTFS  P/M RB IB  T350D GM  16 4 53000 3 6 92600 102000
60                                 YTFS  P/M RB IB  T370D CUM 16 4 53000 3 6 95500 105000
--------------------- 1967 BOATS -----------------------------------------------------
24  7                        EXP   P/M RB IB  185       9  6       2       6550   7550
24  7                        FSH   P/M RB IB  185       9  6       2       6650   7650
26                      ST   EXP   P/M RB IB  250 PACE  9  6  5480 2       6250   7200
26  6                        EXP   P/M RB IB  250       9  9       2       7050   8150
26  6                        FSH   P/M RB IB  250       9  9       2       7150   8200
28                           EXP   P/M RB IB  250       10 2       2       8300   9550
28                           EXP   P/M RB IB  T190 PACE 10 2       2       9000  10300
28                           SDNSF P/M RB IB  250       10 2       2       8350   9600
28                           SDNSF P/M RB IB  T190 PACE 10 2       2       9100  10300
28                           SF    P/M RB IB  250       10 2       2       8450   9700
28                           SF    P/M RB IB  T190 PACE 10 2       2       9150  10400

29                      HT   EXP   P/M RB IB  250       10 2  8115 2       9050  10300
29                      HT   EXP   P/M RB IB  T190 PACE 10 2  9015 2      10000  11400
29                      HT   SF    P/M RB IB  250       10 2  7865 2       8900  10100
29                      HT   SF    P/M RB IB  T190 PACE 10 2  8765 2       9950  11300
31                      HT   SF    P/M RB IB  250 PACE  10 10 8795 2  4  12700  14400
31                      HT   SF    P/M RB IB  T190 PACE 10 10 8795 2  4  13500  15300
31                      FB   SF    P/M RB IB  250 PACE  10 10 8795 2  4  12700  14400
31                      FB   SF    P/M RB IB  T190 PACE 10 10 8795 2  4  13500  15300
31    2 SLEEPER             HT   SDNSF P/M RB IB  T190 PACE 10 10 8795 2  4 10700  12200
31    2 SLEEPER             HT   SDNSF P/M RB IB  170D CRUS 10 10 8795 2  4 14900  16900

31    2 SLEEPER             HT   SDNSF P/M RB IB  T190 PACE 10 10 9795 2  4 12400  14100
31    2 SLEEPER             FB   SDNSF P/M RB IB  250 PACE  10 10 8795 2  4 14000  16200
31    2 SLEEPER             FB   SDNSF P/M RB IB  T190 PACE 10 10 9795 2  4 16400  18600
31    4 SLEEPER             HT   EXP   P/M RB IB  T190 PACE 10 10 9765 2  4 12100  13700
31    4 SLEEPER             HT   EXP   P/M RB IB  170D CRUS 10 10 9765 2  4 11900  13500
31    4 SLEEPER             HT   EXP   P/M RB IB  T190 PACE 10 10 10765 2 4 17300  19600
31    4 SLEEPER             HT   EXP   P/M RB IB  250 PACE  10 10 10765 2 4 12900  14600
31    4 SLEEPER             FB   EXP   P/M RB IB  250 PACE  10 10 9765 2  4 11900  13500
```

```
LOA  NAME AND/          TOP/ BOAT  -HULL-  ----ENGINE---  BEAM  WGT  DRAFT RETAIL RETAIL
FT IN  OR MODEL         RIG TYPE   MTL TP TP # HP  MFG  FT IN  LBS  FT IN  LOW   HIGH
---------------------- 1967 BOATS ------------------------------------------------------
31  4 SLEEPER          FB  EXP   P/M RB IB  170D CRUS 10 10  9765  2  4  17300  19600
31  4 SLEEPER          FB  EXP   P/M RB IB  T190 PACE 10 10 10765  2  4  12900  14700
31  4 SLEEPER          HT  SDNSF P/M RB IB  250  PACE 10 10  8795  2  4  11300  12900
31  4 SLEEPER          HT  SDNSF P/M RB IB  170D CRUS 10 10  8795  2  4  15500  17700
31  4 SLEEPER          HT  SDNSF P/M RB IB  T190 PACE 10 10  9795  2  4  13000  14800
31  4 SLEEPER          FB  SDNSF P/M RB IB  250  PACE 10 10  8795  2  4  11300  12900
31  4 SLEEPER          FB  SDNSF P/M RB IB  170D CRUS 10 10  8795  2  4  15200  17300
31  4 SLEEPER          FB  SDNSF P/M RB IB  T190 PACE 10 10  9795  2  4  12700  14400
31  6 SLEEPER          HT  EXP   P/M RB IB  250  PACE 10 10  9765  2  4  12100  13800
31  6 SLEEPER          HT  EXP   P/M RB IB  T190 PACE 10 10 10765  2  4  13100  14900
31  6 SLEEPER          FB  EXP   P/M RB IB  250  PACE 10 10  9765  2  4  12100  13800
31  6 SLEEPER          FB  EXP   P/M RB IB  T190 PACE 10 10 10765  2  4  13100  14900

31  6 SLEEPER CNV      HT  SDN   P/M RB IB  250  PACE 10 10  8795  2  4  11300  12800
31  6 SLEEPER CNV      HT  SDN   P/M RB IB  170D CRUS 10 10  9795  2  4  18600  20700
31  6 SLEEPER CNV      HT  SDN   P/M RB IB  T190 PACE 10 10  8795  2  4  12200  13800
31  6 SLEEPER CNV      FB  SDN   P/M RB IB  250  CRUS 10 10  8795  2  4  11300  12800
31  6 SLEEPER CNV      FB  SDN   P/M RB IB  170D CRUS 10 10  8795  2  4  16300  18500
31  6 SLEEPER CNV      FB  SDN   P/M RB IB  T190 PACE 10 10  9795  2  4  13800  15700
33  4 SLEEPER          HT  EXP   FBG RB IB  250  PACE 13  2 13500  2  6   **     **
33  4 SLEEPER          HT  EXP   FBG RB IB  170D CRUS 13  2 13500  2  6  24000  26600
33  4 SLEEPER          FB  EXP   FBG RB IB  250  PACE 13  2 13500  2  6   **     **
33  4 SLEEPER          FB  EXP   FBG RB IB  170D CRUS 13  2 13500  2  6  24000  26600
33  6 SLEEPER CNV      HT  SDN   FBG RB IB  250  PACE 13  2 13500  2  6   **     **
33  6 SLEEPER CNV      HT  SDN   FBG RB IB  170D CRUS 13  2 13500  2  6  24700  27500

33  6 SLEEPER CNV      FB  SDN   FBG RB IB  250  PACE 13  2 13500  2  6   **     **
33  6 SLEEPER CNV      FB  SDN   FBG RB IB  170D CRUS 13  2 13500  2  6  24700  27500
34                     HT  DC    P/M RB IB  T190 PACE 11 10 13095  2  6  18400  20500
34                     FB  DC    P/M RB IB  T190 PACE 11 10 13095  2  6  18400  20500
34                     HT  SF    P/M RB IB  T190-T250 11 10 13095  2  6  18400  21400
34                     HT  SF    P/M RB IB  T170D CRUS 11 10 13095  2  6  26500  29500
34                     FB  SF    P/M RB IB  T190-T250 11 10 13095  2  6  18900  21300
34                     FB  SF    P/M RB IB  T170D CRUS 11 10 13095  2  6  26500  29400
34  6 SLEEPER CNV      HT  SDN   P/M RB IB  T190-T250 11 10 13095  2  6  19100  22000
34  6 SLEEPER CNV      HT  SDN   P/M RB IB  T170D CRUS 11 10 13095  2  6  27900  31000
34  6 SLEEPER CNV      FB  SDN   P/M RB IB  T190-T250 11 10 13095  2  6  19100  21200
34  6 SLEEPER CNV      FB  SDN   P/M RB IB  T170D CRUS 11 10 13095  2  6  27900  31000

34  6 SLEEPER DELUXE   HT  EXP   P/M RB IB  T190-T250 11 10 13095  2  6  18400  21000
34  6 SLEEPER DELUXE   FB  EXP   P/M RB IB  T190-T250 11 10 13095  2  6  18400  21000
34  TOURNAMENT FISHERMAN HT SF   P/M RB IB  T190-T250 10 10 13095  2  6  16800  20400
34  TOURNAMENT FISHERMAN HT SF   P/M RB IB  T170D CRUS 11 10 13095  2  6  25100  27900
34  TOURNAMENT FISHERMAN FB SF   P/M RB IB  T190-T250 11 10 13095  2  6  17500  20400
34  TOURNAMENT FISHERMAN FB SF   P/M RB IB  T170D CRUS 11 10 13095  2  6  25200  28000
36                         SF    P/M RB IB  T250 PACE 10 10 13095  2  6  22400  24900
36                         SF    P/M RB IB  T320 PACE 10 10 13095  2  6  24000  26700
36                         SF    P/M RB IB  T170D CRUS 11 10 13095  2  6  25000  27800
36  6 SLEEPER CNV          SDN   P/M RB IB  T250 PACE 12  8            2  7  25100  27900
36  6 SLEEPER CNV          SDN   P/M RB IB  T320 PACE 12  8            2  7  25700  28500
36  6 SLEEPER CNV          SDN   P/M RB IB  T170D CRUS 12  8           2  7  28900  32100

36  6 SLEEPER DELUXE       EXP   P/M RB IB  T250 PACE 12  8            2  7  24700  27500
36  6 SLEEPER DELUXE       EXP   P/M RB IB  T320 PACE 12  8            2  7  25300  28100
36  6 SLEEPER DELUXE       EXP   P/M RB IB  T170D CRUS 12  8           2  7  28200  31300
36  8 SLEEPER CNV          SDN   P/M RB IB  T250 PACE 12  8            2  7  25300  28400
36  8 SLEEPER CNV          SDN   P/M RB IB  T320 PACE 12  8            2  7  26100  29000
36  8 SLEEPER CNV          SDN   P/M RB IB  T170D CRUS 12  8           2  7  29300  32500
36  TOURNAMENT FISHERMAN   SF    P/M RB IB  T250 CRUS 12  8            2  7  23900  26500
36  TOURNAMENT FISHERMAN   SF    P/M RB IB  T320 PACE 12  8            2  7  24200  26900
36  TOURNAMENT FISHERMAN   SF    P/M RB IB  T170D CRUS 12  8           2  7  27000  30000
37                     HT  SF    P/M RB IB  T250 PACE 12  8 17500      2  7  28200  31300
37                     HT  SF    P/M RB IB  T320 PACE 12  8 17500      2  7  28700  31900
37                     HT  SF    P/M RB IB  T170D CRUS 12  8 17500     2  7  31200  34700

37                     FB  SF    P/M RB IB  T250 PACE 12  8 17500      2  7  28200  31300
37                     FB  SF    P/M RB IB  T320 PACE 12  8 17500      2  7  28700  31900
37                     FB  SF    P/M RB IB  T170D CRUS 12  8 17500     2  7  31200  34700
37  6 SLEEPER CNV      HT  SDN   P/M RB IB  T250 PACE 12  8 17500      2  7  28300  31400
37  6 SLEEPER CNV      HT  SDN   P/M RB IB  T320 PACE 12  8 17500      2  7  28800  32000
37  6 SLEEPER CNV      HT  SDN   P/M RB IB  T170D CRUS 12  8 17500     2  7  31500  35000
37  6 SLEEPER CNV      FB  SDN   P/M RB IB  T250 PACE 12  8 17500      2  7  28300  31400
37  6 SLEEPER CNV      FB  SDN   P/M RB IB  T320 PACE 12  8 17500      2  7  28800  32000
37  6 SLEEPER CNV      FB  SDN   P/M RB IB  T170D CRUS 12  8 17500     2  7  31500  35000
37  6 SLEEPER DELUXE   HT  EXP   P/M RB IB  T250 PACE 12  8 17500      2  7  28200  31300
37  6 SLEEPER DELUXE   HT  EXP   P/M RB IB  T320 PACE 12  8 17500      2  7  28700  31900
37  6 SLEEPER DELUXE   HT  EXP   P/M RB IB  T170D CRUS 12  8 17500     2  7  31200  34700

37  8 SLEEPER CNV      HT  SDN   P/M RB IB  T250 PACE 13  8 17500      2  7  28800  32000
37  8 SLEEPER CNV      HT  SDN   P/M RB IB  T320 PACE 13  8 17500      2  7  29300  32500
37  8 SLEEPER CNV      HT  SDN   P/M RB IB  T170D CRUS 13  8 17500     2  7  31900  35500
37  8 SLEEPER CNV      FB  SDN   P/M RB IB  T250 PACE 13  8 17500      2  7  28800  31900
37  8 SLEEPER CNV      FB  SDN   P/M RB IB  T320 PACE 13  8 17500      2  7  29300  32500
37  8 SLEEPER CNV      FB  SDN   P/M RB IB  T170D PACE 13  8 17500     2  7  31900  35500
37  DELUXE            FB  EXP   P/M RB IB  T250 PACE 12  8 17500      2  7  28200  31300
37  DELUXE            FB  EXP   P/M RB IB  T320 PACE 12  8 17500      2  7  28700  31900
37  DELUXE            FB  EXP   P/M RB IB  T170D CRUS 12  8 17500     2  7  31200  34700
37  TOURNAMENT FISHERMAN HT SF  P/M RB IB  T250 PACE 12  8 17500      2  7  28200  31300
37  TOURNAMENT FISHERMAN HT SF  P/M RB IB  T320 PACE 12  8 17500      2  7  28700  31900
37  TOURNAMENT FISHERMAN HT SF  P/M RB IB  T170D CRUS 12  8 17500     2  7  31200  34700

37  TOURNAMENT FISHERMAN FB SF  P/M RB IB  T250 PACE 12  8 17500      2  7  28200  31300
37  TOURNAMENT FISHERMAN FB SF  P/M RB IB  T320 PACE 12  8 17500      2  7  28700  31900
37  TOURNAMENT FISHERMAN FB SF  P/M RB IB  T170D CRUS 12  8 17500     2  7  31200  34700
39                     HT  MY    P/M RB IB  T250 PACE 13 10 22560  3      35900  39900
    IB T320 PACE 36300 40300, IB T170D CRUS 39400 43700, IB T195D GM 39800 44200

39                     FB  MY    P/M RB IB  T250 PACE 13 10 22560  3      35900  39900
    IB T320 PACE 36300 40300, IB T170D CRUS 39400 43700, IB T195D GM 39800 44200

39                     HT  SDNSF P/M RB IB  T250 PACE 13 10 22560  3      35800  39800
    IB T320 PACE 36200 40300, IB T170D CRUS 39300 43700, IB T195D GM 39700 44100

39                     FB  SDNSF P/M RB IB  T250 PACE 13 10 22560  3      35800  39800
    IB T320 PACE 36200 40300, IB T170D CRUS 39300 43700, IB T195D GM 39700 44100

39  6 SLEEPER          HT  SF    P/M RB IB  T250 PACE 13 10 22560  3      35800  39800
    IB T320 PACE 36200 40300, IB T170D CRUS 39300 43700, IB T195D GM 39700 44100

39  6 SLEEPER          FB  SF    P/M RB IB  T250 PACE 13 10 22560  3      35800  39800
    IB T320 PACE 36200 40300, IB T170D CRUS 39300 43700, IB T195D GM 39700 44100

39  PILOTHOUSE         HT  MYDKH P/M RB IB  T250 PACE 13 10 22560  3      35900  39900
    IB T320 PACE 36400 40400, IB T170D CRUS 39400 43800, IB T195D GM 39800 44300

39  PILOTHOUSE         FB  MYDKH P/M RB IB  T250 PACE 13 10 22560  3      35900  39900
    IB T320 PACE 36400 40400, IB T170D CRUS 39400 43800, IB T195D GM 39800 44300

44                     HT  MY    P/M RB IB  T320 PACE 14  4 24600  3      42300  47000
    IB T215D CUM 46300 50900, IB T216D GM  46500 51100, IB T280D CUM 49300 54200
    IB T280D GM 49400 54300

44                     HT  SDNSF P/M RB IB  T320 PACE 14  4 24600  3      41800  46400
    IB T215D PACE 44100 49000, IB T216D PACE 44200 49100, IB T280D PACE 48300 53100
    IB T300D CUM 49600 54500

44                     FB  SDNSF P/M RB IB  T320 PACE 14  4 24600  3      41600  46200
    IB T215D CUM 44000 48800, IB T216D CUM 44000 48800, IB T280D CUM 48000 52800
    IB T300D CUM 49400 54300

44                     HT  SF    P/M RB IB  T320 PACE 14  4 24600  3      41300  45900
    IB T215D CUM 44200 49200, IB T216D CUM 44300 49200, IB T280D CUM 47900 52700
    IB T300D CUM 49000 53800

44                     FB  SF    P/M RB IB  T320 PACE 14  4 24600  3      41100  45900
    IB T215D CUM 44100 49100, IB T216D CUM 44200 49100, IB T280D CUM 47800 52500
    IB T300D CUM 48800 53600

44  COCKPIT            HT  DCCPT P/M RB IB  T320 PACE 14  4 24600  3      39700  44100
    IB T215D CUM 42700 47500, IB T216D CUM 42800 47500, IB T280D CUM 46200 50800

44  CONV SUN BRIDGE    FB  MY    P/M RB IB  T320 PACE 14  4 24600  3      42200  46900
    IB T215D CUM 46200 50700, IB T216D CUM 46200 50800, IB T280D CUM 49100 54000

44  EXTENDED PILOTHOUSE HT MYDKH P/M RB IB  T320 PACE 14  4 24600  3      43700  48600
    IB T215D CUM 47700 52400, IB T216D CUM 47700 52400, IB T280D CUM 50900 55900

44  PILOTHOUSE         HT  DCCPT P/M RB IB  T320 PACE 14  4 24600  3      41000  45600
    IB T215D CUM 43600 48400, IB T216D CUM 43600 48500, IB T280D CUM 47500 52200

44  PILOTHOUSE         FB  DCCPT P/M RB IB  T320 PACE 14  4 24600  3      40500  45000
    IB T215D CUM 43100 47900, IB T216D CUM 43200 48000, IB T280D CUM 47000 51600

44  PILOTHOUSE         FB  MYDKH P/M RB IB  T320 PACE 14  4 24600  3      43500  48400
    IB T215D CUM 47500 52200, IB T216D CUM 47600 52300, IB T280D CUM 50700 55700
```

```
 LOA   NAME AND/     TOP/ BOAT -HULL-  ----ENGINE---  BEAM   WGT  DRAFT RETAIL RETAIL
FT IN  OR MODEL      RIG  TYPE MTL TP TP # HP MFG    FT IN  LBS  FT IN  LOW    HIGH
-------------------- 1967 BOATS -------------------------------------------------------
 53                       DC   P/M RB IB T350D GM  16  4 48000 3  6 78400  86200
 53                       DC   P/M RB IB T370D CUM 16  4 48000 3  6 80400  88400
 53                       MY   P/M RB IB T350D GM  16  4 48000 3  6 76900  84500
 53                       MY   P/M RB IB T370D CUM 16  4 48000 3  6 78800  86600
 53                       SDNSF P/M RB IB T350D GM  16  4 48000 3  6 79600  87400
 53                       SDNSF P/M RB IB T370D CUM 16  4 48000 3  6 81700  89700
 53    FISHERMAN          DC   P/M RB IB T350D GM  16  4 48000 3  6 78400  86200
 53    FISHERMAN          DC   P/M RB IB T370D CUM 16  4 48000 3  6 80400  88400
 60    PILOTHOUSE     FB  MYDKH P/M RB IB T350D CUM 16  4 53000 3  6 91400 100500
 60    PILOTHOUSE     FB  MYDKH P/M RB IB T370D CUM 16  4 53000 3  6 92700 102000
-------------------- 1966 BOATS -------------------------------------------------------
 24  7 PACER              EXP  P/M RB IB  185  PACE  9  6          2      6350   7300
 24  7 PACER          SF  P/M RB IB  185  PACE  9  6          2      6400   7400
 25 10 CUTLAS        ST   CUD  WD  IB  185  PACE        4000         4800   5500
 28                       EXP  P/M RB IB 185-220 10  2           2      7750   9050
 28                       EXP  P/M RB IB T185  PACE 10  2        2      8550   9850
 28                       SF   P/M RB IB 185-220 10  2           2      7850   9200
 28    PLAN A             EXP  P/M RB IB T185 PACE 10  2         2      8700  10000
 28    PLAN A             SF   P/M RB IB T185 PACE 10  2         2      8700  11000
 31                   HT  SDNSF P/M RB IB  220  PACE 10 10 8795 2  4 10500  11900
 31                   HT  SDNSF P/M RB IB 170D CRUS 10 10 8795 2  4 15000  17000
 31                   HT  SDNSF P/M RB IB T185 PACE 10 10 9795 2  4 12200  13800
 31  4 SLEEPER        HT  EXP  P/M RB IB 170D CRUS 10 10      2  4 17100  19400
 31  4 SLEEPER        HT  EXP  P/M RB IB  220 PACE 10 10 9795 2  4 11400  12900

 31  4 SLEEPER        HT  EXP  P/M RB IB T185 PACE 10 10 10765 2 4 12500  14200
 31    CONVERTIBLE    HT  SDN  P/M RB IB  220 PACE 10 10 8795 2  4 10700  12100
 31    CONVERTIBLE    HT  SDN  P/M RB IB 170D CRUS 10 10 8795 2  4 16000  18200
 31    CONVERTIBLE    HT  SDN  P/M RB IB T185 PACE 10 10 9795 2  4 13300  15100
 31    PLAN A         HT  SF   P/M RB IB  220 PACE 10 10 8795 2  4  9300  10600
 31    PLAN A         HT  SF   P/M RB IB 170D CRUS 10 10 8795 2  4 13300  15100
 31    PLAN A         HT  SF   P/M RB IB T185 PACE 10 10 9795 2  4 12300  13800
 34                   FB  SF   P/M RB IB T185-T220 11 10 13045 2 6 17300  20000
 34                   FB  SF   P/M RB IB T170D CRUS 11 10 13045 2 6 25400  28200
 34    CONVERTIBLE    FB  SDN  P/M RB IB T185-T220 11 10 13045 2 6 18600  21000
 34    CONVERTIBLE    FB  SDN  P/M RB IB T170D CRUS 11 10 13045 2 6 27400  30500
 34    DELUXE         FB  EXP  P/M RB IB T185-T220 11 10 13045 2 6 17300  20000

 36                       SF   P/M RB IB T280 PACE 12  8        2  6 23200  25800
 36                       SF   P/M RB IB T320 PACE 12  8        2  6 23500  26200
 36                       SF   P/M RB IB T170D CRUS 12  8       2  6 26300  29200
 36                   FB  SF   P/M RB IB T220 PACE 12  8        2  6 22900  25500
 36                       SDN  P/M RB IB T220 PACE 12  8        2  6 24200  26900
 36    6 SLEEPER CNV
       IB T280  PACE  24600  27300, IB T320  PACE  24900  27700, IB T170D CRUS  28100  31200

 36    8 SLEEPER CNV       SDN  P/M RB IB T220 PACE 12  8       2  6 24600  27400
       IB T280  PACE  25000  27800, IB T320  PACE  25400  28200, IB T170D CRUS  28500  31600

 36    DELUXE             EXP  P/M RB IB T220 PACE 12  8        2  6 23900  26600
       IB T280  PACE  24200  26900, IB T320  PACE  24600  27300, IB T170D CRUS  27400  30400

 36    TOURNAMENT FISHERMAN SF P/M RB IB T220 PACE 12  8        2  6 22900  25500
       IB T280  PACE  23200  25800, IB T320  PACE  23500  26200, IB T170D CRUS  26300  29200

 39                       MY   P/M RB IB T220 PACE 13 10 22560 3   34800  38700
       IB T280  PACE  35000  38900, IB T320  PACE  35300  39200, IB T170D CRUS  38300  42500
       IB T216D GM   39000  43400

 39                       SDNSF P/M RB IB T220 PACE 13 10 22560 3  34800  38600
       IB T280  PACE  35000  38800, IB T320  PACE  35200  39100, IB T170D CRUS  38200  42400
       IB T216D GM   38900  43300

 39                       SF   P/M RB IB T220 PACE 13 10 22560 3   34800  38600
       IB T280  PACE  35000  38800, IB T320  PACE  35200  39100, IB T170D CRUS  38200  42400
       IB T216D GM   38900  43300

 39    DELUXE PILOTHOUSE  MYDKH P/M RB IB T220 PACE 13 10 22560 3  34900  38700
       IB T280  PACE  35100  39000, IB T320  PACE  35300  39300, IB T170D CRUS  38300  42600
       IB T216D GM   39100  43500

 44                       MY   P/M RB IB T220 PACE 14  4 24600 3   39400  43800
       IB T320  PACE  40900  45400, IB T215D CRUS  43300  48100, IB T216D GM  44400  49300
       IB T280D CUM  47800  52500, IB T283D GM  48100  52800

 44                       SDNSF P/M RB IB T280 PACE 14  4 24600 3  38100  42400
       IB T320  PACE  40300  44800, IB T215D GM  42700  47400, IB T216D GM  42700  47500
       IB T280D GM  46900  51500, IB T283D GM  47100  51700, IB T300D GM  48000  52700

 44                       SF   P/M RB IB T280 PACE 14  4 24600 3   38000  42300
       IB T320  PACE  39900  44300, IB T215D GM  42900  47700, IB T216D GM  43600  47700
       IB T280D GM  46400  51000, IB T283D GM  46600  51200, IB T300D GM  47600  52300

 44    COCKPIT            DC   P/M RB IB T280 PACE 14  4 24600 3   39000  43400
       IB T320  PACE  40600  45100, IB T215D GM  44000  48800, IB T216D GM  44000  48900
       IB T280D GM  47600  52300, IB T283D GM  47800  52500

 44    CONV SUN BRIDGE    MY   P/M RB IB T215D GM 14  4 26200 3    46000  50500
 44    CONV SUN BRIDGE FB MY   P/M RB IB T280 PACE 14  4 24600 3   39500  43800
       IB T320  PACE  41000  45500, IB T216D GM  44500  49500, IB T280D GM  48000  52800
       IB T283D GM  48000  52700

 44    EXTENDED PILOTHOUSE HT MYDKH P/M RB IB T280 PACE 14  4 24600 3 40800  45300
       IB T320  PACE  42500  47200, IB T215D GM  46400  51000, IB T216D GM  46500  51100
       IB T280D GM  49600  54500, IB T283D GM  49700  54600

 44    PILOTHOUSE     HT  DCCPT P/M RB IB T280 PACE 14  4 26200 3  39000  43800
       IB T320  PACE  39400  43800, IB T215D GM  42100  46800, IB T216D GM  42100  46800
       IB T280D GM  45900  50500

 44    PILOTHOUSE         MYDKH P/M RB IB T280 PACE 14  4 24600 3  40500  45000
       IB T320  PACE  42200  46900, IB T215D GM  46200  51000, IB T216D GM  46200  50800
       IB T280D GM  49200  54100, IB T283D GM  49400  54300

 53                       DC   P/M RB IB T350D GM  16  4 48000 3  6 76100  83700
 53                       DC   P/M RB IB T370D CUM 16  4 48000 3  6 78100  85800
 53                       MY   P/M RB IB T350D GM  16  4 48000 3  6 74700  82100
 53                       MY   P/M RB IB T370D CUM 16  4 48000 3  6 76600  84100
 53                       SDNSF P/M RB IB T350D GM  16  4 48000 3  6 77300  85000
 53                       SDNSF P/M RB IB T370D CUM 16  4 48000 3  6 79400  87200
 53    FISHERMAN          DC   P/M RB IB T350D GM  16  4 48000 3  6 76100  83700
 53    FISHERMAN          DC   P/M RB IB T370D CUM 16  4 48000 3  6 78100  85800
-------------------- 1965 BOATS -------------------------------------------------------
 25 11                    EXP  P/M RB IB  190              6250   7200
 25 11                    EXP  P/M RB IB  150              6750   7750
 25 11 CUSTOM             SF   P/M RB IB  190              6350   7250
 25 11 CUSTOM             SF   P/M RB IB  150              6800   7800
 30                       SDNSF P/M RB IB  220             9950  11300
 30                       SDNSF P/M RB IB T185            10600  12100
 30                       SF   P/M RB IB  220             9000  10200
 30                       SF   P/M RB IB T185             9550  10900
 30    4 SLEEPER          EXP  P/M RB IB  220            10200  11600
 30    4 SLEEPER          EXP  P/M RB IB T185            11000  12500
 30    6 SLEEPER          EXP  P/M RB IB  220            10600  12100
 30    6 SLEEPER          EXP  P/M RB IB T185            11300  12900

 30    CONVERTIBLE        SDN  P/M RB IB  220            10100  11400
 30    CONVERTIBLE        SDN  P/M RB IB T185            10900  12400
 32                       SF   P/M RB IB T220            11800  13400
 32                       SF   P/M RB IB T185            11800  12500
 32    IB  180D   18200  20200, IB T185   11600  13100, IB T 97D GM  18100  20100

 32    CONVERTIBLE        SDN  P/M RB IB  220            12100  13800
 32    IB  180D   20300  22500, IB T185-T220   13000  15300, IB T 97D GM  20400  22700

 32    DELUXE             EXP  P/M RB IB  220            13000  14800
 32    DELUXE             EXP  P/M RB IB T185-T220       13800  16100
 33                       SDNSF P/M RB IB T185-T220      15500  17900
 33                       SDNSF P/M RB IB T 97D GM       26900  29900
 33                       SF   P/M RB IB T185-T220       13800  15900
 33                       SF   P/M RB IB T 97D GM        23900  26500
 36                       SF   P/M RB IB T220            21800  24200
 36                       SF   P/M RB IB T280            22100  24500
 36                       SF   P/M RB IB T180D           25200  28000
 36    6 SLEEPER CNV      SDN  P/M RB IB T220            23400  26000
 36    6 SLEEPER CNV      SDN  P/M RB IB T280            23800  26500
 36    6 SLEEPER CNV      SDN  P/M RB IB T180D           27300  30400

 36    8 SLEEPER CNV      SDN  P/M RB IB T220            23900  26600
 36    8 SLEEPER CNV      SDN  P/M RB IB T280            24300  27000
 36    8 SLEEPER CNV      SDN  P/M RB IB T180D           27700  30800
 36    CUSTOM CONVERTIBLE SDN  P/M RB IB T220            22300  24800
 36    CUSTOM CONVERTIBLE SDN  P/M RB IB T280            22700  25200
 36    CUSTOM CONVERTIBLE SDN  P/M RB IB T180D           26300  29300
 36    DELUXE             EXP  P/M RB IB T220            22700  25200
 36    DELUXE             EXP  P/M RB IB T280            23100  25600
 36    DELUXE             EXP  P/M RB IB T180D           26300  29200
 38                       DCFD P/M RB IB T220            30800  34200
```

                    CONTINUED ON NEXT PAGE

```
LOA   NAME AND/          TOP/ BOAT  -HULL- ----ENGINE---  BEAM   WGT  DRAFT RETAIL RETAIL
FT IN  OR MODEL              RIG TYPE MTL TP TP # HP  MFG  FT IN  LBS  FT IN  LOW   HIGH
-------------------- 1965 BOATS -----------------------------------------------------
38                         DCFD P/M RB IB T280                     31000 34500
38                         DCFD P/M RB IB T180D                    34500 38300
38                         DCFD P/M RB IB T195D                    34700 38600
38                        SDNSF P/M RB IB T220                     30800 34200
   IB T280  31000 34500, IB T180D    34500 38300, IB T195D GM    34700 38600
38                          SF  P/M RB IB T220                     30400 33800
   IB T280  30600 34000, IB T180D    34000 37800, IB T195D GM    34200 38000
44             HT          DCCPT P/M RB IB T280     14 4 24600 3   35400 39400
44             HT          DCCPT P/M RB IB T195D GM 14 4 26200 3   39300 43700
44             HT          DCCPT P/M RB IB T280D GM 14 4 26200 3   42800 47500
44             HT             MY  P/M RB IB T280     14 4 24600 3   38200 42500
44             HT             MY  P/M RB IB T195D GM 14 4 26200 3   42400 47100
44             HT             MY  P/M RB IB T280D GM 14 4 26200 3   46700 51300
44                        SDNSF P/M RB IB T280     14 4 24600 3    37100 41200
   IB T195D GM 40500 45000, IB T280D GM  45600 50100, IB T300D CUM  46800 51500
44                          SF  P/M RB IB T280     14 4 24600 3    37000 41100
   IB T195D GM 40800 45400, IB T280D GM  44700 49700, IB T300D CUM  46200 50800
44 EXTENDED PILOT HOUSE HT DCCPT P/M RB IB T280     14 4 24600 3   37600 41800
44 EXTENDED PILOT HOUSE HT DCCPT P/M RB IB T195D GM 14 4 26200 3   40900 45500
44 EXTENDED PILOT HOUSE HT DCCPT P/M RB IB T280D GM 14 4 26200 3   45900 50400
44 EXTENDED PILOT HOUSE HT    MY  P/M RB IB T280     14 4 24600 3   39100 43400
44 EXTENDED PILOT HOUSE HT    MY  P/M RB IB T195D GM 14 4 26200 3   43100 47800
44 EXTENDED PILOT HOUSE HT    MY  P/M RB IB T280D GM 14 4 26206 3   47000 51600
44 PILOT HOUSE          HT DCCPT P/M RB IB T280     14 4 24600 3   36500 40500
44 PILOT HOUSE          HT DCCPT P/M RB IB T195D GM 14 4 26200 3   40100 44500
44 PILOT HOUSE          HT    MY  P/M RB IB T280     14 4 24600 3   37900 42100
44 PILOT HOUSE          HT    MY  P/M RB IB T195D GM 14 4 26200 3   42100 46800
44 PILOT HOUSE          HT    MY  P/M RB IB T280D GM 14 4 26200 3   47000 51600
44 PILOT HUSE           HT DCCPT P/M RB IB T280D GM 14 4 26200 3   44500 49400
53                          DC  P/M RB IB T280D GM 16 4 48000 3 6  68800 75600
53                          DC  P/M RB IB T350D GM 16 4 48000 3 6  74000 81400
53                          DC  P/M RB IB T370D CUM 16 4 48000 3 6 75900 83400
53             HT           MY  P/M RB IB T280D GM 16 4 48000 3 6  68200 75000
53             HT           MY  P/M RB IB T350D GM 16 4 48000 3 6  74000 81300
53             HT           MY  P/M RB IB T370D CUM 16 4 48000 3 6 75900 83400
53 FISHERMAN                DC  P/M RB IB T350D GM 16 4 48000 3 6  74000 81400
53 FISHERMAN                DC  P/M RB IB T370D CUM 16 4 48000 3 6 75900 83400
53 FISHERMAN    HT          DC  P/M RB IB T280D GM 16 4 48000 3 6  69600 76400
-------------------- 1964 BOATS -----------------------------------------------------
25 11 CUSTOM    HT         SF  P/M RB IB 185       10    7493 1 11  6800 7800
25 11 CUSTOM    HT         SF  P/M RB IB T100-T185 10    8453 1 11  7550 9300
25 11 CUSTOM    FB         SF  P/M RB IB 185       10    7493 1 11  6800 7800
25 11 CUSTOM    FB         SF  P/M RB IB T100-T185 10    8453 1 11  7550 9300
30             HT        SDNSF P/M RB IB T185      10 10 10722 2 4 10800 12200
30             HT        SDNSF P/M RB IB T 97D GM  10 10 10722 2 4 16600 18900
30             FB        SDNSF P/M RB IB T185      10 10  9700     10800 12200
30             FB        SDNSF P/M RB IB T 97D GM  10 10 10722 2 4 16600 18900
30             HT          SF  P/M RB IB  220      10 10  8755 2 4  7950  9100
30             HT          SF  P/M RB IB T185      10 10  9755 2 4 10400 11800
30             HT          SF  P/M RB IB T 97D GM  10 10  9755 2 4 15400 17600
30             FB          SF  P/M RB IB  220      10 10  8755 2 4  7950  9100
30             FB          SF  P/M RB IB T185      10 10  9755 2 4 10400 11800
30             FB          SF  P/M RB IB T 97D     10 10  9755 2 4 15400 17600
30 4 SLEEPER    HT        EXP  P/M RB IB  220      10 10  9722 2 4  9500 10800
30 4 SLEEPER    HT        EXP  P/M RB IB T185      10 10 10722 2 4 10600 12200
30 4 SLEEPER    HT        EXP  P/M RB IB T 97D GM  10 10 10722 2 4 16600 18900
30 4 SLEEPER    FB        EXP  P/M RB IB  220      10 10  9722 2 4  9500 10800
30 4 SLEEPER    FB        EXP  P/M RB IB T185      10 10 10722 2 4 10600 12100
30 4 SLEEPER    FB        EXP  P/M RB IB T 97D GM  10 10 10722 2 4 16600 18900
30 6 SLEEPER    HT        EXP  P/M RB IB  220      10 10  9722 2 4  9900 11200
30 6 SLEEPER    HT        EXP  P/M RB IB T185      10 10 10722 2 4 10900 12400
30 6 SLEEPER    FB        EXP  P/M RB IB  220      10 10  9722 2 4  9850 11200
30 6 SLEEPER    FB        EXP  P/M RB IB T185      10 10 10722 2 4 10900 12400
30 CONVERTIBLE  HT        SDN  P/M RB IB  220      10 10  9722 2 4 10400 11800
30 CONVERTIBLE  HT        SDN  P/M RB IB T185      10 10 10722 2 4 11600 13200
30 CONVERTIBLE  HT        SDN  P/M RB IB T 97D GM  10 10 10722 2 4 18600 20700
30 CONVERTIBLE  FB        SDN  P/M RB IB  220      10 10  9722 2 4 10400 11800
30 CONVERTIBLE  FB        SDN  P/M RB IB T185      10 10 10722 2 4 11600 13200
30 CONVERTIBLE  FB        SDN  P/M RB IB T 97D GM  10 10 10722 2 4 18600 20700
30 CONVERTIBLE  HT       SDNSF P/M RB IB  220      10 10  9722 2 4  9700 11000
32             HT          SF  P/M RB IB T185-T220 10 10 13195 2 3 13300 15600
32             HT          SF  P/M RB IB T 97D GM  10 10 13195 2 3 21100 23400
32             FB          SF  P/M RB IB T185-T220 11 4 13195 2 3 13400 15600
32             FB          SF  P/M RB IB T 97D GM  11 4 13195 2 3 21200 23600
32 CONVERTIBLE  HT        SDN  P/M RB IB T185-T220 11 4 13195 2 3 14400 16800
32 CONVERTIBLE  HT        SDN  P/M RB IB T 97D GM  11 4 13195 2 3 22600 25100
32 CONVERTIBLE  FB        SDN  P/M RB IB T185-T220 11 4 13195 2 3 14400 16800
32 CONVERTIBLE  FB        SDN  P/M RB IB T 97D GM  11 10 13195 2 3 22500 25000
32 DELUXE       HT        EXP  P/M RB IB T185-T220 11 4 13195 2 3 13400 15600
32 DELUXE       HT        EXP  P/M RB IB T185-T220 11 4 13195 2 3 13400 15600
33             HT          SF  P/M RB IB T 97D GM  12 8 12185 2 3 14400 16700
33             HT          SF  P/M RB IB T185-T220 12 8 12185 2 3 21300 23700
33             FB          SF  P/M RB IB T 97D GM  12 8 12185 2 3 21300 23700
33             FB          SF  P/M RB IB T185-T220 12 8 12185 2 3 14400 16700
36             HT          SF  P/M RB IB T220      12   13400 2 6 20500 22800
36             HT          SF  P/M RB IB T151D GM  12   14800 2 6 24200 26900
36             FB          SF  P/M RB IB T220      12   13400 2 6 20500 22800
36             FB          SF  P/M RB IB T151D GM  12   14800 2 6 24200 26900
36 CONVERTIBLE  HT        SDN  P/M RB IB T220      12   13400 2 6 21100 23400
36 CONVERTIBLE  HT        SDN  P/M RB IB T151D GM  12   14800 2 6 25100 27800
36 CONVERTIBLE  FB        SDN  P/M RB IB T220      12   13400 2 6 21100 23400
36 CONVERTIBLE  FB        SDN  P/M RB IB T151D GM  12   14800 2 6 25100 27800
36 DELUXE       HT        EXP  P/M RB IB T220      12   13400 2 6 20500 22800
36 DELUXE       FB        EXP  P/M RB IB T220      12   13400 2 6 20500 22800
38             OP        DCFD  P/M RB IB T220      13 10 22160 3   30900 34300
   IB T280 31100 34500, IB T151D GM 35700 39700, IB T195D GM 34800 38600
38             FB        DCFD  P/M RB IB T220      13 10 22160 3   30900 34300
   IB T280 31100 34500, IB T151D GM 35200 39100, IB T195D GM 35700 39700
38             HT          SF  P/M RB IB T220      13 10 21090 3   29600 32900
   IB T280 29800 33100, IB T151D GM 34400 38200, IB T195D GM 34900 38800
38             FB          SF  P/M RB IB T220      13 10 21090 3   29600 32900
   IB T280 29800 33100, IB T151D GM 34400 38200, IB T195D GM 34900 38800
43             HT        DCFD  P/M RB IB T280      14 4 24400 3    38200 42400
43             HT        DCFD  P/M RB IB T195D GM  14 4 24400 3    42400 47100
43             FB        DCFD  P/M RB IB T280      14 4 24400 3    38100 42300
43             FB        DCFD  P/M RB IB T195D GM  14 4 26000 3    76500 83000
43             HT          SF  P/M RB IB T280      14 4 22400 3    35100 39000
   IB T195D GM 39300 43700, IB T280D GM 43400 48200, IB T300D CUM 44400 49300
43             FB          SF  P/M RB IB T280      14 4 22400 3    35000 38900
   IB T195D GM 39300 43600, IB T280D GM 43300 48100, IB T300D CUM 44200 49100
43 COCKPIT      OP        DCCPT P/M RB IB T280      14 4 24600 3   36000 40000
43 COCKPIT      OP        DCCPT P/M RB IB T195D GM  14 4 24600 3   39400 43800
43 COCKPIT      FB        DCCPT P/M RB IB T280      14 4 24600 3   36200 40200
43 COCKPIT      FB        DCCPT P/M RB IB T195D GM  14 4 26000 3   40000 44400
-------------------- 1963 BOATS -----------------------------------------------------
30             HT        SDNSF P/M RB IB T185 PACE 10 2  9950 2 2 10000 11400
30             FB        SDNSF P/M RB IB T185 PACE 10 2  8950 2 2  8500  9750
30             HT        SDNSF P/M RB IB T185 PACE 10 2  9950 2 2 10000 11400
30             FB        SDNSF P/M RB IB T185 PACE 10 2  8950 2 2  8500  9750
30             HT          SF  P/M RB IB T185 PACE 10 2  9450 2 2  8400  9650
30             FB          SF  P/M RB IB T185 PACE 10 2  8450 2 2  7500  8600
30             HT          SF  P/M RB IB T185 PACE 10 2  9450 2 2  8400  9650
30             FB          SF  P/M RB IB T185 PACE 10 2  8450 2 2  7500  8600
30 CONVERTIBLE  HT        SDN  P/M RB IB  220 PACE 10 2  9950 2 2  8700 10000
30 CONVERTIBLE  FB        SDN  P/M RB IB  220 PACE 10 2  8950 2 2 10900 12400
30 CONVERTIBLE  HT        SDN  P/M RB IB  220 PACE 10 2  9950 2 2  9700 11000
30 CONVERTIBLE  FB        SDN  P/M RB IB  220 PACE 10 2  8950 2 2 10900 12400
30 CONVERTIBLE  HT       SDNSF P/M RB IB  220 PACE 10 2  9950 2 2  8500  9750
30 STANDARD     HT        EXP  P/M RB IB  220 PACE 10 2  8950 2 2  9050 10300
30 STANDARD     FB        EXP  P/M RB IB  220 PACE 10 2  9950 2 2 10000 11400
30 STANDARD     HT        EXP  P/M RB IB T185 PACE 10 2  9450 2 2 10000 11400
30 STANDARD     FB        EXP  P/M RB IB T185 PACE 10 2  9450 2 2 10000 11400
32             HT          SF  P/M RB IB T220 PACE 11   13195 2 2 12900 15100
32             HT          SF  P/M RB IB T185-T220 PACE 11 13195 2 2 13200 15000
32 CONVERTIBLE  HT        SDN  P/M RB IB T185-T220 PACE 11 13195 2 2 13900 16200
32 CONVERTIBLE  FB        SDN  P/M RB IB T185-T220 PACE 11 13195 2 2 13900 16200
32 CONVERTIBLE  FB          SF P/M RB IB T185 PACE 11 13195 2 2 12900 15100
32 DELUXE       HT        EXP  P/M RB IB T185-T220 PACE 11 13195 2 2 14200 14700
36             HT          SF  P/M RB IB T220 PACE 12   13400 2 6 12900 15000
36             HT          SF  P/M RB IB T220 PACE 12   13400 2 6 20000 22300
```

```
LOA  NAME AND/           TOP/ BOAT -HULL- ----ENGINE---  BEAM    WGT  DRAFT RETAIL RETAIL
FT IN OR MODEL           RIG  TYPE MTL TP TP # HP  MFG   FT IN   LBS  FT IN  LOW   HIGH
------------------- 1963 BOATS ------------------------------------------------------------
 36                      HT  SF  P/M RB IB T151D GM   12  14800 22  6  23600  26200
 36                      FB  SF  P/M RB IB T220  PACE 12  13400  2  6  20000  22300
 36                      FB  SF  P/M RB IB T151D GM   12  14800  2  6  23600  26200
 36   CONVERTIBLE        HT  SDN P/M RB IB T220  PACE 12  13400  2  6  20600  22900
 36   CONVERTIBLE        HT  SDN P/M RB IB T130D GM   12  14800  2  6  24200  26800
 36   CONVERTIBLE        FB  SDN P/M RB IB T220  PACE 12  13400  2  6  20600  22900
 36   CONVERTIBLE        FB  SDN P/M RB IB T130D GM   12  14800  2  6  24200  26800
 36   DELUXE             HT  EXP P/M RB IB T220  PACE 12  13400  2  6  20200  22500
 36   DELUXE             FB  EXP P/M RB IB T220  PACE 12  13400  2  6  20200  22500
 36   STANDARD           HT  EXP P/M RB IB T220  PACE 12  13400  2  6  19900  22100
 36   STANDARD           HT  EXP P/M RB IB T151D GM   12  14800  2  6  23600  26300

 36   STANDARD           FB  EXP P/M RB IB T220  PACE 12  13400  2  6  19900  22100
 36   STANDARD           FB  EXP P/M RB IB T151D GM   12  14800  2  6  23600  26300
 43                      OP  DC  P/M RB IB T280  PACE 14  4 24400  3     37000  41100
 43                      OP  DC  P/M RB IB T101D GM   14  4 26000  3     40300  44800
 43                      OP  DCFD P/M RB IB T280 PACE 14  4 24400  3     37000  41100
 43                      OP  DCFD P/M RB IB T181D GM  14  4 26000  3     40300  44800
 43                      HT  SDNSF P/M RB IB T280 PACE 14 4 22400  3     34500  38400
 43                      HT  SDNSF P/M RB IB T195D GM 14  4 24400  3     38100  42300
 43                      FB  SDNSF P/M RB IB T280 PACE 14 4 22400  3     34400  38300
 43                      FB  SDNSF P/M RB IB T195D GM 14 4 24400  3     38000  42300
 43                      HT  SF  P/M RB IB T280  PACE 14  4 22400  3     34300  38100
 43                      HT  SF  P/M RB IB T181D GM   14  4 24400  3     37900  42100

 43                      FB  SF  P/M RB IB T280  PACE 14  4 22400  3     34200  38000
 43                      FB  SF  P/M RB IB T181D GM   14  4 24400  3     37800  42000
------------------- 1962 BOATS ------------------------------------------------------------
 30                      FB  SF  P/M RB IB  220  PACE 10  2  6500  2  2   6750   7750
 30                      FB  SF  P/M RB IB T185  PACE 10  2  6500  2  2   7400   8500
 30   STANDARD           HT  EXP P/M RB IB  220  PACE 10  2  6500  2  2   7900   9100
 30   STANDARD           FB  EXP P/M RB IB T185  PACE 10  2  6500  2  2   8700  10000
 30   STANDARD           FB  EXP P/M RB IB  220  PACE 10  2  6506  2  2   7900   9100
 30   STANDARD           FB  EXP P/M RB IB T185  PACE 10  2  6506  2  2   8700  10000
 35                      FB  SDNSF P/M RB IB T220 PACE 12  10800  2  6  14900  17000
 35   CONVERTIBLE        FB  SDN P/M RB IB T220  PACE 12  10800  2  6  22800  25300
 35   CONVERTIBLE        FB  SDN P/M RB IB T120D GM  12  10800  2  6  15000  17000
 35   STANDARD           FB  EXP P/M RB IB T220  PACE 12  10800  2  6  23300  25900
 35   STANDARD           FB  EXP P/M RB IB T220  PACE 12  10800  2  6  15600  17800
 35   STANDARD           HT  EXP P/M RB IB T120D GM  12  10800  2  6  23800  26400

 40                      FB  SDNSF P/M RB IB T220 PACE 12 7 14200  2 11 25000  27800
      IB T280  PACE 25200 28000, IB T120D GM   28500 31600, IB T181D GM  29300  32500

 40   STANDARD           HT  EXP P/M RB IB T220  PACE 12 7 14200  2 11 25000  27800
      IB T280  PACE 25200 28000, IB T120D GM   28500 31600, IB T181D GM  29300  32500

 43                      DC  P/M RB IB T280  GM              35300  39200
 43                      DC  P/M RB IB T181D GM              38800  43100
 43                      FB  SF  P/M RB IB T280  PACE        37400  41500
 43                      FB  SF  P/M RB IB T181D GM          39900  44400
------------------- 1961 BOATS ------------------------------------------------------------
 30                      SF  P/M RB IB 195-215  10  2  6500  2  2   6500   7550
 30                      SF  P/M RB IB T110-T125 10  2  6500  2  2   6600   7750
 30                      SF  P/M RB IB T195-T215 10  2  6500  2  2   7300   8550
 30   STANDARD           EXP P/M RB IB 195-215   10  2  6500  2  2   7600   8850
 30   STANDARD           EXP P/M RB IB T110-T125 10  2  6500  2  2   7750   9100
 30   STANDARD           EXP P/M RB IB T195-T215 10  2  6500  2  2   8600  10100
 35                      SF  P/M RB IB T177      12    10800  2  6  13100  14800
      IB T195  13200 15000, IB T200          13200 15000, IB T215       13300  15100
      IB T225  13300 15100, IB T130D         20700 23000

 35   DELUXE             EXP P/M RB IB T177      12    10800  2  6  15000  17100
      IB T195  15300 17400, IB T200          15300 17400, IB T215       15300  17400
      IB T225  15500 17600

 35   DELUXE CONVERTIBLE SDN P/M RB IB T177      12    10800  2  6  14300  16300
      IB T195  14500 16500, IB T200          14500 16500, IB T215       14600  16600
      IB T225  14700 16700, IB T130D         23300 25900

 35   STANDARD           EXP P/M    IB T225     12    10800  2  6  15200  17300
 35   STANDARD           EXP P/M RB IB T177     12    10800  2  6  15000  17100
      IB T195  15000 17100, IB T200          15100 17100, IB T215       18600  20700
      IB T130D 23800 26400

 40                      SDNSF P/M RB IB T210    12 7 14200  2 11 24500  27200
      IB T225  22200 24600, IB T240          24500 27300, IB T260       24600  27300
      IB T275  24600 27400, IB T280          24700 27400, IB T130D      27000  30000
      IB T195D 28800 32000

 40                      SF  P/M    IB T240     12 7 14200  2 11 24500  27300
 40                      SF  P/M RB IB T210     12 7 15000  2 11 25400  28300
      IB T225  24500 27200, IB T260          24600 27300, IB T275       24600  27400
      IB T280  24700 27400, IB T130D         27000 30000, IB T195D      28800  32000

 40   DELUXE             SDN P/M RB IB T210     12 7 15000  2 11 25500  28300
      IB T225  24500 27300, IB T240          24600 27300, IB T260       24600  27400
      IB T275  24700 27400, IB T280          24700 27400, IB T130D      28000  31100
      IB T195D 28900 32100

 40   STANDARD           EXP P/M RB IB T210     12 7 15000  2 11 25400  28300
      IB T225  24500 27200, IB T240          24500 27300, IB T260       24600  27300
      IB T275  24700 27400, IB T280          25600 28500, IB T130D      28000  31100
      IB T195D 28800 32000
------------------- 1960 BOATS ------------------------------------------------------------
 30   DAY BOAT           CR  P/M RB IB 125-188   10  2  6500  2  2   6350   7700
 30   DAY BOAT           CR  P/M RB IB T110-T177 10  2  6500  2  2   6850   8550
 30   DAY BOAT           CR  P/M RB IB T188 GRAY 10  2  6500  2  2   7550   8700
 30   STANDARD           OP  EXP P/M RB IB 125-188 10 2  6500  2  2   7050   8550
 30   STANDARD           OP  EXP P/M RB IB T110-T177 10 2 6500  2  2   7600   9500
 30   STANDARD           OP  EXP P/M RB IB T188 GRAY 10 2 6500  2  2   8350   9600
 30   DELUXE             FB  EXP P/M    IB  170 GRAY 10 2  6500  2  2   7300   8400
 30   STANDARD           FB  EXP P/M RB IB 125-188 10 2  6500  2  2   7050   8550
 30   STANDARD           FB  EXP P/M RB IB T110-T177 10 2 6500  2  2   7600   9500
 30   STANDARD           FB  EXP P/M RB IB T188 GRAY 10 2 6500  2  2   8350   9600
 33   CONVERTIBLE        SDN P/M RB IB 125-188             12500  14300
 33   CONVERTIBLE        SDN P/M RB IB T125-T188           12900  15300

 33   CONVERTIBLE        FB  SDN P/M RB IB 125-188         12500  14300
 33   CONVERTIBLE        FB  SDN P/M RB IB T125-T188       12900  15300
 33   EXPRESS            HT  EXP L/P    IB  125   10  2    14300  16200
 33   EXPRESS            HT  EXP L/P    IB  188   10  2  2  6 14700  16700
 33   STANDARD           OP  EXP P/M RB IB 125-188         13900  15800
 33   STANDARD           OP  EXP P/M RB IB T125-T188       14000  16300
 33   STANDARD           FB  EXP P/M RB IB 125-188         13900  15800
 33   STANDARD           FB  EXP P/M RB IB T125-T188       14000  16300
 40   STANDARD           FB  SDN P/M RB IB T225 CHRY 12 7 14200  2  4 23600  26200
 40   STANDARD           FB  SDN P/M RB IB T225 CHRY 12 7 14200  2  4 24000  26600

 40   CONVERTIBLE        SDN P/M RB IB T125 CHRY  12 7 14200  2  4 23600  26200
      IB T170 GRAY 23900 26600, IB T177 CHRY 23900 26500, IB T188 GRAY  24000  26700
      IB T225 CHRY 24000 26600, IB T120D GM  27300 30400, IB T151D GM   27700  30800
      IB T197D GM  28300 31500

 40   CONVERTIBLE        FB  SDN P/M RB IB T170 GRAY 12 7 14200  2  4 23900  26600
      IB T177 CHRY 23900 26500, IB T188 GRAY 24000 26700, IB T120D GM   27300  30400
      IB T151D GM  27700 30800, IB T197D GM  28300 31500

 40   SPORT FISH         SF  L/P    IB T125     12 7      2 11 29100  32400
 40   SPORT FISH         SF  L/P    IB T225     12 7      2 11 29500  32800
 40   STANDARD           EXP P/M    IB T125 CHRY 12 7 14200  2  4 23600  26200
      IB T170 GRAY 23900 26600, IB T177 CHRY 23900 26500, IB T188 GRAY  24000  26600
      IB T225 CHRY 24000 26600, IB T120D GM  27300 30300, IB T151D GM   27700  30800
      IB T197D GM  28300 31400

 40                      FB  EXP P/M    IB T125 CHRY 12 7 14200  2  4 23600  26200
      IB T170 GRAY 23900 26600, IB T177 CHRY 23900 26500, IB T188 GRAY  24000  26600
      IB T225 CHRY 24000 26600, IB T120D GM  27300 30300, IB T151D GM   27700  30800
      IB T197D GM  28300 31400
------------------- 1959 BOATS ------------------------------------------------------------
 29   STANDARD           EXP P/M RB IB  125      9  9               6500   7450
 29   STANDARD           EXP P/M RB IB T 95      9  9               6850   7900
 33   DELUXE             SDN P/M RB IB  125      10 10             12900  14700
 33   DELUXE             SDN P/M RB IB  125      10 10             14000  15900
 40   DELUXE-CONV        SDN P/M RB IB  125      12 7 14200  2 11 23200  25800
 40   STANDARD           EXP P/M RB IB  125      12 7 14200  2 11 23200  25800
------------------- 1958 BOATS ------------------------------------------------------------
 29   STANDARD           EXP WD     IB  135                        6500   7450
 29   STANDARD           EXP P/M RB IB 125-225                     6750   7900
 29   STANDARD           EXP P/M RB IB T 95-T110                   6750   7900
 33   DELUXE             SDN P/M RB IB T125                       12400  14100
 33   STANDARD           EXP P/M RB IB 125-225                    13400  15300
 33   STANDARD           EXP P/M RB IB 125                        13500  15300
 33   STANDARD           HT  EXP P/M RB IB T125-T225              13500  16000
```

450   CONTINUED ON NEXT PAGE   96th ed. - Vol. III

LOA FT	LOA IN	NAME AND/ OR MODEL	TOP/ RIG	BOAT TYPE	-HULL- MTL	-HULL- TP	ENGINE TP	ENGINE # HP	ENGINE MFG	BEAM FT	BEAM IN	WGT LBS	DRAFT FT	DRAFT IN	RETAIL LOW	RETAIL HIGH
		1958 BOATS														
33		STANDARD	FB	EXP	P/M	RB	IB	125-225							13400	15300
33		STANDARD	FB	EXP	P/M	RB	IB	T125-T225							13500	16000
		1957 BOATS														
29		STANDARD		EXP	P/M	RB	IB	125							6400	7350
33		STANDARD		EXP	P/M	RB	IB	125							13200	15000
		1956 BOATS														
29		STANDARD		EXP	P/M	RB	IB	125							6350	7300
33		DELUXE		SDN	P/M	RB	IB	T125							12000	13700
33		STANDARD		EXP	P/M	RB	IB	125							13000	14700
		1955 BOATS														
29		STANDARD		EXP	P/M	RB	IB	125-200							6200	7450
29		STANDARD		EXP	P/M	RB	IB	T 95-T110							6500	7650
33		SPECIAL		EXP	P/M	RB	IB	T125							12800	14600
33		STANDARD		EXP	P/M	RB	IB	130-200							12800	14500
33		STANDARD		EXP	P/M	RB	IB	T125-T155							12800	14700
		1954 BOATS														
29		STANDARD		EXP	P/M	RB	IB	125							6450	7400
33			HT	EXP	WD	RB	IB								**	**
		1953 BOATS														
29			HT	EXP	WD		IB	115	CHRY						6400	7350
29			HT	EXP	WD		IB	T 95	CHRY						6550	7550
29		STANDARD	FB	EXP	P/M	RB	IB	125	PACE	10	2	6506	2	2	5400	6200
33			HT	EXP	WD		IB	130	NORD						12400	14100
33			HT	EXP	WD		IB	T115	CHRY						12500	14200
		1952 BOATS														
29		STANDARD		EXP	P/M	RB	IB	125							6000	6900
		1951 BOATS														
29		STANDARD		EXP	P/M	RB	IB	125							5900	6800
		1950 BOATS														
28	2	SKIFF	HT	UTL	WD		IB			9	4				**	**

PACESHIP YACHTS

DIV AMF INTERNATIONAL
WATERBURY CT 06720 COAST GUARD MFG ID- PAY

See inside cover to adjust price for area

LOA FT	LOA IN	NAME AND/ OR MODEL	TOP/ RIG	BOAT TYPE	-HULL- MTL	-HULL- TP	ENGINE TP	ENGINE # HP	ENGINE MFG	BEAM FT	BEAM IN	WGT LBS	DRAFT FT	DRAFT IN	RETAIL LOW	RETAIL HIGH
		1980 BOATS														
22	7	PY23	SLP	SA/RC	FBG	KC				8		2950			4100	4800
22	7	PY23	SLP	SA/RC	FBG	KL				8		2950			4100	4800
26	4	PY26	SLP	SA/RC	FBG	KC				9	6	6900			10400	11800
26	4	PY26	SLP	SA/RC	FBG	KL				9	6	6900			10400	11800
		1979 BOATS														
21	1	AMF 2100	SLP	SAIL	FBG	KL	OB			8		2200	5		3200	3700
22	7	PY23	SLP	SA/CR	FBG	KC	OB			8		2950	1	9	4000	4650
22	7	PY23	SLP	SA/CR	FBG	KL	OB			8		2950	3	9	4000	4650
26	4	PY26	SLP	SA/CR	FBG	KC	OB			9	6	6900	2	7	10500	12000
26	4	PY26	SLP	SA/CR	FBG	KC	IB	8D	YAN	9	6	6900	2	7	11000	12400
26	4	PY26	SLP	SA/CR	FBG	KL	OB			9	6	6400	4	6	9700	11000
26	4	PY26	SLP	SA/CR	FBG	KL	IB	8D	YAN	9	6	6400	4	6	10100	11500
		1978 BOATS														
22	7	PY23	SLP	SA/CR	FBG	KC	OB			8			1	9	4000	4650
22	7	PY23	SLP	SA/CR	FBG	KL	OB			8			3	9	4000	4650
26	4	PY26	SLP	SA/CR	FBG	KC	OB			9	6	6000	2	7	8850	10100
26	4	PY26	SLP	SA/CR	FBG	KC	IB	8D		9	6	6000	2	7	9250	10500
26	4	PY26	SLP	SA/CR	FBG	KL	OB			9	6	6000	4	6	8850	10100
26	4	PY26	SLP	SA/CR	FBG	KL	IB	8D		9	6	6000	4	6	9250	10500
		1977 BOATS														
22	7	PY23	SLP	SA/CR	FBG	KC	OB			8		3200	1	9	4000	4650
22	7	PY23K	SLP	SA/CR	FBG	KL	OB			8		3200	3	9	4000	4650
26	4	PY26	SLP	SA/CR	FBG	KL	OB			9	6	6800	4	6	9800	11100
26	4	PY26	SLP	SA/CR	FBG	KL	IB	8D	YAN	9	6	6800	4	6	10200	11600
		1976 BOATS														
22	7	PY23	SLP	SAIL	FBG	KC	OB			8			1	9	3800	4400
22	7	PY23K	SLP	SAIL	FBG	KL	OB			8			3	9	3800	4400
26	4	PY26	SLP	SAIL	FBG	KL	OB			9	6	6000	4	6	8300	9550
26	4	PY26	SLP	SAIL	FBG	KL	IB	8D	YAN	9	6	6000	4	6	8700	10000
		1975 BOATS														
19	3	PACESHIP 20	SLP	SAIL	FBG	CB	OB			7	9	800	4		1700	2000
22	7	PY23	SLP	SAIL	FBG	KC	OB			8		2600	4	9	3250	3800
26	4	PY26	SLP	SAIL	FBG	KL	IB	7D	PETT	9	6	6000	4	6	8450	9750
28	8	CHANCE P29-25	SLP	SAIL	F/S	KL	IB	30	UNIV	9	4	7500	5	7	11100	12600
28	8	CHANCE P29-25	SLP	SAIL	F/S	KL	IB	23D	VLVO	9	4		5	7	11400	12900
32	1	CHANCE P32-28	SLP	SAIL	FBG	KL	IB	30	UNIV	10		12025	5	9	18500	20500
32	1	CHANCE P32-28	SLP	SAIL	FBG	KL	IB	23D	VLVO	10			5	9	19100	21200
		1974 BOATS														
22	7	PY 23	SLP	SAIL	FBG		OB			8			1	9	3650	4200
22	9	PACESHIP 23	SLP	SAIL	FBG		OB			7	6	2800	3	6	3400	3950
28	7	CHANCE P29/25	SLP	SAIL	FBG		IB	30	UNIV	9	1	7500	5	1	10900	12300
28	10	PACESHIP 29	SLP	SAIL	FBG	CB	IB	30	UNIV	9	1	6500	6	9	9400	10700
28	10	PACESHIP 29	SLP	SAIL	FBG	KL	IB	30	UNIV	9	1	6500	6	9	9400	10700
32	1	CHANCE P32/28	SLP	SAIL	FBG		IB	30	UNIV	10		12025	5	9	18100	20100
		1973 BOATS														
22	9	PACESHIP 23	SLP	SAIL	FBG		OB			7	6	2800	3	6	3350	3850
22	10	BLUEJACKET	SLP	SAIL	FBG		OB			7		2000	3	9	2700	3100
23	11	WESTWIND 24	SLP	SAIL	FBG		OB			8		4630	5	6	5350	6150
28	10	NORTHWIND 29	SLP	SAIL	FBG		IB	30	UNIV	9	2	6600	6	9	9450	10700
28	10	PACESHIP 29	SLP	SAIL	FBG	KC	IB	30	UNIV	9	1	6500	6	9	9300	10500
28	10	PACESHIP 29	SLP	SAIL	FBG	KL	IB	30	UNIV	9	1	6500	6	9	9300	10500
30		ACADIAN 30 MK II	SLP	SAIL	FBG		IB	30	UNIV	8	6	6800	4	4	9800	11100
30		ACADIAN 30 MK II	SLP	SAIL	FBG		IB	20D	PALM	9	1	6800	4	4	9850	11200
30		ACADIAN 30 MK II	YWL	SAIL	FBG		IB	30	UNIV	8	6	6800	4	4	9800	11100
30		ACADIAN 30 MK II	YWL	SAIL	FBG		IB	20D	PALM	9	1	6800	4	4	9850	11200
31	10	PACESHIP 32	SLP	SAIL	FBG		IB	30	UNIV	10	6	9000	4	8	13100	14900
32	1	CHANCE 32/28		SAIL	FBG		IB	30	UNIV	10		13000	5	9	19200	21300
		1972 BOATS														
22	9	PACESHIP 23	SLP	SAIL	FBG		OB			7	6	2800	3	6	3250	3800
22	10	BLUEJACKET 23		SAIL	FBG		OB			7		2000	3	9	2650	3050
23	11	WESTWIND 24	SLP	SAIL	FBG		OB			8		4630	5	6	5250	6050
28	10	NORTHWIND 29		SAIL	FBG		IB	30	UNIV	9	2	6600	6	9	9250	10500
28	10	PACESHIP 29	SLP	SAIL	FBG		IB	30	UNIV	9	1	6450	6	9	9000	10200
30		ACADIAN 30 MK II	SLP	SAIL	FBG		IB	30	UNIV	8	6	6800	4	4	9600	10900
30		ACADIAN 30 MK II	SLP	SAIL	FBG		IB	20D	PALM	8	6	6800	4	4	9650	11000
30		ACADIAN 30 MK II	YWL	SAIL	FBG		IB	30	UNIV	8	6	6800	4	4	9600	10900
30		ACADIAN 30 MK II	YWL	SAIL	FBG		IB	20D	PALM	8	6	6800	4	4	9650	11000
31	10	PACESHIP 32	SLP	SAIL	FBG		IB	30	UNIV	10	6	9000	4	8	12800	14500
		1971 BOATS														
16	7	ATLANTIC-CLIPPER	FB		FBG		OB			6	5				2350	2700
16	7	ATLANTIC-CLIPPER		UTL	FBG		OB			6	5	700			1750	2050
22	9	PACESHIP 23	SLP	SAIL	FBG		OB			7	6	2800	3	6	3200	3700
22	10	BLUEJACKET		SAIL	FBG		OB			7		2000	3	9	2450	2850
22	10	BLUEJACKET MORCEE		SAIL	FBG		OB			7		2000	3	9	2650	3100
23	11	WESTWIND 24	SLP	SAIL	FBG		OB			8		4630	5	6	5150	5900
28	10	NORTHWIND		SAIL	FBG		OB			9	2	6200	6	9	8250	9450
28	10	NORTHWIND		SAIL	FBG		IB	30	UNIV	9	2	6600	6	9	9000	10200
30		ACADIAN MARK II	SLP	SAIL	FBG		IB	30	UNIV	8	6	6800	4	4	9400	10700
30		ACADIAN MARK II	YWL	SAIL	FBG		IB	30	UNIV	8	6	6800	4	4	9400	10700
		1970 BOATS														
16	7	ATLANTIC-CLIPPER	FB		FBG		OB			6	5	700			1800	2100
16	7	ATLANTIC-CLIPPER		UTL	FBG		OB			6	5	700			1750	2100
19	6	CRUISETTE	SLP	SAIL	FBG	KL	OB			6	10	1500	3	10	2050	2400
22	10	BLUEJACKET		SA/OD	FBG	KL	OB			7		2000	3	9	2500	2900
22	10	BLUEJACKET MORCEE	SLP	SAIL	FBG	KL	OB			7		2000	3	9	2500	2900
23	11	WESTWIND	SLP	SAIL	FBG	KC	OB			8		4630	2	1	5000	5750
28	10	NORTHWIND	SLP	SAIL	FBG	KL	OB			9	2	6200	3	1	8050	9250
28	10	NORTHWIND	SLP	SAIL	FBG	KL	IB	30	UNIV	9	2	6200	3	1	8150	9350
30		ACADIAN MARK II	SLP	SAIL	FBG	KL	IB	30	UNIV	8	6	6800	4	4	9150	10400
30		ACADIAN MARK II	YWL	SAIL	FBG	KL	IB	30	UNIV	8	6	6800	4	4	9150	10400
		1969 BOATS														
16	6	ATLANTIC-CLIPPER	FB		FBG		OB								2350	2700
16	6	ATLANTIC-CLIPPER		UTL	FBG		OB								1750	2100
19	6	CRUISETTE	SLP	SAIL	FBG	KL	OB			6	10	1200	3	10	1750	2100
22	10	BLUEJACKET	SLP	SAIL	FBG	KL	OB			7		2000	5	6	2450	2850
23	11	WESTWIND	SLP	SAIL	FBG	KC	OB			8		4630	5	6	4900	5600
24	7	EAST-WIND	SLP	SAIL	FBG	KL	OB			7	1	4600	3	7	5050	5800
24	7	EAST-WIND	SLP	SAIL	FBG	KL	IB	8	PALM	7	1	4600	3	7	5200	6000
30		ACADIAN MARK II	SLP	SAIL	FBG	KL	IB	30	UNIV	8	6	6800	4	4	8950	10200
30		ACADIAN MARK II	YWL	SAIL	FBG	KL	IB	30	UNIV	8	6	6800	4	4	8950	10200
		1968 BOATS														
23	11	WESTWIND BCB	SLP	SAIL	FBG	CB	OB			8				2	3300	3850
24	7	EAST-WIND	SLP	SAIL	FBG		OB								7050	8100
30		ACADIAN	SLP	SAIL	FBG	KL	OB			8	6		4	4	7950	9150
30		ACADIAN	YWL	SAIL	FBG	KL	OB			8	6		4	4	7950	9150
		1967 BOATS														
23	11	WESTWIND BCB	SLP	SAIL	FBG	CB	OB			7	11				3250	3750
24	7	EAST-WIND	SLP	SAIL	FBG	KL	OB			7	1		3	7	6900	7950
24	7	EAST-WIND	SLP	SAIL	FBG	KL	IB	7D		7	1		3	7	7250	8350
30		ACADIAN	SLP	SAIL	FBG	KL	OB			8	6		4	4	7800	9000
30		ACADIAN	SLP	SAIL	FBG	KL	IB	15D		8	6		4	4	11200	12800
30		ACADIAN	YWL	SAIL	FBG	KL	OB			8	6		4	4	7800	9000
30		ACADIAN	YWL	SAIL	FBG	KL	IB	15D		8	6		4	4	11200	12800
31	7	PACESHIP 32	SLP	SAIL	FBG	KL	IB	25		10	2		5		15300	17300
31	7	PACESHIP 32	SLP	SAIL	FBG	KL	IB	15D		10	2		5		15800	18000

 CONTINUED ON NEXT PAGE

PACESHIP YACHTS   -CONTINUED   See inside cover to adjust price for area

LOA FT IN	NAME AND/ OR MODEL	TOP/ RIG	BOAT TYPE	MTL	-HULL- TP	TP	#	-ENGINE- HP	MFG	BEAM FT IN	WGT LBS	DRAFT FT IN	RETAIL LOW	RETAIL HIGH
					1966 BOATS									
24 7	EAST-WIND	SLP	SAIL	FBG	KL	OB				7 1		3 7	6800	7800
24 7	EAST-WIND	SLP	SAIL	FBG	KL	IB		7D		7 1		3 7	7150	8200
30	ACADIAN	SLP	SAIL	FBG	KL	OB				8 6		3 7	7700	8850
30	ACADIAN	SLP	SAIL	FBG	KL	IB		15D		8 6		4 4	11000	12600
30	ACADIAN	YWL	SAIL	FBG	KL	OB				8 6		4 4	7700	8850
30	ACADIAN	YWL	SAIL	FBG	KL	IB		15D		8 6		4 4	11000	12600
31 7	PACESHIP 32	SLP	SAIL	FBG	KL	IB		25		10 2		4 4	15000	17100
31 7	PACESHIP 32	SLP	SAIL	FBG	KL	IB		15D		10 2		4 4	15500	17700
					1965 BOATS									
24 7	EAST-WIND 24	SLP	SAIL	FBG		IB		8	PALM				4550	5200
31 7	PACESHIP	SLP	SAIL	FBG	CB	IB		25	PALM				14800	16800
31 7	PACESHIP	SLP	SAIL	FBG	KL	IB		25	PALM				14800	16800
					1964 BOATS									
24 7	EAST-WIND	SLP	SAIL	FBG		OB							6600	7600
32	PACESHIP 32	SLP	SAIL	FDC		OB							9300	10600
					1963 BOATS									
24 7	EAST-WIND	SLP	SAIL	FBG		OB							6500	7500
32	PACESHIP 32	SLP	SAIL	FBG		OB							9200	10500

PACIFIC BOATS INC
SANTA CRUZ CA 95062   COAST GUARD MFG ID- PCX See inside cover to adjust price for area

For more recent years, see the BUC Used Boat Price Guide, Volume 1 or Volume 2

LOA FT IN	NAME AND/ OR MODEL	TOP/ RIG	BOAT TYPE	MTL	-HULL- TP	TP	#	-ENGINE- HP	MFG	BEAM FT IN	WGT LBS	DRAFT FT IN	RETAIL LOW	RETAIL HIGH
					1983 BOATS									
30	OLSON 30	SLP	SA/RC	F/S	KL	OB				9 3	3600	5 1	13400	15200
30	OLSON 30	SLP	SA/RC	F/S	KL	IB		7D		9 3	3600	5 1	13700	15500
40 4	OLSON 40	SLP	SA/RC	F/S	KL	IB		23D	YAN	11 6	10350	6 6	59200	65000
					1982 BOATS									
30	OLSON 30	SLP	SA/RC	F/S	KL	OB				9 3	3600	5 1	12700	14400
40 4	OLSON 40	SLP	SA/RC	F/S	KL	IB		18D		11 4	9500	5 9	52500	57700
					1981 BOATS									
30	OLSON 30	SLP	SA/RC	F/S	KL	OB				9 3	3600	5 6	12000	13700
					1980 BOATS									
30	OLSON 30	SLP	SA/CR	F/S	KL	OB				9 6	3600	5 6	11600	13200
					1979 BOATS									
22 6	PB-22	CUT	SA/CR	WD	KL	IB		D		7 2		4	10000	11400

PACIFIC DOLPHIN INC
COAST GUARD MFG ID- PDM

Call 1-800-327-6929 for BUC Personalized Evaluation Service
Or, for 1976 to 1979 boats, sign onto www.BUCValuPro.com

PACIFIC EAST COMPANY
SEATTLE WA 38101   See inside cover to adjust price for area

LOA FT IN	NAME AND/ OR MODEL	TOP/ RIG	BOAT TYPE	MTL	-HULL- TP	TP	#	-ENGINE- HP	MFG	BEAM FT IN	WGT LBS	DRAFT FT IN	RETAIL LOW	RETAIL HIGH
					1971 BOATS									
33	COASTER 34	MY	FBG	SV	IB			70		11 9		2 10	16600	18900
35 6	SEA-WITCH	KTH	SA/CR	FBG	KL	IB		D		11 4		4 6	34900	38800
36 9	SEA-BIRD	SLP	SA/CR	FBG	KL	IB		D		11 6	19200	4	36600	40700
40	SEA-WOLF	KTH	SA/CR	FBG	KL	IB		D		12	27000	6	54500	59900
50 10	PACIFIC-EAST 50	KTH	SA/CR	FBG	KL	IB		D		14 1	51000	6 2	87900	96600
					1970 BOATS									
33	COASTER 34	CR	FBG		IB			120D		11 9		2 10	28400	31600
33 11	SEA-SPIRIT	KTH	SA/CR	FBG	KL	IB		D		11 3		4 5	32600	36200
33 11	SEA-SPIRIT	KTH	SA/CR	WD	KL	IB		D		11 3		4 5	32500	36100
40	SEA-WOLF	MS	FBG	KL	IB			D		12		6	48500	53300
40	SEA-WOLF	MS	WD	KL	IB			D		12		6	48500	53300
40	SEA-WOLF	KTH	SA/CR	FBG	KL	IB		D		12		6	53200	58500
40	SEA-WOLF	KTH	SA/CR	WD	KL	IB		D		12		6	53200	58500
50 10	PACIFIC-EAST 50	KTH	SA/CR	FBG	KL	IB		D		14 1		6 2	85800	94300
50 10	PACIFIC-EAST 50	KTH	SA/CR	WD	KL	IB		D		14 1		6 2	85800	94300
					1969 BOATS									
33	COASTER 34	MY	FBG		IB			72D	PERK	11 9	17500	3 6	27600	30700
33 8	MYSTIC 34	SLP	MS	WD	IB			47D	PERK	10 6	16000	4 3	28500	31700
33 8	MYSTIC 34	SLP	MS	FBG	KL	IB		47D	PERK	10 6	16000	4 3	28600	31800
33 11	SEA-SPIRIT	CUT	SAIL	WD	IB			20D	ALBN	11 3	18000	4 5	31900	35500
33 11	SEA-SPIRIT GAFF	KTH	SAIL	WD	IB			20D	ALBN	11 3	18000	4 5	32500	36100
33 11	SEA-SPIRIT MARCONI	KTH	SAIL	WD	IB			20D	ALBN	11 3	18000	4 5	32500	36100
36 9	SEA-BIRD	SLP	MS	FBG	IB			47D	PERK	11 6	18000	4	32800	36400
38	SEA-DREAM	KTH	SAIL	WD	IB			47D	PERK	12	20000	6	38500	42700
40	SEA-WOLF	KTH	SAIL	FBG	IB			47D	PERK	12	27000	6	52000	57100
50 10	PACIFIC-EAST 50	KTH	SAIL	WD	IB			72D	PERK	14 1	51000	6 2	83400	91700
50 10	PACIFIC-EAST 50	KTH	SAIL	FBG	KL	IB		72D	PERK	14 1	51000	6 2	83400	91700
					1968 BOATS									
33 11	SEA-SPIRIT	CUT	SAIL	WD	KL	IB		20D		11 3	18000	4 5	33300	36900
33 11	SEA-SPIRIT GAFF	KTH	SAIL	WD	KL	IB		20D		11 3	18000	4 5	33800	37600
33 11	SEA-SPIRIT MARCONI	KTH	SAIL	WD	KL	IB		20D		11 3	18000	4 5	33800	37600
34	MYSTIC 34	SLP	SAIL	WD	IB			40D		10 6	16000	4 3	30000	33400
36	SEA-BIRD	SLP	SAIL	WD	IB			40D		11 6	18000	4	33900	37600
38	SEA-DREAM	KTH	SAIL	WD	IB			20D		12	20000	6	39900	44400
38 4	PE	SLP	SAIL	WD	IB			20D		12 10	16000	5 3	32500	36100
40	SEA-WOLF	KTH	SAIL	WD	KL	IB		40D		12	27000	6	53300	58600
					1967 BOATS									
33 11	SEA-SPIRIT	KTH	SA/CR	WD	KL	IB				11 3		4 5	29300	32500
33 11	SEA-SPIRIT MARCONI	KTH	SAIL	WD	KL	IB		20D			18000		33300	37000
34			CR	WD	IB			110D		11		4	28300	31500
38			CR	WD	IB	T		70D		13		4	29900	33300
38	SEA-DREAM	KTH	SAIL	WD	IB			40D			20000		39300	43700
38 4	PACIFIC-EAST 38	KTH	SA/CR	WD	KL	IB				10 10		5 3	35300	39200
40	SEA-WOLF	KTH	SAIL	WD	IB					12	27000	6 2	35400	39400
40	SEA-WOLF	KTH	SAIL	WD	IB			40D					52500	57700
44			CR	WD	IB	T		110D		15		4 4	38400	42700
50	PACIFIC-EAST 50	KTH	SA/CR	WD	KL	IB		D		14		5 6	75600	83100
51			CR	WD	IB			D		15		4 2	**	**
					1966 BOATS									
33 11	SEA-SPIRIT	KTH	SAIL	WD	IB			20D			18000		32900	36500
40	SEA-WOLF	KTH	SAIL	WD	IB			40D			27000		51800	56900
					1965 BOATS									
33 11	SEA-SPIRIT GAFF	KTH	SAIL	WD	IB			20D			18000		32500	36100
33 11	SEA-SPIRIT MARCONI	KTH	SAIL	WD	IB			20D			18000		32500	36100
38	SEA-DREAM	KTH	SAIL	WD	IB			20D			20000		38400	42600
40	SEA-WOLF	KTH	SAIL	WD	IB			40D			27000		51300	56300

PACIFIC MARINER
SEATTLE WA 98114   See inside cover to adjust price for area

LOA FT IN	NAME AND/ OR MODEL	TOP/ RIG	BOAT TYPE	MTL	-HULL- TP	TP	#	-ENGINE- HP	MFG	BEAM FT IN	WGT LBS	DRAFT FT IN	RETAIL LOW	RETAIL HIGH
					1967 BOATS									
16 1	BOLO DELUXE		FBG	DV	IO			120		6 7	805		2350	2750
16 1	BOLO STANDARD		FBG	DV	IO			120			775		2300	2700
18 2	MACHETE DELUXE		FBG	DV	IO			120-160		7 4	940		3650	4300
18 2	MACHETE STD		FBG	DV	IO			120-160			915		3650	4300
21 4	CUTLASS		RNBT	FBG	DV	OB				8	1664		1950	2300
21 4	CUTLASS	OP	RNBT	FBG	DV	IO		155-225		8	1664		5900	7050
21 4	CUTLASS TRUNK CABIN	CR	FBG	DV	IO			155-225		8	1664		6150	7400
					1966 BOATS									
16 1	BOLO DELUXE		FBG		IO			110-120					2450	2850
16 1	BOLO STANDARD		FBG		IO			110-120					2350	2750
18 2	MACHETE DELUXE		FBG		IO			110-150					3850	4500
18 2	MACHETE STANDARD		FBG		IO			110-150					3850	4500
21 4	CUTLASS	OP	FBG	DV	OB					8			1750	2100
21 4	CUTLASS	OP	FBG	DV	IO			150		8			6100	7000
21 4	CUTLASS	HT	FBG	DV	IO			150		8			6100	7000
21 4	CUTLASS TRUNK CABIN	CR	FBG	DV	IO			150		8			6400	7400
					1965 BOATS									
16 1	BOLO DELUXE		FBG		IO			110-120					2550	2950
16 1	BOLO STANDARD		FBG		IO			110-120					2450	2850
18 2	MACHETE DELUXE		FBG		IO			120-150					3900	4500
18 2	MACHETE STANDARD		FBG		IO			120-150					3850	4500
					1964 BOATS									
17 6	RAPIER		FBG		IO			110					3700	4300
17 6	RAPIER	HT	FBG		IO			110					3700	4300
18 2	MACHETE		FBG		IO			110-140					4050	4700
18 2	MACHETE	HT	FBG		IO			110-140					4050	4700
					1961 BOATS									
20 4	ALASKAN	CBNCR	FBG		OB					8			1900	2250
20 4	CABIN CR	CBNCR	FBG		OB					8			1900	2250

PACIFIC SAILBOATS
PELAGIC CONST & DES LTD

Call 1-800-327-6929 for BUC Personalized Evaluation Service
Or, for 1965 boats, sign onto www.BUCValuPro.com

PACIFIC SEACRAFT CORP

FULLERTON CA 92831 COAST GUARD MFG ID- PCS See inside cover to adjust price for area

For more recent years, see the BUC Used Boat Price Guide, Volume 1 or Volume 2

LOA FT	LOA IN	NAME AND/ OR MODEL	TOP/ RIG	BOAT TYPE	-HULL- MTL	-HULL- TP	ENGINE TP	ENGINE # HP	ENGINE MFG	BEAM FT	BEAM IN	WGT LBS	DRAFT FT	DRAFT IN	RETAIL LOW	RETAIL HIGH
		1983 BOATS														
24		FLICKA	SLP	SAIL	FBG	KL	OB			8		6000	3	3	15800	17900
24		FLICKA GAFF	CUT	SAIL	FBG	KL	IB	8D	YAN	8		6000	3	3	16900	19200
27	4	ORION	SLP	SAIL	FBG	KL	IB	15D	YAN	9	3	10000	4		34800	38700
27	4	ORION	CUT	SAIL	FBG	KL	IB	15D	YAN	9	3	10000	4		34800	38700
27	4	ORION	YWL	SAIL	FBG	KL	IB	15D	YAN	9	3	10000	4	3	34800	38700
36	11	CREALOCK	SLP	SAIL	FBG	KL	IB	40D	UNIV	10	10	16000	5	4	63400	69600
36	11	CREALOCK	CUT	SAIL	FBG	KL	IB	40D	UNIV	10	10	16000	5	4	63400	69600
36	11	CREALOCK	YWL	SAIL	FBG	KL	IB	40D	UNIV	10	10	16000	5	4	63400	69600
		1982 BOATS														
24		FLICKA	SLP	SAIL	FBG	KL	OB			8		6000	3	3	14900	17000
24	6	MK II	SLP	SA/CR	FBG	KL	IB	D		8		5700	3	4	15800	17900
24	6	MK II	CUT	SA/CR	FBG	KL	IB	D		8		5700	3	4	15800	17900
27	4	ORION	SLP	SAIL	FBG	KL	IB	15D	YAN	9	3	10000	4		33000	36700
27	4	ORION	CUT	SAIL	FBG	KL	IB	15D	YAN	9	3	10000	4		33000	36700
36	11	CREALOCK	SLP	SAIL	FBG	KL	IB	40D	UNIV	10	10	16000	5	4	60100	66000
36	11	CREALOCK	CUT	SAIL	FBG	KL	IB	40D	UNIV	10	10	16000	5	4	60100	66000
36	11	CREALOCK	YWL	SAIL	FBG	KL	IB	40D	UNIV	10	10	16000	5	4	60100	66000
		1981 BOATS														
24		FLICKA GAFF	CUT	SA/CR	FBG	KL	IB	8D	YAN	8		6000	3	3	15200	17200
24		FLICKA MARCONI	SLP	SA/CR	FBG	KL	OB			8		6000	3	3	14200	16100
24		FLICKA MARCONI	SLP	SA/CR	FBG	KL	IB	8D	YAN	8		6000	3	3	15200	17200
24	6	PACIFIC-SEACRAFT 25	SLP	SA/CR	FBG	KL	IB	8D	YAN	8		4750	3	3	12400	14100
24	6	PACIFIC-SEACRAFT 25	CUT	SA/CR	FBG	KL	IB	8D	YAN	8		4750	3	3	12400	14100
27	4	ORION	SLP	SA/CR	FBG	KL	IB	15D	YAN	9	3	10000	4		31300	34700
27	4	ORION	CUT	SA/CR	FBG	KL	IB	15D	YAN	9	3	10000	4		31300	34700
36		MARIAH	CUT	SA/CR	FBG	KL	IB	22D	YAN	10	9	16000	4	5	55500	61000
36		MARIAH	CUT	SA/CR	FBG	KL	IB	33D	YAN	10	9	16000	4	5	55700	61200
36	11	CREALOCK 37	SLP	SA/CR	FBG	KL	IB	D		10	10	16000	5	4	56800	62400
36	11	CREALOCK 37	CUT	SA/CR	FBG	KL	IB	D		10	10	16000	5	4	56800	62400
36	11	CREALOCK 37	YWL	SA/CR	FBG	KL	IB	D		10	10	16000	5	4	56800	62400
		1980 BOATS														
20		FLICKA 20	SLP	SA/CR	FBG	KL	IB	D		8		4500	3	3	10100	11500
24		FLICKA GAFF	CUT	SA/CR	FBG	KL	OB			8		6000	3	3	13600	15500
24		FLICKA GAFF	CUT	SA/CR	FBG	KL	IB	8D	YAN	8		6000	3	3	14600	16600
24		FLICKA MARCONI	SLP	SA/CR	FBG	KL	OB			8		6000	3	3	13600	15500
24		FLICKA MARCONI	SLP	SA/CR	FBG	KL	IB	8D	YAN	8		6000	3	3	14600	16600
24	6	PACIFIC-SEACRAFT 25	SLP	SA/CR	FBG	KL	IB	8D	YAN	8		4750	3	3	11900	13600
24	6	PACIFIC-SEACRAFT 25	CUT	SA/CR	FBG	KL	IB	8D	YAN	8		4750	3	3	11900	13600
27	4	ORION	SLP	SA/CR	FBG	KL	IB	15D		9	3	10000	4		30000	33400
27	4	ORION	CUT	SA/CR	FBG	KL	IB	15D		9	3	10000	4		30000	33400
27	4	ORION	YWL	SA/CR	FBG	KL	IB	15D		9	3	10000	4		30000	33400
36		MARIAH	CUT	SA/CR	FBG	KL	IB	22D	YAN	10	9	16000	4	5	53400	58700
36		MARIAH	CUT	SA/CR	FBG	KL	IB	33D	YAN	10	9	16000	4	5	53600	58900
36	11	CREALOCK 37	CUT	SA/CR	FBG	KL	IB	32D		10	10	16000	5	4	54600	60000
		1979 BOATS														
24		FLICKA GAFF	CUT	SA/CR	FBG	KL	OB			8		6000	3	3	13200	15000
24		FLICKA GAFF	CUT	SA/CR	FBG	KL	IB	8D	YAN	8		6000	3	3	14100	16100
24		FLICKA MARCONI	SLP	SA/CR	FBG	KL	OB			8		6000	3	3	13200	15000
24		FLICKA MARCONI	SLP	SA/CR	FBG	KL	IB	8D	YAN	8		6000	3	3	14100	16100
24	6	PACIFIC-SEACRAFT 25	SLP	SA/CR	FBG	KL	IB	8D	YAN	8		4750	3	3	11600	13100
24	6	PACIFIC-SEACRAFT 25	CUT	SA/CR	FBG	KL	IB	8D	YAN	8		4750	3	3	11600	13100
26	3	PACIFIC-SEACRAFT 25	SLP	SA/CR	FBG	KL				8		4750	3	3	10900	12400
36		MARIAH	CUT	SA/CR	FBG	KL	IB	22D	YAN	10	9	16000	4	5	51800	56900
36		MARIAH	CUT	SA/CR	FBG	KL	IB	33D	YAN	10	9	16000	4	5	51900	57000
		1978 BOATS														
20		FLICKA KIT	SLP	SA/CR	FBG	KL	IB	8D	YAN	8		5200	3	3	10900	12400
24	6	PACIFIC-SEACRAFT 25	SLP	SA/CR	FBG	KL	IB	8D	YAN	8		5500	3	4	12900	14700

PACIFIC SEACRAFT PHILIPPINES

Call 1-800-327-6929 for BUC Personalized Evaluation Service
Or, for 1981 to 1982 boats, sign onto www.BUCValuPro.com

PACIFIC TRAWLER CORP

COAST GUARD MFG ID- PTL

Call 1-800-327-6929 for BUC Personalized Evaluation Service
Or, for 1974 to 1977 boats, sign onto www.BUCValuPro.com

PACIFICA YACHTS

HONOLULU HI 96822-4667 COAST GUARD MFG ID- PYU See inside cover to adjust price for area
FORMERLY PACIFICA BY KIPPER YACHTS

For more recent years, see the BUC Used Boat Price Guide, Volume 1 or Volume 2

LOA FT	LOA IN	NAME AND/ OR MODEL	TOP/ RIG	BOAT TYPE	-HULL- MTL	-HULL- TP	ENGINE TP	ENGINE # HP	ENGINE MFG	BEAM FT	BEAM IN	WGT LBS	DRAFT FT	DRAFT IN	RETAIL LOW	RETAIL HIGH
		1983 BOATS														
41		PACIFICA 41	FB	SF	FBG	SV	IB	T400D	GM	14		24000	3	11	148500	163500
44		PACIFICA 44	FB	SF	FBG	SV	IB	T525D	GM	15		33000	4	2	176000	193500
50		PACIFICA 50	FB	SF	FBG	SV	IB	T570D	GM	15		45000	4	7	210500	231500
63		PACIFICA 63	FB	SF	FBG	SV	IB	T675D	GM	20	6	75000	5		393000	431500
67		PACIFICA 67	FB	MY	FBG	SV	IB	T675D	GM	20	6	80000	5		466500	512500
67		PACIFICA 67	FB	SF	FBG	SV	IB	T675D	GM	20	6	77000	5		439000	482500
67		PACIFICA 67	FB	YTFS	FBG	SV	IB	T675D	GM	20	6	73000	5		441000	485000
77		PACIFICA 77	FB	YTFS	FBG	SV	IB	T675D	GM	20	6	85000	5		**	**
		1982 BOATS														
41		PACIFICA 41	FB	SF	FBG	SV	IB	T400D	GM	14		24000	3	11	142000	156000
44		PACIFICA 44	FB	SF	FBG	SV	IB	T462D	GM	15		33000	4	2	158500	174500
48		PACIFICA 48		SF	FBG	SV	IB	T570D		15	3				190500	209500
50		PACIFICA 50	FB	SF	FBG	SV	IB	T570D	GM	15		50000	4	7	212500	233000
62		PACIFICA 62		SF	FBG	SV	IB	T675D	GM	20	6				375500	412500
63		PACIFICA 63	FB	MY	FBG	SV	IB	T675D	GM	20	6	78000	5		422500	464000
63		PACIFICA 63	FB	SF	FBG	SV	IB	T675D	GM	20	6	75000	5		376000	413000
67		PACIFICA 67	FB	MY	FBG	SV	IB	T675D	GM	20	6	80000	5		445000	489000
67		PACIFICA 67	FB	SF	FBG	SV	IB	T675D	GM	20	6	77000	5		420500	462000
77		PACIFICA 77	FB	YTFS	FBG	SV	IB	T675D	GM	20	6	85000	5		**	**
		1981 BOATS														
41		PACIFICA 41	FB	SDNSF	FBG	SV	IB	T400D	GM	14		24000	3	11	136000	149000
44		PACIFICA 44	FB	SDNSF	FBG	SV	IB	T450D	GM	15		33000	4	2	152000	167000
44		PACIFICA 44		SF	FBG	SV	IB	T435D		15					147000	161500
50		PACIFICA 50	FB	SDNSF	FBG	SV	IB	T550D	GM	15		50000	4	7	202500	222500
50		PACIFICA 50		SF	FBG	SV	IB	T570D		15	3				189000	207500
62		PACIFICA 62		SF	FBG	SV	IB	T675D		20	6				357500	393000
63		PACIFICA 63	FB	MY	FBG	SV	IB	T675D	GM	20	6	78000	5		402500	442000
63		PACIFICA 63	FB	YTFS	FBG	SV	IB	T675D	GM	20	6	75000	5		389000	427500
67		PACIFICA 67	FB	MY	FBG	SV	IB	T675D	GM	20	6	80000	5		424000	466000
67		PACIFICA 67	FB	YTFS	FBG	SV	IB	T675D	GM	20	6	77000	5		414000	455000
		1980 BOATS														
36		PACIFICA		SF	FBG	SV	IB	T216D		13		16000			72000	79200
41		PACIFICA		SF	FBG	SV	IB	T310D		14		24000			119500	131500
41		PACIFICA 41	FB	SDN	FBG	SV	IB	T400D	GM	14		24000	3	11	128500	141000
44		PACIFICA		SF	FBG	SV	IB	T350D		15		33000			129000	142000
44		PACIFICA		SF	FBG	SV	IB	T435D		15		33000			140500	154500
44		PACIFICA 44	FB	SDNSF	FBG	SV	IB	T325D	GM	15		33000	4	2	127500	140000
44		PACIFICA 44	FB	SDNSF	FBG	SV	IB	T450D	GM	15		33000	4	2	145000	159500
50		PACIFICA		SF	FBG	SV	IB	T570D		15		42000			191500	210500
50		PACIFICA 50	FB	SDNSF	FBG	SV	IB	T375D	GM	15		50000	4	7	167000	183500
50		PACIFICA 50	FB	SDNSF	FBG	SV	IB	T550D	GM	15		50000	4	7	193500	212500
		1979 BOATS														
36		PACIFICA 36		SF	FBG	SV	IB	T216D		13					64500	70800
41		PACIFICA 41		SF	FBG	SV	IB	T400D		14					126000	138500
44		PACIFICA 44		SF	FBG	SV	IB	T435D		15					134000	147000
48		PACIFICA 48		SF	FBG	SV	IB	T570D		15					165500	182000
		1978 BOATS														
36		PACIFICA 36		SF	FBG	SV	IB	T216D		13					61700	67800
36		PACIFICA 36		SF	FBG	SV	IB	T310D		13					65800	72400
41		PACIFICA 41		SF	FBG	SV	IB	T310D		14					112000	123000
41		PACIFICA 41		SF	FBG	SV	IB	T400D		14					120500	132500
44		PACIFICA 44		SF	FBG	SV	IB	T435D		15	2	34000	3	4	130000	143000
		1977 BOATS														
36		PACIFICA 36	FB	SF	FBG	SV	IB	T216D	GM	13		16000	2	11	63100	69300
36		PACIFICA 36 ST	FB	SF	FBG	SV	IB	T305D	GM	13		16000	2	11	67000	73700
44		PACIFICA 44	FB	SF	FBG	SV	IB	T435D	GM	15		33000	3		123000	135000
44		PACIFICA 44 N	FB	SF	FBG	SV	IB	T350D	GM	15		33000	3		118000	129500
55		PACIFICA 55	FB	SF	FBG	SV	IB	T435D	GM	18	6	45000	4		165500	182000
61		PACIFICA 60	FB	SF	FBG	SV	IB	T475D	GM	21		68000	5		243500	267500
		1976 BOATS														
36		PACIFICA ST 36	FB	SF	FBG	SV	IB	T310D	GM	13		16000	2	11	64500	70900
36		PACIFICA SUPER 36	FB	SF	FBG	SV	IB	T216D	GM	13		16000	2	11	60500	66500
44		PACIFICA 44N	FB	SF	FBG	SV	IB	T350D	GM	15		33000	3		114500	126000
44		PACIFICA 44TI	FB	SF	FBG	SV	IB	T435D	GM	15		33000	3		120000	131500
44		PACIFICA TC-TI	FB	MYDKH	FBG	SV	IB	T435D	GM	15		34000	3		123500	136000
44		PACIFICA TRIPLE CBN	FB	MYDKH	FBG	SV	IB	T350D	GM	15		34000	3		118500	130000
60		PACIFICA 60	FB	SF	FBG	SV	IB	T675D	GM	21		58000	5		226000	248000
		1975 BOATS														
36		PACIFICA 36	FB	SF	FBG	SV	IB	T216D	GM	13	3	17000	2	11	59700	65600
44		PACIFICA 44	FB	SF	FBG	SV	IB	T350D	GM	15	2	34000	3		106000	116500

CONTINUED ON NEXT PAGE

LOA FT IN	NAME AND/ OR MODEL	TOP/ RIG	BOAT TYPE	-HULL- MTL TP	----ENGINE--- TP # HP MFG	BEAM FT IN	WGT LBS	DRAFT FT IN	RETAIL LOW	RETAIL HIGH
					1975 BOATS					
44	PACIFICA 44	FB	SF	FBG SV	IB T435D GM	15 2	34000	3	115000	126500
60	PACIFICA 60 CUSTOM		SF	FBG SV	IB T650D GM	21	79000	4	276500	304000
					1974 BOATS					
35	PACIFICA 35	FB	SF	FBG SV	IB T216D GM	13 3	17000	3	60500	66500
44	PACIFICA 44	FB	SF	FBG SV	IB T350D GM	15 2	34000	3 4	102000	112000
44	PACIFICA 44	FB	SF	FBG SV	IB T435D GM	15 2	34000	3 4	110500	121500
					1973 BOATS					
44	PACIFICA 44	FB	SF	FBG SV	IB T350D GM	15 2	34000	3 4	98100	108000
					1969 BOATS					
36	PACIFICA		CR	FBG	IB T D				**	**
48	PACIFICA	FB	SF	FBG	IB T350D	17		3 10	93200	102500
54	PACIFICA		MY	FBG	IB T350D	17		4	106000	116000

PACKANACK MARINE CORP

Call 1-800-327-6929 for BUC Personalized Evaluation Service
Or, for 1966 to 1971 boats, sign onto www.BUCValuPro.com

PADEBCO CUSTOM BOATS

Call 1-800-327-6929 for BUC Personalized Evaluation Service
Or, for 1966 boats, sign onto www.BUCValuPro.com

C W PAINE YACHT DESIGN CO

Call 1-800-327-6929 for BUC Personalized Evaluation Service
Or, for 1980 boats, sign onto www.BUCValuPro.com

PALM BEACH BOAT BLDRS INC

RIVIERA BEACH FL   COAST GUARD MFG ID- PBB See inside cover to adjust price for area

LOA FT IN	NAME AND/ OR MODEL	TOP/ RIG	BOAT TYPE	-HULL- MTL TP	----ENGINE--- TP # HP MFG	BEAM FT IN	WGT LBS	DRAFT FT IN	RETAIL LOW	RETAIL HIGH
					1979 BOATS					
39	ARISTOCRAT	FB	SDNSF	FBG SV	IB T225D CAT	14 4	24000	3	141000	155000
39	ARISTOCRAT T	FB	SDNSF	FBG SV	IB T225D CAT	14 4	24000	3	147000	161500
39	ARISTOCRAT T	FB	SDNSF	FBG SV	IB T260D	14 4	24000	3	133500	146500
39	OFFSHORE	FB	SDNSF	FBG SV	IB T225D CAT	14 4	24000	3	120500	132000
39	OFFSHORE T	FB	SDNSF	FBG SV	IB T225D CAT	14 4	24000	3	126500	139000
39	OFFSHORE T	FB	SDNSF	FBG SV	IB T260D	14 4	24000	3	133500	146500
					1978 BOATS					
39	ARISTOCRAT	FB	SDNSF	FBG SV	IB T225D CAT	14 4	24000	3	138000	152000
39	ARISTOCRAT	FB	SDNSF	FBG SV	IB T270D CAT	14 4	24000	3	141000	155000
39	OFFSHORE	FB	SDNSF	FBG SV	IB T225D CAT	14 4	24000	3	117500	129500
39	OFFSHORE	FB	SDNSF	FBG SV	IB T270D CAT	14 4	24000	3	121000	133000
					1977 BOATS					
39	ARISTOCRAT	FB	SDNSF	FBG SV	IB T225D CAT	14 4	24000	3	132500	145500
39	ARISTOCRAT	FB	SDNSF	FBG SV	IB T275D CAT	14 4	24000	3	135500	149000
39	OFFSHORE	FB	SDNSF	FBG SV	IB T225D CAT	14 4	24000	3	112500	124000
39	OFFSHORE	FB	SDNSF	FBG SV	IB T275D CAT	14 4	24000	3	116500	128000
					1976 BOATS					
39	ARISTOCRAT 39	FB	SDNSF	FBG SV	IB T225D CAT	14 4	24000	3	127000	139500
39	OFFSHORE 39	FB	SDNSF	FBG SV	IB T225D CAT	14 4	24000	3	108000	119000
					1975 BOATS					
34	PALM-BEACH 34	FB	OPFSH	FBG SV	IB T225D CAT	11 6	18000	3	79100	86900
39	PALM BEACH 39	FB	SDNSF	FBG SV	IB T225D CAT	14 4	24000	3	113000	124000
39	PALM-BEACH 39	FB	SDNSF	FBG SV	IB T210D	14 4		3	110000	121000
					1974 BOATS					
34	PALM-BEACH 34		SDNSF	FBG SV	IB T225D CAT	11 6		3	77900	85600
39	PALM-BEACH 39	FB	SDNSF	FBG SV	IB T225D CAT	14 5		3	108000	119000

PALMER

Call 1-800-327-6929 for BUC Personalized Evaluation Service
Or, for 1905 to 1967 boats, sign onto www.BUCValuPro.com

PALMER JOHNSON INC

STURGEON BAY WI 54235   COAST GUARD MFG ID- PAJ See inside cover to adjust price for area

For more recent years, see the BUC Used Boat Price Guide, Volume 1 or Volume 2

LOA FT IN	NAME AND/ OR MODEL	TOP/ RIG	BOAT TYPE	-HULL- MTL TP	----ENGINE--- TP # HP MFG	BEAM FT IN	WGT LBS	DRAFT FT IN	RETAIL LOW	RETAIL HIGH
					1983 BOATS					
56	P-J ALDEN 56	SLP	SA/RC AL	KC	IB 150D VLVO		44000	5 6	288500	317000
75	P-J ALDEN 75	KTH	SA/RC AL	KC	IB 286D VLVO		50T	6 6	**	**
77	P-J FRERS 77	SLP	SA/RC AL	KL	IB 200D GM		80000	10 4	**	**
					1982 BOATS					
56	P-J ALDEN 56	SLP	SA/RC AL	KC	IB 150D VLVO		44000	5 6	271500	298500
75	P-J ALDEN 75	KTH	SA/RC AL	KC	IB 270D VLVO		50T	6 6	**	**
77	P-J FRERS 77	SLP	SA/RC AL	KL	IB 200D GM		80000	10 4	**	**
					1981 BOATS					
39 6	NEW-YORK-YACHT-CLUB	SLP	SA/RC FBG	KL	IB D	12 10	17000	6 10	52300	57400
56	P-J ALDEN 56	SLP	SA/RC AL	KC	IB 150D VLVO		44000	5 6	255500	280500
56	P-J ALDEN 56	SLP	SA/RC AL	KC	IB 150D VLVO		44000	5 6	255500	281000
75	P-J ALDEN 75	KTH	SA/RC AL	KC	IB 270D VLVO		50T	6 6	**	**
77	P-J FRERS 77	SLP	SA/RC AL	KL	IB 200D GM		80000	10 4	**	**
77	P-J FRERS 77	KTH	SA/RC AL	KL	IB 200D GM		80000	10 4	**	**
					1980 BOATS					
39 6	NEW-YORK 40	SLP	SA/RC FBG	VD	IB 23D VLVO	12 10	17000	6 10	49500	54400
43	PALMER-JOHNSON 43	SLP	SA/CR FBG	KL	IB 41D WEST	13	17800	7 6	62600	68800
43	PALMER-JOHNSON 43	SLP	SA/RC FBG	KL	IB 41D WEST	13	19500	7 6	65800	72300
					1979 BOATS					
39 6	NEW-YORK 40	SLP	SA/CR FBG	VD	IB 23D VLVO	12 10	17000	6 10	47700	52500
					1978 BOATS					
39 6	NEW-YORK-YACHT-CLUB	SLP	SAIL FBG	KL	IB 23D VLVO	12 10	17000	6 10	46000	50500
					1977 BOATS					
36	STANDFAST 36	SLP	SAIL F/S	KL	IB 25D VLVO	12 4	17200	6 9	42700	47400
40	STANDFAST 40	SLP	SAIL F/S	KL	IB 25D VLVO	13 2	20900	7 5	51900	57000
42 9	AMPHITRITE 43CR	KTH	SA/CR FBG	KL	IB 50D PERK	13 8	26000	5 10	68200	74900
47	STANDFAST 47	SLP	SAIL	KL	IB 26D	14 2	33000	8 1	95900	105500
47	STANDFAST 47	SLP	SAIL	KL	IB 37D PERK	14	33000	8 1	95800	105500
57	P-J 57		MY	AL	SV IB 250D	17	60000	5 8	175500	193000
63	P-J 63		MY	AL	SV IB 250D	17	80000	5 3	316000	347500
63	P-J 63		MY	AL	SV IB 250D	17	80000	5 3	324500	356500
72	P-J 72		MY	AL	SV IB T350D	18		4 8	**	**
					1976 BOATS					
36	STANDFAST 36	SLP	SAIL FBG	KL	IB 25D VLVO	12 4	17100	6 9	41100	45700
40	STANDFAST 40	SLP	SAIL FBG	KL	IB 25D VLVO	13 2	21000	7 5	50300	55300
42	AMPHITRITE	KTH	SAIL FBG	KL	IB D	13 10	26000	7 11	64400	70300
47	STANDFAST 47	SLP	SAIL FBG	KL	IB 26D	14 2	33000	8 1	92800	102000
47	STANDFAST 47	SLP	SAIL FBG	KL	IB 37D PERK	14 2	33000	8 1	92800	102000
57	P-J 57		MY	AL	SV IB 250D	17	60000	5 8	168000	184500
63	P-J 63		MY	AL	SV IB 250D	17	80000	5 3	303000	332500
63	P-J 63		MY	AL	SV IB 250D	17	80000	5 3	311000	341500
72	P-J 72		MY	AL	SV IB T350D	18		4 8	**	**
					1975 BOATS					
36	STANDFAST 36	SLP	SAIL F/S	KL	IB 25D VLVO	12 4	17500	6 9	40800	45300
40	STANDFAST 40	SLP	SA/CR FBG	KL	IB 25D VLVO	13 2	20900	7 5	50100	55300
42	AMPHITRITE	KTH	SAIL AL	KL	IB D	13 10	26000	7 11	62100	68200
42 9	P-J 43	SLP	SA/CR FBG	KL	IB 36D VLVO	12	19500	7 1	51700	56800
47	STANDFAST 47	SLP	SAIL F/S	KL	IB 50D PERK	13 8	25000	5 10	62600	69300
47	STANDFAST 47	SLP	SAIL	KL	IB 37D PERK	14 2	33000	8 1	90300	99300
57	P-J 57		MY	AL	SV IB 250D	17	60000	5 8	161000	177000
63	P-J 63		MY	AL	SV IB 335	17	80000	5 3	292000	320500
63	P-J 63		MY	AL	SV IB 250D	17	80000	5 3	298000	327500
72	P-J 72		MY	AL	SV IB T350D	18		4 8	**	**
					1974 BOATS					
29 11	P-J HALF TONNER		SAIL FBG		IB 10D VLVO	9 6	7800	5 3	19200	21300
36	STANDFAST 36	SLP	SAIL FBG		IB 25D	12 4	17100	6 9	38900	44300
39 6	P-J 40	SLP	SAIL FBG		IB 36D VLVO	10 10	16800	6 7	39900	44400
40	P-J STANDFAST 40	SLP	SAIL FBG		IB 25D VLVO	13 2	20000	7 5	46200	50700
42	P-J 44	SLP	SAIL FBG		IB 36D PERK	14	23800	7 3	63300	69600
47	STANDFAST 47	SLP	SAIL FBG		IB 26D	14 2	33000	8 1	87700	96400
48	P-J 48	SLP	SAIL FBG		IB 75D VLVO	14 3	34000	9	94400	104000
55	P-J 55	YWL	SAIL FBG		IB 75D VLVO	14 3	37180	8 1	177500	195500
57	P-J 57		MY	AL	SV IB 250D	17	60000	5 8	154500	169500
63	P-J 63		MY	AL	SV IB 250D	17	80000	5 3	278000	305500
63	P-J 63		MY	AL	SV IB 250D	17	80000	5 3	285500	314000
72	P-J 72		MY	AL	SV IB T350D	18		4 8	**	**
					1973 BOATS					
29 11	P-J 1/2 TON	SLP	SAIL FBG		IB 10D VLVO	9 6	7800	5 3	19000	21100
33 7	P-J 34	SLP	SAIL FBG		IB 25D	10	9200	5 10	21800	24200
35 5	P-J 37	SLP	SAIL FBG		IB 25D	10	14300	5 8	32600	36100
39 6	P-J 40	SLP	SAIL FBG		IB 36D VLVO	10 10	16800	6 7	38900	43300
40	P-J 40	SLP	SAIL FBG		IB 25D VLVO	13 2	20000	7 5	44500	49000
43	P-J 43	SLP	SAIL FBG		IB 36D	11 8	19750	8	52700	57900
44	CHANCE 44	SLP	SAIL FBG	KC	IB D	12 6			75400	82900
44	P-J 44	SLP	SAIL FBG		IB 37D PERK	13	23800	8	61800	67900

LOA FT	LOA IN	NAME AND/ OR MODEL	TOP/ RIG	BOAT TYPE	HULL MTL	HULL TP	ENGINE TP	ENGINE # HP	ENGINE MFG	BEAM FT	BEAM IN	WGT LBS	DRAFT FT	DRAFT IN	RETAIL LOW	RETAIL HIGH
1973 BOATS																
47		P-J 47		MY	AL	DV	IB	T250D		14		32000	2	5	118500	130500
48		P-J 48	SLP	SAIL	FBG		IB	75D	VLVO	13	8	34000	7	9	92100	101500
54		P-J 54	KTH	SAIL	AL	KC	IB	86D		12	9	33520	5	9	156000	171500
55	4	P-J 55	YWL	SAIL	FBG		IB	75D	PERK	14	3	37180	8	1	178500	196000
57		P-J 57		MY	AL	DV	IB	T250D		17		60000	5	8	162000	178000
63		P-J 63		MY	AL	DV	IB	T250D		17		80000	5	3	274000	301000
64	7	P-J 65	SLP	SAIL	FBG	KL	IB	106D		16	4	57000	9	8	255000	280000
72		P-J 72		MY	AL	DV	IB	T350D		18			4	8	**	**
1972 BOATS																
33	7	P-J 34		SAIL	FBG		IB	25D	VLVO	10	1	9185	5	10	21300	23600
36	6	P-J 37		SAIL	FBG		IB	25D	VLVO	10	10	12000	6	2	27100	30100
39	6	P-J 40		SAIL	FBG		IB	25D	VLVO	10	10	15000	6	7	34900	38800
43		P-J 43		SAIL	FBG		IB	36D	PERK	11	8	19850	6	11	51500	56600
45		CHANCE 45	SLP	SA/RC	FBG	KC	IB	D		12	6		4	3	65400	71900
45		CHANCE 45	KTH	SA/RC	FBG	KC	IB	D		12	6		4	3	65900	72400
47		P-J 47		MY	FBG	DV	IB	T250D		14		32000	2	5	114000	125500
47		P-J 47		MY	FBG	DV	IB	T350D		14		32000	2	5	120500	132000
48	1	P-J 48		SAIL	FBG		IB	36D	VLVO	13	8	34000	7	9	90200	99100
54		P-J 54	KTH	SA/CR	FBG	KC	IB	86		12	9	33000	5	9	150500	165500
55	4	P-J 55		SAIL	FBG		IB	80D	PERK	14	3	38000	8		175000	192000
57		P-J 57 TRAWLER		MY	AL	DS	IB	250D		17		60000	5	8	142000	156000
63		P-J 63		MY	AL	DS	IB	250D		17		80000	5	3	255500	281000
63		P-J 63		MY	AL	DS	IB	T250D		17		80000	5	3	263000	289000
63		P-J 63 TRAWLER		MY	AL	DS	IB	T335		17		80000	5	3	267000	293500
72		P-J72		MY	AL	DS	IB	T350D		19			4	8	**	**
1971 BOATS																
33	7	P-J 34		SAIL	FBG		IB	16D	VLVO	10	1	9185	5	10	20800	23100
36		P-J 36	SLP	SA/CR	FBG	KL	IB	17		9	8	14300	6		30700	34100
36	6	P-J 37		SAIL	FBG		IB	16D	VLVO	10	10	12000	6	2	26500	29400
39	6	P-J 40		SAIL	FBG		IB	45D	PERK	10	10	15000	6	7	34300	38100
43		P-J 43		SAIL	FBG		IB	36D	PERK	11	8	19850	6	11	50400	55400
47		P-J 47		MY	FBG	DS	IB	T350D	GM	14		32000	2	5	116500	128000
54		P-J 54	KTH	SA/CR	AL	KC	IB	86		12	9	33000	5	9	147500	162500
55	4	P-J 55		SAIL	FBG		IB	80D	PERK	14	3	38000	8		171500	188000
57		P-J 57		DC	AL	DS	IB	250D	CAT	17		60000	5		140000	154000
57		P-J 57		MY	AL	DS	IB	250D	CAT	18		65000	5	8	140000	154000
63		P-J 63		DC	AL	DS	IB	250D	CAT	17	6	80000	6		254500	279500
63		P-J 63		MY	AL	DS	IB	245D	CAT	17		83400	5	3	249000	273500
72		P-J 72		DC	AL	DS	IB	T350D	GM	18		85000	5	6	**	**
72		P-J 72		MY	AL	DS	IB	T350D	GM	19		84000	4	8	**	**
1970 BOATS																
33	7	P-J 34	SLP	SAIL	FBG	KL	IB	D		10	1	9200	5	11	20500	22800
36		P-J 36	SLP	SA/CR	FBG	KL	IB	D		9	8	14300	6		30500	33900
39		P-J 39	SLP	SA/CR	FBG	KL	IB	D		11			6	4	40800	45300
43		P-J 43	SLP	SA/CR	FBG	KL	IB	36D		11	8	19750	6	8	49600	54500
43		P-J 43	YWL	SA/CR	FBG	KL	IB	36D		10	8	19750	6	8	49600	54500
47		P-J 47		MY	FBG	DV	IB	T350D		14		32000	2	10	112000	123000
50		P-J 50	SLP	SA/CR	AL	KL	IB	D		11	10		7	2	104500	114500
52		P-J 52	SLP	SA/CR	AL	KL	IB	D		11	10		7	2	127500	140000
52		P-J 52	KTH	SA/CR	AL	KL	IB	D		11	10		7	2	127500	140000
54		P-J 54	KTH	SA/CR	AL	KL	IB	D		12	9	33000	5	6	146500	161000
57		P-J 57		MY	AL	DS	IB	250D		18		65000			138000	151500
57		PALMER-JOHNSON 57		DC	AL	RB	IB	250D	CAT	17		60000	5		134500	148000
63		P-J 63		MY	AL	DS	IB	250D		19		83400			258500	284000
63		PALMER-JOHNSON 63		DC	AL	RB	IB	250D	CAT	17	6	80000	6		244000	268500
72		P-J 72		MY	AL	DS	IB	T350D		19					**	**
72		PALMER-JOHNSON 72		DC	AL	RB	IB	T350D	GM	18		85000	5	6	**	**
1969 BOATS																
43		P-J 43	SLP	SAIL	FBG	KL	IB	D		11	8		6	2	60000	65900
43		P-J 43	YWL	SAIL	AL	KL	IB	36		10	8	19750	6	8	48200	53000
54		P-J 54	KTH	SA/CR	AL	KC	IB	86		12	9	33000	5	9	143000	157000
57		P-J 57		MY	AL	DS	IB	250D	CAT	18		65000	5	8	129500	142000
63		P-J 63		MY	AL	DS	IB	250D	CAT	19		83400	5	3	248000	272500
1968 BOATS																
54		P-J 54	KTH	SA/CR	AL	KC	IB	86		12	9	33000	5	6	141000	155000
57		P-J 57		MY	AL		IB	250D	CAT	17		60000	5		117500	129000
1965 BOATS																
44		P-J 44	SLP	SAIL	AL		IB	D	WEST	10	11	23800	6	2	55300	60800
54		P-J 54	SLP	SAIL	AL		IB	86D	GM	14	3	33500	8	1	138000	152000
1961 BOATS																
30		ALDEN-PRISCILLA	SLP	SA/CR	WD	KL	OB			8	6		4	3	13000	14800
33	3	ALDEN-MALABAR	SLP	SA/CR	WD	KL	OB			9	9		5		22500	25000
35	11	JOHNSON 36 EXP		EXP	WD		IB	T125		11	8		2	6	26000	28900
35	11	JOHNSON 36 EXP		EXP	WD		IB	T300		11	8		2	6	27500	30600
38	6	ALDEN-CHALLENGER	YWL	SA/CR	FBG	CB	OB			11					31300	34800
1960 BOATS																
33	3	MALABAR-SR	SLP	SA/CR	WD	KL	OB			9	9		5		22600	25100
35	11	JOHNSON 36		EXP	WD		IB	T125		11	8		2	6	25500	28400
35	11	JOHNSON 36		EXP	WD		IB	T275		11	8		2	6	26800	29700
38	6	ALDEN-CHALLENGER	YWL	SA/CR	FBG	CB	OB			11					31400	34900
39		ALDEN-PRISCILLA	SLP	SA/CR	WD	KL	OB			8	6		4	3	31700	35300
1959 BOATS																
30		ALDEN-PRISCILLA	SLP	SA/CR	WD	KL	OB			8	6		4	3	13100	14800
33	3	ALDEN-MALABAR	SLP	SA/CR	WD	KL	OB			9	9		5		22600	25200
36		JOHNSON		EXP	WD		IB	T300		11	8				29200	32500

BRIAN W PALMER

Call 1-800-327-6929 for BUC Personalized Evaluation Service
Or, for 1967 boats, sign onto www.BUCValuPro.com

PAN OCEANIC MARINE INC

MIAMI FL 33136 COAST GUARD MFG ID- FSL See inside cover to adjust price for area

For more recent years, see the BUC Used Boat Price Guide, Volume 1 or Volume 2

LOA FT	LOA IN	NAME AND/ OR MODEL	TOP/ RIG	BOAT TYPE	HULL MTL	HULL TP	ENGINE TP	ENGINE # HP	ENGINE MFG	BEAM FT	BEAM IN	WGT LBS	DRAFT FT	DRAFT IN	RETAIL LOW	RETAIL HIGH
1983 BOATS																
41	3	OCEANIC 41 PH	CUT	SA/CR	FBG	KL	IB	50D	PERK	12	11	23500	6	6	72700	79800
41	3	OCEANIC 41 PH SHOAL	CUT	SA/CR	FBG	KL	IB	50D	PERK	12	11	23500	5	9	72700	79800
43		OCEANIC 43 CC	CUT	SA/CR	FBG	KL	IB	50D	PERK	13	1	27500	5	7	80400	88400
43		OCEANIC 43 CC	KTH	SA/CR	FBG	KC	IB	50D	PERK	13	1	27500	4	4	82900	91100
43		OCEANIC 43 CC	KTH	SA/CR	FBG	KL	IB	50D	PERK	13	1	27500	5	7	82900	91100
43		OCEANIC 43 PH	CUT	SA/CR	FBG	KC	IB	50D	PERK	13	1	27500	4	4	85100	93500
43		OCEANIC 43 PH	CUT	SA/CR	FBG	KL	IB	50D	PERK	13	1	27500	5	7	82800	90900
43		OCEANIC 43 PH	KTH	SA/CR	FBG	KC	IB	50D	PERK	13	1	27500	4	4	82900	91100
43		OCEANIC 43 PH	KTH	SA/CR	FBG	KL	IB	50D	PERK	13	1	27500	5	7	82900	91100
45	10	OCEANIC 46 PH	CUT	SA/CR	FBG	KL	IB	62D	PERK	13	6	33500	5	10	97900	107500
54	6	OCEANIC 55 PH	CUT	SA/CR	FBG	KC	IB	135D	PERK	15	9	51500	5	6	172500	189500
54	6	OCEANIC 55 PH	CUT	SA/CR	FBG	KL	IB	135D	PERK	15	9	51500	6	6	172500	189500
1982 BOATS																
41	3	OCEANIC 41	CUT	SA/CR	FBG	KL	IB	52D	PERK	12	11	23500	6	6	68400	75100
43		OCEANIC 43	CUT	SA/CR	FBG	KC	IB	52D	PERK	13	1	27500	4	4	77900	85600
43		OCEANIC 43	CUT	SA/CR	FBG	KL	IB	52D	PERK	13	1	27500	5	7	77900	85600
43		OCEANIC 43	KTH	SA/CR	FBG	KC	IB	52D	PERK	13	1	27500	4	4	78100	85800
43		OCEANIC 43	KTH	SA/CR	FBG	KL	IB	52D	PERK	13	1	27500	5	7	78100	85800
45	10	OCEANIC 46	CUT	SA/CR	FBG	KL	IB	62D	PERK	13	6	33500	5	10	92100	101000
54	6	OCEANIC 55	KTH	SA/CR	FBG	KC	IB	120D	LEHM	15	9	51500	5	6	162500	179000
54	6	OCEANIC 55	KTH	SA/CR	FBG	KL	IB	120D	LEHM	15	9	51500	6	6	162500	179000
1981 BOATS																
41	3	OCEANIC 41	CUT	SA/CR	FBG	KL	IB	52D	PERK	12	11	23500	6	6	64300	70700
41	3	OCEANIC 41 SHOAL	CUT	SA/CR	FBG	KL	IB	52D	PERK	12	11	23500	5	9	64300	70700
43		OCEANIC 43	CUT	SA/CR	FBG	KC	IB	52D	PERK	13		27500	5	7	73200	80500
43		OCEANIC 43	CUT	SA/CR	FBG	KL	IB	52D	PERK	13	3	27500	5	7	73200	80500
43		OCEANIC 43	KTH	SA/CR	FBG	KC	IB	52D	PERK	13		27500	5	7	73500	80700
43		OCEANIC 43	KTH	SA/CR	FBG	KL	IB	52D	PERK	13		27500	5	7	73500	80700
45	8	OCEANIC 46	CUT	SA/CR	FBG	KL	IB	62D	PERK	13	6	33500	5	10	86300	94900
54	6	OCEANIC 55	KTH	SA/CR	FBG	KL	IB	120D	FORD	15	9	51500	6	6	153000	168000
1980 BOATS																
36	2	OCEANIC 36	CUT	SA/CR	FBG	KL	IB	52D	PERK	11	2	28000	5	9	63700	70000
37	9	OCEANIC 38	SLP	SA/CR	FBG	KL	IB	32D	YAN	11	6	16500	6	2	42300	47000
41		OCEANIC 41	KTH	SA/CR	FBG	KL	IB	52D	PERK	12	3	23000	4	10	60500	66500
42		OCEANIC 42	SLP	SA/CR	FBG	KL	IB	52D	PERK	12	2	19500	6	6	55900	61400
43		OCEANIC 43	CUT	SA/CR	FBG	KL	IB	52D	PERK	13	6	27500	5	7	70000	76900
45	10	OCEANIC 46	CUT	SA/CR	FBG	KL	IB	62D	PERK	13	6	34000	5	10	83300	91600

PANTERA USA INC

N MIAMI BEACH FL 33180 COAST GUARD MFG ID- WCW See inside cover to adjust price for area

For more recent years, see the BUC Used Boat Price Guide, Volume 1 or Volume 2

LOA FT	LOA IN	NAME AND/ OR MODEL	TOP/ RIG	BOAT TYPE	HULL MTL	HULL TP	ENGINE TP	ENGINE # HP	ENGINE MFG	BEAM FT	BEAM IN	WGT LBS	DRAFT FT	DRAFT IN	RETAIL LOW	RETAIL HIGH
1982 BOATS																
24		PANTERA 24 SPECIAL	OP	RACE	FBG	DV	OB			7		2800	1	6	9700	11000
24		PANTERA 24 SPECIAL	OP	RACE	FBG	DV	IO	260		7			1	6	6450	7450
24		PANTERA 24 SPORTS	OP	RACE	FBG	DV	OB			7		2500	1	6	8850	10100
24		PANTERA 24 SPORTS	OP	RACE	FBG	DV	IO	260		7			1	6	5750	6600
28		PANTERA 28	OP	RACE	KEV	DV	OB			8		2000	1	10	18600	20700

CONTINUED ON NEXT PAGE

PANTERA USA INC -CONTINUED

See inside cover to adjust price for area

LOA FT IN	NAME AND/OR MODEL	TOP/RIG	BOAT TYPE	HULL MTL	TP	TP	ENGINE # HP	MFG	BEAM FT IN	WGT LBS	DRAFT FT IN	RETAIL LOW	RETAIL HIGH
1982 BOATS													
28	PANTERA 28	OP	RACE	KEV	DV	IO	800		8		1 10	**	**
28	PLEASURE 28	OP	RACE	FBG	DV	OB			8	3500		18600	20700
28	PLEASURE 28	OP	RACE	FBG	DV	IO	T260		8			9400	10700
38	PANTERA 38	OP	RACE	FBG	DV	OB			8			**	**
38	PANTERA 38	OP	RACE	FBG	DV	IO	13C		8			**	**
38	PLEASURE 38	OP	RACE	KEV	DV	OB			8	5000		37500	41700
38	PLEASURE 38	OP	RACE	KEV	DV	IO	T330		8			21100	23400
1981 BOATS													
23 7	PANTERA 24 SPECIAL	OP	RACE	FBG	DV	OB			7	3800	1 6	11700	13300
23 7	PANTERA 24 SPECIAL	OP	RACE	FBG	DV	IO	260-280		7		1 6	6200	7600
23 7	PANTERA 24 SPECIAL	OP	RACE	FBG	DV	IO	330	MRCR	7		1 6	6800	7800
23 7	PANTERA 24 SPECIAL	OP	RACE	FBG	DV	IO	T170	MRCR	7	3800	1 6	6800	7800
23 7	PANTERA 24 SPORTS	OP	RACE	FBG	DV	OB			7		1 6	11700	13300
23 7	PANTERA 24 SPORTS	OP	RACE	FBG	DV	IO	260-280		7		1 6	5550	6600
23 7	PANTERA 24 SPORTS	OP	RACE	FBG	DV	IO	330	MRCR	7		1 6	6100	7000
23 7	PANTERA 24 SPORTS	OP	RACE	FBG	DV	IO	T170	MRCR	7		1 6	5950	6850
28	PANTERA 28	OP	RACE	FBG	DV	OB			8		1 10	18300	20300
28	PANTERA 28	OP	RACE	FBG	DV	IO	330	MRCR	8	5500	1 10	8200	9450
28	PANTERA 28	OP	RACE	FBG	DV	IO	T260-T330		8	5500	1 10	9150	11300
28	PLEASURE 28	OP	RACE	FBG	DV				8	3500		18300	20300
38	CUSTOM	OP	RACE	FBG	DV	IO	T330		8			20700	23000
38	PLEASURE 38		RACE	KEV	DV	OB			8	5000		36900	41000
1979 BOATS													
23 7	PANTERA LTD EDITION	OP	RACE	FBG	DV	IO	260-330		7	3800	1 6	6400	7950
23 7	PANTERA LTD EDITION	OP	RACE	FBG	DV	IO	T170	MRCR	7	3800	1 6	6850	7850
23 7	PANTERA SPEC EDITION	OP	RACE	FBG	DV	IO	260-280		7	3800	1 6	5600	6800
23 7	PANTERA SPEC EDITION	OP	RACE	FBG	DV	IO	330	MRCR	7	3800	1 6	6150	7050
23 7	PANTERA SPEC EDITION	OP	RACE	FBG	DV	IO	T170	MRCR	7	3800	1 6	6100	7050
23 7	PANTERA SPORTS	OP	RACE	FBG	DV	OB			7	3800	1 6	11300	12900
23 7	PANTERA SPORTS	OP	RACE	FBG	DV	IO	260-280		7	3800	1 6	4950	6000
23 7	PANTERA SPORTS	OP	RACE	FBG	DV	IO	330	MRCR	7	3800	1 6	5500	6300
23 7	PANTERA SPORTS	OP	RACE	FBG	DV	IO	T170	MRCR	7	3800	1 6	5550	6350
1978 BOATS													
23 7	PANTERA	OP	RACE	FBG	DV	IO	260	MRCR	7	3800	1 6	5600	6450
23 7	PANTERA	OP	RACE	FBG	DV	IO	330	MRCR	7	3800	1 6	6200	7100
23 7	PANTERA	OP	RACE	FBG	DV	IO	T170	MRCR	7	3800	1 6	6150	7100
1977 BOATS													
23 8	PANTERA 7.1 METERS	OP	RACE	FBG	DV	IO		MRCR	7	3200	1 6	**	**
23 8	PANTERA 7.1 METERS	OP	RACE	FBG	DV	IO	T165-T170		7	3200	1 6	5650	6450

PAR-CRAFT LAMINATES INC

Call 1-800-327-6929 for BUC Personalized Evaluation Service
Or, for 1966 to 1967 boats, sign onto www.BUCValuPro.com

PARADISE CRAFTSMAN

Call 1-800-327-6929 for BUC Personalized Evaluation Service
Or, for 1959 boats, sign onto www.BUCValuPro.com

PARKER DAWSON CORP

COAST GUARD MFG ID- PHR
FOR OLDER MODELS SEE PARKER HOPKINS

Call 1-800-327-6929 for BUC Personalized Evaluation Service
Or, for 1982 to 1984 boats, sign onto www.BUCValuPro.com

PARKER RIVER YACHT YARD INC

COAST GUARD MFG ID- WPV

Call 1-800-327-6929 for BUC Personalized Evaluation Service
Or, for 1963 to 1987 boats, sign onto www.BUCValuPro.com

PARKER YACHTS

WINGA BOATS

See inside cover to adjust price for area

ROCKLAND ME 04841-2546

For more recent years, see the BUC Used Boat Price Guide, Volume 1 or Volume 2

LOA FT IN	NAME AND/OR MODEL	TOP/RIG	BOAT TYPE	HULL MTL	TP	TP	ENGINE # HP	MFG	BEAM FT IN	WGT LBS	DRAFT FT IN	RETAIL LOW	RETAIL HIGH
1977 BOATS													
25	WINGA MS-25	SLP	SAIL	FBG	KL	IB	25D		9	5020	2 11	11400	12900
1976 BOATS													
25	WINGA MS-25	SLP	SA/CR	FBG	KL	IB	25D		9	5020	2 11	11100	12600

PARKINS MARINE INC

FT LAUDERDALE FL 33315   COAST GUARD MFG ID- PKN See inside cover to adjust price for area

For more recent years, see the BUC Used Boat Price Guide, Volume 1 or Volume 2

LOA FT IN	NAME AND/OR MODEL	TOP/RIG	BOAT TYPE	HULL MTL	TP	TP	ENGINE # HP	MFG	BEAM FT IN	WGT LBS	DRAFT FT IN	RETAIL LOW	RETAIL HIGH
1983 BOATS													
32 9	SPIRIT H-28	SLP	SA/CR	FBG	KL	IB	15D	YAN	8 11	10500	3 6	27800	30900
1982 BOATS													
32 9	SPIRIT H-28	SLP	SA/CR	FBG	KL	IB	13D	VLVO	8 11	10000	3 6	24900	27700

PASSAMAQUODDY YACHT CO

Call 1-800-327-6929 for BUC Personalized Evaluation Service
Or, for 1970 to 1971 boats, sign onto www.BUCValuPro.com

PASSPORT YACHT & SHIPBUILDERS

LAWNSIDE NJ 08045   COAST GUARD MFG ID- PSX See inside cover to adjust price for area

LOA FT IN	NAME AND/OR MODEL	TOP/RIG	BOAT TYPE	HULL MTL	TP	TP	ENGINE # HP	MFG	BEAM FT IN	WGT LBS	DRAFT FT IN	RETAIL LOW	RETAIL HIGH
1982 BOATS													
18 4	MULE	OP	UTL	FBG	TR	OB			8			1950	2300
18 9	HERCULES 19		UTL	FBG	SV	OB			8			2500	2950
41 8	ROVER 42RT	HT	PH	FBG	DS	IB	T190D	GM	14	23000		87000	95600
41 8	ST-TROPEZ 42ST	FB	TRWL	FBG	DS	IB	T165D	PERK	14	23000		90000	98900
41 8	TOBAGO 42T	FB	TRWL	FBG	DS	IB	235D	VLVO	14	23000	3 6	84400	92800
41 8	TOBAGO 42T	FB	TRWL	FBG	DS	IB	T165D	PERK	14	23000		90000	98900
1981 BOATS													
18 4	MULE	OP	UTL	FBG	TR	OB			8			1900	2250
18 9	HERCULES 19		UTL	FBG	SV	OB			8			2500	2900
41 8	ROVER 42RT	HT	PH	FBG	DS	IB	T190D	GM	14	23000		82800	91000
41 8	ST-TROPEZ 42ST	FB	TRWL	FBG	DS	IB	235D	VLVO	14	23000		80400	88400
41 8	ST-TROPEZ 42ST	FB	TRWL	FBG	DS	IB	T165D	PERK	14	23000		85700	94200
41 8	TOBAGO 42T	FB	TRWL	FBG	DS	IB	235D	VLVO	14	23000	3 6	80400	88400
41 8	TOBAGO 42T	FB	TRWL	FBG	DS	IB	T165D	PERK	14	23000	3	85700	94200
1980 BOATS													
41 8	ROVER	HT	PH	FBG	SV	IB	190D		14	23000		76200	83700
41 8	ROVER	HT	PH	FBG	SV	IB	T190D		14	23000		78500	86200
41 8	TOBAGO	FB	TRWL	FBG	SV	IB	220D		14	23000		76000	83500
41 8	TOBAGO	FB	TRWL	FBG	SV	IB	T130D		14	23000		78500	86300

G A PATTEN BOATBUILDING INC

COAST GUARD MFG ID- GAP

Call 1-800-327-6929 for BUC Personalized Evaluation Service
Or, for 1983 to 1986 boats, sign onto www.BUCValuPro.com

PATTERSON YACHT MFG

Call 1-800-327-6929 for BUC Personalized Evaluation Service
Or, for 1970 boats, sign onto www.BUCValuPro.com

GORDON PAYNE LTD

ROMANY WORKS   COAST GUARD MFG ID- RMF

Call 1-800-327-6929 for BUC Personalized Evaluation Service
Or, for 1972 to 1973 boats, sign onto www.BUCValuPro.com

PEARSON BROTHERS LTD

Call 1-800-327-6929 for BUC Personalized Evaluation Service
Or, for 1968 to 1979 boats, sign onto www.BUCValuPro.com

PEARSON YACHT CORP

PORTSMOUTH RI 02871 COAST GUARD MFG ID- PEA See inside cover to adjust price for area

For more recent years, see the BUC Used Boat Price Guide, Volume 1 or Volume 2

LOA FT	LOA IN	NAME AND/ OR MODEL	TOP/ RIG	BOAT TYPE	-HULL- MTL	-HULL- TP	ENGINE TP	ENGINE # HP	ENGINE MFG	BEAM FT	BEAM IN	WGT LBS	DRAFT FT	DRAFT IN	RETAIL LOW	RETAIL HIGH
		1983 BOATS														
22	6	ENSIGN	SLP	SA/OD	FBG	KL	OB			7		3000	3		6350	7300
23		PEARSON 23 C	CAT	SA/CR	FBG	KL	OB			8		3000	4		6450	7450
26	2	PEARSON 26 OD	SLP	SA/OD	FBG	KL	OB			8	8	5200	4		12500	14200
30		PEARSON-FLYER	SLP	SA/OD	F/S	KL	IB	6D	BMW	12		6135	5	9	16700	19000
30	3	PEARSON 303	SLP	SA/CR	FBG	KL	IB	15D	YAN	10	11	10000	4	4	27900	31100
32	3	PEARSON 323	SLP	SA/CR	FBG	KL	SD	23D	VLVO	10	3	12800	4	5	35600	39600
33	10	PEARSON 34	SLP	SA/CR	FBG	KC	IB	16D	UNIV	11	3	11750	3	10	33000	36700
33	10	PEARSON 34	SLP	SA/RC	FBG	KL	IB	16D	UNIV	11	3	11240	5	11	31600	35200
36	5	PEARSON 367	CUT	SA/CR	FBG	KL	IB	44D		11	6	17700	5	6	50500	55500
36	11	PEARSON 37	SLP	SA/RC	F/S	KL	IB	25D	UNIV	11	10	12800	6	5	38500	42800
42	2	PEARSON 422	SLP	SA/CR	FBG	KL	IB	58D	WEST	13		22000	5	3	73600	80900
42	4	PEARSON 424	CUT	SA/CR	F/S	KL	IB	58D	WEST	13		21000	5	3	72200	79300
42	4	PEARSON 424	KTH	SA/CR	F/S	KL	IB	58D	WEST	13		21000	5	3	72200	79300
42	4	PEARSON 424 PLANC	CUT	SA/CR	FBG	KL	IB	58D	WEST	13		21000	5	3	72200	79300
42	4	PEARSON 424 PLANC	KTH	SA/CR	FBG	KL	IB	58D	WEST	13		21000	5	3	72200	79300
53		PEARSON 530	KTH	SA/CR	F/S	KC	IB	85D	PERK	15		43000	5	9	166000	182000
53		PEARSON 530	KTH	SA/CR	F/S	KL	IB	85D	PERK	15		43000	6	10	166000	182000
		1982 BOATS														
22	6	ENSIGN	SLP	SA/OD	FBG	KL	OB			7		3000	3		6050	6950
26	2	PEARSON 26	SLP	SA/CR	FBG	KL	OB			8	8	5400	4		12300	14000
26	2	PEARSON 26 OD	SLP	SA/OD	FBG	KL	OB			8	8	5200	4		11800	13500
28		PEARSON 28	SLP	SA/CR	FBG	KL	IB	11D	UNIV	9	3	7850	5		20100	22300
30		PEARSON-FLYER	SLP	SA/OD	F/S	KL	IB	6D	BMW	12		6135	5	9	15800	18000
31	9	PEARSON 32	SLP	SA/CR	F/S	KL	IB	11D	UNIV	10	7	9400	5	6	24900	27700
32	3	PEARSON 323	SLP	SA/CR	FBG	KL	IB	23D	VLVO	10	3	12800	4	5	33800	37500
35		PEARSON 35	SLP	SA/CR	FBG	KC	IB	24D	UNIV	10		13000	3	9	35000	38900
35		PEARSON 35	YWL	SA/CR	FBG	KC	IB	24D	UNIV	10		13000	3	9	35000	38900
36	5	PEARSON 36	CUT	SA/CR	FBG	KL	IB	44D		11	6	17700	5	6	47900	52600
36	5	PEARSON 365	SLP	SA/CR	FBG	KL	IB	44D		11	6	17700	4	6	47900	52600
36	5	PEARSON 365	KTH	SA/CR	FBG	KL	IB	44D		11	6	17700	4	6	47900	52600
36	11	PEARSON 37	SLP	SA/RC	F/S	KL	IB	25D	UNIV	11	10	12800	6	5	36500	40500
42	4	PEARSON 424	SLP	SA/CR	F/S	KL	IB	58D	WEST	13		21000	5	3	68400	75200
42	4	PEARSON 424	KTH	SA/CR	F/S	KL	IB	58D	WEST	13		21000	5	3	68400	75200
53		PEARSON 530	KTH	SA/CR	F/S	KC	IB	85D	PERK	15		43000	5	9	157000	172500
53		PEARSON 530	KTH	SA/CR	F/S	KL	IB	85D	PERK	15		43000	6	10	157000	172500
		1981 BOATS														
22	6	ENSIGN	SLP	SA/OD	FBG	KL	OB			7		3000	3		5700	6550
23		PEARSON 23	SLP	SA/RC	FBG	KC				7	11	3500	5	2	6600	7550
26	2	PEARSON 26	SLP	SA/CR	FBG	KL	OB			8	8	5400	4		11700	13300
26	2	PEARSON 26 OD	SLP	SA/OD	FBG	KL	OB			8	8	5200	4		11200	12800
28		PEARSON 28	SLP	SA/CR	FBG	KL	IB	11D	UNIV	9	3	7850	5		19000	21200
30		PEARSON-FLYER	SLP	SA/OD	FBG	KL	IB	7D	BMW	11		6135	5	9	15000	17100
31		PEARSON 31	SLP	SA/RC	FBG	KL	OB			10	7	9400	5	6	23500	26100
31	9	PEARSON 32	SLP	SA/CR	FBG	KL	IB	11D	UNIV	10	7	9400	5	6	23600	26300
32	3	PEARSON 323	SLP	SA/CR	FBG	KL	IB	23D	VLVO	10	3	12000	4	5	30100	33400
35		PEARSON 35	SLP	SA/CR	FBG	KC	IB	24D	UNIB	10		13000	3	9	33200	36900
35		PEARSON 35	YWL	SA/CR	FBG	KC	IB	24D	UNIV	10		13000	3	9	33200	36900
36	5	PEARSON 36	CUT	SA/CR	FBG	KL	IB	37D	WEST	11	6	17700	5	6	45700	50200
36	5	PEARSON 36 PILOTHOUS	SLP	MS	FBG	KL	IB	43D	WEST	11	6	17500	4	6	44800	49800
36	5	PEARSON 365	SLP	SA/CR	FBG	KL	IB	37D	WEST	11	6	17700	4	6	45700	50200
36	5	PEARSON 365	KTH	SA/CR	FBG	KL	IB	37D	WEST	11	6	17700	4	6	45700	50200
39	11	PEARSON 40	SLP	SA/CR	FBG	KC	IB	37D	WEST	12	6	22800	4	3	62200	68400
42	4	PEARSON 424	SLP	SA/CR	FBG	KL	IB	58D	WEST	13		21000	5	3	64800	71200
42	4	PEARSON 424	KTH	SA/CR	FBG	KL	IB	58D	WEST	13		21000	5	3	64900	71300
53		PEARSON 530	KTH	SA/CR	FBG	KC	IB	85D	PERK	15		43000	5	9	149000	163500
		1980 BOATS														
22	6	ENSIGN	SLP	SA/OD	FBG	KL	OB			7		3000	3		5500	6300
23		PEARSON 23	SLP	SA/CR	FBG	KL	OB			8		3500	5	2	6350	7300
26	2	PEARSON 26	SLP	SA/CR	FBG	KL	OB			8	8	5400	4		11200	12800
26	2	PEARSON ONE DESIGN	SLP	SA/OD	FBG	KL	OB			8	8	5200	4		10800	12300
28		PEARSON 28	SLP	SA/CR	FBG	KL	IB	11D	UNIV	9	3	7850	5		18500	20600
29	10	PEARSON 30	SLP	SA/CR	FBG	KL	IB	11D	UNIV	9	6	8320	5		19900	22100
31	9	PEARSON 32	SLP	SA/CR	FBG	KL	IB	11D	UNIV	10	7	9400	5	6	22800	25300
32	3	PEARSON 323	SLP	SA/CR	FBG	KL	IB	23D	VLVO	10	3	12800	4	5	30800	34200
33	1	PEARSON 10M	SLP	SA/CR	FBG	KL	IB	23D	VLVO	11		12441	5	11	30000	33400
35		PEARSON 35	SLP	SA/CR	FBG	KC	IB	24D	UNIV	10		13000	3	9	32000	35500
35		PEARSON 35	YWL	SA/CR	FBG	KC	IB	24D	UNIV	10		13000	3	9	32000	35500
36	5	PEARSON 365	SLP	SA/CR	FBG	KL	IB	40D	WEST	11	6	17700	4	6	43500	48300
36	5	PEARSON 365	KTH	SA/CR	FBG	KL	IB	40D	WEST	11	6	17700	4	6	43500	48300
39	11	PEARSON 40	SLP	SA/CR	FBG	KC	IB	40D	WEST	12	6	22800	4	3	59900	65800
42	4	PEARSON 424	SLP	SA/CR	FBG	KL	IB	60D	WEST	13		21000	5	3	62400	68600
42	4	PEARSON 424	KTH	SA/CR	FBG	KL	IB	60D	WEST	13		21000	5	3	62400	68600
		1979 BOATS														
22	6	ENSIGN	SLP	SA/OD	FBG	KL	OB			7		3000	3		5350	6100
23		PEARSON 23	SLP	SA/CR	FBG	KL	OB			8		3500	5	2	6150	7050
26	2	PEARSON 26	SLP	SA/CR	FBG	KL	OB			8	8	5400	4		10900	12400
26	2	PEARSON ONE DESIGN	SLP	SA/OD	FBG	KL	OB			8	8	5200	4		10500	11900
28		PEARSON 28	SLP	SA/CR	FBG	KL	IB	10D-	30D	9	3	7850	5		17600	20200
29	10	PEARSON 30	SLP	SA/CR	FBG	KL	IB	10D-	30D	9	6	8320	5		19300	21600
31		PEARSON 31	SLP	SA/CR	FBG	KL	IB	D		10	7	9400	5	6	22000	24500
31	9	PEARSON 32	SLP	SA/CR	FBG	KL	IB	D		10	7	9400	5	6	22000	24500
32	3	PEARSON 323	SLP	SA/CR	FBG	KL	IB	23D	UNIV	10	3	12800	4	5	29800	33200
33	1	PEARSON 10M	SLP	SA/CR	FBG	KL	IB	23D-	30D	11		12441	5	11	29100	32400
35		PEARSON 35	SLP	SA/CR	FBG	KC	IB	25D	WEST	10		13000	3	9	31000	34400
35		PEARSON 35	SLP	SA/CR	FBG	KC	IB	30D	UNIV	10		13000	3	9	31000	34400
35		PEARSON 35	YWL	SA/CR	FBG	KC	IB	25D	WEST	10		13000	3	9	31000	34400
35		PEARSON 35	YWL	SA/CR	FBG	KC	IB	30D	UNIV	10		13000	3	9	31000	34400
36	5	PEARSON 365	SLP	SA/CR	FBG	KL	IB	37D	WEST	11	6	17700	4	6	42100	46800
36	5	PEARSON 365	KTH	SA/CR	FBG	KL	IB	37D	WEST	11	6	17700	4	6	42100	46800
39	11	PEARSON 40	SLP	SA/CR	FBG	KC	IB	40D	WEST	12	6	22800	4	3	58000	63800
39	11	PEARSON 40	YWL	SA/CR	FBG	KC	IB	40D	WEST	12	6	22800	4	3	58000	63800
42	4	PEARSON 424	KTH	SA/CR	FBG	KL	IB	60D	WEST	13		21000	5	3	60500	66400
		1978 BOATS														
22	6	ENSIGN	SLP	SA/OD	FBG	KL	OB			7		3000	3		5150	5950
26	2	PEARSON 26	SLP	SA/CR	FBG	KL	OB			8	8	5400	4		10600	12000
26	2	PEARSON ONE DESIGN	SLP	SA/OD	FBG	KL	OB			8	8	5200	4		10200	11500
28		PEARSON 28	SLP	SA/CR	FBG	KL	IB	30	UNIV	9	3	7850	5		16900	19200
28		PEARSON 28	SLP	SA/CR	FBG	KL	IB	10D	WEST	9	3	7850	5		17100	19400
29	10	PEARSON 30	SLP	SA/CR	FBG	KL	IB	30	UNIV	9	6	8320	5		18900	21000
29	10	PEARSON 30	SLP	SA/CR	FBG	KL	IB	10D	WEST	9	6	8320	5		19000	21100
31		PEARSON 31	SLP	SA/CR	FBG	KL	IB	30	UNIV	10	7	9400	5	6	21300	23700
31		PEARSON 31	SLP	SA/CR	FBG	KL	IB	D		10	7	9400	5	6	21400	23800
32	3	PEARSON 323	SLP	SA/CR	FBG	KL	IB	30	UNIV	10	3	12800	4	5	29000	32200
32	3	PEARSON 323	SLP	SA/CR	FBG	KL	IB	23D	VLVO	10	3	12800	4	5	29000	32200
33	1	PEARSON 10M	SLP	SA/CR	FBG	KL	IB	30	UNIV	11		12441	5	11	28200	31300
33	1	PEARSON 10M	SLP	SA/CR	FBG	KL	IB	23D	VLVO	11		12441	5	11	28300	31400
35		PEARSON 35	SLP	SA/CR	FBG	KC	IB	30	UNIV	10		13000	3	9	29800	33100
35		PEARSON 35	SLP	SA/CR	FBG	KC	IB	25D	WEST	10		13000	3	9	30100	33400
35		PEARSON 35	YWL	SA/CR	FBG	KC	IB	30	UNIV	10		13000	3	9	29800	33100
35		PEARSON 35	YWL	SA/CR	FBG	KC	IB	25D	WEST	10		13000	3	9	30100	33400
36	5	PEARSON 365	SLP	SA/CR	FBG	KL	IB	37D	WEST	11	6	17700	4	6	40900	45400
36	5	PEARSON 365	KTH	SA/CR	FBG	KL	IB	37D	WEST	11	6	17700	4	6	40900	45400
39	3	PEARSON 39	SLP	SA/CR	FBG	KC	IB	30	UNIV	11	8	17000	4	8	43300	48100
39	3	PEARSON 39	YWL	SA/CR	FBG	KC	IB	30	UNIV	11	8	17000	4	8	43300	48100
42	4	PEARSON 424	KTH	SA/CR	FBG	KL	IB	53D	WEST	13		21000	5	3	58600	64400
		1977 BOATS														
22	6	ENSIGN	SLP	SA/OD	FBG	KL	OB			7		3000	3		5050	5800
26	2	PEARSON 26	SLP	SA/CR	FBG	KL	OB			8	8	5400	4		10300	11700
28		PEARSON 28	SLP	SA/CR	FBG	KL	OB			9	3	7850	4	6	16200	18400
28		PEARSON 28	SLP	SA/CR	FBG	KL	IB	30	UNIV	9	3	7850	4	6	16400	18700
28		PEARSON 28	SLP	SA/CR	FBG	KL	IB	10D	WEST	9	3	7850	4	6	16600	18900
29	10	PEARSON 30	SLP	SA/CR	FBG	KL	IB	30	UNIV	9	6	8320	5		18400	20400
29	10	PEARSON 30	SLP	SA/CR	FBG	KL	IB	10D	WEST	9	6	8320	5		18500	20500
32	3	PEARSON 323	SLP	SA/CR	FBG	KL	IB	30	UNIV	10	3	12800	4	5	28200	31300
32	3	PEARSON 323	SLP	SA/CR	FBG	KL	IB	D		10	3	12800	4	5	28200	31300
33	1	PEARSON 10M	SLP	SA/CR	FBG	KL	IB	30	UNIV	11		12441	5	11	27400	30500
33	1	PEARSON 10M	SLP	SA/CR	FBG	KL	IB	24D	FARY	11		12441	5	11	27500	30600
35		PEARSON 35	SLP	SA/CR	FBG	KC	IB	30	UNIV	10		13000	3	9	29000	32300
35		PEARSON 35	SLP	SA/CR	FBG	KC	IB	25D	WEST	10		13000	3	9	29300	32500
35		PEARSON 35	YWL	SA/CR	FBG	KC	IB	30	UNIV	10		13000	3	9	29000	32300
35		PEARSON 35	YWL	SA/CR	FBG	KC	IB	25D	WEST	10		13000	3	9	29300	32500
36	5	PEARSON 365	KTH	SA/CR	FBG	KL	IB	37D	WEST	11	5	17700	4	6	39800	44200
39	3	PEARSON 39	SLP	SA/CR	FBG	KC	IB	37D	WEST	11	8	17000	4	8	43000	47700
39	3	PEARSON 39	YWL	SA/CR	FBG	KC	IB	37D	WEST	11	8	17000	4	8	43000	47700
41	9	PEARSON 424	KTH	SA/CR	FBG	KL	IB	D		13		21000	5	3	55400	60900
		1976 BOATS														
22	6	ENSIGN	SLP	SA/OD	FBG	KL	OB			7		3000	3		4900	5650
26	2	PEARSON 26	SLP	SA/CR	FBG	KL	OB			8	8	5400	4		10000	11400
26	2	PEARSON 26W	SLP	SA/CR	FBG	KL	OB			8	8	5200	4		9650	11000
28		PEARSON 28	SLP	SAIL	FBG	KL	OB			9	3	7850	4	6	15800	18000
29	10	PEARSON 30	SLP	SAIL	FBG	KL	IB	30	UNIV	9	6	8320	5		17500	19900
29	10	PEARSON 30	SLP	SAIL	FBG	KL	IB	10D	WEST	9	6	8320	5		18000	20000
32	3	PEARSON 320	SLP	SAIL	FBG	KL	IB	30	UNIV	10			4	3	13800	15700
33	1	PEARSON 10M	SLP	SAIL	FBG	KL	IB	30	UNIV	11		12441	5	11	26800	29700
33	1	PEARSON 10M	SLP	SAIL	FBG	KL	IB	20D	WEST	11		12441	5	11	26800	29800

CONTINUED ON NEXT PAGE

LOA FT	LOA IN	NAME AND/ OR MODEL	TOP/ RIG	BOAT TYPE	-HULL- MTL	-HULL- TP	ENGINE TP	ENGINE # HP	ENGINE MFG	BEAM FT	BEAM IN	WGT LBS	DRAFT FT	DRAFT IN	RETAIL LOW	RETAIL HIGH
		1976 BOATS														
35		PEARSON 35	SLP	SAIL	FBG	KC	IB	30	UNIV	10		13000	3	9	28300	31500
35		PEARSON 35	SLP	SAIL	FBG	KC	IB	25D	WEST	10		13000	3	9	28600	31800
35		PEARSON 35	YWL	SAIL	FBG	KC	IB	30	UNIV	10		13000	3	9	28300	31500
35		PEARSON 35	YWL	SAIL	FBG	KC	IB	25D	WEST	10		13000	3	9	28600	31800
36	5	PEARSON 365	KTH	SAIL	FBG	KL	VD	37D	FARY	11	6	17700	4	6	38800	43100
36	7	PEARSON 36	SLP	SAIL	FBG	KL	IB	30	UNIV	11	1	13500	6		30400	33800
36	7	PEARSON 36	SLP	SAIL	FBG	KL	IB	D	FARY	11	1	13500	6		30800	34200
39	3	PEARSON 39	SLP	SAIL	FBG	KC	VD	37D	FARY	11	8	17000	4	8	41800	46500
39	3	PEARSON 39	YWL	SAIL	FBG	KC	VD	37D	FARY	11	8	17000	4	8	41800	46500
41	9	PEARSON 419	SLP	SAIL	FBG	KL	IB	53D	WEST	13		21000	5	3	54300	59600
41	9	PEARSON 419	KTH	SAIL	FBG	KL	IB	53D	WEST	13		21000	5	3	54300	59600
43		PORTSMOUTH 43	FB	MY	FBG	SV	IB	T220D		14	10	22000	3		59700	65600
		1975 BOATS														
22	6	ENSIGN	SLP	SA/OD	FBG	KL	OB			7		3000	3		4800	5500
26	2	PEARSON 26	SLP	SA/CR	FBG	KL	OB			8	8	5400	4		9800	11100
26	2	PEARSON 26W	SLP	SA/CR	FBG	KL	OB			8	8	5200	4		9450	10700
28		PEARSON 28	SLP	SAIL	FBG	KL	IB	30	UNIV	9	3	7850	4	6	15700	17800
28		PEARSON 28	SLP	SAIL	FBG	KL	IB	12D	FARY	9	3	7850	4	6	15800	18000
29	10	PEARSON 30	SLP	SAIL	FBG	KL	IB	30	UNIV	9	6	8320	5		17100	19500
29	10	PEARSON 30	SLP	SAIL	FBG	KL	IB	12D	FARY	9	6	8320	5		17200	19600
32	11	PEARSON 33	SLP	SAIL	FBG	KC	IB	30	UNIV	10		10900	4		23000	25600
32	11	PEARSON 33	SLP	SAIL	FBG	KC	IB	24D	FARY	10		10900	4		23100	25600
33	1	PEARSON 10M	SLP	SAIL	FBG	KL	IB	30	UNIV	11		12441	5	11	26200	29100
33	1	PEARSON 10M	SLP	SAIL	FBG	KL	IB	24D	FARY	11		12441	5	11	26200	29200
35		PEARSON 35	SLP	SAIL	FBG	KC	IB	30	UNIV	10		13000	3	9	27700	30800
35		PEARSON 35	SLP	SAIL	FBG	KC	IB	24D	FARY	10		13000	3	9	27900	31000
36	7	PEARSON 36	SLP	SAIL	FBG	KL	IB	30	UNIV	11	1	13500	6		29700	33000
36	7	PEARSON 36	SLP	SAIL	FBG	KL	IB	26D	FARY	11	1	13500	6		30100	33400
36	7	PEARSON 36	YWL	SAIL	FBG	KC	IB	30	UNIV	10		13000	3	9	28700	31900
39	3	PEARSON 39	SLP	SAIL	FBG	KC	IB	30	UNIV	11	8	17000	4	8	40200	44700
39	3	PEARSON 39	SLP	SAIL	FBG	KC	IB	25D	WEST	11	8	17000	4	8	40800	45300
39	3	PEARSON 39	YWL	SAIL	FBG	KC	IB	30	UNIV	11	8	17000	4	8	40200	44700
39	3	PEARSON 39	YWL	SAIL	FBG	KC	IB	25D	WEST	11	8	17000	4	8	40800	45300
41	9	PEARSON 419	SLP	SAIL	FBG	KL	IB	70D	CHRY	13		21000	5	3	53100	58400
41	9	PEARSON 419	KTH	SAIL	FBG	KL	IB	70D	CHRY	13		21000	5	3	53100	58400
43		PORTSMOUTH 43	FB	MY	FBG	SV	IB	T220D		14	10	22000	3		57300	62900
43		PORTSMOUTH 43	FB	MY	FBG	SV	IB	T250D		14	10	22000	3		58500	64300
43		PORTSMOUTH 43	FB	MY	FBG	SV	IB	T330D		14	10	22000	3		62500	68700
		1974 BOATS														
22	6	ENSIGN	SLP	SA/OD	FBG	KL	OB			7		3000	3		4700	5400
26	2	PEARSON 26	SLP	SA/CR	FBG	KL	OB			8	8	5400	4		9600	10900
29	10	PEARSON 30	SLP	SAIL	FBG		IB	30	UNIV	9	6	8320	5		16800	19100
32	11	PEARSON 33	SLP	SA/CR	FBG	CB	IB	30	UNIV	10		10900	4		22500	25000
32	11	PEARSON 33	SLP	SAIL	FBG	CB	IB	30	UNIV	10		10900	4		22500	25000
33	1	PEARSON 10M	SLP	SAIL	FBG		IB	30	UNIV	11		12441	5	11	25600	28500
35		PEARSON 35	SLP	SAIL	FBG	CB	IB	30	UNIV	10		13000	3	9	27100	30100
35		PEARSON 35	YWL	SAIL	FBG	CB	IB	30	UNIV	10		13000	3	9	27100	30100
36	7	PEARSON 36	SLP	SAIL	FBG		IB	30	UNIV	11	1	13500	6		29100	32400
39	3	PEARSON 39	SLP	SAIL	FBG	CB	IB	30	UNIV	11	8	17000	4	8	39400	43800
39	3	PEARSON 39	YWL	SAIL	FBG	CB	IB	30	UNIV	11	8	17000	4	8	39400	43800
43		PORTSMOUTH 43	FB	MY	FBG		IB	T185D	PERK	14	10	22000	3		54700	60100
		IB T225D CAT 56200 61700, IB T250D CHRY 56200 61800, IB T330D CHRY													60100	66000
		1973 BOATS														
22	6	ENSIGN	SLP	SA/OD	FBG	KL	OB			7		3000	3		4650	5350
26	2	PEARSON 26	SLP	SA/CR	FBG	KL	OB			8	8	5400	4		9450	10700
29	10	PEARSON 30	SLP	SAIL	FBG	KL	IB	30	UNIV	9	6	8320	5		16500	18700
32	11	PEARSON 33	SLP	SA/CR	FBG	CB	IB	30	UNIV	10		10900	4		22100	24600
32	11	PEARSON 33 COMP	SLP	SAIL	FBG	CB	IB	30	UNIV	10		10900	4		22100	24600
35		PEARSON 35	SLP	SAIL	FBG	CB	IB	30	UNIV	10		13000	3	9	26600	29600
36	7	PEARSON 36	SLP	SAIL	FBG	KL	IB	30	UNIV	11	1	13650	6		28900	32100
39		PEARSON 390	SLP	SAIL	FBG	CB	IB	37D	WEST	13		20600	4	3	44700	49700
39	3	PEARSON 39	SLP	SAIL	FBG	CB	IB	30	UNIV	11	8	17000	4	8	38700	42900
43		PORTSMOUTH 43	HT	MY	FBG		IB	T212D	PALM	14	10	22000	3		52700	57900
43		PORTSMOUTH 43	FB	MY	FBG		IB	T212D	PALM	14	10	22000	3		52700	57900
		1972 BOATS														
22	3	PEARSON 22	SLP	SAIL	FBG	KL	OB			7	7	2600	3	5	4000	4700
22	6	ENSIGN	SLP	SA/OD	FBG	KL	OB			7		3000	3		4550	5250
26	2	PEARSON 26	SLP	SA/CR	FBG	KL	OB			8	8	5400	4		9300	10600
29	10	PEARSON 30	SLP	SAIL	FBG	KL	IB	22	PALM	9	6	8320	5		16100	18300
32	11	PEARSON 33	SLP	SA/CR	FBG	CB	IB	30	UNIV	10		10900	4		21600	24100
32	11	PEARSON 33 COMP	SLP	SAIL	FBG	CB	IB	30	UNIV	10		10900	4		21600	24100
35		PEARSON 35	SLP	SAIL	FBG	CB	IB	30	UNIV	10		13000	3	9	26100	29000
39		PEARSON 390	SLP	SAIL	FBG	CB	IB	72	UNIV	13		20600	4	3	43200	48000
39	3	PEARSON 39	SLP	SAIL	FBG	CB	IB	30	UNIV	11	8	17000	4	8	37800	42000
43		PORTSMOUTH 43	HT	MY	FBG		IB	T212	PALM	14	10	22000	3		44200	49100
43		PORTSMOUTH 43	FB	MY	FBG	SV	IB	T212	PALM	14	10	22000	3		44100	49000
		1971 BOATS														
22	3	PEARSON 22	SLP	SAIL	FBG	KL	OB			7	7	2600	3	5	3900	4550
22	6	ENSIGN	SLP	SA/OD	FBG	KL	OB			7		3000	3		4450	5100
26	2	PEARSON 26	SLP	SA/CR	FBG	KL	OB			8	9	5400	4		9050	10300
29	10	PEARSON 30	SLP	SAIL	FBG	KL	IB	22	PALM	9	6	8320	5		15700	17800
30	3	WANDERER 30	SLP	SAIL	FBG	CB	IB	30	UNIV	9	4	9800	3	6	19100	21200
32	11	PEARSON 33	SLP	SA/CR	FBG	CB	IB	20	PALM	10		10900	4		21100	23400
32	11	PEARSON 33 COMP	SLP	SAIL	FBG	CB	IB	20	PALM	10		10900	4		21100	23400
35		PEARSON 35	YWL	SA/CR	FBG	KC	IB	30		10		13000	3	9	25400	28200
35		PEARSON 35	SLP	SAIL	FBG	CB	IB	20	UNIV	10		13000	3	9	25400	28200
39	3	PEARSON 39	YWL	SA/CR	FBG	KC	IB	30		11	8	17000	4	7	36900	41000
39	3	PEARSON 39	SLP	SAIL	FBG	CB	IB	30	UNIV	11	8	17000	4	8	36900	41000
42	9	PEARSON 43	YWL	SA/CR	FBG	KL	IB	30		11	9	21796	6	3	50900	56000
42	9	PEARSON 43		SAIL	FBG	KL	IB	72	UNIV	11	9	21300	6	3	50500	55500
43		PORTSMOUTH 43	HT	MY	FBG		IB	T212	PALM	14	10	22000	3		42600	47300
43		PORTSMOUTH 43	FB	MY	FBG		IB	T212	PALM	14	10	22000	3		42600	47300
44	6	COUNTESS 44	KTH	SA/CR	FBG	KL	IB	110		12		28000	5	4	63300	69600
		1970 BOATS														
22	3	PEARSON 22	SLP	SA/OD	FBG	CB				7	7	2600	1	1	3800	4450
22	3	PEARSON 22	SLP	SA/OD	FBG	KL	OB			7	7	2600	3	5	3800	4450
22	6	ENSIGN	SLP	SA/OD	FBG	KL	OB			7		3000	3		4300	4950
26	2	PEARSON 26	SLP	SA/CR	FBG	KL	OB			8	9	5354	4		8650	9950
29	10	COASTER 30	SLP	SAIL	FBG	KL	IB	30	UNIV	9	4	9500	4	7	17600	20000
30	3	PEARSON 300	SLP	SAIL	FBG	KL	IB	22	PALM	9	4	10000	3	6	19000	21100
30	3	WANDERER 30	SLP	SAIL	FBG	KC	IB	30	UNIV	9	4	9800	6	9	18600	20700
32	11	PEARSON 33	SLP	SAIL	FBG	KC	IB	30	UNIV	10		10930	4		20600	22900
35		PEARSON 35	YWL	SA/CR	FBG	CB	IB	30	UNIV	10		13000	3	9	24800	27500
35		PEARSON 35	SLP	SAIL	FBG	KC	IB	30	UNIV	10		13000	3	9	24800	27500
39	3	PEARSON 39	YWL	SA/CR	FBG	CB	IB	30	UNIV	11	8	17000	4	7	36000	40000
39	3	PEARSON 39	SLP	SAIL	FBG	KC	IB	30	UNIV	11	8	11700	4	7	27100	30200
42	9	PEARSON 43	YWL	SA/CR	FBG	KL	IB	30	UNIV	11	9	21796	6	3	49700	54600
42	9	PEARSON 43 AFT CABIN	SLP	SAIL	FBG	KL	IB	72	UNIV	11	9	21796	6	3	49900	54800
42	9	PEARSON 43 STD INT	SLP	SAIL	FBG	KL	IB	72	UNIV	11	9	21796	6	3	49900	54800
44	6	COUNTESS 44 INT A	KTH	SAIL	FBG	KL	IB	110D	LATH	12		28000	5	4	62300	68400
44	6	COUNTESS 44 INT B	KTH	SAIL	FBG	KL	IB	110D	LATH	12		28000	5	4	62300	68400
44	6	COUNTESS 44 INT C	KTH	SAIL	FBG	KL	IB	110D	LATH	12		28000	5	4	62300	68400
44	6	COUNTESS 44 INT E	KTH	SAIL	FBG	KL	IB	110D	LATH	12		28000	5	4	64800	71300
		1969 BOATS														
22	3	PEARSON 22	SLP	SA/OD	FBG	CB				7	7	2600	1	1	3750	4350
22	3	PEARSON 22	SLP	SAIL	FBG	KL	OB			7	7	2600	3	5	3750	4350
22	6	ENSIGN	SLP	SA/OD	FBG	KL	OB			7		3000	3		4200	4850
23	6	PEARSON 24	SLP	SAIL	FBG	KL	OB			8		4300	4		6000	6900
27	2	RENEGADE 27	SLP	SAIL	FBG	KL	OB			8	7	6500	4	3	10800	12300
27	2	RENEGADE 27	SLP	SAIL	FBG	KL	IB	30	UNIV	8	7	6500	4	3	11000	12500
27	10	RENDOVA		EXP	FBG	SV	IB	195	CHRY	10	5	9800	2	6	11700	13300
28	6	TRITON	SLP	SAIL	FBG	KL	IB	30		8	3	8400	4		14900	16900
28	6	TRITON	YWL	SAIL	FBG	KL	IB	30		8	3	8600	4		15200	17300
29	10	COASTER 30	SLP	SAIL	FBG	KL	IB	30	UNIV	9	4	9500	4	7	17200	19500
30	3	PEARSON 300	SLP	SAIL	FBG	KL	IB	22	PALM	9	4	10000	3	6	18600	20700
30	3	WANDERER 30	SLP	SAIL	FBG	CB	IB	30	UNIV	9	4	9800	6	9	18200	20200
35		PEARSON 35	SLP	SAIL	FBG	CB	IB	30	UNIV	10		13000	7	6	24200	26900
35		PEARSON 35	YWL	SAIL	FBG	CB	IB	30	UNIV	10		13000	7	6	24200	26900
37	8	INVICTA II DIN	SLP	SAIL	FBG	CB	IB	30	UNIV	10	8	17750	8	7	34300	38100
37	8	INVICTA II DIN	YWL	SAIL	FBG	CB	IB	30	UNIV	10	8	17750	8	7	34300	38100
37	8	INVICTA II STD	SLP	SAIL	FBG	CB	IB	30	UNIV	10	8	17750	8	7	33700	37500
37	8	INVICTA II STD	YWL	SAIL	FBG	CB	IB	30	UNIV	10	8	17750	8	7	33700	37500
42	9	PEARSON 43	YWL	SAIL	FBG	KL	IB	72	UNIV	11	9	21796	6	3	48800	53600
42	9	PEARSON 43 AFT CABIN	SLP	SAIL	FBG	KL	IB	72	UNIV	11	9	21796	6	3	48800	53600
42	9	PEARSON 43 STD INT	SLP	SAIL	FBG	KL	IB	72	UNIV	11	9	21796	6	3	48800	53600
44	6	COUNTESS 44 INT A	KTH	SAIL	FBG	KL	IB	110D	LATH	12		28000	5	4	60900	66900
44	6	COUNTESS 44 INT B	KTH	SAIL	FBG	KL	IB	110D	LATH	12		28000	5	4	60900	66900
44	6	COUNTESS 44 INT C	KTH	SAIL	FBG	KL	IB	110D	LATH	12		28000	5	4	60900	66900
44	6	COUNTESS 44 INT E	KTH	SAIL	FBG	KL	IB	110D	LATH	12		28000	5	4	63400	69700
		1968 BOATS														
22	3	PEARSON 22	SLP	SAIL	FBG	KL	OB			7	9	3100	3	5	4150	4850
22	6	ENSIGN	SLP	SA/OD	FBG	KL	OB			7		3000	3	2	4100	4750
23	6	PEARSON 24	SLP	SAIL	FBG	KL	OB			8		4100	4		5600	6450
24		LARK	SLP	SAIL	FBG	KL	OB			8		4300	4		5950	6850
27	2	RENEGADE	SLP	SAIL	FBG	KL	OB			8	7	6500	4	3	10600	12000
27	2	RENEGADE	SLP	SAIL	FBG	KL	IB	30		8	7	6800	4	3	11300	12900
29	10	COASTER	SLP	SAIL	FBG	KL	IB	30		9	4	9500	4	7	16800	19100
30	3	WANDERER	SLP	SAIL	FBG	CB	IB	30		9	4	9800	3	6	17500	19800
35		PEARSON 35	SLP	SAIL	FBG	CB	IB	30		10		13000	3	9	23700	26400

CONTINUED ON NEXT PAGE

LOA FT	LOA IN	NAME AND/ OR MODEL	TOP/ RIG	BOAT TYPE	-HULL- MTL	-HULL- TP	ENGINE TP	ENGINE # HP	ENGINE MFG	BEAM FT	BEAM IN	WGT LBS	DRAFT FT	DRAFT IN	RETAIL LOW	RETAIL HIGH
		1968 BOATS														
35		PEARSON 35	YWL	SAIL	FBG	CB	IB	30		10		13000	3	9	23700	26400
37	8	INVICTA	SLP	SAIL	FBG	CB	IB	30		10	8	17750	4	6	33300	37000
37	8	INVICTA	YWL	SAIL	FBG	CB	IB	30		10	8	18100	4	6	33800	37600
42	9	PEARSON 43	SLP	SAIL	FBG	KL	IB	72		11	9	21796	6	3	47800	52500
42	9	PEARSON 43	YWL	SAIL	FBG	KL	IB	72		11	9	21796	6	3	47800	52500
44	6	COUNTESS 44	KTH	SAIL	FBG	KL	IB	110D		12		28000	5	4	60200	66200
		1967 BOATS														
22	6	ENSIGN	SLP	SA/OD	FBG	KL	OB			7		3000	3		4000	4700
24		LARK	SLP	SAIL	FBG	KL	OB			8		4300	4		5850	6700
25	7	ARIEL	SLP	SAIL	FBG	KL	OB			8		5500	3	8	8150	9400
25	7	ARIEL	SLP	SAIL	FBG	KL	IB	30		8		5800	3	8	9000	10200
25	7	COMMANDER	SLP	SAIL	FBG	KL	OB			8		5100	3	8	7550	8650
25	7	COMMANDER	SLP	SAIL	FBG	KL	IB	30		8		5400	3	8	8300	9550
27	2	RENEGADE	SLP	SAIL	FBG	KL	OB			8	7	6500	4	3	10400	11800
27	2	RENEGADE	SLP	SAIL	FBG	KL	IB	30		8	7	6800	4	3	11100	12600
27	10	RENDOVA		EXP	FBG		IB	210		10	5		2	6	9100	10300
28	6	TRITON	SLP	SAIL	FBG	KL	IB	30		8	3	8400	4		14300	16200
28	6	TRITON	YWL	SAIL	FBG	KL	IB	30		8	3	8600	4		14700	16700
29	10	COASTER	SLP	SAIL	FBG		IB	30		9	4	9500	4	7	16500	18800
30	3	WANDERER	SLP	SAIL	FBG	KC	IB	30		9	4	9800	3	6	17100	19500
32	6	VANGUARD	SLP	SAIL	FBG	KL	IB	30		9	3	10300	4	6	18500	20600
32	6	VANGUARD	YWL	SAIL	FBG	KL	IB	30		9	3	10500	4	6	18900	21000
34	1	SUNDERLAND		SDN	FBG		IB	T290		12	9		2	10	20500	22800
34	9	ALBERG 35	SLP	SAIL	FBG	KL	IB	30		9	8	12600	5	2	22600	25100
34	9	ALBERG 35	YWL	SAIL	FBG	KL	IB	30		9	8	12850	5	2	23000	25500
36	9	ARENDAL		SDN	FBG	SV	IB	T290		12			2	6	38700	43000
37	8	INVICTA	SLP	SAIL	FBG	KC	IB	30		10	8	17750	4	6	32700	36300
37	8	INVICTA	YWL	SAIL	FBG	KC	IB	30		10	8	18100	4	6	33200	36900
44	6	COUNTESS 44	KTH	SAIL	FBG	KL	IB	110D		12		28000	5	4	59100	65000
		1966 BOATS														
19	7	RESOLUTE	SLP	SAIL	FBG	KL	OB			6	7	1880	3	5	2750	3200
22	6	ELECTRA	SLP	SAIL	FBG	KL	OB			7		3000	3		3950	4600
22	6	ENSIGN	SLP	SA/OD	FBG	KL	OB			7		3000	3		3950	4600
24		LARK	SLP	SA/CR	FBG	KL				8			4		4750	5450
25	7	ARIEL	SLP	SAIL	FBG	KL	OB			8		5100	3	8	8350	9600
25	7	ARIEL	SLP	SAIL	FBG	KL	IB	30		8		5100	3	8	8500	9750
25	7	COMMANDER	SLP	SAIL	FBG	KL	OB			8		5100	3	8	6500	7450
25	7	COMMANDER	SLP	SAIL	FBG	KL	IB	30		8		5100	3	8	6900	7950
28	6	TRITON	SLP	SAIL	FBG	KL	IB	30		8	3	6930	4		11500	13100
28	6	TRITON	YWL	SAIL	FBG	KL	IB	30		8	3	6930	4		11500	13100
29	10	COASTER	SLP	SA/CR	FBG	KL	IB			9	4		4	7	11900	13500
29	10	GYPSY	SLP	SA/CR	FBG	KL	IB			9	4		4	7	8500	9800
30	3	WANDERER	SLP	SA/CR	FBG	KC	IB			9	4		3	6	10300	11700
32	6	VANGUARD	SLP	SAIL	FBG	KL	IB	30		9	3	10300	4	6	18200	20200
32	6	VANGUARD	YWL	SAIL	FBG	KL	IB	30		9	3	10300	4	6	18200	20200
34	9	ALBERG 35	SLP	SAIL	FBG	KL	IB	30		9	8	12600	5	2	22200	24600
34	9	ALBERG 35	YWL	SAIL	FBG	KL	IB	30		9	8	12600	5	2	22200	24600
37	8	INVICTA	SLP	SAIL	FBG	CB	IB	30		10	8	17750	4	6	32100	35700
37	8	INVICTA	YWL	SAIL	FBG	CB	IB	30		10	8	18100	4	6	32600	36300
41		RHODES 41	SLP	SAIL	FBG	KL	IB	30		10	3	18800	5	8	38700	42900
41		RHODES 41	YWL	SAIL	FBG	KL	IB	30		10	3	18800	5	8	38700	42900
44	6	COUNTESS 44	KTH	SAIL	FBG	KL	IB	95		12		25000	5	4	54000	59300
44	6	COUNTESS 44	KTH	SAIL	FBG	KL	IB	60D		12		25000	5	4	54600	60000
44	6	COUNTESS 44	KTH	SAIL	FBG	KL	IB	110D		12		25000	5	4	55100	60500
		1965 BOATS														
18		PACKET	OP	LNCH	FBG		IB	30		6	5		1	6	2550	2950
18		PACKET LAUNCH	SLP	SAIL	FBG	CB	IB			6	5		1	6	2750	3200
19	7	RESOLUTE	SLP	SAIL	FBG	KL	OB					1880			2700	3150
22	6	ELECTRA	SLP	SAIL	FBG	KL	OB					3000			3900	4550
22	6	ENSIGN	SLP	SA/OD	FBG	KL	OB					3000			3900	4550
25	7	ARIEL	SLP	SAIL	FBG	KL	IB	30				5100			8550	9800
25	7	COMMANDER	SLP	SAIL	FBG	KL	IB	30				5100			6600	7850
26	8	PEARSON 27	HT	SF	FBG		IB	210							6750	7800
26	8	PEARSON 27	HT	SF	FBG		IB	T145							7300	8350
26	8	PEARSON 27	FB	SF	FBG		IB	210							6800	7800
26	8	PEARSON 27	FB	SF	FBG		IB	T145							7300	8400
27	10	PEARSON 28	OP	EXP	FBG		IB	210				6500			7950	9150
27	10	PEARSON 28	OP	EXP	FBG		IB	T190				6500			9000	10200
27	10	PEARSON 28	HT	EXP	FBG		IB	210				6500			8000	9200
27	10	PEARSON 28	HT	EXP	FBG		IB	T190				6500			9000	10200
28	6	TRITON	SLP	SAIL	FBG	KL	IB	30				6930			11300	12900
28	6	TRITON	YWL	SAIL	FBG	KL	IB	30				6930			11300	12900
32	6	VANGUARD	SLP	SAIL	FBG	KL	IB	30				10300			17500	19900
32	6	VANGUARD	YWL	SAIL	FBG	KL	IB	30				10300			17500	19900
34	9	ALBERG 35	SLP	SAIL	FBG	KL	IB	30				12600			21900	24300
34	9	ALBERG 35	YWL	SAIL	FBG	KL	IB	30				12600			21900	24300
36	9	PEARSON 36	HT	SDNSF	FBG	SV	IB	T290				17000			27000	30000
36	9	PEARSON 36	FB	SDNSF	FBG	SV	IB	T290				17000			27000	30000
37	8	INVICTA	SLP	SAIL	FBG	CB	IB	30				17750			31700	35200
37	8	INVICTA	YWL	SAIL	FBG	CB	IB	30				18100			32200	35700
41	10	RHODES 41	SLP	SAIL	FBG	KL	IB	30				18800			39500	43900
41	10	RHODES 41	SLP	SAIL	FBG	KL	IB	30D				18800			40100	44500
41	10	RHODES 41	YWL	SAIL	FBG	KL	IB	30				18800			39500	43900
41	10	RHODES 41	YWL	SAIL	FBG	KL	IB	30D				18800			40100	44500
44	6	COUNTESS 44	KTH	SAIL	FBG	KL	IB	109		12		25000			53200	58500
44	6	COUNTESS 44	KTH	SAIL	FBG	KL	IB	60D		12		25000			53800	59100
44	6	COUNTESS 44	KTH	SAIL	FBG	KL	IB	95D		12		25000			54100	59500
		1964 BOATS														
17		TIGER-CAT		SAIL	FBG		OB								1700	2000
18		PACKET		LNCH	FBG		IB	30							2850	3300
18		PACKET		OVNTR	FBG		OB								2800	3300
18		PACKET SAIL LAUNCH		SAIL	FBG		IB	30							2750	3200
22	6	ELECTRA	SLP	SAIL	FBG	KL	OB					3000			3850	4450
22	6	ENSIGN	SLP	SA/OD	FBG	KL	OB					3000			3850	4450
25	7	ARIEL	SLP	SAIL	FBG	KL	OB					5100			7200	8300
25	7	ARIEL	SLP	SAIL	FBG	KL	IB	30				5100			7500	8600
26	8	PEARSON 27	HT	SF	FBG		IB	210							6550	7550
26	8	PEARSON 27	HT	SF	FBG		IB	T190							7400	8500
27	10	PEARSON 28	OP	EXP	FBG		IB	210				6500			7700	8850
27	10	PEARSON 28	OP	EXP	FBG		IB	T145				6500			8250	9450
28	6	TRITON	SLP	SAIL	FBG	KL	IB	30				6930			11200	12700
28	6	TRITON	YWL	SAIL	FBG	KL	IB	30				6930			11200	12700
32	6	VANGUARD	SLP	SAIL	FBG	KL	IB	30				10300			17300	19700
34	9	ALBERG 35	SLP	SAIL	FBG	KL	IB	30				12600			21600	24000
34	9	ALBERG 35	YWL	SAIL	FBG	KL	IB	30				12600			21600	24000
36	9	PEARSON 37	HT	SDNSF	FBG		IB	T290				17000			26300	29200
37	8	INVICTA	SLP	SAIL	FBG	CB	IB	30				17750			31300	34700
37	8	INVICTA	YWL	SAIL	FBG	CB	IB	30				18100			31800	35300
40	10	RHODES 41	SLP	SAIL	FBG	KL	IB	30				18800			37300	41500
40	10	RHODES 41	SLP	SAIL	FBG	KL	IB	30D				18800			37900	42100
40	10	RHODES 41	YWL	SAIL	FBG	KL	IB	30				18800			37300	41500
40	10	RHODES 41	YWL	SAIL	FBG	KL	IB	30D				18800			37900	42100
		1963 BOATS														
18		PACKET		LNCH	FBG		IB	30							2750	3200
20	6	PEARSON 21		SF	FBG		IO	120							8000	9200
22	6	ELECTRA	SLP	SA/CR	FBG		OB								4350	5000
22	6	ELECTRA-ENSIGN	SLP	SAIL	FBG	KL	OB					3000			3800	4400
25	7	ARIEL	SLP	SAIL	FBG	KL	OB					5100			7150	8200
26	8	PEARSON 27	HT	SF	FBG		IB	185-215							6200	7300
26	8	PEARSON 27	HT	SF	FBG		IO	T120							20400	22600
27	10	PEARSON 28	OP	EXP	FBG		IB	215-230				6500			7450	8650
27	10	PEARSON 28	OP	EXP	FBG		IB	T185				6500			8300	9550
28	6	TRITON	SLP	SAIL	FBG	KL	IB	30				6930			11100	12600
32	6	VANGUARD	SLP	SAIL	FBG	KL	IB	30				10300			17100	19500
34	9	ALBERG 35	SLP	SAIL	FBG	KL	IB	30				12600			21300	23700
36	9	PEARSON 37	HT	SDNSF	FBG		IB	T215				17000			25300	28100
		IB T240 25400 28200, IB T260 25500 28300, IB T120D													27800	30900
37	8	INVICTA	SLP	SAIL	FBG	CB	IB	30				17750			30900	34400
40	10	RHODES 41	SLP	SAIL	FBG	KL	IB	30				18800			36900	41000
		1962 BOATS														
20	6			SF	FBG		IB	120							2450	2850
22	6	ELECTRA 201	SLP	SAIL	FBG		OB								4250	4950
22	6	ELECTRA 227	SLP	SAIL	FBG		OB								4250	4950
24		AERO 24		SAIL	FBG		OB								4550	5250
25	7	ARIEL MORC 307		SA/CR	FBG		OB								5250	6050
25	7	ARIEL MORC 307		SA/RC	FBG		OB								5250	6050
26	8		HT	SF	FBG		IB	185-230							6050	7150
26	8		HT	SF	FBG		IO	T120							21000	23400
28	6	TRITON 372	SLP	SAIL	FBG	KL	OB					6930			10800	12300
28	6	TRITON 382	YWL	SAIL	FBG	KL	OB					6930			10800	12300
34	9	ALBERG 35 536	SLP	SAIL	FBG	KL	OB					12600			21000	23400
34	9	ALBERG 35 582	YWL	SAIL	FBG	KL	OB					12600			21000	23400
36	9		HT	SDNSF	FBG		IB	T215				17000			24700	27400
		IB T225 24700 27500, IB T230 24800 27500, IB T260													24900	27700
		IB T280 25000 27800, IB T120D 27200 30200														
37	8	INVICTA 614	YWL	SAIL	FBG	CB	OB					18100			30900	34300
40	10	BOUNTY 11-661		SAIL	FBG		OB								30000	33400

CONTINUED ON NEXT PAGE

LOA FT IN	NAME AND/ OR MODEL	TOP/ RIG	BOAT TYPE	HULL MTL TP	ENGINE TP # HP MFG	BEAM FT IN	WGT LBS	DRAFT FT IN	RETAIL LOW	RETAIL HIGH
1962 BOATS										
40 10	BOUNTY 746	YWL	SAIL	FBG	OB				30000	33400
1961 BOATS										
20 6	PEARSON 21		SF	FBG	IB 80	8		1 8	2350	2700
22 6	ELECTRA 227	SLP	SAIL	FBG KL	OB	7		3	4250	4950
26 8	PEARSON 27	HT	SF	FBG	IB 135	9 1		2 3	5700	6550
28 6	TRITON 372	SLP	SAIL	FBG KL	OB		6930		10700	12200
28 6	TRITON 372	YWL	SAIL	FBG KL	OB		6930		10700	12200
30	PEARSON 30		EXP	FBG	IB 185	10		2	9150	10400
34 9	ALBERG 540	SLP	SAIL	FBG KL	OB	9 8	12600	5 2	20900	23200
34 9	ALBERG 540	YWL	SAIL	FBG KL	OB	9 8		5 2	21400	23800
35	INVICTA	SLP	SA/CR	FBG KC	OB	10 9		4 6	21500	23800
35	INVICTA	YWL	SA/CR	FBG KC	OB	10 9		4 6	21500	23800
36 9	PEARSON 37	HT	SDNSF	FBG	IB T225	12	17000	2	25900	28700
37 8	INVICTA 614	SLP	SAIL	FBG CB	OB		17750		30200	33500
1960 BOATS										
20 3	CHALLENGER MK1		SF	FBG	OB	8	1200		3950	4600
20 3	CHALLENGER MK5		CR	FBG	OB	8	1200		3950	4600
21	CHALLENGER MK2		SF	FBG	IB 109	8			2400	2800
21	CHALLENGER MK3		SF	FBG	IB 109	8		1 9	2400	2800
21	CHALLENGER MK6		CR	FBG	IB 109				2650	3050
22	ELECTRA A-205	SLP	SAIL	FBG	OB				4150	4800
28 6	TRITON A-372	SLP	SAIL	FBG KL	OB		6930		10700	12100
28 6	TRITON A-372	YWL	SAIL	FBG KL	OB		6930		10700	12100
30	PEARSON 30		EXP	FBG	IB 185				9100	10300
37 6	VICTORY A-660	SLP	SAIL	FBG	OB				13000	14700
37 6	VICTORY A-740	YWL	SAIL	FBG	OB				13000	14700
1959 BOATS										
20 3	CHALLENGER		CR	FBG	OB	8	1200		2200	2550
20 3	CHALLENGER DLX		CR	FBG	OB	8	1200		5850	6700
20 6	CHALLENGER		BASS	FBG	IB 125	8			1900	2300
20 6	CHALLENGER		CBNCR	FBG	IB 180	8			2600	3050
28 3	TRITON A-231	SLP	SAIL	FBG KL	OB	8 3	6930	4	10600	12000
28 3	TRITON A-392	YWL	SAIL	FBG KL	OB	8 3	6930	4	10600	12000

CRAIG PEASE ENTERPRISES
SHERWOOD BOATS

Call 1-800-327-6929 for BUC Personalized Evaluation Service
Or, for 1965 boats, sign onto www.BUCValuPro.com

PELAGIC CONST & DESIGN LTD

Call 1-800-327-6929 for BUC Personalized Evaluation Service
Or, for 1965 boats, sign onto www.BUCValuPro.com

PEMBROKE P HUCKINS
TEXAS DORY

Call 1-800-327-6929 for BUC Personalized Evaluation Service
Or, for 1966 boats, sign onto www.BUCValuPro.com

PEMBROKE YACHT CORP
SUNCOOK NH 03275   COAST GUARD MFG ID- PEM See inside cover to adjust price for area

LOA FT IN	NAME AND/ OR MODEL	TOP/ RIG	BOAT TYPE	HULL MTL TP	ENGINE TP # HP MFG	BEAM FT IN	WGT LBS	DRAFT FT IN	RETAIL LOW	RETAIL HIGH
1969 BOATS										
33 3			SDN	FBG RB	IB T195 PALM	11 11	11500	2 7	13900	15800
33 3		FB	SDN	FBG	IB T195-T210	11 11	11500	2 7	13900	16000
34 2			CNV	FBG	IB T195-T210	12	12500	2 7	15300	17600
34 2			SDN	FBG SV	IB T195-T210	12	12500	2 7	15200	17500
34 2		FB	SDN	FBG SV	IB T195-T210	12	12500	2 7	15300	17500
38 2		FB	SDN	MHG	IB T265 PALM	13 3	15500	3	19700	21900
1968 BOATS										
33 3	PEMBROKE 33		EXP	MHG	IB T195-T210	11 11	11500	2 7	12700	14500
33 3	PEMBROKE 33	FB	EXP	MHG	IB T195-T210	11 11	11500	2 7	12700	14500
33 3	PEMBROKE 33		SDN	MHG	IB T195-T210	11 11	11500	2 7	13400	15400
33 3	PEMBROKE 33	FB	SDN	MHG	IB T195-T210	11 11	11500	2 7	13400	15400
37 3			SDN	MHG	IB T265	13	15500	3	19000	21100
1967 BOATS										
28 3			EXP	WD	IB 250	10 6	8025	2 10	6300	7200
28 3			EXP	WD	IB T190	10 6	8025	2 10	6800	7800
28 3		FB	EXP	WD	IB 250	10 6	9050	2 10	6700	7700
28 3		FB	EXP	WD	IB T190	10 6	9050	2 10	7200	8300
28 3			SPTCR	WD	IB 250	10 6	8025	2 10	6850	7850
28 3		FB	SPTCR	WD	IB 250	10 6	9050	2 10	6750	7750
28 3		FB	SPTCR	WD	IB T190	10 6	9050	2 10	7300	8350
31 9			EXP	WD	IB 250	11	8850	2 10	9400	10700
31 9			EXP	WD	IB T190	11	8850	2 10	9950	11300
31 9		FB	EXP	WD	IB 250	11	9825	2 10	9650	10900
31 9		FB	EXP	WD	IB T190	11	9825	2 10	10200	11600
31 9			SDN	WD	IB 250	11	8850	2 10	9100	10400
31 9			SDN	WD	IB T190	11	8850	2 10	9800	11100
31 9		FB	SDN	WD	IB 250	11	9825	2 10	9250	10500
31 9		FB	SDN	WD	IB T190	11	9825	2 10	9900	11300
31 9		FB	SPTCR	WD	IB T190	11 7	9825	2 10	9150	10400
37 2		FB	SDN	WD	IB T250	13	15500	3	18300	20400
1966 BOATS										
23	SPORTSMAN			WD	IB 185	8		2 1	2350	2750
27 6			EXP	WD	IB 215	9 7		2 7	5700	6550
27 6	DELUXE	FB	EXP	WD	IB 215	9 7		2 7	5800	6650
27 6	STANDARD	FB	EXP	WD	IB 215	9 7		2 7	5650	6500
27 9			SF	WD	IB 215	9 9		2 7	5750	6650
27 9		FB	SF	WD	IB 215	9 9		2 7	6050	6950
27 9	W/DLX FB	FB	SF	WD	IB 215	9 9		2 7	6200	7100
31 9			EXP	WD	IB 250	11		3 2	9150	10400
31 9			EXP	WD	IB T185	11		3 2	9650	11000
31 9			SDN	WD	IB 250	11		3 2	9450	10800
31 9		FB	SDN	WD	IB T185	11		3 2	9450	10800
31 9	DELUXE	FB	EXP	WD	IB 250	11		3 2	9200	10400
31 9	DELUXE	FB	EXP	WD	IB T185	11		3 2	9700	11000
31 11		FB	SF	WD	IB T185	11 6		2 10	8350	9550
37 2		FB	SDNSF	WD	IB T225	13		3	16900	19200
1965 BOATS										
27 5			SF	WD	IB 215				5550	6350
27 5		FB	SF	WD	IB 215				5550	6350
27 9			SF	WD	IB 215				5600	6400
27 9		FB	SF	WD	IB 215				5950	6800
30 8			EXP	WD	IB 250				7850	9050
30 8			EXP	WD	IB T185				8350	9600
30 8		FB	EXP	WD	IB 250				7850	9050
30 8		FB	EXP	WD	IB T185				8350	9600
31 8			SDN	WD	IB T225				7900	9100
34 8			EXP	WD	IB T210				13100	14900
34 8			SDN	WD	IB T210				12400	14100
1964 BOATS										
23	SPORTSMAN	FB		WD	IB 150-210				2200	2600
27 9			EXP	WD	IB 210				5400	6200
30 11			EXP	WD	IB 210				7650	8750
30 11			EXP	WD	IB T150				8000	9200
34 8			EXP	WD	IB T210				12700	14400
34 8			SDN	WD	IB T210				12000	13600
1963 BOATS										
23	SPORTSMAN			WD	IB 145-210				2050	2500
27 6			SF	WD	IB 210				5150	5900
27 6			SF	WD	IB T145				5400	6250
30 2			EXP	WD	IB 210				6550	7500
30 2			EXP	WD	IB T145-T210				6850	8400
34 8			EXP	WD	IB T210				12200	13900
34 8			EXP	WD	IB T210				21300	23700
34 8			SDN	WD	IB T110D				11600	13200
34 8			SDN	WD	IB T110D				21500	23900
1962 BOATS										
22 10	SF-23		SF	WD	IB 100-190				2350	2850
27 1	FC 28		CR	WD	IB 190				4950	5700
32 11	FC 33		CR	WD	IB 210				9050	10300
1961 BOATS										
24	SEA-SKIFF		CR	MHG	IB 135	8 2		2	2450	2850
28	SEA-SKIFF		CR	MHG	IB 188	9 2		2 6	5050	5800
1960 BOATS										
23			EXP	MHG	IB 135				2350	2750
23	EXPRESS 23		EXP	MHG	IB 188	8		2	2350	2750
27			EXP	MHG	IB 188				4700	5400
27	EMPRESS 27		CR	WD	IB 215				4800	5500
27	EXPRESS 27		EXP	MHG	IB T109	9		2 6	6800	7800
31			EXP	WD	IB 188				7050	8100
31	EXPRESS 31		EXP	MHG	IB T135	10 6		3	7050	8100
1959 BOATS										
17	SEA-SKIFF		RNBT	L/P	OB	6 2			3200	3700
18	SEA-SKIFF		RNBT	L/P	OB	6 2			3750	4400

```
  LOA  NAME AND/            TOP/ BOAT  -HULL- ----ENGINE--- BEAM  WGT  DRAFT RETAIL RETAIL
  FT IN OR MODEL            RIG  TYPE  MTL TP TP # HP  MFG  FT IN LBS  FT IN  LOW   HIGH
------------------- 1959 BOATS -----------------------------------------------------------
  19    SEA-SKIFF SEMI-ENCL           L/P   OB                            3900  4550
  25                             EXP  L/P   IB 185      9                 2900  3400
------------------- 1958 BOATS -----------------------------------------------------------
  25                             EXP  WD    IB 110                        2700  3100
------------------- 1957 BOATS -----------------------------------------------------------
  22    SEA-SKIFF            RNBT WD   IB  95                             1700  2000
```

PENINSULA MARINE PLASTICS

Call 1-800-327-6929 for BUC Personalized Evaluation Service
Or, for 1961 boats, sign onto www.BUCValuPro.com

PENINSULAR MARINE ENTERPRISES
COAST GUARD MFG ID- PMB

Call 1-800-327-6929 for BUC Personalized Evaluation Service
Or, for 1981 boats, sign onto www.BUCValuPro.com

PENN YAN BOAT CO
OAK HALL VA 23416-0127 COAST GUARD MFG ID- PYB See inside cover to adjust price for area

For more recent years, see the BUC Used Boat Price Guide, Volume 1 or Volume 2

```
  LOA  NAME AND/            TOP/ BOAT  -HULL-  ----ENGINE--- BEAM  WGT  DRAFT RETAIL RETAIL
  FT IN OR MODEL            RIG  TYPE  MTL TP TP # HP  MFG  FT IN LBS  FT IN  LOW   HIGH
------------------- 1983 BOATS -----------------------------------------------------------
  18    GAMEFISHER         OP  RNBT FBG DV IO 185  MRCR 7  4 2094  2  2  3200  3750
  21  3 TOURNAMENT         OP  RNBT FBG DV IO 188  MRCR 8    3200  2  6  4150  4800
  22  8 AVENGER 23         OP  FSH  FBG DV TD 220-270    9  5 3800  1  2  7100  8250
  22  8 PENN-YAN 23        FB  SF   FBG DV TD 260-270    9  5 4600  1  2  8050  9450
  25    ANGLER 25          OP  CUD  FBG DV IO 188-260    9    5200  2  8  7650  9150
  25    ANGLER 25          ST  CUD  FBG DV TD 220-350   10    6500  1  5 11700 14000
  26    PENN-YAN 26        FB  SF   FBG DV TD 260-350   10    6500  1  5 12100 14500
      TD 150D-225D  15700 18900, TD 270D CUM   17300 19600, TD T165-T228  12900 15200

  26    TOURNAMENT 26      OP  SF   FBG DV TD 260-270   10    6200  1  5 11700 13400
      TD 150D-225D  15100 18200, TD 270D-350D  16700 20800, TD T165-T228  12500 14800

  29 11 PENN-YAN 30        FB  SF   FBG DV TD 350   CRUS 11 10 12000 1 10 21100 23400
  29 11 PENN-YAN 30        FB  SF   FBG DV TD T260-T270 11 10 12000 1 10 22200 24900
  29 11 PENN-YAN 30        FB  SF   FBG DV TDT150D-T270D 11 10 12000 1 10 28900 35600
  32  8 PENN-YAN 33        FB  SF   FBG DV TD T260-T350  12    13700 1 10 28200 32900
  32  8 PENN-YAN 33        FB  SF   FBG DV TDT150D-T270D 12    13700 1 10 34100 41500
------------------- 1982 BOATS -----------------------------------------------------------
  20  5 EXPLORER 21        OP  OPFSH FBG DV TD 165-270    8    2650 1  2  4450  5300
  21  3 PENN-YAN 22M       OP  RNBT FBG DV TD 260         8    3250       5350  6150
  21  3 PENN-YAN 22R       OP  CUD  FBG DV IB  260        8    3600       5650  6500
  22  8 AVENGER 23         OP  FSH  FBG DV TD 220-270     9  5 4200 1  2  7300  8450
  22  8 AVENGER 23         HT  FSH  FBG DV TD 220-270     9  5 4200 1  2  7300  8450
  22  8 AVENGER 23         FB  FSH  FBG DV TD 220-270     9  5 4600 1  2  7800  9000
  22  8 PENN-YAN 23        OP  OVNTR FBG DV TD 220-270    9  5 4200 1  2  7300  8450
  22  8 PENN-YAN 23        ST  SF   FBG DV TD 220-270     9  5 4600 1  2  7800  9050
  23 10 PENN-YAN 24        OP  OFF  FBG DV TD 220-270     8    3600 1  2  6550  7600
  23 10 PENN-YAN 24        FB  SF   FBG DV TD 220-270     8    4300 1  2  7450  8650
  25    ANGLER 25          ST  CUD  FBG DV TD 220-270     9  4 4500 1  5  8400  9900
  25    ANGLER 25          ST  CUD  FBG DV TD 225D CRUS   9  4 4500 1  5 12000 13700

  26    PENN-YAN 26        FB  CR   FBG DV TD 220-270    10    7600 1  5 12800 14800
  26    PENN-YAN 26        OP  EXP  FBG DV TD 220-270    10    7600 1  5 12800 14800
  26    PENN-YAN 26        HT  EXP  FBG DV TD 220-270    10    7600 1  5 12800 14800
  26    PENN-YAN 26        FB  SF   FBG DV TD 220-270    10    6500 1  5 11400 13300
      TD  D CAT  **  **  , TD 195D-225D  15400 18100, TD T165-T270  13500 16300

  26    TOURNAMENT 26      OP  SF   FBG DV TD 220-270    10    5200 1  5  9850 11500
      TD  D CAT  **  **  , TD 195D-225D  14800 17500, TD T165-T270  10900 13400

  28  2 PENN-YAN 28E       FB  SDN  FBG DV IB T260       11    9000      18100 20100
  29 11 PENN-YAN 30        FB  SDN  FBG DV TD T220-T270  11 10 12000 1 10 22400 25900
  29 11 PENN-YAN 30        FB  SDN  FBG DV TD T  D CAT   11 10 12000 1 10  **    **
  29 11 PENN-YAN 30        FB  SDN  FBG DV TDT195D-T225D 11 10 12000 1 10 31900 36800
  29 11 PENN-YAN 30        FB  SF   FBG DV TD T220-T270  11 10 12000 1 10 20800 23800
  29 11 PENN-YAN 30        FB  SF   FBG DV TDT195D-T225D 11 10 12000 1 10  **    **
  32  8 PENN-YAN 33        FB  SDN  FBG DV TD T220-T270  12    13500 1 10 28700 32900
  32  8 PENN-YAN 33        FB  SDN  FBG DV TD T  D CAT   12    13500 1 10 28200 32400
  32  8 PENN-YAN 33        FB  SDN  FBG DV TDT195D-T225D 12    13500 1 10  **    **
  32  8 PENN-YAN 33        FB  SF   FBG DV TD T220-T270  12    13500 1 10 37000 42400
  32  8 PENN-YAN 33        FB  SF   FBG DV TD T  D CAT   12    13500 1 10 26400 30100
  32  8 PENN-YAN 33        FB  SF   FBG DV TD T  D CAT   12    13500 1 10  **    **

  32  8 PENN-YAN 33        FB  SF   FBG DV TDT195D-T225D 12    13500 1 10 33500 38100
------------------- 1981 BOATS -----------------------------------------------------------
  20  5 PENN-YAN ERM       OP  CUD  FBG DV TD 225-255     8    2650 1  2  4150  5150
  20  5 PENN-YAN EWG       OP  RNBT FBG DV TD 225-255     8    2790 1  2  4450  5400
  21  3 PENN-YAN 22M       OP  RNBT FBG DV TD 225-255     8    3250 1  2  5050  6100
  21  3 PENN-YAN 22R       OP  CUD  FBG DV TD 225-255     8    3600 1  2  5300  6400
  22  8 PENN-YAN 23M       FB  FSH  FBG DV TD 225-255     9  5 3800 1  2  6350  7600
  22  8 PENN-YAN 23M       HT  FSH  FBG DV TD 225-255     9  5 3800 1  2  6350  7600
  22  8 PENN-YAN 23M       FB  FSH  FBG DV TD 225-255     9  5 3800 1  2  6350  7600
  22  8 PENN-YAN 23R       OP  CUD  FBG DV TD 225-255     9  5 4200 1  2  6850  8150
  22  8 PENN-YAN 23S       HT  CR   FBG DV TD 225-255          1  2  6350  7600
  22  8 PENN-YAN 23SF      FB  SF   FBG DV TD 225-255     9  5 4600 1  2  7150  8600
  22  8 PENN-YAN 23SFT     FB  SF   FBG DV TD 225-255     9  5 4600 1  2  7400  8850
  23 10 PENN-YAN 24M       OP  RNBT FBG DV TD 225-255     8    3600 1  2  6100  7350

  23 10 PENN-YAN 24R       OP  CUD  FDG DV TD 225-255     8    4100 1  2  6750  8050
  23 10 PENN-YAN 24SFT     FB  SF   FBG DV TD 225-255     8    4300 1  2  7000  8350
  23 10 PENN-YAN 24XE      OP  SPTCR FBG DV TD 225-255    8    4100 1  2  6750  8050
  26    PENN-YAN 26CR      OP  CR   FBG DV TD 225-255         11200     13000
  26    PENN-YAN 26CR      HT  CR   FBG DV TD 225-255         11200     13000
  26    PENN-YAN 26M       OP  SF   FBG DV TD 225-255    10    5200 1  5  9400 11000
  26    PENN-YAN 26R       OP  CR   FBG DV TD 225-255    10    7600     12100 14100
  26    PENN-YAN 26R       HT  CR   FBG DV TD 225-255    10    7600     12100 14100
  26    PENN-YAN 26RF      FB  EXP  FBG DV TD 225-255    10    7600 1  5 12100 14100
  26    PENN-YAN 26SF      FB  SF   FBG DV TD 225-255    10    6500 1  5 10900 12700
  26    PENN-YAN 26SF      FB  SF   FBG DV TD 225-255    10    6500 1  5 12100 14300
  28  2 PENN-YAN 28E       FB  SDN  FBG DV TD T225-T255  11    9000 1 10 16500 19300

  29 11 PENN-YAN 30E       FB  SDN  FBG DV TD T225-T255  11 10 12000 1 10 21500 24500
  29 11 PENN-YAN 30SF      FB  SF   FBG DV TD T225-T255  11 10 12000 1 10 19900 22600
  32  8 PENN-YAN 33E       FB  SDN  FBG DV TD T225-T255  12    13500 1 10 27000 30700
  32  8 PENN-YAN 33SF      FB  SF   FBG DV TD T225-T255  12    13700 1 10 25400 28700
------------------- 1980 BOATS -----------------------------------------------------------
  20  5 PENN-YAN ERM       OP  CUD  FBG DV TD 225-255     8    2650       4000  4700
  20  5 PENN-YAN EWG       OP  RNBT FBG DV TD 225-255     8    2970       4450  5150
  21  3 PENN-YAN 22M       OP  RNBT FBG DV TD 225-255     8    3250       4850  5600
  21  3 PENN-YAN 22R       OP  CUD  FBG DV TD 225-255     8               5250  5600
  22  8 PENN-YAN 23HF      FB  FSH  FBG DV TD  255  MRCR  9  5 4350 1  2  6800  7900
  22  8 PENN-YAN 23M       OP  FSH  FBG DV TD 225-255     9  5 3800       6150  7100
  22  8 PENN-YAN 23R       OP  CUD  FBG DV TD 225-255     9  5 4200       6600  7600
  22  8 PENN-YAN 23S       HT  CR   FBG DV TD  255  MRCR  9  5 4300 1  2  6750  7800
  22  8 PENN-YAN 23SF      FB  SF   FBG DV TD 225-255     9  5 4300       6700  8000
  22  8 PENN-YAN 23SFT     FB  SF   FBG DV TD 225-255     9  5 4300       6700  8250
  23 10 PENN-YAN 24M       OP  RNBT FBG DV TD 225-255     8    3600       5900  6800
  23 10 PENN-YAN 24R       OP  CUD  FBG DV TD 225-255     8    4100       6500  7500

  23 10 PENN-YAN 24SFT     OP  SF   FBG DV TD 225-255     8    4000       6350  7350
  23 10 PENN-YAN 24XE      OP  SPTCR FBG DV TD 225-255    8    4200       6450  7400
  26    PENN-YAN 26CR      HT  CR   FBG DV TD 225        10  5 7700      11800 13500
  26    PENN-YAN 26R       OP  CR   FBG DV TD 225-255    10    7600      11800 13400
  26    PENN-YAN 26RF      HT  EXP  FBG DV TD 225-255    10    7600      11700 13400
  26    PENN-YAN 26SF      FB  SF   FBG DV TD  255  MRCR 10    6500 1  5 10600 12200
  26    PENN-YAN 26SF      FB  SF   FBG DV TD 225-255    10    6500      11700 13300
  28  2 PENN-YAN 28E       FB  SDN  FBG DV TD T225-T228  11    9000      15800 18400
  29 11 PENN-YAN 30E       FB  SDN  FBG DV TD T225-T255  11    12000     20600 23400
  29 11 PENN-YAN 30SF      FB  SF   FBG DV TD T225-T255  11 10 12000     19100 21600
------------------- 1979 BOATS -----------------------------------------------------------
  20  5 PENN-YAN ERM       OP  CUD  FBG DV TD 225-255     8    2650 1  2  3800  4700
  20  5 PENN-YAN EWG       OP  RNBT FBG DV TD 225-255     8    2970 1  2  4150  5100
  21  3 PENN-YAN 22M       OP  RNBT FBG DV TD 225-255     8    3250 1  2  4650  5600
  21  3 PENN-YAN 22R       OP  CUD  FBG DV TD 225-255     8    3600 1  2  4950  5950
  22  8 PENN-YAN 23HF      FB  FSH  FBG DV TD 225-330     9  5 4350 1  2  6450  7950
  22  8 PENN-YAN 23HF      HT  FSH  FBG DV TD  200D CHRY  9  5 4350 1  2  9500 10800
  22  8 PENN-YAN 23M       HT  FSH  FBG DV TD 225-330     9  5 3800 1  2  5850  7250
  22  8 PENN-YAN 23M       HT  FSH  FBG DV TD  200D CHRY  9  5 3800 1  2  8900 10100
  22  8 PENN-YAN 23R       OP  OPFSH FBG DV TD 225-330    9  5 3800 1  2  5850  7250
  22  8 PENN-YAN 23R       OP  OPFSH FBG DV TD  200D CHRY 9  5 3800 1  2  8900 10100
  22  8 PENN-YAN 23R       OP  CUD  FBG DV TD 225-330     9  5 4200 1  2  6250  7750
  22  8 PENN-YAN 23R       HT  CUD  FBG DV TD 225-330     9  5 4200 1  2  6250  7750

  22  8 PENN-YAN 23S       HT  CR   FBG DV TD 225-330     9  5 4300 1  2  6400  7900
  22  8 PENN-YAN 23SF      FB  SF   FBG DV TD 225-330     9  5 4600 1  2  6600  8100
  22  8 PENN-YAN 23SFT     FB  SF   FBG DV TD 225-330     9  5 4600 1  2  6850  8400
  23 10 PENN-YAN 24M       OP  RNBT FBG DV TD 225-330     8    3600 1  2  5600  7000
```

LOA FT	LOA IN	NAME AND/ OR MODEL	TOP/ RIG	BOAT TYPE	HULL MTL	HULL TP	ENGINE TP	ENGINE # HP MFG	BEAM FT	BEAM IN	WGT LBS	DRAFT FT	DRAFT IN	RETAIL LOW	RETAIL HIGH
		1979 BOATS													
23	10	PENN-YAN 24M	HT	RNBT	FBG	DV	TD	225-330	8		3600	1	2	5600	7000
23	10	PENN-YAN 24M	FB	RNBT	FBG	DV	TD	225-330	8		3600	1	2	5600	7000
23	10	PENN-YAN 24R	OP	CUD	FBG	DV	TD	225-330	8		4100	1	2	6200	7650
23	10	PENN-YAN 24SFT	FB	SF	FBG	DV	TD	225-330	8		4300	1	2	6400	7900
23	10	PENN-YAN 24XE	OP	SPTCR	FBG	DV	TD	225-330	8		4100	1	2	6200	7650
26		PENN-YAN 26CR	OP	CR	FBG	DV	TD	225-330	10	6	7600	1	5	11200	13500
26		PENN-YAN 26CR	HT	CR	FBG	DV	TD	225-330	10	6	7600	1	5	11200	13500
26		PENN-YAN 26SF	FB	SF	FBG	DV	TD	225-330	10		6500	1	5	10000	12100
26		PENN-YAN 26SF	FB	SF	FBG	DV	TD	200D CHRY	10		6500	1	5	13900	15800
26		PENN-YAN 26SF	FB	SF	FBG	DV	TD	T225-T255	10		6500	1	5	11100	13200
29	11	PENN-YAN 30SF	FB	SF	FBG	DV	TD	T225-T255	11	10	12000	1	10	18500	21000
29	11	PENN-YAN 30SF	FB	SF	FBG	DV	TD	T200D CHRY	11	10	12000	1	10	25700	28600
		1978 BOATS													
18		SABRE SI	OP	RNBT	FBG	DV	IO	140-185	7	4	2094			3000	3500
18	8	IMPERIAL II	OP	RNBT	FBG	DV	IO	140-185	7	6	2198			3200	3750
20	5	EXPLORER ERI	OP	CUD	FBG	DV	IO	140-185	8		2475			3400	4000
20	5	EXPLORER ERM	OP	CUD	FBG	DV	TD	225-255	8		2600	1	2	3600	4500
20	5	EXPLORER EWI	OP	FSH	FBG	DV	IO	140-185	8		2300			3500	4050
20	5	EXPLORER EWM	OP	RNBT	FBG	DV	TD	225-255	8		2600	1	2	3700	4600
21	3	PENN-YAN 22	OP	CUD	FBG	DV	TD	225-255	8		3250	1	2	4400	5300
22	8	AVENGER AHF	FB	SF	FBG	DV	TD	225-255	9	5	4300	1	2	6100	7300
22	8	AVENGER AM	OP	OPFSH	FBG	DV	TD	225-255	9	5	4300	1	2	6100	7300
22	8	AVENGER AM	HT	SF	FBG	DV	TD	225-255	9	5	4300	1	2	6100	7300
22	8	AVENGER AR	OP	CUD	FBG	DV	TD	225-255	9	5	4200	1	2	6000	7200
22	8	AVENGER AR	HT	CUD	FBG	DV	TD	225-255	9	5	4200	1	2	6000	7200
22	8	AVENGER AS	HT	SPTCR	FBG	DV	TD	225-255	9	5	4200	1	2	6000	7200
22	8	AVENGER ASF	FB	SF	FBG	DV	TD	225-255	9	5	4200	1	2	5900	7050
22	8	AVENGER ASFT	FB	SF	FBG	DV	TD	225-255	9	5	4200	1	2	6100	7350
23	10	PENN-YAN 24HM	HT	CUD	FBG	DV	TD	225-255	8		3600	1	2	5400	6450
23	10	PENN-YAN 24HM	FB	SF	FBG	DV	TD	225-255	8		3600	1	2	5400	6450
23	10	PENN-YAN 24M	OP	CUD	FBG	DV	TD	225-255	8		3600	1	2	5400	6450
23	10	PENN-YAN 24R	HT	CUD	FBG	DV	TD	225-255	8		4100	1	2	5950	7100
23	10	PENN-YAN 24S	HT	CR	FBG	DV	TD	225-255	8		4000	1	2	5800	6950
23	10	PENN-YAN 24SFT	FB	CR	FBG	DV	TD	225-255	8		4000	1	2	5800	6950
26		PENN-YAN 26CR	OP	CR	FBG	DV	TD	225-255	10	6	7600	1	5	10800	12500
26		PENN-YAN 26CR	HT	CR	FBG	DV	TD	225-255	10	6	7600	1	5	10800	12500
26		PENN-YAN 26SFT	FB	CR	FBG	DV	TD	225-255	10		6500	1	5	9550	11100
29	11	PENN-YAN 30SF	FB	SF	FBG	DV	TD	225-255	11	10	12000	1	5	16000	18400
29	11	PENN-YAN 30SF	FB	SF	FBG	DV	TD	T225-T255	11	10	12000	1	5	17400	20100
		1977 BOATS													
18		SABRE SI	OP	RNBT	FBG	DV	IO	165-175	7	4	2095			3050	3550
19		IMPERIAL II	OP	RNBT	FBG	DV	IO	165-175	7	6	2198			3300	3850
20	5	EXPLORER EI	OP	RNBT	FBG	DV	IO	165-175	8		2300			3300	3800
20	5	EXPLORER EI	HT	RNBT	FBG	DV	IO	165-175	8		2300			3250	3750
20	5	EXPLORER EM	OP	RNBT	FBG	DV	TD	225-255	8		2550	1	2	3600	4400
20	5	EXPLORER EM	HT	RNBT	FBG	DV	TD	225-255	8		2550	1	2	3500	4350
20	5	EXPLORER ERI	OP	CUD	FBG	DV	IO	165-175	8		2475			3500	4050
20	5	EXPLORER ERM	OP	CUD	FBG	DV	TD	225-255	8		2650	1	2	3500	4350
20	5	EXPLORER EWI	OP	RNBT	FBG	DV	IO	165-175	8		2300			3200	3700
20	5	EXPLORER EWM	OP	RNBT	FBG	DV	TD	225-255	8		2550	1	2	3450	4300
21	3	MONTEGO M2	OP	RNBT	FBG	DV	TD	225-255	8		3200	1	2	4200	5100
21	3	MONTEGO MR2	OP	CUD	FBG	DV	TD	225-255	8		3550	1	2	4500	5350
22	8	AVENGER AM	OP	RNBT	FBG	DV	TD	225-255	9	5	3600	1	2	5200	6250
22	8	AVENGER AM	HT	RNBT	FBG	DV	TD	225-255	9	5	3600	1	2	5200	6250
22	8	AVENGER AM	FB	RNBT	FBG	DV	TD	225-255	9	5	3600	1	2	5200	6250
22	8	AVENGER AR	OP	CUD	FBG	DV	TD	225-255	9	5	4200	1	2	5750	6900
22	8	AVENGER AR	HT	CUD	FBG	DV	TD	225-255	9	5	4200	1	2	5750	6900
22	8	AVENGER AS	HT	SPTCR	FBG	DV	TD	225-255	9	5	4000	1	2	5550	6650
22	8	AVENGER ASF	FB	SF	FBG	DV	TD	225-255	9	5	4300	1	2	5900	7000
22	8	AVENGER ASFT	FB	SF	FBG	DV	TD	225-255	9	5	4350	1	2	5950	7050
23	10	PENN-YAN 24C	OP	CR	FBG	DV	TD	225-255	8		3900	1	2	5500	6550
23	10	PENN-YAN 24CF	FB	CR	FBG	DV	TD	225-255	8		4000	1	2	5600	6650
23	10	PENN-YAN 24M	OP	CUD	FBG	DV	TD	225-255	8		3500	1	2	5050	6050
23	10	PENN-YAN 24S	HT	SPTCR	FBG	DV	TD	225-255	8		3800	1	2	5400	6450
23	10	PENN-YAN SFT	FB	SF	FBG	DV	TD	225-255	8		3850	1	2	5450	6500
26		PENN-YAN 26C	OP	CR	FBG	DV	TD	T225-T255	10	6	7700	1	7	11500	13500
26		PENN-YAN 26CF	FB	CR	FBG	DV	TD	T225-T255	10	6	7800	1	7	11600	13600
26		PENN-YAN 26CR	OP	CR	FBG	DV	TD	225-255	10	6	6000	1	5	8850	10300
26		PENN-YAN 26CR	HT	CR	FBG	DV	TD	225-255	10	6	6000	1	5	8850	10300
26		PENN-YAN 26M	OP	RNBT	FBG	DV	TD	225-255	10	6	6200	1	5	8900	10400
26		PENN-YAN 26M	HT	RNBT	FBG	DV	TD	225-255	10	6	6200	1	5	8900	10400
26		PENN-YAN 26M	FB	RNBT	FBG	DV	TD	225-255	10	6	6200	1	5	8900	10400
26		PENN-YAN 26SF	FB	SF	FBG	DV	TD	T225-T255	10	6	7800	1	7	11600	13600
29	11	PENN-YAN 30SF	FB	SF	FBG	DV	TD	T225-T255	10	6	11700	1	10	16200	18800
		1976 BOATS													
18		SABRE SI	OP	RNBT	FBG	DV	IO	165	7	4	2094			3100	3600
18		SABRE SM	OP	RNBT	FBG	DV	TD	225-255	7	4	2350	1	2	3300	4100
18		SABRE SM	OP	RNBT	FBG	DV	TD	260 OMC	7	4	2350	1	2	3550	4150
18	8	IMPERIAL II	OP	RNBT	FBG	DV	IO	165	7	6	2198			3300	3850
19	7	MONTEGO MO	OP	RNBT	FBG	DV	TD	225-260	7	8	2600	1	2	3850	4800
20	5	EXPLORER EI	OP	RNBT	FBG	DV	IO	165-225	8		2300			3350	4000
20	5	EXPLORER EM	OP	RNBT	FBG	DV	TD	225-260	8		2550	1	2	3450	4250
20	5	EXPLORER ERI	OP	CUD	FBG	DV	IO	165-225	8		2475			3550	4250
20	5	EXPLORER ERM	OP	CUD	FBG	DV	TD	225-260	8		2650	1	2	3350	4200
20	5	EXPLORER EWI	OP	RNBT	FBG	DV	IO	165-225	8		2300			3250	3850
20	5	EXPLORER EWM	OP	RNBT	FBG	DV	TD	225-260	8		2550	1	2	3350	4150
21	3	MONTEGO M2	OP	RNBT	FBG	DV	TD	225-260	8		3200	1	2	4000	4950
21	3	MONTEGO MR2	OP	CUD	FBG	DV	TD	225-260	8		3550	1	2	4250	5200
22	8	AVENGER AM	OP	RNBT	FBG	DV	TD	225-260	9	5	3600	1	2	5000	6000
22	8	AVENGER AR	OP	CUD	FBG	DV	TD	225-260	9	5	4200	1	2	5550	6650
22	8	AVENGER AR	HT	CUD	FBG	DV	TD	225-260	9	5		1	2	5250	6300
22	8	AVENGER AS	HT	FSH	FBG	DV	TD	225-260	9	5	4000	1	2	5350	6400
22	8	AVENGER ASF	FB	SF	FBG	DV	TD	225-260	9	5	4300	1	2	5650	6750
23	10	PENN-YAN 24 C	OP	CR	FBG	DV	TD	225-260	8		3900	1	2	5250	6300
23	10	PENN-YAN 24 CF	HT	CR	FBG	DV	TD	225-260	8		4000	1	2	5350	6400
26		PENN-YAN 26 C	OP	CR	FBG	DV	TD	T225-T260	10	6	7700	1	7	11000	13000
26		PENN-YAN 26 CF	FB	CR	FBG	DV	TD	T225-T260	10	6	7800	1	7	11100	13100
26		PENN-YAN 26 CR	OP	CR	FBG	DV	TD	225-260	10	6	6300	1	5	8650	10300
26		PENN-YAN 26 CR	HT	CR	FBG	DV	TD	225-260	10	6		1	5	9250	10700
26		PENN-YAN 26 M	OP	UTL	FBG	DV	TD	225-260	10	6	6200	1	2	8550	10100
26		PENN-YAN 26 S	HT	SF	FBG	DV	TD	T225-T260	10	6	7500	1	7	10800	12800
26		PENN-YAN 26 SF	FB	SF	FBG	DV	TD	T225-T260	10	6	7800	1	7	11100	13100
29	11	PENN-YAN 30 SF	FB	SF	FBG	DV	TD	T225-T260	11	10	12000	1	10	16000	18600
		1975 BOATS													
18		SABRE SI	OP	RNBT	FBG	DV	IO	165	7	4	2095	2	2	3200	3700
18		SABRE SM	OP	RNBT	FBG	DV	TD	225-255	7	4	2350	1	2	3150	3900
18		SABRE SM	OP	RNBT	FBG	DV	TD	260 OMC	7	4	2350	1	2	3400	3950
18	8	IMPERIAL II	OP	RNBT	FBG	DV	IO	165	7	6	2198			3400	3950
19	7	MONTEGO MO	OP	RNBT	FBG	DV	TD	225-260	7	8	2600	1	2	3700	4600
20	5	BLUEFIN EF	OP	OPFSH	FBG	DV	TD	225-260	8		2950	1	2	3450	4250
20	5	EXPLORER EI	OP	RNBT	FBG	DV	IO	165-225	8		2300	2	2	3400	4050
20	5	EXPLORER EM	OP	RNBT	FBG	DV	TD	225-260	8		2550	1	2	3250	4050
20	5	EXPLORER EM	HT	RNBT	FBG	DV	TD	225-260	8		2850	1	2	3450	4250
20	5	EXPLORER ER	OP	CUD	FBG	DV	IO	165-225	8		2475	2	2	3700	4350
20	5	EXPLORER ERM	OP	CUD	FBG	DV	TD	225-260	8		2650	1	2	3250	4000
21	3	MONTEGO M2	OP	RNBT	FBG	DV	TD	225-260	8		3200	1	2	3850	4750
21	3	MONTEGO MR	OP	CUD	FBG	DV	TD	225-260	8		3550	1	2	4100	5000
22	8	AVENGER AM	OP	RNBT	FBG	DV	TD	225-260	9	5	3600	1	2	4800	5750
22	8	AVENGER AM	HT	RNBT	FBG	DV	TD	225-260	9	5	3900	1	2	5100	6100
22	8	AVENGER AM	FB	RNBT	FBG	DV	TD	225-260	9	5	3900	1	2	5100	6100
22	8	AVENGER AR	OP	CUD	FBG	DV	TD	225-260	9	5	4200	1	2	5350	6350
22	8	AVENGER AR	HT	CUD	FBG	DV	TD	225-260	9	5	4500	1	2	5600	6700
22	8	AVENGER AS	HT	EXP	FBG	DV	TD	225-260	9	5	4000	1	2	5150	6150
22	8	AVENGER ASF	FB	SF	FBG	DV	TD	225-260	9	5	4300	1	2	5400	6500
22	8	AVENGER ASFT	FB	SF	FBG	DV	TD	225-260	9	5	4300	1	2	5400	6500
22	8	BLUEFIN AF	OP	OPFSH	FBG	DV	TD	225-260	9	5	3520	1	2	4700	5650
23	10	PENN-YAN 24C	OP	CR	FBG	DV	TD	225-260	8		3900	1	2	5050	6050
23	10	PENN-YAN 24CF	FB	CR	FBG	DV	TD	225-260	8		4300	1	2	5450	6500
26		PENN-YAN 26C	OP	CR	FBG	DV	TD	T225-T260	10	6	7700	1	7	11000	13000
26		PENN-YAN 26CF	FB	CR	FBG	DV	TD	T225-T260	10	6	7800	1	7	10700	12600
26		PENN-YAN 26M	OP	CR	FBG	DV	TD	T225-T260	10	6	7700	1	7	10100	12000
26		PENN-YAN 26M	HT	CR	FBG	DV	TD	T225-T260	10	6	8000	1	7	10800	12800
26		PENN-YAN 26M	FB	CR	FBG	DV	TD	T225-T260	10	6	8000	1	7	10800	12800
26		PENN-YAN 26S	HT	SF	FBG	DV	TD	T225-T260	10	6	7500	1	7	10400	12300
26		PENN-YAN 26SF	FB	SF	FBG	DV	TD	T225-T260	10	6	7800	1	7	10700	12600
		1974 BOATS													
18		SABRE SI			FBG		IO	165	7	4	2094	1	2	3150	3700
18		SABRE SM			FBG		TD	225	7	4	2350	1	2	2900	3600
18		SABRE SM			FBG		TD	250-255	7	4	2350	1	2	2950	3650
18	8	IMPERIAL II			FBG		IO	165	7	6	2198	1	2	3400	3950
19	7	MONTEGO M20			FBG		TD	225-255	7	8	2600	1	2	3450	4300
20	5	EXPLORER EI	OP		FBG		IO	165-225	8		2300	1	2	3500	4150
20	5	EXPLORER EI	HT		FBG		IO	165-225	8		2600	1	2	3700	4400
20	5	EXPLORER EM	OP		FBG		TD	225-255	8		2550	1	2	3050	3750
20	5	EXPLORER EM	HT		FBG		TD	225-255	8		2850	1	2	3250	4000
20	5	EXPLORER ER		CUD	FBG		IO	165-225	8		2475	1	2	3800	4500
20	5	EXPLORER ERM		CUD	FBG		TD	225-255	8		2650	1	2	3100	3850

 CONTINUED ON NEXT PAGE

```
     LOA  NAME AND/              TOP/ BOAT  -HULL-  ----ENGINE--- BEAM   WGT  DRAFT RETAIL RETAIL
     FT IN OR MODEL              RIG  TYPE  MTL TP TP # HP  MFG   FT IN  LBS  FT IN  LOW   HIGH
-------------------- 1974 BOATS --------------------------------------------------------------
21  3 MONTEGO M22                     FBG   TD 225-255      8     3200  1  2  3650   4500
21  3 MONTEGO MR              CUD     FBG   TD 225-255      8     3550  1  2  3900   4800
21  7 BARRACUDA BRM                   FBG   TD 225-255      8     2850  1  2  3450   4250
21  7 BLUEFIN BF                      FBG   TD 225         8            1  2  3450   4200
22  8 AVENGER AM              OP      FBG   TD 225-255    9 5     3600  1  2  4600   5500
22  8 AVENGER AM              HT      FBG   TD 225-255    9 5     3900  1  2  4850   5800
22  8 AVENGER AM              FB      FBG   TD 225-255    9 5     4200  1  2  5100   6100
22  8 AVENGER ARM             CUD     FBG   TD 225-255    9 5     4200  1  2  5100   6100
22  8 AVENGER ARM             HT CUD  FBG   TD 225-255    9 5     4500  1  2  5400   6400
22  8 AVENGER ARM             FB CUD  FBG   TD 225-255    9 5     4800  1  2  5650   6750
22  8 AVENGER ASFM            FB SF   FBG   TD 225-255    9 5     4300  1  2  5200   6200
22  8 AVENGER ASM SPT                 FBG   TD 225-255    9 5     4000  1  2  4950   5900

22  8 AVENGER AF                      FBG   TD 225        9 5     3520  1  2  4550   5400
26    VINDICATOR VM           OP      FBG   TD T225-T255 10 6           1  7  8850  10500
26    VINDICATOR VM           HT      FBG   TD T225-T255 10 6           1  7  8850  10500
26    VINDICATOR VRFM         FB      FBG   TD T225-T255 10 6     7800  1  7  10200 11800
26    VINDICATOR VRM          CUD     FBG   TD T225-T255 10 6     7700  1  7  10200 12000
26    VINDICATOR VSFM         FB      FBG   TD T225-T255 10 6     7800  1  7  10700 12400
26    VINDICATOR VSM SPT              FBG   TD T225-T255 10 6     7500  1  7  10000 11800
-------------------- 1973 BOATS --------------------------------------------------------------
18    SABRE SI                        FBG   IO 165        7 4     2094        3250   3750
18    SABRE SM                        FBG   TD 225        7 4     2350  1  2  2800   3500
18    SABRE SM                        FBG   TD 250-255    7 4     2350  1  2  2800   3500
18  8 IMPERIAL II                     FBG   IO 165        7 6     2198        3500   4050
19  7 MONTEGO M200                    FBG   TD 225-255    7 8     2950  1  2  3600   4400
20  5 EXPLORER EI                     FBG   IO 165-225    8       2300        3600   4300
20  5 EXPLORER EM                     FBG   TD 225-255    8       2450  1  2  2850   3550
20  5 EXPLORER EM              HT      FBG   TD 225-255    8       2450  1  2  2850   3550
20  5 EXPLORER ER             CUD     FBG   IO 165-225    8       2475        3950   4650
20  5 EXPLORER ERM            CUD     FBG   TD 225-255    8       2575  1  2  2950   3650
21  7 BARRACUDA BRM                   FBG   TD 225-255    8       2850  1  2  3350   4100
21  7 MONTEGO M220                    FBG   TD 225-255    8       3300  1  2  3650   4450

21  7 MONTEGO MR              CUD     FBG   TD 225-255    8       3550  1  2  3850   4700
22  8 AVENGER AM              OP      FBG   TD 225-255    9 5     3200  1  2  4050   4950
22  8 AVENGER ARM             CUD     FBG   TD 225-255    9 5     4200  1  2  4900   5850
22  8 AVENGER ARM             HT CUD  FBG   TD 225-255    9 5     4200  1  2  4900   5850
22  8 AVENGER ARM             FB CUD  FBG   TD 225-255    9 5     4200  1  2  4900   5850
22  8 AVENGER ASFM            FB SF   FBG   TD 225-255    9 5     4500  1  2  5200   6150
22  8 AVENGER ASM SPT                 FBG   TD 225-255    9 5     4050  1  2  4400   5700
26    VINDICATOR VRFM         FB      FBG   TD T225-T255 10 6     8200  1  7  10200 12000
26    VINDICATOR VRM          CUD     FBG   TD T225-T255 10 6     7700  1  7  9850  11600
26    VINDICATOR VSFM         FB      FBG   TD T225-T255 10 6     8000  1  7  10000 11800
26    VINDICATOR VSM SPT              FBG   TD T225-T255 10 6     7500  1  7  9600  11300
-------------------- 1972 BOATS --------------------------------------------------------------
18    SABRE SI                        FBG   IO 155-165    7 4     2094        3300   3900
18    SABRE SM                        FBG   TD 210-250    7 4     2350  1  2  2850   3400
18  8 IMPERIAL II                     FBG   IO 155-165    7 6     2198        3550   4200
19  7 MONTEGO M200                    FBG   TD 210-250    7 8     2950  1  2  3600   4250
20  5 EXPLORER EI                     FBG   IO 155-225    8       2300        3700   4450
20  5 EXPLORER EM                     FBG   TD 210-250    8       2450  1  2  2900   3400
20  5 EXPLORER ER             CUD     FBG   IO 155-225    8       2475        4050   4800
20  5 EXPLORER ERM            CUD     FBG   TD 210-250    8       2575  1  2  3000   3500
21  7 BARRACUDA BRM                   FBG   TD 210-250    8       2850  1  2  3350   3950
21  7 MONTEGO M220                    FBG   TD 210-270    8       3300  1  2  3650   4300
22  8 AVENGER AM              OP      FBG   TD 210-270    9 5     3200  1  2  4050   4750
22  8 AVENGER AM              OP      FBG   TD 100D CHRY  9 5     3200  1  2  5850   6700

22  8 AVENGER AM              FB      FBG   TD 210-270    9 5           1  2  4500   5150
22  8 AVENGER AM              FB      FBG   TD 100D CHRY  9 5           1  2  6300   7250
22  8 AVENGER ARM             CUD     FBG   TD 210-270    9 5     4200  1  2  4900   5650
22  8 AVENGER ARM             CUD     FBG   TD 100D CHRY  9 5     4200  1  2  6750   7800
22  8 AVENGER ARM             FB CUD  FBG   TD 210-270    9 5           1  2  4650   5350
22  8 AVENGER ARM             FB CUD  FBG   TD 100D CHRY  9 5           1  2  6500   7450
22  8 AVENGER SPT ASM                 FBG   TD 210-270    9 5     4050  1  2  4750   5500
22  8 AVENGER SPT ASM                 FBG   TD 100D CHRY  9 5     4050  1  2  6650   7600
22  8 AVENGER SPT ASM         FB      FBG   TD 210-270    9 5           1  2  4800   5500
22  8 AVENGER SPT ASM         FB      FBG   TD 100D CHRY  9 5           1  2  6700   7700
26    VINDICATOR VSM                  FBG   TD T210-T250 10 6     7500  1  7  9450  10900
26    VINDICATOR VSM                  FBG   TD T100D CHRY 10 6    7500  1  7  13400 15200

26    VINDICATOR VSM          FB      FBG   TD T210-T250 10 6           1  7  8200   9650
26    VINDICATOR VSM          FB      FBG   TD T100D CHRY 10 6          1  7  11400 13000
-------------------- 1971 BOATS --------------------------------------------------------------
16    TORNADO                         FBG   IO 120        6 5           2250   2650
18    SABRE                           FBG   TD 210-225    7 4     2350        2750   3200
18    SABRE                   RNBT    FBG SV IO 155-165   7 4     1700  2 8  3300   3850
18  8 IMPERIAL                        FBG   IO 155-215    7 6     2198        3650   4400
20  5 EXPLORER                OP      FBG   IO 155-165    8       2200        3750   4400
      TD 210  OMC   2650      3100, IO  215 MRCR  3850  4500, IO  215   OMC     3850   4450
      TD 215-225    2550      2950

20  5 EXPLORER                HT      FBG   IO 155-165    8                    4250   5000
      TD 210  OMC   3000      3500, IO  215 MRCR  4400  5100, IO  215   OMC     4400   5050
      TD 215-225    2900      3350

20  5 EXPLORER                FB      FBG   IO 155-165    8                    4250   5000
      TD 210  OMC   3000      3500, IO  215 MRCR  4400  5100, IO  215   OMC     4400   5050
      TD 215-225    2900      3350

20  5 EXPLORER                CUD     FBG   IO 155-165    8       2375        4100   4800
      TD 210  OMC   2750      3200, IO  215 MRCR  4200  4900, IO  215   OMC     4150   4850
      TD 215-225    2650      3050

21  7 BARRACUDA               CUD     FBG TR IO 155-215   8       2850  2 10  4850   5700
21  7 BARRACUDA               CUD     FBG TR IB 225       8       2850  1  2  3100   3600
21  7 BARRACUDA               CUD     FBG TR IB T210      8       2850  1  2  3600   4200
22  8 AVENGER                 OP      FBG   IO 155-165    9 5     3200        5600   6450
      TD 210  OMC   3900      4550, IO  215 MRCR  5700  6550, IO  215   OMC     5650   6500

22  8 AVENGER                 CUD     FBG   TD 210-270    9 5           4450   5150
22  8 AVENGER                 FB CUD  FBG   TD 210-270    9 5           4450   5150
22  8 AVENGER SPORTSMAN               FBG   TD 155-165    9 5     4050        6500   7550
      TD 210  OMC   4600      5300, IO  215 MRCR  6650  7650, IO  215   OMC     6600   7600
      TD 215-270    4500      5300

22  8 AVENGER SPTMAN          FB      FBG   TD 155-165    9 5     4050        6500   7550
      TD 210  OMC   4600      5300, IO  215 MRCR  6650  7650, IO  215   OMC     6600   7600
      TD 215-270    4500      5300

26    VINDICATOR VSM                  FBG   IB 250-325   10 6     6600  1  7  7400   8850
26    VINDICATOR VSM                  FBG   IB T210-T225 10 6     7500  1  7  9050  10300
26    VINDICATOR VSM          FB      FBG   IB 250-325   10 6           1  7  7000   8350
26    VINDICATOR VSM          FB      FBG   IB T210-T225 10 6           1  7  7900   9050
-------------------- 1970 BOATS --------------------------------------------------------------
16    TORNADO                 RNBT    FBG DV IO 120        6 5    1363  4    2650   2900
18    SABRE                   RNBT    FBG DV TD 210-225    7 4           2650   3050
18  8 IMPERIAL                CUD     FBG SV IO 120-215    7 6    1850  2 4  3650   4400
20  5 EXPLORER                        FBG   IO 120-165    8       2375  2 4  4250   4950
      IO 210  OMC   4300      5000, TD  210  OMC  2650  3100, IO  215   MRCR    4400   5050

20  5 EXPLORER                OP RNBT FBG DV IO 120-165    8       2200  2 4  3950   4600
      IO 210  OMC   4000      4650, TD  210  OMC  2650  3050, IO  215   MRCR    4050   4700
      TD 215-225    2500      2950

20  5 EXPLORER                HT RNBT FBG DV IO 120-165    8       2200  2 4  3950   4600
      IO 210  OMC   4000      4650, TD  210  OMC  2650  3050, IO  215   MRCR    4050   4700
      TD 215-225    2500      2950

21  7 BARRACUDA               CUD     FBG TR IO 120-165    8       2650  2 4  4800   5550
      IO 210  OMC   4850      5600, TD  210  OMC  3000  3450, IO  215   MRCR    4900   5650
      TD 215-225    2850      3350

21  7 BLUEFIN                 FSH     FBG TR TD 225  CHRY  8       2860  2 4  2950   3450
22  8 AVENGER                 HT      FBG DV IO 155-165    9 5    3120  2 6  5700   6550
      IO 210  OMC   5750      6600, TD  210  OMC  3700  4300, IO  215   MRCR    5800   6650
      TD 215-260    3600      4350

22  8 AVENGER                 FB      FBG DV IO 155-165    9 5           2 6  6550   7550
      IO 210  OMC   6600      7600, TD  210  OMC  4250  4950, IO  215   MRCR    6650   7650
      TD 215-260    4150      4350

22  8 AVENGER                 OP CR   FBG DV IO 155-165    9 5    3120  2 6  6000   6900
      IO 210  OMC   6050      6950, TD  210  OMC  3700  4300, IO  215   MRCR    6100   7000
      TD 215-260    3600      4350

22  8 AVENGER                 CUD     FBG DV IO 155-165    9 5    4500  2 6  7650   8850
      IO 210  OMC   7700      8900, TD  210  OMC  4750  5450, IO  215   MRCR    7750   8950
      TD 215-260    4650      5500

22  8 AVENGER SPORTS          FB      FBG DV IO 155-165    9 5    4400  2 6  7150   8250
      IO 210  OMC   7250      8300, TD  210  OMC  4700  5350, IO  215   MRCR    7250   8350
      TD 215-260    4600      5400
```

```
 LOA  NAME AND/            TOP/ BOAT -HULL- ----ENGINE--- BEAM   WGT  DRAFT RETAIL RETAIL
FT IN OR MODEL             RIG  TYPE MTL TP TP  # HP  MFG  FT IN  LBS  FT IN  LOW   HIGH
--------------------- 1970 BOATS -----------------------------------------------------------
22  8 AVENGER SPORTSMAN          FBG DV IO 155-165      9  5 4400  2  6 7150  8250
         IO 210  OMC   7250  8300, TD 210 OMC   4700  5350, IO 215 MRCR 7250  8350
         TD 215-260    4600  5400
--------------------- 1969 BOATS -----------------------------------------------------------
16    TORNADO            RNBT FBG SV IO 120       6  5 1363  2  6 2600  3000
18  8 IMPERIAL           RNBT FBG SV IO 120-210   7  6 1850  2  6 3750  4500
18  8 IMPERIAL        HT RNBT FBG SV IO 120-210   7  6 1850  2  6 3750  4500
20  5 EXPLORER           CUD  FBG    IO 120-210   8    2375  2  6 4400  5150
20  5 EXPLORER           CUD  FBG DV TD 225  CHRY 8    2375  2  6 2450  2800
20  5 EXPLORER        OP RNBT FBG SV IO 120-210   8    2200  2  6 4050  4800
20  5 EXPLORER        OP RNBT FBG SV TD 225  CHRY 8    2200  2  6 2400  2800
20  5 EXPLORER        HT RNBT FBG    IO 120-210   8    2200  2  6 4050  4800
20  5 EXPLORER        HT RNBT FBG DV TD 225  CHRY 8    2200  2  6 2400  2800
21  7 BARRACUDA          CUD  FBG TR IO 120-210   8    2650  2  6 4950  5800
21  7 BARRACUDA          CUD  FBG TR IO 225  MRCR 8    2650  2  6 5100  5850
21  7 BARRACUDA          CUD  FBG TR TD 225  CHRY 8    2650  2  6 2750  3200

22  8 AVENGER             CR    FBG    IO 155-210  9  5 4250      7600  8850
22  8 AVENGER             CR    FBG    IO 225  MRCR 9  5 4250      7750  8900
22  8 AVENGER             CR    FBG    TD 225  CHRY 9  5 4250      4250  4900
22  8 AVENGER          OP CR    FBG    IO 155-225  9  5 3200  2  6 6250  7400
22  8 AVENGER          OP CR    FBG DV TD 225  CHRY 9  5 3200  2  6 3500  4050
22  8 AVENGER             CUD   FBG    IO 155-210  9  5      7100  8250
22  8 AVENGER             CUD   FBG    IO 225  MRCR 9  5      7250  8350
22  8 AVENGER             CUD   FBG    TD 225  CHRY 9  5      3950  4600
22  8 AVENGER          HT SPTCR FBG    IO 160-225  9  5 3200 6300  7400
22  8 AVENGER          HT SPTCR FBG DV IO 155  OMC 9  5 3200 6300  7200
22  8 AVENGER          HT SPTCR FBG DV TD 225  CHRY 9  5 3200 3500  4050

22  8 AVENGER          FB SPTCR FBG    IO 155-210  9  5      7150  8300
22  8 AVENGER          FB SPTCR FBG    IO 225  MRCR 9  5      7300  8400
22  8 AVENGER          FB SPTCR FBG    TD 225  CHRY 9  5      3950  4600
22  8 AVENGER SPORTS    FB SPTCR FBG    IO 155-210 9  5 3450 6600  7700
22  8 AVENGER SPORTS    FB SPTCR FBG    IO 225  MRCR 9 5 3450 6750  7750
22  8 AVENGER SPORTS    FB SPTCR FBG    TD 225  CHRY 9 5 3450 3650  4250
22  8 AVENGER SPORTSMEN       FBG    IO 200-210  9  5      6850  7850
22  8 AVENGER SPORTSMEN       FBG    IO 225  MRCR 9  5      6900  7950
22  8 AVENGER SPORTSMEN       FBG    IO 225  CHRY 9  5      3950  4600
22  8 AVENGER SPORTSMEN SPTCR FBG    IO 155-160  9  5      7150  8250
--------------------- 1968 BOATS -----------------------------------------------------------
16  1 CUTLAS CI        OP RNBT  FBG SV IO 120       6  9 1360  2  4 2750  3200
17    RIVIERA RSI      OP RNBT  FBG SV IO 120-160   7    1500  2  4 3150  3800
18  8 IMPERIAL IHI     HT RNBT  FBG    IO 120-185   7  6 1925      3950  4900
18  8 IMPERIAL IHI     HT RNBT  FBG    IO 200       7  6 2175      4250  4950
18  8 IMPERIAL II      OP UTL   FBG    IO 120-210   7  6 1850  2  4 4350  5450
20  5 EXPLORER EGI     OP UTL   FBG    IO 120-210   8    2200  2  4 4650  5800
20  5 EXPLORER EGIC    OP CR    FBG    IO 120-160   8    2650  2  4 4800  5800
20  5 EXPLORER EGIH    HT CBNCR FBG    IO 120       8    2200  2  4 4700  5400
20  5 EXPLORER EGIH    HT CBNCR FBG    IO 155-210   8    2700  2  4 5250  6000
21  7 BARRACUDA BI        UTL   FBG    IO 155-225   8    3025  2  4 5850  6750
22  8 AVENGER             CR    FBG    IO 155-210   9  5 4250  2  4 7850  9150
22  8 AVENGER          HT SF    FBG    IO 120-225   9  5 3300  2  6 7450  8750

22  8 AVENGER          OP UTL   FBG    IO 120-225   9  5 3200  2  6 6850  8050
--------------------- 1967 BOATS -----------------------------------------------------------
16  1 COBRA               RNBT FBG    IO 120       6  9      2800  3300
17    RIVIERA             RNBT FBG    IO 120       7         3100  3650
18  8 IMPERIAL            RNBT FBG    IO 120-200   7  6 1282 3650  4350
20  5 EXPLORER         HT      FBG    IO 120-225   8         4850  5800
20  5 EXPLORER            CR   FBG    IO 120-160   8         5150  5950
20  5 EXPLORER         HT UTL  FBG    IO 120  MRCR 8         4950  5650
20  5 EXPLORER         HT RNBT FBG    IO 120-225   8    2200 4800  5700
22  8 AVENGER          HT      FBG    IO 120-225   9  5      7250  8500
22  8 AVENGER             CR   FBG    IO 155-200   9  5      7600  8800
22  8 AVENGER             UTL  FBG    IO 120-225   9  5 3200 7100  8350
--------------------- 1966 BOATS -----------------------------------------------------------
17    RIVIERA            RNBT FBG   IO 150-200  7        3200  3800
17 10 STARFIRE 18        RNBT WD    IO 110-225  7  1     4050  4900
17 10 STARFIRE 18        RNBT WD    IO T 60D    7  1     6100  7000
18  8 IMPERIAL           RNBT FBG   IO 110-225  7  6     4400  5300
20  3 EXPLORER           CR   WD    IO 120      8        5250  6050
20  5 EXPLORER           CR   FBG   IO 110      8        5300  6100
20  5 EXPLORER           CR   WD    IO 120      8        5300  6100
20  5 EXPLORER           CR   FBG   IO 120      8        5300  6100
20  5 EXPLORER           CR   FBG   IO 120  OMC 8        5300  6050
20  5 EXPLORER           CR   WD    IO 120  OMC 8        5300  6050
20  5 EXPLORER           CR   FBG   IO 150      8        5350  6150
20  5 EXPLORER           CR   WD    IO 150      8        5350  6150

20  5 EXPLORER           CR   WD    IO 150  OMC 8        5300  6100
20  5 EXPLORER           CR   FBG   IO 150  OMC 8        5300  6100
20  5 EXPLORER           CR   FBG   IO 165      8        5350  6150
20  5 EXPLORER           CR   WD    IO 165      8        5350  6150
20  5 EXPLORER           CR   FBG   IO 200      8        5400  6200
20  5 EXPLORER           CR   WD    IO 200      8        5400  6200
20  5 EXPLORER           CR   FBG   IO 200  OMC 8        5350  6150
20  5 EXPLORER           CR   WD    IO 200  OMC 8        5350  6150
20  5 EXPLORER           CR   FBG   IO 225      8        5500  6300
20  5 EXPLORER           CR   WD    IO 225      8        5500  6300
20  5 EXPLORER           CR   FBG   IO 60D      8        6550  7550
20  5 EXPLORER           CR   WD    IO 60D      8        6550  7550

20  5 EXPLORER        OP RNBT WD    IO 110-225  8        5100  6050
20  5 EXPLORER        OP RNBT WD    IO T 60D    8        8100  9300
20  5 EXPLORER        HT RNBT WD    IO 110      8        5100  5850
20  5 EXPLORER        HT RNBT FBG   IO 110      8        5100  5850
20  5 EXPLORER        HT RNBT WD    IO 120      8        5100  5850
20  5 EXPLORER        HT RNBT FBG   IO 120      8        5050  5800
20  5 EXPLORER        HT RNBT WD    IO 120  OMC 8        5050  5800
20  5 EXPLORER        HT RNBT FBG   IO 120  OMC 8        5050  5800
20  5 EXPLORER        HT RNBT WD    IO 150      8        5100  5850
20  5 EXPLORER        HT RNBT FBG   IO 150      8        5100  5850
20  5 EXPLORER        HT RNBT WD    IO 150  OMC 8        5050  5850
20  5 EXPLORER        HT RNBT FBG   IO 150  OMC 8        5050  5850
20  5 EXPLORER        HT RNBT FBG   IO 165      8        5100  5900

20  5 EXPLORER        HT RNBT FBG   IO 165      8        5100  5900
20  5 EXPLORER        HT RNBT WD    IO 200      8        5150  5950
20  5 EXPLORER        HT RNBT FBG   IO 200      8        5150  5950
20  5 EXPLORER        HT RNBT WD    IO 200  OMC 8        5150  5900
20  5 EXPLORER        HT RNBT FBG   IO 200  OMC 8        5150  5900
20  5 EXPLORER        HT RNBT WD    IO 225      8        5250  6050
20  5 EXPLORER        HT RNBT FBG   IO 225      8        5250  6050
20  5 EXPLORER        HT RNBT FBG   IO 60D      8        6250  7200
20  5 EXPLORER        HT RNBT WD    IO 60D      8        6250  7200
20  5 EXPLORER           UTL  FBG   IO 110-225  8        5600  6650
20  5 EXPLORER           UTL  FBG   IO 60D      8        8200  9400
22  8 AVENGER            CR   WD    IO 150-225  9  5     7900  9250

22  8 AVENGER         OP RNBT WD    IO 120-225  9  5     7400  8700
22  8 AVENGER         OP RNBT WD    IO 60D      9  5     8800 10000
22  8 AVENGER         HT RNBT WD    IO 120-225  9  5     7400  8700
22  8 AVENGER         HT RNBT WD    IO 60D      9  5     8800 10000
25 10 AVENGER 26        CR   WD    IO 150-225  9  7    13100 15400
--------------------- 1965 BOATS -----------------------------------------------------------
17    RIVIERA R1              FBG   IO 110-150           2950  3550
17    RIVIERA SPORT-RSI       FBG   IO 110-120           2900  3500
17 10 MARINER MAI             WD    IO 110-150           3800  4650
17 10 STARFIRE SI             WD    IO 110-150           4250  5100
20  3 EXPLORER EI       OP    WD    IO 110-165           5150  6000
20  3 EXPLORER EIC          CR WD   IO 110-165           5450  6300
20  3 EXPLORER EIH      HT    WD    IO 110-165           5150  6000
22  8 AVENGER AI             WD    IB 110-225           3250  4000
--------------------- 1964 BOATS -----------------------------------------------------------
17    RIVIERA                FBG   IO 110-150           3050  3800
17  1 TAHITI                 WD    IO 110               3100  3600
17  8 STARFIRE MK VIII       WD    IO 110-160           4200  5150
17 10 MARINER                WD    IO 110  MRCR         4000  4650
17 10 STARFIRE               WD    IO 110-160           4050  5050
17    STARFIRE               WD    IO 110-160           4400  5450
20  3 EXPLORER               WD    IB 185               2250  2600
20  3 EXPLORER          OP   WD    IO 110-160           5350  6350
20  3 EXPLORER          HT   WD    IO 110-160           5350  6350
20  3 EXPLORER         CR    WD    IO 110-160           5600  6700
23  3 VOYAGER                WD    IB 185               3350  3900
23  3 VOYAGER          OP   WD    IO 110-160           8050  9450

23  3 VOYAGER          HT   WD    IO 110-160           8050  9450
23  3 VOYAGER          HT   WD    IB 185               3350  3900
23  3 VOYAGER         CR    WD    IO 110-160           8500 10000
--------------------- 1963 BOATS -----------------------------------------------------------
16  7 TAHITI                 WD    IO 80-110            3050  3550
17    STARFIRE               WD    IO 100-140           4300  5000
17  7 STARFIRE MARK VII      WD    IO 110-140           4350  5000
19  7 NOMAD             RNBT WD    IB 109-188           2400  2950
19  7 NOMAD NI               WD    IB 100-110           2300  2700
```

LOA FT	LOA IN	NAME AND/ OR MODEL	TOP/ RIG	BOAT TYPE	HULL MTL	HULL TP	ENGINE TP	ENGINE # HP	ENGINE MFG	BEAM FT	BEAM IN	WGT LBS	DRAFT FT	DRAFT IN	RETAIL LOW	RETAIL HIGH
		1963 BOATS														
19	7	NOMAD NI			WD		IO	140							6000	6900
19	7	NOMAD NIC			WD		IO	100-140							6000	6900
19	7	NOMAD NIH			WD		IO	100-140							6000	6900
23	3	VOYAGER	HT		WD		IB	109-188							3100	3750
23	3	VOYAGER		CR	WD		IB	109-188							3100	3750
23	3	VOYAGER		RNBT	WD		IB	109-188							3100	3750
23	3	VOYAGER VI			WD		IO	100-140							8300	9550
23	3	VOYAGER VIC			WD		IO	100-140							8300	9550
23	3	VOYAGER VIH			WD		IO	100-140							8300	9550
		1962 BOATS														
17	4	MAGELLAN M18			WD		IO	80-100							3350	3900
19	6	ALL-SEAS A120			WD		IO	80-100							6150	7100
19	6	ALL-SEAS A1C20			WD		IO	80-100							6150	7100
19	6	ALL-SEAS A1H 20			WD		IO	80-100							6150	7100
19	6	ALL-SEAS AM			WD		IB	109-188							2300	2800
23	3	OCEANIC			WD		IO	80-100							8600	9850
23	3	OCEANIC C4			WD		IO	80-100							8600	9850
23	3	OCEANIC H4			WD		IO	80-100							8600	9850
23	3	OCEANIC OMC	HT	CR	WD		IB	109-188							3050	3650
23	3	OCEANIC OMC		RNBT	WD		IB	109-188							3050	3650
23	3	OCEANIC OMH	HT	RNBT	WD		IB	109-188							3050	3650
		1961 BOATS														
18	10	ALL-SEAS		RNBT	WD		IB	109		7	9		1	6	1800	2150
22	6	OCEANIC	HT		WD		IB	109		7	11		1	6	2700	3150
22	6	OCEANIC		CR	WD		IB	199		7	11		1	6	2850	3300
22	6	OCEANIC		RNBT	WD		IB	109		7	11		1	6	2750	3200
22	6	OCEANIC	HT	RNBT	WD		OB			7	11				1900	2250
		1937 BOATS														
24			SLP	SAIL	WD	KL									8300	9550
		1931 BOATS														
17	6			CR	WD		OB			5					3100	3600
17	6			RNBT	WD		VD		GRAY						**	**

PENNANT CLASS SLOOPS INC

Call 1-800-327-6929 for BUC Personalized Evaluation Service
Or, for 1960 to 1962 boats, sign onto www.BUCValuPro.com

PENOBSCOT BOAT WORKS

ROCKPORT ME 04856 COAST GUARD MFG ID- PBW See inside cover to adjust price for area

LOA FT	LOA IN	NAME AND/ OR MODEL	TOP/ RIG	BOAT TYPE	HULL MTL	HULL TP	ENGINE TP	ENGINE # HP	ENGINE MFG	BEAM FT	BEAM IN	WGT LBS	DRAFT FT	DRAFT IN	RETAIL LOW	RETAIL HIGH
		1982 BOATS														
25	9	LUBEC BOAT	SLP	SA/CR	WD	KL	IB	26D	PISC	8	9	11500	4		22400	24900
30	9	SCHEEL 30	CUT	SA/RC	WD	KL	IB	15	OMC	8		7400	3	10	15900	18100
32	9	QUODDY-PILOT	SLP	SA/CR	WD	KL	IB	25D	WEST	10	6	22500	5		48200	53000
44	10	PINKY SCHOONER	SCH	SA/CR	WD	KL	IB	45D	WEST	13	5	45000	6	3	82100	90200
		1981 BOATS														
25	9	LUBEC BOAT GAFF RIG	SLP	SAIL	P/C	KL	IB	26D	PISC	8	8	11500	4		21600	24000
30	9	SCHEEL 30	SLP	SAIL	P/M	KL	SD	15	OMC	8		7400	3	10	15100	17200
32	9	QUODDY-PILOT GAFF RG	SLP	SAIL	P/C	KL	IB	25D	WEST	10	6	22500	5		45600	50100
53	9	PINKY GAFF RIG	SCH	SAIL	P/C	KL	IB	45D	WEST	13	5	45000	6	3	106000	116500
		1980 BOATS														
25	9	LUBEC BOAT GAFF RIG	SLP	SAIL	P/C	KL	IB	26D	PISC	8	8	11500	4		20600	22800
30	9	SCHEEL 30	SLP	SAIL	P/M	KL	SD	15	OMC	8		7400	3	10	14400	16300
32	9	QUODDY-PILOT GAFF RG	SLP	SAIL	P/C	KL	IB	25D	WEST	10	6	22500	5		42900	47700
53	9	PINKY GAFF RIG	SCH	SAIL	P/C	KL	IB	45D	WEST	13	5	45000	6	3	101000	111000
		1977 BOATS														
53	9	PINKY SCHOONER	SCH	SA/CR	P/C	KL	IB	50D	WEST	13	5	45000	6	3	88800	97600
		1976 BOATS														
25	9	LUBEC BOAT	GAF	SAIL	P/C	KL	IB	20D	PISC	8	9	11500	4		16900	19200
37	1	QUODDY-PILOT	GAF	SAIL	P/C	KL	IB	25D	WEST	10	6	21120	5		34700	38500
45		PINKY SCHOONER	SCH	SAIL	P/C	KL	IB	50D	WEST	13		45000	6	6	63000	69300
		1975 BOATS														
31	7	QUODDY-PILOT	GAF	SAIL	WD	KL	IB	20D	WEST	10	6	21120	5		34000	37700
		1967 BOATS														
36		OFFSHORE CRUISER		OFF	WD		IB	100		11	6		3		28700	31900
40		CHB CRUISER		CR	WD		IB	140		13			3	9	51400	56500
40		TRAWLER YT		TRWL	WD		IB	140		13			3	9	63800	70100
42		50-FATHOM LONG-RANGE		CR	WD		IB	140		13	6		4		54900	60400
		1966 BOATS														
32		OFFSHORE		CR	WD	RB	IB	125		10	6		3	3	18900	21000
36		CHB		CR	WD	RB	IB	110		11			3	6	35400	39300
38		CC		CR	WD	RB	IB	110		12			3	9	43000	47800
		1965 BOATS														
36		PENBO		HB	WD		IB			12			3	6	16800	19100
		1961 BOATS														
16	10	SEA-O-RAMIC		RNBT	L/P		OB			6	7	740			2200	2550
19	8	CRUISE-O-RAMIC		CR	L/P		OB			7	4	1000			3150	3650
19	8	SEA-O-RAMIC		UTL	L/P		OB			7	4	900			2400	2800
		1960 BOATS														
19	3	CRUISE-O-RAMIC	HT	CR	L/P	DV	OB			7	3	1100			3400	3950
19	3	SEA-O-RAMIC 19		RNBT	L/P	DV	OB			7	3	990			3100	3600
		1959 BOATS														
16	9	SEA-O-RAMIC		RNBT	L/P		OB			6	4	790			2350	2750
19	3	CRUISE-O-RAMIC	HT	CR	L/P		OB			7		1010			3200	3700
19	3	SEA-O-RAMIC		RNBT	L/P		OB			7		970			3100	3600
		1953 BOATS														
22		BIG-WATER	OP	EXP	WD	RB	IB	90							3900	4550
24		BIG-WATER	OP	EXP	WD	RB	IB	90							4800	5500
26				SF	WD		IB								**	**
27			SLP	MS	WD		IB								**	**
31			SLP	MS	WD		IB								10600	12000
35			SLP	MS	WD		IB								24700	27400

PENRYN BOATBUILDING & ENG LTD

Call 1-800-327-6929 for BUC Personalized Evaluation Service
Or, for 1967 boats, sign onto www.BUCValuPro.com

PEQUOD OF MAINE

YORK ME 03909 COAST GUARD MFG ID- PYC See inside cover to adjust price for area

LOA FT	LOA IN	NAME AND/ OR MODEL	TOP/ RIG	BOAT TYPE	HULL MTL	HULL TP	ENGINE TP	ENGINE # HP	ENGINE MFG	BEAM FT	BEAM IN	WGT LBS	DRAFT FT	DRAFT IN	RETAIL LOW	RETAIL HIGH
		1982 BOATS														
34	4	MKII SEDAN	FB	SDN	FBG	SV	IB	T235D		12					37500	41600
34	4	NEW-ENGLANDER	FB	EXP	FBG	SV	IB	270D		12					36700	40700
34	4	PEQUOD 34	FB	SPTCR	FBG	SV	IB	T270	CRUS	12		16000	2	8	29600	32900
34	4	PEQUOD 34	FB	SPTCR	FBG	SV	IB	T225D	CRUS	12		16000	2	8	37200	41300
34	4	SPORT FISHERMAN	FB	SF	FBG	SV	IB	T240D		12					40800	45300
34	4	SPORT SEDAN	FB	SDN	FBG	SV	IB	T210D		12					36700	40800
		1981 BOATS														
34	4	MK II SEDAN	FB	SDN	FBG	SV	IB	T235D	VLVO	12		19600			41900	46600
34	4	NEW-ENGLANDER		EXP	FBG	SV	IB	270D		12					35200	39100
34	4	SPORT FISHERMAN		SF	FBG	SV	IB	T240D		12					39100	43400
34	4	SPORT SEDAN	FB	SDN	FBG	SV	IB	T270	CRUS	12		16600	2	8	29700	33000
34	4	SPORT SEDAN	FB	SDN	FBG	SV	IB	T210D	CRUS	12		19000	2	8	40900	45400
		1980 BOATS														
34	4	MKII SEDAN	FB	SDN	FBG	SV	IB	T270-T350		12		16600	2	8	28700	31900
34	4	MKII SEDAN	FB	SDN	FBG	SV	IB	T235D	VLVO	12		19600	2	8	40400	44900
34	4	NEW-ENGLANDER	FB	SDN	FBG	SV	IB	350	CRUS	12		16000	2	8	26800	29700
34	4	NEW-ENGLANDER	FB	SDN	FBG	SV	IB	289D	VLVO	12		19000	2	8	37200	41300
34	4	NEW-ENGLANDER	FB	SDN	FBG	SV	IB	T270D	CUM	12		14309	2	8	35900	39900
34	4	PEQUOD 34		CR	FBG	SV	IB	T225		12		16000			26600	29500
34	4	PEQUOD 34		CR	FBG	SV	IB	T200D		12		18000			37200	41300
34	4	SPORT FISHERMAN	FB	SF	FBG	SV	IB	T350	CRUS	12		16600	2	8	28200	31400
34	4	SPORT FISHERMAN	FB	SF	FBG	SV	IB	T235D	VLVO	12		19600	2	8	38900	43200
34	4	SPORT SEDAN	FB	SDN	FBG	SV	IB	T270-T350		12		16600	2	8	28300	31400
34	4	SPORT SEDAN	FB	SDN	FBG	SV	IB	T210D	REN	12		19000	2	8	39300	43700
		1979 BOATS														
34	4	PEQUOD 34		SDN	FBG	SV	IB	T225-T330		12		13000			24700	29100
		1978 BOATS														
34	4	PEQUOD 34	HT	SDN	FBG	SV	VD	T225		12		13000	2	8	23700	26400
34	4	PEQUOD 34	HT	SDN	FBG	SV	VD	T200D	CHRY	12		13000	2	8	30200	33500
34	4	PEQUOD 34	FB	SDN	FBG	SV	VD	T225		12		13000	2	8	23700	26400
34	4	PEQUOD 34	FB	SDN	FBG	SV	VD	T200D	CHRY	12		13000	2	8	30200	33500
		1977 BOATS														
34	4	PEQUOD 34	HT	SDN	FBG	SV	VD	T220		12		13000	2	8	22700	25200
34	4	PEQUOD 34	HT	SDN	FBG	SV	VD	T160D-T200D		12		13000	2	8	28200	32300
34	4	PEQUOD 34	FB	SDN	FBG	SV	VD	T220		12		13000	2	8	22700	25200
34	4	PEQUOD 34	FB	SDN	FBG	SV	VD	T160D-T200D		12		13000	2	8	28300	32300
		1976 BOATS														
34	4	PEQUOD 34	HT	SDN	FBG	SV	IB	T225		12		13000	2	8	21900	24300
		1975 BOATS														
34	4	PEQUOD 34	HT	SDN	FBG	SV	IB	T225		12		13000	2	8	21000	23300
		1974 BOATS														
34	4	PEQUOD 34 SPORT		SDN	FBG	SV	IB	T225	CHRY	12		13000	2	8	20100	22400
34	4	PEQUOD 34 SPORT		SDN	FBG	SV	IB	T160D	PERK	12		13000	2	8	25600	28500

CONTINUED ON NEXT PAGE

LOA NAME AND/	TOP/ BOAT	-HULL-	----ENGINE---	BEAM	WGT	DRAFT	RETAIL	RETAIL
FT IN OR MODEL	RIG TYPE	MTL TP TP	# HP MFG	FT IN	LBS	FT IN	LOW	HIGH

-------------------- 1973 **BOATS** ---
| 33 2 PEQUOD 33 | SDN | P/M SV IB | T225 CHRY | 11 11 | 11500 | 2 7 | 17200 | 19600 |
| 34 2 PEQUOD 34 | SF | FBG SV IB | T225 CHRY | 11 11 | 12500 | 2 8 | 18200 | 20200 |

-------------------- 1971 **BOATS** ---
| 33 PEQUOD | WD | IB | T195 PALM | | | | 13700 | 15500 |

PEREGRIN MRNE DESIGN LTD
COAST GUARD MFG ID- ZPE

Call 1-800-327-6929 for BUC Personalized Evaluation Service
Or, for 1977 to 1978 boats, sign onto www.BUCValuPro.com

PERFECTION INDUSTRIES
COAST GUARD MFG ID- PFT

Call 1-800-327-6929 for BUC Personalized Evaluation Service
Or, for 1982 boats, sign onto www.BUCValuPro.com

PERFORMANCE BOATS OF AMER

Call 1-800-327-6929 for BUC Personalized Evaluation Service
Or, for 1973 boats, sign onto www.BUCValuPro.com

PERFORMANCE CRUISING INC
TELSTAR   See inside cover to adjust price for area
ANNAPOLIS MD 21403

For more recent years, see the BUC Used Boat Price Guide, Volume 1 or Volume 2

LOA NAME AND/	TOP/ BOAT	-HULL-	----ENGINE---	BEAM	WGT	DRAFT	RETAIL	RETAIL
FT IN OR MODEL	RIG TYPE	MTL TP TP	# HP MFG	FT IN	LBS	FT IN	LOW	HIGH

-------------------- 1982 **BOATS** ---
| 30 6 GEMINI 31 | SLP SA/RC FBG | | | 14 | 6520 | 1 6 | 12900 | 14700 |

PERFORMANCE MARINE
COAST GUARD MFG ID- PFJ

Call 1-800-327-6929 for BUC Personalized Evaluation Service
Or, for 1975 to 1979 boats, sign onto www.BUCValuPro.com

PERFORMANCE MARINE INC

Call 1-800-327-6929 for BUC Personalized Evaluation Service
Or, for 1970 to 1972 boats, sign onto www.BUCValuPro.com

PERFORMER
AN ALLFIN INDUSTRIES COMPANY   See inside cover to adjust price for area
FT LAUDERDALE FL 33314   COAST GUARD MFG ID- PER

LOA NAME AND/	TOP/ BOAT	-HULL-	----ENGINE---	BEAM	WGT	DRAFT	RETAIL	RETAIL
FT IN OR MODEL	RIG TYPE	MTL TP TP	# HP MFG	FT IN	LBS	FT IN	LOW	HIGH

-------------------- 1981 **BOATS** ---
28 3 CENTER CONSOLE CUDDY OP	CTRCN FBG DV IO	330 MRCR 10	1	8000	2 6	22200	24700
28 3 FISHER CRUISER A	CR	FBG DV IO	330 MRCR 10	1	8000	2 6	21000	22300
IB 350 CRUS 23600	26300, IO	370 MRCR	20800 23200, IO	200D S&S			23000	25500
IB 200D S&S 29700	33100, IO	210D REN	23300 25800, IB	210D-235D			30100	33900
IO 240D REN 23900	26600, IB	240D-260D	31000 35300, IB	T270 CRUS			25600	28400
28 3 FISHER CRUISER B	CR	FBG DV IO	330 MRCR 10	1	8000	2 6	21000	23400
IB 350 CRUS 24900	27600, IO	370 MRCR	21700 24200, IO	200D S&S			23700	26300
IB 200D S&S 30800	34200, IO	210D REN	24000 26700, IB	210D-235D			31200	35100
IO 240D REN 24700	27400, IB	240D-260D	32000 36500, IB	T270 CRUS			27000	30000
28 3 FISHER CRUISER C	CR	FBG DV IO	330 MRCR 10	1	8000	2 6	22000	24500
IB 350 CRUS 26100	29000, IO	370 MRCR	22600 25100, IO	200D S&S			24400	27200
IB 200D S&S 31800	35400, IO	210D REN	24800 27600, IB	210D-235D			32300	36200
IO 240D REN 25400	28300, IB	240D-260D	33100 37600, IB	T270 CRUS			28400	31500
28 3 OPEN FISHERMAN OP	CTRCN FBG DV IB	T270 CRUS 10	1	8000	2 6	26600	29600
IO T330 MRCR 25800	28700, IB	T350 CRUS	28700 31900, IO	T370 MRCR			30100	30200
IO T200D S&S 35100	39000, IB	T200D S&S	36900 41000, IO	T210D REN			35900	39900
IBT210D-T235D 37700	42600, IO	T240D REN	37300 41500, IB	T240D REN			39200	43600
28 3 TOURNAMENT FISHERMAN OP	SF	FBG DV IB	T270 CRUS 10	1	9000	2 6	28300	31500
IO T330 MRCR 29100	32300, IB	T350 CRUS	30000 33300, IO	T370 MRCR			30500	33900
IO T200D S&S 37600	41800, IB	T200D S&S	39700 44100, IO	T210D REN			38400	42700
IBT210D-T235D 40500	45600, IO	T240D REN	39500 43900, IBT240D-T260D				42000	48600
32 COBRA 10 METER	OP	CTRCN FBG DV OB	8				17400	19800
32 COBRA 10 METER	OP	CTRCN FBG DV IO	330 MRCR 8			2 6	27400	30500
IB 350 CRUS 31200	34700, IO	370 MRCR	28000 31100, IB	240D-286D			32200	37500
IO T330-T370 31600	36300							
32 COBRA 10 METER	OP	SPTCR FBG DV OB	8				18800	20900
32 COBRA 10 METER	OP	SPTCR FBG DV IO	T330-T370 8			2 6	30000	34300
32 COBRA 10 METER	OP	SPTCR FBG DV IOT200D-T240D	8			2 6	33200	38600
32 CONQUEST	FB	SF	FBG IO	11			2 6	**	**
32 RAISED BRIDGE FSH	OP	SF	FBG SV IO	11			2 6	**	**
32 RAISED BRIDGE FSH	TT	SF	FBG SV IO	11			2 6	**	**
32 TOURNAMENT FISHERMAN OP	SF	FBG SV IO	11			2 6	**	**
32 TOURNAMENT FISHERMAN TT	SF	FBG SV IO	11			2 6	**	**
36 LIGHT TACKLE FISH	OP	CTRCN FBG DV OB	9	3	11000	2 10	19700	21800
36 PERFORMER 36	OP	CTRCN FBG DV IO	T330 MRCR	9	3 11000	2 10	39300	43600
IO T370 MRCR 40500	45000, IO	T210D REN	46200 50800, IO	T240D REN			47100	51700
36 PERFORMER 36 SPORT	OP	SPTCR FBG DV IO	T330 MRCR	9	3 11000	2 10	32500	36100
IO T370 MRCR 34000	37800, IO	T210D REN	39300 43700, IO	T240D REN			40300	44800
IO R330 MRCR 38500	42700, IO	R370 MRCR	40600 45200					
40 4 SPORT	OP	SPTCR FBG DV IO	T240D REN	9	3 12000	2 10	63500	69700
IO R370 MRCR 55100	60600, IO	R370 MRCR	58500 64300, IO	R210D REN			62900	69100
IO R240D REN 68900	75700							
40 4 SPORT CRUISER	OP	SPTCR FBG DV IO	T240D REN	9	3 11000	2 10	61800	67900
IB R330 MRCR 77300	84900, IO	R370 MRCR	56600 62200, IO	R210D REN			67600	74300
IO R240D REN 67000	73700							

-------------------- 1980 **BOATS** ---
23 7 CONVERTIBLE	RNBT	FBG DV OB	8				6600	7600
23 7 FISHERMAN	FSH	FBG DV OB	8				6700	7700
23 7 PERFORMER 24 CONV	RNBT	FBG DV IB	260	8			9100	10400
23 7 PERFORMER 24 CONV	RNBT	FBG DV IB	270	8			10700	12200
23 7 PERFORMER 24 FSH	FSH	FBG DV IB	260	8			10600	12000
23 7 PERFORMER 24 FSH	FSH	FBG DV IB	270	8			11100	12600
23 7 PERFORMER 24 SPT	RNBT	FBG DV IB	260	8			9800	11100
23 7 PERFORMER 24 SPT	RNBT	FBG DV IB	270	8			11600	13100
28 3 CENTER CONSOLE CUDDY OP	CTRCN FBG DV IO	330 MRCR 10	1	8000	2 6	22000	24500
IB 350 CRUS 23800	26500, IO	370 MRCR	22700 25300, IO	200D S&S			24300	32600
IB 200D S&S 29700	33300, IO	210D REN	29200 32500, IB	210D-235D			30000	33800
IO 240D REN 30000	33300, IB	240D-260D	30900 34300, IB	T270 CRUS			26300	29100
28 3 FISHER CRUISER A	CR	FBG DV IO	330 MRCR 10	1	8000	2 6	19900	22200
IB 350 CRUS 22200	25200, IO	370 MRCR	20600 22900, IO	200D S&S			22800	25300
IB 200D S&S 28600	31800, IO	210D REN	23000 25600, IB	210D-235D			23000	33600
IO 240D REN 26300	26300, IB	240D-260D	29800 34000, IB	T270 CRUS			24500	27200
28 3 FISHER CRUISER B	CR	FBG DV IO	330 MRCR 10	1	8000	2 6	20800	23200
IB 350 CRUS 23800	26500, IO	370 MRCR	21500 23900, IO	200D S&S			23500	26100
IB 200D S&S 29600	32900, IO	210D REN	23800 26400, IB	210D-235D			30000	33700
IO 240D REN 24400	27200, IB	240D-260D	30800 35100, IB	T270 CRUS			25800	28700
28 3 FISHER CRUISER C	CR	FBG DV IO	370 MRCR 10	1	8000	2 6	21800	24200
IB 350 CRUS 25000	27800, IO	370 MRCR	22400 24900, IO	200D S&S			24800	26900
IB 200D S&S 30600	34000, IO	210D REN	24600 27300, IB	210D-235D			31100	34900
IO 240D REN 25200	28000, IB	240D-260D	31900 36200, IB	T270 CRUS			28400	30200
28 3 OPEN FISHERMAN	CTRCN FBG DV OB	10	1				11700	13200
28 3 OPEN FISHERMAN	OP	CTRCN FBG DV IB	T270 CRUS 10	1	8000	2 6	25500	28300
IO T330 MRCR 25800	28700, IB	T350 CRUS	27800 30600, IO	T370 MRCR			29000	29900
IO T200D S&S 34700	38600, IB	T200D S&S	35500 39400, IO	T210D REN			35300	39300
IBT210D-T235D 36800	41000, IO	T240D REN	36700 40800, IB	T240D REN			37700	42100
28 3 TOURNAMENT FISHERMAN OP	SF	FBG DV IB	T270 CRUS 10	1	9000	2 6	27200	30200
IO T330 MRCR 28800	32000, IB	T350 CRUS	28700 31900, IO	T370 MRCR			30300	33600
IO T200D S&S 36900	41000, IB	T200D S&S	38200 42400, IO	T210D REN			37700	41900
IBT210D-T235D 38900	43900, IO	T240D REN	39100 43400, IBT240D-T260D				40400	46800
32 COBRA 10 METER	OP	CTRCN FBG DV OB	8				17100	19400
32 COBRA 10 METER	OP	CTRCN FBG DV IO	330 MRCR 8			2 6	27200	30200
IB 350 CRUS 29900	33900, IO	370 MRCR	27700 30800, IB	240D-286D			31000	36100
IO T330-T370 31300	35900							

```
LOA  NAME AND/      TOP/ BOAT -HULL- ----ENGINE--- BEAM  WGT  DRAFT RETAIL RETAIL
FT IN OR MODEL      RIG TYPE MTL TP TP # HP  MFG  FT IN LBS  FT IN  LOW   HIGH
----------------------- 1980 BOATS ---------------------------------------------
32  COBRA 10 METER        OP SPTCR FBG DV OB         8                       18400 20400
32  COBRA 10 METER        OP SPTCR FBG DV IO T330-T370  8            2  6    29700 34000
32  COBRA 10 METER        OP SPTCR FBG DV IOT200D-T240D 8            2  6    32900 38200
36  LIGHT TACKLE FISH     OP CTRCN FBG DV OB         9 3 11000       2 10    19200 21300
36  PERFORMER 36          OP SPTCR FBG DV IO T330   MRCR 9 3 11000   2 10    38900 43200
    IO T370   MRCR  40100 44600, IO T210D REN  45800 50300, IO T240D REN  46600 51200

36  PERFORMER 36 SPORT    OP SPTCR FBG DV IO T330   MRCR 9 3 11000   2 10    32100 35700
    IO T370   MRCR  33600 37400, IO T210D REN  39000 43300, IO T240D REN  39900 44300
    IO R330   MRCR  38000 42300, IO R370  MRCR  40200 44700

36  TOURNAMENT FISHERMAN OP SF  FBG DV IB T350  CRUS 11 9 11000      2 10    44800 49700
    IB T200D S&S   48400 53200, IB T235D VLVO 49200 54000, IB T240D REN  50200 55200
    IB T260D CAT   52100 57300, IB T260D GM   51000 56100, IB T277D S&S  51300 56400
    IB T286D VLVO  51100 56200

40  4 SPORT               OP SPTCR FBG DV IO T240D  REN  9 3 12000   2 10    62800 69100
    IO R330   MRCR  54200 59600, IO R370  MRCR  57500 63200, IO R210D REN  62000 68200
    IO R240D REN   68000 74700

40  4 SPORT CRUISER       OP SPTCR FBG DV IO T240D  REN  9 3 11000   2 10    61100 67200
    IB R330   MRCR  73800 81100, IO R370  MRCR  55600 61100, IO R210D REN  66600 73200
    IO R240D REN   66100 72600
----------------------- 1979 BOATS ---------------------------------------------
28  3 CHARTER FISHERMAN   OP SF  FBG DV IO T260   MRCR 10 1 8500     2  6    26100 29000
    IB T270   CRUS  25400 28200, IO T330   MRCR  28000 31100, IB T350  CRUS  26900 29900
    IO T370   MRCR  29500 32800, IBT210D-T240D  36100 41700

28  3 CHARTER FISHERMAN   TT SF  FBG DV IO T260   MRCR 10 1 8500     2  6    26200 29100
    IB T270   CRUS  25400 28200, IO T330   MRCR  28100 31200, IB T350  CRUS  26900 29900
    IO T370   MRCR  29500 32800, IBT210D-T240D  36100 41700

28  3 OPEN FISHERMAN      OP CTRCN FBG DV IO T260   MRCR 10 1 8000   2  6    23700 26300
    IB T270   CRUS  24800 27500, IO T330   MRCR  25500 28300, IB T350  CRUS  26400 29300
    IO T370   MRCR  26800 29800, IBT210D-T240D  34900 40400

28  3 OPEN FISHERMAN      TT CTRCN FBG DV IO T260   MRCR 10 1 8000   2  6    23700 26300
    IB T270   CRUS  24800 27500, IO T330   MRCR  25500 28300, IB T350  CRUS  26400 29300
    IO T370   MRCR  26800 29800, IBT210D-T240D  34900 40400

28  3 SPORT CRUISER       OP SPTCR FBG DV IO T260-T330 10 1 8500     2  6    23000 27500
28  3 SPORT CRUISER       OP SPTCR FBG DV IO T370  MRCR 10 1 8500    2  6    26000 28900
28  3 SPORT CRUISER       TT SPTCR FBG DV IO T260-T330 10 1 8500     2  6    23000 27500
28  3 SPORT CRUISER       TT SPTCR FBG DV IO T370  MRCR 10 1 8500    2  6    26000 28900
28  3 TOURNAMENT FISHERMAN OP SF  FBG DV IB T270-T350 10 1 9000      2  6    26000 30600
28  3 TOURNAMENT FISHERMAN OP SF  FBG DV IBT210D-T240D 10 1 9000     2  6    37500 43200
28  3 TOURNAMENT FISHERMAN TT SF  FBG DV IB T270-T350 10 1 9000      2  6    26000 30600
28  3 TOURNAMENT FISHERMAN TT SF  FBG DV IBT210D-T240D 10 1 9000     2  6    37500 43200
36  PERFORMER 36          OP SPTCR FBG DV IO T330   MRCR 9 3 11000   3  2    35400 39400
36  PERFORMER 36          OP SPTCR FBG DV IO T350   CRUS 9 3 10000   3  2    49200 54100
36  PERFORMER 36          OP SPTCR FBG DV IO T370   MRCR 9 3 11000   3  2    36800 40900

40  4 SPORT               OP SPTCR FBG DV IO T330   MRCR 9 3 11000   2  8    51100 56200
    IO T370   MRCR  55200 60700, IO R330  MRCR  54100 59400, IO R370  MRCR  57000 62600

40  4 SPORT CRUISER       OP SPTCR FBG DV IB T350  CRUS 9 3 11000    2  8    71400 78400
40  4 TOURNAMENT FISHERMAN OP SF  FBG DV IB T350  CRUS 9 3 11000     2  8    69600 76400
----------------------- 1978 BOATS ---------------------------------------------
17  4 BABY-PERFORMER      RNBT FBG  OB            6 10                       2050  2450
28  3 PERFORMER 28        OP SPTCR FBG DV IO T260-T330 10 1 8500     2  6    23200 27600
28  3 PERFORMER 28        OP SPTCR FBG DV IO T370  MRCR 10 1 8500    2  6    26100 29000
28  3 TOURNAMENT FISHERMAN OP CTRCN FBG DV IB T270-T350 10 1 8500    2  6    24400 28700
28  3 TOURNAMENT FISHERMAN OP CTRCN FBG DV IBT210D-T210D 10 1 8500   2  6    34300 38700
28  3 TOURNAMENT FISHERMAN TT CTRCN FBG DV IB T270-T350 10 1 8500    2  6    24400 28700
28  3 TOURNAMENT FISHERMAN TT CTRCN FBG DV IBT197D-T210D 10 1 8500   2  6    34300 38700
36  FISHER CRUISER           SF  FBG DV IB T       9 3 12000                 **    **
40  4 SPORT               OP SPTCR FBG DV IO T330   MRCR 9 3 10700   2  8    50600 55700
    IO T370   MRCR  53000 58300, IO R330  MRCR  51400 56500, IO R370  MRCR  54300 59700
----------------------- 1977 BOATS ---------------------------------------------
28  3 PERFORMER 28        OP SPTCR FBG DV IO T250-T330 10 1 9500     2  6    24500 29300
28  3 TOURNAMENT FISHERMAN OP SF  FBG DV IB T270-T350 10 1 7500      2  6    22200 26300
28  3 TOURNAMENT FISHERMAN OP SF  FBG DV IBT197D-T210D 10 1 7500     2  6    30500 34600
28  3 TOURNAMENT FISHERMAN TT SF  FBG DV IB T270-T350 10 1 7500      2  6    22200 26300
28  3 TOURNAMENT FISHERMAN TT SF  FBG DV IBT197D-T210D 10 1 7500     2  6    30500 34600
40  4 404 FISHER/CRUISER  OP CR  FBG DV IO T330   MRCR 9 3 14000     3  2    57300 62900
    IB T350   CRUS  73200 80500, IO T370   MRCR  59200 65000, IO T390  MRCR  60500 66500
    IB T400   MRCR  74100 81400, IB T197D GM   78800 86600, IB T210D REN  79300 87100

40  4 404 FISHER/CRUISER  TT CR  FBG DV IO T330   MRCR 9 3 14000            58100 63900
    IB T350   CRUS  73600 80900, IO T370   MRCR  60300 66300, IO T390  MRCR  61700 67800
    IB T400   MRCR  74500 81900, IB T197D GM   78600 86400, IB T210D REN  79100 86900

40  4 SPORT               OP SPTCR FBG DV IO T370   MRCR 9 3 12000          55900 61400
40  4 SPORT               OP SPTCR FBG DV IO R280   MRCR 9 3 12000          51600 56700
40  4 SPORT               OP SPTCR FBG DV IO R330   MRCR 9 3 12000          54300 59700
----------------------- 1976 BOATS ---------------------------------------------
23  6 PERFORMER           ST CUD FBG    IB           4000                    **    **
23  6 PERFORMER           ST CUD FBG    IB    D      4000                    **    **
23  6 PERFORMER           ST CUD FBG    IO T         4000                    **    **
23  6 PERFORMER           ST CUD FBG DV IO           4000                    **    **
----------------------- 1975 BOATS ---------------------------------------------
23  6 PERFORMER 24 CONV   OP CUD FBG DV IO 188-190   8   4000        2  8    10400 11800
    IO  225   OMC  10500 11900, IO 225   VLVO 10800 12300, IB 225   OMC  9250 10500
    VD  225   OMC   9250 10500, IO 233   MRCR 10600 12000, IB 233   MRCR 9000 10200
    VD  233   MRCR  9000 10200, IO 235-280  10500 12500, IO 225D  14400 16300
    IO T140-T170   11500 13800

23  6 PERFORMER 24 HARDTOP HT SDN FBG DV IO 188-190  8   4000        2  8    10400 11800
    IO  225   OMC  10500 11900, IO 225   VLVO 10800 12300, IB 225   OMC  9250 10500
    VD  225   OMC   9250 10500, IO 233   MRCR 10600 12000, IB 233   MRCR 9000 10200
    VD  233   MRCR  9000 10200, IO 235-280  10500 12500, IO T140-T170  11500 13800

23  6 PERFORMER 24 HI-PERF OP RNBT FBG DV IO T225-T280 8             2  8    11100 13700
23  6 PERFORMER 24 HI-PERF OP RNBT FBG DV IO T300  CC 8              2  8    12600 14300
23  6 PERFORMER 24 SPTCR  OP OPFSH FBG DV IO 188-190  8   4000       2  8    11000 12500
    IO  225   OMC  11100 12600, IO 225   VLVO 11400 13000, IB 225   OMC  9250 10500
    VD  225   OMC   9250 10500, IO 233   MRCR 11200 12700, IB 233   MRCR 9000 10200
    VD  233   MRCR  9000 10200, IO 235-280  11100 13200, IO 225D  17500 19900
    IO T140-T170   12200 14500

28  3 PERFORMER 28        OP EXP FBG DV IO T233-T330 10 1 7500       2  8    23000 28200
28  3 PERFORMER 28        OP EXP FBG DV IO T350  MRCR 10 1 7500      2  8    26000 28900
----------------------- 1974 BOATS ---------------------------------------------
23  6 PERFORMER 24        FB  FBG    IO 188   MRCR 8    4700         1  4    11600 13200
    IO  225   OMC  11700 13300, IO 225D  15500 17600, IB T115  VLVO 10700 12200
    IO T165   MRCR  13800 15600

23  6 PERFORMER 24        CNV FBG    IO 165-225  8     3800         1  2    11600 13300
    IB 106D  VLVO  14500 16500, IO T140-T170  13600 16800, IO T115D 20000 22200

23  6 PERFORMER 24        HT SDN FBG    IO 188-225 8    4200         1  3    11200 12800
    IB T115  VLVO  10100 11400, IO T165-T170  13600 16100, IO T115D 18000 20000

23  6 PERFORMER 24        SPTCR FBG    IO 165-225  8    3800         1  2    10300 11900
23  6 PERFORMER 24        SPTCR FBG    IO T170  VLVO 8   4300        1  2    13300 14900
23  6 PERFORMER 24 TWNBD  FBG    IB T115  VLVO 8        4200         1 11     9400 10700
----------------------- 1973 BOATS ---------------------------------------------
23  6 PERFORMER 24        FBG    IO 188-235  8         3800                  10200 11800
23  6 PERFORMER 24        FBG    IO T130-T170 8        4300                  12800 15300
23  6 PERFORMER 24        HT FBG    IO 130-225                               10700 12200
23  6 PERFORMER 24        HT FBG    IO 107D VLVO                             12500 14200
23  6 PERFORMER 24        HT FBG    IO T140-T170                             11700 14000
```

PERFORMER BOAT CORP

Call 1-800-327-6929 for BUC Personalized Evaluation Service
Or, for 1960 to 1981 boats, sign onto www.BUCValuPro.com

PERKINS BOAT & MFG CO

Call 1-800-327-6929 for BUC Personalized Evaluation Service
Or, for 1965 boats, sign onto www.BUCValuPro.com

PERMA-CRAFT BOAT CORP

HOLLYWOOD FL 33020   COAST GUARD MFG ID- PLB See inside cover to adjust price for area

```
LOA  NAME AND/      TOP/ BOAT -HULL- ----ENGINE--- BEAM  WGT  DRAFT RETAIL RETAIL
FT IN OR MODEL      RIG TYPE MTL TP TP # HP  MFG  FT IN LBS  FT IN  LOW   HIGH
----------------------- 1979 BOATS ---------------------------------------------
25 10 MOTORSAILER 26  SLP MS  FBG KL IB 22D YAN  9 3 6500    3  2    13300 15100
25 10 TRAWLER 26      HT TRWL FBG DV IB 22D YAN  9 3 6500    3  2    11600 13200
```

PERMA-CRAFT BOAT CORP -CONTINUED See inside cover to adjust price for area

LOA FT	LOA IN	NAME AND/ OR MODEL	TOP/ RIG	BOAT TYPE	-HULL- MTL	-HULL- TP	ENGINE TP	ENGINE # HP	ENGINE MFG	BEAM FT	BEAM IN	WGT LBS	DRAFT FT	DRAFT IN	RETAIL LOW	RETAIL HIGH
		1979 BOATS														
29	1	TAHITI 29	SLP	SA/CR	FBG	KL	IB	22D	YAN	8	11	7800	3	8	17300	19600
29	1	TAHITI 30	SLP	SA/CR	FBG	KL	IB	25D	YAN	8	11	7800	3	8	17300	19700
32		DC CUSTOM	FB	DC	FBG	SV	IB	T160D	PERK	11			2	4	22000	24400
32		SEDAN CRUISER	HT	SDN	FBG	SV	IB	T160D	PERK	11		10500	2	4	29700	33000
32		SPORT EXPRESS	OP	EXP	FBG	SV	IB	T185D	PERK	11		9500	2	4	22900	25500
32		SPORTFISHERMAN	FB	SF	FBG	SV	IB	T185D	PERK	11		11500	2	4	23500	26100
		1978 BOATS														
25	10	MOTORSAILER 26	SLP	MS	FBG	KL	IB	50D	PERK	9	3	6500	3	2	12800	14600
25	10	TRAWLER 26	HT	TRWL	FBG	DV	IB	50D	PERK	9	3	6500	3	2	11700	13300
32		SEDAN CRUISER	HT	SDN	FBG	SV	IB	160D	PERK	11		10500	2	4	25400	28200
		IB 225D CAT 26700 29700, IB T225 23700 26300, IB T225D CAT													31100	34600
32		SPORT EXPRESS	OP	EXP	FBG	SV	IB	160D	PERK	11		9500	2	4	20200	22500
		IB 225D CAT 20600 22900, IB T225 18500 20500, IB T225D CAT													23100	25700
32		SPORTFISHERMAN	FB	SF	FBG	SV	IB	160D	PERK	11		11500	2	4	21600	24000
		IB 225D CAT 21500 23900, IB T225 19000 21100, IB T225D CAT													23500	26100
		1977 BOATS														
25	10	MOTORSAILER 26	SLP	MS	FBG	KL	IB	50D	PERK	9	3	7500	3	2	14400	16400
25	10	TRAWLER 26	HT	TRWL	FBG	DV	IB	50D	PERK	9	3	7200	3	2	12400	14100
32		SEDAN CRUISER	HT	SDN	FBG	SV	IB	225D	CAT	11		10500	2	4	25700	28500
32		SEDAN CRUISER	HT	SDN	FBG	SV	IB	T225	CHRY	11		10500	2	4	22900	25400
32		SEDAN CRUISER	HT	SDN	FBG	SV	IB	T160D-T225D		11		10500	2	4	27500	33300
32		SPORT EXPRESS	OP	EXP	FBG	SV	IB	225D	CAT	11		9500	2	4	20200	22400
32		SPORT EXPRESS	OP	EXP	FBG	SV	IB	T225	CHRY	11		9500	2	4	17300	19700
32		SPORT EXPRESS	OP	EXP	FBG	SV	IB	T160D-T225D		11		9500	2	4	21000	24700
32		SPORTFISHERMAN	FB	SF	FBG	SV	IB	225D	CAT	11		11500	2	4	20700	23000
32		SPORTFISHERMAN	FB	SF	FBG	SV	IB	T225	CHRY	11		11500	2	4	18200	20200
32		SPORTFISHERMAN	FB	SF	FBG	SV	IB	T160D-T225D		11		11500	2	4	21700	25100
		1976 BOATS														
25	10	MOTORSAILER 26	SLP	MS	FBG	KL	IB	50D	PERK	9	3	7500	3	2	14000	15900
25	10	TRAWLER 26	HT	TRWL	FBG	DV	IB	50D	PERK	9	3	7200	3	2	11900	13600
32		SEDAN CRUISER	HT	SDN	FBG	SV	IB	225D	CAT	11		10500	2	4	24700	27500
32		SEDAN CRUISER	HT	SDN	FBG	SV	IB	T225	CHRY	11		10500	2	4	22000	24400
32		SEDAN CRUISER	HT	SDN	FBG	SV	IB	T160D-T225D		11		10500	2	4	26500	32100
32		SPORT EXPRESS	ST	EXP	FBG	SV	IB	225D	CAT	11		9500	2	4	19500	21600
32		SPORT EXPRESS	ST	EXP	FBG	SV	IB	T225	CHRY	11		9500	2	4	16600	18900
32		SPORT EXPRESS	ST	EXP	FBG	SV	IB	T160D-T225D		11		9500	2	4	20300	24300
32		SPORTFISHERMAN	FB	SF	FBG	SV	IB	225D	CAT	11		11500	2	4	19900	22100
32		SPORTFISHERMAN	FB	SF	FBG	SV	IB	T225	CHRY	11		11500	2	4	17100	19400
32		SPORTFISHERMAN	FB	SF	FBG	SV	IB	T160D-T225D		11		11500	2	4	20900	24700
		1975 BOATS														
25	10		SLP	MS	FBG	KL	IB	45D- 50D		9	3	10000	2	3	19000	21200
25	10		HT	TRWL	FBG	DV	IB	45D- 50D		9	3	10000	2	10	15900	18300
32			OP	EXP	FBG	SV	IB	T225	CHRY	11		9500	2	4	16000	18100
32			HT	SDN	FBG	SV	IB	T225	CHRY	11		10000	2	4	18700	20800
32			FB	SDNSF	FBG	SV	IB	T225	CHRY	11		11500	2	4	16400	18600
		1974 BOATS														
25	10		SLP	MS	FBG	KL	IB	50D	PERK	9	3	10000	2	10	18600	20700
32			OP	EXP	FBG	SV	IB	T225	CHRY	11		9500	2	4	15300	17400
32			HT	SDN	FBG	SV	IB	T225	CHRY	11		10000	2	4	18100	20100
32			FB	SF	FBG	SV	IB	T225	CHRY	11		11000	2	4	15600	17800
32			FB	SF	FBG	SV	IB	T160D	PERK	11		12000	2	4	19900	22100
		1973 BOATS														
32			OP	EXP	FBG	SV	IB	T225	CHRY	11		9500	2	4	14700	16800
32			HT	SDN	FBG	SV	IB	T225	CHRY	11		10000	2	4	17000	19300
32			FB	SF	FBG	SV	IB	T225	CHRY	11		11000	2	4	15000	17100
32			FB	SF	FBG	SV	IB	T130D-T160D		11		12000	2	5	19200	21900
		1972 BOATS														
32			OP	EXP	FBG		IB	T225	CHRY	11		9500	2	4	14200	16100
32			HT	SDN	FBG	SV	IB	T225	CHRY	11		10000	2	4	16300	18500
32			FB	SF	FBG		IB	T225	CHRY	11		11000	2	4	14400	16400
32			FB	SF	FBG		IB	T130D-T170D		11		12000	2	5	18700	21500
32		SPORT	OP	SPTCR	FBG		IB	T225	CHRY	11		9000	2	4	14700	16700
32		SPORT	HT	SPTCR	FBG		IB	T225	CHRY	11		9800	2	4	14800	16800
		1971 BOATS														
32				EXP	FBG		IB	T225	CHRY	11		9500	2	4	13600	15500
32			HT	SDN	FBG	SV	IB	T225	CHRY	11		10000	2	4	15700	17800
32			FB	SF	FBG		IB	T225	CHRY	11		11000	2	4	13900	15800
32			FB	SF	FBG		IB	T130D-T170D		11		12000	2	5	18200	21000
32		SPORT	OP	CR	FBG		IB	T225	CHRY	11		9000	2	4	12100	13800
32		SPORT	HT	CR	FBG		IB	T225	CHRY	11		9800	2	4	12200	13900
32		SPORT	FB	CR	FBG		IB	T225	CHRY	11		10000	2	4	12300	13900
		1970 BOATS														
32				EXP	FBG	SV	IB	T225	CHRY	11		9500	2	4	13200	15000
32			HT	SDN	FBG	SV	IB	T225	CHRY	11		10000	2	4	15100	17200
32			FB	SF	FBG	SV	IB	T225	CHRY	11		11000	2	4	13400	15300
32		SPORT	OP	CR	FBG	SV	IB	T225	CHRY	11		9000	2	4	11700	13200
32		SPORT	HT	CR	FBG	SV	IB	T225	CHRY	11		9800	2	4	11800	13400
32		SPORT	FB	CR	FBG	SV	IB	T225	CHRY	11		10000	2	4	11800	13400
		1969 BOATS														
32				EXP	FBG	SV	IB	T225	CHRY	11		9500	2	4	12700	14400
32			HT	SDN	FBG	SV	IB	T225	CHRY	11		10000	2	4	14500	16500
32			FB	SF	FBG	SV	IB	T225	CHRY	11		11000	2	4	12900	14700
32		SPORT	OP	CR	FBG	SV	IB	T225	CHRY	11		9000	2	4	11200	12700
32		SPORT	HT	CR	FBG	SV	IB	T225	CHRY	11		9800	2	4	11300	12900
32		SPORT	FB	CR	FBG	SV	IB	T225	CHRY	11		10000	2	4	11400	12900
		1968 BOATS														
32				EXP	FBG		IB	T210		11		9500	2	4	12200	13900
32			HT	SDN	FBG		IB	T210		11		10000	2	4	13800	15700
32			FB	SF	FBG		IB	T210		11		11000	2	4	12400	14100
32		SPORT	OP	CR	FBG		IB	T210		11		9000	2	4	10800	12200
32		SPORT	HT	CR	FBG		IB	T210		11		9800	2	4	10900	12400
32		SPORT	FB	CR	FBG		IB	T210		11		10000	2	4	10900	12400
		1967 BOATS														
32				EXP	FBG		IB	T210		11		9500	2	4	11800	13400
32			HT	SDN	FBG		IB	T210		11		10000	2	4	13300	15100
32			FB	SF	FBG		IB	T210		11		11000	2	4	12000	13600
32		SPORT	OP	CR	FBG		IB	T210		11		9000	2	4	10400	11800
32		SPORT	HT	CR	FBG		IB	T210		11		9800	2	4	10500	11900
32		SPORT	FB	CR	FBG		IB	T210		11		10000	2	4	10500	12000
		1966 BOATS														
32			HT	EXP	FBG		IB	T210		11		9500	2	4	11300	12900
32			HT	SDN	FBG		IB	T210		11		10000	2	4	12800	14600
32			FB	SDN	FBG		IB	T210		11			2	4	13000	14800
32			HT	SF	FBG		IB	T210		11		11000	2	4	11500	13100
32			FB	SF	FBG		IB	T210		11			2	4	9700	11000
32		SPORT	ST	CR	FBG		IB	T210		11			2	4	10200	11600
32		SPORT	HT	CR	FBG		IB	T210		11		9800	2	4	10100	11500
		1965 BOATS														
32			HT	EXP	FBG		IB	T210		11		9500	2	4	11000	12500
32			HT	SDN	FBG		IB	T210		11		10000	2	4	12300	14000
32			FB	SF	FBG		IB	T210		11		11000	2	4	11200	12800
32		SPORT	ST	CR	FBG		IB	T210		11			2	4	9900	11300
32		SPORT	HT	CR	FBG		IB	T210		11		9800	2	4	9850	11200
		1964 BOATS														
32			HT	EXP	FBG		IB	T210		11		9500	2	4	10600	12100
32			HT	SDN	FBG		IB	T210		11		10000	2	4	12000	13600
32			FB	SF	FBG		IB	T210		11		11000	2	4	10800	12300
32		SPORT	ST	CR	FBG		IB	T210		11		9000	2	4	9400	10700
		1963 BOATS														
32			HT	EXP	FBG		IB	T210		11		9500	2	4	10200	11600
32			HT	SDN	FBG		IB	T210		11		10000	2	4	11600	13200
32			FB	SF	FBG		IB	T210		11		11000	2	4	10400	11900
32		SPORT	ST	CR	FBG		IB	T210		11		9000	2	4	9050	10300
		1962 BOATS														
32			FB	EXP	FBG		IB	225		11					9150	10400
32			FB	EXP	FBG		IB	T280		11					10400	11800
32			FB	SF	FBG		IB	225		11					7700	8850
32			FB	SF	FBG		IB	T280		11					8700	10000
32		ENCLOSED	HT	SDN	FBG		IB	225		11		10278			11500	13100
32		ENCLOSED	HT	SDN	FBG		IB	T280		11		10278			13400	15200
32		SPORT	ST	CR	FBG		IB	225		11		9571			8000	9200
32		SPORT	ST	CR	FBG		IB	T280		11		9571			9250	10500
		1961 BOATS														
30			ST	CR	FBG		IB	200		10	8	7811	2	4	7300	8400
30			ST	CR	FBG		IB	T240		10	8	7811	2	4	8400	9650
30			HT	CR	FBG		IB	200		10	8		2	4	7350	8450
30			HT	CR	FBG		IB	T240							8450	9750
30			FB	EXP	FBG		IB	200		10	8	7913	2	4	8100	9300
30			FB	EXP	FBG		IB	T240		10	8	7913	2	4	9400	10700
30			HT	SDN	FBG		IB	200		10	8	9037	2	4	8250	9500
30			HT	SDN	FBG		IB	T240		10	8	9037	2	4	9700	11000
30			FB	SF	FBG		IB	200		10	8	8393	2	4	7100	8150
30			FB	SF	FBG		IB	T240		10	8	8393	2	4	8100	9300
		1960 BOATS														
28		CABIN CRUISER		CBNCR	F/W		IB	140		9	3		2	6	6250	7200
28		CABIN CRUISER		CBNCR	F/W		IB	280		9	3		2	6	7150	8250
		1959 BOATS														
28		SEA-SHELL	FB	CR	FBG		IB			9	3				**	**
28		SEA-SHELL		FSH	FBG		IB			9	3				**	**
28		SEA-SHELL		SDN	FBG		IB			9	3				**	**

PETERSON BUILDERS INC
STURGEON BAY WI 54235   See inside cover to adjust price for area

LOA FT IN	NAME AND/ OR MODEL	TOP/ RIG	BOAT TYPE	-HULL- MTL TP	ENGINE TP # HP	MFG	BEAM FT IN	WGT LBS	DRAFT FT IN	RETAIL LOW	RETAIL HIGH
					1961 BOATS						
52 3	R52		CR	AL	IB 200		12 9		3 6	49700	54600
63	R63		CR	STL	IB 300		15 10		3 6	**	**
64	R65		CR	AL	IB 600		15 10		4 6	111500	122500
					1960 BOATS						
52 3	R52		CR	AL	IB 200		12 9		3 6	48700	53500
63	R63		CR	STL	IB 300		15 10		3 6	**	**
64 10	R65		CR	AL	IB 600		15 10		4 6	113000	124500

PETERSON CUSTOM YACHTS
Call 1-800-327-6929 for BUC Personalized Evaluation Service
Or, for 1973 to 1982 boats, sign onto www.BUCValuPro.com

PELLE PETTERSON A B
MOLNLYCKE MARIN A B
543600 ASKIM SWEDEN   COAST GUARD MFG ID- PFA   See inside cover to adjust price for area

SVEN-ERIK EKLUND
SAN DIEGO CA 92101

For more recent years, see the BUC Used Boat Price Guide, Volume 1 or Volume 2

LOA FT IN	NAME AND/ OR MODEL	TOP/ RIG	BOAT TYPE	-HULL- MTL TP	ENGINE TP # HP	MFG	BEAM FT IN	WGT LBS	DRAFT FT IN	RETAIL LOW	RETAIL HIGH
					1983 BOATS						
22 4	MAX 1	OP	CTRCN	FBG DV	IO	VLVO	8 3	2200	2 7	**	**
22 4	MAXI 68	SLP	SA/CR	FBG KL	OB		7 9	2970	4 2	6650	7650
25	MAXIM	ST	EXP	FBG DV	IO	61D VLVO	9 10	4620	2 7	15600	17700
25 3	MAXI 77	SLP	SA/CR	FBG KL	SD	8D VLVO	8 2	4400	4 9	12000	13600
26	MAX 11			FBG DV	IO	D VLVO				**	**
26 1	MAXI RACER	SLP	SA/RC	FBG	IB					11200	12700
26 2	MAXI 777	SLP	SA/CR	FBG KL	SD	8D VLVO	8 2	9400	5 1	27700	30800
27 7	MAXI 84	SLP	SA/CR	FBG KL	SD	13D VLVO	9 8	6600	4 11	19900	22100
27 11	FENIX DINETTE	SLP	SA/CR	FBG KL	SD	8D VLVO	9 4	6160	4 11	18800	20900
28 7	MAXI 87	SLP	SA/CR	FBG KL	IB	D	8 3	7700	4 10	24000	26600
32	MAXI 95	SLP	SA/CR	FBG KL	IB	D	10 7	9460	4 10	31200	34600
33	MAXI 100	SLP	SA/CR	FBG KL	IB					33700	37500
34 5	MAXI 100 P/S	SLP	SA/CR	FBG KL	SD	25D VLVO	10 7	9680	5 1	32900	36500
34 7	MIXER CRUSING	SLP	SA/CR	FBG KL	IB	17D VLVO	10 8	9900	6 1	33600	37400
34 7	MIXER EXCLUSIVE	SLP	SA/RC	FBG KL	SD	17D VLVO	10 8	9900	6 1	35500	39400
34 7	MIXER RACING	SLP	SA/RC	FBG KL	SD	17D VLVO	10 8	9900	6 1	31800	35400
35 3	MAXI 108	SLP	SA/CR	FBG KL	SD	23D VLVO	11 2	13200	5 9	44900	49900
39 4	MAXI 120	SLP	SA/CR	FBG KL	IB	64D VLVO	12 6	21560	5 6	79200	87000
39 4	MAXI 120	KTH	SA/CR	FBG KL	IB	64D VLVO	12 6	21560	5 6	79200	87000
42	MAXI 130	SLP	SA/CR	FBG KL	IB	D VLVO	12 6	23100	6 3	90800	99700
42	MAXI 130	KTH	SA/CR	FBG KL	IB	D VLVO	12 6	23100	6 3	91200	100000
					1982 BOATS						
22 4	MAXI 68	SLP	SA/CR	FBG KL	OB		7 9	2970	4 2	6250	7200
26	MAXI 77	SLP	SA/CR	FBG KL	OB		8 3	4400	4 8	11000	12500
26	MAXI 77	SLP	SA/CR	FBG KL	IB	D	8 3	4400	4 8	11000	12500
26 6	MAXI 80	SLP	SA/RC	FBG KL	IB	D	9 2	3080	4 10	8650	9950
28 7	MAXI 87	SLP	SA/CR	FBG KL	IB	D	8 3	7700	4 10	22600	25100
32	MAXI 95	SLP	SA/CR	FBG KL	IB	D	10 7	9460	4 10	29300	32600
36	MAXI 108	SLP	SA/CR	FBG KL	IB	D	11 1	13200	5 7	43200	48000
40	MAXI 120	SLP	SA/CR	FBG KL	IB	D	12 4	19800	5 5	72400	79600
40	MAXI 120	KTH	SA/CR	FBG KL	IB	D	12 4	19800	5 5	72400	79600
					1981 BOATS						
22 4	MAXI 68	SLP	SA/CR	FBG KL	OB		7 9	2970	4 2	5900	6750
26	MAXI 77	SLP	SA/CR	FBG KL	OB		8 3	4400	4 8	10300	11700
26 6	MAXI 80	SLP	SA/RC	FBG KL	IB	D	9 2	3080	4 10	8150	9400
28 7	MAXI 87	SLP	SA/CR	FBG KL	IB	D	8 3	7700	4 10	18100	20100
32	MAXI 95	SLP	SA/CR	FBG KL	IB	D	10 7	9460	4 10	21200	23600
36	MAXI 108	SLP	SA/CR	FBG KL	IB	D	11 1	13200	5 7	40700	45200
40	MAXI 120	SLP	SA/CR	FBG KL	IB	D	12 4	19800	5 5	68100	74900
40	MAXI 120	KTH	SA/CR	FBG KL	IB	D	12 4	19800	5 5	68100	74900
					1979 BOATS						
22 4	MAXI 68	SLP	SA/CR	FBG KL	OB		7 9	2936	4 2	5350	6150
22 4	MAXI 68	SLP	SA/CR	FBG KL	IB	8D VLVO	7 9	3417	4 2	7050	8100
26	MAXI 77	SLP	SA/CR	FBG KL	IB		8 3	4409	4 8	9500	10800
26	MAXI 77	SLP	SA/CR	FBG KL	IB	8D VLVO	8 3	4740	4 8	10800	12300
26	MAXI 77 SHOAL	SLP	SA/CR	FBG KL	OB		8 3	4409	3 6	9500	10800
26	MAXI 77 SHOAL	SLP	SA/CR	FBG KL	IB	8D VLVO	8 3	4740	3 6	10800	12300
28 7	MAXI 87	SLP	SA/CR	FBG KL	SD	10D VLVO	9 10	7700	4 10	19400	21600
32	MAXI 95	SLP	SA/CR	FBG KL	IB	23D VLVO	10 7	8400	4 10	22500	25000
36	MAXI 108	SLP	SA/CR	FBG KL	IB	23D VLVO	11 1	13200	5 7	37300	41400
40	MAXI 120	SLP	SA/CR	FBG KL	IB	50D VLVO	12 6	20000	5 7	63100	69300
40	MAXI 120	KTH	SA/CR	FBG KL	IB	50D VLVO	12 6	20000	5 7	63100	69300
					1978 BOATS						
22 4	MAXI 68	SLP	SA/CR	FBG KL	OB		7 9	2976	4 2	5200	6000
26	MAXI 77	SLP	SA/CR	FBG KL	IB		8 3	4480	4 8	9350	10600
26	MAXI 77	SLP	SA/CR	FBG KL	IB	8D VLVO	8 3	4480	4 8	9850	11200
26	MAXI 77 SHOAL	SLP	SA/CR	FBG KL	OB		8 3	4480	3 6	9350	10600
26	MAXI 77 SHOAL	SLP	SA/CR	FBG KL	IB	8D VLVO	8 3	4480	3 6	9850	11200
28 7	MAXI 87	SLP	SA/CR	FBG KL	SD	10D VLVO	9 10	7840	4 10	19100	21200
32	MAXI 95	SLP	SA/CR	FBG KL	IB	23D VLVO	10 7	8512	4 10	22000	24400
40	MAXI 120	KTH	SA/CR	FBG KL	IB	50D VLVO	12 6	20160	5 8	61200	67200
45 3	MAXI 140	SLP	SA/RC	FBG KL	IB		13 3	22000	7 5	78600	86400
					1977 BOATS						
23	MAXI 68	SLP	SA/CR	FBG KL	OB		7 9	2976	4 2	5200	5950
23	MAXI 68	SLP	SA/CR	FBG KL	IB	8D VLVO	7 9	3417	4 2	6650	7650
26	MAXI 77	SLP	SA/CR	FBG KL	OB		8 3	4409	4 8	9450	11400
26	MAXI 77 SHOAL	SLP	SA/CR	FBG KL	OB		8 3	4409	3 6	9450	10700
29	MAXI 87	SLP	SA/CR	FBG KL	IB	10D VLVO	9 10	6614	4 10	15500	17600
32	MAXI 95	SLP	SA/CR	FBG KL	IB	23D VLVO	10 7	8377	4 10	20900	23200
					1976 BOATS						
26	MAXI 77	SLP	SAIL	FBG KL	OB		8 3	4400	4 8	8500	9800
26	MAXI 77	SLP	SAIL	FBG KL	IB	8D VLVO	8 3	4800	4 8	9850	11200
28 7	MAXI 87	SLP	SAIL	FBG KL	IB	10D VLVO	9 10	7700	4 10	17300	19700
32	MAXI 95	SLP	SAIL	FBG KL	IB	25D VLVO	10 7	8400	4 10	20300	22600
					1975 BOATS						
25 7	NIMBUS 26	HT	MY	FBG SV	IB	75D VLVO	9 1	4405	2 7	15100	17200
26	MAXI 77	SLP	SAIL	FBG KL	OB		8 3	4405	4 8	8900	10100
28 7	MAXI 87	SLP	SAIL	FBG KL	IB	10D VLVO	9 10	7710	4 10	16800	19100
32	MAXI 77	SLP	SAIL	FBG KL	IB	15D VLVO	10 8	4800	4 8	11000	12500
32	MAXI 95	SLP	SAIL	FBG KL	IB	25D VLVO	10 6	9030	4 11	21200	23600

PHANTOM BOATS
COAST GUARD MFG ID- PJI

Call 1-800-327-6929 for BUC Personalized Evaluation Service
Or, for 1977 to 1998 boats, sign onto www.BUCValuPro.com

PHANTOM CORPORATION
COAST GUARD MFG ID- PHA

Call 1-800-327-6929 for BUC Personalized Evaluation Service
Or, for 1973 to 1976 boats, sign onto www.BUCValuPro.com

PHILBROOKS SHIPYARD LTD
SIDNEY BC CANADA   COAST GUARD MFG ID- ZPS See inside cover to adjust price for area

LOA FT IN	NAME AND/ OR MODEL	TOP/ RIG	BOAT TYPE	-HULL- MTL TP	ENGINE TP # HP	MFG	BEAM FT IN	WGT LBS	DRAFT FT IN	RETAIL LOW	RETAIL HIGH
					1979 BOATS						
39 6	FAST-PASSAGE	CUT	SAIL	F/S KL	IB	50D PERK	11 10	21000	5 6	89800	98700

PHOENIX MARINE ENT INC
DIV OF AMERICAN MARINE HOLDING
HIALEAH FL 33010   COAST GUARD MFG ID- PMG   See inside cover to adjust price for area

For more recent years, see the BUC Used Boat Price Guide, Volume 1 or Volume 2

LOA FT IN	NAME AND/ OR MODEL	TOP/ RIG	BOAT TYPE	-HULL- MTL TP	ENGINE TP # HP	MFG	BEAM FT IN	WGT LBS	DRAFT FT IN	RETAIL LOW	RETAIL HIGH
					1983 BOATS						
27 3	PHOENIX 27	OP	RNBT	FBG DV	OB		9 10	5400	1 10	16200	18400
27 3	PHOENIX 27	OP	RNBT	FBG DV	IB 350	CRUS	9 10	6500	1 10	18500	20500
27 3	PHOENIX 27	OP	RNBT	FBG DV	IB 235D-300D		9 10	6500	1 10	22400	27600
27 3	PHOENIX 27	OP	RNBT	FBG DV	IB T165	CRUS	9 10	6500	1 10	18600	20700
27 3	PHOENIX 27	OP	RNBT	FBG DV	SE T205	OMC	9 10	6500	1 10	16300	18500
27 3	PHOENIX 27	OP	RNBT	FBG DV	IB T220-T270		9 10	7200	1 10	20200	23200
27 3	PHOENIX 27	OP	RNBT	FBG DV	IB IBT124D-T205D		9 10	7200	1 10	22500	27200
28 10	PHOENIX 29	FB	CR	FBG DV	IB T165-T270		10	8500	2 4	22000	26500
28 10	PHOENIX 29	FB	CR	FBG DV	IB IBT124D-T165D		10	8500	2 4	28600	33600
28 10	PHOENIX 29	FB	CR	FBG DV	IB T205D GM		10	8500	2 4	32300	35900

LOA FT IN	NAME AND/ OR MODEL	TOP/ RIG	BOAT TYPE	HULL MTL TP	ENGINE TP # HP MFG	BEAM FT IN	WGT LBS	DRAFT FT IN	RETAIL LOW	RETAIL HIGH
------ 1983 BOATS ------										
28 10	PHOENIX 29	FB	SF	FBG DV	IB T165-T270	10	8500	2 4	22200	26500
28 10	PHOENIX 29	FB	SF	FBG DV	IBT124D-T165D	10	8500	2 4	28600	33600
28 10	PHOENIX 29	FB	SF	FBG DV	IB T205D GM	10	8500	2 4	32300	35900
28 10	PHOENIX 29 CHARTER	FB	SF	FBG DV	IB T165-T270	10	8500	2 4	22200	26500
28 10	PHOENIX 29 CHARTER	FB	SF	FBG DV	IBT124D-T165D	10	8500	2 4	28600	33600
28 10	PHOENIX 29 CHARTER	FB	SF	FBG DV	IB T205D GM	10	8500	2 4	32300	35900
38	PHOENIX 38 CNV	FB	SDNSF	FBG DV	IB T350 CRUS	14	25000	3 7	76800	84400
	IB T286D VLVO 84700 93100, IB T300D CAT 89100 97900, IB T410D J&T 94500 104000									
------ 1982 BOATS ------										
27 3	PHOENIX 27	OP	RNBT	FBG DV	OB	9 10	5400	1 6	15800	18000
27 3	PHOENIX 27	OP	RNBT	FBG DV	IB 350 CRUS	9 10	5400	1 6	17300	19600
27 3	PHOENIX 27	OP	RNBT	FBG DV	IB 235D-300D	9 10	6500	2 5	21500	26500
27 3	PHOENIX 27	OP	RNBT	FBG DV	IB T165-T170	9 10	6500	2 5	17400	20800
27 3	PHOENIX 27	OP	RNBT	FBG DV	SE T205 OMC	9 10	6500	1 10	15900	18100
27 3	PHOENIX 27	OP	RNBT	FDC DV	IB T220-T270	9 10	7200	1 10	19400	22200
27 3	PHOENIX 27	OP	RNBT	FBG DV	IBT124D-T205D	9 10	7200	1 10	24500	29400
28 10	PHOENIX 29	FB	CR	FBG DV	IB T165-T270	10	8500	2 4	21100	25300
28 10	PHOENIX 29	FB	CR	FBG DV	IBT124D-T148D	10	8500	2 4	27500	31600
28 10	PHOENIX 29	FB	CR	FBG DV	IB T205D GM	10	8500	2 4	31100	34500
28 10	PHOENIX 29	FB	SF	FBG DV	IB T165-T270	10	8500	2 4	21200	25400
28 10	PHOENIX 29	FB	SF	FBG DV	IBT124D-T148D	10	8500	2 4	27500	31600
28 10	PHOENIX 29	FB	SF	FBG DV	IB T205D GM	10	8500	2 4	31100	34500
28 10	PHOENIX 29	FB	SF	FBG DV	IB T165-T270	10	8500	2 4	21200	25400
28 10	PHOENIX 29 CHARTER	FB	SF	FBG DV	IBT124D-T148D	10	8500	2 4	27500	31600
28 10	PHOENIX 29 CHARTER	FB	SF	FBG DV	IB T205D GM	10	8500	2 4	31100	34500
38	PHOENIX 38 CNV	FB	SDNSF	FBG DV	IB T286D VLVO	14	25000	3 2	80800	88800
38	PHOENIX 38 CNV	FB	SDNSF	FBG DV	IB T300D CAT	14	25000	3 2	85000	93400
38	PHOENIX 38 CNV	FB	SDNSF	FBG DV	IB T410D J&T	14	25000	3 2	90100	99100
------ 1981 BOATS ------										
27 3	PHOENIX 27	OP	RNBT	FBG DV	OB	9 10	5400	1 6	15500	17700
27 3	PHOENIX 27	OP	RNBT	FBG DV	IB 330-350	9 10	6500	2 5	16200	18800
	IB 235D-300D 20700 25500, IB T170-T270 17500 21300, IBT124D-T148D 23600 27200									
28 10	PHOENIX 29	FB	CR	FBG DV	IB T170-T270	10	8500	2 4	20200	24300
28 10	PHOENIX 29	FB	CR	FBG DV	IBT124D-T148D	10	8500	2 4	26400	30400
28 10	PHOENIX 29	FB	SF	FBG DV	IB T170-T270	10	8500	2 4	20300	24300
28 10	PHOENIX 29	FB	SF	FBG DV	IBT124D-T148D	10	8500	2 4	26400	30400
28 10	PHOENIX 29 CHARTER	FB	SF	FBG DV	IB T170-T270	10	8500	2 4	20300	24300
28 10	PHOENIX 29 CHARTER	FB	SF	FBG DV	IBT124D-T148D	10	8500	2 4	26400	30400
------ 1980 BOATS ------										
27 3	PHOENIX 27	OP	RNBT	FBG DV	OB	9 10	5400	1 6	15300	17300
27 3	PHOENIX 27	OP	RNBT	FBG DV	IB 330-350	9 10	6500	2 5	15600	18000
	IB 197D-250D 19400 23200, IB T225-T270 18300 21200, IB T130D VLVO 23900 26500									
28 10	PHOENIX 29	FB	CR	FBG DV	IB T225-T270	10	8500	2 4	20100	23200
28 10	PHOENIX 29	FB	CR	FBG DV	IBT124D-T130D	10	8500		25700	28500
28 10	PHOENIX 29	HT	RNBT	FBG DV	IB T225-T270	10	8000		19300	22200
28 10	PHOENIX 29	HT	RNBT	FBG DV	IBT124D-T130D	10	8000		23900	26600
28 10	PHOENIX 29	FB	RNBT	FBG DV	IB T228-T270	10	8000		19300	22200
28 10	PHOENIX 29	FB	RNBT	FBG DV	IB T130D VLVO	10	8000	2 4	23800	26500
38	PHOENIX 38		SF	FBG DV	IB T370D	13 11	26000		81600	89600
------ 1979 BOATS ------										
27 3	PHOENIX	OP	RNBT	FBG DV	IB T228-T270	9 10	7200	1 10	16800	19800
27 3	PHOENIX	OP	RNBT	FBG DV	IB T130D VLVO	9 10	7200	1 10	22000	24500
28 10	PHOENIX	HT	RNBT	FBG DV	IB T130D VLVO	10	8000	2 4	23000	25500
28 10	PHOENIX	HT	RNBT	FBG DV	IB T225D	10	8000	2 4	26500	29500
28 10	PHOENIX	FB	SF	FBG DV	IB T228-T270	10	8500	2 4	19400	22300
28 10	PHOENIX	FB	SF	FBG DV	IBT130D-T225D	10	8500	2 4	24700	30500
------ 1978 BOATS ------										
28 10	PHOENIX 29	HT	RNBT	FBG DV	IB T225-T228	10	8000	2 4	17500	20000
28 10	PHOENIX 29	HT	RNBT	FBG DV	IB T130D VLVO	10	8000	2 4	22100	24600
28 10	PHOENIX 29	FB	SF	FBG DV	IB T225-T270	10	8500	2 4	18700	21400
28 10	PHOENIX 29	FB	SF	FBG DV	IB T130D VLVO	10	8500	2 4	23800	26400
------ 1977 BOATS ------										
28 10	PHOENIX 29	HT	RNBT	FBG DV	IB T228 MRCR	10	7200	2 4	16200	18400
28 10	PHOENIX 29	FB	SF	FBG DV	IB T225-T228	10	8500	2 4	17600	20100

PIPESTONE-MARINER CORP

PIPESTONE MN   FOR MORE RECENT YEARS SEE BAYLINER   See inside cover to adjust price for area

LOA FT IN	NAME AND/ OR MODEL	TOP/ RIG	BOAT TYPE	HULL MTL TP	ENGINE TP # HP MFG	BEAM FT IN	WGT LBS	DRAFT FT IN	RETAIL LOW	RETAIL HIGH
------ 1972 BOATS ------										
16 4	MARAUDER			FBG	OB	7 3	1460		2500	2900
16 4	MARAUDER			FBG	IO 120-170	7 3			3000	3500
16 4	SABRE			FBG	OB	7 3	1480		2550	2950
16 4	SABRE			FBG	IO 120-170	7 3			2950	3450
16 11	CAPTAIN DELUXE			FBG	OB	6 10	1050		1900	2250
16 11	CAPTAIN DELUXE			FBG	IO 120-245	6 10			2900	3600
17 2	DELTA-RALLYE DLX			FBG	OB	6 10	1590		2700	3100
17 2	DELTA-RALLYE DLX			FBG	IO 120-245	6 10			2950	3650
17 2	GT-RALLYE DLX			FBG	OB	6 10	1490		2550	2950
17 2	GT-RALLYE DLX			FBG	IO 120-245	6 10			2950	3650
17 2	RALLYE SPORT DELUXE			FBG	OB	6 10	1515		2600	3000
17 2	RALLYE SPORT DELUXE			FBG	IO 120-245	6 10			2950	3650
18 3	WAVEMASTER			FBG	IO 120-245	7 5	1925		3550	4350
18 10	SPORTSMASTER			FBG	IO 155-265	7 7	2560		4350	5400
19 1	SURFMASTER			FBG	IO 155-245	7 7	2390		4200	5100
19 1	SURFMASTER			FBG	IO 265 CHRY	7 7	2390		4600	5300
23	IMPERIAL			FBG	IO 155-265	8	3770		7800	9400
------ 1971 BOATS ------										
16 5	CAPTAIN	OP	RNBT	FBG DV IO		6 9	1090		1950	2300
16 5	CAPTAIN	OP	RNBT	FBG DV IO	120	6 9			3100	3600
17 1	RALLYE SPORT	OP	RNBT	FBG TR OB		6 10	1050		1900	2300
17 1	RALLYE SPORT	OP	RNBT	FBG TR OB	120	6 10			3150	3650
17 2	DELTA-RALLYE	OP	RNBT	FBG TR OB		6 11			1900	2250
17 2	DELTA-RALLYE	OP	RNBT	FBG TR OB	120	6 11	1130		3200	3700
17 2	GT-RALLYE	OP	RNBT	FBG TR OB		6 11			2050	2450
17 2	GT-RALLYE	OP	RNBT	FBG TR OB	120	6 11			3200	3700
18 10	SPORTMASTER	OP	RNBT	FBG DV IO	120	7 7			4250	4950
19 3	SURFMASTER		CR	FBG DV IO	120	7 5			4500	5150
23	IMPERIAL		CR	FBG TR IO	215	7 9			8500	9750
------ 1970 BOATS ------										
16 5	CAPTAIN			FBG SV IO	120-140	6 9	1050		1850	2050
16 5	CAPTAIN			FBG TR OB		6 9	1820		3050	3550
17 1	RALLYE SPORT			FBG TR OB	120-160	6 10			1850	2200
17 1	RALLYE SPORT			FBG TR OB		6 11	1655		3100	3600
17 2	GT-RALLYE SPORT			FBG TR OB	120-160	6 11	1100		2000	2200
17 2	GT-RALLYE SPORT			FBG TR OB	120-160	6 11	1745		3200	3750
18 10	RALLYE SPORTMASTER			FBG TR OB	120-215	7 7	1750		3850	4650
19 3	SURFMASTER			FBG SV IO	120-215	7 5	2150		4250	5050
23	IMPERIAL		CR	FBG TR IO	215 OMC	7 9			8850	10000
------ 1969 BOATS ------										
16	BRAVE DELUXE			FBG	OB	5			2350	2700
16 5	CAPTAIN			FBG SV OB		6 9			2350	2700
16 5	CAPTAIN			FBG SV IO	120-160	6 9			3150	3700
16 10	GT-RALLYE SPORT			FBG TR OB		6 11			2300	2650
16 10	GT-RALLYE SPORT			FBG TR OB	80-210	6 10			3150	3800
16 10	RALLYE SPORT			FBG TR OB		6 10			2300	2650
16 10	RALLYE SPORT			FBG TR OB	80-210	6 11			3100	3750
18 10	RALLYE SPORTMASTER			FBG TR IO	120-210	7 7			4500	5200
19	SURFMASTER			FBG SV IO	120-210	7 4			4450	5200
------ 1968 BOATS ------										
16 8	CHIEFTAIN		RNBT	FBG	IO 120-160	6 5			3300	3850
17 4	SIOUXLINER		RNBT	FBG	IO 120-210	7 4			3700	4450
18	WAVEMASTER		RNBT	FBG	IO 120-210	7 4			4050	4850
------ 1967 BOATS ------										
16 8	CHIEFTAIN DELUXE			FBG	OB				2500	2900
16 8	CHIEFTAIN DELUXE			FBG	60-120				3500	4050
16 8	CHIEFTAIN STANDARD			FBG	OB				2250	2600
16 8	CHIEFTAIN STANDARD			FBG	60-120				3200	3850
17	WARRIOR DELUXE			FBG	OB				2500	2900
17	WARRIOR DELUXE			FBG	80-160				3450	4100
17	WARRIOR SPORTSMAN			FBG	OB				2300	2650
17	WARRIOR SPORTSMAN			FBG	80-160				2450	4000
17	WARRIOR STANDARD			FBG	OB				2200	2550
17	WARRIOR STANDARD			FBG	80-160				3300	3900
17 4	SIOUXLINER DELUXE			FBG	OB				2550	3000
17 4	SIOUXLINER DELUXE			FBG	80-200				3600	4250
17 4	SIOUXLINER STANDARD			FBG	OB				2050	2450
17 4	SIOUXLINER STANDARD			FBG	80-160				4250	4950
18	WAVEMASTER DELUXE			FBG	OB				2250	2600
18	WAVEMASTER STANDARD			FBG	80-160				3900	4300
------ 1966 BOATS ------										
17	WARRIOR			FBG	OB				2000	2400
17	WARRIOR			FBG	IO 60-200				3350	4050
17	WARRIOR			FBG	225				3600	4150
17	WARRIOR DELUXE			FBG	OB				2250	2750
17	WARRIOR DELUXE			FBG	60-225				3550	4250
17	WARRIOR SPORTSMAN			FBG	OB				2250	2600
17	WARRIOR SPORTSMAN			FBG	60-225				3450	4300

LOA FT IN	NAME AND/ OR MODEL	TOP/ RIG	BOAT TYPE	-HULL- MTL TP	TP	#	---ENGINE--- HP	MFG	BEAM FT IN	WGT LBS	DRAFT FT IN	RETAIL LOW	RETAIL HIGH
---	--- 1966 BOATS ---												
17	WAVEMASTER		FBG	OB								2250	2600
17	WAVEMASTER		FBG	IO			60-225					3450	4300
17	WAVEMASTER DELUXE		FBG	OB								2700	3150
17	WAVEMASTER DELUXE		FBG	IO			60-225					3850	4600
17 4	SIOUXLINER		FBG	OB								2050	2450
17 4	SIOUXLINER		FBG	IO			60-225					3450	4300
17 4	SIOUXLINER DELUXE		FBG	OB								2550	3000
17 4	SIOUXLINER DELUXE		FBG	IO			60-225					3800	4600
18 6	APACHE	FSH	FBG	IO			60-225					5350	6400
---	--- 1965 BOATS ---												
17	WAVEMASTER		FBG	OB								2350	2700
17	WAVEMASTER		FBG	IO			110-150					3650	4250
17 2	WARRIOR DELUXE		FBG	OB								2450	2850
17 2	WARRIOR DELUXE		FBG	IO			110-150					3800	4450
17 2	WARRIOR SPORTSMAN		FBG	OB								2350	2750
17 2	WARRIOR SPORTSMAN		FBG	IO			110-150					3700	4400
17 2	WARRIOR STANDARD		FBG	OB								2200	2550
17 2	WARRIOR STANDARD		FBG	IO			110-150					3600	4300
18 4	APACHE	FSH	FBG	IO			110-150					5000	5750
---	--- 1964 BOATS ---												
16 3	ARROW		FBG	OB								2400	2750
17 2	WARRIOR DELUXE		FBG	IO								**	**
17 2	WARRIOR DELUXE		FBG	OB			10- 40					3950	4600
17 2	WARRIOR STANDARD		FBG	OB								2350	2750
17 2	WARRIOR STANDARD		FBG	IO			10- 40					3650	4300
18 4	APACHE	FSH	FBG	IO			10- 40					5150	5900
---	--- 1963 BOATS ---												
16 3	ARROW		FBG	OB								2400	2800
17 2	WARRIOR		FBG	OB								2150	2500
17 2	WARRIOR		FBG	IO			110-140					3950	4600
17 2	WARRIOR DELUXE		FBG	OB								2550	2950
17 2	WARRIOR DELUXE		FBG	IO			110-140					3950	4600
18 4	APACHE	CR	FBG	IO			110-140					5050	5800
18 4	APACHE	FSH	FBG	IO			110-140					5300	6150
18 4	APACHE SPORTSMAN		FBG	IO			110-140					4800	5550
---	--- 1961 BOATS ---												
18 4	APACHE	CBNCR	FBG	OB					7	1260		2400	2800
---	--- 1959 BOATS ---												
18 4	APACHE AP195	RNBT	FBG	OB					7	1160		2400	2800
18 4	APACHE STD AP190	RNBT	FBG	OB					7	1160		2200	2550

PIRANHA BOAT CORP
COAST GUARD MFG ID- PRN

Call 1-800-327-6929 for BUC Personalized Evaluation Service
Or, for 1967 to 1975 boats, sign onto www.BUCValuPro.com

ARTHUR PIVER SAILBOATS
PI-CRAFT
MILL VALLEY CA 94942   See inside cover to adjust price for area

LOA FT IN	NAME AND/ OR MODEL	TOP/ RIG	BOAT TYPE	-HULL- MTL TP	TP	#	---ENGINE--- HP	MFG	BEAM FT IN	WGT LBS	DRAFT FT IN	RETAIL LOW	RETAIL HIGH
---	--- 1965 BOATS ---												
24	PI 24	SLP	SAIL	F/W	TM				14		1 6	3750	4400
25	PI 25	SLP	SAIL	F/W	TM				15		1 7	4250	4950
30	PI 30	SLP	SAIL	F/W	TM				18		2	9950	11300
35	PI 35	KTH	SAIL	F/W	TM				20		2 6	18100	20200
40	PI 40	KTH	SAIL	F/W	TM				22		2 9	25400	28200
46	TRIDENT	KTH	SAIL	F/W	TM				24		3	39700	44100
53	DIADEM	KTH	SAIL	F/W	TM				28		3 3	61300	67400
64	EMPRESS	KTH	SAIL	F/W	TM				32		3 8	81500	89600

PLACE CRAFT BOATS
COAST GUARD MFG ID- PCJ

Call 1-800-327-6929 for BUC Personalized Evaluation Service
Or, for 1982 boats, sign onto www.BUCValuPro.com

PLASTREND
FT WORTH TX 76131   COAST GUARD MFG ID- PTN See inside cover to adjust price for area
                              SEE COMPOSITE TECHNOLOGY INC

LOA FT IN	NAME AND/ OR MODEL	TOP/ RIG	BOAT TYPE	-HULL- MTL TP	TP	#	---ENGINE--- HP	MFG	BEAM FT IN	WGT LBS	DRAFT FT IN	RETAIL LOW	RETAIL HIGH
---	--- 1968 BOATS ---												
21 11	INTERNATL-TEMPEST	SLP	SA/OD	FBG	KL				6 5	1035	3 7	2300	2700
22	MUSTANG	SLP	SA/CR	FBG	KC	OB			7	2000	2 4	3100	3600
40	PT 40	SLP	SA/RC	FBG	KL	IB	25		11	15500	5 6	33700	37500

PLAY-CRAFT PONTOON CO
DIV RICHLAND DIVERSIFIE COAST GUARD MFG ID- PLF

Call 1-800-327-6929 for BUC Personalized Evaluation Service
Or, for 1969 to 2008 boats, sign onto www.BUCValuPro.com

PLAYMATE

Call 1-800-327-6929 for BUC Personalized Evaluation Service
Or, for 1970 to 1972 boats, sign onto www.BUCValuPro.com

PLEASURE CRAFT INC

Call 1-800-327-6929 for BUC Personalized Evaluation Service
Or, for 1959 to 1965 boats, sign onto www.BUCValuPro.com

PLUCKEBAUM CUSTOM BOATS
PROSPECT KY 40059   COAST GUARD MFG ID- PRP See inside cover to adjust price for area
                          FORMERLY PROSPECT BOAT WORKS INC

For more recent years, see the BUC Used Boat Price Guide, Volume 1 or Volume 2

LOA FT IN	NAME AND/ OR MODEL	TOP/ RIG	BOAT TYPE	-HULL- MTL TP	TP	#	---ENGINE--- HP	MFG	BEAM FT IN	WGT LBS	DRAFT FT IN	RETAIL LOW	RETAIL HIGH
---	--- 1983 BOATS ---												
54	APOLLO	ST	SPTCR	AL	DV	IB	T570D	GM	16	25000		178000	195500
55	PLUCKEBAUM	HT	HB	AL	SV	IB	T260D	CAT	17	40000		205000	225500
67	PLUCKEBAUM	HT	HB	AL	SV	IB	T435D	GM	18	50000		258500	284000
75	PLUCKEBAUM	HT	HB	AL	SV	IB	T570D	GM	19	60000		**	**
---	--- 1981 BOATS ---												
55	PLUCKEBAUM	HT	HB	AL	SV	IB	260D		17			144000	158000
75	PLUCKEBAUM	HT	HB	AL	SV	IB	T260D	CAT	18	54000		**	**
75	PLUCKEBAUM	HT	HB	AL	SV	IB	T400D	CUM	18	54000		**	**
75	PLUCKEBAUM	HT	HB	AL	SV	IB	T435D	GM	18	54000		**	**
---	--- 1980 BOATS ---												
52	PLUCKEBAUM	HT	HB	AL	SV	IB	260D		17			131500	144500
55	PLUCKEBAUM	HT	HB	AL	SV	IB	260D		17			141500	155500
55	PLUCKEBAUM	HT	HB	AL	SV	IB	T260D		17			161500	177500
57	PLUCKEBAUM	HT	HB	AL	SV	IB	260D		17			157000	172500
65	PLUCKEBAUM	HT	HB	AL	SV	IB	435D		18			184000	202500
71	PLUCKEBAUM	HT	HB	AL	SV	IB	435D		18			211500	232500
75	PLUCKEBAUM	HT	HB	AL	SV	IB	435D		18			**	**
---	--- 1979 BOATS ---												
52	PLUCKEBAUM	FB	HB	AL	SV	IB	T330	CHRY	17		3 9	137000	150500
52	PLUCKEBAUM	HT	HB	AL	SV	IB	T210D		17		3 9	143500	158000
55	PLUCKEBAUM	HT	HB	AL	SV	VD	T330	CHRY	17		3 9	141500	155500
55	PLUCKEBAUM	FB	HB	AL	SV	IB	T330	CHRY	17		3 9	141500	155500
55	PLUCKEBAUM	HT	HB	AL	SV	IB	T210D		17		3 9	153500	169000
57	PLUCKEBAUM	FB	HB	AL	SV	VD	T330	CHRY	17		3 9	156500	171500
57	PLUCKEBAUM	HT	HB	AL	SV	IB	T210D		17		3 9	168500	185500
64 10	PLUCKEBAUM	HT	HB	AL	SV	VD	T330	CHRY	18		3 11	170500	187500
64 10	PLUCKEBAUM	HT	HB	AL	SV	IB	T210D	CAT	18		3 11	185000	203000
64 10	PLUCKEBAUM	FB	HB	AL	SV	VD	T330	CHRY	18		3 11	170500	187500
64 10	PLUCKEBAUM	FB	HB	AL	SV	IB	T210D	CAT	18		3 11	185000	203000
71	PLUCKEBAUM	FB	HB	AL	SV	VD	T330	CHRY	18		3 11	180000	198500
71	PLUCKEBAUM	FB	HB	AL	SV	IB	T210D		18		3 11	207500	228000
73	PLUCKEBAUM	FB	HB	AL	SV	IB	T330	CHRY	18		3 11	201000	221500
73	PLUCKEBAUM	FB	HB	AL	SV	IB	T210D		18		3 11	**	**
---	--- 1978 BOATS ---												
52	BAYMASTER	FB	HB	AL	SV	VD	T830	CHRY	17		3 9	187500	206500
55	BAYMASTER	HT	HB	AL	SV	IB	T330	CHRY	17		3 9	139500	153500
55	BAYMASTER	FB	HB	AL	SV	VD	T330	CHRY	17		3 9	139500	153500
57	BAYMASTER	FB	HB	AL	SV	VD	T330	CHRY	17		3 9	154000	169500
64 10	BAYMASTER	HT	HB	AL	SV	IB	T210D		18		3 11	168500	185000
64 10	BAYMASTER	HT	HB	AL	SV	IB	T210D	CAT	18		3 11	182500	200500
64 10	BAYMASTER	FB	HB	AL	SV	IB	T210D	CAT	18		3 11	168500	185000
64 10	BAYMASTER	FB	HB	AL	SV	IB	T330	CHRY	18		3 11	182500	200500

LOA FT IN	NAME AND/ OR MODEL	TOP/ RIG	BOAT TYPE	HULL MTL	HULL TP	ENG TP	ENG #	ENG HP	ENG MFG	BEAM FT IN	WGT LBS	DRAFT FT IN	RETAIL LOW	RETAIL HIGH
1978 BOATS														
71	BAYMASTER	FB	HB	AL	SV	VD		T330	CHRY	18		3 11	178500	196000
73	BAYMASTER	FB	HB	AL	SV	VD		T330	CHRY	18		3 11	**	**
1977 BOATS														
52	RIVERMASTER	HT	HB	AL	DV	VD		T330	CHRY	17			138000	151500
52	RIVERMASTER	HT	HB	AL	DV	VD		T210D	CAT	17			149500	164500
52	RIVERMASTER	FB	HB	AL	DV	VD		T330	CHRY	17			138000	151500
52	RIVERMASTER	FB	HB	AL	DV	VD		T210D	CAT	17			149500	164500
55	RIVERMASTER	HT	HB	AL	DV	VD		T330	CHRY	17			142500	156500
55	RIVERMASTER	HT	HB	AL	DV	VD		T210D	CAT	17			159500	175500
55	RIVERMASTER	FB	HB	AL	DV	VD		T330	CHRY	17			142500	156500
55	RIVERMASTER	FB	HB	AL	DV	VD		T210D	CAT	17			159500	175500
64 10	BAYMASTER	HT	HB	AL	DV	VD		T330	CHRY	18			173500	190500
64 10	BAYMASTER	HT	HB	AL	DV	VD		T210D	CAT	18			188000	206500
64 10	BAYMASTER	FB	HB	AL	DV	VD		T330	CHRY	18			173500	190500
64 10	BAYMASTER	FB	HB	AL	DV	VD		T210D	CAT	18			188000	206500
1976 BOATS														
52	RIVERMASTER	HT	HB	AL	DV	VD		T330	CHRY	17	26000	3 6	137000	150500
52	RIVERMASTER	HT	HB	AL	DV	VD		T210D	CAT	17	26000	3 6	161000	177000
52	RIVERMASTER	FB	HB	AL	DV	VD		T330	CHRY	17	26000	3 6	137000	150500
52	RIVERMASTER	FB	HB	AL	DV	VD		T210D	CAT	17	26000	3 6	161000	177000
55	RIVERMASTER	HT	HB	AL	DV	VD		T330	CHRY	17	27000	3 6	143500	158000
55	RIVERMASTER	HT	HB	AL	DV	VD		T210D	CAT	17	27000	3 6	168000	184500
55	RIVERMASTER	FB	HB	AL	DV	VD		T330	CHRY	17	27000	3 6	143500	158000
55	RIVERMASTER	FB	HB	AL	DV	VD		T210D	CAT	17	27000	3 6	168000	184500
64	BAYMASTER	FB	CR	AL	DV	VD		T210D	CAT	18	29000	4	**	**
1974 BOATS														
52	RIVERMASTER	HT	FH	AL		VD		T330	CHRY	17		3 6	**	**
52	RIVERMASTER	FB	FH	AL		VD		T330	CHRY	17		3 6	**	**
1972 BOATS														
44	PANORAMIC	HT	HB	AL	SV	IB		T600		16			114500	126000
52	LIVABLE	HT	HB	AL	SV	IB		T600		18			159000	174500
62	SPACIOUS	HT	HB	AL	SV	IB		T450D		20			**	**

PLYMOUTH BOAT YARD

Call 1-800-327-6929 for BUC Personalized Evaluation Service
Or, for 1966 boats, sign onto www.BUCValuPro.com

GEO POCOCK RACING SHELLS INC
COAST GUARD MFG ID- EPR

Call 1-800-327-6929 for BUC Personalized Evaluation Service
Or, for 1983 to 1986 boats, sign onto www.BUCValuPro.com

POINTER MARINE CO INC
COAST GUARD MFG ID- PTR
FORMERLY POINTER CORP

Call 1-800-327-6929 for BUC Personalized Evaluation Service
Or, for 1975 to 1994 boats, sign onto www.BUCValuPro.com

POLAR KRAFT MFG CO
GODFREY MARINE   COAST GUARD MFG ID- PLR

Call 1-800-327-6929 for BUC Personalized Evaluation Service
Or, for 1959 to 2008 boats, sign onto www.BUCValuPro.com

POLLARD ENTERPRISES INC
FUN MASTER   COAST GUARD MFG ID- PLD

Call 1-800-327-6929 for BUC Personalized Evaluation Service
Or, for 1977 to 1978 boats, sign onto www.BUCValuPro.com

PORALI MARIN AB
COAST GUARD MFG ID- PXA

Call 1-800-327-6929 for BUC Personalized Evaluation Service
Or, for 1980 boats, sign onto www.BUCValuPro.com

PORT CITY FIBERGLASS
COAST GUARD MFG ID- POR

Call 1-800-327-6929 for BUC Personalized Evaluation Service
Or, for 1983 to 1986 boats, sign onto www.BUCValuPro.com

PORT HAMBLE LTD

Call 1-800-327-6929 for BUC Personalized Evaluation Service
Or, for 1966 boats, sign onto www.BUCValuPro.com

PORTMAN MARINE
COAST GUARD MFG ID- AJC

Call 1-800-327-6929 for BUC Personalized Evaluation Service
Or, for 1979 boats, sign onto www.BUCValuPro.com

PORTSMOUTH YACHT CO
PORTSMOUTH RI 02871   COAST GUARD MFG ID- PYA See inside cover to adjust price for area

LOA FT IN	NAME AND/ OR MODEL	TOP/ RIG	BOAT TYPE	HULL MTL	HULL TP	ENG TP	ENG #	ENG HP	ENG MFG	BEAM FT IN	WGT LBS	DRAFT FT IN	RETAIL LOW	RETAIL HIGH
1981 BOATS														
23 8	EASTWARD-HO 24	SLP	SA/CR	FBG	KL	IB		15D	YAN	8 8	7000	3 10	10200	11600
31	EASTWARD-HO 31	SLP	SA/CR	FBG	KL	IB		15D	YAN	9 10	11000	4 2	19100	21200
1980 BOATS														
23 8	EASTWARD-HO 24	SLP	SA/CR	FBG	KL	IB		15D	YAN	8 8	7000	3 10	9750	11100
31	EASTWARD-HO 31	SLP	SA/CR	FBG	KL	IB		15D	YAN	9 10	11000	4 2	18400	20500
1979 BOATS														
23 8	EASTWARD-HO 24	SLP	SA/CR	FBG	KL	IB	13D-	15D	YAN	8 8	7000	3 10	9400	10700
31	EASTWARD-HO 31	SLP	SA/CR	FBG	KL	IB		15D	YAN	9 10	11000	4 2	17300	19700
1978 BOATS														
23 8	EASTWARD-HO 24	SLP	SA/CR	FBG	KL	IB	13D-	22D	WEST	8 8	7000	3 10	9050	10500
31	EASTWARD-HO 31	SLP	SA/CR	FBG	KL	IB		22D	WEST	9 10	11000	4 2	16700	19000
1977 BOATS														
23 8	EASTWARD-HO	SLP	SA/CR	FBG	KL	IB		22D	WEST	8 10	7000	3 10	8900	10100
1976 BOATS														
23 8	EASTWARD-HO	SLP	SAIL	FBG	KL	IB	22D-	27D		8 8	7000	3 10	8500	9800
1975 BOATS														
23 8	EASTWARD-HO	SLP	SAIL	FBG	KL	OB				8 8	7000	3 10	7650	8750
23 8	EASTWARD-HO	SLP	SAIL	FBG	KL	IB		20D		8 8	7000	3 10	8200	9500

POSEIDON CORP

Call 1-800-327-6929 for BUC Personalized Evaluation Service
Or, for 1971 to 1972 boats, sign onto www.BUCValuPro.com

POSEIDON MARINE INC
COAST GUARD MFG ID- PMJ

Call 1-800-327-6929 for BUC Personalized Evaluation Service
Or, for 1977 boats, sign onto www.BUCValuPro.com

GEORGE POST & ASSOCIATES INC

Call 1-800-327-6929 for BUC Personalized Evaluation Service
Or, for 1969 boats, sign onto www.BUCValuPro.com

POST MARINE CO INC
MAYS LANDING NJ 08330   COAST GUARD MFG ID- PMC See inside cover to adjust price for area

For more recent years, see the BUC Used Boat Price Guide, Volume 1 or Volume 2

LOA FT IN	NAME AND/ OR MODEL	TOP/ RIG	BOAT TYPE	HULL MTL	HULL TP	ENG TP	ENG #	ENG HP	ENG MFG	BEAM FT IN	WGT LBS	DRAFT FT IN	RETAIL LOW	RETAIL HIGH
1983 BOATS														
42	POST 42	FB	SDNSF	FBG	SV	IB		T310D	GM	15 9	30000	3 6	110500	121000
46	POST 46	FB	SDNSF	FBG	SV	IB		T310D	GM	15 9	33000	3 6	119000	131000
46	POST 46	FB	SDNSF	FBG	SV	IB		T450D	GM	15 9	33000	3 6	137000	150500
1982 BOATS														
42	POST 42	FB	SDNSF	FBG	SV	IB		T310D	GM	15 9	30000	3	105500	115500
42	POST 42	FB	SDNSF	FBG	SV	IB		T450D	GM	15 9	30000	3	119000	130500

LOA FT	IN	NAME AND/ OR MODEL	TOP/ RIG	BOAT TYPE	-HULL- MTL	TP	TP	----ENGINE--- # HP	MFG	BEAM FT	IN	WGT LBS	DRAFT FT	IN	RETAIL LOW	RETAIL HIGH
		1982 BOATS														
46		POST 46	FB	SDNSF	FBG	SV	IB	T310D	GM	15	9	33000	3	6	114000	125500
46		POST 46	FB	SDNSF	FBG	SV	IB	T450D	GM	15	9	33000	3	6	131000	143500
		1981 BOATS														
42		POST 42	FB	SDNSF	FBG	SV	IB	T310D	GM	15	9	30000	3		100500	110000
42		POST 42	FB	SDNSF	FBG	SV	IB	T410D	GM	15	9	30000	3		109500	120500
46		POST 46	FB	SDNSF	FBG	SV	IB	T310D	GM	15	9	33000	3	6	109000	119500
46		POST 46	FB	SDNSF	FBG	SV	IB	T410D	GM	15	9	33000	3	6	119500	131500
		1980 BOATS														
42		POST 42	FB	SDNSF	FBG	SV	IB	T310D	GM	15	9	29000	3		93400	102500
42		POST 42	FB	SDNSF	FBG	SV	IB	T410D	GM	15	9	30000	3		104500	114500
46		POST 46	FB	SDNSF	FBG	SV	IB	T310D	GM	15	9	33000	3	6	103500	114000
46		POST 46	FB	SDNSF	FBG	SV	IB	T410D	GM	15	9	33000	3	6	114000	125500
		1979 BOATS														
42		POST 42	FB	SDNSF	FBG	SV	IB	T270D	CUM	15	9	29000	3		85700	94200
42		POST 42	FB	SDNSF	FBG	SV	IB	T295D	CUM	15	9	29000	3		87700	96300
42		POST 42	FB	SDNSF	FBG	SV	IB	T310D	J&T	15	9	29000	3		89600	98400
46		POST 46	FB	SDNSF	FBG	SV	IB	T295D	CUM	15	9	33000	3	6	97600	107000
46		POST 46	FB	SDNSF	FBG	SV	IB	T310D	J&T	15	9	33000	3	6	99300	109000
		1978 BOATS														
42		POST 42	FB	SDNSF	FBG	SV	IB	T350		15	9	28000	3		74200	81600
42		POST 42	FB	SDNSF	FBG	SV	IB	T310D	GM	15	9	28000	3		83300	91500
46		POST 46	FB	SDNSF	FBG	SV	IB	T310D	GM	15	9	33000			94600	104000
		1977 BOATS														
42		POST 42		SF	FBG	SV	IB	T350	CRUS	15	9	22000	3		60000	66000
		1976 BOATS														
42		POST 42	FB	SDNSF	FBG	SV	IB	T350	CRUS	15	9	20000	3		54900	60400
42		POST 42	FB	SDNSF	FBG	SV	IB	T310D	GM	15	9	22500	3		66700	73300
		1975 BOATS														
39	11	POST 40		SDN	WD	SV	IB	350		14	9	16500	2	10	39400	43800
39	11	POST 40		SDN	WD	SV	IB	T330		14	9	16500	2	10	41000	45500
39	11	POST 40		SDN	WD	SV	IB	T350		14	9	16500	2	10	41300	45900
42		POST 42	FB	SDNSF	FBG	SV	IB	T330	CHRY						78700	86500
		IB T350 CRUS 80100 88100, IB T310D GM 99000 109000, IB T320D CUM													99400	109000
		1974 BOATS														
39	11	POST 40		CR	WD		IB	T250	WAUK	14	9	16500	2	10	38700	43000
		IB T325 MRCR 41000 45600, IB T330 CHRY 40900 45400, IB T350 CRUS													41800	46500
		IB T350 PALM 41400 46000, IB T350 WAUK 41400 46000, IB T210D CUM													51200	56200
		IB T216D GM 51600 56700, IB T225D CAT 53000 58300, IB T240D CUM													51900	57100
		IB T320D CUM 54600 60000														
39	11	POST 40		FSH	WD		IB	T250	WAUK	14	9	16500	2	10	38600	42900
		IB T330 CHRY ** **, IB T350 CRUS ** **, IB T350 PALM													**	**
		IB T350 WAUK ** **, IB T210D CUM 40100 44500, IB T216D GM													40500	45000
		IB T225D CAT 41900 46600, IB T240D CUM 40900 45400, IB T320D CUM													43500	48300
39	11	POST 40		SPTCR	WD		IB	T250	WAUK	14	9	16500	2	10	38700	43000
		IB T325 MRCR 28700 31900, IB T330 CHRY 28600 31800, IB T350 CRUS													29500	32800
		IB T350 PALM 29100 32300, IB T350 WAUK 29100 32300, IB T210D CUM													47800	52600
		IB T216D GM 48300 53000, IB T225D CAT 49700 54600, IB T240D CUM													48600	53400
		IB T320D CUM 51300 56300														
		1973 BOATS														
39	11	POST 40		CR	WD		IB	250D		14	9	16500	2	10	39300	43700
39	11	POST 40		FSH	WD		IB	250D		14	9	16500	2	10	39300	43700
39	11	POST 40		SPTCR	WD		IB	250D		14	9	16500	2	10	39300	43700
		1972 BOATS														
39	11			CR	WD		IB	T250	MRCR	14	9	16500	2	10	35900	39900
39	11			CR	WD		IB	T210D	CUM	14	9	17600	2	10	43000	47800
39	11			SF	WD		IB	T250	MRCR	14	9	16500	2	10	35900	39900
39	11			SF	WD		IB	T210D	CUM	14	9	17600	2	10	43000	47800
39	11			SPTCR	WD		IB	T250	MRCR	14	9	16500	2	10	35900	39900
39	11			SPTCR	WD		IB	T210D	CUM	14	9	17600	2	10	43000	47800
		1971 BOATS														
39	11			FSH	WD		IB	T225	PALM	14	9	16500	2	10	34600	38400
39	11			FSH	WD		IB	T170D	CUM	14	9	17000	2	10	39600	44100
39	11			SF	WD		IB	T225	PALM	14	9	16500	2	10	34600	38500
39	11			SF	WD		IB	T170D	CUM	14	9	17000	2	10	39600	44100
		1970 BOATS														
39	11	POST 40		FSH	WD	RB	IB	T225	PALM	14	9	16000	2	10	32600	36200
39	11	POST 40		MY	WD	RB	IB	T225	PALM	14	9	16000	2	10	32700	36300
39	11	POST 40		SF	WD	RB	IB	T225	PALM	14	9	16000	2	10	32600	36200
		1969 BOATS														
37	8	POST 38		SF	WD	SV	IB	T225	PALM	12	6	13000	2	10	27800	30900
		1968 BOATS														
36	8	POST 37		DC	WD		IB	T250	PALM	12	6	13000	2	10	26800	29700
36	8	POST 37		SDN	WD		IB	T225	PALM	12	6	13000	2	10	27200	30200
36	8	POST 37		SF	WD		IB	T250	PALM	12	6	13000	2	10	26800	29700
		1967 BOATS														
37			FB	SPTCR	WD		IB	T250	PALM	12	6	13000	2	10	26200	29200
37		DECKHOUSE	FB	DC	WD		IB	T250	PALM	12	6	13000	2	10	26200	29100
37		DECKHOUSE	FB	SDN	WD		IB	T250	PALM	12	6	13000	2	10	26700	29600
		1966 BOATS														
34				DC	WD		IB	T195	CHRY	12		11500	2	10	19600	21800
34			FB	DC	WD		IB	T195	CHRY	12		11500	2	10	19600	21800
34			FB	SF	WD		IB	T210	CHRY	12		11000	2	10	19500	21600
34			FB	SPTCR	WD		IB	T210	CHRY	12		11000	2	10	19500	21600
34		DECKHOUSE		DC	WD		IB	T195	CHRY	12		11500	2	10	20000	22200
34		DECKHOUSE	FB	DC	WD		IB	T195	CHRY	12		11500	2	10	20000	22200
34		DECKHOUSE	FB	SF	WD		IB	T210	CHRY	12		11000	2	10	19900	22200
34		DECKHOUSE	FB	SPTCR	WD		IB	T210	CHRY	12		11000	2	10	20000	22200
		1965 BOATS														
34		POST 34		SPTCR	WD		IB	T210	CHRY	12		11000	2	10	19200	21300
		1964 BOATS														
38		POST 38 CUSTOM		FSH	WD		IB	T290	CHRY	12	6	13500	2	10	25400	28200
		1963 BOATS														
38		POST 38 CUSTOM		FSH	WD		IB	280	CHRY	12	6	13500	2	10	23800	26400
38		POST 38 CUSTOM		FSH	WD		IB	T155D		12	6	13500	2	10	27800	30800
38		SEA-DAN POST 38		SDN	WD		IB	280	CHRY	12	6	13500	2	10	23900	26600
38		SEA-DAN POST 38		SDN	WD		IB	T155D		12	6	13500	2	10	28000	31100
		1962 BOATS														
38		POST 38 CUSTOM		FSH	WD		IB	T155D		12	6	13500	2	10	27100	30200
38		SEA-DAN POST 38		SDN	WD		IB	T155D		12	6	13500	2	10	27400	30400
		1961 BOATS														
37		POST 37 CUSTOM		SF	WD		IB	280	CHRY	12	6	13500	2	10	22200	24600
		1960 BOATS														
37		POST 37 CUSTOM		SF	WD		IB	225	PALM	12	6	13500	2	10	21600	24000
37		POST 37 CUSTOM		SF	P/C		IB	T200		13			2	10	24400	27200
37		POST 37 CUSTOM		SF	P/M		IB	T200		13			2	10	24400	27200
		1959 BOATS														
34		POST 34		SDN	WD		IB	195	CHRY	12		11500	2	10	15700	17900
34		POST 34		SF	WD		IB	195	CHRY	12		11500	2	10	15100	17200
		1958 BOATS														
34		POST 34		SF	WD		IB	150	PALM	12		11500	2	10	14900	16900

POWER CAT BOAT CORP

Call 1-800-327-6929 for BUC Personalized Evaluation Service
Or, for 1960 to 1969 boats, sign onto www.BUCValuPro.com

JACK POWLES INTL MRNE LTD

NORFOLK ENGLAND COAST GUARD MFG ID- JPW See inside cover to adjust price for area

LOA FT	IN	NAME AND/ OR MODEL	TOP/ RIG	BOAT TYPE	-HULL- MTL	TP	TP	----ENGINE--- # HP	MFG	BEAM FT	IN	WGT LBS	DRAFT FT	IN	RETAIL LOW	RETAIL HIGH
		1980 BOATS														
33		POWLES 33	FB	SPTCR	FBG	DV	IB	T180D	VLVO	12	3	14550	3	7	47100	51800
38		POWLES 38	FB	EXP	FBG	DV	IB	T150D	FIAT	12	3	19485	3		70700	77700
38		POWLES 38	FB	EXP	FBG	DV	IB	T212D	FORD	12	3	19485	3		72600	79700
38		POWLES 38	FB	EXP	FBG	DV	IB	T220D	VLVO	12	3	19485	3		71500	78500
40		POWLES 40 AFT CABIN	FB	EXP	FBG	DV	IB	T220D	VLVO	13		20829	3	6	79300	87100
40		POWLES 40 AFT CABIN	FB	EXP	FBG	DV	IB	T270D	VLVO	13		20829	3	6	81100	89100
40		POWLES 40 AFT COCKPT	FB	EXP	FBG	DV	IB	T220D	VLVO	13		20829	3	6	79300	87100
40		POWLES 40 AFT COCKPT	FB	EXP	FBG	DV	IB	T270D	VLVO	13		20829	3	6	81100	89100
46		POWLES 46	FB	EXP	FBG	DV	IB	T270D	VLVO	15	2	28000	3	10	103000	113000
46		POWLES 46	FB	EXP	FBG	DV	IB	T435D	GM	15	2	28000	3	10	114000	125500
53		POWLES 53	FB	EXP	FBG	DV	IB	T450D	GM	15	2	36000	3	10	155500	171000
53		POWLES 53	FB	EXP	FBG	DV	IB	T680D	MTU	15	2	36000	4		190500	209500
65		POWLES 65	FB	EXP	FBG	DV	IB	T550D	GM	17	6	64000	4	9	324000	356000
75		POWLES 75	FB	EXP	FBG	DV	IB	T800D	GM	19	10		5	2	**	**
		1979 BOATS														
31	6	NANTUCKET-CLIPPER 31	YWL	SA/CR	FBG	KL	IB	13D	VLVO	9	6	8247	4	3	22100	24600
33		POWLES 33	FB	SPTCR	FBG	DV	IB	T180D	FORD	12	3	14550	3	1	45500	50000
36		POWLES 36	FB	SPTCR	FBG	DV	IB	T150D	FIAT	12	3	16799	3	1	53900	59200
36		POWLES 36	FB	SPTCR	FBG	DV	IB	T212D	FORD	12	3	16799	3	1	55700	61200
36		POWLES 36	FB	SPTCR	FBG	DV	IB	T220D	VLVO	12	3	16799	3	1	55200	60600
38		POWLES 36+2	FB	EXP	FBG	DV	IB	T150D	FIAT	12	3	20159	3	1	69300	76100
38		POWLES 36+2	FB	EXP	FBG	DV	IB	T212D	FORD	12	3	20159	3	1	71000	78000
38		POWLES 36+2	FB	EXP	FBG	DV	IB	T220D	VLVO	12	3	20159	3	1	70000	76900
40		POWLES 40 AFT CABIN	FB	EXP	FBG	DV	IB	T220D	VLVO	13		20829	3	6	78900	86700
40		POWLES 40 AFT CABIN	FB	EXP	FBG	DV	IB	T270D	VLVO	13		20829	3	6	80500	88500
40		POWLES 40 AFT COCKPT	FB	EXP	FBG	DV	IB	T220D	VLVO	13		20829	3	6	72700	79900
40		POWLES 40 AFT COCKPT	FB	EXP	FBG	DV	IB	T270D	VLVO	13		20829	3	6	74500	81800

 CONTINUED ON NEXT PAGE

LOA FT	LOA IN	NAME AND/ OR MODEL	TOP/ RIG	BOAT TYPE	-HULL- MTL	-HULL- TP	TP	ENGINE # HP	ENGINE MFG	BEAM FT	BEAM IN	WGT LBS	DRAFT FT	DRAFT IN	RETAIL LOW	RETAIL HIGH
		1979 BOATS														
46		POWLES 46	FB	EXP	FBG	DV	IB	T270D	VLVO	16		33289	4		108000	118500
46		POWLES 46	FB	EXP	FBG	DV	IB	T435D	GM	16		33289	4		118500	130000
53		POWLES 53	FB	EXP	FBG	DV	IB	T435D	GM	16		46175	4		162000	178000
65		POWLES 65	FB	EXP	FBG	DV	IB	T550D	GM	17	6	64000	4	9	310000	340500
		1978 BOATS														
38		POWLES 36+2	FB	EXP	FBG	SV	IB	T212D	FORD	12	3	18000	3		62900	69100
46		POWLES 46	FB	EXP	FBG	SV	IB	T D							**	**
53		POWLES 53	FB	EXP	FBG	SV	IB	T435D	GM	15		19000	3	10	106000	116500
		1977 BOATS														
33		POWLES 33	HT	SPTCR	FBG	SV	VD	T164D-T180D		12	3	13000	3		38600	43500
36		POWLES 36	FB	SPTCR	FBG	SV	VD	T164D	BED	12	3	15000	3		46900	51500
36		POWLES 36	FB	SPTCR	FBG	SV	VD	T175D	PERK	12	3	15000	3		47600	52300
36		POWLES 36	FB	SPTCR	FBG	SV	VD	T210D	SABR	12	3	15000	3		47000	51600
38		POWLES 38	FB	EXP	FBG	SV	IB	T175D	PERK	13	2	17000	3		55500	61000
38		POWLES 38	FB	EXP	FBG	SV	IB	T250D	SABR	13	2	17000	3		54300	59600
38		POWLES 38	FB	EXP	FBG	SV	IB	T270D	VLVO	13	2	17000	3		56000	61500
41		POWLES 41	FB	EXP	FBG	SV	IB	T175D	PERK	14	6	20400	3	4	66900	73500
41		POWLES 41	FB	EXP	FBG	SV	IB	T250D	SABR	14	6	20400	3	4	66100	72700
41		POWLES 41	FB	EXP	FBG	SV	IB	T270D	VLVO	14	6	20400	3	4	67900	74700
45		POWLES 45	FB	EXP	FBG	SV	IB	385D	GM	14	10		3	7	62100	68200
53		POWLES 53	FB	EXP	FBG	SV	IB	T425D	GM	15		38800	2	2	135500	148500
65		POWLES 65	FB	EXP	FBG	SV	IB	T550D	GM	17	6	64000	4	9	284500	312500
		1976 BOATS														
33		POWLES 33	HT	EXP	FBG	DV	VD	T138D-T210D		12	3	14560	3		39300	45900
36		POWLES 36	FB	EXP	FBG	DV	VD	T138D	GM	12	3	16800	3		47500	52200
36		POWLES 36	FB	EXP	FBG	DV	VD	T175D	PERK	12	3	16800	3		48700	53500
36		POWLES 36	FB	EXP	FBG	DV	VD	T210D	FORD	12	3	16800	3		48900	53700
38		POWLES 38	FB	EXP	FBG	DV	IB	T175D	PERK	13	2	19000	3		57400	63100
38		POWLES 38	FB	EXP	FBG	DV	IB	T210D	FORD	13	2	19000	3		57200	62900
38		POWLES 38	FB	EXP	FBG	DV	IB	T270D	VLVO	13	2	19000	3		57900	63600
41	10	POWLES 41	FB	EXP	FBG	DV	IB	T175D	PERK	14	6	23250	3	4	71600	78700
41	10	POWLES 41	FB	EXP	FBG	DV	IB	T250D	FORD	14	6	23250	3	4	73700	81000
41	10	POWLES 41	FB	EXP	FBG	DV	IB	T270D	VLVO	14	6	23250	3	4	73300	80600
53		POWLES 53	FB	EXP	FBG	DV	IB	T425D	GM	15	6	35800			127000	140000
53		POWLES 53	FB	EXP	FBG	DV	IB	T650D	MTU	15	6	35800			156500	172000
		1975 BOATS														
33		POWLES 33	FB	SPTCR	FBG	DV	IB	T175D	PERK	12	3	13440	3		37200	41400
36		POWLES 36		CR	FBG	DV	IB	T175D	PERK	12	3	16240	3		45900	50500
38		POWLES 38		CR	FBG	DV	IB	T175D	PERK	13	2	18480	3		54000	59400
41	10	POWLES 41		CR	FBG	DV	IB	T175D	PERK	14	6	22644	3	4	66100	72600
45		POWLES 45 FISHERMAN		CR	FBG	DV	IB	T250D	VLVO	14	10	27552	3	7	76000	83500
45		POWLES 45 TRAVELLER		CR	FBG	DV	IB	T250D	VLVO	14	10	27552	3	7	84200	92500
		1973 BOATS														
37		POWLES 37		EXP	FBG	SV	IB	T145D		12			3		44800	49800
37		POWLES 37		SF	FBG	SV	IB	T145D		12			3		42600	47300
38		POWLES 38		EXP	FBG	SV	IB	T175D		13	2	18480	3		49200	54100
38		POWLES 38		SF	FBG	SV	IB	T175D		13	2	18480	3		48600	53400
41	10	POWLES 41		EXP	FBG	SV	IB	T175D		14	6	22644	3	4	61300	67400
45		POWLES 45		EXP	FBG	SV	IB	T250D		14	10	27552	3	7	66100	72600
45		POWLES 45		SF	FBG	SV	IB	T250D		14	10	27552	3	7	59800	65800
		1972 BOATS														
37		POWLES 37		EXP	FBG	SV	IB	T145D		12			3		43200	48000
37		POWLES 37		EXP	FBG	SV	IB	T175D		12			3		43800	48700
37		POWLES 37		SF	FBG	SV	IB	T145D		12			3		41100	45600
37		POWLES 37		SF	FBG	SV	IB	T175D		12			3		41600	46300
41	6	POWLES 41		EXP	FBG	SV	IB	T175D		13	10		3	3	55100	60600
41	6	POWLES 41		EXP	FBG	SV	IB	T300D		13	10		3	3	60300	66200
45		POWLES 45		EXP	FBG	SV	IB	T250D		15			3	7	53100	58400
45		POWLES 45		EXP	FBG	SV	IB	T370D		15			3	7	57500	63200
45		POWLES 45		SF	FBG	SV	IB	T250D		15			3	7	57600	63300
45		POWLES 45		SF	FBG	SV	IB	T370D		15			3	7	69000	75800
		1971 BOATS														
37		POWLES 37		EXP	FBG	SV	IB	T160		12	3		3		33000	36600
37		POWLES 37		SF	FBG	SV	IB	T160		12	3		3		35500	39400
45		POWLES 45		SF	FBG	SV	IB	T210		15			3	7	47800	52500

PRAIRIE BOAT WORKS INC

CLEARWATER FL 33520 COAST GUARD MFG ID- PBJ See inside cover to adjust price for area

LOA FT	LOA IN	NAME AND/ OR MODEL	TOP/ RIG	BOAT TYPE	-HULL- MTL	-HULL- TP	TP	ENGINE # HP	ENGINE MFG	BEAM FT	BEAM IN	WGT LBS	DRAFT FT	DRAFT IN	RETAIL LOW	RETAIL HIGH
		1982 BOATS														
29		PRAIRIE 29	FB	TRWL	FBG	DS	IB	62D- 85D		11	11	12000	3		44300	49400
36		PRAIRIE 36	FB	TRWL	FBG	DS	IB	T 85D	PERK	13	9	16750	3	3	72200	79300
		IB T135D PERK 74700 82100, IB T160D PERK 76000 83500, IB T200D PERK													78300	86100
42	9	PRAIRIE 42	FB	TRWL	FBG	DS	IB	T135D	PERK	16		28000	3	9	129500	142500
42	9	PRAIRIE 42	FB	TRWL	FBG	DS	IB	T160D	PERK	16		28000	3	9	130500	143500
42	9	PRAIRIE 42	FB	TRWL	FBG	DS	IB	T200D	PERK	16		28000	3	9	133000	146000
46	9	PRAIRIE 46	FB	TRWL	FBG	DS	IB	T135D	PERK	16		31000	3	9	139500	153500
46	9	PRAIRIE 46	FB	TRWL	FBG	DS	IB	T160D	PERK	16		31000	3	9	141000	155000
46	9	PRAIRIE 46	FB	TRWL	FBG	DS	IB	T200D	PERK	16		31000	3	9	143000	157000
46	9	PRAIRIE 46 COCKPIT	FB	TRWL	FBG	DS	IB	T135D	PERK	16		31000	3	9	125500	138000
46	9	PRAIRIE 46 COCKPIT	FB	TRWL	FBG	DS	IB	T160D	PERK	16		31000	3	9	127000	139500
46	9	PRAIRIE 46 COCKPIT	FB	TRWL	FBG	DS	IB	T200D	PERK	16		31000	3	9	129500	142500
		1981 BOATS														
29		PRAIRIE 29	FB	TRWL	FBG	DS	IB	62D- 85D		11	11	12000	3		42600	47500
36		PRAIRIE 36	FB	TRWL	FBG	DS	IB	T 85D	PERK	13		16000	3	3	68600	75400
36		PRAIRIE 36	FB	TRWL	FBG	DS	IB	T115D	PERK	13		16000	3	3	70000	76900
36		PRAIRIE 36	FB	TRWL	FBG	DS	IB	T130D	PERK	13		16000	3	3	70800	77800
42	9	PRAIRIE 42	FB	TRWL	FBG	DS	IB	T130D	PERK	16		28000	3	9	123000	135500
42	9	PRAIRIE 42	FB	TRWL	FBG	DS	IB	T160D	PERK	16		28000	3	9	124500	137000
42	9	PRAIRIE 42	FB	TRWL	FBG	DS	IB	T200D	PERK	16		28000	3	9	126500	139000
46	9	PRAIRIE 46	FB	TRWL	FBG	DS	IB	T130D	PERK	16		31000	3	9	129000	141500
46	9	PRAIRIE 46	FB	TRWL	FBG	DS	IB	T160D	PERK	16		31000	3	9	130500	143500
46	9	PRAIRIE 46	FB	TRWL	FBG	DS	IB	T200D	PERK	16		31000	3	9	132500	145500
46	9	PRAIRIE 46 COCKPIT	FB	TRWL	FBG	DS	IB	T130D	PERK	16		31000	3	9	123500	136000
		IB T160D PERK 125000 137500, IB T200D PERK 127500 140000, IB T240D PERK													132000	145000
		1980 BOATS														
29		PRAIRIE 29	FB	TRWL	FBG	DS	IB	170	MRCR	11	11	12000	3		30400	33800
29		PRAIRIE 29	FB	TRWL	FBG	DS	IB	62D- 85D		11	11	12000			40800	45700
29		PRAIRIE 29	FB	TRWL	FBG	DS	IB	130D-225D		11	11	12000	3		46500	54700
31	8	PRAIRIE 32	CUT	SA/CR	FBG	KL	IB	D		11		17300	4	6	27300	30400
34	8	PRAIRIE 32/2	CUT	SA/CR	FBG	KL	IB	D		11		17300	4	6	26900	29900
36		PRAIRIE 36	FB	TRWL	FBG	DS	IB	T 85D	PERK	13		16000	3	3	65400	71900
		IB T130D PERK 67500 74200, IB T160D PERK 69000 75800, IB T185D PERK													70300	77200
		IB T225D PERK 72600 79700														
42	9	PRAIRIE 42	FB	TRWL	FBG	DS	IB	T130D	PERK	15	6	28000	3	9	118000	130000
		IB T160D PERK 119500 131500, IB T200D PERK 121500 133500, IB T225D PERK													123000	135000
46	9	PRAIRIE 46	FB	TRWL	FBG	DS	IB	T130D	PERK	15	6	31000	3	9	120500	132500
46	9	PRAIRIE 46	FB	TRWL	FBG	DS	IB	T160D	PERK	15	6	31000	3	9	122000	134500
46	9	PRAIRIE 46	FB	TRWL	FBG	DS	IB	T225D	PERK	15	6	31000	3	9	125500	138000
		1979 BOATS														
29		COASTAL-CRUISER 29	FB	TRWL	FBG	DS	IB	50D- 85D		11	11	12000	3		39400	44000
29		COASTAL-CRUISER 29	FB	TRWL	FBG	DS	IB	130D-160D		11	11	12000	3		44300	50400
31	8	PRAIRIE 32	SLP	SA/CR	FBG	KL	IB	33D- 50D		11		17300	4	6	26500	29400
34	8	PRAIRIE 32/2	SLP	SA/CR	FBG	KL	IB	50D	PERK	11		17300	4	6	26000	28900
36		COASTAL-CRUISER 36	FB	TRWL	FBG	DS	IB	T 85D	PERK	13		16000	3	3	62500	68700
		1978 BOATS														
27		OSPREY 27	SLP	SAIL	FBG	KL	OB			9	2	6000	4	3	8550	9850
27		OSPREY 27	SLP	SAIL	FBG	KL	IB	8D	YAN	9	2	6000	4	3	9000	10200
31	8	PRAIRIE 32	CUT	SA/CR	FBG	KL	IB	33D- 50D		11		17300	4	6	25700	28600
		1977 BOATS														
31	8	PRAIRIE 32	CUT	SA/CR	FBG	KL	IB	D		11		17000	4	6	24600	27300

PRECISION BOAT WORKS

PALMETTO FL 34221 COAST GUARD MFG ID- PCW See inside cover to adjust price for area

For more recent years, see the BUC Used Boat Price Guide, Volume 1 or Volume 2

LOA FT	LOA IN	NAME AND/ OR MODEL	TOP/ RIG	BOAT TYPE	-HULL- MTL	-HULL- TP	TP	ENGINE # HP	ENGINE MFG	BEAM FT	BEAM IN	WGT LBS	DRAFT FT	DRAFT IN	RETAIL LOW	RETAIL HIGH
		1983 BOATS														
24		SEAFORTH	SLP	SA/CR	FBG	KL	OB			7	4	4000	2	6	7200	8250
24		SEAFORTH	SLP	SA/CR	FBG	KL	IB	D	YAN	7	4	4000	2	6	8050	9250
		1982 BOATS														
24		SEAFORTH	SLP	SA/CR	FBG	KL	OB			7	4	4000	2	6	6750	7750
24		SEAFORTH	SLP	SA/CR	FBG	KL	IB	8D	REN	7	4	4000	2	6	7450	8550
		1981 BOATS														
24		SEAFORTH	SLP	SA/CR	FBG	KL	OB			7	4	4000	2	6	6350	7300
24		SEAFORTH	SLP	SA/CR	FBG	KL	IB	8D	REN	7	4	4000	2	6	7000	8050
24		SEAFORTH COASTAL CR	SLP	SAIL	FBG	KL	IB	8D		7	4	4000	2	6	7000	8050
		1980 BOATS														
22		SEAFORTH	SLP	SA/CR	FBG	KL	OB			7	4	4000	2	6	5700	6550
22		SEAFORTH	SLP	SA/CR	FBG	KL	IB	8D	FARY	7	4	4000	2	6	6300	7250
		1979 BOATS														
22		SEAFORTH	SLP	SA/CR	FBG	KL	OB			7	4	3800	2	6	5100	5900

PRECISIONCRAFT YTS INC

Call 1-800-327-6929 for BUC Personalized Evaluation Service
Or, for 1977 boats, sign onto www.BUCValuPro.com

PRESENT YACHTS INC

ROCHESTER NY 14607-1619   See inside cover to adjust price for area

For more recent years, see the BUC Used Boat Price Guide, Volume 1 or Volume 2

LOA FT IN	NAME AND/ OR MODEL	TOP/ RIG	BOAT TYPE	MTL	-HULL- TP	TP	ENGINE #	HP	MFG	FT IN	WGT LBS	DRAFT FT IN	RETAIL LOW	RETAIL HIGH
					1983 BOATS									
30 6	SEDAN	FB	TRWL	FBG	DS	IB	80D	LEHM	11 6	14771	3 4	46700	51300
37 10	DOUBLE CABIN	FB	TRWL	FBG	DS	IB	120D	LEHM	12 10	18739	3 5	70300	77300
37 10	DOUBLE CABIN	FB	TRWL	FBG	DS	IB	T120D	LEHM	12 10	18739	3 5	74800	82200
37 10	SEDAN	FB	TRWL	FBG	DS	IB	120D	LEHM	12 10	18739	3 5	70300	77300
37 10	SEDAN	FB	TRWL	FBG	DS	IB	T120D	LEHM	12 10	18739	3 5	74800	82200
41 2	DOUBLE CABIN	FB	TRWL	FBG	DS	IB	120D	LEHM	13 8	25365	3 6	94300	103500
41 2	DOUBLE CABIN	FB	TRWL	FBG	DS	IB	T120D	LEHM	13 8	25365	3 6	99000	108500
41 2	SEDAN	FB	TRWL	FBG	DS	IB	120D	LEHM	13 8	25365	3 6	94800	104000
41 2	SEDAN	FB	TRWL	FBG	DS	IB	T120D	LEHM	13 8	25365	3 6	99500	109500

41 2	SUNDECK	FB	TRWL	FBG	DS	IB	120D	LEHM	13 8	25353	3 6	97500	107000
	IB T120D LEHM 102000 112000, IB T135D LEHM 100500 110500, IB T200D PERK 104500 115000												
	IB T210D CAT 105000 115500, IB T225D LEHM 104000 114000, IB T235D VLVO 103000 113000												
	IB T240D PERK 106500 117000, IB T270D CUM 105500 116000												

41 2	TRI-CABIN	FB	TRWL	FBG	DS	IB	120D	LEHM	13 8	25353	3 6	92300	101500
41 2	TRI-CABIN	FB	TRWL	FBG	DS	IB	T120D	LEHM	13 8	25353	3 6	97200	107000
44 10	PILOTHOUSE	FB	TRWL	FBG	DS	IB	T120D	LEHM	15 10	30864	4 2	108500	119000
44 10	SEDAN	FB	TRWL	FBG	DS	IB	210D	LEHM	15 10	30864	4 2	104500	114500
44 10	SEDAN	FB	TRWL	FBG	DS	IB	270D	CUM	15 10	30864	4 2	105000	115500
44 10	SEDAN	FB	TRWL	FBG	DS	IB	T120D	LEHM	15 10	30864	4 2	105000	115500
					1982 BOATS									
30	SEDAN	FB	TRWL	FBG	DS	IB	80D-120D	LEHM	11 6	14000	3 6	42000	50800
37 8	DOUBLE CABIN	FB	TRWL	FBG	DS	IB	120D	LEHM	12 10	22000	3 5	75700	83200
37 8	DOUBLE CABIN	FB	TRWL	FBG	DS	IB	T120D	LEHM	12 10	23500	3 5	83700	92000
37 8	SEDAN	FB	TRWL	FBG	DS	IB	120D	LEHM	12 10	22000	3 5	75700	83200
37 8	SEDAN	FB	TRWL	FBG	DS	IB	T120D	LEHM	12 10	23500	3 5	83700	92000
41 2	DOUBLE CABIN	FB	TRWL	FBG	DS	IB	120D	LEHM	13 8	25300	3 6	88600	97400
41 2	DOUBLE CABIN	FB	TRWL	FBG	DS	IB	T120D	LEHM	13 8	26800	3 6	97800	107500
41 2	SEDAN	FB	TRWL	FBG	DS	IB	120D	LEHM	13 8	25300	3 6	89100	97900
41 2	SEDAN	FB	TRWL	FBG	DS	IB	T120D	LEHM	13 8	26800	3 6	98400	108000
41 2	TRI-CABIN	FB	TRWL	FBG	DS	IB	120D	LEHM	13 8	25300	3 6	92300	101500
41 2	TRI-CABIN	FB	TRWL	FBG	DS	IB	T120D	LEHM	13 8	26800	3 6	99900	109500
44 10	PILOTHOUSE	FB	TRWL	FBG	DS	IB	T120D	LEHM	15 10	26500	4 2	94800	104000

44 10	SEDAN	FB	TRWL	FBG	DS	IB	210D	CAT	15 10	26500	4 2	91100	100000
44 10	SEDAN	FB	TRWL	FBG	DS	IB	270D	CUM	15 10	26500	4 2	91900	101000
44 10	SEDAN	FB	TRWL	FBG	DS	IB	T120D	LEHM	15 10	26500	4 2	91900	101000
					1981 BOATS									
30	SEDAN	FB	TRWL	FBG	DS	IB	65D-120D		11 6	14000	3 6	40300	48800
37 8	DOUBLE CABIN	FB	TRWL	FBG	DS	IB	120D	LEHM	12 10	22000	3 5	72200	79300
37 8	DOUBLE CABIN	FB	TRWL	FBG	DS	IB	T120D	LEHM	12 10	23500	3 5	79800	87600
37 8	SEDAN	FB	TRWL	FBG	DS	IB	120D	LEHM	12 10	22000	3 5	72200	79300
37 8	SEDAN	FB	TRWL	FBG	DS	IB	T120D	LEHM	12 10	23500	3 5	79800	87600
41 2	DOUBLE CABIN	FB	TRWL	FBG	DS	IB	120D	LEHM	13 8	25300	3 6	84800	93100
41 2	DOUBLE CABIN	FB	TRWL	FBG	DS	IB	T120D	LEHM	13 8	26800	3 6	93200	102500
41 2	SEDAN	FB	TRWL	FBG	DS	IB	120D	LEHM	13 8	25300	3 6	85200	93700
41 2	SEDAN	FB	TRWL	FBG	DS	IB	T120D	LEHM	13 8	26800	3 6	93700	103000
41 2	TRI-CABIN	FB	TRWL	FBG	DS	IB	120D	LEHM	13 8	25300	3 6	87200	95900
41 2	TRI-CABIN	FB	TRWL	FBG	DS	IB	T120D	LEHM	13 8	26800	3 6	95100	104500
44 10	PILOTHOUSE	FB	TRWL	FBG	DS	IB	T120D	LEHM	15 10	26500	4 2	90300	99300

44 10	SEDAN	FB	TRWL	FBG	DS	IB	210D	CAT	15 10	26500	4 2	86800	95400
44 10	SEDAN	FB	TRWL	FBG	DS	IB	270D	CUM	15 10	26500	4 2	87600	96200
44 10	SEDAN	FB	TRWL	FBG	DS	IB	T120D	LEHM	15 10	26500	4 2	87600	96200
54	MOTOR YACHT	FB	TRWL	FBG	DS	IB	T210D	CAT	16 10	50000	4 6	133500	146500

PRESIDENT YACHTS

FT LAUDERDALE FL 33316   COAST GUARD MFG ID- MYI See inside cover to adjust price for area

For more recent years, see the BUC Used Boat Price Guide, Volume 1 or Volume 2

LOA FT IN	NAME AND/ OR MODEL	TOP/ RIG	BOAT TYPE	MTL	-HULL- TP	TP	ENGINE #	HP	MFG	BEAM FT IN	WGT LBS	DRAFT FT IN	RETAIL LOW	RETAIL HIGH
					1983 BOATS									
40 6	PRESIDENT 41 DC	FB	MY	FBG	SV	IB	T120D	LEHM	13 5	22500	2 10	81500	89600
					1982 BOATS									
40 6	PRESIDENT 41 DC	FB	MY	FBG	SV	IB	T120D	LEHM	13 5	22500	2 10	77800	85500
					1981 BOATS									
40 6	PRESIDENT 41 DC	FB	MY	FBG	SV	IB	T120D	LEHM	13 5	22500	2 10	74100	81400

RICHARD PRICE YACHT YARD

Call 1-800-327-6929 for BUC Personalized Evaluation Service
Or, for 1959 to 1969 boats, sign onto www.BUCValuPro.com

PRIVATEER MFG CO INC

CHOCOWINITY NC 27817   COAST GUARD MFG ID- PVT See inside cover to adjust price for area

For more recent years, see the BUC Used Boat Price Guide, Volume 1 or Volume 2

LOA FT IN	NAME AND/ OR MODEL	TOP/ RIG	BOAT TYPE	MTL	-HULL- TP	TP	ENGINE #	HP	MFG	BEAM FT IN	WGT LBS	DRAFT FT IN	RETAIL LOW	RETAIL HIGH
					1983 BOATS									
18 4	RETRIEVER 1800	OP	CBNCR	FBG	SV	OB				7 2	900	6	2250	2600
20 2	REVENGE 2002	ST	CBNCR	FBG	SV	OB				7 10	1400	7	3450	4000
20 2	REVENGE 2002	ST	CBNCR	FBG	SV	IO	145D	VLVO		7 10	2200	7	7800	9000
20 2	REVENGE 2002	OP	CTRCN	FBG	SV	OB				7 10	1200	7	3050	3550
20 2	REVENGE 2002	OP	CTRCN	FBG	SV	IO	145D	VLVO		7 10	2000	8	8500	9750
24 4	RENEGADE 2400	HT	CBNCR	FBG	SV	OB				9 1	2400	11	6700	7250
24 4	RENEGADE 2400	HT	CTRCN	FBG	SV	IO	290D-305D			9 1	3900	2	15800	18200
24 4	RENEGADE 2400	OP	CTRCN	FBG	SV	OB				9 1	2150	11	5450	6250
24 4	RENEGADE 2400	OP	CTRCN	FBG	SV	IO	290D-305D			9 1	3500	2	15500	18100
					1982 BOATS									
18 4	RETRIEVER 1800	OP	CTRCN	FBG	SV	OB				7 2	900	6	2200	2550
20 2	REVENGE 2002	ST	CTRCN	FBG	SV	OB				7 10	1400	7	3350	3900
20 2	REVENGE 2002	ST	CTRCN	FBG	SV	IO	145D	VLVO		7 10	2200	8	7600	8700
20 2	REVENGE 2002	OP	CTRCN	FBG	SV	OB				7 10	1200	7	2950	3450
20 2	REVENGE 2002	OP	CTRCN	FBG	SV	IO	145D	VLVO		7 10	2000	8	8200	9450
24 4	RENEGADE 2400	HT	CBNCR	FBG	SV	OB				9 1	2400	11	6150	7050
24 4	RENEGADE 2400	HT	CTRCN	FBG	SV	IO	290D	VLVO		9 1	3900	1	15300	17400
24 4	RENEGADE 2400	OP	CTRCN	FBG	SV	OB				9 1	2150	11	5350	6100
24 4	RENEGADE 2400	OP	CTRCN	FBG	SV	IO	290D	VLVO		9 1	3500	1	15000	17000
					1980 BOATS									
20 2	REVENGE 2002	OP	CTRCN	FBG	SV	OB				7 10	1200	8	2800	3300
24 4	RENEGADE 2400	HT	CTRCN	FBG	SV	OB				9 1		9	5850	6700
24 4	RENEGADE 2400	OP	CTRCN	FBG	SV	OB				9 1	2000	10	5050	5850
24 4	RENEGADE 2400	HT	PH	FBG	SV	OB				9 1		9	5400	6200

PRO-CAT ENGINEERING INC

Call 1-800-327-6929 for BUC Personalized Evaluation Service
Or, for 1977 boats, sign onto www.BUCValuPro.com

PRO-LINE BOATS INC

CRYSTAL RIVER FL 34423- COAST GUARD MFG ID- PLC See inside cover to adjust price for area

For more recent years, see the BUC Used Boat Price Guide, Volume 1 or Volume 2

LOA FT IN	NAME AND/ OR MODEL	TOP/ RIG	BOAT TYPE	MTL	-HULL- TP	TP	ENGINE #	HP	MFG	BEAM FT IN	WGT LBS	DRAFT FT IN	RETAIL LOW	RETAIL HIGH
					1983 BOATS									
16 10	PRO 17	ST	CTRCN	FBG	SV	OB				7 2	1100	8	2000	2400
16 10	PRO 17 TWIN CONSOLE	ST	OPFSH	FBG	SV	OB				7 2	1100	8	2000	2350
20 1	PRO 20	ST	CUD	FBG	DV	OB				7 8	1590	10	3650	4250
20 1	PRO 20	ST	OPFSH	FBG	SV	OB				7 8	1740	10	4000	4650
20 1	PRO 20 TWIN CONSOLE	ST	OPFSH	FBG	SV	OB				7 8	1590	10	3700	4300
20 6	PRO 21 WALKAROUND	ST	CTRCN	FBG	DV	OB				8	1830	1	4150	4800
20 6	PRO 21 WALKAROUND	ST	CTRCN	FBG	DV	IO	185	MRCR		8	2940	1	5450	6300
20 6	PRO 21 WALKAROUND	ST	CUD	FBG	DV	OB				8	2150	1	4800	5550
20 6	PRO 21 WALKAROUND	ST	CUD	FBG	DV	IO	140	MRCR		8	2940	1	5150	5900
23	PRO 23	ST	CTRCN	FBG	DV	OB				8	1920	1 6	4800	5500
23	PRO 23	ST	CTRCN	FBG	DV	IO	170	MRCR		8	2430	1 8	5650	6500
23	PRO 23	ST	CUD	FBG	DV	IO	185	MRCR		8	2650	1 8	5600	6450
23	PRO 23 TWIN CONSOLE	ST	OPFSH	FBG	DV	OB				8	1880	1 6	4750	5500
23	PRO 23 TWIN CONSOLE	ST	OPFSH	FBG	DV	IO	170	MRCR		8	2430	1 8	5650	6500
23	PRO 23 WALKAROUND	ST	CUD	FBG	DV	OB				8	2650	1 6	6400	7350
23	PRO 23 WALKAROUND	ST	CUD	FBG	DV	IO	185	MRCR		8	2300	1 8	5250	6050

PRO-LINE BOATS INC -CONTINUED See inside cover to adjust price for area

LOA FT	IN	NAME AND/ OR MODEL	TOP/ RIG	BOAT TYPE	-HULL- MTL	TP	TP	----ENGINE--- # HP	MFG	BEAM FT	IN	WGT LBS	DRAFT FT	IN	RETAIL LOW	RETAIL HIGH
		1982 BOATS														
16	10	PRO 17	ST	CTRCN	FBG	SV	OB			7	2	1100		8	1950	2350
16	10	PRO 17 TWIN CONSOLE	ST	OPFSH	FBG	SV	OB			7	2	1100		8	1950	2350
20	1	PRO 20	ST	CTRCN	FBG	SV	OB			7	8	1590		10	3550	4150
20	1	PRO 20	ST	CUD	FBG	SV	OB			7	8	1740		10	3900	4550
20	1	PRO 20 TWIN CONSOLE	ST	OPFSH	FBG	SV	OB			7	8	1590		10	3600	4200
20	6	PRO 6.2	ST	CTRCN	FBG	DV	OB			8		1830	1		4050	4700
20	6	PRO 6.2	ST	CTRCN	FBG	DV	IO	140	MRCR	8		2940	1		5300	6100
20	6	PRO 6.2 WALKAROUND	ST	CUD	FBG	DV	OB			8		2150	1		4700	5400
20	6	PRO 6.2 WALKAROUND	ST	CUD	FBG	DV	IO	140	MRCR	8		2940	1		5050	5800
23		PRO 23	ST	CTRCN	FBG	DV	OB			8		1920	1	6	4700	5400
23		PRO 23	ST	CTRCN	FBG	DV	IO	170	MRCR	8		2430	1	8	5500	6350
23		PRO 23	ST	CUD	FBG	DV	OB			8		2100	1	6	5150	5950
23		PRO 23	ST	CUD	FBG	DV	IO	170	MRCR	8		2650	1	8	5450	6250
23		PRO 23 TWIN CONSOLE	ST	OPFSH	FBG	DV	OB			8		1880	1	6	4650	5350
23		PRO 23 TWIN CONSOLE	ST	OPFSH	FBG	DV	IO	170	MRCR	8		2430	1	8	5500	6350
23		PRO 23 WALKAROUND	ST	CUD	FBG	DV	OB			8		2650	1	6	6250	7200
23		PRO 23 WALKAROUND	ST	CUD	FBG	DV	IO	170	MRCR	8		2300	1	8	5100	5850
24		PRO 24	ST	CTRCN	FBG	SV	OB			7	8	1850	1		4600	5300
24		PRO 24	ST	CTRCN	FBG	SV	IO	130		7	8		1		6750	7750
24		PRO 24 TWIN CONSOLE	ST	OPFSH	FBG	SV	OB			7	8	1850	1		4700	5400
		1981 BOATS														
16	10	PRO 17		CTRCN	FBG	SV	OB			7	2	1100			1950	2300
16	10	PRO 17	ST	CTRCN	FBG	SV	OB			7	2	1100		8	1950	2300
16	10	PRO 17		SF	FBG	SV	OB			7	2	1100			1950	2300
16	10	PRO 17 TWIN CONSOLE		OPFSH	FBG	SV	OB			7	2	1100			1900	2300
16	10	PRO 17 TWIN CONSOLE	ST	OPFSH	FBG	SV	OB			7	2	1100		8	1900	2300
20	1	PRO 20	ST	CTRCN	FBG	SV	OB			7	8	1590		10	3500	4050
20	1	PRO 20	ST	CUD	FBG	SV	OB			7	8	1740		10	3850	4450
20	1	PRO 20		SF	FBG	SV	OB			7	8	1590			3550	4100
20	1	PRO 20		SF	FBG	SV	IO	140		7	8				4800	5550
20	1	PRO 20 TWIN CONSOLE	ST	OPFSH	FBG	SV	OB			7	8	1590		10	3500	4100
23		PRO 23	ST	CTRCN	FBG	DV	OB			8		1920	1	6	4550	5250
23		PRO 23	ST	CTRCN	FBG	DV	IO	170	MRCR	8		2430	1	8	5450	6250
23		PRO 23		CUD	FBG	DV	OB			8		2300			5450	6250
23		PRO 23	ST	CUD	FBG	DV	OB			8		2100	1	6	5050	5800
23		PRO 23	ST	CUD	FBG	DV	IO	170	MRCR	8		2650	1	8	5350	6150
23		PRO 23 TWIN CONSOLE	ST	OPFSH	FBG	DV	OB			8		1880	1	6	4550	5250
23		PRO 23 TWIN CONSOLE	ST	OPFSH	FBG	DV	IO	170	MRCR	8		2430	1	8	5450	6250
23		PRO 23 WALKAROUND	ST	CUD	FBG	DV	OB			8		2650	1	6	6100	7000
23		PRO 23 WALKAROUND	ST	CUD	FBG	DV	IO	170	MRCR	8		2300	1	8	5050	5800
23	1	PRO 23		CUD	FBG	DV	OB			8		2170			5200	6000
23	1	PRO 23		SF	FBG	DV	IO	170		8					6900	7950
24		PRO 24	ST	CTRCN	FBG	SV	OB			7	8	2100	1		5000	5750
24		PRO 24		SF	FBG	SV	OB			7	8	1850			4600	5300
24		PRO 24		SF	FBG	SV	IO	130		7	8				7150	8250
		1980 BOATS														
16	10	PRO 17	ST	CTRCN	FBG	SV	OB			7	2	1100		8	1900	2250
16	10	PRO 17 TWIN CONSOLE	ST	OPFSH	FBG	SV	OB			7	2	1100		8	1900	2250
20	1	PRO 20	ST	CTRCN	FBG	SV	OB			7	8	1740		10	3650	4250
20	1	PRO 20	ST	CUD	FBG	SV	OB			7	8	1740		10	3750	4350
20	1	PRO 20	ST	CUD	FBG	SV	IO	140		7	8	2290		11	4050	4900
20	1	PRO 20 TWIN CONSOLE	ST	OPFSH	FBG	SV	OB			7	8	1590		10	3450	4000
20	1	PRO 20 TWIN CONSOLE	ST	OPFSH	FBG	SV	IO	140		7	8	2140		11	4150	5050
23		PRO 23	ST	CTRCN	FBG	DV	OB			8		1880	1	6	4400	5050
23		PRO 23	ST	CTRCN	FBG	DV	IO	170	MRCR	8		2430	1	8	5400	6200
23		PRO 23	ST	CUD	FBG	DV	OB			8		2100	1	6	4950	5700
23		PRO 23	ST	CUD	FBG	DV	IO	170	MRCR	8		2650	1	8	5300	6100
23		PRO 23 TWIN CONSOLE	ST	OPFSH	FBG	DV	OB			8		1880	1	6	4450	5150
23		PRO 23 TWIN CONSOLE	ST	OPFSH	FBG	DV	IO	170	MRCR	8		2430	1	8	5400	6200
24		PRO 24	ST	CTRCN	FBG	SV	OB			7	8	2100	1		4950	5700
24		PRO 24	ST	CUD	FBG	SV	OB			7	8	2100	1		5100	5850
24		PRO 24	ST	CUD	FBG	SV	IO	140-170		7	8	2650	1	1	5550	6550
24		PRO 24	ST	OPFSH	FBG	SV	IO	140-170		7	8	2400	1	1	5550	6600
24		PRO 24 TWIN CONSOLE	ST	OPFSH	FBG	SV	OB			7	8	1850	1		4500	5200
		1979 BOATS														
16	10	PRO-17 DELUXE	OP	OPFSH	FBG	SV	OB			7	2	1140		8	1950	2300
16	10	PRO-17 SPORTSMAN	OP	CTRCN	FBG	SV	OB			7	2	1140		8	1950	2300
20		PRO-20 CUDDY CABIN	ST	CUD	FBG	SV	OB			7	8	1740		10	3650	4250
20		PRO-20 CUDDY CABIN	ST	CUD	FBG	SV	IO	140		7	8	2290		11	4050	4700
20		PRO-20 DELUXE	ST	OPFSH	FBG	SV	OB			7	8	1590		10	3400	3950
20		PRO-20 DELUXE	ST	OPFSH	FBG	SV	IO	140		7	8	2140		11	4150	4800
20		PRO-20 SPORTSMAN	ST	OPFSH	FBG	SV	OB			7	8	1590		10	3350	3900
20		PRO-20 SPORTSMAN	ST	OPFSH	FBG	SV	IO	140		7	8	2140		11	4150	4800
23		PRO-23 CUDDY CABIN	ST	CUD	FBG	SV	OB			8		2166	1	3	5000	5750
23		PRO-23 DELUXE	ST	OPFSH	FBG	SV	OB			8		2100	1	3	4900	5650
23		PRO-23 SPORTSMAN	ST	OPFSH	FBG	SV	OB			8		2100	1	3	4700	5400
24		PRO-24 CUDDY CABIN	ST	CUD	FBG	SV	OB			7	8	2100	1		5000	5750
24		PRO-24 CUDDY CABIN	ST	CUD	FBG	SV	IO	140-185		7	8	2650	1	1	5500	6400
24		PRO-24 DELUXE	ST	OPFSH	FBG	SV	OB			7	8	1850	1		4500	5150
24		PRO-24 DELUXE	ST	OPFSH	FBG	SV	IO	140-185		7	8	2400	1	1	5550	6450
24		PRO-24 SPORTSMAN	ST	OPFSH	FBG	SV	OB			7	8	1850	1		4300	5000
24		PRO-24 SPORTSMAN	ST	OPFSH	FBG	SV	IO	140-185		7	8	2400	1	1	5550	6450
		1978 BOATS														
16	10	PRO-17 DELUXE	OP	OPFSH	FBG	SV	OB			7	2	1240		8	2050	2450
16	10	PRO-17 SPORTSMAN	OP	CTRCN	FBG	SV	OB			7	2	1240		8	2050	2450
20	1	PRO-20 CUDDY CABIN	ST	CUD	FBG	SV	OB			7	8	1740		10	3600	4200
20	1	PRO-20 CUDDY CABIN	ST	CUD	FBG	SV	IO	130-140		7	8	2290		11	4250	4950
20	1	PRO-20 DELUXE	ST	CTRCN	FBG	SV	IO	130-140		7	8	2140		11	4400	5050
20	1	PRO-20 DELUXE	ST	OPFSH	FBG	SV	OB			7	8	1590		10	3300	3850
20	1	PRO-20 SPORTSMAN	ST	CTRCN	FBG	SV	OB			7	8	1590		10	3300	3800
20	1	PRO-20 SPORTSMAN	ST	CTRCN	FBG	SV	IO	130-140		7	8	2140		11	4400	5050
24		PRO-24 CUDDY CABIN	ST	CUD	FBG	SV	OB			7	8	2100	1		4900	5650
24		PRO-24 CUDDY CABIN	ST	CUD	FBG	SV	IO	130-185		7	8	2650	1	1	5750	6600
24		PRO-24 DELUXE	ST	OPFSH	FBG	SV	OB			7	8	1850	1		4250	4950
24		PRO-24 DELUXE	ST	OPFSH	FBG	SV	IO	130-185		7	8	2400	1	1	5800	6650
24		PRO-24 SPORTSMAN	ST	CTRCN	FBG	SV	OB			7	8	1850	1		4200	4900
24		PRO-24 SPORTSMAN	ST	CTRCN	FBG	SV	IO	130-185		7	8	2400	1	1	5800	6650
		1977 BOATS														
16	10	PRO-17 DELUXE	OP	OPFSH	FBG	SV	OB			7	2	1000		6	1750	2050
20	1	PRO-20	ST	OPFSH	FBG	SV	IO	130-140		7	8	2340		8	4650	5350
20	1	PRO-20 CUDDY CABIN	ST	CUD	FBG	SV	OB			7	8	1740		8	3550	4150
20	1	PRO-20 CUDDY CABIN	ST	CUD	FBG	SV	IO	130-140		7	8	2490		8	4550	5250
20	1	PRO-20 DELUXE	ST	OPFSH	FBG	SV	OB			7	8	1590		8	3300	3850
20	1	PRO-20 SPORTSMAN	ST	OPFSH	FBG	SV	OB			7	8	1590		8	3250	3750
24		PRO-24	ST	OPFSH	FBG	SV	IO	130-175		7	8	2600		11	6100	7050
24		PRO-24 CUDDY CABIN	ST	CUD	FBG	SV	OB			7	8	2100		11	4850	5600
24		PRO-24 CUDDY CABIN	ST	CUD	FBG	SV	IO	130-175		7	8	2850		11	6050	7000
24		PRO-24 DELUXE	ST	OPFSH	FBG	SV	OB			7	8	1850		11	4250	4950
24		PRO-24 SPORTSMAN	ST	OPFSH	FBG	SV	OB			7	8	1850		11	4150	4850
		1976 BOATS														
17		SPORTSMAN	OP	FSH	FBG	SV	OB			7	2	1020			1700	2050
20		CUDDY	ST	CUD	FBG	SV	OB			7	9	1610			3300	3850
20		CUDDY	ST	CUD	FBG	SV	IO	140	OMC	7	8	2210			4150	4800
20		SPORTSMAN	ST	OPFSH	FBG	SV	OB			7	9	1570			3200	3700
20		SPORTSMAN	ST	OPFSH	FBG	SV	IO	140	OMC	7	8	2145			4350	5000
24		CUDDY	ST	CUD	FBG	SV	OB			7	9	1940			4500	5150
24		CUDDY	ST	CUD	FBG	SV	IO	165	OMC	7	9	3150			6400	7350
24		SPORTSMAN	ST	OPFSH	FBG	SV	OB			7	9	1890			4250	4900
24		SPORTSMAN	ST	OPFSH	FBG	SV	IO	140-165		7	9	2630			6900	7550
24		SPORTSMAN	ST	OPFSH	FBG	SV	IB	225	CHRY	7	8	2940			5650	6450
		1975 BOATS														
20		PRO-20	OP	OPFSH	FBG	SV	OB			7	8	1400		8	2900	3350
20		PRO-20	OP	OPFSH	FBG	SV	IO	140		7	8	1650		8	4100	4800
24	2	PRO-24	OP	OPFSH	FBG	SV	OB			7	8	1750		7	4000	4650
24	2	PRO-24	OP	OPFSH	FBG	SV	IO	140-170		7	8	2000		7	5700	6650
24	2	PRO-24	OP	OPFSH	FBG	SV	IB	225		7	8	2000		7	4700	5400
		1974 BOATS														
16	10	PRO 17 DLX		OPFSH	FBG	SV	OB			7	2	1000		6	1700	2050
20		PRO 20 DLX		OPFSH	FBG	SV	OB			7	8	1400		8	2900	3400
20		PRO 20 DLX		OPFSH	FBG	SV	IO	140		7	8			8	5000	5750
20		PRO 20 SPORTSMAN		OPFSH	FBG	SV	OB			7	8	1400		8	2800	3250
20		PRO 20 SPORTSMAN		OPFSH	FBG	SV	IO	140		7	8			8	5000	5750
24	2	PRO 24 DLX		OPFSH	FBG	SV	OB			7	8	1750		7	4000	4650
24	2	PRO 24 DLX		OPFSH	FBG	SV	IO	130-170		7	8			7	7650	8850
24	2	PRO 24 SPORTSMAN		OPFSH	FBG	SV	OB			7	8	1750		7	3900	4550
24	2	PRO 24 SPORTSMAN		OPFSH	FBG	SV	IO	130-170		7	8			7	7550	8750
		1973 BOATS														
16	10	PRO 17 DLX		OPFSH	FBG	SV	OB			7	2	1000		6	1700	2050
20		PRO 20 DLX		OPFSH	FBG	SV	OB			7	8	1400		8	2900	3350
20		PRO 20 SPORTSMAN		OPFSH	FBG	SV	OB			7	8	1400		8	2800	3250
24	2	PRO 24 DLX		OPFSH	FBG	SV	OB			7	8	1750		7	4000	4650
24	2	PRO 24 DLX		OPFSH	FBG	SV	IO	130-170		7	8			7	7850	9100
24	2	PRO 24 SPORTSMAN		OPFSH	FBG	SV	OB			7	8	1750		7	3850	4500
24	2	PRO 24 SPORTSMAN		OPFSH	FBG	SV	IO	130-170		7	8			7	7850	9100
		1972 BOATS														
20		PRO 20			FBG	SV	OB			7	8	1400			2800	3300
20		PRO 20			FBG	SV	IB	100-140		7	8	1400			2600	3200
24		PRO 24			FBG	SV	OB			7	8	1750			3800	4400
24		PRO 24			FBG	SV	IB	130-160		7	8	1750			3800	4550

 CONTINUED ON NEXT PAGE

PRO-LINE BOATS INC   -CONTINUED   See inside cover to adjust price for area

LOA FT IN	NAME AND/ OR MODEL	TOP/ RIG	BOAT TYPE	-HULL- MTL TP	----ENGINE--- TP # HP MFG	BEAM FT IN	WGT LBS	DRAFT FT IN	RETAIL LOW	RETAIL HIGH

------------------ 1971 BOATS ------------------

LOA FT IN	NAME AND/ OR MODEL	TOP/ RIG	BOAT TYPE	MTL	TP	TP	# HP	MFG	BEAM FT IN	WGT LBS	DRAFT FT IN	RETAIL LOW	RETAIL HIGH
20	PRO-20	SF	FBG	SV	OB				7 8	1400	8	2800	3300
24	PRO-24	SF	FBG	SV	OB				7 8	1700	8	3700	4300
24	PRO-24	SF	FBG	SV	IO	120	MRCR		7 8	2300	8	7300	8400

PRODUCTION YACHTS LTD

Call 1-800-327-6929 for BUC Personalized Evaluation Service
Or, for 1980 boats, sign onto www.BUCValuPro.com

PROPER YACHT CO

Call 1-800-327-6929 for BUC Personalized Evaluation Service
Or, for 1980 boats, sign onto www.BUCValuPro.com

PROUT CATAMARANS LTD
CANVEY ISLAND ESSEX ENG COAST GUARD MFG ID- PRV See inside cover to adjust price for area

For more recent years, see the BUC Used Boat Price Guide, Volume 1 or Volume 2

LOA FT IN	NAME AND/ OR MODEL	TOP/ RIG	BOAT TYPE	-HULL- MTL TP	TP	#	HP	MFG	BEAM FT IN	WGT LBS	DRAFT FT IN	RETAIL LOW	RETAIL HIGH

------------------ 1983 BOATS ------------------

25 11	SIROCCO 26	SLP	SA/CR	FBG	CT	IB		15D	YAN	12 9	5000	2 4	18200	20200
31	QUEST 31	CUT	SA/CR	FBG	CT	IB		15D	YAN	14 3	7300	2 7	35000	38900
31	QUEST 31 PH	CUT	MS	FBG	CT	IB	T	36D	VW	14 3	7300	2 7	35000	38900
37	SNOWGOOSE 37	CUT	SA/CR	FBG	CT	IB		22D	YAN	15 3	9600	2 8	61500	67600
37	SNOWGOOSE 37 PH	CUT	MS	FBG	CT	IB	T	36D	VW	15 3	9600	2 8	61600	67600
49 6	QUASAR 50	CUT	SA/CR	FBG	CT	IB	T	22D	YAN	20	20000	3	175500	192500

------------------ 1982 BOATS ------------------

25 11	SIROCCO 26	SLP	SA/CR	FBG	CT	IB		D	YAN	12 9	5000	2 4	16800	19000
31	QUEST 31	CUT	SA/CR	FBG	CT	IB		15D	YAN	14 3	7300	2 7	32900	36600
31	QUEST MS	SLP	SA/CR	FBG	CT	IB		D		14 3	7800	2 7	33500	37200
37	SNOWGOOSE 37	CUT	SA/CR	FBG	CT	IB		15D	YAN	15 3	9600	2 8	57900	63600
37	SNOWGOOSE MS	CUT	MS	FBG	CT	IB		D		15 3	10000	2 8	58500	64300
49 6	QUASAR 50	CUT	SA/CR	FBG	CT	IB	T	20D	YAN	20	20000	3	165000	181000

------------------ 1978 BOATS ------------------

31	QUEST 31	CUT	SA/CR	FBG	CT	IB		12D	HYDR	14 1	7000	2 6	27100	30100
35 3	SNOWGOOSE	CUT	SA/CR	FBG	CT	IB		25D	HYDR	15 3	8000	2 8	39700	44100
45	QUASAR	CUT	SA/CR	FBG	CT	IB	T	25D	HYDR	20	14500	3	87700	96400

------------------ 1977 BOATS ------------------

| 35 3 | SNOWGOOSE | CUT | SA/CR | FBG | CT | IB | | 25D | VLVO | 15 3 | 8500 | 2 6 | 39000 | 43300 |

------------------ 1976 BOATS ------------------

| 35 3 | SNOWGOOSE 34 | CUT | SAIL | FBG | CT | OB | | | | 15 3 | 8500 | 2 6 | 37800 | 42000 |
| 35 3 | SNOWGOOSE 34 | CUT | SAIL | FBG | CT | IB | | 25D | VLVO | 15 3 | 8500 | 2 6 | 37800 | 42000 |

------------------ 1975 BOATS ------------------

| 35 2 | SNOWGOOSE | CUT | SAIL | FBG | CT | IB | | 25D | VLVO | 15 3 | 8000 | 2 9 | 35900 | 39800 |
| 45 | OCEAN-RANGER | CUT | SA/CR | FBG | CT | IB | | D | | 20 | 16000 | 3 | 80700 | 88700 |

------------------ 1974 BOATS ------------------

| 34 | SNOWGOOSE | | SAIL | FBG | CT | IB | | 25D | VLVO | 15 | | 2 3 | 33700 | 37400 |

------------------ 1973 BOATS ------------------

| 34 3 | SNOWGOOSE 34 | CUT | SAIL | | CT | IB | | 25D | VLVO | 15 | 5000 | 2 9 | 28000 | 31100 |

------------------ 1972 BOATS ------------------

| 18 9 | COUGAR MARK III | SLP | SA/OD | FBG | CT | | | 8 | | | 620 | 5 | 2300 | 2700 |

------------------ 1971 BOATS ------------------

| 18 9 | COUGAR MARK III | SLP | SA/OD | FBG | CT | | | 8 | | | 620 | 5 | 2300 | 2650 |

------------------ 1970 BOATS ------------------

| 17 | COUGAR MARK III | SLP | SA/OD | | CT | | | 7 8 | | | 620 | 5 | 2050 | 2450 |

------------------ 1969 BOATS ------------------

| 18 9 | COUGAR MARK III | SLP | SA/OD | FBG | CT | | | 8 | | | 620 | 5 | 2200 | 2550 |

------------------ 1968 BOATS ------------------

| 18 9 | COUGAR MK III | SLP | SA/OD | F/W | CT | | | 8 | | | 620 | 5 | 2200 | 2550 |

------------------ 1967 BOATS ------------------

| 18 9 | COUGAR MARK III | SLP | SA/OD | FBG | CT | | | 8 | | | 620 | 5 | 2150 | 2550 |

------------------ 1966 BOATS ------------------

| 27 3 | RANGER | SLP | SA/CR | FBG | CT | | | 12 6 | | | | | 12000 | 13600 |
| 37 | PROUT 37 | SLP | SA/CR | MHG | CT | | | 16 3 | | | 1 6 | 38600 | 42900 |

PROVIDENCE MARINE LTD

Call 1-800-327-6929 for BUC Personalized Evaluation Service
Or, for 1966 to 1967 boats, sign onto www.BUCValuPro.com

PRW CORP

Call 1-800-327-6929 for BUC Personalized Evaluation Service
Or, for 1967 boats, sign onto www.BUCValuPro.com

PUGET SOUND BOAT WKS LTD
SEATTLE WA 98109   COAST GUARD MFG ID- PUG See inside cover to adjust price for area

LOA FT IN	NAME AND/ OR MODEL	TOP/ RIG	BOAT TYPE	-HULL- MTL TP	TP	#	HP	MFG	BEAM FT IN	WGT LBS	DRAFT FT IN	RETAIL LOW	RETAIL HIGH

------------------ 1979 BOATS ------------------

32 6	PUGET DC SDN	FB	TRWL	FBG	DS	IB		120D	LEHM	12	15300	3 6	37000	41100
32 6	PUGET SDN	FB	TRWL	FBG	DS	IB		120D	LEHM	12	15300	3 6	37000	41100
36 6	PUGET DC	FB	TRWL	FBG	DS	IB		120D	LEHM	13	23500	3 9	53600	58900
36 6	PUGET DC	FB	TRWL	FBG	DS	IB	T	120D	LEHM	13	25200	3 10	58200	64000
36 6	PUGET SDN	FB	TRWL	FBG	DS	IB		120D	LEHM	13	23500	3 9	53600	58900
36 6	PUGET SDN	FB	TRWL	FBG	DS	IB	T	120D	LEHM	13	25200	3 10	58200	64000
38 10	PUGET DC	FB	TRWL	FBG	DS	IB		120D	LEHM	13	29800	4	70200	77100
38 10	PUGET DC	FB	TRWL	FBG	DS	IB		120D	LEHM	13	31200	4	76100	83600
38 10	PUGET SDN	FB	TRWL	FBG	DS	IB		120D	LEHM	13	29800	4	70200	77100
38 10	PUGET SDN	FB	TRWL	FBG	DS	IB		120D	LEHM	13	31200	4	76100	83600
43 6	PUGET TC	FB	TRWL	FBG	DS	IB		120D	LEHM	14	33800	4	81700	89800
43 6	PUGET TC	FB	TRWL	FBG	DS	IB		120D	LEHM	14	35200	4 4	87300	95900
44 3	PUGET PH	HT	TRWL	FBG	DS	IB	T	120D	LEHM	14	35900	4 4	100000	110000
44 3	PUGET PH	FB	TRWL	FBG	DS	IB	T	120D	LEHM	14	36200	4 4	100000	110000

------------------ 1978 BOATS ------------------

27 8	PUGET SDN	FB	TRWL	FBG	DS	IB		80D	LEHM	10 6	10500	3 3	19500	21600
31 2	MONTEREY DIESEL CR	HT	DC	FBG	DS	IB		75D	VLVO	10	15200	3 6	29200	32500
31 2	MONTEREY SPORTS TRWL	FB	TRWL	FBG	DS	IB		75D	VLVO	10	15200	3 6	29300	32600
31 3	MONTEREY WORKBOAT	HT	PH	FBG		IB		D	VLVO	10	15200	4	**	**
32	MONTEREY MOTOR SAIL	CUT	MS	FBG	KL	IB		40D	VLVO	14	17000	4	48300	53100
32 6	PUGET DC SDN	FB	TRWL	FBG	DS	IB		120D	LEHM	12	15300	3 6	35600	39600
33 6	PUGET DC	FB	TRWL	FBG	DS	IB		120D	LEHM	11 9	17500	3 6	40200	44700
33 6	PUGET SDN	FB	TRWL	FBG	DS	IB		120D	LEHM	11 9	17500	3 6	40900	45400
36 6	PUGET DC OR DC SDN	FB	TRWL	FBG	DS	IB		120D	LEHM	13 2	23500	3 9	51300	56300
36 6	PUGET DC OR DC SDN	FB	TRWL	FBG	DS	IB	T	120D	LEHM	13 2	23500	3 9	52900	58100
49	CUSTOM CRUISER	HT	MY	FBG	DS	IB				15	60000	5	**	**
49	TROLLER	HT	PH	FBG	DS	IB				15	60000	5 3	**	**

------------------ 1977 BOATS ------------------

30	BYSTEDT 30	SLP	SAIL	FBG	KL	IB		10D	VLVO	10	7400	5 4	19000	21100
30	BYSTEDT 30 DELUXE	SLP	SAIL	FBG	KL	IB		10D	VLVO	10	7400	5 4	21700	24100
31 2	MONTEREY DIESEL CR	HT	CR	FBG		IB		40D- 75D	VLVO	10 3	15200	4	28100	31300
31 2	MONTEREY DIESEL CR	FB	CR	FBG		IB		40D- 75D	VLVO	10 3	15200	4	28200	31300
31 2	MONTEREY SPORTS TRWL	FB	TRWL	FBG		IB		40D- 75D	VLVO	10 3	15200	4	28200	31400
32	MONTEREY MOTOR SAIL	CUT	MS	FBG	KL	IB		36D	VLVO	14	17000	4	46400	51000
32 6	PUGET DC	FB	TRWL	FBG	DS	IB		120D	FORD	12	15200	3 6	34700	41900
32 6	PUGET SDN	FB	TRWL	FBG	DS	IB		120D	FORD	12	15300	3 6	37700	41900
33 6	PUGET DC	FB	TRWL	FBG	DS	IB	T	80D	FORD	11 9	17500	3 6	38800	43100
33 6	PUGET DC	FB	TRWL	FBG	DS	IB		120D	FORD	11 9	17500	3 6	39400	43700
36 6	PUGET DC	FB	TRWL	FBG	DS	IB		120D	FORD	13	21500	3 9	45800	50300
36 6	PUGET SDN	FB	TRWL	FBG	DS	IB		120D	FORD	13 2	21500	3 9	45800	50300
36 6	PUGET SDN	FB	TRWL	FBG	DS	IB	T	120D	FORD	13 2	21500	3 9	47600	52300
48	PACIFIC CRUISER	HT	MY	FBG	DS	IB		195D	VLVO	14	60000	5 3	120000	141000

------------------ 1976 BOATS ------------------

30	BYSTEDT 30	SLP	SAIL	FBG	KL	IB		10D	VLVO	10	7400	5 4	19700	21900
31 2	MONTEREY DIESEL CR	HT	CR	FBG		IB		50D- 85D	VLVO	10 3	15200	4	27100	30200
31 2	MONTEREY DIESEL CR	FB	CR	FBG		IB		50D- 85D	VLVO	10 3	15200	4	27100	30200
31 2	MONTEREY SPORTS TRWL	FB	TRWL	FBG		IB		50D- 85D	VLVO	10 3	15200	4	27200	30300
31 2	MONTEREY WORK BOAT G	HT	PH	FBG		IB		75D	VLVO	10 3	15200	4	27100	30100
31 2	MONTEREY WORK BOAT T	HT	PH	FBG		IB		75D	VLVO	10 3	15200	4	27300	30100
32	MONTEREY MOTOR SAIL	CUT	MS	FBG	KL	IB		40D	VLVO	14	18000	4	46900	51600
32	MONTEREY MOTOR SAIL	CUT	MS	FBG	KL	IB		40D	VLVO	14	18000	4	46200	50700
47	PACIFIC CRUISER	HT	MY	FBG	DS	IB		150		14 6	60000	6	96600	106000
47	PACIFIC CRUISER	HT	MY	FBG	DS	IB		232		14 6	60000	6	97400	107000
47	PACIFIC CRUISER	HT	MY	FBG	DS	IB		100D	VLVO	14 6	60000	6	122500	134500
47	PACIFIC TROLLER	HT	PH	FBG	DS	IB		150		14 6	60000	6	93900	103000
47	PACIFIC TROLLER	HT	PH	FBG	DS	IB		232		14 6	60000	6	94400	103500
47	PACIFIC TROLLER	HT	PH	FBG	DS	IB		100D	VLVO	14 6	60000	6	116500	128000

PURDY

Call 1-800-327-6929 for BUC Personalized Evaluation Service
Or, for 1927 boats, sign onto www.BUCValuPro.com

PURSUIT
DIV OF S2 YACHTS INC
FT PIERCE FL 34946   See inside cover to adjust price for area

         ALSO TIARA YACHTS

For more recent years, see the BUC Used Boat Price Guide, Volume 1 or Volume 2

LOA FT IN	NAME AND/ OR MODEL	TOP/ RIG	BOAT TYPE	MTL	HULL TP	ENG TP	# HP	MFG	BEAM FT IN	WGT LBS	DRAFT FT IN	RETAIL LOW	RETAIL HIGH
1983 BOATS													
20 2	PURSUIT 2000 C/C	OP	CTRCN	FBG	DV	OB			8	1950	1 3	5700	6550
20 2	PURSUIT 2000 CUDDY	ST	FSH	FBG	DV	OB			8	1950	1 3	5700	6550
20 2	PURSUIT 2000 CUDDY	ST	FSH	FBG	DV	IO	170-230		8	2950	2 3	6300	7750
21 7	PURSUIT 2200	OP	FSH	FBG	DV	OB			8	2400	1 3	7200	8250
21 7	PURSUIT 2200	OP	FSH	FBG	DV	SE	155-205		8	2760		7900	9050
21 7	PURSUIT 2200 C/C	OP	CTRCN	FBG	DV	OB			8	2400	1 3	7150	8250
21 7	PURSUIT 2200 C/C	OP	CTRCN	FBG	DV	SE	155-205		8	2760		7850	9050
24 7	PURSUIT 2500	ST	FSH	FBG	DV	OB			8	3200	1 4	10400	11800
24 7	PURSUIT 2500	ST	FSH	FBG	DV	OB	205	OMC	8	4200	2 5	12300	14000
24 7	PURSUIT 2500	ST	FSH	FBC	DV	IO	225-260		8	4200	2 5	10700	12500
24 7	PURSUIT 2500 C/C	ST	CTRCN	FBG	DV	OB			8	3200	1 4	10300	11700
24 7	PURSUIT 2500 C/C	ST	CTRCN	FBG	DV	SE	205	OMC	8	4200		12200	13900
27	PURSUIT 2700	OP	SF	FBG	DV	SE	205	OMC	10	7500		15800	17900
27	PURSUIT 2700	OP	SF	FBG	DV	SE	220-270		10	7500		20900	23700
27	PURSUIT 2700	TT	SF	FBG	DV	SE	205	OMC	10	7500		16100	18200
27	PURSUIT 2700	TT	SF	FBG	DV	SE	220-270		10	7500		20900	23700
31 3	PURSUIT 3100	OP	SF	FBG	DV	SE	205	OMC	12	9200	2 9	29500	32700
31 3	PURSUIT 3100	OP	SF	FBG	DV	SE	220-350		12	9200	2 9	27100	32000
31 3	PURSUIT 3100	OP	SF	FBG	DV	IB	158D-240D		12	9200	2 9	32400	38200
31 3	PURSUIT 3100	HT	SF	FBG	DV	SE	205	OMC	12	9500	2 10	30000	33300
31 3	PURSUIT 3100	HT	SF	FBG	DV	SE	220-350		12	9500	2 10	27400	32300
	IB D GM ** ** , IB D PERK ** **, IB 158D VLVO											33300	37000
31 3	PURSUIT 3100	FB	SF	FBG	DV	IB	220-230		12	10000	2 10	33200	37100
	IO 260 MRCR 31000 34500, IB 270-350 34000 39100, IB D VLVO ** **												
	IB 210D-240D 40100 45500												
31 3	PURSUIT 3100	TT	SF	FBG	DV	SE	205	OMC	12	10500	2 9	30000	33400
31 3	PURSUIT 3100	TT	SF	FBG	DV	IB	220-350		12	10500	2 9	33700	39600
31 3	PURSUIT 3100	TT	SF	FBG	DV	IB	158D-240D		12	10500	2 9	41000	46800
1982 BOATS													
20 2	PURSUIT 2000 CUDDY	ST	FSH	FBG	DV	OB			8	2000	1 3	5650	6500
20 2	PURSUIT 2000 CUDDY	ST	FSH	FBG	DV	IO	170-230		8	2950	2 3	6150	7550
21 7	PURSUIT 2200 C/C	OP	CTRCN	FBG	DV	IO		OMC	8	3650		**	**
21 7	PURSUIT 2200 C/C	OP	CTRCN	FBG	DV	IO			8	2400		7000	8050
24 7	PURSUIT 2500	ST	FSH	FBG	DV	OB			8	3250	1 4	10200	11600
24 7	PURSUIT 2500	ST	FSH	FBG	DV	IO		OMC	8	4200	2 5	9900	12200
24 7	PURSUIT 2500	ST	FSH	FBG	DV	IO	170-260		8	4200	2 5	9900	12200
24 7	PURSUIT 2500 C/C	ST	CTRCN	FBG	DV	OB			8	3200	1 4	10100	11500
31 3	PURSUIT 3100	OP	SF	FBG	DV	IO	205	OMC	12	9200	2 9	24100	26800
	IB 220-255 26000 29300, IO 260 24800 27500, IB 270-350											26600	30700
31 3	PURSUIT 3100	HT	SF	FBG	DV	IB	220-228		12	9500	2 10	26200	29200
	IO 260 MRCR 25000 27800, IB 270-350 26800 30900, IB T220 CRUS											28800	32000
	IO T228-T255 27100 30800, IB T270-T350 29800 35000, IO T D VLVO ** **												
31 3	PURSUIT 3100	FB	SF	FBG	DV	IO	260		12	10000	2 10	30300	33700
	IB 270-350 32500 37400, IB T220 CRUS 34900 38800, IO T228-T255											32800	37200
	IB T270-T350 36100 42300, IO T D VLVO ** **												
31 3	PURSUIT 3100	TT	SF	FBG	DV	IB	220-255		12	10500	2 9	32200	36400
31 3	PURSUIT 3100	TT	SF	FBG	DV	IB	270-350		12	10500	2 9	33000	37900
1981 BOATS													
20 2	PURSUIT 2000 CUDDY	ST	FSH	FBG	DV	OB			8	2000	1 3	5550	6400
20 2	PURSUIT 2000 CUDDY	ST	FSH	FBG	DV	IO	170-230		8	2950	2 3	6100	7450
24 7	PURSUIT 2500	ST	FSH	FBG	DV	OB			8	3250	1 4	10000	11400
24 7	PURSUIT 2500	ST	FSH	FBG	DV	IO	170-260		8	4200	2 5	9750	12000
24 7	PURSUIT 2500 C/C	ST	CTRCN	FBG	DV	OB			8	3200	1 4	9850	11200
31 3	PURSUIT 3100	OP	SF	FBG	DV	IB	220-350		12	9200	2 9	24900	29400
31 3	PURSUIT 3100	HT	SF	FBG	DV	IO	T220-T350		12	9500	2 10	26500	32400
31 3	PURSUIT 3100	HT	SF	FBG	DV	IO	T D VLVO		12	9500	2 10	**	**
31 3	PURSUIT 3100	FB	SF	FBG	DV	IO	T220-T350		12	10000	2 10	32100	39100
31 3	PURSUIT 3100	FB	SF	FBG	DV	IO	T D VLVO		12	10000	2 10	**	**
31 3	PURSUIT 3100	TT	SF	FBG	DV	IB	220-350		12	10500	2 9	30900	36300
1980 BOATS													
20 2	PURSUIT 2000 CUDDY	ST	FSH	FBG	DV	OB			8	2000		5450	6250
20 2	PURSUIT 2000 CUDDY	ST	FSH	FBG	DV	IO	170-230		8	2950	2 3	6100	7400
20 2	PURSUIT 2000 CUDDY	ST	FSH	FBG	DV	IO	260		8	2950	2 3	6400	7700
24 7	PURSUIT 2500	ST	FSH	FBG	DV	OB			8	3200		9750	11100
24 7	PURSUIT 2500	ST	FSH	FBG	DV	IO	198-260		8	4200	2 5	9800	11900
31 3	PURSUIT 3100	OP	SF	FBG	DV	IO	170-350		12	9200	2 9	23200	28100
31 3	PURSUIT 3100	TT	SF	FBG	DV	IO	170-350		12	10500	2 9	29000	34700
1979 BOATS													
20 2	PURSUIT 2000	ST	FSH	FBG	DV	IO	170-230		8	2950	2 3	6000	7400
20 2	PURSUIT 2000	ST	FSH	FBG	DV	IO	260		8	2950	2 3	6350	7650
24 7	PURSUIT 2500	ST	FSH	FBG	DV	IO	198-260		8	4200	2 5	9800	11900
30 10	PURSUIT 3100	ST	FSH	FBG	DV	IB			11 11	10500	3 3	**	**
30 10	PURSUIT 3100	FB	FSH	FBG	DV	IB			11 11	10500	3 3	**	**
1978 BOATS													
20 2	PURSUIT 2000	ST	FSH	FBG	DV	IO	170-228		8	2950	1 3	6050	7450
24 7	PURSUIT 2500	ST	FSH	FBG	DV	IO	185-260		8	4200	1 5	9800	11900

PYRAMID BOATWORKS
COAST GUARD MFG ID- PHZ

Call 1-800-327-6929 for BUC Personalized Evaluation Service
Or, for 1982 to 1983 boats, sign onto www.BUCValuPro.com

QUEENS OF THE SEA

Call 1-800-327-6929 for BUC Personalized Evaluation Service
Or, for 1974 boats, sign onto www.BUCValuPro.com

R & L YACHT CONSULTANTS

Call 1-800-327-6929 for BUC Personalized Evaluation Service
Or, for 1981 to 1986 boats, sign onto www.BUCValuPro.com

R K INDUSTRIES INC
STRASBURG VA 22657   COAST GUARD MFG ID- RKA See inside cover to adjust price for area

LOA FT IN	NAME AND/ OR MODEL	TOP/ RIG	BOAT TYPE	MTL	HULL TP	ENG TP	# HP	MFG	BEAM FT IN	WGT LBS	DRAFT FT IN	RETAIL LOW	RETAIL HIGH
1981 BOATS													
20	RK20	SLP	SAIL	FBG	KL	OB			7 1	2220	3 3	1800	2150
20	RK20S	SLP	SAIL	FBG	KL	OB			7 1	2220	3 3	1800	2150
1980 BOATS													
20	RK20	SLP	SAIL	FBG	KL	OB			7 1	2220	3 3	1750	2050
20	RK20S	SLP	SAIL	FBG	KL	OB			7 1	2220	3 3	1750	2050
21	RK-21	SLP	SA/CR	FBG	CB	OB			7 11	2100		1700	2050

R K L BOATWORKS
COAST GUARD MFG ID- RKL

Call 1-800-327-6929 for BUC Personalized Evaluation Service
Or, for 1979 to 1985 boats, sign onto www.BUCValuPro.com

RACING SAILBOAT SERV LTD

Call 1-800-327-6929 for BUC Personalized Evaluation Service
Or, for 1979 boats, sign onto www.BUCValuPro.com

RADON BOATS
ABALONE BOATS
SANTA BARBARA CA   COAST GUARD MFG ID- RAB   See inside cover to adjust price for area

LOA FT IN	NAME AND/ OR MODEL	TOP/ RIG	BOAT TYPE	MTL	HULL TP	ENG TP	# HP	MFG	BEAM FT IN	WGT LBS	DRAFT FT IN	RETAIL LOW	RETAIL HIGH
1976 BOATS													
19	EXPLORER	OP	UTL	FBG	SV	IO	165	MRCR	7 8	3250	1 6	8200	9400
19	STANDARD	OP	CUD	FBG	SV	IO	165	MRCR	7 8	3500	1 6	7900	9050
24	EXPLORER 24	OP	UTL	FBG	SV	IO	255	MRCR	8	4250	2	13800	15700
24	STANDARD	OP	CUD	FBG	SV	IO	200D	CHRY	8	4250	2	18200	20200
24	SEA-RAM 24	OP	CR	FBG	SV	IO	255	MRCR	8	4500	2	13600	15400
32	STANDARD 24	OP	CUD	FBG	SV	IO	255	MRCR	8	9000	2 6	32600	36200
32	32 STANDARD	OP	CUD	FBG	SV	IO	T255	MRCR	10	9500	2 6	35200	39100
32	32 TROLLER	OP	CR	FBG	SV	IO	T255	MRCR	10	9500	2 6	35200	39100
32	32 UTILITY	OP	UTL	FBG	SV	IO	T255	MRCR	10	9000	2 6	39400	43800
1975 BOATS													
19		OP		FBG		IO	165	MRCR				7400	8550
24		OP		FBG		IO	255	MRCR	8			14200	16100
32		OP		FBG		IO	T255	MRCR	10			38200	42400

RADON BOATS   -CONTINUED   See inside cover to adjust price for area

LOA FT IN	NAME AND/ OR MODEL	TOP/ RIG	BOAT TYPE	-HULL- MTL TP	ENGINE TP # HP	MFG	BEAM FT IN	WGT LBS	DRAFT FT IN	RETAIL LOW	RETAIL HIGH
				1974 BOATS							
18	RADON-CRAFT		F/W	IO	120	MRCR	8	3000	2	6850	7850
20	RADON-CRAFT		F/W	IO	165	MRCR	8	3500	2	9300	10600
22	RADON-CRAFT		F/W	IO	255	MRCR	8	4000	2	11900	13500
24	RADON-CRAFT		F/W	IO	255	MRCR	9	6000	2	18900	21000
24	RADON-CRAFT		FBG	IO	255	MRCR	8	4200	2	13100	14900
26	RADON-CRAFT		F/W	IO	255	MRCR	8	6500	2	21700	24100
28	RADON-CRAFT		F/W	IO	255	MRCR	9	7000	2	24300	27000
28	RADON-CRAFT		F/W	VD	210D	CAT	10	8000	2 6	28300	31500
30	RADON-CRAFT		F/W	VD	210D	CAT	10	8500	2 6	27900	31000
32	RADON-CRAFT		FBG	IO	210D	CAT	10	9000	2 6	42100	46800
32	RADON-CRAFT		F/W	VD	210D	CAT	10	9000	2 6	31500	35000
32	RADON-CRAFT		F/W	VD	T210D	CAT	12	10000	2 6	38600	42900
34	RADON-CRAFT		F/W	VD	T210D	CAT	12	11000	2 6	52800	58100
36	RADON-CRAFT		F/W	VD	T210D	CAT	12	12000	2 6	54900	60300
				1973 BOATS							
18	RADON-CRAFT		FBG	IO	188	MRCR				7150	8200
20	RADON-CRAFT		FBG	IO	188	MRCR				9500	10800
22	RADON-CRAFT		FBG	IO	255	MRCR				11900	13500
24	RADON-CRAFT		FBG	IO	255	MRCR				15200	17300
25	RADON-CRAFT		FBG	IO	255	MRCR				16400	18700
26	RADON-CRAFT		FBG	IO	255	MRCR				19900	22100
28	RADON-CRAFT		FBG	IO	T255	MRCR				27500	30500
29	RADON-CRAFT		FBG	IO	T255	MRCR				28200	31400
30	RADON-CRAFT		FBG	IO	T255	MRCR				32800	36400

RADOVCICH BOATWORKS
WILMINGTON CA 90744   COAST GUARD MFG ID- RDW See inside cover to adjust price for area

LOA FT IN	NAME AND/ OR MODEL	TOP/ RIG	BOAT TYPE	-HULL- MTL TP	ENGINE TP # HP	MFG	BEAM FT IN	WGT LBS	DRAFT FT IN	RETAIL LOW	RETAIL HIGH
				1981 BOATS							
32	RADOVCICH 32	HT	CR	FBG DV	IBT200D-T270D		13	11000	3	71800	84600
32	RADOVCICH 32	FB	FSH	FBG DV	IB 310D	GM	13	18000	3	93900	103000
42	RADOVCICH 42	HT	FSH	FBG DV	IB 430D	GM	14 6	28000	3 6	154000	169000
42	RADOVCICH 42	FB	FSH	FBG DV	IB T270D	VLVO	14 6	25000	3 6	146500	160500
42	RADOVCICH 42	FB	FSH	FBG DV	IB T350D	GM	14 6	30000	3 6	179500	197500
42	RADOVCICH 42	FB	FSH	FBG DV	IB T430D	GM	14 6	30000	3 6	191000	210000
				1980 BOATS							
32	RADOVCICH 32	HT	FSH	FBG DV	IB 260D-273D		13		3 6	79200	87000
32	RADOVCICH 32	FB	FSH	FBG DV	IB T130D		13		3 6	79200	87000
39 10	RADOVCICH 40	FB	FSH	FBG DV	IB 350D	GM	13 4		3 6	90300	99200
	IB 435D GM	94600	104000,	IB T200D	PERK	96000 105500,	IB T210D	CAT		96500	106000
	IB T217D GM	94400	104000,	IB T221D	VLVO	92300 101500					

RAINBOW CO INC

Call 1-800-327-6929 for BUC Personalized Evaluation Service
Or, for 1962 to 1963 boats, sign onto www.BUCValuPro.com

RAMPONE BOATS
EAST COAST MARINE INC

Call 1-800-327-6929 for BUC Personalized Evaluation Service
Or, for 1978 to 1984 boats, sign onto www.BUCValuPro.com

RAND L MARINE ENTERPRISES INC
COAST GUARD MFG ID- RML

Call 1-800-327-6929 for BUC Personalized Evaluation Service
Or, for 1980 boats, sign onto www.BUCValuPro.com

RANGER BOAT CO
KENT WA 98032   COAST GUARD MFG ID- RFB See inside cover to adjust price for area
     SEE MARTINI MARINE

For more recent years, see the BUC Used Boat Price Guide, Volume 1 or Volume 2

LOA FT IN	NAME AND/ OR MODEL	TOP/ RIG	BOAT TYPE	-HULL- MTL TP	ENGINE TP # HP	MFG	BEAM FT IN	WGT LBS	DRAFT FT IN	RETAIL LOW	RETAIL HIGH
				1983 BOATS							
17	RANGER SAILING CANOE	SLP	CANOE	FBG			2 11		4	**	**
18	RANGER 18	OP	ROW	FBG	SV OB		6 8		2	**	**
18 2	RANGER CRUISER	SLP	SA/CR	FBG CB	OB		6 8	1300	1 2	2400	2750
18 2	RANGER DAYSAILER	SLP	SA/CR	FBG CB	OB		6 8	1200	1 2	2300	2650
18 2	RANGER SPRIT	CAT	SA/CR	FBG CB	OB		6 8	1200	1 2	2350	2700
18 2	RANGER TROLLER	HT	PH	FBG DS	OB		6 8	1550	1 6	4100	4750
18 2	RANGER TROLLER	HT	PH	FBG DS	IB	8D YAN	6 8	1550	1 6	3450	4050
20	RANGER 20	SLP	SA/OD	FBG CB	OB		7 10	1550	1 10	2500	2900
23 11	RANGER 24	SLP	SA/RC	FBG KL	OB		8 4	3150	4 1	5050	5800
26	RANGER 26	SLP	SA/CR	FBG KC	OB		8	4750	2 4	8800	10000
28	RANGER 8.5	SLP	SA/RC	FBG KL	IB	8D YAN	9 6	5000	5 1	10600	12000
				1982 BOATS							
17	RANGER SAILING CANOE	OP	SAIL	FBG FL			2 11		4	2000	2350
18	RANGER CRUISER	SLP	SA/CR	FBG CB	OB		6 8	1300	1 2	2250	2600
18	RANGER DAYSAILER	SLP	SA/CR	FBG CB	OB		6 8	1200	1 2	2150	2500
18	RANGER SPRIT	CAT	SA/CR	FBG CB	OB		6 8	1200	1 2	2200	2550
18 2	RANGER TROLLER	HT	PH	FBG DS	OB		6 8	1550	1 6	4050	4700
18 2	RANGER TROLLER	HT	PH	FBG DS	IB	8D YAN	6 8	1550	1 6	3350	3850
20	RANGER 20	SLP	SA/OD	FBG CB	OB		7 10	1550	1 10	2350	2750
23 11	RANGER 24	SLP	SA/RC	FBG KL	OB		8 4	2950	4 1	4550	5250
26	RANGER 26	SLP	SA/CR	FBG KC	OB		8	4750	2 4	6300	7500
28	RANGER 8.5	SLP	SA/CR	FBG KL	IB	8D YAN	9 6	5000	5 1	10100	11400
				1981 BOATS							
17	RANGER 17		SAIL	FBG	OB		2 11			1900	2250
18	RANGER TROLLER			FBG	IB	8D YAN	6 8	1550	1 6	3150	3650
18 2	RANGER 18	SLP	SA/OD	FBG CB	OB		6 8	1000	1 2	1750	2100
18 2	RANGER 18 SPRIT	GAF	SA/OD	FBG CB	OB		6 8	1200	1 2	1750	2100
18 2	RANGER TROLLER			FBG	OB		6 8	1400	1 2	3700	4300
20	RANGER 20	SLP	SA/OD	FBG KC	OB		7 10	1550	1 9	2200	2550
23 11	RANGER 24	SLP	SA/CR	FBG KL	OB		8 4	3200	4 1	4600	5300
26	RANGER 26	SLP	SA/CR	FBG KC	OB		8	4750	2 4	7850	9050
28	RANGER 8.5	SLP	SA/OD	FBG KL	IB	D	9 8	5000	5 1	9650	11000
				1980 BOATS							
18	RANGER TROLLER			FBG	OB		6 8	1400	1 2	3600	4200
18	RANGER TROLLER			FBG	IB	8D YAN	6 8	1550	1 2	3050	3500
18 2	RANGER 18	SLP	SA/OD	FBG CB	OB		6 8	1450	1 2	2050	2450
20	RANGER 20	SLP	SA/OD	FBG KC	OB		7 10	1550	1 9	2050	2450
23 11	RANGER 24	SLP	SA/CR	FBG KL	OB		8 4	3200	4 1	4400	5050
26	RANGER 26	SLP	SA/CR	FBG KC	OB		8	4750	2 4	7450	8550
28	RANGER 8.5	SLP	SA/OD	FBG KL	IB	D	9 8	5000	5 1	9200	10500
				1979 BOATS							
20	RANGER 20	SLP	SA/OD	FBG KC	OB		7 10	1550		1950	2350
23 11	RANGER 24	SLP	SA/OD	FBG KL	OB		8 4	2950	4 1	3900	4500
26	RANGER 26	SLP	SA/OD	FBG KC	OB		8	4750	2 4	7100	8200
				1978 BOATS							
20	RANGER 20	SLP	SA/OD	FBG KC	OB		7 10	1550		1750	2250
23 11	RANGER 24	SLP	SAIL	FBG KL	OB		8 4	3300	4 1 11	4100	4750
26	RANGER 26	SLP	SAIL	FBG KC	OB		8	4750	2 4	6850	7850
26	RANGER 26	SLP	SAIL	FBG KC	IB	15 OMC	8	4750	2 4	7050	8100
26	RANGER 26	SLP	SAIL	FBG KC	IB	8D YAN	8	4750	2 4	7250	8300
				1977 BOATS							
20	RANGER 20	SLP	SA/OD	FBG KC	OB		7 10	1550	1 9	1800	2100
23 11	RANGER 24	SLP	SA/RC	FBG KL	OB		8 4	3150	4 1	3800	4400
26	RANGER 26	SLP	SA/CR	FBG KL	OB		8	4750	2 4	6500	7500
				1976 BOATS							
20	RANGER 20	SLP	SA/OD	FBG KC	OB		7 10	1550	1 9	1750	2050
23 11	RANGER 24	SLP	SAIL	FBG KL	OB		8 4	3150	4 1	3650	4200
				1975 BOATS							
19	FLYING-SCOT	SLP	SA/OD	FBG CB	OB		6 9		4	1700	2000
23 11	RANGER 24	SLP	SAIL	FBG KL	OB		8 4	3150	4	3500	4050
				1974 BOATS							
24	K I-24	SLP	SAIL	FBG KL	OB		8 4	3100	4 4	3350	3900

RANGER BOATS
RANGER BOATS
WOOD MFG
FLIPPIN AR 72634   COAST GUARD MFG ID- RNG   See inside cover to adjust price for area
     FORMERLY WOOD MFG CO INC

For more recent years, see the BUC Used Boat Price Guide, Volume 1 or Volume 2

LOA FT IN	NAME AND/ OR MODEL	TOP/ RIG	BOAT TYPE	-HULL- MTL TP	ENGINE TP # HP	MFG	BEAM FT IN	WGT LBS	DRAFT FT IN	RETAIL LOW	RETAIL HIGH
				1983 BOATS							
16	CHIEF 1600V	OP	RNBT	FBG SV	OB		5 8			2500	2900
16	CHIEF 1600V-3	OP	RNBT	FBG SV	OB		5 8	675		1900	2300
16 10	CHIEF 330	OP	BASS	FBG SV	OB		6 10	1025		2950	3400
16 10	CHIEF 335	OP	RNBT	FBG SV	OB		6 10	1045		3000	3500
17 10	CHIEF 350	OP	BASS	FBG SV	OB		6 10			3800	4400

LOA FT	LOA IN	NAME AND/ OR MODEL	TOP/ RIG	BOAT TYPE	HULL MTL	HULL TP	ENGINE TP	ENGINE # HP	ENGINE MFG	BEAM FT	BEAM IN	WGT LBS	DRAFT FT	DRAFT IN	RETAIL LOW	RETAIL HIGH
1983 BOATS																
17	10	CHIEF 370	OP	BASS	FBG	SV	OB								3800	4400
17	10	CHIEF 375	OP	RNBT	FBG	SV	OB			7	4	1200			3500	4050
17	10	CHIEF 375	OP	RNBT	FBG	SV	IO			7	4				**	**
17	10	RANGER 372		BASS	FBG	DV	OB			7	4	1190			3450	4000
18	8	CHIEF 380	OP	BASS	FBG	SV	OB								4200	4850
18	8	RANGER 380		SF	FBG	DV	IO	160		7	6				4050	4700
20		RANGER 395		BASS	FBG	SV	OB			7	6				5200	6000
20		RANGER 395		FSH	FBG	SV	IO			7	6				**	**
22		RANGER 622		OFF	FBG	DV	OB			8		2700			8100	9300
1982 BOATS																
16	10	RANGER 330		BASS	FBG	DV	OB			6	10	1025			2900	3350
16	10	RANGER 335		BASS	FBG	DV	OB			6	10	1045			2950	3400
17	10	RANGER 350		BASS	FBG	DV	OB			6	10	1050			3050	3550
17	10	RANGER 370		BASS	FBG	DV	OB			7	4	1190			3350	3900
17	10	RANGER 375		BASS	FBG	DV	OB			7	4	1200			3400	3950
17	10	RANGER 375		BASS	FBG	DV	IO	160		7	4				3300	3800
18	8	RANGER 380 CHIEF		FSH	FBG	DV	IO	160		7	6				3650	4250
1981 BOATS																
16		RANGER 1600V		RNBT	FBG		OB			5	8				2400	2800
16		RANGER 1600V3		BASS	FBG		OB			5	8	675			1850	2200
16	10	RANGER 230V		BASS	FBG		OB			6	10	1025			2850	3300
16	10	RANGER 235V		BASS	FBG		OB			6	10	1045			2850	3350
17		RANGER 1750V		RNBT	FBG		OB			6					3000	3500
17		RANGER 178V		RNBT	FBG	DV	OB			6					3000	3500
17	10	RANGER 168V		BASS	FBG		OB			6	10	1050			3000	3450
17	10	RANGER 198V		BASS	FBG		OB			7	4	1190			3300	3850
17	10	RANGER 275V		BASS	FBG		OB			7	4	1200			3350	3850
17	10	RANGER 275V		BASS	FBG		IO	170		7	4				3250	3750
18		RANGER 1850		RNBT	FBG	TR	IO			6	3				**	**
18		RANGER 1850V		RNBT	FBG		OB			7					3700	4300
1980 BOATS																
16		RANGER 1600V-3	OP	BASS	FBG	DV	OB			5	8	1100			2900	3400
16	10	RANGER 230V	OP	BASS	FBG	DV	OB			6	10	1045			2850	3300
16	10	RANGER 235V	OP	BASS	FBG	DV	OB			6	10	1045			2850	3300
17		RANGER 1750V	OP	RNBT	FBG	DV	OB			6					2950	3450
17		RANGER 178V	OP	RNBT	FBG	DV	OB			6	1	900			2500	2900
17	10	RANGER 168V	OP	BASS	FBG	DV	OB			6	10	1050			2950	3400
17	10	RANGER 188V	OP	BASS	FBG	DV	OB			6	6	995			2800	3250
17	10	RANGER 198V	OP	BASS	FBG	DV	OB			7	4	1190			3250	3800
17	10	RANGER 275V	OP	BASS	FBG	DV	OB			7	4	1200			3250	3800
17	10	RANGER 275V	OP	BASS	FBG	DV	IO	170		7	4				3200	3750
18		RANGER 1850V	OP	RNBT	FBG	DV	OB			6	6	1350			3600	4200
18		RANGER 1850V	OP	RNBT	FBG	DV	IO	170		6	6				2850	3300
1978 BOATS																
16		RANGER 1600 V-1		BASS	FBG	SV	OB			5	8				2300	2700
16	4	RANGER TR-3	OP	BASS	FBG	FL	OB			5	3	715			1900	2250
17		RANGER 175	OP	BASS	FBG	TR	IO	140		6	1				2400	2800
17		RANGER 1750 V		BASS	FBG	SV	OB			6					2850	3300
17		RANGER 175A	OP	BASS	FBG	TR	OB			6	1	900			2450	2800
17		RANGER 178V	OP	BASS	FBG	DV	OB			6	1	900			2450	2800
18		RANGER 1850	OP	BASS	FBG	TR	IO	170		6	6				3000	3500
18		RANGER 1850 V		BASS	FBG	SV	OB			7					3500	4100
18		RANGER 185A	OP	BASS	FBG	TR	OB			6	6	995			2750	3200
18		RANGER 185V	OP	BASS	FBG	DV	OB			6	6	995			2750	3200
20		RANGER 205A	OP	BASS	FBG	TR	OB			6	6	1200			3600	4150
1977 BOATS																
16	4	RANGER TR-10	OP	BASS	FBG	TR	OB			5	4	770			2000	2400
17		RANGER 1700 W/T	OP	RNBT	FBG	TR	OB			6	2	900			2400	2800
17		RANGER 175	OP	BASS	FBG	TR	IO	140		6	2				2450	2850
17		RANGER 175A	OP	BASS	FBG	TR	OB			6	2	900			2400	2800
18	2	RANGER 18-10	OP	BASS	FBG	TR	OB			5	8	925			2550	3000
18	5	RANGER 185A	OP	BASS	FBG	TR	OB			6	5	995			2750	3200
20	2	RANGER 205A	OP	BASS	FBG		OB			6	5	1200			3550	4150
1976 BOATS																
16	4	RANGER TR-10	OP	BASS	FBG	TR	OB			5	4	770			2000	2350
17		RANGER 175	OP	BASS	FBG	TR	IO	140		6	2				2500	2950
17		RANGER 175A	OP	BASS	FBG	TR	OB			6	2	900			2400	2750
18	2	RANGER 18	OP	BASS	FBG	TR	IO	140		5	8				2950	3400
18	2	RANGER 18-10	OP	BASS	FBG	TR	OB			5	8	925			2550	2950
18	5	RANGER 185A	OP	BASS	FBG	TR	OB			6	5	995			2750	3200
1975 BOATS																
16	4	RANGER TR-10	OP	BASS	FBG	TR	OB			5	3	770			2000	2350
16	5	RANGER DTR-11	OP	BASS	FBG	TR	OB			5	3	735	2	5	1900	2250
16	5	RANGER DTR-12	OP	BASS	FBG	TR	OB			5	3	790	2	5	2050	2400
16	5	RANGER DTR-3	OP	BASS	FBG	TR	OB			5	3	745	2	5	1900	2300
16	5	RANGER DTR-4	OP	BASS	FBG	TR	OB			5	3	745	2	5	1900	2300
16	5	RANGER DTR-7	OP	BASS	FBG	TR	OB			5	3	745	2	5	1900	2300
16	5	RANGER TR-11	OP	BASS	FBG	TR	OB			5	3	705	2	2	1800	2150
16	5	RANGER TR-12	OP	BASS	FBG	TR	OB			5	3	760	2	2	1950	2350
16	5	RANGER TR-3	OP	BASS	FBG	TR	OB			5	3	715	2	2	1850	2200
16	5	RANGER TR-4	OP	BASS	FBG	TR	OB			5	3	715	2	2	1850	2200
17		RANGER 170A	OP	BASS	FBG	TR	OB			6	2	825			2200	2600
17		RANGER 175 I/O	OP	BASS	FBG	TR	IO	140	MRCR	6	2	1665			3250	3800
17		RANGER 175A	OP	BASS	FBG	TR	OB			6	2	900			2350	2750
18	2	RANGER 18 I/O	OP	BASS	FBG	TR	IO	120-140		5	7	1640			3350	3900
18	2	RANGER 18-10	OP	BASS	FBG	TR	OB			5	7	925			2550	2950
18	2	RANGER 18-5	OP	BASS	FBG	TR	OB			5	7	925			2550	2950

RANGER SAILBOATS

A BANGOR PUNTA COMPANY
JENSEN MARINE
FALL RIVER MA 02722 COAST GUARD MFG ID- RAY

See inside cover to adjust price for area

For more recent years, see the BUC Used Boat Price Guide, Volume 1 or Volume 2

LOA FT	LOA IN	NAME AND/ OR MODEL	TOP/ RIG	BOAT TYPE	HULL MTL	HULL TP	ENGINE TP	ENGINE # HP	ENGINE MFG	BEAM FT	BEAM IN	WGT LBS	DRAFT FT	DRAFT IN	RETAIL LOW	RETAIL HIGH
1981 BOATS																
22	6	RANGER 22	SLP	SA/RC	FBG	KL	OB			8		2182	4	3	3350	3900
25	6	RANGER 26	SLP	SA/RC	FBG	KL	OB			8		3000	4	9	4900	5650
1980 BOATS																
22	6	RANGER 22	SLP	SA/RC	FBG	KL	OB			8		2182	4	3	3200	3750
25	6	RANGER 26	SLP	SA/RC	FBG	KL	OB			8		3000	1	8	4700	5400
1979 BOATS																
22	6	RANGER 22	SLP	SA/RC	FBG	KL	OB			8		2182	4	3	3100	3600
25	6	RANGER 26	SLP	SA/CR	FBG	CB	OB			8		3288	1	9	4850	5600
29	11	RANGER 30	SLP	SA/CR	FBG	KL	IB	30	UNIV	10	9	9000	5	6	15400	17500
29	11	RANGER 30	SLP	SA/CR	FBG	KL	IB	16D	UNIV	10	9	9000	5	6	15500	17600
33	2	RANGER 33	SLP	SA/CR	FBG	KL	IB	30	UNIV	9	7	10300	5	2	18200	20300
33	2	RANGER 33	SLP	SA/CR	FBG	KL	IB	16D	UNIV	9	7	10300	5	2	18300	20300
1978 BOATS																
22	6	RANGER 22	SLP	SA/RC	F/S	KL	OB			7	10	2182	4	3	3000	3450
22	11	RANGER 23	SLP	SA/CR	F/S	KL	OB			8		3394	3	9	4200	4850
28		RANGER 28	SLP	SA/RC	F/S	KL	IB	30	UNIV	9	8	5081	4	6	7950	9150
29	11	RANGER 30	SLP	SA/CR	F/S	KL	IB	30		10	9	9000	5	6	14800	16900
33	1	RANGER 33	SLP	SA/CR	F/S	KL	IB	30		9	7	10300	5	2	17200	19500
1977 BOATS																
23		RANGER 23	SLP	SA/CR	FBG	KL				7	11	3400	3	9	4050	4750
28		RANGER 28	SLP	SA/CR	FBG	KL	IB			9	7	6000	4	6	9150	10400
1976 BOATS																
23		RANGER 23	SLP	SAIL	FBG	KL	OB			7	11	3400	3	9	3950	4600
26	3	RANGER 26	SLP	SA/CR	FBG	KL	OB			8	8	5860	4	4	7950	9100
28		RANGER 28	SLP	SA/RC	FBG	KL	IB	10	UNIV	9	7	5108	4	6	7450	8550
28	7	RANGER 29	SLP	SAIL	FBG	KL	IB	25	UNIV	9	4	6700	4	5	10000	11400
32	7	RANGER 32	SLP	SAIL	FBG	KL	IB	25	UNIV	10	10	9500	5	3	14800	16900
33	2	RANGER 33	SLP	SAIL	FBG	KL	IB	25	UNIV	9	7	10500	5		16400	18600
33	2	RANGER 33	SLP	SAIL	FBG	KL	IB	D		9	7	10500	5		16500	18700
37		RANGER 37	SLP	SAIL	FBG	KL	IB	25	UNIV	11	4	15200	6		24900	27600
1975 BOATS																
23		RANGER 23	SLP	SAIL	FBG	KL	OB			7	11	3400	3	9	3800	4450
26	3	RANGER 26	SLP	SA/CR	FBG	KL	OB			8	8	5860	4	4	7700	8850
28		RANGER 28	SLP	SA/RC	FBG	KL	IB			9	7	5108	4	6	7250	8350
28	7	RANGER 29	SLP	SAIL	FBG	KL	IB			9	4	6700	4	5	9750	11100
28	7	RANGER 29	SLP	SAIL	FBG	KL	IB	D		9	4	6700	4	5	9900	11200
32	7	RANGER 32	SLP	SAIL	FBG	KL	IB	25		10	10	9500	5	3	14400	16400
33	2	RANGER 33	SLP	SAIL	FBG	KL	IB	25		9	7	10500	5		15900	18100
33	2	RANGER 33	SLP	SAIL	FBG	KL	IB	D		9	7	10500	5		16000	18200
37		RANGER 37	SLP	SAIL	FBG	KL	IB	25		11	4	15200	6		24200	26800
37		RANGER 37	SLP	SAIL	FBG	KL	IB	D		11	4	15200	6		24500	27200
1974 BOATS																
23		RANGER 23	SLP	SAIL	FBG		OB			7	11	3400	3	9	3700	4350
26	3	RANGER 26	SLP	SA/CR	FBG		OB			8	8	5860	4	4	7500	8600
28	7	RANGER 29	SLP	SAIL	FBG		IB	30	UNIV	9	4	6700	4	5	9500	10800
32	7	RANGER 32	SLP	SAIL	FBG	KL	IB	30		10	10	9500	5	3	14000	15900
33	2	RANGER 33	SLP	SAIL	FBG		IB	30	UNIV	9	7	10500	5		15500	17600
37		RANGER ONE TON	SLP	SAIL	FBG		IB	30	UNIV	11	4	15200	6		23500	26100
1973 BOATS																
23		RANGER 23	SLP	SAIL	FBG		OB			7	11	3400	3	9	3650	4200
26	3	RANGER 26	SLP	SA/CR	FBG		OB			8	8	5860	4	4	7300	8400
28	7	RANGER 29	SLP	SAIL	FBG		IB	25	UNIV	9	4	6700	4	5	9300	10600
33	2	RANGER 33	SLP	SAIL	FBG		IB	25	UNIV	9	7	10500	5		15100	17200
37		RANGER ONE TON	SLP	SAIL	FBG		IB	25D	VLVO	11	4	15200	6		23200	25800

CONTINUED ON NEXT PAGE

RANGER SAILBOATS   -CONTINUED   See inside cover to adjust price for area

LOA FT IN	NAME AND/ OR MODEL	TOP/ RIG	BOAT TYPE	-HULL- MTL TP	----ENGINE--- TP # HP MFG	BEAM FT IN	WGT LBS	DRAFT FT IN	RETAIL LOW	RETAIL HIGH

------------------ 1972 BOATS ------------------

23	RANGER 23	SAIL	FBG	OB		7 11	3400	3 9	3550	4150
26	3 RANGER 26	SA/CR	FBG	OB		8 8	5860	4 4	7150	8200
28	7 RANGER 29	SAIL	FBG	IB	25 UNIV	9 4	6700	4 5	9100	10300
33	2 RANGER 33	SAIL	FBG	IB	25 UNIV	9 7	10500	5	14800	16800

------------------ 1971 BOATS ------------------

26	3 RANGER 26	SA/CR	FBG	OB		8 8	5860	4 4	7000	8050
28	7 RANGER 29	SAIL	FBG	IB	25 UNIV	9 4	6700	4 5	8900	10100
33	2 RANGER 33	SAIL	FBG	IB	25 UNIV	9 7	10500	5	14500	16500

RON RAWSON INC
REDMOND WA 98052   COAST GUARD MFG ID- RRW See inside cover to adjust price for area

For more recent years, see the BUC Used Boat Price Guide, Volume 1 or Volume 2

LOA FT IN	NAME AND/ OR MODEL	TOP/ RIG	BOAT TYPE	-HULL- MTL TP	----ENGINE--- TP # HP MFG	BEAM FT IN	WGT LBS	DRAFT FT IN	RETAIL LOW	RETAIL HIGH

------------------ 1982 BOATS ------------------

| 30 | 6 RAWSON CRUISING 30 | SLP | SA/CR | FBG KL | IB D | 9 | 12000 | 5 | 23400 | 26000 |
| 30 | 6 RAWSON PILOTHOUSE 30 | SLP | SA/CR | FBG KL | IB D | 9 | 12500 | 5 | 24400 | 27100 |

------------------ 1981 BOATS ------------------

| 30 | 6 RAWSON CRUISING 30 | SLP | SA/CR | FBG KL | IB D | 9 | 12000 | 5 | 22000 | 24500 |
| 30 | 6 RAWSON PILOTHOUSE 30 | SLP | SA/CR | FBG KL | IB D | 9 | 12500 | 5 | 23000 | 25500 |

------------------ 1980 BOATS ------------------

| 30 | 6 RAWSON CRUISING 30 | SLP | SA/CR | FBG KL | IB D | 9 | 12000 | 5 | 21000 | 23400 |
| 30 | 6 RAWSON PILOTHOUSE 30 | SLP | SA/CR | FBG KL | IB D | 9 | 12500 | 5 | 21900 | 24400 |

------------------ 1979 BOATS ------------------

| 30 | 6 RAWSON CRUISING 30 | SLP | SA/CR | FBG KL | IB D | 9 | 12000 | 5 | 20200 | 22500 |
| 30 | 6 RAWSON PILOTHOUSE 30 | SLP | SA/CR | FBG KL | IB D | 9 | 12500 | 5 | 21100 | 23400 |

------------------ 1978 BOATS ------------------

30	6 RAWSON CRUISING 30	SLP	SA/CR	FBG KL	IB 23D- 40D	9	12500	5	19100	21300
30	6 RAWSON PILOTHOUSE 30	SLP	SA/CR	FBG KL	IB 23D- 40D	9	12500	5	21600	24000
32	1 TRAVELLER 32	CUT	SA/CR	FBG KL	IB D	10 2	15200	5	24500	27200
32	1 TRAVELLER 32	KTH	SA/CR	FBG KL	IB D	10 2	15200	5	24500	27200

------------------ 1977 BOATS ------------------

30	6 RAWSON CRUISING 30	SLP	SA/CR	FBG KL	OB	9	12000	5	18900	21000
30	6 RAWSON CRUISING 30	SLP	SA/CR	FBG KL	IB 27 PALM	9	12000	5	19000	21100
30	6 RAWSON CRUISING 30	SLP	SA/CR	FBG KL	IB 25D- 40D	9	12000	5	19100	21200
30	6 RAWSON PILOTHOUSE 30	SLP	SA/CR	FBG KL	OB	9	12500	5	19500	21700
30	6 RAWSON PILOTHOUSE 30	SLP	SA/CR	FBG KL	IB 27 PALM	9	12500	5	19600	21800
30	6 RAWSON PILOTHOUSE 30	SLP	SA/CR	FBG KL	IB 25D- 40D	9	12500	5	19700	23000
32	PUGET-SOUNDER	FSH	FBG	DS	IB 130-160	11	14000	2 6	29000	32200
32	PUGET-SOUNDER	FSH	FBG	DS	IB 130D	11	14000	2 6	41500	46100
32	SEKIU	SF	FBG	DS	IB 220D	11	11500	2 6	34600	38400
37	6 COASTAL CRUISER	CR	FBG	DS	IB 160	13 6	28500	3 6	81000	89000
37	6 COASTAL CRUISER	CR	FBG	DS	IB 225	13 6	28500	4	81200	89200
37	6 COASTAL CRUISER	CR	FBG	DS	IB 220D	13 6	28500	3 6	87800	96500
42	GULF CRUISER	CR	FBG	IB	185	14	34000	4	103500	113500
42	GULF CRUISER	CR	FBG	IB	300	14	34000	4	105500	115500
42	GULF CRUISER	CR	FBG	IB	220D	14	34000	4	110000	121000

------------------ 1976 BOATS ------------------

30	6 RAWSON 30	SLP	SA/CR	FBG KL	OB	9	12000		18300	20400
32	BRISTOL-BAY	FSH	FBG	DS	IB 130-225	11		2 6	19500	22700
32	COMBINATION	FSH	FBG	DS	IB 130-225	11		3	19500	22700
32	PUGET-SOUNDER	FSH	FBG	DS	IB 130D	11	14000	2 6	40000	44500
32	RAWSON	CR	FBG	DS	IB 130-160	11		3	21500	23900
32	SEKIU	SF	FBG	DS	IB 220D	11	11500	2 6	33300	37000
37	6 COASTAL CRUISER	CR	FBG	DS	IB 220D	13 6	28500	4	84200	92600
37	6 SEINER	FSH	FBG	DS	IB 225	13 6	28500	4	76200	83700
37	6 TROLLER	FSH	FBG	DS	IB 225	13 6	28500	4	76200	83700
42	GULF CRUISER	CR	FBG	DS	IB 220D	14	34000	5	106500	117000
42	TROLLER	FSH	FBG	DS	IB 225	14		5	**	**

------------------ 1975 BOATS ------------------

21	3 LUDERS 21	SLP	SA/OD	FBG KL	OB	5 7	1400	3	1900	2250
25	4 RAWSON 25	SLP	SAIL	FBG KL	OB	6		4	4500	5200
30	6 RAWSON 30	SLP	SA/CR	FBG KL	OB	9	12000		17400	19800
32	DOUBLE CABIN	SF	FBG	DS	IB	11		2 6	**	**
32	PUGET-SOUNDER	FSH	FBG	DS	IB D	11	14000	2 6	**	**
32	SEKIU	SF	FBG	DS	IB D	11	11500	2 6	**	**
37	6 COASTAL CRUISER	CR	FBG	DS	IB D	13 6	28500	4	**	**
37	6 TRI CABIN	SF	FBG	DS	IB	13 6		4	**	**
40	RAWSON 40	SLP	SA/CR	FBG KL	IB D	12		6 6	34000	37800
42	GULF-CRUISER TRI CBN	CR	FBG	DS	IB D	14	42000	5	**	**
42	TRI CABIN	SF	FBG	DS	IB	14		5	**	**
48	GULF-CRUISER TRI CBN	CR	FBG	DS	IB	14		5	**	**

------------------ 1974 BOATS ------------------

21	3 LUDERS 21	SLP	SA/OD	FBG KL	OB	5 7	1400	3	1850	2200
25	4 RAWSON 25	SLP	SAIL	FBG KL	OB	6		4	4400	5050
30	6 RAWSON 30	SLP	SA/CR	FBG KL	OB	9	12000	5	17000	19300
40	RAWSON 40	SLP	SA/CR	FBG KL	IB D	12		6 6	33100	36800

------------------ 1973 BOATS ------------------

21	3 LUDERS 21	SLP	SA/OD	FBG KL	OB	5 6	1400	3	1800	2150
25	4 RAWSON 25	SLP	SAIL	FBG KL	OB	6		4	4250	4900
30	6 RAWSON 30	SLP	SAIL	FBG KL	IB 22D	9	12000	5	16600	18900
30	6 RAWSON 30	YWL	SAIL	FBG KL	IB 22D	9	12000	5	16600	18900
32	PUGET-SOUNDER	FSH	FBG	DS	IO	11	14000	2 6	**	**
37	6 COASTAL CRUISER	MY	FBG	DS	IB 220D	13 6	28500	4	74900	82300
42	GULF CRUISER	MY	FBG	DS	IB 300D	14	42000	5	117500	129000
48	GULF CRUISER	MY	FBG	DS	IB 300D	14		5	108500	119500

------------------ 1972 BOATS ------------------

21	LUDERS	SLP	SAIL	FBG KL		5 7	1400	3	1750	2050
32	RAWSON 32	CR	FBG	DS	IO	11		2 6	**	**
32	SEKIU	SF	FBG	IB	11		2 6	**	**

------------------ 1971 BOATS ------------------

21	LUDERS 21	SLP	SA/RC	FBG KL		5 7		3	1950	2300
25	5 RAWSON 25	SLP	SA/RC	FBG KL		6		4	4150	4800
30	RAWSON 30	SLP	SA/RC	FBG KL	IB	9		5	7100	8150
32	BRISTOL-GILLNETTER	FSH	FBG	IB	11		1 10	**	**
32	PUGET-SOUNDER	FSH	FBG	IB	11		2 6	**	**
32	SE-GILLNETTER	FBG	IB	11		2 6	**	**
32	SEKIU	SF	FBG	IB	11		2 6	**	**
32	SPORT FISHERMAN	SF	FBG	IB 225	13 6		3 6	16800	19100
37	6 CRUISER	CR	FBG	IB 325D	13 6		3 6	50400	55300
37	6 SPORT FISHERMAN	SF	FBG	IB 325	13 6		4	47100	51700
38	SALMON-SEINER	FSH	FBG	IB 300	13 6	7000	3 6	21700	24100
42	GULF-CRUISER	CR	FBG	IB	14		**	**
42	SPORT FISHERMAN	SF	FBG	IB D	14		5	**	**

------------------ 1970 BOATS ------------------

21	2 LUDERS	SLP	SA/OD	FBG KL	IB	5 7		3	2650	3050
26	RAWSON 26	SLP	SA/CR	FBG KL		8		4 9	4650	5350
30	6 RAWSON 30	SLP	SA/CR	FBG KL	IB 22D	9		5	16000	18200
30	6 RAWSON 30	YWL	SA/CR	FBG KL	IB 22D	9		5	16000	18200
32	BRISTOL-GILLNETTER	FSH	FBG	IB	11		1 10	**	**
32	PUGET-SOUNDER	CR	FBG	DS	IB	11		2 6	**	**
32	RAWSON 32	CR	FBG	DS	IO	11		2 6	**	**
32	RAWSON 32	CR	FBG	DS	IO T	11		2 6	**	**
32	SE-GILLNETTER	FSH	FBG	IB	11		2 6	**	**
32	SEKIU FISHERMAN	FSH	FBG	IB	11		2 6	**	**
32	SPORT FISHERMAN	SF	FBG	IB	11		2 6	**	**
37	PUGET SOUNDER	CR	FBG	IB	11		2 6	**	**
37	6 DIESEL CRUISER	SF	FBG	IB D	13 6		3 8	**	**
37	6 SPORT FISHERMAN	SF	FBG	IB D	13 6		4	**	**
42	GULF CRUISER	CR	FBG	IB	14		5	**	**
42	SPORT FISHERMAN	SF	FBG	IB D	14		5	**	**

------------------ 1969 BOATS ------------------

| 30 | 6 RAWSON 30 | SLP | SA/RC | FBG KL | IB 22D | 9 | 12000 | 5 | 15400 | 17500 |

------------------ 1967 BOATS ------------------

26	RAWSON 26	SLP	SAIL	FBG KL		7 1	4 9	4450	5100
30	6 RAWSON 30	SLP	SA/CR	FBG KL	IB 22	9		5	11700	13300
42	GULF-CRUISER	FSH	CR	FBG	IB 300D CUM	14	25000	5	61100	67200

------------------ 1966 BOATS ------------------

26	RAWSON 26	SLP	SAIL	FBG KL		7 1	4 6	4400	5100
30	6 RAWSON 30	SLP	SA/CR	FBG KL	IB 22	9		5	7300	8350
32	PUGET-SOUNDER	SF	FBG	IB 150	10 6		4 6	14400	16300
42	SPORT FISHERMAN	SF	FBG	IB 150	10 6		3 6	13400	15200
42	SPORT FISHERMAN	CR	FBG	IB 165	14		4	45000	50000
42	SPORT FISHERMAN	SF	FBG	IB 165	14		4	32500	36100

------------------ 1965 BOATS ------------------

26	RAWSON 26	SLP	SAIL	FBG KL		8	4 6	4400	5050
30	6 RAWSON	SLP	SA/OD	FBG KL	IB 22	9		5	19000	21100
32	SPORT FISHERMAN	SF	FBG	IB 100	14		4	12900	14700
42	GULF CRUISER	CR	FBG	IB 125	14		5	57300	63000
42	SOUND-CRUISER	CR	FBG	IB D	14		**	**

------------------ 1961 BOATS ------------------

30	RAWSON 30	SLP	SA/OD	FBG KL		9		4 9	14700	16700
32	GILLNETTER	FBG	IB	10 6			**	**
32	RAWSON	SF	FBG	IB 165	10 6		2 3	11500	13100

------------------ 1960 BOATS ------------------

| 30 | 6 RAWSON 30 | SLP | SA/CR | WD | KL OB | 9 | | 5 | 15000 | 17000 |

RAY PLASTICS INC
COAST GUARD MFG ID- RPS

Call 1-800-327-6929 for BUC Personalized Evaluation Service
Or, for 1908 to 1986 boats, sign onto www.BUCValuPro.com

RAYSON CRAFT BOAT CO

Call 1-800-327-6929 for BUC Personalized Evaluation Service
Or, for 1961 to 1968 boats, sign onto www.BUCValuPro.com

REBEL INDUSTRIES INC
TALLEVAST FL 33588   COAST GUARD MFG ID- RRR See inside cover to adjust price for area
FORMERLY RAY GREENE & CO INC

For more recent years, see the BUC Used Boat Price Guide, Volume 1 or Volume 2

LOA FT IN	NAME AND/ OR MODEL	TOP/ RIG	BOAT TYPE	-HULL- MTL TP	TP #	----ENGINE--- HP MFG	BEAM FT IN	WGT LBS	DRAFT FT IN	RETAIL LOW	RETAIL HIGH
--- 1982 BOATS ---
16 1	REBEL MARK IV	SLP	SA/OD	FBG CB			6 6	700	6	1900	2250
19 2	MARINER	SLP	SA/OD	FBG CB			7	1200	10	2550	2950
19 2	RHODES 19	SLP	SA/OD	FBG CB			7	1355	10	2700	3100
19 2	RHODES 19	SLP	SA/OD	FBG KL			7	1355	3 3	2700	3100
--- 1981 BOATS ---
16 1	REBEL IV	SLP	SA/OD	FBG CB			6 6	700	6	1800	2150
19 2	MARINER	SLP	SA/OD	FBG CB			7	1600	10	2550	2950
19 2	RHODES 19	SLP	SA/OD	FBG KL			7	1355	10	2550	2950
19 2	RHODES 19	SLP	SA/OD	FBG KL			7	1355	3 3	2550	2950
--- 1980 BOATS ---
16 1	REBEL IV	SLP	SA/OD	FBG CB			6 6	700	6	1700	2050
19 2	MARINER	SLP	SA/OD	FBG CB			7	1600	10	2650	3050
19 2	RHODES 19	SLP	SA/OD	FBG CB			7	1355	10	2400	2800

RED WING MARINE CORP

Call 1-800-327-6929 for BUC Personalized Evaluation Service
Or, for 1959 to 1966 boats, sign onto www.BUCValuPro.com

DAVE REED & CO
COAST GUARD MFG ID- DVR

Call 1-800-327-6929 for BUC Personalized Evaluation Service
Or, for 1980 to 1999 boats, sign onto www.BUCValuPro.com

ROLAND REED ASSOCIATES INC

Call 1-800-327-6929 for BUC Personalized Evaluation Service
Or, for 1961 to 1968 boats, sign onto www.BUCValuPro.com

REED'S INC

Call 1-800-327-6929 for BUC Personalized Evaluation Service
Or, for 1965 to 1973 boats, sign onto www.BUCValuPro.com

REGAL FIBERGLASS
MIAMI FL 33142   See inside cover to adjust price for area
FOR OLDER MODELS SEE HEWES BOAT COMPANY

LOA FT IN	NAME AND/ OR MODEL	TOP/ RIG	BOAT TYPE	-HULL- MTL TP	TP #	----ENGINE--- HP MFG	BEAM FT IN	WGT LBS	DRAFT FT IN	RETAIL LOW	RETAIL HIGH
--- 1977 BOATS ---
17	BONEFISHER	OP	OPFSH	FBG SV	OB		6 6	1080		2100	2500
17	TARPON	OP	OPFSH	FBG SV	OB		7 1	1260		2400	2800
21	MARLIN	OP	OPFSH	FBG DV	OB		7 9	1810		3650	4200
21	SAILFISHER	SF		FBG DV	OB			1830		3650	4250

REGAL MARINE INDS INC
ORLANDO FL 32809   COAST GUARD MFG ID- RGM See inside cover to adjust price for area

For more recent years, see the BUC Used Boat Price Guide, Volume 1 or Volume 2

LOA FT IN	NAME AND/ OR MODEL	TOP/ RIG	BOAT TYPE	-HULL- MTL TP	TP #	----ENGINE--- HP MFG	BEAM FT IN	WGT LBS	DRAFT FT IN	RETAIL LOW	RETAIL HIGH
--- 1983 BOATS ---
16 5	DUCHESS 166 XL	ST	RNBT	FBG DV	IO	185-188	6 10	1750		2050	2450
16 5	DUCHESS 166XL VBR	ST	RNBT	FBG DV	OB		6 10	1150		2050	2450
16 5	DUCHESS 166XL VBR	ST	RNBT	FBG DV	IO	120 MRCR	6 10	1750		2000	2400
16 5	DUCHESS 166XL VBR	ST	RNBT	FBG DV	IO	120 OMC	6 10	1750		2000	2400
16 5	DUCHESS 166XL VBR	ST	RNBT	FBG DV	IO	120-175	6 10	1750		2200	2600
17 10	COUNTESS 180 VBR	ST	RNBT	FBG DV	OB		7 2	1450		2550	3000
17 10	COUNTESS 180 VBR&RAB	ST	RNBT	FBG DV	IO	120-188	7 2	2250		2600	3200
17 10	PRINCESS 180	ST	CUD	FBG DV	IO	120-175	7 3	2250		2650	3300
19 8	EMPRESS 190 VBR&RAB	ST	RNBT	FBG DV	OB		7 4	1500		2750	3200
19 8	EMPRESS 190 VBR&RAB	ST	RNBT	FBG DV	IO	120-200	7 4	2600		3100	3850
19 8	EMPRESS 190 VBR&RAB	ST	RNBT	FBG DV	IO	225-260	7 4	2600		3400	4100
20 6	MAJESTIC 207XL	ST	CUD	FBG DV	IO	138-260	8	3075		5050	6250
20 6	MAJESTIC 207XL	ST	CUD	FBG DV	IO	330 MRCR	8	3075		5900	6800
20 6	MAJESTIC 207XL	ST	CUD	FBG DV	IO	T120-T175	8	3075		5700	7050
20 11	REGENCY 21FF	ST	FSH	FBG DV	OB		8	2450		3850	4500
20 11	REGENCY 21FF	ST	FSH	FBG DV	IO		8	3450		3800	4400
20 11	REGENCY 21FF	ST	FSH	FBG DV	IO	138-200	8	3450		5900	6850
20 11	REGENCY 21FF	ST	FSH	FBG DV	SE	205 OMC	8	3450		4400	5050
20 11	REGENCY 21FF	ST	FSH	FBG DV	IO	225-260	8	3450		6050	7200
24	AMBASSADOR 245XL	ST	CUD	FBG DV	IO	130D VLVO	8	3400		7850	9000
24	AMBASSADOR 245XL	ST	OVNTR	FBG DV	IO	120-260	8	4200		7550	9050
IO 330 MRCR	8350		9600, IO 130D-165D	9000	10500, IO T120-T188	8150	9850
24 7	ROYAL 25 FF	ST	FSH	FBG DV	IO	170-200	8	4200		7950	9450
24 7	ROYAL 25 FF	ST	FSH	FBG DV	SE	205 OMC	8	4200		6650	7650
24 7	ROYAL 25 FF	ST	FSH	FBG DV	IO	225-260	8	4200		8350	9900
IO 330 MRCR	9250		10500, IO 130D-165D	11100	13200, IO T120-T188	8900	10700
24 7	ROYAL 250 XL	ST	CUD	FBG DV	IO	170-200	8	4200		7550	8950
24 7	ROYAL 250 XL	ST	CUD	FBG DV	SE	205 OMC	8	4200		6800	7800
24 7	ROYAL 250 XL	ST	CUD	FBG DV	IO	225-260	8	4200		7900	9300
IO 330 MRCR	8650		9950, IO 130D-165D	8950	10600, IO T120-T188	8350	10200
27 4	COMMODORE 277 XL	ST	OVNTR	FBG DV	IO	260-330	10	8000		14100	16800
27 4	COMMODORE 277 XL	ST	OVNTR	FBG DV	IO	T138-T188	10	8000		14600	17000
--- 1982 BOATS ---
16 5	DUCHESS 166XL VBR	ST	RNBT	FBG DV	OB		6 10	1150		2000	2400
16 5	DUCHESS 166XL VBR	ST	RNBT	FBG DV	IO	120 MRCR	6 10	1750		2000	2400
16 5	DUCHESS 166XL VBR	ST	RNBT	FBG DV	IO	120 OMC	6 10	1750		1950	2350
16 5	DUCHESS 166XL VBR	ST	RNBT	FBG DV	IO	120-170	6 10	1750		2150	2500
17 10	COUNTESS 180 VBR	ST	RNBT	FBG DV	OB		7 2	1450		2500	2900
17 10	COUNTESS 180 VBR&RAB	ST	RNBT	FBG DV	IO	120-185	7 2	2250		2550	3100
19 8	EMPRESS 190 VBR&RAB	ST	RNBT	FBG DV	OB		7 4	1500		2700	3150
19 8	EMPRESS 190 VBR&RAB	ST	RNBT	FBG DV	IO	120-200	7 4	2600		3050	3750
19 8	EMPRESS 190 VBR&RAB	ST	RNBT	FBG DV	IO	225-260	7 4	2600		3300	4000
20 6	MAJESTIC 207XL	ST	CUD	FBG DV	IO	140-230	8	3075		4800	5900
IO 260	5100		6100, IO 330 MRCR	5800	6650, IO 130D VLVO	6150	7050
IO T120-T140	5550		6800, IO T155D VLVO	8650	9900
20 6	MEDALLION 209XL	OP	OPFSH	FBG DV	OB		8	2400		3600	4150
20 11	REGENCY 210XL	ST	FSH	FBG DV	OB		8	2450		3800	4400
20 11	REGENCY 21FF	ST	FSH	FBG DV	OB		8	2450		3700	4300
20 11	REGENCY 21FF	ST	FSH	FBG DV	IO		8	3450		**	**
IO 140-230	5600		6800, IO 260	5900 OMC	7050, IO 330 MRCR	6600	7600
IO 130D VLVO	8300		9550
24	AMBASSADOR 245XL	ST	CUD	FBG DV	IO	130D VLVO	8	3400		8400	9650
24	AMBASSADOR 245XL	ST	OVNTR	FBG DV	IO	145-260	8	4200		7350	8850
IO 330 MRCR	8150		9400, IO 130D VLVO	8700	10000, IO T120-T185	7950	9550
IO T155D VLVO	11400		12900
24	ROYAL 24FF	ST	CUD	FBG DV	IO		8	3400		**	**
IO 140-260	6150		7700, IO 330 MRCR	7150	8200, IO 130D VLVO	6900	7950
IO T120-T140	6950		8350, IO T155D VLVO	10300	11800
--- 1981 BOATS ---
16 5	DUCHESS 166XL VBR	ST	RNBT	FBG DV	OB		6 10	1150		1950	2350
16 5	DUCHESS 166XL VBR	ST	RNBT	FBG DV	IO	120 MRCR	6 10	1750		1900	2300
16 5	DUCHESS 166XL VBR	ST	RNBT	FBG DV	IO	120 OMC	6 10	1750		1900	2300
16 5	DUCHESS 166XL VBR	ST	RNBT	FBG DV	IO	120-170	6 10	1750		2050	2450
17 10	COUNTESS 180 VBR	ST	RNBT	FBG DV	OB		7 2	1450		2450	2850
17 10	COUNTESS 180 VBR&RAB	ST	RNBT	FBG DV	IO	120-185	7 2	2250		2500	3050
18 8	EMPRESS 190 VBR&RAB	ST	RNBT	FBG DV	OB		7 4	1500		2550	2950
18 8	EMPRESS 190 VBR&RAB	ST	RNBT	FBG DV	IO	120-200	7 4	2600		3050	3550
18 8	EMPRESS 190 VBR&RAB	ST	RNBT	FBG DV	IO	225-260	7 4	2600		3300	3950
20 6	MAJESTIC 206XL	ST	CUD	FBG DV	OB		8	2200		3400	3950
20 6	MAJESTIC 206XL	ST	CUD	FBG DV	IO	140-230	8	3075		4650	5700

REGAL MARINE INDS INC -CONTINUED See inside cover to adjust price for area

LOA FT	IN	NAME AND/ OR MODEL	TOP/ RIG	BOAT TYPE	-HULL- MTL	TP	ENGINE TP	# HP	MFG	BEAM FT	IN	WGT LBS	DRAFT FT IN	RETAIL LOW	RETAIL HIGH
		1981 BOATS													
20	6	MAJESTIC 206XL	ST	CUD	FBG	DV	IO	260		8		3075		4900	5900
		IO 330 MRCR 5600 6450, IO 130D VLVO 5950 6850, IO T120-T140												5400	6550
20	6	MAJESTIC 207XL	ST	CUD	FBG	DV	IO	140-230		8		3075		4800	5900
		IO 260 5100 6100, IO 330 MRCR 5800 6650, IO 130D VLVO												6150	7050
		IO T120-T140 5550 6800													
20	6	MEDALLION 209XL	OP	OPFSH	FBG	DV	OB			8		2400		3500	4100
20	11	REGENCY 210XL	ST	CUD	FBG	DV	OB			8		2450		3700	4300
20	11	REGENCY 210XL	ST	CUD	FBG	DV	IO	140-260		8		3450		5200	6250
		IO 330 MRCR 5900 6800, IO 130D VLVO 6300 7250, IO T120-T140												5700	6900
20	11	REGENCY 211XL	ST	CUD	FBG	DV	IO	145-260		8		3450		5650	6900
		IO 330 MRCR 6450 7400, IO 130D VLVO 6800 7800, IO T120-T140												6250	7550
20	11	REGENCY 21FF	ST	FSH	FBG	DV	OB			8		2450		3650	4250
20	11	REGENCY 21FF	ST	FSH	FBG	DV	IO	140-230		8		3450		5500	6700
		IO 260 5800 6950, IO 330 MRCR 6500 7500, IO 130D VLVO												8150	9400
24		AMBASSADOR 245XL	ST	OVNTR	FBG	DV	IO	145-260		8		4200		7250	8700
		IO 330 MRCR 8050 9250, IO 130D VLVO 8550 9850, IO T120-T185												7850	9400
24		ROYAL 240XL	ST	CUD	FBG	DV	OB			8		2500		4100	4750
24		ROYAL 240XL	ST	CUD	FBG	DV	IO	140-260		8		3400		6050	7550
		IO 330 MRCR 7050 8100, IO 130D VLVO 7550 8650, IO T120-T140												6850	8200
24		ROYAL 244XL	ST	CUD	FBG	DV	IO	145-260		8		3600		6500	7850
		IO 330 MRCR 7250 8350, IO 130D VLVO 7800 8950, IO T120-T140												7050	8500
		1980 BOATS													
16	3	DUCHESS 166	OP	RNBT	FBG	DV	IO	120-140		6	10			2200	2550
17	10	COUNTESS 180 VBR&RAB	ST	RNBT	FBG	DV	OB			7	2	1450		2400	2800
17	10	COUNTESS 180 VBR&RAB	ST	RNBT	FBG	DV	IO	120-170		7	2	2250		2450	2900
18	8	EMPRESS 190 VBR&RAB	ST	RNBT	FBG	DV	OB			7	4	1500		2500	2900
18	8	EMPRESS 190 VBR&RAB	ST	RNBT	FBG	DV	IO	120-230		7	4	2600		2800	3400
18	8	EMPRESS 190 VBR&RAB	ST	RNBT	FBG	DV	IO	260		7	4	2600		3050	3550
19		IMPERIAL 190	OP	RNBT	FBG	DV	OB			7	4			2600	3000
19		IMPERIAL 190	OP	RNBT	FBG	DV	IO	140		7	4			2950	3400
20	6	MAJESTIC 206XL	ST	CUD	FBG	DV	OB			8		3000		3850	4450
20	6	MAJESTIC 206XL	ST	CUD	FBG	DV	IO	140-260		8		3000		4650	5600
20	6	MAJESTIC 206XL	ST	CUD	FBG	DV	IO	330	MRCR	8		3000		5550	6400
20	6	MAJESTIC 206XL	ST	CUD	FBG	DV	IO	T120-T140		8		3000		5350	6200
20	6	MAJESTIC 207XL	ST	CUD	FBG	DV	IO	140-260		8		3075		4650	5700
20	6	MAJESTIC 207XL	ST	CUD	FBG	DV	IO	330	MRCR	8		3075		5650	6500
20	6	MAJESTIC 207XL	ST	CUD	FBG	DV	IO	T120-T140		8		3075		5450	6250
20	6	MEDALLION 209XL	OP	OPFSH	FBG	DV	OB			8		2400		3450	4000
20	11	REGENCY 210XL	ST	CUD	FBG	DV	OB			8		2450		3600	4200
20	11	REGENCY 210XL	ST	CUD	FBG	DV	IO	170-260		8		3450		5200	6250
20	11	REGENCY 210XL	ST	CUD	FBG	DV	IO	330	MRCR	8		3450		6100	7050
20	11	REGENCY 210XL	ST	CUD	FBG	DV	IO	T120-T140		8		3450		5900	6800
20	11	REGENCY 211XL	ST	CUD	FBG	DV	IO	170-260		8		3550		5300	6350
20	11	REGENCY 211XL	ST	CUD	FBG	DV	IO	330	MRCR	8		3550		6200	7150
20	11	REGENCY 211XL	ST	CUD	FBG	DV	IO	T120-T140		8		3550		6000	6950
20	11	REGENCY 21FF	ST	FSH	FBG	DV	IO	170-260		8		3450		5450	6600
20	11	REGENCY 21FF	ST	FSH	FBG	DV	IO	330	MRCR	8		3450		6450	7400
20	11	REGENCY 21FF	ST	FSH	FBG	DV	IO	T120-T140		8		3450		6250	7200
20	11	REGENCY 21FF		SF	FBG	DV	OB			8				3100	3600
24		AMBASSADOR 245XL	ST	OVNTR	FBG	DV	IO	198-260		8		4200		7100	8400
24		AMBASSADOR 245XL	ST	OVNTR	FBG	DV	IO	330	MRCR	8		4200		7950	9150
24		AMBASSADOR 245XL	ST	OVNTR	FBG	DV	IO	T120-T170		8		4200		7750	9000
24		ROYAL 240XL	ST	CUD	FBG	DV	OB			8		3600		5350	6150
24		ROYAL 240XL	ST	CUD	FBG	DV	IO	170-260		8		3600		6300	7500
24		ROYAL 240XL	ST	CUD	FBG	DV	IO	330	MRCR	8		3600		7200	8300
24		ROYAL 240XL	ST	CUD	FBG	DV	IO	T120-T140		8		3600		7000	8050
24		ROYAL 244XL	ST	CUD	FBG	DV	IO	170-260		8		3650		6350	7600
24		ROYAL 244XL	ST	CUD	FBG	DV	IO	330	MRCR	8		3650		7250	8350
24		ROYAL 244XL	ST	CUD	FBG	DV	IO	T120-T140		8		3650		7050	8150
		1979 BOATS													
17	10	COUNTESS 180 VBR&RAB	ST	RNBT	FBG	DV	OB			7	2	1450		2400	2750
17	10	COUNTESS 180 VBR&RAB	ST	RNBT	FBG	DV	IO	120-230		7	2	2250		2450	3000
18	8	IMPERIAL 190 VBR&RAB	ST	RNBT	FBG	DV	OB			7	4	1500		2450	2850
18	8	IMPERIAL 190 VBR&RAB	ST	RNBT	FBG	DV	IO	120-230		7	4	2300		2650	3200
18	8	IMPERIAL 190 VBR&RAB	ST	RNBT	FBG	DV	IO	260		7	4	2300		2850	3350
20	6	MAJESTIC 206XL	ST	CUD	FBG	DV	OB			8		2200		3250	3800
20	6	MAJESTIC 206XL	ST	CUD	FBG	DV	IO	140-260		8				4800	5850
20	6	MAJESTIC 206XL	ST	CUD	FBG	DV	IO	330	MRCR	8				5750	6600
20	6	MAJESTIC 206XL	ST	CUD	FBG	DV	IO	T120-T140		8				5550	6400
20	6	MEDALLION 209	OP	OPFSH	FBG	DV	OB			8		2400		3350	3900
20	11	REGENCY 210XL	ST	CUD	FBG	DV	IO	140-260		8		2250		3850	4800
20	11	REGENCY 210XL	ST	CUD	FBG	DV	IO	330	MRCR	8		2250		4850	5550
20	11	REGENCY 210XL	ST	CUD	FBG	DV	IO	T120-T140		8		2250		4650	5400
20	11	REGENCY 211XL	ST	CUD	FBG	DV	IO	140-260		8		2250		4200	5200
20	11	REGENCY 211XL	ST	CUD	FBG	DV	IO	330	MRCR	8		2250		5200	5950
20	11	REGENCY 211XL	ST	CUD	FBG	DV	IO	T120-T140		8		2250		4950	5700
24		ROYAL 240XL	ST	CUD	FBG	DV	OB			8		2500		3950	4600
24		ROYAL 240XL	ST	CUD	FBG	DV	IO	140-260		8		3400		6000	7250
24		ROYAL 240XL	ST	CUD	FBG	DV	IO	330	MRCR	8		3400		6950	8000
24		ROYAL 240XL	ST	CUD	FBG	DV	IO	T120-T165		8		3400		6750	7800
24		ROYAL 244XL	ST	CUD	FBG	DV	IO	140-260		8		3600		6250	7500
24		ROYAL 244XL	ST	CUD	FBG	DV	IO	330	MRCR	8		3600		7200	8300
24		ROYAL 244XL	ST	CUD	FBG	DV	IO	T120-T165		8		3600		7000	8100
27	9	AMBASSADOR 280		SF	FBG	DV	IO	260		9	8			13100	14900
27	9	AMBASSADOR 280		SF	FBG	DV	IO	T170		9	8			13900	15800
		1978 BOATS													
17	5	DUCHESS 176	ST	RNBT	FBG	TR	OB			7	2	1500		2400	2750
17	5	DUCHESS 176	ST	RNBT	FBG	TR	IO	120-198		7	2	2300		2450	3000
17	5	DUCHESS 176	ST	RNBT	FBG	TR	IO	200	VLVO	7	2	2300		2650	3050
17	10	COUNTESS 180	ST	RNBT	FBG	DV	OB			6	5	1300		2150	2500
17	10	COUNTESS 180	ST	RNBT	FBG	DV	IO	120-140		6	5	2000		2250	2700
18	8	IMPERIAL 190 VBR&RAB	ST	RNBT	FBG	DV	OB			7	4	1500		2450	2850
18	8	IMPERIAL 190 VBR&RAB	ST	RNBT	FBG	DV	IO	120-228		7	4	2300		2650	3300
20	6	MAJESTIC 206	ST	CUD	FBG	DV	OB			8		2200		3200	3700
20	6	MAJESTIC 206	ST	CUD	FBG	DV	IO	140-260		8		3100		4750	5750
		IB 305 5100 5850, IO 330 MRCR 5700 6550, IO T120-T140												5500	6700
20	6	MEDALLION 209	OP	OPFSH	FBG	DV	OB			8		2400		3300	3850
20	11	REGENCY 210	ST	CUD	FBG	DV	OB			8				3850	4450
20	11	REGENCY 210	ST	CUD	FBG	DV	IO	140-260		8		3400		5150	6250
		IB 305 5500 6350, IO 330 MRCR 6100 7000, IB 350												5700	6550
		IO T120-T140 5900 7150													
24		ROYAL 240	ST	CUD	FBG	DV	OB			8		2500		3850	4500
24		ROYAL 240	ST	CUD	FBG	DV	IO	140-260		8		3800		6550	7850
		IB 305 7000 8050, IO 330 MRCR 7500 8650, IB 350												7200	8250
		IO T120-T165 7300 8800													
27	7	AMBASSADOR 280	FB	SF	FBG	DV	IO	255		9	8			12900	14700
		1977 BOATS													
17	4	EMPRESS 177TBR	ST	RNBT	FBG	TR	OB			6	6	1300		2050	2450
17	4	EMPRESS 177TBR	ST	RNBT	FBG	TR	IO	120-140		6	6	2000		2200	2600
17	5	DUCHESS 1976TBR	ST	RNBT	FBG	TR	OB			7	2	1500		2350	2750
17	5	DUCHESS 1976TBR	ST	RNBT	FBG	TR	IO	120-190		7	2	2300		2500	2950
17	10	COUNTESS 180VBR	ST	RNBT	FBG	DV	OB			6	5	1300		2100	2500
17	10	COUNTESS 180VBR	ST	RNBT	FBG	DV	IO	120-140		6	5	2000		2250	2650
18	8	IMPERIAL 190	ST	RNBT	FBG	DV	OB			7	4	1500		2400	2800
18	8	IMPERIAL 190	ST	RNBT	FBG	DV	IO	120-190		7	4	2300		2700	3200
20	6	MAJESTIC 206	ST	CUD	FBG	DV	OB			8		2000		3000	3450
20	6	MAJESTIC 206	ST	CUD	FBG	DV	IO	140-235		8		3100		4800	5700
20	6	MAJESTIC 206	ST	CUD	FBG	DV	IO	300	CC	8		3100		5400	6250
20	11	REGENCY 210	ST	CUD	FBG	DV	IO	165-235		8		3100		4950	6150
20	11	REGENCY 210	ST	CUD	FBG	DV	IO	300	CC	8		3400		5850	6700
20	11	REGENCY 210	ST	CUD	FBG	DV	IO	T120-T140		8		3400		6000	6900
24		ROYAL 240	ST	CUD	FBG	DV	IO	188-300		8		3800		6700	8350
24		ROYAL 240	ST	CUD	FBG	DV	IO	T120-T170		8		3800		7450	8600
		1976 BOATS													
17	5	DUCHESS 1976	ST	RNBT	FBG	TR	OB			7	10	1500		2300	2700
17	5	DUCHESS 1976	ST	RNBT	FBG	TR	IO	120-190		7	10	2350		2750	3200
17	5	EMPRESS 177	ST	RNBT	FBG	TR	OB			6	6	1350		2100	2500
17	5	EMPRESS 177	ST	RNBT	FBG	TR	IO	120-140		6	6	2050		2300	2700
17	10	COUNTESS 180	ST	RNBT	FBG	DV	OB			6	5	1350		2150	2500
17	10	COUNTESS 180	ST	RNBT	FBG	DV	IO	120-140		6	5	2050		2300	2700
18	8	IMPERIAL 190 RAB	ST	RNBT	FBG	DV	OB			7		1500		2400	2750
18	8	IMPERIAL 190 RAB	ST	RNBT	FBG	DV	IO	120-190		7		2350		2750	3200
18	8	IMPERIAL 190 VBR	ST	RNBT	FBG	DV	OB			7		1500		2400	2750
18	8	IMPERIAL 190 VBR	ST	RNBT	FBG	DV	IO	120-190		7		2350		2750	3200
20	11	REGENCY 210/21	ST	CUD	FBG	DV	OB			8		2200		3200	3700
20	11	REGENCY 210/21	ST	CUD	FBG	DV	IO	165-235		8		3400		5400	6350
20	11	REGENCY 210/21	ST	CUD	FBG	DV	IO	300	CC	8		3400		6000	6900
20	11	REGENCY 210/21	ST	CUD	FBG	DV	IO	T120-T140		8		3400		6150	7100

 CONTINUED ON NEXT PAGE

LOA FT	LOA IN	NAME AND/ OR MODEL	TOP/ RIG	BOAT TYPE	HULL MTL	HULL TP	ENGINE TP	ENGINE # HP	ENGINE MFG	BEAM FT	BEAM IN	WGT LBS	DRAFT FT	DRAFT IN	RETAIL LOW	RETAIL HIGH
		1976 BOATS														
24		ROYAL 240/24	ST	CUD	FBG	DV	IO	165-235		8		3800			6850	8050
24		ROYAL 240/24	ST	CUD	FBG	DV	IO	300	CC	8		3800			7450	8550
24		ROYAL 240/24	ST	CUD	FBG	DV	IO	T120-T140		8		3800			7600	8800
		1975 BOATS														
17	4	EMPRESS 177	ST	RNBT	FBG	TH	OB			6	10	1350			2050	2450
17	4	EMPRESS 177	ST	RNBT	FBG	TH	IO	120-140		6	10				2500	2900
17	10	COUNTESS 180	ST	RNBT	FBG	DV	OB			6	10	1350			2100	2500
17	10	COUNTESS 180	ST	RNBT	FBG	DV	IO	140	MRCR	6	10				2650	3050
18	8	IMPERIAL 190	ST	RNBT	FBG	DV	OB			7	4	1500			2350	2750
18	8	IMPERIAL 190	ST	RNBT	FBG	DV	IO	140-165		7	4				3150	3650
20	11	REGENCY 21	ST	CUD	FBG	DV	OB			8					3700	4300
20	11	REGENCY 21	ST	CUD	FBG	DV	IO	165-188		8					5350	6150
		1974 BOATS														
17	4	EMPRESS 177	OP	RNBT	FBG	TR	OB			6	10	1100			1750	2100
17	4	EMPRESS 177	OP	RNBT	FBG	TR	IO	120		6	10				2550	3000
18	8	IMPERIAL 190	OP	RNBT	FBG	DV	OB			7	4	1400			2200	2600
18	8	IMPERIAL 190	OP	RNBT	FBG	DV	IO	140		7	4				3250	3750
20	11	REGENCY 21		CUD	FBG	DV	IO	165		8					5500	6350

REGATTA BOATS

COAST GUARD MFG ID- REG

Call 1-800-327-6929 for BUC Personalized Evaluation Service
Or, for 1972 to 1980 boats, sign onto www.BUCValuPro.com

REGATTA PLASTICS CO

Call 1-800-327-6929 for BUC Personalized Evaluation Service
Or, for 1965 to 1972 boats, sign onto www.BUCValuPro.com

REGENT MARINE

Call 1-800-327-6929 for BUC Personalized Evaluation Service
Or, for 1969 to 1970 boats, sign onto www.BUCValuPro.com

REINELL BOATS INC

REINELL MARINE CORP
SALEM OR 97302 COAST GUARD MFG ID- REN

See inside cover to adjust price for area

LOA FT	LOA IN	NAME AND/ OR MODEL	TOP/ RIG	BOAT TYPE	HULL MTL	HULL TP	ENGINE TP	ENGINE # HP	ENGINE MFG	BEAM FT	BEAM IN	WGT LBS	DRAFT FT	DRAFT IN	RETAIL LOW	RETAIL HIGH
		1983 BOATS														
16	9	B1701	OP	RNBT	FBG	DV	IO	120	MRCR	6	10	1850			2000	2400
16	9	SPRINT V1701	OP	RNBT	FBG	DV	OB			6	10				2350	2750
16	9	SPRINT V1701	OP	RNBT	FBG	DV	IO	120-188		6	10	1850			2000	2450
16	10	SPRINT T-1701	OP	RNBT	FBG	TR	OB			6	9				2350	2750
16	10	SPRINT T-1701	OP	RNBT	FBG	TR	IO	120	MRCR	6	9	1700			1850	2200
16	10	SPRINT T-1701	OP	RNBT	FBG	TR	IO	120	OMC	6	9	1700			1850	2200
16	10	SPRINT T-1701	OP	RNBT	FBG	TR	IO	120-170		6	9	1700			1950	2350
16	10	SPRINT T1701	OP	RNBT	FBG	DV	IO	170	OMC	6	9	1700			1850	2200
16	10	SPRINT T1701	OP	RNBT	FBG	DV	IO	175	VLVO	6	9	1700			2000	2400
18	4	SPRINT B/R B1901	OP	RNBT	FBG	DV	IO	120-200		7	6	1950			2350	2950
18	4	SPRINT B/R B1901	OP	RNBT	FBG	DV	IO	225-260		7	6	1950			2600	3000
18	4	SPRINT V1901	OP	RNBT	FBG	DV	OB			7	10				2750	3200
18	4	SPRINT V1901	OP	RNBT	FBG	DV	IO	120-200		7	6	1950			2350	2900
18	4	SPRINT V1901	OP	RNBT	FBG	DV	IO	225-260		7	6	1950			2550	3100
19		L2031	OP	CUD	FBG	DV	IO	120-200		7	10	2750			3050	3750
19		L2031	OP	CUD	FBG	DV	IO	225-260		7	10	2750			3300	3800
19	7	V2101 6 METER	OP	SPTCR	FBG	DV	IO	138-230		7	11	2600			3250	3900
19	7	V2101 6 METER	OP	SPTCR	FBG	DV	IO	260		7	11	2600			3300	4100
20	7	L2101	OP	RNBT	FBG	DV	OB			8					4450	5100
20	7	L2101	OP	RNBT	FBG	DV	IO	120-230		8		2770			3450	4350
20	7	L2101	OP	RNBT	FBG	DV	IO	260		8		2770			3700	4500
20	7	L2171	HT	CBNCR	FBG	DV	IO	138-260		8		2920			4200	5250
20	9	C2201	OP	RNBT	FBG	DV	IO	138-260		8		2700			3600	4450
24		B2471	FB	SPTCR	FBG	DV	IO	198-260		7	11	4200			5850	7150
24		B2471	FB	SPTCR	FBG	DV	IO	T120-T170		7	11	4200			6450	7750
24		C2421 7.4 METER	OP	SPTCR	FBG	DV	IO	170-260		7	11	4000			5600	6900
24		C2421 7.4 METER	OP	SPTCR	FBG	DV	IO	T120-T200		7	11	4000			6250	7650
24		V2401	OP	RNBT	FBG	DV	IO	170-260		7	11	3100			4450	5500
24		V2401	OP	RNBT	FBG	DV	IO	T120-T230		7	11	3100			5000	6000
25	9	C2621 8 METER	OP	SPTCR	FBG	DV	IO	225-260		8		5200			7600	9000
25	9	C2621 8 METER	OP	SPTCR	FBG	DV	IO	T138-T230		8		5200			8250	10200
		1982 BOATS														
16	9	B1701	OP	RNBT	FBG	DV	IO	120-170		6	10	1850			1900	2300
16	9	SPRINT V1701	OP	RNBT	FBG	DV	OB			6	10				2350	2700
16	9	SPRINT V1701	OP	RNBT	FBG	DV	IO	120		6	10	1850			1900	2250
16	9	SPRINT V1701	OP	RNBT	FBG	DV	IO	125-170		6	10	1850			2000	2400
16	10	SPRINT T-1701	OP	RNBT	FBG	TR	OB			6	9				2350	2700
16	10	SPRINT T-1701	OP	RNBT	FBG	TR	IO	120		6	9	1700			1800	2150
16	10	SPRINT T-1701	OP	RNBT	FBG	TR	IO	125-170		6	9	1700			1900	2300
18	3	SPRINT TR T1901	OP	RNBT	FBG	TR	IO	120-200		7	6	1950			2300	2850
18	3	SPRINT TR T1901	OP	RNBT	FBG	TR	IO	225-260		7	6	1950			2500	2900
18	4	SPRINT B/R B1901	OP	RNBT	FBG	DV	IO	120-200		7	6	1950			2350	2850
18	4	SPRINT B/R B1901	OP	RNBT	FBG	DV	IO	225-260		7	6	1950			2500	2950
18	4	SPRINT V1901	OP	RNBT	FBG	DV	OB			7	10				2700	3150
18	4	SPRINT V1901	OP	RNBT	FBG	DV	IO	120-200		7	6	1950			2300	2800
18	4	SPRINT V1901	OP	RNBT	FBG	DV	IO	225-260		7	6	1950			2500	2900
19		L2001	OP	RNBT	FBG	DV	IO	120-200		7	10	2430			2700	3300
19		L2001	OP	RNBT	FBG	DV	IO	225-260		7	10	2430			2900	3400
19		L2031	OP	CUD	FBG	DV	IO	120-200		7	10	2750			2950	3650
19		L2031	OP	CUD	FBG	DV	IO	225-260		7	10	2750			3200	3750
19		L2041	HT	CUD	FBG	DV	IO	120-200		7	10	2800			3000	3700
19		L2041	HT	CUD	FBG	DV	IO	225-260		7	10	2800			3250	3750
19	7	V2101 6 METER	OP	SPTCR	FBG	DV	IO	140-200		7	11	2600			3050	3750
19	7	V2101 6 METER	OP	SPTCR	FBG	DV	IO	225-260		7	11	2600			3300	4000
20	7	L2101	OP	RNBT	FBG	DV	OB			8					4300	5000
20	7	L2101	OP	RNBT	FBG	DV	IO	120-230		8		2770			3400	4250
20	7	L2101	OP	RNBT	FBG	DV	IO	260		8		2770			3600	4400
20	7	L2111	HT	RNBT	FBG	DV	IO	140-230		8		2820			3450	4250
20	7	L2111	HT	RNBT	FBG	DV	IO	260		8		2820			3650	4450
20	7	L2131	OP	CUD	FBG	DV	IO	140-230		8		2820			3600	4450
20	7	L2131	OP	CUD	FBG	DV	IO	260		8		2820			3800	4650
20	7	L2141	HT	CUD	FBG	DV	IO	140-230		8		2870			3600	4500
20	7	L2141	HT	CUD	FBG	DV	IO	260		8		2870			3850	4700
20	7	L2171	HT	CBNCR	FBG	DV	IO	140-230		8		2920			3950	4900
20	7	L2171	HT	CBNCR	FBG	DV	IO	260		8		2920			4200	5100
20	9	C2201	OP	RNBT	FBG	DV	IO	140-230		8		2700			3400	4200
20	9	C2201	OP	RNBT	FBG	DV	IO	260		8		2700			3600	4350
20	9	C2211	HT	RNBT	FBG	DV	IO	140-230		8		2730			3400	4250
20	9	C2211	HT	RNBT	FBG	DV	IO	260		8		2730			3600	4400
20	9	C2231	OP	CAMPR	FBG	DV	IO	140-230		8		2750			3550	4450
20	9	C2231	OP	CAMPR	FBG	DV	IO	260		8		2750			3800	4600
20	9	C2241	HT	CAMPR	FBG	DV	IO	140-230		8		2770			3600	4450
20	9	C2241	HT	CAMPR	FBG	DV	IO	260		8		2770			3800	4650
24		B2441	FB	EXP	FBG	DV	IO	170-260		7	11	4100			5600	6850
24		B2441	FB	EXP	FBG	DV	IO	T120-T170		7	11	4100			6200	7400
24		B2471	FB	SPTCR	FBG	DV	IO	198-260		7	11	4200			5750	7000
24		B2471	FB	SPTCR	FBG	DV	IO	T120-T170		7	11	4200			6300	7550
24		C2421 7.4 METER	OP	SPTCR	FBG	DV	IO	170-260		7	11	4000			5500	6750
24		C2421 7.4 METER	OP	SPTCR	FBG	DV	IO	T120-T200		7	11	4000			6100	7450
24		C2441	HT	EXP	FBG	DV	IO	170-260		7	11	3700			5150	6400
24		C2441	HT	EXP	FBG	DV	IO	T120-T170		7	11	3700			5750	6950
24		C2471	HT	CBNCR	FBG	DV	IO	170-260		7	11	3800			6000	7400
24		C2471	HT	CBNCR	FBG	DV	IO	T120-T170		7	11	3800			6700	8050
24		V2401	OP	RNBT	FBG	DV	IO	170-230		7	11	3100			4300	5250
24		V2401	OP	RNBT	FBG	DV	IO	260		7	11	3100			4550	5400
24		V2401	OP	RNBT	FBG	DV	IO	T120-T230		7	11	3100			4850	5900
25	9	C2621 8 METER	OP	SPTCR	FBG	DV	IO	225-260		8		5200			7450	8800
25	9	C2621 8 METER	OP	SPTCR	FBG	DV	IO	T140-T200		8		5200			7850	9700
25	9	C2621 8 METER	OP	SPTCR	FBG	DV	IO	T225-T230		8		5200			8650	9950
		1981 BOATS														
16	9	SPRINT V1701	OP	RNBT	FBG	DV	IO	120		6	10	1850			1850	2200
16	10	SPRINT T-1701	OP	RNBT	FBG	TR	IO	120		6	9	1700			1800	2100
18	4	SPRINT B/R B1901	OP	RNBT	FBG	DV	IO	120		7	6	1950			2300	2650
18	4	SPRINT V1901	OP	RNBT	FBG	DV	IO	120		7	6	1950			2250	2600
19		L2001	OP	RNBT	FBG	DV	IO	120		7	10	2430			2650	3050
19		L2041	HT	CUD	FBG	DV	IO	120		7	10	2800			2950	3400
19	7	V2101 6 METER	OP	SPTCR	FBG	DV	IO	140		7	11	2600			3000	3450
20	7	L2101	OP	RNBT	FBG	DV	IO	140		8		2770			3350	3900
20	7	L2171	HT	CBNCR	FBG	DV	IO	140		8		2920			3900	4500
20	9	C2231	OP	CAMPR	FBG	DV	IO	140		8		2750			3500	4100
24		B2471	FB	SPTCR	FBG	DV	IO	200		7	11	4200			5650	6500
24		C2421 7.4 METER	OP	SPTCR	FBG	DV	IO	230		7	11	4000			5500	6300
25	9	C2621 8 METER	OP	SPTCR	FBG	DV	IO	230		8		5200			7250	8300

LOA FT	IN	NAME AND/ OR MODEL	TOP/ RIG	BOAT TYPE	-HULL- MTL	TP	ENGINE TP	# HP	MFG	BEAM FT	IN	WGT LBS	DRAFT FT	IN	RETAIL LOW	RETAIL HIGH
		1979 BOATS														
16	9	T-1701	OP	RNBT	FBG	DV	IO	120		6	10				1800	2150
16	9	V-1700	OP	RNBT	FBG	DV	OB			6	10	1135			2100	2500
16	9	V-1700	OP	RNBT	FBG	DV	IO	120		6	10	1765			1800	2150
16	10	T-1700	OP	RNBT	FBG	DV	OB			6	8	1135			2100	2500
16	10	T-1701	OP	RNBT	FBG	DV	IO	120		6	8				1800	2150
16	10	T-180		RNBT	FBG	DV	IO	140		7	3	2028			2000	2350
18	2	V-180		RNBT	FBG	DV	IO	140		7	3	1801			2050	2450
18	3	T-1901	OP	RNBT	FBG	DV	IO	120		7	4	2135			2300	2650
18	4	B-1901 W/T	OP	RNBT	FBG	DV	IO	120		7	4				2200	2550
18	4	V-1901	OP	RNBT	FBG	DV	IO	140		7	6	2146			2350	2700
19		L-2001	OP	RNBT	FBG	DV	IO	120		7	10	2128			2450	2850
19		L-2031		CUD	FBG	DV	IO	120		7	10				2900	3350
19	4	V-1900	OP	RNBT	FBG	DV	OB			7	6	1573			2950	3400
19	7	6 METER		CUD	FBG	DV	IO	140		7	11	2638			2950	3400
19	7	V-2101 W/T	OP	RNBT	FBG	DV	IO	120		7	11				3100	3600
20	7	L-2100	OP	RNBT	FBG	DV	OB			8		2050			4100	4750
20	7	L-2101	OP	RNBT	FBG	DV	IO	120		8					3300	3800
20	7	L-2131		CUD	FBG	DV	IO	120		8					3800	4400
20	7	L-214		CR	FBG	DV	IO	140		8		3075			3700	4300
20	7	L-2171	HT	CUD	FBG	DV	IO	120		8					3800	4400
20	10	C-2201		CUD	FBG	DV	IO	120		8					3850	4450
20	10	C-2221	HT	CUD	FBG	DV	IO	120		8					3850	4450
20	10	C-2241	HT	CAMPR	FBG	DV	IO	120		8					3500	4050
24		2471 BRIDGE CR	FB	CR	FBG	DV	IO	165		8		3925			5250	6050
24		B-247		CR	FBG	DV	IO	200		8		4150			5550	6350
24		C-2241	HT	SDN	FBG	DV	IO	165		8					5250	6050
24		C-2421 7.4 METER		SPTCR	FBG	DV	IO	165		8		4100			5450	6250
24		V-2401		CUD	FBG	DV	IO	140		8		3545			4900	5600
25	9	B-267		CR	FBG	DV	IO	240		8		5500			7450	8600
25	9	C-2671		SDN	FBG	DV	IO	240		8		5000			7550	8650
25	9	V-2621 8 METER		SPTCR	FBG	DV	IO	240		8		5200			7200	8300
29	9	B-3072 BRIDGE CR	FB	SDN	FBG	DV	IO	T225		11	2	11500			16600	18800
		1978 BOATS														
16	9	V-170	ST	RNBT	FBG	DV	OB			6	10	1135			2050	2450
16	9	V-170	ST	RNBT	FBG	DV	IO	120		6	10	1765			1800	2150
		IO 140 MRCR 1800 2150, IO 140 OMC 1800 2100, IO 140-185													1900	2300
16	10	T-180	ST	RNBT	FBG	TR	OB			7	3	1460			2550	3000
16	10	T-180	ST	RNBT	FBG	TR	IO	120		7	3	2028			2000	2400
		IO 140 MRCR 2000 2400, IO 140 OMC 2000 2350, IO 140-198													2150	2500
18	2	V-180	OP	RNBT	FBG	DV	IO	140	MRCR	7	3	1801			2050	2450
		IO 140 OMC 2050 2450, IO 140-240 2250 2700, IO 255-260													2400	2800
18	3	T-190	ST	RNBT	FBG	TR	IO	120-200		7	4	2135			2300	2850
18	3	T-190	ST	RNBT	FBG	TR	IO	225-228		7	4	2135			2350	2900
18	4	B-190	ST	RNBT	FBG	DV	IO	120-200		7	6	2160			2350	2900
18	4	B-190	ST	RNBT	FBG	DV	IO	225-228		7	6	2160			2400	2950
18	4	V-190	ST	RNBT	FBG	DV	OB			7	6	1573			2800	3250
18	4	V-190	ST	RNBT	FBG	DV	IO	120-200		7	6	2146			2350	2900
18	4	V-190	ST	RNBT	FBG	DV	IO	225-228		7	6	2146			2400	2950
19		L-200	ST	RNBT	FBG	DV	IO	120-200		7	10	2128			2450	3050
19		L-200	ST	RNBT	FBG	DV	IO	225-228		7	10	2128			2550	3150
19	7	V-210 6 METER	ST	SPTCR	FBG	DV	IO	140-200		7	11	2638			2950	3650
19	7	V-210 6 METER	ST	SPTCR	FBG	DV	IO	225-240		7	11	2638			3050	3750
20	7	L-210	ST	RNBT	FBG	DV	OB			8		2050			4050	4700
20	7	L-210	ST	RNBT	FBG	DV	IO	120-240		8		2660			3250	4050
20	7	L-213	ST	CR	FBG	DV	IO	140-240		8		2875			3550	4450
20	7	L-214		CR	FBG	DV	IO	140-240		8		3075			3700	4600
20	7	L-217	HT	CR	FBG	DV	IO	140-240		8		3200			3800	4700
24		B-244	FB	CR	FBG	DV	IO	185-260		8		4150			5550	6800
24		B-244	FB	CR	FBG	DV	IO	T140-T170		8		4150			6150	7350
24		B-247	FB	CR	FBG	DV	IO	185-260		8		4200			5600	6850
24		B-247	FB	CR	FBG	DV	IO	T140-T170		8		4200			6200	7400
24		C-242 7.4 METER	ST	SPTCR	FBG	DV	IO	165-260		7	11	4100			5500	6700
24		C-242 7.4 METER	ST	SPTCR	FBG	DV	IO	T140-T200		7	11	4100			6100	7400
24		C-244	HT	CUD	FBG	DV	IO	140-260		8		3925			5300	6500
24		C-244	HT	CUD	FBG	DV	IO	T140		8		3925			5900	7100
24		C-247	HT	CR	FBG	DV	IO	140-260		8		4025			5400	6650
24		C-247	HT	CR	FBG	DV	IO	T140		8		4025			6000	7200
24		V-240	ST	RNBT	FBG	DV	IO	140-260		7	11	3545			4650	5700
24		V-240	ST	RNBT	FBG	DV	IO	T140		7	11	3545			5150	6200
25	9	B-267	FB	CR	FBG	DV	IO	240-260		8		5500			7500	8900
25	9	B-267	FB	CR	FBG	DV	IO	T140-T200		8		5500			7950	9800
25	9	B-267	FB	CR	FBG	DV	IO	T225	VLVO	8		5500			8850	10000
25	9	C-262 8 METER	ST	SPTCR	FBG	DV	IO	198-260		8		5200			7050	8550
25	9	C-262 8 METER	ST	SPTCR	FBG	DV	IO	T140-T240		8		5200			7700	9600
25	9	C-267	HT	CR	FBG	DV	IO	198-260		8		5000			6850	8350
25	9	C-267	HT	CR	FBG	DV	IO	T140-T200		8		5000			7500	9300
25	9	C-267	HT	CR	FBG	DV	IO	T225		8		5000			8050	9550
29	9	B-307		SDN	FBG	DV	IB	T225		11	2	11500	2		17400	19800
		1977 BOATS														
16	9	V-170	ST	RNBT	FBG	DV	OB			6	10	1135			2050	2450
16	9	V-170	ST	RNBT	FBG	DV	IO	120		6	10	1697			1800	2150
16	9	V-170	ST	RNBT	FBG	DV	IO	130-190		6	10	1697			1900	2300
16	10	T-180	ST	RNBT	FBG	TR	OB			7	3	1162			2100	2500
16	10	T-180	ST	RNBT	FBG	TR	IO	120		7	3	1724			1900	2250
16	10	T-180	ST	RNBT	FBG	TR	IO	130-190		7	3	1724			2000	2400
18	3	T-190	ST	RNBT	FBG	TR	OB			7	4	1400			2550	2950
18	3	T-190	ST	RNBT	FBG	TR	IO	120-200		7	4	1970			2250	2800
18	4	B-190	ST	RNBT	FBG	DV	IO	120-200		7	6	1780			2200	2750
18	4	V-180	OP	RNBT	FBG	DV	IO	120		7	3	1670			2050	2450
18	4	V-180	OP	RNBT	FBG	DV	IO	130-235		7	3	1670			2250	2650
18	4	V-190	ST	RNBT	FBG	DV	OB			7	6	1185			2250	2650
18	4	V-190	ST	RNBT	FBG	DV	IO	120-200		7	6	1787			2200	2750
19		C-208	ST	CR	FBG	DV	IO	120-200		7	10	2730			2950	3650
19		F-208	ST	FSH	FBG	DV	IO	120-200		7	10	2730			3100	3850
19		V-200	ST	RNBT	FBG	DV	IO	120-200		7	10	2433			2650	3300
19		V-200	HT	RNBT	FBG	DV	IO	120-200		7	10	2433			2650	3300
19	7	C-214	HT	SDN	FBG	DV	IO	140-235		8		3500			3550	4350
19	7	C-214	HT	SDN	FBG	DV	IO	240	VLVO	8		3500			3850	4450
19	7	C-217 BULKHEAD	HT	SDN	FBG	DV	IO	140-235		8		3500			3650	4450
19	7	C-217 BULKHEAD	HT	SDN	FBG	DV	IO	240	VLVO	8		3500			3950	4600
19	7	V-210 6 METER	ST	RNBT	FBG	DV	IO	120-235		7	11	3100			3150	3900
19	7	V-211 6 METER	HT	RNBT	FBG	DV	IO	120-235		7	11	3100			3150	3900
21		V-220	ST	CUD	FBG	DV	IO	140-240		7	11	3450			4150	5150
21		V-220	ST	CUD	FBG	DV	IO	255	VLVO	7	11	3450			4550	5250
21		V-220	ST	CUD	FBG	DV	IO	T140		7	11	3450			4800	5500
21		V-224	HT	CUD	FBG	DV	IO	140-240		7	11	3450			4100	5100
21		V-224	HT	CUD	FBG	DV	IO	255	VLVO	7	11	3450			4500	5200
21		V-224	HT	CUD	FBG	DV	IO	T140		7	11	3450			4850	5550
21		V-227 BULKHEAD	HT	CUD	FBG	DV	IO	140-240		7	11	3450			4200	5250
21		V-227 BULKHEAD	HT	CUD	FBG	DV	IO	255	VLVO	7	11	3450			4600	5300
21		V-227 BULKHEAD	HT	CUD	FBG	DV	IO	T140		7	11	3450			4950	5700
21	11	SUN 22	SLP	SA/CR	FBG	KL				7	2	2300	1	7	3300	3850
22	8	C-237	HT	SDN	FBG	DV	IO	235-255		8		4300			5500	6600
22	8	C-237	HT	SDN	FBG	DV	IO	T140-T190		8		4300			6000	7300
24		C-240	OP	CUD	FBG	DV	IO	140-255		7	11	3600			5050	6250
24		C-240	OP	CUD	FBG	DV	IO	T130-T190		7	11	3600			5900	6800
24		C-242 7.4 METER	ST	RNBT	FBG	DV	IO	165-255		7	11	4000			5100	6300
24		C-242 7.4 METER	ST	RNBT	FBG	DV	IO	T130-T190		7	11	4000			5900	6900
24		C-244	FB	CR	FBG	DV	IO	140-255		7	11	4350			5800	7000
24		C-244	FB	CR	FBG	DV	IO	T130-T190		7	11	4350			6700	7700
24		C-244	HT	CUD	FBG	DV	IO	140-255		7	11	4000			5400	6600
24		C-244	HT	CUD	FBG	DV	IO	T130-T190		7	11	4000			6250	7200
24		C-245 7.4 BULKHEAD	HT	CR	FBG	DV	IO	165-255		7	11	4000			5550	6800
24		C-245 7.4 BULKHEAD	HT	CR	FBG	DV	IO	T130-T190		7	11	4000			6400	7450
24		C-246 7.4 METER	HT	CR	FBG	DV	IO	165-255		7	11	4000			5400	6650
24		C-246 7.4 METER	HT	CR	FBG	DV	IO	T130-T190		7	11	4000			6250	7300
24		C-247 BULKHEAD	FB	CR	FBG	DV	IO	175-255		7	11	4350			5750	7200
24		C-247 BULKHEAD	FB	CR	FBG	DV	IO	T140-T190		7	11	4350			6550	7850
24		C-247 BULKHEAD	HT	CUD	FBG	DV	IO	140-255		7	11	4000			5550	6800
24		C-247 BULKHEAD	HT	CUD	FBG	DV	IO	T130-T190		7	11	4000			6400	7350
25	9	B-267	FB	CR	FBG	DV	IO	235-255		8		5550			7650	9050
25	9	B-267	FB	CR	FBG	DV	IO	T140-T190		8		5550			8150	9950
25	9	C-262 8 METER	ST	CR	FBG	DV	IO	188-255		8		5200			7100	8700
25	9	C-262 8 METER	ST	CR	FBG	DV	IO	T140-T190		8		5200			7800	9550
25	9	C-267	HT	CR	FBG	DV	IO	235-255		8		5000			7150	8500
25	9	C-267	HT	CR	FBG	DV	IO	T140-T190		8		5000			7650	9350
27	6	SUN 27	SLP	SA/RC	FBG	KL				9		6000	4	4	9050	10300
29	9	B-307	FB	CR	FBG	DV	IO	255	MRCR	11		11500	2		14500	16500
		VD T230 OMC 15500 17700, IO T240 VLVO 15900 18000, VD T260 OMC													15800	18000
		1976 BOATS														
16	8	T-1800	OP	RNBT	FBG	TR	OB			7	3	1162			2050	2450
16	8	T-1801	OP	RNBT	FBG	TR	IO	120	OMC	7	3	1724			1900	2250
16	9	V-1700	OP	RNBT	FBG	DV	OB			6	11	1135			2000	2400

CONTINUED ON NEXT PAGE

LOA FT IN	NAME AND/ OR MODEL	TOP/ RIG	BOAT TYPE	HULL MTL TP TP#	ENGINE HP	MFG	BEAM FT IN	WGT LBS	DRAFT FT IN	RETAIL LOW	RETAIL HIGH
1976 BOATS											
16 9	V-1701	OP	RNBT	FBG DV IO	120	OMC	6 11	1697		1850	2200
18 3	T-1900	OP	RNBT	FBG TR OB			7 3	1400		2500	2950
18 3	T-1901	OP	RNBT	FBG TR IO	120	OMC	7 3	1970		2250	2650
18 5	F-1901	OP	RNBT	FBG DV IO	120	OMC	7 6	1800		2250	2650
18 5	V-1900	OP	RNBT	FBG DV OB			7 6	1185		2250	2600
18 5	V-1901	OP	RNBT	FBG DV IO	120	OMC	7 6	1787		2250	2600
19 9	C-2081	HT	EXP	FBG DV IO	120	OMC	7 10	2700		2950	3450
19	C-2001	OP	RNBT	FBG DV IO	120	OMC	7 10	2563		2800	3250
19	F-2011	OP	RNBT	FBG DV IO	120	OMC	7 10	2430		2700	3150
19	F-2081	HT	EXP	FBG DV IO	120	OMC	8	2830		3100	3600
19	V-2001	OP	RNBT	FBG DV IO	120	OMC	7 10	2433		2700	3150
19	V-2011	HT	RNBT	FBG DV IO	120	OMC	7 10	2513		2750	3200
19 7	C-2141	HT	SDN	FBG DV IO	120	OMC	7 11	3500		3650	4250
19 7	C-2171	HT	CDN	FBG DV IO	120	OMC	7 11	3600		3700	4300
19 7	V-2101 METER	OP	CR	FBG DV IO	120	OMC	7 11	3100		3350	3900
19 7	V-2111 METER	HT	CR	FBG DV IO	120	OMC	7 11	3200		3450	4000
19 7	X-2101 METER	OP	CR	FBG DV IO	120	OMC	8	3300		3500	4100
19 7	X-2111 METER	HT	CR	FBG DV IO	120	OMC	8	3330		3550	4100
21	C-2201	OP	CUD	FBG DV IO	140	OMC	7 11	3450		4200	4900
21	C-2281	HT	EXP	FBG DV IO	140	OMC	7 11	4200		4900	5650
21	X-2201	OP	CUD	FBG DV IO	140	OMC	7 11	3650		4450	5100
21 11	S-2240	SLP	SAIL	FBG KC OB			7 2	2300	1 7	3200	3750
22 8	B-2371	FB	SDNSF	FBG DV IO	190	OMC	8	4800		6900	7900
22 8	C-2371	HT	SDN	FBG DV IO	190	OMC	8	4300		5550	6350
24	B-2471	FB	SDNSF	FBG DV IO	175	OMC	7 11	4700		7250	8300
24	C-2401	OP	CUD	FBG DV IO	140	OMC	7 11	3600		5150	5900
24	C-2421 METER	HT	CR	FBG DV IO	165	OMC	7 11	4100		5700	6550
24	C-2451 METER	HT	CR	FBG DV IO	165	OMC	7 11	4700		6350	7300
24	C-2461 METER	HT	CR	FBG DV IO	165	OMC	7 11	4600		6250	7150
24	C-2481	HT	EXP	FBG DV IO	140	OMC	7 11	4400		6000	6900
24	X-2401	OP	CUD	FBG DV IO	140	OMC	7 11	3825		5400	6200
25 8	B-2671	FB	SDNSF	FBG DV IO	190	OMC	8	5500		8600	9900
25 8	C-2671	HT	SDN	FBG DV IO	190	OMC	8	5100		7600	8750
25 8	S-2690	SLP	SAIL	FBG KC OB			8	4675	2 6	6900	7950
25 8	S-2691	SLP	SAIL	FBG KC IB	25	BALD	8	4750	2 6	7300	8350
25 11	S-2790	SLP	SAIL	FBG KC OB			9	5200	4 4	7800	9000
29 9	B-3071	FB	CR	FBG DV IO	255	MRCR	11	9500		13700	15600
29 9	B-3072	FB	CR	FBG DV VD	T230	OMC	11	10000		14100	16100
1975 BOATS											
16 8	1750	ST	RNBT	FBG SV OB			6 11	1135		2000	2400
16 8	1750	ST	RNBT	FBG SV IO	120		6 11	1697		1900	2250
16 8	1750	ST	RNBT	FBG SV IO	130-170		6 11	1697		2050	2450
16 8	1800	ST	RNBT	FBG TR OB			7 3	1162		2050	2450
16 8	1800	ST	RNBT	FBG TR IO	120		7 3	1724		2000	2350
16 8	1800	ST	RNBT	FBG TR IO	130-170		7 3	1724		2150	2550
18 3	1900	ST	RNBT	FBG TR OB			7 3	1408		2500	2900
18 3	1900	ST	RNBT	FBG TR IO	120-188		7 6	1970		2400	2950
18 3	1900	ST	RNBT	FBG TR IO	200-225		7 6	1970		2600	3050
18 5	1900	ST	RNBT	FBG DV OB			7 6	1172		2200	2600
18 5	1900	ST	RNBT	FBG DV IO	120-188		7 6	1787		2350	2850
18 5	1900	ST	RNBT	FBG DV IO	200-225		7 6	1787		2500	3000
19	2000	ST	RNBT	FBG SV IO	120-200		8	2433		2850	3550
19	2000	ST	RNBT	FBG SV IO	225		8	2433		2950	3600
19	2000	HT	RNBT	FBG SV IO	120-200		8	2433		2850	3550
19	2000	HT	RNBT	FBG SV IO	225		8	2433		2950	3600
19 7	6 METER INTERNAT	OP	CUD	FBG SV IO	120-225		8	3100		3500	4400
19 7	6 METER INTERNAT	HT	CUD	FBG SV IO	120-225		8	3200		3600	4450
21	2200	OP	CUD	FBG SV IO	120-225		8	3450		4450	5400
21	2200	OP	CUD	FBG SV IO	T120-T170		8	3450		5100	6200
21	2200	HT	CUD	FBG SV IO	120-225		8	4100		5000	6100
21	2200	HT	CUD	FBG SV IO	T120-T170		8	4100		5650	6900
21	2200	HT	SDN	FBG SV IO	120-225		8	4350		5250	6350
21	2200	HT	SDN	FBG SV IO	T120-T170		8	4350		5850	7150
21	2250	FB	CR	FBG SV IO	120-225		8	4200		5100	6200
21	2250	FB	CR	FBG SV IO	T120-T170		8	4200		5750	7000
21	6.4 METER INTERNAT	OP	CUD	FBG DV IO	120-225		8	3950		4900	5950
21	6.4 METER INTERNAT	OP	CUD	FBG DV IO	T120-T170		8	3950		5550	6750
21	6.4 METER INTERNAT	HT	CUD	FBG DV IO	120-225		8	4300		5200	6300
21	6.4 METER INTERNAT	HT	CUD	FBG DV IO	T120-T170		8	4300		5850	7100
21 11	2200 SAILBOAT	SLP	SAIL	FBG KL OB			7 2	2300	1 7	3100	3650
24	2400	OP	CUD	FBG SV IO	120-225		8	3600		5500	6450
24	2400	OP	CUD	FBG SV IO	T120-T170		8	3600		6000	7250
24	2400	HT	CUD	FBG SV IO	130-225		8	4100		6050	7100
24	2400	HT	CUD	FBG SV IO	T120-T170		8	4100		6550	7900
24	2400	FB	CUD	FBG SV IO	175-225		8	4400		6250	7500
24	2400	FB	CUD	FBG SV IO	T120-T170		8	4400		6900	8300
24	2400	HT	SDN	FBG SV IO	130-225		8	4350		6300	7400
24	2400	HT	SDN	FBG SV IO	T120-T170		8	4350		6800	8200
24	2400	FB	SDN	FBG SV IO	175-225		8	4700		6550	7850
24	2400	FB	SDN	FBG SV IO	T120-T170		8	4700		7200	8650
24	2500	FB	SDN	FBG SV IO	130-225		8	4400		6350	7500
24	2500	FB	CR	FBG SV IO	T120-T170		8	4400		6900	8300
24	7.4 METER INTERNAT	OP	CUD	FBG DV IO	130-225		8	4100		6050	7100
24	7.4 METER INTERNAT	OP	CUD	FBG DV IO	T120-T170		8	4100		6550	7900
24	7.4 METER INTERNAT	HT	CUD	FBG DV IO	130-225		8	4600		6600	7750
24	7.4 METER INTERNAT	HT	CUD	FBG DV IO	T120-T170		8	4600		7100	8550
25 8	2600 SAIL CRUISER	SLP	SAIL	FBG KL IB	25	BALD	8	5600	2 6	8250	9500
25 8	2600 SAILBOAT	SLP	SAIL	FBG KL OB			8	5600	2 6	9000	9200
25 11	2700 SAILBOAT	SLP	SAIL	FBG KL OB			9	5800	4 4	8450	9700
1974 BOATS											
16 9	RT 1800		RNBT	FBG OB			7 3	1400		2400	2800
16 9	RT 1810			FBG OB	120	MRCR	7 3	2300		2350	2700
16 10	RV 1750		RNBT	FBG OB			6 11	1200		2100	2500
16 10	RV 1760			FBG IO	120	OMC	6 11	1850		1950	2350
18 3	RT 1950		RNBT	FBG OB			7 3	1500		2600	3000
18 3	RT 1960			FBG IO	130	VLVO	7 4	2750		2950	3450
18 5	RV 1900		RNBT	FBG OB			7 5	1400		2500	2900
18 5	RV 1910			FBG IO	120	OMC	7 5	2690		2800	3250
19	RV 2000			FBG IO	140	MRCR	8	2200		2750	3200
19	RV 2010			FBG IO	140	OMC	8	2900		2900	3350
19 7	6-METER			FBG IO	140	OMC	7 11	3100		3400	3950
19 7	6-METER	HT		FBG IO	140	OMC	7 11	3240		3550	4100
21	RV 2200			FBG IO	165	MRCR	8	3600		4550	5200
21	RV 2210			FBG IO	170	VLVO	8	3800		4800	5550
21	RV 2220			FBG IO	165	MRCR	8	4100		4000	4650
21	RV 2230			FBG IO	165	OMC	8	3950		4800	5500
21	RV 2240			FBG IO	165	MRCR	8	4100		5850	6750
21	RV 2250			FBG IO	225	OMC	8	4200		5100	5850
21	RV 2260			FBG IO	165	MRCR	8	4200		5000	5750
21	RV 2270			FBG IO	170	VLVO	8	4350		5150	5900
21	RV 2280			FBG IO	165	OMC	8	4675		5450	6300
21	RV 3230			FBG IO	165	MRCR	8	4660		5450	6300
21	RV 3240			FBG IO	225	MRCR	8	4660		5500	6300
21	RV 3270			FBG IO	188	MRCR	8	4690		5500	6350
24	RV 2400			FBG IO	165	OMC	8	3600		5250	6050
24	RV 2410			FBG IO	165	MRCR	8	3800		5500	6300
24	RV 2420			FBG IO	165	OMC	8	4200		5900	6800
24	RV 2430			FBG IO	165	OMC	8	3950		5600	6450
24	RV 2440			FBG IO	170	VLVO	8	4100		5950	6850
24	RV 2460			FBG IO	225	MRCR	8	4400		6200	7150
24	RV 2470			FBG IO	165	OMC	8	4350		6050	6950
24	RV 2500			FBG IO	188	MRCR	8	4400		6150	7100
24	RV 3440			FBG IO	225	OMC	8	4675		6500	7450
24	RV 3470			FBG IO	225	OMC	8	4660		6500	7450
24				FBG IO	188	MRCR	8	4690		6500	7450
1973 BOATS											
16 6	RV 1710			FBG IO	120	MRCR	6 11	1600		1850	2200
17	RV 1810			FBG IO	120	OMC	7	1800		2050	2450
17	RV 1820			FBG IO	120	OMC	7	1900		2100	2500
17 8	RT 1750		RNBT	FBG OB			7	1200		2200	2500
17 8	RT 1760		RNBT	FBG OB	120	OMC	7	1850		2200	2600
18	RV 1900			FBG IO	120	MRCR	7 8	1300		2350	2700
18	RV 1910			FBG IO	120	MRCR	7 8	2100		2450	2800
18	RV 1920			FBG IO	120	OMC	7 8	2200		2600	2950
18	RV 1930		RNBT	FBG OB			7 8	1400		2450	2850
18 6	RT 1860			FBG IO	120	OMC	7 6	2200		2500	2900
19	RV 2000			FBG IO	140	MRCR	8	2200		2850	3300
19	RV 2010			FBG IO	130	VLVO	8	2400		2950	3450
19	RV 2020			FBG IO	140	MRCR	7 8	2200		2800	3250
19	RV 2030			FBG IO	140	OMC	8	2300		2850	3300
19	RV 2050			FBG IO	130	VLVO	8	2400		3300	3800
21	RV 2200			FBG IO	140	MRCR	8	3600		4650	5350
21	RV 2210			FBG IO	140	OMC	8	3800		4800	5500
21	RV 2220			FBG IO	165	MRCR	8	3750		4800	5500
21	RV 2230			FBG IO	165	OMC	8	3950		4950	5700
21	RV 2240			FBG IO	165	OMC	8	4100		5100	5850

LOA FT IN	NAME AND/ OR MODEL	TOP/ RIG	BOAT TYPE	HULL MTL TP	TP	# HP	MFG	BEAM FT IN	WGT LBS	DRAFT FT IN	RETAIL LOW	RETAIL HIGH
1973 BOATS												
21	RV 2250		FBG	IO	165	MRCR	8	4200		5200	6000
21	RV 2260		FBG	IO	165	OMC	8	4150		5150	5900
21	RV 2270		FBG	IO	165	MRCR	8	4350		5350	6150
21	RV 2280		FBG	IO	165	MRCR	8	4400		5400	6200
21	RV 3210		FBG	IO	165-188	MRCR	8	4650		5650	6500
21	RV 3230		FBG	IO	165	MRCR	8	4675		5650	6500
21	RV 3240		FBG	IO	165	MRCR	8	4660		5650	6500
21	RV 3270		FBG	IO	165	MRCR	8	4690		5650	6500
24	RV 2400		FBG	IO	188	MRCR	8	3600		5500	6300
24	RV 2410		FBG	IO	188	MRCR	8	3800		5700	6550
24	RV 2420		FBG	IO	188	MRCR	8	3750		5650	6500
24	RV 2430		FBG	IO	188	MRCR	8	3950		5850	6750
24	RV 2440		FBG	IO	188	MRCR	8	4100		6050	6950
24	RV 2450		FBG	IO	165	OMC	8	4200		6100	7000
24	RV 2460		FBG	IO	170	VLVO	8	4150		6200	7150
24	RV 2470		FBG	IO	188	MRCR	8	4350		6300	7250
24	RV 2500		FBG	IO	188	MRCR	8	4400		6350	7300
25 9	RV2680	CR	FBG DV	IO	246		8			6400	9650
1972 BOATS												
16	RV1710	RNBT	FBG	IO	130	VLVO	6 11	1600		2100	2500
17	RV1810	RNBT	FBG	IO	120	MRCR	7	1800		2300	2650
17 8	RT1720	RNBT	FBG	OB			7	1200		2200	2550
17	RT1730	RNBT	FBG	IO	155	OMC	7	1850		2400	2800
18	RT1860	RNBT	FBG	IO	120	OMC	7 6	2000		2600	3000
18	RV1910	RNBT	FBG	IO	130	VLVO	7 8	2000		2800	3250
18	RV1920	HT RNBT	FBG	IO	120	MRCR	7 4	2200		2700	3150
18 2	RV1900	RNBT	FBG	OB			7 4	1250		2300	2650
18 2	RV1930	HT RNBT	FBG	OB			7 4	1450		2500	2950
19	RV2000	RNBT	FBG	IO	165	MRCR	8	2200		3050	3550
19	RV2010	HT RNBT	FBG	IO	165	OMC	8	2400		3150	3650
19	RV2020	RNBT	FBG	IO	165	MRCR	7 8	2200		2950	3450
19	RV2050	EXP	FBG	IO	165	OMC	8	2400		3250	3750
21 4	RV2100	SDN	FBG	IO	165	MRCR	8	2600		4200	4850
21 4	RV2110	SDN	FBG	IO	215	MRCR	8	2800		4500	5150
21 4	RV2120	SDN	FBG	IO	165	OMC	8	2750		4300	5000
21 4	RV2130	SDN	FBG	IO	215	MRCR	8	2950		4600	5300
21 4	RV2150	EXP	FBG	IO	170	VLVO	8	3400		5100	5850
21 4	RV2200	SDN	FBG	IO	170	VLVO	8	3000		4700	5450
21 4	RV2210	SDN	FBG	IO	225	OMC	8	3200		4800	5550
21 4	RV2220	SDN	FBG	IO	170	VLVO	8	3150		4850	5600
21 4	RV2230	SDN	FBG	IO	215	MRCR	8	3350		5000	5700
21 4	RV2250	EXP	FBG	IO	225	OMC	8	3450		5050	5800
24	RV2400	SDN	FBG	IO	170	VLVO	8	3600		6100	7000
24	RV2410	SDN	FBG	IO	225	OMC	8	3800		6250	7150
24	RV2420	SDN	FBG	IO	165	MRCR	8	3750		6100	7000
24	RV2430	SDN	FBG	IO	225	OMC	8	3950		6400	7350
24	RV2440	SDN	FBG	IO	225	OMC	8	4100		6600	7600
24	RV2450	EXP	FBG	IO	188	MRCR	8	4200		6650	7650
24	RV2460	EXP	FBG	IO	170	VLVO	8	4150		6750	7750
24	RV2500	CBNCR	FBG	IO	188	MRCR	8	4400		7900	9050
1971 BOATS												
16	RV-1700		FBG	IO	120-165		6 7	1450	3 5	1750	2100
16 6	RT-1650		FBG	IO	120		7 6	1800	3 6	2300	2650
16 6	RT-1650	RNBT	FBG	OB			7 6	1245	3 6	2200	2550
17	RV-1800		FBG	IO	120-165		7 4	1700	3 6	2250	2650
18	XR-18		FBG	IO	165	MRCR	7	1350	2 6	2200	2600
18 2	RV-1900		FBG	IO	120-165		7	1850	3 8	2450	2850
18 2	RV-1900	RNBT	FBG	OB			7 4	1250	3 8	2300	2650
18 5	RT-1850		FBG	IO	140-165		7 6	2000	4	2700	3150
18 5	RT-1850	RNBT	FBG	OB			7 6	1450	4	2550	2950
19	RV-2000		FBG	IO	120-165		8	2200	4	3050	3600
19	RV-2050	CR	FBG	IO	120-165		8	2400	4	3350	3900
21 4	RV-2100		FBG	IO	120-215		8	2600	3 6	4100	4850
21 4	RV-2150	CR	FBG	IO	120-215		8	3400	4 6	5050	6050
21 4	RV-2200		FBG	IO	120-215		8	3000	4 2	4500	5250
21 4	RV-2250	CR	FBG	IO	120-215		8	3400	3 6	5150	6150
24	RV-2400		FBG	IO	155-215		8	3600	4 4	5800	6800
24	RV-2430		FBG	IO	155-215		8	3800	4 4	6000	7050
24	RV-2450	CR	FBG	IO	155-215		8	4200	4 10	6850	8000
24	RV-2500	CR	FBG	IO	155-215		8	4400	4 10	7100	8300
24	V-I-P		FBG	IO	155-215		8	3700	4 4	5900	6900
1970 BOATS												
16	RV 1700	RNBT	FBG DV	OB				985		1700	2050
16 6	RV 1700	RNBT	FBG DV	IO	165	MRCR	6 7	1450	3 5	1950	2350
16 6	RT 1650	RNBT	FBG TR	OB			7 6	1090		1900	2250
16 6	RT 1650	RNBT	FBG TR	IO	140	MRCR	7 6	1800	3 6	2450	2850
17	RV 1800	RNBT	FBG DV	OB			7 6	1165		2050	2400
17	RV 1800	RNBT	FBG DV	IO	165	MRCR	6 11	1700	3 6	2350	2750
18	RV 1900		FBG	IO			7 4	1285		2300	2700
18	XR-18		FBG	IO	165	MRCR	6 6	1350	2 6	2200	2550
18 2	RV 1900	RNBT	FBG DV	IO	165	MRCR	7 4	1850	3 8	2700	3150
18 6	RT 1850	RNBT	FBG TR	OB			7	1400		2500	2900
18 6	RT 1850	RNBT	FBG TR	IO	165	MRCR	7 6	2000	4	2900	3350
19	RV 2000	RNBT	FBG DV	IO	225	MRCR	8	2200	4	3300	3900
21 4	RV 2100	RNBT	FBG DV	IO	T165	MRCR	8	2600	4	5000	5750
21 4	RV 2150	CR	FBG DV	IO	T165	MRCR	8	3400	3 6	6050	7000
21 4	RV 2200	CR	FBG DV	IO	T165	MRCR	8	3400	4 6	6050	7000
23 1	RV 2300	CR	FBG DV	IO	T225	MRCR	8	3100	4 6	6450	7450
23 1	RV 2350	CR	FBG DV	IO	T225	MRCR	8	3800	4 6	7250	8300
23 1	RV 2400	CR	FBG DV	IO	T210-T225		8	3500	5 2	6750	8450
1967 BOATS												
17	SEA-ROBIN	RNBT	FBG	IO	80		6 11			2650	3050
19	SEA-GULL	RNBT	FBG	OB			8	1200		2250	2650
19	SEA-GULL	RNBT	FBG	IO	110		8			3650	4250
23 4	SEA-HAWK	CR	FBG	IB	285		10 9			4100	4800
25 8	SUCIA	CR	WD SV	IO	150		9 9			10000	11400
25 8	SUCIA	CR	WD SV	IO	210		9 9			5000	5700
27 6	SEA-HAWK	CR	FBG	IB	500		11 9			7800	8950
28	SEA-HAWK	CR	FBG	IO	225		10 9			13300	15100
33	SEA-HAWK	CR	FBG	IO	450		11 6			26000	28900
1946 BOATS												
18		HT RNBT	WD	IB						**	**
20		HT CBNCR	WD	IB		KERM				**	**

REISINGER MARINE SALES CO

Call 1-800-327-6929 for BUC Personalized Evaluation Service
Or, for 1959 to 1961 boats, sign onto www.BUCValuPro.com

RELIANCE SAILING CRAFT CO LTD

BEACONSFIELD MON PQ CANADA   See inside cover to adjust price for area

For more recent years, see the BUC Used Boat Price Guide, Volume 1 or Volume 2

LOA FT IN	NAME AND/ OR MODEL	TOP/ RIG	BOAT TYPE	HULL MTL TP	TP	# HP	MFG	BEAM FT IN	WGT LBS	DRAFT FT IN	RETAIL LOW	RETAIL HIGH
1982 BOATS												
44 4	RELIANCE 44 KIT	CUT	SA/CR FBG KL	IB	40D	PERK	11 8	28000	6 2	71900	79000
44 4	RELIANCE 44 KIT	KTH	SA/CR FBG KL	IB	40D	PERK	11 8	28000	6 2	77200	84800
1981 BOATS												
44 4	RELIANCE 44 KIT	CUT	SA/CR FBG KL	IB	40D	PERK	11 8	28000	6 2	68500	75200
44 4	RELIANCE 44 KIT	KTH	SA/CR FBG KL	IB	40D	PERK	11 8	28000	6 2	73500	80800
1980 BOATS												
44 4	RELIANCE 44 KIT	CUT	SA/CR FBG KL	IB	40D	PERK	11 8	28000	6 2	65300	71800
44 4	RELIANCE 44 KIT	KTH	SA/CR FBG KL	IB	40D	PERK	11 8	28000	6 2	70100	77100
1979 BOATS												
44 4	RELIANCE 44	CUT	SA/CR FBG KL	IB	40D	PERK	11 8	28000	6 2	62800	69000
44 4	RELIANCE 44	KTH	SA/CR FBG KL	IB	40D	PERK	11 8	28000	6 2	67100	73800
1978 BOATS												
44 4	RELIANCE 44	CUT	SA/CR FBG KL	IB	40D	PERK	11 8	28000	6 2	60300	66300
44 4	RELIANCE 44	KTH	SA/CR FBG KL	IB	40D	PERK	11 8	28000	6 2	64400	70800
1977 BOATS												
44 4	RELIANCE 44	CUT	SA/CR FBG KL	IB	40D	PERK	11 8	28000	6 2	58500	64300
44 4	RELIANCE 44	KTH	SA/CR FBG KL	IB	40D	PERK	11 8	28000	6 2	62200	68400
1976 BOATS												
44 4	RELIANCE 44	CUT	SAIL F/S	IB	40D	PERK	11 8	28000	6 2	56400	62000
44 4	RELIANCE 44	KTH	SAIL F/S	IB	40D	PERK	11 8	28000	6 2	60300	66300
1975 BOATS												
44 4	RELIANCE 44	KTH	SAIL FBG	IB	40D	PERK	11 8	28000	6 2	58500	64300
44 4	RELIANCE 44	SLP	SAIL FBG	IB	40D	PERK	11 8	28000	6 2	55700	61300
1974 BOATS												
44 4	RELIANCE 44		SAIL FBG	IB	40D	PERK	11 8	20000	6 2	46700	51300
1973 BOATS												
44 4	RELIANCE 44	KTH	SAIL FBG KL	IB	40D	PERK	11 8	28000	6 2	55000	60500

RENKEN

UNITED MARINE CORPORATION
WATSEKA IL 60907 COAST GUARD MFG ID- RBM

See inside cover to adjust price for area

For more recent years, see the BUC Used Boat Price Guide, Volume 1 or Volume 2

LOA FT	LOA IN	NAME AND/ OR MODEL	TOP/ RIG	BOAT TYPE	-HULL- MTL	-HULL- TP	ENGINE TP	ENGINE # HP	ENGINE MFG	BEAM FT	BEAM IN	WGT LBS	DRAFT FT	DRAFT IN	RETAIL LOW	RETAIL HIGH
		1983 BOATS														
16	8	750 B/R	OP	RNBT	FBG	SV	IO	120	OMC	6	11	1200			1800	2100
17	4	795 B/R	OP	RNBT	FBG	SV	OB			7	2	1160			1900	2250
17	6	RENKEN 18	SLP	SA/CR	FBG	KL	OB			6	4	1220	2		2350	2750
18	2	950 B/R	OP	RNBT	FBG	SV	IO	120-228		7	9	1450			2400	2900
18	2	950 B/R	OP	RNBT	FBG	SV	IO	260	MRCR	7	9	1450			2600	3050
18	2	950 C/C	OP	CUD	FBG	SV	IO	120	OMC	7	9	1500			2400	2800
18	8	1095 B/R	OP	RNBT	FBG	SV	IO	120	OMC	7	2	1400			2300	2700
18	8	900 FISH	OP	FSH	FBG	DV	OB			7		1220			2000	2400
18	8	900 FISH	OP	FSH	FBG	DV	IO	120-228		7		1500			2500	3050
18	8	900 FISH	OP	FSH	FBG	DV	IO	260	MRCR	7		1500			2750	3200
18	8	900 STD	OP	RNBT	FBG	SV	OB			7		1220			2050	2450
18	8	900 STD	OP	RNBT	FBG	SV	IO	120-228		7		1420			2300	2850
18	8	900 STD	OP	RNBT	FBG	SV	IO	260	MRCR	7		1500			2550	2950
18	8	995 B/R	OP	RNBT	FBG	SV	OB			7	2	1220			2050	2450
18	8	995 B/R	OP	RNBT	FBG	SV	IO	120-228		7	2	1420			2350	2850
18	8	995 B/R	OP	RNBT	FBG	SV	IO	260	MRCR	7	2	1420			2550	3000
19	7	2095 B/R	OP	RNBT	FBG	SV	IO	120-228		8		1875			2900	3500
19	7	2095 B/R	OP	RNBT	FBG	SV	IO	260	MRCR	8		1875			3100	3600
19	7	2095 C/C	OP	CUD	FBG	SV	IO	120-228		8		1900			3000	3600
19	7	2095 C/C	OP	CUD	FBG	SV	IO	260	MRCR	8		1900			3250	3750
21	2	2100 C/C	OP	CUD	FBG	DV	IO	120-260		8		1900			3550	4300
21	2	2100 STD	OP	RNBT	FBG	DV	IO	120-228		8		1650			3250	3950
21	2	2100 STD	OP	RNBT	FBG	DV	IO	260	MRCR	8		1650			3500	4100
21	2	2200 EXP	OP	EXP	FBG	DV	IO	140-230		8		2700			4100	5100
21	2	2200 EXP	OP	EXP	FBG	DV	IO	260		8		2700			4400	5300
21	2	2200 FISH	OP	FSH	FBG	DV	IO	120-200		8		2300			4000	4900
21	2	2200 FISH	OP	FSH	FBG	DV	IO	225-260		8		2300			4350	5200
23	1	2400 FISH	OP	FSH	FBG	DV	IO	170-230		8		2900			5050	6150
23	1	2400 FISH	OP	FSH	FBG	DV	IO	260		8		2900			5300	6350
		1982 BOATS														
16	8	170 B/R	OP	RNBT	FBG	SV	IO	120		7					1850	2200
16	8	750 B/R	OP	RNBT	FBG	SV	IO	120-198		7		1100			1750	2150
16	8	750 B/R	OP	RNBT	FBG	SV	IO	228	MRCR	7		1100			1850	2200
16	8	750 B/R	OP	RNBT	FBG	SV	IO	260	MRCR	7		1100			1950	2350
16	9	695 B/R	OP	RNBT	FBG	SV	OB			7		1100			1750	2050
17	2	795 B/R	OP	RNBT	FBG	SV	IO	120		7					1950	2300
17	4	795 B/R	OP	RNBT	FBG	SV	OB			7	4	1160			1850	2200
17	4	795 B/R	OP	RNBT	FBG	SV	IO	120		7	2	1160			1900	2300
		IO 140 MRCR 1950 2300, IO 140-230 2000 2500, IO 260													2200	2650
17	4	795 STD	OP	RNBT	FBG	SV	IO	120		7	2	1420			1900	2250
17	4	795 STD	OP	RNBT	FBG	SV	IO	140-198		7	2	1420			2000	2450
17	4	795 STD	OP	RNBT	FBG	SV	IO	228-260		7	2	1420			2200	2700
17	10	750 B/R	OP	RNBT	FBG		IO	120	OMC	6	11	1200			1950	2350
17	10	750 B/R	OP	RNBT	FBG	DV	IO	120-140		7		1200			1950	2350
18	2	950 B/R	OP	RNBT	FBG	SV	IO	120-228		7	9	1500			2350	2850
18	2	950 B/R	OP	RNBT	FBG	SV	IO	260	MRCR	7	9	1500			2600	3000
18	2	950 C/C	OP	CUD	FBG	DV	IO	120	OMC	7	9	1050			2250	2600
18	4	795 B/R	OP	RNBT	FBG	SV	OB			7	2	1160			1900	2250
18	8	1095 B/R	OP	RNBT	FBG	DV	IO	120	OMC	7	2	1220			2200	2600
18	8	900	OP	RNBT	FBG	SV	OB			7	2	1220			1900	2250
18	8	900 STD	OP	RNBT	FBG	SV	OB			7		1110			1850	2200
18	8	900 STD	OP	RNBT	FBG	SV	IO	120-260		7		1500			2300	2800
18	8	995 B/R	OP	RNBT	FBG	SV	OB			7	4	1220			2000	2350
18	8	995 B/R	OP	RNBT	FBG	SV	IO	120-228		7	2	1420			2300	2800
18	8	995 B/R	OP	RNBT	FBG	SV	IO	260	MRCR	7	2	1420			2500	2900
19	3	1095 B/R	OP	RNBT	FBG		IO	120	OMC	7	2	1220			2350	2700
19	3	950 B/R	OP	RNBT	FBG	SV	IO	120-230		7	9	1500			2500	3100
19	3	950 B/R	OP	RNBT	FBG	SV	IO	260	MRCR	7	9	1500			2750	3200
19	3	950 C/C		CUD	FBG		IO	120	OMC	7	9	1050			2500	2900
19	3	995 B/R	OP	RNBT	FBG	SV	IO	260	OMC	7	2	1420			2600	3000
19	4	2095 B/R	OP	RNBT	FBG	SV	IO	120		8		1900			2800	3250
19	4	2095 C/C	OP	CUD	FBG	SV	IO	120		8		1900			2850	3350
19	7	2095 B/R	OP	RNBT	FBG	SV	IO	120-198		8		1900			2700	3350
19	7	2095 B/R	OP	RNBT	FBG	SV	IO	228-260		8		1900			2950	3550
19	7	2095 C/C	OP	CUD	FBG	SV	IO	120-228		8		1900			2900	3550
19	7	2095 C/C	OP	CUD	FBG	SV	IO	260	MRCR	8		1900			3150	3700
19	7	2095 C/C	OP	RNBT	FBG	DV	IO	120	OMC	8		1900			3100	3600
20	9	2095 B/R	OP	RNBT	FBG	SV	IO	120-260		8		1900			3200	4000
20	9	2095 C/C	OP	CUD	FBG	SV	IO	120-260		8		1900			3350	4150
21		2100 C/C	OP	CUD	FBG	DV	IO	120-228		8		1900			3400	4100
21		2100 C/C	OP	CUD	FBG	DV	IO	260	MRCR	8		1900			3700	4300
21		2100 C/C	OP	RNBT	FBG	DV	OB			8		1900			3800	4400
21		2100 STD	OP	RNBT	FBG	DV	IO	120-260		8		1900			3250	4100
21	2	2100 C/C	OP	CUD	FBG	DV	OB			8		1875			3800	4400
22	4	2100 C/C	OP	CUD	FBG	DV	IO	120-260		8		1900			3700	4550
22	4	2100 FSH	OP	RNBT	FBG	DV	IO			8		1900			**	**
22	4	2100 FSH	OP	RNBT	FBG	DV	IO	120-260		8		1900			4450	5250
22	4	2100 STD	OP	RNBT	FBG	DV	IO	120-140		8		1900			2550	3000
22	4	2100 STD	OP	RNBT	FBG	DV	IO	170-260		8		1900			3500	4100
		1981 BOATS														
16	6	695 B/R W/T		RNBT	FBG	SV	IO	120		7					1800	2150
16	7	167 B/R W/T		RNBT	FBG	TR	IO	120		6	6				1750	2050
16	8	695 B/R	OP	RNBT	FBG	SV	OB			7		1100			1700	2000
16	8	795 B/R	OP	RNBT	FBG	SV	OB			7	2	1160			1750	2100
16	8	795 B/R	OP	RNBT	FBG	SV	IO	120	MRCR	7	2	1420			1900	2250
16	9	695 B/R	OP	RNBT	FBG	SV	OB			7		1100			1700	2000
17	4	795 B/R	OP	RNBT	FBG	SV	OB			7	2	1160			1800	2150
17	4	795 B/R	OP	RNBT	FBG	SV	IO	120-198		7	2	1420			2000	2450
17	4	795 B/R	OP	RNBT	FBG	SV	IO	228-260		7	2	1420			2150	2650
17	4	795 STD	OP	RNBT	FBG	SV	IO	120-198		7	2	1420			2000	2450
17	4	795 STD	OP	RNBT	FBG	SV	IO	228	MRCR	7	2	1420			2100	2500
17	4	795 STD	OP	RNBT	FBG	SV	IO	260	MRCR	7	2	1420			2250	2650
17	5	174 B/R W/T		RNBT	FBG	TR	IO	120		6	8				1900	2250
18	2	950 B/R	OP	RNBT	FBG	SV	IO	120-228		7	9	1500			2350	2800
18	2	950 B/R	OP	RNBT	FBG	SV	IO	260	MRCR	7	9	1500			2550	2950
18	8	900 STD	OP	RNBT	FBG	SV	OB			7		1110			1800	2150
18	8	900 STD	OP	RNBT	FBG	SV	IO	120-170		7		1500			2250	2650
19	3	2095 B/R	OP	RNBT	FBG	SV	IO	170-230		8		1900			2700	3300
19	3	2095 B/R	OP	RNBT	FBG	SV	IO	260	MRCR	8		1900			2950	3450
19	3	995 B/R	OP	RNBT	FBG	SV	IO	140-228		7	2	1420			2300	2800
19	7	2095 B/R	OP	RNBT	FBG	SV	IO	198-260		8		1900			2850	3500
19	7	2095 C/C	OP	CUD	FBG	SV	IO	120-228		8		1900			2850	3500
19	7	2095 C/C	OP	CUD	FBG	SV	IO	260	MRCR	8		1900			3100	3600
19	7	900 STD	OP	RNBT	FBG	SV	IO	120-228		7		1500			2350	2850
19	7	900 STD	OP	RNBT	FBG	SV	IO	260	OMC	7		1500			2600	3000
19	7	995 B/R	OP	RNBT	FBG	SV	OB			7	2	1220			2000	2400
19	7	995 B/R	OP	RNBT	FBG	SV	IO	170-230		7	2	1420			2400	2900
21		2100 C/C	OP	CUD	FBG	DV	IO	120-228		8		1900			3350	4050
21		2100 C/C	OP	CUD	FBG	DV	IO	260	MRCR	8		1900			3600	4200
21		2100 STD	OP	RNBT	FBG	DV	IO	120-260		8		1900			3200	4000
		1980 BOATS														
16	8	750 B/R	OP	RNBT	FBG	SV	IO	120-170		6	11	1200			1750	2100
16	9	695 B/R	OP	RNBT	FBG	SV	IO	120-170		7		1200			1750	2100
17	4	795 B/R	OP	RNBT	FBG	SV	OB			7	2	1160			1750	2100
17	4	795 B/R	OP	RNBT	FBG	SV	IO	120-198		7	2	1420			2000	2400
17	4	795 B/R	OP	RNBT	FBG	SV	IO	228	MRCR	7	2	1420			2100	2500
17	4	795 B/R	OP	RNBT	FBG	SV	IO	260	MRCR	7	2	1420			2250	2650
17	4	795 STD	OP	RNBT	FBG	SV	IO	120-198		7	2	1420			1950	2400
17	4	795 STD	OP	RNBT	FBG	SV	IO	228	MRCR	7	2	1420			2100	2500
17	4	795 STD	OP	RNBT	FBG	SV	IO	260	MRCR	7	2	1420			2250	2600
18	8	900 STD	OP	RNBT	FBG	SV	OB			7		1110			1750	2100
18	8	900 STD	OP	RNBT	FBG	SV	IO	120-228		7		1500			2250	2700
18	8	900 STD	OP	RNBT	FBG	SV	IO	260	MRCR	7		1500			2450	2850
18	8	995 B/R	OP	RNBT	FBG	SV	OB			7	2	1220			1900	2250
18	8	995 B/R	OP	RNBT	FBG	SV	IO	120-228		7	2	1420			2250	2750
18	8	995 B/R	OP	RNBT	FBG	SV	IO	260	MRCR	7	2	1420			2450	2850
18	8	995 STD	OP	RNBT	FBG	SV	IO	120-228		7	2	1420			2200	2700
18	8	995 STD	OP	RNBT	FBG	SV	IO	260	MRCR	7	2	1420			2400	2800
19	7	2095 B/R	OP	RNBT	FBG	SV	IO	120-228		8		1900			2750	3350
19	7	2095 B/R	OP	RNBT	FBG	SV	IO	260	MRCR	8		1900			3000	3450
19	7	2095 C/C	OP	CUD	FBG	SV	IO	120-228		8		1900			2850	3450
19	7	2095 C/C	OP	CUD	FBG	SV	IO	260	MRCR	8		1900			3100	3600
21		2100 C/C	OP	CUD	FBG	DV	IO	120-228		8		1900			3350	4000
21		2100 C/C	OP	CUD	FBG	DV	IO	260	MRCR	8		1900			3600	4150
21		2100 STD	OP	RNBT	FBG	DV	IO	120-260		8		1900			3200	4000
		1979 BOATS														
16	9	695 B/R	OP	RNBT	FBG	SV	IO	120-170		7		1200			1750	2100
17	4	795 B/R	OP	RNBT	FBG	SV	OB			7	2	1160			1700	2050
17	4	795 B/R	OP	RNBT	FBG	SV	IO	120-198		7	2	1290			1900	2350
17	4	795 B/R	OP	RNBT	FBG	SV	IO	228	MRCR	7	2	1290			2050	2400
17	4	795 B/R	OP	RNBT	FBG	SV	IO	260	MRCR	7	2	1290			2200	2550

CONTINUED ON NEXT PAGE

LOA FT	LOA IN	NAME AND/ OR MODEL	TOP/ RIG	BOAT TYPE	-HULL- MTL	-HULL- TP	ENGINE TP	ENGINE # HP	ENGINE MFG	BEAM FT	BEAM IN	WGT LBS	DRAFT FT	DRAFT IN	RETAIL LOW	RETAIL HIGH
		1979 BOATS														
17	5	174 B/R	OP	RNBT	FBG	TR	IO	120-140		6	9	1140			1800	2150
18	8	900 STD	OP	RNBT	FBG	SV	OB			7		1220			1850	2200
18	8	900 STD	OP	RNBT	FBG	SV	IO	120-228		7		1420			2200	2700
18	8	900 STD	OP	RNBT	FBG	SV	IO	260	MRCR	7		1420			2400	2800
18	8	995 B/R	OP	RNBT	FBG	SV	OB			7	2	1220			1900	2250
18	8	995 B/R	OP	RNBT	FBG	SV	IO	120-228		7	2	1420			2250	2700
18	8	995 B/R	OP	RNBT	FBG	SV	IO	260	MRCR	7	2	1420			2450	2850
18	8	995 STD	OP	RNBT	FBG	SV	OB			7	2	1220			1850	2200
18	8	995 STD	OP	RNBT	FBG	SV	IO	120-228		7	2	1420			2250	2700
18	8	995 STD	OP	RNBT	FBG	SV	IO	260	MRCR	7	2	1420			2450	2850
19	4	2095 B/R	OP	RNBT	FBG	SV	IO	120-228		8		1875			2700	3250
19	4	2095 B/R	OP	RNBT	FBG	SV	IO	260	MRCR	8		1875			2900	3400
19	4	2095 C/C	OP	CUD	FBG	SV	IO	120-228		8		1900			2800	3400
19	4	2095 C/C	OP	CUD	FBG	SV	IO	260	MRCR	8		1900			3050	3550
21		2100 C/C	OP	CUD	FBG	DV	IO	120-228		8		1900			3350	4000
21		2100 C/C	OP	CUD	FBG	DV	IO	260	MRCR	8		1900			3600	4150
21		2100 STD	OP	RNBT	FBG	DV	IO	120-260		8		1900			3200	4000
23	1	2300 C/C	ST	CUD	FBG	SV	IO	170-260		8		3600			5250	6300
		1978 BOATS														
16	6	695 B/R	OP	RNBT	FBG	SV	IO	140		6	11	1200			1700	2050
17	4	795 B/R	OP	RNBT	FBG	SV	OB			7	2	1600			2200	2600
17	4	795 B/R	OP	RNBT	FBG	SV	IO	120-198		7	2	1500			2000	2450
17	4	795 B/R	OP	RNBT	FBG	SV	IO	228-260		7	2	1500			2200	2700
17	5	174 B/R	OP	RNBT	FBG	TR	OB			6	9	1550			2150	2550
17	5	174 B/R	OP	RNBT	FBG	TR	IO	120-140		6	9	1100			1800	2150
18	8	900 STD	OP	RNBT	FBG	SV	OB			7		1700			2400	2750
18	8	900 STD	OP	RNBT	FBG	SV	IO	120-228		7		1500			2250	2700
18	8	900 STD	OP	RNBT	FBG	SV	IO	260	MRCR	7		1500			2450	2850
18	8	995 B/R	OP	RNBT	FBG	SV	OB			7	1	1700			2400	2800
18	8	995 B/R	OP	RNBT	FBG	SV	IO	120-228		7	2	1500			2300	2750
18	8	995 B/R	OP	RNBT	FBG	SV	IO	260	MRCR	7	2	1500			2500	2900
18	8	995 STD	OP	RNBT	FBG	SV	OB			7	1	1700			2350	2750
18	8	995 STD	OP	RNBT	FBG	SV	IO	120-228		7	2	1500			2250	2750
21	1	2100 C/C	OP	CUD	FBG	SV	IO	140-260		8		3600			4750	5700
21	1	2100 STD	OP	RNBT	FBG	SV	IO	120-228		8		1700			3100	3800
21	1	2100 STD	OP	RNBT	FBG	SV	IO	260	MRCR	8		1700			3400	3950
23	1	2300 C/C	OP	CUD	FBG	SV	IO	170-260		8		3600			5300	6350
		1977 BOATS														
16	6	695 B/R	OP	RNBT	FBG	SV	IO	120-140		6	11	1900			2150	2500
16	7	167 B/R	OP	RNBT	FBG	TR	IO	120-140		6	7	1200			1700	2000
17	4	795 B/R	OP	RNBT	FBG	SV	IO	120-188		7	2	1290			1950	2400
17	4	795 B/R	OP	RNBT	FBG	SV	IO	233	MRCR	7	2	1290			2100	2500
17	5	174 B/R	OP	RNBT	FBG	TR	IO	120-140		6	9	1300			1900	2250
18	8	900 STD	OP	RNBT	FBG	SV	OB			7		1220			1800	2150
18	8	900 STD	OP	RNBT	FBG	SV	IO	120-233		7		1420			2250	2750
18	8	995 B/R	OP	RNBT	FBG	SV	OB			7	1	1220			1800	2150
18	8	995 B/R	OP	RNBT	FBG	SV	IO	120-233		7	2	1420			2300	2800
18	8	995 C/C	OP	RNBT	FBG	SV	OB			7	1	1300			1900	2250
18	8	995 C/C	OP	RNBT	FBG	SV	IO	120-233		7	2	1470			2300	2800
18	8	995 STD	OP	RNBT	FBG	SV	OB			7	1	1220			1800	2100
18	8	995 STD	OP	RNBT	FBG	SV	IO	120-188		7	2	1420			2300	2700
18	8	995 STD	OP	RNBT	FBG	SV	IB	233	MRCR	7	2	1420			2400	2800
21	1	2100	OP	RNBT	FBG	SV	IO	120		8		3600			4600	5300
23	1	2300	ST	CUD	FBG	SV	IO	170-233		8		3600			5350	6300
		1976 BOATS														
17	4	795 B/R	OP	RNBT	FBG	SV	IO	120-190		7	1	1290			2000	2450
17	4	795 B/R	OP	RNBT	FBG	SV	IO	233-235		7	1	1290			2200	2550
17	5	174 B/R	OP	RNBT	FBG	TH	IO	120-140		6	9	1100			1900	2250
18	8	900 STD	OP	RNBT	FBG	SV	OB			7		1220			1750	2100
18	8	900 STD	OP	RNBT	FBG	SV	IO	120-235		7		1220			2250	2750
18	8	995 B/R	OP	RNBT	FBG	SV	IO	120-190		7	1	1420			2250	2750
18	8	995 B/R	OP	RNBT	FBG	SV	IO	233-235		7	1	1420			2450	2850
18	8	995 C/C	OP	RNBT	FBG	SV	OB			7	1	1220			2050	2400
18	8	995 C/C	OP	RNBT	FBG	SV	IO	120-140		7	1	1420			2450	2850
18	8	995 STD	OP	RNBT	FBG	SV	IO	120-190		7	1	1420			2250	2700
18	8	995 STD	OP	RNBT	FBG	SV	IO	233-235		7	1	1420			2450	2850
		1975 BOATS														
16	4	700	OP	RNBT	FBG	DV	IO	120-165		6	2		1	6	1800	2150
16	7	167 B/R	OP	RNBT	FBG	TH	OB			6	8	1668			2200	2550
16	7	167 B/R	OP	RNBT	FBG	TH	IO	120-140		6	8	1668			2050	2450
16	10	800 B/R	OP	RNBT	FBG	DV	OB			6	2	1650			2200	2550
16	10	800 B/R	OP	RNBT	FBG	DV	IO	120-165		6	2		1	6	1850	2250
16	10	800 STD	OP	RNBT	FBG	SV	OB			6	2	1693			2200	2600
17	1	170 B/R	OP	RNBT	FBG	TH	OB			6	10	1670			2200	2550
17	1	170 B/R	OP	RNBT	FBG	TH	IO	120-140		6	10	1670			2200	2600
17	4	795 B/R	OP	RNBT	FBG	SV	OB			7	2	2271			2600	3000
17	4	795 B/R	OP	RNBT	FBG	SV	IO	120-233		7	2	2271			2650	3250
18	6	900 STD	OP	RNBT	FBG	TH	OB			6	10	2493			2650	3100
18	6	900 STD	OP	RNBT	FBG	TH	IO	120-188		6	10	2493			2900	3400
18	6	995 B/R	OP	RNBT	FBG	TH	OB			7	2	2385			2700	3100
18	6	995 B/R	OP	RNBT	FBG	TH	IO	120-233		7	2	2385			2900	3550
18	6	995 STD	OP	RNBT	FBG	TH	OB			7	2	2385			2600	3000
18	6	995 STD	OP	RNBT	FBG	TH	IO	120-233		7	2	2385			2850	3500
		1974 BOATS														
16	4	RENKEN 700			FBG		IO	165	MRCR	6	2	1260			1700	2000
16	7	RENKEN 167			FBG		IO	120-165		6	8	1190			1750	2100
16	10	RENKEN 800V			FBG		IO	120-165		6	2	1220			1750	2100
17	1	RENKEN 170			FBG		IO	120-140		6	10	1270			1950	2300
18	7	RENKEN 900V			FBG		OB			6	10	1220			1700	2050
18	7	RENKEN 900V			FBG		IO	120-188		6	10	1220			2300	2750
		1973 BOATS														
16	4	RENKEN 700			FBG		IO	120-165		6	2	1260			1700	2050
16	7	RENKEN 167			FBG		IO	120-165		6	8	1190			1800	2200
16	10	RENKEN 800V			FBG		IO	120-165		6	2	1220			1800	2150
17	1	RENKEN 170			FBG		IO	120-140		6	10	1270			2000	2400
18	7	RENKEN 900V			FBG		OB			6	10	1220			1700	2050
18	7	RENKEN 900V			FBG		IO	120-188		6	10	1220			2350	2850
		1972 BOATS														
16	4	RENKEN 700			FBG		IO	120-165		6	5	1100			1700	2050
16	10	800V B/R		RNBT	FBG		IO	120-188		6	6				2150	2550
17	4	170 B/R		RNBT	FBG		IO	120-165		6	10	1600			2400	2900
18	7	RENKEN 190			FBG		IO	120-165		7	2	1600			2650	3150
18	7	RENKEN 900V			FBG		IO	120-188		6	10				2700	3200
		1971 BOATS														
17	3	DELUXE B/R		RNBT	FBG		IO	120-165				1600			2600	3150
17	7	RENKEN B/R		RNBT	FBG	TR	IO	120		6	8	1375	1	8	2400	2750
18	7	RENKEN 190			FBG		IO	120-165		7	2	1600			2700	3250
		1970 BOATS														
17	3	175V		RNBT	FBG		IO	160		6	7				2400	2800
17	3	RENKEN 175V		RNBT	FBG	SV	IO	120		6	7	1200	1	7	2300	2700
17	7	RENKEN 18 B/R			FBG	TR	IO	120	OMC	6	8	1375	1	8	2300	2700
17	7	RENKEN 18 B/R		RNBT	FBG	TR	IO	120	MRCR	6	8	1375	1	8	2450	2850
17	7	RENKEN B/R		RNBT	FBG		IO	160		6	8				2450	2900
18	7	RENKEN 190V		RNBT	FBG	SV	IO	120		7	10	1450	2	1	3000	3500
		1969 BOATS														
17	3	RENKEN 175		RNBT	FBG		IO	160		6	7				2450	2850
17	7	RENKEN 18		RNBT	FBG	TR	IO	160		6	8				2550	2950
		1968 BOATS														
16	2			RNBT	FBG	TR	IO	120		6	2				2250	2650
16	7	1700		RNBT	FBG		IO	120		6	7				2400	2800
17	7			RNBT	FBG	TR	IO	195		6	8				2700	3100
18	6	1900		RNBT	FBG	DV	OB			7					2200	2600
18	6	1900		RNBT	FBG	DV	IO	195		7					3500	4050
		1966 BOATS														
16	6	MODEL 1700		RNBT	FBG		IO	60							2700	3150
18	5	MODEL 1900		RNBT	FBG		IO	110							3150	3700
20	5	2100		RNBT	FBG		IO	110							4800	5550
		1965 BOATS														
20	3	2100		RNBT	FBG		OB			7	6	1500			2650	3100
		1963 BOATS														
17		SEA-VOYAGER			FBG		OB								1700	2050

REVEL CRAFT INC

REVLINE
ARNOLD MD 21013 COAST GUARD MFG ID- RCM

See inside cover to adjust price for area

LOA FT	LOA IN	NAME AND/ OR MODEL	TOP/ RIG	BOAT TYPE	-HULL- MTL	-HULL- TP	ENGINE TP	ENGINE # HP	ENGINE MFG	BEAM FT	BEAM IN	WGT LBS	DRAFT FT	DRAFT IN	RETAIL LOW	RETAIL HIGH
		1975 BOATS														
24		KEY-LARGO	HT	EXP	FBG	DV	IB	215-225		8		5000	2	4	4200	4900
26	10	KEY-BISCAYNE	HT	EXP	FBG	DV	IB	215-225		10		5800			5500	6350
26	10	KEY-BISCAYNE	FB	SPTCR	FBG	DV	IB	215-255		10		5800	2		5500	6500
29	10	KEY-WEST	HT	EXP	FBG	DV	IB	225-255		10	10	6800	2		8250	9700
29	10	KEY-WEST	HT	EXP	FBG	DV	IB	T155	WAUK	10	10	6800	2		8850	10100
29	10	KEY-WEST	FB	EXP	FBG	DV	IB	225-255		10	10	6800	2		8250	9700
29	10	KEY-WEST	FB	EXP	FBG	DV	IB	T155	WAUK	10	10	6800	2		8850	10100
29	10	KEY-WEST	HT	SDN	FBG	DV	IB	225-255		10	10	7000	2		8250	9700
29	10	KEY-WEST	HT	SDN	FBG	DV	IB	T155	WAUK	10	10	7000	2		8950	10200
29	10	KEY-WEST	FB	SDN	FBG	DV	IB	225-255		10	10	7000	2		8250	9700
29	10	KEY-WEST	FB	SDN	FBG	DV	IB	T155	WAUK	10	10	7000	2		8950	10200

CONTINUED ON NEXT PAGE

LOA FT	LOA IN	NAME AND/ OR MODEL	TOP/ RIG	BOAT TYPE	HULL MTL	HULL TP	ENGINE TP	ENGINE # HP	ENGINE MFG	BEAM FT	BEAM IN	WGT LBS	DRAFT FT	DRAFT IN	RETAIL LOW	RETAIL HIGH
		1974 BOATS														
24		KEY-LARGO	HT	EXP	FBG	DV	IB	185-225		8		5000	2	4	4050	4700
26	10	KEY-BISCAYNE	HT	EXP	FBG	DV	IB	225D	CHRY	10		5800	2		7500	8600
26	10	KEY-BISCAYNE	FB	SPTCR	FBG	DV	IB	215-225		10		5800	2		5300	6100
29	10	KEY-WEST		EXP	FBG		IB	225	CHRY	10	10	6800	2		7950	9150
29	10	KEY-WEST	HT	EXP	FBG	DV	IB	255	WAUK	10	10	6800	2		8100	9300
29	10	KEY-WEST	HT	EXP	FBG	DV	IB	T155	WAUK	10	10	6800	2		8450	9700
29	10	KEY-WEST	FB	EXP	FBG		IB	225-255		10	10		2		7950	9300
29	10	KEY-WEST	FB	EXP	FBG		IB	T155	WAUK	10	10		2		8400	9650
29	10	KEY-WEST	HT	SDN	FBG	DV	IB	225-255		10	10	7000	2		7950	9350
29	10	KEY-WEST	HT	SDN	FBG	DV	IB	T155	WAUK	10	10	7000	2		8500	9750
29	10	KEY-WEST	FB	SDN	FBG		IB	225-255		10	10		2		7900	9300
29	10	KEY-WEST	FB	SDN	FBG		IB	T155	WAUK	10	10		2		8500	9750
		1973 BOATS														
24		AVALON	HT	EXP	FBG	DV	IO	185	WAUK	8		4400	2	4	4800	5500
24		KEY-LARGO	HT	EXP	FBG	DV	IO	185	WAUK	8		5000	2	4	5300	6100
24		KEY-LARGO	HT	EXP	FBG	DV	IB	215-255		8		5000	2	4	3900	4550
26	10	KEY-BISCAYNE	HT	EXP	FBG	DV	IB	215-255		10		5800	2		5100	6000
29	10	SEAMATE	HT	EXP	FBG	DV	IB	215-255		10	10	6800	2		7600	8950
29	10	SEAMATE	HT	EXP	FBG	DV	IB	T155	WAUK	10	10	6800	2		8100	9300
29	10	SEAMATE	FB	EXP	FBG		IB	215-255		10	10		2		7600	8950
29	10	SEAMATE	FB	EXP	FBG		IB	T155	WAUK	10	10		2		8100	9300
29	10	SEAMATE	HT	SDN	FBG	DV	IB	215-255		10	10	7000	2		7550	8950
29	10	SEAMATE	HT	SDN	FBG	DV	IB	T155	WAUK	10	10	7000	2		8150	9400
29	10	SEAMATE	FB	SDN	FBG		IB	215-255		10	10		2		7550	8950
29	10	SEAMATE	FB	SDN	FBG		IB	T155	WAUK	10	10		2		8150	9350
		1972 BOATS														
24		KEY-LARGO 24			FBG		IB	215-255		8		5000			3750	4400
24		KEY-LARGO 24	HT		FBG		IB	215-255		8					3700	4300
26	10	SEAMATE		EXP	FBG		IB	215-255		10		5800			4900	5750
26	10	SEAMATE	FB	EXP	FBG		IB	215-255		10					4800	5650
29	10	SEAMATE		EXP	FBG		IB	215-255		10	10	6800			7300	8600
29	10	SEAMATE	FB	EXP	FBG		IB	215-255		10	10				7300	8600
29	10	SEAMATE		SDN	FBG		IB	215-255		10	10	7000			7300	8600
29	10	SEAMATE	FB	SDN	FBG		IB	215-255		10	10				7250	8600
		1971 BOATS														
17	6	BREAKWATER	OP	RNBT	FBG	TR	OB			7		980			2300	2700
17	8	SEA-CRUISE	OP	CR	FBG	SV	OB			7		975			2000	2400
17	8	SEA-CRUISE CUSTOM	OP	CR	FBG	SV	OB			7		975			2550	2950
17	8	SEA-SCOUT	OP	RNBT	FBG	SV	OB			7		850			2000	2400
24		AVALON			FBG		IB	225	CHRY	8		4400	2	4	3250	3750
24		AVALON	HT		FBG		IB	225	CHRY	8			2	4	3300	3850
24		KEY-LARGO			FBG		IB	225	CHRY	8		5000	2	4	3500	4100
24		KEY-LARGO	HT		FBG		IB	225	CHRY	8			2	4	3550	4150
24		KEY-LARGO CUSTOM			FBG		IB	225	CHRY	8		5000	2	4	3650	4250
24		KEY-LARGO CUSTOM	HT		FBG		IB	225	CHRY	8			2	4	3700	4300
26	10	SEAMATE		EXP	FBG		IB	225	CHRY	10		5000	2		4400	5050
26	10	SEAMATE	HT	EXP	FBG		IB	225	CHRY	10			2		4650	5350
26	10	SEAMATE	FB	EXP	FBG		IB	225	CHRY	10			2		4650	5350
26	10	SEAMATE	FB	FSH	FBG		IB	225	CHRY	10		5000	2		4400	5050
26	10	SEAMATE CUSTOM	FB		FBG		IB	225	CHRY	10			2		4600	5250
26	10	SEAMATE CUSTOM		EXP	FBG		IB	225	CHRY	10		5300	2		4550	5200
29	10	SEAMATE		EXP	FBG		IB	225	CHRY	10	10	6200	2		6900	7950
29	10	SEAMATE	HT	EXP	FBG		IB	225	CHRY	10	10		2		7050	8100
29	10	SEAMATE	FB	EXP	FBG		IB	225	CHRY	10	10		2		7050	8100
29	10	SEAMATE	FB	SDN	FBG		IB	225	CHRY	10	10		2		7050	8100
29	10	SEAMATE CUSTOM	FB		FBG		IB	225	CHRY	10	10		2		6050	6950
29	10	SEAMATE CUSTOM		EXP	FBG		IB	225	CHRY	10	10	6500	2		7000	8050
29	10	SEAMATE CUSTOM		SDN	FBG		IB	225	CHRY	10	10	6800	2		7000	8050
33		SEA-SKIFF		SDN	WD		IB	T225	CHRY	12		9200	2	6	11400	12900
36	10	SEA-SKIFF		SDN	WD		IB	T225	CHRY	12		9200	2	6	13700	15500
		1970 BOATS														
17	6	BREAKWATER		RNBT	FBG	TR	OB			7		980			2300	2700
17	8	SEA-CRUISE		CR	FBG	SV	OB			7		975			2300	2700
17	8	SEA-SCOUT		RNBT	FBG	SV	OB			7		850			2000	2400
24		AVALON		EXP	FBG	DV	IB	200	CHRY	8		4500	2	4	3150	3700
24		KEY-LARGO		EXP	FBG	DV	IB	200	CHRY	8		5000	2	4	3450	4000
24		SEAMATE		EXP	FBG	DV	IB	200	CHRY	8			2	4	3400	4000
25	6	PLAYMATE		EXP	PLY	SV	IB	200	CHRY	10			2		3450	4000
26	10	PLAYMATE		EXP	PLY	SV	IB	200	CHRY	10			2		4450	5100
26	10	PLAYMATE		FSH	PLY	SV	IB	200	CHRY	10			2		4100	4800
26	10	SEAMATE		EXP	FBG	DV	IB	200	CHRY	10		5200	2		4200	4900
29	10	PLAYMATE		EXP	PLY	SV	IB	200	CHRY	10	10		2		6700	7700
29	10	PLAYMATE		SDN	PLY	SV	IB	200	CHRY	10	10		2		6650	7650
29	10	SEAMATE		EXP	FBG	DV	IB	200	CHRY	10	10		2		6700	7700
29	10	SEAMATE		SDN	FBG	DV	IB	200	CHRY	10	10		2		6650	7650
33		PLAYMATE		EXP	L/P	SV	IB	T200	CHRY	12			2	6	11000	12500
33		PLAYMATE		SDN	L/P	SV	IB	T200	CHRY	12			2	6	10700	12200
36	10	PLAYMATE		EXP	L/P	SV	IB	T200	CHRY	12			2	6	13400	15200
36	10	PLAYMATE		SDN	L/P	SV	IB	T200	CHRY	12			2	6	13700	15500
		1969 BOATS														
17	6	BREAKWATER	OP	RNBT	FBG	TR	OB			6	3	980			2300	2700
17	6	RIPTIDE	OP	RNBT	FBG	TR	OB			6	3	985			2300	2700
17	8	SEA-CRUISE	OP	RNBT	FBG		OB			7		975			2300	2700
17	8	SEA-SCOUT	OP	RNBT	FBG		OB			7		850			2000	2400
24		AVALON		EXP	FBG	DV	IO	155	CHRY	8		4700	2	4	5750	6600
24		BISCAYNE		CR	FBG	DV	IB	200	CHRY	8			2	4	3250	3750
24		BISCAYNE		EXP	FBG	DV	IO	175	CHRY	8		5200	2	4	6250	7150
24		KEY-LARGO		CR	FBG	DV	IB	200	CHRY	8			2	4	3400	3950
24		KEY-LARGO		EXP	FBG	DV	IO	175	CHRY	8		5400	2	4	6450	7400
24		REVELAIRE		CR	FBG	DV	IB	200	CHRY	8		5000	2	4	3300	3850
24		REVELAIRE SPORTS		SF	FBG	DV	IB	200	CHRY	8		4600	2	4	3100	3600
25	6	PLAYMATE		CR	PLY	SV	IB	200	CHRY	10		4400	2		3400	3950
25	6	REVELATION		CR	PLY	DV	IB	200	CHRY	10		4200	2		3300	3800
26	10			SF	PLY	SV	IB	200	CHRY	10		4000	2		3600	4150
26	10	FIESTA		CR	PLY	SV	IB	200	CHRY	10		5200	2		3550	4100
26	10	PLAYMATE		CR	PLY	SV	IB	200	CHRY	10		5200	2		4600	5300
26	10	VACATIONER		CR	PLY	SV	IB	200	CHRY	10		3800	2		3500	4100
29	10	HOLIDAY		CR	PLY	SV	IB	200	CHRY	10	10	6200	2		5700	6550
29	10	PLAYMATE		CR	PLY	SV	IB	200	CHRY	10	10	6500	2		5750	6600
29	10	PLAYMATE		SDN	PLY	SV	IB	200	CHRY	10	10	6800	2		6350	7300
33		ESCAPADE		SDN	PLY	SV	IB	T200	CHRY	12		9200	2	6	10300	11700
33		EXPLORER		CR	PLY	SV	IB	T200	CHRY	12		8300	2	6	9450	10700
33		PLAYMATE		CR	PLY	SV	IB	T200	CHRY	12		8700	2	6	9450	10700
36	10	ADVENTURER		EXP	PLY	SV	IB	T200	CHRY	12		10000	2	6	13000	14800
36	10	ADVENTURER		SDN	PLY	SV	IB	T200	CHRY	12		10800	2	6	13700	15600
		1968 BOATS														
16	11	SEA-CRUISE		CR	FBG		OB			7		975			2250	2600
16	11	SEA-SCOUT		CR	FBG		OB			7		850			1950	2300
17	6	BREAKWATER CUST		RNBT	FBG		OB			6	3	1225			2750	3200
17	6	BREAKWATER DLX		RNBT	FBG		OB			6	3	1175			2650	3100
24		BISCAYNE		CR	FBG	DV	IB	195-210		8			2	4	3200	3750
24		KEY-LARGO		CR	FBG	DV	IB	210		8			2	4	3200	3750
25	6	PLAYMATE		EXP	WD		IB	210	CHRY	10		4400	2		3250	3800
25	6	REVELATION		EXP	WD		IB	195	CHRY	10		4200	2		3150	3650
26	10			SF	WD		IB	210	CHRY	10		4000	2		3500	4050
26	10	FIESTA		EXP	WD		IB	195	CHRY	10		5200	2		3900	4500
26	10	PLAYMATE		EXP	WD		IB	210	CHRY	10		5400	2		4000	4650
26	10	VACATIONER		CR	WD		IB	195	CHRY	10		3800	2		3350	3900
29	10	HOLIDAY		EXP	WD		IB	195	CHRY	10	10	6200	2		6050	6950
29	10	PLAYMATE		EXP	WD		IB	210	CHRY	10	10	6500	2		6150	7100
29	10	PLAYMATE		SDN	WD		IB	210	CHRY	10	10	7300	2		6300	7200
32		EXPLORER		EXP	WD		IB	T195	CHRY	12		8500	2	6	9450	10800
32		EXPLORER		SDN	WD		IB	T195	CHRY	12		8900	2	6	9300	10500
32		PLAYMATE		EXP	WD		IB	T210	CHRY	12		9000	2	6	9650	11000
32		PLAYMATE		SDN	WD		IB	T210	CHRY	12		9400	2	6	9450	10700
		1967 BOATS														
25	2	REVELATION		EXP	P/P		IB	195		10		4200	2		3000	3500
25	2	REVELATION	HT	EXP	P/P		IB	195-210		10		4200	2		3000	3500
26	10	FIESTA		EXP	P/P		IB	195-210		10		5200	2		3750	4400
26	10	FIESTA	HT	EXP	P/P		IB	195-210		10		5200	2		3750	4400
26	10	VACATIONER		FSH	P/P		IB	195-210		10		3800	2		3250	3850
29	10	EXPLORER			P/P		IB	210				8500			5550	6400
29	10	EXPLORER	FB		P/P		IB	210				8500			5550	6400
29	10	EXPLORER SKIFF			P/P		IB	T195-T210							5750	6700
29	10	EXPLORER SKIFF	FB		P/P		IB	T195-T210							5750	6700
29	10	HOLIDAY		EXP	P/P		IB	195-210		10	10	6200	2		5800	6750
29	10	HOLIDAY	HT	EXP	P/P		IB	195-210		10	10	6200	2		5800	6750
29	10	PLAYMATE		EXP	P/P		IB	195-210		10	10	6800	2		5950	6950
32		EXPLORER		EXP	L/P		IB	195		12			2	6	8300	9550
34	10	ESCAPADE		EXP	P/P		IB	T195-T210		12		9000	2	6	11200	12800
34	10	ESCAPADE	FB	EXP	P/P		IB	T195-T210		12		9000	2	6	11200	12800
34	10	ESCAPADE		SDN	P/P		IB	T195-T210		12			2	6	13100	14900
34	10	ESCAPADE	FB	SDN	P/P		IB	T195-T210		12			2	6	13100	14900
36	10	ADVENTURER		SDN	P/P		IB	T195		12		10500	2	6	12800	14500
36	10	ADVENTURER		SDN	P/P		IB	T210		12		10500	2	6	12800	14600
36	10	ADVENTURER	FB	SDN	P/P		IB	T195		12		10500	2	6	12800	14500
36	10	ADVENTURER	FB	SDN	P/P		IB	T210		12		10500	2	6	12800	14600

 CONTINUED ON NEXT PAGE

REVEL CRAFT INC -CONTINUED See inside cover to adjust price for area

LOA FT	LOA IN	NAME AND/ OR MODEL	TOP/ RIG	BOAT TYPE	-HULL- MTL	-HULL- TP	ENGINE TP	ENGINE # HP	ENGINE MFG	BEAM FT	BEAM IN	WGT LBS	DRAFT FT	DRAFT IN	RETAIL LOW	RETAIL HIGH
		1966 BOATS														
24	10	REVELATION		CNV	PLY		IB	195		9	4		1	10	3250	3750
24	10	REVELATION		CR	PLY		IB	195		9	4		1	10	3150	3650
24	10	REVELATION	HT	CR	PLY		IB	195		9	4		1	10	3150	3650
24	10	VACATIONER		FSH	PLY		IB	165		9	4		1	10	3100	3600
26	10	FIESTA		CNV	PLY		IB	195		10			2		4000	4650
26	10	FIESTA		CR	PLY		IB	195		10			2		3450	4000
26	10	FIESTA	HT	CR	PLY		IB	195		10			2		3450	4000
26	10	RIPTIDE	FB	CR	L/P		IB	195		10			2		3450	4000
29	10	HOLIDAY		CNV	PLY		IB	195		10	10		2		5500	6300
29	10	HOLIDAY		CNV	PLY		IB	T165		10	10		2		6150	7100
29	10	HOLIDAY		CR	PLY		IB	195		10	10		2		4950	5650
29	10	HOLIDAY		CR	PLY		IB	T165		10	10		2		5450	6250
29	10	HOLIDAY	HT	CR	PLY		IB	195		10	10		2		4950	5700
29	10	HOLIDAY	HT	CR	PLY		IB	T165		10	10		2		5450	6250
29	10	HOLIDAY	FB	CR	PLY		IB	195		10	10		2		4950	5700
29	10	HOLIDAY	FB	CR	PLY		IB	T165		10	10		2		5450	6300
29	10	MARDI-GRAS		CR	PLY		IB	195		10	10		2		5300	6050
29	10	MARDI-GRAS		CR	PLY		IB	T165		10	10		2		5750	6600
29	10	MARDI-GRAS	HT	CR	PLY		IB	195		10	10		2		5250	6050
29	10	MARDI-GRAS	HT	CR	PLY		IB	T165		10	10		2		5750	6600
29	10	MARDI-GRAS	FB	CR	PLY		IB	195		10	10		2		5250	6050
29	10	MARDI-GRAS	FB	CR	PLY		IB	T165		10	10		2		5700	6600
29	10	MARDI-GRAS W/CONV		CNV	PLY		IB	195		10	10		2		5850	6750
29	10	MARDI-GRAS W/CONV		CNV	PLY		IB	T165		10	10		2		6450	7450
29	10	PLAYMATE		SDN	PLY		IB	195		10	10		2		5700	6550
29	10	PLAYMATE		SDN	PLY		IB	T165		10	10		2		6350	7300
29	10	PLAYMATE	FB	SDN	PLY		IB	195		10	10		2		5700	6550
29	10	PLAYMATE	FB	SDN	PLY		IB	T165		10	10		2		6350	7300
32		EXPLORER		CR	PLY		IB	T195		12			2	6	7700	8850
32		EXPLORER	FB	CR	PLY		IB	T195		12			2	6	7700	8850
32		EXPLORER LAPSTRAKE	HT	CR	PLY		IB	T195		12			2	6	7700	8850
32		EXPLORER W/CONV		CNV	PLY		IB	T195		12			2	6	8500	9800
33	10	ESCAPADE		CR	L/P		IB	T195		12			2	6	9000	10300
36	10	ADVENTURER	HT	EXP	L/P		IB	T195		12			2	6	11900	13500
36	10	ADVENTURER	FB	EXP	L/P		IB	T195		12			2	6	11900	13500
36	10	ADVENTURER		SDN	L/P		IB	T195		12			2	6	12100	13800
36	10	ADVENTURER	FB	SDN	L/P		IB	T195		12			2	6	12100	13800
		1965 BOATS														
23	10	HOLIDAY			WD		IB	185							2800	3250
23	10	HOLIDAY	HT		WD		IB	185							2800	3250
23	10	HOLIDAY		CNV	WD		IB	185							2800	3250
24	10	REVELATION			WD		IB	185							2900	3400
24	10	REVELATION	HT		WD		IB	185							2900	3400
24	10	REVELATION		CNV	WD		IB	185							3000	3500
26	10	FIESTA			WD		IB	185							3550	4100
26	10	FIESTA	HT		WD		IB	185							3550	4100
26	10	FIESTA		CNV	WD		IB	185							3800	4450
29	10	MARDI-GRAS			WD		IB	185							4450	5100
29	10	MARDI-GRAS	HT		WD		IB	185							4350	5000
29	10	MARDI-GRAS		CNV	WD		IB	185							5100	5900
29	10	PLAYMATE			WD		IB	185							5050	5800
29	10	PLAYMATE	HT		WD		IB	185							5100	5850
29	10	PLAYMATE		CNV	WD		IB	185							5750	6600
32	9	ESCAPADE			WD		IB	T185							7350	8450
32	9	ESCAPADE	HT		WD		IB	T185							7350	8450
32	9	ESCAPADE	FB		WD		IB	T185							7350	8450
32	9	ESCAPADE		CNV	WD		IB	T185							8550	9850
35	9		HT	SDN	WD		IB	T185							10700	12200
35	9		FB	SDN	WD		IB	T185							10700	12200
35	9	ADVENTURER		SDN	WD		IB	T185							10700	12200
		1964 BOATS														
24		SEA-SKIFF		EXP	WD		IB	110							2650	3100
24		SEA-SKIFF		WKNDR	WD		IB	110							2650	3100
25	4	REVELATION		EXP	WD		IB	110							2650	3050
25	4	REVELATION		EXP	WD		IB	190							2850	3300
25	4	REVELATION	FB	EXP	WD		IB	110-190							2650	3300
25	4	SEA-SKIFF		EXP	WD		IB	110-190							2800	3400
25	4	SEA-SKIFF	FB	EXP	WD		IB	110-190							2750	3400
25	10	REVELATION		EXP	WD		IB	190-210							2750	3250
25	10	REVELATION	FB	EXP	WD		IB	190-210							2750	3250
25	10	SEA-SKIFF		EXP	WD		IB	190-210							2900	3400
25	10	SEA-SKIFF	FB	EXP	WD		IB	190-210							2850	3400
28	4			EXP	WD		IB	210							4450	5100
28	4			EXP	WD		IB	T185							4900	5650
28	4		FB	EXP	WD		IB	210							4400	5050
28	4		FB	EXP	WD		IB	T185							4850	5600
28	4	REVELATION		EXP	WD		IB	190-210							3950	4600
28	4	REVELATION		EXP	WD		IB	T185							4450	5100
28	4	REVELATION	FB	EXP	WD		IB	190-210							3950	4600
28	4	REVELATION	FB	EXP	WD		IB	T185							4500	5150
28	4	SEA-SKIFF		EXP	WD		IB	190-210							4100	4800
28	4	SEA-SKIFF		EXP	WD		IB	T185							4600	5300
28	4	SEA-SKIFF	FB	EXP	WD		IB	190-210							4100	4750
28	4	SEA-SKIFF	FB	EXP	WD		IB	T185							4600	5300
30	9			EXP	WD		IB	T185							7400	8500
30	9		FB	EXP	WD		IB	T185							7500	8600
30	9	REVELATION		EXP	WD		IB	190-210							5800	6800
30	9	REVELATION		EXP	WD		IB	T185							6150	7050
30	9	REVELATION	FB	EXP	WD		IB	190-210							5850	6800
30	9	REVELATION	FB	EXP	WD		IB	T185							5850	6700
30	9	SEA-SKIFF		EXP	WD		IB	190-210							6100	7100
30	9	SEA-SKIFF		EXP	WD		IB	T185							6400	7350
30	9	SEA-SKIFF	FB	EXP	WD		IB	190-210							6100	7100
30	9	SEA-SKIFF	FB	EXP	WD		IB	T185							6600	7600
32	9			EXP	WD		IB	T210							9800	11100
32	9		FB	EXP	WD		IB	T210							9700	11000
32	9	REVELATION		EXP	WD		IB	T190-T210							8400	9700
32	9	REVELATION	FB	EXP	WD		IB	T190-T210							8450	9700
32	9	SEA-SKIFF		EXP	WD		IB	T190-T210							8850	10100
32	9	SEA-SKIFF	FB	EXP	WD		IB	T190-T210							8850	10000
35	9			EXP	WD		IB	T210							11300	12800
35	9		FB	EXP	WD		IB	T210							11100	12700
35	9	REVELATION		EXP	WD		IB	T190							9800	11200
35	9	REVELATION		EXP	WD		IB	T210							9350	10600
35	9	REVELATION	FB	EXP	WD		IB	T190							9850	11200
35	9	REVELATION	FB	EXP	WD		IB	T210							9400	10700
35	9	SEA-SKIFF		EXP	WD		IB	T190							10100	11500
35	9	SEA-SKIFF		EXP	WD		IB	T210							9600	10900
35	9	SEA-SKIFF	FB	EXP	WD		IB	T190							10100	11500
35	9	SEA-SKIFF	FB	EXP	WD		IB	T210							9650	11000
		1963 BOATS														
24	9			WKNDR	WD		OB								8650	9950
24	9			WKNDR	WD		IB	190							2750	3200
24	9	FAMILY CRUISER		CR	WD		IB	195							2750	3200
24	9	REVEL QUEEN			WD		OB								4900	5650
25	10			SF	WD		IB	210							2750	3200
25	10	REVEL EMPRESS			WD		IB	210							2750	3200
25	10	REVEL FRIENDSHIP			WD		IB	190							2700	3150
27	10	REVELATION 4 SLPR			WD		IB	210							3350	3900
27	10	REVELATION 6 SLPR			WD		IB	210							3900	4500
30		REVELINER			WD		IB	210							4550	5250
30		REVELINER			WD		IB	T210							5100	5900
		1962 BOATS														
20	9	COMPACT		EXP	WD		OB								3400	3950
20	9	COMPACT		EXP	WD		IO	100							4350	5000
20	9	COMPACT		FSH	WD		OB								4200	4900
20	9	COMPACT		FSH	WD		IO	100							4450	5100
20	9	COMPACT		WKNDR	WD		OB								4900	5650
20	9	COMPACT		WKNDR	WD		IO	100							4750	5500
23	3		HT		WD		OB								4800	5550
23	3		HT		WD		IO	100							6800	7800
23	3		HT		WD		IB	100-110							2350	2800
23	3	QUEEN			WD		OB								4800	5550
24	9	EMPRESS		EXP	WD		IB	100-185							2500	3100
27			HT		WD		IB	110							3000	3500
27			HT		WD		IB	185							3250	3750
27		REVELATION			WD		IB	110							3000	3500
27		REVELATION			WD		IB	T110							3350	3900
30				SDN	WD		IB	185							5050	5800
30				SDN	WD		IB	T110							5200	6000
30				SDN	WD		IB	T185							5800	6650
30		REVELINER			WD		IB	185							4400	5050
30		REVELINER			WD		IB	T110-T185							4500	5600
		1961 BOATS														
19		REVELER	ST	CNV	PLY		OB			6	11	800			2050	2450
19		REVILLE	HT		PLY		OB			6	11	950			2400	2800
23		REVEL QUEEN		CBNCR	PLY		OB			8		1800			4850	5600

 CONTINUED ON NEXT PAGE

REVEL CRAFT INC   -CONTINUED   See inside cover to adjust price for area

LOA FT IN	NAME AND/ OR MODEL	TOP/ RIG	BOAT TYPE	HULL MTL TP	ENGINE TP # HP MFG	BEAM FT IN	WGT LBS	DRAFT FT IN	RETAIL LOW	RETAIL HIGH
--- 1961 BOATS ---
23	REVELUX		CR	MHG	IB 100-185	8		11	2350	2800
25	REVEL EMPRESS		CR	MHG	IB 110-185	8		1 8	2500	3050
30	REVELINER		CR	MHG	IB 185	10		2	4400	5050
30	REVELINER		CR	MHG	IB T185	10		2	4900	5650
--- 1960 BOATS ---
17	SEA-SKIFF SS			WD	OB				1750	2100
17	SEA-SKIFF SS			PLY DV	OB	6 9	750		1800	2150
19	C C		CNV	WD	OB				2400	2800
19	C U		CNV	WD	OB				2400	2800
19	CC		CR	PLY DV	OB	7	800		2050	2450
19	CU		UTL	PLY DV	OB	7	800		1750	2100
19	HC	HT	CR	WD	OB				2450	2850
19	HC	HT	UTL	PLY DV	OB	7	1000		2250	2600
19	HU	HT	CR	PLY DV	OB	7	1000		2500	2950
19	HU	HT	UTL	WD	OB				2100	2500
22	C 4		SDN	WD	OB				4100	4750
22	C 4		SDN	PLY DV	OB	7 10	1500		4050	4700
22	C C		CNV	WD	OB				5150	5950
22	CC		CR	PLY DV	OB	7 10	1400		3800	4400
22	E C 2		EXP	WD	OB				5350	6150
22	EC 2		EXP	PLY DV	OB	7 10	1600		4250	4950
22	HC	HT	CR	WD	OB				4850	5600
22	HC	HT	CR	PLY DV	OB	7 10	1400		3800	4400
25	REVEL EMPRESS		CR	WD	IB 110				2450	2850
27	REVELINER		CR	WD	IB 110				2700	3100
--- 1959 BOATS ---
18			CR	WD	OB				2400	2800
20		HT	CR	WD	OB				3850	4450
23			EXP	WD	IB 110				2250	2650
25			CR	WD	IB 110				2400	2800
--- 1958 BOATS ---
19		HT	CR	WD	OB				2500	2900
22			CR	WD	OB				4900	5650
23			EXP	WD	IB 109				2200	2600
--- 1957 BOATS ---
21			CR	WD	OB				4550	5200
--- 1956 BOATS ---
19			CR	WD	OB				2500	2900
21			CR	WD	OB				4550	5200

REYNOCO INC
SAVAGE AMERICAN

Call 1-800-327-6929 for BUC Personalized Evaluation Service
Or, for 1967 to 1968 boats, sign onto www.BUCValuPro.com

RHODE ISLAND MRNE SERV INC
DIV OF U S YACHT CHARTERS   See inside cover to adjust price for area
WAKEFIELD RI 02880   COAST GUARD MFG ID- RXD

For more recent years, see the BUC Used Boat Price Guide, Volume 1 or Volume 2

LOA FT IN	NAME AND/ OR MODEL	TOP/ RIG	BOAT TYPE	HULL MTL TP	ENGINE TP # HP MFG	BEAM FT IN	WGT LBS	DRAFT FT IN	RETAIL LOW	RETAIL HIGH
--- 1982 BOATS ---
20	CLASSIC 20 ELEGANCE		UTL	WD	DS IB 45	5 4	1900		8200	9450
20	CLASSIC 20 NANCY		UTL	FBG	DS IB 55	4 8	1200		7000	8050
22 6	CLASSIC 22 DOREEN		UTL	WD	DS IB 55	6 7	2400		13100	14900
25	CLASSIC 25 AID		UTL	WD	SV IB T 45	5 2	3000		17300	19700
28	CLASSIC 28 PRESTON		CR	AL	IB 105	8 2	5000		24100	26700
47	CLASSIC 47 ANN LEE		CR	STL	SV IB 220D	15	40000		257000	282000
55	CLASSIC 55		MY	STL	SV IB 325D	16 4	60000		319500	351000
70	CLASSIC 70 WOOD PECK		MY	STL	SV IB T165D	14 4	50000		610000	670500
--- 1978 BOATS ---
26	WASQUE 26		FSH	FBG	SV IB 135D PERK	8 7	4800	2 3	33400	37100
32	WASQUE 32		FSH	FBG	SV IB 160D PERK	9 8	9000	2 6	44900	49900
50	SNUG-HARBOR 50		OFF	STL	SV IB 325D CAT	14 6	24000	4 3	196500	216000
55	SNUG-HARBOR 55		OFF	STL	SV IB 475D CAT	16 8	32000	5	210000	230500
65	SNUG-HARBOR 65	HT	OFF	STL	SV IB 500D CAT	18 6	50000	5	540000	593500
70	SNUG-HARBOR 70	HT	OFF	STL	SV IB 530D CAT	19	55000	5 6	669500	736500

RHYAN-CRAFT BOAT MFG CO
COAST GUARD MFG ID- RHY

Call 1-800-327-6929 for BUC Personalized Evaluation Service
Or, for 1973 to 1983 boats, sign onto www.BUCValuPro.com

RICH LINE
RIVER MARINE CORP   COAST GUARD MFG ID- RCH

Call 1-800-327-6929 for BUC Personalized Evaluation Service
Or, for 1959 to 1977 boats, sign onto www.BUCValuPro.com

RICHARDSON BOAT COMPANY
N TONAWANDA NY   COAST GUARD MFG ID- RBH See inside cover to adjust price for area

LOA FT IN	NAME AND/ OR MODEL	TOP/ RIG	BOAT TYPE	HULL MTL TP	ENGINE TP # HP MFG	BEAM FT IN	WGT LBS	DRAFT FT IN	RETAIL LOW	RETAIL HIGH
--- 1962 BOATS ---
36			EXP	AL	IB T225				22400	24900
36			SDN	AL	IB T225				24400	27100
40		FB	DC	AL	IB T225				50300	55300
43			DC	AL	IB T225				36300	40400
43			MY	AL	IB T225				41000	45600
46			MY	AL	IB T225				44400	49300
--- 1961 BOATS ---
28			EXP	WD	IB 177	10 4		2 3	7500	8650
31			EXP	WD	IB 109	10 10		2 6	12500	14200
32			EXP	AL	IB 188	10 10		2 6	13600	15500
36			EXP	WD	IB T225	11 10		2 8	21700	24100
36			SDN	AL	IB 188	12		2 8	22400	24900
36			SDN	WD	IB T225	11 10		2 8	23800	26500
36	CUSTOM		SPTCR	WD	IB T225	11 10		2 8	21100	23500
40		FB	DC	AL	IB T225	12 10		3 1	48400	53200
40		FB	DC	WD	IB T225	12 4		3 1	49500	54300
40			EXP	WD	IB T225	12 4		3 1	32300	35900
40			SDN	WD	IB T225	12 4		3 1	37500	41600
40	CUSTOM		SPTCR	WD	IB T225	12 4		3 1	23900	26600
43		FB	DC	WD	IB T225	13 10		3 6	38700	43000
43	SALON		DC	AL	IB T225	13 10		3 1	38700	42900
46			MY	AL	IB T225	13 10		3 1	43800	48700
46			MY	WD	IB T225	13 10		3 6	43800	48700
46	MARK I		MY	WD	IB T130D	13 10		3 6	53100	58300
--- 1960 BOATS ---
24			EXP	WD	IB 188				3900	4550
24			UTL	WD	IB 188				3750	4350
28	SEA-SKIFF		CR	WD	IB 188				7150	8250
31			EXP	WD	IB T188				13200	15000
31			EXP	WD	DS IB T150	INT 11	12000	3 6	12800	14500
31	CUSTOM		UTL	WD	IB T188				12500	14200
35			EXP	WD	IB T177				19100	21300
35			SDN	WD	IB T177				20300	22600
40			DC	WD	IB T225				48300	53000
40			EXP	WD	IB T225				31600	35200
40			SDN	WD	IB T225				36700	40800
40			SPTCR	WD	IB T225				23500	26100
43			DC	WD	IB T275				36300	40300
46			MY	WD	IB T275				42800	47600
--- 1959 BOATS ---
24	GOLDEN		UTL	WD	IB 170				3650	4250
27	GOLDEN		UTL	WD	IB 170				5250	6000
31	GOLDEN		EXP	WD	IB 170				12800	14600
31	GOLDEN COMMUTER			WD	IB 170				10200	11600
35	GOLDEN-JUBILEE		EXP	WD	IB T170				18700	20800
35	GOLDEN-JUBILEE		SDN	WD	IB T170				19900	22100
40	GOLDEN CUSTOM SPORT			WD	IB T225				31000	34400
40	GOLDEN-JUBILEE		EXP	WD	IB T225				31100	34500
40	GOLDEN-JUBILEE		SDN	WD	IB T225				36000	40100
43	GOLDEN-JUBILEE		DC	WD	IB T225				34000	37800
46	GOLDEN-ANNIVERSARY		MY	WD	IB T225				41600	46200
53	GOLDEN-ANNIVERSARY		MY	WD	IB T225				63700	70000
--- 1958 BOATS ---
27			CBNCR	WD	IB 170				5900	6800
27			EXP	WD	IB 160				5950	6850
30			EXP	WD	IB T160				11700	13300
30			SF	WD	IB T177				10200	11500
35			EXP	WD	IB T150				18200	20300
35			SDN	WD	IB T150				19400	21500

LOA FT	IN	NAME AND/ OR MODEL	TOP/ RIG	BOAT TYPE	HULL MTL	HULL TP	ENG TP	ENG #	HP	MFG	BEAM FT	IN	WGT LBS	DRAFT FT	IN	RETAIL LOW	RETAIL HIGH
1958 BOATS																	
40				EXP	WD		IB		T225							30500	33900
40		CUSTOM		SDN	WD		IB		T225							35400	39400
40				SPTCR	WD		IB		T225							22600	25100
43				MY	WD		IB		T225							37900	42100
43		SALON		DC	WD		IB		T225							33400	37100
1957 BOATS																	
25					WD		IB		125	CHRY						**	**
27				CBNCR	WD		IB		100							5100	5850
34			FB	SDN	WD		IB		T135							15800	17900
40				SF	WD		IB		T225							34200	38000
43			FB	CR	WD		IB		T165							26200	29100
43		SALON		DC	WD		IB		T225							32900	36500
1956 BOATS																	
26				EXP	WD		IB		100							4650	5350
30				EXP	WD		IB		T100							10800	12300
36				SDN	WD		IB		T165							21500	23900
38				EXP	WD		IB		T165							24900	27700
40				SDN	WD		IB		T200							34300	38100
1955 BOATS																	
25				CBNCR	WD		IB		100							4050	4750
30				EXP	WD		IB		T125							10800	12300
34				EXP	WD		IB		150							15300	17400
40				EXP	WD		IB		T165							29100	32300
40				SDN	WD		IB		T200							33900	37600
43				DCMY	WD		IB		T200							32400	36000
1954 BOATS																	
25				CR	WD		IB		95							4100	4800
29				EXP	WD		IB		T125							8150	9400
33			HT	**	WD	RB	IB										**	**
33				SDN	WD		IB		T125							12900	14700
37				EXP	WD		IB		T200							22200	24600
37			HT	SDN	WD	RB	IB										**	**
40				SDN	WD		IB		T165							33400	37100
1953 BOATS																	
28			HT	EXP	WD	RB	IB					9	6				**	**
33			HT	EXP	WD	RB	IB	T									**	**
33			HT	SDN	WD	RB	IB	T									**	**
36			HT	SDN	WD	RB	IB	T									**	**
40			FB	DC	WD	RB	IB	T				12	2				**	**
41			FB	DC	WD		IB		T285								36900	41000
1952 BOATS																	
26				CBNCR	WD		IB		125							4600	5300
27		LITTLE-GIANT	OP	EXP	WD		IB										**	**
27		LITTLE-GIANT	HT	SDN	WD		IB										**	**
32					WD		IB		T115	CHRY						**	**
32			OP	EXP	WD		IB	T									**	**
33			HT	SDN	WD		IB	T									**	**
36			FB	SDN	WD		IB		T165							20600	22900
40				DCMY	WD		IB		T225							42600	47300
40				SDN	WD		IB		T145							32600	36200
1951 BOATS																	
27		LITTLE-GIANT			WD		IB		95							4450	5100
32			HT	CR	WD		IB		T 95							10400	11800
32				SDN	WD		IB		T100							11000	12400
35				EXP	WD		IB		T135							16000	18200
1950 BOATS																	
26				CBNCR	WD		IB		185							4850	5550
31			HT	SDN	WD	RB	IB		100	GRAY	10	6		2	6	9400	10700
31			OP	SPTCR	WD	RB	IB		100	GRAY	10	6		2	6	9400	10700
35			HT	DC	WD	RB	IB		T100	GRAY	11			2	8	17200	19600
1949 BOATS																	
25				EXP	WD		IB										**	**
25				SDN	WD		IB										**	**
31			HT	SDN	WD	RB	IB		93	GRAY	10	6		2	6	9350	10600
31			OP	SPTCR	WD	RB	IB		93	GRAY	10	6		2	6	9350	10600
1948 BOATS																	
26				CBNCR	WD		IB		100							4200	4850
31				SDN	WD		IB		165							9650	10900
1946 BOATS																	
25				CBNCR	WD		IB		185							4100	4750
1941 BOATS																	
26				CBNCR	WD		IB		91							4450	5100
31			HT	SDN	WD		IB			GRAY						**	**
33			HT	CR	WD		IB			GRAY						**	**
34				EXP	WD		IB										**	**
36			HT	CR	WD		IB			GRAY						**	**
1940 BOATS																	
26				CBNCR	WD		IB		91							4550	5250
1939 BOATS																	
25	11	LITTLE-GIANT	HT	SDN	WD		IB			GRAY	8	6				**	**
32				EXP	WD		IB										**	**
33		CRUISABOUT DECKHOUSE	HT	CBNCR	WD		IB			GRAY	10	8				**	**
33		CRUISABOUT OPEN CPT	OP	CBNCR	WD		IB			GRAY	10	8				**	**
36		SUPER-CRUISABOUT	HT	CBNCR	WD		IB	T		GRAY	10	8				**	**
36		SUPER-CRUISABOUT	HT	DC	WD		IB	T		GRAY	10	8				**	**
1938 BOATS																	
26				CBNCR	WD		IB										**	**
33				SDN	WD		IB		177							11000	12600
1937 BOATS																	
25	11	LITTLE-GIANT	HT	CBNCR	WD		IB		51		8	6				4700	5400
30		JUNIOR	HT	CR	WD		IB		71		9	4				8150	9350
32					WD		IB		105	CHRY						**	**
32		CRUISABOUT	HT	CR	WD		IB			GRAY	10	1				**	**
1936 BOATS																	
25			HT	CR	WD		IB										**	**
26				CBNCR	WD		IB		130							5000	5750
30			HT	CR	WD		IB										**	**
32		CRUISABOUT	HT	CR	WD		IB			GRAY						**	**
1935 BOATS																	
31		AFT CABIN			WD		IB		90	GRAY						8250	9500
1934 BOATS																	
28				EXP	WD		IB										**	**
32					WD		IB		140	NORD						**	**
1933 BOATS																	
22		LITTLE-GIANT	HT	CR	WD		IB										**	**
26		RICHARDSON-JR	HT	CR	WD		IB										**	**
32				SDN	WD		IB		100							9600	10900
1932 BOATS																	
24	6	BABY-RICHARDSON	HT	CBNCR	WD		IB		50	GRAY	8	2		2	2	4650	5350
24	6	BABY-RICHARDSON	HT	FSH	WD		IB			GRAY	8	2		2	2	**	**
30		CRUISABOUT	HT	CBNCR	WD		IB			GRAY	9			2	4	**	**
30		CRUISABOUT	HT	DC	WD		IB			GRAY				2	4	**	**
1931 BOATS																	
24		BABY-RICHARDSON		CR	WD		IB					8					**	**
30				EXP	WD		IB		155							9450	10700
1928 BOATS																	
29	8				WD		IB		125	CC						**	**
1925 BOATS																	
23					WD		IB			GRAY						**	**
1917 BOATS																	
67					WD		IB		455							**	**

RICHARDSON BOAT SHOPS

Call 1-800-327-6929 for BUC Personalized Evaluation Service
Or, for 1961 to 1967 boats, sign onto www.BUCValuPro.com

RICHARDSON BOATS & PLASTICS

Call 1-800-327-6929 for BUC Personalized Evaluation Service
Or, for 1966 to 1969 boats, sign onto www.BUCValuPro.com

CLIFF RICHARDSON

Call 1-800-327-6929 for BUC Personalized Evaluation Service
Or, for 1950 boats, sign onto www.BUCValuPro.com

RICKBORN INDUSTRIES INC
COAST GUARD MFG ID- RCK

Call 1-800-327-6929 for BUC Personalized Evaluation Service
Or, for 1961 to 1986 boats, sign onto www.BUCValuPro.com

RIDGWAY MARINE INC
COAST GUARD MFG ID- RWM

Call 1-800-327-6929 for BUC Personalized Evaluation Service
Or, for 1971 boats, sign onto www.BUCValuPro.com

RIEHL MFG CO

CLINTON STEEL BOATS   COAST GUARD MFG ID- RHL

Call 1-800-327-6929 for BUC Personalized Evaluation Service
Or, for 1959 to 1985 boats, sign onto www.BUCValuPro.com

RINKER BOAT CO INC

SYRACUSE IN 46567   COAST GUARD MFG ID- RNK See inside cover to adjust price for area

For more recent years, see the BUC Used Boat Price Guide, Volume 1 or Volume 2

LOA FT	LOA IN	NAME AND/ OR MODEL	TOP/ RIG	BOAT TYPE	-HULL- MTL	-HULL- TP	ENGINE TP	ENGINE # HP	ENGINE MFG	BEAM FT	BEAM IN	WGT LBS	DRAFT FT	DRAFT IN	RETAIL LOW	RETAIL HIGH
		1983 BOATS														
16	5	V165 BR	OP	RNBT	FBG	SV	IO	120		6	9	1500			1850	2250
17	3	V173 BR	OP	RNBT	FBG	DV	IO	120		7	2	1700			2200	2600
19		V190 BR	OP	RNBT	FBG	DV	IO	120		7	5	2000			2650	3100
19		V190 CB	OP	RNBT	FBG	DV	IO	120		7	5	2000			2650	3100
20	5	V205	OP	CUD	FBG	DV	IO	120		8		2400			3600	4150
		1981 BOATS														
16	5	WEDGE	OP	RNBT	FBG	DV	IO	120		6	9	1500	1	7	1800	2150
17	3	RAIDER	OP	RNBT	FBG	DV	IO	140		7	2	1800	1	8	2200	2550
18	11	RIDEAU	OP	RNBT	FBG	DV	IO	140		7	5	2200	1	10	2650	3100
		1980 BOATS														
17		RAIDER	OP	RNBT	FBG	DV	IO	120		7	2	1675			2000	2400
17		RAMERO	OP	RNBT	FBG	TR	IO	120		6	9	1650			1950	2300
19		RIDEAU	OP	RNBT	FBG	DV	IO	120		7	5	2100			2600	3000
20		CUDDY CABIN		CUD	FBG	DV	IO	120		8	1	2700			3550	4150
		1979 BOATS														
16	9	RAMERO II	OP	RNBT	FBG	TR	IO	140		6	9	1700			1950	2300
17	3	RAIDER	OP	RNBT	FBG	DV	IO	185	OMC	7	2	1800			2150	2550
18	11	RIDEAU	OP	RNBT	FBG	DV	IO	185	OMC	7	5	2200	1	10	2650	3050
		1978 BOATS														
16	9	RAMERO II	OP	RNBT	FBG	TR	IO	120-140		6	9	1700			1950	2300
17	3	RAIDER	OP	RNBT	FBG	DV	IO	120-185		7	2	1800			2200	2550
18	11	RIDEAU	OP	RNBT	FBG	DV	IO	120-185		7	5	2200			2650	3100
		1977 BOATS														
16	9	RAMERO	OP	RNBT	FBG	TR	IO	120-140		6	9	1680			1950	2350
17		RAIDER	OP	RNBT	FBG	DV	IO	120-170		7	1	1700			2050	2550
17		RAIDER	OP	RNBT	FBG	DV	IO	175	OMC	7	1	1900			2200	2600
18	9	RIDEAU	OP	RNBT	FBG	DV	IO	120-175		7	4	1875			2500	3000
		1976 BOATS														
16	7	RAMERO	OP	SKI	FBG	TR	IO	120-140		6	7	1700			1850	2200
17		RAIDER	OP	SKI	FBG	DV	IO	120-140		7	2	1750			2050	2450
18	5	RIDEAU	OP	SKI	FBG	DV	IO	120-175		7	5	1875			2400	2800
		1975 BOATS														
16	7	RAMERO W/T	OP	RNBT	FBG	TR	IO	140		6	7	1700			2050	2450
17		RAIDER	OP	SKI	FBG	DV	IO	140		7	8	1750			2250	2650
18	5	RIDEAU	OP	SKI	FBG	DV	IO	165		7	11	1875			2650	3050
		1970 BOATS														
16	10	RAIDER 17		RNBT	FBG		IO	160						11	2900	3350
16	10	RAIDER 17		RNBT	FBG	DV	IO	160		6	9			11	2750	3200
16	10	RAMARO 17		RNBT	FBG		IO	160						8	2900	3400
16	10	RAMARO 17		RNBT	FBG	TR	IO	160		6	10			8	2750	3200
18	7				FBG		IO	250					1	7	4000	4650
		1967 BOATS														
16	8	RAIDER		RNBT	FBG		IO	110		6	9			9	3000	3450
		1966 BOATS														
16	10	DEEP VEE HULL			FBG	DV	IO	120		7					3050	3550

RIVA S P A

FERRETTI GROUP
24067 SARNICO ITALY   COAST GUARD MFG ID- RVA   See inside cover to adjust price for area

For more recent years, see the BUC Used Boat Price Guide, Volume 1 or Volume 2

LOA FT	LOA IN	NAME AND/ OR MODEL	TOP/ RIG	BOAT TYPE	-HULL- MTL	-HULL- TP	ENGINE TP	ENGINE # HP	ENGINE MFG	BEAM FT	BEAM IN	WGT LBS	DRAFT FT	DRAFT IN	RETAIL LOW	RETAIL HIGH
		1983 BOATS														
19	3	RUDY SUPER	OP	RNBT	FBG	FL	IB	210	RIVA	7	1	2425	1	6	7200	8300
21	6	OLYMPIC	OP	RNBT	MHG	FL	IB	270	RIVA	7	4	2865	1	6	38400	42600
28	8	AQUARAMA-SPECIAL	OP	RNBT	MHG	FL	IB	T350	RIVA	8	5	6614	2		**	**
31	3	ST-TROPEZ	OP	RNBT	FBG	DV	IB	T350	RIVA	8	10	7060	2	4	67400	74100
34	4	SUMMERTIME-SPECIAL	FB	CR	FBG	DV	IB	T210D	CUM	11	4	15000	2	8	135500	149000
37		RIVA 2000	HT	OFF	FBG	DV	IB	R350	RIVA	9	4	11900	2	3	93000	102000
38	4	BRAVO SPECIAL	HT	CBNCR	FBG	DV	IB	T320D	CUM	12	6	15870	3	2	110500	121000
42	8	CARIBE	FB	SF	FBG	DV	IB	T320D	CUM	12	7	19000	3	4	147500	162000
42	8	MALIBU	FB	MY	FBG	DV	IB	T320D	CUM	12	7	21000	3	4	158500	174000
49	10	SUPERAMERICA	FB	MY	FBG	DV	IB	T400D	CUM	13	9	31000	3	8	199500	219500
60		CORSARO	FB	MY	FBG	DV	IB	T650D	J&T	17	4				347000	381500
66		MONTECARLO	FB	MY	FBG	DV	IB	T725D	S&S	18		85120	5	1	607500	667500
		1982 BOATS														
19	3	RUDY SUPER	OP	RNBT	FBG	DV	IB	210	RIVA	7	1	2425	1	6	6900	7950
21	6	OLYMPIC	OP	RNBT	MHG	DV	IB	270	RIVA	7	4	2865	1	6	37900	42100
28	8	AQUARAMA-SPECIAL	OP	RNBT	MHG	DV	IB	T350	RIVA	8	5	6614	2		**	**
31	3	ST-TROPEZ	OP	RNBT	FBG	DV	IB	T350	RIVA	8	10	7060	2	4	64500	70900
34	4	SUMMERTIME-SPECIAL	FB	CR	FBG	DV	IB	T210D	CUM	11	4	15000	2	8	130500	143500
37		RIVA 2000	OP	OFF	FBG	DV	IB	R350	RIVA	9	4	11900	2	3	88800	97600
38	4	BRAVO	OP	CBNCR	FBG	DV	IB	T320D	CUM	12	6	15870	3	2	105500	115500
42	8	CARIBE	FB	SF	FBG	DV	IB	T320D	CUM	12	7	19000	3	4	141000	155000
49	10	SUPERAMERICA	FB	MY	FBG	DV	IB	T400D	CUM	13	9	31000	3	8	190500	209500
60		CORSARO	FB	MY	FBG	DV	IB	T650D	GM	17	4				334000	367000
66		MONTECARLO	FB	MY	FBG	DV	IB	T725D	GM	18		85120	5	1	587500	645500
		1981 BOATS														
19	3	RUD-SUPER	OP	RNBT	FBG	FL	IB	210	RIVA	7	1	2425	1	9	6600	7600
21	6	OLYMPIC	OP	RNBT	MHG	FL	IB	270	RIVA	7	4	2450	1	9	34500	38300
28	8	AQUARAMA-SPECIAL	OP	RNBT	MHG	FL	IB	T350	RIVA	8	5	6640	1	9	**	**
31	3	ST-TROPEZ	OP	RNBT	FBG	DV	IB	T350	RIVA	8	10	7060	2	4	61800	67900
34	3	SUMMERTIME SPECIAL	FB	CR	FBG	DV	IB	T350	RIVA	11	3	12600	2	6	95200	104500
34	3	SUMMERTIME SPECIAL	FB	CR	FBG	DV	IB	T210D	CUM	11	3	14330	3	1	122000	134000
37		RIVA 2000	HT	OFF	FBG	DV	IB	R350	RIVA	9	2	11900	2	10	85600	94000
39	8	BRAVO SPECIAL	HT	CBNCR	FBG	DV	IB	T320D	CUM	12	7	16720	3	1	109000	119500
42	8	CARIBE	FB	SF	FBG	DV	IB	T320D	CUM	12	7	21110	3	3	139500	153500
49	10	SUPERAMERICA	FB	MY	FBG	DV	IB	T400D	CUM	13	9	30860	3	6	181000	199000
50		SUPERAMERICA		MY	FBG	DV	IB	T425D		13	9				206000	226500
55		RIVA 55		MY	FBG	DV	IB	T650D		17	2				230500	253000
66		MONTECARLO		MY	FBG	DV	IB	T999D		18					500000	549500
66		MONTECARLO	FB	MY	FBG	DV	IB	T725D	GM	18		85000	6	2	559000	614500
		1980 BOATS														
19	3	RUDY-SUPER	OP	RNBT	FBG	FL	IB	210	RIVA	7	1	2425	1	9	6350	7300
21	6	OLYMPIC	OP	RNBT	MHG	FL	IB	270	RIVA	7	4	2450	1	9	34100	37900
28	8	AQUARAMA-SPECIAL	OP	RNBT	MHG	FL	IB	T350	RIVA	8	5	6640	1	9	**	**
31	3	ST-TROPEZ	OP	RNBT	FBG	DV	IB	T350	RIVA	8	10	7060	2	4	59200	65000
34	3	PORTOFINO	FB	FSH	FBG	DV	IB	T350	RIVA	11	3	11500	2	4	89100	98000
34	3	PORTOFINO	FB	FSH	FBG	DV	IB	T210D	CUM	11	3	13200	3	1	113000	124000
34	3	SUMMERTIME	FB	CR	FBG	DV	IB	T350	RIVA	11	3	12600	2	6	91200	100500
34	3	SUMMERTIME	FB	CR	FBG	DV	IB	T210D	CUM	11	3	14330	3	1	117500	129000
37		RIVA 2000	HT	OFF	FBG	DV	IB	R350	RIVA	9	2	11900	2	10	81600	89700
39	8	BRAVO	HT	CBNCR	FBG	DV	IB	T350	RIVA	12	7	14500	2	9	79800	87700
39	8	BRAVO	HT	CBNCR	FBG	DV	IB	T270D	CUM	12	7	16720	3	1	100500	110500
48		SUPERAMERICA	FB	MY	FBG	DV	IB	T400D	CUM	13	9	30860	3	6	175500	192500
66		MONTECARLO	FB	MY	FBG	DV	IB	T D		18					**	**
66		MONTECARLO	FB	MY	FBG	DV	IB	T725D		18					423500	465000
		1979 BOATS														
19	3	RUDY-SUPER	OP	RNBT	FBG	FL	IB	210	RIVA	7	1	2425	1	9	6050	6950
21	6	OLYMPIC	OP	RNBT	MHG	FL	IB	220	RIVA	7	4	2450	1	9	33300	37000
28	8	AQUARAMA-SPECIAL	OP	RNBT	MHG	FL	IB	T350	RIVA	8	5	6640	1	9	**	**
31	3	ST-TROPEZ	OP	RNBT	FBG	DV	IB	T350	RIVA	8	10	7060	2	4	56700	62300
34	3	PORTOFINO	FB	FSH	FBG	DV	IB	T350	RIVA	11	3	11500	2	4	85500	93900
34	3	PORTOFINO	FB	FSH	FBG	DV	IB	T210D	CUM	11	3	13200	3	1	108500	119500
34	3	SUMMERTIME	FB	CR	FBG	DV	IB	T350	RIVA	11	3	12600	2	6	87500	96100
34	3	SUMMERTIME	FB	CR	FBG	DV	IB	T210D	CUM	11	3	14330	3	1	113000	124000
37		RIVA 2000	HT	OFF	FBG	DV	IB	R350	RIVA	9	4	11900	2	10	77000	84700
39	3	BRAVO	HT	CBNCR	FBG	DV	IB	T350	RIVA	12	7	14500	2	9	74500	81900
39	3	BRAVO	HT	CBNCR	FBG	DV	IB	T270D	CUM	12	7	16720	3	1	94100	103500
48		SUPERAMERICA	FB	MY	FBG	DV	IB	T400D	CUM	13	9	30860	3	6	167500	184000
		1978 BOATS														
19	3	RUDY	OP	RNBT	FBG	FL	IB	190	RIVA	7	1	2425	1	9	5800	6650
19	3	RUDY-SUPER	OP	RNBT	FBG	FL	IB	210	RIVA	7	1	2450	1	9	5850	6750
21	6				WD		IB	270	CHEV						**	**
21	6	OLYMPIC	OP	RNBT	MHG	FL	IB	270	RIVA	7	4	2876	1	6	36500	40600
24	9	SPORTFISHERMAN 25	FB	SF	FBG	DV	IB	T210	RIVA	9	10	7050	2	9	30200	33500
28	8	AQUARAMA-SPECIAL	ST	RNBT	MHG	FL	IB	T350	RIVA	8	5	6640	1	10	**	**
31	3	ST-TROPEZ	OP	RNBT	FBG	DV	IB	T350	RIVA	8	10	7060	2	4	54400	59800
34	3	PORTOFINO 34	FB	SF	FBG	DV	IB	T350	RIVA	11	3	11500	2	4	81900	90000
34	3	PORTOFINO 34	FB	SF	FBG	DV	IB	T210D	CUM	11	3	13200	3	1	104500	115000
34	3	SUMMERTIME SPECIAL	FB	CR	FBG	DV	IB	T350	RIVA	11	3	12600	2	6	83900	92200
34	3	SUMMERTIME SPECIAL	FB	CR	FBG	DV	IB	T210D	CUM	11	3	14330	3	1	108500	119500
37		RIVA 2000	OP	CR	FBG	DV	IB	R350	RIVA	9	4	11900	2	10	74400	81800
45	2	SUPERAMERICA 45	FB	MY	FBG	DV	IB	T400D	CUM	13	9	28660	3	6	130500	143500
48	6	SUPERAMERICA 48	FB	MY	FBG	DV	IB	T400D	CUM	13	9	30860	3	6	135500	149000
		1977 BOATS														
19	4	RUDY	OP	RNBT	FBG	FL	IB	190	CRUS	6	10	2280	1	6	5450	6300
19	4	RUDY-SUPER	OP	RNBT	FBG	FL	IB	210	CRUS	6	10	2340	1	6	5550	6400
21	6	OLYMPIC	OP	RNBT	MHG	FL	IB	270	CRUS	6	10	2970	1	6	36800	40800

CONTINUED ON NEXT PAGE

LOA FT	LOA IN	NAME AND/ OR MODEL	TOP/ RIG	BOAT TYPE	HULL MTL	HULL TP	TP	ENGINE # HP	ENGINE MFG	BEAM FT	BEAM IN	WGT LBS	DRAFT FT	DRAFT IN	RETAIL LOW	RETAIL HIGH
		1977 BOATS														
24	8	SPORTFISHERMAN 25	FB	SF	FBG	DV	IB	T210	CRUS	10	3	7000	2	3	29300	32600
28	10	AQUARAMA-SPECIAL	ST	RNBT	MHG	FL	IB	T350	CRUS	8	2	6620	1	10	**	**
31		ST-TROPEZ	OP	RNBT	FBG	DV	IB	T350	CRUS	9		6400	1	10	50600	55700
34	2	PORTOFINO 34	FB	SF	FBG	DV	IB	T225-T350		11	1	12700	2	10	76200	86400
34	2	SUMMERTIME 34	FB	CR	FBG	DV	IB	T225-T350		11	1	15500	2	10	81500	90500
37		RIVA 2000	OP	CR	FBG	DV	IB	R350	CRUS	9	2	12780	2	4	75200	82700
44	6	SUPERAMERICA 45	FB	MY	FBG	DV	IB	T400D	CUM	13	7	28600	4	7	125000	137500
		1976 BOATS														
19		RUDY	OP	RNBT	FBG	FL	IB	190	RIVA	7		2200	1	9	5000	5700
19		RUDY SUPER	OP	RNBT	FBG	FL	IB	210	RIVA	7		2200	1	9	5000	5750
22		OLYMPIC	OP	CR	WD	FL	IB	270	RIVA	7		2900	1	6	36000	40000
25		25 SPORT FISHERMAN	FB	SF	FBG	DV	IB	T210	RIVA	10		6800	2	8	27300	30400
28		AQUARAMA SPECIAL	OP	CR	WD	FL	IB	T350	RIVA	8		6600	1	10	**	**
31		ST-TROPEZ	OP	CR	FBG	DV	IB	T350	RIVA	9		6400	2	4	50100	55100
34		PORTOFINO	FB	SF	FBG	DV	IB	T225-T350		11		13600	2	5	73400	84500
34		SUMMERTIME	FB	CR	FBG	DV	IB	T225-T350		11		15800	2	6	77300	88600
37		RIVA 2000	OP	CR	FBG	DV	IB	R350	RIVA	9		12700	2	10	71900	79000
45		SUPERAMERICA	FB	MY	FBG	DV	IB	T400D	CUM	14		30000	3	6	132500	145500
		1969 BOATS														
18	8	RIVA JUNIOR		RNBT	P/M		IB	180		7	2	1927	1	6	15200	17300
20	6	SUPER-FLORIDA		RNBT	P/M		IB	220		7	3	2731	1	6	31100	34500
22	4	ARISTON		RNBT	P/M		IB	220		7	3	2995	1	7	36300	40300
22	10	ARISTON SUPER		RNBT	P/M		IB	320		7	3	3175	1	7	40100	44600
27		AQUARAMA		CR	P/M		IB	T220		8	6	6162	1	10	**	**
27	8	AQUARAMA SUPER		CR	P/M		IB	T220		8	5	7092	1	10	**	**
		1968 BOATS														
19	11	SUPER-FLORIDA	OP		WD		IB	185	CC	7	1	2371	1	6	17300	19600
21	8	ARISTON	OP		WD		IB	185	CC	7	1	2995	1	6	33800	37500
22	2	SUPER-ARISTON	OP		WD		IB	290	CHRY	7	1	3127	1	6	36400	40500
26	4	AQUARAMA	OP		WD		IB	T185	CC	8	7	5347	1	9	**	**
26	4	TRITONE	OP		WD		IB	T185	CC	8	7	5792	1	9	80800	88800
27	1	SUPER-AQUARAMA	OP		WD		IB	T290	CHRY	8	7	6277	1	9	**	**
		1967 BOATS														
18	2	RIVA JUNIOR		RNBT	P/M		IB	180		7	1	1927	1	6	14500	16500
19	11	SUPER-FLORIDA		RNBT	P/M		IB	185		7	1	2731	1	6	19300	21500
22	4	ARISTON		RNBT	P/M		IB	220		7	1	2995	1	6	35600	39600
22	4	ARISTON SUPER		RNBT	P/M		IB	320		7	1	3175	1	6	38400	42700
26	4	TRITONE		CR	P/M		IB	T185		8	7	5792	1	9	80400	88400
27		AQUARAMA		CR	P/M		IB	T220		8	7	6162	1	9	**	**
27	8	AQUARAMA SUPER		CR	P/M		IB	T320		8	7	7092	1	9	**	**
		1966 BOATS														
19	11	SUPER-FLORIDA		SKI	WD		IB	185		7	1		1	6	17300	19600
21	8	ARISTON		RNBT	WD		IB	185		7	1		1	6	36800	40900
22	2	ARISTON SUPER		RNBT	WD		IB	290		7	1		1	6	38700	43100
26	4	AQUARAMA		RNBT	WD		IB	T185		8	7		1	9	**	**
26	4	TRITONE		RNBT	WD		IB	T185		8	7		1	9	**	**
27					WD		IB	T285	CHEV						**	**
27	1	AQUARAMA SUPER		RNBT	WD		IB	T290		8	7		1	9	**	**
73	10	CARAVELLE		MY	STL		IB	T330		16	9		5	9	**	**
		1965 BOATS														
16	4	TRITONE			WD		IB	T185							**	**
17	11	SUPER-FLORIDA			WD		IB	185							12900	14600
21	8	ARISTON			WD		IB	185							38800	43100
22	2	ARISTON SUPER			WD		IB	290							40800	45300
27		SUPER-AQUARAMA	HT	CR			IB	T							**	**
27	1	AQUARAMA SUPER			WD		IB	T290							**	**
73	10	CARAVELLA DEVRIES		MY	STL		IB	T330D		16	9		5	9	**	**
		1964 BOATS														
19	11	SUPER-FLORIDA			WD		IB	185							18400	20400
21	8	ARISTON			WD		IB	185							38600	42900
22	8	ARISTON SUPER			WD		IB	290							40700	45300
26	4	AQUARAMA			WD		IB	T185							**	**
26	4	TRITONE			WD		IB	T185							**	**
27	1	AQUARAMA SUPER			WD		IB	T290							**	**

RIVAL BOWMAN YACHT LTD

SOUTHAMPTON ENGLAND SO14 5QY
ALSO SADLER INTL

See inside cover to adjust price for area

For more recent years, see the BUC Used Boat Price Guide, Volume 1 or Volume 2

LOA FT	LOA IN	NAME AND/ OR MODEL	TOP/ RIG	BOAT TYPE	HULL MTL	HULL TP	TP	ENGINE # HP	ENGINE MFG	BEAM FT	BEAM IN	WGT LBS	DRAFT FT	DRAFT IN	RETAIL LOW	RETAIL HIGH
		1983 BOATS														
25	9	SADLER 26	SLP	SA/RC	FBG	KL	IB	D		9	5	4800	4	8	18000	20000
28	5	SADLER 29	SLP	SA/RC	FBG	KL	IB	D		9	6	6500	5		26400	29300
31	6	SADLER 32	SLP	SA/RC	FBG	KL	IB	D		10	6	9500	6	6	40800	45400
		1982 BOATS														
25		SADLER 25	SLP	SA/RC	FBG	KL	IB	D		8	9	4400	4	7	14800	16800
28	3	SADLER 28	SLP	SA/RC	FBG	KC	IB	D		9	6	6500	4	11	24700	27500
31	6	SADLER 32	SLP	SA/RC	FBG	KL	IB	D		10	6	9500	6	6	38400	42700
		1981 BOATS														
25		SADLER 25	SLP	SA/RC	FBG	KL	IB	D		8	9	4400	4	7	13900	15800
28	3	SADLER 28	SLP	SA/RC	FBG	KC	IB	D		9	6	6500	4	11	23200	25800
31	6	SADLER 32	SLP	SA/RC	FBG	KL	IB	D		10	6	9500	6	6	36100	40100
		1980 BOATS														
25		SADLER 25	SLP	SA/RC	FBG	KL	IB	D		8	9	4400	4	7	13300	15100
31	6	SADLER 32	SLP	SA/RC	FBG	KL	IB	D		10	6	9500	6	6	34500	38300
		1979 BOATS														
25		SADLER 25	SLP	SA/CR	FBG	KL	IB	D		8	9	4000	5	6	11700	13300
32		SADLER 32	SLP	SA/CR	FBG	KL	IB	D		10	6	8500	4	7	29800	33100

RIVAL YACHTS LTD

SOUTHERN BOATBUILDING CO LTD
SOUTHAMPTON ENGLAND

See inside cover to adjust price for area

LOA FT	LOA IN	NAME AND/ OR MODEL	TOP/ RIG	BOAT TYPE	HULL MTL	HULL TP	TP	ENGINE # HP	ENGINE MFG	BEAM FT	BEAM IN	WGT LBS	DRAFT FT	DRAFT IN	RETAIL LOW	RETAIL HIGH
		1982 BOATS														
34		RIVAL 34	SLP	SA/CR	FBG	KC	IB	20D	BUKH	9	8	10900	4	8	50400	55400
34		RIVAL 34	SLP	SA/CR	FBG	KL	IB	20D	BUKH	9	8	10900	5	10	50300	55300
35	10	RIVAL 36D	SLP	SA/CR	FBG	KL	IB	20D	BUKH	11		14250	6	1	66100	72700
35	10	RIVAL 36S	SLP	SA/CR	FBG	KC	IB	20D	BUKH	11		13700	3	9	64000	70300
37	7	RIVAL 38A	SLP	SA/CR	FBG	KL	IB	36D	BUKH	11	3	17196	5	4	79800	87700
37	7	RIVAL 38A	CUT	SA/CR	FBG	KL	IB	36D	BUKH	11	3	17196	5	4	79300	87200
37	7	RIVAL 38C	SLP	SA/CR	FBG	KL	IB	36D	BUKH	11	3	17196	5	4	84000	92400
37	7	RIVAL 38C	CUT	SA/CR	FBG	KL	IB	36D	BUKH	11	3	17196	5	4	83600	91800
37	7	RIVAL 38CK	KTH	SA/CR	FBG	KL	IB	36D	BUKH	11	3	17196	5	4	82700	90800
41		RIVAL 41A	SLP	SA/CR	FBG	KL	IB	50D	PERK	12	3	22046	5	11	110000	121000
41		RIVAL 41A	CUT	SA/CR	FBG	KL	IB	50D	PERK	12	3	22046	5	11	109000	119500
41		RIVAL 41C	SLP	SA/CR	FBG	KL	IB	50D	PERK	12	3	22046	5	11	112000	123500
41		RIVAL 41C	CUT	SA/CR	FBG	KL	IB	50D	PERK	12	3	22046	5	11	111000	122000
41		RIVAL 41CK	KTH	SA/CR	FBG	KL	IB	50D	PERK	12	3	22046	5	11	112500	123500
		1981 BOATS														
34		RIVAL 34	SLP	SA/CR	FBG	KL	IB	20D		9	8	10900	4	8	47600	52300
35	10	RIVAL 36D	SLP	SA/CR	FBG	KL	IB	20D	BUKH	11		14250	6	1	62400	68600
35	10	RIVAL 36S	SLP	SA/CR	FBG	KL	IB	20D	BUKH	11		13700	3	9	60300	66300
37	7	RIVAL 38A	SLP	SA/CR	FBG	KL	IB	36D	BUKH	11	3	17196	5	4	75300	82800
37	7	RIVAL 38A	CUT	SA/CR	FBG	KL	IB	36D	BUKH	11	3	17196	5	4	75000	82400
37	7	RIVAL 38C	SLP	SA/CR	FBG	KL	IB	36D	BUKH	11	3	17196	5	4	79300	87200
37	7	RIVAL 38C	CUT	SA/CR	FBG	KL	IB	36D	BUKH	11	3	17196	5	4	79000	86800
37	7	RIVAL 38CK	KTH	SA/CR	FBG	KL	IB	36D	BUKH	11	3	17196	5	4	77800	85500
41		RIVAL 41A	SLP	SA/CR	FBG	KL	IB	50D	PERK	12	3	22046	5	11	104000	114000
41		RIVAL 41A	CUT	SA/CR	FBG	KL	IB	50D	PERK	12	3	22046	5	11	103000	113000
41		RIVAL 41C	SLP	SA/CR	FBG	KL	IB	50D	PERK	12	3	22046	5	11	106000	116500
41		RIVAL 41C	CUT	SA/CR	FBG	KL	IB	50D	PERK	12	3	22046	5	11	105000	115500
41		RIVAL 41CK	KTH	SA/CR	FBG	KL	IB	50D	PERK	12	3	22046	5	11	106000	116500
		1980 BOATS														
34		RIVAL 34	SLP	SA/CR	FBG	KL	IB	20D		9	8	10900	4	8	45000	50000
37	7	RIVAL 38A	SLP	SA/CR	FBG	KL	IB	36D	BUKH	11	3	17196	5	4	73100	80400
37	7	RIVAL 38A	CUT	SA/CR	FBG	KL	IB	36D	BUKH	11	3	17196	5	4	72800	80000
37	7	RIVAL 38C	SLP	SA/CR	FBG	KL	IB	36D	BUKH	11	3	17196	5	4	74500	81800
37	7	RIVAL 38C	CUT	SA/CR	FBG	KL	IB	36D	BUKH	11	3	17196	5	4	74100	81400
37	7	RIVAL 38CK	KTH	SA/CR	FBG	KL	IB	36D	BUKH	11	3	17196	5	4	74300	81700
41		RIVAL 41A	SLP	SA/CR	FBG	KL	IB	50D	THOR	12	3	22046	5	11	99800	109500
41		RIVAL 41A	CUT	SA/CR	FBG	KL	IB	50D	THOR	12	3	22046	5	11	99100	109000
41		RIVAL 41C	SLP	SA/CR	FBG	KL	IB	50D	THOR	12	3	22046	5	11	101500	111500
41		RIVAL 41C	CUT	SA/CR	FBG	KL	IB	50D	THOR	12	3	22046	5	11	100500	110500
41		RIVAL 41CK	KTH	SA/CR	FBG	KL	IB	50D	THOR	12	3	22046	5	11	101500	111500
		1979 BOATS														
34		RIVAL 34	SLP	SA/CR	FBG	KL	IB	20D		9	8	10900	4	8	43200	48000
37	7	RIVAL 38A	SLP	SA/CR	FBG	KL	IB	36D	BUKH	11	3	17196	5	4	70800	77800
37	7	RIVAL 38A	CUT	SA/CR	FBG	KL	IB	36D	BUKH	11	3	17196	5	4	70400	77400
37	7	RIVAL 38CK	KTH	SA/CR	FBG	KL	IB	36D	BUKH	11	3	17196	5	4	71400	78500
41		RIVAL 41A	SLP	SA/CR	FBG	KL	IB	50D	THOR	12	3	22046	5	11	96500	106000
41		RIVAL 41A	CUT	SA/CR	FBG	KL	IB	50D	THOR	12	3	22046	5	11	95600	105000
41		RIVAL 41CK	KTH	SA/CR	FBG	KL	IB	50D	THOR	12	3	22046	5	11	97600	107500
		1978 BOATS														
34		RIVAL 34	SLP	SA/CR	FBG	KL	IB	20D	BUKH	9	8	10900	4	8	41600	46200
37	7	RIVAL 38A	SLP	SA/CR	FBG	KL	IB	36D	BENZ	11	3	17196	5	4	64500	70800
37	7	RIVAL 38C	SLP	SA/CR	FBG	KL	IB	36D	BENZ	11	3	17196	5	4	71400	78500
37	7	RIVAL 38CK	KTH	SA/CR	FBG	KL	IB	36D	BENZ	11	3	17196	5	4	68600	75400

CONTINUED ON NEXT PAGE

LOA FT IN	NAME AND/ OR MODEL		TOP/ RIG	BOAT TYPE	-HULL- MTL TP TP	----ENGINE--- # HP MFG	BEAM FT IN	WGT LBS	DRAFT FT IN	RETAIL LOW	RETAIL HIGH
		1978 BOATS									
41	RIVAL 41		SLP	SA/CR	FBG KL IB	36D BENZ	12 3	22046	5 11	92500	101500
41	RIVAL 41		KTH	SA/CR	FBG KL IB	36D BENZ	12 3	22046	5 11	93700	103000

RIVER CITY SAILCRAFT INC
COAST GUARD MFG ID- RVY

Call 1-800-327-6929 for BUC Personalized Evaluation Service
Or, for 1976 to 1980 boats, sign onto www.BUCValuPro.com

RIVER QUEEN BOAT WORKS
DIV OF U S I INC
GARY IN 46403   COAST GUARD MFG ID- RVB   See inside cover to adjust price for area

LOA FT IN	NAME AND/ OR MODEL		TOP/ RIG	BOAT TYPE	-HULL- MTL TP TP	----ENGINE--- # HP MFG	BEAM FT IN	WGT LBS	DRAFT FT IN	RETAIL LOW	RETAIL HIGH
		1976 BOATS									
40	RIVER-QUEEN		HT	HB	STL FL IO	50	13 6			18300	20300
40	RIVER-QUEEN		HT	HB	STL SV IO	T225	13 6			19900	22100
		1974 BOATS									
40	STAR-STREAM MK II			HB	STL	IO 225 MRCR	13	14000	1 7	18400	20400
	IO 225 VLVO 18700	20800,	IO	T225	MRCR	20400 22700,	IO T225	VLVO		21100	23400
	VD T225 CHRY 19800	22000									
50	NEWPORT			HB	STL	VD T330 CHRY	15	27500	2 8	36100	40100
50	NEWPORT			HB	STL	VD T250D VLVO	15	27500	2 8	41400	46000
		1973 BOATS									
40	STAR-STREAM MK II			HB	STL	IO 225 CHRY	13	14000	2 6	18200	20200
	IO T155 CHRY 19500	21700,	IO	T225	CHRY	20300 22500,	VD T225	CHRY		19700	21900
40	STAR-STREAM MK II	FB	HB	STL	IO T155 CHRY	13	14500	2 6	19500	21700
40	STAR-STREAM MK II	FB	HB	STL	IO T225 CHRY	13	15000	2 6	20300	22500
40	STAR-STREAM MK II	FB	HB	STL	VD T225 CHRY	13	15000	2 6	19700	21900
50	NEWPORT			HB	STL	VD T225 CHRY	15	28500	3 8	35400	39300
50	NEWPORT			HB	STL	VD T280 CHRY	15	28500	3 8	35600	39600
50	NEWPORT			HB	STL	VD T330 CHRY	15	28500	3 8	36200	40300
60	RIVER-QUEEN		HT	HB	STL SV IB	T330	15			38300	42500
		1972 BOATS									
38			HT	HB	STL SV IO	225	12			18100	20100
38			HT	HB	STL SV IO	225	12			17500	19800
40	STAR-STREAM			HB	STL	IO 225 CHRY	13	12000		16000	18100
	VD 225 CHRY 15700	17800,	IO	T155	CHRY	17000 19400,	VD T155	CHRY		16600	18800
	IO T225 CHRY 17400	19800,	VD	T225	CHRY	16800 19100					
40	STAR-STREAM	FB	HB	STL	IO 225 CHRY	13			17500	19900
	VD 225 CHRY 17200	19500,	IO	T155	CHRY	19000 21100,	VD T155	CHRY		18500	20600
	IO T225 CHRY 19200	21300,	VD	T225	CHRY	18800 20900					
43			HT	HB	STL SV IO	225	12			18800	20900
43			HT	HB	STL SV IO	225	12			18600	20700
50			HT	HB	STL SV IB	225	12			32800	36500
50			HT	HB	STL SV IB	225	12			32100	35600
		1971 BOATS									
38	RIVER-QUEEN			HB	STL IO	225 CHRY	12	13000	1 8	18200	20200
38	RIVER-QUEEN			HB	STL IO	T225 CHRY	12	14000	1 8	20300	22500
38	UTILITY RIVER	HT	HB	STL SV IO	225 CHRY	12	11000	2	16000	18200
43 6	RIVER-QUEEN			HB	STL IO	225 CHRY	12	17500	1 8	19400	21600
43 6	RIVER-QUEEN			HB	STL IO	T225 CHRY	12	18500	1 8	21500	23800
50	RIVER-QUEEN			HB	STL IO	T225 CHRY	12	22500	1 8	32700	36300
		1970 BOATS									
32	RIVER-QUEEN			HB	FBG IO	120 CHRY	12			16300	18500
36		HT		HB	FBG SV IO	150 CHRY	12	6000	2	9700	11500
37	RIVER-QUEEN			HB	STL SV IO	225 CHRY	12	11000	1 8	15900	18100
37	RIVER-QUEEN			HB	STL SV IO	T225 CHRY	12	11000	1 8	17400	19800
37	UTILITY RIVER	HT	HB	STL SV IO	225 CHRY	12	11000	2	15900	18100
38	RIVER-QUEEN	HT		HB	STL SV IO	225 CHRY	12	13000	2	18000	20000
40	RIVER-QUEEN			HB	STL SV IO	T225 CHRY	12		2	19100	21200
43	RIVER-QUEEN	HT		HB	STL SV IO	225 CHRY	12	16000	2	18500	20400
50	RIVER-QUEEN			HB	STL SV IO	T225 CHRY	15	20000	2 6	29700	33000
55	RIVER-QUEEN			HB	FBG IO	T225 CHRY	15			35500	39400
		1969 BOATS									
37	RIVER QUEEN	HT	HB	STL IO	225	12	13000	1 8	17500	19900
37	RIVER-QUEEN	HT	UTL	STL IO	225	12	11000	1 8	13600	15500
37	RIVER-QUEEN PH	HT	UTL	STL SV IB	210 CHRY	12		1 8	**	**
37	RIVER-QUEEN STD	HT	HB	STL SV IB	210 CHRY	12		1 8	15500	17600
37	RIVER-QUEEN STD	HT	HB	STL SV IB	T210 CHRY	12		1 8	16600	18900
40	RIVER-QUEEN	HT	HB	STL IO	T225	12	16000	2	20400	22600
40	RIVER-QUEEN DLX	HT	HB	STL SV IB	210 CHRY	12		2	16800	19100
40	RIVER-QUEEN DLX	HT	HB	STL SV IB	T210 CHRY	12		2	18300	20400
50	RIVER-QUEEN	HT	HB	STL IO	T225	14	2000	2	**	**
50	RIVER-QUEEN	HT	HB	STL SV IB	T260 CHRY	14		2 6	32800	36400
		1968 BOATS									
35	RIVER-QUEEN ECONO	HT	HB	STL DV IO	210	12	12000	1 8	16300	18500
35	RIVER-QUEEN PH		UTL	STL	IO 210	12	10000	1 8	12600	14400
35	RIVER-QUEEN PH		UTL	STL	IO 95D	12	10000	1 8	15500	17600
40	RIVER-QUEEN		HB	STL DV IO	210	12	15000	2	18200	20300
40	RIVER-QUEEN		HB	STL IO	T210	12	16000	2	20100	22300
50	RIVER-QUEEN		HB	STL DV IO	T210	14	24000	2 6	32700	36300
		1967 BOATS									
32	RIVER-QUEEN	HT	HB	STL	IO 150	9		2	14600	16600
38	RIVER-QUEEN		HB	STL	IO 150	9	13000	2	17100	19400
38	RIVER-QUEEN		HB	STL	IO 150	9	13000	2	17200	19600
38	RIVER-QUEEN		HB	STL	IO T210	9	13000	2	19000	21100
		1966 BOATS									
38	RIVER-QUEEN		HT	HB	STL DV IO	150			16800	19100
	IO 210 16900	19200,	IO	T150		18500 20500,	IO T210			18700	20800
		1961 BOATS									
28	SUWANNE		HT	HB	STL	OB	11			**	**
28	SUWANNE		HT	HB	STL	IB 30	11	5000		**	**
34	OHIO		HT	HB	STL	OB	11			7750	8900
34	OHIO		HT	HB	STL	OB 70	11	6000		8350	9600
43	MISSISSIPPI		HT	HB	STL	OB	13	12000		12900	14600
		1959 BOATS									
32	OHIO		HT	HB	STL	IB 35	6	5000	6	6450	7400
35	MISSISSIPPI		HT	HB	STL	IB 35	6	8000	6	10700	12200

RIVERSIDE BOAT WORKS

Call 1-800-327-6929 for BUC Personalized Evaluation Service
Or, for 1965 to 1978 boats, sign onto www.BUCValuPro.com

RIVERTON BOAT WORKS
RIVERTON NJ 08077   COAST GUARD MFG ID- LPP See inside cover to adjust price for area
                           FORMERLY LIPPINCOTT BOAT WORKS INC

For more recent years, see the BUC Used Boat Price Guide, Volume 1 or Volume 2

LOA FT IN	NAME AND/ OR MODEL		TOP/ RIG	BOAT TYPE	-HULL- MTL TP TP	----ENGINE--- # HP MFG	BEAM FT IN	WGT LBS	DRAFT FT IN	RETAIL LOW	RETAIL HIGH
		1983 BOATS									
30 4	LIPPINCOTT 30		SLP	SA/CR	FBG KL IB	15D YAN	10	8600	4 11	17000	19300
30 4	LIPPINCOTT 30 SHOAL		SLP	SA/CR	FBG KL IB	15D YAN	10	8600	4 2	17000	19300
35 11	LIPPINCOTT 36		SLP	SA/CR	FBG KL IB	23D YAN	11 1	12500	5	25900	28800
		1982 BOATS									
30 4	LIPPINCOTT 30		SLP	SA/CR	FBG KL IB	15D YAN	10	8600	4 11	15900	18100
30 4	LIPPINCOTT 30 SHOAL		SLP	SA/CR	FBG KL IB	15D YAN	10	8600	4 2	15900	18100
		1981 BOATS									
22 9	STAR		SLP	SA/OD	FBG KL		5 8		3 4	4150	4850
30 4	LIPPINCOTT 30		SLP	SA/CR	FBG KL IB	15D YAN	10	8600	4 11	14900	16900
30 4	LIPPINCOTT 30 SHOAL		SLP	SA/CR	FBG KL IB	15D YAN	10	8600	4 2	14900	16900
		1980 BOATS									
22 9	STAR		SLP	SA/OD	F/S KL		5	1480	3 10	2400	2800
30 4	LIPPINCOTT 30		SLP	SA/CR	FBG KL IB	15D YAN	10	8600	4 11	14200	16100
		1979 BOATS									
30 4	LIPPINCOTT 30		SLP	SA/CR	FBG KL IB	15D YAN	10	8600	4 11	13600	15400
		1978 BOATS									
22 9	STAR		SLP	SA/OD	FBG KL		5 9	1480	3 6	2250	2600
		1977 BOATS									
22 9	STAR		SLP	SA/OD	FBG KL		5 8	1480	3 6	2150	2500
		1976 BOATS									
22 9	STAR		SLP	SA/OD	FBG KL		5 8	1480	3 6	2050	2400
		1975 BOATS									
22 9	STAR		SLP	SA/OD	FBG KL		5 8	1480	3 6	1950	2350
		1974 BOATS									
22 9	STAR		SLP	SA/OD	FBG KL		5 8	1480	3 6	1900	2300
		1973 BOATS									
22 9	STAR		SLP	SA/OD	FBG KL		5 8	1480	3 6	1850	2200
		1972 BOATS									
22 9	STAR		SLP	SA/OD	FBG KL		5 8	1460	3 4	1800	2150
		1971 BOATS									
22 8	STAR		SLP	SA/OD	FBG KL		5 8	1460	3 4	1800	2100

RIVERTON BOAT WORKS   -CONTINUED   See inside cover to adjust price for area

LOA FT IN	NAME AND/ OR MODEL	TOP/ RIG	BOAT TYPE	-HULL- MTL TP	----ENGINE--- TP # HP MFG	BEAM FT IN	WGT LBS	DRAFT FT IN	RETAIL LOW	RETAIL HIGH
----------------- 1970 BOATS ---
22 9	STAR	SLP	SA/OD	FBG KL		5 8	1460	3 4	1750	2100
----------------- 1969 BOATS ---
22 9	STAR	SLP	SA/OD	FBG KL		5 8	1460	3 4	1750	2050
----------------- 1968 BOATS ---
22 7	STAR	SLP	SA/OD	FBG KL		5 8		3 4	2400	2800
22 7	STAR	SLP	SA/OD	WD KL		5 8		3 4	2400	2800
----------------- 1967 BOATS ---
22 9	STAR	SLP	SA/OD	FBG KL		5 8	1460	3 4	1700	2050
----------------- 1965 BOATS ---
22 9	STAR	SLP	SA/OD	WD KL		5 8		3 4	2350	2700
----------------- 1961 BOATS ---
22 9	STAR	SLP	SA/OD	KL		5 8		3 4	2300	2650
----------------- 1960 BOATS ---
22 8	STAR	SLP	SA/OD	WD KL		5 8	1460	3 4	1700	2050

RIVIERA CRUISER
DIV OF L M L CORPORATION   See inside cover to adjust price for area
COLUMBIA CITY IN 46725   COAST GUARD MFG ID- RCD

For more recent years, see the BUC Used Boat Price Guide, Volume 1 or Volume 2

LOA FT IN	NAME AND/ OR MODEL	TOP/ RIG	BOAT TYPE	-HULL- MTL TP	----ENGINE--- TP # HP MFG	BEAM FT IN	WGT LBS	DRAFT FT IN	RETAIL LOW	RETAIL HIGH
----------------- 1979 BOATS ---
28	HB-28	HT	HB	AL PN	OB	8	2695	11	**	**
----------------- 1978 BOATS ---
28	HOUSEBOAT HB-28	HT	HB	AL PN	OB	8	2695	11	**	**

RO-MO-SAIL
Call 1-800-327-6929 for BUC Personalized Evaluation Service
Or, for 1960 to 1961 boats, sign onto www.BUCValuPro.com

ROBALO BOATS LLC
DIV OF MARINE PRODUCTS CORP   See inside cover to adjust price for area
NASHVILLE GA 31639   COAST GUARD MFG ID- FGBR
                         FORMERLY ROBALO MARINE

For more recent years, see the BUC Used Boat Price Guide, Volume 1 or Volume 2

LOA FT IN	NAME AND/ OR MODEL	TOP/ RIG	BOAT TYPE	-HULL- MTL TP	----ENGINE--- TP # HP MFG	BEAM FT IN	WGT LBS	DRAFT FT IN	RETAIL LOW	RETAIL HIGH
----------------- 1983 BOATS ---
18 1	ROBALO 1820	OP	CTRCN	FBG DV	OB	7 3	2215		3800	4400
19 4	ROBALO 2020	OP	CTRCN	FBG DV	OB	8	2230		4000	4650
21 4	ROBALO 2120	OP	CTRCN	FBG DV	OB	8	2420		5800	6700
21 4	ROBALO 2160	OP	CUD	FBG DV	OB	8	3070		6650	7650
21 4	ROBALO 2163	OP	CUD	FBG DV	SE 205 OMC	8	4020		7200	8300
21 4	ROBALO 2165	OP	CUD	FBG DV	IO 170-200	8	4020		6000	6950
23 2	ROBALO 2320	OP	CTRCN	FBG DV	OB	8	3100		7700	8850
25 6	ROBALO 2520	OP	CUD	FBG DV	OB	8	3350		9550	10800
26	ROBALO 2660	OP	CUD	FBG DV	OB	8	4700		11300	12900
26	ROBALO 2660	OP	CUD	FBG DV	SE 205 OMC	8	4700		11300	12900
26	ROBALO 2663	OP	CUD	FBG DV	SE T155 OMC	8	5600		11800	13400
26 5	SPORTSFISHERMAN	OP	SF	FBG DV	SE T205 OMC	10 2	7780		12700	14400
26 5	SPORTSFISHERMAN	OP	SF	FBG DV	SE T225 OMC	10 2	7780		18700	20700
	IO T228 MRCR 16800	19100,	IB T250-T260	18900	21000, IO T 35D VLVO		19900		22100
----------------- 1982 BOATS ---
18 1	ROBALO 1820	OP	CTRCN	FBG DV	OB	7 3	1840		3350	3900
19 4	ROBALO 2020	OP	CTRCN	FBG DV	OB	8	1900		3600	4200
21 4	ROBALO 2120	OP	CTRCN	FBG DV	OB	8	2150		5250	6050
21 4	ROBALO 2160	OP	CUD	FBG DV	OB	8	1960		4900	5650
21 4	ROBALO 2163	OP	CUD	FBG DV	OB	8	4014		7050	8150
21 4	ROBALO 2165	OP	CUD	FBG DV	IO 170-200	8	4014		5800	6750
23 2	ROBALO 2320	OP	CTRCN	FBG DV	OB	8	2786		6950	8000
25 6	ROBALO 2520	OP	CTRCN	FBG DV	OB	8	3220		9250	10500
26 5	SPORTSFISHERMAN	OP	SF	FBG DV	OB	10 2	7000		12300	14000
26 5	SPORTSFISHERMAN	OP	SF	FBG DV	IB T225-T255	10 2	7000		16600	19100
26 5	SPORTSFISHERMAN	OP	SF	FBG DV	IB T 40D VLVO	10 2	7000		18600	20700
26 5	SPORTSFISHERMAN	OP	SF	FBG DV	IB T148D VLVO	10 2	7000		22500	25100
----------------- 1981 BOATS ---
18 1	ROBALO 1820	OP	CTRCN	FBG DV	OB	7 3	1840		3300	3850
19 4	ROBALO 2020	OP	CTRCN	FBG DV	OB	8	1900		3550	4150
21 4	ROBALO 2120	OP	CTRCN	FBG DV	OB	8	2344		5500	6300
21 4	ROBALO 2160	OP	CUD	FBG DV	OB	8	2655		5950	6850
21 4	ROBALO 2165	OP	CUD	FBG DV	IO 170-230	8	4014		5750	6700
23	ROBALO 2360	OP	CUD	FBG DV	IO 200	8	2712		6650	7650
23 2	ROBALO 2365	OP	CUD	FBG DV	IO 200	8	3367		5550	6400
23 2	ROBALO 2320	OP	CTRCN	FBG DV	OB	8	2686		6650	7650
25 6	ROBALO 2520	OP	CTRCN	FBG DV	OB	8	3220		9100	10300
26 5	SPORTSFISHERMAN	OP	SF	FBG DV	IB T170-T255	10 2	7000		14800	18300
26 5	SPORTSFISHERMAN	OP	SF	FBG DV	IB T 40D VLVO	10 2	7000		17500	19900
----------------- 1980 BOATS ---
18 1	ROBALO 181	OP	OPFSH	FBG DV	OB	7 3	2000		3450	4000
19 5	ROBALO 200	OP	OPFSH	FBG DV	OB	8	2130		3750	4400
23	ROBALO 232	ST	OPFSH	FBG DV	OB	8	2760		6600	7600
23	ROBALO 236	ST	OPFSH	FBG DV	OB	8	2620		6350	7300
23	ROBALO 236	OP	OPFSH	FBG DV	IO 170-260	8	3820		6400	7600
25 6	ROBALO 256	OP	OPFSH	FBG DV	OB	8	3220		8950	10100
26 4	ROBALO 260	OP	SF	FBG DV	IB 255-330	10 1	7000		13200	15600
26 4	ROBALO 260	OP	SF	FBG DV	IB T170-T255	10 1	7000		14100	16900

ARTHUR ROBB
Call 1-800-327-6929 for BUC Personalized Evaluation Service
Or, for 1969 boats, sign onto www.BUCValuPro.com

ROBERTS & MATTHEWS YT CORP
COAST GUARD MFG ID- RAR

Call 1-800-327-6929 for BUC Personalized Evaluation Service
Or, for 1976 to 1982 boats, sign onto www.BUCValuPro.com

ROBERTS & OLTHOUSE
BARRACUDA

Call 1-800-327-6929 for BUC Personalized Evaluation Service
Or, for 1959 boats, sign onto www.BUCValuPro.com

ROBERTSON'S OF SANDBANK
Call 1-800-327-6929 for BUC Personalized Evaluation Service
Or, for 1971 to 1979 boats, sign onto www.BUCValuPro.com

ALEXANDER ROBERTSON
Call 1-800-327-6929 for BUC Personalized Evaluation Service
Or, for 1970 boats, sign onto www.BUCValuPro.com

ROBINHOOD MARINA INC
Call 1-800-327-6929 for BUC Personalized Evaluation Service
Or, for 1967 boats, sign onto www.BUCValuPro.com

ROBINSON YACHTS INC
COAST GUARD MFG ID- RBY

Call 1-800-327-6929 for BUC Personalized Evaluation Service
Or, for 1975 to 1977 boats, sign onto www.BUCValuPro.com

JEROME ROBINSON
Call 1-800-327-6929 for BUC Personalized Evaluation Service
Or, for 1959 to 1966 boats, sign onto www.BUCValuPro.com

ROCS MARINE
Call 1-800-327-6929 for BUC Personalized Evaluation Service
Or, for 1980 boats, sign onto www.BUCValuPro.com

RODGERS YACHT & DESIGN

COAST GUARD MFG ID- RYH

Call 1-800-327-6929 for BUC Personalized Evaluation Service
Or, for 1980 to 1984 boats, sign onto www.BUCValuPro.com

ROGERS MARINE

Call 1-800-327-6929 for BUC Personalized Evaluation Service
Or, for 1974 to 1979 boats, sign onto www.BUCValuPro.com

JEREMY ROGERS

LYMINGTON ENGLAND

See inside cover to adjust price for area

LOA FT	LOA IN	NAME AND/ OR MODEL	TOP/ RIG	BOAT TYPE	-HULL- MTL	-HULL- TP	ENGINE TP	# HP	MFG	BEAM FT	BEAM IN	WGT LBS	DRAFT FT	DRAFT IN	RETAIL LOW	RETAIL HIGH
		1983 BOATS														
27	8	CONTESSA 28	SLP	SA/RC	FBG	KL	IB	D		9	5	6970	4	10	21600	24000
32		CONTESSA 32	SLP	SA/RC	FBG	KL	IB	D		9	6	9500	5	6	33100	36700
33	8	ONE-DESIGN 34	SLP	SA/RC	FBG	KL	IB	D		11	1	8050	6	4	28100	31200
38	2	CONTESSA 38	SLP	SA/CR	FBG	KL	IB	D		11	3	15900	6	1	59600	65500
38	8	ROGERS 39	SLP	SA/RC	FBG	KL	IB	D		12	3	14250	7	3	56200	61800
42	9	CONTESSA 43	SLP	SA/RC	FBG	KL	IB	D		12	6	21000	7	3	85100	93500
		1982 BOATS														
27	8	CONTESSA 28	SLP	SA/RC	FBG	KL	IB	D		9	5	6970	4	10	20500	22800
32		CONTESSA 32	SLP	SA/RC	FBG	KL	IB	D		9	6	9500	5	6	31400	34900
33	8	ONE DESIGN 34	SLP	SA/RC	FBG	KL	IB	D		11	1	8050	6	4	26700	29600
38	2	CONTESSA 38	SLP	SA/CR	FBG	KL	IB	D		11	3	15900	6	1	56600	62200
38	8	ROGERS 39	SLP	SA/RC	FBG	KL	IB	D		12	3	14250	7	3	53600	58900
42	9	CONTESSA 43	SLP	SA/RC	FBG	KL	IB	D		12	6	21000	7	3	80800	88700
		1981 BOATS														
27	8	CONTESSA 28	SLP	SA/RC	FBG	KL	IB	D		9	5	6970	4	10	19800	22000
32		CONTESSA 32	SLP	SA/RC	FBG	KL	IB	D		9	6	9500	5	6	29800	33200
33	8	ONE DESIGN 34	SLP	SA/RC	FBG	KL	IB	D		11	1	8050	6	4	25400	28300
35	6	CONTESSA 35	SLP	SA/RC	FBG	KL	IB	D		11	5	14000	6	4	44400	49300
38	8	ROGERS 39	SLP	SA/RC	FBG	KL	IB	D		12	3	14250	7	3	50800	55800
42	9	CONTESSA 43	SLP	SA/RC	FBG	KL	IB	D		12	6	21000	7	3	76800	84400
		1980 BOATS														
27	8	CONTESSA 28	SLP	SA/RC	FBG	KL	IB	D		9	5	6970	4	10	18900	21000
32		CONTESSA 32	SLP	SA/RC	FBG	KL	IB	D		9	6	9500	5	6	28500	31600
33	8	ONE-DESIGN 34	SLP	SA/RC	FBG	KL	IB	D		11	1	8050	6	4	24300	27000
35	6	CONTESSA 35	SLP	SA/RC	FBG	KL	IB	D		11	5	14000	6	4	42400	47100
38	8	ROGERS 39	SLP	SA/RC	FBG	KL	IB	D		12	3	13500	7	3	46800	51400
42	9	CONTESSA 43	SLP	SA/RC	FBG	KL	IB	D		12	6	21000	7	3	73200	80500

ROSBOROUGH BOATS LTD

HALIFAX NS CANADA B3P 1B3

See inside cover to adjust price for area

For more recent years, see the BUC Used Boat Price Guide, Volume 1 or Volume 2

LOA FT	LOA IN	NAME AND/ OR MODEL	TOP/ RIG	BOAT TYPE	-HULL- MTL	-HULL- TP	ENGINE TP	# HP	MFG	BEAM FT	BEAM IN	WGT LBS	DRAFT FT	DRAFT IN	RETAIL LOW	RETAIL HIGH
		1983 BOATS														
18	4	RF-18	HT	CUD	FBG	SV	OB			7	5			7	4600	5300
18	4	RF-18	OP	UTL	FBG	SV	OB			7	5			7	4150	4800
28	3	RF-28 BANKS-CRUISER	HT	TRWL	FBG	DS	IB			9	8	6500	3	2	**	**
28	3	RF-28 CRUISER	HT	TRWL	FBG	DS	IB			9	8	6500	3	2	**	**
28	3	RF-28 SEDAN	HT	TRWL	FBG	DS	IB			9	8	6500	3	2	**	**
28	3	RF28	OP	TRWL	FBG	DS	IB			9	8	6500	3	2	**	**
28	3	RF28	HT	TRWL	FBG	DS	IB			9	8	6500	3	2	**	**
30		R-30	KTH	SA/CR	WD	KL	IB	12D	WEST	8	10	9850	3	8	22000	24500
31	3	TERN	KTH	SA/CR	WD	KL	IB	D		9	8	13600	5		30700	34100
32		DESTINY	KTH	SA/CR	WD	KL	IB	50D	PERK	11		14000	4	5	31400	34800
34	4	PILGRIM	CUT	SA/CR	WD	KL	IB	50D	PERK	11		22000	5		47600	52300
37	8	JOLLY-ROGER	KTH	SA/CR	WD	KL	IB	85D	PERK	12		28000	5		58100	63900
39	7	NOMAD	KTH	SA/CR	WD	KL	IB	85D	PERK	12		36000	6	3	70900	77900
45	8	NOR'EASTER	KTH	SA/CR	WD	KL	IB			12	9	36000	5	9	76000	83600
45	10	BUCCANEER	SCH	SA/CR	WD	KL	IB	85D	PERK	13	3	42000	5	11	82600	90800
45	10	DISTANT-STAR	SCH	SA/CR	WD	KL	IB	85D	PERK	13	3	46000	6	1	86100	94600
45	10	PRIVATEER	KTH	SA/CR	WD	KL	IB	85D	PERK	13	3	42000	5	11	82600	90800
45	10	SEA-SONG	SCH	SA/CR	WD	KL	IB	85D	PERK	13	3	42000	5	11	82600	90800
55	6	AQUARIUS	SQ	SA/CR	WD	KL	IB	85D	PERK	15	9	75000	6	3	141500	155500
56		LOYALIST	SQ	SA/CR	WD	KL	IB	85D	PERK	14	6	76000	6	6	145500	160000
64	6	VAGABOND	KTH	SA/CR	WD	KL	IB	85D	PERK	17		55T	7	2	263000	289000
79	6	VIKING	SQ	SA/CR	WD	KL	IB	85D	PERK	21	6	78T	9	9	**	**
		1982 BOATS														
30		R-30	KTH	SA/CR	WD	KL	IB	12D	WEST	8	10	10000	3	8	21100	23400
32		DESTINY	KTH	SA/CR	WD	KL	IB	50D	PERK	11		14000	4	5	29500	32800
35		PILGRIM	KTH	SA/CR	WD	KL	IB	50D	PERK	11		28000	5	6	54900	60300
38		JOLLY-ROGER	KTH	SA/CR	WD	KL	IB	85D	PERK	12		28000	5	6	54800	60300
40		NOMAD	KTH	SA/CR	WD	KL	IB	85D	PERK	12		36000	6	3	67000	73700
43		SEA-SONG	SCH	SA/CR	WD	KL	IB	85D	PERK	13	3	42000	5	11	74600	82000
46		BUCCANEER	SCH	SA/CR	WD	KL	IB	85D	PERK	13	3	42000	5	11	77900	85600
46		DISTANT-STAR	SCH	SA/CR	WD	KL	IB	85D	PERK	13	3	46000	6	1	81200	89200
46		PRIVATEER	KTH	SA/CR	WD	KL	IB	85D	PERK	13	3	42000	5	11	77900	85700
55	6	AQUARIUS	SQ	SA/CR	WD	KL	IB	85D	PERK	15	9	75000	6	3	133500	146500
56		LOYALIST	SQ	SA/CR	WD	KL	IB	85D	PERK	14	6	76000	6	6	137500	151000
65		VAGABOND	KTH	SA/CR	WD	KL	IB	85D	PERK	17		55T	7	2	244500	269000
		1981 BOATS														
30		R-30	KTH	SA/CR	WD	KL	IB	12D	WEST	8	10	10000	3	8	19800	22000
32		DESTINY	KTH	SA/CR	WD	KL	IB	50D	PERK	11		14000	4	5	27800	30800
35		PILGRIM	KTH	SA/CR	WD	KL	IB	50D	PERK	11		28000	5	6	51700	56800
38		JOLLY ROGER	KTH	SA/CR	WD	KL	IB	85D	PERK	12		28000	5	6	51600	56700
40		NOMAD	KTH	SA/CR	WD	KL	IB	85D	PERK	12		36000	6	3	63100	69300
43		SEA-SONG	SCH	SA/CR	WD	KL	IB	85D	PERK	13	3	42000	5	11	70200	77100
46		BUCCANEER	SCH	SA/CR	WD	KL	IB	85D	PERK	13	3	42000	5	11	73300	80600
46		DISTANT-STAR	SCH	SA/CR	WD	KL	IB	85D	PERK	13	3	46000	6	1	76400	83900
46		PRIVATEER	KTH	SA/CR	WD	KL	IB	85D	PERK	13	3	42000	5	11	73300	80600
55	6	AQUARIUS	SQ	SA/CR	WD	KL	IB	85D	PERK	15	9	75000	6	3	126000	138500
56		LOYALIST	SQ	SA/CR	WD	KL	IB	85D	PERK	14	6	76000	6	6	130000	142500
65		VAGABOND	KTH	SA/CR	WD	KL	IB	85D	PERK	17		55T	7	2	230000	253000
		1980 BOATS														
30		R-30	KTH	SA/CR	WD	KL	IB	12D	WEST	8	10	10000	3	8	19100	21300
31		TERN	SCH	SA/CR	WD	KL	IB	50D	PERK	9	8	14000	4	10	26700	29700
32		DESTINY	KTH	SA/CR	WD	KL	IB	50D	PERK	11		14000	4	5	26500	29400
35		PILGRIM	KTH	SA/CR	WD	KL	IB	50D	PERK	11		28000	5	6	49300	54200
38		JOLLY ROGER	KTH	SA/CR	WD	KL	IB	85D	PERK	12		28000	5	6	49300	54100
43		SEA-SONG	SCH	SA/CR	WD	KL	IB	85D	PERK	13	3	42000	5	11	67000	73700
45		NOR'EASTER	KTH	SA/CR	WD	KL	IB	85D	PERK	12	9	36000	5	9	63900	70300
46		BUCCANEER	SCH	SA/CR	WD	KL	IB	85D	PERK	13	3	42000	5	11	70000	76900
46		DISTANT-STAR	SCH	SA/CR	WD	KL	IB	85D	PERK	13	3	46000	6	1	73000	80200
46		PRIVATEER	KTH	SA/CR	WD	KL	IB	85D	PERK	13	3	42000	5	11	70000	77000
55	6	AQUARIUS	SQ	SA/CR	WD	KL	IB	85D	PERK	15	9	75000	6	3	120000	132000
56		LOYALIST	SQ	SA/CR	WD	KL	IB	85D	PERK	14	6	76000	6	6	124000	136000
65		VAGABOND	KTH	SA/CR	WD	KL	IB	85D	PERK	17		55T	7	2	217500	239000
		1979 BOATS														
30		R-30	KTH	SA/CR	WD	KL	IB	12D	YAN	8	10	10000	3	8	18400	20400
32		DESTINY	KTH	SA/CR	WD	KL	IB	50D	PERK	11		14000	4	5	25500	28300
35		PILGRIM	KTH	SA/CR	WD	KL	IB	50D	PERK	11		28000	5		47700	52400
43		SEA-SONG	SCH	SA/CR	WD	KL	IB	85D	PERK	13	3	42000	5	11	64500	70800
46		BUCCANEER	SCH	SA/CR	WD	KL	IB	85D	PERK	13	3	42000	5	11	67300	74000
46		DISTANT-STAR BRIG	SQ	SA/CR	WD	KL	IB	85D	PERK	13	3	42000	5	11	67300	74000
46		PRIVATEER	KTH	SA/CR	WD	KL	IB	85D	PERK	13	3	42000	5	11	67300	74000
55	6	AQUARIUS BRIG/BARQ	SQ	SA/CR	WD	KL	IB	160D	PERK	15	9	74000	6	3	115500	127000
64	6	VAGABOND BRIG/BARQ	SQ	SA/CR	WD	KL	IB	160D	PERK	17		55T	7	2	211500	232000
		1978 BOATS														
30		R-30	KTH	SAIL	WD	KL	IB	10D	WEST	8	10	10000	3	8	17300	19700
32		DESTINY	KTH	SAIL	WD	KL	IB	50D	PERK	11		14000	4	5	24600	27300
34		PILGRIM	CUT	SAIL	WD	KL	IB	50D	PERK	11		22000	5		37000	41100
38		JOLLY-ROGER	KTH	SAIL	WD	KL	IB	85D	PERK	12		28000	5	6	45900	50400
43		SEA-SONG	SCH	SAIL	WD	KL	IB	85D	PERK	13	3	42000	5	11	62100	68300
46		BUCCANEER	SCH	SAIL	WD	KL	IB	85D	PERK	13	3	42000	5	11	64900	71300
46		DISTANT-STAR	SQ	SAIL	WD	KL	IB	85D	PERK	13	3	46000	5	11	67600	74300
46		PRIVATEER	KTH	SAIL	WD	KL	IB	85D	PERK	13	3	42000	5	11	64900	71300
55		AQUARIUS	SQ	SAIL	WD	KL	IB	160D	PERK	15	9	70000	6	6	106500	117500
55	8	LOYALIST	SCH	SAIL	WD	KL	IB	160D	PERK	14	6	78000	6	6	113000	124000
65		VAGABOND	SCH	SAIL	WD	KL	IB	210D	CAT	17		55T	7	5	201500	221500
65		VAGABOND	SCH	SAIL	WD	KL	IB	T160D	PERK	17		55T	7	5	200500	220500
65		VAGABOND	SQ	SAIL	WD	KL	IB	210D	CAT	17		55T	7	5	201500	221500
65		VAGABOND	SQ	SAIL	WD	KL	IB	T160D	PERK	17		55T	7	5	200500	220500
		1977 BOATS														
30		R-30	KTH	SA/CR	WD	KL	IB	10D	WEST	8	10	9850	3	8	16500	18700
31	3	TERN	SCH	SA/CR	WD	KL	IB	50D	PERK	9	8	13600	5		23200	25800
32		DESTINY	SCH	SA/CR	WD	KL	IB	50D	PERK	11		14000	4	5	23700	26400
32		DESTINY	CUT	SA/CR	WD	KL	IB	50D	PERK	11		14000	4	5	23700	26400
32		DESTINY	KTH	SA/CR	WD	KL	IB	50D	PERK	11		14000	4	5	23700	26400
35		PILGRIM	CUT	SA/CR	WD	KL	IB	50D	PERK	11		22000	5		35500	39500
38		JOLLY-ROGER	KTH	SA/CR	WD	KL	IB	85D	PERK	12		28000	5	6	43900	48700
43		SEA-SONG	SCH	SA/CR	WD	KL	IB	85D	PERK	13	3	42000	5	11	60100	66000
45	8	NOR-EASTER	KTH	SA/CR	WD	KL	IB	D		12	9	36000	5	9	58300	64000
46		BUCCANEER	SCH	SA/CR	WD	KL	IB	85D	PERK	13	3	42000	5	11	62700	68900
46		DISTANT-STAR	SQ	SA/CR	WD	KL	IB	85D	PERK	13	3	46000	5	11	65300	71800
46		PRIVATEER	KTH	SA/CR	WD	KL	IB	85D	PERK	13	3	42000	5	11	62700	68900

CONTINUED ON NEXT PAGE

ROSBOROUGH BOATS LTD   -CONTINUED   See inside cover to adjust price for area

LOA FT IN	NAME AND/ OR MODEL	TOP/ RIG	BOAT TYPE	-HULL- MTL TP TP	----ENGINE--- # HP MFG	BEAM FT IN	WGT LBS	DRAFT FT IN	RETAIL LOW	RETAIL HIGH
			---- 1977 BOATS							
55	AQUARIUS	SQ	SA/CR WD	KL IB	160D PERK	15 9	76000	6 6	104500	115000
55 8	LOYALIST	SCH	SA/CR WD	KL IB	160D PERK	14 6	78000	6 6	109000	119500
65	VAGABOND	SQ	SA/CR WD	KL IB	210D CAT	21 6	55T	9 9	194500	213500
65	VAGABOND	SQ	SA/CR WD	KL IB	T160D PERK	21 6	55T	9 9	193500	213000
			---- 1976 BOATS							
30	R-30	KTH	SAIL WD	KL IB	10D WEST	8 10	10000	3 8	16200	18400
31 3	TERN	KTH	SAIL WD	KL IB	D	9 8	15000	4 10	24800	27500
32	DESTINY	KTH	SAIL WD	KL IB	50D PERK	11	14000	4 5	23000	25500
34	PILGRIM	CUT	SAIL WD	KL IB	50D PERK	11	22000	5	34600	38500
38	JOLLY-ROGER	KTH	SAIL WD	KL IB	85D PERK	12	28000	5 6	42500	47200
43	SEA-SONG	SCH	SAIL WD	KL IB	85D PERK	13 3	42000	5 11	58200	63900
45 8	NOR-EASTER	KTH	SAIL WD	KL IB	D	12 9	40000	5 9	59300	65100
46	BUCCANEER	SCH	SAIL WD	KL IB	85D PERK	13 3	42000	5 11	60700	66700
46	DISTANT-STAR	SQ	SAIL WD	KL IB	85D PERK	13 3	46000	5 11	63300	69500
46	PRIVATEER	KTH	SAIL WD	KL IB	85D PERK	13 3	42000	5 11	60800	66800
55	AQUARIUS	SQ	SAIL WD	KL IB	160D PERK	15 9	76000	6 6	101000	111000
55 8	LOYALIST	SCH	SAIL WD	KL IB	160D PERK	14 6	78000	6 6	105000	115500
65	VAGABOND	SCH	SAIL WD	KL IB	210D CAT	17	55T	7 5	188000	206500
65	VAGABOND	SQ	SAIL WD	KL IB	T160D PERK	17	55T	7 5	187500	206000
			---- 1975 BOATS							
30	R-30	KTH	SAIL WD	KL IB	10D WEST	8 10	10000	3 8	15800	17900
31	TERN	SCH	SAIL WD	KL IB	50D PERK	9 8	14000	4 10	22500	25000
32	DESTINY	SCH	SAIL WD	KL IB	50D PERK	11	14000	4 5	22300	24800
32	DESTINY	CUT	SAIL WD	KL IB	50D PERK	11	14000	4 5	22300	24800
32	DESTINY	KTH	SAIL WD	KL IB	50D PERK	11	14000	4 5	22300	24800
34	PILGRIM	CUT	SAIL WD	KL IB	50D PERK	11	22000	5	33600	37400
38	JOLLY-ROGER	KTH	SAIL WD	KL IB	85D PERK	12	28000	5 6	41300	45900
43	SEA-SONG	SCH	SAIL WD	KL IB	85D PERK	13 3	42000	5 11	56500	62100
45	NOR-EASTER	KTH	SAIL WD	KL IB	85D PERK	12 9	36000	5 9	53900	59200
46	BUCCANEER	SCH	SAIL WD	KL IB	85D PERK	13 3	42000	5 11	58900	64700
46	DISTANT-STAR	SQ	SAIL WD	KL IB	85D PERK	13 3	46000	5 11	61400	67500
46	PRIVATEER	KTH	SAIL WD	KL IB	85D PERK	13 3	42000	5 11	59000	64800
55	AQUARIUS	SQ	SAIL WD	KL IB	160D PERK	15 9	76000	6 6	97500	107000
55	AQUARIUS	SQ	SAIL WD	KL IB	T 85D PERK	15 9	76000	6 6	98100	108000
65	VAGABOND	SCH	SAIL WD	KL IB	210D CAT	17	55T	7 5	182500	200500
65	VAGABOND	SCH	SAIL WD	KL IB	T160D PERK	17	55T	7 5	181500	199500
			---- 1974 BOATS							
29 6	R-30	KTH	SAIL WD	OB		8 10		3 8	9400	10700
30	DESTINY		SAIL WD	IB	50D PERK	11		4 5	13500	15400
31 3	TERN		SAIL WD	OB		8		4 10	12300	14000
45 8	NOR-EASTER		SAIL WD	IB	85D PERK	12 9		5 9	47300	52200
46	BUCCANEER		SAIL WD	IB	85D PERK	15 3		5 11	47500	52200
46	DISTANT-STAR		SAIL WD	IB	85D PERK	15 3		6 1	49600	54500
46	PRIVATEER		SAIL WD	IB	85D PERK	15 3		5 11	46200	50800
50 5	AQUARIUS		SAIL WD	IB	85D PERK	15 9		6 3	62500	68700
65	VAGABOND		SAIL WD	IB	T 85D PERK	17		7 5	97700	107500
			---- 1972 BOATS							
30	DESTINY	SCH	SA/CR WD	KL IB	D	11		4 5	12900	14600
30	DESTINY	KTH	SA/CR WD	KL IB	D	11		4 5	12900	14600
31 3	TERN	SCH	SA/CR WD	KL IB	D	9 8		5	15100	17100
31 3	TERN	KTH	SA/CR WD	KL IB	D	9 8		5	15100	17100
45 10	BUCCANEER	SCH	SA/CR WD	KL IB	D	13 3		5 11	44800	49700
45 10	DISTANT-STAR BRIG	SQ	SA/CR WD	KL IB	D	13 3		5 11	44900	49900
45 10	PRIVATEER	KTH	SA/CR WD	KL IB	D	13 3		5 11	45000	50000
50	AQUARIUS BARQ	SQ	SA/CR WD	KL IB	D	14 6		6 2	58600	64400
			---- 1971 BOATS							
30	DESTINY	SCH	SA/CR WD	KL IB	D	11		4 5	12600	14300
30	DESTINY	KTH	SA/CR WD	KL IB	D	11		4 5	12600	14300
31 3	TERN	SCH	SA/CR WD	KL IB	D	9 8		5	14800	16800
31 3	TERN	KTH	SA/CR WD	KL IB	D	9 8		5	14800	16800
45 10	BUCCANEER	SCH	SA/CR WD	KL IB	D	13 3		5 11	43800	48700
45 10	DISTANT-STAR	SQ	SA/CR WD	KL IB	D	13 3		5 11	43900	48900
45 10	PRIVATEER	KTH	SA/CR WD	KL IB	D	13 3		5 11	44100	49000
			---- 1970 BOATS							
45	BUCCANEER	SCH	SA/CR WD	KL IB	D	13 3		5 11	43800	48700
45	DISTANT-STAR	SQ	SA/CR WD	KL IB	D	13 3		6 1	43900	48700
45	PRIVATEER	KTH	SA/CR WD	KL IB	D	13 3		5 11	44000	48800
			---- 1969 BOATS							
45 10	BUCCANEER	SCH	SA/CR WD	KL IB	D	13 3		5 11	42200	46900
45 10	DISTANT-STAR BRIG	SQ	SA/CR WD	KL IB	D	13 3		5 11	42400	47100
45 10	PRIVATEER	KTH	SA/CR WD	KL IB	D	13 3		5 11	42600	47300

ED ROSS INDUSTRIES INC
COAST GUARD MFG ID- ERS

Call 1-800-327-6929 for BUC Personalized Evaluation Service
Or, for 1982 boats, sign onto www.BUCValuPro.com

ROSS MARINE INC

Call 1-800-327-6929 for BUC Personalized Evaluation Service
Or, for 1981 to 1992 boats, sign onto www.BUCValuPro.com

ROSSITER YACHTS LTD
COAST GUARD MFG ID- PUR
FORMERLY PURBROOK ROSSITER

Call 1-800-327-6929 for BUC Personalized Evaluation Service
Or, for 1979 to 1993 boats, sign onto www.BUCValuPro.com

MCKIE W ROTH JR BOATBUILDER

Call 1-800-327-6929 for BUC Personalized Evaluation Service
Or, for 1965 boats, sign onto www.BUCValuPro.com

ROUGHWATER BOATS
MARINE DEL REY CA 90292 COAST GUARD MFG ID- RWB See inside cover to adjust price for area
FORMERLY ROUGHWATER YACHTS INC

For more recent years, see the BUC Used Boat Price Guide, Volume 1 or Volume 2

LOA FT IN	NAME AND/ OR MODEL	TOP/ RIG	BOAT TYPE	-HULL- MTL TP TP	----ENGINE--- # HP MFG	BEAM FT IN	WGT LBS	DRAFT FT IN	RETAIL LOW	RETAIL HIGH
			---- 1983 BOATS							
32 1	ROUGHWATER 33	SLP	SA/CR FBG	KL IB	20D YAN	9 9	15000	4 9	27500	30500
37	ROUGHWATER 37	FB	CR FBG	DS IB	215D GM	11 7	16400	4	54200	59600
37	ROUGHWATER 37	HT	SDN FBG	DS IB	215D GM	11 7	16400	4	54200	59600
41	ROUGHWATER 41	HT	TCMY FBG	DS IB	215D GM	13	21000	4	69100	75900
			---- 1982 BOATS							
32 1	ROUGHWATER 33	SLP	SA/CR FBG	KL IB	22D YAN	9 9	15000	4 9	25800	28700
37	ROUGHWATER 37	FB	CR FBG	DS IB	240D PERK	11 7	16400	4	52500	57700
37	ROUGHWATER 37	HT	SDN FBG	DS IB	240D PERK	11 7	16400	4	52700	57900
41	ROUGHWATER 41	HT	TCMY FBG	DS IB	240D PERK	13	21000	4	67500	74100
			---- 1981 BOATS							
29 6	ROUGHWATER 29	HT	CR FBG	DS IB	80D LEHM	8	6300	3	13400	15200
32 1	ROUGHWATER 33	SLP	SA/CR FBG	KL IB	22D YAN	9 9	15000	4 9	23200	27000
35 9	ROUGHWATER 36		CR FBG	KL IB	200D	11 5			47900	52700
35 9	ROUGHWATER 36	SLP	MS FBG	KL IB	200D	11 5	15000	3 8	24700	27500
37	ROUGHWATER 37	FB	CR FBG	DS IB	200D PERK	11 7	16400	4	49700	54600
37	ROUGHWATER 37	HT	SDN FBG	DS IB	200D PERK	11 7	16400	4	49700	54600
41	ROUGHWATER 41	HT	TCMY FBG	DS IB	200D PERK	13	22000	4	67500	74200
			---- 1980 BOATS							
29 6	ROUGHWATER 29	HT	CR FBG	DS IB	80D FORD	8	6300	3	12900	14600
32 1	ROUGHWATER 33	SLP	SA/CR FBG	KL IB	22D YAN	9 9	15000	4 9	23200	25800
35 9	ROUGHWATER 36	MS	FBG	KL IB	185D	11 5			24200	26800
36 6	ROUGHWATER 36	FB	CR FBG	DS IB	185D	11 5	14000		40900	45400
36 6	ROUGHWATER 36	FB	SDN FBG	DS IB	185D	11 5	16000	3 4	45400	50000
41	ROUGHWATER 41	HT	TCMY FBG	DS IB	185D	13	21000		61500	67600
41	ROUGHWATER 41	HT	TCMY FBG	DS IB	200D PERK	13	22000	4	64400	70800
58	ROUGHWATER 58		OFF FBG	DS IB	265D	13 8			99500	109500
			---- 1979 BOATS							
32 1	ROUGHWATER 33	SLP	SA/CR FBG	KL IB	22D YAN	9 9	15000	4 9	22800	24800
35 9	ROUGHWATER 36	SLP	MS FBG	KL IB	85D PERK	11 5	15000	3 4	22000	24400
35 9	ROUGHWATER 36	SPTCR	HT FBG	DS IB	185D PERK	11 5	14000	3 4	34300	43800
41	ROUGHWATER 41	HT	TCMY FBG	DS IB	185D PERK	13	21000		59300	65100
			---- 1978 BOATS							
32 1	ROUGHWATER 33	SLP	SA/CR FBG	KL IB	22D YAN	9 9	15000	4 9	21500	23900
35 9	ROUGHWATER 36	SLP	MS FBG	KL IB	85D PERK	11 5	15000	3 4	22000	24400
35 9	ROUGHWATER 36	SPTCR	HT FBG	DS IB	185D PERK	11 5	14000	3 4	34900	43800
41	ROUGHWATER 41	HT	TCMY FBG	DS IB	185D PERK	13	21000	4	56700	62300
58	ROUGHWATER 58	HT	TRWL FBG	DS IB	265D GM	13 6	64000	5 6	85500	94000
			---- 1977 BOATS							
32 1	ROUGHWATER 33	SLP	SDN FBG	KL IB	25D WEST	9 9	15000	4 9	20800	23100
35 9	ROUGHWATER 36	SPTCR	HT FBG	DS IB	185D PERK	11 5	14000	3 4	38000	42200
41	ROUGHWATER 41	HT	TCMY FBG	DS IB	185D PERK	13	21000	4	53400	59700
58	ROUGHWATER 58	HT	TRWL FBG	DS IB	174D GM	13	64000	5 6	72700	79900
58	ROUGHWATER 58	HT	TRWL FBG	DS IB	265D	13	64000	6	81900	90000

LOA FT IN		NAME AND/ OR MODEL		TOP/ RIG	BOAT TYPE	-HULL- MTL TP	TP	ENGINE #	HP	MFG	BEAM FT	IN	WGT	DRAFT FT	IN	RETAIL LOW	RETAIL HIGH
								1976	BOATS								
32	1	ROUGHWATER 33		SLP	SA/CR	FBG	KL	IB	25D	FARY	9	6	15000	4	9	20100	22300
35	9	ROUGHWATER 35	SPTCR	HT	SDN	FBG	DS	IB	185D	PERK	11	5	14000	3	4	36600	40700
41		ROUGHWATER 41		HT	TCMY	FBG	DS	IB	185D	PERK	13		21000	4		52100	57300
58		ROUGHWATER 58		HT	TRWL	FBG	DS	IB	265D	GM	13		64000	5	6	78900	86700
								1975	BOATS								
32	1	ROUGHWATER 33		SLP	SA/CR	FBG	KL	IB	25D	FARY	9	9	15000	4	9	19500	21700
35	9	ROUGHWATER 35		HT	FSH	FBG	DS	IB	185D	PERK	11	5	14000	3	4	34700	38500
35	9	ROUGHWATER 35		HT	PH	FBG	DS	IB	185D	PERK	11	5	14000	3	4	34900	38800
35	9	ROUGHWATER 35		HT	SDN	FBG	DS	IB	185D	PERK	11	5	14000	3	4	35500	39400
35	9	ROUGHWATER 35		HT	SF	FBG	DS	IB	185D	PERK	11	5	14000	3	4	34900	38800
41		ROUGHWATER 41		HT	TCMY	FBG	DS	IB	160D	PERK	13		21000	4		49700	54700
58		ROUGHWATER 58		HT	TRWL	FBG	DS	IB	280D	GM	13		64000	5	6	77100	84700
								1974	BOATS								
35	8	ROUGHWATER 35		HT	FSH	FBG	DS	IB	120D	FORD	11	5	14000	3	4	33700	37400
35	8	ROUGHWATER 35		HT	FCH	FBG	DS	IB	185D	PERK	11	5	14000	3	4	33500	37200
35	8	ROUGHWATER 35		HT	PH	FBG	DS	IB	120D	FORD	11	5	14000	3	4	33800	37600
35	8	ROUGHWATER 35		HT	PH	FBG	DS	IB	185D	PERK	11	5	14000	3	4	33700	37400
35	8	ROUGHWATER 35		HT	SDN	FBG	DS	IB	120D	FORD	11	5	14000	3	4	33800	37500
35	8	ROUGHWATER 35		HT	SDN	FBG	DS	IB	185D	PERK	11	5	14000	3	4	34200	38000
35	8	ROUGHWATER 35		HT	SF	FBG	DS	IB	120D	FORD	11	5	14000	3	4	33800	37600
35	8	ROUGHWATER 35		HT	SF	FBG	DS	IB	185D	PERK	11	5	14000	3	4	33700	37400
40	7	ROUGHWATER 41		HT	TCMY	FBG	DS	IB	160D	PERK	13		21000	4		47700	52400
58		NORTHSEA RW 58		HT	TRWL	FBG	DS	IB	280D	GM	13		64000	5	6	74100	81500
								1973	BOATS								
33	3	BOUNTY 34		FB	CR	FBG	DV	IB	120		11	9			3	18100	20100
35	9	ROUGHWATER 35		HT	FSH	FBG	DS	IB	120D	FORD	11	5	14000	3	4	32900	36600
35	9	ROUGHWATER 35		HT	PH	FBG	DS	IB	120D	FORD	11	5	14000	3	4	33100	36800
35	9	ROUGHWATER 35		HT	SDN	FBG	DS	IB	120D	FORD	11	5	14000	3	4	33100	36800
35	9	ROUGHWATER 35		HT	SF	FBG	DS	IB	120D	FORD	11	5	14000	3	4	33100	36800
35	9	ROUGHWATER 35		HT	SF	FBG	DS	IB	185D	PERK	11	5	14000	3	4	33000	36700
40	7	ROUGHWATER 41		HT	TCMY	FBG	DS	IB	160D	PERK	12	11	19000	3	11	42400	47100
40	7	ROUGHWATER 41		HT	TCMY	P/M	DS	IB	160D	PERK	12	11	19000	3	11	42400	47100
								1972	BOATS								
35	9	ROUGHWATER 35		HT	CR	MHG	DS	IB	85D	PERK	11		11500	3	2	28300	31400

ROYAL SYSTEM YACHT YARD

Call 1-800-327-6929 for BUC Personalized Evaluation Service
Or, for 1965 to 1967 boats, sign onto www.BUCValuPro.com

ROYAL THAI YACHTS NA
PACIFIC SAILING YACHTS   COAST GUARD MFG ID- PYP

Call 1-800-327-6929 for BUC Personalized Evaluation Service
Or, for 1983 boats, sign onto www.BUCValuPro.com

RUMERYS BOAT YARD INC

Call 1-800-327-6929 for BUC Personalized Evaluation Service
Or, for 1965 to 1999 boats, sign onto www.BUCValuPro.com

RUSSELL BOATS INC

Call 1-800-327-6929 for BUC Personalized Evaluation Service
Or, for 1960 to 1961 boats, sign onto www.BUCValuPro.com

WILLIAM F RUSSELL CO

Call 1-800-327-6929 for BUC Personalized Evaluation Service
Or, for 1972 boats, sign onto www.BUCValuPro.com

RYBO RUNNER BOATS LLC
ROYAL PALM BEACH FL 334 COAST GUARD MFG ID- RBV See inside cover to adjust price for area
FORMERLY RYBOVICH BOAT WORKS INC

For more recent years, see the BUC Used Boat Price Guide, Volume 1 or Volume 2

LOA FT IN	NAME AND/ OR MODEL	TOP/ RIG	BOAT TYPE	-HULL- MTL TP	TP	ENGINE #	HP	MFG	BEAM FT	IN	WGT LBS	DRAFT FT	IN	RETAIL LOW	RETAIL HIGH
							1983	BOATS							
30	RYBO-RUNNER		CTRCN	FBG	SV	SE	T205	OMC	10	8	6500		3	32100	35700
30	RYBO-RUNNER	OP	SF	FBG	SV	OB			10	8	6500	3		32100	35600
30	RYBO-RUNNER	OP	SF	FBG	SV	SE	T205	OMC	10	8	6500	3		32100	35700
30	RYBO-RUNNER	HT	SF	FBG	SV	OB			10	8	6500	3		32100	35600
30	RYBO-RUNNER	HT	SF	FBG	SV	SE	T205	OMC	10	8	6500	3		32100	35700
30	RYBO-RUNNER	TT	SF	FBG	SV	OB			10	8	6500	3		32100	35700
30	RYBO-RUNNER	TT	SF	FBG	SV	SE	T205	OMC	10	8	6500	3		32100	35700

RYBOVICH
WEST PALM BEACH FL 33407   See inside cover to adjust price for area

For more recent years, see the BUC Used Boat Price Guide, Volume 1 or Volume 2

LOA FT IN		NAME AND/ OR MODEL	TOP/ RIG	BOAT TYPE	-HULL- MTL TP	TP	ENGINE #	HP	MFG	BEAM FT	IN	WGT LBS	DRAFT FT	IN	RETAIL LOW	RETAIL HIGH
								1981	BOATS							
50		CONVERTIBLE	F+T	CNV	WCM	SV	IB	T735D	DD	16	4		4		324500	356500
								1977	BOATS							
43			FB	CNV	MHG		IB	T	D						**	**
								1975	BOATS							
48		SPORTFISH	F+T	SF	WCM	SV	IB	T800D	DD	15	5		4		258000	283500
								1972	BOATS							
75			HT	MYCPT	F/W	SV	IB	T750D	GM	18	5		6		**	**
								1971	BOATS							
45			TT	SF	F/W	SV	IB	T500D	CUM	15			4		165500	182000
								1970	BOATS							
54		SPORT FISHERMAN	F+T	SF	WCM	SV	IB	T800D	MAN	15	8		3	6	239000	262500
								1969	BOATS							
45		SPORTCRUISER	TT	SF	F/W	SV	IB	T500D	CUM	15			4		155000	170000
								1967	BOATS							
45			F+T	CNV	F/W	SV	IB	T450D	CUM	13	6		4		182500	200500
53			FB	CNV	MHG		IB	T550D	GM	14	2		3	6	198500	218000
								1966	BOATS							
44			F+T	CNV	F/W	SV	IB	T	D						**	**
53		SPORT FISHERMAN	H+T	SF	FBC	SV	IB	T425D	CUM	15			4	6	182000	200000
								1965	BOATS							
37	4		F+T	SF	WD	SV	IB	T350D	CAT	11	3		3	5	81400	89500
43		SPORTFISH 43		SF	WD		IB	T	D	13	4		3	6	**	**
								1964	BOATS							
36		SPORTFISH	TT	SF	WCM	SV	IB	T		12			2	5	**	**
37	4		F+T	SF	WD	SV	IB	T350D	CAT	11	3		2	5	79400	87200
50		SPORT FISHERMAN	F+T	SF	F/W		IB	T425D	GM	14	6		4	6	141000	155000
								1963	BOATS							
45		SPORT FISHERMAN	F+T	SF	F/W		IB	T	D						**	**
								1962	BOATS							
30		SPORTFISH	TT	SF	WCM	SV	IB	T							**	**
36		SPORTFISH	TT	SF	WCM	SV	IB	T		12			2	5	**	**
42		SPORTFISH	TT	SF	F/W	SV	IB	T425D	CUM	15			4		117500	129000
								1961	BOATS							
30		SPORTFISH	TT	SF	WCM	SV	IB	T							**	**
36		SPORTFISH	TT	SF	WCM	SV	IB	T		12			2	5	**	**
40		SPORTFISH		SF	WD		IB	T	D						**	**
48		SPORTFISH		SF	WD		IB	T355D		16	1		4	2	119500	131500
								1960	BOATS							
30		EXPRESS FISHERMAN	HT	EXPSF	F/W	SV	IB	T240D	CUM	11	6				39000	43300
36			ST	SDNSF	F/W	SV	IB	T350	CRUS				2	6	24200	26900
40		SPORTFISH		SF	WD		IB	T	D						**	**
42		SPORTFISH		SF	WD		IB	T	D						**	**
44		SPORTFISH		SF	WD		IB	T	D	15	2		4	4	**	**
								1959	BOATS							
36		SPORTFISH	TT	SF	WCM	SV	IB	T350	CRUS	12			2	5	45000	50000
44		SPORTFISH	F+T	SF	WCM	SV	IB	T	D	13			3	6	**	**
46			TT	SDNSF	F/W	SV	IB	T435D	GM	14			4		124000	136000
								1958	BOATS							
36			F+T	SF	WD	SV	IB	T	D	12			3		**	**
42		SPORTFISH	F+T	SF	WCM	SV	IB	T350D	CAT	12	7		3	6	110500	121500
								1957	BOATS							
36			TT	SF	WD	SV	IB	T	D	12			3		**	**
43			TT	SF	WD	SV	IB	T	D	12			3		**	**
								1956	BOATS							
31			TT	SF	WD	SV	IB	T	D	12			3		**	**
36			TT	SF	WD	SV	IB	T	D	12			3		**	**
42			TT	SF	WD	SV	IB	T	D	12			3		**	**
								1955	BOATS							
36		SPORTFISHER	TT	SF	WD	SV	IB	T300D	SABR	12			3		50700	55700
40			FB	SF	WD		IB	T216D	GM	13	2		3		77600	85300
43		SPORT FISHERMAN		SF	WD		IB	T370D		12	5		3	4	107500	118500

RYBOVICH   -CONTINUED   See inside cover to adjust price for area

LOA FT IN	NAME AND/ OR MODEL	TOP/ RIG	BOAT TYPE	-HULL- MTL TP TP	----ENGINE--- # HP MFG	BEAM FT IN	WGT LBS	DRAFT FT IN	RETAIL LOW	RETAIL HIGH
			1954 BOATS							
28	EXPRESS SPORTFISH	HT	SF	WCM SV IB	260D GM	9 9			23300	25900
36	FLYBRIDGE SPORTFISH	TT	SF	F/W SV IB	T350 MERC	12 2		3 6	41000	45600
40	FLYBRIDGE SPORTFISH	TT	SF	F/W SV IB	T350 MERC	12 2		3 6	66300	72800
			1953 BOATS							
36	FLYBRIDGE SPORTFISH	TT	SF	F/W SV IB	T350 MERC	12 2		3 6	40600	45100
			1952 BOATS							
34		F+T	SF	WD SV IB	T D	11		3	**	**
			1950 BOATS							
36		F+T	SF	WD SV IB	T D	11		3	**	**
37		F+T	SF	WD SV IB	T D	11		3	**	**
			1949 BOATS							
28	SPORTFISH	OP	SF	WD IB	175 HERC	9 9		1 5	10000	11400
37		F+T	SF	WD SV IB	T300D CUM	11		3	58300	64100
			1946 BOATS							
34		F+T	SF	WD SV IB	T D	11		3	**	**

C E RYDER CORP

BRISTOL RI 02809   COAST GUARD MFG ID- CER See inside cover to adjust price for area

For more recent years, see the BUC Used Boat Price Guide, Volume 1 or Volume 2

LOA FT IN	NAME AND/ OR MODEL	TOP/ RIG	BOAT TYPE	-HULL- MTL TP TP	----ENGINE--- # HP MFG	BEAM FT IN	WGT LBS	DRAFT FT IN	RETAIL LOW	RETAIL HIGH
			1983 BOATS							
22 6	SEA-SPRITE 23	SLP	SAIL	FBG KL OB	7		3350	3	6800	7800
22 6	SEA-SPRITE 23	SLP	SAIL	FBG KL IB	8D YAN 7		3350	3	8000	9200
23	SONAR	SLP	SAIL	FBG KL OB	7 10		2100	3 11	5050	5800
23 11	QUICKSTEP	SLP	SAIL	FBG KL OB	7 11		4000	3 5	8550	9800
27 11	SEA-SPRITE 27	SLP	SAIL	FBG KL IB	11D UNIV 8 10		7600	4 3	20900	23300
30	SEA-SPRITE	SLP	SA/CR	FBG KL IB	16D UNIV 9 6		10000	4 9	28600	31800
30 5	SOUTHERN-CROSS 28	CUT	SA/CR	FBG KL VD	11D UNIV 8 6		8500	4 8	24300	27000
33 11	SEA-SPRITE 34	SLP	SAIL	FBG KL IB	24D UNIV 10 3		12800	5	36600	40700
34 6	SOUTHERN-CROSS 31	CUT	SA/CR	FBG KL IB	21D UNIV 9 6		13600	4 7	39000	43300
35 3	SOUTHERN-CROSS 35	CUT	SA/CR	FBG KL IB	24D UNIV 11 5		14461	4 11	46400	51000
39 6	NEW-YORK 40	SLP	SA/OD	FBG KL	12 10		17000	6 10	54800	60200
41	SOUTHERN-CROSS 39	CUT	SA/CR	FBG KL VD	50D PERK 12 1		21000	5 4	68200	74900
			1982 BOATS							
22 6	SEA-SPRITE 23	SLP	SAIL	FBG KL OB	7		3350	3	6400	7350
23	SONAR	SLP	SAIL	FBG KL OB	7 10		2100	3 11	4750	5450
27 11	SEA-SPRITE 27	SLP	SAIL	FBG KL IB	11D UNIV 8 10		7600	4 3	19800	22000
30 5	SOUTHERN-CROSS 28	CUT	SA/CR	FBG KL IB	11D UNIV 8 6		8500	4 8	22800	25400
33 11	SEA-SPRITE 34	SLP	SAIL	FBG KL IB	24D UNIV 10 3		12800	5	34500	38300
34 6	SOUTHERN-CROSS 31	CUT	SA/CR	FBG KL IB	22D YAN 9 6		13600	4 7	36700	40800
35 3	SOUTHERN-CROSS 35	CUT	SA/CR	FBG KL IB	24D UNIV 11 4		14500	4 11	43300	48100
39 6	NEW-YORK 40	SLP	SA/RC	FBG KL	D		17000	6 10	52700	57900
43	SOUTHERN-CROSS 39	CUT	SA/CR	FBG KL VD	50D PERK 12 1		21000	5 4	69700	76500
			1981 BOATS							
22 6	SEA-SPRITE 23	SLP	SAIL	FBG KL OB	7		3350	3	6050	6950
22 6	SEA-SPRITE 23	SLP	SAIL	FBG KL IB	8D YAN 7		3350	3	7100	8150
27 11	SEA-SPRITE 27	SLP	SA/RC	FBG KL IB	D 8 10		7500	4 2	18600	20700
27 11	SEA-SPRITE 27	SLP	SAIL	FBG KL IB	11D UNIV 8 10		7600	4 3	18800	20900
30 5	SOUTHERN-CROSS 28	CUT	SA/CR	FBG KL IB	11D UNIV 8 6		8500	4 8	21500	23900
34 6	SOUTHERN-CROSS 31	CUT	SA/CR	FBG KL IB	22D YAN 9 6		13600	4 7	34500	38400
43	SOUTHERN-CROSS 39	CUT	SA/CR	FBG KL VD	50D WEST 12 1		21000	5 4	66200	72800
			1980 BOATS							
22 6	SEA-SPRITE	SLP	SAIL	FBG KL IB	8D YAN 7		3350	3	6750	7750
22 6	SEA-SPRITE 23	SLP	SAIL	FBG KL OB	7		3350	3	5750	6600
27 9	SOUTHERN-CROSS	SLP	SA/CR	FBG KL IB	12D YAN 8 6		8500	3 10	20000	22200
27 11	SEA-SPRITE 27	SLP	SAIL	FBG KL IB	11D UNIV 8 10		7500	4 3	17300	19700
30 5	SOUTHERN-CROSS 28	SLP	SA/CR	FBG KL IB	12D YAN 8 6		8500	4 8	20500	22800
30 5	SOUTHERN-CROSS 28	CUT	SA/CR	FBG KL IB	12D YAN 8 6		8500	4 8	20500	22800
32 7	RESOLUTE	CUT	SA/CR	FBG KL IB	D 10		8200	4 6	19900	22100
34 6	SOUTHERN-CROSS 31	CUT	SA/CR	FBG KL IB	22D YAN 9 6		13600	4 7	33000	36600
34 6	SOUTHERN-CROSS 31	SLP	SA/CR	FBG KL IB	22D YAN 9 6		13600	4 7	33000	36600
43	SOUTHERN-CROSS 39	SLP	SA/CR	FBG KL VD	50D WEST 12 1		21000	5 4	63400	69700
43	SOUTHERN-CROSS 39	CUT	SA/CR	FBG KL VD	50D WEST 12 1		21000	5 4	63200	69400
			1978 BOATS							
23	SEA-SPRITE	SLP	SA/CR	FBG KL IB	D 7		3350	3	6250	7200
28	SOUTHERN-CROSS	SLP	SA/CR	FBG KL IB	8D 8 6		7885	3 10	16900	19200
28	SOUTHERN-CROSS	SLP	SA/CR	FBG KL IB	8D 8 6		7885	3 10	16900	19200
34	SOUTHERN-CROSS	SLP	SA/CR	FBG KL IB	22D 9 6		13600	4 7	30400	33800
34	SOUTHERN-CROSS	SLP	SA/CR	FBG KL IB	22D 9 6		13600	4 7	30400	33800
34	SOUTHERN-CROSS	CUT	SA/CR	FBG KL IB	22D 9 6		13600	4 7	30400	33800
34	SOUTHERN-CROSS	KTH	SA/CR	FBG KL IB	22D 9 6		13600	4 7	30400	33800
			1977 BOATS							
31	SOUTHERN-CROSS	CUT	SA/CR	FBG KL IB	20D 9 6		13600	4 7	29600	32900
			1976 BOATS							
31	SOUTHERN-CROSS	CUT	SA/CR	FBG KL IB	20D 9 6		13600	4 7	28600	31800

S & J BOATBUILDERS

Call 1-800-327-6929 for BUC Personalized Evaluation Service
Or, for 1974 boats, sign onto www.BUCValuPro.com

S E B MARINE

Call 1-800-327-6929 for BUC Personalized Evaluation Service
Or, for 1972 boats, sign onto www.BUCValuPro.com

S L C CORP
COAST GUARD MFG ID- SHC

Call 1-800-327-6929 for BUC Personalized Evaluation Service
Or, for 1973 to 1974 boats, sign onto www.BUCValuPro.com

SABRE
AMERICAN MARINE IND INC   See inside cover to adjust price for area
TACOMA WA 98421   COAST GUARD MFG ID- AMM

LOA FT IN	NAME AND/ OR MODEL	TOP/ RIG	BOAT TYPE	-HULL- MTL TP TP	----ENGINE--- # HP MFG	BEAM FT IN	WGT LBS	DRAFT FT IN	RETAIL LOW	RETAIL HIGH
			1976 BOATS							
18	XL195 HI-PERF	OP	RNBT	FBG DV IO	140 OMC	7 1	2400		2400	2800
18	XL196 HI-PERF	OP	RNBT	FBG DV IO	140-235	7 1	2400		2350	2900
18	XL196 HI-PERF	OP	RNBT	FBG DV JT	290 BERK	7 1	2400		2700	3150
18 6	SV1900	OP	RNBT	FBG DV OB		7 4	1400		2150	2550
18 6	SV1900	ST	RNBT	FBG DV OB		7 4	1400		2150	2550
18 6	SV1905	OP	RNBT	FBG DV IO	120-200	7 4	2500		2550	3200
18 6	SV1905	ST	RNBT	FBG DV IO	120-200	7 4	2500		2550	3200
18 6	SV1910	HT	RNBT	FBG DV OB		7 4	1500		2300	2650
18 6	SV1910	HT	RNBT	FBG DV IO	120-200	7 4	2600		2600	3200
18 6	SV1915	HT	RNBT	FBG DV OB		7 4	1600		2350	2750
18 6	SV1915	HT	RNBT	FBG DV IO	120-200	7 4	2700		2700	3300
20 6	SV2100	OP	RNBT	FBG DV IO	120-235	8	2800		3450	4250
20 6	SV2100	OP	RNBT	FBG DV IO	240 VLVO	8	2800		3750	4350
20 6	SV2105	ST	RNBT	FBG DV IO	120-235	8	2800		3450	4250
20 6	SV2105	ST	RNBT	FBG DV IO	240 VLVO	8	2800		3750	4350
20 6	SV2115	HT	RNBT	FBG DV IO	120-235	8	2900		3500	4300
20 6	SV2115	HT	RNBT	FBG DV IO	240 VLVO	8	2900		3800	4400
20 6	SV2120	OP	CUD	FBG DV IO	120-235	8	3000		3750	4600
20 6	SV2120	OP	CUD	FBG DV IO	240 VLVO	8	3000		4100	4750
20 6	SV2140	HT	CUD	FBG DV IO	120-235	8	2900		3700	4500
20 6	SV2140	HT	CUD	FBG DV IO	240 VLVO	8	2900		4000	4650
22 3	SV2300	HT	SDN	FBG DV IO	175-240	8	4400		5450	6650
22 3	SV2300	HT	SDN	FBG DV IO	T120-T140	8	4400		6100	7300
22 3	SV2350	HT	OFF	FBG DV IO	175-240	8	4500		5550	6750
22 3	SV2350	HT	OFF	FBG DV IO	T120-T140	8	4500		6200	7400
24 3	SV2520	HT	EXP	FBG DV IO	170-240	8	5000		6850	8050
24 3	SV2520	HT	EXP	FBG DV IO	T120-T140	8	5000		7300	8700
24 3	SV2530	FB	SDN	FBG DV IO	170-240	8	5000		6900	8150
24 3	SV2530	FB	SDN	FBG DV IO	T120-T140	8	5000		7400	8800
			1975 BOATS							
17 1	SV1800	ST	RNBT	FBG DV OB		7 1	1300		1900	2300
17 1	SV1800	ST	RNBT	FBG DV IO	120-190	7 1	2050		2200	2600
17 1	SV1805	ST	RNBT	FBG DV OB		7 1	1350		2000	2350
17 1	SV1805	ST	RNBT	FBG DV IO	120-190	7 1	2100		2250	2650
17 1	SV1810	HT	RNBT	FBG DV OB		7 1	1450		1950	2300
17 1	SV1810	HT	RNBT	FBG DV IO	120-190	7 1	2200		2300	2600
17 1	SV1815	HT	RNBT	FBG DV OB		7 1	1500		2300	2750
17 1	SV1815	HT	RNBT	FBG DV IO	120-190	7 1	2250		2350	2750
18	EX190	OP	RNBT	FBG DV IO	140-235	7 1	2400		2400	2950
18	EX190	OP	RNBT	FBG DV JT	140-235	7 1	2400		2550	3000
18	EX191	OP	RNBT	FBG DV IO	140-235	7 1	2400		2350	2900
18	EX191	OP	RNBT	FBG DV JT	295-330	7 1	2400		2500	2900
18	XL195	OP	RNBT	FBG DV IO	140-235	7 1	2400		2550	3150
18	XL195	OP	RNBT	FBG DV JT	295-330	7 1	2400		2700	3150
18	XL196	OP	RNBT	FBG DV IO	140-235	7 1	2400		2500	3050
18	XL196	OP	RNBT	FBG DV JT	295-330	7 1	2400		2650	3100
18	XL197	OP	RNBT	FBG DV IO	140-235	7 1	2400		2450	3050

LOA FT	LOA IN	NAME AND/ OR MODEL	TOP/ RIG	BOAT TYPE	-HULL- MTL	-HULL- TP	ENGINE TP	ENGINE # HP	ENGINE MFG	BEAM FT	BEAM IN	WGT LBS	DRAFT FT	DRAFT IN	RETAIL LOW	RETAIL HIGH
1975 BOATS																
18		XL197	OP	RNBT	FBG	DV	JT	295-330		7	1	2400			2600	3050
19	1	SV2000	ST	RNBT	FBG	DV	IO	120-235		7	7	2400			2750	3300
19	1	SV2005	ST	RNBT	FBG	DV	IO	120-235		7	7	2450			2750	3350
19	1	SV2010	HT	RNBT	FBG	DV	IO	120-235		7	7	2550			2750	3350
19	1	SV2015	HT	RNBT	FBG	DV	IO	120-235		7	7	2550			2950	3500
19	1	SV2040	HT	RNBT	FBG	DV	IO	120-235		7	7	2650			2900	3450
19	1	SV2050	HT	RNBT	FBG	DV	IO	120-235		7	7	2650			2950	3550
21	3	SV2220	HT	CUD	FBG	DV	IO	120-235		8		2850			3950	4750
22	3	SV2300	HT	SDN	FBG	DV	IO	175-235		8		4000			5250	6200
22	3	SV2300	HT	SDN	FBG	DV	IO	T120-T140		8		4000			5900	6750
22	3	SV2330	FB	SPTCR	FBG	DV	IO	175-235		8		4300			5550	6500
22	3	SV2330	FB	SPTCR	FBG	DV	IO	T120-T140		8		4300			6200	7100
22	3	SV2340	ST	OFF	FBG	DV	IO	175-235		8		4000			5250	6200
22	3	SV2340	ST	OFF	FBG	DV	IO	T120-T140		8		4000			5900	6800
22	3	SV2350	HT	OFF	FBG	DV	IO	175-235		8		4000			5250	6200
22	3	SV2350	HT	OFF	FBG	DV	IO	T120-T140		8		4000			5900	6800
24	3	SV2500	OP	SDN	FBG	DV	IO	175-235		8		4500			6450	7600
24	3	SV2500	OP	SDN	FBG	DV	IO	T120-T140		8		4500			7100	8200
24	3	SV2520	HT	EXP	FBG	DV	IO	175-235		8		4500			6350	7500
24	3	SV2520	HT	EXP	FBG	DV	IO	T120-T140		8		4500			7000	8100
24	3	SV2530	FB	SPTCR	FBG	DV	IO	175-235		8		4650			6500	7700
24	3	SV2530	FB	SPTCR	FBG	DV	IO	T120-T140		8		4650			7150	8300
1974 BOATS																
17	1	SV1800	ST	RNBT	FBG	DV	OB			7	1	1300			1900	2250
17	1	SV1800	ST	RNBT	FBG	DV	IO	120-200		7	1	2100			2300	2850
17	1	SV1800	ST	RNBT	FBG	DV	JT	270	BERK	7	1	2100			2300	2650
17	1	SV1800	HT	RNBT	FBG	DV	IO	130-200		7	1	2175			2450	2900
17	1	SV1800	HT	RNBT	FBG	DV	JT	270	BERK	7	1	2175			2300	2700
17	1	SV1805	ST	RNBT	FBG	DV	OB			7	1	1325			1950	2300
17	1	SV1805	ST	RNBT	FBG	DV	IO	120-200		7	1	2125			2300	2900
17	1	SV1805	ST	RNBT	FBG	DV	JT	270	BERK	7	1	2125			2300	2650
17	1	SV1810	HT	RNBT	FBG	DV	OB			7	1	1375			2000	2350
17	1	SV1810	HT	RNBT	FBG	DV	IO	120-190		7	1	2175			2350	2700
17	1	SV1815	HT	RNBT	FBG	DV	OB			7	1	1395			2000	2400
17	1	SV1815	HT	RNBT	FBG	DV	IO	120-190		7	1	2200			2350	2900
17	1	SV1815	HT	RNBT	FBG	DV	IO	200	VLVO	7	1	2200			2500	2950
17	1	SV1815	HT	RNBT	FBG	DV	IO	270	VLVO	7	1	2200			2800	3250
18		SABRE EX-190		RNBT	FBG	DV	IO	140-225		7	1				2450	3000
18		SABRE EX-190		RNBT	FBG	DV	IO	255	WAUK	7	1				2700	3150
18		SABRE EX-190		RNBT	FBG	DV	JT	445	BERK	7	1				2500	2900
18		SABRE EX-191		RNBT	FBG	DV	IO	140-225		7	1				2400	2950
18		SABRE EX-191		RNBT	FBG	DV	IO	255	WAUK	7	1				2650	3050
18		SABRE EX-191		RNBT	FBG	DV	JT	455	BERK	7	1				2400	2750
18		SABRE XL-195		RNBT	FBG	DV	IO	140-225		7	1				2650	3200
18		SABRE XL-195		RNBT	FBG	DV	IO	255	WAUK	7	1				2850	3350
18		SABRE XL-195		RNBT	FBG	DV	JT	455	BERK	7	1				2600	3050
18		SABRE XL-196		RNBT	FBG	DV	IO	140-255		7	1				2650	3250
18		SABRE XL-196		RNBT	FBG	DV	JT	455	BERK	7					2500	2900
18		SABRE XL-197		RNBT	FBG	DV	IO	140-255		7	1				2650	3200
18		SABRE XL-197		RNBT	FBG	DV	JT	455	BERK	7	1				2500	2900
19	1	SV2000	ST	RNBT	FBG	DV	IO	120-200		7	9	2435			2900	3550
19	1	SV2000	ST	RNBT	FBG	DV	IO	225		7	9	2435			2950	3650
19	1	SV2000	ST	RNBT	FBG	DV	JT	270	BERK	7	9	2435			2800	3250
19	1	SV2005	ST	RNBT	FBG	DV	IO	120-200		7	9	2460			2900	3600
19	1	SV2005	ST	RNBT	FBG	DV	IO	225		7	9	2460			3000	3650
19	1	SV2005	ST	RNBT	FBG	DV	JT	270	BERK	7	9	2460			2800	3250
19	1	SV2010	HT	RNBT	FBG	DV	IO	120-200		7	9	2535			2950	3650
19	1	SV2010	HT	RNBT	FBG	DV	IO	225		7	9	2535			3000	3700
19	1	SV2010	HT	RNBT	FBG	DV	JT	270	BERK	7	9	2535			2850	3300
19	1	SV2015	HT	RNBT	FBG	DV	IO	120-200		7	9	2560			2950	3650
19	1	SV2015	HT	RNBT	FBG	DV	IO	225		7	9	2560			3050	3750
19	1	SV2015	HT	RNBT	FBG	DV	JT	270	BERK	7	9	2560			2850	3300
19	1	SV2040	HT	RNBT	FBG	DV	IO	120-200		7	9	2600			3000	3650
19	1	SV2040	HT	RNBT	FBG	DV	IO	225		7	9	2600			3000	3750
19	1	SV2040	HT	RNBT	FBG	DV	JT	270	BERK	7	9	2600			2850	3300
19	1	SV2050	HT	RNBT	FBG	DV	IO	120-225		7	9	2600			3050	3800
19	1	SV2050	HT	RNBT	FBG	DV	JT	270	BERK	7	9	2600			2900	3350
22	3	SV2300		SDN	FBG	DV	IO	140-255		8		4200			5600	6800
22	3	SV2300		SDN	FBG	DV	IO	T120-T140		8		4200			6300	7550
22	3	SV2310		SF	FBG		IO	T120	MRCR	8		4000			6950	7950
22	3	SV2310		SF	FBG	DV	IO	140-255		8		4000			6150	7450
22	3	SV2310		SF	FBG	DV	IO	T120-T140		8		4000			6850	8350
22	3	SV2320		EXP	FBG	DV	IO	140-255		8		4400			5850	7000
22	3	SV2320		EXP	FBG	DV	IO	T120-T140		8		4400			6500	7800
22	3	SV2330	FB		FBG	DV	IO	255	WAUK	8		4500			5850	6750
22	3	SV2330	FB	RNBT	FBG	DV	IO	188-190		8		4500			5650	6500
22	3	SV2330	FB	SDN	FBG	DV	IO	140-225		8		4500			5950	7150
22	3	SV2330	FB	SDN	FBG	DV	IO	T120-T140		8		4500			6600	7900
24	3	SV2500		SDN	FBG	DV	IO	165-255		8		4400			6550	7850
24	3	SV2500		SDN	FBG	DV	IO	T120-T140		8		4400			7200	8650
24	3	SV2510		SF	FBG	DV	IO	165-255		8		4500			7500	9000
24	3	SV2510		SF	FBG	DV	IO	T120-T140		8		4500			8250	9850
24	3	SV2520		EXP	FBG	DV	IO	165-255		8		4600			6700	8000
24	3	SV2520		EXP	FBG	DV	IO	T120-T140		8		4600			7350	8750
24	3	SV2530	FB	SDN	FBG	DV	IO	165-255		8		4700			6900	8250
24	3	SV2530	FB	SDN	FBG	DV	IO	T120-T140		8		4700			7550	9000
24	3	SV2540 OFFSHORE		OFF	FBG	DV	IO	165-255		8		4200			6200	7450
24	3	SV2540 OFFSHORE		OFF	FBG	DV	IO	T120-T140		8		4200			6850	8200
1973 BOATS																
17	1	SV1800	ST	RNBT	FBG	DV	OB			7	1	1275			1850	2250
17	1	SV1800	ST	RNBT	FBG	DV	IO	120-165		7	1	2075			2350	2750
17	1	SV1800	HT	RNBT	FBG	DV	OB			7	1	1350			1950	2350
17	1	SV1800	HT	RNBT	FBG	DV	IO	120-165		7	1	2150			2400	2800
17	6	ST1800		RNBT	FBG	DV	OB			7	2	1300			1900	2300
17	6	ST1800		RNBT	FBG	DV	IO	120-140		7	2	2100			2400	2800
19	1	SV2000	ST	RNBT	FBG	DV	OB			7	7				2250	2650
19	1	SV2000	ST	RNBT	FBG	DV	IO	120-225		7	7	2400			2900	3500
19	1	SV2000	HT	RNBT	FBG	DV	OB			7	7				2250	2650
19	1	SV2000	HT	RNBT	FBG	DV	IO	120-225		7	7	2500			3000	3550
21	3	SV2200	HT	RNBT	FBG	DV	IO	120-225		8		2650			3800	4500
21	3	SV2210	HT	RNBT	FBG	DV	IO	120-225		8		2650			3900	4600
21	3	SV2220		OVNTR	FBG	DV	IO	120-225		8		2850			4200	5000
21	3	SV2230		EXP	FBG	DV	IO	120-225		8		3000			4450	5200
21	3	SV2240		EXP	FBG	DV	IO	120-225		8		3000			4300	5050
24	3	SV2500	HT	SDN	FBG	DV	IO	165-255		8		4400			6750	8100
24	3	SV2500	HT	SDN	FBG	DV	IO	100D	CHRY	8		4400			8100	9300
24	3	SV2510		SF	FBG	DV	IO	165-255		8		4450			7650	9150
24	3	SV2510		SF	FBG	DV	IO	100D	CHRY	8		4450			10100	11400
24	3	SV2510		SF	FBG	DV	IO	T120-T140		8		4450			8450	9750
24	3	SV2520		EXP	FBG	DV	IO	165-255		8		4500			6800	8100
24	3	SV2520		EXP	FBG	DV	IO	100D	CHRY	8		4500			8100	9300
24	3	SV2520		EXP	FBG	DV	IO	T120-T140		8		4500			7500	8650
24	3	SV2530	FB	SDN	FBG	DV	IO	165-255		8		4800			7250	8650
24	3	SV2530	FB	SDN	FBG	DV	IO	100D	CHRY	8		4800			8600	9850
24	3	SV2530	FB	SDN	FBG	DV	IO	T120-T140		8		4800			7950	9150
1972 BOATS																
17	1	SV 1800	HT		FBG		IO	120	OMC	7	1	2150			2400	2800
17	1	SV1800	ST		FBG		OB			7	1	1275			1850	2200
17	1	SV1800	ST		FBG		IO	120-165		7	1	2075			2350	2800
17	1	SV1800	HT		FBG		OB			7	1	1350			1950	2300
17	1	SV1800	HT		FBG		IO	120-165		7	1	2150			2400	2850
17	6	ST1800			FBG	TR	IO	120-140		7	9	1600			2300	2700
19	1	SV2000	ST		FBG		OB			7	9	1600			2350	2750
19	1	SV2000	ST		FBG		IO	120-225		7	9	2400			3050	3750
19	1	SV2000	ST		FBG		IO	255	WAUK	7	9	2600			3350	3900
19	1	SV2000	HT		FBG		OB			7	9	1700			2450	2850
19	1	SV2000	HT		FBG		IO	120-225		7	9	2500			3100	3800
19	1	SV2000	HT		FBG		IO	255	WAUK	7	9	2700			3400	4000
21	3	SV2200	ST		FBG		IO	120-225		8		2550			3900	4800
21	3	SV2200	ST		FBG		IO	255	WAUK	8		2750			4250	4950
21	3	SV2200	HT		FBG		IO	120-225		8		2650			4000	4850
21	3	SV2200	HT		FBG		IO	255	WAUK	8		2825			4400	5050
21	3	SV2200		EXP	FBG		IO	120-255		8		3000			4550	5600
21	3	SV2200	HT	EXP	FBG		IO	120-255		8		3000			4500	5450
21	3	SV2200		OVNTR	FBG		IO	120-255		8		2850			4400	5450
21	3	SV2200	HT	OVNTR	FBG		IO	120-255		8					4450	5350
24	3	SV2500		EXP	FBG		IO	165-255		8		4425			6950	8400
24	3	SV2500		EXP	FBG		IO	T120-T140		8		5150			8550	9850
24	3	SV2500	HT	EXP	FBG		IO	165-255		8					7250	8650
24	3	SV2500	HT	EXP	FBG		IO	T120-T140		8					8000	9300
25	11	SABRE V2600		EXP	F/W		IO	165-255		9	2	5000	2	6	8200	10100
25	11	SABRE V2600		EXP	F/W		IO	T120-T140		9	2	5800	2	6	9900	11400
25	11	SABRE V2600	HT	EXP	F/W		IO	165-255		9	2		2	6	8400	10200
25	11	SABRE V2600	HT	EXP	F/W		IO	T120-T140		9	2		2	6	9250	10700

 CONTINUED ON NEXT PAGE

LOA FT	LOA IN	NAME AND/ OR MODEL	TOP/ RIG	BOAT TYPE	-HULL- MTL	-HULL- TP	ENGINE TP	ENGINE # HP	ENGINE MFG	BEAM FT	BEAM IN	WGT LBS	DRAFT FT	DRAFT IN	RETAIL LOW	RETAIL HIGH
		1971 BOATS														
16	1	SV 1700			FBG		IO	140	MRCR	6	6	1750			1950	2300
17	1	SV 1800	ST		FBG		OB			7	1	1275			1850	2200
17	1	SV 1800	ST		FBG		IO	155-165		7	1	2075			2400	2800
17	1	SV 1800	HT		FBG		OB			7	1	1350			1950	2300
17	1	SV 1800	HT		FBG		IO	155-165		7	1	2150			2450	2850
17	6	1800	ST		FBG	TR	IO	140-155		7	2	1900			2400	2750
19	1	SV 2000	ST		FBG		OB			7	9	1500			2300	2650
19	1	SV 2000	ST		FBG		IO	215		7	9	2400			3200	3700
19	1	SV 2000	HT		FBG		OB			7	9	1600			2350	2750
19	1	SV 2000	HT		FBG		IO	215		7	9	2500			3250	3800
21	3	SV 2200	ST		FBG		IO	215		8		2550			4100	4750
21	3	SV 2200	HT		FBG		IO	215		8		2650			4200	4850
21	3	SV 2200		EXP	FBG		IO	215		8		3000			4750	5450
21	3	SV 2200		OVNTR	FBG		IO	215		8		2850			4650	5300
24	3	SV 2500		EXP	FBG		IO	215		8		4500			7350	8450
25	11	SABRE V-2600			F/W		IO	215	OMC	9	2	5000			8950	10200
25	11	SABRE V-2600			F/W		IO	T140	MRCR	9	2	5000			9650	11000
26	1	V2600		EXP	F/W		IB	225	CHRY	9	2	5000	2	6	5700	6550
26	1	V2600		EXP	F/W		IB	T140		9	2	5000	2	6	6050	6950
		1970 BOATS														
17	1	RIVIERA		RNBT	FBG	SV	OB			7	1	1200			1750	2100
17	1	RIVIERA	ST	RNBT	FBG	SV	IO	120		7	1				2600	3050
18	8	MARLIN		RNBT	FBG	TR	IO	120		7	11				3350	3850
19	1	VIKING			FBG	SV	OB			7	10	1500			2300	2650
19	1	VIKING	ST		FBG	SV	IO	120		7	10				3300	3850
21	3	SUNLINER	ST		FBG	SV	IO	120		7	11				4200	4900
21	3	SUNLINER		EXP	FBG	SV	IO	120		7	11				4800	5500
21	3	SUNLINER		OVNTR	FBG	SV	IO	120		7	11				4700	5400
25	10	SABRE V2600		EXP	F/W	DV	IB	275	CHRY	9	2	5000	2	6	5550	6350
		1969 BOATS														
17	1	RIVIERA	ST	RNBT	FBG	SV	IO	120		7	1			11	2700	3150
17	1	RIVIERA	HT	RNBT	FBG	SV	OB			7	1	1125			1700	2000
19	1	VIKING	ST		FBG	SV	IO	120	OMC	7	10		1		3400	3950
19	1	VIKING	ST	RNBT	FBG	SV	OB			7	10	1500			2300	2650
19	1	VIKING	HT	RNBT	FBG	SV	OB			7	10	1500			2300	2650
21	3	SUNLINER	ST	CR	FBG	SV	IO	120	OMC	7	11		1	1	4750	5450
21	3	SUNLINER	HT	CR	FBG	SV	IO	120	OMC	7	11		1	3	4750	5450
21	3	SUNLINER		EXP	FBG	SV	IO	120	OMC	7	11		1	3	4900	5650
21	3	SUNLINER		OVNTR	FBG	SV	IO	120	OMC	7	11		1	3	4800	5500
25	10	SABRE V2600		EXP	PLY	DV	IB	210	CHRY	9	2	5000	2	6	5150	5900
		1968 BOATS														
17	1	RIVIERA	ST		FBG		IO	80-160		7	1				2700	3150
17	1	RIVIERA	HT		FBG		IO	80-160		7	1				2700	3150
17	1	RIVIERA	ST	RNBT	FBG		OB			7	1	1200			1800	2100
17	1	RIVIERA	HT	RNBT	FBG		OB			7	1	1200			1800	2100
19	1	VIKING	ST		FBG		IO	120-210		7	10				3550	4200
19	1	VIKING	HT		FBG		IO	120-210		7	10				3550	4200
19	1	VIKING	ST	RNBT	FBG		OB			7	10	1500			2300	2650
19	1	VIKING	HT	RNBT	FBG		OB			7	10	1500			2300	2650
21	3	SUNLINER	ST		FBG		IO	120-210		7	11				4550	5350
21	3	SUNLINER	HT		FBG		IO	120-210		7	11				4550	5350
21	3	SUNLINER		EXP	FBG		IO	120-210		7	11				5100	6000
21	3	SUNLINER		OVNTR	FBG		IO	120-210		7	11				4950	5800
26	1	SABRE V 2600			FBG		IO	160		9	2	5000	2	6	9600	10900
26	1	SABRE V 2600			FBG		IO	210		9	2	5000	2	6	9950	11300
26	1	SABRE V 2600			FBG		IB	210		9	2	5000	2	6	5050	5800
		1967 BOATS														
16	4	RIVIERA 17 CUSTOM			FBG		IO	80-160							2300	2750
16	4	RIVIERA SPORT 17			FBG		IO	80-160							2250	2650
18	6	VIKING CUSTOM			FBG		IO	120-200							3450	4250
18	6	VIKING CUSTOM		RNBT	FBG		OB								2300	2650
18	6	VIKING SPORT 19			FBG		IO	120-200							3350	4100
18	6	VIKING SPORT 19		RNBT	FBG		OB								2100	2500
19	9	SUNLINER		EXP	FBG		IO	120-200							4550	5250
19	9	SUNLINER 20 CUSTOM			FBG		IO	120-200							3700	4550
19	9	SUNLINER SPORT 20			FBG		IO	120-200							3600	4450
		1966 BOATS														
16	4	IMPELLA 17 CUSTOM		SKI	FBG		IO	60-120		6	10				2450	3050
16	4	IMPELLA CUSTOM	HT	SKI	FBG		IO	60-120		6	10				2350	2950
16	4	IMPELLA SPORT 17		SKI	FBG		IO	60-120		6	10				2350	2900
18	4	COMMANDER 19			FBG		IO	110-150							2950	3600
18	4	SARATOGA CUS	HT	SKI	FBG		OB			7	4				1750	2100
18	4	SARATOGA CUS	HT	SKI	FBG		IO	110-150		7	4				3300	4000
18	4	SARATOGA CUSTOM		SKI	FBG		OB			7	4	1250			1900	2250
18	4	SARATOGA CUSTOM		SKI	FBG		IO	110-150		7	4				3300	4100
18	4	SARATOGA SPORT 19		SKI	FBG		OB			7	4				1750	2100
18	4	SARATOGA SPORT 19		SKI	FBG		IO	110-150		7	4				3200	3950
18	6	VIKING CUSTOM		SKI	FBG		OB			7	4				2250	2650
18	6	VIKING CUSTOM		SKI	FBG		IO	110-200		7	4				3450	4200
18	6	VIKING CUSTOM	HT	SKI	FBG		OB			7	4				2250	2650
18	6	VIKING CUSTOM	HT	SKI	FBG		IO	110-200		7	4				3450	4200
18	6	VIKING SPORT 19			FBG		OB			7	4				2300	2700
18	6	VIKING SPORT 19			FBG		IO	110-200		7	4				3500	4250
19	9	SUNLINER 20 CUSTOM			FBG		OB								2500	2950
19	9	SUNLINER 20 CUSTOM			FBG		IO	110-200							3950	4850
19	9	SUNLINER CUS	HT		FBG		OB								2450	2850
19	9	SUNLINER CUS	HT		FBG		IO	110-200							3900	4700
19	9	SUNLINER SPORT 20			FBG		OB								2350	2750
19	9	SUNLINER SPORT 20			FBG		IO	110-200							3800	4650
23		MARLIN		CR	FBG		IO			8					**	**
25	7	SABRE V2600			FBG		IO	150-200							9850	11500
25	7	SABRE V2600			FBG		IB	210							4600	5250
25	7	SABRE V2600			FBG		IO	T110-T120							10800	12500
25	7	SABRE V2600	HT		FBG		IO	150-200							9850	11500
25	7	SABRE V2600	HT		FBG		IB	210							4600	5250
25	7	SABRE V2600	HT		FBG		IO	T110-T120							10800	12500
		1965 BOATS														
16		RAIDER 16			FBG		IO	110-120							2350	2950
17		IMPELLA 17 CUSTOM			FBG		OB								2000	2400
17		IMPELLA 17 CUSTOM			FBG		IO	110							2950	3400
17		IMPELLA 17 CUSTOM			FBG		IO	110-120							3250	3800
17		IMPELLA CUSTOM	HT		FBG		OB								1900	2300
17		IMPELLA CUSTOM	HT		FBG		IO	110-120							2950	3600
17		IMPELLA SPORT 17			FBG		OB								1800	2150
17		IMPELLA SPORT 17			FBG		IO	110							2800	3250
17		IMPELLA SPORT 17			FBG		IO	110-120							3100	3650
19		SARATOGA CUS	HT		FBG		OB								2300	2700
19		SARATOGA CUS	HT		FBG		IO	110							3700	4350
19		SARATOGA CUS	HT		FBG		IO	110-150							4050	4700
19		SARATOGA CUSTOM			FBG		OB								2400	2800
19		SARATOGA CUSTOM			FBG		IO	110							3800	4400
19		SARATOGA CUSTOM			FBG		IO	110-150							4150	4800
19		SARATOGA SPORT 19			FBG		OB								2200	2550
19		SARATOGA SPORT 19			FBG		IO	110							3650	4200
19		SARATOGA SPORT 19			FBG		IO	110-150							3950	4600
19		VIKING CUSTOM			FBG		OB								2500	2950
19		VIKING CUSTOM			FBG		IO	110							3900	4550
19		VIKING CUSTOM			FBG		IO	110-150							4250	4950
19		VIKING CUSTOM	HT		FBG		OB								2400	2800
19		VIKING CUSTOM	HT		FBG		IO	110							3800	4450
19		VIKING CUSTOM	HT		FBG		IO	110-150							4150	4850
19		VIKING SPORT 19			FBG		OB								2350	2700
19		VIKING SPORT 19			FBG		IO	110							3750	4350
19		VIKING SPORT 19			FBG		IO	110-150							4100	4750
23		MARLIN 23			FBG		IO	150							7900	9050
26		SABRE V2600			FBG		IO	150							10400	11900
26		SABRE V2600			FBG		IB	210							4500	5200
26		SABRE V2600			FBG		IO	T110-T120							11500	13300
26		SABRE V2600	HT		FBG		IO	150							10400	11900
26		SABRE V2600	HT		FBG		IB	210							4500	5200
26		SABRE V2600	HT		FBG		IO	T110-T120							11500	13300
		1964 BOATS														
17		IMPELLA CUSTOM			FBG		OB								2200	2550
17		IMPELLA CUSTOM			FBG		IO	80-120							3200	3750
17		IMPELLA LUXURY SPORT			FBG		OB								1950	2300
17		IMPELLA LUXURY SPORT			FBG		IO	80-120							3050	3550
17		IMPELLA SPORT			FBG		IO	80-120							2850	3350
19		COMMANDER			FBG		OB								2950	3400
19		COMMANDER			FBG		IO	80-150							4550	5250
19		DEBUTANTE CUSTOM			FBG		OB								2550	3000
19		DEBUTANTE CUSTOM			FBG		IO	80-150							4150	4850
19		SARATOGA CUSTOM			FBG		OB								2400	2800
19		SARATOGA CUSTOM			FBG		IO	80-150							4000	4700
19		SARATOGA LUXURY SPT			FBG		OB								2200	2550
19		SARATOGA LUXURY SPT			FBG		IO	80-150							3800	4500
19		SARATOGA SPORT			FBG		OB								1900	2250
19		SARATOGA SPORT			FBG		IO	80-150							3600	4300
19		VIKING CUSTOM			FBG		OB								2500	2900
19		VIKING CUSTOM			FBG		IO	80-150							4100	4800

CONTINUED ON NEXT PAGE

LOA FT	LOA IN	NAME AND/ OR MODEL	TOP/ RIG	BOAT TYPE	HULL MTL	HULL TP	ENGINE TP	# HP	MFG	BEAM FT	BEAM IN	WGT LBS	DRAFT FT	DRAFT IN	RETAIL LOW	RETAIL HIGH
		1964 BOATS														
19		VIKING LUXURY SPORT			FBG		OB								2350	2700
19		VIKING LUXURY SPORT			FBG		IO	80-150							3950	4600
19		VIKING SPORT			FBG		OB								2050	2400
19		VIKING SPORT			FBG		IO	80-150							3700	4350
		1963 BOATS														
16	4	IMPELLA 17 CUSTOM			FBG		IO	80-110							2600	3000
16	4	IMPELLA SPORT 17			FBG		IO	80-110							2600	3000
18	4	COMMANDER 19			FBG		OB								2250	2600
18	4	COMMANDER 19			FBG		IO	80-140							3250	3800
18	4	DEBUTANTE CUSTOM			FBG		IO	80-140							3250	3800
18	4	DEBUTANTE SPORT 19			FBG		IO	80-140							3250	3800
18	4	SARATOGA CUSTOM			FBG		IO	80-140							3250	3800
18	4	SARATOGA SPORT 19			FBG		IO	80-140							3250	3800
21	6	VAGABOND 22			FBG		OB								2450	2850
21	6	VAGABOND 22			FBG		IO	80-140							7750	8900
24	8	SKYLARK 26			FBG		OB								3150	3650
24	8	SKYLARK 26			FBG		IO	80-140							10100	11700
24	8	SKYLARK 26			FBG		IB	185							3900	4500
24	8	SKYLARK 26			FBG		IO	T 80							11100	12600
		1962 BOATS														
16	4	IMPELLA CUSTOM			FBG		IO	80-100							2650	3100
16	4	IMPELLA SPORT			FBG		IO	80-100							2650	3100
18	4	COMMANDER			FBG		IO	80-100							3350	3900
18	4	DEBUTANTE CUSTOM			FBG		IO	80-100							3350	3900
18	4	DEBUTANTE SPORT			FBG		IO	80-100							3350	3900
18	4	SARATOGA CUSTOM			FBG		IO	80-100							3350	3900
18	4	SARATOGA SPORT			FBG		IO	80-100							3350	3900
21	6	VAGABOND			WD		OB								2450	2850
21	6	VAGABOND			FBG		IO	80-111							8000	9200
21	6	VAGABOND JET		RNBT	WD		IB	188							2950	3400
24	8	SKYLARK			WD		OB								3150	3650
24	8	SKYLARK			FBG		IO	80-111							10400	11900
		IB 135 3700 4300, IO 188 10800 12300, IB 188													3800	4400
		IO T 80 11500 13100														
		1961 BOATS														
17		IMPELLA 17 CUSTOM			FBG		OB			6	7				2000	2400
17		IMPELLA CUSTOM 17			FBG		IO	80							3400	3950
17		IMPELLA SPORT 17			FBG		OB			6	7				1850	2200
17		IMPELLA SPORT 17			FBG		IO	80							3300	3850
19		DEBUTANTE CUSTOM			FBG		OB			7	4				2400	2800
19		DEBUTANTE CUSTOM 19			FBG		IO	80	t	7	4			8	4300	5000
19		DEBUTANTE SPORT 19			FBG		OB			7	4				2400	2800
19		DUBUTANTE SPORT 19			FBG		IO	80		7	4			8	4200	4850
19		SARATOGA CUSTOM			FBG		OB								2450	2850
19		SARATOGA CUSTOM 19			FBG		IO	80							4500	5150
19		SARATOGA SPORT 19			FBG		OB								2350	2700
19		SARATOGA SPORT 19			FBG		IO	80							4350	5050
21		VAGABOND		CR	PLY		OB			7	9				2950	3400
21		VAGABOND		CR	PLY		IO	85	VLVO	7	9			7	6250	7200
24		SKYLARK		CR	PLY		OB			8					5100	5850
24		SKYLARK 25		CR	PLY		IO	85	VLVO	8				10	10400	11800
		1960 BOATS														
17		IMPELLA		CNV	FBG		OB								1950	2350
17		IMPELLA		CNV	FBG	DV	OB			6	7				1950	2350
17		IMPELLA	HT	CNV	FBG		OB								1950	2350
17		IMPELLA	HT	CNV	FBG	DV	OB			6	7				1950	2350
17		PACER			FBG		OB								1950	2300
17		PACER			FBG	DV	OB			6	7				1800	2100
17		SARATOGA			FBG		OB								1950	2300
17		SARATOGA			FBG	DV	OB			6	7				2150	2500
19		CATALINA		CR	FBG		OB								2350	2750
19		CATALINA		CR	FBG	DV	OB			7	4				2350	2750
19		DEBUTANTE		CNV	FBG		OB								2350	2750
19		DEBUTANTE		CNV	FBG	DV	OB			7	4				2350	2750
19		DEBUTANTE	HT	CNV	FBG		OB								2350	2750
19		DEBUTANTE	HT	CNV	FBG	DV	OB			7	4				2350	2750
20		SUNLINER		CNV	WD		OB								2550	2950
20		SUNLINER	HT	CNV	WD		OB								2550	2950
21		VAGABOND		CR	WD		OB								2950	3450
21		VAGABOND		CR	PLY	DV	IB	85		7	9			7	1800	2100
24		SKYLARK		CR	WD		OB								5100	5850
24		SKYLARK		CR	PLY	DV	IB	85		8				10	3100	3600
		1959 BOATS														
18	2	CATALINA		CBNCR	FBG		OB			7	4	1250			1950	2300
18	2	DEBUTANTE		CR	FBG		OB			7	4	1100			1750	2100
19	6	SUNLINER		CR	PLY		OB			7	2	1020			1700	2050
20	9	VAGABOND		CBNCR	PLY		OB			7	9	1200			2200	2550

SABRE CORPORATION

SOUTH CASCO ME 04077 COAST GUARD MFG ID- HWS See inside cover to adjust price for area
FORMERLY SABRE YACHTS

For more recent years, see the BUC Used Boat Price Guide, Volume 1 or Volume 2

LOA FT	LOA IN	NAME AND/ OR MODEL	TOP/ RIG	BOAT TYPE	HULL MTL	HULL TP	ENGINE TP	# HP	MFG	BEAM FT	BEAM IN	WGT LBS	DRAFT FT	DRAFT IN	RETAIL LOW	RETAIL HIGH
		1983 BOATS														
28	5	SABRE 28	SLP	SA/CR	FBG	KL	IB	13D	WEST	9	2	7800	4	8	25100	27900
28	5	SABRE 28 SHOAL	SLP	SA/CR	FBG	KL	IB	13D	WEST	9	2	7900	3	10	25500	28300
29	11	SABRE 30	SLP	SA/CR	FBG	KL	IB	13D	WEST	10		8600	5	2	28500	31700
29	11	SABRE 30 SHOAL	SLP	SA/CR	FBG	KL	IB	13D	WEST	10		8800	4		29200	32400
33	8	SABRE 34	SLP	SA/CR	FBG	KC	IB	27D	WEST	10	6	11700	3	11	39700	44100
33	8	SABRE 34	SLP	SA/CR	FBG	KL	IB	27D	WEST	10	6	11400	5	6	38700	43000
37	10	SABRE 38	SLP	SA/CR	FBG	KC	IB	33D	WEST	11	6	15600	4	3	55700	61200
37	10	SABRE 38	SLP	SA/CR	FBG	KL	IB	33D	WEST	11	6	15200	6	6	54500	59900
37	10	SABRE 38 AFT-CABIN	SLP	SA/CR	FBG	KC	IB	33D	WEST	11	6	15600	4	3	58400	64200
37	10	SABRE 38 AFT-CABIN	SLP	SA/CR	FBG	KL	IB	33D	WEST	11	6	15200	6	6	57300	62900
		1982 BOATS														
28	5	SABRE 28	SLP	SA/CR	FBG	KL	IB	13D	WEST	9	2	7900	4	4	23700	26300
28	5	SABRE 28 SHOAL	SLP	SA/CR	FBG	KC	IB	13D	WEST	9	2	7900	3	10	24000	26700
29	11	SABRE 30	SLP	SA/CR	FBG	KL	IB	13D	WEST	10		8600	5		26700	29600
29	11	SABRE 30 SHOAL	SLP	SA/CR	FBG	KC	IB	13D	WEST	10		8800	4		27300	30300
33	8	SABRE 34	SLP	SA/CR	FBG	KC	IB	27D	WEST	10	6	11700	3	11	37100	41200
33	8	SABRE 34	SLP	SA/CR	FBG	KL	IB	27D	WEST	10	6	11400	5	6	36200	40200
37	10	SABRE 38	SLP	SA/CR	FBG	KL	IB	33D	WEST	11	6	15200	6	6	52300	57500
37	10	SABRE 38 SHOAL	SLP	SA/CR	FBG	KC	IB	33D	WEST	11	6	15600	4	3	53400	58700
		1981 BOATS														
28	5	SABRE 28	SLP	SA/CR	FBG	KL	IB	13D	VLVO	9	2	7900	4	4	22300	24800
29	11	SABRE 30	SLP	SA/CR	FBG	KL	IB	13D		10		8600	5		25000	27700
29	11	SABRE 30 SHOAL	SLP	SA/CR	FBG	KL	IB	13D	WEST	10		8800	4		25600	28400
33	8	SABRE 34	SLP	SA/CR	FBG	KC	IB	27D	WEST	10	6	11700	3	11	34800	38600
33	8	SABRE 34	SLP	SA/CR	FBG	KL	IB	27D-	30D	10	6	11400	5	6	33900	37700
		1980 BOATS														
28	5	SABRE 28	SLP	SA/CR	FBG	KL	IB	13D	VLVO	9	2	7900	4	4	21100	23400
28	5	SABRE 28 SHOAL	SLP	SA/CR	FBG	KL	IB	13D	VLVO	9	2	7900	3	10	21300	23700
29	11	SABRE 30	SLP	SA/CR	FBG	KL	IB	13D	VLVO	10		8600	5		23700	26400
29	11	SABRE 30 SHOAL	SLP	SA/CR	FBG	KL	IB	13D	VLVO	10		8700	4		24000	26700
33	8	SABRE 34	SLP	SA/CR	FBG	KC	IB	23D-	30D	10	6	12000	3	11	33800	37600
33	8	SABRE 34	SLP	SA/CR	FBG	KL	IB	23D-	30D	10	6	11400	5	6	32200	35800
		1979 BOATS														
28	5	SABRE 28	SLP	SA/CR	FBG	KL	IB	13D	VLVO	9	2	7900	4	4	20200	22400
28	5	SABRE 28 SHOAL	SLP	SA/CR	FBG	KL	IB	13D	VLVO	9	2	7900	3	10	20400	22700
29	11	SABRE 30	SLP	SA/CR	FBG	KL	IB	13D	VLVO	10		8400	5		22200	24600
33	8	SABRE 34	SLP	SA/CR	FBG	KC	IB	23D	VLVO	10	6	12000	3	11	32400	36000
33	8	SABRE 34	SLP	SA/CR	FBG	KL	IB	23D	VLVO	10	6	11400	5	6	30800	34200
		1978 BOATS														
28	5	SABRE 28	SLP	SA/CR	FBG	KL	IB	13D	VLVO	9	2	7900	4	4	19400	21500
28	5	SABRE 28 SHOAL	SLP	SA/CR	FBG	KL	IB	13D	VLVO	9	2	7900	3	10	19600	21800
33	8	SABRE 34	SLP	SA/CR	FBG	KL	IB	20D-	23D	10	6	11800	5	6	30600	34000
		1977 BOATS														
28	5	SABRE 28	SLP	SA/CR	FBG	KL	IB	30	UNIV	9	2	7400	4	4	17100	19400
28	5	SABRE 28	SLP	SA/CR	FBG	KL	IB	10D	VLVO	9	2	7400	4	4	17200	19600
28	5	SABRE 28	KTH	SA/CR	FBG	KL	IB	30	UNIV	9	2	7400	4	4	17100	19400
28	5	SABRE 28	KTH	SA/CR	FBG	KL	IB	10D	VLVO	9	2	7400	4	4	17200	19600
28	5	SABRE 28 SHOAL DRAFT	SLP	SA/CR	FBG	KL	IB	30	UNIV	9	2	7400	3	10	17200	19600
28	5	SABRE 28 SHOAL DRAFT	SLP	SA/CR	FBG	KL	IB	10D	VLVO	9	2	7400	3	10	17400	19800
28	5	SABRE 28 SHOAL DRAFT	KTH	SA/CR	FBG	KL	IB	30	UNIV	9	2	7400	3	10	17200	19600
28	5	SABRE 28 SHOAL DRAFT	KTH	SA/CR	FBG	KL	IB	10D	VLVO	9	2	7400	3	10	17400	19800
33	8	SABRE 34	SLP	SA/CR	FBG	KL	IB	30	UNIV	10	6	10500	5	6	26200	29100
33	8	SABRE 34	SLP	SA/CR	FBG	KL	IB	22D	WEST	10	6	10500	5	6	26300	29200
		1976 BOATS														
28	5	SABRE 28	SLP	SAIL	FBG	KL	IB	30	UNIV	9	2	7400	4	4	16500	18800
28	5	SABRE 28	SLP	SAIL	FBG	KL	IB	10D	VLVO	9	2	7400	4	4	16700	18900
28	5	SABRE 28	KTH	SAIL	FBG	KL	IB	30	UNIV	9	2	7400	4	4	16500	18800
28	5	SABRE 28	KTH	SAIL	FBG	KL	IB	10D	VLVO	9	2	7400	4	4	16700	18900
28	5	SABRE 28 SHOAL DRAFT	SLP	SAIL	FBG	KL	IB	30	UNIV	9	2	7400	3	10	16700	18900
28	5	SABRE 28 SHOAL DRAFT	SLP	SAIL	FBG	KL	IB	10D	VLVO	9	2	7400	3	10	16800	19100
28	5	SABRE 28 SHOAL DRAFT	KTH	SAIL	FBG	KL	IB	30	UNIV	9	2	7400	3	10	16700	18900
28	5	SABRE 28 SHOAL DRAFT	KTH	SAIL	FBG	KL	IB	10D	VLVO	9	2	7400	3	10	16800	19100

SABRE CORPORATION   -CONTINUED   See inside cover to adjust price for area

LOA FT IN	NAME AND/ OR MODEL	TOP/ RIG	BOAT TYPE	MTL	-HULL- TP	TP	----ENGINE--- # HP	MFG	BEAM FT IN	WGT LBS	DRAFT FT IN	RETAIL LOW	RETAIL HIGH
			1975 BOATS										
28	SABRE 28	SLP	SAIL	FBG	KL	IB	30	UNIV	9	7400	4 4	15900	18100
28	SABRE 28	SLP	SAIL	FBG	KL	IB	10D	VLVO	9	7400	4 4	16000	18200
			1974 BOATS										
28 5	SABRE 28	SLP	SAIL	FBG	KL	IB	30	UNIV	9 2	7400	4 4	15600	17700
			1970 BOATS										
28	SABRE 28	SLP	SA/RC	FBG	KL	OB			9	6500	4 3	12300	14000
28	SABRE 28	SLP	SA/RC	FBG	KL	IB		UNIV	9	6500	4 3	12500	14200

SABRE JET
COAST GUARD MFG ID- SDJ

Call 1-800-327-6929 for BUC Personalized Evaluation Service
Or, for 1977 to 1979 boats, sign onto www.BUCValuPro.com

SABRE MARINE INC
COAST GUARD MFG ID- XSF

Call 1-800-327-6929 for BUC Personalized Evaluation Service
Or, for 1977 to 1980 boats, sign onto www.BUCValuPro.com

SAFARI MARINE INC
COSTA MESA CA 92627   COAST GUARD MFG ID- SFK See inside cover to adjust price for area

LOA FT IN	NAME AND/ OR MODEL	TOP/ RIG	BOAT TYPE	MTL	-HULL- TP	TP	----ENGINE--- # HP	MFG	BEAM FT IN	WGT LBS	DRAFT FT IN	RETAIL LOW	RETAIL HIGH
			1978 BOATS										
28 3	SAFARI 28	FB	SDN	FBG	SV	IO	T225	VLVO	8	6700	2 2	15300	17300
36 8	SAFARI 37 FD	CUT	SA/CR	FBG	KL	IB	25D	VLVO	11	17800	5 9	38200	42500

SAIL CRAFT LTD
COLCHESTER ENGLAND   See inside cover to adjust price for area

LOA FT IN	NAME AND/ OR MODEL	TOP/ RIG	BOAT TYPE	MTL	-HULL- TP	TP	----ENGINE--- # HP	MFG	BEAM FT IN	WGT LBS	DRAFT FT IN	RETAIL LOW	RETAIL HIGH
			1981 BOATS										
20	TORNADO	SLP	SA/OD	FBG	CT				10	427	7	3100	3600
25	TYPHOON	SLP	SAIL	FBG	TM				17 5	600	1	9900	11200
31 6	IROQUOIS MKII	SLP	SA/CR	FBG	CT				13 6	6800	1 3	36400	40500
32 2	COMMANCHE	SLP	MS	FBG	CT	IB	T 15D	YAN	13 10	8400	3 2	51200	56300
32 2	COMMANCHE	SLP	SA/CR	FBG	CT	OB			13 10	8400	3 2	51200	56300
35	CHEROKEE	SLP	SA/CR	FBG	CT	IB	42D	PERK	16 6	11100	3 6	69400	76200
40	APACHE	KTH	SA/CR	FBG	CT	IB	T 31D	VLVO	19 6	13500	3 4	103500	114000
45	APACHE	KTH	SA/CR	FBG	CT	IB	T 31D	VLVO	19 6	14000	3 4	134000	147000
			1980 BOATS										
20	TORNADO	SLP	SA/OD	FBG	CT				10	427	7	2950	3450
25	TYPHOON	SLP	SAIL	FBG	TM				17 5	600	1	9450	10700
30	IROQUOIS	SLP	SA/CR	FBG	CT	OB			13 6	6650	1 3	30300	33700
31 6	IROQUOIS MKII	SLP	SA/CR	FBG	CT				13 6	6800	1 3	34800	38600
32 2	COMANCHE	SLP	MS	FBG	CT	IB	T 15D	YAN	13 10	8400	3 2	48900	53800
32 2	COMANCHE	SLP	SA/CR	FBG	CT				13 10	8400	3 2	48900	53800
32 2	COMMANCHE	SLP	MS	FBG	CT	IB	T 15D	YAN	13 10	8400	3 2	48900	53800
32 2	COMMANCHE	SLP	SA/CR	FBG	CT	OB			13 10	8400	3 2	48900	53800
35	CHEROKEE	SLP	SA/CR	FBG	CT	IB	42D	PERK	16 6	11100	3 6	66200	72800
38	VAL 38	SLP	SA/RC	FBG	TM	OB			25	13000	1 6	85400	93800
38	VAL 38	SLP	SA/RC	FBG	TM	SD	8D	VLVO	25	13000	1 6	85400	93800
40	APACHE	KTH	SA/CR	FBG	CT	IB	T 31D	VLVO	19 6	13500	3 4	99000	109000
45	APACHE	KTH	SA/CR	FBG	CT	IB	T 31D	VLVO	19 6	14000	3 4	128000	140500
			1978 BOATS										
16 8	MYSTERE	SLP	SA/RC	FBG	CT				7 6	320	5	1950	2300
20	TORNADO	SLP	SA/OD	F/S	CT				10	427	7	2750	3200
20	TORNADO	SLP	SA/OD	FBG	CT				10	427	7	2750	3200
23	AZTEC 23	SLP	SA/RC	FBG	CT	OB			11 3	900	8	7750	8900
30	IROQUOIS MKII	SLP	SA/CR	FBG	CT	OB			13 6	6560	1 3	28000	31100
31 6	IROQUOIS MKIIA	SLP	SA/CR	FBG	CT	OB			13 6	6800	1 3	33200	35800
31 6	IROQUOIS MKIIAM	SLP	SA/CR	FBG	CT	IB	T	D	VLVO	13 6	6800	1 3	33200	35800
32 2	COMMANCHE	SLP	SA/CR	FBG	CT	OB			13 10		3 4	43500	48300
32 2	COMMANCHE	SLP	SA/CR	FBG	CT	IB		8D- 25D		13 10		3 4	42600	47400
35	CHEROKEE	SLP	SA/CR	FBG	CT	IB	T	D		16 6	11100	3 6	61400	67500
41	APACHE	SLP	SA/CR	FBG	CT	IB		D		19 6	13350	3 6	97800	107500
41	APACHE	CUT	SA/CR	FBG	CT	IB		D		19 6	13350	3 6	97800	107500
41	APACHE	KTH	SA/CR	FBG	CT	IB		D		19 6	13350	3	97800	107500
42	MEDALLION-OLYMPIC	KTH	SA/CR	FBG	KL	IB	72D	THOR	12 6	20000		90900	99900
			1977 BOATS										
16 4	MYSTERE	SLP	SA/RC	FBG	CT				7 6	320	6	1850	2200
20	TORNADO	SLP	SA/OD	FBG	CT				10	375	6	2450	2850
20	TORNADO	SLP	SA/OD	PLY	CT				10	375	6	2450	2850
20	TORNADO	SLP	SA/OD	WD	CT				10	375	6	2450	2850
23	AZTEC 23	SLP	SA/OD	FBG	CT	OB			11	650	9	6850	7900
30	IROQUOIS	SLP	MS	FBG	CT	IB	T 10D	VLVO	13 6	7800	1 9	28300	31500
30	IROQUOIS	SLP	SA/CR	FBG	CT	OB			13 6	6800	1 4	27300	30300
35	CHEROKEE	SLP	SA/CR	FBG	CT	HD	38D	THOR	16 6	11100	3 6	59300	65200
41	APACHE	SLP	SA/CR	FBG	CT	IB	T 38D	PERK	19 6	13350	3 6	94500	104000
41	APACHE	CUT	SA/CR	FBG	CT	IB	T 38D	PERK	19 6	13350	3 6	94500	104000
41	APACHE	YWL	SA/CR	FBG	CT	IB	T 38D	PERK	19 6	13350	3 6	94900	104500
			1976 BOATS										
16 4	MYSTERE	SLP	SAIL	FBG	CT				7 6	320		1800	2150
20	TORNADO	SLP	SA/OD	FBG	CT				10	300	6	2050	2400
20	TORNADO	SLP	SA/OD	WD	CT				10	300	6	2050	2400
26 6	AZTEC	SLP	SAIL	FBG	CT				15			16700	19000
26 6	AZTEC	SLP	SAIL	FBG	TM				15			16700	19000
30	IROQUOIS FF CR	SLP	SAIL	FBG	CT	OB			13 6	5600	1 4	26100	27900
35	CHEROKEE	SLP	SA/CR	FBG	CT		D		16 6	11100	3 6	57500	63200
41	APACHE 40	SLP	SAIL	FBG	CT	IB		D		19 6	16800	3	97400	107000
41	APACHE 40	CUT	SAIL	FBG	CT	IB		D		19 6	16800	3	97400	107000
41	APACHE 40	YWL	SAIL	FBG	CT	IB		D		19 6	16800	3	97400	107000
			1975 BOATS										
31 6	IROQUOIS MKII	SLP	MS	FBG	CT	OB		D		13 6	5600	1 4	27800	30900
31 6	IROQUOIS MKII	SLP	SA/CR	FBG	CT	OB		D		13 6	5600	1 4	27800	30900
35	CHEROKEE	CUT	SA/CR	FBG	CT		D		16 6	11000	2 2	55700	61200
40 10	APACHE	SLP	SA/CR	FBG	CT	IB		D		19 6	13000	3 6	87300	96000
40 10	APACHE	CUT	SA/CR	FBG	CT	IB		D		19 6	13000	3 6	87300	96000
40 10	APACHE	KTH	SA/CR	FBG	CT	IB		D		19 6	13000	3 6	87300	96000
			1974 BOATS										
31 6	IROQUOIS MKII	SLP	SA/CR	FBG	CT	OB		D		13 6	5600	1 4	23700	26400
31 6	IROQUOIS MKII	SLP	MS	FBG	CT		D		13 6	5600	1 4	27100	30100
35	CHEROKEE	SLP	SA/CR	FBG	CT		D		16 6	11000	2 9	54200	59600
40 10	APACHE	SLP	SA/CR	FBG	CT	IB		D		19 6	13000	3 6	85000	93400
40 10	APACHE	CUT	SA/CR	FBG	CT	IB		D		19 6	13000	3 6	85000	93400
40 10	APACHE	KTH	SA/CR	FBG	CT	IB		D		19 6	13000	3 6	85000	93400
			1973 BOATS										
20	SHARK	SLP	SA/OD	FBG	CT				10	510		2650	3050
20	TORNADO	SLP	SAIL	FBG	CT				10	380		2250	2600
30	IROQUOIS MKII	SLP	SAIL	FBG	CT	OB			13 6	5000	1 4	22500	25000
31 6	IROQUOIS	SLP	MS	FBG	CT	IB		D		13 6	5600	1 4	26400	29300
35	CHEROKEE	SLP	SA/CR	FBG	CT				17	11000	2 2	52900	58100
40 10	APACHE	SLP	SAIL	FBG	CT	IB		D		19 6	13000	2 10	82900	91100
40 10	APACHE	KTH	SAIL	FBG	CT	IB		D		19 6	13000	2 10	82900	91100
			1970 BOATS										
20	SHARK	SLP	SA/OD		CT				10	450	6	2350	2700
20	SHARK	SLP	SA/OD	FBG	CT				10	450	6	2350	2700
20	TORNADO	SLP	SA/OD	WD	CT				10		6	2350	2700
25	HELLCAT	SLP	SA/OD	PLY	CT				14		7	7050	8150
30	IROQUOIS MKII	SLP	SA/CR	FBG	CT	OB			13 6	5000	1 4	21100	23500
			1969 BOATS										
20	SHARK	SLP	SA/OD	FBG	CT				10	450	6	2300	2700
20	TORNADO	SLP	SA/OD	FBG	CT				10	380	6	2200	2400
25	HELLCAT	SLP	SA/OD	PLY	CT				14		6	6950	8000
			1968 BOATS										
20	SHARK	SLP	SA/OD	FBG	CT				10		6	2300	2650
20	TORNADO	SLP	SA/OD	FBG	CT				10		6	2150	2550
25	HELLCAT	SLP	SA/OD	FBG	CT				14		6	6850	7900
			1967 BOATS										
20	SHARK	SLP	SA/OD	FBG	CT				10	450	9	2250	2600
25	HELLCAT	SLP	SA/OD	WD	CT				14		6	6800	7800

SAIL CRAFT OF CANADA

Call 1-800-327-6929 for BUC Personalized Evaluation Service
Or, for 1971 to 1986 boats, sign onto www.BUCValuPro.com

SAIL FAST INC

Call 1-800-327-6929 for BUC Personalized Evaluation Service
Or, for 1970 to 1978 boats, sign onto www.BUCValuPro.com

SAIL/POWER YACHTS LTD
SOLOMON IS MD 20688   COAST GUARD MFG ID- TVZ See inside cover to adjust price for area

For more recent years, see the BUC Used Boat Price Guide, Volume 1 or Volume 2

LOA FT IN	NAME AND/ OR MODEL	TOP/ RIG	BOAT TYPE	-HULL- MTL TP	ENGINE TP # HP MFG	BEAM FT IN	WGT LBS	DRAFT FT IN	RETAIL LOW	RETAIL HIGH
				--- 1983 **BOATS** ---						
38	OCEAN 38 DC		TRWL	FBG DS	IB 135D PERK	12 10	22000	3 5	77000	84600

SAILAND INC
LEON IRISH CO

Call 1-800-327-6929 for BUC Personalized Evaluation Service
Or, for 1959 to 1974 boats, sign onto www.BUCValuPro.com

SAILBOAT WORKS INC
COAST GUARD MFG ID- SQG

Call 1-800-327-6929 for BUC Personalized Evaluation Service
Or, for 1983 boats, sign onto www.BUCValuPro.com

SAILBOATS BY MCCULLOCH
COAST GUARD MFG ID- AWM

Call 1-800-327-6929 for BUC Personalized Evaluation Service
Or, for 1965 to 1983 boats, sign onto www.BUCValuPro.com

SAILCRAFT

Call 1-800-327-6929 for BUC Personalized Evaluation Service
Or, for 1968 to 1969 boats, sign onto www.BUCValuPro.com

SAILING CRAFT BY ROTH

Call 1-800-327-6929 for BUC Personalized Evaluation Service
Or, for 1961 boats, sign onto www.BUCValuPro.com

SAILMASTER INC
SHELTER ISLAND NY   See inside cover to adjust price for area

LOA FT IN	NAME AND/ OR MODEL	TOP/ RIG	BOAT TYPE	-HULL- MTL TP	ENGINE TP # HP MFG	BEAM FT IN	WGT LBS	DRAFT FT IN	RETAIL LOW	RETAIL HIGH
				--- 1970 **BOATS** ---						
22	SAILMASTER 22	SLP	SA/CR	FBG KC		7	3640	2 4	3550	4100
22	SAILMASTER 22D	SLP	SA/OD	FBG KC		7 1	3640	2 4	3550	4100
26 3	SAILMASTER 26	SLP	SA/CR	FBG KC		7 9	5400	3	6100	7050
				--- 1969 **BOATS** ---						
22	SAILMASTER 22	SLP	SA/CR	FBG KC		7	3640	2 4	3500	4050
22	SAILMASTER 22D	SLP	SA/OD	FBG KC		7 1	3640	2 4	3500	4050
26 3	SAILMASTER 26	SLP	SA/CR	FBG KC		7 9	5400	3	6000	6900
45 1	SAILMASTER 45	SLP	SA/CR	FBG KL		11	26000	6 5	39400	43700
45 1	SAILMASTER 45	YWL	SA/CR	FBG KL		11	26000	6 5	39300	43700
				--- 1968 **BOATS** ---						
22	SAILMASTER 22D	SLP	SAIL	FBG KC		7 1	3640	2 4	3450	4000
26 3	SAILMASTER 26	SLP	SA/CR	FBG KC		7 9	5400	3	5950	6850
45 1	SAILMASTER 45	SLP	SAIL	FBG KL		11	26000	6 5	41400	46000
45 1	SAILMASTER 45	YWL	SAIL	FBG KL		11	26000	6 5	41300	45900
				--- 1967 **BOATS** ---						
22	SAILMASTER 22	SLP	SA/OD	FBG KC		7	3640	2 4	3400	3950
26 3	SAILMASTER 26	SLP	SA/CR	FBG KC		7 9	5400	3	5850	6750
45 1	SAILMASTER 45	SLP	SA/CR	FBG KL		11	26000	6 5	40700	45200
45 1	SAILMASTER 45	YWL	SA/CR	FBG KL	IB	11	26000	6 5	41400	46000
				--- 1966 **BOATS** ---						
22	SAILMASTER 22	SLP	SAIL	FBG KC		7	3640	2 4	3350	3900
22	SAILMASTER 22D	SLP	SA/CR	FBG KC		7	3640	2 4	3350	3900
26 3	SAILMASTER 26	SLP	SA/CR	FBG KC		7 9	5400	2 2	5800	6700
45 1	SAILMASTER 45	SLP	SA/CR	FBG KL		11	26000	6 5	40100	44600
45 1	SAILMASTER 45	YWL	SA/CR	FBG KL		11	26000	6 5	40100	44600
				--- 1965 **BOATS** ---						
22	SAILMASTER 22	SLP	SA/RC	FBG KC	OB	7	3640	2 4	3350	3900
22	SAILMASTER 22O	SLP	SA/RC	FBG KC	OB	7	3640	2 4	3350	3900
26 3	SAILMASTER 26	SLP	SAIL	FBG KC		7 9	5400	2 2	5800	6650
29 11	SAILMASTER 30	SLP	SAIL	FBG KL		9		4 10	7350	8450
45 1	SAILMASTER 45	YWL	SAIL	FBG KL	22D	11	26000	6 5	39700	44100
				--- 1963 **BOATS** ---						
22	SAILMASTER 22		SAIL	FBG	OB	7	3640	2 4	3300	3850
26 3	SAILMASTER 26		SAIL	FBG	OB	7 9	5400	2 4	6100	7000
45 1	SAILMASTER 45		SAIL	FBG	IB	11	26000	6 5	39600	44000

SAILSTAR BOATS INC
BRISTOL RI 02809   See inside cover to adjust price for area
FOR MORE RECENT YEARS SEE BRISTOL YACHT COMPANY

LOA FT IN	NAME AND/ OR MODEL	TOP/ RIG	BOAT TYPE	-HULL- MTL TP	ENGINE TP # HP MFG	BEAM FT IN	WGT LBS	DRAFT FT IN	RETAIL LOW	RETAIL HIGH
				--- 1971 **BOATS** ---						
19 7	CORINTHIAN	SLP	SA/CR	FBG KL	OB	6 6		2 9	2200	2550
22	CARAVEL	SLP	SAIL	FBG	OB				2700	3150
24 7	CORSAIR	SLP	SA/RC	FBG KL	OB	8		3 5	5000	5750
26	SAILSTAR	SLP	SA/RC	FBG KL	OB	8		3 10	5050	5800
32 1		SLP	SAIL	FBG	IB 30 UNIV				8150	9350
				--- 1970 **BOATS** ---						
19 7	CORINTHIAN	SLP	SAIL	FBG KL	OB	6 6	2724	2 9	2150	2500
22	CARAVEL	SLP	SAIL	FBG CB	OB	7 2	3500	3 4	2650	3100
24 7	CORSAIR DINETTE	SLP	SAIL	FBG KL	OB	8	5920	3 5	5150	5900
24 7	CORSAIR STD	SLP	SAIL	FBG KL	OB	8	5920	3 5	4850	5550
26	COURIER	SLP	SAIL	FBG KC	OB	8	5500	2 10	4850	5550
26	COURIER C	SLP	SAIL	FBG KC	OB	8	5500	2 10	5050	5800
26	HERRESHOFF 25	SLP	SAIL	FBG	OB	8	5600	2 10	5050	5800
26	HERRESHOFF 25	SLP	SAIL	FBG CB	OB	8	5600	2 10	5050	5800
				--- 1969 **BOATS** ---						
19 7	CORINTHIAN	SLP	SAIL	FBG KL	OB	6 6	2724	2 9	2050	2450
22	CARAVEL	SLP	SAIL	FBG KC	OB			2 8	2650	3050
22	CAVALIER	SLP	SAIL	FBG KC	OB	8	3500	2 8	2450	2850
22	CAVALIER DINETTE	SLP	SAIL	FBG KC	OB		3500	2 8	2600	3050
22	SAILSTAR 22	SLP	SAIL	FBG KC	OB	7 2	3500	2 8	2600	3050
24 7	CORSAIR DINETTE	SLP	SAIL	FBG KL	OB	8	5920	3 5	5050	5800
24 7	CORSAIR STD	SLP	SAIL	FBG KL	OB	8	5920	3 5	4750	5500
26	COURIER	SLP	SAIL	FBG KC	OB	8	5500	2 10	4850	5600
26	COURIER	SLP	SAIL	FBG KL	OB	8	5500	3 10	4850	5600
				--- 1968 **BOATS** ---						
19 6	CORINTHIAN	SLP	SAIL	FBG KL	OB	6 6	2724	2 9	2050	2450
24 7	CORSAIR	SLP	SAIL	FBG KL	OB	8	5920	3 5	4850	5600
26	COURIER	SLP	SAIL	FBG CB	OB	8	5500	2 10	4800	5500
				--- 1967 **BOATS** ---						
19 6	CORINTHIAN	SLP	SAIL	FBG					2050	2450
24 7	CORSAIR	SLP	SAIL	FBG					4800	5500
				--- 1966 **BOATS** ---						
19 6	CORINTHIAN	SLP	SAIL	FBG KL	OB	6 6		2 9	2000	2400
24 7	CORSAIR	SLP	SAIL	FBG KL	OB	7 11		3 3	4750	5450
				--- 1965 **BOATS** ---						
19 6	CORINTHIAN	SLP	SAIL	FBG KL	OB				2000	2400
22 6	SEA-SPRITE		SA/CR	FBG KL	OB				2550	3000
22 6	SEA-SPRITE DAY SA		SAIL	FBG KL	OB				2550	3000
25 5	AMPHIBI-CON	SLP	SA/OD	FBG KC	IB	7 9		5 4	4000	4650
				--- 1964 **BOATS** ---						
19	ORION DAY SAILER		SAIL	FBG	OB				1700	2000
22 6	SEA-SPRITE		SAIL	FBG	OB				2550	2950

SALERNO BOAT BUILDERS

Call 1-800-327-6929 for BUC Personalized Evaluation Service
Or, for 1980 boats, sign onto www.BUCValuPro.com

SALERNO SHIPYARD INC
GOLDCOAST FIBERCRAFT

Call 1-800-327-6929 for BUC Personalized Evaluation Service
Or, for 1959 to 1960 boats, sign onto www.BUCValuPro.com

SALT MARINE INC
COAST GUARD MFG ID- KSM

Call 1-800-327-6929 for BUC Personalized Evaluation Service
Or, for 1975 to 1981 boats, sign onto www.BUCValuPro.com

SALT SHAKER MARINE
PUNTA GORDA FL 33951   See inside cover to adjust price for area
For more recent years, see the BUC Used Boat Price Guide, Volume 1 or Volume 2

LOA FT IN	NAME AND/ OR MODEL	TOP/ RIG	BOAT TYPE	-HULL- MTL TP	----ENGINE--- TP # HP	MFG	BEAM FT IN	WGT LBS	DRAFT FT IN	RETAIL LOW	RETAIL HIGH
					1980 BOATS						
53	SALT-SHAKER 53	TT	CTRCN	FBG	IB T570D	GM	16	32000	3 11	178000	195500

SALTAIR YACHT SALES
Call 1-800-327-6929 for BUC Personalized Evaluation Service
Or, for 1970 boats, sign onto www.BUCValuPro.com

SAMOA FIBERGLASS INC
COAST GUARD MFG ID- SOF

Call 1-800-327-6929 for BUC Personalized Evaluation Service
Or, for 1983 boats, sign onto www.BUCValuPro.com

SAMSEL SUPPLY COMPANY
COAST GUARD MFG ID- S0S

Call 1-800-327-6929 for BUC Personalized Evaluation Service
Or, for 1983 boats, sign onto www.BUCValuPro.com

SAN AUGUSTINE FBG PROD
RAY-CRAFT   COAST GUARD MFG ID- SAG

Call 1-800-327-6929 for BUC Personalized Evaluation Service
Or, for 1971 to 1986 boats, sign onto www.BUCValuPro.com

SAN JUAN CRUISERS INC
KENT WA 98031   See inside cover to adjust price for area

LOA FT IN	NAME AND/ OR MODEL	TOP/ RIG	BOAT TYPE	-HULL- MTL TP	----ENGINE--- TP # HP	MFG	BEAM FT IN	WGT LBS	DRAFT FT IN	RETAIL LOW	RETAIL HIGH
					1971 BOATS						
31 9	SPOILER 30	FB	CR	FBG SV	IB T270		11 6		3	18500	20500
32 6	SPOILER 30		SDN	FBG SV	IB T270	MRCR	11 6	10000	3	21100	23500
32 6	SPOILER 30		SF	FBG SV	IB 170D	CRUS	11 6	11000	3	25700	28500
40	SPOILER 40		TCMY	FBG SV	IB T325		15 3		4	42900	47700
40	SPOILER COHO 40		DC	FBG SV	IB T325	MRCR	15 3	21000	4	42900	47700
					1970 BOATS						
31 9	SPOILER 30	FB	CR	FBG DV	IB T270		11 6	11000	3 6	19800	22000
31 9	SPOILER 30	FB	SF	FBG DV	IB T270		11 6	11000	3 6	19800	22000
41 10	SPOILER 40	FB	MY	FBG DV	IB T325		14 10	21000	3 11	45000	50000
					1969 BOATS						
29 9	CORSAIR 29	FB	SDN	FBG	IO 250		11 6		2 6	22400	24900
29 9	CORSAIR 29	FB	SDN	FBG	IO T210		11 6		2 6	25000	27800

SAN JUAN MANUFACTURING
AUBURN WA 98001   COAST GUARD MFG ID- CLK See inside cover to adjust price for area
For more recent years, see the BUC Used Boat Price Guide, Volume 1 or Volume 2

LOA FT IN	NAME AND/ OR MODEL	TOP/ RIG	BOAT TYPE	-HULL- MTL TP	----ENGINE--- TP # HP	MFG	BEAM FT IN	WGT LBS	DRAFT FT IN	RETAIL LOW	RETAIL HIGH
					1983 BOATS						
20 6	SAN-JUAN 21	SLP	SA/RC	FBG KC	OB		7	1250	1	2650	3050
23	SAN-JUAN 23	SLP	SA/RC	FBG KC	OB		8	2700	1 11	4550	5250
23	SAN-JUAN 23	SLP	SA/RC	FBG KL	OB		8	2700	4	4550	5250
24	SAN-JUAN 24	SLP	SA/RC	FBG KL	OB		8	3200	4	5450	6250
25 9	SAN-JUAN 7.7	SLP	SA/RC	FBG KL	IB 7D		9 6	3200	4	6350	7300
28 8	SAN-JUAN 28	SLP	SA/RC	FBG KL	IB 12D		10	6200	4 6	12300	14000
33	SAN-JUAN 33S	SLP	SA/RC	FBG KL	IB 20D		7 9	5700	5 8	11200	12700
33 10	SAN-JUAN 34	SLP	SA/RC	FBG KL	IB 20D	YAN	11	10500	5 11	21200	23600
33 10	SAN-JUAN 34 SHOAL	SLP	SA/RC	FBG KL	IB 20D	YAN	11	11000	4 9	22200	24700
					1982 BOATS						
20 6	SAN-JUAN 21	SLP	SA/RC	FBG SK	OB		7	1250	1	2450	2850
23	SAN-JUAN 23	SLP	SA/RC	FBG KC	OB		8	2700	1 11	4250	4950
23	SAN-JUAN 23	SLP	SA/RC	FBG KL	OB		8	2700	4	4250	4950
24	SAN-JUAN 24	SLP	SA/RC	FBG KL	OB		8	3200	4	5100	5850
25 9	SAN-JUAN 7.7	SLP	SA/RC	FBG KL	OB		9 6	3200	4	5500	6300
28 8	SAN-JUAN 28	SLP	SA/RC	FBG KL	IB 15D	YAN	10	6200	4 6	11600	13200
33	SAN-JUAN 33S	SLP	SA/RC	FBG KL	IB 8D		7 11	6000	5 11	11100	12600
33 10	SAN-JUAN 34	SLP	SA/CR	FBG KL	IB 16D		11	11000	4 11	20900	23200
					1981 BOATS						
20 6	SAN-JUAN 21	SLP	SA/RC	FBG SK	OB		7	1250	1	2300	2700
23	SAN-JUAN 23	SLP	SA/RC	FBG KC	OB		8	2700	1 11	4000	4650
24	SAN-JUAN 24	SLP	SA/RC	FBG KL	OB		8	3200	4	4800	5500
25 9	SAN-JUAN 7.7	SLP	SA/RC	FBG KL	OB		9 6	3200	4	5150	5950
25 9	SAN-JUAN 7.7	SLP	SA/RC	FBG KL	SD	OMC	9 6	3200	4	5450	6250
28 8	SAN-JUAN 28	SLP	SA/RC	FBG KL	IB 15D	YAN	10	6200	4 6	10900	12400
33	SAN-JUAN 335	SLP	SA/RC	FBG KL	IB D	YAN	7 10	6000	5 10	10500	11900
33 10	SAN-JUAN 34	SLP	SA/RC	FBG KL	IB 15D	YAN	10 11	10500	5 11	19000	21100
					1980 BOATS						
20 6	SAN-JUAN 21	SLP	SA/RC	FBG SK	OB		7	1250	1	2250	2600
23	SAN-JUAN 23	SLP	SA/RC	FBG KC	OB		8	2700	1 11	3800	4450
24	SAN-JUAN 24	SLP	SA/RC	FBG KL	OB		8	3200	4	4600	5300
24	SAN-JUAN 24	SLP	SA/RC	FBG KL	SD	OMC	8	3200	4	4900	5650
25 9	SAN-JUAN 7.7	SLP	SA/RC	FBG KL	OB		9 6	3200	4	5200	5700
25 9	SAN-JUAN 7.7	SLP	SA/RC	FBG KL	SD	OMC	9 6	3200	4	5250	6000
28 8	SAN-JUAN 28	SLP	SA/RC	FBG KL	SD	OMC	10	6200	4 6	10300	11700
28 8	SAN-JUAN 28	SLP	SA/RC	FBG KL	IB 15D- 30D		10	6200	4 6	10400	11900
30	SAN-JUAN 30	SLP	SA/RC	FBG KL	IB D		10	7200	5 4	12200	13900
34	SAN-JUAN 34	SLP	SA/RC	FBG KL	IB 15D	YAN	10 11	10500	5 11	18100	20100
					1979 BOATS						
20 6	SAN-JUAN 21 MK II	SLP	SA/RC	FBG SK	OB		7	1250	1	2150	2500
23	SAN-JUAN 23	SLP	SA/CR	FBG KC	OB		8	2700	1 11	3650	4250
24	SAN-JUAN 24	SLP	SA/RC	FBG KL	OB		8	3200	4	4450	5100
25 9	SAN-JUAN 7.7	SLP	SA/RC	FBG KL	OB		9 6	3200	4	4750	5450
25 9	SAN-JUAN 7.7	SLP	SA/RC	FBG KL	SD	OMC	9 6	3200	4	5000	5750
25 11	SAN-JUAN 26	SLP	SA/CR	FBG KC	SD		8	4400	2 3	6400	7350
25 11	SAN-JUAN 26	SLP	SA/CR	FBG KC	SD	OMC	8	4400	2 3	6650	7600
28 8	SAN-JUAN 28	SLP	SA/CR	FBG KL	IB		10	6200	4 6	9750	11100
28 8	SAN-JUAN 28	SLP	SA/CR	FBG KL	SD	OMC	10	6200	4 6	9850	11200
28 8	SAN-JUAN 28	SLP	SA/CR	FBG KL	IB 15D- 30D		10	6200	4 6	10000	11500
30	SAN-JUAN 30	SLP	SA/CR	FBG KL	IB		10	7200	5 4	11700	13400
					1978 BOATS						
20 6	SAN-JUAN 21 MK I	SLP	SA/RC	FBG SK			7	1250	1	2050	2400
20 6	SAN-JUAN 21 MK II	SLP	SA/RC	FBG SK			7	1250	1	2050	2400
23	SAN-JUAN 23	SLP	SA/CR	FBG KC			8	2700	1 11	3550	4100
24 2	SAN-JUAN 24	SLP	SA/CR	FBG KC			8	3700	4	4850	5550
24 2	SAN-JUAN 24M	SLP	SA/CR	FBG KL			8	3700	4	4850	5550
25 11	SAN-JUAN 26	SLP	SA/CR	FBG KC	OB		8	4500	2	6300	7250
28 8	SAN-JUAN 28	SLP	SA/CR	FBG KL	IB		10	6200	4 6	9100	10300
30	SAN-JUAN 30	SLP	SA/CR	FBG KL	IB 25D		10	7200	5	11300	12900
					1977 BOATS						
20 6	SAN-JUAN 21	SLP	SA/RC	F/S KC	OB		7	1250	1	1950	2350
20 6	SAN-JUAN 21	SLP	SA/RC	F/S KC	OB		7	1250	1	1950	2350
23	SAN-JUAN 23	SLP	SA/RC	F/S KC	OB		8	2700	1 11	3400	3950
24	SAN-JUAN 24	SLP	SA/RC	F/S KC	OB		8	3200	4	4100	4750
25 11	SAN-JUAN 26	SLP	SA/CR	F/S KC			8	4400	2 3	5950	6850
25 11	SAN-JUAN 26	SLP	SA/CR	F/S KC	25 UNIV		8	4400	2 3	6200	7100
25 11	SAN-JUAN 26	SLP	SA/CR	F/S KC	6D FARY		8	4400	2 3	6300	7200
25 11	SAN-JUAN 26	SLP	SA/CR	F/S KL	25 UNIV		8	4400	4	5950	6850
25 11	SAN-JUAN 26	SLP	SA/CR	F/S KL	6D FARY		8	4400	4	6300	7200
30	SAN-JUAN 30	SLP	SA/CR	F/S KL	IB 25 UNIV		10	7200	5 4	10800	12300
30	SAN-JUAN 30	SLP	SA/CR	F/S KL	IB 10D- 12D		10	7200	5	10900	12400
					1976 BOATS						
20 6	SAN-JUAN 21 I	SLP	SAIL	FBG KL			7			1800	2150
20 6	SAN-JUAN 21 I	SLP	SAIL	FBG SK			7	1250	1	1800	2150
20 6	SAN-JUAN 21 II	SLP	SAIL	FBG KL			7			2000	2400
20 6	SAN-JUAN 21 II	SLP	SAIL	FBG SK			7	1250	1	2000	2400
24 2	SAN-JUAN 24	SLP	SAIL	FBG KL			8	3700	4	4550	5250
25 11	SAN-JUAN 26	SLP	SAIL	FBG KC	OB		8	4500	2	5900	6750
25 11	SAN-JUAN 26	SLP	SAIL	FBG KC	25 UNIV		8		4	4550	5250
25 11	SAN-JUAN 26	SLP	SAIL	FBG KL	6D FARY		8		4	4700	5400
30	SAN-JUAN 30	SLP	SAIL	FBG KL	IB 10 UNIV		10	7200	5	10500	11900
30	SAN-JUAN 30	SLP	SAIL	FBG KL	IB 10D- 12D		10		5	10600	12000
					1975 BOATS						
20 6	SAN-JUAN MK I	SLP	SAIL	FBG SK	OB		8	1250		1750	2050
20 6	SAN-JUAN MK II	SLP	SAIL	FBG SK	OB		8	1950		1950	2300
24	SAN-JUAN 24	SLP	SAIL	FBG SV	OB		8	3900	4	4600	5300
25 11	SAN-JUAN 26	SLP	SAIL	FBG KL	OB D		8	4400	5	5100	5850
25 11	SAN-JUAN 26	SLP	SAIL	FBG KL	OB 14D		8	4400	5	5600	6450
25 11	SAN-JUAN 26	SLP	SAIL	FBG KL	OB		8	4400	5	5600	6900
25 11	SAN-JUAN 26	SLP	SAIL	FBG KL	OB 14D		8	4400	5	5600	6900
25 11	SAN-JUAN 26	SLP	SAIL	FBG KL	OB		8		5	5950	6900
30	SAN-JUAN 30	SLP	SAIL	FBG KL	IB 10D VLVO		10	7200	5 4	10300	11700

LOA (FT IN)	NAME AND/OR MODEL	TOP/RIG	BOAT TYPE	HULL MTL	HULL TP	ENG TP	# HP	MFG	BEAM (FT IN)	WGT LBS	DRAFT (FT IN)	RETAIL LOW	RETAIL HIGH
1974 BOATS													
20 6	SAN-JUAN 21		SAIL	FBG		OB			7	1250	4	1800	2150
24 2	SAN-JUAN 24		SAIL	FBG		OB			8	3800	4	4450	5100
1973 BOATS													
20 6	SAN-JUAN 21	SLP	SAIL	FBG		OB			7	1250	4	1750	2100
24 2	SAN-JUAN 24	SLP	SAIL	FBG		OB			8	3300	4	3800	4400
1972 BOATS													
20 6	SAN-JUAN 21		SAIL	FBG		OB			7	1250	4	1700	2050
1971 BOATS													
20 6	SAN-JUAN 21		SAIL	FBG		OB			7	1250	4	1700	2000

SANFORD-WOOD
FORMERLY SANFORD BOAT CO INC

Call 1-800-327-6929 for BUC Personalized Evaluation Service
Or, for 1980 to 1985 boats, sign onto www.BUCValuPro.com

SANGER BOAT
FRESNO CA 93725   COAST GUARD MFG ID- SAN   See inside cover to adjust price for area

For more recent years, see the BUC Used Boat Price Guide, Volume 1 or Volume 2

LOA (FT IN)	NAME AND/OR MODEL	TOP/RIG	BOAT TYPE	HULL MTL	HULL TP	ENG TP	# HP	MFG	BEAM (FT IN)	WGT LBS	DRAFT (FT IN)	RETAIL LOW	RETAIL HIGH
1983 BOATS													
18	BUBBLEDECK	OP	SKI	FBG	DV	JT			6 7			**	**
18	BUBBLEDECK OUTBOARD	OP	SKI	FBG	DV	OB			6 7			2450	2850
18	DRAG-RUNNER	OP	RACE	FBG	DV	VD	333	CHEV	6 1			3350	3850
18	SKI-HYDRO	OP	SKI	FBG	DV	VD	333	CHEV	7 8			4150	4850
18	SUPER-JET	OP	SKI	FBG	DV	JT	320-333	CHEV	6 7			4100	4800
18 3	CIRCLE-RUNNER	OP	RNBT	FBG	DV	VD	333	CHEV	6 6			4250	4950
19 6	FAMILY SKI	OP	SKI	FBG	DV	VD	333	CHEV	6 9			4800	5500
20	MINI-CRUISER	OP	RNBT	FBG	DV	JT	320	FORD	8			6350	7250
20	MINI-CRUISER	OP	RNBT	FBG	DV	VD	333	CHEV	8			6000	6900
20	MINI-CRUISER	OP	SKI	FBG	DV	IO	260	MRCR	8			4500	5150
20 1	ALLEY-CAT	OP	SKI	FBG	TH	OB			7			3600	4150
21	CLASSIC OUTBOARD	OP	SKI	FBG	DV	OB			7 10			4600	5300
23	ALLEY-CAT	OP	SKI	FBG	TH	OB			8			8000	9200
23	CLASSIC STERNDRIVE	OP	SKI	FBG	DV	IO	260	MRCR	7 10			5650	6500
24 6	SANGER 24	OP	OVNTR	FBG	DV	IO	330	CHEV	8	4275		9300	10600
26	SPRINT CRUISER	OP	OVNTR	FBG	DV	IO	330	MRCR	8			10900	12400
26	TAHOE CRUISER	OP	OVNTR	FBG	DV	IO	330	CHEV	8			11800	13400
1982 BOATS													
18	BUBBLEDECK OUTBOARD	OP	SKI	FBG	DV	OB			6 7			2400	2750
18	DRAG-RUNNER	OP	RACE	FBG	DV	VD	333	CHEV	6 1			3200	3700
18	SKI-HYDRO	OP	SKI	FBG	DV	VD	333	CHEV	7 8			4000	4650
18	SUPER-JET	OP	SKI	FBG	DV	JT	320-333	CHEV	6 7			3950	4700
18 3	CIRCLE-RUNNER	OP	RNBT	FBG	DV	VD	333	CHEV	6 6			4050	4700
19 6	FAMILY SKI	OP	SKI	FBG	DV	VD	333	CHEV	6 9			4600	5300
20	MINI-CRUISER	OP	RNBT	FBG	DV	JT	320	FORD	8			6050	6950
20	MINI-CRUISER	OP	RNBT	FBG	DV	VD	333	CHEV	8			5750	6600
20	MINI-CRUISER	OP	SKI	FBG	DV	IO	260	MRCR	8			4400	5050
20 1	ALLEY-CAT	OP	SKI	FBG	TH	OB			7			3500	4050
21	CLASSIC OUTBOARD	OP	SKI	FBG	DV	OB			7 10			4500	5150
23	ALLEY-CAT		SKI	FBG	TH	OB			8			7800	8950
23	CLASSIC STERNDRIVE	OP	SKI	FBG	DV	IO	260	MRCR	7 10			5550	6350
24 6	SANGER 24	OP	OVNTR	FBG	DV	IO	330	CHEV	8	4275		9100	10400
26	SPRINT CRUISER	OP	OVNTR	FBG	DV	IO	330	MRCR	8			10900	12400
26	TAHOE CRUISER	OP	OVNTR	FBG	DV	IO	330	MRCR	8			11300	12900
1981 BOATS													
18	DRAG-RUNNER	OP	RACE	FBG	DV	VD	333	CHEV	6 1			3050	3550
18	SKI-HYDRO	OP	SKI	FBG	DV	VD	333	CHEV	7 8			3800	4450
18	SUPER-JET	OP	SKI	FBG	DV	JT	320-333	CHEV	6 7			3800	4400
18 3	CIRCLE-RUNNER	OP	RNBT	FBG	DV	VD	333	CHEV	6 6			3900	4500
19 6	FAMILY SKI	OP	SKI	FBG	DV	VD	333	CHEV	6 9			4400	5050
20	MINI-CRUISER	OP	RNBT	FBG	DV	JT	320	FORD	8			5800	6650
20	MINI-CRUISER	OP	RNBT	FBG	DV	VD	333	CHEV	8			5500	6300
20	MINI-CRUISER	OP	SKI	FBG	DV	IO	260	MRCR	8			4250	4950
20 1	ALLEY-CAT	OP	SKI	FBG	TH	OB			7			3400	3950
21	CLASSIC OUTBOARD	OP	SKI	FBG	DV	OB			7 10			4400	5050
23	ALLEY-CAT	OP	SKI	FBG	TH	OB			8			7600	8750
23	CLASSIC STERNDRIVE	OP	SKI	FBG	DV	IO	260	MRCR	7 10			5450	6250
26	SPRINT CRUISER	OP	OVNTR	FBG	DV	IO	330	MRCR	8			10700	12200
26	TAHOE CRUISER	OP	OVNTR	FBG	DV	IO	330	MRCR	8			11100	12700
1980 BOATS													
18	DRAG-RUNNER	OP	RACE	FBG	DV	VD	360	CHEV	6 1			3050	3550
18	SKI-HYDRO	OP	SKI	FBG	DV	JT	320	FORD	7 8			3950	4600
18	SKI-HYDRO	OP	SKI	FBG	DV	JT	360	CHEV	7 8			3950	4600
18	SKI-HYDRO	OP	SKI	FBG	DV	VD	360	CHEV	7 8			3800	4450
18	SPRINT JET	OP	RNBT	FBG	DV	JT	320-360	CHEV	6 7			4000	4650
18	SUPER-JET	OP	SKI	FBG	DV	JT	320-360	CHEV	6 7			3600	4200
18 3	CIRCLE-RUNNER	OP	RNBT	FBG	DV	VD	360	CHEV	6 6			3850	4500
19 6	FAMILY SKI	OP	SKI	FBG	DV	VD	360	CHEV	6 9			4350	5050
20	MINI-CRUISER	OP	RNBT	FBG	DV	JT	320	FORD	8			**	**
20	MINI-CRUISER	OP	RNBT						8			5550	6400
1978 BOATS													
18	BUBBLEDECK SKI JET	OP	SKI	FBG	DV	JT	320-360					3450	4000
18	JET HYDRO	OP	RNBT	FBG	TR	JT	320	FORD	7 8			3950	4600
18	PICKLEFORK SKI HYDRO	OP	SKI	FBG	TR	VD	360	CHEV	7 8			3500	4100
18	SPRINT JET	OP	RNBT	FBG	DV	JT	320-360		6 7			3650	4250
18 3	CIRCLE-RUNNER	OP	RNBT	FBG	DV	VD	360	CHEV	6 6			3550	4150
18 6	CLIMAX DRAG HULL	OP	RACE	FBG	TR	JT						**	**
18 6	DRAG-RUNNER	OP	RACE	FBG	DV	VD			6 6			**	**
19 6	FAMILY SKI	OP	SKI	FBG	DV	VD	360	CHEV	6 9			3950	4600
20	MINI-CRUISER	OP	RNBT	FBG	DV	JT	320-360		8			5100	5850
1977 BOATS													
18	BUBBLEDECK SUPERJET	OP	SKI	FBG	DV	JT	320-360		6 7			3200	3700
18	CLIMAX DRAG HULL	OP	RACE	FBG	TR	JT			6 7			**	**
18	JET SKI HYDRO	OP	SKI	FBG	TR	JT	320	FORD	7 8			3500	4050
18	PICKLEFORK SKI HYDRO	OP	SKI	FBG	TR	VD	360	CHEV	7 8			3350	3900
18	SPRINT JET	OP	RNBT	FBG	DV	JT	320-360		6 7			3500	4100
18 3	CIRCLE-RUNNER	OP	RNBT	FBG	DV	VD	360	CHEV	6 6			3400	4000
18 6	DRAG-RUNNER	OP	RACE	FBG	DV	VD	360	CHEV	6 6			3550	4150
19 6	FAMILY SKI	OP	SKI	FBG	DV	VD	360	CHEV	6 9			3800	4450
20	MINI-CRUISER	OP	RNBT	FBG	DV	JT	320-330		8			4900	5650
20	MINI-CRUISER	OP	RNBT	FBG	DV	VD	360	CHEV	8			4900	5650
20	MINI-CRUISER	OP	RNBT	FBG	DV	VD	360	CHEV	8			4800	5500
1975 BOATS													
17 10	SUPER-SANGER	OP	SKI	FBG	FL	VD			6 4			**	**
18	BUBBLEDECK SUPER JET	OP	SKI	FBG	FL	VD	330-360		7 7			2950	3450
18	CLIMAX DRAG HYDRO	OP	SKI	FBG	FL	VD			7			**	**
18	PICKLEFORK SKI HYDRO	OP	SKI	FBG	FL	VD			7 8			**	**
18 3	CIRCLE-RUNNER	OP	SKI	FBG	FL	VD			6 6			**	**
18 6	DRAG-RUNNER	OP	SKI	FBG	FL	VD			6 7			**	**
19	FAMILY SKI BOAT	OP	SKI	FBG	FL	VD			6			**	**
20	MINI CRUISER JET	OP	SKI	FBG	FL	JT	330-360		8			4450	5100
1973 BOATS													
17 10	SUPER-SANGER	OP	SKI	FBG	FL	VD	250		6 4		1 11	2300	2650
18	HYDRO	OP	SKI	FBG	FL	VD	360		7 7		1 11	2850	3350
18	SUPER JET	OP	SKI	FBG	FL	VD	360		7 8			2700	3150
18 3	CIRCLE-RUNNER	OP	RNBT	FBG	FL	VD	360		6 6		1 6	2900	3400
19	CATALINA	OP	RNBT	FBG	DV	VD	360		8		2 4	3650	4250
19	FAMILY SKI	OP	SKI	FBG	FL	VD	360		6 7		1 6	3100	3650

SANTA BARBARA YACHTS INC
SANTA BARBARA CA 93103   See inside cover to adjust price for area

LOA (FT IN)	NAME AND/OR MODEL	TOP/RIG	BOAT TYPE	HULL MTL	HULL TP	ENG TP	# HP	MFG	BEAM (FT IN)	WGT LBS	DRAFT (FT IN)	RETAIL LOW	RETAIL HIGH
1971 BOATS													
39 9	CEDROS-ISLAND 40	EXP		FBG	DS	IB	160D	PERK	12 2	22000	4	58600	64400
39 9	OCEAN CRUISER 40	DC		FBG	DS	IB	160D	PERK	12 2	24000		62300	68500
39 11	CEDROS-ISLAND 40	EXP		FBG	SV	IB	T160D	PERK	13 10	20000	2 4	54300	59600
39 11	MARLIN 40	EXP		FBG	SV	IB	T160D	PERK	13 10			53600	58900
39 11	OCEAN CRUISER 40	EXP		FBG	SV	IB	T160D	PERK	13 10			57700	63400
42 8	FORCE-TEN 43	EXP		FBG	SV	IB	T160D	PERK	13 10			60000	65900
42 8	MARLIN 43	EXP		FBG	SV	IB	T160D	PERK	13 10			52000	57200
42 8	MARLIN 43	EXP		FBG	SV	IB	T160D	PERK	13 10			59000	76700
42 8	OCEAN CRUISER 43	EXP		FBG	SV	IB	T210D	CUM	13 10	26000	2 4	55400	60900
46	OCEAN CRUISER 46	EXP		FBG	SV	IB	T283D	GM	15	30000	3	83000	91200
46	OCEAN CRUISER 46	DC		FBG	SV	IB	T283D	GM	15	32000	3	82000	90200
50 9	FORCE-TEN 51	TCMY		FBG	SV	IB	T283D	CUM	15	36000	3	91600	100500
50 9	MARLIN 51	EXP		FBG	SV	IB	T300D		16		3	82200	90400
1970 BOATS													
39 9	CEDROS-ISLAND 40	EXP		FBG	RB	IB	160D	PERK	12 2	22000	4	56700	62300
39 9	OCEAN CRUISER 40	DC		FBG	RB	IB	160D	PERK	12 2	24000		60300	66200
39 11	CEDROS-ISLAND 40	EXP		FBG	SV	IB	T160D	PERK	13 10	20000	2 4	52500	57600
39 11	MARLIN 40	EXP		FBG		IB	T160D	PERK	13 10			57100	62800
39 11	OCEAN CRUISER 40	EXP		FBG		IB	T160D	PERK	13 10			55300	60700
39 11	SANTA-CRUZ 40	EXP		FBG		IB	T160D	PERK	13 10			54300	59700

LOA FT IN	NAME AND/ OR MODEL	TOP/ RIG	BOAT TYPE	-HULL- MTL TP	TP	----ENGINE--- # HP MFG	BEAM FT IN	WGT LBS	DRAFT FT IN	RETAIL LOW	RETAIL HIGH
						1970 BOATS					
42 7	CEDROS-ISLAND 43		EXP	FBG	IB	T160D PERK	13 10		2 4	54200	59600
42 7	FORCE-TEN 43			FBG	IB	T160D PERK	13 10		2 4	56100	61700
42 7	MARLIN 43			FBG	IB	T160D PERK	13 10		2 4	54900	60400
42 7	OCEAN CRUISER 43		EXP	FBG	IB	T160D PERK	13 10		2 4	55200	60700
46	CEDROS-ISLAND 46		EXP	FBG SV	IB	T283D GM	15 3	30000	3	80200	88100
46	FORCE-TEN 46		EXP	FBG	IB	T283D GM	15 3		3	64800	71200
46	OCEAN CRUISER 46		EXP	FBG SV	IB	T283D GM	15 3	32000	3	84900	93300
46	SANTA-CRUZ 46		EXP	FBG	IB	T283D GM	15 3		3	60100	66000
						1969 BOATS					
39 9	CEDROS-ISLAND 40		EXP	FBG RB	IB	160D PERK	12 2	22000	4	54900	60400
39 9	OCEAN CRUISER 40		CR	FBG RB	IB	160D PERK	12 2	24000	4	58600	64400
39 11	CEDROS-ISLAND 40		EXP	FBG SV	IB	T160D PERK	13 10	20000	2 4	50800	55800
39 11	OCEAN CRUISER 40		EXP	FBG	IB	T160D PERK	13 10		2 4	54200	59500
39 11	SANTA-CRUZ 40		EXP	FBG	IB	T160D PERK	13 10		2 4	51900	57100
46	CEDROS-ISLAND 46		EXP	FBG SV	IB	T283D GM	15 3	30000	3	77600	85300
46	OCEAN CRUISER 46		EXP	FBG SV	IB	T283D GM	15 3	32000	3	82200	90300
46	SANTA-CRUZ 46		EXP	FBG	IB	T283D GM	15 3		3	60400	66300
						1968 BOATS					
39 9	CEDROS-ISLAND 40		CR	FBG	IB	130D	12 2	22000	4	52500	57700
39 9	CEDROS-ISLAND 40		CR	FBG	IB	T130D	12 2	24000	4	58100	63800
39 9	CEDROS-ISLAND 40		EXP	FBG	IB	T110D	13 10	24000	4	54200	59600
	IB T160D PERK	51000		56100, IB T170D CUM		48100 52900, IB T283D GM				53100	58400
39 9	OCEAN CRUISER 40		TCMY	FBG	IB	T130D	12 2	24000	4	59000	64800
39 9	OCEAN CRUISER 40		TCMY	FBG	IB	T160D PERK	12 2		4	60500	66500
46	CEDROS-ISLAND 46		EXP	FBG	IB	T160D PERK	15	30000	3	69500	76400
46	CEDROS-ISLAND 46		EXP	FBG	IB	T170D CUM	15	30000	3	69700	76600
46	OCEAN CRUISER		TCMY	FBG	IB	T160D PERK	15	32000	3	69500	76400
						1967 BOATS					
39 9	OCEAN CRUISER 40			FBG	IB	160D	12 2	22500	4	52200	57300
39 9	OCEAN CRUISER 40		CR	FBG	IB	160D	12 2	24500	4	55600	61100
46			CR	FBG	IB	T160D	15	36000	3	71800	78900
46	CEDROS-ISLAND 46		EXP	FBG	IB	T160D	15	32000	3	70200	77100
						1966 BOATS					
36	CATALINA 36	KTH	SA/CR	MHG KL	IB	40D	12		5	24800	27500
39 9	CEDROS-ISLAND 40		CR	FBG	IB	160D	12 4		4	49900	54800
39 9	OCEAN CRUISER 40		CR	FBG	IB	160D	12 4		4	53900	59200
45	OCEAN CRUISER 45		CR	P/M	IB	180	14		4	41700	46400
46	CEDROS-ISLAND 46		CR	P/M	IB	T160	15		3	48500	53300
46	CEDROS-ISLAND 46		CR	FBG	IB	T160D	15		3	52800	58100
46	OCEAN CRUISER 46		CR	FBG	IB	T160D	15		3	57500	63200
49 11	CATALINA 49	KTH	SA/CR	MHG KL	IB	85D	13 6		6	73400	80700
						1965 BOATS					
36	CATALINA	KTH	SAIL	WD KC	IB		12		5	17000	19400
39 9	CEDROS-ISLAND 40		CR	FBG	IB	160D				47400	52100
39 9	OCEAN CRUISER 40		CR	FBG	IB	160D				50800	55900
45 3			SF	WD	IB	300D	14		4	51900	57100
45 3	OCEAN CRUISER		MY	WD	IB	180D	14		4	65400	71800
46 3			EXP	FBG	IB	T160D				50400	55400
49 10	CALIFORNIA-49ER	KTH	SAIL	WD KL	IB		13 6		6	70500	77500
						1964 BOATS					
39			FSH	WD	IB	160D				42600	47300
40			FSH	WD	IB	160D				44700	49600
40	OCEAN CRUISER		CR	WD	IB	160D				50100	55000
45	OCEAN CRUISER		CR	WD	IB	175D				48600	53400
						1963 BOATS					
38	OCEAN CRUISER		CR	WD	IB	130D				35900	39900
39			FSH	WD	IB	130D				41300	45900
43	OCEAN CRUISER		CR	WD	IB	160D				39100	43500
45	OCEAN CRUISER		CR	WD	IB	175D				47300	52000
						1962 BOATS					
38	OCEAN CRUISER		CR	WD	IB	100D				34600	38400
43	OCEAN CRUISER		CR	WD	IB	160D				38100	42300
45	OCEAN CRUISER		CR	WD	IB	175D				46200	50800
49	CALIFORNIA 49ER	KTH	MS	WD	IB					66000	72500
						1961 BOATS					
38			CR	P/C	IB	160D	12		4 3	36200	40200
42			CR	P/C	IB	T130D	13		4 6	43600	48400
46	MONK	KTH	MS	P/C KL	IB		13		5 6	49500	54400
						1960 BOATS					
38			CR	WD	IB	160D				33800	37500
42			CR	WD	IB	T130D				41400	46000
46	MONK 46	KTH	MS	P/C KL			13		5 6	**	**
						1959 BOATS					
27			CR	WD	IB	177				7250	8350
38			CR	WD	IB	T180				28100	31200
						1957 BOATS					
35			CR	WD	IB	155				17600	19900
						1956 BOATS					
24			CR	WD	IB	145				4250	4950
						1954 BOATS					
26 4	BERTH		CR	WD	IB	160				6100	7050
						1950 BOATS					
48 9	BERTH		CR	WD	IB	T225				43200	48000
						1948 BOATS					
31			CR	WD	IB	115				9250	10500

SANTA CRUZ MARINE & CONST INC

Call 1-800-327-6929 for BUC Personalized Evaluation Service
Or, for 1965 to 1968 boats, sign onto www.BUCValuPro.com

SANTA CRUZ YACHTS LLC

LA SELUA BEACH CA 95026 COAST GUARD MFG ID- SYM See inside cover to adjust price for area

For more recent years, see the BUC Used Boat Price Guide, Volume 1 or Volume 2

LOA FT IN	NAME AND/ OR MODEL	TOP/ RIG	BOAT TYPE	-HULL- MTL TP	TP	----ENGINE--- # HP MFG	BEAM FT IN	WGT LBS	DRAFT FT IN	RETAIL LOW	RETAIL HIGH
						1983 BOATS					
40	SANTA-CRUZ 40	SLP	SA/RC	FBG KL	IB	18D	12	10000	7	53400	58700
50	SANTA-CRUZ 50	SLP	SA/RC	FBG KL	IB	42D PATH	12	16000	8	151500	166500
50	SANTA-CRUZ 50	SLP	SA/RC	FBG KL	IB	42D PATH	12	16000	8	139000	153000
50	SANTA-CRUZ 50	SLP	SA/RC	FBG KL	IB	82D PATH	12	16000	8	146500	160500
67	SANTA-CRUZ 70	SLP	SA/RC	FBG KL	IB	138 BMW	15	25800	8 5	284000	312500
						1982 BOATS					
27	SANTA-CRUZ 27	SLP	SA/RC	FBG KL	OB		8	3000	4 6	8200	9450
40	SANTA-CRUZ 40	SLP	SA/RC	FBG KL	IB		12	10000	7	49800	54700
40	SANTA-CRUZ 40	SLP	SA/RC	FBG KL	IB	18D TRID	12	10500	7	52400	57600
50	SANTA-CRUZ 50	SLP	SA/RC	FBG KL	IB	42D PATH	12	16000	8	138000	151500
50	SANTA-CRUZ 50	SLP	SA/RC	FBG KL	IB	82D PATH	12	16000	8	138500	152500
						1981 BOATS					
50	SANTA-CRUZ 50	SLP	SA/RC	FBG KL	IB	42D PATH	12	16000	8	130500	143500
50	SANTA-CRUZ 50	SLP	SA/RC	FBG KL	IB	85D PATH	12	16000	8	131500	144500
						1980 BOATS					
27	SANTA-CRUZ 27	SLP	SA/RC	FBG KL	OB		8	3000	4 6	7500	8600
50	SANTA-CRUZ 50	SLP	SA/CR	FBG KL	IB	40D	12	16000	8	125500	138000
						1979 BOATS					
27	SANTA-CRUZ 27	SLP	SA/RC	FBG KL	OB		8	3000	4 6	7250	8350
50	SANTA-CRUZ 50	SLP	SA/CR	F/S KL	IB	40D PATH	12	16000	8	120000	132000
						1978 BOATS					
27	SANTA-CRUZ 27	SLP	SA/RC	FBG KL	OB		8	3000	4 6	7050	8100
27	SANTA-CRUZ 27	SLP	SA/RC	FBG KL	IB		8	3000	4 6	7300	8400
33	SANTA-CRUZ 33	SLP	SA/RC	FBG KL	IB	16D REN	10	6400	6	19400	21500
						1977 BOATS					
27	SANTA-CRUZ 27	SLP	SA/RC	FBG KL	OB		8	3000	4 6	6850	7850
27	SANTA-CRUZ 27	SLP	SA/RC	FBG KL	IB	8 BALD	8	3000	4 6	7050	8100
27	SANTA-CRUZ 27	SLP	SA/RC	FBG KL	D		8	3000	4 6	7250	8350
29 11	SANTA-CRUZ 30	SLP	SA/RC	FBG KL	OB		10	5000		13100	14900
29 11	SANTA-CRUZ 30	SLP	SA/RC	FBG KL	IB	8 BALD	10	5000		13200	14900
29 11	SANTA-CRUZ 30	SLP	SA/RC	FBG KL	D		10	5000		13300	15100
33	SANTA-CRUZ 33	SLP	SA/RC	FBG KL	IB		10	5000	6	13900	15800
33	SANTA-CRUZ 33	SLP	SA/RC	FBG KL	IB	8 BALD	10	5000	6	13900	15800
33	SANTA-CRUZ 33	SLP	SA/RC	FBG KL	D		10	5000	6	14000	15900
						1976 BOATS					
27	SANTA-CRUZ	SLP	SAIL	FBG KL	OB		8	3000	4 6	6650	7650
27	SANTA-CRUZ	SLP	SAIL	FBG KL	IB	8 BALD	8	3000	4 6	6900	7950
27	SANTA-CRUZ	SLP	SAIL	FBG KL	D		8	3000	4 6	7050	8150
						1975 BOATS					
27	SANTA-CRUZ 27	SLP	SA/CR	FBG KL	OB		8	2800	3 7	6150	7050

SARASOTA MARINE IND
WATERBIRD

Call 1-800-327-6929 for BUC Personalized Evaluation Service
Or, for 1959 boats, sign onto www.BUCValuPro.com

SAVAGE FIBREGLASS BTS LTD

Call 1-800-327-6929 for BUC Personalized Evaluation Service
Or, for 1975 to 1978 boats, sign onto www.BUCValuPro.com

SAVANNAH ENT INC

Call 1-800-327-6929 for BUC Personalized Evaluation Service
Or, for 1969 boats, sign onto www.BUCValuPro.com

TOM SAWYER BOATS INC

STANDARD BOAT CORP   See inside cover to adjust price for area
LEBANON MO 65536   COAST GUARD MFG ID- TMR

LOA FT IN	NAME AND/ OR MODEL	TOP/ RIG	BOAT TYPE	-HULL- MTL TP	ENGINE TP # HP MFG	BEAM FT IN	WGT LBS	DRAFT FT IN	RETAIL LOW	RETAIL HIGH
--- 1974 BOATS ---
16 1	160-T	RNBT	FBG TR	IO	120	6 4			2750	3200
16 2	160-V W/T	RNBT	FBG TR	IO	120-140	6 4			2750	3200
17 11	180-T	RNBT	FBG TR	IO	165-188	7			3500	4150
17 11	180-T	RNBT	FBG TR	JT	455	7			3400	4000
18 2	180-V W/T	RNBT	FBG	IO	165-188	7 4			3650	4300
18 2	180-V W/T	RNBT	FBG	JT	455	7 4			3550	4100
20 2	200-V W/T	RNBT	FBG	IO	165-225	7 7			4900	5800
20 2	200-V W/T	RNBT	FBG	JT	455	7 7			4650	5350
--- 1973 BOATS ---
16 1	160T	RNBT	FBG	IO	120-140	6 4			2850	3300
16 2	160V	RNBT	FBG	IO	120-140	6 4			2850	3300
16 2	160V W/T	RNBT	FBG	IO	120-140	6 4			2850	3350
17 11	180T	RNBT	FBG	IO	165-188	7	2300		3500	4100
17 11	180T	RNBT	FBG	JT	270 BERK	7	2300		3200	3700
18 2	180V STD	RNBT	FBG	IO	165-188	7 4	2500		3800	4450
18 2	180V STD	RNBT	FBG	JT	270 BERK	7 4	2500		3400	3950
18 2	180V W/T	RNBT	FBG	IO	165-188	7 4	2500		3850	4500
18 2	180V W/T	RNBT	FBG	JT	270 BERK	7 4	2500		3450	4050
20 2	200V	RNBT	FBG	IO	165-215	7 7	2800		5000	5900
20 2	200V	RNBT	FBG	JT	270 BERK	7 7	2800		4450	5100
--- 1972 BOATS ---
16 1	W/T	RNBT	FBG TR	IO	120-140	6 4	1700		2650	3100
16 2	LARK STD	RNBT	FBG	OB		6 4	1600		2000	2400
16 2	LARK STD	RNBT	FBG	IO	120-140	6 4			2950	3400
16 2	LARK W/T	RNBT	FBG	OB		6 4	1600		2100	2500
16 2	LARK W/T	RNBT	FBG	IO	120-140	6 4			2950	3450
17 11	W/T	RNBT	FBG TR	IO	140-188	7	2300		3600	4225
18 2	FUNLINER 18 STD	RNBT	FBG	IO	165-215	7 4	2500		3900	4650
18 2	FUNLINER W/T	RNBT	FBG	IO	165-215	7 4	2500		4000	4750
20 2	SEAFARER 20	RNBT	FBG	IO	165-215	7 7	2800		5200	6100
--- 1971 BOATS ---
16 2	LARK	RNBT	FBG DV	IO	120-140	6 4	2200	1 6	3150	3650
16 2	LARK W/T	RNBT	FBG DV	IO	120-140	6 4	2200	1 6	3200	3700
17 8	SPORTSTER	RNBT	FBG TR	IO	140 MRCR	7 1	2500	2	3900	4500
17 8	SPORTSTER W/T	RNBT	FBG TR	IO	120	7 1	2500	1 6	3900	4500
18 2	FUNLINER	RNBT	FBG DV	IO	165-215	7 4	2500	1 6	4050	4800
18 2	FUNLINER W/T	RNBT	FBG DV	IO	165-215	7 4	2500	1 6	4100	4900
20 2	SEAFARER	RNBT	FBG DV	IO	215 MRCR	7 7	3000	2	5700	6550
20 2	SEAFARER W/T	RNBT	FBG DV	IO	165	7 7	3000	1 6	5600	6400
--- 1969 BOATS ---
16 2	LARK	RNBT	FBG DV	IO	120	6 4	2200	1 6	3400	3950
18 2	FUNLINER	RNBT	FBG DV	IO	160	7 4	2500	1 6	4400	5050

SAYBROOK YACHT YD INC
COAST GUARD MFG ID- SYY

Call 1-800-327-6929 for BUC Personalized Evaluation Service
Or, for 1959 to 1983 boats, sign onto www.BUCValuPro.com

SCANAMERICAN MARKETNG GRP INC

Call 1-800-327-6929 for BUC Personalized Evaluation Service
Or, for 1979 boats, sign onto www.BUCValuPro.com

SCANDIA MARINE

Call 1-800-327-6929 for BUC Personalized Evaluation Service
Or, for 1959 to 1961 boats, sign onto www.BUCValuPro.com

SCANDIA PLAST BOAT WORKS LTD
COAST GUARD MFG ID- SPS

Call 1-800-327-6929 for BUC Personalized Evaluation Service
Or, for 1981 to 1987 boats, sign onto www.BUCValuPro.com

SCANDINAVIAN YACHTS & MARINE
COAST GUARD MFG ID- VER

Call 1-800-327-6929 for BUC Personalized Evaluation Service
Or, for 1983 to 1986 boats, sign onto www.BUCValuPro.com

SCANDINAVIAN YACHTS LTD
COAST GUARD MFG ID- XCY

Call 1-800-327-6929 for BUC Personalized Evaluation Service
Or, for 1979 to 1988 boats, sign onto www.BUCValuPro.com

SCAT-CRAFT MARINE INC
COAST GUARD MFG ID- SCC

Call 1-800-327-6929 for BUC Personalized Evaluation Service
Or, for 1974 to 1975 boats, sign onto www.BUCValuPro.com

SCEPTRE YACHTS LTD

W VANCOUVER BC CANADA V COAST GUARD MFG ID- ZSZ See inside cover to adjust price for area

For more recent years, see the BUC Used Boat Price Guide, Volume 1 or Volume 2

LOA FT IN	NAME AND/ OR MODEL	TOP/ RIG	BOAT TYPE	-HULL- MTL TP	ENGINE TP # HP MFG	BEAM FT IN	WGT LBS	DRAFT FT IN	RETAIL LOW	RETAIL HIGH
--- 1982 BOATS ---
35 6	SCEPTRE 36	SLP	SA/RC FBG KL	IB	20D YAN	11 5	12000	6	42300	47000
35 6	SCEPTRE 36 SHOAL	SLP	SA/RC FBG KL	IB	20D YAN	11 5	12000	4 11	42300	47000
IB	23D YAN	42400	47100, IB	30D YAN	42400	47200, IB	42D PATH	42500	47200
--- 1981 BOATS ---
41	SCEPTRE 41	SLP	SA/CR FBG KL	IB	45D BMW	12 8	21500	5 8	90000	98900
35 6	SCEPTRE 36	SLP	SA/RC FBG KL	IB	20D YAN	11 5	12000	6	39800	44200
35 6	SCEPTRE 36	SLP	SA/RC FBG KL	IB	50D PATH	11 5	12000	6	40100	44500
41	SCEPTRE 41	SLP	SAIL FBG KL	IB	50D BMW	12 8	21500	5 8	84800	93200

SCHEEL YACHTS
ROCKLAND ME 04841   COAST GUARD MFG ID- SCY See inside cover to adjust price for area

LOA FT IN	NAME AND/ OR MODEL	TOP/ RIG	BOAT TYPE	-HULL- MTL TP	ENGINE TP # HP MFG	BEAM FT IN	WGT LBS	DRAFT FT IN	RETAIL LOW	RETAIL HIGH
--- 1976 BOATS ---
29 11		SAIL	FBG KL			7 11	7400		18300	20300
--- 1974 BOATS ---
44	SCHEEL 44	SLP	SA/CR FBG KC	IB	D	13 6		4 6	92700	102000
44	SCHEEL 44	SLP	SA/CR FBG KL	IB	D	13 6		4 6	92700	102000
45	DECK HOUSE	KTH	SAIL FBG KC	IB	80D FORD	13 6	30000	4 8	100500	110500
48 5	BIRD-OF-PASSAGE	KTH	MS FBG KL	IB	120D	15 4	48500	5	130500	143500
--- 1973 BOATS ---
45	SCHEEL 45	SLP	SA/CR FBG KC	IB	75D	13 6	30000	4 8	93000	102000
45	SCHEEL 45	KTH	SA/CR FBG KC	IB	75D	13 6	30000	4 8	97400	107000

SCHENKEL BROS MFG CO
COAST GUARD MFG ID- XUL

Call 1-800-327-6929 for BUC Personalized Evaluation Service
Or, for 1959 to 1980 boats, sign onto www.BUCValuPro.com

OSCAR SCHLEIN

Call 1-800-327-6929 for BUC Personalized Evaluation Service
Or, for 1966 to 1967 boats, sign onto www.BUCValuPro.com

SCHNEIDER BOAT CO INC

Call 1-800-327-6929 for BUC Personalized Evaluation Service
Or, for 1961 boats, sign onto www.BUCValuPro.com

W D SCHOCK CORP

CORONA CA 92883 COAST GUARD MFG ID- WDS See inside cover to adjust price for area

For more recent years, see the BUC Used Boat Price Guide, Volume 1 or Volume 2

LOA FT	LOA IN	NAME AND/ OR MODEL	TOP/ RIG	BOAT TYPE	-HULL- MTL	-HULL- TP	ENGINE TP	# HP	MFG	BEAM FT	BEAM IN	WGT LBS	DRAFT FT	DRAFT IN	RETAIL LOW	RETAIL HIGH
		1983 BOATS														
18		EDISON 18	OP	LNCH	FBG	DS	EL	3		6	5	1650			**	**
18		HARD TOP	HT	LNCH	FBG	DS	EL	3		6	5	1650			**	**
18		SURREY	OP	LNCH	FBG	DS	EL	3		6	5	1650			**	**
20	3	SANTANA 20	SLP	SA/OD	FBG	KL				8		1350	4		2750	3200
23	4	SANTANA 23	SLP	SA/RC	FBG	DB				8	10	2600		10	4750	5450
24		WAVELENGTH 24	SLP	SA/RC	FBG	KL				9		2500	4	5	4800	5550
24	7	SANTANA 525	SLP	SA/RC	FBG	KL				9	4	2400	4	6	4800	5550
29	11	SANTANA 30/30	SLP	SA/CR	FBG	KL	IB	15D	VLVO	10	3	6500	5	6	13200	15000
29	11	SANTANA 30/30 GP	SLP	SA/RC	FBG	KL	IB	7D	BMW	10	3	6000	5	6	12200	13800
29	11	WAVELENGTH 30	SLP	SA/RC	FBG	KL	IB	7D	BMW	10		7000	5	3	14200	16100
35		SANTANA 35	SLP	SA/RC	F/S	KL	IB	15D	VLVO	11	11	8500	6	3	20700	23000
35	8	NEW-YORK 36	SLP	SA/RC	F/S	KL	IB	15D	VLVO	11	8	10000	6	4	25500	28400
40	9	GRAND-PRIX	SLP	SA/RC	FBG	KL	IB	42D	PATH	12	11	15800	7	6	58200	63900
		1982 BOATS														
18		EDISON 18	OP	LNCH	FBG	DS	EL			6	5	1650	1	8	**	**
18		NEWPORT-PACKET	HT	LNCH	FBG	DS	EL			6	5	1650	1	8	**	**
18		NEWPORT-PACKET SURRY	OP	LNCH	FBG	DS	EL	3		6	5	1650			**	**
18		NEWPORT-PACKET-CLASS	OP	LNCH	FBG	DS	EL			6	5	1650	1	8	**	**
20	3	SANTANA 20	SLP	SA/OD	FBG	KL				8		1350	4		2600	3000
23	4	SANTANA 23	SLP	SA/RC	FBG	DB				8	10	2600		10	4500	5150
24	7	SANTANA 525	SLP	SA/RC	FBG	KL				9	4	2400	4	6	4550	5250
29	11	SANTANA 30/30	SLP	SA/CR	FBG	KL	IB	13D	VLVO	10	3	6500	5	6	12400	14100
30		WAVELENGTH 30	SLP	SA/RC	FBG	KL	IB	7D	BMW	10		7000	5	3	13400	15200
35		SANTANA 35	SLP	SA/RC	F/S	KL	IB	13D	VLVO	11	11	8500	6	3	19400	21600
35	8	NEW-YORK 36	SLP	SA/RC	F/S	KL	IB	13D	VLVO	11	8	10000	6	4	24000	26700
39		SANTANA 39	SLP	SA/CR	FBG	KL	IB	D		11	8	18000	5	7	53000	58200
		1981 BOATS														
20	3	SANTANA 20	SLP	SA/OD	FBG	KL				8		1300	4		2400	2800
23	4	SANTANA 23	SLP	SA/RC	FBG	DB				8	10	2600		10	4150	4850
24	7	SANTANA 525	SLP	SA/RC	FBG	KL				9	4	2400	4	6	4250	4950
28	4	SANTANA 228	SLP	SA/CR	FBG	KL	IB	13D	VLVO	9	3	6500	5		11700	13300
29	11	SANTATA 30	SLP	SA/RC	FBG	KL	IB	D		10		8000	6		14500	16400
35	5	SANTANA 35	SLP	SA/RC	F/S	KL	IB	13D	VLVO	11	11	8500	6	3	19100	21200
35	8	NEW-YORK 36	SLP	SA/RC	F/S	KL	IB	13D	VLVO	11	8	10200	6	4	23000	25600
39		SANTANA 39	SLP	SA/CR	F/S	KL	IB	37D	PERK	11	8	18000	5	7	49500	54400
		1980 BOATS														
20	3	SANTANA 20	SLP	SA/OD	FBG	KL				8			4		2500	2900
20	3	SANTANA 20	SLP	SA/RC	FBG	KL				8		1350	4		2350	2700
22		SANTANA 22	SLP	SA/RC	FBG	KL				7	10	2600	3	6	3700	4300
24	7	SANTANA 525	SLP	SA/RC	FBG	KL				9	4	2400	4	6	4050	4700
28	4	SANTANA 228	SLP	SA/RC	FBG	KL	IB	D		9	3	6800	5		11800	13400
29	11	SANTANA 30	SLP	SA/RC	FBG	KL	IB	D		10		8000	6		13800	15700
35		SANTANA 35	SLP	SA/RC	FBG	KL	IB	D		11	11	8500	6	3	17300	19700
39		SANTANA 39	SLP	SA/CR	F/S	KL	IB	50D	PERK	11	8	18000	5	7	47600	52300
		1979 BOATS														
20	3	SANTANA 20	SLP	SA/OD	FBG	KL	OB			8		1300	4		2200	2550
20	4	NEW-ENGLAND-DORY	OP	ROW	FBG	FL	OB			5	10	300			**	**
22		SANTANA 22	SLP	SA/OD	FBG	KL				7	10	2600	3	6	3550	4100
24	7	SANTANA 525	SLP	SA/RC	FBG	KL	OB			9	4	2400	4	6	3850	4500
28	4	SANTANA 28	SLP	SA/CR	FBG	KL	IB	8D	VLVO	9	3	6500	5		10700	12200
28	4	SANTANA 28 SHOAL	SLP	SA/CR	FBG	KL	IB	8D	VLVO	9	3	6500	3	6	10700	12200
29	11	SANTANA 30	SLP	SA/RC	F/S	KL	IB	10D	VLVO	10		8000	5		13200	15000
35	5	SANTANA 35	SLP	SA/RC	F/S	KL	IB	10D	VLVO	11	11	8500	6	3	17100	19400
39		SANTANA 39	SLP	SA/CR	F/S	KL	IB	36D	VLVO	11	8	18000	5	7	45900	50400
		1978 BOATS														
20	3	SANTANA 20	SLP	SA/OD	FBG	KL	OB			8		1300	4		2050	2450
22		SANTANA 22	SLP	SA/OD	FBG	KL				7	10	2600	3	6	3400	3950
24	7	SANTANA 525	SLP	SA/RC	FBG	KL	OB			9	4	2400	4	6	3700	4350
28	4	SANTANA 28	SLP	SA/CR	FBG	KL	IB	8D	VLVO	9	3	6500	5		10300	11700
28	4	SANTANA 28 SHOAL	SLP	SA/CR	FBG	KL	IB	8D	VLVO	9	3	6500	3	6	10300	11700
29	11	SANTANA 30	SLP	SA/RC	F/S	KL	IB	10D	VLVO	10		8000	5		12700	14500
35	5	SANTANA 35	SLP	SA/RC	F/S	KL	IB	10D	VLVO						19500	21700
39		SANTANA 39	SLP	SA/CR	F/S	KL	IB	36D	VLVO	11	8	18000	5	7	43700	48600
		1977 BOATS														
20	3	SANTANA 20	SLP	SA/OD	FBG	KL				8		1300	4		2000	2400
21	3	SANTANA 21	SLP	SA/OD	FBG	KL	OB			7	6	2150	1	6	2800	3250
22		SANTANA 22	SLP	SA/OD	FBG	KL				7	10	2600	3	6	3300	3850
24	7	SANTANA 25	SLP	SA/RC	FBG	KL	OB			7	10	4050	4	1	5500	6350
24	7	SANTANA 25	SLP	SA/RC	FBG	KL	IB	7D	WEST	7	10	4050	4	1	6050	6950
28	4	SANTANA 28	SLP	SA/CR	FBG	KL	IB	8D		9	3	6500	3	6	10000	11300
29	11	SANTANA 30	SLP	SA/RC	F/S	KL	IB	10D	VLVO	10		8000	5		12300	14000
39		SANTANA 39	SLP	SA/CR	F/S	KL	IB	36D	VLVO	11	8	18000	5	7	42200	46900
		1976 BOATS														
21	3	SANTANA 21	SLP	SA/OD	FBG	KL				7	6	2150	1	6	2700	3150
22		SANTANA 22	SLP	SA/OD	FBG	KL				7	10	2600	3	6	3200	3700
24	7	SANTANA 25	SLP	SAIL	FBG	KL	OB			7	10	4050	4	1	5350	6150
24	7	SANTANA 25	SLP	SAIL	FBG	KL	IB	7D	WEST	7	10	4050	4	1	5850	6700
28		SANTANA 28	SLP	SAIL	FBG	KL	IB	8D	VLVO						10500	12000
29	11	SANTANA 30	SLP	SAIL	FBG	KL	IB	10D	VLVO	10		8000	5		11900	13600
39		SANTANA 39	SLP	SAIL	F/S	KL	IB	35D	VLVO	11	8	18000	5	7	40900	45500
		1975 BOATS														
21	3	SANTANA 21	SLP	SA/OD	FBG	KL	OB			7	6		1	6	2250	2600
22		SANTANA 22	SLP	SA/OD	FBG	KL				7	10		3	6	3100	3600
24	7	SANTANA 25	SLP	SAIL	FBG	KL	OB			7	10	4050	4	1	5200	5950
24	7	SANTANA 25	SLP	SAIL	FBG	KL	IB	7D	WEST	7	10	4050	4	1	5700	6550
25	11	SANTANA 26	SLP	SAIL	FBG	KL	OB			7	11		4	2	5900	6750
25	11	SANTANA 26	SLP	SAIL	FBG	SK	OB			7	11		5	6	5900	6750
27	2	SANTANA 27	SLP	SAIL	FBG	KL	OB			9			4	3	6600	7550
29	11	SANTANA 30	SLP	SAIL	FBG	KL	IB	10D	VLVO	10		8000	5		11600	13200
39		SANTANA 39	SLP	SAIL	FBG	KL	IB	36D	VLVO	11	9	18000	5	6	39700	44200
		1974 BOATS														
21	3	SANTANA 21	SLP	SA/OD	FBG	KL	OB			7	6	2150	1	6	2550	2950
22		SANTANA 22	SLP	SA/OD	FBG	KL	OB			7	10	2150	1	6	2650	3100
22		SANTANA 22	SLP	SA/OD	FBG	KL	OB			7	10	2600	3	6	3000	3500
24	7	SANTANA 25	SLP	SAIL	FBG	KL	OB			7	10	4050	4	1	5050	5800
24	7	SANTANA 25	SLP	SAIL	FBG	SK	OB			7	10	3600	2	7	4550	5250
25	11	SANTANA 26	SLP	SAIL	FBG	KL	IB	5D	WEST	7	11	5060	4	2	6900	7950
25	11	SANTANA 26	SLP	SAIL	FBG	SK	IB	5D	WEST	7	11	4460			6150	7050
27	1	SANTANA 27	SLP	SAIL	FBG	KL	IB	30	UNIV	9		5000	4	3	6850	7850
27	1	SANTANA 27	SLP	SAIL	FBG	KL	IB	5D	WEST	9		5000	4	3	6950	8000
		1973 BOATS														
21	3	SANTANA 21	SLP	SA/OD	FBG	KL	OB			7	6	1900	5		2350	2700
22		SANTANA 22	SLP	SA/OD	FBG	KL	OB			7		2600	3	6	2950	3400
25	11	SANTANA 26	SLP	SAIL	FBG	KL	OB			7	11	5000	5		6300	7250
25	11	SANTANA 26	SLP	SAIL	FBG	SK	OB			7	11	5000	5		6300	7250
25	11	SANTANA 26	SLP	SAIL	FBG	SK	IB	10D	KERM	7	11	5000	5		6700	7700
27	1	SANTANA 27	SLP	SAIL	FBG	KL	OB			9		5000	4	3	6500	7450
27	1	SANTANA 27	SLP	SAIL	FBG	KL	IB	30	UNIV	9		5000	4	3	6700	7650
27	1	SANTANA 27	SLP	SAIL	FBG	KL	IB	10D	KERM	9		5000	4	3	6800	7800
37			SLP	SAIL	FBG	CT	IB	25D	JOHN	17		5500	1	7	30300	33700
37	8	SANTANA 39	SLP	SAIL	FBG	KL	IB	30	UNIV	11	8	6600	5	7	13700	15600
40	6	SCHOCK 41	KTH	MS	FBG		IB	50D	PERK	11	10	22000	5	10	48300	53100
		1972 BOATS														
21	3	SANTANA 21	SLP	SA/OD	FBG	KL	OB			7	6	2150	1	6	2450	2850
21	11	TEMPEST	SLP	SA/OD	FBG	KL	OB			6	3	943	3	7	1700	2050
22		SANTANA 22	SLP	SA/OD	FBG	KL	OB			7		2600	3	6	2900	3350
26	2	SANTANA 26	SLP	SAIL	FBG	SK	OB			7	11	5000	5	6	6200	7150
26	2	SANTANA 26	SLP	SAIL	FBG	SK	IB	10	KERM	7	11	5000	5	6	6350	7350
27	1	SANTANA 27	SLP	SAIL	FBG	KL	OB			9		5000	4	3	6350	7300
27	1	SANTANA 27	SLP	SAIL	FBG	KL	IB	10- 30		9		5000	4	3	6500	7500
37		POLYNESIAN	SLP	SAIL	FBG	CT	IB	25	JOHN	17		5500	1	7	29600	32900
37	8	SANTANA 37	SLP	SAIL	FBG		IB	30	UNIV	11	8	15000	5	7	28100	31300
		1971 BOATS														
21	3	SANTANA 21	SLP	SA/OD	FBG	KL	OB			7	6	2150	5		2400	2800
22		SANTANA 22	SLP	SA/OD	FBG	KL	OB			7	10	2600	3	6	2800	3300
27	1	SANTANA 27	SLP	SAIL	FBG	KL	OB			9		5000	4	3	6200	7150
27	1	SANTANA 27	SLP	SAIL	FBG	KL	IB	10- 30		9		5000	4	3	6350	7350
37		POLYNESIAN-CONCEPT	SLP	SA/CR	FBG	CT				17		6000	1	7	29700	33000
37	8	SANTANA 37	SLP	SAIL	FBG		IB	30	UNIV	11	8	15000	5	7	27600	30700
		1970 BOATS														
22		SANTANA 22	SLP	SA/OD	FBG	KL	OB			7	10	2600	2	6	2750	3200
24		INTERNATIONAL	SLP	SA/OD	FBG	KL	OB			4	2	900	3		1950	2350
27	1	SANTANA 27	SLP	SAIL	FBG	KL	OB			9		5000	4	3	6100	7000
27	1	SANTANA 27	SLP	SAIL	FBG	KL	IB	30	UNIV	9		5000	4	3	6300	7250
37	8	SANTANA 37	SLP	SAIL	FBG	KL	IB	30	UNIV	11	8	15000	5	7	27100	30100
		1969 BOATS														
22		SANTANA 22	SLP	SA/OD	FBG	KL	OB			7	10	2600	2	6	2750	3150
24		INTERNATIONAL	SLP	SA/OD	FBG	KL	OB			4	2	900	3		1950	2300
25		SCHOCK 25	SLP	SAIL	FBG	KL	OB			7		2200	4		2850	3300
27		TARTAN 27	SLP	SAIL	FBG	KC	OB			8	7	6875	3	2	8350	9600
27		TARTAN 27	YWL	SAIL	FBG	KC	OB			8	7	6875	3	2	8350	9600
27	1	SANTANA 27	SLP	SAIL	FBG	KL	OB			9		5000	4	3	6000	6900
		1968 BOATS														
22		SANTANA 22	SLP	SA/OD	FBG	KC	OB			7	10	2600	3	6	2700	3150
24		INTERNATIONAL	SLP	SA/OD	FBG	KL	OB			4	2	900	3		1900	2250
25		SCHOCK 25	SLP	SA/CR	FBG	KL	OB			7		2200	4	1	2800	3250
25	9	ENDEAVOR	SLP	SA/CR	FBG	KL	OB			7	2	3200	4		3800	4400
27		TARTAN	SLP	SAIL	FBG	KC	IB	30		8	7	6875	3	2	8450	9700
27	5	SANTANA 27	SLP	SAIL	FBG	KL	OB			9		5000	4	3	5950	6850

CONTINUED ON NEXT PAGE

LOA FT	LOA IN	NAME AND/ OR MODEL	TOP/ RIG	BOAT TYPE	HULL MTL	HULL TP	ENGINE TP	# HP	MFG	BEAM FT	BEAM IN	WGT LBS	DRAFT FT	DRAFT IN	RETAIL LOW	RETAIL HIGH
		1967 BOATS														
22		SANTANA 22	SLP	SA/OD	FBG	KL	OB					2600			2650	3100
24		INTERNATIONAL	SLP	SA/OD	FBG	KL	OB					900			1900	2250
25		SCHOCK 25		SAIL	FBG		OB					2200			2750	3200
25	9	ENDEAVOR		SAIL	FBG		OB					3200			3750	4350
27		TARTAN		SAIL	FBG		IB	30				6875			8350	9600
		1966 BOATS														
22		SANTANA 22	SLP	SA/OD	FBG	KL	OB			7	10	2600	3	6	2650	3050
25		SCHOCK 25	SLP	SA/OD	FBG	KL	OB			7		2200	4	1	2750	3200
25	9	ENDEAVOR	SLP	SA/OD	FBG	KL	OB			7	2	3200	4		3700	4300
27		TARTAN	SLP	SA/OD	FBG	KC	IB	30		8	8	6875	3	2	8250	9500
		1965 BOATS														
17	6	CATALINA	SLP	SAIL	FBG	CT	OB								2050	2450
25		SCHOCK 25		SAIL	FBG		OB								4100	4750
25	9	ENDEAVOR		SAIL	FBG		OB								4950	5700
27		TARTAN	SLP	SAIL	FBG		OB								5550	6350
27		TARTAN	YWL	SAIL	FBG	CB	OB								5550	6350
		1964 BOATS														
17		CATALINA		SAIL	FBG	CT	OB								1750	2100
22		SCHOCK		SAIL	FBG		OB								2600	3050
25		SCHOCK 25		SAIL	FBG		OB								4050	4750
		1963 BOATS														
17		CATALINA		SAIL	FBG	CT	OB								1750	2100
22		SCHOCK 22		SAIL	FBG		OB								2600	3000
25		SCHOCK 25		SAIL	FBG		OB								4050	4700
		1961 BOATS														
22		OCEAN-RACER S-22-JR	SLP	SA/RC	FBG	KC				7	6		4	6	2600	3000
22		S-22	SLP	SA/OD	FBG	KC				7	6		2	1	2600	3000
		1960 BOATS														
22		S-22 JR OCEAN RACER	SLP	SA/RC	FBG	KC				7	6		4	6	2600	3000
		1959 BOATS														
22		SCHOCK 22	SLP	SA/CR	FBG	CB				7	6		2	1	2600	3050

SCHUCKER YACHT CORP

CAPE CORAL FL 33904 COAST GUARD MFG ID- SYB See inside cover to adjust price for area

LOA FT	LOA IN	NAME AND/ OR MODEL	TOP/ RIG	BOAT TYPE	HULL MTL	HULL TP	ENGINE TP	# HP	MFG	BEAM FT	BEAM IN	WGT LBS	DRAFT FT	DRAFT IN	RETAIL LOW	RETAIL HIGH
		1982 BOATS														
40		SCHUCKER 330	HT	CR	FBG	DS	IB	50D	PERK	14		20000	2	10	47100	51800
40		SCHUCKER 430	SLP	MS	FBG	KL	IB	50D	PERK	14		25000	3	1	70000	76900
40		SCHUCKER 430	SLP	MS	FBG	KL	IB	62D	PERK	14		25000	3	1	70100	77100
40		SCHUCKER 430	SLP	MS	FBG	KL	IB	85D	PERK	14		25000	3	1	70400	77400
40		SCHUCKER 436	CUT	MS	FBG	KL	IB	62D	PERK	14		26000	3	2	72000	79100
40		SCHUCKER 436	CUT	MS	FBG	KL	IB	85D	PERK	14		26000	3	2	71200	78200
40		SCHUCKER 438	FB	TRWL	FBG	DS	IB	85D	PERK	14		26000	3	2	59000	64800
40		SCHUCKER 440	CUT	MS	FBG	KL	IB	85D	PERK	14		26000	3	2	73300	80600
50		SCHUCKER 50	CUT	MS	FBG	KL	IB	85D	PERK	14	10	46000	3	6	136000	149000
50		SCHUCKER 50	CUT	MS	FBG	KL	IB	130D	PERK	14	10	46000	3	6	134500	148000
50		SCHUCKER 50	KTH	MS	FBG	KL	IB	85D	PERK	14	10	46000	3	6	137000	150500
50		SCHUCKER 50	KTH	MS	FBG	KL	IB	130D	PERK	14	10	46000	3	6	137500	151000
50		SCHUCKER 50	FB	TRWL	FBG	DS	IB	85D	PERK	14	10	46000	3	6	89400	98200
50		SCHUCKER 50	FB	TRWL	FBG	DS	IB	130D	PERK	14	10	46000	3	6	92600	101500
		1981 BOATS														
40		SCHUCKER 330	HT	CR	FBG	DS	IB	50D	PERK	14		20000	2	10	44400	49300
40		SCHUCKER 430	SLP	MS	FBG	KL	IB	50D	PERK	14		25000	3	1	65800	72300
40		SCHUCKER 436	CUT	MS	FBG	KL	IB	62D	PERK	14		26000	3	2	67700	74400
40		SCHUCKER 438	FB	TRWL	FBG	DS	IB	85D	PERK	14		26000	3	2	56200	61700
40		SCHUCKER 440	CUT	MS	FBG	KL	IB	85D	PERK	14		26000	3	2	68000	74700
48		SCHUCKER 48	CUT	MS	FBG	KL	IB	D		14	9	30000	3	2	99300	109000
48		SCHUCKER 48	KTH	MS	FBG	KL	IB	D		14	9	30000	3	2	100500	110500
48		TRAWLER		TRWL	FBG	DS	IB	106D		14	9				84900	93300
50		SCHUCKER 50	CUT	MS	FBG	KL	IB	85D	PERK	14	10	36000	3	2	119000	131000
50		SCHUCKER 50	CUT	MS	FBG	KL	IB	130D	PERK	14	10	36000	3	2	118500	130000
50		SCHUCKER 50	KTH	MS	FBG	KL	IB	85D	PERK	14	10	36000	3	2	120000	131500
50		SCHUCKER 50	KTH	MS	FBG	KL	IB	130D	PERK	14	10	36000	3	2	120000	132000
50		SCHUCKER 50	FB	TRWL	FBG	DS	IB	85D	PERK	14	10	36000	3	2	92000	101000
50		SCHUCKER 50	FB	TRWL	FBG	DS	IB	130D	PERK	14	10	36000	3	2	92400	101500
		1980 BOATS														
40		SCHUCKER 430	SLP	MS	FBG	KL	IB	50D	PERK	14		25000	3	1	62900	69100
40		SCHUCKER 436	CUT	MS	FBG	KL	IB	62D	PERK	14		26000	3	2	64700	71100
40		SCHUCKER 437 CHART I	CUT	SA/CR	FBG	KL	IB	50D	PERK	14		26000	3	2	64500	70900
40		SCHUCKER 437C CHR II	CUT	SA/CR	FBG	KL	IB	50D	PERK	14		26000	3	2	64500	70900
40		SCHUCKER 438	FB	TRWL	FBG	DS	IB	85D	PERK	14		26000	3	2	53600	58900
40		SCHUCKER 439		TRWL	FBG	DS	IO	270		14		20000			35800	39700
40		SCHUCKER 440	CUT	MS	FBG	KL	IB	85D	PERK	14		26000	3	2	64900	71300
48		SCHUCKER 48	CUT	MS	FBG	KL	IB	85D	PERK	15		30000	3	2	95500	105000
48		SCHUCKER 48	KTH	MS	FBG	KL	IB	85D	PERK	15		30000	3	2	95900	105500
48		SCHUCKER 48	FB	TRWL	FBG	DS	IB	85D	PERK	15		30000	3	2	79600	87500
		1979 BOATS														
40		SCHUCKER 430	SLP	MS	FBG	KL	IB	50D	PERK	14		25000	3	2	60500	66400
40		SCHUCKER 436	CUT	MS	FBG	KL	IB	50D	CHRY	14		26000	3	2	62300	68500
40		SCHUCKER 437	CUT	SA/CR	FBG	KL	IB	50D	PERK	14		26000	3	2	62000	68200
40		SCHUCKER 438	FB	TRWL	FBG	DS	IB	85D	PERK	14		26000	3	2	51200	56200
40		SCHUCKER 440	CUT	MS	FBG	KL	IB	62D	PERK	14		26000	3	2	62200	68300
		1978 BOATS														
40		SCHUCKER 436	SLP	MS	FBG	KL	IB	70	CHRY	14		26000	3	2	58100	63900
40		SCHUCKER 436	SLP	MS	FBG	KL	IB	85D	PERK	14		26000	3	2	59000	64900
40		SCHUCKER 436T	SLP	MS	FBG	KL	IB	70	CHRY	14		26000	3	2	60500	66500
40		SCHUCKER 436T	SLP	MS	FBG	KL	IB	50D	PERK	14		26000	3	2	59800	65700
40		SCHUCKER 436T	SLP	MS	FBG	KL	IB	85D	PERK	14		26000	3	2	61300	67400
40		SCHUCKER 437	CUT	SA/CR	FBG	KC	IB	50D	PERK	14		26800	3	2	61000	67000
40		SCHUCKER 438	HT	TRWL	FBG	DS	IB	85D	PERK	14		26000	3	2	49000	53800
40		SCHUCKER 438	FB	TRWL	FBG	DS	IB	85D	PERK	14		26000	3	2	49000	53800
40		SCHUCKER 439	HT	TRWL	FBG	SV	IB	200D	PERK	14		26000	3	2	50100	55100
40		SCHUCKER 439	FB	TRWL	FBG	SV	IB	200D	PERK	14		26000	3	2	50100	55100
40		SCHUCKER 440	CUT	MS	FBG	KL	IB	85D	PERK	14		26000	3	2	60200	66100
44		SCHUCKER 444	KTH	SA/CR	FBG	KL	IB	50D	PERK	14		32000	5	6	76600	84200
		1977 BOATS														
37	6	SCHUCKER 436	CUT	MS	FBG	KC	IB	37D	WEST	14		16000	3		36800	40900
37	6	SCHUCKER 436	CUT	MS	FBG	KL	IB	37D	WEST	14		16000	3		36800	40900
37	6	SCHUCKER 437	CUT	SA/CR	FBG	KC	IB	37D	WEST	14		16800	3		38300	42500
37	6	SCHUCKER 438	FB	TRWL	FBG	DS	IB	130D	CHRY	14		16000	3		28300	31500
44		SCHUCKER 444	SLP	SA/CR	FBG	KC	IB	50D	PERK	14		32000	4	6	74000	81300
44		SCHUCKER 444	SLP	SA/CR	FBG	KL	IB	50D	PERK	14		32000	5	9	74000	81300
44		SCHUCKER 444	KTH	SA/CR	FBG	KC	IB	50D	PERK	14		32000	4	6	74000	81300
44		SCHUCKER 444	KTH	SA/CR	FBG	KL	IB	50D	PERK	14		32000	5	9	74000	81300
		1976 BOATS														
36	7	SCHUCKER 437	CUT	SA/CR	FBG	KC	IB	30D	VLVO	14		16000	3		34500	38400
44		SCHUCKER 444	KTH	SA/CR	FBG	KC	IB	50D	PERK	14		30000	4	6	69400	76200
44		SCHUCKER 444	KTH	SA/CR	FBG	KL	IB	50D	PERK	14		30000	5	9	69400	76200

SCHULZ BOAT CO LLC

BRISTOL RI 02809 COAST GUARD MFG ID- NHN See inside cover to adjust price for area
FORMERLY SHANNON YACHTS

For more recent years, see the BUC Used Boat Price Guide, Volume 1 or Volume 2

LOA FT	LOA IN	NAME AND/ OR MODEL	TOP/ RIG	BOAT TYPE	HULL MTL	HULL TP	ENGINE TP	# HP	MFG	BEAM FT	BEAM IN	WGT LBS	DRAFT FT	DRAFT IN	RETAIL LOW	RETAIL HIGH
		1983 BOATS														
28	2	SHANNON 28	CUT	SA/CR	FBG	KL	IB	15D	YAN	9	6	9300	4	3	48200	53000
37	9	SHANNON 38	CUT	SA/CR	FBG	KL	IB	40D	PERK	11	6	18500	5		98200	108000
37	9	SHANNON 38	KTH	SA/CR	FBG	KL	IB	40D	PERK	11	6	18500	5		99800	109500
37	9	SHANNON-PILOT 38	CUT	SA/CR	FBG	KL	IB	40D	PERK	11	6	18500	5		101500	111500
50	11	SHANNON 50	KTH	SA/CR	FBG	KC	IB	85D	PERK	14	3	39000	5	7	246500	270500
50	11	SHANNON AEGEAN 51	KTH	SA/CR	FBG	KL	IB	85D	PERK	14	3	39000	7		253000	278000
		1982 BOATS														
28	2	SHANNON 28	CUT	SA/CR	FBG	KL	IB	15D	YAN	9	6	9300	4	3	46000	50500
37	9	SHANNON 38	CUT	SA/CR	FBG	KL	IB	40D	PERK	11	6	18500	5		91400	100500
37	9	SHANNON 38	KTH	SA/CR	FBG	KL	IB	40D	PERK	11	6	18500	5		94500	104000
37	9	SHANNON-PILOT 38	CUT	SA/CR	FBG	KL	IB	40D	PERK	11	6	18500	5		97700	107500
50	9	SHANNON 50	KTH	SA/CR	FBG	KC	IB	85D	PERK	14		39000	5	7	234500	257500
		1981 BOATS														
28	2	SHANNON 28	CUT	SA/CR	FBG	KL	IB	15D	YAN	9	6	9300	4	3	43100	47900
37	9	SHANNON 38	CUT	SA/CR	FBG	KL	IB	40D	PERK	11	6	18500	5		87200	95800
37	9	SHANNON 38	KTH	SA/CR	FBG	KL	IB	40D	PERK	11	6	18500	5		89600	98500
37	9	SHANNON-PILOT 38	CUT	SA/CR	FBG	KL	IB	40D	PERK	11	6	18500	5		92000	101000
50	9	SHANNON 50	KTH	SA/CR	FBG	KC	IB	85D	PERK	14		39000	6	6	222000	244000
		1980 BOATS														
28		SHANNON	CUT	SA/CR	FBG	KL	IB	15D	YAN	9	6	9300	4	3	41400	46000
37	9	SHANNON	CUT	SA/CR	FBG	KL	IB	40D	PERK	11	6	18500	5		82800	91000
37	9	SHANNON	KTH	SA/CR	FBG	KL	IB	40D	PERK	11	6	18500	5		86200	94800
37	9	SHANNON-PILOT	CUT	SA/CR	FBG	KL	IB	40D	PERK	11	6	18500	5		89700	98500
		1979 BOATS														
28		SHANNON 28	CUT	SA/CR	FBG	KL	IB	15D	YAN	9	6	9300	4	3	40100	44500
37	9	PILOT 38	CUT	SA/CR	FBG	KL	IB	40D	PERK	11	6	18500	5		87600	96300
37	9	PILOT 38	KTH	SA/CR	FBG	KL	IB	40D	PERK	11	6	18500	5		87500	96100
37	9	SHANNON 38	CUT	SA/CR	FBG	KL	IB	40D	PERK	11	6	18500	5		79400	87300
37	9	SHANNON 38	KTH	SA/CR	FBG	KL	IB	40D	PERK	11	6	18500	5		79600	87500
		1978 BOATS														
28		SHANNON 28	CUT	SA/CR	FBG	KL	IB	15D	YAN	9	4	9300	4	3	38900	43200
38		SHANNON 38	CUT	SA/CR	FBG	KL	IB	40D	PERK	11	6	18500	5		81700	89800

 CONTINUED ON NEXT PAGE

LOA FT IN	NAME AND/ OR MODEL	TOP/ RIG	BOAT TYPE	-HULL- MTL TP TP	----ENGINE--- # HP MFG	BEAM FT IN	WGT LBS	DRAFT FT IN	RETAIL LOW	RETAIL HIGH
--- 1978 BOATS ---										
38	SHANNON 38	KTH	SA/CR	FBG KL IB	40D PERK	11 6	18500	5	81700	89800
--- 1977 BOATS ---										
38	SHANNON	CUT	SA/CR	FBG KL IB	40D PERK	11 6	18500	5	79600	87400
38	SHANNON	KTH	SA/CR	FBG KL IB	40D PERK	11 6	18500	5	79600	87400
--- 1976 BOATS ---										
38	SHANNON	CUT	SA/CR	FBG KL IB	40D PERK	11 6	18500	5	77600	85300
38	SHANNON	KTH	SA/CR	FBG KL IB	40D PERK	11 6	18500	5	77600	85300

SCHUSTER BOATS INC

Call 1-800-327-6929 for BUC Personalized Evaluation Service
Or, for 1974 boats, sign onto www.BUCValuPro.com

PALMER SCOTT & COMPANY INC
COAST GUARD MFG ID- XCY

Call 1-800-327-6929 for BUC Personalized Evaluation Service
Or, for 1937 to 1954 boats, sign onto www.BUCValuPro.com

SCOTT BOAT CO INC
COAST GUARD MFG ID- SCT

Call 1-800-327-6929 for BUC Personalized Evaluation Service
Or, for 1974 to 1979 boats, sign onto www.BUCValuPro.com

SCOTT PRODUCT CO
COAST GUARD MFG ID- TAD

Call 1-800-327-6929 for BUC Personalized Evaluation Service
Or, for 1983 boats, sign onto www.BUCValuPro.com

SCOTTIE CRAFT
N MIAMI BEACH FL 33180   COAST GUARD MFG ID- SCB See inside cover to adjust price for area

LOA FT IN	NAME AND/ OR MODEL	TOP/ RIG	BOAT TYPE	-HULL- MTL TP TP	----ENGINE--- # HP MFG	BEAM FT IN	WGT LBS	DRAFT FT IN	RETAIL LOW	RETAIL HIGH
--- 1973 BOATS ---										
23	KEY-LARGO 23		SF	FBG DV IO	165	8			7400	8500
25 6	KEY-LARGO		SF	FBG DV IO	225	8			13000	14800
27	KEY-LARGO		SF	FBG DV IO	245	8 6		2 6	14900	16900
29	MIAMI 29		SF	FBG DV IB	T225	11 10		1 11	16900	19200
36 11	MIAMI 37		SF	FBG DV IB	T330	13 2		3	32000	35500
--- 1972 BOATS ---										
23	KEY-LARGO 23			FBG	IO 130-225	8			6550	7550
25 6	KEY-LARGO	HT		FBG	IO 165-225	8 6			11300	13400
25 6	KEY-LARGO	HT		FBG	IO T120-T170	8 6			12400	15100
25 6	KEY-LARGO	RNBT		FBG	IO 165-225	8 6	5000		10500	12400
25 6	KEY-LARGO	RNBT		FBG	IO T120-T170	8 6			11500	13900
25 6	KEY-LARGO	SF		FBG	IO 165-225	8 6			13000	15200
25 6	KEY-LARGO	SF		FBG	IO T120-T170	8 6			14100	17200
27	KEY-LARGO	HT		FBG	IO 165-225	8 6			12200	14600
27	KEY-LARGO	HT		FBG	IO T130-T170	8 6			13900	16500
27	KEY-LARGO	RNBT		FBG	IO 165-225	8 6			11100	13200
27	KEY-LARGO	RNBT		FBG	IO T130-T170	8 6	5500		13300	15800
27	KEY-LARGO	SF		FBG	IO 165-225	8 6			14500	17200
27	KEY-LARGO	SF		FBG	IO T130-T170	8 6			16200	19200
29	MIAMI 29	HT		FBG	IO T215-T255	11 10			25300	28800
29	MIAMI 29	HT		FBG	IO T185D CUM	11 10			32000	35500
29	MIAMI 29	RNBT		FBG	IO T215-T250	11 10	9300		19100	21800
29	MIAMI 29	RNBT		FBG	IO T185D CUM	11 10	9300		24200	26900
29	MIAMI 29	SF		FBG	IO T215-T250	11 10			26900	30700
29	MIAMI 29	SF		FBG	IO T185D CUM	11 10			37300	41400
36 11	MARLIN	HT		FBG	IO T270	SEA 13			33500	37200
	IO T325 MRCR 34900	38800, IO T330	CHRY	35100	39000, IO T180D PERK		40900		45400	
	IO T210D CUM 40600	45200, IO T216D	GM	42000	46700, IO T225D CAT		42100		44800	
36 11	MARLIN	SF		FBG	IO T270	SEA 13			43600	48400
	IO T325 MRCR 45800	50300, IO T330	CHRY	46000	50500, IO T180D PERK		49100		53900	
	IO T210D CUM 51400	56500, IO T216D	GM	50600	55700, IO T225D CAT		50500		55500	
36 11	MIAMI 37	HT		FBG	IO T270	SEA 13			35400	39300
	IO T325 MRCR 37100	41200, IO T330	CHRY	37300	41500, IO T180D PERK		42900		47700	
	IO T210D CUM 42600	47300, IO T216D	GM	42000	46700, IO T225D CAT		44500		49500	
36 11	MIAMI 37	SF		FBG	IO T270	SEA 13			46900	51500
	IO T325 MRCR 48800	53700, IO T330	CHRY	49100	54000, IO T180D PERK		52100		57300	
	IO T210D CUM 49000	53800, IO T216D	GM	50600	55700, IO T225D CAT		53800		59100	
--- 1971 BOATS ---										
25 5	MIAMI 25	OP	RNBT	FBG	IO 170	VLVO 8	4400	1 10	10900	11400
27	MIAMI 27	HT		FBG	IO 210-215	8 6	5700	2 6	14600	16700
27	MIAMI 27	HT		FBG	IO T155-T170	8 6	5700	2 6	16000	18800
27	MIAMI 27	HT		FBG	IO T106D VLVO	8 6	5700	2 6	19400	21600
27	MIAMI 27	RNBT		FBG	IO 210-215	8 6	5500	2 6	12700	14500
27	MIAMI 27	RNBT		FBG	IO T155-T170	8 6	5500	2 6	13900	16300
27	MIAMI 27	RNBT		FBG	IO T106D VLVO	8 6	5500	2 6	15700	17800
27	MIAMI 27	OP	RNBT	FBG	IO T160	8	4800	2 6	13000	14800
27	MIAMI 27	HT	SDN	FBG	IO T160	8	5800	2 6	16300	18500
27	MIAMI 27	SF		FBG	IO T155-T170	8 6	5800	2 6	18000	20700
27	MIAMI 27	SF		FBG	IO T106D VLVO	8 6	5800	2 6	22600	25100
27	MIAMI 27	FB	SF	FBG	IO T160	8	5800	2 7	18000	20500
29	MIAMI 29	HT		FBG	VD T215-T280	11 10	8900	3 1	15400	18300
29	MIAMI 29	HT		FBG	VD T160D PERK	11 10	8900	3 1	23100	25700
29	MIAMI 29	RNBT		FBG	VD T215-T280	11 10	8700	3 1	15000	17700
29	MIAMI 29	RNBT		FBG	VD T160D PERK	11 10	8700	3 1	22100	24600
29	MIAMI 29	OP	RNBT	FBG	IO T210	11 8	6500	2 10	17100	19400
29	MIAMI 29	HT	SDN	FBG	IO T210	11 8	6500	2 10	24400	27100
29	MIAMI 29	FB	SDN	FBG	IO T210	11 8	6500	2 10	24400	27100
29	MIAMI 29	SF		FBG	VD T215-T280	11 10	9000	3 1	15500	18400
29	MIAMI 29	SF		FBG	VD T160D PERK	11 10	9000	3 1	23300	25900
36 11	MARLIN 37	HT		FBG	IB T270	SEA 13 2 12500	3		28200	31300
	IB T325 MRCR 28700	31900, IB T330	CHRY	28700	31900, IB T225D CAT		32200		35800	
	IB T210D CUM 32000	35500, IB T216D	GM	32300	35900, IB T225D CAT		33300		37000	
36 11	MARLIN 37	SF		FBG	IB T270	SEA 13 2 12600	3		28300	31500
	IB T325 MRCR 28900	32100, IB T330	CHRY	28800	32000, IB T 16D GM		28100		31200	
	IB T180D PERK 32200	35800, IB T210D	CUM	32000	35600, IB T225D CAT		33300		37000	
36 11	MIAMI 37	HT		FBG	IB T270	SEA 13 2 13000	3		28800	32100
	IB T325 MRCR 29400	32700, IB T330	CHRY	29400	32600, IB T180D PERK		31200		34700	
	IB T210D CUM 31000	34400, IB T216D	GM	33000	36700, IB T225D CAT		32300		35900	
36 11	MIAMI 37	SF		FBG	IB T270	SEA 13 2 13100	3		29000	32200
	IB T325 MRCR 29500	32800, IB T350	CHRY	29800	33100, IB T180D PERK		33000		36600	
	IB T210D CUM 32700	36400, IB T216D	GM	33000	36700, IB T225D CAT		34100		37800	
37 1	MARLIN 37	HT	SDN	FBG DV IB	T300	CHRY 13 2 14850	2 6		31100	34600
37 1	MARLIN 37	FB	SF	FBG DV IB	T300	CHRY 13 2 16000	2 6		32100	35600
37 1	MIAMI 37	HT	SDN	FBG DV IB	T300	CHRY 13 2 14850	2 6		33100	36800
37 1	MIAMI 37	FB	SF	FBG DV IB	T300	CHRY 13 2 16000	2 6		34500	38300
--- 1970 BOATS ---										
24	1 V-226 DELUXE		CBNCR	FBG DV IO	120-225	8	3400	2 1	9900	11500
24	1 V-226 DELUXE		CBNCR	FBG DV IO	T110-T120	8	3400	2 1	11600	13200
28	5 MIAMI 27	HT		FBG	IO 210-225	8	5000	2 6	16200	18600
28	5 MIAMI 27	HT		FBG	IO T120-T160	8	5000	2 6	17400	20300
28	5 MIAMI 27	FB		FBG	IO 210-225	8	5000	2 6	16200	18600
28	5 MIAMI 27	FB		FBG	IO T120-T160	8	5000	2 6	17400	20300
28	5 MIAMI 27		RNBT	FBG	IO 210-225	8	5000	2 6	12600	14500
28	5 MIAMI 27		RNBT	FBG	IO T120-T160	8	5000	2 6	13200	15700
29	MIAMI 29	HT		FBG	IB T225 MRCR 12		9000	1 11	27200	30200
29	MIAMI 29	HT		FBG	IB T225-T325 12		9000	1 11	16300	18300
29	MIAMI 29	FB		FBG	IB T225 MRCR 12		9000	1 11	16300	18300
29	MIAMI 29	FB		FBG	IB T225-T325 12		9000	1 11	15000	18300
29	MIAMI 29		RNBT	FBG	IB T225 MRCR 12		9000	1 11	20300	22600
29	MIAMI 29		RNBT	FBG	IB T225-T325 12		9000	1 11	14700	17900
37	MIAMI 37		SF	FBG	IB T300	CHRY 13	16000	2 6	36500	39200
37	MIAMI 37		SF	FBG	IB T170D CRUS 13	16000	2 6	40400	44100	
37	MIAMI 37		SF	FBG	IB T220D CRUS 13	16000	2 6	36300	40400	
37	MIAMI 37	FB	SF	FBG	IB T170D CRUS 13	16000	2 6	35300	39300	
37	MIAMI 37	FB	SF	FBG	IB T220D CRUS 13	16000	2 6	35300	39300	
37	1 BLUE-MARLIN	HT	SDN	FBG DV IB	T300	CHRY 13	14850	2 6	36300	40400
37	1 BLUE-MARLIN	FB	SF	FBG DV IB	T300	CHRY 13 2 16000	2 6		32200	35700
--- 1969 BOATS ---										
16 9	MIAMI-PLAYMATE	OP		FBG DV IO	165	6 11	1800	2 1	2950	3450
19 8	V-182		CBNCR	FBG IO	110-160	7 8	2400	1 11	5100	5900
19 8	V-182		RNBT	FBG IO	110-160	7 8	2400	1 11	4650	5350
19 8	V-182		SF	FBG IO	110-160	7 8	2400	1 11	5500	6300
22 2	MIAMI TRI 21	FSH		FBG	OB	8	2750	1 8	7400	8500

LOA FT IN	NAME AND/ OR MODEL	TOP/ RIG	BOAT TYPE	HULL MTL	HULL TP	ENGINE TP	ENGINE # HP	ENGINE MFG	BEAM FT IN	WGT LBS	DRAFT FT IN	RETAIL LOW	RETAIL HIGH
					1969 BOATS								
22 2	MIAMI TRI 21		RNBT	FBG		IO	120-200		8	2750	1 8	6650	7700
22 2	MIAMI TRI 21		TCMY	FBG		IO	120-200		8	2750	1 8	8000	9300
24 1	V-226		FSH	FBG		IO	120-225		8	3400	2 1	9400	11000
24 1	V-226		FSH	FBG		IO	T110-T120		8	3400	2 1	11100	12600
24 1	V-226 DELUXE		CBNCR	FBG		IO	120-225		8	3400	2 1	10200	11900
24 1	V-226 DELUXE		CBNCR	FBG		IO	T110-T120		8	3400	2 1	12000	13600
28 5	MIAMI 27	HT		FBG		IO	120-225		8	5000	2 6	15900	19200
28 5	MIAMI 27	HT		FBG		IO	T120-T210		8	5000	2 6	18400	21500
28 5	MIAMI 27	FB		FBG		IO	120-225		8	5000	2 6	15900	19200
28 5	MIAMI 27	FB		FBG		IO	T120-T210		8	5000	2 6	18400	21500
28 5	MIAMI 27		RNBT	FBG		IO	120-225		8	5000	2 6	12000	15000
28 5	MIAMI 27		RNBT	FBG		IO	T120-T160		8	5000	2 6	13600	16200
28 5	MIAMI 27		RNBT	FBG		IO	T210	CHRY	8	5000	2 6	15100	17200
29	MIAMI 29	HT		FBG		TR	T210	CHRY	12			14300	16200
29	MIAMI 29	HT		FBG		IO	T225	MRCR	12			27900	31000
29	MIAMI 29	HT		FBG		IB	T320-T325		12			15400	17600
29	MIAMI 29	FB		FBG		IB	T210	CHRY	12			14300	16200
29	MIAMI 29	FB		FBG		IO	T225	MRCR	12			27900	31000
29	MIAMI 29	FB		FBG		IB	T320-T325		12			15400	17600
29	MIAMI 29		RNBT	FBG		IB	T210-T325		12			13900	17100
37	MIAMI 37	SF		FBG		IB	T300	CHRY	13	2	14850	29600	32800
37	MIAMI 37	SF		FBG		IB	T170D	CRUS	13	2	14850	32600	36200
37	MIAMI 37	SF		FBG		IB	T220D	CRUS	13	2	14850	33600	37300
37	MIAMI 37	FB	SF	FBG		IB	T300	CHRY	13	2	16000	31000	34500
37	MIAMI 37	FB	SF	FBG		IB	T170D	CRUS	13	2	16000	34200	38000
37	MIAMI 37	FB	SF	FBG		IB	T220D	CRUS	13	2	16000	35200	39100
37 1	BLUE-MARLIN		CR	FBG	DV	IB	T300	CHRY	13	2	14850	2 6	29600	32900
					1968 BOATS								
19 8	V-182		CBNCR	FBG		IO	110-150		7 8	2500	1	5200	6000
19 8	V-182	OP	RNBT	FBG		IO	110-150		7 8	2400	1	4600	5350
19 8	V-182	OP	SF	FBG		IO	110-150		7 8	2400	1	5450	6250
22 2	MIAMI TRI 21			FBG	TR	IO	110-200		8	2750	1 8	8300	9650
22 2	MIAMI TRI 21		TCMY	FBG	TR	IO	110-200		8	2750	1 8	8300	9650
24 1	V-226		CBNCR	FBG		IO	110-225		8	3400	2 1	10500	12300
24 1	V-226		CBNCR	FBG		IO	T110-T150		8	3900	2 1	12900	14800
24 1	V-226		FSH	FBG		IO	110-225		8	3200	2 1	9400	10900
24 1	V-226		FSH	FBG		IO	T110-T150		8	3800	2 1	11700	13400
26 8	MIAMI 27	HT		FBG		IO	110-200		8	4400	2 6	12300	15300
26 8	MIAMI 27	HT		FBG		IO	225		8	4400	2 6	13700	15600
26 8	MIAMI 27	HT		FBG		IO	T110-T150		8	4800	2 6	14900	17700
26 8	MIAMI 27	HT	CBNCR	FBG		IO	110		8	5000	2 6	15800	17900
26 8	MIAMI 27	HT	CBNCR	FBG		IO	200		8	5000	2 6	17500	19900
26 8	MIAMI 27	HT	CBNCR	FBG		IO	T110-T150		8	5600	2 6	19600	22100
26 8	MIAMI 27		RNBT	FBG		IO	200-225		8	4800	2 6	12500	14500
26 8	MIAMI 27		RNBT	FBG		IO	T110-T150		8	4800	2 6	13300	15700
26 8	MIAMI 27	OP	RNBT	FBG		IO	110-200		8	4200	2 6	10800	13300
26 8	MIAMI 27	FB	SF	FBG		IO	110-200		8	4600	2 6	14000	17300
26 8	MIAMI 27	FB	SF	FBG		IO	225		8	4600	2 6	15600	17700
26 8	MIAMI 27	FB	SF	FBG		IO	T110-T150		8	5300	2 6	17300	20500
37 1	MIAMI 37		SF	FBG		IB	T290	CHRY	13	2	14850	2 6	26800	31800
37 1	MIAMI 37	FB	SF	FBG		IB	T290	CHRY	13	2	16000	2 6	30100	33500
					1967 BOATS								
18 3	MIAMI PLAYMATE			FBG		IO	110-165			1800		3500	4100
19 8	V-182		CBNCR	FBG		IO	110-150			2400		5250	6050
19 8	V-182		RNBT	FBG		IO	110-150		7 8	2400		4750	5500
19 8	V-182		SF	FBG		IO	110-150			2400		5600	6450
22 2	MIAMI TRI 21	OP		FBG		IO	150-200		8	2750		7150	8300
22 2	MIAMI TRI 21	OP	FSH	FBG		IO	110		8	2750		7900	9100
22 2	MIAMI TRI 21		TCMY	FBG		IO	110-200		8	2750		10500	12200
24 1	V-226		CBNCR	FBG		IO	110-225		8	3200		11800	14100
24 1	V-226		CBNCR	FBG		IO	T110-T150		8	3200		11800	14100
24 1	V-226		FSH	FBG		IO	110-225		8	3200		9650	11300
24 1	V-226		FSH	FBG		IO	T110-T150		8	3200		10900	13000
26 8	MIAMI 25	HT		FBG		IO	110-200		8	4200		12400	15500
26 8	MIAMI 25	HT		FBG		IO	225		8	4200		13900	15800
26 8	MIAMI 25	HT		FBG		IO	T110-T150		8	4200		14500	17300
26 8	MIAMI 25	FB		FBG		IO	110-200		8	4200		12400	15500
26 8	MIAMI 25	FB		FBG		IO	225		8	4200		13900	15800
26 8	MIAMI 25	FB		FBG		IO	T110-T150		8	4200		14500	17300
26 8	MIAMI 25	HT	CBNCR	FBG		IO	200 INT		8	4200		16700	19000
26 8	MIAMI 25	HT	CBNCR	FBG		IO	T110	VLVO	8	4200		18200	20200
26 8	MIAMI 25	HT	EXP	FBG		IO	110-200		8	4200		12100	15000
26 8	MIAMI 25	HT	EXP	FBG		IO	T110-T150		8	4200		14000	16800
26 8	MIAMI 25		RNBT	FBG		IO	110-200		8	4200		11100	13800
26 8	MIAMI 25		RNBT	FBG		IO	225		8	4200		12400	14100
26 8	MIAMI 25		RNBT	FBG		IO	T110-T150		8	4200		12900	15300
37	MIAMI 37		SF	FBG		IB	T290		13	2		26000	28900
37	MIAMI 37	FB	SF	FBG		IB	T290		13	2		26000	28900
					1966 BOATS								
18 2	V-181		RNBT	FBG		IB	110		7 9			1750	2100
21	MIAMI TRI 21		FSH	FBG		IB	110		8			3100	3500
21	MIAMI TRI 21		TCMY	FBG		IB	110		8			3100	3600
22 6	V-226		CBNCR	FBG		IB	110		8			3850	4500
22 6	V-226		FSH	FBG		IB	110		8			3350	3900
25 5	MIAMI 25		CBNCR	FBG		IB	110		8			5800	6700
25 5	MIAMI 25		FSH	FBG		IB	110		8			5300	6100
					1965 BOATS								
16 10	BISCAYNE		RNBT	FBG		OB			6 9	840		2000	2350
17 9	PLAYBOY		RNBT	FBG		OB			7 6	900		2250	2600
18 2	KEY-LARGO		RNBT	FBG		OB	60		7 9			4150	4800
20	VW 20		CR	FBG	CT	IO			8		2	**	**
22 6	V-226 FISHERMAN		RNBT	FBG		IO	90		8		2 3	7700	8850
25	V-25		CBNCR	FBG		IO	150		8		2 3	15100	17200
34	MIAMI 34		SF	FBG		IB	T275		12 6		2 10	19200	21400
34	MIAMI 34		SF	FBG		IB	T150D		12 6		2 10	31500	35000
					1962 BOATS								
16 10	BISCAYNE		UTL	FBG		OB						1700	2000
16 10	KEY-LARGO		CBNCR	FBG		OB						2050	2450
16 10	PRESIDENT		RNBT	FBG		OB						2600	3050
17 10	PLAYBOY		SF	FBG		OB						2600	3050
19 2	SPORTSMAN		RNBT	FBG		IO	125					5450	6250
19 2	SPORTSMAN		SF	FBG		IO	150					6450	7400
22 6	SEA-MASTER		SF	FBG		IO	125					10300	11700
					1961 BOATS								
16 10	BISCAYNE		UTL	FBG		OB			6 9	890		2150	2500
16 10	KEY-LARGO		CR	FBG		OB			6 9	1200		2850	3300
17 10	PLAYBOY		SF	FBG		OB			7 6	900		2300	2700
19 2	SPORTSMAN		SF	FBG		OB			8	1300		3250	3750
					1960 BOATS								
17		HT	RNBT	FBG		OB						2700	3100
17	BISCAYNE		RNBT	FBG		OB						2700	3100
					1959 BOATS								
16 7	BISCAYNE		CR	FBG		OB			6 9			2700	3100
16 7	MIAMI CUSTOM		CR	FBG		OB			6 9			2000	2350
16 7	PRESIDENT	HT	CR	FBG		OB						2700	3100
17	CORSAIR CUSTOM		RNBT	FBG		OB						2700	3150
					1957 BOATS								
19			CR	FBG		OB						3100	3600
					1956 BOATS								
18			CR	FBG		OB						2750	3200

SEA & AIR PRODUCTS
COAST GUARD MFG ID- SAA

Call 1-800-327-6929 for BUC Personalized Evaluation Service
Or, for 1972 to 1975 boats, sign onto www.BUCValuPro.com

SEA CAMPER INDS INC
HOLLAND MI 49423   COAST GUARD MFG ID- FAR See inside cover to adjust price for area

For more recent years, see the BUC Used Boat Price Guide, Volume 1 or Volume 2

LOA FT IN	NAME AND/ OR MODEL	TOP/ RIG	BOAT TYPE	HULL MTL	HULL TP	ENGINE TP	ENGINE # HP	ENGINE MFG	BEAM FT IN	WGT LBS	DRAFT FT IN	RETAIL LOW	RETAIL HIGH
					1983 BOATS								
18 6	HOBO		CR	FBG	DV	IO	150		8			2700	3150
24 1	SEA-CAMPER 24		FSH	FBG	DV	IO			8	4720		**	**
24 1	SEA-CAMPER 24	HT	HB	FBG	DV	IO			8	4720		**	**
					1982 BOATS								
24 2	SEA-CAMPER 24	HT	HB	FBG	DV	IO			8	4720		**	**
24 2	SEA-CAMPER 24 FSH	HT	HB	FBG	DV	IO			8	4720		**	**
					1981 BOATS								
24 2	SEA-CAMPER 24	HT	HB	FBG	DV	IO			8			**	**
24 2	SEA-CAMPER 24 FSH	HT	CR	FBG	DV	IO			8			**	**
					1980 BOATS								
24	SEA-CAMPER	HT	HB	FBG	SV	IO			8			**	**
					1979 BOATS								
24	SEA-CAMPER	HT		FBG	SV	IO	190		8			**	**
24 2	SEA-CAMPER	HT	CAMPR	FBG	SV	IO	190-225		8	4720	1 3	6300	7350
24 2	SEA-CAMPER	HT	CAMPR	FBG	SV	IO	130D	VLVO	8	4720	1 3	7300	8400

LOA FT	IN	NAME AND/ OR MODEL	TOP/ RIG	BOAT TYPE	-HULL- MTL	TP	----ENGINE--- TP	# HP	MFG	BEAM FT	IN	WGT LBS	DRAFT FT	IN	RETAIL LOW	RETAIL HIGH
		1979 BOATS														
24	2	SEA-CAMPER	HT	CAMPR	FBG	SV	IO	T140	VLVO	8		4720	1	3	7000	8050
24	2	SEA-CAMPER	FB	CAMPR	FBG	SV	IO	190-225		8		4720	1	3	6300	7350
24	2	SEA-CAMPER	FB	CAMPR	FBG	SV	IO	130D	VLVO	8		4720	1	3	7300	8400
24	2	SEA-CAMPER	FB	CAMPR	FBG	SV	IO	T140	VLVO	8		4720	1	3	7000	8050
		1978 BOATS														
24	2	SEA-CAMPER	HT	CAMPR	FBG	DV	IO	190-225		8		4720	1	3	6350	7400
24	2	SEA-CAMPER	HT	CAMPR	FBG	DV	IO	130D	VLVO	8		4720	1	3	7350	8450
24	2	SEA-CAMPER	FB	CAMPR	FBG	DV	IO	190-225		8		4720	1	3	6350	7400
24	2	SEA-CAMPER	FB	CAMPR	FBG	DV	IO	130D	VLVO	8		4720	1	3	7350	8450
		1974 BOATS														
24		SEA-CAMPER DLX			FBG		IO	188-225		8		4700	1	3	6800	8000
24		SEA-CAMPER DLX			FBG		IO	T140-T165		8		4750	1	3	7500	8650
24		SEA-CAMPER DLX	FB		FBG		IO	188-225		8		4250	1	3	6050	7050
24		SEA-CAMPER DLX	FB		FBG		IO	T140-T165		8		4250	1	3	6650	7700
24		SEA-CAMPER STD			FBG		IO	140-225		8		4250	1	2	6000	7400
24		SEA-CAMPER STD			FBG		IO	T130-T170		8		4750	1	3	7450	8650
		1973 BOATS														
24	1	SEA-CAMPER		CBNCR	FBG	TR	IO	T170		8			1	3	9100	10300
24	1	SEA-CAMPER II		CBNCR	FBG	TR	OB			8		3850			10800	12300
24	1	SEASPORT		OPFSH	FBG	TR	OB			8		2865			8650	9900
		1972 BOATS														
24	1	SEA-CAMPER			FBG		OB			8		4250		10	11500	13100
24	1	SEA-CAMPER			FBG		IO	165-245		8		4250		10	6450	7600
24	2	SEA-CAMPER II			FBG		OB			8		3390	1	1	9900	11200
24	2	SEASPORT			FBG		OB			8		2500			7750	8900
		1971 BOATS														
24	1	SEA-CAMPER	HT	CAMPR	FBG	TR	IO	120		7		4250	2	6	6800	7800
		1970 BOATS														
24		SEA-CAMPER		HB	FBG	TR	IO	120-160		8		4000	1	6	**	**

SEA CHIEF YACHT COMPANY

KAOHSIUNG TAIWAN COAST GUARD MFG ID- XCV See inside cover to adjust price for area

LOA FT	IN	NAME AND/ OR MODEL	TOP/ RIG	BOAT TYPE	-HULL- MTL	TP	----ENGINE--- TP	# HP	MFG	BEAM FT	IN	WGT LBS	DRAFT FT	IN	RETAIL LOW	RETAIL HIGH
		1980 BOATS														
37	11	HOLLMANN 38	CUT	SA/RC	FBG	KL	IB	35D	VLVO	11	6	12000	6		46900	51500
38	5	SEA-EXPLORER SE-38	FB	TRWL	FBG	DS	IB	120D	LEHM	13	1	21300	3	8	52400	57600
38	5	SEA-EXPLORER SE-38	FB	TRWL	FBG	DS	IB	T120D	LEHM	13	1	26100	3	8	65000	71400
38	5	SEA-EXPLORER SE-38	FB	TRWL	FBG	DS	IB	T120D	LEHM	13	1	25100	3	11	63000	69200
41	8	VAGABOND V-42	CUT	SA/CR	FBG	KL	IB	65D	LEHM	12	10	28500	5	6	96400	106000
41	8	VAGABOND V-42	KTH	SA/CR	FBG	KL	IB	65D	LEHM	12	10	28500	5	6	103500	114000

SEA CRAFT

FOREST CITY NC 28043 COAST GUARD MFG ID- SXC See inside cover to adjust price for area
FORMERLY SEACRAFT INDUSTRIES INC

For more recent years, see the BUC Used Boat Price Guide, Volume 1 or Volume 2

LOA FT	IN	NAME AND/ OR MODEL	TOP/ RIG	BOAT TYPE	-HULL- MTL	TP	----ENGINE--- TP	# HP	MFG	BEAM FT	IN	WGT LBS	DRAFT FT	IN	RETAIL LOW	RETAIL HIGH
		1983 BOATS														
18	2	FAMILY 18	OP	CTRCN	FBG	SV	OB			7	5	1800		11	4400	5050
19	8	MASTER-ANGLER 20	OP	CTRCN	FBG	SV	OB			7	6	2000	1		5100	5850
20	4	BOWRIDER 20	OP				OB			7	6	2000			6100	7000
20	4	SPORT DIVER 20	OP	CTRCN	FBG	SV	OB			7	6	2100			6300	7200
20	4	SUPERFISHERMAN 20	OP	CTRCN	FBG	SV	OB			7	6	2100			6300	7200
23	3	SAVAGE 23					OB			8		3200			10300	11700
23	3	SCEPTRE 23		RNBT	FBG	SV	IO	200		8		4300	1	5	13500	15300
23	3	SCEPTRE 23		RNBT	FBG	SV	IB	220		8		4100	1	5	17000	19400
23	3	SCEPTRE 23	HT	RNBT	FBG	SV	OB			8		3200	1	4	10400	11800
23	3	SUPERFISHERMAN 23	OP	CTRCN	FBG	SV	OB			8		3100			9950	11300
23	3	SUPERFISHERMAN 23		FSH	FBG	SV	IO	200		8		4200	1	5	14900	16900
23	3	SUPERFISHERMAN 23		FSH	FBG	SV	IB	220		8		4000	1	5	16700	18900
27		OVERNIGHTER 27					OB			10		7000			10300	11700
		1982 BOATS														
18	2	SF18	OP	CTRCN	FBG	SV	OB			7	5	1400			3600	4150
19	8	MASTER-ANGLER 20		CTRCN	FBG	SV	OB			7	6	1600			4300	5000
19	8	SCEPTRE 20		OVNTR	FBG	SV	OB			7	6	1800			4700	5400
19	8	SEAFARI 20		CR	FBG	SV	OB			7	6	1800			4800	5500
19	8	SF20	OP	OPFSH	FBG	SV	OB			7	6	1600			4350	5000
23	3	SCEPTRE 23		RNBT	FBG	SV	OB			8		2650			8850	10100
23	3	SF23		OPFSH	FBG	SV	OB			8		2650			8650	9950
		1981 BOATS														
18	2	SF18	OP	CTRCN	FBG	SV	OB			7	5	1400		11	3500	4100
19	8	MASTER-ANGLER 20	OP	CTRCN	FBG	SV	OB			7	6	1600	1		4200	4850
19	8	SCEPTRE 20	ST	OVNTR	FBG	SV	OB			7	6	1800	1		4600	5300
19	8	SCEPTRE 20	ST	OVNTR	FBG	SV	IO	140-200		7	6		1	2	8150	9850
19	8	SCEPTRE 20	ST	OVNTR	FBG	SV	IO	260		7	6		1	2	8650	10400
23	3	SCEPTRE 23	ST	RNBT	FBG	SV	OB			8		2800	1	4	9050	10300
23	3	SCEPTRE 23	HT	RNBT	FBG	SV	OB			8		3150	1	4	9850	11200
23	3	SF23	OP	OPFSH	FBG	SV	OB			8		2650	1	4	8500	9800
23	4	SCEPTRE 23	ST	RNBT	FBG	SV	IO	198-260		8			1	5	11500	14000
		IO 330 MRCR 13100 14900, IO 130D VLVO 14300 16300, IO T140-T170													12800	15200
23	4	SCEPTRE 23	HT	RNBT	FBG	SV	IO	198-260		8			1	5	11500	14000
		IO 330 MRCR 13100 14900, IO 130D VLVO 14300 16300, IO T140-T170													12800	15200
23	4	SF23	OP	OPFSH	FBG	SV	IO	198-260		8			1	5	11600	14300
23	4	SF23	OP	OPFSH	FBG	SV	IO	330	MRCR	8			1	5	13500	15300
23	4	SF23	OP	OPFSH	FBG	SV	IO	130D	VLVO	8			1	5	17200	19500
		1980 BOATS														
18	2	SF18	OP	CTRCN	FBG	SV	OB			7	5	1400		11	3450	4000
19	8	MASTER-ANGLER 20	OP	CTRCN	FBG	SV	OB			7	6	1600	1		4100	4750
19	8	SCEPTRE 20	ST	OVNTR	FBG	SV	OB			7	6	1800	1		4500	5200
19	8	SCEPTRE 20	ST	OVNTR	FBG	SV	IO	140-200		7	6		1	2	8050	9750
19	8	SCEPTRE 20	ST	OVNTR	FBG	SV	IO	260		7	6		1	2	8600	10300
19	8	SEAFARI 20		CR	FBG	SV	OB			7	6	1800			4600	5250
19	8	SEAFARI 20		CR	FBG	SV	IO	140		7	6				6750	7750
23	3	SCEPTRE 23	ST	RNBT	FBG	SV	OB			8		2800	1	4	8900	10100
23	3	SCEPTRE 23	HT	RNBT	FBG	SV	OB			8		3150	1	4	9650	11000
23	3	SF23	OP	OPFSH	FBG	SV	OB			8		2650	1	4	8350	9600
23	4	SAVAGE 23		FSH	FBG	SV	OB			8		2900			9050	10300
23	4	SCEPTRE 23	ST	RNBT	FBG	SV	IO	198-260		8			1	5	11400	13900
		IO 330 MRCR 13000 14800, IO 130D VLVO 14200 16100, IO T140-T170													12700	15100
23	4	SCEPTRE 23	HT	RNBT	FBG	SV	IO	198-260		8			1	5	11400	13900
		IO 330 MRCR 13000 14800, IO 130D VLVO 14200 16100, IO T140-T170													12700	15100
23	4	SCEPTRE 23	FB	RNBT	FBG	SV	IO	228		8					11500	13100
23	4	SEAVETTE 23		RNBT	FBG	SV	OB			8		2975			9350	10600
23	4	SEAVETTE 23		RNBT	FBG	SV	IO	225		8					11500	13100
23	4	SF23	OP	OPFSH	FBG	SV	IO	198-260		8			1	5	11500	14100
23	4	SF23	OP	OPFSH	FBG	SV	IO	330	MRCR	8			1	5	13400	15200
23	4	SF23	OP	OPFSH	FBG	SV	IO	130D	VLVO	8			1	5	17000	19300
		1979 BOATS														
18	2	SF18	OP	CTRCN	FBG	SV	OB			7	5	1400		11	3400	3950
19	8	MASTER-ANGLER 20	OP	CTRCN	FBG	SV	OB			7	6	1600	1		4150	4800
19	8	SCEPTRE 20	OP	OVNTR	FBG	SV	OB			7	6	1800	1		4450	5100
19	8	SCEPTRE 20	OP	OVNTR	FBG	SV	IO	140-170		7	6		1	2	8050	9600
19	8	SCEPTRE 20	OP	OVNTR	FBG	SV	IO	255-260		7	6		1	2	9000	10200
19	8	SEAFARI 20	OP	CUD	FBG	SV	OB			7	6	1800	1		4500	5200
19	8	SEAFARI 20	OP	CUD	FBG	SV	IO	140-170		7	6		1	2	7250	8650
19	8	SEAFARI 20	OP	CUD	FBG	SV	IO	255-260		7	6		1	2	8100	9300
19	8	SF20	OP	CTRCN	FBG	SV	OB			7	6	1600	1		3900	4550
19	8	SF20	OP	CTRCN	FBG	SV	IO	140-170		7	6		1	2	7250	8700
19	8	SF20	OP	CTRCN	FBG	SV	IO	255-260		7	6		1	2	8200	9400
23	3	SCEPTRE 23	OP	RNBT	FBG	SV	OB			8		2800	1	4	8650	9950
23	3	SCEPTRE 23	HT	RNBT	FBG	SV	OB			8		3150	1	4	9500	10800
23	3	SEAVETTE 23	OP	RACE	FBG	SV	OB			8		2975	1	4	9150	10400
23	3	SF23	OP	OPFSH	FBG	SV	OB			8		2650	1	4	8250	9450
23	4	SCEPTRE 23	OP	OPFSH	FBG	SV	OB			8		2900	1	4	8950	10200
23	4	SCEPTRE 23	OP	OPFSH	FBG	SV	IO	255	VLVO	8			1	5	13200	15000
		IB 255-260 12700 14900, IO 290 VLVO 13800 15700, IB 330													13100	15500
		IB 124D VLVO 17200 19600, IO 130D VLVO 18300 20300														
23	4	SCEPTRE 23	OP	RNBT	FBG	SV	IO	255	VLVO	8			1	5	12100	13800
		IB 255 MRCR 13300 15100, IO 260 MRCR 11800 13400, IO 260 OMC													11700	13300
		IB 260 OMC 13700 15600, IO 290 VLVO 12700 14400, IO 330 MRCR													13000	14800
		IB 330 13700 16200, IO 130D VLVO 14200 16100, IO T140-T170													12700	15100
23	4	SCEPTRE 23	HT	RNBT	FBG	SV	IO	255	VLVO	8			1	5	12100	13800
		IB 255 MRCR 13300 15100, IO 260 MRCR 11800 13400, IO 260 OMC													11700	13300
		IB 260 OMC 13700 15600, IO 290 VLVO 12700 14400, IO 330 MRCR													13000	14800
		IB 330 13700 16200, IO 130D VLVO 14200 16100, IO T140-T170													12700	15100
23	4	SCEPTRE 23	FB	RNBT	FBG	SV	IO	255-330		8			1	5	12100	14800
23	4	SCEPTRE 23	FB	RNBT	FBG	SV	IO	130D	VLVO	8			1	5	14200	16100
23	4	SCEPTRE 23	FB	RNBT	FBG	SV	IO	T140-T170		8			1	4	12700	15100
23	4	SEAVETTE 23	OP	RACE	FBG	SV	IO	255-330		8			1	5	10200	12600
23	4	SEAVETTE 23	OP	RACE	FBG	SV	IO	130D	VLVO	8			1	5	**	**

 CONTINUED ON NEXT PAGE

SEA CRAFT -CONTINUED See inside cover to adjust price for area

```
 LOA  NAME AND/              TOP/ BOAT  -HULL- ----ENGINE--- BEAM   WGT  DRAFT RETAIL RETAIL
FT IN  OR MODEL               RIG TYPE  MTL TP TP # HP   MFG  FT IN  LBS  FT IN   LOW   HIGH
--------------------- 1979 BOATS ---------------------------------------------------------------
23  4 SEAVETTE 23             OP  RACE  FBG SV IO T170   MRCR  8            1  5  10800  12300
23  4 SF23                    OP  OPFSH FBG SV IO  255   VLVO  8            1  5  11600  13100
   IB 255-260      11200  13200, IO  290  VLVO  12200  13800, IB  330         11600  13700
   IB  124D VLVO   15600  17700, IO  130D VLVO  16100  18300

26  9 MASTER-ANGLER 27        HT  SF    FBG SV IB T255-T260    9 10         2  4  26300  29900
26  9 MASTER-ANGLER 27        HT  SF    FBG SV IB T124D VLVO   9 10         2  4  39000  43400
26  9 MASTER-ANGLER 27        TT  SF    FBG SV IB T255-T260    9 10         2  4  26300  29900
26  9 MASTER-ANGLER 27        TT  SF    FBG SV IB T124D VLVO   9 10         2  4  39000  43400
--------------------- 1978 BOATS ---------------------------------------------------------------
18  2 SF18                    OP  OPFSH FBG SV OB              7  5  1400     11   3300   3850
19  8 MASTER-ANGLER 20        OP  OPFSH FBG SV OB              7  6  1600  1       4100   4750
19  8 SCEPTRE 20              OP  RNBT  FBG SV OB              7  6  1650  1       4150   4850
19  8 SCEPTRE 20              OP  RNBT  FBG SV IO 140-198      7  6  1650  1  2    5700   6900
19  8 SCEPTRE 20              OP  RNBT  FBG SV IO 225-228      7  6  1650  1  2    5900   7200
19  8 SEAFARI 20              OP  CUD   FBG SV OB              7  6  1800  1       4450   5100
19  8 SEAFARI 20              OP  CUD   FBG SV IO 140-198      7  6  1800  1  2    6050   7300
19  8 SEAFARI 20              OP  CUD   FBG SV IO 225-228      7  6  1800  1  2    6200   7600
19  8 SF20                    OP  OPFSH FBG SV OB              7  6  1600  1       3850   4500
19  8 SF20                    OP  OPFSH FBG SV IO 140-198      7  6  1600  1  2    6200   7450
19  8 SF20                    OP  OPFSH FBG SV IO 225-228      7  6  1600  1  2    6350   7800
23  3 SAVAGE 23               OP  OPFSH FBG SV OB              8     2900  1  4    8850  10000

23  3 SCEPTRE 23              OP  RNBT  FBG SV OB              8     2800  1  4    8550   9800
23  3 SCEPTRE 23              HT  RNBT  FBG SV OB              8     2800  1  4    8550   9800
23  3 SCEPTRE 23              FB  RNBT  FBG SV OB              8     2800  1  4    8550   9800
23  3 SEAVETTE 23             OP  SPTCR FBG SV OB              8     2975  1  4    9000  10200
23  3 SF23                    OP  OPFSH FBG SV OB              8     2650  1  4    8150   9350
23  4 SAVAGE 23               OP  OPFSH FBG SV IO 165-185      8     2900  1  5   11000  12500
   IO  198  MRCR   11100  12600, IB  198  MRCR  10800  12300, IO  225         11200  13200
   IO  228  MRCR   11300  12800, IB  228  MRCR  10900  12400, IO  240  OMC    11300  12800
   IO  255  VLVO   12000  13600, IB  255  MRCR  10900  12400, IO  260  MRCR   11600  13200
   IB 305-350      11400  13800, IB  454  OMC   14000  15900, IO T140-T170     12600  15100

23  4 SCEPTRE 23              OP  RNBT  FBG SV IO 165-185      8     2800  1  5    9650  11000
   IO  198  MRCR    9700  11000, IB  198  MRCR  10700  12100, IO  225          9750  11600
   IO  228  MRCR    9850  11200, IB  228  MRCR  10700  12200, IO  240  OMC     9850  11200
   IO  255  VLVO   10500  11900, IB  255  MRCR  10800  12200, IO  260  MRCR   10100  11500
   IB 305-350      11200  13600, IB  454  OMC   13800  15700, IO T140-T170     11000  13200

23  4 SCEPTRE 23              HT  RNBT  FBG SV IO 165-185      8     2800  1  5    9650  11000
   IO  198  MRCR    9700  11000, IB  198  MRCR  10700  12100, IO  225          9750  11600
   IO  228  MRCR    9850  11200, IB  228  MRCR  10700  12200, IO  240  OMC     9850  11200
   IO  255  VLVO   10500  11900, IB  255  MRCR  10800  12200, IO  260  MRCR   10100  11500
   IB 305-350      11200  13600, IB  454  OMC   13800  15700, IO T140-T170     11000  13200

23  4 SCEPTRE 23              FB  RNBT  FBG SV IO 165-185      8     2800  1  5    9650  11000
   IO  198  MRCR    9700  11000, IB  198  MRCR  10700  12100, IO  225          9750  11600
   IO  228  MRCR    9850  11200, IB  228  MRCR  10700  12200, IO  240  OMC     9850  11200
   IO  255  VLVO   10500  11900, IB  255  MRCR  10800  12200, IO  260  MRCR   10100  11500
   IB 305-350      11700  13600, IB  454  OMC   13800  15700, IO T140-T170     11000  13200

23  4 SEAVETTE 23             OP  SPTCR FBG SV IO 165-260      8     2975  1  5   10600  13100
23  4 SEAVETTE 23             OP  SPTCR FBG SV IO  330   MRCR  8     2975  1  5   12500  14200
23  4 SEAVETTE 23             OP  SPTCR FBG SV IO T140-T170    8     2975  1  5   12100  14400
23  4 SF23                    OP  OPFSH FBG SV IO 165-185      8     2650  1  5   10500  11900
   IO  198  MRCR   10600  12000, IB  198  MRCR  10300  11700, IO  225         10600  12600
   IO  228  MRCR   10700  12200, IB  228  MRCR  10400  11800, IO  240  OMC    10800  12200
   IO  255  VLVO   11400  13000, IB  255  MRCR  10400  11800, IO  260  MRCR   11000  12600
   IB 305-350      10800  13200, IB  454  OMC   13500  15300, IB  124D VLVO   14700  16700
   IO T140-T170    12100  14500

24 10 SEAFARI 25              OP  CUD   FBG DV IO T140-T170    8     3000  1  8   13500  15800
26  9 MASTER-ANGLER 27        OP  SF    FBG SV IB T198-T305    9 10  7000  2  4   27000  32500
26  9 MASTER-ANGLER 27        OP  SF    FBG SV IB T350   OMC   9 10  7000  2  4   30800  34200
26  9 MASTER-ANGLER 27        OP  SF    FBG SV IB T124D VLVO   9 10  7000  2  4   36400  40400
26  9 MASTER-ANGLER 27        TT  SF    FBG SV IB T198-T305    9 10  7000  2  4   27000  32600
26  9 MASTER-ANGLER 27        TT  SF    FBG SV IB T350   OMC   9 10  7000  2  4   30800  34200
26  9 MASTER-ANGLER 27        TT  SF    FBG SV IB T124D VLVO   9 10  7000  2  4   36400  40400
--------------------- 1977 BOATS ---------------------------------------------------------------
18  2 SF18                    OP  OPFSH FBG DV OB              7  5  1400     11   3300   3800
19  8 MASTER-ANGLER 20        OP  OPFSH FBG DV OB              7  6           11   4750   5500
19  8 SCEPTRE 20              OP  RNBT  FBG DV OB              7  6  1650  1       4100   4750
19  8 SCEPTRE 20              OP  RNBT  FBG DV IO 120-235      7  6        1  2    7100   8500
19  8 SCEPTRE 20              OP  RNBT  FBG DV JT  245   OMC   7  6        1  2    8400   9650
19  8 SEAFARI 20              OP  CUD   FBG DV OB              7  6  1800  1       4400   5050
19  8 SEAFARI 20              OP  CUD   FBG DV IO 120-235      7  6        1  2    7400   8850
19  8 SEAFARI 20              OP  CUD   FBG DV JT  245   OMC   7  6        1  2    8200   9450
19  8 SF20                    OP  OPFSH FBG DV OB              7  6  1600  1       3950   4550
19  8 SF20                    OP  OPFSH FBG DV IO 120-235      7  6        1  2    7350   8800
19  8 SF20                    OP  OPFSH FBG DV JT  245   OMC   7  6        1  2    7800   8950
23  3 SAVAGE 23               OP  OPFSH FBG DV OB              8     2900  1  4    8650   9950

23  3 SCEPTRE 23              OP  RNBT  FBG DV OB              8     2800  1  4    8450   9700
23  3 SF23                    OP  OPFSH FBG DV OB              8     2650  1  4    8050   9250
23  4 SAVAGE 23               OP  OPFSH FBG DV IO 165-190      8           1  5   12700  14400
   IB  230  OMC    12100  13800, IO  233  MRCR  12900  14700, IB  233  MRCR   11700  13300
   IO  235  OMC    12900  14600, IO  255  MRCR  13200  15000, IB 255-260      11800  13800
   IO  280  MRCR   13500  15300, IO T120-T165   14200  16100

23  4 SCEPTRE 23              OP  RNBT  FBG DV IO 165-190      8           1  5   11600  13200
   IB  230  OMC    12500  14200, IO  233  MRCR  11800  13400, IB  233  MRCR   12200  13800
   IO  235  OMC    11800  13400, IO  255  MRCR  12000  13600, IB 255-260      12200  14300
   IO  280  MRCR   12300  14000, IO T120-T165   12900  14800

23  4 SF23                    OP  OPFSH FBG DV IO 165-190      8           1  5   10700  12300
   IB  230  OMC    10500  11900, IO  233  MRCR  11100  12600, IB  233  MRCR   10100  11500
   IO  235  OMC    11000  12500, IO  255  MRCR  11200  12800, IB 255-260      10200  12000
   IO  280  MRCR   11600  13200, IB  200D CHRY  17300  19700, IO T120-T165    12300  14200

24 10 SEAFARI 25              ST  CUD   FBG DV IO  255   MRCR  8     3000  1  8   12800  14500
24 10 SEAFARI 25              ST  CUD   FBG DV IO  280   MRCR  8           1  8   16300  18600
24 10 SEAFARI 25              ST  CUD   FBG DV IO T120-T165    8           1  8   16700  19500
26  9 MASTER-ANGLER 27        HT  SF    FBG DV IB T233   MRCR  9 10  6500  2  4   25500  28400
26  9 MASTER-ANGLER 27        TT  SF    FBG DV IB T233   MRCR  9 10  6500  2  4   25500  28400
--------------------- 1976 BOATS ---------------------------------------------------------------
18  2 SF18                    OP  FSH   FBG    OB              7  5  1400     11   3250   3800
19  8 MASTER-ANGLER 20        OP  FSH   FBG    OB              7  6  1600  1       4000   4650
19  8 SCEPTRE 20              OP  RNBT  FBG    OB              7  6  1650  1       3700   4300
19  8 SCEPTRE 20              OP  RNBT  FBG    IO 120-235      7  6        1  2    6850   8300
19  8 SCEPTRE 20              OP  RNBT  FBG    JT  290   OMC   7  6        1  2    8000   9200
19  8 SEAFARI 20              OP  RNBT  FBG    OB              7  6  1650  1       4450   5100
19  8 SEAFARI 20              OP  RNBT  FBG    IO 120-235      7  6        1  2    7700   9100
19  8 SEAFARI 20              OP  RNBT  FBG    JT  290   OMC   7  6        1  2    8100   9300
19  8 SF20                    OP  FSH   FBG    OB              7  6  1600  1       3750   4350
19  8 SF20                    OP  FSH   FBG    IO 120-235      7  6        1  2    8600  10200
19  8 SF20                    OP  FSH   FBG    JT  290   OMC   7  6        1  2    8400   9650
23  3 SCEPTRE 23              OP  RNBT  FBG    OB              8     2800  1  4    8400   9650

23  3 SCEPTRE 23              OP  RNBT  FBG    IO 140-190      8           1  5   11800  13500
   IB  230  OMC    12000  13600, IO  233  MRCR  12100  13700, IB  233  MRCR   11600  13200
   IO  235  OMC    12000  13700, IO  255  MRCR  12300  13900, IB 255-260      11700  13700
   IO  280  MRCR   12600  14300, IO T120-T165   13200  15100

23  3 SF 23                   OP  FSH   FBG    OB              8     2650  1  4    8000   9200
23  3 SF 23                   OP  FSH   FBG    IO 140-190      8           1  5   13500  15500
   IB  230  OMC    12200  13900, IO  233  MRCR  13900  15800, IB  233  MRCR   11900  13500
   IO  235  OMC    13800  15700, IO  255  MRCR  14100  16000, IB 255-260      11900  14000
   IO  280  MRCR   14500  16400, IO T120-T165   15200  17400

24 10 SEAFARI 25              ST  RNBT  FBG    IO 255-280      8           1  8   14500  16900
24 10 SEAFARI 25              ST  RNBT  FBG    IO T120-T233    8           1  8   15300  18800
--------------------- 1975 BOATS ---------------------------------------------------------------
18  2 SF18 FISHERMAN          OP  OPFSH FBG    OB              7  5           11   2950   3450
19  8 SCEPTRE 20              OP  RNBT  FBG    OB              7  6        1       4250   4950
19  8 SCEPTRE 20              OP  RNBT  FBG    IO 140-245      7  6        1  2    7100   8550
19  8 SCEPTRE 20              OP  RNBT  FBG    JT  290   OMC   7  6        1  2    7300   8400
19  8 SEAFARI 20              OP  RNBT  FBG    OB              7  6        1       5200   6000
19  8 SEAFARI 20              OP  RNBT  FBG    IO 140-245      7  6        1  2    7950   9500
19  8 SEAFARI 20              OP  RNBT  FBG    JT  290   OMC   7  6        1  2    8150   9400
19  8 SF20 FISHERMAN          OP  OPFSH FBG    OB              7  6        1       4700   5400
19  8 SF20 FISHERMAN          OP  OPFSH FBG    IO 140-245      7  6        1  2    7800   9350
19  8 SF20 FISHERMAN          OP  OPFSH FBG    JT  290   OMC   7  6        1  2    7150   8250
23  3 SCEPTRE 23              OP  RNBT  FBG    OB              8           1  4    9000  10200

23  3 SCEPTRE 23              OP  RNBT  FBG    IO 165-280      8           1  5   12200  14800
   IO  115D S&S    15500  17600, JT  150D S&S   16500  18800, IO  150D S&S    16000  18200
   JT  155D S&S    16600  18900, IO  155D S&S   16100  18300, JT  200D S&S    17300  19700
   IO  200D S&S    16800  19100, IO T140-T165   13700  15600

23  3 SF23 SUPER FISHERMAN OP     FSH   FBG    OB              8           1  4    9000  10200
23  3 SF23 SUPER FISHERMAN OP     FSH   FBG    IO 165-225      8           1  5   14000  16100
   IB  230  OMC    11700  13300, IO  233  MRCR  14300  16300, IB  233  MRCR   11400  13000
   IO 245-280      14400  17000, IO  115D S&S   20800  23100, JT  150D S&S    16500  18700
   IO  150D S&S    21500  23900, JT  155D S&S   16600  18800, IO  155D S&S    21600  24000
   JT  200D S&S    17300  19700, IO  200D S&S   22600  25100, IO T140-T165    15700  17900
```


CONTINUED ON NEXT PAGE

SEA CRAFT — CONTINUED

See inside cover to adjust price for area

LOA FT	IN	NAME AND/OR MODEL	TOP/RIG	BOAT TYPE	HULL MTL	HULL TP	ENGINE TP	HP	MFG	BEAM FT	IN	WGT LBS	DRAFT FT	IN	RETAIL LOW	RETAIL HIGH
1975 BOATS																
23	3	TSUNAMI 23	RNBT	FBG	DV		OB			8		2800			8300	9550
23	3	TSUNAMI 23	RNBT	FBG	DV		IO	165		8		3650			12200	13900
23	3	TSUNAMI 23	RNBT	FBG	DV		IO	T165		8		3650			13800	15700
24	10	SEAFARI 25	OP	RNBT	FBG		IO	255-280		8			1	8	15000	17400

JT 150D S&S 18800 20900, IO 150D S&S 18300 20300, JT 155D S&S 19000 21100
IO 155D S&S 18400 20400, JT 200D S&S 19800 22000, IO 200D S&S 19200 21300
IO T140-T233 15900 19400

LOA FT	IN	NAME AND/OR MODEL	TOP/RIG	BOAT TYPE	HULL MTL	HULL TP	ENGINE TP	HP	MFG	BEAM FT	IN	WGT LBS	DRAFT FT	IN	RETAIL LOW	RETAIL HIGH
1974 BOATS																
19	8	SEAFARI 20		FBG			OB			7	6	1800		10	4150	4850
19	8	SEAFARI 20		FBG			IO	140-245		7	6			10	7350	8850
19	8	SUPERFISHERMAN 20	FSH	FBG			OB			7	6	1650		10	3900	4550
19	8	SUPERFISHERMAN 20	FSH	FBG			IO	140-245		7	6			10	9300	10900
19	8	TSUNAMI 20		FBG			OB			7	6	1700		10	4000	4650
19	8	TSUNAMI 20		FBG			IO	140-245		7	6			10	6950	8350
23	3	SUPERFISHERMAN 23	FSH	FBG			OB			8		2500	1	2	7550	8700
23	3	SUPERFISHERMAN 23	FSH	FBG			IO	165-255		8			1	2	14500	17100
23	3	SUPERFISHERMAN 23	FSH	FBG			IO	T140-T170		8			1	2	16200	19400
23	3	TSUNAMI 23		FBG			OB			8		2800	1	2	8250	9500
23	3	TSUNAMI 23		FBG			IO	165-255		8			1	2	12000	14200
23	3	TSUNAMI 23		FBG			IO	T140-T170		8			1	2	13600	16300
24	10	SEAFARI 25		FBG			IO	T140-T188		8		4500	1	8	18800	21300
24	10	SEAFARI 25		FBG			IO	T300 CC		8		4500	1	8	21900	24300
1973 BOATS																
19	8	SEAFARI 20	CR	FBG			OB			7	6	1882			4300	5000
19	8	SEAFARI 20	CR	FBG			IO	130-140		7	6	2493	1	2	8350	9600
19	8	SUPERFISHERMAN	FSH	FBG			OB			7	6	1650			3900	4550
19	8	SUPERFISHERMAN	FSH	FBG			IO	130-245		7	6	2260	1	2	8400	10300
23	3	SUPERFISHERMAN	FSH	FBG			OB			8		2110	1	4	6550	7500
23	3	SUPERFISHERMAN	FSH	FBG			IO	165-255		8		3925	1	6	15500	19100
23	3	SUPERFISHERMAN	FSH	FBG			IO	T140-T170		8		4436	1	7	19000	22300
23	3	TSUNAMI 23 SPT		FBG			OB			8		2800	1	4	6250	9500
23	3	TSUNAMI 23 SPT		FBG			IO	165-245		8		3615	1	5	13100	16300
23	3	TSUNAMI 23 SPT		FBG			IO	255	MRCR	8		4085	1	6	14900	16900
23	3	TSUNAMI 23 SPT		FBG			IO	T140-T170		8		4126	1	6	16100	19300
24	10	SEAFARI 25	CR	FBG			IO	188-255		8		4615	1	8	18200	21900
24	10	SEAFARI 25	CR	FBG			IO	T140-T170		8		4996	1	8	21000	24500
1972 BOATS																
19	8	F-20	FSH	FBG			OB			7	6	1470			3550	4150
19	8	F-20	FSH	FBG			IO	120-140		7	6	2070			7900	9600
19	8	SEAFARI 20	CR	FBG			OB			7	6	1700			4000	4650
19	8	SEAFARI 20	CR	FBG			IO	120-140		7	6	2400			8050	9700
19	8	SF-20	FSH	FBG			OB			7	6	1500			3600	4200
19	8	SF-20	FSH	FBG			IO	120-140		7	6	2100			7950	9650
23	3	F-23	FSH	FBG			OB			8		2500			7550	8650
23	3	F-23	FSH	FBG			IO	165-245		8		3250			14000	17400
23	3	F-23	FSH	FBG			IO	250	CHRY	8					15000	17600
23	3	F-23	FSH	FBG			IO	T130-T170		8					18000	20200
23	3	SF-23	FSH	FBG			OB			8					8950	10100
23	3	SF-23	FSH	FBG			IO	165-250		8					15500	18800
23	3	SF-23	CR	FBG			IO	T130-T170		8					19000	21300
24	10	SEAFARI	CR	FBG			IO	188-250		8					19500	22500
26	9	SEAVILLA	EXP	FBG			IO	T165-T235		9	9				27900	33000
1971 BOATS																
19	8		FSH	FBG			OB			7	6	1400	1		3450	4000
19	8		FSH	FBG			IO	120-140		7	6	2150	1	2	8300	9650
19	8	SEAFARI 20		FBG			OB			7	6	1600	1	2	4250	4950
19	8	SEAFARI 20		FBG			IO	120-140		7	6	2300	1	2	7700	8950
19	8	SEAQUARIUS 20		FBG			OB			7	6	1600	1	8	3350	3900
23			FSH	FBG			OB			8		1800	1	8	5650	6500
24	10	SEAFARI 25		FBG			IO	215-325		8		5500	1	8	21800	26500
24	10	SEAFARI 25		FBG			IO	T130-T215		8		5500	1	8	23300	27100
26	9			FBG			IO	T155-T188		9	10	7500	1	8	36600	41700

IO T215 OMC 38200 42400, VD T215 21500 24200, IO T235 38800 43100

LOA FT	IN	NAME AND/OR MODEL	TOP/RIG	BOAT TYPE	HULL MTL	HULL TP	ENGINE TP	HP	MFG	BEAM FT	IN	WGT LBS	DRAFT FT	IN	RETAIL LOW	RETAIL HIGH
26	9	SEAVILLA 27		FBG			IO	T155-T188		9	10	7200	1	8	32300	36900

IO T215 OMC 33900 37600, VD T215 21000 23700, IO T235 34500 38300

LOA FT	IN	NAME AND/OR MODEL	TOP/RIG	BOAT TYPE	HULL MTL	HULL TP	ENGINE TP	HP	MFG	BEAM FT	IN	WGT LBS	DRAFT FT	IN	RETAIL LOW	RETAIL HIGH
1970 BOATS																
19	8		OP	OPFSH	FBG	SV	OB			7	6	1400	1		3450	4000
19	8		OP	OPFSH	FBG	SV	IO	120-140		7	6	2150	1	2	8600	9950
19	8	SEAFARI 20	CR	FBG	SV		OB			7	6	1800	1	1	4150	4850
19	8	SEAFARI 20	CR	FBG	SV		IO	120-140		7	6	2300	1	2	8400	9750
26	10	SEACRAFT 27	EXP	FBG	SV		IB	T230	MRCR	9	10	7500	2	6	20900	23200
26	10	SEACRAFT 27	SF	FBG	SV		IO	T160	MRCR	9	10	7200	1	8	37200	41300
26	10	SEACRAFT 27	SF	FBG	SV		IB	T230	MRCR	9	10	7500	2	6	20900	23200
1969 BOATS																
19		B/R	OP	RNBT	FBG	SV	OB			7	4	1300		11	3200	3700
19	8			CUD	FBG		IO	120		6	6	2250		11	8000	9150
19	8			FSH	FBG		OB			7	4	1200		11	3050	3550
19	8			FSH	FBG		IO	120		6	6	2100		11	8150	9350
19	8	FISHERMAN	OP	FSH	FBG	SV	OB			7	6	1200		11	3050	3550
26	9	SEACRAFT 27	FB	CR	FBG	SV	IO	T160		9	10	7200	1	8	33600	37400
1968 BOATS																
19		B/R	OP	FSH	FBG		OB			7	4	1300		11	3200	3700
19		B/R	OP	FSH	FBG		IO	120-160		7	4	2300		11	8650	10400
26	9	SEAMASTER	FB	EXP	FBG		IO	T160		9	10	7200	1	8	34800	38600
26	9	SEAMASTER	FB	EXP	FBG		VD	T210		9	10	7800	2	10	19500	21700
1967 BOATS																
19		B/R		RNBT	FBG		OB			7	4	1300			3250	3750
19		B/R		RNBT	FBG		IO	120		7	4	2300	2	6	8600	9850
19		B/R		SKI	FBG		IO	160		10		2500	2	7	11000	12500
27		SEAMASTER	FB	CR	FBG		IO	T160		10		7500	2	7	37200	41300
27		SEAMASTER	FB	CR	FBG		IB	T210		10		7800	2	7	19000	21200
1966 BOATS																
19		BOW RIDER		RNBT	FBG	DV	OB			7	4				4600	5250
19		BOW RIDER		RNBT	FBG	DV	IO	110-150		7	4				9300	10600
21		SEA-CRAFT		OVNTR	FBG	DV	IO	150-225		8			2	6	15000	17500
21		SEA-CRAFT		OVNTR	FBG	DV	IO	T110-T120		8			1	11	17200	19600
21		SEA-CRAFT		UTL	FBG	DV	IO	150-225		8			2	6	11700	13700
21		SEA-CRAFT		UTL	FBG	DV	IO	T110-T120		8			1	11	14000	15900
21		SEA-CRAFT SPORTSMAN	CR	FBG	DV		IO	150-225		8			2	6	13800	16100
21		SEA-CRAFT SPORTSMAN	CR	FBG	DV		IO	T110-T120		8			1	11	15900	18100
1965 BOATS																
21		SPORTSMAN 21		OVNTR	FBG		IO	140		8			1	11	15500	17700
21				CR	FBG		IO	140		8			1	11	14200	16200

SEA CROWN MARINE INC
COAST GUARD MFG ID- XUX

Call 1-800-327-6929 for BUC Personalized Evaluation Service
Or, for 1980 to 1983 boats, sign onto www.BUCValuPro.com

SEA DOO SPORT BOATS
BOMBARDIER
VALCOURT QUE CANADA   COAST GUARD MFG ID- ZZN

See inside cover to adjust price for area

BOMBARDIER SEA DOO
GRANT FL 32949

For more recent years, see the BUC Used Boat Price Guide, Volume 1 or Volume 2

LOA FT	IN	NAME AND/OR MODEL	TOP/RIG	BOAT TYPE	HULL MTL	HULL TP	ENGINE TP	HP	MFG	BEAM FT	IN	WGT LBS	DRAFT FT	IN	RETAIL LOW	RETAIL HIGH
1983 BOATS																
25	4	BOMBARDIER 7.6	SLP	SA/RC	F/W	KL	OB			8	6	3300	4	6	6350	7300
1982 BOATS																
25	4	BOMBARDIER 7.6	SLP	SA/RC	FBG	KL	OB			8	6	3300	4	6	6000	6850
1981 BOATS																
25	4	BOMBARDIER 7.6	SLP	SA/OD	F/W	KL				8	6	3300	4	6	5450	6300
25	4	BOMBARDIER 7.6	SLP	SA/RC	FBG	KL	OB			8	6	3300	4	6	5600	6450

SEA FEVER YACHTS

Call 1-800-327-6929 for BUC Personalized Evaluation Service
Or, for 1980 to 1985 boats, sign onto www.BUCValuPro.com

SEA FURY

Call 1-800-327-6929 for BUC Personalized Evaluation Service
Or, for 1966 to 1970 boats, sign onto www.BUCValuPro.com

SEA HAWK MARINE
DAVIDSONVILLE MD   See inside cover to adjust price for area

LOA FT IN	NAME AND/ OR MODEL	TOP/ RIG	BOAT TYPE	-HULL- MTL TP	----ENGINE--- TP # HP MFG	BEAM FT IN	WGT LBS	DRAFT FT IN	RETAIL LOW	RETAIL HIGH
			1974 BOATS							
28	SEA-HAWK		SF	FBG IB	225	10 3		2 2	12700	14400

SEA HUNTER BOATS
Call 1-800-327-6929 for BUC Personalized Evaluation Service
Or, for 1965 to 1966 boats, sign onto www.BUCValuPro.com

SEA LANE'S
Call 1-800-327-6929 for BUC Personalized Evaluation Service
Or, for 1977 boats, sign onto www.BUCValuPro.com

SEA LARK MARINE
COAST GUARD MFG ID- SAK

Call 1-800-327-6929 for BUC Personalized Evaluation Service
Or, for 1967 to 1980 boats, sign onto www.BUCValuPro.com

SEA LINE BOATS INC
COAST GUARD MFG ID- SLN

Call 1-800-327-6929 for BUC Personalized Evaluation Service
Or, for 1973 to 1974 boats, sign onto www.BUCValuPro.com

SEA MAC INC
COAST GUARD MFG ID- EST

Call 1-800-327-6929 for BUC Personalized Evaluation Service
Or, for 1960 to 1962 boats, sign onto www.BUCValuPro.com

SEA NYMPH BOATS
SYRACUSE IN 46567   COAST GUARD MFG ID- SEA See inside cover to adjust price for area

DIV OMC ALUMINUM BOAT GROUP
LEBANON MO 65536

For more recent years, see the BUC Used Boat Price Guide, Volume 1 or Volume 2

LOA FT IN	NAME AND/ OR MODEL	TOP/ RIG	BOAT TYPE	-HULL- MTL TP	---ENGINE--- TP # HP MFG	BEAM FT IN	WGT LBS	DRAFT FT IN	RETAIL LOW	RETAIL HIGH
			1983 BOATS							
16	SS165	RNBT	AL	SV OB		6 4	800		1900	2250
16 7	BASS-STRIPER CC170	RNBT	AL	DV OB		6 10			2300	2650
16 7	BAY-STRIPER CC171	RNBT	AL	DV OB		6 10			1850	2200
16 7	FISH-&-SKI SS175	RNBT	AL	DV OB		6 10			2200	2550
16 7	FISH-TRACKER SC170	RNBT	AL	DV OB		6 10			1850	2200
16 7	SKI-SPORT SS171	RNBT	AL	DV OB		6 10			2150	2500
			1982 BOATS							
16	SS165	OP RNBT	AL	DV OB		6 4	800		1850	2200
			1981 BOATS							
16	SS165	RNBT	AL	DV OB		6 4	800		1800	2150
			1980 BOATS							
16 3	FISH-FUN-SKI SS165	OP RNBT	AL	DV OB		6 10	844		1850	2250
16 7	SEA-SPORT SS170	OP RNBT	AL	DV OB		6 10	820		1850	2200
			1979 BOATS							
16 5	FISH-FUN-SKI SS165	OP RNBT	AL	SV OB		6 10	800		1750	2100
16 10	SEA-SPORT SS170	OP RNBT	AL	SV OB		6 6	800		1750	2100
			1978 BOATS							
16 10	SEA-SPORT SS-170	OP RNBT	AL	SV OB		6 6	775		1700	2000
16 10	SPORT-DECK SD-170	OP RNBT	AL	SV OB		6 6	795		1750	2050
			1977 BOATS							
16 10	SPORT DECK SD-170	OP RNBT	AL	SV OB		6 6	795		1700	2050

SEA RAIDER BOATS INC
SANDUSKY OH 44870   COAST GUARD MFG ID- PEV See inside cover to adjust price for area

LOA FT IN	NAME AND/ OR MODEL	TOP/ RIG	BOAT TYPE	-HULL- MTL TP	----ENGINE--- TP # HP MFG	BEAM FT IN	WGT LBS	DRAFT FT IN	RETAIL LOW	RETAIL HIGH
			1980 BOATS							
16 3	MARK 165	ST RNBT	FBG	TH OB		6 3	850	8	1750	2100
16 4	MARK 170	ST RNBT	FBG	TH OB		7 3	1000	9	2050	2450

SEA RANGER YACHT SALES INC
WILMINGTON CA 90748   See inside cover to adjust price for area

For more recent years, see the BUC Used Boat Price Guide, Volume 1 or Volume 2

LOA FT IN	NAME AND/ OR MODEL	TOP/ RIG	BOAT TYPE	-HULL- MTL TP	----ENGINE--- TP # HP MFG	BEAM FT IN	WGT LBS	DRAFT FT IN	RETAIL LOW	RETAIL HIGH
			1983 BOATS							
35 8	SEA-RANGER	TRWL	FBG DS	IB	T120D FORD	13 10	19000	3 3	75200	82600
35 8	SEA-RANGER	TRWL	FBG DS	IB	T124D VLVO	13 10	19000	3 3	74700	82100
36 6	SEA-RANGER	TRWL	FBG DS	IB	T120D FORD	13 1	26000	3 10	90000	98900
36 6	SEA-RANGER	TRWL	FBG DS	IB	T124D VLVO	13 1	26000	3 10	89300	98100
38 3	SEA-RANGER	TRWL	FBG DS	IB	T120D FORD	13 8	23000	3 3	87100	95700
38 3	SEA-RANGER	TRWL	FBG DS	IB	T124D VLVO	13 8	23000	3 3	86000	94500
44 10	SEA-RANGER	TRWL	FBG DS	IB	T120D FORD	14 2	31000	4 4	117500	129500
44 10	SEA-RANGER	TRWL	FBG DS	IB	T124D VLVO	14 2	31000	4 4	117500	129000
45	SEA-RANGER	TRWL	FBG DS	IB	T D VLVO	15 3	32400	4	**	**
45	SEA-RANGER	TRWL	FBG DS	IB	T120D FORD	15 3	32400	4	120500	132000
45 3	EXPLORER 45	SA/CR	FBG KL	IB	50D PERK	13	30000	6 8	105500	116000
46 10	SEA-RANGER	TRWL	FBG DS	IB	T120D FORD	14 2	32400	4 4	127000	139500
46 10	SEA-RANGER	TRWL	FBG DS	IB	T124D VLVO	14 2	32400	4 4	127000	139500
47 3	SEA-RANGER	TRWL	FBG DS	IB	T235D VLVO	14 8	29000	4 4	127000	139500
51	SEA-RANGER	MY	FBG DS	IB	T265D GM	16 8	52000	4 3	154500	169500
55	SEA-RANGER	MY	FBG DS	IB	T265D GM	18 7	64900	4 9	187500	206000
59 3	SEA-RANGER	MY	FBG DS	IB	T350D GM	19	72000	4 9	243500	268000
65	SEA-RANGER	MY	FBG DS	IB	T462D GM	19	76000	4 9	291000	320000
72	SEA-RANGER	MY	FBG DS	IB	T675D GM	19	85000	4 9	**	**
			1981 BOATS							
39 3	SEA RANGER 39 SDN	FB	TRWL	FBG DS	IB 120D LEHM	13 8	23000	3 6	78200	85900
60 3	SEA RANGER 60	FB	MY	FBG SV	IB T350D GM	19	72000	4 9	206500	227000
			1980 BOATS							
35 9	SEA RANGER 35 DC	FB	TRWL	FBG DS	IB 120D LEHM	13 10	19500	3 3	68000	74800
35 9	SEA RANGER 35 DC	FB	TRWL	FBG DS	IB 130D VLVO	13 10	19200	3 3	67200	73800
35 9	SEA RANGER 35 DC	FB	TRWL	FBG DS	IB 160D PERK	13 10	19800	3 3	71000	78000
39 3	SEA RANGER 39 DC	FB	TRWL	FBG DS	IB 120D LEHM	13 8	23000	3 3	74600	81900
39 3	SEA RANGER 39 DC	FB	TRWL	FBG DS	IB 130D VLVO	13 8	24800	3 3	83600	91900
39 3	SEA RANGER 39 DC	FB	TRWL	FBG DS	IB 160D PERK	13 8	25000	3 3	86700	95300
39 3	SEA RANGER 39 SDN	FB	TRWL	FBG DS	IB 120D LEHM	13 8	23000	3 3	74600	81900
39 3	SEA RANGER 39 SDN	FB	TRWL	FBG DS	IB 130D VLVO	13 8	24800	3 3	83600	91900
39 3	SEA RANGER 39 SDN	FB	TRWL	FBG DS	IB 160D PERK	13 8	25000	3 3	86700	95300
60 3	SEA-RANGER 60	FB	MY	FBG SV	IB T350D GM	19	72000	4 9	197000	216500

SEA RAY BOATS
KNOXVILLE TN 37914   COAST GUARD MFG ID- SER See inside cover to adjust price for area

SEA RAY BOATS
MERRITT ISLAND FL 32953

For more recent years, see the BUC Used Boat Price Guide, Volume 1 or Volume 2

LOA FT IN	NAME AND/ OR MODEL	TOP/ RIG	BOAT TYPE	-HULL- MTL TP	----ENGINE--- TP # HP MFG	BEAM FT IN	WGT LBS	DRAFT FT IN	RETAIL LOW	RETAIL HIGH
			1983 BOATS							
17 3	SRV190	OP	RNBT	FBG DV	IO 188 MRCR	7 5		1	1700	2000
17 3	SRV192	OP	RNBT	FBG DV	IO 140-188	7 5		1 1	1750	2100
18 6	SEVILLE 5.6 BR	OP	RNBT	FBG DV	IO 120	7 6	1950	2	2200	2550
18 6	SEVILLE 5.6 CB	OP	RNBT	FBG DV	IO 120	7 6	1950		2050	2450
18 6	SEVILLE 5.6 CC	OP	RNBT	FBG DV	IO 120	7 6	2000		2200	2550
18 11	SRV195	OP	RNBT	FBG DV	IO 140-260	8		1 1	2750	3400
18 11	SRV197	OP	RNBT	FBG DV	IO 140-260	8		1 1	2850	3500
20 5	SRV200	OP	RNBT	FBG DV	IO 170-260	8		1 1	3450	4300
20 5	SRV207	OP	RNBT	FBG DV	IO 170-260	8		1 1	3550	4400
20 5	SRV210 CC	OP	CUD	FBG DV	IO 170-260	8		1 2	3650	4550
20 5	SRV210 FSH	OP	RNBT	FBG DV	IO 170-260	8		1 2	3850	4750
22 4	SRV225 CC	OP	CUD	FBG DV	IO 170-260	8		1 3	5650	6650
22 4	SRV225 EC	OP	EXP	FBG DV	IO 198-260	8		1 3	5000	5950
22 4	SRV225 SXL	OP	RNBT	FBG DV	IO 198-260	8		1 3	5800	6850
22 4	SRV225 SXL	OP	RNBT	FBG DV	IO 330 MRCR	8		1 3	6450	7400
24 7	SRV245	OP	CUD	FBG DV	IO 198-260	8		1 3	7200	7950
24 7	SRV245	OP	CUD	FBG DV	IO T120-T185	8		1 3	7200	8600
24 7	SRV245 FSH	OP	CUD	FBG DV	IO 198-260	8		1 3	6700	7950

```
LOA    NAME AND/            TOP/ BOAT -HULL- ----ENGINE--- BEAM WGT  DRAFT RETAIL RETAIL
FT IN  OR MODEL             RIG  TYPE MTL TP TP # HP  MFG  FT IN LBS  FT IN  LOW   HIGH
------------------------- 1983 BOATS --------------------------------------------------
24  7 SRV245 FSH            OP CUD   FBG DV IO T120-T185  8        1  3  7300  8600
24  7 SUNDANCER SRV245      OP CBNCR FBG DV IO 198-260    8        1  3  7500  8850
24  7 SUNDANCER SRV245      OP CBNCR FBG DV IO T120-T185  8        1  3  8100  9400
25  5 AMBERJACK SRV255      OP CUD   FBG DV IO 260-330    9 10     1  3  7550  9400
25  5 AMBERJACK SRV255      OP CUD   FBG DV IO T120-T198  9 10     1  3  7800  9500
25  5 AMBERJACK SRV255      OP CUD   FBG DV IO T228 MRCR  9 10     1  3  8500  9800
25  5 SRV255               FB SDN   FBG DV IO 260-330    9 10     1  3  7800  9600
25  5 SRV255               FB SDN   FBG DV IO T120-T228  9 10     1  3  8000  9650
26  3 SRV260 EC            OP EXP   FBG DV IO 198-260    8        1  4  8600 10300
26  3 SRV260 EC            OP EXP   FBG DV IO 330 MRCR   8        1  4  9600 10900
26  3 SRV260 EC            OP EXP   FBG DV IO T120-T185  8        1  4  9250 11000

26  3 SRV260 SXL           OP CUD   FBG DV IO 198-260    8        1  6  7900  9500
      IO 330 MRCR 8950 10200, IO T120-T198  8400 10400, IO T228 MRCR 9400 10700

26  3 SRV360 EC            OP EXP   FBG DV IO T185 OMC   8        1  4  9650 11000
26  3 SUNDANCER SRV260      OP CBNCR FBG DV IO 198-260    8        1  4  9500 11200
26  3 SUNDANCER SRV260      OP CBNCR FBG DV IO T120-T185  8        1  4 10100 11600
27  7 SUNDANCER SRV270      OP EXP   FBG DV IO 260-330   10        1  3 10700 12800
27  7 SUNDANCER SRV270      OP EXP   FBG DV IO T120-T198 10        1  3 10800 13100
27  7 SUNDANCER SRV270      OP EXP   FBG DV IO T228-T260 10        1  3 11900 13900
30  6 SRV310               OP EXP   FBG DV IB T230-T350  11 11     2  5 21300 25900
30  6 SRV310               OP EXP   FBG DV IBT165D-T205D 11 11 9500 2  5 27800 32400
30  6 SRV310               FB SPTCR FBG DV IB T230-T350  11 11     2  5 19900 24000
30  6 SRV310               FB SPTCR FBG DV IBT165D-T205D 11 11     2  5 25400 29500
30  6 SUNDANCER SRV310            CBNCR FBG DV IB T230-T350  11 11  2  6 24400 27700

33  7 SRV340               FB SDN   FBG DV IB T260-T350  11 11 11400 2  6 32700 38600
33  7 SRV340               FB SDN   FBG DV IBT165D-T205D 11 11 11400 2  6 38200 44300
36  3 355T                 FB SDN   FBG DV IB 165 CRUS   12  6 13000 2 10 33220 36900
      IB 200D PERK 40500 45100, IB 200D S&S 40000 44500, IB T165 CRUS 35000 38900
      IB T230 MRCR 35600 39500, IB T260 MRCR 35900 39900, IB T270 CRUS 36300 40300
      IB T340 MRCR 37200 41300, IB T350 CRUS 37700 41800, IB T 95D CRUS 41300 45900
      IB T135D PERK 43000 47800, IB T200D PERK 45700 50200

36  3 355T AFT CABIN       FB TRWL  FBG DV IB 165 CRUS   12  6 13500 2 10 34400 38200
      IB 200D PERK 42500 47300, IB 205D S&S 42100 46700, IB T165 CRUS 36300 40400
      IB T230 MRCR 37100 41200, IB T260 MRCR 37500 41600, IB T270 CRUS 37800 42000
      IB T340 MRCR 38300 42600, IB T350 CRUS 38700 43100, IB T 95D CRUS 43200 48000
      IB T135D PERK 45700 50200, IB T200D PERK 47900 52700

36  6 SRV360               HT EXP   FBG DV IB T340 MRCR  13 11     2  4 29900 33300
36  6 SRV360               HT EXP   FBG DV IB T350 CRUS  13 11     2  4 30400 33800
36  6 SRV360               FB EXP   FBG DV IB T340 MRCR  13 11     2  4 29900 33300
      IB T350 CRUS 30400 33800, IB T300D CAT 44600 49600, IB T305D GM 43700 48500

39    SRV390               FB SF    FBG DV IB T340 MRCR  13 11     2  4 47000 51600
      IB T350 CRUS 47600 52400, IB T300D CAT 56700 62300, IB T325D PERK 57900 63600

------------------------- 1982 BOATS --------------------------------------------------
17  3 SRV192               OP RNBT  FBG DV IO 140-185    7  5      1  1  1700  2050
18 11 SRV195               OP RNBT  FBG DV IO 140-260    8        1  1  2700  3300
18 11 SRV195 SXL           OP RNBT  FBG DV IO 170-230    8        1  1  2700  3250
18 11 SRV195 SXL           OP RNBT  FBG DV IO 260        8        1  1  2900  3350
18 11 SRV197               OP RNBT  FBG DV IO 140-260    8        1  3  2800  3450
18 11 SRV197 SXL           OP RNBT  FBG DV IO 170-260    8        1  3  2800  3450
20  5 SRV200               OP RNBT  FBG DV IO 170-260    8        1  3  3350  4200
20  5 SRV207               OP CUD   FBG DV IO 170-260    8        1  3  3500  4300
20  5 SRV210 CC            OP CUD   FBG DV IO 170-260    8        1  3  3550  4400
20  5 SRV210 FSH           OP CUD   FBG DV IO 170-260    8        1  2  3800  4650
22  4 SRV225 CC            OP CUD   FBG DV IO 170-260    8        1  3  5550  6600
22  4 SRV225 CR            OP EXP   FBG DV IO 198-260    8        1  3  4850  5800

22  4 SRV225 SXL           OP CBNCR FBG DV IO 198-260    8        1  3  5550  6600
22  4 SRV225 SXL           OP CBNCR FBG DV IO 330 MRCR   8        1  3  6350  7300
24  7 SRV245               FB SDN   FBG DV IO 198-260    8        1  3  6400  7650
24  7 SRV245               OP CUD   FBG DV IO 198-260    8        1  3  6550  7800
24  7 SRV245 FSH           OP CUD   FBG DV IO T120-T185  8        1  3  6950  8200
24  7 SRV245 FSH           OP CUD   FBG DV IO T120-T185  8        1  3  6550  7800
24  7 SUNDANCER SRV245      OP CBNCR FBG DV IO 198-260    8        1  3  7100  8400
24  7 SUNDANCER SRV245      OP CBNCR FBG DV IO T120-T185  8        1  3  7900  9200
25  5 AMBERJACK SRV255      OP SF    FBG DV IO 260-330    9 10     1  3  8050 10100
25  5 AMBERJACK SRV255      OP SF    FBG DV IO T120-T198  9 10     1  3  8350 10200
25  5 AMBERJACK SRV255      OP SF    FBG DV IO T228 MRCR  9 10     1  3  9250 10500

25  5 SRV255               FB SDN   FBG DV IO 260-330    9 10     1  3  7600  9350
25  5 SRV255               FB SDN   FBG DV IO T120-T228  9 10     1  3  7800  9450
26  3 SRV260 CR            OP EXP   FBG DV IO 198-260    8        1  4  8450 10100
26  3 SRV260 CR            OP EXP   FBG DV IO 330 MRCR   8        1  4  9400 10700
26  3 SRV260 SXL           OP EXP   FBG DV IO T120-T185  8        1  4  9050 10800
26  3 SRV260 SXL           OP CBNCR FBG DV IO 198-260    8        1  6  8850 10400
26  3 SRV260 SXL           OP CBNCR FBG DV IO 330 MRCR   8        1  6 10000 11400
26  3 SRV260 SXL           OP CBNCR FBG DV IO T120-T228  8        1  6  9650 11500
26  3 SUNDANCER SRV260      OP EXP   FBG DV IO 198-260    8        1  4  9450 11500
26  3 SUNDANCER SRV260      OP CBNCR FBG DV IO T120-T185  8        1  4 10300 11700
27  7 SUNDANCER SRV270      OP EXP   FBG DV IO 260-330   10        1  3 10400 12500
27  7 SUNDANCER SRV270      OP EXP   FBG DV IO T120-T198 10        1  3 10500 12800

27  7 SUNDANCER SRV270      OP EXP   FBG DV IO T228-T260 10        1  3 11600 13600
30  6 VANGUARD SRV310       OP EXP   FBG DV IB T230-T350  11 11     2  5 20300 24800
30  6 VANGUARD SRV310       FB SDN   FBG DV IB T230-T350  11 11     2  5 18200 25100
30  6 VANGUARD SRV310       FB SPTCR FBG DV IB T230-T350  11 11     2  5 19100 23300
30  6 VANGUARD-SUNDANCER    OP CBNCR FBG DV IB T230-T350  11 11     2  6 23300 26500
34    SRV 34+              OP EXP   FBG DV IB T134        12        2  5 27500 30600
36  3 355T                 FB SDN   FBG DV IB            12  6     2 10   **    **
36  6 VANGUARD SRV360       HT EXP   FBG DV IB T330 MRCR  13 11     2  4 28400 31600
36  6 VANGUARD SRV360       HT EXP   FBG DV IB T350 CRUS  13 11     2  4 29000 32300
36  6 VANGUARD SRV360       FB SF    FBG DV IB T330 MRCR  13 11     2  7 27600 30600
36  6 VANGUARD SRV360       FB SF    FBG DV IB T350 CRUS  13 11     2  7 28200 31300

------------------------- 1981 BOATS --------------------------------------------------
17  3 SRV190               ST RNBT  FBG DV IO 120-170    7  5 2600     2100  2500
17  3 SRV192               ST RNBT  FBG DV IO 120-185    7  5 2600     2250  2650
18 11 SRV195               ST RNBT  FBG DV IO 140-260    8    2800     2550  3200
18 11 SRV195 SXL           OP RNBT  FBG DV IO 140-260    8              2700  3300
18 11 SRV197               ST RNBT  FBG DV IO 140-260    8    2800     2650  3300
18 11 SRV197SXL            OP RNBT  FBG DV IO 198-260    8              2800  3400
19 11 SRV200               ST RNBT  FBG DV IO 165-260    8    2900     2850  3500
19 11 SRV207               ST CUD   FBG DV IO 165-260    8    3000     2900  3550
20  5 SRV210 CC            ST CUD   FBG DV IO 165-260    8    3200     3750  4600
22  4 EXPRESS SRV225        ST EXP   FBG DV IO 165-260    8    4000     5000  5995
22  4 EXPRESS SRV225        HT EXP   FBG DV IO 130-260    8              4700  5700

22  4 SRV225 CC            ST CUD   FBG DV IO 165-170    8    3605     4600  5395
22  4 SRV225 CC            ST CUD   FBG DV IO 185-260    8              5450  6300
22  4 SRV225 VGXL          OP       FBG DV IO 228-260    8              4750  5550
22  4 SRV225 VGXL          OP       FBG DV IO 330 MRCR   8              5350  6150
22  4 SUNDOWNER SRV225      HT CBNCR FBG DV IO 198-260    8    3875     5400  6400
24  4 CUDDY CABIN SRV240    ST CUD   FBG DV IO 198-260    8    4000     5600  6850
24  4 CUDDY CABIN SRV240    ST CUD   FBG DV IO T120-T170  8    4000     6150  7200
24  7 WEEKENDER SRV240      ST WKNDR FBG DV IO 198-260    8    4400     6050  7100
24  7 WEEKENDER SRV240      ST WKNDR FBG DV IO T120-T170  8    4400     6600  7700
24  7 SEDANBRIDGE SRV245    FB SDN   FBG DV IO 200-260    8              6250  7550
24  7 SEDANBRIDGE SRV245    FB SDN   FBG DV IO T120-T198  8              6850  8100

24  7 SUNDANCER SRV245      OP CBNCR FBG DV IO 198-260    8    4500     7300  8600
24  7 SUNDANCER SRV245      OP       FBG DV IO 330 MRCR   8    4500     7850  9150
24  7 SUNDANCER SRV245      OP       FBG DV IO T120-T185  8    4500     7850  9200
25  5 SEDANBRIDGE SRV255    FB SDN   FBG DV IO 260-330    9 10           7500  9200
25  5 SEDANBRIDGE SRV255    FB SDN   FBG DV IO T120-T228  9 10           7700  9300
25  5 SEDANBRIDGE SRV270    FB SDN   FBG DV IO 260-330    9 10 6000      9000 10900
25  5 SEDANBRIDGE SRV270    FB SDN   FBG DV IO T120-T228  9 10 6000      9200 11200
25  5 SRV255 AJ            ST SF    FBG DV IO 165-260    9 10           7450  9150
      IO 330 MRCR 8600 9900, IO T120-T198 8200 10100, IO T228 MRCR 9100 10400

25  5 SRV255 AJ DUAL SP BR  FB SF    FBG DV IO 260-330    9 10           8000  9950
25  5 SRV255 AJ DUAL SP BR  FB SF    FBG DV IO T120-T198  9 10           8300 10100
25  5 SRV255 AJ DUAL SP BR  FB SF    FBG DV IO T228 MRCR  9 10           9150 10400
25  5 SRV255 AJ SING SPBR   FB SF    FBG DV IO 260-330    9 10           7900  9850
25  5 SRV255 AJ SING SPBR   FB SF    FBG DV IO T120-T198  9 10           8200 10000
25  5 SRV255 AJ SING SPBR   FB SF    FBG DV IO T228 MRCR  9 10           9100 10300
26  3 EXPRESS SRV260        ST EXP   FBG DV IO 198-260    8    5200     7400  8900
      IO 330 MRCR 8350 9600, IO T120-T170 7900 9550, IB T185 MRCR 9350 10600

26  3 SUNDANCER SRV260 VGXL ST CBNCR FBG DV IO T228-T260  8              9900 11500
26  3 SUNDANCER SRV260      ST CBNCR FBG DV IO 198-260    8    5300     9350 11000
26  3 SUNDANCER SRV260      ST CBNCR FBG DV IO T120-T185  8    5300     9950 11300
26  3 WEEKENDER SRV260      ST WKNDR FBG DV IO 198-260    8    5100     7600  9100
      IO 330 MRCR 8600 9850, IO T120-T198 8100 10100, IO T228 MRCR 9150 10400

29  7 EXPRESS SRV300        ST EXP   FBG DV IB T228-T255  11  6 10000   19000 21300
      IO T270 CRUS 15400 17600, IB T330  20100 22400, IB T350 CRUS 16700 18900

29  7 SEDANBRIDGE SRV300    FB SDN   FBG DV IB T228-T330  11  6 11300   21400 25600
29  7 SPORTBRIDGE SRV300    FB SPTCR FBG DV IB T228-T330  11  6 10300   19100 22600
29  7 WEEKENDER SRV300      ST WKNDR FBG DV IB T228-T350  11  6 9500    18700 22000
```

SEA RAY BOATS -CONTINUED See inside cover to adjust price for area

LOA FT	LOA IN	NAME AND/ OR MODEL	TOP/ RIG	BOAT TYPE	-HULL- MTL	-HULL- TP	----ENGINE--- TP	# HP	MFG	BEAM FT	BEAM IN	WGT LBS	DRAFT FT	DRAFT IN	RETAIL LOW	RETAIL HIGH
		1981 BOATS														
30	4	EXPRESS SRV310VG	ST	EXP	FBG	DV	IO	T228	MRCR	11	6				16000	18200
30	4	EXPRESS SRV310VG	ST	EXP	FBG	DV	IB	T250-T350		11	6				19400	23300
30	4	SEDANBRIDGE SRV310VG	FB	SDN	FBG	DV	IB	T228-T350		11	9				19000	22200
30	4	SPORTBRIDGE SRV310VG	FB	SPTCR	FBG	DV	IB	T228-T350		11	9				16900	21100
36	6	EXPRESS SRV360	ST	EXP	FBG	DV	IB	T330	CHRY	14					26800	29800
36	6	EXPRESS SRV360	ST	EXP	FBG	DV	IB	T330	MRCR	14					26900	29900
36	6	EXPRESS SRV360	ST	EXP	FBG	DV	IB	T350	CRUS	14					27500	30600
36	6	SRV360 VGSSF	FB	EXP	FBG	DV	IB	T330	CHRY	14					26800	29800
36	6	SRV360 VGSSF	FB	EXP	FBG	DV	IB	T330	MRCR	14					26900	29900
36	6	SRV360 VGSSF	FB	EXP	FBG	DV	IB	T350	CRUS	14					27500	30600
		1980 BOATS														
17	3	SRV190	ST	RNBT	FBG	DV	IO	120-170		7	5	2600			2050	2500
17	3	SRV192	ST	RNBT	FBG	DV	IO	120-170		7	5	2600			2250	2600
18	6	SRV195	ST	RNBT	FBG	DV	IO	140-230		8		2800			2500	3000
18	6	SRV195	ST	RNBT	FBG	DV	IO	260		8		2800			2700	3300
18	6	SRV197	ST	RNBT	FBG	DV	IO	140-230		8		2800			2600	3100
18	6	SRV197	ST	RNBT	FBG	DV	IO	260		8		2800			2800	3400
19	11	SRV200	ST	RNBT	FBG	DV	IO	165-230		8		2900			2800	3350
19	11	SRV200	ST	RNBT	FBG	DV	IO	260		8		2900			3000	3650
19	11	SRV207	ST	RNBT	FBG	DV	IO	165-230		8		3000			2850	3450
19	11	SRV207	ST	RNBT	FBG	DV	IO	260		8		3000			3050	3700
19	11	SRV210 CC	ST	CUD	FBG	DV	IO	165-230		8		3200			3100	3700
19	11	SRV210 CC	ST	CUD	FBG	DV	IO	260		8		3200			3300	4000
22	4	EXPRESS SRV225	ST	EXP	FBG	DV	IO	198-260		8		4000			4950	6100
22	4	SRV225 CC	ST	CUD	FBG	DV	IO	165-260		8		3605			4550	5650
22	4	SUNDOWNER SRV225	OP	CBNCR	FBG	DV	IO	198-260		8		3875			5350	6600
24	4	CUDDY CABIN SRV240	ST	CUD	FBG	DV	IO	198-260		8		4000			5550	6800
24	4	CUDDY CABIN SRV240	ST	CUD	FBG	DV	IO	T120-T170		8		4000			6100	7150
24	4	WEEKENDER SRV240	ST	WKNDR	FBG	DV	IO	198-260		8		4400			6000	7300
24	4	WEEKENDER SRV240	ST	WKNDR	FBG	DV	IO	T120-T170		8		4400			6550	7650
24	7	SUNDANCER SRV245	OP	CBNCR	FBG	DV	IO	198-260		8		4500			7250	8700
24	7	SUNDANCER SRV245	OP	CBNCR	FBG	DV	IO	330	MRCR	8		4500			7950	9150
24	7	SUNDANCER SRV245	OP	CBNCR	FBG	DV	IO	T120-T170		8		4500			7800	9000
25	5	SEDANBRIDGE SRV270	FB	SDN	FBG	DV	IO	260-330		9	10	6000			8900	10800
25	5	SEDANBRIDGE SRV270	FB	SDN	FBG	DV	IO	T120-T228		9	10	6000			9150	11100
26	3	EXPRESS SRV260	ST	EXP	FBG	DV	IO	198-260		8		5200			7350	8950
26	3	EXPRESS SRV260	ST	EXP	FBG	DV	IO	330	MRCR	8		5200			8250	9500
26	3	EXPRESS SRV260	ST	EXP	FBG	DV	IO	T120-T170		8		5200			7850	9450
26	3	SUNDANCER SRV260	OP	CBNCR	FBG	DV	IO	198-260		8		5300			9300	11000
26	3	SUNDANCER SRV260	OP	CBNCR	FBG	DV	IO	T120-T170		8		5300			9850	11200
26	3	WEEKENDER SRV260	ST	WKNDR	FBG	DV	IO	198-260		8		5100			7500	9200
		IO 330 MRCR 8500 9800, IO T120-T198 8050 10000, IO T228-T260													9100	10700
29	7	EXPRESS SRV300	ST	EXP	FBG	DV	IB	T228-T330		11	6	10000	2	5	18200	21400
29	7	SEDANBRIDGE SRV300	FB	SDN	FBG	DV	IB	T228-T330		11	6	11300	2	5	20500	24500
29	7	SPORTBRIDGE SRV300	FB	SPTCR	FBG	DV	IB	T228-T330		11	6	10300	2	5	18500	21700
29	7	WEEKENDER SRV300	ST	WKNDR	FBG	DV	IB	T228-T330		11	6	9500	2	5	17500	21300
30	4	SRV310		CR	FBG	DV	IB	T330		11	9				17500	19900
30	6	VANGUARD EXP SRV310		EXP	FBG	DV	IB	T250-T330		11	11				19200	22400
36	6	EXPRESS SRV360		EXP	FBG	DV	IB	T330	CHRY	14		15400			31700	35200
36	6	EXPRESS SRV360		EXP	FBG	DV	IB	T330	MRCR	14		15400			31800	35300
36	6	SRV360		CR	FBG	DV	IB	T330		14		15400			31800	35300
36	6	SRV360		EXP	FBG	DV	IB	T330		14		15400			31800	35300
36	6	VANGUARD SDN SRV360		SDN	FBG	DV	IB	T330	CHRY	14		15400			32500	36100
36	6	VANGUARD SDN SRV360		SDN	FBG	DV	IB	T330	MRCR	14		15400			32600	36200
		1979 BOATS														
17	3	SRV190	ST	RNBT	FBG	DV	IO	120-170		7	5	2600			2050	2500
17	3	SRV192	ST	RNBT	FBG	DV	IO	120-170		7	5	2600			2250	2600
18	6	SRV195	ST	RNBT	FBG	DV	IO	140-230		8		2800			2450	3000
18	6	SRV195	ST	RNBT	FBG	DV	IO	260		8		2800			2650	3200
18	6	SRV197	ST	RNBT	FBG	DV	IO	140-230		8		2800			2600	3100
18	6	SRV197	ST	RNBT	FBG	DV	IO	260		8		2800			2750	3350
19	11	SRV200	ST	RNBT	FBG	DV	IO			8		2900			**	**
19	11	SRV200	ST	RNBT	FBG	DV	IO	165-230		8		2900			2800	3350
19	11	SRV200	ST	RNBT	FBG	DV	IO	260		8		2900			3000	3650
19	11	SRV200 CC	ST	CUD	FBG	DV	IO	165-230		8		3200			3100	3700
19	11	SRV200 CC	ST	CUD	FBG	DV	IO	260		8		3200			3300	4000
19	11	SRV207	ST	RNBT	FBG	DV	IO	165-230		8		3000			2850	3450
19	11	SRV207	ST	RNBT	FBG	DV	IO	260		8		3000			3050	3700
21	7	OVERNIGHTER SRV220	HT	OVNTR	FBG	DV	IO	170-260		8		3600			4350	5450
21	7	SRV220 CC	ST	CUD	FBG	DV	IO	165-230		8		3400			4150	4950
21	7	SRV220 CC	ST	CUD	FBG	DV	IO	260		8		3400			4400	5250
22	4	EXPRESS SRV220	ST	EXP	FBG	DV	IO	198-260		8		4000			4950	6100
24	4	CUDDY CABIN SRV240	ST	CUD	FBG	DV	IO	198-260		8		4000			5550	6800
24	4	CUDDY CABIN SRV240	ST	CUD	FBG	DV	IO	T120-T170		8		4000			6100	7100
24	4	SUNDANCER SRV240	OP	CBNCR	FBG	DV	IO	198-260		8		4500			7050	8500
24	4	SUNDANCER SRV240	OP	CBNCR	FBG	DV	IO	T120-T170		8		4500			7650	8800
24	4	WEEKENDER SRV240	ST	WKNDR	FBG	DV	IO	198-260		8		4400			6000	7300
24	4	WEEKENDER SRV240	ST	WKNDR	FBG	DV	IO	T120-T170		8		4400			6550	7650
26	3	EXPRESS SRV260	ST	EXP	FBG	DV	IO	198-260		8		5200			7350	8950
26	3	EXPRESS SRV260	ST	EXP	FBG	DV	IO	T120-T170		8		5200			7850	9450
26	3	SUNDANCER SRV260	OP	CBNCR	FBG	DV	IO	198-260		8		5300			9250	11000
26	3	SUNDANCER SRV260	OP	CBNCR	FBG	DV	IO	T120-T170		8		5300			9850	11200
26	3	WEEKENDER SRV260	ST	WKNDR	FBG	DV	IO	198-260		8		5100			7500	9200
26	3	WEEKENDER SRV260	ST	WKNDR	FBG	DV	IO	T120-T198		8		5100			8050	10000
26	3	WEEKENDER SRV260	ST	WKNDR	FBG	DV	IO	T228	MRCR	8		5100			9050	10300
29	7	EXPRESS SRV300	ST	EXP	FBG	DV	IB	T225-T330		11	6	10000	2	5	17100	20800
29	7	EXPRESS SRV300	ST	EXP	FBG	DV	IB	T130D	VLVO	11	6	10000	2	5	21500	23900
29	7	SEDANBRIDGE SRV300	FB	SDN	FBG	DV	IB	T225-T330		11	6	11300	2	5	19600	23500
29	7	SPORTBRIDGE SRV300	FB	SPTCR	FBG	DV	IB	T225-T330		11	6	10300	2	5	17300	21000
29	7	SPORTBRIDGE SRV300	FB	SPTCR	FBG	DV	IB	T130D	VLVO	11	6	10300	2	5	22000	24400
29	7	SUNBRIDGE SRV300	FB	SDN	FBG	DV	IB	T225-T330		11	6	11500			19700	23600
29	7	WEEKENDER SRV300	ST	WKNDR	FBG	DV	IB	T225-T330		11	6	9500	2	5	16700	20500
29	7	WEEKENDER SRV300	ST	WKNDR	FBG	DV	IB	T130D	VLVO	11	6	9500	2	5	20700	23000
36	6	EXPRESS SRV360		EXP	FBG	DV	IB	T330	CHRY	14		20000	2	7	35800	39700
		IB T330 MRCR 35900 39800, IB T210D CAT 44800 49700, IB T230D VLVO													43800	48700
		IB T260D CAT 46700 51300														
		1978 BOATS														
16	8	SRV185	ST	RNBT	FBG	DV	OB			7	5	2500			3050	3550
16	8	SRV185	ST	RNBT	FBG	DV	IO	140-170		7	5	2500			2000	2350
16	8	SRV187	ST	RNBT	FBG	DV	OB			7	5	2500			3050	3550
16	8	SRV187	ST	RNBT	FBG	DV	IO	140-170		7	5	2500			2050	2450
18	6	SRV195	ST	RNBT	FBG	DV	OB			8		2800			2950	3450
18	6	SRV195	ST	RNBT	FBG	DV	IO	140-260		8		2800			2500	3100
18	6	SRV197	ST	RNBT	FBG	DV	OB			8		2800			2950	3450
18	6	SRV197	ST	RNBT	FBG	DV	IO	140-260		8		2800			2600	3250
19	11	SEARUNNER SRV200	ST	CUD	FBG	DV	OB			8		3100			3450	4000
19	11	SEARUNNER SRV200	ST	CUD	FBG	DV	IO	140-240		8		3100			3050	3700
19	11	SEARUNNER SRV200	ST	CUD	FBG	DV	IO	255-260		8		3100			3400	3950
19	11	SRV200	ST	RNBT	FBG	DV	OB			8		2900			3450	4000
19	11	SRV200	ST	RNBT	FBG	DV	IO	140-240		8		2900			2800	3400
19	11	SRV200	ST	RNBT	FBG	DV	IO	255-260		8		2900			3100	3650
21	7	CUDDY CABIN SRV220	ST	CUD	FBG	DV	OB			8		3400			5350	6150
21	7	CUDDY CABIN SRV220	ST	CUD	FBG	DV	IO	170-240		8		3400			4200	5000
21	7	CUDDY CABIN SRV220	ST	CUD	FBG	DV	IO	255-260		8		3400			4600	5300
21	7	OVERNIGHTER SRV220	HT	OVNTR	FBG	DV	OB			8		3600			5450	6250
21	7	OVERNIGHTER SRV220	HT	OVNTR	FBG	DV	IO	185-260		8		3600			4400	5450
24	4	CUDDY CABIN SRV240	ST	CUD	FBG	DV	OB			8		4000			7150	8250
24	4	CUDDY CABIN SRV240	ST	CUD	FBG	DV	IO	185-260		8		4000			5550	6800
24	4	CUDDY CABIN SRV240	ST	CUD	FBG	DV	IO	T120-T170		8		4000			6150	7200
24	4	CUDDY CABIN SRV240	HT	CUD	FBG	DV	IO	185-260		8		4000			5550	6800
24	4	CUDDY CABIN SRV240	HT	CUD	FBG	DV	IO	T120-T170		8		4000			6150	7200
24	4	CUDDY CABIN SRV240	FB	CUD	FBG	DV	IO	185-260		8		4000			5550	6800
24	4	CUDDY CABIN SRV240	FB	CUD	FBG	DV	IO	T120-T170		8		4000			6150	7200
24	4	SEDAN BRIDGE SRV240	FB	SDN	FBG	DV	IO	185-260		8		4700			6350	7800
24	4	SEDANBRIDGE SRV240	FB	SDN	FBG	DV	OB			8		4700			7850	9050
24	4	SEDANBRIDGE SRV240	FB	SDN	FBG	DV	IO	T120-T170		8		4700			6950	8150
24	4	SEDANCRUISER SRV240	HT	SDN	FBG	DV	OB			8		4500			7700	8850
24	4	SEDANCRUISER SRV240	HT	SDN	FBG	DV	IO	185-240		8		4500			6150	7300
24	4	SEDANCRUISER SRV240	HT	SDN	FBG	DV	IO	255-260		8		4700			6750	7800
24	4	SEDANCRUISER SRV240	HT	SDN	FBG	DV	IO	T120-T170		8		4500			6750	7900
24	4	SUNDANCER SRV240	ST	CBNCR	FBG	DV	OB			8		4500			7700	8850
24	4	SUNDANCER SRV240	ST	CBNCR	FBG	DV	IO	185-260		8		4500			7050	8550
24	4	SUNDANCER SRV240	ST	CBNCR	FBG	DV	IO	T120-T170		8		4500			7700	8900
24	4	WEEKENDER SRV240	ST	WKNDR	FBG	DV	OB			8		4400			7600	8700
24	4	WEEKENDER SRV240	ST	WKNDR	FBG	DV	IO	185-260		8		4400			6000	7350
24	4	WEEKENDER SRV240	ST	WKNDR	FBG	DV	IO	T120-T170		8		4400			6600	7700
26	3	EXPRESS SRV260	ST	EXP	FBG	DV	IO	185-260		8		5100			7250	8900
26	3	EXPRESS SRV260	ST	EXP	FBG	DV	IO	T120-T170		8		5100			7800	9450
26	3	SUNDANCER SRV260	ST	CBNCR	FBG	DV	OB			8		5100			8850	10000
26	3	SUNDANCER SRV260	ST	CBNCR	FBG	DV	IO	185-260		8		5100			9050	10800
26	3	SUNDANCER SRV260	ST	CBNCR	FBG	DV	IO	T120-T198		8		5100			9700	11100
29	7	EXPRESS SRV300	ST	EXP	FBG	DV	IO	T228	MRCR	11	6	10000			15700	17900
29	7	SEDAN	HT	SDN	FBG	DV	IO	T228	MRCR	11	6	10900			18100	20100
29	7	SEDANBRIDGE	FB	SDN	FBG	DV	IO	T228	MRCR	11	6	11300			18300	20300
29	7	SPORTBRIDGE SRV300	FB	SPTCR	FBG	DV	IO	T228	MRCR	11	6	10300			15900	18100

 CONTINUED ON NEXT PAGE

LOA FT	LOA IN	NAME AND/ OR MODEL	TOP/ RIG	BOAT TYPE	-HULL- MTL	-HULL- TP	ENGINE TP	ENGINE # HP	ENGINE MFG	BEAM FT	BEAM IN	WGT LBS	DRAFT FT	DRAFT IN	RETAIL LOW	RETAIL HIGH
		1978 BOATS														
29	7	SUNBRIDGE	FB	SDN	FBG	DV	IO	T228	MRCR	11	6	11500			18400	20400
29	7	WEEKENDER SRV300	ST	WKNDR	FBG	DV	IO	T228	MRCR	11	6	9500			15500	17600
		1977 BOATS														
16	8	SRV185	OP	RNBT	FBG	DV	OB			7	5	2500	1		2900	3400
16	8	SRV185	ST	RNBT	FBG	DV	IO	120-190		7	5	2500	1		2050	2450
16	8	SRV187	OP	RNBT	FBG	DV	OB			7	5	2500	1		3100	3600
16	8	SRV187	ST	RNBT	FBG	DV	IO	120-190		7	5	2500	1		2150	2500
18	6	SRV195	OP	RNBT	FBG	DV	OB			8		2800	1	1	2850	3300
18	6	SRV195	ST	RNBT	FBG	DV	IO	120-235		8		2800	1	1	2550	3100
18	6	SRV197	OP	RNBT	FBG	DV	OB			8		2800	1	1	3000	3500
18	6	SRV197	ST	RNBT	FBG	DV	IO	120-235		8		2800	1	1	2650	3150
19	11	SEARUNNER SRV200	ST	CUD	FBG	DV	IO	120-235		8		3100	1	1	3100	3750
19	11	SRV200	ST	RNBT	FBG	DV	IO	120-235		8		2900	1	1	2850	3450
21	7	CUDDY CABIN SRV220	ST	CUD	FBG	DV	IO	165-235		8		3400	1	2	4250	5050
21	7	CUDDY CABIN SRV220	ST	CUD	FBG	DV	IO	255		8		3400	1	2	4500	5350
21	7	HARDTOP SRV200	HT	CUD	FBG	DV	IO	165-235		8		3600	1	2	4450	5250
21	7	OVERNIGHTER SRV220	HT	OVNTR	FBG	DV	IO	188-235		8		3600	1	2	4500	5250
24	4	CUDDY CABIN SRV240	ST	CUD	FBG	DV	IO	188-255		8		4000	1	4	5650	6950
24	4	CUDDY CABIN SRV240	ST	CUD	FBG	DV	IO	T120-T170		8		4000	1	4	6250	7300
24	4	SEDAN BRIDGE SRV240	FB	SDN	FBG	DV	IO	188-255		8		4700	1	4	6500	7900
24	4	SEDAN BRIDGE SRV240	FB	SDN	FBG	DV	IO	T120-T170		8		4700	1	4	7100	8250
24	4	SEDAN CRUISER SRV240	HT	SDN	FBG	DV	IO	188-255		8		4500	1	4	6300	7650
24	4	SEDAN CRUISER SRV240	HT	SDN	FBG	DV	IO	T120-T170		8		4500	1	4	6850	8000
24	4	SUNDANCER SRV240	OP	CUD	FBG	DV	IO	188-255		8		4500	1	4	6150	7500
24	4	SUNDANCER SRV240	OP	CUD	FBG	DV	IO	T120-T170		8		4500	1	4	6750	7900
24	4	WEEKENDER SRV240	ST	WKNDR	FBG	DV	IO	188-255		8		4400	1	4	6100	7450
24	4	WEEKENDER SRV240	ST	WKNDR	FBG	DV	IO	T120-T170		8		4400	1	4	6700	7800
29	7	HARDTOP SRV300	HT	CR	FBG	DV	IB	330	MRCR	11	6	9900			14900	16900
		IO T188 MRCR 15500 17600, IO T233 MRCR 16000 18200, IB T233-T260													15700	18300
		IO T280 MRCR 16600 18800, IB T330 16800 19200														
29	7	SEDAN BRIDGE SRV300	FB	SDN	FBG	DV	IB	330	MRCR	11	6	11300			16900	19200
29	7	SEDAN BRIDGE SRV300	FB	SDN	FBG	DV	IB	T233-T260		11	6	11300			18400	20900
29	7	SEDAN SRV300	HT	SDN	FBG	DV	IB	330	MRCR	11	6	10900			16700	18900
29	7	SEDAN SRV300	HT	SDN	FBG	DV	IB	T233-T260		11	6	10900			18100	20700
29	7	SPORT BRIDGE SRV300	FB	CR	FBG	DV	IB	330	MRCR	11	6	10300			15200	17200
29	7	SPORT BRIDGE SRV300	FB	CR	FBG	DV	IB	T233-T330		11	6	10300			16000	19400
29	7	SUN BRIDGE SRV300	FB	SDN	FBG	DV	IB	330	MRCR	11	6	11500			17000	19300
29	7	SUN BRIDGE SRV300	FB	SDN	FBG	DV	IB	T233-T260		11	6	11500			18500	21000
29	7	WEEKENDER SRV300	ST	WKNDR	FBG	DV	IB	330	MRCR	11	6	9500			14700	16700
		IO T188 MRCR 15200 17300, IO T233 MRCR 15800 17900, IB T233-T260													15500	18000
		IO T280 MRCR 16400 18600, IB T330 16600 18900														
		1976 BOATS														
16	7	SRV180	OP	RNBT	FBG	DV	OB			6	11	1350			1900	2300
18	1	SRV190	OP	RNBT	FBG	DV	OB			7	5	1500			2200	2550
18	1	SRV190	OP	RNBT	FBG	DV	IO	120-190		7	5	1500			1850	2250
18	1	SRV190	OP	RNBT	FBG	DV	IO	233-235		7	5	1500			1950	2350
18	2	SRV193	OP	RNBT	FBG	TR	IO	120-235		7	5	2750			2450	3000
18	6	SRV195	OP	RNBT	FBG	DV	IO	120-235		8		2800			2650	3200
19	11	AMBERJACK SRV200	OP	FSH	FBG	DV	OB			8		2625			3250	3800
19	11	AMBERJACK SRV200	OP	FSH	FBG	DV	IO	120-235		8		3150			3400	4100
19	11	SRV200	OP	RNBT	FBG	DV	IO	120-235		8		2900			2950	3550
19	11	SRV200	OP	RNBT	FBG	DV	IO	280	MRCR	8		2900			3200	3750
19	11	SUNCHASER SRV200	OP	CUD	FBG	DV	IO	120-235		8		3100			3200	3850
21	7	CUDDY SRV220	OP	CUD	FBG	DV	IO	165-280		8		3400			4400	5400
21	7	HARDTOP SRV220	HT	CUD	FBG	DV	IO	175-235		8		3600			4400	5250
21	7	OVERNIGHTER SRV220	HT	CUD	FBG	DV	IO	175-235		8		3600			4700	5550
24	4	CUDDY SRV240	OP	CUD	FBG	DV	IO	165-280		8		4200			5950	7350
24	4	CUDDY SRV240	OP	CUD	FBG	DV	IO	T120-T165		8		4200			6600	7700
24	4	HARDTOP SRV240	OP	CUD	FBG	DV	IO	T120-T165		8		4400			6400	7550
24	4	HARDTOP SRV240	HT	CUD	FBG	DV	IO	188-280		8		4400			6200	7550
24	4	SPORTBRIDGE SRV240	OP	CUD	FBG	DV	IO	T120-T165		8		4400			7100	8300
24	4	SPORTBRIDGE SRV240	FB	CUD	FBG	DV	IO	188-280		8		4400			6200	7550
24	4	SUNDANCER SRV240	OP	CUD	FBG	DV	IO	188-255		8		4500			6350	7550
24	4	SUNDANCER SRV240	OP	CUD	FBG	DV	IO	T120-T140		8		4400			6950	8050
24	4	WEEKENDER SRV240	OP	CUD	FBG	DV	IO	188-280		8		4400			6200	7550
24	4	WEEKENDER SRV240	OP	CUD	FBG	DV	IO	T120-T165		8		4400			6800	8000
29	7	HARDTOP SRV300	HT	CUD	FBG	DV	IB	350	MRCR	11	6	9400			14200	16100
		IO T188 MRCR 15600 17700, IO T233 MRCR 16100 18300, IB T233-T260													14900	17300
		IO T280 MRCR 16700 19000, IB T350 MRCR 16100 18300														
29	7	SEDAN BRIDGE SRV300	FB	SDN	FBG	DV	IB	350	MRCR	11	6	10800			16100	18300
29	7	SEDAN BRIDGE SRV300	FB	SDN	FBG	DV	IB	T233-T260		11	6	10800			17000	19800
29	7	SEDAN SRV300	HT	SDN	FBG	DV	IB	350	MRCR	11	6	10400			15900	18100
29	7	SEDAN SRV300	HT	SDN	FBG	DV	IB	T233-T260		11	6	10400			16800	19600
29	7	SPORTBRDIGE SRV300	FB	CUD	FBG	DV	IB	350	MRCR	11	6	9800			14400	16400
29	7	SPORTBRDIGE SRV300	FB	CUD	FBG	DV	IB	T233-T350		11	6	9800			15100	18500
29	7	WEEKENDER SRV300	OP	CUD	FBG	DV	IB	350	MRCR	11	6	9000			12000	13700
		IO T188 MRCR 13300 15100, IO T233 MRCR 13700 15600, IB T233-T260													12600	14700
		IO T280 MRCR 14300 16200, IB T350 MRCR 13700 15600														
		1975 BOATS														
16	7	SRV180	OP	RNBT	FBG	DV	OB			6	11	1350			1900	2250
16	7	SRV180	ST	RNBT	FBG	DV	IO	120-190		6	11	2300			2000	2400
18	2	SRV190	OP	RNBT	FBG	DV	OB					1500			2200	2550
18	2	SRV190	ST	RNBT	FBG	DV	IO	120-245		7	5	2600			2450	3000
18	2	SRV190	ST	RNBT	FBG	DV	JT	330	BERK	7	5	2600			2550	3000
18	2	SRV193	ST	RNBT	FBG	TR	IO	120-235		7	5	2750			2550	3100
19	11	AMBERJACK SRV200	OP	FSH	FBG	DV	OB			8		2100			2900	3400
19	11	AMBERJACK SRV200	OP	FSH	FBG	DV	IO	175-190		8		3150			3500	4150
19	11	SRV200	ST	RNBT	FBG	DV	IO	120-245		8		2900			3050	3650
19	11	SRV200	ST	RNBT	FBG	DV	JT	330	BERK	8		2900			3100	3600
21	7	SRV220 CUDDY	ST	CUD	FBG	DV	IO	165-280		8		3400			4550	5600
21	7	SRV220 OVERNIGHTER	HT	CUD	FBG	DV	IO	175-235		8		3600			4700	5550
24	4	SRV240 CUDDY	ST	CUD	FBG	DV	IO	165-280		8		3900			5850	7200
24	4	SRV240 CUDDY	ST	CUD	FBG	DV	IO	T120-T165		8		3900			6500	7600
24	4	SRV240 HARDTOP	HT	CUD	FBG	DV	IO	188-280		8		4200			6200	7550
24	4	SRV240 HARDTOP	HT	CUD	FBG	DV	IO	T120-T165		8		4200			6850	7950
24	4	SRV240 SPORT BRIDGE	FB	CUD	FBG	DV	IO	255-280		8		4400			6650	7800
24	4	SRV240 SPORT BRIDGE	FB	CUD	FBG	DV	IO	T120-T165		8		4400			7050	8200
24	4	SRV240 WEEKENDER	ST	CUD	FBG	DV	IO	188-280		8		4400			6450	7800
24	4	SRV240 WEEKENDER	ST	CUD	FBG	DV	IO	T120-T165		8		4400			7050	8200
24	4	SUNDANCER SRV240	OP	CR	FBG	DV	IO	188-255		8		4500			6550	7800
24	4	SUNDANCER SRV240	OP	CR	FBG	DV	IO	T120-T140		8		4500			7150	8250
24	4	SUNDOWNER SRV240	HT	CUD	FBG	DV	IO	188-280		8		4600			6650	8100
24	4	SUNDOWNER SRV240	HT	CUD	FBG	DV	IO	T120-T165		8		4600			7250	8450
29	7	SRV300 HARDTOP	HT	CR	FBG	DV	IO	350	MRCR	11	6	10000			16400	18700
		IO T188 MRCR 16500 18700, IO T233 MRCR 17000 19300, VD T233-T350													14600	17900
29	7	SRV300 SPORT BRIDGE	FB	CR	FBG	DV	IO	350	MRCR	11	6	10000			16400	18700
29	7	SRV300 SPORT BRIDGE	FB	CR	FBG	DV	VD	T233-T350		11	6	10000			14600	17900
29	7	SRV300 WEEKENDER	ST	CUD	FBG	DV	IO	350	MRCR	11	6	9800			16300	18500
		IO T188 MRCR 16400 18600, IO T233 MRCR 16900 19200, VD T233-T350													14500	17800
		1974 BOATS														
16	7	SRV 180			FBG		OB			6	11	1200			1700	2050
16	7	SRV 180			FBG		IO	120-190		6	11	2100			1850	2250
16	7	SRV 180			FBG		IO	225	MRCR	6	11	2100			1950	2350
18	2	SRV 190			FBG		OB			7	5	1400			2000	2400
18	2	SRV 190			FBG		IO	120-245		7	5	2400			2400	2900
18	2	SRV 190			FBG		JT	455	BERK	7	5	2400			2300	2700
18	2	SRV 193			FBG		OB			7	5	1500			2150	2500
18	2	SRV 193			FBG		IO	120-225		7	5	2500			2450	2950
19	11	SRV 200			FBG		IO	120-245		8		2700			3000	3600
19	11	SRV 200			FBG		JT	455	BERK	8		2700			2800	3250
21	7	SRV 220 CC			FBG		IO	165-190		8		3400			4500	5150
21	7	SRV 220 CC			FBG		IO	225	MRCR	8		3400			4550	5250
21	7	SRV 220 CC			FBG		IO	225-255		8					5000	5900
21	7	SRV 220 OV			FBG		IO	170-225		8		3600			4650	5450
24	4	SRV 240 CC			FBG		IO	165-255		8		3900			5800	7000
24	4	SRV 240 CC			FBG		IO	T120-T165		8		3900			6450	7550
24	4	SRV 240 HT			FBG		IO	165-255		8		4200			6150	7350
24	4	SRV 240 HT			FBG		IO	T120-T165		8		4200			6800	7950
24	4	SRV 240 SBII			FBG		IO	225-255		8		4400			6600	7600
24	4	SRV 240 SBII			FBG		IO	T120-T165		8		4400			7150	8300
24	4	SRV 240 SD			FBG		IO	188-255		8		4600			6600	7850
24	4	SRV 240 SD			FBG		IO	T120-T165		8		4600			7250	8450
24	4	SRV 240 WE			FBG		IO	165-255		8		4400			6350	7600
24	4	SRV 240 WE			FBG		IO	T120-T165		8		4400			6850	8050
		1973 BOATS														
16	7	SRV 180			FBG		OB			6	11		2	4	2500	2900
16	10	SRV 183			FBG		OB			6	11		2	4	2450	2850
18	2	SRV 190 B			FBG		OB			7	5		2	6	2500	2900
18	2	SRV 190 B			FBG		IO	120-245		7	5		2	6	2300	2850
19		SRV 193			FBG		IO	120-225		7	5		2	4	2850	3400
19	11	SRV 200			FBG		IO	120-245		8			2	6	3200	3850
21	7	CC SRV220			FBG		IO	165-255		8			2	6	5100	6100
21	7	CC SRV220			FBG		IO	T120-T140		8			2	6	5750	6600
21	7	SRV220		OVNTR	FBG		IO	188	MRCR	8			2	6	5400	6200
24	4	CC SRV240			FBG		IO	165-255		8			2	9	6600	7900
24	4	CC SRV240			FBG		IO	T120-T165		8			2	9	7300	8500

CONTINUED ON NEXT PAGE

LOA FT	LOA IN	NAME AND/ OR MODEL	TOP/ RIG	BOAT TYPE	-HULL- MTL	-HULL- TP	ENGINE TP	ENGINE # HP	ENGINE MFG	BEAM FT	BEAM IN	WGT LBS	DRAFT FT	DRAFT IN	RETAIL LOW	RETAIL HIGH
		1973 BOATS														
24	4	SRV 240	FB	SPTCR	FBG		IO	225-255		8			2	9	7000	8200
24	4	SRV 240	FB	SPTCR	FBG		IO	T120-T165		8			2	9	7550	8800
24	4	SRV240	HT		FBG		IO	165-255		8			2	9	6600	7900
24	4	SRV240	HT		FBG		IO	T120-T165		8			2	9	7300	8500
24	4	SRV240		WKNDR	FBG		IO	165-255		8			2	9	6900	8250
24	4	SRV240		WKNDR	FBG		IO	T120-T165		8			2	9	7600	8900
		1972 BOATS														
16	7	SRV 180			FBG		IO	120-165		6	11	1800			1850	2200
16	10	SRV 183			FBG		OB			7		1200			1700	2050
16	10	SRV 183			FBG		IO	120-140		7		2050			2000	2400
18	1	SRV 190			FBG		OB			7	2	1300			1900	2250
18	1	SRV 190			FBG		IO	120-245		7	2	1950			2250	2750
18	1	SRV 190			FBG		JT	270	BERK	7	2	1950			1850	2200
19		SRV 193			FBG		IO	120-225		7	5	2350			2650	3200
19	7	SRV 200			FBG		IO	120-245		7	5	2350			2750	3350
19	7	SRV 200			FBG		JT	270	BERK	7	5	2350			2300	2700
21	7	SRV 220 CC			FBG		IO	165-245		8		3400			4750	5600
21	7	SRV 220 CC			FBG		IO	T120-T140		8		4050			6050	6950
24	4	SRV 240 CC		CUD	FBG		IO	165-245		8		3900			6450	7650
24	4	SRV 240 CC		CUD	FBG		IO	T120-T165		8		4550			7950	9250
24	4	SRV 240 FB	FB	CR	FBG		IO	165-245		8		4400			7050	8350
24	4	SRV 240 WE		WKNDR	FBG		IO	165-245		8		4400			7100	8400
24	4	SRV 240 WE		WKNDR	FBG		IO	T120-T165		8		5100			8700	10100
		1971 BOATS														
16	7	SRV 180			FBG		IO	120-165		6	11	1800			1900	2300
16	10	SRV 183			FBG		OB			7		1200			1700	2050
16	10	SRV 183			FBG		IO	120-140		7		2050			2100	2500
18		PACHANGA			FBG		IO	235	OMC	7	2	2300			3800	4400
18		PACHANGA			FBG		JT	260	BERK	7	2	2300			2850	3300
18	1	SRV 190			FBG		OB			7	2	1300			1900	2250
18	1	SRV 190			FBG		IO	120-235		7	2	1950			2350	2800
18	1	SRV 190			FBG		JT	260	BERK	7	2	1950			1800	2150
19		SRV 193			FBG		IO	120-235		7	5	2350			2750	3300
19		SRV 193			FBG		JT	260	BERK	7	5	2350			2100	2500
19	7	SRV 200			FBG		IO	120-235		7	5	2350			2850	3450
19	7	SRV 200			FBG		JT	260	BERK	7	5	2350			2200	2600
21	7	SRV 220 CC			FBG		IO	155-235		8		3400			4900	5750
21	7	SRV 220 CC			FBG		IO	T120-T140		8		4050			6250	7200
21	7	SRV 220 CR			FBG		IO	155-235		8		3900			5400	6350
24	4	SRV 240 CC		CUD	FBG		IO	155-235		8		3900			6600	7850
24	4	SRV 240 CC		CUD	FBG		IO	T120-T165		8		4550			8200	9600
24	4	SRV 240 WE		WKNDR	FBG		IO	165-235		8		4400			7300	8600
24	4	SRV 240 WE		WKNDR	FBG		IO	T120-T165		8		5100			9100	10500
		1970 BOATS														
16	5	SRV 370		RNBT	FBG	TR	OB			6	11	1200			1700	2050
16	7	SRV 180		RNBT	FBG	DV	IO	120-165		6	11	1800			2050	2500
18		PACHANGA		RNBT	FBG	DV	IO	155-215		7	2	2300			3850	4650
18	1	SRV 190		RNBT	FBG	DV	OB			7	2	1300			1900	2250
18	1	SRV 190		RNBT	FBG	DV	IO	120-215		7	2	1950			2450	2950
18	3	SRV 380		RNBT	FBG	TR	OB			7	3	1400			2000	2400
18	3	SRV 380		RNBT	FBG	TR	IO	120-165		7	3	2450			2800	3250
19	7	SRV 200		RNBT	FBG	DV	IO	120-215		7	5	2350			3000	3600
20	7	SRV 210	OP	RNBT	FBG	DV	IO	155-215		7	10	3200			4550	5350
20	7	SRV 210	OP	RNBT	FBG	DV	IO	T120-T140		7	10	3200			5250	6050
20	7	SRV 210 CC		CR	FBG	DV	IO	155-215		7	10	3200			4750	5600
20	7	SRV 210 CC		CR	FBG	DV	IO	T120-T140		7	10	3200			5500	6350
23	10	SRV 240	HT	CR	FBG	DV	IO	155-215		8		4200			7050	8250
23	10	SRV 240	HT	CR	FBG	DV	IO	T120-T165		8		4200			7850	9100
23	10	SRV 240 CC		CR	FBG	DV	IO	155-215		8		3600			6300	7400
23	10	SRV 240 CC		CR	FBG	DV	IO	T120-T165		8		3600			7100	8200
		1969 BOATS														
17	4	SRV 170 PT	OP	RNBT	FBG		IO	120	OMC	6	10	1200			1950	2300
17	4	SRV 170 TT	OP	RNBT	FBG		IO	120-160		6	10	1200			1950	2350
18	10	SRV 185	OP	RNBT	FBG	SV	OB			7	1	1150			1750	2100
18	10	SRV 185 PT	OP	RNBT	FBG	SV	IO	120-155		7	1	1150			2350	2700
18	10	SRV 185 TT	OP	RNBT	FBG	SV	IO	120-160		7	1	1150			2300	2750
18	11	PACHANGA SRX PT			FBG		IO	155-210		7	2	1200			3400	4050
18	11	PACHANGA SRX TT			FBG		IO	160-225		7	2	1200			3400	4150
20	4	SRV 190 PT	OP	RNBT	FBG		IO	120-210		7	5	1500			3250	3850
20	4	SRV 190 TT	OP	RNBT	FBG		IO	120-225		7	5	1500			3250	3950
20	8	SRV 380	OP	RNBT	FBG	TR	OB			7	3	1350			2600	3050
20	8	SRV 380 PT	OP	RNBT	FBG	TR	IO	120-210		7	3	1500			3300	3900
20	8	SRV 380 TT	OP	RNBT	FBG	TR	IO	120-200		7	3	1500			3250	3900
22	1	SRV 210 PT		CR	FBG		IO	155-210		7	10	2000			4250	5000
22	1	SRV 210 TT		CR	FBG		IO	160-210		7	10	2000			4250	5050
23	10	SRV 240 PT		CR	FBG		IO	155-210		8		2600			5350	6200
23	10	SRV 240 PT		CR	FBG		IO	T120-T210		8		2600			6100	7200
23	10	SRV 240 TT		CR	FBG		IO	160-250		8		2600			5350	6450
23	10	SRV 240 TT		CR	FBG		IO	325	MRCR	8		2600			6300	7250
23	10	SRV 240 TT		CR	FBG		IO	T120-T160		8		2600			6100	7100
24		SRV 150	OP	CR	FBG		IO	125		7	10				7700	8850
		1968 BOATS														
16	2	SRV 170	OP	RNBT	FBG		IO	120-160		6	10				1900	2250
16	5	SRV 370	OP	RNBT	FBG	TR	IO	120	MRCR	6	11				1950	2300
17	7	SRV 180	OP	RNBT	FBG	SV	OB			7	1	1150			1700	2050
17	7	SRV 180	OP	RNBT	FBG	SV	IO	120-160		7	1				2600	3050
17	7	SRV 185	OP	RNBT	FBG		IO	120-160		7	1				2650	3100
18	3	SRV 380	OP	RNBT	FBG	TR	OB			7	3	1350			2000	2350
18	3	SRV 380	OP	RNBT	FBG	TR	IO	120-210		7	3				2750	3300
19		SRV 190	OP	RNBT	FBG		IO	120-255		7	5				3500	4350
19		SRV 190 SPORTSMAN		CR	FBG		IO	120-210		7	5				3550	4250
23	10	SRV 240		CR	FBG		IO	155-255		8					7900	9400
		1967 BOATS														
16		SRV 170		RNBT	FBG		IO	120-160		6	8				1900	2250
17	6	SRV 180		RNBT	FBG		OB			7		1150			1700	2050
17	6	SRV 180		RNBT	FBG		IO	120-160		7					2650	3150
19		SRV 190		RNBT	FBG		IO	120-225		7	4				3600	4300
19		SRV 190 DELUXE		RNBT	FBG		OB			7	4	1300			2000	2350
19		SRV 190 SPORTSMAN		CR	FBG		IO	120-200		7	4				3650	4300
22	2	SRV 230		CR	FBG		IO	155-225		8					6750	7900
24	4	SRV 240			FBG		IO	185-225							8200	9550
		1966 BOATS														
16		SRV 170		RNBT	FBG	DV	IO	110-150		6	8				1950	2350
16	2	DELUXE		RNBT	FBG		IO	110-150		6	8				1950	2350
17	6	SRV 180		RNBT	FBG	DV	OB			7		1150			1700	2050
17	6	SRV 180		RNBT	FBG	DV	IO	110-150		7					2750	3200
19		SRV 190		RNBT	FBG	DV	OB			7	4	1300			2000	2350
19		SRV 190		RNBT	FBG	DV	IO	110-225		7	4				3700	4450
22	2	SRV 230		CR	FBG	DV	IO	150-225		8			2		6950	8150
22	2	SRV 230		CR	FBG	DV	IO	T110-T150		8			2		7800	9000
24	4	SRV 240			FBG	DV	IO	200-225							8500	9900
24	4	SRV 240			FBG	DV	IO	T110-T150							9350	10700
		1965 BOATS														
16	2	DELUXE			FBG		IO	110-150							1950	2350
17	2	SRX-17			FBG		IO	110-150							2250	2600
18		DELUXE			FBG		OB								2550	2950
18		DELUXE			FBG		IO	110-225							2950	3550
22	2	SR-230			FBG		IO	150-225							7000	8200
22	2	SR-230			FBG		IO	T110-T150							7850	9050
		1964 BOATS														
16	2	SEA-RAY 800 DELUXE			FBG		IO	88-150							2050	2450
18		SEA-RAY 900 DELUXE			FBG		OB								2250	2600
18		SEA-RAY 900 DELUXE			FBG		IO	110-150							2800	3300
18		SEA-RAY 900 DELUXE			FBG		IO	225							3150	3700
18		SEA-RAY 990 DELUXE			FBG		OB								2950	3400
18		SEA-RAY 990 DELUXE			FBG		IO	110-150							3250	3800
		1963 BOATS														
16	2	SEA-RAY 800 DELUXE			FBG		IO	80-110							2100	2500
17	8	SEA-RAY 900 DELUXE			FBG		OB								2550	3000
17	8	SEA-RAY 900 DELUXE			FBG		IO	80-140							3050	3550
17	8	SEA-RAY 990		CR	FBG		OB								2550	3000
17	8	SEA-RAY 990		CR	FBG		IO	80							3200	3750
		1962 BOATS														
17	8			RNBT	FBG		OB								2550	3000

SEA ROVER MARINE

DIV OF APECO CORP
ST PETERSBURG FL 33701 COAST GUARD MFG ID- SRM

See inside cover to adjust price for area

LOA FT	LOA IN	NAME AND/ OR MODEL	TOP/ RIG	BOAT TYPE	-HULL- MTL	-HULL- TP	ENGINE TP	ENGINE # HP	ENGINE MFG	BEAM FT	BEAM IN	WGT LBS	DRAFT FT	DRAFT IN	RETAIL LOW	RETAIL HIGH
		1973 BOATS														
37	9	SEA-ROVER 36	FB	HB	FBG		IO	T165		12		15000	1	7	23500	26100
		1972 BOATS														
32		SEA-ROVER 32		HB	FBG		IO			12		12000	1	7	20900	23200
37	9	SEA-ROVER 36		HB	FBG		IO	270	MRCR	12		15000	1	7	22400	24900
		IO T165 MRCR 23300 25900, IO T215 MRCR 23600 26200, IO T215 OMC 22700 25300														
		IO T225 CHRY 23700 26400, VD T225 CHRY 23500 26100														
37	9	SEA-ROVER 36	FB	HB	FBG		IO	270	MRCR	12		15000	1	7	22400	24900
		IO T165 MRCR 23300 25900, IO T215 MRCR 24100 26800, IO T215 OMC 23000 25500														

CONTINUED ON NEXT PAGE

```
LOA  NAME AND/              TOP/ BOAT  -HULL- ----ENGINE---  BEAM    WGT  DRAFT RETAIL RETAIL
FT IN  OR MODEL             RIG  TYPE  MTL TP TP # HP  MFG   FT IN   LBS  FT IN  LOW   HIGH
------------------- 1972 BOATS ---------------------------------------------------------------
37  9 SEA-ROVER 36          FB  HB    FBG    IO  T225 CHRY 12      15000  1 7  23700 26400
37  9 SEA-ROVER 36          FB  HB    FBG    VD  T225 CHRY 12             1 7  23500 26100
37  9 SEA-ROVER 36 EXEC         HB    FBG    IO  270  MRCR 12      15000  1 7  22400 24900
      IO T165 MRCR 23300 25900, IO T215 MRCR 24000 26700, IO T215 OMC   23900 26500
      IO T225 CHRY 23700 26400, VD T225 CHRY      23500 26100

37  9 SEA-ROVER 36 EXEC     FB  HB    FBG    IO  270  MRCR 12      15000  1 7  22400 24900
      IO T165 MRCR 23300 25900, IO T215 MRCR 24100 26800, IO T215 OMC   23000 25500
      IO T225 CHRY 23700 26400, VD T225 CHRY      23500 26100
------------------- 1971 BOATS ---------------------------------------------------------------
32    SEA-ROVER 32              HB    FBG    IO  215       12      12000  1 7  20800 23100
      IO  225 CHRY 20800 23200, IB  225 CHRY 20700 23000, IO  270 MRCR 21100 23500
      IO T140-T165 22000 24500

32    SEA-ROVER 32          FB  HB    FBG    IO  215       12      12000  1 7  20800 23100
      IO  225 CHRY 20800 23200, IB  225 CHRY 20700 23000, IO  270 MRCR 21100 23500
      IO T140-T165 22000 24500

36    SEA-ROVER 36              HB    FBG    IO  T165 MRCR 12      15000  1 7  23100 25700
      IO T215 MRCR 23400 26000, IO T215 OMC  23300 25900, IO T225 CHRY 23500 26200
      IB T225 CHRY 23200 25800

36    SEA-ROVER 36          FB  HB    FBG    IO  T165 MRCR 12      15000  1 7  23100 25700
      IO T215 MRCR 23400 26000, IO T215 OMC  23300 25900, IO T225 CHRY 23500 26200
------------------- 1970 BOATS ---------------------------------------------------------------
31  3 SEA-ROVER SPRITE         HB    FBG TR IO  160-250   12      12000  1 7  20400 23200
31  3 SEA-ROVER SPRITE         HB    FBG TR IO  T120-T160 12      12000  1 7  21800 24300
35  3 SEA-ROVER 36             HB    FBG TR IO  250  MRCR 12      14000  1 4  22500 25100
      IO T160 MRCR 23700 26300, IO T200 MRCR 23900 26500, IO T225 CHRY 24100 26800
      IB T225 CHRY 23800 26500
```

SEA SAFE MARINE INC
COAST GUARD MFG ID- SSF

Call 1-800-327-6929 for BUC Personalized Evaluation Service
Or, for 1974 to 1980 boats, sign onto www.BUCValuPro.com

SEA SLED INDUSTRIES

Call 1-800-327-6929 for BUC Personalized Evaluation Service
Or, for 1961 boats, sign onto www.BUCValuPro.com

SEA SPRITE
UNITED MARINE CORP   See inside cover to adjust price for area
WATSEKA IL 60970   COAST GUARD MFG ID- SSB

For more recent years, see the BUC Used Boat Price Guide, Volume 1 or Volume 2

```
LOA  NAME AND/              TOP/ BOAT  -HULL- ----ENGINE---  BEAM    WGT  DRAFT RETAIL RETAIL
FT IN  OR MODEL             RIG  TYPE  MTL TP TP # HP  MFG   FT IN   LBS  FT IN  LOW   HIGH
------------------- 1983 BOATS ---------------------------------------------------------------
16    COUGAR 672            ST  RNBT  FBG TR OB            6       780        1750 2050
16  1 STINGER 678           OP  SKI   FBG DV OB            6       780        1700 2050
16  1 VEE 1600              RNBT  FBG DV IB  120           6  6   1100        2200 2550
16  3 SEA-HAWK 1779         RNBT  FBG TR IO  120           6  7               2350 2700
16  3 SEA-HAWK 1779         RNBT  FBG DV IB  120           6  7   1300        2400 2800
16  8 VEE 1700              RNBT  FBG DV IO  120           6 10              2650 3050
16  8 VEE 1700              RNBT  FBG DV IB  120           6 10   1150        2450 2850
16  9 SEA-RAVEN 780 XL      OP  SKI   FBG IO  120-140      6  8   1690        2250 2600
16  9 SEA-RAVEN 780 XL      ST  SKI   FBG DV OB            6  8    995        2250 2600
17    FISH-N-SKI 1784       OP  RNBT  FBG TR OB            7       960        2200 2600
17  2 BASS-RANGER II 784    OP  BASS  FBG TR OB            7  1    935        2150 2550
17  9 SANDPIPER 1789        ST  RNBT  FBG DV IO  120-200   7  5   1950        2850 3400

17  9 SANDPIPER 889 XL      ST  RNBT  FBG DV OB            8  9   1200        2700 3150
17  9 SANDPIPER 889 XL      ST  RNBT  FBG DV IO  120       7  5   1950        2850 3350
18  1 VEE 1900              OP  RNBT  FBG TR IB  120       7  4   1050        3000 3500
18  2 SEA-GULL 1886         RNBT  FBG TR IB  120           7  1   1405        3100 3600
18  3 SEA-SPIRIT 895        ST  RNBT  FBG DV IO  120-170   7 11  2250        3300 3850
19  5 WBV 1895              RNBT  FBG DV IB  120           8               4650 5350
19  5 WBV 1995              RNBT  FBG DV IO  120           8               4650 5350
19  8 SEA-SKIFF 2095        ST  CUD   FBG DV IO  120-200   7 11  2450        3850 4550
19  8 SEA-SKIFF 2095 B/R    ST  RNBT  FBG DV IO  120-170   7 11  2450        3700 4350
21    CAPRICE 2196          OP  CR    FBG DV IO  198-260   8      3400        4650 5550
23 10 CRUISER 2496          CR    FBG DV IB  228          8      2600        5650 6500
25  9 CRUISER 2696          CR    FBG DV IB  260          8      2600        7350 8450
------------------- 1982 BOATS ---------------------------------------------------------------
16  1 VEE 1600 B/R          OP  SKI   FBG DV OB            6  6    995        2150 2500
16  1 VEE 1600 B/R          OP  SKI   FBG DV IO  120-140   6  6   1650        2000 2400
16  3 SEA-HAWK 1779         ST  RNBT  FBG TR OB            6  6   1165        2500 2900
16  3 SEA-HAWK 1779         ST  RNBT  FBG TR IO  120-170   6  7   1950        2400 2800
17    1784 BASS             OP  BASS  FBG TR OB            7       960        2150 2500
17    1784 FISH N SKI       OP  RNBT  FBG TR OB            7       960        2200 2550
17  4 COUGAR 1782           ST  RNBT  FBG TR IO           6 10   1140        2500 2900
17  9 1789 VEE              ST  RNBT  FBG DV OB            7  5   1025        2350 2750
17  9 1789 VEE              ST  RNBT  FBG DV IO  120-170   7  5   2000        2850 3300
18  2 SEA-GULL 1886         ST  RNBT  FBG TR IB  120-170   7  1   2100        2900 3400
18  3 1895                  ST  RNBT  FBG DV OB            7 11  1350        2950 3450
18  3 1895                  ST  RNBT  FBG DV IO  120-170   7 11  2250        3200 3750

19  8 1995                  ST  RNBT  FBG DV IO  120-170   7 11  2450        3600 4200
19  8 1995 CUDDY            ST  RNBT  FBG DV IO  120-170   7 11  2450        3600 4350
21    CAPRICE 2196          OP  CR    FBG DV IO  260       8      3600        4700 5350
23 10 CRUISER 2496          OP  CR    FBG DV IO  260       8      4400        6550 7550
25  9 CRUISER 2696          OP  CR    FBG DV IO  260       8      5400        8300 9550
25  9 CRUISER 2696          OP  CR    FBG DV IO  T170  MRCR 8     5400        8950 10200
------------------- 1981 BOATS ---------------------------------------------------------------
16    COUGAR 1672           ST  RNBT  FBG TR IO  120-140   6      1650        2000 2400
16  1 VEE 1600 B/R          OP  SKI   FBG DV OB            6  6    995        2050 2450
16  1 VEE 1600 B/R          OP  SKI   FBG DV IO  120-140   6  6   1650        1950 2350
16  3 SEA-HAWK 1779         ST  RNBT  FBG TR OB            6  7   1165        2450 2850
16  3 SEA-HAWK 1779         ST  RNBT  FBG TR IO  140-170   6  7   1950        2350 2750
16  8 VEE 1700 B/R          ST  RNBT  FBG SV OB            6 10   1090        2400 2800
16  8 VEE 1700 B/R          ST  RNBT  FBG SV IO  120-170   6 10   1850        2400 2800
17  4 COUGAR 1782           ST  RNBT  FBG TR OB            6 10   1090        2400 2750
18  1 1900                  ST  RNBT  FBG DV OB            7  4              2850 3300
18  1 1900                  ST  RNBT  FBG DV IO  120       7  4              3350 3900
18  1 VEE 1888              ST  RNBT  FBG SV OB            7  4   1200        3600 3050
18  1 VEE 1888              ST  RNBT  FBG SV IO  120-250   7  4   2050        2850 3550

18  2 SEA-GULL 1886         ST  RNBT  FBG TR OB            7 11  2100        2850 3350
18  3 1895                  ST  RNBT  FBG DV IO  120-170   7 11  1350        2900 3350
18  3 1895                  ST  RNBT  FBG DV IO  120-170   7 11  2250        3150 3700
19  5 1995                  ST  RNBT  FBG DV IB  120       8               4200 4900
19  8 1995                  ST  RNBT  FBG DV IO  170  MRCR 7 11  2450        3600 4150
19 10 SEA-SKIFF 2095        ST  CUD   FBG SV IO  185-250   7 11  2600        3900 4700
19 10 SEA-SKIFF 2095 B/R    ST  RNBT  FBG DV IO  185-230   7 11  2600        3750 4450
21    CAPRICE 2196          OP  CR    FBG DV IO  170       8               4200 4900
21    CAPRICE 2196          OP  CR    FBG DV IO  185-228   8      3600        4600 5400
23 10 CRUISER 2496          CR    FBG DV IO  198          8               6050 6950
23 10 CRUISER 2496          OP  CR    FBG DV IO  228-260   8      4400        6300 7400
25  9 CRUISER 2696          OP  CR    FBG DV IO  260       8      5400        6150 9350
------------------- 1980 BOATS ---------------------------------------------------------------
16  1 VEE 1600 B/R          OP  SKI   FBG DV OB            6  6    995        2050 2400
16  1 VEE 1600 B/R          OP  SKI   FBG DV IO  120-140   6  6   1650        1950 2300
16  3 SEA-HAWK 1779         ST  RNBT  FBG DV OB            6  7   1165        2400 2800
16  3 SEA-HAWK 1779         ST  RNBT  FBG DV IO  120-170   6  7   1950        2350 2750
16  8 VEE 1700 B/R          ST  RNBT  FBG SV OB            6 10   1090        2400 2700
16  8 VEE 1700 B/R          ST  RNBT  FBG SV IO  120-170   6 10   1850        2350 2750
17  4 COUGAR 1782           ST  RNBT  FBG TR OB            6 10   1090        2350 2750
18  1 VEE 1900              ST  RNBT  FBG DV OB            7  4   1200        2600 3000
18  1 VEE 1900              ST  RNBT  FBG DV IO  120-250   7  4   2050        2850 3300
18  2 SEA-GULL 1886         ST  RNBT  FBG TR IO  120-250   7  1   2100        2800 3300
18  3 1895                  ST  RNBT  FBG DV OB            7 11  1350        2800 3300
18  3 1895                  ST  RNBT  FBG DV IO  120-250   7 11  2250        3150 3850

19  8 1995                  ST  RNBT  FBG DV IO  170-250   7 11  2450        3550 4100
19 10 SEA-SKIFF 2095        ST  CUD   FBG DV IO  170  MRCR 7 11              3850 4650
19 10 SEA-SKIFF 2095 B/R    OP  RNBT  FBG DV IO  170-250   7 11              3700 4450
21    CAPRICE 2196          OP  CR    FBG DV IO  185-260   8               4600 5500
23 10 CRUISER 2496          OP  CR    FBG DV IO  228-260   8      3600        6250 7250
23 10 SEA-SPRITE 2500       OP  CR    FBG DV IO           8      4400        3100 3600
25  9 CRUISER 2696          OP  CR    FBG DV IO  250-260   8               5000 9300
25  9 CRUISER 2696          OP  CR    FBG DV IO  T170-T185 8      5400        8650 10000
26    SEA-SPRITE 2600       RNBT  FBG DV IO  260          8               6150 7100
------------------- 1979 BOATS ---------------------------------------------------------------
16  1 VEE 1600              ST  RNBT  FBG DV OB            6  6    995        2000 2400
16  3 SEA-HAWK 1779         ST  RNBT  FBG DV OB            6  7   1165        2400 2750
16  3 SEA-HAWK 1779         ST  RNBT  FBG DV IO  120-170   6  7   1950        2250 2750
16  8 VEE 1700              ST  RNBT  FBG DV OB            6 10   1090        2250 2650
16  8 VEE 1700              ST  RNBT  FBG DV IO  140-170   6 10   1850        2400 2800
```

LOA FT IN	NAME AND/ OR MODEL	TOP/ RIG	BOAT TYPE	-HULL- MTL TP	----ENGINE--- TP # HP MFG	BEAM FT IN	WGT LBS	DRAFT FT IN	RETAIL LOW	RETAIL HIGH
					1979 BOATS					
17 4	COUGAR 1782	ST	RNBT	FBG TR	OB	6 10	1140		2400	2800
18 1	VEE 1900	ST	RNBT	FBG DV	IO 140-230	7 4	2050		2850	3400
18 2	SEA-GULL 1886	ST	RNBT	FBG TR	IO 120-230	7 1	2100		2800	3400
19 10	SEA-SKIFF 2095	ST	CUD	FBG DV	IO 170-260	7 11	2600		3850	4750
19 10	SEA-SKIFF 2095 B/R	ST	RNBT	FBG DV	IO 170-260	7 11	2600		3700	4550
21	CAPRICE 2100	ST	CR	FBG DV	IO 185-260	8	3650		4600	5550
23 10	CRUISER 2500	ST	CUD	FBG TR	IO 185-260	8	4400		6150	7350
					1978 BOATS					
16 3	SEA-HAWK 1779	ST	RNBT	FBG TR	OB	6 7	1165		2350	2750
16 3	SEA-HAWK 1779	ST	RNBT	FBG TR	IO 120	6 7	1730		2250	2600
16 8	VEE 1700	ST	RNBT	FBG DV	OB	6 10	1170		2350	2750
16 8	VEE 1700	ST	RNBT	FBG DV	IO 140	6 10	1980		2500	2900
17	WRANGLER 1775	OP	BASS	FBG TR	OB	6 3	980		2000	2400
17 4	COUGAR 1782	ST	RNBT	FBG TR	OB	6 10	1150		2400	2750
18 1	VEE 1900	ST	RNBT	FBG DV	IO 140	7 4	2130		2900	3400
18 2	SEA-GULL 1886	ST	RNBT	FBG TR	OB	7 1	1385		2800	3250
18 2	SEA-GULL 1886	ST	RNBT	FBG TR	IO 140	7 1	1970		2750	3200
19 8	SEA-STINGER 2088	OP	RNBT	FBG DV	OB	6 11	1060		2400	2800
19 10	SEA-SKIFF 2095	ST	RNBT	FBG DV	IO 198 MRCR	7 11	2600		3750	4350
21	CAPRICE 2100	ST	CBNCR	FBG DV	IO 198 MRCR	8	3660		5100	5850
					1977 BOATS					
16 3	SEA-HAWK 1779	ST	RNBT	FBG TR	OB	6 5	1165		2300	2700
16 3	SEA-HAWK 1779	ST	RNBT	FBG TR	IO 120-140	6 5	1740		2250	2650
16 3	SEA-SWINGER 1680	ST	RNBT	FBG TR	OB	6 6	960		1900	2250
16 8	1700 VEE	ST	RNBT	FBG DV	OB	6 8	1170		2350	2750
16 8	1700 VEE	ST	RNBT	FBG DV	IO 140 MRCR	6 8	1980		2500	2900
17	WRANGLER 1775	OP	BASS	FBG TR	OB	6 2	980		2000	2350
17 4	COUGAR 1782	ST	RNBT	FBG TR	OB	6 8	1150		2350	2750
18 1	1900 VEE	ST	RNBT	FBG DV	IO 165-188	7 3	2130		2950	3450
18 2	SEA-GULL 1886	ST	RNBT	FBG TR	OB	7 8	1385		2750	3200
18 2	SEA-GULL 1886	ST	RNBT	FBG TR	IO 140-188	7 8	2000		2950	3500
18 11	SEA-SWINGER II 1993	ST	RNBT	FBG TR	IO 140-165	7 9	2000		3100	3650
19 8	SEA-STINGER 2082	OP	RNBT	FBG DV	OB	6 9	1060		2350	2750
19 10	SEA-SKIFF 2095	ST	RNBT	FBG DV	IO 188 MRCR	7 9	2600		3750	4350
21	CAPRICE 2100	ST	RNBT	FBG DV	IO 188 MRCR	8	3660		4550	5200
					1976 BOATS					
16 1	SEA-LANCER 1681BR	ST	RNBT	FBG DV	OB	6 9	900		1750	2100
16 1	SEA-LANCER 1681CD	OP	RNBT	FBG DV	OB	6 9	900		1750	2100
16 3	SEA-HAWK 1779	ST	RNBT	FBG TR	OB	6 7	1165		2300	2650
16 3	SEA-HAWK 1779	ST	RNBT	FBG TR	IO 120-140	6 7	1830		2400	2750
16 3	SEA-SWINGER 1680	ST	RNBT	FBG TR	OB	6 8	960		1900	2250
16 8	VEE 1700	ST	RNBT	FBG DV	OB	6 10	1140		2500	2650
16 8	VEE 1700	ST	RNBT	FBG DV	IO 140-165	6 10	1820		2500	2900
17	WRANGLER 1775	ST	BASS	FBG TR	OB	6 3	980		1950	2350
17 4	COUGAR 1782	ST	RNBT	FBG TR	OB	6 10	1150		2350	2700
18 1	VEE 1900	ST	RNBT	FBG DV	IO 165-233	7 4	2030		2950	3600
18 2	SEA-GULL 1886	ST	RNBT	FBG TR	OB	7 1	1385		2700	3150
18 2	SEA-GULL 1886	ST	RNBT	FBG TR	IO 140-233	7 1	2070		2950	3600
19 10	SEA-SKIFF 2095	ST	RNBT	FBG DV	IO 188-233	7 11	2600		3900	4650
21	CAPRICE 2100	ST	CR	FBG DV	IO 190-233	8	3060		4250	5100
					1975 BOATS					
16 1	SEA-LANCER BR	OP	RNBT	FBG DV	OB	6 11	900		1800	2150
16 1	SEA-LANCER CD	OP	RNBT	FBG DV	OB	6 11	900		1700	2000
16 3	SEA-HAWK	OP	RNBT	FBG TR	OB	6 7	1165		2300	2650
16 3	SEA-HAWK	OP	RNBT	FBG TR	IO 120-140	6 7	1730		2400	2800
18 2	SEA-GULL	OP	RNBT	FBG DV	IO 140-233	7	1970		2950	3600
18 2	SEA-GULL	OP	RNBT	FBG DV	390 OLDS	7	1970		4950	5700
18 2	SEA-GULL	OP	RNBT	FBG TR	OB	7	1385		2700	3100
19 10	SEA-SKIFF	OP	RNBT	FBG DV	IO 165-233	7 10	2600		3950	4750
19 10	SEA-SKIFF	OP	RNBT	FBG DV	390 OLDS	7 10	2600		5950	6850
					1974 BOATS					
16 3	SEA-HAWK 1679	OP	RNBT	FBG TR	OB	6 7	1685		3050	3550
16 3	SEA-HAWK 1679	OP	RNBT	FBG TR	IO 120-140	6 7	1780		2500	2900
18 3	SEA-GULL 1886	OP	RNBT	FBG TR	IO 140-188	7 2	1920		3050	3600
18 3	SEA-GULL 1886	OP	RNBT	FBG TR	OB	7 2	1525		2850	3300
20	SEA-SKIFF 2095	OP	RNBT	FBG DV	IO 165-188	8	2035		3400	3950
					1973 BOATS					
16	BASS-CHARGER	OP	BASS	FBG TR	OB	5 2	1200		2300	2650
16 3	SEA-HAWK 1679	OP	RNBT	FBG TR	OB	6 7	1185		2300	2650
16 3	SEA-HAWK 1679	OP	RNBT	FBG TR	IO 120-140	6 7	1185		2200	2550
18 3	SEA-GULL	OP	RNBT	FBG TR	IO 140-188	7 2	1920		3150	3750
					1972 BOATS					
16 1	SEA-LANCER 1681	OP	RNBT	FBG DV	IO 120-140	6 9	1650		2550	2950
16 1	SEA-LANCER 1681 BR	OP	RNBT	FBG DV	IO 120-140	6 9	1650		2600	3050
16 3	SEA-HAWK 1679	OP	RNBT	FBG TR	OB	6 7	1040		1950	2350
16 3	SEA-HAWK 1679	OP	RNBT	FBG TR	IO 120-140	6 7			2650	3100
18 3	SEA-GULL 1886	OP	RNBT	FBG DV	IO 120-165	7 2	1685		3100	3800
18 3	SEA-GULL 1886	OP	RNBT	FBG TR	OB	7 2	975		2000	2350
					1971 BOATS					
16 1	SEA-LANCER	OP	RNBT	FBG DV	IO 120-140	6 9	1650		2600	3250
16 1	SEA-LANCER BR	OP	RNBT	FBG DV	IO 120-140	6 9	1650		2700	3150
18 3	SEA-GULL	OP	RNBT	FBG DV	IO 120-165	7 2	1685		3200	3950
18 3	SEA-GULL	OP	RNBT	FBG TR	OB	7 2	975		2000	2350
					1970 BOATS					
16 1	SEA-LANCER 1681	OP	RNBT	FBG DV	IO 120	6 9	1590		2700	3150
17 4	SEA-GULL 1882	OP	RNBT	FBG TR	OB	6 10	975		1900	2300
17 4	SEA-GULL 1882	OP	RNBT	FBG TR	IO 120	6 10	1750		3100	3600
					1969 BOATS					
17 4	SEA-GULL	OP	RNBT	FBG TR	OB	6 10	950		1900	2250
17 4	SEA-GULL 1882	OP	RNBT	FBG TR	IO 120 MRCR	6 10	1750	7	3200	3700
					1968 BOATS					
16	SEA-LANCER 80C	OP	RNBT	FBG DV	IO 80 MRCR	6 6	1300	5	2550	3000
16	SEA-LANCER 80M	OP	RNBT	FBG DV	IO 80 CHRY	6 6	1300	5	2550	2950
17	SEA-SKIFF	OP	RNBT	FBG SV	OB	7	875	5	1750	2050
17 4	SEA-GULL	OP	RNBT	FBG SV	IO 120 OMC	7	1650	5	3150	3650
17 4	SEA-GULL	OP	RNBT	FBG TR	OB	6 10	1050	5	1900	2250
17 4	SEA-GULL	OP	RNBT	FBG TR	IO 120 OMC	6 10	1750	5	3250	3800
					1967 BOATS					
16	SEA-LANCER	OP	RNBT	FBG DV	IO 120	6 6	1300		2650	3050
16	SEA-LANCER 80C	OP	RNBT	FBG DV	IO 80	6 6	1300		2650	3100
16	SEA-LANCER 80M	OP	RNBT	FBG DV	IO 80	6 6	1300		2600	3050
17	SEA-SKIFF	OP	RNBT	FBG SV	OB	7	875		1750	2050
17	SEA-SKIFF	OP	RNBT	FBG SV	IO 120	7	1650		3300	3850
					1966 BOATS					
16	SEA-LANCER II	OP	RNBT	FBG DV	IO 120	6 6	800		2300	2650
17	SEA-SKIFF	OP	RNBT	FBG SV	OB	7	875		1750	2050
17	SEA-SKIFF	OP	RNBT	FBG SV	IO 120	7	1050		2950	3450
17 8	SEAFARER	OP	RNBT	FBG	OB	7	875		1800	2100
					1965 BOATS					
17	SEA-SKIFF	OP	RNBT	FBG SV	OB	7	875		1750	2050
17	SEA-SKIFF	OP	RNBT	FBG SV	IO 120	7	1050		3050	3550
17 9	CATALINA	OP	CBNCR	FBG DV	OB	6 10	950		1900	2250

SEA SPRITE COMPANY

WICKFORD SHIPYARD
N KINGSTOWN RI 02852   COAST GUARD MFG ID- WSY   See inside cover to adjust price for area

LOA FT IN	NAME AND/ OR MODEL	TOP/ RIG	BOAT TYPE	-HULL- MTL TP	----ENGINE--- TP # HP MFG	BEAM FT IN	WGT LBS	DRAFT FT IN	RETAIL LOW	RETAIL HIGH
					1979 BOATS					
22 6	SEA-SPRITE	SLP	SA/CR	FBG KL	OB	7	3350	3	6000	6900
					1978 BOATS					
22 6	SEA-SPRITE	SLP	SA/CR	FBG KL	OB	7	3350	3	5750	6650
					1977 BOATS					
22 6	SEA-SPRITE	SLP	SA/CR	FBG KL	OB	7	3350	3	5550	6400
22 6	SEA-SPRITE	SLP	SA/CR	FBG KL	IB 7D WEST	7	3350	3	6500	7450
					1976 BOATS					
22 6	ALBERG	SLP	SAIL	FBG KL	OB	7	3350	3	5400	6200
22 6	ALBERG	SLP	SAIL	FBG KL	IB 5D WEST	7	3350	3	6250	7200
					1975 BOATS					
22 6	SEA-SPRITE	SLP	SAIL	FBG KL	OB	7	3350	3	5200	6000
					1974 BOATS					
22 6	SEA-SPRITE	SLP	SAIL	FBG KL	OB	7	3350	3	5050	5850
					1973 BOATS					
22 6	SEA-SPRITE	SLP	SAIL	FBG KL	OB	7	3350	3	4950	5650
					1972 BOATS					
22 6	SEA-SPRITE	SLP	SAIL	FBG KL	OB	7	3350	3	4200	4900
22 6	SEA-SPRITE RACER	SLP	SAIL	FBG KL	OB	7	3350	3	5400	6200
					1970 BOATS					
22 6	SEA-SPRITE	SLP	SAIL	FBG KL	OB	7	3350	3	4650	5300
22 6	SEA-SPRITE	SLP	SAIL	FBG KL	IB D	7	3350	3	5400	6250
					1969 BOATS					
22 6	SEA-SPRITE	SLP	SAIL	FBG KL	OB	7	3350	3	4550	5250

SEA STAR BOATS INC

MIAMI FL 33166   COAST GUARD MFG ID- SSR See inside cover to adjust price for area

LOA FT IN	NAME AND/ OR MODEL	TOP/ RIG	BOAT TYPE	-HULL- MTL TP	----ENGINE--- TP # HP MFG	BEAM FT IN	WGT LBS	DRAFT FT IN	RETAIL LOW	RETAIL HIGH
					1975 BOATS					
23 2	24 CONV BASIC	OP	CUD	FBG SV	IO 165 OMC	7 10	3300	2 2	4250	4950
23 2	24 CONV CUSTOM	OP	CUD	FBG SV	IO 165 OMC	7 10	3300	2 2	4650	5350

```
SEA STAR BOATS INC          -CONTINUED     See inside cover to adjust price for area
  LOA   NAME AND/            TOP/ BOAT  -HULL- ----ENGINE--- BEAM   WGT  DRAFT RETAIL RETAIL
FT IN   OR MODEL             RIG  TYPE  MTL TP TP # HP  MFG  FT IN  LBS  FT IN  LOW   HIGH
------------------- 1975 BOATS ---------------------------------------------------------
23  2 24 CONV DELUXE         OP   CUD   FBG SV IO 225  OMC  7 10   3300  2  2   4700  5400
23  2 24 FB BASIC            FB   SF    FBG SV IO 225  OMC  7 10   4300  2  2   5900  6750
23  2 24 FB CUSTOM           FB   SF    FBG SV IO 225  OMC  7 10   4300  2  2   6550  7500
23  2 24 FB DELUXE           FB   SF    FBG SV IO 225  OMC  7 10   4300  2  2   7000  8050
23  2 24 HT BASIC            HT   EXP   FBG SV IO 165  OMC  7 10   3900  2  2   5000  5750
23  2 24 HT CUSTOM           HT   EXP   FBG SV IO 165  OMC  7 10   3900  2  2   5350  6150
23  2 24 HT DELUXE           HT   EXP   FBG SV IO 225  OMC  7 10   3900  2  2   5300  6050
23  2 24 SDN CONV BASIC      OP   CUD   FBG SV IO 165  OMC  7 10   3500  2  2   4800  5500
23  2 24 SDN CONV CUSTOM     OP   CUD   FBG SV IO 165  OMC  7 10   3300  2  2   4850  5600
23  2 24 SDN CONV DELUXE     OP   CUD   FBG SV IO 225  OMC  7 10   3500  2  2   4900  5600
28  7 29 CONVERTIBLE         OP   CUD   FBG SV VD T230 OMC 10 10   8500  2 10  11900 13500
28  7 29 FLYBRIDGE           FB   SF    FBG SV VD T230 OMC 10 10  10500  2 10  13000 14800

28  7 29 HARDTOP             HT   EXP   FBG SV VD T230 OMC 10 10   9000  2 10  12100 13800
```

SEA VEE BOATS

```
MIAMI FL 33150              COAST GUARD MFG ID- SXJ See inside cover to adjust price for area

        For more recent years, see the BUC Used Boat Price Guide, Volume 1 or Volume 2

  LOA   NAME AND/            TOP/ BOAT  -HULL- ----ENGINE--- BEAM   WGT  DRAFT RETAIL RETAIL
FT IN   OR MODEL             RIG  TYPE  MTL TP TP # HP  MFG  FT IN  LBS  FT IN  LOW   HIGH
------------------- 1982 BOATS ---------------------------------------------------------
25      SEA-VEE 25           OP   CUD   FBG DV OB        8          5000  2  8  13200 15000
25      SEA-VEE 25           OP   CUD   FBG DV IB 270-350  8        5000  2  8  14200 16900
        IB 200D PERK  20100 22400, IB  300D CAT  22900   25400, IB T170 MRCR 15100 17100

25      SEA-VEE 25           TT   CUD   FBG DV OB        8          5000  2  8  13600 15400
25      SEA-VEE 25           TT   CUD   FBG DV IB 270-350  8        5000  2  8  14200 16900
        IB 200D PERK  20100 22400, IB  300D CAT  22900   25400, IB T170 MRCR 15100 17100

25      SEA-VEE 25           OP   OPFSH FBG DV OB        8          5000  2  8  12000 13700
25      SEA-VEE 25           OP   OPFSH FBG DV IB 270-350  8        5000  2  8  14100 16700
        IB 200D PERK  19800 22000, IB  300D CAT  22500   25000, IB T170 MRCR 14900 17000

25      SEA-VEE 25           TT   OPFSH FBG DV OB        8          5000  2  8  13400 15200
25      SEA-VEE 25           TT   OPFSH FBG DV IB 220-350  8        5000  2  8  13800 16700
        IB 200D PERK  19800 22000, IB  300D CAT  22500   25000, IB T170 MRCR 14900 17000

25      SEA-VEE 25           ST   RNBT  FBG DV OB        8          5000  2  8  13400 15300
25      SEA-VEE 25           ST   RNBT  FBG DV IB 270-350  8        5000  2  8  14100 16700
        IB 200D PERK  19800 22000, IB  300D CAT  22500   25000, IB T170 MRCR 14900 17000
------------------- 1981 BOATS ---------------------------------------------------------
25  6 SEA-VEE 25             OP   CUD   FBG DV OB        8          5000  2  8  13600 15400
25  6 SEA-VEE 25             OP   CUD   FBG DV IB 270-350  8        5000  2  8  14000 16700
        IB 200D PERK  19400 21500, IB  300D CAT  22100   24600, IB T170 MRCR 14900 16900

25  6 SEA-VEE 25             TT   CUD   FBG DV OB        8          5000  2  8  13600 15500
25  6 SEA-VEE 25             TT   CUD   FBG DV IB 270-350  8        5000  2  8  14000 16700
        IB 200D PERK  19400 21500, IB  300D CAT  22100   24600, IB T170 MRCR 14900 16900

25  6 SEA-VEE 25             OP   OPFSH FBG DV OB        8          5000  2  8  12900 14700
25  6 SEA-VEE 25             OP   OPFSH FBG DV IB 270-350  8        5000  2  8  13800 16400
        IB 200D PERK  19200 21300, IB  300D CAT  21600   24100, IB T170 MRCR 14600 16600

25  6 SEA-VEE 25             TT   OPFSH FBG DV OB        8          5000  2  8  13200 15000
25  6 SEA-VEE 25             TT   OPFSH FBG DV IB 220-350  8        5000  2  8  13400 16400
        IB 200D PERK  19200 21300, IB  300D CAT  21600   24100, IB T170 MRCR 14600 16600

25  6 SEA-VEE 25             ST   RNBT  FBG DV OB        8          5000  2  8  13600 15500
25  6 SEA-VEE 25             ST   RNBT  FBG DV IB 270-350  8        5000  2  8  13800 16400
        IB 200D PERK  19200 21300, IB  300D CAT  21600   24100, IB T170 MRCR 14600 16600
------------------- 1977 BOATS ---------------------------------------------------------
25      RAMPONE 25           OP   OPFSH FBG DV IO 185-215  8        4500  2  5  10800 12500
        IO 225  COMM  11000 12500, IB 225  COMM 10300 11700, IO 250  CC  11300 12800
        IB 250  CC    10400 11800, IO 255  COMM 11200 12800, IB 255  COMM 10400 11800
        IO 300  CC    11900 13500, IB 330  CC   10800 12300
```

SEA VIEW FLOATING HOMES INC
COAST GUARD MFG ID- SVH

Call 1-800-327-6929 for BUC Personalized Evaluation Service
Or, for 1970 to 1977 boats, sign onto www.BUCValuPro.com

SEABIRD
```
DIV OF P & L INDUSTRIES                     See inside cover to adjust price for area
PEMBROKE PARK FL           COAST GUARD MFG ID- VSL
                           FORMERLY SEABIRD INDUSTRIES

        For more recent years, see the BUC Used Boat Price Guide, Volume 1 or Volume 2

  LOA   NAME AND/            TOP/ BOAT  -HULL- ----ENGINE--- BEAM   WGT  DRAFT RETAIL RETAIL
FT IN   OR MODEL             RIG  TYPE  MTL TP TP # HP  MFG  FT IN  LBS  FT IN  LOW   HIGH
------------------- 1983 BOATS ---------------------------------------------------------
23  6 SEA-HAWK 24+           OP   CTRCN FBG DV OB        8          3000  2  7   7550  8650
23  6 SEA-HAWK 24+           OP   RNBT  FBG DV OB        8          3000  2  7   7550  8650
23  6 SEA-HAWK 24+           OP   RNBT  FBG DV SE      OMC          3900  2  7    **    **
23  6 SEA-HAWK 24+           OP   RNBT  FBG DV IO 225-228  8        3900  2  7   6300  7250
        IO 260  MRCR  6250  7200, IO 260  VLVO  6450  7450, IB 260-270  VLVO  8150  9400
        IB 124D VLVO 10600 12000, IO 130D VLVO  7350  8450, IO T138  VLVO  7000  8050

26      FALCON               FB   DV    FBG DV OB                            10800 12300
29  1 CONDOR 29+             FB   SF    FBG DV SE T    OMC 10  3   9500  2  4   **    **
29  1 CONDOR 29+             FB   SF    FBG DV IB T225-T270 10  3  9500  2  4  21900 25100
29  1 CONDOR 29+             FB   SF    FBG DV IBT124D-T210D 10  3 9500  2  4  27800 34600
29  1 CUSTOM 29+             OP   OPFSH FBG DV SE T    OMC 10  3        2  4   **    **
29  1 CUSTOM 29+             OP   OPFSH FBG DV IB T225-T270 10  3       2  4  19500 22400
29  1 CUSTOM 29+             OP   OPFSH FBG DV IBT200D-T158D 10 3       2  4  23000 26900
29  1 CUSTOM 29+             OP   OPFSH FBG DV IBT200D-T210D 10 3       2  4  23000 29300
36  1 EAGLE 36+              FB   SF    FBG DV IB T350  CRUS 13  6     2  6  56900 63300
        IB T270D CUM 66600 73200, IB T300D CAT  69200 76000, IB T320D CUM  68700 75500

42  1 GOLDEN-EAGLE           FB   CR    FBG DV IB T300D CAT 14       28500  3  5 107000 117500
42  1 GOLDEN-EAGLE           FB   CR    FBG DV IB T320D     14       28500  3  5 106500 117000
42  1 GOLDEN-EAGLE           FB   SF    FBG DV IB T435D GM  14       28500  3  5 114000 125500
42  1 GOLDEN-EAGLE           FB   SF    FBG DV IB T300D CAT 14       28500  3  5 106500 117000
------------------- 1982 BOATS ---------------------------------------------------------
23  3 SEA-HAWK 24+           OP   SF    FBG DV IO 225-228  8        3900  2  7   7350  8450
        IO 260  MRCR  7350  8450, IO 260  VLVO  7550  8700, IB 260-270  VLVO  7650  8850
        IB 124D VLVO 10000 11400, IO 130D VLVO  9450 10700, IO T145  VLVO  8200  9450

23  6 SEA-HAWK 24+           OP   SF    FBG DV OB        8          3000  2  7   7400  8500
29      CONDOR 29+           FB   SF    FBG DV IB T220-T270 10  3   9500  2  4  20800 23900
29      CONDOR 29+           FB   SF    FBG DV IBT124D-T200D 10  3  9500  2  4  26700 32800
36      EAGLE 36+            FB   SF    FBG DV IB T270D CUM 13  6  22000  3  7  63300 69900
36      EAGLE 36+            FB   SF    FBG DV IB T320D CUM 13  6  22000  3  7  65200 71600
36  1 EAGLE 36+              FB   SF    FBG DV IB T350  CRUS 13  6 22000  3  6  55000 60500
42      SEABIRD-SPORT 42     FB   SF    FBG DV IO R370  CHEV 10  9 12500  3  5  54900 60300
42  1 GOLDEN-EAGLE           FB   CR    FBG DV IB T320D CUM 14      28500  3  5 101000 111000
42  1 GOLDEN-EAGLE           FB   CR    FBG DV IB T435D GM  14      28500  3  5 109000 119500
42  1 GOLDEN-EAGLE           FB   SF    FBG DV IB T300D CAT 14      28500  3  5 101500 111500
------------------- 1981 BOATS ---------------------------------------------------------
23  3 SEA-HAWK 24+           OP   SF    FBG DV OB        8          3900  2  7   8550  9800
23  3 SEA-HAWK 24+           OP   SF    FBG DV IO 220  BMW  8       3900  2  7   7300  8400
        IB 220  BMW   7150  8250, IO 225-228    7250  8350, IO 260  MRCR  7200  8300
        IO 260  VLVO  7450  8550, IB 260-270    7450  8450, IB 124D VLVO  9600 10900
        IO 130D VLVO  9350 10600, IB 200D CHRY 10800 12300, IO T145  VLVO  8100  9300

29      CONDOR 29+           FB   SF    FBG DV IB T220-T270 10  3   9500  2  4  19900 22900
29      CONDOR 29+           FB   SF    FBG DV IBT124D-T200D 10  3  9500  2  4  25700 31600
36      EAGLE 36+            FB   SF    FBG DV IB T350  CRUS 13  6  22000  3  7  52100 57200
        IB T270D CUM 60300 66300, IB T285D REN  61100 67100, IB T320D CUM  62200 68300

42      GOLDEN-EAGLE         FB   CR    FBG DV IB T300D CAT 14      28500  3  5  97400 107000
42      GOLDEN-EAGLE         FB   CR    FBG DV IB T320D CUM 14      28500  3  5 104000 114000
42      GOLDEN-EAGLE         FB   CR    FBG DV IB T435D GM  14      28500  3  5 103500 114000
------------------- 1980 BOATS ---------------------------------------------------------
23  3 SEA-HAWK 23+           FB   CUD   FBG DV IO        8                         8400  9700
23  3 SEA-HAWK 23+           OP   SF    FBG DV IO 130D   8                         7650  8800
23  8 SEA-HAWK 24+           TT   SF    FBG DV OB        8          4300  2  4   9300 10600
23  8 SEA-HAWK 24+           TT   SF    FBG DV IO 270  CRUS 8       4500  2  4   8200  9400
23  8 SEA-HAWK 24+           TT   SF    FBG DV IO 234D VLVO 8       4700  2  4  10600 12000
29      CONDOR 29+           FB   SF    FBG DV IB T220-T270 10  3   9500  2  4  19100 21900
29      CONDOR 29+           FB   SF    FBG DV IBT124D-T150D 10  3  9500  2  4  24700 28600
36      EAGLE 36             FB   SF    FBG DV IB 235     13  6            3  7  42400 47100
36      EAGLE 36             FB   SF    FBG DV IB T260D BENZ 13  6 19000  3  7  52300 57500
        IB T260D GM  52300 57500, IB T270D CUM 52400 57600, IB T270D VLVO 51800 56900
------------------- 1979 BOATS ---------------------------------------------------------
23  3 SEA-HAWK 23+           ST   RNBT  FBG DV IO 225-260  8        3900  2  7   8300  9550
23  3 SEA-HAWK 23+           ST   RNBT  FBG DV OB        8          3900  2  7   5750  6950
        IO 290-330    6300  7450, IO 130D VLVO  6900  7950, IO T140-T225  6600  7900


96th ed. - Vol. III          CONTINUED ON NEXT PAGE                           525
```

```
    LOA  NAME AND/        TOP/ BOAT  -HULL-  ----ENGINE---  BEAM  WGT   DRAFT RETAIL RETAIL
    FT IN  OR MODEL        RIG TYPE  MTL TP TP # HP  MFG    FT IN LBS   FT IN  LOW   HIGH
---------------------------- 1979 BOATS ----------------------------------------
29   CONDOR 29+          FB  SF   FBG DV IB T220-T270  10  3  8500  2 4 17200 20200
29   CONDOR 29+          FB  SF   FBG DV IBT124D-T130D 10  3  8500  2 4 21900 24800
36   EAGLE 36            FB  SF   FBG DV IB T      OMC 13  6 19000  3 7  **    **
     IB T330 MRCR 42800  47500, IB T350  CRUS 43300 48100, IB T  D GM   **    **
     IB T240D REN 49400  54200, IB T270D CAT  51100 56100
---------------------------- 1978 BOATS ----------------------------------------
28  3 CRUISER            FB  CR   FBG DV TD T220-T270   10 2  8500  2 2 15600 18200
28  3 CRUISER            FB  CR   FBG DV TDT124D-T200D  10 2  8500  2 2 20500 25600
28  3 CRUISER            FB  CR   FBG DV TD T210D REN   10 2  8500  2 2 23300 25900
28  3 RUNABOUT           OP  CUD  FBG DV TD T220-T270   10 2  8000  2 2 15100 17800
28  3 RUNABOUT           OP  CUD  FBG DV TDT124D-T130D  10 2  8000  2 2 19500 22200
28  3 RUNABOUT           OP  CUD  FBG DV TDT200D-T210D  10 2  8000  2 2 22100 24900
---------------------------- 1976 BOATS ----------------------------------------
20  9 FISHERMAN          OP  FSH  F/S DV OD           /  4  1810  2 4  4100  4750
20  9 FISHERMAN          OP  FSH  F/S DV IO  165      7  4  2560  2 4  4250  5200
20  9 FISHERMAN          OP  FSH  F/S DV IO 170-235   7  4        2 4  4700  5400
20  9 RUNABOUT           ST  RNBT F/S DV OB           7  4  1920  2 4  4250  4950
20  9 RUNABOUT           ST  RNBT F/S DV IO  165      7  4  2670  2 4  3950  4800
20  9 RUNABOUT           ST  RNBT F/S DV IO 170-235   7  4        2 4  4350  5000
22    FISHERMAN          OP  FSH  FBG SV OB           8     1975        9  4650  5350
22    FISHERMAN          OP  FSH  FBG SV IO  165 MRCR 8     2725        9  4650  5350
22    FISHERMAN          OP  FSH  FBG SV IO 165-235   8                 9  5850  6950
22    FISHERMAN DELUXE   OP  FSH  FBG SV OB           8                 9  7100  8150
22    FISHERMAN DELUXE   OP  FSH  FBG SV IO  165 MRCR 8     2725        9  5200  6000
22    FISHERMAN DELUXE   OP  FSH  FBG SV IO 165-235   8                 9  6550  7800

23  3 23 PLUS            ST  RNBT FBG DV IO 188-280   8     3900  2 8  5950  7250
23  3 23 PLUS            ST  RNBT FBG DV IO T140-T170 8     4325  2 8  8450  8450
26    WEEKEND FISHERMAN      FSH  FBG DV IB  255      9  9        8550  9800
28  3 FISHERMAN          FB  SF   FBG DV IB T230-T233 10        2 4 14600 16500
28  3 FLYBRIDGE CRUISER  FB  CR   FBG DV IB T230      10           14200 16200
28  3 RUNABOUT           ST  RNBT FBG DV IO T230-T233 10        2 4 12800 14600
28  3 RUNABOUT FISH LTD ED ST RNBT FBG DV IO T230-T233 10      2 4 11400 16300
28  3 RUNABOUT SPORT     ST  RNBT FBG DV IO T230-T233 10        2 4 13600 15500
28  3 RUNABOUT SPORT SPEC ST RNBT FBG DV IO T230-T233 10       2 4 14700 16800
36    CONVERTIBLE            CR   FBG DV IB T350      13           38500 42400
36    SEA-BIRD 36           SF   FBG DV IB T350      13  6     3 6 36300 40400
---------------------------- 1975 BOATS ----------------------------------------
20  9 CORMORANT V21      OP  FSH  FBG DV OB           7  4  1400  2 4  3300  3850
20  9 CORMORANT V21      OP  FSH  FBG DV IO 140-165   7  4  2150  2 4  4000  4700
20  9 GULL V21           OP  RNBT FBG DV OB           7  4  2100  2 4  4050  4750
20  9 GULL V21           OP  RNBT FBG DV IO 120-165   7  4  2800  2 4  4100  4850
20  9 SHEARWATER V21     OP  RNBT FBG DV IO 165       7  4  2100  2 4  5000  5750
20  9 SHEARWATER V21     OP  RNBT FBG DV IO 165       7  4  2800  2 4  4550  5200
22    MARINER 22         OP  FSH  FBG SV OB           8        1778        9  4200  4900
22    MARINER 22         OP  FSH  FBG SV IO 165-170   8        1778        9  4350  5250
23  3 CORMORANT V24      OP  FSH  FBG DV IO 165-233   8        3000  2 7  6700  7700
23  3 CORMORANT V24      OP  FSH  FBG DV IO T140      8        3000  2 7  5750  6800
23  3 CORMORANT V24      OP  FSH  FBG DV IO T140      8        3000  2 7  6600  7550

23  3 SEA-FALCON SEV24   ST  RNBT FBG DV IO 225-233   8        3500  2 8  6150  7050
23  3 SEA-FALCON SEV24   ST  RNBT FBG DV IO T140      8        3500  2 8  6750  7750
23  3 SEA-FALCON V24     ST  RNBT FBG DV IO 225-233   8        3500  2 8  5550  6500
23  3 SEA-FALCON V24     ST  RNBT FBG DV IO T140      8        3500  2 8  6350  7300
23  3 SEA-FALCON WKNDR V24 ST RNBT FBG DV IO 225-233  8        3500  2 8  5600  6550
23  3 SEA-FALCON WKNDR V24 ST RNBT FBG DV IO T140     8        3500  2 8  6400  7350
23  3 SHEARWATER V24     ST  RNBT FBG DV OB           8        3200  2 7  7050  8100
23  3 SHEARWATER V24     ST  RNBT FBG DV IO 188-233   8        3200  2 7  5400  6300
23  3 SHEARWATER V24     ST  RNBT FBG DV IO T140      8        3200  2 7  6050  7000
23  3 SHEARWATER V24     HT  SDN  FBG DV IO 225-233   8        4000  2 8  6750  7800
23  3 SHEARWATER V24     HT  SDN  FBG DV IO T140      8        4000  2 8  7450  8550

23  3 SHEARWATER V24     FB  SDN  FBG DV IO 225-233   8        4500  2 8  7350  8550
23  3 SHEARWATER V24     FB  SDN  FBG DV IO T140      8        4500  2 8  8050  9250
28  3 ALBATROSS V28      ST  RNBT FBG DV IO T225 OMC  10       7500  2 8 11900 13500
     VD T230  OMC 12800  14600, IO T233 MRCR 12000 13700, VD T233  MRCR 14400 14440

28  3 ALBATROSS V28      HT  SDN  FBG DV IO T225 OMC  10       8400  2 8 17200 19600
     VD T230  OMC 15100  17100, IO T233 MRCR 17400 19700, VD T233  MRCR 14900 17000

28  3 ALBATROSS V28      FB  SF   FBG DV IO T225 OMC  10       8800  2 8 18800 20900
     VD T230  OMC 14300  16300, IO T233 MRCR 19000 21100, VD T233  MRCR 14200 16100

36    EAGLE V36          FB  SDN  FBG DV IO           14  4 19000  3 7  **    **
---------------------------- 1974 BOATS ----------------------------------------
20  9 CORMORANT V-21                 FBG       OB           7  4  1400  2 4  3300  3800
20  9 CORMORANT V-21                 FBG       OB 165-225   7  4  2150  2 4  3750  4500
20  9 MARINER             FSH        FBG       OB           7  4  1400  2 4  3300  3800
20  9 MARINER             FSH        FBG       IO  165      7  4        2 4  4850  5550
20  9 MARINER             FSH        FBG       IO  340      7  4        2 4  6050  6950
20  9 SHEARWATER V-21                FBG       OB           7  4  2100  2 4  4550  5250
20  9 SHEARWATER V-21                FBG       IO 165-225   7  4  2800  2 4  4300  5100
23  3 CORMORANT V-24                 FBG       OB           8     3000  2 7  6700  7700
23  3 CORMORANT V-24                 FBG       IO 165-188   8     3200  2 7  5450  6300
     IO 225 CHRY  5500  6350, IO 225 OMC  5350  6150, VD 225 CHRY 4550 5200
     IO 245 OMC   5600  6400, IO 250 CHRY 5650  6500, VD 250 CHRY 4550 5250
     IO T130-T170 6500  7450

23  3 MARINER             FSH        FBG       IO  165      8        2 7  7150  8200
23  3 MARINER             FSH        FBG       IO  340      8        2 7  8350  9600
23  3 SEA-FALCON S/E V-24            FBG       IO  188 MRCR 8   3500 2 8  6600  7600
     IO 225 CHRY  6650  7600, IO 225 MRCR 6800  7800, IO 225 OMC  6500 7450
     VD 225 CHRY  5400  6200, IO 245 OMC  6700  7700, IO 250 CHRY 6750 7750
     VD 250 CHRY  5400  6250, IO T130-T170 7200 8350

23  3 SEA-FALCON V-24                FBG       OB           8     3500  2 8  7450  8550
23  3 SEA-FALCON V-24                FBG       IO 165-188   8     3500  2 8  5950  6850
     IO 225 CHRY  5450  6250, IO 225 MRCR 5600  6450, IO 225 OMC  5300 6050
     VD 225 CHRY  4500  5150, IO 245 OMC  5500  6300, IO 250 CHRY 5550 6400
     VD 250 CHRY  4500  5200, IO T130-T170 6150 7300

23  3 SHEARWATER S/C V-24            FBG       IO 225-250   8     4000  2 8  6650  7750
23  3 SHEARWATER S/C V-24            FBG       IO T130-T170 8     4000  2 8  7300  8450
23  3 SHEARWATER V-24                FBG       OB           8     3200  2 7  7000  8050
23  3 SHEARWATER V-24                FBG       IO 165-188   8     3200  2 7  5850  6700
     IO 225 CHRY  5850  6700, IO 225 MRCR 6050  6950, IO 225 OMC  5700 6550
     VD 225 CHRY  4800  5500, IO 245 OMC  5900  6800, IO 250 CHRY 5950 6850
     VD 250 CHRY  4800  5500, IO T130-T170 6200 7600

28    MARABOU             EXP        FBG       IO T225     10       15900 18100
28    MARABOU             EXP        FBG       IB T225     10       12700 14500
28    MARABOU             SF         FBG       IO T225     10       18600 20600
28    MARABOU             SF         FBG       IB T225     10       12700 14400
28  3 ALBATROSS E/C V-28             FBG       IO T225 CHRY 10    8400 2 8 18200 20300
     IO T225 MRCR 18600 20700, IO T225 OMC  17500 19800, VD T225     13400 15400

28  3 ALBATROSS S/C V-28             FBG       IO T225 CHRY 10    8400 2 8 16800 19100
     IO T225 MRCR 17200 19500, IO T225 OMC  16400 18700, VD T225     12600 14500
     VD T210D SABR 21600

28  3 ALBATROSS V-28     RNBT        FBG       IO T170 CHRY 10    7500 2 8 11800 13400
     IO T225 CHRY 12300 14000, VD T225 MRCR 12300 14000, IO T225 OMC  12300 14000
     VD T225      12100 14000

28  3 ALBATROSS V-28     SF          FBG       IO T225 CHRY 10    8800 2 8 19100 21300
     IO T225 MRCR 19100 21300, IO T225 OMC  19100 21200, VD T225     13200 15200
     VD T210D SABR 20000 22200

28  3 MARINER             FSH        FBG       IO T225     10       2 8 17100 19400
36    EAGLE V-36          FB         FBG       IB T300  CC 13  6 19000 3 6 34900 38800
     IB T330 CHRY 35200 39100, IB T203D CAT  40700 45200, IB T210D SABR 39400 43700
     IB T250D SABR 40200 44600
---------------------------- 1973 BOATS ----------------------------------------
20  9 MARINER V-21                   FBG       OB           7  4        2 4  3250  3800
20  9 MARINER V-21                   FBG       OB 165-260   7  4  2150  2 4  3850  4800
20  9 V21                 RNBT       FBG       IO 165-260   7  4  2800  2 4  4550  5200
20  9 V21                 RNBT       FBG       IO 165-260   7  4  2800  2 4  5450  5450
23  3 ISLANDIA V24                   FBG       IO 225-245   8     3300  2 7  5850  5100
23  3 MARINER V-24                   FBG       IO 165-260   8     3000  2 7  5650  6550
23  3 MARINER V-24                   FBG       IO T120-T170 8     3000  2 7  6250  7300
23  3 SUPERSPORT V24                 FBG       IO 188-260   8     3500  2 8  6150  7350
23  3 SUPERSPORT V24                 FBG       IO T120-T170 8     3500  2 8  6900  8000
23  3 V24                 RNBT       FBG       IO 165-260   8     3200  2 7  5700  6900
23  3 V24                 RNBT       FBG       IO T120-T170 8     3200  2 7  6450  7500

23  3 V24             HT  RNBT       FBG       IO 225-260   8              2 7  6700  7850
23  3 V24             HT  RNBT       FBG       IO T120-T170 8              2 7  7300  8450
23  3 V24             FB  RNBT       FBG       IO 225-260   8     3700  2 7  6450  7550
23  3 V24             FB  RNBT       FBG       IO T120-T170 8     3700  2 7  7050  8200
23  3 V24                 SDN        FBG       IO 225-255   8     4000  2 8  7250  8450
23  3 V24                 SDN        FBG       IO T120-T170 8     4000  2 8  7900  9150
23  3 V24             FB  SDN        FBG       IO 225-260   8     4500  2 8  7900  9300
23  3 V24             FB  SDN        FBG       IO T120-T170 8     4500  2 8  8600  9950
23  6 V24             FB  SDN        FBG       IO  188 MRCR 8     4500  2 8  7950  9100
28  3 V28                 EXP        FBG       IO 260 CHRY 10     8400  2 8 15400 17500
```

```
  LOA  NAME AND/         TOP/ BOAT -HULL- ----ENGINE--- BEAM  WGT  DRAFT RETAIL RETAIL
  FT IN OR MODEL         RIG  TYPE MTL TP TP # HP MFG    FT IN  LBS  FT IN  LOW   HIGH
------------------ 1973 BOATS ----------------------------------------------------------
28  3 V28              EXP   FBG    IO T225 MRCR 10       8400  2 8 16800 19100
28  3 V28              EXP   FBG    IO T225 OMC  10       8400  2 8 16800 19100
28  3 V28              EXP   FBG    VD T225      10       8400  2 8 12500 14400
28  3 V28              RNBT  FBG    IO 235  CHRY 10       7500  2 8 11400 13000
      IO T170  CHRY 12200 13900, IO T225 MRCR 12800 14500, IO T225 OMC 12700 14500
      VD T225-T255 11700 13600

28  3 V28              SDN   FBG    IO 235  CHRY 10       8400  2 8 16200 18500
      IO T225  MRCR 18800 20900, IO T225 OMC 18800 20900, VD T225 13700 15700

28  3 V28              FB SF FBG    IO T225 MRCR 10       8800  2 8 20000 22200
      IO T225  OMC  19900 22100, VD T225 13100 15000, IO T235 CHRY 20100 22400

36    V-36             FB SDN FBG   VD T280  CHRY 13 6 19000  3 7 33500 37200
36    V-36             FB SDN FBG   VD T330  CHRY 13 6 19000  3 7 34100 37900
36    V-36             FB SDN FBG   VD T225D CAT  13 6 20000  3 8 41000 45500
------------------ 1972 BOATS ----------------------------------------------------------
19    ANGLER V-19           FBG    OB           6 3  1600    10  3200  3700
19    SCORPION              FBG    IO 165-245   6 3  2000  2 1  2900  3550
19    SCORPION              FBG    IO 265  CHRY 6 3  2000  2 1  3200  3750
20  9 MARINER V-21          FBG    OB           7 4  2150  2 4  4600  5300
20  9 MARINER V-21          FBG    IO 120-265   7 4        2 4  4650  5700
20  9 V-21             RNBT FBG    OB           7 4  2800  2 4  5300  6100
20  9 V-21             RNBT FBG    IO 120-265   7 4        2 4  4750  5800
23  3 ISLANDIA V 24         FBG    IO 165-270   8    3300  2 7  6100  7400
23  3 ISLANDIA V 24         FBG    IO T120-T170 8    3300  2 7  6900  8000
23  3 MARINER V-24          FBG    IO 165-270   8    3200  2 7  5950  7250
23  3 MARINER V-24          FBG    IO T120-T170 8    3200  2 7  6750  7850
23  3 SUPERSPORT V-24   HT  FBG    IO 165-270   8         2 8  6850  8300

23  3 SUPERSPORT V-244      FBG    IO 165-270   8    3500  2 8  6350  7700
23  3 SUPERSPORT V-244      FBG    IO T120-T170 8         2 8  7650  8850
23  3 V-24             RNBT FBG    IO 165-270   8    3000  2 7  5700  6950
23  3 V-24             RNBT FBG    IO T120-T170 8         2 7  7550  8750
23  3 V-24         HT  RNBT FBG    IO 165-270   8         2 7  6800  8200
23  3 V-24         FB  RNBT FBG    IO 165-270   8         2 7  6800  8200
23  3 V-24         FB  RNBT FBG    IO T120-T170 8         2 7  7550  8750
23  3 V-24             SDN  FBG    IO 225-270   8    4000  2 8  7450  8850
23  3 V-24             SDN  FBG    IO T120-T170 8    4000  2 8  8200  9450
23  3 V-24         FB  SDN  FBG    IO 225-270   8    4500  2 8  8150  9700
23  3 V-24         FB  SDN  FBG    IO T120-T170 8    4500  2 8  9000  10300

28  3 V-28             FB CR FBG   IO T215 MRCR 10       8400  2 8 17300 19700
      VD T215  OMC  12200 13800, IO T225 OMC 17400 19800, VD T225 CHRY 12100 13800
      IO T235-T245 18000 20100, VD T250 OMC 12400 14100, IO T265 CHRY 12500 20500
      IO T270  MRCR 18600 20600, IO T270-T280 12500 14300, IO T325 MRCR 19400 21600

28  3 V-28             EXP   FBG   VD T215      10       8400  2 8 12000 13700
      IO T225  OMC  17300 19700, VD T225 CHRY 12000 13600, IO T235-T245 17500 20000
      VD T250  OMC  12400 14000, IO T265 CHRY 18400 20400, IO T270 MRCR 18500 20500
      VD T270-T280 12400 14200, IO T325 MRCR 19300 21500

28  3 V-28             HT EXP FBG  IO T215      10       8400  2 8 11900 13600
      IO T225  OMC  17200 19500, VD T225 CHRY 11900 13500, IO T235-T245 17400 19900
      VD T250  OMC  12300 13900, IO T265 CHRY 18200 20300, IO T270 MRCR 18300 20400
      VD T270  MRCR 12300 14000, IO T325 MRCR 19200 21300

28  3 V-28             RNBT  FBG   IO T165-T170 10            2 8 13100 15000
      VD T215  11600 13400, IO T225 OMC 13700 15600, VD T225 CHRY 11700 13300
      IO T235-T245 13800 15800, VD T250 OMC 12000 13700, IO T265 CHRY 14200 16100
      IO T270  MRCR 14300 16200, IO T270-T280 12100 13800, IO T325 MRCR 15100 17100

28  3 V-28             SDN   FBG   VD T215      10       8400  2 8 13100 15000
      IO T225  OMC  19200 21300, VD T225 CHRY 13200 15000, IO T235-T245 19400 21700
      VD T250  OMC  13600 15400, IO T265 CHRY 20000 22200, VD T270-T280 13700 15600
      IO T325  MRCR 20700 23000

28  3 V-28             SF    FBG   VD T215      10       8800  2 8 12200 14000
      IO T225  OMC  20400 22700, VD T225 CHRY 12200 13900, IO T235-T245 20600 23000
      VD T250  OMC  12600 14300, IO T265 CHRY 21100 23500, IO T270 MRCR 21200 23600
      VD T270-T280 12600 14400, IO T325 MRCR 22400 24900

35  9 V-36             SF    FBG   IB 270  MRCR 13 16000  3 1 26700 29600
      IB 280  CHRY 26700 29700, IB 325 MRCR 27000 29900, IB 330 CHRY 26900 29900
      IB 225D CAT 35000 38800
------------------ 1971 BOATS ----------------------------------------------------------
19    ANGLER V-19           FBG    OB           6 3  1600    10  3200  3700
19    SCORPION V-19         FBG    IO 155-235   6 3  2000  2 1  2950  3700
20  9 MARINER V-21          FBG    OB           7 4  2400  2 4  4900  5600
20  9 MARINER V-21          FBG    IO 120-215   7 4  2800  2 4  4750  5550
20  9 V-21             RNBT FBG    OB           7 4  2400  2 4  4900  5600
20  9 V-21             RNBT FBG    IO 120-215   7 4        2 4  4750  5600
23  3 ISLANDIA V 24         FBG    IO 155-215   8    3300  2 7  6250  7350
23  3 ISLANDIA V 24         FBG    IO T 90-T165 8    3300  2 7  7050  8250
23  3 MARINER V-24          FBG    IO 155  OMC  2    3300  2 7  4750  5500
23  3 MARINER V-24          FBG    IO 165-215   8    3200  2 7  6150  7200
23  3 MARINER V-24          FBG    IO T 90-T165 8    3200  2 7  6900  8100

23  3 SUPERSPORT V-244      FBG    IO 155-215   8    3500  2 8  6500  7650
23  3 SUPERSPORT V-244      FBG    IO T 90-T165 8    3500  2 8  7300  8500
23  3 V-24             RNBT FBG    IO 155-215   8    3000  2 7  5850  6850
23  3 V-24             RNBT FBG    IO T 90-T165 8    3000  2 7  6600  7700
23  3 V-24         HT  RNBT FBG    IO 155-215   8    3000  2 7  5850  6850
23  3 V-24         HT  RNBT FBG    IO T 90-T165 8    3000  2 7  6600  7700
23  3 V-24             SDN  FBG    IO 200-215   8    4000  2 8  7650  8850
23  3 V-24             SDN  FBG    IO T 90-T165 8    4000  2 8  7650  8850
23  3 V-24         FB  SDN  FBG    IO 200-215   8    4000  2 8  8350  9750
23  3 V-24         FB  SDN  FBG    IO T 90-T165 8    4000  2 8  8350  9750

28  3                  HT EXP FBG  IO T200 CHRY 10       8550  2 8 18100 20200
      VD T210  OMC  11700 13300, IO T215 MRCR 18400 20400, VD T215 OMC 18300 20400
      VD T215-T225 11600 13200, IO T235 OMC 18600 20700, VD T250 OMC 12000 13600
      IO T270  MRCR 19000 21100, IO T270-T280 12000 13700, IO T325 MRCR 20100 22300

28  3 V-28             FB CR FBG   IO T200 CHRY 10       8400  2 8 18100 20100
      IO T215  OMC  18300 20300, IO T215 MRCR 18300 20300, VD T215-T225 11600 13300
      IO T235  OMC  18600 20600, VD T250 OMC 12000 13600, IO T270 MRCR 19100 21300
      VD T270-T280 12000 13700, IO T325 MRCR 20000 22300

28  3 V-28             EXP   FBG   IO T200 CHRY 10       8400  2 8 17600 20000
      VD T210  OMC  11700 13100, IO T215 MRCR 18200 20200, VD T215 OMC 18200 20200
      VD T215-T225 11500 13100, IO T235 OMC 18500 20500, VD T250 OMC 11900 13500
      IO T270  MRCR 19100 21200, IO T270-T280 11900 13600, IO T325 MRCR 19900 22200

28  3 V-28             HT EXP FBG DV IB T155   10                10900 12300
28  3 V-28             EXP   FBG DV IB T155    10                10900 12300
28  3                  RNBT  FBG DV IB T155    10                11100 12300
28  3                  SDN   FBG   IO T200 CHRY 10       8400  2 8 19400 21600
      VD T210  OMC  12600 14400, IO T215 MRCR 19700 21900, VD T215 OMC 19600 21800
      VD T215-T225 12600 14400, IO T235 OMC 20000 22200, VD T250 OMC 13100 14800
      IO T270  MRCR 20800 23100, IO T270-T280 13200 15000, IO T325 MRCR 21400 23700

28  3 V-28             SDN   FBG DV IB T155    10       8800  2 8 11800 13400
28  3 V-28             SF    FBG   IO T200 CHRY 10            2 8 20700 23000
      IO T215  OMC  21000 23300, VD T215 OMC 23600, VD T215-T225 11700 13400
      IO T235  OMC  21200 23600, VD T250 OMC 12100 13900, IO T270 MRCR 21900 24300
      VD T270-T280 12200 13900, IO T325 MRCR 23100 25700

28  3 V-28             SF    FBG DV IB T155    10            2 8 10800 12300
------------------ 1970 BOATS ----------------------------------------------------------
19    ANGLER V-19           FBG DV OB          6 3  1600    10  3200  3700
19    SCORPION V-19    SKI  FBG DV OB           6 3  2000  2 1  3450  4250
19    SCORPION V-19    SKI  FBG    IO 155-235   6 3  2000  2 1  3050  3750
20  9 V-21             RNBT FBG DV OB           7 4  2400  2 4  4900  5600
20  9 V-21             RNBT FBG DV IO 90-215    7 4  2800  2 4  4900  5800
23  3 ISLANDIA V 24    FSH  FBG DV IO 155-215   8    3300  2 7  7150  8400
23  3 ISLANDIA V 24    FSH  FBG DV IO T 90-T160 8    3300  2 7  8050  9450
23  3 MARINER V-24     FSH  FBG DV IO 155-215   8    3200  2 7  7050  8250
23  3 MARINER V-24     FSH  FBG DV IO T 90-T160 8    3200  2 7  7950  9250
23  3 SUPERSPORT V-244 FSH  FBG DV IO 155-215   8    3500  2 7  7450  8750
23  3 SUPERSPORT V-244 FSH  FBG DV IO T 90-T160 8    3500  2 8  8350  9750

23  3 V-24             EXP  FBG DV  IO 200  CHRY 8    4500  2 8  7900  9100
23  3 V-24             EXP  FBG DV  IO 210-270   8    4500  2 8  8650  10300
23  3 V-24             EXP  FBG DV  IO T120-T160 8    4500  2 8  9550  10900
23  3 V-24             RNBT FBG DV  IO 155-215   8    3000  2 7  6800  7950
23  3 V-24             RNBT FBG DV  IO T 90-T160 8    3000  2 7  6800  7950
23  3 V-24             SDN  FBG DV  IO 200-215   8    4000  2 8  8650  10100
23  3 V-24             SDN  FBG DV  IO T 90-T160 8    4000  2 8  8650  10100
23  3 V-24             SPTCR FBG DV IO 200-215   8    4800  2 8  9200  10500
23  3 V-24 2 SLEEPER   SPTCR FBG DV IO T120-T160 8    4800  2 8  10100 11400
23  3 V-24 2 SLEEPER   SPTCR FBG DV IO 200-215   8    4700  2 8  9050  10300
23  3 V-24 3 SLEEPER   SPTCR FBG DV IO T120-T160 8    4700  2 8  9850  11200

23  3 V-24 4 SLEEPER   SPTCR FBG DV IO 200-215   8    4500  2 8  8650  10000
23  3 V-24 4 SLEEPER   SPTCR FBG DV IO T120-T160 8    4500  2 8  9550  10900
```

```
LOA  NAME AND/        TOP/ BOAT -HULL- ----ENGINE--- BEAM  WGT  DRAFT RETAIL RETAIL
FT IN OR MODEL        RIG TYPE  MTL TP TP # HP  MFG   FT IN  LBS  FT IN  LOW    HIGH
----------------------- 1970 BOATS -----------------------------------------------
25 3 STILETTO V-25    RNBT FBG DV IO 200-270    8    4300 3 3   8500 10300
25 3 STILETTO V-25    RNBT FBG DV IO 325  MRCR  8    4300 3 3   9700 11000
28   V-28             EXP  FBG DV IB 390  MRCR 10    6000 3 4   9300 10600
28   V-28             EXP  FBG DV IB T    OMC  10    6000 3 4    **    **
----------------------- 1969 BOATS -----------------------------------------------
18 5 SKIFF V-185      RNBT FBG DV IO 120-175  7 2  2200 1 7   3550  4400
18 5 SKIFF V-185      RNBT FBG DV IO 200-210  7 2  2500 1 8   3900  4550
18 5 V-185            RNBT FBG    OB          7 2  1600        3150  3650
19   ANGLER V-19           FBG    IO 120 MRCR 7 3        2     3650  4250
19   ANGLER V-19      FSH  FBG    IO 120-225  7 3        2     3900  4800
19   SCORPION V-19    SKI  FBG DV IO 120-225  7 3  2000  2     3450  4200
20 2                  RNBT FBG DV IO 250 MRCR 8    3500 2 1   6000  6900
20 2 CATALINA V-202   RNBT FBG    IO 155-210  8    3200 2 1   5600  6900
     IO 225-260  6100 7450, IO 325  MRCR 7300  8400, IO 107D-111D  7500  8950
     IO T120     6100 7000

20 2 V-202            RNBT FBG DV IO 120-210  8    3000 2 1   5400  6700
     IO 225-260  6000 7000, IO 325  MRCR 6900  7900, IO 107D-141D  7100  8500
     IO T120     5750 6650

23 3 ISLANDIA V 24      CR  FBG DV IO 155-260  8    3300 2 6   7000  8500
     IO 325  MRCR 8150  9350, IO 107D-141D 9100 10700, IO T120-T160  8000  9250

23 3 MARINER V-24       CR  FBG DV IO 200  CHRY 8   3200 2 6   7000  8050
23 3 MARINER V-24       FSH FBG DV IO 155-210   8   3100 2 6   7100  8500
23 3 SUPERSPORT V-244   CR  FBG DV IO 155-260   8   3500 2 6   7300  8850
     IO 325  MRCR 8450  9700, IO 107D-141D 9400 11000, IO T120-T160  8250  9550

23 3 V-24               EXP FBG DV IO 155-260   8   4300 2 6   8500 10200
     IO 325  MRCR 9700 11000, IO 107D-141D 10600 12400, IO T120-T160  9550 10900

23 3 V-24               RNBT FBG DV IO 155-260  8   3000 2 6   6200  7550
     IO 325  MRCR 7300  8350, IO 107D-141D 8050  9650, IO T120-T160  7100  8250

23 3 V-24               SDN FBG DV IO 155-260   8   4200 2 6   8350 10100
     IO 325  MRCR 9550 10900, IO 107D-141D 10400 12200, IO T120-T160  9400 10700

25 3 STILETTO V-25      RNBT FBG DV IO 210-300  8   4200 2 7   8800 10800
     IO 325  MRCR 9850 11200, IO 107D-141D 9500 11400, IO T120-T225  9500 11700

26   V-26               RNBT FBG    IO 155-260  8          2 6  9200 11300
     IO 325  MRCR 10700 12100, IO 107D-141D 10900 13100, IO T120-T160 10200 12000

26   V-26               SDN FBG IO 210-325      8          2 6 14900 18500
26   V-26               SDN FBG IO 107D-141D    8          2 6 18100 20900
26   V-26               SDN FBG IO T120-T160    8          2 6 15600 18300
----------------------- 1968 BOATS -----------------------------------------------
18 5 SKIFF V-185    OP RNBT FBG IO 120-160  7 2  2200 1 7   3650  4400
18 5 SKIFF V-185    OP RNBT FBG IO 200      7 2  2500 1 8   4000  4700
18 5 V-185                FBG    OB         7 2  1600        3150  3650
20 2 CATALINA SKIFF    RNBT FBG IO 155-210  8    3200 2 1   5750  7050
20 2 CATALINA SKIFF    RNBT FBG IO 225      8    3500 2 1   6300  7250
20 2 SKIFF V-202    OP RNBT FBG IO 120-160  8    3000 2 1   5500  6550
20 2 SKIFF V-202    OP RNBT FBG IO 210-225  8    3300 2 1   6000  7100
23   BAHAMA SUPER SPORT RNBT FBG IO 155-225    8  3700 2 2   7300  9100
23   BAHAMA SUPER SPORT RNBT FBG IO T120-T160  8  4200 2 3   9050 10700
23   GULFSTREAM SKIFF FSH FBG IO 155-210       8  3200 2 1   7400  9050
23   GULFSTREAM SKIFF FSH FBG IO 225           8  3500 2 1   8050  9300
23   GULFSTREAM SKIFF FSH FBG IO T120-T160     8  3700 2 2   9350 11000

23   KEY-LARGO          SDN FBG IO 155-225     8  4300 2 3   8700 10700
23   KEY-LARGO          SDN FBG IO T120-T160   8  4800 2 4  10500 12400
23   KEY-LARGO SKIFF    RNBT FBG IO 155-210    8  3300 2 2   6750  8200
23   KEY-LARGO SKIFF    RNBT FBG IO 225        8  3600 2 2   7350  8450
23   KEY-LARGO SKIFF    RNBT FBG IO T120-T160  8  3800 2 3   8400 10000
26   KEY-LARGO          SDN FBG IO 210-225     8  5000 2 4  12300 14300
26   KEY-LARGO          SDN FBG IO T120-T160   8  5300 2 5  13500 16300
26   KEY-LARGO SKIFF    RNBT FBG IO 155-225    8  4000 2 3   8850 11100
26   KEY-LARGO SKIFF    RNBT FBG IO T120-T160  8  4500 2 4  10600 12700
----------------------- 1967 BOATS -----------------------------------------------
18 5 V-185                 FBG OB          1600   3150  3650
20 2 SKIFF V-202      RNBT  FBG IO 110     2600   5250  6000
23   BAHAMA SUPER SPORT    FBG IO 110      3400   7200  8250
23   GULFSTREAM SKIFF FSH  FBG IO 110      3000   7350  8450
23   KEY-LARGO        HT RNBT FBG IO 110   3500   7250  8350
23   KEY-LARGO             FBG IO 110      3800   8200  9400
23   KEY-LARGO        FB SF FBG IO 110     3800   9450 10700
23   KEY-LARGO SKIFF    RNBT FBG IO 110    3200   6850  7850
26   KEY-LARGO        FB CR FBG IO 110     4500  10600 12000
26   KEY-LARGO        HT RNBT FBG IO 110   3900   8850 10100
26   KEY-LARGO           SDN FBG IO 110    4200  10900 12400

26   KEY-LARGO        FB SF FBG IO 110     4200  11600 13200
26   KEY-LARGO SKIFF    RNBT FBG IO 110    3600   8400  9650
----------------------- 1966 BOATS -----------------------------------------------
18 5 V-185             RNBT FBG OB          7 2 1300   2750  3150
18 5 V-185             RNBT FBG IO 60-200   7 2        3900  4750
23   BAHAMA SUPER SPORT SPTCR FBG IO 165-225    8  2 2  8150  9550
23   BAHAMA SUPER SPORT SPTCR FBG IO 110-225    8  2 2  8650 10100
23   GULFSTREAM      HT SF FBG IO T 80-T120     8  2 2  9900 11500
23   GULFSTREAM      HT SF FBG IO 110-225       8  2 2  9700 11500
23   GULFSTREAM      FB SF FBG IO 110-225       8  2 2 11100 13100
23   GULFSTREAM      FB SF FBG IO T 80-T120     8  2 2  9950 11500
23   GULFSTREAM DELTA FB FBG IO 110-225         8  2 2 11100 13200
23   GULFSTREAM DELTA FB FBG IO T 80-T120       8  2 2  9300  9650

23   GULFSTREAM DELTA  CR FBG IO 110-225        2 2   9050 10400
23   GULFSTREAM DELTA  CR FBG IO T 80-T120      2 2  10000 12200
23   GULFSTREAM SKIFF FSH FBG IO 110-225        2 2   9200 10700
23   GULFSTREAM SKIFF FSH FBG IO T 80-T120      2 2  10200 12200
23   KEY-LARGO        EXP FBG IO 110-225        2 2   8600 10100
23   KEY-LARGO        EXP FBG IO T 80-T120      2 2   9700 11500
23   KEY-LARGO     FB EXP FBG IO 110-225        2 2   9800 10100
23   KEY-LARGO     FB EXP FBG IO T 80-T120      2 2   9700 11500
23   KEY-LARGO     HT RNBT FBG IO 110-150       2 2   8100  9350
23   KEY-LARGO     HT RNBT FBG IO T 80-T120     2 2   9100 10900
23   KEY-LARGO     FB RNBT FBG IO 110-225       2 2   8200  9550
23   KEY-LARGO     FB RNBT FBG IO T 80-T120     2 2   9100 10900

23   KEY-LARGO        SDN FBG IO 110-225        2 2   8650 10100
23   KEY-LARGO        SDN FBG IO T 80-T120      2 2   9700 11500
23   KEY-LARGO     FB SDN FBG IO 110-225        2 2   8650 10100
23   KEY-LARGO     FB SDN FBG IO T 80-T120      2 2   9700 11500
23   KEY-LARGO SKIFF   RNBT FBG IO 110-225      2 2   8100  9550
23   KEY-LARGO SKIFF   RNBT FBG IO T 80-T120    2 2   9200 10900
23   NASSAU CRUISETTE  CR FBG IO 110-225        2 2   8300  9800
23   NASSAU CRUISETTE  CR FBG IO T 80-T120      2 2   9450 11500
----------------------- 1965 BOATS -----------------------------------------------
18 5 V-185             RNBT FBG IO 110   8    4400  5050
23   V-23              RNBT FBG IO 110   8    8400  9650
```

SEABREEZE MARINE CORP

LYN-CRAFT   See inside cover to adjust price for area
TAMPA FL 33609   COAST GUARD MFG ID- SEM

```
LOA  NAME AND/        TOP/ BOAT -HULL- ----ENGINE--- BEAM  WGT  DRAFT RETAIL RETAIL
FT IN OR MODEL        RIG TYPE  MTL TP TP # HP  MFG   FT IN  LBS  FT IN  LOW    HIGH
----------------------- 1975 BOATS -----------------------------------------------
17 6 DYNAMAGLAS 180T  RNBT FBG OB        6 8   970   1900 2300
17 6 PRINCESS         CR   FBG OB        6 8  1110   2100 2450
17 6 SURFRIDER W/T    RNBT FBG OB        6 8   970   1800 2150
18   180T          OP      FBG TR OB     6 8        1800 2150
18   CONTESSA         CR   FBG OB        7    1096   2100 2500
18   CONTESSA         CR   FBG OB 120    7          2500 2900
18   OCEANIC          RNBT FBG OB        7     860   1700 2000
19   190V          OP      FBG DV OB     7 2        2450 2850
19   190V          OP      FBG DV OB 165 7 2        2750 3200
19   200T          OP      FBG DV OB     6 9        2450 2850
19   DYNAMAGLAS 190V  RNBT FBG TR OB     6 11 1260  2650 3100
19   DYNAMAGLAS 200T  RNBT FBG TR OB     6 11 1260  2400 2800

19   LUCAYAN W/T      RNBT FBG TR OB     6 11 1260  2300 2700
19   LUCAYAN W/T      RNBT FBG OB 120    6 11       2750 3200
20   DYNAMAGLAS 210V  RNBT FBG DV OB     7 6  2000  3750 4350
20   VISCOUNT         RNBT FBG DV OB     7 6  2000  3550 4150
21   EMPRESS          CR   FBG OB        7 6  2000  3900 4550
21   EMPRESS          CR   FBG OB 120    7 6        4200 4900
----------------------- 1974 BOATS -----------------------------------------------
17 6 PRINCESS 1850    CR FBG OB          6 8  1110  2050 2450
17 6 SEA-WAGON 1850   CR FBG OB          6 8   970  1850 2200
17 6 SURF-RIDER 1850  CR FBG OB          6 8   970  1850 2200
18   CONTESSA 1900    CR FBG OB          7    1096  2100 2450
18   CONTESSA 1900    CR FBG OB 120      7          2550 3000
```

LOA FT	IN	NAME AND/ OR MODEL	TOP/ RIG	BOAT TYPE	HULL MTL	HULL TP	ENGINE TP	# HP	MFG	BEAM FT	BEAM IN	WGT LBS	DRAFT FT	DRAFT IN	RETAIL LOW	RETAIL HIGH
		1974 BOATS														
18		OCEANIC 1900			FBG		OB			7		860			1700	2000
19		LUCAYAN 2000			FBG	TR	OB			6	11	1260			2450	2850
19		LUCAYAN 2000			FBG	TR	IO			6	11	1260			**	**
20		EMPRESS 2100		CR	FBG		OB			7	6	2200			3850	4500
20		EMPRESS 2100		CR	FBG		IO			7	6	2000			**	**
20		VISCOUNT 2100			FBG		OB			7	6	2000			3650	4250
20		VISCOUNT 2100			FBG		IO			7	6	2000			**	**
		1973 BOATS														
17	6	OCEANIC 1900			FBG		IO			7		860			**	**
17	6	SEA-WAGON 1850			FBG		OB			6	8	960			1800	2150
17	6	SURF-RIDER TRI 1850			FBG		OB			6	8	960			1800	2150
18		CONTESSA 1900		CR	FBG		OB			7		960			1850	2200
19		LUCAYAN 2000			FBG		IO								**	**
19		LUCAYAN TRI 2000			FBG		OB								2400	2800
20		EMPRESS 2100			FBG		IO	120		7	6	2200			4100	4750
20		VISCOUNT 2100			FBG		IO	120		7	6	2200			4100	4750
		1972 BOATS														
17	6	SEA-WAGON 1850			FBG		OB			6	8	960			1800	2150
17	6	SURF-RIDER TRI 1850			FBG		OB			6	8	960			1800	2150
18		CONTESSA 1900		CR	FBG		OB			7		960			1850	2200
18		OCEANIC 1900			FBG		IO			7		860			**	**
19		LUCAYAN 2000			FBG		IO								**	**
19		LUCAYAN TRI 2000			FBG		OB								2400	2800
20		EMPRESS 2100			FBG		IO	120-225		7	6	2200			4250	5100
20		VISCOUNT 2100			FBG		IO	120-225		7	6	2000			4050	4900
		1971 BOATS														
17	6	PRINCESS		CR	FBG		OB			6	8	1080			2000	2400
17	6	SURF-RIDER TRI			FBG		OB			6	8	960			1800	2150
17	6	TRI		B/R	FBG		OB			6	8	960			1800	2150
18		CONTESSA		CR	FBG		OB			7		960			1850	2200
18		OCEANIC			FBG		IO			7		860			**	**
19		CONTESSA		EXP	FBG	SV	IO	120		7					3250	3750
19		LUCAYAN			FBG		IO								**	**
19		LUCAYAN TRI			FBG		OB								2400	2800
19	9	SEA-WAGON	OP		FBG	TR	OB			6	8	980			2000	2350
20		EMPRESS			FBG		IO	120		7	6	2200			4450	5100
20		VISCOUNT			FBG		IO	120		7	6	2000			4200	4900
		1970 BOATS														
17	6	PRINCESS		CR	FBG		OB			6	8	1080			2000	2400
17	6	SURF-RIDER TRI			FBG		OB			6	8	960			1800	2150
17	6	TRI		B/R	FBG		OB			6	8	960			1800	2150
18		CONTESSA		CR	FBG		OB			7		960			1850	2200
18		OCEANIC 1900			FBG	SV	IO			7		860			**	**
19		LUCAYAN 2000			FBG	TR	IO			6	9				**	**
19		LUCAYAN TRI			FBG	TR	OB			6	9				2400	2800
20		EMPRESS			FBG	DV	IO	120		7	6	2200			4600	5250
20		VISCOUNT			FBG	DV	IO	120		7	6	2000			4400	5050
		1969 BOATS														
17	6	PRINCESS		CR	FBG		OB			6	8	1080			2000	2400
17	6	SURF-RIDER TRI	OP		FBG	TR	OB			6	8	960			1800	2150
17	6	TRI		B/R	FBG		OB			6	8	960			1850	2200
18		CONTESSA 1900		CR	FBG	RB	OB			7		960			1850	2200
18		OCEANIC 1900	OP		FBG	SV	IO	110		7		860			2850	3350
19		CONTESSA 1900		CR	FBG	SV	IO	110		7					3450	4000
19		LUCAYAN 2000			FBG	TR	IO	80		6	9				3200	3700
19		LUCAYAN TRI	OP		FBG	TR	OB			6	1				2400	2800
19	9	PRINCESS		CR	FBG	TR	OB			6	8				3700	4300
20		EMPRESS 2100		CR	FBG	DV	IO	120		7	6	2200			4950	5700
20		VISCOUNT 2100	OP		FBG	DV	IO	120		7	6	2000			4550	5200
		1968 BOATS														
18				EXP	FBG	SV	OB			7					1850	2200
19		CONTESSA		CBNCR	FBG		OB			7		960			1900	2300
19		CONTESSA	OP	EXP	FBG		IO	110		7					3550	4150
19		LUCYAN		RNBT	FBG	TR	OB			7	4	1010			2000	2400
19		LUCYAN		RNBT	FBG	TR	IO	160		7	4				3600	4200
19		OCEANIC			FBG		OB			7		840			1700	2050
19		OCEANIC 1900		RNBT	FBG		IO	60-110		7					3500	4050
19	9	SURF-RIDER	OP	RNBT	FBG	TR	OB			6	8	960			1950	2350
19	9	SURF-RIDER 4+4		RNBT	FBG		OB			6	8	980			2000	2400
20		EMPRESS		OVNTR	FBG		IO	160		7	6				5050	5800
20		VISCOUNT	OP	RNBT	FBG		IO	160		7	6				4850	5600
21	7	VISCOUNT	OP	RNBT	FBG		IO	110		8					7000	8050
		1967 BOATS														
18		CONTESSA		CR	FBG		OB			7		960			1850	2200
18	2	OCEANIC		RNBT	FBG		IO	80					1		3250	3800
20	3	VISCOUNT		RNBT	FBG	DV	IO	110					1	6	5050	5800
		1966 BOATS														
17		OFFSHORE 1800		RNBT	FBG		IO	60		7				5	2850	3350
18		CONTESSA 1900		CR	FBG		OB			7		960			1850	2250
18		OCEANIC 1900		RNBT	FBG		IO	110		7				6	3300	3850
19	2	LAPSTRAKE 2000		RNBT	FBG		OB			6	11	1115			2250	2650
20		VISCOUNT 2100		RNBT	FBG		OB			8	2				3650	4250
20		VISCOUNT 2100		RNBT	FBG		IO	110		8	2				5450	6250
		1965 BOATS														
18		1800 EXPRESS		RNBT	FBG		OB			7		860			1700	2050
19		1900 OFFSHORE		RNBT	FBG		OB			7	2	810			1700	2000
19		1900 OFFSHORE		RNBT	FBG		IO	110		7	2				3900	4550
20	2	2000 OFFSHORE		RNBT	FBG		OB			7	2	1125			2400	2800
20	2	2000 OFFSHORE		RNBT	FBG		IO	110		7	2				5250	6000

SEAFARER FIBERGLASS YACHTS

HUNTINGTON NY 11743 COAST GUARD MFG ID- SFR See inside cover to adjust price for area

For more recent years, see the BUC Used Boat Price Guide, Volume 1 or Volume 2

LOA FT	IN	NAME AND/ OR MODEL	TOP/ RIG	BOAT TYPE	HULL MTL	HULL TP	ENGINE TP	# HP	MFG	BEAM FT	BEAM IN	WGT LBS	DRAFT FT	DRAFT IN	RETAIL LOW	RETAIL HIGH
		1983 BOATS														
21	8	SKYLARK 22 HIGH PERF	SLP	SA/RC	FBG	KL	OB			7	5	2400	2	10	3850	4450
21	8	SKYLARK 22 SHOAL	SLP	SA/RC	FBG	KL	OB			7	5	2400	2	1	3850	4450
22	8	CHALLENGER 23 H PERF	SLP	SA/RC	FBG	KL	OB			7	7	2750	3	3	4400	5050
22	8	CHALLENGER 23 SHOAL	SLP	SA/RC	FBG	KL	OB			7	7	2750	2	4	4450	5150
25	9	CENTURY 26 HIGH PERF	SLP	SA/RC	FBG	KL	OB			8	3	5200	4		9300	10500
25	9	CENTURY 26 HIGH PERF	SLP	SA/RC	FBG	KL	IB	8D	YAN	8	3	5200	4		9750	11100
25	9	CENTURY 26 SHOAL	SLP	SA/RC	FBG	KL	OB			8	3	5200	3	6	9300	10500
25	9	CENTURY 26 SHOAL	SLP	SA/RC	FBG	KL	IB	8D	YAN	8	3	5200	3	6	9750	11100
29	11	SWIFTSURE 30	SLP	SA/RC	FBG	KL	IB	12D		10		8600	4	9	18300	20300
29	11	SWIFTSURE 30 SHOAL	SLP	SA/RC	FBG	KC	IB	12D		10		8600	3	6	18300	20300
36	8	SEAFARER 37 H PERF	SLP	SA/RC	FBG	KL	IB	20D	YAN	11	9	16500	6	3	34800	38700
36	8	SEAFARER 37 H PERF	SLP	SA/RC	FBG	KL	IB	30D	WEST	11	9	16500	6	3	34900	38800
36	8	SEAFARER 37 SHOAL	SLP	SA/RC	FBG	KL	IB	20D	YAN	11	9	17100	5		35900	39900
36	8	SEAFARER 37 SHOAL	SLP	SA/RC	FBG	KL	IB	30D	WEST	11	9	17100	5		36000	40000
		1982 BOATS														
21	8	SKYLARK 22 HIGH PERF	SLP	SA/RC	FBG	KL	OB			7	5	2300	2	10	3500	4050
22	8	CHALLENGER 23 H PERF	SLP	SA/RC	FBG	KL	OB			7	7	2750	3	3	4100	4750
22	8	CHALLENGER 23 SHOAL	SLP	SA/RC	FBG	KL	OB			7	7	2750	2	4	4150	4850
25	9	CENTURY 26 HIGH PERF	SLP	SA/RC	FBG	KL	OB			8	3	4600			7600	8750
25	9	CENTURY 26 HIGH PERF	SLP	SA/RC	FBG	KL	IB	8D	YAN	8	3	4600			8150	9350
29	11	SWIFTSURE 30	SLP	SA/RC	FBG	KL	IB	13D-	15D	10		8600	4	9	16800	19100
36	8	SEAFARER 37 H PERF	SLP	SA/RC	FBG	KL	IB	29D	WEST	11	9	16500	6	3	32900	36500
36	8	SEAFARER 37 H PERF	SLP	SA/RC	FBG	KL	IB	30D	YAN	11	9	16500	6	3	32900	36500
36	8	SEAFARER 37 SHOAL	SLP	SA/RC	FBG	KL	IB	29D	WEST	11	9	17100	5		33900	37600
36	8	SEAFARER 37 SHOAL	SLP	SA/RC	FBG	KL	IB	30D	YAN	11	9	17100	5		33900	37600
		1981 BOATS														
21	8	SKYLARK 22 HIGH PERF	SLP	SA/RC	FBG	KL	OB			7	5	2300	2	10	3300	3850
22	8	CHALLENGER 23 H PERF	SLP	SA/RC	FBG	KL	OB			7	7	2750	3	3	3850	4500
22	8	CHALLENGER 23 SHOAL	SLP	SA/RC	FBG	KL	OB			7	7	2750	2	4	3900	4550
25	9	CENTURY 26 HIGH PERF	SLP	SA/RC	FBG	KL	OB			8	3	4600	3	9	7150	8250
25	9	CENTURY 26 HIGH PERF	SLP	SA/RC	FBG	KL	IB	8D	YAN	8	3	4600	3	9	7650	8800
29	11	SWIFTSURE 30	SLP	SA/RC	FBG	CB	IB	12D		10		8600	3	6	15800	17900
29	11	SWIFTSURE 30	SLP	SA/RC	FBG	KL	IB	12D		10		8600	4	9	15800	17900
36	8	SEAFARER 37 H PERF	SLP	SA/RC	FBG	KL	IB	22D	YAN	11	9	15700	6	3	29600	32800
36	8	SEAFARER 37 H PERF	SLP	SA/RC	FBG	KL	IB	30D	WEST	11	9		6	3	31000	34500
36	8	SEAFARER 37 SHOAL	SLP	SA/RC	FBG	KL	IB	22D	YAN	11	9		5		31000	34400
36	8	SEAFARER 37 SHOAL	SLP	SA/RC	FBG	KL	IB	30D	WEST	11	9		5		31100	34500
		1980 BOATS														
21	8	SKYLARK 22	SLP	SA/RC	FBG	KL	OB			7	5	2300	2	10	3150	3650
22	8	CHALLENGER 23	SLP	SA/RC	FBG	KL	OB			7	7	2550	3	3	3500	4100
25	9	CENTURY 26	SLP	SA/RC	FBG	KL	IB	D		8	3	4600	3	9	7300	8400
29		SWIFTSURE 30	SLP	SA/RC	FBG	KL	IB	D		10		8200	4	9	14200	16200
36	9	SEAFARER 37	SLP	SA/RC	FBG	KL	IB	D		11	9	14000	6		25700	28500
37	9	SEAFARER 38	SLP	SA/CR	FBG	KL	IB	D		10	6	16500	4	6	30400	33700
37	9	SEAFARER 38	CUT	SA/CR	FBG	KL	IB	D		10	6	16500	4	6	30400	33700
37	9	SEAFARER 38	KTH	SA/CR	FBG	KL	IB	D		10	6	16500	4	6	30400	33800
		1979 BOATS														
21	8	SKYLARK 22 HIGH PERF	SLP	SAIL	FBG	KL	OB			7	5	2300	2	10	3000	3500
22	8	CHALLENGER 23 H PERF	SLP	SA/CR	FBG	KL	OB			7	7	2550	3	3	3350	3900
22	8	CHALLENGER 23 SHOAL	SLP	SA/CR	FBG	KL	OB			7	7	2550	2	4	3400	3950
25	9	CENTURY 26 HIGH PERF	SLP	SA/CR	FBG	KL	OB			8	3	4110	3	9	5900	6750
25	9	CENTURY 26 HIGH PERF	SLP	SA/CR	FBG	KL	IB	8D	YAN	8	3	4110	3	9	6350	7250
25	9	CENTURY 26 SHOAL	SLP	SA/CR	FBG	KL	OB			8	3	4110	2	7	5950	6800
25	9	CENTURY 26 SHOAL	SLP	SA/CR	FBG	KL	IB	8D	YAN	8	3	4110	2	7	6350	7300
29	11	SWIFTSURE 30	SLP	SA/CR	FBG	KL	IB	12D	YAN	10		7520	4	9	12600	14400
37	9	RHODES 38	SLP	SA/CR	FBG	KL	IB	50D	PERK	10	6	16500	4	6	29200	32400

 CONTINUED ON NEXT PAGE

SEAFARER FIBERGLASS YACHTS -CONTINUED See inside cover to adjust price for area

LOA FT	LOA IN	NAME AND/ OR MODEL	TOP/ RIG	BOAT TYPE	HULL MTL	HULL TP	ENGINE TP	ENGINE # HP	ENGINE MFG	BEAM FT	BEAM IN	WGT LBS	DRAFT FT	DRAFT IN	RETAIL LOW	RETAIL HIGH
		1979 BOATS														
37	9	RHODES 38	KTH	SA/CR	FBG	KL	IB	50D	PERK	10	6	16500	4	6	29700	33000
37	9	RHODES 38 BOWSPRIT	CUT	SA/CR	FBG	KL	IB	50D	PERK	10	6	16500	4	6	29200	32400
37	9	RHODES 38 BOWSPRIT	KTH	SA/CR	FBG	KL	IB	50D	PERK	10	6	16500	4	6	28700	31800
		1978 BOATS														
21	8	SKYLARK 22 HIGH PERF	SLP	SAIL	FBG	KL	OB			7	5	2300	2	10	2900	3350
21	8	SKYLARK 22 SHOAL	SLP	SAIL	FBG	KL	OB			7	5	2300	2	1	2950	3450
22	8	CHALLENGER 23 H PERF	SLP	SA/CR	FBG	KL	OB			7	7	2550	3	3	3250	3750
22	8	CHALLENGER 23 SHOAL	SLP	SA/CR	FBG	KL	OB			7	7	2550	2	4	3300	3800
25	9	CENTURY 26 HIGH PERF	SLP	SA/CR	FBG	KL	OB			8	3	4100	3	9	5650	6500
25	9	CENTURY 26 HIGH PERF	SLP	SA/CR	FBG	KL	IB	8D	YAN	8	3	4100	3	9	6100	7000
25	9	CENTURY 26 SHOAL	SLP	SA/CR	FBG	KL	OB			8	3	4100	2	7	5700	6550
25	9	CENTURY 26 SHOAL	SLP	SA/CR	FBG	KL	IB	8D	YAN	8	3	4100	2	7	6150	7050
29	11	SWIFTSURE 30 HI PERF	SLP	SA/CR	FBG	KL	IB	12D	YAN	10		7520	4	9	12100	13800
29	11	SWIFTSURE 30 SHOAL	SLP	SA/CR	FBG	KL	IB	12D	YAN	10		7520	3	6	12200	13900
37	9	RHODES 38	SLP	SA/CR	FBG	KL	IB	72	UNIV	10	6	16500	4	6	27900	31000
37	9	RHODES 38	SLP	SA/CR	FBG	KL	IB	20D	YAN	10	6	16500	4	6	28000	31200
37	9	RHODES 38	SLP	SA/CR	FBG	KL	IB	50D	PERK	10	6	16500	4	6	28100	31200
37	9	RHODES 38	CUT	SA/CR	FBG	KL	IB	72	UNIV	10	6	16500	4	6	27900	31000
37	9	RHODES 38	CUT	SA/CR	FBG	KL	IB	20D	YAN	10	6	16500	4	6	28000	31200
37	9	RHODES 38	CUT	SA/CR	FBG	KL	IB	50D	PERK	10	6	16500	4	6	28100	31200
37	9	RHODES 38	KTH	SA/CR	FBG	KL	IB	72	UNIV	10	6	16500	4	6	27900	31000
37	9	RHODES 38	KTH	SA/CR	FBG	KL	IB	20D	YAN	10	6	16500	4	6	28100	31200
37	9	RHODES 38	KTH	SA/CR	FBG	KL	IB	50D	PERK	10	6	16500	4	6	28100	31300
		1977 BOATS														
21	8	SEAFARER 22 HP	SLP	SAIL	FBG	KL	OB			7	5	2300	2	10	2650	3100
21	8	SEAFARER 22 SD	SLP	SAIL	FBG	KL	OB			7	5	2300	2	1	2950	3450
25	9	SEAFARER 26 HP	SLP	SAIL	FBG	KL	OB			8	3	4110	3	9	5450	6250
25	9	SEAFARER 26 HP	SLP	SAIL	FBG	KL	IB	8D	YAN	8	3	4110	3	9	5900	6800
25	9	SEAFARER 26 SD	SLP	SAIL	FBG	KL	OB			8	3	4110	2	7	5550	6400
25	9	SEAFARER 26 SD	SLP	SAIL	FBG	KL	IB	8D	YAN	8	3	4110	2	7	5900	6800
28	7	SEAFARER 29 HP	SLP	SAIL	FBG	KL	OB			9		6610	4	6	9800	11200
28	7	SEAFARER 29 HP	SLP	SAIL	FBG	KL	IB	8D	YAN	9		6610	4	6	10100	11400
28	7	SEAFARER 29 SD	SLP	SAIL	FBG	KL	OB			9		6610	3	3	9950	11300
28	7	SEAFARER 29 SD	SLP	SAIL	FBG	KL	IB	8D	YAN	9		6610	3	3	10200	11600
31		SEAFARER MARK II HP	SLP	SAIL	FBG	KL	IB	30	UNIV	9	9	10300	5	3	16300	18500
31		SEAFARER MARK II HP	SLP	SAIL	FBG	KL	IB	12D	YAN	9	9	10300	5	3	16300	18600
31		SEAFARER MARK II SD	SLP	SAIL	FBG	KL	IB	30	UNIV	9	9	10300	4	11	16300	18500
31		SEAFARER MARK II SD	SLP	SAIL	FBG	KL	IB	12D	YAN	9	9	10300	4	11	16300	18600
33	9	SEAFARER 34	SLP	SAIL	FBG	KC	IB	30	UNIV	10		12300	3	9	19500	21600
33	9	SEAFARER 34	SLP	SAIL	FBG	KC	IB	10D	WEST	10		12300	3	9	19500	21700
33	9	SEAFARER 34	YWL	SAIL	FBG	KC	IB	30	UNIV	10		12300	3	9	19500	21600
33	9	SEAFARER 34	YWL	SAIL	FBG	KC	IB	10D	WEST	10		12300	3	9	19500	21700
33	9	SEAFARER 34 HP	SLP	SAIL	FBG	KL	IB	30	UNIV	10		11700	5	3	18800	20900
33	9	SEAFARER 34 HP	SLP	SAIL	FBG	KL	IB	10D	WEST	10		11700	5	3	18800	20900
33	9	SEAFARER 34 HP	YWL	SAIL	FBG	KL	IB	30	UNIV	10		11700	5	3	18800	20900
33	9	SEAFARER 34 HP	YWL	SAIL	FBG	KL	IB	10D	WEST	10		11700	5	3	18800	20900
37	9	SEAFARER 38	SLP	SAIL	FBG	KL	IB	72	UNIV	10	6	16500	4	6	26900	29900
37	9	SEAFARER 38	SLP	SAIL	FBG	KL	IB	20D	YAN	10	6	16500	4	6	27100	30100
37	9	SEAFARER 38	CUT	SAIL	FBG	KL	IB	72	UNIV	10	6	16500	4	6	26900	29900
37	9	SEAFARER 38	CUT	SAIL	FBG	KL	IB	20D	YAN	10	6	16500	4	6	27100	30100
37	9	SEAFARER 38	KTH	SAIL	FBG	KL	IB	72	UNIV	10	6	16500	4	6	26900	29900
37	9	SEAFARER 38	KTH	SAIL	FBG	KL	IB	20D	YAN	10	6	16500	4	6	27100	30100
		1976 BOATS														
24		SEAFARER 24	SLP	SA/CR	FBG	KL	IB	D		7	10	3910	3	9	5150	5900
28	7	SEAFARER 29	SLP	SA/CR	FBG	KL	IB	D		9		6610	4	6	9850	11200
30	7	SEAFARER ATLANTIC	SLP	SA/CR	FBG	KL	IB	D		6	6	4559	4	9	6900	7950
31		SEAFARER 31-MKII	SLP	SA/CR	FBG	KL	IB	30D		9	9	10300	5	3	15800	18000
31	2	SEAFARER 31-MKI	SLP	SA/CR	FBG	KL	IB	D		8	10	8750	4	6	13400	15300
33	9	SEAFARER 34	SLP	SA/CR	FBG	KC	IB	30D		10		12300	3	9	19200	21300
37	9	SEAFARER 38	SLP	SA/CR	FBG	KL	IB	72D		10	6	16500	4	6	26600	29500
		1975 BOATS														
21	8	SEAFARER 22	SLP	SAIL	FBG	KL	OB			7	5	2300	2	1	2650	3100
24		SEAFARER 24	SLP	SAIL	FBG	CB	OB			7	10	3920	1	9	4550	5200
24		SEAFARER 24	SLP	SAIL	FBG	KL	OB			7	10	3910	3	9	4500	5200
28	8	SEAFARER 29	SLP	SAIL	FBG	CB	OB			9		6665	2	6	9400	10700
28	8	SEAFARER 29	SLP	SAIL	FBG	CB	IB	D		9		6665	2	6	9650	11000
28	8	SEAFARER 29	SLP	SAIL	FBG	KL	OB			9		6610	4	6	9400	10700
28	8	SEAFARER 29	SLP	SAIL	FBG	KL	IB	D		9		6610	4	6	9600	10900
30	7	ATLANTIC	SLP	SAIL	FBG	KL	OB			6	6	4559	4	9	6600	7550
31		MARK II	SLP	SAIL	FBG	KL	IB	30	UNIV	9	9	10300	5	3	15300	17400
31	2	MARK I	SLP	SAIL	FBG	KL	OB			8	10	8750	4	6	13000	14800
31	2	MARK I	SLP	SAIL	FBG	KL	IB	D		8	10	8750	4	6	13100	14800
31	2	MARK I	YWL	SAIL	FBG	KL	OB			8	10	8750	4	6	13000	14800
31	2	MARK I	YWL	SAIL	FBG	KL	IB	D		8	10	8750	4	6	13100	14800
33	9	SEAFARER 34	SLP	SAIL	FBG	KC	IB	30	UNIV	10		12300	3	9	18500	20600
33	9	SEAFARER 34	SLP	SAIL	FBG	KC	IB	25D	PALM	10		12300	3	9	18600	20700
33	9	SEAFARER 34	SLP	SAIL	FBG	KL	IB	30	UNIV	10		11700	5	3	17300	19600
33	9	SEAFARER 34	SLP	SAIL	FBG	KL	IB	25D	PALM	10		11700	5	3	17400	19700
33	9	SEAFARER 34	YWL	SAIL	FBG	KC	IB	30	UNIV	10		12300	3	9	18500	20600
33	9	SEAFARER 34	YWL	SAIL	FBG	KC	IB	25D	PALM	10		12300	3	9	18600	20700
33	9	SEAFARER 34	YWL	SAIL	FBG	KL	IB	30	UNIV	10		11700	5	3	17300	19600
33	9	SEAFARER 34	YWL	SAIL	FBG	KL	IB	25D	PALM	10		11700	5	3	17400	19700
37	9	SEAFARER 38	SLP	SAIL	FBG	KL	IB	72	UNIV	10	6	16500	4	6	25300	28100
37	9	SEAFARER 38	KTH	SAIL	FBG	KL	IB	72	UNIV	10	6	16500	4	6	25300	28100
		1974 BOATS														
24		SEAFARER	SLP	SAIL	FBG	CB	IB	6D	OMC	7	10	3920	1	9	4800	5500
24		SEAFARER	SLP	SAIL	FBG	KL	IB	6D	OMC	7	10	3860	3	9	4750	5450
28	7	SEAFARER	SLP	SAIL	FBG	CB	OB			9		5950	2	6	8100	9300
28	7	SEAFARER	SLP	SAIL	FBG	CB	IB	25D	OMC	9		5950	2	6	8350	9600
28	7	SEAFARER	SLP	SAIL	FBG	KL	OB			9		5850	4	6	7950	9100
28	7	SEAFARER	SLP	SAIL	FBG	KL	IB	25D	OMC	9		5850	4	6	8200	9450
30	7	SEAFARER ATLANTIC	SLP	SAIL	FBG	KL	OB			6	6	4559	4	9	6400	7350
31		MARK II	SLP	SAIL	FBG	KL	IB	30	UNIV	9	9	4850	5	3	6900	7950
31		MARK II	SLP	SAIL	FBG	KL	IB	25D	VLVO	9	9	4850	5	3	6950	8000
31	2	MARK I	SLP	SAIL	FBG	KL	IB	25	OMC	8	10	8750	4	6	12600	14300
31	2	MARK I	SLP	SAIL	FBG	KL	IB	22D-	25D	8	10	8750	4	6	12600	14300
31	2	MARK I	YWL	SAIL	FBG	KL	IB	25	OMC	8	10	8750	4	6	12700	14400
31	2	MARK I	YWL	SAIL	FBG	KL	IB	22D-	25D	8	10	8750	4	6	12700	14400
31	2	MARK I IOR	SLP	SAIL	FBG	KL	IB	25	OMC	8	10	8750	4	6	12800	14500
31	2	MARK I IOR	SLP	SAIL	FBG	KL	IB	22D-	25D	8	10	8750	4	6	12800	14500
33	9	SEAFARER	SLP	SAIL	FBG	KC	IB	22D-	25D	10		12300	3	9	18100	20100
33	9	SEAFARER	SLP	SAIL	FBG	KL	IB	22D-	25D	10		11700	5	3	16900	19200
33	9	SEAFARER	YWL	SAIL	FBG	KC	IB	22D-	25D	10		12300	3	9	18100	20100
33	9	SEAFARER	YWL	SAIL	FBG	KL	IB	22D-	25D	10		11700	5	3	16900	19200
37	9	SEAFARER STD	SLP	SAIL	FBG	KL	IB	30D	PALM	10	6	16500	4	6	23500	26100
37	9	SEAFARER STD	SLP	SAIL	FBG	KL	IB	44D	PERK	10	6	16500	4	6	23600	26200
37	9	SEAFARER STD	KTH	SAIL	FBG	KL	IB	30D	PALM	10	6	16500	4	6	24300	27100
37	9	SEAFARER STD	KTH	SAIL	FBG	KL	IB	44D	PERK	10	6	16500	4	6	24400	27100
37	9	SEAFARER STD BW	KTH	SAIL	FBG	KL	IB	30D	PALM	10	6	16500	4	6	25000	27800
37	9	SEAFARER STD BW	KTH	SAIL	FBG	KL	IB	44D	PERK	10	6	16500	4	6	25000	27800
37	9	SEAFARER STD BWT	SLP	SAIL	FBG	KL	IB	30D	PALM	10	6	16500	4	6	25600	28500
37	9	SEAFARER STD BWT	SLP	SAIL	FBG	KL	IB	44D	PERK	10	6	16500	4	6	25600	28400
37	9	SEAFARER TALL	SLP	SAIL	FBG	KL	IB	30D	PALM	10	6	16500	4	6	25900	28800
37	9	SEAFARER TALL	SLP	SAIL	FBG	KL	IB	44D	PERK	10	6	16500	4	6	25800	28700
37	9	SEAFARER TALL	KTH	SAIL	FBG	KL	IB	30D	PALM	10	6	16500	4	6	24700	27400
37	9	SEAFARER TALL	KTH	SAIL	FBG	KL	IB	44D	PERK	10	6	16500	4	6	24700	27400
37	9	SEAFARER TALL/BW	SLP	SAIL	FBG	KL	IB	30D	PALM	10	6	16500	4	6	24500	27200
37	9	SEAFARER TALL/BW	SLP	SAIL	FBG	KL	IB	44D	PERK	10	6	16500	4	6	24500	27200
37	9	SEAFARER TALL/BW	KTH	SAIL	FBG	KL	IB	30D	PALM	10	6	16500	4	6	25400	28200
37	9	SEAFARER TALL/BW	KTH	SAIL	FBG	KL	IB	44D	PERK	10	6	16500	4	6	25300	28200
48	2	SEAFARER 48	SLP	SA/CR	FBG	KL	IB	70D		11	10	33000	6	9	57000	62600
48	2	SEAFARER 48	YWL	SA/CR	FBG	KL	IB	70D		11	10	33000	6	9	57000	62600
		1973 BOATS														
24		SEAFARER 24	SLP	SAIL	FBG	CB	OB			7	10	3920	1	9	4250	4950
24		SEAFARER 24	SLP	SAIL	FBG	KL	OB			7	10	3860	3	10	4200	4850
28	8	SEAFARER 29	SLP	SAIL	FBG	CB	OB			9		5950	2	6	7900	9100
28	8	SEAFARER 29	SLP	SAIL	FBG	KL	OB			9		5850	4	6	7750	8900
30	7	SEAFARER ATLANTIC	SLP	SAIL	FBG	KL	OB			6	6	4559	4	9	6250	7200
31	2	SEAFARER 31	SLP	SAIL	FBG	KL	OB			8	10	8750	4	7	12300	14000
31	2	SEAFARER 31	SLP	SAIL	FBG	KL	IB	25D-	30D	8	10	8750	4	7	12400	14100
31	2	SEAFARER 31	YWL	SAIL	FBG	KL	OB			8	10	8750	4	7	12300	14000
31	2	SEAFARER 31	YWL	SAIL	FBG	KL	IB	25D-	30D	8	10	8750	4	7	12400	14100
33	9	SEAFARER	SLP	SAIL	FBG	KC	IB	25D-	30D	10		12300	3	9	17300	19700
33	9	SEAFARER	YWL	SAIL	FBG	KC	IB	25D-	30D	10		12300	3	9	17300	19700
37	9	SEAFARER	SLP	SAIL	FBG	KL	IB	72	UNIV	10	6	16500	4	6	24100	26700
37	9	SEAFARER	SLP	SAIL	FBG	KL	IB	50D	PERK	10	6	16500	4	6	24300	27000
37	9	SEAFARER	KTH	SAIL	FBG	KL	IB	72	UNIV	10	6	16500	4	6	24100	26700
37	9	SEAFARER	KTH	SAIL	FBG	KL	IB	50D	PERK	10	6	16500	4	6	24300	27000
48	2	SEAFARER	SLP	SAIL	FBG	KL	IB	42D	BENZ	11	10	33000	6	9	55200	60700
48	2	SEAFARER	SLP	SAIL	FBG	KL	IB	50D	PERK	11	10	33000	6	9	55100	60600
48	2	SEAFARER	YWL	SAIL	FBG	KL	IB	42D	BENZ	11	10	33000	6	9	55200	60700
48	2	SEAFARER	YWL	SAIL	FBG	KL	IB	50D	PERK	11	10	33000	6	9	55100	60600
		1972 BOATS														
23	1	SEAFARER	SLP	SAIL	FBG	KC	OB			7	2	3500	2	4	3600	4150
24		SEAFARER R/K	SLP	SAIL	FBG	CB	OB			7	10	3350	1	9	3600	4200
25	7	SEAFARER	SLP	SAIL	FBG		OB			7	3	5000	3	7	5800	6650
28	8	SEAFARER R/K	SLP	SAIL	FBG	CB	OB			9		6300	2	9	8200	9400
30	7	SEAFARER ATLANTIC	SLP	SAIL	FBG	KL	OB			6	6	4559	4	9	6100	7050

CONTINUED ON NEXT PAGE

LOA FT	LOA IN	NAME AND/ OR MODEL	TOP/ RIG	BOAT TYPE	-HULL- MTL	-HULL- TP	ENGINE TP	ENGINE # HP	ENGINE MFG	BEAM FT	BEAM IN	WGT LBS	DRAFT FT	DRAFT IN	RETAIL LOW	RETAIL HIGH
		1972 BOATS														
31	2	SEAFARER	SLP	SAIL	FBG	KL	OB			8	10	8750	4	7	12100	13700
33	9	SEAFARER	YWL	SAIL	FBG	KC	IB	30	UNIV	10		12300	3	9	16800	19100
33	9	SEAFARER	YWL	SAIL	FBG	KC	IB	25D	VLVO	10		12300	3	9	16900	19200
33	9	SEAFARER R/K	SLP	SAIL	FBG	KC	IB	30	UNIV	10		12300	3	9	16800	19100
33	9	SEAFARER R/K	SLP	SAIL	FBG	KC	IB	25D	VLVO	10		12300	3	9	16900	19200
37	9	SEAFARER	SLP	SAIL	FBG	KL	IB	72	UNIV	10	6	16500	4	6	23500	26100
37	9	SEAFARER	SLP	SAIL	FBG	KL	IB	50D	PERK	10	6	16500	4	6	23700	26400
37	9	SEAFARER	KTH	SAIL	FBG	KL	IB	72	UNIV	10	6	16500	4	6	23500	26100
37	9	SEAFARER	KTH	SAIL	FBG	KL	IB	50D	PERK	10	6	16500	4	6	23700	26400
48	2	SEAFARER	SLP	SAIL	FBG	KL	IB	70	UNIV	11	10	33000	6	9	53500	58800
48	2	SEAFARER	SLP	SAIL	FBG	KL	IB	50D	PERK	11	10	33000	6	9	53800	59100
48	2	SEAFARER	YWL	SAIL	FBG	KL	IB	70	UNIV	11	10	33000	6	9	53500	58800
48	2	SEAFARER	YWL	SAIL	FBG	KL	IB	50D	PERK	11	10	33000	6	9	53800	59100
		1971 BOATS														
23	1	SEAFARER 23	SLP	SAIL	FBG	KC	OB			7	2	3500	2	4	3500	4100
24		SEAFARER 24 R/K	SLP	SAIL	FBG	CB	OB			7	10	3350	1	9	3550	4100
25	7	SEAFARER 26	SLP	SAIL	FBG		OB			7	3	5000	3	7	5650	6500
28	8	SEAFARER 28 R/K	SLP	SAIL	FBG	CB	OB			9		6300	2	9	8050	9250
30	3	SEAFARER 30R		SAIL	FBG		IB			8	10	8800	4	7	11800	13400
30	7	SEAFARER ATLANTIC	SLP	SAIL	FBG	KL	OB			6	6	4559	4	9	6000	6900
31	2	SEAFARER 31	SLP	SAIL	FBG	KL	OB			8	10	8750	4	7	11800	13400
31	2	SEAFARER 31	YWL	SAIL	FBG	KL	OB			8	10	8750	4	7	11800	13400
33	9	SEAFARER 34	YWL	SA/CR	FBG	KC	IB	30		10		12300	3	9	16500	18700
33	9	SEAFARER 34	SLP	SAIL	FBG	KC	IB	22- 30		10		12300	3	9	16500	18700
33	9	SEAFARER 34	SLP	SAIL	FBG	KC	IB	20D- 25D		10		12300	3	9	16600	18800
36	4	SEAFARER 36C R/K		SAIL	FBG		IB	70	UNIV	10	6	16500	4	6	22300	24800
36	4	SEAFARER 36C R/K		SAIL	FBG		IB	50D	PERK	10	6	16500	4	6	22500	25000
39		SEAFARER 39	SLP	SA/CR	FBG	KL	IB	30		10		17500	5	7	25200	28000
39		SEAFARER 39	YWL	SA/CR	FBG	KL	IB	30		10		17500	5	7	25200	28000
48	2	SEAFARER 48	SLP	SAIL	FBG	KL	IB	70	UNIV	11	10	33000	6	9	52500	57700
48	2	SEAFARER 48	SLP	SAIL	FBG	KL	IB	42D	BENZ	11	10	33000	6	9	52900	58200
48	2	SEAFARER 48	SLP	SAIL	FBG	KL	IB	50D	PERK	11	10	33000	6	9	52800	58100
48	2	SEAFARER 48	YWL	SAIL	FBG	KL	IB	70	UNIV	11	11	33000	6	9	52500	57700
48	2	SEAFARER 48	YWL	SAIL	FBG	KL	IB	42D	BENZ	11	11	33000	6	9	52900	58200
48	2	SEAFARER 48	YWL	SAIL	FBG	KL	IB	50D	PERK	11	11	33000	6	9	52800	58100
		1970 BOATS														
23	1	SEAFARER 23	SLP	SA/OD	FBG	KC	OB			7	2	3500	2	4	3450	4000
24		SEAFARER 24 R/K	SLP	SAIL	FBG	CB	OB			7	10	3350	1	9	3500	4050
25	7	SEAFARER 26	SLP	SA/OD	FBG	KL	OB			7	3	5000	3	7	5550	6400
28	8	SEAFARER 28 R/K	SLP	SAIL	FBG	CB	OB			9		6300	2	9	7900	9050
30	3	SEAFARER 30R		SAIL	FBG		IB			8	10	8800	4	7	11600	13200
30	7	SEAFARER ATLANTIC	SLP	SA/OD	FBG	KL	OB			6	6	4559	4	9	5900	6750
31	2	SEAFARER 31	SLP	SA/OD	FBG	KL	OB			8	10	8750	4	7	11600	13200
31	2	SEAFARER 31	YWL	SA/OD	FBG	KL	OB			8	10	8750	4	7	11600	13200
33	9	SEAFARER 34	SLP	SAIL	FBG	KC	IB	22- 30		10		12300	3	9	16200	18400
33	9	SEAFARER 34	SLP	SAIL	FBG	KC	IB	20D- 25D		10		12300	3	9	16300	18500
36	4	SEAFARER 36C R/K	SLP	SAIL	FBG	KL	IB	70	UNIV	10	6	16500	4	6	21900	24400
36	4	SEAFARER 36C R/K	SLP	SAIL	FBG	KL	IB	50D	PERK	10	6	16500	4	6	22100	24500
48	2	SEAFARER 48	SLP	SAIL	FBG	KL	IB	70	UNIV	11	10	33000	6	9	51400	56500
48	2	SEAFARER 48	SLP	SAIL	FBG	KL	IB	42D	BENZ	11	10	33000	6	9	51900	57000
48	2	SEAFARER 48	SLP	SAIL	FBG	KL	IB	50D	PERK	11	10	33000	6	9	51700	56800
48	2	SEAFARER 48	YWL	SAIL	FBG	KL	IB	70	UNIV	11	11	33000	6	9	51400	56500
48	2	SEAFARER 48	YWL	SAIL	FBG	KL	IB	42D	BENZ	11	11	33000	6	9	51900	57000
48	2	SEAFARER 48	YWL	SAIL	FBG	KL	IB	50D	PERK	11	11	33000	6	9	51700	56800
		1969 BOATS														
23	1	CATALINA DAYSAILER	SLP	SAIL	FBG	KC	OB			7	2	3700	2	4	3200	3700
23	1	CATALINA PLAN 1	SLP	SAIL	FBG	KC	OB			7	2	3700	2	4	3750	4400
23	1	CATALINA PLAN 2	SLP	SAIL	FBG	KC	OB			7	2	3700	2	4	3900	4550
23	1	NANTUCKET DAYSAILER	SLP	SAIL	FBG	KC	OB			7	2	3700	2	4	3350	3900
23	1	NANTUCKET PLAN 1	SLP	SAIL	FBG	KC	OB			7	2	3700	2	4	3950	4600
23	1	NANTUCKET PLAN 2	SLP	SAIL	FBG	KC	OB			7	2	3700	2	4	4100	4750
23	1	OLYMPIC	SLP	SAIL	FBG	KC	OB			7	2	3700	2	4	3250	3800
23	1	OLYMPIC DAYSAILER	SLP	SAIL	FBG	KC	OB			7	2	3700	2	4	3000	3450
25	7	BERMUDA	SLP	SAIL	FBG		OB			7	3	4690	3	7	5100	5850
25	7	BERMUDA DAYSAILER	SLP	SAIL	FBG		OB			7	3	4690	3	7	4150	4850
25	7	CHESAPEAKE DAYSAILER	SLP	SAIL	FBG		OB			7	3	4690	3	7	4450	5100
25	7	CHESAPEAKE PLAN 1	SLP	SAIL	FBG		OB			7	3	4690	3	7	5600	6450
25	7	CHESAPEAKE PLAN 2	SLP	SAIL	FBG		OB			7	3	4690	3	7	5950	6850
25	7	STRATFORD DAYSAILER	SLP	SAIL	FBG		OB			7	3	4690	3	7	4500	5150
25	7	STRATFORD PLAN 1	SLP	SAIL	FBG		OB			7	3	4690	3	7	5450	6250
25	7	STRATFORD PLAN 2	SLP	SAIL	FBG		OB			7	3	4690	3	7	6000	6900
30	7	ATLANTIC	SLP	SA/OD	FBG	KL	OB			6	6	4559	4	9	5800	6650
31	1	FASTNET #1	SLP	SAIL	FBG	KL	OB			8	10	8750	4	7	10700	12200
31	1	FASTNET #1	YWL	SAIL	FBG	KL	OB			8	10	8750	4	7	10300	11700
31	1	FASTNET #2	SLP	SAIL	FBG	KL	OB			8	10	8750	4	7	11700	13300
31	1	FASTNET #2	YWL	SAIL	FBG	KL	OB			8	10	8750	4	7	11300	12800
31	1	FASTNET #3	SLP	SAIL	FBG	KL	OB			8	10	8750	4	7	11900	13500
31	1	FASTNET #3	YWL	SAIL	FBG	KL	OB			8	10	8750	4	7	11500	13000
31	1	FASTNET #4	SLP	SAIL	FBG	KL	OB			8	10	8750	4	7	12200	13900
31	1	FASTNET #4	YWL	SAIL	FBG	KL	OB			8	10	8750	4	7	11800	13400
31	1	FASTNET #5	SLP	SAIL	FBG	KL	OB			8	10	8750	4	7	12400	14100
31	1	FASTNET #5	YWL	SAIL	FBG	KL	OB			8	10	8750	4	7	11900	13600
31	1	FASTNET #6	SLP	SAIL	FBG	KL	OB			8	10	8750	4	7	12800	14500
31	1	FASTNET #6	YWL	SAIL	FBG	KL	OB			8	10	8750	4	7	12300	14000
31	1	FASTNET #7	SLP	SAIL	FBG	KL	OB			8	10	8750	4	7	13000	14700
31	1	FASTNET #7	YWL	SAIL	FBG	KL	OB			8	10	8750	4	7	12500	14200
31	1	FASTNET DAYSAILER	SLP	SAIL	FBG	KL	OB			8	10	8750	4	7	8900	10100
31	1	NEWPORT #1	SLP	SAIL	FBG	KL	OB			8	10	8750	4	7	10500	11900
31	1	NEWPORT #1	YWL	SAIL	FBG	KL	OB			8	10	8750	4	7	10100	11500
31	1	NEWPORT #2	SLP	SAIL	FBG	KL	OB			8	10	8750	4	7	11500	13000
31	1	NEWPORT #2	YWL	SAIL	FBG	KL	OB			8	10	8750	4	7	11000	12600
31	1	NEWPORT #3	SLP	SAIL	FBG	KL	OB			8	10	8750	4	7	11700	13300
31	1	NEWPORT #3	YWL	SAIL	FBG	KL	OB			8	10	8750	4	7	11200	12700
31	1	NEWPORT #4	SLP	SAIL	FBG	KL	OB			8	10	8750	4	7	12000	13600
31	1	NEWPORT #4	YWL	SAIL	FBG	KL	OB			8	10	8750	4	7	11500	13100
31	1	NEWPORT #5	SLP	SAIL	FBG	KL	OB			8	10	8750	4	7	12200	13800
31	1	NEWPORT #5	YWL	SAIL	FBG	KL	OB			8	10	8750	4	7	11700	13300
31	1	NEWPORT DAYSAILER	SLP	SAIL	FBG	KL	OB			8	10	8750	4	7	8550	9800
33	11	SEAFARER 34	SLP	SAIL	FBG	KC	IB			10		12300	3	9	16000	18100
33	11	SEAFARER 34	YWL	SAIL	FBG	KC	IB			10		12300	3	9	16000	18100
36	4	SEAFARER 36C #1	SLP	SAIL	FBG		OB			10	6	16500	4	6	21000	23400
36	4	SEAFARER 36C #1	KTH	SAIL	FBG		OB			10	6	16500	4	6	21000	23400
36	4	SEAFARER 36C #2	SLP	SAIL	FBG		OB			10	6	16500	4	6	21700	24100
36	4	SEAFARER 36C #2	KTH	SAIL	FBG		OB			10	6	16500	4	6	21700	24100
39		SEAFARER 39	SLP	SAIL	FBG	KL	IB			10		16500	5	7	23300	25900
39		SEAFARER 39	YWL	SAIL	FBG	KL	IB			10		16500	5	7	23300	25900
48	2	SEAFARER 48	SLP	SAIL	FBG	KL	IB			11	11	33000	6	9	50500	55500
48	2	SEAFARER 48	YWL	SAIL	FBG	KL	IB			11	11	33000	6	9	50500	55500
		1968 BOATS														
23	1	CATALINA	SLP	SAIL	FBG	KL	OB			7	2	3700			3500	4100
23	1	MONHEGAN	SLP	SAIL	FBG	KL	OB			7	2	3700			3950	4600
23	1	NANTUCKET	SLP	SAIL	FBG	KL	OB			7	2	3700			3850	4450
23	1	NASSAU	SLP	SAIL	FBG	KL	OB			7	2	3700			3650	4250
23	1	OLYMPIC	SLP	SAIL	FBG	KL	OB			7	2	3700			3000	3500
23	1	SEAFARER 23	SLP	SAIL	FBG	KL	OB			7	2	3700			3150	3650
25	7	BERMUDA	SLP	SAIL	FBG	KL	OB			7	3	5500	3	9	5600	6400
25	7	CHESAPEAKE	SLP	SAIL	FBG	KL	OB			7	3	5500	3	9	6500	7450
25	7	MACKINAC	SLP	SAIL	FBG	KL	OB			7	3	5500	3	9	5950	6850
25	7	SEAFARER 26	SLP	SAIL	FBG	KL	OB			7	3	5500	3	9	4900	5600
25	7	STRATFORD	SLP	SAIL	FBG	KL	OB			7	3	5500	3	9	6250	7200
25	7	VINEYARD	SLP	SAIL	FBG	KL	OB			7	3	5500	3	9	6650	7650
31		COMPETITOR	SLP	SAIL	FBG	KL	OB			8	9	8800	4	7	9950	11300
31		ENSENADA	SLP	SAIL	FBG	KL	OB			8	9	8800	4	7	12000	13700
31		FASTNET	SLP	SAIL	FBG	KL	OB			8	9	8800	4	7	11800	13400
31		HALIFAX	SLP	SAIL	FBG	KL	OB			8	9	8800	4	7	11500	13100
31		NEWPORT	SLP	SAIL	FBG	KL	OB			8	9	8800	4	7	11300	12800
31		SEAFARER 31	SLP	SAIL	FBG	KL	OB			8	9	8800	4	7	11300	12900
31		TAHITI	SLP	SAIL	FBG		OB					8800			11300	12900
33	8	SEAFARER 34	SLP	SAIL	FBG	KL	OB			10		11400	3	6	14600	16600
36	4	SEAFARER 36C	SLP	SAIL	FBG	KL	OB			10	6	16350	4	6	20900	23200
39	3	SEAFARER 39	SLP	SAIL	FBG	KL	OB			10		17500	5	5	24000	26700
39	3	SEAFARER 39	YWL	SAIL	FBG	KL	OB			10			5	5	22500	25000
46		SEAFARER 46	YWL	SAIL	FBG	KL	IB	30		10		27000	6	7	42300	47000
46		SEAFARER 46C	SLP	SAIL	FBG	KL	IB	30		10		27500	6	7	42600	47400
		1967 BOATS														
23	1	KESTREL CATALINA	SLP	SAIL	FBG		OB					3700			3450	4050
23	1	KESTREL DAYSAIL	SLP	SAIL	FBG		OB					3700			3100	3600
23	1	KESTREL MONHEGAN	SLP	SAIL	FBG		OB					3700			3750	4350
23	1	KESTREL NASSAU	SLP	SAIL	FBG		OB					3700			3550	4150
23	1	NANTUCKET		SAIL	FBG		OB					3700			3450	4050
25	7	CHESAPEAKE MERIDIAN	SLP	SAIL	FBG		OB					5400			6300	7250
25	7	MACKINAC MERIDIAN	SLP	SAIL	FBG		OB					5400			5750	6600
25	7	MERIDIAN BERMUDA	SLP	SAIL	FBG		OB					5400			5350	6150
25	7	MERIDIAN DAYSAIL	SLP	SAIL	FBG		OB					5400			4850	5550
25	7	STRATFORD MERIDIAN	SLP	SAIL	FBG		OB					5400			6100	7000
25	7	VINEYARD MERIDIAN	SLP	SAIL	FBG		OB					5400			6400	7350
31		ENSENADA	SLP	SAIL	FBG		OB					8700			11500	13100

CONTINUED ON NEXT PAGE

LOA FT IN	NAME AND/ OR MODEL	TOP/ RIG	BOAT TYPE	-HULL- MTL TP	----ENGINE--- TP # HP MFG	BEAM FT IN	WGT LBS	DRAFT FT IN	RETAIL LOW	RETAIL HIGH
			1967 BOATS							
31	FASTNET	SLP	SAIL	FBG	OB		8700		11300	12800
31	HALIFAX	SLP	SAIL	FBG	OB		8700		11000	12500
31	NEWPORT	SLP	SAIL	FBG	OB		8700		10800	12200
31	SEAFARER 31	SLP	SAIL	FBG KL	OB	8 8	8700	4 8	11100	12600
31	SEAFARER COMPETITOR	SLP	SAIL	FBG	OB		8700		9800	11100
31	TAHITI	SLP	SAIL	FBG	OB		8700		12100	13800
35	BAHAMA		MS	FBG KL	IB	70 4 6	16350		20600	22900
39 1	SEAFARER 39	SLP	SAIL	FBG	IB	30	17500		23800	26500
39 1	SEAFARER 39	YWL	SAIL	FBG KL	IB	10			30100	33400
45 1	SEAFARER 45	SLP	SAIL	FBG	IB	70	25024		38800	43100
45 1	SEAFARER 45	YWL	SAIL	FBG KL	IB	11			45900	50400
			1966 BOATS							
23 1	CATALINA	SLP	SAIL	FBG	OB				2400	2800
23 1	CATALINA	SLP	SAIL	FBG	IB	15- 24			2750	3250
23 1	KESTREL	SLP	SA/OD	FBG	CB	7		2 4	2700	3100
23 1	MONHEGAN	SLP	SAIL	FBG	OB				2700	3150
23 1	MONHEGAN	SLP	SAIL	FBG	IB	15- 24			3000	3550
23 1	NANTUCKET	SLP	SAIL	FBG	OB				2600	3050
23 1	NANTUCKET	SLP	SAIL	FBG	IB	15- 24			2950	3450
23 1	NASSAU	SLP	SAIL	FBG	OB				2550	2950
23 1	NASSAU	SLP	SAIL	FBG	IB	15- 24			2850	3400
25 7	MERIDIAN	SLP	SA/CR	FBG KL		7		3 9	4150	4850
26 5	BERMUDA	SLP	SAIL	FBG	OB				4150	4800
26 5	BERMUDA	SLP	SAIL	FBG	IB	15- 24			5500	6350
26 5	MACKINAC	SLP	SAIL	FBG	OB				4500	5200
26 5	MACKINAC	SLP	SAIL	FBG	IB	15- 24			5900	6800
26 5	STRATFORD	SLP	SAIL	FBG	OB				4600	5300
26 5	STRATFORD	SLP	SAIL	FBG	IB	15- 24			6000	6900
26 5	VINEYARD	SLP	SAIL	FBG	OB				4900	5650
26 5	VINEYARD	SLP	SAIL	FBG	IB	15- 24			6400	7350
28 6	RANGER	SLP	SA/CR	FBG KL		8		4	5150	5900
31	COMPETITOR	SLP	SAIL	FBG	OB				9150	10400
31	COMPETITOR	SLP	SAIL	FBG	IB	15- 24			10800	12300
31	ENSENADA	SLP	SAIL	FBG	OB				10600	12000
31	ENSENADA	SLP	SAIL	FBG	IB	15- 24			12400	14100
31	FASTNET	SLP	SAIL	FBG	OB				10200	11600
31	FASTNET	SLP	SAIL	FBG	IB	15- 24			12000	13700
31	HALIFAX	SLP	SAIL	FBG	OB				10100	11500
31	HALIFAX	SLP	SAIL	FBG	IB	15- 24			11900	13500
31	NEWPORT	SLP	SAIL	FBG	OB				9750	11100
31	NEWPORT	SLP	SAIL	FBG	IB	15- 24			11500	13100
31	SEAFARER 31	SLP	SA/OD	FBG KL		8 6		4 8	5450	6300
31	TAHITI	SLP	SAIL	FBG	OB				10900	12400
31	TAHITI	SLP	SAIL	FBG	IB	15- 24			12800	14500
33	SWIFTSURE	SLP	SAIL	FBG CB	IB	15- 24 10		3 6	12900	14600
35	BAHAMA	SLP	SAIL	FBG KL	IB	15 10 6		4 6	18200	20200
35	BAHAMA	SLP	SAIL	FBG KL	IB	24 10 6		4 6	18200	20300
39 3	SEAFARER 39	SLP	SAIL	FBG KL	IB	24 10		5 5	29900	33200
45 1	SEAFARER 45	SLP	SA/CR	FBG KL		11		6 5	38800	43100
			1965 BOATS							
22	KESTREL	SLP	SAIL	FBG	OB				2350	2700
25 7	MERIDIAN	SLP	SAIL	FBG	OB				4350	5000
26 5	POLARIS	SLP	SAIL	FBG	OB				4550	5200
28 6	RANGER II	SLP	SA/RC	FBG	OB				3850	4450
31	SEAFARER	SLP	SAIL	FBG	OB		10000		10000	11400
33	SWIFTSURE	SLP	SAIL	FBG	IB		12800		12800	14500
35	BAHAMA	SLP	SAIL	FBG	IB		18100		18100	20100
38	SEAFARER	SLP	SAIL	FBG	IB		22500		22500	25000
45 1	SEAFARER 45	SLP	SAIL	FBG	IB	11		6 5	44600	49500
45 1	SEAFARER 45	YWL	SAIL	FBG	IB	11		6 5	44600	49500
			1964 BOATS							
22	KESTREL		SAIL	FBG	OB				2300	2700
24 9	MERIDIAN		SAIL	FBG	OB				4100	4800
26 5	POLARIS		SAIL	FBG	OB				4500	5200
28 6	RANGER II		SA/RC	FBG	OB				3800	4450
28 6	SEAFARER 28		SAIL	FBG	IB	30			9450	10700
30 6	SEAFARER 30		SAIL	FBG	IB	30			11700	13300
33	SWIFTSURE 33	SLP	SAIL	FBG	IB	30			12700	14400
35	BAHAMA		SAIL	FBG	IB	70			18000	20100
38	SEAFARER 38	SLP	SAIL	FBG	IB	30			22300	24800
			1963 BOATS							
22	KESTREL		SAIL	FBG	OB				2300	2700
24 9	MERIDIAN		SAIL	FBG	OB				4100	4750
26 5	POLARIS		SAIL	FBG	OB				4500	5150
28 6	RANGER II		SA/RC	FBG	OB				3800	4400
28 6	SEAFARER 28		SAIL	FBG	IB	30			9450	10700
30 6	SEAFARER 30	SLP	SAIL	FBG	IB	30			11700	13300
33	SWIFTSURE	SLP	SAIL	FBG	IB	30			12700	14400
35	BAHAMA		SAIL	FBG	IB	70			17600	20000
38	SEAFARER 38	SLP	SAIL	FBG	IB	30			22300	24700
45	SEAFARER 45	SLP	SAIL	FBG	IB	30D			41200	45800
			1962 BOATS							
22 3	KESTREL	SLP	SAIL	FBG	OB				2350	2700
24 9	MERIDIAN	SLP	SAIL	FBG	OB				4100	4750
26 3	POLARIS	SLP	SAIL	FBG	OB				4450	5100
26 3	POLARIS	SLP	SAIL	FBG	IB	30			5850	6700
28 6	RANGER II	SLP	SA/RC	FBG	OB				3800	4400
28 6	RANGER II	SLP	SA/RC	FBG	IB	30			8400	9700
30 4	TRIPP	SLP	SAIL	FBG	IB	30			7350	8450
33 6	SWIFTSURE	SLP	SAIL	FBG	IB	30			19400	21500
37 10	JAVELIN	SLP	SAIL	FBG	IB	30			22100	24600
45 1	SEAFARER	SLP	SAIL	FBG	IB	20D			41200	45800
			1961 BOATS							
22	KESTRAL		SA/RC	FBG	CB		7		2 4	2300	2700
24 9	MERIDIAN	SLP	SAIL	FBG	OB		7		3 3	4100	4750
26 3	POLARIS	SLP	SAIL	FBG CB	OB		7 9		2 2	4450	5100
28 6	RANGER II	SLP	SA/RC	FBG KL	OB		8		3 10	3800	4400
30 4	TRIPP 30	SLP	SAIL	FBG KL	OB		8 6		4 6	8800	8800
30 4	TRIPP 30	YWL	SAIL	FBG KL	OB		8 6		4 6	8800	8800
33 6	SWIFTSURE	SLP	SAIL	FBG CB	OB		10		3 6	13300	15200
37 10	JAVELIN	SLP	SAIL	FBG KL	OB		10		5 3	9800	11100
37 10	JAVELIN	YWL	SAIL	FBG KL	OB		10		5 3	9800	11100
45 1	SEAFARER	SLP	SA/CR	FBG	OB		11		6 5	38100	42300
45 1	SEAFARER	YWL	SA/CR	FBG	OB		11		6 5	38100	42300
			1960 BOATS							
26 3	POLARIS	SLP	SA/CR	FBG	CB OB		7 9			4450	5150
28 6	RANGER	SLP	SA/CR	FBG KL	OB		8		3 10	5450	6250
30 4	TRIPP 30	SLP	SA/CR	FBG KL	OB		8 6		4 6	7650	8800
30 4	TRIPP 30	YWL	SA/CR	FBG KL	OB		8 6		4 6	7650	8800
33 6	SWIFTSURE	SLP	SA/CR	FBG CB	OB		10			13400	15200
34	BAHAMA		MS	FBG KL	OB		10		4 3	**	**
37 10	JAVELIN	SLP	SA/CR	FBG KL	OB		10		5 3	9800	11200
37 10	JAVELIN	YWL	SA/CR	FBG KL	OB		10		5 3	9800	11200

SEAFERRO INC

Call 1-800-327-6929 for BUC Personalized Evaluation Service
Or, for 1969 to 1970 boats, sign onto www.BUCValuPro.com

SEAGOING HOUSEBOATS INC

A BANGOR PUNTA COMPANY
FLORENCE AL 35630   COAST GUARD MFG ID- SEG   See inside cover to adjust price for area

LOA FT IN	NAME AND/ OR MODEL	TOP/ RIG	BOAT TYPE	-HULL- MTL TP	----ENGINE--- TP # HP MFG	BEAM FT IN	WGT LBS	DRAFT FT IN	RETAIL LOW	RETAIL HIGH
			1972 BOATS							
42		HT	HB	FBG	IO				13600	15400
			1971 BOATS							
32		HT	HB	FBG	IO	11			9450	10700
32		HT	HB	STL	IO	11			9400	10700
39 9		HT	HB	FBG	IO				14000	15900
52		HT	HB	STL	IO				19900	22200
			1970 BOATS							
32			HB	STL	IO	215 MRCR 11			9400	10700
35		HT	HB	FBG SV	IO	225 12	9000	1	9450	10700
35			HB	STL SV	IO	225 12	8800	1	9300	10600
41			HB	FBG SV	IO	225 CHRY 12	15000	1 10	13500	15400
41			HB	FBG SV	IO	T200 MRCR 12	15000	1 10	14400	16400
41		HT	HB	STL SV	IO	T225 12	15000	1 10	12800	14500
45			HB	FBG	IO	225 CHRY 12			13600	15400
45			HB	FBG	IO	225 CHRY 12			14700	16700
48		HT	HB	FBG SV	IO	T225 12	17000	2 3	16300	18500
48		HT	HB	STL SV	IO	T225 12	16500	2 3	14800	16900
55		HT	HB	FBG SV	IO	T225 12	19000	2 3	22300	24800
55		HT	HB	STL SV	IO	T225 12	17000	2 3	19900	22100
			1969 BOATS							
32		HT	HB	FBG SV	IO	120 VLVO 11	9000	1 6	9400	10700
32		HT	HB	STL SV	IO	210 11	8800	1 4	9150	10400
32		HT	HB	FBG SV	IO	225 CHRY 11	9000	1 6	9400	10700
38		HT	HB	FBG SV	IO	225 CHRY 12	11800	1 8	12400	14100

CONTINUED ON NEXT PAGE

LOA FT IN	NAME AND/OR MODEL	TOP/RIG	BOAT TYPE	HULL MTL	TP	TP#	ENGINE # HP	MFG	BEAM FT IN	WGT LBS	DRAFT FT IN	RETAIL LOW	RETAIL HIGH
— 1969 BOATS —													
38		HT	HB	FBG	SV	IO	260	CHRY	12	11800	1 8	12600	14400
38		HT	HB	STL	SV	IO	T120		12	10450	2 4	10600	12000
38		HT	HB	FBG	SV	IO	T120	VLVO	12	11800	1 8	13600	15500
40		HT	HB	FBG	SV	IO	T120		12		2 4	13700	15600
41		HT	HB	FBG	SV	IO	225	CHRY	12	12000	1 8	11600	13200
41		HT	HB	FBG	SV	IO	T200	MRCR	12	12000	1 8	12500	14200
44		HT	HB	FBG	SV	IO	225	CHRY	12	15500	2 2	13600	15500
44		HT	HB	FBG	SV	IO	T200	MRCR	12	15500	2 2	14500	16500
45		HT	HB	STL	SV	IO	225		12	14000	2 2	11700	13300
45		HT	HB	FBG	SV	IO	225	CHRY	12	14200	2 2	12900	14700
45		HT	HB	FBG	SV	IO	T260	CHRY	12	14200	2 2	14300	16300
47		HT	HB	FBG		IO	T					16500	18700
— 1968 BOATS —													
50		HT	HB	STL		IO	T		12			19200	21300
52		HT	HB	STL	SV	IO	225		12	19000	2 6	19200	21400
60		HT	HB	STL	SV	IO	225		12	23000	2 6	19500	21600
65		HT	HB	STL	SV	IO	225		12	32000	2 6	21900	24300
— 1967 BOATS —													
32			HB	STL	DV	IO	210		12	8800	1 6	9200	10400
32			HB	FBG	DV	IO	210	CHRY	12			9250	10500
38			HB	STL	DV	IO	T210		12	10450	1 8	10500	11900
38			HB	FBG	DV	IO	T265	CHRY	12			13900	15800
45			HB	FBG	DV	IO	210	CHRY	12			14500	16500
45			HB	STL	DV	IB	T160	CHRY	12	14000	2	12100	13800
50			HB	STL	DV	IO	210		12			17300	19600
52			HB	STL	DV	IO	T290		12	19000	2	21800	24200
60			HB	STL	DV	IO	T290		12	23000	2 4	21600	24100
65			HB	STL	DV	IO	T290		14	32000	2 4	24300	27000
— 1967 BOATS —													
38			HB	FBG		IO	T210	CHRY	11			13800	15700
45			HB	FBG		IO	T210	CHRY	12			14300	16200

SEAGULL MARINE SALES

Call 1-800-327-6929 for BUC Personalized Evaluation Service
Or, for 1970 to 1972 boats, sign onto www.BUCValuPro.com

SEAHORSE PLASTICS CORP
COAST GUARD MFG ID- SET

Call 1-800-327-6929 for BUC Personalized Evaluation Service
Or, for 1973 to 1993 boats, sign onto www.BUCValuPro.com

SEAIR MARINE LTD

Call 1-800-327-6929 for BUC Personalized Evaluation Service
Or, for 1981 to 1985 boats, sign onto www.BUCValuPro.com

SEAJAY BOATS INC
SPEEDLINER BOATS   COAST GUARD MFG ID- SEJ

Call 1-800-327-6929 for BUC Personalized Evaluation Service
Or, for 1959 to 1994 boats, sign onto www.BUCValuPro.com

SEAL COVE BOAT YARD
COAST GUARD MFG ID- SVB

Call 1-800-327-6929 for BUC Personalized Evaluation Service
Or, for 1965 to 1968 boats, sign onto www.BUCValuPro.com

SEALANDER

Call 1-800-327-6929 for BUC Personalized Evaluation Service
Or, for 1972 boats, sign onto www.BUCValuPro.com

SEALION SALES

Call 1-800-327-6929 for BUC Personalized Evaluation Service
Or, for 1975 to 1976 boats, sign onto www.BUCValuPro.com

SEAMAN SEACRAFT CO INC

Call 1-800-327-6929 for BUC Personalized Evaluation Service
Or, for 1960 to 1965 boats, sign onto www.BUCValuPro.com

SEAMASTER BOATS
DUXBURY MA 02332   COAST GUARD MFG ID- VFH   See inside cover to adjust price for area

LOA FT IN	NAME AND/OR MODEL	TOP/RIG	BOAT TYPE	HULL MTL	TP	TP#	ENGINE # HP	MFG	BEAM FT IN	WGT LBS	DRAFT FT IN	RETAIL LOW	RETAIL HIGH
— 1980 BOATS —													
22 6	SEAMASTER	OP	CUD	FBG	SV	OB			5 10	950	7	3250	3800
— 1979 BOATS —													
22 6	SEAMASTER	OP	CUD	FBG	SV	OB			5 10	950	7	3250	3750
— 1978 BOATS —													
22 6	SEAMASTER	OP	CUD	FBG	SV	OB			5 10	950	7	3200	3700
— 1967 BOATS —													
22	SEAMASTER 22	CR		FBG		OB			5 4	950		3050	3550

SEAMASTER LTD

Call 1-800-327-6929 for BUC Personalized Evaluation Service
Or, for 1965 to 1967 boats, sign onto www.BUCValuPro.com

SEAMASTER YACHTS
FT LAUDERDALE FL 33312   COAST GUARD MFG ID- EYT   See inside cover to adjust price for area

For more recent years, see the BUC Used Boat Price Guide, Volume 1 or Volume 2

LOA FT IN	NAME AND/OR MODEL	TOP/RIG	BOAT TYPE	HULL MTL	TP	TP#	ENGINE # HP	MFG	BEAM FT IN	WGT LBS	DRAFT FT IN	RETAIL LOW	RETAIL HIGH
— 1983 BOATS —													
45 1	SEAMASTER 45	KTH	SA/RC	F/S	KL	IB	62D	PERK	13 3	28000	5	94100	103500
— 1982 BOATS —													
28 10	SEAMASTER 29	SLP	SA/RC	F/S	KL	IB	9D	REN	9	5500	4 6	12600	14300
45 1	SEAMASTER 45	KTH	SA/RC	F/S	KL	IB	62D	PERK	13 3	28000	5	89100	97900

SEAMASTER YACHTS INC
NO MIAMI FL 33161   See inside cover to adjust price for area

For more recent years, see the BUC Used Boat Price Guide, Volume 1 or Volume 2

LOA FT IN	NAME AND/OR MODEL	TOP/RIG	BOAT TYPE	HULL MTL	TP	TP#	ENGINE # HP	MFG	BEAM FT IN	WGT LBS	DRAFT FT IN	RETAIL LOW	RETAIL HIGH
— 1983 BOATS —													
47 11	MOTOR YACHT 48	F+H	MYFD	F/S	DV	IB	T355D	CAT	15 9	44000	3 10	126000	138500
— 1982 BOATS —													
47 11	MOTOR YACHT 48	F+H	MYFD	F/S	DV	IB	T355D	CAT	15 9	44000	3 10	120500	132000

SEARIDER YACHTS LTD

Call 1-800-327-6929 for BUC Personalized Evaluation Service
Or, for 1970 boats, sign onto www.BUCValuPro.com

JOHN SEARS INT'L

Call 1-800-327-6929 for BUC Personalized Evaluation Service
Or, for 1976 boats, sign onto www.BUCValuPro.com

SEARS ROEBUCK & CO
CHICAGO IL 60684   COAST GUARD MFG ID- SES   See inside cover to adjust price for area

For more recent years, see the BUC Used Boat Price Guide, Volume 1 or Volume 2

LOA FT IN	NAME AND/OR MODEL	TOP/RIG	BOAT TYPE	HULL MTL	TP	TP#	ENGINE # HP	MFG	BEAM FT IN	WGT LBS	DRAFT FT IN	RETAIL LOW	RETAIL HIGH
— 1959 BOATS —													
18 11	6266	HT	CR	PLY		OB			6 4	760		1900	2250

SEASTREAM YACHTS LTD

Call 1-800-327-6929 for BUC Personalized Evaluation Service
Or, for 1980 to 1982 boats, sign onto www.BUCValuPro.com

SEASWIRL BOATS INC

SEASWIRL BOATS
CULVER OR 97734

COAST GUARD MFG ID- GSS
FORMERLY BRAMCO INC

See inside cover to adjust price for area

For more recent years, see the BUC Used Boat Price Guide, Volume 1 or Volume 2

LOA FT IN	NAME AND/ OR MODEL	TOP/ RIG	BOAT TYPE	HULL MTL TP	ENGINE TP # HP MFG	BEAM FT IN	WGT LBS	DRAFT FT IN	RETAIL LOW	RETAIL HIGH
			1983 BOATS							
16	SPIRIT B/R	ST	RNBT	FBG SV	IO 120 MRCR	6 9	1750		2000	2350
17	SPITFIRE	ST	RNBT	FBG DV	IO 120-170	7	1865		2300	2700
17	SPITFIRE SPORT	ST	RNBT	FBG DV	IO 170	7	1975		2700	2700
18	SIERRA	ST	RNBT	FDG DV	IO 120-230	7 6	2150		2750	3250
18	SIERRA	ST	RNBT	FBG DV	IO 260	7 6	2150		2900	3400
18	SIERRA B/R	OP	RNBT	FBG DV	OB	7 6	1450		2400	2800
18 9	CHALLENGER	ST	RNBT	FBG DV	IO 120-230	7 2	2250		2750	3350
18 9	CHALLENGER	ST	RNBT	FBG DV	IO 260	7 2	2250		3000	3500
19 2	CONTENDER	ST	RNBT	FBG DV	IO 120-230	7 6	2350		2950	3600
19 2	CONTENDER	ST	RNBT	FBG DV	IO 260	7 6	2350		3200	3750
			1982 BOATS							
16 4	SV-175	ST	FSH	FBG DV	IO 120-170	6 9	1725		2050	2450
16 4	SV-175 B/R CUSTOM	OP	RNBT	FBG DV	OB	6 9	1000		1700	2000
16 4	SV-175 B/R CUSTOM	ST	RNBT	FBG DV	IO 120-170	6 9	1850		2000	2450
16 4	SV-175 B/R CUSTOM	ST	RNBT	FBG DV	IO 260 OMC	6 9	1850		2300	2650
16 4	SV-175 C/D CUSTOM	ST	RNBT	FBG DV	IO	6 9	1750		**	**
16 8	SPITFIRE C/D FUTURA	ST	RNBT	FBG DV	IO 140-170	7	1975		2250	2600
16 8	SPITFIRE FUTURA	ST	RNBT	FBG DV	IO 140-170	7	2000		2250	2600
16 11	VENTURE	ST	RNBT	FBG TR	IO 120-170	6 8	2300		2300	2700
18	LANCER	OP	FSH	FBG DV	OB	7 2	1475		2400	2750
18	LANCER	ST	FSH	FBG DV	IO 120-170	7 2	2025		2600	3100
18	LANCER	ST	FSH	FBG DV	IO 230-260	7 2	2310		2950	3600
18	LANCER B/R CUSTOM	OP	RNBT	FBG DV	OB	7 2	1555		2450	2850
18	LANCER B/R CUSTOM	ST	RNBT	FBG DV	IO 120-230	7 2	1500		2200	2700
18	LANCER B/R CUSTOM	ST	RNBT	FBG DV	IO 260 OMC	7 6	2280		2900	3350
18	LANCER C/D CUSTOM	OP	RNBT	FBG DV	OB	7 2	1500		2400	2800
18	LANCER C/D CUSTOM	ST	RNBT	FBG DV	IO 120-200	7 2	2030		2450	2900
18	LANCER C/D CUSTOM	ST	RNBT	FBG DV	IO 230-260	7 2	2310		2700	3300
18	LANCER C/R CUSTOM	ST	RNBT	FBG DV	IO 200 OMC	7 2	1500		2250	2650
18 9	CHALLENGER DLX	ST	RNBT	FBG DV	IO	7 2	2250		**	**
18 9	CHALLENGER STD	ST	RNBT	FBG DV	IO	7 2	2250		**	**
19 2	CONTENDER	ST	RNBT	FBG DV	IO 120-260	7 6	2550		3000	3750
19 2	POLARIS	ST	RNBT	FBG DV	IO 140-200	7 6	2280		2850	3350
19 2	POLARIS	ST	RNBT	FBG DV	IO 230-260	7 6	2560		3100	3800
			1980 BOATS							
16 4	SV-175	OP	RNBT	FBG DV	OB	6 9			2650	3050
16 4	SV-175	ST	RNBT	FBG DV	IO 120-170	6 9	1692		1900	3250
16 4	SV-175 OPEN BOW	OP	RNBT	FBG DV	OB	6 9			2850	3300
16 4	SV-175 OPEN BOW	ST	RNBT	FBG DV	IO 120-170	6 9	1732		1950	2400
16 11	VENTURE	ST	RNBT	FBG TR	IO 120-185	6 8	2030		2200	2700
16 11	VENTURE	ST	RNBT	FBG TR	IO 198 MRCR	6 8	2325		2400	2800
18	LANCER	OP	RNBT	FBG DV	OB	7 2	1750		2550	2950
18	LANCER	ST	RNBT	FBG DV	IO 120-185	7 2	2030		2350	2950
18	LANCER	ST	RNBT	FBG DV	IO 198-260	7 2	2325		2600	3250
18	LANCER OPEN BOW	OP	RNBT	FBG DV	OB	7 2	1855		2650	3050
18	LANCER OPEN BOW	ST	RNBT	FBG DV	IO 120-185	7 2	2030		2450	3050
18	LANCER OPEN BOW	ST	RNBT	FBG DV	IO 198-260	7 2	2325		2650	3300
19 2	POLARIS CUDDY	ST	CUD	FBG DV	IO 120-185	7 6	2280		2900	3550
19 2	POLARIS CUDDY	ST	CUD	FBG DV	IO 198-260	7 6	2575		3100	3850
19 2	POLARIS OPEN	ST	RNBT	FBG DV	IO 120-185	7 6	2280		2800	3450
19 2	POLARIS OPEN	ST	RNBT	FBG DV	IO 198-260	7 6	2575		3000	3750
			1979 BOATS							
16 4	SV-175	ST	RNBT	FBG DV	IO 120-170	6 9	1750		1900	2300
16 4	SV-175 OPEN BOW	ST	RNBT	FBG DV	IO 120-170	6 9	1750		2000	2400
16 11	VENTURE	ST	RNBT	FBG TR	IO 120-198	6 8	2300		2300	2750
18	LANCER	ST	RNBT	FBG DV	IO 120-230	7 2	2300		2550	3050
18	LANCER	ST	RNBT	FBG DV	IO 260	7 2	2300		2800	3250
18	LANCER OPEN BOW	ST	RNBT	FBG DV	IO 120-230	7 2	2300		2650	3150
18	LANCER OPEN BOW	ST	RNBT	FBG DV	IO 260	7 2	2300		2900	3350
19 2	POLARIS CUDDY	ST	CUD	FBG DV	IO 120-230	7 6	2550		3050	3700
19 2	POLARIS CUDDY	ST	CUD	FBG DV	IO 260	7 6	2550		3300	3850
19 2	POLARIS OPEN	ST	RNBT	FBG DV	IO 120-230	7 6	2500		2900	3550
19 2	POLARIS OPEN	ST	RNBT	FBG DV	IO 260	7 6	2500		3150	3650
			1978 BOATS							
16 4	SSV-175	ST	RNBT	FBG DV	IO 120-140	6 9	1692		1900	2300
16 11	VENTURE	ST	RNBT	FBG TR	IO 120-185	6 8	2030		2200	2750
16 11	VENTURE	ST	RNBT	FBG TR	IO 198 MRCR	6 8	2325		2400	2800
17 8	FALCON	OP	RNBT	FBG TR	OB	7 2	1400		2050	2450
17 8	FALCON	ST	RNBT	FBG TR	IO 120-185	7 2	2180		2450	3050
17 8	FALCON	ST	RNBT	FBG TR	IO 198-260	7 2	2475		2700	3350
18	LANCER	OP	RNBT	FBG DV	OB	7 2	1250		1900	2300
18	LANCER	ST	RNBT	FBG DV	IO 120-185	7 2	2030		2400	3000
18	LANCER	ST	RNBT	FBG DV	IO 198-260	7 2	2325		2650	3300
19 2	POLARIS CUDDY	ST	CUD	FBG DV	IO 120-185	7 6	2280		2900	3600
19 2	POLARIS CUDDY	ST	CUD	FBG DV	IO 198-260	7 6	2575		3150	3900
19 2	POLARIS OPEN	ST	RNBT	FBG DV	IO 120-185	7 6	2280		2800	3450
19 2	POLARIS OPEN	ST	RNBT	FBG DV	IO 198-260	7 6	2575		3050	3750
19 9	CITATION	ST	RNBT	FBG TR	IO 185-240	7 8	2750		3250	3950
19 9	CITATION	ST	RNBT	FBG TR	IO 260 MRCR	7 8	2805		3500	4050
			1977 BOATS							
16 3	RANGER	ST	RNBT	FBG SV	IO 120-140	6 8	1700		1950	2300
16 11	VENTURE	ST	RNBT	FBG TR	IO 120-190	6 8	2200		2300	2900
17 8	FALCON	OP	RNBT	FBG TR	OB	7 2	1400		2200	2550
17 8	FALCON	ST	RNBT	FBG TR	IO 120-190	7 2	2350		2600	3200
17 8	FALCON	ST	RNBT	FBG TR	IO 233-235	7 2	2650		2900	3400
18	LANCER	OP	RNBT	FBG DV	OB	7 2	1350		2000	2400
18	LANCER	ST	RNBT	FBG DV	IO 120-190	7 2	2350		2650	3150
18	LANCER	ST	RNBT	FBG DV	IO 233-235	7 2	2500		2850	3350
19 2	POLARIS	ST	RNBT	FBG DV	IO 120-190	7 6	2450		2950	3650
19 2	POLARIS	ST	RNBT	FBG DV	IO 233-235	7 6	2700		3300	3800
19 9	CITATION	ST	RNBT	FBG TR	IO 165-190	7 8	2700		3250	3950
19 9	CITATION	ST	RNBT	FBG TR	IO 233-235	7 8	2950		3550	4150
			1976 BOATS							
16 3	RANGER	OP	RNBT	FBG DV	IO 120-140	7 2	1700		1950	2300
17 8	FALCON	OP	RNBT	FBG TR	OB	7 2	1350		1950	2350
17 8	FALCON	OP	RNBT	FBG TR	IO 120-190	7 2	2100		2500	3100
18	LANCER	OP	RNBT	FBG DV	OB	7 2	1250		1850	2200
18	LANCER	OP	RNBT	FBG DV	IO 120-190	7 2	2000		2500	3100
19 2	POLARIS	OP	RNBT	FBG DV	IO 120-190	7 6	2250		2900	3550
19 9	CITATION	OP	RNBT	FBG TR	IO 165-190	7 8	2530		3250	3850
			1975 BOATS							
16 3	RANGER	ST	RNBT	FBG DV	IO 120-140	6 8	1600		2000	2400
17 7	ROGUE	OP	RNBT	FBG DV	OB	7 1	1750		1750	2100
17 7	ROGUE	ST	RNBT	FBG DV	IO 120-175	7 1	1950		2500	3050
17 7	ROGUE	ST	RNBT	FBG DV	IO 188-190	7 1	2210		2700	3100
17 8	FALCON	OP	RNBT	FBG TR	OB	7 2	1350		1950	2300
17 8	FALCON	ST	RNBT	FBG TR	IO 120-175	7 2	2100		2600	3150
17 8	FALCON	ST	RNBT	FBG TR	IO 188-190	7 2	2360		2800	3250
19 2	POLARIS	ST	RNBT	FBG DV	IO 120-190	7 6	2250		3000	3650
19 9	CITATION	ST	RNBT	FBG TR	IO 165-190	7 8	2540		3350	4050
			1974 BOATS							
16 3	RANGER		RNBT	FBG DV	IO 120-140	6 8			2550	3000
16 3	RANGER		RNBT	FBG DV	IO 120-140	6 8			2550	3000
17 7	FALCON		RNBT	FBG TR	OB	7 2			2600	3050
17 7	FALCON		RNBT	FBG TR	IO 120-225	7 2			2850	3450
17 9	ROGUE		RNBT	FBG DV	OB	7 1			2650	3050
17 9	ROGUE		RNBT	FBG DV	IO 120-188	7 1			2900	3400
18 7	MARLIN		CUD	FBG	IO 120-188	7 6			3850	4500
18 7	MARLIN		RNBT	FBG	OB	7 6			2800	3250
18 7	MARLIN		RNBT	FBG	IO 120-188	7 6			3400	4000
19 8	CITATION		RNBT	FBG TR	IO 165-225	7 8			3800	4500
			1968 BOATS							
17 1	SS-17	ST		FBG	IO 80-120		1450		2650	3200

SEAWARD INDUSTRIES INC

COAST GUARD MFG ID- SWD

Call 1-800-327-6929 for BUC Personalized Evaluation Service
Or, for 1973 to 1974 boats, sign onto www.BUCValuPro.com

SEAWAY BOATS INC
WINTHROP ME 04101   COAST GUARD MFG ID- XKX See inside cover to adjust price for area

For more recent years, see the BUC Used Boat Price Guide, Volume 1 or Volume 2

LOA FT IN	NAME AND/ OR MODEL	TOP/ RIG	BOAT TYPE	MTL	HULL TP	TP	ENGINE # HP	MFG	BEAM FT IN	WGT LBS	DRAFT FT IN	RETAIL LOW	RETAIL HIGH
--- 1983 BOATS ---													
16 6	COMMERCIAL	OP	UTL	FBG	SV	OB			6 8	800	6	**	**
16 6	SEASPRAY	OP	RNBT	FBG	SV	OB			6 8	825	6	2500	2900
16 6	SKIFF	OP	UTL	FBG	SV	OB			6 8	650	6	1950	2300
16 6	SPORTSMAN	OP	OPFSH	FBG	SV	OB			6 8	825	6	2500	2900
18 10		OP	CUD	FBG	RB	OB			7 5	1300	5	3950	4600
18 10		ST	RNBT	FBG	RB	OB			7 5	1150	5	3600	4150
18 10		ST	RNBT	FBG	RB	IO	120	MRCR	7 5		5	4400	5050
18 10	COMMERCIAL	OP	CTRCN	FBG	RB	OB			7 5	1100	5	**	**
18 10	COMMERCIAL	OP	CTRCN	FBG	RB	IO	120		7 5	1100	5	**	**
18 10	COMMERCIAL CUDDY	ST	CBNCR	FBG	RB	OB			7 5	1250	5	**	**
18 10	COMMERCIAL CUDDY	ST	CBNCR	FBG	RB	IO	120		7 5	1250	5	**	**
18 10	OPEN FISHERMAN	OP	CTRCN	FBG	RB	OB			7 5	1250	5	3800	4450
18 10	OPEN FISHERMAN	OP	CTRCN	FBG	RB	IO	120		7 5	1250	5	4700	5400
18 10	SEAFARER		CUD	FBG	RB	OB			7 5	1250	5	3800	4450
18 10	SEAFARER		CUD	FBG	RB	IO	120		7 5	1250	5	4500	5150
18 10	VOYAGER	ST	RNBT	FBG	RB	OB			7 5	1250	5	3800	4450
18 10	VOYAGER	ST	RNBT	FBG	RB	IO	120		7 5	1250	5	4400	5050
20	SALTY-DOG	OP	RNBT	FBG	SV	OB			8	1700	9	5900	6800
20	SALTY-DOG	OP	RNBT	FBG	SV	IO	120-170		8	1700	9	5700	6900
22 10	COMMERCIAL	OP	UTL	FBG	RB	OB			7 9	1600		**	**
22 10	COMMERCIAL	OP	UTL	FBG	RB	IO	120-170		7 9	1600		**	**
22 10	COMMERCIAL CUDDY	HT	CBNCR	FBG	RB	OB			7 9	2000		**	**
22 10	COMMERCIAL CUDDY	HT	CBNCR	FBG	RB	IO	120-170		7 9	2000		**	**
22 10	SEA HAVEN	OP	CUD	FBG	RB	OB			7 9	2200		8200	9400
22 10	SEA HAVEN	OP	CUD	FBG	RB	IO	120-170		7 9	2200		7500	8950
22 10	SPORT FISHERMAN	OP	CTRCN	FBG	RB	OB			7 9	1900		7100	8200
22 10	SPORT FISHERMAN	OP	CTRCN	FBG	RB	IO	120-170		7 9	1900		7550	9050
25 11	COMMERCIAL		UTL	FBG		OB			10	4500	2 7	**	**
25 11	COMMERCIAL		UTL	FBG		SE	115	OMC	10	4500	2 7	**	**
25 11	COMMERCIAL		UTL	FBG		IB	220		10	4500	2 7	**	**
25 11	EXPLORER		CTRCN	FBG		OB			10	4500	2 7	15000	17000
25 11	EXPLORER		CTRCN	FBG		IB		VLVO	10	4500	2 7	**	**
25 11	EXPLORER		CTRCN	FBG		SE	115	OMC	10	4500	2 7	15000	17000
25 11	EXPLORER		CTRCN	FBG		IB	220	CRUS	10	4500	2 7	18900	21000
25 11	FULL HOUSE COMM		FH	FBG		OB			10	4500	2 7	**	**
IB 40 VLVO **		**	, SE	115	OMC	**		** , IB 220 CRUS		**		**	**
25 11	NORTH STAR		CUD	FBG		OB			10	4500	2 7	15500	17700
25 11	NORTH STAR		CUD	FBG		IB	40	VLVO	10	4500	2 7	15800	18000
25 11	NORTH STAR		CUD	FBG		SE	115	OMC	10	4500	2 7	15500	17700
25 11	NORTH STAR		CUD	FBG		IB	220	CRUS	10	4500	2 7	18900	21000
--- 1982 BOATS ---													
16 6	COMMERCIAL	OP	UTL	FBG	SV	OB			6 8	800	6	**	**
16 6	SKIFF	OP		FBG	SV	OB			6 8	650	6	1900	2300
16 6	SPORTSMAN	OP	OPFSH	FBG	SV	OB			6 8	825	6	2450	2850
18 10		OP	CUD	FBG	RB	OB			7 5	1300	5	3850	4450
18 10		OP	RNBT	FBG	RB	IB	68D		7 5			9050	10300
18 10		ST	RNBT	FBG	RB	OB			7 5	1150	5	3050	4050
18 10	COMMERCIAL	OP	CTRCN	FBG	RB	IB			7 5	1100	5	**	**
18 10	COMMERCIAL	OP	CTRCN	FBG	RB	IB	42D		7 5			**	**
18 10	COMMERCIAL CUDDY	ST	CBNCR	FBG	RB	OB			7 5	1250	5	**	**
18 10	OPEN FISHERMAN	OP	CTRCN	FBG	RB	OB			7 5	1150	5	3450	4050
18 10	OPEN FISHERMAN	OP	CTRCN	FBG	RB	IB	68D		7 5			9250	10500
20	COMMERCIAL	OP	UTL	FBG	SV	OB			8	1400		**	**
20	SALTY-DOG	OP	CTRCN	FBG	SV	OB			8	1600		5400	6200
22 10	COMMERCIAL	OP	UTL	FBG	RB	OB			8	2000		**	**
22 10	COMMERCIAL	OP	UTL	FBG	RB	IB	170	MRCR	8			**	**
22 10	COMMERCIAL	OP	UTL	FBG	RB	IB	82D		8			**	**
22 10	COMMERCIAL CUDDY	HT	CBNCR	FBG	RB	OB			8	2400		**	**
22 10	COMMERCIAL CUDDY	HT	CBNCR	FBG	RB	IB	82D		8			7850	9000
22 10	SPORT FISHERMAN	OP	CTRCN	FBG	RB	OB			8	2200		15200	17300
22 10	SPORT FISHERMAN	OP	CTRCN	FBG	RB	IB	82D		8			8550	9850
22 10	SPORT FISHERMAN	OP	CUD	FBG	RB	OB			8	2400		9100	10400
22 10	SPORT FISHERMAN	OP	CUD	FBG	RB	IB	170	MRCR	8			16100	18300
22 10	SPORT FISHERMAN	OP	CUD	FBG	RB	IB	82D		8				
--- 1981 BOATS ---													
18 10	SEAWAY 19		OPFSH	FBG		OB			7 5	1500	5	4150	4800
22 10	SEAWAY 23			FBG		IO	170	MRCR	7 11	2400	2 1	7600	8750

SEAWIND BOAT MFG CO
POMPANO BEACH FL 33060   See inside cover to adjust price for area

LOA FT IN	NAME AND/ OR MODEL	TOP/ RIG	BOAT TYPE	MTL	HULL TP	TP	ENGINE # HP	MFG	BEAM FT IN	WGT LBS	DRAFT FT IN	RETAIL LOW	RETAIL HIGH
--- 1972 BOATS ---													
21 6	SPORT V-22		RNBT	FBG		IO	120-225		8		2 5	4850	5700
21 6	V-21	OP	RNBT	FBG		IO	120-225		8		2 5	4850	5700
23 6	GALAXY V-24			FBG		IO	155-245		8		1 8	6200	7350
23 6	GALAXY V-24			FBG		IO	T120	OMC	8		1 8	6850	7900
23 6	V-24		CR	FBG		IO	120-245		8		1 8	6550	7750
23 6	V-24		CR	FBG		IO	T120	OMC	8			7250	8350
23 6	V-24 CUSTOM	HT		FBG		IO	120-245		8		1 8	6200	7350
23 6	V-24 CUSTOM	HT		FBG		IO	T120	OMC	8			6850	7900
23 6	V-24 CUSTOM	FB		FBG		IO	120-245		8		1 8	6200	7350
23 6	V-24 CUSTOM	FB		FBG		IO	T120	OMC	8			6850	7900
28	V-28 CUSTOM	HT		FBG		IO	245	OMC	10		2 6	13100	14900
IB 225 CHRY 8450		9700, IO	245	OMC	13300	15100,	IO T120-T155		13400	15900			
IO T225 OMC 15000		17000, IB T225	CHRY	9650	10900								
28	V-28 CUSTOM	FB		FBG		IO	245	OMC	10		2 6	13100	14900
IB 225 CHRY 8450		9700, IO	245	OMC	13300	15100,	IO T120-T155		13400	15900			
IO T225 OMC 15000		17000, IB T225	CHRY	9650	10900								
28	V-28 CUSTOM	CNV		FBG		IO	245	OMC	10		2	16800	19100
IB 225 CHRY 10200		11600, IO	245	OMC	17100	19400,	IO T120-T155		17300	20400			
IO T225 OMC 19400		21600, IB T225	CHRY	11600	13100								

SEAY-CRAFT
Call 1-800-327-6929 for BUC Personalized Evaluation Service
Or, for 1959 to 1960 boats, sign onto www.BUCValuPro.com

SEIYEN ENTERPRISES CO LTD
COAST GUARD MFG ID- SYE

Call 1-800-327-6929 for BUC Personalized Evaluation Service
Or, for 1980 boats, sign onto www.BUCValuPro.com

SELJE BRUK A/S
SAGA BOATS

LAUDERDALE MARINA

Call 1-800-327-6929 for BUC Personalized Evaluation Service
Or, for 1973 to 1977 boats, sign onto www.BUCValuPro.com

SEMICAT INC
Call 1-800-327-6929 for BUC Personalized Evaluation Service
Or, for 1960 boats, sign onto www.BUCValuPro.com

SERENDIPITY YACHTS
CORTE MADERA CA 94925-1238   See inside cover to adjust price for area

For more recent years, see the BUC Used Boat Price Guide, Volume 1 or Volume 2

LOA FT IN	NAME AND/ OR MODEL	TOP/ RIG	BOAT TYPE	MTL	HULL TP	TP	ENGINE # HP	MFG	BEAM FT IN	WGT LBS	DRAFT FT IN	RETAIL LOW	RETAIL HIGH
--- 1983 BOATS ---													
40 8	SERENDIPITY 41	SLP	SA/RC	FBG	KL	IB	D		12 8	15400	7 4	53500	58800
42 4	SERENDIPITY 43	SLP	SA/RC	FBG	KL	IB	D		13 3	17800	7 4	63800	70100
--- 1982 BOATS ---													
42 4	SERENDIPITY 43	SLP	SA/RC	FBG	KL	IB	50D	PERK	13 3	17800	7 4	59700	65600
--- 1981 BOATS ---													
42 4	SERENDIPITY 43	SLP	SA/RC	FBG	KL	IB	50D	PERK	13 3	17800	7 4	56200	61700
--- 1980 BOATS ---													
42 6	SERENDIPITY 43	SLP	SA/RC	FBG	KL	IB	50D	PATH	13 3	17800	7 6	54400	59800

SETTON BOATS
COAST GUARD MFG ID- XTT

Call 1-800-327-6929 for BUC Personalized Evaluation Service
Or, for 1980 to 1983 boats, sign onto www.BUCValuPro.com

SEVEN EYES YACHTS INC

Call 1-800-327-6929 for BUC Personalized Evaluation Service
Or, for 1982 boats, sign onto www.BUCValuPro.com

SEVEN SEAS BOAT WORKS
FIBERGLASS FABRICATORS INC

Call 1-800-327-6929 for BUC Personalized Evaluation Service
Or, for 1983 to 1988 boats, sign onto www.BUCValuPro.com

SEVERN VALLEY CRUISERS

Call 1-800-327-6929 for BUC Personalized Evaluation Service
Or, for 1979 to 1980 boats, sign onto www.BUCValuPro.com

SEVILLE BOAT COMPANY
CUSTOM COMPONENTS   COAST GUARD MFG ID- CXW

Call 1-800-327-6929 for BUC Personalized Evaluation Service
Or, for 1979 boats, sign onto www.BUCValuPro.com

SEYLER MARINE INC
COAST GUARD MFG ID- SIG

Call 1-800-327-6929 for BUC Personalized Evaluation Service
Or, for 1983 to 1986 boats, sign onto www.BUCValuPro.com

SHAMROCK
BLADEN COMPOSITES LLC   See inside cover to adjust price for area
DIV OF PALMBER MARINE OF WA
BLADENBORO NC 28320   COAST GUARD MFG ID- OPA

For more recent years, see the BUC Used Boat Price Guide, Volume 1 or Volume 2

LOA FT IN	NAME AND/ OR MODEL	TOP/ RIG	BOAT TYPE	HULL MTL	HULL TP	ENGINE TP	#	HP	MFG	BEAM FT IN	WGT LBS	DRAFT FT IN	RETAIL LOW	RETAIL HIGH
			1983 BOATS											
20	CENTER CONSOLE	OP	CTRCN	FBG	SV	IO			PCM	7 11	2400	1 10	**	**
20	CON-WALK	OP	OPFSH	FBG	SV	IO			PCM	7 11	2650	1 10	**	**
20	CON-WALK	OP	OPFSH	FBG	SV	IO		185	PCM	7 11	2650	1 10	5150	5900
20	CON-WALK	OP	OPFSH	FBG	SV	IB		85D	PERK	7 11	2650	1 10	9100	10300
20	CUDDY CABIN	OP	CUD	FBG	SV	IO		220	PCM	7 11	3000	1 11	5350	6150
20	CUDDY CABIN	OP	CUD	FBG	SV	IB		85D	PERK	7 11	3000	1 11	9500	10800
20	PILOT-HOUSE	HT	UTL	FBG	SV	IO		200	PCM	7 11	2650	1 10	5200	5950
20	PILOT-HOUSE	HT	UTL	FBG	SV	IB		85D	PERK	7 11	2650	1 10	9100	10300
20	WALK-THRU	OP	OPFSH	FBG	SV	IO		220	PCM	7 11	2750	1 10	5350	6150
20	WALK-THRU	OP	OPFSH	FBG	SV	IB		85D	PERK	7 11	2750	1 10	9200	10500
25 9	CENTER CONSOLE	OP	CTRCN	FBG	SV	IB		250	PCM	8	4000	2	9800	11200
25 9	CENTER CONSOLE	OP	CTRCN	FBG	SV	IB		200D	PERK	8	4000	2	15300	17300
25 9	CUDDY CABIN	OP	CUD	FBG	SV	IO		250	PCM	8	4400	2	9800	11100
25 9	CUDDY CABIN	OP	CUD	FBG	SV	IB		200D	PERK	8	4400	2	16200	18400
25 9	PILOT-HOUSE	HT	UTL	FBG	SV	IO		250	PCM	8	4300	2	10200	11600
25 9	PILOT-HOUSE	HT	UTL	FBG	SV	IB		200D	PERK	8	4300	2	16000	18100
			1982 BOATS											
20	CENTER CONSOLE	OP	CTRCN	FBG	SV	IO		170-200	PCM	7 11	2400	1 10	4750	5550
20	CENTER CONSOLE	OP	CTRCN	FBG	SV	IO		80D	PERK	7 11	2400	1 10	8250	9450
20	CON-WALK	OP	OPFSH	FBG	SV	IO		170-200	PCM	7 11	2650	1 10	5000	5800
20	CON-WALK	OP	OPFSH	FBG	SV	IB		80D	PERK	7 11	2650	1 10	8550	9850
20	CUDDY CABIN	OP	CUD	FBG	SV	IO		170-220	PCM	7 11	3000	1 11	5100	6000
20	CUDDY CABIN	OP	CUD	FBG	SV	IB		80D	PERK	7 11	3000	1 11	9100	10400
20	PILOT-HOUSE	HT	UTL	FBG	SV	IO		170-200	PCM	7 11	2650	1 10	5000	5800
20	PILOT-HOUSE	HT	UTL	FBG	SV	IB		80D	PERK	7 11	2650	1 10	8550	9850
20	WALK-THRU	OP	OPFSH	FBG	SV	IO		170-220	PCM	7 11	2750	1 10	5100	6000
20	WALK-THRU	OP	OPFSH	FBG	SV	IB		80D	PERK	7 11	2750	1 10	8700	10000
25 9	CENTER CONSOLE	OP	CTRCN	FBG	SV	IB		250	PCM	8	4000	2	9600	10900
25 9	CENTER CONSOLE	OP	CTRCN	FBG	SV	IB		200D	PERK	8	4000	2	14700	16700
25 9	CUDDY CABIN	OP	CUD	FBG	SV	IO		250	PCM	8	4400	2	9550	10900
25 9	CUDDY CABIN	OP	CUD	FBG	SV	IB		200D	PERK	8	4400	2	15600	17700
25 9	PILOT-HOUSE	HT	UTL	FBG	SV	IO		250	PCM	8	4300	2	9950	11300
25 9	PILOT-HOUSE	HT	UTL	FBG	SV	IB		200D	PERK	8	4300	2	15300	17400
			1981 BOATS											
20	CENTER CONSOLE	OP	CTRCN	FBG	SV	IB		170-220	PCM	7 11	2400	1 10	5150	6000
20	CENTER CONSOLE	OP	CTRCN	FBG	SV	IB		80D	PERK	7 11	2400	1 10	7900	9100
20	CON-WALK	OP	OPFSH	FBG	SV	IB		170-220	PCM	7 11	2650	1 10	5500	6400
20	CON-WALK	OP	OPFSH	FBG	SV	IB		80D	PERK	7 11	2650	1 10	8300	9500
20	CUDDY CABIN	OP	CUD	FBG	SV	IB		170-220	PCM	7 11	2900	1 10	5750	6650
20	CUDDY CABIN	OP	CUD	FBG	SV	IB		80D	PERK	7 11	2900	1 10	8550	9800
20	PILOT-HOUSE	HT	UTL	FBG	SV	IB		170-220	PCM	7 11	2550	1 10	5300	6200
20	PILOT-HOUSE	HT	UTL	FBG	SV	IB		80D	PERK	7 11	2550	1 10	8100	9300
20	WALK-THRU	OP	OPFSH	FBG	SV	IB		170-220	PCM	7 11	2650	1 10	5400	6200
20	WALK-THRU	OP	OPFSH	FBG	SV	IB		80D	PERK	7 11	2650	1 10	8150	9350
25 9	CENTER CONSOLE	OP	CTRCN	FBG	SV	IB		250	PCM	8	4000	2	10400	11800
25 9	CENTER CONSOLE	OP	CTRCN	FBG	SV	IB		200D	PERK	8	4600	2	15400	17500
25 9	CUDDY CABIN	OP	CUD	FBG	SV	IB		250	PCM	8	4400	2	11000	12400
25 9	CUDDY CABIN	OP	CUD	FBG	SV	IB		200D	PERK	8	5000	2	16300	18500
25 9	PILOT-HOUSE	HT	UTL	FBG	SV	IB		250	PCM	8	4300	2	10800	12300
25 9	PILOT-HOUSE	HT	UTL	FBG	SV	IB		200D	PERK	8	4900	2	16100	18300
			1980 BOATS											
20	CENTER CONSOLE	OP	CTRCN	FBG	SV	IB		185-215	PCM	7 11	2400	1 10	4950	5750
20	CENTER CONSOLE	OP	CTRCN	FBG	SV	IB		80D	PERK	7 11	2400	1 10	7600	8750
20	CON-WALK	OP	OPFSH	FBG	SV	IB		185-215	PCM	7 11	2650	1 10	5250	6050
20	CON-WALK	OP	OPFSH	FBG	SV	IB		80D	PERK	7 11	2650	1 10	7850	9000
20	CUDDY CABIN	OP	CUD	FBG	SV	IB		215	PCM	7 11	2900	1 10	5550	6350
20	CUDDY CABIN	OP	CUD	FBG	SV	IB		80D	PERK	7 11	2900	1 10	8200	9450
20	PILOT-HOUSE	HT	UTL	FBG	SV	IB		185-215	PCM	7 11	2550	1 10	5100	5900
20	PILOT-HOUSE	HT	UTL	FBG	SV	IB		80D	PERK	7 11	2550	1 10	7800	8950
20	WALK-THRU	OP	OPFSH	FBG	SV	IB		215	PCM	7 11	2650	1 10	5250	6050
20	WALK-THRU	OP	OPFSH	FBG	SV	IB		80D	PERK	7 11	2650	1 10	8000	9150
25 9	CENTER CONSOLE	OP	CTRCN	FBG	SV	IB		250	PCM	8	4300	2	10400	11800
25 9	CENTER CONSOLE	OP	CTRCN	FBG	SV	IB		185D	PERK	8	4300	2	13800	15700
25 9	PILOT-HOUSE	HT	UTL	FBG	SV	IB		250	PCM	8	4450	2	10600	12000
25 9	PILOT-HOUSE	HT	UTL	FBG	SV	IB		185D	PERK	8	4450	2	14200	16100
			1979 BOATS											
20	CENTER CONSOLE	OP	CTRCN	FBG	SV	IB		185-215	PCM	7 11	2400	1 10	4750	5500
20	CENTER CONSOLE	OP	CTRCN	FBG	SV	IB		80D-105D	PERK	7 11	2400	1 10	7350	8400
20	CON-WALK	OP	OPFSH	FBG	SV	IB		215	PCM	7 11	2650	1 10	5150	5950
20	CON-WALK	OP	OPFSH	FBG	SV	IB		80D-105D	PERK	7 11	2650	1 10	7750	8900
20	CUDDY CABIN	OP	CUD	FBG	SV	IB		215	PCM	7 11	2900	1 10	5300	6100
20	CUDDY CABIN	OP	CUD	FBG	SV	IB		80D-105D	PERK	7 11	2900	1 10	7900	9100
20	PILOT-HOUSE	OP	UTL	FBG	SV	IB		80D	PERK	7 11	2550	1 10	7500	8600
20	PILOT-HOUSE	HT	UTL	FBG	SV	IB		185-215	PCM	7 11	2550	1 10	4900	5700
20	PILOT-HOUSE	HT	UTL	FBG	SV	IB		105D	CHRY	7 11	2550	1 10	7500	8600
20	WALK-THRU	OP	OPFSH	FBG	SV	IB		215	PCM	7 11	2650	1 10	4900	5650
20	WALK-THRU	OP	OPFSH	FBG	SV	IB		80D-105D	PCM	7 11	2650	1 10	7450	8600
			1978 BOATS											
20	CENTER CONSOLE	OP	OPFSH	FBG	SV	IB		200	PCM	7 11	2400	1 10	4600	5300
20	CUDDY-CABIN	OP	CUD	FBG	SV	IB		225	PCM	7 11	2900	1 10	5100	5850
20	WALK-THRU	OP	OPFSH	FBG	SV	IB		225	PCM	7 11	2650	1 10	4850	5550
			1977 BOATS											
20	SHAMROCK	OP	CUD	FBG	SV	IB		185-255	PCM	7 10	2900	1 10	4850	5650
20	SHAMROCK	OP	CUD	FBG	SV	IB		105D	CHRY	7 10	2900	1 10	7200	8300
20	SHAMROCK	OP	OPFSH	FBG	SV	IB		185-255	PCM	7 10	2400	1 10	4400	5100
20	SHAMROCK	OP	OPFSH	FBG	SV	IB		105D	CHRY	7 10	2400	1 10	6650	7650
20	SHAMROCK WALK-THRU	OP	RNBT	FBG	SV	IB		215-255	PCM	7 10	2650	1 10	4750	5500
20	SHAMROCK WALK-THRU	OP	RNBT	FBG	SV	IB		105D	CHRY	7 10	2650	1 10	7050	8100
			1976 BOATS											
20	SHAMROCK	OP	OPFSH	FBG	SV	IB		165-185		7 10	2400	1 10	4100	4850
20	SHAMROCK	ST	OPFSH	FBG	SV	IB		165-185		7 10	2400	1 10	4100	4850

SHARK BOATS LTD

Call 1-800-327-6929 for BUC Personalized Evaluation Service
Or, for 1965 to 1969 boats, sign onto www.BUCValuPro.com

SHARK SHOP

Call 1-800-327-6929 for BUC Personalized Evaluation Service
Or, for 1982 boats, sign onto www.BUCValuPro.com

SHELCRAFT INC

Call 1-800-327-6929 for BUC Personalized Evaluation Service
Or, for 1958 to 1960 boats, sign onto www.BUCValuPro.com

SHELL LAKE BOAT CO

Call 1-800-327-6929 for BUC Personalized Evaluation Service
Or, for 1961 to 1969 boats, sign onto www.BUCValuPro.com

SHELL LAKE FIBERGLAS

DIV OF LUND AMERICAN IN COAST GUARD MFG ID- SLB

Call 1-800-327-6929 for BUC Personalized Evaluation Service
Or, for 1959 to 1980 boats, sign onto www.BUCValuPro.com

SHELTER ISLAND BOAT YARD

COAST GUARD MFG ID- XSX

Call 1-800-327-6929 for BUC Personalized Evaluation Service
Or, for 1961 to 1965 boats, sign onto www.BUCValuPro.com

SHEPHERD BOATS LTD

NIAGARA ON LAKE ONTARIO CANADA See inside cover to adjust price for area
FOR MORE RECENT MODELS SEE TROJAN YACHTS

LOA FT IN	NAME AND/ OR MODEL			TOP/ RIG	BOAT TYPE	-HULL- MTL TP	TP	----ENGINE--- # HP MFG		BEAM FT IN	WGT LBS	DRAFT FT IN	RETAIL LOW	RETAIL HIGH
				---- 1970	BOATS ----									
42				MY	MHG	IB	T300	CHRY 13 11	21000	3	4	30700	34100
46				MY	MHG	IB	T300	CHRY 15 4	30000	3	10	40300	44800
	IB T300 INT	40300	44800, IB	T320	CRUS	41600	46200,	IB T270D	GM			46300	50900
	IB T280D GM	46900	51600, IB	T300D	CUM	47800	52600,	IB T370D	CUM			51300	56300
50				DCMY	MHG SV	IB	T300	CHRY 15 4	46000	3	10	58300	64000
	IB T320 CRUS	58400	64200, IB	T270D	GM	59900	65900,	IB T280D	GM			60300	66300
	IB T300D CUM	61100	67200, IB	T370D	CUM	63300	69500						
50				MY	MHG	IB	T300	INT 15 4	46000	3	10	58200	64000
				---- 1969	BOATS ----									
41				MY	MHG	IB	T165	13 11	19000	3	4	25600	28400
42				MY	MHG SV	IB	T300	CHRY 13 11	21000	3	4	29700	33000
	IB T300 INT	29800	33100, IB	T320	CRUS	30200	33500,	IB T165D	PERK			33400	37100
	IB T215D CUM	33600	37300, IB	T216D	GM	33700	37500,	IB T270D	GM			34800	38600
	IB T300D CUM	35200	39100										
46				MY	MHG SV	IB	T300	CHRY 15 4	30000	3	10	38900	43400
	IB T300 INT	39100	43400, IB	T320	CRUS	40300	44700,	IB T270D	GM			44300	49200
	IB T280D GM	44900	49900, IB	T300D	CUM	46600	51200,	IB T370D	CUM			49600	54500
50				MY	MHG SV	IB	T300	CHRY 15 4	46000	3	10	56300	61800
	IB T300 INT	56300	61900, IB	T320	CRUS	56800	62400,	IB T270D	GM			58800	64600
	IB T280D GM	59200	65100, IB	T300D	CUM	59600	65500,	IB T370D	CUM			62200	68300
60				MY	MHG	IB	T350D	16 3		4	2	85400	93900
				---- 1968	BOATS ----									
41				DCMY	MHG	IB	T300	CHRY 13 11	21000	3	4	26800	29800
	IB T320	27000	30000, IB	T165D		30300	33700,	IB T215D				31000	34500
	IB T216D GM	31100	34500, IB	T270D		32000	35500,	IB T300D				32600	36200
46				DCMY	MHG	IB	T300	CHRY 15 4	30000	3	10	38900	43300
	IB T320	40000	44400, IB	T270D	GM	43900	48700,	IB T280D				44300	49300
	IB T300D	45700	50200, IB	T370D		48100	52800						
50				DCMY	MHG	IB	T300	CHRY 15 4	46000	3	10	54600	60000
	IB T320	55500	61000, IB	T270D	CHRY	56800	62400,	IB T280D				57600	63300
	IB T300D	58300	64100, IB	T370D		60200	66200						
				---- 1967	BOATS ----									
26	SEA-BREEZE			EXP	MHG	IB	190					4600	5300
26	SEA-SKIFF			EXP	MHG	IB	190					4750	5450
28	SEA-SKIFF			EXP	MHG	IB	210-250					6400	7450
31	SEA-VOYAGER			EXP	MHG	IB	T210					10700	12100
36				EXP	MHG	IB	T210	12	14000	2	9	16900	19300
	IB T210 INT	16900	19300, IB	T290		17300	19700,	IB T300				17400	19700
	IB T320	17500	19900, IB	T165D		19900	22100,	IB T216D				20600	22800
41				MY	MHG	IB	T290	13	19000	3	4	25600	28400
	IB T300	25600	28500, IB	T320		25700	28600,	IB T165D				28600	31800
	IB T215D	29300	32600, IB	T270D		30200	33600,	IB T300D				30800	34200
46				MY	MHG	IB	T290	14	26000	3	8	37600	41800
	IB T300	38100	42300, IB	T320		38800	43100,	IB T270D				42200	46900
	IB T280D	42600	47300, IB	T300D		43200	48000,	IB T370D				45800	50300
50				MY	MHG	IB	T290	14	34000	3	10	44700	49600
	IB T300	46000	50600, IB	T320		47600	52300,	IB T270D				48700	53500
	IB T280D	49500	54400, IB	T300D		50800	55900,	IB T370D				54400	59700
				---- 1966	BOATS ----									
19	4			RNBT	P/M	IO	200	6 9		2	1	3300	3850
	IB 200	1700	2050, VD	200		1750	2050,	IO 210				3300	3850
	IB 210	1700	2050, VD	210		1750	2050,					1750	2050
	VD 240	1750	2050, VD	290		1750	2100,	VD 290				1800	2100
	IB 320	1800	2150, VD	320		1850	2200,	IB 325				1850	2150
	VD 325	1850	2200										
22	4			RNBT	P/M	IO	200	7 4		2	2	5100	5900
	IB 200	2750	3200, VD	200		2800	3250,	IO 210				5150	5900
	IB 210	2750	3200, VD	210		2800	3250,	IO 240				2750	3200
	VD 240	2800	3250, VD	290		2800	3250,	VD 290				2850	3300
	IB 320	2850	3300, VD	320		2900	3350,	IB 325				2850	3300
	VD 325	2900	3350										
26	EXPLORER			EXP	P/M	IB	175	9 8		2	4	4500	5200
	IO 200	9200	10500, IB	200		4550	5250,	IO 210				9250	10500
	IB 210-320	4600	5600										
26	VENTURER			CR	P/M	IB	175	9 8		2	3	5000	5750
	IO 200	10200	11600, IB	200		5100	5850,	IO 210				10300	11700
	IB 210-320	5100	6200										
31				EXP	P/M	IB	T200-T320	11 2		2	7	10200	12500
36	3			EXP	P/M	IB	T200	12		2	9	16600	18900
	IB T210	16700	19000, IB	T240		16800	19100,	IB T250				16800	19100
	IB T290	17000	19300, IB	T320		17200	19500,	IB T160D				19900	22100
	IB T216D	20300	22500, IB	T220D		20300	22600,	IB T240D				20600	22900
41				MY	P/M	IB	T210	13		3	4	24500	27200
	IB T240	24600	27300, IB	T290		24800	27500,	IB T320				25000	27800
	IB T215D	28400	31600, IB	T216D		28400	31600,	IB T220D				28500	31700
	IB T240D	28800	32000, IB	T270D		29300	32600,	IB T300D				29900	33200
46	4			MY	P/M	IB	T290	14		3	8	38800	43100
	IB T320	39900	44300, IB	T240D		42000	46700,	IB T270D				43200	48000
	IB T280D	43600	48400, IB	T300D		44200	49100,	IB T370D				46700	51300
				---- 1965	BOATS ----									
19	4			RNBT	WD	IO	210-225					3350	3950
	VD 230 CRUS	1700	2050, VD	230		3650	4200,	IB 280				1700	2000
	IB 280 CRUS	1750	2100, VD	280		1700	2000,	IO 290				3700	4300
	IB 290	1700	2050, VD	290	CHRY	1700	2000,	IB 325				1750	2100
	VD 325 CHRY	1750	2100										
22	4			RNBT	WD	IB	190					2650	3050
	VD 190 CHRY	2650	3100, IO	210		5300	6100,	IB 210				2650	3100
	VD 210 CHRY	2650	3100, IO	220		2650	3100,	VD 220	GRAY			2650	3100
	IO 225	5350	6150, IO	230		2650	3100,	VD 230	CRUS			2750	3200
	VD 280	5650	6450, IB	280		2700	3150,	IB 280	CRUS			2750	3200
	VD 280	2700	3200, IO	290		5650	6500,	IB 290				2700	3150
	VD 290 CHRY	2700	3150, IB	325		2750	3200,	VD 325	CHRY			2700	3200
26	6 STANDARD			EXP	WD	IB	190					4750	5450
	IO 210	10200	11600, IB	210-220		4800	5550,	IO 225				10400	11800
	IB 230	4850	5550, IB	T190		5400	6400						
26	6 SUNLINER			EXP	WD	IB	190					5050	5800
	IO 210	11000	12500, IB	210-220		5100	5900,	IO 225				11000	12500
	IB 230	5150	5950, IB	T190		5700	6500						
31				EXP	WD	IB	130D					14700	16800
31				EXP	WD	IB	T190-T280					9900	11800
35	6			EXP	WD	IB	T190					15700	17900
	IB T210	15800	18000, IB	T220		15900	18100,	IB T230				15900	18100
	IB T280	16200	18400, IB	T280	CRUS	16300	18500,	IB T290				16300	18500
	IB T170D	23500	26100, IB	T195D		23800	26500						

LOA FT IN	NAME AND/ OR MODEL	TOP/ RIG	BOAT TYPE	HULL MTL	TP	ENGINE TP # HP MFG	BEAM FT IN	WGT LBS	DRAFT FT IN	RETAIL LOW	RETAIL HIGH

------------------- 1965 BOATS -------------------

41			MY	WD	IB T210					24100	26800
	IB T280	24400	27100, IB T280	CRUS	24600	27300, IB T280 GRAY				24400	27100
	IB T290	24400	27100, IB T290		24600	27400, IB T195D				27300	30400
	IB T215D	27600	30700, IB T270D		28500	31600, IB T280D				28600	31800
	IB T300D	29000	32200								
46	4		MY	WD	IB T280					27600	30700
	IB T280 CRUS	27700	30700, IB T290		28000	31100, IB T325				29700	33000
	IB T270D	33100	36800, IB T280D		33700	37500, IB T300D				34900	38700
	IB T370D	38600	42800								

------------------- 1964 BOATS -------------------

16	COMBO			WD	IO 88-140					2000	2400
22	1		RNBT	WD	IB 190-225					2500	2950
22	1		RNBT	WD	VD 230					2550	3000
22	1		RNBT	WD	IB 280-325					2550	3050
26	1		EXP	WD	IB 185-230					3850	4750
26	1		EXP	WD	IB T145					4500	5200
26	1 SUNLINER		EXP	WD	IB 185-230					4950	5650
26	1 SUNLINER		EXP	WD	IB T145					4850	5600
30			EXP	WD	IB T185-T230					8150	9650
35	6		EXP	WD	IB 215					14600	16600
	IB T190	15200	17200, IB T225		15300	17400, IB T230				15400	17500
	IB T280	15600	17700, IB T280D		24400	27100					
40			MY	WD	IB T225					22300	24800
	IB T230	22300	24800, IB T280		22400	24900, IB T280 CHRY				22300	24800
45			MY	WD	IB T280					29500	32700
	IB T280 CHRY	29400	32700, IB T325		31300	34700, IB T235D				32900	36600

------------------- 1963 BOATS -------------------

16	COMBO			WD	IO 88-140					2100	2500
22	4		RNBT	WD	IB 190					2500	2900
	VD 190	2500	2900, IB 210		2500	2900, VD 210				2500	2950
	IB 215	2500	2900, VD 215		2500	2950, IB 225				2500	2900
	VD 225	2550	2950, VD 280		2500	2950, VD 280				2550	3000
25	4 STANDARD 25		EXP	WD	IB 185-225					3750	4400
25	4 STANDARD 25		EXP	WD	IB T145					4150	4800
25	4 SUNLINER 25		EXP	WD	IB 185-225					3750	4400
25	4 SUNLINER 25		EXP	WD	IB T145					4150	4800
28	7		EXP	WD	IB 185-210					6200	7250
33			EXP	WD	IB T190-T280					11400	13600
38			MY	WD	IB T225					20100	22300
38			MY	WD	IB T280					20200	22400
45			MY	WD	IB T280					28700	31900
45			MY	WD	IB T235D					32100	35700

------------------- 1962 BOATS -------------------

16				WD	OB					1700	2000
19			RNBT	WD	VD 280					1700	2000
22			RNBT	WD	IB 190					2500	2900
	VD 190	2500	2900, IB 210		2500	2900, VD 210				2500	2900
	IB 215	2500	2900, VD 215		2500	2900, IB 225				2500	2950
	VD 225	2500	2900, VD 280		2500	2900, VD 280				2550	2950
25			FB CR	WD	IB 188-225					3700	4350
25			FB CR	WD	IB T145					4100	4800
33			FB CR	WD	IB T190-T225					10800	12400
38	AFT STATEROOM 38		FB CR	WD	IB T225					18300	20400
38	AFT STATEROOM 38		FB CR	WD	IB T280					18500	20500
45			FB DCFD	WD	IB T280					28800	32000
45			FB DCFD	WD	IB T181D					29500	32800
45			FB DCFD	WD	IB T235D					32300	35800

------------------- 1961 BOATS -------------------

16	55		RNBT	P/M	OB		6 4	750		2100	2500
22	110		RNBT	P/M	IB 177		7 4		2 1	2500	2900
	IB 190	2500	2900, VD 190		2500	2900, IB 215				2450	2900
	VD 215	2500	2900, IB 225		2500	2900, VD 225				2500	2950
	IB 280	2500	2900, VD 280		2600	3000					
25	4 170		FB CR	P/M	IB 177-195		9 4		2 3	3900	4500
25	4 170		FB CR	P/M	IB T135-T170		9 4		2 3	4250	5100
27	130 COMMUTER		EXP	P/M	IB T135		9 4		2 6	4900	5650
27	130 COMMUTER		EXP	P/M	VD T190-T280		9 4		2 6	5650	6700
27	150 SPORTSMAN			WD	VD T190-T280					5600	6600
30	155-A COMMUTER			WD	IB T190-T280					6500	7900
30	160		HT	WD	VD T190-T280					7200	8700
33	180		FB CR	P/M	IB T177-T255		11 9		2 6	9900	11500

------------------- 1960 BOATS -------------------

16	55			WD	OB					1700	2050
22	110		UTL	WD	IB 177					2350	2750
	VD 177	2400	2800, IB 215		2400	2750, IB 225				2400	2800
	IB 225 CHRY	2350	2750, VD 225	GRAY	2400	2800, IB 300				2450	2850
	VD 300	2500	2900								
25	170		FB CR	WD	IB 177					4000	4650
25	170		FB CR	WD	IB T177					4600	5300
27	130 COMMUTER			WD	VD T135-T215					5700	6750
27	130 COMMUTER			WD	IB T225 CHRY					5050	5850
27	130 COMMUTER			WD	VD T225-T300					5900	6950
27	150 SPORTSMAN			WD	VD T135-T215					5700	6750
27	150 SPORTSMAN			WD	IB T225 CHRY					5050	5850
27	150 SPORTSMAN			WD	VD T225-T300					5900	6950
30	155-A COMMUTER			WD	VD T135-T215					6800	8350
30	155-A COMMUTER			WD	IB T225					6500	7500
30	160		HT	WD	VD T135-T215					6800	8350
30	160		HT	WD	IB T225 CHRY					6500	7500
30	160		HT	WD	VD T225 GRAY					7300	8400
32	180		FB CR	WD	IB T177-T225					8150	9700

------------------- 1959 BOATS -------------------

16	55		UTL	MHG	OB		6 4	850		2450	2850
22	110		UTL	MHG	IB 275		7 4			2400	2800
24	120		SDN	MHG	IB T135		8 4			4850	5550
27	130			MHG	IB T225		9 4			5250	6050
30	155-A			MHG	IB T225		9 10			6300	7250

------------------- 1958 BOATS -------------------

| 18 | | | | WD | IB 135 CHRY | | | | | ** | ** |

------------------- 1956 BOATS -------------------

18				WD	IB 135 CHRY					**	**
22				WD	IB 135 CHRY					**	**
27				WD	IB T275 CHRY					**	**

------------------- 1955 BOATS -------------------

| 22 | | | | WD | IB 300 CHRY | | | | | ** | ** |

------------------- 1954 BOATS -------------------

| 22 | | | | WD | IB 135 CHRY | | | | | ** | ** |
| 24 | | | | WD | IB 225 CHRY | | | | | ** | ** |

------------------- 1953 BOATS -------------------

18			OP RNBT	WD	IB 140					2100	2450
22			OP RNBT	WD	IB 165					3550	4150
27			OP EXP	WD	IB 125 CHRY					6750	7750

------------------- 1952 BOATS -------------------

18			OP RNBT	MHG	VD					**	**
22			OP RNBT	MHG	VD 125 CHRY					3600	4150
22			OP UTL	MHG	IB					**	**

------------------- 1950 BOATS -------------------

| 22 | UTILITY | | OP RNBT | WD | IB GRAY | | | | | ** | ** |

SHETLAND BOATS LTD
COAST GUARD MFG ID- SBL

Call 1-800-327-6929 for BUC Personalized Evaluation Service
Or, for 1974 to 1977 boats, sign onto www.BUCValuPro.com

SHIP-WRIGHT YACHTS

Call 1-800-327-6929 for BUC Personalized Evaluation Service
Or, for 1966 to 1968 boats, sign onto www.BUCValuPro.com

SICA SKIFFS
COAST GUARD MFG ID- SCA

Call 1-800-327-6929 for BUC Personalized Evaluation Service
Or, for 1959 to 1963 boats, sign onto www.BUCValuPro.com

SIDEWINDER OF WISCONSIN

PESHTIGO WI 54157   COAST GUARD MFG ID- SWM See inside cover to adjust price for area

Yr	LOA FT IN	Name/Model	Top/Rig	Boat Type	Hull MTL	Hull TP	Eng TP	# HP	MFG	Beam FT IN	Wgt LBS	Draft FT IN	Retail Low	Retail High
1976	17 8	SUPER 18	OP	RNBT	FBG	DV	OB			7	950		2600	3000
1976	17 8	SUPER 18	OP	RNBT	FBG	DV	IO	188-233			1900		2700	3250
1976	17 8	SUPER 18	OP	RNBT	FBG	DV	JT	454-455			1900		3050	3550
1976	17 9	SK LO-PROFILE 18	OP	RNBT	FBG	DV	JT	454-455			1880		3050	3550
1976	21	DAYCRUISER 21	OP	CR	FBG	DV	IO	188-233			2700		4650	5450
1976	21	DAYCRUISER 21	OP	CR	FBG	DV	JT	454-455			2700		4700	5400
1975	17 8	18 SUPER	OP	RNBT	FBG	DV	OB			7	1095		2900	3350
1975	17 8	18 SUPER	OP	RNBT	FBG	DV	JT	325-405		7	1950		2950	3400
1975	17 9	18 SK LO PROFILE	OP	RNBT	FBG	DV	JT	325		7	1250		2600	3050
1975	17 9	18 SK LO PROFILE	OP	RNBT	FBG	DV	JT	405	CHEV	7	1900		2950	3400
1974	16 10	DUNES 17			FBG		IO	120-140		7 1			2600	3050
1974	17 4	FRONTIER			FBG		IO	120-140		6 11			2650	3100
1974	17 4	XL-17			FBG	DV	OB			7	1200		3000	3500
1974	17 4	XL-17			FBG	DV	IO	120-165		7	1800		2600	3050
1974	17 4	XL-17			FBG	DV	JT	225-400		7	2010		2700	3150
1974	17 4	XL-17			FBG	TR	OB			7	1460		3500	4100
1974	17 4	XL-17			FBG	TR	IO	120-188		7	2020		2750	3250
1974	17 8	SUPER 18			FBG		OB			7	950		2550	2950
1974	17 8	SUPER 18			FBG		JT	390-400		7	1900		2700	3100
1974	17 9	SIDEWINDER SK			FBG		OB			7			2400	2800
1974	17 9	SIDEWINDER SK			FBG		JT	390-400		7	1880		2700	3100
1974	19	XL-19			FBG	DV	IO	165-245		7 8	2040		3250	4000
1974	19	XL-19			FBG	DV	JT	390-400		7 8	2250		3250	3800
1973	16 10	DUNES 17			FBG		IO	120-140		7 1			2700	3150
1973	17 4	FRONTIER			FBG		IO	120-140		6 11			2750	3200
1973	17 4	XL-17			FBG	DV	OB			7	1200		3000	3500
1973	17 4	XL-17			FBG	DV	IO	120-165		7	1800		2650	3150
1973	17 4	XL-17			FBG	DV	JT	390-400		7	2010		2600	3000
1973	17 4	XL-17			FBG	TR	OB			7	1460		3500	4050
1973	17 4	XL-17			FBG	TR	IO	120-188		7	2020		2800	3350
1973	17 8	SIDEWINDER SK			FBG		OB			6 5			2400	2800
1973	17 8	SIDEWINDER SK			FBG		JT	390-400		6 5			2400	2800
1973	17 8	SUPER 18			FBG		OB			7	950		2500	2900
1973	17 8	SUPER 18			FBG		JT	454-455		7	1900		2600	3000
1973	18 11	STARDUST			FBG		IO	140-245		7 8			3400	4150
1973	18 11	STARDUST			FBG		IO	390-400		7 8			5500	6600
1973	19	XL-19			FBG	DV	IO	165-245		7 8	2040		3400	4100
1973	19	XL-19			FBG	DV	IO	390-400		7 8	2250		5600	6700
1971	16 10	LAS-VEGAS-DUNES			FBG		IO	120	MRCR	7 1	1680	2 6	2700	3100
1971	16 10	LAS-VEGAS-DUNES			FBG		JT	260	OLDS	7 1	1950	1 7	2350	2700
1971	16 10	LAS-VEGAS-RIVIERA			FBG		OB			7			2350	2700
1971	17 4	LAS-VEGAS-FRONTIER			FBG		IO	120	MRCR	6 11	2020	2 6	3000	3500
1971	17 4	LAS-VEGAS-SAHARA			FBG		OB			6 11	1640		3800	4400
1971	17 8	SIDEWINDER JET	RNBT		FBG		JT	260	BERK	7	1720	1 5	2400	2800
1971	17 8	SIDEWINDER LOW PROFI			FBG	DV	JT	360	BERK	7		1 5	2200	2600
1971	17 8	SIDEWINDER SUPER			FBG		IO	120		7	1485		3000	3150
1971	17 8	SIDEWINDER SUPER			FBG	DV	IO	165		7		2 4	2900	3400
1971	17 8	SIDEWINDER SUPER JET			FBG		JT	260	BERK	7	1580	1 5	2250	2650
1971	17 8	SIDEWINDER SUPER JET			FBG	DV	JT	360	OLDS	7		1 5	2450	2850
1971	18 11	LAS-VEGAS-STARDUST			FBG		IO	120	MRCR	7 6	2040	2 5	3500	4100
1971	18 11	LAS-VEGAS-STARDUST			FBG		JT	260	OLDS	7 6	2250	1 6	3850	4300
1971	18 11	LAS-VEGAS-STARDUST			FBG	DV	IO	165		7 6		2 5	3600	4200
1971	18 11	LAS-VEGAS-STARDUST			FBG	DV	JT	360		7 6		1 6	2800	3250
1971	20 2	SIDEWINDER	CR		FBG	DV	JT	260	BERK	7 9		1 5	3350	4100
1971	20 3	SIDEWINDER	CR		FBG		JT	120	BERK	7 9	2535	1 2	3350	3900
1970	16 10	DUNES			FBG	DV	IO	155-160		7 1			2950	3500
1970	16 10	DUNES			FBG	DV	JT	475	AERO	7			2250	2600
1970	16 10	RIVIERA			FBG	DV	OB			6 11	1050		2650	3050
1970	17 4	FRONTIER			FBG	TR	IO	155-160		6 11			3000	3550
1970	17 4	FRONTIER			FBG	TR	IO	475	AERO	6 11			2300	2650
1970	17 4	SAHARA			FBG	TR	OB			6 11	990		2550	3000
1970	17 8	SIDEWINDER 18	OP		FBG	DV	OB			7	800		2200	2550
1970	17 8	SIDEWINDER 18	OP		FBG	DV	IO	120		7			3000	3500
1970	17 8	SIDEWINDER 18	OP		FBG	DV	IB	240		7			1850	2250
1970	17 8	SUPER-SIDEWINDER 18	OP		FBG	DV	IO	160		7			3000	3500
1970	18 11	STARDUST			FBG	DV	IO	210-215		7 8			3800	4500
1970	18 11	STARDUST			FBG	DV	JT	475	AERO	7 8			2700	3150
1969	17	SIDEWINDER TUNNEL 17	SKI		FBG	TH	OB			7 1	650		1700	2050
1969	17 8	SIDEWINDER	RNBT		FBG	DV	IO	120		7	1480		3000	3500
1969	17 8	SIDEWINDER	SKI		FBG	DV	OB	225		7	1480		3000	3500
1969	17 8	SIDEWINDER 18 DLX	SKI		FBG	DV	OB			7	950		2500	2900
1969	17 8	SIDEWINDER JET 18	SKI		FBG	DV	JT	150		7	1850		2050	2450
1969	17 8	SIDEWINDER STD 18	RACE		FBG		OB			7	850		2300	2700
1969	18	COMPETITION	RACE		FBG		OB			8	650		1900	2250

THE SIDNEY COMPANY

SABOT SAILBOATS   COAST GUARD MFG ID- SDN
SEE CAL BOATS WEST

Call 1-800-327-6929 for BUC Personalized Evaluation Service
Or, for 1965 to 1984 boats, sign onto www.BUCValuPro.com

SIERRA BOAT COMPANY

Call 1-800-327-6929 for BUC Personalized Evaluation Service
Or, for 1979 boats, sign onto www.BUCValuPro.com

SIGNA CORPORATION

A FUQUA INDUSTRIES COMPANY   See inside cover to adjust price for area
DECATUR IN 46733   COAST GUARD MFG ID- SGN
FOR MORE RECENT YEARS SEE THUNDERBIRD PROD CORP

Yr	LOA FT IN	Name/Model	Top/Rig	Boat Type	Hull MTL	Hull TP	Eng TP	# HP	MFG	Beam FT IN	Wgt LBS	Draft FT IN	Retail Low	Retail High
1975	16 2	S-16	ST	RNBT	FBG	TR	OB			6 6	1260	2	2950	3000
1975	16 2	S-16	ST	RNBT	FBG	TR	IO	120-140		6 6	2050	2	3000	3050
1975	18 2	S-18	ST	RNBT	FBG	TR	OB			7 1	1350	2	3250	3750
1975	18 2	S-18	ST	RNBT	FBG	TR	IO	120-175		7 3	2290	2 1	3250	3900
1975	18 2	SF-18	ST	RNBT	FBG	TR	IO	140-225		7 8	1690	2 6	3800	4400
1975	18 2	SF-18	ST	RNBT	FBG	TR	IO	140-225		7 8	2470	2 6	3500	4300
1975	20 2	SF-20	ST	RNBT	FBG	DV	IO	165-233		8	2850	2 8	4700	5700
1975	20 2	SF-20	ST	RNBT	FBG	DV	IO	280	MRCR	8	3100	2 8	5400	6200
1975	20 3	S-20	ST	RNBT	FBG	TR	IO	120-233		7	2970	2 3	4500	5400
1975	20 3	S-20-C	ST	CUD	FBG	DV	IO	120-233		7	3300	2 3	5200	6450
1975	23 3	SF-233-C	ST	CUD	FBG	DV	IO	165-255		8	4680	2 10	8250	10200
1975	23 3	SF-233-C	ST	CUD	FBG	DV	IO	280	MRCR	8	4940	2 10	9150	10400
1975	23 3	SF-233-C	ST	CUD	FBG	DV	IO	T120-T233		8	4940	2 10	9500	11700
1975	23 3	SF-233-H	ST	CUD	FBG	DV	IO	165-255		8	4880	2 10	8500	10500
1975	23 3	SF-233-H	ST	CUD	FBG	DV	IO	280	MRCR	8	5200	2 10	9000	11000
1975	23 3	SF-233-H	ST	CUD	FBG	DV	IO	T120-T233		8	5235	2 10	9900	12000
1975	26 2	SF-26-C	ST	CR	FBG	DV	IO	255-280		9	6340	3 2	12300	14300
1975							IO	T165-T233					13100	15900
1975							IO	T255	MRCR				14500	16500
1975							VD	T255	MRCR				12200	13900
1975							IO	T280	MRCR				15000	17000
1974	16 3	ECHO 16		W/T	FBG		OB			6 6	1100		2350	2700
1974	16 3	YANKEE 16		W/T	FBG		IO	120-140		6 6	1750		2350	2700
1974	18 2	DELTA 18		W/T	FBG		OB			7 3	1350		3200	3700
1974	18 2	VICTOR 18		W/T	FBG		IO	120-245		7 3	2150		3200	4000
1974	20 3	BRAVO 20		W/T	FBG		IO	120-245		7 6	2400		5050	6100
1974	23 3	SIERRA 20		W/T	FBG		IO	120-245		7 6	2700		5900	7100
1973	16 3	ECHO 16		W/T	FBG		OB			6 6	1100		2550	3000
1973	16 3	YANKEE 16		W/T	FBG		IO	120-140		6 6	1750		2400	2800
1973	18 2	DELTA 18		W/T	FBG		OB			7 3	1350		3200	3700
1973	18 2	VICTOR 18		W/T	FBG		IO	120-225		7 3	2150		3350	4000
1973	18 2	VICTOR 18		W/T	FBG		IO	245	OMC	7 3	2150		2950	3450
1973	23 3	SIERRA 20		W/T	FBG		IO	120-225		7 6	2700		6100	7150
1973	23 3	SIERRA 20		W/T	FBG		IO	245	OMC	7 6	2700		4800	5500
1973	23 3	SIERRA 20		W/T	FBG		IO	245	OMC	7 6	2700		6300	7250
1972	16 3	ECHO		W/T	FBG	TR	OB			6 6	1100		2550	3000
1972	16 3	YANKEE	OP	W/T	FBG		IO	120-165		6 6			2500	2900
1972	16 3	YANKEE	OP	W/T	FBG		IO	240		6 6			2700	3150
1972	18 2	DELTA	OP	W/T	FBG	TR	OB			7 3	1350		3150	3700
1972	18 2	VICTOR	OP	W/T	FBG		IO	120-165		7 3			3450	4050

SIGNATURE MARINE CO
COAST GUARD MFG ID- SXV

Call 1-800-327-6929 for BUC Personalized Evaluation Service
Or, for 1977 to 1981 boats, sign onto www.BUCValuPro.com

SIGNET MARINE DIV
S L KAYE CO INC

Call 1-800-327-6929 for BUC Personalized Evaluation Service
Or, for 1963 to 1971 boats, sign onto www.BUCValuPro.com

SILHOUETTE MARINE LTD

Call 1-800-327-6929 for BUC Personalized Evaluation Service
Or, for 1959 to 1963 boats, sign onto www.BUCValuPro.com

SILVER QUEEN INC
NASHVILLE TN 37211

See inside cover to adjust price for area

LOA FT	LOA IN	NAME AND/ OR MODEL	TOP/ RIG	BOAT TYPE	HULL MTL	HULL TP	ENGINE TP	# HP	MFG	BEAM FT	BEAM IN	WGT LBS	DRAFT FT	DRAFT IN	RETAIL LOW	RETAIL HIGH
1972 BOATS																
35		SILVER-QUEEN			FBG		IO			12					**	**

SILVER TOWN CO INC

Call 1-800-327-6929 for BUC Personalized Evaluation Service
Or, for 1971 boats, sign onto www.BUCValuPro.com

SILVERLINE
DIV OF LUND AMERICAN INC
LIL FALLS MN 56345 COAST GUARD MFG ID- SLV

See inside cover to adjust price for area

LOA FT	LOA IN	NAME AND/ OR MODEL	TOP/ RIG	BOAT TYPE	HULL MTL	HULL TP	ENGINE TP	# HP	MFG	BEAM FT	BEAM IN	WGT LBS	DRAFT FT	DRAFT IN	RETAIL LOW	RETAIL HIGH
1982 BOATS																
16	1	GRENADA 16GTL		RNBT	FBG	DV	IO	170		7	1	1850			2500	2900
16	2	CATALINA 16V		RNBT	FBG	DV	IO	140		7	1	1880			2500	2900
16	2	CATALINA 16VBR		RNBT	FBG	DV	IO	140		7	1	2125			2650	3100
16	2	NANT SEA BREEZE 16BR	ST	RNBT	FBG	DV	IO	120-140		7	1	2075			2650	3050
16	2	NANTUCKET 16V	OP	RNBT	FBG	DV	IO	120-185		7	1	1880			2500	3100
16	2	NANTUCKET 16VBR	OP	RNBT	FBG	DV	IO	120-185		7	1	2125			2650	3300
16	2	NANTUCKET 16VBR	ST	RNBT	FBG	DV	IO	120	OMC	7	1	2125			2650	3050
16	7	COMORO 17T		RNBT	FBG	TR	IO	165		7	2	2415			2950	3450
16	7	SCRAMBLER 16GTL	OP	RNBT	FBG	TR	IO	140	MRCR	7	1	1345			2250	2650
17	2	NANT SEA BREEZE 17BR	ST	RNBT	FBG	DV	IO	120-170		6	11	2400			2950	3500
17	2	NANTUCKET 17V	OP	RNBT	FBG	DV	IO	120-185		6	11	2500			3050	3600
17	2	NANTUCKET 17V	ST	RNBT	FBG	DV	IO	145	VLVO	6	11	2500			3200	3750
17	2	NANTUCKET 17V SPT	OP	RNBT	FBG	DV	IO	120-200		6	10	2500			3050	3700
17	2	NANTUCKET 17V SPT	ST	RNBT	FBG	DV	IO	170		6	10	2500			3050	3550
17	2	NANTUCKET 17VBR	OP	RNBT	FBG	DV	IO	120-185		6	11	2590			3100	3750
17	2	NANTUCKET 17VBR SPT	OP	RNBT	FBG	DV	IO	120-200		6	11	2590			3150	3800
19	5	FARALLON 19-1/2GTL	OP	RNBT	FBG	DV	IO	170	MRCR	7	8	3060			4100	4750
19	5	FARALLON 19-1/2GTL	ST	RNBT	FBG	DV	IO	170-230		7	8	3060			4100	5100
19	5	FARALLON 19-1/2GTL	ST	RNBT	FBG	DV	IO	260		7	8	3060			4400	5300
19	5	FARALLON CONCORD	OP	RNBT	FBG	DV	IO	170-198		7	8	3060			4000	4850
19	5	FARALLON CONCORD	OP	RNBT	FBG	DV	IO	200-230		7	8	3060			4100	5100
19	5	FARALLON CONCORD	OP	RNBT	FBG	DV	IO	260		7	8	3060			4400	5300
19	5	NANTUCKET 19-1/2 EXP	OP	EXP	FBG	DV	IO	170-230		7	8	3175			4400	5400
19	5	NANTUCKET 19-1/2 EXP	OP	EXP	FBG	DV	IO	260		7	8	3175			4650	5600
19	5	NANTUCKET 19-1/2V		RNBT	FBG	DV	IO	260		7	8	2985			4300	5000
19	5	NANTUCKET 19-1/2VBR		RNBT	FBG	DV	IO	260		7	8	2755			4100	4750
19	5	NANTUCKET 19-1/2VC	OP	CUD	FBG	DV	IO	170	MRCR	7	8	3110			4350	5000
19	5	NANTUCKET 19-1/2VC	ST	CUD	FBG	DV	IO	170-230		7	8	3110			4350	5350
19	5	NANTUCKET 19-1/2VC	ST	CUD	FBG	DV	IO	260		7	8	3110			4650	5550
19	5	NANTUCKET 19-1/2VHT	HT	RNBT	FBG	DV	IO	198		7	8	3120			4200	4850
19	5	NANTUCKET 19.5VBR	ST	RNBT	FBG	DV	IO	170-230		7	8	3040			4100	4900
19	6	NANTUCKET 19-1/2V		RNBT	FBG	DV	OB			7	8	1890			2000	2400
22		NANTUCKET 22	OP	EXP	FBG	DV	IO	170-260		7	11	4500			7150	8850
24		NANTUCKET 24VC		CUD	FBG	DV	IO	260		7	11	4900			8950	10200
24		NANTUCKET 24VCB		SPTCR	FBG	DV	IO	260		7	11	4750			8650	9950
24		NANTUCKET 24VSD		SPTCR	FBG	DV	IO	260		7	11	4680			8550	9850
1981 BOATS																
16	1	GRENADA 16GTL	OP	RNBT	FBG	SV	IO	120-185		7	1	1850			2450	2900
16	2	CATALINA 16V	OP	RNBT	FBG	DV	IO	120-185		7	1	1880			2450	2900
16	2	CATALINA 16VBR	OP	RNBT	FBG	DV	IO	120-185		7	1	2125			2650	3100
16	7	COMORO 17T	OP	RNBT	FBG	TR	IO	140-185		7	2	2415			2900	3400
17	2	NANTUCKET 17V	OP	RNBT	FBG	DV	IO	140-200		6	11	2500			3000	3550
17	2	NANTUCKET 17V SPT	OP	RNBT	FBG	DV	IO	140	MRCR	6	10	2500			3000	3450
17	2	NANTUCKET 17VBR	OP	RNBT	FBG	DV	IO	140-185		6	11	2590			3050	3600
19	5	FARALLON 19-1/2GTL	ST	RNBT	FBG	DV	IO	170-260		7	8	3060			4050	5000
19	5	NANTUCKET 19-1/2V	OP	RNBT	FBG	DV	OB			7	8	1930			2000	2400
19	5	NANTUCKET 19-1/2V	ST	RNBT	FBG	DV	IO	170-260		7	8	2985			4000	4900
19	5	NANTUCKET 19-1/2VBR	ST	RNBT	FBG	DV	IO	170-260		7	8	2755			3800	4700
19	5	NANTUCKET 19-1/2VC	ST	CUD	FBG	DV	IO	170-260		7	8	3110			4250	5250
19	5	NANTUCKET 19-1/2VHT	HT	RNBT	FBG	DV	IO	170-260		7	8	3120			4100	5050
22		NANTUCKET 22VC	ST	CUD	FBG	DV	IO	198-260		7	11	4260			6800	8100
22		NANTUCKET 22VC	ST	CUD	FBG	DV	IO	T120-T140		7	11	4260			7500	8650
22		NANTUCKET 22VCX	ST	CUD	FBG	DV	IO	200-260		7	11	4550			7150	8500
22		NANTUCKET 22VCX	ST	CUD	FBG	DV	IO	T120-T198		7	11	4550			7900	9200
22		NANTUCKET 22VHT	HT	CR	FBG	DV	IO	200-260		7	11	4930			7600	9050
22		NANTUCKET 22VHT	HT	CR	FBG	DV	IO	T120-T140		7	11	4930			8400	9650
22		NANTUCKET 22VSD	HT	CR	FBG	DV	IO	200-260		7	11	4960			7650	9100
24		NANTUCKET 24VC	ST	CUD	FBG	DV	IO	228-260		7	11	4900			8550	10000
24		NANTUCKET 24VC	ST	CUD	FBG	DV	IO	T120-T140		7	11	4900			9300	10600
24		NANTUCKET 24VCB	FB	SPTCR	FBG	DV	IO	260		7	11	4750			8500	9800
24		NANTUCKET 24VSD	FB	SPTCR	FBG	DV	IO	260		7	11	4680			8400	9650
1980 BOATS																
16	1	GRENADA 16GTL	OP	RNBT	FBG	SV	IO	120-170		7	1	1850			2400	2850
16	2	CATALINA 16V	OP	RNBT	FBG	DV	IO	120-170		7	1	1880			2450	2850
16	2	CATALINA 16VBR	OP	RNBT	FBG	DV	IO	120-170		7	1	2125			2600	3050
16	7	COMORO 17T	OP	RNBT	FBG	TR	IO	140-170		7	2	2415			2900	3350
17	2	NANTUCKET 17V	OP	RNBT	FBG	DV	IO	140-200		6	11	2500			3000	3500
17	2	NANTUCKET 17VBR	OP	RNBT	FBG	DV	IO	140-170		6	11	2590			3050	3550
19	5	FARALLON 19-1/2GTL	ST	RNBT	FBG	DV	IO	170-260		7	8	3060			4000	4950
19	5	NANTUCKET 19-1/2V	OP	RNBT	FBG	DV	OB			7	8	1930			1950	2350
19	5	NANTUCKET 19-1/2V	ST	RNBT	FBG	DV	IO	170-260		7	8	2985			3950	4850
19	5	NANTUCKET 19-1/2VBR	ST	RNBT	FBG	DV	IO	170-260		7	8	2755			3750	4650
19	5	NANTUCKET 19-1/2VC	ST	CUD	FBG	DV	IO	170-260		7	8	3110			4200	5200
19	5	NANTUCKET 19-1/2VHT	HT	RNBT	FBG	DV	IO	170-260		7	8	3120			4050	5000
22		NANTUCKET 22SDN	HT	SDN	FBG	DV	IO	200-260		7	11	4960			7550	9000
22		NANTUCKET 22VC	ST	CUD	FBG	DV	IO	198-260		7	11	4260			6750	8000
22		NANTUCKET 22VC	ST	CUD	FBG	DV	IO	T120-T140		7	11	4260			7450	8550
22		NANTUCKET 22VHT	HT	CR	FBG	DV	IO	200-260		7	11	4930			7550	9000
22		NANTUCKET 22VHT	HT	CR	FBG	DV	IO	T120-T140		7	11	4930			8300	9550
24		NANTUCKET 24SDN	HT	SDN	FBG	DV	IO	260		7	11	4680			8300	9550
24		NANTUCKET 24VC	ST	CUD	FBG	DV	IO	228-260		7	11	4900			8450	9900
24		NANTUCKET 24VC	ST	CUD	FBG	DV	IO	T120-T140		7	11	4900			9250	10500
24		NANTUCKET 24VCB	FB	SPTCR	FBG	DV	IO	260		7	11	4750			8450	9700
1979 BOATS																
16	1	GRENADA 16GTL	OP	RNBT	FBG	SV	IO	120-170		7	1	1685			2350	2700
16	2	HILO 16V	OP	RNBT	FBG	SV	IO	120-140		6	8	1750			2300	2700
16	2	HILO 16VBR	OP	RNBT	FBG	SV	IO	120-140		6	8	1850			2350	2750
16	7	COMORO 17T	OP	RNBT	FBG	TR	IO	140-170		7	2	2265			2800	3250
17	2	NANTUCKET 17V	OP	RNBT	FBG	DV	IO	140-200		6	11	2410			2900	3450
17	2	NANTUCKET 17VBR	OP	RNBT	FBG	DV	IO	140-170		6	11	2480			2950	3450
18		COMORO 18T	OP	RNBT	FBG	TR	IO	165-228		7	4	2820			3450	4150
19	5	FARALLON 19-1/2GTL	ST	RNBT	FBG	DV	IO	170-260		7	8	3060			4000	4950
19	5	NANTUCKET 19-1/2V	OP	RNBT	FBG	DV	OB			7	8	1930			1950	2300
19	5	NANTUCKET 19-1/2V	ST	RNBT	FBG	DV	IO	170-260		7	8	2900			3850	4800
19	5	NANTUCKET 19-1/2VBR	ST	RNBT	FBG	DV	IO	170-260		7	8	2755			3750	4650
19	5	NANTUCKET 19-1/2VC	ST	CUD	FBG	DV	IO	170-260		7	8	3020			4100	5100
19	5	NANTUCKET 19-1/2VHT	HT	RNBT	FBG	DV	OB			7	8				1750	2050
19	5	NANTUCKET 19-1/2VHT	HT	RNBT	FBG	DV	IO	170-260		7	8	2835			3800	4700
22		NANTUCKET 22VC	ST	CUD	FBG	DV	IO	198-260		7	11	4050			6450	7700
22		NANTUCKET 22VC	ST	CUD	FBG	DV	IO	T120-T140		7	11	4050			7150	8250
22		NANTUCKET 22VHT	HT	CR	FBG	DV	IO	200-260		7	11	4530			7050	8400
22		NANTUCKET 22VHT	HT	CR	FBG	DV	IO	T120-T140		7	11	4530			7800	8950
24		NANTUCKET 24VC	ST	CUD	FBG	DV	IO	228-260		7	11	4400			7750	9050
24		NANTUCKET 24VC	ST	CUD	FBG	DV	IO	T120-T140		7	11	4400			8400	9700
25	8	NANTUCKET 26V	ST	CBNCR	FBG	DV	IO	260		7	11	5975			12700	14500
25	8	NANTUCKET 26V	ST	CBNCR	FBG	DV	IO	T120-T170		7	11	5975			13100	15100
1978 BOATS																
16	2	HILO 16V	OP	RNBT	FBG	DV	IO	120-140		6	7	1750			2300	2700
16	2	HILO 16VBR	OP	RNBT	FBG	DV	IO	120-140		6	7	1890			2350	2750
16	7	COMORO 17T	ST	RNBT	FBG	TR	IO	140-170		7	2	2300			2800	3300
16	9	DOLPHIN 17	SLP	SAIL	FBG	CB				6		575		8	2350	2700

LOA FT	LOA IN	NAME AND/ OR MODEL	TOP/ RIG	BOAT TYPE	-HULL- MTL	-HULL- TP	ENGINE TP	ENGINE # HP	ENGINE MFG	BEAM FT	BEAM IN	WGT LBS	DRAFT FT	DRAFT IN	RETAIL LOW	RETAIL HIGH
		1978 BOATS														
17	3	NANTUCKET 17V	ST	RNBT	FBG	DV	IO	140-198		6	11	2445			2950	3500
17	3	NANTUCKET 17VBR	ST	RNBT	FBG	DV	IO	140-170		6	11	2480			3000	3500
18		COMORO 18T	ST	RNBT	FBG	TR	IO	165-240		7	4	2820			3450	4200
19	5	NANTUCKET 19-1/2V	ST	RNBT	FBG	DV	IO	165-260		7	8	2745			3750	4650
19	5	NANTUCKET 19-1/2VBR	OP	RNBT	FBG	DV	OB			7	8	1770			1800	2150
19	5	NANTUCKET 19-1/2VBR	ST	RNBT	FBG	DV	IO	165-260		7	8	2795			3800	4700
19	5	NANTUCKET 19-1/2VC	ST	CUD	FBG	DV	IO	170-260		7	8	2865			4000	4950
21	3	TIBURON 21V	OP	OPFSH	FBG	DV	OB			7	7	1775			2100	2500
22		NANTUCKET 22VC	ST	CUD	FBG	DV	IO	228-260		7	11	4050			6600	7750
22		NANTUCKET 22VC	ST	CUD	FBG	DV	IO	T120-T140		7	11	4050			7200	8300
22		NANTUCKET 22VHT	HT	CR	FBG	DV	IO	228-260		7	11	4530			7200	8450
22		NANTUCKET 22VHT	HT	CR	FBG	DV	IO	T120-T140		7	11	4530			7800	9000
25	8	NANTUCKET 26V	ST	CBNCR	FBG	DV	IO	240-260		7	11	5975			12500	14500
25	8	NANTUCKET 26V	ST	CBNCR	FBG	DV	IO	T120-T170		7	11	5975			13100	15100
		1977 BOATS														
16	7	COMORO 17T	ST	RNBT	FBG	TR	IO	140-175		7	2	2175			2800	3250
16	7	NANTUCKET 16-1/2V	ST	RNBT	FBG	DV	IO	120-140		7	1	1900			2600	3000
16	9	DOLPHIN 17 CUDDY	SLP	SAIL	FBG	CB				6		725		8	2500	2900
16	9	DOLPHIN 17 OPEN	SLP	SAIL	FBG	CB				6		575		8	2250	2600
16	10	KODIAK 17T	ST	FSH	FBG	TR	IO	120-140		6	4	1900			2600	3050
17	3	NANTUCKET 17V	OP	RNBT	FBG	DV	OB			6	11	2340			1950	2350
17	3	NANTUCKET 17V	ST	RNBT	FBG	DV	IO	140-190		6	11	2340			2950	3450
17	3	NANTUCKET 17VBR	OP	RNBT	FBG	DV	OB			6	11	2210			1900	2300
17	3	NANTUCKET 17VBR	ST	RNBT	FBG	DV	IO	140-175		6	11	2210			2850	3350
18		COMORO 18T	ST	RNBT	FBG	TR	IO	165-235		7	4	2250			3100	3750
19	6	NANTUCKET 19-1/2V	ST	RNBT	FBG	DV	IO	165-235		7	8	2580			3700	4450
22		NANTUCKET 22VC	ST	CUD	FBG	DV	IO	233-235		7	11	3240			5750	6600
22		NANTUCKET 22VC	ST	CUD	FBG	DV	IO	T120-T140		7	11	3240			6350	7300
22		NANTUCKET 22VHT	HT	CR	FBG	DV	IO	233-235		7	11	3900			6550	7500
22		NANTUCKET 22VHT	HT	CR	FBG	DV	IO	T120-T140		7	11	3900			7150	8200
25	10	NANTUCKET 26V	ST	CR	FBG	DV	IO	233-235		7	11	6260			11100	12600
25	10	NANTUCKET 26V	ST	CR	FBG	DV	IO	T120-T170		7	11	6260			11600	13600
		1976 BOATS														
16	7	COMORO 16-1/2V	OP	RNBT	FBG	DV	IO	120-140		7	1				3000	3500
16	7	COMORO 17T	OP	RNBT	FBG	TR	IO	120-175		7	2				3000	3550
16	9	DOLPHIN 17 CUDDY	SLP	SAIL	FBG	CB				6		725		8	2400	2800
16	9	DOLPHIN 17 OPEN	SLP	SAIL	FBG	CB				6		575		8	2200	2550
16	10	KODIAK 17T	OP	BASS	FBG	TR	IO	120-140		6	4				3050	3550
18		COMORO 18T	OP	RNBT	FBG	TR	IO	165-235		7	4				3450	4150
19	6	NANTUCKET 19-1/2V	OP	RNBT	FBG	DV	IO	165-235		7	8				3800	4600
22		NANTUCKET 22VC	OP	CUD	FBG	DV	IO	175-235		7	11				6750	7950
22		NANTUCKET 22VC	OP	CUD	FBG	DV	IO	T140		7	11				7550	8650
22		NANTUCKET 22VHT	HT	EXP	FBG	DV	IO	175-235		7	11				7150	8400
22		NANTUCKET 22VHT	HT	EXP	FBG	DV	IO	T140		7	11				7950	9100
		1975 BOATS														
16	7	COMORO 16 1/2V	OP	RNBT	FBG	DV	IB	140		7	1	1900			2350	2900
16	7	COMORO 16 1/2VS	OP	RNBT	FBG	DV	IO	140				1900			2700	3150
16	7	COMORO 17T	OP	RNBT	FBG	TR	IO	140-165		7	2	2175			2850	3350
16	7	COMORO 17TS	OP	RNBT	FBG	TR	IO	140-165		7	2	2175			3000	3500
17	7	COMORO 18V	OP	RNBT	FBG	DV	IO	140-233		7	1	2000			2950	3650
17	7	COMORO 18V	OP	RNBT	FBG	DV	JT	330	BERK	7	1	2000			3150	3700
18		ANTIGUA 18TD	OP	RNBT	FBG	TR	IO	140-165		7	4	2540			3500	4100
18		COMORO 18T	OP	RNBT	FBG	TR	IO	140-233		7	4	2250			3250	4000
18		COMORO 18T	OP	RNBT	FBG	TR	JT	330	BERK	7	4	2250			3450	4000
19	6	NANTUCKET 19 1/2V	OP	RNBT	FBG	DV	IO	140-225		7	8	2580			3900	4650
19	6	NANTUCKET 19 1/2V	OP	RNBT	FBG	DV	JT	330	BERK	7	8	2580			4050	4700
22		GRAND-BAHAMA 22T	HT	CR	FBG	TR	IO	188-233		8		3950			6850	8000
22		NANTUCKET 22VC	OP	CUD	FBG	DV	IO	188-233		7	11	3240			5950	6950
		1974 BOATS														
16	7	COMORO 16-1/2V	OP	RNBT	FBG		IO	140		7	1	1900			2800	3300
16	7	COMORO 17T	OP	RNBT	FBG		IO	140-165		7	2	1850			2800	3300
17	7	COMORO 18V	OP	RNBT	FBG		IO	140-188		7	1	2000			3050	3600
18		ANTIGUA 18T	OP	RNBT	FBG		IO	140-225		7	4	2200			3450	4050
18		COMORO 18T	OP	RNBT	FBG		IO	140-188		7	4	2200			3200	3850
18		COMORO 18T	OP	RNBT	FBG		IO	225		7	4	2200			3450	4050
19	6	NANTUCKET 19V	OP	RNBT	FBG		IO	140-225		7	8	2300			3800	4600
22		GRAND-BAHAMA 22'T	HT	RNBT	FBG		IO	188-225		8		3950			6700	7750
		1973 BOATS														
16	7	ARUBA 16 1/2 GTV	OP	RNBT	FBG		IO	120-140		7	1	1900			2900	3400
16	7	COMORO 17T	OP	RNBT	FBG		IO	120-165		7	2	1850			2900	3350
17	7	ARUBA 18 GTV	OP	RNBT	FBG		IO	140-225		7	1	2000			3150	3800
17	7	ARUBA 18 GTV	OP	RNBT	FBG		IO	260	BERK	7	1	2000			3450	4000
18		ANTIGUA	OP	RNBT	FBG		IO	120-188		7	2	2200			3400	4000
18		COMORO 18T	OP	RNBT	FBG		IO	120-225		7	4	2200			3450	4150
18	7	COMORO 19V	OP	RNBT	FBG		IO	120-188		7	4	1900			3350	3950
18	7	COMORO 19V	OP	RNBT	FBG		IO	260	BERK	7	4	1900			3650	4250
22		GRAND-BAHAMA	HT	RNBT	FBG		IO	188	MRCR	8		3740			6650	7650
		1972 BOATS														
16	1	COMORO 16V			FBG		IO	120-140		6	8	1600			2450	2850
16	7	COMORO 17T			FBG		IO	120-165		7	4	1850			2900	3400
18		ANTIGUA 18T		CAMPR	FBG		IO	120-165		7	4	2200			3650	4250
18		COMORO 18T			FBG		IO	120-225		7	4				3800	4550
18	8	COMORO 19V			FBG		IO	120-225		7	4	1900			3350	4050
18	8	COMORO 19V			FBG		JT	270	BERK	7	4	1900			2850	3350
22		GRAND-BAHAMA		CR	FBG		IO	188-225		8		3500			6950	8050
		1971 BOATS														
16	1	CATALINA 16 V			FBG		IO	120		6	8	1600			2550	2950
16	1	COMORO 16V			FBG		IO	140	MRCR	6	8	1600			2550	2950
16	7	COMORO 16T			FBG		IO	165	MRCR	7	4	1850			3000	3500
16	8	ARUBA		RNBT	FBG	DV	IO	165		7	1	1850			3100	3600
17		COMORO 17V			FBG		IO	165	MRCR	6	11	1740			2900	3400
18		ANTIGUA 18T		CAMPR	FBG		IO	165	MRCR	7	4	2200			3800	4400
18		COMORO 18T			FBG		IO	165	MRCR	7	4	2200			3600	4200
18	8	COMORO 19V			FBG		IO	165	MRCR	7	4	1900			3500	4100
18	8	SAMOA 19V			FBG		IO	215	OMC	7	4	1900			3550	4150
22		GRAND-BAHAMA		CR	FBG		IO	250	MRCR	8		3500			7400	8500
		1970 BOATS														
16	2	CATALINA 16 V		RNBT	FBG	DV	IO	120		6	6	1600			2650	3100
16	2	COMORO 16 V		RNBT	FBG	DV	IO	120		6	6	1600			2850	3300
16	8	ARUBA 16V			FBG	DV	IO			7	1	1850			**	**
17		CATALINA 17 V		RNBT	FBG	DV	IO	120		6	11	1740			3000	3500
17		COMORO 17 V		RNBT	FBG	DV	IO	120		6	11	1740			3200	3750
17	6	COMORO 18T			FBG	TR	IO		MRCR	7	1				**	**
17	10	CATALINA 18 V		RNBT	FBG	DV	IO	120		6	11	1750			3300	3800
18	8	COMORO 18 V		RNBT	FBG	DV	IO	120		7	6	1900			3550	4100
18	8	SAMOA 18 V		RNBT	FBG	DV	IO	120		7	6	1900			3950	4600
20		BAHAMA 20		RNBT	FBG	DV	IO	120		7	4	2400			4800	5550
		1969 BOATS														
16	8	BEL-AIRE 15.6	OP	RNBT	FBG	DV	IO	120		6	5	1263			2650	3100
16	8	DEVILLE 15.6			FBG		IO	120							3600	4150
17	2	BEL-AIRE 16	OP	RNBT	FBG	DV	IO	120		6	8	1325			2900	3350
17	2	DEVILLE 16			FBG		IO	120							3700	4300
17	2	IMPERIAL 16	OP		FBG	DV	IO	120		6	6	1425			2750	3200
17	9	BEL-AIRE 17	OP		FBG	SV	IO	120		6	9	1430			3000	3450
17	9	DEVILLE 17			FBG		IO	160							4150	4800
17	9	IMPERIAL 17	OP		FBG	DV	IO	160		6	9	1525			3050	3550
18	11	RIVIERA 18GS	OP	RNBT	FBG	TR	IO	160		7	1				4850	5550
18	11	RIVIERA 18SS	OP	RNBT	FBG	TR	IO	160		7		1680			3650	4250
19	2	BEL-AIRE 18	OP		FBG	DV	IO	160		7	1	1625			3600	4150
19	2	DEVILLE 18			FBG		IO	160							5050	5800
19	2	IMPERIAL 18	OP		FBG	DV	IO	160		7	1	1675			3600	4200
21	5	DEVILLE 20			FBG		IO	160							5700	6550
21	5	ELDORADO	OP		FBG	DV	IO	160		7	6	2200			5250	6000
21	5	IMPERIAL 20	OP		FBG	DV	IO	160		7	6	2000			5050	5800
		1968 BOATS														
16		BEL-AIRE 16	OP	RNBT	FBG		IO	80-120		6	8	1325			2700	3150
16		DEVILLE 16	OP	RNBT	FBG		IO	80-120		6	8	1375			2750	3200
16		IMPERIAL 16	OP		FBG		IO	80-120				1425			2650	3100
16		MAVERICK 16	OP		FBG		IO	80-120		6	8				3050	3550
16	9	BEL-AIRE 17	OP		FBG		IO	120-160		6	9	1430			2800	3300
16	9	DEVILLE 17	OP		FBG		IO	120-160		6	9	1480			2850	3350
16	9	IMPERIAL 17	OP		FBG		IO	120-160		6	9	1525			2900	3400
16	9	MAVERICK 17	OP		FBG		IO	120		6	9	1425			2800	3250
17	6	RIVIERA W/T	OP	RNBT	FBG	TR	IO	120-160		7		1725			3450	4000
17	11	BEL-AIRE 18	OP		FBG		IO	120-160		6	11	1625			3300	3850
17	11	DEVILLE 18	OP		FBG		IO	120-160		6	11	1675			3350	3900
17	11	IMPERIAL	OP		FBG		IO	120-160		6	11	1725			3350	3950
17	11	MAVERICK 18	OP		FBG		IO	120		6	11	1525			3250	3750
		1967 BOATS														
16		DART			FBG		IO	80							3200	3750
16		DEVILLE			FBG		IO	80							3200	3750
16		IMPERIAL			FBG		IO	80							3200	3750
16	9	DART			FBG		IO	120							3850	4450
16	9	DEVILLE			FBG		IO	120							3850	4450
16	9	IMPERIAL			FBG		IO	120							3850	4450
16	9	STAR			FBG		IO	120							3850	4450
17	11	DART			FBG		IO	120							4500	5150
17	11	DEVILLE			FBG		IO	120							4500	5150
17	11	IMPERIAL			FBG		IO	120							4500	5150

CONTINUED ON NEXT PAGE

LOA FT	LOA IN	NAME AND/ OR MODEL	TOP/ RIG	BOAT TYPE	HULL MTL	HULL TP	ENGINE TP	ENGINE # HP	ENGINE MFG	BEAM FT	BEAM IN	WGT LBS	DRAFT FT	DRAFT IN	RETAIL LOW	RETAIL HIGH
		1966 BOATS														
16		DART DAYTONA			FBG		IO	110							2650	3100
16		DAYTONA DEVILLE			FBG		IO	110-150							3600	4150
16		IMPERIAL DAYTONA			FBG		IO	110-150							3950	4550
16		RIVIERA			FBG		IO	110							3050	3550
16	9	DAYTONA DEVILLE			FBG		IO	110-150							3800	4450
16	9	IMPERIAL DAYTONA			FBG		IO	110-150							4100	4800
17		DART DAYTONA			FBG		IO	110-150							4000	4700
17	11	DAYTONA DEVILLE			FBG		IO	110-150							4450	5200
17	11	IMPERIAL DAYTONA			FBG		IO	110-150							4800	5500
18		DART DAYTONA			FBG		IO	110-120							4000	4700
18		DART DAYTONA			FBG		IO	150							4650	5350
18		NEWPORT DAYTONA			FBG		IO								**	**
18		NEWPORT DAYTONA			FBG		IO	110-120							5250	6050
		1965 BOATS														
16		RAMBLER DAYTONA			FBG		IO	90							3250	3800
16		RIVIERA DAYTONA			FBG		IO	90							3550	4150
17		BEL-AIRE DAYTONA			FBG		IO	110-150							4150	4850
18		NEWPORT DAYTONA			FBG		IO	110-150							4800	5550

SILVERTON MARINE CORP

MILLVILLE NJ 08332 COAST GUARD MFG ID- STN See inside cover to adjust price for area

For more recent years, see the BUC Used Boat Price Guide, Volume 1 or Volume 2

LOA FT	LOA IN	NAME AND/ OR MODEL	TOP/ RIG	BOAT TYPE	HULL MTL	HULL TP	ENGINE TP	ENGINE # HP	ENGINE MFG	BEAM FT	BEAM IN	WGT LBS	DRAFT FT	DRAFT IN	RETAIL LOW	RETAIL HIGH
		1983 BOATS														
31		CONVERTIBLE	FB	CNV	FBG	DV	VD	T220-T270		11	11	11400	2	11	31600	36500
31		CONVERTIBLE	FB	CNV	FBG	DV	VD	T155D	VLVO	11	11	11400	2	11	40300	44800
31		GULFSTREAM	OP	CR	FBG	DV	IB	T270-T350		11	11	9500	2	10	25800	30200
34		CONVERTIBLE	FB	CNV	FBG	DS	VD	T205D	J&T	12	6	12500	3	1	50700	55700
34		CONVERTIBLE	FB	CNV	FBG	DV	VD	T250-T270		12	6	12500	3	1	40600	45800
34		LUHRS 340	OP	SF	FBG		IB	T350	CRUS	12	6	12100	3	4	40100	44600
34		LUHRS 340	OP	SF	FBG		IB	T205D	J&T	12	6	12100	3	4	45900	50500
37		CONVERTIBLE	FB	CNV	FBG	DV	VD	T350	CRUS	14		20000	3		54400	59800
37		CONVERTIBLE	FB	CNV	FBG	DV	IB	T240D	PERK	14		20000	3		62200	68300
40		AFT CABIN	FB	DC	FBG	DV	IB	T350	CRUS	14		24000	3		72300	79500
40		AFT CABIN	FB	DC	FBG	DV	IB	T240D	PERK	14		24000	3		80600	88500
		1982 BOATS														
31		CONVERTIBLE	FB	CNV	FBG	DV	IB	T220-T270		11	11	11400	2	10	30300	35000
31		CONVERTIBLE	FB	CNV	FBG	DV	IB	T155D	VLVO	11	11	11400	2	10	38800	43100
34		CONVERTIBLE	FB	CNV	FBG	DV	IB	T250-T270		12	6	12500	3	1	38900	43900
34		CONVERTIBLE	FB	CNV	FBG	DV	IB	T200D	PERK	12	6	12500	3	1	48700	53500
37		CONVERTIBLE	FB	CNV	FBG	DV	VD	T350	CRUS	14		20000	3		51900	57000
37		CONVERTIBLE	FB	CNV	FBG	DV	IB	T240D	PERK	14		20000	3		59300	65200
40		AFT CABIN	FB	DC	FBG	DV	IB	T350	CRUS	14		24000	3		69000	75800
40		AFT CABIN	FB	DC	FBG	DV	IB	T240D	PERK	14		24000	3		76900	84500
		1981 BOATS														
31		CONVERTIBLE	FB	CNV	FBG	DV	VD	T220-T270		11	11	11400	2	11	29000	33500
31		CONVERTIBLE	FB	CNV	FBG	DV	VD	T155D	VLVO	11	11	11400	2	11	37300	41400
31		GULFSTREAM	OP	SPTCR	FBG	DV	VD	T250-T350		11	11	9340	2	11	23200	27700
34		CONVERTIBLE	FB	CNV	FBG	DS	VD	T200D	PERK	12	6	12500	3	1	47100	51800
34		CONVERTIBLE	FB	CNV	FBG	DV	VD	T250-T270		12	6	12500	3	1	37300	42000
37		CONVERTIBLE	FB	CNV	FBG	DV	VD	T350	CRUS	14		18400	3		46900	51500
37		CONVERTIBLE	FB	CNV	FBG	DV	VD	T200D	PERK	14		18400	3		52000	57200
		1980 BOATS														
31		CONVERTIBLE SEDAN	FB	CNV	FBG	DV	VD	T220-T225		11	11	11400	2	11	27800	30900
31		GULFSTREAM	OP	SPTCR	FBG	DV	VD	T250-T270		11	11	9340	2	11	22200	25100
31		SPORT SEDAN	FB	SDN	FBG	DV	VD	T220-T225		11	11	11400	2	11	27800	30900
34		CONVERTIBLE SEDAN	FB	CNV	FBG	DV	VD	T250-T270		12	6	12500	3	1	35700	40200
34		SPORT SEDAN	FB	SDN	FBG	DV	VD	T250-T270		12	6	12500	3	1	35700	40200
37		CONVERTIBLE	FB	CNV	FBG	DV	VD	T350	CRUS	14		18400	3		44200	49200
37		CONVERTIBLE	FB	CNV	FBG	DV	VD	T200D	PERK	14		18400	3		49600	54600
		1979 BOATS														
26	1	EXPRESS	HT	EXP	FBG	SV	VD	220-270		10	6	6925	3		10600	12300
26	1	FLYBRIDGE	FB	CR	FBG	SV	VD	220-270		10	6	6925	3		10600	12300
31		CONVERTIBLE SEDAN	FB	CNV	FBG	SV	VD	T220-T270		11	11	11400	2	11	26600	30700
31		GULFSTREAM		SPTCR	FBG	SV	VD	T250-T270		11	11	10800	3		24600	27700
31		SPORT SEDAN	FB	SDN	FBG	SV	VD	T220-T270		11	11	11400	2	11	26600	30700
34		CONVERTIBLE SEDAN	FB	CNV	FBG	SV	VD	T250-T270		12	6	12500	3	1	34200	38600
34		SPORT SEDAN	FB	SDN	FBG	SV	VD	T250-T270		12	6	12500	3	1	34200	38600
		1978 BOATS														
26	1	EXPRESS	HT	EXP	FBG	SV	VD	220-225		10	6	6925	3		10200	11600
26	1	FLYBRIDGE	FB	CR	FBG	SV	VD	220-225		10	6	6925	3		10200	11600
28		SEDAN	FB	SDN	FBG	SV	VD	330-350		10	6	9000	3		17000	19700
28		SEDAN	FB	SDN	FBG	SV	VD	T220-T225		10	6	9500	2	8	19000	21100
31		CONVERTIBLE	FB	SDN	FBG	SV	VD	T220-T225		11	11	11400	2	11	25900	28900
31		SEDAN	FB	SDN	FBG	SV	VD	T220-T225		11	11	11400	2	11	25100	28000
34		SEDAN	FB	SDN	FBG	SV	VD	T250-T270		12	6	12500	3	1	32800	37000
		1977 BOATS														
26	1	EXPRESS	OP	EXP	FBG	SV	VD	220-225		10	6	6925	3		9800	11100
26	1	FLYBRIDGE	FB	CR	FBG	SV	VD	220-225		10	6	6925	3		9800	11100
28		SEDAN	FB	SDN	FBG	SV	VD	330-350		10	6	9000	3		16300	18900
28		SEDAN	FB	SDN	FBG	SV	VD	T220-T225		10	6	9700	2	8	18400	20500
31		CONVERTIBLE SEDAN	FB	CNV	FBG	SV	VD	T220-T225		11	11	11400	2	11	24500	27300
31		SPORT SEDAN	FB	SDN	FBG	SV	VD	T220-T225		11	11	11400	2	11	24500	27300
34		CONVERTIBLE SEDAN	FB	CNV	FBG	SV	VD	T250-T270		12	6	12500	3	1	31500	35500
34		SPORT SEDAN	FB	SDN	FBG	SV	VD	T250-T270		12	6	12500	3	1	31500	35500
		1976 BOATS														
26	1	EXPRESS	OP	EXP	FBG	SV	IB	220-225		10	6	7000	3		9450	10800
26	1	FLYBRIDGE	FB	CR	FBG	SV	IB	220-225		10	6	7000	3		9450	10800
27		SEDAN	FB	SDN	FBG	SV	IB			10	1	7675	2	6	**	**
28		CUDDY CRUISER		CUD	FBG	SV	IB	250		10	6				11900	13600
28		SEDAN	FB	SDN	FBG	SV	IB	250-270		10	6	9000	3		15000	17300
28		SEDAN	FB	SDN	FBG	SV	IB	T220-T225		10	6	9600	3		17200	19500
31		SEDAN	FB	SDN	FBG	SV	IB	T220-T250		11	11	11400	2	10	23500	26700
33	8	SEDAN	FB	SDN	FBG	SV	IB	T220-T250		12	6	11400	2	10	28600	32300
33	8	SPORT SEDAN	FB	SDN	FBG	SV	IB	T225-T250		12	6	11400	2	10	28600	32300
		1975 BOATS														
26		EXPRESS	OP	EXP	FBG	SV	IB			10	6	7000	3		**	**
27		SEDAN	FB	SDN	FBG	SV	IB	225	CHRY	10	1	7675	2	6	10400	11800
28		SEDAN	FB	SDN	FBG	SV	IB	225	CHRY	10	6	9000	3		14200	16200
28		SEDAN	FB	SDN	FBG	SV	IB	T225	CHRY	10	6	9300	3		16200	18500
28		SUPER SPORT	TT	EXP	FBG	SV	IB	225	CHRY	10	6	8700	3		13100	14900
28		SUPER SPORT	TT	EXP	FBG	SV	IB	T225	CHRY	10	6	9000	3		14700	16800
30	10	SEDAN	FB	SDN	FBG	SV	IB	T225	CHRY	10	6	9900	2	6	21300	23700
33	8	SPORT	FB	SDN	FBG	SV	IB	T225	CHRY	12	6	11400	2	10	27500	30500
		1974 BOATS														
25	6	SPORTSTER			FBG	SV	IB	220-250		10	6	6800	3		8350	9700
27	4			SDN	FBG	SV	IB	220-250		10	1	7800	2	6	10200	11800
28		SILVERTON 28			FBG	SV	IB	250	PALM	10	6	8500	3		13500	15300
28		SILVERTON 28			FBG	SV	IB	T200	CHRY	10	6	9500	3		15200	17300
28		SUPER SPORT			FBG	SV	IB	250	CHRY	10	6	8500	3		11700	13300
28		SUPER SPORT			FBG	SV	IB	T200	CHRY	10	6	9500	3		13500	15300
30	10			SPTCR	FBG	SV	IB	350	PALM	11	11	10000	3	2	18600	20600
30	10			SPTCR	FBG	SV	IB	T220	PALM	11	11	10000	2	10	19000	21100
33	8			SDN	FBG	SV	IB	T220-T250		12	6	12000	2	10	26600	30100
33	8			SDN	FBG	SV	IB	T160D-T185D		12	6	12000	2	10	33700	38400
		1973 BOATS														
25	6	SPORTSTER			FBG	SV	IB	220-255		10	6	6800	3		8050	9350
27	2			SF	FBG	SV	IB	220-255		10	1	7000	2	6	8550	10000
27	4	27-4		SDN	FBG	SV	IB	220-255		10	1	7800	2	6	9850	11400
28		SILVERTON 28			FBG	SV	IO	250-255		10	6	8500	3		17300	19800
28		SILVERTON 28			FBG	SV	IO	T190-T200		10	6	9500	2	6	19800	22200
30	10			SPTCR	FBG	SV	IB	330-350		11	11	10000	3	2	17300	19800
30	10			SPTCR	FBG	SV	IB	T220-T225		11	11	10000	2	10	18500	21100
33	8			SDN	FBG	SV	IB	T220-T255		12	6	12000	2	10	25600	29100
33	8			SDN	FBG	SV	IB	T160D-T185D		12	6	12700	2	10	33800	38600
		1972 BOATS														
25	6	SPORTSTER	FB		FBG		IB	225	CHRY	10	6		3		6300	7250
27	2			SDN	FBG		IB	225-250		10	3	7800	2	6	9450	10900
27	2			SF	FBG		IB	225-250		10	3	7000	2	6	8250	9600
30	10			SPTCR	FBG		IB	330	CHRY	11	11	10000	3	2	16600	18900
30	10			SPTCR	FBG		IB	T225-T250		11	11	11200	2	10	18400	20800
33	8			SDN	FBG		IB	T225-T250		12	7	12000	2	10	24700	27800
33	8			SDN	FBG		IB	T160D-T185D		12	7	12700	2	10	32900	37600
		1971 BOATS														
27			FB	SDN	FBG		IB	225	CHRY						9100	10400
27			FB	SF	FBG		IB	225	PALM						6850	7850
33			FB	SDN	FBG		VD	T225	CHRY						19800	22000
		1970 BOATS														
27			FB	SDN	FBG		IB	225							8700	10000
		1968 BOATS														
27	2		FB	SDN	FBG		IB	210	CHRY	9	10	6000	3	2	6950	7950
		1967 BOATS														
20		SEA-SPRITE		RNBT	L/P		IB	120		7	8		1	4	2250	2650
23	2	SEA-SPORT	HT		L/P		IB	120-175		9			1	8	3250	3900
23	2	SEE-OPEN SKIFF			L/P		IB	120-175		9			1	8	3250	3900
24	4	SEA-MATE	HT		L/P		IB	120-175		9	2	3200	1	8	3300	4000
26	4	SEA-MASTER	FB		L/P		IB	195		9	7		2		5300	6050
		1966 BOATS														
20	1	SEA-SPRITE		RNBT	L/P		IB	100		7	8		1	4	2150	2500
20	1	VIKING-RAIDER		SKI	L/P		IB	110		7	8		1	4	1950	2300

 CONTINUED ON NEXT PAGE

SILVERTON MARINE CORP — CONTINUED

See inside cover to adjust price for area

1966 BOATS

LOA	NAME AND/OR MODEL	TOP/RIG	BOAT TYPE	MTL	HULL TP	ENG TP	#HP	MFG	BEAM	WGT LBS	DRAFT	RETAIL LOW	RETAIL HIGH
23 2	SEA-SPORT		SF	L/P		IB	120		8 2		1 8	3650	4200
23 2	SEA-VEE	OP	SF	L/P		IB	120		8 2		1 8	3650	4200
24 4	BASS-MASTER	OP	SF	L/P		IB	120		8 6		1 8	3800	4400
24 4	SEA-MATE		SF	L/P		IB	120		8 6		1 8	3800	4400

1963 BOATS

LOA	NAME AND/OR MODEL	TOP/RIG	BOAT TYPE	MTL	HULL TP	ENG TP	#HP	MFG	BEAM	WGT LBS	DRAFT	RETAIL LOW	RETAIL HIGH
20	SEA-SPRITE DELUXE			WD		IB	85					1700	2000
20	SEA-SPRITE DELUXE			WD		IB	150					1800	2150
20	SEA-SPRITE STD			WD		IB	85					1700	2000
23	SEA-SPORT			WD		IB	120					2650	3100
23	SEA-SUN			WD		IB	178					2750	3200
23	SEA-VEE			WD		IB	120					2650	3100
24	SEA-MATE			WD		IB	120-178					3250	3900
27	SUN-LINER	OP		WD		IB	178					4600	5300
27	SUN-LINER	OP		WD		IB	T178					5300	6100
27	SUN-LINER	CR		WD		IB	178					5450	6250
27	SUN-LINER	CR		WD		IB	T178					6100	7000
27	SUN-LINER SHELTER	CR		WD		IB	178					5450	6250
27	SUN-LINER SHELTER	CR		WD		IB	T178					6100	7000

1962 BOATS

LOA	NAME AND/OR MODEL	TOP/RIG	BOAT TYPE	MTL	HULL TP	ENG TP	#HP	MFG	BEAM	WGT LBS	DRAFT	RETAIL LOW	RETAIL HIGH
23 2	SEA-SPORT SKIFF			WD		IB	110					2600	3000
23 2	SEA-VEE SKIFF			WD		IB	110					2600	3000
24 2	SHELTER CABIN SKIFF	CR		WD		IB	110					3200	3700
30 2	ALL-SEAS			WD		IB	195					7800	9000

1961 BOATS

LOA	NAME AND/OR MODEL	TOP/RIG	BOAT TYPE	MTL	HULL TP	ENG TP	#HP	MFG	BEAM	WGT LBS	DRAFT	RETAIL LOW	RETAIL HIGH
23 11	SEAFARER		SF	L/P		IB	60-177		8		2	3050	3800
24 7	SEA-CRUISER	CR		L/P		IB	110-177		8 8		2	3700	4450
24 7	SEAROVER		SF	L/P		IB	110-177		8 8		2	3250	3950

1960 BOATS

LOA	NAME AND/OR MODEL	TOP/RIG	BOAT TYPE	MTL	HULL TP	ENG TP	#HP	MFG	BEAM	WGT LBS	DRAFT	RETAIL LOW	RETAIL HIGH
23	SEAFARER		SF	L/P		IB	60		8 3		2	2900	3400
23	SEAFARER		SF	WD		IB	60-150					3000	3700
24	SEAROVER		SF	L/P		IB	109		8 8		2	3150	3700
24	SEAROVER		SF	WD		IB	109-188					3100	3750

1959 BOATS

LOA	NAME AND/OR MODEL	TOP/RIG	BOAT TYPE	MTL	HULL TP	ENG TP	#HP	MFG	BEAM	WGT LBS	DRAFT	RETAIL LOW	RETAIL HIGH
23	SEAFARER SKIFF	HT		L/P		IB	109-150		8 2			2450	2950
24	SEAROVER	CR		L/P		IB	170		8 5			3150	3650

SIMON BOATS LTD
COAST GUARD MFG ID- ZSA

Call 1-800-327-6929 for BUC Personalized Evaluation Service
Or, for 1978 to 1983 boats, sign onto www.BUCValuPro.com

L J SIMONDS BOATS
COAST GUARD MFG ID- SMB

Call 1-800-327-6929 for BUC Personalized Evaluation Service
Or, for 1965 to 1975 boats, sign onto www.BUCValuPro.com

SIMPSON WILD INTL INC
SIMPSON WILD MARINE LIM COAST GUARD MFG ID- SXX

OCEAN PLASTICS INDUSTRIES

Call 1-800-327-6929 for BUC Personalized Evaluation Service
Or, for 1976 to 1978 boats, sign onto www.BUCValuPro.com

SINO AMERICA YT IND CO LTD
TAIPEI TAIWAN   COAST GUARD MFG ID- SGY See inside cover to adjust price for area

1980 BOATS

LOA	NAME AND/OR MODEL	TOP/RIG	BOAT TYPE	MTL	HULL TP	ENG TP	#HP	MFG	BEAM	WGT LBS	DRAFT	RETAIL LOW	RETAIL HIGH
39 2	LANDFALL 39	CUT	SA/CR	FBG	KL	IB	35D	PERK	11 6	23500	5 7	51700	56800

1973 BOATS

LOA	NAME AND/OR MODEL	TOP/RIG	BOAT TYPE	MTL	HULL TP	ENG TP	#HP	MFG	BEAM	WGT LBS	DRAFT	RETAIL LOW	RETAIL HIGH
36	SEA-PHOENIX	SLP	SAIL	FBG	KL	IB	D		9 10		4 6	27100	30100
40 11	SEA-DRAGON	KTH	SAIL	FBG	KL	IB	D		12 2		6 2	44000	48800

SIROCCO BOATWORKS LTD
COAST GUARD MFG ID- SBF

Call 1-800-327-6929 for BUC Personalized Evaluation Service
Or, for 1972 to 1976 boats, sign onto www.BUCValuPro.com

SISU BOAT INC
DOVER NH 03820   COAST GUARD MFG ID- SGH See inside cover to adjust price for area

For more recent years, see the BUC Used Boat Price Guide, Volume 1 or Volume 2

1983 BOATS

LOA	NAME AND/OR MODEL	TOP/RIG	BOAT TYPE	MTL	HULL TP	ENG TP	#HP	MFG	BEAM	WGT LBS	DRAFT	RETAIL LOW	RETAIL HIGH
21 9	SISU 22	OP	CTRCN	F/S	RB	OB			7 10	2000	1 9	9250	10500
21 9	SISU 22	OP	CTRCN	F/S	RB	IO	120	VLVO	7 10	3000	1 9	7900	9100
21 9	SISU 22	OP	CTRCN	F/S	RB	IB	145	VLVO	7 10	3000	1 9	9050	10300
21 9	SISU 22	OP	CTRCN	F/S	RB	IB	50D-85D		7 10	3200	1 9	12700	15900
21 9	SISU 22	OP	FSH	F/S	RB	OB			7 10	2200	1 9	9900	11300
21 9	SISU 22	OP	FSH	F/S	RB	IO	120	VLVO	7 10	3600	2 2	9000	10200
21 9	SISU 22	OP	FSH	F/S	RB	IB	125	VLVO	7 10	3600	2 2	10000	11400
21 9	SISU 22	OP	FSH	F/S	RB	IB	50D-85D		7 10	3600	2 2	13600	16400
21 9	SISU 22	HT	FSH	F/S	RB	OB			7 10	2200	1 9	9700	11300
21 9	SISU 22	HT	FSH	F/S	RB	IO	120	VLVO	7 10	3600	2 2	9000	10200
21 9	SISU 22	HT	FSH	F/S	RB	IB	125	VLVO	7 10	3600	2 2	10000	11400
21 9	SISU 22	HT	FSH	F/S	RB	IB	50D-85D		7 10	3600	2 2	13600	16400
25 6	SISU 26	OP	FSH	F/S	RB	OB			9 8	4500	3 4	19200	21300
25 6	SISU 26	OP	FSH	F/S	RB	IB	165D-200D		9 8	7500	3	31100	35600
25 6	SISU 26	OP	FSH	F/S	RB	OB			9 8	4500	3 4	19400	21500
25 6	SISU 26	HT	FSH	F/S	RB	IB	225	CHRY	9 8	7500	3	22500	25000
25 6	SISU 26	HT	FSH	F/S	RB	IB	D	VLVO	9 8	7500	3	**	**
25 6	SISU 26	HT	FSH	F/S	RB	IB	85D-200D		9 8	7500	3	29100	35600
29 9	SISU 30	HT	CBNCR	F/S	RB	IB	225	CHRY	10 6	10000	3	33400	37100
29 9	SISU 30	HT	CBNCR	F/S	RB	IB	D	VLVO	10 6	10000	3	**	**
29 9	SISU 30	HT	CBNCR	F/S	RB	IB	135D-200D		10 6	10000	3	42800	50900

1982 BOATS

LOA	NAME AND/OR MODEL	TOP/RIG	BOAT TYPE	MTL	HULL TP	ENG TP	#HP	MFG	BEAM	WGT LBS	DRAFT	RETAIL LOW	RETAIL HIGH
21 9	SISU 22	OP	FSH	F/S	RB	OB			7 10	2200	1 9	9700	11000
21 9	SISU 22	OP	FSH	F/S	RB	IO	125	VLVO	7 10	3600	2 2	9550	10900
21 9	SISU 22	OP	FSH	F/S	RB	IO	140		7 10	3600		8450	9750
21 9	SISU 22	OP	FSH	F/S	RB	IB	85D	PERK	7 10	3600	2 2	13900	15800
21 9	SISU 22	HT	FSH	F/S	RB	OB			7 10	2200	1 9	9700	11000
21 9	SISU 22	HT	FSH	F/S	RB	IB	125	VLVO	7 10	3600	2 2	9550	10900
21 9	SISU 22	HT	FSH	F/S	RB	IB	85D	PERK	7 10	3600	2 2	13900	15800
25 6	SISU 26	HT	CBNCR	F/S	RB	IB			9 8	6000	3	20600	22800
25 6	SISU 26	HT	FSH	F/S	RB	IB	225	CHRY	9 8	7500	3	21500	23900
25 6	SISU 26	HT	FSH	F/S	RB	IB	85D-200D		9 8	7500	3	27900	34200
29 9	SISU 30	HT	CBNCR	F/S	RB	IB	225	CHRY	10 6	10000	3	32000	35600
29 9	SISU 30	HT	CBNCR	F/S	RB	IB	135D-200D		10 6	10000	3	41100	49000

1981 BOATS

LOA	NAME AND/OR MODEL	TOP/RIG	BOAT TYPE	MTL	HULL TP	ENG TP	#HP	MFG	BEAM	WGT LBS	DRAFT	RETAIL LOW	RETAIL HIGH
21 9	SISU 22		FSH	FBG	RB	OB			7 10	2400		10000	11400
21 9	SISU 22		FSH	FBG	RB	IO	140		7 10			8300	9600
21 9	SISU 22		FSH	FBG	RB	IB	85D		7 10			12800	14500
21 9	SISU 22	OP	FSH	F/S	RB	OB			7 10	2200	1 9	9500	10800
21 9	SISU 22	OP	FSH	F/S	RB	IO	125	VLVO	7 10	3600	2 2	9200	10500
21 9	SISU 22	OP	FSH	F/S	RB	IB	85D	PERK	7 10	3600	2 2	13300	15200
21 9	SISU 22	HT	FSH	F/S	RB	OB			7 10	2200	1 9	9500	10800
21 9	SISU 22	HT	FSH	F/S	RB	IO	125	VLVO	7 10	3600	2 2	9200	10500
21 9	SISU 22	HT	FSH	F/S	RB	IB	85D	PERK	7 10	3600	2 2	13300	15200
25 6	SISU 26	HT	FSH	F/S	RB	IB	85D		9 8	6000	3	20600	29400
25 6	SISU 26	HT	FSH	FBG	RB	IB	225	CHRY	9 8	7500	3	20600	22900
25 6	SISU 26	HT	FSH	FBG	RB	IB	85D-165D		9 8	7500	3	26900	31900
29 9	SISU 30	HT	CBNCR	F/S	RB	IB	165D-200D		10 6	10000	3	40800	47100
29 9	SISU 30			FBG	RB	IB	225		10 6			23400	26000

1980 BOATS

LOA	NAME AND/OR MODEL	TOP/RIG	BOAT TYPE	MTL	HULL TP	ENG TP	#HP	MFG	BEAM	WGT LBS	DRAFT	RETAIL LOW	RETAIL HIGH
21 9	SISU 22	OP	FSH	F/S	RB	OB			7 10	2200	1 9	9250	10500
21 9	SISU 22	OP	FSH	F/S	RB	IO	125	VLVO	7 10	3400	2 2	8150	9400
21 9	SISU 22	OP	FSH	F/S	RB	IO	125		7 10	3400	2 2	8400	9650
21 9	SISU 22	OP		FBG	RB	IO	140		7 10	3400		7950	9100
21 9	SISU 22	OP		FBG	RB	OB			7 10			8800	10100
21 9	SISU 22	HT	FSH	F/S	RB	IB	125	VLVO	7 10	3600	2 2	12800	14600
21 9	SISU 22	HT	FSH	F/S	RB	IO	125		7 10	3400	2 2	8400	9650
21 9	SISU 22	HT	FSH	F/S	RB	IO	125	VLVO	7 10	3600	2 2	8150	9400
21 9	SISU 22	HT	FSH	F/S	RB	IB	85D	PERK	7 10	3600	2 2	13300	15200
21 9	SISU 22	HT		FBG	RB	IB	85D		7 10			12800	14600
25 6	SISU 26	HT	FSH	F/S	RB	IB	225	CHRY	9 8	7500	3	19700	21300
25 6	SISU 26	HT	FSH	F/S	RB	IB	85D-118D		9 8	7500	3	25900	28800
29 9	SISU 30	HT	CBNCR	F/S	RB	IB	225-330		10 6	10000	3	29400	35000
29 9	SISU 30	HT	CBNCR	F/S	RB	IB	118D-228D		10 6	10000	3	37000	46100

SISU BOAT INC   -CONTINUED   See inside cover to adjust price for area

LOA FT IN	NAME AND/ OR MODEL	TOP/ RIG	BOAT TYPE	-HULL- MTL TP TP	----ENGINE--- # HP MFG	BEAM FT IN	WGT LBS	DRAFT FT IN	RETAIL LOW	RETAIL HIGH
---	---	---	---	--- 1979 BOATS	---	---	---	---	---	---
21 9	SISU 22	ST	FSH	FBG RB OB		7 10	2400	1 9	9650	11000
21 9	SISU 22	HT	FSH	FBG RB OB		7 10	2400	1 9	9650	11000
21 9	SISU 22	HT	FSH	FBG RB IO	140 VLVO	7 10	3400	1 9	8150	9400
21 9	SISU 22	HT	FSH	FBG RB IB	140 VLVO	7 10	3400	2 2	8150	9350
21 9	SISU 22	HT	FSH	FBG RB IB	85D PERK	7 10	3400	2 2	12000	13600
26	SISU 26		FSH	FBG RB IB					**	**
26	SISU 26		FSH	FBG RB IB	118D VLVO	9 8	7200	2 9	24000	26600
29 9	SISU 30	HT	CBNCR	FBG RB IB	225-330	10 6	8500	3	25600	30800
29 9	SISU 30	HT	CBNCR	FBG RB IB	118D VLVO	10 6	8500	3	32100	35700
29 9	SISU 30	HT	CBNCR	FBG RB IB	228D VLVO	10 6	9500	3	39000	43300
---	---	---	---	--- 1978 BOATS	---	---	---	---	---	---
21 9	SISU 22	ST	FSH	F/S RB OB		7 10	2400	1 9	9500	10800
21 9	SISU 22	ST	FSH	F/S RB OB		7 10	2400	1 9	9500	10800
21 9	SISU 22	HT	FSH	F/S RB IB	115 VLVO	7 10	3400	2 2	7650	8750
IO 140 VLVO		8250	9450, IB	155 CHRY	8050 9250, IO	61D VLVO			11000	12500
ID	61D VLVO	10200	11600							
29 9	SISU 30	HT	FSH	F/S RB IB	225 CHRY	10 6	8500	3	19300	21400
29 9	SISU 30	HT	FSH	F/S RB IB	120D VLVO	10 6	8500	3	23900	26600
29 9	SISU 30	HT	FSH	F/S RB IB	192D VLVO	10 6	9500	3	29600	32900
---	---	---	---	--- 1977 BOATS	---	---	---	---	---	---
21 9	SISU 22	ST	FSH	F/S RB OB		7 10	2400	1 9	9350	10600
21 9	SISU 22	HT	FSH	F/S RB OB		7 10	2400	1 9	9350	10600
21 9	SISU 22	HT	FSH	F/S RB IO	61 VLVO	7 10	3400	1 9	8350	9600
IB 115-155		7250	8950, IB	61D VLVO	9850 11200, IO	105D VLVO			11800	13500
IB 106D		11200	12800							

SKAGIT PLASTICS INC

Call 1-800-327-6929 for BUC Personalized Evaluation Service
Or, for 1959 to 1960 boats, sign onto www.BUCValuPro.com

SKALLERUD & SONS
WILMINGTON CA 90744   See inside cover to adjust price for area

LOA FT IN	NAME AND/ OR MODEL	TOP/ RIG	BOAT TYPE	-HULL- MTL TP TP	----ENGINE--- # HP MFG	BEAM FT IN	WGT LBS	DRAFT FT IN	RETAIL LOW	RETAIL HIGH
---	---	---	---	--- 1966 BOATS	---	---	---	---	---	---
43	BAHA 43	CR	STL	IB		14		5	**	**
65	CRUISER	CR	STL	IB T333D		18		7	746000	819500
---	---	---	---	--- 1965 BOATS	---	---	---	---	---	---
54		KTH	SA/CR	STL KL IB	D				132500	146000
54	STEEL CRUISER	MY	STL	IB	D	17		7	**	**
56		KTH	SA/CR	STL KL IB	D				152500	167500

SKEE-CRAFT BOAT CO
COAST GUARD MFG ID- SKR

Call 1-800-327-6929 for BUC Personalized Evaluation Service
Or, for 1958 to 1963 boats, sign onto www.BUCValuPro.com

SKEETER BOATS INC
A SUBDIVISION OF GARLOCK
DIV OF STEMCO MARINE
KILGORE TX 75662   COAST GUARD MFG ID- STE

See inside cover to adjust price for area

For more recent years, see the BUC Used Boat Price Guide, Volume 1 or Volume 2

LOA FT IN	NAME AND/ OR MODEL	TOP/ RIG	BOAT TYPE	-HULL- MTL TP TP	----ENGINE--- # HP MFG	BEAM FT IN	WGT LBS	DRAFT FT IN	RETAIL LOW	RETAIL HIGH
---	---	---	---	--- 1983 BOATS	---	---	---	---	---	---
17 11	STARFIRE 18	OP	BASS	FBG DV OB		7 2	1400		2500	2900
---	---	---	---	--- 1982 BOATS	---	---	---	---	---	---
17 11	STARFIRE 18	OP	BASS	FBG DV OB		7 2	1400		2400	2800
---	---	---	---	--- 1981 BOATS	---	---	---	---	---	---
16 2	WRANGLER 16	OP	BASS	FBG DV OB		7 5	1100		1800	2150
17 11	STARFIRE 18	OP	BASS	FBG DV OB		7 2	1400		2350	2750
---	---	---	---	--- 1980 BOATS	---	---	---	---	---	---
16 2	WRANGLER 16	OP	BASS	FBG DV OB		7 5	1100		1750	2100
17 11	STARFIRE 18	OP	BASS	FBG DV OB		7 2	1400		2300	2650
---	---	---	---	--- 1975 BOATS	---	---	---	---	---	---
18 4	EAGLE III	OP	FSH	FBG OB		7 1	1400		2100	2500
---	---	---	---	--- 1974 BOATS	---	---	---	---	---	---
18 3	EAGLE I E-111	OP	FSH	FBG FL OB		6 10	1500		2200	2550

SKI BOATS OF WISC INC
COAST GUARD MFG ID- XSW

Call 1-800-327-6929 for BUC Personalized Evaluation Service
Or, for 1977 boats, sign onto www.BUCValuPro.com

SKIFF CRAFT
HENRY BOATS
PLAIN CITY OH 43064   See inside cover to adjust price for area
              FORMERLY HENRY BOATS INC   COAST GUARD MFG ID- HEN

For more recent years, see the BUC Used Boat Price Guide, Volume 1 or Volume 2

LOA FT IN	NAME AND/ OR MODEL	TOP/ RIG	BOAT TYPE	-HULL- MTL TP TP	----ENGINE--- # HP MFG	BEAM FT IN	WGT LBS	DRAFT FT IN	RETAIL LOW	RETAIL HIGH
---	---	---	---	--- 1983 BOATS	---	---	---	---	---	---
21 10	X-220	OP	CBNCR	L/P SV IO	170 MRCR	8	2700		7950	9150
21 10	X-220	HT	CBNCR	L/P SV IO	170 MRCR	8	2700		7950	9150
24 3	X-240	OP	CBNCR	L/P SV IO	198 MRCR	8	3500		11300	12900
24 3	X-240	HT	CBNCR	L/P SV IO	198 MRCR	8	3500		11300	12900
24 3	X-240	HT	RNBT	L/P SV IO	198 MRCR	8	3500		9200	10500
25 10	X-260	OP	CBNCR	L/P SV IO	198 MRCR	10	5500		18700	20700
25 10	X-260	OP	RNBT	L/P SV IO	198 MRCR	10	5500		13900	15800
25 10	X-260	HT	RNBT	L/P SV IO	198 MRCR	10	5500		13900	15800
25 10	X-260	FB	SDNSF	L/P SV IO	198 MRCR	10	5500		17100	19400
25 10	X-260	FB	SF	L/P SV IO	198 MRCR	10	5500		17100	19400
30	X-300	OP	RNBT	L/P SV IB	T225 CHRY	12	8200		32000	35600
30	X-300	HT	RNBT	L/P SV IB	T225 CHRY	12	8600		32500	36100
30	X-300	FB	SF	L/P SV IB	T225 CHRY	12	8900		31700	35200
---	---	---	---	--- 1982 BOATS	---	---	---	---	---	---
21 10	X-220	OP	CBNCR	WD SV IO	120	8			8150	9400
21 10	X-220	OP	CBNCR	L/P SV IO	170 MRCR	8	2700		7800	8950
21 10	X-220	HT	CBNCR	L/P SV IO	170 MRCR	8	2700		7800	8950
24 3	X-240	OP	CBNCR	WD SV IO	170	8			11800	13400
24 3	X-240	OP	CBNCR	L/P SV IO	198 MRCR	8	3500		11100	12600
24 3	X-240	OP	CBNCR	WD SV IO	170	8			11800	13400
24 3	X-240	HT	CBNCR	L/P SV IO	198 MRCR	8	3500		11100	12600
24 3	X-240	HT	CBNCR	WD SV IO	170	8			12700	14400
24 3	X-240	OP	RNBT	WD SV IO	170	8			9500	10800
24 3	X-240	HT	RNBT	L/P SV IO	198 MRCR	8	3500		9000	10200
25 10	X-260	HT	CBNCR	WD SV IO	225	10			18200	20300
25 10	X-260	HT	CBNCR	WD SV IB	225	10			20100	22300
25 10	X-260	OP	RNBT	WD SV IO	198 MRCR	10			13000	14700
25 10	X-260	OP	RNBT	L/P SV IO	198 MRCR	10	5500		13500	15400
25 10	X-260	HT	RNBT	L/P SV IO	198 MRCR	10	5500		13500	15400
25 10	X-260	FB	SDNSF	L/P SV IO	198 MRCR	10	5500		16700	19000
25 10	X-260	FB	SF	L/P SV IO	198 MRCR	10	5500		16700	19000
30 3	X-300	OP	RNBT	L/P SV IB	225 CHRY	12	8100		28100	31300
---	---	---	---	--- 1981 BOATS	---	---	---	---	---	---
21 10	220	HT	CBNCR	WD SV IO	120	8			8050	9250
21 10	220	HT	RNBT	WD SV IO	120	8			6900	7950
21 10	X-220	OP	CBNCR	L/P SV IO	170 MRCR	8	2700		7650	8800
21 10	X-220	HT	CBNCR	L/P SV IO	170 MRCR	8	2700		7650	8800
24 3	240		CBNCR	WD SV IO	170	8			11600	13200
24 3	240	HT	CBNCR	WD SV IO	170	8			11600	13200
24 3	240	HT	CBNCR	WD SV IO	225	8			12300	13800
24 3	240		RNBT	WD SV IO	170	8			9400	10700
24 3	X-240	OP	CBNCR	L/P SV IO	198 MRCR	8	3500		10900	12400
24 3	X-240	HT	CBNCR	L/P SV IO	198 MRCR	8	3500		10900	12400
24 3	X-240	HT	RNBT	L/P SV IO	198 MRCR	8	3500		8850	10100
25 10	X-260	OP	RNBT	L/P SV IO	198 MRCR	8	5500		13300	15200
25 10	X-260	HT	RNBT	L/P SV IO	198 MRCR	10	5500		13300	15200
25 10	X-260	FB	SDNSF	L/P SV IO	198 MRCR	10	5500		16400	18700
25 10	X-260	FB	SF	L/P SV IO	198 MRCR	10	5500		16400	18700
25 11	260	HT	CBNCR	WD SV IO	170	10			16900	19200
25 11	260	HT	CBNCR	WD SV IO	170	10			16900	19200
25 11	260	HT	RNBT	WD SV IO	170	10			19400	21900
25 11	260		RNBT	WD SV IO	170	10			12800	14500
25 11	260		SF	WD SV IO	170	10			15900	18000
---	---	---	---	--- 1980 BOATS	---	---	---	---	---	---
21 10	X-220	OP	CBNCR	L/P SV IO	120-170	8			7950	9150
21 10	X-220	HT	CBNCR	L/P SV IO	170 MRCR	8	2700		7600	8750

SKIFF CRAFT -CONTINUED See inside cover to adjust price for area

LOA FT	LOA IN	NAME AND/ OR MODEL	TOP/ RIG	BOAT TYPE	-HULL- MTL	-HULL- TP	ENGINE TP	ENGINE # HP	ENGINE MFG	BEAM FT	BEAM IN	WGT LBS	DRAFT FT	DRAFT IN	RETAIL LOW	RETAIL HIGH
1980 BOATS																
21	10	X-220	HT	CR	L/P	SV	IO	120		8					7250	8300
21	10	X-220		RNBT	L/P	SV	IO	120		8					6850	7900
24	3	X-240	OP	CBNCR	L/P	SV	IO	170-198		8					11500	13100
24	3	X-240	HT	CBNCR	L/P	SV	IO	198	MRCR	8		3500			10800	12300
24	3	X-240	HT	CR	L/P	SV	IO	170		8					9950	11300
24	3	X-240		RNBT	L/P	SV	IO	170		8					9350	10600
24	3	X-240	HT	RNBT	L/P	SV	IO	198	MRCR	8		3500			8700	9950
25	10	X-260		CBNCR	L/P	SV	IO	170		10					16700	18900
25	10	X-260	HT	CBNCR	L/P	SV	IO	198	MRCR	10		5000			16500	18800
25	10	X-260	HT	CR	L/P	SV	IO	170		10					13700	15600
25	10	X-260		RNBT	L/P	SV	IO	170		10					12700	14400
25	10	X-260	OP	RNBT	L/P	SV	IO	198	MRCR	10		5000			12400	14100
25	10	X-260	HT	RNBT	L/P	SV	IO	198	MRCR	10		5000			12400	14100
25	10	X-260	FB	SDNSF	L/P	SV	IO	198	MRCR	10		5000			15300	17400
25	10	X-260		SF	L/P	SV	IO	170		10					15700	17800
25	10	X-260	FB	SF	L/P	SV	IO	198	MRCR	10		5000			15300	17400
1979 BOATS																
22		SC-22		CBNCR	L/P	SV	IO	120-233		8					8050	9550
22		SC-22	HT	CR	L/P	SV	IO	120-233		8					7300	8650
22		SC-22		RNBT	L/P	SV	IO	120-233		8					6900	8200
26		SC-26		CBNCR	L/P	SV	IO	188-233		10					17100	20100
26		SC-26	HT	CR	L/P	SV	IO	188		10					13900	15800
26		SC-26	HT	CR	L/P	SV	IB	225		10					15500	17700
26		SC-26	HT	CR	L/P	SV	IO	233		10					14400	16300
26		SC-26		RNBT	L/P	SV	IO	188		10					12800	14600
26		SC-26		RNBT	L/P	SV	IB	225		10					15300	17400
26		SC-26		RNBT	L/P	SV	IO	233		10					13200	15000
26		SC-26		SF	L/P	SV	IO	188-233		10					15900	18700
1978 BOATS																
21	10	X-220	OP	CBNCR	L/P	SV	IO	120-260		8		2700			7600	9300
21	10	X-220	HT	CBNCR	L/P	SV	IO	120-260		8		2700			7600	9300
21	10	X-220	OP	RNBT	L/P	SV	IO	120-260		8		2300			6050	7450
21	10	X-220	OP	RNBT	L/P	SV	IO	T120	OMC	8		2300			7050	8100
21	10	X-220	HT	RNBT	L/P	SV	IO	120-260		8		2600			6450	7850
24	3	X-240	OP	CBNCR	L/P	SV	IO	120-260		8		3500			10600	12800
24	3	X-240	HT	CBNCR	L/P	SV	IO	120-260		8		3500			10600	12800
24	3	X-240	OP	RNBT	L/P	SV	IO	120-260		8		3500			8500	10400
24	3	X-240	HT	RNBT	L/P	SV	IO	120-260		8		3500			8500	10400
25	10	X-260	OP	CBNCR	L/P	SV	IO	120-240		10		5000			15500	19300
25	10	X-260	OP	CBNCR	L/P	SV	IO	260	MRCR	10		5000			17100	19500
25	10	X-260	HT	CBNCR	L/P	SV	IO	120-240		10		5000			15500	19300
25	10	X-260	HT	CBNCR	L/P	SV	IO	260	MRCR	10		5000			17100	19500
25	10	X-260	HT	FSH	L/P	SV	IB	225		10		5000			14300	16200
25	10	X-260	OP	RNBT	L/P	SV	IO	120-260		10		5000			11900	14800
25	10	X-260	HT	RNBT	L/P	SV	IO	120-198		10		5000			11900	14200
25	10	X-260	HT	RNBT	L/P	SV	IB	225		10		5000			14100	16000
25	10	X-260	HT	RNBT	L/P	SV	IO	228-260		10		5000			12700	14800
25	10	X-260	FB	SDNSF	L/P	SV	IO	120-240		10		5000			14600	18000
25	10	X-260	FB	SDNSF	L/P	SV	IO	260	MRCR	10		5000			16100	18300
25	10	X-260	FB	SF	L/P	SV	IO	120-240		10		5000			14600	18000
25	10	X-260	FB	SF	L/P	SV	IO	260	MRCR	10		5000			16100	18300
1977 BOATS																
22		X-22	OP	CR	L/P	SV	IO	190	OMC	8		2700			7100	8200
22		X-220	HT	CBNCR	L/P	SV	IO	120-235		8		2700			7800	9300
22		X-220	OP	CR	L/P	SV	IO	120-235		8		2700			7100	8400
22		X-220	OP	RNBT	L/P	SV	IO	120-235		8		2300			6200	7400
22		X-220	HT	RNBT	L/P	SV	IO	120-235		8		2500			6450	7700
24		X-240	HT	CBNCR	L/P	SV	IO	120-235		8		3600			10800	12600
24		X-240	OP	CR	L/P	SV	IO	120-235		8		3600			9450	11100
24		X-240	OP	RNBT	L/P	SV	IO	120-235		8		3300			8300	9850
24		X-240	HT	RNBT	L/P	SV	IO	120-235		8		3500			8650	10200
26		X-260	HT	CBNCR	L/P	SV	IO	120-190		10		5000			15900	19300
26		X-260	HT	CBNCR	L/P	SV	IO	233-235		10		5000			17500	19900
26		X-260	HT	CBNCR	L/P	SV	IO	T120	OMC	10		5000			18500	20600
26		X-260	OP	CR	L/P	SV	IO	120-235		10		5000			13100	16100
26		X-260	OP	CR	L/P	SV	IO	T120	OMC	10		5000			14800	16800
26		X-260	HT	CR	L/P	SV	IB	225		10		4500			13000	14800
26		X-260	HT	FSH	L/P	SV	IB	225		10		5000			13800	15700
26		X-260	OP	RNBT	L/P	SV	IO	120-235		10		4500			11300	14000
26		X-260	OP	RNBT	L/P	SV	IO	T120	OMC	10		4500			12900	14600
26		X-260	HT	RNBT	L/P	SV	IO	120-235		10		4700			11700	14400
26		X-260	HT	RNBT	L/P	SV	IO	T120	OMC	10		4700			13200	15000
26		X-260	FB	SDNSF	L/P	SV	IO	120-235		10		5400			15700	19300
26		X-260	FB	SDNSF	L/P	SV	IO	T120	OMC	10		5400			18000	20000
26		X-260	FB	SF	L/P	SV	IO	120-235		10		5000			14900	18400
26		X-260	FB	SF	L/P	SV	IO	T120	OMC	10		5000			16900	19200
1976 BOATS																
21	10	X-220	OP	CR	L/P	SV	IO	120-235		8		2700			7200	8600
21	10	X-220	OP	RNBT	L/P	SV	IO	120-235		8		2300			6350	7600
21	10	X-220	HT	RNBT	L/P	SV	IO	120-235		8		2600			6700	8000
24	3	X-240	OP	CR	L/P	SV	IO	120-235		8		3700			9950	11800
24	3	X-240	OP	RNBT	L/P	SV	IO	120-235		8		3700			9350	11000
24	3	X-240	HT	RNBT	L/P	SV	IO	120-235		8		3700			9350	11000
25	10	X-260	HT		L/P	SV	IB	215		10		5000			13100	14900
25	10	X-260	HT	CR	L/P	SV	IO	120-235		10		5000			13400	16400
25	10	X-260	HT	CR	L/P	SV	IO	T120-T165		10		5000			15100	17900
25	10	X-260	HT	FSH	L/P	SV	IB	215		10		5000			13100	14900
25	10	X-260	OP	RNBT	L/P	SV	IO	120-235		10		5000			12400	15100
25	10	X-260	OP	RNBT	L/P	SV	IO	T120-T165		10		5000			13900	16500
25	10	X-260	HT	RNBT	L/P	SV	IO	120-235		10		5000			12400	15100
25	10	X-260	HT	RNBT	L/P	SV	IO	T120-T165		10		5000			13900	16500
25	10	X-260	FB	SDNSF	L/P	SV	IO	120-235		10		5000			15200	18700
25	10	X-260	FB	SDNSF	L/P	SV	IO	T120-T165		10		5000			17200	20300
25	10	X-260	FB	SF	L/P	SV	IO	120-235		10		5000			15300	18700
25	10	X-260	FB	SF	L/P	SV	IO	T120-T165		10		5000			17200	20400
1975 BOATS																
21	10	V-220	OP	RNBT	L/P	SV	IO	120-190		8		2300			6550	7600
21	10	X-220	OP	CR	L/P	SV	IO	120-190		8		2700			7450	8650
21	10	X-220	HT	CR	L/P	SV	IO	120-190		8		2700			7450	8650
21	10	X-220	HT	RNBT	L/P	SV	IO	120-190		8		2600			6950	8050
24	3	X-240	OP	CR	L/P	SV	IO	120-255		8		3700			10300	12400
24	3	X-240	HT	CR	L/P	SV	IO	120-255		8		3700			10300	12400
24	3	X-240	OP	RNBT	L/P	SV	IO	120-255		8		3500			9300	11100
24	3	X-240	HT	RNBT	L/P	SV	IO	120-255		8		3700			9650	11500
24	10	X-260	HT	RNBT	L/P	SV	IO	120-255		8		4600			11400	13800
25	10	X-260	OP	CR	L/P	SV	IO	120-255		8		5000			13300	16600
25	10	X-260	HT	CR	L/P	SV	IO	120-255		8		5000			13300	16600
25	10	X-260	FB	CR	L/P	SV	IO	120-255		8		5000			13300	16600
25	10	X-260	OP	SF	L/P	SV	IO	120-255		8		5000			15100	18900
1974 BOATS																
21	10	X-220	HT		L/P		IO	120-190		8		2600			7150	8300
21	10	X-220		CBNCR	L/P		IO	120-190		8		2700			8450	9850
21	10	X-220	HT	CBNCR	L/P		IO	120-190		8		2700			8450	9850
21	10	X-220		RNBT	L/P		IO	120-190		8		2300			6750	7850
24	3	X-240	HT		L/P		IO	120-245		8		3700			10200	12100
24	3	X-240		CBNCR	L/P		IO	120-245		8		3700			12300	14500
24	3	X-240		RNBT	L/P		IO	120-245		8		3500			9600	11300
24	10	X-260	HT		L/P		IO	120-245		8		4600			12300	14900
25	10	X-260	FB		L/P		IO	120-245		8					14300	17700
25	10	X-260		CBNCR	L/P		IO	120-245		8		5000			16500	20600
25	10	X-260		SF	L/P		IO	120-245		8		5000			15600	19300
1973 BOATS																
21	8	X-220	HT		L/P		IO	140-188		8					7900	9150
21	8	X-220		CBNCR	L/P		IO	140-165		8		2400			8150	9400
21	8	X-220	HT	CBNCR	L/P		IO	140-170		8		2400			8150	9400
21	8	X-220		RNBT	L/P		IO	120-188		8		2400			7050	8200
24		X-240	HT		L/P		IO	165-188		8					10800	12300
24		X-240		CBNCR	L/P		IO	165-225		8		3500			12000	13900
24		X-240	HT	CBNCR	L/P		IO	165-188		8					12900	14800
24		X-240		RNBT	L/P		IO	170-188		8		3500			9900	11300
26		X-260	HT		L/P		IO	188-245		10		4000			14000	16700
26		X-260		SF	L/P		IO	188-225		10		4500			16700	19500
1972 BOATS																
19		X-190	OP	RNBT	WD	SV	IO	120		7					5500	6300
21	8	X-220	HT		L/P		IO	140-188		8		2400			7300	8450
21	8	X-220		CBNCR	L/P		IO	120-188		8		2400			8400	9800
21	8	X-220	HT	CBNCR	L/P		IO	120-188		8		2400			8400	9800
21	8	X-220		RNBT	L/P		IO	120-188		8		2400			7300	8450
24		X-240	HT		L/P		IO	165-245		8		3500			10400	12100
24		X-240	HT	CBNCR	L/P		IO	165-188		8		3500			12400	14200
24		X-240		RNBT	L/P		IO	225	OMC	8		3500			10400	11800
26		X-260	HT		L/P		IO	165-245		10		4000			14200	17300
26		X-260		CBNCR	L/P		IO	188-245		10		4200			18700	21000
26		X-260		RNBT	L/P		IO	188	MRCR	10					15400	17500
26		X-260		SF	L/P		IO	188-245		10		4500			17200	20400
1971 BOATS																
19		X-190			L/P		IO	120-170		7	8	1800			5100	5900
21	2	X-210			L/P		IO	120-170		8		2010			6800	7900
21	2	X-210		CBNCR	L/P		IO	120-170		8		2200			8050	9350

CONTINUED ON NEXT PAGE

SKIFF CRAFT   -CONTINUED   See inside cover to adjust price for area

LOA FT IN	NAME AND/ OR MODEL	TOP/ RIG	BOAT TYPE	HULL MTL TP	TP	# HP	MFG	BEAM FT IN	WGT LBS	DRAFT FT IN	RETAIL LOW	RETAIL HIGH
1971 BOATS												
24	X-240			L/P	IO	120-235		8			11500	13300
24	X-240	HT		L/P	IO	120-235		8	3500		10700	12400
24	X-240		CBNCR	L/P	IO	120-235		8	3500		12800	14900
26	X-260			L/P	IO	120-235		10			16600	20400
26	X-260			L/P	IO	120-220		10	4000		14000	17500
26	X-260	HT		L/P	IO	235	OMC	10	4000		15500	17700
26	X-260	HT		L/P	IO			10	4000		15500	17700
26	X-260		CBNCR	L/P	IO	120-235		10	4200		17600	21400
26	X-260		SF	L/P	IO	120-235		10	4500		16900	20900
1970 BOATS												
19	X-190			WD	IO	120-155		7 8	1800		5250	6050
21 2	X-210			WD	IO	120-170		8	2010		7050	8150
21 2	X-210		CBNCR	WD	IO	120-170		8	2200		8350	8650
24	X-240			WD	IO	120-220		8	3300		10600	12300
24	X-240	HT		WD	IO	120-220		8	3500		11100	12800
26	X-260			WD	IO	130-220		10	3800		14200	17600
26	X-260	HT		WD	IO	130-220		10	4000		14600	18100
26	X-260		CBNCR	WD	IO	130-220		10	4200		18800	22100
1969 BOATS												
18	180		RNBT	PLY	RB	OB		7 1	940		3200	3750
18	X-180		RNBT	PLY	RB	IO	120	7 1	1600		4750	5500
19	190		RNBT	PLY	RB	OB		7 8	1060		3650	4250
19	X-190		RNBT	MHG	RB	IO	120 MRCR	7 8	1710		5500	6300
21 2	210		RNBT	PLY	RB	OB		8	1340		4950	5650
21 2	210C		CR	PLY	RB	OB		8	1460		5250	6050
21 2	X-210		CBNCR	MHG	RB	IO	120-160	8	2130		8500	9800
21 2	X-210		RNBT	MHG	RB	IO	120-160	8	2010		7300	8450
24	X-240			PLY	DV	IO	130 CHRY	8			12300	14000
25 7	X-260		CBNCR	MHG	DV	IO	160-200	10	3800		18500	20800
25 7	X-260			PLY	DV	IO	160 MRCR	10	4100		15200	17200
1968 BOATS												
19	X-190	OP	RNBT	WD		IO	120 MRCR	7 8	1710		5650	6500
21 2	X-210		CBNCR	WD		IO	120-160	8	2010		8600	9950
21 2	X-210	OP	RNBT	WD		IO	120-160	8	2010		7550	8700
21 2	X-210		WKNDR	WD		IO	120-160	8	2010		7900	9150
25 7	X-260		CBNCR	WD		IO	160-200	10	3800		19100	21300
25 7	X-260			WD		IO	160-200	10	3800		15000	17700
1967 BOATS												
17	ROCKET I			PLY	CT	OB		7 9	1800		5150	5900
17	ROCKET I		CBNCR	WD	CT	IO	80	7 9		6	4550	5250
17	ROCKET I		RNBT	WD	CT	IO	80	7 9		6	5500	6350
17	ROCKET II		CBNCR	PLY	CT	OB		7 9	2200		5800	6650
18	180		RNBT	L/P		OB		7	940		3200	3750
18	X-180		RNBT	L/P		IO	120	7 1			5750	6600
19	190		CBNCR	L/P		OB		7 8	1060		3650	4250
19	SNOW-GOOSE	SLP	SA/CR	P/P	CB			7 4		1	3100	3600
19	X-190		CBNCR	L/P		IO	120	7 8			6750	7750
19	X-190		RNBT	L/P		IO	120	7 8			6800	7800
21 2	210		CBNCR	L/P		OB		8	1460		4350	5000
21 2	210		RNBT	L/P		OB		8	1340		4150	4800
21 2	X-210		CBNCR	L/P		IO	120-160	8			10800	12300
21 2	X-210		RNBT	L/P		IO	120-160	8			9400	10700
21 2	X-210		WKNDR	L/P		IO	120-160	8			9900	11300
22	ROCKET II		CBNCR	WD	CT	IO	240	11		1	14000	15900
22	ROCKET II		CBNCR	WD	CT	IO	200	11		1	11800	13400
24	SILVER-WING	SLP	SA/CR	PLY	KL			7 9		3 4	5800	6650
24	SILVER-WING	SLP	SA/CR	PLY	KL	IB		7 9		3 9	6200	7150
25 7	X-260		CBNCR	L/P		IO	160-200	10			23100	26500
25 7	X-260		RNBT	L/P		IO	160-200	10			18000	20400
31	EAGLE		SCH	SA/CR	WD	KL IB		10		4 4	20300	22500
1966 BOATS												
18	180		RNBT	WD		OB		7 1	940		3200	3750
18	X-180			WD		IO	100-120	7 8			5200	5950
19	190		CBNCR	WD		OB		7 8	1180		4000	4650
19	190		RNBT	WD		OB		7 8	1060		3650	4250
19	X-190			WD		IO	100	7 8	1180		5500	6350
19	X-190			WD		IO	110-140	7 8			6500	7500
19	X-190			WD		IO	100-140	7 8			7000	8050
21 2	210		CBNCR	WD		OB		8	1460		4350	5050
21 2	210		RNBT	WD		OB		8	1340		4200	4900
21 2	X-210		CBNCR	WD		IO	110-165	8			11100	12700
21 2	X-210		RNBT	WD		IO	100-165	8			9700	11100
21 2	X-210		WKNDR	WD		IO	100-165	8			10200	11700
25 7	X-260			WD		IO	165		9 10			19800	22000
25 7	X-260		CBNCR	WD		IO	100-225	9 10			22700	27800
25 7	X-260		RNBT	WD		IO	110-225	9 10			18100	21100
1965 BOATS												
18	180			WD		OB					3300	3800
18	X-180			WD		OB					5350	6150
19	190			WD		OB					4250	4950
19	190		CBNCR	WD		OB					3900	4500
19	X-190			WD		IO	110-140				6600	7600
19	X-190		CBNCR	WD		IO	110-140				7150	8200
21 2	210			WD		OB					4600	5250
21 2	210		CBNCR	WD		OB					5250	6050
21 2	X-210			WD		IO	110-165				10100	11500
21 2	X-210		CBNCR	WD		IO	110-165				11600	13200
1964 BOATS												
17 6	180			WD		OB					3250	3750
17 6	X-180			WD		OB	100				5300	6100
18 5	190			WD		OB					3350	3850
18 5	X-190			WD		IO	100				5700	6550
20 8	210			WD		OB					5200	6000
20 8	X-210			WD		IO	100				10100	11500
1963 BOATS												
17 6	HENRY XVIII			WD		OB					3250	3750
17 6	HENRY XVIII			WD		OB	100				5500	6300
18 5	HENRY XIX			WD		OB					3350	3850
18 5	HENRY XIX			WD		IO	100-120				5900	6750
20 6	HENRY XXI			WD		OB					5100	5850
20 6	HENRY XXI			WD		IO	100-120				10400	11800
20 6	HENRY XXI	HT		WD		IO	100				10400	11800
20 6	HENRY XXI		CBNCR	WD		IO	100				11800	13400
1962 BOATS												
17 6	HENRY XVII		RNBT			OB					4150	4800
20 6	HENRY XXI		SF			OB					6300	7250
1961 BOATS												
17 2	HENRY XVII		RNBT	L/P		OB		6 6	750		2600	3000
17 5	HENRY		RNBT	L/P		OB		6 8	750		2600	3050
20 6	HENRY XXI		RNBT	L/P		OB		8	1000		3800	4400

SKIPPER BOATS LTD

Call 1-800-327-6929 for BUC Personalized Evaluation Service
Or, for 1964 to 1986 boats, sign onto www.BUCValuPro.com

SKIPPERLINER INDUSTRIES

LACROSSE WI 54603-1533   COAST GUARD MFG ID- SGU See inside cover to adjust price for area

For more recent years, see the BUC Used Boat Price Guide, Volume 1 or Volume 2

LOA FT IN	NAME AND/ OR MODEL	TOP/ RIG	BOAT TYPE	HULL MTL TP	TP	# HP	MFG	BEAM FT IN	WGT LBS	DRAFT FT IN	RETAIL LOW	RETAIL HIGH
1983 BOATS												
35	FI 35	HT	HB	STL	IO	120		14	19000	2 10	44800	49700
39	FI 39	HT	HB	STL	IO	120		14	19500	2 10	40100	44500
40	FI 40	HT	HB	STL	IO	120		14	20500	2 10	40700	45300
42	SLV 42	HT	HB	STL	IO	120		14	22000	2 11	41900	46600
44	FI 44	HT	HB	STL	IO	120		14	21000	2 11	46900	51500
47	SLV 47	HT	HB	STL	IO	T120		14	26000	3	55700	61200
52	SLV 52	HT	HB	STL	IO	T120		14	28000	3	76900	84600
57	SLV 57	HT	HB	STL	IO	T120		14	31000	3	83900	92200
1982 BOATS												
42	SLV 42	HT	HB	STL	SV IO	120		14	26000		42100	46700
47	SLV 47	HT	HB	STL	SV IO	120		14			44500	49500
52	SLV 52	HT	HB	STL	SV IO	T120		14			70200	77200
57	SLV 57	HT	HB	STL	SV IO	T120		14			80300	88300
1981 BOATS												
42	SLV 42	HT	HB	STL	SV IO	120		14	26000		41300	45900
47	SLV 47	HT	HB	STL	SV IO	165		14			43800	48700
52	SLV 52	HT	HB	STL	SV IO	T120		14			68900	75700
57	SLV 57	HT	HB	STL	SV IO	T120		14			78800	86600
1980 BOATS												
37	SLV 37	HT	HB	STL	SV IO	120		12			31200	34700
42	SLV 42	HT	HB	STL	SV IO	120		14			31600	35200
47	SLV 47	HT	HB	STL	SV IO	120		14			43100	47900
47	SLV 47	HT	HB	STL	SV IO	165		14			43200	47900
52	SLV 52	HT	HB	STL	SV IO	200		14			65200	71600
52	SLV 52	HT	HB	STL	SV IO	T120		14			67800	74500
57	SLV 57	HT	HB	STL	SV IO	200		14			74900	82300
57	SLV 57	HT	HB	STL	SV IO	T165		14			77700	85400

```
     LOA  NAME AND/              TOP/ BOAT  -HULL- ----ENGINE--- BEAM    WGT  DRAFT RETAIL RETAIL
     FT IN OR MODEL               RIG TYPE  MTL TP TP # HP  MFG  FT IN   LBS  FT IN  LOW   HIGH
     ----------------------- 1979 BOATS -------------------------------------------------------
      37   SLP 37                 HT  HB    STL SV IO 120      12               30800  34200
      37   SLP 37                 HT  HB    STL SV IO T228     12               33600  37400
      37   SLV 37                 HT  HB    STL DV IO 120      12               32900  36600
      37   SLV 37                 HT  HB    STL DV IO T228     12               36000  40000
      42   SLF 42                 HT  HB    STL SV IO 120      14               31200  34700
      42   SLF 42                 HT  HB    STL SV IO T228     14               34000  37800
      42   SLV 42                 HT  HB    STL DV IO 120      14               33000  36700
      42   SLV 42                 HT  HB    STL DV IO 165      14               33100  36700
      42   SLV 42                 HT  HB    STL DV IO T228     14               36000  40000
      47   SLF 47                 HT  HB    STL SV IO 120      14               42500  47200
      47   SLF 47                 HT  HB    STL SV IO T260     14               47100  51700

      47   SLV 47                 HT  HB    STL DV IO 120      14               44400  49300
      47   SLV 47                 HT  HB    STL DV IO T120     14               47300  52000
      47   SLV 47                 HT  HB    STL DV IO T260     14               49200  54100
      52   SLF 52                 HT  HB    STL SV IO T120     14               66800  73400
      52   SLF 52                 HT  HB    STL SV IO T260     14               69000  75900
      52   SLV 52                 HT  HB    STL DV IO T120     14               69800  76800
      52   SLV 52                 HT  HB    STL DV IO T200     14               70400  77400
      52   SLV 52                 HT  HB    STL DV IO T260     14               72100  79300
      57   SLF 57                 HT  HB    STL SV IO T228     14               77500  85200
      57   SLF 57                 HT  HB    STL SV IO T260     14               78600  86400
      57   SLV 57                 HT  HB    STL DV IO T200     14               80400  88400
      57   SLV 57                 HT  HB    STL DV IO T228     14               81000  89000

      57   SLV 57                 HT  HB    STL DV IO T260     14               82200  90300
     ----------------------- 1978 BOATS -------------------------------------------------------
      32   SLF 32                 HT  HB    STL SV OB          12                9150  10400
      32   SLF 32                 HT  HB    STL SV IO 120-228  12               26100  30200
      32   SLF 32                 HT  HB    STL SV IO T120-T225 12              28500  33900
      32   SLF 32                 FB  HB    STL SV OB          12                9250  10500
      32   SLF 32                 FB  HB    STL SV IO 120-228  12               26300  30400
      32   SLF 32                 FB  HB    STL SV IO T120-T225 12              28700  34000
      32   SLV 32                 HT  HB    STL DV OB          12               10700  12100
      32   SLV 32                 HT  HB    STL DV IO 120-228  12               30300  34700
      32   SLV 32                 HT  HB    STL DV IO T120-T225 12              32600  38500
      32   SLV 32                 FB  HB    STL DV OB          12               10600  12000
      32   SLV 32                 FB  HB    STL DV IO 120-228  12               30100  34500
      32   SLV 32                 FB  HB    STL DV IO T120-T225 12              32500  38300

      40   SLF 40                 HT  HB    STL SV OB          12               17000  19300
             IO  120  MRCR 27500 30600, IO 130  VLVO 27900 31100, IO 165  MRCR 27600 30700
             IO  200  VLVO 28200 31400, IO 225  VLVO 28400 31600, IO 228  MRCR 28000 31100
             IO  T120 MRCR 29600 32900, IO T130 VLVO 30500 33900, IO T165 MRCR 29800 33100
             IO  T200 VLVO 31000 34400, IO T225 VLVO 31400 34900, IO T228 MRCR 30600 34000
      40   SLF 40                 FB  HB    STL SV OB          12               18100  20200
             IO  120  MRCR 27700 30700, IO 130  VLVO 28100 31200, IO 165  MRCR 27800 30800
             IO  200  VLVO 28300 31400, IO 225  VLVO 28600 31700, IO 228  MRCR 28100 31300
             IO  T120 MRCR 29800 33100, IO T130 VLVO 30600 34000, IO T165 MRCR 29900 33200
             IO  T200 VLVO 31100 34600, IO T225 VLVO 31500 35000, IO T228 MRCR 30700 34100
      40   SLV 40                 HT  HB    STL DV OB          12               20200  22400
             IO  120  MRCR 31600 35200, IO 130  VLVO 32100 35700, IO 165  MRCR 31700 35200
             IO  200  VLVO 32300 35900, IO 225  VLVO 32500 36100, IO 228  MRCR 31900 35500
             IO  T120 MRCR 33700 37500, IO T130 VLVO 34700 38600, IO T165 MRCR 33800 37600
             IO  T200 VLVO 35100 39000, IO T225 VLVO 35500 39500, IO T228 MRCR 34400 38200
      40   SLV 40                 FB  HB    STL DV OB          12               19300  21500
             IO  120  MRCR 31500 35000, IO 130  VLVO 32000 35500, IO 165  MRCR 31500 35000
             IO  200  VLVO 32200 35800, IO 225  VLVO 32400 36000, IO 228  MRCR 31800 35400
             IO  T120 MRCR 33600 37300, IO T130 VLVO 34600 38400, IO T165 MRCR 33700 37400
             IO  T200 VLVO 35000 38900, IO T225 VLVO 35400 39400, IO T228 MRCR 34300 38100
      45   SLF 45                 HT  HB    STL SV IO 120  MRCR 14             33300  37000
             IO  130  VLVO 33800 37500, IO 165  MRCR 33400 37100, IO 200  VLVO 32000 35500
             IO  225  VLVO 33200 35800, IO 228  MRCR 31800 35300, IO 255  VLVO 32800 36500
             IO  T120 MRCR 33600 37300, IO T130 VLVO 34500 38300, IO T165 MRCR 33800 37600
             IO  T200 VLVO 35100 39000, IO T225 VLVO 35100 39000, IO T228 MRCR 34800 38700
             IO  T255 VLVO 36600 40700
      45   SLF 45                 FB  HB    STL SV IO 120  MRCR 14             33400  37100
             IO  130  VLVO 33900 37700, IO 165  MRCR 33500 37200, IO 200  VLVO 32300 35800
             IO  225  VLVO 32500 36100, IO 228  MRCR 32100 35700, IO 255  VLVO 32900 36800
             IO  T120 MRCR 33900 37600, IO T130 VLVO 34700 38600, IO T165 MRCR 34100 37900
             IO  T200 VLVO 35400 39300, IO T225 VLVO 35400 39300, IO T228 MRCR 35000 38900
             IO  T255 VLVO 36900 41000
      45   SLV 45                 HT  HB    STL DV IO 120  MRCR 14             37200  41300
             IO  130  VLVO 37700 41900, IO 165  MRCR 37200 41300, IO 200  VLVO 35600 39600
             IO  225  VLVO 35900 39900, IO 228  MRCR 35400 39300, IO 255  VLVO 36400 40500
             IO  T120 MRCR 37200 41400, IO T130 VLVO 38200 42500, IO T165 MRCR 37500 41600
             IO  T200 VLVO 38800 43100, IO T225 VLVO 39600 44000, IO T228 MRCR 38300 42600
             IO  T255 VLVO 40300 44800
      45   SLV 45                 FB  HB    STL DV IO 120  MRCR 14             37100  41200
             IO  130  VLVO 37600 41800, IO 165  MRCR 37100 41200, IO 200  VLVO 35700 39700
             IO  225  VLVO 36000 40000, IO 228  MRCR 35500 39400, IO 255  VLVO 36500 40500
             IO  T120 MRCR 37400 41500, IO T130 VLVO 38400 42600, IO T165 MRCR 37500 41700
             IO  T200 VLVO 38900 43300, IO T225 VLVO 39700 44100, IO T228 MRCR 38400 42700
             IO  T255 VLVO 40500 44900
      45   SLV 45CC               HT  HB    STL DV IO 200  VLVO 14             41300  45900
             IO  225  VLVO 41500 46200, IO 228  MRCR 40700 45300, IO 255  VLVO 41800 46500
             IO  T120 MRCR 42400 47600, IO T130 VLVO 44000 48900, IO T165 MRCR 42800 47500
             IO  T200 VLVO 44300 49200, IO T225 VLVO 45500 50000, IO T228 MRCR 43200 48000
             IO  T255 VLVO 46100 50600
      45   SLV 45CC               FB  HB    STL DV IO 200  VLVO 14             40900  45400
             IO  225  VLVO 41100 45700, IO 228  MRCR 40300 44800, IO 255  VLVO 41500 46100
             IO  T120 MRCR 42400 47200, IO T130 VLVO 43600 48500, IO T165 MRCR 42400 47200
             IO  T200 VLVO 43900 48400, IO T225 VLVO 44600 49600, IO T228 MRCR 42900 47700
             IO  T255 VLVO 45700 50200
      52   SLF 52                 HT  HB    STL SV IO 200  VLVO 14             59100  65000
             IO  225  VLVO 59400 65300, IO 228  MRCR 59000 64800, IO 255  VLVO 59100 65000
             IO  T120 MRCR 62000 67200, IO T130 VLVO 62300 68500, IO T165 MRCR 61500 67600
             IO  T200 VLVO 63100 69300, IO T225 VLVO 63700 70000, IO T228 MRCR 62800 69000
             IO  T255 VLVO 65100 71500
      52   SLF 52                 FB  HB    STL SV IO 200  VLVO 14             59500  65400
             IO  225  VLVO 59800 65700, IO 228  MRCR 59400 65200, IO 255  VLVO 60600 66600
             IO  T120 MRCR 61500 67600, IO T130 VLVO 62300 68000, IO T165 MRCR 61900 68000
             IO  T200 VLVO 63400 69700, IO T225 VLVO 64100 70400, IO T228 MRCR 63100 69300
             IO  T255 VLVO 65400 71900
      52   SLV 52                 HT  HB    STL DV IO 200  VLVO 14             65200  71600
             IO  225  VLVO 65500 72000, IO 228  MRCR 64900 71500, IO 255  VLVO 66300 72700
             IO  T120 MRCR 67200 73900, IO T130 VLVO 68500 75300, IO T165 MRCR 67500 74200
             IO  T200 VLVO 69200 76000, IO T225 VLVO 69800 76700, IO T228 MRCR 68600 75300
             IO  T255 VLVO 71200 78200
      52   SLV 52                 FB  HB    STL DV IO 200  VLVO 14             65200  71800
             IO  225  VLVO 65600 72100, IO 228  MRCR 65000 71500, IO 255  VLVO 66300 72900
             IO  T120 MRCR 67300 74000, IO T130 VLVO 68600 75400, IO T165 MRCR 67600 74200
             IO  T200 VLVO 69300 76100, IO T225 VLVO 69900 76900, IO T228 MRCR 68600 75400
             IO  T255 VLVO 71300 78300
      52   SLV 52CC               HT  HB    STL DV IO 200  VLVO 14             73700  81000
             IO  225  VLVO 74000 81300, IO 228  MRCR 73000 80300, IO 255  VLVO 74300 81600
             IO  T120 MRCR 75600 83000, IO T130 VLVO 77000 84600, IO T165 MRCR 75500 83000
             IO  T200 VLVO 77300 84900, IO T225 VLVO 77900 85600, IO T228 MRCR 76000 83500
             IO  T255 VLVO 78600 86400
      52   SLV 52CC               FB  HB    STL DV IO 200  VLVO 14             73200  80500
             IO  225  VLVO 73400 80700, IO 228  MRCR 72500 79700, IO 255  VLVO 73800 81100
             IO  T120 MRCR 75000 82400, IO T130 VLVO 76400 84000, IO T165 MRCR 75000 82400
             IO  T200 VLVO 76800 84400, IO T225 VLVO 77400 85000, IO T228 MRCR 75600 83000
             IO  T255 VLVO 78300 86000
      60   SLF 60                 HT  HB    STL SV IO 200  VLVO 14             66600  73200
             IO  225  VLVO 66900 73500, IO 228  MRCR 66400 73000, IO 255  VLVO 67400 74100
             IO  T200 VLVO 70200 77100, IO T225 VLVO 70700 77700, IO T228 MRCR 69700 76600
             IO  T255 VLVO 71900 79000
      60   SLF 60                 FB  HB    STL SV IO 200  VLVO 14             66800  73400
             IO  225  VLVO 67200 73800, IO 228  MRCR 66600 73200, IO 255  VLVO 67700 74400
             IO  T200 VLVO 69500 76400, IO T225 VLVO 69900 76800, IO T228 MRCR 67700 74400
             IO  T255 VLVO 72100 79200
      60   SLV 60                 HT  HB    STL DV IO 200  VLVO 14             72800  80000
             IO  225  VLVO 73000 80300, IO 228  MRCR 72400 79600, IO 255  VLVO 73700 81000
             IO  T200 VLVO 76500 84000, IO T225 VLVO 77100 84700, IO T228 MRCR 75800 83300
             IO  T255 VLVO 78300 86000
      60   SLV 60                 FB  HB    STL DV IO 200  VLVO 14             72800  80000
```

```
                          LOA   NAME AND/              TOP/ BOAT  -HULL-  ----ENGINE---  BEAM     WGT   DRAFT  RETAIL  RETAIL
                          FT IN OR MODEL               RIG  TYPE  MTL TP TP # HP  MFG    FT IN    LBS   FT IN  LOW     HIGH
----------------- 1978 BOATS -------------------------------------------------------------------------
 60      SLV 60                       FB  HB   STL DV IO 225  VLVO 14               73100   80300
         IO  228  MRCR  72500  79600, IO  255  VLVO 73700 81000, IO T200  VLVO 77000 84600
         IO T225  VLVO  77700  85400, IO T228  MRCR 77000 84600, IO T255  VLVO 78300 86100

 60      SLV 60CC                     HT  HB   STL DV IO 200  VLVO 14               79800   87700
         IO  225  VLVO  80100  88100, IO  228  MRCR 79300 87100, IO  255  VLVO 80500 88500
         IO T200  VLVO  83400  91600, IO T225  VLVO 84000 92300, IO T228  MRCR 82300 90400
         IO T255  VLVO  85000  93400

 60      SLV 60CC                     FB  HB   STL DV IO 200  VLVO 14               79500   87400
         IO  225  VLVO  79800  87700, IO  228  MRCR 78900 86700, IO  255  VLVO 80200 88100
         IO T200  VLVO  83500  91800, IO T225  VLVO 84200 92600, IO T228  MRCR 83200 91400
         IO T255  VLVO  84700  93100
----------------- 1977 BOATS -------------------------------------------------------------------------
 32      SLF 32                       HT  HB   STL FL IO          12                27700   30700
 32      SLV 32                       HT  HB   STL SV IO          12                28300   31500
 40      SLF 40                       HT  HB   STL FL IO          12                28700   31900
 40      SLV 40                       HT  HB   STL SV IO          12                30000   33300
 45      SLF 45                       HT  HB   STL FL IO          14                35500   39400
 45      SLV 45                       HT  HB   STL SV IO          14                34600   38400
 52      SLF 52                       HT  HB   STL FL IO          14                64000   70300
 52      SLV 52                       HT  HB   STL SV IO          14                64100   70400
 60      SLF/SLV 60                   HT  HB   STL    IO          14                72500   79700
----------------- 1976 BOATS -------------------------------------------------------------------------
 31      LITTLE-SKIPPER               HT  HB   STL FL OB          12                10400   11900
 31      LITTLE-SKIPPER               HT  HB   STL FL IO          12                28200   31300
 41      SL 41                        HT  HB   STL FL OB          12                18200   20300
 41      SL 41                        HT  HB   STL FL IO          12                33300   37000
 45      SL 45                        HT  HB   STL FL OB          14                30300   33600
 45      SL 45                        HT  HB   STL FL IO          14                35400   39400
 52      SL 52                        HT  HB   STL FL OB          14                53100   58300
 52      SL 52                        HT  HB   STL FL IO T        14                68100   74800
 60      SL 60                        HT  HB   STL FL IO          15   6            71700   78800
```

SKJOL MARINE

Call 1-800-327-6929 for BUC Personalized Evaluation Service
Or, for 1967 boats, sign onto www.BUCValuPro.com

SKOOKUM DORIES
COAST GUARD MFG ID- SKU

Call 1-800-327-6929 for BUC Personalized Evaluation Service
Or, for 1979 to 1982 boats, sign onto www.BUCValuPro.com

SKOOKUM MARINE CONSTRUCTION
PORT TOWNSEND WA 98368   COAST GUARD MFG ID- SKK See inside cover to adjust price for area

For more recent years, see the BUC Used Boat Price Guide, Volume 1 or Volume 2

```
                          LOA   NAME AND/              TOP/ BOAT  -HULL-  ----ENGINE---  BEAM     WGT   DRAFT  RETAIL  RETAIL
                          FT IN OR MODEL               RIG  TYPE  MTL TP TP # HP  MFG    FT IN    LBS   FT IN  LOW     HIGH
----------------- 1983 BOATS -------------------------------------------------------------------------
 28      SKOOKUM 28           SLP SA/CR FBG KL SD   15D VLVO  9      8450   4  6  29200   32400
 34    2 SKOOKUM 34           SLP SA/CR FBG KL IB   30D       10 10 18000   5      61700   67800
 47      SKOOKUM 47           SLP SA/CR FBG KL IB   60D       13  2 38000   6     115500  127000
 50      SKOOKUM 50           SLP SA/CR FBG KL IB   60D       13  6 38000   6  4 137500  151000
 53      SKOOKUM 53           KTH SA/CR FBG KL IB  120D       15  6 55000   7     189000  208000
 70      SKOOKUM 70           CUT SA/CR FBG KL IB  160D       18  2   55T   8     450500  495000
----------------- 1982 BOATS -------------------------------------------------------------------------
 28      SKOOKUM 28           SLP SA/CR FBG KL IB   15D VLVO  9      8450   4  6  27600   30600
 34    2 SKOOKUM 34           SLP SA/CR FBG KL IB   30D       10 10 18000   5      58100   63800
 47      SKOOKUM 47           SLP SA/CR FBG KL IB   60D       13  2 38000   6     108500  119500
 50      SKOOKUM 50           SLP SA/CR FBG KL IB   60D       13  6 38000   6  4 129000  142000
 53      SKOOKUM 53           KTH SA/CR FBG KL IB  120D       15  6 55000   7     178500  196000
 70      SKOOKUM 70           CUT SA/CR FBG KL IB  160D       18  2   55T   8     423500  465500
```

SKYLINE DISTRIBUTING CO

Call 1-800-327-6929 for BUC Personalized Evaluation Service
Or, for 1960 boats, sign onto www.BUCValuPro.com

SLICKCRAFT
AMF POWERBOAT
HOLLAND MI 49423   COAST GUARD MFG ID- SLK   See inside cover to adjust price for area
                           FOR LATER YEARS SEE S2 YACHTS

```
                          LOA   NAME AND/              TOP/ BOAT  -HULL-  ----ENGINE---  BEAM     WGT   DRAFT  RETAIL  RETAIL
                          FT IN OR MODEL               RIG  TYPE  MTL TP TP # HP  MFG    FT IN    LBS   FT IN  LOW     HIGH
----------------- 1981 BOATS -------------------------------------------------------------------------
 26    4 SEDAN 26            FB  SDN  FBG DV IB T170  MRCR 10  1  7140   2 11 13800  15700
 28      EXPRESS 28          FB  EXP  FBG DV IB T228-T255 10  6  8050   2  7 14600  16900
 28      EXPRESS 28          FB  EXP  FBG DV IB T124D VLVO 10  6  8050   2  7 19100  21200
----------------- 1980 BOATS -------------------------------------------------------------------------
 17    7 SL177               OP  RNBT FBG DV IO 170-200     6  5  2700      2650   3300
 17    7 SL177               OP  RNBT FBG DV IO 225-260     6  5  2700      2900   3550
 17    7 SL177               OP  RNBT FBG DV IO  290  VLVO  6  5  2700      3250   3800
 17    7 SS177               ST  RNBT FBG DV IO 140-200     6  5  2700      2650   3300
 17    7 SS177               ST  RNBT FBG DV IO 225-230     6  5  2700      2900   3400
 18      R-181               OP  OPFSH FBG SV OB  170       7    2000      4300   5000
 18      SB180               OP  RNBT FBG SV IO  170        7  3  2000      2500   2900
 18      SB180 B/R           ST  RNBT FBG DV IO 170-200     7  3  2000      2750   3400
 18      SB180 B/R           ST  RNBT FBG DV IO 225-260     7  2  2517      3000   3650
 18      SL177               OP  RNBT FBG SV IO  260        7    2700      3050   3550
 18      SS177               OP  RNBT FBG SV IO  170        7    2700      2850   3300

 19    7 SB196 B/R           ST  RNBT FBG DV IO 170-200     7  5  2750      3200   3950
 19    7 SB196 B/R           ST  RNBT FBG DV IO 225-260     7  5  2750      3450   4200
 19    7 SB196 B/R           ST  RNBT FBG DV IO  290  VLVO  7  5  2750      3800   4450
 20      R-200               OP  OPFSH FBG SV OB            8    2130      5150   5950
 20    2 SC200               ST  CUD  FBG DV IO 198-230     7  8  3320      3950   4800
 20    2 SC200               ST  CUD  FBG DV IO  260        7  8  3320      4100   5000
 20    2 SCS200              ST  CUD  FBG DV IO 198-230     7  7  3320      3900   4800
 20    2 SCS200              ST  CUD  FBG DV IO  260        7  7  3320      4100   4950
 20    2 SL200               ST  CR   FBG DV IO 225-260     7  7  3020      3900   4700
 20    2 SL200               ST  CR   FBG DV IO  290  VLVO  7  7  3020      4250   4950
 20    2 SS200               ST  RNBT FBG DV IO 170-230     7  7  2780      3300   4150
 20    2 SS200               ST  RNBT FBG DV IO  290  VLVO  7  7  2780      3550   4300

 20    2 SS200               ST  RNBT FBG DV IO  290  VLVO  7  7  2780      3900   4550
 22   10 SS235               ST  OVNTR FBG DV IO 198-260    9    3700      5050   6200
 22   10 SS235               ST  OVNTR FBG DV IO  290  VLVO 9    3700      5600   6450
 22   10 SS235               HT  OVNTR FBG DV IO 185-260    9    3700      5000   6200
 22   10 SS235               HT  OVNTR FBG DV IO  290  VLVO 9    3700      5600   6450
 23      R-232               OP  FSH  FBG SV OB             8    2560      7000   8050
 24      R-236               OP  FSH  FBG RB OB             8    2620      7400   8500
 24    2 SCF240              ST  CUD  FBG DV IO 225-290     8    4100      6000   7300
 24    2 SCF240              ST  CUD  FBG DV IO  330  MRCR  8    4100      6500   7500
 24    2 SCF240              ST  CUD  FBG DV IO T140-T170   8    4632      7050   8150
 24    2 SF240               ST  CR   FBG DV IO 225-290     8    4000      5950   7300
 24    2 SF240               ST  CR   FBG DV IO  330  MRCR  8    4000      6500   7500

 24    2 SF240               ST  CR   FBG DV IO T140-T170   8    4000      6450   7450
 24    2 SF240               HT  CR   FBG DV IO 225-290     8    4000      5950   7300
 24    2 SF240               HT  CR   FBG DV IO  330  MRCR  8    4000      6500   7500
 24    2 SF240               HT  CR   FBG DV IO T140-T170   8    4000      6450   7450
 24    2 SL240               ST  CR   FBG DV IO 260-290     8    4632      6600   8100
         IO  330  MRCR  7200  8300, IO T260      8500 10200, IO T290  VLVO 9400 10700

 24    2 SS240               ST  CUD  FBG DV IO 225-290     8    4000      5850   7200
 24    2 SS240               ST  CUD  FBG DV IO  330  MRCR  8    4000      6400   7350
 24    2 SS240               ST  CUD  FBG DV IO T140-T170   8    4000      6350   7300
 24    2 SS240               HT  CUD  FBG DV IO 225-290     8    4000      5850   7200
 24    2 SS240               HT  CUD  FBG DV IO  330  MRCR  8    4000      6400   7350
 24    2 SS240               HT  CUD  FBG DV IO T140-T170   8    4000      6350   7350
 25      R-256               OP  OPFSH FBG SV OB            8    3220      9400  10700
 25    4 CONVERTIBLE 25      OP  CR   FBG DV IO 260-330     9  8  6000      8800  10700
 25    4 CONVERTIBLE 25      OP  CR   FBG DV IO T140-T170   9  8  6000      9300  10800
 25    4 CONVERTIBLE 25      HT  CR   FBG DV IO 260-330     9  8  6000      8800  10700
 25    4 CONVERTIBLE 25      HT  CR   FBG DV IO T140-T170   9  8  6000      9300  10800

 25    4 CONVERTIBLE 25      FB  CR   FBG DV IO T140-T170   9  8  6000      8800  10200
 25    4 CONVERTIBLE 25      FB  CR   FBG DV IO 260-330     9  8  6000      9300  10800
 25    4 SEDAN 25            HT  SDN  FBG DV IO 260-330     9  8  5660      8700  10900
 25    4 SEDAN 25            HT  SDN  FBG DV IO T140-T170   9  8  5660      9200  11200
 25    4 SEDAN 25            FB  SDN  FBG DV IO 260-330     9  8  6000      9600  11200
 25    4 SEDAN 25            FB  SDN  FBG DV IO T140-T170   9  8  6000      9600  11200
 26    4 SEDAN 26            FB  SDN  FBG DV IB  255-330   10  1  7140     11100  12700
 26    4 SEDAN 26            FB  SDN  FBG DV IB T170-T255  10  1  7140     12200  14500
 26    4 SEDAN 26            FB  SDN  FBG DV IB T170-T255  10  1  7140     13200  15800
 28      EXPRESS 28          FB  EXP  FBG DV IB T228-T255  10  6  8050     13900  16100
```

LOA FT	LOA IN	NAME AND/ OR MODEL	TOP/ RIG	BOAT TYPE	-HULL- MTL	-HULL- TP	ENGINE TP	ENGINE # HP	ENGINE MFG	BEAM FT	BEAM IN	WGT LBS	DRAFT FT	DRAFT IN	RETAIL LOW	RETAIL HIGH
		1980 BOATS														
28		EXPRESS 28	FB	EXP	FBG	DV	IB	T124D	VLVO	10	6	8050			18300	20400
28		LIMITED 28	FB	SDN	FBG	DV	IB	T228-T255		10	6	8050			15400	17700
28		LIMITED 28	FB	SDN	FBG	DV	IB	T125D	VLVO	10	6	8050			20600	22900
		1979 BOATS														
17	6	SX176	OP	SKI	FBG	DV	IO	170-200		7		2700			2650	3300
17	6	SX176	OP	SKI	FBG	DV	IO	225-260		7		2700			2900	3500
17	6	SX176	OP	SKI	FBG	DV	IO	290	VLVO	7		2700			3250	3750
18	1	ROBALO 181	OP	OPFSH	FBG	SV	OB			7	3	2000			4250	4950
19	5	ROBALO 200	OP	OPFSH	FBG	SV	OB			8		2130			4700	5400
19	6	SB196 B/R	ST	RNBT	FBG	DV	IO	170-200		7	6	2750			3200	3900
19	6	SB196 B/R	ST	RNBT	FBG	DV	IO	225-260		7	6	2750			3450	4200
19	6	SB196 B/R	ST	RNBT	FBG	DV	IO	290	VLVO	7	6	2750			3800	4400
20	2	SC200	ST	CUD	FBG	DV	IO	185-230		7	8	3320			3850	4800
20	2	SC200	ST	CUD	FBG	DV	IO	260		7	8	3320			4100	4950
20	2	SC200	ST	CUD	FBG	DV	IO	290	VLVO	7	8	3320			4550	5250
20	2	SL200	ST	CR	FBG	DV	IO	225-260		7	8	3320			4150	5000
20	2	SL200	ST	CR	FBG	DV	IO	290	VLVO	7	8	3320			4550	5250
20	2	SS200	ST	RNBT	FBG	DV	IO	170-230		7	8	2780			3300	4150
20	2	SS200	ST	RNBT	FBG	DV	IO	260		7	8	2780			3550	4300
20	2	SS200	ST	RNBT	FBG	DV	IO	290	VLVO	7	8	2780			3900	4550
21	5	ROBALO 210	OP	FSH	FBG	SV	OB			8					4900	5650
21	5	ROBALO 210	OP	FSH	FBG	SV	IO		MRCR	8		3050			**	**
21	5	ROBALO 210	OP	FSH	FBG	SV	IO		OMC	8		3050			**	**
21	5	ROBALO 210	OP	FSH	FBG	SV	IO		VLVO	8		3050			**	**
22	10	SS235	ST	OVNTR	FBG	DV	IO	185-230		8		3160			4450	5450
22	10	SS235	ST	OVNTR	FBG	DV	IO	260-290		8		3160			4700	5850
22	10	SS235	HT	OVNTR	FBG	DV	IO	185-230		8		3160			4450	5450
22	10	SS235	HT	OVNTR	FBG	DV	IO	260-290		8		3160			4700	5850
23		ROBALO 232	ST	FSH	FBG	SV	OB			8					6800	7800
23		ROBALO 236	ST	FSH	FBG	SV	OB			8		2620			7050	8100
23		ROBALO 236	ST	FSH	FBG	SV	IO	170-260		8		3620			5350	6650
23	1	ROBALO 230	OP	OPFSH	FBG	SV	OB			8		2560			6950	8000
24	2	SC240	ST	OVNTR	FBG	DV	IO	225-330		8		4632			6550	8200
24	2	SC240	ST	OVNTR	FBG	DV	IO	T140-T170		8		4632			7100	8200
24	2	SF240	ST	CR	FBG	DV	IO	225-290		8					5950	7300
24	2	SF240	ST	CR	FBG	DV	IO	330	MRCR	8					6500	7500
24	2	SF240	ST	CR	FBG	DV	IO	T140-T170		8					6450	7500
24	2	SF240	HT	CR	FBG	DV	IO	225-290		8					5950	7300
24	2	SF240	HT	CR	FBG	DV	IO	330	MRCR	8					6500	7500
24	2	SF240	HT	CR	FBG	DV	IO	T140-T170		8					6450	7500
24	2	SL240	ST	CR	FBG	DV	IO	260-290		8		4632			6600	8050
		IO 330 MRCR 7200 8250, IO T260 7650 9250, IO T290 VLVO													8500	9750
24	2	SS240	ST	CUD	FBG	DV	IO	225-290		8		3800			5650	6900
24	2	SS240	ST	CUD	FBG	DV	IO	330	MRCR	8		3800			6200	7100
24	2	SS240	ST	CUD	FBG	DV	IO	T140-T170		8		3800			6100	7050
24	2	SS240	HT	CUD	FBG	DV	IO	225-290		8		3800			5650	6900
24	2	SS240	HT	CUD	FBG	DV	IO	330	MRCR	8		3800			6200	7100
24	2	SS240	HT	CUD	FBG	DV	IO	T140-T170		8		3800			6100	7050
25	4	CONVERTIBLE 25	OP	CR	FBG	DV	IO	260		9	8	6000			8650	10100
25	4	CONVERTIBLE 25	OP	CR	FBG	DV	IO	T140-T170		9	8	6000			9250	10700
25	4	CONVERTIBLE 25	HT	CR	FBG	DV	IO	260		9	8	6000			8650	10100
25	4	CONVERTIBLE 25	HT	CR	FBG	DV	IO	T140-T170		9	8	6000			9250	10700
25	4	CONVERTIBLE 25	FB	CR	FBG	DV	IO	260		9	8	6000			8650	10100
25	4	CONVERTIBLE 25	FB	CR	FBG	DV	IO	T140-T170		9	8	6000			9250	10700
25	4	SEDAN 25	HT	SDN	FBG	DV	IO	260		9	8	6000			9100	10500
25	4	SEDAN 25	HT	SDN	FBG	DV	IO	T140-T170		9	8	6000			9550	11100
25	4	SEDAN 25	FB	SDN	FBG	DV	IO	260		9	8	6000			9100	10500
25	4	SEDAN 25	FB	SDN	FBG	DV	IO	T140-T170		9	8	6000			9550	11100
25	6	ROBALO 256	OP	OPFSH	FBG	SV	OB			8		3220			9850	11200
26	4	SEDAN 26	FB	SDN	FBG	DV	IB	255-330		10	1	6000			10600	12700
28		EXPRESS 28	FB	EXP	FBG	DV	IB	T228	MRCR	10	6	8050			13300	15100
28		EXPRESS 28	FB	EXP	FBG	DV	IB	T125D	VLVO	10	6	8050			17300	19600
28		LIMITED 28	FB	SDN	FBG	DV	IB	T228	MRCR	10	6	8050			14700	16700
28		LIMITED 28	FB	SDN	FBG	DV	IB	T125D	VLVO	10	6	8050			19800	22100
		1978 BOATS														
17	6	ROBALO 180	OP	OPFSH	FBG	TR	OB			7	4	1290		9	3100	3600
17	6	SS-176	ST	RNBT	FBG	DV	IO	165-235		7		2160			2450	2950
17	6	SS-176	ST	RNBT	FBG	DV	IO	260	MRCR	7		2160			2650	3100
17	6	SX-176	OP	SKI	FBG	DV	IO	165-235		7		2700			2650	3200
17	6	SX-176	OP	SKI	FBG	DV	IO	260	MRCR	7		2700			2850	3350
19	1	ROBALO 190	OP	OPFSH	FBG	SV	OB			8		2100		9	4500	5200
19	5	ROBALO 200	OP	OPFSH	FBG	SV	OB			8		2130		9	4650	5350
19	6	SB-196	ST	RNBT	FBG	DV	IO	165-260		7	7	2750			3200	4000
20	2	SC-200	ST	CUD	FBG	DV	IO	175-260		7	8	3320			3850	4800
20	2	SS-200	ST	RNBT	FBG	DV	IO	165-260		7	8	2780			3350	4150
21	5	ROBALO 210	ST	FSH	FBG	SV	OB			8					4850	5600
21	5	ROBALO 210	ST	FSH	FBG	SV	IO	165-260		8		3050	1	1	4350	5300
22	10	SS-235	ST	OVNTR	FBG	DV	IO	190-260		8		3160			4500	5400
22	10	SS-235	ST	OVNTR	FBG	DV	IO	T140-T170		8		3160			5100	5900
22	10	SS-235	HT	OVNTR	FBG	DV	IO	190-260		8		3160			4500	5400
22	10	SS-235	HT	OVNTR	FBG	DV	IO	T140-T170		8		3160			5100	5900
23	1	ROBALO 230	OP	OPFSH	FBG	SV	OB			8		2560		9	6900	7900
23	7	ROBALO 236	ST	FSH	FBG	SV	OB			8		2620	2		7150	8200
23	7	ROBALO 236	ST	FSH	FBG	SV	IO	165-260		8		3620	2		5550	6700
23	7	ROBALO 236	ST	FSH	FBG	SV	IO	T140-T170		8		3620	2		6350	7350
24		SC-240	ST	OVNTR	FBG	DV	IO	190-260		8		3500			5100	6100
24		SC-240	ST	OVNTR	FBG	DV	IO	T140-T170		8		3500			5800	6700
24	2	SS-240	ST	CUD	FBG	DV	IO			8			1	8	**	**
25	4	CONVERTIBLE 25	OP	CR	FBG	DV	IO	235-260		9	8	5000	2	6	7500	8800
25	4	CONVERTIBLE 25	OP	CR	FBG	DV	IO	T140-T170		9	8	5000	2	6	8100	9550
25	4	CONVERTIBLE 25	HT	CR	FBG	DV	IO	235-260		9	8	5000	2	6	7500	8800
25	4	CONVERTIBLE 25	HT	CR	FBG	DV	IO	T140-T170		9	8	5000	2	6	8100	9550
25	4	CONVERTIBLE 25	FB	CR	FBG	DV	IO	235-260		9	8	5000	2	6	7500	8800
25	4	CONVERTIBLE 25	FB	CR	FBG	DV	IO	T140-T170		9	8	5000	2	6	8100	9550
25	4	SEDAN 25	HT	SDN	FBG	DV	IO	235-260		9	8	6000	2	6	8950	10400
25	4	SEDAN 25	HT	SDN	FBG	DV	IO	T140-T170		9	8	6000	2	6	9550	11100
25	4	SEDAN 25	FB	SDN	FBG	DV	IO	235-260		9	8	6000	2	6	8950	10400
25	4	SEDAN 25	FB	SDN	FBG	DV	IO	T140-T170		9	8	6000	2	6	9550	11100
25	6	ROBALO 256		OPFSH	FBG	DV	OB			8					9750	11100
28		EXPRESS 28	OP	EXP	FBG	DV	IB	T228	MRCR	10	6	8050	2	7	12700	14500
28		EXPRESS 28	HT	EXP	FBG	DV	IB	T228	MRCR	10	6	8050	2	7	12700	14500
28		EXPRESS 28	FB	EXP	FBG	DV	IB	T228	MRCR	10	6	8050	2	7	12700	14500
		1977 BOATS														
17	6	ROBALO 180	OP	OPFSH	FBG	TR	OB			7	4	1290		9	3050	3550
17	6	SS-176	ST	RNBT	FBG	DV	IO	165-235		7		2160			2450	3000
17	6	SX-176	OP	SKI	FBG	DV	IO	165-235		7		2160			2350	2850
19	1	ROBALO 190	OP	OPFSH	FBG	SV	OB			8		2100		9	4500	5150
19	5	ROBALO 200	OP	OPFSH	FBG	SV	OB			8		2160		9	4650	5350
19	6	SS-204	ST	RNBT	FBG	DV	IO	165-235		7	7	2700			3250	3900
19	6	SS-205 B/R	ST	RNBT	FBG	DV	IO	165-235		7	7	2750			3250	3900
19	6	SS-206	ST	CUD	FBG	DV	IO	165-235		7	7	2920			3500	4200
20	3	SS-215	ST	OVNTR	FBG	DV	IO	165-235		7	10	2900			3650	4400
20	3	SS-215	HT	OVNTR	FBG	DV	IO	165-235		7	10	2900			3650	4400
22	10	SS-235	ST	OVNTR	FBG	DV	IO	188-235		8		3160			4600	5350
22	10	SS-235	ST	OVNTR	FBG	DV	IO	T140-T165		8		3160			5150	5950
22	10	SS-235	HT	OVNTR	FBG	DV	IO	188-235		8		3160			4600	5350
22	10	SS-235	HT	OVNTR	FBG	DV	IO	T140-T165		8		3160			5150	5950
23		ROBALO 236	ST	CUD	FBG	SV	OB			8		2620		9	6950	7950
23		ROBALO 236	ST	CUD	FBG	SV	IO	188-235		8		3620	1	3	5050	5900
23		ROBALO 236	ST	CUD	FBG	SV	IO	T140		8		3620	1	3	5650	6500
23		ROBALO 236	TT	CUD	FBG	SV	OB			8		2620		9	6950	7950
23		ROBALO 236	TT	CUD	FBG	SV	IO	188-235		8		3620		9	5050	5900
23		ROBALO 236	TT	CUD	FBG	SV	IO	T140		8		3620		9	5650	6500
23		SS-236	ST	FSH	FBG	SV	OB			8		2620	1	3	6950	7950
23		SS-236	ST	FSH	FBG	SV	IO	188-235		8		3620	1	3	5450	6400
23		SS-236	ST	FSH	FBG	SV	IO	T140		8		3620	1	3	6150	7050
23		SS-236	TT	FSH	FBG	SV	OB			8		2620	1	3	6950	7950
23		SS-236	TT	FSH	FBG	SV	IO	188-235		8		3620	1	3	5450	6400
23		SS-236	TT	FSH	FBG	SV	IO	T140		8		3620	1	3	6150	7050
23	1	ROBALO 230	OP	OPFSH	FBG	SV	OB			8		2560		9	6800	7850
24		SS-245	ST	CR	FBG	DV	IO	233-255		8		3620	1	6	5450	6350
24		SS-245	ST	CR	FBG	DV	IO	T140-T175		8		3620	1	6	6050	6950
24		SS-245	HT	CR	FBG	DV	IO	233-255		8		3620	1	6	5450	6350
24		SS-245	HT	CR	FBG	DV	IO	T140-T175		8		3620	1	6	6050	6950
24		SS-245 SEDAN	HT	SDN	FBG	DV	IO	233-255		8		4370	1	6	6150	7200
24		SS-245 SEDAN	HT	SDN	FBG	DV	IO	T140-T175		8		4370	1	6	6750	7800
25	4	COMMAND 25	OP	CR	FBG	DV	IO	255	MRCR	9	8	5000	2	6	7700	8850
25	4	COMMAND 25	OP	CR	FBG	DV	IO	T165		9	8	5000	2	6	8350	9600
25	4	CONVERTIBLE 25	OP	CNV	FBG	DV	IO	255	MRCR	9	8	5000	2	6	9250	10500
25	4	CONVERTIBLE 25	OP	CNV	FBG	DV	IO	T165		9	8	5000	2	6	10000	11400
25	4	CONVERTIBLE 25	HT	CNV	FBG	DV	IO	255	MRCR	9	8	5000	2	6	9200	10500
25	4	CONVERTIBLE 25	HT	CNV	FBG	DV	IO	T165		9	8	5000	2	6	9900	11300
25	4	CONVERTIBLE 25	FB	CNV	FBG	DV	IO	255	MRCR	9	8	5000	2	6	10100	11500
25	4	CONVERTIBLE 25	FB	CNV	FBG	DV	IO	T165		9	8	5000	2	6	11100	12600
25	4	SEDAN 25	HT	SDN	FBG	DV	IO	255	MRCR	9	8	6000	2	6	9200	10400

 CONTINUED ON NEXT PAGE

LOA FT	LOA IN	NAME AND/ OR MODEL	TOP/ RIG	BOAT TYPE	-HULL- MTL	-HULL- TP	ENGINE TP	ENGINE # HP	ENGINE MFG	BEAM FT	BEAM IN	WGT LBS	DRAFT FT	DRAFT IN	RETAIL LOW	RETAIL HIGH
		1977 BOATS														
25	4	SEDAN 25	HT	SDN	FBG	DV	IO	T165		9	8	6000	2	6	9850	11200
25	4	SEDAN 25	FB	SDN	FBG	DV	IO	255	MRCR	9	8	6000	2	6	9200	10400
25	4	SEDAN 25	FB	SDN	FBG	DV	IO	T165		9	8	6000	2	6	9850	11200
28		EXPRESS 28	OP	EXP	FBG	DV	IB	T233	MRCR	10	6	8050	2	7	12300	13900
28		EXPRESS 28	HT	EXP	FBG	DV	IO	T233	MRCR	10	6	8050	2	7	12300	14000
28		EXPRESS 28	FB	EXP	FBG	DV	IO	T233	MRCR	10	6	8050	2	7	12300	14000
		1976 BOATS														
17	3	ROBALO 180	OP	FSH	FBG	TR	OB			7	2	1300		9	3050	3500
17	3	ST-190	OP	UTL	FBG	TR	OB			7	2	1230			2800	3250
17	6	SS-190	OP	RNBT	FBG	DV	OB			7		1550			3500	4050
17	6	SS-194	OP	UTL	FBG	DV	IO	165-235		7		2160			2750	3350
17	6	SS-195	OP	RNBT	FBG	DV	IO	165-235		7		2160			2500	3050
19		ROBALO 190	OP	FSH	FBG	DV	OB			8		1700		9	3850	4500
19	6	ROBALO 200	OP	FSH	FBG	DV	OB			8		1800		9	4150	4800
19	6	SS-204	OP	RNBT	FBG	DV	IO	165-235		7	7	2700			3300	3950
19	6	SS-205	OP	RNBT	FBG	DV	IO	165-235		7	7	2750			3350	4000
19	6	SS-206	OP	RNBT	FBG	DV	IO	165-235		7	7	2920			3450	4150
19	8	ST-203	OP	UTL	FBG	TR	IO	165-235		7	7	2800			3800	4550
20	3	SS-215	OP	CUD	FBG	DV	IO	165-235		7	10	2900			3750	4500
22	10	SS-235	OP	CUD	FBG	DV	IO	188-235		8		3160			4650	5450
22	10	SS-235	OP	CUD	FBG	DV	IO	T140-T165		8		3160			5250	6050
23		ROBALO 230	OP	FSH	FBG	DV	OB			8		2050		9	5600	6450
23		ROBALO 236	OP	FSH	FBG	DV	OB			8		2712	1	2	7100	8150
23		ROBALO 236	OP	FSH	FBG	DV	IO	188-235		8		3620	1	2	5600	6550
23		ROBALO 236	OP	FSH	FBG	DV	IO	T140		8		3620	1	2	6250	7200
23		SS-236	OP	FSH	FBG	DV	OB			8		2712	1	2	7050	8100
23		SS-236	OP	FSH	FBG	DV	IO	188-235		8		3620	1	2	5500	6450
23		SS-236	OP	FSH	FBG	DV	IO	T140-T165		8		3620	1	2	6200	7200
24		SS-245	OP	EXP	FBG	DV	IO	233-255		8		3720	1	6	5600	6550
24		SS-245	OP	EXP	FBG	DV	IO	T140-T175		8		3720	1	6	6200	7150
24		SS-245 SEDAN	HT	SDN	FBG	DV	IO	233-255		8		3720	1	6	5600	6550
24		SS-245 SEDAN	HT	SDN	FBG	DV	IO	T140-T175		8		3720	1	6	6200	7150
25	4	COMMAND 25	HT	EXP	FBG	DV	IB	255	MRCR	9	8	5000	2	6	7250	8300
25	4	COMMAND 25	HT	EXP	FBG	DV	IO	T165		9	8	5000	2	6	8450	9700
25	4	OFFSHORE 25	OP	EXP	FBG	DV	IO	255	MRCR	9	8	5000	2	6	7800	8950
25	4	OFFSHORE 25	OP	EXP	FBG	DV	IO	T165		9	8	5000	2	6	8450	9700
25	4	SEDAN 25	FB	SDN	FBG	DV	IO	255	MRCR	9	8	6000	2	6	9400	10700
25	4	SEDAN 25	FB	SDN	FBG	DV	IO	T165		9	8	6000	2	6	10100	11400
28		EXPRESS 28	OP	EXP	FBG	DV	IB	T233	MRCR	10	6	8050	2	7	11800	13400
		1975 BOATS														
17	3	ROBALO 180	OP	FSH	FBG	TR	OB			7	2	1300		9	3000	3500
17	3	ST190 W/T	OP	UTL	FBG	TR	OB			7	2	1230			2800	3250
17	4	ST195 W/T	OP	UTL	FBG	TR	IO	130-165		7	1	2530			3250	3750
17	6	SS190 W/T	OP	RNBT	FBG	DV	OB			7		1550			3450	4050
17	6	SS194 W/T	OP	RNBT	FBG	DV	IO	130-235		7		2160			2700	3300
17	6	SS195	OP	RNBT	FBG	DV	IO	130-235		7		2160			2700	3300
19		ROBALO 190	OP	FSH	FBG	DV	OB			8		1700		9	3850	4500
19	6	ROBALO 200	OP	FSH	FBG	DV	OB			8		1800		9	4100	4800
19	6	SS204 W/T	OP	RNBT	FBG	DV	IO	165-200		7	7	2700			3400	4150
19	6	SS204 W/T	OP	RNBT	FBG	DV	IO	225-235		7	7	2700			3450	4250
19	6	SS206	OP	RNBT	FBG	DV	IO	165-235		7	7	2920			3550	4450
19	8	ST203 W/T	OP	UTL	FBG	TR	IO	165-235		7	7	2800			3900	4850
20	3	SS215	OP	CUD	FBG	DV	IO	165-235		7	10	2900			3850	4800
20	3	SS215	OP	CUD	FBG	DV	IO	280	MRCR	7	10	2900			4200	4900
22	10	SS235	OP	CUD	FBG	DV	IO	165-280		8		3160			4750	5900
22	10	SS235	OP	CUD	FBG	DV	IO	T130-T140		8		3160			5700	6550
23		ROBALO 230	OP	FSH	FBG	DV	OB			8		2050		9	5600	6400
23		ROBALO 236	OP	CUD	FBG	DV	OB			8		2900	1	3	7400	8500
23		ROBALO 236	OP	CUD	FBG	DV	IO	165-235		8		3620	1	3	5250	6350
23		ROBALO 236	OP	CUD	FBG	DV	IO	T130-T140		8		3620	1	3	6200	7150
24	1	SS245	OP	CR	FBG	DV	IO	170-280		8		3720	1	6	5700	7000
24	1	SS245	OP	CR	FBG	DV	IO	T130-T190		8		3720	1	6	6750	7850
25	4	SPORT COMMAND 255	OP	SPTCR	FBG	DV	IO	233-255		9	8	5000	2	6	8050	9400
25	4	SPORT COMMAND 255	OP	SPTCR	FBG	DV	IO	T140-T190		9	8	5000	2	6	8800	10500
25	4	SPORT COMMAND 255	OP	SPTCR	FBG	DV	IB	T106D	VLVO	9	8	5000	2	6	10800	12300
25	4	SPORT CONVERTIBLE255	OP	SPTCR	FBG	DV	IO	233-235		9	8	5000	2	6	8050	9250
		IO 255 MRCR 8200 9400, IB 255 MRCR 7100 8150, IO T140													8800	10000
		IB T155 CHRY 7550 8700, IO T165-T190 8950 10500, IB T106D VLVO													10800	12300
25	4	SPORT OFFSHORE 256	OP	CUD	FBG	DV	IO	233-255		9	8	6000	2	6	9100	10500
25	4	SPORT OFFSHORE 256	OP	CUD	FBG	DV	IO	T140-T190		9	8	6000	2	6	9700	11500
25	4	SPORT OFFSHORE 256	OP	CUD	FBG	DV	IB	T106D	VLVO	9	8	6000	2	6	12000	13600
25	4	SPORT OFFSHORE 256	FB	CUD	FBG	DV	IO	233-255		9	8	6000	2	6	9100	10500
25	4	SPORT OFFSHORE 256	FB	CUD	FBG	DV	IO	T140-T190		9	8	6000	2	6	9700	11500
25	4	SPORT OFFSHORE 256	FB	CUD	FBG	DV	IB	T106D	VLVO	9	8	6000	2	6	12000	13600
25	4	SPORT SEDAN 255	HT	SPTCR	FBG	DV	IO	233-255		9	8	6000	2	6	9250	10700
25	4	SPORT SEDAN 255	HT	SPTCR	FBG	DV	IO	T140-T190		9	8	6000	2	6	9900	11700
25	4	SPORT SEDAN 255	HT	SPTCR	FBG	DV	IB	T106D	VLVO	9	8	6000	2	6	12300	14000
25	4	SPORT SEDAN 255	FB	SPTCR	FBG	DV	IO	233-255		9	8	6000	2	6	9250	10700
25	4	SPORT SEDAN 255	FB	SPTCR	FBG	DV	IO	T140-T190		9	8	6000	2	6	9900	11700
25	4	SPORT SEDAN 255	FB	SPTCR	FBG	DV	IB	T106D	VLVO	9	8	6000	2	6	12300	14000
28		SPORT EXP SALON A285	OP	EXP	FBG	DV	IB	T200-T233		10	6	8050	2	7	11200	13000
28		SPORT EXP SALON A285	HT	EXP	FBG	DV	IB	T200-T233				8050			11200	13000
28		SPORT EXP SALON B285	OP	EXP	FBG	DV	IB	T200-T233		10	6	8050	2	7	10900	12700
28		SPORT EXP SALON B285	HT	EXP	FBG	DV	IB	T200-T233				8050			10900	12700
28		SPORT SEDAN 285	HT	SDN	FBG	DV	IB	T200-T233		10	6	8500	2	7	12300	14400
28		SPORT SEDAN 285	FB	SDN	FBG	DV	IB	T200-T233				8500			12300	14400
		1974 BOATS														
17	3	ROBALO 180		FSH	FBG		OB			7	2	1300		9	3000	3500
17	3	ST-190	ST	FSH	FBG	TR	OB			7	2	1230			2850	3350
17	4	ST-195	ST	UTL	FBG	TR	IO	140-165		7	1	2530			3200	3750
17	6	SS-194	ST	RNBT	FBG	DV	IO	140-165		7		2160			2700	3150
17	6	SS-194	ST	RNBT	FBG	DV	IO	170	OMC	7		2160			2650	3100
17	6	SS-194	ST	RNBT	FBG	DV	IO	170-245		7		2160			2900	3550
17	6	SS-195	ST	RNBT	FBG	DV	IO	140-165		7		2160			2600	3050
17	6	SS-195	ST	RNBT	FBG	DV	IO	170	OMC	7		2160			2550	3000
17	6	SS-195	ST	RNBT	FBG	DV	IO	170-245		7		2160			2850	3450
19		ROBALO 190	OP	FSH	FBG		OB			8		1700		9	3850	4450
19	6	SS-204	ST	RNBT	FBG	DV	IO	165-225		7	7	2700			3500	4400
19	6	SS-206	ST	RNBT	FBG	DV	IO	165-225		7	7	2920			3700	4600
19	8	ST-203	ST	UTL	FBG	TR	IO	165-225		7	7	2800			4050	5000
20	3	SS-215	ST	CUD	FBG	DV	IO	165-225		7	10	2900			4000	4950
20	3	SS-215	HT	CUD	FBG	DV	IO	165-225		7	10	2900			4000	4950
22	10	SS-235	ST	CUD	FBG	DV	IO	165-225		8		3160			4900	5950
22	10	SS-235	ST	CUD	FBG	DV	IO	T130-T140		8		3160			5900	6750
22	10	SS-235	HT	CUD	FBG	DV	IO	165-225		8		3160			4900	5950
22	10	SS-235	HT	CUD	FBG	DV	IO	T130-T140		8		3160			5900	6750
23		ROBALO 230	OP	FSH	FBG	DV	OB			8		2050		9	5550	6400
25	4		HT	SDN	FBG	DV	IO	188-255		9	8	6000	2	6	9600	11300
25	4		HT	SDN	FBG	DV	IO	T140-T170		9	8	6000	2	6	10500	12500
25	4	SPORT	FB	SDN	FBG	DV	IO	188-255		9	8				9550	11300
25	4	SPORT	FB	SDN	FBG	DV	IO	T140-T170		9	8				10500	12400
25	4	SPORT	OP	SPTCR	FBG	DV	IO	188-255		9	8	5000	2	6	8100	9750
25	4	SPORT	OP	SPTCR	FBG	DV	IO	T140-T170		9	8	5000	2	6	9100	10800
25	4	SPORT OFFSHORE	OP	OFF	FBG	DV	IO	188-255		9	8	5000	2	6	7900	9500
25	4	SPORT OFFSHORE	OP	OFF	FBG	DV	IO	T140-T170		9	8	5000	2	6	8850	10500
25	4	SPORT OFFSHORE	HT	OFF	FBG	DV	IO	188-255		9	8	5000			7900	9500
25	4	SPORT OFFSHORE	HT	OFF	FBG	DV	IO	T140-T170		9	8	5000			8850	10500
25	4	SPORT OFFSHORE	FB	OFF	FBG	DV	IO	188-255		9	8	5000			7900	9500
25	4	SPORT OFFSHORE	FB	OFF	FBG	DV	IO	T140-T170		9	8	5000			8850	10500
28			OP	EXP	FBG	DV	IB	T200-T225		10	6	8050	2	7	10600	12300
28			HT	SDN	FBG	DV	IB	T200-T225		10	6	8500	2	7	11900	13800
28		SPORT	HT	EXP	FBG	DV	IB	T200-T225		10	6	8050	2	7	10600	12300
28		SPORT	FB	SDN	FBG	DV	IB	T200-T225		10	6	8500	2	7	11900	13800
		1973 BOATS														
17	3	ROBALO 180	OP	SF	FBG		OB			7	2	1300		9	3000	3500
17	3	ST190	OP	RNBT	FBG	TR	OB			7	2	1230			2850	3350
17	4	ST195	OP	RNBT	FBG	TR	IO	140-165		7	1	2530			3000	3500
17	6	SS194	OP	RNBT	FBG	DV	IO	140-225		7		2160			2750	3300
17	6	SS194	OP	RNBT	FBG	DV	JT	245	OMC	7		2160			2650	3100
17	6	SS195	OP	RNBT	FBG	DV	IO	140-225		7		2160			2700	3250
17	6	SS195	OP	RNBT	FBG	DV	JT	245	OMC	7		2160			2600	3050
19		ROBALO 190	OP	SF	FBG		OB			8		1700		9	3800	4450
19	6	SS204	OP	RNBT	FBG	DV	IO	165-245		7	7	2700			3650	4400
19	6	SS206 CBN	OP	RNBT	FBG	DV	IO	165-245		7	7	2920			3800	4600
19	8	ST203	OP	UTL	FBG	TR	IO	165-245		7	7	2800			4150	5050
20	3	SS210 CBN	OP	CUD	FBG	DV	OB			7	10	2100			4950	5700
20	3	SS210 CBN	HT	CUD	FBG	DV	OB			7	10	2900			5800	6650
20	3	SS215 CBN	OP	CUD	FBG	DV	IO	165-245		7	10	2900			4150	5000
20	3	SS215 CBN	HT	CUD	FBG	DV	IO	165-245		7	10	2900			4150	5000
22	10	SF235	OP	SF	FBG	DV	IO	165-245		8		3560			6250	7350
22	10	SF235	OP	SF	FBG	DV	IO	T130-T140		8		3560			7350	8450
22	10	SS235	OP	CUD	FBG	DV	IO	165-245		8		3160			5100	6000
22	10	SS235	OP	CUD	FBG	DV	IO	T130-T140		8		3160			6100	7000
22	10	SS235 CBN CR	HT	CUD	FBG	DV	IO	165-245		8		3160			5050	6000
22	10	SS235 CBN CR	HT	CUD	FBG	DV	IO	T130-T140		8		3160			6100	7000
22	10	SS235 CNB CR	HT	CUD	FBG	DV	IO	165	OMC	8		3160			5100	5850
23		ROBALO 230	OP	SF	FBG	DV	OB			8		2300		9	6100	7000

CONTINUED ON NEXT PAGE

LOA FT	LOA IN	NAME AND/ OR MODEL	TOP/ RIG	BOAT TYPE	-HULL- MTL	-HULL- TP	ENGINE TP	ENGINE # HP	ENGINE MFG	BEAM FT	BEAM IN	WGT LBS	DRAFT FT	DRAFT IN	RETAIL LOW	RETAIL HIGH
		1973 BOATS														
25	4	SF255 CBN	OP	SF	FBG	DV	IO	225-255		9	8	5400			10100	11700
25	4	SF255 CBN	OP	SF	FBG	DV	IO	T130-T170		9	8	5400			11100	12900
28		SC 285	OP	SF	FBG		IB	T200-T225		10	8	8050			10200	11800
28		SC285	HT	EXP	FBG	DV	IB	T200-T225		10	8				10200	11800
28		SC285 CBN	OP	EXP	FBG	DV	IB	T200-T225		10	8	8050			10200	11800
		1972 BOATS														
17	3	SS180	OP	UTL	FBG		OB			7	2	1230			2750	3200
17	6	SS190	OP	RNBT	FBG	DV	OB			7		1255			2950	3400
17	6	SS194	OP	UTL	FBG	DV	IO	140-225		7		2160	1		3100	3750
17	6	SS195	OP	RNBT	FBG	DV	IO	140-225		7		2160	1		2850	3400
19		ROBALO CUSTOM		SF	FBG		OB			8		1700		9	4200	4900
19		ROBALO STD		SF	FBG		OB			8		1700		9	3450	4000
19	6	SS204	OP	RNBT	FBG	DV	IO	155-245		7	7	2700	1	3	3700	4300
19	6	SS205 DLX	OP	RNBT	FBG	DV	IO	165-245		7	7	2700	1	2	3950	4750
19	8	SS203	OP	UTL	FBG		IO	155-245		7	7	2800	1	3	4250	5200
20	3	SS214	OP	SF	FBG		IO	155-245		7	10	2800	1	3	4750	5700
20	3	SS215	HT	RNBT	FBG	DV	IO	155-245		7	10	2900	1	3	4050	4900
20	3	SS215 CBN		RNBT	FBG		IO	155-245		7	10	2900	1	3	4050	4950
22	10	SF235	FB	SF	FBG	DV	IO	155-245		8		3160	1	2	6450	7700
22	10	SS235	OP	CUD	FBG	DV	IO	155-245		8		3160	1	2	5200	6200
22	10	SS235	OP	CUD	FBG	DV	IO	T120-T140		8		3160	1	2	5950	6850
22	10	SS235 CBN CR	HT	CUD	FBG	DV	IO	155-245		8		3160	1	2	5200	6200
22	10	SS235 CBN CR	HT	CUD	FBG	DV	IO	T120-T140		8		3160	1	2	5950	6850
25	4	SF255	FB	SF	FBG		IO	215-225		9	8	5400	1	4	11500	13100
		IB 300 CC 7300 8350, IO 325 MRCR 12600 14300, IO T140-T165													12600	14500
28		SC285	OP	EXP	FBG		IB	T200-T215		10	8	8050	2	2	9850	11300
28		SC285	HT	EXP	FBG		IB	T200-T215		10	8	8050	2	2	9850	11300
		1971 BOATS														
17		SF-180	OP	UTL	FBG	TR	OB			6	11	1140	2	2	2650	3100
17		SS180	OP	UTL	FBG	TR	OB			6	11	1140			2550	2950
17		SS185	OP	UTL	FBG	TR	IO	120-140		6	11	2055	2	2	3000	3500
17	6	SS-195		RNBT	FBG	DV	IO	120		7			2	5	3050	3550
17	6	SS190	OP	RNBT	FBG		OB			7		1255			2950	3400
17	6	SS195	OP	RNBT	FBG		IO	140-165		7		2000	2	4	2850	3450
17	6	SS195	OP	RNBT	FBG		IO	215	OMC	7		2300	2	4	3100	3600
19		ROBALO CUSTOM		SF	FBG		OB			8		1700		9	4050	4750
19		ROBALO DELUXE		SF	FBG		OB			8		1700		9	3550	4150
19	6	SS-205	OP	RNBT	FBG	DV	IO	165-235		7	7	2700	3	7	3850	4650
19	6	SS204	OP	RNBT	FBG	DV	IO	140-235		7	7	2800	2	6	3950	4900
19	8	SS-203		RNBT	FBG	TR	IO	140		7	7		2	8	3950	4600
19	8	SS-203	OP	UTL	FBG	TR	IO	155-235		7	7	2800	3	7	4450	5300
20	3	SS214	OP	SF	FBG		IO	155-235		7	10	2600	2	8	4700	5800
20	3	SS215		RNBT	FBG		IO	155-235		7	10	2700	2	8	4050	5000
22	10	SS235	OP	CUD	FBG		IO	155-235		8		3000	2	7	5250	6450
22	10	SS235	OP	CUD	FBG		IO	T120-T140		8		4100	2	6	7300	8400
28		SC-285	OP	EXP	FBG		IO	T215-T230		10	8	8050	2	2	14700	16900
28		SF-285	OP	SF	FBG		IO	T215-T230		10	8	8050	2	2	16700	19200
28		SFH-285	HT	SF	FBG		IO	T215-T230		10	8	8050	2	2	16700	19200
28		SH-285	HT	EXP	FBG		IO	T215-T230		10	8	8050	2	2	14700	16900
		1970 BOATS														
17		SF 180	OP	UTL	FBG	TR	OB			6	11	1140			2650	3100
17		SS 180	OP	UTL	FBG	TR	OB			6	11	1140			2550	2950
17		SS 185	OP	UTL	FBG	TR	IO	120-140		6	11	2055	2	2	3100	3650
17	6	SS 190	OP	RNBT	FBG		OB			7		1255			2950	3400
17	6	SS 195V	OP	RNBT	FBG	DV	IO	120-165		7		2000	2	4	2900	3600
17	6	SS 195V	OP	RNBT	FBG	DV	IO	210-215		7		2300	2	4	3200	3750
19		ROBALO 190		SF	FBG	SV	OB			8		1800		9	3950	4600
19	6	SS 204	OP	RNBT	FBG	DV	IO	140-215		7	7	2800	2	6	4100	4850
19	6	SS 205	OP	RNBT	FBG	DV	IO	165	MRCR	7	7	2850	2	6	4150	4800
19	6	SS 205	OP	RNBT	FBG	DV	IO	210-215		7	7	3000	2	6	4700	5450
20	3	SS 210			FBG	DV	OB			7		2000			4800	5500
20	3	SS 214	OP	SF	FBG	DV	IO	155-215		7	10	2600	2	8	4850	5950
20	3	SS 215V		RNBT	FBG	DV	IO	155-215		7	10	2700	2	8	4150	5150
22	3	SH 235V		SF	FBG	DV	IO	155		8			2	7	6000	6900
22	3	SS 235			FBG	DV	IO	210	OMC	8		3200	2	7	5250	6050
22	3	SS 235		CUD	FBG	DV	IO	165-215		8		3000	2	7	5250	6400
22	3	SS 235		CUD	FBG	DV	IO	T120-T140		8		4100	2	7	7300	8400
22	3	SS 235	OP	CUD	FBG	DV	IO	155	OMC	8		3000	2	7	5250	6000
28		SC 285		EXP	FBG	DV	IB	230	CC	10	8	8050	2	2	8250	9450
		1969 BOATS														
16	6	SS170V	OP	RNBT	FBG	SV	OB			6	8	1025			2400	2800
16	6	SS175V	OP	RNBT	FBG	DV	IO	120		6	8	1675	2	5	2550	2950
16	6	SS175V	OP	RNBT	FBG	DV	IO	140-160		6	8		2	5	3200	3700
17		SF-180T	OP	RNBT	FBG	TR	OB			6	11	1140			2750	3200
17		SS180T	OP	RNBT	FBG	TR	OB			6	11	1140			2600	3050
18	2	SS195V	OP	RNBT	FBG	DV	IO	120-210		7	2	2200	2	6	3300	4100
20	3	SS210V		RNBT	FBG	DV	OB			7	10	2000			4800	5550
20	3	SS215V		RNBT	FBG	DV	IO	140-210		7	10	2700	2	8	4350	5200
22	3	SF-235	OP	SF	FBG	DV	IO	155-210		8		3000	2	7	6100	7200
22	3	SF-235	OP	SF	FBG	DV	IO	T120-T140		8			2	7	7100	8150
22	3	SH235	HT	SF	FBG	DV	IO		OMC	8		3200			**	**
22	3	SH235	HT	SF	FBG	DV	IO	160-210		8		3200			6350	7350
22	3	SH235	HT	SF	FBG	DV	IO	T120-T140		8					7050	8150
22	3	SS235	OP	CUD	FBG	DV	IO	155-160		8		3000			5400	6250
22	3	SS235	OP	CUD	FBG	DV	IO	200-210		8					5950	6850
22	3	SS235	OP	CUD	FBG	DV	IO	T120-T140		8					6650	7700
		1968 BOATS														
16		SS160V	OP	RNBT	FBG	SV	OB			6	5	950			2250	2600
16		SS165V	OP	RNBT	FBG	SV	IO	120	MRCR	6	5	1620	2	3	2450	2850
16	6	SS170V	OP	RNBT	FBG	DV	OB			6	8	1025			2400	2800
16	6	SS175V	OP	RNBT	FBG	DV	IO	120-160		6	8	1675	2	5	2650	3200
17		SS180T	OP	RNBT	FBG	TR	OB			6	11	1140			2700	3150
17		SS185T	OP	RNBT	FBG	TR	IO	120-160		6	11	1925			2950	3550
18	2	SS195V	OP	RNBT	FBG	DV	IO	120-210		7	2	2120	2	6	3350	4200
22	3	SF-235V	OP	SF	FBG	DV	IO	155-210		8		3015	2	7	6200	7400
22	3	SS235V	OP	SF	FBG	DV	IO	155-210		8		3015	2	7	6450	7650
22	3	SS235V	OP	SF	FBG	DV	IO	T120	MRCR	8		3525	2	7	7950	9150
		1967 BOATS														
16		SS 160	OP	RNBT	FBG	SV	OB			6	5	790			1850	2200
16		SS 160 V	OP	RNBT	FBG	SV	OB			6	5	920			2200	2550
16		SS 165 V	OP	RNBT	FBG	SV	IO	120	MRCR	6	5	1650	2	3	2550	3000
16	6	SS 170 V	OP	RNBT	FBG	DV	OB			6	8	1090			2550	3000
16	6	SS 175 V	OP	RNBT	FBG	DV	IO	120	MRCR	6	8	1700	2	5	2750	3200
17		SS 180 T	OP	RNBT	FBG	TR	OB			6	11	1100			2600	3050
17		SS 185 T	OP	RNBT	FBG	TR	IO	120							3600	4150
17	10	SS 190	OP	RNBT	FBG		OB			7	2	1100			2700	3150
18	2	SS 195 V	OP	RNBT	FBG	DV	IO	120-200		7	2		2	6	3650	4350
22	3	SS 235 V	OP	SF	FBG	DV	IO	150-200		8		2900	2	7	6450	7700
22	3	SS 235 V	OP	SF	FBG	DV	IO	T120	MRCR	8			2	7	7600	8700
		1966 BOATS														
16		SS 160	OP	RNBT	FBG	SV	OB			6	5	790			1850	2200
16		SS 160 V	OP	RNBT	FBG	SV	OB			6	2	800			1900	2250
16		SS 165 V	OP	RNBT	FBG	SV	IO	80-110		6	2				2650	3300
16	6	SS 170 V	OP	RNBT	FBG	DV	OB			6	8	925			2250	2600
16	6	SS 175 V	OP	RNBT	FBG	DV	IO	110-120		6	8				3500	4300
17	10	SS 180	OP	RNBT	FBG	TR	OB			7	2	1100			2700	3150
17	10	SS 195 V	OP	RNBT	FBG	TR	IO	120-200		7	2				3750	4450
22	3	SS 235 V	OP	SF	FBG	DV	IO	T110-T225		8			2	7	7850	9500
		1965 BOATS														
16		SS 160			FBG		OB								2600	3050
16	6	SS 170			FBG		OB								2950	3400
16	6	SS 175			FBG		IO	110-120							3600	4150
17	10	SS 180			FBG		OB								3600	4200
17	10	SS 185			FBG		IO	110-120							3700	4300
17	10	SS 195			FBG		IO	150-165							3700	4300
22	3	SS 235			FBG		IO	150-225							5950	7000
22	3	SS 235			FBG		IO	T120							6800	7800
		1964 BOATS														
16		PREMIERE			FBG		OB								2600	3050
16		PREMIERE SPORT			FBG		OB								2600	3050
16		SEA-SPORT			FBG		IO	110-120							2750	3200
17	9	CUSTOM OFFSHORE		OFF	FBG		OB								3650	4200
17	9	SEA-SPORT			FBG		IO	140-190							3800	4500
17	9	SPORT OFFSHORE		OFF	FBG		OB								3650	4200
17	9	SPORT OFFSHORE		OFF	FBG		IO	110-140							4150	4850
17	9	SURFCASTER			FBG		OB								3650	4200
		1961 BOATS														
17	6	ROYAL-EXPRESS		CR	FBG		OB			7		1050			2650	3050
17	6	SPORTSMAN		RNBT	FBG		OB			7		850			2250	2600
		1960 BOATS														
17		CAPITAN		CR	PLY	DV	OB			6	6	830			2100	2500
17		SPORTSMAN		UTL	PLY	DV	OB			6	6	775			1900	2250
		1959 BOATS														
17		CAPITAN		RNBT	PLY		OB			6	6	825			2150	2550
17		SPORTSMAN		RNBT	PLY		OB			6	6	775			2000	2400

SMITH & RHULAND LTD

Call 1-800-327-6929 for BUC Personalized Evaluation Service
Or, for 1961 boats, sign onto www.BUCValuPro.com

SMITH BROS

Call 1-800-327-6929 for BUC Personalized Evaluation Service
Or, for 1960 to 1970 boats, sign onto www.BUCValuPro.com

SMOKER CRAFT INC

NEW PARIS IN 46553   COAST GUARD MFG ID- SMK See inside cover to adjust price for area

For more recent years, see the BUC Used Boat Price Guide, Volume 1 or Volume 2

LOA FT IN	NAME AND/ OR MODEL	TOP/ RIG	BOAT TYPE	MTL	TP	ENG TP	HP	MFG	BEAM FT IN	WGT LBS	DRAFT FT IN	RETAIL LOW	RETAIL HIGH
1983 BOATS													
18 6	CHALLANGER	OP	RNBT	AL	SV	OB	7			1020		2200	2550
1976 BOATS													
18 2	T-BIRD 180R	OP	RNBT	AL	SV	OB			6 10	952		1850	2200
1973 BOATS													
18 2	T-BIRD	OP	RNBT	AL	SV	IO			6 10	952		1800	2150
18 10	T-BIRD	OP	RNBT	AL	SV	IO	140		6 10	1325		2250	2600
1972 BOATS													
18	T-BIRD		RNBT	AL	SV	IO	100-140		6 10	760		2000	2400
1971 BOATS													
18 5	T-BIRD	OP	RNBT	AL	SV	IO	120	MRCR	6 10	1325		2300	2650
1970 BOATS													
18 5	T-BIRD	OP	RNBT	AL	SV	IO	120	MRCR	6 10	1325		2350	2700
1969 BOATS													
16 5	T-BIRD	OP	RNBT	AL	SV	IO	60	MRCR	6 10			2200	2550
18 5	T-BIRD	OP	RNBT	AL	SV	IO	120	MRCR	6 10	1325		2400	2800
1968 BOATS													
16 5	T-BIRD	OP	RNBT	AL		IO	80	MRCR	6 3	925		1750	2050
18 10	T-BIRD	OP	RNBT	AL		IO	120	MRCR	7 10	1325		2850	3300
1967 BOATS													
16 5	THUNDERBIRD 16		RNBT	AL		IO	80		6 3	925		1800	2150
18 5	THUNDERBIRD W/TILT		RNBT	AL		IO	120		6 10	1325		2600	3000
1966 BOATS													
16 5	T-BIRD 16		RNBT	AL		IO	60		6 3			2300	2700
18 5	T-BIRD 18		RNBT	AL		IO	110		6 10			2700	3150
1965 BOATS													
18 5	THUNDERBIRD 18			AL		OB						2000	2400
18 5	VEE 18 DELUXE			AL		OB						2400	2800

SNAPIR SAILING CRAFT LTD

COAST GUARD MFG ID- SNP

Call 1-800-327-6929 for BUC Personalized Evaluation Service
Or, for 1970 to 1975 boats, sign onto www.BUCValuPro.com

SNARK BOATS

ADRIAN MI 49221   COAST GUARD MFG ID- SNA See inside cover to adjust price for area
FORMERLY LOCKLEY MFG CO INC

For more recent years, see the BUC Used Boat Price Guide, Volume 1 or Volume 2

LOA FT IN	NAME AND/ OR MODEL	TOP/ RIG	BOAT TYPE	MTL	TP	ENG TP	MFG	BEAM FT IN	WGT LBS	DRAFT FT IN	RETAIL LOW	RETAIL HIGH
1982 BOATS												
17 8	NEWPORT 17	SLP	SAIL	FBG	CB	OB		6 4	1000	9	3250	3800
1981 BOATS												
17 8	NEWPORT 17	SLP	SAIL	FBG	CB	OB		6 4	1000		3100	3600
18	WHITECAP	SLP	SA/OD	FBG	CB	OB		6 7		8	2400	2800
18	WHITECAP	SLP	SAIL	FBG	CB	OB		6 7	760		2750	3200
22 10	LN 23	SLP	SAIL	FBG	CB	OB		8	2700		6100	7000
1980 BOATS												
17 8	NEWPORT 17	SLP	SAIL	FBG	CB	OB		6 4	1000	9	2950	3450
18	WHITECAP	SLP	SAIL	FBG	CB	OB		6 7	760	8	2650	3050
22 10	LN 23	SLP	SAIL	FBG	KC	OB		8	2700	1 11	5850	6700
1979 BOATS												
17 8	NEWPORT 17	SLP	SAIL	FBG	CB	OB		6 4	1000	9	2850	3300
18	WHITECAP	SLP	SAIL	FBG	CB	OB		6 7	760	8	2550	2950
22 10	LN 23	SLP	SAIL	FBG	KC	OB		8	2700	1 11	5650	6450
1978 BOATS												
17 8	NEWPORT 17	SLP	SAIL	FBG	CB	OB		6 4	1000	9	2750	3200
18	WHITECAP	SLP	SAIL	FBG	CB	OB		6 7	760	8	2450	2850
1977 BOATS												
17 8	NEWPORT 17	SLP	SA/CR	FBG	SK	OB		6 4	1000	9	2650	3100
21 4	NEWPORT 214	SLP	SA/CR	FBG	SK	OB		7 8	1500	9	3450	4050

SNUG HARBOR BOAT WORKS

ST PETERSBURG FL 33702   COAST GUARD MFG ID- SNU See inside cover to adjust price for area

For more recent years, see the BUC Used Boat Price Guide, Volume 1 or Volume 2

LOA FT IN	NAME AND/ OR MODEL	TOP/ RIG	BOAT TYPE	MTL	TP	BEAM FT IN	WGT LBS	DRAFT FT IN	RETAIL LOW	RETAIL HIGH
1983 BOATS										
23	SNUG-HARBOR 23	SLP	SA/CR	FBG	KL	8	4500	3	6650	7650
1982 BOATS										
23	SNUG-HARBOR 23	SLP	SA/CR	FBG	KL	8	4500	3	6250	7200
1981 BOATS										
23	SNUG-HARBOR 23	SLP	SA/CR	FBG	KL	8	4500	3	5900	6750
1980 BOATS										
23	SNUG-HARBOR 23	SLP	SA/CR	FBG	KL	8	4500	3	5600	6450

SOL CATAMARANS INC

COAST GUARD MFG ID- SXL

Call 1-800-327-6929 for BUC Personalized Evaluation Service
Or, for 1974 to 1984 boats, sign onto www.BUCValuPro.com

SOLARIS YACHTS

SOUTHAMPTON ENGLAND   COAST GUARD MFG ID- SLY See inside cover to adjust price for area

For more recent years, see the BUC Used Boat Price Guide, Volume 1 or Volume 2

LOA FT IN	NAME AND/ OR MODEL	TOP/ RIG	BOAT TYPE	MTL	TP	ENG TP	#	HP	MFG	BEAM FT IN	WGT LBS	DRAFT FT IN	RETAIL LOW	RETAIL HIGH
1979 BOATS														
42	SOLARIS 42	KTH	SA/CR	FBG	CT	HD	T	42D	BENZ	17 9	25200	4	94000	103500
51	SOLARIS 51	SLP	SA/CR	FBG	CT	IB	T	150D	FORD	24	56000	5 3	137000	151000
51	SOLARIS 51	SCH	SA/CR	FBG	CT	IB	T	150D	FORD	24	56000	5 3	137000	151000
51	SOLARIS 51	KTH	SA/CR	FBG	CT	IB	T	150D	FORD	24	56000	5 3	137000	151000
1978 BOATS														
42	SOLARIS 42	KTH	SA/CR	FBG	CT	HD	T	42D	BENZ	17 9	24640	4	89600	98500
51	SOLARIS 51	SCH	SA/CR	FBG	CT	IB	T	125D	BENZ	24	56000	5 3	131500	144500
61 3	SOLARIS 60	SCH	SA/CR	FBG	CT	IB	T	D	BENZ	25 3		5 6	196000	215500

SOLING YACHTS A/S

Call 1-800-327-6929 for BUC Personalized Evaluation Service
Or, for 1970 to 1972 boats, sign onto www.BUCValuPro.com

SOLNA MARIN

SOLNA SWEDEN   COAST GUARD MFG ID- SNM See inside cover to adjust price for area

LOA FT IN	NAME AND/ OR MODEL	TOP/ RIG	BOAT TYPE	MTL	TP	ENG TP	HP	BEAM FT IN	WGT LBS	DRAFT FT IN	RETAIL LOW	RETAIL HIGH
1976 BOATS												
27	SOLNA 27	SLP	SA/CR	FBG	KL	IB	12D	8 10	4620	4 6	9450	10700
29 9	SCAMPI 30	SLP	SA/CR	FBG	KL	IB	12D	9 9	6600	5 3	14200	16100
1974 BOATS												
29 9	SCAMPI 30	SLP	SAIL	FBG	KL	OB		9	6600	5 2	13200	14800
33 6	NORLIN 34	SLP	SAIL	FBG	KL	IB		11	9900	6 2	20500	22800
36 2	NORLIN 37	SLP	SA/CR	FBG	KL	IB	D	12		6 5	32800	36400
40 6	NORLIN 41	SLP	SA/CR	FBG	KL	IB	D	12 10		6 5	52500	57700
1973 BOATS												
29 9	SCAMPI 30	SLP	SAIL	FBG	KL	IB	12D	9	6600	5 2	13100	14800
33 6	NORLIN 34	SLP	SAIL	FBG	KL	IB	12D	11	9900	6 2	20200	22400
1972 BOATS												
29 5	SCAMPI 30	SLP	SA/CR	FBG	KL	IB	D	9 9		5 6	12700	14500
33 10	SCAMPI 34	SLP	SA/CR	FBG	KL	IB	D	10 10		6 6	19800	22000
1971 BOATS												
26	SM 44	SLP	SA/RC	FBG	KL	IB		7 8		4 11	6900	7950
29 7	SCAMPI	SLP	SA/RC	FBG	KL	IB		9 9		4 9	10300	11700

SOMERSET BOAT CO
SOMERSET KY 42501   See inside cover to adjust price for area

For more recent years, see the BUC Used Boat Price Guide, Volume 1 or Volume 2

LOA FT IN	NAME AND/ OR MODEL	TOP/ RIG	BOAT TYPE	-HULL- MTL TP	TP	----ENGINE--- # HP MFG	BEAM FT IN	WGT LBS	DRAFT FT IN	RETAIL LOW	RETAIL HIGH
1983 BOATS											
46		HT	HB	AL	SV IO	140	14			40700	45200
58		HT	HB	AL	SV IO	140	14			59900	65800
62		HT	HB	AL	SV IO	140	15			63100	69300
70		HT	HB	AL	SV IO	140	18			72700	79900

SONAR INTERNATIONAL
Call 1-800-327-6929 for BUC Personalized Evaluation Service
Or, for 1981 boats, sign onto www.BUCValuPro.com

SONDERBERG YACHT WORKS
COAST GUARD MFG ID- SGR

INTERNATIONAL YACHT AGY LTD

Call 1-800-327-6929 for BUC Personalized Evaluation Service
Or, for 1976 to 1977 boats, sign onto www.BUCValuPro.com

W A SOUTER LTD
ADMIRALTY GATE/COWES   See inside cover to adjust price for area
ISLE WIGHT ENGLAND

For more recent years, see the BUC Used Boat Price Guide, Volume 1 or Volume 2

LOA FT IN	NAME AND/ OR MODEL	TOP/ RIG	BOAT TYPE	-HULL- MTL TP	TP	----ENGINE--- # HP MFG	BEAM FT IN	WGT LBS	DRAFT FT IN	RETAIL LOW	RETAIL HIGH
1969 BOATS											
25 9	MERMAID	SLP	SAIL	WD	KL		6		3 5	7100	8150

SOUTH BAY MULTIHULLS INC
Call 1-800-327-6929 for BUC Personalized Evaluation Service
Or, for 1978 boats, sign onto www.BUCValuPro.com

SOUTH COAST BOATYARD LTD
COAST GUARD MFG ID- XBY

Call 1-800-327-6929 for BUC Personalized Evaluation Service
Or, for 1977 to 1979 boats, sign onto www.BUCValuPro.com

SOUTH COAST CO
NEWPORT BEACH CA 92663   See inside cover to adjust price for area

LOA FT IN	NAME AND/ OR MODEL	TOP/ RIG	BOAT TYPE	-HULL- MTL TP	TP	----ENGINE--- # HP MFG	BEAM FT IN	WGT LBS	DRAFT FT IN	RETAIL LOW	RETAIL HIGH
1961 BOATS											
33 4	RHODES 33	SLP	SA/OD	KL			6 10		5	15400	17500

SOUTH COAST SEACRAFT CORP
SHREVEPORT LA 71165   COAST GUARD MFG ID- SCS See inside cover to adjust price for area

LOA FT IN	NAME AND/ OR MODEL	TOP/ RIG	BOAT TYPE	-HULL- MTL TP	TP	----ENGINE--- # HP MFG	BEAM FT IN	WGT LBS	DRAFT FT IN	RETAIL LOW	RETAIL HIGH
1979 BOATS											
21 4	SOUTH-COAST 21	SLP	SA/RC	FBG KL	OB		6 11	1750	3	2750	3200
22	SOUTH-COAST 22	SLP	SA/CR	FBG SK	OB		7 1	1800		2850	3350
23	SOUTH-COAST 23	SLP	SA/RC	FBG KL	OB		7 3	3750	2 10	5050	5850
24	SOUTH-COAST 24	SLP	SA/CR	FBG SK	IB		8	3200		5000	5750
25 10	SOUTH-COAST 26	SLP	SA/CR	FBG SK	IB		8	4200		6850	7900
1978 BOATS											
21 4	SOUTH-COAST 21	SLP	SA/CR	FBG KL	OB		6 11	1800	3	2700	3150
22	SOUTH-COAST 22	SLP	SA/CR	FBG SK	OB		7 1	1800	10	2750	3200
23	SOUTH-COAST 23	SLP	SA/CR	FBG KL	OB		7 3	3750	2 10	4900	5600
25 10	SOUTH-COAST 26-A	SLP	SA/CR	FBG SK	OB		8	3800	1 10	5800	6650
25 10	SOUTH-COAST 26-A	SLP	SA/CR	FBG SK	IB	9D	8	3800	1 10	6250	7150
1977 BOATS											
25 8	SOUTH-COAST 26	SLP	SAIL	FBG CB	OB		7 11	2700	1 8	4150	4800
25 8	SOUTH-COAST 26 DC	SLP	SAIL	FBG CB	OB		7 11	2700	1 8	4150	4800
25 10	SOUTH-COAST AFT CPT	SLP	SAIL	FBG CB	OB		8	3300	1 10	4950	5700
1976 BOATS											
21 4	SOUTH-COAST 21	SLP	SAIL	FBG KL	OB		6 11	1750	3	2500	2900
22	SOUTH-COAST 22	SLP	SAIL	FBG SK	OB		7 1	1750	10	2550	3000
25 8	SOUTH-COAST 26	SLP	SAIL	FBG SK	OB		7 11	2700	1 8	4000	4650
1975 BOATS											
21 4	SOUTH-COAST 21	SLP	SAIL	FBG KL	OB		6 11	1750	3	2400	2800
22	SOUTH-COAST 22	SLP	SAIL	FBG SK	OB		7 1	1750	10	2500	2900
25 8	SOUTH-COAST 26	SLP	SAIL	FBG SK	OB		7 11	2700	3 8	3900	4500
1974 BOATS											
22	SC-22	SLP	SAIL	FBG SK	OB		7 1	1750		2400	2800
1973 BOATS											
21 4	SOUTH-COAST 21	SLP	SAIL	FBG KL	OB		6 11	1750	3	2300	2700
22	SC-22	SLP	SAIL	FBG SK	OB		7 1	1750	10	2350	2750
23	SOUTH-COAST 2 BERTH	SLP	SAIL	FBG KL	OB		7 3	3750	2 10	3700	4300
23	SOUTH-COAST 4 BERTH	SLP	SAIL	FBG KL	OB		7 3	3750	2 10	4650	5350
25 6	SOUTH-COAST 25	SLP	SAIL	FBG KL	OB		8	4200	3 6	5350	6200
1972 BOATS											
21	SOUTH-COAST 21	SLP	SAIL	FBG KL	OB		7 3		2 10	2250	2650
21 4	SOUTH-COAST 21	SLP	SA/OD	FBG KL			6 6	1750	3	2250	2600
22	SC-22	SLP	SAIL	FBG SK	OB		7 1	1750	10	2300	2700
23	SOUTH-COAST 23	SLP	SA/CR	FBG KL	OB		7 3		2 10	4050	4700
23	SOUTH-COAST 23	SLP	SA/OD	FBG KL			7 3	3750		4050	4700
25 6	SOUTH-COAST 25	SLP	SA/CR	FBG KL	OB		8		3 6	4800	5500
1971 BOATS											
21 4	SC-21	SLP	SAIL	FBG KL	OB		6 11	1750	3	2200	2550
22	SC-22	SLP	SAIL	FBG SK	OB		7 1	1800	10	2300	2700
23	SC-23 2 BERTH	SLP	SAIL	FBG KL	OB		7 3	3750	2 10	3500	4100
23	SC-23 4 BERTH	SLP	SAIL	FBG KL	OB		7 3	3750	2 10	4450	5100
25 6	SC-25	SLP	SAIL	FBG KL	OB		8	4400	3 6	5350	6150
1970 BOATS											
21 4	SOUTH-COAST 21	SLP	SA/OD	FBG KL	OB		6 11	2000	3	2300	2700
23	SOUTH-COAST 2 BERTH	SLP	SA/OD	FBG KL	OB		7 3	3750	2 10	3450	4000
23	SOUTH-COAST 4 BERTH	SLP	SA/OD	FBG KL	OB		7 3	3750	2 10	4350	5000
25 6	SOUTH-COAST 25	SLP	SAIL	FBG KL	OB		8	4200	3 6	5050	5800
1969 BOATS											
21 4	SOUTH-COAST 21	SLP	SAIL	FBG KL	OB		6 11	2000	3	2300	2650
23	SOUTH-COAST 23	SLP	SAIL	FBG KL	OB		7 3	3750	2 10	3800	4400
25 6	SOUTH-COAST 25	SLP	SAIL	FBG KL	OB		8	4200	3 6	5000	5700
28	ROZINANTE	KTH	SA/OD	FBG			6 4	6650	3 9	8900	10100
1968 BOATS											
21 4	SOUTH-COAST 21	SLP	SAIL	FBG KL	OB		6 11	2000	3	2250	2600
23	SOUTH-COAST 2 BERTH	SLP	SAIL	FBG KL	OB		7 3	3750	2 10	3250	3800
23	SOUTH-COAST 4 BERTH	SLP	SAIL	FBG KL	OB		7 3	3750	2 10	4100	4750
25 6	SOUTH-COAST 25	SLP	SAIL	FBG KL	OB		8	4200	3 6	4850	5550
28	ROZINANTE	KTH	SA/OD	FBG KL	OB		6 4	6650	3 9	8600	9900
1967 BOATS											
21 4	SOUTH-COAST 21	SLP	SAIL	FBG KL	OB		6 11	2000	3	2200	2550
23	SOUTH-COAST 23 DAYSA	SLP	SAIL	FBG KL	OB		7 3	3750	2 10	3050	3550
23	SOUTH-COAST 23 DAYSA	SLP	SAIL	FBG KL	IB	8	7 3	3750	2 10	3350	3900
23	SOUTH-COAST 4 BERTH	SLP	SAIL	FBG KL	OB		7 3	3750	2 10	4150	4800
23	SOUTH-COAST 4 BERTH	SLP	SAIL	FBG KL	IB	8	7 3	3750	2 10	4450	4950
25 6	SOUTH-COAST 25	SLP	SAIL	FBG KL	OB		8	4200	3 6	4750	5450
28	ROZINANTE	KTH	SA/OD	FBG KL	OB		6 4	6650	3 9	4500	9750
1966 BOATS											
21 4	SOUTH-COAST 21	SLP	SAIL	FBG KL	OB		6 11	2000	3	2000	2400
23	SOUTH-COAST	SLP	SAIL	FBG KL	OB		7 3		2 10	3250	3750
23	SOUTH-COAST	SLP	SAIL	FBG KL	IB	8	7 3		2 10	3050	3550
23	SOUTH-COAST 4 SLPR	SLP	SAIL	FBG KL	OB	7D	7 3		2 10	4050	4700
23	SOUTH-COAST 4 SLPR	SLP	SAIL	FBG KL	IB	8	7 3		2 10	3450	4200
23	SOUTH-COAST 4 SLPR	SLP	SAIL	FBG KL	IB	7D	7 3		2 10	3650	4200
28	ROZINANTE	KTH	SA/OD	FBG KL	OB		6 4		3 9	4600	5300
1965 BOATS											
21 4	SOUTH-COAST 21	SLP	SAIL	FBG KL	OB		6 11			2000	2350
23	SOUTH-COAST	SLP	SAIL	FBG	OB					3550	4100
23	SOUTH-COAST 23	SLP	SAIL	FBG	OB					3550	4100
28	ROZINANTE	KTH	SA/OD	FBG KL			6 4		3 9	4450	5100
1946 BOATS											
33 8	RHODES 33	SLP	SAIL	WD	KL		6 10		5	17500	19900

SOUTH FREEPORT YACHT BASN INC

Call 1-800-327-6929 for BUC Personalized Evaluation Service
Or, for 1965 to 1966 boats, sign onto www.BUCValuPro.com

SOUTH HANTS MARINE

Call 1-800-327-6929 for BUC Personalized Evaluation Service
Or, for 1979 to 1983 boats, sign onto www.BUCValuPro.com

SOUTH SEAS BOAT CO INC

Call 1-800-327-6929 for BUC Personalized Evaluation Service
Or, for 1960 to 1961 boats, sign onto www.BUCValuPro.com

SOUTHAMPTON MARINE CO

BAJA
BERLIN NJ 08033   COAST GUARD MFG ID- SMP   See inside cover to adjust price for area

LOA FT IN	NAME AND/ OR MODEL	TOP/ RIG	BOAT TYPE	-HULL- MTL TP	TP	----ENGINE--- # HP	MFG	BEAM FT IN	WGT LBS	DRAFT FT IN	RETAIL LOW	RETAIL HIGH

--------------- 1975 BOATS ---------------

31	1 BAJA 31 FISHERMAN	FB	SDNSF	FBG SV	IB	250	CHRY	11 2	11000	3	16900	19200
31	1 BAJA 31 SPORTSMAN	OP	UTL	FBG SV	IB	225-350		11 2	10000	3	16200	19500
	IB 216D GM 20700		23000, IB T230-T260			18400 20800, IBT140D-T225D					21700	26600

--------------- 1974 BOATS ---------------

| 31 | 1 | SDN | | FBG | IB | 225 | MRCR | 11 | 1 | 3 | 15100 | 17100 |
| 31 | 1 SPORTSMAN | | | FBG | IB | 225 | MRCR | 11 | 1 | 3 | 13200 | 15000 |

--------------- 1973 BOATS ---------------

31	1 BAJA 31	SF		FBG SV	IB	225		11 2		3	12700	14500
31	1 BARNEGAT	SDN		FBG SV	IB	225		11 2		3	14500	16500
31	1 CANYON-RUNNER	SF		FBG SV	IB	225		11 2		3	12700	14500

SOUTHCOAST BOATS

COAST GUARD MFG ID- TSA

Call 1-800-327-6929 for BUC Personalized Evaluation Service
Or, for 1980 boats, sign onto www.BUCValuPro.com

SOUTHERN MARINE CO

Call 1-800-327-6929 for BUC Personalized Evaluation Service
Or, for 1960 to 1961 boats, sign onto www.BUCValuPro.com

SOUTHERN MARINE LTD

Call 1-800-327-6929 for BUC Personalized Evaluation Service
Or, for 1967 to 1977 boats, sign onto www.BUCValuPro.com

SOUTHERN OCEAN SHIPYARD

DORSET ENGLAND   See inside cover to adjust price for area

LOA FT IN	NAME AND/ OR MODEL	TOP/ RIG	BOAT TYPE	-HULL- MTL TP	TP	----ENGINE--- # HP	MFG	BEAM FT IN	WGT LBS	DRAFT FT IN	RETAIL LOW	RETAIL HIGH

--------------- 1981 BOATS ---------------

29 8	CONTENTION 30	SLP	SA/RC	FBG KL	IB	9D		10 4	6000	5 8	19100	21200
32 10	CONTENTION 33	SLP	SA/RC	FBG KL	IB	10D	BUKH	10 6	10080	6	32800	36400
35 11	HIGH-TENSION 36	SLP	SA/RC	FBG KL	IB	30D	FORD	11 8	15120	6 9	50000	54900
60	OCEAN 60	SCH	SA/CR	FBG KL	IB	80D	FORD	15	38000	7 7	248000	272500
75	OCEAN 75	KTH	SA/CR	FBG KL	IB	100D	PERK	17	87360	8 6	**	**

--------------- 1980 BOATS ---------------

29 8	CONTENTION 30	SLP	SA/RC	FBG KL	IB	9D	SOLU	10 4	6000	5 8	18500	20600
32 10	CONTENTION 33	SLP	SA/RC	FBG KL	IB	10D	BUKH	10 6	10080	6	31500	35100
35 11	HIGH-TENSION 36	SLP	SA/RC	FBG KL	IB	30D	WATE	11 8	15120	6 9	48100	52800
60	OCEAN 60	SCH	SA/CR	FBG KL	IB	80D	FORD	15	42560	7 7	247500	272000
75	OCEAN 75	KTH	SA/CR	FBG KL	IB	115D	PERK	17	87360	8 6	**	**

--------------- 1979 BOATS ---------------

29 8	CONTENTION 30	SLP	SA/CR	FBG KL	IB	9D	SOLU	10 4	6000	5 8	17600	20000
32 10	CONTENTION 33	SLP	SA/CR	FBG KL	IB	10D	BUKH	10 6	10080	6	30600	34000
35 11	HIGH-TENSION 36	SLP	SA/CR	FBG KL	IB	30D	WATE	11 8	15120	6 9	46800	51500
60	OCEAN 60	SCH	SA/CR	FBG KL	IB	80D	FORD	15	42560	7 7	239500	263500
75	OCEAN 75	KTH	SA/CR	FBG KL	IB	115D	PERK	17	87360	8 6	**	**

--------------- 1978 BOATS ---------------

29 8	CONTENTION 30	SLP	SA/CR	FBG KL	IB	D		10	6000		17100	19500
31 10	PIONIER 10	SLP	SA/CR	FBG KL	IB	D		9 10	9000	5 11	26500	29500
32 10	CONTENTION 33	SLP	SA/CR	FBG KL	IB	D		10	10000		29500	32700
35 11	HIGH-TENSION 36	SLP	SA/CR	FBG KL	IB	D		11 8	13000		39300	43700
42 3	SPANKER 42	SLP	SA/CR	FBG KL	IB	D		12 3	22500	7 1	74700	82000
75	OCEAN 75	KTH	SA/CR	FBG KL	IB	D		17	90000		**	**

--------------- 1975 BOATS ---------------

31 10	PIONIER 10	SLP	SA/CR	FBG KL	IB	D		9 10	8960	5 11	24500	27200
35 9	HIGH-TENSION 36	SLP	SA/CR	FBG KL	IB	D		11 7		6 7	39000	43400
42 3	SPANKER 42	SLP	SA/CR	FBG KL	IB	D		12 3	24640	7 1	73100	80300
71	OCEAN 71	KTH	SA/CR	FBG KL	IB	D		17 5	64064	8 1	310000	340500

--------------- 1974 BOATS ---------------

31 10	PIONIER 10	SLP	SA/CR	FBG KL	IB	D		9 10	8960	5 11	24000	26700
42 3	SPANKER 12.8	SLP	SA/CR	FBG KL	IB	D		12 3	24640	7 1	71600	78700
53 2	GALLANT 53	SLP	SA/CR	FBG KL	IB	D		13 1		7 4	140500	154500
71	OCEAN 71	KTH	SA/CR	FBG KL	IB	D		17 5	64064	8 1	303000	333000

--------------- 1973 BOATS ---------------

31 10	PIONIER 10	SLP	SA/RC	FBG KL	IB	D		9 10	8960	5 11	23600	26200
42 3	SPANKER 42	SLP	SA/CR	FBG KL	IB	D		12 3	24640	7 1	70300	77300
53 2	GALLANT 53	SLP	SA/CR	FBG KL	IB	D		13 1		7 4	138500	152500
53 2	GALLANT 53	KTH	SA/CR	FBG KL	IB	D		13 1		7 4	139000	152500
71	OCEAN 71	KTH	SA/RC	FBG KL	IB	D		17 5	64064	8 1	296500	326000
71 5	ESCAPE	KTH	MS	FBG KL	IB	D		19 9		7 10	300000	329500

--------------- 1972 BOATS ---------------

32	PIONIER 10	SLP	SA/CR	FBG KL	IB	D		10	8960	5 11	23100	25700
41 2	REBEL 41	SLP	SA/CR	FBG KL	IB	D		10 11	700	6 7	4000	4650
53 2	GALLANT 53	SLP	SA/CR	FBG KL	IB	D		13 1	1050	7 4	102500	112500
53 2	GALLANT 53	KTH	SA/CR	FBG KL	IB	D		13 1	1050	7 4	102500	112500
71	OCEAN 71	KTH	SA/CR	FBG KL	IB	D		17 5	64064	8 1	290000	319000

--------------- 1971 BOATS ---------------

32	PIONIER 10	SLP	SA/RC	FBG KL	IB	D		10		5	22600	25100
36	EXCALIBUR 36	SLP	SA/RC	FBG KL	IB	D		10		5 11	38300	42600
41 2	REBEL 41	SLP	SA/RC	FBG KL	IB	D		10 11		6 7	63500	69700
53 2	GALLANT 53	SLP	SA/RC	FBG KL	IB	D		13 1		7 4	132500	145500
53 2	GALLANT 53	KTH	SA/RC	FBG KL	IB	D		13 1		7 4	132500	145500
71	OCEAN 71	KTH	SA/RC	FBG KL	IB	D		17		8	283500	311500

--------------- 1969 BOATS ---------------

30	PIONIER 30	SLP	SA/RC	FBG KL	IB			8		4 8	12700	14400
31	HARMONY 31	SLP	SA/RC	FBG KL	IB			9 2		4 8	22900	25500
36	EXCALIBUR 36	SLP	SA/RC	FBG KL	IB			10		5 11	15800	18000
41 2	REBEL 41	SLP	SA/RC	FBG KL	IB			10 11		6 7	45900	50400
53 2	GALLANT 53	SLP	SA/RC	FBG KL	IB			13 1		7 4	**	**
53 2	GALLANT 53	KTH	SA/RC	FBG KL	IB			13 1		7 4	**	**
71	OCEAN 71	KTH	SA/RC	FBG KL	IB			17	64000	8 1	268000	294500

SOUTHERN OFFSHORE LTD

TARPON SPRINGS FL 34286   See inside cover to adjust price for area
FORMERLY SOUTHERN OFFSHORE YACHTS INC

For more recent years, see the BUC Used Boat Price Guide, Volume 1 or Volume 2

LOA FT IN	NAME AND/ OR MODEL	TOP/ RIG	BOAT TYPE	-HULL- MTL TP	TP	----ENGINE--- # HP	MFG	BEAM FT IN	WGT LBS	DRAFT FT IN	RETAIL LOW	RETAIL HIGH

--------------- 1983 BOATS ---------------

| 25 7 | DAWSON 26 | SCH | SA/CR | FBG KC | IB | D | | 8 | 5700 | 5 4 | 14300 | 16300 |

SOUTHERN SAILS INC

SKIPPER YACHTS   See inside cover to adjust price for area
SEMINOLE FL 33542   COAST GUARD MFG ID- XUT

For more recent years, see the BUC Used Boat Price Guide, Volume 1 or Volume 2

LOA FT IN	NAME AND/ OR MODEL	TOP/ RIG	BOAT TYPE	-HULL- MTL TP	TP	----ENGINE--- # HP	MFG	BEAM FT IN	WGT LBS	DRAFT FT IN	RETAIL LOW	RETAIL HIGH

--------------- 1983 BOATS ---------------

17 2	SKIPPERS-MATE	SLP	SAIL	FBG SK	OB			7 1	1200	1	2000	2400
18 9	SKIPPER CUDDY SHOAL	SLP	SAIL	FBG DS	OB			6 8	1900	2	2650	3100
19	SKIFFIE	OP	RNBT	FBG DS	OB			6 8	2000	2	2600	3050
19	SKIFFIE	OP	RNBT	FBG DS	IB	D		6 8	2000	2	**	**
20	SKIPPER 20 SHOAL	SLP	SAIL	FBG KL	OB			6 8	2000	2	2850	3300

--------------- 1982 BOATS ---------------

17 2	SKIPPERS-MATE	SLP	SAIL	FBG SK	OB			7 1	1200	1	1900	2250
18 9	SKIPPER CUDDY SHOAL	SLP	SAIL	FBG DS	OB			6 8	1900	2	2550	2950
19	SKIFFIE	OP	RNBT	FBG DS	OB			6 8	2000	2	2600	3050
19	SKIFFIE	OP	RNBT	FBG DS	IB	D		6 8	2000	2	**	**
20	SKIPPER 20 SHOAL	SLP	SAIL	FBG KL	OB			6 8	2000	2	2700	3100

--------------- 1981 BOATS ---------------

18 9	SKIPPER CUDDY SHOAL	SLP	SAIL	FBG DS	OB			6 8	1900	2	2400	2750
19	SKIFFIE	OP	RNBT	FBG DS	OB			6 8	2000	2	2600	3000
19	SKIFFIE	OP	RNBT	FBG DS	IB	D		6 8	2000	2	**	**
20	SKIPPER 20 SHOAL	SLP	SAIL	FBG KL	OB			6 8	2000	2	2500	2950

--------------- 1980 BOATS ---------------

| 18 9 | SKIPPER CUDDY | SLP | SAIL | FBG DS | OB | | | 6 8 | 1900 | 2 | 2300 | 2650 |
| 19 | SKIFFIE | | | FBG DS | OB | | | 6 8 | 1800 | 2 | 2400 | 2800 |

LOA FT IN	NAME AND/ OR MODEL	TOP/ RIG	BOAT TYPE	-HULL- MTL TP	----ENGINE--- TP # HP MFG	BEAM FT IN	WGT LBS	DRAFT FT IN	RETAIL LOW	RETAIL HIGH
---	--- 1980 BOATS									
20	SKIPPER	SLP	SAIL	FBG KL	OB	6 8	2000	2	2400	2800
---	--- 1979 BOATS									
18 9	SKIPPER CUDDY	SLP	SAIL	FBG KL	OB	6 8	1850	2	2150	2550
20	SKIPPER	SLP	SAIL	FBG KL	OB	6 8	2000	2	2350	2700
---	--- 1978 BOATS									
20	SKIPPER	SLP	SAIL	FBG KL	OB	6 8	1950	1 11	2200	2600
20	SKIPPER	SLP	SAIL	FBG KL	IB 8D	6 8		1 11	3750	4350

SOUTHERN YACHTS
COAST GUARD MFG ID- SDY

Call 1-800-327-6929 for BUC Personalized Evaluation Service
Or, for 1972 to 1986 boats, sign onto www.BUCValuPro.com

SOUTHWEST BOAT CORP

Call 1-800-327-6929 for BUC Personalized Evaluation Service
Or, for 1960 to 1961 boats, sign onto www.BUCValuPro.com

SOUTHWEST MFG CO
ARKANSAS TRAVELER - RESORTER

Call 1-800-327-6929 for BUC Personalized Evaluation Service
Or, for 1959 to 1961 boats, sign onto www.BUCValuPro.com

SOUTHWIND YACHTS
COAST GUARD MFG ID- XTS

Call 1-800-327-6929 for BUC Personalized Evaluation Service
Or, for 1980 boats, sign onto www.BUCValuPro.com

SOVEREIGN YACHT CO INC
LARGO FL 33540   COAST GUARD MFG ID- XVG See inside cover to adjust price for area

For more recent years, see the BUC Used Boat Price Guide, Volume 1 or Volume 2

LOA FT IN	NAME AND/ OR MODEL	TOP/ RIG	BOAT TYPE	-HULL- MTL TP	----ENGINE--- TP # HP MFG	BEAM FT IN	WGT LBS	DRAFT FT IN	RETAIL LOW	RETAIL HIGH
---	--- 1983 BOATS									
17	ADVENTURE 17-A	SLP	SA/CR FBG KL	OB	7		1350	1 10	2000	2350
17	ADVENTURE 17-B	SLP	SA/CR FBG KL	OB	7		1350	1 10	2100	2500
18	SOVEREIGN 18	SLP	SA/CR FBG KL	OB	7		1900	2 4	2500	2900
23	ADVENTURE 23	SLP	SA/CR FBG KL	OB	8		3250	3 8	4150	4850
23	ADVENTURE 23	SLP	SA/CR FBG KL	OB 7D BMW	8		3350	3 8	4900	5650
23	ADVENTURE 23 SHOAL	SLP	SA/CR FBG KL	OB	8		3250	2 4	4150	4850
23	ADVENTURE 23 SHOAL	SLP	SA/CR FBG KL	OB 7D BMW	8		3600	2 4	5200	5950
24	PRINCESS 24	SLP	SA/CR FBG KL	OB	8		3350	3 8	4550	5200
24	PRINCESS 24	SLP	SA/CR FBG KL	OB 7D BMW	8		3600	3 8	5300	6100
24	PRINCESS SHOAL 24	SLP	SA/CR FBG KL	OB	8		3350	2 4	4550	5200
24	PRINCESS SHOAL 24	SLP	SA/CR FBG KL	OB 7D BMW	8		3600	2 4	5300	6100
---	--- 1982 BOATS									
17	ADVENTURE 17	SLP	SA/CR FBG KL	OB	7		1350	1 10	1700	2000
17	SOVEREIGN 5.0	SLP	SA/CR FBG KL	OB	7		1350	1 10	2200	2550
23	ADVENTURE 23	SLP	SA/CR FBG KL	OB	8		3350	2 4	3800	4400
23	ADVENTURE 23 DEEP	SLP	SA/CR FBG KL	OB	8		3250	3 8	3900	4550
23	ADVENTURE 23 SHOAL	SLP	SA/CR FBG KL	OB	8		3250	2 4	3900	4550
23	SOVEREIGN 7.0	SLP	SA/CR FBG KL	OB	8		3350	2 4	4200	4900
23	SOVEREIGN 7.0	SLP	SA/CR FBG KL	OB 8D REN	8		3600	2 4	4900	5600
24	PRINCESS 24	SLP	SA/CR FBG KL	OB	8		3350	2 4	4200	4900
24	PRINCESS SHOAL 24	SLP	SA/CR FBG KL	IB 8D REN	8		3600	2 4	5000	5750
---	--- 1981 BOATS									
17	SOVEREIGN 5.0	SLP	SA/CR FBG KL	OB	7		1350	1 10	1800	2150
23	SOVEREIGN 7.0	SLP	SA/CR FBG KL	OB	8		3350	2 4	3750	4400
23	SOVEREIGN 7.0	SLP	SA/CR FBG KL	IB 8D REN	8		3600	2 4	4600	5300
---	--- 1980 BOATS									
17	SOVEREIGN 5.0	SLP	SA/CR FBG KL	OB	7		1350	1 10	1750	2050
23	SOVEREIGN 7.0	SLP	SA/CR FBG KL	OB	8		3350	2 4	3600	4200
23	SOVEREIGN 7.0	SLP	SA/CR FBG KL	IB 8D REN	8		3600	2 4	4400	5050
---	--- 1979 BOATS									
23	SOVEREIGN 7.0	SLP	SA/CR FBG KL	OB	8		3200	2 2	3350	3900

SOVEREIGN YACHTS INC
DIV OF KALIK INC   See inside cover to adjust price for area
STAMFORD CT 06902   COAST GUARD MFG ID- XVE

LOA FT IN	NAME AND/ OR MODEL	TOP/ RIG	BOAT TYPE	-HULL- MTL TP	----ENGINE--- TP # HP MFG	BEAM FT IN	WGT LBS	DRAFT FT IN	RETAIL LOW	RETAIL HIGH
---	--- 1981 BOATS									
30	KALIK 30	SLP	SAIL F/S KL	IB 15D YAN	10 5	7582	5 7	18400	20400
32 9	KALIK 33	SLP	SAIL F/S KL	IB 22D YAN	11	10700	6	25300	28100
39 6	KALIK 40	SLP	SAIL F/S KL	IB 47D PATH	12 9	18500	6 8	46100	50700
43 9	KALIK 44	CUT	SAIL F/S KL	IB 47D PATH	13 9	25000	6 6	60700	66700
---	--- 1980 BOATS									
30	KALIK 30	SLP	SAIL F/S KL	IB 15D YAN	10 5	7582	5 7	17200	19500
32 9	KALIK 33	SLP	SAIL F/S KL	IB 22D YAN	11	10988	6	24800	27500
39 6	KALIK 40	SLP	SAIL F/S KL	IB 47D PATH	12 9	18000	6 8	42700	47500
41 4	KALIK 414	SLP	SA/RC F/S KL	IB 35D YAN	11 9	16000		42300	47000
44	KALIK 44	SLP	SAIL F/S KL	IB 52D PERK	13 9	22000	6	56400	62000
---	--- 1979 BOATS									
30	KALIK 30	SLP	SAIL F/S KL	IB 15D YAN	10 5	7582	5 7	16400	18700
32 9	KALIK 33	SLP	SAIL F/S KL	IB 22D YAN	11	10700	6	23600	26300
39	KALIK 39	SLP	SAIL F/S KC	IB D PERK				40300	44700
42	KALIK 42	SLP	SAIL F/S KL	IB 47D PERK	13 9	20900	6	49300	54200

SOVEREL MARINE INC
N PALM BEACH FL 33410   COAST GUARD MFG ID- SVM See inside cover to adjust price for area

For more recent years, see the BUC Used Boat Price Guide, Volume 1 or Volume 2

LOA FT IN	NAME AND/ OR MODEL	TOP/ RIG	BOAT TYPE	-HULL- MTL TP	----ENGINE--- TP # HP MFG	BEAM FT IN	WGT LBS	DRAFT FT IN	RETAIL LOW	RETAIL HIGH
---	--- 1983 BOATS									
33	SOVEREL 33-15/16	SLP	SA/RC FBG KL	IB	11	11000	5 10	21600	24000
35 10	SOVEREL 36	SLP	SA/RC FBG KC	IB 16D REN	10 8	14500	3 9	29100	32400
35 10	SOVEREL 36	SLP	SA/RC FBG KL	IB 30D WEST	10 8	14500	3 9	29300	32500
35 10	SOVEREL 36	SLP	SA/RC FBG KC	IB 16D REN	10 8	14500	3 9	29100	32400
43	SOVEREL 43	SLP	SA/RC FBG KL	IB D	14	18000	8	47700	52400
48	SOVEREL 48	KTH	SA/CR FBG KC	IB 85D FORD	13	28000	5	73600	80800
---	--- 1982 BOATS									
29 11	SOVEREL 30 3/4-RIG	SLP	SA/RC FBG KL	OB	11	7000	5 4	12400	14100
29 11	SOVEREL 30 3/4-RIG	SLP	SA/RC FBG KL	IB 11D- 16D	11	7000	5 4	12600	14300
29 11	SOVEREL 30 MASTHEAD	SLP	SA/RC FBG KL	OB	11	7000	5 4	12400	14100
29 11	SOVEREL 30 MASTHEAD	SLP	SA/RC FBG KL	IB 11D- 16D	11	7000	5 4	12600	14300
35 10	SOVEREL 36	SLP	SA/RC FBG KC	IB 16D REN	10 8	14500	3 9	27800	30700
35 10	SOVEREL 36	SLP	SA/RC FBG KL	IB 30D WEST	10 8	14500	3 9	27800	30800
35 10	SOVEREL 36	SLP	SA/RC FBG KC	IB 16D REN	10 8	14500	3 9	27800	30700
48	SOVEREL 48	KTH	SA/CR FBG KC	IB 85D FORD	13	28000	5	69700	76600
---	--- 1981 BOATS									
29 11	SOVEREL 30 3/4-RIG	SLP	SA/RC FBG KL	IB 11D UNIV	11	7000	5 4	12000	13600
29 11	SOVEREL 30 MASTHEAD	SLP	SA/RC FBG KL	IB 11D- 16D	11	7000	5 4	12000	13600
35 10	SOVEREL 36 FIN KEEL	SLP	SA/RC FBG KL	IB 16D REN	10 8	14500	3 9	26200	29100
39	SOVEREL 39	SLP	SA/RC FBG KL	IB D	12	13500	7 6	28500	31700
42	SOVEREL 42	SLP	SA/RC FBG KL	IB D	13	16000	7 6	37800	41800
48	SOVEREL 48	KTH	SA/CR FBG KC	IB 85D FORD	13	28000	5	66100	72600
---	--- 1980 BOATS									
29 11	SOVEREL 30 3/4-RIG	SLP	SA/RC FBG KL	IB	11	7000	5 4	11400	12900
29 11	SOVEREL 30 3/4-RIG	SLP	SA/RC FBG KL	IB 11D UNIV	11	7000	5 4	11500	13100
29 11	SOVEREL 30 MASTHEAD	SLP	SA/RC FBG KL	IB	11	7000	5 4	11400	12900
29 11	SOVEREL 30 MASTHEAD	SLP	SA/RC FBG KL	IB 11D UNIV	11	7000	5 4	11500	13100
35 10	SOVEREL 36	SLP	SA/RC FBG KL	IB 30D WEST	10 8	14500	3 9	24900	27700
35 10	SOVEREL 36 FIN KEEL	SLP	SA/RC FBG KL	IB 30D WEST	10 8	14500	4	25700	28600
48	SOVEREL 48	KTH	SA/CR FBG KC	IB 85D FORD	13	28000	5	63500	69800
---	--- 1979 BOATS									
30	SOVEREL 30	SLP	SA/RC FBG CB	IB D	11	7000	5 6	11200	12700
30	SOVEREL 30	SLP	SA/RC FBG CB	IB D	11	7000		11200	12700
36	SOVEREL 36	SLP	SA/RC FBG KL	IB D	10 10	16000		26800	29800
36	SOVEREL 36	SLP	SA/RC FBG CB	IB D	10 10	16000	6 6	26800	29800
48	SOVEREL 48	KTH	SA/RC FBG KC	IB D	13	29000		62200	68400
---	--- 1978 BOATS									
29 11	SOVEREL 36	SLP	SA/RC FBG KL	IB 16D REN	10 8	14000	4	10800	12300
35 10	SOVEREL 36	SLP	SA/RC FBG KL	IB 26D WEST	10 8	14000	4	23100	25600
35 10	SOVEREL 36	SLP	SA/RC FBG KL	IB 26D WEST	10 8	14000	4	23100	25600
36 7	SOVEREL 37	SLP	SA/RC FBG KL	IB D	9 4	12000	3	20500	22800
36 7	SOVEREL 37	KTH	SA/RC FBG KL	IB D	9	12000	3	20500	22800
48	SOVEREL 48	KTH	SA/RC FBG KC	IB 85D FORD	13	28000	5	59800	65700
---	--- 1977 BOATS									
26	SOVEREL MORC RACER	SLP	SA/RC FBG KL	OB	10	5000	4 9	6450	7400
26	SOVEREL MORC RACER	SLP	SA/RC FBG KL	IB 7D WEST	10	5000	4 9	6800	7850
36	SOVEREL 36	SLP	SA/RC FBG KC	IB 30D WEST	11	16000	4	25400	28200

LOA FT	LOA IN	NAME AND/ OR MODEL	TOP/ RIG	BOAT TYPE	HULL MTL	HULL TP	ENGINE TP	ENGINE # HP	ENGINE MFG	BEAM FT	BEAM IN	WGT LBS	DRAFT FT	DRAFT IN	RETAIL LOW	RETAIL HIGH
		1977 BOATS														
36		SOVEREL 36	SLP	SA/RC	FBG	KL	IB	30D	WEST	11		16000	6	6	25400	28200
36	7	SOVEREL 37	SLP	SA/CR	FBG	KC	IB	30	UNIV	9	4	12000	3	6	19700	21900
36	7	SOVEREL 37	SLP	SA/CR	FBG	KC	IB	25D	WEST	9	4	12000	3	6	20000	22300
36	7	SOVEREL 37	KTH	SA/CR	FBG	KC	IB	30	UNIV	9	4	12000	3	6	19700	21900
36	7	SOVEREL 37	KTH	SA/CR	FBG	KC	IB	25D	WEST	9	4	12000	3	6	20000	22300
41	3	SOVEREL 41	SLP	SA/CR	FBG	KC	IB	30	UNIV	11		18000	4		33800	37600
41	3	SOVEREL 41	SLP	SA/CR	FBG	KC	IB	17D	VLVO	11		18000	4		34200	37900
41	3	SOVEREL 41	SLP	SA/CR	FBG	KC	IB	45D	WEST	11		18000	4		34600	38400
41	3	SOVEREL 41	YWL	SA/CR	FBG	KC	IB	30	UNIV	11		18000	4		33800	37600
41	3	SOVEREL 41	YWL	SA/CR	FBG	KC	IB	17D	VLVO	11		18000	4		34200	37900
41	3	SOVEREL 41	YWL	SA/CR	FBG	KC	IB	45D	WEST	11		18000	4		34600	38400
48		SOVEREL 48	KTH	SA/CR	FBG	KL	IB	80D	LEHM	13		28000	5		58100	63900
		1976 BOATS														
26		SOVEREL 26	SLP	SA/RC	FBG	KL	OB			10		5000	4	9	6300	7250
30		MARK III 30	CUT	SA/RC	FBG	KC	IB	30	UNIV	9	4	9500			14000	15900
30		MARK III 30	CUT	SA/RC	FBG	KC	IB	20D-	25D	9	4	9500			14100	16000
30		SOVEREL 30 MK III	CUT	SAIL	FBG	KC	IB	30	UNIV	9	4	9580	3	6	14100	16000
30		SOVEREL 30 MK III	CUT	SAIL	FBG	KC	IB	20D-	25D	9	4	9580	3	6	14200	16200
35	10	SOVEREL 36	SLP	SAIL	FBG	KC	IB	25D	WEST	10	8	15000	6	6	23300	25900
36	7	SOVEREL 37	SLP	SA/RC	FBG	CB	IB	30	UNIV	9	4	12000	3	6	19300	21400
36	7	SOVEREL 37	SLP	SA/RC	FBG	CB	IB	25D	VLVO	9	4	12000	3	6	19500	21700
36	7	SOVEREL 37	SLP	SA/RC	FBG	CB	IB	25D	WEST	9	4	12000	3	6	19500	21700
36	7	SOVEREL 37	KTH	SA/RC	FBG	CB	IB	30	UNIV	9	4	12000	3	6	19300	21400
36	7	SOVEREL 37	KTH	SA/RC	FBG	CB	IB	25D	VLVO	9	4	12000	3	6	19500	21700
36	7	SOVEREL 37	KTH	SA/RC	FBG	CB	IB	25D	WEST	9	4	12000	3	6	19500	21700
36	7	SOVEREL 37	SLP	SAIL	FBG	KC	IB	30	UNIV	9	4	12000	3	6	19300	21400
36	7	SOVEREL 37	SLP	SAIL	FBG	KC	IB	25D	VLVO	9	4	12000	3	6	19500	21700
36	7	SOVEREL 37	SLP	SAIL	FBG	KC	IB	25D	WEST	9	4	12000	3	6	19500	21700
36	7	SOVEREL 37	KTH	SAIL	FBG	KC	IB	30	UNIV	9	4	12000	3	6	19300	21400
36	7	SOVEREL 37	KTH	SAIL	FBG	KC	IB	25D	VLVO	9	4	12000	3	6	19500	21700
36	7	SOVEREL 37	KTH	SAIL	FBG	KC	IB	25D	WEST	9	4	12000	3	6	19500	21700
41	3	SOVEREL 41	SLP	SA/RC	FBG	KC	IB	30	UNIV	11		18000			33000	36700
41	3	SOVEREL 41	SLP	SA/RC	FBG	KC	IB	17D	VLVO	11		18000			33300	37000
41	3	SOVEREL 41	SLP	SA/RC	FBG	KC	IB	45D	WEST	11		18000			33700	37500
41	3	SOVEREL 41	YWL	SA/RC	FBG	KC	IB	30	UNIV	11		18000			33000	36700
41	3	SOVEREL 41	YWL	SA/RC	FBG	KC	IB	17D	VLVO	11		18000			33300	37000
41	3	SOVEREL 41	YWL	SA/RC	FBG	KC	IB	45D	WEST	11		18000			33700	37500
41	3	SOVEREL 41	SLP	SAIL	FBG	CB	IB	30	UNIV	11		18000	4		33000	36700
41	3	SOVEREL 41	SLP	SAIL	FBG	CB	IB	17D	VLVO	11		18000	4		33300	37000
41	3	SOVEREL 41	SLP	SAIL	FBG	CB	IB	45D	WEST	11		18000	4		33700	37500
41	3	SOVEREL 41	YWL	SAIL	FBG	CB	IB	30	UNIV	11		18000	4		33000	36700
41	3	SOVEREL 41	YWL	SAIL	FBG	CB	IB	17D	VLVO	11		18000	4		33300	37000
41	3	SOVEREL 41	YWL	SAIL	FBG	CB	IB	45D	WEST	11		18000	4		33700	37500
48		SOVEREL 48	KTH	SA/CR	FBG	KC	IB	85D	LEHM	13		28000	5		56800	62400
		1975 BOATS														
30		SOVEREL 30 MK III	SLP	SAIL	FBG	KC	IB	30	UNIV	9	4	9580	3	6	13800	15700
30		SOVEREL 30 MK III	SLP	SAIL	FBG	KC	IB	20D-	25D	9	4	9580	3	6	13900	15800
35	10	SOVEREL 36	SLP	SAIL	FBG	KC	IB	25D	WEST	10	8	15080	6	6	22900	25400
36	7	SOVEREL 37	SLP	SAIL	FBG	KC	IB	25D	VLVO	9	4	12000	9	6	19100	21200
36	7	SOVEREL 37	SLP	SAIL	FBG	KC	IB	25D	WEST	9	4	12000	9	6	19100	21200
36	7	SOVEREL 37	KTH	SAIL	FBG	KC	IB	25D	VLVO	9	4	12000	9	6	19100	21200
36	7	SOVEREL 37	KTH	SAIL	FBG	KC	IB	25D	WEST	9	4	12000	9	6	19100	21200
41	3	SOVEREL 41	SLP	SAIL	FBG	CB	IB	30	UNIV	11		18000	10		32300	35900
41	3	SOVEREL 41	SLP	SAIL	FBG	CB	IB	25D	VLVO	11		18000	10		32700	36300
41	3	SOVEREL 41	SLP	SAIL	FBG	CB	IB	45D	WEST	11		18000	10		33000	36600
41	3	SOVEREL 41	YWL	SAIL	FBG	CB	IB	30	UNIV	11		18000	10		32300	35900
41	3	SOVEREL 41	YWL	SAIL	FBG	CB	IB	25D	VLVO	11		18000	10		32700	36300
41	3	SOVEREL 41	YWL	SAIL	FBG	CB	IB	45D	WEST	11		18000	10		33000	36600
48		SOVEREL 48	KTH	SA/CR	FBG	KC	IB	75D	WEST	13		28000			55500	61000
		1974 BOATS														
30		SOVEREL 30 MK III	SLP	SAIL	FBG	KC	IB	30	UNIV	9	4	9500	3	6	13400	15200
30		SOVEREL 30 MK III	SLP	SAIL	FBG	KC	IB	25D	WEST	9	4	9500	3	6	13500	15400
36	7	SOVEREL 37	SLP	SAIL	FBG	KC	IB	30	UNIV	9	4	12000	9	6	18700	20700
36	7	SOVEREL 37	SLP	SAIL	FBG	KC	IB	25D	WEST	9	4	12000	9	6	18900	21000
36	7	SOVEREL 37	KTH	SAIL	FBG	KC	IB	30	UNIV	9	4	12000	9	6	18700	20700
36	7	SOVEREL 37	KTH	SAIL	FBG	KC	IB	25D	WEST	9	4	12000	9	6	18900	21000
41	3	SOVEREL 41	SLP	SAIL	FBG	CB	IB	30	UNIV	11		18000	10		31600	35100
41	3	SOVEREL 41	SLP	SAIL	FBG	CB	IB	25D	VLVO	11		18000	10		32000	35600
41	3	SOVEREL 41	SLP	SAIL	FBG	CB	IB	45D	WEST	11		18000	10		32300	35900
41	3	SOVEREL 41	YWL	SAIL	FBG	CB	IB	30	UNIV	11		18000	10		31600	35100
41	3	SOVEREL 41	YWL	SAIL	FBG	CB	IB	25D	VLVO	11		18000	10		32000	35600
41	3	SOVEREL 41	YWL	SAIL	FBG	CB	IB	45D	WEST	11		18000	10		32300	35900
48		SOVEREL 48	KTH	SA/CR	FBG	CB	IB	85D	WEST	13	3	28000	4		54500	59900
		1973 BOATS														
29	11	SOVEREL 30 MK III	SLP	SAIL	FBG	KC	IB	25D	VLVO	9	6	9580	4		13400	15200
36	8	SOVEREL 37		SAIL	FBG	KC	IB	25D	VLVO	9	6	13000	3		19800	21900
41	3	SOVEREL 41		SAIL	FBG	CB	IB	16D	VLVO	11		18000	4		31300	34800
41	3	SOVEREL 41		SAIL	FBG	CB	IB	45D	WEST	11		18000	4		31700	35200
41	3	SOVEREL 41	YWL	SAIL	FBG	CB	IB	30	UNIV	11		18000	4		31000	34500
41	3	SOVEREL 41	YWL	SAIL	FBG	CB	IB	16D	VLVO	11		18000	4		31300	34800
41	3	SOVEREL 41	YWL	SAIL	FBG	CB	IB	45D	WEST	11		18000	4		31700	35200
48		SOVEREL 48	KTH	SA/CR	FBG	KC	IB	85D		13		28000	5		53400	58700
		1972 BOATS														
29	11	SOVEREL 30	SLP	SAIL	FBG		IB	15D	VLVO	8	4	9000	4		12200	13900
29	11	SOVEREL 30	CUT	SAIL	FBG		IB	15D	VLVO	8	4	9000	4		12200	13900
36	8	SOVEREL 37	SLP	SAIL	FBG		IB	25D	VLVO	9	6	13000	3	6	19300	21500
36	8	SOVEREL 37	KTH	SAIL	FBG		IB	25D	VLVO	9	6	13000	3	6	19300	21500
41	3	SOVEREL 41	CUT	SAIL	FBG		IB	16	VLVO	11		18000	4		30300	33700
41	3	SOVEREL 41	CUT	SAIL	FBG		IB	45D	WEST	11		18000	4		31000	34500
41	3	SOVEREL 41	YWL	SAIL	FBG		IB	16	VLVO	11		18000	4		30300	33700
41	3	SOVEREL 41	YWL	SAIL	FBG		IB	45D	WEST	11		18000	4		31000	34500
45		SOVEREL 45	KTH	SA/CR	FBG	KC	IB			12		22000	4		40400	44900
		1971 BOATS														
29	11	SOVEREL 30	SLP	SAIL	FBG		IB	30	UNIV	8	4	9000	4		11900	13500
29	11	SOVEREL 30	SLP	SAIL	FBG		IB	15D	VLVO	8	4	9000	4		11900	13500
35		SOVEREL 35	SLP	SA/RC	FBG	KC	IB	D		9	4		3	6	19800	22000
35		SOVEREL 35	KTH	SA/RC	FBG	KC	IB	D		9	4		3	6	19800	22000
36	8	SOVEREL 37		SAIL	FBG		IB	25D	VLVO	9	6	13000	3	6	19100	21200
41	3	SOVEREL 41		SAIL	FBG		IB	16	VLVO	11		18000	4		29500	32800
41	3	SOVEREL 41		SAIL	FBG		IB	30	UNIV	11		18000	4		29600	32900
41	3	SOVEREL 41		SAIL	FBG		IB	45D	WEST	11		18000	4		30200	33600
41	3	SOVEREL 41	YWL	SAIL	FBG		IB	16	VLVO	11		18000	4		29500	32800
41	3	SOVEREL 41	YWL	SAIL	FBG		IB	30	UNIV	11		18000	4		29600	32900
41	3	SOVEREL 41	YWL	SAIL	FBG		IB	45D	WEST	11		18000	4		30200	33600
		1970 BOATS														
28	9	SOVEREL 28	SLP	SA/CR	FBG	KC	IB	30		8	4	7500	3		9400	10700
28	9	SOVEREL 28	YWL	SA/CR	FBG	KC	IB	30		8	4	7500	3		9400	10700
28	9	SOVEREL MORC	SLP	SA/RC	FBG	KC	IB	30		8	4	7500	3		9400	10700
28	9	SOVEREL MORC	YWL	SA/RC	FBG	KC	IB	30		8	4	7500	3		9400	10700
29	11	SOVEREL 30	SLP	SAIL	FBG	KC	IB	30	UNIV	8	4	8900	4		11400	13000
29	11	SOVEREL 30	SLP	SAIL	FBG	KC	IB	15D	VLVO	8	4	9000	4		11600	13200
32	10	SOVEREL 33	SLP	SAIL	FBG	KC	IB	30	UNIV	9	4	11000	3	6	14400	16300
32	10	SOVEREL 33	SLP	SAIL	FBG	KC	IB	15D	VLVO	9	4	11000	3	6	14400	16400
38	7	SOVEREL 38	SLP	SAIL	FBG	KC	IB	15D	VLVO	11		16000	4		23700	26300
38	7	SOVEREL 38	YWL	SAIL	FBG	KC	IB	15D	VLVO	11		16000	4		23700	26300
		1969 BOATS														
28	9	SOVEREL 28	SLP	SAIL	FBG	KC	IB	15D	VLVO	8	4	7500	3		9350	10600
28	9	SOVEREL 28	YWL	SAIL	FBG	KC	IB	15D	VLVO	8	4	7500	3		9350	10600
28	9	SOVEREL MORC	SLP	SA/RC	FBG	KC	OB			8	4	7500	3		9150	10400
28	9	SOVEREL MORC	SLP	SA/RC	FBG	KC	IB			8	4	7500	3		9250	10500
28	9	SOVEREL MORC	SLP	SA/RC	FBG	KC	IB	15D	VLVO	8	4	7500	3		9350	10600
28	9	SOVEREL MORC	YWL	SA/RC	FBG	KC	OB			8	4	7500	3		9150	10400
28	9	SOVEREL MORC	YWL	SA/RC	FBG	KC	IB			8	4	7500	3		9250	10500
29	11	SOVEREL 30	SLP	SAIL	FBG	KC	IB	15D	VLVO	8	4	9000	4		11400	12900
32	10	SOVEREL 33	SLP	SAIL	FBG	KC	IB	30	UNIV	9	4	11000	3	6	14100	16000
32	10	SOVEREL 33	SLP	SAIL	FBG	KC	IB	15D	VLVO	9	4	11000	3	6	14100	16000
38	7	SOVEREL 38	SLP	SAIL	FBG	KC	IB	30	UNIV	11		16000	4		22900	25500
38	7	SOVEREL 38	SLP	SAIL	FBG	KC	IB	15D	VLVO	11		16000	4		23100	25700
38	7	SOVEREL 38	YWL	SAIL	FBG	KC	IB	30	UNIV	11		16000	4		22900	25500
		1968 BOATS														
28	7	SOVEREL MORC	SLP	SA/RC	FBG		OB			8	4	6500	3		7600	8750
28	7	SOVEREL MORC	SLP	SA/RC	FBG		IB	10-	30	8	4	6500	3		7650	8850
28	7	SOVEREL MORC	YWL	SA/RC	FBG		OB			8	4	6500	3		7600	8750
28	7	SOVEREL MORC	YWL	SA/RC	FBG		IB	10-	30	8	4	6500	3		7650	8850
28	9	SOVEREL 28	SLP	SAIL	FBG	KC	OB			8	4	7000	3		8250	9450
28	9	SOVEREL 28	SLP	SAIL	FBG	KC	IB	30		8	4	7000	3		8350	9600
28	9	SOVEREL 28	SLP	SAIL	FBG	KC	IB	15D		8	4	7000	3		8400	9700
28	9	SOVEREL 28	YWL	SAIL	FBG	KL	OB			8	4	7000	3		8250	9450
28	9	SOVEREL 28	YWL	SAIL	FBG	KL	IB	30		8	4	7000	3		8350	9600
28	9	SOVEREL 28	YWL	SAIL	FBG	KL	IB	15D		8	4	7000	3		8400	9700
32	10	SOVEREL 33	SLP	SAIL	FBG	KC	IB	30		9	4	11000	3	6	13800	15700
32	10	SOVEREL 33	SLP	SAIL	FBG	KC	IB	15D		9	4	11000	3	6	13800	15700
32	10	SOVEREL 33	YWL	SAIL	FBG	KC	IB	30		9	4	11000	3	6	13800	15700
32	10	SOVEREL 33	YWL	SAIL	FBG	KC	IB	15D		9	4	11000	3	6	13800	15700
36	7	SOVEREL 36	SLP	SAIL	FBG	KC	IB	30		11		16000	4	6	20800	23100
36	7	SOVEREL 36	SLP	SAIL	FBG	KC	IB	30D		11		16000	4	6	21000	23400
36	7	SOVEREL 36	YWL	SAIL	FBG	KC	IB	30		11		16000	4	6	20800	23100
36	7	SOVEREL 36	YWL	SAIL	FBG	KC	IB	30D		11		16000	4	6	21000	23400

 CONTINUED ON NEXT PAGE

LOA FT IN	NAME AND/ OR MODEL	TOP/ RIG	BOAT TYPE	-HULL- MTL TP	TP	----ENGINE--- # HP MFG	BEAM FT IN	WGT LBS	DRAFT FT IN	RETAIL LOW	RETAIL HIGH
						1967 BOATS					
28 7	SOVEREL MORC S	SLP	SA/RC FBG		OB		8 4	6500	3	7450	8550
28 9	SOVEREL 28	SLP	SA/CR FBG	KC	OB		8 4		3	8100	9300
28 9	SOVEREL 28	SLP	SA/CR FBG	KC	IB	30	8 4		3	9300	10600
28 9	SOVEREL 28	SLP	SA/CR FBG	KC	IB	15D	3	7000		8250	9500
28 9	SOVEREL 28	YWL	SA/CR FBG	KC	OB		8 4		3	8100	9300
28 9	SOVEREL 28	YWL	SA/CR FBG	KC	IB	30	8 4		3	9300	10600
32 11	SOVEREL 33	SLP	SA/CR FBG	KC	IB		9 4	11000	3 6	13500	15400
36 7	SOVEREL 36	SLP	SA/CR FBG	KC	IB	30	11	16000	4	20400	22700
						1966 BOATS					
28 9	SOVEREL 28	SLP	SAIL FBG	KC	IB	10- 30	8 4		3	9100	10400
29 9	SOVEREL MORC S	SLP	SA/RC FBG	KC	IB	15D	3			8250	9500
36 7	SOVEREL 36	SLP	SAIL FBG	KC	IB	30	11	16000	4	20100	22300
36 7	SOVEREL 36	SLP	SAIL FBG	KC	IB	D	11	16000	4	20300	22600
						1965 BOATS					
28 9	SOVEREL 28	SLP	SAIL FBG		IB	30				9000	10200
28 9	SOVEREL 28	YWL	SAIL FBG		IB	30				9000	10200
28 9	SOVEREL MORC S		SA/RC FBG		IB	30				8050	9250
28 9	SOVEREL MORC Y		SA/RC FBG		IB	10				8000	9200
36 7	SOVEREL 36	SLP	SAIL FBG		IB	30		16000		19800	22000
36 7	SOVEREL 36	YWL	SAIL FBG		IB	30		16000		19800	22000
						1964 BOATS					
28 9	SOVEREL 28	SLP	SAIL FBG		IB	30				8900	10100
28 9	SOVEREL 28	YWL	SAIL FBG		IB	30				8900	10100
28 9	SOVEREL MORC S		SA/RC FBG		IB	10				7900	9100
						1963 BOATS					
28 9	SOVEREL 28	SLP	SAIL FBG		IB	30				8700	10000
28 9	SOVEREL 28	YWL	SAIL FBG		IB	30				8700	10000
28 9	SOVEREL MORC		SA/RC FBG		IB	30				7850	9050
						1962 BOATS					
28 9	SOVEREL 28	SLP	SAIL FBG		IB	30				8600	9900
28 9	SOVEREL 28	YWL	SAIL FBG		IB	30				8600	9900
						1961 BOATS					
28 9	SOVEREL 28	SLP	SAIL FBG		IB	30				8550	9850

SPACE CRUISERS INC

Call 1-800-327-6929 for BUC Personalized Evaluation Service
Or, for 1968 to 1969 boats, sign onto www.BUCValuPro.com

SPACECRAFT BOATWORKS INC
COAST GUARD MFG ID- SPA

Call 1-800-327-6929 for BUC Personalized Evaluation Service
Or, for 1981 to 1990 boats, sign onto www.BUCValuPro.com

SPAN-AMERICA BOAT CO INC

Call 1-800-327-6929 for BUC Personalized Evaluation Service
Or, for 1960 to 1961 boats, sign onto www.BUCValuPro.com

SPARCRAFT INC

Call 1-800-327-6929 for BUC Personalized Evaluation Service
Or, for 1974 boats, sign onto www.BUCValuPro.com

SPAULDING CRAFT
COAST GUARD MFG ID- XUD

Call 1-800-327-6929 for BUC Personalized Evaluation Service
Or, for 1979 to 1983 boats, sign onto www.BUCValuPro.com

MYRON SPAULDING

Call 1-800-327-6929 for BUC Personalized Evaluation Service
Or, for 1960 to 1967 boats, sign onto www.BUCValuPro.com

R H SPEAS
SEE TORTOLA TRAWLERS

Call 1-800-327-6929 for BUC Personalized Evaluation Service
Or, for 1980 boats, sign onto www.BUCValuPro.com

SPECTRA BOATS
SPECTRA LEISURE PRODUCTS

Call 1-800-327-6929 for BUC Personalized Evaluation Service
Or, for 1970 boats, sign onto www.BUCValuPro.com

SPECTRA MARINE
COAST GUARD MFG ID- SPE

Call 1-800-327-6929 for BUC Personalized Evaluation Service
Or, for 1974 to 1977 boats, sign onto www.BUCValuPro.com

SPEED-CRAFT BOATS
RAUL ENTERPRISES   COAST GUARD MFG ID- SPB

Call 1-800-327-6929 for BUC Personalized Evaluation Service
Or, for 1971 to 1980 boats, sign onto www.BUCValuPro.com

SPENCER BOATS LTD
RICHMOND BC CANADA   COAST GUARD MFG ID- SBD See inside cover to adjust price for area

For more recent years, see the BUC Used Boat Price Guide, Volume 1 or Volume 2

LOA FT IN	NAME AND/ OR MODEL	TOP/ RIG	BOAT TYPE	-HULL- MTL TP	TP	----ENGINE--- # HP MFG	BEAM FT IN	WGT LBS	DRAFT FT IN	RETAIL LOW	RETAIL HIGH
						1983 BOATS					
31	SPENCER 31	SLP	SA/CR FBG	KL	IB	D	9 2	9350	5	38900	43200
33 9	SPENCER 34	SLP	SA/RC FBG	KL	IB	D	11 2	10000	6	41900	46500
35	SPENCER 35	SLP	SA/CR FBG	KL	IB	D	9 6	12000	5 3	50900	55900
42 3	SPENCER 42	SLP	SA/CR FBG	KL	IB	D	11 4	19000	6	97400	107000
43 9	SPENCER 44	SLP	SA/CR FBG	KL	IB	D	11 6	20000	6 6	107500	118000
43 9	SPENCER 44	KTH	SA/CR FBG	KL	IB	D	11 6	20000	6 6	110000	121000
44	SPENCER 1330	SLP	SA/CR FBG	KL	IB	D	13	24000	7	119500	131500
44	SPENCER 1330	KTH	SA/CR FBG	KL	IB	D	13	24000	7	122500	134500
53	SPENCER 53	SLP	SA/CR FBG	KL	IB	D	13 2	30000	7 6	194000	213500
53	SPENCER 53	KTH	SA/CR FBG	KL	IB	D	13 2	30000	7 6	198500	218000
						1982 BOATS					
31	SPENCER 31	SLP	SA/CR FBG	KL	IB	D	9 2	9350	5	36900	41000
33 9	SPENCER 34	SLP	SA/CR FBG	KL	IB	D	11 2	10000	6	39700	44100
35	SPENCER MKII 35	SLP	SA/CR FBG	KL	IB	D	9 6	12000	5 3	48200	53000
42 3	SPENCER 42	SLP	SA/CR FBG	KL	IB	D	11 4	19000	6	92600	102000
43 9	SPENCER 44	SLP	SA/CR FBG	KL	IB	D	11 6	20000	6 6	102500	112500
43 9	SPENCER 44	KTH	SA/CR FBG	KL	IB	D	11 6	20000	6 6	104500	114500
44	SPENCER 1330	SLP	SA/CR FBG	KL	IB	D	13	24000	7	114000	125000
44	SPENCER 1330	KTH	SA/CR FBG	KL	IB	D	13	24000	7	116500	128000
53	SPENCER 53	SLP	SA/CR FBG	KL	IB	D	13 2	30000	7 6	185000	203000
53	SPENCER 53	KTH	SA/CR FBG	KL	IB	D	13 2	30000	7 6	189000	207500
						1981 BOATS					
31	SPENCER 31	SLP	SA/CR FBG	KL	IB	D	9 2	9350	5	35000	38800
33 9	SPENCER 34	SLP	SA/RC FBG	KL	IB	D	11 2	10000	6	37600	41800
35	SPENCER 35	SLP	SA/CR FBG	KL	IB	D	9 6	12000	5 3	46000	50500
42 3	SPENCER 42	SLP	SA/CR FBG	KL	IB	D	11 4	19000	6	88100	96800
43 9	SPENCER 44	SLP	SA/CR FBG	KL	IB	D	11 6	20000	6 6	97500	107000
43 9	SPENCER 44	KTH	SA/CR FBG	KL	IB	D	11 6	20000	6 6	99100	109000
44	SPENCER 1330	SLP	SA/CR FBG	KL	IB	D	13	24000	7	108500	119000
44	SPENCER 1330	KTH	SA/CR FBG	KL	IB	D	13	24000	7	110500	121500
53	SPENCER 53	SLP	SA/CR FBG	KL	IB	D	13 2	30000	7 6	176000	193500
53	SPENCER 53	KTH	SA/CR FBG	KL	IB	D	13 2	30000	7 6	179500	197500
						1980 BOATS					
31	SPENCER 31	SLP	SA/CR FBG	KL	IB	D	9 2	9350	5	33600	37400
33 9	SPENCER 34	SLP	SA/RC FBG	KL	IB	D	11 2	10000	6	36200	40200
35	SPENCER 35	SLP	SA/CR FBG	KL	IB	D	9 6	12000	5 3	43800	48600
42 3	SPENCER 42	SLP	SA/CR FBG	KL	IB	D	11 4	19000	6	84600	93000
43 9	SPENCER 44	SLP	SA/CR FBG	KL	IB	D	11 6	20000	6 6	93600	103000
43 9	SPENCER 44	KTH	SA/CR FBG	KL	IB	D	11 6	20000	6 6	95100	104500
44	SPENCER 1330 AFT CPT	SLP	SA/CR F/S	KL	IB	D	13	24000	7	104000	114500
44	SPENCER 1330 AFT CPT	KTH	SA/CR F/S	KL	IB	D	13	24000	7	106000	116500
44	SPENCER 1330 CTR CPT	KTH	SA/CR F/S	KL	IB	D	13	24000	7	104000	114500
53	SPENCER 53 AFT CPT	SLP	SA/CR F/S	KL	OB	D	13 2	30000	7 6	168500	185000
53	SPENCER 53 AFT CPT	KTH	SA/CR F/S	KL	IB	D	13 2	30000	7 6	172000	189000
53	SPENCER 53 CTR CPT	SLP	SA/CR F/S	KL	IB	D	13 2	30000	7 6	168500	185000

SPENCER BOATS LTD   -CONTINUED   See inside cover to adjust price for area

LOA FT IN	NAME AND/ OR MODEL	TOP/ RIG	BOAT TYPE	HULL MTL TP	ENGINE TP # HP	MFG	BEAM FT IN	WGT LBS	DRAFT FT IN	RETAIL LOW	RETAIL HIGH
1980 BOATS											
53	SPENCER 53 CTR CPT	KTH	SA/CR	F/S KL IB	D		13 2	30000	7 6	172000	189000
1979 BOATS											
31	SPENCER 31	SLP	SA/RC	F/S KL IB	D		9 2	9350	5	32600	36200
33 8	SPENCER 34	SLP	SA/CR	F/S KL IB	D		11 2	9500	5 10	33300	37000
35	SPENCER 35	SLP	SA/CR	F/S KL IB	D		9 6	12000	5 3	42400	47100
42 3	SPENCER 42	SLP	SA/CR	F/S KL IB	D		11 4	19000	6	81800	89900
43 8	SPENCER 1330	SLP	SA/CR	F/S KL IB	D		13	24000	7	99200	109000
43 8	SPENCER 1330	KTH	SA/CR	F/S KL IB	D		13	24000	7	101000	111000
43 9	SPENCER 44	SLP	SA/CR	F/S KL IB	D		11 6	24000	6 6	99400	109000
43 9	SPENCER 44	KTH	SA/CR	F/S KL IB	D		11 6	24000	6 6	101500	111500
51	SPENCER 51	SLP	SA/RC	F/S KL IB	D		13 2	30000	7 5	146000	160500
51	SPENCER 51	KTH	SA/RC	F/S KL IB	D		13 2	30000	7 5	150000	165000
1978 BOATS											
31	SPENCER 31	SLP	SAIL	F/S KL IB	23D VLVO		9 2	9350	5	31700	35200
33 8	SPENCER 34	SLP	SAIL	F/S KL IB	12D		11 2	9500	5 10	32300	35900
35	SPENCER 35	SLP	SA/CR	F/S KL IB	23D VLVO		9 6	12000	5 3	41100	45700
35	SPENCER 35	KTH	SA/CR	F/S KL IB	60D VLVO		9 6	12000	5 3	41500	46100
42 3	SPENCER 42	SLP	SA/CR	F/S KL IB	60D PISC		11 4	19000	6	79600	87500
42 3	SPENCER 42	KTH	SA/CR	F/S KL IB	60D PISC		11 4	19000	6	80600	88600
43 8	SPENCER 1330 AFT CPT	SLP	SA/CR	F/S KL IB	60D PISC		13	24000	7	96100	105500
43 8	SPENCER 1330 AFT CPT	KTH	SA/CR	F/S KL IB	60D PISC		13	24000	7	98100	108000
43 9	SPENCER 44	SLP	SA/CR	F/S KL IB	60D PISC		11 6	24000	6 6	96400	106000
43 9	SPENCER 44	KTH	SA/CR	F/S KL IB	60D PISC		11 6	24000	6 6	98500	108500
44 4	SPENCER 1330 CTR CPT	SLP	SA/CR	F/S KL IB	60D PISC		13	24000	7	98700	108500
44 4	SPENCER 1330 CTR CPT	KTH	SA/CR	F/S KL IB	60D PISC		13	24000	7	101000	111000
51	SPENCER 51 AFT CPT	SLP	SA/CR	F/S KL IB	75D PISC		13 2	30000	7 5	141000	155000
51	SPENCER 51 AFT CPT	KTH	SA/CR	F/S KL IB	75D PISC		13 2	30000	7 5	145000	159500
51	SPENCER 51 CTR CPT	SLP	SA/CR	F/S KL IB	75D PISC		13 2	30000	7 5	141000	155000
51	SPENCER 51 CTR CPT	KTH	SA/CR	F/S KL IB	75D PISC		13 2	30000	7 5	145000	159500
1975 BOATS											
31	SPENCER 31	SLP	SAIL	F/S KL IB	D		9 2	9000	5	28300	31400
35	SPENCER 35	SLP	SAIL	F/S KL IB	D		9 6	12000	5 3	38200	42500
42 3	SPENCER 42	SLP	SAIL	F/S KL IB	D		11 4	19000	6	72900	80200
43 9	SPENCER 44	SLP	SAIL	F/S KL IB	D		11 6	24000	6 6	88400	97100
43 9	SPENCER 44	KTH	SAIL	F/S KL IB	D		11 6	24000	6 6	90800	99800
44 4	SPENCER 1330	SLP	SAIL	F/S KL IB	D		13	24000	7	90600	99600
44 4	SPENCER 1330	KTH	SAIL	F/S KL IB	D		13	24000	7	93400	102500
51	SPENCER 51	SLP	SAIL	F/S KL IB	D		13 2	30000	7 5	129500	142000
51	SPENCER 51	KTH	SAIL	F/S KL IB	D		13 2	30000	7 5	133000	146500
1971 BOATS											
35	S-35	SLP	SA/OD	FBG KL			9 6		5 3	**	**
1970 BOATS											
35	SPENCER 35		SA/OD	FBG KL			9 6		5 3	**	**
1969 BOATS											
35	SPENCER 35	SLP	SA/OD	FBG KL			9 6		5 3	**	**
1968 BOATS											
31	S-31	SLP	SAIL	FBG KL IB			9 2		4 9	25300	28100
35	S-35	SLP	SAIL	FBG KL IB			9 6		5 3	33600	37400
42 3	S-42	SLP	SAIL	FBG KL IB			11 4		6	62600	68800
42 3	S-42	KTH	SAIL	FBG KL IB			11 4		6	64700	71100
45	S-45	SLP	SAIL	FBG KL IB			11 7		6 4	93400	102500
45	S-45	KTH	SAIL	FBG KL IB			11 7		6 4	96700	106000
1967 BOATS											
16 7	SPENCER 17		RNBT	F/S	OB		6 2	850		2300	2700
18 9	SPENCER 19		RNBT	F/S	OB		6	1250		3450	4050
21 6	SPENCER 21		CR	F/S	IO	110		8		7950	9150
25 7	SPENCER 26		CR	F/S	IB	200		9		7100	8150
30	SPENCER 30		CR	F/S	IB	250		10 8		10900	12400
31	SPENCER 31	SLP	SA/CR	F/S KL IB	D		9 2		4 8	24800	27600
32	SPENCER 32		CR	F/S	IB	250		10 8		13700	15600
34	SPENCER 34		CR	F/S	IB	300		10 8		18600	20700
35	SPENCER 35	SLP	SA/CR	F/S KL IB	30		9 6		5 3	37500	41700
42 3	SPENCER 42	SLP	SA/CR	F/S KL IB	D		11 4		6	63800	70100
42 3	SPENCER 42	KTH	SA/CR	F/S KL IB	D		11 4		6	64500	70900
45 3	SPENCER 45		CR	F/S	IB	520		13 8		48400	53200
1966 BOATS											
35	SPENCER 35	SLP	SA/CR	FBG KL IB	30		9 6	12000	5 3	31400	34900
42 3	SPENCER 42	SLP	SA/CR	FBG KL IB			11 4	19000	6	60000	65900

SPENCER YACHTS INC

Call 1-800-327-6929 for BUC Personalized Evaluation Service
Or, for 1982 to 1983 boats, sign onto www.BUCValuPro.com

SPINDRIFT ONE DESIGNS
TALLEVAST FL 33588   See inside cover to adjust price for area

For more recent years, see the BUC Used Boat Price Guide, Volume 1 or Volume 2

LOA FT IN	NAME AND/ OR MODEL	TOP/ RIG	BOAT TYPE	HULL MTL TP	ENGINE TP # HP	MFG	BEAM FT IN	WGT LBS	DRAFT FT IN	RETAIL LOW	RETAIL HIGH
1983 BOATS											
16 1	REBEL	SLP	SA/OD	FBG CB			6 6	675	6	2700	3150
16 9	DAYSAILER I	SLP	SA/OD	FBG CB			6 3	525	7	2400	2800
19 2	MARINER	SLP	SA/OD	FBG CB			7	1200	10	3700	4300
19 2	RHODES 19	SLP	SA/OD	FBG CB			7	1000	10	3450	4000
21 6	SPINDRIFT 22	SLP	SA/OD	FBG			8			5750	6600
1982 BOATS											
16 1	REBEL	SLP	SA/OD	FBG CB			6 6	675	6	2550	2950
16 9	DAYSAILER I	SLP	SA/OD	FBG CB			6 3	525	7	2300	2700
19 2	MARINER	SLP	SA/OD	FBG CB			7	1200	10	3500	4100
19 2	RHODES 19	SLP	SA/OD	FBG CB			7	1000	10	3250	3800
19 2	RHODES 19	SLP	SA/OD	FBG KL			7	1240	3 3	3550	4150
1975 BOATS											
33	DRIFTER		TRWL	FBG	IB T 80D		10 3			26500	29500

SPIRIT YACHTS BY GLASTRON
A CONROY COMPANY   See inside cover to adjust price for area
AUSTIN TX 78759   COAST GUARD MFG ID- CEC
                         FORMERLY NORTH AMERICAN YACHTS

LOA FT IN	NAME AND/ OR MODEL	TOP/ RIG	BOAT TYPE	HULL MTL TP	ENGINE TP # HP	MFG	BEAM FT IN	WGT LBS	DRAFT FT IN	RETAIL LOW	RETAIL HIGH
1982 BOATS											
21 3	SPIRIT 6.5	SLP	SA/RC	FBG CB			7 10	2100	5	4200	4900
23	SPIRIT 23	SLP	SA/RC	FBG CB			7 11	2800	2 11	5500	6350
23	SPIRIT 23K	SLP	SA/RC	FBG KL			7 11	3150	3 6	6050	6950
28	SPIRIT 28	SLP	SA/RC	FBG KL IB	D		10	6900	4 10	17100	19400
1981 BOATS											
21 3	SPIRIT 6.5	SLP	SA/RC	FBG CB			7 10	2100	5	4000	4650
23	SPIRIT 23	SLP	SA/RC	FBG CB			7 11	2800	2 11	5250	6000
23	SPIRIT 23K	SLP	SA/RC	FBG KL			7 11	3150	3 6	5700	6550
28	SPIRIT 28	SLP	SA/RC	FBG KL IB	D		10	6900	4 10	16200	18400
1980 BOATS											
21 3	SPIRIT 6.5	SLP	SA/CR	FBG SK OB			7 10	2100	5	3800	4400
23	SPIRIT 23	SLP	SA/CR	FBG CB			7 11	2800	2 11	5000	5750
23	SPIRIT 23K	SLP	SA/CR	FBG KL			7 11	3150	3 6	5450	6250
28	SPIRIT 28 FIN	SLP	SA/CR	FBG KL IB	D		10	6900	4 10	15400	17500
28	SPIRIT 28 SHOAL	SLP	SA/CR	FBG KL IB	D		10	6900	4 10	15400	17500
1979 BOATS											
21 3	SPIRIT 6.5	SLP	SA/CR	FBG SK OB			7 10	2100		3650	4250
23	SPIRIT 23	SLP	SA/CR	FBG KC OB			7 11	2800		4800	5500
23	SPIRIT 23K	SLP	SA/RC	FBG KC OB			7 11	3150	3 6	5250	6000
27 11	SPIRIT 28	SLP	SA/CR	FBG KL IB	D		10	6300	4 8	13400	15300
1978 BOATS											
21 3	SPIRIT 6.5	SLP	SA/CR	FBG SK OB			7 10	2150	1 8	3550	4150
23	SPIRIT 23	SLP	SA/CR	FBG KC OB			7 11	2800	2 4	4600	5300
23	SPIRIT 23K	SLP	SA/CR	FBG KC OB			7 11	3150	3 6	5050	5800
1977 BOATS											
21	NORTH-AMERICAN	SLP	SA/CR	FBG SK OB			7 7	1800	1 9	3100	3600
23	NORTH-AMERICAN	SLP	SA/CR	FBG KC OB			7 11	2800	2	4450	5150
1976 BOATS											
23	NORTH-AMERICAN	SLP	SA/CR	FBG KC OB			7 11	2800	2	4250	4950

SPLENDOR CRAFT MFG CO INC
COAST GUARD MFG ID- SNC

Call 1-800-327-6929 for BUC Personalized Evaluation Service
Or, for 1980 boats, sign onto www.BUCValuPro.com

SPOILER YACHTS INC
COSTA MESA CA 92626   COAST GUARD MFG ID- SPY See inside cover to adjust price for area

For more recent years, see the BUC Used Boat Price Guide, Volume 1 or Volume 2

LOA FT IN	NAME AND/ OR MODEL	TOP/ RIG	BOAT TYPE	HULL MTL TP	ENGINE TP # HP	MFG	BEAM FT IN	WGT LBS	DRAFT FT IN	RETAIL LOW	RETAIL HIGH
1976 BOATS											
31 4	SPOILER 30	FB	SDNSF	FBG DV VD			11 6	10000	3	**	**
31 4	SPOILER 30 COHO	FB	SDN	FBG DV VD			11 6	10000	3	**	**

LOA FT	IN	NAME AND/ OR MODEL	TOP/ RIG	BOAT TYPE	-HULL- MTL	TP	TP	----ENGINE--- # HP	MFG	BEAM FT	IN	WGT LBS	DRAFT FT	IN	RETAIL LOW	RETAIL HIGH
		1975 BOATS														
31	4	SPOILER 30	FB	SDN	FBG	SV	VD	270-350		11	6	10000	3		19100	22200
		VD 120D-225D 23800 28600, VD T220-T255 21100 24100, VD T120D FORD													27900	31000
31	4	SPOILER 30	FB	SDNSF	FBG	SV	VD	390	OLDS	11	6	10000	3		18800	20900
31	4	SPOILER 30	FB	SDNSF	FBG	SV	VD	T233-T255		11	6	11000	3		19600	22100
		1974 BOATS														
32	4	SPOILER	FB	SDN	FBG		IO	255	MRCR	11	6	10000	3		21900	24300
		VD 255 MRCR 18000 20000, IO 325 MRCR 22800 25300, VD 325 MRCR													18700	20800
		IO 350 WAUK 23100 25600, VD 350 WAUK 18900 21000, IO 212D GM													27800	30900
		VD 212D GM 25600 28500, IO 225D CAT 25700 28500, VD 225D CAT													23700	26300
		IO 240D CUM 26000 28800, VD 240D CUM 24000 26600, IO T215 WAUK													23800	26500
		VD T215 WAUK 19400 21500, IO T220 CRUS 23900 26600, VD T220 CRUS													22100	24600
		IO T225 MRCR 24000 26700, IO T225 OMC 24000 26700, VD T225													19500	21700
		IO T255 MRCR 24600 27400, IO T255 WAUK 24600 27400, VD T255 MRCR													20000	22300
		VD T255 WAUK 22700 25300, IO T140D FORD 26800 29800, VD T140D FORD													24800	27500
		IO T180D FORD 28400 31600, VD T180D FORD 26200 29100														
32	4	SPOILER	FB	SF	FBG		IO	255	MRCR	11	6	10000	3		21700	24200
		VD 255 MRCR 15300 17400, IO 325 MRCR 22400 24900, VD 325 MRCR													15800	17900
		IO 350 WAUK 22600 25200, VD 350 WAUK 15900 18100, IO 212D GM													31100	34500
		VD 212D GM 23000 25600, IO 225D CAT 31300 34800, VD 225D CAT													23200	25800
		IO 240D CUM 31500 35000, VD 240D CUM 23300 25900, IO T215 WAUK													23200	25800
		VD T215 WAUK 16400 18600, IO T220 CRUS 23300 25900, VD T220 CRUS													16400	18700
		IO T225 MRCR 23400 26000, IO T225 OMC 23400 26000, VD T225													16500	18700
		IO T255 MRCR 23900 26500, IO T255 WAUK 23900 26500, VD T255													16800	19100
		IO T140D FORD 27500 30600, VD T140D FORD 20400 22600, IO T180D FORD													28800	32000
		VD T180D FORD 21300 23700														
40		SPOILER	FB	TCMY	FBG		VD	T325	MRCR	15	3	21000	3	10	44500	49400
40		SPOILER	FB	TCMY	FBG		IO	T225D	CAT	15	3	21000	3	10	63500	69800
47		SPOILER	FB	SF	FBG		IB	T225D	CAT	16	7	34000	4	6	75000	82400
47		SPOILER	FB	TRWL	FBG		IB	T225D	CAT	16	7	34000	4	6	89200	98000
47		SPOILER FORMAL	FB	MY	FBG		IB	T225D	CAT	16	7	34000	4	6	90000	98900
		1973 BOATS														
32	4	SPOILER	FB	SDN	FBG		IO	255	MRCR	11	6	10000	3		22600	25100
		VD 255 MRCR 16900 19200, IO 325 MRCR 23500 26100, VD 325 MRCR													17600	20000
		IO 350 WAUK 23800 26500, VD 350 WAUK 18200 20200, IO 212D GM													28700	31900
		VD 212D GM 24900 27700, IO 225D CAT 26500 29500, VD 225D CAT													23100	25600
		IO 240D CUM 26800 29800, VD 240D CUM 23300 25900, IO T140 FORD													22900	25500
		VD T140 FORD 17100 19500, IO T180 FORD 23800 26500, VD T180 FORD													18200	20300
		IO T215 WAUK 24600 27300, VD T215 WAUK 18800 20900, IO T220 CRUS													24700	27500
		VD T220 CRUS 18900 21000, IO T225 MRCR 24800 27600, IO T225 OMC													24800	27600
		VD T225 19000 21100, IO T255 MRCR 25500 28300, IO T255 WAUK													29000	32200
		VD T255 19300 21400														
32	4	SPOILER	FB	SF	FBG		IO	255	MRCR	11	6	10000	3		22500	25000
		VD 255 MRCR 14700 16700, IO 325 MRCR 23200 25700, VD 325 MRCR													15200	17200
		IO 350 WAUK 23400 26000, VD 350 WAUK 15300 17400, IO 212D GM													32100	35700
		VD 212D GM 22400 24900, IO 225D CAT 32400 36000, VD 225D CAT													22600	25100
		IO 240D CUM 32600 36200, VD 240D CUM 22700 25200, IO T215 WAUK													24000	26600
		VD T215 WAUK 15700 17900, IO T220 CRUS 24100 26700, VD T220 CRUS													15800	17900
		IO T225 MRCR 24100 26800, IO T225 OMC 24100 26800, VD T225													15800	18000
		IO T255 MRCR 24600 27400, IO T255 WAUK 30300 33600, VD T255 MRCR													16200	18400
		VD T255 WAUK 20000 22300, IO T140D FORD 28500 31600, VD T140D FORD													19900	22100
		IO T180D FORD 29800 33100, VD T180D FORD 20700 23000														
40		SPOILER	FB	TCMY	FBG		VD	T325	MRCR	15	3	21000	3	10	42800	47600
40		SPOILER	FB	TCMY	FBG		IO	T225D	CAT	15	3	21000	3	10	65600	72100
47		SPOILER	FB	SF	FBG		IB	T225D	CAT	16	7	34000	4	6	72200	79400
47		SPOILER	FB	TRWL	FBG		IB	T225D	CAT	16	7	34000	4	6	85800	94300
47		SPOILER FORMAL	FB	MY	FBG		IB	T225D	CAT	16	7	34000	4	6	86600	95200
		1972 BOATS														
32		SPOILER		SDN	FBG		VD	270	MRCR	11	6	10000	3		15900	18100
32		SPOILER		SDN	FBG		IO	212D-240D		11	6	10500	3		29200	33100
32		SPOILER		SDN	FBG		VD	T215-T255		11	6	11000	3		20000	22900
32		SPOILER		SF	FBG		VD	270	MRCR	11	6	10000	3		13700	15600
32		SPOILER		SF	FBG		IO	212D-240D		11	6	10500	3		32400	36600
32		SPOILER		SF	FBG		VD	T215-T255		11	6	11000	3		18500	21100
40		SPOILER		TCMY	FBG		VD	T325	MRCR	15	3	21000	3	10	41200	45700
40		SPOILER		TCMY	FBG		IO	T225D	CAT	15	3	21000	3	10	67700	74400
		1971 BOATS														
31	9	SPOILER 30		SDN	FBG		IO	270-325		11	6	8500	3		22600	26000
		IB 220D GM 21300 23600, IO T225 MRCR 25200 28000, IB T270 CHRY													17000	19300
31	9	SPOILER 30		SF	FBG		IO	270-325		11	6	8500	3		22000	25100
31	9	SPOILER 30		SF	FBG		IB	220D	GM	11	6	10000	3		17400	19700
31	9	SPOILER 30		SF	FBG		IB	T225	CHRY	11	6	10000	3		13900	15800
39	11	SPOILER 40		OFF	FBG		IB	128D	FORD	13	6	26000	4		52800	58000
39	11	SPOILER 40		OFF	FBG		IB	T128D	FORD	13	6	27000	4		57100	62800
41	9	COHO		TCMY	FBG		IB	T325	MRCR	14	10	19000	4	2	43200	48000
41	9	COHO		TCMY	FBG		IB	T225D	CAT	14	10	20000	4	2	49400	54300
		1970 BOATS														
31	9	SPOILER 30	FB	SDN	FBG		IO	270-325		11	6	8200	3		23300	26800
31	9	SPOILER 30	FB	SDN	FBG		IO	T155	OMC	11	6	8200	3		23900	26500
31	9	SPOILER 30	FB	SDN	FBG		IO	T170D	CRUS	11	6	8500	3		29600	32900
31	9	SPOILER 30	FB	SF	FBG		IO	270-325		11	6	8150	3		22600	26000
31	9	SPOILER 30	FB	SF	FBG		IO	T127D	AERO	11	6	8700	3		27800	30900
41	9	SPOILER 40		TCMY	FBG		IO	T325	MRCR	14	10	19000	4	2	73300	80500
41	9	SPOILER 40		TCMY	FBG		IB	T325	MRCR	14	10	19000	4	2	41000	45600
41	9	SPOILER 40		TCMY	FBG		IB	T225D	CAT	14	10	20000	4	2	47100	51800

SPORT-CRAFT BOATS

PERRY FL 32347 COAST GUARD MFG ID- SXK See inside cover to adjust price for area

For more recent years, see the BUC Used Boat Price Guide, Volume 1 or Volume 2

LOA FT	IN	NAME AND/ OR MODEL	TOP/ RIG	BOAT TYPE	-HULL- MTL	TP	TP	----ENGINE--- # HP	MFG	BEAM FT	IN	WGT LBS	DRAFT FT	IN	RETAIL LOW	RETAIL HIGH
		1983 BOATS														
16	1	ADVENTURER 170	ST	RNBT	FBG	DV	OB			6	4	955			1800	2150
16	1	FISHERMAN 170	OP	FSH	FBG	SV	OB			6	2	1050			1950	2300
16	4	C-GULL 170	ST	RNBT	FBG	TR	OB			6	4	1150			2200	2550
16	4	C-GULL 170	ST	RNBT	FBG	TR	IO	120	MRCR	6	4				1950	2350
16	4	C-GULL 170	ST	RNBT	FBG	TR	IO	120	OMC	6	4				1950	2300
16	4	C-GULL 170	ST	RNBT	FBG	TR	IO	120-140		6	4				2150	2500
17	1	SPORTSMAN 180	ST	RNBT	FBG	DV	OB			7	2	1300			2350	2750
17	1	SPORTSMAN 180 B/R	ST	RNBT	FBG	DV	OB			7	2	1300			2550	2950
17	1	SPORTSMAN 180 B/R	ST	RNBT	FBG	DV	IO	120-188		7	2				2350	2900
18	2	SPORTSMAN 190	ST	RNBT	FBG	DV	OB			7	8	1700			2950	3450
18	2	SPORTSMAN 190	ST	RNBT	FBG	DV	IO	120-200		7	8				2700	3400
18	2	SPORTSMAN 190 B/R	ST	RNBT	FBG	DV	OB			7	8	1700			3150	3650
18	2	SPORTSMAN 190 B/R	ST	RNBT	FBG	DV	IO	120-200		7	8				2750	3400
18	11	CAPRICE 190	ST	CUD	FBG	DV	OB			7		1540			2900	3400
20		FISHERMAN 200	OP	CTRCN	FBG	DV	OB			7	6	1800			3500	4100
20	9	C-EAGLE 210	ST	CUD	FBG	DV	IO	120-230		8	1	3300			4750	5850
20	9	FISHERMAN 210	ST	FSH	FBG	DV	IO	120-230		8	1	3300			5050	6150
22	2	FISHERMAN 222	ST	CUD	FBG	DV	OB			7	6	2800			5700	6550
22	2	FISHERMAN 222	ST	CUD	FBG	DV	IO	138-260		7	6				4550	5600
22	2	FISHERMAN 222	ST	CUD	FBG	DV	IO	130D-165D		7	6				5700	6850
22	2	FISHERMAN 230	ST	FSH	FBG	DV	IO	138-140		8		3434			5700	6550
22	2	FISHERMAN 230	ST	FSH	FBG	DV	SE	155	OMC	8		3434			6250	7150
22	2	FISHERMAN 230	ST	FSH	FBG	DV	IO	170-200		8		3434			5600	6650
22	2	FISHERMAN 230	ST	FSH	FBG	DV	SE	205	OMC	8		3434			6250	7150
22	2	FISHERMAN 230	ST	FSH	FBG	DV	IO	225-260		8		3434			5900	6950
22	2	FISHERMAN 230	ST	FSH	FBG	DV	IO	130D-165D		8		3434			8200	9800
22	2	FISHERMAN 230	ST	FSH	FBG	DV	SE	T155-T205		8		3434			6250	7150
22	2	SPORTSMAN 230	ST	RNBT	FBG	DV	IO	138-140		8		3434			5100	5900
22	2	SPORTSMAN 230	ST	RNBT	FBG	DV	SE	155	OMC	8		3434			6400	7350
22	2	SPORTSMAN 230	ST	RNBT	FBG	DV	IO	170-200		8		3434			5000	5950
22	2	SPORTSMAN 230	ST	RNBT	FBG	DV	SE	205	OMC	8		3434			6400	7350
22	2	SPORTSMAN 230	ST	RNBT	FBG	DV	IO	225-260		8		3434			5250	6250
22	2	SPORTSMAN 230	ST	RNBT	FBG	DV	IO	130D-165D		8		3434			6200	7400
22	2	SPORTSMAN 230	ST	RNBT	FBG	DV	SE	T155-T205		8		3434			6400	7350
24	2	C-EAGLE 250	ST	CUD	FBG	DV	IO	138-140		8		4830			7700	8850
24	2	C-EAGLE 250	ST	CUD	FBG	DV	SE	155	OMC	8		4400			8600	9900
24	2	C-EAGLE 250	ST	CUD	FBG	DV	IO	170-200		8		4830			7550	8950
24	2	C-EAGLE 250	ST	CUD	FBG	DV	SE	205	OMC	8		4400			8600	9900
24	2	C-EAGLE 250	ST	CUD	FBG	DV	IO	225-260		8		4830			7850	9250
24	2	C-EAGLE 250	ST	CUD	FBG	DV	IO	130D-165D		8		4830			9050	10600
24	2	C-EAGLE 250	ST	CUD	FBG	DV	IO	T120-T140		8		4830			8300	9900
24	2	C-EAGLE 250	ST	CUD	FBG	DV	SE	T155	OMC	8		4400			8600	9900
24	2	C-EAGLE 250	ST	CUD	FBG	DV	IO	T170-T188		8		4830			8350	9650
24	2	C-EAGLE 250	ST	CUD	FBG	DV	SE	T205	OMC	8		4400			8600	9900
24	2	C-EAGLE 250	HT	CUD	FBG	DV	IO	138-140		8		4830			7700	8850
24	2	C-EAGLE 250	HT	CUD	FBG	DV	SE	155	OMC	8		4830			9150	10400
24	2	C-EAGLE 250	HT	CUD	FBG	DV	IO	170-200		8		4830			7550	8950
24	2	C-EAGLE 250	HT	CUD	FBG	DV	SE	205	OMC	8		4830			9150	10400
24	2	C-EAGLE 250	HT	CUD	FBG	DV	IO	225-260		8		4830			7850	9250
24	2	C-EAGLE 250	HT	CUD	FBG	DV	IO	130D-165D		8		4830			9050	10600
24	2	C-EAGLE 250	HT	CUD	FBG	DV	IO	T120-T140		8		4830			8300	9900

96th ed. - Vol. III CONTINUED ON NEXT PAGE 559

LOA FT	IN	NAME AND/ OR MODEL	TOP/ RIG	BOAT TYPE	-HULL- MTL	TP	ENGINE TP	# HP	MFG	BEAM FT	IN	WGT LBS	DRAFT FT	IN	RETAIL LOW	RETAIL HIGH
		1983 BOATS														
24	2	C-EAGLE 250	HT	CUD	FBG	DV	SE	T155	OMC	8		4830			9100	10400
24	2	C-EAGLE 250	HT	CUD	FBG	DV	IO	T170-T188		8		4830			8350	9650
24	2	C-EAGLE 250	HT	CUD	FBG	DV	SE	T205	OMC	8		4830			9100	10400
24	2	C-EAGLE 250	FB	CUD	FBG	DV	IO	138-140		8		4830			7700	8850
24	2	C-EAGLE 250	FB	CUD	FBG	DV	SE	155	OMC	8		4830			9150	10400
24	2	C-EAGLE 250	FB	CUD	FBG	DV	IO	170-200		8		4830			7550	8950
24	2	C-EAGLE 250	FB	CUD	FBG	DV	SE	205	OMC	8		4830			9150	10400
24	2	C-EAGLE 250	FB	CUD	FBG	DV	IO	225-260		8		4830			7850	9250
24	2	C-EAGLE 250	FB	CUD	FBG	DV	IO	130D-165D		8		4830			9050	10600
24	2	C-EAGLE 250	FB	CUD	FBG	DV	IO	T120-T140		8		4830			8300	9900
24	2	C-EAGLE 250	FB	CUD	FBG	DV	SE	T155	OMC	8		4830			9150	10400
24	2	C-EAGLE 250	FB	CUD	FBG	DV	IO	T170-T188		8		4830			8350	9650
24	2	C-EAGLE 250	FB	CUD	FBG	DV	SE	T205	OMC	8		4830			9150	10400
24	2	FAMILY CRUISER 242	ST	CR	FBC	DV	IO	138-260		8		4400			7150	8650
24	2	FAMILY CRUISER 242	ST	CR	FBG	DV	IO	130D-165D		8		4400			8400	9950
24	2	FAMILY CRUISER 242	ST	CR	FBG	DV	IO	T120-T185		8		4400			7750	9250
24	2	FISHERMAN 242	ST	FSH	FBG	DV	IO	138-260		8		4400			7550	9100
24	2	FISHERMAN 242	ST	FSH	FBG	DV	IO	130D-165D		8		4400			10500	12300
24	2	FISHERMAN 242	ST	FSH	FBG	DV	IO	T120-T185		8		4400			8150	9750
24	2	FISHERMAN 250	ST	CUD	FBG	DV	SE	155-205		8		4400			8600	9900
24	2	FISHERMAN 250	ST	CUD	FBG	DV	SE	T155-T205		8		4400			8600	9900
24	2	FISHERMAN 250	OP	FSH	FBG	DV	IO	138-260		8		5210			8600	10400
24	2	FISHERMAN 250	OP	FSH	FBG	DV	IO	130D-165D		8		5210			11900	13900
24	2	FISHERMAN 250	OP	FSH	FBG	DV	IO	T120-T188		8		5210			9350	10900
24	2	FISHERMAN 250	HT	FSH	FBG	DV	IO	138-260		8		5210			8600	10400
24	2	FISHERMAN 250	HT	FSH	FBG	DV	IO	130D-165D		8		5210			11900	13900
24	2	FISHERMAN 250	HT	FSH	FBG	DV	IO	T120-T188		8		5210			9350	10900
24	2	SPORT FISHERMAN 250	FB	SF	FBG	DV	IO	170-260		8		5210			9300	11100
24	2	SPORT FISHERMAN 250	FB	SF	FBG	DV	IO	T120-T170		8		5210			10100	11900
24	2	SPORTFISHERMAN 250	HT	SF	FBG	DV	SE	155-205		8		5210			9000	10600
24	2	SPORTFISHERMAN 250	HT	SF	FBG	DV	SE	T155-T205		8		5210			9000	10200
24	2	SPORTFISHERMAN 250	FB	SF	FBG	DV	IO	138-140		8		5210			9450	10700
24	2	SPORTFISHERMAN 250	FB	SF	FBG	DV	SE	155	OMC	8		5210			8600	9900
24	2	SPORTFISHERMAN 250	FB	SF	FBG	DV	IO	200	VLVO	8		5210			9500	10800
24	2	SPORTFISHERMAN 250	FB	SF	FBG	DV	SE	205	OMC	8		5210			8650	9900
24	2	SPORTFISHERMAN 250	FB	SF	FBG	DV	IO	225	VLVO	8		5210			9600	10900
24	2	SPORTFISHERMAN 250	FB	SF	FBG	DV	IO	130D-165D		8		5210			11900	13900
24	2	SPORTFISHERMAN 250	FB	SF	FBG	DV	SE	T155	OMC	8		5210			9300	10500
24	2	SPORTFISHERMAN 250	FB	SF	FBG	DV	IO	T188	MRCR	8		5210			10300	11700
24	2	SPORTFISHERMAN 250	FB	SF	FBG	DV	SE	T205	OMC	8		5210			9300	10500
27		C-EAGLE	ST	CUD	FBG	DV	OB			10		6185			11300	12800
27		C-EAGLE 270	ST	CUD	FBG	DV	SE	205	OMC	10		6185			11300	12800
27		C-EAGLE 270	ST	CUD	FBG	DV	IO	225	VLVO	10		6185			10800	12300
		IB 225 VLVO 13300 15100, IO 228-230 10700 12200, IO 260 MRCR 11000 12500														
		IO 260 OMC 10900 12400, IO 260 VLVO 11100 12600, IB 260 13500 15400														
		IO 330 MRCR 11600 13200, IB 158D VLVO 16100 18300, IO 165D VLVO 12000 13700														
		IB 200D-235D 17200 20000, IO T138-T140 11400 13000														
27		C-EAGLE 270	ST	CUD	FBG	DV	SE	T155	OMC	10		6185			11300	12800
27		C-EAGLE 270	ST	CUD	FBG	DV	IO	T170-T200		10		6185			11600	13500
27		C-EAGLE 270	ST	CUD	FBG	DV	SE	T205	OMC	10		6185			11300	12800
27		C-EAGLE 270	ST	CUD	FBG	DV	IO	T225-T230		10		6185			12400	14100
27		C-EAGLE 270	ST	CUD	FBG	DV	IO	T130D-T165D		10		6185			14000	16900
27		C-EAGLE 270	HT	CUD	FBG	DV	OB			10		6185			11300	12800
27		C-EAGLE 270	HT	CUD	FBG	DV	SE	205	OMC	10		6185			11300	12800
27		C-EAGLE 270	HT	CUD	FBG	DV	IO	225-230		10		6185			10800	12300
		IO 260 MRCR 11000 12500, IO 260 OMC 10900 12400, IO 260 VLVO 11100 12600														
		IB 260 MRCR 13500 15300, IO 330 MRCR 11600 13200, IB 158D VLVO 16100 18300														
		IO 165D VLVO 12000 13700, IB 235D VLVO 18000 20000, IO T140 11300 12800														
27		C-EAGLE 270	HT	CUD	FBG	DV	SE	T155	OMC	10		6185			11300	12800
27		C-EAGLE 270	HT	CUD	FBG	DV	IO	T170-T200		10		6185			11600	13500
27		C-EAGLE 270	HT	CUD	FBG	DV	SE	T205	OMC	10		6185			11300	12800
27		C-EAGLE 270	HT	CUD	FBG	DV	IO	T225-T230		10		6185			12400	14100
27		C-EAGLE 270	HT	CUD	FBG	DV	IO	T130D-T165D		10		6185			14000	16900
27		C-EAGLE 270	FB	CUD	FBG	DV	OB			10		6185			11100	12600
27		C-EAGLE 270	FB	CUD	FBG	DV	SE	205	OMC	10		6185			11100	12600
27		C-EAGLE 270	FB	CUD	FBG	DV	IB	158D	VLVO	10		6185			16100	18300
27		C-EAGLE 270	FB	CUD	FBG	DV	IO	165D	VLVO	10		6185			12000	13700
27		C-EAGLE 270	FB	CUD	FBG	DV	IB	235D	VLVO	10		6185			18000	20000
27		C-EAGLE 270	FB	CUD	FBG	DV	SE	T155-T205		10		6185			11100	12600
27		C-EAGLE 270	FB	CUD	FBG	DV	IO	T130D-T165D		10		6185			14000	16900
27		FAMILY CRUISER 270	ST	CR	FBG	DV	SE	205	OMC	10		6800			11400	12900
27		FAMILY CRUISER 270	ST	CR	FBG	DV	IO	225	VLVO	10		6800			11400	12900
		IB 225 VLVO 14000 15900, IO 228-230 11300 12800, IO 260 MRCR 11500 13100														
		IO 260 OMC 11500 13100, IO 260 VLVO 11700 13200, IB 260 14200 16200														
		IO 330 MRCR 12200 13900, IB 158D VLVO 17500 19900, IO 165D VLVO 13100 14800														
		IB 200D-235D 19000 21300, IO T138-T140 12000 13700														
27		FAMILY CRUISER 270	ST	CR	FBG	DV	SE	T155	OMC	10		6800			11400	12900
27		FAMILY CRUISER 270	ST	CR	FBG	DV	IO	T170-T200		10		6800			12200	14200
27		FAMILY CRUISER 270	ST	CR	FBG	DV	SE	T205	OMC	10		6800			11400	12900
27		FAMILY CRUISER 270	ST	CR	FBG	DV	IO	T225-T230		10		6800			12900	14700
27		FAMILY CRUISER 270	ST	CR	FBG	DV	IO	T130D-T165D		10		6800			15000	18000
27		FISHERMAN 270	ST	FSH	FBG	DV	OB			10		6185			11000	12500
27		FISHERMAN 270	ST	FSH	FBG	DV	SE	205	OMC	10					10900	12400
27		FISHERMAN 270	ST	FSH	FBG	DV	IO	225	VLVO	10		6185			11400	12900
		IB 225 VLVO 13300 15100, IO 228-230 11300 12800, IO 260 MRCR 11600 13100														
		IO 260 OMC 11500 13100, IO 260 VLVO 11700 13300, IB 260 13500 15400														
		IO 330 MRCR 12300 14000, IB 158D VLVO 16100 18300, IO 165D VLVO 15000 17100														
		IB 200D-235D 17200 20000, IO T138-T140 12100 13700														
27		FISHERMAN 270	ST	FSH	FBG	DV	SE	T155	OMC	10					10900	12400
27		FISHERMAN 270	ST	FSH	FBG	DV	IO	T170-T200		10		6185			12300	14300
27		FISHERMAN 270	ST	FSH	FBG	DV	SE	T205	OMC	10					10900	12400
27		FISHERMAN 270	ST	FSH	FBG	DV	IO	T225-T230		10		6185			13100	14900
27		FISHERMAN 270	ST	FSH	FBG	DV	IO	T130D-T165D		10		6185			17500	21100
27		FISHERMAN 270	HT	FSH	FBG	DV	OB			10		6185			11000	12500
27		FISHERMAN 270	HT	FSH	FBG	DV	SE	205	OMC	10		6185			11000	12500
27		FISHERMAN 270	HT	FSH	FBG	DV	IO	225	VLVO	10		6185			11400	12900
		IB 225 VLVO 13300 15100, IO 228-230 11300 12800, IO 260 MRCR 11600 13100														
		IO 260 OMC 11500 13100, IO 260 VLVO 11700 13300, IB 260 13500 15400														
		IO 330 MRCR 12300 14000, IB 158D VLVO 16100 18300, IO 165D VLVO 15000 17100														
		IB 200D-235D 17200 20000, IO T138-T140 12100 13700														
27		FISHERMAN 270	HT	FSH	FBG	DV	SE	T155	OMC	10		6185			11000	12500
27		FISHERMAN 270	HT	FSH	FBG	DV	IO	T170-T200		10		6185			12300	14300
27		FISHERMAN 270	HT	FSH	FBG	DV	SE	T205	OMC	10		6185			11000	12500
27		FISHERMAN 270	HT	FSH	FBG	DV	IO	T225-T230		10		6185			13100	14900
27		FISHERMAN 270	HT	FSH	FBG	DV	IO	T130D-T165D		10		6185			17500	21100
27		SPORT FISHERMAN 270	FB	SF	FBG	DV	OB			10		6670			10200	11600
27		SPORT FISHERMAN 270	FB	SF	FBG	DV	SE	205	OMC	10		6670			10200	11600
27		SPORT FISHERMAN 270	FB	SF	FBG	DV	IO	225	VLVO	10		6670			12800	14600
		IB 225 VLVO 13800 15700, IO 228-230 12700 14500, IO 260 MRCR 13000 14800														
		IO 260 OMC 13000 14800, IO 260 VLVO 13100 14900, IB 260 14000 16000														
		IO 330 MRCR 13800 15700, IB 158D VLVO 11100 12600, IO 165D VLVO 10500 11900														
		IB 200D-235D 18700 20700, IO T138-T140 13600 15400														
27		SPORT FISHERMAN 270	FB	SF	FBG	DV	SE	T155	OMC	10		6670			10200	11600
27		SPORT FISHERMAN 270	FB	SF	FBG	DV	IO	T170-T200		10		6670			13700	16000
27		SPORT FISHERMAN 270	FB	SF	FBG	DV	SE	T205	OMC	10		6670			10200	11600
27		SPORT FISHERMAN 270	FB	SF	FBG	DV	IO	T225-T230		10		6670			14600	16600
27		SPORT FISHERMAN 270	FB	SF	FBG	DV	IO	T130D	VLVO	10					13400	15200
27		SPORT FISHERMAN 270	FB	SF	FBG	DV	IO	T165D	VLVO	10		6670			19700	21900
30		C-EAGLE 300	ST	CUD	FBG	DV	SE	205	OMC	10		7255			15300	17400
30		C-EAGLE 300	ST	CUD	FBG	DV	VD	228	MRCR	10		7255			15500	17600
		IO 260 MRCR 12800 14500, IO 260 OMC 12700 14500, IO 260 VLVO 12800 14500														
		VD 260 MRCR 15800 17900, IO 330 MRCR 13300 15200, VD 330 MRCR 16400 18600														
		IB 158D VLVO 17500 19900, IO 165D VLVO 13100 14900, VD 200D CHRY 18900 21000														
		IB 235D VLVO 19200 21400, IO T138-T140 13000 14800														
30		C-EAGLE 300	ST	CUD	FBG	DV	SE	T155	OMC	10		7255			15300	17400
30		C-EAGLE 300	ST	CUD	FBG	DV	IO	T170-T200		10		7255			13400	15600
30		C-EAGLE 300	ST	CUD	FBG	DV	SE	T205	OMC	10		7255			15300	17400
30		C-EAGLE 300	ST	CUD	FBG	DV	IO	T225	VLVO	10		7255			14100	16100
		IO T228 MRCR 14100 16000, VD T228 MRCR 17500 19800, IO T230 OMC 14100 16000														
		VD T260-T330 18300 21300, IOT130D-T165D 14700 17700														
30		C-EAGLE 300	HT	CUD	FBG	DV	SE	205	OMC	10		7255			15300	17400
30		C-EAGLE 300	HT	CUD	FBG	DV	VD	228	MRCR	10		7255			15500	17600
		IO 260 MRCR 12800 14500, IO 260 OMC 12700 14500, IO 260 VLVO 12800 14500														
		VD 260 MRCR 15800 17900, IO 330 MRCR 13300 15200, VD 330 MRCR 16400 18600														
		IB 158D VLVO 17500 19900, IO 165D VLVO 13100 14900, VD 200D CHRY 18900 21000														
		IB 235D VLVO 19200 21400, IO T138-T140 13000 14800														
30		C-EAGLE 300	HT	CUD	FBG	DV	SE	T155	OMC	10		7255			15300	17400
30		C-EAGLE 300	HT	CUD	FBG	DV	IO	T170-T200		10		7255			13400	15600
30		C-EAGLE 300	HT	CUD	FBG	DV	SE	T205	OMC	10		7255			15300	17400
30		C-EAGLE 300	HT	CUD	FBG	DV	IO	T225	VLVO	10		7255			14100	16100
		IO T228 MRCR 14100 16000, VD T228 MRCR 17500 19800, IO T230 OMC 14100 16000														
		VD T260-T330 18300 21300, IOT130D-T165D 14700 17700														

CONTINUED ON NEXT PAGE

```
     LOA  NAME AND/             TOP/ BOAT  -HULL- ----ENGINE--- BEAM  WGT  DRAFT RETAIL RETAIL
     FT IN  OR MODEL            RIG  TYPE  MTL TP TP # HP MFG   FT IN LBS  FT IN  LOW    HIGH
------------------------- 1983 BOATS -----------------------------------------------------------
30   C-EAGLE 300              FB  CUD  FBG DV IO        10      7255              **     **
30   FISHERMAN 300            ST  FSH  FBG DV VD  228 MRCR 10   7255            15500  17600
     IO 260 MRCR 13500   15300, IO 260 OMC   13400 15300, IO 260 VLVO 13500   15300
     VD 260 MRCR 15800   17900, IO 330 MRCR  14100 16000, VD 330 MRCR 16400   18600
     VD 200D CHRY 18900  21000, IO T138-T225 13700 16900, IO T228 MRCR 14900   16900
     VD T228 MRCR 17500  19800, IO T230 OMC  14900 16900, VD T260-T330 18300  21300

30   FISHERMAN 300            HT  FSH  FBG DV SE  205 OMC  10   7255            15200  17300
30   FISHERMAN 300            HT  FSH  FBG DV VD  228 MRCR 10   7255            15500  17600
     IO 260 MRCR 13500   15300, IO 260 OMC   13400 15300, IO 260 VLVO 13500   15300
     VD 260 MRCR 15800   17900, IO 330 MRCR  14100 16000, VD 330 MRCR 16400   18600
     IB 158D VLVO 17500  19900, IO 165D VLVO 16400 18600, VD 200D CHRY 18900  21000
     IB 235D VLVO 19200  21400, IO T138-T140 13700 15600

30   FISHERMAN 300            HT  FSH  FBG DV SE  T155 OMC  10  7255            15200  17300
30   FISHERMAN 300            HT  FSH  FBG DV IO  T170-T200 10  7255            14100  16500
30   FISHERMAN 300            HT  FSH  FBG DV SE  T205 OMC  10  7255            15200  17300
30   FISHERMAN 300            HT  FSH  FBG DV IO  T225 VLVO 10  7255            14900  16900
     IO T228 MRCR 14900  16900, VD T228 MRCR 17500 19800, IO T230 OMC 14900  16900
     VD T260-T330 18300  21300, IOT130D-T165D 18700 21800

30   FISHRMAN 300             ST  FSH  FBG DV IB  205 OMC  10   7255            15200  17300
30   FISHRMAN 300             ST  FSH  FBG DV IB  158D VLVO 10  7255            17500  19900
30   FISHRMAN 300             ST  FSH  FBG DV IB  165D VLVO 10  7255            16400  18600
30   FISHRMAN 300             ST  FSH  FBG DV IB  235D VLVO 10  7255            19200  21400
30   FISHRMAN 300             ST  FSH  FBG DV SE  T155-T205 10  7255            15200  17300
30   FISHRMAN 300             ST  FSH  FBG DV IOT130D-T165D 10 7255            18700  21800
30   SPORT FISHERMAN 300      FB  SF   FBG DV SE  205 OMC  10   7800            14200  16100
30   SPORT FISHERMAN 300      FB  SF   FBG DV VD  228 MRCR 10   7800            15900  18000
     IO 260 MRCR 14800   16900, IO 260 OMC   14800 16900, IO 260 VLVO 14900  16900
     VD 260 MRCR 16100   18300, IO 330 MRCR  15500 17600, VD 330 MRCR 16700  19000
     IB 158D VLVO 18800  20900, IO 165D VLVO 17200 19500, VD 200D CHRY 19500  21700
     IB 235D VLVO 20000  22200, IO T138-T140 15100 17200

30   SPORT FISHERMAN 300      FB  SF   FBG DV SE  T155 OMC  10  7800            14200  16100
30   SPORT FISHERMAN 300      FB  SF   FBG DV IO  T170-T200 10 7800            18100  18100
30   SPORT FISHERMAN 300      FB  SF   FBG DV SE  T225 VLVO 10 7800            14200  16100
30   SPORT FISHERMAN 300      FB  SF   FBG DV IO  T225 VLVO 10 7800            16400  18600
     IO T228 MRCR 16300  18600, VD T228 MRCR 18100 20200, IO T230 OMC 16300  18600
     VD T260-T330 18600  21500, IOT130D-T165D 19200 22600
------------------------- 1982 BOATS -----------------------------------------------------------
16   1 ADVENTURER 170         ST  RNBT FBG SV OB            6  4  955          1750   2100
16   1 FISHERMAN 170          OP  FSH  FBG SV OB            6  2 1050          1900   2250
16   4 C-GULL 170             ST  RNBT FBG TR OB            6  4 1150          2150   2500
16   4 C-GULL 170             ST  RNBT FBG TR IO 120-140    6  4              1950   2300
17   1 SPORTSMAN 180          ST  RNBT FBG DV OB            7  2 1300          2300   2700
17   1 SPORTSMAN 180  B/R     ST  RNBT FBG DV IO 120-185    7  2 1300          2500   2900
17   1 SPORTSMAN 180  B/R     ST  RNBT FBG DV OB            7  2              2350   2850
18   2 SPORTSMAN 190          ST  RNBT FBG DV IO 120-200    7  8 1700          2900   3350
18   2 SPORTSMAN 190          ST  RNBT FBG DV OB            7  8              2650   3300
18   2 SPORTSMAN 190  B/R     ST  RNBT FBG DV IO 120-200    7  8 1700          3100   3600
18   2 SPORTSMAN 190  B/R     ST  RNBT FBG DV OB            7  8              2700   3350
18  11 CAPRICE 190                CUD  FBG DV OB            7     1540          2850   3350

20     FISHERMAN 200          OP  CTRCN FBG DV OB           7  6 1800          3400   3950
20   9 C-EAGLE 210            ST  CUD  FBG DV IO 120-230    8  1 3300          4700   5700
22   9 FISHERMAN 210          ST  FSH  FBG DV IO 120-230    8  1 3300          4900   6000
22   2 FISHERMAN 222          ST  CUD  FBG DV OB            7  6 2800          5550   6350
22   2 FISHERMAN 222          ST  CUD  FBG DV IO 140-230    7  6              4250   5300
22   2 FISHERMAN 222          ST  CUD  FBG DV IO 260        7  6              4600   5450
22   2 FISHERMAN 222          ST  CUD  FBG DV IO 130D-155D  7  6              5600   6600
22   2 FISHERMAN 230          ST  FSH  FBG DV OB            8                 5100   5850
22   2 FISHERMAN 230          ST  FSH  FBG DV IO 140-230    8    3434          5450   6500
22   2 FISHERMAN 230          ST  FSH  FBG DV IO 260        8    3434          5700   6800
22   2 FISHERMAN 230          ST  FSH  FBG DV IO 130D-155D  8    3434          8050   9450
22   2 SPORTSMAN 230          ST  RNBT FBG DV OB            8                 5250   6050

22   2 SPORTSMAN 230          ST  RNBT FBG DV IO 140-230    8    3434          4850   5850
22   2 SPORTSMAN 230          ST  RNBT FBG DV IO 260        8    3434          5100   6100
24   2 C-EAGLE 250            ST  CUD  FBG DV IO 140-225    8    4830          7350   8850
     IO 228 MRCR 7550   8650, IB 228 MRCR 9100 10400, IO 230-260 7500  9050
     IO 130D-155D 8850  10300, IO T120-T185 8100 9450

24   2 C-EAGLE 250            HT  CUD  FBG DV IO 140-260    8    4830          7350   9050
     IO 280 VLVO 8050    9200, IO 130D-155D 8850 10300, IO T120-T185 8100  9450

24   2 FISHERMAN 250          OP  FSH  FBG DV IO 140-260    8    5210          8250  10100
24   2 FISHERMAN 250          OP  FSH  FBG DV IO 130D-155D  8    5210         11600  13400
24   2 FISHERMAN 250          OP  FSH  FBG DV IO T120-T185  8    5210          9150  10500
24   2 FISHERMAN 250          HT  FSH  FBG DV IO 140-260    8    5210          8250  10100
24   2 FISHERMAN 250          HT  FSH  FBG DV IO 130D-155D  8    5210         11600  13400
24   2 FISHERMAN 250          HT  FSH  FBG DV IO T120-T185  8    5210          9150  10500
24   2 SPORT FISHERMAN 250    FB  SF   FBG DV IO 165-280    8    5210          9100  11100
24   2 SPORT FISHERMAN 250    FB  SF   FBG DV IO 330 MRCR   8    5210         10100  11400
24   2 SPORT FISHERMAN 250    FB  SF   FBG DV IO T120-T170  8    5210          9850  11300

27     C-EAGLE 270            ST  CUD  FBG DV IO  225 VLVO 10   6185          10500  12000
     IB 225 VLVO 12700  14400, IO 228 MRCR 10500 11900, IB 228 MRCR 12700  14400
     IO 230-260 10500  12300, IO 330 MRCR  11400 12900, IB 330-350 13400  15600
     IB 454 OMC 14800   16900, IB 200D CHRY 16500 18800, IO T140-T230 11000  13800

27     C-EAGLE 270            HT  CUD  FBG DV IO  225 VLVO 10   6185          10500  12000
     IB 225 VLVO 12700  14400, IO 228 MRCR 10500 11900, IB 228 MRCR 12700  14400
     IO 230-280 10500  12500, IO 330 MRCR  11400 12900, IB 330-350 13400  15600
     IB 454 OMC 14800   16900, IB 200D CHRY 16500 18800, IO T140-T230 11000  13800

27     C-EAGLE 270            FB  CUD  FBG DV IB  225 VLVO 10   6185          12700  14400
     IO 228 MRCR 10500  11900, IB 228 MRCR 12700 14400, IO 230-260 10500  12300
     IO 330 MRCR 11400  12900, IB 330-350 13400 15600, IB 454 OMC 14800  16900
     IB 200D CHRY 16500 18800, IO T140-T230 11000 13800

27     FAMILY CRUISER 270     ST  CR   FBG DV IO  225 VLVO 10   6800          11100  12600
     IO 228 MRCR 11000  12500, IB 228 MRCR 13400 15200, IO 230-260 11000  12900
     IO 330 MRCR 11900  13600, IB 330-454 14100 17600, IB 200D CHRY 18200  20200
     IO T140-T230 11600 14400

27     FISHERMAN 270          ST  FSH  FBG DV IB            OMC 10  6185      **     **
     IB 200 CHRY 12400  14100, IO 225 VLVO 11100 12600, IB 225 VLVO 12700  14400
     IO 228 MRCR 11000  12600, IB 228 MRCR 12700 14400, IO 230-260 11000  13000
     IO 330 MRCR 12000  13600, IB 330-350 13400 15600, IO T140-T230 11700  14500

27     FISHERMAN 270          HT  FSH  FBG DV IB            CHRY 10  6185     **     **
     IB OMC **    **, IO 225 VLVO 11100 12600, IB 225 VLVO 12700  14400
     IO 228 MRCR 11000  12600, IB 228 MRCR 12700 14400, IO 230-280 11000  13200
     IO 330 MRCR 12000  13600, IB 330-350 13400 15600, IO T140-T230 11700  14500

27     SPORT FISHERMAN 270    FB  SF   FBG DV IB            OMC 10  6670      **     **
     IB 200-225 13000  15100, IO 228 MRCR 12400 14100, IB 228 MRCR 13200  15000
     IO 230-260 12400  14400, IO 330 MRCR  13500 15300, IB 330-350 13900  16200
     IO T140-T230 13100 16200

30     C-EAGLE 300            ST  CUD  FBG DV VD            OMC 10  7255      **     **
     VD 200-228 14600  16900, IO 260 MRCR  15200 14200, IO 260 OMC 12500  14200
     VD 260 VLVO 12500  14200, VD 260      15100 17200, IO 330 MRCR 13000  14800
     VD 330-350 15700  18100, IO 200D CHRY 18100 20200, IB T        OMC **   **
     VD T OMC  **    **, IO T140      12700 14400, IO T145 VLVO 15500  17500
     IO T170 MRCR 13100 14900, IO T170 OMC 13100 14800, IO T170 MRCR 15900  18000
     IO T185-T200 13300 15300, IO T225 VLVO 13600 15700, IO T225 VLVO 16700  19000
     IO T228 MRCR 13800 15700, IO T228 MRCR 16700 19000, IO T230 OMC 13800  15700
     VD T255-T260 17100 19500, IB T330 MRCR 18500 20600, VD T330-T350 18500  21100

30     C-EAGLE 300            HT  CUD  FBG DV IB            CHRY 10  7255      **     **
     VD OMC  **    **, VD 225-228 14800 16900, IO 260 MRCR 12500  14200
     IO 260 OMC 12500   14200, IO 260 VLVO 14200 16900, IO 330 MRCR 13000  14700
     VD 280 VLVO 12700  14400, IO 330 MRCR  15100 17200, IB T        OMC **   **
     VD 200D CHRY 18100 20200, IB T OMC  **   **, VD 330-350   **    OMC **   **
     IO T140 12700    14400, IO T145 VLVO  15500 17600, IO T165 MRCR 13000  14800
     IO T170 MRCR 13100 14900, IO T170 OMC 13100 14800, IO T170 MRCR 15900  18000
     IO T185-T200 13300 15300, IO T225 VLVO 13600 15700, IO T225 VLVO 16700  19000
     IO T228 MRCR 13800 15700, IO T228 MRCR 16700 19000, IO T230 OMC 13800  15700
     VD T255-T260 17100 19500, IB T330 MRCR 18500 20600, VD T330-T350 18500  21100

30     C-EAGLE 300            FB  CUD  FBG DV IO            10      7255      **     **
30     FISHERMAN 300          ST  FSH  FBG DV IO            10      7255      **     **
     VD 225 VLVO 14800  16900, IB 228 MRCR 14800 16900, VD 228 MRCR 14800  16900
     IB 260 OMC 14900   16400, IO 260 MRCR 13100 14800, IO 330 MRCR 13100  14500
     IO 260 VLVO 13200  15000, IO 260      15100 17200, IB 330 MRCR 13800  15600
     VD 330-350 15700  18100, IO 200D CHRY 18100 20200, VD 200D CHRY 18100  20200
     IB T OMC  **    **, VD T       **    **, IO T140      13400  15200
     IO T170 MRCR 13800 15700, IO T170 OMC 13800 15700, IO T165 MRCR 15900  18000
     IO T185-T200 14000 16100, IO T225 VLVO 14300 16500, IO T225 VLVO 16700  19000
     IO T228 MRCR 14500 16400, IO T228 MRCR 16700 19000, IO T230 OMC 14500  16500
     VD T255-T260 17100 19500, IB T330 MRCR 18500 20600, VD T330-T350 18500  21100

30     FISHERMAN 300          HT  FSH  FBG DV IO            CHRY 10 7255      **     **
     VD OMC  **    **, VD 225-228 14800 16900, IO 260 MRCR 13200  14900
```

```
 LOA  NAME AND/                TOP/ BOAT  -HULL-  ----ENGINE--- BEAM    WGT   DRAFT RETAIL RETAIL
FT IN  OR MODEL                 RIG TYPE  MTL TP TP # HP   MFG  FT IN   LBS   FT IN  LOW    HIGH
------------------- 1982 BOATS --------------------------------------------------------------------
30       FISHERMAN 300          HT  FSH   FBG DV IO  260  OMC  10       7255          13100  14900
      IO  260  VLVO  13200   15000, VD  260        15100  17200, IO  280  VLVO   13400  15200
      IO  330  MRCR  13800   15600, VD 330-350     15700  18100, VD  200D CHRY   18100  20200
      IB T     OMC     **       **, VD T     OMC      **     **, IO T140-T165    13400  15600
      IO T170  MRCR  13800   15700, IO T170  OMC   13800  15700, VD T170  MRCR   15900  18000
      IO T185-T200   14000   16100, IO T225  VLVO  14600  16600, VD T225  VLVO   16700  19000
      IO T228  MRCR  14500   16500, VD T228  MRCR  16700  19000, IO T230  OMC    14500  16500
      VD T255-T260   17100   19500, IB T330  MRCR  18500  20600, VD T330-T350    18500  21100

30       SPORT FISHERMAN 300    FB  SF    FBG DV VD       OMC  10       7800             **     **
      VD 200-228     14900   17200, IO  260  MRCR  14500  16500, IO  260  OMC    14500  16500
      IO  260  VLVO  14600   16500, VD  260  MRCR  15400  17500, IO  330  MRCR   15100  17200
      VD 330-350     16000   18400, VD  200D CHRY  19000  21100, VD T     OMC       **     **
      IO T140-T145   14800   16900, IO T170  MRCR  15200  17200, IO T170  OMC    15200  17200
      VD T170  MRCR  16200   18400, IO T185-T200   15400  17700, IO T225  VLVO   16000  18200
      VD T225  VLVO  17000   19300, IO T228  MRCR  16000  18100, VD T228  MRCR   17000  19300
      IO T230  OMC   16000   18100, VD T255-T260   17300  19800, IB T330  MRCR   18800  20800
      VD T330-T350   18800   21300
------------------- 1981 BOATS --------------------------------------------------------------------
16  1 ADVENTURER 170             RNBT  FBG DV IO  120          6  4                1850   2250
16  1 ADVENTURER 170        ST   RNBT  FBG DV OB               6  4    955         1750   2050
16  1 FISHERMAN 170         OP   FSH   FBG SV OB               6  2   1050         1850   2200
16  4 C-GULL 170            ST   RNBT  FBG TR OB               6  4   1150         2100   2450
16  4 C-GULL 170            ST   RNBT  FBG TR IO 120-140       6  4                1900   2250
17  1 SPORTSMAN 180         ST   RNBT  FBG DV OB               7  2   1300         2050   2450
17  1 SPORTSMAN 180 B/R     ST   RNBT  FBG DV OB               7  2   1300         2300   2700
17  1 SPORTSMAN 180 B/R     ST   RNBT  FBG DV IO 120-170       7  2                2200   2600
17  1 SPORTSMAN 180 BR LTD  ST   RNBT  FBG DV OB               7  2   1300         2700   3150
17  1 SPORTSMAN 180 BR LTD  ST   RNBT  FBG DV IO 120-170       7  2                2350   2750
18  2 SPORTSMAN 190         ST   RNBT  FBG DV OB               7  8   1700         2900   3350
18  2 SPORTSMAN 190         ST   RNBT  FBG DV IO 120-198       7  8                2600   3050

18  2 SPORTSMAN 190 B/R     ST   RNBT  FBG DV OB               7  8   1700         3000   3500
18  2 SPORTSMAN 190 B/R     ST   RNBT  FBG DV IO 120-198       7  8                2650   3150
18 11 CAPRICE 190           ST   CUD   FBG DV OB               7      1540         2800   3250
20  2 SPORTSMAN 200              RNBT  FBG DV IO  140          7  3                3500   4100
20  9 C-EAGLE 210           ST   CUD   FBG DV IO 120-230       8  1   3300         4600   5450
20  9 C-EAGLE 210           ST   CUD   FBG DV IO  280  VLVO    8  1   3300         5200   6000
20  9 FISHERMAN 210         ST   FSH   FBG DV IO 120-230       8  1   3300         4850   5700
20  9 FISHERMAN 210         ST   FSH   FBG DV IO  280  VLVO    8  1   3300         5500   6300
22  2 FISHERMAN 230         ST   FSH   FBG DV OB               8                   4950   5700
22  2 FISHERMAN 230         ST   FSH   FBG DV IO 140-260       8      3434         5350   6450
22  2 FISHERMAN 230         ST   FSH   FBG DV IO  280  VLVO    8      3434         6000   6900
22  2 FISHERMAN 230         ST   FSH   FBG DV IO T120  MRCR    8      3434         6100   7000

22  2 SPORTSMAN 230         ST   RNBT  FBG DV OB               8                   5150   5900
22  2 SPORTSMAN 230         ST   RNBT  FBG DV IO 140-260       8      3434         4800   5800
22  2 SPORTSMAN 230         ST   RNBT  FBG DV IO  280  VLVO    8      3434         5350   6150
22  2 SPORTSMAN 230         ST   RNBT  FBG DV IO T120  MRCR    8      3434         5450   6250
24  2 C-EAGLE 250           ST   CUD   FBG DV IO 140-200       8      4830         7250   8400
      IB  228  MRCR   8650    9900, IO 230-280      7400   9100, IO T120-T170     7950   9250

24  2 C-EAGLE 250           HT   CUD   FBG DV IO 140-260       8      4830         7250   8700
24  2 C-EAGLE 250           HT   CUD   FBG DV IO  280  VLVO    8      4830         7900   9100
24  2 C-EAGLE 250           HT   CUD   FBG DV IO T120-T170     8      4830         7950   9250
24  2 C-EAGLE 250           FB   CUD   FBG DV IO 165-280       8      4830         7250   9100
24  2 C-EAGLE 250           FB   CUD   FBG DV IO  330  MRCR    8      4830         8150   9400
24  2 C-EAGLE 250           FB   CUD   FBG DV IO T120-T170     8      4830         7950   9250
24  2 FISHERMAN 250         OP   FSH   FBG DV IO 140-280       8      5210         8150  10100
24  2 FISHERMAN 250         OP   FSH   FBG DV IO T120-T170     8      5210         9000  10300
24  2 FISHERMAN 250         HT   FSH   FBG DV IO 140-280       8      5210         8150  10100
24  2 FISHERMAN 250         HT   FSH   FBG DV IO T120-T170     8      5210         9000  10300
24  2 SPORT FISHERMAN 250   FB   SF    FBG DV IO 165-280       8      5210         8950  10900
24  2 SPORT FISHERMAN 250   FB   SF    FBG DV IO  330  MRCR    8      5210         9900  11300

24  2 SPORT FISHERMAN 250   FB   SF    FBG DV IO T120-T170     8      5210         9700  11100
27      C-EAGLE 270         ST   CUD   FBG DV IO  228  MRCR 10        6185        10300  11700
      IB  228  MRCR  12100   13800, IO  230  OMC   10300  11700, IB  255  MRCR   12300  14000
      IO 260-280     10500   12300, IB  305  OMC   12800  14500, IO  330  MRCR   11200  12700
      IB 330-350     12800   15000, IB  454  OMC   14200  16200, IB  655  CHRY   15900  18000
      IO T140-T230   10900   13400

27      C-EAGLE 270         HT   CUD   FBG DV IO  228  MRCR 10        6185        10300  11700
      IB  228  MRCR  12100   13800, IO  230  OMC   10300  11700, IB  255  MRCR   12300  14000
      IO 260-280     10500   12300, IB  305  OMC   12800  14500, IO  330  MRCR   11200  12700
      IB 330-350     12800   15000, IB  454  OMC   14200  16200, IB  655  CHRY   15900  18000
      IO T140-T230   10900   13400

27      C-EAGLE 270         FB   CUD   FBG DV IO  228  MRCR 10        6185        10300  11700
      IB  228  MRCR  12100   13800, IO  230  OMC   10300  11700, IB  255  MRCR   12300  14000
      IO 260-280     10500   12300, IB  305  OMC   12800  14500, IO  330  MRCR   11200  12700
      IB 330-350     12800   15000, IB  454  OMC   14200  16200, IB  655  CHRY   15900  18000
      IO T140-T230   10900   13400

27      FAMILY CRUISER 270  ST   CR    FBG DV IO  228  MRCR 10        6800        10900  12300
      IB  228  MRCR  12800   14500, IO  230  OMC   10900  12300, IB  255  MRCR   13000  14700
      IO  260        11100   12600, IB  305  OMC   13400  15300, IO  330  MRCR   11700  13300
      IB 330-454     13500   16900, IB  200D CHRY  17100  19500, IO T140-T230    11400  14000

27      FISHERMAN 270       ST   FSH   FBG DV IO  228  MRCR 10        6185        10900  12400
      IB  228  MRCR  12100   13800, IO  230  OMC   10900  12300, IB  255  MRCR   12300  14000
      IO 260-280     11100   13000, IB  305  OMC   12800  14500, IO  330  MRCR   11800  13400
      IB 330-350     12800   15000, IB  454  OMC   14200  16200, IB  655  CHRY   15900  18000
      IO T140-T230   11500   14100

27      FISHERMAN 270       HT   FSH   FBG DV IO  228  MRCR 10        6185        10900  12400
      IB  228  MRCR  12100   13800, IO  230  OMC   10900  12300, IB  255  MRCR   12300  14000
      IO 260-280     11100   13000, IB  305  OMC   12800  14500, IO  330  MRCR   11800  13400
      IB 330-350     12800   15000, IB  454  OMC   14200  16200, IB  655  CHRY   15900  18000
      IO T140-T230   11500   14100

27      SPORT FISHERMAN 270 FB   SF    FBG DV IO  228  MRCR 10        6670        12200  13900
      IB  228  MRCR  12700   14400, IO  230  OMC   12200  13900, IB  255  MRCR   12800  14600
      IO 260-280     12500   14600, IB  305  OMC   13300  15100, IO  330  MRCR   13300  15100
      IB 330-350     13400   15500, IB  454  OMC   14700  16700, IB  655  CHRY   16300  18500
      IO T140-T230   12900   15800

30      C-EAGLE 300         ST   CUD   FBG DV VD 228-255       10     7255        14200  16400
      IO 260-280     12300   14200, VD  305  OMC   14900  16900, IO  330  MRCR   12800  14600
      VD 330-454     15000   18400, VD  655  CHRY  18100  20100, IO T140-T200    12500  15000
      IO T228  MRCR  13600   15400, VD T228  MRCR  16000  18200, IO T230  OMC    13600  15400
      VD T255-T350   16300   20200, VD T454  OMC   19400  21600

30      C-EAGLE 300         HT   CUD   FBG DV VD 228-255       10     7255        14200  16400
      IO 260-280     12300   14200, VD  305  OMC   14900  16900, IO  330  MRCR   12800  14600
      VD 330-454     15000   18400, VD  655  CHRY  18100  20100, IO T140-T200    12500  15000
      IO T228  MRCR  13600   15400, VD T228  MRCR  16000  18200, IO T230  OMC    13600  15400
      VD T255-T350   16300   20200, VD T454  OMC   19400  21600

30      FISHERMAN 300       ST   FSH   FBG DV IO  140          10     7255        11900  13600
      IB  228  MRCR  14200   16100, VD  255  MRCR  14400  16400, IO 260-280      12900  15000
      IB  305  OMC   14900   16900, IO  330  MRCR  13500  15400, VD 330-454      15000  18400
      IB  655  CHRY  18100   20100, IO T165-T185   13500  15600, VD T198  MRCR   15600  17700
      IO T200  OMC   13900   15800, IO T228  MRCR  14300  16300, VD T228  MRCR   16000  18200
      IO T230  OMC   14300   16300, VD T255-T305   16300  19400, IB T330  MRCR   17300  19700
      VD T350  OMC   18100   20200, IB T454  OMC   19400  21600

30      FISHERMAN 300       HT   FSH   FBG DV VD 228-255       10     7255        14200  16400
      IO 260-280     12900   15000, VD  305  OMC   14900  16900, IO  330  MRCR   13500  15400
      VD 330-454     15000   18400, VD  655  CHRY  18100  20100, IO T140-T200    13200  15800
      IO T228  MRCR  14300   16300, VD T228  MRCR  16000  18200, IO T230  OMC    14300  16300
      VD T255-T350   16300   20200, VD T454  OMC   19400  21600

30      SPORT FISHERMAN 300 FB   SF    FBG DV VD 228-255       10     7800        14500  16800
      IO 260-280     14300   16500, VD  305  OMC   15200  17300, IO  330  MRCR   14900  16900
      VD 330-454     15300   18700, VD  655  CHRY  18300  20300, IO T140-T200    14500  17400
      IO T228  MRCR  15700   17800, VD T228  MRCR  16300  18500, IO T230  OMC    15700  17900
      VD T255-T350   16600   20400, VD T454  OMC   19800  22000
------------------- 1980 BOATS --------------------------------------------------------------------
16  1 ADVENTURER 170        ST   RNBT  FBG DV OB               6  4    955         1700   2050
16  1 ADVENTURER 170        ST   RNBT  FBG DV IO 120-140       6  4                1850   2200
16  1 FISHERMAN 170         OP   FSH   FBG SV OB               6  2   1050         1800   2150
16  4 C-GULL 170            ST   RNBT  FBG TR OB               6  4   1150         2050   2450
16  4 C-GULL 170            ST   RNBT  FBG TR IO 120-140       6  4                1900   2250
17  1 SPORTSMAN 180         ST   RNBT  FBG DV OB               7  2   1300         2250   2600
17  1 SPORTSMAN 180 B/R     ST   RNBT  FBG DV OB               7  2   1300         2450   2800
17  1 SPORTSMAN 180 B/R     ST   RNBT  FBG DV IO 120-170       7  2                2300   2700
18  2 SPORTSMAN 190         ST   RNBT  FBG DV OB               7  8   1700         2850   3300
18  2 SPORTSMAN 190         ST   RNBT  FBG DV IO 120-198       7  8                2600   3000
18  2 SPORTSMAN 190 B/R     ST   RNBT  FBG DV OB               7  8   1700         2950   3400
18  2 SPORTSMAN 190 B/R     ST   RNBT  FBG DV IO 120-198       7  8                2600   3150

18 11 CAPRICE 190           ST   CUD   FBG DV OB               7      1540         2750   3200
20  2 SPORTSMAN 200         ST   RNBT  FBG DV OB               7  3   1580         3100   3650
20  2 SPORTSMAN 200         ST   RNBT  FBG DV IO 140-198       7  3                3500   4100
20  9 C-EAGLE 210           ST   CUD   FBG DV IO 165-230       8  1   3300         4600   5400
```

 CONTINUED ON NEXT PAGE

LOA FT	LOA IN	NAME AND/ OR MODEL	TOP/ RIG	BOAT TYPE	-HULL- MTL	-HULL- TP	ENGINE TP	ENGINE # HP	ENGINE MFG	BEAM FT	BEAM IN	WGT LBS	DRAFT FT IN	RETAIL LOW	RETAIL HIGH
		1980 BOATS													
20	9	C-EAGLE 210	ST	CUD	FBG	DV	IO	124D-145D		8	1	3300		5750	7100
20	9	FISHERMAN 210	ST	FSH	FBG	DV	IO	165-230		8	1	3300		4800	5700
20	9	FISHERMAN 210	ST	FSH	FBG	DV	IO	124D-145D		8	1	3300		7150	8850
22	2	FISHERMAN 230	ST	FSH	FBG	DV	OB			8				4900	5600
22	2	FISHERMAN 230	ST	FSH	FBG	DV	IO	165-260		8		3434		5300	6400
22	2	FISHERMAN 230	ST	FSH	FBG	DV	IO	124D-145D		8		3434		7800	9600
22	2	SPORTSMAN 230	ST	RNBT	FBG	DV	OB			8				5000	5750
22	2	SPORTSMAN 230	ST	RNBT	FBG	DV	IO	165-260		8		3434		4750	5750
22	2	SPORTSMAN 230	ST	RNBT	FBG	DV	IO	124D-145D		8		3434		5900	7250
24	2	C-EAGLE 250	ST	CUD	FBG	DV	IO	165-200		8		4830		7200	8350
		IB 228 MRCR 8250 9500, IO 230-260 7300 8600, IO 124D-145D												8500	10300
		IO T120-T170 7900 9150													
24	2	C-EAGLE 250	HT	CUD	FBG	DV	IO	165-260		8		4830		7200	8600
24	2	C-EAGLE 250	HT	CUD	FBG	DV	IO	124D-145D		8		4830		8500	10300
24	2	C-EAGLE 250	HT	CUD	FBG	DV	IO	T120-T170		8		4830		7900	9150
24	2	C-EAGLE 250	FB	CUD	FBG	DV	IO	185-260		8		4830		7200	8600
		IO 330 MRCR 8100 9300, IO 124D-145D 8500 10300, IO T120-T170												7900	9150
24	2	FISHERMAN 250	OP	FSH	FBG	DV	IO	165-260		8		5210		8100	9650
24	2	FISHERMAN 250	OP	FSH	FBG	DV	IO	124D-145D		8		5210		11300	13400
24	2	FISHERMAN 250	OP	FSH	FBG	DV	IO	T120-T170		8		5210		8900	10200
24	2	FISHERMAN 250	HT	FSH	FBG	DV	IO	165-260		8		5210		8100	9650
24	2	FISHERMAN 250	HT	FSH	FBG	DV	IO	124D-145D		8		5210		11300	13400
24	2	FISHERMAN 250	HT	FSH	FBG	DV	IO	T120-T170		8		5210		8900	10200
24	2	SPORT FISHERMAN 250	FB	SF	FBG	DV	IO	185-300		8		5210		8850	10700
24	2	SPORT FISHERMAN 250	FB	SF	FBG	DV	IO	124D-145D		8		5210		11300	13500
24	2	SPORT FISHERMAN 250	FB	SF	FBG	DV	IO	T120-T170		8		5210		9600	11000
27		C-EAGLE 270	ST	CUD	FBG	DV	IO	228	MRCR	10		6185		10200	11600
		IB 228 MRCR 11600 13200, IO 230 OMC 10200 11600, IB 255 MRCR												11800	13400
		IO 260 10400 11900, IB 305 OMC 12300 13900, IO 330 MRCR												11100	12600
		IB 330-350 12300 14300, IB 454 OMC 13600 15500, IO T140-T230												10800	13300
27		C-EAGLE 270	HT	CUD	FBG	DV	IO	228	MRCR	10		6185		10200	11600
		IB 228 MRCR 11600 13200, IO 230 OMC 10200 11600, IB 255 MRCR												11800	13400
		IO 260 10400 11900, IB 305 OMC 12300 13900, IO 330 MRCR												11100	12600
		IB 330-350 12300 14300, IB 454 OMC 13600 15500, IO T140-T230												10800	13300
27		C-EAGLE 270	FB	CUD	FBG	DV	IB	255	MRCR	10		6185		11800	13400
		IO 330 MRCR 11100 12600, IB 330-350 12300 14300, IB 454 OMC												13600	15500
		IO T140-T230 10800 13300													
27		FISHERMAN 270	ST	FSH	FBG	DV	IO	228	MRCR	10		6185		10800	12200
		IB 228 MRCR 11600 13200, IO 230 OMC 10800 12200, IB 255 MRCR												11800	13400
		IO 260 11000 12500, IB 305 OMC 12300 13900, IO 330 MRCR												11700	13300
		IB 330-350 12300 14300, IB 454 OMC 13600 15500, IO T140-T230												11400	14000
27		FISHERMAN 270	HT	FSH	FBG	DV	IO	228	MRCR	10		6185		10800	12200
		IB 228 MRCR 11600 13200, IO 230 OMC 10800 12200, IB 255 MRCR												11800	13400
		IO 260 11000 12500, IB 305 OMC 12300 13900, IO 330 MRCR												11700	13300
		IB 330-350 12300 14300, IB 454 OMC 13600 15500, IO T140-T230												11400	14000
27		SPORT FISHERMAN 270	FB	SF	FBG	DV	IB	255	MRCR	10		6670		12300	14000
		IO 330 MRCR 13100 14900, IB 330-350 12800 14900, IB 454 OMC												14100	16000
		IO T140-T230 12800 15700													
30		FISHERMAN 300	ST	FSH	FBG	DV	VD	255	MRCR	10		7255		13800	15700
		IO 330 MRCR 13400 15300, VD 330-454 14400 17600, IO T165-T185												13400	15500
		VD T198 MRCR 14900 17000, IO T200 OMC 13800 15700, IO T228 MRCR												14200	16100
		VD T228 MRCR 15300 17400, IO T230 OMC 14200 16100, VD T255-T350												15700	19300
30		SPORT FISHERMAN 300	FB	SF	FBG	DV	VD	255	MRCR	10		7800		14100	16100
		IO 330 MRCR 14800 16800, VD 330 MRCR 14700 16700, IB 350-454												14900	17900
		IO T165-T200 14700 17300, IO T228 MRCR 15600 17700, VD T228 MRCR												15600	17700
		IO T230 OMC 15600 17700, VD T255 MRCR 15900 18100, IB T305 OMC												16600	18900
		VD T350 OMC 17200 19600													
		1979 BOATS													
16	1	ADVENTURE 170		RNBT	FBG	DV	OB			6	4	955		1700	2000
16	1	ADVENTURER 170	OP	RNBT	FBG	DV	IO	120-140		6	4			1850	2200
16	1	SAFARI 170		RNBT	FBG	DV	OB			6	4	955		1700	2000
16	4	C-GULL 170	OP	RNBT	FBG	TR	OB			6	4	1150		2000	2400
16	4	C-GULL 170	OP	RNBT	FBG	TR	IO	120		6	4			1900	2250
16	4	C-GULL 170	OP	RNBT	FBG	TR	IB	120		6	4			2000	2400
17	1	SPORTSMAN 180		RNBT	FBG	DV	IO	165		7	2			2300	2650
17	1	SPORTSMAN 180	OP	RNBT	FBG		IO	185		7	2			2300	2700
17	1	SPORTSMAN 180	OP	RNBT	FBG	DV	OB			6	11	1430		2450	2900
17	1	SPORTSMAN 180	OP	RNBT	FBG	DV	IO	120		7	2			2300	2650
17	1	SPORTSMAN 180 BR	OP	RNBT	FBG	DV	IO	120		7	2			2300	2650
17	2	C-GULL 180		RNBT	FBG	TR	OB			7	2	1600		2700	3150
17	2	C-GULL 180		RNBT	FBG	TR	IO	140-185		7	2			2300	2700
18	2	SPORTSMAN 190		RNBT	FBG	DV	IO	140-198		7	8			2600	3100
18	2	SPORTSMAN 190		RNBT	FBG	DV	IO	270		7	8			2850	3350
18	2	SPORTSMAN 190	OP	RNBT	FBG	DV	IO	120		7	8			2600	3000
18	2	SPORTSMAN 190 BR	OP	RNBT	FBG	DV	IO			7	8			**	**
18	11	CAPRICE 190	OP	CUD	FBG	DV	OB			7		1540		2700	3150
20	2	SPORTSMAN 200		RNBT	FBG	DV	IO	170		7	3			3500	4100
20	2	SPORTSMAN 200	OP	RNBT	FBG	DV	OB			7	3	1580		3050	3550
20	2	SPORTSMAN 200	OP	RNBT	FBG	DV	IO	165-185		7	3			3500	4100
21		C-EAGLE 210		CUD	FBG	DV	IO	165		8				4050	4700
21		FISHERMAN		FSH	FBG	DV	OB			8		3300		4900	5650
22	2	FISHERMAN		FSH	FBG	DV	OB			8		3434		5700	6550
22	2	FISHERMAN 230		FSH	FBG	DV	IO	165		8				4600	5250
22	2	FISHERMAN 230		SF	FBG	SV	IB	165		8				4700	5400
22	2	SPORTSMAN 230		RNBT	FBG	DV	IO	170-240		8				4050	4900
24	2	SPORT FISHERMAN 250		SF	FBG	DV	IO	200		8				6850	7850
24	6	C-EAGLE 250		CUD	FBG	DV	IO	185-240		8				6250	7400
26	2	IMPERIAL 260		EXP	FBG	DV	IB	330		10	6			9250	10500
26	2	IMPERIAL 260	FB	EXP	FBG	DV	IO	228		10	6			7800	8950
26	2	IMPERIAL 260	FB	EXP	FBG	DV	IO	330		10	6			8850	10000
26	2	IMPERIAL 260	FB	EXP	FBG	SV	IB	330		10	6			9250	10500
27		C-EAGLE 270		CUD	FBG	DV	IO	228		10				8550	9800
27		C-EAGLE 270		CUD	FBG	DV	IO	330		10				9550	10900
27		C-EAGLE 270	FB	CUD	FBG	DV	IB	255		10				9550	10900
27		SPORT FISHERMAN 270		SF	FBG	DV	IO	228		10				9350	10600
27		SPORT FISHERMAN 270		SF	FBG	SV	IB	255		10				9150	10400
30		C-EAGLE 300		CUD	FBG	SV	IB	255		10				12800	14500
30		C-EAGLE 300		EXP	FBG	DV	IO	330		10				14500	16400
30		SPORT FISH 300		SF	FBG	DV	IO	330		10				14000	15900
30		SPORT FISHERMAN 300		SF	FBG	DV	IB	255		10				12800	14500
		1978 BOATS													
16	1	ADVENTURER 170	OP	RNBT	FBG	DV	OB			6	4	955		1700	2050
16	1	ADVENTURER 170	OP	RNBT	FBG	DV	IO	120-140		6	4			1850	2250
16	4	C-GULL 170	ST	RNBT	FBG	TR	OB			6	4	1150		2000	2400
16	4	C-GULL 170	ST	RNBT	FBG	TR	IO	120-140		6	4			1900	2250
17	1	SPORTSMAN 180	ST	RNBT	FBG	DV	OB			7	2	1300		2250	2600
17	1	SPORTSMAN 180	ST	RNBT	FBG	DV	IO	120-198		7	2			2300	2700
17	1	SPORTSMAN 180 B/R	ST	RNBT	FBG	DV	OB			7	2	1300		2350	2700
17	1	SPORTSMAN 180 B/R	ST	RNBT	FBG	DV	IO	120-198		7	2			2300	2700
17	2	C-GULL 180		RNBT	FBG	TR	OB			7	2	1600		2650	3100
17	2	C-GULL 180		RNBT	FBG	TR	IO	120-198		7	2			2300	2700
18	2	SPORTSMAN 190		RNBT	FBG	DV	OB			7	8	1700		2750	3250
18	2	SPORTSMAN 190		RNBT	FBG	DV	IO	140-198		7	8			2600	3100
18	2	SPORTSMAN 190 B/R		RNBT	FBG	DV	OB			7	8	1700		2850	3350
18	2	SPORTSMAN 190 B/R		RNBT	FBG	DV	IO	140-198		7	8			2650	3100
18	11	CAPRICE 190		CUD	FBG	DV	OB			7	8			3100	3600
20	2	SPORTSMAN 200	OP	RNBT	FBG	DV	OB			7	3	1580		3000	3500
20	2	SPORTSMAN 200	OP	RNBT	FBG	DV	IO	140-198		7	3			3500	4150
22	2	FISHERMAN 230	ST	FSH	FBG	DV	IO	165-185		8		3434		5350	6150
		IO 198 MRCR 5400 6200, VD 198 MRCR 5250 6050, IO 225 OMC												5400	6250
		IO 228 MRCR 5450 6300, VD 228 MRCR 5300 6050, IO 240 OMC												5450	6300
		VD 305 OMC 5700 6550													
22	2	SPORTSMAN 230	OP	RNBT	FBG	DV	IO	165-185		8		3434		4800	5500
		IO 198 MRCR 4850 5550, VD 198 MRCR 5300 6100, IO 225 OMC												4850	5600
		IO 228 MRCR 4900 5650, VD 228 MRCR 5350 6150, IO 240 OMC												4900	5650
		VD 305 OMC 5700 6550													
24	2	C-EAGLE 250	HT	CUD	FBG	DV	IO	165-185		8		4300		6600	7600
		IO 198 MRCR 6700 7650, IB 198 MRCR 6900 7950, IO 225 OMC												6700	7700
		IO 228 MRCR 6750 7750, IB 228 MRCR 6950 7950, IO 240 OMC												6750	7800
		IB 255-350 6950 8650, IO T140-T170 7350 8500													
24	2	SPORT FISHERMAN 250	FB	SF	FBG	DV	IO	185-240		8		5210		8900	10300
24	2	SPORT FISHERMAN 250	FB	SF	FBG	DV	IO	T140-T170		8		5210		9700	11100
26	2	IMPERIAL 260	OP	EXP	FBG	DV	IO	225	OMC	10	6	7400		11200	12800
		IO 228 MRCR 11300 12800, VD 228 MRCR 11700 13300, IO 240 OMC												11300	12900
		VD 255 MRCR 11800 13400, IO 260 MRCR 11500 13000, VD 305 OMC												12200	13900
		IO 330 MRCR 12100 13800, VD 330-454 12200 15200													
26	2	IMPERIAL 260	FB	EXP	FBG	DV	IO	228	MRCR	10	6	7700		11600	13200
		VD 228 MRCR 12000 13700, IO 240 OMC 11600 13200, VD 255 MRCR												12200	13800

96th ed. - Vol. III CONTINUED ON NEXT PAGE 563

SPORT-CRAFT BOATS -CONTINUED See inside cover to adjust price for area

LOA FT	IN	NAME AND/ OR MODEL	TOP/ RIG	BOAT TYPE	-HULL- MTL	TP	ENGINE TP	# HP	MFG	BEAM FT	IN	WGT LBS	DRAFT FT	IN	RETAIL LOW	RETAIL HIGH
		1978 BOATS														
26	2	IMPERIAL 260	FB	EXP	FBG	DV	IO	260	MRCR	10	6	7700			11800	13400
		VD 305 OMC 12500 14300, IO 330 MRCR 12400 14100, VD 330-454													12500	15600
27		C-EAGLE 270	HT	CUD	FBG	DV	IO	225	OMC	10		6185			10200	11600
		IO 228 MRCR 10300 11700, IB 228 MRCR 10700 12100, IO 240 OMC													10300	11800
		IB 255-305 10800 12800, IO 330 MRCR 11200 12700, IB 330-350													11300	13200
		IB 454 OMC 12500 14200, IO T165-T240 11100 13500														
27		SPORT FISHERMAN 270	FB	SF	FBG	DV	IO	225	OMC	10		6670			12200	13800
		IO 228 MRCR 12200 13900, IB 228 MRCR 11100 12700, IO 240 OMC													12300	14000
		IB 255-305 11300 13300, IO 330 MRCR 13200 15000, IB 330-350													11800	13700
		IB 454 OMC 12900 14700, IO T165-T240 13100 15900														
30		C-EAGLE 300	HT	EXP	FBG	DV	IO	228-330		10		7255			14100	17100
		IO T165-T185 15000 17300, IO T198 MRCR 15500 17600, VD T198 MRCR													16100	18300
		IO T225 OMC 15800 18000, IO T228 MRCR 15900 18100, VD T228-T330													16600	20400
30		SPORT FISHERMAN 300	FB	SF	FBG	DV	VD	255	MRCR	10		7800			13000	14800
		IO 330 MRCR 14900 16900, VD 330 MRCR 13500 15300, IO T165-T185													14800	17100
		IO T198 MRCR 15300 17400, VD T198 MRCR 14000 15900, IO T225 OMC													15600	17700
		IO T228 MRCR 15700 17800, VD T228-T330 14300 17600														
		1977 BOATS														
16	1	ADVENTURER 170	ST	RNBT	FBG	DV	OB			6	4	955			1700	2000
17	1	ADVENTURER 180	ST	RNBT	FBG	DV	OB			7		1240			2200	2550
17	1	SPORTSMAN 180	ST	RNBT	FBG	DV	OB			6	9	1430			2400	2800
17	1	SPORTSMAN 180	ST	RNBT	FBG	DV	IO	120-175		6	9	1430			1900	2300
17	2	C-GULL 180	ST	RNBT	FBG	TR	OB			7	2	1600			2650	3050
17	2	C-GULL 180	ST	RNBT	FBG	TR	IO	120-175		7	2	1600			2100	2500
18	2	SPORTSMAN 190	ST	RNBT	FBG	DV	OB			7	8	1700			2800	3250
18	2	SPORTSMAN 190	ST	RNBT	FBG	DV	IO	120-175		7	8	1700			2400	2850
18	11	CAPRICE 190	ST	CUD	FBG	DV	OB			7		1540			2650	3100
18	11	CAPRICE 190	HT	CUD	FBG	DV	OB			7		1540			2650	3100
20	2	SPORTSMAN 200	ST	RNBT	FBG	DV	OB			7	3	1580			2950	3450
20	2	SPORTSMAN 200	ST	RNBT	FBG	DV	IO	120-235		7	3	1580			2900	3550
20	11	C-EAGLE 210	ST	CUD	FBG	DV	IO	165-235		7	8	3500			4800	5650
20	11	C-EAGLE 210	HT	CUD	FBG	DV	IO	165-235		7	8	3500			4800	5650
22	2	C-EAGLE 230	ST	CUD	FBG	DV	IO	165-235		8		3500			5200	6150
22	2	C-EAGLE 230	HT	CUD	FBG	DV	IO	165-235		8		3500			5200	6150
22	2	SPORTSMAN 230	ST	RNBT	FBG	DV	IO	165-235		8		3434			4850	5750
24	2	C-EAGLE 250	ST	CUD	FBG	DV	IO	165-190		8		4830			7400	8500
		IB 225-230 7250 8600, IO 233 MRCR 7550 8650, IB 233 MRCR													7300	8400
		IO 235 OMC 7500 8650, IO T120-T170 8050 9400														
24	2	C-EAGLE 250	HT	CUD	FBG	DV	IO	165-190		8		4830			7400	8500
		IB 225-230 7250 8600, IO 233 MRCR 7550 8650, IB 233 MRCR													7300	8400
		IO 235 OMC 7500 8650, IO T120-T170 8050 9400														
24	2	IMPERIAL 250	ST	EXP	FBG	DV	IO	165-255		8		6830			9950	11600
24	2	IMPERIAL 250	ST	EXP	FBG	DV	IO	T120-T170		8		6830			10600	12200
24	2	IMPERIAL 250	HT	EXP	FBG	DV	IO	165-255		8		6830			9950	11600
24	2	IMPERIAL 250	HT	EXP	FBG	DV	IO	T120-T170		8		6830			10600	12200
24	2	SPORT FISHERMAN 250	FB	SF	FBG	DV	IO	165-255		8		5210			9050	10600
24	2	SPORT FISHERMAN 250	FB	SF	FBG	DV	IO	T120-T170		8		5210			9800	11200
27		C-EAGLE 270	ST	CUD	FBG	DV	IB	225-230		10		6185			10200	11800
		IO 233 MRCR 10500 11900, IB 233 MRCR 10300 11700, IO 235 OMC													10500	11900
		IB 250 CHRY 10400 11800, IO 255 MRCR 10600 12100, IB 255-330													10400	12500
		IO T140-T235 11000 13600														
27		C-EAGLE 270	HT	CUD	FBG	DV	IB	225-230		10		6185			10200	11800
		IO 233 MRCR 10500 11900, IB 233 MRCR 10300 11700, IO 235 OMC													10500	11900
		IB 250 CHRY 10400 11800, IO 255 MRCR 10600 12100, IB 255-330													10400	12500
		IO T140-T235 11000 13600														
27		SPORT FISHERMAN 270	FB	SF	FBG	DV	IB	225-230		10		6670			10700	12300
		IO 233 MRCR 12500 14200, IB 233 MRCR 10700 12200, IO 235 OMC													12500	14200
		IB 250 CHRY 10800 12300, IO 255 MRCR 12600 14400, IB 255-330													10800	13000
		IO T140-T235 13000 16100														
30		C-EAGLE 300	ST	EXP	FBG	DV	VD	250	CHRY	10		7255			14300	16200
		IO 255 MRCR 14500 16500, VD 255-330 14300 17000, IO T140-T190													14800	17700
		VD T225-T230 15800 18200, IO T233 MRCR 16200 18400, VD T233 MRCR													16000	18100
		IO T235 OMC 16200 18400														
30		C-EAGLE 300	HT	EXP	FBG	DV	VD	250	CHRY	10		7255			14300	16200
		IO 255 MRCR 14500 16500, VD 255-330 14300 17000, IO T140-T190													14800	17700
		VD T225-T230 15800 18200, IO T233 MRCR 16200 18400, VD T233 MRCR													16000	18100
		IO T235 OMC 16200 18400														
30		SPORT FISHERMAN 300	FB	SF	FBG	DV	VD	250	CHRY	10		7800			12400	14100
		IO 255 MRCR 14400 16400, VD 255-330 12500 14800, IO T165-T190													15100	17500
		VD T225-T230 13700 15700, IO T233 MRCR 16000 18200, VD T233 MRCR													13800	15700
		IO T235 OMC 16000 18200														
30		SPORT SEDAN 300	ST	SDN	FBG	DV	VD	250-330		10		8120			14500	17400
		IO T165-T190 15500 18100, VD T230 OMC 16500 18700, IO T233 MRCR													16700	19000
		VD T233 MRCR 16400 18700, IO T235 OMC 16700 19000														
30		SPORT SEDAN 300	HT	SDN	FBG	DV	VD	250-330		10		8120			14500	17400
		IO T165-T190 15500 18100, VD T230 OMC 16500 18700, IO T233 MRCR													16700	19000
		VD T233 MRCR 16400 18700, IO T235 OMC 16700 19000														
30		SPORT SEDAN 300	FB	SDN	FBG	DV	VD	250-330		10		8120			14500	17400
		IO T165-T190 15500 18100, VD T230 OMC 16500 18700, IO T233 MRCR													16700	19000
		VD T233 MRCR 16400 18700, IO T235 OMC 16700 19000														
		1976 BOATS														
16	8	SPORTSMAN 170	ST	RNBT	FBG	DV	IO	120-140		6	8				2250	2750
17	1	ADVENTURER 180	ST	RNBT	FBG	DV	OB			7		1240			2200	2550
17	1	SPORTSMAN 180	ST	RNBT	FBG	DV	OB			7		1240			2100	2450
17	1	SPORTSMAN 180	ST	RNBT	FBG	DV	IO	120-170		7					2350	2900
17	2	FISHERMAN 180	ST	FSH	FBG	TR	OB			7	2	1600			2500	2900
17	2	FISHERMAN 180	ST	FSH	FBG	TR	IO	120		7	2				2100	2500
17	2	FISHERMAN 180	ST	FSH	FBG	TR	IO	130-170		7	2				2300	2700
18	11	CAPRICE 190	ST	CUD	FBG	SV	OB			7		1540			2600	3050
19	10	SPORTSMAN 200	ST	RNBT	FBG	DV	OB			7	5	1580			2800	3250
19	10	SPORTSMAN 200	ST	RNBT	FBG	DV	IO	120-190		7	5				3250	4000
20	2	ADVENTURER 200	ST	RNBT	FBG	DV	IO	120-190		7	6	3210			4150	5050
20	9	C-EAGLE 210	ST	CUD	FBG	DV	IO	165-245		7	6	3905			5200	6200
20	9	C-EAGLE 210	HT	CUD	FBG	DV	IO	165-245		7	6				4050	4850
22	2	C-EAGLE 230	ST	CUD	FBG	DV	IO	165-245		8		3500			5350	6350
22	2	C-EAGLE 230	HT	CUD	FBG	DV	IO	165-245		8					4550	5400
22	2	SPORTSMAN 230	ST	RNBT	FBG	DV	IO	165-245		8		3434			5000	5900
24	2	C-EAGLE 250	ST	CUD	FBG	DV	IO	165-255		8		4830			7550	9000
24	2	C-EAGLE 250	ST	CUD	FBG	DV	IO	T120-T140		8		4830			8300	9850
24	2	C-EAGLE 250	HT	CUD	FBG	DV	IO	165-255		8					6250	7450
24	2	C-EAGLE 250	HT	CUD	FBG	DV	IO	T120-T140		8					6950	8350
24	2	IMPERIAL 250	ST	EXP	FBG	DV	IO	165-245		8		5405			8300	9750
24	2	IMPERIAL 250	ST	EXP	FBG	DV	IO	T120-T140		8		5405			9100	10700
24	2	IMPERIAL 250	HT	EXP	FBG	DV	IO	165-245		8					6250	7350
24	2	IMPERIAL 250	HT	EXP	FBG	DV	IO	T120-T140		8					6950	8350
24	2	SPORT FISHERMAN 250	FB	SF	FBG	DV	IO	165-255		8		5210			9300	10800
24	2	SPORT FISHERMAN 250	FB	SF	FBG	DV	IO	T120-T140		8		5210			10100	11800
27		C-EAGLE 270	ST	CUD	FBG	DV	IO	225	OMC	10		6185			10700	12100
		IB 225 CHRY 9800 11100, IO 233 MRCR 10700 12200, IB 233 MRCR													9850	11200
		IO 255 MRCR 10900 12400, IB 255 MRCR 10000 11400, IO T140-T190													11300	13400
		IO T225 OMC 12200 13800, IB T225 CHRY 11100 12700, IO T233 MRCR													12300	14000
		IB T233 MRCR 11200 12800														
27		C-EAGLE 270	HT	CUD	FBG	DV	IO	225	OMC	10					9000	10300
		IB 225 CHRY 8200 9400, IO 233 MRCR 9100 10400, IB 233 MRCR													8250	9500
		IO 255 MRCR 9300 10600, IB 255 MRCR 8400 9650, IO T140-T190													9650	11600
		IO T225 OMC 10700 12100, IB T225 CHRY 9750 11100, IO T233 MRCR													10800	12300
		IB T233 MRCR 9850 11200														
27		IMPERIAL 270	ST	EXP	FBG	DV	IO	233-255		10		6830			11400	13100
27		IMPERIAL 270	ST	EXP	FBG	DV	IO	T140-T233		10		6830			11900	14600
27		IMPERIAL 270	HT	EXP	FBG	DV	IO	233-255		10					8900	10300
27		IMPERIAL 270	HT	EXP	FBG	DV	IO	T140-T190		10					9450	11400
27		IMPERIAL 270	HT	EXP	FBG	DV	IO	T225-T233		10					10500	12100
27		IMPERIAL 270	FB	EXP	FBG	DV	IO	233-255		10					8900	10300
27		IMPERIAL 270	FB	EXP	FBG	DV	IO	T140-T190		10					9450	11400
27		IMPERIAL 270	FB	EXP	FBG	DV	IO	T225-T233		10					10500	12100
27		SPORT FISHERMAN 270	FB	SF	FBG	DV	IO	255	MRCR	10		6670			13000	14700
		IB 255 MRCR 10400 11800, IO T140-T190 13400 15900, IO T225 OMC													14400	16300
		IB T225 CHRY 11500 13100, IO T233 MRCR 14500 16500, IB T233 MRCR													11600	13200
30		C-EAGLE 300	ST	EXP	FBG	DV	VD	225-233		10		7255			13500	15400
30		C-EAGLE 300	ST	EXP	FBG	DV	IO	255	MRCR	10		7255			14900	16900
30		C-EAGLE 300	ST	EXP	FBG	DV	IO	T140-T233		10		7255			15200	18900
30		C-EAGLE 300	HT	EXP	FBG	DV	VD	225-233		10					13000	14900
		IO 255 MRCR 14400 16400, IO T140-T225 14700 18300, IO T233 MRCR													16200	18400
30		SPORT FISHERMAN 300	FB	SF	FBG	DV	IO	255	MRCR	10		7800			14800	16800

CONTINUED ON NEXT PAGE

```
     LOA  NAME AND/           TOP/ BOAT -HULL- ----ENGINE--- BEAM   WGT  DRAFT RETAIL RETAIL
     FT IN  OR MODEL          RIG  TYPE MTL TP TP # HP  MFG   FT IN  LBS  FT IN  LOW   HIGH
-------------------- 1976 BOATS -------------------------------------------------------------
30    SPORT FISHERMAN 300    FB  SF   FBG DV IO T140-T190  10      7800        15100  18000
      IO T225  OMC   16300   18500, VD T225  CHRY 13200 14900, IO T233   MRCR 16400  18600
      VD T233  MRCR  13200   15100

30    SPORT SEDAN 300        ST  SDN  FBG DV IO T165-T190  10      8120        15900  18600
      IO T225  OMC   17000   19300, VD T225  CHRY 15600 17800, IO T233   MRCR 17100  19500
      VD T233  MRCR  15800   17900

30    SPORT SEDAN 300        HT  SDN  FBG DV IO T165-T190  10                  15300  17900
      IO T225  OMC   16100   18300, VD T225  CHRY 14800 16900, IO T233   MRCR 16100  18300
      VD T233  MRCR  14900   16900

30    SPORT SEDAN 300        FB  SDN  FBG DV IO T165-T190  10                  15300  17900
      IO T225  OMC   16100   18300, VD T225  CHRY 14800 16900, IO T233   MRCR 16100  18300
      VD T233  MRCR  14900   16900
-------------------- 1975 BOATS -------------------------------------------------------------
16 10 SPORTSMAN 170          ST  RNBT FBG SV IO 120-140   6   8           1300  2350   2850
17  4 FISHERMAN 180          ST  FSH  FBG TR OB           7   4           1300  2150   2550
17  6 ADVENTURER 180         ST  RNBT FBG SV OB           6  10           1240  2200   2600
17  6 SPORTSMAN 180          ST  RNBT FBG DV OB           6  10           1240  2100   2500
17  6 SPORTSMAN 180          ST  RNBT FBG DV IO 120-170   6  10                 2550   3150
18  6 SPORTSMAN 190          ST  RNBT FBG DV OB           6   9           1315  2300   2700
18  6 SPORTSMAN 190          ST  RNBT FBG DV IO 120-170   6   9                 2850   3500
18 11 CAPRICE 190            ST  CUD  FBG DV OB           7           1540        2600   3000
19 10 ADVENTURER 200         ST  RNBT FBG DV IO 120-190   7   6           3210  3800   4600
19 10 SPORTSMAN 200          ST  RNBT FBG DV OB           7   6           1580  2750   3250
19 10 SPORTSMAN 200          ST  RNBT FBG DV IO 120-190   7   6                 3400   4150
20  9 C-EAGLE 210            ST  CUD  FBG DV IO 165-245   7   6           3905  5400   6400

22  2 SPORTSMAN 230          ST  RNBT FBG DV IO 165-245   8           3640  5400   6350
24  6 C-EAGLE 250            ST  CUD  FBG DV IO 165-255   8           4830  7850   9450
24  6 C-EAGLE 250            ST  CUD  FBG DV IO T120-T140 8           4830  8650  10300
24  6 C-EAGLE 250            HT  CUD  FBG DV IO 165-255   8           4830  7850   9450
24  6 C-EAGLE 250            HT  CUD  FBG DV IO T120-T140 8           4830  8650  10300
24  6 IMPERIAL 250           ST  EXP  FBG DV IO 165-245   8           5405  8600  10200
24  6 IMPERIAL 250           ST  EXP  FBG DV IO T120-T140 8           5405  9400  11100
24  6 IMPERIAL 250           HT  EXP  FBG DV IO 165-245   8           5405  8600  10200
24  6 IMPERIAL 250           HT  EXP  FBG DV IO T120-T140 8           5405  9400  11100
24  6 SPORT FISHERMAN 250    FB  SF   FBG DV IO 165-255   8           5210  9600  11300
24  6 SPORT FISHERMAN 250    FB  SF   FBG DV IO T120-T140 8           5210 10500  12300

27    C-EAGLE 270            ST  CUD  FBG DV IO 225  OMC  10      6185        11000  12500
      IB  225  CHRY  9400   10700, IO  233  MRCR 11100 12600, IB  233   MRCR  9500  10800
      IO  255  MRCR 11300   12800, IB  255  MRCR  9600 10900, IO T140-T190 11700  13900
      IO T225  OMC   12600   14300, IB T225  CHRY 10700 12200, IO T233   MRCR 12700  14500
      IB T233  MRCR  10800   12300

27    C-EAGLE 270            HT  CUD  FBG DV IO 225  OMC  10      6185        11000  12500
      IB  225  MRCR  9450   10700, IO  233  MRCR 11100 12600, IB  233   MRCR  9500  10800
      IO  255  MRCR 11300   12800, IB  255  MRCR  9600 10900, IO T140-T190 11700  13900
      IO T225  OMC   12600   14300, IB T225  CHRY 10700 12200, IO T233   MRCR 12700  14500
      IB T233  MRCR  10800   12300

27    IMPERIAL 270           ST  EXP  FBG DV IO 233-255   10      6830        11700  13500
27    IMPERIAL 270           ST  EXP  FBG DV IO T140-T233 10      6830        12300  15100
27    IMPERIAL 270           HT  EXP  FBG DV IO 233-255   10      6830        11700  13500
27    IMPERIAL 270           HT  EXP  FBG DV IO T140-T233 10      6830        12300  15100
27    IMPERIAL 270           FB  EXP  FBG DV IO 233-255   10      6830        11700  13500
27    IMPERIAL 270           FB  EXP  FBG DV IO T140-T233 10      6830        12300  15100
27    SPORT FISHERMAN 270    FB  SF   FBG DV IO 255  MRCR 10      6670        13400  15700
      IB  255  MRCR 10000   11400, IO T140-T190 13900 16400, IO T225   OMC  14900  16900
      IB T225  CHRY 11100   12600, IO T233  MRCR 15000 17100, IB T225   MRCR 11200  12700

30    C-EAGLE 300            ST  EXP  FBG DV IO 225  MRCR 10      7255        15100  17200
      IO T140-T190  15700   18800, IO T225  OMC  17100 19400, VD T225   CHRY 14600  16600
      IO T233  MRCR  17200   19500, IO T233  MRCR 14700 16700

30    C-EAGLE 300            HT  EXP  FBG DV IO 225  MRCR 10      7255        15100  17200
      IO T140-T190  15700   18800, IO T225  OMC  17100 19400, VD T225   CHRY 14600  16600
      IO T233  MRCR  17200   19500, IO T233  MRCR 14700 16700

30    SPORT FISHERMAN 300    FB  SF   FBG DV IO 255  MRCR 10      7800        15300  17400
      IO T140-T190  15600   18600, IO T225  OMC  16800 19100, VD T225   CHRY 12600  14400
      IO T233  MRCR  17000   19300, IO T233  MRCR 12700 14500

30    SPORT SEDAN 300        ST  SDN  FBG DV IO T165-T190 10      8120        16500  19200
      IO T225  OMC   17500   19900, VD T225  CHRY 15000 17100, IO T233   MRCR 18100  20100
      VD T233  MRCR  15100   17200

30    SPORT SEDAN 300        HT  SDN  FBG DV IO T165-T190 10      8120        16500  19200
      IO T225  OMC   17500   19900, VD T225  CHRY 15000 17100, IO T233   MRCR 18100  20100
      VD T233  MRCR  15100   17200

30    SPORT SEDAN 300        FB  SDN  FBG DV IO T165-T190 10      8120        16500  19200
      IO T225  OMC   17500   19900, VD T225  CHRY 15000 17100, IO T233   MRCR 18100  20100
      VD T233  MRCR  15100   17200
-------------------- 1974 BOATS -------------------------------------------------------------
17  4 FISHERMAN 180          ST  FSH  FBG TR OB           7   4           1300  2150   2500
17  4 FISHERMAN 180          ST  FSH  FBG DV IO 120-165   7   4           1300  2350   2900
17  4 FISHERMAN 180          ST  FSH  FBG DV IO 170  VLVO 7   4           1300  2550   2900
17  6 ADVENTURER 180         ST  RNBT FBG DV OB           6  10           1240  2200   2550
17  6 SPORTSMAN 180          ST  RNBT FBG DV OB           6  10           1240  2050   2450
18  6 SPORTSMAN 190          ST  RNBT FBG DV OB           6   9           1315  2300   2650
18 11 C-EAGLE 190            ST  CUD  FBG SV OB           7           1640        2700   3150
18 11 CAPRICE 190            ST  CUD  FBG SV OB           7           1540        2600   3000
19 10 ADVENTURER 200         ST  RNBT FBG DV IO 120-188   7   6           3210  3900   4750
19 10 SPORTSMAN 200          ST  RNBT FBG DV OB           7   6           1580  2750   3200
19 10 SPORTSMAN 200          ST  RNBT FBG DV IO 120-188   7   6           2367  3300   4000
20  9 C-EAGLE 210            ST  CUD  FBG DV IO 165-188   7   6           3905  5550   6600

22  2 SPORTSMAN 230          ST  RNBT FBG DV IO 140-225   8           3640  5550   6550
24  6 250                    FB  SF   FBG DV IO 165-255   8           5210  9900  11700
24  6 250                    FB  SF   FBG DV IO T120-T140 8           5210 10800  12700
24  6 C-EAGLE 250            ST  CUD  FBG DV IO 165-255   8           4830  8150   9750
24  6 C-EAGLE 250            ST  CUD  FBG DV IO T120-T140 8           4830  9000  10600
24  6 C-EAGLE 250            HT  CUD  FBG DV IO 165-255   8           4830  8150   9750
24  6 C-EAGLE 250            HT  CUD  FBG DV IO T120-T140 8           4830  9000  10600
24  6 IMPERIAL 250           ST  EXP  FBG DV IO 165-255   8           5405  9000  10600
24  6 IMPERIAL 250           ST  EXP  FBG DV IO T120-T140 8           5405  9750  11400
24  6 IMPERIAL 250           HT  EXP  FBG DV IO 165  MRCR 8          5405  9000  10200
24  6 IMPERIAL 250           HT  EXP  FBG DV IO 165-255  14   5       5405 10200  11500
24  6 IMPERIAL 250           HT  EXP  FBG DV IO T120-T140 8           5405  9750  11400

27    270                    FB  SF   FBG DV IO 225  MRCR 10      6670        13600  15600
      IO  225  OMC   13600   15400, IB  225  MRCR  9450 10800, IO  245   OMC  13700  15600
      IB  250  CHRY  9550   10900, IO  255  MRCR 13900 15700, IB 255-350       9600  11300
      IO T140-T188  14300   16900, IO T225  MRCR 15400 17500, IO T225   OMC  15400  17400
      IB T225        10600   12100

27    C-EAGLE 270            ST  CUD  FBG DV IO 225  MRCR 10      6185        11400  13000
      IO  225  OMC   11400   12900, IB  225  MRCR  9100 10400, IO  245   OMC  11600  13100
      IB  250  CHRY  9250   10500, IO  255  MRCR 11700 13200, IB 255-350       9250  11100
      IO T140-T188  12100   14300, IO T225  MRCR 13000 14800, IO T225   OMC  13000  14800
      IB T225        10300   11700

27    C-EAGLE 270            HT  CUD  FBG DV IO 225  MRCR 10      6185        11400  13000
      IO  225  OMC   11400   12900, IB  225  MRCR  9100 10400, IO  245   OMC  11600  13100
      IB  250  CHRY  9250   10500, IO  255  MRCR 11700 13200, IB 255-350       9250  11100
      IO T140-T188  12100   14300, IO T225  MRCR 13000 14800, IO T225   OMC  13000  14800
      IB T225        10300   11700

27    IMPERIAL 270           ST  EXP  FBG DV IO 225-255   10      6830        12100  14000
27    IMPERIAL 270           ST  EXP  FBG DV VD 330-350   10      6830        10100  11700
27    IMPERIAL 270           ST  EXP  FBG DV IO T140-T225 10      6830        12700  15500
27    IMPERIAL 270           HT  EXP  FBG DV IO 225-255   10      6830        12100  14000
27    IMPERIAL 270           HT  EXP  FBG DV IO 330-350   10      6830        10100  11700
27    IMPERIAL 270           HT  EXP  FBG DV IO T140-T225 10      6830        12700  15500
27    IMPERIAL 270           FB  EXP  FBG DV IO 225-255   10      6830        12100  14000
27    IMPERIAL 270           FB  EXP  FBG DV IO 330-350   10      6830        10100  11700
27    IMPERIAL 270           FB  EXP  FBG DV IO T140-T225 10      6830        12700  15500

30    300                    FB  SF   FBG DV IO 225  MRCR 10      7800        15500  17600
      VD  225        10900   12400, IO  245  OMC  15700 17800, VD  250   CHRY 11000  12500
      IO  255  MRCR 13400   18000, VD 255-350 11100 13200, IO T140-T188 16100  19200
      IO T225  MRCR  17400   19800, VD T225  OMC  17400 19700, VD T225       12100  13800

30    C-EAGLE 300            ST  EXP  FBG DV IO 225  MRCR 10      7255        15600  17700
      IO  225  OMC   15600   17700, IO  225  MRCR 12500 14200, IO  245   OMC  15800  18000
      VD  250  CHRY  14400   16300, IO  255  MRCR 15900 18100, VD 255-350 12700  15200
      IO T140-T188  16300   19400, IO T225  MRCR 18000 20000, IO T225   OMC  18000  20000
      VD T225        14000   16000

30    C-EAGLE 300            HT  EXP  FBG DV IO 225  MRCR 10      7255        15600  17700
      IO  225  OMC   15600   17700, IO  225  MRCR 12500 14200, IO  245   OMC  15800  18000
      VD  250  CHRY  12600   14400, IO  255  MRCR 15900 18100, VD 255-350 12700  15200
```

```
SPORT-CRAFT BOATS          -CONTINUED      See inside cover to adjust price for area
LOA  NAME AND/         TOP/ BOAT  -HULL- ----ENGINE--- BEAM  WGT  DRAFT RETAIL RETAIL
FT IN  OR MODEL        RIG  TYPE  MTL TP TP # HP  MFG  FT IN  LBS  FT IN  LOW   HIGH
-------------------- 1974 BOATS---------------------------------------------------------
30   C-EAGLE 300           HT   EXP  FBG DV IO T140-T188  10    7255       16300  19400
     IO T225 MRCR  18000   20000, IO T225 OMC   18000 20000, VD T225       14000  16000

30   SPORT SEDAN 300       ST   SDN  FBG DV VD 330-350  10     8126       13500  15500
     IO T165-T188  17000   19800, IO T225 MRCR 18500 20600, IO T225 OMC   18500  20600
     VD T225  14400        16400

30   SPORT SEDAN 300       HT   SDN  FBG DV VD 330-350  10     8126       13500  15500
     IO T165-T188  17000   19800, IO T225 MRCR 18500 20600, IO T225 OMC   18500  20600
     VD T225  14400        16400

30   SPORT SEDAN 300       FB   SDN  FBG DV VD 330-350  10     8126       13500  15500
     IO T165-T188  17000   19800, IO T225 MRCR 18500 20600, IO T225 OMC   18500  20600
     VD T225  14400        16400

-------------------- 1973 BOATS---------------------------------------------------------
16   3 C-GULL 170          ST   RNBT FBG    IO 100-140  5   9               2050   2500
16  10 SPORTSMAN 170       ST   RNBT FBG    IO 100-140  6   8               2450   2900
17   4 180                 ST   RNBT FBG       OB       7   4   1250        2150   2500
17   4 180                 ST   RNBT FBG    IO 120-170  7   4               2700   3150
17   6 ADVENTURER 180      ST   RNBT FBG       OB       6  10   1275        2200   2550
17   6 ADVENTURER 180      ST   RNBT FBG    IO 120-170  6  10   1275        2250   2600
17   6 SPORTSMAN 180       ST   RNBT FBG       OB       6  10   1250        2150   2500
17   6 SPORTSMAN 180       ST   RNBT FBG    IO 120-165  6  10               2700   3150
18   4 ADVENTURER 190      ST   RNBT FBG    IO 120-170  6  10               2850   3300
18   6 SPORTSMAN 190       ST   RNBT FBG       OB       6   9   1400        2400   2800
18   6 SPORTSMAN 190       ST   RNBT FBG    IO 120-188  6   9               3050   3600
18  10 C-KING 190          OP   FSH  FBG       OB       8       2100        3000   3450

18  11 C-EAGLE 190         ST   CUD  FBG    IO 120-170  7       1400        2600   3100
18  11 CAPRICE 190         ST   CUD  FBG       OB       7       1400        2400   2800
18  11 CAPRICE 190         ST   CUD  FBG    IO 120-140  7                   3350   3900
20   2 ADVENTURER 200      ST   RNBT FBG    IO 120-255  7   6               4200   5100
20   2 C-EAGLE 200         ST   CUD  FBG    IO 120-188  7   6   2888        4500   5250
20   2 C-EAGLE 210         ST   CUD  FBG    IO 165-255  7   6   3250        4900   5900
20   2 SPORTSMAN 200       ST   RNBT FBG       OB       7   6   1580        2850   3300
20   2 SPORTSMAN 200       ST   RNBT FBG    IO 120-188  7   6               4100   4750
20   2 SPORTSMAN 210       ST   RNBT FBG    IO 140-255  7   6   2800        4200   5200
20  11 C-GULL 210          ST   CUD  FBG    IO 165-255  8       2800        4600   5550
22   2 C-EAGLE 230         ST   CUD  FBG    IO 165-255  8       3500        5900   7100
22   2 C-EAGLE 230         ST   CUD  FBG    IO T120-T140 8      3500        6700   7700

22   2 C-EAGLE 230         HT   CUD  FBG    IO 165-255  8                   5000   6050
22   2 C-EAGLE 230         HT   CUD  FBG    IO T120-T140 8                  5800   6650
22   2 C-EAGLE 230         FB   CUD  FBG    IO 165-255  8                   5000   6050
22   2 C-EAGLE 230         FB   CUD  FBG    IO T120-T140 8                  5800   6650
22   2 SPORT FISHERMAN 230      SF   FBG    IO 165-255  8   4100           7550   9700
22   2 SPORT FISHERMAN 230      SF   FBG    IO T120-T140 8  4100           8450   9700
22   2 SPORT FISHERMAN 230 HT   SF   FBG    IO 165-255  8                   5700   6900
22   2 SPORT FISHERMAN 230 HT   SF   FBG    IO T120-T140 8                  6600   7600
22   2 SPORT FISHERMAN 230 FB   SF   FBG    IO 165-255  8                   5700   6900
22   2 SPORT FISHERMAN 230 FB   SF   FBG    IO T120-T140 8                  6600   7600
22   2 SPORTSMAN 230       ST   RNBT FBG    IO 140-255  8   3200           5250   6300
22   2 SPORTSMAN 230       ST   RNBT FBG    IO T120-T140 8  3200           6000   6900

22   2 SPORTSMAN 230       HT   RNBT FBG    IO 140-255  8                   4750   5700
22   2 SPORTSMAN 230       HT   RNBT FBG    IO T120-T140 8                  5450   6300
22   2 SPORTSMAN 230       FB   RNBT FBG    IO 140-255  8                   4750   5700
22   2 SPORTSMAN 230       FB   RNBT FBG    IO T120-T140 8                  5450   6300
24   6 250                      SF   FBG    IO 165-255  8   5000           9900  11700
24   6 250                      SF   FBG    IO T120-T140 8  5000          10800  12400
24   6 C-EAGLE 250         ST   CUD  FBG    IO 165-255  8   4400           7850   9400
24   6 C-EAGLE 250         ST   CUD  FBG    IO T120-T140 8  4400           8650  10000
24   6 C-EAGLE 250         HT   CUD  FBG    IO 165-255  8                   7200   8700
24   6 C-EAGLE 250         HT   CUD  FBG    IO T120-T140 8                  8000   9300
24   6 C-EAGLE 250         FB   CUD  FBG    IO 165-255  8                   7200   8700
24   6 C-EAGLE 250         FB   CUD  FBG    IO T120-T140 8                  8000   9300

24   6 IMPERIAL 250        ST   EXP  FBG    IO 165-255  8   4900           8500  10200
24   6 IMPERIAL 250        ST   EXP  FBG    IO T120-T140 8  4900           9400  10700
24   6 IMPERIAL 250        HT   EXP  FBG    IO 165-255  8                   7000   8450
24   6 IMPERIAL 250        HT   EXP  FBG    IO T120-T140 8                  7800   9050
24   6 SPORT FISHERMAN 250 HT   SF   FBG    IO 165-275  8                   7600   9400
24   6 SPORT FISHERMAN 250 HT   SF   FBG    IO T120-T140 8                  8550   9900
24   6 SPORT FISHERMAN 250 FB   SF   FBG    IO 165-275  8                   7600   9400
24   6 SPORT FISHERMAN 250 FB   SF   FBG    IO T120-T140 8                  8550   9900

27     270                      SF   FBG    IO 225 MRCR 10   6300          13600  15400
     IB   225       8850   10100, IO  245 CHRY 13800 15600, IB  250 CHRY   8950  10500
     IO  255 MRCR 13900   15700, IB  255 MRCR  9000 10200, IO 275 CHRY    14100  16000
     IB 325-330  9350     10600, IO T140-T200  14300 17200, IB T225 MRCR  15500  17600
     IB T225        9950   11500, IO T245 CHRY 15800 17900, IB T250 CHRY  10100  11500
     IO T255 MRCR 15900   18100, IB T255 MRCR 10200 11600, IO T275 CHRY   16300  18500
     IB T325-T330 10800   12300

27     C-EAGLE 270         ST   CUD  FBG    IO 225 MRCR 10   5600          11200  12700
     IO  225 OMC  11200   12700, IB  225     8200 9450, IO 245             11400  12900
     IB  250 CHRY  8300    9550, IO 255 MRCR 11400 13000, IB  255 MRCR     8350   9600
     IO  275 CHRY 11600   13200, IB 325-330  8850 10100, IO T140-T200     11900  14300
     IO T225 MRCR 12900   14700, IO T250 OMC 12900 14600, IB T225         9450  10800
     IO T245       13200   15000, IB T250 CHRY 9650 11000, IO T255 MRCR   13400  15200
     IB T255 MRCR  9750   11100, IO T275 CHRY 13700 15500, IB T325-T330   10400  11800

27     C-EAGLE 270         HT   CUD  FBG    IO 225 MRCR 10                  9900  11300
     IO  225 OMC   9900   11200, IB  225     7250 8350, IO  245           10100  11500
     IB  250 CHRY  7400    8500, IO 255 MRCR 10200 11600, IB  255 MRCR     7450   8550
     IO  275 CHRY 10400   11800, IB 325-330  7850 9050, IO T140-T200      10700  13000
     IO T225 MRCR 11800   13400, IO T250 OMC 11800 13400, IB T225         8600   9900
     IO T245       12100   13800, IB T250 CHRY 8900 10100, IO T255 MRCR   12300  14000
     IB T255 MRCR  9000   10200, IO T275 CHRY 12500 14200, IB T325-T330    9250  10500

27     C-EAGLE 270         FB   CUD  FBG    IO 225 MRCR 10                  9900  11300
     IO  225 OMC   9900   11200, IB  225     7250 8350, IO  245           10100  11500
     IB  250 CHRY  7400    8500, IO 255 MRCR 10200 11600, IB  255 MRCR     7450   8550
     IO  275 CHRY 10400   11800, IB 325-330  7850 9050, IO T140-T200      10700  13000
     IO T225 MRCR 11800   13400, IO T250 OMC 11800 13400, IB T225         8600   9900
     IO T245       12100   13800, IB T250 CHRY 8900 10100, IO T255 MRCR   12300  14000
     IB T255 MRCR  9000   10200, IO T275 CHRY 12500 14200, IB T325-T330    9250  10500

27     SPORT FISHERMAN 270 HT   SF   FBG    IO 225 MRCR 10                 10700  12200
     IB  225       6900    7950, IO 245 CHRY 11000 12500, IB  250 CHRY     7050   8100
     IO  255 MRCR 11100   12600, IB 255 MRCR 7100 8150, IO 275 CHRY       11300  12900
     IB 325-330    7550    8650, IO T140-T200 11600 14300, IO T225 MRCR   13000  14800
     IB T225       8300    9750, IO T245 CHRY 13200 15000, IB T250 MRCR    8400   9650
     IO T255 MRCR 13300   15100, IB T255 MRCR 8450 9700, IO T275 CHRY     13500  15300
     IB T325-T330  8650    9950

27     SPORT FISHERMAN 270 FB   SF   FBG    IO 225 MRCR 10                 10800  12200
     IB  225       6900    7950, IO 245 CHRY 11000 12500, IB  250 CHRY     7050   8100
     IO  255 MRCR 11100   12600, IB 255 MRCR 7100 8150, IO 275 CHRY       11300  12900
     IB 325-330    7550    8650, IO T165-T200 11600 14300, IO T225 MRCR   13000  14800
     IB T225       8300    9750, IO T245 CHRY 13200 15100, IB T250 MRCR    8400   9650
     IO T255 MRCR 13300   15200, IB T255 MRCR 8450 9700, IO T275 CHRY     13500  15400
     IB T325-T330  8650    9950

27   1 IMPERIAL 270        ST   EXP  FBG    IO 225-275  10   6500          12200  14300
     VD 325-330    9500   10800, IO T140-T245 12800 16000, IO T255-T275   14300  16600

27   1 IMPERIAL 270        HT   EXP  FBG    IO 225-275  10                  9750  11700
     VD 325-330    7800    8950, IO T140-T200 10500 12900, IO T225-T275   11700  14000

27   1 IMPERIAL 270        FB   EXP  FBG    IO 225-275  10                  9750  11700
     VD 325-330    7800    8950, IO T140-T200 10500 12900, IO T255-T275   11700  14000

30     300                 HT   HB   FBG    IO 275 CHRY 12                 15000  17000
30     300                 HT   HB   FBG    IO T165-T188 12                15600  17900
30     300                 ST   SDN  FBG    IO 275 CHRY 12     8200        17000  19300
     VD 325-330   13000   14800, IO T165-T200 20800, IO T225 MRCR         19000  21100
     IO T225 OMC  19000   21100, VD T225     13900 15800, IO T245         19400  21500
     VD T225 CHRY 14200   16200, IO T255 MRCR 14900 21700, IO T255 MRCR   14300  16300
     IO T275 CHRY 19800   22000, VD T325-T330 14600 16600

30     300                 HT   SDN  FBG    IO T165-T275 10    8200        17000  19300
30     300                 FB   SDN  FBG    IO T165-T275 10    8200        18000  22000
30     300                      SF   FBG    IO 225-255  10     8200        16000  20000
     IO  275 CHRY 16800   19100, VD 325-330  11200 12700, IO T165-T200    17300  20300
     IB T225 MRCR 18600   20700, VD T225     19100 21200, IO T225-T330    14500  14500
     VD T250 CHRY 12000   13700, IO T255 MRCR 19100 21200, IO T255-T330   12100  14500

30     C-EAGLE 300         HT   CUD  FBG    IO 225     9000              13300  15300
     IO  225 OMC  13200   15100, IO  245 MRCR 9850 11200, IO  245         13400  15300
     IO  250 CHRY 13000   14800, IO 275     9500 15400, IO  275 CHRY     10000  11400
     IO T225 MRCR 13700   15600, VD 325-330 10500 11900, IO T140-T200    13800  16700
     IO T245       15100   17500, IO T250 OMC 10500 17100, IO T225        16500  17700
     IO T245 MRCR 15400   17500, IO T250 CHRY 11400 13100, IO T255 MRCR  15500  17700
     VD T255 MRCR 11500   13000, IO T275 CHRY 15800 18000, VD T325-T330  12200  13900

566                    CONTINUED ON NEXT PAGE                96th ed. - Vol. III
```

```
LOA   NAME AND/       TOP/ BOAT -HULL- ----ENGINE--- BEAM  WGT DRAFT RETAIL RETAIL
FT IN  OR MODEL       RIG TYPE MTL TP TP # HP  MFG  FT IN  LBS FT IN  LOW   HIGH
--------------------- 1973 BOATS ---------------------------------------------------
30   C-EAGLE 300      FB  CUD  FBG      IO  225  MRCR 10          13300 15100
  IO  225   OMC  13200 15100, VD  225        9850 11200, IO  245        13400 15300
  VD  250   CHRY 10000 11400, IO  255  MRCR 13500 15400, VD  255  MRCR 10000 11400
  IO  275   CHRY 13700 15600, VD 325-330    10500 11900, IO T140-T200  13800 16700
  IO T225   MRCR 15100 17200, IO T225  OMC  15100 17100, VD T225       11200 12700
  IO T245        15400 17500, VD T250  CHRY 11400 13000, IO T255  MRCR 15500 17700
  VD T255   MRCR 11500 13000, IO T275  CHRY 15800 18000, VD T325-T330  12200 13900

30   C-EAGLE 300      ST  EXP  FBG      IO  225  MRCR 10     8200  16800 19100
  IO  225   OMC  16800 19000, VD  225        12400 14100, IO  245       17000 19300
  VD  250   CHRY 12600 14300, IO  255  MRCR 17100 19400, VD  255  MRCR 12700 14400
  IO  275   CHRY 17300 19600, VD 325-330    13100 14900, IO T140-T200  17400 20900
  IO T225   MRCR 19200 21300, IO T225  OMC  19200 21300, VD T225       13900 15800
  IO T245        19300 21400, VD T250  CHRY 14200 16100, IO T255  MRCR 19500 21600
  VD T255   MRCR 14200 16200, IO T275  CHRY 19800 22000, VD T325-T330  15000 17100

30   IMPERIAL 300     ST  EXP  FBG      IO  275  CHRY 10     7200  16600 18900
  IB  325   MRCR 12700 14400, VD  325  MRCR 12700 14400, IB  330  CHRY 12700 14400
  VD  330   CHRY 12700 14400, IO T165-T200  17200 20200, IO T225  MRCR 18600 20700
  IO T225   OMC  18600 20700, IB T225       13500 15300, IO T245       18900 21000
  IB T250   CHRY 13800 15600, IO T255  MRCR 19100 21200, IB T255  MRCR 13800 15700
  IO T275   CHRY 19300 21400, IB T325-T330  14600 16700

30   IMPERIAL 300     HT  EXP  FBG      IO  275  CHRY 10           16100 18300
  IB  325   MRCR 12300 14000, VD  325  MRCR 12300 14000, IB  330  CHRY 12300 14000
  VD  330   CHRY 12300 14000, IO T165-T200  16700 19700, IO T225  MRCR 18200 20200
  IO T225   OMC  18200 20200, IB T225       13200 15000, IO T245       18500 20600
  IB T250   CHRY 13500 15300, IO T255  MRCR 18700 20800, IB T255  MRCR 13500 15400
  IO T275   CHRY 19100 21200, IB T325-T330  14400 16400

30   IMPERIAL 300     FB  EXP  FBG      IO  275  CHRY 10           16100 18300
  IB  325   MRCR 12300 14000, VD  325  MRCR 12300 14000, IB  330  CHRY 12300 14000
  VD  330   CHRY 12300 14000, IO T165-T200  16700 19700, IO T225  MRCR 18200 20200
  IO T225   OMC  18200 20200, IB T225       13200 15000, IO T245       18500 20600
  IB T250   CHRY 13500 15300, IO T255  MRCR 18700 20800, IB T255  MRCR 13500 15400
  IO T275   CHRY 19100 21200, IB T325  MRCR 14400 16300

30   SPORT FISHERMAN 300  HT  SF  FBG   VD 225-255    10           9800 11400
  IO  275   CHRY 15600 17800, VD 325-330    10400 11900, IO T165-T200  16200 19100
  IO T225   MRCR 17200 19500, VD T225       11200 12700, IO T245  CHRY 17500 19900
  VD T250   CHRY 11400 13000, IO T255  MRCR 18100 20100, VD T255-T330  11500 13900

30   SPORT FISHERMAN 300  FB  SF  FBG   VD 225-255    10           9800 11400
  IO  275   CHRY 15600 17800, VD 325-330    10400 11900, IO T165-T200  16200 19100
  IO T225   MRCR 17200 19500, VD T225       11200 12700, IO T245  CHRY 17500 19900
  VD T250   CHRY 11400 13000, IO T255  MRCR 18100 20100, VD T255-T330  11500 13900

30   SPORT SEDAN 300  HT  SDN  FBG      IO  275  CHRY 10           16100 18300
  VD 325-330     12400 14100, IO T165-T200  16800 20000, IO T225  MRCR 18200 20200
  IO T225   OMC  18200 20200, VD T225       13200 15000, IO T245       18200 20300
  VD T250   CHRY 13200 15000, IO T255  MRCR 18300 20300, VD T255  MRCR 13200 15000
  IO T275   CHRY 18400 20400, VD T325-T330  13400 15200

30   SPORT SEDAN 300  FB  SDN  FBG      IO  275  CHRY 10           16100 18300
  VD 325-330     12400 14100, IO T165-T200  16800 20000, IO T225  MRCR 18200 20200
  IO T225   OMC  18200 20200, VD T225       13200 15000, IO T245       18200 20300
  VD T250   CHRY 13200 15000, IO T255  MRCR 18300 20300, VD T255  MRCR 13200 15000
  IO T275   CHRY 18400 20400, VD T325-T330  13400 15200
--------------------- 1972 BOATS ---------------------------------------------------
16  3 C-GULL 170      ST  RNBT FBG      IO  90-140    5  9          2200  2550
16  3 SAFARI 170      ST  RNBT FBG      IO  90-140    6  6          2300  2700
16  6 SPORTSMAN 170   ST  RNBT FBG      IO  90-140    8  4          2450  2900
17  4 180             ST  FSH  FBG      OB           8  4  1250     2000  2350
17  4 180             ST  FSH  FBG      OB  120-188   8  4  2800    2800  3300
17  6 ADVENTURER 180  ST  RNBT FBG      IO  120-188   6 10  1275    2200  2550
17  6 ADVENTURER 180  ST  RNBT FBG      OB  120-188   6 10         2850  3350
17  6 SPORTSMAN 180   ST  RNBT FBG      IO  120-188   6 10  1250    2150  2500
17  6 SPORTSMAN 180   ST  RNBT FBG      OB  120-188   6 10         2750  3250
18  4 ADVENTURER 190  ST  RNBT FBG      IO  120-188   6  9  1400    2450  2850
18  4 ADVENTURER 190  ST  RNBT FBG      OB  120-188   6  9         2950  3500
18  4 SPORTSMAN 190   ST  RNBT FBG      OB           6  9  1400     2300  2650

18  4 SPORTSMAN 190   ST  RNBT FBG      IO  120-188   6  9          2850  3400
18  6 C-GULL 190      ST  RNBT FBG      IO  120-188   6 10          3150  3750
18  6 C-HAWK 190      ST  RNBT FBG      IO  120-188   6 10  2600    3250  3900
18 11 C-EAGLE 190     ST  CUD  FBG      OB           7     1400     2450  2850
18 11 C-EAGLE 190     ST  CUD  FBG      IO  120-188   7          3500  4100
18 11 CAPRICE 190     ST  CUD  FBG      OB           7     1400     2350  2750
18 11 CAPRICE 190     ST  CUD  FBG      IO  90-140    7          3450  4050
20  2 C-EAGLE 200     ST  CUD  FBG      IO  120-188   7  6  2800    4600  5250
20  2 C-EAGLE 210     ST  CUD  FBG      IO  155-188   8     2400    4350  5400
20  2 C-EAGLE 210     ST  CUD  FBG      IO  215-245   8          4750  5550
20  2 C-GULL 210      ST  RNBT FBG      IO  155-245   7  6  1580    3450  4250
20  2 SPORTSMAN 200   ST  RNBT FBG      OB           7  6  1580     2850  3300

20  2 SPORTSMAN 200   ST  RNBT FBG      IO  120-188   7  6          4250  5000
20  2 SPORTSMAN 210   ST  RNBT FBG      IO  140-245   7 10  2800    4500  5250
20 11 ADVENTURER 200  ST  RNBT FBG      OB           8  3         4400  5050
20 11 ADVENTURER 200  ST  RNBT FBG      IO  120-245   8  3  2800    4800  5550
22  2 230             SF        FBG      IO  155-245   8     4100    7750  9200
22  2 230             SF        FBG      IO T120-T140 8     4100    8800 10000
22  2 C-EAGLE 230     ST  CUD  FBG      IO  155-245   8     3500    6050  6900
22  2 C-EAGLE 230     HT  CUD  FBG      IO T120-T140 8          5950  6900
22  2 C-EAGLE 230     ST  CUD  FBG      IO  155-245   8          5150  6150
22  2 C-EAGLE 230     HT  CUD  FBG      IO T120-T140 8          5950  6900
22  2 C-EAGLE 230     FB  CUD  FBG      IO  155-245   8          5150  6150
22  2 C-EAGLE 230     FB  CUD  FBG      IO T120-T140 8          5950  6900

22  2 SPORTSMAN 230   ST  RNBT FBG      IO  140-270   8     3200    5400  6250
22  2 SPORTSMAN 230   ST  RNBT FBG      IO T120-T140 8          5650  6500
24  6 240             HT  HB   FBG      OB           8          **    **
24  6 C-EAGLE 250     ST  CUD  FBG      IO  155-270   8     4400    8050  9250
24  6 C-EAGLE 250     ST  CUD  FBG      IO T120-T140 8          8300  9600
24  6 C-EAGLE 250     HT  CUD  FBG      IO  155-270   8          7400  9100
24  6 C-EAGLE 250     HT  CUD  FBG      IO T120-T140 8          8300  9600
24  6 C-EAGLE 250     FB  CUD  FBG      IO  155-270   8          7400  9100
24  6 C-EAGLE 250     FB  CUD  FBG      IO T120-T140 8          8300  9600
24  6 IMPERIAL 250    ST  EXP  FBG      IO  155-245   8     4800    8600  9850
24  6 IMPERIAL 250    ST  EXP  FBG      IO T120-T140 8          8050  9350

24  6 IMPERIAL 250    HT  EXP  FBG      IO  155-245   8          7150  8600
24  6 IMPERIAL 250    HT  EXP  FBG      IO T120-T140 8          8050  9350
25    SPORT FISHERMAN 250  SF  FBG      IO  155-270   8     5000   10300 12500
25    SPORT FISHERMAN 250  SF  FBG      IO  325  MRCR 8     5000   11700 13300
25    SPORT FISHERMAN 250  SF  FBG      IO T120-T140 8     5000   11300 13000
27    C-EAGLE 270     ST  CUD  FBG      IO  215  MRCR 9 10          10100 11500
  IB  215   MRCR  6900  7950, IO  225  OMC  10200 11600, IB 225-255  8200  9200
  IO  270   MRCR 10700 12100, IB  270  MRCR  7200  8300, IO  325  MRCR 11300 12900
  IB 325-330      7550  8700, IO T120-T188 10700 13200, IB T215-T330 11300 13000

27    C-EAGLE 270     HT  CUD  FBG      IO  215  MRCR 9 10          10100 11500
  IB  215   MRCR  6900  7950, IO  225  OMC  10200 11600, IB 225-255  6950  8200
  IO  270   MRCR 10700 12100, IB  270  MRCR  7200  8300, IO  325  MRCR 11300 12900
  IB 325-330      7550  8700, IO T120-T188 10700 13200, IB T215-T330 11300 13000

27    C-EAGLE 270     FB  CUD  FBG      IO  215  MRCR 9 10          10100 11500
  IB  215   MRCR  6900  7950, IO  225  OMC  10200 11600, IB 225-255  6950  8200
  IO  270   MRCR 10700 12100, IB  270  MRCR  7200  8300, IO  325  MRCR 11300 12900
  IB 325-330      7550  8700, IO T120-T188 10700 13200, IB T215-T330  8200 10100

27    SPORT FISHERMAN 270  SF  FBG      IO  215  MRCR 9 10  6300   13900 15800
  IB  215   MRCR  6600  7550, IO  270  OMC  11900 12600, IB 225-255  6600  7800
  IO  225   OMC  11600 13200, IB  270  MRCR  6900  7900, IO  325  MRCR 14400 14100
  IB 325-330      7200  8200, IO T120-T188 11600 14500, IB T215-T330 13200 15800
  IB T215   MRCR  7900  9100, IO T120-T188 11600 14500, IB T215-T330  7950  9250

27  1 IMPERIAL 270    ST  EXP  FBG      IO  215-270   9 10          9950 12000
  IO  325   MRCR 11200 12700, IO T120-T165 10500 13100, IO T215-T225 11900 13700

27  1 IMPERIAL 270    HT  EXP  FBG      IO  215-270   9 10          9950 12000
  IO  325   MRCR 11200 12700, IO T120-T188 10500 13100, IO T215-T225 11900 13700

27  1 IMPERIAL 270    FB  EXP  FBG      IO  215-270   9 10          9950 12000
  IO  325   MRCR 11200 12700, IO T120-T188 10500 13100, IO T215-T225 11900 13700

30    300             HT  HB   FBG      IO  215-325  12     8700   13300 15200
30    300             HT  HB   FBG      IO  225-325  12          14800 16800
30    300             HT  HB   FBG      IO T155-T188 12     8700   14400 16400
30    300             ST  SDN  FBG      IO  270  MRCR 9 10  8200   17400 19800
  IO  325   MRCR 18600 20600, VD 325-330    11900 13500, IO T155-T188 18400 20800
  IO T215   MRCR 18700 20800, VD T215  MRCR 12600 14300, IO T215-T330 18700 20800
  VD T225-T330    12600 14600

30    300             FB  SDN  FBG      IO  270-325   9 10  8200   17400 19800
30    300             FB  SDN  FBG      IO T155-T225 9 10         16900 20500
```

1972 BOATS

LOA FT	IN	NAME AND/ OR MODEL	TOP/ RIG	BOAT TYPE	-HULL- MTL	TP	TP	ENGINE # HP	MFG	BEAM FT	IN	WGT LBS	DRAFT FT IN	RETAIL LOW	RETAIL HIGH
30		IMPERIAL 300	ST	EXP	FBG		IO	270	MRCR	9	10	7200		17100	19400
		IB 270 MRCR 11400 13000, IO 325 MRCR 18100 20100, IB 325-330												11800	13400
		IO T155-T188 17500 20600, IO T215 MRCR 19000 21100, IB T215 MRCR												12500	14200
		IO T225 OMC 19200 21300, IB T225-T330 12600 15700													
30		IMPERIAL 300	HT	EXP	FBG		IO	270	MRCR	9	10			16600	18800
		IB 270 MRCR 11400 13000, IO 325 MRCR 17200 19500, IB 325-330												11800	13400
		IO T155-T188 17000 20100, IO T215 MRCR 18500 20600, IB T215 MRCR												12500	14200
		IO T225 OMC 18700 20800, IB T225-T330 12600 15700													
30		IMPERIAL 300	FB	EXP	FBG		IB	270-330		9	10			11400	13400
30		IMPERIAL 300	FB	EXP	FBG		IB	T155-T225		9	10			11800	14400
30		IMPERIAL 300	FB	EXP	FBG		IB	T270-T330		9	10			13200	15700
30		SPORT FISHERMAN 300		SF	FBG		VD	225	MRCR	9	10			9450	10700
		IO 270 MRCR 17300 19600, VD 270 MRCR 9700 11000, IO 325 MRCR												16700	18900
		VD 325-330 10000 11400, IO T155-T188 16500 19400, VD T215-T325												10600	13300
		VD T330 CHRY 11700 13300													
30		SPORT SEDAN 300	HT	SDN	FBG		IO	270	MRCR	9	10			16600	18800
		IO 325 MRCR 17300 19700, VD 325-330 11900 13500, IO T155-T188												17100	20300
		IO T215 MRCR 18700 20800, VD T215 MRCR 12600 14300, IO T225 OMC												18700	20800
		VD T225-T330 12600 14600													
30		SPORT SEDAN 300	FB	SDN	FBG		IO	270	MRCR	9	10			16600	18800
		VD 325-330 11900 13500, IO T155-T188 17300 21300, IO T215 MRCR												18900	21100
		VD T215 MRCR 12600 14300, IO T225 OMC 19100 21200, VD T225-T270												12600	14400
		IO T325 MRCR 19100 21200, VD T325-T330 12800 14600													
30	1	C-EAGLE 300	ST	EXP	FBG		IO	215	MRCR	9	10	6500		16200	18400
		VD 215 MRCR 11100 12600, IO 225 OMC 16200 18400, VD 225-255												11200	13000
		IO 270 MRCR 16700 19000, VD 270-300 11500 13300, IO 325 MRCR												17400	19700
		VD 325 MRCR 11900 13500, IO T140-T188 16900 20300, VD T215-T270												12600	15100
		VD T325-T330 13900 15900													
30	1	C-EAGLE 300	HT	EXP	FBG		IO	215	MRCR	9	10			16100	18300
		VD 215 MRCR 11100 12600, IO 225 OMC 16200 18400, VD 225-255												11200	13000
		IO 270 MRCR 16700 19000, VD 270-300 11500 13300, IO 325 MRCR												17400	19700
		VD 325 MRCR 11900 13500, IO T140-T188 16900 20300, VD T215-T270												12600	15100
		VD T325-T330 13900 15900													
30	1	C-EAGLE 300	FB	EXP	FBG		IO	215	MRCR	9	10			16100	18300
		VD 215 MRCR 11100 12600, IO 225 OMC 16200 18400, VD 225-255												11200	13000
		IO 270 MRCR 16700 19000, VD 270-300 11500 13300, IO 325 MRCR												17400	19700
		VD 325 MRCR 11900 13500, IO T140-T188 16900 20300, VD T215-T270												12600	15100
		VD T325-T330 13900 15900													

1971 BOATS

LOA FT	IN	NAME AND/ OR MODEL	TOP/ RIG	BOAT TYPE	-HULL- MTL	TP	TP	ENGINE # HP	MFG	BEAM FT	IN	WGT LBS	DRAFT FT IN	RETAIL LOW	RETAIL HIGH
16	3	C-GULL 170	ST	RNBT	FBG		IO	90-120		5	9			2250	2650
16	3	SAFARI 170	ST	RNBT	FBG		IO	90-140		6	6			2350	2750
16	6	SPORTSMAN 170	ST	RNBT	FBG		IO	90-140		6	6			2550	3000
17	4	180	ST	FSH	FBG		OB			8	4	1250		2150	2500
17	4	180	ST	FSH	FBG		IO	120-165		8	4			2900	3400
17	4	C-HAWK 180	ST	RNBT	FBG		OB			6	10	1400		2300	2700
17	4	STANDARD 180	ST	FSH	FBG		OB			8	4	1250		1900	2250
17	6	ADVENTURER 180	ST	RNBT	FBG		OB			6	10	1275		2200	2550
17	6	ADVENTURER 180	ST	RNBT	FBG		IO	120-165		6	10			2900	3450
17	6	SPORTSMAN 180	ST	RNBT	FBG		OB			6	10	1250		2150	2500
17	6	SPORTSMAN 180	ST	RNBT	FBG		IO	120-165		6	10			2800	3300
17	9	C-GULL 180	ST	RNBT	FBG		OB			6	10	1050		1800	2150
17	9	C-GULL 180	ST	RNBT	FBG		IO	120-165		6	10			2900	3400
18	4	ADVENTURER 190	ST	RNBT	FBG		OB			6	9	1400		2450	2850
18	4	ADVENTURER 190	ST	RNBT	FBG		IO	120-165		6	9			3050	3550
18	4	SPORTSMAN 190	ST	RNBT	FBG		OB			6	9	1400		2250	2650
18	4	SPORTSMAN 190	ST	RNBT	FBG		IO	120-165		6	9			2950	3450
18	6	C-GULL 190	ST	RNBT	FBG		IO	120-165		6	10			3250	3800
18	6	C-HAWK 190	ST	RNBT	FBG		IO	120-165		6	10	2600		3350	4050
18	11	C-EAGLE 190	ST	CUD	FBG		OB			7		1400		2450	2800
18	11	C-EAGLE 190	ST	CUD	FBG		IO	120-165		7				3600	4200
18	11	CAPRICE CBN 190	ST	CUD	FBG		OB			7		1400		2350	2750
18	11	CAPRICE CBN 190	ST	CUD	FBG		IO	90-140		7				3600	4150
18	11	SAFARI 190	ST	RNBT	FBG		OB			7				2950	3400
20	2	C-EAGLE 200	ST	CUD	FBG		IO	120-165		7	6	2800		4700	5400
20	2	C-EAGLE 210		CUD	FBG		IO	155-165		8		2400		4500	5550
20	2	C-EAGLE 210		CUD	FBG		IO	215-235		8				4900	5700
20	2	C-GULL 210	ST	RNBT	FBG		IO	155-235		7	6	1580		3550	4350
20	2	SPORTSMAN 200	ST	RNBT	FBG		OB			7	6	1580		2800	3300
20	2	SPORTSMAN 200	ST	RNBT	FBG		IO	120-165		7	6			4450	5150
20	2	SPORTSMAN 210	ST	RNBT	FBG		IO	140-235		7	10	2800		4650	5350
20	11	ADVENTURER 200	ST	RNBT	FBG		OB			8	3			4350	5000
20	11	ADVENTURER 200	ST	RNBT	FBG		IO	120-235		8	3	2800		4950	5700
20	11	ADVENTURER 210		RNBT	FBG		IO	155-235		8	3			4800	5700
22	2	C-EAGLE 230		CUD	FBG		IO	155-235		8		3500		6250	7200
22	2	C-EAGLE 230		CUD	FBG		IO	T120		8				6150	7100
22	2	C-EAGLE 230	HT	CUD	FBG		IO	155-235		8				5300	6300
22	2	C-EAGLE 230	HT	CUD	FBG		IO	T120		8				6150	7100
22	2	C-EAGLE 230	FB	CUD	FBG		IO	155-235		8				5300	6300
22	2	C-EAGLE 230	FB	CUD	FBG		IO	T120		8				6150	7100
22	2	SPORTSMAN 230	ST	RNBT	FBG		IO	140-270		8		3200		5600	6450
22	2	SPORTSMAN 230	ST	RNBT	FBG		IO	T120		8				5850	6700
24	6	C-EAGLE 250		CUD	FBG		IO	155-270		8		4400		8300	9550
24	6	C-EAGLE 250		CUD	FBG		IO	T120-T140		8				8550	9950
24	6	C-EAGLE 250	HT	CUD	FBG		IO	155-270		8				7650	9400
24	6	C-EAGLE 250	HT	CUD	FBG		IO	T120-T140		8				8550	9950
24	6	C-EAGLE 250	FB	CUD	FBG		IO	155-270		8				7650	9400
24	6	C-EAGLE 250	FB	CUD	FBG		IO	T120-T140		8				8550	9950
24	6	IMPERIAL 250	ST	EXP	FBG		IO	155-235		8		4800		9000	10200
24	6	IMPERIAL 250	ST	EXP	FBG		IO	T120-T140		8				8350	9650
24	6	IMPERIAL 250	HT	EXP	FBG		IO	155-235		8				7400	8850
24	6	IMPERIAL 250	HT	EXP	FBG		IO	T120-T140		8				8350	9650
27		C-EAGLE 270		CUD	FBG		IO	215	MRCR	9	10			10500	11900
		IO 215 OMC 11800 13400, IB 215-225 6650 7750, IO 235 OMC												10600	12100
		IB 250 OMC 6900 7950, IO 270 MRCR 11000 12500, IB 270 MRCR												6950	8000
		IO 325 MRCR 11700 13300, IB 325-330 7250 8350, IO T120-T165												11000	13300
		IB T215-T330 7900 9700													
27		C-EAGLE 270	HT	CUD	FBG		IO	215	MRCR	9	10			10500	11900
		IO 215 OMC 10400 11900, IB 215-225 6650 7750, IO 235 OMC												10600	12100
		IB 250 OMC 6900 7950, IO 270 MRCR 11000 12500, IB 270 MRCR												6950	8000
		IO 325 MRCR 11700 13300, IB 325-330 7250 8350, IO T120-T165												11000	13300
		IB T215-T330 7900 9700													
27		C-EAGLE 270	FB	CUD	FBG		IO	215	MRCR	9	10			10500	11900
		IO 215 OMC 10400 11900, IB 215-225 6650 7750, IO 235 OMC												10600	12100
		IB 250 OMC 6900 7950, IO 270 MRCR 11000 12500, IB 270 MRCR												6950	8000
		IO 325 MRCR 11700 13300, IB 325-330 7250 8350, IO T120-T165												11000	13300
		IB T215-T330 7900 9700													
27	1	IMPERIAL 270	ST	EXP	FBG		IO	215	MRCR	9	10			10300	11700
		IO 215-325 12900 14600, IO T120-T165 10900 13100, IO T215												12300	14000
27	1	IMPERIAL 270	HT	EXP	FBG		IO	215-270		9	10			10300	12400
		IO 325 MRCR 11600 13200, IO T120-T165 10900 13100, IO T215												12300	14000
27	1	IMPERIAL 270	FB	EXP	FBG		IO	215-270		9	10			10300	12400
		IO 325 MRCR 11600 13200, IO T120-T165 10900 13100, IO T215												12300	14000
30		300	ST	SDN	FBG		IO	270-325		9	10	8200		18400	20500
		IB 330 CHRY 11500 13000, IO T155-T215 18100 21200, IB T225-T330												12100	14000
30		300	FB	SDN	FBG		IO	270-325		9	10	8200		18400	20500
30		300	FB	SDN	FBG		IO	T155-T215		9	10			17400	21100
30		IMPERIAL 300		EXP	FBG	DV	IB	300		9	10			11200	12700
30		IMPERIAL 300	ST	EXP	FBG		IB	250	OMC	9	10			10900	12400
		IO 270 MRCR 18100 20100, IB 270 MRCR 11000 12500, IO 325 MRCR												18200	20200
		IB 325-330 11400 12900, IO T155-T165 17600 20200, IO T215 MRCR												19200	21300
		IO T215 OMC 19100 21300, IB T215-T225 12000 13800, IB T330 CHRY												13300	15100
30		IMPERIAL 300	HT	EXP	FBG		IB	250	OMC	9	10			10900	12400
		IO 270 MRCR 17100 19400, IB 270 MRCR 11000 12500, IO 325 MRCR												18200	20200
		IB 325-330 11400 12900, IO T155-T165 17600 20200, IO T215 MRCR												19200	21300
		IO T215 OMC 19100 21300, IB T215-T225 12000 13800, IB T330 CHRY												13300	15100
30		IMPERIAL 300	FB	EXP	FBG		IB	250	OMC	9	10			10900	12400
		IO 270 MRCR 17100 19400, IB 270 MRCR 11000 12500, IO 325 MRCR												18200	20200
		IB 325-330 11400 12900, IO T155-T165 17600 20200, IO T215 MRCR												19200	21300
		IO T215 OMC 19100 21300, IB T215-T225 12000 13800, IB T330 CHRY												13300	15100
30		PILOTHOUSE 300		HB	FBG		IO	155-235		12		8700		13000	16200
30		PILOTHOUSE 300		HB	FBG		IO	270-325		12				14700	17700
30		PILOTHOUSE 300		HB	FBG		IO	T155-T165		12				15300	17500
30		SPORT SEDAN 300		SDN	FBG	DV	IB	300		9	10			11200	12800
30		SPORT SEDAN 300	HT	SDN	FBG		IO	270-325		9	10			17100	20300

 CONTINUED ON NEXT PAGE

LOA FT	LOA IN	NAME AND/ OR MODEL	TOP/ RIG	BOAT TYPE	HULL MTL	HULL TP	ENGINE TP	ENGINE # HP	ENGINE MFG	BEAM FT	BEAM IN	WGT LBS	DRAFT FT	DRAFT IN	RETAIL LOW	RETAIL HIGH
		1971 BOATS														
30		SPORT SEDAN 300	HT	SDN	FBG		IB	330	CHRY	9	10				11500	13000
30		SPORT SEDAN 300	HT	SDN	FBG		IO	T155-T215		9	10				18100	21200
30		SPORT SEDAN 300	HT	SDN	FBG		IB	T225-T330		9	10				12100	14000
30		SPORT SEDAN 300	FB	SDN	FBG		IO	270-325		9	10				17100	20500
		IB 330 CHRY 11500 13000, IO T155-T215 18300 21700, IB T225-T330													12100	14000
30	1	C-EAGLE 300	ST	EXP	FBG		IO	215		9	10				16600	19000
		IB 225 CHRY 10800 12200, IO 235 OMC 16900 19200, IB 250 OMC													11000	12500
		IO 270 MRCR 17300 19600, IB 270 MRCR 11100 12600, IO 325 MRCR													18400	20400
		IB 325-330 11500 13100, IO T120-T165 17000 20400, IO T215 MRCR													19100	21300
		IO T215 OMC 19100 21200, IB T215-T270 12200 14500, IB T330 CHRY													13400	15300
30	1	C-EAGLE 300	HT	EXP	FBG		IO	215		9	10				16600	18900
		IB 225 CHRY 10800 12200, IO 235 OMC 16900 19200, IB 250 OMC													11000	12500
		IO 270 MRCR 17300 19600, IB 270 MRCR 11100 12600, IO 325 MRCR													18400	20400
		IB 325-330 11500 13100, IO T120-T165 17000 20400, IO T215 MRCR													19100	21300
		IO T215 OMC 19100 21200, IB T215-T270 12200 14500, IB T330 CHRY													13400	15300
30	1	C-EAGLE 300	FB	EXP	FBG		IO	215		9	10				16600	18900
		IB 225 CHRY 10800 12200, IO 235 OMC 16900 19200, IB 250 OMC													11000	12500
		IO 270 MRCR 17300 19600, IB 270 MRCR 11100 12600, IO 325 MRCR													18400	20400
		IB 325-330 11500 13100, IO T120-T165 17000 20400, IO T215 MRCR													19100	21300
		IO T215 OMC 19100 21200, IB T215-T270 12200 14500, IB T330 CHRY													13400	15300
34		300	HT	HB	FBG	SV	IO	270		12					15400	17500
		1970 BOATS														
16	3	C-GULL	ST	RNBT	FBG	TR	IO	90-120		5	9				2300	2700
16	3	SAFARI	ST	RNBT	FBG		OB			6	6				2200	2550
16	3	SAFARI	ST	RNBT	FBG		IO	90-140		6	6				2400	2850
16	6	SPORTSMAN	ST	RNBT	FBG	DV	IO	90-140		6	6				2650	3100
17	6	SPORTSMAN	ST	RNBT	FBG	DV	OB			6	10				2850	3300
17	6	SPORTSMAN	ST	RNBT	FBG	DV	IO	120-165		6	10				3000	3500
17	9	C-GULL		RNBT	FBG	TR	OB			6	10	1050			1800	2150
17	9	C-GULL		RNBT	FBG	TR	IO	120-165		6	10				3000	3550
17	9	C-HAWK	ST	RNBT	FBG		OB			6	10	1400			2350	2700
18	4	C-EAGLE	ST	CUD	FBG		OB			6	9	1650			2600	3050
18	4	C-EAGLE	ST	CUD	FBG		IO	120-165		6	9				3200	3750
18	4	SPORTSMAN	ST	RNBT	FBG	DV	OB			6	9	1400			2350	2750
18	4	SPORTSMAN	ST	RNBT	FBG	DV	IO	120-165		6	9				3100	3650
18	6	C-GULL	ST	RNBT	FBG	TR	IO	120		6	10	1150			2600	3050
18	6	C-GULL	ST	RNBT	FBG	TR	IO	140-165		6	10				3200	3750
18	6	C-HAWK	ST	RNBT	FBG		IO	120-165		6	10	2600			3500	4150
18	11	CAPRICE	ST	CUD	FBG		OB			7		1400			2400	2800
18	11	CAPRICE	ST	CUD	FBG		IO	90-140		7					3700	4300
18	11	SAFARI	ST	RNBT	FBG	TR	OB			7		1200			2150	2500
18	11	SAFARI	ST	RNBT	FBG	TR	IO	90-140		7					3500	4050
20	2	C-EAGLE	ST	CUD	FBG		IO	120-225		7	6	2800			4850	5850
20	2	SPORTSMAN	ST	RNBT	FBG	DV	OB			7	6	1580			2800	3300
20	2	SPORTSMAN	ST	RNBT	FBG	DV	IO	120-215		7	6				4600	5500
22	2	C-EAGLE		CUD	FBG	DV	IO	155-215		8		3500			6450	7450
22	2	C-EAGLE		CUD	FBG	DV	IO	T120		8					6400	7350
22	2	SPORTSMAN	ST	RNBT	FBG	DV	IO	140-270		8		3200			5800	6650
22	2	SPORTSMAN	ST	RNBT	FBG	DV	IO	T120		8					6050	6950
23	4	ROAMER	HT	HB	FBG		IO	80-120		8					**	**
24	6	C-EAGLE	ST	CUD	FBG	DV	IO	155-270		8		4800			9300	10500
24	6	C-EAGLE	ST	CUD	FBG	DV	IO	T120-T140		8					8950	10300
24	6	IMPERIAL	ST	EXP	FBG	DV	IO	155-215		8		4800			9250	10500
24	6	IMPERIAL	ST	EXP	FBG	DV	IO	T120-T140		8					8600	10000
27	1	C-EAGLE	ST	CUD	FBG	DV	IO	210-215		9	10	5600			12200	13900
		IB 225 CHRY 7300 8400, IO 270 MRCR 11500 13000, IB 300 CHRY													7650	8800
		IO 325-390 12200 15200, IO T120-T165 11500 13900, IB T225-T300													7700	9300
27	1	IMPERIAL	ST	EXP	FBG	DV	IO	210-215		9	10	4800			11300	12900
		IB 225 CHRY 6800 7800, IO 270 MRCR 11200 12800, IB 300 CHRY													7150	8250
		IO 325-390 12000 14900, IO T120-T165 11200 13600, IO T210-T215													12600	14500
		IB T225-T300 7550 9050														
27	1	IMPERIAL		RNBT	FBG	DV	IO	T155	OMC	9	10				10700	12200
30		C-EAGLE		CUD	FBG	DV	IO	210-215		10					14500	16500
		IB 225 CHRY 8800 10000, IO 270 MRCR 15100 17100, IB 300 CHRY													9200	10500
		IO 325-390 15700 18700, IO T120-T210 14900 18600, IO T215 MRCR													16500	18700
		IB T225-T300 9950 12100														
30	1			SDN	FBG		IB	300	CHRY	9	10				10900	12400
30	1		ST	SDN	FBG		IO	270-390		9	10				18200	22100
		IO T120-T165 17500 21200, IO T210-T215 19900 22100, IB T225-T300													11800	13500
30	1	IMPERIAL	ST	EXP	FBG	DV	IO	270	MRCR	9	10	7200			18800	20900
		IB 300 CHRY 11200 12700, IO 325-390 19000 21800, IO T120-T215													18000	22000
		IB T225-T300 11800 14300														
40				SF	FBG		IB	T300	CHRY	14	6				27400	30500
		IB T165D CHRY 32000 35600, IB T185D CUM 32200 35800, IB T230D CHRY													33100	36800
		IB T300D CUM 34400 38200														
		1969 BOATS														
16		ADVENTURER	ST	RNBT	FBG		IO	80		6	8		1	6	2500	2950
16	4	C-GULL	ST	RNBT	FBG	TR	IO	80		6			1	9	2450	2850
16	6	SAFARI	ST	RNBT	FBG	SV	IO	80-120		6	11		1	6	2800	3250
16	7	SPORTSMAN	ST	RNBT	FBG	DV	IO	80-140		6	7		1	6	2750	3200
17	6	C-GULL	ST	RNBT	FBG	TR	OB			7	3	1050			1800	2150
17	6	C-GULL	ST	RNBT	FBG	TR	IO	120-160		7	3		2		3200	3700
17	6	IMPERIAL C-GULL		CBNCR	FBG		OB			7	3	1450			2300	2700
18	6	SPORTSMAN	ST	RNBT	FBG	DV	OB			6	10	1400			2400	2750
18	6	SPORTSMAN	ST	RNBT	FBG	DV	IO	120-160		6	10		2	1	3500	4100
18	8	C-GULL	ST	RNBT	FBG	TR	OB			7	3	1150			2000	2400
18	8	C-GULL	ST	RNBT	FBG	TR	IO	120-200		7	3	1150	1	11	2850	3400
18	8	IMPERIAL C-GULL		CBNCR	FBG	DV	IO	120-200		7	3	1450			3150	3800
18	10	IMPERIAL			FBG	DV	IO	120-160		7	6	1350	1	10	2950	3450
18	10	IMPERIAL		CR	FBG	DV	OB			7	6	1350			2300	2700
18	10	IMPERIAL SPORTS		EXP	FBG		OB			7	6	1350			2300	2650
18	10	SAFARI		RNBT	FBG	SV	IO	120-160		7	6	1200	2		3000	3500
18	10	SAFARI	ST	RNBT	FBG	SV	OB			7	6	1200			2150	2500
20	2	C-EAGLE		CUD	FBG	DV	IO	155-225		8		2500	2	1	4900	5800
20	2	IMPERIAL			FBG		IO	120-200		7	8	2640			4700	5450
20	2	SPORTSMAN		RNBT	FBG	DV	OB			8		1580	2	1	2800	3300
20	2	SPORTSMAN		RNBT	FBG	DV	IO	120-160		8		1580	2	1	4000	4650
20	2	SPORTSMAN		RNBT	FBG	DV	IO	200-225		8		2200	2	1	4550	5300
22	2	C-EAGLE		CUD	FBG	DV	IO	155-225		8		3600	2	1	6800	8050
22	2	C-EAGLE		CUD	FBG	DV	IO	T120-T140		8			2	1	6600	7600
22	2	SPORTSMAN		RNBT	FBG	DV	IO	155-225		8		3200	2	3	5950	7050
22	2	SPORTSMAN		RNBT	FBG	DV	IO	T120		8			2	3	6250	7150
23	11	C-EAGLE		CUD	FBG	DV	IO	155-250		8		4000	2	3	8100	9500
23	11	C-EAGLE		CUD	FBG	DV	IO	325	MRCR	8			2	3	8900	10100
23	11	C-EAGLE		CUD	FBG	DV	IO	T120-T200		8			2	3	8650	10100
24			HT	HB	FBG		IO	80-120		8					**	**
25		IMPERIAL		CR	FBG	DV	IO	155-325		8		4600	2	5	9400	11000
25		IMPERIAL		CR	FBG	DV	IO	T120-T140		8			2	5	9250	10700
27		C-EAGLE		CUD	FBG		IO	T140	MRCR	9	10		2	8	12100	13800
27		C-EAGLE		CUD	FBG	DV	IO	200-325		9	10	5500	2	8	12400	14300
27		C-EAGLE		CUD	FBG	DV	IO	T120-T160		9	10		2	8	11800	14100
27		C-EAGLE		CUD	FBG	DV	IO	T200	MRCR	9	10		2	8	13000	14800
27		IMPERIAL		CR	FBG	DV	IO	200-325		9	10	6100	2	10	13100	15100
27		IMPERIAL		CR	FBG	DV	IO	T120-T160		9	10		2	10	11500	13800
27		IMPERIAL		CR	FBG	DV	IO	T200-T225		9	10		2	10	12800	15000
30		C-EAGLE		CUD	FBG		IO	T120-T200		10					15400	19100
30		C-EAGLE		CUD	FBG		IO	T225	MRCR	10					17200	19600
30		IMPERIAL		CR	FBG	DV	IO	200-325		9	10	7200	2	10	16300	19500
30		IMPERIAL		CR	FBG	DV	IO	T120-T200		9	10		2	10	16300	20200
30		IMPERIAL		CR	FBG	DV	IO	T225	MRCR	9	10		2	10	18600	20700
30	1	C-EAGLE		CUD	FBG		IO	200-325		10		7600			15800	18500
		1968 BOATS														
16		ADVENTURER	OP	RNBT	FBG	FL	IO	60- 90		6	8	1150			2150	2500
16	4	C-GULL	OP	RNBT	FBG	DV	IO	80-120		6					2550	2950
16	6	SAFARI	OP	RNBT	FBG	SV	IO	80-120		6	11	1200			2350	2700
16	7	C-EAGLE		CUD	FBG	DV	IO	80-120		6	7				2800	3250
17	6	GULL-WING	OP	RNBT	FBG	TR	OB			7	3	1050			1800	2150
17	6	GULL-WING	OP	RNBT	FBG	TR	IO	120	MRCR	7	3	1400			2750	3200
18		C-EAGLE	OP	CUD	FBG	DV	IO	120-160		6	10	1400			2800	3300
18	8	C-EAGLE	OP	CUD	FBG	DV	OB			6	10	1400			2400	2750
18	8	C-EAGLE	OP	CUD	FBG	DV	IO	120-160		6	10	1400			2950	3500
18	8	C-GULL	OP	RNBT	FBG		OB			7	3	1250			2250	2600
18	8	C-GULL	OP	RNBT	FBG		IO	120-160		7	3	1800			3250	3800
18	10	IMPERIAL		CR	FBG	SV	OB			7	6	1350			2300	2700
18	10	IMPERIAL		CR	FBG	SV	IO	120-155		7	6	1875			3500	4100
18	10	SAFARI	OP	RNBT	FBG	SV	OB			7	6	1200			2150	2500
18	10	SAFARI	OP	RNBT	FBG	SV	IO	120-160		7	6	1800			3350	3950
20	2	C-EAGLE		CUD	FBG	DV	IO	155-160		8		2400			5000	5750
20	2	C-EAGLE		CUD	FBG	DV	IO	T 80		8		2400			5900	6800
22	2	C-EAGLE		CUD	FBG	DV	IO	155-225		8		2400			5600	6600

CONTINUED ON NEXT PAGE

LOA FT IN	NAME AND/ OR MODEL	TOP/ RIG	BOAT TYPE	HULL MTL	TP	TP #	ENGINE HP	MFG	BEAM FT IN	WGT LBS	DRAFT FT IN	RETAIL LOW	RETAIL HIGH
						1968 BOATS							
22 2	C-EAGLE		CUD	FBG	DV	IO	T 80-T120		8	2400		6500	7450
23 10	C-EAGLE		CUD	FBG	DV	IO	155-225		8	3000		6850	8050
23 10	C-EAGLE		CUD	FBG	DV	IO	T155-T160		8	3000		7800	9000
25 1	IMPERIAL DELUXE		EXP	FBG	DV	IO	155-225		8 10	4400		9600	11400
25 1	IMPERIAL DELUXE		EXP	FBG	DV	IO	T120-T160		8 10	4400		10700	12500
27 1	C-EAGLE		CUD	FBG		IO	155-225		8			10800	13100
27 1	C-EAGLE		CUD	FBG		IO	T120-T160		8			12100	14500
						1967 BOATS							
16	ADVENTURER	RNBT	FBG		IO		60-100		6 7			2650	3100
16 7	C-EAGLE	CUD	FBG		IO		80-120		6 10			2950	3500
16 7	SAFARI	RNBT	FBG		IO		60-120		6 11			3000	3500
16 8	GULL-WING	RNBT	FBG		IO		80-120		6 11			3050	3550
17 6	GULL-WING	RNBT	FBG		OB				7 3	1050		1800	2150
17 6	GULL-WING	RNBT	FBG		IO		100		7 3	1050		2700	3150
17 6	GULL-WINC	RNBT	FBG		IO		110-120		7 3			3400	3950
18	C-EAGLE	CUD	FBG		IO		110-175		7 6			3650	4300
18 10	IMPERIAL		FBG		OB				7 6			2850	3300
18 10	IMPERIAL		FBG		IO		110-175		7 6			3700	4350
18 10	SAFARI		FBG		OB				7 6			2950	3400
18 10	SAFARI	RNBT	FBG		IO		110-175		7 6			4000	4700
20 2	C-EAGLE	CUD	FBG		IO		155-210		8			5500	6400
20 2	C-EAGLE	CUD	FBG		IO		T110-T120		8			6450	7400
22 2	C-EAGLE	CUD	FBG		IO		155-225		8			6100	7150
22 2	C-EAGLE	CUD	FBG		IO		T110-T120		8			7050	8100
23 10	C-EAGLE	CUD	FBG		IO		155-225		8			8250	9650
23 10	C-EAGLE	CUD	FBG		IO		T110-T120		8			9300	10600
23 10	IMPERIAL	CR	FBG		IO		155-225		8			8250	9650
23 10	IMPERIAL	CR	FBG		IO		T110-T120		8			9300	10600
						1966 BOATS							
16	ADVENTURER	RNBT	FBG		IO		60		6 8			2800	3250
16 5	C-EAGLE	CUD	FBG		IO		110		6 11			3050	3350
16 6	SAFARI	RNBT	FBG		IO		60		6 11			3100	3600
17	IMPERIAL	CR	FBG		OB				7	1300		2050	2450
17	IMPERIAL	CR	FBG		IO		60		7			3500	4050
17	SPORTSMAN	RNBT	FBG		OB				7	995		1700	2050
17	SPORTSMAN	RNBT	FBG		IO		60		7			3200	3750
18	C-EAGLE	CUD	FBG		OB				7 1	1500		2450	2850
18	C-EAGLE	CUD	FBG		IO		120-150		7 1			3650	4250
18 10	SAFARI	RNBT	FBG		OB				7 6	1200		2200	2550
18 10	SAFARI	RNBT	FBG		IO		110-120		7 6			4150	4800
20 2	C-EAGLE	CUD	FBG		OB				8	1700		3000	3450
20 2	C-EAGLE	CUD	FBG		IO		150		8			5650	6500
20 2	C-EAGLE	HT	CUD	FBG		OB			8			3800	4400
22 2	C-EAGLE 23		CUD	FBG		OB			8	1900		3550	4100
22 2	C-EAGLE 23		CUD	FBG		IO		150		8			6250	7200
23 8	IMPERIAL DELUXE		EXP	FBG		OB			8	4200		6650	7650
23 8	IMPERIAL DELUXE		EXP	FBG		IO		150		8			8450	9700
						1965 BOATS							
17	IMPERIAL	ST	RNBT	FBG		IO		110		7			3300	3850
17	IMPERIAL	HT	RNBT	FBG		IO		110		7			3300	3850
17	SPORTSMAN		RNBT	FBG		IO		110		7	995		2600	3050
18	C-EAGLE	ST	RNBT	FBG		IO		110		7			3650	4250
20 2	C-EAGLE	ST	RNBT	FBG		IO		110		8			5550	6400
22 2	C-EAGLE	ST	RNBT	FBG		IO		110		8			6150	7050
						1964 BOATS							
16	ADVENTURER		RNBT	FBG		OB						2250	2600
16 4			FSH	FBG		OB						2050	2400
16 4	CAPRI		RNBT	FBG		OB						2200	2600
17	IMPERIAL			FBG		OB						2050	2400
17	IMPERIAL			FBG		IO		110-150					3050	3550
17	SPORTSMAN		RNBT	FBG		OB						2250	2600
17	SPORTSMAN		RNBT	FBG		IO		88-120					3450	4000
18 9	SAFARI		RNBT	FBG		OB						2950	3450
18 9	SAFARI		RNBT	FBG		IO		88-120					4500	5150
20 2	C-EAGLE		CUD	FBG		OB						3800	4400
20 2	C-EAGLE		CUD	FBG		IO		110-150					5950	6900
						1963 BOATS							
16	IMPERIAL		CBNCR	WD		OB						2050	2450
16	IMPERIAL		CBNCR	WD		IO		80-140					2250	2650
16	SAFARI 17 DELUXE		RNBT	WD		OB						2250	2650
16	SAFARI 17 DELUXE		RNBT	WD		IO		80-140					3100	3600
16	SPORTSMAN 17		RNBT	WD		OB						2250	2650
16	SPORTSMAN 17		RNBT	WD		IO		80-140					3100	3600
16	SUNLINER SLEEPER 17		RNBT	WD		OB						2250	2650
16	SUNLINER SLEEPER 17		RNBT	WD		IO		80-140					3100	3600
17 4			FSH	WD		OB						2150	2500
17 4			FSH	WD		IO		80-140					3150	3650
17 4	CRUISETTE 18		RNBT	WD		OB						2250	2650
17 4	CRUISETTE 18		RNBT	WD		IO		80-140					3600	4250
17 4	IMPERIAL		CBNCR	WD		OB						2150	2500
17 4	IMPERIAL		CBNCR	WD		IO		80-140					2850	3350
17 4	IMPERIAL DLX		EXP	WD		OB						2150	2500
17 4	IMPERIAL DLX		EXP	WD		IO		80-140					4400	5050
17 4	SAFARI 18 DELUXE		RNBT	WD		OB						2250	2650
17 4	SAFARI 18 DELUXE		RNBT	WD		IO		80-140					3600	4250
17 4	SPORTSMAN 18		RNBT	WD		OB						2250	2650
17 4	SPORTSMAN 18		RNBT	WD		IO		80-140					3600	4250
17 4	SUNLINER SLEEPER 18		RNBT	WD		OB						2250	2650
17 4	SUNLINER SLEEPER 18		RNBT	WD		IO		80-140					3600	4250
19 3	CRUISETTE 20		RNBT	WD		OB						3050	3550
19 3	CRUISETTE 20		RNBT	WD		IO		80-140					4750	5450
19 3	IMPERIAL		EXP	WD		OB						2950	3400
19 3	IMPERIAL DLX		EXP	WD		IO		80-140					5650	6500
19 3	SPORTSMAN 20		RNBT	WD		OB						3050	3550
19 3	SPORTSMAN 20		RNBT	WD		IO		80-140					4750	5450
24	IMPERIAL		EXP	WD		OB						5950	6850
24	IMPERIAL DLX		EXP	WD		IO		80-140					9650	11000
						1962 BOATS							
16	IMPERIAL		CBNCR	WD		OB						2050	2450
16	SAFARI		RNBT	WD		OB						2250	2650
17 4	IMPERIAL		CBNCR	WD		OB						2150	2500
17 4	SAFARI DELUXE		RNBT	WD		OB						2250	2650
17 4	SAFARI DELUXE		RNBT	WD		IO		80	VLVO				3950	4600
17 4	SPORTSMAN		RNBT	WD		OB						2250	2650
19 3	IMPERIAL			WD		IO		110	VLVO				4650	5350
19 3	IMPERIAL DELUXE		EXP	WD		OB						2950	3400
19 3	SPORTSMAN		RNBT	WD		OB						3050	3550
19 3	SPORTSMAN		RNBT	WD		IO		80	VLVO				5100	5850
						1961 BOATS							
18	IMPERIAL DELUXE		EXP	PLY		OB				7 1	1027		1750	2100
19 2	IMPERIAL DELUXE		EXP	PLY		OB				7 6			2900	3400
19 2	SPORTSMAN SLEEPER		RNBT	PLY		OB				7 6	1200		2200	2600
19 3	IMPERIAL DLX		CR	PLY		IO		80	VLVO	7 6			5450	6250
19 3	SPORTSMAN		CR	PLY		IO		80	VLVO	7 6			4900	5600
						1960 BOATS							
17 4	VOYAGER SLEEPER		RNBT	WD		IO		80		7 4			4100	4750

SPORTSHIP BOAT CO

Call 1-800-327-6929 for BUC Personalized Evaluation Service
Or, for 1959 to 1970 boats, sign onto www.BUCValuPro.com

SPORTSHIP-HAMBURG

Call 1-800-327-6929 for BUC Personalized Evaluation Service
Or, for 1968 boats, sign onto www.BUCValuPro.com

SQUADRON YACHTS INC
PROVIDENCE RI 02903   COAST GUARD MFG ID- XUH See inside cover to adjust price for area
SEE ALSO NOWAK & WILLIAMS CO

LOA FT IN	NAME AND/ OR MODEL	TOP/ RIG	BOAT TYPE	HULL MTL	TP	TP #	ENGINE HP	MFG	BEAM FT IN	WGT LBS	DRAFT FT IN	RETAIL LOW	RETAIL HIGH
						1982 BOATS							
18	SEA-OTTER	OP	CTRCN	FBG	DV	IB	120	MRCR	7 10	1800	1	4100	4750
18 2	HERRESHOFF BAY FISH	OP	FSH	FBG	DS	IB	15D	YAN	8	2200	1 10	6400	7350
18 2	HERRESHOFF HBR PILOT	HT	PH	FBG	DS	IB	15D	YAN	8	2200	1 10	6400	7350
18 2	HERRESHOFF YCHT CLUB	OP	LNCH	FBG	DS	IB	30D	WEST	8	2200	1 10	10700	12200
18 2	HERRESHOFF-AMERICA	GAF	SAIL	FBG	CB	OB			8	2500	1 10	6100	7000
18 2	HERRESHOFF-AMERICA	GAF	SAIL	FBG	CB	IB	8D	YAN	8	2500	1 10	8650	9900
18 2	HERRESHOFF-SCOUT	KTH	SAIL	FBG	CB	OB			8	2000	1 10	5300	6100
22	HERRESHOFF-EAGLE	GAF	SAIL	FBG	CB	OB			8	2700	1 10	6950	8000
22	HERRESHOFF-EAGLE	GAF	SAIL	FBG	CB	IB	8D	YAN	8	2700	1 10	8550	9850
24	BAHAMA-SANDPIPER	SLP	SAIL	FBG	CB	OB			8	4147	1 6	10900	12400
24	BAHAMA-SANDPIPER	SLP	SAIL	FBG	CB	IB	8D	YAN	8	4147	1 6	12000	13700
24	BAHAMA-SANDPIPER	CUT	SAIL	FBG	CB	OB			8	4147	1 6	10900	12400
24	BAHAMA-SANDPIPER	CUT	SAIL	FBG	CB	IB	8D	YAN	8	4147	1 6	12000	13700
24	BAHAMA-SANDPIPER	KTH	SAIL	FBG	CB	OB			8	4147	1 6	10900	12400

```
LOA   NAME AND/           TOP/ BOAT  -HULL- ----ENGINE--- BEAM  WGT  DRAFT RETAIL RETAIL
FT IN OR MODEL            RIG  TYPE  MTL TP TP # HP  MFG   FT IN LBS  FT IN LOW    HIGH
--------------------- 1982 BOATS ----------------------------------------------------
24    BAHAMA-SANDPIPER    KTH  SAIL  FBG CB IB 8D    YAN   8     4147 1  6  12000  13700
36    SQUADRON 36         SLP  SA/CR FBG KL IB D           5  6  16000 5  6  46900  51500
--------------------- 1981 BOATS ----------------------------------------------------
18    SEA-OTTER           OP   CTRCN FBG DV IO 120   MRCR  7 10  1800 1     4000   4700
18 2  HERRESHOFF BAY FISH OP   FSH   FBG DS IB 15D   YAN   8     2200 1 10  6150   7050
18 2  HERRESHOFF HBR PILOT HT  PH    FBG DS IB 15D   YAN   8     2200 1 10  6150   7050
18 2  HERRESHOFF YCHT CLUB OP  LNCH  FBG DS IB 30D   WEST  8     2600 1 10  10300  11700
18 2  HERRESHOFF-AMERICA  GAF  SAIL  FBG CB OB              8     2500 1 10  5750   6600
18 2  HERRESHOFF-AMERICA  GAF  SAIL  FBG CB IB 8D    YAN   8     2500 1 10  8100   9350
18 2  HERRESHOFF-SCOUT    KTH  SAIL  FBG CB OB              8     2000 1 10  5000   5750
22    HERRESHOFF-EAGLE    GAF  SAIL  FBG CB OB              8     2700 1 10  6550   7500
22    HERRESHOFF-EAGLE    GAF  SAIL  FBG CB IB 8D    YAN   8     2700 1 10  8050   9250
24    BAHAMA-SANDPIPER    SLP  SAIL  FBG CB IB              8     4147 1  6  10200  11600
24    BAHAMA-SANDPIPER    SLP  SAIL  FBG CB IB 8     YAN   8     4147 1  6  10700  12100
24    BAHAMA-SANDPIPER    CUT  SAIL  FBG CB OB              8     4147 1  6  10200  11600
24    BAHAMA-SANDPIPER    CUT  SAIL  FBG CB OB 8     YAN   8     4147 1  6  10700  12100
24    BAHAMA-SANDPIPER    KTH  SAIL  FBG CB OB              8     4147 1  6  10200  11600
24    BAHAMA-SANDPIPER    KTH  SAIL  FBG CB IB 8     YAN   8     4147 1  6  10700  12100
--------------------- 1980 BOATS ----------------------------------------------------
18    HERRESHOFF BAY FISH OP   FSH   FBG DS IB 40D         8     2200       6450   7400
18    HERRESHOFF HBR PILOT HT  PH    FBG DS IB 40D         8     2200       6450   7400
18    HERRESHOFF YCHT CLUB OP  LNCH  FBG DS IB 40D- 50D    8     2600       10000  11600
18    SEA-OTTER           OP   CTRCN FBG DV IO 120   MRCR  7 10  1800 1     4000   4650
18 2  HERRESHOFF BAY FISH OP   FSH   FBG DS IB 15D   YAN   8     2200 1 10  5900   6800
18 2  HERRESHOFF HBR PILOT HT  PH    FBG DS IB 15D   YAN   8     2200 1 10  5900   6800
18 2  HERRESHOFF YCHT CLUB OP  LNCH  FBG DS IB 30D   WEST  8     2600 1 10  9900   11200
18 2  HERRESHOFF-AMERICA  GAF  SAIL  FBG CB OB              8     2500 1 10  5450   6300
18 2  HERRESHOFF-AMERICA  GAF  SAIL  FBG CB IB 8D    YAN   8     2500 1 10  7750   8900
18 2  HERRESHOFF-SCOUT    KTH  SAIL  FBG CB OB              8     2000 1 10  4750   5500
22    HERRESHOFF-EAGLE    GAF  SAIL  FBG CB OB              8     2700 1 10  6250   7200
22    HERRESHOFF-EAGLE    GAF  SAIL  FBG CB IB 8D    YAN   8     2700 1 10  7700   8850
24    BAHAMA-SANDPIPER    SLP  SAIL  FBG CB OB              8     4147 1  6  9800   11100
24    BAHAMA-SANDPIPER    SLP  SAIL  FBG CB OB 8     YAN   8     4147 1  6  10200  11600
24    BAHAMA-SANDPIPER    CUT  SAIL  FBG CB OB              8     4147 1  6  9800   11100
24    BAHAMA-SANDPIPER    CUT  SAIL  FBG CB OB 8     YAN   8     4147 1  6  10200  11600
24    BAHAMA-SANDPIPER    KTH  SAIL  FBG CB OB              8     4147 1  6  9800   11100
24    BAHAMA-SANDPIPER    KTH  SAIL  FBG CB OB 8     YAN   8     4147 1  6  10200  11600
--------------------- 1979 BOATS ----------------------------------------------------
18    SEA-OTTER           OP   RNBT  FBG DV IO 120   MRCR  7 10  1800 1     3700   4300
18 2  HERRESHOFF BAY FISH OP   FSH   FBG DS IB 15D   YAN   8     2200 1 10  5700   6550
18 2  HERRESHOFF HBR PILOT HT  PH    FBG DS IB 15D   YAN   8     2200 1 10  5700   6550
18 2  HERRESHOFF YCHT CLUB OP  UTL   FBG DS IB 30D   WEST  8     2600 1 10  6600   7600
18 2  HERRESHOFF-AMERICA  GAF  SAIL  FBG CB OB              8     2500 1 10  5250   6050
18 2  HERRESHOFF-AMERICA  GAF  SAIL  FBG CB IB 8D    YAN   8     2500 1 10  7450   8550
18 2  HERRESHOFF-SCOUT    KTH  SAIL  FBG CB OB              8     2000 1 10  4600   5300
22    HERRESHOFF-EAGLE    GAF  SAIL  FBG CB OB              8     2700 1 10  6000   6900
22    HERRESHOFF-EAGLE    GAF  SAIL  FBG CB IB 8D    YAN   8     2700 1 10  7400   8500
--------------------- 1978 BOATS ----------------------------------------------------
18    SEA-OTTER           OP   UTL   FBG DV IO 120-140     7 10  1800 1     4000   4700
18 2  AMERICA             CAT  SAIL  FBG CB OB              8     2500 1 10  5050   5850
18 2  AMERICA             CAT  SAIL  FBG CB IB 8D    YAN   8     2500 1 10  7200   8250
18 2  HERRESHOFF-PILOT    HT   PH    FBG RB IB 42    VLVO  8     2200 1 10  3700   4350
18 2  HERRESHOFF-SCOUT    KTH  SAIL  FBG CB OB              8     2000 1 10  4450   5100
18 2  YACHT CLUB          OP   LNCH  FBG DS IB 30D   WEST  8     2600 1 10  9200   10500
22    HERRESHOFF-EAGLE    SLP  SAIL  FBG CB OB              8     2700 1 10  5800   6650
22    HERRESHOFF-EAGLE    SLP  SAIL  FBG CB IB 8D    YAN   8     2700 1 10  7150   8200
--------------------- 1977 BOATS ----------------------------------------------------
18    SEA-OTTER           ST   RNBT  FBG DV IO 120   MRCR  7 10  1800 1     3800   4400
18 2  HERRESHOFF BAY FISH ST   FSH   FBG RB IB 42    VLVO  8     2200 1 10  3550   4150
18 2  HERRESHOFF-AMERICA  CAT  SAIL  FBG CB IB 8D    YAN   8     2500 1 10  6950   8000
18 2  HERRESHOFF-PILOT    HT   PH    FBG RB IB 42    VLVO  8     2400 1 10  3750   4400
18 2  HERRESHOFF-SCOUT    KTH  SAIL  FBG RB OB              8     2000 1 10  4250   4950
18 2  YACHT CLUB          OP   LNCH  FBG RB IB 30D   WEST  8     2600 1 10  8900   10100
22    HERRESHOFF-EAGLE    SLP  SAIL  FBG CB IB 8D    YAN   8     2700 1 10  6900   7900
```

ST CLOUD MARINE MFG CO
REGAL LINE

Call 1-800-327-6929 for BUC Personalized Evaluation Service
Or, for 1959 boats, sign onto www.BUCValuPro.com

STAMAS YACHTS INC
TARPON SPRINGS FL 34689
FORMERLY STAMAS BOATS INC

For more recent years, see the BUC Used Boat Price Guide, Volume 1 or Volume 2

```
LOA   NAME AND/           TOP/ BOAT  -HULL- ----ENGINE---- BEAM  WGT  DRAFT RETAIL RETAIL
FT IN OR MODEL            RIG  TYPE  MTL TP TP # HP   MFG   FT IN LBS  FT IN LOW    HIGH
--------------------- 1983 BOATS -----------------------------------------------------
21 3  STAMAS 21           OP   CR    FBG SV OB              7 9  3100 1  6  9200   10400
21 3  STAMAS 21           OP   CR    FBG SV IO 170-185      7 9  4100 1  6  7550   8700
23 3  STAMAS 24           OP   FSH   FBG SV OB              8     3500 2  4  11500  13100
23 3  STAMAS 24           OP   FSH   FBG SV SE 205    OMC   8     3500 2  4  11500  13100
23 3  STAMAS 24           OP   FSH   FBG SV IO 228-260      8     4500 2  4  9850   11400
23 3  STAMAS 24           OP   FSH   FBG SV IO T138-T140    8     4900 2  4  11800  13400
23 3  STAMAS 24           HT   FSH   FBG SV OB              8     3500 2  4  11500  13100
23 3  STAMAS 24           HT   FSH   FBG SV SE 205    OMC   8     3500 2  4  11500  13100
23 3  STAMAS 24           HT   FSH   FBG SV IO 228-260      8     4500 2  4  9850   11400
23 3  STAMAS 24           HT   FSH   FBG SV IO T138-T140    8     4900 2  4  11800  13400
23 3  STAMAS 24           OP   SPTCR FBG SV SE 205    OMC   8     5000 2  4  13700  15500
23 3  STAMAS 24           OP   SPTCR FBG SV IO 228-260      8     4600 2  4  9500   11000
23 3  STAMAS 24           OP   SPTCR FBG SV IO T138-T140    8     5000 2  4  11400  12900
23 3  STAMAS 24           HT   SPTCR FBG SV SE 205    OMC   8     5000 2  4  13700  15500
23 3  STAMAS 24           HT   SPTCR FBG SV IO 228-260      8     4600 2  4  9500   11000
23 3  STAMAS 24           HT   SPTCR FBG SV IO T138-T140    8     5000 2  4  11400  12900
25 3  STAMAS-TARPON 24    OP   OPFSH FBG SV OB              8          2  4  12900  14600
25 3  STAMAS-TARPON 24    OP   OPFSH FBG SV SE        OMC   8          2  4  **     **
25 3  STAMAS-TARPON 24    OP   OPFSH FBG SV IO 228-260      8          2  4  9300   10800
26    STAMAS 26           OP   FSH   FBG SV SE 205    OMC   9 7             9300   10800
26    STAMAS 26           OP   FSH   FBG SV IO 228-330      9 7  6500      14800  18300
26    STAMAS 26           OP   FSH   FBG SV IB 340    OMC   9 7  6500      19000  21100
26    STAMAS 26           OP   FSH   FBG SV IB T138   VLVO  9 7  7500      17500  19900
26    STAMAS 26           OP   FSH   FBG SV SE T155   OMC   9 7             15000  17000
26    STAMAS 26           OP   FSH   FBG SV IO T170   MRCR  9 7  7500      17500  19900
26    STAMAS 26           OP   FSH   FBG SV IO T170   OMC   9 7  7500      17500  19900
26    STAMAS 26           OP   FSH   FBG SV IO T170-T175    9 7  7500      20700  23100
26    STAMAS 26           HT   FSH   FBG SV SE 205    OMC   9 7             15000  17000
26    STAMAS 26           HT   FSH   FBG SV IO 228-330      9 7  6500      13200  16400
26    STAMAS 26           HT   FSH   FBG SV IB 340    OMC   9 7  6500      16600  18900
26    STAMAS 26           HT   FSH   FBG SV IB T138   VLVO  9 7  7500      14300  16200
26    STAMAS 26           HT   FSH   FBG SV SE T155   OMC   9 7             15000  17000
26    STAMAS 26           HT   FSH   FBG SV IO T170   MRCR  9 7             14300  16300
26    STAMAS 26           HT   FSH   FBG SV IO T170   OMC   9 7  7500      14300  16300
26    STAMAS 26           HT   FSH   FBG SV IB T170-T175    9 7             16800  19100

26    STAMAS 26                HT SDN  FBG SV IB 255  MRCR  9 7             2 6  16800 19000
  IO 260 MRCR 13700 15600, IO 340  OMC  13700 15600, IB 260  OMC         17000 19300
  IO 330 MRCR 14800 16800, IB 340  OMC  18400 20500, IB T138 VLVO        14500 16500
  IO T170 MRCR 14700 16700, IO T170 OMC 14700 16700, IB T170-T175         18600 20700

26    STAMAS 26                FB SDN  FBG SV IB 255  MRCR  9 7             2 6  16800 19000
  IO 260 MRCR 13700 15600, IB 340  OMC  13700 15600, IB 260  OMC         17000 19300
  IO 330 MRCR 14800 16800, IB 340  OMC  18400 20500, IB T138 VLVO        14500 16500
  IO T170 MRCR 14700 16700, IO T170 OMC 14700 16700, IB T170-T175         18600 20700

26    STAMAS 26                OP SPTCR FBG SV IO 228-230  9 7  7500  2 8  15500 17700
  IB 255 MRCR 19600 21800, IO 260  MRCR 15800 18000, IO 260  OMC         15800 17900
  IB 260 OMC  19800 22000, IO 330  MRCR 16700 19000, IB 340  OMC         20600 22900
  IO T138 VLVO 16600 18800, IO T170 MRCR 16600 18900, IO T170 OMC        16600 18800
  IB T170-T175 20700 23100

26    STAMAS 26                HT SPTCR FBG SV IO 228-230  9 7  7500  2 6  15500 17700
  IB 255 MRCR 19600 21800, IO 260  MRCR 15800 18000, IO 260  OMC         15800 17900
  IB 260 OMC  19800 22000, IO 330  MRCR 16700 19000, IB 340  OMC         20600 22900
  IO T138 VLVO 16600 18800, IO T170 MRCR 16600 18900, IO T170 OMC        16600 18800
  IB T170-T175 20700 23100

26    STAMAS 26                FB SPTCR FBG SV IO 228-230  9 7  6900  2 8  14600 16600
  IB 255 MRCR 18700 20800, IO 260  MRCR 14900 17000, IO 260  OMC         14900 16900
  IB 260 OMC  18900 21000, IB 340  OMC  18400 20500, IB 340  OMC          22300 24700
  IO T138 VLVO 18300 20400, IO T170 MRCR 18300 20400, IO T170 OMC        18300 20300
  IB T170-T175 25000

26    STAMAS-RIVIERA 26        ST CR   FBG SV IO 228-230  9 7  6500  2 6  14000 16000
  IB 255 MRCR 17500 19900, IO 260  MRCR 14300 16300, IO 260  OMC         14300 16200
  IB 260 OMC  18200 20200, IO 330  MRCR 15200 17300, IB 340  OMC         18800 20900
  IO T138 VLVO 16600 18800, IO T170 MRCR 16600 18900, IO T170 OMC        16500 18800
  IB T170 MRCR 20700 23000
```

```
STAMAS YACHTS INC          -CONTINUED      See inside cover to adjust price for area
 LOA  NAME AND/          TOP/ BOAT -HULL- ----ENGINE--- BEAM  WGT  DRAFT RETAIL RETAIL
FT IN OR MODEL           RIG TYPE MTL TP TP # HP  MFG  FT IN  LBS  FT IN  LOW    HIGH
------------------- 1983 BOATS-------------------------------------------------------
26    STAMAS-TARPON 26      OP  FSH  FBG SV OB           9  7  6400  2       16700  18900
26    STAMAS-TARPON 26      OP  FSH  FBG SV SE  205  OMC 9  7  6400  2       16700  18900
26    STAMAS-TARPON 26      OP  FSH  FBG SV IO 228-230   9  7  6400  2       14700  16700
      IB  255  MRCR 17300 19700, IO 260  MRCR 15000 17000, IO 260  OMC  14900  17000
      IB  260  OMC  17600 20000, IO 330  MRCR 15900 18100, IB 330  OMC  18700  20700
      IO T138  VLVO 15800 17900
26    STAMAS-TARPON 26      OP  FSH  FBG SV SE T155  OMC 9  7  6400  2       16700  18900
26    STAMAS-TARPON 26      OP  FSH  FBG SV IO T170  MRCR 9  7  6400  2       15800  18000
26    STAMAS-TARPON 26      OP  FSH  FBG SV IO T170  OMC 9  7  6400  2       15800  17900
26    STAMAS-TARPON 26      OP  FSH  FBG SV IB T170  MRCR 9  7  6400  2       18900  21000
32  3 STAMAS 32             HT  SDN  FBG SV IB T255-T260 12    13300  2  9    44500  49600
32  3 STAMAS 32             HT  SDN  FBG SV IO T330  MRCR 12   13300  2  9    37700  41900
32  3 STAMAS 32             FB  SDN  FBG SV IB T255-T260 12           2  9    36200  40300
32  3 STAMAS 32             FB  SDN  FBG SV IO T330  MRCR 12          2  9    29500  32800
32  3 STAMAS 32             OP  SF   FBG SV IB T255-T260 12    12800  2  9    40800  45500
32  3 STAMAS 32             OP  SF   FBG SV IO T330  MRCR 12   12800  2  9    39100  43500
32  3 STAMAS 32             HT  SF   FBG SV IB T255-T260 12           2  9    31000  34700
32  3 STAMAS 32             HT  SF   FBG SV IO T330  MRCR 12          2  9    30200  33600

32  3 STAMAS 32             FB  SF   FBG SV IB T255-T260 12           2  9    31000  34700
32  3 STAMAS 32             FB  SF   FBG SV IO T330  MRCR 12          2  9    30200  33600
32  3 STAMAS-CONTINENTAL    ST  CR   FBG SV IB T255-T260 12    12000  2  9    40200  44900
32  3 STAMAS-CONTINENTAL    ST  CR   FBG SV IO T330  MRCR 12   12000  2  9    33900  37700
32  3 STAMAS-CONTINENTAL    HT  CR   FBG SV IB T255-T260 12           2  9    33400  37300
32  3 STAMAS-CONTINENTAL    HT  CR   FBG SV IO T330  MRCR 12          2  9    28500  31700
32  3 STAMAS-CONTINENTAL    FB  CR   FBG SV IB T255      12           2  9    33400  37100
32  3 STAMAS-CONTINENTAL    FB  CR   FBG SV IO T330  MRCR 12          2  9    28500  31700
44    STAMAS 44             KTH SA/CR FBG KL IB   62D PERK 14  30000  5  1 104000 114000
------------------- 1982 BOATS-------------------------------------------------------
21  3 STAMAS 21             OP  CR   FBG SV OB           7  9  3100  1  6     9050  10300
21  3 STAMAS 21             OP  CR   FBG SV IO 170-185   7  9  4100  1  6     7350   8500
23  3 STAMAS 24             OP  FSH  FBG SV OB           8        4  2  4     9950  11300
23  3 STAMAS 24             OP  FSH  FBG SV IO 228-260   8        4  2  4     8350   9850
23  3 STAMAS 24             OP  FSH  FBG SV IO T140-T145 8        4  2  4     9300  11000
23  3 STAMAS 24             HT  FSH  FBG SV OB           8        4  2  4     9950  11300
23  3 STAMAS 24             HT  FSH  FBG SV IO 228-260   8  4500  4  2  4     9600  11200
23  3 STAMAS 24             HT  FSH  FBG SV IO T140-T145 8  4900  4  2  4    11100  12600
23  3 STAMAS 24             OP  SPTCR FBG SV IO 228-260  8        4  2  4     7750   9100
23  3 STAMAS 24             OP  SPTCR FBG SV IO T140-T145 8       4  2  4     8550  10300
23  3 STAMAS 24             HT  SPTCR FBG SV IO 228-260  8  4600  4  2  4     9350  10700
23  3 STAMAS 24             HT  SPTCR FBG SV IO T140-T145 8 5000  4  2  4    10700  12200

26    STAMAS 26             OP  FSH  FBG SV IO 228-260   9  7      2  8    12900  15000
      IB 330-340  17200 19500, IO T145  VLVO 14000 16000, IO T170  MRCR  14000  16000
      IO T170  OMC  14000 15900, IB T170-T175 19800 22100
26    STAMAS 26             HT  FSH  FBG SV IO 228-260   9  7      2  8    12900  15000
      IB 330-340  15600 18100, IO T145  VLVO 14000 16000, IO T170  MRCR  14000  16000
      IO T170  OMC  14000 15900, IB T170-T175 16000 18300
26    STAMAS 26             HT  SDN  FBG SV IB  255  MRCR 9  7      2  6    16000  18200
      IO  260  MRCR 13400 15300, IO 260  MRCR 13400 15200, IB 260  OMC  16300  18500
      IO T145  VLVO 14300 16300, IO T170  MRCR 14400 16400, IO T170  OMC  14400  16300
      IB T170-T175 17400 19900
26    STAMAS 26             FB  SDN  FBG SV IB  255  MRCR 9  7      2  6    16000  18200
      IO  260  MRCR 13400 15300, IO 260  MRCR 13400 15200, IB 260  OMC  16300  18500
      IO T145  VLVO 14300 16300, IO T170  MRCR 14400 16400, IO T170  OMC  14400  16300
      IB T170-T175 17400 19900
26    STAMAS 26             OP  SPTCR FBG SV IO 228-230  9  7  7500  2  6    15200  17300
      IB  255  MRCR 19000 21100, IO 260  MRCR 15500 17600, IO 260  OMC  15400  17500
      IB  260  OMC  19000 21100, IO T145  VLVO 16300 18500, IO T170  MRCR  16200  18400
      IO T170  OMC  16200 18400, IB T170-T175 19800 22100
26    STAMAS 26             HT  SPTCR FBG SV IO 228-230  9  7  7500  2  6    15200  17300
      IB  255  MRCR 19000 21100, IO 260  MRCR 15500 17600, IO 260  OMC  15400  17500
      IB  260  OMC  19000 21100, IO T145  VLVO 16300 18500, IO T170  MRCR  16200  18400
      IO T170  OMC  16200 18400, IB T170-T175 19800 22100
26    STAMAS 26             FB  SPTCR FBG SV IO 228-230  9  7  6900  2  6    14300  16500
      IB  255  MRCR 17500 19900, IO 260  MRCR 14600 16600, IO 260  OMC  14600  16500
      IB  260  OMC  18100 20100, IO T145  VLVO 16800 19100, IO T170  MRCR  16800  19100
      IO T170  OMC  16800 19000, IB T170  MRCR 16000 18200, IB T175  PCM  19000  21200
26    STAMAS-RIVIERA 26     ST  CR   FBG SV IO  228  MRCR 9  7      2  6    12200  13800
      IO  230  MRCR 13700 15600, IB  255  MRCR 14900 16900, IO 260  MRCR  14000  15900
      IO  260  OMC  14000 15900, IB 260-330   15100 18000, IO T145  VLVO  16300  18500
      IO T170  MRCR 16200 18400, IO T170  OMC  16100 18400, IB T170  MRCR  16000  18200
26    STAMAS-TARPON 26      OP  FSH  FBG SV OB           9  7      2  6    13800  15600
26    STAMAS-TARPON 26      OP  FSH  FBG SV IO 228-230   9  7  6400  2  6    14300  16300
      IB  255  MRCR 16600 18900, IO 260  MRCR 14600 16600, IO 260  OMC  14600  16600
      IB 260-330   16800 19000, IO T145  VLVO 15500 17600, IO T170  MRCR  15500  17600
      IO T170  OMC  15400 17500, IB T170  MRCR 18100 20100
32  3 STAMAS 32             HT  SDN  FBG SV IB T255-T330 12    13300  2  9    42600  49700
32  3 STAMAS 32             FB  SDN  FBG SV IB T255-T330 12           2  9    34600  38900
32  3 STAMAS 32             OP  SF   FBG SV IB T255-T330 12    12800  2  9    39000  45300
32  3 STAMAS 32             HT  SF   FBG SV IB T255-T330 12           2  9    30000  35000
32  3 STAMAS 32             FB  SF   FBG SV IB T255-T330 12           2  9    29700  35000
32  3 STAMAS-CONTINENTAL    ST  CR   FBG SV IB T255-T330 12    12000  2  9    38500  44700
32  3 STAMAS-CONTINENTAL    HT  CR   FBG SV IB T255-T330 12           2  9    31900  37600
32  3 STAMAS-CONTINENTAL    FB  CR   FBG SV IB T255-T330 12           2  9    31900  37600
44    STAMAS 44             KTH SA/CR FBG KL IB   62D PERK 14  30000  5  1  97600 107500
------------------- 1981 BOATS-------------------------------------------------------
21  3 STAMAS 21             OP  CR   FBG SV OB           7  9  3100  1  6     8900  10100
21  3 STAMAS 21             OP  CR   FBG SV IO 170-185   7  9  4100  1  6     7250   8300
23  3 STAMAS 24             OP  FSH  FBG SV OB           8        4  2  4     8250   9700
23  3 STAMAS 24             OP  FSH  FBG SV IO 228-260   8        4  2  4     9150  10400
23  3 STAMAS 24             HT  FSH  FBG SV IO T140      8        4  2  4     9450  11300
23  3 STAMAS 24             HT  FSH  FBG SV IO 228-260   8  4500  4  2  4     7600  10900
23  3 STAMAS 24             HT  FSH  FBG SV IO T140      8  4900  4  2  4    10900  12400
23  3 STAMAS 24             OP  SPTCR FBG SV IO 228-260  8        4  2  4     7200  10600
23  3 STAMAS 24             OP  SPTCR FBG SV IO T140     8        4  2  4     8400   9650
23  3 STAMAS 24             HT  SPTCR FBG SV IO 228-260  8  4600  4  2  4     9200  10600
23  3 STAMAS 24             HT  SPTCR FBG SV IO T140     8  5000  4  2  4    10500  12100
26    STAMAS 26             OP  FSH  FBG SV IO 228-260   9  7      2  8    12700  14700
      IB  330  16500 18700, IO T145  VLVO 13800 15700, IO T170  MRCR  13800  15700
      IO T170  OMC  13800 15600, IB T170-T175 19800 21200
26    STAMAS 26             HT  FSH  FBG SV IO 228-260   9  7      2  8    12700  14700
      IB  330  14900 17200, IO T145  VLVO 13800 15700, IO T170  MRCR  13800  15700
      IO T170  OMC  13800 15600, IB T170-T175 15400 17500
26    STAMAS 26             HT  SDN  FBG SV IB  255  MRCR 9  7      2  6    15400  17500
      IO  260  MRCR 13200 15000, IO 260  MRCR 13200 15000, IB 260  OMC  15600  17700
      IO T145  VLVO 14100 16000, IO T170  MRCR 14200 16100, IO T170  OMC  14100  16000
      IB T170-T175 16600 19000
26    STAMAS 26             FB  SDN  FBG SV IB  255  MRCR 9  7      2  6    15400  17500
      IO  260  MRCR 13200 15000, IO 260  MRCR 13200 15000, IB 260  OMC  15600  17700
      IO T145  VLVO 14100 16000, IO T170  MRCR 14200 16100, IO T170  OMC  14100  16000
      IB T170-T175 16600 19000
26    STAMAS 26             OP  SPTCR FBG SV IO 228-230  9  7      2  6    12000  13500
      IB  255  MRCR 18200 20200, IO 260  MRCR 12300 14000, IO 260  OMC  12300  13900
      IB  260  OMC  18400 20400, IO T145  VLVO 13100 14900, IO T170  MRCR  13100  14900
      IO T170  OMC  13000 14800, IB T170-T175 19000 21200
26    STAMAS 26             HT  SPTCR FBG SV IO 228-230  9  7      2  6    12300  13900
      IB  255  MRCR 18200 20200, IO 260  MRCR 12300 14000, IO 260  OMC  12300  13900
      IB  260  OMC  18400 20400, IO T145  VLVO 13100 14900, IO T170  MRCR  13100  14900
      IO T170  OMC  13000 14800, IB T170-T175 19000 21200
26    STAMAS 26             FB  SPTCR FBG SV IO 228-230  9  7  6900  2  6    14100  16300
      IB  255  MRCR 16700 19000, IO 260  MRCR 14400 16300, IO 260  OMC  14300  16300
      IB  260  OMC  18400 19300, IO T145  VLVO 16800 18800, IO T170  MRCR  16500  18800
      IO T170  OMC  16500 18700, IB T170  MRCR 15400 17500, IB T175  PCM  18200  20300
26    STAMAS-RIVIERA 26     ST  CR   FBG SV IO  228  MRCR 9  7      2  6    12000  13500
26    STAMAS-RIVIERA 26     ST  CR   FBG SV IO  230-260 9  7  6500  2  6    13500  15700
26    STAMAS-TARPON 26      OP  FSH  FBG SV IO T145-T170 9  7      2  6    15900  15900
26    STAMAS-TARPON 26      OP  FSH  FBG SV IB T255-330  9  7  6400  2  6    15900  19000
32  3 STAMAS 32             HT  SDN  FBG SV IB T255-T340 12    13300  2  9    40800  45500
32  3 STAMAS 32             FB  SDN  FBG SV IB T255-T340 12           2  9    33200  37300
32  3 STAMAS 32             OP  SF   FBG SV IB T255-T340 12    12800  2  9    38400  44700
32  3 STAMAS 32             HT  SF   FBG SV IB T255-T340 12           2  9    28400  33700
32  3 STAMAS 32             FB  SF   FBG SV IB T255-T340 12           2  9    28400  33700
32  3 STAMAS-CONTINENTAL    ST  CR   FBG SV IB T255-T340 12    12000  2  9    36900  41100
32  3 STAMAS-CONTINENTAL    HT  CR   FBG SV IB T255-T340 12           2  9    30600  36300
32  3 STAMAS-CONTINENTAL    FB  CR   FBG SV IB T255-T340 12           2  9    30600  36300
44    STAMAS 44             KTH SA/CR FBG KL IB   62D PERK 14  30000  5  1  91900 101500
```

```
LOA   NAME AND/         TOP/ BOAT -HULL- ----ENGINE--- BEAM    WGT  DRAFT RETAIL RETAIL
FT IN OR MODEL          RIG  TYPE MTL TP TP #  HP   MFG  FT IN  LBS  FT IN  LOW   HIGH
-------------------- 1980 BOATS ----------------------------------------------------
21  3 STAMAS 21          OP  CR    FBG SV OB           7  9 3100  1  6  8700   9950
21  3 STAMAS 21          OP  CR    FBG SV IO 170-200   7  9 4100  1  6  7200   8250
23  3 STAMAS 24          OP  CR    FBG SV IO 228-260   8    4250  2  4  8450   9950
23  3 STAMAS 24          OP  CR    FBG SV IO T140      8    4250  2  4  9350  10600
23  3 STAMAS 24          HT  CR    FBG SV IO 228-260   8    4250  2  4  8450   9950
23  3 STAMAS 24          HT  CR    FBG SV IO T140      8    4250  2  4  9350  10600
23  3 STAMAS 24          OP  FSH   FBG SV IO 228-260   8    4500  2  4  9400  10900
23  3 STAMAS 24          OP  FSH   FBG SV IO T140      8    4900  2  4 10900  12300
23  3 STAMAS 24          HT  FSH   FBG SV IO 228-260   8    4500  2  4  9400  10900
23  3 STAMAS 24          HT  FSH   FBG SV IO T140      8    4900  2  4 10900  12300
23  3 STAMAS 24          OP  SPTCR FBG SV IO 228-260   8    4600  2  4  9100  10500
23  3 STAMAS 24          OP  SPTCR FBG SV IO T140      8    4550  2  4  9750  11100

23  3 STAMAS 24          HT  SPTCR FBG SV IO 228-260   8    4600  2  4  9100  10500
23  3 STAMAS 24          HT  SPTCR FBG SV IO T140      8    5000  2  4 10400  11900
26    STAMAS 26          OP  FSH   FBG SV IO 228  MRCR 9  7 5500  2  4 12700  14400
      IO 230-260   14100 16400, IB 330       16000 18400, IO T170  MRCR 16700 19000
      IB T170-T175 18400 20500, IO T200  OMC 17000 19300

26    STAMAS 26          HT  FSH   FBG SV IO 228-260   9  7 6500  2  4 14100  16400
      IB 330       18400, IO T170  MRCR 16700 19000, IB T170-T175 18400 20500
      IO T200  OMC 17000 19300

26    STAMAS 26          HT  SDN   FBG SV IB 255       9  7 7400  2  4 18100  20100
      IO 260   MRCR 15700 17900, IO 260  OMC  15700 17800, IB 260  OMC 18400 20400
      IO T170  MRCR 15300 17400, IB T175 PCM  17500 19900, IO T200 OMC 15700 17800
      IO T260  MRCR 19400 21600

26    STAMAS 26          FB  SDN   FBG SV IB 255       9  7 7400  2  4 18100  20100
      IO 260   MRCR 15700 17900, IO 260  OMC  14500 16500, IB 260  OMC 18400 20400
      IO T170  MRCR 15400 17500, IB T175 PCM  18000 20000, IO T200 OMC 15800 17900

26    STAMAS 26          OP  SPTCR FBG SV IO 228-230   9  7 6900  2  4 14000  15900
      IB 255   MRCR 16000 18200, IO 260  MRCR 14200 16200, IO 260  OMC 14200 16100
      IB 260   OMC  16200 18500, IO T170 MRCR 16400 18600, IB T175 PCM 19100 21200
      IO T200  OMC  16600 18900

26    STAMAS 26          ST  SPTCR FBG SV IO 228  MRCR 9  7 5500  2  4 12000  13600
      IB 255       13800 15900, IO 260  OMC  12300 14000, IO T170 MRCR 13100 14900
      IB T175  PCM 14900 16900, IO T200 OMC  13400 15200

26    STAMAS 26          HT  SPTCR FBG SV IO 228-230   9  7 6900  2  4 14000  15900
      IB 255       16000 18200, IO 260  MRCR 12800 14500, IO 260  OMC 12700 14500
      IB 260   OMC 16200 18500, IO T170 MRCR 16400 18600, IB T175 PCM 15400 17600
      IO T200  OMC 13800 15700

26    STAMAS 26          FB  SPTCR FBG SV IO 228  MRCR 9  7 5930  2  4 12600  14300
      IO 230   OMC 14000 15900, IB 255      16000 18200, IO 260  MRCR 12900 14600
      IO 260   OMC 12800 14600, IB 260 OMC  16200 18500, IO T170 MRCR 13700 15500
      IB T175  PCM 15600 17700, IO T200 OMC  13900 15800

26    STAMAS-RIVIERA 26  ST  CR    FBG SV IO 228-260    9  7 6500  2  4 13400  15500
26    STAMAS-RIVIERA 26  ST  CR    FBG SV IO T170-T200  9  7 7500  2  4 15800  18300
26    STAMAS-TARPON 26   OP  FSH   FBG SV IB 255-330    9  7 6400  2  4 15200  18200
26    STAMAS-TARPON 26   ST  FSH   FBG SV IB 255-330    9  7 6500  2  4 15400  18600
32  3 STAMAS-CONTINENTAL ST  CR    FBG SV IB T255-T260  12   12000 2  9 30200  33700
32  3 STAMAS 32          HT  SDN   FBG SV IB T255-T260  12   12500 2  9 38600  43600
32  3 STAMAS 32          FB  SDN   FBG SV IB T255-T260  12   13300 2  9 39100  43600
32  3 STAMAS 32          OP  SF    FBG SV IB T255-T260  12   12800 2  9 35800  40000
32  3 STAMAS 32          HT  SF    FBG SV IB T255-T260  12   11000 2  9 35800  40000
32  3 STAMAS 32          FB  SF    FBG SV IB T255-T260  12   11000 2  9 38400  40000
32  3 STAMAS-CONTINENTAL ST  SF    FBG SV IB T255-T260  12   12000 2  9 35300  39400
32  3 STAMAS-CONTINENTAL HT  CR    FBG SV IB T255-T260  12   12000 2  9 35300  39400
-------------------- 1979 BOATS ----------------------------------------------------
21  3 STAMAS 21          OP  CR    FBG SV OB           7  9 2500  2  2  7600   8750
21  3 STAMAS 21          OP  CR    FBG SV IO 165-220   7  9 3500  2  2  6400   7450
23  3 STAMAS 24          OP  CR    FBG SV IO 228-260   8    4250  2  4  8450   9900
23  3 STAMAS 24          OP  CR    FBG SV IO T140      8    4250  2  4  9300  10600
23  3 STAMAS 24          HT  CR    FBG SV IO 228-260   8    4250  2  4  8450   9900
23  3 STAMAS 24          HT  CR    FBG SV IO T140      8    4250  2  4  9300  10600
23  3 STAMAS 24          OP  SPTCR FBG SV IO 228-260   8    4550  2  4  9000  10400
23  3 STAMAS 24          OP  SPTCR FBG SV IO T140      8    4550  2  4  9750  11100
23  3 STAMAS 24          HT  SPTCR FBG SV IO 228-260   8    4550  2  4  9000  10400
23  3 STAMAS 24          HT  SPTCR FBG SV IO T140      8    4550  2  4  9750  11100

26    STAMAS 26          OP  FSH   FBG SV IO 228-260   9  7 5500  2  4 12700  14700
      IB 330   MRCR 15700, IO    D    **    **, IO T170 MRCR 13800 15700
      IB T175      14600 16600, IO T185 OMC 13900 15800

26    STAMAS 26          HT  SDN   FBG SV IO 250  OMC  9  7 6440  2  4 14300  16200
      IB 255       15600, IO 260  MRCR 14400 16400, IO    D    **    **
      IO T170  MRCR 15300 17400, IB T175 17100 19400, IO T185 OMC 15500 17600

26    STAMAS 26          FB  SDN   FBG SV IO 250  OMC  9  7 6520  2  4 14400  16300
      IB 255       18000, IO 260  MRCR 14500 16500, IO    D    **    **
      IO T170  MRCR 15400 17500, IB T175 17200 19500, IO T185 OMC 15600 17700

26    STAMAS 26          ST  SPTCR FBG SV IO 228-250   9  7 5500  2  4 12000  13800
      IB 255       15200, IO 260  MRCR 12300 14000, IO    D    **    **
      IO T170  MRCR 13200 15000, IB T175 14600 16600, IO T185 OMC 13200 15000

26    STAMAS 26          HT  SPTCR FBG SV IO 228-250   9  7 5850  2  4 12500  14400
      IB 255       15800, IO 260  MRCR 12800 14500, IO    D    **    **
      IO T170  MRCR 13600 15400, IB T175 15100 17200, IO T185 OMC 13700 15500

26    STAMAS 26          FB  SPTCR FBG SV IO 228-250   9  7 5930  2  4 12600  14500
      IB 255       16000, IO 260  MRCR 12900 14600, IO    D    **    **
      IO T170  MRCR 13700 15500, IB T175 15200 17300, IO T185 OMC 13800 15600

32  3 STAMAS 32          HT  SDN   FBG SV IB T255   MRCR 12  12500 2  9 37000  41200
32  3 STAMAS 32          HT  SDN   FBG SV IB T      D    12  12500 2  9   **     **
32  3 STAMAS 32          FB  SDN   FBG SV IB T255   MRCR 12  12500 2  9 37000  41200
32  3 STAMAS 32          FB  SDN   FBG SV IB T      D    12  12500 2  9   **     **
32  3 STAMAS 32          OP  SF    FBG SV IB T255   MRCR 12  11000 2  9 33300  37000
32  3 STAMAS 32          OP  SF    FBG SV IB T      D    12  11000 2  9   **     **
32  3 STAMAS 32          HT  SF    FBG SV IB T255   MRCR 12  11000 2  9 33300  37000
32  3 STAMAS 32          HT  SF    FBG SV IB T      D    12  11000 2  9   **     **
32  3 STAMAS 32          FB  SF    FBG SV IB T255   MRCR 12  11000 2  9 33300  37000
32  3 STAMAS 32          FB  SF    FBG SV IB T      D    12  11000 2  9   **     **
-------------------- 1978 BOATS ----------------------------------------------------
21  3 STAMAS 21          OP  CR    FBG SV OB           7  9 2500  2  2  7550   8650
21  3 STAMAS 21          OP  CR    FBG SV IO 165-185   7  9 3500  2  2  5900   6800
23  3 STAMAS 24          OP  CR    FBG SV IO 228-240   8    4250  2  4  8500   9800
23  3 STAMAS 24          OP  CR    FBG SV IO T140      8    4250  2  4  9400  10700
23  3 STAMAS 24          HT  CR    FBG SV IO 228-240   8    4250  2  4  8500   9800
23  3 STAMAS 24          HT  CR    FBG SV IO T140      8    4250  2  4  9400  10700
23  3 STAMAS 24          OP  SPTCR FBG SV IO 228-240   8    4550  2  4  9100  10300
23  3 STAMAS 24          OP  SPTCR FBG SV IO T140      8    4550  2  4  9800  11100
23  3 STAMAS 24          HT  SPTCR FBG SV IO 228-240   8    4550  2  4  9100  10300
23  3 STAMAS 24          HT  SPTCR FBG SV IO T140      8    4550  2  4  9800  11100

26    STAMAS 26          HT  SDN   FBG SV IO 228-240   9  7 6440  2  4 14200  16200
      IB 255   CHRY 14900 17200, IO 260  MRCR 14500 16500, IO 130D VLVO 16500 18700
      IB T155  CHRY 15700 17800

26    STAMAS 26          FB  SDN   FBG SV IO 228-240   9  7 6520  2  4 14300  16300
      IB 255   CHRY 15000 17300, IO 260  MRCR 14600 16600, IO 130D VLVO 16600 18900
      IB T155  CHRY 15800 18000

26    STAMAS 26          ST  SPTCR FBG SV IO 228-240   9  7 5500  2  4 12100  13800
      IB 255   CHRY 12700 14600, IO 260  MRCR 12400 14100, IO 130D VLVO 13200 15000
      IB T155  CHRY 13400 15100

26    STAMAS 26          HT  SPTCR FBG SV IO 228-240   9  7 5850  2  4 12600  14400
      IB 255   CHRY 13300 15300, IO 260  MRCR 12900 14700, IO 130D VLVO 13900 15800
      IB T155  CHRY 13900 15800

26    STAMAS 26          FB  SPTCR FBG SV IO 228-240   9  7 5930  2  4 12700  14500
      IB 255   CHRY 15300 15900, IO 260  MRCR 12900 14700, IO 130D VLVO 14100 16000
      IB T155  CHRY 14100 15900

32  3 STAMAS 32          HT  SDN   FBG SV IB T255        12  12500 2  9 35500  39500
32  3 STAMAS 32          HT  SDN   FBG SV IB T200D CHRY  12  12500 2  9 47000  51600
32  3 STAMAS 32          FB  SDN   FBG SV IB T255        12  12500 2  9 35500  39500
32  3 STAMAS 32          FB  SDN   FBG SV IB T200D CHRY  12  12500 2  9 47000  51600
32  3 STAMAS 32          OP  SF    FBG SV IB T255        12  11000 2  9 32000  35500
32  3 STAMAS 32          OP  SF    FBG SV IB T200D CHRY  12  11000 2  9 38800  43100
32  3 STAMAS 32          HT  SF    FBG SV IB T255        12  11000 2  9 33200  35500
32  3 STAMAS 32          HT  SF    FBG SV IB T255        12  11000 2  9 38800  43100
32  3 STAMAS 32          FB  SF    FBG SV IB T255        12  11000 2  9 33300  35500
32  3 STAMAS 32          FB  SF    FBG SV IB T200D CHRY  12  11000 2  9 38800  43100
-------------------- 1977 BOATS ----------------------------------------------------
21  3 CRUISER           OP  EXP   FBG SV OB            7  9 2500  2  2  7450   8600
21  3 CRUISER           OP  EXP   FBG SV OB  165-175   7  9 3500  2  2  6550   7500
21  3 SPORT FISHERMAN   OP  OFSH  FBG SV OB            7  9 2275  2  2  7000   8050
23  6 CRUISER           OP  EXP   FBG SV IO 188-235    8    4500  2  4  9150  10600
```

STAMAS YACHTS INC -CONTINUED See inside cover to adjust price for area

LOA FT	LOA IN	NAME AND/ OR MODEL	TOP/ RIG	BOAT TYPE	HULL MTL	HULL TP	ENGINE TP	ENGINE # HP	ENGINE MFG	BEAM FT	BEAM IN	WGT LBS	DRAFT FT	DRAFT IN	RETAIL LOW	RETAIL HIGH
		1977 BOATS														
23	6	CRUISER	OP	EXP	FBG	SV	IO	T140		8		4500	2	4	10000	11400
23	6	CRUISER	HT	EXP	FBG	SV	IO	188-235		8		4500	2	4	9150	10600
23	6	CRUISER	HT	EXP	FBG	SV	IO	T140		8		4500	2	4	10000	11400
23	6	RUNABOUT	OP	RNBT	FBG	SV	IO	188-235		8		4250	2	4	8150	9500
23	6	RUNABOUT	OP	RNBT	FBG	SV	IO	T140		8		4250	2	4	9050	10300
23	6	SPORT CRUISER	OP	EXP	FBG	SV	IO	188-235		8		4550	2	4	9250	10700
23	6	SPORT CRUISER	OP	EXP	FBG	SV	IO	T140		8		4550	2	4	10100	11500
26		SPORT CRUISER	OP	EXP	FBG	SV	IO	233-235		9	7	5500	2	4	12300	14000
		IO 255 MRCR 12500 14200, IB 255-260 12200 14100, IB T155 CHRY 12800 14600														
		IO T165-T175 13300 15200														
26		SPORT CRUISER	HT	EXP	FBG	SV	IO	233-235		9	7	5500	2	4	12300	14000
		IO 255 MRCR 12500 14200, IB 255-260 12200 14100, IB T155 CHRY 12800 14600														
		IO T165-T175 13300 15200														
26		SPORT CRUISER	FB	EXP	FBG	SV	IO	233-235		9	7	5500	2	4	12300	14000
		IO 255 MRCR 12500 14200, IB 255-260 12200 14100, IB T155 CHRY 12800 14600														
		IO T165-T175 13300 15200														
26		SPORT SEDAN	FB	SDN	FBG	SV	IO	233-235		9	7	5930	2	4	13800	15600
		IO 255 MRCR 14000 15900, IB 255-260 13600 15700, IB T155 CHRY 14400 16400														
		IO T165-T175 15000 17100														
32		SPORT CRUISER	OP	SPTCR	FBG	SV	IB	T255	MRCR	12		11500	2	9	30300	33700
32		SPORT CRUISER	OP	SPTCR	FBG	SV	IB	T200D	CHRY	12		11500	2	9	37700	41900
32		SPORT CRUISER	HT	SPTCR	FBG	SV	IB	T255	MRCR	12		11500	2	9	30300	33700
32		SPORT CRUISER	HT	SPTCR	FBG	SV	IB	T200D	CHRY	12		11500	2	9	37700	41900
32		SPORT CRUISER	FB	SPTCR	FBG	SV	IB	T255	MRCR	12		11500	2	9	30300	33700
32		SPORT CRUISER	FB	SPTCR	FBG	SV	IB	T200D	CHRY	12		11500	2	9	37700	41900
32		SPORT SEDAN	HT	SDN	FBG	SV	IB	T200D	CHRY	12		12500	2	9	44400	49400
32		SPORT SEDAN	FB	SDN	FBG	SV	IB	T200D	CHRY	12		12500	2	9	44400	49400
32		SPORT SEDAN 4 SLPR	HT	SDN	FBG	SV	IB	D		12		12500	2	9	**	**
32		SPORT SEDAN 4 SLPR	HT	SDN	FBG	SV	IB	T255	MRCR	12		12500	2	9	33300	37000
32		SPORT SEDAN 4 SLPR	FB	SDN	FBG	SV	IB	D		12		12500	2	9	**	**
32		SPORT SEDAN 4 SLPR	FB	SDN	FBG	SV	IB	T255	MRCR	12		12500	2	9	33300	37000
32		SPORT SEDAN 6 SLPR	HT	SDN	FBG	SV	IB	D		12		12500	2	9	**	**
32		SPORT SEDAN 6 SLPR	HT	SDN	FBG	SV	IB	T255	MRCR	12		12500	2	9	33800	37600
32		SPORT SEDAN 6 SLPR	FB	SDN	FBG	SV	IB	D		12		12500	2	9	**	**
32		SPORT SEDAN 6 SLPR	FB	SDN	FBG	SV	IB	T255	MRCR	12		12500	2	9	33800	37500
		1976 BOATS														
21	3	CRUISER	OP	EXP	FBG	SV	OB			7	9	2500	2	2	7400	8500
21	3	CRUISER	OP	EXP	FBG	SV	IO	165-235		7	9	3500	2	2	6700	7900
21	3	SPORTS FISHERMAN	OP	SF	FBG	SV	OB			7	9	2275	2	2	6950	8000
23	6	CRUISER	OP	EXP	FBG	SV	IO	188-235		8		4250	2	4	9000	10400
23	6	CRUISER	OP	EXP	FBG	SV	IO	T140		8		4250	2	4	9850	11200
23	6	CRUISER	HT	EXP	FBG	SV	IO	188-235		8		4250	2	4	9000	10400
23	6	CRUISER	HT	EXP	FBG	SV	IO	T140		8		4250	2	4	9850	11200
23	6	RUNABOUT	ST	RNBT	FBG	SV	IO	188-235		8		4250	2	4	8350	9750
23	6	RUNABOUT	ST	RNBT	FBG	SV	IO	T140		8		4250	2	4	9300	10600
23	6	RUNABOUT	HT	RNBT	FBG	SV	IO	188-235		8		4550	2	4	8900	10300
23	6	RUNABOUT	HT	RNBT	FBG	SV	IO	T140		8		4550	2	4	9700	11000
23	6	RUNABOUT	FB	RNBT	FBG	SV	IO	188-235		8		4630	2	4	9000	10400
26		SPORTS CRUISER	ST	EXP	FBG	SV	VD	225	MRCR	9	7	5500	2	4	11500	13100
		IO 233-250 12600 14500, VD 260 OMC 11900 13500, VD T155 CHRY 12300 14000														
		IO T165 13700 15500														
26		SPORTS CRUISER	HT	EXP	FBG	SV	VD	225	MRCR	9	7	5850	2	4	12000	13600
		IO 233-250 13100 15100, VD 260 OMC 12300 14000, VD T155 CHRY 12800 14500														
		IO T165 14200 16100														
26		SPORTS CRUISER	FB	EXP	FBG	SV	VD	225	MRCR	9	7	5930	2	4	12100	13700
		IO 233-250 13300 15200, VD 260 OMC 12400 14100, VD T155 CHRY 12900 14600														
		IO T165 14300 16200														
32		SPORTS SEDAN	HT	SDN	FBG	SV	IB	T255	MRCR	12		12500	2	9	32200	35800
32		SPORTS SEDAN	HT	SDN	FBG	SV	IB	T210D	CUM	12		13000	2	9	44000	48900
32		SPORTS SEDAN	FB	SDN	FBG	SV	IB	T255	MRCR	12		12950	2	9	32400	36000
32		SPORTS SEDAN	FB	SDN	FBG	SV	IB	T210D	CUM	12		13450	2	9	44700	49600
		1975 BOATS														
21	3	APOLLO V21	HT	EXP	FBG	SV	OB			7	9	2489	2	2	7350	8450
21	3	APOLLO V21	HT	EXP	FBG	SV	IO	140-225		7	9	3400	2	2	6750	7900
21	3	ORION V21	OP	FSH	FBG	SV	OB			7	9	1750	2	2	5650	6500
23	6	AEGEAN V-24	OP	EXP	FBG	SV	IO	188-233		8		4850	2	4	10200	11800
23	6	AEGEAN V-24	OP	EXP	FBG	SV	IO	T140		8		4850	2	4	11200	12700
23	6	AEGEAN V-24	HT	EXP	FBG	SV	IO	188-233		8		4850	2	4	10200	11800
23	6	AEGEAN V-24	HT	EXP	FBG	SV	IO	T140		8		4850	2	4	11200	12700
23	6	AEGEAN V-24	FB	EXP	FBG	SV	IO	188-233		8		5200	2	4	10900	12500
23	6	CLEARWATER V-24	OP	EXP	FBG	SV	IO	188-233		8		4295	2	4	9350	10700
23	6	CLEARWATER V-24	OP	EXP	FBG	SV	IO	T140		8		4295	2	4	10300	11700
23	6	CLEARWATER V-24	HT	EXP	FBG	SV	IO	188-233		8		4295	2	4	9350	10700
23	6	CLEARWATER V-24	HT	EXP	FBG	SV	IO	T140		8		4295	2	4	10300	11700
26		AMERICANA V-26	OP	EXP	FBG	SV	IO	225-233		9	7	6126	2	4	13900	15900
26		AMERICANA V-26	OP	EXP	FBG	SV	IO	T165		9	7	6126	2	4	15100	17100
26		AMERICANA V-26	HT	EXP	FBG	SV	IO	225-233		9	7	6126	2	4	13900	15900
26		AMERICANA V-26	HT	EXP	FBG	SV	IO	T165		9	7	6126	2	4	15100	17100
26		AMERICANA V-26	FB	EXP	FBG	SV	IO	T165		9	7	6556	2	4	15700	17800
32	3	V-32 SPORTS SEDAN	HT	SDN	FBG	SV	IB	T225-T255		12		12500	2	9	30800	34900
32	3	V-32 SPORTS SEDAN	HT	SDN	FBG	SV	IB	T210D	CUM	12		14200	2	9	44700	49600
32	3	V-32 SPORTS SEDAN	FB	SDN	FBG	SV	IB	T225-T255		12		12500	2	9	30800	34900
32	3	V-32 SPORTS SEDAN	FB	SDN	FBG	SV	IB	T210D	CUM	12		14200	2	9	44700	49600
		1974 BOATS														
21	3	APOLLO V-21 DLX		CR	FBG		OB			7	9	1850	2	2	5900	6800
21	3	APOLLO V-21 DLX		CR	FBG		IO	140-225		7	9		2	2	6550	7650
21	3	ORION DELUXE		SF	FBG		OB			7	9	1750	2	2	5650	6500
23	6	AEGEAN V-24 DELUXE	HT		FBG		IO	165-225		8			2	4	8800	10200
23	6	AEGEAN V-24 DELUXE	HT		FBG		IO	T140		8			2	4	9750	11100
23	6	AEGEAN V-24 DLX	FB		FBG		IO	188-225		8		5150	2	4	10600	12100
23	6	AEGEAN V-24 DLX		RNBT	FBG		IO	165-225		8		4850	2	4	9900	11400
23	6	AEGEAN V-24 DLX		RNBT	FBG		IO	T140		8		4850	2	4	10900	12400
23	6	CLEARWATER V-24		CR	FBG		IO	165-225		8		4850	2	4	10600	12200
23	6	CLEARWATER V-24		CR	FBG		IO	T140		8		4850	2	4	11600	13200
23	6	CLEARWATER V-24	HT	CR	FBG		IO	165-225		8		4850	2	4	10600	12200
23	6	CLEARWATER V-24	HT	CR	FBG		IO	T140		8		4850	2	4	11600	13200
26		AMERICANA V-26	FB		FBG		IO	T165		9	7		2	4	14700	16700
26		AMERICANA V-26		CR	FBG		IO	140-225		9	7	6125	2	5	13700	16400
26		AMERICANA V-26	HT	CR	FBG		IO	225		9	7		2	5	13300	15100
26		AMERICANA V-26	HT	CR	FBG		IO	T140-T165		9	7		2	5	14200	16500
32	3	V-32		SDNSF	FBG		IB	T225		12		12500	2	9	27400	30400
32	3	V-32		SDNSF	FBG		IB	T210D	CUM	12		12500	2	9	36500	40600
32	3	V-32	FB	SDNSF	FBG		IB	T225		12			2	9	23800	26400
32	3	V-32	FB	SDNSF	FBG		IB	T210D	CUM	12			2	9	29100	32400
		1973 BOATS														
16	7	SPARTAN V-18 DLX	OP	RNBT	FBG	SV	OB			7		1000	2	2	2900	3350
21	3	APOLLO V-21 DLX		CR	FBG		OB			7	9	1850	2	2	5900	6800
21	3	APOLLO V-21 DLX		CR	FBG		IO	140-225		7	9		2	2	6750	7900
21	3	ORION DELUXE		SF	FBG		OB			7	9	1750	2	2	5650	6500
23	6	AEGEAN V-24 DELUXE	HT		FBG		IO	188-225		8			2	4	9150	10500
23	6	AEGEAN V-24 DELUXE	HT		FBG		IO	T120-T140		8			2	4	10000	11400
23	6	AEGEAN V-24 DLX	FB		FBG		IO	188-225		8		5150	2	4	10900	12600
23	6	AEGEAN V-24 DLX		RNBT	FBG		IO	165-225		8		4850	2	4	10200	11800
23	6	AEGEAN V-24 DLX		RNBT	FBG		IO	T120-T140		8		4850	2	4	11200	12800
23	6	CLEARWATER V-24		CR	FBG		IO	165-225		8		4850	2	4	10900	12600
23	6	CLEARWATER V-24		CR	FBG		IO	T120-T140		8		4850	2	4	11900	13600
23	6	CLEARWATER V-24	HT	CR	FBG		IO	165-225		8		4850	2	4	10900	12600
23	6	CLEARWATER V-24	HT	CR	FBG		IO	T120-T140		8		4850	2	4	11900	13600
26		AMERICANA V-26	FB		FBG		IO	T165		9	7		2	4	15200	17300
26		AMERICANA V-26		CR	FBG		IO	225		9	7	6125	2	5	14900	16900
26		AMERICANA V-26		CR	FBG		IO	T140-T165		9	7	6125	2	5	15800	18300
26		AMERICANA V-26	HT	CR	FBG		IO	225		9	7		2	5	13700	15600
26		AMERICANA V-26	HT	CR	FBG		IO	T140-T165		9	7		2	5	14700	17000
		1972 BOATS														
16	7	SPARTAN V-18 DLX			FBG		OB			7		1000	2	2	2850	3350
16	7	SPARTAN V-18 DLX			FBG		IO	120		7		1000	2	2	2550	2950
21	3	APOLLO V-21 DLX		CR	FBG		OB			7	9	1850	2	2	5900	6750
21	3	APOLLO V-21 DLX		CR	FBG		IO	120-225		7	9		2	2	7000	8200
21	3	ORION DELUXE		SF	FBG		OB			7	9	1750	2	2	5650	6450
23	6	AEGEAN V-24 DELUXE	HT		FBG		IO	120-225		8			2	4	9350	10800
23	6	AEGEAN V-24 DELUXE	HT		FBG		IO	T120-T140		8			2	4	10400	11800
23	6	AEGEAN V-24 DLX	FB		FBG		IO	165-225		8		4850	2	4	10700	12300
23	6	AEGEAN V-24 DLX		RNBT	FBG		IO	120-225		8		4850	2	4	10500	12200
23	6	AEGEAN V-24 DLX		RNBT	FBG		IO	T120-T140		8		4850	2	4	11600	13200
23	6	CLEARWATER V-24		CR	FBG		IO	120-225		8		4850	2	4	11200	12900
23	6	CLEARWATER V-24		CR	FBG		IO	T120-T140		8		4850	2	4	12300	14000
23	6	CLEARWATER V-24	HT	CR	FBG		IO	120-225		8		4850	2	4	11200	12900
23	6	CLEARWATER V-24	HT	CR	FBG		IO	T120-T140		8		4850	2	4	12300	14000
23	6	TARPON SF V-24 DLX			FBG		IO	120-225		8		4250	2	4	9600	11100
23	6	TARPON SF V-24 DLX			FBG		IO	T120-T140		8		4250	2	4	10700	12100
26		AMERICANA V-26	FB		FBG		IO	T140-T165		9	7		2	4	15400	17900
26		AMERICANA V-26		CR	FBG		IO	215-225		9	7	7000	2	5	16800	19100
26		AMERICANA V-26		CR	FBG		IO	T120-T165		9	7	7000	2	5	17500	20500

CONTINUED ON NEXT PAGE

LOA FT	LOA IN	NAME AND/ OR MODEL	TOP/ RIG	BOAT TYPE	-HULL- MTL	-HULL- TP	ENGINE TP	ENGINE # HP	ENGINE MFG	BEAM FT	BEAM IN	WGT LBS	DRAFT FT	DRAFT IN	RETAIL LOW	RETAIL HIGH
		1972 BOATS														
26		AMERICANA V-26	HT	CR	FBG		IO	215-225		9	7		2	5	14100	16100
26		AMERICANA V-26	HT	CR	FBG		IO	T120-T165		9	7		2	5	14900	17600
		1971 BOATS														
16	7	SPARTAN V-18 DLX			FBG		OB			7		1000	2	2	2850	3350
16	7	SPARTAN V-18 DLX			FBG		IO	120		7		1000	2	2	2650	3050
21	3	APOLLO V-21 DLX		CR	FBG		OB			7	9	1850	2	2	5900	6750
21	3	APOLLO V-21 DLX		CR	FBG		IO	120-215		7	3	1850	2	2	5450	6450
23	6	AEGEAN V-24 DLX		RNBT	FBG		IO	120-215		8		4650	2	4	10500	12100
23	6	AEGEAN V-24 DLX		RNBT	FBG		IO	T120-T140		8		4650	2	4	11600	13200
23	6	CLEARWATER V-24		CR	FBG		IO	120-215		8		4850	2	4	11600	13400
23	6	CLEARWATER V-24		CR	FBG		IO	T120-T140		8		4850	2	4	12800	14500
23	6	CLEARWATER V-24	HT	CR	FBG		IO	120-215		8		4850	2	4	11600	13400
23	6	CLEARWATER V-24	HT	CR	FBG		IO	T120-T140		8		4850	2	4	12800	14500
23	6	TARPON SF V-24 DLX			FBG		IO	120-215		8		4250	2	4	9950	11500
23	6	TARPON SF V-24 DLX			FBG		IO	T120-T140		8		4250	2	4	11000	12500
26		AMERICANA V-26	FB		FBG		IO	T155	OMC	9	7	6450	2	4	18200	20200
26		AMERICANA V-26		CR	FBG		IO	215		9	7	6125	2	4	15800	17900
26		AMERICANA V-26		CR	FBG		IO	T120-T165		9	7	6125	2	4	16600	19500
26		AMERICANA V-26	FB	SDN	FBG		IO	T155	OMC	9	7	7000	2	4	19800	22000
		1970 BOATS														
16	7	SPARTAN V-18 DELUXE			FBG	DV	IO	80-120		7		1000			2700	3150
16	7	SPARTAN V-18 DELUXE			FBG	DV	IO	130	VLVO	7		1000			2950	3400
16	7	SPARTAN V-18 DELUXE		CR	FBG	DV	OB			7		900			2600	3050
21	2	APOLLO V-21		CR	FBG	DV	OB			7	8				5650	6450
21	2	APOLLO V-21		CR	FBG	DV	IO	120-160		7	8				7400	8500
23	6	AEGEAN V-24		RNBT	FBG		IO	225	MRCR	8		4650	2	4	11100	12600
23	6	AEGEAN V-24		RNBT	FBG	DV	IO	120-225		8		4650	2	4	10900	12600
23	6	CLEARWATER		CR	FBG		IO	120-225		8		4850	2	4	12000	13900
23	6	CLEARWATER		CR	FBG	DV	IO	155-225		8		4850	2	4	12000	13900
23	6	TARPON V-24		SF	FBG	DV	IO	120-225		8		4250	2	4	12300	14300
25	11	AMERICANA	FB	SDN	FBG	DV	IO	210-350		9	7	7000	2	4	19100	23600
25	11	AMERICANA	FB	SDN	FBG	DV	IO	T155	OMC	9	7	7000	2	4	20400	22600
25	11	AMERICANA V26		CBNCR	FBG	DV	IO	210-325		9	7	6450	2	4	20400	24500
25	11	AMERICANA V26		CBNCR	FBG	DV	IO	T120-T160		9	7	6450	2	4	21600	24600
		1969 BOATS														
16	7	SPARTAN V-18 DELUXE	OP	RNBT	FBG	DV	OB			7		900			2650	3050
16	7	SPARTAN V-18 DELUXE	OP	RNBT	FBG	DV	IO	80-120		7		1000	2		3000	3500
19	3	ORION V-20	OP	SPTCR	FBG		OB			7	6		2		3150	3650
19	3	ORION V-20	OP	SPTCR	FBG		IO	80		7	6	1300	2		4450	5100
23	6	CLEARWATER V-24	OP	CUD	FBG		IO	200-225		8		4050	2	4	10900	12500
23	6	CLEARWATER V-24	OP	CUD	FBG	DV	IO	120-160		8		4050	2	4	10700	12200
23	6	TARPON V-24	OP	FSH	FBG		IO	155-225		8		4250	2	4	11700	13600
23	6	V-24	OP	RNBT	FBG		IO	155-160		8		4250	2	4	10400	11900
23	6	V-24	OP	RNBT	FBG	DV	IO	200-225		8		4250	2	4	10600	12100
25	11	AMERICANA V-26	OP	CR	FBG	DV	IO	200-290		9	7	5000	2	4	14600	17800
25	11	AMERICANA V-26	OP	CR	FBG	DV	IO	T110-T160		9	7	5000	2	4	15800	18400
		1968 BOATS														
16	7	SPARTAN V-18 DELUXE	OP	RNBT	FBG		OB			7		900	2	4	2650	3050
16	7	SPARTAN V-18 DELUXE	OP	RNBT	FBG		IO	80-120		7		1000	2	4	3100	3600
19	3	ORION V-20	OP	SPTCR	FBG		OB			7	6	1400	2	4	4150	4850
19	3	ORION V-20	OP	SPTCR	FBG		IO	110-160		7	6	1400	2	4	4650	5350
23	6	CLEARWATER V-24	OP	CUD	FBG		IO	120-225		8		3800	2	4	10600	12300
23	6	TARPON V-24	OP	FSH	FBG		IO	120-225		8		3850	2	4	11300	13100
25	11	AMERICANA V-26	OP	CR	FBG		IO	155-225		9	7	5000	2	4	14600	17400
25	11	AMERICANA V-26	OP	CR	FBG		IO	290		9	7	5000	2	4	16200	18400
25	11	AMERICANA V-26	OP	CR	FBG		IO	T110-T120		9	7	5000	2	4	16000	18400
25	11	AMERICANA V-26	HT	CR	FBG		IO	155-225		9	7	5000	2	4	14600	17400
25	11	AMERICANA V-26	HT	CR	FBG		IO	290		9	7	5000	2	4	16200	18400
25	11	AMERICANA V-26	HT	CR	FBG		IO	T110-T120		9	7	5000	2	4	16000	18400
		1967 BOATS														
16	7	SPARTAN V-18 DELUXE	OP	RNBT	FBG		OB			8		900			2650	3100
16	7	SPARTAN V-18 DELUXE	OP	RNBT	FBG		IO	80	CHRY	2		1000			2450	2900
16	7	SPARTAN V-18 DELUXE	OP	RNBT	FBG		IO	80-120		7		1000	2		3200	3700
19	3	ORION V-20	OP	SPTCR	FBG		OB			7	6	1350			4050	4700
19	3	ORION V-20	OP	SPTCR	FBG		IO	120-160		7	6	1400	2		4750	5500
23	6	CLEARWATER V-24	OP	CUD	FBG		IO	120-225		8		3800	2	4	10900	12700
23	6	CLEARWATER V-24	OP	CUD	FBG		IO	T120-T155		8		3800	2	4	12200	14500
23	6	CLEARWATER V-24	OP	CUD	FBG		IO	T 60D		8		3800	2	4	16200	18400
25	11	AMERICANA V-26	OP	CR	FBG		IO	200-225		9	7	5000	2	4	15600	18000
25	11	AMERICANA V-26	OP	CR	FBG		IO	T110-T160		9	7	5000	2	4	16900	19600
25	11	AMERICANA V-26	OP	CR	FBG		IO	T 60D		9	7	5000	2	4	19100	21200
		1966 BOATS														
16	7	SPARTAN V-18	OP	RNBT	FBG		OB			7		900			2650	3100
16	7	SPARTAN V-18	ST	RNBT	FBG		IO	90-120		7					4250	5300
19	3	ORION V-20	OP	SPTCR	FBG		OB			7	6	1350			4050	4750
19	3	ORION V-20	OP	SPTCR	FBG		IO		OMC	7	6	1300			**	**
19	3	ORION V-20	OP	SPTCR	FBG		IO	110-150		7	6	1300			4900	5900
23	6	CLEARWATER V-24	OP	CUD	FBG		OB			8		3800			11300	12900
23	6	CLEARWATER V-24	OP	CUD	FBG		IO	110-225		8		3800			11600	13200
23	6	CLEARWATER V-24	OP	CUD	FBG		IO	T110-T120		8		3800			12600	15000
23	6	CLEARWATER V-24	OP	CUD	FBG		IO	T 60D	MRCR	8		3800			16700	19000
25	11	AMERICANA V-26	OP	CR	FBG		OB			9	7	5000			14400	16400
25	11	AMERICANA V-26	OP	CR	FBG		IO	190-225		9	7	5000			16000	18600
25	11	AMERICANA V-26	OP	CR	FBG		IO	T110-T150		9	7	5000			17100	20100
25	11	AMERICANA V-26	OP	CR	FBG		IO	T 60D	MRCR	9	7	5000			19500	21700
		1965 BOATS														
16	7	SPARTAN V-18			FBG		IO	120							3900	4550
16	7	SPARTAN V-18	OP	RNBT	FBG		IO			7		900			**	**
16	7	SPARTAN V-18	ST	RNBT	FBG		OB			7					3200	3750
16	7	SPARTAN V-18	ST	RNBT	FBG		IO	90-110		7					4450	5100
19	3	ORION V-20	OP	SPTCR	FBG		OB			7	6	1350			4100	4750
19	3	ORION V-20	OP	SPTCR	FBG		IO	90-150		7	6	1300			5000	6100
23	6	CLEARWATER V-24	OP	CUD	FBG		IO	120-225		8		3800	2	4	11600	13500
23	6	CLEARWATER V-24	OP	CUD	FBG		IO	T110-T120		8		3800	2	4	12900	14700
25	11	AMERICANA V-26	OP	CR	FBG		IO	190-225		9	7	5000	2	4	16500	19200
25	11	AMERICANA V-26	OP	CR	FBG		IO	T110	OMC	9	7	5000	2	4	17600	20000
		1964 BOATS														
16	7	SPARTAN V 18	OP	RNBT	FBG		OB			7		900			2700	3150
16	7	SPARTAN V 18	ST	RNBT	FBG		IO	88-110		7					4600	5300
19	3	ORION V 20	OP	SPTCR	FBG		OB			7	6	1350			4100	4800
19	3	ORION V 20	OP	SPTCR	FBG		IO	88-110		7	6				5950	7250
25	11	AMERICANA V-26	OP	CR	FBG		IO	190-225		9	7	5000			17100	19900
25	11	AMERICANA V-26	OP	CR	FBG		IO	T110	MRCR	9	7	5000			18700	20700
		1963 BOATS														
16	7	GALATEA SPORT		RNBT	FBG		OB			7		800			2450	2850
19	3	ORION V-20	ST	SPTCR	FBG		OB			7	6	1300			4000	4700
19	3	ORION V-20	ST	SPTCR	FBG		IB	80		7	6	1300			1700	2000
19	3	TITAN	OP	CBNCR	FBG		OB			7	6	1450			4400	5100
26			HT	EXP	FBG		IB	215		9	7	6500			7800	8950
26			FB	SF	FBG		IB	215		9	7	6500	1	9	7800	8950
		1962 BOATS														
16	7	GALATEA	ST	OVNTR	FBG		OB			7		800			2450	2850
19	3	ORION V-20	ST	SPTCR	FBG		OB			7	6	1300			4050	4700
19	3	ORION V-20	ST	SPTCR	FBG		IO	80-111		7	6	1300			5550	6750
19	3	TITAN	OP	CBNCR	FBG		OB			7	6	1450			4450	5100
19	3	TITAN	OP	CBNCR	FBG		IO	80-111		7	6				6650	8000
26			HT	EXP	FBG		IB	185-188		9	7	6500	1	9	7500	8650
26			HT	EXP	FBG		IB	T100-T138		9	7	6500	1	9	7600	9200
26			FB	SF	FBG		IB	185-188		9	7	6500	1	9	7500	8650
26			FB	SF	FBG		IB	T100-T138		9	7	6500	1	9	7600	9200
		1961 BOATS														
16	7	GALATEA	OP	OVNTR	FBG		OB			7		800			2450	2850
19	3	ORION V-20	OP	SPTCR	FBG		OB			7	6	1450			4450	5150
19	3	TITAN		CBNCR	FBG		OB			7	6	1450			4450	5150
22	1	CLEARWATER		CR	FBG		OB			8		1475			5200	5950
22	1	CLEARWATER		CR	PLY		OB			8		1475			5200	5950
36		SEA-COTTAGE	HT	HB	PLY		OB			14		10000			13600	15400
		1960 BOATS														
16	6	AMERICANA SLEEPER		RNBT	PLY	DV	OB			6	9	625			1950	2300
18	3	FLORIDA		SPTCR	PLY	DV	OB			7	2	725			2450	2800
20	4	CLEARWATER		SPTCR	PLY	DV	OB			8		1200			4150	4800
26		SEA-COTTAGE	HT	HB	PLY		OB			14				11	**	**
27		SEA-COTTAGE	HT	HB	PLY		OB			10				10	**	**
36		SEA-COTTAGE	HT	HB	PLY		OB			16			1		13700	15500
		1959 BOATS														
16		AMERICANA		CR	PLY		OB			6	9	580			1750	2100
18		FLORIDA		RNBT	PLY		OB			7	2	695			2350	2700
19		CLEARWATER		CR	PLY		OB			8		1100			3550	4150

STAMM BOAT CO INC

DELAFIELD WI 53018 COAST GUARD MFG ID- STB See inside cover to adjust price for area

LOA FT	LOA IN	NAME AND/ OR MODEL	TOP/ RIG	BOAT TYPE	-HULL- MTL	-HULL- TP	ENGINE TP	ENGINE # HP	ENGINE MFG	BEAM FT	BEAM IN	WGT LBS	DRAFT FT	DRAFT IN	RETAIL LOW	RETAIL HIGH
		1974 BOATS														
16		X-SCOW	SLP	SA/OD	FBG	BB	OB			6	3	500	1	4	2050	2450
18		ARROW	SLP	SA/OD	FBG	CB	OB			6	4	685	2	3	2550	2950
19		LIGHTNING	SLP	SA/OD	FBG	CB	OB			6	6	725	2	10	2700	3150
20		C-SCOW	CAT	SA/OD	FBG	BB	OB			6	8	650	1	8	2700	3150
28		E-SCOW	SLP	SA/OD	FBG	BB	OB			6	9	900	1	6	3200	3750

 CONTINUED ON NEXT PAGE

STAMM BOAT CO INC   -CONTINUED   See inside cover to adjust price for area

LOA FT IN	NAME AND/ OR MODEL	TOP/ RIG	BOAT TYPE	-HULL- MTL TP	----ENGINE--- TP # HP MFG	BEAM FT IN	WGT LBS	DRAFT FT IN	RETAIL LOW	RETAIL HIGH
1973 BOATS										
16	X-SCOW	SLP	SA/OD	FBG BB	OB	6 3	500	1 4	2000	2400
18	ARROW	SLP	SA/OD	FBG CB	OB	6 4	685	2 3	2500	2900
19	LIGHTNING	SLP	SA/OD	FBG CB	OB	6 6	725	2 10	2650	3050
20	C-SCOW	CAT	SA/OD	FBG BB	OB	6 8	650	1 8	2650	3100
28	E-SCOW	SLP	SA/OD	FBG BB	OB	6 9	900	1 6	3150	3650
1972 BOATS										
16	X-SCOW	SLP	SA/OD	FBG BB	OB	6 3	500	1 4	1950	2350
18	ARROW	SLP	SA/OD	FBG CB	OB	6 4	685	2 3	2450	2850
19	LIGHTNING	SLP	SA/OD	FBG CB	OB	6 6	725	2 10	2600	3000
20	C-SCOW	CAT	SA/OD	FBG BB	OB	6 8	650	1 8	2600	3000
28	E-SCOW	SLP	SA/OD	FBG BB	OB	6 9	900	1 6	3050	3550
1971 BOATS										
16	X-SCOW	SLP	SA/OD	FBG BB	OB	6 3			1850	2200
18	ARROW	SLP	SA/OD	FBG CB	OB	6 4			2400	2750
19	LIGHTNING	SLP	SA/OD	FBG CB	OB	6 6			2500	2950
20	C-SCOW	CAT	SA/OD	FBG BB	OB	6 8			2350	2750
28	INLAND CLASS E		SAIL	FBG	OB	3 9			3050	3550
1970 BOATS										
16	X-SCOW	SLP	SA/OD	FBG BB	OB	6 3		6	1800	2150
18	ARROW	SLP	SA/OD	FBG CB	OB	6 3		1 3	2350	2750
19	LIGHTNING	SLP	SA/OD	FBG CB	OB	6 6		9	2450	2900
20	C-SCOW	CAT	SA/OD	FBG BB	OB	6 8		1 6	2350	2700
28	INLAND CLASS E	SLP	SA/OD	FBG BB	OB	3 9		1 8	2950	3450
1969 BOATS										
16	X-SCOW	SLP	SA/OD	FBG BB	OB	6 3		2	1800	2150
18	ARROW	SLP	SA/OD	FBG CB	OB	6 4		1 2	2350	2700
19	LIGHTNING	SLP	SA/OD	FBG CB	OB	6 6		5	2450	2850
20	C-SCOW	CAT	SA/OD	FBG BB	OB	6 8		5	2300	2650
28	INLAND CLASS E	SLP	SAIL	FBG BB	OB	6 9		3	2950	3400
1968 BOATS										
16	X-SCOW	SLP	SA/OD	FBG BB	OB	6 3	500	6	1850	2200
18	ARROW	SLP	SA/OD	FBG CB	OB	6 4		1 2	2300	2650
19	LIGHTNING	SLP	SA/OD	FBG CB	OB	6 6	700	9	2350	2750
20	C-SCOW	CAT	SA/OD	FBG BB	OB	6 8	50	1 6	2050	2450
28	INLAND CLASS E	SLP	SAIL	FBG BB	OB	6 8	965	1 8	3000	3500
1967 BOATS										
16	X-SCOW	SLP	SA/OD	FBG BB	OB				1750	2050
18	ARROW	SLP	SA/OD	FBG CB	OB				2250	2650
19	LIGHTNING	SLP	SA/OD	FBG CB	OB				2350	2750
20	C-SCOW	CAT	SA/OD	FBG BB	OB				2250	2600
28	INLAND CLASS E		SAIL	FBG	OB				2850	3350
1966 BOATS										
16	X-SCOW	SLP	SA/OD	FBG BB	OB	6 1	500	5	1800	2150
18	ARROW	SLP	SA/OD	FBG CB	OB	6 4	1100	1 2	2750	3200
19	LIGHTNING	SLP	SA/OD	FBG CB	OB	6 6	700	6	2300	2700
20	C-SCOW	CAT	SA/OD	FBG BB	OB	6 6	650	6	2350	2750
28	E-SCOW	SLP	SA/OD	FBG BB	OB	6 7		4 1	2800	3250
1965 BOATS										
16	X-SCOW	SLP	SA/OD	FBG BB	OB				1700	2050
18	ARROW	SLP	SA/OD	FBG CB	OB				2200	2600
19	LIGHTNING	SLP	SA/OD	FBG CB	OB				2300	2700
20	C-SCOW	CAT	SA/OD	FBG BB	OB				2200	2550
28	INLAND CLASS E		SAIL	FBG	OB				2800	3300
1964 BOATS										
16	X-SCOW	SLP	SA/OD	FBG BB	OB				1700	2000
18	ARROW	SLP	SA/OD	FBG CB	OB				2200	2550
19	LIGHTNING	SLP	SA/OD	FBG CB	OB				2300	2700
20	C-SCOW	CAT	SA/OD	FBG BB	OB				2200	2550
28	INLAND CLASS E		SAIL	FBG	OB				2800	3250
1963 BOATS										
16	X-SCOW	SLP	SA/OD	FBG BB	OB				1700	2000
18	ARROW	SLP	SA/OD	FBG CB	OB				2200	2550
19	LIGHTNING	SLP	SA/OD	FBG CB	OB				2300	2700
20	C-SCOW	CAT	SA/OD	FBG BB	OB				2150	2550
1962 BOATS										
16	X-SCOW	SLP	SA/OD	FBG BB	OB				1700	2000
18	ARROW	SLP	SA/OD	FBG CB	OB				2200	2550
19	LIGHTNING	SLP	SA/OD	FBG CB	OB				2300	2700
1961 BOATS										
19	LIGHTNING	SLP	SA/OD	FBG CB		6 6	700	5	2300	2650
21 9	ARROW	SLP	SA/OD	FBG KL		6 4		2 4	3500	4100
1960 BOATS										
16	D-SCOW	SLP	SAIL	FBG CB		6 3			1700	2000
18	ARROW	SLP	SAIL	FBG KL		6 4			2200	2550
20	C-SCOW	CAT	SAIL	FBG BB		6 8			2200	2550
1959 BOATS										
16	X-SCOW		SA/OD	FBG BB		6 3			1700	2000
20	C-SCOW		SA/OD	FBG BB		6 8			2200	2550

STANCRAFT BOAT COMPANY
COAST GUARD MFG ID- SFT

Call 1-800-327-6929 for BUC Personalized Evaluation Service
Or, for 1946 to 1979 boats, sign onto www.BUCValuPro.com

STANDARD BOAT WORKS

Call 1-800-327-6929 for BUC Personalized Evaluation Service
Or, for 1978 to 1981 boats, sign onto www.BUCValuPro.com

STANGATE MARINE LTD
SUSSEX ENGLAND   See inside cover to adjust price for area

IMPEX ENTERPRISES LTD
READING PA 19603

LOA FT IN	NAME AND/ OR MODEL	TOP/ RIG	BOAT TYPE	-HULL- MTL TP	----ENGINE--- TP # HP MFG	BEAM FT IN	WGT LBS	DRAFT FT IN	RETAIL LOW	RETAIL HIGH
1979 BOATS										
28	STAG 28	SLP	SA/CR	FBG CB	IB D PERK	9 10	7500	6 9	23600	26300
35	ROGGER 35	KTH	MS	FBG KL	IB 72D PERK	11 4	12012	4	42300	47000
36 6	BANJER 36	KTH	MS	FBG KL	IB 95D PERK	11 5	31360	4 7	99800	109500
37 10	FINISTERRE 38	KTH	MS	FBG KL	IB 48D PERK	10 6	16680	5 2	61600	67700
40	SALAR-BUCCANEER 40	KTH	MS	FBG KL	IB D PERK	11 3	23520	5 6	87300	96000
41	USHANT 41	KTH	MS	FBG KL	IB 108D PERK	13	38080	4 9	120000	132000
46	ATLAS 46	KTH	MS	FBG KL	IB 120D PERK	14	47040	5	141500	156000
1978 BOATS										
35	ROGGER AFT CABIN ENC	KTH	MS	FBG KL	IB 72D PERK	11 4	20160	4	66900	73500
35	ROGGER AFT CABIN OPN	KTH	MS	FBG KL	IB 72D PERK	11 4	20160	4	63600	69900
35	ROGGER OPEN COCKPIT	KTH	MS	FBG KL	IB 72D PERK	11 4	20160	4	65100	71600
36 6	BANJER AFT CABIN	KTH	MS	FBG KL	IB 95D PERK	11 5	31360	4 7	98000	107500
36 6	BANJER OPEN COCKPIT	KTH	MS	FBG KL	IB 95D PERK	11 5	31360	4 7	93800	103000
37 10	FINISTERRE 38	KTH	MS	FBG KL	IB 48D PERK	10	15680	5 2	56500	62000
41	USHANT	KTH	MS	FBG KL	IB 108D PERK	13	36080	4 9	112000	123000
41 10	FINISTERRE 42	KTH	MS	FBG KL	IB 72D PERK	12 3	22400	5 6	85700	94200
46	ATLAS	KTH	MS	FBG KL	IB 120D PERK	14	47040	5	136000	149500
1977 BOATS										
35	ROGGER	CUT	MS	FBG KL	IB 72D PERK	11 2	19000	4	58900	64700
37	BANJER	KTH	MS	FBG KL	IB 108D PERK	11 6	27000	4 7	82400	90600
41	USHANT-ROGGER	KTH	MS	FBG KL	IB 108D PERK	13	40000	4 9	115000	126500
46	ATLAS-ROGGER	KTH	MS	FBG KL	IB 120D PERK	14	50000	5	134000	147500
1976 BOATS										
35 2	ROGGER FD	CUT	MS	FBG KL	IB 72D PERK	11 4	19000	4	56800	62400
36 6	BANJER TRANSOCEANIQU	KTH	MS	FBG KL	IB 108D PERK	11 6	27000	4 7	79100	86900
1975 BOATS										
35 2	ROGGER FD	CUT	MS	FBG KL	IB D	11 4	19000	3 9	54900	60300
36 6	BANJER-TRANSOCEANIQU	KTH	MS	FBG KL	IB D	11 6	27000	4 7	76400	83900
1973 BOATS										
36 6	BANJER	KTH	MS	FBG KL	IB 108D PERK	11 6	27000	4 6	72100	79200
1972 BOATS										
34 6	ROGGER MKI	SLP	MS	FBG KL	IB D	11 4		4	49700	54600
34 6	ROGGER MKII	SLP	MS	FBG KL	IB D	11 4		4	48700	53500
36 6	BANJER	KTH	MS	FBG KL	IB D	11 5		4 7	73900	81200
1971 BOATS										
36 6	BANJER	KTH	MS	FBG KL	IB 85D	11 5	24000	4 7	62300	68400
1970 BOATS										
36 6	BANJER PH	KTH	MS	FBG KL	IB 85D PERK	11 8	24000	4 7	60600	66600

STAR CATAMARANS INC
COAST GUARD MFG ID- XTJ

Call 1-800-327-6929 for BUC Personalized Evaluation Service
Or, for 1979 to 1984 boats, sign onto www.BUCValuPro.com

STARBOARD YACHT CO
STUART FL 34997   COAST GUARD MFG ID- SYX See inside cover to adjust price for area

For more recent years, see the BUC Used Boat Price Guide, Volume 1 or Volume 2

LOA FT IN	NAME AND/ OR MODEL	TOP/ RIG	BOAT TYPE	-HULL- MTL TP	TP	# HP	ENGINE MFG	BEAM FT IN	WGT LBS	DRAFT FT IN	RETAIL LOW	RETAIL HIGH
----- 1983 BOATS -----												
16 10	SLIPPER 17 DH	SLP	SAIL	FBG CB	OB			8	1250	1 7	3050	3550
16 10	SLIPPER 17 FD	SLP	SAIL	FBG CB	OB			8	1250	1 7	2700	3100
24	STARBOARD 24	SLP	SAIL	FBG CB	OB			8	3000	2	7150	8250
----- 1982 BOATS -----												
16 10	SLIPPER 17 DH	SLP	SAIL	FBG CB	OB			8	1250	1 7	2900	3350
16 10	SLIPPER 17 FD	SLP	SAIL	FBG CB	OB			8	1250		2500	2900
----- 1981 BOATS -----												
16 10	SLIPPER 17	SLP	SAIL	FBG CB	OB			8	1250	1 7	2650	3050
16 10	SLIPPER 17	CUT	SAIL	FBG CB	OB			8	1250	1 7	2500	2950
16 10	SLIPPER 17 FD	SLP	SAIL	FBG CB	OB			8	1250		2400	2800
----- 1980 BOATS -----												
16 10	SLIPPER 17	SLP	SAIL	FBG KL	OB			8	1400	1 7	2550	2950

STARBOARD YACHTS INC
HOUSTON TX 77058   COAST GUARD MFG ID- TYA See inside cover to adjust price for area

For more recent years, see the BUC Used Boat Price Guide, Volume 1 or Volume 2

LOA FT IN	NAME AND/ OR MODEL	TOP/ RIG	BOAT TYPE	-HULL- MTL TP	TP	# HP	ENGINE MFG	BEAM FT IN	WGT LBS	DRAFT FT IN	RETAIL LOW	RETAIL HIGH
----- 1983 BOATS -----												
29 2	VANCOUVER 25	SLP	SAIL	FBG KL	IB	8D		8 6	7000	4	22000	24400
33 11	NASSAU 34	CUT	SAIL	FBG KL	IB	33D	YAN	11 6	14250	5	47800	52500
41 10	NASSAU 42	SLP	SAIL	FBG KL	IB	50D	PERK	12 9	21000	5 10	80800	88800

STARCRAFT MARINE L L C
TOPEKA IN 46571   COAST GUARD MFG ID- STR See inside cover to adjust price for area

For more recent years, see the BUC Used Boat Price Guide, Volume 1 or Volume 2

LOA FT IN	NAME AND/ OR MODEL	TOP/ RIG	BOAT TYPE	-HULL- MTL TP	TP	# HP	ENGINE MFG	BEAM FT IN	WGT LBS	DRAFT FT IN	RETAIL LOW	RETAIL HIGH
----- 1983 BOATS -----												
16 10	ST171	ST	RNBT	FBG	TR	IO	120-200	6 11	1085		1800	2200
17 3	WV170B	OP	RNBT	FBG	TR	OB		6 11	1095		1800	2150
17 3	WV171	OP	RNBT	FBG		IO	140-185	6 11	1170		1950	2350
17 3	WV171 B/R	OP	RNBT	FBG		IO	140-185	6 11	1170		1950	2350
18 3	HOLIDAY 181	OP	RNBT	AL	SV	IO	120	6 9	960		2050	2450
18 3	HOLIDAY 181	OP	RNBT	AL	SV	JT	140 OMC	6 9	960		3150	3650
18 3	HOLIDAY 181	OP	RNBT	AL	SV	IO	140	6 9	960		2050	2450
18 3	SUPER-SPORT 181	OP	RNBT	AL	SV	IO	120	6 7	960		2000	2400
18 3	SUPER-SPORT 181	OP	RNBT	AL	SV	JT	140 OMC	6 7	960		3100	3600
18 3	SUPER-SPORT 181	OP	RNBT	AL	SV	IO	140	6 7	960		2050	2400
18 6	V190B	OP	RNBT	FBG	SV	OB		7 2	1325		2250	2600
18 6	V191	OP	RNBT	FBG	SV	IO	140-230	7 2	1225		2300	2800
18 6	V191B	OP	RNBT	FBG	SV	IO	140-230	7 2	1225		2300	2800
18 10	SF191V	OP	RNBT	FBG		IO	185	8	1280		2600	3000
21 2	MARINER 210	OP	CTRCN	AL	SV	OB		7 2	900		1800	2100
22	SF220V	OP	RNBT	AL		OB		8	1600		3050	3550
22	SF221V		CR	FBG		IO	240	8	1600		3550	4150
22 2	SC221	OP	RNBT	FBG		IO		8	2500		**	**
22 3	MARINER V220	OP	CTRCN	AL	SV	OB		8	1250		2450	2850
25 10	CR261V		CR	FBG		IO	280	8	3340		6600	7600
25 10	SF261V		CR	FBG		IO	280	8	2400		6050	6950
----- 1982 BOATS -----												
16 3	V161B	OP	RNBT	FBG		IO	120-170	6 5			2050	2450
16 11	ST171	ST	RNBT	FBG	TR	IO	120-200	6 11	1085		1750	2150
17 3	WV170B	OP	RNBT	FBG	TR	OB		6 11	1095		1800	2100
17 3	WV171	OP	RNBT	FBG		IO	140-170	6 11	1170		1850	2200
17 3	WV171B	OP	RNBT	FBG		IO	140-170	6 11	1170		1900	2250
18 6	HOLIDAY 181	OP	RNBT	AL	SV	IO	120	6 11	965		2100	2500
18 6	HOLIDAY 181	OP	RNBT	AL	SV	JT	140 OMC	6 11	965		3100	3600
18 6	HOLIDAY 181	OP	RNBT	AL	SV	IO	140	6 11	965		2100	2500
18 6	V190B	OP	RNBT	FBG	SV	OB		7 2	1325		2200	2550
18 6	V191	OP	RNBT	FBG	SV	IO	140-230	7 2	1225		2200	2700
18 6	V191B	OP	RNBT	FBG	SV	IO	140-230	7 2	1225		2300	2750
18 7	SUPER-SPORT 181	OP	RNBT	AL	SV	IO	120	6 9	951		2100	2450
18 7	SUPER-SPORT 181	OP	RNBT	AL	SV	JT	140 OMC	6 9	951		3100	3600
18 7	SUPER-SPORT 181	OP	RNBT	AL	SV	IO	140	6 9	951		2100	2500
21 2	MARINER 210	OP	CTRCN	AL	SV	OB		7 2	900		1750	2100
21 5	ISLANDER 221	ST	CUD	AL	SV	IO	120	7 6	1438		3000	3500
21 5	ISLANDER 221	ST	CUD	AL	SV	JT	140 OMC	7 6	1438		4000	4650
21 5	ISLANDER 221	ST	CUD	AL	SV	IO	140-170	7 6	1438		3000	3550
22	HOLIDAY V221	OP	RNBT	AL	DV	JT	140 OMC	7 10	1500		4350	5050
22	HOLIDAY V221	OP	RNBT	AL	DV	IO	140-230	7 10	1500		3100	3700
22	ISLANDER V220	ST	CUD	AL	DV	OB		8	1600		3000	3450
22	ISLANDER V221	ST	CUD	AL	DV	JT	140 OMC	8	1600		4400	5050
22	ISLANDER V221	ST	CUD	AL	DV	IO	140-170	8	1600		3300	3850
22 3	SC221	ST	RNBT	FBG	DV	IO	170-260	8	2500		3850	4750
22 4	MARINER V220	OP	CTRCN	AL	SV	OB		8	1250		2400	2800
25 10	ISLANDER V251	ST	CUD	AL	DV	IO	170-230	8	3340		6400	7750
25 10	ISLANDER V251	ST	CUD	AL	DV	IO	260	8	3340		7000	8050
25 10	SF261V	ST	CUD	AL	DV	IO	170-230	8	3340		5050	6150
25 10	SF261V	ST	CUD	AL	DV	IO	260	8	3340		5600	6450
25 10	SF261V	ST	CUD	AL	DV	IO	170 MRCR	8	3340		5000	5750
----- 1981 BOATS -----												
16 11	ST171	ST	RNBT	FBG	TR	IO	120-200	6 11	1085		1750	2100
17 3	WV171	OP	RNBT	FBG		IO	140-185	6 11	1170		1800	2200
17 3	WV171 B/R	OP	RNBT	FBG		IO	140-185	6 11	1170		1850	2200
18 1	HOLIDAY V181	OP	RNBT	AL	DV	IO	120-140	6 11	975		1950	2350
18 6	HOLIDAY 181	OP	RNBT	AL	SV	JT		6 11	965		**	**
18 6	HOLIDAY 181	OP	RNBT	AL	SV	IO	120-140	6 11	965		2100	2450
18 6	STARCRAFT 191	OP	RNBT	FBG	SV	IO	140	7 2	1315		2200	2550
18 6	STARCRAFT 191 B/R	OP	RNBT	FBG	SV	IO	140	7 2	1315		2200	2550
18 6	V191		RNBT	FBG	SV	IO	140-230	7 2	1225		2000	2350
18 6	V191B	OP	RNBT	FBG	SV	IO	140-230	7 2	1225		2200	2700
18 7	SUPER-SPORT 181	OP	RNBT	AL	SV	JT		6 9	951		**	**
18 7	SUPER-SPORT 181	OP	RNBT	AL	SV	IO	120-140	6 9	951		2050	2450
20 7	QUESTSTAR 211		CUD	FBG		IO		8			**	**
21 2	MARINER 210	OP	CTRCN	AL	SV	OB		7 2	900		1700	2050
21 5	ISLANDER 221	ST	CUD	AL	SV	IO	120-170	7 6	1438		2950	3500
21 5	ISLANDER 221	OP	RNBT	AL	DV	OB		7 10	1475		2750	3200
22	HOLIDAY V220		CR	AL		IO	120	7 9			4850	5550
22	HOLIDAY V221		RNBT	AL	DV	JT		7 10			**	**
22	HOLIDAY V221	OP	RNBT	AL	DV	IO	140-230	7 10	1500		3050	3650
22	ISLANDER V220	ST	CUD	AL	DV	OB		8	1600		2950	3400
22	ISLANDER V221	ST	CUD	AL	DV	JT		8	1600		**	**
22	ISLANDER V221	ST	CUD	AL	DV	IO	140-185	8	1600		3250	3800
22 4	MARINER V220	OP	CTRCN	AL	SV	OB		8	1250		2400	2750
----- 1980 BOATS -----												
16 11	ST171		RNBT	FBG	TR	IO	120-200	6 11	1085		1700	2100
18 1	HOLIDAY V181	ST	RNBT	AL	DV	IO	120-170	6 11	975		1950	2300
18 1	SUPER-SPORT V180	ST	RNBT	AL	DV	OB		6 11	1100		1800	2100
18 1	SUPER-SPORT V181	ST	RNBT	AL	DV	IO	120-170	6 11			2400	2800
18 6	HOLIDAY 181	ST	CUD	AL	SV	IO	120-140	6 11			2500	2900
18 6	HOLIDAY 190	ST	CUD	AL	DV	IO		6 10	1030		1700	2050
18 6	HOLIDAY 190	ST	CUD	AL	DV	IO	120-140	6 10	1110		2050	2450
18 6	STARCRAFT 191	ST	CUD	FBG	DV	IO	140	7 2	1315		2150	2550
18 6	STARCRAFT 191 B/R	ST	CUD	FBG	DV	IO	140	7 2	1315		2150	2550
18 7	QUESTSTAR 190	ST	RNBT	AL	DV	OB		7 2	1325		2300	2700
18 7	QUESTSTAR 191	ST	RNBT	AL	DV	IO	140-230	7 2	1580		2100	2500
18 7	QUESTSTAR 191 B/R	ST	RNBT	AL	DV	IO		7 2	1325		2100	2500
18 7	QUESTSTAR 191 B/R	ST	RNBT	FBG	DV	IO	140-170	7 2	1580		2300	2750
18 7	SUPER-SPORT 181	OP	RNBT	FBG	DV	IO	120-140	6 9	951		2000	2350
20 1	CAN-AM 2000	OP	RNBT	AL	SV	JT	454-460	7	1380		4400	5100
20 1	CAN-AM 2000	OP	RNBT	AL	SV	IO		7			4700	5400
20 1	CAN-AM 2001	OP	RNBT	AL	SV	IO	260 MRCR	7	1640		3700	4300
20 1	CAN-AM 2001	OP	RNBT	AL	SV	IO		7			3700	4300
20 1	CAN-AM 2001	OP	RNBT	AL	SV	JT	454-460	7			4850	5550
20 7	QUESTSTAR 211	OP	RNBT	FBG	DV	IO	170-260	7 6	1830		3050	3800
21 2	MARINER 210	OP	CTRCN	AL	SV	OB		7 2	900		1700	2000
21 5	ISLANDER 221	ST	CUD	AL	SV	IO	120-170	7 6	1438		2950	3500
22	HOLIDAY V220	OP	RNBT	AL	DV	OB		7 10	1475		2700	3150
22	HOLIDAY V221	ST	RNBT	AL	DV	IO	140-230	7 10	1500		3000	3600
22	ISLANDER V220	ST	CUD	AL	DV	OB		8	1600		2900	3350
22	ISLANDER V221	ST	CUD	AL	DV	IO	140-185	8	1600		4700	5400
22 4	MARINER V220	ST	CTRCN	AL	SV	OB		8	1250		2350	2750
22 4	SUPER-SPORT V220	ST	RNBT	AL	DV	OB		8	1380		2550	3000
22 4	SUPER-SPORT V221	ST	RNBT	AL	DV	IO	140-230	8	1400		3100	3750

STARCRAFT MARINE L L C -CONTINUED See inside cover to adjust price for area

LOA FT	LOA IN	NAME AND/ OR MODEL	TOP/ RIG	BOAT TYPE	-HULL- MTL	-HULL- TP	ENGINE TP	ENGINE # HP	ENGINE MFG	BEAM FT	BEAM IN	WGT LBS	DRAFT FT IN	RETAIL LOW	RETAIL HIGH
		1979 BOATS													
16	10	TRISTAR 17		RNBT	FBG	TR	IO	120-200		6	11	1085		1700	2050
18		HOLIDAY 18 V-5		RNBT	AL	DV	OB			6	10	1050		1700	2050
18	1	HOLIDAY 18 V-5		RNBT	AL	DV	IO	120-170		6	10	975		1900	2300
18	1	SUPER-PORT 18 V-5		RNBT	AL	DV	IO	120-170		6	10	1025		1900	2300
18	3	MONTEGO 18		RNBT	FBG	TR	IO	140		6	10	1235		2000	2350
18	3	MONTEGO 18		RNBT	FBG	TR	IO	250		6	10	1235		2200	2550
18	5	QUESTSTAR 18 B/R		RNBT	FBG	SV	OB			7	2			2550	2950
18	6	CHIEFTAIN 18		CR	AL	SV	OB			6	10	1030		1700	2000
18	6	HOLIDAY 18		RNBT	AL	SV	IO	120-140		6	11	965		2000	2400
18	6	QUESTSTAR 18 B/R		RNBT	FBG	SV	IO	140-230		7	2	1580		2250	2750
18	7	CHIEFTAIN 18 MK4		CR	AL	SV	IO	120-140		6	11	1110		2050	2450
18	7	SUPER-PORT 18		RNBT	AL	SV	IO	120-140		6	9	951		2000	2400
20	7	QUESTSTAR 20 B/R		RNBT	FBG	SV	IO	170-250		8		1830		2900	3550
21	5	ISLANDER 22 MK4		CUD	AL	SV	IO	120-170		7	6	1465		2950	3450
21	5	ISLANDER 22 STD		CUD	AL	SV	IO	120-170		7	6	1438		2950	3450
21	6	CHIEFTAIN 22 MK4		CR	AL	SV	IO	120-170		7	7	1745		3050	3600
21	7	CHIEFTAIN 22 MK4		CR	AL	SV	OB			7	7	1410		2550	2950
22		HOLIDAY 22 V-5		RNBT	AL	DV	OB			7	10	1475		2650	3100
22		HOLIDAY 22 V-5		RNBT	AL	DV	IO	120-250		7	10	1500		3000	3700
22		ISLANDER 22 V-5 OFF		CUD	AL	DV	OB			8		1600		2850	3350
22		ISLANDER 22 V-5 OFF		CUD	AL	DV	IO	120-170		8		1600		3200	3750
22	3	AMERICAN OFF 22		OFF	FBG	DV	IO	185		8		2650		3900	4500
22	3	AMERICAN OFF 22		OFF	FBG	DV	IO	340		8		2650		4800	5500
22	3	AMERICAN SPTCR 22		CR	FBG	DV	IO	185		8		2500		3800	4400
22	3	AMERICAN SPTCR 22		CR	FBG	DV	IO	340		8		2500		4700	5400
22	4	FISHMASTER 22 V-5		FSH	AL	DV	OB			8		1320		2450	2850
22	4	MARINER 22 V-5		FSH	AL	SV	OB			8		1250		2350	2700
22	4	SUPER-PORT 22 V-5		RNBT	AL	DV	OB			8		1380		2550	2950
22	4	SUPER-PORT 22 V-5		RNBT	AL	DV	IO	120-250		8		1400		3100	3800
24	8	CHIEFTAIN 25 MK4		CR	AL	SV	IO	170		8		2600		4500	5200
24	8	CHIEFTAIN 25 MK4		CR	AL	SV	IO	280		8		2600		5000	5700
25	2	STARCRUISER 25		CBNCR	FBG	DV	IO	185		11	2			7400	8500
25	2	STARCRUISER 25		CBNCR	FBG	DV	IO	340		11	2			8150	9400
25	2	STARCRUISER 25	FB	CBNCR	FBG	DV	IO	185		11	2			7400	8500
25	2	STARCRUISER 25	FB	CBNCR	FBG	DV	IB	225		11	2			7350	8450
25	2	STARCRUISER 25	FB	CBNCR	FBG	DV	IO	340		11	2			8150	9400
25	2	STARCRUISER 25SF		CBNCR	FBG	DV	IB	225		11	2			7350	8450
		1978 BOATS													
16	10	TRISTAR 17	OP	RNBT	FBG	SV	IO	120-198		6	11	1085		1700	2100
18	3	MONTEGO 18 B/R	OP	RNBT	FBG	TR	IO	140-225		6	10	1235		2000	2450
18	3	MONTEGO 18 B/R	OP	RNBT	FBG	TR	IO	228-240		6	10	1235		2100	2500
18	5	AMERICAN 18	ST	RNBT	FBG	SV	OB			7	2	1325		2050	2400
18	5	AMERICAN 18 B/R	ST	RNBT	FBG	SV	OB			7	2	1350		2050	2450
18	6	AMERICAN 18	ST	RNBT	FBG	SV	IO	140-240		7	2	1315		2150	2650
18	6	AMERICAN 18 B/R	ST	RNBT	FBG	SV	IO	140-240		7	2	1545		2250	2750
18	6	FIRESTAR 1900	OP	SKI	FBG		JT			6	11	1750		**	**
18	6	HOLIDAY 18	ST	RNBT	AL	SV	IO	120-140		6	11	965		2000	2400
18	7	CHIEFTAIN MARK IV 18	OP	CR	AL	SV	IO	120-140		6	11	1110		2050	2450
18	7	SUPER-SPORT 18 B/R	ST	RNBT	AL	SV	IO	120-140		6	9	951		2000	2400
19	1	FIRESTAR 1900	OP	SKI	FBG		OB			7	2	1200		1950	2300
19	4	STINGER 19	OP	RNBT	FBG	DV	OB			7	3	1210		1950	2350
20	7	AMERICAN 20	ST	RNBT	FBG	SV	IO	165-240		8		1605		2850	3400
21		FIRESTAR 2100	OP	SKI	FBG		JT			7	8	2700		**	**
21	5	HOLIDAY 22	ST	RNBT	AL	SV	OB			7	6	1275		2350	2700
21	5	HOLIDAY 22	ST	RNBT	AL	SV	IO	120-240		7	6	1345		2800	3400
21	5	ISLANDER 22	ST	RNBT	AL	DV	OB			7	6	1325		2400	2750
21	5	ISLANDER 22	ST	RNBT	AL	DV	IO	120-170		7	6	1438		2850	3300
21	5	ISLANDER MARK IV 22	ST	RNBT	AL	SV	IO	120-170		7	6	1468		2850	3300
21	6	CHIEFTAIN MARK IV 22	OP	CR	AL	SV	IO	120-170		7	7	1745		3050	3600
21	7	CHIEFTAIN MARK IV 22	OP	CR	AL	SV	OB			7	7	1410		2500	2950
21	7	SUPER-SPORT 22 B/R	ST	RNBT	AL	SV	OB			7	4	1210		2250	2600
21	7	SUPER-SPORT 22 B/R	ST	RNBT	AL	SV	IO	120-170		7	4	1220		2850	3300
22		HOLIDAY 22	ST	RNBT	AL	SV	OB			7	10	1475		2650	3050
22		HOLIDAY 22	ST	RNBT	AL	SV	IO	120-240		7	10	1500		3000	3650
22		ISLANDER MARK IV 22	ST	RNBT	AL	DV	OB			8		1550		2750	3200
22		ISLANDER MARK IV 22	ST	RNBT	AL	DV	IO	120-240		8		1600		3100	3700
22	3	AMERICAN 22	HT	EXP	FBG	DV	IO	185-260		8		2750		3950	4850
22	3	AMERICAN 22	HT	EXP	FBG	DV	IO	T120-T170		8		2750		4600	5350
22	3	AMERICAN 22	ST	OFF	FBG	DV	IO	185-260		8		2650		3900	4800
22	3	AMERICAN 22	ST	OFF	FBG	DV	IO	T120-T170		8		2650		4550	5300
22	3	AMERICAN 22	ST	SPTCR	FBG	DV	IO	185-260		8		2500		3800	4700
22	3	AMERICAN 22	ST	SPTCR	FBG	DV	IO	T120-T170		8		2500		4450	5150
22	4	SUPER-SPORT 22 B/R	ST	RNBT	AL	SV	OB			8		1380		2500	2900
22	4	SUPER-SPORT 22 B/R	ST	RNBT	AL	SV	IO	120-240		8		1400		3100	3750
24	8	CHIEFTAIN MARK IV 25	OP	CR	AL	SV	IO	165-240		8		2600		4550	5450
24	8	CHIEFTAIN MARK IV 25	OP	CR	AL	SV	IO	T120-T140		8		2600		5200	6050
25	2	STARCRUISER 25	ST	CUD	FBG	SV	IO	185-260		9	4			5950	7250
25	2	STARCRUISER 25	ST	CUD	FBG	SV	IO	T120-T170		9	4			6600	7900
25	2	STARCRUISER 25	FB	OFF	FBG	SV	IO	185-260		9	4			5700	7000
25	2	STARCRUISER 25	FB	OFF	FBG	SV	IO	T120-T170		9	4			6350	7600
		1977 BOATS													
16	4	MONTEGO 16	OP	RNBT	FBG	TR	OB			6	7			2050	2450
17	1	CAPRI 17	ST	RNBT	FBG	TR	OB			6	10	1213		1800	2150
17	1	CAPRI 17	ST	RNBT	FBG	TR	IO	120-140		6	10	1295		1850	2200
18	3	MONTEGO 18	OP	RNBT	FBG	TR	OB			6	9			2500	2900
18	3	MONTEGO 18	OP	RNBT	FBG	TR	IO	140-190		6	9	1235		2000	2400
18	3	MONTEGO 18	OP	RNBT	FBG	TR	IO	233-235		6	9	1235		2150	2500
18	5	AMERICAN 18	ST	RNBT	FBG	SV	OB			7	2	1315		2000	2400
18	6	AMERICAN 18	ST	RNBT	FBG	SV	IO	140-235		7	2	1325		2200	2700
18	6	AMERICAN 18 B/R	ST	RNBT	FBG	SV	IO	140-235		7	2	1345		2200	2700
18	6	HOLIDAY 18	ST	RNBT	AL	SV	IO	120-140		6	11	965		2050	2450
18	7	SUPER-SPORT 18	ST	RNBT	AL	SV	IO	120-140		6	9	951		2050	2400
19	4	AMERICAN S19	OP	RNBT	FBG	SV	OB			7	3	1210		1950	2300
20	7	AMERICAN 20	ST	RNBT	FBG	SV	IO	165-235		8		1605		2900	3500
21	5	HOLIDAY 22	ST	RNBT	AL	SV	OB			7	6	1275		2300	2700
21	5	HOLIDAY 22	ST	RNBT	AL	SV	IO	120-170		7	6	1340		2850	3350
21	5	ISLANDER 22	OP	CUD	AL	SV	OB			7	6	1438		2550	2950
21	5	ISLANDER 22	OP	CUD	AL	SV	IO	120-170		7	6	1438		3000	3500
21	5	ISLANDER-MARK-IV 22	OP	CUD	AL	SV	IO	120-170		7	6	1468		3000	3500
21	6	CHIEFTAIN-MARK-IV 22	OP	CR	AL	SV	IO	120-170		7	7	1745		3100	3650
21	6	CHIEFTAIN-MARK-IV 22	ST	EXP	AL	SV	IO	120-170		7	7	2020		3250	3800
21	6	CHIEFTAIN-MARK-IV 22	HT	EXP	AL	SV	IO	120-170		7	7	2080		3300	3850
21	7	CHIEFTAIN 22	OP	CR	AL	SV	OB			7	7	1410		2500	2900
21	7	SUPER-SPORT 22	ST	RNBT	AL	SV	OB			7	4	1210		2200	2550
21	7	SUPER-SPORT 22	ST	RNBT	AL	SV	IO	120-170		7	4	1220		2900	3400
22	3	AMERICAN 22	HT	EXP	FBG	DV	IO	188-255		8		2750		4050	4900
22	3	AMERICAN 22	HT	EXP	FBG	DV	IO	280	MRCR	8		2750		4400	5050
22	3	AMERICAN 22	HT	EXP	FBG	DV	IO	T120-T170		8		2750		4650	5400
22	3	AMERICAN 22	ST	SPTCR	FBG	DV	IO	188-255		8		2500		3900	4700
22	3	AMERICAN 22	ST	SPTCR	FBG	DV	IO	280	MRCR	8		2500		4200	4900
22	3	AMERICAN 22	ST	SPTCR	FBG	DV	IO	T120-T170		8		2500		4500	5250
24	8	CHIEFTAIN-MARK-IV 25	OP	CR	AL	SV	IO	165-235		8		2600		4600	5550
24	8	CHIEFTAIN-MARK-IV 25	OP	CR	AL	SV	IO	T120-T140		8		2600		5300	6150
24	8	CHIEFTAIN-MARK-IV 25	ST	EXP	AL	SV	IO	165-235		8		2575		4550	5500
24	8	CHIEFTAIN-MARK-IV 25	ST	EXP	AL	SV	IO	T120-T140		8		2575		5250	6100
24	8	CHIEFTAIN-MARK-IV 25	HT	EXP	AL	SV	IO	165-235		8		2635		4600	5550
24	8	CHIEFTAIN-MARK-IV 25	HT	EXP	AL	SV	IO	T120-T140		8		2635		5300	6150
25	3	AMERICAN 25	HT	CR	FBG	DV	IO	188-255		8		3400		5550	6800
25	3	AMERICAN 25	HT	CR	FBG	DV	IO	280	MRCR	8		3400		6050	7000
25	3	AMERICAN 25	HT	CR	FBG	DV	IO	T120-T170		8		3400		6200	7450
		1976 BOATS													
16	4	AMERICAN 16	ST	RNBT	FBG	DV	IO	120-140		6	6	2170		2250	2600
17	1	CAPRI 17	ST	RNBT	FBG	TR	OB			6	10	1213		1800	2150
17	1	CAPRI 17	ST	RNBT	FBG	TR	IO	120-140		6	10	1857		2200	2600
18	3	MONTEGO 18	OP	RNBT	FBG	TR	IO	140-190		6	9	1823		2350	2900
18	3	MONTEGO 18	OP	RNBT	FBG	TR	IO	233-235		6	9	2135		2600	3050
18	3	MONTEGO 18	OP	RNBT	FBG	TR	JT	245-290		6	9	2095		2900	3400
18	5	AMERICAN 18	ST	RNBT	FBG	DV	OB			7	2	1325		2000	2400
18	6	AMERICAN 18	ST	RNBT	FBG	DV	IO	140-190		7	2	1903		2450	3100
18	6	AMERICAN 18	ST	RNBT	FBG	DV	IO	233-235		7	2	2215		2750	3200
18	6	AMERICAN 18	ST	RNBT	FBG	DV	JT	245-290		7	2	2175		3050	3600
18	6	AMERICAN OPEN BOW 18	ST	RNBT	FBG	DV	IO	140-190		7	2	1928		2500	3100
18	6	AMERICAN OPEN BOW 18	ST	RNBT	FBG	DV	IO	233-235		7	2	2240		2800	3250
18	6	AMERICAN OPEN BOW 18	ST	RNBT	FBG	DV	JT	245-290		7	2	2200		3100	3600
18	6	HOLIDAY 18	OP	RNBT	AL	SV	IO	120-140		6	11	1527		2250	2650
18	7	SUPER-SPORT 18	ST	RNBT	AL	SV	IO	120-140		6	9	1513		2250	2600
19	4	AMERICAN S19	OP	RNBT	FBG	DV	OB			7	3	1210		1950	2300
19	4	AMERICAN S19	OP	RNBT	FBG	DV	IO	165-190		7	3	1940		2650	3200
19	4	AMERICAN S19	OP	RNBT	FBG	DV	IO	233-235		7	3	2125		2850	3350
19	4	AMERICAN S19	OP	RNBT	FBG	DV	JT	245-290		7	3	2085		3150	3700
20	3	CAPRI 20	ST	RNBT	FBG	TR	IO	165-235		7	11	2430		3300	4150
20	3	CAPRI 20	ST	RNBT	FBG	TR	JT	245-290		7	11	2575		3750	4400
20	3	CAPRI-SPORT 20	ST	SPTCR	FBG	TR	IO	188-235		6	10	2977		3650	4400
20	3	CAPRI-SPORT 20	ST	SPTCR	FBG	TR	JT	290	OMC	6	10	2997		3800	4450
20	7	AMERICAN 20	ST	RNBT	FBG	DV	IO	165-235		7	11	2320		3300	4100

 CONTINUED ON NEXT PAGE

STARCRAFT MARINE L L C -CONTINUED See inside cover to adjust price for area

LOA FT	LOA IN	NAME AND/ OR MODEL	TOP/ RIG	BOAT TYPE	-HULL- MTL	-HULL- TP	ENGINE TP	ENGINE # HP MFG	BEAM FT	BEAM IN	WGT LBS	DRAFT FT	DRAFT IN	RETAIL LOW	RETAIL HIGH
		1976 BOATS													
20	7	AMERICAN 20	ST	RNBT	FBG	DV	JT	245-290	7	11	2465			3750	4350
21	5	HOLIDAY 22	ST	RNBT	AL	SV	OB		7	6	1275			2300	2650
21	5	HOLIDAY 22	ST	RNBT	AL	SV	IO	120-165	7	6	1922			3100	3750
21	5	ISLANDER 22	OP	CR	AL	SV	IO	120-165	7	6	2000			3300	3950
21	5	ISLANDER MKIV 22	OP	CR	AL	SV	IO	120-165	7	6	2030			3300	3950
21	6	CHIEFTAIN EXPRESS 22	ST	EXP	AL	SV	IO	120-165	7	7	2582			3700	4500
21	6	CHIEFTAIN EXPRESS 22	HT	EXP	AL	SV	IO	120-165	7	7	2642			3750	4550
21	6	CHIEFTAIN MKIV 22	OP	EXP	AL	SV	IO	120-165	7	7	2277			3500	4200
21	7	CHIEFTAIN 22	OP	CR	AL	SV	OB		7	7	1410			2500	2900
21	7	SUPER-SPORT 22	ST	RNBT	AL	SV	OB		7	4	1210			2200	2550
21	7	SUPER-SPORT 22	ST	RNBT	AL	SV	IO	120-165	7	4	1782			3050	3600
22	3	AMERICAN SPORT 22	ST	SPTCR	AL	SV	IO	188-235	8		3345			4750	5600
22	3	AMERICAN SPORT 22	ST	SPTCR	AL	SV	JT	290 OMC	8		3365			4850	5550
22	3	AMERICAN SPORT 22	ST	SPTCR	AL	SV	IO	T120-T140	8		3624			5600	6550
24	8	CHIEFTAIN EXPRESS 25	ST	EXP	AL	SV	IO	165-235	8		3290			5300	6550
24	8	CHIEFTAIN EXPRESS 25	ST	EXP	AL	SV	IO	280	8		3290			5800	6650
24	8	CHIEFTAIN EXPRESS 25	ST	EXP	AL	SV	IO	T120-T140	8		3699			6350	7500
24	8	CHIEFTAIN EXPRESS 25	HT	EXP	AL	SV	IO	165-235	8		3350			5350	6600
24	8	CHIEFTAIN EXPRESS 25	HT	EXP	AL	SV	IO	280	8		3350			5850	6700
24	8	CHIEFTAIN EXPRESS 25	HT	EXP	AL	SV	IO	T120-T140	8		3759			6450	7550
24	8	CHIEFTAIN MKIV 25	OP	CR	AL	SV	IO	165-235	8		3315			5300	6550
24	8	CHIEFTAIN MKIV 25	OP	CR	AL	SV	IO	280	8		3315			5800	6700
24	8	CHIEFTAIN MKIV 25	OP	CR	AL	SV	IO	T120-T140	8		3724			6400	7550
24	8	CHIEFTAIN MKIV 25	HT	CR	AL	SV	IO	280	8					6150	7050
		1975 BOATS													
16	4	AMERICAN 16	ST	RNBT	FBG	DV	IO	120-140	6	6	1570			1900	2300
17	1	CAPRI 17	ST	RNBT	FBG	TR	OB		6	10	1213			1800	2150
17	1	CAPRI 17	ST	RNBT	FBG	TR	IO	120-140	6	10	1854			2250	2650
18	3	MONTEGO 18	OP	RNBT	FBG	TR	IO	120-165	6	9	1190			2100	2500
		JT 185 WAUK 2350 2750, IO 185-233 2150 2650, JT 245-255												2400	2800
18	5	AMERICAN B/R18	OP	RNBT	FBG	DV	IO	120-165	7	2	1672			2400	3000
		JT 185 WAUK 2800 3250, IO 185-233 2600 3150, JT 245-255												2850	3350
18	6	AMERICAN 18	ST	RNBT	FBG	DV	IO	120-165	7	2	1926			2550	3150
		JT 185 WAUK 2950 3400, IO 185-233 2750 3350, JT 245-255												3000	3550
18	6	HOLIDAY 18	ST	RNBT	AL	SV	IO	120-140	6	11	1527			2350	2750
18	7	SUPER-SPORT 18	ST	RNBT	AL	SV	IO	120-140	6	9	1513			2300	2700
19	5	AMERICAN S19	OP	RNBT	FBG	DV	OB		7	3	1210			1950	2300
19	5	AMERICAN S19	OP	RNBT	FBG	DV	IO	165	7	3	1940			2750	3250
		JT 185 WAUK 3000 3500, IO 185-233 2800 3450, JT 255 WAUK												3100	3600
		IO 255-290 3050 3700													
20	7	AMERICAN 20	ST	RNBT	FBG	DV	IO	140-165	8		2193			3350	4000
		JT 185 WAUK 3600 4150, IO 185-233 3500 4250, JT 245 OMC												3600	4200
		JT 255 WAUK 3700 4300, IO 255 WAUK 3750 4350													
20	8	CAPRI 20	ST	RNBT	FBG	TR	IO	140-225	7	11	2664			3650	4550
20	8	CAPRI 20	ST	RNBT	FBG	TR	IO	233-255	7	11	2976			4000	4750
20	8	CAPRI SPRT CRUISER20	ST	CUD	FBG	TR	IO	185-255	8		2970			4100	5100
21	5	HOLIDAY 22	ST	RNBT	AL	SV	OB		7	5	1249			2250	2600
21	6	ISLANDER 22 CRUISER	OP	CUD	AL	SV	IO	120-165	7	7	1939			3400	4100
21	7	CHIEFTAIN MKIV22	OP	CR	AL	SV	OB		7	7	1598			2750	3200
21	7	SUPER-SPORT 22	ST	RNBT	AL	SV	OB		7	4	1210			2200	2550
21	7	SUPER-SPORT 22	ST	RNBT	AL	SV	IO	120-165	7	4	1782			3150	3750
21	11	CHIEFTAIN MKIV EXP22	OP	CR	AL	SV	IO	120-165	7	7	2142			3600	4350
22	1	CHIEFTAIN MKIV22	OP	CR	AL	SV	IO	120-165	7	7	2212			3700	4450
22	1	ISLANDER MKIV22	ST	CR	AL	SV	IO	120-165	7	8	2030			3600	4300
22	2	HOLIDAY 22	ST	RNBT	AL	SV	IO	120-165	7	5	1907			3300	3950
25		CHIEFTAIN MKIV25	OP	CR	AL	SV	IO	140-188	8		3158			5350	6650
25		CHIEFTAIN MKIV25	OP	CR	AL	SV	IO	215-255	8		3400			5900	7100
25		CHIEFTAIN MKIV25	OP	CR	AL	SV	IO	T120 MRCR	8		3694			6700	7700
25	2	CHIEFTAIN MKIVEXP25	OP	EXP	AL	SV	IO	140-188	8		3046			5350	6600
25	2	CHIEFTAIN MKIVEXP25	OP	EXP	AL	SV	IO	215-255	8		3288			5850	7100
25	2	CHIEFTAIN MKIVEXP25	OP	EXP	AL	SV	IO	T120 MRCR	8		3582			6650	7650
		1974 BOATS													
16	3	AMERICAN	ST	RNBT	FBG	DV	IO	120-140	6	5	1405			1850	2200
17	1	CAPRI	OP	RNBT	FBG	TR	IO	120-140	6	10	1705			2250	2650
18	4	HOLIDAY	OP	RNBT	AL	SV	IO	140 MRCR	6	11	1600			2400	2800
18	4	HOLIDAY	ST	RNBT	AL	SV	IO	120 MRCR	6	11	1600			2400	2800
18	4	SUPER-SPORT	ST	RNBT	AL	SV	IO	120-140	6	9	1610			2350	2750
18	5	AMERICAN	OP	RNBT	FBG	DV	IO	140-165	7	2	1785			2550	3000
		JT 185 STAR 2600 3000, IO 188 MRCR 2600 3000, JT 255-270												2650	3050
18	5	AMERICAN	ST	RNBT	FBG	DV	OB		7	2	1100			1700	2050
18	5	AMERICAN OPEN BOW	OP	RNBT	FBG	DV	IO	140-165	7	2	1835			2600	3000
		JT 185 STAR 2600 3050, IO 188 MRCR 2600 3050, JT 255-270												2650	3100
19	5	STINGER	OP	SPTCR	FBG	SV	OB		7	3	1050			1700	2050
19	5	STINGER	OP	SPTCR	FBG	SV	IO	188 MRCR	7	3				3050	3550
19	5	STINGER	OP	SPTCR	FBG	SV	JT	255-350	7	3				2950	3400
20	3	CAPRI	OP	RNBT	FBG	TR	IO	165-188	8		2356			3500	4100
20	3	CAPRI	OP	RNBT	FBG	TR	JT	255-350	8		2356			3350	3900
20	3	CAPRI	OP	SPTCR	FBG	TR	IO	188 MRCR	8					4350	5000
20	3	CAPRI	OP	SPTCR	FBG	TR	JT	255-350	8					3850	4500
20	5	AMERICAN	OP	RNBT	FBG	DV	IO	165-188	7	11	2406			3550	4150
20	5	AMERICAN	OP	RNBT	FBG	DV	JT	250-350	7	11	2406			3400	3950
21	5	SUPER-SPORT	OP	RNBT	AL	SV	OB		7	4	1080			1900	2300
21	5	SUPER-SPORT	OP	RNBT	AL	SV	IO	120-165	7	4	1770			3200	3750
21	7	CHIEFTAIN MARK IV	OP	EXP	AL	SV	IO	120-165	7	8	2305			3800	4450
21	7	HOLIDAY	OP	RNBT	AL	SV	OB		7	5	1180			2100	2450
21	7	HOLIDAY	OP	RNBT	AL	SV	IO	120-165	7	5	1845			3150	3700
21	7	HOLIDAY MARK IV	OP	RNBT	AL	SV	IO	120-165	7	5	1845			3400	3950
21	7	ISLANDER	OP	CUD	AL	SV	IO	120-165	7	8	1985			3600	4200
21	7	ISLANDER MARK IV	ST	CUD	AL	SV	IO	120-165	7	8	2015			3600	4200
24	9	CHIEFTAIN MARK IV	OP	EXP	AL	SV	IO	140-188	8		3395			5700	6700
24	9	CHIEFTAIN MARK IV	OP	EXP	AL	SV	IO	T120 MRCR	8		3395			6500	7500
		1973 BOATS													
16	3	AMERICAN	OP	RNBT	FBG		IO	120 MRCR	6	5	1250		6	1800	2150
16	3	AMERICAN	OP	RNBT	FBG		IO	130-140	6	5	1250		6	1950	2350
17	1	CAPRI	OP	RNBT	FBG	TR	IO	120-140	6	9	2100		6	2550	3100
18	2	NOVA	OP	RNBT	AL		IO	120-140	6	11	1650		6	2450	2900
18	3	HOLIDAY	OP	RNBT	AL		IO	120-140	6	11	1800		6	2550	3150
18	4	AMERICAN	OP	RNBT	FBG		IO	140-188	7	1	1900		8	2700	3150
18	4	AMERICAN	OP	RNBT	FBG		JT	270 BERK	7	1	1900		8	2550	2950
18	4	AMERICAN OPEN BOW	OP	RNBT	FBG		OB		7	1	1150		8	1850	2250
18	4	AMERICAN OPEN BOW	OP	RNBT	FBG		IO	140-188	7	1	2000		8	2750	3200
18	4	AMERICAN OPEN BOW	OP	RNBT	FBG		JT	270 BERK	7	1	2000		8	2600	3050
18	4	SUPER-SPORT	OP	RNBT	AL		IO	120-140	6	11	1850		6	2600	3050
18	5	CHEIFTAIN	OP	CUD	AL		IO	120-140	6	10	1900		8	2700	3300
20	2	SUNCRUISER	OP	RNBT	FBG		IO	140-188	7	11	2200		8	3450	4100
20	2	SUNCRUISER	OP	RNBT	FBG		IO	T130 VLVO	7	11	2200		8	4500	5150
20	3	CAPRI	OP	RNBT	FBG	TR	OB		7	11	1700		10	2700	3150
20	3	CAPRI	OP	RNBT	FBG	TR	IO	165-188	7	11	2500		10	3700	4350
20	3	CAPRI	OP	RNBT	FBG	TR	JT	270 BERK	7	11	2500		10	3300	3850
20	4	AMERICAN	OP	RNBT	FBG		IO	165-188	7	11	2500		10	3700	4350
20	4	AMERICAN	OP	RNBT	FBG		JT	270 BERK	7	11	2500		10	3300	3850
21	7	CHIEFTAIN	OP	EXP	AL		OB		7	8	1590		10	2700	3150
21	7	CHIEFTAIN	OP	EXP	AL		IO	120-165	7	8	2340		10	3950	4750
21	7	CHIEFTAIN 21 MK IV	OP	EXP	AL		IO	120-165	7	8	2400		10	4000	4800
21	7	ISLANDER	OP	CUD	AL		IO	120-165	7	8	2060		10	3750	4550
24	9	CHIEFTAIN 24 MK IV	OP	EXP	AL		IO	140-188	7	11	3660	1		6150	7250
24	9	CHIEFTAIN 24 MK IV	OP	EXP	AL		IO	T130 VLVO	7	11	3660	1		7300	8400
		1972 BOATS													
16	2	AMERICAN	OP	RNBT	FBG		IO	120-140	6	4				2350	2700
17		CAPRI SPORT	OP	CTRCN	FBG		OB		6	10	1140			1700	2000
17		CAPRI SPORT	OP	CTRCN	FBG		IO	120-170	6	10				2850	3300
18		HOLIDAY	OP	RNBT	AL		IO	120-140	6	10				2750	3200
18		NOVA	OP	RNBT	AL		IO	120-140	6	10				2800	3300
18		STARCHIEF	OP	CUD	AL		IO	120-140	6	10	1035			2300	2700
18		SUPER-SPORT	OP	RNBT	AL		IO	120-140	6	10	965			2300	2650
18	2	AMERICAN	OP	RNBT	FBG		OB		7	2	1100			1700	2000
18	2	AMERICAN	OP	RNBT	FBG		IO	130-185	7	2				2900	3400
18	2	AMERICAN	OP	RNBT	FBG		JT	250 BERK	7	2				2550	2950
20		AMERICAN	OP	RNBT	FBG		IO	165-215	7	9				4400	5150
20		AMERICAN	OP	RNBT	FBG		JT	250 BERK	7	9				3550	4150
21	1	CHIEFTAIN	OP	EXP	AL		OB		7	6	1590			2700	3100
21	1	CHIEFTAIN	OP	EXP	AL		IO	120-165	7	6				3550	4150
21	1	HOLIDAY	OP	RNBT	AL		OB		7	6	1440			2450	2850
21	1	HOLIDAY	OP	RNBT	AL		IO	120-140	7	6				3400	3950
21	1	ISLANDER	OP	CUD	AL		IO	120-165	7	6	1540			3450	4050
		1971 BOATS													
16	2	V-160	OP	RNBT	FBG	SV	IO	120-140	6	4	1385	1	4	2000	2400
17		SPORT TR-170	OP	RNBT	FBG	TR	IO	120-165	6	10	1785	1	4	2500	3000
17		SPORT TR-170 DLX	OP	RNBT	FBG	TR	OB		6	10	1140	1	4	1700	2000
18		V OFFSHORE	OP	UTL	AL	SV	IO	120-140	6	10	1550	1	4	2750	3250
18	2	HOLIDAY V	OP	RNBT	AL	SV	IO	120-140	7	9	1450	1	4	2750	3200
18	2	STARCHIEF V	OP	CUD	AL	SV	IO	120-140	6	9	1620	1	4	2600	3050

96th ed. - Vol. III
CONTINUED ON NEXT PAGE
579

LOA FT	LOA IN	NAME AND/ OR MODEL	TOP/ RIG	BOAT TYPE	-HULL- MTL	-HULL- TP	ENGINE TP	# HP	MFG	BEAM FT	BEAM IN	WGT LBS	DRAFT FT	DRAFT IN	RETAIL LOW	RETAIL HIGH
		1971 BOATS														
18	2	V-180	OP	RNBT	FBG	SV	OB			7	2	1100	1	4	1700	2000
18	2	V-180	OP	RNBT	FBG	SV	IO	120-165		7	2	1765	1	4	2750	3300
20		V-200	OP	RNBT	FBG	SV	IO	155-215		7	9	2110	1	4	3550	4300
20		V-200	OP	RNBT	FBG	SV	IO	235	OMC	7	9	2325	1	4	3850	4450
21	1	CHIEFTAIN V	OP	EXP	AL	SV	IO	120-165		7	6	2225	1	4	3950	4700
21	1	ISLANDER V	OP	CUD	AL	SV	IO	120-165		7	6	2125	1	4	3850	4600
		1970 BOATS														
16	2	V-160	OP	RNBT	FBG	SV	IO	120-140		6	4	1385	1	4	2050	2450
16	5	UPSTART	SLP	SAIL	FBG	CB	OB			6	5	720		6	1800	2150
17		TR-170	OP	RNBT	FBG	TR	OB			6	10	1140	1	4	1700	2000
17		TR-170	OP	RNBT	FBG	TR	IO	120-140		6	10	1785	1	4	2600	3000
17		TR-170	ST	RNBT	FBG	TR	IO	155-165		6	10	1910	1	4	2650	3100
18		OFFSHORE V		OFF	AL	DV	IO	120-140		6	10	1550	1	4	2750	3200
18	2	HOLIDAY V		RNBT	AL	DV	IO	120-140		7	9	1450	1	4	2850	3300
18	2	STARCHIEF V		CR	AL	DV	IO	120-140		6	9	1620	1	4	2700	3150
18	2	V-180	ST	RNBT	FBG	SV	OB			7	2	1100	1	4	1700	2000
18	2	V-180	ST	RNBT	FBG	SV	IO	120-165		7	2	1765	1	4	2850	3400
20		V-200	ST	RNBT	FBG	SV	IO	120-210		7	9	1985	1	4	3600	4400
20		V-200	ST	RNBT	FBG	SV	IO	215	MRCR	7	9	2325	1	4	3950	4550
21	1	CHIEFTAIN V		EXP	AL	DV	IO	120-165		7	6	2000	1	4	3900	4650
21	1	ISLANDER V		CUD	AL	DV	IO	120-165		7	6	1955	1	4	3900	4600
		1969 BOATS														
16	2	TRIDENT	OP	RNBT	FBG	SV	IO	120		6	9	1840	2		2550	3000
16	3	NEWPORT V	OP	RNBT	FBG	SV	IO	120		6	7	1600	2		2350	2750
16	5	UPSTART	SLP	SAIL	FBG	CB	OB			6	5	720		8	1750	2100
18		OFFSHORE V	OP	OFF	AL	SV	IO			6	10	1550	2		**	**
18		OFFSHORE V	OP	OFF	AL	SV	IO	120	MRCR	6	10	1550			2850	3300
18		V-180	OP	RNBT	FBG	SV	IO	120		6	11	1720	2		2800	3300
18	2	HOLIDAY V	OP	RNBT	AL	SV	IO			7		1550			**	**
18	2	HOLIDAY V	OP	RNBT	AL	SV	IO	120	MRCR	7		1550	2		2800	3250
18	2	STARCHIEF V	OP	RNBT	AL	SV	IO			6	9	1620			**	**
18	2	STARCHIEF V	OP	RNBT	AL	SV	IO	120	MRCR	6	9	1620	2		2750	3200
20	1	SUNCRUISER V	OP	RNBT	FBG	SV	IO	155-160		8		2350			4050	4750
21	2	CHIEFTAIN V	OP	CR	AL	SV	OB			7	6	1250			2200	2600
21	2	CHIEFTAIN V	OP	CR	AL	SV	IO	120	MRCR	7	6	2000			4050	4750
21	2	ISLANDER V	OP	CR	AL	SV	OB			7	6	1400			2400	2800
21	2	ISLANDER V	OP	CR	AL	SV	IO	120	MRCR	7	6	1955			4050	4700
		1968 BOATS														
16		NEWPORT V	OP	RNBT	FBG	SV	IO	120	MRCR	6	7	1400			2300	2650
16	1	JUPITER V	OP	RNBT	AL	SV	IO	80	MRCR	6	9	1000			2000	2350
16	6	UPSTART	SLP	SAIL	FBG	CB	OB			6	3	720			1750	2100
18	4	HOLIDAY V	OP	RNBT	AL	SV	IO	120	MRCR	7	1	1600			2950	3450
18	4	STARCHIEF V		CR	AL	SV	IO	120	MRCR	7	1	1600			3000	3500
18	5	IMPERIAL V	OP	RNBT	FBG	SV	IO	160	MRCR	7	2	1900			3200	3700
20	3	SUNCRUISER V		RNBT	FBG	SV	IO	160	MRCR	7	11	2400			4250	4950
21	7	CHIEFTAIN V		CR	AL	SV	IO	120	MRCR	7	8	2000			4550	5250
21	7	ISLANDER V		CR	AL	SV	IO	120	MRCR	7	8	2000			4200	4900
		1967 BOATS														
16		NEWPORT V	OP	RNBT	FBG	SV	IO	120		6	7	1400			2350	2750
16	1	JUPITER	OP	RNBT	AL	SV	IO	80		6	9	1000			2050	2450
16	6	UPSTART	SLP	SAIL	FBG	CB	OB			6	3	720			1750	2050
18	4	HOLIDAY V	OP	RNBT	AL	SV	IO	110		7	1	1550			3050	3500
18	4	HOLIDAY V DELUXE	OP	RNBT	AL	SV	IO	120		7	1	1600			3050	3550
18	4	STARCHIEF V	OP	CR	AL	SV	IO	120		7	1	1600			3100	3600
18	5	IMPERIAL V	OP	RNBT	FBG	SV	OB			7	2	1200			1850	2200
18	5	IMPERIAL V	OP	RNBT	FBG	SV	IO	150		7	2	1900			3300	3850
20	3	SUNCRUISER V	OP	RNBT	FBG	SV	IO	150		7	11	2400			4450	5150
21	7	CHIEFTAIN V	OP	CR	AL	SV	OB			7	8	1500			2600	3050
21	7	CHIEFTAIN V	OP	CR	AL	SV	IO	120		7	8	2000			4550	5250
21	7	ISLANDER V	OP	CR	AL	SV	OB			7	8	1400			2450	2850
21	7	ISLANDER V	OP	CR	AL	SV	IO	120		7	8	1900			4500	5150
		1966 BOATS														
16		NEWPORT V	OP	RNBT	FBG	DV	IO	110		6	7	1400			2400	2800
16	1	JUPITER V	OP	RNBT	AL	SV	IO	60		6	9	1000			2150	2500
18	4	HOLIDAY V	OP	RNBT	AL	SV	IO	110		7	1	1550			3150	3650
18	4	STARCHIEF V	OP	CR	AL	SV	IO	110		7	1	1600			3200	3750
18	5	IMPERIAL	OP	RNBT	FBG	DV	IO	150		7	2	1900			3400	3950
18	5	IMPERIAL V	OP	RNBT	FBG	DV	OB			7	2	1200			1850	2250
20	3	SUNCRUISER	OP	RNBT	FBG	SV	IO	150		7	11	2800			4950	5700
21	7	CHIEFTAIN V	OP	CR	AL	SV	OB			7	8	1250			2250	2650
21	7	CHIEFTAIN V	OP	CR	AL	SV	IO	110		7	8	2000			4700	5400
21	7	SUNCHIEF V	OP	RNBT	AL	SV	OB			7	8	950			1750	2050
21	7	SUNCHIEF V	OP	RNBT	AL	SV	IO	110		7	8	1700			4250	4950
		1965 BOATS														
16		NEWPORT	OP	RNBT	FBG	SV	IO	110		6	7	1400			2500	2900
18	4	HOLIDAY V	OP	RNBT	AL	SV	IO	110		7	1	1550			3250	3750
18	4	HOLIDAY V HULL	OP	RNBT	AL	SV	IO			7	1	900			**	**
18	4	STARCHIEF V	OP	CR	AL	SV	IO	110		7	1	1640			3350	3900
18	4	STARCHIEF V HULL	OP	CR	AL	SV	IO			7	1	1140			**	**
20	3	SUNCRUISER	OP	RNBT	FBG	SV	IO	150		7	11	2800			5150	5900
21	7	CHIEFTAIN	OP	CR	AL	SV	IO			7	8	2600			**	**
21	7	CHIEFTAIN V	OP	CR	AL	SV	OB			7	8	2600			4050	4700
21	7	CHIEFTAIN V	OP	CR	AL	SV	IO	110		7	8	2100			4950	5650
21	7	SUNCHIEF	OP	CR	AL	SV	IO			7	8	2050			**	**
21	7	SUNCHIEF V	OP	RNBT	AL	SV	OB			7	8	1300			2350	2700
21	7	SUNCHIEF V	OP	RNBT	AL	SV	IO	110		7	8	1850			4550	5200
		1964 BOATS														
18	4	HOLIDAY	OP	RNBT	AL	SV	IO	110		7	1	1550			3350	3900
18	4	STARCHIEF	OP	CR	AL	SV	IO	110		7	1	1640			3450	4000
21	7	CHIEFTAIN	OP	CR	AL	SV	OB			7	8	1850			3150	3700
21	7	CHIEFTAIN	OP	CR	AL	SV	IO	110		7	8	2600			5600	6450
21	7	SUNCHIEF	OP	RNBT	AL	SV	OB			7	8	1250			2300	2650
21	7	SUNCHIEF	OP	RNBT	AL	SV	IO	110		7	8	2050			4800	5550
		1963 BOATS														
21	7	CHIEFTAIN	OP	CR	AL	SV	IB	100		7	8	1850			1700	2000
		1960 BOATS														
16		VISCOUNT	OP	RNBT	AL		OB								2200	2600
17		COMMANDER	OP	RNBT	FBG		OB								2400	2750
18		HOLIDAY	OP	CR	AL		OB								2100	2450

STARDUST CRUISER MFG CO

SUB OF ALASKA INTERSTATE CO
CHATTANOOGA TN 37404 COAST GUARD MFG ID- SCM

See inside cover to adjust price for area

LOA FT	LOA IN	NAME AND/ OR MODEL	TOP/ RIG	BOAT TYPE	-HULL- MTL	-HULL- TP	ENGINE TP	# HP	MFG	BEAM FT	BEAM IN	WGT LBS	DRAFT FT	DRAFT IN	RETAIL LOW	RETAIL HIGH
		1980 BOATS														
46		STARDUST	HT	HB	AL	SV	IO			14		15000			21100	23400
46		STARDUST	HT	HB	FBG	SV	IO			14					24200	26800
46		STARDUST	HT	HB	STL	SV	IO			14		18000			21600	24100
53		STARDUST	HT	HB	AL	SV	IO			14		19000			33100	36800
53		STARDUST	HT	HB	FBG	SV	IO			14					34200	38000
53		STARDUST	HT	HB	STL	SV	IO			14		24000			33500	37300
54		STARDUST	HT	HB	FBG	SV	IO			14					39900	44300
58		STARDUST	HT	HB	AL	SV	IO			14		25000			39600	44000
58		STARDUST	HT	HB	STL	SV	IO			14		30000			38700	43000
		1979 BOATS														
36		SILVER-QUEEN	HT	HB	FBG	SV	IO	120	VLVO	12		13000	3		18700	20800
		IO 165 MRCR 18500 20500, IO 200 VLVO 18900 21000, IO 225 VLVO 19000 21100														
		IO 228 MRCR 18700 20800, IO 260 VLVO 19300 21500, VD 260 MRCR 19300 21500														
		VD 260 OMC 19700 21900, VD 325 OMC 20100 22300, IO 330 MRCR 20100 22400														
		IO 130D CHRY 21600 24000, IO 130D VLVO 21200 23600, VD 200D CHRY 23200 25800														
		VD 200D VLVO 22800 25300														
36		SILVER-QUEEN	FB	HB	FBG	SV	IO	120	VLVO	12		13000	3		18700	20800
		IO 165 MRCR 18500 20500, IO 200 VLVO 18900 21000, IO 225 VLVO 19000 21100														
		IO 228 MRCR 18700 20800, IO 260 VLVO 19300 21500, VD 260 MRCR 19300 21500														
		VD 260 OMC 19700 21900, VD 325 OMC 20100 22300, IO 330 MRCR 20100 22400														
		IO 130D CHRY 21600 24000, IO 130D VLVO 21200 23600, VD 200D CHRY 23200 25800														
		VD 200D VLVO 22800 25300														
42		STARDUST-CRUISER	HT	HB	FBG	SV	IB	165		12					17100	19400
46		SILVER-QUEEN	HT	HB	FBG	SV	IO	120	VLVO	14		24000	2	8	26600	29600
		IO 165 MRCR 26400 29300, IO 200 VLVO 26800 29700, IO 225 VLVO 26900 29900														
		IO 228 MRCR 26600 29500, IO 260 VLVO 27200 30300, VD 260 MRCR 25200 28000														
		VD 260 OMC 25600 28400, VD 325 OMC 25900 28800, IO 330 MRCR 28000 31100														
		IO 130D CHRY 28100 31200, IO 130D VLVO 27700 30700, VD 200D CHRY 27500 30600														
		VD 200D VLVO 27000 30000														
46		SILVER-QUEEN	HT	HB	AL	SV	IB	T260		14		24000			26800	29800
46		SILVER-QUEEN	HT	HB	STL	SV	IB	T260		14		24000			24800	27600
46		SILVER-QUEEN	FB	HB	FBG	SV	IO	120	VLVO	14		24000	2	8	26600	29600
		IO 165 MRCR 26400 29300, IO 200 VLVO 26800 29700, IO 225 VLVO 26900 29900														
		IO 228 MRCR 26600 29500, IO 260 VLVO 27200 30300, VD 260 MRCR 25200 28000														
		VD 260 OMC 25600 28400, VD 325 OMC 25900 28800, IO 330 MRCR 28000 31100														
		IO 130D CHRY 28100 31200, IO 130D VLVO 27700 30700, VD 200D CHRY 27500 30600														
		VD 200D VLVO 27000 30000														
46		SILVER-QUEEN	FB	HB	AL	SV	IB	T260		14		24000			26800	29800
46		SILVER-QUEEN	FB	HB	STL	SV	IB	T260		14		24000			24800	27600
46		STARDUST-CRUISER	HT	HB	AL	SV	IO	120	VLVO	13		15000	2	3	20900	23200

CONTINUED ON NEXT PAGE

580 96th ed. - Vol. III

LOA FT	LOA IN	NAME AND/ OR MODEL	TOP/ RIG	BOAT TYPE	-HULL- MTL	-HULL- TP	ENGINE TP	ENGINE # HP	ENGINE MFG	BEAM FT	BEAM IN	WGT LBS	DRAFT FT	DRAFT IN	RETAIL LOW	RETAIL HIGH
		1979 BOATS														
46		STARDUST-CRUISER	HT	HB	STL	SV	IO	120	VLVO	13		18000	2	5	21500	23800
46		STARDUST-CRUISER	HT	HB	AL	SV	IO	165	MRCR	13		15000	2	3	20700	23000
46		STARDUST-CRUISER	HT	HB	STL	SV	IO	165	MRCR	13		18000	2	5	21200	23600
46		STARDUST-CRUISER	HT	HB	AL	SV	IO	200	VLVO	13		15000	2	3	21100	23400
46		STARDUST-CRUISER	HT	HB	STL	SV	IO	200	VLVO	13		18000	2	5	21600	24000
46		STARDUST-CRUISER	HT	HB	AL	SV	IO	225	VLVO	13		15000	2	3	21200	23600
46		STARDUST-CRUISER	HT	HB	STL	SV	IO	225	VLVO	13		18000	2	5	21700	24100
46		STARDUST-CRUISER	HT	HB	AL	SV	IO	228	MRCR	13		15000	2	3	20900	23200
46		STARDUST-CRUISER	HT	HB	STL	SV	IO	228	MRCR	13		18000	2	5	21400	23800
46		STARDUST-CRUISER	HT	HB	AL	SV	IO	260	VLVO	13		15000	2	3	21500	23900
46		STARDUST-CRUISER	HT	HB	STL	SV	IO	260	VLVO	13		18000	2	5	22000	24500
46		STARDUST-CRUISER	HT	HB	AL	SV	VD	260	MRCR	13		15000	2	3	19800	22000
46		STARDUST-CRUISER	HT	HB	STL	SV	VD	260	MRCR	13		18000	2	5	20500	22700
46		STARDUST-CRUISER	HT	HB	AL	SV	VD	260	OMC	13		15000	2	3	20100	22400
46		STARDUST-CRUISER	HT	HB	STL	SV	VD	260	OMC	13		18000	2	5	20800	23100
46		STARDUST-CRUISER	HT	HB	AL	SV	VD	325	OMC	13		15000	2	3	20500	22800
46		STARDUST-CRUISER	HT	HB	STL	SV	VD	325	OMC	13		18000	2	5	21100	23500
46		STARDUST-CRUISER	HT	HB	AL	SV	IO	330	MRCR	13		15000	2	3	22400	24800
46		STARDUST-CRUISER	HT	HB	STL	SV	IO	330	MRCR	13		18000	2	5	22800	25300
46		STARDUST-CRUISER	HT	HB	AL	SV	IO	130D	CHRY	13		15000	2	3	22400	24900
46		STARDUST-CRUISER	HT	HB	STL	SV	IO	130D	CHRY	13		18000	2	5	22800	25300
46		STARDUST-CRUISER	HT	HB	AL	SV	IO	130D	VLVO	13		15000	2	3	22000	24400
46		STARDUST-CRUISER	HT	HB	STL	SV	IO	130D	VLVO	13		18000	2	5	22400	24900
46		STARDUST-CRUISER	HT	HB	AL	SV	VD	200D	CHRY	13		15000	2	3	22100	24500
46		STARDUST-CRUISER	HT	HB	STL	SV	VD	200D	CHRY	13		18000	2	5	22600	25100
46		STARDUST-CRUISER	HT	HB	AL	SV	VD	200D	VLVO	13		15000	2	3	21600	24000
46		STARDUST-CRUISER	HT	HB	STL	SV	VD	200D	VLVO	13		18000	2	5	22100	24600
46		STARDUST-CRUISER	FB	HB	AL	SV	IO	120	VLVO	13		15000	2	3	20900	23200
46		STARDUST-CRUISER	FB	HB	STL	SV	IO	120	VLVO	13		18000	2	5	21500	23800
46		STARDUST-CRUISER	FB	HB	AL	SV	IO	165	MRCR	13		15000	2	3	20700	23000
46		STARDUST-CRUISER	FB	HB	STL	SV	IO	165	MRCR	13		18000	2	5	21200	23600
46		STARDUST-CRUISER	FB	HB	AL	SV	IO	200	VLVO	13		15000	2	3	21100	23400
46		STARDUST-CRUISER	FB	HB	STL	SV	IO	200	VLVO	13		18000	2	5	21600	24000
46		STARDUST-CRUISER	FB	HB	AL	SV	IO	225	VLVO	13		15000	2	3	21200	23600
46		STARDUST-CRUISER	FB	HB	STL	SV	IO	225	VLVO	13		18000	2	5	21700	24100
46		STARDUST-CRUISER	FB	HB	AL	SV	IO	228	MRCR	13		15000	2	3	20900	23200
46		STARDUST-CRUISER	FB	HB	STL	SV	IO	228	MRCR	13		18000	2	5	21400	23800
46		STARDUST-CRUISER	FB	HB	AL	SV	IO	260	VLVO	13		15000	2	3	21500	23900
46		STARDUST-CRUISER	FB	HB	STL	SV	IO	260	VLVO	13		18000	2	5	22000	24500
46		STARDUST-CRUISER	FB	HB	AL	SV	VD	260	MRCR	13		15000	2	3	19800	22000
46		STARDUST-CRUISER	FB	HB	STL	SV	VD	260	MRCR	13		18000	2	5	20500	22700
46		STARDUST-CRUISER	FB	HB	AL	SV	VD	260	OMC	13		15000	2	3	20100	22400
46		STARDUST-CRUISER	FB	HB	STL	SV	VD	260	OMC	13		18000	2	5	20800	23100
46		STARDUST-CRUISER	FB	HB	AL	SV	VD	325	OMC	13		15000	2	3	20500	22800
46		STARDUST-CRUISER	FB	HB	STL	SV	VD	325	OMC	13		18000	2	5	21100	23500
46		STARDUST-CRUISER	FB	HB	AL	SV	IO	330	MRCR	13		15000	2	3	22400	24800
46		STARDUST-CRUISER	FB	HB	STL	SV	IO	330	MRCR	13		18000	2	5	22800	25300
46		STARDUST-CRUISER	FB	HB	AL	SV	IO	130D	CHRY	13		15000	2	3	22400	24900
46		STARDUST-CRUISER	FB	HB	STL	SV	IO	130D	CHRY	13		18000	2	5	22800	25300
46		STARDUST-CRUISER	FB	HB	AL	SV	IO	130D	VLVO	13		15000	2	3	22000	24400
46		STARDUST-CRUISER	FB	HB	STL	SV	IO	130D	VLVO	13		18000	2	5	22400	24900
46		STARDUST-CRUISER	FB	HB	AL	SV	VD	200D	CHRY	13		15000	2	3	22100	24500
46		STARDUST-CRUISER	FB	HB	STL	SV	VD	200D	CHRY	13		18000	2	5	22600	25100
46		STARDUST-CRUISER	FB	HB	AL	SV	VD	200D	VLVO	13		15000	2	3	21600	24000
46		STARDUST-CRUISER	FB	HB	STL	SV	VD	200D	VLVO	13		18000	2	5	22100	24600
53		STARDUST-CRUISER	HT	HB	AL	SV	IO	120	VLVO	14		19000	2	4	32800	36400
53		STARDUST-CRUISER	HT	HB	STL	SV	IO	120	VLVO	14		24000	2	7	33200	36900
53		STARDUST-CRUISER	HT	HB	AL	SV	IO	165	MRCR	14		19000	2	4	32500	36100
53		STARDUST-CRUISER	HT	HB	STL	SV	IO	165	MRCR	14		24000	2	7	32900	36600
53		STARDUST-CRUISER	HT	HB	AL	SV	IO	200	VLVO	14		19000	2	4	33000	36600
53		STARDUST-CRUISER	HT	HB	STL	SV	IO	200	VLVO	14		24000	2	7	33400	37100
53		STARDUST-CRUISER	HT	HB	AL	SV	IO	225	VLVO	14		19000	2	4	33100	36800
53		STARDUST-CRUISER	HT	HB	STL	SV	IO	225	VLVO	14		24000	2	7	33500	37200
53		STARDUST-CRUISER	HT	HB	AL	SV	IO	228	MRCR	14		19000	2	4	32800	36400
53		STARDUST-CRUISER	HT	HB	STL	SV	IO	228	MRCR	14		24000	2	7	33200	36800
53		STARDUST-CRUISER	HT	HB	AL	SV	IO	260	VLVO	14		19000	2	4	33600	37300
53		STARDUST-CRUISER	HT	HB	STL	SV	IO	260	VLVO	14		24000	2	7	33900	37700
53		STARDUST-CRUISER	HT	HB	AL	SV	VD	260	MRCR	14		19000	2	4	31000	34500
53		STARDUST-CRUISER	HT	HB	STL	SV	VD	260	MRCR	14		24000	2	7	31400	34900
53		STARDUST-CRUISER	HT	HB	AL	SV	VD	260	OMC	14		19000	2	4	31400	34900
53		STARDUST-CRUISER	HT	HB	STL	SV	VD	260	OMC	14		24000	2	7	31800	35400
53		STARDUST-CRUISER	HT	HB	AL	SV	VD	325	OMC	14		19000	2	4	31900	35400
53		STARDUST-CRUISER	HT	HB	STL	SV	VD	325	OMC	14		24000	2	7	32200	35800
53		STARDUST-CRUISER	HT	HB	AL	SV	IO	330	MRCR	14		19000	2	4	34500	38400
53		STARDUST-CRUISER	HT	HB	STL	SV	IO	330	MRCR	14		24000	2	7	34800	38700
53		STARDUST-CRUISER	HT	HB	AL	SV	IO	130D	CHRY	14		19000	2	4	34600	38400
53		STARDUST-CRUISER	HT	HB	STL	SV	IO	130D	CHRY	14		24000	2	7	34800	38700
53		STARDUST-CRUISER	HT	HB	AL	SV	IO	130D	VLVO	14		19000	2	4	34100	37900
53		STARDUST-CRUISER	HT	HB	STL	SV	IO	130D	VLVO	14		24000	2	7	34400	38200
53		STARDUST-CRUISER	HT	HB	AL	SV	VD	200D	CHRY	14		19000	2	4	33800	37600
53		STARDUST-CRUISER	HT	HB	STL	SV	VD	200D	CHRY	14		24000	2	7	34000	37800
53		STARDUST-CRUISER	HT	HB	AL	SV	VD	200D	VLVO	14		19000	2	4	33300	37000
53		STARDUST-CRUISER	HT	HB	STL	SV	VD	200D	VLVO	14		24000	2	7	33500	37200
53		STARDUST-CRUISER	HT	HB	AL	SV	IB	T228		14		19000			32500	36200
53		STARDUST-CRUISER	HT	HB	STL	SV	IB	T228		14		24000			32800	36500
53		STARDUST-CRUISER	FB	HB	STL	SV		T228		14		24000			30000	33400
53		STARDUST-CRUISER	FB	HB	AL	SV	IO	120	VLVO	14		19000	2	4	32800	36400
53		STARDUST-CRUISER	FB	HB	STL	SV	IO	120	VLVO	14		24000	2	7	33200	36900
53		STARDUST-CRUISER	FB	HB	AL	SV	IO	165	MRCR	14		19000	2	4	32500	36100
53		STARDUST-CRUISER	FB	HB	STL	SV	IO	165	MRCR	14		24000	2	7	32900	36600
53		STARDUST-CRUISER	FB	HB	AL	SV	IO	200	VLVO	14		19000	2	4	33000	36600
53		STARDUST-CRUISER	FB	HB	STL	SV	IO	200	VLVO	14		24000	2	7	33400	37100
53		STARDUST-CRUISER	FB	HB	AL	SV	IO	225	VLVO	14		19000	2	4	33100	36800
53		STARDUST-CRUISER	FB	HB	STL	SV	IO	225	VLVO	14		24000	2	7	33500	37200
53		STARDUST-CRUISER	FB	HB	AL	SV	IO	228	MRCR	14		19000	2	4	32800	36400
53		STARDUST-CRUISER	FB	HB	STL	SV	IO	228	MRCR	14		24000	2	7	33200	36800
53		STARDUST-CRUISER	FB	HB	AL	SV	IO	260	VLVO	14		19000	2	4	33600	37300
53		STARDUST-CRUISER	FB	HB	STL	SV	IO	260	VLVO	14		24000	2	7	33900	37700
53		STARDUST-CRUISER	FB	HB	AL	SV	VD	260	MRCR	14		19000	2	4	31000	34500
53		STARDUST-CRUISER	FB	HB	STL	SV	VD	260	MRCR	14		24000	2	7	31400	34900
53		STARDUST-CRUISER	FB	HB	AL	SV	VD	260	OMC	14		19000	2	4	31400	34900
53		STARDUST-CRUISER	FB	HB	STL	SV	VD	260	OMC	14		24000	2	7	31800	35400
53		STARDUST-CRUISER	FB	HB	AL	SV	VD	325	OMC	14		19000	2	4	31900	35400
53		STARDUST-CRUISER	FB	HB	STL	SV	VD	325	OMC	14		24000	2	7	32200	35800
53		STARDUST-CRUISER	FB	HB	AL	SV	IO	330	MRCR	14		19000	2	4	34500	38400
53		STARDUST-CRUISER	FB	HB	STL	SV	IO	330	MRCR	14		24000	2	7	34800	38700
53		STARDUST-CRUISER	FB	HB	AL	SV	IO	130D	CHRY	14		19000	2	4	34600	38400
53		STARDUST-CRUISER	FB	HB	STL	SV	IO	130D	CHRY	14		24000	2	7	34800	38700
53		STARDUST-CRUISER	FB	HB	AL	SV	IO	130D	VLVO	14		19000	2	4	34100	37900
53		STARDUST-CRUISER	FB	HB	STL	SV	IO	130D	VLVO	14		24000	2	7	34400	38200
53		STARDUST-CRUISER	FB	HB	AL	SV	VD	200D	CHRY	14		19000	2	4	33800	37600
53		STARDUST-CRUISER	FB	HB	STL	SV	VD	200D	CHRY	14		24000	2	7	34000	37800
53		STARDUST-CRUISER	FB	HB	AL	SV	VD	200D	VLVO	14		19000	2	4	33300	37000
53		STARDUST-CRUISER	FB	HB	STL	SV	VD	200D	VLVO	14		24000	2	7	33500	37200
53		STARDUST-CRUISER	FB	HB	AL	SV	IB	T228		14		19000			32500	36200
54		SILVER-QUEEN	HT	HB	FBG	SV	IO	120	VLVO	14		30000	2	8	39600	44000
		IO 165 MRCR 39400 43700, IO 200 VLVO 39700 44100, IO 225 VLVO 39800 44300														
		IO 228 MRCR 39600 44000, IO 260 VLVO 40200 44700, VD 260 MRCR 37300 41400														
		VD 260 OMC 38000 42200, VD 325 OMC 38400 42700, IO 330 MRCR 41600 46200														
		IO 130D CHRY 41600 46200, IO 130D VLVO 40700 45200, VD 200D CHRY 40100 44600														
		VD 200D VLVO 39600 44000														
54		SILVER-QUEEN	FB	HB	FBG	SV	IO	120	VLVO	14		30000	2	8	39600	44000
		IO 165 MRCR 39400 43700, IO 200 VLVO 39700 44100, IO 225 VLVO 39800 44300														
		IO 228 MRCR 39600 44000, IO 260 VLVO 40200 44700, VD 260 MRCR 37300 41400														
		VD 260 OMC 38000 42200, VD 325 OMC 38400 42700, IO 330 MRCR 41600 46200														
		IO 130D CHRY 41600 46200, IO 130D VLVO 40700 45200, VD 200D CHRY 40100 44600														
		VD 200D VLVO 39600 44000														
58		STARDUST-CRUISER	HT	HB	AL	SV	IO	120	VLVO	14		25000	2	4	39400	43700
58		STARDUST-CRUISER	HT	HB	STL	SV	IO	120	VLVO	14		30000	2	8	38300	42500
58		STARDUST-CRUISER	HT	HB	AL	SV	IO	165	MRCR	14		25000	2	4	39100	43400
58		STARDUST-CRUISER	HT	HB	STL	SV	IO	165	MRCR	14		30000	2	8	38000	42200
58		STARDUST-CRUISER	HT	HB	AL	SV	IO	200	VLVO	14		25000	2	4	39500	43900
58		STARDUST-CRUISER	HT	HB	STL	SV	IO	200	VLVO	14		30000	2	8	38500	42700
58		STARDUST-CRUISER	HT	HB	AL	SV	IO	225	VLVO	14		25000	2	4	39600	44000
58		STARDUST-CRUISER	HT	HB	STL	SV	IO	225	VLVO	14		30000	2	8	38600	42900
58		STARDUST-CRUISER	HT	HB	AL	SV	IO	228	MRCR	14		25000	2	4	39300	43700
58		STARDUST-CRUISER	HT	HB	STL	SV	IO	228	MRCR	14		30000	2	8	38300	42500
58		STARDUST-CRUISER	HT	HB	AL	SV	IO	260	VLVO	14		25000	2	4	39900	44400
58		STARDUST-CRUISER	HT	HB	STL	SV	IO	260	VLVO	14		30000	2	8	39000	43300
58		STARDUST-CRUISER	HT	HB	AL	SV	VD	260	MRCR	14		25000	2	4	37000	41100
58		STARDUST-CRUISER	HT	HB	STL	SV	VD	260	MRCR	14		30000	2	8	36000	40000
58		STARDUST-CRUISER	HT	HB	AL	SV	VD	260	OMC	14		25000	2	4	37400	41600
58		STARDUST-CRUISER	HT	HB	STL	SV	VD	260	OMC	14		30000	2	8	36400	40400

CONTINUED ON NEXT PAGE

LOA FT	IN	NAME AND/ OR MODEL	TOP/ RIG	BOAT TYPE	-HULL- MTL	TP	ENGINE TP	# HP	MFG	BEAM FT	IN	WGT LBS	DRAFT FT	IN	RETAIL LOW	RETAIL HIGH
		1979 BOATS														
58		STARDUST-CRUISER	HT	HB	AL	SV	VD	325	OMC	14		25000	2	4	38200	42400
58		STARDUST-CRUISER	HT	HB	STL	SV	VD	325	OMC	14		30000	2	8	36800	40900
58		STARDUST-CRUISER	HT	HB	AL	SV	IO	330	MRCR	14		25000	2	4	41300	45900
58		STARDUST-CRUISER	HT	HB	STL	SV	IO	330	MRCR	14		30000	2	8	39700	44100
58		STARDUST-CRUISER	HT	HB	AL	SV	IO	130D	CHRY	14		25000	2	4	41400	45900
58		STARDUST-CRUISER	HT	HB	STL	SV	IO	130D	CHRY	14		30000	2	8	39800	44200
58		STARDUST-CRUISER	HT	HB	AL	SV	IO	130D	VLVO	14		25000	2	4	40500	44900
58		STARDUST-CRUISER	HT	HB	STL	SV	IO	130D	VLVO	14		30000	2	8	39500	43900
58		STARDUST-CRUISER	HT	HB	AL	SV	VD	200D	CHRY	14		25000	2	4	39900	44300
58		STARDUST-CRUISER	HT	HB	STL	SV	VD	200D	CHRY	14		30000	2	8	38900	43200
58		STARDUST-CRUISER	HT	HB	AL	SV	VD	200D	VLVO	14		25000	2	4	39500	43900
58		STARDUST-CRUISER	HT	HB	STL	SV	VD	200D	VLVO	14		30000	2	8	38300	42600
58		STARDUST-CRUISER	HT	HB	AL	SV	IB	T260		14		25000			39000	43300
58		STARDUST-CRUISER	HT	HB	STL	SV	IB	T260		14		30000			37500	41700
58		STARDUST-CRUISER	FB	HB	AL	SV	IO	120	VLVO	14		25000	2	4	39400	43700
58		STARDUST-CRUISER	FB	HB	STL	SV	IO	120	VLVO	14		30000	2	8	38300	42500
58		STARDUST-CRUISER	FB	HB	AL	SV	IO	165	MRCR	14		25000	2	4	39100	43400
58		STARDUST-CRUISER	FB	HB	STL	SV	IO	165	MRCR	14		30000	2	8	38000	42200
58		STARDUST-CRUISER	FB	HB	AL	SV	IO	200	VLVO	14		25000	2	4	39500	43900
58		STARDUST-CRUISER	FB	HB	STL	SV	IO	200	VLVO	14		30000	2	8	38500	42700
58		STARDUST-CRUISER	FB	HB	AL	SV	IO	225	VLVO	14		25000	2	4	39600	44000
58		STARDUST-CRUISER	FB	HB	STL	SV	IO	225	VLVO	14		30000	2	8	38600	42900
58		STARDUST-CRUISER	FB	HB	AL	SV	IO	228	MRCR	14		25000	2	4	39300	43700
58		STARDUST-CRUISER	FB	HB	STL	SV	IO	228	MRCR	14		30000	2	8	38300	42500
58		STARDUST-CRUISER	FB	HB	AL	SV	IO	260	VLVO	14		25000	2	4	39900	44400
58		STARDUST-CRUISER	FB	HB	STL	SV	IO	260	VLVO	14		30000	2	8	39000	43300
58		STARDUST-CRUISER	FB	HB	AL	SV	VD	260	MRCR	14		25000	2	4	37000	41100
58		STARDUST-CRUISER	FB	HB	STL	SV	VD	260	MRCR	14		30000	2	8	36000	40000
58		STARDUST-CRUISER	FB	HB	AL	SV	VD	260	OMC	14		25000	2	4	37400	41600
58		STARDUST-CRUISER	FB	HB	STL	SV	VD	260	OMC	14		30000	2	8	36400	40400
58		STARDUST-CRUISER	FB	HB	AL	SV	VD	325	OMC	14		25000	2	4	38200	42400
58		STARDUST-CRUISER	FB	HB	STL	SV	VD	325	OMC	14		30000	2	8	36800	40900
58		STARDUST-CRUISER	FB	HB	AL	SV	IO	330	MRCR	14		25000	2	4	41300	45900
58		STARDUST-CRUISER	FB	HB	STL	SV	IO	330	MRCR	14		30000	2	8	39700	44100
58		STARDUST-CRUISER	FB	HB	AL	SV	IO	130D	CHRY	14		25000	2	4	41400	45900
58		STARDUST-CRUISER	FB	HB	STL	SV	IO	130D	CHRY	14		30000	2	8	39800	44200
58		STARDUST-CRUISER	FB	HB	AL	SV	IO	130D	VLVO	14		25000	2	4	40500	44900
58		STARDUST-CRUISER	FB	HB	STL	SV	IO	130D	VLVO	14		30000	2	8	39500	43900
58		STARDUST-CRUISER	FB	HB	STL	SV	IO	200D	CHRY	14		30000	2	8	40500	45000
58		STARDUST-CRUISER	FB	HB	STL	SV	IO	200D	VLVO	14		30000	2	8	40000	44400
58		STARDUST-CRUISER	FB	HB	AL	SV	VD	200D	CHRY	14		25000	2	4	39900	44300
58		STARDUST-CRUISER	FB	HB	AL	SV	VD	200D	VLVO	14		25000	2	4	39500	43900
58		STARDUST-CRUISER	FB	HB	AL	SV	IB	T260		14		25000			39000	43300
58		STARDUST-CRUISER	FB	HB	STL	SV	IB	T260		14		30000			37500	41700
		1978 BOATS														
36		SILVER-QUEEN 36	HT	HB	FBG	SV	IO	120		12					16000	18200
		IO 140 MRCR 16000 18200, IO 140 OMC 16000 18100, IO 140 VLVO 16300 18500														
		IO 165 MRCR 16000 18200, IO 185 OMC 16000 18200, IO 200 VLVO 16400 18700														
		IO 225 OMC 16200 18400, IO 228 MRCR 16200 18500, IO 255 MRCR 16400 18700														
		VD 255 MRCR 16800 19100, VD 260 OMC 17200 19500														
36		SILVER-QUEEN 36	FB	HB	FBG	SV	IO	120		12					16000	18200
		IO 140 MRCR 16000 18200, IO 140 OMC 16000 18100, IO 140 VLVO 16300 18500														
		IO 165 MRCR 16000 18200, IO 185 OMC 16000 18200, IO 200 VLVO 16400 18700														
		IO 225 OMC 16200 18400, IO 228 MRCR 16200 18500, IO 255 MRCR 16400 18700														
		VD 255 MRCR 16800 19100, VD 260 OMC 17200 19500														
42		STARDUST-CRUISER	HT	HB	STL	SV	IO	120		12					15200	17300
		IO 140 MRCR 15200 17300, IO 140 OMC 15200 17200, IO 140 VLVO 15400 17500														
		IO 165 MRCR 15200 17300, IO 185 OMC 15200 17300, IO 200 VLVO 15500 17700														
		IO 225 OMC 15300 17400, IO 228 MRCR 15400 17500, IO 255 MRCR 15600 17700														
		VD 255 MRCR 15300 17300, VD 260 OMC 15600 17700														
42		STARDUST-CRUISER	FB	HB	STL	SV	IO	120		12					15200	17300
		IO 140 MRCR 15200 17300, IO 140 OMC 15200 17200, IO 140 VLVO 15400 17500														
		IO 165 MRCR 15200 17300, IO 185 OMC 15200 17300, IO 200 VLVO 15500 17700														
		IO 225 OMC 15300 17400, IO 228 MRCR 15400 17500, IO 255 MRCR 15600 17700														
		VD 255 MRCR 15300 17300, VD 260 OMC 15600 17700														
46		SILVER-QUEEN 46	HT	HB	FBG	SV	IO	120		14					23300	25900
		IO 140 MRCR 23400 25900, IO 140 OMC 23300 25900, IO 140 VLVO 23600 26300														
		IO 165 MRCR 23400 26000, IO 185 OMC 23400 26000, IO 200 VLVO 23800 26400														
		IO 225 OMC 23500 26100, IO 228 MRCR 23600 26200, IO 255 MRCR 23800 26400														
		VD 255 MRCR 22400 24800, VD 260 OMC 22700 25200														
46		SILVER-QUEEN 46	FB	HB	FBG	SV	IO	120		14					23300	25900
		IO 140 MRCR 23400 25900, IO 140 OMC 23300 25900, IO 140 VLVO 23600 26300														
		IO 165 MRCR 23400 26000, IO 185 OMC 23400 26000, IO 200 VLVO 23800 26400														
		IO 225 OMC 23500 26100, IO 228 MRCR 23600 26200, IO 255 MRCR 23800 26400														
		VD 255 MRCR 22400 24800, VD 260 OMC 22700 25200														
46		STARDUST-CRUISER	HT	HB	STL	SV	IO	120		13					21700	24100
		IO 140 MRCR 21700 24100, IO 140 OMC 21600 24000, IO 140 VLVO 22000 24400														
		IO 165 MRCR 21700 24100, IO 185 OMC 21700 24100, IO 200 VLVO 22100 24500														
		IO 225 OMC 21800 24300, IO 228 MRCR 21900 24400, IO 255 MRCR 22100 24600														
		VD 255 MRCR 20900 23200, VD 260 OMC 21200 23600														
46		STARDUST-CRUISER	FB	HB	STL	SV	IO	120		13					21700	24100
		IO 140 MRCR 21700 24100, IO 140 OMC 21600 24000, IO 140 VLVO 22000 24400														
		IO 165 MRCR 21700 24100, IO 185 OMC 21700 24100, IO 200 VLVO 22100 24500														
		IO 225 OMC 21800 24300, IO 228 MRCR 21900 24400, IO 255 MRCR 22100 24600														
		VD 255 MRCR 20900 23200, VD 260 OMC 21200 23600														
53		STARDUST-CRUISER	HT	HB	STL	SV	IO	120		14					30600	34000
		IO 140 MRCR 30600 34000, IO 140 OMC 30500 33900, IO 140 VLVO 30900 34400														
		IO 165 MRCR 30600 34000, IO 185 OMC 30600 34000, IO 200 VLVO 31100 34500														
		IO 225 OMC 30800 34200, IO 228 MRCR 30900 34300, IO 255 MRCR 31100 34600														
		VD 255 MRCR 29300 32500, VD 260 OMC 29600 32900														
53		STARDUST-CRUISER	FB	HB	STL	SV	IO	120		14					30600	34000
		IO 140 MRCR 30600 34000, IO 140 OMC 30500 33900, IO 140 VLVO 30900 34400														
		IO 165 MRCR 30600 34000, IO 185 OMC 30600 34000, IO 200 VLVO 31100 34500														
		IO 225 OMC 30800 34200, IO 228 MRCR 30900 34300, IO 255 MRCR 31100 34600														
		VD 255 MRCR 29300 32500, VD 260 OMC 29600 32900														
58		STARDUST-CRUISER	HT	HB	STL	SV	IO	120		14					35900	39900
		IO 140 MRCR 35900 39900, IO 140 OMC 35800 39800, IO 140 VLVO 36200 40200														
		IO 165 MRCR 35900 39900, IO 185 OMC 35900 39900, IO 200 VLVO 36400 40400														
		IO 225 OMC 36100 40100, IO 228 MRCR 36200 40200, IO 255 MRCR 36400 40400														
		VD 255 MRCR 34300 38100, VD 260 OMC 34700 38500														
58		STARDUST-CRUISER	FB	HB	STL	SV	IO	120		14					35900	39900
		IO 140 MRCR 35900 39900, IO 140 OMC 35800 39800, IO 140 VLVO 36200 40200														
		IO 165 MRCR 35900 39900, IO 185 OMC 35900 39900, IO 200 VLVO 36400 40400														
		IO 225 OMC 36100 40100, IO 228 MRCR 36200 40200, IO 255 MRCR 36400 40400														
		VD 255 MRCR 34300 38100, VD 260 OMC 34700 38500														
		1977 BOATS														
36		STARDUST-CRUISER	HT	HB	STL	SV	IO	120		11					13800	15600
43		STARDUST-CRUISER	HT	HB	STL	SV	IO	140	OMC	12		12500			13700	15600
		IO 170 MRCR 13800 15700, IO 175 OMC 13700 15600, IO 188 MRCR 13800 15700														
		IO 233 MRCR 14000 15900, IO 235 OMC 13900 15800, IO 255 MRCR 14100 16000														
		VD 260 OMC 14000 15900														
43		STARDUST-CRUISER	FB	HB	STL	SV	IO	140	OMC	12		12500			13700	15600
		IO 170 MRCR 13800 15700, IO 175 OMC 13700 15600, IO 188 MRCR 13800 15700														
		IO 233 MRCR 14000 15900, IO 235 OMC 13900 15800, IO 255 MRCR 14100 16000														
		VD 260 OMC 14000 15900														
44	6	STARDUST-CRUISER	HT	HB	STL	SV	IO	140	OMC	13		17500	1	1	19800	22000
		IO 170 MRCR 19900 22100, IO 175 OMC 19800 22000, IO 188 MRCR 19900 22100														
		IO 233 MRCR 20100 22300, IO 235 OMC 20000 22300, IO 255 MRCR 20200 22500														
		VD 260 OMC 19800 22000														
44	6	STARDUST-CRUISER	FB	HB	STL	SV	IO	140	OMC	13		17500	1	1	19800	22000
		IO 170 MRCR 19900 22100, IO 175 OMC 19800 22000, IO 188 MRCR 19900 22100														
		IO 233 MRCR 20100 22300, IO 235 OMC 20000 22300, IO 255 MRCR 20200 22500														
		VD 260 OMC 19800 22000														
51	6	STARDUST-CRUISER	HT	HB	STL	SV	IO	140	OMC	14		23930	1	3	25800	28700
		IO 170 MRCR 25900 28800, IO 175 OMC 25800 28700, IO 188 MRCR 25900 28800														
		IO 233 MRCR 26100 29000, IO 235 OMC 26100 28900, IO 255 MRCR 26300 29200														
		VD 260 OMC 25200 28000														
51	6	STARDUST-CRUISER	FB	HB	STL	SV	IO	140	OMC	14		23930	1	3	25800	28700
		IO 170 MRCR 25900 28800, IO 175 OMC 25800 28700, IO 188 MRCR 25900 28800														
		IO 233 MRCR 26100 29000, IO 235 OMC 26100 28900, IO 255 MRCR 26300 29200														
		VD 260 OMC 26800 29700														
53		STARDUST-CRUISER	HT	HB	STL	DV	IO	260		13					32200	35700
58		STARDUST-CRUISER	HT	HB	STL	SV	IO	140	OMC	14		28000	1	3	35800	39800
		IO 170 MRCR 35900 39900, IO 175 OMC 35900 39800, IO 188 MRCR 36000 39900														
		IO 233 MRCR 36200 40200, IO 235 OMC 36100 40100, IO 255 MRCR 36400 40400														

CONTINUED ON NEXT PAGE

```
  LOA  NAME AND/            TOP/ BOAT  -HULL- ----ENGINE--- BEAM   WGT  DRAFT RETAIL RETAIL
  FT IN OR MODEL            RIG  TYPE  MTL TP TP # HP  MFG  FT IN  LBS  FT IN  LOW   HIGH
-------------------- 1977 BOATS --------------------------------------------------------
  58   STARDUST-CRUISER     HT  HB    STL SV VD 260 OMC  14    28000 1 3   34700  38500
  58   STARDUST-CRUISER     FB  HB    STL SV IO 140 OMC  14    28000 1 3   35800  39800
       IO 170 MRCR  35900   39900, IO 175 OMC  35900 39800, IO 188 MRCR  36000  39900
       IO 233 MRCR  36200   40200, IO 235 OMC  36100 40100, IO 255 MRCR  36400  40400
       VD 260 OMC   34700   38500
-------------------- 1976 BOATS --------------------------------------------------------
  36   STARDUST-CRUISER     HT  HB    STL SV IO 120      11          13600  15500
  42   STARDUST-CRUISER     HT  HB    STL SV IO 165 MRCR 12    13000 2     14000  16000
       IO 165 OMC   14000   15900, IO 175 OMC  14000 15900, IO 188 MRCR  14100  16000
       IO 225 OMC   14100   16100, IO 233 MRCR 14200 16200, IO 255 MRCR  14400  16300
       VD 260 OMC   14400   16300
  42   STARDUST-CRUISER     FB  HB    STL SV IO 165 MRCR 12    13000 2     14000  16000
       IO 165 OMC   14000   15900, IO 175 OMC  14000 15900, IO 188 MRCR  14100  16000
       IO 225 OMC   14100   16100, IO 233 MRCR 14200 16200, IO 255 MRCR  14400  16300
       VD 260 OMC   14400   16300
  47   STARDUST-CRUISER     HT  HB    STL SV IO 165 MRCR 12    14000 2 6   17500  19900
       IO 165 OMC   17400   19800, IO 175 OMC  17400 19800, IO 188 MRCR  17500  19900
       IO 225 OMC   17600   20000, IO 233 MRCR 18100 20100, IO 255 MRCR  18300  20300
       VD 260 OMC   17200   19500
  47   STARDUST-CRUISER     FB  HB    STL SV IO 165 MRCR 12    14000 2 6   17500  19900
       IO 165 OMC   17400   19800, IO 175 OMC  17400 19800, IO 188 MRCR  17500  19900
       IO 225 OMC   17600   20000, IO 233 MRCR 18100 20100, IO 255 MRCR  18300  20300
       IO 260 OMC   18200   20300
  50   STARDUST-CRUISER     HT  HB    STL SV IO T165 MRCR 14   20000 2 6   24400  27100
       IO T165 OMC  24300   27000, IO T175 OMC  24300 27000, IO T188 MRCR 24400  27200
       IO T225 OMC  24600   27300, IO T233 MRCR 24800 27600, IO T255 MRCR 25100  27900
       VD T260 OMC  24100   26800
  50   STARDUST-CRUISER     FB  HB    STL SV IO T165 MRCR 14   20000 2 6   24400  27100
       IO T165 OMC  24300   27000, IO T175 OMC  24300 27000, IO T188 MRCR 24400  27200
       IO T225 OMC  24600   27300, IO T233 MRCR 24800 27600, IO T255 MRCR 25100  27900
       VD T260 OMC  24100   26800
  53   STARDUST-CRUISER     HT  HB    STL SV IO T165 MRCR 13   18000 2 6   29300  32600
       IO T165 OMC  29200   32500, IO T175 OMC  29300 32500, IO T188 MRCR 29500  32700
       IO T225 OMC  29600   32900, IO T233 MRCR 29900 33200, IO T255 MRCR 30300  33600
       VD T260 OMC  28800   32000
  53   STARDUST-CRUISER     FB  HB    STL SV IO T165 MRCR 13   18000 2 6   29300  32600
       IO T165 OMC  29200   32500, IO T175 OMC  29300 32500, IO T188 MRCR 29500  32700
       IO T225 OMC  29600   32900, IO T233 MRCR 29900 33200, IO T255 MRCR 30300  33600
       VD T260 OMC  28800   32000
  58   STARDUST-CRUISER     HT  HB    STL SV IO T165 MRCR 14   24000 2 6   35100  39000
       IO T165 MRCR 34000   37800, IO T165 OMC  35000 38900, IO T165 OMC  33900  37600
       IO T175 OMC  35000   38900, IO T175 OMC  33900 37700, IO T188 MRCR 35200  39100
       IO T188 OMC  34100   37900, IO T225 OMC  35400 39300, IO T225 OMC  34300  38100
       IO T233 MRCR 35600   39600, IO T233 MRCR 34500 38400, IO T255 MRCR 36000  40000
       IO T255 MRCR 34900   38800, VD T260 OMC  34300 38100, VD T260 OMC  33200  36900
  58   STARDUST-CRUISER     FB  HB    STL SV IO T165 MRCR 14   24000 2 6   35100  39000
       IO T165 MRCR 34000   37800, IO T165 OMC  35000 38900, IO T165 OMC  33900  37600
       IO T175 OMC  35000   38900, IO T175 OMC  33900 37700, IO T188 MRCR 35200  39100
       IO T188 OMC  34100   37900, IO T225 OMC  35400 39300, IO T225 OMC  34300  38100
       IO T233 MRCR 35600   39600, IO T233 MRCR 34500 38400, IO T255 MRCR 36000  40000
       IO T255 MRCR 34900   38800, VD T260 OMC  34300 38100, IO T260 OMC  33200  36900
-------------------- 1975 BOATS --------------------------------------------------------
  36   STARDUST CRUISER     HT  HB    STL SV OB       11    6500        7800   8950
       IO 120 MRCR  9000    10200, IO 120 OMC  9000 10200, IO 165 MRCR  9050  10300
       IO 165 OMC   9000    10200, IO 170 OMC  9000 10200, IO 225 CHRY  9200  10500
       IO 225 MRCR  9200    10500, IO 225 OMC  9150 10400, VD 250 OMC   9500  10800
  42   STARDUST CRUISER     HT  HB    STL SV OB       12    16000       14500  16500
       IO 120 MRCR  15900   18100, IO 120 OMC  15900 18100, IO 165 MRCR 16000  18100
       IO 165 OMC   15900   18100, IO 170 OMC  15900 18100, IO 225 CHRY 16300  18500
       IO 225 MRCR  16300   18500, IO 225 OMC  16200 18400, VD 250 OMC  16400  18600
  47   STARDUST CRUISER     HT  HB    STL SV OB       12    19000       19300  21400
       IO 120 MRCR  21200   23500, IO 120 OMC  21100 23500, IO 165 MRCR 21200  23600
       IO 165 OMC   21200   23500, IO 170 OMC  21200 23500, IO 225 CHRY 21400  23800
       IO 225 MRCR  21400   23800, IO 225 OMC  21300 23700, VD 250 OMC  20700  23000
  53   STARDUST CRUISER     HT  HB    STL SV OB       13    24000       28300  31500
       IO 120 MRCR  31300   34700, IO 120 OMC  31200 34700, IO 165 MRCR 31300  34800
       IO 165 OMC   31200   34700, IO 170 OMC  31300 34700, IO 225 CHRY 31500  35000
       IO 225 MRCR  31500   35000, IO 225 OMC  31400 34900, VD 250 OMC  30300  33600
  58   STARDUST CRUISER     HT  HB    STL SV OB       15    36000       34500  38400
       IO 120 MRCR  35400   39400, IO 120 OMC  38000 42300, IO 165 MRCR 35500  39400
       IO 165 OMC   35400   39400, IO 170 OMC  38000 42300, IO 225 CHRY 35700  39700
       IO 225 MRCR  38300   40700, IO 225 OMC  35600 39600, VD 250 OMC  36400  40500
-------------------- 1974 BOATS --------------------------------------------------------
  34   STARDUST             HT  HB    FBG   OB        12    8000  1     12200  13900
  34   STARDUST             HT  HB    FBG IO 120 MRCR 12    8000  1     14200  16100
  40   STARDUST             HT  HB    STL   OB        11    9000     11  9700   11000
  40   STARDUST             HT  HB    STL IO 120 MRCR 11    9000     11  11100  12600
  40   STARDUST             HT  HB    STL IO 225      11    9000     11  11300  12800
  42   STARDUST             HT  HB    FBG   OB        12    14000 1     15200  17300
  42   STARDUST             HT  HB    STL   OB        11    10000  1    12000  11500
  42   STARDUST             HT  HB    FBG IO 120 MRCR 12    10000 1     17300  17900
  42   STARDUST             HT  HB    STL IO 120      11    10000     11 11600  13200
  45   STARDUST             HT  HB    STL   OB        11    10000 1     15200  17300
  45   STARDUST             HT  HB    STL IO 120 MRCR 12    14000     11 17100  19400
  45   STARDUST             HT  HB    STL IO 225      12    14000     11 17300  19700
  47   STARDUST             HT  HB    STL   OB        12    14000     11 15700  17800
  47   STARDUST             HT  HB    STL IO 120 MRCR 12    14000     11 18200  20200
  52   STARDUST             HT  HB    FBG   OB        12    20000 1     28800  32000
  52   STARDUST             HT  HB    FBG IO 120 MRCR 12    20000 1     31900  35500
  52   STARDUST             HT  HB    FBG IO T275     12    20000 1     35200  39100
  53   STARDUST             HT  HB    STL   OB        13    18000     11 25600  28500
  53   STARDUST             HT  HB    STL IO 120 MRCR 13    18000     11 28500  31600
  53   STARDUST             HT  HB    STL IO 225      13    18000     11 28700  31900
  58   STARDUST             HT  HB    STL   OB        15    22000     11 30100  33500
  58   STARDUST             HT  HB    STL IO 120 MRCR 15    22000     11 33200  36900
  58   STARDUST             HT  HB    STL IO T245     15    22000     11 35500  39500
-------------------- 1973 BOATS --------------------------------------------------------
  40   STARDUST             HT  HB    STL   OB        11    8000        8450   9700
       IO 120 MRCR  9850    11200, IO 120 OMC  9800 11100, IO 165 MRCR  9900  11200
       IO 188 MRCR  9900    11300, IO 225 MRCR 10000 11400, IO 225 OMC  10000  11300
       IO 245 OMC   10100   11500
  40   STARDUST             FB  HB    FBG   OB        11                10900  12300
       IO 120 MRCR  12500   14300, IO 120 OMC  12500 14200, IO 165 MRCR 12600  14300
       IO 188 MRCR  12600   14300, IO 225 MRCR 12800 14500, IO 225 OMC  12700  14400
       IO 245 OMC   12800   14600
  44   STARDUST             HT  CR    STL IO 188 MRCR 12    12000       33300  37000
  44   STARDUST             HT  HB    STL   OB        12    12000       13000  14800
       IO 120 MRCR  14800   16900, IO 120 OMC  14800 16800, IO 165 MRCR 14900  16900
       IO 225 MRCR  15000   17100, IO 225 OMC  15000 17000, IO 245 OMC   15100  17200
  44   STARDUST             HT  HB    STL   OB        12                14900  16900
       IO 120 MRCR  15300   17400, IO 120 OMC  15300 17400, IO 165 MRCR 15400  17500
       IO 188 MRCR  15400   17600, IO 245 OMC  15400 17500, IO 225 OMC   15500  17600
  52   STARDUST             HT  HB    STL   OB        13    16000       23400  26000
       IO 120 MRCR  26100   29000, IO 120 OMC  26000 28900, IO 165 MRCR 26100  29000
       IO 188 MRCR  26200   29100, IO 225 MRCR 26300 29300, IO 225 OMC   26300  29200
       IO 245 OMC   26400   29300
  52   STARDUST             HT  HB    FBG DV OB       12                28500  31700
       IO 120 MRCR  34000   37800, IO 120 OMC  34000 37700, IO 165 MRCR 34100  37900
       IO 188 MRCR  34100   37900, IO 225 MRCR 34300 38100, IO 225 OMC   34200  38000
       IO 245 OMC   34400   38200
  52   STARDUST             FB  HB    STL   OB        13                26400  29300
       IO 120 MRCR  31500   35000, IO 120 OMC  31400 34900, IO 165 MRCR 31500  35000
       IO 188 MRCR  31600   35100, IO 225 MRCR 31700 35300, IO 225 OMC   31700  35200
       IO 245 OMC   31800   35300
  52   STARDUST             FB  HB    FBG DV OB       12                28500  31700
       IO 120 MRCR  34000   37800, IO 120 OMC  34000 37700, IO 165 MRCR 34100  37900
       IO 188 MRCR  34100   37900, IO 225 MRCR 34300 38100, IO 225 OMC   34200  38000
       IO 245 OMC   34400   38200
  57   STARDUST 57          HT  HB    STL   OB        13    20000       28300  31400
       IO 120 MRCR  31200   34700, IO 120 OMC  31200 34600, IO 165 MRCR 31300  34700
```

STARDUST CRUISER MFG CO   -CONTINUED   See inside cover to adjust price for area

```
       LOA  NAME AND/          TOP/ BOAT  -HULL-  ----ENGINE---   BEAM    WGT  DRAFT  RETAIL RETAIL
       FT IN OR MODEL          RIG  TYPE  MTL TP TP # HP  MFG     FT IN   LBS  FT IN   LOW   HIGH
------------------- 1973 BOATS -------
57    STARDUST 57              HT  HB   STL   IO  188 MRCR 13      20000         31300 34800
      IO 225 MRCR 31500 35000, IO 225 OMC  31400 34900, IO 245       OMC        31600 35100

57    STARDUST 57              FB  HB   STL   OB       13                        32700 36400
      IO 120 MRCR 35100 39000, IO 120 OMC  35000 38900, IO 165 MRCR             35100 39000
      IO 188 MRCR 35200 39100, IO 225 MRCR 35300 39300, IO 225 OMC              35300 39200
      IO 245 OMC  35400 39400
------------------- 1972 BOATS -------
34                             HT  HB   STL SV IO 120     12            11100 12600
40                             HT  HB   STL SV IO 225     12            10600 12100
42                             HT  HB   STL SV IO 225     12            14300 16300
50                             HT  HB   STL SV IO T225    13            23800 26400
52                             HT  HB   FBG SV IO T270    12            35200 39100
57                             HT  HB   STL SV IO T245    13            35400 39400
------------------- 1971 BOATS -------
34    STARDUST                 HT  HB   STL   OB         11    8000  2 10 10200 11500
34    STARDUST                 HT  HB   FBG   IO  215 OMC 12  12000  2 10 19300 21500
40    STARDUST 40              HT  HB   STL   OB         11   10000  2 10 10400 11800
      IO 120 MRCR 10800 12300, IO 120 OMC  10700 12200, IO 165 MRCR        10800 12300
      IO 215 MRCR 10900 12400, IO 215 OMC  10900 12400, IO 270 MRCR        11300 12800

41    STARDUST                 HT  HB   STL   OB         11   10000  2 10 10100 11500
42    STARDUST 42              HT  HB   FBG   IO         12   16000  2 10 16400 18600
      IO 120 MRCR 16800 19100, IO 120 OMC  16700 19000, IO 165 MRCR        16800 19100
      IO 215 MRCR 17000 19300, IO 215 OMC  16900 19200, IO 270 MRCR        17400 19700

50    STARDUST 50              HT  HB   STL   OB         12   12000  2 10 14400 16400
      IO 120 MRCR 16500 18800, IO 120 OMC  16500 18700, IO 165 MRCR        16500 18800
      IO 215 MRCR 16700 18900, IO 215 OMC  16600 18900, IO 270 MRCR        17100 19400

52    STARDUST 52              HT  HB   FBG   IO         12   20000  2 10 28000 31100
      IO 120 MRCR 33400 37200, IO 120 OMC  33400 37100, IO 165 MRCR        33500 37200
      IO 215 MRCR 33700 37400, IO 215 OMC  33600 37300, IO 270 MRCR        34200 38000
------------------- 1970 BOATS -------
34                             HT  HB   STL   OB    210               1   10100 11400
34                             HT  HB   STL   IO    210               1   11800 13400
40                             HT  HB   STL   OB         11    6000        5650  6500
      IO             6950 8000, IO 120 MRCR 6850 7850, IO 120     OMC       6800  7800
      IO 160 MRCR 6850 7900, IO 210 OMC  6900 7950, IO 225     CHRY        7000  8050
      IO 250 MRCR 7200 8250, IO T120 MRCR 7900 9100, IO T120    OMC        7800  8950
      IO T160 MRCR 7950 9150, IO T210 OMC  8100 9300, IO T225   CHRY       8300  9550
      IO T250 MRCR 8600 9850

42                             HT  HB   FBG DV IO        12            16800 19100
      IO 120 MRCR 16700 18900, IO 120 OMC  16600 18900, IO 160 MRCR        16700 19000
      IO 210 OMC  16800 19000, IO 225 CHRY 16900 19200, IO 250 MRCR        17000 19400
      IO T120 MRCR 18300 20300, IO T120 OMC 18200 20200, IO T160 MRCR       18300 20400
      IO T210 OMC  18500 20500, IO T225 CHRY 18700 20800, IO T250 MRCR      19100 21200

50                             HT  HB   STL   IO        12            22900 25500
      IO 120 MRCR 22800 25300, IO 120 OMC  22700 25300, IO 160 MRCR        22800 25400
      IO 210 OMC  22900 25400, IO 225 CHRY 23000 25600, IO 250 MRCR        23200 25700
      IO T160 MRCR 24000 26700, IO T210 MRCR 24300 27000, IO T210 OMC       24200 26800
      IO T225 CHRY 24400 27100, IO T250                 27500

50                             HT  HB   STL DV IO       12            22900 25500
      IO 120 MRCR 22800 25300, IO 120 OMC  22700 25300, IO 160 MRCR        22800 25400
      IO 210 OMC  22900 25400, IO 225 CHRY 23000 25600, IO 250 MRCR        23200 25700
      IO T120 MRCR 24000 26600, IO T120 OMC 23900 26500, IO T160 MRCR       24000 26600
      IO T210 OMC  24200 26800, IO T225 CHRY 24400 27100, IO T250 MRCR      24700 27500

52                             HT  HB   FBG DV IO       12            33300 37000
      IO 120 MRCR 33200 36900, IO 120 OMC  33100 36800, IO 160 MRCR        33200 36900
      IO 210 OMC  33300 37000, IO 225 CHRY 33400 37200, IO 250 MRCR        33700 37400
      IO T120 MRCR 34700 38600, IO T120 OMC 34600 38400, IO T160 MRCR       34800 38700
      IO T210 OMC  35000 38800, IO T225 CHRY 35300 39200, IO T250 MRCR      35700 39700
------------------- 1969 BOATS -------
32    LAKE-CRAFT               HT  HB   STL   OB          8             4650  5300
40    STARDUST                 HT  HB   STL   OB          8             9350 10600
42    STARDUST                 HT  HB   FBG   IO 120      9 6          16500 18800
42    STARDUST                 HT  HB   STL   IO 120      9 6          14600 16600
50    STARDUST                 HT  HB   STL   IO 120      9 6          22600 25100
------------------- 1968 BOATS -------
40    STARDUST                 HT  HB   STL DV IO         8        1 8 10700 12100
40    STARDUST                 HT  HB   STL   IO          8        1 8 10700 12100
40    STARDUSY                 HT  HB   STL   OB          8        1 8  9300 10500
50    STARDUST                 HT  HB   STL   IO         10        3   22600 25100
50    STARDUST                 HT  HB   STL DV IO        10        3   22600 25100
------------------- 1967 BOATS -------
40    STARDUST 40              HT  HB   STL   OB         11        1 8  9200 10500
42    STARDUST 42              HT  HB   STL   OB         12        3   12400 14000
50    STARDUST 50              HT  HB   STL   OB         12        3   17200 19600
------------------- 1966 BOATS -------
40    STARDUST 40              HT  HB   STL   OB         11        2 6  9150 10400
50    STARDUST 50              HT  HB   STL   OB         13        2 6 17100 19400
```

STARFIRE BOATS
WEST JORDAN UT 84088   COAST GUARD MFG ID- SRF See inside cover to adjust price for area

For more recent years, see the BUC Used Boat Price Guide, Volume 1 or Volume 2

```
       LOA  NAME AND/          TOP/ BOAT  -HULL-  ----ENGINE---   BEAM   WGT  DRAFT RETAIL RETAIL
       FT IN OR MODEL          RIG  TYPE  MTL TP TP # HP   MFG    FT IN  LBS  FT IN  LOW   HIGH
------------------- 1983 BOATS -------
17  4 LAGUNA 174        ST RNBT FBG DV IO 120-185   6 2 2100         2950  3700
17  4 MALIBU 174        ST RNBT FBG DV IO 120-185   6 2 2100         2800  3500
18  3 MONTEREY 183      ST RNBT F/S DV IO 170-200   7 6 2450         3550  4350
18  3 MONTEREY 183      ST RNBT F/S DV IO 225-260   7 6 2450         3850  4700
18  3 NEWPORT 183       ST RNBT F/S DV IO 170-200   7 6 2450         3700  4600
18  3 NEWPORT 183       ST RNBT F/S DV IO 225-260   7 6 2450         4000  4900
18  3 SPORTSTER 183     ST RNBT F/S DV IO 170-230   7 6 2450         3950  4950
18  3 SPORTSTER 183     ST RNBT F/S DV IO 260       7 6 2450         4200  5150
19  4 DEL-REY 194       ST RNBT F/S DV IO 170-230   7 7 2600         4100  5100
19  4 DEL-REY 194       ST RNBT F/S DV IO 260       7 7 2600         4400  5350
19  4 SALTAIRE 194      ST RNBT F/S DV IO 170-230   7 7 2600         4150  5150
19  4 SALTAIRE 194      ST RNBT F/S DV IO 260       7 7 2600         4450  5400

19  4 SKYLINER          HT RNBT F/S DV IO 170-230   7 7 2750         4250  5300
19  4 SKYLINER          HT RNBT F/S DV IO 260       7 7 2750         4550  5500
20  7 FISHERMAN 207     ST CUD  F/S DV IO 198-260   7 11 3600        6150  7700
20  7 FISHERMAN 207     ST CUD  F/S DV IO T170-T185 7 11 3600        6300  7850
20  7 FISHERMAN 207     HT CUD  F/S DV IO 198-260   7 11 3600        7000  8500
20  7 FISHERMAN 207     HT CUD  F/S DV IO T170-T185 7 11 3600        7150  8700
20  7 NEW-YORKER 207    ST CUD  F/S DV IO 198-230   7 11 3400        5900  7150
20  7 NEW-YORKER 207    ST CUD  F/S DV IO 260       7 11 3400        6200  7400
20  7 NEW-YORKER 207    ST CUD  F/S DV IO T170-T185 7 11 3400        6350  7600
20  7 NEW-YORKER 207    HT CUD  F/S DV IO 198-260   7 11 3400        6700  8200
20  7 NEW-YORKER 207    HT CUD  F/S DV IO 260       7 11 3400        6800  8300
21  2 SANTA CRUZ 212    ST CUD  F/S DV IO 225-260   8   3800         6950  8250

21  2 SANTA CRUZ 212    HT CUD  F/S DV IO 225-260   8   4000         7200  8550
24  1 ENTERTAINER 241   ST CUD  F/S DV IO 225-260   8   4600         9400 10900
24  1 ENTERTAINER 241   ST CUD  F/S DV IO T170-T230 8   4600        10100 12000
24  1 ENTERTAINER 241   ST CUD  F/S DV IO T260      8   4600        10700 12800
24  1 ENTERTAINER 241   HT CUD  F/S DV IO 225-260   8   4800         9450 10900
24  1 ENTERTAINER 241   HT CUD  F/S DV IO T170-T230 8   4800         9950 12300
24  1 ENTERTAINER 241   HT CUD  F/S DV IO T260      8   4800        10800 12800
24  1 FISHERMAN 241     ST CUD  F/S DV IO 225-260   8   4800         9650 11200
24  1 FISHERMAN 241     ST CUD  F/S DV IO T170-T230 8   4800        10400 12600
24  1 FISHERMAN 241     ST CUD  F/S DV IO T260      8   4800        11000 13100
24  1 FISHERMAN 241     HT CUD  F/S DV IO 225-260   8   4800         9800 11500
24  1 FISHERMAN 241     HT CUD  F/S DV IO T170-T260 8   4800        10800 13400
------------------- 1982 BOATS -------
17  4 MALIBU 174           RNBT FBG DV IO 140       7    2100        3000  3500
18  3 MONTEREY 183 B/R     RNBT FBG DV IO 228       7 5  2600        3750  4350
19  4 SALTAIRE 194 B/R     RNBT FBG DV IO 228       7 6  2700        4150  4800
20  7 NEW-YORKER 207    ST CUD  FBG DV IO 228       7 11 3700        6150  7100
21  2 SANTA-CRUZ 212    HT CUD  FBG DV IO 228       8    4400        7250  8350
24  1 FISHERMAN 241     ST CUD  FBG DV IO 228       8    5400       10000 11400
------------------- 1981 BOATS -------
17  4 MALIBU 174           RNBT FBG DV IO 140       7    2950  3450
18  3 MONTEREY 183 B/R     RNBT FBG DV IO 228       7 5  3550  4100
19  4 SALTAIRE 194 B/R     RNBT FBG DV IO 228       7 6  4050  4650
20  7 FISHERMAN 207        CUD  FBG DV IO 228       7 11 6200  7100
20  7 NEW-YORKER 207       CUD  FBG DV IO 228       7 11 5850  6700
21  2 SANTA-CRUZ 212       CUD  FBG DV IO 228       8    6200  7150
24  1 ENTERTAINER 241      CUD  FBG DV IO 228       8    8850 10100
------------------- 1980 BOATS -------
17  4 MALIBU 174           RNBT FBG DV IO 140       7    2900  3400
18  3 MONTEREY 183         RNBT FBG DV IO 198       7    3350  4050
19  4 SALTAIRE 194         RNBT FBG DV IO 228       7 6  3950  4600
20  7 FISHERMAN 207     ST CUD  FBG DV IO 228       7 11 6100  7000
20  7 NEW-YORKER 207    ST CUD  FBG DV IO 228       7 11 5800  6650
21  2 SANTA-CRUZ 212    ST CUD  FBG DV IO 228       8    6150  7100
```

```
  LOA  NAME AND/           TOP/ BOAT -HULL- ----ENGINE---   BEAM  WGT  DRAFT RETAIL RETAIL
  FT IN  OR MODEL          RIG  TYPE MTL TP TP # HP   MFG   FT IN LBS  FT IN  LOW    HIGH
---------------------- 1980 BOATS ------------------------------------------------------------
21 2 SANTA-CRUZ 212        HT CUD     DV IO 228          8              6150  7100
24 1 ENTERTAINER 241       ST CUD FBG DV IO 228          8              8450  9750
24 1 FISHERMAN 241         ST CUD FBG DV IO 228          8              8950 10200
---------------------- 1979 BOATS ------------------------------------------------------------
17 4 MALIBU 174            ST RNBT FBG DV IO 140-185   7    2100        2850  3450
17 4 MALIBU 174            ST RNBT FBG DV IO 228        7    2200        3100  3600
18 3 MONTEREY 183          ST RNBT F/S DV IO 200-250   7 5  2600        3600  4400
18 3 MONTEREY 183          ST RNBT F/S DV IO 280        7 5  2600        4000  4650
19 4 DELRAY 194 W/T        ST RNBT F/S DV IO 230-280   7 6  2800        4100  5050
19 4 SALTAIRE 194 B/R      ST RNBT F/S DV IO 230-280   7 6  2700        4000  5000
19 4 SKYLINER 194          HT RNBT F/S DV IO 230        7 6  2900        4200  4850
19 4 SKYLINER 194          HT RNBT F/S DV IO 250-280   7 6  2900        4250  5150
20 7 FISHERMAN 207         ST FSH  F/S DV IO 250   OMC 7 11 3700        6450  7400
20 7 NEW-YORKER 207        ST CUD  F/S DV IO 250   OMC 7 11 3700        6100  7000
20 7 NEW-YORKER 207        ST CUD  F/S DV IO T230      7 11 3700        7000  8050
21 2 SANTA-CRUZ 212        ST CUD  F/S DV IO 230-250   8    4200        6850  7950

21 2 SANTA-CRUZ 212        HT CUD  F/S DV IO 230-250   8    4400        7100  8200
22 8 228V                  HT CR   FBG    IO 250       8                6500  7500
22 8 228V                  HT CR   FBG    IO T230      8                7400  8550
24 1 ENTERTAINER 241       ST CUD  F/S DV IO 250-280   8    5400        9850 11500
24 1 ENTERTAINER 241       ST CUD  F/S DV IO T230-T280 8    6400       12400 14800
24 1 ENTERTAINER 241       HT CUD  F/S DV IO 250-280   8    5600       10200 11900
24 1 ENTERTAINER 241       HT CUD  F/S DV IO T230-T280 8    6600       12700 15200
24 1 FISHERMAN 241         ST FSH  F/S DV IO 250   OMC 8    5400       10700 12100
24 1 FISHERMAN 241         ST FSH  F/S DV IO T230  OMC 8    6400       13500 15300
28   280V                     CR   FBG    IO 370       8               13200 15000
28   280V                     CR   FBG    IO T280      8               14300 16300
---------------------- 1978 BOATS ------------------------------------------------------------
17 4 MALIBU 174            ST RNBT FBG DV IO 185-198   6 11 2100        2900  3450
17 4 MALIBU 174            ST RNBT FBG DV IO 200  VLVO 6 11 2100        3100  3650
18 3 MONTEREY 183 W/T      ST RNBT F/S DV IO 225-240   7 5  2600        3650  4500
19 4 DELRAY 194 W/T        ST RNBT F/S DV IO 225-240   7 6  2700        3900  4600
19 4 SALTAIRE 194 B/R      ST RNBT F/S DV IO 225-240   7 6  2700        4100  4800
19 4 SKYLINER 194          HT RNBT F/S DV IO 225-240   7 6  2900        4150  4900
20 7 NEW-YORKER 207        ST CUD  F/S DV IO 240   OMC 7 11 3700        6050  6950
20 7 NEW-YORKER 207        HT CUD  F/S DV IO 240   OMC 7 11 3900        6300  7250
21 2 OVERNIGHTER 2125      HT OVNTR F/S DV IO 240   OMC 8    4100        6750  7800
21 2 SANTA-CRUZ 212        ST CUD  F/S DV IO 240   OMC 8    4200        6900  7900
24 1 ENTERTAINER 241       ST CUD  F/S DV IO 240   OMC 8    5300        9750 11100
24 1 ENTERTAINER 241       ST CUD  F/S DV IO T140-T240 8    5300       10400 12300

24 1 ENTERTAINER 241       HT CUD  F/S DV IO 240   OMC 8    5400        9900 11200
24 1 ENTERTAINER 241       HT CUD  F/S DV IO T140-T240 8    5400       10600 12500
24 1 FISHERMAN 241         ST FSH  F/S DV IO 240   OMC 8    5400       10600 12100
---------------------- 1977 BOATS ------------------------------------------------------------
17 4 STARFIRE 180          ST RNBT FBG DV IO 165-235   6 11 2000        2850  3500
17 4 STARFIRE 180          ST RNBT FBG DV IO 255  VLVO 6 11 2000        3300  3850
17 4 STARFIRE 180          ST RNBT FBG DV JT 320   BERK 6 11 2000       3650  4200
18 3 STARFIRE 190          ST RNBT FBG DV IO 165-235   7 5  2500        3650  4250
18 3 STARFIRE 190          ST RNBT FBG DV IO 255  VLVO 7 5  2500        4000  4650
18 3 STARFIRE 190          ST RNBT FBG DV JT 320   BERK 7 5  2500       4350  5000
19 4 STARFIRE 200          ST RNBT FBG DV IO 165-235   7 6  2700        3950  4750
19 4 STARFIRE 200          ST RNBT FBG DV IO 255  VLVO 7 6  2700        4400  5050
19 4 STARFIRE 200          ST RNBT FBG DV JT 320   BERK 7 6  2700       4800  5500
19 4 STARFIRE 200          HT RNBT FBG DV IO 165-235   7 6  2900        4100  4900
19 4 STARFIRE 200          HT RNBT FBG DV IO 255  VLVO 7 6  2900        4550  5250
19 4 STARFIRE 200          HT RNBT FBG DV JT 320   BERK 7 6  2900       4950  5700

20 7 STARFIRE 210          ST CUD  FBG DV IO 175-235   7 11 3500        5750  6800
20 7 STARFIRE 210          ST CUD  FBG DV IO 255  VLVO 7 11 3500        6300  7250
20 7 STARFIRE 210          HT CUD  FBG DV IO 175-235   7 11 3700        6000  7100
20 7 STARFIRE 210          HT CUD  FBG DV IO 255  VLVO 7 11 3700        6550  7500
21 2 STARFIRE 220          ST CUD  FBG DV IO 175-255   8    3700        6550  8200
21 2 STARFIRE 225          HT OVNTR FBG DV IO 188-255  8    3900        6500  8050
24 1 STARFIRE 240          ST CUD  FBG DV IO 175-255   8    4500        8400 10300
24 1 STARFIRE 240          ST CUD  FBG DV IO T255 VLVO 8    4500        9350 11100
24 1 STARFIRE 240          HT CUD  FBG DV IO 175-255   8    4700        8800 10600
24 1 STARFIRE 240          ST CUD  FBG DV IO T120-T235 8    4700        9600 11400
24 1 STARFIRE 240          HT CUD  FBG DV IO T255 VLVO 8    4700       10700 12200
---------------------- 1975 BOATS ------------------------------------------------------------
18 3 STARFIRE 190          ST RNBT FBG DV IO 165        7 5  2500        3650  4250
18 3 STARFIRE 190          ST RNBT FBG DV IO 255        7 5  2500        3950  4600
18 3 STARFIRE 190          ST RNBT FBG DV JT 270-330   7 5  2500        3800  4600
18 3 STARFIRE 190 W/T      ST RNBT FBG DV IO 165-255   7 5  2500        4050  4700
18 3 STARFIRE 190 W/T      ST RNBT FBG DV JT 270-330   7 5  2500        4050  5100
19 4 STARFIRE 200          ST RNBT FBG DV IO 165-255   7 6  2700        4350  5050
19 4 STARFIRE 200          ST RNBT FBG DV JT 270-330   7 6  2700        4600  5250
19 4 STARFIRE 200          HT RNBT FBG DV IO 165-255   7 6  2900        4300  5300
19 4 STARFIRE 200          HT RNBT FBG DV JT 270-330   7 6  2900        4600  5250
19 4 STARFIRE 200 W/T      ST RNBT FBG DV IO 165-255   7 6  2700        4200  5100
19 4 STARFIRE 200 W/T      ST RNBT FBG DV JT 270-330   7 6  2700        4500  5150
20 7 STARFIRE 210          ST CR   FBG DV IO 165-255   7 11 3500        6100  7350

20 7 STARFIRE 210          HT CR   FBG DV IO 165-255   7 11 3700        6350  7650
21 2 STARFIRE 220          ST CR   FBG DV IO 165        8    4000        7000  8050
21 2 STARFIRE 220          ST CR   FBG DV IO T255       8    4000        8500  9800
21 2 STARFIRE 220          HT CR   FBG DV IO 165        8    4500        9050 10300
24 1 STARFIRE 240          ST CR   FBG DV IO T255       8    4500       10600 12000
24 1 STARFIRE 240          ST CR   FBG DV IO 165        8    4500        9350 10600
24 1 STARFIRE 240          HT CR   FBG DV IO T255       8    4700       10900 12400
---------------------- 1974 BOATS ------------------------------------------------------------
18 3 STARFIRE 190          ST       FBG    IO 188   MRCR 7 5  2500        3750  4400
18 3 STARFIRE 190 WT                FBG    IO 225   OMC  7 5  2500        3850  4450
18 6 STARFIRE 195 T        ST       FBG    IO 188   MRCR 7 9  2700        4250  4850
19 4 STARFIRE 200                   FBG    IO 225   OMC  7 6  2700        4250  4900
19 4 STARFIRE 200 WT       HT       FBG    IO 255   WAUK 7 6  2700        4500  5200
20 7 STARFIRE 210          ST       FBG    IO 225   OMC  7 6  2700        4300  5000
20 7 STARFIRE 210          HT       FBG    IO 225   OMC  7 11 3500        6150  7050
21 2 STARFIRE 220          HT       FBG    IO 225   WAUK 7 11 3500        6350  7300
24 1 SALTAIRE 240          ST       FBG    IO 225   OMC  8    4500        6950  8000
24 1 STARFIRE 240          HT       FBG    IO 225   OMC  8    4800        9000 10200
24 1 STARFIRE 240          HT       FBG    IO 255   WAUK 8    4800        9650 10900
24 1 STARFIRE 240          SF       FBG    IO 255   WAUK 8    5000       11900 13500
---------------------- 1973 BOATS ------------------------------------------------------------
18 3 STARFIRE 190          ST       FBG    IO 165-255 7 5 2500        3850  4800
18 3 STARFIRE 190          ST       FBG JT 165-450 7 5 2500           3550  4150
18 3 STARFIRE 190          HT       FBG    IO 165-255 7 5 2500        3850  4800
18 3 STARFIRE 190          HT       FBG JT 365-450 7 5 2500           3550  4150
18 6 STARFIRE 195 TRI      ST       FBG    IO 165-255 7 9 2700        4200  5200
18 6 STARFIRE 195 TRI      HT       FBG JT 365-450 7 9 2700           3850  4450
19 4 STARFIRE 200          ST       FBG    IO 165-255 7 6 2700        4400  5350
19 4 STARFIRE 200          ST       FBG JT 365-450 7 6 2700           3950  4600
19 4 STARFIRE 200          HT       FBG    IO 165-255 7 6             3900  4500
19 4 STARFIRE 200          HT       FBG JT 365-450 7 6                3900  4500
20 7 STARFIRE 210          ST       FBG    IO 165-255 7 11 3500       6200  7500
20 7 STARFIRE 210          ST       FBG JT 365-450 7 11 3500          5350  6150

21 2 STARFIRE 220          ST       FBG    IO 165-255 8 4000         7100  8500
21 2 STARFIRE 220          ST       FBG JT 365-450 8 4000            6000  6900
21 2 STARFIRE 220          ST       FBG    IO T255    8 4000         8000  9950
24 1 STARFIRE 240          ST       FBG    IO 165-255 8 4500         9200 10800
24 1 STARFIRE 240          ST       FBG JT 365-450 8 4500            7600  8750
24 1 STARFIRE 240          HT       FBG    IO 165-255 8              10100 12200
24 1 STARFIRE 240          HT       FBG    IO T120-T255 8            9450 11100
24 1 STARFIRE 240          HT       FBG JT 365-450 8                 7850  9050
24 1 NEW-YORKER 240        SF       FBG    IO T120-T255 8 4500       10900 12900
24 1 NEW-YORKER 240        SF       FBG JT 365-450 8 4500            7600  8700
24 1 NEW-YORKER 240        SF       FBG    IO T120-T255 8 4500       12000 14600
---------------------- 1972 BOATS ------------------------------------------------------------
18 3 STARFIRE 190          ST RNBT FBG DV IO 165-245 7 6            4100  5000
18 3 STARFIRE 190 W/T         RNBT FBG DV IO 165-245 7 6            4100  5000
18 6 STARFIRE 195T            RNBT FBG DV IO 165-245 7 9            4450  5350
19 4 STARFIRE 200          ST RNBT FBG DV IO 165-245 7 7            4550  5500
19 4 STARFIRE 200          HT RNBT FBG DV IO 165-245 7 7            4550  5500
19 4 STARFIRE 200 W/T         RNBT FBG DV IO 165-245 7 7            4550  5500
21   STARFIRE 220             CR   FBG DV IO 188      8             7050  8100
21   STARFIRE 240             CR   FBG DV IO T165     8             8050  9900
24   STARFIRE 240             CR   FBG DV IO 188      8            10300 11700
24   STARFIRE 240             CR   FBG DV IO T188     8            11800 13400
24   STARFIRE 240          HT CR   FBG DV IO T248     8            10300 11700
24   STARFIRE 240          HT CR   FBG DV IO T245     8            11800 13400
---------------------- 1965 BOATS ------------------------------------------------------------
17 4 SX-1800 DLX           RNBT FBG    IO 71                        4250  4900
```

STARRATT & JENKS YT CO
LARGO FL 33540   COAST GUARD MFG ID- SJK See inside cover to adjust price for area

LOA FT IN	NAME AND/ OR MODEL	TOP/ RIG	BOAT TYPE	-HULL- MTL TP	----ENGINE--- TP # HP MFG	BEAM FT IN	WGT LBS	DRAFT FT IN	RETAIL LOW	RETAIL HIGH
--- 1980 BOATS ---										
45 8	STARRATT 45	SLP	SA/CR	FBG KL IB	D 11		25000	6 1	54400	59700
45 8	STARRATT 45	YWL	SA/CR	FBG KL IB	D 11		25000	6 1	54400	59700
--- 1979 BOATS ---										
45 8	STARRATT	SLP	SA/CR	FBG KL IB	35D VLVO 11		25000	6 1	52100	57300
	IB 40D PERK 52000	57100, IB		42D WEST	52300 57500, IB	60D PERK			52200	57300
45 8	STARRATT	CUT	SA/CR	FBG KL IB	35D VLVO 11		25000	6 1	52100	57300
	IB 40D PERK 52000	57100, IB		42D WEST	52300 57500, IB	60D PERK			52200	57300
45 8	STARRATT	YWL	SA/CR	FBG KL IB	35D VLVO 11		25000	6 1	52100	57300
	IB 40D PERK 52000	57100, IB		42D WEST	52300 57500, IB	60D PERK			52200	57300
45 8	STARRATT CRUISING KL	SLP	SA/CR	FBG KL IB	35D VLVO 11		25000	5 9	52100	57300
	IB 40D PERK 52000	57100, IB		42D WEST	52300 57500, IB	60D PERK			52200	57300
45 8	STARRATT CRUISING KL	CUT	SA/CR	FBG KL IB	35D VLVO 11		25000	5 9	52100	57300
	IB 40D PERK 52000	57100, IB		42D WEST	52300 57500, IB	60D PERK			52200	57300
45 8	STARRATT CRUISING KL	YWL	SA/CR	FBG KL IB	35D VLVO 11		25000	5 9	52100	57300
	IB 40D PERK 52000	57100, IB		42D WEST	52300 57500, IB	60D PERK			52200	57300
45 8	STARRATT SHOAL KL	SLP	SA/CR	FBG KL IB	35D VLVO 11		25000	4 11	52100	57300
	IB 40D PERK 52000	57100, IB		42D WEST	52300 57500, IB	60D PERK			52200	57300
45 8	STARRATT SHOAL KL	CUT	SA/CR	FBG KL IB	35D VLVO 11		25000	4 11	52100	57300
	IB 40D PERK 52000	57100, IB		42D WEST	52300 57500, IB	60D PERK			52200	57300
45 8	STARRATT SHOAL KL	YWL	SA/CR	FBG KL IB	35D VLVO 11		25000	4 11	52100	57300
	IB 40D PERK 52000	57100, IB		42D WEST	52300 57500, IB	60D PERK			52200	57300
--- 1978 BOATS ---										
45	STARRATT	SLP	SA/CR	FBG KL IB	40D 11		25500	6 1	49100	54000
45	STARRATT	YWL	SA/CR	FBG KL IB	40D 11		25500	5 9	49100	54000

STARWIND SAILBOATS
DIV OF REBEL INDUSTRIES   See inside cover to adjust price for area
SARASOTA FL 34243

For more recent years, see the BUC Used Boat Price Guide, Volume 1 or Volume 2

LOA FT IN	NAME AND/ OR MODEL	TOP/ RIG	BOAT TYPE	-HULL- MTL TP	----ENGINE--- TP # HP MFG	BEAM FT IN	WGT LBS	DRAFT FT IN	RETAIL LOW	RETAIL HIGH
--- 1983 BOATS ---										
18	STARWIND 18 CHAMP	SLP	SA/OD	FBG		6			1700	2050
18 8	STARWIND 19	SLP	SA/OD	FBG		7 10			2550	3000
19 6	FREESTYLE 195	SLP	SA/OD	FBG CT		8	380	6	1900	2250
22	STARWIND 22	SLP	SA/OD	FBG		7 9			3950	4600
22	WEEKENDER	SLP	SA/OD	FBG		7 9			3950	4600

STATES MARINE INC
COAST GUARD MFG ID- STT

Call 1-800-327-6929 for BUC Personalized Evaluation Service
Or, for 1973 boats, sign onto www.BUCValuPro.com

STAYSAIL YACHTS LTD
COAST GUARD MFG ID- XYL

Call 1-800-327-6929 for BUC Personalized Evaluation Service
Or, for 1978 to 1980 boats, sign onto www.BUCValuPro.com

STEEL CRUISER MFG CO INC

Call 1-800-327-6929 for BUC Personalized Evaluation Service
Or, for 1961 to 1967 boats, sign onto www.BUCValuPro.com

STEELCRAFT BOAT CO
CHURCHWARD & CO INC   COAST GUARD MFG ID- STC

Call 1-800-327-6929 for BUC Personalized Evaluation Service
Or, for 1946 to 1954 boats, sign onto www.BUCValuPro.com

STEPHENS MARINE INC
STOCKTON CA 95201   COAST GUARD MFG ID- RTS See inside cover to adjust price for area

LOA FT IN	NAME AND/ OR MODEL	TOP/ RIG	BOAT TYPE	-HULL- MTL TP	----ENGINE--- TP # HP MFG	BEAM FT IN	WGT LBS	DRAFT FT IN	RETAIL LOW	RETAIL HIGH
--- 1977 BOATS ---										
60	OCEAN CRUISER	HT	MY	AL DS IB	T350D GM	17	70000	6	241000	265000
--- 1976 BOATS ---										
60	FLUSH DECK CRUISER	HT	FD	AL DS IB	T350D GM	16 6	60000	3	194000	213000
60	MOTORSAILER	KTH	MS	AL KL IB	350D GM		65000	6	360500	396500
65	MOTORYACHT	HT	MY	AL DS IB	T525D GM	17	70000	3 6	293000	322000
72	MOTORYACHT	HT	MY	AL DS IB	T525D GM	17 6	85000	4 6	**	**
--- 1975 BOATS ---										
60	FLUSH DECK CRUISER	HT	FD	AL DS IB	T350D GM	16 6	60000	3	186000	204500
60	MOTORSAILER	KTH	MS	AL KL IB	350D GM		65000	6	347500	382000
65	MOTORYACHT	HT	MY	AL DS IB	T525D GM	17	70000	3 6	281500	309500
72	MOTORYACHT	HT	MY	AL DS IB	T525D GM	17 6	85000	4 6	**	**
--- 1974 BOATS ---										
56 6		HT		AL DS IB	T700D GM	16		3	174500	192000
72		HT	MY	AL DS IB	T600D GM	17 6	81000	5	**	**
--- 1972 BOATS ---										
45	STEPHENS 45		MY	AL DS IB	T283D	13 9		3	100500	110500
50	STEPHENS 50		MY	AL DS IB	T350D	15		4	123500	135500
55	STEPHENS 55		MY	AL DS IB	T350D	15 6		4	130500	143500
60	STEPHENS 60		MY	AL DS IB	T525D	16		4	193500	212500
65	STEPHENS 65		MY	AL DS IB	T525D	17		4 2	246500	271000
75	STEPHENS 75		MY	AL DS IB	T525D	17 6		4 4	**	**
--- 1971 BOATS ---										
51		FB	MY	WD DS IB	T350D GM				113000	124000
--- 1970 BOATS ---										
45	STEPHENS		HT	AL DS IB	T215D GM	13 9	26000	3	75600	83100
50		FB	SF	WD DS IB	T370D CUM			3	117500	129000
50	STEPHENS		FD	AL DS IB	T280D GM	15	37000	3 4	106000	116500
55	STEPHENS		FD	AL DS IB	T280D GM	15 6	47000	4	110500	121500
60		FB	MY	WD DS IB	T D GM				**	**
60		FB	MY	WD DS IB	T D GM				**	**
65	STEPHENS		FD	AL DS IB	T350D GM	16	55500	4	140000	153500
65	STEPHENS		FD	AL DS IB	T525D GM	16 6	65000	4	219000	241000
75	STEPHENS		MY	AL DS IB	T525D GM	17	93000	4 4	**	**
--- 1969 BOATS ---										
42		SLP	MS	AL KL IB	130D PERK				82600	90800
44 5		SLP	SAIL	FBG KL IB	D				82900	91100
45	STEPHENS		FD	DS IB	T195D	13 9	26000	3	72200	79400
50	STEPHENS		FD	DS IB	T270D	15	36000	4	114000	125000
55	STEPHENS		FD	DS IB	T320D	15 6	47000	4	129000	141500
60	STEPHENS		FD	DS IB	T320D	16	55300	4	129000	141500
65	STEPHENS		FD	DS IB	T320D	16 6	61500	4	178500	196500
75	STEPHENS		FD	DS IB	T456D	17	93000	4 6	**	**
--- 1968 BOATS ---										
45	STEPHENS 45		MY	AL DS IB	T195D GM	13 9	26000	3	73600	80900
50	STEPHENS 50		MY	AL DS IB	T165D GM	15	37000	3 4	89500	98300
50	STEPHENS 50		MY	AL DS IB	T280D GM	15	37000	3 4	93600	103000
55	STEPHENS 55		SF	AL DS IB	T320 GM	15 6	52000	4	115500	127000
55	STEPHENS 55		SF	AL DS IB	T270D GM	15 6	52000	4	109000	120000
60	STEPHENS 60		SF	AL DS IB	T320D GM	16	55000	4	119500	131000
61	STEPHENS 61		MY	AL DS IB	T320 GM				159500	175000
65	STEPHENS 65		MY	AL DS IB	T320D GM	16 6	62000	4	173000	190000
65	STEPHENS 65		MY	AL DS IB	T320D GM	16 6	62000	4	187500	206000
75	STEPHENS 75		MY	AL DS IB	T456D GM	17 6	93000	4 4	**	**
--- 1967 BOATS ---										
38	FARALLONE-CLIPPER	SLP	SAIL	WD KL IB		9 6		5 7	40200	44700
45	STEPHENS 45		FD	WD DS IB	T280D	13 9		3	**	**
45	STEPHENS 45		FD	WD DS IB	T280D	13 9		3	**	**
50	STEPHENS 50		FD	WD DS IB	T165D	15		3 4	**	**
50	STEPHENS 50		FD	WD DS IB	T280D	15		4	**	**
61				WD DS IB	T330D GM				136000	149500
65	STEPHENS 65		FD	WD DS IB	T640	16 6		5	170000	186500
65	STEPHENS 65		FD	WD DS IB	T912				203000	223000
66			MY	WD DS IB	T470D GM				207000	227500
75	STEPHENS 75		MY	WD DS IB	T	17 6		5 6	**	**
--- 1966 BOATS ---										
38	FARALLONE-CLIPPER	SLP	SA/CR	WD KL SJK	25	9 6		5 6	48600	53400
43	RIVER-CRUISER	HT	HB	WD IO	210	13 4		8	14000	21600
45	STEPHENS 45			WD IB	T290				72100	79200
45	STEPHENS 45			WD IB	T195D				71300	78300
45	STEPHENS 45			WD IB	T280D				73900	81200
50	STEPHENS 50			WD IB	T290				86100	94600

STEPHENS MARINE INC   -CONTINUED   See inside cover to adjust price for area

LOA FT IN	NAME AND/ OR MODEL	TOP/ RIG	BOAT TYPE	-HULL- MTL TP	ENGINE TP	# HP	MFG	BEAM FT IN	WGT LBS	DRAFT FT IN	RETAIL LOW	RETAIL HIGH

———————————— 1966 BOATS ————————————
50	STEPHENS 50			WD	IB	T165D					**	**
50	STEPHENS 50			WD	IB	T280D					**	**
55	STEPHENS 55			WD	IB	T280D					99700	109500
60	STEPHENS 60			WD	IB	T280D					125500	138000
60	STEPHENS 60			WD	IB	T350D					133000	146000
61		FD		WD	IB	T330D	GM				132000	145000
65	STEPHENS 65			WD	IB	T350D					177000	194500
65	STEPHENS 65			WD	IB	T530D					199000	218500

———————————— 1965 BOATS ————————————
25 7	JUNIOR-CLIPPER	SLP	SA/OD	WD KL				7 4		4 9	7300	8400
38	FARALLONE-CLIPPER	SLP	SAIL	WD KL				9 6		5 7	20500	22700
45	STEPHENS 45			WD	IB	T290					70000	76900
45	STEPHENS 45			WD	IB	T195D					69300	76100
45	STEPHENS 45			WD	IB	T258D					**	**
48 8		FB	SF	WD	RB IB	T300D	CUM				94500	104000
50	STEPHENS 50			WD	IB	T290					83700	91900
50	STEPHENS 50			WD	IB	T165D					**	**
50	STEPHENS 50			WD	IB	T270D	GM				**	**
55	STEPHENS 55			WD	IB	T280D					96900	106500
60	STEPHENS 60			WD	IB	T280D					122500	134500
60	STEPHENS 60			WD	IB	T350D					129500	142500
65	STEPHENS 65			WD	IB	T350D					172000	189000
65	STEPHENS 65			WD	IB	T530D					193500	213000

———————————— 1963 BOATS ————————————
| 60 | | FD | | WD | IB | T325D | GM | | | | 117500 | 129500 |

———————————— 1962 BOATS ————————————
| 42 | | TCMY | WD | | IB | T265 | CHRY | | | | 54800 | 60200 |
| 50 | | HT | TCMY | WD | DS IB | T270D | GM | | | | 79800 | 87700 |

———————————— 1961 BOATS ————————————
25 10	JUNIOR-CLIPPER	SLP	SA/OD	KL						4 9	7250	8350
36	FLUSH DECK CR		FD	WD	IB	354		11 9		2 10	**	**
36	SPORT FISH		SF	WD	IB	354		11 9		2 10	33200	36900
38	FARALLONE-CLIPPER	SLP	SA/OD	WD KL				9 6		5 7	30600	34000
42	FLUSH DECK CR		FD	WD	DS IB	450		12 10		3	53200	58400
47	FLUSH DECK CR		FD	WD	DS IB	450		13 2		3	62600	68800

———————————— 1960 BOATS ————————————
36	FLUSH DECK		FD	WD	IB	177		11 9		2 7	**	**
36	FLUSH DECK		FD	WD	IB	225		11 9		2 7	**	**
37 10	FARALLONE-CLIPPER		SA/OD	WD KL				9 8		5 6	30300	33600
42		FB	SDN	WD	DS IB	T330	CHRY				62300	68500
42	FLUSH DECK		FD	WD	IB	225		12 10		2 9	48300	53100
42	FLUSH DECK		FD	WD	IB	275		12 10		2 9	48800	53600
42	MARK I		SDN	WD	IB	225		12 10		2 9	57500	63200
42	MARK I		SDN	WD	IB	275		12 10		2 9	59500	65300
42	MARK II		SDN	WD	IB	225		12 10		2 9	60200	66200
42	MARK II		SDN	WD	IB	275		12 10		2 9	59500	65300
47	FLUSH DECK		FD	WD	IB	225		13 2		3	58900	64700
47	FLUSH DECK		FD	WD	IB	275		13 2		3	59300	65100
50		HT	FD	WD	RB IB	T275	CHRY				70000	76900

———————————— 1959 BOATS ————————————
36			FD		IB			11 9			**	**
36			SDN		IB			11 3			**	**
42			FD		IB			12 10			**	**
42	MARK I		SDN		IB			12 10			**	**
47	MARK I		FD		IB			13			**	**
48		MY		WD	IB	T300	CC				65600	72000

———————————— 1958 BOATS ————————————
| 32 | | HT | EXP | WD | IB | T135 | CHRY | | | | 16900 | 19200 |
| 36 | | HT | SDN | WD | IB | T135 | CHRY | | | | 30700 | 34200 |

———————————— 1956 BOATS ————————————
| 36 | | FB | CR | WD | IB | T125 | CHRY | | | | 29300 | 32500 |
| 36 | | HT | SDN | WD | RB IB | T125 | CHRY | | | | 29800 | 33100 |

———————————— 1954 BOATS ————————————
32		HT	SDN	MHG SV	IB		CHRY				**	**
36		HT	SDN	MHG SV	IB		CHRY				**	**
38	FARALLONE-CLIPPER	SLP	SAIL	MHG	IB		CHRY				40400	44900
42		HT	SDN	MHG SV	IB		CHRY				**	**
47		HT	SDN	MHG SV	IB		CHRY				**	**
52		HT	MY	MHG SV	IB		CHRY				**	**

———————————— 1953 BOATS ————————————
| 32 | | HT | EXP | WD | IB | T135 | CHRY | | | | 15400 | 17500 |

———————————— 1952 BOATS ————————————
30		HT	SDN	WD	IB						**	**
34		HT	SDN	WD	IB						**	**
46		HT	MY	WD	IB						**	**
52		HT	MY	WD	IB						**	**

———————————— 1950 BOATS ————————————
30		HT	DC	WD	IB						**	**
34		HT	DC	WD	IB	T	CHRY				**	**
38		HT	MY	WD	IB						**	**
38	FARALLONE-CLIPPER	SLP	SAIL	WD	IB			9 6		5 7	43000	47800
46		FB	CR	WD	RB IB	T275	CHRY				50000	55000
48		HT	MY	WD	IB						**	**
52		HT	MY	WD	IB						**	**

———————————— 1949 BOATS ————————————
34		HT	DC	WD	IB		CHRY				**	**
38			SDN	WD	IB	T130	CHRY				40500	45000
43	CUSTOM		HT	MY	WD	IB					**	**
48	CUSTOM		HT	MY	WD	IB					**	**
50	CUSTOM		HT	MY	WD	IB					**	**
52	CUSTOM		HT	MY	WD	IB					**	**

———————————— 1941 BOATS ————————————
| 38 | | | | WD | DS IB | T220 | WAUK | 10 10 | 26000 | 3 | 54000 | 59400 |
| 38 | | | SDN | WD | IB | T220 | WAUK | 10 10 | | 3 6 | 48100 | 52800 |

———————————— 1931 BOATS ————————————
30			DC	WD	IB						**	**
32			SPTCR	WD	IB						**	**
38			MYDKH	WD	IB						**	**
38			SPTCR	WD	IB						**	**
43		HT	DC	WD	IB	T200					53700	59000
45	RAISED DECK		CR	WD	IB						**	**
48	COMMUTER	FB	MY	WD	IB	T200					68700	75500
55		HT	MY	WD	IB	T200					86400	95000

———————————— 1929 BOATS ————————————
| 50 | | | | WD | IB | 220 | CHRY | | | | ** | ** |

———————————— 1926 BOATS ————————————
| 45 | | | | WD | IB | 60 | BUDA | | | | ** | ** |

JO STEPHENS YACHTS OF NEWPORT

Call 1-800-327-6929 for BUC Personalized Evaluation Service
Or, for 1970 to 1971 boats, sign onto www.BUCValuPro.com

STERNCRAFT BOAT CO
DIV OF DECKBOAT CORP   COAST GUARD MFG ID- STF

Call 1-800-327-6929 for BUC Personalized Evaluation Service
Or, for 1966 to 1979 boats, sign onto www.BUCValuPro.com

STEURY CORPORATION
GOSHEN IN 46526   COAST GUARD MFG ID- SRC See inside cover to adjust price for area

LOA FT IN	NAME AND/ OR MODEL	TOP/ RIG	BOAT TYPE	-HULL- MTL TP	ENGINE TP	# HP	MFG	BEAM FT IN	WGT LBS	DRAFT FT IN	RETAIL LOW	RETAIL HIGH

———————————— 1981 BOATS ————————————
16 6	S1700 W/T		RNBT	FBG DV	IO	120		7			1800	2150
17	V170 SC		RNBT	FBG TR	IO	140		7 6			1950	2300
18	S1900 W/T		CR	FBG DV	IO	120		7 5			2150	2500
22	S2200		CR	FBG DV	IO	170		8			3500	4050
22	S2200		CUD	FBG DV	IO	170		8			3600	4150
22	S2200		OFF	FBG DV	OB			8			2500	2900
23	T523	HT	HB	FBG TR	OB			8	3700		**	**
23	T523	HT	HB	FBG TR	IO	170		8	4200		**	**
25	S2500		EXP	FBG DV	IO	228		8			5700	6500
25	S2500		SDN	FBG DV	IO	228		8			6150	7100
25	S2500		SPTCR	FBG DV	IO	228		8			5150	5950

———————————— 1980 BOATS ————————————
16 6	S1700		RNBT	FBG DV	IO	120		7 4			1800	2100
17 6	S1800		RNBT	FBG TR	IO	120		7 4			1950	2300
18	S1900		CR	FBG DV	IO	120		7 5			2300	2700
18	S1900 W/T		CR	FBG DV	IO	120		7 5			1900	2300
22	S2200		CR	FBG DV	IO	170		8			3450	4000
22	S2200		CUD	FBG DV	IO	170		8			3550	4150
22	S2200		OPFSH	FBG DV	OB			8			2500	2900
23	T523	HT	HB	FBG TR	OB			8	3700		**	**
23	T523	HT	HB	FBG TR	IO	170		8	4200		**	**
25	S2500		EXP	FBG DV	IO	228		8			5600	6450
25	S2500		SDN	FBG DV	IO	228		8			6100	7000
25	S2500		SPTCR	FBG DV	IO	228		8			5100	5850

LOA FT	IN	NAME AND/ OR MODEL	TOP/ RIG	BOAT TYPE	-HULL- MTL	TP	ENGINE TP	# HP	MFG	BEAM FT	IN	WGT LBS	DRAFT FT	IN	RETAIL LOW	RETAIL HIGH
		1979 BOATS														
16	6	S1700BR	ST	RNBT	FBG	DV	IO	120-170		7		2250			1850	2250
16	6	S1700RAB	ST	RNBT	FBG	DV	IO	120-170		7		2250			1800	2200
17	6	S1800	OP	RNBT	FBG	TR	IO	120-170		7	4	2100			1950	2300
18		S1900BR	ST	RNBT	FBG	DV	IO	120-230		7	4	2330			2150	2600
18		S1900CR	ST	CBNCR	FBG	DV	IO	120-230		7	4	2560			2350	2850
18		S1900RAB	ST	RNBT	FBG	DV	IO	120-230		7	4	2330			2050	2550
22		S2200CC	ST	CUD	FBG	DV	IO	170-230		8		3460			3550	4200
22		S2200CR	ST	CBNCR	FBG	DV	IO	170-230		8		3750			4150	4900
22		S2200OSF	ST	FSH	FBG	DV	OB			8		2426			2400	2750
23		T523HB	HT	HB	FBG	TR	OB			8		3700			**	**
23		T523HB	HT	HB	FBG	TR	IO	170-230		8		4200			**	**
25		S2500EC	ST	EXP	FBG	DV	IO	228-260		8		5100			5650	6600
25		S2500EC	ST	EXP	FBG	DV	IO	T170	MRCR	8		5100			6150	7050
25		S2500EC	HT	EXP	FBG	DV	IO	228-260		8		5100			5650	6600
25		S2500EC	HT	EXP	FBG	DV	IO	T170	MRCR	8		5100			6150	7050
25		S2500FB	FB	CR	FBG	DV	IO	228-260		8		5000			5550	6500
25		S2500FB	FB	CR	FBG	DV	IO	T170	MRCR	8		5000			6050	6950
25		S2500SAB	ST	SPTCR	FBG	DV	IO	228-260		8		4405			5100	6000
25		S2500SAB	ST	SPTCR	FBG	DV	IO	T170	MRCR	8		4405			5600	6450
25		S2500SD	HT	SDN	FBG	DV	IO	228-260		8		5350			6050	7150
25		S2500SD	HT	SDN	FBG	DV	IO	T170	MRCR	8		5350			6650	7650
		1978 BOATS														
16	6	S1700	OP	RNBT	FBG	DV	IO	120-170		7		2250			1850	2250
17	6	S1800	OP	RNBT	FBG	TR	IO	120-225		7	4	2100			1950	2400
18		S1900CC	ST	CUD	FBG	DV	IO	120-225		7	5	2330			2200	2650
18		S1900CR	ST	CBNCR	FBG	DV	IO	120-225		7	5	2560			2400	2850
18		S1900RAB	OP	RNBT	FBG	DV	IO	120-225		6	11	2330			2000	2500
18	2	V518F	OP	CTRCN	FBG	DV	IO	120-190		7	4	1200			1800	2200
18	2	X180	OP	RNBT	FBG	SV	IO	165-225		7	3	1890			1950	2350
18	2	X180	OP	RNBT	FBG	SV	JT	320		7	3	1890			2550	2950
21	2	V521		RNBT	FBG	DV	IO	120-235		8					2650	3200
21	2	V521CR		CR	FBG	DV	IO	120-235		8					3250	3900
22		S2200CC	ST	CUD	FBG	DV	IO	170-240		8		3460			3550	4250
22		S2200OSF	OP	FSH	FBG	DV	OB			7	11	2426			2350	2750
22		SS2200CR	ST	RNBT	FBG	DV	IO	170-240		8		3750			3550	4250
23		T523HB	HT	HB	FBG	TR	OB			8		3700			**	**
23		T523HB	HT	HB	FBG	TR	IO	140-228		8		4200			**	**
25		S2500EC	ST	EXP	FBG	DV	IO	185-240		8		5100			5500	6550
25		S2500EC	ST	EXP	FBG	DV	IO	T120-T170		8		5100			6000	7100
25		S2500FB	FB	CR	FBG	DV	IO	185-240		8		5000			5450	6450
25		S2500FB	FB	CR	FBG	DV	IO	T120-T170		8		5000			5900	7000
25		S2500SAB	ST	SPTCR	FBG	DV	IO	185-240		8		4405			4950	5900
25		S2500SAB	ST	SPTCR	FBG	DV	IO	T120-T170		8		4405			5450	6500
25		S2500SD	HT	SDN	FBG	DV	IO	185-240		8		5350			5950	7050
25		S2500SD	HT	SDN	FBG	DV	IO	T120-T170		8		5350			6450	7650
		1977 BOATS														
17	6	S1800	ST	RNBT	FBG	TR	IO	120-190		7	4	2100			1950	2400
18		S1900	ST	RNBT	FBG	DV	IO	120-190		7	5	2330			2200	2550
18		S1900CC	ST	CUD	FBG	DV	IO	120-190		7	5	2330			2250	2650
18		S1900CR	ST	CBNCR	FBG	DV	IO	120-190		7	5				2350	2800
18	2	V518C	ST	RNBT	FBG	DV	IO	120-190		7	4	2060			2050	2450
18	2	V518CR	ST	CBNCR	FBG	DV	IO	120-190		7	4	2358			2350	2750
18	2	X180	OP	RNBT	FBG	SV	IO	165-235		7	3	1890			1950	2400
18	2	X180	OP	RNBT	FBG	SV	JT	320	BERK	7	3	1890			2450	2850
21	2	V521	ST	RNBT	FBG	DV	IO	120-235		8		2450			2650	3200
21	2	V521CR	ST	CR	FBG	DV	IO	120-235		8		3250			3300	3950
22		S2200CR	ST	CBNCR	FBG	DV	IO	170-235		8					4200	5000
23		T523HB	HT	HB	FBG	TR	OB			8		3700			**	**
23		T523HB	HT	HB	FBG	TR	IO	140-235		8		4200			**	**
25		S2500	FB	CR	FBG	DV	IO	233-235		8		5000			5650	6500
25		S2500	FB	CR	FBG	DV	IO	T120-T170		8		5000			6000	7100
25		S2500	ST	EXP	FBG	DV	IO	233-235		8		5100			5750	6600
25		S2500	ST	EXP	FBG	DV	IO	T120-T170		8		5100			6100	7200
25		S2500	ST	SPTCR	FBG	DV	IO	188-235		8		4405			5050	5950
		1976 BOATS														
17		T517	ST	RNBT	FBG	TR	IO	120-165		7	1	2010			1900	2250
18		S1800	ST	RNBT	FBG	TR	IO	120-190		7	4	2100			2050	2500
18		S1900	ST	RNBT	FBG	DV	IO	120-190		7	5	2330			2250	2650
18		S1900 CC	ST	CUD	FBG	DV	IO	120-190		7	5	2330			2300	2700
18		V518	ST	RNBT	FBG	DV	IO	120-190		7	4	2060			2050	2450
18		V518CR	ST	CBNCR	FBG	DV	IO	120-190		7	4	2358			2350	2800
18		X180	OP	RNBT	FBG	SV	IO	175-235		7	3	1890			1950	2450
18		X180	OP	RNBT	FBG	SV	JT	320		7	3	1890			2350	2700
21		S2200 CR	ST	CBNCR	FBG	DV	IO	140-235		8		3250			3650	4350
21		V521	ST	RNBT	FBG	DV	IO	120-235		8		2450			2700	3250
21		V521 CR	ST	CR	FBG	DV	IO	120-235		8		3250			3350	4000
21	2	S2200 CC	ST	CUD	FBG	DV	OB			8		2400			2250	2650
21	2	S2200 CC	ST	CUD	FBG	DV	IO	140-235		8		3250			3350	4050
23		T523CR	ST	CR	FBG	TR	IO	140-235		8		3730			4100	4900
23		T523HB	HT	HB	FBG	TR	OB			8		3300			**	**
23		T523HB	HT	HB	FBG	TR	IO	140-235		8		4200			**	**
25		S2500 EXP	ST	EXP	FBG	DV	IO	233-255		8		4645			5500	6450
		1975 BOATS														
16		S1600IO	ST	RNBT	FBG	TR	IO	120-165		6	11	1780			1700	2000
17		T517IO	ST	RNBT	FBG	TR	IO	120-165		7	1	2010			1950	2350
18		S1800IO	ST	RNBT	FBG	TR	IO	120-190		7	4	2200			2200	2600
18		V518CRIO	ST	CBNCR	FBG	DV	IO	120-190		7	4	2358			2450	2850
18		V518IO	ST	RNBT	FBG	DV	IO	120-190		7	4	2060			2150	2550
18		X180 JET	OP	RNBT	FBG	SV	IO	175-235		7	3	1890			2050	2500
18		X180 JET	OP	RNBT	FBG	SV	JT	270-330		7	3	1890			2250	2600
21		V521CRIO	ST	CR	FBG	DV	IO	120-235		8		3250			3450	4150
21		V521IO	ST	RNBT	FBG	DV	IO	120-235		8		2450			2800	3350
22		S2200IO	ST	CR	FBG	DV	IO	140-233		8		3250			3650	4350
22		S2200IO	ST	CR	FBG	DV	IO	235	OMC	8		3730			4100	4800
23		T523CR	ST	CR	FBG	DV	IO	140-235		8		3730			4200	5050
23		T523HB	HT	HB	FBG	TR	IO	140-235		8		4200			**	**
		1974 BOATS														
17	2	T517 CUS		RNBT	FBG		IO	120-165		7	1	2010			2000	2450
18	2	V518		RNBT	FBG		IO	120-225		7	4	2358			2400	2850
18	2	V518 CUS		RNBT	FBG		IO	120-225		7	4	2060			2250	2700
18	2	X180		RNBT	FBG		IO	188-225		7	3				2300	2700
18	2	X180		RNBT	FBG		JT	260	BERK	7	3	1890			2150	2550
21	2	V521		CBNCR	FBG		IO	120-225		8		3250			3950	4700
21	2	V521 CUS		RNBT	FBG		IO	120-225		8		2450			2900	3500
23		T523		CBNCR	FBG		IO	120-225		8		3730			4950	5800
23		T523	HT	HB	FBG		IO	120-225		8		4200			**	**
		1973 BOATS														
17	2	T517		RNBT	FBG		IO	120-165		7	1	2010			2050	2500
18	2	V518		RNBT	FBG		IO	120-225		7	4	2358			2450	2950
18	2	V518 CUS		RNBT	FBG		IO	120-225		7	4	2060			2300	2800
18	2	X180		RNBT	FBG		IO	188-225		7	3				2350	2800
18	2	X180		RNBT	FBG		JT	260	BERK	7	3	1890			2050	2450
21	2	V521		CBNCR	FBG		IO	120-225		8		3250			4050	4850
21	2	V521 CUS		RNBT	FBG		IO	120-225		8		2450			3000	3600
23		T523		CBNCR	FBG		IO	120-225		8		3730			5100	6000
23		T523	HT	HB	FBG		IO	120-225		8		4200			**	**
		1972 BOATS														
16	1	CUSTOM		RNBT	FBG		IO	120-140		6	7	1552	3	7	1700	2050
17	2			RNBT	FBG	TR	IO	120-165		7	1	2010	3	8	2200	2550
18	2	CUSTOM		RNBT	FBG		IO	120-165		7	4	2060	3	10	2400	3000
18	2	CUSTOM		RNBT	FBG		IO	215		7	4	2358	3	10	2650	3050
21	2			CR	FBG		IO	120-225		8		3250	4	6	3850	4550
21	2	CUSTOM		RNBT	FBG		IO	120-225		8		2450	4	6	3100	3700
23			HT	HB	FBG		IO	120-165		8		4200	4	11	**	**
23		CUSTOM		RNBT	FBG		IO	120-270		8		2930	4	11	3750	4650
		1971 BOATS														
16	1	V416IO CUSTOM		RNBT	FBG		IO	120-140		6	7	1552	3	7	1750	2100
17	2	T517IO		RNBT	FBG	TR	IO	120-165		7	1	2010	3	8	2250	2650
18	2	V518CRIO CUS		CBNCR	FBG		IO	120-215		7	4	2358	3	10	2800	3350
18	2	V518IO CUS		RNBT	FBG		IO	120-215		7	4	2060	3	10	2450	2950
23		T523CRIO CUS		CBNCR	FBG		IO	120-270		8		3730	4	11	5450	6600
23		T523HBIO	HT	HB	FBG		IO	120-165		8		4200	4	11	**	**
23		T523IO CUS		RNBT	FBG		IO	120-270		8		2930	4	11	3900	4800
		1970 BOATS														
16	1	V416IO CUSTOM		RNBT	FBG	DV	IO	120-140		6	7	1552	3	7	1800	2150
17	2	T517IO		RNBT	FBG	TR	IO	120-165		7	1	2010	3	8	2350	2750
18	2	V518CRIO CUS		CBNCR	FBG	DV	IO	120-215		7	4	2358	3	10	2900	3500
18	2	V518IO CUS		RNBT	FBG	DV	IO	120-215		7	4	2060	3	10	2550	3050
23		T523CRIO CUS		CBNCR	FBG	TR	IO	120-270		8		3730	4	11	5600	6800
23		T523IO CUS		RNBT	FBG	TR	IO	120-270		8		2930	4	11	4000	4950
		1969 BOATS														
16	1	V416	OP	RNBT	FBG	DV	IO	120		6	7	1552		6	1900	2250
17	2	T517	OP	RNBT	FBG	TR	IO	120-160		7	1	1858		9	2350	2850
18	2	V518	OP	RNBT	FBG	DV	IO	120-160		7	4	1905		10	2550	3100
18	2	V518	OP	RNBT	FBG	DV	IO	210-225		7	4	2205		10	2750	3300
18	2	V518CR		CBNCR	FBG	DV	IO	155-210		7	4	2350	1		2950	3700
18	2	V518CR		CBNCR	FBG	DV	IO	225	MRCR	7	4	2550	1		3250	3800
18	2	V518CR		CBNCR	FBG	DV	IO	T120		7	4	2210	1		3500	4050
23		T523	OP	RNBT	FBG	TR	IO	120-225		8			1	3	4900	5750
23		T523	OP	RNBT	FBG	TR	IO	T120-T160		8			1	3	5500	6350
23		T523CR		CR	FBG	TR	IO	120-225		8			1	4	5200	6100

 CONTINUED ON NEXT PAGE

LOA FT IN	NAME AND/ OR MODEL	TOP/ RIG	BOAT TYPE	-HULL- MTL TP	----ENGINE--- TP # HP MFG	BEAM FT IN	WGT LBS	DRAFT FT IN	RETAIL LOW	RETAIL HIGH
					1969 BOATS					
23	T523CR		CR	FBG TR	IO T120-T160	8		1 4	5850	6750
					1968 BOATS					
16 1	V416	OP	RNBT	FBG SV	IO 120 OMC	6 7	1552	8	1900	2300
17 2	T517	OP	RNBT	FBG TR	IO 120-160	7 1	2010	8	2450	2900
18 2	V518	OP	RNBT	FBG	IO 120-225	7 4	2060	10	2700	3300
18 2	V518CR		CBNCR	FBG SV	IO 120-225	7 4	2358	1	3100	3750
					1967 BOATS					
16 1	CUSTOM		RNBT	FBG	IO 80	6 7			2100	2500
16 1	V416 CUSTOM		RNBT	FBG	IO 120				2200	2550
18 2	V518 CUS		RNBT	FBG	IO 120-225	7 4			2850	3450
18 2	V518CR10		CBNCR	FBG	IO 120	7 4			3250	3800
18 2	V518DC10		CR	FBG	IO 120	7 4			2950	3450
					1966 BOATS					
16 1	V416		RNBT	FBG	IO 110-120	6 7		3 7	2200	2550
18 2	V518 CUS		RNBT	FBG	IO 120-150	7 4		3 10	2950	3450
					1965 BOATS					
16 1	SUPER DELUXE		RNBT	FBG	IO 110-120				2300	2700
18 2	SUPER DELUXE		RNBT	FBG	IO 120-150				3050	3550
					1964 BOATS					
16 1			RNBT	FBG	IO 110				2400	2800
					1963 BOATS					
16			RNBT	FBG	IO				**	**

STEVENS BOAT MFG

Call 1-800-327-6929 for BUC Personalized Evaluation Service
Or, for 1961 to 1971 boats, sign onto www.BUCValuPro.com

STINGRAY BOAT COMPANY

HARTSVILLE SC 29551   COAST GUARD MFG ID- PNY See inside cover to adjust price for area

For more recent years, see the BUC Used Boat Price Guide, Volume 1 or Volume 2

LOA FT IN	NAME AND/ OR MODEL	TOP/ RIG	BOAT TYPE	-HULL- MTL TP	----ENGINE--- TP # HP MFG	BEAM FT IN	WGT LBS	DRAFT FT IN	RETAIL LOW	RETAIL HIGH
					1983 BOATS					
17 3	SVB 175	OP	FSH	FBG DV	OB	7	1100		1750	2100
17 3	SVB 175		RNBT	FBG DV	IO 120	7			2400	2750
17 3	SVB 175	OP	RNBT	FBG DV	OB	7	1100		1750	2100
18 7	SVB 190		RNBT	FBG DV	IO 120	7			2800	3250
18 7	SVC 195		CR	FBG DV	IO 120	7			2850	3300
					1982 BOATS					
17 3	SVB 175	OP	FSH	FBG DV	OB	7	1100		1700	2000
17 3	SVB 175	OP	RNBT	FBG DV	OB	7	1100		1750	2050
					1981 BOATS					
17 3	SVB 175 B/R	OP	RNBT	FBG DV	IO 120-185	7			2300	2700
17 3	SVBF 175	OP	FSH	FBG DV	IO 120-185	7	1900		2300	2850
17 3	SVBO 175	OP	RNBT	FBG DV	OB	7	1100		1700	2000
17 3	SVBO 175 B/R	OP	RNBT	FBG DV	OB	7	1100		1700	2000
17 3	SVBS 175 SE	OP	RNBT	FBG DV	IO 120-185	7	1940		2250	2700
17 3	SVC 175	OP	RNBT	FBG DV	IO 120-185	7	1925		2200	2700
17 3	SVC 175 B/R	OP	RNBT	FBG DV	OB	7	1925		2550	3000
17 3	SVCF 175	OP	FSH	FBG DV	IO 120-185	7	1900		2300	2850
17 3	SVCS 175 SE	OP	RNBT	FBG DV	IO 120-185	7	1940		2250	2700
18 7	SVB 190 B/R	OP	RNBT	FBG DV	IO 120-185	7	2030		2450	2950
18 7	SVBF 190	OP	RNBT	FBG DV	IO 120-185	7	2005		2400	2950
18 7	SVBS 190 SE	OP	RNBT	FBG DV	IO 120-140	7	2045		2450	2850
18 7	SVBS 190 SE	OP	RNBT	FBG DV	IO 470-485	7	2180		5650	6850
18 7	SVC 190	OP	RNBT	FBG DV	IO 120-185	7	2030		2450	2950
18 7	SVC 195 CUDDY CABIN	OP	SPTCR	FBG DV	IO 120-185	7			2750	3250
18 7	SVCC 190	OP	SPTCR	FBG DV	IO 120-185	7	2280		2650	3200
18 7	SVCCF 190	OP	FSH	FBG DV	IO 120-185	7	2265		2750	3400
18 7	SVCF 190	OP	RNBT	FBG DV	IO 120-185	7	2005		2400	2950
18 7	SVCS 190 SE	OP	RNBT	FBG DV	IO 120-185	7	2045		2450	2950

STOKEY

Call 1-800-327-6929 for BUC Personalized Evaluation Service
Or, for 1913 boats, sign onto www.BUCValuPro.com

R S STOKVIS & SONS

Call 1-800-327-6929 for BUC Personalized Evaluation Service
Or, for 1959 boats, sign onto www.BUCValuPro.com

W F STONE & SON

Call 1-800-327-6929 for BUC Personalized Evaluation Service
Or, for 1965 boats, sign onto www.BUCValuPro.com

STONINGTON BOAT WORKS

STONINGTON CT 06378   COAST GUARD MFG ID- SYR See inside cover to adjust price for area

LOA FT IN	NAME AND/ OR MODEL	TOP/ RIG	BOAT TYPE	-HULL- MTL TP	----ENGINE--- TP # HP MFG	BEAM FT IN	WGT LBS	DRAFT FT IN	RETAIL LOW	RETAIL HIGH
					1965 BOATS					
37 6	STONINGTON	SLP	SAIL	WD KL		12 4		4 5	11000	12500
41 8	STONINGTON	KTH	MS	WD	IB D FORD			4	46600	51200
41 8	STONINGTON	KTH	SAIL	WD KL		12 4		4 5	34700	38600
44 3	FISHER-ISLAND	KTH	SAIL	WD CB		13		4 3	43000	47800
					1963 BOATS					
37 6	STONINGTON L		SAIL	WD	OB				11700	13300
41 8	STONINGTON		SAIL	WD	OB				33800	37600
44 3	FISHER-ISLAND CPT		SAIL	WD	OB				43400	48300
44 3	FISHER-ISLAND DKHS		SAIL	WD	OB				43400	48300
					1962 BOATS					
37 6	STONINGTON		SAIL	WD	IB				23000	25500
41 8	STONINGTON		SAIL	WD	IB				29900	33300
42 3	FISHER-ISLAND 42		SAIL	WD	IB				31200	34700
46	FISHER-ISLAND 44		SAIL	WD	IB				49100	54000
					1961 BOATS					
41 8	STONINGTON		SAIL	WD KL	IB	12 4		4 6	29700	33000
42 3	FISHER-ISLAND	SLP	SAIL	WD CB	IB	13		4 3	30700	34200
					1960 BOATS					
37 6	STONINGTON		SAIL	WD	IB				23000	25500
41 8	STONINGTON		SAIL	WD	IB				29600	32900
42 3	FISHER-ISLAND		SAIL	WD	IB				30600	34000
					1954 BOATS					
39		HT	MY	WD SV	IB				**	**
40		SLP	MS	WD	IB				31200	34700
					1953 BOATS					
37		SLP	MS	WD KL	IB				26100	29000
					1951 BOATS					
44	FISHER-ISLAND		SAIL	WD	IB 30 UNIV				48100	52900
					1950 BOATS					
32		HT	CR	WD	IB				**	**
36		FB	SF	WD	RB IB	11 2		3 10	**	**
39 8		HT	CR	WD	IB T135 CHRY	12 2		4	27600	30700
					1949 BOATS					
35 11		HT	FSH	WD	IB CHRY	11 2		4	**	**
					1937 BOATS					
37 6	STONINGTON		SAIL	WD	IB				37200	41300

STOREBRO BRUKS AB

POMPANO BEACH FL 33062 COAST GUARD MFG ID- XBF See inside cover to adjust price for area

For more recent years, see the BUC Used Boat Price Guide, Volume 1 or Volume 2

LOA FT IN	NAME AND/ OR MODEL	TOP/ RIG	BOAT TYPE	-HULL- MTL TP	----ENGINE--- TP # HP MFG	BEAM FT IN	WGT LBS	DRAFT FT IN	RETAIL LOW	RETAIL HIGH
					1983 BOATS					
30 6	STOREBRO-ROYAL ADRIA	OP	CBNCR	FBG RB	IBT124D-T158D	10 6	12000	3 1	59000	68300
30 6	STOREBRO-ROYAL ADRIA	OP	CBNCR	FBG RB	IB T235D VLVO	10 6	12000	3 1	71400	78500
30 6	STOREBRO-ROYAL BALTC	OP	CBNCR	FBG RB	IBT124D-T158D	10 6	11500	3 1	59000	68300
30 6	STOREBRO-ROYAL BALTC	OP	CBNCR	FBG RB	IB T235D VLVO	10 6	11500	3 1	71400	78500
30 6	STOREBRO-ROYAL BALTC	HT	CBNCR	FBG RB	IBT124D-T158D	10 6	11500	3 1	60300	68300
30 6	STOREBRO-ROYAL BALTC	HT	CBNCR	FBG RB	IB T235D VLVO	10 6	12000	3 1	72600	79800
30 6	STOREBRO-ROYAL BISCY	HT	CBNCR	FBG RB	IBT124D-T158D	10 6	12000	3 1	61600	71000
30 6	STOREBRO-ROYAL BISCY	HT	CBNCR	FBG RB	IB T235D VLVO	10 6	13000	3 1	73800	81100
30 6	STOREBRO-ROYAL BISCY	FB	CBNCR	FBG RB	IBT124D-T158D	10 6	12500	3 1	63000	72500
30 6	STOREBRO-ROYAL BISCY	FB	CBNCR	FBG RB	IB T235D VLVO	10 6	13000	3 1	75000	82400
30 6	STOREBRO-ROYAL PATRL	HT	CR	FBG	IB T235D VLVO	10 10	11000		54700	60100
33 1	STOREBRO-ROYAL 33	SLP	SA/CR	FBG KL	SD 35D VLVO	11 2	10600	5 5	43400	48100
34	STOREBRO-ROYAL BALTC	OP	CBNCR	FBG DS	IBT124D-T235D	10 6		3 1	74400	92000
34	STOREBRO-ROYAL BALTC	HT	CBNCR	FBG DS	IBT124D-T158D	10 6	13000	3 1	70300	80300
34	STOREBRO-ROYAL BALTC	HT	CBNCR	FBG DS	IB T235D VLVO	10 6	13000	3 1	81200	89300
34	STOREBRO-ROYAL BALTC	FB	CBNCR	FBG DS	IBT124D-T158D	10 6	12500	3 1	71500	81500

LOA FT	LOA IN	NAME AND/ OR MODEL	TOP/ RIG	BOAT TYPE	-HULL- MTL	-HULL- TP	ENGINE TP	ENGINE # HP	ENGINE MFG	BEAM FT	BEAM IN	WGT LBS	DRAFT FT	DRAFT IN	RETAIL LOW	RETAIL HIGH
		1983 BOATS														
34		STOREBRO-ROYAL BALTC	FB	CBNCR	FBG	DS	IB	T235D	VLVO	10	6	13500	3	1	82200	90400
34		STOREBRO-ROYAL BISCY	HT	CBNCR	FBG	DS	IB	T124D-T235D		10	6		3	1	74400	92000
34		STOREBRO-ROYAL WORK	HT	PH	FBG	RB	IB	79D-235D		10	10	12000	3	3	58000	67500
34		STOREBRO-ROYAL WORK	HT	PH	FBG	RB	IB	T79D-T235D		10	10	12000	3	3	61200	73300
36	1	STOREBRO-ROYAL BALTC	HT	CBNCR	FBG	RB	IB	T235D	VLVO	12	6	19845	3	11	92400	101500
36	1	STOREBRO-ROYAL BALTC	FB	CBNCR	FBG	RB	IB	T235D	VLVO	12	6	19845	3	11	95100	104500
39	8	STOREBRO-ROYAL BALTC	HT	CBNCR	FBG	DS	IB	T235D	VLVO	12	10	25000	3	11	123500	135500
39	8	STOREBRO-ROYAL BALTC	HT	CBNCR	FBG	DS	IB	T286D	VLVO	12	10	26000	3	11	129500	142500
39	8	STOREBRO-ROYAL BALTC	FB	CBNCR	FBG	DS	IB	T235D	VLVO	12	10	26000	3	11	135500	149000
39	8	STOREBRO-ROYAL BALTC	FB	CBNCR	FBG	DS	IB	T286D	VLVO	12	10	27000	3	11	142000	156500
39	8	STOREBRO-ROYAL BISCY	HT	CBNCR	FBG	DS	IB	T235D	VLVO	12	10	25000	3	11	123500	135500
39	8	STOREBRO-ROYAL BISCY	HT	CBNCR	FBG	DS	IB	T286D	VLVO	12	10	26000	3	11	129500	142500
39	8	STOREBRO-ROYAL BISCY	FB	CBNCR	FBG	DS	IB	T235D	VLVO	12	10	26000	3	11	135500	149000
39	8	STOREBRO-ROYAL BISCY	FB	CBNCR	FBG	DS	IB	T286D	VLVO	12	10	27000	3	11	142000	156500
		1982 BOATS														
30	6	STOREBRO-ROYAL ADRIA	OP	CBNCR	FBG	RB	IB	T124D-T148D		10	6	11000	3	1	55000	62900
30	6	STOREBRO-ROYAL ADRIA	OP	CBNCR	FBG	RB	IB	T225D	VLVO	10	6	12000	3	1	66000	72600
30	6	STOREBRO-ROYAL BALTC	OP	CBNCR	FBG	RB	IB	T124D-T148D		10	6	11000	3	1	58300	66500
30	6	STOREBRO-ROYAL BALTC	OP	CBNCR	FBG	RB	IB	T225D	VLVO	10	6	12000	3	1	69600	76500
30	6	STOREBRO-ROYAL BALTC	HT	CBNCR	FBG	RB	IB	T124D-T148D		10	6	11500	3	1	57900	64700
30	6	STOREBRO-ROYAL BALTC	HT	CBNCR	FBG	RB	IB	T225D	VLVO	10	6	12500	3	1	68900	75700
30	6	STOREBRO-ROYAL BISCY	HT	CBNCR	FBG	RB	IB	T124D-T148D		10	6	12000	3	1	59200	67300
30	6	STOREBRO-ROYAL BISCY	HT	CBNCR	FBG	RB	IB	T225D	VLVO	10	6	13000	3	1	70100	77000
30	6	STOREBRO-ROYAL BISCY	FB	CBNCR	FBG	RB	IB	T124D-T148D		10	6	12500	3	1	60500	68700
30	6	STOREBRO-ROYAL BISCY	FB	CBNCR	FBG	RB	IB	T225D	VLVO	10	6	13500	3	1	71300	78300
33	1	STOREBRO-ROYAL 33	SLP	SA/CR	FBG	KL	IB	35D	VLVO	11	2	10600	4	11	40900	45400
34		STOREBRO-ROYAL BALTC	OP	CBNCR	FBG	DS	IB	T124D-T225D		10	6	12000	3	1	67600	83000
34		STOREBRO-ROYAL BALTC	HT	CBNCR	FBG	DS	IB	T124D-T148D		10	6	12000	3	1	67600	76300
34		STOREBRO-ROYAL BALTC	HT	CBNCR	FBG	DS	IB	T225D	VLVO	10	6	13000	3	1	77300	84900
34		STOREBRO-ROYAL BALTC	FB	CBNCR	FBG	DS	IB	T124D-T148D		10	6	12500	3	1	68700	77500
34		STOREBRO-ROYAL BALTC	FB	CBNCR	FBG	DS	IB	T225D	VLVO	10	6	13500	3	1	78300	86000
34		STOREBRO-ROYAL BISCY	HT	CBNCR	FBG	DS	IB	T124D-T225D		10	6		3	1	71500	87500
39	8	STOREBRO-ROYAL BALTC	HT	CBNCR	FBG	DS	IB	T225D	VLVO	12	10	25000	3	11	119500	131000
39	8	STOREBRO-ROYAL BALTC	HT	CBNCR	FBG	DS	IB	T270D	VLVO	12	10	26000	3	11	125000	137500
39	8	STOREBRO-ROYAL BALTC	FB	CBNCR	FBG	DS	IB	T225D	VLVO	12	10	26000	3	11	131000	144000
39	8	STOREBRO-ROYAL BALTC	FB	CBNCR	FBG	DS	IB	T270D	VLVO	12	10	27000	3	11	137000	150500
39	8	STOREBRO-ROYAL BISCY	HT	CBNCR	FBG	DS	IB	T225D	VLVO	12	10	25000	3	11	115000	126500
39	8	STOREBRO-ROYAL BISCY	HT	CBNCR	FBG	DS	IB	T270D	VLVO	12	10	26000	3	11	120500	132500
39	8	STOREBRO-ROYAL BISCY	FB	CBNCR	FBG	DS	IB	T225D	VLVO	12	10	26000	3	11	126500	139000
39	8	STOREBRO-ROYAL BISCY	FB	CBNCR	FBG	DS	IB	T270D	VLVO	12	10	27000	3	11	132500	145500
		1981 BOATS														
30	6	STOREBRO-ROYAL ADRIA	OP	CBNCR	FBG	RB	IB	T124D-T148D		10	6	11000	3	1	52900	60400
30	6	STOREBRO-ROYAL ADRIA	OP	CBNCR	FBG	RB	IB	T225D	VLVO	10	6	12000	3	1	63500	69800
30	6	STOREBRO-ROYAL BALTC	OP	CBNCR	FBG	RB	IB	T124D-T148D		10	6	11000	3	1	56100	63900
30	6	STOREBRO-ROYAL BALTC	OP	CBNCR	FBG	RB	IB	T225D	VLVO	10	6	12000	3	1	66900	73500
30	6	STOREBRO-ROYAL BALTC	HT	CBNCR	FBG	RB	IB	T124D-T148D		10	6	11500	3	1	55700	62200
30	6	STOREBRO-ROYAL BALTC	HT	CBNCR	FBG	RB	IB	T225D	VLVO	10	6	12500	3	1	66300	72800
30	6	STOREBRO-ROYAL BISCY	HT	CBNCR	FBG	RB	IB	T124D-T148D		10	6	12000	3	1	56900	64700
30	6	STOREBRO-ROYAL BISCY	HT	CBNCR	FBG	RB	IB	T225D	VLVO	10	6	13000	3	1	67400	74000
30	6	STOREBRO-ROYAL BISCY	FB	CBNCR	FBG	RB	IB	T124D-T148D		10	6	12500	3	1	58200	66100
30	6	STOREBRO-ROYAL BISCY	FB	CBNCR	FBG	RB	IB	T225D	VLVO	10	6	13500	3	1	68500	75300
33	1	STOREBRO-ROYAL 33	SLP	SA/CR	FBG	KL	IB	35D	VLVO	11	2	10600	4	11	38600	42900
34		STOREBRO-ROYAL BALTC	OP	CBNCR	FBG	DS	IB	T124D-T148D		10	6		3	1	68700	77500
34		STOREBRO-ROYAL BALTC	HT	CBNCR	FBG	DS	IB	T124D-T148D		10	6	12000	3	1	65000	73400
34		STOREBRO-ROYAL BALTC	HT	CBNCR	FBG	DS	IB	T225D	VLVO	10	6	13000	3	1	74300	81600
34		STOREBRO-ROYAL BALTC	FB	CBNCR	FBG	DS	IB	T124D-T225D		10	6		3	1	68800	82700
34		STOREBRO-ROYAL BISCY	HT	CBNCR	FBG	DS	IB	T124D-T225D		10	6		3	1	68400	83700
39	8	STOREBRO-ROYAL BALTC	HT	CBNCR	FBG	DS	IB	T225D	VLVO	12	10	25000	3	11	113500	125000
39	8	STOREBRO-ROYAL BALTC	HT	CBNCR	FBG	DS	IB	T270D	VLVO	12	10	26000	3	11	119000	131000
39	8	STOREBRO-ROYAL BALTC	FB	CBNCR	FBG	DS	IB	T225D	VLVO	12	10	26000	3	11	125000	137500
39	8	STOREBRO-ROYAL BALTC	FB	CBNCR	FBG	DS	IB	T270D	VLVO	12	10	27000	3	11	131000	144000
39	8	STOREBRO-ROYAL BISCY	HT	CBNCR	FBG	DS	IB	T225D	VLVO	12	10	25000	3	11	109500	120500
39	8	STOREBRO-ROYAL BISCY	HT	CBNCR	FBG	DS	IB	T270D	VLVO	12	10	26000	3	11	115000	126500
39	8	STOREBRO-ROYAL BISCY	FB	CBNCR	FBG	DS	IB	T225D	VLVO	12	10	26000	3	11	121000	132500
39	8	STOREBRO-ROYAL BISCY	FB	CBNCR	FBG	DS	IB	T270D	VLVO	12	10	27000	3	11	126500	139000
		1980 BOATS														
30	6	STOREBRO-ROYAL ADRIA	OP	CBNCR	FBG	RB	IB	T124D	VLVO	10	6	11000	3	1	50700	55800
30	6	STOREBRO-ROYAL ADRIA	OP	CBNCR	FBG	RB	IB	T225D	VLVO	10	6	12000	3	1	60900	66900
30	6	STOREBRO-ROYAL BALTC	OP	CBNCR	FBG	RB	IB	T124D	VLVO	10	6	11000	3	1	54100	59400
30	6	STOREBRO-ROYAL BALTC	OP	CBNCR	FBG	RB	IB	T225D	VLVO	10	6	12000	3	1	64500	70900
30	6	STOREBRO-ROYAL BALTC	HT	CBNCR	FBG	RB	IB	T124D	VLVO	10	6	11500	3	1	53600	58900
30	6	STOREBRO-ROYAL BALTC	HT	CBNCR	FBG	RB	IB	T225D	VLVO	10	6	12500	3	1	63800	70100
30	6	STOREBRO-ROYAL BISCY	HT	CBNCR	FBG	RB	IB	T124D	VLVO	10	6	12000	3	1	54800	60200
30	6	STOREBRO-ROYAL BISCY	HT	CBNCR	FBG	RB	IB	T225D	VLVO	10	6	13000	3	1	64800	71200
30	6	STOREBRO-ROYAL BISCY	FB	CBNCR	FBG	RB	IB	T124D	VLVO	10	6	12500	3	1	56000	61500
30	6	STOREBRO-ROYAL BISCY	FB	CBNCR	FBG	RB	IB	T225D	VLVO	10	6	13500	3	1	65900	72400
33	1	STOREBRO-ROYAL 33	SLP	SA/CR	FBG	KL	IB	35D	VLVO	11	2	10600	5	5	36900	41000
34		STOREBRO-ROYAL 34	HT	CBNCR	FBG	DS	IB	T124D	VLVO	10	6	12000	3	1	62500	68700
34		STOREBRO-ROYAL 34	HT	CBNCR	FBG	DS	IB	T225D	VLVO	10	6	13000	3	1	71500	78500
34		STOREBRO-ROYAL 34	FB	CBNCR	FBG	DS	IB	T124D	VLVO	10	6	12500	3	1	63500	69800
34		STOREBRO-ROYAL 34	FB	CBNCR	FBG	DS	IB	T225D	VLVO	10	6	13500	3	1	72400	79500
39	8	STOREBRO-ROYAL BALTC	HT	CBNCR	FBG	DS	IB	T225D	VLVO	12	10	25000	3	11	108500	119500
39	8	STOREBRO-ROYAL BALTC	HT	CBNCR	FBG	DS	IB	T270D	VLVO	12	10	26000	3	11	113500	125000
39	8	STOREBRO-ROYAL BALTC	FB	CBNCR	FBG	DS	IB	T225D	VLVO	12	10	26000	3	11	120000	131500
39	8	STOREBRO-ROYAL BALTC	FB	CBNCR	FBG	DS	IB	T270D	VLVO	12	10	27000	3	11	125000	137500
39	8	STOREBRO-ROYAL BISCY	HT	CBNCR	FBG	DS	IB	T225D	VLVO	12	10	25000	3	11	104500	114500
39	8	STOREBRO-ROYAL BISCY	HT	CBNCR	FBG	DS	IB	T270D	VLVO	12	10	26000	3	11	109500	120500
39	8	STOREBRO-ROYAL BISCY	FB	CBNCR	FBG	DS	IB	T225D	VLVO	12	10	26000	3	11	115000	126500
39	8	STOREBRO-ROYAL BISCY	FB	CBNCR	FBG	DS	IB	T270D	VLVO	12	10	27000	3	11	121000	132500
		1979 BOATS														
31		ADRIATIC		EXP	FBG		IB	124D		10	6				47700	52400
31		ADRIATIC		EXP	FBG		IB	T192D		10	6				50200	55200
31		BALTIC		CR	FBG		IB	124D		10	6				38400	42600
31		BISCAY		CR	FBG		IB	124D		10	6				40700	45200
31		BISCAY		CR	FBG		IB	T192D		10	6				42800	47500
33	1	STORE-ROYAL	SLP	SA/CR	FBG	KL	IB	D		11	2	11000	4	11	36700	40700
34		ROYAL-CRUISER		CR	FBG		IB	T124D-T192D		10	6				61300	70100
38	6			CR	FBG		IB	T270D		12	7				107500	118000
38	6	ROYAL-CRUISER		CR	FBG		IB	T192D		12	7				104000	114000
42	7	ROYAL-CRUISER		MY	WD		IB	T270D		14	1				124000	136000
47	3	ROYAL-CRUISER		MY	WD		IB	T342		14	3				151500	166500
47	3	ROYAL-CRUISER	HT	MY	WD		IB	T270D		14	3				158000	173500
		1966 BOATS														
23	11	SEA-CHASER		CBNCR	MHG		IO	100		8	2		2	2	15300	17400
28	9	EAGLE	SLP	SA/CR	P/M	KL	IB			7	10		4	3	18400	20400
29	9	ROYAL-CRUISER		CR	MHG		IB	T100		10	2		2	4	13700	15500
34		SEA-EAGLE	SLP	SA/CR	P/M	KL	IB			9	8		5	8	37000	41200
40	3	GOLDEN-EAGLE		CR	MHG		IB	T115		12	7		3	5	45600	50100
		1965 BOATS														
23	9	SEA-CHASER		CBNCR	WD		IB	100		8	2		2	2	5500	6350
28	9	EAGLE	SLP	SAIL	WD	KL	IB	7D		7	10		4	3	17300	19600
29	9	ROYAL-CRUISER		CR	WD		IB	T100		10			2	4	13100	14900
33	10	SEA-EAGLE II	SLP	SAIL	WD	KL	IB	14D		9	6		5	7	25300	28200
40		GOLDEN-EAGLE		CR	WD		IB	T115		12	2		3	6	44500	49500

STOWMAN SHIPBUILDING CORP

Call 1-800-327-6929 for BUC Personalized Evaluation Service
Or, for 1957 to 1970 boats, sign onto www.BUCValuPro.com

STREBLOW BOATS INC

Call 1-800-327-6929 for BUC Personalized Evaluation Service
Or, for 1961 to 1984 boats, sign onto www.BUCValuPro.com

STRIK COAST GUARD MFG ID- SAY

See inside cover to adjust price for area
For more recent years, see the BUC Used Boat Price Guide, Volume 1 or Volume 2

LOA FT	LOA IN	NAME AND/ OR MODEL	TOP/ RIG	BOAT TYPE	-HULL- MTL	-HULL- TP	ENGINE TP	ENGINE # HP	ENGINE MFG	BEAM FT	BEAM IN	WGT LBS	DRAFT FT	DRAFT IN	RETAIL LOW	RETAIL HIGH
		1983 BOATS														
32	6	STRIKER 33	FB	SF	AL	SV	IB	T250D		14		12500			79900	87800
41		STRIKER 41	FB	SDNSF	AL	SV	IB	T410D		14	10	16250			130000	142500
50		STRIKER 50	FB	SDNSF	AL	SV	IB	T550D		16	5	30000			207500	228500
60		STRIKER 60	FB	SDNSF	AL	SV	IB	T670D	GM	19	6	45000	3	6	281000	308500
60		STRIKER 60	FB	SDNSF	AL	SV	IB	T900D	MTU	19	6	45000	3	6	332000	364500
70		STRIKER 70	FB	SDNSF	AL	SV	IB	T13CD	MTU			80000			721500	793000
		1982 BOATS														
26		STRIKER 26	TT	OPFSH	FBG	SV	IB	130D	VLVO	8			2	2	13800	15700
33		STRIKER 33	FB	SF	AL	SV	IB	T310D	GM	14		12500	2	4	82200	90300
41		STRIKER 41	FB	SDNSF	AL	SV	IB	T325D	GM	14	9	16250	2	4	112500	124000
50		STRIKER 50	FB	SDNSF	AL	SV	IB	T550D	GM	17		30000	2	11	196000	215500
60		STRIKER 60	FB	SDNSF	AL	SV	IB	T670D	GM	19	6	45000	3	6	269000	295500
60		STRIKER 60	FB	SDNSF	AL	SV	IB	T900D	MTU	19	6	45000	3	6	317500	349000
70	6	STRIKER 70	FB	SDNSF	AL	SV	IB	T12CD	MTU	23	6	75000	3	4	674000	740500

CONTINUED ON NEXT PAGE

LOA FT	LOA IN	NAME AND/ OR MODEL	TOP/ RIG	BOAT TYPE	HULL MTL	HULL TP	ENGINE TP	ENGINE # HP	ENGINE MFG	BEAM FT	BEAM IN	WGT LBS	DRAFT FT	DRAFT IN	RETAIL LOW	RETAIL HIGH
		1981 BOATS														
26		STRIKER 26	TT	OPFSH	FBG	SV	IB	130D	VLVO	8			2	2	13300	15100
33		STRIKER 33	FB	SF	AL	SV	IB	T310D	GM	14		12500	2	4	79000	86800
41		STRIKER 41	F+T	SDNSF	AL	SV	IB	T325D	GM	14	9	16250	2	4	106500	117000
50		STRIKER 50	F+T	SDNSF	AL	SV	IB	T550D	GM	17		30000	2	11	185000	203500
60		STRIKER 60	F+T	SDNSF	AL	SV	IB	T670D	GM	19	6		3	6	257500	282500
60		STRIKER 60	F+T	SDNSF	AL	SV	IB	T900D	MTU	19	6		3	6	303000	333000
70	6	STRIKER 70	F+T	SDNSF	AL	SV	IB	T12CD	GM	23	6	75000	3	4	605000	665000
		1980 BOATS														
26		STRIKER 26	TT	OPFSH	FBG	SV	IB	130D	VLVO	8		5500	2	2	15700	17800
33		STRIKER 33	FB	SF	AL	SV	IB	T310D	GM	14		12500	2	4	76000	83500
40		STRIKER 40	FB	SDNSF	AL	SV	IB	T325D	GM	14	10	16250	2	5	94200	103500
50		STRIKER 50	FB	SDNSF	AL	SV	IB	T510D	GM	17		30000	2	11	173000	190500
60		STRIKER 60	FB	SDNSF	AL	SV	IB	T675D	GM	19	6		3	6	247000	271500
70	6	STRIKER 70	FB	SDNSF	AL	SV	IB	T725D	GM	23	6	75000	3	4	521000	572500
		1979 BOATS														
26		STRIKER 26	TT	OPFSH	FBG	SV	IB	130D	VLVO	8		5500	2	3	15200	17200
29		STRIKE 29	OP	OPFSH	FBG	SV	IB	T130D	VLVO	11			2	3	37600	41800
33		STRIKER 33	FB	SF	AL	SV	IB	T D	GM	14		12500	2		**	**
40		STRIKER 40	FB	SDNSF	AL	SV	IB	T325D	GM	14	4	15000	2	5	87500	96200
50		STRIKER 50	FB	SDNSF	AL	SV	IB	T510D	GM	16	3	28000	2	11	163000	179000
60		STRIKER 60	FB	SDNSF	AL	SV	IB	T675D	GM	17	10		3	6	227000	249500
70		STRIKER 70	FB	SDNSF	AL	SV	IB	T725D	GM	23	6				501500	551000
		1978 BOATS														
32	8	SPORT FISHERMAN	FB	SF	AL	SV	IB	T197D	GM	13		13500	2	3	65600	72100
38		CANYON-RUNNER	FB	CR	AL	SV	IB	T375D	GM	14	4	16250	2	5	85400	93800
38		SPORT FISHERMAN CNV	FB	SF	AL	SV	IB	T375D	GM	14	4	16250	2	5	84200	92500
48	9	SPORT FISHERMAN	FB	SF	AL	SV	IB	T425D	GM	16	3	28000	2	11	147500	162000
48	9	SPORT FISHERMAN	FB	SF	AL	SV	IB	T510D		16	3	28000	2	11	156500	172000
58		SPORT FISHERMAN	FB	SF	AL	SV	IB	T650D	GM	17	10	51480	3	6	230500	253000
58		SPORT FISHERMAN	FB	SF	AL	SV	IB	T820D		17	10	51480	3	6	258000	283500
68		YACHT FISHERMAN	FB	YTFS	AL		IB	T625D		19	9	75000	3	4	393000	431500
68		YACHT FISHERMAN	FB	YTFS	AL		IB	T820D		19	9	75000	3	4	417000	458000
		1977 BOATS														
38		CANYON-RUNNER	FB	SF	AL	SV	IB	T310D	GM	14	4	15000	2	5	72000	79100
38		SPORT FISHERMAN CNV	FB	SF	AL	SV	IB	T310D	GM	14	4	16000	2	5	75200	82600
48		SPORT FISHERMAN CNV	FB	SF	AL	SV	IB	T435D	GM	16	3	28000	2	11	143000	157000
58		SPORT FISHERMAN CNV	FB	SF	AL	SV	IB	T650D	GM	17	10		3	6	202000	222000
68		YACHT FISHERMAN	FB	YTFS	AL	SV	IB	T650D	GM	19	6	75000	3	4	382000	419500
		1976 BOATS														
30	10	SPORT FISHERMAN	FB	SF	AL	SV	IB	265D	GM	11	4	9500	2		37500	41700
30	10	SPORT FISHERMAN	FB	SF	AL	SV	IB	T175D-T235D		11	4		2		40800	48500
34		CANYON-RUNNER	FB	SF	AL	SV	IB	T230D	CUM	13	7	14000	2	4	67000	73600
38		SPORT FISHERMAN	FB	SF	AL	SV	IB	T265D	GM	14	4	15000	2	5	66500	73100
38		SPORT FISHERMAN	FB	SF	AL	SV	IB	T310D		14	4	15000	2	5	69000	75900
38		SPORT FISHERMAN	FB	SF	AL	SV	IB	T450D		14	4	15000	2	5	79600	87500
48	9	SPORT FISHERMAN	FB	SF	AL	SV	IB	T435D	GM	16	3	28000	2	11	136500	150000
48	9	SPORT FISHERMAN	FB	SF	AL	SV	IB	T675D		16	3	28000	2	11	159500	175000
54		SPORT FISHERMAN	FB	SF	AL	SV	IB	T650D	GM	17	10	40000	3	6	181000	199000
58		SPORT FISHERMAN	FB	SF	AL	SV	IB	T650D	GM	17	10		3	6	193500	212500
58		SPORT FISHERMAN	FB	SF	AL	SV	IB	T900D	BENZ	17	10		3	6	223500	246000
68		YACHT FISHERMAN	FB	YTFS	AL	SV	IB	T675D	GM	19	9	75000	3	4	370500	407000
68		YACHT FISHERMAN	FB	YTFS	AL	SV	IB	T900D		19	9	75000	3	4	392000	430500
		1975 BOATS														
34		CANYON-RUNNER	FB	SF	AL		IB	T225D	CUM	13	7	14000	2	4	64700	71100
44		SPORT FISHERMAN	FB	SF	AL		IB	T310D	GM	15	9	20000	2	9	85600	94000
		IB T350D GM 88600 97400, IB T370D CUM 89900 98800, IB T435D GM													97000	106500
54		SPORT FISHERMAN	FB	SF	AL		IB	T675D	GM	17	10	40000	3	6	179000	197000
		1974 BOATS														
34		CANYON-RUNNER			AL		IB	T225D-T240D		13	7	14500	2	4	64800	71300
44			FB	SF	AL		IB	T310D	GM	15	9	20000	2	10	83600	91800
		IB T350D GM 87900 96500, IB T370D CUM 89900 98800, IB T425D GM													97400	107000
54			FB	SF	AL		IB	T510D	GM	17	10	34000	3	6	141500	155500
54			FB	SF	AL		IB	T620D	GM	17	10	34000	3	6	161500	177500
		1973 BOATS														
34			FB	SF	AL		IB	T210D-T240D		13	7	14000	2	4	60700	70600
40			FB	SF	AL		IB	T310D	GM	14	11	19000	6		77300	84900
44			FB	SF	AL		IB	T310D	GM	15	9	22575	2	9	84600	92900
44			FB	SF	AL		IB	T350D	GM	15	9	23790	2	9	90100	99000
44			FB	SF	AL		IB	T370D	CUM	15	9	23125	2	9	90700	99700
54			FB	MY	AL		IB	T400D	GM	16	8	62000	3	11	172000	189000
54			FB	SF	AL		IB	T350D	GM	17	10	40000	3	6	116500	128000
54			FB	SF	AL		IB	T525D	GM	17	10	45000	3	6	157000	172500
		1972 BOATS														
34			FB	SF	AL		IB	T210D-T240D		13	7	14000	2	4	59200	68800
39			FB	SF	AL		IB	T210D	GM	14	11	17000	2	6	61000	67100
39			FB	SF	AL		IB	T310D	GM	14	11	19000	2	6	71000	78000
44			FB	SF	AL		IB	T240D	DAF	15	9	19000	2	9	71000	78000
		IB T310D GM 81500 89500, IB T350D GM 86800 95400, IB T370D CUM													87500	96100
54			FB	MY	AL		IB	T400D	GM	16	8	62000	3	11	166000	182500
54			FB	SF	AL		IB	T350D	GM	17	10	40000	3	6	112000	123500
54			FB	SF	AL		IB	T530D	GM	17	10	45000	3	6	152000	167000
		1971 BOATS														
36	7		FB	SF	AL		IB	T185D	DAF	13	9	14000	2	6	48800	53700
36	7		FB	SF	AL		IB	T190D	GM	13	9	14000	2	6	49000	53800
36	7		FB	SF	AL		IB	T210D	CUM	13	9	14000	2	6	49400	54300
36	10			SF	AL	DS	IB	T185D	DAF	13	9	12000	2	6	44500	49500
36	10			SF	AL	DS	IB	T190D	GM	13	9	12000	2	6	44700	49600
44			FB	SF	AL		IB	T240D	DAF	15	9	19000	2	9	68500	75200
		IB T290D GM 71600 78700, IB T350D GM 77600 85200, IB T370D CUM													79600	87500
54			FB	MY	AL		IB	T400D	GM	16		62000	3	11	161500	177500
54			FB	SF	AL		IB	T350D	GM	18		30000	2	9	95600	105000
54			FB	SF	AL		IB	T400D	GM	18		35000	3	9	109000	119500
54			FB	SF	AL		IB	T530D	GM	18		40000	3	5	138000	151500
65				TRWL	AL	DS	IB	T290D	GM	20		78000	5		240000	263500
		1970 BOATS														
36	6		FB	SF	AL	SV	IB	T185D	DAF	13	9	13000	2	6	44800	49800
36	6		FB	SF	AL	SV	IB	T216D	GM	13	9	13000	2	6	46200	50800
36	6			UTL	AL	SV	IB	T185D	DAF	13	9	12000	2	6	42700	47400
36	6			UTL	AL	SV	IB	T216D	GM	13	9	12000	2	6	43700	48500
44			FB	SF	AL	SV	IB	T240D	DAF	15	9	19000	2	9	66100	72600
		IB T283D GM 68700 75500, IB T290D GM 69200 76000, IB T350D GM													75000	82400
47				TCMY	AL	SV	IB	T240D	DAF	15	9	23000	2	9	87900	96600
		IB T283D GM 90000 98900, IB T290D GM 90300 99300, IB T350D GM													94200	103500
54				MY	AL	SV	IB	T300D	CAT	16		62000	3	11	140000	154000
54				MY	AL	SV	IB	T350D	GM	16		62000	3	11	148000	162500
54				MY	AL	SV	IB	T525D	GM	16		62000	3	11	169500	186000
54			FB	SF	AL	SV	IB	T300D	CAT	18		30000	3	2	88700	97400
54			FB	SF	AL	SV	IB	T350D	GM	18		30000	3	2	91800	101000
54			FB	SF	AL	SV	IB	T525D	GM	18		30000	3	2	121000	133000
68	4			MY	AL	SV	IB	T525D	GM	18		78000	4		283500	311500
		1969 BOATS														
34				SF	AL	SV	IB	T		11					**	**
36	6	FIRE SCUBA RESCUE		CR	AL	SV	IB	T D		13	9		2	6	**	**
36	6	POLICE BOAT		CR	AL	SV	IB	T D		13	9		2	9	**	**
36	7		FB	SF	AL		IB	T165D		13	9		2	6	49500	54400
36	7		FB	SF	AL		IB	T216D		13	9		2	6	51000	56000
44			FB	SF	AL		IB	T216D		15	6		2	9	85100	93500
44			FB	SF	AL		IB	T283D		15	6		2	9	88500	97300
53				MY	AL	SV	IB	T350D	CAT	16		28500	3	11	88800	97600
53			FB	SF	AL	SV	IB	T335D	CAT	16		28500	3	11	88600	97300
		1968 BOATS														
36	4	STRIKER 37	FB	SF	AL		IB	T165D		13	9	13228	2	6	41700	46300
44		STRIKER 44		DCFD	AL		IB	T215D		15	6	16372	2	9	56800	62400
44		STRIKER 44	FB	SF	AL		IB	T185D	CUM	15	6	16372	2	9	55500	61000
53		STRIKER 53		MY	AL		IB	T350D		16		28500	3	11	86500	95000
53		STRIKER 53	FB	SF	AL		IB	T350D		16		28500	3	11	87600	96300
		1967 BOATS														
27	2			SF	AL		IB	165D		10	6	7283	2	6	15000	17000
27	2	DELUXE		SF	AL		IB	165D		10	6	7283	2	6	16200	18400
36	4		FB	SF	AL		IB	T165D		13	9	13228	2	6	40500	45000
44			FB	SF	AL		IB	T185D		15	6	16372	3		54000	59400
		1966 BOATS														
27	2			SF	AL		IB	T165D	DAF			7283	2	6	18500	20600
28	11	SPORTFISHERMAN		SF	AL		IB	108D		11			2	2	28900	32100
34		SPORTFISHERMAN		SF	AL		IB	T108D		12	2		2	6	41900	46600
36	4			SF	AL		IB	T165D	DAF	13	9	14000	2	6	40700	45200
43		SPORTFISHERMAN		SF	AL		IB	T165D		14			2	7	80700	88700
44				SF	AL		IB	T165D	DAF			17000	2	9	53000	58200
		1965 BOATS														
34	8			SF	AL		IB	T108D	FORD	12	7	12500	2	6	47900	52600
36	4			SF	AL		IB	T165D	DAF	13	9	13228	2	6	38300	42600
44				SF	AL		IB	T165D	DAF	15	6	16372	2	9	50100	55100
		1964 BOATS														
28	11			SF	AL		IB	98D							26400	29300
34	8			SF	AL		IB	T165D							50200	55200
43				SF	AL		IB	T160D							75700	83200
56				MY	AL		IB								**	**
66				MY	AL		IB								**	**

CONTINUED ON NEXT PAGE

STRIKER YACHTS   -CONTINUED   See inside cover to adjust price for area

LOA FT IN	NAME AND/ OR MODEL	TOP/ RIG	BOAT TYPE	-HULL- MTL TP	TP	----ENGINE--- # HP	MFG	BEAM FT IN	WGT LBS	DRAFT FT IN	RETAIL LOW	RETAIL HIGH
--- 1963 BOATS ---
28 11		SF	AL	IB		98D					26100	29000
34 8		SF	AL	IB T		98D					49500	54400
43		SF	AL	IB T		160D					73700	81000
--- 1962 BOATS ---
28 11		SF	STL	IB		98D					25800	28700
34 8		SF	STL	IB T		98D					49000	53800
--- 1961 BOATS ---
27 10		CR	STL	IB		98D	FORD	10 6	15500	2 8	15500	17600
27 10		FB CR	STL	IB		98D	FORD	10 6	15500	2 8	15500	17600
33 8		SF	STL	IB T		98D	FORD	11 9	38900	3 2	38900	43200
36 10		SF	STL	IB T		98D	FORD	12 9	41700	3 4	41700	46400
42 4		SF	STL	IB T		98D	FORD	13 6	48900	3 10	48900	53700
--- 1960 BOATS ---
28		SF	STL	IB		98D					19900	22100
33		OP	STL	IB T		98D					35500	39400
42		SF	STL	IB T		98D					44800	49800
--- 1959 BOATS ---
26		SF	STL	IB		98D					10200	11500
29		SF	STL	IB		98D					25300	28100
33		SF	STL	IB T		98D					35300	39200
--- 1958 BOATS ---
33		SF	STL	IB T		98D					35100	39000

STRINGARI SKIFFS
FIBERGLASSING SHOP   COAST GUARD MFG ID- TFL
FORMERLY FIBERGLASS SHOP*THE

Call 1-800-327-6929 for BUC Personalized Evaluation Service
Or, for 1983 to 1986 boats, sign onto www.BUCValuPro.com

STUART ANGLER CORP
MIAMI FL 33054   COAST GUARD MFG ID- XAL See inside cover to adjust price for area

For more recent years, see the BUC Used Boat Price Guide, Volume 1 or Volume 2

LOA FT IN	NAME AND/ OR MODEL	TOP/ RIG	BOAT TYPE	-HULL- MTL TP	TP	----ENGINE--- # HP	MFG	BEAM FT IN	WGT LBS	DRAFT FT IN	RETAIL LOW	RETAIL HIGH
--- 1978 BOATS ---
33 2	COMMERCIAL	HT	FSH	FBG RB	IB	120D	FORD	11	7000	2 6	23700	26400
33 2	FLYBRIDGE	FB	SF	FBG RB	IB	120D-230D		11	8000	2 6	25700	29900
33 2	OPEN	OP	FSH	FBG RB	IB	120D-230D		11	7000	2 6	23700	28600
33 2	WORKBOAT	OP	UTL	FBG RB	IB	295	OLDS	11	6000	2 6	25500	28400
33 2	WORKBOAT	OP	UTL	FBG RB	IB	120D	FORD	11	6000	2 6	25200	28000
--- 1977 BOATS ---
33 2	STUART ANGLER	OP	FSH	FBG RB	IB	D		11	8000	2 6	**	**
--- 1976 BOATS ---
31 4	STUART SAILER	SLP	SA/CR	FBG CB	IB	D		9	7867	6 6	19100	21200
33 2	STUART ANGLER	OP	FSH	FBG	IB	120D-180D		10 4	7000	2 10	22200	25800

STUART YACHT BUILDERS
STUART FL 33497   See inside cover to adjust price for area

For more recent years, see the BUC Used Boat Price Guide, Volume 1 or Volume 2

LOA FT IN	NAME AND/ OR MODEL	TOP/ RIG	BOAT TYPE	-HULL- MTL TP	TP	----ENGINE--- # HP	MFG	BEAM FT IN	WGT LBS	DRAFT FT IN	RETAIL LOW	RETAIL HIGH
--- 1983 BOATS ---
31	STUART 31	FB	SF	FBG	OB			11			32300	35900
31	STUART 31	FB	SF	FBG	IO	T200		11			25600	28400
31	STUART 31	FB	SF	FBG	IB	T124D		11			38200	42400
34	STUART 34		CR	FBG	IB	T124D		11			55800	61300
34 8	STUART 35	SLP	SA/CR	FBG SK	IB	D		11 4	14250	4 2	52500	57700
43	STUART 43	KTH	SA/CR	FBG KL	IB	D		12 6	30000	6	116000	127000
55	STUART 55	CUT	SA/RC	FBG KL	IB	D		15	33000	6 6	218500	240000
58 6	STUART 60	SCH	SA/CR	FBG CT	IB	D		24	30000	4	276500	304000
63	STUART 63	KTH	SA/CR	FBG KC	IB	D		16	80000	6 6	477500	525000
--- 1982 BOATS ---
31	STUART 31		SF	FBG SV	OB			11			31200	34700
31	STUART 31		SF	FBG SV	IO	T200		11	10000		25200	28000
31	STUART 31		SF	FBG SV	IB	T124D		11	11000		34700	38600
32	STUART 32		CTRCN	FBG SV	OB			11			34500	38400
32	STUART 32		CTRCN	FBG SV	IO	300		11	9500		22100	24600
32	STUART 32		CTRCN	FBG SV	IB	300D		11	9000		31700	35200
34	STUART 34		EXP	FBG SV	IB	T124D		11	13000		53100	58400
35		SLP	SA/CR	FBG KL	IB	D		11 4	14250	4 2	49600	54500
42	STUART 42		MY	FBG SV	IB	T310D		15	28500		110000	120500
48	STUART 48	CUT	SA/RC	FBG KL	IB	D		15	30000	6 6	166000	182000
52	OCEAN		MY	FBG KL	IB	D		15	40000		156500	172000
52	STUART 52		EXP	FBG SV	IB	T221D		13	39000		156000	171500
60	CARIBBEAN	KTH	SA/CR	FBG CT	IB	D		24	30000	3 6	275500	302500
60	STUART 60		MY	FBG DS	IB	T150D		17	65000		233500	256500
63	CARIBBEAN	KTH	SA/CR	FBG KL	IB	D		16	70000	5 6	399000	438000
63	OCEAN	KTH	SA/CR	FBG KL	IB	D		16	70000	6 6	399000	438000
--- 1981 BOATS ---
31	STUART 31		SF	FBG	OB			11			30700	34100
31	STUART 31		SF	FBG	IO	T200		11			21200	23600
31	STUART 31		SF	FBG	IB	T124D		11			29800	33100
34	STUART 34		CR	FBG	IB	T124D		11			51400	56500
34 8		SLP	SA/CR	FBG KL	IB	D		11 4	14250	4 2	46700	51300
42	STUART 42		SF	FBG	IB	T310D		15			105000	115000
48	STUART 48		MY	FBG	IB	T310D		15			149500	164000
52	STUART 52		EXP	FBG	IB	T221D		13			149500	164500
60	STUART 60	KTH	SA/CR	FBG KL	IB	D			30000	3 6	256500	281500
60			MY	FBG DS	IB	T150D		17			223500	245500
63		KTH	SA/CR	FBG KL	IB	D		16	80000	5 6	428000	470000
--- 1980 BOATS ---
34 6	SPORTFISH 10.5		SF	FBG	OB			11			**	**
34 8		SLP	SA/CR	FBG KL	IB	D		11 4	14250	4 3	44100	49000
38	SPORTFISH 11.5		SF	FBG	OB			14			**	**

STUR-DEE BOAT COMPANY
TIVERTON RI 02878   COAST GUARD MFG ID- SDB See inside cover to adjust price for area

For more recent years, see the BUC Used Boat Price Guide, Volume 1 or Volume 2

LOA FT IN	NAME AND/ OR MODEL	TOP/ RIG	BOAT TYPE	-HULL- MTL TP	TP	----ENGINE--- # HP	MFG	BEAM FT IN	WGT LBS	DRAFT FT IN	RETAIL LOW	RETAIL HIGH
--- 1983 BOATS ---
18 5	THE FOX	CAT	SAIL	FBG KL				6			7100	8200
--- 1982 BOATS ---
18 5	FOX	CAT	SA/RC	FBG KL				6	855	3 3	5250	6000
--- 1973 BOATS ---
20	VIKING	OP	RNBT	FBG SV	OB			7 9	900		1750	2100
--- 1972 BOATS ---
20		OP	PLY SV	OB				7 9	900		1750	2100
--- 1970 BOATS ---
18	VIKING 18	OP	RNBT	PLY SV	IO	90	MRCR	7 2			2400	2800
20	VIKING 20	OP	RNBT	PLY SV	IO	120	MRCR	7 2			3000	3500
--- 1969 BOATS ---
18	VIKING 18	OP	RNBT	PLY SV	IO	60	MRCR	7 2			2500	2900
20	VIKING 20	OP	RNBT	PLY SV	IO	110	MRCR	7 2			3100	3600
--- 1968 BOATS ---
18	VIKING 18	OP	RNBT	WD	IO	60	MRCR	7 2			2600	3000
20	VIKING 20	OP	RNBT	WD	IO	110	MRCR	7 2			3200	3700

SUBURBAN INDUSTRIES
COAST GUARD MFG ID- SUC

Call 1-800-327-6929 for BUC Personalized Evaluation Service
Or, for 1972 to 1976 boats, sign onto www.BUCValuPro.com

SUMERSET CRUISERS

Call 1-800-327-6929 for BUC Personalized Evaluation Service
Or, for 1978 to 1982 boats, sign onto www.BUCValuPro.com

SUMNER BOAT CO INC
AMITYVILLE NY 11701   COAST GUARD MFG ID- SBC See inside cover to adjust price for area

For more recent years, see the BUC Used Boat Price Guide, Volume 1 or Volume 2

LOA FT IN	NAME AND/ OR MODEL	TOP/ RIG	BOAT TYPE	-HULL- MTL TP	TP	----ENGINE--- # HP	MFG	BEAM FT IN	WGT LBS	DRAFT FT IN	RETAIL LOW	RETAIL HIGH
--- 1983 BOATS ---
17	ISLANDS 17		SAIL	FBG	OB			6 2	475		1900	2300
--- 1973 BOATS ---
36	MOTORSAILER	SLP	MS	F/W KC	IB	170D		10 6	12000	5	22600	25100

SUMNER BOAT CO INC (continued)

LOA FT IN	NAME AND/OR MODEL	TOP/RIG	BOAT TYPE	HULL MTL	HULL TP	ENG TP	#	HP	MFG	BEAM FT IN	WGT LBS	DRAFT FT IN	RETAIL LOW	RETAIL HIGH
1972 BOATS														
36			MS	F/W		IB		170D	GM	10 6		5	29600	32900
36			MS	F/W		IB		220D	GM	10 6		5	29800	33100
1971 BOATS														
36			MS	F/W		IB		170D	GM	10 6		5	28900	32100
36			MS	F/W		IB		220D	GM	10 6		5	29100	32300
1970 BOATS														
36		SLP	MS	F/W	KC	IB		170D	GM	10 6	11500	3 2	20500	22800
36		SLP	MS	F/W	KC	IB		220D	GM	10 6	11500	3 2	20700	23000
1969 BOATS														
36		YWL	MS	F/W	KC	IB		170		10 6	11500	3 2	19800	22000
1968 BOATS														
31			EXP	F/W		IB		108D	FORD				15800	18000
31		CUT	MS	F/W	KL	IB		108D	FORD	10 2	9000	3 2	14600	16600
31			SDN	F/W		IB		108D	FORD	10 2		2 10	13700	15600
35		CUT	MS	F/W	KL	IB		160D		10 6		3 2	25900	28800
37			MS	F/W		IB		T108D	FORD				37500	41600
1967 BOATS														
31			EXP	F/W		IB		108D		10 2		2 10	15300	17400
31		CUT	MS	F/W	KL	IB		108D		10 2		3 1	19600	21800
31			SDN	F/W		IB		108D		10 2		2 10	13500	15300
35		CUT	MS	F/W	KL	IB		160D		10 2		3 2	25700	28600
37			MS	F/W		IB		T108D					36900	41000
1966 BOATS														
31			EXP	F/W		IB		108D		10 2		2 10	15100	17100
31		CUT	MS	F/W	KL	IB		108D		10 2		3 1	19400	21600
31			SDN	F/W		IB		108D		10 2		2 10	13300	15100
35		CUT	MS	F/W	KL	IB		160D		10 6		3 2	25400	28200
37			MS	F/W		IB		T108D					36400	40500
1965 BOATS														
31			EXP	F/W		IB		108D					15100	17100
31			MS	F/W		IB		108D					19200	21400
31			SDN	F/W		IB		108D					13300	15100
34			MS	F/W		IB		108D					26100	29000
37			MS	F/W		IB		108D					35200	39100
1964 BOATS														
26	SKIFF			FBG		IB		70D					5650	6500
31			EXP	FBG		IB		108D					14900	16900
31			MS	FBG		IB		108D					19100	21200
31			SDN	FBG		IB		108D					13100	14900
31			SDN	FBG		IB		T 70D					13200	15000
34			MS	FBG		IB		108D					25900	28800
34			MS	FBG		IB		T 70D					26100	29000
34			SDN	FBG		IB		T108D					19400	21500
37			MS	FBG		IB		T108D					35700	39700
42			SDN	FBG		IB		T130D					45900	50500
42			SDN	FBG		IB		T130D					29500	32700
1963 BOATS														
20	SKIFF			FBG		IB		60D					5550	6350
30			EXP	FBG		IB		108D					10600	12100
31			EXP	FBG		IB		108D					14700	16700
31		CUT		FBG		IB		108D					19000	21100
31			SDN	FBG		IB		108D					13000	14700
31			SDN	FBG		IB		T 60D					12900	14700
34			SDN	FBG		IB		T108D					19100	21300
36		CUT	MS	FBG		IB		T108D					26100	29000
36			SDN	FBG		IB		T108D					19500	21600
1962 BOATS														
30			EXP	FBG		IB		215					6150	7050
30			EXP	FBG		IB		T 96D					10700	12200
30		CUT	MS	FBG		IB		215					11200	12700
30		CUT	MS	FBG		IB		96D					19300	21400
1961 BOATS														
25	ADVENTURER SKIFF			WD		IB		125		8		2	2700	3150
25	ADVENTURER SKIFF			WD		IB		135		8		2	2750	3200
25	RESOLUTE	CR		WD		IB		109		8		2	2750	3200
25	RESOLUTE	CR		FBG		IB		T170		8		2	3300	3850
29 6	CRUSADER	CBNCR		WD		IB		135		9 10		2 8	6000	6900
29 6	CRUSADER	CBNCR		FBG		IB		170		9 10		2 8	6250	7150
29 6	CRUSADER	CBNCR		FBG		IB		96D		9 10		2 8	10400	11800
29 6	CRUSADER	CBNCR		WD		IB		96D		9 10		2 8	10400	11800
29 6	MOTORSAILER	MS		PLY				D		9 10		2 8	**	**
36	MOTORSAILER	MS		PLY						11 6		3	**	**
36	OCEAN CRUISER	CR		FBG		IB		T170		11 6		3	13100	14900
36	OCEAN CRUISER	CR		WD		IB		T 96D		11 6		3	16000	18200
43	MOTORSAILER	MS		PLY				D		12 6		3	**	**
43	OCEAN VOYAGER	CR		FBG		IB		T170		12 6		3	19100	21200
43	OCEAN VOYAGER	CR		WD		IB		T180		12 6		3	19200	21300
43	OCEAN VOYAGER	CR		FBG		IB		T 96D		12 6		3	22500	25000
43	OCEAN VOYAGER	CR		WD		IB		T 96D		12 6		3	22500	25000
1960 BOATS														
23	DAUNTLESS			F/W		IB		120		8		2	1850	2250
24	ADVENTURER			F/W		IB		120		8		2	2400	2750
25	RESOLUTE	CBNCR		F/W		IB		120		8 2		2 4	2700	3150
28	CRUSADER	CBNCR		F/W		IB		140		9 6		2 5	4550	5250
28	EXPLORER			F/W		IB		140		9 6		2 5	4050	4700
30	INTREPID	CBNCR		F/W		IB		D		9 8		2	**	**
32	OCEANIC	CBNCR		F/W		IB		D		9 8		3	**	**
33	EL-PRESIDENTE	CBNCR		F/W		IB		T130		11 2		2 6	9550	10900
1959 BOATS														
23	ADVENTURER			F/W		IB				8			**	**
24		CR		F/W		IB							**	**
25		CR		F/W		IB							**	**
25 11	CRUSADER I	CBNCR		F/W		IB				9 2			**	**
25 11	EXPLORER	CBNCR		F/W		IB				9 2			**	**
28	COMMANDO	CBNCR		F/W		IB				9 4			**	**
28	CRUSADER II	CBNCR		F/W		IB				9 4			**	**
33	EL-PRESIDENTE	CBNCR		F/W		IB				11 2			**	**
1958 BOATS														
23		CBNCR		FBG		IB							**	**
23		HT	CR	FBG		IB							**	**
23	ADVENTURER	CR		FBG		IB							**	**
26			CR	FBG		IB		95D					6350	7300
28	COMMANDO II			FBG		IB							**	**
28	CRUSADER II	EXP		FBG		IB		170D					8950	10200
33	EL-PRESIDENTE	CR		FBG		IB		T130					7850	9050

SUN RAY BOATS INC
COAST GUARD MFG ID- BED
FORMERLY BEDOUIN BOAT MFG

SUN RUNNER MARINE INC
SPOKANE WA 99205-3600   COAST GUARD MFG ID- XUE   See inside cover to adjust price for area

For more recent years, see the BUC Used Boat Price Guide, Volume 1 or Volume 2

LOA FT IN	NAME AND/OR MODEL	TOP/RIG	BOAT TYPE	HULL MTL	HULL TP	ENG TP	#	HP	MFG	BEAM FT IN	WGT LBS	DRAFT FT IN	RETAIL LOW	RETAIL HIGH
1983 BOATS														
16 6	175 B	ST	RNBT	FBG	DV	IO		120	MRCR	7 3	1650		1700	2000
16 6	175 F	ST	RNBT	FBG	DV	OB				7 3	970		1800	2150
18 3	195 B	ST	RNBT	FBG	DV	IO		120-230		7 8	2050		2100	2600
18 3	195 CV	OP	RNBT	FBG	DV	IO		120-230		7 8	2150		2200	2650
18 3	200 CF	ST	RNBT	FBG	DV	IO		120-230		7 8	2150		2250	2700
18 3	200 S	ST	CUD	FBG	DV	IO		120-230		7 8	2050		2300	2750
18 3	SABRE 195	ST	CUD	FBG	DV	IO		140-230		7 8	2050		3050	3750
20 2	215 CF	ST	CUD	FBG	DV	IO		140-260		8	2500		3350	4100
20 2	215 CV	ST	CUD	FBG	DV	IO		140-260		8	2500		3300	4100
20 2	215 CV	HT	CUD	FBG	DV	IO		140-260		8	2500		3450	4300
20 2	220 S	ST	CUD	FBG	DV	IO		140-260		8	2750		3650	4400
20 2	SABRE 215	ST	CUD	FBG	DV	IO		140-260		8	2500		3650	4400
22 2	225 CF	ST	CUD	FBG	DV	IO		140-260		8	3225		4250	5200
22 2	225 CF	ST	CUD	FBG	DV	IO		T120-T140		8	3225		4900	5650
22 2	225 CF	HT	CUD	FBG	DV	IO			VLVO	8	3225		**	**
22 2	225 CF	HT	CUD	FBG	DV	IO		138-260		8	3225		4450	5250
22 2	COASTAL-CRUISER 230	HT	CBNCR	FBG	DV	IO		140-260		8	3650		5150	6250
22 2	COASTAL-CRUISER 230	HT	CBNCR	FBG	DV	IO		T120-T140		8	3650		5850	6750
22 2	SUNBRIDGE	ST	CR	FBG	DV	IO		170	OMC	8	3650		5400	
22 6	SUNBRIDGE 230	ST	CR	FBG	DV	IO		140-260		8	3650		4700	5650
22 2	SUNBRIDGE 230	ST	CR	FBG	DV	IO		T120-T140		8	3650		5300	6100
23 6	SUNBRIDGE 245	ST	CR	FBG	DV	IO		170-260		8	3980		5350	6400
23 6	SUNBRIDGE 245	ST	CR	FBG	DV	IO		T120-T188		8	3980		5950	6950
26 3	SABRE 275	ST	CUD	FBG	DV	IO		260-330		9 7	7500		10100	12100
26 3	SABRE 275	ST	CUD	FBG	DV	IO		T170-T260		9 7	7500		10600	12900
26 6	SUNBRIDGE 275	ST	CR	FBG	DV	IO		260-330		9 7	7500		10200	12200
26 6	SUNBRIDGE 275	ST	CR	FBG	DV	IO		T170-T260		9 7	7500		10700	13000
29 6	SUNBRIDGE 310	ST	CR	FBG	DV	IO		260-330		11 6	10000		13200	15500

IO 130D-165D 15300 17300, IO T140-T260 13500 16800, IO T288-T330 15000 17700

LOA FT IN	NAME AND/ OR MODEL	TOP/ RIG	BOAT TYPE	-HULL- MTL TP	TP	----ENGINE--- # HP MFG	BEAM FT IN	WGT LBS	DRAFT FT IN	RETAIL LOW	RETAIL HIGH
						--- 1982 BOATS ---					
16 6	175 B	ST	RNBT		IO	VLVO	7 3	1750		**	**
16 6	175 B	ST	RNBT		IO	125-145	7 3	1750		1750	2100
16 6	175 F	ST	RNBT		OB		7 3	970		1700	2050
16 6	175 V	ST	RNBT		OB		7 3	970		1850	2200
16 6	175 V	ST	RNBT		IO	VLVO	7 3	1650		**	**
16 6	175 V	ST	RNBT		IO	125-145	7 3	1650		1750	2100
16 6	SABRE 175	ST	RNBT		IO	VLVO	7 3	1650		**	**
16 6	SABRE 175	ST	RNBT		IO	120 MRCR	7 3	1650		1700	2000
16 6	SABRE 175	ST	RNBT		IO	120-185	7 3	1650		1800	2200
18 3	195 B	ST	RNBT		IO	OMC	7 8	2050		**	**
	IO VLVO	**	**	, IO 120-140		2050 2550, IO 145-230				2200	2650
	IO 260	2300	2800								
18 3	195 CF	ST	RNBT		IO	OMC	7 8	1950		**	**
	IO VLVO	**	**	, IO 120-140		2000 2500, IO 145-230				2150	2600
	IO 260	2250	2750								
18 3	195 CV	ST	CUD		IO	OMC	7 8	2050		**	**
	IO VLVO	**	**	, IO 120		2000 2400, IO 125-260				2250	2800
18 3	200 OS	ST	CUD		IO	OMC	7 8	1950		**	**
	IO 120 MRCR	2050	2450, IO 120	OMC		2050 2400, IO 120-230				2200	2700
	IO 260	2300	2800								
18 3	200 S	ST	CUD		IO	OMC	7 8	2050		**	**
18 3	200 S	ST	CUD		IO	120-200	7 8	2050		2200	2750
18 3	200 S	ST	CUD		IO	225-260	7 8	2050		2400	3000
18 3	SABRE 195	ST	CUD		IO	OMC	7 8	2100		**	**
	IO VLVO	**	**	, IO 120-198		2150 2650, IO 200				2200	2700
18 3	SABRE 195	HT	CUD		IO	260	7 8	2100		2350	2900
20 2	215 CF	ST	CUD		IO	OMC	8	2500		**	**
20 2	215 CF	ST	CUD		IO	140-200	8	2500		3200	3950
20 2	215 CF	ST	CUD		IO	225-260	8	2500		3450	4200
20 2	215 CF	HT	CUD		IO	OMC	8	2500		**	**
20 2	215 CF	HT	CUD		IO	85-200	8	2500		3200	3950
20 2	215 CF	HT	CUD		IO	225-260	8	2500		3450	4200
20 2	215 CF	ST	RNBT		OB		8	1500		3250	3200
20 2	215 CF	HT	RNBT		OB		8	1500		2750	3200
20 2	215 CV	ST	CUD		IO	OMC	8	2550		**	**
20 2	215 CV	ST	CUD		IO	140-200	8	2550		3250	4000
20 2	215 CV	ST	CUD		IO	225-260	8	2550		3500	4250
20 2	215 CV	HT	CUD		IO	OMC	8	2550		**	**
20 2	215 CV	HT	CUD		IO	140-200	8	2550		3250	4000
20 2	215 CV	HT	CUD		IO	225-260	8	2550		3500	4250
20 2	215 SD	ST	CUD		IO	OMC	8	2900		**	**
20 2	215 SD	ST	CUD		IO	140-230	8	2900		3500	4350
20 2	215 SD	ST	CUD		IO	260	8	2900		3700	4550
20 2	220 OS	ST	CUD		IO	OMC	8	2700		**	**
20 2	220 OS	ST	CUD		IO	140-230	8	2700		3350	4200
20 2	220 OS	ST	CUD		IO	260	8	2700		3600	4350
20 2	220 OS	HT	CUD		IO	OMC	8	2700		**	**
20 2	220 OS	HT	CUD		IO	140-230	8	2700		3350	4200
20 2	220 OS	HT	CUD		IO	260	8	2700		3600	4350
20 2	220 S	ST	CUD		IO	OMC	8	2750		**	**
20 2	220 S	ST	CUD		IO	140-230	8	2750		3400	4250
20 2	220 S	ST	CUD		IO	260	8	2750		3600	4400
20 2	220 S	HT	CUD		IO	OMC	8	2750		**	**
20 2	220 S	HT	CUD		IO	140-230	8	2750		3400	4250
20 2	220 S	HT	CUD		IO	260	8	2750		3600	4400
20 2	220 SD	HT	CUD		IO	OMC	8	2900		**	**
20 2	220 SD	HT	CUD		IO	140-230	8	2900		3500	4350
20 2	220 SD	HT	CUD		IO	260	8	2900		3700	4550
20 2	SABRE 215	ST	CUD		IO	OMC	8	2600		**	**
20 2	SABRE 215	ST	CUD		IO	140-200	8	2600		3300	4050
20 2	SABRE 215	ST	CUD		IO	225-260	8	2600		3550	4300
22 2	225 CF	ST	CUD		IO	OMC	8	3225		**	**
	IO VLVO	**	**	, IO 140-230		4200 5150, IO 260				4450	5350
22 2	225 CF	HT	CUD		IO	OMC	8	3225		**	**
	IO VLVO	**	**	, IO 140-230		4150 5050, IO 260				4400	5250
22 2	225 CV	ST	CUD		IO	OMC	8	3225		**	**
	IO VLVO	**	**	, IO 140-230		4200 5100, IO 260				4450	5300
22 2	225 CV	HT	CUD		IO	OMC	8	3225		**	**
	IO VLVO	**	**	, IO 140-230		4250 5200, IO 260				4500	5400
22 2	225 SD	HT	CR	FBG	IO	OMC	8	3450		**	**
22 2	225 SD	HT	CR	FBG	IO	140-260	8	3450		4400	5500
22 2	230 CC	HT	CR	FBG	IO	OMC	8	3650		**	**
22 2	230 CC	HT	CR	FBG	IO	140-260	8	3650		4600	5700
22 2	230 OS	ST	CR	FBG	IO	OMC	8	3450		**	**
22 2	230 OS	ST	CR	FBG	IO	140-230	8	3450		4300	5250
22 2	230 OS	ST	CR	FBG	IO	260	8	3450		4550	5450
22 2	230 SB	ST	CR	FBG	IO	OMC	8	3450		**	**
22 2	230 SB	ST	CR	FBG	IO	140-260	8	3450		4500	5650
23 6	245 CB	HT	CR	FBG	IO	OMC	8	4350		**	**
23 6	245 CB	HT	CR	FBG	IO	170-260	8	4350		5600	6900
23 6	245 SB	ST	CR	FBG	IO	OMC	8	3380		**	**
23 6	245 SB	ST	CR	FBG	IO	170-260	8	3380		4700	5800
23 6	245 SD	HT	CR	FBG	IO	OMC	8	3990		**	**
23 6	245 SD	HT	CR	FBG	IO	170-260	8	3990		5250	6450

SUN YACHTS

LOA FT IN	NAME AND/ OR MODEL	TOP/ RIG	BOAT TYPE	-HULL- MTL TP	TP	----ENGINE--- # HP MFG	BEAM FT IN	WGT LBS	DRAFT FT IN	RETAIL LOW	RETAIL HIGH
						--- 1979 BOATS ---					
27 6	SUN 838	SLP	SA/CR	FBG KL	OB		9	6200	4 4	11100	12600
27 6	SUN 838	SLP	SA/CR	FBG KL	SD	15 OMC	9	6200	4 4	11300	12800
27 6	SUN 838	SLP	SA/CR	FBG KL	IB	8D- 15D	9	6200	4 4	11400	13100
33 10	SUN 1030	SLP	SA/CR	FBG KL	IB	15D- 20D	11	10500	5 11	22800	25400
						--- 1978 BOATS ---					
27 6	SUN YACHT 27	SLP	SAIL	FBG KL	OB		9	6300	4 4	10900	12400
27 6	SUN YACHT 27	SLP	SAIL	FBG KL	SD	15 OMC	9	6300	4 4	11000	12500
27 6	SUN YACHT 27	SLP	SAIL	FBG KL	IB	8D YAN	9	6300	4 4	11200	12700

SUNBIRD YACHTS LTD
Call 1-800-327-6929 for BUC Personalized Evaluation Service
Or, for 1979 to 1985 boats, sign onto www.BUCValuPro.com

SUNDANCE MARINE INC
COAST GUARD MFG ID- SNX

Call 1-800-327-6929 for BUC Personalized Evaluation Service
Or, for 1977 to 1979 boats, sign onto www.BUCValuPro.com

SUNLINER

LOA FT IN	NAME AND/ OR MODEL	TOP/ RIG	BOAT TYPE	-HULL- MTL TP	TP	----ENGINE--- # HP MFG	BEAM FT IN	WGT LBS	DRAFT FT IN	RETAIL LOW	RETAIL HIGH
						--- 1969 BOATS ---					
36	MARK III	HT	HB	STL DV	IO	T210 OMC	12	13500	2 6	25300	28100
36	MARK III A	HT	HB	STL DV	IO	T250 MRCR	12	13750	2 6	26300	29300
36	MARK III B	HT	HB	STL DV	IO	T325 MRCR	12	14500	2 6	29000	32300
45	MARK IV	HT	HB	STL DV	IO	T210 OMC	13	19300	3	29400	32600
45	MARK IV A	HT	HB	STL DV	IO	T250 MRCR	13	19300	3	30400	33800
45	MARK IV B	HT	HB	STL DV	IO	T250 MRCR	13	19800	3	30800	34200
57	MARK V	HT	HB	STL DV	IO	T325 MRCR	14	21500	3	41400	46000
						--- 1968 BOATS ---					
32	SUNLINER 32		HB	STL DV	IO	210-235	12	11300	1 2	21700	24300
32	SUNLINER 32 T		HB	STL DV	IO	T150	12	11300		22700	25300
42	SUNLINER 42		HB	STL DV	IO	T210	13	16500	1 4	27000	30300
42	SUNLINER 42C		HB	STL DV	IO	T235	13	16500	1 4	27300	30300
42	SUNLINER 42M		HB	STL DV	IO	T225	13	16500	1 4	27200	30200
						--- 1967 BOATS ---					
32	SUNLINER 32		HB	STL	IO	210-235	12	11300		25100	24100
32	SUNLINER 32T		HB	STL	IO	T150	12	11300		25600	25100
42	SUNLINER 42		HB	STL	IO	T210	13	16500		26800	29700
42	SUNLINER 42C		HB	STL	IO	T235	13	16500		27100	30100
42	SUNLINER 42M		HB	STL	IO	T225	13	16500		27000	29900

LOA FT IN	NAME AND/ OR MODEL	TOP/ RIG	BOAT TYPE	-HULL- MTL TP	--ENGINE--- TP # HP MFG	FT IN	WGT LBS	FT IN	RETAIL LOW	RETAIL HIGH
1966 BOATS
32	SUNLINER 32	HT	HB	STL	IO 210	12	11300	1	21300	23700
42	SUNLINER 42	HT	HB	STL	IO T210	13	16500	1	26600	29500

SUNRAY
ST ANNE DE LA PERADE QU COAST GUARD MFG ID- ZSU See inside cover to adjust price for area

For more recent years, see the BUC Used Boat Price Guide, Volume 1 or Volume 2

LOA FT IN	NAME AND/ OR MODEL	TOP/ RIG	BOAT TYPE	-HULL- MTL TP TP	--ENGINE--- # HP MFG	BEAM FT IN	WGT LBS	DRAFT FT IN	RETAIL LOW	RETAIL HIGH
1978 BOATS
16 4	SW-165	OP	RNBT	FBG TR OB		6 6	1025		1800	2100
16 10	SV-169	OP	RNBT	FBG DV OB		6 9	1000		1750	2100
16 10	SV-170	ST	RNBT	FBG DV IO	120-175	6 9	1960		2550	2950
18 6	SV-184	ST	RNBT	FBG DV OB		8	1650		2750	3200
18 6	SV-185	ST	WKNDR	FBG DV IO	175-240	8	2630		3700	4450
19 11	SV-200	ST	WKNDR	FBG DV IO	175-240	8	2920		4250	5100
1977 BOATS
16 4	SW165	OP	RNBT	FBG TR OB		6 6	1025		1750	2100
16 10	SV169	OP	RNBT	FBG DV OB		6 9	1000		1750	2100
16 10	SV170	ST	RNBT	FBG DV IO	120-175	6 9	1960		2600	3000
18 6	SV184	ST	RNBT	FBG DV OB		8	1650		2700	3150
18 6	SV185	ST	RNBT	FBG DV IO	165-235	8	2630		3650	4400
19 11	SV200	ST	RNBT	FBG DV IO	188-235	8	2920		4200	5000
19 11	SV200	ST	RNBT	FBG DV IO	280 MRCR	8	2920		4600	5300
1976 BOATS
16 4	SW165	OP	RNBT	FBG TR OB		6 6	1000		1700	2000
16 5	AS-165	OP	ROW	AL FL OB		5 10	1505		**	**
16 10	SV169	OP	RNBT	FBG SV OB		6 9	1250		2100	2500
16 10	SV170	ST	RNBT	FBG DV IO	120-175	6 9	1500		2350	2750
18	AS-180	OP	RNBT	AL FL OB		6 9	1870		2900	3350
19 11	SV200	ST	RNBT	FBG DV IO	165-235	8	2350		3800	4600
1975 BOATS
16 4	SW165	OP	RNBT	FBG TR OB		6 6	1000		1700	2000
16 10	SV169	OP	RNBT	FBG SV OB		6 9	1250		2050	2450
16 10	SV170	OP	RNBT	FBG SV IO	120-140	6 9	1500		2400	2800
16 10	SV170	OP	RNBT	FBG SV IO	165 VLVO	6 9	1500		2600	3050
1974 BOATS
16 10	SV-170	OP	RNBT	FBG SV IO		6 9	1500	3 1	**	**
1973 BOATS
16 10	SV-170	OP	RNBT	FBG SV IO	120 OMC	6 9	1500	3 1	2550	2950
1972 BOATS
16 10	SV-170			FBG IO		6 9	1500	3 1	**	**

SUNSATION PERFORMANCE BOATS
ANCHORVILLE MI 48004   COAST GUARD MFG ID- SP3 See inside cover to adjust price for area
FORMERLY SUNSATION PRODUCTS

For more recent years, see the BUC Used Boat Price Guide, Volume 1 or Volume 2

LOA FT IN	NAME AND/ OR MODEL	TOP/ RIG	BOAT TYPE	-HULL- MTL TP TP	--ENGINE--- # HP MFG	BEAM FT IN	WGT LBS	DRAFT FT IN	RETAIL LOW	RETAIL HIGH
1983 BOATS
16	MINI RACER	OP	OFF	FBG SV OB		6 4	789	8	2350	2700

SUNWARD YACHT CORP
WILMINGTON NC 28405   COAST GUARD MFG ID- SJW See inside cover to adjust price for area

For more recent years, see the BUC Used Boat Price Guide, Volume 1 or Volume 2

LOA FT IN	NAME AND/ OR MODEL	TOP/ RIG	BOAT TYPE	-HULL- MTL TP TP	--ENGINE--- # HP MFG	BEAM FT IN	WGT LBS	DRAFT FT IN	RETAIL LOW	RETAIL HIGH
1983 BOATS
48	SUNWARD 48	KTH	SA/CR	FBG KL IB	100D WEST	14 3	48000	5 7	160000	176000
1982 BOATS
48	SUNWARD 48	KTH	SA/CR	FBG KL IB	85D PERK	14 3	48000	5 7	149500	164500
1981 BOATS
48	SUNWARD 48	KTH	SA/CR	FBG KL IB	85D PERK	14 3	48000	5 7	140500	154500
1980 BOATS
48	SUNWARD 48	KTH	SA/CR	FBG KL IB	85D PERK	14 3	48000	5 7	134500	147500
1979 BOATS
48	SUNWARD 48	KTH	SA/CR	FBG KL IB	85D PERK	14 3	48000	5 7	129000	142000
1978 BOATS
48	SUNWARD 48	KTH	SA/CR	FBG KL IB	100D GM	14 3	48000	5 7	125000	137500

SUPER CRAFT BOAT MFG CO
COAST GUARD MFG ID- SSJ

Call 1-800-327-6929 for BUC Personalized Evaluation Service
Or, for 1969 to 1971 boats, sign onto www.BUCValuPro.com

SUPER CRAFT BOATS INC
COAST GUARD MFG ID- SVS

Call 1-800-327-6929 for BUC Personalized Evaluation Service
Or, for 1978 to 1980 boats, sign onto www.BUCValuPro.com

SUPERBOATS
COAST GUARD MFG ID- SBY

Call 1-800-327-6929 for BUC Personalized Evaluation Service
Or, for 1982 to 1999 boats, sign onto www.BUCValuPro.com

SUPERCAT CATAMARANS
DIV OF ERICSON YACHTS   COAST GUARD MFG ID- FMS

Call 1-800-327-6929 for BUC Personalized Evaluation Service
Or, for 1981 to 1990 boats, sign onto www.BUCValuPro.com

SUPERIOR MARINE CO

Call 1-800-327-6929 for BUC Personalized Evaluation Service
Or, for 1966 to 1968 boats, sign onto www.BUCValuPro.com

SUPERIOR PLASTICS INC
DIV HOOKER INDUSTRIES   See inside cover to adjust price for area
MARLIN BOATS
WHITE CITY OR 97501   COAST GUARD MFG ID- SPR

LOA FT IN	NAME AND/ OR MODEL	TOP/ RIG	BOAT TYPE	-HULL- MTL TP TP	--ENGINE--- # HP MFG	BEAM FT IN	WGT LBS	DRAFT FT IN	RETAIL LOW	RETAIL HIGH
1975 BOATS
16 3	VENUS	OP	CUD	FBG TR OB		6 5	975		2300	2700
16 3	VENUS	OP	RNBT	FBG TR IO	120-165	6 5	1747		2100	2500
17 2	JUPITER	OP	RNBT	FBG DV IO	120-188	6 9	1935		2400	2850
17 2	JUPITER	OP	RNBT	FBG DV JT	365	6 9	1935		2600	3050
17 2	JUPITER	OP	RNBT	FBG TR OB		6 9	1140		2700	3150
17 6	MERCURY	OP	RNBT	FBG DV OB		7 2	1290		3000	3500
17 6	MERCURY	OP	RNBT	FBG DV IO	120-188	7 2	2090		2650	3100
17 10	AQUARIUS	OP	SKI	FBG DV OB		7 3	750		1900	2250
17 10	AQUARIUS	OP	SKI	FBG DV JT	365	7 3	1600		2500	2900
17 10	LEO	OP	SKI	FBG DV IO	165-188	7 3	1830		2450	2900
17 10	LEO	OP	SKI	FBG DV JT	365	7 3	1830		2600	3050
17 10	MARS	OP	RNBT	FBG TR IO	165	6 11	1710		2450	2850
17 10	MARS	OP	RNBT	FBG TR JT	365	6 11	1710		2750	3200
17 10	TAURUS	OP	SKI	FBG DV IO	365	7 3	845		2150	2500
17 10	TAURUS	OP	SKI	FBG DV JT	365	7 3	1810		2600	3050
20 4	LIBRA	OP	CUD	FBG DV JT	390	7 7			3650	4250
1974 BOATS
16 3	VENUS	OP	CUD	FBG TR OB		6 5	975		2300	2650
16 3	VENUS	ST	CUD	FBG TR IO	120-165	6 5	1747		2200	2600
17 2	JUPITER	ST	RNBT	FBG TR OB		6 9	1140		2700	3100
17 2	JUPITER	ST	RNBT	FBG TR IO	120-188	6 9	1935		2500	2950
17 2	JUPITER	ST	RNBT	FBG DV JT	365-390	6 9	2140		2600	3050
17 2	SATURN	ST	RNBT	FBG TR OB		6 9	1140		2700	3100
17 6	MERCURY	ST	RNBT	FBG DV OB		7 2	1290		3000	3500
17 6	MERCURY	ST	RNBT	FBG DV IO	120-188	7 2	2090		2750	3250
17 10	AQUARIUS III		SKI	FBG DV OB		7 3	750		1900	2250
17 10	AQUARIUS III		SKI	FBG DV IO	140-165	7 3	1600		2400	2800
17 10	AQUARIUS III		SKI	FBG DV JT	330-450	7 6	1740		2550	2950
17 10	AQUARIUS IV		SKI	FBG DV JT	330-450	7 6	1790		2550	2950
17 10	LEO		RNBT	FBG DV IO	165-188	7 6	1830		2700	3200
17 10	LEO		RNBT	FBG DV JT	330-450	7 6	1865		2700	3150
17 10	MARS	ST	RNBT	FBG TR IO	165-188	6 11	1710		2500	2950
17 10	MARS	ST	RNBT	FBG TR JT	330-450	6 11	2315		2800	3300

```
SUPERIOR PLASTICS INC        -CONTINUED      See inside cover to adjust price for area
  LOA  NAME AND/             TOP/ BOAT  -HULL-  ----ENGINE---  BEAM   WGT  DRAFT RETAIL RETAIL
FT IN  OR MODEL              RIG  TYPE  MTL TP TP # HP  MFG   FT IN   LBS  FT IN  LOW   HIGH
----------------- 1974 BOATS -----------------------------------------------------------------
17 10  TAURUS                SKI  FBG DV OB               7  3   845         2100  2500
17 10  TAURUS                SKI  FBG DV IO 165-188       7  6  1810         2600  3050
17 10  TAURUS                SKI  FBG DV JT 330-450       7  6  1835         2550  3000
20  4  LIBRA                 CUD  FBG DV IO 188   MRCR    7  7  2265         3900  4550
20  4  LIBRA                 CUD  FBG DV JT 390-450       7  7  2300         3500  4100
----------------- 1973 BOATS -----------------------------------------------------------------
16     BLUEWATER                  FBG    IO 120   MRCR    5  4  1935         2050  2450
16  3  VENUS                      FBG    OB               6  5   975         2300  2650
16  3  VENUS                      FBG    IO 120   MRCR    6  5  1747         2150  2500
17  2  JUPITER                    FBG    JT 330   BERK    7  7  2140         2550  2950
17  2  SATURN                     FBG    OB               7  7  1140         2650  3100
17 10  AQUARIUS                   FBG    OB               7  3   750         1850  2250
17 10  AQUARIUS III               FBG    IO 140-165          1600         2500  2900
17 10  AQUARIUS III               FBG    JT 330   BERK       1740         2350  2750
17 10  AQUARIUS IV                FBG    JT 330   BERK    7  3  1790         2400  2800
17 10  LEO                        FBG    IO 165-188       7  3  1830         2650  3100
17 10  LEO                        FBG    JT 330   BERK    7  3  1865         2450  2850

17 10  MARS                       FBG    IO 188   MRCR    6 11  2270         2900  3350
17 10  MARS                       FBG    JT 330   BERK    6 11  2315         2600  3050
17 10  TAURUS                     FBG    OB               7  3   845         2100  2500
17 10  TAURUS                     FBG    IO 165   MRCR    7  3  1810         2650  3100
17 10  TAURUS                     FBG    JT 330   BERK    7  3  1835         2400  2800
20  4  LIBRA                      FBG    IO 188   MRCR    7  7  2265         3850  4500
20  4  LIBRA                      FBG    JT 330   BERK    7  7  2300         3400  3950
----------------- 1972 BOATS -----------------------------------------------------------------
17  2  JUPITER                    FBG    IO 120-188       6  9  1530         2300  2750
17  2  JUPITER                    FBG    JT 330   OLDS    6  9               2000  2400
17  2  SATURN                     FBG    OB               6  9  1140         2650  3050
17 10  AQUARIUS                   FBG    OB               7  3   730         1800  2150
17 10  AQUARIUS                   FBG    IO 140-188       7  3  1590         2600  3050
17 10  AQUARIUS                   FBG    JT 330   OLDS    7  3  1730         2300  2700
17 10  LEO                        FBG    IO 140-230       7  3  1620         2600  3200
17 10  LEO                        FBG    JT 330   OLDS    7  3  1785         3650  4250
17 10  TAURUS                     FBG    IO 140-188       7  3  1605         2600  3050
17 10  TAURUS                     FBG    JT 330   OLDS    7  3  1755         2300  2700
17 11  MARS                       FBG    IO 165-230       6 11  1637         2550  3150
17 11  MARS                       FBG    JT 330   OLDS    6 11  1840         3600  4200

20  3  LIBRA                      FBG    IO 165   MRCR    7 11  1840         3750  4350
20  3  LIBRA                      FBG    JT 330   OLDS    7 11  2020         3150  3650
```

SUPRA SPORTS INC
GREENBACK TN 37742   COAST GUARD MFG ID- XKB See inside cover to adjust price for area

For more recent years, see the BUC Used Boat Price Guide, Volume 1 or Volume 2

```
  LOA  NAME AND/             TOP/ BOAT  -HULL-  ----ENGINE---  BEAM   WGT  DRAFT RETAIL RETAIL
FT IN  OR MODEL              RIG  TYPE  MTL TP TP # HP  MFG   FT IN   LBS  FT IN  LOW   HIGH
----------------- 1983 BOATS -----------------------------------------------------------------
19  6  SUPRA-BEAST           OP   SKI  FBG SV IB 330       7 11  2875  2  3  5500  6800
19  6  SUPRA-RIDER           OP   SKI  FBG SV IB 255-330   7 11  2750  2  3  5500  6600
19  6  SUPRA-SPORT           OP   SKI  FBG SV IB 255-260   7 11  2750  2  3  5300  6150
19  6  SUPRA-SPORT           OP   SKI  FBG SV IB 330       7 11  2875  2  3  5500  6800
19  6  SUPRA-STAR            OP   SKI  FBG SV IB 255-260   7 11  2750  2  3  5300  6150
19  6  SUPRA-STAR            OP   SKI  FBG SV IB 330       7 11  2875  2  3  5500  6800
----------------- 1982 BOATS -----------------------------------------------------------------
19  6  SUPRA-BEAST           OP   SKI  FBG SV IB 330   PCM 7 11  2965  2  3  5600  6450
19  6  SUPRA-SPORT           OP   SKI  FBG SV IB 255-330   7 11  2850  2  3  5250  6450
19  6  SUPRA-STAR            OP   SKI  FBG SV IB 255-330   7 11  2850  2  3  5250  6450
----------------- 1981 BOATS -----------------------------------------------------------------
19  6  SUPRA-BEAST           OP   SKI  FBG SV IB 330   PCM 7 11  2965  2  3  5350  6150
19  6  SUPRA-SPORT           OP   SKI  FBG SV IB 255-330   7 11  2850  2  3  5000  6150
```

SUPREME INDUSTRIES INC
LOUISVILLE TN 37777   COAST GUARD MFG ID- XTB See inside cover to adjust price for area

For more recent years, see the BUC Used Boat Price Guide, Volume 1 or Volume 2

```
  LOA  NAME AND/             TOP/ BOAT  -HULL-  ----ENGINE---  BEAM   WGT  DRAFT RETAIL RETAIL
FT IN  OR MODEL              RIG  TYPE  MTL TP TP # HP  MFG   FT IN   LBS  FT IN  LOW   HIGH
----------------- 1983 BOATS -----------------------------------------------------------------
17  8  SKI-SEVILLE           OP   SKI  FBG SV IB        CHEV 6  4  1925  1  8   **    **
17  8  SKI-SEVILLE           OP   SKI  FBG SV IB 225D   CHEV 6  4  1925  1  8  7900  9100
17  8  SKI-SPRINT            OP   SKI  FBG SV IB        CHEV 6  4  1925  1  8   **    **
17  8  SKI-SPRINT            OP   SKI  FBG SV IB 225D   PCM  6  4  1925  1  8  7200  8250
18 11  SKI-SUPREME           OP   SKI  FBG SV IB 255    PCM  6  8  2275  2     4600  5300
----------------- 1982 BOATS -----------------------------------------------------------------
18 11  SKI-SUPREME           OP   SKI  FBG SV IB 255    PCM  6  9  2275  2     4450  5100
----------------- 1981 BOATS -----------------------------------------------------------------
17  8  SKI-SEVILLE           OP   SKI  FBG SV IB        CHEV 6  4  1925  1  8   **    **
17  8  SKI-SEVILLE           OP   SKI  FBG SV IB 225    CHEV 6  4  1925  1  8  3550  4150
17  8  SKI-SPRINT            OP   SKI  FBG SV IB        CHEV 6  4  1925  1  8   **    **
17  8  SKI-SPRINT            OP   SKI  FBG SV IB 225    PCM  6  4  1925  1  8  3250  3750
18 11  SKI-SUPREME           OP   SKI  FBG SV IB 255    PCM  6  8  2275  2     4200  4850
----------------- 1980 BOATS -----------------------------------------------------------------
17  8  SKI-SEVILLE           OP   SKI  FBG SV IB 225    PCM  6  4  1925  1 10  3450  4000
17  8  SKI-SPRINT            OP   SKI  FBG SV IB 225    PCM  6  4  1925  1 10  3100  3600
18 11  SKI-SUPREME           OP   SKI  FBG SV IB 255    PCM  6  9  2275  2     4050  4700
----------------- 1979 BOATS -----------------------------------------------------------------
17  8  SKI-SEVILLE           OP   SKI  FBG SV IB 215-220     6  3  2075  2  1  3250  3750
17  8  SKI-SPRINT            OP   SKI  FBG SV IB 215-220     6  3  2025  2  1  3200  3700
18 11  SKI-SUPREME           OP   SKI  FBG SV IB 255-270     6  9  2275  2  3  3850  4500
----------------- 1978 BOATS -----------------------------------------------------------------
19     SKI-SUPREME           OP   SKI  FBG SV IB 255    PCM  6  9  2200  1  8  3650  4250
```

SURF HUNTER CORP
FAIRHAVEN MA 02719   COAST GUARD MFG ID- SJJ See inside cover to adjust price for area
                        FORMERLY FAIRHAVEN MARINE INC

For more recent years, see the BUC Used Boat Price Guide, Volume 1 or Volume 2

```
  LOA  NAME AND/             TOP/ BOAT  -HULL-  ----ENGINE---  BEAM   WGT  DRAFT RETAIL RETAIL
FT IN  OR MODEL              RIG  TYPE  MTL TP TP # HP  MFG   FT IN   LBS  FT IN  LOW   HIGH
----------------- 1983 BOATS -----------------------------------------------------------------
25     SURF-HUNTER           OP   FSH  FBG DV OB              9  2        2  6  12900 14600
25     SURF-HUNTER           OP   FSH  FBG DV IB 225   CHRY   9  2  6250  2  6  26500 29400
       IO 260  VLVO 21500  23900, IB 200D PERK 41200  45700, IO T170         22400 24900
25     SURF-HUNTER           OP   WKNDR FBG DV IO 330         9  2  7000  2  6  25800 28700
25     SURF-HUNTER           OP   WKNDR FBG DV OB             9  2  5000  2  6  12100 13800
25     SURF-HUNTER           OP   WKNDR FBG DV IO 260  VLVO   9  2  7000  2  6  24800 27500
----------------- 1982 BOATS -----------------------------------------------------------------
25     SURF-HUNTER           OP   FSH  FBG DV OB              9  2  5000  2  6  11800 13400
25     SURF-HUNTER           OP   FSH  FBG DV VD 225   CHRY   9  2  5500  2  6  23000 25500
       IO 228  MRCR 20200  22500, VD 250  CHRY 23200  25700, IO 260  VLVO 21000 23400
       VD 200D PERK 39600  44000, IO T170 MRCR 21900  24400
25     SURF-HUNTER           OP   WKNDR FBG DV IO 228-260     9  2  7250  2  6  24100 26900
25     SURF-HUNTER           OP   WKNDR FBG DV IO T170  MRCR  9  2  7000  2  6  25000 27800
----------------- 1981 BOATS -----------------------------------------------------------------
25     SURF-HUNTER           OP   FSH  FBG DV VD 225          9  2  5500  2  6  22000 24400
25     SURF-HUNTER           OP   FSH  FBG DV IO T140-T170    9  2  5500  2  6  21300 24000
25     SURF-HUNTER           OP   FSH  FBG DV VD 200D PERK    9  2  5500  2  6  41400 46000
25     SURF-HUNTER           OP   WKNDR FBG DV IO 260  VLVO   9  2  7000  2  6  23800 26500
25     SURF-HUNTER           OP   WKNDR FBG DV IO T170  MRCR  9  2  7000  2  6  24600 27400
----------------- 1980 BOATS -----------------------------------------------------------------
25     SURF-HUNTER           OP   FSH  FBG DV IO 225   OMC    9  2  5500  2  6  19700 21800
       VD 225-228 21100  23500, IO 330  MRCR 21600  24000, VD 330  MRCR 22100 24600
       VD 200D 30500  33900, IO T140-T170 21100  23800, IO T185D PERK 38900 43200
25     SURF-HUNTER           OP   WKNDR FBG DV IO 225   OMC    9  2  7000  2  6  22800 25300
       VD 225-228 25800  28800, IB 250 26700  29600, IO 330  MRCR 24600 27400
       VD 330  MRCR 29800  32800, VD 200D 37300  41400, IO T140-T170 24100 27100
       VD T185D PERK 46100  50700
----------------- 1979 BOATS -----------------------------------------------------------------
25     SURF-HUNTER           OP   FSH  F/S DV IB 225   CHRY   9  2  5500  2  9  20300 22500
25     SURF-HUNTER           OP   FSH  F/S DV IB 200D  CAT    9  2  6000  2  9  31300 34700
25     SURF-HUNTER           OP   WKNDR F/S DV IB 330   MRCR  9  2  6500  2  9  23300 25900
25     SURF-HUNTER           OP   WKNDR F/S DV IO T170  MRCR  9  2  6500  2  9  23100 25700
----------------- 1978 BOATS -----------------------------------------------------------------
25     SURF-HUNTER           OP   FSH  F/S DV IB 198   MRCR   9  2  6000  2  9  20900 23300
       IB 225  CHRY 16700  18900, IO 228-260 17100  19900, IB 200D-210D 23800 27700
25     SURF-HUNTER           OP   WKNDR F/S DV IO 198   MRCR  9  2  6500  2  9  21500 23800
       IB 225  CHRY 22400  24900, IO 228-260 21700  24600, IB 200D-210D 31800 36600
```

SURFGLAS INC

PERFORMANCE CATAMARANS INC
SANTA ANA CA 92705   COAST GUARD MFG ID- SUR   See inside cover to adjust price for area
SEE STARCRAFT SAILBOAT PROD

For more recent years, see the BUC Used Boat Price Guide, Volume 1 or Volume 2

LOA FT IN	NAME AND/ OR MODEL	TOP/ RIG	BOAT TYPE	-HULL- MTL TP	TP	----ENGINE--- # HP MFG	BEAM FT IN	WGT LBS	DRAFT FT IN	RETAIL LOW	RETAIL HIGH
--------------------- 1983 BOATS ---
16	PRINDLE 16	SLP	SA/OD	F/S	CT		7 11	300	10	1750	2100
18	PRINDLE 18	SLP	SA/OD	F/S	CT		7 11	335	10	2200	2550
--------------------- 1982 BOATS ---
18	PRINDLE 18	SLP	SA/OD	F/S	CT		8	335	10	2050	2400
--------------------- 1981 BOATS ---
18	PRINDLE 18	SLP	SA/OD	F/S	CT		7 11		9	1900	2250
--------------------- 1980 BOATS ---
18	PRINDLE 18	SLP	SA/OD	F/S	CT		7 11	335		1800	2150
--------------------- 1979 BOATS ---
18	PRINDLE 18	SLP	SA/OD	F/S	CT		8	335	10	1750	2100
--------------------- 1978 BOATS ---
18	PRINDLE 18	SLP	SA/OD	F/S	CT		8	335	10	1700	2000

SURFLINER CORP

Call 1-800-327-6929 for BUC Personalized Evaluation Service
Or, for 1959 to 1969 boats, sign onto www.BUCValuPro.com

SUTPHEN MARINE CORP

CAPE CORAL FL 33990   COAST GUARD MFG ID- SUT See inside cover to adjust price for area

For more recent years, see the BUC Used Boat Price Guide, Volume 1 or Volume 2

LOA FT IN	NAME AND/ OR MODEL	TOP/ RIG	BOAT TYPE	-HULL- MTL TP	TP	----ENGINE--- # HP MFG	BEAM FT IN	WGT LBS	DRAFT FT IN	RETAIL LOW	RETAIL HIGH
--------------------- 1983 BOATS ---
17 3	SPORT-PACER 173		RNBT	FBG SV	JT	360	6 8	820		2550	3000
20 1	SUPER-PACER 200		RNBT	FBG SV	IO	260	8			4900	5650
20 1	SUPER-PACER 200	OP	RNBT	FBG SV	OB		8	1600		6750	7750
25 6	RUM-RUNNER 260		RNBT	FBG	IO	260	8			8900	10100
25 6	RUM-RUNNER 260		RNBT	FBG	IO	T260	8			10400	11900
25 6	RUM-RUNNER 260	OP	RNBT	FBG	OB		8	2800		14900	16900
29 5	OCEAN-PACER 300		RNBT	FBG DV	IO	T260	8			14900	17000
29 5	OCEAN-PACER 300	OP	RNBT	FBG DV	OB		8	3600		23500	26100
33	OUTRAGEOUS 330		RNBT	FBG	IO	T330	8			24300	27000
38 1	DOMINATOR 380		RNBT	FBG	IO	T370	8			38800	43100
38 1	ELEGANTE 380		RNBT	FBG	IO	T370	8			44400	49400
--------------------- 1982 BOATS ---
17 3	SPORT-PACER 173	OP	RNBT	FBG SV	JT	360	6 8	1850		2950	3400
20 1	SUPER-PACER 200	OP	RNBT	FBG SV	OB		7	1625		6700	7700
20 1	SUPER-PACER 200	OP	RNBT	FBG DV	IO	330	7	2700		5200	5950
29 5	OCEAN-PACER 300	OP	EXP	FBG DV	IO	T330	8	5800	2 8	19200	21300
33	HIPERF	OP	RNBT	FBG DV	IO	T400	8			24100	26800
38 1	DOMINATOR	OP	EXP	FBG DV	IO	T370	8	7200	2 8	32500	36100
--------------------- 1981 BOATS ---
17 3	SPORT-PACER 173		RNBT	FBG SV	IB	360	6 8			2800	3250
20 1	SUPER-PACER 200		RNBT	FBG SV	OB		7	1625		6550	7500
20 1	SUPER-PACER 200		RNBT	FBG DV	IO	330	7			5050	5850
29 5	OCEAN-PACER 300		EXP	FBG DV	IO	T370	8			20500	22800
38 1	DOMINATOR 380		EXP	FBG DV	IO	T370	8			44300	49200
--------------------- 1980 BOATS ---
17 3	SPORT-PACER 173	OP	RNBT	FBG SV	JT	320-360	6 8	1850		2700	3150
20 1	SUPER-PACER 200	OP	RNBT	FBG SV	OB		7	1625		6400	7350
20 1	SUPER-PACER 200	OP	RNBT	FBG SV	IO	240-260	7	2700		4150	5000
JT 320 BERK	5600	6450,	IO	330		MRCR 5000	5750, JT 360		BERK	6600	6450
29 5	OCEAN-PACER 300	OP	OFF	FBG DV	IO	T240-T260	8	5800	2 8	16200	18800
29 5	OCEAN-PACER 300	OP	OFF	FBG DV	IO	T330 MRCR	8	5800	2 8	18500	20600
38 1	DOMINATOR 380	OP	OFF	FBG DV	IO	T330 MRCR	8	7200	2 8	29600	32900
38 1	DOMINATOR 380	OP	OFF	FBG DV	IO	T370 MRCR	8	7200	2 8	31500	35000
--------------------- 1979 BOATS ---
20 1	SUPER-PACER 200	OP	RNBT	FBG DV	OB		7	1600		6200	7150
20 1	SUPER-PACER 200	OP	RNBT	FBG DV	IO	260 MRCR	7	2625		4150	4850
20 1	SUPER-PACER 200	OP	RNBT	FBG DV	IO	330 MRCR	7	2625		4900	5650
29 5	INTIMIDATOR 300	OP	OFF	FBG DV	IO	T260 MRCR	8	5900		16400	18600
29 5	INTIMIDATOR 300	OP	OFF	FBG DV	IO	T330 MRCR	8	6100		18600	20600
38 4	DOMINATOR	OP	OFF	FBG DV	IO	T370 MRCR	8	7100		31200	34600
--------------------- 1978 BOATS ---
17 3	SPORT-PACER 173	OP	RNBT	FBG SV	OB		6 8	960		3250	3800
17 3	SPORT-PACER II	OP	RNBT	FBG SV	OB		6 8	960		3850	4450
17 3	SPORT-PACER JET	OP	SKI	FBG SV	JT	320 BERK	6 8	1890		2400	2750
18 2	GRAN-SPORT	OP	RNBT	FBG SV	IO	300 MPC	7	2300		2250	2600
18 2	GRAN-SPORT	OP	RNBT	FBG SV	JT	320 BERK	7	2200		2850	3300
18 2	GRAN-SPORT	OP	RNBT	FBG SV	IO	330 MPC	7	2325		2950	3450
20 1	SUPER-PACER 200	OP	RNBT	FBG DV	IO	300 MPC	7	2600		3800	4400
20 1	SUPER-PACER 200	OP	RNBT	FBG SV	JT	320 BERK	7	2500		4950	5700
20 1	SUPER-PACER 200	OP	RNBT	FBG DV	IO	330 MRCR	7	2625		4900	5600
20 1	SUPER-PACER 200II	OP	RNBT	FBG DV	OB		7	1600		6100	7050
29 5	INTIMIDATOR 300	OP	OFF	FBG DV	IO	T260 MRCR	8	5850		16100	18300
29 5	INTIMIDATOR 300	OP	OFF	FBG DV	IO	T330 MRCR	8	6050		18300	20400
38 4	DOMINATOR	OP	OFF	FBG DV	IO	T330 MRCR	8	7100		28900	32100
--------------------- 1977 BOATS ---
17 3	SPORT-PACER 173	OP	SKI	FBG SV	OB		6 8	860		3150	3650
17 3	SPORT-PACER 173-II	OP	SKI	FBG SV	OB		6 8	910		3300	3850
17 3	SPORT-PACER JET	OP	SKI	FBG SV	JT	300-400	6 8	1850		2300	2650
18 2	GRAN-SPORT 182	OP	RACE	FBG SV	IO	250-280	7	2200		2300	2850
JT 300 FORD	2700	3150,	IO	300	CC	2600	3000, JT 400		CHEV	2700	3150
20 1	SUPER-PACER 200	OP	OFF	FBG SV	IO	250-280	7	2680		4500	5400
JT 300 FORD	4850	5550,	IO	300	CC	4900	5600, JT 400		CHEV	4850	5550
29 4	OCEAN-PACER	OP	OFF	FBG DV	IO	T250-T300	8			15800	19600
29 4	OCEAN-PACER	OP	OFF	FBG DV	IO	T400 CHEV	8			20400	22700
--------------------- 1975 BOATS ---
17 3	JET-PACER	OP	RNBT	FBG SV	IB	330	6 8	1850	8	2000	2350
17 3	SPORT-PACER	OP	RNBT	FBG SV	OB		6 8	860	8	3100	3600
18 2	GRANSPORT	OP	RNBT	FBG SV	IO		7	2200	8	**	**
18 2	GRANSPORT	OP	RNBT	FBG SV	IB	330	7	2200	8	2350	2750
--------------------- 1974 BOATS ---
17 3	SPORT-PACER	OP	RNBT	FBG SV	OB		6 8	860		3100	3600
17 3	SPORT-PACER	OP	RNBT	FBG SV	IB	330	6 8		1	2000	2350
18 2	GRAN-SPORT	OP	RNBT	FBG SV	IB	330	7		1	2250	2650
--------------------- 1973 BOATS ---
17 3	SPORT-PACER	OP	SKI	FBG SV	OB		6 8	860		3000	3500
17 3	SPORT-PACER	OP	SKI	FBG SV	JT	330	6 8		8	1750	2100
18 2	GRAN-SPORT	OP	RACE	FBG SV	IO	250	7		2 8	1950	2300
24 1	SEA-SPORT	OP	OFF	FBG SV	IO	275	7		2 8	7150	8250
28 2	SPORT-CHALLENGER	OP	OFF	FBG SV	IO	T250	8		2 8	14500	16500
--------------------- 1972 BOATS ---
17 3	COMPETITION-PACER		SKI	FBG	OB		6 8	860		3250	3800
17 3	SPORT-PACER		OP	SKI FBG SV	OB		6 8	860		2750	3200
18 2	GRAN-SPORT		RNBT	FBG SV	JT	200	7		2 2	2250	2600
IO 200	2650	3100,	JT	500		2250	2600, IO 500			6600	7550
--------------------- 1971 BOATS ---
17 3	PACER		SKI	FBG	OB		6 8	860		3000	3500
17 3	PACER-COMPETITION		RNBT	FBG DV	OB	300	6 8	550		2400	2750
17 3	SPORT-PACER		SKI	FBG DV	IO	140	6 8		2 4	2000	2350
18 2	GRAN-SPORT		RNBT	FBG DV	IO	200	7		2 6	2750	3200

SWALLOW CRAFT COMPANY

NEWPORT BEACH CA 92659   COAST GUARD MFG ID- XWW See inside cover to adjust price for area

LOA FT IN	NAME AND/ OR MODEL	TOP/ RIG	BOAT TYPE	-HULL- MTL TP	TP	----ENGINE--- # HP MFG	BEAM FT IN	WGT LBS	DRAFT FT IN	RETAIL LOW	RETAIL HIGH
--------------------- 1981 BOATS ---
32 9	SWIFT 33	SLP	SA/CR FBG KL	IB		D	11 3	14740	5 3	32200	35800
39 1	SWIFT 40	KTH	SA/CR FBG KL	IB		D	13 4	24300	5 3	54400	59700
--------------------- 1980 BOATS ---
32 9	SWIFT 33	SLP	SA/CR FBG KL	SD		23D VLVO	11 3	14740	5 3	30800	34200
39 2	SWIFT 40	KTH	SA/CR FBG KL	IB		50D PERK	13 4	24300	5 3	51700	56800
--------------------- 1979 BOATS ---
32 9	SWIFT 33	SLP	SA/CR FBG KL	IB		D	11 3	14740	5 3	29600	32900
39 1	SWIFT 40	KTH	SA/CR FBG KL	IB		D	13 4	24300	5 3	49900	54800

SWEDEN YACHTS

STENUNGSUND SWEDEN   See inside cover to adjust price for area

For more recent years, see the BUC Used Boat Price Guide, Volume 1 or Volume 2

LOA FT IN	NAME AND/ OR MODEL	TOP/ RIG	BOAT TYPE	-HULL- MTL TP	TP	----ENGINE--- # HP MFG	BEAM FT IN	WGT LBS	DRAFT FT IN	RETAIL LOW	RETAIL HIGH
--------------------- 1983 BOATS ---
33 6	COMFORT 34	SLP	SA/RC FBG KL	IB		D	11 5	13000	6	55400	60800
34	SWEDEN Y 34	SLP	SA/RC FBG KL	IB		D VLVO	11 5	12600	6 4	53800	59100
41	COMFORT 41	SLP	SA/RC FBG KL	IB		D	13	18700	7 3	90400	99300

```
SWEDEN YACHTS        -CONTINUED    See inside cover to adjust price for area
  LOA   NAME AND/      TOP/ BOAT  -HULL-  ----ENGINE---  BEAM   WGT  DRAFT RETAIL RETAIL
FT IN   OR MODEL       RIG  TYPE  MTL TP  TP # HP  MFG  FT IN   LBS  FT IN  LOW   HIGH
------------------------ 1983 BOATS -----------------------------------------------------
41    S30               SLP SA/RC FBG KL  SD    17D VLVO  8  2  7934  4 10  50800 55800
------------------------ 1982 BOATS -----------------------------------------------------
33  6 COMFORT 34        SLP SA/RC FBG KL  IB     D       11  5 13000  6      51800 56900
41    COMFORT 41        SLP SA/RC FBG KL  IB     D       13    18700  7  3  84600 93000
------------------------ 1980 BOATS -----------------------------------------------------
38    SWEDE 38          SLP SA/RC FBG KL  IB     D        9     9900  6      39800 44200
------------------------ 1979 BOATS -----------------------------------------------------
33  6 COMFORT 34        SLP SA/CR FBG KL  IB    23D VLVO 11  5 12200  6      41300 45900
------------------------ 1978 BOATS -----------------------------------------------------
33  6 COMFORT 34        SLP SA/CR FBG KL  IB    23D VLVO 11  5 12200  6      39700 44100
```

SWEDISH QUALITY YTS INC
DIV OF SCANDANAVIAN HOL COAST GUARD MFG ID- SDY
SEE ALSO OY FISKARS A/B & STOREBORO BRUKS AD

Call 1-800-327-6929 for BUC Personalized Evaluation Service
Or, for 1975 to 1978 boats, sign onto www.BUCValuPro.com

SWIFT BOAT COMPANY
Call 1-800-327-6929 for BUC Personalized Evaluation Service
Or, for 1954 to 1962 boats, sign onto www.BUCValuPro.com

SWIFT MARINE INC
Call 1-800-327-6929 for BUC Personalized Evaluation Service
Or, for 1966 to 1986 boats, sign onto www.BUCValuPro.com

SWIFTWATER INDUSTRIES INC
Call 1-800-327-6929 for BUC Personalized Evaluation Service
Or, for 1960 boats, sign onto www.BUCValuPro.com

SWITZER CRAFT INC
CRYSTAL LAKE IL 60014   COAST GUARD MFG ID- SWT See inside cover to adjust price for area

For more recent years, see the BUC Used Boat Price Guide, Volume 1 or Volume 2

```
  LOA   NAME AND/      TOP/ BOAT  -HULL-  ----ENGINE---  BEAM   WGT  DRAFT RETAIL RETAIL
FT IN   OR MODEL       RIG  TYPE  MTL TP  TP # HP  MFG  FT IN   LBS  FT IN  LOW   HIGH
------------------------ 1983 BOATS -----------------------------------------------------
16  3 160H              OP  RNBT  FBG SV  OB             6  8    740         1850  2200
17 11 170 SS            OP  RNBT  FBG SV  OB             7  3    840         2250  2650
17 11 BOW RIDER 193B    ST  RNBT  FBG TR  IO    185             2150        2950  3400
17 11 SKIER SK175       OP  SKI   FBG SV  OB             7  3    900         2400  2750
20  1 GL-21             OP  RACE  FBG SV  OB             8      1000        2900  3350
20  1 SS20B             OP        FBG SV  OB                    1100        3100  3600
20  1 SS20C             OP  CUD   FBG SV  OB             7  4   1100        3100  3600
------------------------ 1981 BOATS -----------------------------------------------------
16  3 HUGGER 160        OP  RNBT  F/S SV  OB             6  8    740         1750  2100
17 11 193 BR            OP  RNBT  F/S SV  IO 120-185     7  5   2150        2800  3300
17 11 193 BR            OP  RNBT  F/S SV  IO 198-260     7  5   2400        3050  3750
17 11 SKIER 175         OP  SKI   F/S SV  OB             7  3    900         2300  2650
17 11 SUPER-SPORT 170   OP  RNBT  F/S SV  OB             7  3    840         2150  2550
20  1 GL-21             OP  SKI   F/S SV  OB             8      1000        2750  3200
20  1 SS20 BR           OP  RNBT  F/S SV  OB             8      1100        2950  3450
20  1 SS20 CUDDY        OP  CUD   F/S SV  OB             8      1100        2950  3450
------------------------ 1980 BOATS -----------------------------------------------------
16  3 HUGGER 160        OP  RNBT  F/S SV  OB             6  8    740         1750  2050
17    SK 175            SF        FBG DV  OB             7  4    875         2050  2450
17    SUPER-SPORT 170   SF        FBG DV  OB             7  4    740         1800  2100
17 11 193 BR            OP  RNBT  F/S SV  IO 120-200     7  5   2150        2800  3450
17 11 193 BR            OP  RNBT  F/S SV  IO 228-260     7  5   2400        3050  3700
17 11 SKIER 175         OP  RNBT  F/S SV  OB             7  3    900         2250  2600
17 11 SUPER-SPORT 170   OP  RNBT  F/S SV  OB             7  3    840         2100  2500
19    BOWRIDER 193      OP  RNBT  FBG TR  IO             7  5   2000         **    **
20    2001              SF        FBG DV  OB             8      1100        2900  3350
20    GL 21             SF        FBG DV  OB             8      1000        2650  3100
20  1 GL-21             OP  SKI   F/S SV  OB             7  8   1000        2700  3100
20  1 SS20 BR           OP  RNBT  F/S SV  OB             8      1100        2900  3400

20  1 SS20 CUDDY        OP  CUD   F/S SV  OB             8      1100        2900  3400
------------------------ 1978 BOATS -----------------------------------------------------
18    183 BR            OP  RNBT  FBG TR  IO    170             2800        3250
19    GL-20             OP  RNBT  FBG DV  IO    188      7  8    900        2250  2650
19    GL-20             OP  RNBT  FBG DV  IO    188      7  8    900        2700  3100
20    202 BR            OP  RNBT  FBG DV  IO    233             3850        4500
20    202 CC            OP  RNBT  FBG DV  IO    165             3750        4350
------------------------ 1977 BOATS -----------------------------------------------------
18    183-BR            OP  RNBT  FBG TR  IO    170             2850        3350
19    GL-20             OP  RNBT  FBG DV  OB             7  8    900        2250  2600
20    202-BR            OP  RNBT  FBG DV  IO    233             3950        4600
20    202-CC            OP  CUD   FBG DV  IO    165             3900        4550
20    GL-20             OP  RNBT  FBG DV  IO    188             3850        4450
------------------------ 1975 BOATS -----------------------------------------------------
18    183               OP  CUD   FBG DV  IO    120      6 10              2950  3450
------------------------ 1974 BOATS -----------------------------------------------------
17  7 183R STD          OP  RNBT  FBG     IO 90-140      6 10   1300        2400  2950
17  7 STD 183B          B/R       FBG     IO 90-140      6 10   1400        2350  2850
17  7 SUPER-SPORT DLX 170          FBG     OB             7  2    675        1750  2050
------------------------ 1970 BOATS -----------------------------------------------------
17  6 PLAYDAY 175                 FBG     IO    90 MRCR         1500  1 10  2750  3200
------------------------ 1969 BOATS -----------------------------------------------------
17    EXECUTIVE 170     OP        FBG DV  IO 80-160      6 10   1200        2500  2900
20    HYDRO-KAT UNLTD   OP        FBG CT  OB             8      1000        2450  2850
------------------------ 1968 BOATS -----------------------------------------------------
16  1 PACEMAKER         OP        FBG     IO    60 MRCR  6  3              2350  2750
17    EXECUTIVE 170     OP        FBG TR  OB    120 MRCR 7  4              3450  4000
17    HOLIDAY 170       OP        FBG DV  OB             7  4    900        2350  2750
18  3 HYDRO-KAT         OP        FBG     OB             8      1000        2300  2650
18  9 EXECUTIVE 190     OP        FBG TR  IO    160 MRCR 7  4              3900  4500
18  9 HOLIDAY 190       OP        FBG DV  OB             7  4   1000        2350  2700
------------------------ 1967 BOATS -----------------------------------------------------
16    PACEMAKER 60      RNBT      FBG     IO    60       6  3              2900  3400
17    EXECUTIVE 170     RNBT      FBG     IO    120      7  4              3700  4300
17    HOLIDAY 170       RNBT      FBG     OB             7  4    900        2000  2350
18  9 EXECUTIVE 190     RNBT      FBG     IO    150      7  4              4100  4750
18  9 HOLIDAY 190       RNBT      FBG     OB             7  4   1000        2350  2750
19    HYDRO-KAT         RACE      FBG     OB             7 10              2400  2800
------------------------ 1966 BOATS -----------------------------------------------------
17  1 EXECUTIVE 170     RNBT      FBG TR  OB             7  7               **    **
17  1 HOLIDAY 170       RNBT      FBG TR  OB             7  7    900        2000  2350
19  1 EXECUTIVE 190     RNBT      FBG TR  OB             7  7               **    **
19  1 HOLIDAY 190       RNBT      FBG TR  OB             7  7   1050        2450  2850
------------------------ 1965 BOATS -----------------------------------------------------
16    DELUXE 110        RACE      PLY     OB    110      6  7              2850  3300
18    SHOOTING-STAR     RNBT      FBG     OB             7  5    900        2050  2450
19    HYDRO-CAT         RNBT      FBG CT  OB             8      1000        2400  2750
------------------------ 1963 BOATS -----------------------------------------------------
18  6 HYDRO-KAT         OP        WD      OB                               2500  2900
18 10                   OP        CBNCR   WD  OB                           2050  2450
18 10                   CR        WD      OB                               2050  2450
------------------------ 1962 BOATS -----------------------------------------------------
18 10                   CR        WD      OB                               2050  2450
18 10                   OVNTR     WD  OB                                   2050  2450
------------------------ 1961 BOATS -----------------------------------------------------
16                      CBNCR     PLY     OB             6  8    790        1700  2000
18                      CBNCR     PLY     OB             7  7    990        2300  2650
18                      OP  RNBT  PLY     OB             7  7    920        2150  2500
------------------------ 1960 BOATS -----------------------------------------------------
17    COMBO 17          CR        PLY DV  OB             7      800        1800  2100
17    GYPSY             CBNCR     PLY DV  OB             7      850        1900  2250
------------------------ 1959 BOATS -----------------------------------------------------
17    COMBO 17 DLX      RNBT      PLY     OB             7      650        1700  2050
------------------------ 1958 BOATS -----------------------------------------------------
17    LIGHTNING         RNBT      WD      OB                               1700  2000
```

SYLVAN MARINE
SMOKER CRAFT INC   See inside cover to adjust price for area
NEW PARIS IN 46553   COAST GUARD MFG ID- SYL

For more recent years, see the BUC Used Boat Price Guide, Volume 1 or Volume 2

```
  LOA   NAME AND/      TOP/ BOAT  -HULL-  ----ENGINE---  BEAM   WGT  DRAFT RETAIL RETAIL
FT IN   OR MODEL       RIG  TYPE  MTL TP  TP # HP  MFG  FT IN   LBS  FT IN  LOW   HIGH
------------------------ 1983 BOATS -----------------------------------------------------
16  8 V-171 B/R         ST  RNBT  FBG DV  IO 120-170     7  6   1450        2500  2950
18  6 SKIPPER           ST  RNBT  AL  SV  IO 120-140     7     1594        2850  3350
18  6 SPORTSTER         ST  RNBT  AL  SV  IO 120-140     7     1610        2850  3350
18  7 V-190 B/R         ST  RNBT  FBG DV  IO 140-200     8     1650        3200  3750
```

LOA FT IN	NAME AND/ OR MODEL	TOP/ RIG	BOAT TYPE	-HULL- MTL TP	----ENGINE--- TP # HP MFG	BEAM FT IN	WGT LBS	DRAFT FT IN	RETAIL LOW	RETAIL HIGH
\-\-\- 1983 BOATS										
18 7	V-190 B/R	ST	RNBT	FBG DV	IO 228-230	8	2246		3700	4300
21 7	OFFSHORE	ST	CBNCR AL	SV	OB	7 10	1300		1700	2050
21 7	OFFSHORE	ST	CBNCR AL	SV	IO 120-170	7 10	1970		4800	5650
21 7	SKIPPER	ST	RNBT AL	SV	IO 120-170	7 7	1250		3850	4750
\-\-\- 1982 BOATS										
17 3	V-170 B/R	ST	RNBT	FBG DV	IO 120-170	6 11	1770		2650	3200
18 6	SKIPPER	ST	RNBT AL	SV	IO 120-140	7	1594		2800	3250
18 6	SPORTSTER	ST	RNBT AL	SV	IO 120-140	7	1610		2800	3250
18 7	V-190 B/R	ST	RNBT	FBG DV	IO 140-170	8	2246		3500	4150
18 7	V-190 B/R	ST	RNBT	FBG DV	IO 198 MRCR	8	2530		3750	4350
21 7	OFFSHORE		CBNCR AL	SV	OB	7 10	1400		1800	2100
21 7	OFFSHORE		CBNCR AL	SV	IO 120-185	7 10	1970		4700	5600
21 7	SKIPPER	ST	RNBT AL	SV	IO 120-140	7 7	1820		3900	4550
21 7	SKIPPER	ST	RNBT AL	SV	IO 470	7 7	1927		8100	9300
\-\-\- 1981 BOATS										
16 3	T-160 B/R	ST	RNBT	FBG TR	IO 120-170	7 2	1565		2350	2850
17 3	V-170 B/R	ST	RNBT	FBG DV	IO 120-170	6 11	1770		2600	3150
18 6	SKIPPER	ST	RNBT AL	SV	IO 120-140	7	1594		2750	3200
18 6	SPORTSTER	ST	RNBT AL	SV	IO 120-140	7	1610		2750	3200
18 7	V-190 B/R	ST	RNBT	FBG DV	IO 140-170	8	2246		3450	4100
18 7	V-190 B/R	ST	RNBT	FBG DV	IO 198 MRCR	8	2530		3700	4300
21 7	OFFSHORE		CBNCR AL	SV	OB	7 10	1400		1750	2050
21 7	OFFSHORE		CBNCR AL	SV	IO 120-185	7 10	1970		4650	5500
21 7	SKIPPER	ST	RNBT AL	SV	IO 120-140	7 7	1820		3850	4500
21 7	SKIPPER	ST	RNBT AL	SV	IO 470	7 7	1927		7950	9150
\-\-\- 1980 BOATS										
17	V-170		RNBT	FBG DV	IO 140	6 10	1700		2450	2900
18	SKIPPER		RNBT AL	DV	IO 140	6 11	1400		2500	2900
18	SPORTSTER		RNBT AL	DV	IO 140	6 11	1400		2500	2900
19	V-190		RNBT	FBG DV	IO 198	8	2200		3500	4050
22	OFFSHORE		CR	AL	DV	IO 140	7 10	2200		4500	5150
\-\-\- 1979 BOATS										
16 3	T-160	ST	RNBT	FBG TR	IO 120 MRCR	6 10	1035		1900	2250
17 3	V-170	ST	RNBT	FBG DV	IO	6 10	1200		**	**
18 7	V-190	ST	RNBT	FBG DV	IO 165 MRCR	8	3700		4600	5300
18 10	DELUXE	ST	RNBT	FBG TR	IO 180 OMC	7 10	1400		2900	3400
\-\-\- 1978 BOATS										
16 3	T-160 B/R	ST	RNBT	FBG TR	IO 120-170	6 10	1035		1900	2300
17 3	V-170 B/R	ST	RNBT	FBG DV	IO 120-140	6 10	1200		2300	2650
18 3	T-180	ST	RNBT	FBG DV	IO 140-198	6 10			2550	3050
18 4	SPORTSTER B/R	ST	RNBT AL	DV	IO 120-140	6 11	1551		2650	3100
18 7	SKIPPER	ST	RNBT AL	DV	IO 120-140	6 9	1565		2650	3100
18 7	V-190	ST	RNBT	FBG DV	IO 165-240	8	3700		4650	5450
\-\-\- 1977 BOATS										
16 3	SYLVAN T160	ST	RNBT	FBG TR	IO 120-188	6 10	1600		2350	2750
17 3	SYLVAN V170	ST	RNBT	FBG DV	IO 120-188	6 10	1800		2650	3100
18 3	SYLVAN T180	ST	RNBT	FBG DV	IO 140-188	6 10	2145		3050	3550
18 6	SPORTSTER	ST	RNBT AL	DV	IO 120-140	6 11			2650	3100
18 7	SKIPPER	ST	RNBT	FBG DV	IO 120-140	6 9			2650	3050
\-\-\- 1974 BOATS										
28	SYLVAN 1024	HT	HB	AL	PN OB	10			**	**
28	SYLVAN 1024	HT	HB	AL	PN OB	120	10		**	**
28	SYLVAN 1024	FB	HB	AL	PN OB	10			**	**
28	SYLVAN 1024	FB	HB	AL	PN OB	120	10		**	**
\-\-\- 1971 BOATS										
40	SYLVAN-PRINCESS	HT	HB	AL	PN OB	14			7550	8700
40	SYLVAN-PRINCESS	HT	HB	STL	PN OB	14	8000	1 3	6000	6850
\-\-\- 1970 BOATS										
37	SYLVAN-PRINCESS		HB	AL	PN OB	14	7750	1 3	7500	8500
37	SYLVAN-PRINCESS		HB	STL	PN OB	14	7750	1 3	6500	7450
37	SYLVAN-PRINCESS	HT	HB	AL	IO	14		11	12900	14600
37	SYLVAN-PRINCESS	HT	HB	STL	IO	14	8000	11	7500	8600
40	SYLVAN 40	HT	HB	AL	IO	14			11900	13500
40	SYLVAN-PRINCESS		HB	AL	PN OB	14	8000	1 3	6800	7800
40	SYLVAN-PRINCESS		HB	STL	PN OB	14	8000	1 3	5950	6800
40	SYLVAN-PRINCESS	HT	HB	AL	IO	14		11	11900	13500
40	SYLVAN-PRINCESS	HT	HB	STL	IO	14	7750	11	6550	7550
\-\-\- 1969 BOATS										
37	SYLVAN-PRINCESS	HT	HB	STL	PN OB	14	7750	1 3	6450	7400
37	SYLVAN-PRINCESS	HT	HB	STL	PN OB	65	14	8000	1 3	7650	8800
40	SYLVAN-PRINCESS	HT	HB	STL	PN IO	14	7750	1 3	5700	6600
40	SYLVAN-PRINCESS	HT	HB	STL	PN IO	65	14	8000	1 3	6900	7950
\-\-\- 1968 BOATS										
40	SYLVAN	HT	HB	STL	PN OB	14	77500		20000	22200
40	SYLVAN	HT	HB	STL	PN IO	14	8000		6950	7950
40	SYLVAN-PRINCESS	HT	HB	STL	PN OB	14	7750	1 3	5700	6550
\-\-\- 1966 BOATS										
37	PRINCESS 37	HT	HB	AL	OB	14	7750	1 8	7050	8100
37	PRINCESS 37	HT	HB	STL	OB	14	7750	1 8	6050	6950
40	PRINCESS 40	HT	HB	AL	OB	14	8000	1 8	6400	7350
40	PRINCESS 40	HT	HB	STL	OB	14	8000	1 8	5600	6450

SYMBOL YACHTS
WARWICK RI 02889   See inside cover to adjust price for area

For more recent years, see the BUC Used Boat Price Guide, Volume 1 or Volume 2

LOA FT IN	NAME AND/ OR MODEL	TOP/ RIG	BOAT TYPE	-HULL- MTL TP	----ENGINE--- TP # HP MFG	BEAM FT IN	WGT LBS	DRAFT FT IN	RETAIL LOW	RETAIL HIGH
\-\-\- 1983 BOATS										
44 2		FB	MY	FBG SV	IB T310D CUM	14 9	36000	3 8	112000	123000
44 2		FB	MY	FBG SV	IB T410D	14 9	38000	3 8	125500	138000
44 2		FB	SF	FBG SV	IB T460D	14 9	34000	3 8	122500	135000
44 2		FB	TCMY	FBG SV	IB T310D CUM	14 9	34000	3 8	117500	129000

SYMONS CHOICE
ST PETERSBURG FL 33702   COAST GUARD MFG ID- SYM See inside cover to adjust price for area
FORMERLY SYMONS SAILING INC

For more recent years, see the BUC Used Boat Price Guide, Volume 1 or Volume 2

LOA FT IN	NAME AND/ OR MODEL	TOP/ RIG	BOAT TYPE	-HULL- MTL TP	----ENGINE--- TP # HP MFG	BEAM FT IN	WGT LBS	DRAFT FT IN	RETAIL LOW	RETAIL HIGH
\-\-\- 1983 BOATS										
23	AZTEC 23	SLP	SA/RC FBG	CT		11 3	900	3	8800	10000
24	HIRONDELLE 24	SLP	SA/RC FBG	CT		10	2600	2 6	13100	14800
25 11	SIROCCO 26	SLP	SA/RC FBG	CT OB		12 9	5100	2 4	19500	21600
25 11	SIROCCO 26	SLP	SA/RC FBG	CT IB	D	12 9	5100	2 4	19500	21600
27	CATALAC 27	SLP	SA/CR FBG	CT		13 8	5200	2	21400	23300
27	CATALAC 8M	SLP	SA/CR FBG	CT OB		13 10	4850	2 1	21400	23800
27	CATALAC 8M	SLP	SA/CR FBG	CT IB	D	13 10	4850	2 1	21400	23800
29 6	CATALAC 30	SLP	SA/CR FBG	CT OB		13 10	5900	2 6	27500	30500
29 6	CATALAC 30	SLP	SA/CR FBG	CT IB	D	13 10	5900	2 6	27500	30700
31	QUEST 31	SLP	SA/CR FBG	CT IB	15D YAN	14 3	6500	2 6	32600	36200
32	CATFISHER	SLP	SA/CR FBG	CT IB	30D YAN	13 1	7800	2 6	37400	41600
35	CHEROKEE 35	SLP	SA/CR FBG	CT		17	11000	3 6	52500	57600
37	SNOW-GOOSE 37	CUT	SA/RC FBG	CT IB	15D YAN	15	10000	2 8	59100	64900
37	SNOW-GOOSE 37	CUT	SA/CR FBG	CT IB		15	10000	2 8	59100	64900
40	CATALAC 40	SLP	SA/CR FBG	CT		17 6		3	80600	88600
45	APACHE 45 MKII	SLP	SA/CR FBG	CT IB T	D				137500	151000
45	APACHE 45 MKII	CUT	SA/CR FBG	CT IB T	D				137500	151000
45	APACHE 45 MKII	KTH	SA/CR FBG	CT IB T	D				137500	151000
49	QUASAR 50	CUT	SA/RC FBG	CT IB		19 8	14500	3	180000	198000
50	QUASAR 50	SLP	SA/CR FBG	CT IB					192000	211000
\-\-\- 1982 BOATS										
23	AZTEC 23	SLP	SA/RC FBG	CT		11 3	900	3	8200	9400
24	HIRONDELLE MK III	SLP	SA/CR FBG	CT		10	2600	2 6	12300	14000
25 11	SIROCCO 26	SLP	SA/RC FBG	CT OB		12 9	5100	2 4	18300	20600
25 2	HEAVENLY-TWINS 26	SLP	SA/CR FBG	CT		13 9	4400	2 3	18300	20300
26 3	TELSTAR 26	SLP	SA/CR FBG	CT TM		16	2200	1	15000	17000
27	CATALAC 27	SLP	SA/CR FBG	CT		13 8	5200	2	20600	22800
28	CATFISHER 28	SLP	SA/CR FBG	CT IB	D	13 1	7600	2 4	24100	26800
28	CATFISHER 28	KTH	SA/CR FBG	CT IB	D	13 1	7600	2 4	24100	26800
29 6	CATALAC 30	SLP	SA/CR FBG	CT OB		13 10	5900	2 6	25800	28700
29 6	CATALAC 30	SLP	SA/CR FBG	CT IB	D	13 10	5900	2 6	26000	28900
30	IROQUOIS MK II	SLP	SA/CR FBG	CT OB		13 6	5000	1 4	26000	28900
31	QUEST 31	SLP	SA/RC FBG	CT IB	D	14 3	6500	2 6	30500	33900
32 2	COMANCHE 32	SLP	SA/RC FBG	CT		13 10	7900	3 6	35400	39300
32 2	COMANCHE 32	SLP	SA/CR FBG	CT IB	D	13 10	7900	3 6	35400	39700
33	OCEAN-WINDS 33	SLP	SA/RC FBG	CT		16	7900	3 8	38400	42700
35	CHEROKEE 35	SLP	SA/CR FBG	CT IB	D	17	11000	3 6	49700	54700
37	TELSTAR 35	SLP	SA/CR FBG	CT		25	13000	2 3	52500	57200
37	SNOW-GOOSE 37	CUT	SA/CR FBG	CT IB	D	15	10000	2 8	55500	61000
40	APACHE 41	SLP	SA/CR FBG	CT IB		19 6	13500	3 6	78500	86300
40 10	APACHE 41	SLP	SA/CR FBG	CT IB		19 6	13500	3 6	78500	86300
40 10	APACHE 41	CUT	SA/CR FBG	CT IB		19 6	13500	3 6	78500	86300
40 10	APACHE 41	KTH	SA/CR FBG	CT IB		19 6	13500	3 6	78500	86300
49	QUASAR 50	CUT	SA/RC FBG	CT IB T	20D YAN	19 8	14500	3	172500	189500
\-\-\- 1981 BOATS										
23	AZTEC 23	SLP	SA/RC FBG	CT		11 3	900	3	7700	8850
24	HIRONDELLE MKIII	SLP	SA/CR FBG	CT		10	2600	2 6	11600	13100
24	HIRONDELLE MKIII	SLP	SA/CR FBG	CT		10	2600	2 6	11600	13100
25 11	SIROCCO 26	SLP	SA/RC FBG	CT OB		12 9	5100	2 4	17000	19400

LOA FT	LOA IN	NAME AND/ OR MODEL	TOP/ RIG	BOAT TYPE	-HULL- MTL	-HULL- TP	ENGINE TP	ENGINE #	ENGINE HP	ENGINE MFG	BEAM FT	BEAM IN	WGT LBS	DRAFT FT	DRAFT IN	RETAIL LOW	RETAIL HIGH
		1981 BOATS															
25	11	SIROCCO 26	SLP	SA/RC	FBG	CT	IB		D		12	9	5100	2	4	17000	19400
26		SIROCCO	SLP	SA/CR	FBG	CT	OB									16500	18800
26	2	HEAVENLY-TWINS 26	SLP	SA/CR	FBG	CT	OB				13	9	4400	2	3	16800	19100
26	3	TELSTAR 26	SLP	SA/RC	FBG	CT	OB				16		2200	1	7	14100	16000
27		CATALAC 27	SLP	SA/CR	FBG	CT	OB				13	8	5200	2		19300	21500
27		CATALAC 8M	SLP	SA/CR	FBG	CT	OB				13	10	4850	2	1	19000	21100
27		CATALAC 8M	SLP	SA/CR	FBG	CT	IB		D		13	10	4850	2	1	19000	21100
28		CATFISHER 28	SLP	SA/CR	FBG	CT	IB		D		13	1	7600	3	4	22700	25300
28		CATFISHER 28	KTH	SA/CR	FBG	CT					13	1	7600	3	4	22600	25100
29	6	CATALAC 30	SLP	SA/CR	FBG	CT	OB				13	10	5900	2	6	24300	27000
29	6	CATALAC 30	SLP	SA/CR	FBG	CT	IB		D		13	10	5900	2	6	24500	27200
30		CATALAC 9M	SLP	SA/CR	FBG	CT	OB				13	10	7720	2	4	27400	30400
30		CATALAC 9M	SLP	SA/CR	FBG	CT	IB		D		13	10	7720	2	1	27600	30600
30		IROQUOIS MKII	SLP	SA/RC	FBG	CT	OB				13	6	5000	1	4	24300	27000
30		IROQUOIS MKIIS	SLP	SA/RC	FBG	CT	IB				13	6	5000	5	8	24300	27000
31		QUEST 31	SLP	SA/CR	FBG	CT	IB		15D	YAN	14	3	6500	2	6	28800	31900
31		QUEST 31	SLP	SA/RC	FBG	CT	IB		D		14	3	6500	2	6	28800	31900
32	2	COMANCHE 32	SLP	SA/RC	FBG	CT	OB				13	10	7900	3	2	33400	37100
32	2	COMANCHE 32	SLP	SA/RC	FBG	CT	IB		D		13	10	7900	3	2	33700	37400
33		OCEAN-WINDS 33	SLP	SA/CR	FBG	CT	IB		30D		16		7900	3	3	36200	40200
33		OCEAN-WINDS 33	SLP	SA/CR	FBG	CT	IB	T	13D	VLVO	16		7900	3	3	36600	40600
35		CHEROKEE 35	SLP	SA/CR	FBG	CT	IB				17		11000	3	6	46700	51300
35		CHEROKEE 35	SLP	SA/CR	FBG	CT	IB		D		17		11000	3	6	47300	51900
35		TELSTAR 35	SLP	SA/RC	FBG	TM	IB		D		20		13000	2	3	49300	54200
37		SNOW-GOOSE 37	CUT	SA/CR	FBG	CT	IB		15D	YAN	15		10000	2	8	52300	57400
37		SNOW-GOOSE 37	CUT	SA/RC	FBG	CT	IB		D		15		10000	2	8	52300	57400
40	10	APACHE 41	SLP	SA/RC	FBG	CT	IB		D		19	6	13500	3		73900	81200
40	10	APACHE 41	CUT	SA/RC	FBG	CT	IB		D		19	6	13500	3		73900	81200
40	10	APACHE 41	KTH	SA/RC	FBG	CT	IB		D		19	6	13500	3		73900	81200
45		APACHE 45 MKII	SLP	SA/CR	FBG	CT	IB	T	D							121500	133500
45		APACHE 45 MKII	CUT	SA/CR	FBG	CT	IB	T	D							121500	133500
45		APACHE 45 MKII	KTH	SA/CR	FBG	CT	IB	T	D							121500	133500
49		QUASAR 50	CUT	SA/RC	FBG	CT	IB		D		19	8	14500	3		159500	175000
50		QUASAR 50	SLP	SA/CR	FBG	CT	IB	T	20D							170000	186500
		1980 BOATS															
20		CRACKSMAN 20	SLP	SA/CR	FBG	CT	OB				10		1000			4050	4700
23		AZTEC 23	SLP	SA/CR	FBG	CT					11	3	900			7350	8450
24		HIRONDELLE 24 MKIII	SLP	SA/RC	FBG	CT	OB				10		2700	2	6	11100	12700
26	2	HEAVENLY-TWINS 26	SLP	SA/CR	FBG	CT	IB		D		13	9	4400	2	3	16000	18200
26	3	TELSTAR 25	SLP	SA/RC	FBG	TM	OB				16		2200			13400	15300
27		CATALAC 27	SLP	SA/CR	FBG	CT	OB				13	8	4600	2		18100	20100
28		CATFISHER 28	SLP	SA/CR	FBG	CT	IB		D		13	1	7600	3	4	21700	24100
29	6	CATALAC 30	SLP	SA/CR	FBG	CT	IB		D		13	10	5900	2	6	23300	25900
30		IROQUOIS MKII	SLP	SA/RC	FBG	CT	IB		D		13	6	5200	1	4	23600	26200
31		QUEST 31	SLP	SA/RC	FBG	CT	IB		D		14	3	6500	2	6	27400	30500
32	2	COMANCHE 32	SLP	SA/RC	FBG	CT	IB		D		13	10	7800	3	4	32000	35500
33		OCEAN-WINDS 33	SLP	SA/CR	FBG	CT	IB		D		16		7900	3	3	34400	38200
35		CHEROKEE 35	SLP	SA/CR	FBG	CT	IB		D		17		11000	3	6	44500	49400
35		TELSTAR 35	SLP	SA/RC	FBG	TM	IB		D		20		13000			47000	51700
37		SNOW-GOOSE 37	CUT	SA/RC	FBG	CT	IB		D		15		10000	2	8	49800	54700
40	10	APACHE 41	SLP	SA/RC	FBG	CT	IB		D		19	6	13500			70400	77400
40	10	APACHE 41	CUT	SA/RC	FBG	CT	IB		D		19	6	13500			70400	77400
40	10	APACHE 41	KTH	SA/RC	FBG	CT	IB		D		19	6	13500			70400	77400
49		QUASAR 50	CUT	SA/RC	FBG	CT	IB		D		19	8	14500	3		152500	167500
		1979 BOATS															
23		AZTEC 23	SLP	SA/CR	FBG	CT	OB				11	3	900	3		7050	8150
23	2	CAT 26	SLP	SA/CR	FBG	CT	IB		D		13	9	4400	2	3	11100	12600
24		HIRONDELLE	SLP	SA/CR	FBG	CT	OB				10		2600	2	6	10600	12100
26	2	HEAVENLY-TWINS 26	SLP	SA/CR	FBG	CT	OB				13	9	4400	2	3	15400	17500
26	2	HEAVENLY-TWINS 26	SLP	SA/CR	FBG	CT	IB		D		13	9	4400	2	3	15400	17500
28		CATFISHER 28	SLP	SA/CR	FBG	CT	IB		D		13	1	7600	3	4	20800	23100
30		IROQUOIS	SLP	SA/CR	FBG	CT	IB		D		13	6	5000	5	8	22400	24900
31		QUEST 31	SLP	SA/CR	FBG	CT	IB		D		14	3	6500	2	6	26300	29200
32	2	COMANCHE 32	SLP	SA/CR	FBG	CT	IB		D		13	10	7800	5	6	30600	33900
33		OCEAN-WINDS 33	SLP	SA/CR	FBG	CT	IB		D		16		7900	3	3	32900	36600
35		CHEROKEE 35	SLP	SA/CR	FBG	CT	IB		D		17		11000	3	6	42500	47300
37		SNOW-GOOSE 37	CUT	SA/CR	FBG	CT	IB		D		15		10000	2	8	47900	52600
40	10	APACHE 41	SLP	SA/CR	FBG	CT	IB		D		19	6	13500	6	9	67700	74400
40	10	APACHE 41	CUT	SA/CR	FBG	CT	IB		D		19	6	13500	6	9	67700	74400
40	10	APACHE 41	KTH	SA/CR	FBG	CT	IB		D		19	6	13500	6	9	67700	74400
49		QUASAR 49	CUT	SA/CR	FBG	CT	IB		D		19	8	14500	3		146500	161000
		1978 BOATS															
24		HIRONDELLE	SLP	SA/CR	FBG	CT	OB				10		2600	1	3	10200	11600
26	2	HEAVENLY-TWINS 26	SLP	SA/CR	FBG	CT	OB				13	9	3400	2	3	13900	15800
31		QUEST 31	SLP	SA/CR	FBG	CT	IB		12D		14	3	7000	2	6	25800	28700
		1977 BOATS															
24		HIRONDELLE	SLP	SA/CR	FBG	CT	OB				10		2600	1	3	9900	11200
26	2	HEAVENLY-TWINS 26	SLP	SA/CR	FBG	CT	OB				13	9	5000	2	3	14900	16900
		1976 BOATS															
20		CRACKSMAN	SLP	SA/CR	FBG	CT	OB				8		1000		10	3500	4050
24		HIRONDELLE	SLP	SA/CR	FBG	CT	OB				10		2600	1	3	9550	10900
26	2	HEAVENLY-TWINS	SLP	SA/CR	FBG	CT	OB				13	9	5000	2	3	14400	16400
26	2	HEAVENLY-TWINS	SLP	SA/CR	FBG	CT	IB		10D		13	9	5000	2	3	14400	16400
26	3	TELSTAR	SLP	SA/CR	FBG	CT	OB				15		2000	1	6	11400	12900
26	3	TELSTAR	SLP	SA/CR	FBG	CT	IB		24D		15		2000	1	6	11400	12900
		1975 BOATS															
24		HIRONDELLE	SLP	SA/CR	FBG	CT	OB				10		2600	1	3	9350	10600
30		TROGUOIS MKII	SLP	SA/CR	FBG	CT	OB				13	6	5000	1	4	19500	21700
31		SYMONS 31	SLP	SA/CR	F/W	TM	IB		D		18		3800	2	2	19800	22000
34		SNOW-GOOSE 34	CUT	SA/CR	FBG	CT	IB		25D	VLVO	15		8000	2	3	31100	34500
35		CHEROKEE 35	SLP	SA/CR	FBG	CT	IB		50D		17		11000	2	9	36700	40700
36		SYMONS 36	CUT	SA/CR	F/W	TM	IB		D		20		7200	2	6	35400	39300
42		SYMONS 42	KTH	SA/CR	F/W	TM	IB		D		22	2	12500	2	10	62600	68800
49		SYMONS 49	KTH	SA/CR	F/W	TM	IB		D		24	2	24000	3	6	128000	141000
		1974 BOATS															
24		HIRONDELLE	SLP	SA/CR	FBG	CT	OB				10		2600	1	3	9100	10300
30		IROQUOIS MKII	SLP	SA/CR	FBG	CT	OB				13	6	5000	1	4	19000	21100
31		SYMONS 31	KTH	SA/CR	F/W	TM	IB		D		18		3800	2	10	19300	21400
35		CHEROKEE	SLP	SA/CR	FBG	CT	IO				17			2	2	38200	42400
36		SYMONS 36	KTH	SA/CR	F/W	TM	IB		D		20		7200	2	6	34500	38300
42		SYMONS 42	SLP	SA/CR	F/W	TM	IB		D		22	2	12500	2	2	60900	66900
42		TAHITI TRAWLER		TRWL	FBG	RB	IB		160D		13	8				36900	41000
49		SYMONS 49	KTH	SA/CR	F/W	TM	IB		D		24	2	24000	3	6	125000	137000
		1973 BOATS															
24		HIRONDELLE	SLP	SA/CR	FBG	CT	OB				10		2600	1	3	8900	10100
31		SYMONS 31	SLP	SA/CR	F/W	TM	IB		D		18		3800	2	2	19000	21100
36		SYMONS 36	SLP	SA/CR	F/W	TM	IB		D		20		7200	2	6	33600	37400
42		SYMONS 42	KTH	SA/CR	F/W	TM	IB		D		22	2	12500	2	10	59400	65300
42		TAHITI TRAWLER		TRWL	FBG	RB	IB		160D		13	8				35500	39500
49	3	SYMONS 49	KTH	SA/CR	F/W	TM	IB		D		24	2	24000	3	6	123500	135500
		1972 BOATS															
24		HIRONDELLE	SLP	SA/CR	FBG	CT	OB				10		2600	1	3	8600	9850
30		IROQUOIS	SLP	SA/CR	FBG	CT	OB				13	6	5000	1	4	18300	20300
31		SYMONS 31	SLP	SA/CR	WD	TM	IB		D		18		3800	2	2	18600	20700
32		IROQUOIS	SLP	SA/CR	FBG	CT	IB		D		13	6	5600	1	4	22200	24700
32	8	SYMONS 33	SLP	SA/CR	FBG	TM	IB		D		18	8	6160	3		24100	26800
32	8	SYMONS 33	CUT	SA/CR	FBG	TM	IB		D		18	8	6160	3		24100	26800
35		CHEROKEE 35	SLP	SA/CR	FBG	CT	IB		D		17			2	2	36500	40500
36		SYMONS 36	SLP	SA/CR	WD	TM	IB		D		20		7200	2	7	32900	36500
36		SYMONS 36	KTH	SA/CR	WD	TM	IB		D		20		7200	2	7	32900	36500
40	10	APACHE 41	SLP	SA/CR	FBG	CT	IB		D		19	6		2	10	63800	70100
40	10	APACHE 41	CUT	SA/CR	FBG	CT	IB		D		19	6		2	10	63800	70100
40	10	APACHE 41	KTH	SA/CR	FBG	CT	IB		D		19	6		2	10	63800	70100
42		SYMONS 42	KTH	SA/CR	WD	TM	IB		D		22	2	12500	2	10	58100	63900
43	6	TAHITI TRAWLER		TRWL	FBG	RB	IB		160D		13	8	31629	3	8	36500	40500
43	6	TAHITI TRAWLER		TRWL	FBG	RB	IB	T	95D		13	8	31629	3	8	37200	41300
49	3	SYMONS 49	KTH	SA/CR	WD	TM	IB		D		24	2	24000	3	6	120500	132500
		1971 BOATS															
30		DUTCH-TREAT 30	SLP	SA/CR	STL	KL	IB		15D		11	2		3	3	19100	21300
30	6	IROQUOIS	SLP	SA/CR	FBG	CT	OB				13	6	5000	1	4	18800	20900
31		SYMONS 31	SLP	SA/CR	WD	TM	IB		D		18	8	5150	2	2	19500	21700
32	8	SYMONS 33	CUT	SA/CR	FBG	TM	IB		D		18	8	7030	3		24500	27200
36		SYMONS 36	SLP	SA/CR	WD	TM	IB		D		20		7200	2	6	32200	35800
42		SYMONS 42	KTH	SA/CR	WD	TM	IB		D		23		12500	3	2	57000	62600
49	3	SYMONS 49	KTH	SA/CR	WD	TM	IB		D		24	2	22100	3	6	118000	130000
		1970 BOATS															
25		PI	SLP	SA/CR	F/W	TM					15			1	7	10200	11600
30		DUTCH-TREAT 30	SLP	SA/CR	STL		IB		15D		11	2	12200	3	3	26300	29200
30		IROQUOIS	SLP	SA/CR	FBG	CT	OB				13	6		1	4	18500	20500
30		PI	SLP	SA/CR	F/W	TM					18			2		18500	20500
30		PI	SLP	SA/CR	FBG	TM					18		3800	2		16000	18200
32	8	SYMONS 33	SLP	SA/CR	FBG	TM	IB				18	6	6160	3		23200	25800
35		PI	SLP	SA/CR	F/W	TM	IB		D		20			2	6	35100	39000
36		SYMONS 36	SLP	SA/CR	FBG	TM	IB				20		6850	2	7	31200	34700
36		SYMONS 36	KTH	SA/CR	FBG	TM	IB				20		6850	2	7	31200	34700
40		PI	KTH	SA/CR	FBG	TM							8220	2	9	43600	48400
40		PI	KTH	SA/CR	F/W	TM	IB		D		22			2	9	56500	62100
49		SYMONS 49	KTH	SA/CR	F/W	TM	IB		D		24			3	3	114500	126000
49	3	SYMONS 49	KTH	SA/CR	FBG	TM	IB				24	2	24000	3	6	116000	127500

 CONTINUED ON NEXT PAGE

LOA FT IN	NAME AND/ OR MODEL	TOP/ RIG	BOAT TYPE	-HULL- MTL TP	----ENGINE--- TP # HP MFG	BEAM FT IN	WGT LBS	DRAFT FT IN	RETAIL LOW	RETAIL HIGH
---	---	--- 1969	BOATS	---	---	---	---	---	---	---
30	P 30	SLP	SA/CR	FBG TM	IB D	18	3800	2	15800	17900
35	P 35	KTH	SA/CR	FBG TM	IB D	20	5000	2 6	26000	28900
40	P 40	KTH	SA/CR	FBG TM	IB D	22	8220	2 9	42900	47700
41	CORINTHIAN 41 STD	KTH	SA/CR	F/W TM	IB 50	23 9	12000	2 2	51000	56100
47	P 47	KTH	SA/CR	FBG TM	IB 55D	24		3	102000	112000
---	---	--- 1968	BOATS	---	---	---	---	---	---	---
30	PI	SLP	SAIL	F/W TM	OB	18		2	17500	19900
35	PI	KTH	SAIL	F/W TM	OB	20		2 6	33100	36800
40	PI	KTH	SAIL	F/W TM	OB	22		2 9	49800	54700
41	CORINTHIAN 41	KTH	SAIL	F/W TM	IB 50	23 9	12000	2 2	50400	55300
47	PI	KTH	SAIL	F/W TM	IB	24		3	98500	108500
---	---	--- 1967	BOATS	---	---	---	---	---	---	---
30	PI	SLP	SA/CR	F/W TM	IB	18	2200	2	13300	15100
34	CORINTHIAN 34	SLP	SA/CR	FBG TM	IB 55D	20		1 10	30800	34300
35	PI	KTH	SA/CR	F/W TM		20	5000	2 6	25400	28200
40	PI	KTH	SA/CR	F/W TM		22		2 9	49200	54100
41	CORINTHIAN 41	KTH	SA/CR	FBG TM	IB 55D	23 9	10000	2 2	47700	52400
47	PI	KTH	SA/CR	F/W TM	IB 48D	24		3 3	99100	109000
---	---	--- 1966	BOATS	---	---	---	---	---	---	---
25	PI	SLP	SA/CR	F/W TM		15		3 6	9700	11000
30	PI	SLP	SA/CR	F/W TM		18		2	17200	19500
32	1 CORINTHIAN 32	SLP	SA/CR	FBG TM	IB	18 6		1 8	21300	23700
35	LODESTAR	KTH	SA/CR	F/W TM		20		2 6	32400	36100
35	PI	KTH	SA/CR	F/W TM	OB	20		2 6	32400	36100
40	PI	KTH	SA/CR	F/W TM	OB	22		2 9	52300	57500
40	VICTRESS	KTH	SA/CR	F/W TM		22		2 9	44900	49900
41	CORINTHIAN 41	KTH	SA/CR	FBG TM	IB	23		1 10	50000	54900
47	PI	KTH	SA/CR	F/W TM	IB	24		3 3	96500	106000
---	---	--- 1965	BOATS	---	---	---	---	---	---	---
24	NUGGET	SLP	SAIL	F/W TM		14		1 6	8450	9750
25	PI 25	SLP	SAIL	F/W TM		15		1 7	9600	10900
30	NIMBLE	SLP	SAIL	F/W TM		18			17000	19400
35	LODESTAR	SLP	SAIL	F/W TM		20			32200	35800
40	VICTRESS	KTH	SAIL	F/W TM		22			48400	53200
46	TRIDENT	KTH	SAIL	F/W TM		24			89200	98100
55	DIADEM	KTH	SAIL	F/W TM		28			153500	168500
64	EMPRESS	KTH	SAIL	F/W TM		32			184000	202500

T B I PRODUCTS INC
TUGBOATS   COAST GUARD MFG ID- TBX

Call 1-800-327-6929 for BUC Personalized Evaluation Service
Or, for 1973 to 1975 boats, sign onto www.BUCValuPro.com

T C & T T COMPANY
NILS LUCANDER

Call 1-800-327-6929 for BUC Personalized Evaluation Service
Or, for 1970 boats, sign onto www.BUCValuPro.com

T-CRAFT BOAT CO INC
DIV THOMPSON INDUSTRIES INC   See inside cover to adjust price for area
TITUSVILLE FL 32780   COAST GUARD MFG ID- TCB

LOA FT IN	NAME AND/ OR MODEL	TOP/ RIG	BOAT TYPE	-HULL- MTL TP	----ENGINE--- TP # HP MFG	BEAM FT IN	WGT LBS	DRAFT FT IN	RETAIL LOW	RETAIL HIGH
---	---	--- 1983	BOATS	---	---	---	---	---	---	---
21 3	GULFSTREAM	OP	CTRCN	FBG SV	OB	7 8		2 6	4550	5200
23 9	GULFSTREAM	OP	CTRCN	FBG SV	OB	7 8		2 6	5700	6550
23 9	GULFSTREAM	TT	CTRCN	FBG SV	OB	7 8		2 6	5700	6550
23 9	T-CRAFT FLAT	OP	FSH	FBG FL	IO 330	9 2			6150	7100
23 9	T-CRAFT FLAT	OP	FSH	FBG FL	IO 340	9 2			6800	7800
23 9	T-CRAFT FLAT CAB		FSH	FBG FL	IO 330	9 2			6150	7100
23 9	T-CRAFT FLAT CAB		FSH	FBG FL	IB 340	9 2			6800	7800
29 8		ST	CBNCR	FBG DV	IO 330 MRCR 10			3	14400	16400
	IB 340 MRCR 17400		19700,	IO T155 OMC	14200 16200,	IB T188	MRCR	18200	20300
	IO T205 OMC 14900		17000,	IOT130D-T165D	19500 22900				
29 8		HT	CBNCR	FBG DV	IB 235D-350D 10			3	24200	30200
29 8		FB	CBNCR	FBG DV	IB 235D-350D 10			3	24200	30200
29 8		F+T	CBNCR	FBG DV	IB 235D-350D 10			3	24200	30200
29 8		OP	CTRCN	FBG DV	IO 115-155 10			3	8100	9800
	IO 205 OMC 9050		10300,	IO 330 MRCR	10100 11500,	IB 340	MRCR	11800	13400
	IO T188 MRCR 10400		11800,	IOT130D-T165D	12600 15600				
29 8	GULFSTREAM	OP	CTRCN	FBG DV	OB	10	6000	3	13000	14800
29 8	SPORTS CABIN	ST	CBNCR	FBG DV	OB	10		3	13000	14800
29 8	SPORTS CABIN	ST	CBNCR	FBG DV	IB 235D-350D 10			3	24200	30200
29 8	SPORTS CABIN	HT	CTRCN	FBG DV	OB	10		3	13000	14800
29 8	SPORTS CABIN	FB	CBNCR	FBG DV	OB	10		3	13000	14800
29 8	SPORTS CABIN	OP	CTRCN	FBG DV	IB 235D-286D 10			3	12900	15800
29 8	SPORTS CABIN	ST	CBNCR	FBG DV	IB 300D-350D 10			3	14500	17500
29 8	SPORTS CABIN	TT	CTRCN	FBG DV	IB 235D-286D 10			3	12900	15800
29 8	SPORTS CABIN	TT	CTRCN	FBG DV	IB 300D-350D 10			3	14500	17500
---	---	--- 1982	BOATS	---	---	---	---	---	---	---
21 3	GULFSTREAM	OP	CTRCN	FBG SV	OB	7 8		2 6	4450	5150
23 9	GULFSTREAM	OP	CTRCN	FBG SV	OB	7 8		2 6	5600	6450
29 8	OFFSHORE CABIN	OP	CBNCR	FBG DV	OB	10 8	4800	3	14300	16200
29 8	OFFSHORE CABIN	OP	CBNCR	FBG DV	IO 330 MRCR 10 8			3	14300	16200
	IB 340 MRCR 16800		19100,	IB 240D-300D	23800 28000,	IOT130D-T155D		19200	22300
29 8	OFFSHORE CABIN	HT	CBNCR	FBG DV	IB 240D-300D 10 8			3	12800	14600
29 8	OFFSHORE CABIN	HT	CBNCR	FBG DV	IO 240D-300D 10 8			3	23800	28000
29 8	OFFSHORE CABIN	HT	CBNCR	FBG DV	IO T185 MRCR 10 8			3	14500	16500
29 8	OFFSHORE CABIN	HT	CBNCR	FBG DV	IO T130D VLVO 10 8			3	19200	21400
29 8	OFFSHORE CABIN	FB	CBNCR	FBG DV	OB	10 8		3	12800	14600
29 8	OFFSHORE CABIN	FB	CBNCR	FBG DV	IO 330 MRCR 10 8			3	14300	16200
	IB 340 MRCR 16800		19100,	IB 240D-300D	23800 28000,	IO T130D VLVO		19200	21400
29 8	OFFSHORE CTRCN	OP	OPFSH	FBG DV	OB	10 8	6000	3	12800	14600
29 8	OFFSHORE CTRCN	OP	OPFSH	FBG DV	IO 330 CAT 10 8			3	9950	11300
	IB 340 MRCR 11400		12900,	IB 300D CAT	13000 14800,	IO T130D VLVO		11600	13100
29 8	OFFSHORE CTRCN	TT	OPFSH	FBG DV	OB	10 8		3	12800	14600
29 8	OFFSHORE CTRCN	TT	OPFSH	FBG DV	IO 330 MRCR 10 8			3	9950	11300
29 8	OFFSHORE CTRCN	TT	OPFSH	FBG DV	IO 340 MRCR 10 8			3	11400	12900
29 8	OFFSHORE CTRCN	TT	OPFSH	FBG DV	IB 300D CAT 10 8			3	13000	14800
---	---	--- 1981	BOATS	---	---	---	---	---	---	---
21 3	GULFSTREAM	OP	CTRCN	FBG SV	OB	7 8		2 6	4400	5050
23 9		OP	OPFSH	FBG FL	OB	9 2	2100		4550	5250
23 9		OP	OPFSH	FBG FL	IO 120	9 2			5000	5750
23 9		OP	OPFSH	FBG FL	IO 170	9 2			5600	6400
23 9	CABIN FISHERMAN	FSH	FBG FL	IO 120	9 2	2350		5000	5750
23 9	CABIN FISHERMAN	FSH	FBG FL	IO 120	9 2			5250	6050
23 9	CABIN FISHERMAN	FSH	FBG FL	IO 170	9 2			5950	6800
29 8	GULFSTREAM	OP	CBNCR	FBG DV	OB	10 8	6000	3	12600	14300
29 8	OFFSHORE CABIN	OP	CBNCR	FBG DV	OB	10 8		3	12600	14300
	IO 260 MRCR 13300		15100,	IO 330 MRCR	13300 14800,	IB 260 OMC		15300	17400
	IO 330 MRCR 14000		15900,	IB 330 MRCR	16000 18200,	IB 200D-260D		22000	26000
29 8	OFFSHORE CABIN	HT	CBNCR	FBG DV	OB	10 8		3	12600	14300
29 8	OFFSHORE CABIN	HT	CBNCR	FBG DV	IO 330 MRCR 10 8			3	15200	17300
	IO 260 13300		15100,	IO 330 MRCR	14000 15900,	IB 330 MRCR		16000	18200
	IB 200D-260D 22000		26000						
29 8	OFFSHORE CABIN	FB	CBNCR	FBG DV	OB	10 8		3	12600	14300
29 8	OFFSHORE CABIN	FB	CBNCR	FBG DV	IO 330 MRCR 10 8			3	15200	17300
	IO 260 13300		15100,	IO 330 MRCR	14000 15900,	IB 330 MRCR		16000	18200
	IB 200D-260D 22000		26000						
29 8	OFFSHORE CTRCN	OP	OPFSH	FBG DV	OB	10 8	6000	3	12600	14300
29 8	OFFSHORE CTRCN	OP	OPFSH	FBG DV	IO 330 MRCR 10 8			3	10300	11700
	IO 260 MRCR 9300		10600,	IO 260 OMC	9300 10600,	IB 260 OMC		10400	11800
	IO 330 MRCR 9800		11100,	IO 330 MRCR	10800 12300,	IB 200D-260D		10800	12300
---	---	--- 1980	BOATS	---	---	---	---	---	---	---
21 3	BEACHCOMBER	OP	CBNCR	FBG SV	OB	7 8	2550	2	4700	5400
21 3	BEACHCOMBER	OP	CBNCR	FBG SV	IO 120-265	7 8		2	4350	4950
21 3	BEACHCOMBER	HT	CBNCR	FBG SV	IO T120-T170	7 8	2700	2	4850	5550
21 3	BEACHCOMBER	HT	CBNCR	FBG SV	OB	7 8		2	3900	4550
21 3	BEACHCOMBER	HT	CBNCR	FBG SV	IO 120-265	7 8		2	3350	4150
21 3	BEACHCOMBER	HT	CBNCR	FBG SV	IO T120-T170	7 8		2	3850	4150
21 3	EXPLORER	OP	CUD	FBG SV	OB	7 8	2300	2	4400	5050
21 3	EXPLORER	OP	CUD	FBG SV	IO 120-265	7 8		2	4050	4650
21 3	EXPLORER	HT	CUD	FBG SV	IO T120-T170	7 8	2625	2	4550	4300
21 3	EXPLORER	HT	CUD	FBG SV	OB	7 8		2	3650	4300
21 3	EXPLORER	HT	CUD	FBG SV	IO 120-265	7 8		2	3150	3900
21 3	EXPLORER	HT	CUD	FBG SV	IO T120-T170	7 8		2	3650	4300
21 3	GULFSTREAM	OP	RNBT	FBG SV	OB	7 8	1875	2 6	3750	4350
21 3	GULFSTREAM	OP	RNBT	FBG SV	IO 120-265	7 8		2 6	2900	3300
21 3	GULFSTREAM	OP	RNBT	FBG SV	IO T120-T170	7 8		2 6	3350	3950
21 3	PLAYBOY	OP	RNBT	FBG SV	OB	7 8	1900	2 6	3800	4400

T-CRAFT BOAT CO INC -CONTINUED See inside cover to adjust price for area

LOA FT	LOA IN	NAME AND/ OR MODEL	TOP/ RIG	BOAT TYPE	-HULL- MTL	-HULL- TP	ENGINE TP	ENGINE # HP	ENGINE MFG	BEAM FT	BEAM IN	WGT LBS	DRAFT FT	DRAFT IN	RETAIL LOW	RETAIL HIGH
		1980 BOATS														
21	3	PLAYBOY	OP	RNBT	FBG	SV	IO	120-265		7	8		2	6	2900	3600
21	3	PLAYBOY	OP	RNBT	FBG	SV	IO	T120-T170		7	8		2	6	3350	3950
21	3	PLAYBOY	HT	RNBT	FBG	SV	OB			7	8	2100	2	6	4100	4750
21	3	PLAYBOY	HT	RNBT	FBG	SV	IO	120-265		7	8		2	6	2900	3600
21	3	PLAYBOY	HT	RNBT	FBG	SV	IO	T120-T170		7	8		2	6	3350	3950
22	10	ADVENTURER	ST	CUD	FBG	DV	OB			8		3300	3		6150	7050
22	10	ADVENTURER	ST	CUD	FBG	DV	IO	170-265		8			3		4000	4900
22	10	ADVENTURER	ST	CUD	FBG	DV	IO	T120-T170		8			3		4550	5250
22	10	ADVENTURER	HT	CUD	FBG	DV	OB			8		3300	3		6150	7050
22	10	ADVENTURER	HT	CUD	FBG	DV	IO	170-265		8			3		4000	4900
22	10	ADVENTURER	HT	CUD	FBG	DV	IO	T120-T170		8			3		4550	5250
23	9	BEACHCOMBER	OP	CBNCR	FBG	SV	OB			7	8	2850	2	6	5800	6650
23	9	BEACHCOMBER	OP	CBNCR	FBG	SV	IO	120-265		7	8		2	6	4750	5750
23	9	BEACHCOMBER	OP	CBNCR	FBG	SV	IO	T120-T170		7	8		2	6	5300	6150
23	9	BEACHCOMBER	HT	CBNCR	FBG	SV	OB			7	8	3000	2	6	6050	6950
23	9	BEACHCOMBER	HT	CBNCR	FBG	SV	IO	120-265		7	8		2	6	4750	5750
23	9	BEACHCOMBER	HT	CBNCR	FBG	SV	IO	T120-T170		7	8		2	6	5300	6150
23	9	EXPLORER	OP	CUD	FBG	SV	OB			7	8	2600	2	6	5400	6200
23	9	EXPLORER	OP	CUD	FBG	SV	IO	120-265		7	8		2	6	4500	5400
23	9	EXPLORER	OP	CUD	FBG	SV	IO	T120-T170		7	8		2	6	5000	5750
23	9	EXPLORER	HT	CUD	FBG	SV	OB			7	8	2800	2	6	5700	6550
23	9	EXPLORER	HT	CUD	FBG	SV	IO	120-265		7	8		2	6	4500	5400
23	9	EXPLORER	HT	CUD	FBG	SV	IO	T120-T170		7	8		2	6	5000	5750
23	9	EXPLORER	FB	CUD	FBG	SV	OB			7	8	2925	2	6	5900	6800
23	9	EXPLORER	FB	CUD	FBG	SV	IO	120-265		7	8		2	6	4500	5400
23	9	EXPLORER	FB	CUD	FBG	SV	IO	T120-T170		7	8		2	6	5000	5750
23	9	PLAYBOY	OP	RNBT	FBG	SV	OB			7	8	2200	2	6	4650	5350
23	9	PLAYBOY	OP	RNBT	FBG	SV	IO	120-265		7	8		2	6	4100	5000
23	9	PLAYBOY	OP	RNBT	FBG	SV	IO	T120-T170		7	8		2	6	4600	5350
23	9	PLAYBOY	HT	RNBT	FBG	SV	OB			7	8	2400	2	6	5050	5800
23	9	PLAYBOY	HT	RNBT	FBG	SV	IO	120-265		7	8		2	6	4100	5000
23	9	PLAYBOY	HT	RNBT	FBG	SV	IO	T120-T170		7	8		2	6	4600	5350
23	9	PLAYBOY	FB	RNBT	FBG	SV	OB			7	8	2525	2	6	5250	6050
23	9	PLAYBOY	FB	RNBT	FBG	SV	IO	120-265		7	8		2	6	4100	5000
23	9	PLAYBOY	FB	RNBT	FBG	SV	IO	T120-T170		7	8		2	6	4600	5350
29	8	OFFSHORE CABIN	OP	CBNCR	FBG	DV	OB			10	8	6000	3		12400	14100
29	8	OFFSHORE CABIN	OP	CBNCR	FBG	DV	IB	255	MRCR	10	8		3		14600	16500
		IO 260 MRCR 13200 15000, IO 260 OMC 13200 15000, IB 260 OMC													14700	16700
		IO 330 MRCR 13900 15800, IB 330 MRCR 15300 17400, IB 200D-260D													21200	25000
29	8	OFFSHORE CABIN	HT	CBNCR	FBG	DV	OB			10	8		3		12500	14200
29	8	OFFSHORE CABIN	HT	CBNCR	FBG	DV	IB	255	MRCR	10	8		3		14600	16500
		IO 260 13200 15000, IO 330 MRCR 13900 15800, IB 330 MRCR													15300	17400
		IB 200D-260D 21200 25000														
29	8	OFFSHORE CABIN	FB	CBNCR	FBG	DV	OB			10	8		3		12400	14100
29	8	OFFSHORE CABIN	FB	CBNCR	FBG	DV	IB	255	MRCR	10	8		3		14600	16500
		IO 260 13200 15000, IO 330 MRCR 13900 15800, IB 330 MRCR													15300	17400
		IB 200D-260D 21200 25000														
29	8	OFFSHORE CTRCN	OP	OPFSH	FBG	DV	OB			10	8	6000	3		12400	14100
29	8	OFFSHORE CTRCN	OP	OPFSH	FBG	DV	IB	255	MRCR	10	8		3		9900	11200
		IO 260 MRCR 9250 10500, IO 260 OMC 9200 10500, IB 260 OMC													9950	11300
		IO 330 MRCR 9700 11000, IB 330 MRCR 10400 11800, IB 200D-260D													10400	12900
		1979 BOATS														
21	3	BEACHCOMBER	OP	CBNCR	FBG	SV	OB			7	8	2550	1	8	4650	5350
21	3	BEACHCOMBER	OP	CBNCR	FBG	SV	IO	120-265		7	8		2		3350	4150
21	3	BEACHCOMBER	OP	CBNCR	FBG	SV	IO	T120-T170		7	8		2		3900	4550
21	3	BEACHCOMBER	HT	CBNCR	FBG	SV	OB			7	8	2700	1	8	4800	5500
21	3	BEACHCOMBER	HT	CBNCR	FBG	SV	IO	120-265		7	8		2		3350	4150
21	3	BEACHCOMBER	HT	CBNCR	FBG	SV	IO	T120-T170		7	8		2		3900	4550
21	3	EXPLORER	OP	CUD	FBG	SV	OB			7	8	2300	1	8	4300	5000
21	3	EXPLORER	OP	CUD	FBG	SV	IO	120-265		7	8		2		3150	3900
21	3	EXPLORER	OP	CUD	FBG	SV	IO	T120-T170		7	8		2		3650	4300
21	3	EXPLORER	HT	CUD	FBG	SV	OB			7	8	2625	1	8	4700	5400
21	3	EXPLORER	HT	CUD	FBG	SV	IO	120-265		7	8		2		3150	3900
21	3	EXPLORER	HT	CUD	FBG	SV	IO	T120-T170		7	8		2		3650	4300
21	3	GULFSTREAM	OP	RNBT	FBG	SV	OB			7	8	1875	1	8	3700	4300
21	3	GULFSTREAM	OP	RNBT	FBG	SV	IO	120-265		7	8		2		2850	3550
21	3	GULFSTREAM	OP	RNBT	FBG	SV	IO	T120-T170		7	8		2		3350	3950
21	3	GULFSTREAM	HT	RNBT	FBG	SV	OB			7	8	1875	1	8	3700	4300
21	3	GULFSTREAM	HT	RNBT	FBG	SV	IO	120-265		7	8		2		2900	3550
21	3	GULFSTREAM	HT	RNBT	FBG	SV	IO	T120-T170		7	8		2		3350	3950
21	3	PLAYBOY	OP	RNBT	FBG	SV	OB			7	8	1900	1	8	3750	4350
21	3	PLAYBOY	OP	RNBT	FBG	SV	IO	120-265		7	8		2		2900	3600
21	3	PLAYBOY	OP	RNBT	FBG	SV	IO	T120-T170		7	8		2		3350	3950
21	3	PLAYBOY	HT	RNBT	FBG	SV	OB			7	8	2100	1	8	4050	4700
21	3	PLAYBOY	HT	RNBT	FBG	SV	IO	120-265		7	8		2		2900	3600
21	3	PLAYBOY	HT	RNBT	FBG	SV	IO	T120-T170		7	8		2		3350	3950
22	10	ADVENTURER	ST	CUD	FBG	DV	OB			8		3300	2	1	6050	7000
22	10	ADVENTURER	ST	CUD	FBG	DV	IO	170-265		8			2	10	4000	4900
22	10	ADVENTURER	ST	CUD	FBG	DV	IO	T120-T170		8			2	10	4550	5250
22	10	ADVENTURER	HT	CUD	FBG	DV	OB			8		3300	2	1	6050	7000
22	10	ADVENTURER	HT	CUD	FBG	DV	IO	170-265		8			2	10	4000	4900
22	10	ADVENTURER	HT	CUD	FBG	DV	IO	T120-T170		8			2	10	4550	5250
23	9	BEACHCOMBER	OP	CBNCR	FBG	SV	OB			7	8	2850	1	8	5750	6600
23	9	BEACHCOMBER	OP	CBNCR	FBG	SV	IO	120-265		7	8		2		4750	5700
23	9	BEACHCOMBER	OP	CBNCR	FBG	SV	IO	T120-T170		7	8		2		5300	6150
23	9	BEACHCOMBER	HT	CBNCR	FBG	SV	OB			7	8	3000	1	8	5950	6850
23	9	BEACHCOMBER	HT	CBNCR	FBG	SV	IO	120-265		7	8		2		4750	5700
23	9	BEACHCOMBER	HT	CBNCR	FBG	SV	IO	T120-T170		7	8		2		5300	6150
23	9	EXPLORER	OP	CUD	FBG	SV	OB			7	8	2600	1	8	5300	6100
23	9	EXPLORER	OP	CUD	FBG	SV	IO	120-265		7	8		2		4500	5400
23	9	EXPLORER	OP	CUD	FBG	SV	IO	T120-T170		7	8		2		5000	5750
23	9	EXPLORER	HT	CUD	FBG	SV	OB			7	8	2800	1	8	5650	6500
23	9	EXPLORER	HT	CUD	FBG	SV	IO	120-265		7	8		2		4500	5400
23	9	EXPLORER	HT	CUD	FBG	SV	IO	T120-T170		7	8		2		5000	5750
23	9	EXPLORER	FB	CUD	FBG	SV	OB			7	8	2925	1	8	5850	6700
23	9	EXPLORER	FB	CUD	FBG	SV	IO	120-265		7	8		2		4500	5400
23	9	EXPLORER	FB	CUD	FBG	SV	IO	T120-T170		7	8		2		5000	5750
23	9	PLAYBOY	OP	RNBT	FBG	SV	OB			7	8	2200	1	8	4650	5350
23	9	PLAYBOY	OP	RNBT	FBG	SV	IO	120-265		7	8		2		4100	5000
23	9	PLAYBOY	OP	RNBT	FBG	SV	IO	T120-T170		7	8		2		4600	5350
23	9	PLAYBOY	HT	RNBT	FBG	SV	OB			7	8	2400	1	8	4950	5700
23	9	PLAYBOY	HT	RNBT	FBG	SV	IO	120-265		7	8		2		4100	5000
23	9	PLAYBOY	HT	RNBT	FBG	SV	IO	T120-T170		7	8		2		4600	5350
23	9	PLAYBOY	FB	RNBT	FBG	SV	OB			7	8	2525	1	8	5200	5950
23	9	PLAYBOY	FB	RNBT	FBG	SV	IO	120-265		7	8		2		4100	5000
23	9	PLAYBOY	FB	RNBT	FBG	SV	IO	T120-T170		7	8		2		4600	5350
29	8	OFFSHORE CABIN	OP	CBNCR	FBG	SV	OB			10		6000	3		12300	14000
29	8	OFFSHORE CABIN	OP	CBNCR	FBG	SV	IO	170-260		10			3		12200	14800
29	8	OFFSHORE CABIN	OP	CBNCR	FBG	SV	IB	210D-260D		10			3		20400	23800
29	8	OFFSHORE CABIN	OP	CBNCR	FBG	SV	IO	T170-T225		10			3		13800	16200
29	8	OFFSHORE CABIN	HT	CBNCR	FBG	SV	OB			10		6500	3		12300	14000
29	8	OFFSHORE CABIN	HT	CBNCR	FBG	SV	IO	170-260		10			3		12200	14800
29	8	OFFSHORE CABIN	HT	CBNCR	FBG	SV	IB	210D-260D		10			3		20400	23800
29	8	OFFSHORE CABIN	HT	CBNCR	FBG	SV	IO	T170-T225		10			3		13800	16200
29	8	OFFSHORE CABIN	FB	CBNCR	FBG	SV	OB			10		6750	3		12300	14000
29	8	OFFSHORE CABIN	FB	CBNCR	FBG	SV	IO	170-260		10			3		12200	14800
29	8	OFFSHORE CABIN	FB	CBNCR	FBG	SV	IB	210D-260D		10			3		20400	23800
29	8	OFFSHORE CABIN	FB	CBNCR	FBG	SV	IO	T170-T225		10			3		13800	16200
29	8	OFFSHORE CTRCN	OP	OPFSH	FBG	SV	OB			10		6000		3	12300	14000
29	8	OFFSHORE CTRCN	OP	OPFSH	FBG	SV	IO	170-260		10				3	8400	10400
29	8	OFFSHORE CTRCN	OP	OPFSH	FBG	SV	IB	210D-260D		10				3	10100	12300
29	8	OFFSHORE CTRCN	OP	OPFSH	FBG	SV	IO	T170-T225		10				3	9600	11600
		1978 BOATS														
21	3	BEACHCOMBER	OP	CR	FBG	SV	OB			7	8	2550			4600	5300
21	3	BEACHCOMBER	OP	CR	FBG	SV	IO	120-240		7	8				3150	3800
21	3	BEACHCOMBER	HT	CR	FBG	SV	OB			7	8				4650	5350
21	3	BEACHCOMBER	HT	CR	FBG	SV	IO	120-240		7	8				3150	3800
21	3	EXPLORER	OP	CUD	FBG	SV	OB			7	8	2300			4250	4950
21	3	EXPLORER	OP	CUD	FBG	SV	IO	120-240		7	8				3200	3800
21	3	EXPLORER	HT	CUD	FBG	SV	OB			7	8	2625			4650	5350
21	3	EXPLORER	HT	CUD	FBG	SV	IO	120-240		7	8				3200	3800
21	3	GULFSTREAM	OP	RNBT	FBG	SV	OB			7	8	1875			3650	4250
21	3	GULFSTREAM	OP	RNBT	FBG	SV	IO	120-240		7	8				2900	3450
21	3	GULFSTREAM	HT	RNBT	FBG	SV	OB			7	8	1875			3650	4250
21	3	GULFSTREAM	HT	RNBT	FBG	SV	IO	120-240		7	8				2900	3450
21	3	PLAYBOY	OP	RNBT	FBG	SV	OB			7	8	1900			3700	4300
21	3	PLAYBOY	OP	RNBT	FBG	SV	IO	120-240		7	8				2900	3500
21	3	PLAYBOY	HT	RNBT	FBG	SV	OB			7	8	2100			4000	4650
21	3	PLAYBOY	HT	RNBT	FBG	SV	IO	120-240		7	8				2900	3500
22	10	ADVENTURER	ST	OFF	FBG	DV	OB			8		3300			6000	6900
22	10	ADVENTURER	ST	OFF	FBG	DV	IO	198-240		8					3500	4150
22	10	ADVENTURER	HT	OFF	FBG	DV	OB			8		3300			6000	6900
22	10	ADVENTURER	HT	OFF	FBG	DV	IO	198-240		8					3500	4150
23	7	BEACHCOMBER	OP	CR	FBG	SV	OB			7	8	2850			5600	6450

CONTINUED ON NEXT PAGE

LOA FT	LOA IN	NAME AND/ OR MODEL	TOP/ RIG	BOAT TYPE	HULL MTL	HULL TP	ENGINE TP	ENGINE # HP MFG	BEAM FT	BEAM IN	WGT LBS	DRAFT FT	DRAFT IN	RETAIL LOW	RETAIL HIGH
1978 BOATS															
23	7	BEACHCOMBER	OP	CR	FBG	SV	IO	120-240	7	8				4450	5250
23	7	BEACHCOMBER	HT	CR	FBG	SV	OB		7	8	3000			5850	6750
23	7	BEACHCOMBER	HT	CR	FBG	SV	IO	120-240	7	8				4450	5250
23	7	PLAYBOY	OP	RNBT	FBG	SV	OB		7	8	2200			4550	5250
23	7	PLAYBOY	OP	RNBT	FBG	SV	IO	120-240	7	8				4100	4900
23	7	PLAYBOY	HT	RNBT	FBG	SV	OB		7	8	2400			4900	5600
23	7	PLAYBOY	HT	RNBT	FBG	SV	IO	120-240	7	8				4100	4900
23	9	EXPLORER	OP	CUD	FBG	SV	OB		7	8	2600			5250	6050
23	9	EXPLORER	OP	CUD	FBG	SV	IO	120-240	7	8				4550	5350
23	9	EXPLORER	HT	CUD	FBG	SV	OB		7	8	2800			5600	6400
23	9	EXPLORER	HT	CUD	FBG	SV	IO	120-240	7	8				4550	5350
1977 BOATS															
17		GULFSTREAM	OP	RNBT	FBG	SV	OB		7	8	1525			2500	2950
17		GULFSTREAM	OP	RNBT	FBG	SV	IO	120-140	7	8				1750	2100
18		TS-18	SLP	SA/CR	FBG	SK			7	1		4	8	3000	3450
18	6	GULFSTREAM	OP	RNBT	FBG	SV	OB		7	8	1750			2850	3300
18	6	GULFSTREAM	OP	RNBT	FBG	SV	IO	120-190	7	8				2200	2600
18	6	GULFSTREAM	HT	RNBT	FBG	SV	OB		7	8	1750			2850	3300
18	6	GULFSTREAM	HT	RNBT	FBG	SV	IO	120-190	7	8				2200	2600
21	3	BEACHCOMBER	OP	CR	FBG	SV	OB		7	8	2550			4550	5250
21	3	BEACHCOMBER	OP	CR	FBG	SV	IO	120-233	7	8				3200	3850
21	3	BEACHCOMBER	OP	CR	FBG	SV	IO	T120-T140	7	8				3700	4300
21	3	BEACHCOMBER	HT	CR	FBG	SV	OB		7	8	2700			4700	5400
21	3	BEACHCOMBER	HT	CR	FBG	SV	IO	120-233	7	8				3200	3850
21	3	BEACHCOMBER	HT	CR	FBG	SV	IO	T120-T140	7	8				3700	4300
21	3	EXPLORER	OP	CUD	FBG	SV	OB		7	8	2300			4200	4900
21	3	EXPLORER	OP	CUD	FBG	SV	IO	120-233	7	8				3250	3900
21	3	EXPLORER	OP	CUD	FBG	SV	IO	T120-T140	7	8				3750	4350
21	3	EXPLORER	HT	CUD	FBG	SV	OB		7	8	2500			4500	5150
21	3	EXPLORER	HT	CUD	FBG	SV	IO	120-233	7	8				3250	3900
21	3	EXPLORER	HT	CUD	FBG	SV	IO	T120-T140	7	8				3750	4350
21	3	EXPLORER	FB	CUD	FBG	SV	OB		7	8	2625			4650	5350
21	3	EXPLORER	FB	CUD	FBG	SV	IO	120-233	7	8				3250	3900
21	3	EXPLORER	FB	CUD	FBG	SV	IO	T120-T140	7	8				3750	4350
21	3	GULFSTREAM	OP	RNBT	FBG	SV	OB		7	8	1875			3600	4200
21	3	GULFSTREAM	OP	RNBT	FBG	SV	IO	120-233	7	8				2900	3500
21	3	GULFSTREAM	OP	RNBT	FBG	SV	IO	T120-T140	7	8				3400	3950
21	3	GULFSTREAM	HT	RNBT	FBG	SV	OB		7	8	1875			3600	4200
21	3	GULFSTREAM	HT	RNBT	FBG	SV	IO	120-233	7	8				2900	3500
21	3	GULFSTREAM	HT	RNBT	FBG	SV	IO	T120-T140	7	8				3400	3950
21	3	PLAYBOY	OP	RNBT	FBG	SV	OB		7	8	1900			3650	4250
21	3	PLAYBOY	OP	RNBT	FBG	SV	IO	120-233	7	8				3000	3600
21	3	PLAYBOY	OP	RNBT	FBG	SV	IO	T120-T140	7	8				3450	4000
21	3	PLAYBOY	HT	RNBT	FBG	SV	OB		7	8	2100			3950	4600
21	3	PLAYBOY	HT	RNBT	FBG	SV	IO	120-233	7	8				3000	3600
21	3	PLAYBOY	HT	RNBT	FBG	SV	IO	T120-T140	7	8				3450	4000
21	3	PLAYBOY	FB	RNBT	FBG	SV	OB		7	8	2225			4100	4800
21	3	PLAYBOY	FB	RNBT	FBG	SV	IO	120-233	7	8				2950	3550
21	3	PLAYBOY	FB	RNBT	FBG	SV	IO	T120-T140	7	8				3450	4000
22	10	ADVENTURER	ST	OFF	FBG	DV	OB		8		3300			5950	6850
22	10	ADVENTURER	ST	OFF	FBG	DV	IO	188-233	8					3550	4200
22	10	ADVENTURER	ST	OFF	FBG	DV	IO	T120-T140	8					4050	4700
23	7	BEACHCOMBER	OP	CR	FBG	SV	OB		7	8	2850			5550	6400
23	7	BEACHCOMBER	OP	CR	FBG	SV	IO	120-233	7	8				4550	5350
23	7	BEACHCOMBER	OP	CR	FBG	SV	IO	T120-T140	7	8				5000	5800
23	7	BEACHCOMBER	HT	CR	FBG	SV	OB		7	8	3000			5800	6650
23	7	BEACHCOMBER	HT	CR	FBG	SV	IO	120-233	7	8				4550	5350
23	7	BEACHCOMBER	HT	CR	FBG	SV	IO	T120-T140	7	8				5000	5800
23	7	PLAYBOY	OP	RNBT	FBG	SV	OB		7	8	2200			4500	5200
23	7	PLAYBOY	OP	RNBT	FBG	SV	IO	120-233	7	8				4150	4950
23	7	PLAYBOY	OP	RNBT	FBG	SV	IO	T120-T140	7	8				4650	5400
23	7	PLAYBOY	HT	RNBT	FBG	SV	OB		7	8	2400			4850	5550
23	7	PLAYBOY	HT	RNBT	FBG	SV	IO	120-233	7	8				4150	4950
23	7	PLAYBOY	HT	RNBT	FBG	SV	IO	T120-T140	7	8				4650	5400
23	7	PLAYBOY	FB	RNBT	FBG	SV	OB		7	8	2525			5050	5800
23	7	PLAYBOY	FB	RNBT	FBG	SV	IO	120-233	7	8				4150	4950
23	7	PLAYBOY	FB	RNBT	FBG	SV	IO	T120-T140	7	8				4650	5400
23	9	EXPLORER	OP	CUD	FBG	SV	OB		7	8	2600			5200	6000
23	9	EXPLORER	OP	CUD	FBG	SV	IO	120-233	7	8				4600	5400
23	9	EXPLORER	OP	CUD	FBG	SV	IO	T120-T140	7	8				5100	5850
23	9	EXPLORER	HT	CUD	FBG	SV	OB		7	8	2800			5550	6350
23	9	EXPLORER	HT	CUD	FBG	SV	IO	120-233	7	8				4600	5400
23	9	EXPLORER	HT	CUD	FBG	SV	IO	T120-T140	7	8				5100	5850
23	9	EXPLORER	FB	CUD	FBG	SV	OB		7	8	2925			5700	6600
23	9	EXPLORER	FB	CUD	FBG	SV	IO	120-233	7	8				4600	5400
23	9	EXPLORER	FB	CUD	FBG	SV	IO	T120-T140	7	8				5100	5850
1976 BOATS															
17		GULFSTREAM	ST	RNBT	FBG	SV	OB		7	8		2		2500	2900
17		GULFSTREAM	ST	RNBT	FBG	SV	IO	140	7	8		2		1800	2150
18	6	GULFSTREAM	ST	RNBT	FBG	SV	OB		7	8		2		2850	3300
18	6	GULFSTREAM	ST	RNBT	FBG	SV	IO	120-190	7	8		2		2250	2650
18	6	GULFSTREAM	HT	RNBT	FBG	SV	OB		7	8		2		2850	3300
18	6	GULFSTREAM	HT	RNBT	FBG	SV	IO	120-190	7	8		2		2250	2650
21	3	BEACHCOMBER	ST	CR	FBG	SV	OB		7	8		2		4550	5250
21	3	BEACHCOMBER	HT	CR	FBG	SV	OB		7	8		2		4550	5250
21	3	EXPLORER	ST	CUD	FBG	SV	OB		7	8		2		4450	5100
21	3	EXPLORER	ST	CUD	FBG	SV	IO	120-233	7	8		2		3300	4000
21	3	EXPLORER	ST	CUD	FBG	SV	IO	T120-T140	7	8		2		3850	4450
21	3	EXPLORER	HT	CUD	FBG	SV	OB		7	8		2		4450	5100
21	3	EXPLORER	HT	CUD	FBG	SV	IO	120-233	7	8		2		3300	4000
21	3	EXPLORER	HT	CUD	FBG	SV	IO	T120-T140	7	8		2		3850	4450
21	3	EXPLORER	FB	CUD	FBG	SV	IO	120-233	7	8		2		3300	4000
21	3	EXPLORER	FB	CUD	FBG	SV	IO	T120-T140	7	8		2		3850	4450
21	3	EXPLORER	FB	SF	FBG	SV	OB		7	8		2		4550	5250
21	3	GULFSTREAM	ST	RNBT	FBG	SV	OB		7	8		2		3700	4300
21	3	GULFSTREAM	ST	RNBT	FBG	SV	IO	120-233	7	8		2		3000	3600
21	3	GULFSTREAM	ST	RNBT	FBG	SV	IO	T120-T140	7	8		2		3500	4050
21	3	GULFSTREAM	HT	RNBT	FBG	SV	OB		7	8		2		3700	4300
21	3	GULFSTREAM	HT	RNBT	FBG	SV	IO	120-233	7	8		2		3000	3600
21	3	GULFSTREAM	HT	RNBT	FBG	SV	IO	T120-T140	7	8		2		3500	4050
21	3	PLAYBOY	ST	RNBT	FBG	SV	OB		7	8		2		3700	4300
21	3	PLAYBOY	ST	RNBT	FBG	SV	IO	120-233	7	8		2		3050	3650
21	3	PLAYBOY	ST	RNBT	FBG	SV	IO	T120-T140	7	8		2		3550	4150
21	3	PLAYBOY	HT	RNBT	FBG	SV	OB		7	8		2		3700	4300
21	3	PLAYBOY	HT	RNBT	FBG	SV	IO	120-233	7	8		2		3050	3650
21	3	PLAYBOY	HT	RNBT	FBG	SV	IO	T120-T140	7	8		2		3550	4150
21	3	PLAYBOY	FB	SF	FBG	SV	OB		7	8		2		3700	4300
21	3	PLAYBOY	FB	SF	FBG	SV	IO	120-233	7	8		2		3450	4150
21	3	PLAYBOY	FB	SF	FBG	SV	IO	T120-T140	7	8		2		4000	4700
23	1	ADVENTURER	ST	OFF	FBG	DV	OB		8			3		6000	6900
23	1	ADVENTURER	ST	OFF	FBG	DV	IO	188-233	8			3		3700	4400
23	1	ADVENTURER	ST	OFF	FBG	DV	IO	T120-T140	8			3		4200	4900
23	9	BEACHCOMBER	ST	CR	FBG	SV	OB		7	8		2		5700	6500
23	9	BEACHCOMBER	ST	CR	FBG	SV	IO	120-233	7	8		2		4650	5500
23	9	BEACHCOMBER	ST	CR	FBG	SV	IO	T120-T140	7	8		2		5200	6000
23	9	BEACHCOMBER	HT	CR	FBG	SV	OB		7	8		2		5700	6500
23	9	BEACHCOMBER	HT	CR	FBG	SV	IO	120-233	7	8		2		4650	5500
23	9	BEACHCOMBER	HT	CR	FBG	SV	IO	T120-T140	7	8		2		5200	6000
23	9	EXPLORER	ST	CUD	FBG	SV	OB		7	8		2		5400	6250
23	9	EXPLORER	ST	CUD	FBG	SV	IO	120-233	7	8		2		4700	5550
23	9	EXPLORER	ST	CUD	FBG	SV	IO	T120-T140	7	8		2		5250	6000
23	9	EXPLORER	HT	CUD	FBG	SV	OB		7	8		2		5400	6250
23	9	EXPLORER	HT	CUD	FBG	SV	IO	120-233	7	8		2		4700	5550
23	9	EXPLORER	HT	CUD	FBG	SV	IO	T120-T140	7	8		2		5250	6000
23	9	EXPLORER	FB	SF	FBG	SV	OB		7	8		2		5500	6300
23	9	EXPLORER	FB	SF	FBG	SV	IO	120-233	7	8		2		5400	6350
23	9	EXPLORER	FB	SF	FBG	SV	IO	T120-T140	7	8		2		6000	6900
23	9	PLAYBOY	ST	RNBT	FBG	SV	OB		7	8		2		4750	5450
23	9	PLAYBOY	ST	RNBT	FBG	SV	IO	120-233	7	8		2		4350	5150
23	9	PLAYBOY	ST	RNBT	FBG	SV	IO	T120-T140	7	8		2		4850	5550
23	9	PLAYBOY	HT	RNBT	FBG	SV	OB		7	8		2		4750	5450
23	9	PLAYBOY	HT	RNBT	FBG	SV	IO	120-233	7	8		2		4350	5150
23	9	PLAYBOY	HT	RNBT	FBG	SV	IO	T120-T140	7	8		2		4850	5550
23	9	PLAYBOY	FB	SF	FBG	SV	OB		7	8		2		4950	5650
1975 BOATS															
19		GULFSTREAM SHORT DK	ST	RNBT	FBG	SV	OB		7	8				2850	3350
19		GULFSTREAM SHORT DK	ST	RNBT	FBG	SV	IO	120-225	7	8				2350	2800
19		GULFSTREAM SHORT DK	ST	RNBT	FBG	SV	IO	T120-T140	7	8				2850	3300
19		GULFSTREAM SHORT DK	HT	RNBT	FBG	SV	OB		7	8				2850	3350
19		GULFSTREAM SHORT DK	HT	RNBT	FBG	SV	IO	120-225	7	8				2350	2800
19		GULFSTREAM SHORT DK	HT	RNBT	FBG	SV	IO	T120-T140	7	8				2850	3300
21	3	BEACHCOMBER	ST	CR	FBG	SV	OB		7	8				4550	5200
21	3	BEACHCOMBER	ST	CR	FBG	SV	IO	120-225	7	8				3400	4000
21	3	BEACHCOMBER	ST	CR	FBG	SV	IO	T120-T140	7	8				3950	4600
21	3	BEACHCOMBER	HT	CR	FBG	SV	OB		7	8				4550	5200
21	3	BEACHCOMBER	HT	CR	FBG	SV	IO	120-225	7	8				3400	4000
21	3	BEACHCOMBER	HT	CR	FBG	SV	IO	T120-T140	7	8				3950	4600

CONTINUED ON NEXT PAGE

T-CRAFT BOAT CO INC —CONTINUED   See inside cover to adjust price for area

LOA FT IN	NAME AND/OR MODEL	TOP/RIG	BOAT TYPE	HULL MTL	HULL TP	ENG TP	# HP	MFG	BEAM FT IN	DRAFT FT IN	RETAIL LOW	RETAIL HIGH
1975 BOATS												
21 3	EXPLORER	ST	CUD	FBG	SV	OB			7 8		4400	5050
21 3	EXPLORER	ST	CUD	FBG	SV	IO	120-225		7 8		3400	4050
21 3	EXPLORER	ST	CUD	FBG	SV	IO	465	MRCR	7 8		6250	7150
21 3	EXPLORER	ST	CUD	FBG	SV	IO	T120-T140		7 8		3950	4600
21 3	EXPLORER	HT	CUD	FBG	SV	OB			7 8		4400	5050
21 3	EXPLORER	HT	CUD	FBG	SV	IO	120-225		7 8		3400	4050
21 3	EXPLORER	HT	CUD	FBG	SV	IO	T120-T140		7 8		3950	4600
21 3	EXPLORER	FB	CUD	FBG	SV	OB			7 8		4400	5050
21 3	EXPLORER	FB	CUD	FBG	SV	IO	120-225		7 8		3400	4050
21 3	EXPLORER	FB	CUD	FBG	SV	IO	T120-T140		7 8		3950	4600
21 3	GULFSTREAM SHORT DK	HT	RNBT	FBG	SV	IO	120-225		7 8		3150	3700
21 3	GULFSTREAM SHORT DK	HT	RNBT	FBG	SV	IO	T120-T140		7 8		3650	4250
21 3	GULFSTREAM SHORT DK	FB	RNBT	FBG	SV	OB			7 8		3700	4300
21 3	GULFSTREAM SHORT DK	FB	RNBT	FBG	SV	IO	120-225		7 8		3150	3700
21 3	GULFSTREAM SHORT DK	FB	RNBT	FBG	SV	IO	T120-T140		7 8		3650	4250
21 3	PLAYBOY LONG DECK	ST	RNBT	FBG	SV	OB			7 8		3700	4300
21 3	PLAYBOY LONG DECK	ST	RNBT	FBG	SV	IO	120-225		7 8		3150	3700
21 3	PLAYBOY LONG DECK	ST	RNBT	FBG	SV	IO	T120-T140		7 8		3650	4250
21 3	PLAYBOY LONG DECK	HT	RNBT	FBG	SV	OB			7 8		3700	4300
21 3	PLAYBOY LONG DECK	HT	RNBT	FBG	SV	IO	120-225		7 8		3150	3700
21 3	PLAYBOY LONG DECK	HT	RNBT	FBG	SV	IO	T120-T140		7 8		3650	4250
23	ADVENTURER V			FBG	SV	IO	165-225		7 8		3750	4450
23	ADVENTURER V			FBG	SV	IO	T120-T140		7 8		4250	5000
23 9	BEACHCOMBER	ST	CR	FBG	SV	OB			7 8		5650	6500
23 9	BEACHCOMBER	ST	CR	FBG	SV	IO	120-225		7 8		4850	5650
23 9	BEACHCOMBER	ST	CR	FBG	SV	IO	T120-T140		7 8		5350	6200
23 9	BEACHCOMBER	HT	CR	FBG	SV	OB			7 8		5650	6500
23 9	BEACHCOMBER	HT	CR	FBG	SV	IO	120-225		7 8		4850	5650
23 9	BEACHCOMBER	HT	CR	FBG	SV	IO	T120-T140		7 8		5350	6200
23 9	EXPLORER	ST	CUD	FBG	SV	OB			7 8		5400	6200
23 9	EXPLORER	ST	CUD	FBG	SV	IO	120-225		7 8		4850	5650
23 9	EXPLORER	ST	CUD	FBG	SV	IO	T120-T140		7 8		5400	6200
23 9	EXPLORER	HT	CUD	FBG	SV	OB			7 8		5400	6200
23 9	EXPLORER	HT	CUD	FBG	SV	IO	120-225		7 8		4850	5650
23 9	EXPLORER	HT	CUD	FBG	SV	IO	T120-T140		7 8		5400	6200
23 9	EXPLORER	FB	CUD	FBG	SV	OB			7 8		5400	6200
23 9	EXPLORER	FB	CUD	FBG	SV	IO	120-225		7 8		4850	5650
23 9	EXPLORER	FB	CUD	FBG	SV	IO	T120-T140		7 8		5400	6200
23 9	GULFSTREAM SHORT DK	ST	RNBT	FBG	SV	OB			7 8		4750	5450
23 9	GULFSTREAM SHORT DK	ST	RNBT	FBG	SV	IO	120-225		7 8		4500	5250
23 9	GULFSTREAM SHORT DK	ST	RNBT	FBG	SV	IO	T120-T140		7 8		5000	5750
23 9	GULFSTREAM SHORT DK	HT	RNBT	FBG	SV	OB			7 8		4750	5450
23 9	GULFSTREAM SHORT DK	HT	RNBT	FBG	SV	IO	120-225		7 8		4500	5250
23 9	GULFSTREAM SHORT DK	HT	RNBT	FBG	SV	IO	T120-T140		7 8		5000	5750
23 9	GULFSTREAM SHORT DK	FB	RNBT	FBG	SV	OB			7 8		4750	5450
23 9	GULFSTREAM SHORT DK	FB	RNBT	FBG	SV	IO	120-225		7 8		4500	5300
23 9	GULFSTREAM SHORT DK	FB	RNBT	FBG	SV	IO	T120-T140		7 8		5000	5750
23 9	PLAYBOY LONG DECK	ST	RNBT	FBG	SV	OB			7 8		4750	5450
23 9	PLAYBOY LONG DECK	ST	RNBT	FBG	SV	IO	120-225		7 8		4500	5250
23 9	PLAYBOY LONG DECK	ST	RNBT	FBG	SV	IO	T120-T140		7 8		5000	5750
23 9	PLAYBOY LONG DECK	HT	RNBT	FBG	SV	OB			7 8		4750	5450
23 9	PLAYBOY LONG DECK	HT	RNBT	FBG	SV	IO	120-225		7 8		4500	5250
23 9	PLAYBOY LONG DECK	FB	RNBT	FBG	SV	IO	T120-T140		7 8		5000	5750
23 9	PLAYBOY LONG DECK	FB	RNBT	FBG	SV	OB			7 8		4750	5450
23 9	PLAYBOY LONG DECK	FB	RNBT	FBG	SV	IO	120-225		7 8		4450	5250
23 9	PLAYBOY LONG DECK	FB	RNBT	FBG	SV	IO	T120-T140		7 8		5000	5750
1974 BOATS												
18 6	GULFSTREAM			FBG		OB			7 8		2800	3250
18 6	GULFSTREAM			FBG		IO	120-225		7 8		2200	2650
18 6	GULFSTREAM			FBG		IO	T120-T140		7 8		2700	3150
18 6	GULFSTREAM	HT		FBG		OB			7 8		2800	3250
18 6	GULFSTREAM	HT		FBG		IO	120-225		7 8		2200	2650
18 6	GULFSTREAM	HT		FBG		IO	T120-T140		7 8		2700	3150
21 3	BEACHCOMBER	HT		FBG		OB			7 8		5250	6000
21 3	BEACHCOMBER	HT		FBG		IO	120-225		7 8		3700	4300
21 3	BEACHCOMBER	HT		FBG		IO	T120-T140		7 8		4150	4850
21 3	BEACHCOMBER		CBNCR	FBG		OB			7 8		4550	5200
21 3	BEACHCOMBER		CBNCR	FBG		IO	120-225		7 8		3750	4450
21 3	BEACHCOMBER		CBNCR	FBG		IO	T120-T140		7 8		4400	5050
21 3	EXPLORER	FB		FBG		OB			7 8		4450	5100
21 3	EXPLORER	FB		FBG		IO	120-225		7 8		3350	3950
21 3	EXPLORER	FB		FBG		IO	T120-T140		7 8		3850	4500
21 3	EXPLORER		CUD	FBG		OB			7 8		4350	5050
21 3	EXPLORER		CUD	FBG		IO	120-225		7 8		3550	4200
21 3	EXPLORER		CUD	FBG		IO	T120-T140		7 8		4100	4800
21 3	GULFSTREAM			FBG		OB			7 8		4050	4700
21 3	GULFSTREAM			FBG		IO	120-225		7 8		3200	3750
21 3	GULFSTREAM			FBG		IO	T120-T140		7 8		3700	4300
21 3	GULFSTREAM	HT		FBG		OB			7 8		3450	4050
21 3	GULFSTREAM	HT		FBG		IO	120-225		7 8		2900	3500
21 3	GULFSTREAM	HT		FBG		IO	T120-T140		7 8		3500	4100
21 3	GULFSTREAM	FB		FBG		OB			7 8		3700	4300
21 3	GULFSTREAM	FB		FBG		IO	120-225		7 8		3000	3600
21 3	GULFSTREAM	FB		FBG		IO	T120-T140		7 8		3550	4150
21 3	PLAYBOY			FBG		OB			7 8		4050	4700
21 3	PLAYBOY			FBG		IO	120-225		7 8		3200	3750
21 3	PLAYBOY			FBG		IO	T120-T140		7 8		3700	4300
21 3	PLAYBOY	HT		FBG		OB			7 8		3450	4050
21 3	PLAYBOY	HT		FBG		IO	120-225		7 8		2900	3500
21 3	PLAYBOY	HT		FBG		IO	T120-T140		7 8		3500	4100
23 1	ADVENTURER			FBG		IO	165-225		8		3950	4700
23 1	ADVENTURER			FBG		IO	T120-T140		8		4550	5250
23 9	BEACHCOMBER	HT		FBG		OB			7 8		6400	7350
23 9	BEACHCOMBER	HT		FBG		OB			7 8		5450	6250
23 9	BEACHCOMBER	HT		FBG		IO	120-225		7 8		5850	6750
23 9	BEACHCOMBER		CBNCR	FBG		OB			7 8		5600	6450
23 9	BEACHCOMBER		CBNCR	FBG		IO	120-225		7 8		5300	6200
23 9	BEACHCOMBER		CBNCR	FBG		IO	T120-T140		7 8		5950	6850
23 9	EXPLORER	FB		FBG		OB			7 8		5650	6500
23 9	EXPLORER	FB		FBG		IO	120-225		7 8		5050	5850
23 9	EXPLORER		CUD	FBG		OB			7 8		5350	6150
23 9	EXPLORER		CUD	FBG		IO	120-225		7 8		5050	5850
23 9	EXPLORER		CUD	FBG		IO	T120-T140		7 8		5600	5850
23 9	GULFSTREAM			FBG		OB			7 8		5150	5900
23 9	GULFSTREAM			FBG		OB			7 8		4700	5500
23 9	GULFSTREAM			FBG		IO	T120-T140		7 8		5250	6050
23 9	GULFSTREAM	HT		FBG		OB			7 8		4450	5250
23 9	GULFSTREAM	HT		FBG		IO	120-225		7 8		4350	5150
23 9	GULFSTREAM	HT		FBG		IO	T120-T140		7 8		4950	5600
23 9	GULFSTREAM	FB		FBG		OB			7 8		4900	5600
23 9	GULFSTREAM	FB		FBG		IO	120-225		7 8		4550	5600
23 9	GULFSTREAM	FB		FBG		IO	T120-T140		7 8		5100	5900
23 9	PLAYBOY			FBG		OB			7 8	2	5150	5900
23 9	PLAYBOY			FBG		IO	120-225		7 8	2	4700	5900
23 9	PLAYBOY	HT		FBG		IO	T120-T140		7 8	2	5250	6050
23 9	PLAYBOY	HT		FBG		IO	120-225		7 8	2	4550	5250
23 9	PLAYBOY	HT		FBG		OB			7 8	2	4350	5100
23 9	PLAYBOY	HT		FBG		IO	T120-T140		7 8	2	4950	5700
23 9	PLAYBOY	FB		FBG		OB			7 8	2	4900	5600
23 9	PLAYBOY	FB		FBG		IO	120-225		7 8	2	4550	5350
23 9	PLAYBOY	FB		FBG		IO	T120-T140		7 8	2	5100	5900
1973 BOATS												
18 6	GULFSTREAM			FBG		OB			7 8		2800	3250
18 6	GULFSTREAM			FBG		IO	120-225		7 8		2300	2700
18 6	GULFSTREAM			FBG		IO	T120-T140		7 8		2800	3250
21 3	BEACHCOMBER	HT		FBG		OB			7 8		5350	6150
21 3	BEACHCOMBER	HT		FBG		IO	120-225		7 8		3900	4500
21 3	BEACHCOMBER	HT		FBG		IO	T120-T140		7 8		4400	5050
21 3	BEACHCOMBER		CBNCR	FBG		OB			7 8		4550	5200
21 3	BEACHCOMBER		CBNCR	FBG		IO	120-225		7 8		3850	4600
21 3	BEACHCOMBER		CBNCR	FBG		IO	T120-T140		7 8		4550	5350
21 3	EXPLORER			FBG		OB			7 8		4650	5350
21 3	EXPLORER			FBG		IO	120-225		7 8		3500	4100
21 3	EXPLORER			FBG		IO	T120-T140		7 8		4000	4700
21 3	EXPLORER	HT		FBG		OB			7 8		4150	4850
21 3	EXPLORER	HT		FBG		IO	120-225		7 8		3350	3900
21 3	EXPLORER	HT		FBG		IO	T120-T140		7 8		3900	4500
21 3	EXPLORER	FB		FBG		OB			7 8		4450	5100
21 3	EXPLORER	FB		FBG		IO	120-225		7 8		3450	4100
21 3	EXPLORER	FB		FBG		IO	T120-T140		7 8		4000	4650
21 3	GULFSTREAM			FBG		OB			7 8		3750	4350
21 3	GULFSTREAM			FBG		IO	120-225		7 8		3150	3800
21 3	GULFSTREAM			FBG		IO	T120-T140		7 8		3750	4350
21 3	GULFSTREAM	HT		FBG		IO	T120-T140		7 8		3300	3850

```
LOA   NAME AND/       TOP/ BOAT -HULL- ----ENGINE--- BEAM  WGT  DRAFT RETAIL RETAIL
FT IN OR MODEL        RIG  TYPE MTL TP  TP # HP  MFG  FT IN LBS  FT IN  LOW   HIGH
-------------------- 1973 BOATS --------------------------------------------------
21 3 GULFSTREAM       HT        FBG     IO 120-225    7 8         2950   3600
21 3 GULFSTREAM       HT        FBG     IO T120-T140  7 8         3550   4150
21 3 GULFSTREAM       FB        FBG     OB            7 8         3700   4300
21 3 GULFSTREAM       FB        FBG     IO 120-225    7 8         3100   3700
21 3 GULFSTREAM       FB        FBG     IO T120-T140  7 8         3650   4300
21 3 PLAYBOY                    FBG     OB            7 8         3750   4400
21 3 PLAYBOY                    FBG     IO 120-225    7 8         3150   3800
21 3 PLAYBOY                    FBG     IO T120-T140  7 8         3750   4350
21 3 PLAYBOY          HT        FBG     OB            7 8         3300   3850
21 3 PLAYBOY          HT        FBG     IO 120-225    7 8         2950   3600
21 3 PLAYBOY          HT        FBG     IO T120-T140  7 8         3550   4150
23 9 BEACHCOMBER      HT        FBG     OB            7 8         6500   7500

23 9 BEACHCOMBER      HT        FBG     IO 120-225    7 8         5700   6900
23 9 BEACHCOMBER      HT        FBG     IO T120-T140  7 8         6100   7000
23 9 BEACHCOMBER      CBNCR     FBG     OB            7 8         5600   6400
23 9 BEACHCOMBER      CBNCR     FBG     IO 120-225    7 8         5500   6400
23 9 BEACHCOMBER      CBNCR     FBG     IO T120-T140  7 8         6150   7100
23 9 EXPLORER                   FBG     OB            7 8         5650   6500
23 9 EXPLORER                   FBG     IO 120-225    7 8         5150   6000
23 9 EXPLORER                   FBG     IO T120-T140  7 8         5650   6500
23 9 EXPLORER         HT        FBG     OB            7 8         5250   6050
23 9 EXPLORER         HT        FBG     IO 120-225    7 8         4950   5750
23 9 EXPLORER         HT        FBG     IO T120-T140  7 8         5500   6300
23 9 EXPLORER         FB        FBG     OB            7 8         5500   6350

23 9 EXPLORER         FB        FBG     IO 120-188    7 8         4850   5900
23 9 EXPLORER         FB        FBG     IO 225  OMC   7 8         5350   6150
23 9 EXPLORER         FB        FBG     IO T120-T140  7 8         5400   6250
23 9 GULFSTREAM                 FBG     OB            7 8         4850   5600
23 9 GULFSTREAM                 FBG     IO 120-225    7 8         4700   5550
23 9 GULFSTREAM                 FBG     IO T120-T140  7 8         5300   6100
23 9 GULFSTREAM       HT        FBG     OB            7 8         4400   5050
23 9 GULFSTREAM       HT        FBG     IO 120-225    7 8         4450   5300
23 9 GULFSTREAM       HT        FBG     IO T120-T140  7 8         5050   5800
23 9 PLAYBOY                    FBG     OB            7 8     2   4850   5600
23 9 PLAYBOY                    FBG     IO 120-225    7 8     2   4700   5550
23 9 PLAYBOY                    FBG     IO T120-T140  7 8     2   5300   6100

23 9 PLAYBOY          HT        FBG     OB            7 8     2   4400   5050
23 9 PLAYBOY          HT        FBG     IO 120-225    7 8     2   4450   5200
23 9 PLAYBOY          HT        FBG     IO T120-T140  7 8     2   5050   5800
23 9 PLAYBOY          FB        FBG     OB            7 8     2   4750   5450
23 9 PLAYBOY          FB        FBG     IO 140-225    7 8     2   4650   5400
-------------------- 1972 BOATS --------------------------------------------------
18 6 GULFSTREAM                 FBG     OB            7 8         2750   3200
18 6 GULFSTREAM                 FBG     IO 120-215    7 8         2350   2800
18 6 GULFSTREAM                 FBG     IO T120-T140  7 8         2900   3350
18 6 GULFSTREAM       HT        FBG     OB            7 8         2750   3200
18 6 GULFSTREAM       HT        FBG     IO 120-215    7 8         2350   2800
18 6 GULFSTREAM       HT        FBG     IO T120-T140  7 8         2900   3350
21 3 BEACHCOMBER      HT        FBG     OB            7 8         5350   6150
21 3 BEACHCOMBER      HT        FBG     IO 120-215    7 8         4000   4700
21 3 BEACHCOMBER      HT        FBG     IO T120-T140  7 8         4550   5200
21 3 BEACHCOMBER      CBNCR     FBG     OB            7 8         4500   5200
21 3 BEACHCOMBER      CBNCR     FBG     IO 120-215    7 8         4000   4750
21 3 BEACHCOMBER      CBNCR     FBG     IO T120-T140  7 8         4650   5400

21 3 EXPLORER                   FBG     OB            7 8         4600   5300
21 3 EXPLORER                   FBG     IO 120-215    7 8         3650   4300
21 3 EXPLORER                   FBG     IO T120-T140  7 8         4150   4850
21 3 EXPLORER         HT        FBG     OB            7 8         4150   4850
21 3 EXPLORER         HT        FBG     IO 120-215    7 8         3450   4150
21 3 EXPLORER         HT        FBG     IO T120-T140  7 8         4050   4700
21 3 EXPLORER         FB        FBG     OB            7 8         4450   5100
21 3 EXPLORER         FB        FBG     IO 120-215    7 8         3600   4250
21 3 EXPLORER         FB        FBG     IO T120-T140  7 8         4150   4800
21 3 GULFSTREAM                 FBG     OB            7 8         3750   4350
21 3 GULFSTREAM                 FBG     IO 120-215    7 8         3250   3950
21 3 GULFSTREAM                 FBG     IO T120-T140  7 8         3850   4500

21 3 GULFSTREAM       HT        FBG     OB            7 8         3300   3850
21 3 GULFSTREAM       HT        FBG     IO 120-215    7 8         3050   3700
21 3 GULFSTREAM       HT        FBG     IO T120-T140  7 8         3650   4300
21 3 GULFSTREAM       FB        FBG     OB            7 8         3700   4300
21 3 GULFSTREAM       FB        FBG     IO 120-215    7 8         3200   3850
21 3 GULFSTREAM       FB        FBG     IO T120-T140  7 8         3800   4450
21 3 PLAYBOY                    FBG     OB            7 8         3750   4350
21 3 PLAYBOY                    FBG     IO 120-215    7 8         3250   3950
21 3 PLAYBOY                    FBG     IO T120-T140  7 8         3850   4500
21 3 PLAYBOY          HT        FBG     OB            7 8         3300   3850
21 3 PLAYBOY          HT        FBG     IO 120-215    7 8         3050   3700
21 3 PLAYBOY          HT        FBG     IO T120-T140  7 8         3650   4300

23   WORKBOAT         CUD       FBG     IB D          9 2         **     **
23   WORKBOAT         OPFSH     FBG     IB D          9 2         **     **
23 9 BEACHCOMBER      HT        FBG     OB            7 8         6200   7100
23 9 BEACHCOMBER      HT        FBG     IO 120-215    7 8         5700   6650
23 9 BEACHCOMBER      HT        FBG     IO T120-T140  7 8         6150   7100
23 9 BEACHCOMBER      CBNCR     FBG     OB            7 8         5550   6400
23 9 BEACHCOMBER      CBNCR     FBG     IO 120-215    7 8         5700   6650
23 9 BEACHCOMBER      CBNCR     FBG     IO T120-T140  7 8         6350   7300
23 9 EXPLORER                   FBG     OB            7 8         5500   6350
23 9 EXPLORER                   FBG     IO 120-215    7 8         5250   6150
23 9 EXPLORER                   FBG     IO T120-T140  7 8         5800   6650
23 9 EXPLORER         HT        FBG     OB            7 8         5000   5750

23 9 EXPLORER         HT        FBG     IO 120-215    7 8         4950   5850
23 9 EXPLORER         HT        FBG     IO T120-T140  7 8         5550   6400
23 9 EXPLORER         FB        FBG     OB            7 8         5100   5900
23 9 EXPLORER         FB        FBG     IO 120-215    7 8         5050   5850
23 9 EXPLORER         FB        FBG     IO T120-T140  7 8         5600   6450
23 9 GULFSTREAM                 FBG     OB            7 8         4700   5450
23 9 GULFSTREAM                 FBG     IO T120-T140  7 8         4800   5700
23 9 GULFSTREAM                 FBG     IO 120-215    7 8         5400   6250
23 9 GULFSTREAM       HT        FBG     OB            7 8         4150   4800
23 9 GULFSTREAM       HT        FBG     IO 120-215    7 8         4450   5300
23 9 GULFSTREAM       HT        FBG     IO T120-T140  7 8         5100   5900
36   COMMERCIAL BOAT  COMM      FBG     IB D         13           **     **
44   COMMERCIAL BOAT  COMM      FBG     IB D         15           **     **
-------------------- 1971 BOATS --------------------------------------------------
18 6 GULFSTREAM                 FBG     OB            7 8         2750   3200
18 6 GULFSTREAM                 FBG     IO 120-215    7 8         2400   2900
18 6 GULFSTREAM                 FBG     IO T120-T140  7 8         2950   3450
18 6 GULFSTREAM       HT        FBG     OB            7 8         2750   3200
18 6 GULFSTREAM       HT        FBG     IO 120-215    7 8         2400   2900
18 6 GULFSTREAM       HT        FBG     IO T120-T140  7 8         2950   3450
21 3 BEACHCOMBER      HT        FBG     OB            7 8         5350   6150
21 3 BEACHCOMBER      HT        FBG     IO 120-215    7 8         4150   4850
21 3 BEACHCOMBER      HT        FBG     IO T120-T140  7 8         4700   5400
21 3 BEACHCOMBER      CBNCR     FBG     OB            7 8         4500   5200
21 3 BEACHCOMBER      CBNCR     FBG     IO 120-215    7 8         4100   4900
21 3 BEACHCOMBER      CBNCR     FBG     IO T120-T140  7 8         4800   5550

21 3 EXPLORER                   FBG     OB            7 8         4600   5300
21 3 EXPLORER                   FBG     IO 120-165    7 8         3750   4350
21 3 EXPLORER         HT        FBG     OB            7 8         4150   4850
21 3 EXPLORER         HT        FBG     IO 120-215    7 8         3600   4300
21 3 EXPLORER         HT        FBG     IO T120-T140  7 8         4150   4850
21 3 EXPLORER         FB        FBG     OB            7 8         4450   5100
21 3 EXPLORER         FB        FBG     IO 120-215    7 8         4250   4950
21 3 EXPLORER         FB        FBG     IO T120-T140  7 8         3750   4350
21 3 GULFSTREAM                 FBG     OB            7 8         3400   4200
21 3 GULFSTREAM                 FBG     IO 120-215    7 8         4100   4750
21 3 GULFSTREAM       HT        FBG     OB            7 8         3300   3850

21 3 GULFSTREAM       HT        FBG     OB            7 8         3150   3850
21 3 GULFSTREAM       HT        FBG     IO 120-215    7 8         3800   4450
21 3 GULFSTREAM       HT        FBG     IO T120-T140  7 8         3300   4300
21 3 GULFSTREAM       FB        FBG     OB            7 8         3900   4600
21 3 GULFSTREAM       FB        FBG     IO 120-215    7 8         3750   4350
21 3 GULFSTREAM       FB        FBG     IO T120-T140  7 8         3400   4200
21 3 PLAYBOY                    FBG     OB            7 8         4100   4750
21 3 PLAYBOY                    FBG     IO 120-215    7 8         3300   3850
21 3 PLAYBOY                    FBG     IO T120-T140  7 8         3400   4200
21 3 PLAYBOY          HT        FBG     OB            7 8         3150   3850
21 3 PLAYBOY          HT        FBG     IO 120-215    7 8         3800   4450
21 3 PLAYBOY          HT        FBG     IO T120-T140  7 8         3300   4300
23 9 BEACHCOMBER      HT        FBG     OB            7 8         6200   7100

23 9 BEACHCOMBER      HT        FBG     IO 120-215    7 8         5900   6850
23 9 BEACHCOMBER      HT        FBG     IO T120-T140  7 8         6350   7300
23 9 BEACHCOMBER      CBNCR     FBG     OB            7 8         5550   6400
23 9 BEACHCOMBER      CBNCR     FBG     IO 120-215    7 8         5850   6850
23 9 BEACHCOMBER      CBNCR     FBG     IO T120-T140  7 8         6550   7550
```

T-CRAFT BOAT CO INC -CONTINUED   See inside cover to adjust price for area

LOA FT	IN	NAME AND/ OR MODEL	TOP/ RIG	BOAT TYPE	HULL MTL	HULL TP	ENG TP	#	HP	ENG MFG	BEAM FT	IN	WGT LBS	DR FT	IN	RETAIL LOW	RETAIL HIGH
		--- 1971 BOATS ---															
23	9	EXPLORER		FBG			OB				7	8				5500	6350
23	9	EXPLORER		FBG			IO		120-215		7	8				5450	6350
23	9	EXPLORER		FBG			IO		T120-T140		7	8				5950	6850
23	9	EXPLORER	HT	FBG			OB				7	8				5000	5750
23	9	EXPLORER	HT	FBG			IO		120-215		7	8				5150	6050
23	9	EXPLORER	HT	FBG			IO		T120-T140		7	8				5750	6600
23	9	EXPLORER	FB	FBG			OB				7	8				5500	6300
23	9	EXPLORER	FB	FBG			IO		120-215		7	8				5450	6400
23	9	EXPLORER	FB	FBG			IO		T120-T140		7	8				6000	6900
23	9	GULFSTREAM		FBG			OB				7	8				4700	5450
23	9	GULFSTREAM		FBG			IO		120-215		7	8				4950	5900
23	9	GULFSTREAM		FBG			IO		T120-T140		7	8				5600	6450
23	9	GULFSTREAM	HT	FBG			OB				7	8				4150	4800
23	9	GULFSTREAM	HT	FBG			IO		120-215		7	8				4600	5450
23	9	GULFSTREAM	HT	FBG			IO		T120-T140		7	8				5250	6050
23	9	GULFSTREAM	FB	FBG			OB				7	8				4750	5450
23	9	GULFSTREAM	FB	FBG			IO		120-215		7	8				4950	5850
23	9	GULFSTREAM	FB	FBG			IO		T120-T140		7	8				5550	6400
41	3	EXPLORER		FBG			IO		215	MRCR	7	8				45900	50400

IO 215 OMC 45800 50300, IO T120 MRCR 47000 51600, IO T120 OMC 46900 51600
IO T140 MRCR 47100 51800

LOA FT	IN	NAME AND/ OR MODEL	TOP/ RIG	BOAT TYPE	HULL MTL	HULL TP	ENG TP	HP	ENG MFG	BEAM FT	IN	WGT LBS	DR FT	IN	RETAIL LOW	RETAIL HIGH
		--- 1970 BOATS ---														
18	6	CHALLENGER	RNBT	FBG		SV	OB			7	8	1600	1	10	2650	3050
18	6	CHALLENGER	RNBT	FBG		SV	OB			7	8	1600	1	10	2650	3050
18	6	GULFSTREAM	RNBT	FBG		SV	OB	120	MRCR	7	8	2400	2		2650	3100
21	3	BEACHCOMBER	CBNCR	FBG		SV	OB			7	8	2600			4500	5150
21	3	BEACHCOMBER	CBNCR	FBG		SV	OB	160	MRCR	7	8	3000	2		4350	5000
21	3	CUDDY	ST	CUD	FBG	SV	OB			7	8	2200	2		4000	4600
21	3	CUDDY	HT	CUD	FBG	SV	OB			7	8	2300			4100	4750
21	3	EXPLORER		CUD	FBG	SV	IO	160	MRCR	7	8	2800	2		3800	4400
21	3	GULFSTREAM	RNBT	FBG		SV	OB			7	8	1800			3400	3950
21	3	GULFSTREAM	RNBT	FBG		SV	IO	120	MRCR	7	8	2600	2		3450	4000
21	3	GULFSTREAM	HT	RNBT	FBG	SV	OB			7	8	2100	2		3850	4450
21	3	GULFSTREAM	FB	RNBT	FBG	DV	IO	160	MRCR	7	8	3100	2		3850	4450
21	3	GULFSTREAM	FB	RNBT	FBG	SV	OB			7	8	2300			4100	4750
21	3	PLAYBOY		RNBT	FBG	SV	OB			7	8	1800			3400	3950
21	3	PLAYBOY		RNBT	FBG	SV	IO	120	MRCR	7	8	2600	2		3450	4000
23	9	BEACHCOMBER		CBNCR	FBG	SV	IO	160	MRCR	7	8	3200	2		5400	6200
23	9	EXPLORER	FB	CUD	FBG	SV	IO	160	MRCR	7	8	3000	2		4600	5300
23	9	GULFSTREAM		RNBT	FBG	SV	OB			7	8	2300			4600	5300
23	9	GULFSTREAM		RNBT	FBG	SV	IO	160	MRCR	7	8	2700	2		4000	4650
23	9	GULFSTREAM	HT	RNBT	FBG	SV	OB			7	8	2400			4750	5450
23	9	GULFSTREAM	FB	RNBT	FBG	SV	OB			7	8	2600			5100	5850
		--- 1969 BOATS ---														
18	6	CHALLENGER		RNBT	FBG		OB			7	8	1600	1	10	2650	3050
18	6	CHALLENGER		RNBT	FBG	DV	IO	120	MRCR	7	8	2400	2		2750	3200
21	3	BEACHCOMBER	OP	CR	FBG	DV	IO	120	MRCR	7	8	3000	2		4000	4650
21	3	BEACHCOMBER	OP	CR	FBG	DV	IO	160	MRCR	7	8	3000	2		4050	4700
21	3	GULFSTREAM		CBNCR	FBG	DV	IO	160	MRCR	7	8	3000	2		4450	5150
21	3	GULFSTREAM	HT	CR	FBG	DV	OB			7	8	2000	2		3700	4300
21	3	GULFSTREAM	HT	CR	FBG	DV	IO	120	MRCR	7	8	2800	2		3900	4500
21	3	GULFSTREAM	FB	CR	FBG	DV	OB			7	8	2200	2		4000	4650
21	3	GULFSTREAM	FB	CR	FBG	DV	IO	160	MRCR	7	8	3000	2		4050	4750
21	3	GULFSTREAM		CUD	FBG	DV	IO			7	8	2000	2		3700	4300
21	3	GULFSTREAM		CUD	FBG	DV	IO	120	MRCR	7	8	2800	2		3900	4500
21	3	GULFSTREAM		RNBT	FBG		OB			7	8	2300	1	8	4100	4800
21	3	GULFSTREAM		RNBT	FBG		IB	60D		7	8		2		3450	4000
21	3	GULFSTREAM		RNBT	FBG	DV	IO	120	MRCR	7	8	3050	2		4050	4150
21	3	GULFSTREAM JET		CR	FBG	DV	IO	450	MRCR	7	8	3000	1		7150	8200
21	3	PLAYBOY	OP		FBG	DV	OB			7	8	1800	1	8	3400	4000
21	3	PLAYBOY	OP		FBG	DV	IO	120	MRCR	7	8	2600	1	8	3550	4150

LOA FT	IN	NAME AND/ OR MODEL	TOP/ RIG	BOAT TYPE	HULL MTL	ENG TP	HP	BEAM FT	IN	WGT LBS	RETAIL LOW	RETAIL HIGH
		--- 1967 BOATS ---										
18	6	CHALLENGER		FBG		OB				1600	2650	3050
18	6	CHALLENGER		FBG		IO	120-225			1600	2450	2950
18	6	CHALLENGER		FBG		IO	60D			1600	3250	3750
21	3	BEACHCOMBER	CR	FBG		OB				2600	4000	4600
21	3	BEACHCOMBER	CR	FBG		IO	120-225			2600	4000	4800
21	3	BEACHCOMBER	CR	FBG		IO	T 80-T120			2600	4700	5400
21	3	GULFSTREAM	FB	FBG		OB				2300	4150	4800
21	3	GULFSTREAM	FB	FBG		IO	120-225			2300	3550	4300
21	3	GULFSTREAM	FB	FBG		IO	T 80-T120			2300	4250	4950
21	3	GULFSTREAM	HT SDN	FBG		OB				2200	4000	4650
21	3	GULFSTREAM	HT SDN	FBG		IO	120-225			2200	3700	4400
21	3	GULFSTREAM	HT SDN	FBG		IO	T 60-T120			2200	4450	5100
		--- 1966 BOATS ---										
21	3	GULFSTREAM/PLAYBOY		FBG		OB				2000	3750	4350
21	3	GULFSTREAM/PLAYBOY		FBG		IO	120-225			2000	3400	4050
21	3	GULFSTREAM/PLAYBOY		FBG		IO	60D			2000	4400	5050
21	3	GULFSTREAM/PLAYBOY		FBG		IO	T 60-T120			2000	4050	4700
		--- 1966 BOATS ---										
18	4	T-CRAFT 19	RNBT	FBG		OB		7	6	2400	3250	3800
18	4	T-CRAFT 19	RNBT	FBG		IO	110	7	6		2800	3250
21	3	T-CRAFT 21	RNBT	FBG		OB		7	8	2600	4550	5200
21	3	T-CRAFT 21	RNBT	FBG		IO	110	7	8		4200	4900
		--- 1965 BOATS ---										
21	3	PLAYBOY		FBG		IO	120				4250	4950

TA CHIAO BROS YACHT BLDG CO

TA CHIAO USA
SEABROOK TX 77586   COAST GUARD MFG ID- TAC   See inside cover to adjust price for area
ALSO SEE SEABOARD MARINE

For more recent years, see the BUC Used Boat Price Guide, Volume 1 or Volume 2

LOA FT	IN	NAME AND/ OR MODEL	TOP/ RIG	BOAT TYPE	HULL MTL	HULL TP	ENG TP	HP	ENG MFG	BEAM FT	IN	WGT LBS	DR FT	IN	RETAIL LOW	RETAIL HIGH
		--- 1983 BOATS ---														
33	3	CT-34	CUT	SA/CR	FBG	KL	IB	22D	YAN	10	3	16100	5		51300	56300
37	9	CT-38	SLP	SA/CR	FBG	KL	IB	33D	YAN	11	6	16755	5	7	53700	59100
40	8	CT-41	KTH	SA/CR	FBG	KL	IB	33D	YAN	12	2	27500	6		82400	90600
41	5	CT-42	KTH	SA/CR	FBG	KL	IB	33D	YAN	13	2	23900	6		76400	83900
43	2	CT-43	KTH	SA/CR	FBG	KL	IB	50D	PERK	13	2	20216	4	9	73000	80200
43	2	CT-44	CUT	SA/CR	FBG	KL	IB	50D	PERK	13	2	20216	4	9	72900	80100
46	11	CT-47	CUT	SA/CR	FBG	KL	IB	62D	PERK	13	2	29395	6		100500	110000
46	11	CT-47	KTH	SA/CR	FBG	KL	IB	62D	PERK	13	2	29395	6		100500	110000
47	7	CT-48	KTH	SA/CR	FBG	KL	IB	D	VLVO	13	4	39500	5	11	115500	127000
49		CT-49	CUT	SA/CR	FBG	KL	IB	62D	PERK	13	2	29395	6		111000	122000
49		CT-49	KTH	SA/CR	FBG	KL	IB	62D	PERK	13	2	29395	6		111000	122000
		--- 1982 BOATS ---														
34	6	CT 35	KTH	SA/CR	FBG	KL	IB	D		11	2	16900	4	10	49900	54800
40	8	CT 41	KTH	SA/CR	FBG	KL	IB	D		12	2	27500	6		78100	85800
41	5	CT 42	KTH	SA/CR	FBG	KL	IB	D		12	2	29300	6		81900	90000
43	2	EXPLORER 43	KTH	SA/CR	FBG	KL	IB	D	PATH	13	6	22216	5		72700	79900
46	11	CT 47	CUT	SA/CR	FBG	KL	IB	D	PERK	13	2	29395	6		94400	104000
46	11	CT 47	KTH	SA/CR	FBG	KL	IB	D	PERK	13	2	29395	6		94400	104000
47	7	CT 48	CUT	SA/CR	FBG	KL	IB	D		13	4	39500	5	11	109000	119500
47	7	CT 48	KTH	SA/CR	FBG	KL	IB	D		13	4	39500	5	11	109000	119500
53	7	CT 54	CUT	SA/CR	FBG	KL	IB	D		15	1	57000	6		165000	181000
53	7	CT 54	KTH	SA/CR	FBG	KL	IB	D		15	1	57000	6		166500	183000
		--- 1981 BOATS ---														
33	3	CT 34	CUT	SA/CR	FBG	KL	IB	D		10	3	16100	5		45600	50200
34	6	CT 35	KTH	SA/CR	FBG	KL	IB	D		11	2	16900	4	10	47200	51900
40	8	CT 41	KTH	SA/CR	FBG	KL	IB	D		12	2	27500	6		73600	80900
41	5	CT 42 AFT COCKPIT	KTH	SA/CR	FBG	KL	IB	D		12	2	29300	6		77100	84800
41	5	CT 42 CENTER COCKPIT	KTH	SA/CR	FBG	KL	IB	D		12	2	29300	6		77100	84800
43	2	TANTON 43	KTH	SA/CR	FBG	KL	IB	D		13	6	22216	5		68400	75200
43	2	TANTON 43	KTH	SA/CR	FBG	KL	IB	D	PERK	13	2	20216	4	10	64600	71000
46	11	CT 47	KTH	SA/CR	FBG	KL	IB	D		13	2	29395	6		89200	98000
47	7	CT 48	CUT	SA/CR	FBG	KL	IB	D		13	4	39500	5	11	102500	112500
47	7	CT 48	KTH	SA/CR	FBG	KL	IB	D		13	4	39500	5	11	102500	112500
53	7	CT 54	CUT	SA/CR	FBG	KL	IB	D		15	1	57000	6		155500	170500
53	7	CT 54	KTH	SA/CR	FBG	KL	IB	D		15	1	57000	6		156500	172000
		--- 1980 BOATS ---														
33	3	CT 34	CUT	SA/CR	FBG	KL	IB	20D	YAN	10	3	16100	5		43100	47900
34	6	CT 35	KTH	SA/CR	FBG	KL	IB	33D	YAN	11	2	16900	4	10	44600	49500
37	9	PRINCESS CT 38	SLP	SA/CR	FBG	KL	IB	33D	YAN	11	6	16755	5		45700	50200
40	8	CT 41	KTH	SA/CR	FBG	KL	IB	49D	PERK	12	2	27500	6		69700	76600
41	5	MERMAID CT 42	KTH	SA/CR	FBG	KL	IB	49D	PERK	13	2	29300	6		73000	80200
47	7	CT 48	KTH	SA/CR	FBG	KL	IB	75D	VLVO	13	4	39000	5	11	97200	107000
53	7	CT 54	KTH	SA/CR	FBG	KL	IB	120D	LEHM	15	1	57000	6		149500	164500
		--- 1979 BOATS ---														
33	3	CT 34	CUT	SA/CR	FBG	KL	IB	24D	VLVO	10	3	16100	5		41400	45700
34	6	CT 35	KTH	SA/CR	FBG	KL	IB	24D	YAN	11	2	16900	4	10	42800	47500
36	8	CT 37 PILOT HOUSE	CUT	SA/CR	FBG	KL	IB	33D	YAN	11	6	24000	8		59500	65400
36	8	CT 37 PILOT HOUSE	CUT	SA/CR	FBG	KL	IB	33D	YAN	11	6	24000	8		59600	65500
36	8	CT 37 PILOT HOUSE	KTH	SA/CR	FBG	KL	IB	49D	PERK	11	6	24000	8		59600	65500
36	8	CT 37 PILOT HOUSE	KTH	SA/CR	FBG	KL	IB	49D	PERK	11	6	24000	8		59600	65500
36	8	CT 37 TRUNK CABIN	CUT	SA/CR	FBG	KL	IB	33D	YAN	11	6	24000	8		56400	61900
36	8	CT 37 TRUNK CABIN	CUT	SA/CR	FBG	KL	IB	33D	YAN	11	6	24000	8		56300	61900
36	8	CT 37 TRUNK CABIN	KTH	SA/CR	FBG	KL	IB	33D	YAN	11	6	24000	8		56400	62000
36	8	CT 37 TRUNK CABIN	KTH	SA/CR	FBG	KL	IB	49D	PERK	11	6	24000	8		56400	62000
40	8	CT 41	KTH	SA/CR	FBG	KL	IB	D		12	2	28100	6		68300	75100

LOA FT	LOA IN	NAME AND/ OR MODEL	TOP/ RIG	BOAT TYPE	-HULL- MTL	-HULL- TP	ENGINE TP	ENGINE # HP	ENGINE MFG	BEAM FT	BEAM IN	WGT LBS	DRAFT FT	DRAFT IN	RETAIL LOW	RETAIL HIGH
		1979 BOATS														
41	5	CT 42 AFT COCKPIT	KTH	SA/CR	FBG	KL	IB	33D	YAN	12	2	29300	6		69100	75900
41	5	CT 42 CENTER COCKPIT	KTH	SA/CR	FBG	KL	IB	33D	YAN	12	2	29300	6		71500	78500
47	7	CT 48	KTH	SA/CR	FBG	KL	IB	60D	VLVO	13	4	39500	5	11	93800	103000
53	7	CT 54	KTH	SA/CR	FBG	KL	IB	120D	FORD	15	1	57000	6	6	144000	158000
		1978 BOATS														
33	3	CT 34	CUT	SA/CR	FBG	KL	IB	D		10	3	16100	5		40000	44400
34	6	CT 35	KTH	SA/CR	FBG	KL	IB	D		11	2	16900	4	10	41300	45900
36	8	CT 37	CUT	SA/CR	FBG	KL	IB	D		11	6	24000	5	8	55900	61500
36	8	CT 37	KTH	SA/CR	FBG	KL	IB	D		11	6	24000	5	8	56000	61500
40	8	CT 41	KTH	SA/CR	FBG	KL	IB	D		12	2	27500	6		64800	71300
41	5	CT 42	KTH	SA/CR	FBG	KL	IB	D		12	2	29000			67600	74300
47	7	CT 48	KTH	SA/CR	FBG	KL	IB	D		13	4	39500	5	11	90600	99600
53	7	CT 54	KTH	SA/CR	FBG	KL	IB	D		15	1	57000	6	6	138500	152000
		1977 BOATS														
33	3	CT-34	CUT	SA/CR	FBG	KL	IB	24D-	36D	10	3	16100	5		38600	42900
34	6	CT-35	SLP	SA/CR	FBG	KL	IB	24D-	36D	11	2	16900	4	10	39900	44300
34	6	CT-35	KTH	SA/CR	FBG	KL	IB	34D-	36D	11	2	16900	4	10	39900	44300
34	6	FANTASIA	SLP	SA/CR	FBG	KL	IB	D		11		22000	5		51000	56100
36	8	CT-37 PILOT HOUSE	CUT	SA/CR	FBG	KL	IB	36D	VLVO	11	6	24000	5	8	55700	61200
36	8	CT-37 PILOT HOUSE	CUT	SA/CR	FBG	KL	IB	49D	PERK	11	6	24000	5	8	55700	61200
36	8	CT-37 PILOT HOUSE	CUT	SA/CR	FBG	KL	IB	75D	VLVO	11	6	24000	5	8	54300	59600
36	8	CT-37 PILOT HOUSE	KTH	SA/CR	FBG	KL	IB	36D	VLVO	11	6	24000	5	8	55700	61200
36	8	CT-37 PILOT HOUSE	KTH	SA/CR	FBG	KL	IB	49D	PERK	11	6	24000	5	8	55600	61100
36	8	CT-37 PILOT HOUSE	KTH	SA/CR	FBG	KL	IB	75D	VLVO	11	6	24000	5	8	54300	59600
36	8	CT-37 TRUNK CABIN	CUT	SA/CR	FBG	KL	IB	36D	VLVO	11	6	24000	5	8	52200	57300
36	8	CT-37 TRUNK CABIN	CUT	SA/CR	FBG	KL	IB	49D	PERK	11	6	24000	5	8	52100	57300
36	8	CT-37 TRUNK CABIN	KTH	SA/CR	FBG	KL	IB	36D	VLVO	11	6	24000	5	8	52200	57400
36	8	CT-37 TRUNK CABIN	KTH	SA/CR	FBG	KL	IB	49D	PERK	11	6	24000	5	8	52200	57300
37	1	PRINCESS CT-38	SLP	SA/CR	FBG	KL	IB	24D	VLVO	11	11	20320	5	10	47200	51900
37	1	PRINCESS CT-38	SLP	SA/CR	FBG	KL	IB	36D	VLVO	11	11	20320	5	10	47300	52000
37	4	CT 38	CUT	SA/CR	FBG	KL	IB	36D	VLVO	11	9	29400	6	3	63400	69600
37	4	CT-38	SLP	SA/CR	FBG	KL	IB	36D	VLVO	11	9	29400	6	3	63400	69600
37	4	CT-38	SLP	SA/CR	FBG	KL	IB	49D	PERK	11	9	29400	6	3	63300	69600
37	4	CT-38	SLP	SA/CR	FBG	KL	IB	75D	VLVO	11	9	29400	6	3	63700	70000
40	8	AFT CABIN OR PH	KTH	SA/CR	FBG	KL	IB	36D	VLVO	12	2	27500	6		62800	69000
40	8	AFT CABIN OR PH	KTH	SA/CR	FBG	KL	IB	49D	PERK	12	2	27500	6		62600	68800
40	8	AFT CABIN OR PH	KTH	SA/CR	FBG	KL	IB	75D	VLVO	12	2	27500	6		63300	69500
40	8	CT 41	KTH	SA/CR	FBG	KL	IB	50D		12	2	28100	6		63300	69600
40	8	CT-41 STANDARD DKHS	KTH	SA/CR	FBG	KL	IB	36D	VLVO	12	2	27500	6		60400	66400
40	8	CT-41 STANDARD DKHS	KTH	SA/CR	FBG	KL	IB	49D	PERK	12	2	27500	6		60400	66300
40	8	CT-41 STANDARD DKHS	KTH	SA/CR	FBG	KL	IB	75D	VLVO	12	2	27500	6		61000	67000
40	8	CTR CPT/PH-C/EXT CBN	KTH	SA/CR	FBG	KL	IB	36D	VLVO	12	2	27500	6		63600	69900
40	8	CTR CPT/PH-C/EXT CBN	KTH	SA/CR	FBG	KL	IB	49D	PERK	12	2	27500	6		63500	69800
40	8	CTR CPT/PH-C/EXT CBN	KTH	SA/CR	FBG	KL	IB	75D	VLVO	12	2	27500	6		64200	70500
45	10	CT-46	KTH	SA/CR	FBG	KL	IB	75D	VLVO	13	6	34100	5	11	78700	86500
47	7	CT 48	CUT	SA/CR	FBG	KL	IB	61D	VLVO	13	4	39500	5	11	87300	95900
47	7	CT 48	CUT	SA/CR	FBG	KL	IB	80D	LEHM	13	4	39500	5	11	87500	96100
47	7	CT 48	KTH	SA/CR	FBG	KL	IB	61D	VLVO	13	4	39500	5	11	87400	96000
47	7	CT 48	KTH	SA/CR	FBG	KL	IB	80D	LEHM	13	4	39500	5	11	87500	96200
47	7	CT-48	KTH	SA/CR	FBG	KL	IB	75D	VLVO	13	4	39500	5	11	87500	96200
53	7	CT-54	KTH	SA/CR	FBG	KL	IB	120D	LEHM	15	1	57000	6	6	134000	147000
		1976 BOATS														
34	6	FANTASIA	SLP	SAIL	FBG	KL	IB	40D	PISC	11		23000	5		51400	56500
		1975 BOATS														
34	6	CT 35	KTH	SA/CR	FBG	KL	IB	25D		11	2	17000	4	10	37700	41900
40	8	CT 41	KTH	SA/CR	FBG	KL	IB	30D		12	2	27500	6		58400	64100
42		CT 42	FB	TRWL	FBG	SV	IB	120D	YAN	14	7				51900	57000
53	7	CT 54	KTH	SA/CR	FBG	KL	IB	120D		15	1	57000	6	6	126000	138500
		1974 BOATS														
41		CT 41	KTH	SA/CR	FBG	KL	IB	30D		12	2	27500	6	2	57000	62600
		1973 BOATS														
41	8	TORTUGA 42 DLX			FBG		IB	T120D	FORD	14	4	34000	4	5	79500	87400
41	8	TORTUGA 42 STD			FBG		IB	T120D	FORD	14	4	34000	4	5	70200	77200

TA SHING YACHT BLDG CO

AN PING INDUSTRIAL DIST
TAINAN TAIWAN
COAST GUARD MFG ID- TSQ
See inside cover to adjust price for area

For more recent years, see the BUC Used Boat Price Guide, Volume 1 or Volume 2

LOA FT	LOA IN	NAME AND/ OR MODEL	TOP/ RIG	BOAT TYPE	-HULL- MTL	-HULL- TP	ENGINE TP	ENGINE # HP	ENGINE MFG	BEAM FT	BEAM IN	WGT LBS	DRAFT FT	DRAFT IN	RETAIL LOW	RETAIL HIGH
		1983 BOATS														
29	9	BABA 30	CUT	SA/CR	FBG	KL	SD	23D	YAN	10	3	12500	4	9	52200	57400
34	11	BABA 35	CUT	SA/CR	FBG	KL	SD	33D	YAN	11	2	20000	5	6	80300	88300
34	11	BABA 35 PH	CUT	SA/CR	FBG	KL	SD	33D	YAN	11	2	20000	5	6	85500	93900
53	9	MASON 53	CUT	SA/CR	FBG	KC	IB	85D	PERK	14	5	38600	5	9	242500	266500
53	9	MASON 53	KTH	SA/CR	FBG	KC	IB	85D	PERK	14	5	38600	5	9	243000	267000
63	7	MASON 63	KTH	SA/CR	FBG	KL	IB	140D	GM	16	6	64400	7		437000	480500
		1982 BOATS														
29	9	BABA 30	CUT	SA/CR	FBG	KL	IB	23D	VLVO	10	3	12500	4	9	49100	54000
34	10	BABA 35	CUT	SA/CR	FBG	KL	IB	36D		11	2	21140	5	6	81900	90000
34	11	FLYING DUTCHMAN BABA	CUT	SA/CR	FBG	KL	IB	36D	VLVO	11	2	21140	5	6	80200	88100
34	11	PILOTHOUSE 35	CUT	SA/CR	FBG	KL	IB	36D	VLVO	11	2	21140	5	6	83600	91900
39	10	PANDA 40	CUT	SA/CR	FBG	KL	IB	D	VLVO	12	10	29000	6		118500	130000
39	10	PANDA 40	KTH	SA/CR	FBG	KL	IB	D	VLVO	12	10	29000	6		118500	130000
43	11	MASON 43	CUT	SA/CR	FBG	KL	IB	50D	PERK	12	3	24000	6	3	119500	131000
43	11	MASON 43	KTH	SA/CR	FBG	KL	IB	50D	PERK	12	3	24000	6	3	119500	131500
44	7	NORSEMAN 447	SLP	SA/CR	FBG	KL	IB	61D		13		28617	6	4	135000	148000
44	7	NORSEMAN 447	CUT	SA/CR	FBG	KL	IB	61D		13		28617	6	4	135000	148000
53	9	MASON 53	CUT	SA/CR	FBG	KC	IB	85D	PERK	14	5	38600	6	8	228500	251000
53	9	MASON 53	KTH	SA/CR	FBG	KC	IB	85D	PERK	14	5	38600	6	8	228500	251000
63	7	MASON 63	KTH	SA/CR	FBG	KL	IB	140D	GM	16	6	64400	7		411000	452000
		1981 BOATS														
29	9	FLYING-DUTCHMAN 30	CUT	SA/RC	FBG	KL	IB	D		10	6	12500	4	9	46500	51100
34	10	BABA 35	CUT	SA/CR	FBG	KL	IB	D		11	2	21140	5	6	74000	81400
34	10	PILOTHOUSE 35	CUT	SA/CR	FBG	KL	IB	D		11	2	21140	5	6	80100	88000
38	3	PANDA 38	SLP	SA/CR	FBG	KL	IB	D		12	8	22768	5	9	88400	97100
39	9	BABA 40	CUT	SA/CR	FBG	KL	IB	D		12	9	29000	6		111000	122000
39	9	PANDA 40	KTH	SA/CR	FBG	KL	IB	D		12	9	29000	6		111000	122000
43	11	MASON 43	CUT	SA/CR	FBG	KL	IB	50D	PERK	12	3	25000	6	3	114500	126000
43	11	MASON 43	KTH	SA/CR	FBG	KL	IB	50D	PERK	12	3	25000	6	3	115000	126000
63	7	MASON 63	KTH	SA/CR	FBG	KL	IB	140D	GM	16	6	64400			387000	425000
		1980 BOATS														
29	9	BABA 30	CUT	SA/CR	FBG	KL	IB	D		10	3	12500	4	9	43900	48800
34	11	FLYING-DUTCHMAN 35	CUT	SA/CR	FBG	KL	IB	36D	VLVO	11	2	21140	5	6	73600	80800
34	11	PILOT 35	CUT	SA/CR	FBG	KL	IB	40D	PERK	11	2	21600	5	6	74900	82300
38	3	PANDA 38	SLP	SA/CR	FBG	KL	IB	40D	PERK	12	8	22770	5	9	83800	92100
39	10	BABA 40	CUT	SA/CR	FBG	KL	IB	52D	VLVO	13		28500	6		105000	115500
39	10	BABA 40	KTH	SA/CR	FBG	KL	IB	52D	VLVO	13		28500	6		105000	115500
39	11	QUICKSILVER 40	CUT	SA/CR	FBG	KL	IB	D		12	10	29000	6		106500	117500
39	11	QUICKSILVER 40	KTH	SA/CR	FBG	KL	IB	D		12	10	29000	6		106500	117500
41	10	QUICKSILVER 42	SLP	SA/CR	FBG	KL	IB	40D	PERK	12	9	21258	5	10	91600	100500
43	10	MASON 43	CUT	SA/CR	FBG	KL	IB	D		12	3	24000	6	3	107500	118000
43	10	MASON 43	KTH	SA/CR	FBG	KL	IB	D		12	3	24000	6	3	107500	118000
		1979 BOATS														
29	9	BABA 30	CUT	SA/CR	FBG	KL	IB	D		10	3	12500	4	9	42200	46900
34	11	BABA 35	CUT	SA/CR	FBG	KL	IB	D		11	2		5	6	49900	54900
		1978 BOATS														
29	9	BABA 30	CUT	SA/CR	FBG	KL	IB	23D		10	3	12500	4	9	40700	45200

TA YANG YACHT BUILDING CO LTD

LIN YAN KAOHSING HSN TA COAST GUARD MFG ID- TYA See inside cover to adjust price for area

For more recent years, see the BUC Used Boat Price Guide, Volume 1 or Volume 2

LOA FT	LOA IN	NAME AND/ OR MODEL	TOP/ RIG	BOAT TYPE	-HULL- MTL	-HULL- TP	ENGINE TP	ENGINE # HP	ENGINE MFG	BEAM FT	BEAM IN	WGT LBS	DRAFT FT	DRAFT IN	RETAIL LOW	RETAIL HIGH
		1983 BOATS														
35	10	TAYANA MARINER 36	CUT	SA/CR	FBG	KL	IB	33D	YAN	11		21000	5		62300	68500
35	10	TAYANA MARINER 36	KTH	SA/CR	FBG	KL	IB	33D	YAN	11		21000	5		63100	69400
36	8	TAYANA 37	CUT	SA/CR	FBG	KL	IB	36D	YAN	11	6	24000	5	8	66800	73400
36	8	TAYANA 37	KTH	SA/CR	FBG	KL	IB	33D	YAN	11	6	22500	5	8	67600	74300
36	8	TAYANA 37 LONG PH	CUT	SA/CR	FBG	KL	IB	36D	YAN	11	6	24000	5	8	73600	80800
36	8	TAYANA 37 PH	CUT	SA/CR	FBG	KL	IB	36D	YAN	11	6	24000	5	8	70400	77400
40	4	TAYANA MARINER 40	KTH	SA/CR	FBG	KL	IB	D	YAN	11	5	26500	5	8	83600	91900
41	9	TAYANA 42	CUT	SAIL	FBG	KL	IB	50D	PERK	12	6	29000	5	10	90100	99000
41	9	TAYANA V-42 AFT	SLP	SA/CR	FBG	KL	IB	49D	PERK	12	6	29147	5	10	87600	96200
41	9	TAYANA V-42 CTR	SLP	SA/CR	FBG	KL	IB	49D	PERK	12	6	29147	5	10	93200	102500
41	10	SOUTHERN OFFSHORE 42	SLP	SA/CR	FBG	KL	IB	50D	PATH	12	9	21258	5	10	75500	83000
43		LA BELLE 43 DC		MY	FBG	SV	IB	T124D	VLVO	14	2	26850	4	2	114000	125000
45	11	SURPRISE 45	KTH	SA/CR	FBG	KL	IB	52D	PUEG	13	5	26400	6	5	102500	113000
46	7	VAGABOND 47	KTH	SA/CR	FBG	KL	IB	80D	FORD	13	5	40000	5	3	127000	139500
48		LA BELLE 48 DC		MY	FBG	SV	IB	T D		16			4	6	**	**
52	6	TAYANA 52	CUT	SA/CR	FBG	KL	IB	72D	PERK			38570	5	4	167500	184000
55		SOUTHERN-OFFSHORE 55	CUT	SA/CR	FBG	CB	IB	135D	PERK	16	1	48400	5	3	205500	225500
55		SOUTHERN-OFFSHORE 55	CUT	SA/CR	FBG	KL	IB	135D	PERK	16	1	48400	6	6	205500	225500
55		SOUTHERN-OFFSHORE 55	KTH	SA/CR	FBG	CB	IB	135D	PERK	16	1	48400	5	3	206500	226500
55		SOUTHERN-OFFSHORE 55	KTH	SA/CR	FBG	KL	IB	135D	PERK	16	1	48400	6	6	206500	226500

 CONTINUED ON NEXT PAGE

LOA FT IN	NAME AND/ OR MODEL	TOP/ RIG	BOAT TYPE	-HULL- MTL TP TP	---ENGINE--- # HP MFG	BEAM FT IN	WGT LBS	DRAFT FT IN	RETAIL LOW	RETAIL HIGH

------------------- 1982 BOATS -------------------

30 6	TANTON 30	SLP	SA/CR	AL KL IB	D	10 9		5 2	28900	32100
30 6	TANTON 30	CUT	SA/CR	AL KL IB	D	10 9		5 2	28900	32100
34	TANTON 34	SLP	SA/CR	AL KC IB	D	12 6		5 6	40200	44700
34	TANTON 34	CUT	SA/CR	AL KC IB	D	12 6		5 6	40100	44600
36 8	TAYANA 37	CUT	SA/CR	FBG KL OB	D	11 6 22500		5 8	62700	68900
IB 30D YAN 63200	69500, IB 35D VLVO 63200	69500, IB 50D PERK							63200	69400
36 8	TAYANA 37	KTH	SA/CR	FBG KL OB	D	11 6 22500		5 8	64300	70700
IB 30D YAN 64400	70800, IB 35D VLVO 64400	70800, IB 60D PERK							63200	70800
37	TANTON 37		SA/CR	AL KC IB	D	13		5 6	66100	72600
37	TANTON 37		SA/CR	STL KL IB	D	13		5 6	66100	72600
37	TANTON 37	CUT	SA/CR	AL KC IB	D	13		5 6	65800	72300
37	TANTON 37	CUT	SA/CR	STL KL IB	D	13		5 6	65800	72300
41	TANTON 41		SA/CR	AL KL ID	D	13 6		5 6	86100	94600
41	TANTON 41		SA/CR	STL KL IB	D	13 6		5 6	86100	94600
41	TANTON 41	CUT	SA/CR	AL KL IB	D	13 6		5 6	86100	94600
41	TANTON 41	CUT	SA/CR	STL KL IB	D	13 6		5 6	86100	94600
41 9	TAYANA LONG CABIN PN	KTH	SA/CR	FBG KL IB	D	12 6 29147		5 10	86800	95400
41 9	TAYANA V42	CUT	SA/CR	FBG KL IB	50D PERK	12 6 29147		5 10	85900	94100
43	TANTON 43		SA/CR	AL KL IB	D	13		4 10	91500	100500
43	TANTON 43	CUT	SA/CR	AL KL IB	D	13		4 10	91500	100500
45 3	TAYANA 41 PLUS 2	FB	TRWL	FBG DV IB	120D PERK	14 11	33069	3 11	110000	121000
45 11	SURPRISE 45	KTH	SA/CR	FBG KL IB	50D PERK	13 5	26400	6 5	97000	106500
45 11	TAYANA V-24 AFTCPT	KTH	SA/CR	FBG KL IB	D	12 6	29147	5 10	102000	112000
50 4	FD-12	CUT	SA/CR	FBG KL IB	61D LEHM	14 3	35175	6 6	136000	149500

------------------- 1981 BOATS -------------------

36 8	TAYANA 37	SLP	SA/CR	FBG KL IB	D	11 6	24000	5 8	63600	69900
36 8	TAYANA 37	KTH	SA/CR	FBG KL IB	D	11 6	24000	5 8	65000	71500
41 9	TAYANA V-42	CUT	SA/CR	FBG KL IB	D	12 6	29147	5 10	81700	89800

------------------- 1980 BOATS -------------------

28	TANTON 28	SLP	SA/RC	FBG KL IB	D	10 5	6500	5 6	15500	17600
31	TANTON 31	SLP	SA/RC	F/W KL IB	D	10 3	7000	5 7	18300	20400
34	TANTON 34	SLP	SA/CR	FBG KL IB	D	11	12500	5 1	33200	36900
36 8	TAYANA 37	CUT	SA/CR	FBG KL IB	33D YAN	11 6	24000	5 8	59100	65000
36 8	TAYANA 37	KTH	SA/CR	FBG KL IB	33D YAN	11 6	24000	5 8	60500	66500
36 8	TAYANA 37 PH	CUT	SA/CR	FBG KL IB	33D YAN	11 6	24000	5 8	62900	69100
36 8	TAYANA 37 PH	KTH	SA/CR	FBG KL IB	33D YAN	11 6	24000	5 8	64300	70600
37	TANTON 37	STP	SA/RC	FBG KC IB	D	12 6	10000		29000	32200
39	TANTON 38	SLP	SA/CR	FBG KL IB	D	12 6	22000	5 6	60200	66100
39	TANTON 39	SLP	SA/RC	FBG KL IB	D	12 8	16000	7 1	47800	52500
41 9	TAYANA V-42	CUT	SA/CR	FBG KL IB	49D PERK	12 6	29147	5 10	78100	85800
43 2	TANTON 43	KTH	SA/CR	FBG KL IB	D	13 2	22000	4 11	70700	77700
45	TAYANA 41+2	FB	TRWL	F/S DS IB	T180D FORD	14 10	33000	3 11	115500	127000
45 9	TAYANA-SURPRISE	KTH	SA/CR	F/S KL IB	49D PERK	13 5	26400	6 5	87700	96400
50	10D-50-CRD	SLP	SA/RC	FBG KL IB	D	14	15000	7 5	97800	107500
57 5	TANTON 57	SLP	SA/RC	FBG KL IB	D	14	21000	8 6	175500	192500
67	TANTON 67	SLP	SA/RC	FBG KL IB	D	14	22000	9	162500	178500

------------------- 1979 BOATS -------------------

28	TANTON 28	SLP	SA/CR	F/W KL IB	D	10 5	6500	5 6	15000	17000
31	TANTON 31	SLP	SA/CR	F/W KL IB	D	10 3	7000	5 7	17400	19800
34	TANTON 34	SLP	SA/CR	F/W KL IB	D	11	12500	5 1	32100	35600
36 8	TAYANA 37	CUT	SA/CR	FBG KL IB	33D YAN	11 6	24000	5 8	59100	64900
36 8	TAYANA 37	KTH	SA/CR	FBG KL IB	33D YAN	11 6	24000	5 8	60300	66200
37	TANTON 37	SLP	SA/RC	F/W KC IB	D	12 6	10000		28100	31200
39	TANTON 39	SLP	SA/CR	F/W KL IB	D	12 8	17000	7 1	48200	52900
41 9	TAYANA V-42	KTH	SA/CR	FBG KL IB	50D PERK	12 6	29147	5 10	75900	83400
50	IOD 50	SLP	SA/RC	FBG KL IB	D	12 5	15000	7 5	94600	104000
57 5	TANTON 57	SLP	SA/CR	FBG KL IB	D	13 9	21000	8 6	170000	186500
66 8	TANTON 66	SLP	SA/CR	F/W KL IB	D	15	22000	8 6	157500	173000

TAIWAN YACHT INDUSTRIES INC
TAIPEI TAIWAN CHINA   See inside cover to adjust price for area

LOA FT IN	NAME AND/ OR MODEL	TOP/ RIG	BOAT TYPE	-HULL- MTL TP TP	---ENGINE--- # HP MFG	BEAM FT IN	WGT LBS	DRAFT FT IN	RETAIL LOW	RETAIL HIGH

------------------- 1968 BOATS -------------------

25	MARINER	SAIL	F/W	TM		15		1 7	10300	11700
30	NIMBLE	SAIL	F/W	TM		18		2	24100	26700
31	AA-31	SAIL	F/W	TM		18		2	27500	30500
35	LODESTER	SAIL	F/W	TM		20		2 6	43300	48100
43 9		MS	P/M	KL IB	D	12		5	65800	72300
46	TRIDENT	SAIL	F/W	TM IB	D	24		3	87600	96300
48	AA-48	SAIL	F/W	TM IB	D	24		2 9	102500	112500
72	HARRIS	SAIL	P/M	CT		30		5	**	**

TALISMAN YACHTS

Call 1-800-327-6929 for BUC Personalized Evaluation Service
Or, for 1972 boats, sign onto www.BUCValuPro.com

TALMAN YACHT CO
WARREN RI 02806   COAST GUARD MFG ID- TYC See inside cover to adjust price for area

LOA FT IN	NAME AND/ OR MODEL	TOP/ RIG	BOAT TYPE	-HULL- MTL TP TP	---ENGINE--- # HP MFG	BEAM FT IN	WGT LBS	DRAFT FT IN	RETAIL LOW	RETAIL HIGH

------------------- 1982 BOATS -------------------

| 24 2 | MENEMSHA | SLP | SA/CR | FBG KC IB | 7D FARY | 8 | 6000 | 2 9 | 19400 | 21600 |
| 24 8 | KATAMA | SLP | SA/CR | FBG KC IB | 7D FARY | 8 | 6000 | 2 9 | 20100 | 22300 |

------------------- 1973 BOATS -------------------

| 24 2 | MENEMSHA | SLP | SAIL | FBG KC IB | 7D FARY | 8 | | 2 9 | 13500 | 15300 |
| 24 8 | KATAMA | SLP | SAIL | FBG KC IB | 7D FARY | 8 | | 2 9 | 13800 | 15700 |

------------------- 1972 BOATS -------------------

| 24 2 | MENEMSHA | SLP | SAIL | FBG KC IB | D | 8 | | 2 9 | 13300 | 15100 |
| 24 8 | KATAMA | SLP | SAIL | FBG KC IB | D | 8 | | 2 6 | 13600 | 15500 |

------------------- 1971 BOATS -------------------

| 24 2 | MENEMSHA | SLP | SA/RC | FBG KC IB | D | 8 | | 2 9 | 13000 | 14800 |
| 24 8 | KATAMA | SLP | SA/RC | FBG KC IB | D | 8 | | 2 6 | 13400 | 15200 |

------------------- 1970 BOATS -------------------

| 24 2 | MENEMSHA | SLP | SAIL | FBG KC IB | D | 8 | | 2 9 | 12700 | 14500 |
| 24 8 | KATAMA | SLP | SAIL | FBG KC IB | D | 8 | | 2 6 | 13100 | 14900 |

ROY TANNER ENTERPRISES

Call 1-800-327-6929 for BUC Personalized Evaluation Service
Or, for 1971 to 1972 boats, sign onto www.BUCValuPro.com

TANTON INC
NEWPORT RI 02840   See inside cover to adjust price for area

For more recent years, see the BUC Used Boat Price Guide, Volume 1 or Volume 2

LOA FT IN	NAME AND/ OR MODEL	TOP/ RIG	BOAT TYPE	-HULL- MTL TP TP	---ENGINE--- # HP MFG	BEAM FT IN	WGT LBS	DRAFT FT IN	RETAIL LOW	RETAIL HIGH

------------------- 1983 BOATS -------------------

30 6	TANTON 30	CUT	SA/CR	AL KL IB	D	10 9		5 2	27300	30400
30 6	TANTON 30	KTH	SA/CR	AL KL IB	D	10 9		5 2	27300	30400
34	TANTON 34	CUT	SA/CR	AL KC IB	D	12 6		5 6	48000	52800
34	TANTON 34	KTH	SA/CR	AL KC IB	D	12 6		5 6	48000	52800
37	TANTON 37	CUT	SA/CR	AL KC IB	D	13		5 6	31900	35400
37	TANTON 37	CUT	SA/CR	STL KC IB	D	13		5 6	31900	35400
37	TANTON 37	KTH	SA/CR	AL KC IB	D	13		5 6	31900	35400
37	TANTON 37	KTH	SA/CR	STL KC IB	D	13		5 6	31900	35400
41	TANTON 41	CUT	SA/CR	AL KL IB	D	13 6		5 6	56200	61800
41	TANTON 41	CUT	SA/CR	STL KL IB	D	13 6		5 6	56300	61800
41	TANTON 41	KTH	SA/CR	AL KL IB	D	13 6		5 6	56300	61800
41	TANTON 41	KTH	SA/CR	STL KL IB	D	13 6		5 6	56300	61800
43	TANTON 43	CUT	SA/CR	FBG KL IB	D	13		4 10	112500	123500
43	TANTON 43	KTH	SA/CR	FBG KL IB	D	13		4 10	113000	124000

TANZER INDUSTRIES INC
DORION QUE CANADA   COAST GUARD MFG ID- ZTI See inside cover to adjust price for area

TANZER YACHTS INC
EDENTON NC 27932

For more recent years, see the BUC Used Boat Price Guide, Volume 1 or Volume 2

LOA FT IN	NAME AND/ OR MODEL	TOP/ RIG	BOAT TYPE	-HULL- MTL TP TP	---ENGINE--- # HP MFG	BEAM FT IN	WGT LBS	DRAFT FT IN	RETAIL LOW	RETAIL HIGH

------------------- 1983 BOATS -------------------

22 6	TANZER 22	SLP	SAIL	FBG KC OB		7 10	3100	2 4	4600	5300
22	TANZER 22	SLP	SAIL	FBG KL OB		7 10	2900	3 5	4350	5000
24 7	TANZER 7.5	SLP	SAIL	FBG KL OB		8	3800	4	6000	6900
24 7	TANZER 7.5 SHOAL	SLP	SAIL	FBG KL OB		8	4150	2 8	6550	7500
26 4	TANZER 26	SLP	SAIL	FBG KL OB		8 8	4350	3 10	7550	8700
26 4	TANZER 26	SLP	SAIL	FBG KL IB	8D	8 8	4350	3 10	8000	9200

LOA FT	LOA IN	NAME AND/ OR MODEL	TOP/ RIG	BOAT TYPE	-HULL- MTL	-HULL- TP	ENGINE TP	ENGINE # HP	ENGINE MFG	BEAM FT	BEAM IN	WGT LBS	DRAFT FT	DRAFT IN	RETAIL LOW	RETAIL HIGH
		1983 BOATS														
26	7	TANZER 27	SLP	SAIL	FBG	KC	OB			9	6	6700	2	7	12000	13600
26	7	TANZER 27	SLP	SAIL	FBG	KC	IB	8D		9	6	6700	2	7	12400	14100
26	7	TANZER 27	SLP	SAIL	FBG	KL	OB			9	6	6200	4	6	11000	12600
26	7	TANZER 27	SLP	SAIL	FBG	KL	IB	8D		9	6	6200	4	6	11500	13000
27	11	TANZER 8.5	SLP	SAIL	FBG	KL	OB			9	6	7400	4	4	14100	16000
27	11	TANZER 8.5	SLP	SAIL	FBG	KL	IB	12D- 15D		9	6	7400	4	4	14400	16400
34	5	TANZER 10.5PH	SLP	SAIL	FBG	KL	IB	30D	YAN	11	6	13000	5	10	27600	30700
34	5	TANZER 10.5PH	SLP	SAIL	FBG	SK	IB	30D		11	6	13000	2	1	27600	30700
		1982 BOATS														
22	6	TANZER 22	SLP	SAIL	FBG	KC	OB			7	10	3100	2		4250	4950
22	6	TANZER 22	SLP	SAIL	FBG	KL	OB			7	10	2900	3	5	4050	4700
24	7	TANZER 7.5	SLP	SAIL	FBG	KL	OB			8		3800	4		5650	6500
24	7	TANZER 7.5 SHOAL	SLP	SAIL	FBG	KL	OB			8		4150	2	8	6150	7050
26	4	TANZER 26	SLP	SAIL	FBG	KL	OB			8	8	4350	3	10	7100	8200
26	4	TANZER 26	SLP	SAIL	FBG	KL	IB	8D		8	8	4350	3	10	7500	8650
26	7	TANZER 27	SLP	SAIL	FBG	KC	OB			9	6	6700	2	7	11300	12800
26	7	TANZER 27	SLP	SAIL	FBG	KC	IB	13D	VLVO	9	6	6700	2	7	11700	13300
26	7	TANZER 27	SLP	SAIL	FBG	KL	OB			9	6	6200	4	6	10400	11800
26	7	TANZER 27	SLP	SAIL	FBG	KL	IB	13D	VLVO	9	6	6200	4	6	10800	12300
27	11	TANZER 8.5	SLP	SAIL	FBG	KL	IB	12D- 15D		9	6	7400	4	4	13600	15500
34	5	TANZER 10.5	SLP	SAIL	FBG	KL	IB	30D	YAN	11	6	13000	5	10	26000	28900
34	5	TANZER 10.5	SLP	SAIL	FBG	SK	IB	30D	YAN	11	6	13000	2	1	26000	28900
		1981 BOATS														
22	6	TANZER 22	SLP	SAIL	FBG	KC	OB			7	10	3100	2		4000	4650
22	6	TANZER 22	SLP	SAIL	FBG	KL	OB			7	10	2900	3	5	3800	4450
24	7	TANZER 7.5	SLP	SAIL	FBG	KL	OB			8		3800	4		5300	6100
24	7	TANZER 7.5 SHOAL	SLP	SAIL	FBG	KL	OB			8		4150	2	8	5800	6650
26	4	TANZER 26	SLP	SAIL	FBG	KL	OB			8	8	4350	3	10	6700	7700
26	4	TANZER 26	SLP	SAIL	FBG	KL	IB	8D		8	8	4350	3	10	7050	8150
27	11	TANZER 8.5	SLP	SAIL	FBG	KL	OB			9	6	7400	4	4	12400	14100
27	11	TANZER 8.5	SLP	SAIL	FBG	KL	IB	12D- 15D		9	6	7400	4	4	12800	14500
		1980 BOATS														
22	6	TANZER 22	SLP	SAIL	FBG	KC	OB			7	10	3100	2		3850	4450
22	6	TANZER 22	SLP	SAIL	FBG	KL	OB			7	10	2900	3	5	3650	4250
24	7	TANZER 7.5	SLP	SAIL	FBG	KL	OB			8		3800	4		5100	5850
24	7	TANZER 7.5 SHOAL	SLP	SAIL	FBG	KL	OB			8		4150	2	8	5500	6350
26	4	TANZER 26	SLP	SAIL	FBG	KL	OB			8	8	4350	3	10	6400	7350
26	4	TANZER 26	SLP	SAIL	FBG	KL	IB	8D		8	8	4350	3	10	6750	7750
27	11	TANZER 8.5	SLP	SAIL	FBG	KL	OB			9	6	7400	4	4	11900	13500
27	11	TANZER 8.5	SLP	SAIL	FBG	KL	IB	12D- 15D		9	6	7400	4	4	12200	13900
		1979 BOATS														
22	6	TANZER 22	SLP	SAIL	FBG	KC	OB			7	10	3100	2		3700	4300
22	6	TANZER 22	SLP	SAIL	FBG	KL	OB			7	10	2900	3	5	3500	4100
24	7	TANZER 7.5	SLP	SAIL	FBG	KL	OB			8		3800	4		4900	5600
24	7	TANZER 7.5 SHOAL	SLP	SAIL	FBG	KL	OB			8		4150	2	8	5300	6100
26	4	TANZER 26	SLP	SAIL	FBG	KL	OB			8	8	4350	3	10	6150	7050
27	11	TANZER 8.5	SLP	SAIL	FBG	KL	IB	12D- 15D		9	6	7400	4	4	11700	13300
		1978 BOATS														
22	6	TANZER 22	SLP	SAIL	FBG	KC	OB			7	10	3100	2		3550	4150
22	6	TANZER 22	SLP	SAIL	FBG	KL	OB			7	10	2900	3	5	3400	3950
24	7	TANZER 7.5	SLP	SAIL	FBG	KL	OB			8		3800	4		4700	5400
24	7	TANZER 7.5 SHOAL	SLP	SAIL	FBG	KL	OB			8		4150	2	8	5100	5900
26	4	TANZER 26	SLP	SAIL	FBG	KL	OB			8	8	4350	3	10	5950	6800
26	4	TANZER 26	SLP	SAIL	FBG	KL	IB	8D	YAN	8	8	4350	3	10	6300	7250
27	7	TANZER 8.5	SLP	SA/CR	FBG	KL	IB	D		9	10	6800	4	4	10300	11700
		1977 BOATS														
22	6	TANZER 22	SLP	SAIL	FBG	KC	OB			7	10	3100	2		3450	4000
22	6	TANZER 22	SLP	SAIL	FBG	KL	OB			7	10	2900	3	5	3250	3800
26	4	TANZER 26	SLP	SAIL	FBG	KL	OB			8	8	4350	3	10	5750	6600
26	4	TANZER 26	SLP	SAIL	FBG	KL	IB	8D	YAN	8	8	4350	3	10	6100	7000
27	7	TANZER 28	SLP	SAIL	FBG	KL	OB			9	10	6800	4	4	9600	10900
27	7	TANZER 28	SLP	SAIL	FBG	KL	IB	12D	VLVO	9	10	6800	4	4	9900	11300
		1976 BOATS														
22	6	TANZER 22	SLP	SAIL	FBG	KC				7	10	3100	2		3350	3850
22	6	TANZER 22	SLP	SAIL	FBG	KL				7	10	2900	3	5	2650	3100
22	6	TANZER QUARTER TON	SLP	SAIL	FBG	KL				7	10	2900	3	5	3650	4250
26	4	TANZER 26	SLP	SAIL	FBG	KL				8	8	4350	3	10	5150	5900
27	7	TANZER 28	SLP	SAIL	FBG	KL	OB			9	10	6800	4	4	9350	10600
27	7	TANZER 28	SLP	SAIL	FBG	KL	IB	12D	VLVO	9	10	6800	4	4	9600	10900
		1975 BOATS														
22	6	TANZER 22	SLP	SAIL	FBG	KC				7	10	3100	4		3250	3750
22	6	TANZER 22	SLP	SAIL	FBG	KL				7	10	2900	3	5	2750	3200
22	6	TANZER QUARTER TON	SLP	SAIL	FBG	KL				7	10	2900	3	5	3400	3950
26	6	TANZER 26	SLP	SAIL	FBG	KL				8	8	4350	3	10	5000	5750
27	7	TANZER 28	SLP	SAIL	FBG	KL	OB			9	10	6800	4	4	9100	10300
27	7	TANZER 28	SLP	SAIL	FBG	KL	IB	15	VLVO	9	10	6800	4	4	9200	10500
		1974 BOATS														
22	6	TANZER 22	SLP	SAIL	FBG	KC	OB			7	10	3100	2		3150	3650
22	6	TANZER 22	SLP	SAIL	FBG	KL	OB			7	10	2900	3	5	2600	3000
22	6	TANZER QUARTER TON	SLP	SAIL	FBG		OB			7	10	2900	3	5	3400	3950
27	7	TANZER 28	SLP	SAIL	FBG		IB	15D	VLVO	9	10	6500	4	1	8650	9900
		1973 BOATS														
22	6	TANZER 22	SLP	SAIL	FBG	KC	OB			7	10	3100	2		3050	3550
22	6	TANZER 22	SLP	SAIL	FBG	KL	OB			7	10	2900	3	5	2900	3400
27	7	TANZER 28	SLP	SAIL	FBG		IB	15D	VLVO	9	10	6500	4	1	8400	9700
		1972 BOATS														
22	6	TANZER 22	SLP	SAIL	FBG	KC	OB			7	10	3100	2		3000	3500
22	6	TANZER 22	SLP	SAIL	FBG	KL	OB			7	10	2900	3	5	2850	3300
		1971 BOATS														
22	6	TANZER 22	SLP	SAIL	FBG	KC	IB			7	10	3100	2		3200	3700
22	6	TANZER 22	SLP	SAIL	FBG	KL	IB			7	10	2900	3	5	3050	3550
29		CASCADE 29	SLP	SA/OD	FBG	KL				8	2		5	2	8300	9550
		1970 BOATS														
22	4	TANZER 22	SLP	SAIL	FBG	KC				7	10	3100	2		2900	3350
22	4	TANZER 22	SLP	SAIL	FBG	KL				7	10	2900	3	5	2750	3200
29		CASCADE 29	SLP	SA/OD	FBG	KL	OB			8	2	7500	4	9	9400	10700
29		CASCADE 29	SLP	SA/OD	FBG	KL	IB	15D	VLVO	8	2	8000	4	9	10200	11600
		1969 BOATS														
29		CASCADE 29	SLP	SA/OD	FBG	KL	IB			8	2	8000	4	9	10000	11300
32		WILLIAMS 32	SLP	SAIL	FBG	TM	OB			19			2	3	14500	16500
32		WILLIAMS 32	KTH	SAIL	FBG	TM	OB			19			2	3	14500	16500
44		WILLIAMS 44	KTH	SAIL	FBG	TM	OB			22			3		49700	54600
		1965 BOATS														
24		CASCADE NUTMEG		SAIL	FBG		OB								2850	3300

TARGA OY A B

HIMANKA FINLAND

See inside cover to adjust price for area

FINNYACHT USA
S DARTMOUTH MA02748

For more recent years, see the BUC Used Boat Price Guide, Volume 1 or Volume 2

LOA FT	LOA IN	NAME AND/ OR MODEL	TOP/ RIG	BOAT TYPE	-HULL- MTL	-HULL- TP	ENGINE TP	ENGINE # HP	ENGINE MFG	BEAM FT	BEAM IN	WGT LBS	DRAFT FT	DRAFT IN	RETAIL LOW	RETAIL HIGH
		1983 BOATS														
31	6	TARGA 96	SLP	SA/CR	FBG	KL	IB	25D	VLVO	9	10	9000	4	7	24500	27200
		1982 BOATS														
31	6	TARGA 96	SLP	SA/CR	FBG	KL	IB	25D	VLVO	9	10	9000	4	7	23100	25600
		1981 BOATS														
31	6	TARGA 96	SLP	SA/CR	FBG	KL	IB	25D	VLVO	9	10	9000	4	7	21700	24100
		1980 BOATS														
31	6	TARGA 96	SLP	SA/CR	FBG	KL	IB	25D	VLVO	9	10	9000	4	7	20700	23000
		1978 BOATS														
31	9	TARGA 32	SLP	SA/CR	FBG	KL	IB	25D	VLVO	10		9020	4	8	19300	21400

TARQUIN BOAT CO LTD

EMSWORTH HANTS ENGLAND

See inside cover to adjust price for area

For more recent years, see the BUC Used Boat Price Guide, Volume 1 or Volume 2

LOA FT	LOA IN	NAME AND/ OR MODEL	TOP/ RIG	BOAT TYPE	-HULL- MTL	-HULL- TP	ENGINE TP	ENGINE # HP	ENGINE MFG	BEAM FT	BEAM IN	WGT LBS	DRAFT FT	DRAFT IN	RETAIL LOW	RETAIL HIGH
		1983 BOATS														
37	2	JARJOOR 36		FSH	FBG	DV	IB	T140D		8	6				99100	109000
43		TARQUIN 43		MY	FBG	DV	IB	T320D		15					114000	125000
46	3	TARQUIN 46		MY	FBG	DV	IB	T320D		15					123000	135500
53		TARQUIN-GULF 50		MY	FBG	DV	IB	T400D		15					180000	198000
58	8	TARQUIN 57		MY	FBG	DV	IB	T500D		17					220500	242000
63		TARQUIN 63		MY	FBG	DV	IB	T650D		17					324500	356500
69		TARQUIN 66		MY	FBG	DV	IB	T650D		17	6				444500	488500
		1982 BOATS														
37	2	JARJOOR 36		FSH	FBG	DV	IB	T140D		8	6				94600	104000
43		TARQUIN 43		MY	FBG	DV	IB	T320D		15					108500	119500
46	3	TARQUIN 46		MY	FBG	DV	IB	T320D		15					117500	129500
53		TARQUIN-GULF 50		MY	FBG	DV	IB	T400D		15					172500	190000
58	8	TARQUIN 57		MY	FBG	DV	IB	T500D		17					211000	232000
63		TARQUIN 63		MY	FBG	DV	IB	T650D		17					311000	342000
69		TARQUIN 66		MY	FBG	DV	IB	T650D		17	6				426500	468500
		1981 BOATS														
37	2	JARJOOR 36		MY	FBG	DV	IB	T240D		8	6				82100	90300
43	10	TARQUIN 43		MY	FBG	DV	IB	T320D		15	1				104500	115000
46	3	TARQUIN 46		MY	FBG	DV	IB	T320D		15	1				111500	122500

 CONTINUED ON NEXT PAGE

LOA FT	LOA IN	NAME AND/ OR MODEL	TOP/ RIG	BOAT TYPE	-HULL- MTL	-HULL- TP	ENGINE TP	ENGINE # HP	ENGINE MFG	BEAM FT	BEAM IN	WGT LBS	DRAFT FT	DRAFT IN	RETAIL LOW	RETAIL HIGH
1981 BOATS																
54		TARQUIN-GULF 50		MY	FBG	DV	IB	T400D		15	1				165500	182000
57	8	TARQUIN 56		MY	FBG	DV	IB	T500D		17					194000	213500
60	6	TARQUIN 60		MY	FBG	DV	IB	T650D		17					253000	278000
69		TARQUIN 66		MY	FBG	DV	IB	T650D		17	6				408500	449000
1980 BOATS																
37	2	JARJOOR 36		FSH	FBG	DV	IO	T640D		8	6				89900	98800
42	3	BUGGY-CARRIER 42		UTL	FBG	TR	IO	T320D		10	6				**	**
43	10	TARQUIN 43		MY	FBG	DV	IB	T320D		15	1				99700	109500
46	3	TARQUIN 46		MY	FBG	DV	IB	T320D		15	1				106500	117000
54		TARQUIN-GULF 50		MY	FBG	DV	IB	T400D		15	1				158500	174500
56	3	TARQUIN 55		MY	FBG	DV	IB	T650D		16	6				200000	220000
60	6	TARQUIN 60		MY	FBG	DV	IB	T650D		16	6				238000	261500
69		TARQUIN 66		MY	FBG	DV	IB	T650D		17	6				391000	430000
1979 BOATS																
34		TARQUIN 34		SF	FBG	DV	IO	T188D-T330D		8	6				46800	57900
42	10	TARQUIN 42		CR	FBG	DV	IO	T130D		10	6				57700	63400
42	10	TARQUIN 42		CR	FBG	DV	IO	T330D		10	6				68000	74700
43	3			EXP	FBG	DV	IB	T350D		15	1				90200	99100
43	3	TARQUIN 43		EXP	FBG	DV	IB	T280D		15	1				84400	92800
46	3	TARQUIN 46		EXP	FBG	DV	IB	T280D		15	1				78900	86700
46	3	TARQUIN 46		EXP	FBG	DV	IB	T350D		15	1				86400	95000
54		TARQUIN 54		EXP	FBG	DV	IB	T425D		15	2				148000	162500
54		TARQUIN 54		EXP	FBG	DV	IB	T650D		15	2				176000	193500
69		TARQUIN 69		EXP	FBG	DV	IB	T675D		17	6				385000	423000

TARTAN YACHTS INC

FAIRPORT HARBOR OH 4407 COAST GUARD MFG ID- TAR See inside cover to adjust price for area
SEE ALSO DOUGLASS & MCLEOD INC

For more recent years, see the BUC Used Boat Price Guide, Volume 1 or Volume 2

LOA FT	LOA IN	NAME AND/ OR MODEL	TOP/ RIG	BOAT TYPE	-HULL- MTL	-HULL- TP	ENGINE TP	ENGINE # HP	ENGINE MFG	BEAM FT	BEAM IN	WGT LBS	DRAFT FT	DRAFT IN	RETAIL LOW	RETAIL HIGH
1983 BOATS																
30		TARTAN 3000	SLP	SA/RC	FBG	KL	IB	11D	UNIV	10	1	7950	5	2	25400	28300
30		TARTAN 3000 SHOAL	SLP	SA/CR	FBG	KL	IB	11D	UNIV	10	1	7950	4	1	25500	28300
33	1	TARTAN TEN	SLP	SA/RC	FBG	KL	IB	11D	UNIV	9	3	6700	5	10	18300	20300
33	8	TARTAN 33 SHOAL	SLP	SA/CR	FBG	KL	IB	24D	UNIV	11		10000	4	6	34000	37700
33	8	TARTAN 33R	SLP	SA/RC	FBG	KL	IB	24D	UNIV	11		9700	6	3	33000	36600
37	4	TARTAN 37	SLP	SA/CR	FBG	KL	IB	33D	WEST	11	9	15500	6	7	54200	59500
37	4	TARTAN 37 SHOAL	SLP	SA/CR	FBG	KC	IB	33D	WEST	11	9	15500	4	2	54200	59500
42		TARTAN 42	SLP	SA/CR	FBG	KL	IB	41D	WEST	12	3	22700	6	11	85200	93700
42		TARTAN 42 SHOAL	SLP	SA/CR	FBG	KL	IB	41D	WEST	12	3	22000	5		83700	92000
1982 BOATS																
30		TARTAN 3000	SLP	SA/RC	FBG	KL	IB	11D	UNIV	10	1	7950	5	2	23800	26500
30		TARTAN 3000 SHOAL	SLP	SA/CR	FBG	KL	IB	11D	UNIV	10	1	7950	4	1	23800	26500
33	1	TARTAN TEN	SLP	SA/RC	FBG	KL	IB	11D	UNIV	9	3	6700	5	10	16700	19000
33	8	TARTAN 33 SHOAL	SLP	SA/CR	FBG	KL	IB	24D	UNIV	11		10000	4	6	31800	35300
33	8	TARTAN 33R	SLP	SA/RC	FBG	KL	IB	24D	UNIV	11		9700	6	3	30800	34300
37	4	TARTAN 37	SLP	SA/CR	FBG	KL	IB	41D	WEST	11	9	15500	6	7	50800	55800
37	4	TARTAN 37 SHOAL	SLP	SA/CR	FBG	KC	IB	41D	WEST	11	9	15500	4	2	50800	55800
42		TARTAN 42	SLP	SA/CR	FBG	KL	IB	41D	WEST	12	3	22700	6	11	79800	87700
42		TARTAN 42 SHOAL	SLP	SA/CR	FBG	KL	IB	41D	WEST	12	3	22000	5		78300	86100
1981 BOATS																
33	1	TARTAN TEN	SLP	SA/RC	FBG	KL	IB	11D	FARY	9	3	6700	5	10	15700	17800
33	8	TARTAN 33	SLP	SA/CR	FBG	KL	IB	24D	UNIV	11		10000	4	6	29800	33100
37	4	TARTAN 37	SLP	SA/CR	FBG	KC	IB	41D	WEST	11	9	15500	4	2	47800	52600
42		TARTAN 42 FIN KEEL	SLP	SA/CR	FBG	KC	IB	41D	WEST	12	3	21000			71400	78400
42		TARTAN 42 SHOAL	SLP	SA/CR	FBG	KC	IB	41D	WEST	12	3	21000	5		71400	78400
1980 BOATS																
27		TARTAN 27	SLP	SA/RC	FBG	CB	IB	D		8	8	7400			17100	19400
29	11	TARTAN 30	SLP	SA/RC	FBG	KL	OB			10		8750	4	11	23100	25700
33	1	TARTAN TEN	SLP	SA/RC	FBG	KL	IB	11D	FARY	9	3	6700	5	10	14900	16900
33	8	TARTAN 33	SLP	SAIL	FBG	KL	IB	24D	UNIV	11		10000	4	6	28300	31400
37	4	TARTAN 37	SLP	SAIL	FBG	KC	IB	40D	WEST	11	9	15500	4	2	45000	50000
42		TARTAN 42 SHOAL	SLP	SAIL	FBG	KC	IB	50D	WEST	12	3	21000	5		68000	74800
1979 BOATS																
27		TARTAN 27	SLP	SAIL	FBG	KC	IB	12D	FARY	8	8	7400	3	2	16300	18500
27		TARTAN 27	YWL	SAIL	FBG	KC	IB	12D	FARY	8	8	7400	3	2	16300	18500
30		TARTAN 30	SLP	SAIL	FBG	KL	IB	12D- 30D		10		8750	4	11	22400	25000
33	1	TARTAN TEN	SLP	SA/RC	FBG	KL	IB	9D	FARY	9	3	6700	5	10	14300	16200
33	8	TARTAN 33	SLP	SAIL	FBG	KL	IB	25D	WEST	11		10000	4	6	27100	30100
37	4	TARTAN 37	SLP	SAIL	FBG	KC	IB	40D	WEST	11	9	15500	4	2	43100	47800
1978 BOATS																
27		TARTAN 27	SLP	SAIL	FBG	KC	IB	12D	FARY	8	8	7400	3	2	15700	17800
27		TARTAN 27	YWL	SAIL	FBG	KC	IB	30	UNIV	8	8	7400	3	2	15500	17600
30		COMPETITION T-30	SLP	SAIL	FBG	KL	IB	30	UNIV	10		8750	4	11	23000	25500
30		TARTAN 30	SLP	SAIL	FBG	KL	IB	30	UNIV	10		8750	4	11	19800	22000
30		TARTAN 30	SLP	SAIL	FBG	KL	IB	24D	FARY	10		8750	4	11	21500	23900
33	1	TARTAN TEN	SLP	SA/RC	FBG	KL	SD	15D	OMC	9	3	6700	5	10	13700	15600
34	3	TARTAN 34	SLP	SAIL	FBG	KC	IB	30	UNIV	10	2	11200	3	11	28900	32100
34	3	TARTAN 34	SLP	SAIL	FBG	KC	IB	24D	FARY	10	2	11200	3	11	29100	32300
34	3	TARTAN 34	YWL	SAIL	FBG	KC	IB	30	UNIV	10	2	11200	3	11	28900	32100
34	3	TARTAN 34	YWL	SAIL	FBG	KC	IB	24D	FARY	10	2	11200	3	11	29100	32300
37	3	TARTAN 37	SLP	SAIL	FBG	KC	IB	40D	WEST	11	7	15500	4	2	41300	45800
41	3	TARTAN OFFSHORE	KTH	SA/CR	FBG	KL	IB	80D	LEHM	13	3	25000	4	10	67600	74300
1977 BOATS																
27		TARTAN 27	SLP	SAIL	FBG	KC	IB	30	UNIV	8	8	7400	3	2	14900	16900
27		TARTAN 27	SLP	SAIL	FBG	KC	IB	12D	FARY	8	8	7400	3	2	15100	17100
27		TARTAN 27	YWL	SAIL	FBG	KC	IB	12D	FARY	8	8	7400	3	2	15100	17100
30		TARTAN 30	SLP	SAIL	FBG	KL	IB	30	UNIV	10		8750	4	11	20600	22900
30		TARTAN 30	SLP	SAIL	FBG	KL	IB	12D	FARY	10		8750	4	11	20700	23000
34	3	TARTAN 34	SLP	SAIL	FBG	KC	IB	30	UNIV	10	2	11200	3	11	27800	30900
34	3	TARTAN 34	SLP	SAIL	FBG	KC	IB	12D	FARY	10	2	11200	3	11	28000	31100
34	3	TARTAN 34	YWL	SAIL	FBG	KC	IB	30	UNIV	10	2	11200	3	11	27800	30900
34	3	TARTAN 34	YWL	SAIL	FBG	KC	IB	12D	FARY	10	2	11200	3	11	28000	31100
37	3	TARTAN 37	SLP	SAIL	FBG	KC	IB	40D	WEST	11	9	15000	4	2	38700	43000
41	3	TARTAN OFFSHORE 40	KTH	SA/CR	FBG	KL	IB	80D	LEHM	13	3	24500	4	10	64300	70700
1976 BOATS																
27		TARTAN 27	SLP	SAIL	FBG	KC	IB	30	UNIV	8	8	7400	3	2	14400	16400
27		TARTAN 27	SLP	SAIL	FBG	KC	IB	12D	FARY	8	8	7400	3	2	14600	16600
27		TARTAN 27	YWL	SAIL	FBG	KC	IB	30	UNIV	8	8	7400	3	2	14400	16400
27		TARTAN 27	YWL	SAIL	FBG	KC	IB	12D	FARY	8	8	7400	3	2	14600	16600
29	11	TARTAN 30	SLP	SAIL	FBG	KL	IB	30	UNIV	10		8750	4	11	19900	22100
29	11	TARTAN 30	SLP	SAIL	FBG	KL	IB	12D	FARY	10		8750	4	11	19900	22200
34	3	TARTAN 34	SLP	SAIL	FBG	KC	IB	30	UNIV	10	2	11000	3	11	26400	29400
34	3	TARTAN 34	SLP	SAIL	FBG	KC	IB	24D	FARY	10	2	11000	3	11	26600	29600
34	3	TARTAN 34	YWL	SAIL	FBG	KC	IB	30	UNIV	10	2	11000	3	11	26400	29400
34	3	TARTAN 34	YWL	SAIL	FBG	KC	IB	24D	FARY	10	2	11000	3	11	26600	29600
37	4	TARTAN 37	SLP	SAIL	FBG	KC	IB	40D	WEST	11	9	15000	4	2	37400	41600
37	4	TARTAN 37	YWL	SAIL	FBG	KC	IB	40D	WEST	11	9	15000	4	2	37400	41600
41	3	TARTAN OFFSHORE	KTH	SAIL	FBG	KL	IB	80D	LEHM	13	3	24500	4	10	62100	68300
41	8	TARTAN 41	SLP	SA/CR	FBG	KL	IB	20D		12	3	17850	6	4	51300	56400
1975 BOATS																
27		TARTAN 27	SLP	SAIL	F/S	KC	IB	30	UNIV	8	8	7400	6	4	13900	15800
27		TARTAN 27	SLP	SAIL	F/S	KC	IB	12D	FARY	8	8	7400	6	4	14100	16000
27		TARTAN 27	YWL	SAIL	F/S	KC	IB	30	UNIV	8	8	7400	6	4	13900	15800
27		TARTAN 27	YWL	SAIL	F/S	KC	IB	12D	FARY	8	8	7400	6	4	14100	16000
30		TARTAN 30	SLP	SAIL	F/S	KL	IB	30	UNIV	10	2	8750	4	11	19300	21400
30		TARTAN 30	SLP	SAIL	F/S	KL	IB	12D	FARY	10	2	8750	4	11	19400	21500
34	6	TARTAN 34	SLP	SAIL	F/S	KC	IB	30	UNIV	10	2	14000	3	11	32200	35800
34	6	TARTAN 34	SLP	SAIL	F/S	KC	IB	24D	FARY	10	2	14000	3	11	32400	36000
34	6	TARTAN 34	YWL	SAIL	F/S	KC	IB	30	UNIV	10	2	14000	3	11	32200	35800
34	6	TARTAN 34	YWL	SAIL	F/S	KC	IB	24D	FARY	10	2	14000	3	11	32400	36000
40	8	TARTAN 41	SLP	SAIL	F/S	KL	IB	24D	FARY	12	3	17850	6	4	47700	52500
40	8	TARTAN OFFSHORE CR	KTH	SAIL	F/S	KL	IB	75D	FORD	13	3	23000	4	10	56700	62300
1974 BOATS																
26		TARTAN 26	SLP	SAIL	FBG	KL	IB	8D	WEST	8		5200	4	6	9050	10300
27		TARTAN 27	SLP	SAIL	FBG	KC	IB	30	UNIV	8	6	6800	6	4	12400	14100
27		TARTAN 27	YWL	SAIL	FBG	KC	IB	30	UNIV	8	6	6800	6	4	12400	14100
30		TARTAN 30	SLP	SAIL	FBG	KL	IB	30	UNIV	10		8750	4	11	18900	21100
34	5	TARTAN 34	SLP	SAIL	FBG	KC	IB	30	UNIV	10	2	11200	8	4	25300	28100
34	5	TARTAN 34	YWL	SAIL	FBG	KC	IB	30	UNIV	10	2	11200	8	4	25300	28100
41	8	TARTAN 41	SLP	SAIL	FBG	KL	IB	20D	WEST	12	3	17850	3	11	48400	53200
46	8	TARTAN 46		SAIL	FBG	KL	IB	36D	WEST	14		28500	3	11	80200	88100
48		TARTAN 48	SLP	SAIL	FBG	KC	IB	36D	WEST	14		28500	5	6	85600	94100
48		TARTAN 48	YWL	SAIL	FBG	KC	IB	36D	WEST	14		28500	5	6	85600	94100
1973 BOATS																
26		TARTAN 26	SLP	SAIL	FBG	KL	IB	5D	KERM	8		5200	4	6	8650	9950
27		TARTAN 27	SLP	SAIL	FBG	KC	IB	30	UNIV	8	8	6875	3	2	12200	13900
27		TARTAN 27	YWL	SAIL	FBG	KC	IB	30	UNIV	8	8	6875	3	2	12200	13900
30		TARTAN 30	SLP	SAIL	FBG	KL	IB	30	UNIV	10		8750	4	11	18500	20500
34	5	TARTAN 34	SLP	SAIL	FBG	KC	IB	30	UNIV	10	2	11200	3	11	24700	27500
34	5	TARTAN 34	YWL	SAIL	FBG	KC	IB	30	UNIV	10	2	11200	3	11	24700	27500
40	8	TARTAN 41	SLP	SAIL	FBG	KL	IB	20D	WEST	12	3	17850	6	4	44800	49800
46	8	TARTAN 46	SLP	SAIL	FBG	KL	IB	36D	WEST	14		28500	7	7	78300	86000
48	2	TARTAN 48	SLP	SAIL	FBG	KC	IB	40D		14		30000	4	11	85900	94400
48	2	TARTAN 48	YWL	SAIL	FBG	KC	IB	40D		14		30000	4	11	85900	94400
1972 BOATS																
26		TARTAN 26	SLP	SAIL	FBG	KC	IB	5	KERM	8		5200	4	6	8250	9500
27		TARTAN 27	SLP	SAIL	FBG	KC	IB	30	UNIV	8	8	6800	3	2	11800	13400
27		TARTAN 27	YWL	SAIL	FBG	KC	IB	30	UNIV	8	8	6800	3	2	11800	13400

 CONTINUED ON NEXT PAGE

LOA FT	IN	NAME AND/OR MODEL	TOP/RIG	BOAT TYPE	HULL MTL	HULL TP	ENG TP	ENG #	HP	MFG	BEAM FT	IN	WGT LBS	DRAFT FT	IN	RETAIL LOW	RETAIL HIGH
		1972 BOATS															
30		TARTAN 30	SLP	SAIL	FBG	KL	IB		30	UNIV	10		8750	4	11	18100	20100
34	5	TARTAN 34	SLP	SAIL	FBG	KC	IB		30	UNIV	10	2	11000	3	11	23800	26400
34	5	TARTAN 34	YWL	SAIL	FBG	KC	IB		30	UNIV	10	2	11000	3	11	23800	26400
41	3	TARTAN 41	SLP	SAIL	FBG	KL	IB		20D	WEST	12	6	17850	3	4	45600	50100
46	8	TARTAN 46	SLP	SAIL	FBG	KL	IB		40D	WEST	14		28000	7	7	76200	83700
48	2	TARTAN 48	SLP	SAIL	FBG	KC	IB		40D	WEST	14		30000	4	11	84300	92600
48	2	TARTAN 48	YWL	SAIL	FBG	KC	IB		40D	WEST	14		30000	4	11	84300	92600
		1971 BOATS															
26		TARTAN 26	SLP	SAIL	FBG	KC	IB				8		5200	4	6	8200	9450
27		TARTAN 27	SLP	SAIL	FBG	KC	IB		30	UNIV	8	8	6800	3	2	11600	13200
27		TARTAN 27	YWL	SAIL	FBG	KC	IB		30	UNIV	8	8	6800	3	2	11600	13200
29	10	TARTAN 30	SLP	SAIL	FBG	KL	IB		30	UNIV	10		8750	3	11	17600	19600
34	4	TARTAN 34	SLP	SAIL	FBG	KC	IB		30	UNIV	10	2	11000	3	11	23400	26000
34	4	TARTAN 34	YWL	SAIL	FBG	KC	IB		30	UNIV	10	2	11000	2	3	23400	26000
37		BLACK-WATCH	SLP	SAIL	FBG	CB	IB		30	UNIV	10	6	15700	3	10	33500	37300
37		BLACK-WATCH	SLP	SAIL	FBG	KL	IB		30	UNIV	10	6	15700	5	1	33500	37300
37		BLACK-WATCH	YWL	SAIL	FBG	CB	IB		30	UNIV	10	6	15700	3	10	33500	37300
37		BLACK-WATCH	YWL	SAIL	FBG	KL	IB		30	UNIV	10	6	15700	5	1	33500	37300
37		TARTAN 37	SLP	SAIL	FBG	KC	IB		30	UNIV	10	6	14800	3	10	31900	35400
37		TARTAN 37	SLP	SAIL	FBG	KL	IB		30	UNIV	10	6	14800	5	1	31900	35400
37		TARTAN 37	YWL	SAIL	FBG	KC	IB		30	UNIV	10	6	14800	6	3	31900	35400
37		TARTAN 37	YWL	SAIL	FBG	KL	IB		30	UNIV	10	6	14800	5	1	31900	35400
		1970 BOATS															
27		TARTAN 27	SLP	SAIL	FBG	KC	IB		30	UNIV	8	8	6800	3	2	11400	13000
27		TARTAN 27	YWL	SAIL	FBG	KC	IB		30	UNIV	8	8	6800	3	2	11400	13000
34	4	TARTAN 34		SAIL	FBG	KC	IB		30	UNIV	10	2	11000	3	11	23000	25600
37		BLACK-WATCH	SLP	SAIL	FBG	CB	IB		30	UNIV	10	6	15700	3	10	33000	36700
37		BLACK-WATCH	SLP	SAIL	FBG	KL	IB		30	UNIV	10	6	15700	5	1	33000	36700
37		BLACK-WATCH	YWL	SAIL	FBG	CB	IB		30	UNIV	10	6	15700	3	10	33000	36700
37		BLACK-WATCH	YWL	SAIL	FBG	KL	IB		30	UNIV	10	6	15700	5	1	33000	36700
37		TARTAN 37	SLP	SAIL	FBG	KC	IB		30	UNIV	10	6	14800	3	10	31400	34900
37		TARTAN 37	SLP	SAIL	FBG	KL	IB		30	UNIV	10	6	14800	5	1	31400	34900
37		TARTAN 37	YWL	SAIL	FBG	KC	IB		30	UNIV	10	6	14800	3	10	31400	34900
37		TARTAN 37	YWL	SAIL	FBG	KL	IB		30	UNIV	10	6	14800	5	1	31400	34900
		1969 BOATS															
27		TARTAN 27	SLP	SAIL	FBG	KC	IB		30	UNIV	8	8	6800	6	4	11300	12800
27		TARTAN 27	YWL	SAIL	FBG	KC	IB		30	UNIV	8	8	6800	6	4	11300	12800
34	4	TARTAN 34		SAIL	FBG	KC	IB		30	UNIV	10	2	11000	3	11	22800	25300
37		BLACK-WATCH	SLP	SAIL	FBG	CB	IB		30	UNIV	10	6	15700	3	10	32600	36300
37		BLACK-WATCH	SLP	SAIL	FBG	KL	IB		30	UNIV	10	6	15700	5	1	32600	36300
37		BLACK-WATCH	YWL	SAIL	FBG	CB	IB		30	UNIV	10	6	15700	3	10	32600	36300
37		BLACK-WATCH	YWL	SAIL	FBG	KL	IB		30	UNIV	10	6	15700	5	1	32600	36300
37		TARTAN 37	SLP	SAIL	FBG	KC	IB		30	UNIV	10	6	14800	3	10	31000	34500
37		TARTAN 37	SLP	SAIL	FBG	KL	IB		30	UNIV	10	6	14800	5	1	31000	34500
37		TARTAN 37	YWL	SAIL	FBG	KC	IB		30	UNIV	10	6	14800	3	10	31000	34500
37		TARTAN 37	YWL	SAIL	FBG	KL	IB		30	UNIV	10	6	14800	5	1	31000	34500
		1968 BOATS															
27		TARTAN 27	SLP	SAIL	FBG		IB		30				6800			11100	12700
27		TARTAN 27	YWL	SAIL	FBG		IB		30				6800			11100	12700
34	4	TARTAN 34		SAIL	FBG	KC	IB		30		10	2	11000	3	11	22500	25000
37		BLACK-WATCH	SLP	SAIL	FBG	CB	IB		35		10	6	15700	3	11	32300	35900
37		BLACK-WATCH	SLP	SAIL	FBG	KL	IB		35		10	6	15700	3	11	32300	35900
37		BLACK-WATCH	YWL	SAIL	FBG	CB	IB		35		10	6	15700	3	11	32300	35900
37		BLACK-WATCH	YWL	SAIL	FBG	KL	IB		35		10	6	15700	5	1	32300	35900
37		TARTAN 37	SLP	SAIL	FBG	KC	IB		30		10	6	14800	3	10	30700	34200
37		TARTAN 37	SLP	SAIL	FBG	KL	IB		30		10	6	14800	5	1	30700	34200
		1967 BOATS															
27		TARTAN 27	SLP	SAIL	FBG		IB		30				6800			11100	12600
27		TARTAN 27	YWL	SAIL	FBG		IB		30				6800			11100	12600
37		BLACK-WATCH	SLP	SAIL	FBG		IB		30				15700			32100	35700
37		BLACK-WATCH	SLP	SAIL	FBG		IB		30				15700			32100	35700
37		BLACK-WATCH		SAIL	FBG	CB	IB		30				15700			32100	35700
37		BLACK-WATCH	YWL	SAIL	FBG	CB	IB		30				15700			32100	35700
		1966 BOATS															
27		TARTAN 27	SLP	SAIL	FBG		IB		30				6800			11000	12500
27		TARTAN 27	YWL	SAIL	FBG		IB		30				6800			11000	12500
37		BLACK-WATCH	SLP	SAIL	FBG		IB		30				15700			31900	35500
37		BLACK-WATCH	YWL	SAIL	FBG		IB		32				15700			31900	35500
		1965 BOATS															
27		TARTAN 27	SLP	SAIL	FBG		IB		30				6800			11000	12500
27		TARTAN 27	YWL	SAIL	FBG		IB		30				6800			11000	12500
		1964 BOATS															
27		TARTAN 27	SLP	SAIL	FBG		IB		30				6800			10900	12400
27		TARTAN 27	YWL	SAIL	FBG		IB		30				6800			10900	12400
		1963 BOATS															
27		TARTAN 27	SLP	SAIL	FBG		OB						6800			10800	12200
		1962 BOATS															
27		TARTAN 27	SLP	SAIL	FBG		OB						6800			10800	12300

J J TAYLOR & SONS LTD

TORONTO ONTARIO CANADA   COAST GUARD MFG ID- JJT See inside cover to adjust price for area

LOA FT	IN	NAME AND/OR MODEL	TOP/RIG	BOAT TYPE	HULL MTL	HULL TP	ENG TP	ENG #	HP	MFG	BEAM FT	IN	WGT LBS	DRAFT FT	IN	RETAIL LOW	RETAIL HIGH
		1982 BOATS															
25	6	CONTESSA 26	SLP	SA/CR	FBG	KL	IB		7D		7	6	5400	4		9550	10800
32		CONTESSA 32	SLP	SA/OD	FBG	KL	IB		20D	BUIC	9	6		5	6	26900	29800
		1978 BOATS															
25	6	CONTESSA 26	SLP	SA/CR	FBG	KL	OB				7	6	5400	4		7500	8650
25	6	CONTESSA 26	SLP	SA/CR	FBG	KL	IB		6D- 7D		7	6	5400	4		7900	9050
		1977 BOATS															
25	6	CONTESSA 26	SLP	SAIL	F/S	KL	IB		7D	PETT	7	6	5400	4		7600	8750
32		CONTESSA 32	SLP	SAIL	F/S	KL	IB		25D	FARY	9	6	11000	5	6	21600	24000
		1975 BOATS															
25	6	CONTESSA 26	SLP	SAIL	FBG	KL	IB		7D	PETT	7	6	5400	4		7150	8250
32		CONTESSA 32	SLP	SAIL	FBG	KL	IB		25D	FARY	9	6	10200	5	6	19100	21200
		1974 BOATS															
25	6	CONTESSA 26	SLP	SAIL	FBG	KL	IB		7D	WEST	7	6	5500	4		7150	8200
32		CONTESSA 32	SLP	SAIL	FBG	KL	IB		15D		9	6	10100	5	6	18400	20500

TAYLOR BOATS
COAST GUARD MFG ID- DRT

Call 1-800-327-6929 for BUC Personalized Evaluation Service
Or, for 1971 to 1978 boats, sign onto www.BUCValuPro.com

TAYLORCRAFT IND INC
COAST GUARD MFG ID- ATY

Call 1-800-327-6929 for BUC Personalized Evaluation Service
Or, for 1976 boats, sign onto www.BUCValuPro.com

TAYLORMAID BOATS

Call 1-800-327-6929 for BUC Personalized Evaluation Service
Or, for 1959 boats, sign onto www.BUCValuPro.com

TEEL BOAT WORKS
COAST GUARD MFG ID- TBA

Call 1-800-327-6929 for BUC Personalized Evaluation Service
Or, for 1971 to 1981 boats, sign onto www.BUCValuPro.com

TELEDYNE SEACRAFT
COAST GUARD MFG ID- TSS

Call 1-800-327-6929 for BUC Personalized Evaluation Service
Or, for 1972 to 1974 boats, sign onto www.BUCValuPro.com

TEMPEST YACHTS
S E Z MARINE
MIAMI BEACH FL 33280   COAST GUARD MFG ID- SZS   See inside cover to adjust price for area

For more recent years, see the BUC Used Boat Price Guide, Volume 1 or Volume 2

LOA FT	IN	NAME AND/OR MODEL	TOP/RIG	BOAT TYPE	HULL MTL	HULL TP	ENG TP	ENG #	HP	MFG	BEAM FT	IN	WGT LBS	DRAFT FT	IN	RETAIL LOW	RETAIL HIGH
		1983 BOATS															
43	6	TEMPEST 44 OPEN FISH	OP	FSH	FBG		IO		T355D	CAT	9	6	17000	3		65000	71500
43	6	TEMPEST 44 RIVIERA	OP	CR	FBG		IO		T355D	CAT	9	6	15000			50500	55500
43	6	TEMPEST 44 SPORT	OP	SPTCR	FBG		IO		T355D	CAT	9	6	14000	3		49800	54800

TEMPLE MARINE & YACHTS INC

Call 1-800-327-6929 for BUC Personalized Evaluation Service
Or, for 1965 to 1967 boats, sign onto www.BUCValuPro.com

TEXAS MARINE INTL INC

PLANO TX 75074   COAST GUARD MFG ID- GBO See inside cover to adjust price for area
FORMERLY CHRYSLER BOAT CORPORATION

LOA FT IN	NAME AND/ OR MODEL	TOP/ RIG	BOAT TYPE	-HULL- MTL TP	----ENGINE--- TP # HP MFG	BEAM FT IN	WGT LBS	DRAFT FT IN	RETAIL LOW	RETAIL HIGH
					1981 BOATS					
20	OSPREY T20	SLP	SA/OD	FBG CB		7 11		1 11	2650	3100
20	T6.1	SLP	SA/CR	FBG SK OB		7 11	1800	5 7	2500	2900
20	T6.1	SLP	SA/OD	FBG		7 11		1 11	2650	3100
22	SANDPIPER T22	SLP	SA/CR	FBG CB		7 9		1 11	3650	4250
22	T6.7	SLP	SA/RC	FBG SK OB		7 9	3000	4 6	3650	4250
25 11	T8.0	SLP	SA/RC	FBG SK OB		8	5000	3 11	7100	8150
26	TMI-26	SLP	SA/CR	FBG KL OB		8	5500	3 11	7850	8050
26	TMI-26	SLP	SA/CR	FBG KL SD	15 OMC	8		3 11	7700	8900
27 4	TMI-27	SLP	SA/CR	FBG KL OB		9 11	8000	4 11	12500	14200
27 4	TMI-27	SLP	SA/CR	FBG KL SD	VLVO	9 11		4 11	9100	10300
27 4	TMI 27	SLP	SA/CR	FBC KL IB	8D YAN	9 11		4 11	10200	11500
27 4	TMI-27 SHOAL	SLP	SA/CR	FBG KL OB		9 11	8000	3 6	12500	14200
27 4	TMI-27 SHOAL	SLP	SA/CR	FBG KL SD	D VLVO	9 11		3 6	10200	11600
27 4	TMI-27 SHOAL	SLP	SA/CR	FBG KL IB	8D YAN	9 11		3 6	10200	11500
29 11	TMI-30	SLP	SA/CR	FBG KL IB	11D UNIV 11		9600	4 11	16300	18500
29 11	TMI-30 SHOAL	SLP	SA/CR	FBG KL IB	11D UNIV 11		9600	3 11	16300	18500
37 2	T-37	SLP	SA/RC	FBG KL OB		12 2	16220	5 9	28700	31800
					1980 BOATS					
16	CV-165 B/R	OP	RNBT	FBG OB		6 6			2400	2800
16 2	ANGLER	OP	BASS	FBG TR OB		6 4	790		2000	2400
16 2	STRIPER II	OP	RNBT	FBG TR OB		6 4	950		2400	2800
16 2	STRIPER II	OP	RNBT	FBG TR IO	120 MRCR	6 4	958		1850	2200
16 3	FIN-'N-FUN 115	OP	BASS	FBG TR OB		6	860		2250	2600
16 4	CV-164	OP	RNBT	FBG DV OB		6 5	1050		2650	3100
16 4	CV-164	OP	RNBT	FBG DV IO	120-140	6 5	1241		2050	2450
17 3	CV-173	OP	RNBT	FBG DV OB		7 1	1125		2900	3350
17 3	CV-173	OP	RNBT	FBG DV IO	140-195	7 1	1100		2250	2800
17 4	CV-175	OP	RNBT	FBG DV OB		7 2	1265		3200	3700
17 4	CV-175	OP	RNBT	FBG DV IO	140-195	7 2	1616		2700	3200
18 3	CV-186	OP	RNBT	FBG DV IO	195 CHRY	7 8	1200		2850	3350
20	C-20	SLP	SA/CR	FBG SK OB		7 11	2200	1 11	2700	3150
22	C-22	SLP	SA/CR	FBG SK OB		7 9	3000	1 11	3500	4050
22 3	CV-223	OP	WKNDR	FBG DV IO	195-265	8	2681		5500	6650
26	C-26	SLP	SA/CR	FBG KL OB		8	5500	3 11	7500	8600
26	C-26	SLP	SA/CR	FBG SK OB		8	5000	2 3	6800	7800
26	TMI-26	SLP	SA/CR	FBG KL OB		8	5500	3 11	7500	8600
26	TMI-26	SLP	SA/CR	FBG KL SD	15 OMC	8		3 11	7400	8500
27 4	TMI-27	SLP	SA/CR	FBG KL OB		9 11	8000	4 11	11900	13500
27 4	TMI-27	SLP	SA/CR	FBG KL SD	D VLVO	9 11		4 11	9750	11100
27 4	TMI-27	SLP	SA/CR	FBG KL IB	8D YAN	9 11		4 11	9700	11000
27 4	TMI-27 SHOAL	SLP	SA/CR	FBG KL IB		9 11	8000	3 6	11900	13500
27 4	TMI-27 SHOAL	SLP	SA/CR	FBG KL SD	D VLVO	9 11		3 6	9750	11100
27 4	TMI-27 SHOAL	SLP	SA/CR	FBG KL IB	8D YAN	9 11		3 6	9700	11000
29 11	TMI-30	SLP	SA/CR	FBG KL IB	11D UNIV 11		9600	4 11	15500	17600
29 11	TMI-30 SHOAL	SLP	SA/CR	FBG KL IB	11D UNIV 11		9600	3 11	15600	17800

TEXAS TRIMARANS INC

Call 1-800-327-6929 for BUC Personalized Evaluation Service
Or, for 1965 to 1972 boats, sign onto www.BUCValuPro.com

THAMES MARINE LTD

WALSH WAKEFIELD LIMITED COAST GUARD MFG ID- TPM

Call 1-800-327-6929 for BUC Personalized Evaluation Service
Or, for 1971 to 1981 boats, sign onto www.BUCValuPro.com

THERMAFLO METAL PROD INC

Call 1-800-327-6929 for BUC Personalized Evaluation Service
Or, for 1960 to 1961 boats, sign onto www.BUCValuPro.com

THEURER SERVICES

CRAMCO INC

Call 1-800-327-6929 for BUC Personalized Evaluation Service
Or, for 1983 to 1984 boats, sign onto www.BUCValuPro.com

THOMPSON BOAT CO OF NY

SEE CHRIS CRAFT CORPORATION

Call 1-800-327-6929 for BUC Personalized Evaluation Service
Or, for 1937 to 1980 boats, sign onto www.BUCValuPro.com

THOMPSON BOAT WORKS

Call 1-800-327-6929 for BUC Personalized Evaluation Service
Or, for 1965 to 1966 boats, sign onto www.BUCValuPro.com

THOMPSON MARINE PRODUCTS INC

ST CHARLES MI 48655   COAST GUARD MFG ID- TMS See inside cover to adjust price for area

For more recent years, see the BUC Used Boat Price Guide, Volume 1 or Volume 2

LOA FT IN	NAME AND/ OR MODEL	TOP/ RIG	BOAT TYPE	-HULL- MTL TP	----ENGINE--- TP # HP MFG	BEAM FT IN	WGT LBS	DRAFT FT IN	RETAIL LOW	RETAIL HIGH
					1983 BOATS					
17 6	SEA-LANCER 184	OP	RNBT	FBG DV IO	120 MRCR	7	2200		2100	2500
17 8	SEA-RANGER 180	OP	RNBT	FBG DV IO	120-188	7	2200		2050	2550
17 8	SIDEWINDER 18SS	OP	SKI	FBG DV OB		7	1075		3600	4150
17 8	SIDEWINDER 18SS	OP	SKI	FBG DV JT	CHEV	7	1900		**	**
	JT OLDS **	**		IO	185-230 1850 2300, IO	7	260		2050	2450
	JT 320 FORD 2950	3400								
18 9	SEA-RAGE 195	OP	RNBT	FBG DV IO	120-200	7 4	2450		2450	3000
18 9	SEA-RAGE 195	OP	RNBT	FBG DV IO	225-260	7 4	2450		2650	3250
18 9	SEA-RAGE 196	OP	CUD	FBG DV IO	120-200	7 4			2500	3100
18 9	SEA-RAGE 196	OP	CUD	FBG DV IO	225-260	7 4			2700	3300
18 9	SEA-SPORT 191	OP	RNBT	FBG DV IO	120-200	7 4	2450		2450	3000
18 9	SEA-SPORT 191	OP	RNBT	FBG DV IO	225-260	7 4	2450		2650	3200
18 9	SIDEWINDER 195SS	OP	SKI	FBG DV IO	170-230	7 4			2350	2800
18 9	SIDEWINDER 195SS	OP	SKI	FBG DV IO	260	7 4			2500	2950
18 9	SIDEWINDER X-19	OP	SKI	FBG DV IO	170-260	7 4	2260		2300	2850
20 4	FISHERMAN 8322	OP	FSH	FBG SV IO	120-200	8	3125		3200	3900
20 4	FISHERMAN 8322	OP	FSH	FBG SV IO	225-260	8	3125		3450	4150
20 4	FISHERMAN II 8332	OP	FSH	FBG SV IO	120-230	8	3125		3550	4400
20 4	FISHERMAN II 8332	OP	FSH	FBG SV IO	260	8	3125		3800	4550
20 4	FISHERMAN II 8332	HT	FSH	FBG SV IO	120-230	8			3700	4600
20 4	FISHERMAN II 8332	HT	FSH	FBG SV IO	260	8			3950	4750
20 4	FISHERMAN II 8332L	OP	FSH	FBG SV IO	120-230	8	3125		3800	4700
20 4	FISHERMAN II 8332L	OP	FSH	FBG SV IO	260	8	3125		4050	4850
20 4	FISHERMAN II 8332L	HT	FSH	FBG SV IO	120-230	8			4000	4900
20 4	FISHERMAN II 8332L	HT	FSH	FBG SV IO	260	8			4200	5050
20 4	HERITAGE 229	OP	CUD	FBG SV IO	120-230	8	3300		3450	4250
20 4	HERITAGE 229	OP	CUD	FBG SV IO	260	8	3300		3650	4450
20 4	SPORTSMAN 232	OP	CUD	FBG SV IO	120-230	8	3250		3400	4250
20 4	SPORTSMAN 232	OP	CUD	FBG SV IO	260	8	3250		3400	4400
20 4	SPORTSMAN 232	HT	CUD	FBG SV IO	120-230	8			3200	4000
20 4	SPORTSMAN 232	HT	CUD	FBG SV IO	260	8			3400	4150
21	FISHMASTER 8321	OP	FSH	FBG SV IO	120-230	7 8	2500		3100	3850
21	FISHMASTER 8321	OP	FSH	FBG SV IO	260	7 8	2500		3350	4100
21	FISHMASTER 8321L	OP	FSH	FBG SV IO	120-230	7 8	2750		3300	4100
21	FISHMASTER 8321L	OP	FSH	FBG SV IO	260	7 8	2750		3550	4250
21	FISHMASTER II 8321	OP	FSH	FBG DV IO	225 VLVO	7 8	2750		3350	3900
23 4	ADVENTURER 252A	HT	CR	FBG DV IO	170-260	8	5325		5900	7150
23 4	ADVENTURER 252A	HT	CR	FBG DV IO	130D VLVO	8	5325		6900	7950
23 4	ADVENTURER 252A	HT	CR	FBG DV IO	T120-T188	8	5325		6400	7700
23 4	ADVENTURER 252A	FB	CR	FBG DV IO	170-260	8	5880		6400	7750
23 4	ADVENTURER 252A	FB	CR	FBG DV IO	130D VLVO	8	5880		7400	8550
23 4	ADVENTURER 252A	FB	CR	FBG DV IO	T120-T188	8	5880		6900	8300
23 4	EXPLORER 8352L	OP	FSH	FBG DV IO	120-260	8	4325		5250	6450
23 4	EXPLORER 8352L	OP	FSH	FBG DV IO	T120-T188	8	4325		5800	6950
23 4	EXPLORER 8352L	HT	FSH	FBG DV IO	120-260	8	4550		5450	6700
23 4	EXPLORER 8352L	HT	FSH	FBG DV IO	260	8			6000	7200
23 4	EXPLORER 8352L	FB	FSH	FBG DV IO	120-260	8	5850		6050	7300
23 4	EXPLORER 8352L	FB	FSH	FBG DV IO	T120-T188	8	5850		7300	8650
23 4	OFFSHORE 8352	OP	OFF	FBG DV IO	T120-T188	8	4326		4950	6100
23 4	OFFSHORE 8352	OP	OFF	FBG DV IO	120-230	8	4326		5500	6600
23 4	OFFSHORE 8352	HT	OFF	FBG DV IO	T120-T188	8	4326		4950	6100
23 4	OFFSHORE 8352	HT	OFF	FBG DV IO	120-230	8	4550		5350	6350

LOA FT	IN	NAME AND/ OR MODEL	TOP/ RIG	BOAT TYPE	-HULL- MTL	TP	TP	----ENGINE--- # HP	MFG	BEAM FT	IN	WGT LBS	DRAFT FT	IN	RETAIL LOW	RETAIL HIGH
		1983 BOATS														
23	4	OFFSHORE 8352	HT	OFF	FBG	DV	IO	T120-T188		8		4550			5700	6850
23	4	OFFSHORE 8352	FB	OFF	FBG	DV	IO	120-260		8		5850			6350	7750
23	4	OFFSHORE 8352	FB	OFF	FBG	DV	IO	T120-T188		8		5850			6900	8200
23	4	WEEKENDER 252		WKNDR	FBG	DV	IO	170	MRCR	8		4400			5050	5800
23	4	WEEKENDER 252	OP	WKNDR	FBG	DV	IO	170-260		8		4400			5000	6200
23	4	WEEKENDER 252	OP	WKNDR	FBG	DV	IO	130D	VLVO	8		4400			6050	6950
23	4	WEEKENDER 252	OP	WKNDR	FBG	DV	IO	T120-T188		8		4400			5550	6700
23	4	WEEKENDER 252	HT	WKNDR	FBG	DV	IO	170-260		8		5325			5900	7150
23	4	WEEKENDER 252	HT	WKNDR	FBG	DV	IO	130D	VLVO	8		5325			6900	7950
23	4	WEEKENDER 252	HT	WKNDR	FBG	DV	IO	T120-T188		8		5325			6400	7700
23	4	WEEKENDER 252	FB	WKNDR	FBG	DV	IO	170-260		8		5850			6450	7800
23	4	WEEKENDER 252	FB	WKNDR	FBG	DV	IO	130D	VLVO	8		5850			7500	8600
23	4	WEEKENDER 252	FB	WKNDR	FBG	DV	IO	T120-T188		8		5850			7000	8400
23	7	FAMILY EXPRESS 246	OP	EXP	FBG	DV	IO	175-260		8		4200			5050	6050
23	7	FAMILY EXPRESS 246	OP	EXP	FBG	DV	IO	130D	VLVO	8		4200			5950	6850
23	7	FAMILY FLYBRIDGE 247	FB	EXP	FBG	DV	IO	175-260		8		4300			5150	6150
23	7	FAMILY FLYBRIDGE 247	FB	EXP	FBG	DV	IO	130D	VLVO	8		4300			6050	6950
23	7	VACATIONER EXP 246A	OP	EXP	FBG	DV	IO	175-260		8		4550			5350	6450
23	7	VACATIONER EXP 246A	OP	EXP	FBG	DV	IO	130D	VLVO	8		4550			6250	7200
28	2	EXPRESS CRUISER 286	HT	EXP	FBG	DV	OB			10	4	9200			20600	22900
28	2	EXPRESS CRUISER 286	HT	EXP	FBG	DV	IO	260		10	4	8000			10100	11500
		IB T165 CRUS 14100 16000, IO T170 MRCR 11300 12900, IB T170 MRCR													14100	16000
		IO T185-T200 11500 13200, IB T220 CRUS 13700 15600, IO T228 MRCR													11800	13400
		IO T230 OMC 11800 13400, IB T230 13900 16600, IO T250 OMC													12000	13700
		IB T250 PCM 14800 16800, IO T260 MRCR 12100 13800, IB T260-T270													14900	16900
28	2	EXPRESS FB 288	FB	EXP	FBG	DV	IO	260		10	4				9600	11000
		IB T165 CRUS 12500 14200, IO T170 MRCR 10100 11500, IB T170 MRCR													12500	14200
		IO T185-T200 10200 11800, IB T220 13100 14900, IO T228 MRCR													10600	12100
		IO T230 OMC 10600 12100, IB T230-T250 13200 15200, IO T260 MRCR													11000	12500
		IO T260 OMC 10900 12400, IB T260-T270 13500 15500														
28	2	FAMILY FLYBRIDGE 287	FB	EXP	FBG	DV	IO	260		10	4	8000			10100	11500
		IB T165 CRUS 14100 16000, IO T170 MRCR 11300 12900, IB T170 MRCR													14100	16000
		IO T185-T200 11500 13200, IB T220 14600 16600, IO T228 MRCR													11800	13400
		IO T230 OMC 11800 13400, IB T230-T255 14600 16900, IO T260 MRCR													12100	13800
		IO T260 OMC 12100 13800, IB T260-T270 14200 17100														
28	2	OFFSHORE FISH 288L	FB	OFF	FBG	DV	IO	260		10	4				9700	11100
		IB T165 CRUS 12600 14300, IO T170 MRCR 10100 11500, IB T170 MRCR													12600	14300
		IO T185-T200 10200 11800, IB T220 13100 14900, IO T228 MRCR													10600	12100
		IO T230 OMC 10600 12100, IB T230-T250 13100 15100, IO T260 MRCR													10900	12400
		IO T260 OMC 10900 12400, IB T260-T270 13400 15400														
		1982 BOATS														
17	6	SEA-FARER 8284	OP	RNBT	FBG	DV	OB			7		1175			3850	4500
17	6	SEA-FARER 8284	OP	RNBT	FBG	DV	IO	120-140		7		2200			1950	2400
17	6	SEA-FARER 8284	OP	RNBT	FBG	DV	IO	145-170		7		2200			2050	2450
17	6	SEA-LANCER 184	OP	RNBT	FBG	DV	IO	120-185		7		2200			2200	2700
17	6	SEA-LANCER 184	OP	RNBT	FBG	DV	IO	290	VLVO	7		2200			2600	3000
17	6	SEA-RAIDER 8280	OP	RNBT	FBG	DV	OB			7		1175			3750	4350
17	6	SEA-RAIDER 8280	OP	RNBT	FBG	DV	IO	120-140		7		2200			1900	2350
17	6	SEA-RAIDER 8280	OP	RNBT	FBG	DV	IO	145-185		7		2200			2000	2400
17	6	SEA-RANGER 180	OP	RNBT	FBG	DV	IO	120-185		7		2200			2150	2650
17	6	SEA-RANGER 180	OP	RNBT	FBG	DV	IO	290	VLVO	7		2200			2550	2950
17	8	SIDEWINDER 18SS	OP	SKI	FBG	DV	OB			7		1075			3500	4050
17	8	SIDEWINDER 18SS	OP	SKI	FBG	DV	IO	185-230		7		1900			1800	2250
17	8	SIDEWINDER 18SS	OP	SKI	FBG	DV	IO	260		7		1900			2000	2400
17	8	SIDEWINDER 18SS	OP	SKI	FBG	DV	JT	403-460		7		1900			2800	3250
18	9	SEA-COASTER 8291	OP	RNBT	FBG	DV	OB			7	4	1300			4200	4850
18	9	SEA-COASTER 8291	OP	RNBT	FBG	DV	IO	120-200		7	4	2450			2300	2850
18	9	SEA-COASTER 8291	OP	RNBT	FBG	DV	IO	225-260		7	4	2450			2500	3050
18	9	SEA-COASTER 8291	OP	RNBT	FBG	DV	IO	290	VLVO	7	4	2450			2800	3250
18	9	SEA-LANE 8295	OP	RNBT	FBG	DV	OB			7	4	1300			4350	5000
18	9	SEA-LANE 8295	OP	RNBT	FBG	DV	IO	120-200		7	4	2450			2350	2850
18	9	SEA-LANE 8295	OP	RNBT	FBG	DV	IO	225-260		7	4	2450			2500	3100
18	9	SEA-LANE 8295	OP	RNBT	FBG	DV	IO	290	VLVO	7	4	2450			2850	3300
18	9	SEA-RAGE 195	OP	RNBT	FBG	DV	IO	120-200		7	4	2450			2500	3050
18	9	SEA-RAGE 195	OP	RNBT	FBG	DV	IO	225-260		7	4	2450			2700	3250
18	9	SEA-RAGE 195	OP	RNBT	FBG	DV	IO	290	VLVO	7	4	2450			3000	3500
18	9	SEA-SPORT 191	OP	RNBT	FBG	DV	IO	120-200		7	4	2450			2450	3050
18	9	SEA-SPORT 191	OP	RNBT	FBG	DV	IO	225-260		7	4	2450			2650	3250
18	9	SIDEWINDER X-19	OP	SKI	FBG	DV	IO	170-260		7	4	2260			2250	2800
20	4	FISHERMAN 8222	OP	FSH	FBG	SV	IO	120-230		8		3125			3150	3900
20	4	FISHERMAN 8222	OP	FSH	FBG	SV	IO	260		8		3125			3400	4000
20	4	FISHERMAN II 8232	OP	FSH	FBG	SV	IO	120-230		8		3125			3500	4300
20	4	FISHERMAN II 8232	OP	FSH	FBG	SV	IO	260		8		3125			3700	4500
20	4	FISHERMAN II 8232	HT	FSH	FBG	SV	IO	120-200		8		2500			3000	3700
20	4	FISHERMAN II 8232	HT	FSH	FBG	SV	IO	225-260		8		2500			3250	3950
20	4	FISHERMAN II 8232L	OP	FSH	FBG	SV	IO	120-230		8		3125			3750	4600
20	4	FISHERMAN II 8232L	OP	FSH	FBG	SV	IO	260		8		3125			4000	4800
20	4	FISHERMAN II 8232L	HT	FSH	FBG	SV	IO	120-200		8		2500			3000	3700
20	4	FISHERMAN II 8232L	HT	FSH	FBG	SV	IO	225-260		8		2500			3250	3950
20	4	HERITAGE 229	OP	CUD	FBG	SV	IO	120-230		8		3300			3350	4150
20	4	HERITAGE 229	OP	CUD	FBG	SV	IO	260		8		3300			3550	4350
20	4	HERITAGE 229	OP	CUD	FBG	SV	IO	290	VLVO	8		3300			3900	4550
20	4	SPORTSMAN 232	OP	CUD	FBG	SV	IO	120-230		8		3250			3350	4150
20	4	SPORTSMAN 232	OP	CUD	FBG	SV	IO	260		8		3250			3550	4300
20	4	SPORTSMAN 232	OP	CUD	FBG	SV	IO	290	VLVO	8		3250			3850	4500
21		FISHMASTER 8221	OP	FSH	FBG	SV	IO	120-200		7	8	2500			3050	3750
21		FISHMASTER 8221	OP	FSH	FBG	SV	IO	225-260		7	8	2500			3300	4000
21		FISHMASTER 8221L	OP	FSH	FBG	SV	IO	120-230		7	8	2750			3200	4000
21		FISHMASTER 8221L	OP	FSH	FBG	SV	IO	260		7	8	2750			3450	4200
23	4	ADVENTURER 252A	HT	CR	FBG	DV	IO	170-260		8		5325			5750	7000
		IO 290 VLVO 6300 7200, IO 130D VLVO 6750 7750, IO T120-T185													6250	7500
23	4	ADVENTURER 252A	FB	CR	FBG	DV	IO	170-290		8		5880			6250	7800
23	4	ADVENTURER 252A	FB	CR	FBG	DV	IO	130D	VLVO	8		5880			7250	8350
23	4	ADVENTURER 252A	FB	CR	FBG	DV	IO	T120-T185		8		5880			6800	8050
23	4	EXPLORER 8152L	OP	FSH	FBG	DV	IO	120	OMC	8		4325			5100	5900
23	4	EXPLORER 8252L	OP	FSH	FBG	DV	IO	120-260		8		4325			5100	6300
23	4	EXPLORER 8252L	OP	FSH	FBG	DV	IO	T120-T185		8		4325			5650	6800
23	4	EXPLORER 8252L	HT	FSH	FBG	DV	IO	120-260		8		4550			5300	6550
23	4	EXPLORER 8252L	HT	FSH	FBG	DV	IO	T120-T185		8		4550			5900	7050
23	4	EXPLORER 8252L	FB	FSH	FBG	DV	IO	120-260		8		5850			6550	7950
23	4	EXPLORER 8252L	FB	FSH	FBG	DV	IO	T120-T185		8		5850			7100	8500
23	4	OFFSHORE 8252	OP	OFF	FBG	DV	IO	120-260		8		4326			4850	6000
23	4	OFFSHORE 8252	OP	OFF	FBG	DV	IO	T120-T185		8		4326			5400	6450
23	4	OFFSHORE 8252	HT	OFF	FBG	DV	IO	120-230		8		4326			4850	6050
23	4	OFFSHORE 8252	HT	OFF	FBG	DV	IO	260		8		4550			5250	6200
23	4	OFFSHORE 8252	HT	OFF	FBG	DV	IO	T120-T185		8		4550			5550	6700
23	4	OFFSHORE 8252	FB	OFF	FBG	DV	IO	120-260		8		5850			6200	7550
23	4	OFFSHORE 8252	FB	OFF	FBG	DV	IO	T120-T185		8		5850			6750	8050
23	4	WEEKENDER 252	OP	WKNDR	FBG	DV	IO	185-260		8		4400			4950	6050
		IO 290 VLVO 5450 6250, IO T120-T185 5450 6550, IO T130D VLVO													7450	8550
23	4	WEEKENDER 252	HT	WKNDR	FBG	DV	IO	170-260		8		5325			5750	7000
		IO 290 VLVO 6300 7200, IO 130D VLVO 6750 7750, IO T120-T185													6250	7500
23	4	WEEKENDER 252	FB	WKNDR	FBG	DV	IO	170-290		8		5850			6300	7850
23	4	WEEKENDER 252	FB	WKNDR	FBG	DV	IO	130D	VLVO	8		5850			7300	8400
23	4	WEEKENDER 252	FB	WKNDR	FBG	DV	IO	T120-T185		8		5850			6850	8150
23	7	FAMILY EXPRESS 246	OP	EXP	FBG	DV	IO	185-260		8		4200			4800	5900
23	7	FAMILY EXPRESS 246	OP	EXP	FBG	DV	IO	290	VLVO	8		4200			5350	6150
23	7	FAMILY EXPRESS 246	OP	EXP	FBG	DV	IO	130D	VLVO	8		4200			5800	6700
23	7	FAMILY EXPRESS 246	HT	EXP	FBG	DV	IO	185-260		8		4200			4800	5900
		IO 290 VLVO 5350 6150, IO 130D VLVO 5800 6700, IO T120 VLVO													5550	6400
23	7	FAMILY FLYBRIDGE 247	FB	EXP	FBG	DV	IO	185-260		8		4300			4900	6050
23	7	FAMILY FLYBRIDGE 247	FB	EXP	FBG	DV	IO	290	VLVO	8		4300			5450	6250
23	7	FAMILY FLYBRIDGE 247	FB	EXP	FBG	DV	IO	130D	VLVO	8		4300			5900	6800
23	7	VACATIONER EXP 246A	OP	EXP	FBG	DV	IO	185-260		8		4550			5100	6300
23	7	VACATIONER EXP 246A	OP	EXP	FBG	DV	IO	290	VLVO	8		4550			5650	6500
23	7	VACATIONER EXP 246A	OP	EXP	FBG	DV	IO	130D	VLVO	8		4550			6100	7050
23	7	VACATIONER EXP 246A	HT	EXP	FBG	DV	IO	185-260		8		4550			5100	6300
23	7	VACATIONER EXP 246A	HT	EXP	FBG	DV	IO	290	VLVO	8		4550			5650	6500
23	7	VACATIONER EXP 246A	HT	EXP	FBG	DV	IO	130D	VLVO	8		4550			6100	7050
28	2	EXPRESS CRUISER 286	HT	EXP	FBG	DV	IO	260		10	4	8000			9850	11300
		IB T165 CRUS 12600 14300, IO T170 MRCR 11100 12600, IB T170 MRCR													13400	15300
		IO T185-T200 11200 12900, IB T220 13100 15800, IO T228 MRCR													11600	13100
		IB T228 MRCR 14000 15900, IO T230 OMC 11600 13100, IB T230-T255													14100	16200
		IO T260 MRCR 11900 13500, IO T260 OMC 11800 13400, IB T260-T270													14400	16400
28	2	FAMILY FLYBRIDGE 287	FB	EXP	FBG	DV	IO	260		10	4	8000			9850	11300
		IB T165 CRUS 12600 14300, IO T170 MRCR 11100 12600, IB T170 MRCR													13400	15300
		IO T185-T200 11200 12900, IB T220 13100 14900, IO T228 MRCR													11600	13100
		IB T228 MRCR 14000 15900, IO T230 OMC 11600 13100, IB T230-T255													14100	16200
		IO T260 MRCR 11900 13500, IO T260 OMC 11100 12600, VD T260 OMC													14400	16400
		IB T270 CRUS 13600 15400														

 CONTINUED ON NEXT PAGE

LOA FT	LOA IN	NAME AND/ OR MODEL	TOP/ RIG	BOAT TYPE	-HULL- MTL	-HULL- TP	ENGINE TP	ENGINE # HP	ENGINE MFG	BEAM FT	BEAM IN	WGT LBS	DRAFT FT IN	RETAIL LOW	RETAIL HIGH
		1981 BOATS													
17	6	SEA-FARER 8184	OP	RNBT	FBG	DV	OB			7		1175		3750	4350
17	6	SEA-FARER 8184	OP	RNBT	FBG	DV	IO	120-140		7		2200		1900	2350
17	6	SEA-FARER 8184	OP	RNBT	FBG	DV	IO	145-170		7		2200		2000	2400
17	6	SEA-LANCER 184	OP	RNBT	FBG	DV	IO	120-185		7		2200		2150	2650
17	6	SEA-LANCER 184	OP	RNBT	FBG	DV	IO	290	VLVO	7		2200		2500	2950
17	6	SEA-RAIDER 8180	OP	RNBT	FBG	DV	OB			7		1175		3700	4300
17	6	SEA-RAIDER 8180	OP	RNBT	FBG	DV	IO	120-140		7		2200		1850	2350
17	6	SEA-RAIDER 8180	OP	RNBT	FBG	DV	IO	145-185		7		2200		1950	2350
17	6	SEA-RANGER 180	OP	RNBT	FBG	DV	IO	120-140		7		2200		2050	2600
17	6	SEA-RANGER 180	OP	RNBT	FBG	DV	IO	145-185		7		2200		2250	2600
17	6	SEA-RANGER 180	OP	RNBT	FBG	DV	IO	290	VLVO	7		2200		2500	2900
17	8	SIDEWINDER 18SS	OP	SKI	FBG	DV	OB			7		1075		3400	3950
17	8	SIDEWINDER 18SS	OP	SKI	FBG	DV	IO	185-230		7		1900		1800	2200
17	8	SIDEWINDER 18SS	OP	SKI	FBG	DV	IO	260		7		1900		1950	2350
17	8	SIDEWINDER 18SS	OP	SKI	FBG	DV	JT	403-460		7		1900		2700	3100
18	9	SEA-COASTER 8191	OP	RNBT	FBG	DV	OB			7	4	1300		4100	4750
18	9	SEA-COASTER 8191	OP	RNBT	FBG	DV	IO	120-200		7	4	2450		2250	2800
18	9	SEA-COASTER 8191	OP	RNBT	FBG	DV	IO	225-260		7	4	2450		2450	2950
18	9	SEA-COASTER 8191	OP	RNBT	FBG	DV	IO	290	VLVO	7	4	2450		2750	3200
18	9	SEA-LANE 8195	OP	RNBT	FBG	DV	OB			7	4	1300		4200	4900
18	9	SEA-LANE 8195	OP	RNBT	FBG	DV	IO	120-200		7	4	2450		2300	2800
18	9	SEA-LANE 8195	OP	RNBT	FBG	DV	IO	225-260		7	4	2450		2450	2950
18	9	SEA-LANE 8195	OP	RNBT	FBG	DV	IO	290	VLVO	7	4	2450		2800	3250
18	9	SEA-RAGE 195	OP	RNBT	FBG	DV	IO	120-200		7	4	2450		2450	3050
18	9	SEA-RAGE 195	OP	RNBT	FBG	DV	IO	225-260		7	4	2450		2650	3200
18	9	SEA-RAGE 195	OP	RNBT	FBG	DV	IO	290	VLVO	7	4	2450		2950	3450
18	9	SEA-SPORT 191	OP	RNBT	FBG	DV	IO	120-200		7	4	2450		2450	3000
18	9	SEA-SPORT 191	OP	RNBT	FBG	DV	IO	225-260		7	4	2450		2650	3150
18	9	SIDEWINDER X-19	OP	SKI	FBG	DV	IO	170-260		7	4	2260		2200	2750
20	4	FISHERMAN 8122	OP	FSH	FBG	SV	IO	120-230		8		3125		3100	3800
20	4	FISHERMAN 8122	OP	FSH	FBG	SV	IO	260		8		3125		3350	3950
20	4	FISHERMAN II 8132	OP	FSH	FBG	SV	IO	120-230		8		3125		3400	4200
20	4	FISHERMAN II 8132	OP	FSH	FBG	SV	IO	260		8		3125		3650	4300
20	4	FISHERMAN II 8132	HT	FSH	FBG	SV	IO	120-200		8		2500		2850	3500
20	4	FISHERMAN II 8132	HT	FSH	FBG	SV	IO	225-260		8		2500		3050	3700
20	4	FISHERMAN II 8132L	OP	FSH	FBG	SV	IO	120-260		8		3125		3750	4700
20	4	FISHERMAN II 8132L	HT	FSH	FBG	SV	IO	120-200		8		2500		3100	3800
20	4	FISHERMAN II 8132L	HT	FSH	FBG	SV	IO	225-260		8		2500		3350	4000
20	4	HERITAGE 229	OP	CUD	FBG	SV	IO	120-230		8		3300		3300	4100
20	4	HERITAGE 229	OP	CUD	FBG	SV	IO	260		8		3300		3500	4250
20	4	HERITAGE 229	OP	CUD	FBG	SV	IO	290	VLVO	8		3300		3850	4450
20	4	SPORTSMAN 232	OP	CUD	FBG	SV	IO	120-230		8		3250		3300	4050
20	4	SPORTSMAN 232	OP	CUD	FBG	SV	IO	260		8		3250		3500	4200
20	4	SPORTSMAN 232	OP	CUD	FBG	SV	IO	290	VLVO	8		3250		3800	4450
21		FISHMASTER 8121	OP	FSH	FBG	SV	IO	120-200		7	8	2500		3000	3700
21		FISHMASTER 8121	OP	FSH	FBG	SV	IO	225-260		7	8	2500		3250	3900
21		FISHMASTER 8121L	OP	FSH	FBG	SV	IO	120-230		7	8	2750		3150	3950
21		FISHMASTER 8121L	OP	FSH	FBG	SV	IO	260		7	8	2750		3400	4100
23	4	ADVENTURER 252A	HT	CR	FBG	DV	IO	165-260		8		5325		5650	6900
		IO 290 VLVO 6200 7100, IO 130D VLVO 6650 7650, IO T120-T185												6150	7350
23	4	ADVENTURER 252A	FB	CR	FBG	DV	IO	165-290		8		5880		6150	7650
23	4	ADVENTURER 252A	FB	CR	FBG	DV	IO	130D	VLVO	8		5880		7150	8200
23	4	ADVENTURER 252A	FB	CR	FBG	DV	IO	T120-T185		8		5880		6650	7950
23	4	EXPLORER 8152L	OP	FSH	FBG	DV	IO	120-260		8		4325		5050	6200
23	4	EXPLORER 8152L	OP	FSH	FBG	DV	IO	T120-T185		8		4325		5600	6700
23	4	EXPLORER 8152L	HT	FSH	FBG	DV	IO	120-260		8		4550		5250	6450
23	4	EXPLORER 8152L	HT	FSH	FBG	DV	IO	T120-T185		8		4550		5800	6950
23	4	EXPLORER 8152L	FB	FSH	FBG	DV	IO	120-260		8		5850		6450	7850
23	4	EXPLORER 8152L	FB	FSH	FBG	DV	IO	T120-T185		8		5850		7000	8350
23	4	OFFSHORE 8152	OP	OFF	FBG	DV	IO	120-260		8		4326		4750	5900
23	4	OFFSHORE 8152	OP	OFF	FBG	DV	IO	T120-T185		8		4326		5300	6350
23	4	OFFSHORE 8152	HT	OFF	FBG	DV	IO	120-230		8		4326		4750	5950
23	4	OFFSHORE 8152	HT	OFF	FBG	DV	IO	260		8		4550		5150	6100
23	4	OFFSHORE 8152	HT	OFF	FBG	DV	IO	T120-T185		8		4550		5500	6550
23	4	OFFSHORE 8152	FB	OFF	FBG	DV	IO	120-260		8		5850		6100	7450
23	4	OFFSHORE 8152	FB	OFF	FBG	DV	IO	T120-T185		8		5850		6650	7900
23	4	WEEKENDER 252	OP	WKNDR	FBG	DV	IO	165-260		8		4400		4850	5950
		IO 290 VLVO 5350 6150, IO 130D VLVO 5800 6700, IO T120-T185												5350	6400
23	4	WEEKENDER 252	HT	WKNDR	FBG	DV	IO	165-260		8		5325		5650	6900
		IO 290 VLVO 6200 7100, IO 130D VLVO 6650 7650, IO T120-T185												6150	7350
23	4	WEEKENDER 252	FB	WKNDR	FBG	DV	IO	165-290		8		5850		6200	7700
23	4	WEEKENDER 252	FB	WKNDR	FBG	DV	IO	130D	VLVO	8		5850		7150	8250
23	4	WEEKENDER 252	FB	WKNDR	FBG	DV	IO	T120-T185		8		5850		6700	8000
23	7	FAMILY EXPRESS 246	OP	EXP	FBG	DV	IO	185-260		8		4200		4750	5850
		IO 290 VLVO 5250 6050, IO 130D VLVO 5700 6550, IO T120 VLVO												5450	6300
23	7	FAMILY EXPRESS 246	HT	EXP	FBG	DV	IO	185-260		8		4200		4750	5850
		IO 290 VLVO 5250 6050, IO 130D VLVO 5700 6550, IO T120 VLVO												5450	6300
23	7	FAMILY FLYBRIDGE 247	FB	EXP	FBG	DV	IO	185-260		8		4300		4800	5950
23	7	FAMILY FLYBRIDGE 247	FB	EXP	FBG	DV	IO	290	VLVO	8		4300		5350	6150
23	7	FAMILY FLYBRIDGE 247	FB	EXP	FBG	DV	IO	130D	VLVO	8		4300		5800	6650
23	7	VACATIONER EXP 246A	OP	EXP	FBG	DV	IO	185-260		8		4550		5050	6200
23	7	VACATIONER EXP 246A	OP	EXP	FBG	DV	IO	290	VLVO	8		4550		5550	6400
23	7	VACATIONER EXP 246A	OP	EXP	FBG	DV	IO	130D	VLVO	8		4550		6000	6900
23	7	VACATIONER EXP 246A	HT	EXP	FBG	DV	IO	185-260		8		4550		5050	6200
23	7	VACATIONER EXP 246A	HT	EXP	FBG	DV	IO	290	VLVO	8		4550		5550	6400
23	7	VACATIONER EXP 246A	HT	EXP	FBG	DV	IO	130D	VLVO	8		4550		6000	6900
28	2	EXPRESS CRUISER 286	HT	EXP	FBG	DV	IO	260		10	4	8000		9700	11100
		IO T165 MRCR 10900 12400, IO T170 MRCR 10900 12400, VD T170 MRCR												12900	14600
		IO T185-T200 11000 12700, VD T215-T225 13300 15300, IO T228 MRCR												11400	12900
		VD T228 MRCR 13400 15200, IO T230 OMC 11400 12900, VD T250-T255												13700	15600
		IO T260 11700 13300													
28	2	FAMILY FLYBRIDGE 287	FB	EXP	FBG	DV	IO	260		10	4	8000		9700	11100
		IO T165 MRCR 10900 12400, IO T170 MRCR 10900 12400, VD T170 MRCR												12900	14600
		IO T185-T200 11000 12700, VD T215-T225 13300 15300, IO T228 MRCR												11400	12900
		VD T228 MRCR 13400 15200, IO T230 OMC 11400 12900, VD T250-T255												13700	15600
		IO T260 11700 13300													
		1979 BOATS													
16	9	SEA-BIRD 7975	OP	RNBT	FBG	TR	OB			6	10	1350		3900	4550
16	9	SEA-BIRD 7975	OP	RNBT	FBG	TR	IO	120	MRCR	6	10	2000		1750	2100
16	9	SEA-BIRD 7975	OP	RNBT	FBG	TR	IO	120	OMC	6	10	2000		1750	2100
16	9	SEA-BIRD 7975	OP	RNBT	FBG	TR	IO	120-140		6	10	2000		1850	2250
17	6	SEA-FARER 7984	OP	RNBT	FBG	DV	OB			7		1375		4100	4750
17	6	SEA-FARER 7984	OP	RNBT	FBG	DV	IO	120-170		7		2340		2000	2450
17	6	SEA-LANCER 184	OP	RNBT	FBG	DV	IO	120-170		7		2340		2200	2700
17	6	SEA-RAIDER 7980	OP	RNBT	FBG	DV	OB			7		1375		3950	4600
17	6	SEA-RAIDER 7980	OP	RNBT	FBG	DV	IO	120-170		7		2340		1950	2450
17	6	SEA-RANGER 180	OP	RNBT	FBG	DV	IO	120	MRCR	7		2300		2000	2400
17	6	SEA-RANGER 180	OP	RNBT	FBG	DV	IO	120	OMC	7		2300		2000	2350
17	6	SEA-RANGER 180	OP	RNBT	FBG	DV	IO	120-170		7		2300		2150	2500
17	8	SIDEWINDER 18SS	OP	SKI	FBG	SV	OB			7		1075		3250	3800
17	8	SIDEWINDER 18SS	OP	SKI	FBG	SV	IO	170-230		7		1900		1750	2200
17	8	SIDEWINDER 18SS	OP	SKI	FBG	SV	JT	460	FORD	7		1900		2450	2850
18	9	SEA-COASTER 7991	OP	RNBT	FBG	DV	OB			7	4	1480		4450	5100
18	9	SEA-COASTER 7991	OP	RNBT	FBG	DV	IO	120-200		7	4	2410		2250	2750
18	9	SEA-COASTER 7991	OP	RNBT	FBG	DV	IO	225-260		7	4	2410		2400	2950
18	9	SEA-FURY 195	OP	RNBT	FBG	DV	IO	120-200		7	4	2450		2400	2950
18	9	SEA-FURY 195	OP	RNBT	FBG	DV	IO	225-260		7	4	2450		2600	3150
18	9	SEA-LANE 7995	OP	RNBT	FBG	DV	OB			7	4	1510		4500	5150
18	9	SEA-LANE 7995	OP	RNBT	FBG	DV	IO	120-200		7	4	2450		2250	2800
18	9	SEA-LANE 7995	OP	RNBT	FBG	DV	IO	225-260		7	4	2450		2450	2950
18	9	SEA-SPORT 191	OP	RNBT	FBG	DV	IO	120-200		7	4	2410		2400	2950
18	9	SEA-SPORT 191	OP	RNBT	FBG	DV	IO	225-260		7	4	2410		2600	3150
19	8	SIDEWINDER X-19	OP	SKI	FBG	SV	IO	260		7	4	2260		2450	2850
20	4	FISHERMAN 7922	OP	FSH	FBG	SV	IO	120-250		8		3150		3350	4150
20	4	FISHERMAN 7922	OP	FSH	FBG	SV	IO	260		8		3150		3550	4350
20	4	FISHERMAN II 7932	OP	FSH	FBG	SV	IO	120-250		8		3250		3450	4250
20	4	FISHERMAN II 7932	OP	FSH	FBG	SV	IO	260		8		3250		3650	4400
20	4	FISHERMAN II 7932	HT	FSH	FBG	SV	IO	120-250		8		3250		3450	4250
20	4	FISHERMAN II 7932	HT	FSH	FBG	SV	IO	260		8		3250		3650	4400
20	4	HERITAGE 229	OP	CUD	FBG	SV	IO	120-250		8		3350		3300	4100
20	4	HERITAGE 229	OP	CUD	FBG	SV	IO	260		8		3350		3500	4250
20	4	SPORTSMAN 232	OP	CUD	FBG	SV	IO	120-250		8		3250		3250	4050
20	4	SPORTSMAN 232	OP	CUD	FBG	SV	IO	260		8		3250		3450	4200
20	4	SPORTSMAN 232	HT	CUD	FBG	SV	IO	120-250		8		3250		3250	4050
20	4	SPORTSMAN 232	HT	CUD	FBG	SV	IO	260	MRCR	8		2350		2900	3350
20	4	SPORTSMAN 232	HT	CUD	FBG	SV	IO	260		8		3250		3400	4200
23	4	ADVENTURER 252A	HT	CR	FBG	SV	IO	120-260		8		4610		4950	6100
23	4	ADVENTURER 252A	HT	CR	FBG	SV	IO	T120-T170		8		4610		5500	6550
23	4	ADVENTURER 252A	FB	CR	FBG	SV	IO	120-260		8		4610		4950	6100
23	4	ADVENTURER 252A	FB	CR	FBG	SV	IO	T120-T170		8		4610		5500	6550
23	4	EXPLORER 7952L	OP	FSH	FBG	SV	IO	120-260		8		4325		5000	6150

614
CONTINUED ON NEXT PAGE
96th ed. - Vol. III

LOA FT	LOA IN	NAME AND/ OR MODEL	TOP/ RIG	BOAT TYPE	-HULL- MTL	-HULL- TP	ENGINE TP	ENGINE # HP	ENGINE MFG	BEAM FT	BEAM IN	WGT LBS	DRAFT FT	DRAFT IN	RETAIL LOW	RETAIL HIGH
		1979 BOATS														
23	4	EXPLORER 7952L	OP	FSH	FBG	SV	IO	T120-T170		8		4325			5550	6600
23	4	EXPLORER 7952L	HT	FSH	FBG	SV	IO	120-260		8		4325			5000	6150
23	4	EXPLORER 7952L	HT	FSH	FBG	SV	IO	T120-T170		8		4325			5550	6600
23	4	EXPLORER 7952L	FB	FSH	FBG	SV	IO	120-260		8		4325			5000	6150
23	4	EXPLORER 7952L	FB	FSH	FBG	SV	IO	T120-T170		8		4325			5550	6600
23	4	OFFSHORE 7952	OP	OFF	FBG	SV	IO	120-260		8		4225			4650	5750
23	4	OFFSHORE 7952	OP	OFF	FBG	SV	IO	T120-T170		8		4225			5150	6150
23	4	OFFSHORE 7952	HT	OFF	FBG	SV	IO	120-260		8		4225			4650	5750
23	4	OFFSHORE 7952	HT	OFF	FBG	SV	IO	T120-T170		8		4225			5150	6150
23	4	OFFSHORE 7952	FB	OFF	FBG	SV	IO	120-260		8		4225			4650	5750
23	4	OFFSHORE 7952	FB	OFF	FBG	SV	IO	T120-T170		8		4225			5150	6150
23	4	WEEKENDER 252	HT	WKNDR	FBG	SV	IO	120-260		8		4400			4800	5900
23	4	WEEKENDER 252	HT	WKNDR	FBG	SV	IO	T120-T170		8		4400			5300	6350
23	7	FAMILY EXPRESS 246	OP	EXP	FBG	DV	IO	185-260		8		4200			4700	5750
23	7	FAMILY EXPRESS 246	OP	EXP	FBG	DV	IO	130D	VLVO	8		4200			5650	6500
23	7	FAMILY EXPRESS 246	HT	EXP	FBG	DV	IO	185-260		8		4200			4700	5750
23	7	FAMILY EXPRESS 246	HT	EXP	FBG	DV	IO	130D	VLVO	8		4200			5650	6500
23	7	FAMILY FLYBRIDGE 247	FB	EXP	FBG	DV	IO	185-260		8		4200			4700	5750
23	7	FAMILY FLYBRIDGE 247	FB	EXP	FBG	DV	IO	130D	VLVO	8		4200			5650	6500
28	2	EXPRESS 286	HT	EXP	FBG	DV	IO	260		10	4	9200			10400	11800
		IO T165-T200 10800 12500, VD T215-T225 12200 14100, IO T228-T240													11300	12900
		VD T250-T255 12600 14300, IO T260 11600 13100														
28	2	FAMILY FLYBRIDGE 287	FB	EXP	FBG	DV	IO	260		10	4	9200			10400	11800
		IO T165-T200 10800 12500, VD T215-T225 12200 14100, IO T228 MRCR													11300	12800
		VD T228 MRCR 12300 14000, IO T230-T240 11300 12900, VD T250-T255													12600	14300
		IO T260 11600 13100														
31	3	EXPRESS 310	FB	EXP	FBG	DV	IB	T215-T255		11	2	10300			16500	19300
		1978 BOATS														
17	6	SEA-FARER 184	OP	RNBT	FBG	DV	OB			7		1094			3050	3550
17	6	SEA-FARER 184	OP	RNBT	FBG	DV	IO	120		7		2300			1950	2300
17	6	SEA-FARER 184	OP	RNBT	FBG	DV	IO	130-170		7		2300			2050	2450
17	6	SEA-LANCER 184	OP	RNBT	FBG	DV	OB			7		1094			3550	4100
17	6	SEA-LANCER 184	OP	RNBT	FBG	DV	IO	120-170		7		2300			2150	2650
17	6	SEA-RAIDER 180	OP	RNBT	FBG	DV	OB			7		1073			3000	3500
17	6	SEA-RAIDER 180	OP	RNBT	FBG	DV	IO	120		7		2200			1900	2250
17	6	SEA-RAIDER 180	OP	RNBT	FBG	DV	IO	130-170		7		2200			2000	2400
17	6	SEA-RANGER 180	OP	RNBT	FBG	DV	OB			7		1073			3500	4050
17	6	SEA-RANGER 180	OP	RNBT	FBG	DV	IO	120		7		2200			2050	2450
17	6	SEA-RANGER 180	OP	RNBT	FBG	DV	IO	130-170		7		2200			2200	2600
17	8	SIDEWINDER 18SS	OP	SKI	FBG	DV	OB			7		1075			3200	3750
17	8	SIDEWINDER 18SS	OP	SKI	FBG	DV	IO	170-228		7		1900			1800	2200
17	8	SIDEWINDER 18SS	OP	SKI	FBG	DV	JT	320	FORD	7		1900			2350	2750
18	2	CATALINA 190	OP	RNBT	FBG	DV	OB			7	4	1489			4250	4950
18	2	CATALINA 190	OP	RNBT	FBG	DV	IO	120-198		7	4	2300			2050	2600
18	2	CATALINA 190	OP	RNBT	FBG	DV	IO	200-260		7	4	2300			2300	2800
18	2	LAGUNA 190	OP	RNBT	FBG	DV	OB			7	4	1498			4250	4950
18	2	LAGUNA 190	OP	RNBT	FBG	DV	IO	120-200		7	4	2300			2300	2800
18	2	LAGUNA 190	OP	RNBT	FBG	DV	IO	225-240		7	4	2300			2350	2850
18	2	LAGUNA 190	OP	RNBT	FBG	DV	IO	255-260		7	4	2300			2600	3000
20	4	FISHERMAN 222	OP	FSH	FBG	DV	IO	170-240		8		3125			3400	4200
20	4	FISHERMAN 222	OP	FSH	FBG	DV	IO	255-260		8		3125			3700	4300
20	4	FISHERMAN II 232	OP	FSH	FBG	DV	IO	170-240		8		3250			3350	4100
20	4	FISHERMAN II 232	OP	FSH	FBG	DV	IO	255-260		8		3250			3650	4250
20	4	FISHERMAN II 232	HT	FSH	FBG	DV	IO	170-240		8		3375			3450	4250
20	4	FISHERMAN II 232	HT	FSH	FBG	DV	IO	255-260		8		3375			3750	4400
20	4	FISHERMAN II 232L	OP	FSH	FBG	DV	IO	170-240		8		3250			3600	4450
20	4	FISHERMAN II 232L	OP	FSH	FBG	DV	IO	255-260		8		3250			3950	4600
20	4	FISHERMAN II 232L	HT	FSH	FBG	DV	IO	170-198		8		3375			3700	4300
20	4	FISHERMAN II 232L	HT	FSH	FBG	DV	IO	200-260		8		3375			3950	4650
20	4	HERITAGE 229	OP	CUD	FBG	DV	IO	170-240		8		3300			3300	4100
20	4	HERITAGE 229	OP	CUD	FBG	DV	IO	255-260		8		3300			3650	4200
20	4	SPORTSMAN 232	OP	CUD	FBG	DV	IO	170-240		8		3250			3300	4050
20	4	SPORTSMAN 232	OP	CUD	FBG	DV	IO	255-260		8		3250			3600	4200
20	4	SPORTSMAN 232	HT	CUD	FBG	DV	IO	170-240		8		3375			3350	4150
20	4	SPORTSMAN 232	HT	CUD	FBG	DV	IO	255-260		8		3375			3700	4300
20	4	VACATIONER 232	OP	CR	FBG	DV	IO	170-240		8		3375			3350	4150
20	4	VACATIONER 232	OP	CR	FBG	DV	IO	255-260		8		3375			3700	4300
20	4	VACATIONER 232	HT	CR	FBG	DV	IO	170-240		8		3500			3450	4250
20	4	VACATIONER 232	HT	CR	FBG	DV	IO	255-260		8		3500			3750	4400
23	4	ADVENTURER 252	OP	CR	FBG	DV	IO	170-260		8		4325			4800	5850
23	4	ADVENTURER 252	OP	CR	FBG	DV	IO	T120-T170		8		4325			5300	6350
23	4	ADVENTURER 252	HT	CR	FBG	DV	IO	170-260		8		4400			4850	5900
23	4	ADVENTURER 252	HT	CR	FBG	DV	IO	T120-T170		8		4400			5350	6400
23	4	ADVENTURER 252	FB	CR	FBG	DV	IO	170-260		8		5850			6150	7400
23	4	ADVENTURER 252	FB	CR	FBG	DV	IO	T120-T170		8		5850			6650	7900
23	4	EXPLORER 252	OP	CUD	FBG	DV	IO	170-260		8		4325			4800	5850
23	4	EXPLORER 252	OP	CUD	FBG	DV	IO	T120-T170		8		4325			5300	6350
23	4	EXPLORER 252	HT	CUD	FBG	DV	IO	170-260		8		4400			4700	5750
23	4	EXPLORER 252	HT	CUD	FBG	DV	IO	T120-T170		8		4400			5200	6200
23	4	EXPLORER 252	FB	CUD	FBG	DV	IO	170-260		8		5850			5950	7200
23	4	EXPLORER 252	FB	CUD	FBG	DV	IO	T120-T170		8		5850			6450	7700
23	4	EXPLORER 252 BULKHD	HT	CUD	FBG	DV	IO	170-260		8		4400			5000	6100
23	4	EXPLORER 252 BULKHD	HT	CUD	FBG	DV	IO	T120-T170		8		4400			5500	6600
23	4	EXPLORER 252 BULKHD	FB	CUD	FBG	DV	IO	170-260		8		5850			6300	7600
23	4	EXPLORER 252 BULKHD	FB	CUD	FBG	DV	IO	T120-T170		8		5850			6800	8050
23	4	OVERNIGHTER 257	OP	OVNTR	FBG	DV	IO	170-260		8		4300			4750	5800
23	4	OVERNIGHTER 257	OP	OVNTR	FBG	DV	IO	T120-T170		8		4300			5250	6300
23	4	VOYAGER 259	OP	CR	FBG	DV	IO	170-260		8		4625			5050	6150
23	4	VOYAGER 259	OP	CR	FBG	DV	IO	T120-T170		8		4625			5550	6650
23	4	WEEKENDER 252	OP	WKNDR	FBG	DV	IO	170-260		8		4325			4800	5850
23	4	WEEKENDER 252	OP	WKNDR	FBG	DV	IO	T120-T170		8		4325			5300	6350
23	4	WEEKENDER 252	HT	WKNDR	FBG	DV	IO	170-260		8		4400			4700	5750
23	4	WEEKENDER 252	HT	WKNDR	FBG	DV	IO	T120-T170		8		4400			5200	6200
23	4	WEEKENDER 252	FB	WKNDR	FBG	DV	IO	170-260		8		5850			6000	7250
23	4	WEEKENDER 252	FB	WKNDR	FBG	DV	IO	T120-T170		8		5850			6500	7700
23	4	WEEKENDER 252 BULKHD	HT	WKNDR	FBG	DV	IO	170-260		8		4400			5000	6100
23	4	WEEKENDER 252 BULKHD	HT	WKNDR	FBG	DV	IO	T120-T170		8		4400			5500	6600
23	4	WEEKENDER 252 BULKHD	FB	WKNDR	FBG	DV	IO	170-260		8		5850			6300	7600
23	4	WEEKENDER 252 BULKHD	FB	WKNDR	FBG	DV	IO	T120-T170		8		5850			6850	8100
23	4	WEEKENDER SEDAN 252	HT	SDN	FBG	DV	IO	170-260		8		4400			4850	5900
23	4	WEEKENDER SEDAN 252	HT	SDN	FBG	DV	IO	T120-T170		8		4400			5350	6400
23	4	WEEKENDER SEDAN 252	FB	SDN	FBG	DV	IO	170-260		8		5850			6150	7400
23	4	WEEKENDER SEDAN 252	FB	SDN	FBG	DV	IO	T120-T170		8		5850			6650	7900
		1977 BOATS														
17	6	SEA-FARER 7784	OP	RNBT	FBG	DV	OB			7		1150			3450	4050
17	6	SEA-FARER 7784	OP	RNBT	FBG	DV	IO	120-170		7		1700			1750	2200
17	6	SEA-FARER 7784	OP	RNBT	FBG	DV	JT	240	MARI	7		1700			2200	2600
17	6	SEA-LANCER 184	OP	RNBT	FBG	DV	OB			7					3800	4450
17	6	SEA-LANCER 184	OP	RNBT	FBG	DV	IO	120		7		1700			1900	2250
17	6	SEA-LANCER 184	OP	RNBT	FBG	DV	IO	130-170		7		1700			2000	2350
17	6	SEA-LANCER 184	OP	RNBT	FBG	DV	JT	240	MARI	7		1700			2350	2750
17	6	SEA-RAIDER 7780	OP	RNBT	FBG	DV	OB			7		1150			3300	3850
17	6	SEA-RAIDER 7780	OP	RNBT	FBG	DV	IO	120-170		7		1700			1700	2150
17	6	SEA-RAIDER 7780	OP	RNBT	FBG	DV	JT	240	MARI	7		1700			2200	2550
17	6	SEA-RANGER 180	OP	RNBT	FBG	DV	OB			7					3650	4250
17	6	SEA-RANGER 180	OP	RNBT	FBG	DV	IO	120		7		1700			1850	2200
17	6	SEA-RANGER 180	OP	RNBT	FBG	DV	IO	130-170		7		1700			1950	2300
17	6	SEA-RANGER 180	OP	RNBT	FBG	DV	JT	240	MARI	7		1700			2350	2700
17	8	SIDEWINDER 18SS	OP	SKI	FBG	DV	OB			6	5	950			2850	3300
17	8	SIDEWINDER 18SS	OP	SKI	FBG	DV	IO	188-233		6	5	1900			1750	2150
17	8	SIDEWINDER 18SS	OP	SKI	FBG	DV	JT	240-320		6	5	1900			2200	2550
17	11	DEL-RAY 190T	OP	RNBT	FBG	TR	IO	120	OMC	7		2300			2100	2500
17	11	DEL-RAY 190T	OP	RNBT	FBG	TR	IO	130-240		7		2300			2250	2750
17	11	DEL-RAY 190T	OP	RNBT	FBG	TR	JT	320	FORD	7		2300			2600	3000
18	2	CATALINA 7790	OP	RNBT	FBG	DV	OB			7	4	1500			4200	4900
18	2	CATALINA 7790	OP	RNBT	FBG	DV	IO	120-235		7	4	2500			2300	2750
18	2	CATALINA 7790	OP	RNBT	FBG	DV	IO	240	VLVO	7	4	2500			2500	2900
18	2	CATALINA 7790	OP	RNBT	FBG	DV	JT	320	FORD	7	4	2500			2700	3150
18	2	LAGUNA 190V	OP	RNBT	FBG	DV	OB			7	4				3800	4400
18	2	LAGUNA 190V	OP	RNBT	FBG	DV	IO	120	OMC	7	4	2500			2350	2700
18	2	LAGUNA 190V	OP	RNBT	FBG	DV	IO	130-240		7	4	2500			2500	3100
18	2	LAGUNA 190V	OP	RNBT	FBG	DV	JT	320	FORD	7	4	2500			2900	3350
20	4	7722	OP	FSH	FBG	SV	OB			8					7400	8500
20	4	7722	OP	FSH	FBG	SV	IO	165-235		8		3000			3350	4050
20	4	7722	OP	FSH	FBG	SV	IO	240-255		8		3000			3600	4300
20	4	7722	OP	FSH	FBG	SV	JT	320	FORD	8		3000			3450	4000
20	4	7732 HT	HT	FSH	FBG	SV	IO	165-235		8		3250			3550	4250
20	4	7732 HT	HT	FSH	FBG	SV	IO	240-255		8		3250			3800	4500
20	4	7732 HT	HT	FSH	FBG	SV	JT	320	FORD	8		3250			3600	4200
20	4	7732/7732L	OP	FSH	FBG	SV	IO	165-235		8		3250			3550	4250
20	4	7732/7732L	OP	FSH	FBG	SV	IO	240-255		8		3250			3800	4500
20	4	7732/7732L	OP	FSH	FBG	SV	JT	320	FORD	8		3250			3600	4200
20	4	EXECUTIVE 222	OP	RNBT	FBG	SV	IO	165-235		8		3100			3100	3750
20	4	EXECUTIVE 222	OP	RNBT	FBG	SV	IO	240-255		8		3100			3350	3950

CONTINUED ON NEXT PAGE

```
 LOA  NAME AND/           TOP/ BOAT -HULL----ENGINE----  BEAM  WGT DRAFT RETAIL RETAIL
FT IN OR MODEL            RIG  TYPE MTL TP TP # HP  MFG   FT IN LBS FT IN  LOW   HIGH
--------------------- 1977 BOATS ----------------------------------------------------
20  4 EXECUTIVE 222    OP RNBT  FBG SV JT 320   FORD  8  3100       3600 4150
20  4 HERITAGE 229     OP CUD   FBG SV IO 165-235     8  3300       3400 4100
20  4 HERITAGE 229     OP CUD   FBG SV IO 240-255     8  3300       3650 4300
20  4 HERITAGE 229     OP CUD   FBG SV JT 320   FORD  8  3300       3650 4250
20  4 SPORTSMAN 232    OP CUD   FBG SV IO 165-235     8  3250       3350 4050
20  4 SPORTSMAN 232    OP CUD   FBG SV IO 240-255     8  3250       3600 4250
20  4 SPORTSMAN 232    OP CUD   FBG SV JT 320   FORD  8  3250       3600 4200
20  4 SPORTSMAN 232    HT CUD   FBG SV IO 165-235     8  3250       3350 4050
20  4 SPORTSMAN 232    HT CUD   FBG SV IO 240-255     8  3250       3600 4250
20  4 SPORTSMAN 232    HT CUD   FBG SV JT 320   FORD  8  3250       3600 4200
20  4 VACATIONER 233   OP CR    FBG SV IO 165-235     8  3350       3400 4150
20  4 VACATIONER 233   OP CR    FBG SV IO 240-255     8  3350       3650 4350

20  4 VACATIONER 233   OP CR    FBG SV JT 320   FORD  8  3350       3700 4300
20  4 VACATIONER 233   HT CR    FBG SV IO 165-235     8  3350       3400 4150
20  4 VACATIONER 233   HT CR    FBG SV IO 240-255     8  3350       3650 4350
20  4 VACATIONER 233   HT CR    FBG SV JT 320   FORD  8  3350       3700 4300
23  4 ADVENTURER 253   OP CR    FBG SV IO 170-255     8  3900       4500 5500
23  4 ADVENTURER 253   OP CR    FBG SV IO T120-T170   8  3900       5000 6000
23  4 ADVENTURER 253   HT CR    FBG SV IO 170-255     8  3900       4500 5500
23  4 ADVENTURER 253   HT CR    FBG SV IO T120-T170   8  3900       5000 6000
23  4 EXPLORER 7752    OP CUD   FBG SV IO 170-255     8  3800       4450 5400
23  4 EXPLORER 7752    OP CUD   FBG SV IO T120-T170   8  3800       4900 5900
23  4 EXPLORER 7752    HT CUD   FBG SV IO 170-255     8  3800       4450 5400
23  4 EXPLORER 7752    HT CUD   FBG SV IO T120-T170   8  3800       4900 5900

23  4 OVERNIGHTER 7757 OP OVNTR FBG SV IO 170-255     8  3800       4450 5400
23  4 OVERNIGHTER 7757 OP OVNTR FBG SV IO T120-T170   8  3800       4900 5900
23  4 OVERNIGHTER 7757 HT OVNTR FBG SV IO 170-255     8  3800       4450 5400
23  4 OVERNIGHTER 7757 HT OVNTR FBG SV IO T120-T170   8  3800       4900 5900
23  4 VOYAGER 259      FB CR    FBG SV IO 170-255     8  4490       5000 6100
23  4 VOYAGER 259      FB CR    FBG SV IO T120-T170   8  4490       5500 6600
23  4 WEEKENDER 252    OP WKNDR FBG SV IO 170-255     8  3800       4450 5400
23  4 WEEKENDER 252    OP WKNDR FBG SV IO T120-T170   8  3800       4900 5900
23  4 WEEKENDER 252    HT WKNDR FBG SV IO 170-255     8  3800       4450 5900
23  4 WEEKENDER 252    HT WKNDR FBG SV IO T120-T170   8  3800       4900 5900
--------------------- 1976 BOATS ----------------------------------------------------
16  6 SEA-DART 160T    OP RNBT  FBG TR IO 130   VLVO  6 4 1700 3 3  1750 2050
17  6 FUN-BIRD 7683    OP RNBT  FBG DV OB            7   1050       2750 3200
17  6 FUN-BIRD 7683    OP RNBT  FBG DV IO 130   VLVO 7   1050       1700 2050
17  6 FUN-BIRD 7683    OP RNBT  FBG DV IO 245   MRCR 7   1050       1900 2300
17  6 SEA-FARER 7684   OP RNBT  FBG DV IO 130-165     7  1600 3 2   1700 2000
17  6 SEA-FARER 7684   OP RNBT  FBG DV JT 245   OMC  7   1600 3 2   1800 2150
17  6 SEA-LANCER 184   OP RNBT  FBG DV IO 120        7   1600 3 2   1900 2250
17  6 SEA-LANCER 184   OP RNBT  FBG DV IO 130-165     7  1600 3 2   2000 2400
17  6 SEA-LANCER 184   OP RNBT  FBG DV JT 245   OMC  7   1600 3 2   2250 2600
17  6 SEA-RANGER 180   OP RNBT  FBG DV OB            7   1050 3 2   3450 4000

17  6 SEA-RANGER 180   OP RNBT  FBG DV IO 120        7   1600 3 2   1800 2150
17  6 SEA-RANGER 180   OP RNBT  FBG DV IO 130-165     7  1600 3 2   1900 2300
17  6 SEA-RANGER 180   OP RNBT  FBG DV JT 245   OMC  7   1600 3 2   2150 2500
17 11 DEL-RAY 190T     OP RNBT  FBG TR IO 130-190     7  2300 3 6   2300 2700
17 11 DEL-RAY 190T     OP RNBT  FBG TR JT 245-455     7  2300 3 6   2500 2900
18  2 CATALINA 7690    OP RNBT  FBG DV IO 130-190     7 4 2500 3 9  2350 2750
18  2 CATALINA 7690    OP RNBT  FBG DV JT 245-455     7 4 2500 3 9  2550 2950
18  2 LAGUNA 190V      OP RNBT  FBG DV IO 130-190     7 4 2500 3 9  2650 3050
18  2 LAGUNA 190V      OP RNBT  FBG DV JT 245-455     7 4 2500 3 9  2850 3300
20  4 EXECUTIVE 222    OP RNBT  FBG SV IO 165-235     8  2900 4 9   3050 3700
20  4 EXECUTIVE 222    OP RNBT  FBG SV JT 290-455     8  2900 4 9   3300 3850

20  4 EXECUTIVE 222    HT RNBT  FBG SV IO 165-235     8  2900 4 9   3050 3700
20  4 EXECUTIVE 222    HT RNBT  FBG SV JT 290-455     8  2900 4 9   3300 3850
20  4 FISHERMAN 7622   OP SF    FBG SV IO 165-235     8  2900 4 9   3650 4400
20  4 FISHERMAN 7622   OP SF    FBG SV JT 290-455     8  2900 4 9   3250 3800
20  4 FISHERMAN 7622   HT SF    FBG SV IO 165-235     8  2900 4 9   3650 4400
20  4 FISHERMAN 7622   HT SF    FBG SV JT 290-455     8  2900 4 9   3250 3800
20  4 HERITAGE 229     OP CR    FBG SV IO 165-235     8  3050 4 9   3300 3950
20  4 HERITAGE 229     OP CR    FBG SV JT 290-455     8  3050 4 9   3350 3900
20  4 SPORTSMAN 222    OP CUD   FBG SV IO 165-235     8  2900 4 9   3200 3850
20  4 SPORTSMAN 222    OP CUD   FBG SV JT 290-455     8  2900 4 9   3250 3800
20  4 SPORTSMAN 222    HT CUD   FBG SV IO 165-235     8  2900 4 9   3200 3850
20  4 SPORTSMAN 222    HT CUD   FBG SV JT 290-455     8  2900 4 9   3250 3800

21    DAY-CRUISER      OP SKI   FBG SV IO 188-233    7 11 2700       3000 3550
21    DAY-CRUISER      OP SKI   FBG SV IO 454-455    7 11 2700       3250 3750
23  4 ADVENTURER 257   OP CR    FBG SV IO 120-235     8  3900 5 4   4600 5400
23  4 ADVENTURER 257   HT CR    FBG SV IO 120-235     8  3900 5 4   4600 5400
23  4 OVERNIGHTER 7657 OP CUD   FBG SV IO 120-235     8  3700 5 4   4450 5250
23  4 OVERNIGHTER 7657 HT CUD   FBG SV IO 120-235     8  3700 5 4   4450 5250
23  4 VOYAGER 259      OP CR    FBG SV IO 120-235     8  4490       5100 6000
--------------------- 1975 BOATS ----------------------------------------------------
17  6 FUN-BIRD 7583    OP RNBT  FBG DV OB            7   1050       2950 3450
17  6 FUN-BIRD 7583    OP RNBT  FBG DV IB 140-165     7  1650       1700 2100
17  6 FUN-BIRD 7583    OP RNBT  FBG DV IB 175   OMC  7   1650       1800 2150
17  6 FUN-BIRD 7583    OP RNBT  FBG DV JT 245-290     7  1650       2000 2400
17  6 SEA-LANCER 183   OP RNBT  FBG DV IO 120-175     7  1650       1850 2250
17  6 SEA-LANCER 183   OP RNBT  FBG DV JT 245-290     7  1650       2100 2500
17  6 SEA-RANGER 180   OP RNBT  FBG DV OB            7   1050       3250 3800
17  6 SEA-RANGER 180   OP RNBT  FBG DV IB 140-165     7  1650       1700 2150
17  6 SEA-RANGER 180   OP RNBT  FBG DV IB 175   OMC  7   1650       1850 2200
17  6 SEA-RANGER 180   OP RNBT  FBG DV JT 245-290     7  1650       2050 2400
17  6 TRI-GULL 7585    OP RNBT  FBG TR OB            7   1050       2950 3450

17  6 TRI-GULL 7585    OP RNBT  FBG TR IB 140-165     7  1650       1700 2100
17  6 TRI-GULL 7585    OP RNBT  FBG TR IB 175   OMC  7   1650       1800 2150
17  6 TRI-GULL 7585    OP RNBT  FBG TR JT 245-290     7  1650       2000 2400
17 11 DEL-RAY 190T     OP RNBT  FBG TR IO 120-190     7  2300       2200 2700
17 11 DEL-RAY 190T     OP RNBT  FBG TR JT 245-390     7  2300       2400 2800
18  2 LAGUNA 190V      OP RNBT  FBG DV IO 120-190     7  2300       2300 2750
18  2 LAGUNA 190V      OP RNBT  FBG DV JT 245-390     7  2300       2400 2800
20  4 FISHERMAN 7522   OP SF    FBG SV IO 165-235     8  3000       3850 4600
20  4 FISHERMAN 7522   OP SF    FBG SV JT 290-390     8  3000       3200 3700
20  4 HERITAGE 229     OP CR    FBG SV IO 165-235     8  3150       3450 4150
20  4 HERITAGE 229     OP CR    FBG SV JT 290-390     8  3150       3300 3800

20  4 SPORTSMAN 222    OP CUD   FBG SV IO 165-235     8  3000       3350 4050
20  4 SPORTSMAN 222    OP CUD   FBG SV IO 290   OMC  8   3000       3700 4300
20  4 SPORTSMAN 222    OP CUD   FBG SV JT 390   OLDS 8   3000       3200 3700
23  4 ADVENTURER 257   HT CR    FBG SV IO 188-255     8  3950       4800 5700
23  4 ADVENTURER 257   HT CR    FBG SV IO T120-T140   8  3950       5350 6150
23  4 OVERNIGHTER 7557 OP CUD   FBG SV IO 188-255     8  3700       5100 5900
23  4 OVERNIGHTER 7557 OP CUD   FBG SV IO T120-T140   8  3700       5450 6300
23  4 VOYAGER 259      OP CR    FBG SV IO 188-255     8  4500       5350 6300
23  4 VOYAGER 259      OP CR    FBG SV IO T120-T140   8  4500       5850 6750
--------------------- 1974 BOATS ----------------------------------------------------
17  6 FUN-BIRD 7483             FBG    OB             7  1600       3550 4150
17  6 FUN-BIRD 7483             FBG    OB             7  1050       1700 2000
17  6 SEA-LANCER 183            FBG    IO 120   OMC   7  1050       3000 3450
17  6 SEA-LANCER 183            FBG    IO 120-165     7  1600       1900 2300
      JT  185  WAUK 1850  2150, IO 185 WAUK 1900 2250, JT 245 OMC 1850 2200

17  6 SEA-LANE 185              FBG    OB             7  1050       3000 3450
17  6 SEA-LANE 185              FBG    IO 120-165     7  1600       1900 2300
      JT  185  WAUK 1850  2150, IO 185 WAUK 1900 2250, JT 245 OMC 1850 2200

17  6 SEA-RANGER 180            FBG    OB             7  1050       3000 3450
17  6 SEA-RANGER 180            FBG    IO 120-165     7  1600       1850 2200
      JT  185  WAUK 1800  2100, IO 185 WAUK 1850 2200, JT 245 OMC 1800 2150

17  6 TRI-GULL 7485             FBG    OB             7  1600       3550 4150
17  6 TRI-GULL 7485             FBG    IO 120   OMC   7  1700       1700 2000
20  4 7422                      FSH    IO 165   OMC   7  2900       2000 4150
20  4 HERITAGE 229              FBG    IO 165        8   3050       3350 3900
      JT  185  WAUK 3050  3550, IO 185-225  3350 3950, JT 245 OMC 3100 3600
      IO  245  OMC  3450  4000, JT 255 WAUK 3100 3600, IO 255 WAUK 3500 4100
      JT  330  BERK 3100  3600

20  4 SPORTSMAN 222             FBG    IO 165        8   2900       3250 3750
      JT  185  WAUK 2950  3450, IO 185-225  3250 3850, JT 245 OMC 3000 3500
      IO  245  OMC  3350  3900, JT 255 WAUK 3000 3500, IO 255 WAUK 3400 3950
      JT  330  BERK 3000  3500

23  4 257               OVNTR   FBG    IO 165-255     8  3700       4750 5650
23  4 257               OVNTR   FBG    IO T120-T140   8  3700       5300 6100
23  4 VOYAGER 259               FBG    IO 165-255     8  4500       5200 6200
23  4 VOYAGER 259               FBG    IO T120-T140   8  4500       5750 6600
--------------------- 1973 BOATS ----------------------------------------------------
16  6 SEA-SKIFF 173             FBG    OB             7 2 1100      2950 3450
17  6 SEA-LANCER 183            FBG    OB             7  1050       3000 3500
17  6 SEA-LANCER 183            FBG    IO 120-165     7  1600       1900 2300
17  6 SEA-LANCER 183            FBG    JT 245   OMC   7  1600       1800 2150
17  6 SEA-LANE 185              FBG    OB             7  1050       3000 3500
17  6 SEA-LANE 185              FBG    IO 120-165     7  1600       1900 2300
17  6 SEA-LANE 185              FBG    JT 245   OMC   7  1600       1800 2150
17  6 SEA-RANGER 180            FBG    OB             7  1050       2900 3400
```

LOA FT	LOA IN	NAME AND/ OR MODEL	TOP/ RIG	BOAT TYPE	-HULL- MTL	-HULL- TP	ENGINE TP	ENGINE # HP	ENGINE MFG	BEAM FT	BEAM IN	WGT LBS	DRAFT FT IN	RETAIL LOW	RETAIL HIGH
		1973 BOATS													
17	6	SEA-RANGER 180			FBG		IO	120-165		7		1600		1850	2250
17	6	SEA-RANGER 180			FBG		JT	245	OMC	7		1600		1750	2100
20	4	FISHERMAN	OP	SF	FBG	SV	IO	165		8		3000		4100	4750
20	4	HERITAGE 229			FBG		IO	120-225		8		3050		3450	4100
		JT 245 OMC 2950 3450, IO 245 OMC 3550 4150, JT 390 BERK												2950	3450
20	4	SPORTSMAN 222			FBG		IO	120-225		8		2900		3350	3950
		JT 245 OMC 2900 3350, IO 245 OMC 3450 4050, JT 390 BERK												2900	3350
23	4	249		EXP	FBG		IO	188-225		8		3700		4900	5700
23	4	249		EXP	FBG		IO	T120-T140		8		3700		5450	6300
23	4	VOYAGER 259			FBG		IO	188-255		8		4500		5400	6400
23	4	VOYAGER 259			FBG		IO	T120-T140		8		4500		5950	6850
		1972 BOATS													
16		SEA-COASTER 160			FBG		OB			6	4	875		2450	2850
16		SEA-SKIFF 173			FBG		OB			7	2	1100		2950	3450
16		SEA-SKIFF 173			FBG		IO	120-140		7	2	1650		1800	2150
17	6	SEA-LANCER 183			FBG		OB			7		1050		3050	3500
17	6	SEA-LANCER 183			FBG		IO	120-170		7		1600		2000	2400
17	6	SEA-LANE 185			FBG		OB			7		1150		3200	3700
17	6	SEA-LANE 185			FBG		IO	120-170		7		1700		2000	2400
17	6	SEA-RANGER 180			FBG		OB			7		1050		2850	3350
17	6	SEA-RANGER 180			FBG		IO	120-170		7		1600		1900	2300
20	4	OFFSHORE 225		EXP	FBG		IO	120-225		8		2900		3600	4300
20	4	OFFSHORE 225		EXP	FBG		JT	270	BERK	8		2900		2800	3250
20	4	OFFSHORE 229		CR	FBG		IO	120-225		8		3050		3750	4450
20	4	OFFSHORE 229		CR	FBG		JT	270	BERK	8		3050		2850	3300
23	4	249		EXP	FBG		IO	188-225		8		3700		5050	5900
		1971 BOATS													
16		SANDPIPER			FBG		OB			6	2	875		2450	2850
16		SKI-BIRD		SKI	FBG		OB			7	2	1100		2950	3400
16		SKI-BIRD		SKI	FBG		IO	120-165		7	2	1650		1800	2200
17	6	FUN-BIRD			FBG		OB			7		1050		3000	3500
17	6	FUN-BIRD			FBG		IO	120-165		7		1600		2050	2450
17	6	SURF-BIRD			FBG		OB			7		1050		2900	3350
17	6	SURF-BIRD			FBG		IO	120-165		7		1600		1950	2400
17	6	TRI-GULL			FBG		OB			7		1150		3150	3700
17	6	TRI-GULL			FBG		IO	120-165		7		1700		2050	2500
20	4	BRANT			FBG		IO	155-215		8		2900		3550	4250
20	4	MALLARD			FBG		IO	155-215		8		3050		3650	4350
23	4	ALBATROSS			FBG		IO	215		8		3700		5000	5750
23	4	ALBATROSS			FBG		IO	325	MRCR	8		3700		5650	6500
		1970 BOATS													
16		SANDPIPER GV160		RNBT	FBG	DV	OB			6	4	875		2500	2900
16		SKI-BIRD GV173		SKI	FBG	DV	OB			7	2	1100		2950	3400
16		SKI-BIRD GV173		SKI	FBG	DV	IO	120		7	2	1650		1900	2250
16		SUN-BIRD GV170		RNBT	FBG	DV	OB			7	2	950		2650	3050
16		SUN-BIRD GV170		RNBT	FBG	DV	IO	120		7	2	1500		1950	2300
16	7	THOMBOY			WD	RB	OB			6	8	950		2650	3050
16	7	THOMBOY			WD	RB	IO	80		6	8	1350		1750	2050
17	6	SURF-BIRD GV180		RNBT	FBG	DV	OB			7		1050		3000	3450
17	6	SURF-BIRD GV180		RNBT	FBG	DV	IO	120		7		1600		2250	2600
17	6	TRI-GULL GC185		RNBT	FBG	TR	OB			7		1150		3200	3750
17	6	TRI-GULL GC185		RNBT	FBG	TR	IO	120		7		1700		2300	2650
17	11	SEA-LANCER 1850			WD	RB	OB			7	1	1050		3000	3450
17	11	SEA-LANCER 1850			WD	RB	IO	120		7	1	1600		2250	2600
20	1	OFFSHORE 2050		OFF	WD	RB	OB			8		1400		4300	5000
20	1	OFFSHORE 2050		OFF	WD	RB	IO	120		8		2000		3200	3700
20	1	OFFSHORE 2060		CAMPR	WD	RB	OB			8		1450		4450	5150
20	1	OFFSHORE 2060		CAMPR	WD	RB	IO	120		8		2000		3200	3700
20	4	BRANT GV215		RNBT	FBG	DV	IO	155-160		8		2900		3700	4300
20	4	CANVAS BACK GV216			FBG	DV	IO	155-160		8		3000		3750	4400
20	4	MALLARD GV219			FBG	DV	IO	155-160		8		3050		3800	4450
21		SUP OFFSHORE V-2150		CR	WD	DV	IO	120		8		2400		3600	4200
21		SUP OFFSHORE V-2160		CR	WD	DV	IO	120		8		2600		3750	4400
23	4	ALBATROSS GV249		OVNTR	FBG	DV	IO	210-215		8		3700		5400	6250
23	4	ALBATROSS GV249		OVNTR	FBG	DV	IO	135D	PERK	8		4000		7550	8700
23	9	SEA-LANE V2460		CAMPR	WD	DV	IO	155-160		8		3400		5150	5950
		1969 BOATS													
16		SANDPIPER GV160		RNBT	FBG	DV	OB			6	4	875		2500	2900
16		SANDPIPER GV160		RNBT	FBG	DV	IO	80		6	4	1300		1750	2050
16		SUN-BIRD GV170		SKI	FBG	DV	OB			7	2	950		2600	3000
16		SUN-BIRD GV170		SKI	FBG	DV	IO	120		7	2	1500		1850	2200
16	7	THOMBOY 1777		RNBT	WD	RB	OB			6	8	950		2700	3150
16	7	THOMBOY 1777		RNBT	WD	RB	IO	80		6	8	1350		1900	2250
17	6	SURF-BIRD GV180		RNBT	FBG	DV	OB			7		1050		3000	3500
17	6	SURF-BIRD GV180		RNBT	FBG	DV	IO	120	MRCR	7		1600		2300	2700
17	6	SURF-BIRD GV180		RNBT	FBG	DV	IO	120	OMC	7				2600	3050
17	6	TRI-GULL GC185		RNBT	FBG	TR	OB			7		1150		3200	3750
17	6	TRI-GULL GC185		RNBT	FBG	TR	IO	120		7		1700		2350	2700
17	11	SEA-LANCER 1850		RNBT	WD	RB	OB			7	1	1050		3050	3550
17	11	SEA-LANCER 1850		RNBT	WD	RB	IO	120		7	1	1600		2350	2750
20	1	OFFSHORE 2050		CAMPR	WD	RB	OB			8		1450		4450	5150
20	1	OFFSHORE 2050		CAMPR	WD	RB	IO	120		8		2000		3300	3800
20	1	OFFSHORE 2050		OFF	WD	RB	OB			8		1400		4300	5000
20	1	OFFSHORE 2050		OFF	WD	RB	IO	120		8		2000		3300	3800
20	4	BRANT GV205		RNBT	FBG	DV	IO	120		8		2800		3750	4350
20	4	CANVAS BACK GV206		CAMPR	FBG	DV	IO	120		8		2900		4000	4650
20	4	MALLARD GV209		OVNTR	FBG	DV	IO	120		8		2950		4050	4700
21		SUP OFFSHORE V-2150		CR	WD	DV	IO	120		8		2400		3750	4350
21		SUP OFFSHORE V-2160		CR	WD	DV	IO	120		8		2600		3900	4550
23	4	ALBATROSS GV249		OVNTR	FBG	DV	IO	155-160		8		3600		5400	6250
23	9	SEA-LANE V2460		CAMPR	WD	DV	IO	155-160		8		3400		5350	6150
		1968 BOATS													
16		GV160	OP	RNBT	FBG	SV	OB			6	4	875		2500	2900
16		GV160	OP	RNBT	FBG	SV	IO	80-110		6	4			2300	2700
16		GV170	OP	RNBT	FBG	SV	OB			7	2	950		2650	3050
16		GV170	OP	RNBT	FBG	SV	IO	110-120		7	2			2400	2800
16	7	SEA-COASTER	OP	RNBT	WD		OB			6	8	875		2400	2800
16	7	SEA-COASTER	OP	RNBT	WD		IO	110		6	8			2550	2950
16	7	THOMBOY		RNBT	WD		IO	110		6	8			2550	2950
16	7	THOMBOY	OP	RNBT	WD		OB			6	8	875		2650	3100
17	6	GV180	OP	RNBT	FBG	SV	OB			7		1050		3000	3500
17	6	GV180	OP	RNBT	FBG	SV	IO	110-160		7				2700	3200
17	11	SEA-LANCER		EXP	WD		OB			7	1	1150		3200	3750
17	11	SEA-LANCER		EXP	WD		IO	160		7	1			2900	3350
17	11	SEA-LANCER		RNBT	WD		IO	160		7	1			2800	3300
17	11	SEA-LANCER	OP	RNBT	WD		OB			7	1	1030		3000	3450
20	1	OFFSHORE	OP	CAMPR	WD		OB			8		1400		4300	5000
20	1	OFFSHORE	OP	CAMPR	WD		IO	225		8				4700	5350
20	1	OFFSHORE		EXP	WD		OB			8		1530		4650	5350
20	1	OFFSHORE	OP	OFF	WD		OB			8		1400		4300	5000
20	1	OFFSHORE	OP	OFF	WD		IO	225		8				4700	5350
20	4	GV200	OP	RNBT	FBG		IO	155-225		8				4450	5250
20	4	GV206	OP	CAMPR	WD		IO	225		8				4750	5450
20	4	GV209		CBNCR	WD		IO	225		8				5100	5850
21		SUPER OFFSHORE V2100	OP	OFF	WD		IO	225		8		1430		3350	3900
21		SUPER OFFSHORE V2150	OP	OFF	WD		IO	225		8		1430		3600	4200
21		V2160 OFFSHORE	OP	CAMPR	WD		IO	225		8		1460		3500	4050
23	9	SEA-LANE V2460	OP	CAMPR	WD		IO	325		8		1950		5050	5800
23	9	SEA-LANE V2490		CBNCR	WD		IO	325		8		2350		6050	6950
		1967 BOATS													
16		GV160		RNBT	FBG		OB			7	2	1000		2750	3200
16		GV160		RNBT	FBG		IO	110-120		7	2			2500	2950
16	7	SEA-COASTER		RNBT	L/P		OB			6	8	850		2500	2900
16	7	SEA-COASTER DELUXE		RNBT	L/P		OB			6	8	875		2500	2900
16	7	THOMBOY		RNBT	L/P		OB			6	8	920		2600	3050
17	6	GV180		RNBT	FBG		OB			7		1050		3000	3500
17	6	GV180		RNBT	FBG		IO	110-150		7				2800	3300
17	9	V-LANCER		RNBT	L/P		OB			7	3	1070		3050	3550
17	9	V-LANCER		RNBT	L/P		IO	120-150		7	3			2850	3300
17	9	V-LANCER DELUXE		RNBT	L/P		OB			7	3	1090		3100	3650
17	9	V-LANCER DELUXE		RNBT	L/P		IO	120-150		7	3			2950	3450
17	11	SEA-LANCER		CBNCR	L/P		OB			7	1	1100		3100	3600
17	11	SEA-LANCER		CBNCR	L/P		IO	110-150		7	1			3050	3550
17	11	SEA-LANCER		RNBT	L/P		OB			7	1	1010		2950	3400
17	11	SEA-LANCER		RNBT	L/P		IO	110-150		7	1			2850	3350
17	11	SEA-LANCER DELUXE		RNBT	L/P		OB			7	1	1030		3000	3450
17	11	SEA-LANCER DELUXE		RNBT	L/P		IO	110-150		7	1			3000	3450
20	1	CAMPER OFFSHORE		CAMPR	L/P		OB			8		1400		4300	5000
20	1	CAMPER OFFSHORE		CAMPR	L/P		IO	120-225		8				4700	5550
20	1	DELUXE OFFSHORE		OFF	L/P		OB			8		1300		4150	4850
20	1	DELUXE OFFSHORE		OFF	L/P		IO	120-225		8				4750	5600
20	1	OFFSHORE		CBNCR	L/P		OB			8		1500		4600	5300
20	1	OFFSHORE		CBNCR	L/P		IO	120-225		8				5050	5950
20	1	OFFSHORE		OFF	L/P		OB			8		1300		3900	4550
20	1	OFFSHORE		OFF	L/P		IO	120-225		8				4650	5500

 CONTINUED ON NEXT PAGE

THOMPSON MARINE PRODUCTS INC -CONTINUED   See inside cover to adjust price for area

LOA FT IN	NAME AND/ OR MODEL	TOP/ RIG	BOAT TYPE	HULL MTL TP	ENGINE TP	# HP MFG	BEAM FT IN	WGT LBS	DRAFT FT IN	RETAIL LOW	RETAIL HIGH
						1967 BOATS					
21	V		UTL	L/P	OB		8			7300	8400
21	V		UTL	L/P	IO	150-225	8			4850	5700
21	V-SUPER OFFSHORE		OFF	L/P	OB		8	1400		4500	5150
21	V-SUPER OFFSHORE		OFF	L/P	IO	150-225	8			4500	5350
21	V-SUPER OFFSHORE DLX		OFF	L/P	OB		8	1420		4550	5250
21	V-SUPER OFFSHORE DLX		OFF	L/P	IO	150-225	8			4650	5450
23 9	SEA-LANE V2460		RNBT	L/P	IO	150-225	8			6950	8100
23 9	SEA-LANE V2490		CBNCR	L/P	IO	150-225	8			8400	9800
						1966 BOATS					
16	GV160		RNBT	FBG	OB		6 11	950		2650	3050
16	GV160		RNBT	FBG	IO	110-120	6 11			2550	2950
16 7	SEA-COASTER		RNBT	WD	OB		6 8	850		2500	2900
16 7	SEA-COASTER DELUXE		RNBT	WD	OB		6 8	875		2500	2900
16 7	THOMBOY		RNBT	WD	OB		6 8	950		2700	3150
17 6	GV100		RNBT	FBG	OB		7	1050		3000	3500
17 6	GV180		RNBT	FBG	IO	110-150	7			2900	3400
17 9	V LANCER		RNBT	WD	OB		7 3	1070		3050	3550
17 9	V LANCER		RNBT	WD	IO	120-150	7 3			2950	3450
17 9	V LANCER DELUXE		RNBT	WD	OB		7 3			3600	4200
17 9	V LANCER DELUXE		RNBT	WD	IO	120-150	7 3			3050	3550
17 11	SEA-LANCER		CBNCR	WD	OB		7 2	1100		3100	3600
17 11	SEA-LANCER		CBNCR	WD	IO	110-120	7 1			3150	3700
17 11	SEA-LANCER		CBNCR	WD	IO	150	7 1			3150	3950
17 11	SEA-LANCER		RNBT	WD	OB		7 1	1010		2950	3400
17 11	SEA-LANCER		RNBT	WD	IO	110-150	7 1			2950	3450
17 11	SEA-LANCER DELUXE		RNBT	WD	OB		7 1	1030		3000	3450
17 11	SEA-LANCER DELUXE		RNBT	WD	IO	110-150	7 1			3100	3600
20 1	CAMPER OFFSHORE		CAMPR	WD	OB		8			6750	7750
20 1	CAMPER OFFSHORE		CAMPR	WD	IO	120-225	8			4850	5750
20 1	DELUXE OFFSHORE		OFF	WD	OB		8	1350		4150	4850
20 1	DELUXE OFFSHORE		OFF	WD	IO	120-225	8			4950	5800
20 1	OFFSHORE		CBNCR	WD	OB		8	1500		4600	5300
20 1	OFFSHORE		CBNCR	WD	IO	120-225	8			5200	6150
20 1	OFFSHORE		OFF	WD	OB		8	1300		4050	4700
20 1	OFFSHORE		OFF	WD	IO	120-225	8			4800	5650
21 1	V		UTL	WD	OB		8	1400		3800	4400
21 1	V		UTL	WD	IO	150-225	8			5000	5900
21 1	V SUPER OFFSHORE DLX		OFF	WD	OB		8			8000	9150
21 1	V SUPER OFFSHORE DLX		OFF	WD	IO	150-225	8			4750	5650
21 1	V-SUPER OFFSHORE		OFF	WD	OB		8	1400		4500	5150
21 1	V-SUPER OFFSHORE		OFF	WD	IO	150-225	8			4650	5500
23 9	SEA-LANE V2460	OP	CR	WD	IO	150-225	8			7650	8900
23 9	SEA-LANE V2490		CBNCR	WD	IO	150-225	8			8650	10100
						1965 BOATS					
16 7	SEA-COASTER			WD	OB					3100	3600
16 7	SEA-COASTER DELUXE			WD	OB					3500	4050
16 7	SEA-COASTER SPECIAL			WD	OB					3350	3900
16 7	THOMBOY			WD	OB					3800	4450
17 2	SPORTSMAN			WD	OB					3450	4050
17 9	LANCER FULL V			WD	OB					3550	4100
17 9	LANCER FULL V			WD	IO	110-120				3200	3750
17 11	SEA-LANCER			WD	OB					3400	3950
17 11	SEA-LANCER			WD	IO	110-120				3200	3750
17 11	SEA-LANCER		EXP	WD	OB					3550	4150
17 11	SEA-LANCER		EXP	WD	IO	110-120				3400	4000
17 11	SEA-LANCER DELUXE			WD	OB					3700	4300
17 11	SEA-LANCER DELUXE			WD	IO	110-120				3350	3900
18 7			UTL	WD	OB					3350	3900
18 7			UTL	WD	IO	110-190				3950	4650
18 7	SUPER-LANCER			WD	OB					3300	3850
18 7	SUPER-LANCER			WD	IO	110-165				3450	4000
18 7	SUPER-LANCER			WD	IO	190				4250	4950
18 7	SUPER-LANCER DELUXE			WD	OB					3600	4200
18 7	SUPER-LANCER DELUXE			WD	IO	110-165				3600	4150
18 7	SUPER-LANCER DELUXE			WD	IO	190				4450	5100
18 7	SUPER-THOMBOY			WD	OB					3900	4550
18 7	SUPER-THOMBOY			WD	IO	110-190				3700	4350
20 1	CRUISER OFFSHORE		CR	WD	OB					6750	7750
20 1	CRUISER OFFSHORE		CR	WD	OB					5100	5950
20 1	DELUXE OFFSHORE		OFF	WD	OB					6950	8000
20 1	DELUXE OFFSHORE		OFF	WD	IO	110-190				5200	6100
20 1	OFFSHORE		OFF	WD	OB					6500	7500
20 1	OFFSHORE		OFF	WD	IO	110-190				5050	5850
21 1	SUPER OFFSHORE		OFF	WD	OB					8100	9300
21 1	SUPER OFFSHORE		OFF	WD	IO	110-190				5050	5850
22 7	SEA-LANE			WD	OB					10600	12100
22 7	SEA-LANE			WD	IO	110-190				5500	6350
22 7	SEA-LANE		CBNCR	WD	OB					10600	12100
22 7	SEA-LANE		CBNCR	WD	IO	110-190				6450	7450
						1964 BOATS					
16 7	SEA-COASTER			WD	OB					3100	3600
16 7	SEA-COASTER DELUXE			WD	OB					3500	4050
16 7	SEA-COASTER SPECIAL			WD	OB					3350	3900
16 7	THOMBOY			WD	OB					3800	4450
16 8	XL SPORTS			WD	OB					3450	4050
17 2	SPORTSMAN			WD	OB					3450	4050
17 2	SPORTSMAN			WD	IO	80-120				3200	3750
17 11	SEA-LANCER			WD	OB					3400	3950
17 11	SEA-LANCER			WD	IO	80-120				3300	3850
17 11	SEA-LANCER		EXP	WD	OB					3550	4150
17 11	SEA-LANCER		EXP	WD	IO	80-120				3550	4400
17 11	SEA-LANCER DELUXE			WD	OB					3700	4300
17 11	SEA-LANCER DELUXE			WD	IO	80-120				3450	4000
18 4	SUPER-LANCER			WD	IO	80				3450	4000
18 7			UTL	WD	OB					3350	3900
18 7			UTL	WD	IO	80-150				4100	4750
18 7	SUPER-LANCER			WD	OB					3300	3850
18 7	SUPER-LANCER			WD	IO	110-150				3500	4150
18 7	SUPER-LANCER DELUXE			WD	OB					3600	4200
18 7	SUPER-LANCER DELUXE			WD	IO	80-150				3600	4300
18 7	SUPER-THOMBOY			WD	OB					3900	4550
18 7	SUPER-THOMBOY			WD	IO	80-150				3750	4450
20 1	DELUXE OFFSHORE		OFF	WD	OB					6950	8000
20 1	DELUXE OFFSHORE		OFF	WD	IO	110-160				5350	6200
20 1	OFFSHORE		CBNCR	WD	OB					6750	7750
20 1	OFFSHORE		CBNCR	WD	IO	110-160				5650	6550
20 1	OFFSHORE		OFF	WD	OB					6500	7500
20 1	OFFSHORE		OFF	WD	IO	110-160				5200	6000
22 7	SEA-LANE			WD	OB					10400	11800
22 7	SEA-LANE			WD	IO	110-160				5550	6450
22 7	SEA-LANE		CBNCR	WD	OB					10600	12100
22 7	SEA-LANE		CBNCR	WD	IO	110-160				6650	7650
22 7	SEA-LANE DELUXE			WD	OB					10900	12400
22 7	SEA-LANE DELUXE			WD	IO	110-160				5750	6700
						1963 BOATS					
16 6	SEA-COASTER			WD	OB					3450	4000
16 6	SEA-COASTER DELUXE			WD	OB					3450	4000
16 6	SEA-COASTER SPECIAL			WD	OB					3450	4000
16 6	SUPER-THOMBOY			WD	OB					3450	4000
16 6	SUPER-THOMBOY			WD	IO	80-140				3150	3700
16 6	THOMBOY			WD	OB					3450	4000
17	SEA-LANCER		EXP	WD	OB					3450	4050
17 2	SEA-LANCER			WD	OB					3450	4050
17 2	SEA-LANCER			WD	IO	80-110				3300	3850
18 4	SUPER-LANCER			WD	OB					3600	4150
18 4	SUPER-LANCER			WD	IO	80-140				3550	4150
18 4	SUPER-LANCER DELUXE			WD	OB					3600	4150
20 4	DELUXE OFFSHORE		OFF	WD	OB					7100	8150
20 4	OFFSHORE		CBNCR	WD	OB					7100	8150
20 4	OFFSHORE		OFF	WD	OB					7100	8150
20 4	OFFSHORE		OFF	WD	IO	100-160				5550	6400
21 8	SEA-LANE			WD	OB					4550	5200
21 8	SEA-LANE			WD	IO	100-160				5250	6100
21 8	SEA-LANE		CBNCR	WD	OB					5150	5950
						1962 BOATS					
16 4	SEA-COASTER		RNBT	WD	OB					2300	2700
16 4	SEA-COASTER SPECIAL			WD	OB					1700	2050
16 4	THOMBOY			WD	OB					1700	2050
17 2	SEA-LANCER		EXP	WD	OB					3450	4050
17 2	SEA-LANCER			WD	OB					3500	4050
17 2	V SEA LANCER			WD	OB		80			3400	4000
20 4	GE LONGSHORE	OP		WD	IO	111				5450	6250
20 4	OFFSHORE		CBNCR	WD	OB					7100	8150
20 4	OFFSHORE	OP	OFF	WD	OB					7100	8150
20 4	V OFFSHORE	OP	OFF	WD	IO	80				5700	6550
21 8	SEA-LANE	OP		WD	OB					4550	5200
21 8	SEA-LANE		CBNCR	WD	OB					5200	5950

618   CONTINUED ON NEXT PAGE   96th ed. - Vol. III

THOMPSON MARINE PRODUCTS INC   -CONTINUED   See inside cover to adjust price for area

LOA FT IN	NAME AND/ OR MODEL	TOP/ RIG	BOAT TYPE	-HULL- MTL TP	TP	#	ENGINE HP	MFG	BEAM FT IN	WGT LBS	DRAFT FT IN	RETAIL LOW	RETAIL HIGH
--- 1961 BOATS ---
17	LANCER	OP	RNBT	L/P	OB				6 10	830		2450	2850
17	LANCER DELUXE	OP	RNBT	L/P	OB				6 10	830		2450	2850
18 8	OFFSHORE		CBNCR	L/P	OB				7 4	1110		3200	3750
18 8	OFFSHORE	OP	RNBT	L/P	OB				7 4	990		2950	3450
18 8	OFFSHORE DLX		RNBT	L/P	OB				7 4	990		2950	3450
21 7	SEA-LANE		CBNCR	L/P	OB				7 11	1850		5700	6600
21 8	SEA-LANE	OP	RNBT	L/P	OB				7 11	1680		5350	6100
--- 1960 BOATS ---
17	SEA-LANCER		RNBT	L/P RB	OB				6 10	830		2450	2850
17	SEA-LANCER		RNBT	L/P RB	IO	80			6 10			3400	3950
18 8	OFFSHORE		CBNCR	L/P RB	OB				7 4	990		2900	3400
18 8	OFFSHORE		RNBT	L/P RB	OB				7 4	1110		3250	3750
18 8	OFFSHORE	OP	RNBT	L/P RB	IO	80			7 4			4050	4700
21 6	SEA-LANE		CBNCR	L/P RB	OB				7 11	1680		5300	6100
21 6	SEA-LANE	OP	RNBT	L/P RB	OB				7 11	2000		6050	7000
--- 1959 BOATS ---
16 11	473		RNBT	L/P	OB				6			2800	3250
16 11	475		RNBT	L/P	OB				6			2950	3450
16 11	477		RNBT	L/P	OB				6			4900	5650
17	SEA-LANCER		WD		IO	80						3750	4350
18 4	SEA-LANCER		RNBT	L/P	OB				6 10			3650	4250
19	SEA-LANCER		WD		IO	80						4500	5150
19 10	CRUISER OFFSHORE		CR	L/P	OB				7 4			6100	7000
19 10	OFFSHORE		RNBT	L/P	OB				7 4			6100	7050
22 9	SEA-LANE		RNBT	L/P	OB				7 11			10900	12400
--- 1957 BOATS ---
20	CRUISER OFFSHORE		CR	WD	OB							6650	7650
--- 1952 BOATS ---
18	MINNESOTA-GUIDE	OP	UTL	WD	OB				5			3400	3950

THOMPSON TRAWLERS INC
TITUSVILLE FL 32780   COAST GUARD MFG ID- TTR See inside cover to adjust price for area

LOA FT IN	NAME AND/ OR MODEL	TOP/ RIG	BOAT TYPE	-HULL- MTL TP	TP	#	ENGINE HP	MFG	BEAM FT IN	WGT LBS	DRAFT FT IN	RETAIL LOW	RETAIL HIGH
--- 1980 BOATS ---
65	MARAUDER 65		YTFS	FBG SV	IB	325			18	74000		156000	171500
--- 1979 BOATS ---
33 7	FORWARD CABIN		YTFS	FBG DS	IB	175-250			13			**	**
33 7	TRIPLE CABIN	FB	TRWL	FBG DS	IB	85			13			21100	23500
33 7	TRIPLE CABIN	FB	TRWL	FBG DS	IB	T200			13			23600	26200
44	DOUBLE AFT CABIN		YTFS	FBG DS	IB	130			15			**	**
44	DOUBLE AFT CABIN		YTFS	FBG DS	IB	T130			15			**	**
44	DOUBLE FORWARD CABIN		YTFS	FBG DS	IB	130			15			**	**
44	DOUBLE FORWARD CABIN		YTFS	FBG DS	IB	T200			15			**	**
44	TRIPLE CABIN	FB	TRWL	FBG DS	IB	130			15			40000	44500
44	TRIPLE CABIN	FB	TRWL	FBG DS	IB	T200			15			41700	46300
65	AFT SINGLE CABIN		YTFS	FBG DS	IB	250			18	74000		149000	164000
65	AFT SINGLE CABIN		YTFS	FBG DS	IB	T550			18	74000		184000	202500
65	DOUBLE CABIN		YTFS	FBG DS	IB	T250			18	74000		152500	168000
65	DOUBLE CABIN		YTFS	FBG DS	IB	T550			18	74000		184000	202500
--- 1978 BOATS ---
44	MOTOR CRUISER	FB	TRWL	FBG DS	IB		D	GM	15			**	**
44	MOTOR CRUISER	FB	TRWL	FBG DS	IB	120D	FORD	15			66200	72700
--- 1977 BOATS ---
44	MOTOR CRUISER	FB	TRWL	FBG DS	IB	120D	FORD	15		3	63400	69700
44	MOTOR CRUISER	FB	TRWL	FBG DS	IB	425D	GM	15		3	67400	74100
--- 1976 BOATS ---
28		FB	TRWL	FBG SV	IB	250			10	2		11700	13300
36		FB	TRWL	FBG SV	IB	130D			13			32500	36100
--- 1974 BOATS ---
29 8	OFFSHORE	OP	OFF	FBG DV	IB	225	OMC	10		6500	3 4	9300	10600
29 8	OFFSHORE	HT	OFF	FBG DV	IB	225	OMC	10		6500	3 4	9300	10600

THUNDER CRAFT BOATS INC
PIKEVILLE KY 41501   COAST GUARD MFG ID- TCT See inside cover to adjust price for area

For more recent years, see the BUC Used Boat Price Guide, Volume 1 or Volume 2

LOA FT IN	NAME AND/ OR MODEL	TOP/ RIG	BOAT TYPE	-HULL- MTL TP	TP	#	ENGINE HP	MFG	BEAM FT IN	WGT LBS	DRAFT FT IN	RETAIL LOW	RETAIL HIGH
--- 1979 BOATS ---
16 4	ASTRO 165		RNBT	FBG TR	OB				6	970		1750	2100
18	VIKING 180		RNBT	FBG TR	IO	140-170			7			3000	3500
--- 1978 BOATS ---
16 4	ASTRO 165 SS	ST	RNBT	FBG TR	OB				6 4	970	8	1800	2150
18	VIKING 180	ST	RNBT	FBG TR	IO	120-170			6 4	1940	1	2700	3300

THUNDERBIRD PROD CORP
FORMULA
DECATUR IN 46733   COAST GUARD MFG ID- TNR   See inside cover to adjust price for area

For more recent years, see the BUC Used Boat Price Guide, Volume 1 or Volume 2

LOA FT IN	NAME AND/ OR MODEL	TOP/ RIG	BOAT TYPE	-HULL- MTL TP	TP	#	ENGINE HP	MFG	BEAM FT IN	WGT LBS	DRAFT FT IN	RETAIL LOW	RETAIL HIGH
--- 1983 BOATS ---
16 9	FORMULA-ONE	OP	RNBT	FBG DV	OB				7 3	1050	2 8	2250	2600
16 9	FORMULA-ONE	OP	RNBT	FBG DV	IO	120-185			7 3	1950	2 8	2350	2950
18 2	F-18	ST	RNBT	FBG DV	IO				7 8	1650	2 7	3300	3800
18 2	F-18	ST	RNBT	FBG DV	IO	170-200			7 8	2618	2 7	3100	3750
18 2	F-18	ST	RNBT	FBG DV	IO	225-260			7 8	2618	2 7	3350	4050
18 2	F-18 BOW RIDER	ST	RNBT	FBG DV	IO	170-200			7 8	2698	2 7	3150	3800
18 2	F-18 BOW RIDER	ST	RNBT	FBG DV	IO	225-260			7 8	2698	2 7	3400	4100
19 6	FORMULA-TWO B/R	ST	RNBT	FBG DV	OB				8	1913	2 8	3800	4450
19 6	FORMULA-TWO B/R	ST	RNBT	FBG DV	IO				8	2850	2 8	3550	4450
19 6	FORMULA-TWO B/R	ST	RNBT	FBG DV	IO	170-230			8	2850	2 8	3750	4600
19 6	FORMULA-TWO B/R	ST	RNBT	FBG DV	IO	260			8	2850	2 8	4150	4850
19 6	FORMULA-TWO SC	ST	CUD	FBG DV	IO	170-230			8	3050	2 8	3850	4800
19 6	FORMULA-TWO SC	ST	CUD	FBG DV	IO	260			8	3050	2 8	4100	4950
19 6	FORMULA-TWO SC	ST	CUD	FBG DV	IO	290	VLVO		8	3050	2 8	4550	5250
19 6	FORMULA-TWO SPTMN	ST	SF	FBG DV	IO	170-230			8	3050	2 8	4450	5400
19 6	FORMULA-TWO SPTMN	ST	SF	FBG DV	IO	260			8	3050	2 8	4700	5650
20 2	F-20 BOW RIDER	ST	RNBT	FBG DV	IO	170-230			8	2920		4750	5800
20 2	F-20 BOW RIDER	ST	RNBT	FBG DV	IO	260			8	2920		5000	6000
20 2	F-20 SC	ST	CUD	FBG DV	IO	170-230			8	2920		5550	6350
20 2	F-20 SC	ST	CUD	FBG DV	IO	260			8	2970	3	5300	6300
20 2	F-20 SC	ST	CUD	FBG DV	IO	170-230			8	2970	3	5300	6300
21 6	FORMULA-THREE LS	ST	CUD	FBG DV	IO	198-260			8	3500	2 8	6700	7500
21 6	FORMULA-THREE LS	ST	CUD	FBG DV	IO	290	VLVO		8	3500	2 8	6800	7850
23	F-23 SC EXPRESS	ST	EXP	FBG DV	IO	170-260			8	3800	2 8	6850	8500
23	F-23 SC EXPRESS	HT	EXP	FBG DV	IO	170-260			8	3800	2 8	6850	8500
23	FORMULA 23 SPORTSMAN	ST	EXP	FBG DV	OB				8	3500	2 1	7550	8650
23 3	F-233 SPORTSMAN	ST	FSH	FBG DV	IO	198-260			8	4307	3 2	8100	9950
23 3	F-233 SPORTSMAN	ST	FSH	FBG DV	IO	165D	VLVO		8	4307	3 2	11900	13500
23 3	INTERCEPTOR F-233 LS	ST	SPTCR	FBG DV	IO	T170	MRCR		8	4307	3 2	9100	10300
23 3	INTERCEPTOR F-233 LS	ST	SPTCR	FBG DV	IO	260-290			8	4150	3 2	7750	9500
23 3	INTERCEPTOR F-233 LS	ST	SPTCR	FBG DV	IO	T170-T260			8	5100	3 2	9700	11700
25	F-25 SC EXPRESS	ST	EXP	FBG DV	IO	198-260			8	4350	2 11	8400	10300
25	F-25 SC EXPRESS	HT	EXP	FBG DV	IO	198-260			8	4350	2 11	8400	10300
26 2	F-26 SC EXPRESS	ST	EXP	FBG DV	IO	T170-T260			9	6600	2 6	12600	14300
26 2	F-26 SC EXPRESS	ST	EXP	FBG DV	IO	T170-T260			9	6600	2 6	13300	16300
27 2	FORMULA F-272 LS	OP	SPTCR	FBG DV	IO	T260	MRCR		9	5750	3	13900	15800
30 2	F-302 LS	ST	SPTCR	FBG DV	IO	T330-T370			8	6950	3 2	19000	21900
30 2	F-302LS	ST	SPTCR	FBG DV	IO	T400	MRCR		8	6950	3 2	20400	22700
30 2	FORMULA 302SRI	ST	SPTCR	FBG DV	IO	T330-T400			8	6950	3 2	19700	23600
31 6	FORMULA 31SC	FB	EXP	FBG DV	IB	T58D-235D			12	10500	2 6	34800	39400
31 6	FORMULA 31SC	FB	EXP	FBG DV	IB	T255	MRCR	12	10500	2 6	32300	35900
31 6	FORMULA 31SC	FB	EXP	FBG DV	IB	T330	MRCR	12	10500	2 6	27300	30400
40	FORMULA F-402 SC1	ST	SPTCR	FBG DV	IO	T330	MRCR	9	9800	2 10	38900	43200
	IO T330 MRCR 39800 44200, IO T370 MRCR 41700 46300, IB T260D CAT 73700 81000
40 2	FORMULA F-402 SRI	ST	SPTCR	FBG DV	IO	T330	MRCR	9 4	9250	3	38800	43100
40 2	FORMULA F-402 SRI	ST	SPTCR	FBG DV	IO	T370	MRCR	9 4	9250	3	40700	45200
40 2	FORMULA F-402 SRI	ST	SPTCR	FBG DV	IO	T400	MRCR	9 4	9250	3	42400	47100
--- 1982 BOATS ---
16 9	FORMULA-ONE	OP	RNBT	FBG DV	OB				7 3	1350		2700	3150
16 9	FORMULA-ONE	OP	RNBT	FBG DV	IO	120-185			7 3	2145	2 8	2400	3000
18 2	F-18	ST	RNBT	FBG DV	IO				7 8	1650	2 7	3200	3700
18 2	F-18	ST	RNBT	FBG DV	IO	170-200			7 8	2618	2 7	3000	3650
18 2	F-18	ST	RNBT	FBG DV	IO	225-260			7 8	2618	2 7	3200	3900
18 2	F-18 BOW RIDER	ST	RNBT	FBG DV	IO	170-200			7 8	2698	2 7	3050	3700
18 2	F-18 BOW RIDER	ST	RNBT	FBG DV	IO	225-260			7 8	2698	2 7	3300	4000
19 6	FORMULA-TWO B/R	ST	RNBT	FBG DV	OB				8	1913	2 8	3450	4300
19 6	FORMULA-TWO B/R	ST	RNBT	FBG DV	IO	170-230			8	2850	2 8	3450	4300
19 6	FORMULA-TWO B/R	ST	RNBT	FBG DV	IO	260			8	2850	2 8	3650	4450
19 6	FORMULA-TWO B/R	ST	RNBT	FBG DV	IO	290	VLVO		8	2850	2 8	4100	4750
19 6	FORMULA-TWO SC	ST	CUD	FBG DV	IO	170-230			8	3050	2 8	3750	4650

THUNDERBIRD PROD CORP -CONTINUED See inside cover to adjust price for area

LOA FT	LOA IN	NAME AND/ OR MODEL	TOP/ RIG	BOAT TYPE	-HULL- MTL	-HULL- TP	ENGINE TP	ENGINE # HP	ENGINE MFG	BEAM FT	BEAM IN	WGT LBS	DRAFT FT	DRAFT IN	RETAIL LOW	RETAIL HIGH
		1982 BOATS														
19	6	FORMULA-TWO SC	ST	CUD	FBG	DV	IO	260		8		3050	2	8	4000	4850
19	6	FORMULA-TWO SC	ST	CUD	FBG	DV	IO	290	VLVO	8		3050	2	8	4450	5100
19	6	FORMULA-TWO SP	ST	FSH	FBG	DV	IO	170-230		8		3050	2	8	3950	4950
19	6	FORMULA-TWO SP	ST	FSH	FBG	DV	IO	260		8		3050	2	8	4200	5150
19	6	FORMULA-TWO SP	ST	FSH	FBG	DV	IO	290	VLVO	8		3050	2	8	4700	5400
20	2	F-20	ST	RNBT	FBG	DV	IO	170-230		8		2920	3	1	4650	5700
20	2	F-20	ST	RNBT	FBG	DV	IO	260		8		2920	3	1	4900	5900
20	2	F-20	ST	RNBT	FBG	DV	IO	290	VLVO	8		2920	3	1	5400	6200
20	2	F-20 BOW RIDER	ST	RNBT	FBG	DV	IO	170-230		8		2982	3	1	4700	5750
20	2	F-20 BOW RIDER	ST	RNBT	FBG	DV	IO	260		8		2982	3	1	4950	5950
20	2	F-20 BOW RIDER	ST	RNBT	FBG	DV	IO	290	VLVO	8		2982	3	1	5450	6300
20	2	F-20 SC	ST	CUD	FBG	DV	IO	170-230		8		2970	3		4900	6000
20	2	F-20 SC	ST	CUD	FBG	DV	IO	260		8		2970	3		5150	6200
20	2	F-20 SPORTSMAN	ST	FSH	FBG	DV	IO	170-230		8		3070	3		5250	6450
20	2	F-20 SPORTSMAN	ST	FSH	FBG	DV	IO	260		8		3070	3		5550	6700
21	6	FORMULA-THREE LS	ST	SPTCR	FBG	DV	IO	198-260		8		3500	2	8	5900	7300
21	6	FORMULA-THREE LS	ST	SPTCR	FBG	DV	IO	290	VLVO	8		3500	2	8	6650	7650
23		F-23 SC EXPRESS	ST	EXP	FBG	DV	IO	170-260		8		3800	2	8	6700	8300
23		F-23 SC EXPRESS	HT	EXP	FBG	DV	IO	170-260		8		3800	2	8	6700	8300
23		FORMULA 23 SPORTSMAN		FSH	FBG	DV	OB			8		3500	2	1	7400	8500
23	3	F-233 OPEN SPORTSMAN	ST	OPFSH	FBG	DV	IO	198-260		8		4195	3	2	7800	9500
23	3	F-233 SPORTSMAN	ST	FSH	FBG	DV	IO	198-260		8		4307	3	2	7950	9700
23	3	F-233 SPORTSMAN	ST	FSH	FBG	DV	IO	T170-T185		8		4307	3	2	8900	10100
23	3	FORMULA 233 ISLANDER	OP	FSH	FBG	DV	IO	198-260		8		4035	3	2	7550	9250
23	3	INTERCEPTOR F-233 LS	ST	SPTCR	FBG	DV	IO	260-290		8		4150	3	2	7550	9300
23	3	INTERCEPTOR F-233 LS	ST	SPTCR	FBG	DV	IO	T170-T260		8		5100	3	2	9450	11400
25		F-25 SC EXPRESS	ST	EXP	FBG	DV	IO	198-260		8		4350	2	11	8250	10100
25		F-25 SC EXPRESS	ST	EXP	FBG	DV	IO	T170-T185		8		4350	2	11	9350	10700
25		F-25 SC EXPRESS	HT	EXP	FBG	DV	IO	198-260		8		4350	2	11	8250	10100
25		F-25 SC EXPRESS	HT	EXP	FBG	DV	IO	T170-T185		8		4350	2	11	9350	10700
25	5	FREEDOM-CRUISER F255	ST	CR	FBG	DV	IO	198-260		8		4975	3		9300	11200
25	5	FREEDOM-CRUISER F255	ST	CR	FBG	DV	IO	T170-T185		8		4975	3		10300	11900
25	5	LIBERATOR F-255 LS	ST	SPTCR	FBG	DV	IO	T198-T260		8		5622	3		11400	13700
26	2	F-26 SC EXPRESS	ST	EXP	FBG	DV	IO	T170-T260		9	6	6600	2	6	13000	15900
30	2	F-302 LS	OP	SPTCR	FBG	DV	IO	T260-T330		8		6950	3	2	17400	21200
30	2	F-302 LS	ST	SPTCR	FBG	DV	IO	T370	MRCR	8		6950	3	2	19000	21200
30	2	FORMULA 302SRI	ST	SPTCR	FBG	DV	IO	T330-T400		8		6950	3	2	19100	22800
31	6	FORMULA 31SC	FB	EXP	FBG	DV	IB	148D-235D		12		10500	2	6	33600	37900
31	6	FORMULA 31SC	FB	EXP	FBG	DV	IB	T255-T330		12		10500	2	6	30900	36000
40	2	F-402 SC1	ST	SPTCR	FBG	DV	IB			9	4	14500	2	10	**	**
		IO T330 MRCR 38400 42700, IO T370 MRCR 40300 44800, IO T400 MRCR 50200 55200														
		1981 BOATS														
16	9	FORMULA-ONE	OP	RNBT	FBG	DV	IO	170-185		7	3	2145			2350	2800
16	9	FORMULA-ONE	ST	RNBT	FBG	DV	OB			7	3	1350			2650	3100
16	9	FORMULA-ONE	ST	RNBT	FBG	DV	IO	120-170		7	3	2145			2350	2900
18	2	F-18	ST	RNBT	FBG	DV	OB			7	8	1650			3150	3700
18	2	F-18	ST	RNBT	FBG	DV	IO	170-200		7	8	2618			2950	3500
18	2	F-18	ST	RNBT	FBG	DV	IO	225-260		7	8	2618			3200	3900
18	2	F-18 BOW RIDER	ST	RNBT	FBG	DV	IO	170-200		7	8	2698			3000	3550
18	2	F-18 BOW RIDER	ST	RNBT	FBG	DV	IO	225-260		7	8	2698			3250	3950
20	2	F-20	ST	RNBT	FBG	DV	IO	170-230		8		2920			4600	5600
20	2	F-20	ST	RNBT	FBG	DV	IO	260		8		2920			4850	5800
20	2	F-20	ST	RNBT	FBG	DV	IO	290	VLVO	8		2920			5300	6100
20	2	F-20 BOW RIDER	ST	RNBT	FBG	DV	IO	170-230		8		2982			4650	5650
20	2	F-20 BOW RIDER	ST	RNBT	FBG	DV	IO	260		8		2982			4900	5850
20	2	F-20 BOW RIDER	ST	RNBT	FBG	DV	IO	290	VLVO	8		2982			5350	6200
20	2	F-20 SC	ST	CUD	FBG	DV	IO	170-230		8		2970			4800	5900
20	2	F-20 SC	ST	CUD	FBG	DV	IO	260		8		2970			5100	6150
20	2	F-20 SPORTSMAN	ST	FSH	FBG	DV	IO	170-230		8		3070			5200	6350
20	2	F-20 SPORTSMAN	ST	FSH	FBG	DV	IO	260		8		3070			5500	6600
23		F-23 SC EXPRESS	ST	EXP	FBG	DV	IO	170-260		8		3800			6600	8200
23		F-23 SC EXPRESS	ST	EXP	FBG	DV	IO	130D	VLVO	8		3800			8100	9300
23	3	F-233 OPEN SPORTSMAN	ST	OPFSH	FBG	DV	IO	198-260		8		4195			7650	9350
23	3	F-233 OPEN SPORTSMAN	ST	OPFSH	FBG	DV	IO	T170-T185		8		4195			8500	9800
23	3	F-233 SPORTSMAN	ST	FSH	FBG	DV	IO	198-260		8		4307			7800	9550
23	3	F-233 SPORTSMAN	ST	FSH	FBG	DV	IO	140D	VLVO	8		4307			11200	12700
23	3	F-233 SPORTSMAN	ST	FSH	FBG	DV	IO	T170-T185		8		4307			8650	10000
23	3	INTERCEPTOR F-233 LS	ST	SPTCR	FBG	DV	IO	260-290		8		4150			7450	9150
23	3	INTERCEPTOR F-233 LS	ST	SPTCR	FBG	DV	IO	T170-T260		8		5100			9400	11200
25		F-25 SC EXPRESS	OP	EXP	FBG	DV	IO	198-260		8		4350			8100	9950
25		F-25 SC EXPRESS	OP	EXP	FBG	DV	IO	130D	VLVO	8		4350			9300	10600
25		F-25 SC EXPRESS	OP	EXP	FBG	DV	IO	T170-T185		8		4350			9200	10600
25	5	FREEDOM-CRUISER F255	ST	CR	FBG	DV	IO	198-260		8		4975			9150	11000
25	5	FREEDOM-CRUISER F255	ST	CR	FBG	DV	IO	T170-T185		8		4975			10200	11700
25	5	LIBERATOR F-255 LS	ST	SPTCR	FBG	DV	IO	T198-T260		8		5622			11200	13500
26	2	F-26 SC EXPRESS	ST	EXP	FBG	DV	IO	T170-T260		9	6	6600			12800	15700
26	2	F-26 SEDAN	HT	SDN	FBG	DV	IO	T170-T260		9	6	7200			14400	17500
26	2	F-26 SEDAN	FB	SDN	FBG	DV	IO	T170-T260		9	6	7200			14400	17500
26	2	F-26 SEDAN	OP	SF	FBG	DV	IO	T185	MRCR	9	6	7200			15600	17700
30	2	F-302 LS	OP	SPTCR	FBG	DV	IO	T260-T330		8		6950			17100	20800
30	2	F-302 LS	ST	SPTCR	FBG	DV	IO	T370	MRCR	8		6950			19300	21500
40	2	F-402 SC1	ST	SPTCR	FBG	DV	IO	T330	MRCR	9	4	9500			37800	42000
40	2	F-402 SC1	ST	SPTCR	FBG	DV	IO	T370	MRCR	9	4	9500			39600	44000
40	2	F-402 SC1	ST	SPTCR	FBG	DV	IO	T260D	CAT	9	4	14500			56400	62000
		1980 BOATS														
16	9	FORMULA-ONE	ST	RNBT	FBG	DV	OB			7	3	1350			2600	3050
16	9	FORMULA-ONE	ST	RNBT	FBG	DV	IO	120-170		7	3	2145			2350	2900
18	2	F-18	ST	RNBT	FBG	DV	OB			7	8	1650			3150	3650
18	2	F-18	ST	RNBT	FBG	DV	IO	165-200		7	8	2618			2950	3600
18	2	F-18	ST	RNBT	FBG	DV	IO	225-260		7	8	2618			3150	3850
18	2	F-18 BOW RIDER	ST	RNBT	FBG	DV	IO	165-200		7	8	2698			3000	3700
18	2	F-18 BOW RIDER	ST	RNBT	FBG	DV	IO	225-260		7	8	2698			3200	3900
20	2	F-18 BOW RIDER	ST	RNBT	FBG	DV	IO	165-230		8		2982			4600	5600
20	2	F-18 BOW RIDER	ST	RNBT	FBG	DV	IO	260		8		2982			4850	5800
20	2	F-18 BOW RIDER	ST	RNBT	FBG	DV	IO	290	VLVO	8		2982			5350	6100
20	2	F-20	ST	CUD	FBG	DV	IO	170-230		8		2970			4750	5850
20	2	F-20	ST	CUD	FBG	DV	IO	260		8		2970			5050	6050
20	2	F-20	ST	RNBT	FBG	DV	IO	165-230		8		2920			4550	5550
20	2	F-20	ST	RNBT	FBG	DV	IO	260		8		2920			4800	5750
20	2	F-20	ST	RNBT	FBG	DV	IO	290	VLVO	8		2920			5250	6050
20	2	F-20 SPORTSMAN	ST	FSH	FBG	DV	IO	170-230		8		3070			5150	6300
20	2	F-20 SPORTSMAN	ST	FSH	FBG	DV	IO	260		8		3070			5450	6550
23	3	F-233	ST	CUD	FBG	DV	IO	198-260		8		3957			6900	8450
23	3	F-233	ST	FSH	FBG	DV	IO	198-260		8		4307			7750	9450
23	3	F-233	ST	FSH	FBG	DV	IO	130D	VLVO	8		4307			11000	12500
23	3	F-233	ST	FSH	FBG	DV	IO	T165-T170		8		4307			8550	9850
23	3	F-233-F	ST	OPFSH	FBG	DV	IO	198-260		8		4195			7600	9300
23	3	F-233-F	ST	OPFSH	FBG	DV	IO	T165-T170		8		4195			8400	9650
23	3	INTERCEPTOR F-233	ST	SPTCR	FBG	DV	IO	260-330		8		5100			8650	10700
		IO T165-T230 9300 11200, IO T260 9800 11700, IO T290 VLVO 10800 12300														
25	5	CASTAWAY F-255	ST	CBNCR	FBG	DV	IO	198-260		8		5447			11600	13900
25	5	CASTAWAY F-255	ST	CBNCR	FBG	DV	IO	T165-T170		8		5447			12500	14200
25	5	F-255 SPORTSMAN	ST	SF	FBG	DV	IO	198-260		8		4975			10300	12400
25	5	F-255 SPORTSMAN	ST	SF	FBG	DV	IO	T165-T170		8		4975			11400	13100
25	5	FREEDOM-CRUISER F255	OP	CR	FBG	DV	IO	198-260		8		4975			9050	10900
25	5	FREEDOM-CRUISER F255	OP	CR	FBG	DV	IO	T165-T170		8		4975			10000	11500
25	5	LIBERATOR F-255	ST	SPTCR	FBG	DV	IO	T198-T260		8		5622			11100	13800
25	5	LIBERATOR F-255	ST	SPTCR	FBG	DV	IO	T290	VLVO	8		5622			12700	14400
26	2	F-26 EXPRESS	OP	EXP	FBG	DV	IO	T165-T230		9	6	6600			12700	15300
26	2	F-26 EXPRESS	OP	EXP	FBG	DV	IO	T260		9	6	6600			13700	15900
26	2	F-26 SEDAN	HT	SDN	FBG	DV	IO	T165-T260		9	6	7200			14200	17700
26	2	F-26 SEDAN	FB	SDN	FBG	DV	IO	T165-T260		9	6	7200			14200	17700
26	2	F-26 SPORTSMAN	OP	SF	FBG	DV	IO	T165-T230		9	6	6600			14400	17500
26	2	F-26 SPORTSMAN	OP	SF	FBG	DV	IO	T260		9	6	6600			15600	18100
30	2	F-302	OP	SPTCR	FBG	DV	IO	T260-T330		8		6950			17000	20700
30	2	F-302 SPECIAL EDIT	ST	SPTCR	FBG	DV	IO	T260-T330		8		6950			17000	20700
		1979 BOATS														
18	2	F-18	ST	RNBT	FBG	DV	OB			7	8	1650			3100	3600
18	2	F-18	ST	RNBT	FBG	DV	IO	165-200		7	8	2618			2950	3600
18	2	F-18	ST	RNBT	FBG	DV	IO	225-260		7	8	2618			3150	3850
18	2	F-18 BOW RIDER	ST	RNBT	FBG	DV	IO	165-200		7	8	2648			2950	3650
18	2	F-18 BOW RIDER	ST	RNBT	FBG	DV	IO	225-260		7	8	2648			3200	3900
18	2	S-18	ST	RNBT	FBG	TR	OB			7	5	1750			3200	3750
18	2	S-18	ST	RNBT	FBG	TR	IO	165-200		7	5	2572			2850	3500
18	2	S-18	ST	RNBT	FBG	TR	IO	225-260		7	5	2572			3100	3750
20	2	F-20	ST	RNBT	FBG	DV	IO	165-230		8		2712			4350	5350
20	2	F-20	ST	RNBT	FBG	DV	IO	260		8		2712			4600	5550
20	2	F-20	ST	RNBT	FBG	DV	IO	290	VLVO	8		2712			5100	5850
20	2	F-20-CL	ST	CUD	FBG	DV	IO	185-230		8		3070			4850	5950
20	2	F-20-CL	ST	CUD	FBG	DV	IO	260		8		3070			5150	6200
20	2	F-20-CL	ST	CUD	FBG	DV	IO	290	VLVO	8		3070			5650	6500
20	3	S-20	ST	RNBT	FBG	DV	IO	165-230		7	6	2920			4400	5400
20	3	S-20	ST	RNBT	FBG	DV	IO	260		7	6	2920			4650	5600
23	3	F-233-C	ST	CUD	FBG	DV	IO	185-260		8		4550			7600	9350

 CONTINUED ON NEXT PAGE

LOA FT	IN	NAME AND/ OR MODEL	TOP/ RIG	BOAT TYPE	-HULL- MTL	TP	TP	----ENGINE--- # HP	MFG	BEAM FT	IN	WGT LBS	DRAFT FT	IN	RETAIL LOW	RETAIL HIGH
		------------------- 1979 BOATS														
23	3	F-233-C	ST	CUD	FBG	DV	IO	290	VLVO	8		4550			8400	9650
23	3	F-233-C	ST	CUD	FBG	DV	IO	T140-T170		8		4550			8400	9700
23	3	F-233-CL	ST	CUD	FBG	DV	IO	185-260		8		4900			8050	9850
23	3	F-233-CL	ST	CUD	FBG	DV	IO	130D	VLVO	8		4900			9600	10900
23	3	F-233-CL	ST	CUD	FBG	DV	IO	T140-T170		8		4900			8950	10200
23	3	F-233-F	ST	OPFSH	FBG	DV	IO	185-260		8		4228			7550	9350
23	3	F-233-F	ST	OPFSH	FBG	DV	IO	T140-T170		8		4228			8400	9700
23	3	F-233-H	ST	CUD	FBG	DV	IO	185-260		8		4228			7150	8850
23	3	F-233-H	ST	CUD	FBG	DV	IO	T140-T170		8		4228			7950	9200
23	3	INTERCEPTOR F-233	ST	CUD	FBG	DV	IO	260-330		8		5480			9250	11300
23	3	INTERCEPTOR F-233	ST	CUD	FBG	DV	IO	T165-T260		8		5480			9750	11700
25	5	CASTAWAY F-255	ST	CR	FBG	DV	IO	260		8		6324			11100	12800
25	5	CASTAWAY F-255	ST	CR	FBG	DV	IO	T165-T260		8		6324			11700	14300
25	5	FREEDOM CR F-255	OP	CR	FBG	DV	IO			8		6095			**	**
25	5	LIBERATOR F-255	ST	CR	FBG	DV	IO	260		8		5822			10500	12100
25	5	LIBERATOR F-255	ST	CR	FBG	DV	IO	T165-T260		8		5822			11100	13600
25	5	VANGUARD F-255	HT	CR	FBG	DV	IO	260		8		6384			11200	12900
25	5	VANGUARD F-255	HT	CR	FBG	DV	IO	T165-T260		8		6384			11800	14400
26	2	F-26	OP	EXP	FBG	DV	IO			9	6	6600			**	**
26	2	F-26	FB	SDN	FBG	DV	IO			9	6	7200			**	**
30	2	F-302	OP	CR	FBG	DV	IO			8		6950			**	**
		------------------- 1978 BOATS														
16	3	S-16	ST	RNBT	FBG	TR	OB			6	6	1260			2400	2800
16	3	S-16	ST	RNBT	FBG	TR	IO	140		6	6	1412	2		1750	2100
17	1	S-17	ST	RNBT	FBG	TR	OB			7	7	1600			2950	3400
17	1	S-17	ST	RNBT	FBG	TR	IO	140-170		7	7	1562	2		2200	2550
18	2	F-18	ST	RNBT	FBG	DV	OB			7	8	1650			3050	3550
18	2	F-18	ST	RNBT	FBG	DV	IO	165-240		7	8	1711	2	8	2400	2900
18	2	F-18	ST	RNBT	FBG	DV	IO	260	MRCR	7	8	1711	2	8	2600	3050
18	2	F-18 BOW RIDER	ST	RNBT	FBG	DV	IO	165-240		7	8	1711	2	8	2500	3000
18	2	F-18 BOW RIDER	ST	RNBT	FBG	DV	IO	260	MRCR	7	8	1711	2	8	2700	3150
18	2	S-18	ST	RNBT	FBG	TR	OB			7	5	1750			3200	3700
18	2	S-18	ST	RNBT	FBG	TR	IO	165-240		7	5	1855	2	1	2450	2950
18	2	S-18	ST	RNBT	FBG	TR	IO	260	MRCR	7	5	1855	2	1	2650	3100
20	2	F-20	ST	RNBT	FBG	DV	IO	165-260		8		1995	2	8	3800	4700
20	2	F-20	ST	RNBT	FBG	DV	IO	330	MRCR	8		1995	2	8	4750	5450
20	2	F-20-CL	ST	CUD	FBG	DV	IO	185-260		8		2145	2	8	4000	5000
20	2	F-20-CL	ST	CUD	FBG	DV	IO	330	MRCR	8		2145	2	8	5050	5800
20	3	S-20	ST	RNBT	FBG	TR	IO	165-260		7	6	1995	2	3	3650	4550
20	3	S-20-C	ST	CUD	FBG	TR	IO	165-260		7	6	2111	2	3	3850	4800
23	3	F-233-C	ST	CUD	FBG	DV	IO	185-260		8		3020	2	10	5700	6900
		IO 330 MRCR 6700 7700, IO T140-T240 6500 7850, IO T260 MRCR													7100	8150
23	3	F-233-CL	ST	CUD	FBG	DV	IO	185-260		8		3370	2	10	6100	7350
23	3	F-233-CL	ST	CUD	FBG	DV	IO	330	MRCR	8		3370	2	10	7150	8200
23	3	F-233-CL	ST	CUD	FBG	DV	IO	T140-T260		8		3370	2	10	6950	8650
23	3	F-233-F	ST	OPFSH	FBG	DV	IO	185-260		8		3270	2	9	6350	7650
		IO 330 MRCR 7400 8500, IO T140-T240 7200 8650, IO T260 MRCR													7800	9000
23	3	F-233-H	ST	CUD	FBG	DV	IO	185-260		8		3511	2	10	6300	7550
23	3	F-233-H	ST	CUD	FBG	DV	IO	330	MRCR	8		3511	2	10	7300	8400
23	3	F-233-H	ST	CUD	FBG	DV	IO	T140-T260		8		3511	2	10	7100	8850
23	3	INTERCEPTOR F-233	ST	CUD	FBG	DV	IO	185-260		8		3606	2	10	6400	7700
23	3	INTERCEPTOR F-233	ST	CUD	FBG	DV	IO	T140-T260		8		3606	2	10	7200	9000
25	5	CASTAWAY F-255	ST	CR	FBG	DV	IO	240-260		8		4510	2	8	8700	10200
25	5	CASTAWAY F-255	ST	CR	FBG	DV	IO	T165-T240		8		4510	2	8	9550	11600
25	5	CASTAWAY F-255	ST	CR	FBG	DV	IO	T260	MRCR	8		4510	2	8	10500	12000
25	5	FREEDOM CR F-255	ST	CR	FBG	DV	IO	240-260		8		4245	2	8	8350	9850
25	5	FREEDOM CR F-255	ST	CR	FBG	DV	IO	T165-T260		8		4245	2	8	9300	11600
25	5	LIBERATOR F-255	ST	CR	FBG	DV	IO	240-260		8		3948	2	8	8050	9450
25	5	LIBERATOR F-255	ST	CR	FBG	DV	IO	T165-T260		8		3948	2	8	8950	11200
25	5	LIBERATOR F-255	ST	CR	FBG	DV	IO	T330	MRCR	8		3948	2	8	10900	12400
25	5	VANGUARD F-255	HT	CR	FBG	DV	IO	240-260		8		4510	2	8	8700	10200
25	5	VANGUARD F-255	HT	CR	FBG	DV	IO	T165-T240		8		4510	2	8	9550	11600
25	5	VANGUARD F-255	HT	CR	FBG	DV	IO	T260	MRCR	8		4510	2	8	10500	12000
26	2	F-26	ST	CR	FBG	DV	IO	T165-T240		9	6	4750	2	8	10600	13000
26	2	F-26	ST	CR	FBG	DV	IO	T260	MRCR	9	6	4750	2	8	11800	13400
26	2	F-26	ST	CR	FBG	DV	IO	T330	MRCR	9	6	4750	2	8	13000	14700
		------------------- 1977 BOATS														
16	3	S-16	ST	RNBT	FBG	TR	OB			6	6	1260			2400	2800
16	3	S-16	ST	RNBT	FBG	TR	IO	140		6	6	2050	2		2200	2550
17	1	S-17	ST	RNBT	FBG	TR	OB			7	7	1470			2750	3200
17	1	S-17	ST	RNBT	FBG	TR	IO	140		7	7	2140	2		2500	2950
18	2	F-18	ST	RNBT	FBG	DV	OB			7	8	1690			3100	3600
18	2	F-18	ST	RNBT	FBG	DV	IO	165-235		7	8	2720	2	8	3050	3700
18	2	S-18	ST	RNBT	FBG	TR	OB			7	5	1510			2850	3300
18	2	S-18	ST	RNBT	FBG	TR	IO	165-235		7	5	2550	2	1	2900	3450
20	2	F-20	ST	RNBT	FBG	DV	IO	165-280		8		2950	2	8	4700	5800
20	2	F-20-CL	ST	CUD	FBG	DV	IO	175-235		8		3125	2	8	5000	5950
20	2	F-20-CL	ST	CUD	FBG	DV	IO	280	MRCR	8		3125	2	8	5450	6300
20	3	S-20	ST	RNBT	FBG	TR	IO	165-235		7	6	2970	2	3	4550	5350
20	3	S-20-C	ST	CUD	FBG	TR	IO	165-235		7	6	3410	2	3	5200	6150
23	3	F-233-C	ST	CUD	FBG	DV	IO	175-280		8		5580	2	10	9300	11000
23	3	F-233-C	ST	CUD	FBG	DV	IO	T140-T235		8		5580	2	10	10100	11800
23	3	F-233-CL	ST	CUD	FBG	DV	IO	175-280		8		5900	2	10	9700	11500
23	3	F-233-CL	ST	CUD	FBG	DV	IO	T140-T235		8		5900	2	10	10500	12400
23	3	F-233-F	ST	OPFSH	FBG	DV	IO	175-280		8		5590	2	9	9800	11700
23	3	F-233-F	ST	OPFSH	FBG	DV	IO	T140-T235		8		5590	2	9	10700	12500
23	3	F-233-H	ST	CUD	FBG	DV	IO	175-280		8		5855	2	10	9650	11500
23	3	F-233-H	ST	CUD	FBG	DV	IO	T140-T235		8		5855	2	10	10500	12300
25	5	CASTAWAY F-255	ST	CR	FBG	DV	IO	233-280		8		6725	2	8	11700	13700
25	5	CASTAWAY F-255	ST	CR	FBG	DV	IO	T165-T280		8		6725	2	8	12500	15600
25	5	F-255-FC	ST	CR	FBG	DV	IO	233-280		8		6575	2	8	11500	13500
25	5	F-255-FC	ST	CR	FBG	DV	IO	T165-T280		8		6575	2	8	12300	15400
25	5	LIBERATOR F-255	ST	CR	FBG	DV	IO	233-280		8		6450	2	8	11400	13300
25	5	LIBERATOR F-255	ST	CR	FBG	DV	IO	T165-T280		8		6450	2	8	12200	15200
26	2	F-26	ST	CR	FBG	DV	IO	255-280		9	6	6930	2	8	12700	14600
26	2	F-26	ST	CR	FBG	DV	IO	T165-T255		9	6	6930	2	8	13300	16300
26	2	F-26	ST	CR	FBG	DV	IO	T280	MRCR	9	6	6930	2	8	14700	16700
		------------------- 1976 BOATS														
16	3	S-16	ST	RNBT	FBG	TR	OB			6	6	1260			2400	2750
16	3	S-16	ST	RNBT	FBG	TR	IO	140		6	6	2050	2		2250	2600
17	1	S-17	ST	RNBT	FBG	TR	OB			7	7	1470			2700	3150
17	1	S-17	ST	RNBT	FBG	TR	IO	140		7	7	2140	2		2600	3000
18	2	F-18	ST	RNBT	FBG	DV	OB			7	8	1690			3050	3550
18	2	F-18	ST	RNBT	FBG	DV	IO	140-235		7	8	2720	2	8	3100	3800
18	2	S-18	ST	RNBT	FBG	TR	OB			7	5	1510			2850	3300
18	2	S-18	ST	RNBT	FBG	TR	IO	140-235		7	5	2550	2	1	2950	3600
20	2	F-20	ST	RNBT	FBG	DV	IO	165-235		8		2950	2	8	4750	5650
20	2	F-20	ST	RNBT	FBG	DV	IO	280	MRCR	8		2950	2	8	5200	5950
20	3	S-20	ST	RNBT	FBG	TR	IO	140-235		7	6	2970	2	3	4650	5500
20	3	S-20-C	ST	CUD	FBG	TR	IO	165-235		7	6	3410	2	3	5300	6300
23	3	F-233-C	ST	CUD	FBG	DV	IO	175-280		8		5580	2	10	9500	11300
23	3	F-233-C	ST	CUD	FBG	DV	IO	T140-T235		8		5580	2	10	10300	12100
23	3	F-233-COASTAL	ST	CUD	FBG	DV	IO	175-280		8		5900	2	10	9950	11800
23	3	F-233-COASTAL	ST	CUD	FBG	DV	IO	T140-T235		8		5900	2	10	10800	12700
23	3	F-233-F	ST	OPFSH	FBG	DV	IO	175-280		8		5590	2	9	10000	12000
23	3	F-233-F	ST	OPFSH	FBG	DV	IO	T140-T235		8		5590	2	9	10900	12800
23	3	F-233-H	ST	CUD	FBG	DV	IO	175-280		8		5855	2	10	9900	11800
23	3	F-233-H	ST	CUD	FBG	DV	IO	T140-T235		8		5855	2	10	10700	12600
25	5	CASTAWAY F-255	ST	CR	FBG	DV	IO	175-280		8		6725			11700	14100
25	5	CASTAWAY F-255	ST	CR	FBG	DV	IO	T140-T255		8		6725			12700	15600
25	5	CASTAWAY F-255	ST	CR	FBG	DV	IO	T280	MRCR	8		6725			14100	16000
25	5	FREEDOM CR F-255-FC	ST	CR	FBG	DV	IO	188-280		8		6575	2	9	11600	13800
25	5	FREEDOM CR F-255-FC	ST	CR	FBG	DV	IO	T140-T255		8		6575	2	9	12500	15300
25	5	FREEDOM CR F-255-FC	ST	CR	FBG	DV	IO	T280	MRCR	8		6575	2	9	13900	15800
25	5	LIBERATOR F-255	ST	CR	FBG	DV	IO	188-280		8		6450	2	9	11400	13700
25	5	LIBERATOR F-255	ST	CR	FBG	DV	IO	T140-T255		8		6450	2	9	12300	15200
25	5	LIBERATOR F-255	ST	CR	FBG	DV	IO	T280	MRCR	8		6450	2	9	13700	15600
26	2	F-26	ST	CUD	FBG	DV	IO	255-280		9	6	6930	3	2	13000	15000
		IO T165-T235 13700 16400, IO T255 MRCR 14700 16700, VD T255 MRCR													13100	14900
		IO T280 MRCR 15100 17100														
		------------------- 1975 BOATS														
17	1	T-17	ST	RNBT	FBG	TR	OB			7	7	1520	2	3	2750	3200
17	1	T-17	ST	RNBT	FBG	TR	IO	120-165		7	7	2130			2650	3100
18	2	F-18	ST	RNBT	FBG	DV	OB			7	8	1690	2	6	3050	3550
18	2	F-18	ST	RNBT	FBG	DV	IO	140-233		7	8	2650			3150	3950
19		T-19	ST	RNBT	FBG	TR	OB			7	11	1890	2	4	3350	3900
19		T-19	ST	RNBT	FBG	TR	IO	120-190		7	11	2590			3350	4000
19		T-19-C	ST	CUD	FBG	TR	IO	120-190				2600	2	5	3400	4150
20	2	F-20	ST	RNBT	FBG	DV	IO	165-233		8		2850	2	8	4850	5850
20	2	F-20	ST	RNBT	FBG	DV	IO	280	MRCR	8		3100	2	8	5500	6350
23	3	F-233-C	ST	CUD	FBG	DV	IO	165-255		8		4680	2	10	8450	10400
23	3	F-233-C	ST	CUD	FBG	DV	IO	280	MRCR	8		4940	2	10	9400	10700
23	3	F-233-C	ST	CUD	FBG	DV	IO	T120-T233		8		4940	2	10	9850	12000
23	3	F-233-COASTAL	ST	CUD	FBG	DV	IO	165-255		8		4680	2	10	8450	10400
23	3	F-233-COASTAL	ST	CUD	FBG	DV	IO	280	MRCR	8		4940	2	10	9400	10700
23	3	F-233-COASTAL	ST	CUD	FBG	DV	IO	T120-T233		8		4940	2	10	9850	12000

 CONTINUED ON NEXT PAGE

LOA FT	LOA IN	NAME AND/ OR MODEL	TOP/ RIG	BOAT TYPE	HULL MTL	HULL TP	ENGINE TP	ENGINE # HP	ENGINE MFG	BEAM FT	BEAM IN	WGT LBS	DRAFT FT	DRAFT IN	RETAIL LOW	RETAIL HIGH
		1975 BOATS														
23	3	F-233-F	ST	OPFSH	FBG	DV	IO	165-255		8		4380	2	9	8450	10500
23	3	F-233-F	ST	OPFSH	FBG	DV	IO	280	MRCR	8		4690	2	9	9450	10800
23	3	F-233-F	ST	OPFSH	FBG	DV	IO	T120-T233		8		4690	2	9	9850	12000
23	3	F-233-H	ST	CUD	FBG	DV	IO	165-255		8		4880	2	10	8850	10700
23	3	F-233-H	ST	CUD	FBG	DV	IO	280	MRCR	8		5200	2	10	9700	11000
23	3	F-233-H	ST	CUD	FBG	DV	IO	T120-T233		8		5235	2	10	10200	12300
26	2	F-26-C	ST	CUD	FBG	DV	IO	255-280		9	6	6340	3	2	12700	14600
		IO T165-T233 13500 16400, IO T255 MRCR 14900 16900, VD T255 MRCR 12600 14300														
		IO T280 MRCR 15400 17500														
		1974 BOATS														
17	1	T-170		RNBT	FBG		OB			7	7	1180			2300	2650
17	1	T-170		RNBT	FBG		IO	120-165		7	7	1950			2600	3050
18	2	F-180		RNBT	FBG		OB			7	8	1370			2600	3050
18	2	F-180		RNBT	FBG		IO	165-188		7	8	2170			2950	3500
19		T-190		RNBT	FBC		OB			7	10	1680			3100	3600
19		T-190		RNBT	FBG		IO	120-165		7	10	2410			3300	3850
19	2	T-190		CAMPR	FBG		OB			7	11	1850			3350	3900
19	2	T-190		CAMPR	FBG		IO	140-165		7	11	2580			3600	4200
20	2	F-200		CUD	FBG		IO	188	MRCR	8		2420			4800	5500
23	3	F-233		CUD	FBG		IO	188-255		8		3780			7450	8850
23	3	F-233		CUD	FBG		IO	T120-T188		8		3780			8250	9650
23	3	F-233	HT	CUD	FBG	DV	IO	188-255		8		4350			8250	9800
23	3	F-233	HT	CUD	FBG	DV	IO	T120-T188		8		4350			9200	10600
23	3	F-233		FSH	FBG		IO	188-255		8		4200			8500	10100
23	3	F-233		FSH	FBG		IO	T120-T165		8		4200			9450	10800
25		T-250		CUD	FBG		IO	188-255		7	11	3480			7750	9400
25		T-250		CUD	FBG		IO	T120-T140		7	11	3480			8600	10100
26	2	F-260		CBNCR	FBG		IO	225-255		9	6	6050			15200	17700
26	2	F-260		CBNCR	FBG		IO	T165-T225		9	6	6050			16100	18500
		1973 BOATS														
17	1	T-170		RNBT	FBG		OB			7	7	1180			2300	2650
17	1	T-170		RNBT	FBG		IO	120-165		7	7	1910			2700	3150
18	2	F-180		RNBT	FBG		OB			7	8	1570			2900	3350
18	2	F-180		RNBT	FBG		IO	165-188		7	8	2370			3200	3900
19		T-190		RNBT	FBG		OB			7	10	1380			2700	3150
19		T-190		RNBT	FBG		IO	120-188		7	10	2050			3150	3900
19	2	T-190		CAMPR	FBG		OB			7	11	1550			2950	3450
19	2	T-190		CAMPR	FBG		IO	120-188		7	11	2390			3550	4350
20	2	F-200		CUD	FBG		IO	188-265		8		2860			5400	6600
23	3	F-233		CUD	FBG		IO	188-265		8					8200	9800
23	3	F-233		CUD	FBG		IO	T120-T188		8		3780			8550	10400
23	3	F-233	OP	OPFSH	FBG		IO	188-265		8					8200	9800
23	3	F-233	OP	OPFSH	FBG		IO	T120-T170		8		4200			9750	11600
25		T-250		CAMPR	FBG		IO	188	MRCR	7	11	3480			8000	9200
25		T-250		CAMPR	FBG		IO	225-255		7	11	3840			8800	10000
25		T-250		CAMPR	FBG		IO	T120-T140		7	11				10300	11900
26	2	F-260		CBNCR	FBG		IO	225-255		9	6				14700	17000
26	2	F-260		CBNCR	FBG		IO	T165-T225		9	6	5400			15500	18000
		1972 BOATS														
17		FORMULA 1700		RNBT	FBG		OB			6	6	1130			2200	2550
17		SEMINOLE 170		RNBT	FBG		OB								2150	2500
17		SEMINOLE 170		RNBT	FBG		IO	120	MRCR	6	10	1080			2100	2500
17		SEMINOLE 170		RNBT	FBG		IO	120-165		6	10	2095			2700	3150
17	7	FORMULA 177		RNBT	FBG		IO	165-245		7	4	2550			3250	3950
18	7	APACHE 187		RNBT	FBG		OB			7	3	1490			2800	3250
18	7	APACHE 187		RNBT	FBG		IO	120-225		7	3	2735			3500	4200
18	7	COMANCHE 187		RNBT	FBG		OB			7	3	1540			2900	3350
18	7	COMANCHE 187		RNBT	FBG		IO	120-225		7	3	2785			3550	4250
19		FORMULA 190		RNBT	FBG		IO	165-245		7	6	2750			3700	4450
23	3	FORMULA 233		SPTCR	FBG		IO	165-245		8		4100			8400	9850
23	3	FORMULA 233		SPTCR	FBG		IO	T120-T188		8		5300			11300	13000
25		NAVAJO 250		RNBT	FBG		IO	165-245		7	10	4100			8350	10100
25		NAVAJO 250		RNBT	FBG		IO	T120-T160		7	10	5300			11100	12900
		1971 BOATS														
17		SEMINOLE		RNBT	FBG		OB			6	10	1080			2050	2450
17		SEMINOLE		RNBT	FBG		IO	120-165		6	10	2095			2800	3300
17	1	FORMULA 1700		RNBT	FBG		OB			6	6	1130	3	6	2200	2550
17	1	FORMULA 1700		RNBT	FBG		IO	160-170		6	6	2130	3	6	2800	3450
17	5	WARRIOR 700		RNBT	FBG	SV	IO	120		6	8				3150	3650
17	5	WARRIOR 700 W/T		RNBT	FBG	SV	OB			6	8	927			1850	2200
18	7	APACHE		RNBT	FBG		OB			7	3	1490			2800	3250
18	7	APACHE		RNBT	FBG		IO	120-215		7	3	2735			3650	4300
18	7	CHEYENNE		RNBT	FBG		OB			7	3	1430			2750	3150
18	7	CHEYENNE		RNBT	FBG		IO	120-215		7	3	2605			3550	4200
18	7	CHEYENNE DELUXE		RNBT	FBG		OB			7	3	1510			2850	3300
18	7	CHEYENNE DELUXE		RNBT	FBG		IO	120-215		7	3	2705			3600	4300
18	7	COMANCHE DELUXE		RNBT	FBG		OB			7	3	1540			2900	3350
18	7	COMANCHE DELUXE		RNBT	FBG		IO	120-215		7	3	2785			3700	4350
19	2	WARRIOR 900 CAB		RNBT	FBG	SV	OB			7	4	1450			2800	3300
19	2	WARRIOR 900 CAB		RNBT	FBG	SV	IO	120		7	4				4200	4850
19	2	WARRIOR 900 W/T		RNBT	FBG	SV	OB			7	4	1152			2350	2750
19	2	WARRIOR 900 W/T		RNBT	FBG	SV	IO	120		7	4				3750	4350
20	3	FORMULA F-200		CR	FBG		IO	155-215		7	10	3400	5	8	6350	7600
20	3	FORMULA F-200 SPORT		SPTCR	FBG		IO	155-215		7	10	2750	5		5550	6700
21		ARAPAHO		RNBT	FBG		OB			7	4	1800			3800	4400
21		ARAPAHO		RNBT	FBG		IO	155-215		7	4	3400			6100	7200
23	3	FORMULA 233 L-DK DLX		SPTCR	FBG		IO	215		8		4100	5		9950	11300
23	3	FORMULA 233 L-DK DLX		SPTCR	FBG		IO	T120-T170		8		4100	5		10600	12600
23	3	FORMULA 233 S-DK DLX		SPTCR	FBG		IO	215		8		4100	5		9000	10200
23	3	FORMULA 233 S-DK DLX		SPTCR	FBG		IO	T120-T170		8		4100	5		9700	11600
23	3	FORMULA 233 STD		SPTCR	FBG		IO	160-215		8		4100	5		8650	9950
23	3	FORMULA 233 STD		SPTCR	FBG		IO	T120-T170		8		4100	5		8850	10600
25		NAVAJO		RNBT	FBG		IO	160-215		8		4100			8650	10300
25		NAVAJO		RNBT	FBG		IO	T120-T170		8		4100			9700	11800
27		CHEROKEE		CR	FBG		IO	325	MRCR	10		6560			16300	18500
27		CHEROKEE		CR	FBG		IO	T115-T165		10		6560			15500	18500
27		CHEROKEE	HT	CR	FBG		IO	325	MRCR	10		6560			16300	18500
27		CHEROKEE	HT	CR	FBG		IO	T115-T165		10		6560			15500	18500
27		CHEROKEE	FB	CR	FBG		IO	325	MRCR	10					19900	22100
27		CHEROKEE	FB	CR	FBG		IO	T165-T215		10					19800	22700
34		DRIFT-R-CRUZ	HT	HB	FBG		IO	225		11	11		2	6	11800	13400
39	2	DRIFT-R-CRUZ	HT	HB	FBG		IO	225		11	11		2	6	13200	15000
46	8	DRIFT-R-CRUZ	HT	HB	FBG		IB			11	11		2	6	18200	20300
46	8	DRIFT-R-CRUZ	HT	HB	FBG		IO	T225		11	11		2	6	20200	22400
		1970 BOATS														
17		SEMINOLE		RNBT	FBG	TR	OB			6	10	1080	1	6	2050	2450
17		SEMINOLE		RNBT	FBG	TR	IO	120-165		6	10	2095	1	6	2900	3400
17	1	FORMULA F-1700		RNBT	FBG	DV	OB			6	6	1130	1	6	2200	2550
17	1	FORMULA F-1700		RNBT	FBG	DV	IO	140-215		6	6	2130	1	6	2850	3450
17	5	WARRIOR 700		RNBT	FBG	SV	OB			6	8	927	1	6	1850	2200
17	5	WARRIOR 700		RNBT	FBG	SV	IO	120-165		6	8	2000	1	6	2850	3350
18	7	APACHE		RNBT	FBG	TR	OB			7	3	1490	1	10	2800	3250
18	7	APACHE		RNBT	FBG	TR	IO	120-215		7	3	2735	1	10	3750	4500
18	7	CHEYENNE		RNBT	FBG	TR	OB			7	3	1430	1	10	2750	3200
18	7	CHEYENNE		RNBT	FBG	TR	IO	120-215		7	3	2605	1	10	3650	4350
18	7	CHEYENNE DELUXE		RNBT	FBG	TR	OB			7	3	1510			2850	3300
18	7	CHEYENNE DELUXE		RNBT	FBG	TR	IO	120-215		7	3	2705			3750	4450
18	7	COMANCHE DELUXE		RNBT	FBG	TR	OB			7	3	1540	2		2900	3350
18	7	COMANCHE DELUXE		RNBT	FBG	TR	IO	120-215		7	3	2785	2		3800	4550
19	2	WARRIOR 900		CBNCR	FBG	SV	OB			7	4	1450	1	8	2800	3300
19	2	WARRIOR 900		CBNCR	FBG	SV	IO	120-215		7	4	2400	1	8	3950	4700
19	2	WARRIOR 900		RNBT	FBG	SV	OB			7	4	1152	1	8	2350	2750
19	2	WARRIOR 900		RNBT	FBG	SV	IO	120-215		7	4	2360	1	8	3600	4300
20		FORMULA T-2000		CR	FBG	TR	IO	160-165		8		2250			5200	6000
21	10	ARAPAHO		RNBT	FBG	TR	OB			7	4	1800			3900	4550
21	10	ARAPAHO		RNBT	FBG	TR	IO	155-215		7	4	3400			6600	7750
21	10	ARAPAHO		RNBT	FBG	TR	IO	T120	MRCR	7	4	3400			7550	8700
23	3	FORMULA 233 DLX		SPTCR	FBG	DV	IO	210-215		8		3800	2	3	8500	9850
23	3	FORMULA 233 DLX		SPTCR	FBG	DV	IO	T120-T215		8		3800	2	3	9500	11100
23	3	FORMULA 233 STD		SPTCR	FBG	DV	IO	155-215		8		4100	2	3	9000	10400
23	3	FORMULA 233 STD		SPTCR	FBG	DV	IO	T120-T215		8		4100	2	3	10000	11700
23	3	IROQUOIS		RNBT	FBG	TR	IO	155-215		8		4020	2	2	8250	9650
23	3	IROQUOIS		RNBT	FBG	TR	IO	T120	MRCR	8		4020	2	2	9350	10600
23	3	IROQUOIS	HT	RNBT	FBG	TR	IO	T160-T165		8		4220	2	2	9650	11000
27		CHEROKEE		CR	FBG	TR	IO	215-250		10		6560	2	4	15500	18000
27		CHEROKEE		CR	FBG	TR	IO	T160-T215		10		6560	2	4	16700	19900
27		CHEROKEE	HT	CR	FBG	TR	IO	215-250		10			2	4	19300	21800
27		CHEROKEE	HT	CR	FBG	TR	IO	T160-T215		10			2	4	20400	23500
27		CHEROKEE T-BIRD	FB	CR	FBG		IO	215-250		10					19300	21800
27		CHEROKEE T-BIRD	FB	CR	FBG		IO	T160-T215		10					20400	23500
34		DRIFT-R-CRUZ	HT	HB	FBG		IO	210-325		11	11	12000			12200	15100
34		DRIFT-R-CRUZ	HT	HB	FBG		IO	T160-T225		11	11	12000			13100	15300
39	2	DRIFT-R-CRUZ	HT	HB	FBG		IO	325	MRCR	11	11	15000			14800	16800
		IO T210 OMC 14800 16800, IO T215 MRCR 14900 16900, IO T225 CHRY 15000 17000														
		IO T250 MRCR 15200 17300														
47		DRIFT-R-CRUZ	HT	HB	FBG		IO	T215	MRCR	11	11				20000	22300

CONTINUED ON NEXT PAGE

LOA FT	LOA IN	NAME AND/ OR MODEL	TOP/ RIG	BOAT TYPE	-HULL- MTL	-HULL- TP	ENGINE TP	ENGINE # HP	ENGINE MFG	BEAM FT	BEAM IN	WGT LBS	DRAFT FT	DRAFT IN	RETAIL LOW	RETAIL HIGH
		1970 BOATS														
47		DRIFT-R-CRUZ	HT	HB	FBG		IO	T270	MRCR	11	11				20700	23000
		IB T270 MRCR 19400 21500, IO T325 MRCR 21800 24200, IB T325 MRCR 19800 22000														
		1969 BOATS														
16	7	FORMULA 170	OP	RNBT	FBG	DV	OB			6	7	930			1800	2150
16	7	FORMULA 170	OP	RNBT	FBG	DV	IO	120	MRCR	6	7	1795			2650	3050
17		SEMINOLE	OP	RNBT	FBG	TR	OB			6	10	1080			2050	2450
17		SEMINOLE	OP	RNBT	FBG	TR	IO	120-160		6	10	2095			3000	3500
17		SIOUX	OP	RNBT	FBG	TR	OB			6	10	1080			2050	2450
17		SIOUX	OP	RNBT	FBG	TR	IO	120-160		6	10	2095			3000	3500
17	5	WARRIOR 700	OP	RNBT	FBG	SV	OB			6	8	927	1	6	1850	2200
17	5	WARRIOR 700	OP	RNBT	FBG	SV	IO	120	MRCR	6	8	2000	1	6	2950	3400
17	5	WARRIOR 700	OP	RNBT	FBG	SV	IB	120		6	8		1	6	1850	2200
18	7	APACHE	OP	RNBT	FBG	TR	OB			7	3	1490			2800	3300
18	7	APACHE	OP	RNBT	FBG	TR	IO	120-210		7	3	2735			3900	4600
18	7	CHEYENNE	OP	RNBT	FBG	TR	OB			7	3	1430			2750	3200
18	7	CHEYENNE	OP	RNBT	FBG	TR	IO	120-210		7	3	2605			3800	4450
18	7	CHEYENNE DELUXE	OP	RNBT	FBG	TR	OB			7	3	1510			2850	3300
18	7	CHEYENNE DELUXE	OP	RNBT	FBG	TR	IO	120-210		7	3	2705			3850	4550
18	7	COMANCHE DELUXE	OP	RNBT	FBG	TR	OB			7	3	1540			2900	3350
18	7	COMANCHE DELUXE	OP	RNBT	FBG	TR	IO	120-210		7	3	2785			3950	4650
18	7	FORMULA 190	OP	RNBT	FBG	DV	OB			7	2	1200			2400	2800
18	7	FORMULA 190	OP	RNBT	FBG	DV	IO	120-210		7	2	2200			3450	4050
19	2	WARRIOR 900		CR	FBG	SV	OB			7	4	1450	1	8	2850	3300
19	2	WARRIOR 900		CR	FBG	SV	IB	120		7	4		1	8	2050	2450
19	2	WARRIOR 900		CR	FBG	SV	IO	160	MRCR	7	4	2460	1	8	3950	4600
19	2	WARRIOR 900		RNBT	FBG	SV	OB			7	4	1152	1	8	2350	2750
19	2	WARRIOR 900		RNBT	FBG	SV	IB	120		7	4		1	8	2400	2800
19	2	WARRIOR 900	OP	RNBT	FBG	SV	IO	160	MRCR	7	4	2360	1	8	3750	4350
20	9	FORMULA 210	OP	SPTCR	FBG	DV	IO	155-225		7	10	2725			6050	7200
23	3	FORMULA 233 STD		SPTCR	FBG	DV	IO	155-225		8		4100			9300	10800
23	3	FORMULA 233 STD		SPTCR	FBG	DV	IO	T120-T160		8		4100			10300	11800
23	3	IROQUOIS		RNBT	FBG		IO	155-225		8		4020			8550	10000
23	3	IROQUOIS		RNBT	FBG		IO	T120	MRCR	8		4020			9600	10900
23	3	IROQUOIS	HT	RNBT	FBG		IO	T160	MRCR	8		4220			9950	11300
27		CHEROKEE		CR	FBG		IO			10					**	**
34		DRIFT-R-CRUZ	HT	HB	FBG	SV	IO	200-325		11	11	12000	1		11800	14400
34		DRIFT-R-CRUZ	HT	HB	FBG	SV	IO	T200-T250		11	11	12000	1		12700	14900
34		DRIFT-R-CRUZ	HT	HB	FBG	SV	IO	T325	MRCR	11	11	12000	1		14700	16600
39	2	DRIFT-R-CRUZ	HT	HB	FBG	SV	IO	200	MRCR	11	11	15000	1		12900	14700
		IO 210 CHRY 12900 14700, IO 210 OMC 12900 14600, IO 225 MRCR 13000 14700														
		IO 250 MRCR 13100 14900, IO 325 MRCR 13800 15700, IO T200 MRCR 13900 15700														
		IO T210 CHRY 13900 15800, IO T210 OMC 13800 15700, IO T225 MRCR 14000 15900														
		IO T250 MRCR 14200 16200, IO T300 MRCR 15100 17100														
		1968 BOATS														
16	7	FORMULA 170	OP	RNBT	FBG	SV	OB			6	7	930	2		1800	2150
16	7	FORMULA 170	OP	RNBT	FBG	SV	IO	120	MRCR	6	7		2		3300	3850
17		SIOUX	OP	RNBT	FBG	TR	OB			6	10	1080	2		2100	2450
17		SIOUX	OP	RNBT	FBG	TR	IO	80-160		6	10		2		3400	4000
18	7	CHEYENNE	OP	RNBT	FBG	TR	OB			7	1	1360	2	3	2650	3100
18	7	CHEYENNE	OP	RNBT	FBG	TR	IO	120-160		7	1		2	3	3950	4650
18	7	COMANCHE	OP	FSH	FBG	TR	IO	120-160		7	7	2125	2	3	3900	4700
18	7	COMANCHE	OP	FSH	FBG	TR	IO	225		7	7		2	3	4450	5150
18	7	COMANCHE	OP	RNBT	FBG	TR	OB			7	1	1540	2	3	2900	3350
18	7	COMANCHE	OP	RNBT	FBG	TR	IO	120-160		7	1		2	3	4400	5050
18	7	FORMULA 190	OP	RNBT	FBG	SV	OB			7	2	1200	2		2400	2800
18	7	FORMULA 190	OP	RNBT	FBG	SV	IO	120-160		7	2		2		4200	4900
20	2	ARAPAHO		RNBT	FBG	TR	IO	120-160					2	6	6150	7100
20	9	FORMULA 210	OP	SPTCR	FBG		IO	150-225					2	3	6600	7800
22	6	IROQUOIS		RNBT	FBG	TR	IO	T120-T160		8	6		2	8	9450	10800
23	3	FORMULA 233		SPTCR	FBG		IO	150-225		8		3600	2	3	8700	10200
23	3	FORMULA 233		SPTCR	FBG		IO	T120-T160		8		3600	2	3	9800	11200
23	3	FORMULA 233 F&S		SPTCR	FBG		IO	T120-T160		8		3800	2	3	10200	11600
23	3	GULFSTREAM		OPFSH	FBG		IO	160		8		3200	3	3	8450	9750
23	3	GULFSTREAM		OPFSH	FBG		IO	T120-T160		8		3800	3	3	10700	12700
23	3	IROQUOIS		RNBT	FBG		IO	150-160							8650	9950
34		DRIFT-R-CRUZ		HB	FBG	DV	IO	210		11	11	10000	2		10800	12300
40		DRIFT-R-CRUZ		HB	FBG	DV	IO	T210		11	11	15000	2	6	14400	16400
		1967 BOATS														
16	7	FORMULA 170		RNBT	FBG		OB								2150	2500
16	7	FORMULA 170		RNBT	FBG		IO	80-120							3650	4250
17		SIOUX		RNBT	FBG		OB								2200	2550
17		SIOUX		RNBT	FBG		IO	80-160							3750	4400
18	3	CHEYENNE		RNBT	FBG		OB								2550	2950
18	3	CHEYENNE		RNBT	FBG		IO	120-160							4000	4700
18	7	COMANCHE		RNBT	FBG		OB								3150	3650
18	7	COMANCHE		RNBT	FBG		IO	120-160							4550	5350
18	7	FORMULA 190		RNBT	FBG		OB								2700	3150
18	7	FORMULA 190		RNBT	FBG		IO	120-160							4700	5450
20	2	ARAPAHO		RNBT	FBG		IO	120-160							6350	7350
20	9	FORMULA 210		SPTCR	FBG		IO	150-225							6800	8050
22	6	IROQUOIS		RNBT	FBG		IO	150-225							8650	10100
22	6	IROQUOIS		RNBT	FBG		IO	T120-T160							9750	11100
23	3	FORMULA 233		SPTCR	FBG		IO	150-225							9600	11100
23	3	FORMULA 233		SPTCR	FBG		IO	T120-T160							10700	12200
23	3	FORMULA 233 F&S		SPTCR	FBG		IO	T120-T160				3800			10700	12200
30		DRIFT-R-CRUZ		HB	FBG		IO	210							10500	11900
40		DRIFT-R-CRUZ		HB	FBG		IO	T210							13800	15700
40		DRIFT-R-CRUZ		HB	FBG		IO	T225							13900	15800
		1966 BOATS														
16	3	SHAWNEE		RNBT	FBG	TR	IO	60		6	5	725			2000	2350
16	3	SHAWNEE DELUXE		RNBT	FBG	TR	IO	60		6	5				2800	3250
17		SIOUX		RNBT	FBG	TR	IO	60		6	11				3650	4250
17	3	FORMULA JR		SPTCR	FBG	DV	IO	110-200		6	7				3700	4450
17	3	SIOUX		RNBT	FBG	TR	OB			6	11	950			1900	2250
18	3	CHEYENNE		RNBT	FBG		IO	110-200		7	6				4100	5000
18	3	CHEYENNE		RNBT	FBG		IO	T 60		7	6				4750	5450
18	3	CHEYENNE		RNBT	FBG	TR	OB			7	6				2350	2750
18	3	CHEYENNE DELUXE		RNBT	FBG		OB			7	6				2750	3200
20	2	ARAPAHO		RNBT	FBG	TR	OB			7	6				3550	4100
20	2	ARAPAHO		RNBT	FBG	TR	IO	120-200		7	6				6350	7450
20	2	ARAPAHO		RNBT	FBG	TR	IO	T 60		7	6				7450	8550
22	6	IROQUOIS		SPTCR	FBG	TR	IO	150-225		8					9400	10900
22	6	IROQUOIS		SPTCR	FBG	TR	IO	T110-T150		8					10500	12500
23	3	APACHE		RNBT	FBG	DV	IO	150-225		8					9150	10600
23	3	APACHE		RNBT	FBG	DV	IO	T110-T150		8					10200	12100
23	3	FORMULA 233		SPTCR	FBG	DV	IO	225-310		8					9950	12300
23	3	FORMULA 233		SPTCR	FBG	DV	IO	T110-T150		8					10900	12900
		1965 BOATS														
17		SIOUX		RNBT	FBG		OB								2200	2550
17	3	FORMULA JR		SPTCR	FBG		IO	110-160							4200	4900
18	3	CHEYENNE		RNBT	FBG		OB								2600	3000
18	3	CHEYENNE		RNBT	FBG		IO	110-150							4300	5000
20	2	ARAPAHO		RNBT	FBG		IO	150							6800	7850
22	6	IROQUOIS			FBG		IO	110-225							9400	10900
22	6	IROQUOIS			FBG		IO	T110-T150							10500	12000
23	3		OP	OPFSH	FBG		IO	310							12000	13600
23	3		OP	OPFSH	FBG		IO	T150							12100	13800
23	3	FORMULA 233		SPTCR	FBG		IO	210-225							10400	11900
23	3	FORMULA 233 SUPR DLX		SPTCR	FBG		IO	225-310							10400	12900
23	3	FORMULA 233 SUPR DLX		SPTCR	FBG		IO	T110-T150							11400	13000
28		CHEROKEE		SF	FBG	TR	IB	240		10			2		8000	9200
		1964 BOATS														
17		SIOUX		RNBT	FBG		OB								2200	2600
18		CHEYENNE		RNBT	FBG		OB								2600	3000
18		CHEYENNE		RNBT	FBG		IO	110-150							4450	5100
22	6	IROQUOIS			FBG		OB								4050	4700
22	6	IROQUOIS			FBG		IO	110-225							9700	11300
22	6	IROQUOIS			FBG		IO	T110-T150							10900	12400
23	3	FORMULA 233		SPTCR	FBG		IO	225-310							10800	13300
23	3	FORMULA 233		SPTCR	FBG		IO	T110-T150							11800	14000
		1961 BOATS														
18	3	BLACK-HAWK		RNBT	FBG		OB			7	9	1050			2250	2600
18	3	CHEROKEE		RNBT	FBG		OB			7	9	950			2000	2400
18	10	MIAMI		CR	FBG		OB			8		1500			2950	3450
18	10	SCOUT		RNBT	FBG		OB			8		1200			2550	2950
20		APACHE		RNBT	FBG		OB			7	11	1250			2850	3300
20		COMANCHE		FSH	FBG		OB			7	11	1100			2550	2950
20		IROQUOIS		RNBT	FBG		IB	135		7	11		1	6	2600	3000
24	4	HIAWATHA		CR	FBG		OB			8		2300			5550	6350
		1960 BOATS														
18	3	BLACK-HAWK		RNBT	FBG		OB								2650	3100
18	3	CHEROKEE		RNBT	FBG	SV	OB								2650	3100
18	10	MIAMI		CR	FBG		OB								2500	2900
18	10	SCOUT		RNBT	FBG		OB								3050	3550
20		APACHE		RNBT	FBG	SV	OB								3600	4200
20		COMANCHE		FSH	FBG		OB								3350	3900
20		IROQUOIS		RNBT	FBG		IB	109-135							2500	2950
24	4	HIAWATHA		CR	FBG		OB								6800	7850

CONTINUED ON NEXT PAGE

LOA FT	LOA IN	NAME AND/ OR MODEL	TOP/ RIG	BOAT TYPE	HULL MTL	HULL TP	ENGINE TP	ENGINE # HP	ENGINE MFG	BEAM FT	BEAM IN	WGT LBS	DRAFT FT	DRAFT IN	RETAIL LOW	RETAIL HIGH
		1959 BOATS														
18	10	MIAMI		CBNCR	FBG		OB			8		1050			2300	2650
18	10	SCOUT SPORTSMAN		RNBT	FBG		OB			8		1000			2250	2600
20		APACHE		CBNCR	FBG		OB			8		1200			2750	3200
20		COMANCHE		RNBT	FBG		OB			8		1000			2400	2800
20		IROQUOIS		RNBT	FBG		IB	109	VLVO	8					2450	2850

THUNDERCRAFT

THUNDERCRAFT See inside cover to adjust price for area
GRAND MERE QUE CANADA G COAST GUARD MFG ID- ZMC
FORMERLY CADORETTE MARINE

For more recent years, see the BUC Used Boat Price Guide, Volume 1 or Volume 2

LOA FT	LOA IN	NAME AND/ OR MODEL	TOP/ RIG	BOAT TYPE	HULL MTL	HULL TP	ENGINE TP	ENGINE # HP	ENGINE MFG	BEAM FT	BEAM IN	WGT LBS	DRAFT FT	DRAFT IN	RETAIL LOW	RETAIL HIGH
		1977 BOATS														
16		OLYMPIC 0-16	OP	RNBT	FBG	SV	IO	140		6	6	1900			2200	2550
17	4	CYCLONE CC-174	OP	RNBT	FBG	TR	IO	140-165		6	10	1900			2350	2800
18	3	CC-195	OP	RNBT	FBG	DV	OB			7	2	1500			2250	2650
18	3	CC-195	OP	RNBT	FBG	DV	IO	165-190		7	2	2500			3000	3500

THURSTON CO INC

COAST GUARD MFG ID- THU

Call 1-800-327-6929 for BUC Personalized Evaluation Service
Or, for 1973 boats, sign onto www.BUCValuPro.com

TIARA YACHTS INC

DIV OF S2 YACHTS, INC See inside cover to adjust price for area
TIARA & S2 YACHTS
HOLLAND MI 49423 COAST GUARD MFG ID- SSU
ALSO PURSUIT

For more recent years, see the BUC Used Boat Price Guide, Volume 1 or Volume 2

LOA FT	LOA IN	NAME AND/ OR MODEL	TOP/ RIG	BOAT TYPE	HULL MTL	HULL TP	ENGINE TP	ENGINE # HP	ENGINE MFG	BEAM FT	BEAM IN	WGT LBS	DRAFT FT	DRAFT IN	RETAIL LOW	RETAIL HIGH
		1983 BOATS														
18		GRAND-SLAM 5.5	SLP	SA/OD	FBG	SK	OB			7	8	600		6	2500	2900
20	2	CONTINENTAL 2000	ST	CUD	FBG	DV	IO	170-230		8		2950	2	4	5550	6800
20	2	CONTINENTAL 2000	ST	CUD	FBG	DV	IO	260		8		2950	2	4	5850	7050
22		GRAND-SLAM 6.9	SLP	SA/OD	FBG	KC	OB			8		2200		10	4900	5600
22	6	CONTINENTAL 2200	ST	CUD	FBG	DV	IO	198-260		8		3200	2	4	6650	8300
22	6	CONTINENTAL 2200	ST	CUD	FBG	DV	IO	290	VLVO	8		3200	2	4	7550	8650
23	10	S2 7.3 METER DEEP	SLP	SAIL	FBG	KL	OB			8		3250	4		6700	7700
23	10	S2 7.3 METER DEEP	SLP	SAIL	FBG	KL	SE	115	OMC	8		3250	4		7750	8900
23	10	S2 7.3 METER SHOAL	SLP	SAIL	FBG	KL	OB			8		3250	3		6700	7700
23	10	S2 7.3 METER SHOAL	SLP	SAIL	FBG	KL	SE	115	OMC	8		3250	3		7750	8900
25	11	GRAND-SLAM 7.9	SLP	SA/OD	FBG	KC	OB			9		4250	1	2	9400	10700
25	11	GRAND-SLAM 7.9	SLP	SA/OD	FBG	KC	IB	7D	BMW	9		4250	1	2	9950	11300
26		CONTINENTAL 2600	ST	EXP	FBG	DV	IO	260-330		8	9	4600	2	6	11100	13600
26		CONTINENTAL 2600	ST	EXP	FBG	DV	IO	T138-T170		8	9	4600	2	6	11800	13500
26		S2 8.0 METER DEEP	SLP	SAIL	FBG	KL	OB			8		4600	4		10100	11500
26		S2 8.0 METER DEEP	SLP	SAIL	FBG	KL	SE	115	OMC	8		4600	4		10900	12400
26		S2 8.0 METER DEEP	SLP	SAIL	FBG	KL	VD	8D	YAN	8		4600	4		10800	12300
26		S2 8.0 METER SHOAL	SLP	SAIL	FBG	KL	OB			8		4600	3	6	10100	11500
26		S2 8.0 METER SHOAL	SLP	SAIL	FBG	KL	SE	115	OMC	8		4600	3	6	10900	12400
26		S2 8.0 METER SHOAL	SLP	SAIL	FBG	KL	VD	8D	YAN	8		4600	3	6	10800	12300
27	6	CONTINENTAL 2700	ST	EXP	FBG	DV	IO	260-330		9	10	7500	2	8	16000	19200
27	6	CONTINENTAL 2700	ST	EXP	FBG	DV	IO	T170-T260		9	10	7500	2	8	16800	21000
28		S2 8.6 METER	SLP	SAIL	FBG	KL	IB	15D		9	6	7600	4	6	19000	21100
28		S2 8.6 METER SHOAL	SLP	SAIL	FBG	KL	IB	15D		9	6	7600	3	11	19000	21100
29	10	S2 9.1 METER	SLP	SA/RC	FBG	KL	IB	15D	YAN	10	6	7500	5	6	19000	21100
29	11	S2 9.2 METER A DEEP	SLP	SAIL	FBG	KL	IB	15D	YAN	10	3	9800	4	11	23900	26600
29	11	S2 9.2 METER A SHOAL	SLP	SAIL	FBG	KL	IB	15D	YAN	10	3	9800	3	11	23900	26600
29	11	S2 9.2 METER C DEEP	SLP	SAIL	FBG	KL	IB	15D	YAN	10	3	9800	4	11	25400	28200
29	11	S2 9.2 METER C SHOAL	SLP	SAIL	FBG	KL	IB	15D	YAN	10	3	9800	3	11	25400	28200
31	3	CONTINENTAL 3100	OP	EXP	FBG	DV	IB	T220-T350		12		9200	2	9	35600	43300
31	3	CONTINENTAL 3100	OP	EXP	FBG	DV	IB	T158D	VLVO	12		9200	2	9	43000	47700
31	3	CONTINENTAL 3100	HT	EXP	FBG	DV	IB	T220-T350		12		10500	2	9	36400	44100
31	3	CONTINENTAL 3100	HT	EXP	FBG	DV	IB	T158D	VLVO	12		10500	2	9	43500	48300
31	3	CONTINENTAL 3100	FB	SDN	FBG	DV	IB	T225	VLVO	12			2	9	36600	40600
31	3	CONTINENTAL 3100	FB	SDN	FBG	DV	IB	T260-T350		12		11500	2	9	41800	49600
33	9	S2 10.3	SLP	SA/CR	FBG	KL	IB	15D- 23D		11	4	10500	4	11	26200	29100
33	9	S2 10.3	SLP	SA/RC	FBG	KL	IB	15D- 23D		11	4	10500	6	1	26200	29100
36		S2 11 A METER	SLP	SA/CR	FBG	KL	IB	30D	YAN	11	11	15000	5	6	36700	40800
36		S2 11 A SHOAL	SLP	SA/CR	FBG	KL	IB	30D	YAN	11	11	15000	4	8	36700	40800
36		S2 11 C	SLP	SA/CR	FBG	KL	IB	30D	YAN	11	11	15000	4	8	39900	44300
		1982 BOATS														
18		S2 5.5 METER	SLP	SAIL	FBG	SK	OB			7	8	600		6	2350	2750
22		S2 6.7 METER	SLP	SAIL	FBG	KC	OB			8		2200		10	4600	5300
22	6	CONTINENTAL 2200	ST	CUD	FBG	DV	IO	198-260		8		3200	2	4	6500	8100
22	6	CONTINENTAL 2200	ST	CUD	FBG	DV	IO	T145-T170		8			2	4	8550	9850
23	10	S2 7.3 METER DEEP	SLP	SAIL	FBG	KL	OB			8		3250	4		6300	7250
23	10	S2 7.3 METER DEEP	SLP	SAIL	FBG	KL	SD	15	OMC	8		3250	4		6700	7700
23	10	S2 7.3 METER SHOAL	SLP	SAIL	FBG	KL	OB			8		3250	2	10	6300	7250
23	10	S2 7.3 METER SHOAL	SLP	SAIL	FBG	KL	SD	15	OMC	8		3250	2	10	6700	7700
24	7	RIVIERA 2500	ST	CUD	FBG	DV	IO	260		12			2	5	10400	11800
24	7	RIVIERA 2500	ST	CUD	FBG	DV	IO	T145	VLVO	12			2	5	11400	12900
25	11	S2 7.9 METER	SLP	SA/OD	FBG	KC	OB			9		4250	1	2	8850	10100
26		CONTINENTAL 2600	ST	EXP	FBG	DV	IO	260		8	9	4600	2	5	10800	12500
26		CONTINENTAL 2600	ST	EXP	FBG	DV	IO	T145-T170		8	9	4600	2	5	11600	13200
26		S2 8.0 METER B	SLP	SAIL	FBG	KC	OB			8		4600	2	6	9550	10800
26		S2 8.0 METER B	SLP	SAIL	FBG	KC	SD	15	OMC	8		4600	2	6	9850	11200
26		S2 8.0 METER B	SLP	SAIL	FBG	KC	IB	8D	YAN	8		4600	2	6	10200	11500
26		S2 8.0 METER B DEEP	SLP	SAIL	FBG	KL	OB			8		4600	4		9550	10800
26		S2 8.0 METER B DEEP	SLP	SAIL	FBG	KL	SD	15	OMC	8		4600	4		9850	11200
26		S2 8.0 METER B DEEP	SLP	SAIL	FBG	KL	IB	8D	YAN	8		4600	4		10200	11500
26		S2 8.0 METER B SHOAL	SLP	SAIL	FBG	KL	OB			8		4600	2	6	9550	10800
26		S2 8.0 METER B SHOAL	SLP	SAIL	FBG	KL	SD	15	OMC	8		4600	2	6	9850	11200
26		S2 8.0 METER B SHOAL	SLP	SAIL	FBG	KL	IB	8D	YAN	8		4600	2	6	10200	11500
27	6	CONTINENTAL 2700	ST	EXP	FBG	DV	IB	165	CRUS	10		7500	1	9	18500	20500
		IO 205 OMC 15200 17200, IB 220 CRUS 19100 21200, IO 228-330													15400	18700
		IO T145 VLVO 12000 13600, IO T170-T260 16500 20500														
28		S2 8.5 METER	SLP	SAIL	FBG	KL	SD	15	OMC	9	6	7600	4	6	17200	19500
28		S2 8.5 METER	SLP	SAIL	FBG	KL	IB	8D- 13D		9	6	7600	4	6	17400	19800
28		S2 8.5 METER SHOAL	SLP	SAIL	FBG	KL	SD	15	OMC	9	6	7600	3	11	17200	19500
28		S2 8.5 METER SHOAL	SLP	SAIL	FBG	KL	IB	8D- 13D		9	6	7600	3	11	17400	19800
29	11	S2 9.2 METER A DEEP	SLP	SAIL	FBG	KL	IB	12D- 15D		10	3	9800	4	11	22200	25800
29	11	S2 9.2 METER A SHOAL	SLP	SAIL	FBG	KL	IB	12D- 15D		10	3	9800	3	11	23200	25800
29	11	S2 9.2 METER C DEEP	SLP	SAIL	FBG	KL	IB	12D- 15D		10	3	9800	4	11	24200	26900
29	11	S2 9.2 METER C SHOAL	SLP	SAIL	FBG	KL	IB	12D- 15D		10	3	9800	3	11	23200	25800
33	9	S2 10.3/34	SLP	SA/CR	FBG	KL	IB	15D	YAN	11	4	10500	6	2	24600	27300
33	9	S2 10.3/34	SLP	SA/RC	FBG	KL	IB	15D	YAN	11	4	10500	6	2	24600	27300
36		S2 11 METER A	SLP	SA/CR	FBG	KL	SD	D	UNIV	11	11	15000	5	6	35500	39500
36		S2 11 METER A	SLP	SA/CR	FBG	KL	IB	D	UNIV	11	11	15000	5	6	35500	39500
36		S2 11 METER A	SLP	SA/CR	FBG	KL	VD	42D	PATH	11	11	15000	5	6	35600	39500
36		S2 11 METER A SHOAL	SLP	SA/CR	FBG	KL	SD	D	UNIV	11	11	15000	4	8	35500	39500
36		S2 11 METER A SHOAL	SLP	SA/CR	FBG	KL	IB	D	UNIV	11	11	15000	4	8	33600	37300
36		S2 11 METER C	SLP	SA/CR	FBG	KL	IB	D	UNIV	11	11	15000	4	8	37500	41700
		1981 BOATS														
20	2	OVERNITER 2000	ST	OVNTR	FBG	DV	IO	170-260		8		2950	2	3	5250	6500
20	2	TOUCHE' 2000	ST	OVNTR	FBG	DV	IO	170-230		8		2950	2	3	5550	6800
20	2	TOUCHE' 2000	ST	OVNTR	FBG	DV	IO	260		8		2950	2	3	5900	7000
22		S2 6.7 METER	SLP	SAIL	FBG	KC	OB			8		2200		10	4300	5000
23	10	S2 7.3 METER DEEP	SLP	SAIL	FBG	KL	OB			8		3250	4		5900	6800
23	10	S2 7.3 METER DEEP	SLP	SAIL	FBG	KL	SD	15	OMC	8		3250	4		6300	7250
23	10	S2 7.3 METER SHOAL	SLP	SAIL	FBG	KL	OB			8		3250	2	10	5900	6800
23	10	S2 7.3 METER SHOAL	SLP	SAIL	FBG	KL	SD	15	OMC	8		3250	2	10	6300	7250
24	7	SPORT SALON 2500	FB	SDN	FBG	DV	IO	198-260		8		4600			9550	11600
24	7	VACATIONER 2500	ST	CR	FBG	DV	IO	198-260		8		4300			8850	10700
26		S2 8.0 METER B	SLP	SAIL	FBG	KC	OB			8		4600	2	6	9050	10300
26		S2 8.0 METER B	SLP	SAIL	FBG	KC	SD	15	OMC	8		4600	2	6	9300	10600
26		S2 8.0 METER B	SLP	SAIL	FBG	KC	IB	8D	YAN	8		4600	2	6	9550	10900
26		S2 8.0 METER B DEEP	SLP	SAIL	FBG	KL	OB			8		4600	4		9050	10300
26		S2 8.0 METER B DEEP	SLP	SAIL	FBG	KL	SD	15	OMC	8		4600	4		9300	10600
26		S2 8.0 METER B DEEP	SLP	SAIL	FBG	KL	IB	8D	YAN	8		4600	4		9550	10900
26		S2 8.0 METER B SHOAL	SLP	SAIL	FBG	KL	OB			8		4600	2	6	9050	10300
26		S2 8.0 METER B SHOAL	SLP	SAIL	FBG	KL	SD	15	OMC	8		4600	2	6	9300	10600
26		S2 8.0 METER B SHOAL	SLP	SAIL	FBG	KL	IB	8D	YAN	8		4600	2	6	9550	10900
28		S2 8.5 METER	SLP	SAIL	FBG	KC	SD	15	OMC	9	6	7600	4	6	16200	18400
28		S2 8.5 METER	SLP	SAIL	FBG	KC	IB	8D- 13D		9	6	7600	4	6	16400	18600
29	11	S2 9.2 METER A DEEP	SLP	SAIL	FBG	KL	IB	12D- 15D		10	3	9800	4	11	21000	23300
29	11	S2 9.2 METER A SHOAL	SLP	SAIL	FBG	KL	IB	12D- 15D		10	3	9800	3	11	21000	23300
29	11	S2 9.2 METER C DEEP	SLP	SAIL	FBG	KL	IB	12D- 15D		10	3	9800	4	11	22700	25200

 CONTINUED ON NEXT PAGE

LOA FT	IN	NAME AND/ OR MODEL	TOP/ RIG	BOAT TYPE	-HULL- MTL	TP	TP	----ENGINE--- # HP	MFG	BEAM FT	IN	WGT LBS	DRAFT FT	IN	RETAIL LOW	RETAIL HIGH
		1981 BOATS														
29	11	S2 9.2 METER C SHOAL	SLP	SAIL	FBG	KL	IB	12D- 15D		10	3	9800	3	11	22700	25200
36		S2 11 METER A	SLP	SA/CR	FBG	KL	SD	35D	VLVO	11	11	15000	5	6	33400	37100
36		S2 11 METER A	SLP	SA/CR	FBG	KL	IB	35D	VLVO	11	11	15000	5	6	33400	37100
36		S2 11 METER A	SLP	SA/CR	FBG	KL	SD	42D	PATH	11	11	15000	5	6	33500	37200
36		S2 11 METER A SHOAL	SLP	SA/CR	FBG	KL	SD	35D	VLVO	11	11	15000	4	8	33400	37100
36		S2 11 METER A SHOAL	SLP	SA/CR	FBG	KL	IB	35D	VLVO	11	11	15000	4	8	33400	37100
36		S2 11 METER C	SLP	SA/CR	FBG	KL	IB	42D	PATH	11	11	15000	5	6	33500	37200
		1980 BOATS														
20	2	HOLIDAY 2000	ST	CUD	FBG	DV	IO	170-230		8		2950	2	3	5300	6500
20	2	HOLIDAY 2000	ST	CUD	FBG	DV	IO	260		8		2950	2	3	5600	6750
20	2	OVERNITER 2000	ST	OVNTR	FBG	DV	IO	170-230		8		2950	2	3	5300	6500
20	2	OVERNITER 2000	ST	OVNTR	FBG	DV	IO	260		8		2950	2	3	5600	6750
22		S2 6.7 METER	SLP	SAIL	FBG	KC	OB			8		1900		8	3750	4350
23	10	S2 7.3 METER DEEP	SLP	SAIL	FBG	KL	OB			8		3250	4		5650	6500
23	10	S2 7.3 METER DEEP	SLP	SAIL	FBG	KL	SD	15	OMC	8		3250	4		6000	6900
23	10	S2 7.3 METER SHOAL	SLP	SAIL	FBG	KL	OB			8		3250	2	10	5650	6500
23	10	S2 7.3 METER SHOAL	SLP	SAIL	FBG	KL	SD	15	OMC	8		3250	2	10	6000	6900
24	7	GRANDE 2500	ST	CUD	FBG	DV	IO	198-260		8		4200	2	5	8550	10500
24	7	SPORT SALON 2500	FB	SDN	FBG	DV	IO	198-260		8		4600	2	6	9450	11500
24	7	VACATIONER 2500	ST	CR	FBG	DV	IO	198-260		8		4300	2	5	8700	10700
26		S2 8.0 METER B	SLP	SAIL	FBG	KC	OB			8		4600	2	6	8850	10100
26		S2 8.0 METER B	SLP	SAIL	FBG	KC	SD	15	OMC	8		4600	2	6	9100	10300
26		S2 8.0 METER B	SLP	SAIL	FBG	KC	IB	8D	YAN	8		4600	2	6	9400	10700
26		S2 8.0 METER B DEEP	SLP	SAIL	FBG	KL	OB			8		4600	4		8400	9650
26		S2 8.0 METER B DEEP	SLP	SAIL	FBG	KL	SD	15	OMC	8		4600	4		8700	10000
26		S2 8.0 METER B DEEP	SLP	SAIL	FBG	KL	IB	8D	YAN	8		4600	4		9100	10300
26		S2 8.0 METER B SHOAL	SLP	SAIL	FBG	KL	OB			8		4600	2	6	8400	9650
26		S2 8.0 METER B SHOAL	SLP	SAIL	FBG	KL	SD	15	OMC	8		4600	2	6	8700	10000
26		S2 8.0 METER B SHOAL	SLP	SAIL	FBG	KL	IB	8D	YAN	8		4600	2	6	9100	10300
28		S2 8.5 METER	SLP	SAIL	FBG	KC	SD	15	OMC	9	6	7600	4	6	15400	17500
28		S2 8.5 METER	SLP	SAIL	FBG	KC	IB	8D- 13D		9	6	7600	4	6	15600	17800
28		S2 8.5 METER	SLP	SAIL	FBG	KL	SD	13D	VLVO	9	6	7600	4	6	15700	17800
28		S2 8.5 METER	SLP	SAIL	FBG	KL	IB	15D	YAN	9	6	7600	4	6	15700	17800
29	11	S2 9.2 METER A DEEP	SLP	SAIL	FBG	KL	IB	12D- 15D		10	3	9800	4	11	19900	22100
29	11	S2 9.2 METER A SHOAL	SLP	SAIL	FBG	KL	IB	12D- 15D		10	3	9800	3	11	19900	22100
29	11	S2 9.2 METER C DEEP	SLP	SAIL	FBG	KL	IB	12D- 15D		10	3	9800	4	11	21800	24200
29	11	S2 9.2 METER C SHOAL	SLP	SAIL	FBG	KL	IB	12D- 15D		10	3	9800	3	11	21800	24200
36		S2 11 METER A	SLP	SA/CR	FBG	KL	SD	35D	VLVO	11	11	15000	5	6	30400	33700
36		S2 11 METER A	SLP	SA/CR	FBG	KL	IB	35D	VLVO	11	11	15000	5	6	30400	33700
36		S2 11 METER C	SLP	SA/CR	FBG	KL	SD	35D	VLVO	11	11	15000	5	6	33500	37200
36		S2 11 METER C	SLP	SA/CR	FBG	KL	IB	35D	VLVO	11	11	15000	5	6	33500	37200
		1979 BOATS														
20	2	HOLIDAY 2000	ST	CUD	FBG	DV	IO	170-230		8		2950	2	3	5300	6450
20	2	HOLIDAY 2000	ST	CUD	FBG	DV	IO	260		8		2950	2	3	5600	6750
20	2	OVERNITER 2000	ST	OVNTR	FBG	DV	IO	170-230		8		2950	2	3	5300	6450
20	2	OVERNITER 2000	ST	OVNTR	FBG	DV	IO	260		8		2950	2	3	5600	6750
22	4	S2 6.8 METER	SLP	SAIL	FBG	KC	OB			8		2900	2		4800	5550
22	4	S2 6.8 METER	SLP	SAIL	FBG	KL	OB			8		2900	2		4800	5550
23	10	S2 7.3 METER DEEP	SLP	SAIL	FBG	KL	OB			8		3250	4		5450	6250
23	10	S2 7.3 METER DEEP	SLP	SAIL	FBG	KL	SD	15	OMC	8		3250	4		5800	6650
23	10	S2 7.3 METER SHOAL	SLP	SAIL	FBG	KL	OB			8		3250	2	10	5450	6250
23	10	S2 7.3 METER SHOAL	SLP	SAIL	FBG	KL	SD	15	OMC	8		3250	2	10	5800	6650
24	7	OVERNITER 2500	ST	OVNTR	FBG	DV	IO	198-260		8		4200	2	5	8550	10500
24	7	SPORT SALON 2500	FB	SDN	FBG	DV	IO	198-260		8		4600	2	6	9450	11400
24	7	VACATIONER 2500	ST	CR	FBG	DV	IO	198-260		8		4300	2	5	8700	10600
26		S2 8.0 METER	SLP	SAIL	FBG	KC	SD	15	OMC	8		5200	2	6	9600	10900
26		S2 8.0 METER	SLP	SAIL	FBG	KC	IB	8D- 30D		8		5200	2	6	10100	11500
26		S2 8.0 METER B	SLP	SAIL	FBG	KC	OB			8		4600	2	6	8450	9700
26		S2 8.0 METER B	SLP	SAIL	FBG	KC	SD	15	OMC	8		4600	2	6	8650	9950
26		S2 8.0 METER B	SLP	SAIL	FBG	KC	VD	8D	YAN	8		4600	2	6	9050	10300
26		S2 8.0 METER B DEEP	SLP	SAIL	FBG	KL	OB			8		4600	4		8100	9300
26		S2 8.0 METER B DEEP	SLP	SAIL	FBG	KL	SD	15	OMC	8		4600	4		8350	9600
26		S2 8.0 METER B DEEP	SLP	SAIL	FBG	KL	VD	8D	YAN	8		4600	4		8650	9900
26		S2 8.0 METER B SHOAL	SLP	SAIL	FBG	KL	OB			8		4600	2	6	8100	9300
26		S2 8.0 METER B SHOAL	SLP	SAIL	FBG	KL	SD	15	OMC	8		4600	2	6	8350	9600
26		S2 8.0 METER B SHOAL	SLP	SAIL	FBG	KL	VD	8D	YAN	8		4600	2	6	8650	9900
26		S2 8.0 METER C DEEP	SLP	SAIL	FBG	KL	SD	15	OMC	8		5200	4		9600	10900
26		S2 8.0 METER C DEEP	SLP	SAIL	FBG	KL	IB	8D- 30D		8		5200	4		9750	11500
26		S2 8.0 METER SHOAL	SLP	SAIL	FBG	KL	SD	15	OMC	8		5200	2	6	9600	10900
26		S2 8.0 METER SHOAL	SLP	SAIL	FBG	KL	IB	8D- 30D		8		5200	2	6	9750	11500
29	11	S2 9.2 METER A DEEP	SLP	SAIL	FBG	KL	IB	12D- 15D		10	3	9800	4	11	19000	22300
29	11	S2 9.2 METER A SHOAL	SLP	SAIL	FBG	KL	IB	12D- 15D		10	3	9800	3	11	19000	22300
29	11	S2 9.2 METER C DEEP	SLP	SAIL	FBG	KL	IB	12D- 15D		10	3	9800	4	11	21000	23400
29	11	S2 9.2 METER C SHOAL	SLP	SAIL	FBG	KL	IB	12D- 15D		10	3	9800	3	11	21000	23400
30	10	SPORT SALON 3100	FB	SDN	FBG	DV	IB			11	11	10500	3	3	**	**
36		S2 11.0 METER	SLP	SA/CR	FBG	KL	SD	35D	VLVO	11	11	15000	5	6	30700	34100
36		S2 11.0 METER	SLP	SA/CR	FBG	KL	IB	35D	VLVO	11	11	15000	5	6	30700	34100
36		S2 11.0 METER	SLP	SA/CR	FBG	KL	VD	35D	VLVO	11	11	15000	5	6	30700	34100
36		S2 11.0 METER A	SLP	SA/CR	FBG	KL	SD	35D	VLVO	11	11	15000	5	6	30700	34100
36		S2 11.0 METER A	SLP	SA/CR	FBG	KL	IB	35D	VLVO	11	11	15000	5	6	30700	34100
		1978 BOATS														
20	2	HOLIDAY 2000	ST	CUD	FBG	DV	IO	170-228		8		2950	1	3	5300	6500
20	2	OVERNITER 2000	ST	OVNTR	FBG	DV	IO	170-228		8		2950	1	3	5300	6500
22	4	S2 6.8 METER	SLP	SAIL	FBG	KC	OB			8		3050	2		4800	5550
22	4	S2 6.8 METER	SLP	SAIL	FBG	KL	OB			8		3050	2		4800	5550
23	10	S2 7.3 METER DEEP	SLP	SAIL	FBG	KL	OB			8		3250	4		5250	6000
23	10	S2 7.3 METER DEEP	SLP	SAIL	FBG	KL	SD	15	OMC	8		3250	4		5550	6400
23	10	S2 7.3 METER SHOAL	SLP	SAIL	FBG	KL	OB			8		3250	2	10	5250	6000
23	10	S2 7.3 METER SHOAL	SLP	SAIL	FBG	KL	SD	15	OMC	8		3250	2	10	5550	6400
24	7	SPORT SALON 2500	FB	SDN	FBG	DV	IO	225-260		8		4600	1	6	9650	11500
24	7	VACATIONER 2500	ST	CR	FBG	DV	IO	225-260		8		4300	1	5	8300	10300
24	7	VACATIONER II 2500	ST	CR	FBG	DV	IO	225-350		8		4300	1	5	9550	11600
26		S2 8.0 METER B	SLP	SAIL	FBG	KC	OB			8		4600	2	6	8950	10100
26		S2 8.0 METER B	SLP	SAIL	FBG	KC	SD	15	OMC	8		4600	2	6	9100	10300
26		S2 8.0 METER B DEEP	SLP	SAIL	FBG	KL	OB			8		4600	4		7450	8550
26		S2 8.0 METER B DEEP	SLP	SAIL	FBG	KL	SD	15	OMC	8		4600	4		7750	8900
26		S2 8.0 METER B SHOAL	SLP	SAIL	FBG	KL	OB			8		4600	2	6	7450	8550
26		S2 8.0 METER B SHOAL	SLP	SAIL	FBG	KL	SD	15	OMC	8		4600	2	6	7750	8900
26		S2 8.0 METER C	SLP	SAIL	FBG	KC	IB	30	UNIV	8		5200	2	6	9500	10800
26		S2 8.0 METER C	SLP	SAIL	FBG	KC	IB	8D- 13D		8		5200	2	6	9700	11100
26		S2 8.0 METER C DEEP	SLP	SAIL	FBG	KL	IB	30	UNIV	8		5200	4		9250	10500
26		S2 8.0 METER C DEEP	SLP	SAIL	FBG	KL	IB	8D- 13D		8		5200	4		9400	10700
26		S2 8.0 METER C SHOAL	SLP	SAIL	FBG	KL	IB	30	UNIV	8		5200	2	6	9250	10500
26		S2 8.0 METER C SHOAL	SLP	SAIL	FBG	KL	IB	8D- 13D		8		5200	2	6	9400	10700
29	11	S2 9.2 METER A DEEP	SLP	SA/CR	FBG	KL	IB	30	UNIV	10	3	9800	4	11	18400	20500
29	11	S2 9.2 METER A DEEP	SLP	SA/CR	FBG	KL	IB	12D- 13D		10	3	9800	4	11	18500	20600
29	11	S2 9.2 METER A SHOAL	SLP	SA/CR	FBG	KL	IB	30	UNIV	10	3	9800	3	11	18400	20500
29	11	S2 9.2 METER A SHOAL	SLP	SA/CR	FBG	KL	IB	12D- 13D		10	3	9800	3	11	18500	20600
29	11	S2 9.2 METER C DEEP	SLP	SA/CR	FBG	KL	IB	30	UNIV	10	3	9800	4	11	20200	22400
29	11	S2 9.2 METER C DEEP	SLP	SA/CR	FBG	KL	IB	12D- 13D		10	3	9800	4	11	20300	22600
29	11	S2 9.2 METER C SHOAL	SLP	SA/CR	FBG	KL	IB	30	UNIV	10	3	9800	3	11	20200	22400
29	11	S2 9.2 METER C SHOAL	SLP	SA/CR	FBG	KL	IB	12D- 13D		10	3	9800	3	11	20300	22600
		1977 BOATS														
20	2	TIARA 2000	OP	FSH	FBG	SV	IO	188-235		8		3050	1	3	5850	6900
20	2	TIARA 2000	OP	OVNTR	FBG	SV	IO	188-235		8		2950	1	3	5450	6400
22	4	S2 6.8 METER	SLP	SAIL	FBG	KC	OB			8		3050	2		4700	5400
22	4	S2 6.8 METER	SLP	SAIL	FBG	KC	IB	7D	WEST	8		3050	2		5600	6450
22	4	S2 6.8 METER	SLP	SAIL	FBG	KL	OB			8		3050	2		4700	5400
22	4	S2 6.8 METER	SLP	SAIL	FBG	KL	IB	7D	WEST	8		3050	2		5600	6450
23		S2 7.0 METER	SLP	SAIL	FBG	KC	OB			8		3800	2	2	5650	6500
23		S2 7.0 METER	SLP	SAIL	FBG	KC	IB	7D	WEST	8		3800	2	2	6500	7450
23		S2 7.0 METER	SLP	SAIL	FBG	KL	OB			8		3800	2	2	5650	6500
23		S2 7.0 METER	SLP	SAIL	FBG	KL	IB	7D	WEST	8		3800	2	2	6500	7450
24	7	TIARA 2500	OP	CR	FBG	SV	IO	233-235		8		4300	1	5	9150	10400
24	7	TIARA 2500	OP	OVNTR	FBG	SV	IO	233-235		8		4100	1	5	8850	10100
24	7	TIARA 2500	FB	SDN	FBG	SV	IO	233-235		8		4700	1	6	10000	11400
26		S2 8.0 METER B	SLP	SA/CR	FBG	KC	OB			8		4600	2	5	7850	9050
26		S2 8.0 METER B	SLP	SA/CR	FBG	KC	IB	10- 30		8		4600	2	5	8050	9350
26		S2 8.0 METER B	SLP	SA/CR	FBG	KC	IB	8D	YAN	8		4600	2	5	8350	9600
26		S2 8.0 METER B DEEP	SLP	SA/CR	FBG	KL	OB			8		4600	4		7550	8650
26		S2 8.0 METER B DEEP	SLP	SA/CR	FBG	KL	IB	10- 30		8		4600	4		7750	9000
26		S2 8.0 METER B DEEP	SLP	SA/CR	FBG	KL	IB	8D	YAN	8		4600	4		8000	9200
26		S2 8.0 METER B SHOAL	SLP	SA/CR	FBG	KL	OB			8		4600	2	5	7550	8650
26		S2 8.0 METER B SHOAL	SLP	SA/CR	FBG	KL	IB	10- 30		8		4600	2	5	7750	9000
26		S2 8.0 METER B SHOAL	SLP	SA/CR	FBG	KL	IB	8D	YAN	8		4600	2	5	8000	9200
26		S2 8.0 METER C	SLP	SA/CR	FBG	KC	IB	30	UNIV	8		5200	2	5	9250	10500
26		S2 8.0 METER C	SLP	SA/CR	FBG	KC	IB	10D	VLVO	8		5200	2	5	9400	10700
26		S2 8.0 METER C DEEP	SLP	SA/CR	FBG	KL	IB	30	UNIV	8		5200	4		8950	10200
26		S2 8.0 METER C DEEP	SLP	SA/CR	FBG	KL	IB	10D	VLVO	8		5200	4		9150	10400
26		S2 8.0 METER C SHOAL	SLP	SA/CR	FBG	KL	IB	30	UNIV	8		5200	2	5	8950	10200
26		S2 8.0 METER C SHOAL	SLP	SA/CR	FBG	KL	IB	10D	VLVO	8		5200	2	5	9150	10400
29	11	S2 9.2 METER A DEEP	SLP	SA/CR	FBG	KL	IB	30	UNIV	10	3	9800	4	11	17400	19700
29	11	S2 9.2 METER A DEEP	SLP	SA/CR	FBG	KL	IB	10D- 12D		10	3	9800	4	11	17500	19900
29	11	S2 9.2 METER A SHOAL	SLP	SA/CR	FBG	KL	IB	30	UNIV	10	3	9800	3	11	17400	19700
29	11	S2 9.2 METER A SHOAL	SLP	SA/CR	FBG	KL	IB	10D- 12D		10	3	9800	3	11	17500	19900
29	11	S2 9.2 METER C DEEP	SLP	SA/CR	FBG	KL	IB	30	UNIV	10	3	9800	4	11	19600	21700
29	11	S2 9.2 METER C DEEP	SLP	SA/CR	FBG	KL	IB	10D- 12D		10	3	9800	4	11	19600	21900

 CONTINUED ON NEXT PAGE

TIARA YACHTS INC — CONTINUED

LOA FT	IN	NAME AND/OR MODEL	TOP/RIG	BOAT TYPE	MTL	TP	TP	# HP	MFG	BEAM FT	IN	WGT LBS	DRAFT FT	IN	RETAIL LOW	RETAIL HIGH
		1977 BOATS														
29	11	S2 9.2 METER C SHOAL	SLP	SA/CR	FBG	KL	IB	30	UNIV	10	3	9800	3	11	19600	21700
29	11	S2 9.2 METER C SHOAL	SLP	SA/CR	FBG	KL	IB	10D- 12D		10	3	9800	3	11	19600	21900
		1976 BOATS														
22	4	S2 6-METER S	SLP	SAIL	FBG	KC	OB			8		3050	2		4550	5200
22	4	S2 6-METER S	SLP	SAIL	FBG	KL	OB			8		3050	2		4550	5200
23		S2 7-METER S	SLP	SAIL	FBG	KC	OB			8		3800	2	2	5500	6300
23		S2 7-METER S	SLP	SAIL	FBG	KC	IB	10	UNIV	8		3800	2	2	5750	6650
23		S2 7-METER S	SLP	SAIL	FBG	KC	IB	7D	WEST	8		3800	2	2	6300	7200
23		S2 7-METER S	SLP	SAIL	FBG	KL	OB			8		3800	2	2	5500	6300
23		S2 7-METER S	SLP	SAIL	FBG	KL	IB	10	UNIV	8		3800	2	2	5750	6650
23		S2 7-METER S	SLP	SAIL	FBG	KL	IB	7D	WEST	8		3800	2	2	6300	7200
26		S2 8-METER D	SLP	SAIL	FBG	KL	OB			8		4600	4		7500	8650
		IB 7 WEST 7600 8700, VD 30 UNIV 7700 8850, IB 10D VLVO											10D	VLVO	6600	7600
26		S2 8-METER MID S	SLP	SAIL	FBG	KC	IB	30	UNIV	8		4600	2	6	7700	8850
26		S2 8-METER MID S	SLP	SAIL	FBG	KL	IB	10D	VLVO	8		4600	2	6	9400	10700
26		S2 8-METER MID S	SLP	SAIL	FBG	KL	IB	30		8		4600	2	6	7700	8850
26		S2 8-METER MID S	SLP	SAIL	FBG	KL	IB	10D		8		4600	2	6	9150	10700
26		S2 8-METER S	SLP	SAIL	FBG	KC	OB			8		4600	2	6	7550	8650
26		S2 8-METER S	SLP	SAIL	FBG	KC	VD	30	UNIV	8		4600	2	6	7700	8850
26		S2 8-METER S	SLP	SAIL	FBG	KC	IB	7D- 10D		8		4600	2	6	7850	9050
26		S2 8-METER S	SLP	SAIL	FBG	KL	OB			8		4600	2	6	7150	8250
26		S2 8-METER S	SLP	SAIL	FBG	KL	VD	30	UNIV	8		4600	2	6	7700	8850
26		S2 8-METER S	SLP	SAIL	FBG	KL	IB	7D- 10D		8		4600	2	6	7850	9050
		1975 BOATS														
22	4	S2 22	SLP	SAIL	FBG	KL	OB			7	10	3000	2		4300	5000
23		S2 23	SLP	SAIL	FBG	KL	OB			8		3800	2	2	5300	6100
23		S2 23	SLP	SAIL	FBG	KL	IB	7D	WEST	8		3800	2	2	6100	7000
26		S2 26	SLP	SAIL	FBG	KL	OB			8		4600	2	5	7200	8250
26		S2 26	SLP	SAIL	FBG	KL	VD	30	UNIV	8		4600	2	5	7450	8600
26		S2 26 MID COCKPIT	SLP	SAIL	FBG	KL	IB	30	UNIV	8		4600	2	5	7450	8600

TIBURON YACHTS INC
BOULDER CO 80302   COAST GUARD MFG ID- TAE See inside cover to adjust price for area

LOA FT	IN	NAME AND/OR MODEL	TOP/RIG	BOAT TYPE	MTL	TP	TP	# HP	MFG	BEAM FT	IN	WGT LBS	DRAFT FT	IN	RETAIL LOW	RETAIL HIGH
		1983 BOATS														
45	2	HARDIN 45	KTH	SA/CR	FBG	KL	IB	60D	FORD	13	4	32000	5	6	104500	115000
		1982 BOATS														
45	2	HARDIN 45	KTH	SA/CR	FBG	KL	IB	60D	FORD	13	4	32000	5	6	98400	108000
		1981 BOATS														
38		TIBURON 38	CUT	SA/CR	FBG	KL	IB	45D	PERK	11	4	20000	5		48200	53000
44	11	TIBURON 44	KTH	SA/CR	FBG	KL	IB	D		11	4	32000	5	6	91400	101500
45	2	HARDIN 45	KTH	SA/CR	FBG	KL	IB	60D	FORD	13	4	32000	5	6	92600	101500
		1980 BOATS														
38		TIBURON 38	CUT	SA/CR	FBG	KL	IB	45D	PERK	11	4	20000	5		46300	50800
38	2	ANTIGUA 37	SLP	SA/CR	FBG	KL	IB	48D	YAN	11	3	17400	5	7	41600	46200
44	11	HARDIN 44	KTH	SA/CR	FBG	KL	IB	60D	FORD	13	4	32000	5	6	87100	95800
		1979 BOATS														
38		TIBURON 38	CUT	SA/CR	FBG	KL	IB	60D	CHRY	11	4	20000	5		44300	49300
44	6	TIBURON 44	KTH	SA/CR	FBG	KL	IB	60D	PISC	13	4	32000	6		81800	89800
		1978 BOATS														
36	3	TIBURON 36 MKII	KTH	SA/CR	FBG	KL	IB	70D	CHRY	11	4	20000	5		41200	45900
36	8	CREALOCK 37	SLP	SA/CR	FBG	KL	IB	D		10	10	15000	5	3	32300	35900
38		TIBURON 38	CUT	SA/CR	FBG	KL	IB	70D	CHRY	11	4	20000	5		42800	47600
44		TIBURON 44	KTH	SA/CR	FBG	KL	IB	60D	PERK	13	4	32000	5	11	76300	83800

TICON YACHTS
PT CREDIT ONTARIO CANADA   See inside cover to adjust price for area

For more recent years, see the BUC Used Boat Price Guide, Volume 1 or Volume 2

LOA FT	IN	NAME AND/OR MODEL	TOP/RIG	BOAT TYPE	MTL	TP	TP	# HP	MFG	BEAM FT	IN	WGT LBS	DRAFT FT	IN	RETAIL LOW	RETAIL HIGH
		1983 BOATS														
29	11	TICON 30	SLP	SA/CR	FBG	KL	IB	15D- 20D		11		9600	3	11	19700	21900

TIDE CRAFT INC
AFFILIATE OF WOODARD-WA COAST GUARD MFG ID- TDC

Call 1-800-327-6929 for BUC Personalized Evaluation Service
Or, for 1971 to 1979 boats, sign onto www.BUCValuPro.com

TIDEWATCH YACHTS INC
COAST GUARD MFG ID- TYY

Call 1-800-327-6929 for BUC Personalized Evaluation Service
Or, for 1972 to 1973 boats, sign onto www.BUCValuPro.com

TIDEWATER PLASTICS INC
ANNAPOLIS MD 21404   COAST GUARD MFG ID- APJ See inside cover to adjust price for area

LOA FT	IN	NAME AND/OR MODEL	TOP/RIG	BOAT TYPE	MTL	TP	TP	# HP	MFG	BEAM FT	IN	WGT LBS	DRAFT FT	IN	RETAIL LOW	RETAIL HIGH
		1978 BOATS														
24	2	ANNAPOLIS	SLP	SA/CR	FBG	KL	IB	D		6	3	2240	3	6	4450	5150
26	2	ANNAPOLIS	SLP	SA/CR	FBG	KL	IB	6D		6	3	4900	4		8950	10200
		1977 BOATS														
24	2	KNOCKABOUT	SLP	SA/CR	FBG	KL	IB	D		6	3	2240	3	6	4250	4950
24	2	RAINBOW	SLP	SA/CR	FBG	KL	IB	D		6	3	2200	3	4	4200	4900
25	7	ANNAPOLIS 26	SLP	SA/CR	FBG	KL	IB			8		4900	4		8400	9650
		1976 BOATS														
24	2	RAINBOW	SLP	SA/OD	FBG	KL	IB			6	3	2200	3	4	4050	4700
25	7	ANNAPOLIS 26	SLP	SA/OD	FBG	KL	IB	5D		8		5000	4		8150	9350
		1975 BOATS														
24	2	KNOCKABOUT	SLP	SA/OD	FBG	KL	IB			6	3	2250	3	4	3950	4600
24	2	RAINBOW	SLP	SA/OD	FBG	KL	IB			6	3	2250	3	4	3950	4600
25	7	ANNAPOLIS 26	SLP	SAIL	FBG	KL	IB	5D		8		5000	4		7850	9000
		1974 BOATS														
24	2	KNOCKABOUT	SLP	SA/OD	FBG	KL	IB	D		6	3	2250			3800	4450
24	2	RAINBOW	SLP	SA/OD	FBG	KL	IB	D		6	3	2250			3800	4450
25		ANNAPOLIS 25	SLP	SA/OD	FBG	KL	IB			6	5	2600	3	6	4400	5050
25	7	ANNAPOLIS 26	SLP	SA/OD	FBG	KL	IB	5D		8		5000	4		7600	8750
		1973 BOATS														
17		MUSTANG	SLP	SA/OD	FBG	CB	OB			6	6	900	4	7	1750	2100
24	2	KNOCKABOUT	SLP	SA/OD	FBG	KL	OB			6	3	2200	3	4	3300	3850
24	2	RAINBOW	SLP	SA/OD	FBG	KL	OB			6	3	2200	3	4	3300	3850
25		ANNAPOLIS 25	SLP	SA/CR	FBG	KL	OB			6	5	2600	3	6	3850	4450
25	7	ANNAPOLIS 26	SLP	SA/OD	FBG	KL	OB			8		4700	4		6600	7600
25	7	ANNAPOLIS 26	SLP	SA/CR	FBG	KL	IB	5		8		5000	4		7200	8250
		1972 BOATS														
24	2	KNOCKABOUT	SLP	SA/OD	FBG	KL				6	3	2250			3250	3750
24	2	RAINBOW	SLP	SA/OD	FBG	KL				6	3	2500	3	4	3400	3950
25		ANNAPOLIS 25	SLP	SA/CR	FBG	KL	OB			6	5	2600	3	6	3750	4350
25	7	ANNAPOLIS 26	SLP	SA/OD	FBG	KL	OB			8		4500	4		6200	7150
25	7	ANNAPOLIS 26	SLP	SA/CR	FBG	KL	OB	D		8		4500	4		6550	7550
		1971 BOATS														
24	2	RAINBOW	SLP	SA/OD	FBG	KL				6	3	2500	3	4	3300	3850
25		ANNAPOLIS 25	SLP	SA/CR	FBG	KL				6	5	2600	3	6	3500	4100
25	6	ANNAPOLIS 26	SLP	SA/CR	FBG	KL	IB	10		8		4500	4		6200	7100
		1970 BOATS														
24	2	KNOCKABOUT	SLP	SA/OD	FBG	KL				6	3	2200	3	6	3100	3600
24	2	RAINBOW	SLP	SA/OD	FBG	KL				6	3	2200	3	4	3100	3600
25		ANNAPOLIS 25	SLP	SA/CR	FBG	KL				6	5	2600	3	6	3550	4100
		1969 BOATS														
24	2	RAINBOW	SLP	SA/OD	FBG	KL				6	3	2200	3	6	3000	3500
24	2	RAINBOW WEEKENDER	SLP	SA/OD	FBG	KL				6	3	2350	3	4	3150	3650
25		ANNAPOLIS 25	SLP	SAIL	FBG	KL				6	5	2600	3		3500	4050
		1968 BOATS														
24	2	RAINBOW	SLP	SAIL	FBG	KL				6	3	2250	3	6	2900	3400
24	2	WEEKENDER	SLP	SAIL	FBG	KL				6	3	2250	3	6	2900	3400
		1967 BOATS														
24	2		SLP	SAIL	FBG	KL				6	3				2900	3350
24	2	RAINBOW	SLP	SA/OD	FBG	KL				6	3	2200	3		2850	3350
		1966 BOATS														
24	2		SLP	SAIL	FBG	KL				6	3				2850	3300
24	2	RAINBOW	SLP	SA/OD	FBG	KL				6	3		3		2850	3300
		1965 BOATS														
24	2	RAINBOW	SLP	SA/OD	FBG	KL	OB			6	3				2900	3350
24	3			SAIL	FBG	KL									2900	3350
		1963 BOATS														
24	2	RAINBOW	SLP	SA/OD	FBG	KL	OB								2850	3300
		1962 BOATS														
24	2	RAINBOW	SLP	SA/OD	FBG	KL	OB								2850	3300

TIFFANY YACHTS INC
BURGESS VA 22432   COAST GUARD MFG ID- GPB See inside cover to adjust price for area
FORMERLY GLEBE POINT BOAT COMPANY

For more recent years, see the BUC Used Boat Price Guide, Volume 1 or Volume 2

LOA FT IN	NAME AND/ OR MODEL	TOP/ RIG	BOAT TYPE	-HULL- MTL TP	ENGINE TP # HP MFG	BEAM FT IN	WGT LBS	DRAFT FT IN	RETAIL LOW	RETAIL HIGH
					1980 BOATS					
36	GLEBE 36	SF	WD	IB		14			**	**
38	TIFFANY CUSTOM	CR	WD	SV IB	T250	13 6			43300	48100
40	GLEBE 40	SF	WD	IB		14 6			**	**
44	GLEBE 44	SF	WD	IB		15 6			**	**
44	TIFFANY CUSTOM	CR	WD	SV IB	T320D	15			103500	114000
45	TIFFANY CUSTOM	TRWL	WD	SV IB	210D	15			118000	129500
46	TIFFANY CUSTOM	SF	WD	SV IB	T320D	15 6			135500	148500
48	GLEBE 48	MY	WD	IB		16 6			**	**
48	GLEBE 48	SF	WD	IB		15 6			**	**
48	TIFFANY CUSTOM	SF	WD	SV IB	T320D	16			162000	178000
52	GLEBE 52	SF	WD	IB		17 6			**	**
54	GLEBE 54	MY	WD	IB		17 6			**	**
54	TIFFANY CUSTOM	SF	WD	SV IB	T550D	17			253000	278000
60	GLEBE 60	SF	WD	IB		18 6			**	**
60	TIFFANY CUSTOM	SF	WD	SV IB	T650D	18			317500	349000
65	GLEBE 65	MY	WD	IB		18 6			**	**
					1979 BOATS					
38	TIFFANY	FB	SDN	SV IB	T250	13 6	24000		58800	64600
44	TIFFANY	FB	SDN	SV IB	T320D	15	38000		126000	138500
45	TIFFANY	FB	TRWL	SV IB	210D	15	40000		124000	136000
46	TIFFANY	FB	SDNSF	SV IB	T320D	15 6	40000		138500	152500
48	TIFFANY	FB	SDNSF	SV IB	T320D	16	45000		152500	167500
54	TIFFANY	FB	SDNSF	SV IB	T550D	17	56000		283500	312000
60	TIFFANY	FB	SDNSF	SV IB	T650D	18	65000		325500	357500
					1978 BOATS					
38	TIFFANY CUSTOM	FB	SDN	SV IB	T250	13 6	24000		56200	61800
44	TIFFANY CUSTOM	FB	SDN	SV IB	T320D	15	38000		120500	132500
45	TIFFANY CUSTOM	FB	TRWL	DS IB	210D	15	40000		119000	130500
46	TIFFANY CUSTOM	FB	SDNSF	SV IB	T320D	15 6	40000		132500	146000
48	TIFFANY CUSTOM	FB	SDNSF	SV IB	T320D	16	45000		145500	160000
54	TIFFANY CUSTOM	FB	SDNSF	SV IB	T400D	17	56000		241000	265000
60	TIFFANY CUSTOM	FB	SDNSF	SV IB	T400D	18	65000		261000	287000
					1977 BOATS					
38	TIFFANY	FB	SDN	P/M SV IB	T250	13 6	24000		53800	59100
44	TIFFANY	FB	SDN	P/M SV IB	T230D	15	38000		111500	122500
45	TIFFANY	FB	TRWL	P/M DS IB	210D	15	40000		114000	125000
46	TIFFANY	FB	SDNSF	P/M SV IB	T320D	15 6	40000		127000	139500
48	TIFFANY	FB	SDNSF	P/M SV IB	T320D	16	45000		139500	153500
54	TIFFANY	FB	SDNSF	P/M SV IB	T400D	16 6	56000		231000	253500
60	TIFFANY	FB	SDNSF	P/M SV IB	T400D	16	65000		249500	274000
					1976 BOATS					
38	TIFFANY	FB	SDNSF	P/M SV IB	T250	13 6	28000		58100	63800
44	TIFFANY	FB	SDNSF	P/M SV IB	T320D	15			106500	117000
44	TIFFANY	FB	SDNSF	P/M SV IB	T370D CUM	15			109000	119500
45	TIFFANY	FB	TRWL	P/M SV IB	210D	14	40000 4		109500	120500
46	TIFFANY	FB	SDNSF	P/M SV IB	T320D	16	45000		122000	134000
48	TIFFANY	FB	SDNSF	P/M SV IB	T320D	16	45000 3 9		134000	147000
54	TIFFANY	FB	SDNSF	P/M SV IB	T400D	16 6	56000		221000	243000
60	TIFFANY	FB	SDNSF	P/M SV IB	T400D	16 6	65000		239000	262500
					1975 BOATS					
37	TIFFANY CUSTOM	FB	SDNSF	F/W DV IB	T310D GM	14	28000	2 8	63800	70100
40	TIFFANY CUSTOM	FB	SDNSF	P/M SV IB	T310D GM	15	33000	3 2	79400	87300
44	TIFFANY CUSTOM	FB	SDNSF	P/M SV IB	T320D CUM	15 6	38000	3 6	106500	117000
45	CHARACTER BOAT	FB	TRWL	P/M SV IB	T				**	**
48	TIFFANY CUSTOM	FB	SDNSF	P/M SV IB	T400D CUM	16	45000	3 6	132500	146000
50	TIFFANY CUSTOM	FB	YTFS	P/M SV IB	T400D CUM	16	47000	3 8	130500	143500
54	TIFFANY CUSTOM	FB	SDNSF	P/M SV IB	T525D GM	16 9	56000	3 10	227000	249500
60	TIFFANY CUSTOM	FB	SDNSF	P/M SV IB	T525D GM	17	65000	4	253000	278000
64	TIFFANY CUSTOM	FB	MY	P/M SV IB	T525D GM	17 6	73000	4 6	331500	364500
					1974 BOATS					
36	TIFFANY CUSTOM	FB	SDNSF	WD	IB	T330 CHRY	13 6	28000	2 6	47100	51700
38	TIFFANY CUSTOM	FB	SDNSF	WD	IB T240D CUM	14	28000	3 4	61500	67600
42	TIFFANY CUSTOM	FB	SDNSF	WD	IB T300D GM	14 6	30000	3 4	75500	83000
44	TIFFANY CUSTOM	FB	SDNSF	WD	IB T320D CUM	15 6	38000	3 6	102500	112500
46	TIFFANY CUSTOM	FB	SDNSF	WD	IB T320D CUM	15 6	40000	3 6	112000	123000
48	TIFFANY CUSTOM	FB	SDNSF	WD	IB T320D CUM	16	45000	3 8	123000	135500
54	TIFFANY CUSTOM	FB	SDNSF	WD	IB T400D CUM	16 6	56000	4	199000	218500
60	TIFFANY CUSTOM	FB	SDNSF	WD	IB T530D GM	17	65000	4 6	244000	268000
65	TIFFANY CUSTOM	FB	MY	WD	IB T530D GM	17 6	73000	4 6	326500	359000
					1973 BOATS					
36	TIFFANY 36 CUSTOM	FB	SDNSF	WD	IB T330 CHRY	13 6	25000	2 6	41400	46000
38	TIFFANY 38 CUSTOM	FB	SDNSF	P/M SV IB	T250	13 6	28000	3	50500	55500
44	TIFFANY 44 CUSTOM	FB	SDNSF	WD	IB T300D GM	15	38000	3 4	98400	108000
46	TIFFANY 46 CUSTOM	FB	SDNSF	P/M SV IB	T320D	15 6	40000	3 6	108000	118500
48	TIFFANY 48 CUSTOM	FB	SDNSF	P/M SV IB	T320D	16	45000	3 8	118500	130500
54	TIFFANY 54 CUSTOM	FB	SDNSF	WD	IB T370D CUM	16 6	45000	4	174000	191500
60	TIFFANY 60 CUSTOM	FB	SDNSF	P/M SV IB	T530D	17	65000	4 6	234500	257500
65	TIFFANY 65 CUSTOM	FB	MY	WD	IB T530D GM	17 6	65000	4	285000	313000
					1972 BOATS					
27	TIFFANY 27 CUSTOM		CUD	WD	SV IB 210D	10			14900	16900
36	TIFFANY 36 CUSTOM		CR	WD	SV IB T330	13 6			25100	27900
40	TIFFANY 40 CUSTOM		CR	WD	SV IB T330	13 6			37500	41700
46	TIFFANY 46 CUSTOM	FB	SF	WD	SV IB T300D	15	40000	3 6	105000	115000
48	TIFFANY 48 CUSTOM	FB	SF	WD	SV IB T290D	15	40000	3 6	115000	126500
50	TIFFANY 50 CUSTOM	FB	SF	WD	SV IB T300D	16	49500		121500	133500
54	TIFFANY 54 CUSTOM	FB	SF	WD	SV IB T350D	16	53000		174000	191000
58	TIFFANY 58 CUSTOM		CR	WD	SV IB T370D	16 6			169000	185500
60	TIFFANY 60 CUSTOM	FB	SF	WD	SV IB T370D	16 6	68500		214500	236000
64	TIFFANY 64 CUSTOM	FB	MY	WD	SV IB T350D	17	73000		255500	280500
					1971 BOATS					
36 10	GLEBE 36		MHG		IB T300 CHRY	13 6	20000	2 8	36000	40000
40 8	TIFFANY 40 CUSTOM		MHG		IB T300 CHRY	14	30000	3	61300	67300
40 8	TIFFANY 40 CUSTOM		MHG		IB T180D CUM	14	30000	3	68700	75400
45 8	TIFFANY 45 CUSTOM		MHG		IB T300D CUM	15	40000	3	103500	113500
50	TIFFANY 50 CUSTOM		MHG		IB T370D CUM	16	52000	3	122000	134000
58	TIFFANY 58 CUSTOM		MHG		IB T D GM	16 6	65000	4	**	**
58	TIFFANY 58 CUSTOM		MHG		IB T370D CUM	16 6	65000	4	202000	222000
60	TIFFANY 60 CUSTOM		MHG		IB T350D GM	16	72000	4	215000	236500
					1970 BOATS					
36 10	GLEBE 36		SDN	WD	SV IB 300 CHRY	13 6	20000	2 8	31400	34800
40 8	TIFFANY 40 CUSTOM		SDN	WD	SV IB 300 CHRY	14	30000	3	52300	57500
40 8	TIFFANY 40 CUSTOM		SDN	WD	SV IB 180D CUM	14	30000	3	56800	62500
45 8	TIFFANY 45 CUSTOM		SF	WD	SV IB 300D CUM	15	40000	3	89200	98000
50	TIFFANY 50 CUSTOM		SDN	WD	SV IB 370D CUM	16	52000	3	102500	112500
58	TIFFANY 58 CUSTOM		DC	WD	SV IB D GM	16 6	65000	4	**	**
58	TIFFANY 58 CUSTOM		SF	WD	SV IB 370D CUM	16 6	65000	4	165000	181500
					1969 BOATS					
36 10	GLEBE 36		CR	WD	SV IB T250 CRUS	13 6	16000	2 8	27700	30800
40 8	TIFFANY 40 CUSTOM		CR	WD	SV IB T170 CUM	13 6	24000	3	45800	50300
40 8	TIFFANY 40 CUSTOM		CR	WD	SV IB T300 CRUS	14	24000	3	46900	51600
45 8	TIFFANY 45 CUSTOM		SF	WD	SV IB T300 CUM	14 6	36000	3	81000	89100
50	TIFFANY 50 CUSTOM		CR	WD	SV IB T300 CUM	15	48000	3 6	96100	105500
58	TIFFANY 58 CUSTOM		DC	WD	SV IB T370 CUM	16	57000	4	164500	180500
58	TIFFANY 58 CUSTOM		SF	WD	SV IB T370 CUM	16	57000	4	161500	177500
					1968 BOATS					
30	GLEBE 30		CR	WD	IB T200 CRUS	12	12000	2 8	17300	19700
36 10	GLEBE 36		CR	WD	IB T220 CRUS	13 6	16000	2 8	17400	19700
40 8	CUSTOM 40		CR	WD	IB T310 CRUS	13 6	24000	3	44800	49800
40 8	CUSTOM 40		CR	WD	IB T170D CRUS	13 6	24000	3	50700	55800
43 8	CUSTOM 43		CR	WD	IB T300D CUM	14	26000	3	60600	66600
48 8	CUSTOM 48		CR	WD	IB T300D CUM	15	36000	3 6	120000	131500
50	CUSTOM 50		CR	WD	IB T300D CUM	16	38000	3 6	90300	99200
					1967 BOATS					
30	GLEBE 30		SDN	WD	IB T220	12		2 8	13800	15700
36 10	GLEBE 36		SDN	WD	IB T220	13 6		2 8	24700	27400
40 8	CUSTOM 40		SDN	WD	IB T310	13 6		3	41400	46000
43 8	CUSTOM 43		SF	WD	IB T170D	14		3	62100	68200
48 8	CUSTOM 48		DC	WD	IB T300D	15 6		3	95700	105000
50	CUSTOM 50		SDN	WD	IB T300D	16		3 6	91000	100000

TIGER CRAFT CORP
DANIA FL 33004   COAST GUARD MFG ID- TGC See inside cover to adjust price for area

LOA FT IN	NAME AND/ OR MODEL	TOP/ RIG	BOAT TYPE	-HULL- MTL TP	ENGINE TP # HP MFG	BEAM FT IN	WGT LBS	DRAFT FT IN	RETAIL LOW	RETAIL HIGH
					1971 BOATS					
21	BENGAL 21		OFF	FBG	IO 120-215	8	3400	2 6	5450	6400
21	BENGAL OFFSHORE		OFF	FBG	IO 120-215	8	3000	2 6	5300	6200
28 1	OCEAN 28	HT		FBG	IO T225 CHRY	9 4		2 5	17100	19400
28 1	OCEAN 28	FB		FBG	IO T225 CHRY	9 4		2 5	17100	19400
28 1	OCEAN 28 STD			FBG	IO T225 CHRY	9 4		2 5	17100	19400

TOLLYCRAFT YACHT CORP

KELSO WA 98626   COAST GUARD MFG ID- TLY See inside cover to adjust price for area
FORMERLY TOLLYCRAFT CORPORATION

For more recent years, see the BUC Used Boat Price Guide, Volume 1 or Volume 2

```
LOA  NAME AND/          TOP/ BOAT  -HULL-  ----ENGINE--- BEAM   WGT  DRAFT RETAIL RETAIL
FT IN  OR MODEL         RIG  TYPE  MTL TP TP #  HP  MFG  FT IN  LBS  FT IN  LOW   HIGH
--------------------- 1983 BOATS ------------------------------------------------------
25  1 SEDAN             FB   SDN   FBG SV IO  260  MRCR 8       6400 2 10 13700 15500
25  1 SEDAN             FB   SDN   FBG SV IO  130D VLVO 8       6400 2 10 15700 17900
26  8 SEDAN             FB   SDN   FBG SV IB  270  CRUS 10      9000 2 10 23600 26200
   IO  330  MRCR 20000 22200, IB 205D GM   33600 37300, IO T170   MRCR 19900 22100
   IB T170  MRCR 24600 27400

29 11 SEDAN             FB   SDN   FBG SV IB T270  CRUS 11  9 13500 2  6 39900 44300
34    CONVERTIBLE SEDAN FB   SDN   FBG SV IB T270  CRUS 12  6 17000 2 10 56300 61900
34    CONVERTIBLE SEDAN FB   SDN   FBG SV IB T205D GM  12  6 17000 2 10 72200 79300
34    TRI-CABIN         FB   TCMY  FBG SV IB T270  CRUS 12  6 17000 2 10 53800 59100
34    TRI-CABIN         FB   TCMY  FBG SV IB T205D GM  12  6 17000 2 10 67700 74400
37  4 CONVERTIBLE SEDAN FB   SDN   FBG SV IB T350  CRUS 13  2 22000 3     86200 94700
   IB T205D GM  93900 103000, IB T210D CAT  95800 105500, IB T215D CUM 94000 103500
   IB T300D CAT 101000 111500, IB T320D CUM  99800 109500

43  4 MOTOR YACHT       FB   MY    FBG DS IB T350  CRUS 14  2 30000 3  5 122000 134000
   IB T205D GM  123000 135000, IB T210D CAT 125000 137000, IB T215D CUM 124000 136000
   IB T300D CAT 135500 148500, IB T320D CUM 135500 149000

48  2 CONVERTIBLE SEDAN FB   SDN   F/S DS IB T210D CAT 15  2 40000 3  8 147500 162000
   IB T215D CUM 147500 162500, IB T300D CAT 154500 169500, IB T310D GM 155000 170000
   IB T320D CUM 155500 171000, IB T410D GM 161500 177500, IB T435D GM 163000 179500
   IB T550D GM 170500 187500

48  2 MOTOR YACHT       FB   MY    FBG DS IB T210D CAT 15  2 42000 3  8 152000 167000
   IB T300D CAT 159000 175000, IB T310D GM 158500 174500, IB T315D CUM 159000 174500
   IB T320D CUM 159500 175500, IB T410D GM 170500 187500, IB T435D GM 173500 191000

61  2 MOTOR YACHT       FB   MY    F/S DS IB T300D CAT 17  8 52000 4     263000 289000
   IB T310D GM  260500 286000, IB T320D CUM 262500 288500, IB T410D GM 271000 297500
   IB T450D CUM 278000 305000, IB T500D CUM 286000 314500, IB T500D GM 284000 312000
   IB T650D S&S 313000 344000
--------------------- 1982 BOATS ------------------------------------------------------
25  1 SEDAN             FB   SDN   FBG SV IO  260  MRCR 8       6400 2 10 13400 15200
25  1 SEDAN             FB   SDN   FBG SV IO  130D VLVO 8       6400 2 10 15400 17500
26  8 SEDAN             FB   SDN   FBG SV IB  270  CRUS 10      9000 2 10 22600 25100
   IO  330  MRCR 19500 21700, VD 124D VLVO 29900 33200, IO 130D VLVO 22600 25100
   IO T170  MRCR 19500 21600, VD T170  MRCR 23600 26200

29 11 SEDAN             FB   SDN   FBG SV IB T270  CRUS 11  9 13500 2  6 38200 42400
29 11 SEDAN             FB   SDN   FBG SV IB T124D VLVO 11  9 13500 2  6 50400 55400
34    CONVERTIBLE SEDAN FB   SDN   FBG SV IB T270  CRUS 12  6 17000 2 10 53900 59200
34    CONVERTIBLE SEDAN FB   SDN   FBG SV IBT150D-T210D 12  6 17000 2 10 66700 77000
34    TRI-CABIN         FB   TCMY  FBG SV IB T270  CRUS 12  6 17000 2 10 51400 56500
34    TRI-CABIN         FB   TCMY  FBG SV IB T124D VLVO 12  6 17000 2 10 62900 69100
37  4 CONVERTIBLE SEDAN FB   SDN   FBG SV IB T350  CRUS 13  2 22000 3     82200 90400
37  4 CONVERTIBLE SEDAN FB   SDN   FBG SV IB T210D CAT 13  2 22000 3     91400 100500
43  4 MOTOR YACHT       FB   MY    FBG DS IB T350  CRUS 14  2 30000 3  5 116500 128000
   IB T210D CAT 119500 131000, IB T270D GM 124500 136500, IB T300D CAT 129000 142000

48  2 CONVERTIBLE SEDAN FB   SDN   FBG DS IB T210D CAT 15  2 40000 3  8 141000 155000
   IB T300D CAT 147500 162000, IB T310D GM 148000 162500, IB T410D GM 154500 169500
   IB T435D GM 156000 171000, IB T525D GM 161500 177500

48  2 MOTOR YACHT       FB   MY    FBG DS IB T210D CAT 15  2 42000 3  8 145500 160000
   IB T270D GM 148500 163000, IB T300D CAT 152500 167500, IB T310D GM 152000 167000
   IB T435D GM 166000 182500
--------------------- 1981 BOATS ------------------------------------------------------
25  1 TOLLYCRAFT 25          SDN   FBG SV IO  260      8       6400      13100 14900
26  8 TOLLYCRAFT 26      FB   SDN   FBG SV IB  255     10       9000      21400 23800
29 11 TOLLYCRAFT 30          SDN   FBG SV IB T255     11  9 13500      36100 40100
34    TOLLYCRAFT 34          SDN   FBG SV IB T255     12  6 17000      51100 56200
34    TOLLYCRAFT 34          TCMY  FBG SV IB T255     12  6 17000      48900 53700
34    TRI-CABIN         FB   TCMY  FBG SV IB T255     12  6 17000 2 10 48900 53700
37  4 TOLLYCRAFT 37          SDN   FBG SV IB T330     13  2 22000      77200 84800
43  3 TOLLYCRAFT 43          MY    FBG DS IB T330     14  2 30000      116500 128000
43  4 MOTOR YACHT       FB   MY    FBG DS IB T330     14  2 30000      109000 119500
48  2 TOLLYCRAFT 48          MY    FBG DS IB T210D    15  2 44000      169000 185500
--------------------- 1980 BOATS ------------------------------------------------------
25  1 TOLLYCRAFT 25          SDN   FBG SV IO  255      8       6400      13000 14800
25  1 TOLLYCRAFT 25          SDN   FBG SV IO  130D     8       6400      15300 17400
26  8 TOLLYCRAFT 26      FB   SDN   FBG SV IB  255     10       9000      20500 22800
26  8 TOLLYCRAFT 26      FB   SDN   FBG SV IB  330     10       9000      19000 21100
26  8 TOLLYCRAFT 26      FB   SDN   FBG SV IO T170     10       9000      19200 21300
29 11 TOLLYCRAFT 30          SDN   FBG SV IB T255     11  9 13500      34600 38500
33  7 TOLLYCRAFT 34          SDN   FBG SV IB T255     12  3 15000      46100 50700
34    TOLLYCRAFT 34          TCMY  FBG SV IB T255     12  6 17000      47100 51700
37  4 TOLLYCRAFT 37          SDN   FBG SV IB T330     13  2 22000      73600 80900
43  3 TOLLYCRAFT 43          MY    FBG DS IB T330     14  1 30000      111000 122000
48  2 TOLLYCRAFT 48          MY    FBG DS IB T280D    15  2 44000      161000 177000
--------------------- 1979 BOATS ------------------------------------------------------
25  1 SEDAN             FB   SDN   FBG SV IO  255  VLVO 8      6400 2 10 13200 15000
25  1 SEDAN             FB   SDN   FBG SV IO  130D VLVO 8      6500 2 10 15200 17300
26  8 SEDAN             FB   SDN   FBG SV IO  255  MRCR 10     9000 2 10 19600 21800
   IO  330  MRCR 19000 21100, IO 124D VLVO 26600 29500, IO 130D VLVO 22000 24500
   IB T130  MPC  19900 22200, IO T170  MRCR 19200 21300

29 11 SEDAN             FB   SDN   FBG SV IB T255  MRCR 11  9 13500 2  6 33200 36900
29 11 SEDAN             FB   SDN   FBG SV IB T124D VLVO 11  9 13700 2  6 45600 50100
33  7 SEDAN             FB   SDN   FBG SV IB T255  MRCR 12  3 15000 2  8 43700 48600
33  7 SEDAN             FB   SDN   FBG SV IB T124D VLVO 12  3 15400 2  8 54100 59500
34    TRI-CABIN         FB   TCMY  FBG SV IB T255  MRCR 12  6 17000 2 10 44600 49600
34    TRI-CABIN         FB   TCMY  FBG SV IB T124D VLVO 12  6 17400 2 10 56900 62500
37  4 CONVERTIBLE SEDAN FB   SDN   FBG SV IB T330  MRCR 13  2 24000 3     70300 77300
37  4 CONVERTIBLE SEDAN FB   SDN   FBG SV IB T210D CAT 13  2 24000 3     84500 92900
40  2 TRI-CABIN         FB   TCMY  FBG SV IB T330  MRCR 13  4 28000 3  2 97100 106500
40  2 TRI-CABIN         FB   TCMY  FBG SV IB T210D CAT 13  4 30000 3  2 112000 123000
48  2 MOTOR YACHT       FB   MY    FBG DS IB T210D CAT 15  2 42000 3  8 126000 138500
48  2 MOTOR YACHT       FB   MY    FBG DS IB T275D GM 15  2 43000 3  8 130500 143500
--------------------- 1978 BOATS ------------------------------------------------------
24  6 SEDAN                  SDN   FBG SV IO  330  MRCR 8            12600 14300
24  6 SEDAN                  SDN   FBG SV IO T170  MRCR 8            12400 14100
25  1 SEDAN             FB   SDN   FBG SV IO  260  MRCR 8       6000 2 10 12500 14200
26  8 SEDAN             FB   SDN   FBG SV VD  255  MRCR 10      9000 2 10 19000 21100
26  8 SEDAN             FB   SDN   FBG SV IO  330  MRCR 10      9000 2 10 19100 21300
26  8 SEDAN             FB   SDN   FBG SV IO T170  MRCR 10      9000 2 10 19900 22100
29 11 SEDAN             FB   SDN   FBG SV IB T255  MRCR 11  9 13500 2  3 31800 35400
33  7 SEDAN             FB   SDN   FBG SV IB T255  MRCR 12  3 15000 2  7 41900 46600
34    TRI-CABIN         FB   TCMY  FBG SV IB T255  MRCR 12  6 17000 2  9 44600 49600
37  4 LONG RANGE CRUISER FB  TRWL  FBG SV IB T145D GM 13  4 28000 3     87900 96600
37  4 SEDAN             FB   SDNSF FBG SV IB T330  MRCR 13  2 24000 3     66800 73400
37  4 SEDAN             FB   SDNSF FBG SV IB T210D CAT 13  2 24000 3     80100 88000

40  2 TRI-CABIN         FB   TCMY  FBG SV IB T330  MRCR 13  4 25000 3  2 84600 92900
40  2 TRI-CABIN         FB   TCMY  FBG SV IB T210D CAT 13  4 27000 3  2 98900 108500
48  2 MOTOR YACHT       FB   MY    FBG DS IB T210D CAT 15  2 42000 3  8 120500 132500
   IB T235D 121000 133000, IB T260D GM 122500 134500, IB T435D 121500 133500
--------------------- 1977 BOATS ------------------------------------------------------
26  8 SEDAN             FB   SDN   FBG SV IO  255  MRCR 10     9000 2 10 18600 20700
26  8 SEDAN             FB   SDN   FBG SV VD  255  MRCR 10     9000 2 10 18300 20300
26  8 SEDAN             FB   SDN   FBG SV IB  255  MRCR 10     9000 2 10 21500 21500
27  7 SPORTFISHER       FB   SF    FBG SV IB T233  MRCR 10  7 10500 2  2 21100 23500
29 11 SEDAN             FB   SDN   FBG SV IB T255  MRCR 11  5 14000 2  6 30400 34300
33  7 SEDAN             FB   SDN   FBG SV IB T255  MRCR 12  3 15000 2  7 40200 44700
34    TRI-CABIN         FB   TCMY  FBG SV IB T255  MRCR 12  6 17000 2  9 41100 45700
37  4 CONVERTIBLE SEDAN FB   SDNSF FBG SV IB T330  MRCR 13  2 24000 3     63900 70300
37  4 CONVERTIBLE SEDAN FB   SDNSF FBG SV IB T210D CAT 13  2 24000 3     72000 79100
37  4 TRAWLER           FB   TRWL  FBG SV IB T130  GM  13  2 27500 3     82600 90800
40  2 TRI-CABIN         FB   TCMY  FBG SV IB T330  MRCR 13  4 25000 3  2 81000 89000
40  2 TRI-CABIN         FB   TCMY  FBG SV IB T210D CAT 13  4 25000 3  2 89400 98200

48  2 MOTOR YACHT       FB   MY    FBG DS IB T210D CAT 15  2 42000 3  8 115500 127000
--------------------- 1976 BOATS ------------------------------------------------------
26  8 SEDAN 26          FB   SDN   FBG SV IB  255  MRCR 10     6500 2 10 17200 19500
   VD  255  MRCR 17200 19500, VD 200D CHRY 25600 28400, IO T165-T188 19800 22400

27  7 SPORTFISHER 28    FB   SF    FBG SV VD  200D CHRY 10  7 7500 2  2 20600 22900
27  7 SPORTFISHER 28    FB   SF    FBG SV IB T233  MRCR 10  7 7500 2  2 16700 19000
30  2 EXPRESS 30        FB   EXP   FBG SV IB T130  CHRY 11  5 7500 2  3 23700 26300
30  2 EXPRESS 30        FB   EXP   FBG SV IB T130D CHRY 11  5 7500 2  3 29300 32500
33  7 SEDAN 34          FB   SDN   FBG SV IB T255  MRCR 12  3 11000 2  7 36000 40000
33  7 SEDAN 34          FB   SDN   FBG SV IB T130D CHRY 12  3 11000 2  7 41600 46100
34    TRI-CABIN 34      FB   TCMY  FBG SV IB T255  MRCR 12  6 13000 2  7 36000 40000
34    TRI-CABIN 34      FB   TCMY  FBG SV IB T200D-T225D 12 6 13000 2  7 44400 50700
37  4 SPORTFISHER 37    FB   SF    FBG SV IB T350  MRCR 13  4 16000 3     49000 53900
37  4 SPORTFISHER 37    FB   SF    FBG SV IB T210D CAT 13  4 16000 3     56000 61600
40  2 TRI-CABIN 40      FB   TCMY  FBG SV IB T350  MRCR 13  4 20000 3  2 65400 71900
```

TOLLYCRAFT YACHT CORP -CONTINUED See inside cover to adjust price for area

LOA FT	LOA IN	NAME AND/ OR MODEL	TOP/ RIG	BOAT TYPE	-HULL- MTL	-HULL- TP	ENGINE TP	ENGINE # HP	ENGINE MFG	BEAM FT	BEAM IN	WGT LBS	DRAFT FT	DRAFT IN	RETAIL LOW	RETAIL HIGH
1976 BOATS																
40	2	TRI-CABIN 40	FB	TCMY	FBG	SV	IB	T225D	CAT	13	4	20000	3	2	73600	80900
48	2	MOTOR YACHT 48	FB	MY	FBG	DS	IB	T225D	CAT	15	2	34000	3	8	104000	114000
1975 BOATS																
26		SEDAN 26	FB	SDN	FBG	SV	IO	255	MRCR	10		6200	2	2	19300	21400
		VD 255 MRCR 16200 18400, IO T165 MRCR 20200 22400, IO T100D NISS													26500	29400
27	7	SPORTFISHER 28	FB	SF	FBG	SV	IB	T233	MRCR	10	7	7000	2	2	15600	17700
27	7	SPORTFISHER 28	FB	SF	FBG	SV	IB	T100D	NISS	10	7	7000	2	2	19700	21900
30		EXPRESS 30	HT	EXP	FBG	SV	IB	T233	MRCR	11	5	9000	2	3	22400	24900
30		EXPRESS 30	HT	EXP	FBG	SV	IB	T100D	NISS	11	5	9000	2	3	27000	30000
33	7	SPORTS SEDAN 34	FB	SDN	FBG	SV	VD	T255	MRCR	12	3	11000	2	6	34600	38400
34		TRI-CABIN 34	FB	TCMY	FBG	SV	IB	T255	MRCR	12	6	12000	2	9	33800	37600
34		TRI-CABIN 34	FB	TCMY	FBG	SV	IB	T225D	CAT	12	6	12000	2	9	42800	47500
37	4	SPORTFISHER 37	FB	SDNSF	FBG	SV	IB	T350	MRCR	13	2	18000	3		51100	56200
37	4	SPORTFISHER 37	FB	SDNSF	FBG	SV	IB	T225D	CAT	13	2	18000	3		58100	63900
40	2	TRI-CABIN 40	FB	TCMY	FBG	SV	IB	T350	MRCR	13	4	20000	3	2	62900	69100
40	2	TRI-CABIN 40	FB	TCMY	FBG	SV	IB	T225D	CAT	13	4	20000	3	2	70700	77700
1974 BOATS																
26			FB	SDN	FBG	SV	IO	225	OMC	10		5800	2	10	19600	21800
26			FB	SDN	FBG	SV	IB	250	CHRY	10		5800	2	10	15500	17700
26			FB	SDN	FBG	SV	IO	T165	OMC	10		5800	2	10	20800	23100
27	7			EXP	FBG		IB	T225	CHRY	10	7	7000	2	2	14800	16800
27	7			EXP	FBG		IB	T100D	CHRY	10	7	7000	2	2	19100	21300
27	7		FB	SF	FBG		IB	T225	CHRY	10	7	7000	2	2	14800	16900
27	7		FB	SF	FBG		IB	T100D	CHRY	10	7	7000	2	2	19200	21300
30	2			EXP	FBG		IB	T225	CHRY	11	5	9000	2	3	21700	24100
30	2			EXP	FBG		IB	T100D	CHRY	11	5	9000	2	3	26500	29400
33	7		FB	SDN	FBG		IB	T250	CHRY	12	3	11000	2	6	33100	36800
33	7		FB	SDN	FBG		IB	T100D	CHRY	12	3	11000	2	6	37800	42000
37	4		FB	SF	FBG		IB	T330	CHRY	13	2	16000	3		44500	49500
37	4		FB	SF	FBG		IB	T225D	CAT	13	2	18000	3		55900	61400
40	2	TRI-CABIN		TCMY	FBG		IB	T330	CHRY	13	4	20000	3	2	59800	65700
40	2	TRI-CABIN		TCMY	FBG		IB	T225D	CAT	13	4	21000	3	2	70300	77300
1973 BOATS																
23	8			EXP	FBG		IO	165-225		8		4200	2	10	9550	11000
23	8			EXP	FBG		IO	100D	CHRY	8		4200	2	10	11700	13300
23	8			EXP	FBG		IO	T120	OMC	8		4200	2	10	10500	12000
26			FB	SDN	FBG	SV	IO	225	OMC	10		5800	2	10	20200	22500
		IB 250 CHRY 14900 17000, IO T165 OMC 21500 23900, IO T100D CHRY													28300	31400
27	7			EXP	FBG		IB	T225	CHRY	10	7	7000	2	2	14300	16200
27	7			EXP	FBG		IB	T100D	CHRY	10	7	7000	2	2	18800	20900
27	7		FB	SF	FBG		IB	T225	CHRY	10	7	7000	2	2	14300	16200
27	7		FB	SF	FBG		IB	T100D	CHRY	10	7	7000	2	2	18900	20900
30	2			EXP	FBG		IB	T225	CHRY	11	5	9000	2	3	20900	23200
30	2			EXP	FBG		IB	T100D	CHRY	11	5	9000	2	3	25800	28600
30	2		FB	EXP	FBG		IB	T225	CHRY	11	5		2	3	22600	25100
30	2		FB	EXP	FBG		IB	T100D	CHRY	11	5		2	3	25700	28600
33	7		FB	SDN	FBG		IB	T250	CHRY	12	3	11000	2	6	31800	35400
33	7		FB	SDN	FBG		IB	T100D	CHRY	12	3	11000	2	6	36800	40900
40	2	TRI-CABIN		TCMY	FBG		IB	T300	CHRY	13	4	20000	3	2	57200	62800
40	2	TRI-CABIN		TCMY	FBG		IB	T210D	CAT	13	4	20000	3	2	64900	71300
1972 BOATS																
23	8			EXP	FBG		IO	165-225		8		4200	2	10	9850	11400
23	8			EXP	FBG		IO	T100	OMC	8		4200	2	10	10900	12400
23	8		FB	EXP	FBG		IO	165-225		8			2	10	9450	10900
23	8		FB	EXP	FBG		IO	T100	OMC	8			2	10	10500	11900
23	8			SF	FBG		IO	165-225		8		3800	2	10	10400	12000
23	8			SF	FBG		IO	T100	OMC	8		3800	2	10	11600	13100
27	7			EXP	FBG		IB	225	CHRY	10	7	7000	2	2	12200	13800
27	7			EXP	FBG		IB	T225	CHRY	10	7	7000	2	2	13700	15600
27	7			EXP	FBG		IB	T100D	CHRY	10	7	7000	2	2	18400	20400
27	7		HT	EXP	FBG		IB	225	CHRY	10	7	7000	2	2	12200	13800
27	7		HT	EXP	FBG		IB	T225	CHRY	10	7	7000	2	2	13700	15600
27	7		HT	EXP	FBG		IB	T100D	CHRY	10	7	7000	2	2	18400	20400
27	7			SF	FBG		IB	225	CHRY	10	7	7000	2	2	12200	13800
27	7			SF	FBG		IB	T225	CHRY	10	7	7000	2	2	13700	15600
27	7			SF	FBG		IB	T100D	CHRY	10	7	7000	2	2	18400	20400
30	2			DC	FBG		IB	T225	CHRY	11	5	9000	2	3	19000	21200
30	2			DC	FBG		IB	T100D	CHRY	11	5	9000	2	3	23900	26500
30	2			EXP	FBG		IB	T225	CHRY	11	5	9000	2	3	20100	22300
30	2			EXP	FBG		IB	T100D	CHRY	11	5	9000	2	3	25100	27900
33	7			EXP	FBG		IB	T225	CHRY	12	3	10000	2	6	27700	30800
33	7			EXP	FBG		IB	T100D	CHRY	12	3	10000	2	6	33300	37000
33	7			SDNSF	FBG		IB	T225	CHRY	12	3	11000	2	6	28200	31300
33	7			SDNSF	FBG		IB	T100D	CHRY	12	3	11000	2	6	33100	36800
36	2	TOLLYHOME		HB	FBG		IB	T100	CHRY	12		12000	2		20600	22900
36	2	TOLLYHOME		HB	FBG		IO	T225	CHRY	12		12000	2		21700	24100
36	2	TOLLYHOME		HB	FBG		IB	T225	CHRY	12		12000	2		21500	23900
36	2	TOLLYHOME	FB	HB	FBG		IO	T100	CHRY	12		12000	2		21400	23800
36	2	TOLLYHOME	FB	HB	FBG		IO	T225	CHRY	12		12000	2		21700	24100
40	2	TRI-CABIN		TCMY	FBG		IB	T300	CHRY	13	4	20000	3	2	55100	60600
40	2	TRI-CABIN		TCMY	FBG		IB	T210D	CUM	13	4	20000	3	2	61000	67100
40	2	TRI-CABIN		TCMY	FBG		IB	T225D	CAT	13	4	20000	3	2	63100	69400
45				MY	FBG		IB	T330	CHRY	15		30000			78300	86000
45				MY	FBG		IB	T225D	CAT	15		30000			80900	88900
1971 BOATS																
23	8			EXP	FBG		IO	130-215		8		4200	2	10	10200	11700
23	8			EXP	FBG		IO	T 90	OMC	8		4200	2	10	11200	12800
23	8			SF	FBG		IO	130-215		8		3800	2	10	10800	12400
23	8			SF	FBG		IO	T 90	OMC	8		3800	2	10	11900	13600
27	7			EXP	FBG		IB	225	CHRY	10	7	6500	2	2	11300	12800
27	7			EXP	FBG		IB	T225	CHRY	10	7	7000	2	2	13200	15000
27	7			SF	FBG		IB	225	CHRY	10	7	6500	2	2	11300	12800
27	7			SF	FBG		IB	T225	CHRY	10	7	7000	2	2	13200	15000
30	2			DC	FBG		IB	T225	CHRY	11	5	9000	2	3	18500	20600
33	7			EXP	FBG		IB	T225	CHRY	12	3	10000	2	6	26600	29600
33	7			SDNSF	FBG		IB	T225	CHRY	12	3	11000	2	6	27100	30100
33	7			SDNSF	FBG		IB	T100D	CHRY	12	3	11000	2	6	32300	35900
36	2	TOLLYHOME		HB	FBG		IO	240	CHRY	12		12000	2		20100	22400
36	2	TOLLYHOME		HB	FBG		IO	T200	CHRY	12		12000	2		21500	23900
36	2	TOLLYHOME		HB	FBG		IB	T225	CHRY	12		12000	2		21700	24100
40	2	TRI-CABIN		TCMY	FBG		IB	T300	CHRY	13	4	20000	3	2	53200	58500
		IB T160D PERK 58900 64700, IB T210D CUM 58900 64800, IB T225D CAT													61000	67000
45				MY	FBG		IB	T330	CHRY	15		30000			75600	83100
45				MY	FBG		IB	T210D	CUM	15		30000			75900	83400
45				MY	FBG		IB	T225D	CAT	15		30000			78200	85900
1970 BOATS																
23	8	REGENT		EXP	FBG	DV	IO	120-210		8		4200	2	10	10500	12100
23	8	REGENT		EXP	FBG	DV	IB	225	CHRY	8		4200	2	2	6250	7200
23	8	REGENT	HT	EXP	FBG	DV	IO	120-210		8		4200	2	10	10500	12100
23	8	REGENT	HT	EXP	FBG	DV	IB	225	CHRY	8		4200	2	2	6250	7200
23	8	REGENT		SF	FBG	DV	IO	120-210		8		3800	2	10	11100	12800
23	8	REGENT		SF	FBG	DV	IB	225	CHRY	8		3800	2	2	5800	6650
23	8	ROYAL		EXP	FBG	DV	IO	120-210		8		3960	2	10	10000	11600
23	8	ROYAL		EXP	FBG	DV	IB	225	CHRY	8		3960	2	2	6000	6900
23	8	ROYAL	HT	EXP	FBG	DV	IO	120-210		8		3960	2	10	10000	11600
23	8	ROYAL	HT	EXP	FBG	DV	IB	225	CHRY	8		3960	2	2	6000	6900
23	8	ROYAL		SF	FBG	DV	IO	120-210		8		3560	2	10	10600	12200
23	8	ROYAL		SF	FBG	DV	IB	225	CHRY	8		3560	2	2	5550	6350
27	7	REGENT		EXP	FBG	DV	IB	225-300		10	7	7200	2	2	11500	13500
27	7	REGENT		EXP	FBG	DV	IB	T225	CHRY	10	7	7200	2	2	12900	14600
27	7	REGENT	HT	EXP	FBG	DV	IB	225-300		10	7	7200	2	2	11500	13500
27	7	REGENT	HT	EXP	FBG	DV	IB	T225	CHRY	10	7	7200	2	2	12900	14600
27	7	REGENT		SF	FBG	DV	IB	225-300		10	7	7200	2	2	11500	13500
27	7	REGENT		SF	FBG	DV	IB	T225	CHRY	10	7	7200	2	2	12900	14600
27	7	ROYAL		EXP	FBG	DV	IB	225-300		10	7	6500	2	2	10800	12900
27	7	ROYAL		EXP	FBG	DV	IB	T225	CHRY	10	7	6500	2	2	12300	14000
27	7	ROYAL	HT	EXP	FBG	DV	IB	225-300		10	7	6500	2	2	10800	12900
27	7	ROYAL	HT	EXP	FBG	DV	IB	T225	CHRY	10	7	6500	2	2	12300	14000
27	7	ROYAL		SF	FBG	DV	IB	225-300		10	7	6500	2	2	10800	12900
27	7	ROYAL		SF	FBG	DV	IB	T225	CHRY	10	7	6500	2	2	12300	14000
30	2	ROYAL		DC	FBG	DV	IB	T225	CHRY	11	5	9000	2	3	17400	19800
33	7	ROYAL		EXP	FBG	DV	IB	170D	CRUS	12	3	10000	2	6	31100	34500
33	7	ROYAL		EXP	FBG	DV	IB	T225	CHRY	12	3	10000	2	6	25600	28500
33	7	ROYAL	FB	EXP	FBG	DV	IB	170D	CRUS	12	3	10000	2	6	31100	34500
33	7	ROYAL	FB	EXP	FBG	DV	IB	T225	CHRY	12	3	10000	2	6	25600	28500
36	2	TOLLYHOME		HB	FBG	SV	IO	225	CHRY	12		12000	2		19000	21100
36	2	TOLLYHOME		HB	FBG	SV	IO	T225	CHRY	12		12000	2		20300	22500
36	2	TOLLYHOME		HB	FBG	SV	IB	T225	CHRY	12		12000	2		20200	22400
40	2	ROYAL		TCMY	FBG	SV	IB	T225	CHRY	13	4	16000	3	2	42700	47500
		IB T300 CHRY 43400 48300, IB T160D PERK 49000 53900, IB T215D GM													49500	54400
1969 BOATS																
17	2			RNBT	FBG	DV	IO	120-210		7	2	1500	2	6	3850	4650
20	2			RNBT	FBG	DV	IO	120-210		8		1700	2	8	5300	6200
23	8			EXP	FBG	DV	IO	120-210		8		4200	2	10	10900	12500

96th ed. - Vol. III CONTINUED ON NEXT PAGE 629

LOA FT	LOA IN	NAME AND/ OR MODEL	TOP/ RIG	BOAT TYPE	-HULL- MTL	-HULL- TP	ENGINE TP	ENGINE # HP	ENGINE MFG	BEAM FT	BEAM IN	WGT LBS	DRAFT FT	DRAFT IN	RETAIL LOW	RETAIL HIGH
		1969 BOATS														
23	8			SF	FBG	DV	IO	120-210		8		3800	2	10	11500	13200
23	8	ROYAL		EXP	FBG	DV	IO	120-210		8		3960	2	10	10400	11900
23	8	ROYAL		SF	FBG	DV	IO	120-210		8		3560	2	10	10900	12600
27	7			EXP	FBG	DV	IB	210-300		10	7	7200	2	2	10900	13000
27	7			EXP	FBG	DV	IB	T210	CHRY	10	7	7200	2	2	12200	13900
27	7			SF	FBG	DV	IB	210-300		10	7	7200	2	2	10900	13000
27	7			SF	FBG	DV	IB	T210	CHRY	10	7	7200	2	2	12200	13900
27	7	ROYAL		EXP	FBG	DV	IB	210-300		10	7	6500	2	2	10300	12400
27	7	ROYAL		EXP	FBG	DV	IB	T210	CHRY	10	7	6500	2	2	11700	13300
27	7	ROYAL		SF	FBG	DV	IB	210-300		10	7	6500	2	2	10300	12400
27	7	ROYAL		SF	FBG	DV	IB	T210	CHRY	10	7	6500	2	2	11700	13300
30	2	ROYAL		DC	FBG	DV	IO	T155-T210		11	5	9000	2	6	32700	38100
33	7	ROYAL		EXP	FBG	DV	IB	T210-T300		12	3	10000	2	7	24500	28600
33	7	ROYAL		EXP	FBG	DV	IB	T170D	CRUS	12	3	10000	2	7	33300	37100
38	3	ROYAL		TCMY	WD	SV	IB	T210	CHRY	13	2	14000	3	1	34300	38200
38	3	ROYAL		TCMY	WD	SV	IB	T300	CHRY	13	2	14000	3	1	34800	38700
38	3	ROYAL		TCMY	WD	SV	IB	T160D	PERK	13	2	14000	3	1	39800	44200
		1968 BOATS														
17	2	PLI-COR	OP		FBG		IO	120-210		7	2	1500	2	4	3800	4650
20	2	PLI-COR	OP		FBG		IO	120-210		8		1700	2	4	5400	6400
23	8	PLI-COR		CR	FBG		IO	155-210		8		3960	2	8	10700	12400
27	7	PLI-COR		CR	FBG		IB	210-290		10	7	6500	2	11	9950	11900
27	7	PLI-COR		CR	FBG		IB	T210	CHRY	10	7	6500	2	11	11300	12800
27	7	PLI-COR	FB	SF	FBG		IB	210-290		10	7	6500	2	11	10000	11900
27	7	PLI-COR	FB	SF	FBG		IB	T210	CHRY	10	7	6500	2	11	11300	12800
30	2	PLI-COR		CR	FBG		IB	T210		11	5	10000	2	3	17400	19700
33	7	PLI-COR		EXP	FBG		IB	T210-T300		12	3	12000	2	6	24600	28600
38	3	MARINER	FB	TCMY	FBG		IB	T210	CHRY	13	2	14000	2	9	33300	37000
38	3	MARINER	FB	TCMY	FBG		IB	T300		13	2	14000	2	9	33900	37700
49	3	DISCOVERER		DCMY	FBG		IB	T300D		15	8	28500	3	5	74700	82100
		1967 BOATS														
17	1	GL-172		RNBT	FBG		IO	120-150				1450			4050	4750
17	3	173		RNBT	FBG		IO	150							4750	5450
20	2	GL-202		RNBT	FBG		IO	120-185				1650			5600	6500
20	3	203		RNBT	FBG		IO	150					1	10	6800	7800
23	2	232		CR	FBG		IO	200		8					10500	11900
23	8	GL-238	HT	EXP	FBG		IO	150-200				3960			11200	12800
26	1	VACATIONER		EXP	WD		IO	200		9		5000			15200	17300
26	1	VACATIONER		EXP	WD		IB	210		9		5500			7800	8950
27		272		CR	FBG		IB	210		10	9		2	6	9450	10700
27	6	GL-277	HT	EXP	FBG		IB	210-290				6500			9500	11300
27	6	GL-277	HT	EXP	FBG		IB	T210				6500			10800	12200
28	2	VOYAGER		EXP	WD		IB	210-290		10	3	7500			11000	13100
28	2	VOYAGER		EXP	F/W		IO	T150		10	3		2	1	23900	26600
31	7	EXPLORER		EXP	WD		IB	T210			4	11200	2	4	10500	11900
31	7	EXPLORER		SDN	WD		IB	T210		11	4	11900	2	4	21500	23900
38	3	MARINER		TCMY	WD		IB	T210		13	2	14000	2	9	32400	36000
38	3	MARINER		TCMY	WD		IB	T290		13	2	14000	2	9	32800	36500
49	3	DISCOVERER		MY	WD		IB	T300D				36500			78500	86300
51		DISCOVERER		MY	F/W		IB	T290		15	8		3	6	78700	86500
51		DISCOVERER		MY	F/W		IB	T300D		15	8		3	6	87300	96000
		1966 BOATS														
17	1	SPORTABOUT	OP	RNBT	WD		IB	210		6	7				2250	2650
20	4			SF	WD		IO	150-200		7	8				8650	10100
20	4		OP	WKNDR	WD		IO	150-200		7	8				7200	8400
20	4	CRUISETEER	OP	EXP	WD		OB			7	8				2100	2500
26	4	VACATIONER		EXP	WD		IO	200		9					16400	18700
26	4	VACATIONER		EXP	WD		IB	210		9					7400	8550
26	4	VACATIONER		EXP	WD		IO	225		9					16700	19000
26	4	VACATIONER	HT	EXP	WD		IO	200		9					16400	18700
26	4	VACATIONER	HT	EXP	WD		IB	210		9					7400	8550
26	4	VACATIONER	HT	EXP	WD		IO	225		9					16700	19000
28	5	VOYAGER		EXP	WD		IB	210-220		10	3				10500	12000
28	5	VOYAGER	HT	EXP	WD		IB	210-220		10	3				10500	12000
28	5	VOYAGER	HT	EXP	WD		IO	T150		10	3				25100	27900
32	1	EXPLORER		EXP	WD		IB	170D		11	3		2	4	32000	35600
32	1	EXPLORER		EXP	WD		IB	T210-T240		11	3		2	4	20000	22600
32	1	EXPLORER	FB	EXP	WD		IB	T210-T240		11	3		2	4	20000	22600
39	2	MARINER		TCMY	WD		IB	T210		13	2	14000	2	9	32400	36000
		IB T210 EAT 32100 35700, IB T220 32300 35800, IB T240													32400	35900
		IB T170D 36900 40900														
39	2	MARINER W/DUAL CNTRL		TCMY	WD		IB	T210		13	2	14000	2	9	33600	37300
		IB T210 EAT 33400 37100, IB T220 33500 37200, IB T240													33500	37300
		IB T170D 37900 42100														
43		ADVENTURER		MY	WD	RB	IB	T280		13	4		2	10	62900	69100
51		DISCOVERER		MY	WD		IB	T300D		13	2		2	9	97300	107000
		1965 BOATS														
17	1	SPORTABOUT	OP	RNBT	WD		IB	210							2250	2650
20	3			SF	WD		IO	150							9050	10300
20	3		OP	WKNDR	WD		IO	160							7600	8750
20	3	CRUISETEER	OP	EXP	WD		OB								2200	2550
24		VACATIONER		EXP	WD		IO	150							12200	13800
25		VACATIONER		EXP	WD		IB	210							6350	7300
25		VACATIONER		EXP	WD		IO	225							15400	17500
27	2	VOYAGER		EXP	WD		IB	220							8200	9450
32	1	EXPLORER		EXP	WD		IB	T220							19500	21700
36		MARINER		TCMY	WD		IB	T225							28500	31700
43		ADVENTURER		MY	WD		IB	T280							52500	57600
		1964 BOATS														
17	1	SPORTABOUT	OP	RNBT	WD		IB	185-215							2150	2550
17	1	TOLVO	OP	RNBT	WD		IO	110							5100	5900
20	3		OP	WKNDR	WD		IO	110-160							7800	9000
20	3	CRUISETEER	OP	EXP	WD		OB								2200	2550
24	1	TRAVELER		EXP	WD		OB								3600	4200
24	1	VACATIONER		EXP	WD		IO	150							12600	14300
24	1	VACATIONER		EXP	WD		IB	185							4950	5650
27	2	VOYAGER		EXP	WD		IB	220-280							7900	9450
32	1	EXPLORER		EXP	WD		IB	T220							19000	21100
36		MARINER		TCMY	WD		IB	T225							27800	30900
43		ADVENTURER		MY	WD		IB	T280							51100	56200
		1963 BOATS														
17		SPORTABOUT	OP	RNBT	WD		IB	170							2000	2400
21		SEA-ANGLER		FSH	WD		OB								2000	2350
21		SEA-FARER		CR	WD		OB								2250	2600
21		SEA-FISHER		FSH	WD		IO	120							9300	10500
21		SEA-RANGER		CR	WD		IO	120							9200	10500
23		TRAVELER		EXP	WD		OB								2300	2650
23		VACATIONER		EXP	WD		IO	120							13000	14800
26		VOYAGER		EXP	WD		IB	225							6650	7600
31		EXPLORER		EXP	WD		IB	225							15000	17000
31		EXPLORER		EXP	WD		IB	T178							15800	17900
36		MARINER		TCMY	WD		IB	T225							27100	30200
43		ADVENTURER		MY	WD		IB	T225							47900	52600
		1962 BOATS														
17	1	SPORTABOUT	OP	RNBT	WD		IB	170							2000	2350
21	2	SEA-ANGLER		FSH	WD		OB								2050	2450
21	2	SEA-FARER		CR	WD		OB								2300	2650
21	4	SEA-FISHER		FSH	WD		IB	100							2950	3450
21	4	SEA-MASTER		EXP	WD		IB	100							3050	3550
22	3	TRAVELER		EXP	WD		OB								2600	3000
22	7	VACATIONER		EXP	WD		IB	100							4400	5050
25	10	VOYAGER		EXP	WD		IB	225							6400	7350
30	7	EXPLORER		EXP	WD		IB	225							14100	16100
30	7	EXPLORER		EXP	WD		IB	T225							15400	17500
35	10	MARINER		TCMY	WD		IB	T225							23800	26400
44	3	ADVENTURER		MY	WD		IB	T240							47400	52100
		1961 BOATS														
16	11	SPORTABOUT	OP	RNBT	F/W		IB	135		6	7		1	8	1800	2100
22	3	TRAVELER		EXP	F/W		OB			7	9	1800			2450	2800
22	7	VACATIONER		EXP	WD		IB	100		7	9		1	10	4200	4850
25	10	VOYAGER		EXP	WD		IB	170		8	9		1	10	6050	6950
29	7	EXPLORER		EXP	WD		IB	T225		9	7		2		13900	15800
35	10	MARINER		TCMY	WD		IB	T170		11	10		2	4	21500	23800
		1960 BOATS														
16	8	SPORTABOUT		RNBT	PLY		IB	170		6	7		1	10	1800	2150
16	8	SPORTABOUT	OP	RNBT	PLY		IB	135		6	7		1	10	1700	2050
22	3	VACATIONER		EXP	PLY		IB	135-170		7	10		2		3600	4250
22	9	TRAVELER		EXP	PLY	DV	OB			7	10	1725			2150	2500
25	3	VOYAGER		EXP	PLY		IB	170-225		8	9		2	6	5550	6550
28	9	EXPLORER		EXP	PLY		IB	225		9	7		2	9	9850	11200
28	9	EXPLORER		EXP	PLY		IB	T170		9	7		2	9	10500	12000
35		MARINER		TCMY	PLY		IB	T225		11	8		3		23800	26400
		1959 BOATS														
22	10	TRAVELER		EXP	F/W		OB			7	10	1600			2000	2400
22	10	VACATIONER		EXP	F/W		IB	215		7	10				4300	5000
27		EXPLORER		EXP	F/W		IB	225		9	4				7000	8050

TOMAHAWK BOAT MFG CORP

Call 1-800-327-6929 for BUC Personalized Evaluation Service
Or, for 1958 to 1965 boats, sign onto www.BUCValuPro.com

TONE

Call 1-800-327-6929 for BUC Personalized Evaluation Service
Or, for 1928 boats, sign onto www.BUCValuPro.com

TOP SAIL YACHTS INC
COAST GUARD MFG ID- TPG
SEE ALSO AQUARIUS YACHTS INC

Call 1-800-327-6929 for BUC Personalized Evaluation Service
Or, for 1978 to 1979 boats, sign onto www.BUCValuPro.com

TOPAZ MARINE CORP
SWANSBORO NC 21584   COAST GUARD MFG ID- TPP See inside cover to adjust price for area
FORMERLY SEA HAWK MARINE

For more recent years, see the BUC Used Boat Price Guide, Volume 1 or Volume 2

LOA FT IN	NAME AND/ OR MODEL	TOP/ RIG	BOAT TYPE	-HULL- MTL TP	----ENGINE--- TP # HP MFG	BEAM FT IN	WGT LBS	DRAFT FT IN	RETAIL LOW	RETAIL HIGH
					---- 1983 BOATS ----					
29	TOPAZ 29	OP	SF	FBG SV	IB T260 VLVO 10 3	8100	2 6	29800	33100
29	TOPAZ 29	HT	SF	FBG SV	IB T260 VLVO 10 3	8100	2 6	29800	33100
29	TOPAZ 29	HT	SF	FBG SV	IBT124D-T165D 10 3	8100	2 6	35100	41500
29	TOPAZ 29	TT	SF	FBG SV	IB T260 VLVO 10 3	8100	2 6	29800	33100
29	TOPAZ 29	TT	SF	FBG SV	IBT124D-T165D 10 3	8100	2 6	35100	41500
36 2	TOPAZ 36	OP	SF	FBG SV	IB T235D VLVO 13	17800	2 5	76600	84200
36 2	TOPAZ 36	OP	SF	FBG SV	IB T300D CAT 13	17800	2 5	82600	90800
36 2	TOPAZ 36	OP	SF	FBG SV	IB T300D GM 13	17800	2 5	81100	89100
36 2	TOPAZ 36	TT	SF	FBG SV	IB T235D VLVO 13	17800	2 5	76600	84200
36 2	TOPAZ 36	TT	SF	FBG SV	IB T300D CAT 13	17800	2 5	82600	90800
36 2	TOPAZ 36	TT	SF	FBG SV	IB T300D GM 13	17800	2 5	81100	89100
38 2	TOPAZ 38	OP	SF	FBG SV	IO T286D VLVO 13	20800	2 7	76900	84500
	IB T300D CAT 103000 113500, IB T300D GM 100500 110500, IB T410D GM 109000 120000									
38 2	TOPAZ 38	HT	SF	FBG SV	IO T286D VLVO 13	20800	2 7	76900	84500
	IB T300D CAT 103000 113500, IB T300D GM 100500 110500, IB T410D GM 109000 120000									
38 2	TOPAZ 38	TT	SF	FBG SV	IO T286D VLVO 13	20800	2 7	76900	84500
	IB T300D CAT 103000 113500, IB T300D GM 100500 110500, IB T410D GM 109000 120000									
					---- 1982 BOATS ----					
27 8	TOPAZ 28	OP	CUD	FBG SV	IB T228 10 3	7500	2 2	24700	27500
27 8	TOPAZ 28	TT	CUD	FBG SV	IB T228 10 3	7500	2 2	24700	27500
27 8	TOPAZ 28	TT	CUD	FBG SV	IB T128D VLVO 10 3	7500	2 2	35000
29	TOPAZ 29	OP	SF	FBG SV	IB T260 VLVO 10 3	8100	2 6	28500	31700
29	TOPAZ 29	OP	SF	FBG SV	IBT124D-T148D 10 3		2 6	33600	38700
29	TOPAZ 29	TT	SF	FBG SV	IB T260 VLVO 10 3	8100	2 6	28500	31700
29	TOPAZ 29	TT	SF	FBG SV	IBT124D-T148D 10 3		2 6	33600	38700
36 2	TOPAZ 36	OP	SF	FBG SV	IB T235D VLVO 13	17000	2 5	71100	78100
	IB T270D VLVO 75600 83100, IB T300D CAT 79900 87800, IB T300D GM 78400 86200									
36 2	TOPAZ 36	TT	SF	FBG SV	IB T235D VLVO 13	18200	2 5	74100	81500
	IB T270D VLVO 75600 83100, IB T300D CAT 79900 87800, IB T300D GM 75400 82900									
38 2	TOPAZ 38	F+T	SF	FBG SV	IB T270D VLVO 13	20800	2 7	92300	101500
	IB T300D CAT 98500 108500, IB T300D GM 96100 105500, IB T410D GM 108000 118500									
					---- 1981 BOATS ----					
24 4	TOPAZ 24-BIMINI	OP	CUD	FBG SV	IB 228 8	4500	1 11	12300	14000
24 4	TOPAZ 24-BIMINI	OP	CUD	FBG SV	IB 124D VLVO 8	4500	1 11	15800	18000
24 4	TOPAZ 24-CTR	OP	OPFSH	FBG SV	IB 228 8	4500	1 11	12300	14000
24 4	TOPAZ 24-CTR	OP	OPFSH	FBG SV	IB 124D VLVO 8	4500	1 11	15700	17900
24 4	TOPAZ 24-CTR	TT	OPFSH	FBG SV	IB 228 8	4500	1 11	12300	14000
24 4	TOPAZ 24-CTR	TT	OPFSH	FBG SV	IB 124D VLVO 8	4500	1 11	15700	17900
27 8	MAKAIRA 28	OP	FSH	FBG SV	IB 228 10 3	7500	2 2	21100	23500
27 8	MAKAIRA 28	OP	FSH	FBG SV	IB 124D VLVO 10 3	7500	2 2	26100	29000
27 8	MAKAIRA 28	TT	FSH	FBG SV	IB 228 10 3	7500	2 2	21100	23500
27 8	MAKAIRA 28	TT	FSH	FBG SV	IB 124D VLVO 10 3	7500	2 2	26100	29000
27 8	TOPAZ 28-CUDDY	OP	CUD	FBG SV	IB T228 10 3	7500	2 2	23700	26300
27 8	TOPAZ 28-CUDDY	OP	CUD	FBG SV	IB T124D VLVO 10 3	7500	2 2	30100	33500
27 8	TOPAZ 28-CUDDY	TT	CUD	FBG SV	IB T228 10 3	7500	2 2	23700	26300
27 8	TOPAZ 28-CUDDY	TT	CUD	FBG SV	IB T124D VLVO 10 3	7500	2 2	30100	33500
36 2	TOPAZ 36	OP	SF	FBG SV	IB T J&T 13	18000	2 5	**	**
	IB T235D VLVO 70100 77100, IB T260D CAT 73500 80700, IB T286D VLVO 72300 79400									
36 2	TOPAZ 36	TT	SF	FBG SV	IB T J&T 13	18000	2 5	**	**
	IB T235D VLVO 70100 77100, IB T260D CAT 73500 80700, IB T286D VLVO 72300 79400									
					---- 1980 BOATS ----					
24 4	TOPAZ 24-BIMINI	OP	CUD	FBG SV	IB 228 8	4500	1 11	11800	13400
24 4	TOPAZ 24-BIMINI	OP	CUD	FBG SV	IB 124D VLVO 8	4500	1 11	15200	17300
24 4	TOPAZ 24-CTR	OP	OPFSH	FBG SV	IB 228 8	4500	1 11	11800	13400
24 4	TOPAZ 24-CTR	OP	OPFSH	FBG SV	IB 124D VLVO 8	4500	1 11	15100	17200
24 4	TOPAZ 24-CTR	TT	OPFSH	FBG SV	IB 228 8	4500	1 11	11800	13400
24 4	TOPAZ 24-CTR	TT	OPFSH	FBG SV	IB 124D VLVO 8	4500	1 11	15100	17200
27 8	MAKAIRA 28	OP	FSH	FBG SV	IB 228 10 3	7500	2 2	20300	22500
27 8	MAKAIRA 28	OP	FSH	FBG SV	IB 124D VLVO 10 3	7500	2 2	25100	27900
27 8	MAKAIRA 28	TT	FSH	FBG SV	IB 228 10 3	7500	2 2	20300	22500
27 8	MAKAIRA 28	TT	FSH	FBG SV	IB 124D VLVO 10 3	7500	2 2	25100	27900
27 8	TOPAZ 28-CUDDY	OP	CUD	FBG SV	IB T228 10 3	7500	2 2	22700	25200
27 8	TOPAZ 28-CUDDY	OP	CUD	FBG SV	IB T124D VLVO 10 3	7500	2 2	29000	32200
27 8	TOPAZ 28-CUDDY	TT	CUD	FBG SV	IB T228 10 3	7500	2 2	22700	25200
27 8	TOPAZ 28-CUDDY	TT	CUD	FBG SV	IB T124D VLVO 10 3	7500	2 2	29000	32200
36	SPORTFISH		SF	FBG SV	IB T200D 13	15000		59100	65000
					---- 1979 BOATS ----					
24 4	TOPAZ 24-BIMINI	OP	CUD	FBG SV	IB 228 8	4500	1 11	11300	12900
24 4	TOPAZ 24-BIMINI	OP	CUD	FBG SV	IB 124D VLVO 8	4500	1 11	14700	16700
24 4	TOPAZ 24-CTR	OP	OPFSH	FBG SV	IB 228 8	4500	1 11	11300	12800
24 4	TOPAZ 24-CTR	OP	OPFSH	FBG SV	IB 124D VLVO 8	4500	1 11	14600	16600
24 4	TOPAZ 24-CTR	TT	OPFSH	FBG SV	IB 228 8	4500	1 11	11300	12800
24 4	TOPAZ 24-CTR	TT	OPFSH	FBG SV	IB 124D VLVO 8	4500	1 11	14600	16600
27 8	MAKAIRA 28	OP	FSH	FBG SV	IB 228 10 3	7500	2 2	19400	21600
27 8	MAKAIRA 28	OP	FSH	FBG SV	IB 124D VLVO 10 3	7500	2 2	24200	26800
27 8	MAKAIRA 28	TT	FSH	FBG SV	IB 228 10 3	7500	2 2	19400	21600
27 8	MAKAIRA 28	TT	FSH	FBG SV	IB 124D VLVO 10 3	7500	2 2	24200	26800
27 8	TOPAZ 28-CUDDY	OP	CUD	FBG SV	IB T228 10 3	7500	2 2	21800	24200
27 8	TOPAZ 28-CUDDY	OP	CUD	FBG SV	IB T124D VLVO 10 3	7500	2 2	27900	31000
27 8	TOPAZ 28-CUDDY	TT	CUD	FBG SV	IB T228 10 3	7500	2 2	21800	24200
27 8	TOPAZ 28-CUDDY	TT	CUD	FBG SV	IB T124D VLVO 10 3	7500	2 2	27900	31000
					---- 1978 BOATS ----					
24	TOPAZ	OP		FBG SV	IB 228 8		1 11	10700	12100
27 8	TOPAZ		CUD	FBG SV	IB T228 10 3	7500	2 2	20900	23200
33	TOPAZ			FBG SV	IB T350 13			38000	42200
					---- 1977 BOATS ----					
24	TOPAZ	OP	OPFSH	FBG SV	IB 233 8			9650	10900
27 8	TOPAZ		CUD	FBG SV	IB T233 10 3	7500		20100	22300
27 8	TOPAZ		SF	FBG SV	IB T233 10 3	7500		20100	22300
					---- 1976 BOATS ----					
24 8	TOPAZ	OP	OPFSH	FBG SV	IB 233 8			9300	10600
27 8	CUDDY	OP	CUD	FBG	IB 255-350 10 3	7500	2 2	17200	20500
27 8	CUDDY	OP	CUD	FBG	IB D 10 3	7500	2 2	**	**
27 8	CUDDY	OP	CUD	FBG	IB T233 10 3	7500	2 2	19300	21500
27 8	CUDDY	TT	CUD	FBG	IB 255-350 10 3	7500	2 2	17200	20500
27 8	CUDDY	TT	CUD	FBG	IB D 10 3	7500	2 2	**	**
27 8	CUDDY	TT	CUD	FBG	IB T233 10 3	7500	2 2	19300	21500
27 8	SPORT	OP	SF	FBG	IB 255-350 10 3	7500	2 2	17200	20500
27 8	SPORT	OP	SF	FBG	IB D 10 3	7500	2 2	**	**
27 8	SPORT	OP	SF	FBG	IB T233 10 3	7500	2 2	19300	21400
27 8	SPORT	TT	SF	FBG	IB 255-350 10 3	7500	2 2	17200	20500
27 8	SPORT	TT	SF	FBG	IB D 10 3	7500	2 2	**	**
27 8	SPORT	TT	SF	FBG	IB T233 10 3	7500	2 2	19300	21400
					---- 1974 BOATS ----					
27 8	SEA-HAWK 28			FBG	IB 225-325 10 3	7000	2 1	16000	18100
27 8	SEA-HAWK 28			FBG	IB T225-T255 10 3	7000	2 1	17000	19700

TOPPER BOAT COMPANY

Call 1-800-327-6929 for BUC Personalized Evaluation Service
Or, for 1958 to 1963 boats, sign onto www.BUCValuPro.com

TOPPER INTERNATIONAL LTD
COAST GUARD MFG ID- JVD

BOSUN MARINE MARKETING INC
FOR OLDER MODELS SEE J V DUNHILL

Call 1-800-327-6929 for BUC Personalized Evaluation Service
Or, for 1983 to 1986 boats, sign onto www.BUCValuPro.com

TOR TRADING CO INC

Call 1-800-327-6929 for BUC Personalized Evaluation Service
Or, for 1965 boats, sign onto www.BUCValuPro.com

TORTOLA TRAWLERS
KEY LARGO FL 33037   COAST GUARD MFG ID- TTW See inside cover to adjust price for area
                        FORMERLY R H SPEAS

For more recent years, see the BUC Used Boat Price Guide, Volume 1 or Volume 2

LOA FT IN	NAME AND/ OR MODEL	TOP/ RIG	BOAT TYPE	-HULL- MTL TP	ENGINE TP # HP MFG	BEAM FT IN	WGT LBS	DRAFT FT IN	RETAIL LOW	RETAIL HIGH
---	--- 1983 BOATS									
36	TORTOLA 36	SLP	MS	F/W KL	IB 100D WEST	13	22000	4 4	40000	44500
42	TORTOLA 42	FB	TRWL	F/W DS	IB 100D	16	40000	4 4	139500	153500
45	TORTOLA 45	FB	TRWL	F/W DS	IB 145D GM	16	45000	4 4	158500	174000
45	TORTOLA CHARTER	FB	TRWL	F/W DS	IB 145D GM	16	45000	4 4	158500	174000
48	TORTOLA 48	FB	TRWL	F/W DS	IB 145D GM	16	50000	4 4	173500	190500
51	TORTOLA 51	FB	TRWL	F/W DS	IB 265D GM	18	60000	4	187000	205500
54	TORTOLA 54	FB	TRWL	F/W DS	IB 265D GM	18	65000	4	209000	229500
57	TORTOLA 57	FB	TRWL	F/W DS	IB 265D GM	18	70000	4	221000	242500
60	TORTOLA 60	FB	TRWL	F/W DS	IB 265D GM	18	75000	4	272000	299000
---	--- 1982 BOATS									
42	TORTOLA-TRAWLER	FB	TRWL	F/W DS	IB 175D GM	16	40000	3 4	134000	147500
45	TORTOLA-TRAWLER	FB	TRWL	F/W DS	IB 175D GM	16	45000	3 4	152000	167000
48	TORTOLA-TRAWLER	FB	TRWL	F/W DS	IB 175D GM	16	50000	3 4	166000	182500
51	TORTOLA-TRAWLER	FB	TRWL	F/W DS	IB 265D GM	18	60000	3 6	178000	196000
54	TORTOLA-TRAWLER	FB	TRWL	F/W DS	IB 265D GM	18	65000	3 6	199500	219500
57	TORTOLA-TRAWLER	FB	TRWL	F/W DS	IB 265D GM	18	70000	3 6	211500	232500
60	TORTOLA-TRAWLER	FB	TRWL	F/W DS	IB 265D GM	18	75000	3 8	260000	286000
---	--- 1981 BOATS									
50	TORTOLA 50	FB	TRWL	CDR DS	IB 175D GM	18	64000	4	173500	190500
57	TORTOLA	FB	TRWL	CDR DS	IB 265D GM	18	68000	4	198000	218000

TOURNAMENT FISHERMAN INC
COAST GUARD MFG ID- TFB

Call 1-800-327-6929 for BUC Personalized Evaluation Service
Or, for 1976 to 1977 boats, sign onto www.BUCValuPro.com

TOWN CLASS BOATS
COAST GUARD MFG ID- PRM

Call 1-800-327-6929 for BUC Personalized Evaluation Service
Or, for 1960 to 1965 boats, sign onto www.BUCValuPro.com

TRADE RESEARCH CO

Call 1-800-327-6929 for BUC Personalized Evaluation Service
Or, for 1965 to 1967 boats, sign onto www.BUCValuPro.com

TRADE WINDS MARINE INC
FAIRFIELD CT 06430   COAST GUARD MFG ID- TWY See inside cover to adjust price for area

LOA FT IN	NAME AND/ OR MODEL	TOP/ RIG	BOAT TYPE	-HULL- MTL TP	ENGINE TP # HP MFG	BEAM FT IN	WGT LBS	DRAFT FT IN	RETAIL LOW	RETAIL HIGH
---	--- 1974 BOATS									
32	TRAVELLER	SLP	SA/CR	FBG KL	IB D	10	2 15200	5	36400	40500
32	TRAVELLER	KTH	SA/CR	FBG KL	IB D	10	2 15200	5	36400	40500
33 6	TWT 34	FB	TRWL	FBG DS	IB 120D FORD	11	9 14000	3 6	35000	38900
34	COMMITTEE BOAT			FBG SV	IB 80D	11	9		32700	36400
35			TRWL	FBG DS	IB T 80D	12	2		35800	39800
35	TRADEWINDS-CLIPPER	KTH	SA/CR	FBG KL	IB D	11	19000	4 9	45800	50400
40 8	TRADEWINDS-CLIPPER	KTH	SA/CR	FBG KL	IB D	12	2 28000	6 2	68600	75400
41 8	TWT 42 PH	HT	TRWL	FBG DS	IB T120D FORD	14	4 32000	4 5	82500	90700
54	CLIPPER	KTH	SA/CR	FBG KL	IB D	15	1 55000	6 6	129000	141500
---	--- 1973 BOATS									
33 6	TWT 34	FB	TRWL	FBG DS	IB 120D FORD	11	9 14000	3 6	34000	37800
33 6	TWT 34 AFT CBN	FB	TRWL	FBG	IB T 50D VLVO	11	9 15000	3 6	33100	36800
35	TRADEWINDS-CLIPPER	SLP	SA/CR	FBG	IB 37D PERK	11	19000	4 9	43100	47800
35	TRADEWINDS-CLIPPER	KTH	SA/CR	FBG KL	IB 37D PERK	11	19000	4 9	43800	48700
35	TWT 35 AFT CBN		SAIL	FBG	IB 120D FORD	11	9 20000	3 6	44500	49400
40 8	TWC 41 AFT CBN	KTH	SA/CR	FBG	IB 37D PERK	12	2 28000	6 2	73100	80400
40 8	TWC 41 PH	KTH	SAIL	FBG	IB 37D PERK	12	2 28000	6 2	66000	72500
40 8	TWC 41 STD	KTH	SA/CR	FBG	IB 37D PERK	12	2 28000	6 2	58900	64800
40 8	TWT 42 PH	HT	TRWL	FBG DS	IB 210D CAT	14	4 32000	4 5	76000	83500
40 8	TWT 42 PH	HT	TRWL	FBG DS	IB T120D FORD	14	4 32000	4 5	78100	85800
46	TWT 46	KTH	MS	FBG KL	IB 210D CAT	14	4 34000	4 5	79200	87000
46	TWT 46	KTH	MS	FBG KL	IB T120D FORD	14	4 34000	4 5	80400	88400
51	TWC 51 AFT CBN	KTH	SA/CR	FBG KL	IB 85D PERK	13	2 52000	6	107500	118000
54	TWC 54 AFT CBN	KTH	SA/CR	FBG KL	IB 120D FORD	15	1 60000	6 6	127000	140000

TRADEWINDS BOAT CO

Call 1-800-327-6929 for BUC Personalized Evaluation Service
Or, for 1965 to 1967 boats, sign onto www.BUCValuPro.com

TRADEWINDS MARINE INC
FOUNTAIN VALLEY CA 9270 COAST GUARD MFG ID- TML See inside cover to adjust price for area

LOA FT IN	NAME AND/ OR MODEL	TOP/ RIG	BOAT TYPE	-HULL- MTL TP	ENGINE TP # HP MFG	BEAM FT IN	WGT LBS	DRAFT FT IN	RETAIL LOW	RETAIL HIGH
---	--- 1981 BOATS									
40 1	VIGILANTE T-40	SLP	SA/RC	FBG KL	IB D	12	14700	7 8	40000	44500
---	--- 1980 BOATS									
40 1	VIGILANTE T-40	SLP	SA/RC	FBG KL	IB D	12	14700	7 8	38200	42400
54 9	TRADEWINDS T-55	SLP	SA/RC	FBG KL	IB D	14	38000	5 9	122000	134000
54 9	TRADEWINDS T-55	SCH	SA/RC	FBG KL	IB D	14	38000	5 9	122000	134000
54 9	TRADEWINDS T-55	CUT	SA/RC	FBG KL	IB D	14	38000	5 9	122000	134000
---	--- 1977 BOATS									
54 8	TRADE WINDS 55	SLP	SA/CR	FBG KC	IB 60D PERK	14	39000		108000	119000
54 8	TRADE WINDS 55	SLP	SA/CR	FBG KL	IB 60D PERK	14	39000	5 9	108000	119000
54 8	TRADE WINDS 55	CUT	SA/CR	FBG KL	IB 60D PERK	14	39000		108000	119000
54 8	TRADE WINDS 55	CUT	SA/CR	FBG KL	IB 60D PERK	14	39000	5 9	108000	119000
54 8	TRADE WINDS 55	YWL	SA/CR	FBG KL	IB 60D PERK	14	39000		108000	119000
54 8	TRADE WINDS 55	YWL	SA/CR	FBG KL	IB 60D PERK	14	39000	5 9	108000	119000
54 8	TRADE WINDS 55	KTH	SA/CR	FBG KL	IB 60D PERK	14	39000		108000	119000
54 8	TRADE WINDS 55	KTH	SA/CR	FBG KL	IB 60D PERK	14	39000	5 9	108000	119000

TRADITION YACHTS

Call 1-800-327-6929 for BUC Personalized Evaluation Service
Or, for 1963 to 1973 boats, sign onto www.BUCValuPro.com

TRANSMAR

Call 1-800-327-6929 for BUC Personalized Evaluation Service
Or, for 1961 to 1965 boats, sign onto www.BUCValuPro.com

TRANSPAC YACHTS INC
SEATTLE WA 98108   COAST GUARD MFG ID- TYH See inside cover to adjust price for area

LOA FT IN	NAME AND/ OR MODEL	TOP/ RIG	BOAT TYPE	-HULL- MTL TP	ENGINE TP # HP MFG	BEAM FT IN	WGT LBS	DRAFT FT IN	RETAIL LOW	RETAIL HIGH
---	--- 1980 BOATS									
37	TRANSPAC	CR		FBG SV	IB 160D	13	17000		64800	71200
39	TRANSPAC	CR		FBG SV	IB 160D	13	18500		74900	82300

TRANSPACIFIC MARINE CO LTD

TAIPEI TAIWAN ROC 248   COAST GUARD MFG ID- TMU See inside cover to adjust price for area

For more recent years, see the BUC Used Boat Price Guide, Volume 1 or Volume 2

LOA FT IN	NAME AND/ OR MODEL	TOP/ RIG	BOAT TYPE	HULL MTL TP	ENGINE TP # HP MFG	BEAM FT IN	WGT LBS	DRAFT FT IN	RETAIL LOW	RETAIL HIGH
1983 BOATS										
48 6	TRANSPAC 49 MKII	KTH	SA/CR	FBG KL	IB 80D LEHM	13 7	43000	6	172000	189000
1982 BOATS										
48 6	TRANSPAC 49	KTH	SA/CR	FBG KL	IB 80D LEHM	13 7	43000	6	163000	179500
48 6	TRANSPAC 49	KTH	SA/CR	FBG KL	IB 120D LEHM	13 7	43000	6	164000	180000
1981 BOATS										
48 6	TMC-49	KTH	SA/CR	FBG KL	IB D	13 7	44000	5 6	156000	171500
48 6	TRANSPAC 49	KTH	SA/CR	FBG KL	IB 65D LEHM	13 7	41000	6	151500	166500
1980 BOATS										
43 10	MASON 43	CUT	SA/CR	FBG KL	IB 50D PERK	12 3	25000	6 3	96300	106000
48 6	TRANSPAC 49	KTH	SA/CR	FBG KL	IB 65D LEHM	13 6	41000	6	146000	160500
1979 BOATS										
48 6	TRANSPAC 49	KTH	SA/CR	FBG KL	IB 70D LEHM	13 7	44000	5 6	145000	159500
1978 BOATS										
40 1	MASON 40	CUT	SA/CR	FBG KL	IB D	11 11	21000	5 10	71000	78000
48 6	TRANSPAC 49	KTH	SA/CR	FBG KL	IB D	13 7	42000	5 6	139000	152500
1977 BOATS										
31	TRANSPAC	SLP	SA/CR	FBG KL	IB 15D	9 4	11000	4 8	33400	37100
31	TRANSPAC	SCH	SA/CR	FBG KL	IB 15D	9 4	11000	4 8	33400	37100
40 6	TRANSPAC	KTH	SA/CR	FBG KL	IB	12 6	21000	5 6	70300	77200
42 4	TRANSPAC	MY		FBG DS	IB 130D	15		4 9	78000	85700
42 4	TRANSPAC	MY		FBG DS	IB T 80D	15		4 9	81300	89300
48 6	TRANSPAC 49	KTH	SA/CR	FBG KL	IB 80D FORD	13 7	39000	5 6	131500	144500
1976 BOATS										
31	TRANSPAC	SLP	SA/CR	FBG KL	IB 15D	9 4	11000	4 8	32500	36100
31	TRANSPAC	SCH	SA/CR	FBG KL	IB 15D	9 4	11000	4 8	32500	36100
35	TRANSPAC	SLP	SA/CR	FBG KL	IB 30D	11	18500	5	53400	-58700
35	TRANSPAC	KTH	SA/CR	FBG KL	IB 30D	11	18500	5	53800	59100
41	TRANSPAC	SLP	SA/CR	FBG KL	IB 37D	14	23000	5	73300	80500
42 4	TRANSPAC	MY		FBG DS	IB 120D	15		4 9	74600	82000
42 4	TRANSPAC	MY		FBG DS	IB 180D	15		4 9	75600	83100
48 6	TRANSPAC 49	KTH	SAIL	FBG KL	IB 80D LEHM	13 7	39000	5 6	128500	141000
1975 BOATS										
31	MASON	SLP	SA/CR	FBG KL	IB 12D	9 4	11000	4 8	31800	35300
42 4	TRANSPAC	MY		FBG DS	IB 120D	15		4 9	71600	78700
46	TRANSPAC	KTH	SA/CR	FBG KL	IB 72D	15	5 37000	5 6	111500	122500
47 3	TRANSPAC	MY		MHG DS	IB T120	15		4 6	113500	126000
47 3	TRANSPAC	MY		MHG DS	IB T180	15		4 6	115500	127000
49	TRANSPAC	MY		FBG DS	IB 180D	15	6	4 9	126000	138000
1974 BOATS										
35 6	TRANSPAC	OFF		FBG	IB 120D	12 2		3 6	49800	54700
35 8	TRANSPAC ONE TONNER	SLP	SA/CR	FBG KL	IB D	11 8		6 3	43600	48500
38	TRANSPAC		OFF	FBG	IB 120D	13 10		3 3	33100	36800
38	TRANSPAC		OFF	MHG	IB 120D	13 10		3 3	33100	36800
38	TRANSPAC		OFF	FBG	IB 145D	13 10		3 3	33300	37000
38	TRANSPAC		OFF	MHG	IB 145D	13 10		3 3	33300	37000
40 1	TRANSPAC	KTH	SA/CR	WD KL	IB D	11 11	21000	5 10	64800	71200
47	TRANSPAC	MY		FBG DS	IB T120D	15		4 6	100500	110500
47	TRANSPAC	MY		MHG DS	IB T120D	15		4 6	100500	110500
47	TRANSPAC	MY		FBG DS	IB T145D	15		4 6	101500	111500
47	TRANSPAC	MY		MHG DS	IB T145D	15		4 6	101500	111500
50	TRANSPAC	MY		MHG DS	IB T145D	16 3		6	125500	137500
50	TRANSPAC	MY		MHG DS	IB T175D	16 3		6	126500	139500
1973 BOATS										
26	THUNDERBIRD	SAIL	F/W		OB	7 6	3800	4 6	8900	10100
31	TRANSPAC	SAIL	WD		IB 15D FORD	9 4	10400	4 8	28800	32000
36	TRANSPAC		OFF	WD DS	IB 72D	11 3			37300	41400
38	TRANSPAC	SAIL	WD		IB .47D FORD	12 4	26000	5 7	68900	75800
40 1	TRANSPAC	KTH	SA/CR	WD KL	IB 47D	11 11	21000	5 10	63500	69800
45	TRANSPAC	KTH	SA/CR	WD KL	IB 72D	12 8	32000	5 3	96700	106000
47	TRANSPAC	KTH	SA/CR	WD KL	IB 72D	12 1	30000	5 4	102000	112500
50	TRANSPAC	MS	WD		IB T120D FORD	16	70000		160500	176000
50	TRANSPAC	MY	WHG	DS	IB T120D	16			119500	131000
1971 BOATS										
31	MASON 31	SLP	SA/CR	WD KL	IB 22	9 4	10400	4 8	27400	30500
37 9	MASON 38 STERN CAB	KTH	SA/CR	WD KL	IB 39	12 4	26000	5 7	65100	71600
40	MASON 40	KTH	SA/CR	WD KL	IB 39	12	21000	5 10	59500	65400
47 4	ALDEN 47	KTH	SA/CR	WD KL	IB 59	12 1	30000	5 4	97700	107500
1970 BOATS										
40	M-40	KTH	SA/CR	P/M KL	IB D	12		5 8	59400	65300

TRAVELER BOAT DIVISION

DIV OF STANRAY CORP   COAST GUARD MFG ID- TRV

Call 1-800-327-6929 for BUC Personalized Evaluation Service
Or, for 1960 to 1967 boats, sign onto www.BUCValuPro.com

TRAWLER MARINE

Call 1-800-327-6929 for BUC Personalized Evaluation Service
Or, for 1979 to 1980 boats, sign onto www.BUCValuPro.com

TREMOLINO BOAT CO

COAST GUARD MFG ID- TMG

Call 1-800-327-6929 for BUC Personalized Evaluation Service
Or, for 1977 to 1999 boats, sign onto www.BUCValuPro.com

TRI-SONIC INC

FORT WORTH TX 76135   COAST GUARD MFG ID- TRS See inside cover to adjust price for area

LOA FT IN	NAME AND/ OR MODEL	TOP/ RIG	BOAT TYPE	HULL MTL TP	ENGINE TP # HP MFG	BEAM FT IN	WGT LBS	DRAFT FT IN	RETAIL LOW	RETAIL HIGH
1979 BOATS										
16 4	CAPRICE SST BR	ST	RNBT	FBG TR	IO 165 MRCR	6 8	2500		2750	3200
18 2	RIVIERA SST 2+2 BR	ST	RNBT	FBG TR	IO 165-260	7 3	2700		3300	4100
18 2	RIVIERA XLT BR	ST	RNBT	FBG TR	IO 165-260	7 3	2850		3400	4250
18 2	RIVIERA XLT LTD BR	HT	RNBT	FBG TR	IO 165-260	7 3	2875		3400	4250
18 2	VENTURA SST 2+2 BR	ST	RNBT	FBG DV	IO 165-260	7 4	2875		3350	4200
18 2	VENTURA XLT BR	ST	RNBT	FBG DV	IO 165-260	7 4	2875		3450	4300
18 2	VENTURA XLT LTD BR	HT	RNBT	FBG DV	IO 165-260	7 4	2875		3450	4300
19	T-R2 XLT BR	HT	RNBT	FBG TH	IO 228-260	7 6	2925		3800	4550
19	T-R2 XLT LTD BR	HT	RNBT	FBG TH	IO 260	7 6	2925		3900	4550
19 10	VALIANT SST 2+2 BR	ST	RNBT	FBG DV	IO 165-260	7 7	2950		3750	4650
19 10	VALIANT XLT BR	ST	RNBT	FBG DV	IO 165-260	7 7	2950		4000	4900
22	T-R22 XLT BR	ST	RNBT	FBG TH	IO 260	7 9	3150		5200	6000
22	T-R22 XLT BR	HT	RNBT	FBG TH	IO 330 MRCR	7 9	3150		5850	6750
22	T-R22 XLT LTD	ST	RNBT	FBG TH	IO 260	7 9	3300		5350	6200
22	T-R22 XLT LTD	HT	RNBT	FBG TH	IO 330 MRCR	7 9	3300		6000	6900
22	TRC22C XLT	ST	CUD	FBG TH	IO 260	7 9	3300		5650	6500
22	TRC22C XLT	HT	CUD	FBG TH	IO 330 MRCR	7 9	3300		6350	7300
23 6	CARIBBEAN XLT	ST	CR	FBG DV	IO 228-260	8	5840		9400	10900
23 6	CARIBBEAN XLT	ST	CR	FBG DV	IO T170 MRCR	8	5840		10100	11500
1977 BOATS										
16	SPRINT SST	ST	RNBT	FBG DV	IO 140-190	6 4	2224		2500	3000
16	SPRINT SST 2+2	ST	RNBT	FBG DV	IO 140-190	6 4	2540		2750	3200
16	SPRINT XLT	ST	RNBT	FBG DV	IO 140-190	6 4	2590		2750	3250
16 3	CAPRICE SST	ST	RNBT	FBG TR	IO 140-190	6 7	2380		2700	3200
16 3	CAPRICE SST 2+2	ST	RNBT	FBG TR	IO 140-190	6 7	2590		2850	3350
18 3	CAPRICE SST	ST	RNBT	FBG TR	IO 140-190	6 7	2595		2850	3350
18 2	RIVIERA SST	ST	RNBT	FBG TR	IO 165-235	7 3	2634		3350	4000
18 2	RIVIERA SST 2+2	ST	RNBT	FBG TR	JT 460 BERK	7 3	2634		3950	4600
18 2	RIVIERA SST 2+2	ST	RNBT	FBG TR	JT 460 BERK	7 3	2840		3500	4200
18 2	RIVIERA XLT	ST	RNBT	FBG TR	IO 165-235	7 3	2845		3500	4200
18 2	RIVIERA XLT	ST	RNBT	FBG TR	JT 460 BERK	7 3	2845		4100	4800
18 2	RIVIERA XLT LTD	ST	RNBT	FBG TR	IO 188-235	7 3	3010		3650	4350
18 2	RIVIERA XLT LTD	HT	RNBT	FBG TR	JT 460 BERK	7 3	3010		4250	4950
18 2	TORONADO XLT	ST	RNBT	FBG TR	IO 188-235	7 3	3000		3600	4350
18 2	TORONADO XLT	ST	RNBT	FBG TR	JT 460 BERK	7 3	3000		4250	4950
18 2	TORONADO XLT LTD	HT	RNBT	FBG TR	IO 188-235	7 3	3110		4400	5050
18 2	TORONADO XLT LTD	HT	RNBT	FBG TR	JT 460 BERK	7 3	3110		4400	5050
18 2	VENTURA SST	ST	RNBT	FBG DV	IO 165-235	7 4	2600		3300	4000
18 2	VENTURA SST	ST	RNBT	FBG DV	JT 460 BERK	7 4	2600		3950	4600
18 2	VENTURA SST 2+2	ST	RNBT	FBG DV	IO 165-235	7 4	2810		3450	4200
18 2	VENTURA SST 2+2	ST	RNBT	FBG DV	JT 460 BERK	7 4	2810		4100	4800
18 2	VENTURA XLT	ST	RNBT	FBG DV	IO 165-235	7 4	2812		3500	4200
18 2	VENTURA XLT	ST	RNBT	FBG DV	JT 460 BERK	7 4	2812		4100	4800
18 2	VENTURA XLT LTD	HT	RNBT	FBG DV	IO 188-235	7 4	3100		3700	4450
18 2	VENTURA XLT LTD	HT	RNBT	FBG DV	JT 460 BERK	7 4	3100		4400	5050
19 2	T-R2 SST	ST	RNBT	FBG TH	IO 165-235	7 4	3250		4050	4750
19 2	T-R2 SST	ST	RNBT	FBG TH	JT 460 BERK	7 4	3250		4700	5400
19 2	T-R2 SST 2+2	ST	RNBT	FBG TH	IO 165-235	7 4	3350		4100	4900
19 2	T-R2 SST 2+2	ST	RNBT	FBG TH	JT 460 BERK	7 4	3350		4800	5500
19 2	T-R2 XLT	ST	RNBT	FBG TH	IO 165-235	7 4	3450		4200	5000

LOA FT	IN	NAME AND/ OR MODEL	TOP/ RIG	BOAT TYPE	-HULL- MTL	TP	TP	----ENGINE--- # HP	MFG	BEAM FT	IN	WGT LBS	DRAFT FT	IN	RETAIL LOW	RETAIL HIGH
		1977 BOATS														
19	2	T-R2 XLT	ST	RNBT	FBG	TH	JT	460	BERK	7	4	3450			4900	5600
23	6	CARIBBEAN XLT CC	ST	CUD	FBG	DV	IO	188-235		8		5995			9750	11200
23	6	CARIBBEAN XLT CC	ST	CUD	FBG	DV	IO	T165-T235		8		5995			10600	12300
23	6	CARIBBEAN XLT LTD	ST	CUD	FBG	DV	IO	188-235		8		5695			9400	10800
23	6	CARIBBEAN XLT LTD	ST	CUD	FBG	DV	IO	T165-T235		8		5695			10100	11900
23	6	CARIBBEAN XLT RA	ST	CR	FBG	DV	IO	188-235		8		5795			9500	10900
23	6	CARIBBEAN XLT RA	ST	CR	FBG	DV	IO	T165-T235		8		5795			10300	12000
		1976 BOATS														
16	3	CAPRICE BASIC 1700	ST	RNBT	F/W	TR	IO	140-165		6	7	2382			2400	2850
16	3	CAPRICE SST 1700	ST	RNBT	F/W	TR	IO	140-165		6	7	2382			2800	3300
16	3	CAPRICE SST 1700	ST	RNBT	F/W	TR	JT	290	BERK	6	7	2382			3050	3550
16	3	CAPRICE XLT 1700	ST	RNBT	F/W	TR	IO	140-165		6	7	2382			3100	3600
16	3	CAPRICE XLT 1700	ST	RNBT	F/W	TR	JT	290	BERK	6	7	2382			3300	3850
18	2	RIVIERA BASIC 1900	ST	RNBT	F/W	TR	IO	165-190		6	7	2634			3250	3800
18	2	RIVIERA SST 1900	ST	RNBT	F/W	TR	IO	165-235		7	3	2634			3250	3900
18	2	RIVIERA SST 1900	ST	RNBT	F/W	TR	JT	290-320		7	3	2634			3550	4200
18	2	RIVIERA XLT 1900	ST	RNBT	F/W	TR	IO	165-235		7	3	2634			3600	4300
18	2	RIVIERA XLT 1900	ST	RNBT	F/W	TR	JT	290-320		7	3	2634			4050	4700
18	2	RIVIERA XLT 1900	HT	RNBT	F/W	TR	IO	233-235		7	3	2634			3550	4100
18	2	RIVIERA XLT 1900	HT	RNBT	F/W	TR	JT	320	BERK	7	3	2634			3800	4400
18	2	TORONADO XLT 1900	ST	RNBT	F/W	TR	IO	165-235		7	3	2916			3650	4350
18	2	TORONADO XLT 1900	ST	RNBT	F/W	TR	JT	290-320		7	3	2916			4000	4650
18	2	TORONADO XLT 1900	HT	RNBT	F/W	TR	IO	233-235		7	3	2916			3750	4350
18	2	TORONADO XLT 1900	HT	RNBT	F/W	TR	JT	320	BERK	7	3	2916			4000	4650
18	2	VENTURA XLT B/R 1900	ST	RNBT	F/W	DV	IO	165-235		7	4	2600			3400	4100
18	2	VENTURA XLT B/R 1900	ST	RNBT	F/W	DV	JT	290-320		7	4	2600			3800	4400
18	2	VENTURA XLT B/R 1900	HT	RNBT	F/W	DV	IO	233-235		7	4	2600			3550	4100
18	2	VENTURA XLT B/R 1900	HT	RNBT	F/W	DV	JT	320	BERK	7	4	2600			3800	4400
23	6	CC-XLT 2400	ST	CR	F/W	DV	IO	188-235		8		5795			9750	11200
23	6	RA-XLT 2400 RNBT	ST	CUD	F/W	DV	IO	188-235		8		5645			9500	10900
		1975 BOATS														
16	3	CAPRICE	OP	RNBT	F/W	TR	OB			6	7	1320			3300	3800
16	3	CAPRICE	OP	RNBT	F/W	TR	IO	140-165		6	7	2382	3		2650	3150
16	3	CAPRICE	OP	RNBT	F/W	TR	JT	290	OMC	6	7	2382	3		2850	3350
16	3	CAPRICE SST	OP	RNBT	F/W	TR	IO	140-165		6	7	2382			3050	3550
16	3	CAPRICE SST	OP	RNBT	F/W	TR	JT	290	OMC	6	7	2382			3250	3800
18	2	RIVIERA	OP	RNBT	F/W	TR	IO	165-235		7	3	2634			3300	4000
18	2	RIVIERA	OP	RNBT	F/W	TR	JT	290-390		7	3	2634			3450	4000
18	2	RIVIERA SST	OP	RNBT	F/W	TR	IO	165-235		7	3	2634			3750	4550
18	2	RIVIERA SST	OP	RNBT	F/W	TR	JT	290-390		7	3	2634			3850	4500
18	2	RIVIERA XLT	HT	RNBT	F/W	TR	IO	233-235		7	3	3000			3950	4600
18	2	RIVIERA XLT	HT	RNBT	F/W	TR	JT	290-390		7	3	3000			3900	4550
18	2	TORONADO SST	OP	RNBT	F/W	TR	IO	165-235		7	3	2916			3750	4500
18	2	TORONADO SST	OP	RNBT	F/W	TR	JT	290-390		7	3	2916			3850	4500
18	2	TORONADO XLT	HT	RNBT	F/W	TR	IO	233-235		7	3	2916			3900	4500
18	2	TORONADO XLT	HT	RNBT	F/W	TR	JT	290-390		7	3	2916			3850	4500
18	2	VENTURA SST	OP	RNBT	F/W	DV	IO	188-235		7	4	2600			3550	4250
18	2	VENTURA SST	OP	RNBT	F/W	DV	JT	290-390		7	4	2600			3650	4250
18	2	VENTURA XLT	HT	RNBT	F/W	DV	IO	188-235		7	4	2800			3700	4450
18	2	VENTURA XLT	HT	RNBT	F/W	DV	JT	290-390		7	4	2800			3800	4400
23	6	CARIBBEAN	OP	CR	F/W	DV	IO	188-235		8		5795			10100	11600
23	6	CARIBBEAN RNBT	OP	CUD	F/W	DV	IO	188-235		8		5695			9900	11400
23	6	CARIBBEAN XLT RNBT	HT	CUD	F/W	DV	IO	233	MRCR	8		5995			10500	11900
23	6	CARIBBEAN XLT RNBT	HT	CUD	F/W	DV	IO	T233	MRCR	8		5995			11500	13100
		1974 BOATS														
16		SPRINT 1700		RNBT	FBG	DV	IO	120-165		6	4	2223			2750	3250
16		SPRINT 1700		RNBT	FBG	DV	JT	185-245		6	4	2223			2700	3200
16	3	CAPRICE 1700		RNBT	FBG		OB			6	7	1320			3250	3800
16	3	CAPRICE 1700		RNBT	FBG		IO	120-165		6	7	2383			2850	3350
16	3	CAPRICE SST		RNBT	FBG		IO	120-165		6	7	2383			3050	3550
16	3	CAPRICE SST		RNBT	FBG		JT	245	OMC	6	7	2383			2950	3400
18	2	RIVIERA 1900		RNBT	FBG		IO	165-255		7	3	2634			3550	4400
18	2	RIVIERA 1900 SST		RNBT	FBG		IO	165-188		7	3	2634			3750	4350
		JT 245 OMC 3500 4100, JT 255 WAUK 3500 4100, IO 255 WAUK													3950	4600
		JT 365-390 3500 4100														
18	2	TORONADO		RNBT	FBG		IO	165-188		7	3	2916			3850	4550
		JT 245 OMC 3700 4300, JT 255 WAUK 3700 4300, IO 255 WAUK													4100	4800
		JT 365-390 3700 4300														
18	2	VENTURA 1900		RNBT	FBG	DV	IO	165-188		7	4	2600			3650	4250
		JT 245 OMC 3500 4050, JT 255 WAUK 3500 4050, IO 255 WAUK													3900	4500
		JT 360-390 3500 4050														
18	11	1800		WKNDR	FBG	TR	IO	165	MRCR	7	10	3020			4500	5150
22	8	2200		WKNDR	FBG	TR	IO	188-255		7	10	3450			6550	7800
23	6	CARIBBEAN 2400		CR	FBG		IO	188-255		8		5795			10400	12100
23	6	CARIBBEAN 2400		CR	FBG		IO	T165-T188		8		5795			11300	12900
23	6	CARIBBEAN 2400		RNBT	FBG		IO	188-255		8		5645			9550	11100
23	6	CARIBBEAN 2400		RNBT	FBG		IO	T165-T188		8		5645			10400	11800
		1973 BOATS														
16		SPRINT 1700		RNBT	FBG	DV	IO	120-165		6	4	2223			2850	3350
16	3	CAPRICE 1700		RNBT	FBG		OB			6	7	1320			3250	3800
16	3	CAPRICE 1700		RNBT	FBG		IO	120-165		6	7	2383			2950	3500
16	3	CAPRICE SST		RNBT	FBG		IO	120-165		6	7	2383			3150	3650
18	2	RIVIERA 1900		RNBT	FBG		IO	165-215		7	3	2634			3650	4400
		JT 245 OMC 3300 3850, JT 255 WAUK 3300 3850, IO 255 WAUK													3950	4550
		JT 365-390 3350 3900														
18	2	RIVIERA 1900 SST		RNBT	FBG		IO	165-215		7	3	2634			3850	4600
		JT 245 OMC 3450 4000, JT 255 WAUK 3450 4000, IO 255 WAUK													4100	4750
		JT 365-390 3350 3950														
18	2	TORONADO		RNBT	FBG		IO	165-215		7	3	2916			4000	4750
		JT 245 OMC 3550 4150, JT 255 WAUK 3550 4150, IO 255 WAUK													4250	4950
		JT 365-390 3550 4150														
18	2	VENTURA 1900		RNBT	FBG	DV	IO	165		7	4	2600			3750	4350
22	8	2200		WKNDR	FBG	TR	IO	165		7	10	3450			6700	7700
23	6	CARIBBEAN 2400		RNBT	FBG		IO	185-255		8		4780			8550	10100
23	6	CARIBBEAN 2400		RNBT	FBG		JT	365-390		8		4780			7150	8250
		1972 BOATS														
16	3	CAPRICE 1700			FBG		OB			6	3	1335	1		3200	3750
16	3	CAPRICE 1700			FBG		IO	120-165		6	3	2140	1		2750	3250
18	2	RIVIERA 1900			FBG		IO	140-245		7	3	2720	1		3850	4700
23	6	CARIBBEAN 2400			FBG		IO	165-245		8		4140	1		7950	9350
23	6	CARIBBEAN 2400			FBG		IO	T120-T165		8		4140	1		8900	10200
		1971 BOATS														
16	3	CAPRICE			FBG		OB			6	8	1100	1		2700	3150
16	3	CAPRICE			FBG		IO	120-165		6	8	2000	1		2850	3400
18	2	RIVIERA			FBG		IO	140-235		7	3	2500	1		3800	4550

TRI-STAR TRIMARANS

COAST GUARD MFG ID- TST

Call 1-800-327-6929 for BUC Personalized Evaluation Service
Or, for 1967 boats, sign onto www.BUCValuPro.com

TRI-YACHT SALES

Call 1-800-327-6929 for BUC Personalized Evaluation Service
Or, for 1968 boats, sign onto www.BUCValuPro.com

TRIANGLE MARINE CO

Call 1-800-327-6929 for BUC Personalized Evaluation Service
Or, for 1960 to 1967 boats, sign onto www.BUCValuPro.com

TRIDENT MARINE LIMITED

FAREHM/HAMP ENGLAND COAST GUARD MFG ID- TDS See inside cover to adjust price for area
FORMERLY TRIDENT MARINE SALES LIMITED

For more recent years, see the BUC Used Boat Price Guide, Volume 1 or Volume 2

LOA FT	IN	NAME AND/ OR MODEL	TOP/ RIG	BOAT TYPE	-HULL- MTL	TP	TP	----ENGINE--- # HP	MFG	BEAM FT	IN	WGT LBS	DRAFT FT	IN	RETAIL LOW	RETAIL HIGH
		1981 BOATS														
24		ROWAN-CROWN	SLP	SA/CR	FBG	TK	OB			8	9	5340	3	3	10400	11900
27		MACWESTER 27	SLP	SA/CR	FBG	TK	IB	23D	VLVO	9	2	7480			18600	20700
30	6	CHALLENGER 31	SLP	SA/CR	FBG	KL	IB	13D	VLVO	10		9632	4		25200	28000
30	6	VOYAGER 30	SLP	SA/CR	FBG	KL	IB	30D	WATE	10		9632	4		25300	28100
30	6	VOYAGER 30	SLP	SA/CR	FBG	TK	IB	30D	WATE	10		9632	3	6	25400	28300
30	6	WARRIOR 30	SLP	SA/CR	FBG	TK	IB	30D	WATE	10		9632	4		25400	28300
32		MACWESTER-MALIN	KTH	SA/CR	FBG	KL	IB	36D	VLVO	9	5	9120	4	8	24600	27300
32		MACWESTER-MALIN	KTH	SA/CR	FBG	TK	IB	36D	VLVO	9	5	9120	3	3	24700	27500
35		CHALLENGER 35	SLP	SA/CR	FBG	TK	IB	23D	VLVO	10	6	12320	5		33400	37100
35		VOYAGER 35	SLP	SA/CR	FBG	TK	IB	42D	BENZ	10	6	12320	5		33500	37200
35		WARRIOR III	SLP	SA/CR	FBG	TK	IB	42D	BENZ	10	6	12320	5		33500	37200
36		MACWESTER-HEBRIDEAN	KTH	SA/CR	FBG	KL	IB	38D		11	2	13440	4	10	37700	41900

 CONTINUED ON NEXT PAGE

LOA FT IN	NAME AND/ OR MODEL	TOP/ RIG	BOAT TYPE	-HULL- MTL TP	----ENGINE--- TP # HP MFG	BEAM FT IN	WGT LBS	DRAFT FT IN	RETAIL LOW	RETAIL HIGH
			1981 BOATS							
36	MACWESTER-HEBRIDEAN	KTH	SA/CR	FBG TK IB	38D	11 2	13440	4 9	37800	42000
36	MACWESTER-SEAFORTH	KTH	SA/CR	FBG TK IB	42D BENZ	12 2	13440	4 10	37900	42100
38	VOYAGER 38	KTH	SA/CR	FBG TK IB	60D VLVO	13	18816	5	53900	59200
			1980 BOATS							
30 6	CHALLENGER 31	SLP	SA/CR	FBG KL IB	13D VLVO	10	9632	4	24500	27300
30 6	VOYAGER 30	SLP	SA/CR	FBG KL IB	30D WATE	10	9632	4	23900	26600
30 6	WARRIOR 30	SLP	SA/CR	FBG KL IB	30D WATE	10	9632	4	24800	27500
35	CHALLENGER 35	SLP	SA/CR	FBG KL IB	30D WATE	10 6	12320	5	31700	35300
35	VOYAGER 35	SLP	SA/CR	FBG KL IB	42D BENZ	10 6	12320	5	34200	38000
35	WARRIOR III	SLP	SA/CR	FBG KL IB	42D BENZ	10 6	12320	5	29500	32700
38	VOYAGER 38	KTH	SA/CR	FBG KL IB	60D	13	18816	5	51300	56400
			1979 BOATS							
22 3	ROWAN 22	SLP	SA/CR	FBG KL IB	D	8 3	5040	2 9	9300	10600
24	ROWAN-CROWN	SLP	SA/CR	FBG KL IB	D	8 9	5340	3 3	10100	11500
26 6	ROWAN 8 METRE	SLP	SA/CR	FBG KL IB	D	8 3	6720	4 6	14400	16400
27	MACWESTER	SLP	SA/CR	FBG TK IB	D	9 2	7480	3 8	16600	18800
32	MALIN	SLP	SA/CR	FBG KL IB	D	9 5	9120	4 8	23100	25600
32	MALIN	SLP	SA/CR	FBG TK IB	D	9 5	9120	3 3	23200	25800
32	MALIN	KTH	SA/CR	FBG KL IB	D	9 5	9120	4 8	23100	25600
32	MALIN	KTH	SA/CR	FBG TK IB	D	9 5	9120	3 3	23200	25800
36	SEAFORTH	SCH	SA/CR	FBG KL IB	D	11 2	13440	4 10	33400	37100
36	SEAFORTH	SCH	SA/CR	FBG TK IB	D	11 2	13440	3 9	33500	37300
36	SEAFORTH	KTH	SA/CR	FBG KL IB	D	11 2	13440	4 10	34400	38200
36	SEAFORTH	KTH	SA/CR	FBG TK IB	D	11 2	13440	3 9	34500	38300
			1978 BOATS							
22 3	ROWAN 22	SLP	SA/CR	FBG KL IB	6D PETT	8 3	5040	2 9	8650	9950
24	ROWAN-CROWN	SLP	SA/CR	FBG KL IB	6D PETT	8 9	5340	3 3	9650	10900
26 6	ROWAN 8 METRE	SLP	SA/CR	FBG KL IB	12D PETT	8 3	6720	4 6	13800	15700
27	MACWESTER	SLP	SA/CR	FBG TK IB	12D PETT	9 2	7480	3 8	15800	18000
32	MALIN	SLP	SA/CR	FBG KL IB	31D TEMP	9 5	9120	4 8	22200	24700
32	MALIN	KTH	SA/CR	FBG KL IB	31D TEMP	9 5	9120	3 3	22200	24400
32	WIGHT	SLP	SA/CR	FBG KL IB	23D VLVO	9 5	9120	4 8	22200	24700
32	WIGHT	SLP	SA/CR	FBG KL IB	23D VLVO	9 5	9120	3 3	22200	24400
36	SEAFORTH	KTH	SA/CR	FBG KL IB	42D TEMP	11 2	13440	4 10	33000	36700
36	SEAFORTH	KTH	SA/CR	FBG TK IB	42D TEMP	11 2	13440	3 9	33200	36800
			1972 BOATS							
22 6	ROWAN	SLP	SA/CR	FBG KL IB		8 3		3	4100	4750
22 6	ROWAN	SLP	SA/CR	FBG TK IB		8 3		3	4100	4750
27	MACWESTER 27	SLP	SA/CR	FBG TK IB		9 2		3 8	10000	11400
28	MACWESTER 28	SLP	SA/CR	FBG KL IB		9		4 8	12100	13800
30 6	MACWESTER 30	SLP	SA/CR	FBG TK IB		9 4		3 3	18600	20700
30 6	MACWESTER 30	KTH	SA/CR	FBG TK IB		9 4		3 3	18600	20700

TRIDENT MARINE SERVICE
COAST GUARD MFG ID- TDT

Call 1-800-327-6929 for BUC Personalized Evaluation Service
Or, for 1974 boats, sign onto www.BUCValuPro.com

TRIMAR BOATS

Call 1-800-327-6929 for BUC Personalized Evaluation Service
Or, for 1961 to 1966 boats, sign onto www.BUCValuPro.com

TRIMARAN DESIGN CENTER

Call 1-800-327-6929 for BUC Personalized Evaluation Service
Or, for 1970 to 1972 boats, sign onto www.BUCValuPro.com

TRINTELLA SHIPYARD
5231XA HERTOGENBOSCH   See inside cover to adjust price for area
FORMERLY ANN WEVER YACHTYARD BV

For more recent years, see the BUC Used Boat Price Guide, Volume 1 or Volume 2

LOA FT IN	NAME AND/ OR MODEL	TOP/ RIG	BOAT TYPE	-HULL- MTL TP	----ENGINE--- TP # HP MFG	BEAM FT IN	WGT LBS	DRAFT FT IN	RETAIL LOW	RETAIL HIGH
			1983 BOATS							
38	TRINTELLA 38	SLP	SA/CR	FBG KL IB	D	12	20500	8 3	103000	113000
38	TRINTELLA 38	KTH	SA/CR	FBG KL IB	D	12	20500	6 3	107000	117500
42	TRINTELLA 42	SLP	SA/CR	FBG KL IB	D	13 2	19800	7	114000	125500
45	TRINTELLA 45	SLP	SA/CR	FBG KL IB	D	13 5	31900	7 2	162500	178500
45	TRINTELLA 45	KTH	SA/CR	FBG KL IB	D	13 5	31900	7 2	170000	187000
53	TRINTELLA 53	KTH	SA/CR	FBG KC IB	D	15	39000	7 2	243000	267000
53	TRINTELLA 53	KTH	SA/CR	FBG KC IB	D	15	39000	7 2	249500	274500
			1982 BOATS							
38	TRINTELLA 38	SLP	SA/RC	FBG KL IB	D	12	20500	7	97300	107000
38	TRINTELLA 38	KTH	SA/RC	FBG KL IB	D	12	20500	7	101000	111000
42	TRINTELLA 42	SLP	SA/RC	FBG KL IB	D	12	19800	7	108000	119000
44	TRINTELLA 44	SLP	SA/CR	FBG KL IB	D	13 5	31900	7 2	150000	164500
44	TRINTELLA 44	KTH	SA/CR	FBG KL IB	D	13 5	31900	7 2	157000	172500
			1981 BOATS							
37 11	TRINTELLA 38	SLP	SA/CR	FBG KL IB	49D PERK	12 2	21000	6 3	93700	103000
37 11	TRINTELLA 38	KTH	SA/CR	FBG KL IB	49D PERK	12 2	21000	6 3	97300	107000
42 4	TRINTELLA 42	SLP	SA/CR	FBG KL IB	35D VLVO	13 2	18000	7 1	98100	108000
44	TRINTELLA 44	SLP	SA/CR	FBG KL IB	72D PERK	13 5	28000	7 2	132500	146000
44	TRINTELLA 44	KTH	SA/CR	FBG KL IB	72D PERK	13 5	28000	7 2	132500	146000
53	TRINTELLA 53	SLP	SA/CR	FBG KL IB	124D PERK	15 6	36000	7 2	215500	237000
53	TRINTELLA 53	KTH	SA/CR	FBG KL IB	124D PERK	15 6	36000	7 2	221500	243500
			1980 BOATS							
35	TRINTELLA 3	SLP	SA/CR	FBG KL IB	49D	10	15000	4	64000	70400
35	TRINTELLA 3	KTH	SA/CR	FBG KL IB	49D	10	15000	4	65300	71700
37 11	TRINTELLA 38	SLP	SA/CR	FBG KL IB	49D PERK	12 2	22000	6 3	92600	101500
37 11	TRINTELLA 38	KTH	SA/CR	FBG KL IB	49D PERK	12 2	22000	6 3	96100	105500
40	TRINTELLA 41	KTH	SA/CR	FBG KL IB	72D	11 6	20680	7	101000	111000
42 4	TRINTELLA 42	SLP	SA/CR	FBG KL IB	49D PERK	13 2	18000	7 1	93300	102500
44	TRINTELLA 44	SLP	SA/CR	FBG KL IB	72D PERK	13 5	30000	7 2	131000	144000
44	TRINTELLA 44	KTH	SA/CR	FBG KL IB	72D PERK	13 5	30000	7 2	137500	151000
			1977 BOATS							
35 3	TRINTELLA III	SLP	SAIL	FBG KL IB	35D PERK	10 6	15000	4 7	56600	62200
35 3	TRINTELLA III	KTH	SAIL	FBG KL IB	35D PERK	10 6	15000	4 7	57900	63600
40	TRINTELLA IV	KTH	SAIL	FBG KL IB	60D PERK	11 6	21000	4 10	89200	98000
			1975 BOATS							
35 3	TRINTELLA III	SLP	SAIL	FBG KL IB	35D PERK	10 6	15000	4 7	52800	58000
35 3	TRINTELLA III	KTH	SAIL	FBG KL IB	35D PERK	10 6	15000	4 7	53800	59100
40	TRINTELLA IV	KTH	SAIL	FBG KL IB	62D PERK	11 2	21000	4 10	82900	91100
			1973 BOATS							
35 3	TRINTELLA III	SLP	SAIL	FBG KL IB	35D PERK	10 6		4 7	47500	52200
40	TRINTELLA IV	KTH	SAIL	FBG KL IB	62D PERK	11 2		4 10	76100	83600
			1965 BOATS							
53 3		KTH	MS	MHG KL IB	D	14		5 4	153000	168000

TRIPLE C ENT INC
APOLLO BOATS   COAST GUARD MFG ID- TPC

Call 1-800-327-6929 for BUC Personalized Evaluation Service
Or, for 1973 to 1975 boats, sign onto www.BUCValuPro.com

TROJAN EXPRESS YACHTS
CARVER BOAT CORP   See inside cover to adjust price for area
PULASKI WI 54162   COAST GUARD MFG ID- CDR
                         FOR LATER YEARS SEE CARVER BOAT CORPORATION

For more recent years, see the BUC Used Boat Price Guide, Volume 1 or Volume 2

LOA FT IN	NAME AND/ OR MODEL	TOP/ RIG	BOAT TYPE	-HULL- MTL TP	----ENGINE--- TP # HP MFG	BEAM FT IN	WGT LBS	DRAFT FT IN	RETAIL LOW	RETAIL HIGH
			1983 BOATS							
26 4	F-26 261	OP	EXP	FBG SV IB	225 CHRY	10 2	5450	2	10600	12100
26 4	F-26 261	HT	EXP	FBG SV IB	225 CHRY	10 2	5450	2	10600	12100
29 5	902/907 9-METER	OP	SDN	FBG SV IB	T270-T350	11 8		1 1	21500	24300
32	F-32 321	FB	SDN	FBG SV IB	T225-T270	13	13000	2 6	31700	36000
32	F-32 323	FB	SPTCR	FBG SV IB	T225-T250	13	12000	2 6	28800	32500
33	330/335 10-METER	OP	SF	FBG SV IB	T350 CRUS	13	11250	2	32600	36200
33	330/335 10-METER	OP	SF	FBG SV IB	IBT210D-T250D	13	11250	2	36800	42400
33	330/335 10-METER	FB	SDN	FBG SV IB	T350 CRUS	13	11250	2	33500	37200
33	331/336 10-METER	OP	SF	FBG SV IB	T350 CRUS	13	14500	2	43100	47100
33	331/336 10-METER	FB	SDN	FBG SV IB	T350 CRUS	13	14500	2	37100	41300
33	331/336 10-METER	FB	SDN	FBG SV IB	T250D GM	13	14500	2	48000	52700
33	332/337 10-METER	FB	SPTCR	FBG SV IB	T350 CRUS	13	12750	2	33500	37200
33	332/337 10-METER	FB	SPTCR	FBG SV IB	T350 CRUS	13	12750	2	33500	37200
33	333/338 10-METER	MY		FBG SV IB	T330 CRUS	13	15750	2	37900	42100
36	F-36 CONVERTIBLE 460	FB	SDNSF	FBG SV IB	T330 CHRY	13	16000	2 11	44200	49000
36	F-36 CONVERTIBLE 460	HT	SDNSF	FBG SV IB	T330 CRUS	13	16000	2 11	44900	49900
36	F-36 CONVERTIBLE 461	HT	SDNSF	FBG SV IB	T350 CRUS	13	16000	2 11	44900	49900
36	F-36 TRI CABIN 364	FB	TCMY	FBG SV IB	T270 CRUS	13	16500	2 11	44700	48600
36	F-36 TRI CABIN 364	FB	TCMY	FBG SV IB	T270 CRUS	13	16500	2 11	44300	49200
40 3	F-40 400	FB	MY	FBG SV IB	T330 CHRY	14 3	27300	4	77200	84900
44 3	F-44 453/454	HT	MY	FBG SV IB	T350 CRUS	14 11	32000	4	98600	108500

```
LOA   NAME AND/       TOP/ BOAT -HULL- ----ENGINE--- BEAM   WGT  DRAFT RETAIL RETAIL
FT IN OR MODEL        RIG  TYPE MTL TP TP # HP  MFG  FT IN  LBS  FT IN  LOW    HIGH
----------------------- 1983 BOATS -------------------------------------------------
44  3 F-44 454        FB  MY   FBG SV IB T350  CRUS 14 11 32000  4     98700 108500
44  3 F-44 454        FB  MY   FBG SV IB T310D J&T 14 11 32000  4    110000 120500
44  3 F-44 454        FB  MY   FBG SV IB T410D J&T 14 11 32000  4    118500 130000
----------------------- 1982 BOATS -------------------------------------------------
26    C-26 264        OP  CTRCN FBG SV IO 235   OMC  8         2  8  7600   8750
26    CF-26 265 CUD   OP  CTRCN FBG SV IO 235   OMC  8         2  8  8150   9400
26    CF-26 265 CUD   OP  CTRCN FBG SV IB 260   VLVO 8   4500  2  6  8850  10100
26  4 F-26 261        OP  EXP  FBG SV IB 225-228  10 2 5450  2  3 10200  11600
26  4 F-26 261        HT  EXP  FBG SV IB 225-228  10 2 5450  2  3 10200  11600
26  4 F-26 261        FB  EXP  FBG SV IB 225-228  10 2 5450  2  3 10200  11600
32    F-32 321        FB  SDN  FBG SV IB T225-T255 13  13000  2  6 30030  34400
32    F-32 323        FB  SPTCR FBG SV IB T225-T250 13  12000  2  6 27600  31100
32    F 36 363/4      OP  TCMY FBG SV IB T255  MRCR 13 16500 2 11 41900  46500
36    F-36 CONVERTIBLE 460 FB SDN FBG SV IB T330 CHRY 13 16000 2 11 43400 48300
36    F-36 CONVERTIBLE 460 FB SDN FBG SV IB T330 MRCR 13 16000 2 11 43500 48400
36    F-36 CONVERTIBLE 460 FB SDN FBG SV IB T200D CHRY 13 16000 2 11 48300 53100

36    F-36 CONVERTIBLE 461 FB SDNSF FBG SV IB T330 CHRY 13 16000 2 11 42100 46800
      IB T330  MRCR 42200 46900, IB T350  CRUS 42900 47600, IB T200D CHRY 46700 51300
      IB T220D VLVO 46600 51200

36    F-36 TRI CABIN 363   OP  TCMY FBG SV IB T255  MRCR 13 16500 2 11 41900 46500
40  3 F-40 400        FB  MY   FBG SV IB T330  CHRY 14  3 27300  3 10 73700 81000
40  3 F-40 400        FB  MY   FBG SV IB T350  CRUS 14  3 27300  3 10 74900 82300
40  3 F-40 400        FB  MY   FBG SV IB T310D J&T  14  3 27000  3  7 83800 92100
44  3 F-44 454        FB  MY   FBG SV IB T330  CHRY 14 11 32000  4  92700 102000
      IB T350  CRUS 94300 103500, IB T310D J&T 105000 115000, IB T410D J&T 113000 124000
----------------------- 1981 BOATS -------------------------------------------------
26  4 F-26 261        OP  EXP  FBG SV IB 225-228  10 2 5450  2  3  9700  11100
26  4 F-26 261        HT  EXP  FBG SV IB 225-228  10 2 5450  2  3  9700  11100
26  4 F-26 261        FB  EXP  FBG SV IB 225-228  10 2 5450  2  3  9700  11100
28  7 F-29 SPORT SEDAN 292 HT SDNSF FBG SV IB T225-T255 11 5 9700 2 6 18400 20800
28  7 F-29 SPORT SEDAN 292 HT SDNSF FBG SV IB T240D REN 11 5 9700 2 6 27800 30900
28  7 F-29 SPORT SEDAN 292 FB SDNSF FBG SV IB T225-T255 11 5 9700 2 6 18400 20800
28  7 F-29 SPORT SEDAN 292 FB SDNSF FBG SV IB T240D REN 11 5 9700 2 6 27800 30900
28  7 F-29 SPORTSMAN 290  OP SPTCR FBG SV IB T225-T255 11 5 9700 2 6 18400 20900
28  7 F-29 SPORTSMAN 290  OP SPTCR FBG SV IB T240D REN 11 5 9700 2 6 27900 31000
28  7 F-29 SPORTSMAN 290  HT SPTCR FBG SV IB T225-T255 11 5 9700 2 6 18400 20900

28  7 F-29 SPORTSMAN 290  HT SPTCR FBG SV IB T225-T255 11 5  9700 2  6 18400 20900
28  7 F-29 SPORTSMAN 290  HT SPTCR FBG SV IB T240D REN 11 5  9700 2  6 27900 31000
30    F-30 308        FB  SDN  FBG SV IB T155-T255 12 3 10000 2  3 21700 26300
30    F-30 308        FB  SDN  FBG SV IBT140D-T200D 12 3 10000 2  3 29100 35400
32    F-32 321        HT  SDN  FBG SV IB 240D REN 13 12000 2 6 34400 38200
32    F-32 321        HT  SDN  FBG SV IB T225-T255 13 12000 2 6 32600 32600
32    F-32 321        HT  SDN  FBG SV IB T200D CHRY 13 12000 2 6 37800 42000
32    F-32 321        FB  SDN  FBG SV IB T225-T255 13 12000 2 6 28600 32600
32    F-32 321        FB  SDN  FBG SV IB T200D CHRY 13 12000 2 6 37800 42000
32    F-32 323        HT  SPTCR FBG SV IB T225-T255 13 12000 2 6 26400 29900
32    F-32 323        HT  SPTCR FBG SV IB T200D CHRY 13 12000 2 6 33400 37100

32    F-32 323        FB  SPTCR FBG SV IB T225-T255 13 12000 2 6 26400 29900
32    F-32 323        FB  SPTCR FBG SV IB T200D CHRY 13 12000 2 6 33400 37100
36    F-36 363        OP  TCMY FBG SV IB T250  CHRY 13 16500 2 11 39800 44200
36    F-36 363        OP  TCMY FBG SV IB T255  MRCR 13 16500 2 11 39900 44300
36    F-36 363        OP  TCMY FBG SV IB T200D CHRY 13 16500 2 11 44800 49800
36    F-36 CONVERTIBLE 460 FB SDN FBG SV IB T255 MRCR 13 16000 2 11 40300 44800
      IB T330  CHRY 41400 46000, IB T330  MRCR 41500 46100, IB T350  CRUS 42100 46800
      IB T200D CHRY 46300 50800, IB T220D VLVO 46300 50900

36    F-36 CONVERTIBLE 460 FB SDN FBG SV IB T255 MRCR 13 16000 2 11 40300 44800
      IB T330  CHRY 41400 46000, IB T330  MRCR 41500 46100, IB T350  CRUS 42100 46800
      IB T200D CHRY 46300 50800, IB T220D VLVO 46300 50900

36    F-36 CONVERTIBLE 460 FB SDNSF FBG SV IB T255 MRCR 13 16000 2 11 39200 43600
      IB T330  CHRY 40100 44600, IB T330  MRCR 40200 44700, IB T200D CHRY 44000 48900

36    F-36 CONVERTIBLE 461 HT SDNSF FBG SV IB T255 MRCR 13 16000 2 11 39200 43600
      IB T330  CHRY 40100 44600, IB T330  MRCR 40200 44700, IB T200D CHRY 40800 45400
      IB T200D CHRY 44000 48900, IB T220D VLVO 43900 48800

36    F-36 CONVERTIBLE 461 FB SDNSF FBG SV IB T350 CRUS 13 16000 2 11 40800 45400
36    F-36 CONVERTIBLE 461 FB SDNSF FBG SV IB T220D VLVO 13 16000 2 11 43900 48800
36    F-36 TRI CABIN 364 FB TCMY FBG SV IB T250 CHRY 13 16500 2 11 39800 44200
40    F-36 TRI CABIN 364 FB TCMY FBG SV IB T255 MRCR 13 16500 2 11 39900 44300
40  3 F-40 400        FB  MY   FBG SV IB T330  CHRY 14 3 27000 3 7 69600 76400
      IB T350  CRUS 70700 77700, IB T210D J&T 75800 83300, IB T286D CUM 76800 84400
      IB T310D J&T 79800 87700

44  3 F-44 453/454    HT  MY   FBG SV IB T330  CHRY 14 11 32000 4 88300 97000
      IB T350  CRUS 89800 98600, IB T310D J&T 99800 109500, IB T320D CUM 99800 109500

44  3 F-44 454        FB  MY   FBG SV IB T330  CHRY 14 11 32000 4 88400 97200
      IB T350  CRUS 89900 98800, IB T310D J&T 100000 110000, IB T320D CUM 100000 110000

46  9 F-47 470        FB  MY   FBG SV IB T410D J&T 14 3 30000 3 9 116000 127500
----------------------- 1980 BOATS -------------------------------------------------
25    F-25 253        OP  EXP  FBG SV IB 225-228  9 4 4800 2 2 7850 9050
25    F-25 253        HT  EXP  FBG SV IB 225-228  9 4 4800 2 2 7850 9050
26  4 F-26 261        OP  EXP  FBG SV IB 225-228  10 2 5450 2 3 9350 10700
26  4 F-26 261        HT  EXP  FBG SV IB 225-228  10 2 5450 2 3 9350 10700
26  4 F-26 261        FB  EXP  FBG SV IB 225-228  10 2 5450 2 3 9350 10700
26  4 F-26 262        OP  EXP  FBG SV IO T140  VLVO 10 2 5450 2 3 8950 10200
26  4 F-26 262        HT  EXP  FBG SV IO T140  VLVO 10 2 5450 2 3 10200 10200
26  4 F-26 262        FB  EXP  FBG SV IO T140  VLVO 10 2 5450 2 3 8950 10200
28  7 F-29 SPORTSMAN 290  OP SPTCR FBG SV IB T225 CHRY 11 7 10000 2 6 17500 19900
28  7 F-29 SPORTSMAN 290  OP SPTCR FBG SV IB T210D REN 11 7 10000 2 6 26500 29400
28  7 F-29 SPORTSMAN 290  FB SPTCR FBG SV IB T225 CHRY 11 7 10000 2 6 18200 20200
28  7 F-29 SPORTSMAN 290  FB SPTCR FBG SV IB T250 CHRY 11 7 10000 2 6 18200 20200

30    F-30 308        FB  SDN  FBG SV IB T225-T255 12 3 10000 2 3 22100 25200
30    F-30 308        HT  SDN  FBG SV IBT145D-T210D 12 3 10000 2 3 28400 34500
32    F-32 320        HT  EXP  FBG SV IB T225-T250 13 12000 2 6 25300 28500
32    F-32 320        FB  EXP  FBG SV IB T225-T250 13 12000 2 6 25300 28500
32    F-32 321        FB  SDN  FBG SV IB T225-T255 13 12000 2 6 27400 31200
32    F-32 321        HT  SDN  FBG SV IBT145D-T210D 13 12000 2 6 34100 40900
32    F-32 323        HT  SPTCR FBG SV IB T225-T255 13 12000 2 6 24300 28500
32    F-32 323        FB  SDN  FBG SV IB T225-T255 13 12000 2 6 32000 35600
32    F-32 323        FB  SDN  FBG SV IB T255 MRCR 13 12000 2 6 25800 28600
32    F-32 323        FB  SPTCR FBG SV IB T225-T255 13 12000 2 6 24300 36000
36    F-36 363        OP  TCMY FBG SV IBT145D-T210D 13 16500 2 11 37900 42100
      IB T255  MRCR 38000 42300, IB T200D CHRY 42700 47500, IB T210D REN 43000 47800

36    F-36 CONVERTIBLE 460 FB SDN FBG SV IB T255 MRCR 13 16000 2 11 38400 42700
      IB T330  CHRY 39600 43900, IB T330  MRCR 39600 44000, IB T350  CRUS 40200 44700
      IB T195D CUM 43400 48200, IB T200D CHRY 43700 48500, IB T210D REN 44000 48800
      IB T220D VLVO 43700 48500

36    F-36 CONVERTIBLE 461 FB SDNSF FBG SV IB T255 MRCR 13 16000 2 11 37400 41600
      IB T330  CHRY 38400 42700, IB T330  MRCR 38400 42700, IB T350  CRUS 40000 44700
      IB T195D CUM 41700 46300, IB T200D CHRY 42000 46600, IB T210D REN 42200 46900
      IB T220D VLVO 41900 46500

40  3 F-40 400        FB  MY   FBG SV IB T330  CHRY 14 3 27000 3 7 66400 72900
      IB T350  CRUS 67400 74100, IB T210D J&T 72300 79400, IB T310D J&T 76200 83700

44  3 F-44 453        FB  MY   FBG SV IB T330  CHRY 14 11 32000 4 84300 92700
      IB T350  CRUS 85800 94200, IB T310D J&T 95400 105000, IB T320D CUM 95400 105000
----------------------- 1979 BOATS -------------------------------------------------
25    F-25 253        OP  EXP  FBG SV IB 225-228  9 4 4800 2 2 7550 8700
25    F-25 253        HT  EXP  FBG SV IB 225-228  9 4 4800 2 2 7550 8700
26  4 F-26 261        OP  EXP  FBG SV IB 225-228  10 2 5450 2 3 9000 10300
26  4 F-26 261        HT  EXP  FBG SV IB 225-228  10 2 5450 2 3 9000 10300
26  4 F-26 261        FB  EXP  FBG SV IB 225-228  10 2 5450 2 3 9000 10300
26  4 F-26 262        OP  EXP  FBG SV IO T140  VLVO 10 2 5450 2 3 8950 10200
26  4 F-26 262        HT  EXP  FBG SV IO T140  VLVO 10 2 5450 2 3 8950 10200
28  2 F-28 280        HT  SDN  FBG SV IB T225-T228 12 3 7700 2 3 16300 18600
28  2 F-28 280        FB  SDN  FBG SV IB T225-T228 12 3 7700 2 3 16300 18600
28  2 F-28 281        HT  SDN  FBG SV IB 330  CHRY 12 3 6800 2 3 18700 20800

28  2 F-28 281        FB  SDN  FBG SV IB 330  CHRY 12 3 6800 2 3 14500 16500
28  2 F-28 281        FB  SDN  FBG SV IB 200D CHRY 12 3 6800 2 3 18700 20800
30    F-30 306        OP  EXP  FBG SV IB T225-T228 11 9100 2 3 18700 20900
30    F-30 306        HT  EXP  FBG SV IB T225-T228 11 9100 2 3 18700 20900
30    F-30 306        FB  EXP  FBG SV IB T225-T228 11 9100 2 3 18700 20900
30    F-30 307        OP  EXP  FBG SV IB 255-330  11 8100 2 1 16200 19100
30    F-30 307        HT  EXP  FBG SV IB 255-330  11 8100 2 1 16200 19100
30    F-30 307        HT  EXP  FBG SV IB 200D CHRY 11 8100 2 1 20100 22400
30    F-30 307        FB  EXP  FBG SV IB 255-330  11 8100 2 1 16200 19100
30    F-30 307        FB  EXP  FBG SV IB 200D CHRY 11 8100 2 1 20100 22400
```

```
LOA   NAME AND/         TOP/ BOAT -HULL- ----ENGINE--- BEAM  WGT  DRAFT RETAIL RETAIL
FT IN OR MODEL          RIG  TYPE MTL TP TP # HP  MFG  FT IN LBS  FT IN  LOW    HIGH
-------------------- 1979 BOATS -------------------------------------------------
30  2 F-30 304           FB  SPTCR FBG SV IB T225-T228 11 1  9100  2  2  16800  19200
30  2 F-30 305           FB  SPTCR FBG SV IB 255-330   11 1  8100  2  2  14900  17500
30  2 F-30 305           FB  SPTCR FBG SV IB 200D CHRY 11 1  8100  2  2  18600  20700
32    F-32 320           OP  EXP   FBG SV IB T225-T250 13   12000  2  6  24200  27300
32    F-32 320           HT  EXP   FBG SV IB T225-T250 13   12000  2  6  24200  27300
32    F-32 320           FB  EXP   FBG SV IB T225-T250 13   12000  2  6  24200  27300
32    F-32 321           HT  SDN   FBG SV IB T225-T250 13   12000  2  6  26300  29800
32    F-32 321           HT  SDN   FBG SV IB T200D CHRY 13  12000  2  6  35000  38900
32    F-32 321           FB  SDN   FBG SV IB T225-T250 13   12000  2  6  26300  29800
32    F-32 321           FB  SDN   FBG SV IB T200D CHRY 13  12000  2  6  35000  38900
32    F-32 323           FB  SDNSF FBG SV IB T225-T250 13   12000  2  6  24200  27300
32    F-32 323           FB  SDNSF FBG SV IB T200D CHRY 13  12000  2  6  30800  34300

36    F-36 363           OP  TCMY  FBG SV IB T250  CHRY 13  16500  2 11  36200  40300
36    F-36 363           OP  TCMY  FBG SV IB T255  MRCR 13  16500  2 11  36300  40400
36    F-36 363           OP  TCMY  FBG SV IB T200D CHRY 13  16500  2 11  40800  45400
36    F-36 CONVERTIBLE 460 HT  SDN FBG SV IB T255  MRCR 13  16000  2 11  36700  40800
      IB T330  CHRY 37700 41900, IB T330  MRCR 37800 42000, IB T195D CUM  41400  46000
      IB T200D CHRY 41700 46300

36    F-36 CONVERTIBLE 460 FB  SDN FBG SV IB T255  MRCR 13  16000  2 11  36700  40800
      IB T330  CHRY 37700 41900, IB T330  MRCR 37800 42000, IB T195D CUM  41400  46000
      IB T200D CHRY 41700 46300

36    F-36 CONVERTIBLE 461 FB  SDNSF FBG SV IB T255 MRCR 13  16000  2 11  35800  39700
      IB T330  CHRY 36600 40600, IB T330  MRCR 36700 40700, IB T195D CUM  39800  44300
      IB T200D CHRY 40100 44500

40  3 F-40 400           FB  MY    FBG SV IB T330  CHRY 14  3 27000  3  7  63400  69700
      IB T330  MRCR 63600 69800, IB T130D VLVO 66300 72800, IB T192D VLVO 67200 73900
      IB T210D J+T 68800 75600, IB T310D J+T 72400 79500

44  3 F-44 453 454       HT  MY    FBG SV IB T330  CHRY 14 11 32000  4     80200  88100
      IB T330  MRCR 80300 88300, IB T310D GM  90200 99100, IB T320D CUM  90400  99400

44  3 F-44 453 454       FB  MY    FBG SV IB T330  CHRY 14 11 32000  4     80000  87900
      IB T330  MRCR 80200 88100, IB T310D GM  90000 98900, IB T320D CUM  90200  99200
-------------------- 1978 BOATS -------------------------------------------------
25    F-25 253           OP  EXP   FBG SV IB 225-228   9  4  4800  2  2   7200   8350
25    F-25 253           HT  EXP   FBG SV IB 225-228   9  4  4800  2  2   7200   8350
26  4 F-26 261           OP  EXP   FBG SV IB 225-228  10  2  5450  2  3   8500   9850
26  4 F-26 261           HT  EXP   FBG SV IB 225-228  10  2  5450  2  3   8500   9850
26  4 F-26 261           FB  EXP   FBG SV IB 225-228  10  2  5450  2  3   8500   9850
26  4 F-26 262           OP  EXP   FBG SV IO T140  VLVO 10  2 5450  2  3   9050  10300
26  4 F-26 262           HT  EXP   FBG SV IO T140  VLVO 10  2 5450  2  3   9050  10300
26  4 F-26 262           FB  EXP   FBG SV IO T140  VLVO 10  2 5450  2  3   9050  10300
28  2 F-28 280           HT  SDN   FBG SV IB T225-T228 12  3 7700  2  3  15600  17800
28  2 F-28 280           FB  SDN   FBG SV IB T225-T228 12  3 7700  2  3  15600  17800
28  2 F-28 281           HT  SDN   FBG SV IB 330   CHRY 12  3 7700  2  3  14600  16600
28  2 F-28 281           HT  SDN   FBG SV IB 200D CHRY 12  3 7700  2  3  19200  21400

28  2 F-28 281           FB  SDN   FBG SV IB 330   CHRY 12  3 7700  2  3  14600  16600
28  2 F-28 281           FB  SDN   FBG SV IB 200D CHRY 12  3 7700  2  3  19200  21400
30    F-30 306           OP  EXP   FBG SV IB T225-T228 11   8100  2  1  17000  19400
30    F-30 306           HT  EXP   FBG SV IB T225-T228 11   8100  2  1  17000  19400
30    F-30 306           FB  EXP   FBG SV IB T225-T228 11   8100  2  1  17000  19400
30    F-30 307           OP  EXP   FBG SV IB 255-330   11   8100  2  1  15500  18300
30    F-30 307           OP  EXP   FBG SV IB 200D CHRY 11   8100  2  1  19400  21500
30    F-30 307           HT  EXP   FBG SV IB 255-330   11   8100  2  1  15500  18300
30    F-30 307           HT  EXP   FBG SV IB 200D CHRY 11   8100  2  1  19400  21500
30    F-30 307           FB  EXP   FBG SV IB 255-330   11   8100  2  1  15500  18300
30    F-30 307           FB  EXP   FBG SV IB 200D CHRY 11   8100  2  1  19400  21500
30  2 F-30 304           FB  SPTCR FBG SV IB T225-T228 11 1 8100  2  2  15600  17800

30  2 F-30 305           FB  SPTCR FBG SV IB 255-330   11 1 8100  2  2  14200  16800
30  2 F-30 305           FB  SPTCR FBG SV IB 200D CHRY 11 1 8100  2  2  17500  19900
32    F-32 320           OP  EXP   FBG SV IB T225-T250 13   12000  2  6  26200  26200
32    F-32 320           HT  EXP   FBG SV IB T200D CHRY 13  12000  2  6  29700  33000
32    F-32 320           FB  EXP   FBG SV IB T225-T250 13   12000  2  6  23200  26200
32    F-32 320           FB  EXP   FBG SV IB T200D CHRY 13  12000  2  6  29700  33000
32    F-32 321           HT  SDN   FBG SV IB T225-T250 13   12000  2  6  25200  28600
32    F-32 321           HT  SDN   FBG SV IB T200D CHRY 13  12000  2  6  33700  37500
32    F-32 321           FB  SDN   FBG SV IB T225-T250 13   12000  2  6  25200  28600
32    F-32 321           FB  SDN   FBG SV IB T200D CHRY 13  12000  2  6  33700  37500
36    F-36 360           FB  TCMY  FBG SV IB T250  CHRY 13  15500  2 11  33500  37300
36    F-36 360           FB  TCMY  FBG SV IB T255  MRCR 13  15500  2 11  33700  37500

36    F-36 363           OP  TCMY  FBG SV IB T250  CHRY 13  15500  2  6  33500  37300
36    F-36 363           OP  TCMY  FBG SV IB T255  MRCR 13  15500  2  6  33600  37400
36    F-36 363           OP  TCMY  FBG SV IB T200D CHRY 13  15500  2  6  37600  41800
36    F-36 CONVERTIBLE 460 HT  SDN FBG SV IB T250  CHRY 13  16000  2 11  35000  38900
      IB T255  MRCR 35100 39000, IB T330  CHRY 36100 40100, IB T195D CUM  39600  44000
      IB T200D CHRY 39900 44300

36    F-36 CONVERTIBLE 460 FB  SDN FBG SV IB T250  CHRY 13  16000  2 11  35000  38900
      IB T255  MRCR 35100 39000, IB T330  CHRY 36100 40100, IB T195D CUM  39600  44000
      IB T200D CHRY 39900 44300

36    F-36 CONVERTIBLE 461 FB  SDNSF FBG SV IB T250 CHRY 13  16000  2 11  34100  37900
      IB T255  MRCR 34200 38000, IB T330  CHRY 35000 38900, IB T195D CUM  38100  42300
      IB T200D CHRY 38300 42600

44  3 F-44 454           HT  MY    FBG SV IB T330  CHRY 14 11 32000  4     77400  85000
      IB T330  MRCR 77500 85200, IB T310D GM  87200 95800, IB T320D CUM  87500  96200

44  3 F-44 454           FB  MY    FBG SV IB T330  CHRY 14 11 32000  4     77200  84800
      IB T330  MRCR 77300 85000, IB T310D GM  87000 95600, IB T320D CUM  87300  95900

44  3 F-44 CONVERTIBLE 448 FB  SDN FBG SV IB T330  CHRY 14 11 33750  3  9  77200  84800
      IB T330  MRCR 77300 85000, IB T310D GM  85700 94200, IB T320D CUM  85800  94300
      IB T400D CUM 89400 98300
-------------------- 1977 BOATS -------------------------------------------------
25    F-25               OP  EXP   FBG SV IB 225-233   9  4  4800  2  2   6950   8000
25    F-25               HT  EXP   FBG SV IB 225-233   9  4  4800  2  2   6950   8000
26  4 F-26               OP  EXP   FBG SV IB 225-233  10  2  5450  2  3   8150   9450
26  4 F-26               HT  EXP   FBG SV IB 225-233  10  2  5450  2  3   8150   9450
28  2 F-28               HT  SDN   FBG SV IB 280   CHRY 12  3 7700  2  3  13600  15400
28  2 F-28               HT  SDN   FBG SV IB T225-T233 12  3 7700  2  3  13000  15200
28  2 F-28               FB  SDN   FBG SV IB 280   CHRY 12  3 7700  2  3  13600  15400
28  2 F-28               FB  SDN   FBG SV IB T225-T233 12  3 7700  2  3  15000  17200
30    F-30               HT  EXP   FBG SV IB 255-280   11   8100  2  1  14900  17100
30    F-30               HT  EXP   FBG SV IB 200D CHRY 11   8100  2  1  18900  21000
30    F-30               FB  EXP   FBG SV IB T225-T233 11   8100  2  1  16400  18700

30    F-30               FB  EXP   FBG SV IB 255-280   11   8100  2  1  14900  17100
30    F-30               FB  EXP   FBG SV IB 200D CHRY 11   8100  2  1  18900  21000
30    F-30               FB  EXP   FBG SV IB T225-T233 11   8100  2  1  16400  18700
30  2 F-30               FB  SPTCR FBG SV IB 255-280   11   8100  2  1  13700  15700
30  2 F-30               FB  SPTCR FBG SV IB 200D CHRY 11   8100  2  1  16900  19200
32    F-32               HT  EXP   FBG SV IB T225-T250 13   12000  2  6  22300  25200
32    F-32               HT  EXP   FBG SV IB T200D CHRY 13  12000  2  6  27500  27200
32    F-32               FB  EXP   FBG SV IB T225-T250 13   12000  2  6  22300  25200
32    F-32               FB  EXP   FBG SV IB T200D CHRY 13  12000  2  6  27500  30700
32    F-32               HT  SDN   FBG SV IB T225-T250 13   12000  2  6  32500  36100
32    F-32               HT  SDN   FBG SV IB T200D CHRY 13  12000  2  6  24200  27200
32    F-32               FB  SDN   FBG SV IB T200D CHRY 13  12000  2  6  32500  36100

36    F-36 360           FB  TCMY  FBG SV IB T255  MRCR 13  15500  2 11  32200  35800
36    F-36 360           FB  TCMY  FBG SV IB T280  CHRY 13  15500  2 11  32400  36000
36    F-36 361           FB  TCMY  FBG SV IB T280  CHRY 13  15500  2 11  32400  36000
36    F-36 361           OP  TCMY  FBG SV IB T280  CHRY 13  15500  2 11  32400  36000
36    F-36 CONVERTIBLE    FB  SDN  FBG SV IB T255  MRCR 13  16000  2 11  33600  37400
      IB T280  CHRY 33900 37600, IB T330  CHRY 34500 38400, IB T210D CUM  38300  42600

36    F-36 CONVERTIBLE    FB  SDN  FBG SV IB T255  MRCR 13  16000  2 11  33600  37400
      IB T280  CHRY 33900 37600, IB T330  CHRY 34500 38400, IB T210D CUM  38300  42600

44  3 F-44               HT  MY    FBG SV IB T330  CHRY 14 11 32000  3  6  73200  80500
      IB T330  MRCR 73400 80700, IB T310D GM  82400 90500, IB T320D CUM  82500  90700

44  3 F-44               FB  MY    FBG SV IB T330  CHRY 14 11 32000  3  6  73100  80300
      IB T330  MRCR 73300 80500, IB T310D GM  82200 90300, IB T320D CUM  82400  90500

44  3 F-44 CONVERTIBLE    FB  SDN  FBG SV IB T310D GM  14 11 33750  3  9  83000  91400
44  3 F-44 CONVERTIBLE    FB  SDN  FBG SV IB T320D CUM 14 11 33750  3  9  83200  91600
44  3 F-44 CONVERTIBLE    FB  SDN  FBG SV IB T400D CUM 14 11 33750  3  9  86700  95500
47 11 MERIDIAN 48        HT  -TRWL FBG DS IB T185D PERK 14   38000  3  4  98700 108500
47 11 MERIDIAN 48        HT  TRWL  FBG DS IB T185D PERK 14   38000  3  4  98700 108500
47 11 MERIDIAN 48        FB  TRWL  FBG DS IB T185D PERK 14   38000  3  4  98100 108400
47 11 MERIDIAN 48        FB  TRWL  FBG DS IB T185D PERK 14   38000  3  4  98100 108000
54  6 DECKHOUSE SALON    HT  MYDKH FBG SV IB T330  CHRY 16  7 50000  4    118500 130000
      IB T320D CUM 123000 135000, IB T400D CUM 131500 144500, IB T450D CUM 137000 150500

54  6 DECKHOUSE SALON    FB  MYDKH FBG SV IB T330  CHRY 16  7 50000  4    118500 130000
```

TROJAN EXPRESS YACHTS -CONTINUED See inside cover to adjust price for area

LOA FT	LOA IN	NAME AND/ OR MODEL	TOP/ RIG	BOAT TYPE	-HULL- MTL	-HULL- TP	ENGINE TP	ENGINE # HP	ENGINE MFG	BEAM FT	BEAM IN	WGT LBS	DRAFT FT	DRAFT IN	RETAIL LOW	RETAIL HIGH
		1977 BOATS														
54	6	DECKHOUSE SALON	FB	MYDKH	FBG	SV	IB	T320D	CUM	16	7	50000	4		123000	135000
54	6	DECKHOUSE SALON	FB	MYDKH	FBG	SV	IB	T400D	CUM	16	7	50000	4		131000	144000
54	6	DECKHOUSE SALON	FB	MYDKH	FBG	SV	IB	T450D	CUM	16	7	50000	4		136500	150000
		1976 BOATS														
24		F-24	OP	SPTCR	FBG	SV	IO	188	MRCR	8		4000	2		5850	6700
24		F-24	OP	SPTCR	FBG	SV	IB	225	CHRY	8		4000	2		5350	6150
24		F-24	OP	SPTCR	FBG	SV	IO	233	MRCR	8		4000	2		5950	6850
25		F-25	OP	EXP	FBG	SV	IB	225-233		9	4	4800	2	2	6650	7700
25		F-25	HT	EXP	FBG	SV	IB	225-233		9	4	4800	2	2	6650	7700
26	4	F-26	OP	EXP	FBG	SV	IB	225-233		10	2	5450	2	3	7850	9100
26	4	F-26	HT	EXP	FBG	SV	IB	225-233		10	2	5450	2	3	7850	9100
28	2	F-28	HT	SDN	FBG	SV	IB	280	CHRY	12	3	7700	2		13000	14800
28	2	F-28	HT	SDN	FBG	SV	IB	T225-T233		12	3	7700	2		14400	16500
28	2	F-28	FB	SDN	FBG	SV	IB	280	CHRY	12	3	7700	2		13000	14800
28	2	F-28	FB	SDN	FBG	SV	IB	T225-T233		12	3	7700	2		14400	16500
30		F-30	HT	EXP	FBG	SV	IB	280	CHRY	11		8100	2	1	14500	16400
30		F-30	HT	EXP	FBG	SV	IB	200D	CHRY	11		8100	2	1	18200	20200
30		F-30	HT	EXP	FBG	SV	IB	T225-T233		11		8100	2	1	15700	18000
30		F-30	FB	EXP	FBG	SV	IB	280	CHRY	11		8100	2	1	14500	16400
30		F-30	FB	EXP	FBG	SV	IB	200D	CHRY	11		8100	2	1	18200	20200
30		F-30	FB	EXP	FBG	SV	IB	T225-T233		11		8100	2	1	15700	18000
30	2	F-30	FB	SPTCR	FBG	SV	IB	280	CHRY	11	1	8100	2	2	13300	15100
30	2	F-30	FB	SPTCR	FBG	SV	IB	200D	CHRY	11	1	8100	2	2	16300	18500
30	2	F-30	FB	SPTCR	FBG	SV	IB	T225-T233		11	1	8100	2	2	14400	16500
32		F-32	HT	EXP	FBG	SV	IB	T225-T250		13		12000	2	6	21400	24200
32		F-32	FB	EXP	FBG	SV	IB	T225-T250		13		12000	2	6	21400	24200
32		F-32	HT	SDN	FBG	SV	IB	T225-T250		13		12000	2	6	23300	26300
32		F-32	HT	SDN	FBG	SV	IB	T200D	CHRY	13		12000	2	6	31300	34800
32		F-32	FB	SDN	FBG	SV	IB	T225-T250		13		12000	2	6	23300	26300
32		F-32	FB	SDN	FBG	SV	IB	T200D	CHRY	13		12000	2	6	31300	34800
32		F-32	HT	SPTCR	FBG	SV	IB	T225-T250		13		12000	2	6	21400	24200
32		F-32	HT	SPTCR	FBG	SV	IB	T200D	CHRY	13		12000	2	6	27600	30700
32		F-32	FB	SPTCR	FBG	SV	IB	T225-T250		13		12000	2	6	21400	24200
32		F-32	FB	SPTCR	FBG	SV	IB	T200D	CHRY	13		12000	2	6	27600	30700
36		F-36 360	FB	TCMY	FBG	SV	VD	T255	MRCR	13		15500	2	6	30900	34300
36		F-36 360	FB	TCMY	FBG	SV	VD	T280	CHRY	13		15500	2	6	31100	34500
36		F-36 440	OP	TCMY	FBG	SV	VD	T255	MRCR	13		15500	2	6	30900	34300
36		F-36 440	OP	TCMY	FBG	SV	VD	T280	CHRY	13		15500	2	6	31100	34500
36		F-36 CONVERTIBLE	HT	SDN	FBG	SV	IB	T255	MRCR	13		16000	2	11	32300	35800
		IB T280 CHRY 32500 36100, IB T330 CHRY 33100 36800, IB T210D CUM													36800	40800
36		F-36 CONVERTIBLE	FB	SDN	FBG	SV	IB	T255	MRCR	13		16000	2	11	32300	35800
		IB T280 CHRY 32500 36100, IB T330 CHRY 33100 36800, IB T210D CUM													36800	40800
44	3	F-44	HT	MY	FBG	SV	IB	T330	CHRY	14	11	32000	3	6	70200	77200
		IB T350 MRCR 70900 77900, IB T310D GM 79000 86800, IB T320D CUM													79100	86900
44	3	F-44	FB	MY	FBG	SV	IB	T330	CHRY	14	11	32000	3	6	70100	77000
		IB T350 MRCR 70700 77700, IB T310D GM 78800 86600, IB T320D CUM													79000	86800
44	3	F-44 CONVERTIBLE	FB	SDN	FBG	SV	IB	T350	MRCR	14	11	33750	3	9	72600	79800
		IB T310D GM 79600 87500, IB T320D CUM 79800 87700, IB T400D CUM													83100	91300
54	6	F-54 DECKHOUSE	HT	MYDKH	FBG	SV	IB	T330	CHRY	16	7	50000	4		113500	125000
		IB T320D CUM 118000 129500, IB T400D CUM 126000 138500, IB T450D CUM													131000	144000
54	6	F-54 DECKHOUSE	FB	MYDKH	FBG	SV	IB	T330	CHRY	16	7	50000	4		113500	124500
		IB T320D CUM 117500 129500, IB T400D CUM 125500 138000, IB T450D CUM													131000	143500
		1975 BOATS														
24		F-24	OP	SF	FBG	SV	IO	188	MRCR	8		4000	2		6900	7900
25		SEA-RAIDER	OP	EXP	FBG	SV	IB	225-233		9	4	4600	2	1	6200	7200
25		SEA-RAIDER	HT	EXP	FBG	SV	IB	225-233		9	4	4600	2	1	6200	7200
26	4	F-26	OP	EXP	FBG	SV	IB	225-233		10	2	5450	2	3	7550	8750
26	4	F-26	HT	EXP	FBG	SV	IB	225-233		10	2	5450	2	3	7550	8750
26	4	F-26 FISHING CKPIT	OP	EXP	FBG	SV	IB	225-233		10	2	5450	2	3	7550	8750
26	4	F-26 FISHING CKPIT	HT	EXP	FBG	SV	IB	225-233		10	2	5450	2	3	7550	8750
30		F-30	HT	EXP	FBG	SV	IB	280	CHRY	11		8100			13900	15800
30		F-30	HT	EXP	FBG	SV	IB	T225-T233		11		8100			15100	17300
30		F-30	FB	EXP	FBG	SV	IB	280	CHRY	11		8100			13900	15800
30		F-30	FB	EXP	FBG	SV	IB	T225-T233		11		8100			15100	17300
30	2	F-30	FB	SF	FBG	SV	IB	280	CHRY	11	1	8100	2	2	12100	13700
30	2	F-30	FB	SF	FBG	SV	IB	T225-T233		11	1	8100	2	2	13100	14900
32		F-32	HT	EXP	FBG	SV	IB	T225-T250		13		12000	2	6	20600	23200
32		F-32	FB	EXP	FBG	SV	IB	T225-T250		13		12000	2	6	20600	23200
32		F-32	HT	SDN	FBG	SV	IB	T225-T250		13		12000	2	6	22300	25300
32		F-32	HT	SDN	FBG	SV	IB	T210D	CAT	13		12000	2	6	30700	34100
32		F-32	FB	SDN	FBG	SV	IB	T225-T250		13		12000	2	6	22300	25300
32		F-32	FB	SDN	FBG	SV	IB	T210D	CAT	13		12000	2	6	30700	34100
32		F-32	HT	SF	FBG	SV	IB	T225-T233		13		12000	2	6	20600	23000
32		F-32	HT	SF	FBG	SV	IB	T210D	CAT	13		12000	2	6	27000	30000
32		F-32	FB	SF	FBG	SV	IB	T225-T233		13		12000	2	6	20600	23000
32		F-32	FB	SF	FBG	SV	IB	T210D	CAT	13		12000	2	6	27000	30000
36		F-36	HT	SDN	FBG	SV	IB	T255	MRCR	13		16000	2	11	31000	34400
		IB T280 CHRY 31200 34700, IB T330 CHRY 31800 35300, IB T210D CUM													35300	39200
36		F-36	FB	SDN	FBG	SV	IB	T255	MRCR	13		16000	2	11	31000	34400
		IB T280 CHRY 31200 34700, IB T330 CHRY 31800 35300, IB T210D CUM													35300	39200
36		F-36	HT	SF	FBG	SV	IB	T255	MRCR	13		16000	2	11	30200	33500
		IB T280 CHRY 30300 33700, IB T330 CHRY 30900 34300, IB T210D CUM													33900	37700
36		F-36	FB	SF	FBG	SV	IB	T255	MRCR	13		16000	2	11	30200	33500
		IB T280 CHRY 30300 33700, IB T330 CHRY 30900 34300, IB T210D CUM													33900	37700
36		F-36	HT	SPTCR	FBG	SV	IB	T255	MRCR	13		16000	2	11	30200	33500
		IB T280 CHRY 30300 33700, IB T330 CHRY 30900 34300, IB T210D CUM													33900	37700
36		F-36	FB	SPTCR	FBG	SV	IB	T255	MRCR	13		16000	2	11	30200	33500
		IB T280 CHRY 30300 33700, IB T330 CHRY 30900 34300, IB T210D CUM													34000	37700
36		F-36	HT	TCMY	FBG	SV	VD	T255	MRCR	13		15500	2	11	29700	33000
36		F-36	HT	TCMY	FBG	SV	VD	T280	CHRY	13		15500	2	11	29800	33200
44	3	F-44	FB	SF	FBG	SV	IB	T350	MRCR	14	11	33750	3	9	69200	76000
		IB T310D GM 76900 84500, IB T320D CUM 77100 84700, IB T400D CUM													81400	89400
44	3	F-44	HT	TCMY	FBG	SV	IB	T330	CHRY	14	11	32000	3	6	69500	76400
		IB T350 MRCR 70600 77500, IB T310D GM 78600 86400, IB T320D CUM													79000	86800
44	3	F-44	FB	TCMY	FBG	SV	IB	T330	CHRY	14	11	32000	3	6	69300	76200
		IB T350 MRCR 70300 77300, IB T310D GM 78300 86100, IB T320D CUM													78700	86500
53	8	DECKHOUSE	HT	TCMY	F/W	SV	IB	T330	CHRY	16	3	47000	4		111000	122000
53	8	DECKHOUSE	HT	TCMY	MHG	SV	IB	T330	CHRY	16	3	47000	4		105500	116000
53	8	DECKHOUSE	HT	TCMY	F/W	SV	IB	T310D	GM	16	3	47000	4		112500	123500
53	8	DECKHOUSE	HT	TCMY	MHG	SV	IB	T310D	GM	16	3	47000	4		107000	117500
53	8	DECKHOUSE	HT	TCMY	F/W	SV	IB	T320D	CUM	16	3	47000	4		115000	126000
53	8	DECKHOUSE	HT	TCMY	MHG	SV	IB	T320D	CUM	16	3	47000	4		109000	120000
53	8	DECKHOUSE	HT	TCMY	F/W	SV	IB	T350D	GM	16	3	47000	4		116500	128000
53	8	DECKHOUSE	HT	TCMY	MHG	SV	IB	T350D	GM	16	3	47000	4		111000	122000
53	8	DECKHOUSE	HT	TCMY	F/W	SV	IB	T370D	CUM	16	3	47000	4		119500	131500
53	8	DECKHOUSE	HT	TCMY	MHG	SV	IB	T370D	CUM	16	3	47000	4		114000	125500
53	8	DECKHOUSE	HT	TCMY	F/W	SV	IB	T415D	GM	16	3	47000	4		123000	135000
53	8	DECKHOUSE	HT	TCMY	MHG	SV	IB	T415D	GM	16	3	47000	4		118500	130000
53	8	DECKHOUSE	FB	TCMY	F/W	SV	IB	T330	CHRY	16	3	47000	4		110500	121500
53	8	DECKHOUSE	FB	TCMY	MHG	SV	IB	T330	CHRY	16	3	47000	4		105000	115500
53	8	DECKHOUSE	FB	TCMY	F/W	SV	IB	T310D	GM	16	3	47000	4		112000	123500
53	8	DECKHOUSE	FB	TCMY	MHG	SV	IB	T310D	GM	16	3	47000	4		106500	117000
53	8	DECKHOUSE	FB	TCMY	F/W	SV	IB	T320D	CUM	16	3	47000	4		114500	126000
53	8	DECKHOUSE	FB	TCMY	MHG	SV	IB	T320D	CUM	16	3	47000	4		108500	119000
53	8	DECKHOUSE	FB	TCMY	F/W	SV	IB	T350D	GM	16	3	47000	4		116000	127500
53	8	DECKHOUSE	FB	TCMY	MHG	SV	IB	T350D	GM	16	3	47000	4		110000	121000
53	8	DECKHOUSE	FB	TCMY	F/W	SV	IB	T370D	CUM	16	3	47000	4		119000	131000
53	8	DECKHOUSE	FB	TCMY	MHG	SV	IB	T370D	CUM	16	3	47000	4		113500	124500
53	8	DECKHOUSE	FB	TCMY	F/W	SV	IB	T415D	GM	16	3	47000	4		122500	134500
53	8	DECKHOUSE	FB	TCMY	MHG	SV	IB	T415D	GM	16	3	47000	4		117000	128500
		1974 BOATS														
24		F-24	OP	SF	FBG		IO	188	MRCR	8		4000	2		7100	8200
25		SEA-RAIDER	OP	EXP	FBG		IB	225		9	4	4600	2	1	5950	6900
25		SEA-RAIDER	HT	EXP	FBG		IB	225		9	4	4600	2	1	5950	6900
25	5	F-25	OP	EXP	FBG		IB	225		10	2	5300	2	3	6750	7950
25	5	F-25	HT	EXP	FBG		IB	225		10	2	5300	2	3	6750	7950
25	5	F-25 COCKPIT	OP	EXP	FBG		IB	225		10	2	5300	2	3	6750	7950
25	5	F-25 COCKPIT	HT	EXP	FBG		IB	225		10	2	5300	2	3	6750	7950
30		SEA-RAIDER	HT	EXP	FBG		IB	255-280		11		8100	2	1	13200	15200
30		SEA-RAIDER	HT	EXP	FBG		IB	T225		11		8100	2	1	14500	16500
30		SEA-RAIDER	FB	EXP	FBG		IB	255-280		11		8100	2	1	13200	15200
30		SEA-RAIDER	FB	EXP	FBG		IB	T225		11		8100	2	1	14500	16500
30	2	F-30	FB	SF	FBG		IB	255-280		11	1	8100	2	2	11500	13200
30	2	F-30	FB	SF	FBG		IB	T225		11	1	8100	2	2	12500	14300

638
CONTINUED ON NEXT PAGE
96th ed. - Vol. III

```
 LOA  NAME AND/        TOP/ BOAT -HULL- ----ENGINE--- BEAM   WGT  DRAFT RETAIL RETAIL
FT IN OR MODEL         RIG  TYPE MTL TP  TP # HP  MFG  FT IN  LBS  FT IN  LOW   HIGH
------------------- 1974 BOATS -----------------------------------------------------
32 F-32           HT SDN FBG  IB  225D CAT  13  12000  2  6  26600  29500
32 F-32           HT SDN FBG  IB T225-T255  13  12000  2  6  21500  24400
32 F-32           FB SDN FBG  IB T225-T255  13  12000  2  6  21500  24400
32 F-32           FB SDN FBG  IB T225D CAT  13  12000  2  6  30400  33800
32 F-32           HT SF  FBG  IB T225-T255  13  12000  2  6  19800  22400
32 F-32           HT SF  FBG  IB T225D CAT  13  12000  2  6  26600  29600
32 F-32           FB SF  FBG  IB T225-T255  13  12000  2  6  19800  22400
32 F-32           FB SF  FBG  IB T225D CAT  13  12000  2  6  26600  29600
36 F-36           HT SDN FBG  IB T255 MRCR  13  16000  2 11  29800  33100
   IB T280  CHRY 30000  33300, IB T330  CHRY 30600  34000, IB T210D CUM 34000 37700

36 F-36           FB SDN FBG  IB T255 MRCR  13  16000  2 11  29800  33100
   IB T280  CHRY 30000  33300, IB T330  CHRY 30600  34000, IB T210D CUM 34000 37700

36 F-36           HT SF  FBG  IB T255 MRCR  13  16000  2 11  29000  32200
   IB T280  CHRY 29200  32400, IB T330  CHRY 29700  33000, IB T210D CUM 32600 36200

36 F-36           FB SF  FBG  IB T255 MRCR  13  16000  2 11  29000  32200
   IB T280  CHRY 29200  32400, IB T330  CHRY 29700  33000, IB T210D CUM 32600 36200

36 F-36           HT SPTCR FBG IB T255 MRCR 13  16000  2 11  29000  32300
   IB T280  CHRY 29200  32400, IB T330  CHRY 29700  33000, IB T210D CUM 32600 36300

36 F-36           FB SPTCR FBG IB T255 MRCR 13  16000  2 11  29000  32300
   IB T280  CHRY 29200  32400, IB T330  CHRY 29700  33000, IB T210D CUM 32600 36300

36 F-36           OP TCMY FBG  IB T255 MRCR  13  15500  2 11  28500  31700
36 F-36           OP TCMY FBG  IB T280 CHRY  13  15500  2 11  28700  31900
42                HT MY  M/P   IB T330 CHRY  14 10 25000  3      48400  55800
42                HT MY  M/P   IB T210D CUM  14 10 25000  3      51700  56800
42                HT MY  M/P   IB T216D GM   14 10 25000  3      52100  57200
42                FB MY  M/P   IB T330 CHRY  14 10 25000  3      48400  53100
42                FB MY  M/P   IB T210D CUM  14 10 25000  3      51600  56800
42                FB MY  M/P   IB T216D GM   14 10 25000  3      52100  57200
44 3              HT MY  FBG   IB T330 CHRY  14 11 32000  3  6   65300  71700
44 3              HT MY  FBG   IB T310D GM   14 11 32000  3  6   73500  80800
44 3              HT MY  FBG   IB T320D CUM  14 11 32000  3  6   73700  81000
44 3              FB MY  FBG   IB T330 CHRY  14 11 32000  3  6   65100  71600
44 3              FB MY  FBG   IB T310D GM   14 11 32000  3  6   73300  80600
44 3              FB MY  FBG   IB T320D CUM  14 11 32000  3  6   73500  80800
53                HT MY  M/P   IB T330 CHRY  15 10 44000  3 10   92800 102000
   IB T310D GM 94400 104000, IB T320D CUM  96000 105500, IB T350D GM 97700 107500

53                FB MY  FBG   IB T330 CHRY  15 10 44000  3 10   92400 101500
   IB T310D GM 94000 103500, IB T320D CUM  95600 105000, IB T350D GM 97100 106500

53 DECKHOUSE      HT MYDKH M/P  IB T330 CHRY  16  2 47000  4      96900 106500
   IB T310D GM 99200 109000, IB T320D CUM 101000 111000, IB T350D GM 102000 112000

53 DECKHOUSE      FB MYDKH M/P  IB T330 CHRY  16  2 47000  4      96600 106000
   IB T310D GM 98900 108500, IB T320D CUM 100500 110500, IB T350D GM 101500 111500
------------------- 1973 BOATS -----------------------------------------------------
24 F-24           OP SF  FBG   IO  188  MRCR  8      4000         7350   8450
25 SEA-RAIDER     HT EXP FBG   IB  225  CHRY  9  4   4600  2  1   5750   6600
25 SEA-RAIDER     HT EXP M/P   IB  225  MRCR  9  4   4600  2  1   5750   6600
25 SEA-RAIDER     HT EXP FBG   IB  225  MRCR  9  4   4600  2  1   5750   6600
25 5 F-25         OP EXP FBG   IB  225        10 2   5300  2  3   6600   7600
25 5 F-25         HT EXP FBG   IB  225        10 2   5300  2  3   6600   7600
25 5 F-25 COCKPIT OP EXP FBG   IB  225        10 2   5300  2  3   6600   7600
25 5 F-25 COCKPIT HT EXP FBG   IB  225        10 2   5300  2  3   6600   7600
30 SEA-RAIDER     HT EXP FBG   IB 255-280     11     8100  2  1  12700  14600
30 SEA-RAIDER     HT EXP FBG   IB T225        11     8100  2  1  13900  15800
30 SEA-RAIDER     FB EXP FBG   IB 225-280     11     8100  2  1  12500  14600
30 SEA-RAIDER     FB EXP FBG   IB T225        11     8100  2  1  13900  15800
30 2 F-30         FB SF  FBG   IB 225-280     11 1   8100  2  2  10800  12700
30 2 F-30         FB SF  FBG   IB T225        11 1   8100  2  2  12000  13700
31 4 F-31         FB EXP FBG   IB T225        11 9  10450  2  2  16900  19200
32 F-32           HT SDN FBG   IB T225        13  12000 2  6  20600  22900
34 HOUSEBOAT      HT HB  FBG SV IO 225        12     11900 2  8  10800  12300
36 F-36           HT SDN FBG   IB T255 MRCR  13  16000  2 11  28700  31900
   IB T280  CHRY 28900 32100, IB T325 MRCR  29500 32700, IB T330 CHRY 29500 32700
   IB T215D CUM 32800 36500

36 F-36           FB SDN FBG   IB T255 MRCR  13  16000  2 11  28700  31900
   IB T280  CHRY 28900 32100, IB T325 MRCR  29500 32700, IB T330 CHRY 29500 32700
   IB T215D CUM 32800 36500

36 F-36           HT SF  FBG   IB T255 MRCR  13  16000  2 11  27900  31100
   IB T280  CHRY 28100 31200, IB T325 MRCR  28600 31800, IB T330 CHRY 28600 31800
   IB T210D CUM 31400 34900

36 F-36           FB SF  FBG   IB T255 MRCR  13  16000  2 11  27900  31100
   IB T280  CHRY 28100 31200, IB T325 MRCR  28600 31800, IB T330 CHRY 28600 31800
   IB T210D CUM 31400 34900

36 F-36           HT SPTCR FBG IB T255 MRCR  13  16000  2 11  28000  31100
   IB T280  CHRY 28100 31200, IB T325 MRCR  28600 31800, IB T330 CHRY 28600 31800
   IB T215D CUM 31500 35000

36 F-36           FB SPTCR FBG IB T255 MRCR  13  16000  2 11  28000  31100
   IB T280  CHRY 28100 31200, IB T325 MRCR  28600 31800, IB T330 CHRY 28600 31800
   IB T215D CUM 31500 35100

36 F-36           OP TCMY FBG  IB T255 MRCR  13  15500  2 11  27500  30500
36 F-36           OP TCMY FBG  IB T280 CHRY  13  15500  2 11  27600  30700
42 5              HT MY  M/P   IB T325 MRCR  14 10 25000  3      47300  52600
   IB T330 CHRY 47400 52000, IB T210D CUM 50300 55200, IB T216D GM 50700 55700

42 5              FB MY  M/P   IB T325 MRCR  14 10 25000  3      47200  51900
   IB T330 CHRY 47300 51900, IB T210D CUM 50300 55200, IB T216D GM 50600 55700

47                HT MY  M/P   IB T325 MRCR  14 10 27000  3      65400  71900
   IB T330 CHRY 65400 71800, IB T310D GM 71400 78400, IB T320D CUM 71500 78600

47                FB MY  M/P   IB T325 MRCR  14 10 27000  3      65100  71500
   IB T330 CHRY 65000 71500, IB T310D GM 71000 78000, IB T320D CUM 71100 78200

50                HT MY  M/P   IB T325 MRCR  15 10 42000  3 10   82400  90600
   IB T330 CHRY 81700 89800, IB T310D GM 85600 94100, IB T350D GM 87800 96500
   IB T370D CUM 89100 97900

50                FB MY  WD    IB T325 MRCR  15 10 42000  3 10   82000  90100
   IB T330 CHRY 81300 89300, IB T310D GM 85100 93500, IB T350D GM 87200 95900

50                FB MY  WD    IB T370D CHRY 15 10 42000  3 10   91600 100500
53                HT MY  M/P   IB T325 MRCR  15 10 44000  3 10   91000 100000
   IB T330 GM 89100 97900, IB T310D GM 90600 99600, IB T320D CUM 92200 101500
   IB T350D GM 93800 103000, IB T370D CUM 96200 105500

53                FB MY  M/P   IB T325 MRCR  15 10 44000  3 10   90700  99700
   IB T330 CHRY 88700 97500, IB T310D GM 90200 99100, IB T320D CUM 91700 101000
   IB T350D GM 93200 102500, IB T370D CUM 95600 105000

53 8 DECK HOUSE SALON  MYDKH FBG SV IB T330  16  2 46700  4     102500 112500
53 8 DECK HOUSE SALON  MYDKH FBG SV IB T370D 16  2 46700  4     110500 121500
------------------- 1972 BOATS -----------------------------------------------------
25 MARLIN         OP CTRCN FBG IB 215-225     9  4  3000  1 11   4300   5000
25 MARLIN         OP CTRCN FBG IB 85D PERK    9  4  3000  1 11   5300   6100
25 SEA-RAIDER     HT EXP FBG   IB 215-225     9  4  4600  2  1   5500   6350
25 SEA-RAIDER     HT EXP FBG   IB 215-225     9  4  4600  2  1   5500   6350
25 5 F-25         OP EXP FBG   IB 215-225     10 2  5300  2  3   6300   7250
26 F-26           HT EXP FBG   VD 215-225     10    5300  2  4   6450   7400
26 F-26           HT EXP FBG   VD 215-225     10    5300  2  4   6450   7400
30 SEA-RAIDER     HT EXP FBG   IB 270-280     11    8100  2  1  12300  14000
30 SEA-RAIDER     HT EXP FBG   IB T215-T225   11    8100  2  1  13300  15200
30 SEA-RAIDER     FB EXP FBG   IB 270-280     11    8100  2  1  12300  14000
30 SEA-RAIDER     FB EXP FBG   IB T215-T225   11    8100  2  1  13300  15200
31 SEA-VOYAGER    HT SDN M/P   IB T215-T225   11  2  9900  2  4  16800  19200

31 4 F-31         HT EXP FBG   IB T215-T225   11 9 10450  2     16100  18400
31 4 F-31         FB EXP FBG   IB T215-T225   11 9             16000  18300
34 PLAN A         FB HB  FBG   IO 215-280     12    11900 2  8  11300  12800
34 PLAN B         FB HB  FBG   IB 215-225     12    11900 2  8  11400  13400
34 PLAN B         FB HB  FBG   VD 215-225     12    11900 2  8  11900  13600
36 F-36           HT SDN FBG   IB T270 MRCR  13  16000  2 11  27800  30900
   IB T280  CHRY 27900 30900, IB T325 MRCR  28400 30600, IB T330 CHRY 28400 31600
   IB T210D CUM 31500 35000

36 F-36           FB SDN FBG   IB T270 MRCR  13  16000  2 11  22300  24800
   IB T280  CHRY 22300 24800, IB T325 MRCR  22900 25400, IB T330 CHRY 22900 25400
```

LOA FT	LOA IN	NAME AND/ OR MODEL	TOP/ RIG	BOAT TYPE	HULL MTL	HULL TP	ENGINE TP	ENGINE # HP	ENGINE MFG	BEAM FT	BEAM IN	WGT LBS	DRAFT FT	DRAFT IN	RETAIL LOW	RETAIL HIGH
		1972 BOATS														
36		F-36	FB	SDN	FBG		IB	T210D	CUM	13			2	11	25900	28800
36		F-36	HT	SF	FBG		IB	T270	MRCR	13		16000	2	11	27100	30100
		IB T280 CHRY 27100 30100, IB T325 MRCR 27600 30600, IB T330 CHRY 27600 30600														
		IB T210D CUM 30300 33600														
36		F-36	FB	SF	FBG		IB	T270	MRCR	13		16000	2	11	27100	30100
		IB T280 CHRY 27100 30100, IB T325 MRCR 27600 30600, IB T330 CHRY 27600 30600														
		IB T210D CUM 30300 33600														
36		F-36	HT	SPTCR	FBG		IB	T270	MRCR	13		16000	2	11	27100	30100
		IB T280 CHRY 27100 30100, IB T325 MRCR 27600 30600, IB T330 CHRY 27600 30600														
		IB T210D CUM 30300 33700														
36		F-36	FB	SPTCR	FBG		IB	T270	MRCR	13			2	11	21500	23900
		IB T280 CHRY 21500 23900, IB T325 MRCR 22000 24500, IB T330 CHRY 22000 24400														
		IB T210D CUM 24500 27200														
36		SEA-RAIDER	OP	TCMY	FBG		VD	T270	MRCR	13		16500	2	11	27500	30600
36		SEA-RAIDER	OP	TCMY	FBG		VD	T280	CHRY	13		16500	2	11	27500	30600
36		SEA-VOYAGER	HT	SDN	M/P		IB	T270	MRCR	12		13200	2	9	25100	27900
36		SEA-VOYAGER	HT	SDN	M/P		IB	T280	CHRY	12		13200	2	9	25100	27900
42	5		HT	MY	M/P		IB	T325	MRCR	14	10	25000	3		45600	50100
		IB T330 CHRY 45700 50200, IB T210D CUM 48500 53300, IB T216D GM 48900 53700														
42	5		FB	MY	M/P		IB	T325	MRCR	14	10		3		38900	43300
		IB T330 CHRY 39000 43400, IB T210D CUM 41700 46300, IB T216D GM 42000 46700														
47			HT	MY	M/P		IB	T325	MRCR	14	10	27000	3		63000	69200
		IB T330 CHRY 62900 69200, IB T310D GM 68700 75500, IB T320D CUM 68900 75700														
47			FB	MY	M/P		IB	T325	MRCR	14	10		3		73300	80600
		IB T330 CHRY 73400 80600, IB T310D GM 72700 79900, IB T320D CUM 72800 80100														
53			HT	MY	M/P		IB	T325	MRCR	15	10	44000	3	10	87600	96200
		IB T330 CHRY 85700 94200, IB T310D GM 87200 95800, IB T350D GM 90200 99200														
		IB T370D CUM 92600 101500														
53			FB	MY	M/P		IB	T325	MRCR	15	10		3	10	99100	109000
		IB T330 CHRY 96700 106000, IB T310D GM 90200 99100, IB T350D GM 92700 102000														
		IB T370D CUM 94600 104000														
		1971 BOATS														
25		MARLIN	OP	CTRCN	FBG		IB	215-225		9	4	2700	1	9	3950	4600
25		MARLIN	OP	CTRCN	FBG		IB	85D	PERK	9	4	2700		9	4900	5600
25		SEA-RAIDER	OP	EXP	FBG		IB	215-225		9	4	4500	1	10	5250	6000
26		F-26	OP	EXP	FBG		VD	215-225		10		5300	2	1	6200	7150
28		SEA-SKIFF	HT	EXP	L/P		IB	270-280		10	10	6600	2	2	8900	10200
30		SEA-RAIDER	HT	EXP	FBG		IB	270-280		11		8100	2	1	11800	13500
30		SEA-RAIDER	HT	EXP	FBG		IB	T215-T225		11		8100	2	1	12800	14700
31		F-31	HT	EXP	FBG		IB	T215-T225		11	2	9100	2	4	14500	16600
31		F-31	FB	EXP	FBG		IB	T215-T225		11	2	9100	2	4	14500	16600
31		SEA-SKIFF	HT	EXP	L/P		IB	T215-T225		11	2	9100	2	4	14500	16600
31		SEA-VOYAGER	HT	SDN	M/P		IB	T215-T225		11	2	9900	2	4	16200	18400
34			HT	HB	FBG		IO	215-280		12		11900	2	8	11300	13300
		IO T215 MRCR 12300 14000, VD T215 MRCR 12600 14300, IO T225 CHRY 12400 14100														
		VD T225 CHRY 12500 14300														
36			HT	SDN	FBG		IB	T270	MRCR	13		18000	2	11	28500	31700
		IB T280 CHRY 28500 31700, IB T325 MRCR 29100 32300, IB T330 CHRY 29100 32300														
		IB T210D CUM 32500 36100														
36		SEA-RAIDER	OP	TCMY	FBG		VD	T270	MRCR	13		15500	2	11	25700	28600
36		SEA-RAIDER	OP	TCMY	FBG		VD	T280	CHRY	13		15500	2	11	25700	28600
36		SEA-VOYAGER	HT	SDN	M/P		IB	T270	MRCR	12		13200	2	9	24200	26900
36		SEA-VOYAGER	HT	SDN	M/P		IB	T280	CHRY	12		13200	2	9	24200	26900
42	5		HT	MY	M/P		IB	T325	MRCR	14	10	25000	3		43600	48400
42	5		HT	MY	M/P		IB	T330	CHRY	14	10	25000	3		43600	48500
42	5		HT	MY	M/P		IB	T216D	GM	14	10	25000	3		47200	51800
50			HT	MY	M/P		IB	T325	MRCR	15	10	42000	3	10	76500	84000
		IB T330 CHRY 75800 83300, IB T310D GM 79400 87300, IB T350D GM 81500 89600														
		IB T370D CUM 82700 90900														
		1970 BOATS														
25		MARLIN	OP	CTRCN	FBG	SV	IB	155-225		9	4	2700	1	9	3600	4450
25		MARLIN	OP	CTRCN	FBG	SV	IB	85D	PERK	9	4	2700	1	9	4800	5500
25		SEA-RAIDER	OP	EXP	FBG	SV	IB	210-225		9	4	4500	1	10	5050	5850
25		SEA-RAIDER	HT	EXP	FBG	SV	IB	210-225		9	4	4500	1	10	5050	5850
25		SEA-SKIFF	OP	EXP	L/P	SV	IB	210-225		9	4	4600	1	10	5150	5900
25		SEA-SKIFF	HT	EXP	L/P	SV	IB	210-225		9	4	4600	1	10	5150	5900
26		SEA-SKIFF	OP	EXP	L/P	SV	IB	210-225		9	6	4900	1	10	5650	6500
26		SEA-SKIFF	HT	EXP	L/P	SV	IB	210-225		9	6	4900	1	10	5650	6500
28		SEA-SKIFF	HT	EXP	L/P	SV	IB	260		10	10	6600	2	2	8400	9700
30		SEA-RAIDER	HT	EXP	FBG	SV	IB	260		11		8100	2	1	11300	12900
30		SEA-RAIDER	HT	EXP	FBG	SV	IB	T210-T225		11		8100	2	1	12300	14100
30		SEA-RAIDER	FB	EXP	FBG	SV	IB	260		11		8100	2	1	11300	12900
30		SEA-RAIDER	FB	EXP	FBG	SV	IB	T210-T225		11		8100	2	1	12300	14100
31		SEA-SKIFF	HT	EXP	L/P	SV	IB	T210-T225		11	2	9100	2	4	13900	16000
31		SEA-SKIFF	FB	EXP	L/P	SV	IB	T210-T225		11	2	9100	2	4	13900	16000
31		SEA-VOYAGER	HT	EXP	M/P	SV	IB	T210-T225		11	2	9700	2	4	14100	16200
31		SEA-VOYAGER	FB	EXP	M/P	SV	IB	T210-T225		11	2	9700	2	4	14100	16200
31		SEA-VOYAGER	HT	SDN	M/P	SV	IB	T210-T225		11	2	9900	2	4	15500	17800
31		SEA-VOYAGER	FB	SDN	M/P	SV	IB	T210-T225		11	2	9900	2	4	15500	17800
33		SEA-VOYAGER	HT	EXP	M/P	SV	IB	T260		12		11250	2	9	18400	20500
33		SEA-VOYAGER	FB	EXP	M/P	SV	IB	T260		12		11250	2	9	18400	20500
34		SEA-QUEEN	HT	HB	FBG	SV	IO	225-270		12		11900	2	8	10600	12300
		IO T215 MRCR 11500 13000, IO T225 CHRY 11500 13100, IB T225 CHRY 11500 13000														
36		SEA-RAIDER	OP	TCMY	FBG		IB	T260	CHRY	13		15500	2	11	24700	27500
36		SEA-RAIDER	OP	TCMY	FBG		IB	T260	CRUS	13		15500	2	11	24900	27700
36		SEA-VOYAGER	HT	EXP	M/P	SV	IB	T260	CHRY	12		12600	2	9	22100	24600
36		SEA-VOYAGER	HT	EXP	M/P	SV	IB	T260	CRUS	12		12600	2	9	22300	24800
36		SEA-VOYAGER	FB	EXP	M/P	SV	IB	T260	CHRY	12		12600	2	9	22100	24600
36		SEA-VOYAGER	FB	EXP	M/P	SV	IB	T260	CRUS	12		12600	2	9	22300	24800
36		SEA-VOYAGER PLAN C	HT	SDN	M/P	SV	IB	T260	CHRY	12		13200	2	9	22800	25300
36		SEA-VOYAGER PLAN C	HT	SDN	M/P	SV	IB	T260	CRUS	12		13200	2	9	23000	25600
36		SEA-VOYAGER PLAN C	FB	SDN	M/P	SV	IB	T260	CHRY	12		13200	2	9	22800	25300
36		SEA-VOYAGER PLAN C	FB	SDN	M/P	SV	IB	T260	CRUS	12		13200	2	9	23100	25600
36		SEA-VOYAGER PLAN D	HT	SDN	M/P	SV	IB	T260	CHRY	12		13200	2	9	23700	26400
36		SEA-VOYAGER PLAN D	HT	SDN	M/P	SV	IB	T260	CRUS	12		13200	2	9	23900	26600
36		SEA-VOYAGER PLAN D	FB	SDN	M/P	SV	IB	T260	CHRY	12		13200	2	9	23700	26300
36		SEA-VOYAGER PLAN D	FB	SDN	M/P	SV	IB	T260	CRUS	12		13200	2	9	23900	26600
38		SEA-VOYAGER	HT	MY	M/P	SV	IB	T300	CHRY	13		18500	3		31200	34600
38		SEA-VOYAGER	HT	MY	M/P	SV	IB	T320	CRUS	13		18500	3		31700	35200
42	5	SEA-VOYAGER	HT	MY	M/P	SV	IB	T300	CHRY	14	10	25000	3		42200	46900
42	5	SEA-VOYAGER	HT	MY	M/P	SV	IB	T320	CRUS	14	10	25000	3		43200	48000
42	5	SEA-VOYAGER	HT	MY	M/P	SV	IB	T216D	GM	14	10	25000	3		46300	50800
42	5	SEA-VOYAGER	FB	MY	M/P	SV	IB	T300	CHRY	14	10	25000	3		42100	46800
42	5	SEA-VOYAGER	FB	MY	M/P	SV	IB	T320	CRUS	14	10	25000	3		43100	47900
42	5	SEA-VOYAGER	FB	MY	M/P	SV	IB	T216D	GM	14	10	25000	3		46200	50800
		1969 BOATS														
25		SEA-BREEZE	OP	EXP	PLY	SV	IB	190		9	4	4600	1	10	4850	5600
25		SEA-RAIDER		EXP	FBG	SV	IB	190-200		9	4	4500	1	10	4800	5500
25		SEA-SKIFF	OP	EXP	L/P	SV	IB	190-200		9	4	4600	1	10	4850	5600
26		BIMINI SEA SKIFF	HT	SF	PLY	SV	IB	190-200		9	6	4200	1	10	4900	5650
26		SEA-BREEZE	OP	EXP	PLY	SV	IB	200		9	6	4900	1	10	5350	6150
26		SEA-BREEZE	HT	SDN	PLY	SV	IB	190-200		9	6	4900	1	10	5750	6650
26		SEA-SKIFF	OP	EXP	L/P	SV	IB	190-200		9	4	4900	1	10	5300	6150
26		SEA-SKIFF	HT	SDN	L/P	SV	IB	190-200		9	4	4900	1	10	5700	6600
28		BIMINI SEA VOYAGER	HT	SF	M/P	SV	IB	T210-T225		10	10	6800	2	2	9100	10500
28		SEA-BREEZE	HT	EXP	PLY	SV	IB	250-260		10	10	6600	2	2	8050	9300
28		SEA-SKIFF	HT	EXP	L/P	SV	IB	250-260		10	10	6600	2	2	8050	9300
31		SEA-BREEZE	HT	EXP	PLY	SV	IB	250-260		11	2	9100	2	4	12400	14200
31		SEA-BREEZE	HT	EXP	PLY	SV	IB	T210-T225		11	2	9700	2	4	13600	15600
31		SEA-SKIFF	HT	EXP	L/P	SV	IB	250-260		11	2	9100	2	4	12400	14200
31		SEA-SKIFF	HT	EXP	L/P	SV	IB	T210-T225		11	2	9700	2	4	13600	15600
31		SEA-VOYAGER	HT	EXP	M/P	SV	IB	T210-T225		11	2	9700	2	4	13600	15600
31		SEA-VOYAGER	HT	SDN	M/P	SV	IB	T210-T225		11	2	9900	2	4	14900	17200
33		SEA-VOYAGER	HT	EXP	M/P	SV	IB	T210-T260		12		11250	2	9	16900	19700
34		SEA-QUEEN	HT	HB	FBG	SV	IO	210		9		11900	2	8	10500	11900
36		SEA-VOYAGER	HT	EXP	M/P	SV	IB	T210	INT	12		12600	2	9	21200	23500
		IB T225 CHRY 21200 23600, IB T250 INT 21400 23800, IB T260 CHRY 21400 23800														
36		SEA-VOYAGER	HT	SDN	M/P	SV	IB	T210	INT	12		13200	2	9	22200	24700
		IB T225 CHRY 22300 24800, IB T250 INT 22500 25000, IB T260 CHRY 22500 25000														
36		SEA-VOYAGER	FB	SDNSF	M/P	SV	IB	T210	INT	12		13200	2	9	21600	24000
		IB T225 CHRY 21700 24100, IB T250 INT 21900 24300, IB T260 CHRY 21900 24300														
38		SEA-VOYAGER	HT	MY	M/P	SV	IB	T250	INT	13		18500	3		30000	33300
		IB T260 CHRY 29900 33300, IB T300 CHRY 30200 33500, IB T300 INT 30300 33600														
		IB T160D PERK 33800 37500														

CONTINUED ON NEXT PAGE

LOA FT	LOA IN	NAME AND/ OR MODEL	TOP/ RIG	BOAT TYPE	-HULL- MTL	-HULL- TP	ENGINE TP	ENGINE # HP	ENGINE MFG	BEAM FT	BEAM IN	WGT LBS	DRAFT FT	DRAFT IN	RETAIL LOW	RETAIL HIGH
		1969 BOATS														
42	5	SEA-VOYAGER	HT	MY	M/P	SV	IB	T300	CHRY	14	10	25000	3	2	40900	45400
		IB T300 INT 41000 45500, IB T160D PERK 42900 47700, IB T216D GM													44300	49200
		1968 BOATS														
24		BIMINI SEA SKIFF	HT	SF	L/P		IB	165	INT	8		3600	1	10	3600	4150
24		SEA-BREEZE	OP	EXP	PLY		IB	165	INT	8		4200	1	10	4000	4700
24		SEA-SKIFF	OP	EXP	L/P		IB	165	INT	8		4200	1	10	4000	4700
24		SEA-SKIFF	OP	SPTCR	L/P		IB	190-195		8		3600	1	10	3600	4200
26		BIMINI SEA SKIFF	HT	SF	L/P		IB	190-195		9	6	4000	1	10	4600	5300
26		SEA-BREEZE	OP	EXP	PLY		IB	190-195		9	6	4700	1	10	5000	5750
26		SEA-BREEZE	HT	SDN	PLY		IB	190-195		9	6	4700	1	10	5400	6200
26		SEA-SKIFF	OP	EXP	L/P		IB	190-195		9	6	4700	1	10	5000	5750
26		SEA-SKIFF	HT	SDN	L/P		IB	190-195		9	6	4700	1	10	5400	6200
28		BIMINI SEA SKIFF	HT	SF	L/P		IB	250-260		10	10	6000	2	2	7450	8600
28		BIMINI SEA SKIFF	HT	SF	L/P		IB	T210		10	10	6000	2	2	8250	9550
28		BIMINI SEA VOYAGER	HT	SF	M/P		IB	250-260		10	10	6800	2	2	7850	9100
28		BIMINI SEA VOYAGER	HT	SF	M/P		IB	T210		10	10	6800	2	2	8650	10000
28		SEA-BREEZE	HT	EXP	PLY		IB	210-260		10	10	6200	2	2	7350	8700
28		SEA-BREEZE	HT	EXP	PLY		IB	T210		10	10	6200	2	2	8350	9650
28		SEA-SKIFF	HT	EXP	L/P		IB	250-260		10	10	6400	2	2	7650	8850
28		SEA-SKIFF	HT	EXP	L/P		IB	T210		10	10	6400	2	2	8450	9750
28		SEA-VOYAGER	HT	EXP	M/P		IB	250-260		10	10	7200	2	2	8100	9350
28		SEA-VOYAGER	HT	EXP	M/P		IB	T210		10	10	7200	2	2	8950	10200
31		SEA-BREEZE	HT	EXP	PLY		IB	250-260		11	2	8100	2	4	11600	13300
31		SEA-BREEZE	HT	EXP	PLY		IB	T210		11	2	8100	2	4	12600	14300
31		SEA-SKIFF	HT	EXP	L/P		IB	250-260		11	2	8300	2	4	11700	13400
31		SEA-SKIFF	HT	EXP	L/P		IB	T210		11	2	8300	2	4	12700	14400
31		SEA-VOYAGER	HT	EXP	M/P		IB	T210		11	2	9000	2	4	12900	14600
31		SEA-VOYAGER	HT	SDN	M/P		IB	T210		11	2	9500	2	4	12800	14500
33		SEA-SKIFF	HT	EXP	L/P		IB	T210-T260		12		11050	2	8	16200	18900
33		SEA-VOYAGER	HT	EXP	M/P		IB	T210-T260		12		11250	2	8	16200	19000
33		SEA-VOYAGER	FB	SDNSF	M/P		IB	T210-T260		12		11750	2	8	16400	19100
36		SEA-VOYAGER	HT	EXP	M/P		IB	T210		12	3	12200	2	9	21200	23500
		IB T210 CHRY 21100 23500, IB T250 INT 21400 23800, IB T260 CHRY													21400	23800
36		SEA-VOYAGER	HT	SDN	M/P		IB	T210	CHRY	12	3	12800	2	9	22200	24700
		IB T210 INT 22300 24700, IB T250 INT 22600 25100, IB T260 CHRY													22600	25100
38		SEA-VOYAGER	HT	MY	M/P		IB	T250	CHRY	13	4	18500	3		28400	31500
		IB T260 CHRY 28400 31600, IB T300 INT 28700 31900, IB T160D PERK													32100	35700
42				DCMY	WD		IB	T300	INT						34000	37800
42	5	SEA-VOYAGER	HT	DCMY	M/P		IB	T300	INT	14	10	23500	3		38400	42600
42	5	SEA-VOYAGER	HT	DCMY	M/P		IB	T160D	PERK	14	10	23500	3		39700	44200
42	5	SEA-VOYAGER	HT	DCMY	M/P		IB	T216D	GM	14	10	23500	3		41400	46000
		1967 BOATS														
24	3	BIMINI SEA SKIFF	OP	SF	L/P		IO	150	OMC	8		4300	1	10	9500	10800
24	3	BIMINI SEA SKIFF	OP	SF	L/P		IB	165	INT	8		4300	1	10	4000	4650
24	3	BIMINI SEA SKIFF	HT	SF	L/P		IO	150	OMC	8		4300	1	10	9500	10800
24	3	BIMINI SEA SKIFF	HT	SF	L/P		IB	165	INT	8		4300	1	10	4000	4650
24	3	SEA-BREEZE	OP	EXP	PLY		IO	150	OMC	8		4200	1	10	8100	9350
24	3	SEA-BREEZE	OP	EXP	PLY		IB	165	INT	8		4200	1	10	3900	4550
24	3	SEA-SKIFF	OP	EXP	L/P		IO	150	OMC	8		4200	1	10	8100	9350
24	3	SEA-SKIFF	HT	EXP	L/P		IB	165	INT	8		4200	1	10	3900	4550
26		BIMINI SEA SKIFF	HT	SF	L/P		IB	190	INT	9	6	4000	1	10	4450	5100
26		BIMINI SEA SKIFF	FB	SF	L/P		IB	190	INT	9	6	4000	1	10	4450	5100
26		SEA-BREEZE	OP	EXP	PLY		IB	190	INT	9	6	4700	1	10	4850	5550
26		SEA-BREEZE	HT	EXP	PLY		IB	190	INT	9	6	4700	1	10	4850	5550
26		SEA-SKIFF		EXP	L/P		IB	190	INT	9	6	4700	1	10	4850	5550
26		SEA-SKIFF	OP	EXP	L/P		IB	190	INT	9	6	4700	1	10	4850	5550
28		BIMINI SEA SKIFF	HT	SF	L/P		IB	210-250		10	10	6000	2	2	7000	8250
28		BIMINI SEA SKIFF	HT	SF	L/P		IB	T210	INT	10	10	6000	2	2	8000	9200
28		BIMINI SEA SKIFF	FB	SF	L/P		IB	210-250		10	10	6000	2	2	7000	8250
28		BIMINI SEA SKIFF	FB	SF	L/P		IB	T210	INT	10	10	6000	2	2	8000	9200
28		BIMINI SEA VOYAGER	HT	SF	M/P		IB	210-250		10	10	6800	2	2	7400	8700
28		BIMINI SEA VOYAGER	HT	SF	M/P		IB	T210	INT	10	10	6800	2	2	8350	9600
28		BIMINI SEA VOYAGER	FB	SF	M/P		IB	210-250		10	10	6800	2	2	7450	8750
28		BIMINI SEA VOYAGER	FB	SF	M/P		IB	T210	INT	10	10	6800	2	2	8400	9650
28		SEA-BREEZE	OP	EXP	PLY		IB	210-250		10	10	6200	2	2	7100	8350
28		SEA-BREEZE	OP	EXP	PLY		IB	T210	INT	10	10	6200	2	2	8100	9300
28		SEA-BREEZE	HT	EXP	PLY		IB	210-250		10	10	6200	2	2	7100	8350
28		SEA-BREEZE	HT	EXP	PLY		IB	T210	INT	10	10	6200	2	2	8100	9300
28		SEA-BREEZE	FB	EXP	PLY		IB	210-250		10	10	6200	2	2	7100	8350
28		SEA-BREEZE	FB	EXP	PLY		IB	T210	INT	10	10	6200	2	2	8100	9300
28		SEA-SKIFF	OP	EXP	L/P		IB	210-250		10	10	6400	2	2	7200	8500
28		SEA-SKIFF	OP	EXP	L/P		IB	T210	INT	10	10	6400	2	2	8200	9400
28		SEA-SKIFF	HT	EXP	L/P		IB	210-250		10	10	6400	2	2	7200	8500
28		SEA-SKIFF	HT	EXP	L/P		IB	T210	INT	10	10	6400	2	2	8200	9400
28		SEA-SKIFF	FB	EXP	L/P		IB	210-250		10	10	6400	2	2	7200	8500
28		SEA-SKIFF	FB	EXP	L/P		IB	T210	INT	10	10	6400	2	2	8200	9400
28		SEA-VOYAGER	OP	EXP	M/P		IB	210-250		10	10	7200	2	2	7600	8950
28		SEA-VOYAGER	OP	EXP	M/P		IB	T210	INT	10	10	7200	2	2	8550	9850
28		SEA-VOYAGER	HT	EXP	M/P		IB	210-250		10	10	7200	2	2	7600	8950
28		SEA-VOYAGER	HT	EXP	M/P		IB	T210	INT	10	10	7200	2	2	8550	9850
28		SEA-VOYAGER	FB	EXP	M/P		IB	210-250		10	10	7200	2	2	7600	8950
28		SEA-VOYAGER	FB	EXP	M/P		IB	T210	INT	10	10	7200	2	2	8550	9850
31		SEA-BREEZE	OP	EXP	PLY		IB	210-250		11	2	8100	2	4	11000	12700
31		SEA-BREEZE	OP	EXP	PLY		IB	T210	INT	11	2	8100	2	4	12200	13800
31		SEA-BREEZE	HT	EXP	PLY		IB	210-250		11	2	8100	2	4	11000	12700
31		SEA-BREEZE	HT	EXP	PLY		IB	T210	INT	11	2	8100	2	4	12200	13800
31		SEA-BREEZE	FB	EXP	PLY		IB	210-250		11	2	8100	2	4	11000	12700
31		SEA-BREEZE	FB	EXP	PLY		IB	T210	INT	11	2	8100	2	4	12200	13800
31		SEA-SKIFF	OP	EXP	L/P		IB	210-250		11	2	8300	2	4	11000	12800
31		SEA-SKIFF	OP	EXP	PLY		IB	T210	INT	11	2	8300	2	4	12200	13900
31		SEA-SKIFF	HT	EXP	L/P		IB	210-250		11	2	8300	2	4	11000	12800
31		SEA-SKIFF	HT	EXP	L/P		IB	T210	INT	11	2	8300	2	4	12200	13900
31		SEA-SKIFF	FB	EXP	L/P		IB	210-250		11	2	8300	2	4	11000	12800
31		SEA-SKIFF	FB	EXP	L/P		IB	T210	INT	11	2	8300	2	4	12200	13900
31		SEA-VOYAGER	OP	EXP	M/P		IB	T210	INT	11	2	9000	2	4	12400	14100
31		SEA-VOYAGER	HT	EXP	M/P		IB	T210	INT	11	2	9000	2	4	12400	14100
31		SEA-VOYAGER	FB	EXP	M/P		IB	T210	INT	11	2	9000	2	4	12400	14100
31		SEA-VOYAGER	HT	SDN	M/P		IB	T210	INT	11	2	9500	2	4	12300	14000
31		SEA-VOYAGER	FB	SDN	M/P		IB	T210	INT	11	2	9500	2	4	12300	14000
33		SEA-SKIFF	HT	EXP	L/P		IB	210-250		12		11050	2	8	14500	16700
33		SEA-SKIFF	HT	EXP	L/P		IB	T210	INT	12		11050	2	8	15600	17700
33		SEA-SKIFF	FB	EXP	L/P		IB	210-250		12		11050	2	8	14500	16700
33		SEA-SKIFF	FB	EXP	L/P		IB	T210	INT	12		11050	2	8	15600	17700
33		SEA-VOYAGER	HT	EXP	M/P		IB	T210-T285		12		11250	2	8	15600	18500
33		SEA-VOYAGER	FB	EXP	M/P		IB	T210-T285		12		11250	2	8	15600	18500
36		SEA-VOYAGER	HT	EXP	M/P		IB	T210	INT	12	3	12200	2	9	20600	22800
36		SEA-VOYAGER	HT	EXP	M/P		IB	T250	INT	12	3	12200	2	9	20800	23100
36		SEA-VOYAGER	HT	EXP	M/P		IB	T285	INT	12	3	12200	2	9	21100	23400
36		SEA-VOYAGER	FB	EXP	M/P		IB	T210	INT	12	3	12200	2	9	20600	22800
36		SEA-VOYAGER	FB	EXP	M/P		IB	T250	INT	12	3	12200	2	9	20800	23100
36		SEA-VOYAGER	FB	EXP	M/P		IB	T285	INT	12	3	12200	2	9	21100	23400
36		SEA-VOYAGER 4-6 SLPR	HT	SDN	M/P		IB	T210	INT	12	3	12800	2	9	22100	24500
36		SEA-VOYAGER 4-6 SLPR	HT	SDN	M/P		IB	T250	INT	12	3	12800	2	9	22400	24900
36		SEA-VOYAGER 4-6 SLPR	HT	SDN	M/P		IB	T285	INT	12	3	12800	2	9	22700	25200
36		SEA-VOYAGER 4-6 SLPR	FB	SDN	M/P		IB	T210	INT	12	3	12800	2	9	22000	24500
36		SEA-VOYAGER 4-6 SLPR	FB	SDN	M/P		IB	T250	INT	12	3	12800	2	9	22300	24800
36		SEA-VOYAGER 4-6 SLPR	FB	SDN	M/P		IB	T285	INT	12	3	12800	2	9	22600	25200
36		SEA-VOYAGER 6-8 SLPR	HT	SDN	M/P		IB	T210	INT	12	3	12800	2	9	21100	23500
36		SEA-VOYAGER 6-8 SLPR	HT	SDN	M/P		IB	T250	INT	12	3	12800	2	9	21500	23800
36		SEA-VOYAGER 6-8 SLPR	HT	SDN	M/P		IB	T285	INT	12	3	12800	2	9	21800	24200
36		SEA-VOYAGER 6-8 SLPR	FB	SDN	M/P		IB	T210	INT	12	3	12800	2	9	21200	23500
36		SEA-VOYAGER 6-8 SLPR	FB	SDN	M/P		IB	T250	INT	12	3	12800	2	9	21500	23900
36		SEA-VOYAGER 6-8 SLPR	FB	SDN	M/P		IB	T285	INT	12	3	12800	2	9	21800	24200
38		SEA-VOYAGER	HT	MY	M/P		IB	T300	INT	13	4	18500	3		27900	31000
38		SEA-VOYAGER	HT	MY	M/P		IB	T160D	PERK	13	4	18500	3		31200	34700
38		SEA-VOYAGER	HT	MY	M/P		IB	T216D	GM	13	4	18500	3		31500	35000
42	5	SEA-VOYAGER	HT	MY	M/P		IB	T300	INT	14	10	22000	3		34900	38800
42	5	SEA-VOYAGER	HT	MY	M/P		IB	T160D	PERK	14	10	22000	3		36800	40800
42	5	SEA-VOYAGER	HT	MY	M/P		IB	T216D	GM	14	10	22000	3		37900	42100
42	5	SEA-VOYAGER EXT HT	HT	MY	M/P		IB	T300	INT	14	10	22000	3		34700	38600
42	5	SEA-VOYAGER EXT HT	HT	MY	M/P		IB	T160D	PERK	14	10	22000	3		36500	40600
42	5	SEA-VOYAGER EXT HT	HT	MY	M/P		IB	T216D	GM	14	10	22000	3		37800	42100
		1966 BOATS														
24	3	SEA-BREEZE	OP	EXP	PLY		IB	165		8		4200	1	10	3750	4400
24	3	SEA-SKIFF		EXP	L/P		IB	165	INT	8		4300	1	10	3850	4450
26		BIMINI SEA SKIFF	HT	SF	L/P		IB	190-195		9	6	4000	1	10	4250	4950
26		BIMINI SEA SKIFF	FB	SF	L/P		IB	190	INT	9	6	4000	1	10	4250	4950
26		BIMINI SEA SKIFF	FB	SF	L/P		IB	195	GRAY	9	6	4700	1	10	4700	5400
26		SEA-BREEZE	OP	EXP	PLY		IB	190-195		9	6	4700	1	10	4700	5400
26		SEA-BREEZE	HT	EXP	PLY		IB	190-195		9	6	4700	1	10	4700	5400
26		SEA-SKIFF	OP	EXP	L/P		IB	190-195		9	6	4700	1	10	4700	5400
26		SEA-SKIFF	HT	EXP	L/P		IB	190-195		9	6	4700	1	10	4700	5400
27	9	BIMINI SEA SKIFF	HT	SF	L/P		IB	190-220		10	10	5200	2	2	5700	6700
27	9	BIMINI SEA SKIFF	HT	SF	L/P		IB	T165-T195		10	10	5200	2	2	6400	7600

 CONTINUED ON NEXT PAGE

```
TROJAN EXPRESS YACHTS          -CONTINUED    See inside cover to adjust price for area
LOA    NAME AND/        TOP/ BOAT  -HULL-  ----ENGINE---  BEAM   WGT   DRAFT  RETAIL RETAIL
FT IN  OR MODEL         RIG  TYPE  MTL TP  TP # HP  MFG    FT IN  LBS   FT IN  LOW    HIGH
--------------------------- 1966 BOATS -------------------------------------------------
27 9 BIMINI SEA SKIFF   FB SF   L/P   IB 190-220   10 10 5200 2 2  5700  6750
27 9 BIMINI SEA SKIFF   FB SF         IB T165-T195 10 10 5200 2 2  6400  7650
27 9 SEA-BREEZE         OP EXP  PLY   IB 190-220   10 10 5400 2 2  5800  6950
27 9 SEA-BREEZE         OP EXP  PLY   IB T165-T195 10 10 5400 2 2  6500  7700
27 9 SEA-BREEZE         HT EXP  PLY   IB 190  INT  10 10 5400 2 2  5800  6700
27 9 SEA-BREEZE         HT EXP  WD    IB 195  GRAY 10 10 5400 2 2  5850  6700
27 9 SEA-BREEZE         HT EXP  PLY   IB 210-220   10 10 5400 2 2  5900  6850
27 9 SEA-BREEZE         HT EXP  PLY   IB T165-T195 10 10 5400 2 2  6500  7700
27 9 SEA-BREEZE         FB EXP  PLY   IB 190-220   10 10 5400 2 2  5800  6850
27 9 SEA-BREEZE         FB EXP  PLY   IB T165-T195 10 10 5400 2 2  6500  7700
27 9 SEA-SKIFF          OP EXP  L/P   IB 190-220   10 10 5600 2 2  5900  6950
27 9 SEA-SKIFF          OP EXP  L/P   IB T165-T195 10 10 5600 2 2  6600  7800

27 9 SEA-SKIFF          HT EXP  L/P   IB 190-220   10 10 5600 2 2  5900  6950
27 9 SEA-SKIFF          HT EXP  L/P   IB T165-T195 10 10 5600 2 2  6600  7800
27 9 SEA-SKIFF          FB EXP  L/P   IB 190-220   10 10 5600 2 2  5900  6950
27 9 SEA-SKIFF          FB EXP  L/P   IB T165-T195 10 10 5600 2 2  6600  7800
27 9 SEA-VOYAGER        OP EXP  M/P   IB 210-220   10 10 6400 2 2  6350  7350
27 9 SEA-VOYAGER        OP EXP  M/P   IB T165-T195 10 10 6400 2 2  6950  8200
27 9 SEA-VOYAGER        HT EXP  M/P   IB 210-220   10 10 6400 2 2  6350  7350
27 9 SEA-VOYAGER        HT EXP  M/P   IB T165-T195 10 10 6400 2 2  6950  8200
27 9 SEA-VOYAGER        FB EXP  M/P   IB 210-220   10 10 6400 2 2  6350  7350
27 9 SEA-VOYAGER        FB EXP  M/P   IB T165-T195 10 10 6400 2 2  6950  8200
31   SEA-BREEZE         OP EXP  PLY   IB 210-220   11    7300 2 4 10300 11800
31   SEA-BREEZE         OP EXP  PLY   IB T190-T220 11    7300 2 4 11300 13200

31   SEA-BREEZE         HT EXP  PLY   IB 210-220   11    7300 2 4 10300 11800
31   SEA-BREEZE         HT EXP  PLY   IB T190-T220 11    7300 2 4 11300 13200
31   SEA-BREEZE         FB EXP  PLY   IB 210-220   11    7300 2 4 10300 11800
31   SEA-BREEZE         FB EXP  PLY   IB T190-T220 11    7300 2 4 11300 13200
31   SEA-SKIFF          OP EXP  L/P   IB 210-220   11    7500 2 4 10400 11800
31   SEA-SKIFF          OP EXP  L/P   IB T190-T220 11    7500 2 4 11400 13200
31   SEA-SKIFF          HT EXP  L/P   IB 210-220   11    7500 2 4 10400 11800
31   SEA-SKIFF          HT EXP  L/P   IB T190-T220 11    7500 2 4 11400 13200
31   SEA-SKIFF          FB EXP  L/P   IB 210-220   11    7500 2 4 10400 11800
31   SEA-SKIFF          FB EXP  L/P   IB T190-T220 11    7500 2 4 11400 13200
31   SEA-VOYAGER        OP EXP  M/P   IB T190-T220 11    9000 2 4 11800 13700
31   SEA-VOYAGER        HT EXP  M/P   IB T190-T220 11 1  9000 2 4 11800 13700

31   SEA-VOYAGER        FB EXP  M/P   IB T190-T220 11 1  9000 2 4 11800 13700
33   SEA-SKIFF 4 SLPR   HT EXP  L/P   IB T210-T280 12    11050 2 8 15200 18100
33   SEA-SKIFF 4 SLPR   FB EXP  L/P   IB T210-T280 12    11050 2 8 15200 18100
33   SEA-SKIFF 4-6 SLPR HT SDN  L/P   IB T210-T280 12    11650 2 8 16500 19800
33   SEA-SKIFF 4-6 SLPR FB SDN  L/P   IB T210-T280 12    11650 2 8 16500 19700
33   SEA-SKIFF 6 SLPR   FB EXP  L/P   IB T210-T280 12    11050 2 8 14800 17700
33   SEA-SKIFF 6 SLPR   HT EXP  L/P   IB T210-T280 12    11050 2 8 14800 17700
33   SEA-SKIFF 6-8 SLPR FB SDN  L/P   IB T210-T280 12    11650 2 8 16100 19300
33   SEA-SKIFF 6-8 SLPR HT SDN  L/P   IB T210-T280 12    11650 2 8 16100 19300
33   SEA-VOYAGER 4 SLPR FB EXP  WD    IB T210  INT 12    11250 2 8 15100 17100
33   SEA-VOYAGER 4 SLPR FB EXP  M/P   IB T220-T280 12    11250 2 8 15600 18400

33   SEA-VOYAGER 4-6 SLPR HT SDN M/P  IB T210-T280 12    11500 2 8 16700 20000
33   SEA-VOYAGER 4-6 SLPR FB SDN M/P  IB T210-T280 12    11500 2 8 16700 20000
33   SEA-VOYAGER 6 SLPR   FB EXP M/P  IB T210-T280 12    11250 2 8 14600 17400
33   SEA-VOYAGER 6 SLPR   HT EXP M/P  IB T210-T280 12    11250 2 8 15100 17500
33   SEA-VOYAGER 6-8 SLPR HT SDN M/P  IB T210-T280 12    11500 2 8 15800 19000
33   SEA-VOYAGER 6-8 SLPR FB SDN M/P  IB T210-T280 12    11500 2 8 15800 19000
36 4 SEA-SKIFF 4 SLPR    HT EXP  L/P  IB T210  INT 12 3 12000 2 9 20300 22600
     IB T220 GRAY 20400 22600, IB T250 INT 20500 22800, IB T280 GRAY 20900 23200
     IB T280 INT 20600 22900

36 4 SEA-SKIFF 4 SLPR    FB EXP  L/P  IB T210  INT 12 3 12000 2 9 20300 22600
     IB T220 GRAY 20300 22600, IB T250 INT 20300 22500, IB T280 GRAY 20800 23100
     IB T280 INT 20100 22800

36 4 SEA-SKIFF 4-6 SLPR  HT SDN  L/P  IB T210  INT 12 3 12600 2 9 21300 23700
     IB T220 GRAY 21400 23700, IB T250 INT 21600 24000, IB T280 GRAY 21900 24400
     IB T280 INT 21600 24000

36 4 SEA-SKIFF 4-6 SLPR  FB SDN  L/P  IB T210  INT 12 3 12600 2 9 21300 23700
     IB T220 GRAY 21400 23700, IB T250 INT 21300 23700, IB T280 GRAY 21900 24400
     IB T280 INT 21100 23400

36 4 SEA-SKIFF 6 SLPR    HT EXP  L/P  IB T210 GRAY 12 3 12000 2 9 19800 22000
     IB T220 GRAY 19900 22100, IB T250 INT 20000 22300, IB T280 GRAY 20400 22600
     IB T280 INT 20100 22300

36 4 SEA-SKIFF 6 SLPR    FB EXP  L/P  IB T210  INT 12 3 12000 2 9 19800 22000
     IB T220 GRAY 19900 22100, IB T250 INT 20300 22500, IB T280 GRAY 20400 22700
     IB T280 INT 20100 22400

36 4 SEA-SKIFF 6-8 SLPR  HT SDN  L/P  IB T210  INT 12 3 12600 2 9 20800 23100
     IB T220 GRAY 20900 23200, IB T250 INT 21100 23400, IB T280 GRAY 21500 23800
     IB T280 INT 21200 23500

36 4 SEA-SKIFF 6-8 SLPR  FB SDN  L/P  IB T210  INT 12 3 12600 2 9 20800 23100
     IB T220 GRAY 20900 23200, IB T250 INT 20500 22800, IB T280 GRAY 21500 23900
     IB T280 INT 21200 23600

36 4 SEA-VOYAGER 4 SLPR  HT EXP  M/P  IB T210  INT 12 3 12200 2 9 20700 23000
     IB T220 GRAY 20800 23100, IB T250 INT 21000 23300, IB T280 GRAY 21300 23700
     IB T280 INT 21000 23400

36 4 SEA-VOYAGER 4 SLPR  FB EXP  M/P  IB T210  INT 12 3 12200 2 9 20700 23000
     IB T220 GRAY 20800 23100, IB T250 INT 21000 23300, IB T280 GRAY 21200 23600
     IB T280 INT 21000 23300

36 4 SEA-VOYAGER 4-6 SLPR HT SDN  M/P IB T210 GRAY 12 3 12800 2 9 21800 24200
     IB T220 GRAY 21800 24300, IB T250 INT 22000 24500, IB T280 GRAY 22400 24900
     IB T280 INT 22100 24500

36 4 SEA-VOYAGER 4-6 SLPR FB SDN  M/P IB T210  INT 12 3 12800 2 9 21700 24100
     IB T220 GRAY 21800 24200, IB T250 INT 22000 24400, IB T280 GRAY 22300 24800
     IB T280 INT 22100 24500

36 4 SEA-VOYAGER 6 SLPR   HT EXP  M/P IB T210  INT 12 3 12200 2 9 19700 21800
     IB T220 GRAY 19700 21900, IB T250 INT 19900 22100, IB T280 GRAY 20200 22500
     IB T280 INT 19900 22200

36 4 SEA-VOYAGER 6 SLPR   FB EXP  M/P IB T210  INT 12 3 12200 2 9 19700 21900
     IB T220 GRAY 19800 22000, IB T250 INT 19900 22100, IB T280 GRAY 20300 22500
     IB T280 INT 20000 22200

36 4 SEA-VOYAGER 6-8 SLPR HT SDN  M/P IB T210  INT 12 3 12800 2 9 20700 23000
     IB T220 GRAY 20700 23000, IB T250 INT 20900 23200, IB T280 GRAY 21300 23700
     IB T280 INT 21000 23400

36 4 SEA-VOYAGER 6-8 SLPR FB SDN  M/P IB T210  INT 12 3 12800 2 9 20700 23000
     IB T220 GRAY 20800 23100, IB T250 INT 21000 23300, IB T280 GRAY 21300 23700
     IB T280 INT 21100 23400

42 5 SEA-VOYAGER         HT MY   M/P  IB T238 GRAY 14 10 22000 3  32400 36000
     IB T250 INT 32700 36400, IB T280 INT 33600 37300, IB T300 INT 34200 38000
     IB T140D GM 34600 38400, IB T215D GM 37100 41200
--------------------------- 1965 BOATS -------------------------------------------------
21 1 MANHATTAN SEA SKIFF OP RNBT L/P  IB 109-195   8  6 2500 1 10 2200 2700
21 1 MARTINIQUE SEA SKIFF FB SF  L/P  IB 109-195   8  6 2500 1 10 2200 2700
24 6 BIMINI SEA SKIFF    HT SF   L/P  IB 190-195   9  3 3900 2    3650 4250
24 6 SEA-BREEZE          OP EXP  PLY  IB 190-195   9  3 4300    2  3900 4450
24 6 SEA-SKIFF           OP EXP  L/P  IB 190-195   9  3 4300    2  3900 4550
27 9 BIMINI SEA SKIFF    HT SF   L/P  IB 190-220  10 10 5200 2 2  5500 6500
27 9 BIMINI SEA SKIFF    HT SF   L/P  IB T100-T140 10 10 5200 2 2  5600 6400
27 9 BIMINI SEA SKIFF    FB SF   L/P  IB T190-T195 10 10 5200 2 2  6350 7350
27 9 SEA-BREEZE          OP EXP  PLY  IB 190-220  10 10 5400 2 2  5600 6600
27 9 SEA-BREEZE          OP EXP  PLY  IB T140-T195 10 10 5400 2 2  5900 7450
27 9 SEA-SKIFF           OP EXP  L/P  IB 190-220  10 10 5600 2 2  5700 6700
27 9 SEA-SKIFF           OP EXP  L/P  IB T140-T195 10 10 5600 2 2  6150 7550

27 9 SEA-VOYAGER         OP EXP  M/P  IB 190-220  10 10 6400 2 2  6150 7100
27 9 SEA-VOYAGER         OP EXP  M/P  IB T140-T195 10 10 6400 2 2  6500 7900
30 2 SEA-BREEZE          OP EXP  PLY  IB 210-220  11    7200 2 4  9050 10300
30 2 SEA-BREEZE          OP EXP  PLY  IB T190-T220 11    7200 2 4  9900 11600
30 2 SEA-SKIFF           OP EXP  L/P  IB 210-220  11    7400 2 4  9450 10400
30 2 SEA-SKIFF           OP EXP  L/P  IB T190-T220 11    7400 2 4 10400 11600
30 2 SEA-VOYAGER         OP EXP  M/P  IB 210-220  11    8900 2 4  9950 11600
30 2 SEA-VOYAGER         OP EXP  M/P  IB T190-T220 11 1  8900 2 4 10500 12200
33   SEA-SKIFF           HT EXP  L/P  IB T210-T280 12    11050 2 8 14500 17100
33   SEA-SKIFF           HT SDN  L/P  IB T210-T280 12    11650 2 8 15700 18700
33   SEA-VOYAGER 4 SLPR  FB EXP  M/P  IB T210-T280 12    11250 2 8 14700 16900
33   SEA-VOYAGER 6 SLPR  HT EXP  M/P  IB T210-T280 12    11250 2 8 14400 17000

33   SEA-VOYAGER 6-8 SLPR HT SDN M/P  IB T210-T280 12    11500 2 8 15300 18300
36 4 SEA-SKIFF           HT EXP  L/P  IB T210  INT 12 3 12000 2 9 19500 21700
     IB T220 GRAY 19600 21800, IB T240 INT 17900 21900, IB T280 GRAY 19900 22100
```

LOA FT	LOA IN	NAME AND/ OR MODEL	TOP/ RIG	BOAT TYPE	-HULL- MTL	-HULL- TP	ENGINE TP	ENGINE # HP	ENGINE MFG	BEAM FT	BEAM IN	WGT LBS	DRAFT FT	DRAFT IN	RETAIL LOW	RETAIL HIGH
		1965 BOATS														
36	4	SEA-SKIFF	HT	EXP	L/P		IB	T280	INT	12	3	12000	2	9	19900	22100
36	4	SEA-SKIFF	HT	SDN	L/P		IB	T210	INT	12	3	12600	2	9	20500	22800
		IB T220 GRAY 20600 22800, IB T240 INT 20700 23000, IB T280 GRAY 21000 23300														
		IB T280 INT 21000 23300														
36	4	SEA-VOYAGER 4 SLPR	HT	EXP	M/P		IB	T210	INT	12	3	12200	2	8	20100	22300
		IB T220 GRAY 20100 22400, IB T240 INT 20200 22400, IB T280 GRAY 20200 22400														
		IB T280 INT 20200 22500														
36	4	SEA-VOYAGER 4-6 SLPR	HT	SDN	M/P		IB	T210	INT	12	3	12800	2	8	21000	23400
		IB T220 GRAY 21100 23400, IB T240 INT 21200 23600, IB T280 GRAY 21500 23800														
		IB T280 INT 21500 23900														
36	4	SEA-VOYAGER 6 SLPR	HT	EXP	M/P		IB	T210	INT	12	3	12200	2	8	19300	21500
		IB T220 GRAY 19400 21500, IB T240 INT 19500 21700, IB T280 GRAY 19500 21600														
		IB T280 INT 20500 22800														
36	4	SEA-VOYAGER 6-8 SLPR	HT	SDN	M/P		IB	T210	INT	12	3	12800	2	8	20300	22500
		IB T220 GRAY 20300 22600, IB T240 INT 20500 22700, IB T280 GRAY 20700 23000														
		IB T280 INT 20800 23100														
		1964 BOATS														
21	1	MANHATTAN SEA SKIFF	OP	RNBT	L/P		IB	109-140		8	6	2500	1	10	2100	2550
21	1	MARTINIQUE SEA SKIFF	FB	SF	L/P		IB	109-140		8	6	2500	1	10	2050	2550
24	6	BIMINI SEA SKIFF	HT	SF	L/P		IB	190-195		9	3	3900	2		3500	4100
24	6	BIMINI SEA SKIFF	FB	SF	L/P		IB	190-195		9	3	3900	2		3500	4100
24	6	SEA-BREEZE 4 SLPR	OP	EXP	PLY		IB	190-195		9	3	4200	2		3700	4300
24	6	SEA-SKIFF 4 SLPR	OP	EXP	L/P		IB	190-195		9	3	4300	2		3750	4350
27	9	SEA-BREEZE 4 SLPR	OP	EXP	PLY		IB	190-220		10	10	5400	2	2	5400	6350
27	9	SEA-BREEZE 4 SLPR	OP	EXP	PLY		IB	T100-T140		10	10	5400	2	2	5450	6700
27	9	SEA-BREEZE 4 SLPR	OP	EXP	PLY		IB	T190-T195		10	10	5400	2	2	6200	7150
27	9	SEA-BREEZE 4 SLPR	FB	EXP	PLY		IB	190-220		10	10	5400	2	2	5400	6350
27	9	SEA-BREEZE 4 SLPR	FB	EXP	PLY		IB	T100-T140		10	10	5400	2	2	5450	6700
27	9	SEA-BREEZE 4 SLPR	FB	EXP	PLY		IB	T190-T195		10	10	5400	2	2	6200	7150
27	9	SEA-SKIFF 4 SLPR	OP	EXP	L/P		IB	190-220		10	10	5600	2	2	5500	6450
27	9	SEA-SKIFF 4 SLPR	OP	EXP	L/P		IB	T100-T140		10	10	5600	2	2	5550	6800
27	9	SEA-SKIFF 4 SLPR	OP	EXP	L/P		IB	T190-T195		10	10	5600	2	2	6300	7250
27	9	SEA-SKIFF 4 SLPR	FB	EXP	L/P		IB	190-220		10	10	5600	2	2	5500	6450
27	9	SEA-SKIFF 4 SLPR	FB	EXP	L/P		IB	T100-T140				5600	2	2	5500	6800
27	9	SEA-SKIFF 4 SLPR	FB	EXP	L/P		IB	T190-T195		10	10	5600	2	2	6300	7250
27	9	SEA-VOYAGER 4 SLPR	OP	EXP	PLY		IB	190		10	10	6400	2	2	5850	6700
27	9	SEA-VOYAGER 4 SLPR	OP	EXP	WD		IB	195							6150	7050
27	9	SEA-VOYAGER 4 SLPR	OP	EXP	PLY		IB	210-220		10	10	6400	2	2	5950	6850
27	9	SEA-VOYAGER 4 SLPR	OP	EXP	PLY		IB	T138-T195		10	10	6400	2	2	6250	7650
27	9	SEA-VOYAGER 4 SLPR	FB	EXP	PLY		IB	190-220		10	10	6400	2	2	5850	6850
27	9	SEA-VOYAGER 4 SLPR	FB	EXP	PLY		IB	T138-T195		10	10	6400	2	2	6250	7650
30	2	SEA-BREEZE 6 SLPR	OP	EXP	PLY		IB	210-220		11		7200	2	4	8600	9950
30	2	SEA-BREEZE 6 SLPR	OP	EXP	PLY		IB	T190-T220		11		7200	2	4	9550	11200
30	2	SEA-BREEZE 6 SLPR	FB	EXP	PLY		IB	210-220		11		7200	2	4	8600	9950
30	2	SEA-BREEZE 6 SLPR	FB	EXP	PLY		IB	T190-T220		11		7200	2	4	9550	11200
30	2	SEA-SKIFF 6 SLPR	OP	EXP	L/P		IB	210-220		11		7400	2	4	8700	10000
30	2	SEA-SKIFF 6 SLPR	OP	EXP	L/P		IB	T190-T220		11		7400	2	4	9600	11200
30	2	SEA-SKIFF 6 SLPR	FB	EXP	L/P		IB	210-220		11		7400	2	4	8700	10000
30	2	SEA-SKIFF 6 SLPR	FB	EXP	L/P		IB	T190-T220		11		7400	2	4	9600	11200
30	2	SEA-VOYAGER 6 SLPR	OP	EXP	M/P		IB	T190-T220		11	1	8900	2	4	10100	11700
30	2	SEA-VOYAGER 6 SLPR	FB	EXP	M/P		IB	T190-T220		11	1	8900	2	4	10100	11700
33		SEA-VOYAGER 6 SLPR	OP	EXP	M/P		IB	T190-T240		12		11250	2	8	13900	16200
33		SEA-VOYAGER 6 SLPR	FB	EXP	M/P		IB	T190-T240		12		11250	2	8	13900	16200
33		SEA-VOYAGER 6-8 SLPR	HT	SDN	M/P		IB	T190-T240		12		11500	2	8	14900	17500
33		SEA-VOYAGER 6-8 SLPR	FB	SDN	M/P		IB	T190-T240		12		11500	2	8	14900	17500
36	4	SEA-VOYAGER 6 SLPR	HT	EXP	M/P		IB	T190	INT	12	3	12200	2	9	19100	21200
		IB T195 GRAY 19100 21300, IB T210 INT 19200 21300, IB T220 GRAY 19200 21400														
		IB T238 GRAY 19300 21500, IB T240 INT 19300 21500														
36	4	SEA-VOYAGER 6 SLPR	FB	EXP	M/P		IB	T190	INT	12	3	12200	2	9	19100	21200
		IB T195 GRAY 19100 21300, IB T210 INT 19200 21300, IB T220 GRAY 19200 21400														
		IB T238 GRAY 19300 21500, IB T240 INT 19300 21500														
36	4	SEA-VOYAGER 6-8 SLPR	HT	SDN	M/P		IB	T190	INT	12	3	12800	2	9	20000	22200
		IB T195 GRAY 20000 22300, IB T210 INT 20100 22400, IB T220 GRAY 20200 22400														
		IB T238 GRAY 20300 22600, IB T240 INT 20300 22600														
36	4	SEA-VOYAGER 6-8 SLPR	FB	SDN	M/P		IB	T190	INT	12	3	12800	2	9	20000	22200
		IB T195 GRAY 20000 22300, IB T210 INT 20100 22400, IB T220 GRAY 20200 22400														
		IB T238 GRAY 20300 22600, IB T240 GRAY 20300 22600														
		1963 BOATS														
21	1	MANHATTAN SEA SKIFF	OP	RNBT	L/P		IB	100	INT	8	6	2500	1	10	2000	2400
21	1	MARTINIQUE SEA SKIFF	FB	SF	L/P		IB	100	INT	8	6	2500	1	10	1950	2350
24	6	BIMINI SEA SKIFF	HT	SF	L/P		IB	185-188		9	3	3900	1	8	3400	3950
24	6	SEA-BREEZE	OP	EXP	PLY		IB	185-188		9	3	4200	1	8	3550	4150
24	6	SEA-SKIFF	OP	EXP	L/P		IB	185-188		9	3	4200	1	8	3550	4150
27		SEA-BREEZE	OP	EXP	PLY		IB	185-215		9	5	5200	2	1	4700	5500
27		SEA-BREEZE	OP	EXP	PLY		IB	T100-T138		9	5	5200	2	1	4800	5850
27		SEA-BREEZE	OP	EXP	PLY		IB	T185-T188		9	5	5200	2	1	5400	6200
27	4	SEA-SKIFF		EXP	L/P		IB	T135	INT	9	5	5200	2	1	5200	5950
27	4	SEA-SKIFF	OP	EXP	L/P		IB	185-215		9	5	5200	2	1	4800	5650
27	4	SEA-SKIFF	OP	EXP	L/P		IB	T100-T138		9	5	5200	2	1	4900	6000
27	4	SEA-SKIFF	OP	EXP	L/P		IB	T185-T188		9	5	5200	2	1	5550	6400
30	1	SEA-BREEZE	OP	EXP	PLY		IB	215		10	6	7200	2	4	8200	9400
30	1	SEA-BREEZE	OP	EXP	PLY		IB	T185-T215		10	6	7200	2	4	9100	10600
30	1	SEA-SKIFF	OP	EXP	L/P		IB	215		10	6	7200	2	4	8200	9400
30	1	SEA-SKIFF	OP	EXP	L/P		IB	T185-T215		10	6	7200	2	4	9100	10600
		1962 BOATS														
21	1	BIMINI SEA SKIFF	HT	SF	L/P		IB	100-138		8		2800	1	10	1950	2450
21	1	SEA-BREEZE	OP	EXP	PLY		IB	100-138		8		3200	1	10	2200	2650
21	1	SEA-SKIFF	OP	EXP	L/P		IB	100-185		8		3200	1	10	2200	2700
23		SEA-BREEZE	OP	EXP	PLY		IB	135-185		8		3800	1	8	2850	3350
23		SEA-SKIFF	OP	EXP	L/P		IB	135-185		8		3800	1	8	2850	3350
23		SEA-SKIFF	HT	SF	L/P		IB	135-185		8		3400	1	8	2600	3100
26	1	SEA-BREEZE	OP	EXP	PLY		IB	135-215		9	5	4750	2	1	3900	4850
26	1	SEA-BREEZE	OP	EXP	PLY		IB	T100-T138		9	5	4750	2	1	4150	5150
26	1	SEA-SKIFF	OP	EXP	L/P		IB	135-215		9	5	4750	2	1	3900	4850
26	1	SEA-SKIFF	OP	EXP	L/P		IB	T100-T138		9	5	4750	2	1	4150	5150
29		SEA-VOYAGER	OP	EXP	M/P		IB	178-215		10		8000	2		7000	8200
29		SEA-VOYAGER	OP	EXP	M/P		IB	T178-T215		10		8000	2		7750	9150
29		SEA-VOYAGER	HT	SDN	M/P		IB	178-215		10		8000	2		7500	8850
29		SEA-VOYAGER	HT	SDN	M/P		IB	T178-T215		10		8000	2		8500	10100
30	1	SEA-BREEZE	OP	EXP	PLY		IB	178-215		10	6	7200	2	4	7800	9200
30	1	SEA-BREEZE	OP	EXP	PLY		IB	T135-T215		10	6	7200	2	4	8300	10400
30	1	SEA-SKIFF	OP	EXP	L/P		IB	178-215		10	6	7200	2	4	7800	9200
30	1	SEA-SKIFF	OP	EXP	L/P		IB	T135-T185		10	6	7200	2	4	8300	10100
30	1	SEA-SKIFF	OP	EXP	M/P		IB	T215	GRAY	12		11250	2	4	10500	11900
33		SEA-VOYAGER	OP	EXP	M/P		IB	T178-T240		12		11250	2	4	13000	15300
36		SEA-VOYAGER	HT	EXP	M/P		IB	T178	GRAY	12		12000	2	4	16800	19100
		IB T185 INT 16900 19200, IB T215 INT 17000 19300, IB T238 GRAY 19500 21700														
		IB T240 INT 17100 19500														
36		SEA-VOYAGER	HT	SDN	M/P		IB	T178	GRAY	12		12800	2	4	18200	20200
		IB T185 INT 18200 20200, IB T215 INT 18400 20400, IB T238 GRAY 18500 20600														
		IB T240 INT 18600 20600														
		1961 BOATS														
18		MARLIN		FSH	L/P		OB			7	7	1200			2650	3100
18		SEA-BREEZE		CR	PLY		OB			7	7	1800			3600	4150
21		BIMINI		SF	PLY		OB			8		2000			4750	5450
21		BIMINI	HT	SF	PLY		IB	85-100		8			1	9	1850	2200
21		BIMINI	HT	SF	PLY		IB	135-138		8			1	9	1950	2300
21		SEA-BREEZE		CR	PLY		OB			8		2400			5300	6100
21		SEA-BREEZE	OP	EXP	PLY		IB	85-100		8			1	9	1950	2400
21		SEA-BREEZE	OP	EXP	PLY		IB	135-138		8			1	9	2050	2500
23		BIMINI	HT	SF	PLY		IB	135-185		8			1	8	3050	3600
23		SEA-BREEZE	OP	EXP	PLY		IB	135-185		8			1	8	3050	3600
23		SEA-BREEZE	HT	SDN	PLY		IB	135-185		8			1	8	2800	3300
26		SEA-BREEZE	OP	EXP	PLY		IB	135-225		9	4		2	1	4100	5050
26		SEA-BREEZE	OP	EXP	PLY		IB	T 85-T100		9	4		2	1	4200	5000
26		SEA-BREEZE	OP	EXP	PLY		IB	T135	INT	9	4		2	1	4600	5300
29		SEA-BREEZE	OP	EXP	PLY		IB	177-225		10	6		2	3	7100	8400
29		SEA-BREEZE	OP	EXP	PLY		IB	T177-T225		10	6		2	3	7800	9350
33		SEA-BREEZE	HT	EXP	P/P		IB	T177-T240		12			2	4	12700	15000
		1960 BOATS														
18	4	BIMINI	OP	SF	L/P	DV	OB			7	7	2000			3850	4450
18	4	SEA-BREEZE	OP	EXP	PLY	DV	OB			7	7	2150			4000	4650
21			OP	EXP	PLY	DV	OB			8		2000			4750	5500
21			OP	EXP	PLY	DV	IB	135	INT	8			1	9	2050	2400
21		BIMINI		SF	L/P	DV	OB			8		2000			4750	5500
21		BIMINI		SF	L/P	DV	IB	135	INT	8			1	9	1900	2250
23			OP	EXP	PLY		IB	135-170		8			1	8	3000	3550
23			HT	SDN	PLY		IB	135-170		8			1	8	2700	3200
23		BIMINI	HT	SF	L/P		IB	135-170		8			1	8	3000	3550
25			OP	EXP	PLY		IB	135-215		9	4		1	11	3700	4500
29			OP	EXP	P/M		IB	135-225		10			2		6800	8150

 CONTINUED ON NEXT PAGE

TROJAN EXPRESS YACHTS   -CONTINUED   See inside cover to adjust price for area

LOA FT IN	NAME AND/ OR MODEL	TOP/ RIG	BOAT TYPE	HULL MTL TP	ENGINE TP # HP MFG	BEAM FT IN	WGT LBS	DRAFT FT IN	RETAIL LOW	RETAIL HIGH
1960 BOATS										
29		OP	EXP	P/M	IB T185-T225 10			2	7650	9100
33	SIX SLEEPER	HT	EXP	P/M	IB T135-T225 12			2 4	12100	14600
1959 BOATS										
16 4	SEA-QUEEN CUSTOM	OP	RNBT	PLY	OB	6 8			1800	2150
16 4	SEA-QUEEN DELUXE	OP	RNBT	PLY	OB	6 8			1800	2150
18 4	BIMINI	OP	SF	L/P	OB	7 7			2500	2950
18 4	BIMINI 19 SEMI-ENCL	OP	SF	WD	IB 125	7 7			2250	2600
21	SEA-BREEZE	OP	EXP	WD	OB				3350	3850
22 1	BIMINI 23 SEMI-ENCL	SF		WD	IB 170 8				2500	2950
22 1	SEA-BREEZE	CR		WD	IB 170-185 8				2500	2900
22 1	SEA-BREEZE	OP	EXP	WD	IB 135-170 8				2400	2850
25 2	SEA-BREEZE	CR		WD	IB 170-225 8				3600	4450
27 1	SEA-BREEZE	CR		WD	IB 215 9 2				5050	5800
27 1	SEA-BREEZE	CR		WD	IB T225 10				5800	6650
1958 BOATS										
17	MARLIN	OP	FSH	WD	OB				2200	2600
19	BIMINI	SF		WD	OB				3900	4500
19	BIMINI SEMI-ENCL	SF		WD	IB 125				1750	2100
19	SEA-BREEZE FAM CR	CR		WD	OB				2800	3250
22	BIMINI SEMI-ENCL	SF		WD	OB				6300	7250
22	BIMINI SEMI-ENCL	SF		WD	IB 150				2450	2850
22	SEA-BREEZE	EXP		WD	IB 109-150				2350	2800
22	SEA-BREEZE	SDN		WD	IB 150				2750	3200
22	SEA-BREEZE FAM CR	CR		WD	IB				4750	5450
25	SEA-BREEZE	EXP		WD	IB 225				3650	4250
27	SEA-BREEZE	EXP		WD	IB 225				4700	5400
1957 BOATS										
22	BIMINI SPORTSMAN	SF		WD	OB				6350	7300
22	SEA-BREEZE	CR		WD	OB				4800	5500
22	SEA-BREEZE	EXP		WD	IB 120				2350	2950
22	SEA-BREEZE	SDN		WD	IB 100				2600	3050
25	SEA-BREEZE	EXP		WD	IB 170				3550	4100
1956 BOATS										
18	SEA-BREEZE	CR		WD	OB				2500	2900
21	SEA-BREEZE	CR		WD	OB				4450	5100
21	SEA-BREEZE	CR		WD	IB 100				1850	2200
21	SEA-BREEZE	SDN		WD	IB 100				2000	2400
25	SEA-BREEZE	CR		WD	IB 145				3450	4000
1955 BOATS										
18	SEA-BREEZE 218	RNBT		WD	OB				3050	3550
20	SEA-BREEZE 220	RNBT		WD	OB				4100	4800
24	SEA-BREEZE 424	CR		WD	IB 100				2750	3200
1954 BOATS										
20	SEA-BREEZE	CR		WD	OB				3850	4450
1953 BOATS										
16	SEA-QUEEN DELUXE	HT	SDN	FBG	IB 225D CAT 13		12000	2 6	10500	11900
1950 BOATS										
19 8	CAR CARRY	OP		PLY	OB				3000	3500

TROPICAL MARINE INC
COAST GUARD MFG ID- TTV

Call 1-800-327-6929 for BUC Personalized Evaluation Service
Or, for 1968 boats, sign onto www.BUCValuPro.com

A R TRUE INC
COAST GUARD MFG ID- ART

Call 1-800-327-6929 for BUC Personalized Evaluation Service
Or, for 1950 to 1972 boats, sign onto www.BUCValuPro.com

TRUE NORTH MRNE IND INC
COAST GUARD MFG ID- TNS

Call 1-800-327-6929 for BUC Personalized Evaluation Service
Or, for 1977 to 1979 boats, sign onto www.BUCValuPro.com

TRUE WORLD MARINE
HOBY WORLD DEVELOPMENT   COAST GUARD MFG ID- TZO

Call 1-800-327-6929 for BUC Personalized Evaluation Service
Or, for 1982 to 2008 boats, sign onto www.BUCValuPro.com

TRUMP YACHTS
STONINGTON CT 06378   COAST GUARD MFG ID- TMP See inside cover to adjust price for area

For more recent years, see the BUC Used Boat Price Guide, Volume 1 or Volume 2

LOA FT IN	NAME AND/ OR MODEL	TOP/ RIG	BOAT TYPE	HULL MTL TP	ENGINE TP # HP MFG	BEAM FT IN	WGT LBS	DRAFT FT IN	RETAIL LOW	RETAIL HIGH
1983 BOATS										
20 6	COMPANION	SLP	SA/CR	FBG KL	OB	7 1	3000	2 9	7050	8150
1982 BOATS										
20 6	COMPANION	SLP	SA/RC	FBG KL	OB	7 1	3000	2 9	6650	7650
1981 BOATS										
18 3	MINI-CUP	SLP	SA/RC	FBG KL	OB	4 6	1700	3 3	4150	4800
1977 BOATS										
24 7	MARGARET-D	KTH	SAIL	FBG KL IB	7D	8 2	5250	3 4	11600	13200
1976 BOATS										
18 3	MINI-CUP RACER	SLP	SAIL	FBG KL		4 5	1700	3 2	3450	4000
24 7	MARGARET-D	KTH	SAIL	FBG KL OB		8	5250	3 4	10600	12000
24 7	MARGARET-D	KTH	SAIL	FBG KL IB	8	8		3 4	8900	10100
24 7	MARGARET-D	KTH	SAIL	FBG KL IB	5D	8		3 4	9700	11000

TRUMPY & SONS
ANNAPOLIS MD   COAST GUARD MFG ID- JTS See inside cover to adjust price for area

LOA FT IN	NAME AND/ OR MODEL	TOP/ RIG	BOAT TYPE	HULL MTL TP	ENGINE TP # HP MFG	BEAM FT IN	WGT LBS	DRAFT FT IN	RETAIL LOW	RETAIL HIGH
1972 BOATS										
72		HT	MY	WD	IB T D GM				**	**
1970 BOATS										
58		HT	FD	FBG	IB T370D CUM				222500	244500
1969 BOATS										
58		HT	FD	WD	IB T D CUM				**	**
1964 BOATS										
60			FD	WD	IB T325D GM				169000	185500
1962 BOATS										
47			FD	WD	IB T185D GM				107000	117500
1960 BOATS										
57			FD	WD	IB T325D GM				156500	172000
1958 BOATS										
53		HT	FD	MHG	IB T235D GM 14 6			4 6	115500	127000
1957 BOATS										
55			YTFS	WD	IB T370D CUM				145000	159500
1951 BOATS										
50		HT	SF	WD	IB T D GM				**	**
1947 BOATS										
55	CRUISING HOUSEBOAT	HT	HB	WD	IB T140D GM				28300	31500
60	CRUISING HOUSEBOAT	HT	HB	WD	IB T200D GM				**	**

TRUSCOTT BOAT & DOCK CO

Call 1-800-327-6929 for BUC Personalized Evaluation Service
Or, for 1946 boats, sign onto www.BUCValuPro.com

TSUNAMI MARINE INC

Call 1-800-327-6929 for BUC Personalized Evaluation Service
Or, for 1983 to 1985 boats, sign onto www.BUCValuPro.com

TURNER MARINE
COAST GUARD MFG ID- TUN

Call 1-800-327-6929 for BUC Personalized Evaluation Service
Or, for 1975 to 2005 boats, sign onto www.BUCValuPro.com

TYLER BOAT CO LTD
TONBRIDGE KENT ENGLAND   See inside cover to adjust price for area

LOA FT IN	NAME AND/ OR MODEL	TOP/ RIG	BOAT TYPE	HULL MTL TP	ENGINE TP # HP MFG	BEAM FT IN	WGT LBS	DRAFT FT IN	RETAIL LOW	RETAIL HIGH
1983 BOATS										
18 2	NELSON 18			FBG DS	IB	6 11			**	**
27 3	WASP	PH		FBG DS	IB	9 3			**	**
28 3	TYLER 28	SLP	SA/CR	FBG KL	IB D	8 1	8900	5	28100	31200

LOA FT	LOA IN	NAME AND/ OR MODEL	TOP/ RIG	BOAT TYPE	HULL MTL	HULL TP	ENGINE TP	#	HP	MFG	BEAM FT	BEAM IN	WGT LBS	DRAFT FT	DRAFT IN	RETAIL LOW	RETAIL HIGH
		1983 BOATS															
30	3	HORNET		PH	FBG	DS	IB				9	3				**	**
30	4	TYLER 31	SLP	SA/CR	FBG	KL	IB		D		10	1	7000	5	7	22600	25100
33	6	NELSON 34		CBNCR	FBG	DS	IB				9	3		3		**	**
35		TYLER-VORTEX 35		MY	FBG	DS	IB				11	1				**	**
37		ENDURANCE 37	KTH	SA/CR	FBG	KL	IB		D		11	6	17800	5	3	60300	66200
42		SLIPPER 42	KTH	SA/CR	FBG	KL	IB		D		12	3	16500	5	10	71900	79000
43		TYLER-VORTEX 43			FBG	DS	IB				13	11				**	**
44	4	CORSAIR 44	SLP	SA/CR	FBG	KL	IB		D		12	11	10507	7		66900	73500
44	5	NELSON 45		MY	FBG	DS	IB				12	4		3	6	**	**
50		HALBERDIER 50			FBG	DS	IB				15	8				**	**
52	1	POSEIDON MARK I			FBG	DS	IB				15	4				**	**
55		HALBERDIER 55			FBG	DS	IB				15	8				**	**
56	4	NELSON 56		MY	FBG	DS	IB				15	7				**	**
60	4	NELSON 60		MY	FBG	DS	IB				15	7				**	**
70		NELSON 70		MY	FBG	DS	IB				19	11				**	**
74	9	NELSON 75		MY	FBG	DS	IB				19	11				**	**
		1982 BOATS															
18	2	NELSON 18			FBG	DS	IB		D		6	11				**	**
27	3	WASP		PH	FBG	DS	IB		D		9	3				**	**
28	3	TYLER 28	SLP	SA/CR	FBG	KL	IB		D		8	1	8800	5		26100	29000
30	3	HORNET		PH	FBG	DS	IB		D		9	3				**	**
30	4	TYLER 31	SLP	SA/CR	FBG	KL	IB		D		10	1	7000	5	7	21200	23600
33	6	NELSON 34		CBNCR	FBG	DS	IB		D		9	3		3		**	**
37		ENDURANCE 37	KTH	SA/CR	FBG	KL	IB		D		11	6	17800	5	3	56700	62300
42		SLIPPER 42	KTH	SA/CR	FBG	KL	IB		D		12	3	16500	5	10	67600	74300
43		TYLER-VORTEX 43			FBG	DS	IB		D		13	11				**	**
44	4	CORSAIR 44	SLP	SA/CR	FBG	KL	IB		D		12	11	10507	7		62900	69100
44	5	NELSON 45		MY	FBG	DS	IB		D		12	4		3	6	**	**
50		HALBERDIER 50			FBG	DS	IB		D		15	8				**	**
52	1	POSEIDON MARK I			FBG	DS	IB		D		15	4				**	**
55		HALBERDIER 55			FBG	DS	IB		D		15	8				**	**
56	4	NELSON 56		MY	FBG	DS	IB		D		15	7				**	**
60	4	NELSON 60		MY	FBG	DS	IB		D		15	7				**	**
70		NELSON 70		MY	FBG	DS	IB		D		19	11				**	**
74	9	NELSON 75		MY	FBG	DS	IB		D		19	11				**	**
		1981 BOATS															
18	2	NELSON 18			FBG	DS	IB		D		6	11				**	**
27	3	WASP		PH	FBG	DS	IB		D		9	3				**	**
28	3	TYLER 28TG	SLP	SA/CR	FBG	KL	IB		D		8	1		5		24800	27500
30	3	HORNET		PH	FBG	DS	IB		D		9	3				**	**
30	4	TYLER 31TG	SLP	SA/CR	FBG	KL	IB		D		10	1		5	7	19800	22000
33	6	NELSON 34		CBNCR	FBG	DS	IB		D		9	3				**	**
37		ENDURANCE 37	KTH	SA/CR	FBG	KL	IB		D		11	6		5	3	53800	59100
42		SLIPPER 42	KTH	SA/CR	FBG	KL	IB		D		12	3		5	10	63600	69900
43		TYLER-VORTEX 43			FBG	DS	IB		D		13	11				**	**
44	4	CORSAIR 44	SLP	SA/CR	FBG	KL	IB		D		12	11		7		59200	65000
44	5	NELSON 45		MY	FBG	DS	IB		D		12	4				**	**
50		HALBERDIER 50			FBG	DS	IB		D		15	8				**	**
52	1	POSEIDON MARK I			FBG	DS	IB		D		15	4				**	**
55		HALBERDIER 55			FBG	DS	IB		D		15	8				**	**
56	4	NELSON 56		MY	FBG	DS	IB		D		15	7				**	**
60	4	NELSON 60		MY	FBG	DS	IB		D		15	7				**	**
70		NELSON 70		MY	FBG	DS	IB		D		19	11				**	**
74	9	NELSON 75		MY	FBG	DS	IB		D		19	11				**	**
		1980 BOATS															
28	3	TYLER 28	SLP	SA/CR	FBG	KL	IB		D		8	1	8900	5		23800	26400
30	4	TYLER 31	SLP	SA/CR	FBG	KL	IB		D		10	1	7000	5	7	19100	21200
37		ENDURANCE 37	KTH	SA/CR	FBG	KL	IB		D		11	6	17800	5	3	50900	56000
42		SLIPPER 42	KTH	SA/CR	FBG	KL	IB		D		12	3	16500	5	10	60700	66700
		1978 BOATS															
27		HARDY 8.25	HT	PH	FBG	DS	IB		D		9		9400	3	1	**	**
27		HORNET	HT	PH	FBG	DS	IB		D		9	9		2	4	**	**
27		HORNET	HT	PH	FBG	DS	IB	T	D		9	9		2	4	**	**
27		WASP	HT	PH	FBG	DS	IB		D		9	9		2	4	**	**
27		WASP	HT	PH	FBG	DS	IB	T	D		9	9		2	4	**	**
28	3	SLIPPER 28	SLP	SA/RC	FBG	KL	IB		D		8	10	4200	5	6	10300	11700
30		HORNET	HT	PH	FBG	DS	IB		D		9	9		2	4	**	**
30		HORNET	HT	PH	FBG	DS	IB	T	D		9	9		2	4	**	**
30		WASP	HT	PH	FBG	DS	IB		D		9	9		2	4	**	**
30		WASP	HT	PH	FBG	DS	IB	T	D		9	9		2	4	**	**
30	2	HUSTLER 30	SLP	SA/CR	FBG	KL	IB		8D	YAN	9	2	6800	5	6	16900	19200
30	9	HARDY 9.40	HT	PH	FBG	DS	IB		D		10	7	11000	3	3	**	**
32	9	NEPTUNE	SLP	MS	FBG	KL	IB		D	PERK	10		12200	4		31100	34500
32	9	NEPTUNE	KTH	MS	FBG	KL	IB		D	PERK	10		12200	4		31100	34500
32	9	NEPTUNIAN	SLP	SA/CR	FBG	KL	IB		D	PERK	10		12200	4		31100	34500
32	9	NEPTUNIAN	KTH	SA/CR	FBG	KL	IB		D	PERK	10		12200	4		31100	34500
34		NELSON 34 MKI	HT	CBNCR	FBG	DS	VD	T			9	3		3		**	**
34	6	OHLSON 35 MKII	SLP	SA/RC	FBG	KL	IB		12D- 18D		10	6		6	1	50500	55500
35	11	TRINTELLA III A	SLP	SA/CR	FBG	KL	IB		50D	PERK	10	6	20200	4	11	51200	56300
35	11	TRINTELLA III A	KTH	SA/CR	FBG	KL	IB		50D	PERK	10	6	20200	4	11	51200	56300
36	6	DORSET 36	HT	EXP	FBG	DS	IB			SABR	11			2	4	**	**
36	6	DORSET 36	HT	EXP	FBG	DS	IB		T145D	PERK	11			2	4	96200	105500
36	6	DORSET 36	HT	EXP	FBG	DS	IB		T175D	PERK	11			2	4	97600	107000
36	11	ENDURANCE 37	KTH	SA/CR	FBG	KL	IB		62D	PERK	11	6	18600	5	3	48800	53700
37		NORSEMAN 37 PH	HT	TRWL	FBG	DS	IB				13			4	6	**	**
40	3	VICTORY 40	KTH	MS	FBG	KL	IB		62D	PERK	11	6	24000	5	4	66400	72900
40	3	VICTORY 41	KTH	MS	FBG	KL	IB		62D	PERK	11	6	24000	5	4	66400	72900
40	8	POSEIDON 36/40	FB	MY	FBG	DS	IB		T200D	CAT	13	10	6500	4	4	64000	70300
42		SLIPPER 42	KTH	MS	FBG	KL	IB		45D	PERK	12	3	16600	5	10	56300	61800
42	6	LANCER	HT	MY	FBG	DS	IB				12	8		3	8	**	**
44	2	NELSON 45	HT	MY	FBG	DS	IB	T			12	4		3	6	**	**
48	5	VICTORY 48	KTH	MS	FBG	KL	IB		95D	PERK	13	4	36000	6	5	111500	122500
56	3	ENDURANCE 57	KTH	MS	FBG	CB	IB		95D	PERK	15	3		4	6	222000	244000
56	3	ENDURANCE 57	KTH	MS	FBG	KL	IB		95D	PERK	15	3		7	4	222000	244000
60		NELSON 60	HT	MY	FBG	DS	IB		T350D	CAT	16	6		5		123000	135000
71		OCEAN 71	KTH	MS	FBG	KL	IB		95D	PERK	17	5	54000	8	1	247500	272000
75		NELSON 75	HT	MY	FBG	DS	IB				19	9		4	6	**	**
		1974 BOATS															
21	11	INTERNATL-TEMPEST	SLP	SA/OD	FBG	KL	IB		D		6	6	1020	3	7	3600	4200
		1973 BOATS															
21	11	INTERNATL-TEMPEST	SLP	SA/OD	FBG	KL	IB		D		6	6	1020	3	7	3500	4100
		1972 BOATS															
22		INTERNATL-TEMPEST	SLP	SA/OD	FBG	KL					6	6	1020	3	7	2600	3000
26	9	SOLING	SLP	SA/OD	FBG	KL					6	3	2000	4	3	4450	5150
40		TRINTELLA IV	KTH	SA/CR	FBG	KL	IB		D		11	2		4	10	55900	61400
44	3	CORSAIR	SLP	SA/CR	FBG	KC	IB				13	2		5	3	79000	86800
44	3	CORSAIR	SLP	SA/CR	FBG	KL	IB				13	2		7		79000	86800
44	3	CORSAIR	YWL	SA/CR	FBG	KC	IB				13	2		5	3	79000	86800
44	3	CORSAIR	YWL	SA/CR	FBG	KL	IB				13	2		7		79000	86800
46	3	BOWMAN 46	YWL	SA/CR	FBG	KC	IB				13	2		5	3	75700	83200
46	3	BOWMAN 46	YWL	SA/CR	FBG	KL	IB				13	2		7		75700	83200
		1971 BOATS															
22		INTERNATL-TEMPEST	SLP	SA/OD	FBG	KL					6	6	1020	3	7	2550	2950
26	9	SOLING	SLP	SA/OD	FBG	KL					6	3	2200	4	3	4600	5300
		1970 BOATS															
26	9	SOLING	SLP	SA/OD	FBG	KL					6	3	2200	4	3	4500	5200

TYLERCRAFT INC

OAKDALE NY 11769

COAST GUARD MFG ID- TYL See inside cover to adjust price for area
FOR NEWER MODELS SEE CHICHESTER BOAT CO INC

LOA FT	LOA IN	NAME AND/ OR MODEL	TOP/ RIG	BOAT TYPE	HULL MTL	HULL TP	ENGINE TP	#	HP	MFG	BEAM FT	BEAM IN	WGT LBS	DRAFT FT	DRAFT IN	RETAIL LOW	RETAIL HIGH
		1977 BOATS															
24		TYLERCRAFT	SLP	SA/CR	FBG	KL	OB				7	6	4000	3	6	6300	7250
24		TYLERCRAFT	SLP	SA/CR	FBG	TK	OB				7	6	4000	2	2	6300	7250
26	2	TYLERCRAFT	SLP	SA/CR	FBG	KL	IB		D		8		5400	3	10	10200	11500
26	2	TYLERCRAFT	SLP	SA/CR	FBG	TK	IB		D		8		5400	2	7	10200	11600
29	3	TYLERCRAFT	SLP	SA/CR	FBG	KL	IB		D		8	8	7200	4	7	14700	16700
29	3	TYLERCRAFT	SLP	SA/CR	FBG	TK	IB		D		8	8	7200	2	10	14800	16800
40		TYLERCRAFT	SLP	SA/CR	FBG	KL	IB		D		13		22000	4	11	48600	53400
40		TYLERCRAFT	SLP	SA/CR	FBG	TK	IB		D		13		22000	3	8	48600	53400
40		TYLERCRAFT	CUT	SA/CR	FBG	KL	IB		D		13		22000	4	11	47600	52300
40		TYLERCRAFT	CUT	SA/CR	FBG	TK	IB		D		13		22000	3	8	47600	52300
40		TYLERCRAFT	KTH	SA/CR	FBG	KL	IB		D		13		22000	4	11	50900	55900
40		TYLERCRAFT	KTH	SA/CR	FBG	TK	IB		D		13		22000	3	8	50900	55900
		1976 BOATS															
24		TYLERCRAFT	SLP	SA/CR	FBG	KL	OB				7	5	4000	3	6	6100	7000
24		TYLERCRAFT	SLP	SA/CR	FBG	TK	OB				7	5	4000	2	2	6100	7000
26	2	TYLERCRAFT	SLP	SA/CR	FBG	KL	IB		D		8		5400	3	10	9900	11200
26	2	TYLERCRAFT	SLP	SA/CR	FBG	TK	IB		D		8		5400	2	7	9900	11300
29	3	TYLERCRAFT	SLP	SA/CR	FBG	KL	IB		40D		8	8	7200	4	7	14300	16200
29	3	TYLERCRAFT	SLP	SA/CR	FBG	TK	IB		40D		8	8	7200	2	10	14300	16300
40		TYLERCRAFT	SLP	SA/CR	FBG	KL	IB		40D		12	8	22000	4	11	46600	51200
40		TYLERCRAFT	SLP	SA/CR	FBG	TK	IB		40D		12	8	22000	3	8	46600	51200
40		TYLERCRAFT	CUT	SA/CR	FBG	KL	IB		40D		12	8	22000	4	11	45700	50200
40		TYLERCRAFT	CUT	SA/CR	FBG	TK	IB		40D		12	8	22000	3	8	45700	50200
40		TYLERCRAFT	KTH	SA/CR	FBG	KL	IB		40D		12	8	22000	4	11	49300	54200
40		TYLERCRAFT	KTH	SA/CR	FBG	TK	IB		40D		12	8	22000	3	8	49300	54200

 CONTINUED ON NEXT PAGE

LOA FT	LOA IN	NAME AND/ OR MODEL	TOP/ RIG	BOAT TYPE	HULL MTL	HULL TP	ENGINE TP	ENGINE # HP	ENGINE MFG	BEAM FT	BEAM IN	WGT LBS	DRAFT FT	DRAFT IN	RETAIL LOW	RETAIL HIGH
		1975 BOATS														
24		TYLERCRAFT	SLP	SA/CR	FBG	KL	OB			8		4000	3	6	5900	6750
24		TYLERCRAFT	SLP	SA/CR	FBG	TK	OB			8		4000	2	2	5900	6750
26	2	TYLERCRAFT	SLP	SA/CR	FBG	KL	IB	D		8		5200	3	10	9200	10500
26	2	TYLERCRAFT	SLP	SA/CR	FBG	TK	IB	D		8		5200	2	7	9250	10500
29	3	TYLERCRAFT	SLP	SA/CR	FBG	KL	IB	D		8	8	6700	4	7	12800	14500
29	3	TYLERCRAFT	SLP	SA/CR	FBG	TK	IB	D		8	8	6700	2	10	12900	14600
		1974 BOATS														
22		TYLERCRAFT	SLP	SA/CR	FBG	SK				7	7	2000	4	8	3200	3750
22		TYLERCRAFT	SLP	SA/CR	FBG	TK				7	7	2000	2		3200	3750
24		TYLERCRAFT	SLP	SA/CR	FBG	KL	OB			8		4000	3	6	5700	6550
24		TYLERCRAFT	SLP	SA/CR	FBG	TK	OB			8		4000	2	2	5700	6550
26		TYLERCRAFT	SLP	SA/CR	FBG	KL	IB	D		8		5200	3	10	8850	10100
26		TYLERCRAFT	SLP	SA/CR	FBG	TK	IB	D		8		5200	2	7	8900	10100
29	3	TYLERCRAFT	SLP	SA/CR	FBG	KL	IB	D		8	8	6700	4	7	12500	14200
29	3	TYLERCRAFT	SLP	SA/CR	FBG	TK	IB	D		8	8	6700	2	10	12600	14300
		1973 BOATS														
24		TYLERCRAFT	SLP	SA/CR	FBG	TK	OB			8		4000	2	2	5600	6450
26		TYLERCRAFT	SLP	SA/CR	FBG	TK	IB	D		8		5200	2	7	8500	9800
29	3	TYLERCRAFT	SLP	SA/CR	FBG	TK	IB	D		8	8	6500	2	10	11800	13500
		1972 BOATS														
18		TYLERCRAFT 18	SLP	SAIL	FBG	KL	OB			7			2	2	2350	2750
18		TYLERCRAFT 18	SLP	SAIL	FBG	TK	OB			7			2	2	2350	2750
24		TYLERCRAFT 24	SLP	SA/CR	FBG	KL	IB			7	5		3	9	5250	6050
24		TYLERCRAFT 24	SLP	SA/CR	FBG	TK	IB			7	5		2		5250	6050
26		TYLERCRAFT 26	SLP	SA/CR	FBG	KL	IB			8			3	11	8200	9400
26		TYLERCRAFT 26	SLP	SA/CR	FBG	TK	IB			8			2	7	8200	9450
29	3	TYLERCRAFT 29	SLP	SA/CR	FBG	KL	IB			8	6		4	10	13600	15400
29	3	TYLERCRAFT 29	SLP	SA/CR	FBG	TK	IB			8	6		2	10	13600	15400
		1971 BOATS														
17		TYLERCRAFT 17	SLP	SA/CR	FBG	TK	IB	5		7		1500	2		2550	2950
18		TYLERCRAFT 18		SAIL	FBG	KL	OB			7			3	9	2300	2650
18		TYLERCRAFT 18		SAIL	FBG	TK	OB			7			2		2300	2650
24		TYLERCRAFT 24		SAIL	FBG	KL	OB			7	5		3	11	5300	6100
24		TYLERCRAFT 24		SAIL	FBG	TK	OB			7	5		2	7	5300	6100
26		TYLERCRAFT 26		SAIL	FBG	KL	OB			8					6500	7500
26		TYLERCRAFT 26		SAIL	FBG	TK	OB			8			4	6	6550	7500
29	3	TYLERCRAFT 29		SAIL	FBG	KL	OB			8	8		4	6	8100	9300
29	3	TYLERCRAFT 29		SAIL	FBG	KL	IB		UNIV	8	8		4	6	13200	15000
29	3	TYLERCRAFT 29		SAIL	FBG	TK	OB			8	8		2	10	8150	9350
29	3	TYLERCRAFT 29		SAIL	FBG	TK	IB		UNIV	8	8		2	10	13300	15100
		1970 BOATS														
17		TYLERCRAFT 17	SLP	SA/CR	FBG	TK				7					1850	2250
24		TYLERCRAFT 24	SLP	SA/CR	FBG	KL				7	5	3650			4850	5550
24		TYLERCRAFT 24	SLP	SA/CR	FBG	KL	IB			7	5				5000	5750
24		TYLERCRAFT 24	SLP	SA/CR	FBG	TK				7	5	3650	2	1	4850	5550
24		TYLERCRAFT 24	SLP	SA/CR	FBG	TK	IB			7	5		2	1	5000	5750
27	6	TYLERCRAFT 27	SLP	SA/CR	FBG	KL				8					8500	9800
27	6	TYLERCRAFT 27	SLP	SA/CR	FBG	KL	IB			8					10800	12300
27	6	TYLERCRAFT 27	SLP	SA/CR	FBG	TK				8					8500	9800
27	6	TYLERCRAFT 27	SLP	SA/CR	FBG	TK	IB			8					10800	12300
30		TYLERCRAFT 30	SLP	SA/CR	FBG	TK				10		9250			13700	15600
		1969 BOATS														
17		TYLERCRAFT 17	SLP	SA/CR	FBG	TK	IB			7		1500	2		2600	3000
24		TYLERCRAFT 24	SLP	SA/CR	FBG	KL	OB			8			3	8	5100	5850
24		TYLERCRAFT 24	SLP	SA/CR	FBG	TK	OB			8		3650	2		4750	5450
27		TYLERCRAFT 27	SLP	SA/CR	FBG	KL				8		5500	4	2	7350	8450
27		TYLERCRAFT 27	SLP	SA/CR	FBG	TK				8			2	8	6500	7500
30		TYLERCRAFT 30	SLP	SA/CR	FBG	TK				10		9250	2	8	13500	15300
		1968 BOATS														
24		4 BERTH B WKNDR	SLP	SAIL	FBG	TK	OB			7	5	3890	2		5000	5700
24		4 BERTH C	SLP	SA/CR	FBG	TK	OB			7	5		2		5050	5800
24		4 BERTH D	SLP	SA/RC	FBG		OB			7	5	4030	2		5150	5900
24		DAYSAILER B	SLP	SAIL	FBG	TK	OB			7	5		2		5050	5800
		1967 BOATS														
24		4 BERTH B WKNDR	SLP	SAIL	FBG	TK	OB			7	5		2		5150	5900
24		4 BERTH B WKNDR	SLP	SAIL	FBG	TK	JT			7	5		2		4750	5500
24		4 BERTH B WKNDR	SLP	SAIL	FBG	TK	IB	10		7	5		2		4900	5600
24		4 BERTH C	SLP	SA/CR	FBG	TK	OB			7	5		2		5000	5750
24		4 BERTH C	SLP	SA/CR	FBG	TK	IB	10		7	5		2		4750	5450
24		4 BERTH C	SLP	SAIL	FBG	KL	JT			7	5		2		5000	5750
24		4 BERTH D	SLP	SA/RC	FBG	TK	OB			7	5		2		5000	5750
24		4 BERTH D	SLP	SA/RC	FBG	TK	IB	10		7	5		2		5300	6100
24		4 BERTH D	SLP	SAIL	FBG	TK	JT			7	5		2		5400	6250
24		DAYSAILER MDL B	SLP	SAIL	FBG	TK	OB			7	5		2		4850	5550
24		DAYSAILER MDL B	SLP	SAIL	FBG	TK	JT			7	5		2		4500	5150
24		DAYSAILER MDL B	SLP	SAIL	FBG	TK	IB	10		7	5		2		4650	5300
		1966 BOATS														
24		4 BERTH B WKNDR	SLP	SAIL	FBG	KL	OB			7	5		2		5050	5800
24		4 BERTH B WKNDR	SLP	SAIL	FBG	KL	JT			7	5		2		4700	5400
24		4 BERTH B WKNDR	SLP	SAIL	FBG	KL	IB	10		7	5		2		4850	5550
24		4 BERTH C	SLP	SA/CR	FBG	KL	OB			7	5		2		4950	5700
24		4 BERTH C	SLP	SA/CR	FBG	KL	IB	10		7	5		2		4700	5400
24		4 BERTH C	SLP	SAIL	FBG	KL	JT			7	5		2		5000	5750
24		4 BERTH D	SLP	SA/RC	FBG	KL	OB			7	5		2		4950	5700
24		4 BERTH D	SLP	SA/RC	FBG	KL	IB	10		7	5		2		5250	6000
24		4 BERTH D	SLP	SAIL	FBG	KL	JT			7	5		2		5350	6150
24		DAYSAILER MDL B	SLP	SAIL	FBG	KL	OB			7	5		2		4750	5500
24		DAYSAILER MDL B	SLP	SAIL	FBG	KL	JT			7	5		2		4450	5100
24		DAYSAILER MDL B	SLP	SAIL	FBG	KL	IB	10		7	5		2		4550	5250
30		TYLERCRAFT 30	SLP	SA/CR	FBG	TK	IB			10			3		9950	11300
30		TYLERCRAFT 30	YWL	SA/CR	FBG	TK	IB			10			3		9950	11300
40		TYLERCRAFT 40	YWL	SA/CR	FBG	TK	IB			13			3	2	28700	31800
40		TYLERCRAFT 40	KTH	SA/CR	FBG	TK	IB			13			3	2	30300	33700
		1965 BOATS														
24		4 BERTH B WKNDR		SAIL	FBG		JT								4700	5350
24		4 BERTH B WKNDR		SAIL	FBG		IB	10							4900	5600
24		4 BERTH C		SA/CR	FBG		IB	10							4700	5400
24		4 BERTH C		SAIL	FBG		JT								4950	5700
24		4 BERTH D		SA/RC	FBG		IB	10							5250	6050
24		4 BERTH D		SAIL	FBG		JT								5250	6050
24		DAYSAILER MDL B		SAIL	FBG		JT								4400	5050
24		DAYSAILER MDL B		SAIL	FBG		IB	10							4550	5250
		1961 BOATS														
22		T-22	SLP	SA/CR	FBG	TK				7	6		2		2700	3150
26		T-26	SLP	SA/CR	FBG	KC				8			2	6	5550	6350
31		T-31	SLP	SA/CR	FBG	KL				9			4		11200	12700
31		T-31	YWL	SA/CR	FBG	KL				9			4		11200	12700
38		T-38	SLP	SA/CR	FBG	KL				10			4	6	13500	15300
38		T-38	YWL	SA/CR	FBG	KL				10			4	6	13500	15300
		1960 BOATS														
21		TYLERCRAFT 21	SLP	SA/CR	FBG	CB				7					2600	3000
21		TYLERCRAFT 21	SLP	SA/CR	FBG	KL				7			2		2600	3000
21		TYLERCRAFT 21	SLP	SA/CR	FBG	TK				7			2		2600	3000
25	9	TYLERCRAFT 26	SLP	SA/CR	FBG	KC				8			2	9	5500	6350
31		TYLERCRAFT 31	SLP	SA/CR	FBG	KC	OB			8	8		4	6	12900	14600
31		TYLERCRAFT 31	SLP	SA/CR	FBG	KL	OB			8	8		4	6	12700	14500
31		TYLERCRAFT 31	YWL	SA/CR	FBG	KC	OB			8	8		4	6	12900	14600
31		TYLERCRAFT 31	YWL	SA/CR	FBG	KL	OB			8	8		4	6	12700	14500
32		MELODY 32	SLP	SA/CR	FBG	KC				9					**	**
32		MELODY 32	SLP	SA/CR	FBG	KL				9			4	6	**	**
32		MELODY 32	YWL	SA/CR	FBG	KC				9					**	**
32		MELODY 32	YWL	SA/CR	FBG	KL				9			4	6	**	**
36		CREEKMORE 36	SLP	SA/CR	FBG	CB	OB			10					17400	19800
36		CREEKMORE 36	SLP	SA/CR	FBG	KL	OB			10			4		17400	19700
36		CREEKMORE 36	YWL	SA/CR	FBG	CB	OB			10					17400	19800
36		CREEKMORE 36	YWL	SA/CR	FBG	KL	OB			10			4		17400	19700

U S FIBER GLASS CORP

HUSTLER SPORT CENTER COAST GUARD MFG ID- USF

Call 1-800-327-6929 for BUC Personalized Evaluation Service
Or, for 1969 to 1983 boats, sign onto www.BUCValuPro.com

U S YACHTS

BAYLINER MARINE CORP
EVERETT WA 98206

See inside cover to adjust price for area

COAST GUARD MFG ID- BLB
SEE PEARSON YACHTS OF RHODE ISLAND

LOA FT	LOA IN	NAME AND/ OR MODEL	TOP/ RIG	BOAT TYPE	HULL MTL	HULL TP	ENGINE TP	ENGINE # HP	ENGINE MFG	BEAM FT	BEAM IN	WGT LBS	DRAFT FT	DRAFT IN	RETAIL LOW	RETAIL HIGH
		1983 BOATS														
21		U-S 21	SLP	SA/OD	FBG	DB	OB			8		1400	1	3	2500	2900
22		U-S 22	SLP	SA/CR	FBG	KC	OB			7	11	2450	2	1	3500	4100
22		U-S 22	SLP	SA/CR	FBG	KL	OB			7	11	2450	4	1	3500	4100
25		U-S 25	SLP	SA/CR	FBG	KC	OB			8		3750	2	8	5550	6400
25		U-S 25	SLP	SA/CR	FBG	KL	OB			8		3750	4	7	5550	6400
27		U-S 27	SLP	SA/CR	FBG	KL	OB			9	6	6250	5	2	10100	11500
27		U-S 27	SLP	SA/CR	FBG	KL	SE	115	OMC	9	6	6250	5	2	10600	12000
27		U-S 27	SLP	SA/CR	FBG	KL	SD	8D	VLVO	9	6	6250	5	2	10500	11900
27		U-S 27 SHOAL	SLP	SA/CR	FBG	KL	OB			9	6	6250	5	2	10100	11500
27		U-S 27 SHOAL	SLP	SA/CR	FBG	KL	SE	115	OMC	9	6	6250	3	6	10600	12000

 CONTINUED ON NEXT PAGE

LOA FT	LOA IN	NAME AND/ OR MODEL	TOP/ RIG	BOAT TYPE	HULL MTL	HULL TP	ENGINE TP	# HP	ENGINE MFG	BEAM FT	BEAM IN	WGT LBS	DRAFT FT	DRAFT IN	RETAIL LOW	RETAIL HIGH
		1983 BOATS														
27		U-S 27 SHOAL	SLP	SA/CR	FBG	KL	SD	8D	VLVO	9	6	6250	3	6	10500	11900
29		U-S 30 SHOAL	SLP	SA/CR	FBG	KL	SD	15D	VLVO	10	3	7000	3	11	12300	14000
29	11	U-S 30	SLP	SA/CR	FBG	KL	SD	15D	VLVO	10	3	7000	5	7	12500	14100
		1982 BOATS														
21		U-S 21	SLP	SA/OD	FBG	CB	OB			8		1400	1	3	2350	2750
22		U-S 22	SLP	SA/CR	FBG	KC	OB			7	11	2450	2	1	3300	3850
22		U-S 22	SLP	SA/CR	FBG	KL	OB			7	11	2450	4	1	3300	3850
25		U-S 25	SLP	SA/CR	FBG	KC	OB			8		3750	2	8	5250	6000
25		U-S 25	SLP	SA/CR	FBG	KL	OB			8		3750	4	7	5250	6000
27		U-S 27	SLP	SA/CR	FBG	KL	OB			9	6	6250	5	2	9550	10800
27		U-S 27	SLP	SA/CR	FBG	KL	SD	15	OMC	9	6	6250	5	2	9700	11000
27		U-S 27	SLP	SA/CR	FBG	KL	IB	8D	VLVO	9	6	6250	5	2	9850	11200
27		U-S 27 SHOAL	SLP	SA/CR	FBG	KL	OB			9	6	6250	5	2	9550	10800
27		U-S 27 SHOAL	SLP	SA/CR	FBG	KL	SD	15	OMC	9	6	6250	3	6	9700	11000
27		U-S 27 SHOAL	SLP	SA/CR	FBG	KL	IB	8D	VLVO	9	6	6250	3	6	9850	11200
29		U-S 30 SHOAL	SLP	SA/CR	FBG	KL	IB	13D	VLVO	10	3	7000	3	11	11600	13200
29	11	U-S 30	SLP	SA/CR	FBG	KL	IB	13D	VLVO	10	3	7000	5	7	11700	13300
30		U-S 305	SLP	SA/CR	FBG	KL	IB	23D	VLVO	10	2	10000	4		16900	19200
32	10	U-S 33	SLP	SA/CR	FBG	KL	IB	13D	VLVO	10	6	9300	5	6	15700	17800
35	3	U-S 35	SLP	SA/CR	FBG	KL	VD	40D	BMC	12		13250	5	10	22300	24700
41	6	U-S 42	SLP	SA/CR	FBG	KL	IB	60D	BMC	14		24000	6	7	41500	46200
		1981 BOATS														
22		U-S 22	SLP	SA/CR	FBG	KL	OB			7	11	2450	4	8	3100	3600
22		U-S 22 SHOAL	SLP	SA/CR	FBG	KL	OB			7	11	2450	2	7	3100	3600
25		U-S 25	SLP	SA/CR	FBG	KL	OB			8		3750	4	7	4950	5650
25		U-S 25 SHOAL	SLP	SA/CR	FBG	KL	OB			8		3750	2	8	4950	5650
27		U-S 27	SLP	SA/CR	FBG	KL	OB			9	6	5836	5	2	8300	9550
27		U-S 27	SLP	SA/CR	FBG	KL	SD	8	VLVO	9	6	5836	5	2	8450	9700
27		U-S 27	SLP	SA/CR	FBG	KL	IB	13D	VLVO	9	6	5836	5	2	8650	9950
27		U-S 27 SHOAL	SLP	SA/CR	FBG	KL	OB			9	6	5836	5	2	8300	9550
27		U-S 27 SHOAL	SLP	SA/CR	FBG	KL	SD	8D	VLVO	9	6	5836	3	6	8600	9900
27		U-S 27 SHOAL	SLP	SA/CR	FBG	KL	IB	13D	VLVO	9	6	5836	3	6	8650	9950
29		U-S 30 SHOAL	SLP	SA/CR	FBG	KL	IB	13D	VLVO	10	3	7000	3	11	10900	12400
29	11	U-S 30	SLP	SA/CR	FBG	KL	IB	13D	VLVO	10	3	7000	5	7	11000	12500
29	11	U-S 305	SLP	SA/CR	FBG	KL	IB	23D	VLVO	10	2	10000	4		15900	18100
32		U-S 33	SLP	SA/CR	FBG	KL	IB	13D	VLVO	10	6	9300	5	6	14800	16900
35	3	U-S 35	SLP	SA/CR	FBG	KL	IB	40D	BMC	12		13250	5	10	21000	23300
41	6	U-S 42	SLP	SA/CR	FBG	KL	IB	60D	OMC	14		24000	6	7	39000	43400

U S YACHTS INC

EAST NORWALK CT

See inside cover to adjust price for area

LOA FT	LOA IN	NAME AND/ OR MODEL	TOP/ RIG	BOAT TYPE	HULL MTL	HULL TP	ENGINE TP	# HP	ENGINE MFG	BEAM FT	BEAM IN	WGT LBS	DRAFT FT	DRAFT IN	RETAIL LOW	RETAIL HIGH
		1967 BOATS														
22		COMPLEAT-ANGLER		FSH	FBG		IB	150		7	10		2	2	3700	4300
27		EAGLE	SLP	SA/CR	FBG	KL	IB	22		8	5		3	10	11400	13000
32		TRIANGLE	SLP	MS	FBG	KC	IB	70		10			3	5	22900	25400
32		TRIANGLE 32	KTH	SA/CR	FBG	KC	IB	22		10			3	5	14900	17000
45	6	U-S-46	YWL	SA/CR	FBG	KC	IB	40		12			4	11	64400	70800
		1966 BOATS														
20	6	TRIANGLE 20	SLP	SA/CR	FBG	CB				7	1				3500	4100
24	2	DOLPHIN	SLP	SA/CR	FBG	CB				7	8				5750	6600
27	1	EAGLE	SLP	SAIL	FBG	KL	IB	22		8	5		3	10	11200	12800
32		TRIANGLE	SLP	MS	FBG	KL	IB	70		10			3	6	22300	24700
32		TRIANGLE	SLP	MS	FBG	KL	IB	40D		10			3	6	27400	30400
32		TRIANGLE 32	YWL	SAIL	FBG	CB	IB	22- 31		10					14800	16800
32		TRIANGLE 32	YWL	SAIL	FBG	CB	IB	21D		10					26900	29900
40		TRIANGLE 40	SLP	SA/CR	FBG	CB	IB	30D		12	7				48900	53800
40		TRIANGLE 40	KTH	SA/CR	FBG	CB	IB	30D		12	7				51200	56300
41	11	U-S-41	YWL	SA/CR	FBG	CB	IB	D	WEST	12			4	11	54200	59600
41	11	U-S-41	YWL	SAIL	FBG	CB	IB	40D		12			4	11	53900	59300
		1965 BOATS														
20	6	TRIANGLE 20 Z	SLP	SAIL	FBG		OB								3450	4050
24	2	DOLPHIN	SLP	SAIL	FBG		OB								5700	6600
24	2	DOLPHIN	SLP	SAIL	FBG		IB	8- 22							6050	7050
27		EAGLE	SLP	SAIL	FBG		IB	22							11100	12600
32		TRIANGLE 32	KTH	SAIL	FBG		IB	22							14600	16600
32	8	MEDALIST	SLP	SAIL	FBG		IB	30							22300	24700
32	8	MEDALIST	SLP	SAIL	FBG		IB	17D							26200	29100
41	11	U-S-41	YWL	SAIL	FBG		IB	37D							53300	58600
		1963 BOATS														
20		U-S-TRIANGLE 20		SAIL	FBG		OB								3100	3600
24		U-S-DOLPHIN		SAIL	FBG		OB								5600	6450
27		U-S-EAGLE		SAIL	FBG		OB								9200	10500
32		MEDALIST		SAIL	FBG		OB								13400	15200
32		U-S-TRIANGLE 32		SAIL	FBG		OB								13400	15200
35		OHLSON 35		SAIL	WD		OB								24600	27300
41		U-S-YACHTS 41		SAIL	FBG		OB								34600	38400
		1961 BOATS														
24		DOLPHIN	SLP	SA/CR	FBG	KC				7	8		2	10	5600	6450
25		OHLSON 35	YWL	SA/CR	WD	KL	OB			9	4		4	11	6200	7150
32		MEDALIST	SLP	SA/CR	FBG	KL	OB			10			5		16600	18900
32		MEDALIST	YWL	SA/CR	FBG	KL	OB			10			5		16600	18900

ULRICHSEN COMPANY

A BANGOR PUNTA COMPANY
MARLBORO NJ 07746 COAST GUARD MFG ID- ULR

See inside cover to adjust price for area

LOA FT	LOA IN	NAME AND/ OR MODEL	TOP/ RIG	BOAT TYPE	HULL MTL	HULL TP	ENGINE TP	# HP	ENGINE MFG	BEAM FT	BEAM IN	WGT LBS	DRAFT FT	DRAFT IN	RETAIL LOW	RETAIL HIGH
		1970 BOATS														
33			FB	SDN	MHG		IB	300	CHRY	13			3		10700	12100
33				SPTCR	MHG		IB	300	CHRY	13			3		9750	11100
37			FB	SDN	MHG		IB	T225	CHRY	13			3		14600	16600
		1969 BOATS														
25		ALURA	FB	SF	FBG	DV	IB	225	CHRY	9	4		2	6	3450	4000
28		ALURA	FB	SDN	FBG	DV	IB	225	CHRY	11	2		2	10	6250	7200
28		ALURA	FB	SDN	FBG	DV	IB	160D	PERK	11	2		2	10	9750	11100
28		ALURA	FB	SDN	FBG	DV	IB	T225	CHRY	11	2		2	10	7250	8300
29		ULRICHSEN 29		SF	MHG		IB	225	CHRY	10	11		2	2	5750	6600
29		ULRICHSEN 29		SPTCR	MHG		IB	225	CHRY	10	11		2	2	6100	7000
31		ULRICHSEN 31		SDN	MHG		IB	225	CHRY	11	3		2	2	7850	9050
31		ULRICHSEN 31		SPTCR	MHG		IB	225	CHRY	11	3		2	2	7150	8200
33		ULRICHSEN 33		SDN	MHG		IB	300	CHRY	12	4		2	6	10300	11700
33		ULRICHSEN 33		SPTCR	MHG		IB	300	CHRY	12	4		2	6	9450	10700
37		ULRICHSEN 37		SDN	MHG		IB	T225	CHRY	12	6		2	6	14600	16600
37		ULRICHSEN 37		SPTCR	MHG		IB	T160D	PERK	12	6		2	6	18400	20400
		1968 BOATS														
25		ALURA 25	FB	SPTCR	FBG	FL	IB	210	CHRY	9	4		3		3350	3850
27		ULRICHSEN 27		SF	WD		IB	210-235		10	4	6500	2	1	4450	5200
27		ULRICHSEN 27	FB	SF	WD		IB	210-235		10	4	6500	2	1	4900	5700
28		ALURA 28		SDN	FBG	FL	IB	210	CHRY	11	2	8000	2	11	5950	6800
29		ULRICHSEN 29	HT	SF	WD		IB	210-300		10	11	7000	2	2	5400	6450
29		ULRICHSEN 29	HT	SF	WD		IB	T175-T210		10	11	7000	2	2	5950	7000
29		ULRICHSEN 29	FB	SF	WD		IB	210-300		10	11	7000	2	2	5850	7100
29		ULRICHSEN 29	FB	SF	WD		IB	T175-T210		10	11	7000	2	2	6450	7600
29		ULRICHSEN 29	HT	SPTCR	WD		IB	210-300		10	11	7500	2	2	5800	7050
29		ULRICHSEN 29	HT	SPTCR	WD		IB	T175-T210		10	11	7500	2	2	6400	7550
29		ULRICHSEN 29	FB	SPTCR	WD		IB	210-300		10	11	7500	2	2	5800	7050
29		ULRICHSEN 29	FB	SPTCR	WD		IB	T175-T210		10	11	7500	2	2	6400	7550
31		ULRICHSEN 31	FB	SDN	WD		IB	235		11	3	8400	2	2	7550	8700
31		ULRICHSEN 31	HT	SDN	WD		IB	210-300		11	3	8400	2	2	7400	9050
31		ULRICHSEN 31	HT	SDN	WD		IB	T175-T235		11	3	8400	2	2	8200	9800
31		ULRICHSEN 31	FB	SDN	WD		IB	210-300		11	3	8400	2	2	7400	9100
31		ULRICHSEN 31	FB	SDN	WD		IB	T175-T235		11	3	8400	2	2	8200	9950
31		ULRICHSEN 31	HT	SPTCR	WD		IB	210-300		11	3	8000	2	2	6850	8250
31		ULRICHSEN 31	HT	SPTCR	WD		IB	T175-T235		11	3	8000	2	2	7400	9000
31		ULRICHSEN 31	FB	SPTCR	WD		IB	210-300		11	3	8000	2	2	6850	8250
31		ULRICHSEN 31	FB	SPTCR	WD		IB	T175-T235		11	3	8000	2	2	7400	9000
33		ULRICHSEN 33	HT	SDN	WD		IB	300	CHRY	12	4	10200	2	6	9750	11100
33		ULRICHSEN 33	HT	SDN	WD		IB	T175-T235		12	4	10200	2	6	10100	11900
33		ULRICHSEN 33	FB	SDN	WD		IB	300		12	4	10200	2	6	9900	11300
33		ULRICHSEN 33	FB	SDN	WD		IB	T175-T235		12	4	10200	2	6	10200	12000
33		ULRICHSEN 33	HT	SPTCR	WD		IB	300		12	4	9000	2	6	9100	10300
33		ULRICHSEN 33	HT	SPTCR	WD		IB	T175-T235		12	4	9000	2	6	9350	11000
33		ULRICHSEN 33	FB	SPTCR	WD		IB	300		12	4	9000	2	6	9150	10400
33		ULRICHSEN 33	FB	SPTCR	WD		IB	T175-T235		12	4	9000	2	6	9400	11100
37		ULRICHSEN 37	HT	SDN	WD		IB	T210	CHRY	12	6	12500	2	6	14300	16200
37		ULRICHSEN 37	HT	SDN	WD		IB	T235		12	6	12500	2	6	14400	16300
37		ULRICHSEN 37	HT	SDN	WD		IB	T160D		12	6	12500	2	6	17200	19600
37		ULRICHSEN 37	FB	SDN	WD		IB	T210	CHRY	12	6	12500	2	6	14500	16400
37		ULRICHSEN 37	FB	SDN	WD		IB	T235		12	6	12500	2	6	14600	16600
37		ULRICHSEN 37	FB	SDN	WD		IB	T160D		12	6	12500	2	6	17300	19700
37		ULRICHSEN 37	HT	SPTCR	WD		IB	T210	CHRY	12	6	12000	2	6	14400	16400
37		ULRICHSEN 37	HT	SPTCR	WD		IB	T235		12	6	12000	2	6	14500	16500
37		ULRICHSEN 37	HT	SPTCR	WD		IB	T160D		12	6	12000	2	6	17300	19600
37		ULRICHSEN 37	FB	SPTCR	WD		IB	T210	CHRY	12	6	12000	2	6	14900	16900
37		ULRICHSEN 37	FB	SPTCR	WD		IB	T235		12	6	12000	2	6	15000	17000

CONTINUED ON NEXT PAGE

ULRICHSEN COMPANY -CONTINUED

See inside cover to adjust price for area

LOA FT IN	NAME AND/ OR MODEL	TOP/ RIG	BOAT TYPE	HULL MTL TP	ENGINE TP # HP MFG	BEAM FT IN	WGT LBS	DRAFT FT IN	RETAIL LOW	RETAIL HIGH
1968 BOATS										
37	ULRICHSEN 37	FB	SPTCR	WD	IB T160D	12 6	12000	2 6	18200	20200
1967 BOATS										
25	ALURA		SF	FBG	IB 210	10 4		2 1	2800	3300
27	SHELTER		CR	WD	IB 210-290	10 4		2 1	4000	4900
27	TRUNK CABIN		CR	WD	IB 210-290	10 4		2 1	4750	5650
29	SHELTER		CR	WD	IB 235-290	10 11		2 2	5200	6150
29	SHELTER		CR	WD	IB T210	10 11		2 2	5900	6750
29	TRUNK CABIN		CR	WD	IB 235-290	10 11		2 2	5900	7050
29	TRUNK CABIN		CR	WD	IB T210	10 11		2 2	6500	7500
31	SEDAN CRUISER		SDN	WD	IB 238	11 3		2 2	7300	8400
31	SHELTER		CR	WD	IB 235-290	11 3		2 2	6650	7900
31	SHELTER		CR	WD	IB T210	11 3		2 2	7300	8400
31	TRUNK CABIN		CR	WD	IB 238	11 3		2 2	6650	7650
32 6	ALURA	FB	EXP	FBG	IB T210				9300	10600
33			SDN	WD	IB 290	12		3	9550	10800
33			SDN	WD	IB T210	12		3	10100	11500
33	TRUNK CABIN		CR	WD	IB 290	12		3	8800	10000
33	TRUNK CABIN		CR	WD	IB T210	12		3	9300	10500
1966 BOATS										
27	SHELTER CABIN		CR	WD	IB 220				3900	4550
27	SHELTER CABIN	FB	CR	WD	IB 220				4200	4900
27	TRUNK CABIN		CR	WD	IB 220				4550	5250
29	SHELTER CABIN	HT	CR	WD	IB 238				5000	5750
29	SHELTER CABIN	HT	CR	WD	IB T185-T220				5550	6550
29	SHELTER CABIN	FB	CR	WD	IB 238				5000	5750
29	SHELTER CABIN	FB	CR	WD	IB T185-T220				5550	6550
29	TRUNK CABIN	HT	CR	WD	IB 238				5700	6550
29	TRUNK CABIN	HT	CR	WD	IB T185-T220				6150	7300
29	TRUNK CABIN	FB	CR	WD	IB 238				5700	6550
29	TRUNK CABIN	FB	CR	WD	IB T185-T220				6200	7300
31	SHELTER CABIN	HT	CR	WD	IB 238				5800	6650
31	SHELTER CABIN	HT	CR	WD	IB T185-T220				6350	7500
31	SHELTER CABIN	FB	CR	WD	IB 238				5850	6700
31	SHELTER CABIN	FB	CR	WD	IB T185-T220				6400	7550
31	TRUNK CABIN	HT	CR	WD	IB 238				7050	8100
31	TRUNK CABIN	HT	CR	WD	IB T185-T220				7450	8900
31	TRUNK CABIN	FB	CR	WD	IB 238				7000	8050
31	TRUNK CABIN	FB	CR	WD	IB T185-T220				7400	8750
33		HT	SDN	WD	IB 280				9100	10400
33		HT	SDN	WD	IB T185-T220				9500	11100
33		FB	SDN	WD	IB 280				9100	10400
33		FB	SDN	WD	IB T185-T220				9550	11100
33	TRUNK CABIN	HT	CR	WD	IB 280				8400	9650
33	TRUNK CABIN	HT	CR	WD	IB T185-T220				8850	10200
33	TRUNK CABIN	FB	CR	WD	IB 280				8400	9650
33	TRUNK CABIN	FB	CR	WD	IB T185-T220				8850	10200
1965 BOATS										
27	SHELTER CABIN		CR	WD	IB 210-280				3700	4500
27	SHELTER CABIN	FB	CR	WD	IB 210-280				4050	4850
27	TRUNK CABIN		CR	WD	IB 210-280				4350	5200
29	SHELTER CABIN		CR	WD	IB 210-280				4750	5650
29	SHELTER CABIN		CR	WD	IB T175-T225				5300	6350
29	SHELTER CABIN	FB	CR	WD	IB 210-280				4700	5700
29	SHELTER CABIN	FB	CR	WD	IB T175-T225				5300	6350
29	TRUNK CABIN		CR	WD	IB 210-280				5400	6450
29	TRUNK CABIN		CR	WD	IB T175-T225				5850	7050
29	TRUNK CABIN	FB	CR	WD	IB 210-280				5400	6450
29	TRUNK CABIN	FB	CR	WD	IB T175-T225				5850	7100
31	SHELTER CABIN		CR	WD	IB 210-280				5500	6550
31	SHELTER CABIN		CR	WD	IB T175-T238				6100	7350
31	SHELTER CABIN	FB	CR	WD	IB 210-280				5550	6650
31	SHELTER CABIN	FB	CR	WD	IB T175-T238				6150	7450
31	TRUNK CABIN		CR	WD	IB 210-280				6650	7950
31	TRUNK CABIN		CR	WD	IB T175-T238				7100	8500
31	TRUNK CABIN	FB	CR	WD	IB 210-280				6600	7900
31	TRUNK CABIN	FB	CR	WD	IB T175-T238				7100	8450
33			SDN	WD	IB 280				8700	10000
33			SDN	WD	IB T175-T238				9100	10900
33	TRUNK CABIN		CR	WD	IB 280				8100	9300
33	TRUNK CABIN		CR	WD	IB T175-T238				8350	9950
33	TRUNK CABIN	FB	CR	WD	IB 280				8100	9300
33	TRUNK CABIN	FB	CR	WD	IB T175-T238				8350	9950
1964 BOATS										
27	SHELTER CABIN		CR	WD	IB 210-280				3550	4300
27	SHELTER CABIN	FB	CR	WD	IB 210-280				3900	4700
27	TRUNK CABIN		CR	WD	IB 210-280				4150	5000
29	SHELTER CABIN		CR	WD	IB 210-280				4550	5500
29	SHELTER CABIN		CR	WD	IB T178-T225				5100	6100
29	SHELTER CABIN	FB	CR	WD	IB 210-280				4900	5850
29	SHELTER CABIN	FB	CR	WD	IB T178-T225				5400	6450
29	TRUNK CABIN		CR	WD	IB 210-280				5200	6200
29	TRUNK CABIN		CR	WD	IB T178-T225				5650	6750
31	SHELTER CABIN		CR	WD	IB 210-280				5300	6350
31	SHELTER CABIN		CR	WD	IB T178-T238				5850	7100
31	SHELTER CABIN	FB	CR	WD	IB 210-280				5350	6350
31	SHELTER CABIN	FB	CR	WD	IB T178-T238				5850	7150
31	TRUNK CABIN		CR	WD	IB 210-280				6400	7600
31	TRUNK CABIN		CR	WD	IB T178-T238				6900	8250
31	TRUNK CABIN	FB	CR	WD	IB 210-280				6400	7600
31	TRUNK CABIN	FB	CR	WD	IB T178-T238				6900	8200
33	TRUNK CABIN	HT	CR	WD	IB 280				7800	8950
33	TRUNK CABIN	HT	CR	WD	IB T178-T238				8100	9600
33	TRUNK CABIN	FB	CR	WD	IB 280				7800	9000
33	TRUNK CABIN	FB	CR	WD	IB T178-T238				8100	9600
1963 BOATS										
26	SEA-SKIFF SHELTER CB		CR	WD	IB 225				3300	3850
26	TRUNK CABIN		CR	WD	IB 225				3900	4550
28	SEA-SKIFF SHELTER CB		CR	WD	IB 225				4350	5000
28	SEA-SKIFF SHELTER CB		CR	WD	IB 280				4800	5500
28	TRUNK CABIN		CR	WD	IB 225-280				5000	5750
31	SEA-SKIFF SHELTER CB		CR	WD	IB 225-280				5700	6700
31	SEA-SKIFF SHELTER CB		CR	WD	IB T178				6150	7150
31	TRUNK CABIN DLX		CR	WD	IB 225				5700	6550
31	TRUNK CABIN DLX		CR	WD	IB T178				6150	7100
1962 BOATS										
25			CR	WD	IB 170-215				2650	3100
27	SHELTER CABIN		CR	WD	IB 177-230				3500	4200
27	TRUNK CABIN		CR	WD	IB 177-230				3500	4200
1961 BOATS										
24	JR-SURFRIDER S SKIFF			WD	IB 110-215				2050	2500
29	SURFMASTER SEA SKIFF			WD	IB T225				4450	5100
31	SEA-SKIFF	FB		WD	IB T225				5550	6400
1960 BOATS										
24 6	JR-SURFRIDER S SKIFF			L/P	IB 110-170	9 6		1 10	2250	2700
29	SURFMASTER SEA SKIFF			L/P	IB 177	10		2 4	4100	4800
29	SURFMASTER SEA SKIFF			L/P	IB T188	10		2 4	4700	5400
33	SEA-SKIFF	FB		WD	IB T177				6600	7550
1959 BOATS										
27			SF	WD	IB 170				3150	3650
27	SEA-SKIFF			WD	IB 170				3200	3750
31	SEA-SKIFF	FB		WD	IB T177				5150	5900
1958 BOATS										
26	SEA-SKIFF			WD	IB 115				2950	3400
30			EXP	WD	IB T125				4900	5600
36			EXP	WD	IB T145				9950	11300
1957 BOATS										
26	SEA-SKIFF			WD	IB 110				2900	3350
28	SEA-SKIFF			WD	IB 125				3800	4400
1956 BOATS										
28	SEA-SKIFF			WD	IB 125				3700	4300
1955 BOATS										
30	SHELTER SKIFF		CR	WD	IB 145				3900	4550
1954 BOATS										
28			OP	EXP WD	IB	9 4			**	**

ULSTER MARINE INC

Call 1-800-327-6929 for BUC Personalized Evaluation Service
Or, for 1973 boats, sign onto www.BUCValuPro.com

UNIFLITE INC
BRADENTON FL 33506   COAST GUARD MFG ID- UNF See inside cover to adjust price for area
SEE ALSO CHRIS CRAFT

For more recent years, see the BUC Used Boat Price Guide, Volume 1 or Volume 2

```
LOA   NAME AND/        TOP/ BOAT  -HULL- ----ENGINE---   BEAM   WGT  DRAFT RETAIL RETAIL
FT IN OR MODEL         RIG  TYPE  MTL TP TP #  HP   MFG  FT IN  LBS  FT IN  LOW    HIGH
------------------------ 1983 BOATS -------------------------------------------------------
26      SPORT SEDAN          SDN  FBG DV IB    350         9 11  8500        16200  18400
28    2 MEGA            FB   SDN  FBG SV IB T220  CRUS 10 10 10500  2  4  21400  23700
28    2 SALTY-DOG       OP   SF   FBG SV IB T220  CRUS 10 10  9000  2 10  18600  20700
28    2 SALTY-DOG       OP   SF   FBG SV IB T158D VLVO 10 10  9000  2 10  25000  27700
28    2 SALTY-DOG       HT   SF   FBG SV IB T220  CRUS 10 10  9000  2 10  18600  20700
28    2 SALTY-DOG       HT   SF   FBG SV IB T158D VLVO 10 10  9000  2 10  25000  27700
31    8 SPORT SEDAN     FB   SDN  FBG SV IB T270  CRUS 11 11 15000  2  8  31800  35300
31    8 SPORT SEDAN     FB   SDN  FBG SV IBT158D-T205D   11 11 15000  2  8  41800  48500
34    2 CONVERTIBLE     FB   SDN  FBG SV IB T270-T350  11 11 17000  2  9  39800  46000
34    2 CONVERTIBLE     FB   SDN  FBG SV IBT205D-T235D   11 11 17000  2  9  51000  56900
36      DOUBLE CABIN    FB   SDN  FBG SV IB T350  CRUS 12  4 21000  2  8  53800  59100
36      DOUBLE CABIN    FB   SDN  FBG SV IB T205D GM   12  4 21000  2  8  59700  65600

36      DOUBLE CABIN    FB   SDN  FBG SV IB T235D VLVO 12  4 21000  2  8  60000  65900
36      DOUBLE CABIN    FB   SDN  FBG SV IB T205D GM   12  4 21000  2  8  58000  63700
36      SPORT SEDAN     FB   SDN  FBG SV IB T235D VLVO 12  4 20000  2  8  58300  64000
37    9 COASTAL-CRUISER FB   SDN  FBG DS IB  235D VLVO 12  9 21000  3 10  60300  66200
37    9 COASTAL-CRUISER FB   SDN  FBG DS IB T124D VLVO 12  9 21000  3 10  62100  68200
37    9 COASTAL-CRUISER FB   SDN  FBG DS IB T205D GM   12  9 21000  3 10  65100  71500
38      CONVERTIBLE     FB   SDN  FBG SV IB T310D GM   13 11 27000  3  9  79700  87600
38      CONVERTIBLE     FB   SDN  FBG SV IB T320D CUM  13 11 27000  3  9  79700  87600
38      CONVERTIBLE     FB   SDN  FBG SV IB T410D GM   13 11 27000  3  9  85000  93400
41    3 YACHT FISHERMAN FB   YTFS FBG SV IB T350  CRUS 12  4 20000  2  8  70200  77200
41    3 YACHT FISHERMAN FB   YTFS FBG SV IB T205D GM   12  4 20000  2  8  71100  78100
41    3 YACHT FISHERMAN FB   YTFS FBG SV IB T235D VLVO 12  4 20000  2  8  72200  79400

42      CONVERTIBLE     FB   SDN  FBG SV IB T310D GM   14  9 35000  3  9  99400 109000
42      CONVERTIBLE     FB   SDN  FBG SV IB T410D GM   14  9 35000  3  9 105000 115500
42      CONVERTIBLE     FB   SDN  FBG SV IB T425D CUM  14  9 35000  3  9 111500 122500
42      DOUBLE CABIN    FB   SDN  FBG SV IB T310D GM   14  9 35000  3  9 111000 122000
42      DOUBLE CABIN    FB   SDN  FBG SV IB T320D CUM  14  9 35000  3  9 105500 115500
42      DOUBLE CABIN    FB   SDN  FBG SV IB T410D GM   14  9 35000  3  9 116500 128000
45      YACHT HOME      FB   MY   FBG    IB T270  CRUS 13 11 22000  3  4  70100  77000
45      YACHT HOME      FB   MY   FBG    IB T205D GM   13 11 22000  3  4  75400  82900
46    3 MOTOR YACHT     FB   MY   FBG SV IB T410D GM   15  3 46000  4  4 137500 151000
48      YACHT FISHERMAN FB   YTFS FBG SV IB T310D GM   14  9 39000  3  9 119000 131000
48      YACHT FISHERMAN FB   YTFS FBG SV IB T320D CUM  14  9 39000  3  9 123000 135500
48      YACHT FISHERMAN FB   YTFS FBG SV IB T410D GM   14  9 38000  3  9 136500 150000

48   10 CONVERTIBLE     FB   SDN  FBG SV IB T425D CUM  15  9 48000  4  9 156500 172000
48   10 CONVERTIBLE     FB   SDN  FBG SV IB T550D GM   15  9 48000  4  9 163000 179500
53    3 COCKPIT MOTOR YACHT FB MYCPT FBG  IB T500D GM  15  3 55200  4  4 171500 188500
------------------------ 1982 BOATS -------------------------------------------------------
26    2 SEDAN           FB   SDN  FBG    IB    350  CRUS 10     8500  2  8  15700  17900
26    2 SEDAN           FB   SDN  FBG SV IB T190  CRUS 10     8500  2  8  16200  18400
28    2 MEGA            FB   SDN  FBG    IB    270  CRUS 10 10 10500  2 10  19000  21200
28    2 MEGA            FB   SDN  FBG SV IB  210D REN  10 10 10500  2 10  27300  30300
28    2 MEGA            FB   SDN  FBG SV IB T220  CRUS 10 10 10500  2 10  20500  22700
28    2 SALTY-DOG       OP   SF   FBG SV IB 235-270   10 10  9000  2  4  15800  18300
28    2 SALTY-DOG       OP   SF   FBG SV IB T148-T220 10 10  9000  2 10  16500  19800
28    2 SALTY-DOG       HT   SF   FBG SV IB 235-270   10 10  9000  2  4  15800  18300
28    2 SALTY-DOG       HT   SF   FBG SV IB T148-T220 10 10  9000  2 10  16500  19800
31    8 SPORT SEDAN     FB   SDN  FBG SV IB T270  CRUS 11 11 15000  2  8  30400  33800
31    8 SPORT SEDAN     FB   SDN  FBG SV IB T148D VLVO 11 11 15000  2  8  39800  44200

34    2 CONVERTIBLE     FB   SDN  FBG SV IB T270-T350  11 11 17000  2  9  38100  44400
34    2 CONVERTIBLE     FB   SDN  FBG SV IBT140D-T235D   11 11 17000  2  9  46800  54700
36      DOUBLE CABIN    FB   SDN  FBG SV IB T350  CRUS 12  4 21000  2  8  51400  56400
36      DOUBLE CABIN    FB   SDN  FBG SV IB T195D CUM  12  4 21000  2  8  56500  62100
36      DOUBLE CABIN    FB   SDN  FBG SV IB T235D VLVO 12  4 21000  2  8  57300  62900
36      SPORT SEDAN     FB   SDN  FBG SV IB T350  CRUS 12  4 20000  2  8  50100  55000
36      SPORT SEDAN     FB   SDN  FBG SV IB T195D CUM  12  4 20000  2  8  54900  60300
36      SPORT SEDAN     FB   SDN  FBG SV IB T235D VLVO 12  4 20000  2  8  55600  61100
37    9 COASTAL-CRUISER FB   SDN  FBG DS IB  192D VLVO 12  9 21000  3 10  62500  62700
37    9 COASTAL-CRUISER FB   SDN  FBG DS IB T124D VLVO 12  9 21000  3 10  59200  65100
38      CONVERTIBLE     FB   SDN  FBG SV IB T310D GM   13 11 27000  3  9  76100  83600

41    3 YACHT FISHERMAN FB   YTFS FBG SV IB T350  CRUS 12  4 20000  2  8  67000  73700
        IB T195D CUM  66900 73500, IB T235D VLVO  68900 75800, IB T410D GM  117500 129000

42      CONVERTIBLE     FB   SDN  FBG SV IB T310D GM   14  9 35000  3  9  94800 104000
42      CONVERTIBLE     FB   SDN  FBG SV IB T450D CUM  14  9 35000  3  9 108500 118500
42      CONVERTIBLE     FB   SDN  FBG SV IB T450D GM   14  9 35000  3  9 108500 119000
42      DOUBLE CABIN    FB   SDN  FBG SV IB T310D GM   14  9 35000  3  9 106500 117000
42      DOUBLE CABIN    FB   SDN  FBG SV IB T410D GM   14  9 35000  3  9 105500 116000
46    3 MOTOR YACHT     FB   MY   FBG SV IB T410D GM   15  3 41000  4  4 120500 132500
48      YACHT FISHERMAN FB   YTFS FBG SV IB T310D GM   14  9 39000  3  9 116000 127500
48      YACHT FISHERMAN FB   YTFS FBG SV IB T410D GM   14  9 39000  3  9 132000 145000
48   10 CONVERTIBLE     FB   SDN  FBG SV IB T550D GM   15  9 48000  4  9 155500 171000
------------------------ 1981 BOATS -------------------------------------------------------
26    2 SEDAN           FB   SDN  FBG SV IB 270  CRUS 10     8500  2  8  14500  16400
26    2 SEDAN           FB   SDN  FBG SV IB T190 CRUS 10     8500  2  8  15500  17600
28    2 MEGA            FB   SDN  FBG SV IB 270  CRUS 10 10 10500  2 10  18200  20300
28    2 MEGA            FB   SDN  FBG SV IB T220 CRUS 10 10 10500  2 10  19600  21800
28    2 SALTY-DOG       OP   SF   FBG SV IB 235-270 10 10  9000  2  4  15200  17500
        IB  210D CAT  21400 23800, IB T148-T270  15800 19600, IB T124D VLVO  22100 24600

28    2 SALTY-DOG       HT   SF   FBG SV IB 235-270 10 10  9000  2  4  15200  17500
        IB  210D CAT  21400 23800, IB T148-T270  15800 19600, IB T124D VLVO  22100 24600

31    8 SPORT SEDAN     FB   SDN  FBG SV IB T270  CRUS 11 11 15000  2  8  29100  32400
31    8 SPORT SEDAN     FB   SDN  FBG SV IB T148D VLVO 11 11 15000  2  8  38200  42500
34    2 CONVERTIBLE     FB   SDN  FBG SV IB T270-T350  11 11 17000  2  9  36500  42100
34    2 CONVERTIBLE     FB   SDN  FBG SV IBT130D-T235D   11 11 17000  2  9  44300  52600
36      DOUBLE CABIN    FB   SDN  FBG SV IB T350  CRUS 12  4 21000  2  8  48900  53800
        IB T195D CUM  53900 59200, IB T210D CAT  55100 60500, IB T235D VLVO  54500 59900

36      SPORT SEDAN     FB   SDN  FBG SV IB T350  CRUS 12  4 20000  2  8  47900  52600
        IB T195D CUM  52300 57400, IB T210D CAT  53500 58800, IB T215D CUM  52800 58100
        IB T235D VLVO  53000 58200, IB T250D CAT  54800 60300, IB T270D CUM  54600 60000

37    9 COASTAL CRUISER FB   SDN  FBG DS IB  192D VLVO 12  9 21000  3 10  54400  59700
37    9 COASTAL CRUISER FB   SDN  FBG DS IB T124D VLVO 12  9 21000  3 10  56400  62000
38      CONVERTIBLE     FB   SDN  FBG SV IB T310D GM   13 11 27000  3  9  72500  79600
42      CONVERTIBLE     FB   SDN  FBG SV IB T310D GM   14  9 35000  3  9  85000  94000
42      CONVERTIBLE     FB   SDN  FBG SV IB T410D GM   14  9 35000  3  9  99500 110500
42      CONVERTIBLE     FB   SDN  FBG SV IB T450D CUM  14  9 35000  3  9 102500 113300
42      CONVERTIBLE     FB   SDN  FBG SV IB T450D GM   14  9 35000  3  9 103000 113500
42      DOUBLE CABIN    FB   SDN  FBG SV IB T310D GM   14  9 35000  3  9 111000 122000
42      DOUBLE CABIN    FB   SDN  FBG SV IB T410D GM   14  9 35000  3  9 110500 121500
46    3 MOTOR YACHT     FB   MY   FBG SV IB T410D GM   15  3 41000  4  4 115000 126000
48      YACHT FISHERMAN FB   YTFS FBG SV IB T450D GM   14  9 39000  3  9 131500 144500
48   10 CONVERTIBLE     FB   SDN  FBG SV IB T550D GM   15  9 48000  4  9 148500 163000
------------------------ 1980 BOATS -------------------------------------------------------
26    2 SEDAN           FB   SDN  FBG SV IB 270  CRUS 10     8500  2  8  13900  15800
26    2 SEDAN           FB   SDN  FBG SV IB T190 CRUS 10     8500  2  8  14800  16800
28    2 MEGA            FB   SDN  FBG SV IB 270  CRUS 10 10 10500  2 10  17300  19400
28    2 MEGA            FB   SDN  FBG SV IB  210D REN 10 10 10500  2 10  25200  28000
28    2 MEGA            FB   SDN  FBG SV IB T220 CRUS 10 10 10500  2 10  19000  21100
28    2 SALTY-DOG       OP   SF   FBG SV IB 270  CRUS 10 10  9000  2  4  14800  16800
28    2 SALTY-DOG       OP   SF   FBG SV IB  210D REN 10 10  9000  2 10  16000  18200
28    2 SALTY-DOG       HT   SF   FBG SV IB 270  CRUS 10 10  9000  2  4  14800  16800
28    2 SALTY-DOG       HT   SF   FBG SV IB  210D REN 10 10  9000  2 10  16000  18200
31    8 SPORT SEDAN     FB   SDN  FBG SV IB T270 CRUS 11 11 15000  2  8  27900  31100
34    2 CONVERTIBLE     FB   SDN  FBG SV IB T270-T350  11 11 17000  2  9  35500  40400
34    2 CONVERTIBLE     FB   SDN  FBG SV IBT210D-T350D   11 11 17000  2  9  45600  54400

36      DOUBLE CABIN    FB   SDN  FBG SV IB T350  CRUS 12  4 21000  2  8  46900  51500
36      DOUBLE CABIN    FB   SDN  FBG SV IB T210D CAT  12  4 21000  2  8  52500  57700
36      DOUBLE CABIN    FB   SDN  FBG SV IB T210D CUM  12  4 21000  2  8  51800  56900
36      SPORT SEDAN     FB   SDN  FBG SV IB T350  CRUS 12  4 20000  2  8  45700  50300
        IB T210D CAT  51000 56100, IB T210D CUM  50300 55200, IB T240D CUM  51100 56200

37    9 COASTAL CRUISER FB   SDN  FBG DS IB  192D VLVO 12  9 21000  3 10  51900  57000
37    9 COASTAL CRUISER FB   SDN  FBG DS IB T124D VLVO 12  9 21000  3 10  53800  59100
38      CONVERTIBLE     FB   SDN  FBG SV IB T350  CRUS 13 11 27000  3  9  60800  66900
        IB T270D CUM  66900 73500, IB T310D GM  69100 76000
        IB T410D J&T  74200 81600

42      CONVERTIBLE     FB   SDN  FBG SV IB T350  CRUS 14  9 35000  3  9  78000  85700
        IB T270D CUM  84700 93000, IB T295D CUM  85800 94300, IB T310D GM  86400 94900
        IB T410D J&T  91800 101000

42      DOUBLE CABIN    FB   SDN  FBG SV IB T350  CRUS 14  9 35000  3  9  89400  98300
        IB T270D CUM  94200 103500, IB T295D CUM  95100 104500, IB T310D GM  96300 106000
        IB T410D J&T  101000 111000
```

```
     LOA  NAME AND/       TOP/ BOAT  -HULL- ----ENGINE--- BEAM    WGT  DRAFT RETAIL RETAIL
     FT IN OR MODEL       RIG  TYPE  MTL TP TP #  HP  MFG  FT IN  LBS  FT IN LOW    HIGH
-------------------- 1980 BOATS -------------------
48     YACHT FISHERMAN    FB  YTFS  FBG SV IB T350  CRUS 14  9 39000  3  9  96000 105500
       IB T270D CUM  98600 108500, IB T295D CUM 103000 113000, IB T310D GM 105500 115500
       IB T410D J&T 120000 132000

48 10  CONVERTIBLE        FB  SDN   FBG SV IB T550D GM   15  7 48000  4  9 141500 155500
-------------------- 1979 BOATS -------------------
26  2  SEDAN              FB  SDN   FBG SV IB  270  CRUS  9 11  7000  2  8  11700  13300
26  2  SEDAN              FB  SDN   FBG SV IB T190  VLVO .9 11  7000  2  8  12700  14400
28  2  MEGA               FB  SDN   FBG SV IB  270  CRUS 10 10  8500  2 10  14800  16800
28  2  MEGA               FB  SDN   FBG SV IB T220  CRUS 10 10  8500  2  4  16300  18500
28  2  SALTY-DOG          OP  SF    FBG SV IB  220  CRUS 10 10  7000  2 10  12100  13800
28  2  SALTY-DOG          OP  SF    FBG SV IB T220  CRUS 10 10  7000  2  4  13700  15600
28  2  SALTY-DOG          HT  SF    FBG SV IB  220  CRUS 10 10  7000  2 10  12100  13800
28  2  SALTY-DOG          HT  SF    FBG SV IB T220  CRUS 10 10  7000  2  4  13700  15600
32     SPORT SEDAN        FB  SDN   FBG SV IB  270  CRUS 11 11 13500  2  8  26900  29900
34  2  SPORT SEDAN        FB  SDN   FBG SV IB T270-T350 11 11 15000  2  9  32200  37300
34  2  SPORT SEDAN        FB  SDN   FBG SV IBT210D-T310D 11 11 15000  2  9  40900  46900

36     DOUBLE CABIN       FB  SDN   FBG SV IB T350  CRUS 12  4 20000  2  8  45900  50400
36     DOUBLE CABIN       FB  SDN   FBG SV IB T210D CAT  12  4 20000  2  8  50700  55700
36     DOUBLE CABIN       FB  SDN   FBG SV IB T210D CUM  12  4 20000  2  8  49900  54900
36     SPORT SEDAN        FB  SDN   FBG SV IB T350  CRUS 12  4 20000  2  8  41000  45500
       IB T210D CAT  47000  51700, IB T210D CUM  46300  50900, IB T240D CUM  48800  53700

37  9  COASTAL CRUISER    FB  SDN   FBG DS IB  192D VLVO 12  9        3 10  54800  60300
37  9  COASTAL CRUISER    FB  SDN   FBG DS IB T124D VLVO 12  9        3 10  56600  62200
38     CONVERTIBLE        FB  SDN   FBG SV IB T350  CRUS 13 11 24000  3  9  52700  57900
       IB T210D CAT  58300  64100, IB T270D CUM  58700  64500, IB T310D J&T  60800  66800
       IB T410D J&T  65300  71800

42     CONVERTIBLE        FB  SDN   FBG SV IB T350  CRUS 14  9 35000  3  9  75600  83100
       IB T270D CUM  81800  89900, IB T295D CUM  83000  91200, IB T310D J&T  83800  92100
       IB T410D J&T  87800  96500

42     CONVERTIBLE EXT CBN FB SDN   FBG SV IB T350  CRUS 14  9 35000  3  9  79400  87300
       IB T270D CUM  84800  93200, IB T295D CUM  85700  94200, IB T310D J&T  86900  95500
       IB T410D J&T  91900 101000

42     DOUBLE CABIN       FB  SDN   FBG SV IB T350  CRUS 14  9 35000  3  9  84200  92600
       IB T270D CUM  89000  97800, IB T295D CUM  89800  98600, IB T310D J&T  91200 100500
       IB T410D J&T  96100 105500

-------------------- 1978 BOATS -------------------
26  2  SEDAN              FB  SDN   FBG SV IB  270  CRUS  9 11  7000  2  8  11300  12800
26  2  SEDAN              FB  SDN   FBG SV IB T190  CRUS  9 11  7000  2  8  12200  13800
28  2  MEGA               FB  SDN   FBG SV IB  270  CRUS 10 10  8500  2 10  14200  16100
28  2  MEGA               FB  SDN   FBG SV IB T220  CRUS 10 10  8500  2  4  15600  17700
28  2  SALTY-DOG          OP  SF    FBG SV IB  220  CRUS 10 10  7000  2 10  11600  13200
28  2  SALTY-DOG          OP  SF    FBG SV IB T220  CRUS 10 10  7000  2  4  13200  15000
28  2  SALTY-DOG          HT  SF    FBG SV IB  220  CRUS 10 10  7000  2 10  11600  13200
28  2  SALTY-DOG          HT  SF    FBG SV IB T220  CRUS 10 10  7000  2  4  13200  15000
31  8  SPORT SEDAN        FB  SDN   FBG SV IB  270  CRUS 11 11 13500  2  8  25100  27900
34  2  SPORT FISHERMAN    FB SDNSF  FBG SV IB T350  CRUS 11 11 15000  2  9  30500  33800
34  2  SPORT FISHERMAN    FB SDNSF  FBG SV IB T210D      11 11 15000  2  9  37000  41100

34  2  SPORT SEDAN        FB  SDN   FBG SV IB T270  CRUS 11 11 15000  2  9  30900  34300
34  2  SPORT SEDAN        FB  SDN   FBG SV IB T210D      11 11 15000  2  9  39700  44100
36     DOUBLE CABIN       FB  SDN   FBG SV IB T350  CRUS 12  4 20000  2  8  43400  48200
36     DOUBLE CABIN       FB  SDN   FBG SV IB T210D CAT  12  4 20000  2  8  48500  53300
36     DOUBLE CABIN       FB  SDN   FBG SV IB T210D CUM  12  4 20000  2  8  48000  52700
36     SPORT SEDAN        FB  SDN   FBG SV IB T350  CRUS 12  4 20000  2  8  39200  43600
       IB T210D CAT  44600  49600, IB T210D CUM  43700  48600, IB T240D CUM  46900  51600

38     CONVERTIBLE        FB  SDN   FBG SV IB T350  CRUS 13 11 24000  3  9  50400  55400
       IB T210D CAT  55800  61300, IB T210D CUM  54500  59900, IB T240D CUM  55300  60800
       IB T295D CUM  56900  62600, IB T310D J&T  58100  63900

42     DOUBLE CABIN       FB  SDN   FBG SV IB T350  CRUS 14  9 35000  3  9  76400  83900
       IB T210D CAT  80600  88600, IB T210D CUM  79500  87400, IB T240D CUM  80500  88500
       IB T295D CUM  82500  90600, IB T310D J&T  83600  91900

42     SPORT FISHERMAN    FB SDNSF  FBG SV IB T350  CRUS 14  9 35000  3  9  75600  83100
       IB T210D CAT  77700  85300, IB T210D CUM  76600  84200, IB T240D CUM  78400  86200
       IB T295D CUM  81800  89900, IB T310D J&T  83300  91500

-------------------- 1977 BOATS -------------------
28  2  MEGA               FB  SDN   FBG SV VD  270  CRUS 10 10  8500  2 10  13600  15400
28  2  MEGA               FB  SDN   FBG SV VD T220  CRUS 10 10  8500  2  4  15000  17000
28  2  SALTY-DOG          OP  SF    FBG SV IB  220  CRUS 10 10        2 10  12400  14100
28  2  SALTY-DOG          OP  SF    FBG SV IB T220  CRUS 10 10        2 10  13700  15600
28  2  SALTY-DOG          HT  SF    FBG SV IB  220  CRUS 10 10        2 10  12400  14100
28  2  SALTY-DOG          HT  SF    FBG SV IB T220  CRUS 10 10        2 10  13700  15600
28  2  SPORT SEDAN        FB SDNSF  FBG SV IB  220  CRUS 10 10  8600  2  4  12700  14500
28  2  SPORT SEDAN        FB SDNSF  FBG SV IB T220  CRUS 10 10  8600  2  4  13800  15700
31  8  SPORT SEDAN        FB  SDN   FBG SV IB  270  CRUS 11 11 13500  2  8  24100  26800
31  8  SPORT SEDAN        FB  SDN   FBG SV VDT200D-T210D 11 11 13500  2  8  32700  36700
34  2  SPORT FISHERMAN    FB SDNSF  FBG SV IB T350  CRUS 11 11 15000  2  9  29200  32500
34  2  SPORT FISHERMAN    FB SDNSF  FBG SV IBT200D-T210D 11 11 15000  2  9  35100  39600

34  2  SPORT SEDAN        FB  SDN   FBG SV IB T270  CRUS 11 11 15000  2  9  29600  32900
34  2  SPORT SEDAN        FB  SDN   FBG SV IBT200D-T210D 11 11 15000  2  9  37700  42500
36     DOUBLE CABIN       FB  SDN   FBG SV IB T350  CRUS 12  4 20000  2  8  39600  44000
       IB T200D CHRY 43600  48500, IB T210D CAT  44400  49300, IB T210D CUM  43700  48600

37  9  SPORT SEDAN        FB  SDN   FBG SV IB T350  CRUS 12  4 20000  2  8  44100  48900
       IB T200D CHRY 48300  53100, IB T210D CAT  49500  54400, IB T210D CUM  48400  53100
       IB T240D CUM  49100  53900

42     DOUBLE CABIN       FB  SDN   FBG SV IB T350  CRUS 14  9 37000  3  9  76700  84300
       IB T210D CAT  80800  88800, IB T210D CUM  79800  87700, IB T240D CUM  80800  88700
       IB T310D J&T  83700  91900, IB T320D CUM  83500  91800

42     SPORT FISHERMAN    FB SDNSF  FBG SV IB T350  CRUS 14  9 35000  3  9  72400  79600
       IB T210D CAT  74400  81700, IB T210D CUM  73400  80600, IB T240D CUM  75100  82500
       IB T310D J&T  79700  87600, IB T320D CUM  79800  87700

-------------------- 1976 BOATS -------------------
23     SALTY-PUP          OP  CR    FBG SV IO  220  CRUS  8     4800  2      6150   7100
23     SALTY-PUP          OP  CR    FBG    IO  230  OMC   8     4800  2      6700   7700
28  2  MEGA               FB  SDN   FBG SV VD  270  CRUS 10     8500  2 10  12300  14000
28  2  MEGA               FB  SDN   FBG SV IB  270  CRUS 10 10  8500  2 10  12900  14600
28  2  MEGA               FB  SDN   FBG SV IB T220  CRUS 10 10  8500  2 10  14200  16200
28  2  SALTY-DOG          OP  CR    FBG SV IB  220  CRUS 10 10  7000  2 10  10700  12200
       IB  210D  14400  16300, IB T100  NISS 10900  12400, IB T220  CRUS 12100  13800

28  2  SALTY-DOG          HT  CR    FBG SV IB  220  CRUS 10 10  7000  2 10  10700  12200
       IB  210D  14400  16300, IB T100  NISS 10900  12400, IB T220  CRUS 12100  13800

28  2  SPORT SEDAN        FB  SDN   FBG SV IB  270       10 10  8600  2 10  13100  14900
28  2  SPORT SEDAN        FB  SDN   FBG SV IB  210D      11 11 13500  2  8  14500  16400
31  8  SPORT SEDAN        FB  SDN   FBG SV IB  270       11 11 13500  2  8  28500  31600
31  8  SPORT SEDAN        FB  SDN   FBG SV IB T200-T220  11 11 13500  2  8  22000  24800
31  8  SPORT SEDAN        FB  SDN   FBG SV IB  320D CUM  11 11 13500  2  8  31900  35400
34  2  SPORT FISHERMAN    FB SDNSF  FBG SV IB  320D CUM  11 11 15000  2  9  32700  36400
34  2  SPORT FISHERMAN    FB SDNSF  FBG SV IB T350  CRUS 11 11 15000  2  9  28100  31200
34  2  SPORT FISHERMAN    FB SDNSF  FBG SV IBT200D-T210D 11 11 15000  2  9  33900  38200
34  2  SPORT SEDAN        FB  SDN   FBG SV IB T200-T270  11 11 15000  2  9  27400  31600
34  2  SPORT SEDAN        FB  SDN   FBG SV IB  210D      11 11 15000  2  9  36900  41000

36     DOUBLE CABIN       FB  SDN   FBG SV IB  240D CUM  12  4 20000  2  8  41000  45500
       IB  320D CUM  41900  46500, IB T210D CAT  44800  49700

36     SPORT SEDAN        FB  SDN   FBG SV IB  240D CUM  12  4 20000  2  8  37800  42600
       IB  320D CUM  38800  43100, IB T210D CAT  40600  45100

37  9  DOUBLE CABIN       FB  SDN   FBG SV IB T210D CUM  12  4 20000  2  8  46600  51200
42     DOUBLE CABIN       FB  SDN   FBG SV IB T350  CRUS 14  9 37000  3  9  73600  80900
       IB T210D CAT  77500  85200, IB T210D CUM  76600  84200, IB T240D CUM  77400  85100
       IB T310D J&T  80200  88200, IB T320D CUM  80100  88000

42     SPORT FISHERMAN    FB SDNSF  FBG SV IB T350  CRUS 14  9 37000  3  9  72700  79900
       IB T210D CAT  74800  82100, IB T210D CUM  73800  81100, IB T240D CUM  75400  82900
       IB T310D J&T  79800  87800, IB T320D CUM  79900  87800

-------------------- 1975 BOATS -------------------
23     SALTY-PUP          OP  CR    FBG SV IO  225  OMC   8     4800  2      6900   7950
23     SALTY-PUP          OP  CR    FBG    IO  225  CHRY  8     4800  2      5800   6700
28  2  SALTY-DOG          OP  CR    FBG SV IB  225  CHRY 10 10  7000  2 10  10300  11700
       IB  210D CUM  17200  19600, IB  225D CAT  18000  20000, IB T225  CHRY 11600  13200
       IB T100D NISS 18100  20100

28  2  SPORT SEDAN        FB  SDN   FBG SV IB  250  CHRY 10 10  8600  2 10  12400  14100
       IB  210D CUM  21000  23300, IB  225D CAT  21400  23800, IB T225  CHRY 13800  15700
       IB T100D NISS 18700  20800
```

```
UNIFLITE INC                -CONTINUED        See inside cover to adjust price for area
 LOA   NAME AND/             TOP/ BOAT -HULL- ----ENGINE--- BEAM   WGT   DRAFT RETAIL RETAIL
FT IN   OR MODEL             RIG TYPE  MTL TP TP # HP  MFG  FT IN  LBS   FT IN  LOW   HIGH
------------------ 1975 BOATS -----------------------------------------------------------------
31    CRUISER               HT  CR   FBG SV IB T225   CHRY 10  7 12500  2  7 18500 20500
31    CRUISER               FB  CR   FBG SV IB T225   CHRY 10  7 12500  2  7 18500 20500
31  8 SPORT SEDAN           FB  SDN  FBG SV IB 210D  CUM  11 11 13500  2  8 27600 30700
    IB  225D CAT  27800  30900, IB T225-T350   21500 26000, IBT210D-T225D  30900 34900

34  2 SPORT FISHERMAN       FB  SDNSF FBG SV IB T330-T350   11 11 15000  2  6 26600 29800
34  2 SPORT FISHERMAN       FB  SDNSF FBG SV IBT210D-T225D 11 11 15000  2  6 33000 37400
34  2 SPORT SEDAN           FB  SDN  FBG SV IB  320D CUM  11 11 15000  2  6 33800 37600
34  2 SPORT SEDAN           FB  SDN  FBG SV IB T250-T330  11 11 15000  2  6 27000 31200
34  2 SPORT SEDAN           FB  SDN  FBG SV IBT210D-T225D 11 11 15000  2  6 35500 40200
36    DOUBLE CABIN          FB  SDN  FBG SV IB  240D CUM  12  4 20000  2  8 39300 43600
    IB  320D CUM  40100  44600, IB T330   CHRY  37500 41600, IB T210D CUM  41600 46200
    IB T225D CAT  42600  47300, IB T240D CUM  41000 45500

36    SPORT SEDAN           FB  SDN  FBG SV IB  240D CUM  12  4 20000  2  8 36400 40400
    IB  320D CUM  37300  41500, IB T330   CHRY  34300 38100, IB T210D CUM  38900 43300
    IB T225D CAT  39900  44300

42    DOUBLE CABIN          FB  SDN  FBG    IB T330   CHRY 14  9 37000  3  9 69900 76800
    IB T210D CUM  73500  80800, IB T225D CAT  74900 82300, IB T240D CUM  74400 81700
    IB T310D GM   76800  84400, IB T320D CUM  76900 84500

42    SPORT FISHERMAN       FB  SDNSF FBG SV IB T330   CHRY 14  9 37000  3  9 68700 75400
    IB T210D CUM  70900  77900, IB T225D CAT  72600 79800, IB T240D CUM  72400 79600
    IB T310D GM   76400  83900, IB T320D CUM  76700 84300
------------------ 1974 BOATS -----------------------------------------------------------------
23    SALTY-PUP             OP  CR   FBG IO  225   OMC   8      4800  2       7150  8200
23    SALTY-PUP             OP  CR   FBG IO  225   CHRY  8      4800  2       5600  6450
23  2                       HT  CR   FBG IO  225   OMC   8      5400  2       7900  9100
23  2                       HT  CR   FBG IB  225   CHRY  8      5400  2       6200  7150
27  3                       HT  CR   FBG IB  225   CHRY  9  7  8500  2  6 10200 11600
27  3                       HT  CR   FBG IB T225   CHRY  9  7  9700  2  2 12200 13800
27  3                       FB  CR   FBG IB  225   CHRY  9  7  9700  2  2 12200 13800
28  2 SALTY-DOG             OP  CR   FBG IB  225   CHRY 10 10  5700  2 10  9100 10300
    IB T225   CHRY 11300  12800, JT T250  FORD  11800 13400, IB T100D NISS  14000 16000

28  2 SALTY-DOG             HT  CR   FBG IB  225   CHRY 10 10  5700  2 10  9100 10300
    IB T225   CHRY 11300  12800, JT T250  FORD  11800 13400, IB T100D NISS  14000 16000

28  3                       FB  SDN  FBG IB  250   CHRY 10 10  6000  2 10 10400 11900
28  3                       FB  SDN  FBG IB T225   CHRY 10 10  7100  2  4 12600 14300
31                          HT  CR   FBG IB T225   CHRY 10  7 12400  2  7 17300 19700
31                          FB  CR   FBG IB T225   CHRY 10  7 12400  2  7 17300 19700
31                          FB  SDN  FBG IB T225   CHRY 10  7 12500  2  7 19200 21300
31                          FB  SDN  FBG JT T250  FORD  10  7 12500        19400 21600
31                          FB  SDN  FBG IB T100D NISS 10  7 12500  2  7 24500 27200
34  3                       FB  SDN  FBG IB T250-T330  11 11 15800  2  8 26100 30100
34  3 TOURNAMENT FISHERMAN  SF  FBG      IB  320D CUM  11 11 15800  2  8 31900 35500
34  3 TOURNAMENT FISHERMAN  SF  FBG      IB T330-T350  11 11 15800  2  8 26200 29500
34  3 TOURNAMENT FISHERMAN  SF  FBG      IBT175D-T225D 11 11 15800  2  8 32500 37500

36  3 DOUBLE CABIN          FB  SDN  FBG IB T330   CHRY 12  4 20000  2  8 36000 40000
36  3 DOUBLE CABIN          FB  SDN  FBG IB T210D CUM  12  4 20000  2  8 40000 44500
36  3 DOUBLE CABIN          FB  SDN  FBG IB T225D CAT  12  4 20000  2  8 41100 45700
36    SPORT SEDAN           FB  SDN  FBG IB T330   CHRY 12  4 20000  2  8 33000 36700
    IB T210D CUM  37400  41600, IB T225D CAT  38200 42400, IB T240D CUM  39400 43800

36  3 YACHT HOME            HT  HB   FBG IO T225   OMC  12  4 15000  2  6 46300 50900
36  3 YACHT HOME            HT  HB   FBG IB T225   CHRY 12  4 15000  2  8 46500 51100
36  3 YACHT HOME            FB  HB   FBG IB T225   CHRY 12  4 15000  2  8 46500 51100
42                          FB  SF   FBG IB T330   CHRY 14  9 37000  3  9 65500 71900
    IB T210D CUM  67700  74400, IB T225D CAT  69400 76200, IB T240D CUM  69100 76000
    IB T320D CUM  73100  80300

42    DOUBLE CABIN          FB  SDN  FBG IB T330   CHRY 14  9 37000  3  9 67200 73800
    IB T210D CUM  70700  77700, IB T225D CAT  72000 79200, IB T240D CUM  71500 78600
    IB T320D CUM  74000  81300
------------------ 1973 BOATS -----------------------------------------------------------------
23    SALTY-PUP             OP  CR   FBG IO  225   CHRY  8      4800  2       7400  8500
23    SALTY-PUP             OP  CR   FBG IO  225   CHRY  8      4800  2       5350  6200
23  2                       OP  CR   FBG IO  225   CHRY  8      5400  2       8200  9450
23  2                       HT  CR   FBG IB  225   CHRY  8      5400  2       6000  6900
27  3                       HT  CR   FBG IB  225   CHRY  9  7  8500  2  6  9850 11200
27  3                       HT  CR   FBG IB T225   CHRY  9  7  9700  2  2 11700 13330
27  3                       FB  CR   FBG IB T225   CHRY  9  7       2  2 10500 11900
28  2 SALTY-DOG             OP  CR   FBG IB  225   CHRY 10 10  5700  2 10  8650  9950
28  2 SALTY-DOG             OP  CR   FBG IB T100D CHRY 10 10  7200  2  4 10900 12300
28  2 SALTY-DOG             OP  CR   FBG IB T225   CHRY 10 10  7200  2  4 13700 15500
28  2 SALTY-DOG             HT  CR   FBG IB  225   CHRY 10 10  7200  2 10  9650 11000
28  2 SALTY-DOG             HT  CR   FBG IB T225   CHRY 10 10  7200  2  4 10900 12300

28  2 SALTY-DOG             HT  CR   FBG IB T100D CHRY 10 10  7200  2  4 13700 15500
28  3 SPORT                 FB  SDN  FBG IB  250   CHRY 10 10  6000  2 10 10000 11400
28  3 SPORT                 FB  SDN  FBG IB T225   CHRY 10 10  7100  2  4 12100 13700
31                          HT  CR   FBG IB T225   CHRY 10  7 12400  2  7 16600 18900
31                          FB  CR   FBG IB T225   CHRY 10  7 12400  2  7 16600 18900
31    SPORT                 FB  SDN  FBG IB T225   CHRY 10  7 12500  2  7 18400 20500
31    SPORT                 FB  SDN  FBG IB T100D CHRY 10  7 12500  2  7 23800 26500
36                          FB  SDN  FBG IB T330   CHRY 12  4 20000  2  8 33200 36900
36                          FB  SDN  FBG IB T330   CHRY 12  4 20000  2  8 33200 36900
    IB T210D CUM  37300  41400, IB T225D CAT  38200 42400, IB T240D CUM  37900 42200

36  3 YACHT HOME            HT  HB   FBG IO T225   OMC  12  4 15000  2  8 46000 50600
36  3 YACHT HOME            HT  HB   FBG IB T225   CHRY 12  4 15000  2  8 46000 50500
36  3 YACHT HOME            FB  HB   FBG IB T225   CHRY 12  4 15000  2  8 46000 50500
42                          FB  SF   FBG IB T330   CHRY 14  9 37000  3  9 63000 69300
    IB T210D CUM  65200  71600, IB T225D CAT  66800 73400, IB T240D CUM  66600 73200
    IB T300D CUM  69400  76300

42    DOUBLE CABIN          FB  SDN  FBG IB T330   CHRY 14  9 37000  3  9 64700 71100
    IB T210D CUM  68100  74800, IB T225D CAT  69400 76200, IB T240D CUM  68900 75700
    IB T300D CUM  70600  77600
------------------ 1972 BOATS -----------------------------------------------------------------
17                          OP  RNBT FBG IB 150                           1800  2100
17                          HT  RNBT FBG OB                               1900  2250
17                          ST  RNBT FBG OB                               1900  2250
17    CONVERTIBLE           OP  RNBT FBG OB                               2250  2600
18                          OP  CUD  FBG OB                               2850  3300
18                          HT  RNBT FBG OB                               2250  2650
18                          OP  SKI  FBG OB                               2250  2650
18    CONVERTIBLE           ST  CUD  FBG OB 185                           2850  3300
18    CONVERTIBLE           ST  RNBT FBG OB                               2250  2650
19    EXPRESS               OP  RNBT FBG OB                               2650  3050
22    EXPRESS               OP  RNBT FBG OB                               5200  6000

22    EXPRESS               OP  RNBT FBG IB 185                           3800  4450
22    SPORT FISHERMAN       FB  FSH  FBG OB                               4400  5050
22    SPORT FISHERMAN       FB  FSH  FBG IB 185                           3800  4400
23                          OP  FSH  FBG IB  225   OMC   8      4000      6950  8000
23                          OP  CR   FBG IB  225   OMC   8      4000  2  2  4650  5350
23    SALTY-PUP             OP  CR   FBG IO  225   OMC   8      4300      7000  8000
23    SALTY-PUP             OP  CR   FBG IO  225   OMC   8      4400  2  2  4900  5600
23  4                       HT  CR   FBG IO  225   OMC   8      4400  2  3  7250  8300
23  4                       HT  CR   FBG IB  225   OMC   8      4500  2  3  5150  5900
23  4                       HT  SF   FBG IO  225   OMC   8      4300  2  3  8100  9300
23  4                       HT  SF   FBG VD  225   OMC   8      4000  2  3  4700  5400

26                          HT  CR   FBG IB 215-240                       8900 10200
26                          OP  CR   FBG IB T215                          9700 11000
26                          OP  EXP  FBG IB 215-240                      10200 11000
26                          OP  EXP  FBG IB T215                          9700 11000
27  3                       HT  CR   FBG IO T225   OMC   9  7  6500  2  8 11700 13300
27  3                       HT  CR   FBG IB T225   CHRY  9  7  7700  2  8 14400 16400
27  3                       FB  CR   FBG IO T225   OMC   9  7  6500  2  8 14400 16400
27  3                       FB  CR   FBG IB T225   CHRY  9  7  7700  2  8 13300 15100
27  3                       FB  SF   FBG IO 185-210D     9  7  7700  2  8 19900 22700
27  3                       FB  SF   FBG IB T225   OMC   9  7  7700  2  8 16400 18700
28                          OP  EXP  FBG IB T215                         11200 12800
28                          HT  SF   FBG IB T215                         11000 12500

28                          FB  SF   FBG IB T215                         11000 12500
28                          SDN  FBG IB T250   CHRY 10 10  6000  2  8 14000 16000
28  3 SALTY-DOG             OP  CR   FBG IO  225   OMC  10 10  5700  2  8 13600 15500
28  3 SALTY-DOG             OP  CR   FBG IO 185D-210D    10 10  5700  2  8 16000 18200
28  3 SALTY-DOG             OP  CR   FBG IO T225   OMC  10 10  7200  2  6 15300 17400
28  3 SALTY-DOG             FB  SDN  FBG IO  225   OMC  10 10  5700  2  8 15300 17500
28  3 SPORT                 FB  SDN  FBG IO  250   CHRY 10 10  7100  2  8 16900 19000
28  3 SPORT                 HT  CR   FBG IB 240-260     10 10       2  8 10800 12400
29                          HT  CR   FBG IB T215                         11900 13700
29                          OP  EXP  FBG IB 240-260                      10800 12400
29                          OP  EXP  FBG IB T215                         11900 13500

96th ed. - Vol. III              CONTINUED ON NEXT PAGE                              651
```

LOA FT	IN	NAME AND/ OR MODEL	TOP/ RIG	BOAT TYPE	-HULL- MTL	TP	----ENGINE--- TP	# HP	MFG	BEAM FT	IN	WGT LBS	DRAFT FT	IN	RETAIL LOW	RETAIL HIGH
1972 BOATS																
31			HT	CR	FBG		IO	T225	OMC	10	7	10000	2	8	22000	24500
31			FB	CR	FBG		IO	T225	OMC	10	7	10000	2	8	22000	24500
31		SPORT	FB	SDN	FBG		VD	T225	OMC	10	7	10500	2	8	16700	19000
31		SPORT	FB	SDN	FBG		IO	T185D-T210D		10	7	10500	2	8	29200	33500
34			HT	CR	FBG		IB	T260							21400	23800
34			OP	EXP	FBG		IB	T260							23600	26200
34			FB	SF	FBG		IB	T260							20300	22600
36			HT	CR	FBG		IO	T330	CHRY	12	4	15500	3	4	31300	34700
		IO T185D CUM 36500 40600, IO T210D CUM 37100 41200, IO T215D GM 37300 41400														
		IO T225D CAT 38100 42300														
36			FB	CR	FBG		IO	T330	CHRY	12	4	15500	3	4	31300	34700
		IO T185D CUM 36500 40600, IO T210D CUM 37100 41200, IO T215D GM 37300 41400														
		IO T225D CAT 38100 42300														
36		DOUBLE CABIN	FB	SDN	FBG		IO	T330	CHRY	12	4	14700	3	4	31500	35000
36		SPORT SEDAN	HT	SDN	FBG		IO	T330	CHRY	12	4	15700	3	4	32400	36000
36		SPORT SEDAN	FB	SDN	FBG		IO	T330	CHRY	12	4	15700	3	4	32400	36000
		VD T185D CUM 30900 34300, VD T210D CUM 31400 34900, VD T215D GM 31600 35200														
		VD T225D CAT 32300 35900														
36	3	YACHT HOME	HT	HB	FBG		IO	T225	OMC	12	4	11500	3	4	38900	43200
36	3	YACHT HOME	HT	HB	FBG		VD	T225	OMC	12	4	11500	3	4	41600	46200
36	3	YACHT HOME	FB	HB	FBG		VD	T225	OMC	12	4	11500	3	4	41600	46200
42			HT	EXP	FBG		IB	T260							47500	52200
42			HT	SDN	FBG		IB	T260							50800	55800
42			FB	SF	FBG		IB	T260							50800	55900
		IO T330 CHRY 76400 83900, IO T210D CUM 73800 81100, IO T225D CAT 76100 83600														
		IO T300D GM 80500 88500														
42		DOUBLE CABIN	FB	SDN	FBG		IO	T330	CHRY	14	9	30000	3	6	61200	67200
		IO T210D CUM 68500 75300, IO T225D CAT 70100 77000, IO T300D CUM 71600 78700														
42		TRUNK CABIN AFT	HT	EXP	FBG		IB	T260							54900	60400
42		TRUNK CABIN AFT	FB	SF	FBG		IB	T260							59000	64800
48			FB	MY	FBG		IO	T283D	GM	15	8	40000	4	6	93400	102500
1971 BOATS																
23	2		HT	CR	FBG		IO	215	OMC	8			2	3	6500	7450
23	2		HT	CR	FBG		VD	225	CHRY	8			2	3	4100	4750
23	2		OP	SF	FBG		IO	215	OMC	8			2	3	8250	9500
23	2		OP	SF	FBG		VD	225	CHRY	8			2	3	4600	5300
23	2		HT	SF	FBG		IO	215	OMC	8			2	3	8250	9500
23	2		HT	SF	FBG		VD	225	CHRY	8			2	3	4600	5300
23	2	CRUISER		CR	FBG	SV	IO	210	OMC	8		4000	2	3	6850	7850
23	2	SPORTFISHERMAN		SF	FBG	SV	IO	210	OMC	8		3700	2	3	7350	8450
23	2	SPORTFISHERMAN	FB	SF	FBG	SV	IO	210	OMC	8			2	3	8250	9500
27	3		HT	CR	FBG		IB	225	CHRY	9	7	6500	2	8	7700	8850
27	3		HT	CR	FBG		IB	T225	CHRY	9	7	7700	2	8	9500	10800
27	3		FB	SF	FBG		IB	225	CHRY	9	7	7700	2	8	8500	9800
27	3		FB	SF	FBG		IB	T225	CHRY	9	7	7700	2	8	9550	10800
28	3	SALTY-DOG	OP	CR	FBG		IB	225	CHRY	10	10	5700	2	8	8050	9250
28	3	SALTY-DOG	OP	CR	FBG		IB	T225	CHRY	10	10	6800	2	8	9900	11200
31			HT	CR	FBG		IB	T225	CHRY	10	7	10000	3	2	14500	16500
31			FB	CR	FBG		IB	T225	CHRY	10	7	10000	3	2	14500	16500
31		SPORT	FB	SDN	FBG		VD	T225	CHRY	10	7	10500	3	2	16100	18200
36			HT	CR	FBG		IB	T330	CHRY	12	4	15500	3		26500	29400
36			FB	CR	FBG		IB	T330	CHRY	12	4	15500	3	4	26500	29400
36			HT	SDN	FBG		IB	T330	CHRY	12	4	15700	3	4	27400	30500
36		SPORT SEDAN	FB	SDN	FBG		IB	T330	CHRY	12	4	15700	3	4	27400	30500
36	3	YACHT HOME	HT	HB	FBG		IO	T215	OMC	12	4	11500	3		38300	42600
36	3	YACHT HOME	HT	HB	FBG		VD	T225	CHRY	12	4	11500	3		39100	43400
36	3	YACHT HOME	HT	HB	FBG	SV	IO	210	OMC	12	4	10500	3	10	31600	35100
36	3	YACHT HOME	FB	HB	FBG		VD	T225	CHRY	12	4	11500	3		39100	43400
44			FB	SF	FBG		IB	T330	CHRY	14	8	29000	4		46500	51100
44		DOUBLE CABIN	FB	SDN	FBG		IB	T330	CHRY	14	8	30000	4		49000	53900
48	3		FB	MY	FBG		IB	T283D	GM	15	8	40000	4	6	66700	73300
1970 BOATS																
23	2		HT	CR	FBG		IO	210	OMC	8	3		2	3	6750	7750
23	2		HT	CR	FBG		IB	225	CHRY	8	3	3900	2	3	4100	4800
23	2		OP	SF	FBG		IO	210	OMC	8	3		2	3	8600	9850
23	2		OP	SF	FBG		IB	225	CHRY	8	3	3600	2	3	3900	4500
23	2		HT	SF	FBG		IO	210	OMC	8	3		2	3	8600	9850
23	2		HT	SF	FBG		IB	225	CHRY	8	3		2	3	4500	5150
23	2		FB	SF	FBG		IO	210	OMC	8	3		2	3	8600	9900
23	2		FB	SF	FBG		IB	225	CHRY	8	3		2	3	4500	5150
27	3		HT	CR	FBG		IB	225-300		9	7	6500	2	8	7400	8850
27	3		HT	CR	FBG		IB	T225	CHRY	9	7	7700	2	8	9200	10500
27	3		HT	SF	FBG		IB	225-300		9	7	7700	2	8	8200	9750
27	3		HT	SF	FBG		IB	T225	CHRY	9	7	7700	2	8	9200	10500
27	3		FB	SF	FBG		IB	225	CHRY	9	7	7700	2	8	8200	9400
27	3		FB	SF	FBG		IB	T225	CHRY	9	7	7700	2	8	9200	10500
31			HT	CR	FBG		IB	T225	CHRY	10	7	10000	3	2	14000	15900
31			FB	CR	FBG		IB	T225	CHRY	10	7	10000	3	2	14000	15900
31		SPORT	FB	SDN	FBG		IB	T225	CHRY	10	7	15700	3	2	17200	19500
36			HT	CR	FBG		IB	T300	CHRY	12	4	15500	3		25300	28100
36			FB	CR	FBG		IB	T300	CHRY	12	4	15500	3	4	25300	28100
36			HT	SDN	FBG		IB	T300	CHRY	12	4	15700	3	4	26200	29100
36		SPORT SEDAN	FB	SDN	FBG		IB	T300	CHRY	12	4	15700	3	4	26200	29100
36	3	YACHT HOME	HT	HB	FBG		IO	210	OMC	12	4	11500	3		34800	38600
		IB 225 CHRY 35300 39200, IO T210 OMC 37700 41900, IB T225 CHRY 38200 42400														
42		DOUBLE CABIN		SDN	FBG		IB	T300		14	9		3	6	48000	52700
48	3	YACHT HOME	FB	MY	FBG		IB	T283D	GM	15	8	40000	4	6	64300	70700
1969 BOATS																
23	2		HT	CR	FBG	SV	IO	210		8	3		2	3	7050	8100
23	2		HT	CR	FBG	SV	IB	210		8	3	3700	2	3	3800	4550
23	2		OP	SF	FBG	SV	IO	210		8	3		2	3	9000	10300
23	2		OP	SF	FBG	SV	IB	210		8	3	3200	2	3	3450	4250
23	2		HT	SF	FBG	SV	IO	210		8	3		2	3	9000	10300
23	2		HT	SF	FBG	SV	IB	210		8	3	3600	2	3	3750	4500
23	2		FB	SF	FBG	SV	IO	210		8	3		2	3	9050	10300
23	2		FB	SF	FBG	SV	IB	210		8	3	3600	2	3	3750	4500
27	3		HT	CR	FBG	SV	IB	210	CHRY	9	7	5300	2	8	6350	7300
27	3		HT	CR	FBG	SV	IB	T210	CHRY	9	7	6400	2	8	7900	9100
27	3		HT	SF	FBG	SV	IB	210	CHRY	9	7	5600	2	8	6500	7500
27	3		HT	SF	FBG	SV	IB	T210	CHRY	9	7	6530	2	8	8000	9200
27	3		FB	SF	FBG	SV	IB	210	CHRY	9	7	5600	2	8	6550	7500
27	3		FB	SF	FBG	SV	IB	T210	CHRY	9	7	6530	2	8	8000	9200
31			HT	EXP	FBG	SV	IB	T210	CHRY	10	7	7400	3	2	12600	14300
31			FB	EXP	FBG	SV	IB	T210	CHRY	10	7	7400	3	2	12600	14300
31			FB	SDN	FBG	SV	IB	T210	CHRY	10	7	7400	3	2	12500	14200
36			HT	EXP	FBG	SV	IB	T300	CHRY	12	4	12300	3	4	22100	24500
36			FB	EXP	FBG	SV	IB	T300	CHRY	12	4	12300	3	4	22100	24500
36			FB	SF	FBG	SV	IB	T300	CHRY	12	4	15200	3	4	24300	27000
1968 BOATS																
23	2		HT	CR	FBG	SV	IO	210	CHRY	8	3	3800	2	3	7400	8500
23	2		HT	CR	FBG	SV	IB	210	CHRY	8	3	3700	2	3	3650	4250
23	2		OP	SF	FBG	SV	IO	210	CHRY	8	3	3300	2	3	7650	8750
23	2		OP	SF	FBG	SV	IB	210	CHRY	8	3	3200	2	3	3300	3850
23	2		HT	SF	FBG	SV	IO	210	CHRY	8	3	3600	2	3	8100	9300
23	2		HT	SF	FBG	SV	IB	210	CHRY	8	3	3600	2	3	3600	4200
23	2		FB	SF	FBG	SV	IB	210	CHRY	8	3	3600	2	3	3600	4200
27	3		HT	CR	FBG	SV	IB	210	CHRY	9	7	5300	2	8	6100	7050
27	3		HT	CR	FBG	SV	IB	T210	CHRY	9	7	6400	2	8	7650	8750
27	3		HT	SF	FBG	SV	IB	210	CHRY	9	7	5600	2	8	6300	7200
27	3		HT	SF	FBG	SV	IB	T210	CHRY	9	7	6530	2	8	7700	8850
27	3		FB	SF	FBG	SV	IB	210	CHRY	9	7	5600	2	8	6300	7250
27	3		FB	SF	FBG	SV	IB	T210	CHRY	9	7	6530	2	8	7700	8850
31			HT	EXP	FBG	SV	IB	T210	CHRY	10	7	7400	3	2	12100	13800
31			FB	EXP	FBG	SV	IB	T210	CHRY	10	7	7400	3	2	12100	13800
36			HT	EXP	FBG	SV	IB	T300	CHRY	12	4	12300	3	4	21400	23800
36			FB	EXP	FBG	SV	IB	T300	CHRY	12	4	12300	3	4	21400	23800
1967 BOATS																
20	4		OP	EXP	FBG	SV	IO	155	OMC	7	9	2800			5100	5850
23	2		HT	CR	FBG	SV	IO	185	OMC	8	3	3700	2	3	7400	8500
23	2		HT	CR	FBG	SV	IB	210		8	3	3700	2	3	3550	4150
23	2		OP	EXP	FBG	SV	IO	185	OMC	8	3	3700	2	3	7400	8500
23	2		OP	EXP	FBG	SV	IB	210		8	3	3700	2	3	3550	4150
23	2		HT	SF	FBG	SV	IO	185	OMC	8	3	3600	2	3	8250	9500
23	2		HT	SF	FBG	SV	IB	210		8	3	3600	2	3	3500	4050
23	2		FB	SF	FBG	SV	IO	185	OMC	8	3	3600	2	3	8250	9500
23	2		FB	SF	FBG	SV	IB	210		8	3	3600	2	3	3500	4050
27	3		HT	CR	FBG	SV	IB	210		9	7	5300	2	8	5900	6800
27	3		HT	CR	FBG	SV	IB	T210		9	7	6180	2	8	7250	8350
27	3		HT	SF	FBG	SV	IB	210		9	7	5600	2	8	6050	6950
27	3		HT	SF	FBG	SV	IB	T210		9	7	6530	2	8	7450	8550
27	3		FB	SF	FBG	SV	IB	210		9	7	5600	2	8	6050	7000
27	3		FB	SF	FBG	SV	IB	T210		9	7	6530	2	8	7450	8550
31			HT	EXP	FBG	SV	IB	T210		10	7	7200	3	2	11700	13200
31			FB	EXP	FBG	SV	IB	T210		10	7	7200	3	2	11700	13200

CONTINUED ON NEXT PAGE

UNIFLITE INC -CONTINUED See inside cover to adjust price for area

LOA FT	LOA IN	NAME AND/ OR MODEL	TOP/ RIG	BOAT TYPE	HULL MTL	HULL TP	ENGINE TP	ENGINE # HP	ENGINE MFG	BEAM FT	BEAM IN	WGT LBS	DRAFT FT	DRAFT IN	RETAIL LOW	RETAIL HIGH
		1967 BOATS														
36			HT	EXP	FBG	SV	IB	T290		12	4	12300	3	4	20800	23100
36			FB	EXP	FBG	SV	IB	T290		12	4	12300	3	4	20800	23100
36		TRIPLE CABIN	HT	SDN	FBG	SV	IB	T290		12	4	14300	3	4	22900	25400
		1966 BOATS														
18		UNIFLITE 18		EXP	FBG	SV	OB			7	3	1250			2200	2550
18		UNIFLITE 18		SPTCR	FBG		OB			7	3	1000			1800	2150
20	4		OP	EXP	FBG	SV	IO	150		7	9	2800			5300	6100
23	2		OP	EXP	FBG	SV	IO	185		8	3	3800	2	3	7800	9000
23	2		OP	EXP	FBG	SV	IB	210		8	3	3800	2	3	3500	4050
23	2		HT	EXP	FBG	SV	IO	185		8	3	3800	2	3	7800	9000
23	2		HT	EXP	FBG	SV	IB	210		8	3	3800	2	3	3500	4050
23	2		HT	SF	FBG	SV	IO	185		8	3	3800	2	3	9000	10200
23	2		HT	SF	FBG	SV	IB	210		8	3	3800	2	3	3500	4050
23	2		FB	SF	FBG	SV	IO	185		8	3	3800	2	3	9000	10200
23	2		FB	SF	FBG	SV	IB	210		8	3	3800	2	3	3500	4100
27	3		HT	CR	FBG	SV	IB	210		9	7	5080	2	8	5600	6400
27	3		HT	CR	FBG	SV	IB	T210		9	7	5780	2	8	6800	7800
27	3		HT	SF	FBG	SV	IB	210		9	7	5080	2	8	5600	6400
27	3		HT	SF	FBG	SV	IB	T210		9	7	5780	2	8	6800	7800
27	3		FB	SF	FBG	SV	IB	210		9	7	5080	2	8	5600	6400
27	3		FB	SF	FBG	SV	IB	T210		9	7	5780	2	8	6800	7850
31			HT	CR	FBG	SV	IB	T210		10	7	6800	3	2	9950	11300
31			FB	SF	FBG	SV	IB	T210		10	7	6800	3	2	9350	10600
36			HT	CR	FBG	SV	IB	T300		12	4	10000	2	6	17200	19500
36			FB	SF	FBG	SV	IB	T300		12	4	10000	2	6	16600	18800
36		TRIPLE CABIN	HT	SDN	FBG	SV	IB	T300		12	4	12000	2	6	20800	23100
		1965 BOATS														
16	4	SPORTS	OP	RNBT	FBG		IO	100	EAT						2800	3250
18			OP	SPTCR	FBG		OB			7		950			1700	2050
18			OP	SPTCR	FBG		IO	100-225		7		1390			3000	3700
18			HT	SPTCR	FBG		OB			7		950			1700	2050
18			HT	SPTCR	FBG		IO	100-225		7		1390			3000	3700
18		SPORTS	OP	RNBT	FBG		OB			7		950			1750	2050
18		SPORTS	OP	RNBT	FBG		IO	100-225				1390			3050	3600
19	7		OP	EXP	FBG		OB			7	8	1450			2550	3000
19	7		OP	EXP	FBG		IO	100-225		7	8	2095			4100	5000
19	7		OP	SPTCR	FBG		OB			7	8	1495			2650	3050
19	7		OP	SPTCR	FBG		IO	100-225		7	8	1875			3950	4850
19	7		HT	SPTCR	FBG		OB			7	8	1495			2650	3050
19	7		HT	SPTCR	FBG		IO	100-225		7	8	1875			3950	4800
22	10		OP	EXP	FBG		IO	140-190		8		4000			8100	9400
22	10		OP	EXP	FBG		IB	215	INT	8		4000	2		3400	3950
22	10		OP	EXP	FBG		IO	225	MRCR	8		4000	2		8300	9500
22	10		HT	EXP	FBG		IO	140-190		8		4000	2		8100	9400
22	10		HT	EXP	FBG		IB	215	INT	8		4000	2		3400	3950
22	10		HT	EXP	FBG		IO	225	MRCR	8		4000	2		8300	9500
22	10		OP	SPTCR	FBG		IO	140-190		8		4000	2		8100	9400
22	10		OP	SPTCR	FBG		IB	215	INT	8		4000	2		3400	3950
22	10		OP	SPTCR	FBG		IO	225	MRCR	8		4000	2		8300	9500
22	10		HT	SPTCR	FBG		IO	140-190		8		4000	2		8100	9400
22	10		HT	SPTCR	FBG		IB	215	INT	8		4000	2		3400	3950
22	10		HT	SPTCR	FBG		IO	225	MRCR	8		4000	2		8300	9500
26			OP	EXP	FBG		IO	225	MRCR	9	4	4000	2	2	10400	11900
26			OP	EXP	FBG		IB	240		9	4	4000	2	2	4400	5100
26			OP	EXP	FBG		IB	T215	INT	9	4	4000	2	2	5100	5850
26			HT	EXP	FBG		IO	225	MRCR	9	4	4000	2	2	10400	11900
26			HT	EXP	FBG		IB	240		9	4	4000	2	2	4400	5100
26			HT	EXP	FBG		IB	T215	INT	9	4	4000	2	2	5100	5850
29			OP	EXP	FBG		IB	240		9	8	4000	2	2	6350	7350
29			OP	EXP	FBG		IB	T215	INT	9	8	7700	2	4	8450	9750
29			HT	EXP	FBG		IB	240		9	8	6700	2	4	7250	8350
29			HT	EXP	FBG		IB	T215	INT	9	8	7700	2	4	8450	9750
29			HT	SF	FBG		IB	T215	INT	9	8	7700	2	4	8450	9750
29			FB	SF	FBG		IB	T215	INT	9	8	7700	2	4	8450	9750
33	11		OP	CR	FBG		IB	T260	INT	11	8	12100	2	10	16100	18300
33	11		HT	CR	FBG		IB	T260	INT	11	8	12100	2	10	16100	18300
33	11		FB	SPTCR	FBG		IB	T260	INT	11	8	12100	2	10	16100	18300
44	1	ANNAPOLIS	SLP	SAIL	FBG	KL	IB	30		11		22500	6		58700	64500
44	1	ANNAPOLIS	SLP	SAIL	FBG	KL	IB	30D	PERK	11		22500	6		59100	65000
44	1	ANNAPOLIS	YWL	SAIL	FBG	KL	IB	30		11		22500	6		58700	64500
44	1	ANNAPOLIS	YWL	SAIL	FBG	KL	IB	30D	PERK	11		22500	6		59100	65000
		1964 BOATS														
16	4	SPORTS		RNBT	FBG		IO	100	EAT						2900	3400
18			ST	SPTCR	FBG		OB								**	**
18			ST	SPTCR	FBG		IO	100-140		7		950			2950	3600
18			ST	SPTCR	FBG		IO	190-225		7		1390			3150	3800
18			HT	SPTCR	FBG		OB			7		950			1700	2050
18			HT	SPTCR	FBG		IO	100-225		7		1390			3100	3800
18		SPORTS	OP	RNBT	FBG		IO	100-225		7		1350			3050	3700
19	7		ST	EXP	FBG		OB			7	8	1450			2600	3000
19	7		ST	EXP	FBG		IO	100-225		7	8	2075			4250	5150
19	7		ST	SPTCR	FBG		OB			7	8	1495			2650	3050
19	7		ST	SPTCR	FBG		IO	100-225		7	8	1875			4100	4950
19	7		HT	SPTCR	FBG		OB			7	8	1495			2650	3050
19	7		HT	SPTCR	FBG		IO	100-225		7	8	1875			4100	4950
22	10		OP	EXP	FBG		IO	140-190		8		4000	2		8400	9700
22	10		OP	EXP	FBG		IB	215	INT	8		4000	2		3300	3800
22	10		OP	EXP	FBG		IO	225	MRCR	8		4000	2		8550	9850
22	10		HT	EXP	FBG		IO	140-190		8		4000	2		8400	9700
22	10		HT	EXP	FBG		IB	215	INT	8		4000	2		3300	3800
22	10		HT	EXP	FBG		IO	225	MRCR	8		4000	2		8550	9850
22	10		OP	SPTCR	FBG		IO	140-190		8		4000	2		8400	9700
22	10		OP	SPTCR	FBG		IB	215	INT	8		4000	2		3300	3800
22	10		OP	SPTCR	FBG		IO	225	MRCR	8		4000	2		8550	9850
22	10		HT	SPTCR	FBG		IO	140-190		8		4000	2		8400	9700
22	10		HT	SPTCR	FBG		IB	215	INT	8		4000	2		3300	3800
22	10		HT	SPTCR	FBG		IO	225	MRCR	8		4000	2		8550	9850
26			OP	EXP	FBG		IO	225	MRCR	9	4	5800	2	2	13400	15200
26			OP	EXP	FBG		IB	240		9	4	5800	2	2	5250	6000
26			OP	EXP	FBG		IB	T215	INT	9	4	5800	2	2	5850	6700
26			HT	EXP	FBG		IO	225	MRCR	9	4	5800	2	2	13400	15200
26			HT	EXP	FBG		IB	240		9	4	5800	2	2	5250	6000
26			HT	EXP	FBG		IB	T215	INT	9	4	5800	2	2	5850	6700
29			OP	EXP	FBG		IB	240		9	8	6700	2	4	7000	8050
29			OP	EXP	FBG		IB	T215	INT	9	8	7700	2	4	8150	9400
29			HT	EXP	FBG		IB	240		9	8	6700	2	4	7000	8050
29			HT	EXP	FBG		IB	T215	INT	9	8	7700	2	4	8150	9400
29			HT	SF	FBG		IB	T215	INT	9	8	7700	2	4	8150	9400
29			FB	SF	FBG		IB	T215	INT	9	8	7700	2	4	8150	9400
33	11		OP	CR	FBG		IB	T260	INT	11	8	12100	2	10	15500	17600
33	11		HT	CR	FBG		IB	T260	INT	11	8	12100	2	10	15500	17600
33	11		FB	SF	FBG		IB	T260	INT	11	8	12100	2	10	15500	17600
		1963 BOATS														
17			HT	RNBT	FBG		OB								1900	2300
17		CONVERTIBLE	ST	RNBT	FBG		OB								1900	2300
17		EXPRESS	OP	RNBT	FBG		OB								2300	2650
18			HT	CUD	FBG		OB								2900	3350
18			OP	RNBT	FBG		OB								2300	2700
18			HT	RNBT	FBG		OB								2300	2700
18		CONVERTIBLE	ST	CUD	FBG		OB								2900	3350
18		CONVERTIBLE	ST	RNBT	FBG		OB								2300	2700
19		EXPRESS	OP	RNBT	FBG		OB								2650	3100
22		EXPRESS	OP	RNBT	FBG		OB								5250	6050
22		EXPRESS	OP	RNBT	FBG		IB	185							2750	3150
22		SPORT FISHERMAN		FSH	FBG		OB								4450	5100
22		SPORT FISHERMAN		FSH	FBG		IB	185							2700	3150
25				EXP	FBG		IB	215							6250	7200
25				SF	FBG		IB	215							6250	7200
26			HT	CR	FBG		IB	215-240							6300	7300
26			HT	CR	FBG		IB	T215							6900	7950
26			OP	EXP	FBG		IB	215-240							6300	7300
26			OP	EXP	FBG		IB	T215							6900	7950
28			OP	EXP	FBG		IB	T215							8000	9200
28			HT	SF	FBG		IB	T215							7850	9000
29			HT	CR	FBG		IB	T215							8450	9700
29			OP	EXP	FBG		IB	240-260							7700	8950
29			OP	EXP	FBG		IB	T215							8450	9700
34			HT	CR	FBG		IB	T240							15100	17100
34			OP	EXP	FBG		IB	T240							16600	18800
34			FB	SF	FBG		IB	T260							14400	16300
42			HT	EXP	FBG		IB	T260							38500	42800
42			HT	SDN	FBG		IB	T260							38400	42700
42			FB	SF	FBG		IB	T260							41800	46500
42		TRUNK CABIN AFT	HT	EXP	FBG		IB	T260							38500	42800
42		TRUNK CABIN AFT	FB	SF	FBG		IB	T260							41800	46500

 CONTINUED ON NEXT PAGE

LOA FT IN	NAME AND/ OR MODEL	TOP/ RIG	BOAT TYPE	-HULL- MTL TP	TP	----ENGINE--- # HP MFG	BEAM FT IN	WGT LBS	DRAFT FT IN	RETAIL LOW	RETAIL HIGH
				1961 BOATS							
18 7	EXPRESS		EXP	FBG	OB		7 8	1450		2500	2900
21 7	EXPRESS		EXP	FBG	OB		8	2600		4850	5600
21 7	EXPRESS CRUISER		EXP	FBG	IB	185	8		2	2600	3000
21 7	SPORT FISHERMAN		SF	FBG	OB		8	2200		4250	4950
24 10	EXPRESS CRUISER		EXP	FBG	IB	215	8 6		2 4	5900	6750
28	EXPRESS CRUISER		EXP	FBG	IB	215	9 8		2 4	6850	7900
33 11	CRITERION		CR	FBG	IB	240	11 8		2 10	13600	15500
				1960 BOATS							
18 7	EXPRESS CR		EXP	FBG	OB		7 8	1400		2450	2850
21 7	EXPRESS CR		EXP	FBG	OB		8	2600		4850	5600
21 7	EXPRESS CR		EXP	FBG	IB	185	8		2	2550	2950
21 7	SPORTFISH CR		SF	FBG	IB	185	8		2	2600	3050
21 7	SPORTFISHERMAN		SF	FBG	OB		8			5000	5750
24 1	EXPRESS CR		EXP	FBG	OB		8 6	3300		6500	7500
24 1	SPORTFISH CR		SF	FBG	OB		8 6	3000		6050	6950
24 10	EXPRESS CR		EXP	FBG	IB	215	8		2 1	5750	6650
24 10	SPORTFISH CR		SF	FBG	IB	215	8		2 1	5750	6600
28	EXPRESS CR		EXP	FBG	IB	215	9 7		2 2	6700	7700
28	EXPRESS CR		EXP	FBG	IB	T215	9 7		2 2	7400	8500
				1959 BOATS							
18 1	19 EXP		CR	FBG	OB		7 3	1200		2150	2500
18 1	19 RD		RNBT	FBG	OB		7 3	920		1700	2050
23 9			EXP	FBG	IB	215	8 6			3100	3600
23 9	240 B		CR	FBG	OB		8 6			6050	6950
				1958 BOATS							
18 1			EXP	FBG	OB					2200	2550

UNITED BOAT WORKS

Call 1-800-327-6929 for BUC Personalized Evaluation Service
Or, for 1950 boats, sign onto www.BUCValuPro.com

UNIVERSAL MARINE CO LTD
TAIPEI TAIWAN   COAST GUARD MFG ID- LTV See inside cover to adjust price for area
                    FORMERLY RITTUN MARINE

For more recent years, see the BUC Used Boat Price Guide, Volume 1 or Volume 2

LOA FT IN	NAME AND/ OR MODEL	TOP/ RIG	BOAT TYPE	-HULL- MTL TP	TP	----ENGINE--- # HP MFG	BEAM FT IN	WGT LBS	DRAFT FT IN	RETAIL LOW	RETAIL HIGH
				1983 BOATS							
35 8	RITTUN TRI-CABIN	FB	TRWL	FBG DS	IB	120D FORD	12 8	24500	3 10	70300	77300
40 10	PERRY	SLP	SA/CR	FBG KL	IB	50D PERK	12	22300	6	64100	70500
40 10	PERRY	SLP	SA/CR	FBG KL	IB	61D LEHM	12	22300	6	64600	71000
41	RITTUN SEDAN	FB	TRWL	FBG DS	IB	120D FORD	13 8	29000	4	83400	91600
41	RITTUN SEDAN	FB	TRWL	FBG DS	IB	T120D FORD	13 8	29000	4	87100	95800
41	RITTUN TRI-CABIN	FB	TRWL	FBG DS	IB	120D FORD	13 8	29000	4	83400	91600
41	RITTUN TRI-CABIN	FB	TRWL	FBG DS	IB	T120D FORD	13 8	29000	4	87100	95800
46 7	PERRY	CUT	SA/CR	FBG KL	IB	80D LEHM	13 7	30400	6 4	83400	91600
46 7	PERRY	KTH	SA/CR	FBG KL	IB	80D LEHM	13 7	30400	6 4	83400	91600
				1982 BOATS							
35 8	TRI-CABIN 36	FB	TRWL	FBG DS	IB	120D LEHM	12 8	24500	3 10	67600	74200
35 8	TRI-CABIN 36	FB	TRWL	FBG DS	IB	T120D LEHM	12 8	24500	3 10	68500	75300
36	LITTON 36 FSH		TRWL	FBG DS	IB	120D	12 8			57100	62700
36	LITTON 36 TCMY		TRWL	FBG DS	IB	120D	12 8			57100	62700
40 10	PERRY 41	SLP	SA/CR	FBG KL	IB	D	12	22300	6	61100	67100
40 10	PERRY 41	SLP	SA/CR	FBG KL	IB	50D PERK	12	22300	6	60800	66800
40 10	PERRY 41	SLP	SA/CR	FBG KL	IB	65D LEHM	12	22300	6	61300	67400
41	LITTON SDN		TRWL	FBG DS	IB	120D	13 8			81000	89100
41	LITTON TCMY		TRWL	FBG DS	IB	120D	13 8			81000	89100
41	STUART 41		TRWL	FBG DS	IB	120D	13 8			81000	89100
41	TRI-CABIN 41	FB	TRWL	FBG DS	IB	120D LEHM	13 8	29000	4	81600	89700
41	TRI-CABIN 41	FB	TRWL	FBG DS	IB	T120D LEHM	13 8	29000	4	85300	93700
46 7	PERRY 47	CUT	SA/CR	FBG KL	IB	D	13 6	30400	6 4	78900	86700
46 7	PERRY 47	CUT	SA/CR	FBG KL	IB	80D LEHM	13 7	30400	6 4	79000	86800
46 7	PERRY 47	KTH	SA/CR	FBG KL	IB	D	13 6	30400	6 4	78900	86700
46 7	PERRY 47	KTH	SA/CR	FBG KL	IB	80D LEHM	13 7	30400	6 4	79000	86800
				1981 BOATS							
35 8	TRI-CABIN 36	FB	TRWL	FBG DS	IB	120D FORD	12 8	24500	3 10	65900	71400
35 8	TRI-CABIN 36	FB	TRWL	FBG DS	IB	T120D FORD	12 8	24500	3 10	66700	72400
36	LITTON 36 FSH		TRWL	FBG DS	IB	120D	12 8			54400	59700
36	LITTON 36 TCMY		TRWL	FBG DS	IB	120D	12 8			54400	59700
40 10	PERRY 41	SLP	SA/CR	FBG KL	IB	50D PERK	12	22300	6	57600	63300
40 10	PERRY 41	SLP	SA/CR	FBG KL	IB	65D LEHM	12	22300	6	58100	63900
41	LITTON 41 TCMY		TRWL	FBG DS	IB	120D	13 8			77200	84900
41	STUART 41		TRWL	FBG DS	IB	120D	13 8			77200	84900
41	TRI-CABIN 41	FB	TRWL	FBG DS	IB	120D FORD	13 8	29000	4	77800	85500
41	TRI-CABIN 41	FB	TRWL	FBG DS	IB	T120D FORD	13 8	29000	4	81300	89300
46 7	PERRY 47	CUT	SA/CR	FBG KL	IB	80D LEHM	13 7	30400	6 4	74900	82300
46 7	PERRY 47	KTH	SA/CR	FBG KL	IB	80D LEHM	13 7	30400	6 4	74900	82300
				1980 BOATS							
36	LITTON 36 FISH		TRWL	FBG DS	IB	T120	12 8			41400	46000
36	LITTON 36 FISH		TRWL	FBG DS	IB	120	12 8			42300	47000
36	LITTON 36 TRI-CBN		TRWL	FBG DS	IB	T120	12 8			41400	46000
36	LITTON 36 TRI-CBN		TRWL	FBG DS	IB	120	12 8			42300	47000
40 10	PERRY 41	SLP	SA/CR	FBG KL	IB	D	12	22300	6	55700	61200
41	LITTON 41 SDN		TRWL	FBG DS	IB	120	13 8			54900	60300
41	LITTON 41 SDN		TRWL	FBG DS	IB	T120	13 8			55700	61200
41	LITTON 41 TRI-CBN		TRWL	FBG DS	IB	120	13 8			54900	60300
41	LITTON 41 TRI-CBN		TRWL	FBG DS	IB	T120	13 8			55700	61200
41	STUART 41		TRWL	FBG DS	IB	120	13 8			54900	60300
41	STUART 41		TRWL	FBG DS	IB	T120	13 8			55700	61200
46 7	PERRY 47	CUT	SA/CR	FBG KL	IB	D	13 6	30400	6 4	72000	79100
46 7	PERRY 47	KTH	SA/CR	FBG KL	IB	D	13 6	30400	6 4	72000	79100
				1979 BOATS							
35 9	LITTON 36	FB	TRWL	FBG DS	IB	120D LEHM	12 8	19000	3 10	55000	55000
40 8	LITTON 41	FB	TRWL	FBG DS	IB	160D LEHM	13 5	24000	4 2	63600	63900
40 10	PERRY 41	SLP	SA/CR	FBG KL	IB	50D PERK	12	22300	6	53700	59000
46 7	PERRY 47	CUT	SA/CR	FBG KL	IB	85D LEHM	13 6	30400	6 4	69800	76700
46 7	PERRY 47	KTH	SA/CR	FBG KL	IB	85D LEHM	13 6	30400	6 4	69800	76700

UNIVERSAL MARINE CORP
ST PETERSBURG FL 33701 COAST GUARD MFG ID- VMC See inside cover to adjust price for area

For more recent years, see the BUC Used Boat Price Guide, Volume 1 or Volume 2

LOA FT IN	NAME AND/ OR MODEL	TOP/ RIG	BOAT TYPE	-HULL- MTL TP	TP	----ENGINE--- # HP MFG	BEAM FT IN	WGT LBS	DRAFT FT IN	RETAIL LOW	RETAIL HIGH
				1983 BOATS							
19 3	MONTEGO 19	SLP	SAIL	FBG SK	OB		7 2	2150	1 2	2000	2350
19 6	MONTEGO 20	SLP	SAIL	FBG KL	OB		7 2	2300	2	2100	2500
25 3	MONTEGO 25	SLP	SA/RC	FBG KL	OB		9 1	4500	4 6	5050	5800
25 3	MONTEGO 25	SLP	SA/RC	FBG KL	IB	15 OMC	9 1	4500	4 6	5450	6250
25 3	MONTEGO 25	SLP	SA/RC	FBG KL	IB	8D YAN	9 1	4500	4 6	5450	6250
25 3	MONTEGO 25 SHOAL	SLP	SA/RC	FBG KL	OB		9 1	4500	3 6	5050	5800
25 3	MONTEGO 25 SHOAL	SLP	SA/RC	FBG KL	IB	15 OMC	9 1	4500	3 6	5250	6050
25 3	MONTEGO 25 SHOAL	SLP	SA/RC	FBG KL	IB	8D YAN	9 1	4500	3 6	5450	6250
				1982 BOATS							
19 3	MONTEGO 19	SLP	SAIL	FBG SK	OB		7 2	2150	1 2	1850	2200
19 6	MONTEGO 20	SLP	SAIL	FBG KL	OB		7 2	2300	2	1950	2350
25 3	MONTEGO 25	SLP	SA/RC	FBG KL	OB		9 1	4500	4 6	4700	5400
25 3	MONTEGO 25	SLP	SA/RC	FBG KL	IB	15 OMC	9 1	4500	4 6	4850	5600
				1981 BOATS							
25 3	MONTEGO 25	SLP	SA/RC	FBG KL	OB		9 1	4500	4 6	4400	5050
25 3	MONTEGO 25	SLP	SA/RC	FBG KL	IB	15 OMC	9 1	4500	4 6	4600	5250
				1980 BOATS							
19 3	MONTEGO 19	SLP	SA/RC	FBG CB	OB		7 2	2250		1700	2050
25 3	MONTEGO 25	SLP	SA/RC	FBG KL	OB		9	3700	4 6	3450	4000

V I P BOATS
VIVIAN INDUSTRIES INC   See inside cover to adjust price for area
VIVIAN LA 71082   COAST GUARD MFG ID- VVI
                    formerly VIVIAN IND PLAST

For more recent years, see the BUC Used Boat Price Guide, Volume 1 or Volume 2

LOA FT IN	NAME AND/ OR MODEL	TOP/ RIG	BOAT TYPE	-HULL- MTL TP	TP	----ENGINE--- # HP MFG	BEAM FT IN	WGT LBS	DRAFT FT IN	RETAIL LOW	RETAIL HIGH
				1983 BOATS							
16 4	TRI-SONIC 1700	OP	RNBT	FBG TR	IO	140-185	6 6	1785		1700	2050
16 9	V-169	OP	RNBT	FBG SV	IO	120-170	6 10	1850		1800	2200
17 4	V17		RNBT	FBG SV	OB		7 1	1440		1750	2050
17 8	KONA 18		RNBT	FBG SV	JT		7 1			**	**
18 7	V-192	OP	RNBT	FBG SV	IO	170-260	7 8	2475		2550	3150
19 2	HPV-190 F/S	OP	RNBT	FBG SV	IO	170-188	7 8	2300		2500	2900
20 3	KONA 20		RNBT	FBG SV	JT		7 10			**	**
20 3	KONA 20BR	OP	RNBT	FBG TR	IO		7 10	2535		**	**
20 3	KONA 20BR		RNBT	FBG DV	IO	228-260	7 10	2535		3600	4300
20 10	V-210	OP	RNBT	FBG DV	IO	228-260	8	3350		4450	5200

LOA FT	LOA IN	NAME AND/ OR MODEL	TOP/ RIG	BOAT TYPE	-HULL- MTL	-HULL- TP	ENGINE TP	# HP	MFG	BEAM FT	BEAM IN	WGT LBS	DRAFT FT	DRAFT IN	RETAIL LOW	RETAIL HIGH
		1983 BOATS														
20	10	V210	OP	RNBT	FBG	DV	IO	198-260		8		3350			4350	5000
		1982 BOATS														
16	2	V162LTD	OP	RNBT	FBG	TR	IO	120-140		6	2	1810			1700	2050
16	3	PD16	OP	RNBT	FBG	TR	IO	140	OMC	6	10	1825			1700	2000
16	3	PD16LTD	OP	RNBT	FBG	TR	IO	140		6	10	1825			1750	2050
16	3	X6	OP	RNBT	FBG	TR	IO	170	MRCR	6	10	1730			1700	2000
16	3	X6LTD	OP	RNBT	FBG	TR	IO	120-170		6	10	1780			1700	2050
17	4	V17	ST	RNBT	FBG	DV	OB			7	8	1440			1700	2000
17	4	V17	ST	RNBT	FBG	DV	IO	140-230		7	8	2350			2250	2700
17	4	V17LTD	OP	RNBT	FBG	DV	OB			7	8	1440			1700	2000
17	4	V17LTD	OP	RNBT	FBG	DV	IO	140-230		7	8	2350			2250	2700
17	8	KONA 18	OP	RNBT	FBG	TR	IO	120-170		7	1	1687			1850	2200
17	8	KONA 18	OP	RNBT	FBG	TR	JT	330		7	1	2010			3050	3550
18	7	V9	OP	RNBT	FBG	TR	OB			7	8	2475			2400	2800
18	7	V9	OP	RNBT	FBG	TR	IO	140-230		7	8	2475			2400	2900
18	7	V9	OP	RNBT	FBG	TR	IO	260	MRCR	7	8	2475			2600	3050
18	7	V9 COMPETITOR	OP	RNBT	FBG	TR	IO	120-198		7	8	2175			2350	2750
18	7	V9LTD	OP	RNBT	FBG	TR	IO	140-230		7	8	2475			2500	3050
18	7	V9LTD	OP	RNBT	FBG	TR	IO	260	MRCR	7	8	2475			2700	3150
19	2	HPV178FS	OP	BASS	FBG	TR	IO			7		2300			**	**
19	2	HPV190F/S	OP	BASS	FBG	TR	OB			7	6	1400			1750	2100
20	3	KONA 20	OP	RNBT	FBG	TR	OB			7	10	1550			2250	2600
20	3	KONA 20	OP	RNBT	FBG	TR	IO	198-260		7	10				3750	4550
20	3	KONA 20	OP	RNBT	FBG	TR	JT	330		7	10				5300	6100
20	3	KONA 20	OP	RNBT	FBG	TR	IO	330	MRCR	7	10				4500	5200
20	3	KONA 20BR	OP	RNBT	FBG	TR	IO	170		7	10	2535			3400	3950
20	10	V210	OP	RNBT	FBG	DV	IO	198-260		8		3350			4200	4900
24	6	KONA 25	OP	RNBT	FBG	TR	IO	198-260		7	11				5350	6150
24	6	KONA 25	OP	RNBT	FBG	TR	JT	330		7	11	3520			7350	8450
24	6	KONA 25	OP	RNBT	FBG	TR	IO	330	MRCR	7	11	2535			5200	5950
		1981 BOATS														
16	3	PD16	OP	RNBT	FBG	TR	IO	140	MRCR	6	10	1825			1700	2000
17	4	V17	ST	RNBT	FBG	DV	IO	140-230		7	8	2350			2250	2700
17	7	SK17CB	OP	RNBT	FBG	DV	OB			7		1680			1850	2250
17	8	KONA 18	OP	RNBT	FBG	TR	IO	120-170		7	1	1687			1800	2200
17	8	KONA 18		SKI	FBG		JT			7	10				**	**
17	9	LUXURA XR179		RNBT	FBG		IO	140		6	10				2150	2500
17	9	XR179		RNBT	FBG		OB			6	10	1500			1750	2050
18	3	LUXURA V8		RNBT	FBG		IO	170		7	3				2300	2650
18	7	V9	OP	RNBT	FBG	DV	IO	140-230		7	8	2475			2450	2950
18	7	V9	OP	RNBT	FBG	DV	IO	260	MRCR	7	8	2475			2600	3050
19	2	HPV190DC	OP	BASS	FBG	TR	OB			7	6	1400			1750	2050
20	3	KONA 20	OP	RNBT	FBG	TR	OB			7	10	1550			2200	2600
20	3	KONA 20	OP	RNBT	FBG	TR	JT	330		7	10				5100	5850
20	3	KONA 20BR	OP	RNBT	FBG	TR	IO	170		7	10	2535			3350	3900
20	3	KONA 20CB	OP	RNBT	FBG	TR	IO	198-260		7	10	2535			3400	4150
20	3	KONA 20CB	OP	RNBT	FBG	TR	IO	330	MRCR	7	10	2535			4100	4800
20	10	V210	OP	RNBT	FBG	DV	IO	198-260		8		3350			4150	4800
23	6	V242		CR	FBG		IO	T198		7	11				6250	7200
23	10	V240		SF	FBG		IO	198		8					6450	7400
24	6	KONA 25		CR	FBG		IO	198		7	11				5850	6700
24	6	KONA 25	OP	RNBT	FBG	TR	IO	198-330		7	11	3685			5300	6050
		1980 BOATS														
17					FBG	SV	OB			7	6	2350			2300	2650
17			ST	RNBT	FBG	SV	OB			7	6	1680			1850	2200
17		ELITE SK17	ST	RNBT	FBG	SV	OB			6	10	1680			1850	2200
17		ELITE V17		RNBT	FBG	SV	IO	140		7	2	2350			2050	2450
17		LUXURA SK17	OP	RNBT	FBG	SV	IO	140		7	6	2600			2250	2650
17		LUXURA V17	ST	RNBT	FBG	SV	IO	140		7	2	2350			2050	2450
17	2	H17T		UTL	FBG	TR	IO	120		6	10				2200	2600
17	4	V17 W/T		RNBT	FBG	SV	OB			7	6	2350			2250	2650
18		ELITE XR179	OP	RNBT	FBG	TR	IO	140		6	10	2205			2050	2400
18		ELITE XR179	ST	RNBT	FBG	TR	OB			6	10	1500			1700	2000
18		LUXURA V8		RNBT	FBG	TR	IO	170		7	3	2600			2350	2700
18		LUXURA XR179	ST	RNBT	FBG	TR	OB			6	10	1500			1750	2100
18		LUXURA XR179	ST	RNBT	FBG	TR	IO	140		6	10	2205			2050	2400
19		ELITE V9		RNBT	FBG	SV	IO	170		7	8	2475			2450	2850
19		HPV190		FSH	FBG	SV	OB			7	6	1680			1900	2300
19		LUXURA V9		RNBT	FBG	SV	IO	170		7	8	2475			2500	2900
20		KONA 20	OP	SKI	FBG	SV	OB			7	10	1550			2150	2500
20		KONA 20	OP	SKI	FBG	SV	IO	198		7	10	2535			3250	3750
20	2	KONA 20	OP	SKI	FBG	SV	JT			7	10				**	**
21		LUXURA V210	ST	CR	FBG	SV	IO	198		8		3350			4400	5050
24		CARIBBEAN V242	ST	CR	FBG	SV	IO	198		8					5650	6500
24		FISHERMAN 240	OP	FSH	FBG	SV	IO	198		8		4300			6500	7450
24	6	KONA 25	OP	SKI	FBG	SV	JT			7	10				**	**
25		KONA 25	OP	SKI	FBG	SV	IO	198		7	10	3685			5450	6250
		1979 BOATS														
17	2	H17T	OP	BASS	FBG	TR	IO	140		6	2	1800			1750	2100
17	4	V17	ST	RNBT	FBG	DV	OB			7	6	2350			2250	2600
17	4	V17	ST	RNBT	FBG	DV	IO	140-230		7	6	2350			2200	2650
17	7	SK17	OP	RNBT	FBG	TR	IO	140-230		7	6				2250	2700
17	9	XR179	ST	RNBT	FBG	TR	OB			6	10	1500			1700	2000
17	9	XR179	ST	RNBT	FBG	TR	IO	140-230		6	10	2205			2000	2500
18	3	CHALLENGER V8	ST	RNBT	FBG	TR	IO	170-260		7	3	2600			2350	2950
18	7	VIXEN V19	ST	RNBT	FBG	DV	IO	170-260		7	8	2475			2400	3000
20	10	V210	ST	CUD	FBG	DV	IO	198-260		8		3350			4350	5250
23	10	V240	OP	CUD	FBG	DV	IO	198-260		8		4300			6100	7200
		1978 BOATS														
16	3	LUXURA X6	ST	RNBT	FBG	TR	IO	120-170		6	10				1700	2050
17	2	H17T	OP	BASS	FBG	TR	IO	120-170		6	2				2050	2500
17	7	SK17	OP	SKI	FBG	DV	IO	120-228		7	6				2100	2600
17	9	XR179	ST	RNBT	FBG	TR	IO	120-240		6	10				2100	2600
17	9	XR179	ST	RNBT	FBG	TR	IO	260	MRCR	6	10				2350	2700
18	3	CHALLENGER LUXURA	ST	RNBT	FBG	TR	IO	140-260		7	3				2350	2900
18	3	CHALLENGER V8	ST	RNBT	FBG	TR	IO	140-240		7	3				2250	2700
18	3	CHALLENGER V8	ST	RNBT	FBG	TR	IO	260	MRCR	7	3				2400	2800
18	7	VIXEN LUXURA	ST	RNBT	FBG	DV	IO	140-260		7	8				2550	3200
18	7	VIXEN V19	ST	RNBT	FBG	DV	IO	140-240		7	8				2450	3000
18	7	VIXEN V19	ST	RNBT	FBG	DV	IO	260	MRCR	7	8				2650	3100
20	10	CAPRICE V21	ST	CUD	FBG	DV	IO	170-260		8		3100			4100	5050
23	10	V240	OP	CUD	FBG	DV	IO	185-260		8					6300	7550
23	10	V240	OP	CUD	FBG	DV	IO	T120-T170		8					6950	8050
		1977 BOATS														
18	3	CHALLENGER V8I	ST	RNBT	FBG	TR	IO	165-190		7	3	2500			2350	2850
18	7	VIXEN V19	ST	RNBT	FBG	DV	IO	165-190		7	8	2200			2350	2800
18	7	VIXEN V19	ST	RNBT	FBG	DV	IO	233-235		7	8	2400			2500	2950
20	10	CAPRICE V21	ST	RNBT	FBG	DV	IO	188-235		8		3100			4000	4850
		1975 BOATS														
16	3	X6IC	ST	RNBT	FBG	TR	IO	120-140		6	10	1650			1700	2050
16	8	V7IC	ST	RNBT	FBG	TR	IO	120-140		6	7	1650			1750	2050
18	3	CHALLENGER V8IC	ST	RNBT	FBG	TR	IO	165-188		7	3	2500			2500	3000
20	10	CAPRICE V21C		CUD	FBG	DV	IO	165-188		8		3100			4450	5250
		1974 BOATS														
16	8	VIP V7I CUSTOM	OP	RNBT	FBG	TR	IO	120-140		6	7	2060			2000	2400
18	3	CHALLENGER V8I	OP	RNBT	FBG	TR	IO		OLDS	7	3	2500			**	**
18	3	CHALLENGER V8I	OP	RNBT	FBG	TR	IO	165-188		7	3	2500			2600	3050
		1973 BOATS														
16	8	VIP CUSTOM	OP	RNBT	FBG	TR	OB			6	7	2060			2000	2400
16	8	VIP CUSTOM	OP	RNBT	FBG	TR	IO	120-140		6	7				2300	2650
18	3	CHALLENGER	OP	RNBT	FBG	TR	IO	165-188		7	3	2500			2650	3100
18	3	CHALLENGER	OP	RNBT	FBG	TR	IO	455	OLDS	7	3				5350	6200
		1972 BOATS														
16	8	VIP 17 CUSTOM	ST	RNBT	FBG	TR	IO	120-140		6	4	1700			1900	2350
18	3	VIP CHALLENGER	ST	RNBT	FBG	TR	IO	165-188		7	3	2500			2750	3300

V I P MARINE IND INC

COAST GUARD MFG ID- VXP

Call 1-800-327-6929 for BUC Personalized Evaluation Service
Or, for 1973 to 2004 boats, sign onto www.BUCValuPro.com

VAGABOND SAILBOATS INC

SANTA ANA CA 92704 COAST GUARD MFG ID- VAG See inside cover to adjust price for area

LOA FT	LOA IN	NAME AND/ OR MODEL	TOP/ RIG	BOAT TYPE	-HULL- MTL	-HULL- TP	ENGINE TP	# HP	MFG	BEAM FT	BEAM IN	WGT LBS	DRAFT FT	DRAFT IN	RETAIL LOW	RETAIL HIGH
		1982 BOATS														
17		VAGABOND 17	SLP	SAIL	FBG	SK	OB			7	3	950	1	8	3800	4400
17		VAGABOND 17 D/S	SLP	SAIL	FBG	SK	OB			7	3	850	1	8	3600	4150
20	4	HOLDER 20	SLP	SAIL	FBG	KL	OB			7	10	1160	3	4	5000	5750
		1981 BOATS														
17		VAGABOND 17	SLP	SAIL	FBG	SK	OB			7	3	950	1	8	3550	4150
20	4	HOLDER 20	SLP	SAIL	FBG	KL	OB			7	10	1050	3	4	4550	5200
		1978 BOATS														
16	8	VAGABOND 17	SLP	SA/OD	FBG	KC	OB			6	8	750		9	2750	3200

VAGABOND YACHT CORPORATION

HOUSTON TX 77055   COAST GUARD MFG ID- VYC See inside cover to adjust price for area

For more recent years, see the BUC Used Boat Price Guide, Volume 1 or Volume 2

LOA FT IN	NAME AND/ OR MODEL	TOP/ RIG	BOAT TYPE	-HULL- MTL TP	----ENGINE--- TP # HP MFG	BEAM FT IN	WGT LBS	DRAFT FT IN	RETAIL LOW	RETAIL HIGH
------------------- 1983 BOATS --
41 8	WESTWIND 42	KTH	SA/CR	FBG KL	IB 61D LEHM	12 10	28500	5 6	107000	117500
------------------- 1982 BOATS --
41 8	WESTWIND 42	KTH	SA/CR	FBG KL	IB 65D LEHM	12 10	28500	5 6	100500	110500

ALLAN H VAITSES ASSOC INC

Call 1-800-327-6929 for BUC Personalized Evaluation Service
Or, for 1960 to 1972 boats, sign onto www.BUCValuPro.com

VAL-CRAFT INDUSTRIES
COAST GUARD MFG ID- VLC

Call 1-800-327-6929 for BUC Personalized Evaluation Service
Or, for 1972 boats, sign onto www.BUCValuPro.com

VALCO
HULLS INC   COAST GUARD MFG ID- HUL

Call 1-800-327-6929 for BUC Personalized Evaluation Service
Or, for 1960 to 1985 boats, sign onto www.BUCValuPro.com

VALIANT YACHTS

GORDONVILLE TX 76245-37 COAST GUARD MFG ID- VAL See inside cover to adjust price for area

For more recent years, see the BUC Used Boat Price Guide, Volume 1 or Volume 2

LOA FT IN	NAME AND/ OR MODEL	TOP/ RIG	BOAT TYPE	-HULL- MTL TP	----ENGINE--- TP # HP MFG	BEAM FT IN	WGT LBS	DRAFT FT IN	RETAIL LOW	RETAIL HIGH
------------------- 1983 BOATS --
37	ESPRIT 37	SLP	SACAC	FBG KL	IB 30D WEST	11 6	17000	5 9	74000	81300
39 10	VALIANT 40	CUT	SACAC	FBG KL	IB 50D WEST	12 4	22500	6	102000	112000
39 10	VALIANT 40 PH	SLP	SACAC	FBG KL	IB 46D WEST	12 4	22500	6	102000	112000
46 5	VALIANT 47	CUT	SACAC	FBG KL	IB 58D WEST	13 10	30000	6	152000	167000
------------------- 1982 BOATS --
32 1	VALIANT 32	CUT	SACAC	FBG KL	IB 25D WEST	10 5	11800	5 2	47300	51900
37	ESPRIT 37	SLP	SA/RC	FBG KL	IB 30D WEST	11 6	17000	5 9	69600	76500
39 10	VALIANT 40	CUT	SACAC	FBG KL	IB 50D WEST	12 4	22500	6	96000	105500
39 10	VALIANT 40 PH	SLP	SACAC	FBG KL	IB 50D WEST	12 4	22500	6	96000	105500
47	VALIANT 47	CUT	SACAC	FBG KL	IB 58D WEST	13 10	32000	6 3	150500	165000
------------------- 1981 BOATS --
32 1	VALIANT 32	CUT	SACAC	FBG KL	IB 25D WEST	10 5	11800	5 2	44000	48900
37	ESPRIT 37	SLP	SACAC	FBG KL	IB 30D WEST	11 6	17000	5 9	65500	72000
39 10	VALIANT 40	CUT	SACAC	FBG KL	IB 50D WEST	12 4	22500	6	90300	99200
39 10	VALIANT 40 PH	SLP	SACAC	FBG KL	IB 50D WEST	12 4	22500	6	90300	99200
46	VALIANT 46	CUT	SACAC	FBG KL	IB D	14	34000	6 3	139500	153500
46 5	VALIANT 47	CUT	SACAC	FBG KL	IB 58D WEST	13 10		6	124500	136500
------------------- 1980 BOATS --
32 1	VALIANT 32	CUT	SACAC	FBG KL	IB 25D WEST	10 5	11800	5 2	42000	46700
37	ESPRIT 37	SLP	SACAC	FBG KL	IB 30D WEST	11 6	17000	5 9	62600	68700
39 10	VALIANT 40	CUT	SACAC	FBG KL	IB 40D PERK	12 4	22500	6	85400	93800
39 10	VALIANT 40 PH	SLP	SACAC	FBG KL	IB 50D PERK	12 4	22500	6	85600	94000
------------------- 1979 BOATS --
32 1	VALIANT 32	CUT	SACAC	FBG KL	IB 20D- 30D	10 5	11800	5 2	40400	44900
37	ESPRIT 37	SLP	SACAC	FBG KC	IB 30D WEST	11 6	17000	4 6	60100	66100
37	ESPRIT 37	SLP	SACAC	FBG KL	IB 30D WEST	11 6	17000	5 9	60100	66100
39 11	VALIANT 40	CUT	SACAC	FBG KC	IB 40D PERK	12 4	22500	6	82400	90500
39 11	VALIANT 40	CUT	SACAC	FBG KL	IB 40D PERK	12 4	22500	6	83000	91200
39 11	VALIANT 40	CUT	SACAC	FBG KL	IB 40D WEST	12 4	22500	6	82400	90500
39 11	VALIANT 40	CUT	SACAC	FBG KL	IB 40D WEST	12 4	22500	6	83000	91200
------------------- 1978 BOATS --
32 1	VALIANT 32	CUT	SACAC	FBG KL	IB 25D WEST	10 6	11500	5 2	38000	42200
37	VALIANT 37	SLP	SACAC	FBG KL	IB 33D WEST	11 5	17000	5 8	58000	63800
39 11	VALIANT 40	CUT	SACAC	FBG KL	IB 40D WEST	12 4	24000	6	83500	91800
39 11	VALIANT 40	YWL	SACAC	FBG KL	IB 40D WEST	12 4	24000	6	83500	91800
39 11	VALIANT 40	KTH	SACAC	FBG KL	IB 40D WEST	12 4	24000	6	83600	91900
------------------- 1977 BOATS --
32 1	VALIANT 32	CUT	SACAC	FBG KL	IB 40D WEST	10 5	11800	5 2	37600	41800
39 11	VALIANT 40	CUT	SACAC	FBG KL	IB 40D WEST	12 4	23000	6	78400	86200
39 11	VALIANT 40	YWL	SACAC	FBG KL	IB 40D WEST	12 4	23000	6	78400	86200
39 11	VALIANT 40	KTH	SACAC	FBG KL	IB 40D WEST	12 4	23000	6	78500	86300
------------------- 1976 BOATS --
30	VALIANT 30	SLP	SACAC	FBG KL	VD 25D WEST	10	9600	5	29300	32600
39 11	VALIANT 40	CUT	SACAC	FBG KC	VD 40D WEST	12 4	24000	4 6	78200	85900
39 11	VALIANT 40	CUT	SACAC	FBG KL	VD 40D WEST	12 4	23000	6	76000	83500
------------------- 1975 BOATS --
30	VALIANT 30	SLP	SACAC	FBG KL	VD 25D WEST	10	9650	5	28600	31800
39 11	VALIANT 40	CUT	SACAC	FBG KL	VD 50D PERK	12 4	23500	6	74500	81900

VAN DAM NORDIA BV
AALSMEER HOLLAND   See inside cover to adjust price for area

LOA FT IN	NAME AND/ OR MODEL	TOP/ RIG	BOAT TYPE	-HULL- MTL TP	----ENGINE--- TP # HP MFG	BEAM FT IN	WGT LBS	DRAFT FT IN	RETAIL LOW	RETAIL HIGH
------------------- 1982 BOATS --
45	NORDIA	KTH	MS	STL KL	IB 75D VLVO	14 6	42000	6 3	204500	225000
53	NORDIA	KTH	MS	STL KL	IB 300D CAT	20	62000	10	286000	314000
60	NORDIA	KTH	MS	STL KL	IB 165D VLVO	16 5	90000	8 3	604500	664000
61	NORDIA	KTH	MS	STL KL	IB 165D VLVO	16 5	80000	9	555500	610500

PETER D VAN DINE & CO
COAST GUARD MFG ID- VND

Call 1-800-327-6929 for BUC Personalized Evaluation Service
Or, for 1968 to 1979 boats, sign onto www.BUCValuPro.com

VANDESTADT & MC GRUER LTD
OWEN SOUND CANADA   COAST GUARD MFG ID- ZVM See inside cover to adjust price for area

For more recent years, see the BUC Used Boat Price Guide, Volume 1 or Volume 2

LOA FT IN	NAME AND/ OR MODEL	TOP/ RIG	BOAT TYPE	-HULL- MTL TP	----ENGINE--- TP # HP MFG	BEAM FT IN	WGT LBS	DRAFT FT IN	RETAIL LOW	RETAIL HIGH
------------------- 1983 BOATS --
17 2	SIREN	SLP	SA/CR	FBG SK	OB	6 8	750	8	2300	2700
21 2	SIRIUS	SLP	SA/CR	FBG SK	OB	7 11	2000	1 4	4250	4950
28	SIRIUS	SLP	SA/RC	FBG KL	IB 8D YAN	9 8	6700	4 4	18000	20000
------------------- 1982 BOATS --
17 2	SIREN	SLP	SA/CR	FBG SK	OB	6 8	750	8	2200	2550
21 2	SIRIUS	SLP	SA/CR	FBG SK	OB	7 11	2000	1 4	4050	4700
27 11	SIRUS 28	SLP	SA/CR	FBG KL	IB 8D YAN	9 8	5900	4 4	14700	16700
28	SIRIUS 28	SLP	SA/CR	FBG KL	IB 8D YAN	9 8	6700	4 4	16700	19000
------------------- 1981 BOATS --
17 2	SIREN	SLP	SA/CR	FBG SK	OB	6 8	750	8	2050	2400
17 2	SIREN 17	SLP	SAIL	FBG	CB	6 8	750		2050	2400
21 2	SIRIUS	SLP	SA/CR	FBG SK	OB	7 11	2000	1 4	3850	4450
21 2	SIRUS 21	SLP	SA/CR	FBG	CB	7 11	2000		3850	4450
------------------- 1980 BOATS --
17 2	SIREN	SLP	SA/CR	FBG SK	OB	6 8	750	8	1950	2350
21 2	SIRIUS	SLP	SA/CR	FBG SK	OB	7 11	2000	1 4	3700	4300
------------------- 1979 BOATS --
17 2	SIREN	SLP	SAIL	FBG SK	OB	6 8	650	8	1750	2100
21 2	SIRIUS	SLP	SAIL	FBG SK	OB	7 11	2000	1 4	3600	4150
------------------- 1978 BOATS --
17 2	SIREN	SLP	SAIL	FBG SK	OB	6 8	650	8	1700	2050
21 2	SIRIUS	SLP	SAIL	FBG SK	OB	7 11	2000	1 4	3500	4050
------------------- 1977 BOATS --
21 2	SIRIUS	SLP	SA/CR	FBG SK	OB	7 8	1800	10	3200	3700
------------------- 1969 BOATS --
29 6	AFT COCKPIT	SLP	SA/CR	FBG	IB	8 6		4 6	10700	12200
------------------- 1968 BOATS --
21 4	RELIANCE	SLP	SAIL	FBG KC		6 9		1 9	2800	3250

E G VANDESTADT
ZAAN DAM HOLLAND   See inside cover to adjust price for area

LOA FT IN	NAME AND/ OR MODEL	TOP/ RIG	BOAT TYPE	-HULL- MTL TP	----ENGINE--- TP # HP MFG	BEAM FT IN	WGT LBS	DRAFT FT IN	RETAIL LOW	RETAIL HIGH
------------------- 1969 BOATS --
22	TROTTER-PANDORA	SLP	SAIL	FBG KL		7		3 3	3350	3900
------------------- 1967 BOATS --
18 10	SPANKER	SLP	SAIL	PLY	CB	6 3			2550	2950
19 8	ALIZE	SLP	SA/CR	FBG	CB	6 7		1 8	2700	3150
20 7	VARIANTA	SLP	SA/CR	FBG	CB	6 9		2 3	2950	3400
21 3	CAR-A-BO	SLP	SA/CR	PLY	CB	7		1 8	3000	3500

E G VANDESTADT   -CONTINUED   See inside cover to adjust price for area

LOA FT IN	NAME AND/ OR MODEL	TOP/ RIG	BOAT TYPE	HULL MTL	TP	ENGINE TP	#	HP	MFG	BEAM FT IN	WGT LBS	DRAFT FT IN	RETAIL LOW	RETAIL HIGH
---- 1967 BOATS ----
21 3	SPLINTER	SLP	SAIL	FBG	KL					6 8		3 8	3000	3500
21 4	RELIANCE	SLP	SA/OD	FBG	KC					6 11		1 9	2500	2900
21 6	RELIANCE	SLP	SAIL	FBG	CB								3250	3800
21 6	SPURN	SLP	SA/CR	FBG	KL					7 1		2 8	3250	3800
21 6	TROTTER	SLP	SA/CR	FBG	KL	IB				7		2 8	3550	4100
21 6	TROTTER MKII	SLP	SA/CR	FBG	KL					7		2 8	3250	3800
23 4	PRIMAAT	SLP	SA/CR	PLY	KL	IB				7 7		4 4	3850	4500
24 5	HORIZON	SLP	SA/CR	FBG	KL	IB				7 8		4	5050	5800
26 5	INVICTA	SLP	SA/CR	FBG	KL	IB				7 4		3 11	7900	9050
27 3	CLIPPER	SLP	SA/CR	FBG	KL	IB				8 3		4	9150	10400
27 6	ALUMAAT	SLP	SA/CR	AL	KL	OB				8		4 4	9600	10900
29 7	TRINTELLA	SLP	SA/CR	FBG	KL	IB				8 5		4 4	10300	11700
29 10	PIONEER	SLP	SA/CR	FBG	KL	IB				8		4 8	10300	11700
30	AVENIR	SLP	SA/CR	AL	KL	OB				9		4 1	10800	12200
30 9	WEST-HINDER	SLP	SA/CR	FBG	KL	IB				8 6		5 6	16200	18400
31	DOGGER	SLP	SA/CR	PLY	KL	IB				8 6		4 7	16300	18500
31	HARMONY	SLP	SA/CR	FBG	KL	IB				9 2		4 7	16300	18500
32	SPRINTER	SLP	SA/CR	FBG	KL	IB				8 9		5 8	11600	13200
36 1	EXCALIBUR	SLP	SA/CR	FBG	KL	IB				10		5 11	19600	21800
41	REBEL	SLP	SA/CR	FBG	KL	IB				10 10		6 7	27300	30300
48 8	GLASS-SLIPPER	YWL	SA/CR	FBG	KL	IB				12 8		6	68600	75400
---- 1966 BOATS ----
18 10	SPANKER	SLP	SAIL	PLY	CB					6 3			2500	2900
21 4	RELIANCE	SLP	SA/OD	FBG	KC					6 11		1 9	2450	2850
21 4	TROTTER	SLP	SA/CR	FBG	KL					7 2		3	3000	3450
23 4	PRIMAAT	SLP	SA/CR	PLY	KL					7 7		4	4000	4650
24 5	HORIZON	SLP	SA/CR	FBG	KL	IB				7 8		4	4950	5700
26 5	INVICTA	SLP	SA/CR	FBG	KL	IB				7 4		3 11	7800	8950
29 10	PIONEER	SLP	SA/CR	FBG	KL	IB				8		4 8	10200	11600
30	AVENIR	SLP	SA/CR	AL	KL	OB				9		4 1	10600	12100
31 10	SPRINTER	SLP	SA/CR	FBG	KL	IB				8 7		5 7	11600	13000
36	EXCALIBUR	SLP	SA/CR	FBG	KL	IB				10		5 11	19400	21500
41	REBEL	SLP	SA/CR	FBG	KL	IB				10 10		6 7	26900	29900
---- 1965 BOATS ----
18 10	SPANKER	SLP	SAIL	PLY	CB					6 3			2500	2900
21 4	RELIANCE	SLP	SA/OD	FBG	KC					6 11		1 9	2450	2800
21 4	TROTTER	SLP	SAIL	FBG	KL					6 11		3	2950	3400
23 4	PRIMAAT	SLP	SA/RC	PLY	KL					7 7		4	3400	3950
24 5	HORIZON	SLP	SAIL	FBG	KL					7 8		4	4550	5250
26 5	INVICTA	SLP	SAIL	FBG	KL					7 4		3 11	5800	6650
30	AVENIR	SLP	SAIL	AL	KL	OB				9		4 1	10600	12000
30	PIONIER	SLP	SAIL	FBG	KL					8		4 8	8950	10100
32	SPRINTER	SLP	SAIL	FBG	KL					8 7		5 7	**	**
36	EXCALIBUR	SLP	SAIL	FBG	KL					10		5 11	18900	21000
41	REBEL	SLP	SAIL	FBG	KL					10 10		6 7	28300	31400
41	REBEL	YWL	SAIL	FBG	KL					10 10		6 7	28300	31400

VANGUARD SAILBOATS

PORTSMOUTH RI 02871   COAST GUARD MFG ID- OQT See inside cover to adjust price for area
FORMERLY VANGUARD INC

For more recent years, see the BUC Used Boat Price Guide, Volume 1 or Volume 2

LOA FT IN	NAME AND/ OR MODEL	TOP/ RIG	BOAT TYPE	HULL MTL	TP	ENGINE TP	#	HP	MFG	BEAM FT IN	WGT LBS	DRAFT FT IN	RETAIL LOW	RETAIL HIGH
---- 1983 BOATS ----
18	VANGUARD VOLANT	SLP	SA/OD	FBG	CB					6	410	3 4	1800	2150
---- 1982 BOATS ----
18	VANGUARD VOLANT	SLP	SA/OD	FBG	CB					6	410	3 6	1700	2050
19 10	FLYING-DUTCHMAN	SLP	SA/OD	F/S	CB					5 7	353	6	1900	2250
---- 1981 BOATS ----
19 10	FLYING-DUTCHMAN	SLP	SA/OD	F/S						6	365		1800	2100
19 10	FLYING-DUTCHMAN	SLP	SA/OD	FBG						5 7	353	6	1750	2100

VASHON BOAT WORKS INC
COAST GUARD MFG ID- VBW

Call 1-800-327-6929 for BUC Personalized Evaluation Service
Or, for 1979 to 1982 boats, sign onto www.BUCValuPro.com

VAUGHN BOATS
COAST GUARD MFG ID- VAU

Call 1-800-327-6929 for BUC Personalized Evaluation Service
Or, for 1979 to 1984 boats, sign onto www.BUCValuPro.com

VECTOR MARINE ASSOC INC
COAST GUARD MFG ID- VMA

Call 1-800-327-6929 for BUC Personalized Evaluation Service
Or, for 1978 to 1980 boats, sign onto www.BUCValuPro.com

VEGA BOATS
COAST GUARD MFG ID- VEG

Call 1-800-327-6929 for BUC Personalized Evaluation Service
Or, for 1965 to 1966 boats, sign onto www.BUCValuPro.com

VEGA MARINE CORP

LONG BEACH CA 90813   COAST GUARD MFG ID- VEG See inside cover to adjust price for area

LOA FT IN	NAME AND/ OR MODEL	TOP/ RIG	BOAT TYPE	HULL MTL	TP	ENGINE TP	#	HP	MFG	BEAM FT IN	WGT LBS	DRAFT FT IN	RETAIL LOW	RETAIL HIGH
---- 1977 BOATS ----
36	DOUBLE CABIN	CR		FBG	SV	IB		T215		12 6		2 8	38300	42500
36	SPORTFISHERMAN	SF		FBG	SV	IB		T215		12 6		2 8	40500	45000
36	SPORTFISHERMAN	SF		FBG	SV	IB		T250		12 6		2 8	40800	45300
42	DOUBLE CABIN	CR		FBG	SV	IB		T235		13 6		3	78700	86400
42	DOUBLE CABIN	CR		FBG	SV	IB		T350		13 6		3	80600	88500
42	SPORTFISHERMAN	SF		FBG	SV	IB		T235		13 6		3	43100	47900
42	SPORTFISHERMAN	SF		FBG	SV	IB		T350		13 6		3	51900	57100
48	DOUBLE CABIN	CR		FBG	SV	IB		T350		16		3 8	121000	132500
48	DOUBLE CABIN	CR		FBG	SV	IB		T400		16		3 8	122500	135000
48	SPORTFISHERMAN	SF		FBG	SV	IB		T350		16		3 8	113000	124500
48	SPORTFISHERMAN	SF		FBG	SV	IB		T400		16		3 8	115000	126500

VENTNOR BOAT CORP

SOLOMONS MD 20688   COAST GUARD MFG ID- VNT See inside cover to adjust price for area

LOA FT IN	NAME AND/ OR MODEL	TOP/ RIG	BOAT TYPE	HULL MTL	TP	ENGINE TP	#	HP	MFG	BEAM FT IN	WGT LBS	DRAFT FT IN	RETAIL LOW	RETAIL HIGH
---- 1970 BOATS ----
23	PLAYMATE			FBG		IO		200	HOLM	8		1 6	5150	5900
23	VEGA			FBG	DV	IO		200	HOLM	8		1 6	5800	6650
28		EXP		PLY		IB		225-260		10 5	7000	2 3	8100	9450
28		EXP		PLY		IB		T150-T195		10 5	7000	2 3	8550	10200
28		EXP		PLY		IB		260	CHRY	10 5	7000	2 3	9100	10300
28		SDN		PLY		IB		225	CHRY	10 5	7000	2 3	9450	11200
28	CHESAPEAKE		SDN	PLY		IB		225	CHRY	10 5	7000	2 3	8850	10100
31		DCMY		PLY		IB		225-260		10 10	9000	2 6	12300	14300
31		DCMY		PLY		IB		160D	PERK	10 10	9000	2 6	17100	19500
31		DCMY		PLY		IB		T150-T195		10 10	9000	2 6	13000	15500
31		EXP		PLY		IB		225-260		10 10	8500	2 6	11900	13800
31		EXP		PLY		IB		160D	PERK	10 10	8500	2 6	15500	17600
31		EXP		PLY		IB		T150-T195		10 10	8500	2 6	12400	14700
31		SDN		PLY		IB		260	CHRY	10 10	8500	2 6	11800	13400
31		SDN		PLY		IB		160D	PERK	10 10	8500	2 6	15700	17800
31		SDN		PLY		IB		T150-T195		10 10	8500	2 6	12100	14500
31	CHESAPEAKE		SDN	PLY		IB		225	CHRY	10 10	8500	2 6	11500	13100
---- 1969 BOATS ----
23	PLAYMATE	RNBT		FBG	DV	IO		200	HOLM	8	2500	2 6	4900	5650
23	VEGA	EXP		FBG		IO		200	HOLM	8	3200	2 6	6000	6900
28		EXP		PLY		IB		210-260		10 5	7000	2 3	7700	9100
28		EXP		PLY		IB		T150-T195		10 5	7000	2 3	8200	9850
28		SDN		PLY		IB		210-260		10 5	7000	2 3	8350	9950
28		SDN		PLY		IB		T150-T195		10 5	7000	2 3	8800	10800
28		SF		PLY		IB		195	CHRY	10 5	7000	2 3	7650	8900
28		HT	SF	PLY		IB		210-260		10 5	7000	2 3	7700	9100
28		HT	SF	PLY		IB		195	CHRY	10 5	7000	2 3	8200	9450
31		DCMY		PLY		IB		210-260		10 10	9000	2 6	11800	13800
31		DCMY		PLY		IB		160D	PERK	10 10	9000	2 6	16800	19100
31		DCMY		PLY		IB		T150-T195		10 10	9000	2 6	12500	14900
31		EXP		PLY		IB		210-260		10 10	8500	2 6	11400	13300
31		EXP		PLY		IB		160D	PERK	10 10	8500	2 6	15200	17300
31		EXP		PLY		IB		T150-T195		10 10	8500	2 6	12000	14200
31		SDN		PLY		IB		160D	PERK	10 10	8500	2 6	15400	17500

LOA FT IN	NAME AND/ OR MODEL	TOP/ RIG	BOAT TYPE	-HULL- MTL TP	----ENGINE--- TP # HP MFG	BEAM FT IN	WGT LBS	DRAFT FT IN	RETAIL LOW	RETAIL HIGH
---	---	---	1969 BOATS	---	---	---	---	---	---	---
31		SDN	PLY	IB	T150-T195	10 10	8500	2 6	11700	13900
31	CHESAPEAKE	SDN	PLY	IB	210-260	10 10	8500	2 6	11000	12900
---	---	---	1968 BOATS	---	---	---	---	---	---	---
21	SEA-SKIFF		L/P	IB	150		2500		2400	2800
28		HT	CR	L/P	IB	190-240	10 5	7000	2 3	7350	8700
28		HT	CR	L/P	IB	T150-T190	10 5	7000	2 3	7950	9450
28		FB	CR	L/P	IB	190-240	10 5	7000	2 3	7350	8700
28		FB	CR	L/P	IB	T150-T190	10 5	7000	2 3	7950	9450
28			EXP	L/P	IB	190-240	10 5	8500	2 3	8200	9650
28			EXP	L/P	IB	T150-T190	10 5	8500	2 3	8800	10400
28		FB	EXP	L/P	IB	190-240	10 5	8500	2 3	8200	9650
28		FB	EXP	L/P	IB	T150-T190	10 5	8500	2 3	8800	10400
28			SDN	L/P	IB	190-240	10 5	8500	2 3	8700	10300
28			3DN	L/P	IB	T150-T190	10 5	8500	2 3	9450	11200
28		FB	SDN	L/P	IB	190-240	10 5	8500	2 3	8700	10300
28		FB	SDN	L/P	IB	T150-T190	10 5	8500	2 3	9450	11200
31			DC	L/P	IB	160-250	10 10	9000	2 6	10200	12200
31			DC	L/P	IB	T150-T195	10 10	9000	2 6	11000	13000
31			EXP	L/P	IB	190-240	10 10	8000	2 6	10700	12500
31			EXP	L/P	IB	130D-160D	10 10	8000	2 6	14100	16300
31			EXP	L/P	IB	T190	10 10	8000	2 6	11800	13400
31		FB	EXP	L/P	IB	190-240	10 10	8000	2 6	10700	12500
31		FB	EXP	L/P	IB	130D-160D	10 10	8000	2 6	14100	16300
31		FB	EXP	L/P	IB	T190	10 10	8000	2 6	11800	13400
31	CHESAPEAKE		SDN	L/P	IB	190-240	10 10	9500	2 6	10700	12500
31	CHESAPEAKE		SDN	L/P	IB	130D-160D	10 10	9500	2 6	15500	18100
31	CHESAPEAKE		SDN	L/P	IB	T190	10 10	9500	2 6	12000	13600
31	CHESAPEAKE	FB	SDN	L/P	IB	190-240	10 10	9500	2 6	10700	12500
31	CHESAPEAKE	FB	SDN	L/P	IB	130D-160D	10 10	9500	2 6	15500	18100
31	CHESAPEAKE	FB	SDN	L/P	IB	T190	10 10	9500	2 6	12000	13600
---	---	---	1967 BOATS	---	---	---	---	---	---	---
21	SEA-SKIFF		RNBT	L/P	IB	150	8	2500	1 10	2350	2750
24 7	SKIFF	HT	FSH	FBG	IB	150-190	9 4	4000	2 1	3900	4650
24 7	SKIFF	FB	FSH	FBG	IB	150-190	9 4		2 1	3900	4650
28			EXP	L/P	IB	190-240	10 5	8500	2 3	7900	9300
28			EXP	L/P	IB	T150-T190	10 5		2 3	8150	9700
28			EXP	L/P	IB	190-240	10 5		2 3	7600	8950
28		FB	EXP	L/P	IB	T150-T190	10 5		2 3	8150	9700
28		FB	EXP	L/P	IB	190-240	10 5	8500	2 3	8350	9950
28			SDN	L/P	IB	T150-T190	10 5		2 3	8900	10600
28			SDN	L/P	IB	190-240	10 5		2 3	8100	9650
28		FB	SDN	L/P	IB	T150-T190	10 5		2 3	8900	10600
28		FB	SDN	L/P	IB		10 5		2 3		
28		HT	SF	L/P	IB	190-240	10 5	7000	2 3	7100	8400
28		HT	SF	L/P	IB	T150-T190	10 5		2 3	7650	9150
28		FB	SF	L/P	IB	190-240	10 5		2 3	7100	8400
28		FB	SF	L/P	IB	T150-T190	10 5		2 3	7650	9150
30			EXP	L/P	IB	190-240	10 7	8000	2 6	10800	
30			EXP	L/P	IB	130D-160D	10 7		2 6	13100	15100
30			EXP	L/P	IB	T190	10 7		2 6	10300	11700
30		FB	EXP	L/P	IB	190-240	10 7		2 6	9300	10800
30		FB	EXP	L/P	IB	130D-160D	10 7		2 6	13100	15100
30		FB	EXP	L/P	IB	T190	10 7		2 6	10300	11700
30			SDN	L/P	IB	190-240	10 7	9500	2 6	10500	12300
30			SDN	L/P	IB	130D-160D	10 7		2 6	14100	16600
30			SDN	L/P	IB	T190	10 7		2 6	10600	12100
30		FB	SDN	L/P	IB	190-240	10 7		2 6	9500	11200
30		FB	SDN	L/P	IB	130D-160D	10 7		2 6	14100	16600
30		FB	SDN	L/P	IB	T190	10 7		2 6	10600	12100
---	---	---	1966 BOATS	---	---	---	---	---	---	---
21	SEA-SKIFF		RNBT	L/P	IB	150-165	8		1 10	2300	2700
24 7	SEA-SKIFF	HT	CR	FBG	IB	190	9 7		2 4	3900	4500
24 7	SEA-SKIFF	FB	CR	FBG	IB	150-190	9 7		2 4	3800	4500
28			EXP	WD	IB	190-240	10 6		2 3	7350	8650
28		FB	EXP	WD	IB	190-240	10 6		2 3	7350	8650
28			SDN	WD	IB	190-240	10 6		2 3	7800	9300
28		FB	SDN	WD	IB	190-240	10 6		2 3	7800	9300
28		FB	SF	WD	IB	190-240	10 6		2 3	6850	8100
28		FB	SF	WD	IB	T190	10 6		2 3	7650	8800
30			EXP	WD	IB	190-240	10 6		2 6	8950	10500
30			EXP	WD	IB	T190	10 6		2 6	9850	11200
30		FB	EXP	WD	IB	190-240	10 6		2 3	8950	10500
30		FB	EXP	WD	IB	T190	10 6		2 6	9850	11200
30			SDN	WD	IB	190-240	10 6		2 6	9200	10700
30			SDN	WD	IB	T190	10 6		2 6	10200	11600
30		FB	SDN	WD	IB	190-240	10 6		2 6	9200	10700
30		FB	SDN	WD	IB	160D	10 6		2 6	14300	16300
30		FB	SDN	WD	IB	T190	10 6		2 6	10200	11600
31	RAISED DECK		SF	L/P	IB	190	11 2		2 6	8500	9750
---	---	---	1965 BOATS	---	---	---	---	---	---	---
21	SEA-SKIFF			WD	IO	120				5000	5750
21	SEA-SKIFF			WD	IB	120				2050	2450
21	SEA-SKIFF DELUXE			WD	IO	150				2200	5750
21	SEA-SKIFF DELUXE			WD	IB	150				2200	2550
24 7	SEA-SKIFF	HT		FBG	IB	150-190				3650	4350
28		FB	CR	WD	IB	190-240				6550	7800
28			EXP	WD	IB	190-240				7050	8300
28		FB	SF	WD	IB	190-240				6550	7800
28		FB	SF	WD	IB	T190				7350	8450
30		FB	CR	WD	IB	190-240				8000	9450
30		FB	CR	WD	IB	T190				8950	10200
30			EXP	WD	IB	190-240				8600	10200
30			EXP	WD	IB	T190				9600	10900
30			SDN	WD	IB	190-240				8900	10500
30			SDN	WD	IB	T190				9950	11300
31			SF	WD	IB	T190				9150	10400
---	---	---	1964 BOATS	---	---	---	---	---	---	---
21	SEA-SKIFF			WD	IB	120				2000	2350
24			EXP	FBG	IB	150				2850	3300
24			EXP	WD	IB	150				2850	3300
24			EXP	FBG	IB	190				2850	3350
24			EXP	WD	IB	190				2850	3350
24	SEA-SKIFF	HT		FBG	IB	150				2650	3050
24	SEA-SKIFF	HT		WD	IB	150				2650	3050
24	SEA-SKIFF	HT		FBG	IB	190				2700	3100
24	SEA-SKIFF	HT		WD	IB	190				2700	3100
25 9			SDN	WD	IB	150-190				4000	4850
30			EXP	WD	IB	190-210				8250	9650
30			EXP	WD	IB	T190				9300	10600
31	RAISED DECK		SF	WD	IB	195				7950	9150
31	RAISED DECK		SF	WD	IB	T195				8850	10000
---	---	---	1963 BOATS	---	---	---	---	---	---	---
24			OP	BASS	WD	IB	145-190			2550	3000
24			EXP	WD	IB	145-190				2700	3200
24			SDN	WD	IB	145-190				2550	3000
24			SF	WD	IB	145-190				2550	3000
24	SLEEPER	HT		WD	IB	145-190				2550	3000
26			SDN	WD	IB	145-190				3950	4800
30			EXP	WD	IB	190-210				8000	9300
30			EXP	WD	IB	T145-T190				8500	10200
---	---	---	1962 BOATS	---	---	---	---	---	---	---
24 1			BASS	WD	IB	110-190				2400	2950
24 1			EXP	WD	IB	110-190				2600	3150
24 1		FB	SF	WD	IB	110-190				2400	2950
24 1	SEA-SKIFF			WD	IB	110-190				2400	2950
24 1	SEA-SKIFF			WD	IB	110-190				2400	2950
---	---	---	1961 BOATS	---	---	---	---	---	---	---
24 1	SEA-SKIFF	HT	CR	MHG	IB	110	9		1 10	2450	2850
24 1	SEA-SKIFF		EXP	MHG	IB	110	9		1 10	2650	3050
27 10	CRUISING SKIFF			MHG	IB	110	10 2		2	5700	6550
---	---	---	1960 BOATS	---	---	---	---	---	---	---
23 8			CR	L/P	IB	110-177	8 6			2350	2800
23 8			OP	UTL	L/P	IB	110-177	8 6		2350	2800
23 8	SKIFF	HT		L/P	IB	110-177	8 6			2350	2800
27 10	SKIFF		EXP	L/P	IB	110	10 2		2	5700	6550
27 10	SKIFF		EXP	L/P	IB	T177	10 2		2	6500	7450
---	---	---	1959 BOATS	---	---	---	---	---	---	---
25 11	SKIFF		CR	WD	IB	130	10			3300	3850
---	---	---	1946 BOATS	---	---	---	---	---	---	---
22			OP	RNBT	WD	IB	180	10		2200	2550
26			OP	SPTCR	WD	IB				**	**
---	---	---	1927 BOATS	---	---	---	---	---	---	---
25				WD	IB	150 GRAY				**	**

VENTURE BOATS INC
WINCHESTER TN 37398   COAST GUARD MFG ID- VNB See inside cover to adjust price for area

For more recent years, see the BUC Used Boat Price Guide, Volume 1 or Volume 2

LOA FT IN	NAME AND/ OR MODEL	TOP/ RIG	BOAT TYPE	-HULL- MTL TP	----ENGINE--- TP # HP MFG	BEAM FT IN	WGT LBS	DRAFT FT IN	RETAIL LOW	RETAIL HIGH
--- 1979 BOATS ---
16 6	MAGNUM 1650	OP	BASS	FBG TR IO	140 MRCR	6 2	1800		2300	2700
16 6	MAGNUM I 1650	OP	BASS	FBG TR OB		6 2	750		3100	3600
16 6	MAGNUM II 1650	OP	BASS	FBG TR OB		6 2	750		3100	3600
16 6	RENDEZVOUS III	OP	BASS	FBG TR OB		6 2	850		3450	4000
17	MAGNUM XVII	OP	BASS	FBG SV OB		7 2	1050		4250	4950
18	MAGNUM 1800	OP	BASS	FBG TR IO	140-170	6 7	2100		2850	3400
18	MAGNUM IV 1800	OP	BASS	FBG TR OB		6 7	1100		4600	5300
18 2	PHASE V	OP	BASS	FBG SV OB		7 7	1075		4550	5200
18 2	PHASE V	OP	BASS	FBG SV IO	140-170	7 7	2200		3250	3850
--- 1978 BOATS ---
16 6	MAGNUM 1650	OP	BASS	FBG TR OB		6 2	800		3200	3750
16 6	MAGNUM 1650	OP	BASS	FBG TR IO	140 MRCR	6 2	1800		2350	2700
16 6	MAGNUM II 1650	OP	BASS	FBG TR OB		6 2	800		3200	3750
16 6	RENDEZVOUS III	OP	BASS	FBG TR OB		6 2	830		3350	3850
18	MAGNUM IV 1800	OP	BASS	FBG TR OB		6 7	1100		4550	5200
18	MAGNUM IV 1800	OP	BASS	FBG TR IO	140-228	6 7	2100		2900	3500
18	MAGNUM IV 1800	OP	BASS	FBG TR IO	260 MRCR	6 7	2100		3200	3700
18 2	PHASE V	OP	BASS	FBG TR OB		7 7	1150		4700	5400
18 2	PHASE V	OP	BASS	FBG TR IO	140-228	7 7	2150		3200	3900
18 2	PHASE V	OP	BASS	FBG TR IO	260 MRCR	7 7	2150		3500	4100
--- 1977 BOATS ---
16 6	MAGNUM 1650	OP	BASS	FBG TR OB		6 2	750		3000	3450
16 6	MAGNUM 1650	OP	BASS	FBG TR IO	140-175	6 2	1800		2400	2800
18	MAGNUM 1800	OP	BASS	FBG TR OB		6 7	1150		4650	5350
18	MAGNUM 1800	OP	BASS	FBG TR IO	120-235	6 7	2100		2950	3600
--- 1976 BOATS ---
16 6	MAGNUM 1650	OP	BASS	FBG TR OB		6 2	750		2950	3450
16 6	MAGNUM 1650	OP	BASS	FBG TR IO	140 MRCR	6 2	1500		2250	2600
16 6	SPORTABOUT 1650	OP	RNBT	FBG TR OB		6 1	700		2800	3250
18	MAGNUM 1800	OP	BASS	FBG TR OB		6 7	1150		4600	5250
18	MAGNUM 1800	OP	BASS	FBG TR IO	140-165	6 7	1700		2750	3350
18	MAGNUM 1800	OP	BASS	FBG TR IO	188-233	6 7	1980		2950	3650

VERLVALE LTD
Call 1-800-327-6929 for BUC Personalized Evaluation Service
Or, for 1979 to 1980 boats, sign onto www.BUCValuPro.com

VIA MARINE
CMPF
Call 1-800-327-6929 for BUC Personalized Evaluation Service
Or, for 1982 to 1984 boats, sign onto www.BUCValuPro.com

VICTORIA YACHTS INC
DEBARY FL 32713   COAST GUARD MFG ID- VYN See inside cover to adjust price for area

LOA FT IN	NAME AND/ OR MODEL	TOP/ RIG	BOAT TYPE	-HULL- MTL TP	----ENGINE--- TP # HP MFG	BEAM FT IN	WGT LBS	DRAFT FT IN	RETAIL LOW	RETAIL HIGH
--- 1983 BOATS ---
18 6	VICTORIA 18	SLP	SA/OD	FBG KL OB		5 6	1200	2	3750	4350
26 7	VICTORIA 26	SLP	SA/CR	FBG KC IB		8	4000	2 6	16200	18400
--- 1982 BOATS ---
18 6	VICTORIA 18	SLP	SA/OD	FBG KL OB		5 6	1200	2	3500	4100
26 7	VICTORIA 26	SLP	SAIL	FBG KC SD	15 OMC	8	4500	2 6	17100	19400
26 7	VICTORIA 26	SLP	SAIL	FBG KC IB	7D BMW	8	4500	2 6	17500	19900
--- 1981 BOATS ---
18 6	VICTORIA 18	SLP	SA/OD	FBG KL OB		5 6	1200	2	3300	3850
24 10	VICTORIA 25	SLP	SA/CR	FBG KC OB		8	2800	4	9600	10900
24 10	VICTORIA 25	SLP	SA/OD	FBG KL		8		4	10000	11400
26 7	VICTORIA 26	SLP	SAIL	FBG KL IB	15 OMC	8	4500	2 6	16200	18400
--- 1980 BOATS ---
18 6	VICTORIA 18	SLP	SA/OD	FBG KL OB		5 6	1200	2	3150	3650
--- 1979 BOATS ---
18 6	VICTORIA 18	SLP	SA/OD	FBG KL OB		5 6	1200	2	3050	3500
--- 1978 BOATS ---
18 6	VICTORIA 18	SLP	SA/OD	FBG KL OB		5 6	1200	2	2900	3400
--- 1977 BOATS ---
18 6	VICTORIA 18	SLP	SA/OD	FBG KL OB		5 6	1200	2	2800	3300

VIETTI CUSTOM BOATS
COAST GUARD MFG ID- ECA
FORMERLY EMERSON CUSTOM BOATS

Call 1-800-327-6929 for BUC Personalized Evaluation Service
Or, for 1980 to 1985 boats, sign onto www.BUCValuPro.com

VIKENS VARV A B
Call 1-800-327-6929 for BUC Personalized Evaluation Service
Or, for 1976 boats, sign onto www.BUCValuPro.com

VIKING BOAT CO INC
DIV OF COACHMEN INDUSTRIES   See inside cover to adjust price for area
GOSHEN IN 46526   COAST GUARD MFG ID- VBC
FOR MORE RECENT YEARS SEE MURRAY CHRIS CRAFT

LOA FT IN	NAME AND/ OR MODEL	TOP/ RIG	BOAT TYPE	-HULL- MTL TP	----ENGINE--- TP # HP MFG	BEAM FT IN	WGT LBS	DRAFT FT IN	RETAIL LOW	RETAIL HIGH
--- 1983 BOATS ---
20 6	2100SP		CUD	FBG TR IO	198 MRCR	8	2950		7450	8550
--- 1982 BOATS ---
18	1800 BR	ST	RNBT	FBG DV OB		7 4	1420		3200	3700
18	1800 BR	ST	RNBT	FBG DV IO	140-230	7 4	2400		4850	5750
18	1800 CR	ST	CR	FBG DV OB		7 4	1850		3800	4400
18	1800 FI		FSH	FBG DV OB		7 4	1420		3150	3700
18	1800 RA		RNBT	FBG DV OB		7 4	1420		3200	3700
20 5	WAC 2100	ST	OFF	FBG DV OB		8	2500		5700	6550
20 5	WAC 2100	ST	OFF	FBG DV IO	140-230	8	2950		7350	8700
22	2200 CC	ST	OFF	FBG DV IO		8	2426		6250	7200
22	2200 CR	ST	CBNCR	FBG DV IO	170-260	8	3460		9250	11000
22	2200 CU	ST	CUD	FBG DV IO	170-260	8	3460		8500	10200
22	2200 FI		FSH	FBG DV IO	170	8	3350		9200	10500
25	2500 FB	FB	CR	FBG DV IO	198-260	8	5000		13000	15300
25	2500 HB	HT	HB	FBG DV IO	170	8	4900		**	**
25	2500 SU	ST	CR	FBG DV IO	198-260	8	5100		13200	15400
--- 1981 BOATS ---
16 2	1620 BR		RNBT	FBG DV OB		6 11			2200	2550
16 6	1600 BR	ST	RNBT	FBG DV IO	140 MRCR	7	2100		3950	4600
16 6	1660 BR	ST	RNBT	FBG DV OB		7	1330		3050	3550
16 6	1660 BR	ST	RNBT	FBG DV IO	120-198	7	2100		3900	4500
16 6	1660 BR	ST	RNBT	FBG DV IO	198-200	7	2100		4000	4950
16 6	1660 RA	OP	RNBT	FBG DV OB		7	1330		2700	3150
16 6	1660 RA	ST	RNBT	FBG DV IO	120-170	7	2100		3900	4400
17 6	1800	OP	RNBT	FBG DV IO	120-170	7 4	2100		4250	5000
18	1800 BR	OP	RNBT	FBG DV OB		7 4	1650		3450	4050
18	1800 BR	ST	RNBT	FBG DV IO	140-230	7 4	2400		4750	5800
18	1800 CR	ST	CR	FBG DV IO		7 4	1850		3750	4350
18	1800 RA	ST	RNBT	FBG DV IO	140-230	7 4	2400		4750	5800
18	S1900	ST	RNBT	FBG DV OB		7 4	1650		3450	4050
18	S1900	ST	RNBT	FBG DV IO	120 MRCR	7 4	2400		4750	5450
18 2	1820 FI	OP	FSH	FBG DV OB		7 4	1300		2750	3200
18 2	1820 RA	OP	RNBT	FBG DV OB		7 4	1300		2950	3400
18 2	1820 RA	ST	RNBT	FBG DV OB		7 4	1300		2950	3400
18 2	V-518	ST	RNBT	FBG DV IO	120 MRCR	7 4			4700	5450
22	2200 CR	ST	CBNCR	FBG DV IO	170-260	8	3460		9050	11200
22	2200 CU	ST	CUD	FBG DV IO	170-260	8	3460		8300	10100
22	2200 CU	ST	CUD	FBG DV IO	170-260	8	3460		8700	10400
22	2200 FI	OP	FSH	FBG DV IO	260	8	2426		6200	7100
22	2200 FI	OP	FSH	FBG DV IO	260 VLVO	8	2460		7800	8950
22	2200 FI	ST	FSH	FBG DV IO	170-230	8	2460		7450	9100
22	2200 FI	ST	FSH	FBG DV IO	260	8	2460		7850	9450
23	2300 HB	HT	HB	FBG TR IO		8			**	**
23	2300 HB	HT	HB	FBG DV IO	170-230	8	4200		**	**
23	2300 HB	HT	HB	FBG DV IO	260	8	4200		**	**
25	2500 EX	ST	EXP	FBG DV IO	170-260	8	5100		12500	15100
25	2500 FB	FB	CR	FBG DV IO	170-260	8	5000		12600	14900
25	2500 SE		SDN	FBG DV IO	228	8			13700	15600
25	V-2500 HB	HT	HB	FBG DV IO	170-260	8	5100		**	**
--- 1980 BOATS ---
16 2	S1600	ST	RNBT	FBG TR OB		6 11	1180		2550	2950
16 6	S1700	ST	RNBT	FBG DV OB		7	1330		2750	3200

```
LOA  NAME AND/        TOP/ BOAT -HULL- ----ENGINE--- BEAM  WGT DRAFT RETAIL RETAIL
FT IN OR MODEL        RIG  TYPE MTL TP TP # HP  MFG  FT IN  LBS FT IN  LOW   HIGH
--------------------- 1980 BOATS -------------------------------------------------
16  6 S1700           ST  RNBT FBG DV IO 120   MRCR 7      2100        3800  4450
16  6 S1700B/R        ST  RNBT FBG DV OB            7      1330        2950  3400
16  6 S1700B/R        ST  RNBT FBG DV IO 120-170   7      2100        3900  4600
16  6 S1700RAB        ST  RNBT FBG DV IO 120-170   7      2100        3750  4450
17  6 S1800           OP  RNBT FBG TR OB           7  4   1254        2750  3200
17  6 S1800           OP  RNBT FBG TR IO 120-170   7  4   2100        4150  4900
17  6 S1800           ST  RNBT FBG TR IO 120   MRCR 7  4  2100        4200  4850
18    S1900           ST  RNBT FBG DV OB           7  4   1650        3300  3850
18    S1900           ST  RNBT FBG DV IO 120   MRCR 7  4  2400        4600  5300
18    S1900B/R        ST  RNBT FBG DV OB           7  4   1650        3550  4100
18    S1900B/R        ST  RNBT FBG DV IO 120-230   7  4   2400        4650  5650
18    S1900CR         ST  CR   FBG DV OB           7  4   1850        3650  4250

18    S1900CR         ST  CR   FBG DV IO 120-230   7  4   2600        4950  5900
18    S1900RAB        ST  RNBT FBG DV IO 120-230   7  4   2400        4550  5550
18  2 V518            ST  RNBT FBG DV IO 120   MRCR 7  4              4650  5350
18  2 V518F           OP  FSH  FBG DV OB           7  4   1200        2700  3150
18  2 V518R           ST  RNBT FBG DV OB           7  4   1300        2900  3350
18  2 V518R           ST  RNBT FBG DV IO 120-165   7  4              4600  5350
22    S2200CC         ST  CUD  FBG DV IO 170-230   8      3460        8150  9850
22    S2200CC         ST  CUD  FBG DV IO  260      8      3460        8550 10200
22    S2200CC         ST  CUD  FBG DV IO T165-T230 8      3460        9250 10900
22    S2200CR         ST  CBNCR FBG DV IO 170-260  8      3750        9400 11500
22    S2200CR         ST  CBNCR FBG DV IO T165-T230 8     3750       10400 12300
22    S2200OSF        OP  FSH  FBG DV OB           8      2426        6100  7000

22    S2200OSF        ST  FSH  FBG DV IO 170-260   8      3460        9050 11200
22    S2200OSF        ST  FSH  FBG DV IO T165-T230 8      3460       10100 11900
23    T523            HT  HB   FBG TR OB           8      3700         **    **
23    T523            HT  HB   FBG TR IO  230      8      4200         **    **
23    T523            HT  HB   FBG TR IO  260      8      4200         **    **
25    S2500           ST  SPTCR FBG DV IO 198-260   8     4405       11600 14100
25    S2500           ST  SPTCR FBG DV IO  330  MRCR 8    4405       13100 14900
25    S2500           ST  SPTCR FBG DV IO T177-T230 8     4405       13200 15600
25    S2500EC         ST  EXP  FBG DV IO 198-260   8      5100       12500 14900
25    S2500EC         ST  EXP  FBG DV IO T165-T230 8      5100       13900 16500
25    S2500EC         HT  EXP  FBG DV IO 198-260   8      5100       12500 14900
25    S2500EC         HT  EXP  FBG DV IO T165-T230 8      5100       13900 16500

25    S2500FB         FB  CR   FBG DV IO 198-260   8      5000       12500 15000
25    S2500FB         FB  CR   FBG DV IO T165-T230 8      5000       14000 16600
25    S2500SD         HT  SDN  FBG DV IO 198-260   8      5350       13300 16000
25    S2500SD         HT  SDN  FBG DV IO T165-T230 8      5350       15000 17500
--------------------- 1977 BOATS -------------------------------------------------
18  6 V-190 SM        OP  UTL  FBG TR OB           7  6   1250 2  2   2550  2950
18  6 V-190 SM        OP  UTL  FBG TR IO 120-190   7  6   1815 2  2   4750  5850
21  6 V-220 SM        OP  UTL  FBG TR OB           7 10   2050 2 11   4550  5200
21  6 V-220 SM        OP  UTL  FBG TR IO 165-235   7 10   2765 2 11   7350  8800
--------------------- 1974 BOATS -------------------------------------------------
17  8 CAPRICE V-202            FBG    IO 120-188   7  1              4550  5250
17  8 NORSEMAN V-210S          FBG    IO 120-188   7  1              4550  5250
17  8 NORSEMAN V-210SS         FBG    IO 165-188   7  1              4700  5450
17  8 NORSEMAN V-210SS         FBG    JT  245  OMC 7  1              4850  5600
18  4 SPT DECK V-219D          FBG    OB           7  6              3400  3950
18  4 SPT DECK V-219D          FBG    IO 120-140   7  6              5150  5900
18  4 SPT DECK V-219S          FBG    OB           7  6              2700  3100
18  4 SPT DECK V-219S          FBG    IO 120-140   7  6              4650  5400
19  2 CAPRICE V-220            FBG    IO 120-225   7  4              4550  5350
21  6 SPT DECK V-239           FBG    OB           7 10              4900  5650
21  6 SPT DECK V-239           FBG    IO 120-225   7 10              7350  8700
21  6 SPT DECK V-239           FBG    JT  245  OMC 7 10              7450  8550

21  6 SPT DECK V-239D          FBG    OB           7 10              6000  6900
21  6 SPT DECK V-239D          FBG    IO 120-225   7 10              8200  9550
21  6 SPT DECK V-239D          FBG    JT  245  OMC 7 10              8150  9350
--------------------- 1973 BOATS -------------------------------------------------
17  8 CAPRICE V-202      OP RNBT FBG TR IO 120     7  1              4850  5600
17  8 NORSEMAN V-210     OP RNBT FBG SV IO 165     7  1              4900  5650
19  2 CAPRICE V-220      OP RNBT FBG TR IO 120     7  4              4800  5550
21  6 SPORTS DECK V-239     RNBT FBG TR IO 120     7 10              8100  9300
24    MARINER           HT HB   FBG    OB          8                  **    **
24    MARINER DECOR 1   HT HB   FBG    IO 140  MRCR 8                 **    **
24    MARINER DECOR 2   HT HB   FBG    IO 140  MRCR 8                 **    **
24    MARINER ECONOMY   HT HB   FBG    IO 140  MRCR 8                 **    **
--------------------- 1972 BOATS -------------------------------------------------
24    MARINER           HT HB   FBG    OB          8                  **    **
24    MARINER DECOR 1   HT HB   FBG    IO 140  MRCR 8                 **    **
24    MARINER DECOR 2   HT HB   FBG    IO 140  MRCR 8                 **    **
24    MARINER ECONOMY   HT HB   FBG    IO 140  MRCR 8                 **    **
--------------------- 1971 BOATS -------------------------------------------------
17  8 CAPRICE              RNBT FBG TR OB          7  1 1350 1  3    2750  3200
17  8 CAPRICE V-202        RNBT FBG TR IO  90      7  1 2117 1  3    4300  5650
19  2 CAPRICE V-220        RNBT FBG TR IO  90      7  4 2400 1  6    5700  6550
24    MARINER           HT HB   FBG    OB          8                  **    **
24    MARINER DECOR 1   HT HB   FBG    IO 140  MRCR 8                 **    **
24    MARINER DECOR 2   HT HB   FBG    IO 140  MRCR 8                 **    **
24    MARINER ECONOMY   HT HB   FBG    IO 140  MRCR 8                 **    **
--------------------- 1970 BOATS -------------------------------------------------
24    MARINER           HT HB   FBG    OB          8                  **    **
24    MARINER DECOR 1   HT HB   FBG    IO 140  MRCR 8                 **    **
24    MARINER DECOR 2   HT HB   FBG    IO 140  MRCR 8                 **    **
24    MARINER ECONOMY   HT HB   FBG    IO 140  MRCR 8                 **    **
```

VIKING MARINE

Call 1-800-327-6929 for BUC Personalized Evaluation Service
Or, for 1961 to 1971 boats, sign onto www.BUCValuPro.com

VIKING YACHT COMPANY

NEW GRETNA NJ 08244   COAST GUARD MFG ID- VKY See inside cover to adjust price for area

For more recent years, see the BUC Used Boat Price Guide, Volume 1 or Volume 2

```
LOA  NAME AND/        TOP/ BOAT -HULL- ----ENGINE--- BEAM  WGT DRAFT RETAIL RETAIL
FT IN OR MODEL        RIG  TYPE MTL TP TP # HP  MFG  FT IN  LBS FT IN  LOW   HIGH
--------------------- 1983 BOATS -------------------------------------------------
35    CONVERTIBLE     FB  SDNSF FBG SV IB T350  CRUS 13  1 20000 2  5 70200  77100
40  4 VIKING 40       SF   FBG SV IB T350            14  6 34000       130500 143000
41  2 CONVERTIBLE     FB  SDNSF FBG SV IB T350  CRUS 14 10 32000 3  8 122000 134000
  IB T300D CAT 136000 149500, IB T300D J&T 134500 147500, IB T310D J&T 135000 148500
  IB T410D J&T 145000 159500, IB T450D J&T 149500 164000

42  8 VIKING 43       DCMY FBG SV IB T350            14  9 36000       139000 153000
44    DOUBLE CABIN    FB  DCMY FBG SV IB T300D CAT   15    40000 3 10 155000 170500
  IB T300D J&T 154000 169000, IB T310D J&T 155000 170000, IB T410D J&T 165500 181500
  IB T450D J&T 169500 186500

46  6 CONVERTIBLE     FB  SDNSF FBG SV IB T450D J&T  16    44000 4    180000 197500
  IB T462D J&T 181500 199500, IB T500D J&T 186000 204500, IB T675D J&T 207000 227500

50    COCKPIT MOTOR YACHT  FB  DCCPT FBG SV IB T300D CAT 15  43000 3 10 164000 180500
  IB T300D J&T 164000 180500, IB T310D J&T 165000 181500, IB T410D J&T 175000 192500
  IB T450D J&T 179500 197500
--------------------- 1982 BOATS -------------------------------------------------
35    CONVERTIBLE     FB  SDNSF FBG SV IB T350  CRUS 13  1 20000 2  5 67200  73800
35    CONVERTIBLE     FB  SDNSF FBG SV IB T300D CAT 13  1 20000 2  5 86300  95000
40  4 CONVERTIBLE     FB  SDNSF FBG SV IB T350  CRUS 14  6 30000 3  6 111500 123000
  IB T300D CAT 135500 149000, IB T310D J&T 137500 151500, IB T410D J&T 149000 163500

42  8 DOUBLE CABIN    FB  DCMY FBG SV IB T350  CRUS 14  9 34000 3  9 120500 132500
42  8 DOUBLE CABIN    FB  DCMY FBG SV IB T300D CAT 14  9 37000 3  9 143000 157000
42  8 DOUBLE CABIN    FB  DCMY FBG SV IB T310D J&T 14  9 38000 3  9 145500 159500
42  8 DOUBLE CABIN HARDTOP FB  DCMY FBG SV IB T310D J&T 14  9 38000 3  9 152500 167500
44    DOUBLE CABIN    FB  DCMY FBG SV IB T300D CAT 15    40000 3 10 148500 163000
44    DOUBLE CABIN    FB  DCMY FBG SV IB T410D J&T 15    40000 3 10 147000 161500
44    DOUBLE CABIN    FB  DCMY FBG SV IB T450D J&T 15    40000 3 10 158000 173500
46  6 CONVERTIBLE     FB  SDNSF FBG SV IB T450D J&T 16   48000 4    180000 198000
46  6 CONVERTIBLE     FB  SDNSF FBG SV IB T500D J&T 16   48000 4    184500 202500
--------------------- 1981 BOATS -------------------------------------------------
35    CONVERTIBLE     FB  SDNSF FBG SV IB T350  CRUS 13  1 20000 2  5 63400  70700
35    CONVERTIBLE     FB  SDNSF FBG SV IB T300D CAT 13  1 20000 2  5 89600  98500
40  4 CONVERTIBLE     FB  SDNSF FBG SV IB T350  CRUS 14  6 30000 3  6 106500 117500
  IB T300D CAT 129000 142500, IB T310D J&T 131000 144000, IB T410D J&T 142000 156000

42  8 DOUBLE CABIN    FB  DCMY FBG SV IB T300D CAT 14  9 37000 3  9 115000 126500
42  8 DOUBLE CABIN    FB  DCMY FBG SV IB T300D CAT 14  9 37000 3  9 136000 149500
42  8 DOUBLE CABIN    FB  DCMY FBG SV IB T310D J&T 14  9 38000 3  9 138500 152000
42  8 DOUBLE CABIN HARDTOP FB  DCMY FBG SV IB T310D J&T 14  9 40000 3  9 145500 160000
46  6 CONVERTIBLE     FB  SDNSF FBG SV IB T450D GM  16   48000 4    171500 188500
--------------------- 1980 BOATS -------------------------------------------------
35    CONVERTIBLE     FB  SDNSF FBG SV IB T350  CRUS 13  1 20000 2  5 61600  67700
  IB T   D J&T    **    ** , IB T210D CAT 82000 90100, IB T265D CAT 84400 92800
```

```
LOA  NAME AND/            TOP/ BOAT -HULL- ----ENGINE--- BEAM  WGT  DRAFT RETAIL RETAIL
FT IN  OR MODEL           RIG  TYPE MTL TP TP # HP MFG  FT IN  LBS  FT IN  LOW   HIGH
------------------- 1980 BOATS --------------------------------------------------------
40  4 CONVERTIBLE         FB  SDNSF FBG SV IB T350  CRUS 14  6 30000  3  6 101500 111500
40  4 CONVERTIBLE         FB  SDNSF FBG SV IB T210D CAT  14  6 32000  3  6 115000 126500
40  4 CONVERTIBLE         FB  SDNSF FBG SV IB T310D J&T  14  6 34000  3  6 125000 137500
42  8 DOUBLE CABIN        FB  DCMY  FBG SV IB T350  CRUS 14  9 34000  3  9 109500 120500
42  8 DOUBLE CABIN        FB  DCMY  FBG SV IB T210D CAT  14  9 36000  3  9 120000 132000
42  8 DOUBLE CABIN        FB  DCMY  FBG SV IB T310D J&T  14  9 38000  3  9 132000 145000
42  8 DOUBLE CABIN HARDTOP FB DCMY  FBG SV IB T310D J&T  14  9 40000  3  9 138500 152500
------------------- 1979 BOATS --------------------------------------------------------
35    CONVERTIBLE         FB  SDNSF FBG SV IB T350  CRUS 13  1 21100  2  5 60600  66600
35    CONVERTIBLE         FB  SDNSF FBG SV IB T225D CAT  13  1 22300  2  5 80200  88100
40  4 CONVERTIBLE         FB  SDNSF FBG SV IB T350  CRUS 14  6 30000  3  6 97000  106500
40  4 CONVERTIBLE         FB  SDNSF FBG SV IB T225D CAT  14  6 31000  3  6 107500 118500
40  4 CONVERTIBLE         FB  SDNSF FBG SV IB T285D GM   14  6 32000  3  6 112000 123000
42  8 DOUBLE CABIN        FB  DCMY  FBG SV IB T350  CRUS 14  9 34000  3  9 104500 115000
42  8 DOUBLE CABIN        FB  DCMY  FBG SV IB T225D CAT  14  9 35000  3  9 113000 124500
42  8 DOUBLE CABIN        FB  DCMY  FBG SV IB T285D GM   14  9 36000  3  9 118500 130500
------------------- 1978 BOATS --------------------------------------------------------
35    SEDAN FISHERMAN     FB  SDNSF FBG SV IB T350  CRUS 13  1 21100  2  5 58100  63300
35    SEDAN FISHERMAN     FB  SDNSF FBG SV IB T210D CAT  13  1 21100  2  5 74000  81300
40  4 SEDAN FISHERMAN     FB  SDNSF FBG SV IB T350  CRUS 14  6 30000  3  6 92500  101500
40  4 SEDAN FISHERMAN     FB  SDNSF FBG SV IB T210D CAT  14  6 30000  3  6 99500  109500
40  4 SEDAN FISHERMAN     FB  SDNSF FBG SV IB T285D J&T  14  6 30000  3  6 102000 112000
42  8 DOUBLE CABIN        FB  DCMY  FBG SV IB T350  CRUS 14  9 34000  3  9 100000 110000
42  8 DOUBLE CABIN        FB  DCMY  FBG SV IB T210D CAT  14  9 34000  3  9 105000 115000
42  8 DOUBLE CABIN        FB  DCMY  FBG SV IB T285D J&T  14  9 34000  3  9 109000 120000
------------------- 1977 BOATS --------------------------------------------------------
35    SEDAN FISHERMAN     FB  SDNSF FBG SV IB T350  CRUS 13  1 21100  2  5 55800  61300
35    SEDAN FISHERMAN     FB  SDNSF FBG SV IB T225D CAT  13  1 21100  2  5 71800  78900
40  4 SEDAN FISHERMAN     FB  SDNSF FBG SV IB T350  CRUS 14  6 30000  3  6 88600  97400
40  4 SEDAN FISHERMAN     FB  SDNSF FBG SV IB T225D CAT  14  6 30000  3  6 95900  105500
40  4 SEDAN FISHERMAN     FB  SDNSF FBG SV IB T285D J&T  14  6 30000  3  6 97600  107500
42  8 DOUBLE CABIN        FB  DC    FBG SV IB T350  CRUS 14  9 34000  3  9 95500  105000
42  8 DOUBLE CABIN        FB  DC    FBG SV IB T225D CAT  14  9 34000  3  9 101000 111000
42  8 DOUBLE CABIN        FB  DC    FBG SV IB T285D J&T  14  9 34000  3  9 104000 114500
------------------- 1976 BOATS --------------------------------------------------------
35    SEDAN FISHERMAN     FB  SDNSF FBG SV IB T270  CRUS 13  1 20100  2  5 50900  55900
35    SEDAN FISHERMAN     FB  SDNSF FBG SV IB T350  CRUS 13  1 20100  2  5 52300  57500
35    SEDAN FISHERMAN     FB  SDNSF FBG SV IB T225D CAT  13  1 20100  2  5 67100  73800
40  4 SEDAN FISHERMAN     FB  SDNSF FBG SV IB T350  CRUS 14  6 30000  3  6 85000  93400
40  4 SEDAN FISHERMAN     FB  SDNSF FBG SV IB T225D CAT  14  6 30000  3  6 92000  101000
40  4 SEDAN FISHERMAN     FB  SDNSF FBG SV IB T285D J&T  14  6 30000  3  6 93600  103000
42  8 DOUBLE CABIN        FB  DC    FBG SV IB T350  CRUS 14  9 34000  3  9 91600  100500
42  8 DOUBLE CABIN        FB  DC    FBG SV IB T225D CAT  14  9 34000  3  9 96800  106500
42  8 DOUBLE CABIN        FB  DC    FBG SV IB T285D J&T  14  9 34000  3  9 99700  109500
------------------- 1975 BOATS --------------------------------------------------------
35    SEDAN FISHERMAN     FB  SDNSF FBG SV IB T270  CRUS 13  1 20100  2  5 48900  53700
35    SEDAN FISHERMAN     FB  SDNSF FBG SV IB T350  CRUS 13  1 20100  2  5 50300  55300
35    SEDAN FISHERMAN     FB  SDNSF FBG SV IB T225D CAT  13  1 20100  2  5 65100  71600
40  4 SEDAN FISHERMAN     FB  SDNSF FBG SV IB T350  CRUS 14  6 30000  3  6 81600  89700
        IB T225D CAT  88400  97100, IB T255D J&T  87400  96000, IB T320D CUM  90800  99800

42  8 DOUBLE CABIN        FB  DC    FBG SV IB T350  CRUS 14  9 34000  3  9 87900  96600
        IB T225D CUM  91600 100500, IB T255D J&T  93900 103000, IB T320D CUM  97400 107000

------------------- 1974 BOATS --------------------------------------------------------
33                        FB  SDN   FBG    IB T270-T350 12  9 15300  2  7 38300  44600
33                        FB  SF    FBG    IB T270-T350 12  9 15300  2  7 36000  41600
40                        FB  SDNSF FBG    IB T350  CRUS 14  4 25500  3  6 68700  75500
40                        FB  SDNSF FBG    IB T225D CAT  14  4 25500  3  6 75700  83200
------------------- 1973 BOATS --------------------------------------------------------
33                        FB  SDN   FBG    IB T250-T350 12  9 15300  2  7 36300  42800
33                        FB  SDN   FBG    IB T220D PALM 12  9 15300  2  7 51900  57100
33                        FB  SF    FBG    IB T350  CRUS 12  9 15300  2  7 36000  41000
40                        FB  SDN   FBG    IB T225D CAT  14  3 26000  3  1 74300  81600
40                        FB  SDN   FBG    IB T265D GM   14  3 28000  3  1 78700  86500
40                        FB  SDNSF FBG    IB T350  CRUS 14  6 24000  3  1 62400  68600
------------------- 1972 BOATS --------------------------------------------------------
33                        FB  SDNSF FBG    IB T250  PALM 12  9 13100  2  7 31400  34900
38  4                     FB  DC    P/M    IB T250  PALM 13 11 21000  2 11 49600  54500
        IB T277  SEA  49700 54600, IB T210D CUM  55500  61000, IB T160D PERK  55600  61100

38  4                     FB  SDNSF P/M    IB T250  PALM 14  1 21000  2 11 49100  53900
        IB T277  SEA  49300 54100, IB T330  CHRY  49700  54600, IB T160D PERK  55100  60600
        IB T210D CUM  55000  60500

------------------- 1971 BOATS --------------------------------------------------------
38  4                     FB  DC    P/M    IO T250  PALM 13 11 21000  2 11 74700  82100
        IO T277  SEA  75600 83000, IO T330  CHRY  78300  86100, IO T160D PERK  82600  90800

38  4                     FB  SDNSF P/M    IB T250  PALM 14  1 21000  2 11 47700  52400
        IB T277  SEA  47800 52600, IB T330  CHRY  48000  52700, IB T160D PERK  53200  58500
        IB T210D CUM  53100  58400

38  4 DOUBLE CABIN        DC  WD    DS IB T225       13 10    2 11 45600  50100
38  4 SEDAN CRUISER       SDN WD    DS IB T225       13 10    2 11 50100  55100
44  1 MOTOR YACHT         DCMY WD   DS IB T300  PALM 14  6 26000  3  2 62100  68200
------------------- 1970 BOATS --------------------------------------------------------
38  4                     FB  DC    MHG    IB T225  CHRY 13 10 19500  2 11 43200  48000
        IB T250  MRCR  43400 48300, IB T300  CHRY  47800  48500, IB T325  MRCR  44100  49000
        IB T160D PERK  49200  54100

38  4                     FB  SDNSF MHG    IB T225  CHRY 13 10 19500  2 11 43300  48200
        IB T250  MRCR  43600 48400, IB T300  CHRY  43800  48700, IB T325  MRCR  44300  49200
        IB T160D PERK  49400  54300

44  1 MOTOR YACHT         DCMY WD   DS IB T300  CHRY 14  6 26000  3  2 59900  65800
------------------- 1969 BOATS --------------------------------------------------------
37  9 VIKING 37           HT  SF    MHG    IB T210  CHRY 12 10 17000  2  9 38800  43100
        IB T300  CHRY  39300 43700, IB T140D GM   42800  47600, IB T160D PERK  44100  49000

37  9 VIKING 37           FB  SF    MHG    IB T210  CHRY 12 10 17000  2  9 38800  43100
        IB T300  CHRY  39300 43700, IB T140D GM   42800  47600, IB T160D PERK  44100  49000

37  9 VIKING 37           HT  SPTCR MHG    IB T210  CHRY 12 10 17000  2  9 38800  43100
        IB T300  CHRY  39300 43700, IB T140D GM   42800  47600, IB T160D PERK  44100  49000

37  9 VIKING 37           FB  SPTCR MHG    IB T210  CHRY 12 10 17000  2  9 38800  43100
        TR T300  CHRY  39300 43700, IB T140D GM   42800  47600, IB T160D PERK  44100  49000

37  9 VIKING 37 DELUXE    HT  SDN   MHG    IB T210  CHRY 12 10 17000  2  9 39000  43300
        IB T300  CHRY  39600 44000, IB T140D GM   43100  47900, IB T160D PERK  44400  49200

37  9 VIKING 37 DELUXE    FB  SDN   MHG    IB T210  CHRY 12 10 17000  2  9 39000  43300
        IB T300  CHRY  39600 44000, IB T140D GM   43100  47900, IB T160D PERK  44400  49200

44  1                     HT  MY    MHG    IB T277  SEA  14  6 32000  3  2 68300  75100
        IB T300  CHRY  69500 76300, IB T216D GM   73900  81200, IB T225D GM   74500  81900
        IB T283D GM   78700  86400

44  1                     FB  MY    MHG    IB T277  SEA  14  6 32000  3  2 68900  75700
        IB T300  CHRY  70000 77000, IB T216D GM   74400  81700, IB T225D GM   75000  82400
        IB T283D GM   79000  86900

44  1 W/EXT HT            HT  MY    MHG    IB T277  SEA  14  6 32000  3  2 69900  76800
        IB T300  CHRY  71100 78200, IB T216D GM   75300  82800, IB T225D GM   75900  83400
        IB T283D GM   80100  88000

------------------- 1968 BOATS --------------------------------------------------------
37  9 VIKING               FB  SF    MHG    IB T160D PERK 12 10 18000  2  9 44400  49400
37  9 VIKING 37            FB  SF    MHG    IB T210  CHRY 12 10 18000  2  9 39200  43600
37  9 VIKING 37            FB  SF    MHG    IB T210  CHRY 12 10 18000  2  9 39700  44100
37  9 VIKING 37 DELUXE     FB  SDN   MHG    IB T210  CHRY 12 10 18000  2  9 39400  43800
37  9 VIKING 37 DELUXE     FB  SDN   MHG    IB T210  CHRY 12 10 18000  2  9 39900  44300
37  9 VIKING 37 DELUXE     FB  SDN   MHG    IB T160D PERK 12 10 18000  2  9 44800  49800
44  1 W/EXT HT             HT  MY    MHG    IB T290  CHRY 14  6 29000  3  2 62900  69200
44  1 W/EXT HT             HT  MY    MHG    IB T215D GM   14  6 29000  3  2 67600  74200
44  1 W/EXT HT             HT  MY    MHG    IB T283D GM   14  6 29000  3  2 72100  79300
------------------- 1967 BOATS --------------------------------------------------------
37  9 VIKING               FB  SF    MHG    IB T160D PERK 12 10 18000  2  9 43100  47900
37  9 VIKING 37            FB  SF    MHG    IB T210  CHRY 12 10 18000  2  9 38100  42300
37  9 VIKING 37            FB  SF    MHG    IB T210  CHRY 12 10 18000  2  9 38300  42500
37  9 VIKING 37 DELUXE     FB  SDN   MHG    IB T210  CHRY 12 10 18000  2  9 38300  42500
37  9 VIKING 37 DELUXE     FB  SDN   MHG    IB T210  CHRY 12 10 18000  2  9 38500  42700
37  9 VIKING 37 DELUXE     FB  SDN   MHG    IB T160D PERK 12 10 18000  2  9 43500  48300
44  1 W/EXT HT             HT  MY    MHG    IB T290  CHRY 14  6 29000  3  2 61500  67100
44  1 W/EXT HT             HT  MY    MHG    IB T215D GM   14  6 29000  3  2 65600  72100
44  1 W/EXT HT             HT  MY    MHG    IB T283D GM   14  6 29000  3  2 70000  76900
------------------- 1966 BOATS --------------------------------------------------------
37  6                     FB  EXP   MHG    IB T210  CHRY       17000        36800  42800
        IB T290  CHRY  37300 41400, IB T140D GM   37400  41600, IB T170D CRUS  38000  42200

37  6                     FB  EXP   MHG    IB T210  CHRY       17000        36800  40900
        IB T290  CHRY  37300 41400, IB T140D GM   37400  41600, IB T170D CRUS  38000  42200
```

LOA FT IN	NAME AND/ OR MODEL		TOP/ RIG	BOAT TYPE	-HULL- MTL TP	----ENGINE--- TP # HP MFG	BEAM FT IN	WGT LBS	DRAFT FT IN	RETAIL LOW	RETAIL HIGH
--------------------- 1966 BOATS ---------------------
37 6			HT	SF	MHG	IB T210 CHRY		17000		35500	39400
	IB T290 CHRY 35900	39900, IB T140D GM				37500 41600, IB T170D CRUS		38000		38000	42200
37 6			FB	SF	MHG	IB T210 CHRY		17000		35500	39400
	IB T290 CHRY 35900	39900, IB T140D GM				37500 41600, IB T170D CRUS		38000		38000	42200
37 6 DELUXE			HT	SDN	MHG	IB T210 CHRY		17000		34600	38500
37 6 DELUXE			HT	SDN	MHG	IB T290 CHRY		17000		35100	39000
37 6 DELUXE			FB	SDN	MHG	IB T210 CHRY		17000		34600	38500
37 6 DELUXE			FB	SDN	MHG	IB T290 CHRY		17000		35100	39000
--------------------- 1965 BOATS ---------------------
37 6			HT	EXP	MHG	IB T210 CHRY		17000		35900	39800
37 6			HT	EXP	MHG	IB T250		17000		36100	40100
37 6			HT	EXP	MHG	IB T280		17000		36300	40300
37 6			FB	EXP	MHG	IB T210 CHRY		17000		35900	39800
37 6			FB	EXP	MHG	IB T250		17000		36100	40100
37 6			FB	EXP	MHG	IB T280		17000		36300	40300
37 6			HT	SF	MHG	IB T280		17000		35000	38900
37 6			HT	SF	MHG	IB T140D GM		17000		36500	40500
37 6			HT	SF	MHG	IB T170D CRUS		17000		37000	41100
37 6			FB	SF	MHG	IB T250		17000		34800	38600
	IB T280	35000	38900, IB T140D GM			36500 40500, IB T170D CRUS		17000		37000	41100
37 6 DELUXE			HT	SDN	MHG	IB T210 CHRY		17000		33700	37500
37 6 DELUXE			HT	SDN	MHG	IB T250		17000		34000	37800
37 6 DELUXE			HT	SDN	MHG	IB T280		17000		34200	38000
37 6 DELUXE			FB	SDN	MHG	IB T210 CHRY		17000		33700	37500
37 6 DELUXE			FB	SDN	MHG	IB T250		17000		34000	37800
37 6 DELUXE			FB	SDN	MHG	IB T280		17000		34200	38000
--------------------- 1964 BOATS ---------------------
36 5			HT	SPTCR	MHG	IB T210 CHRY				28000	31100
36 5			FB	SPTCR	MHG	IB T210 CHRY				28000	31100
38 2			HT	SF	MHG	IB T210 CHRY				39000	43300
38 2			FB	SF	MHG	IB T210 CHRY				39000	43300
38 2 DELUXE			HT	SDN	MHG	IB T210 CHRY				41500	46200
38 2 DELUXE			FB	SDN	MHG	IB T210 CHRY				41600	46200

VIKSUND BAT
STRUSSHAMN NORWAY

EIKEVIK CO
FT LAUDERDALE FL

For more recent years, see the BUC Used Boat Price Guide, Volume 1 or Volume 2

LOA FT IN	NAME AND/ OR MODEL	TOP/ RIG	BOAT TYPE	-HULL- MTL TP	----ENGINE--- TP # HP MFG	BEAM FT IN	WGT LBS	DRAFT FT IN	RETAIL LOW	RETAIL HIGH
--------------------- 1974 BOATS ---------------------
33	VIKSUND MS33	KTH	SA/CR	FBG KL	IB 36D	10 6	12000	4	25300	28100
--------------------- 1973 BOATS ---------------------
24	BUYABLE 24		CR	FBG	IB 36D				8650	9950
25	COLUMBI 25 D/E		CR	FBG	IB 36D				9700	11000
25	FISHING BOAT 25		CR	FBG	IB 22D				9500	10800
27	COLUMBI 27 D/E		CR	FBG	IB 36D				12000	13600
28	FISHING BOAT 28		CR	FBG	IB 36D				16200	18400
31	VIKSUND-COLUMBI	SLP	MS	FBG KL	IB D	10		3 4	24400	27100
--------------------- 1971 BOATS ---------------------
31	GOLDFISH	KTH	SAIL	FBG KL	IB 36D- 75D	10	12000	3 8	23300	25800

VINDO MARIN
VINDO NORTH AMERICA INC
NEW LONDON NH 03257

For more recent years, see the BUC Used Boat Price Guide, Volume 1 or Volume 2

LOA FT IN	NAME AND/ OR MODEL	TOP/ RIG	BOAT TYPE	-HULL- MTL TP	----ENGINE--- TP # HP MFG	BEAM FT IN	WGT LBS	DRAFT FT IN	RETAIL LOW	RETAIL HIGH
--------------------- 1983 BOATS ---------------------
29 3	VINDO 32	SLP	SA/CR	FBG KL	SD 15D VLVO	9 1	7040	4 3	30100	33400
33 7	VINDO 45	SLP	SA/CR	FBG KL	SD 35D VLVO	10 9	13000	5 2	57000	62700
37 7	VINDO 65 MIX	KTH	SA/CR	FBG KL	SD 61D VLVO	11 9		5 9	86200	94700
37 7	VINDO 65 MS	KTH	MS	FBG KL	SD 61D VLVO	11 9		5 9	90500	99400
37 7	VINDO 65 S	SLP	SA/CR	FBG KL	SD 61D VLVO	11 9	23750	5 9	101500	111500
--------------------- 1979 BOATS ---------------------
29 3	VINDO 32	SLP	SA/CR	FBG KL	IB 10D VLVO	9	7168	4 3	25600	28400
30 8	VINDO 40	SLP	SA/CR	FBG KL	IB 25D VLVO	9 8	10304	4 1	37700	41900
34 11	VINDO 50MS	SLP	MS	FBG KL	IB 36D VLVO	10 2	12140	5 3	45500	50000
34 11	VINDO 50MS	KTH	MS	FBG KL	IB 36D VLVO	10 2	12140	5 3	45500	50000
34 11	VINDO 50S	SLP	SA/CR	FBG KL	IB 36D VLVO	10 2	11480	5 2	42700	47500
34 11	VINDO 50S	KTH	SA/CR	FBG KL	IB 36D VLVO	10 2	11480	5 2	42700	47500
34 11	VINDO 50SL	SLP	SA/CR	FBG KL	IB 36D VLVO	10 2	11480	5 2	42700	47500
34 11	VINDO 50SL	KTH	SA/CR	FBG KL	IB 36D VLVO	10 2	11480	5 2	42700	47500
42 2	VINDO 90	KTH	SA/CR	FBG KL	IB 36D VLVO	13	26880	5 7	104500	115000
--------------------- 1978 BOATS ---------------------
29 3	VINDO 32	SLP	SA/CR	FBG KL	IB 13D VLVO	9 1	7040	4 3	24400	27100
30 8	VINDO 40	SLP	SA/CR	FBG KL	IB 25D VLVO	9 8	10304	4 6	36000	40700
34 11	VINDO 50	SLP	SA/CR	FBG KL	IB 36D VLVO	10 2	12140	5 3	43700	48600
34 11	VINDO 50	KTH	SA/CR	FBG KL	IB 36D VLVO	10 2	12140	5 3	43700	48600
--------------------- 1977 BOATS ---------------------
29 3	VINDO 32	SLP	SA/CR	FBG KL	IB 10D VLVO	9 1	7040	4 3	23800	26400
30 8	VINDO 40	SLP	SA/CR	FBG KL	IB 24D VLVO	9 8	10304	4 6	35700	39600
34 11	VINDO 50K	KTH	SA/CR	FBG KL	IB 37D VLVO	10 2	12140	5 3	41900	46600
34 11	VINDO 50K MIX	KTH	SA/CR	FBG KL	IB 37D VLVO	10 2	12140	5 3	43300	48100
34 11	VINDO 50S	SLP	SA/CR	FBG KL	IB 37D VLVO	10 2	12140	5 3	41800	46500
34 11	VINDO 50S MIX	SLP	SA/CR	FBG KL	IB 37D VLVO	10 2	12140	5 3	43400	48200
43	VINDO 90	KTH	SA/CR	FBG KL	IB D	12 11	24000	5 9	96100	105500

T D VINETTE COMPANY
ESCANABA MI 49829   COAST GUARD MFG ID- TDV

LOA FT IN	NAME AND/ OR MODEL	TOP/ RIG	BOAT TYPE	-HULL- MTL TP	----ENGINE--- TP # HP MFG	BEAM FT IN	WGT LBS	DRAFT FT IN	RETAIL LOW	RETAIL HIGH
--------------------- 1975 BOATS ---------------------
24 2	POOR-MAN		TRWL	STL SV	IB 25D		9	3 4	6100	7000
32 10	MASON 33	SLP	SA/CR	STL KL	IB 25D	10	13000	5	34300	38200
34	NORTH-SHORE 34		TRWL	STL SV	IB 85D	11 3			24300	27000
40	BAYTOWN 40		MY	STL	IB T130D PERK	14	36000	3	60800	66800
40 4	COLVIN-DOXY	SCH	SA/CR	STL KL	IB 25D	11 8	29500	4 2	73800	81100
42 2	COLVIN-GAZELLE	SCH	SA/CR	STL KL	IB 25D	11	18000	3 10	56400	62000
42 7	NORTH-SHORE 42		MY	STL SV	IB 130D	13	34000	4	56900	62600
43	BAYTOWN 43		MY	STL	IB T160D PERK	14	40000	3 4	68400	75200
44 9	NORTH-SHORE 44		MY	STL SV	IB 165D	14	44000	4 6	67300	74000
--------------------- 1974 BOATS ---------------------
24 2	POOR-MAN		TRWL	STL	IB 25D		9	3 4	5900	6800
32 10	MASON 33	SLP	SAIL	STL	IB 25 UNIV	10 7	13000	5	33100	36700
32 10	MASON 33	KTH	SAIL	AL	IB 25 UNIV	10 7	13000	5	33200	36900
34	NORTH-SHORE 34		TRWL	STL SV	IB 85D	11 3			23600	26200
40	BAYTOWN 40		MY	STL	IB T130D BARR	14	36000	3	57800	63500
40 4	COLVIN-DOXIE	SCH	SAIL	STL	IB 30D	11 8	29500	4 2	70000	78800
40 9	MASON 40	SLP	SAIL	STL	IB 50D PERK	12 2		6 3	71700	78800
40 9	MASON 40	KTH	SAIL	AL	IB 50D PERK	12 2		6 3	75700	83200
42 2	COLVIN-GAZELLE	SCH	SAIL	STL	IB 25D	11	18000	3 10	54500	59900
42 7	NORTH-SHORE 42		MY	STL	IB 130D BARR	13	34000	4	54800	60200
43	BAYTOWN 43		MY	STL	IB T160D PERK	14	40000	3 4	65800	72300
44 9	NORTH-SHORE 44		MY	STL	IB 185D PERK	14	44000	4 6	65200	71700
--------------------- 1973 BOATS ---------------------
32 10	MASON 33	SLP	SA/CR	STL KL	IB 25D	10 7	13000	5	32200	35700
40	BAYTOWN 40		MY	STL	IB T130D PERK	14	36000	3	56300	61800
42 2	COLVIN-GAZELLE	SCH	SA/CR	STL KL	IB 25D	11 4	18000	3 10	52800	58000
42 7	NORTH-SHORE 42		MY	STL	IB 130D PERK	13	34000	4	53000	58200
43	BAYTOWN 43		MY	STL	IB T160D PERK	14	40000	3 4	63300	69600
44 9	NORTH-SHORE 44		MY	STL	IB 165D	14	44000	4 6	63000	68300
--------------------- 1972 BOATS ---------------------
43	BAYTOWN 43		MY	STL SV	IB T160D PERK	14	40000	3 4	61000	67000
--------------------- 1971 BOATS ---------------------
30 10	FORD 30		SF	AL SV	IB T265 OMC	11 10	10000	2 4	11800	13400
43	BAYTOWN 43		MY	STL	IB T180D CUM	14	44000	3 10	62400	68600
43	EXPLORER		TRWL	STL SV	IB 160D PERK	13 8	32000	4	47500	52200
45	NAVIGATOR 45	KTH	SA/CR	STL KL	IB 80	14	32000	5	86900	95500
--------------------- 1969 BOATS ---------------------
33	MASON 33	SLP	SA/CR	STL KL	IB	10 7	13000	5	29000	32200
33	MASON 33	KTH	SA/CR	AL KL	IB	10 7	13000	5	29100	32400
37	ADVENTURE 37		CR	STL SV	IB D	13		3 6	**	**
37	ADVENTURE 37		SDN	STL SV	IB D	13		3 6	**	**
41 2	NAVIGATOR 41	KTH	SA/CR	STL KL	IB	12 3		3 10	38300	42500
43 2	BAYTOWN 43		DCMY	STL SV	IB T	14	44000	3 4	**	**
45	NAVIGATOR 45	KTH	SA/CR	STL KL	IB	14 4	42000	5 6	83000	91200
50	EMPRESS 50		DCMY	STL SV	IB	16		4 6	**	**
--------------------- 1968 BOATS ---------------------
33	MASON 33	SLP	SAIL	STL KL	IB	10 7		5	30000	33300
33	MASON 33	KTH	SAIL	AL KL	IB	10 7		5	30200	33500
37	ADVENTURE 37		SDN	STL SV	IB	13		3 6	**	**

T D VINETTE COMPANY — CONTINUED

See inside cover to adjust price for area

LOA FT	IN	NAME AND/OR MODEL	TOP/RIG	BOAT TYPE	HULL MTL	TP	ENG TP	#	HP	MFG	BEAM FT	IN	WGT LBS	DRAFT FT	IN	RETAIL LOW	RETAIL HIGH
1968 BOATS																	
37		BAYTOWN 37		SDN	STL	SV	IB		D		13			3	6	**	**
41	2	NAVIGATOR 41	KTH	SAIL	STL	KL	IB				12	3		3	10	45900	50400
43	2	BAYTOWN 43		DCMY	STL	SV	IB		D		14			3	8	**	**
45		NAVIGATOR 45	KTH	SAIL	STL	KL	IB				13	4		5	6	87500	96200
50		EMPRESS 50		DCMY	STL	SV	IB		D		16			4	6	**	**
1967 BOATS																	
33		MASON 33	SLP	SA/CR	STL	KL	IB				10	7		5		29500	32800
33		MASON 33	KTH	SA/CR	AL	KL	IB				10	7		5		29700	33000
37		ADVENTURE 37		CR	STL	SV	IB		D		13			3	6	**	**
37		BAYTOWN 37		CR	STL	SV	IB		D		13			3	6	**	**
41	2	NAVIGATOR 41	KTH	SA/CR	STL	KL	IB				12	3		3	10	39400	43700
43	2	BAYTOWN 43		DCMY	STL	SV	IB		D		14			3	8	**	**
45		NAVIGATOR 45	KTH	SA/CR	STL	KL	IB				13	4		5	6	86100	94600
50		EMPRESS 50		MY	STL	SV	IB		D		16			4	6	**	**
1965 BOATS																	
32	10	MASON	YWL	SAIL	STL	KL					9	2		5		18900	21000
34	6	WHIPPIT	SLP	SAIL	STL	KL					10			4	9	24200	26900
38		OFFSHORE		CR	STL		IB		100D		13			4		22300	24800
41		NAVIGATOR	KTH	SAIL	STL	KL					12	2		4		36600	40600
44		MONTEREY		CR	STL		IB		165D		15	2		3	8	40400	44900
49	2	SIDEWINDER		CR	STL		IB		250D		16			4	8	39000	43300

VINEYARD SHIP BUILDING CO

Call 1-800-327-6929 for BUC Personalized Evaluation Service
Or, for 1937 to 1952 boats, sign onto www.BUCValuPro.com

VINEYARD YACHTS INC

VINEYARD HAVEN MA 02568 COAST GUARD MFG ID- VNY See inside cover to adjust price for area

LOA FT	IN	NAME AND/OR MODEL	TOP/RIG	BOAT TYPE	HULL MTL	TP	ENG TP	#	HP	MFG	BEAM FT	IN	WGT LBS	DRAFT FT	IN	RETAIL LOW	RETAIL HIGH
1981 BOATS																	
29	4	HAWK 29		SF	FBG	DV	IB		250		11	5				43700	48600
32		WASQUE 32 FSH		CR	FBG	DS	IB		160		9	10				51700	56800
1980 BOATS																	
29	4	HAWK 29		FSH	FBG	DV	IB		330		11	4				46600	51200
29	4	HAWK 29		FSH	FBG	DV	IB		T225		11	4				49100	53900
32	2	WASQUE 32		FSH	FBG	DS	IB		225-330		9	10				50000	57400
1979 BOATS																	
26		WASQUE		UTL	FBG	SV	IB		225		8	7	5000			23800	26500
26		WASQUE		UTL	FBG	SV	IB		D		8	7	5000			**	**
29	4	HAWK		FSH	FBG	DV	IB		330		11	4	8500			44200	49100
29	4	HAWK		FSH	FBG	DV	IB				11	4	8500			**	**
29	4	HAWK		FSH	FBG	DV	IB		T225		11	4	8500			47200	51900
32	2	WASQUE		UTL	FBG	SV	IB		225-330		9	10	8000			53600	61700
32	2	WASQUE		UTL	FBG	SV	IB		D		9	10	8000			**	**
1978 BOATS																	
26		WASQUE 26		UTL	FBG	SV	IB				8	7	5000			**	**
26		WASQUE 26		UTL	FBG	SV	IB		D		8	7	5000			**	**
29		HAWK 29		FSH	FBG	DV	IB				11	6				**	**
32	2	WASQUE 32		UTL	FBG	SV	IB				9	10	8000			**	**
32	2	WASQUE 32		UTL	FBG	SV	IB		D		9	10	8000			**	**
1977 BOATS																	
26		WASQUE		CUD	FBG	SV	IB		225		8	7		2	3	21700	24100
26		WASQUE		CUD	FBG	SV	IB		D		8	7		2	3	**	**
26		WASQUE	OP	FSH	FBG	SV	IB		225		8	7	4750	2	3	21800	24200
26		WASQUE	OP	FSH	FBG	SV	IB		D		8	7	4750	2	3	**	**
27		VY27		FSH	FBG	SV	IB		330-350		11					26300	29600
29		VY29	OP	CUD	FBG		IB				11		7000			**	**
29		VY29			FBG		IB				11		7000			**	**
32	2	WASQUE		FSH	FBG	SV	IB		225-330		9	10	8000	2	6	43100	51500
32	2	WASQUE		FSH	FBG	SV	IB		D		9	10	8000	2	6	**	**
1976 BOATS																	
26		WASQUE		CUD	FBG	SV	IB		225		8	7		2	3	21000	23300
26		WASQUE		CUD	FBG	SV	IB		D		8	7		2	3	**	**
26		WASQUE	OP	FSH	FBG	SV	IB		225		8	7	4750	2	3	20900	23200
26		WASQUE	OP	FSH	FBG	SV	IB		D		8	7	4750	2	3	**	**
32	2	WASQUE		CUD	FBG	SV	IB		225-325		9	10	8000	2	6	41600	48400
32	2	WASQUE		CUD	FBG	SV	IB		D		9	10	8000	2	6	**	**
1975 BOATS																	
26		WASQUE	OP	FSH	FBG	SV	IB		225		8	7	4750	2	3	20100	22400
26		WASQUE	OP	FSH	FBG	SV	IB		105D		8	7	4750	2	3	23400	26000
32	2	WASQUE		FSH	FBG	SV	IB		225-330		9	10	8000	2	6	39700	46400
32	2	WASQUE		FSH	FBG	SV	IB		105D		9	10	8000	2	6	47500	52200
1974 BOATS																	
26		WASQUE 26	OP	FSH	FBG	SV	IB		225		8	7	4750	2	3	19300	21500
26		WASQUE 26	OP	FSH	FBG	SV	IB		100D-106D		8	7	4750	2	3	22000	24800
32	2	WASQUE 32	OP	FSH	FBG	SV	IB				9	9	8500	2	6	**	**
1973 BOATS																	
32	2	WASQUE	OP	FSH	FBG	SV	IB		225		9	9	8000	2	6	36700	40700
1972 BOATS																	
20	7	WASQUE 21			FBG		IB		120	FORD	6	8		1	8	7800	8950
20	7	WASQUE 21	HT		FBG		IB		120	FORD	6	8		1	8	7800	8950
32		WASQUE		BASS	FBG		IB		225	PALM	9	8		2	6	39300	43700
32		WASQUE 4 SLPR			FBG		IB		225	PALM	9	8		2	6	34300	38100
32		WASQUE 4 SLPR			FBG		IB		D	PERK	9	8		2	6	**	**
32		WASQUE LOBSTER BOAT			FBG		IB		150		9	8		2	6	32700	36300
1941 BOATS																	
33			HT	CR	WD		IB									**	**
40			HT	SDN	WD		IB									**	**
47			HT	SDN	WD		IB									**	**

VITA FLOATING HOMES

Call 1-800-327-6929 for BUC Personalized Evaluation Service
Or, for 1960 boats, sign onto www.BUCValuPro.com

VOYAGER MARINE INC

CLEARWATER FL 33520 COAST GUARD MFG ID- SMF See inside cover to adjust price for area

For more recent years, see the BUC Used Boat Price Guide, Volume 1 or Volume 2

LOA FT	IN	NAME AND/OR MODEL	TOP/RIG	BOAT TYPE	HULL MTL	TP	ENG TP	HP	MFG	BEAM FT	IN	WGT LBS	DRAFT FT	IN	RETAIL LOW	RETAIL HIGH
1983 BOATS																
25	9	VOYAGER 26	CUT	SA/CR	FBG	KL	IB	10D	BMW	8	3	6600	3	4	18800	20900
1982 BOATS																
25	9	VOYAGER 26	CUT	SA/CR	FBG	KL	IB	10D	BMW	8	3	6600	3	4	17300	19700
1978 BOATS																
25	9	VOYAGER 26	CUT	SA/CR	FBG	KL	IB	8D	YAN	8	3	6600	3	4	14400	16400

VOYAGER MFG CO

Call 1-800-327-6929 for BUC Personalized Evaluation Service
Or, for 1965 boats, sign onto www.BUCValuPro.com

WACANDA MARINE INC

Call 1-800-327-6929 for BUC Personalized Evaluation Service
Or, for 1965 to 1972 boats, sign onto www.BUCValuPro.com

WADHAM STRINGER LTD

DELL QUAY BOATS   COAST GUARD MFG ID- MPA

DIST BEAVER BOATS N AMER LTD

Call 1-800-327-6929 for BUC Personalized Evaluation Service
Or, for 1977 to 1978 boats, sign onto www.BUCValuPro.com

WAGEMAKER

FOR NEWER MODELS SEE ASHCRAFT

Call 1-800-327-6929 for BUC Personalized Evaluation Service
Or, for 1941 to 1961 boats, sign onto www.BUCValuPro.com

ARNOLD WALKER

Call 1-800-327-6929 for BUC Personalized Evaluation Service
Or, for 1977 boats, sign onto www.BUCValuPro.com

GEORGE B WALTON
ANNAPOLIS MD

See inside cover to adjust price for area

LOA FT	IN	NAME AND/ OR MODEL	TOP/ RIG	BOAT TYPE	HULL MTL	HULL TP	TP	ENG #	HP	MFG	BEAM FT	IN	WGT LBS	DRAFT FT	IN	RETAIL LOW	RETAIL HIGH
		1968 BOATS															
28	11	KINGS-CRUISER	SLP	SAIL	FBG	CB	IB				7	9		4	4	20100	22400
		1967 BOATS															
17	1	ARCOA 520		SA/CR	FBG	KL	IB				7	5			2	3800	4400
28	11	KINGS-CRUISER MODIFD	SLP	SA/CR	FBG	KL	IB				7	9		4	4	20100	22300
		1965 BOATS															
28	4	KINGS-CRUISER		SAIL	WD		IB		7								15700	17800
31	9	CHESAPEAKE 32		SAIL	FBG		IB		30								20700	23000
37	4	WALTON 37	SLP	SAIL	FBG		IB		25								33400	37100
37	4	WALTON 37	YWL	SAIL	FBG		IB		25								33300	37100
		1964 BOATS															
25	3	WALTON 25		SAIL	FBG		IB										9100	10300
28		KINGS-CRUISER		SAIL	WD		IB		8D								17000	19400
31	9	CHESAPEAKE 32		SA/CR	FBG		IB		30								17500	19900
31	9	CHESAPEAKE 32		SA/RC	PDG		ID		30								24500	27200
37	3	WALTON 37	SLP	SAIL	FBG		IB		25								32900	36600
37	3	WALTON 37	YWL	SAIL	FBG		IB		25								32900	36600
		1963 BOATS															
25	3	WALTON 25		SAIL	FBG		OB										7600	8750
28		KINGS-CRUISER		SAIL	WD		OB										13800	15700
31	9	CHESAPEAKE 32		SAIL	FBG		OB										15300	17400
		1962 BOATS															
31	9	CHESAPEAKE		SAIL	FBG		IB		30	GRAY						20300	22500
		1961 BOATS															
17	1	ARCOA 520	SLP	SA/CR	PLY	KL	OB				7	3				2750	3200
17	1	ARCOA 520	SLP	SA/CR	PLY	KL	IB				7	3				3700	4300
25		NORDIC	SLP	SA/CR	P/M	KL	IB		D		7	2		3	11	9600	10900
28		KING'S-CRUISER	SLP	SA/CR	P/M	KL	IB		D		7	3		3	11	16800	19000
32		CHESAPEAKE	SLP	SA/CR	FBG	KL					8	9				**	**
		1960 BOATS															
17	1	ARCOA 520	SLP	SA/CR	PLY	KL	IB		5		7	3		1	6	3500	4100
28		KINGS-CRUISER	SLP	SA/CR	P/M	KL	IB		8D	VLVO	7	3		1	6	16600	18900
39	9	CHESAPEAKE 32	SLP	SA/CR	FBG	KL	IB		25		8	9		4	9	44100	49000
		1959 BOATS															
25	2	NORDIC	SLP	SA/CR	MHG	KL	OB				7	2		3	11	7450	8600
28		KINGS-CRUISER	SLP	SAIL	WD	KL	IB		8D	VLVO	7	3		3	11	16800	19100

WARREN CRAFT BOATS
COAST GUARD MFG ID- WDC

Call 1-800-327-6929 for BUC Personalized Evaluation Service
Or, for 1981 to 1986 boats, sign onto www.BUCValuPro.com

WARREN MARINE

Call 1-800-327-6929 for BUC Personalized Evaluation Service
Or, for 1977 boats, sign onto www.BUCValuPro.com

WARREN PRODUCTS INC
COAST GUARD MFG ID- WAR

Call 1-800-327-6929 for BUC Personalized Evaluation Service
Or, for 1965 to 1979 boats, sign onto www.BUCValuPro.com

WARRIOR CATAMARANS INC
COAST GUARD MFG ID- WAF

Call 1-800-327-6929 for BUC Personalized Evaluation Service
Or, for 1977 to 1984 boats, sign onto www.BUCValuPro.com

WATER HOUSE INC

Call 1-800-327-6929 for BUC Personalized Evaluation Service
Or, for 1968 to 1972 boats, sign onto www.BUCValuPro.com

WATERCRAFT INC
GALLATIN TN 37066   COAST GUARD MFG ID- WAT See inside cover to adjust price for area

LOA FT	IN	NAME AND/ OR MODEL	TOP/ RIG	BOAT TYPE	HULL MTL	HULL TP	TP	ENG #	HP	MFG	BEAM FT	IN	WGT LBS	DRAFT FT	IN	RETAIL LOW	RETAIL HIGH
		1976 BOATS															
42		WATERCRAFT 42	HT	HB	AL	SV	IO		T185		13					25400	28200
46	4	WATERCRAFT 47	HT	HB	AL	SV	IO		T255		14					29700	33000
51	4	WATERCRAFT 52	HT	HB	AL	SV	IO		T255		14					33400	37100
56	4	WATERCRAFT 57	HT	HB	AL	SV	IO		T255		14					46100	50700
		1974 BOATS															
45		WATERCRAFT 45		HB	AL		IB		T165	MRCR	14		13500	1	1	22800	25300
45		WATERCRAFT 45		HB	AL		VD		T225	CHRY	14		13500	1	1	22900	25500
46	4	WATERCRAFT 47		HB	AL		VD		T225	CHRY	14		19000	2	10	27800	30900
46	4	WATERCRAFT 47		HB	AL		VD		T225	OMC	14		19000	2	10	28700	31900
46	4	WATERCRAFT 47		HB	AL		VD		T255	WAUK	14		19000	2	10	28100	31200
50		WATERCRAFT 50		HB	AL		IB		T165	MRCR	14		15000	1		25900	28800
50		WATERCRAFT 50		HB	AL		VD		T225	CHRY	14		15000	1		26200	28900
51	4	WATERCRAFT 52		HB	AL		VD		T225	CHRY	14		21000	2	11	31400	34900
51	4	WATERCRAFT 52		HB	AL		VD		T225	OMC	14		21000	2	11	32400	35900
51	4	WATERCRAFT 52		HB	AL		VD		T255	WAUK	14		21000	2	11	31700	35300
55		WATERCRAFT 55		HB	AL		IB		T165	MRCR	14		16900	1	1	37300	41400
55		WATERCRAFT 55		HB	AL		VD		T225	CHRY	14		16900	1	1	37400	41500
56	4	WATERCRAFT 57		HB	AL		VD		T225	CHRY	14		22500	3		43000	47800
56	4	WATERCRAFT 57		HB	AL		VD		T225	OMC	14		22500	3		44200	49100
56	4	WATERCRAFT 57		HB	AL		VD		T255	WAUK	14		22500	3		43400	48200
		1973 BOATS															
45		WATERCRAFT 45		HB	AL		IB		T165	MRCR	12		13500	2	8	22600	25100
50		WATERCRAFT 50		HB	AL		VD		T225	CHRY	14		15000	1		25800	28600
50		WATERCRAFT 50		HB	AL		VD		T225	OMC	14		15000	1		25700	29600
50		WATERCRAFT 50		HB	AL		VD		T225	WAUK	14		15000	1		26100	29000
55		WATERCRAFT 55		HB	AL		VD		T225	CHRY	14		16900	1	1	37000	41200
55		WATERCRAFT 55		HB	AL		VD		T225	OMC	14		16900	1	1	38200	42400
55		WATERCRAFT 55		HB	AL		VD		T255	WAUK	14		16900	1	1	37400	41500

(1973 WATERCRAFT 45 alternate engines: VD T225 CHRY 22700 25200, VD T225 OMC 23400 26000, VD T255 WAUK 22700 25300)

WATERWAYS BOAT COMPANY
COAST GUARD MFG ID- WWC

Call 1-800-327-6929 for BUC Personalized Evaluation Service
Or, for 1976 to 1980 boats, sign onto www.BUCValuPro.com

WATKINS YACHTS INC
CLEARWATER FL 33520   COAST GUARD MFG ID- WYM See inside cover to adjust price for area

For more recent years, see the BUC Used Boat Price Guide, Volume 1 or Volume 2

LOA FT	IN	NAME AND/ OR MODEL	TOP/ RIG	BOAT TYPE	HULL MTL	HULL TP	TP	ENG #	HP	MFG	BEAM FT	IN	WGT LBS	DRAFT FT	IN	RETAIL LOW	RETAIL HIGH
		1983 BOATS															
24	11	WATKINS 25	SLP	SA/RC	FBG	KL	OB		8		10		4000	2	6	5350	6100
27		WATKINS 27	SLP	SA/RC	FBG	KL	IB		8D	YAN	10		7500	3	8	11700	13300
27		WATKINS 27 PH	SLP	SA/CR	FBG	KL	IB		D		10		8000	3	8	12600	14300
32	6	WATKINS 32	SLP	SA/CR	FBG		IB		15D	YAN	10	2	11000	4		19100	21200
36		WATKINS 36	SLP	SA/CR	FBG	KL	IB		50D	PERK	10	6	18000	4	6	31100	34500
		1982 BOATS															
27		WATKINS 27	SLP	SA/CR	FBG	KL	IB		12D		10		7500	3	8	11000	12500
27		WATKINS 27 PH	SLP	SA/CR	FBG	KL	IB		12D		10		8000	3	8	11800	13400
36		WATKINS 36	SLP	SA/CR	FBG	KL	IB		40D		10	6	18000	4	6	28300	31500
36		WATKINS 36 CC	SLP	SA/CR	FBG	KL	IB		40D		10	6	18000	4	6	30200	33600
		1981 BOATS															
23		WATKINS 23	SLP	SA/CR	FBG	CB			8		10		2500			2850	3350
27		WATKINS 27	SLP	SA/RC	FBG	CB	IB		D		10		7500			10400	11800
36		WATKINS 36	SLP	SA/CR	FBG	KL	IB		D		10	6	18000	4	6	27500	30600
		1980 BOATS															
23		WATKINS 23	SLP	SA/CR	FBG	CB			8		10		2500		6	2750	3200
27		WATKINS 27	SLP	SA/RC	FBG	CB	IB		8		10		7500			9950	11300
		1979 BOATS															
23		WATKINS 23	SLP	SAIL	FBG	KC	OB		8		10		2500			2650	3050
27		WATKINS 27	SLP	SAIL	FBG	KL	IB		15D	YAN	10		7500	3	8	9550	10900
32	3	WATKINS 32	SLP	SA/RC	FBG		IB		D		12		11200			15600	17700
		1978 BOATS															
23		WATKINS 23XL	SLP	SAIL	FBG	KC	OB		8		10		2500	1	6	2550	2950
27		WATKINS 27	SLP	SAIL	FBG	KL	IB		8D	YAN	10		7000	3	8	8500	9750
		1977 BOATS															
23		WATKINS 23XL	SLP	SAIL	FBG	KC	OB		8		10		2500	1	6	2450	2850
27		WATKINS 27	SLP	SAIL	FBG	KL	IB		8D		10		7000	3	3	8200	9400
		1976 BOATS															
23		WATKINS 23XL	SLP	SAIL	FBG	KC	OB		8		10		2500	1	6	2400	2750

LOA FT	LOA IN	NAME AND/ OR MODEL	TOP/ RIG	BOAT TYPE	-HULL- MTL	-HULL- TP	TP	# HP	MFG	BEAM FT	BEAM IN	WGT LBS	DRAFT FT	DRAFT IN	RETAIL LOW	RETAIL HIGH
		1975 BOATS														
23		WATKINS 23	SLP	SAIL	FBG	KC	OB			8		2300	1	6	2200	2550
		1974 BOATS														
23		WATKINS 23	SLP	SAIL	FBG	KC	OB			8		2250	1	6	2050	2450
		1972 BOATS														
27		WATKINS 27 MKII	SLP	SA/CR	FBG	KL	IB	8D- 15D		10		7500	3	8	7700	8900
27		WATKINS 27P	SLP	MS	FBG	KL	IB	15D	YAN	10		8000	3	8	8300	9550
36		WATKINS 36	SLP	SA/CR	FBG	KL	IB	40D	PERK	10	6	17000	4	6	19200	21300
36		WATKINS 36C	SLP	SA/CR	FBG	KL	IB	40D	PERK	10	6	17000	4	6	19800	22000

WAUQUIEZ INTERNATIONAL

DIV OF GROUPE BENETEAU
NEUVILLE EN FERRAIN FRANCE
FORMERLY CHANTIER WAUQUIEZ

See inside cover to adjust price for area

For more recent years, see the BUC Used Boat Price Guide, Volume 1 or Volume 2

LOA FT	LOA IN	NAME AND/ OR MODEL	TOP/ RIG	BOAT TYPE	-HULL- MTL	-HULL- TP	TP	# HP	MFG	BEAM FT	BEAM IN	WGT LBS	DRAFT FT	DRAFT IN	RETAIL LOW	RETAIL HIGH
		1983 BOATS														
33		GLADIATEUR	SLP	SA/RC	FBG	KL	IB	15D	VLVO	11		11000	6		40700	45200
35	1	PRETORIEN	SLP	SA/RC	FBG	KL	IB	23D	VLVO	11	7	14350	6		59100	65000
38		HOOD 38	SLP	SA/CR	FBG	KC	IB	50D	PERK	11	9	22046	4	6	82600	90700
43		AMPHITRITE	KTH	MS	FBG	KL	IB	62D	PERK	13	8	28600	6		114500	126000
47		CENTURION 47	SLP	SA/RC	FBG	KL	IB	62D	PERK	16	7	28600	7	10	135000	148000
		1982 BOATS														
38		HOOD 38	SLP	SA/CR	FBG	KC	IB	47D	PERK	11	9	22046	4	6	78200	86000
		1975 BOATS														
32		CENTURION	SLP	SA/CR	FBG	KL	IB	D		9	10	10560	5	10	29300	32600
32		CHANCE	SLP	SA/CR	FBG	KL	IB	D		9	10	11000	5	10	30500	33900
37		CHANCE	SLP	SA/CR	FBG	KL	IB	D		10	6	14520	5	10	42800	47500
		1974 BOATS														
32		CENTURION	SLP	SA/CR	FBG	KL	IB	D		9	10	10700	5	10	29100	32300
37		CHANCE 37	SLP	SA/CR	FBG	KL	IB	D		10	6	14300	5	10	41400	46000
		1973 BOATS														
32		CENTURION	SLP	SAIL	FBG	KL	IB	25D	VLVO	9	10	10700	5	10	28600	31700
37		CHANCE	SLP	SAIL	FBG	KL	IB	25D	VLVO	10	6	14300	5	10	40500	45000
		1972 BOATS														
32		CENTURION	SLP	SAIL	FBG	KL	IB	D		9	10	10700	5	10	28000	31100
37		CHANCE	SLP	SAIL	FBG	KL	IB	D		10	6	14300	5	10	39700	44100
		1970 BOATS														
27	6	VICTORIAN	SLP	SA/CR	FBG	KL	IB	D		8	7		4	1	16900	19200
32		CENTURIAN	SLP	SA/CR	FBG	KL	IB	D		9	10	10700	5	10	26600	29600
		1969 BOATS														
27	6	VICTORIAN	SLP	SA/CR	FBG	KL	IB	D	VLVO	8	7	5000	4	1	11600	13200
32		CENTURION	SLP	SA/CR	FBG	KL	IB	D		9	10	10700	5	10	26000	28900

WAVERIDER BOATS

COAST GUARD MFG ID- WAY

Call 1-800-327-6929 for BUC Personalized Evaluation Service
Or, for 1981 to 1994 boats, sign onto www.BUCValuPro.com

WEBBCRAFT INC

WEBB BOATS INC
COLLINSVILLE OK 74021 COAST GUARD MFG ID- WBB

See inside cover to adjust price for area

For more recent years, see the BUC Used Boat Price Guide, Volume 1 or Volume 2

LOA FT	LOA IN	NAME AND/ OR MODEL	TOP/ RIG	BOAT TYPE	-HULL- MTL	-HULL- TP	TP	# HP	MFG	BEAM FT	BEAM IN	WGT LBS	DRAFT FT	DRAFT IN	RETAIL LOW	RETAIL HIGH
		1983 BOATS														
17	8	GLIDER 18-V	OP	RNBT	FBG	DV	IO	120	MRCR	7		2500			2800	3250
19	8	WILDCAT	OP	RNBT	FBG	DV	IO	170-260		8		2800			3600	4450
21	2	RIVIERA	OP	CUD	FBG	DV	IO	170-260		8		3000			4100	5000
21	2	RIVIERA	OP	CUD	FBG	DV	IO	330	MRCR	8		3000			4900	5650
21	2	RIVIERA	OP	CUD	FBG	DV	IO	370	MRCR	8		3000			5500	6300
21	2	RIVIERA	OP	RNBT	FBG	DV	IO	170-260		8		3000			3900	4800
21	2	RIVIERA	OP	RNBT	FBG	DV	IO	330	MRCR	8		3000			4700	5400
21	2	RIVIERA	OP	RNBT	FBG	DV	IO	370	MRCR	8		3000			5200	6000
23	9	ENTERPRISE	OP	CUD	FBG	DV	IO	170-260		8		3200			4900	5900
23	9	ENTERPRISE	OP	CUD	FBG	DV	IO	330	MRCR	8		3200			5700	6550
23	9	ENTERPRISE	OP	CUD	FBG	DV	IO	T170-T260		8		3200			5600	6950
23	9	ENTERPRISE	OP	RNBT	FBG	DV	IO	170-260		8		3200			4650	5550
23	9	ENTERPRISE	OP	RNBT	FBG	DV	IO	330	MRCR	8		3200			5350	6150
23	9	ENTERPRISE	OP	RNBT	FBG	DV	IO	T170-T260		8		3200			5250	6500
35		CONCORDE	OP	CR	FBG	DV	IB	T260	MRCR						28600	31800
		IO T330 MRCR 24300 27000, IB T370 MRCR 30000 33400, IB T400 MRCR													30500	33900
		IB T440 MRCR 31200 34700														
		1982 BOATS														
17	8	GLIDER 18-V	OP	RNBT	FBG	DV	IO		OMC	7		2500			**	**
17	8	GLIDER 18-V	OP	RNBT	FBG	DV	IO	120-185		7		2500			2750	3200
19	8	WILDCAT	OP	CUD	FBG	DV	IO		OMC	8		2800			**	**
19	8	WILDCAT	OP	CUD	FBG	DV	IO	170-260		8		2800			3650	4500
19	8	WILDCAT	OP	RNBT	FBG	DV	IO		OMC	8		2800			**	**
19	8	WILDCAT	OP	RNBT	FBG	DV	IO	170-260		8		2800			3500	4350
21	2	COMMANDER	OP	CUD	FBG	DV	IO		OMC	8		3000			**	**
21	2	COMMANDER	OP	CUD	FBG	DV	IO	170-260		8		3000			4000	4900
21	2	COMMANDER	OP	CUD	FBG	DV	IO	330	MRCR	8		3000			4800	5550
21	2	COMMANDER	OP	RNBT	FBG	DV	IO		OMC	8		3000			**	**
21	2	COMMANDER	OP	RNBT	FBG	DV	IO	170-260		8		3000			3800	4650
21	2	COMMANDER	OP	RNBT	FBG	DV	IO	330	MRCR	8		3000			4600	5300
22	9	ENTERPRISE	OP	CUD	FBG	DV	IO	T228-T260		8		3200			5400	6500
22	9	ENTERPRISE	OP	RNBT	FBG	DV	IO		OMC	8		3200			**	**
23	9	ENTERPRISE	OP	CUD	FBG	DV	IO		OMC	8		3200			**	**
		IO 170-260 4800 5800, IO 330 MRCR 5600 6400, IO T OMC													**	**
		IO T170-T200 5450 6350														
23	9	ENTERPRISE	OP	RNBT	FBG	DV	IO	170-260		8		3200			4550	5400
		IO 330 MRCR 5250 6000, IO T MRCR ** ** , IO T170-T260													5150	6350
35		CONCORD	OP	CR	FBG	DV	IB	T330	MRCR						30000	33400
35		CONCORDE	OP	CR	FBG	DV	IB	T260	MRCR						27400	30400
35		CONCORDE	OP	CR	FBG	DV	IB	T330	MRCR						26400	29300
35		CONCORDE	OP	CR	FBG	DV	IB	T370	MRCR						28700	31900
		1981 BOATS														
17	8	WC-18-V B/R	ST	RNBT	FBG	DV	IO	140-230		7		2800			2850	3450
18	2	WC-18 TRI B/R	ST	RNBT	FBG	TR	IO	140-230		7	2	2800			3000	3600
19	11	WC-20-V	ST	RNBT	FBG	DV	IO	170-260		8		3200			3750	4650
19	11	WC-20-V	ST	RNBT	FBG	DV	IO	330	MRCR	8		3200			4550	5250
19	11	WC-20-V CUDDY	ST	CUD	FBG	DV	IO	170-260		8		3200			3950	4850
19	11	WC-20-V CUDDY	ST	CUD	FBG	DV	IO	330	MRCR	8		3200			4750	5500
22	7	WC-22-V	OP	RNBT	FBG	DV	IO	170-260		8					4550	5400
22	7	WC-22-V	OP	RNBT	FBG	DV	IO	330	MRCR	8					5250	6000
22	7	WC-22-V	OP	RNBT	FBG	DV	IO	T140-T260		8					5100	6350
22	7	WC-22-V CUDDY	OP	CUD	FBG	DV	IO	170-260		8					4800	5750
22	7	WC-22-V CUDDY	OP	CUD	FBG	DV	IO	330	MRCR	8					5550	6400
22	7	WC-22-V CUDDY	OP	CUD	FBG	DV	IO	T140-T260		8					5400	6750
23	4	WC-23 LOW DECK	OP	CUD	FBG	DV	IO	228-260		8		4800			6350	7450
23	4	WC-23 LOW DECK	OP	CUD	FBG	DV	IO	330	MRCR	8		4800			7000	8050
23	4	WC-23 LOW DECK	OP	CUD	FBG	DV	IO	T140-T260		8		4800			6850	8400
25	7	WC-26	OP	CR	FBG	DV	IO	260-330		8		6600			9050	10900
25	7	WC-26	OP	CR	FBG	DV	IO	T140-T260		8		6600			9400	11600
25	7	WC-26	OP	CR	FBG	DV	IO	T330	MRCR	8		6600			11300	12800
25	7	WC-26 LOW DECK	OP	CUD	FBG	DV	IO	260-330		8		5800			8150	10100
		IO T140-T230 8500 10400, IO T260 9450 10700, IO T330 MRCR													10500	12000
		1980 BOATS														
17	8	WC-18-V B/R	ST	RNBT	FBG	DV	IO	140-230		7		2800			2850	3400
18	2	WC-18 TRI B/R	ST	RNBT	FBG	TR	IO	140-230		7	2	2800			2950	3550
19	11	WC-20-V	ST	RNBT	FBG	DV	IO	170-260		8		3200			3750	4600
19	11	WC-20-V	ST	RNBT	FBG	DV	IO	330	MRCR	8		3200			4500	5150
19	11	WC-20-V CUDDY	ST	CUD	FBG	DV	IO	170-260		8		3200			3900	4750
19	11	WC-20-V CUDDY	ST	CUD	FBG	DV	IO	330	MRCR	8		3200			4700	5400
23	4	WC-23 LOW DECK	OP	CUD	FBG	DV	IO	228-260		8		4800			6300	7350
		IO 330 MRCR 6950 8000, IO T140-T260 6800 8350, IO T330 MRCR													8350	9600
25	7	WC-26	OP	CR	FBG	DV	IO	260-330		8		6600			9000	10800
25	7	WC-26	OP	CR	FBG	DV	IO	T140-T260		8		6600			9300	11500
25	7	WC-26	OP	CR	FBG	DV	IO	T330	MRCR	8		6600			11200	12700
25	7	WC-26 LOW DECK	OP	CUD	FBG	DV	IO	260-330		8		5800			8100	9950
		IO T140-T230 8450 10300, IO T260 9400 10700, IO T330 MRCR													10400	11900
		1979 BOATS														
17	8	WC-18-V B/R	ST	RNBT	FBG	DV	IO	140-228		7		2800			2800	3400
18	2	WC-18 TRI B/R	ST	RNBT	FBG	TR	IO	140-230		7	2	2800			2950	3550
19	11	WC-20-V	ST	RNBT	FBG	DV	IO	198-260		8		3200			3750	4550
19	11	WC-20-V	ST	RNBT	FBG	DV	IO	330	MRCR	8		3200			4500	5150
19	11	WC-20-V CUDDY	ST	CUD	FBG	DV	IO	198-260		8		3200			3900	4750
19	11	WC-20-V CUDDY	ST	CUD	FBG	DV	IO	330	MRCR	8		3200			4700	5400

CONTINUED ON NEXT PAGE

WEBBCRAFT INC

-CONTINUED   See inside cover to adjust price for area

LOA FT IN	NAME AND/OR MODEL	TOP/RIG	BOAT TYPE	MTL	TP	TP	ENGINE # HP	MFG	BEAM FT IN	WGT LBS	DRAFT FT IN	RETAIL LOW	RETAIL HIGH
1979 BOATS													
23 4	WC-23 LOW DECK	OP	CUD	FBG	DV	IO	228-260		8	4800		6300	7350

IO 330 MRCR 6950 8000, IO T170-T260 6850 8350, IO T330 MRCR 8350

LOA FT IN	NAME AND/OR MODEL	TOP/RIG	BOAT TYPE	MTL	TP	TP	ENGINE # HP	MFG	BEAM FT IN	WGT LBS	DRAFT FT IN	RETAIL LOW	RETAIL HIGH
25 7	WC-26	OP	CR	FBG	DV	IO	260-330		8	6600		8950	10800
25 7	WC-26	OP	CR	FBG	DV	IO	T170-T260		8	6600		9400	11500
25 7	WC-26	OP	CR	FBG	DV	IO	T330	MRCR	8	6600		11100	12700
25 7	WC-26 LOW DECK	OP	CUD	FBG	DV	IO	260-330		8	5800		8100	9950
25 7	WC-26 LOW DECK	OP	CUD	FBG	DV	IO	T170-T260		8	5800		8600	10700
25 7	WC-26 LOW DECK	OP	CUD	FBG	DV	IO	T330	MRCR	8	5800		10400	11800
1978 BOATS													
17 8	WC-18-V B/R	OP	RNBT	FBG	DV	IO	140-228		7	2600		2700	3300
18 2	WC-18 B/R	OP	RNBT	FBG	TR	IO	140-228		7 2	2800		2950	3550
19 10	WC-20	OP	RNBT	FBG	DV	IO	185-260		8	3000		3550	4400
19 10	WC-20	OP	RNBT	FBG	DV	IO	330	MRCR	8	3000		4300	5000
19 10	WC-20 CUDDY	OP	CUD	FBG	DV	IO	185-260		8	3200		3850	4750
19 10	WC-20 CUDDY	OP	CUD	FBG	DV	IO	330	MRCR	8	3200		4700	5400
23 4	WC-23 CUDDY	OP	CUD	FBG	DV	IO	240-260		8	4700		6250	7300
23 4	WC-23 CUDDY	OP	CUD	FBG	DV	IO	330	MRCR	8	4700		6900	7900
25 7	WC-26	OP	CR	FBG	DV	IO	240-260		8	5600		7800	9150

IO 330 MRCR 8550 9800, IO T140-T240 8300 10300, IO T260 MRCR 9300 10500

LOA FT IN	NAME AND/OR MODEL	TOP/RIG	BOAT TYPE	MTL	TP	TP	ENGINE # HP	MFG	BEAM FT IN	WGT LBS	DRAFT FT IN	RETAIL LOW	RETAIL HIGH
1977 BOATS													
17 7	WC-18-V B/R	ST	RNBT	FBG	DV	IO	140-190		6 10	2600		2700	3200
18 1	WC-18 B/R	ST	RNBT	FBG	TR	IO	165-235		7 2	2800		3000	3600
19 10	WC-20	ST	RNBT	FBG	DV	IO	188-235		7 11	3000		3600	4300
19 10	WC-20	ST	RNBT	FBG	DV	IO	280	MRCR	7 11	3000		3900	4550
19 10	WC-20	ST	RNBT	FBG	DV	IO	188-235		7 11	3000		3650	4300
25 8	WC-26 B/R	ST	CUD	FBG	DV	IO	233-235		8	5600		7950	9150
1976 BOATS													
17 7	WC-18-V	OP	RNBT	FBG	DV	IO	120-190		7	2400		2750	3250
18 1	WC-18	OP	RNBT	FBG	TR	IO	165-235		7 2	2600		2900	3550
18 1	WC-18	OP	RNBT	FBG	TR	JT	295	HARD	7 2	2600		3350	3900
19 10	WC-20	OP	RNBT	FBG	DV	IO	188-235		7 11	2900		3600	4300
19 10	WC-20	OP	RNBT	FBG	DV	JT	295	HARD	7 11	2900		4050	4700
19 10	WC-20 B/R	OP	RNBT	FBG	DV	IO	188-235		7 11	2900		3650	4350
1975 BOATS													
18 1	WEBBCRAFT	OP	RNBT	FBG	TR	IO	188		7 2	2600		3050	3550
19 10	WEBBCRAFT	OP	RNBT	FBG	DV	IO	225		7 11	2900		3800	4400
19 10	WEBBCRAFT W/T	OP	RNBT	FBG	DV	IO	225		7 11	2900		3800	4450
1974 BOATS													
18 1	WEBBCRAFT			FBG	TR	IO	165-255		7 2	2500		2950	3700
19 10	WEBBCRAFT			FBG	DV	IO	188-255		7 11	2600		3600	4400
1973 BOATS													
18 1	WEBBCRAFT 18			FBG		IO	188	MRCR	7 2	2500		3100	3600

WEBBERS COVE BOAT YARD INC

BLUE HILL ME 04614-0364 COAST GUARD ID- WBR See inside cover to adjust price for area

For more recent years, see the BUC Used Boat Price Guide, Volume 1 or Volume 2

LOA FT IN	NAME AND/OR MODEL	TOP/RIG	BOAT TYPE	MTL	TP	TP	ENGINE # HP	MFG	BEAM FT IN	WGT LBS	DRAFT FT IN	RETAIL LOW	RETAIL HIGH
1982 BOATS													
33 10	DOWNEAST 34	HT	UTL	FBG	DS	IB	225		10 10		2 6	41100	45600
33 10	DOWNEAST 34	HT	UTL	FBG	DS	IB	130D		10 10		2 6	46100	50700
33 10	DOWNEAST 34	HT	UTL	FBG	DS	IB	T		10 10		2 6	**	**
39 11	DOWNEAST 40	HT	UTL	FBG	DS	IB	D		13 9	29000	3 2	**	**
1981 BOATS													
33 10	DOWNEAST 34	HT	UTL	FBG	DS	IB	225		10 10		2 6	39300	43700
33 10	DOWNEAST 34	HT	UTL	FBG	DS	IB	130D		10 10		2 6	43800	48700
33 10	DOWNEAST 34	HT	UTL	FBG	DS	IB	T		10 10		2 6	**	**
39 11	DOWNEAST 40	HT	UTL	FBG	DS	IB	D		13 9	29000	3 2	**	**
1980 BOATS													
33 10	DOWNEAST 34	HT	UTL	FBG	DS	IB	130D		10 10	9354	2 6	48800	53600
1961 BOATS													
41	BLUEFIN	SF	WD			IB	150		12		3 6	60000	65900
1960 BOATS													
41	BLUEFIN	SF	WD			IB	150		12 6		3 9	57500	63200
41	BLUEFIN	SF	WD			IB	T250		12 6		3 9	56300	61800

PETER WEBSTER LIMITED

Call 1-800-327-6929 for BUC Personalized Evaluation Service
Or, for 1954 to 1976 boats, sign onto www.BUCValuPro.com

WEERES INDUSTRIES CORP

COAST GUARD MFG ID- WRS

Call 1-800-327-6929 for BUC Personalized Evaluation Service
Or, for 1959 to 2008 boats, sign onto www.BUCValuPro.com

WEIST INDUSTRIES INC

LOUISVILLE KY 40206   See inside cover to adjust price for area

LOA FT IN	NAME AND/OR MODEL	TOP/RIG	BOAT TYPE	MTL	TP	TP	ENGINE # HP	MFG	BEAM FT IN	WGT LBS	DRAFT FT IN	RETAIL LOW	RETAIL HIGH
1971 BOATS													
68	CUSTOM	MY		AL	SV	IB	T370D	CUM	18	52000	4	208000	228500
1969 BOATS													
40	ALL-WEATHER-STYLE-CR	CR		AL	SV	IO	T290		13 8	12000	2 6	46300	50900
1968 BOATS													
40	STYLE-CRAFT	CR		AL		IB	210		13 8		2	30200	33600

WELDCRAFT CUSTOM BOATS

COAST GUARD MFG ID- WCD

Call 1-800-327-6929 for BUC Personalized Evaluation Service
Or, for 1980 boats, sign onto www.BUCValuPro.com

WELDCRAFT STEEL & MRNE INC

COAST GUARD MFG ID- WSM

Call 1-800-327-6929 for BUC Personalized Evaluation Service
Or, for 1977 to 1978 boats, sign onto www.BUCValuPro.com

WELIN DAVIT & BOAT DIV

Call 1-800-327-6929 for BUC Personalized Evaluation Service
Or, for 1960 boats, sign onto www.BUCValuPro.com

WELLCRAFT MARINE

DIV OF GENMAR
SARASOTA FL 34243   COAST GUARD MFG ID- WEL   See inside cover to adjust price for area

For more recent years, see the BUC Used Boat Price Guide, Volume 1 or Volume 2

LOA FT IN	NAME AND/OR MODEL	TOP/RIG	BOAT TYPE	MTL	TP	TP	ENGINE # HP	MFG	BEAM FT IN	WGT LBS	DRAFT FT IN	RETAIL LOW	RETAIL HIGH
1983 BOATS													
16	FREEDOM 16	ST	RNBT	FBG	DV	OB			6 9	1250		2100	2450
16	FREEDOM 16	ST	RNBT	FBG	DV	IO	120		6 9	1850		1950	2300
16	FREEDOM 16	ST	RNBT	FBG	DV	IO	138-140		6 9	1850		2100	2500
17 7	BOWRIDER 180	ST	RNBT	FBG	DV	OB			7 2	1500		2500	2900
17 7	BOWRIDER 180	ST	RNBT	FBG	DV	IO	138-188		7 2	2125		2450	2800
17 7	XL 180	ST	RNBT	FBG	DV	IO	138-200		7 2	2125		2650	3050
17 10	FISHERMAN 180	ST	CTRCN	FBG	SV	OB			7 9	1750		3100	3600
19 6	ELITE 200	ST	RNBT	FBG	DV	OB			8	3500		3500	4200
19 6	ELITE 200	ST	RNBT	FBG	DV	IO	138-230		8	2900		3550	4350
19 6	SUN-HATCH 196	ST	CUD	FBG	DV	OB			8	1880		3100	3600
19 6	SUN-HATCH 196	ST	CUD	FBG	DV	IO	138-230		8	2900		3600	4350
19 6	SUN-HATCH 196	ST	CUD	FBG	DV	IO	260		8	2900		3700	4350
20 6	FISHERMAN V20	ST	CTRCN	FBG	DV	OB			8	1920		5550	6400
20 6	STEP-LIFT V20	ST	CUD	FBG	DV	OB			8	1920		5600	6450
20 6	STEP-LIFT V20	ST	CUD	FBG	DV	IO	138-230		8	2620		4050	4900
20 6	STEP-LIFT V20	ST	CUD	FBG	DV	IO	260		8	2620		4200	5100
20 8	SUNCRUISER 210	ST	WKNDR	FBG	DV	IO		OMC	8	3700		**	**
20 8	SUNCRUISER 210	ST	WKNDR	FBG	DV	IO	170-230		8	3700		4950	6000
20 8	SUNCRUISER 210	ST	WKNDR	FBG	DV	IO	260		8	3700		5200	6250
22 9	SUNCRUISER 230	ST	WKNDR	FBG	DV	IO		OMC	8	4200		**	**
22 9	SUNCRUISER 230	ST	WKNDR	FBG	DV	IO	170-260		8	4200		6100	7550
23	AFT CABIN 230	ST	WKNDR	FBG	DV	IO		OMC	8	4200		**	**
23	AFT CABIN 230	ST	WKNDR	FBG	DV	IO	170-260		8	4200		6200	7600
23	NOVA 230	ST	CUD	FBG	DV	IO	170	MRCR	8	2620		4550	5250

IO 170-188 6550 7600, IO 198-200 7400 9200, IO 225-260 8100 9500
IO T170-T188 6600 7650

LOA FT	IN	NAME AND/ OR MODEL	TOP/ RIG	BOAT TYPE	-HULL- MTL	TP	TP	ENGINE # HP	MFG	BEAM FT	IN	WGT LBS	DRAFT FT	IN	RETAIL LOW	RETAIL HIGH
		1983 BOATS														
23		NOVA 230 XL	ST	CUD	FBG	DV	IO	170-260		8		4000			5950	7350
23		NOVA 230 XL	ST	CUD	FBG	DV	IO	T170-T188		8		4000			6750	7800
24	8	FISHERMAN 248 CUD	ST	CTRCN	FBG	DV	OB			8		3150			9950	11300
24	8	FISHERMAN 248 CUD	ST	CTRCN	FBG	DV	IO		OMC	8		4150			**	**
24	8	FISHERMAN 248 CUD	ST	CTRCN	FBG	DV	IO	198-260		8		4150			7050	8700
24	8	FISHERMAN 248 CUD	ST	CTRCN	FBG	DV	IO	130D-165D		8		4150			9700	11500
24	8	OFFSHORE 248	ST	CUD	FBG	DV	OB			8		3750			11200	12700
24	8	OFFSHORE 248	ST	CUD	FBG	DV	IO		OMC	8		4000			**	**
		IO 198-260 6550 8050, IO 130D VLVO 7550 8700, IB 158D VLVO													10600	12100
		IO T138-T188 7500 8600														
24	8	SPORTSMAN 248	ST	SPTCR	FBG	DV	OB			8		3750			11200	12700
24	8	SPORTSMAN 248	ST	SPTCR	FBG	DV	IO		OMC	8		4750			**	**
		IO 198-260 7400 9000, IO 130D VLVO 8600 9850, IB 158D VLVO													12000	13600
		IO T138-T188 8350 9600														
25	3	AFT CABIN 255	ST	WKNDR	FBG	DV	IO		OMC	8		4550			**	**
		IB ** **, IO 198-260 7800 9550, IB 158D VLVO													12100	13800
		IO T138-T188 8850 10200														
25	3	SPORT 255	ST	WKNDR	FBG	DV	IO		OMC	8		4550			**	**
		IO 198-260 7350 9050, IB 158D VLVO 11600 13100, IO T138-T188													8350	9700
25	3	SUNCRUISER 255	ST	WKNDR	FBG	DV	IO		OMC	8		4550			**	**
		IO 198-260 7350 9050, IO 165D VLVO 8900 10100, IO T138-T188													8350	9700
26	2	EXPRESS CRUISER 2600	OP	EXP	FBG	DV	IO	260-330		9	10	7000			11000	13200
26	2	EXPRESS CRUISER 2600	OP	EXP	FBG	DV	IO	165D	VLVO	9	10	7000			12900	14700
26	2	EXPRESS CRUISER 2600	OP	EXP	FBG	DV	IO	T170-T260		9	10	7000			11600	14500
26	2	SEDAN CRUISER 2600	FB	SDN	FBG	DV	IO	260	MRCR	9	10	7750	2	6	12400	14100
		IB T165 CRUS 16300 18500, IO T170 MRCR 13100 14900, IB T170 MRCR													16200	18400
		IO T198-T228 13400 15600, IB T230-T260 16900 19500														
26	3	NOVA II	ST	CUD	FBG	DV	IO	260-330		8		5600			9350	11300
26	3	NOVA II	ST	CUD	FBG	DV	IO	T170-T230		8		5600			9900	12100
26	3	NOVA II	ST	CUD	FBG	DV	IO	T260		8		5600			10800	12600
28	8	EXPRESS CRUISER 2900	ST	EXP	FBG	DV	IO	120	OMC	10	8	9200			13200	15000
28	8	EXPRESS CRUISER 2900	ST	EXP	FBG	DV	IB	T220-T270		10	8	9200			19200	21800
28	8	EXPRESS CRUISER 2900	ST	EXP	FBG	DV	IB	T124D-T158D		10	8	9200			24300	28200
28	8	SPORT BRIDGE 2900	FB	SDN	FBG	DV	IO	T	OMC	10	8	9000			**	**
		IB T220-T270 20500 23700, IO T330 MRCR 18200 20200, IB T350 CRUS													22000	24500
		IBT124D-T158D 26800 31400, IB T235D VLVO 31500 35000														
29	6	SCARAB II	OP	RACE	FBG	DV	IO	T260-T330		8		6400			11400	13900
29	6	SCARAB II	OP	RACE	FBG	DV	IO	T370-T400		8		6400			12800	15100
29	6	SCARAB S TYPE	OP	RACE	FBG	DV	IO	T260-T330		8		6400			11000	13400
29	6	SCARAB S TYPE	OP	RACE	FBG	DV	IO	T370-T400		8		6400			12400	14600
29	6	SCARAB SPORT	ST	OPFSH	FBG	DV	OB			8		2985			21200	23500
31	3	EXPRESS CRUISER 3100	OP	EXP	FBG	DV	IB	T260-T270		11	6	11500			26300	29400
		IO T330 MRCR 22200 24700, IB T350 CRUS 27800 30900, IBT200D-T235D													33100	37900
31	3	SEDAN CRUISER 3100	FB	SDN	FBG	DV	IB	T260-T350		11	6	11500	3	3	28800	34200
33	10	SCARAB 340 III	OP	RACE	FBG	DV	IO	T330-T400		8	4	7750			20900	25600
34	6	CALIFORNIAN CNV	FB	SF	FBG	SV	IB	T210D	CAT	12	4	18000	3	2	50700	55700
34	6	CALIFORNIAN SEDAN		SPTCR	FBG	SV	IB	T210D	CAT	12	4	18000	3	2	50700	55700
37	7	SCARAB 377	OP	RACE	FBG	DV	IO	T330	MRCR	8	9	9100			26200	29100
37	7	SCARAB 377	OP	RACE	FBG	DV	IO	T370	MRCR	8	9	9100			27200	30200
37	7	SCARAB 377	OP	RACE	FBG	DV	IO	T400	MRCR	8	9	9100			27700	30800
37	7	SPECIAL EDITION 377	ST	RACE	FBG	DV	IO	T330	MRCR	8	9	9100			25200	28000
37	7	SPECIAL EDITION 377	ST	RACE	FBG	DV	IO	T370	MRCR	8	9	9100			26300	29200
37	7	SPECIAL EDITION 377	ST	RACE	FBG	DV	IO	T400	MRCR	8	9	8900			27700	30800
37	8	CALIFORNIAN		MY	FBG	SV	IB	T210D	CAT	13		28000	3	6	85300	93700
37	8	CALIFORNIAN CNV	FB	SF	FBG	SV	IB	210D	CAT	13		28000	3	6	80000	87900
37	8	CALIFORNIAN SEDAN		SPTCR	FBG	SV	IB	T210D	CAT	13		28000	3	6	84900	93300
41	8	CALIFORNIAN		OFF	FBG	SV	IB	T210D	CAT	13	8	31000	3	4	99400	109000
50		CALIFORNIAN		OFF	FBG	SV	IB	T300D	CAT	14	2	39000	4		126000	138500
		1982 BOATS														
16		BOWRIDER 160	ST	RNBT	FBG	SV	OB			8		1250			2050	2400
16		BOWRIDER 160	ST	RNBT	FBG	SV	IO	120-170		8		1850			2150	2650
17	7	BOWRIDER 180	ST	RNBT	FBG	DV	OB			7	2	1500			2450	2850
17	7	BOWRIDER 180	ST	RNBT	FBG	DV	IO	140-185		7	2	2125			2350	2900
17	10	FISHERMAN 180	ST	CTRCN	FBG	SV	OB			7	9	1750			3050	3550
19	6	BOWRIDER 196	ST	RNBT	FBG	DV	IO	140-230		8		2900			3300	4100
19	6	BOWRIDER 196	ST	RNBT	FBG	DV	IO	260		8		2900			3500	4250
19	6	SUN-HATCH 196	ST	CUD	FBG	DV	OB			8		1880			3050	3550
19	6	SUN-HATCH 196	ST	CUD	FBG	DV	IO	140-230		8		2900			3400	4250
19	6	SUN-HATCH 196	ST	CUD	FBG	DV	IO	260		8		2900			3650	4450
20	6	FISHERMAN V20	ST	CTRCN	FBG	DV	OB			8		1920			5450	6250
20	6	STEP-LIFT V20	ST	CUD	FBG	DV	OB			8		1920			5500	6350
20	6	STEP-LIFT V20	ST	CUD	FBG	DV	IO	140-230		8		2620			3850	4800
20	6	STEP-LIFT V20	ST	CUD	FBG	DV	IO	260		8		2620			4100	5000
22	9	SUNCRUISER 230	ST	WKNDR	FBG	DV	IO		OMC	8		5600			**	**
		IO 198-260 5650 6950, IO 130D-155D 6900 8100, IO T140-T185													6300	7600
23		NOVA 230	ST	CUD	FBG	DV	IO	170	MRCR	8		2620			4450	5150
		IO 170-185 6400 7400, IO 198-200 7200 9000, IO 225-330													7900	9750
24	8	FISHERMAN 248	ST	CTRCN	FBG	DV	OB			8		3150			9750	11100
24	8	OFFSHORE 248	ST	CUD	FBG	DV	OB			8		3750			11000	12500
24	8	OFFSHORE 248	ST	CUD	FBG	DV	IO		OMC	8		4100			**	**
		IO 198-260 6500 8000, IO 130D VLVO 7500 8650, IB 155D VLVO													10300	11700
		IO T140-T185 7200 8550														
24	8	SPORTSMAN 248	ST	SPTCR	FBG	DV	OB			8		3750			11000	12500
24	8	SPORTSMAN 248	ST	SPTCR	FBG	DV	IO		OMC	8		4750			**	**
		IO 198-260 7250 8800, IO 130D VLVO 8400 9650, IB 155D VLVO													11500	13100
		IO T140-T185 7900 9400														
25	3	AFT CABIN 255	ST	WKNDR	FBG	DV	IO		OMC	8		4550			**	**
		IB ** **, IO 198-260 7650 9350, IO 130D VLVO													8450	9700
		IB 155D VLVO 11600 13200, IO T140-T185 8350 9900														
25	3	SPORT 255	ST	WKNDR	FBG	DV	IO		OMC	8		4550			**	**
		IO 198-260 7200 8850, IO 130D VLVO 8050 9250, IB 155D VLVO													11100	12600
		IO T140-T185 7950 9450														
25	3	SUNCRUISER 255	ST	WKNDR	FBG	DV	IO		OMC	8		4550			**	**
		IO 170-260 7200 8850, IO 130D-155D 8050 9750, IO T140-T185													7950	9450
26	2	SEDAN CRUISER 260	FB	WKNDR	FBG	DV	IO	260	MRCR	9	10	7750	2	6	11900	13600
		IB T165 CRUS 15200 17300, IO T170 MRCR 12500 14200, IB T170													15200	17200
		IO T198 MRCR 12800 14500, IO T228 MRCR 13000 14800, IB T228-T260													15700	18200
26	3	NOVA II	ST	CUD	FBG	DV	IO	198	MRCR	8		5200			8250	9450
		IO 260-330 9100 11000, IO T170-T230 9650 11800, IO T260													10500	12300
28	8	MONACO 288	ST	WKNDR	FBG	DV	IB	T220-T270		10	8	9350	2	6	19400	22300
28	8	MONACO 288	ST	WKNDR	FBG	DV	IB	T130D-T155D		10	8	9350	2	6	25400	29500
28	8	SUNCRUISER 288	ST	WKNDR	FBG	DV	IO	T	OMC	10	8	9200	2	6	**	**
		IB T220-T270 19300 22200, IO T130D VLVO 19100 21300, IB T130D VLVO													25100	27900
		IO T155D VLVO 19500 21700														
29	6	CALIFORNIAN		MY	FBG	DS	IB	135		10	3	9200			16900	19200
29	6	SCARAB II	OP	RACE	FBG	DV	IO	T260-T330		8		6400			11200	13600
29	6	SCARAB II	OP	RACE	FBG	DV	IO	T370-T400		8		6400			12500	14700
29	6	SCARAB II	OP	RACE	FBG	DV	IO	T475	MRCR	8		6400			14100	16000
29	6	SCARAB S TYPE	OP	RACE	FBG	DV	IO	T260-T330		8		6400			10700	13100
29	6	SCARAB S TYPE	OP	RACE	FBG	DV	IO	T370-T400		8		6400			12100	14300
29	6	SCARAB S TYPE	OP	RACE	FBG	DV	IO	T475	MRCR	8		6400			14100	16000
29	6	SCARAB SPORT	ST	OPFSH	FBG	DV	OB			8		2985			20800	23100
31	3	SEDAN BRIDGE 310	FB	WKNDR	FBG	DV	IB	T255-T350		11	6	11500	3	3	25100	29600
31	3	SUNCRUISER 310	ST	WKNDR	FBG	DV	IB	200D	PERK	11	6	10200	3	3	26400	29400
31	3	SUNCRUISER 310	ST	WKNDR	FBG	DV	IB	T255-T350		11	6	10200	3	3	24400	28900
31	3	SUNCRUISER 310	ST	WKNDR	FBG	DV	IB	T235D	VLVO	11	6	10200	3	3	30900	34300
34	4	CALIFORNIAN		MY	FBG	DS	IB	T210D		12	4	18000			50700	55800
35	8	CALIFORNIAN		MY	FBG	DS	IB	T210D		13		25000			65000	71500
37	7	SCARAB 377	OP	RACE	FBG	DV	IO	T330	MRCR	8	9	9100			25300	28100
		IO T370 MRCR 26300 29200, IO T400 MRCR 27100 30100, IO T475 MRCR													30000	33400
		IO R370 MRCR 31300 34800														
37	7	SPECIAL EDITION 377	ST	RACE	FBG	DV	IO	T330	MRCR	8	9	9100			24900	27700
		IO T370 MRCR 26000 28800, IO T400 MRCR 27100 30100, IO T475 MRCR													30200	33600
		IO R370 31600 35100														
37	8	CALIFORNIAN		MY	FBG	DS	IB	T155		13		28000			71600	78700
41	8	CALIFORNIAN		MY	FBG	DS	IB	T210		13	8	31000			83800	92100
46		CALIFORNIAN		MY	FBG	DS	IB	T210		14	8	38000			93600	103000
		1981 BOATS														
16	4	AIRSLOT 170	ST	RNBT	FBG	TR	OB			6	9	1050			1700	2050
16	4	AIRSLOT 170	ST	RNBT	FBG	TR	IO	140	MRCR	6	9	1700			1850	2200
16	4	AIRSLOT 170	ST	RNBT	FBG	TR	IO	140	OMC	6	9	1700			1800	2150
16	4	AIRSLOT 170	ST	RNBT	FBG	TR	IO	140-185		6	9	1700			1950	2350
16	4	STINGER 170	OP	RNBT	FBG	TR	OB			6	9	1050			1700	2050

 CONTINUED ON NEXT PAGE

LOA FT	IN	NAME AND/ OR MODEL	TOP/ RIG	BOAT TYPE	-HULL- MTL	TP	ENGINE TP	# HP	MFG	BEAM FT	IN	WGT LBS	DRAFT FT	IN	RETAIL LOW	RETAIL HIGH
		1981 BOATS														
17	7	BOWRIDER 180	ST	RNBT	FBG	DV	OB			7	2	1800			2700	3150
17	7	BOWRIDER 180	ST	RNBT	FBG	DV	IO		OMC	7	2	2300			**	**
17	7	BOWRIDER 180	ST	RNBT	FBG	DV	IO	140-185		7	2	2300			2400	2950
17	7	XL 180	ST	RNBT	FBG	DV	IO		OMC	7	2	2375			**	**
17	7	XL 180	ST	RNBT	FBG	DV	IO	140-185		7	2	2375			2450	3000
17	10	FISHERMAN 180	ST	CTRCN	FBG	SV	OB			7	9	1750			3000	3450
19	6	200 XL	ST	RNBT	FBG	SV	IO	170-230		8		2900			3450	4200
19	6	200 XL	ST	RNBT	FBG	SV	IO	260		8		2900			3600	4350
19	6	BOWRIDER 196	ST	RNBT	FBG	DV	IO	140-260		8		2900			3250	4000
19	6	SUN-HATCH 196	ST	CUD	FBG	DV	OB			8		1880			3000	3450
19	6	SUN-HATCH 196	ST	CUD	FBG	DV	IO	140-200		8		2900			3350	4100
19	6	SUN-HATCH 196	ST	CUD	FBG	DV	IO	225-260		8		2900			3600	4350
20	6	FISHERMAN V20	ST	CTRCN	FBG	DV	OB			8		1920			5350	6150
20	6	STEP-LIFT V20	ST	CUD	FBG	DV	OB			8		1920			5400	6250
20	6	STEP-LIFT V20	ST	CUD	FBG	DV	IO	140-230		8		2620			3750	4700
20	6	STEP-LIFT V20	ST	CUD	FBG	DV	IO	260		8		2620			4000	4900
21	3	NOVA 210	ST	CUD	FBG	DV	IO	170-230		8		3750			4950	6000
		IO 260 5200 6200, IO 330 MRCR 5800 6700, IO T170-T200													5600	7000
		IO T225-T260 6200 7500														
22	9	SUNCRUISER 225	ST	WKNDR	FBG	DV	IO	170-260		8		3890			5550	6850
24	5	AIRSLOT 24 FISH	ST	CUD	FBG	TR	OB			8		3400			10000	11400
24	5	AIRSLOT 24 FISH	ST	CUD	FBG	TR	IO	170-260		8		4600			6800	8400
24	5	AIRSLOT 24 FISH	ST	CUD	FBG	TR	IO	130D	VLVO	8		4600			8050	9250
24	5	AIRSLOT 24 FISH	ST	CUD	FBG	TR	IO	T140-T185		8		4600			7550	8950
24	8	NOVA OFFSHORE 250	ST	CUD	FBG	DV	IO	198-260		8		5400			7850	9500
24	8	NOVA OFFSHORE 250	ST	CUD	FBG	DV	IO	T170-T230		8		5400			8600	10600
24	8	NOVA OFFSHORE 250	ST	CUD	FBG	DV	IO	T260		8		5400			9350	10900
24	8	OFFSHORE 248	ST	CUD	FBG	DV	OB			8		3750			10800	12300
24	8	OFFSHORE 248	ST	CUD	FBG	DV	IO	198-260		8		4100			6400	7850
24	8	OFFSHORE 248	ST	CUD	FBG	DV	IO	130D	VLVO	8		4100			7400	8500
24	8	OFFSHORE 248	ST	CUD	FBG	DV	IO	T140-T170		8		4100			7050	8400
24	8	SPORTSMAN 248	ST	SPTCR	FBG	DV	OB			8		3750			10800	12300
24	8	SPORTSMAN 248	ST	SPTCR	FBG	DV	IO	198-260		8		4950			7350	8950
24	8	SPORTSMAN 248	ST	SPTCR	FBG	DV	IO	130D	VLVO	8		4950			8550	9800
24	8	SPORTSMAN 248	ST	SPTCR	FBG	DV	IO	T140-T185		8		4950			8000	9500
25	3	AFT CABIN 255	ST	WKNDR	FBG	DV	IO	198-260		8		4550			7500	9200
25	3	AFT CABIN 255	ST	WKNDR	FBG	DV	IO	130D	VLVO	8		4550			8300	9550
25	3	AFT CABIN 255	ST	WKNDR	FBG	DV	IO	T140-T185		8		4550			8200	9750
25	3	SPORT 255	ST	WKNDR	FBG	DV	IO	170-260		8		4550			7050	8700
25	3	SPORT 255	ST	WKNDR	FBG	DV	IO	130D	VLVO	8		4550			7950	9150
25	3	SPORT 255	ST	WKNDR	FBG	DV	IO	T140-T185		8		4550			7800	9300
25	3	SUNCRUISER 255	ST	WKNDR	FBG	DV	IO	170-260		8		4550			7050	8700
25	3	SUNCRUISER 255	ST	WKNDR	FBG	DV	IO	130D	VLVO	8		4550			7950	9150
25	3	SUNCRUISER 255	ST	WKNDR	FBG	DV	IO	T140-T185		8		4550			7800	9300
26	3	NOVA II	ST	CUD	FBG	DV	IO	198-260		8		5600			8500	10300
		IO 330 MRCR 9550 10900, IO T170-T230 9500 11600, IO T260													10400	12100
28	8	MONACO 288	ST	WKNDR	FBG	DV	IB	T228-T270		10	8	9500			19000	21400
28	8	MONACO 288	ST	WKNDR	FBG	DV	IB	T130D	VLVO	10	8	9350			24400	27200
28	8	SUNCRUISER 288	ST	WKNDR	FBG	DV	IB	T228-T270		10	8	9200			18700	21200
28	8	SUNCRUISER 288	ST	WKNDR	FBG	DV	IO	T130D	VLVO	10	8	9200			18800	20900
28	8	SUNCRUISER 288	ST	WKNDR	FBG	DV	IB	T130D	VLVO	10	8	9200			24100	26800
29	6	SCARAB II	OP	RACE	FBG	DV	IO	T260-T330		8		6400			11000	13400
29	6	SCARAB II	OP	RACE	FBG	DV	IO	T370-T400		8		6400			12300	14500
29	6	SCARAB II	OP	RACE	FBG	DV	IO	T475	MRCR	8		6400			14000	15900
29	6	SCARAB S TYPE	OP	RACE	FBG	DV	IO	T260-T330		8		6400			10600	12900
29	6	SCARAB S TYPE	OP	RACE	FBG	DV	IO	T370-T400		8		6400			11900	14000
29	6	SCARAB S TYPE	OP	RACE	FBG	DV	IO	T475	MRCR	8		6400			13700	15500
29	6	SCARAB SPORT	ST	OPFSH	FBG	DV	OB			8		2985			20500	22800
30	3	COUGAR-CAT	ST	RACE	FBG	DV	IO	T260-T330		9	6	7000			12200	14700
30	3	COUGAR-CAT	ST	RACE	FBG	DV	IO	T370-T400		9	6	7000			13500	15800
30	3	COUGAR-CAT	ST	RACE	FBG	DV	IO	T475	MRCR	9	6	7000			15000	17100
31	3	SEDAN BRIDGE 310	ST	WKNDR	FBG	DV	IB	T255-T350		11	6	11500			24000	28300
31	3	SUNCRUISER 310	ST	WKNDR	FBG	DV	IB	T255-T350		11	6	10200			23400	27700
31	3	SUNCRUISER 310	ST	WKNDR	FBG	DV	IB	T235D	VLVO	11	6	10200			29700	33000
37	7	KAAMA EDITION 377	ST	RACE	FBG	DV	IO	T370	MRCR	8	9	8900			25700	28600
		IO T400 MRCR 26700 29600, IO T475 MRCR 29700 33000, IO R370													31100	34600
37	7	SCARAB 377	OP	RACE	FBG	DV	IO	T370	MRCR	8	9	9100			25700	28500
		IO T400 MRCR 26600 29600, IO T475 MRCR 29600 32900, IO R370 MRCR													30800	34200
		1980 BOATS														
16	4	AIRSLOT 165	ST	RNBT	FBG	TR	OB			6	9	1050			1700	2000
16	4	AIRSLOT 165	ST	RNBT	FBG	TR	IO	140	MRCR	6	9	1700			1800	2150
16	4	AIRSLOT 165	ST	RNBT	FBG	TR	IO	140	OMC	6	9	1700			1800	2150
16	4	AIRSLOT 165	ST	RNBT	FBG	TR	IO	140-170		6	9	1700			1950	2300
16	4	STINGER 165	OP	RNBT	FBG	TR	OB			6	9	1050			1700	2000
17	5	175 BOWRIDER	ST	RNBT	FBG	DV	IO	140-198		7	2	2300			2350	2850
17	5	175 BOWRIDER	ST	RNBT	FBG	DV	IO	200		7	2	2300			2400	2950
17	5	175 BOWRIDER	ST	RNBT	FBG	TR	IO	120		7	2				2150	2550
17	5	175 SPORT	ST	RNBT	FBG	DV	IO	140-200		7	2	2300			2350	2900
17	5	175 XL	ST	RNBT	FBG	DV	IO	140-200		7	2	2300			2450	3050
17	10	FISHERMAN 180	ST	CTRCN	FBG	SV	OB			7	9	1750			2900	3400
19	3	AIRSLOT 190	ST	RNBT	FBG	TR	IO	140-200		7	3	2380			2650	3300
19	3	AIRSLOT 190	ST	RNBT	FBG	TR	IO	225-230		7	3	2380			2900	3400
19	5	200 XL	ST	RNBT	FBG	SV	IO	198-230		8		2900			3400	4150
19	5	200 XL	ST	RNBT	FBG	SV	IO	260		8		2900			3550	4300
19	5	BOWRIDER 196	ST	RNBT	FBG	DV	IO	140-260		8		2900			3200	3950
19	5	SUN-HATCH 196	ST	CUD	FBG	DV	OB			8		1880			2900	3400
19	5	SUN-HATCH 196	ST	CUD	FBG	DV	IO	140-200		8		2900			3300	4050
19	5	SUN-HATCH 196	ST	CUD	FBG	DV	IO	225-260		8		2900			3550	4300
19	5	SUNCRUISER 2000	ST	WKNDR	FBG	DV	IO	170-230		8		2900			3300	4150
20	6	FISHERMAN V20	ST	CTRCN	FBG	DV	OB			8		1920			5250	6050
20	6	STEP-LIFT V20	ST	CUD	FBG	DV	OB			8		1920			5350	6150
20	6	STEP-LIFT V20	ST	CUD	FBG	DV	IO	140-230		8		2620			3750	4650
21	3	NOVA 210	ST	CUD	FBG	DV	IO	198-260		8		3750			4750	5900
21	3	NOVA 220 XL	ST	CUD	FBG	DV	IO	198-260		8		3750			5150	6400
22	9	SUNCRUISER 225	ST	WKNDR	FBG	DV	IO	170-260		8		3890			5500	6800
24	5	AIRSLOT 24 FISH	ST	CUD	FBG	TR	OB			8		3400			9900	11200
24	5	AIRSLOT 24 FISH	ST	CUD	FBG	TR	IO	198-260		8		4600			6800	8300
24	5	AIRSLOT 24 FISH	ST	CUD	FBG	TR	IO	130D	VLVO	8		4600			8000	9200
24	5	AIRSLOT 24 FISH	ST	CUD	FBG	TR	IO	T140-T170		8		4600			7450	8900
24	8	MONACO 288	ST	WKNDR	FBG	DV	IB	T255	MRCR	10	8	9500			16100	18300
24	8	NOVA 250 XL	ST	CUD	FBG	DV	IO	198-260		8		5000			7350	8900
		IO 330 MRCR 8200 9400, IO T170-T230 8100 9950, IO T260													8800	10400
24	8	NOVA OFFSHORE 250	ST	CUD	FBG	DV	IO	198-260		8		5400			7800	9450
		IO 330 MRCR 8650 9950, IO T170-T230 8550 10500, IO T260													9250	10800
24	8	SPORTSMAN 248	ST	SPTCR	FBG	DV	IB	170	MRCR	8		4700			7850	9000
		IO 198-260 7000 8550, IO 130D VLVO 8100 9350, IO T140-T170													7650	9100
25	3	SUNCRUISER 255	ST	WKNDR	FBG	DV	IO	198-260		8		4550			7150	8800
25	3	SUNCRUISER 255	ST	WKNDR	FBG	DV	IO	130D	VLVO	8		4550			8000	9200
25	3	SUNCRUISER 255	ST	WKNDR	FBG	DV	IO	T140-T170		8		4550			7850	9300
28	8	MONACO 288	ST	WKNDR	FBG	DV	IB	T228	MRCR	10	8	9500			18200	20200
28	8	SUNCRUISER 288	ST	WKNDR	FBG	DV	IB	T228-T255		10	8	9200			17500	20300
29	6	SCARAB II	OP	RACE	FBG	DV	IO	T260-T330		8		6400			11000	13300
29	6	SCARAB II	OP	RACE	FBG	DV	IO	T370	MRCR	8		6400			12200	13900
29	6	SCARAB S TYPE	OP	RACE	FBG	DV	IO	T260-T330		8		6400			10400	12700
29	6	SCARAB S TYPE	OP	RACE	FBG	DV	IO	T370	MRCR	8		6400			11800	13400
29	6	SCARAB SPORT	ST	OPFSH	FBG	DV	OB			8		2985			20200	22400
31	3	SUNCRUISER 310	ST	WKNDR	FBG	DV	VD	T228-T330		11	6	10200			22000	26200
37	7	KAAMA EDITION 377	ST	RACE	FBG	DV	IO	T370	MRCR	8	10				25400	28200
37	7	SCARAB 377	OP	RACE	FBG	DV	IO	T370	MRCR	8	10	9100			25400	28200
		1979 BOATS														
16	4	AIRSLOT 165	ST	RNBT	FBG	TR	IO	140		6	9	1700			1800	2150
17	10	FISHERMAN 180	ST	CTRCN	FBG	SV	OB			7	11	1800			2850	3350
19	3	AIRSLOT 190	ST	RNBT	FBG	TR	OB			7	3	1650			2650	3050
19	3	AIRSLOT 190	ST	RNBT	FBG	TR	IO	140-230		7	3	2380			2650	3250
19	5	200XL	ST	RNBT	FBG	SV	IO	260		8		3000			3450	4000
19	5	SUN-HATCH 196	ST	CUD	FBG	DV	OB			8		1880			2900	3350
19	5	SUN-HATCH 196	ST	CUD	FBG	DV	IO	170-260		8		2900			3300	4100
19	5	SUN-RIDER 196	ST	RNBT	FBG	DV	IO	170-260		8		2900			3200	3950
19	5	SUNCRUISER 2000	ST	WKNDR	FBG	DV	IO	140-230		8		2900			3300	4000
20	6	FISHERMAN V20	ST	CTRCN	FBG	DV	OB			8		1920			5150	5950
20	6	STEP-LIFT V20	ST	CUD	FBG	DV	OB			8		1920			5250	6050
20	6	STEP-LIFT V20	ST	CUD	FBG	DV	IO	140-230		8		2620			3750	4500
21	3	NOVA XL 210	ST	CUD	FBG	DV	IO	198		8		3750			4950	5700
22	9	SUNCRUISER 225	ST	WKNDR	FBG	DV	IO	170-260		8		3890			5500	6550
24	5	AIRSLOT 24F	ST	CUD	FBG	TR	OB			8		3400			9750	11100
24	5	AIRSLOT 24F	ST	CUD	FBG	TR	IO	198		8		4600			6800	7850
24	5	AIRSLOT 24F	ST	CUD	FBG	TR	IO	T170		8		4600			7550	8650
24	8	NOVA OFFSHORE 250	ST	CUD	FBG	DV	IO	198-260		8		5400			7800	9250
24	8	NOVA OFFSHORE 250	ST	CUD	FBG	DV	IO	T170-T260		8		5400			8550	10500
24	8	NOVA XL 250	ST	CUD	FBG	DV	IO	198		8		5000			7300	8400
24	8	NOVA XL 250	ST	CUD	FBG	DV	IO	330		8		5000			8200	9400
24	8	NOVA XL 250	ST	CUD	FBG	DV	IO	T170-T260		8		5000			8100	10000

CONTINUED ON NEXT PAGE

LOA FT	LOA IN	NAME AND/ OR MODEL	TOP/ RIG	BOAT TYPE	-HULL- MTL	-HULL- TP	ENGINE TP	ENGINE # HP	ENGINE MFG	BEAM FT	BEAM IN	WGT LBS	DRAFT FT	DRAFT IN	RETAIL LOW	RETAIL HIGH
		1979 BOATS														
25	3	SUNCRUISER 255	ST	WKNDR	FBG	DV	IO	200-260		8		4550			7150	8600
25	3	SUNCRUISER 255	ST	WKNDR	FBG	DV	IO	T170		8		4550			8050	9250
25	3	SUNYACHT 255	ST	WKNDR	FBG	DV	IO	260		8		5760			8850	10100
25	3	SUNYACHT 255	ST	WKNDR	FBG	DV	IO	T170		8		5760			9450	10700
29	6	SCARAB 300	OP	RACE	FBG	DV	IO	T330-T370		8		6400			11200	13300
29	6	SCARAB II	OP	RACE	FBG	DV	IO	T330-T370		8		6400			11700	13900
29	6	SCARAB S TYPE	OP	RACE	FBG	DV	IO	T330-T370		8		6400			11500	13700
29	6	SCARAB SPORT	ST	OPFSH	FBG	DV	OB			8		2985			19900	22100
31		SUNCRUISER 310	ST	WKNDR	FBG	DV	IB	T228-T330		11	6	10200			20600	24500
37	7	SCARAB 377	OP	RACE	FBG	DV	IO	T370		8	10	9400			25400	28200
		1978 BOATS														
16	4	AIRSLOT 165	ST	RNBT	FBG	TR	IO	120		6	9	1700			1850	2200
		IO 140 MRCR 1850 2200, IO 140 OMC 1800 2150, IO 140 VLVO													1950	2350
16	4	AIRSLOT 165 FISH	ST	FSH	FBG	TR	OB			6	9	1700			2400	2800
19	3	AIRSLOT 190	ST	RNBT	FBG	TR	OB			7	3	1650			2600	3050
19	3	AIRSLOT 190	ST	RNBT	FBG	TR	IO	120-200		7	3	2380			2700	3350
19	3	AIRSLOT 190	ST	RNBT	FBG	TR	IO	225-228		7	3	2380			2750	3400
19	5	SUN-HATCH 196	ST	CUD	FBG	DV	OB			8		1880			2850	3300
19	5	SUN-HATCH 196	ST	CUD	FBG	DV	IO	140-240		8		2900			3350	4100
19	5	SUN-RIDER 196	ST	RNBT	FBG	DV	OB			8		1880			2850	3300
19	5	SUN-RIDER 196	ST	RNBT	FBG	DV	IO	140-240		8		2900			3200	4000
19	5	SUNCRUISER 2000	ST	CUD	FBG	DV	IO	170-240		8		2900			3650	4400
20	6	STEP-LIFT V20	ST	CUD	FBG	DV	OB			8		1920			5200	6000
20	6	STEP-LIFT V20	ST	CUD	FBG	DV	IO	140-240		8		2620			3750	4700
20	6	STEP-LIFT V20 FISH	ST	OPFSH	FBG	DV	OB			8		1920			5150	5950
21	3	AIRSLOT FISHERMAN 21	ST	FSH	FBG	TR	IO	185-260		8		4000			5500	6800
21	3	NOVA 210 XL	ST	CUD	FBG	DV	IO	185-260		8		3750			4950	6150
22	9	SUNCRUISER 225	ST	WKNDR	FBG	DV	IO	170-260		8		3890			5550	6600
23	10	SKIPJACK 24	FB	CR	FBG	DV	IO	170-260		8		4200			6200	7600
23	10	SKIPJACK 24	FB	CR	FBG	DV	IO	130D	VLVO	8		4200			7450	8600
23	10	SKIPJACK 24	FB	CR	FBG	DV	IO	T120-T140		8		4200			6850	8200
24	5	AIRSLOT FISHERMAN 24	ST	FSH	FBG	TR	IO	185-260		8		4600			7200	8800
24	5	AIRSLOT FISHERMAN 24	ST	FSH	FBG	TR	IO	130D	VLVO	8		4600			10100	11500
24	5	AIRSLOT FISHERMAN 24	ST	FSH	FBG	TR	IO	T120-T170		8		4600			7900	9200
24	8	NOVA CLASSIC 250	ST	CR	FBG	DV	IO	185-260		8					6750	8300
24	8	NOVA CLASSIC 250	ST	CR	FBG	DV	IO	330	MRCR	8					7700	8850
24	8	NOVA CLASSIC 250	ST	CR	FBG	DV	IO	T170-T260		8					7600	9450
24	8	NOVA OFFSHORE 250	ST	OFF	FBG	DV	IO	185-260		8		5400			7750	9400
24	8	NOVA OFFSHORE 250	ST	OFF	FBG	DV	IO	330	MRCR	8		5400			8650	9950
24	8	NOVA OFFSHORE 250	ST	OFF	FBG	DV	IO	T170-T260		8		5400			8550	10500
24	8	NOVA XL 250	ST	CUD	FBG	DV	IO	185-260		8		5000			7300	8950
24	8	NOVA XL 250	ST	CUD	FBG	DV	IO	330	MRCR	8		5000			8250	9500
24	8	NOVA XL 250	ST	CUD	FBG	DV	IO	T170-T260		8		5000			8150	10100
25	3	SUNCRUISER 255	OP	SPTCR	FBG	DV	IO	185-260		8		4550			7000	8600
25	3	SUNCRUISER 255	OP	SPTCR	FBG	DV	IO	130D	VLVO	8		4550			7900	9100
25	3	SUNCRUISER 255	OP	SPTCR	FBG	DV	IO	T140-T170		8		4550			7750	9150
25	3	SUNYACHT 255	FB	CR	FBG	DV	IO	185-260		8					6900	8550
25	3	SUNYACHT 255	FB	CR	FBG	DV	IO	130D	VLVO	8					8450	9700
25	3	SUNYACHT 255	FB	CR	FBG	DV	IO	T140-T170		8					7700	9100
28		SKIPJACK 28	FB	CR	FBG	DV	IO	240-260		8		6600			10300	12000
28		SKIPJACK 28	FB	CR	FBG	DV	IO	130D	VLVO	8		6600			10800	12200
28		SKIPJACK 28	FB	CR	FBG	DV	IO	T170-T225		8		6600			11100	13300
29	6	SCARAB 300	OP	RACE	FBG	DV	IO	T240-T330		8		6400			10600	13100
		1977 BOATS														
16	4	AIRSLOT 165	ST	RNBT	FBG	TR	IO	120-140		6	9	1700			1850	2200
16	4	AIRSLOT 165 FISH	ST	FSH	FBG	TR	IO	120-140		6	9	1700			1950	2350
18	7	AIRSLOT 185	ST	RNBT	FBG	TR	OB			7	3	1550			2400	2800
18	7	AIRSLOT 185	ST	RNBT	FBG	TR	IO	120-170		7	3	2250			2550	3000
19	5	SUN-HATCH 196 SH	ST	CUD	FBG	DV	OB			8		1880			2800	3250
19	5	SUN-HATCH 196 SH	ST	CUD	FBG	DV	IO	140-235		8		2900			3100	3750
19	5	SUN-RIDER 196 SR	ST	RNBT	FBG	DV	OB			8		1880			2800	3250
19	5	SUN-RIDER 196 SR	ST	RNBT	FBG	DV	IO	140-235		8		2900			3250	3950
19	5	SUNCRUISER 2000 SC	ST	CUD	FBG	DV	IO	140-235		8		2900			3700	4400
20	6	STEP-LIFT V20	ST	CUD	FBG	DV	OB			8		1920			5150	5900
20	6	STEP-LIFT V20	ST	CUD	FBG	DV	IO	140-170		8		2620			3800	4450
20	6	STEP-LIFT V20 FISH	ST	OPFSH	FBG	DV	OB			8		1920			5100	5850
21	3	AIRSLOT 21 A/S FISH	ST	FSH	FBG	TR	IO	188-235		8		4000			5600	6550
21	3	NOVA 21	ST	CUD	FBG	DV	IO	188-235		8		3750			5050	5950
21	3	NOVA 21 O/S	ST	OFF	FBG	DV	IO	188-235		8		3900			5200	6100
23	10	SKIPJACK 24	FB	CR	FBG	DV	IO	188-235		8		4200			6350	7400
23	10	SKIPJACK 24	FB	CR	FBG	DV	IO	T120-T233		8		4200			6950	8350
24	5	AIRSLOT 24 A/S FISH	ST	FSH	FBG	TR	IO	188-235		8		4600			7350	8600
24	5	AIRSLOT 24 A/S FISH	ST	FSH	FBG	TR	IO	T120-T170		8		4600			8000	9350
24	8	NOVA 25 O/S	ST	OFF	FBG	DV	IO	188-235		8		5400			7900	9250
24	8	NOVA 25 O/S	ST	OFF	FBG	DV	IO	T165-T235		8		5400			8650	10400
24	8	NOVA CLASSIC 25	ST	CUD	FBG	DV	IO	188-235		8		5000			7450	8750
24	8	NOVA CLASSIC 25	ST	CUD	FBG	DV	IO	T165-T235		8		5000			8250	9950
25	3	SUNCRUISER 255 SC	ST	CR	FBG	DV	IO	188-235		8		4550			7100	8450
25	3	SUNCRUISER 255 SC	ST	CR	FBG	DV	IO	T165-T235		8		4550			8000	9800
28		SCARAB 300	OP	RACE	FBG	DV	IO	T233-T280		8		6400			9550	11300
28		SKIPJACK 28	FB	CR	FBG	SV	IO			8		6600			**	**
		1976 BOATS														
16	4	AIRSLOT SPORT 165	ST	RNBT	FBG	TR	OB			6	9	1150			1750	2050
18	7	AIRSLOT SPORT 185	ST	RNBT	FBG	TR	OB			7	3	1600			2450	2800
18	7	AIRSLOT SPORT 185	ST	RNBT	FBG	TR	IO	120-165		7	3	1600			2350	2700
19	5	BOW RIDER 196	ST	RNBT	FBG	DV	OB			8		1880			2800	3250
19	5	BOW RIDER 196	ST	RNBT	FBG	DV	IO	140-233		8		2100			2850	3450
19	5	SUN-HATCH 196	ST	CUD	FBG	DV	OB			8		1880			2800	3250
19	5	SUN-HATCH 196	ST	CUD	FBG	DV	IO	140-233		8		2100			2950	3550
20	6	FISHERMAN V20	OP	FSH	FBG	DV	OB			8		1920			5000	5750
20	6	FISHERMAN V20	OP	FSH	FBG	DV	IO	140	MRCR	8		1920			3600	4200
20	6	STEP-LIFT V20	OP	CUD	FBG	DV	OB			8		1920			5100	5850
20	6	STEP-LIFT V20	OP	CUD	FBG	DV	IO	140-165		8		1920			3450	4000
21	3	AIRSLOT FISH 21	OP	SF	FBG	TR	IO	188-235		8		3200			5300	6250
21	3	NOVA 21	OP	CUD	FBG	DV	IO	188-235		8		2800			4300	5100
21	3	NOVA FISHERMAN 21	OP	SF	FBG	DV	IO	188-235		8		3050			5150	6050
21	3	NOVA OFFSHORE 21	OP	OFF	FBG	DV	IO	188-235		8		2950			4450	5250
21	3	NOVA WEEKENDER 21	ST	CR	FBG	DV	IO	188-235		8		2950			4450	5250
24	5	AIRSLOT FISH 24	OP	SF	FBG	TR	IO	188-235		8		3700			6950	8150
24	5	AIRSLOT FISH 24	OP	SF	FBG	TR	IO	T140		8		3700			7750	8900
24	8	NOVA 25	OP	CUD	FBG	DV	IO	188-235		8		3400			5850	6950
24	8	NOVA 25	OP	CUD	FBG	DV	IO	T165-T235		8		3400			6700	8150
24	8	NOVA OFFSHORE 25	ST	OFF	FBG	DV	IO	188-235		8		3400			5800	6850
24	8	NOVA OFFSHORE 25	ST	OFF	FBG	DV	IO	T165-T235		8		3400			6600	8050
29	6	SCARAB 300	OP	RACE	FBG	DV	IO	T233-T280		8		6400			11000	13000
		1975 BOATS														
16	4	165 SPORT A/S	OP	SKI	FBG	TR	IO	140	MRCR	6	9				1950	2350
18		KONA JET		RNBT	FBG		JT	445		7	2			8	2950	3450
18	7	185 SPORT A/S	OP	SKI	FBG	TR	OB			7	3	1600			2300	2650
18	7	185 SPORT A/S	OP	SKI	FBG	TR	IO	165		7	3				2900	3350
20	6	V20 FISHERMAN	OP	FSH	FBG	DV	OB			8		1920			4950	5700
20	6	V20 FISHERMAN	OP	FSH	FBG	DV	IO	140	MRCR	8					5150	5950
20	6	V20 STEPLIFT	OP	RNBT	FBG	DV	OB			8		1920			5050	5800
20	6	V20 STEPLIFT	OP	RNBT	FBG	DV	IO	165		8					4100	4800
21		KONA JET		RNBT	FBG		JT	445		8				9	4250	4950
21	3	21 FISHERMAN A/S	OP	FSH	FBG	TR	IO	188-233		8					5450	6350
21	3	21 NOVA	OP	CUD	FBG	DV	IO	188-280		8					4400	5450
21	3	21 NOVA	OP	CUD	FBG	DV	IO	T140	MRCR	8					5050	5800
21	3	21 NOVA WEEKENDER	OP	CR	FBG	DV	IO	188-280		8					4550	5600
21	3	21 NOVA WEEKENDER	OP	CR	FBG	DV	IO	T140	MRCR	8					5200	6000
21	3	21 WEEKENDER A/S	HT	CR	FBG	TR	IO	188-233		8					4550	5350
24	5	24 CABIN A/S	OP	CR	FBG	TR	IO	188-233		8					6900	8100
24	5	24 CABIN A/S	OP	CR	FBG	TR	IO	T140	MRCR	8					7600	8750
24	5	24 FISHERMAN A/S	OP	FSH	FBG	TR	IO	188-233		8					7250	8550
24	5	24 FISHERMAN A/S	OP	FSH	FBG	TR	IO	T140	MRCR	8					8050	9250
24	5	24 WEEKENDER A/S	HT	CR	FBG	TR	IO	188-233		8					6900	8100
24	5	24 WEEKENDER A/S	HT	CR	FBG	TR	IO	T140	MRCR	8					7600	8750
24	8	250 NOVA	OP	CUD	FBG	DV	IO	188-233		8					7700	9050
24	8	250 NOVA	OP	CUD	FBG	DV	IO	T188-T233		8					8650	10300
24	8	250 NOVA OFFSHORE	OP	OFF	FBG	DV	IO	188-233		8					7550	8900
24	8	250 NOVA OFFSHORE	OP	OFF	FBG	DV	IO	T188-T233		8					8500	10100
24	8	250 NOVA WEEKENDER		CR	FBG	DV	IO	188-233		8					7300	8600
24	8	250 NOVA WEEKENDER		CR	FBG	DV	IO	T188-T233		8					8250	9850
		1974 BOATS														
18		KONA			FBG		JT	455	HARD	7	2	1250			2100	2500
18	7	SPORT			FBG		OB			7	3	1550			2300	2650
18	7	SPORT			FBG		IO	165		7	3	1550			2400	2750
20		TUNNEL DRIVE	OP		FBG	DV	IB	225		8					3750	4400
20	2	KONA		CR	FBG		JT	455	HARD	7	10	1600			3050	3550
20	6			FSH	FBG		OB			8		1920			4900	5650
20	6	STEP LIFT			FBG		OB			8		1920			4950	5700
20	6	STEP LIFT			FBG		IO	165-188		8		1920			3500	4100
21	3			EXP	FBG		IO	188-245		8		3100			4900	5750
21	3			EXP	FBG		IO	T140	MRCR	8		3100			5600	6450
21	3			SDN	FBG		IO	188-245		8		3000			4800	5650
21	3			SDN	FBG		IO	T140	MRCR	8		3000			5500	6350

CONTINUED ON NEXT PAGE

WELLCRAFT MARINE -CONTINUED See inside cover to adjust price for area

LOA FT	LOA IN	NAME AND/ OR MODEL	TOP/ RIG	BOAT TYPE	HULL MTL	HULL TP	ENGINE TP	ENGINE # HP	ENGINE MFG	BEAM FT	BEAM IN	WGT LBS	DRAFT FT	DRAFT IN	RETAIL LOW	RETAIL HIGH
		1974 BOATS														
21	3	NOVA		CR	FBG		IO	188-245		8		2800			4600	5450
21	3	NOVA		CR	FBG		IO	T140	MRCR	8		2800			5300	6100
24	5			FSH	FBG		IO	188-245		8		3700			6850	8100
24	5			FSH	FBG		IO	T140	MRCR	8		3700			7650	8800
24	5			OVNTR	FBG		IO	188-245		8		3800			6600	7800
24	5			OVNTR	FBG		IO	T140	MRCR	8		3800			7400	8500
24	5			WKNDR	FBG		IO	188-245		8		3800			6700	7900
24	5			WKNDR	FBG		IO	T140	MRCR	8		3800			7450	8550
24	8	NOVA 250			FBG		IO	188-245		8		3400			6100	7300
24	8	NOVA 250			FBG		IO	T188-T245		8		3400			7150	8550
		1973 BOATS														
16	4	SPT A/S 165			FBG		IO	130	VLVO	6	9	1050			1750	2100
18	7	A/S		CUD	FBG		OB			7	3	1885			2600	3050
18	7	A/S		CUD	FBG		IO	140-170		7	3	1885			2750	3400
18	7	SPORT A/S 185			FBG		OB			7	3	1550			2250	2650
18	7	SPORT A/S 185			FBG		IO	140-170		7	3	1550			2450	3050
20	6	STEP LIFT V-20			FBG		OB			8		1920			4900	5650
20	6	STEP LIFT V-20			FBG		IO	140-188		8		1920			3600	4400
20	6	V20		FSH	FBG		OB			8		1920			4900	5600
24	5	A/S 24		CBNCR	FBG		IO	188-245		8		3800			8000	9350
24	5	A/S 24		CBNCR	FBG		IO	T130-T140		8		3800			9250	10500
24	5	A/S 24		OVNTR	FBG		IO	188-245		8		3800			6850	8100
24	5	A/S 24		OVNTR	FBG		IO	T140	MRCR	8		3800			7650	8750
24	8	NOVA 250			FBG		IO	188-245		8		3000			5900	7050
24	8	NOVA 250			FBG		IO	T188	MRCR	8		3000			7000	8050
		1972 BOATS														
16	4	SPORT 165 A/S			FBG		IO	120-140		6	9				2250	2600
17		17V		RNBT	FBG		IO	120-165		6	9				2400	2850
18	7	18V-A/S		CUD	FBG		OB			7	3	1885			2600	3000
18	7	18V-A/S		CUD	FBG		IO	140-165		7	3				3400	3950
18	7	AIRSLOT 18			FBG		OB			7	3	1475			2200	2550
18	7	AIRSLOT SPT 185			FBG		OB			7	3	1525			2250	2600
18	7	AIRSLOT SPT 185			FBG		IO	140-165		7	3				3200	3750
20	6	STEPLIFT V20			FBG		OB			8		1920			4900	5600
20	6	STEPLIFT V20			FBG		IO	140-188		8					4500	5250
20	6	V20		FSH	FBG		OB			8		1920			4900	5600
24	5	AIRSLOT CABIN 24		CBNCR	FBG		OB			8		3700			9600	10900
24	5	AIRSLOT CABIN 24		CBNCR	FBG		IO	188-225		8					9000	10300
24	5	AIRSLOT CABIN 24		CBNCR	FBG		IO	T120-T140		8					9750	11100
24	8	NOVA 250			FBG		IO	188-245		8					8200	9650
24	8	NOVA 250			FBG		IO	T188	MRCR	8					9350	10600
		1971 BOATS														
16	8	V FISHERMAN		FSH	FBG		IO	120-165		7	5				2750	3250
17		V		RNBT	FBG		IO	120-165		6	9				2500	2950
18	2	V		CUD	FBG		OB			7	4	1280			1900	2300
18	2	V		CUD	FBG		IO	120-165		7	4				2900	3350
18	7	AIRSLOT		CUD	FBG		OB			7	3	1885			2600	3000
18	7	AIRSLOT		CUD	FBG		IO	120-165		7	3				3500	4100
18	7	AIRSLOT COASTAL			FBG		OB			7	3	1475			2200	2550
18	7	AIRSLOT COASTAL			FBG		IO	120-165		7	3				3250	3850
18	7	AIRSLOT DELUXE			FBG		OB			7	3	1525			2250	2600
18	7	AIRSLOT DELUXE			FBG		IO	120-165		7	3				3350	3900
20	6	STEPLIFT V20			FBG		OB			8		1920			4850	5600
20	6	STEPLIFT V20			FBG		IO	140-215		8					4650	5400
20	6	V20		FSH	FBG		OB			8		1920			4850	5600
20	6	V20		FSH	FBG		IO	140	MRCR	8		1920			4250	4950
23	7	V23 DLX	HT		FBG		IO	155-215		7	11				7100	8300
24	5	AIRSLOT		CBNCR	FBG		OB			8		3700			9550	10900
24	5	AIRSLOT		CBNCR	FBG		IO	215-235		8					9350	10700
24	5	AIRSLOT		CBNCR	FBG		IO	T120-T165		8					10100	11500
24	8	NOVA			FBG		IO	215-235		8	5				8650	10000
24	8	NOVA			FBG		IO	T120-T165		8	5				9400	10900
		1970 BOATS														
16		AIRSLOT 16		UTL	FBG	TR	IO	120	MRCR	6	9				2550	3000
17	1	V		RNBT	FBG		IO	165	MRCR	6	9				2600	3050
17	1	V		RNBT	FBG	SV	IO	120-160		6	9				2600	3050
18	2	VC CABIN		CR	FBG		IO	120-165		7	4				2950	3500
18	2	VC CABIN		CUD	FBG	DV	OB			7	4	1200			1800	2150
20	6	V20		CR	FBG	DV	OB			8		1920			4950	5700
20	6	V20		CR	FBG	DV	IO	155-215		8					5000	5950
21		V21		CBNCR	FBG	DV	IO	155-215		7	10				5550	6550
21		V21		CBNCR	FBG	DV	IO	T120	MRCR	7	10				6500	7500
23	4	V23		CBNCR	FBG	DV	IO	155-215		8					8150	9550
23	4	V23		CBNCR	FBG	DV	IO	T120	MRCR	8					9250	10500
23	4	V23	HT	CBNCR	FBG	DV	IO	155-215		8					8150	9550
23	4	V23	HT	CBNCR	FBG	DV	IO	T120	MRCR	8					9250	10500
		1969 BOATS														
17	1	W1850V	OP	RNBT	FBG	SV	IO	120		6	8				2650	3100
18	2	T1975V	OP	RNBT	FBG		OB			7	4	1150			1800	2150
18	2	T1975V	OP	RNBT	FBG	DV	IO	120		7	4				3500	4100
18	2	TCC1975V		CR	FBG	DV	OB			7	4	1240			1850	2200
18	2	TCC1975V		CR	FBG	DV	IO	120		7	4				3050	3550
18	7	W2120T	OP	RNBT	FBG	TR	IO	120		7	3				3550	4150
19	2	W2050V		RNBT	FBG		OB			7	4	1225			1950	2300
19	2	W2050V		RNBT	FBG	SV	IO	120		7	4				3700	4300
19	2	WC2050V		CR	FBG		OB			7	4	1295			2000	2400
21		TCC2265V		CR	FBG	DV	IO	120		7	9				5250	6050
23	4	TCC2475V		CR	FBG	DV	IO	160		8					7500	8650
23	4	TFB2475V		CR	FBG	DV	IO	160		8					7500	8650
23	4	THT2475V		CR	FBG	DV	IO	160		8					7500	8650
		1968 BOATS														
17	1	R1700V		RNBT	FBG	SV	IO	80-160		6	9				2750	3250
17	2	R1700T		RNBT	FBG	TR	IO	80-160		7	1				2850	3350
18	2	C1800V	OP	CUD	FBG	SV	OB			7	2		1		2800	3300
18	2	CC1800V		CUD	FBG	SV	IO	120-160		7	2		1		3100	3650
18	2	R1800V		RNBT	FBG	SV	IO	120-160		7	2				3600	4200
18	2	R1800V	OP	RNBT	FBG	SV	OB			7	2		1		2850	3350
18	9	R1900T		RNBT	FBG	TR	IO	120-160		7	2			11	3700	4300
18	9	R1900T	OP	RNBT	FBG	TR	OB			7	2			11	2900	3350
19	2	R2000V		RNBT	FBG	SV	IO	120-160		7	5		1		3850	4500
19	2	R2000V	OP	RNBT	FBG	SV	OB			7	5		1		3000	3450
21	2	C2100V		CUD	FBG	SV	IO	80-225		8	1				5400	6450
21	2	R2100V		RNBT	FBG	SV	IO	120-225		8	1				5400	6350
21	2	R2100V	OP	RNBT	FBG	SV	IO	T 80		8	1				6250	7150
23	3	C2400V		CUD	FBG	SV	IO	155-225		7	11		1	6	8150	9500
23	3	C2400V		CUD	FBG	SV	IO	T120		7	11		1	6	9150	10400
23	3	HT2400V	FB	CR	FBG	SV	IO	155-225		7	11				7700	9000
23	3	HT2400V	FB	CR	FBG	SV	IO	T		7	11		1	6	**	**
23	3	HT2400V	HT	CUD	FBG	SV	IO	155-225		7	11		1	6	8150	9500
23	3	HT2400V	HT	CUD	FBG	SV	IO	T120		7	11		1	6	9150	10400
23	3	R2400V	OP	RNBT	FBG	SV	IO	155-225		7	11		1	6	7100	8300
23	3	R2400V	OP	RNBT	FBG	SV	IO	T120		7	11		1	6	7900	9100
		1967 BOATS														
17	1	V-1700			FBG		IO	60		6	9				2750	3200
19	2	V-2000			FBG		OB			7	5	2090			2800	3250
19	2	V-2000			FBG		IO	110		7	5				3950	4600
22	6	V-2300			FBG		IO	110		7	10				7200	8300

WELLINGTON BOATS INC

JACKSONVILLE FL 32238-0 COAST GUARD MFG ID- WLN See inside cover to adjust price for area

For more recent years, see the BUC Used Boat Price Guide, Volume 1 or Volume 2

LOA FT	LOA IN	NAME AND/ OR MODEL	TOP/ RIG	BOAT TYPE	HULL MTL	HULL TP	ENGINE TP	ENGINE # HP	ENGINE MFG	BEAM FT	BEAM IN	WGT LBS	DRAFT FT	DRAFT IN	RETAIL LOW	RETAIL HIGH
		1983 BOATS														
44		WELLINGTON 44	CUT	SA/CR	FBG	KC	IB	D		13	6	32000	4	3	91500	100500
47		WELLINGTON 47	CUT	SA/CR	FBG	KC	IB	D		13	6	45000	4	10	118500	130500
47		WELLINGTON 47	KTH	SA/CR	FBG	KC	IB	D		13	6	45000	4	10	118500	130500
57		WELLINGTON 57	SLP	MS	FBG	KL	IB	D		14	6	50000	4	3	282000	310000
57		WELLINGTON 57		MY	FBG	DS	IB	120D		14	6	45000			119500	131500
63	2	WELLINGTON 63	CUT	SA/CR	FBG	KC	IB	D		17		75000	5	9	411000	451500
		1982 BOATS														
44		WELLINGTON 44	CUT	SA/CR	FBG	KC	IB	61D	LEHM	13	6	28000	4	3	80300	88200
44		WELLINGTON 44	CUT	SA/CR	FBG	KC	IB	65D	LEHM	13	6	28000	4	3	80300	88300
47		WELLINGTON 47	CUT	SA/CR	FBG	KC	IB	D		13	6	45000	4	10	111500	122500
47		WELLINGTON 47	CUT	SA/CR	FBG	KC	IB	85D	LEHM	13	6	45000	4	10	111500	122500
47		WELLINGTON 47	KTH	SA/CR	FBG	KC	IB	D		13	6	45000	4	10	111500	122500
47		WELLINGTON 47	KTH	SA/CR	FBG	KC	IB	85D	LEHM	13	6	45000	4	10	111500	122500
57		WELLINGTON 57		MY	FBG	DS	IB	120		14	6	45000			117500	129000
		1981 BOATS														
44		WELLINGTON 44	CUT	SA/CR	FBG	KC	IB	65D	LEHM	13	6	28000	4	3	75600	83000
44		WELLINGTON 44	CUT	SA/CR	FBG	KC	IB	80D	LEHM	13	6	28000	4	3	75800	83200
44		WELLINGTON 44	KTH	SA/CR	FBG	KC	IB	65D	LEHM	13	6	28000	4	3	75600	83100
47		WELLINGTON 44	CUT	SA/CR	FBG	KC	IB	80D	LEHM	13	6	45000	4	10	105000	115000
47		WELLINGTON 47 TRKCBN	CUT	SA/CR	FBG	KC	IB	120D	LEHM	13	6	45000	4	10	105500	115500
		1980 BOATS														
44		WELLINGTON 44	CUT	SA/CR	FBG	KC	IB	D		13	6	28000	4	3	72200	79300
44		WELLINGTON 44	CUT	SA/CR	FBG	KC	IB	65D	LEHM	13	6	28000	4	3	72200	79300

LOA FT IN	NAME AND/ OR MODEL		TOP/ RIG	BOAT TYPE	-HULL- MTL TP	----ENGINE--- TP # HP MFG	BEAM FT IN	WGT LBS	DRAFT FT IN	RETAIL LOW	RETAIL HIGH
					1980 BOATS						
44	WELLINGTON 47		CUT	SA/CR	FBG KC	IB	61D LEHM	13 6	28000	4 3	72100	79200
47	WELLINGTON 47		CUT	SA/CR	FBG KC	IB	D	13 6	24000	4 3	77500	85200
47	WELLINGTON 47		KTH	SA/CR	FBG KC	IB	D	13 6	24000	4 3	77500	85200
47	WELLINGTON 47	TRKCBN	CUT	SA/CR	FBG KC	IB	120D LEHM	13 6	45000	4 10	98600	108500
47	WELLINGTON 47	TRKCRN	CUT	SA/CR	FBG KC	IB	120D LEHM	13 6	45000	4 10	102500	112500
					1979 BOATS						
44	WELLINGTON 44		CUT	SA/CR	FBG KC	IB	65D LEHM	13 6	28000		69400	76300
47	WELLINGTON 47	TRKCBN	CUT	SA/CR	FBG KC	IB	80D LEHM	13 6	45000		96300	106000
47	WELLINGTON 47	TRKCBN	KTH	SA/CR	FBG KC	IB	80D LEHM	13 6	45000		96300	106000
					1978 BOATS						
47	WELLINGTON 47	TRKCBN	CUT	SA/CR	FBG KC	IB	80D LEHM	13 6	45000	4 10	92800	102000
47	WELLINGTON 47	TRKCBN	KTH	SA/CR	FBG KC	IB	120D LEHM	13 6	45000	4 10	93200	102500
					1977 BOATS						
47	WELLINGTON 47		KTH	SA/CR	FBG KC	IB	80D LEHM	13 6	45000	4 10	81200	89200
47	WELLINGTON 47	TRKCBN	KTH	SA/CR	FBG KC	IB	80D LEHM	13 6	45000	4 10	98200	108000
					1976 BOATS						
47	WELLINGTON 47		SLP	MS	FBG KC	IB	85D LEHM	13 6	45000	4 10	86900	95500
47	WELLINGTON 47		CUT	MS	FBG KC	IB	85D LEHM	13 6	45000	4 10	86900	95500
47	WELLINGTON 47		KTH	MS	FBG KC	IB	85D LEHM	13 6	45000	4 10	86900	95500
					1975 BOATS						
47	WELLINGTON 47		KTH	SAIL	FBG KC	IB	85D FORD	13 6	45000	4 10	84400	92800
47	WELLINGTON 47		KTH	SAIL	FBG KC	IB	85D PERK	13 6	45000	4 10	84100	92400
					1974 BOATS						
47	WELLINGTON 47			SAIL	FBG	IB	85D FORD	13 6	45000	4 10	82200	90300
					1973 BOATS						
47	WELLINGTON 47			SAIL	FBG	IB	85D PERK	13 6	45000	4 10	79900	87800
					1972 BOATS						
47	WELLINGTON 47			SAIL	FBG	IB	85D PERK	13 6	45000	4 10	78100	85800

WELLS MARINE

Call 1-800-327-6929 for BUC Personalized Evaluation Service
Or, for 1966 boats, sign onto www.BUCValuPro.com

WELLS YACHT INC

Call 1-800-327-6929 for BUC Personalized Evaluation Service
Or, for 1966 to 1973 boats, sign onto www.BUCValuPro.com

WENZEL FIBERGLASS BOAT CO

C-CRAFT BOATS
MCHENRY MD 21541   COAST GUARD MFG ID- WEN   See inside cover to adjust price for area

For more recent years, see the BUC Used Boat Price Guide, Volume 1 or Volume 2

LOA FT IN	NAME AND/ OR MODEL	TOP/ RIG	BOAT TYPE	-HULL- MTL TP	----ENGINE--- TP # HP MFG	BEAM FT IN	WGT LBS	DRAFT FT IN	RETAIL LOW	RETAIL HIGH
					1981 BOATS					
16 9	WISP	OP	RNBT	FBG DV	IO 120	7	2480	2	2650	3050
16 9	WISP B/R	OP	RNBT	FBG DV	IO 230 OMC	7 8	2670	1	3000	3450
					1980 BOATS					
16 9	WISP	OP	RNBT	FBG DV	IO 240 OMC	7	2480	2	2750	3200
					1979 BOATS					
16 10	WISP	OP	RNBT	FBG DV	IO 225 OMC	8	2300	2	2800	3250
					1978 BOATS					
16 11	WISP	OP	RNBT	FBG DV	OB	8	2400	1 8	3500	4050

WESCO FIBERGLASS

COAST GUARD MFG ID- CES

Call 1-800-327-6929 for BUC Personalized Evaluation Service
Or, for 1983 to 1985 boats, sign onto www.BUCValuPro.com

WESCO MARINE

N HOLLYWOOD CA   See inside cover to adjust price for area
FOR NEWER MODELS SEE COLUMBIA

LOA FT IN	NAME AND/ OR MODEL	TOP/ RIG	BOAT TYPE	-HULL- MTL TP	----ENGINE--- TP # HP MFG	BEAM FT IN	WGT LBS	DRAFT FT IN	RETAIL LOW	RETAIL HIGH
					1968 BOATS					
34 1	CORONADO 34	SLP	SAIL	FBG KL	IB 30	10	9850	5 4	5700	6550
					1967 BOATS					
34	CORONADO 34	SLP	SAIL	FBG KL	IB 30	10	9850	5 4	5600	6450
					1966 BOATS					
34	CORONADO 34	SLP	SAIL	FBG KL	OB	10		5	6150	7050

WESTBROOK BOAT & ENGINE CO

Call 1-800-327-6929 for BUC Personalized Evaluation Service
Or, for 1961 to 1966 boats, sign onto www.BUCValuPro.com

WESTERLY DESIGNS INC

COAST GUARD MFG ID- WDE

Call 1-800-327-6929 for BUC Personalized Evaluation Service
Or, for 1980 to 1982 boats, sign onto www.BUCValuPro.com

WESTERLY MARINE

NEWPORT BEACH CA 92663   See inside cover to adjust price for area

LOA FT IN	NAME AND/ OR MODEL	TOP/ RIG	BOAT TYPE	-HULL- MTL TP	----ENGINE--- TP # HP MFG	BEAM FT IN	WGT LBS	DRAFT FT IN	RETAIL LOW	RETAIL HIGH
					1976 BOATS					
20	FLICKA	SLP	SAIL	FBG KL	IB 6D YAN	8	5500	3 3	16300	18500

WESTERLY YACHTS INC

ANDREW GEMENY & SON   See inside cover to adjust price for area
WESTERLY YACHTS LIMITED
HYATTSVILLE MD 21403   COAST GUARD MFG ID- AGS

WESTERLY MARINE CONSTRUCTION
HANTS ENGLAND

For more recent years, see the BUC Used Boat Price Guide, Volume 1 or Volume 2

LOA FT IN	NAME AND/ OR MODEL		TOP/ RIG	BOAT TYPE	-HULL- MTL TP	----ENGINE--- TP # HP MFG	BEAM FT IN	WGT LBS	DRAFT FT IN	RETAIL LOW	RETAIL HIGH
						1983 BOATS					
26	GRIFFON		SLP	SA/CR	FBG KL	IB 10D- 20D	9 3		4 9	17400	20100
26	GRIFFON		SLP	SA/CR	FBG TK	IB 10D- 20D	9 3	6700	4	22200	24700
28 10	KONSORT		SLP	SA/CR	FBG TK	IB 20D	10 9		5 4	27900	31100
28 10	KONSORT		SLP	SA/CR	FBG TK	IB 20D	10 9		3 3	27900	31100
31 10	FULMAR		SLP	SA/CR	FBG TK	IB 20D	10 11		5 3	34700	38600
31 10	FULMAR		SLP	SA/CR	FBG TK	IB 20D	10 11		4	34700	38600
33 3	WESTERLY 33	(DISCUS)	SLP	SA/CR	FBG KL	IB 20D BUKH	11 2	14343	5 6	49300	54200
33 3	WESTERLY 33	(DISCUS)	SLP	SA/CR	FBG TK	SD 35D VLVO	11 2		5 6	49700	54700
33 3	WESTERLY 33	(DISCUS)	SLP	SA/CR	FBG KL	IB 20D BUKH	11 2	14343	4 4	49300	54200
33 3	WESTERLY 33	(DISCUS)	SLP	SA/CR	FBG TK	SD 35D VLVO	11 2		4 4	49700	54700
33 3	WESTERLY 33	(DISCUS)	KTH	SA/CR	FBG KL	IB 20D BUKH	11 2	14343	5 6	49300	54200
33 3	WESTERLY 33	(DISCUS)	KTH	SA/CR	FBG TK	SD 35D VLVO	11 2		5 6	49700	54700
33 3	WESTERLY 33	(DISCUS)	KTH	SA/CR	FBG KL	IB 20D BUKH	11 2	14343	4 4	49300	54200
33 3	WESTERLY 33	(DISCUS)	KTH	SA/CR	FBG TK	SD 35D VLVO	11 2		4 4	49700	54700
34	VULCAN PH		SLP	SA/CR	FBG TK	SD 61D VLVO	11 10	15500	4 11	53200	58500
34	VULCAN PH		SLP	SA/CR	FBG TK	SD 61D VLVO	11 10	15500	4	53200	58500
35 9	CONWAY		SLP	SA/CR	FBG TK	SD 35D VLVO	11 2	16127	6	55600	61100
35 9	CONWAY		SLP	SA/CR	FBG TK	SD 35D VLVO	11 2	16127	4 6	55600	61100
35 9	CONWAY		KTH	SA/CR	FBG TK	SD 35D VLVO	11 2	16127	6	55600	61200
35 9	CONWAY		KTH	SA/CR	FBG TK	SD 35D VLVO	11 2	16127	4 6	55600	61200
38 6	SEALORD		SLP	SA/CR	FBG TK	SD 35D VLVO	13 2	18500	5 6	66600	73100
38 6	SEALORD		KTH	SA/CR	FBG TK	SD 35D VLVO	13 2	18500	5 6	66600	73200
						1982 BOATS					
26	GRIFFON		SLP	SA/CR	FBG KL	IB 20D BUKH	9 3	6500	4 9	20600	22800
26	GRIFFON		SLP	SA/CR	FBG KL	IB 20D BUKH	9 3	6500	3	20600	22800
28 10	KONSORT		SLP	SA/CR	FBG KL	IB 20D BUKH	10 9	8000	5 4	26200	29100
28 10	KONSORT		SLP	SA/CR	FBG TK	IB 20D BUKH	10 9	8000	3 4	26300	29200
29	GK 29 CLUB RACER		SLP	SA/RC	FBG KL	IB 12D PETT	10 1	6900	5 8	23500	25000
31 10	FULMAR 2 CABIN		SLP	SA/CR	FBG TK	IB 20D BUKH	10 11	10000	2	31900	35500
31 10	FULMAR 2 CABIN		SLP	SA/CR	FBG TK	IB 20D BUKH	10 11	10000	5	32000	35600
31 10	FULMAR 3 CABIN		SLP	SA/CR	FBG TK	IB 20D BUKH	10 11	10000	2	33100	36800
31 10	FULMAR 3 CABIN		SLP	SA/CR	FBG TK	IB 20D BUKH	10 11	10000	5 3	33100	36800
33 3	WESTERLY 33		SLP	SA/CR	FBG KL	IB 20D BUKH	11 2	14800	5 6	47800	52600
33 3	WESTERLY 33		SLP	SA/CR	FBG TK	IB 20D BUKH	11 2	14800	4	47800	52600
33 3	WESTERLY 33		KTH	SA/CR	FBG KL	IB 20D BUKH	11 2	14800	5 6	47800	52600
33 3	WESTERLY 33		KTH	SA/CR	FBG TK	IB 20D BUKH	11 2	14800	6 7	47800	52600
34	GK34		SLP	SA/RC	FBG TK	IB 20D BUKH	11 3	14000	6 7	44000	48900

LOA FT	IN	NAME AND/ OR MODEL	TOP/ RIG	BOAT TYPE	-HULL- MTL	TP	----ENGINE--- TP	# HP	MFG	BEAM FT	IN	WGT LBS	DRAFT FT	IN	RETAIL LOW	RETAIL HIGH
		1982 BOATS														
34		VULCAN PH	SLP	SA/CR	FBG	KL	IB	60D	VLVO	11	10	15500	4	11	49800	54800
34		VULCAN PH	SLP	SA/CR	FBG	TK	IB	60D	VLVO	11	10	15500	4	4	49800	54800
35	9	CONWAY AFT CABIN	SLP	SA/CR	FBG	KL	IB	34D	VLVO	11	2	16127	6		52100	57200
35	9	CONWAY AFT CABIN	SLP	SA/CR	FBG	TK	IB	34D	VLVO	11	2	16127	4	6	52100	57200
35	9	CONWAY AFT CABIN	KTH	SA/CR	FBG	KL	IB	34D	VLVO	11	2	16127	6		52100	57200
35	9	CONWAY AFT CABIN	KTH	SA/CR	FBG	TK	IB	34D	VLVO	11	2	16127	4	6	52100	57200
35	9	CONWAY AFT COCKPIT	SLP	SA/CR	FBG	KL	IB	34D	VLVO	11	2	16127	6		52100	57200
35	9	CONWAY AFT COCKPIT	SLP	SA/CR	FBG	TK	IB	34D	VLVO	11	2	16127	4	6	52100	57200
		1980 BOATS														
23	1	PAGEANT 23	SLP	SA/CR	FBG	TK	IB	D		8		4300	2	10	11000	12500
24		GK-1/4T	SLP	SA/RC	FBG	KL	OB			9	3	4100	5		9750	11100
26		CENTAUR 26	SLP	SA/CR	FBG	TK	IB	D		8	5	6700	3		18900	21000
26		CENTAUR 26	KTH	SA/CR	FBG	TK	IB	D		8	5	6700	3		18900	21000
26		PEMBROKE 26	SLP	SA/CR	FBG	KL	IB	D		0	5	6700	4	3	10900	21000
26		PEMBROKE 26	KTH	SA/CR	FBG	KL	IB	D		8	5	6700	4	3	18900	21000
28	10	KONSORT	SLP	SA/CR	FBG	TK	IB	D		10	9	7900	3	2	23100	25600
29		GK-29	SLP	SA/CR	FBG	KL	IB	D		10	4	6900	5	8	20100	22400
31		BERWICK 31	SLP	SA/CR	FBG	KL	IB	D		9	6	10000	3	7	29200	32500
31		BERWICK 31	KTH	SA/CR	FBG	KL	IB	D		9	6	10000	3	7	29200	32500
31		LONGBOW 31	KTH	SA/CR	FBG	KL	IB	D		9	6	10000	4	6	29200	32500
31		PENTLAND 31	SLP	SA/CR	FBG	TK	IB	D		9	6	10000	3	7	29200	32500
31		PENTLAND 31	KTH	SA/CR	FBG	TK	IB	D		9	6	10000	3	7	29200	32500
31		RENOWN 31	SLP	SA/CR	FBG	KL	IB	D		9	6	10000	4	6	29200	32500
31		RENOWN 31	KTH	SA/CR	FBG	KL	IB	D		9	6	10000	4	6	29200	32500
33	3	WESTERLY 33	SLP	SA/CR	FBG	KL	IB	D		10	11	14800	5		42200	46800
33	3	WESTERLY 33	KTH	SA/CR	FBG	KL	IB	D		10	11	17000	5		48300	53100
35	9	CONWAY 36	SLP	SA/CR	FBG	KL	IB	D		11	2	17000	6		48600	53400
35	9	CONWAY 36	KTH	SA/CR	FBG	KL	IB	D		11	2	17000	6		48600	53400
35	9	GATEWAY 36	SLP	SA/CR	FBG	TK	IB	D		11	2	17000	4	7	48600	53400
35	9	GATEWAY 36	KTH	SA/CR	FBG	TK	IB	D		11	2	17000	4	7	48600	53400
35	9	MEDWAY 36	SLP	SA/CR	FBG	KL	IB	D		11	2	17000	6		48600	53400
35	9	MEDWAY 36	KTH	SA/CR	FBG	KL	IB	D		11	2	17000	6		48600	53400
35	9	SOLWAY 36	SLP	SA/CR	FBG	TK	IB	D		11	2	17000	4	7	48600	53400
35	9	SOLWAY 36	KTH	SA/CR	FBG	TK	IB	D		11	2	17000	4	7	48600	53400
		1979 BOATS														
23	1	PAGEANT	SLP	SA/CR	FBG	TK	IB	13D	VLVO	8		4300	2	10	10500	12000
24		GK 24	SLP	SA/CR	FBG	KL	SD	7D	VLVO	9	3	3500	5		9000	10200
24		GK 24	SLP	SA/RC	FBG	KL	IB	6D	PETT	9	3	3500	5		8950	10200
26		CENTAUR	SLP	SA/CR	FBG	TK	IB	13D-	23D	8	5	6700	3		18100	20300
26		CENTAUR	KTH	SA/CR	FBG	TK	IB	13D-	23D	8	5	6700	3		18100	20300
26		PEMBROKE	SLP	SA/CR	FBG	KL	IB	13D-	23D	8	5	6380	4	3	16800	19300
26		PEMBROKE	KTH	SA/CR	FBG	KL	IB	13D-	23D	8	5	6380	4	3	16800	19300
29		GK 29 CLUB RACER	SLP	SA/RC	FBG	KL	IB	12D	PETT	10	4	6900	5	8	19200	21300
32	6	BERWICK	SLP	SA/CR	FBG	TK	IB	23D	VLVO	9	6	9863	3	7	27300	30300
32	6	BERWICK	KTH	SA/CR	FBG	TK	IB	23D	VLVO	9	6	9863	3	7	27300	30300
32	6	LONGBOW	SLP	SA/CR	FBG	KL	IB	23D	VLVO	9	6	9400	4	6	26000	28900
32	6	LONGBOW	KTH	SA/CR	FBG	KL	IB	23D	VLVO	9	6	9400	4	6	26000	28900
32	6	PENTLAND	SLP	SA/CR	FBG	TK	IB	23D	VLVO	9	6	10163	3	7	28100	31200
32	6	PENTLAND	KTH	SA/CR	FBG	TK	IB	23D	VLVO	9	6	10163	3	7	28100	31200
32	6	RENOWN	SLP	SA/CR	FBG	KL	IB	23D	VLVO	9	6	10080	4	6	27900	31000
32	6	RENOWN	KTH	SA/CR	FBG	KL	IB	23D	VLVO	9	6	10080	4	6	27900	31000
33	3	WESTERLY 33	SLP	SA/CR	FBG	KL	IB	42D	BENZ	11	2	14343	5	6	39200	43600
33	3	WESTERLY 33	SLP	SA/CR	FBG	TK	IB	42D	BENZ	11	2	14343			39200	43600
33	3	WESTERLY 33	KTH	SA/CR	FBG	KL	IB	42D	BENZ	11	2	14343	5	6	39200	43600
33	3	WESTERLY 33	KTH	SA/CR	FBG	TK	IB	42D	BENZ	11	2	14343			39200	43600
35	9	CONWAY	SLP	SA/CR	FBG	KL	IB	42D	BENZ	11	2	16127	6		45000	49900
35	9	CONWAY	KTH	SA/CR	FBG	KL	IB	42D	BENZ	11	2	16127	6		45000	50000
35	9	GALWAY 36	SLP	SA/CR	FBG	TK	IB	D		11	2	17000	4	7	46800	51400
35	9	GALWAY 36	KTH	SA/CR	FBG	TK	IB	D		11	2	17000	4	7	46800	51400
35	9	MEDWAY	SLP	SA/CR	FBG	KL	IB	42D	BENZ	11	2	16127	6		43500	48300
35	9	MEDWAY	SLP	SA/CR	FBG	TK	IB	42D	BENZ	11	2	17350	4	8	46900	51500
35	9	MEDWAY	KTH	SA/CR	FBG	KL	IB	42D	BENZ	11	2	16127	6		43500	48300
35	9	MEDWAY	KTH	SA/CR	FBG	TK	IB	42D	BENZ	11	2	17350	4	8	46900	51500
35	9	SOLWAY	SLP	SA/CR	FBG	TK	IB	42D	BENZ	11	2	17350	4	8	48200	53000
35	9	SOLWAY	KTH	SA/CR	FBG	TK	IB	42D	BENZ	11	2	17350	4	8	48200	53000
		1978 BOATS														
21	6	WARWICK	SLP	SA/CR	FBG	TK				7	9	3695	2	9	7150	8200
23	1	KENDAL	SLP	SA/CR	FBG	KL	IB	13D	VLVO	8		4100	4		9700	11000
23	1	PAGEANT	SLP	SA/CR	FBG	TK	IB	13D	VLVO	8		4300	2	10	10100	11500
24		GK 24	SLP	SA/RC	FBG	KL				9	3	3500	5		7700	8800
26		CENTAUR	SLP	SA/CR	FBG	TK	IB	12D-	23D	8	5	6700	3		17000	19400
26		CENTAUR	KTH	SA/CR	FBG	TK	IB	12D-	23D	8	5	6700	3		17000	19400
26		PEMBROKE	SLP	SA/CR	FBG	KL	IB	12D-	23D	8	5	6380	4	3	16100	18500
26		PEMBROKE	KTH	SA/CR	FBG	KL	IB	12D-	23D	8	5	6380	4	3	16100	18500
29		GK 29	SLP	SA/RC	FBG	KL				10	4	6900	5	8	16500	18800
32	6	BERWICK	SLP	SA/CR	FBG	TK	IB	23D	VLVO	9	6	9863	3	7	26200	29100
32	6	BERWICK	KTH	SA/CR	FBG	TK	IB	23D	VLVO	9	6	9863	3	7	26200	29100
32	6	LONGBOW	SLP	SA/CR	FBG	KL	IB	23D	VLVO	9	6	9400	4	6	25000	27800
32	6	LONGBOW	KTH	SA/CR	FBG	KL	IB	23D	VLVO	9	6	9400	4	6	25000	27800
32	6	PENTLAND	SLP	SA/CR	FBG	TK	IB	23D	VLVO	9	6	10163	3	7	27000	30000
32	6	PENTLAND	KTH	SA/CR	FBG	TK	IB	23D	VLVO	9	6	10163	3	7	27000	30000
32	6	RENOWN	SLP	SA/CR	FBG	KL	IB	23D	VLVO	9	6	10080	4	6	26800	29700
32	6	RENOWN	KTH	SA/CR	FBG	KL	IB	23D	VLVO	9	6	10080	4	6	26800	29700
33	3	WESTERLY 33	SLP	SA/CR	FBG	KL	IB	42D	BENZ	11	2	13400	5	6	35300	39200
33	3	WESTERLY 33	KTH	SA/CR	FBG	KL	IB	42D	BENZ	11	2	13400	5	6	35300	39200
35	9	CONWAY	SLP	SA/CR	FBG	KL	IB	42D	BENZ	11	2	14400	6		39700	44100
35	9	CONWAY	KTH	SA/CR	FBG	KL	IB	42D	BENZ	11	2	14400	6		39500	43900
35	9	GALWAY	SLP	SA/CR	FBG	TK	IB	42D	BENZ	11	2	15600	4	8	40500	45000
35	9	GALWAY	KTH	SA/CR	FBG	TK	IB	42D	BENZ	11	2	15600	4	8	40500	45000
35	9	MEDWAY	SLP	SA/CR	FBG	KL	IB	42D	BENZ	11	2	14400	6		38300	42500
35	9	MEDWAY	KTH	SA/CR	FBG	KL	IB	42D	BENZ	11	2	14400	6		38100	42300
35	9	SOLWAY	SLP	SA/CR	FBG	TK	IB	42D	BENZ	11	2	15600	4	8	42000	46600
35	9	SOLWAY	KTH	SA/CR	FBG	TK	IB	42D	BENZ	11	2	15600	4	8	42000	46600
35	9	WESTERLY 35	SLP	SA/CR	FBG	KL	IB	42D	BENZ	11	2	14400	6		37200	41300
35	9	WESTERLY 35	KTH	SA/CR	FBG	KL	IB	42D	BENZ	11	2	14400	6		37500	41700
		1977 BOATS														
23	1	PAGEANT	SLP	SA/CR	FBG	TK	OB			8		4300	2	10	8650	9950
23	1	PAGEANT	SLP	SA/CR	FBG	TK	IB	10D	VLVO	8		4300	2	10	9600	10900
24		GK 24	SLP	SA/CR	FBG	KL	IB	7D	VLVO	9	3	3500	5		8200	9400
24		GK 24	SLP	SA/RC	FBG	KL	IB			9	3	3500	5		7850	9050
24		GK 24	SLP	SAIL	FBG	KL	OB			9	3	3500	5		7350	8450
25	1	TIGER	SLP	SA/CR	FBG	KL	IB	D		8	9	5264	4	3	12400	14100
26		CENTAUR	SLP	SA/CR	FBG	TK	OB			8	5	6700	3		15500	17700
26		CENTAUR	SLP	SA/CR	FBG	TK	IB	10D-	23D	8	5	6700	3		16200	18700
26		CENTAUR	KTH	SA/CR	FBG	TK	OB			8	5	6700	3		15500	17700
26		CENTAUR	KTH	SA/CR	FBG	TK	IB	10D-	23D	8	5	6700	3		16200	18700
26		CHIEFTAIN	SLP	SA/CR	FBG	TK	IB	D		8	5	7000	3		17100	19400
26		PEMBROKE	SLP	SA/CR	FBG	KL	OB			8	5	6380	4	3	14700	16700
26		PEMBROKE	SLP	SA/CR	FBG	KL	IB	10D-	23D	8	5	6380	4	3	15400	17800
26		PEMBROKE	KTH	SA/CR	FBG	KL	OB			8	5	6380	4	3	14700	16700
26		PEMBROKE	KTH	SA/CR	FBG	KL	IB	10D-	23D	8	5	6380	4	3	15400	17800
31		LONGBOW	SLP	SA/CR	FBG	KL	OB			9	6	8400	4	6	21600	24000
31		LONGBOW	SLP	SA/CR	FBG	KL	IB	23D-	35D	9	6	8400	4	6	21700	24200
31		LONGBOW	KTH	SA/CR	FBG	KL	OB			9	6	8400	4	6	21600	24000
31		LONGBOW	KTH	SA/CR	FBG	KL	IB	23D-	35D	9	6	8400	4	6	21700	24200
32	6	BERWICK	SLP	SA/CR	FBG	TK	OB			9	6	9863	3	7	25200	28000
32	6	BERWICK	SLP	SA/CR	FBG	TK	IB	23D-	35D	9	6	9863	3	7	25200	28100
32	6	BERWICK	KTH	SA/CR	FBG	TK	OB			9	6	9863	3	7	25200	28000
32	6	BERWICK	KTH	SA/CR	FBG	TK	IB	23D-	35D	9	6	9863	3	7	25200	28100
32	6	PENTLAND	SLP	SA/CR	FBG	TK	OB			9	6	10163	3	7	25900	28800
32	6	PENTLAND	SLP	SA/CR	FBG	TK	IB	23D-	35D	9	6	10163	3	7	26000	28900
32	6	PENTLAND	KTH	SA/CR	FBG	TK	OB			9	6	10163	3	7	25900	28800
32	6	PENTLAND	KTH	SA/CR	FBG	TK	IB	23D-	35D	9	6	10163	3	7	26000	28900
32	6	RENOWN	SLP	SA/CR	FBG	KL	OB			9	6	10080	4	6	25700	28600
32	6	RENOWN	SLP	SA/CR	FBG	KL	IB	23D-	35D	9	6	10080	4	6	25800	28700
32	6	RENOWN	KTH	SA/CR	FBG	KL	OB			9	6	10080	4	6	25700	28600
32	6	RENOWN	KTH	SA/CR	FBG	KL	IB	23D-	35D	9	6	10080	4	6	25800	28700
35	9	CONWAY	SLP	SA/CR	FBG	KL	IB	36D	VLVO	11	3	15800	6		40100	44600
35	9	CONWAY	KTH	SA/CR	FBG	KL	IB	36D	VLVO	11	3	15800	6		40100	44600
35	9	GALWAY	SLP	SA/CR	FBG	TK	IB	36D	VLVO	11	3	15500	4	7	38700	43000
35	9	GALWAY	KTH	SA/CR	FBG	TK	IB	36D	VLVO	11	3	15500	4	7	38700	43000
35	9	MEDWAY	SLP	SA/CR	FBG	KL	IB	36D	VLVO	11	3	14400	4	7	36900	41000
35	9	MEDWAY	KTH	SA/CR	FBG	KL	IB	36D	VLVO	11	3	14400	4	7	36900	41000
35	9	SOLWAY	SLP	SA/CR	FBG	TK	IB	36D	VLVO	11	3	15500	4	7	40200	44600
35	9	SOLWAY	KTH	SA/CR	FBG	TK	IB	36D	VLVO	11	3	15500	4	7	40200	44700
		1976 BOATS														
21		JOUSTER	SLP	SAIL	FBG	KL				7	6	2200	3	6	4500	5150
21		JOUSTER	SLP	SAIL	FBG	SK				7	6	2200	3	6	4500	5150
21	6	WARWICK	SLP	SAIL	FBG	TK				7	9	3695	2	9	6600	7600
23	1	PAGEANT	SLP	SAIL	FBG	TK	IB	10D	VLVO	8		4300	2	10	9300	10600
25	1	TIGER	SLP	SAIL	FBG	KL	IB	10D-	25D	8	9	5264	4	3	11900	13800
26		CENTAUR	SLP	SAIL	FBG	TK	IB	10D-	25D	8	5	6700	3		15600	18000
26		CENTAUR	KTH	SAIL	FBG	TK	IB	10D-	25D	8	5	6700	3		15600	18000
26		CHIEFTAIN	SLP	SAIL	FBG	TK	IB	25D		8	5	7000	3		16600	18900
31		LONGBOW	SLP	SAIL	FBG	KL	IB	25D-	36D	9	6	8400	4	6	21000	23400
31		LONGBOW	KTH	SAIL	FBG	KL	IB	25D-	36D	9	6	8400	4	6	21000	23400
32	6	BERWICK	SLP	SAIL	FBG	TK	IB	25D-	36D	9	6	9863	3	7	24400	27100

CONTINUED ON NEXT PAGE

LOA FT IN	NAME AND/ OR MODEL	TOP/ RIG	BOAT TYPE	HULL MTL	TP	TP	ENG #	HP	MFG	BEAM FT IN	WGT LBS	DRAFT FT IN	RETAIL LOW	RETAIL HIGH
1976 BOATS														
32 6	BERWICK	KTH	SAIL	FBG	TK	IB	25D-	36D		9 6	9863	3 7	24400	27100
32 6	PENTLAND	SLP	SAIL	FBG	TK	IB	25D-	36D		9 6	10163	3 7	25100	27900
32 6	PENTLAND	KTH	SAIL	FBG	TK	IB	25D-	36D		9 6	10163	3 7	25100	27900
32 6	RENOWN	SLP	SAIL	FBG	KL	IB	25D-	36D		9 6	10080	4 6	24900	27700
32 6	RENOWN	KTH	SAIL	FBG	KL	IB	25D-	36D		9 6	10080	4 6	24900	27700
35 9	CONWAY	SLP	SAIL	FBG	KL	IB	36D		VLVO	11 3	17412	6	43600	48400
35 9	CONWAY	KTH	SAIL	FBG	KL	IB	36D		VLVO	11 3	17412	6	43600	48500
35 9	GALWAY	SLP	SAIL	FBG	TK	IB	36D		VLVO	11 3	17412	6	40800	45300
35 9	GALWAY	KTH	SAIL	FBG	TK	IB	36D		VLVO	11 3	17412	6	40000	45100
35 9	MEDWAY	SLP	SAIL	FBG	KL	IB	36D		VLVO	11 3	17412	6	39100	43400
35 9	MEDWAY	KTH	SAIL	FBG	KL	IB	36D		VLVO	11 3	17412	6	39100	43400
35 9	SOLWAY	SLP	SAIL	FBG	KL	IB	36D		VLVO	11 3	17412	6	45800	50400
35 9	SOLWAY	KTH	SAIL	FBG	TK	IB	36D		VLVO	11 3	17412	6	45800	50400
1975 BOATS														
21	JOUSTER	SLP	SAIL	FBG	KL	OB				7 6	2200	3 6	4300	5000
21 6	WARWICK	SLP	SAIL	FBG	KL	IB	5D		PETT	7 9	3695	2 9	7450	8550
23 1	PAGEANT	SLP	SAIL	FBG	KL	OB				8	4300	2 10	8050	9250
23 1	PAGEANT	SLP	SAIL	FBG	KL	IB	10D		VLVO	8	4300	2 10	9000	10200
25 1	TIGER	SLP	SAIL	FBG	KL	OB				8 9	5264	4 3	10800	12300
25 1	TIGER	SLP	SAIL	FBG	KL	IB	10D		VLVO	8 9	5264	4 3	11500	13100
26	CENTAUR	SLP	SAIL	FBG	KL	OB				8 5	6700	3	14500	16400
26	CENTAUR	SLP	SAIL	FBG	KL	IB	25D		VLVO	8 5	6700	3	15300	17400
26	CENTAUR	KTH	SAIL	FBG	KL	OB				8 5	6700	3	14500	16400
26	CENTAUR	KTH	SAIL	FBG	KL	IB	25D		VLVO	8 5	6700	3	15300	17400
26	CHIEFTAIN	SLP	SAIL	FBG	KL	OB				8 5	7000	3	15200	17200
26	CHIEFTAIN	SLP	SAIL	FBG	KL	IB	25D		VLVO	8 5	7000	3	16000	18200
31	LONGBOW	SLP	SAIL	FBG	KL	IB	25D-	36D		9 6	8400	4 6	20300	22600
31	LONGBOW	KTH	SAIL	FBG	KL	IB	25D-	36D		9 6	8400	4 6	20300	22600
32 6	BERWICK	SLP	SAIL	FBG	TK	IB	25D-	36D		9 6	9863	3 7	23600	26200
32 6	BERWICK	KTH	SAIL	FBG	TK	IB	25D-	36D		9 6	9863	3 7	23600	26200
32 6	PENTLAND	SLP	SAIL	FBG	KL	IB	25D-	36D		9 6	10163	3 7	24300	27000
32 6	PENTLAND	KTH	SAIL	FBG	KL	IB	25D-	36D		9 6	10163	3 7	24300	27000
32 6	RENOWN	SLP	SAIL	FBG	KL	IB	25D-	36D		9 6	10080	4 6	24100	26800
32 6	RENOWN	KTH	SAIL	FBG	KL	IB	25D-	36D		9 6	10080	4 6	24100	26800
35 9	CONWAY	SLP	SAIL	FBG	KL	IB	36D		VLVO	11 2	17380	6	40800	45300
35 9	CONWAY	KTH	SAIL	FBG	KL	IB	36D		VLVO	11 2	17380	6	40800	45400
1974 BOATS														
21	JOUSTER		SAIL	FBG		OB				7 6	2200	3 6	4150	4850
21 6	WARWICK		SAIL	FBG		OB				7 9	3695	2 9	6200	7100
23 1	PAGEANT		SAIL	FBG		OB				8		2 10	5900	6800
23 1	PAGEANT		SAIL	FBG		IB	10D		VLVO	8	4300	2 10	8600	9900
25 1	TIGER		SAIL	FBG		OB				8 9		2 9	7500	8600
25 1	TIGER		SAIL	FBG		IB	10D-	25D		8 9	5264	4 3	11200	13000
26	CENTAUR		SAIL	FBG		OB				8 5		3	9250	10500
26	CENTAUR		SAIL	FBG		IB	25D		VLVO	8 5	6150	3	13600	15500
26	CHIEFTAIN		SAIL	FBG		IB	25D		VLVO	8 5	6250	3	13800	15700
31	LONGBOW	SLP	SAIL	FBG		IB	25D-	35D		9 6	8400	4 6	19800	22000
31	LONGBOW	KTH	SAIL	FBG		IB	25D-	35D		9 6	8400	4 6	19800	22000
32 6	AFT CABIN	KTH	SAIL	FBG	KL	IB	25D			9 6	8800	4 6	20500	22800
32 6	BERWICK	SLP	SAIL	FBG	TK	IB	25D			9 6	9863	3 7	22900	25500
32 6	BERWICK	KTH	SAIL	FBG	TK	IB	25D			9 6	9863	3 7	22900	25500
32 6	PENTLAND	SLP	SAIL	FBG	TK	IB	25D			9 6	10163	3 7	23600	26200
32 6	PENTLAND	KTH	SAIL	FBG	TK	IB	25D			9 6	10163	3 7	23600	26200
32 6	RENOWN	SLP	SAIL	FBG		IB	25D-	35D		9 6	8700	4 6	20300	22500
32 6	RENOWN	KTH	SAIL	FBG		IB	25D		VLVO	9 6	8700	4 6	20300	22500
1973 BOATS														
21	JOUSTER	SLP	SAIL	FBG		OB				7 6	2200	3 6	4050	4700
21 6	WARWICK	SLP	SAIL	FBG		OB	5D		PETT	7 9	3695	2 9	7050	8100
22 3	CIRRUS	SLP	SAIL	FBG	KL	IB	7D			8	3240	3 6	6550	7500
23 1	PAGEANT	SLP	SAIL	FBG		IB	10D		VLVO	8	4300	2 10	8350	9600
25 1	TIGER	SLP	SAIL	FBG		IB	10D-	25D		8 9	5264	4 3	10900	12600
26	CENTAUR	SLP	SAIL	FBG		IB	25D		VLVO	8 5	6150	3	12600	14400
26	CHIEFTAIN	SLP	SAIL	FBG		IB	25D		VLVO	8 5	6150	3	13900	15800
31	LONGBOW	SLP	SAIL	FBG		IB	25D-	35D		9 6	8400	4 6	19300	21500
31	LONGBOW	KTH	SAIL	FBG		IB	25D-	35D		9 6	8400	4 6	19300	21500
32 6	RENOWN	KTH	SAIL	FBG		IB	25D-	35D		9 6	8700	4 6	19800	22000
1972 BOATS														
17 9	NIMROD		SAIL	FBG		OB				6 6	1000	4	2450	2850
21	JOUSTER		SAIL	FBG		OB				7 6	2200	3 6	3950	4600
21 6	WARWICK		SAIL	FBG		OB				7 9	3695	2 9	5900	6750
21 6	WARWICK		SAIL	FBG		OB	5D			7 9		2 9	5650	6500
22	CIRRUS		SAIL	FBG		OB				8		3 6	5450	6250
22	CIRRUS		SAIL	FBG		OB	7D		VLVO	8	3240	3 6	5750	6600
23 1	PAGEANT		SAIL	FBG		OB				8		2 10	7400	8500
23 1	PAGEANT		SAIL	FBG		OB	7D		VLVO	8	4300	2 10	7800	8950
25 1	TIGER		SAIL	FBG		OB				8 9	5264	4 3	10000	11300
25 1	TIGER		SAIL	FBG		OB				8 9		4 3	10800	12300
26	CENTAUR		SAIL	FBG		OB				8 5	6150	3	12200	13800
26	CENTAUR		SAIL	FBG		OB	7D		VLVO	8 5		3	11100	12600
31	LONGBOW		SAIL	FBG		IB	24D		VLVO	9 6	8400	4 6	19100	21200
32 6	AFT CABIN	KTH	SAIL	FBG		IB	24D		VLVO	9 1	9000	4 6	20000	22300
1971 BOATS														
17 9	NIMROD		SAIL	FBG		OB				6 6	1000	4	2400	2800
21	JOUSTER		SAIL	FBG		OB				7 6	2200	3 6	3850	4500
21 6	WARWICK		SAIL	FBG		OB				7 9	3695	2 9	5750	6650
21 6	WARWICK		SAIL	FBG		IB				7 9		2 9	3950	4600
22	CIRRUS		SAIL	FBG		OB				8		3 6	5300	6100
22	CIRRUS		SAIL	FBG		OB	7		VLVO	8	3240	3 6	3900	4550
23 1	PAGEANT		SAIL	FBG		OB				8		2 10	7250	8350
23 1	PAGEANT		SAIL	FBG		OB	7		VLVO	8	4300	2 10	5250	6050
25 1	TIGER		SAIL	FBG		OB				8 9	5264	4 3	9750	11100
25 1	TIGER		SAIL	FBG		OB	7		VLVO	8 9		4 3	8150	9350
26	CENTAUR		SAIL	FBG		OB				8 5	6150	3	12000	13600
26	CENTAUR		SAIL	FBG		OB	7		VLVO	8 5		3	10400	11900
31	LONGBOW		SAIL	FBG		IB	16		VLVO	9 6	8400	4 6	18700	20700
1970 BOATS														
17 9	NIMROD	SLP	SA/OD	FBG	SK	IB				6 6	1000	8	2300	3250
22	CIRRUS	SLP	SAIL	FBG	KL	IB				8 6	3240	3 6	5600	6450
22 3	NOMAD	SLP	SAIL	FBG	TK	IB				7 5	3150	2 3	5550	6400
23 1	PAGEANT	SLP	SAIL	FBG	TK	IB				8	4350	2 10	7600	8700
25 1	TIGER	SLP	SAIL	FBG	KL	IB				8 9	5600	4 3	10600	12100
25 11	CENTAUR	SLP	SAIL	FBG	KL	IB				8 9	6150	3	12000	13700
28 3	WESTERLY 28	SLP	SAIL	FBG	KL	IB				9	6500	4 4	13500	15300
1969 BOATS														
17 9	NIMROD	SLP	SAIL	FBG	SK	IB				6 6	800	3 6	2550	2950
22	CIRRUS	SLP	SAIL	FBG	KL	IB				8 6	3240	3 6	5550	6350
22 3	NOMAD	SLP	SAIL	FBG	TK	IB				7 5	3900	2 3	6650	7600
26	CENTAUR	SLP	SAIL	FBG	TK	IB				9	5000	3	9700	11000
28 3	WESTERLY 28	SLP	SAIL	FBG	TK	IB				9	7000	4	14400	16300
30 3	WESTERLY 30	SLP	SAIL	FBG	TK	IB				8 8	8000	3	16900	19200
1968 BOATS														
21 6	CIRRUS	SLP	SAIL	FBG	KL	IB	7			8		3 6	3700	4300
22 3	NOMAD	SLP	SAIL	FBG	TK	IB	7			7 5	3300	2 3	6200	7100
25	WINDRUSH	SLP	SAIL	FBG	TK	IB	7			7 5	4500	2 6	8200	9400
28 3	WESTERLY 28	SLP	SAIL	FBG	KL	IB	7			9 4	7000	4 6	14200	16100
30 2	WESTERLY 30	SLP	SAIL	FBG	TK	IB	15			8 8	8400	3	17600	20000
1967 BOATS														
22 3	TWIN KEEL	SLP	SAIL	FBG	TK	IB	7D	7D		7 5		2 3	5350	6150
25 1	TWIN KEEL	SLP	SAIL	FBG	TK	IB	7D	7D		7 5			10100	11400
25 1	WINDRUSH 25	SLP	SA/CR	FBG	TK	OB				7 5		2 6	6600	7600
25 1	WINDRUSH 25	SLP	SA/CR	FBG	TK	OB	7D			7 5			9900	11300
28 3	WESTERLY 28 FIN KEEL	SLP	SAIL	FBG	KL	OB				9		2	12100	13800
30 2	TWIN KEEL	SLP	SAIL	FBG	TK	IB				8 8		3	12500	14200
30 2	TWIN KEEL	SLP	SAIL	FBG	TK	IB	15D			8 8		3	16500	18700
1966 BOATS														
22 3	WESTERLY 22	SLP	SAIL	FBG	TK	OB				7 5		2 3	4250	4900
25 1	WESTERLY 25	SLP	SAIL	FBG	TK	OB				7 5		2 6	6600	7550

WESTERN SAILCRAFT LTD
COAST GUARD MFG ID- WSA

WESTERNER BOAT COMPANY
COAST GUARD MFG ID- WBC

WESTFIELD ENGLAND LTD
WESLEY JONES
FOR OLDER MODELS SEE S GELBER & SON

WESTPHAL BOATS INC
HIALEAH FL 33010   COAST GUARD MFG ID- WES See inside cover to adjust price for area

LOA FT IN	NAME AND/ OR MODEL	TOP/ RIG	BOAT TYPE	-HULL- MTL TP	ENGINE TP	#	HP MFG	BEAM FT IN	WGT LBS	DRAFT FT IN	RETAIL LOW	RETAIL HIGH
--- 1969 BOATS ---												
28 4	WESTPHAL	SLP	SA/OD	FBG KL	OB			6 5	3400	3 11	7500	8650
30	WESTPHAL-DUALER	SLP	SAIL	FBG KL	OB			9	6000	4 3	13800	15700
30	WESTPHAL-DUALER	SLP	SAIL	FBG KL	IB	30		9	6400	4 3	14900	16900
--- 1968 BOATS ---												
28 4	WESTPHAL	SLP	SA/OD	FBG KL	OB			6 5	3400	3 11	7400	8500
30	WESTPHAL-DUALER	SLP	SAIL	FBG KL	OB			9	4700	4	10600	12100
30	WESTPHAL-DUALER C	SLP	SAIL	FBG KL	IB	30		9	5100	4	11700	13300
30	WESTPHAL-DUALER R	SLP	SAIL	FBG KL	IB	30		9	5100	4	11700	13300
--- 1967 BOATS ---												
28 4	WESTPHAL	SLP	SA/OD	FBG KL				6 5	3400	3 11	7100	8150

WESTPORT MARINE INC
COSTA MESA CA 92627   COAST GUARD MFG ID- WPB See inside cover to adjust price for area
FORMERLY WESTPORT PACIFIC

For more recent years, see the BUC Used Boat Price Guide, Volume 1 or Volume 2

LOA FT IN	NAME AND/ OR MODEL	TOP/ RIG	BOAT TYPE	-HULL- MTL TP	ENGINE TP	#	HP MFG	BEAM FT IN	WGT LBS	DRAFT FT IN	RETAIL LOW	RETAIL HIGH
--- 1983 BOATS ---												
18 9	PACIFIC-CAT 2/18	SLP	SA/OD	FBG CT	OB			7 11	450	7	2500	2900
18 9	PACIFIC-CAT 3/18	SLP	SA/OD	FBG CT	OB			7 11	440	7	2450	2850
18 9	PACIFIC-CAT STANDARD	SLP	SA/OD	FBG CT	OB			7 11	540	7	2750	3200
--- 1982 BOATS ---												
18 9	PACIFIC-CAT 2/18	SLP	SA/OD	FBG CT	OB			7 11	450	7	2350	2700
18 9	PACIFIC-CAT 3/18	SLP	SA/OD	FBG CT	OB			7 11	440	7	2350	2700
18 9	PACIFIC-CAT STANDARD	SLP	SA/OD	FBG CT	OB			7 11	540	7	2600	3000
--- 1981 BOATS ---												
18 9	PACIFIC-CAT 2/18	SLP	SA/OD	FBG CT	OB			7 11	450	7	2200	2600
18 9	PACIFIC-CAT STANDARD	SLP	SA/OD	FBG CT	OB			7 11	540	7	2450	2850
--- 1980 BOATS ---												
18 9	PACIFIC-CAT	SLP	SA/OD	FBG CT	OB			7 11	540	7	2350	2700
18 9	PACIFIC-CAT 2/18	SLP	SA/OD	FBG CT	OB			7 11	450	7	2050	2450
--- 1979 BOATS ---												
18 9	PACIFIC-CAT	SLP	SA/OD	FBG CT	OB			7 11	525	7	2250	2600
18 9	PACIFIC-CAT 2/18	SLP	SA/OD	FBG CT	OB			7 11	450	7	2000	2350
--- 1978 BOATS ---												
18 9	PACIFIC-CAT	SLP	SA/OD	FBG CT	OB			7 11	540	7	2200	2550
--- 1977 BOATS ---												
18 9	PACIFIC-CAT	SLP	SA/OD	FBG CT	OB			7 11	540	7	2050	2450
--- 1976 BOATS ---												
18 9	PACIFIC-CAT	SLP	SA/OD	FBG CT	OB			7 11	540	7	2000	2400
--- 1975 BOATS ---												
18 9	PACIFIC-CAT	SLP	SA/OD	FBG CT	OB			7 11	540	7	1950	2300

WESTPORT SHIPYARD
WESTPORT WA 98595   See inside cover to adjust price for area

For more recent years, see the BUC Used Boat Price Guide, Volume 1 or Volume 2

LOA FT IN	NAME AND/ OR MODEL	TOP/ RIG	BOAT TYPE	-HULL- MTL TP	ENGINE TP	#	HP MFG	BEAM FT IN	WGT LBS	DRAFT FT IN	RETAIL LOW	RETAIL HIGH
--- 1983 BOATS ---												
48	WESTPORT	HT	MY	FBG SV	IB	T270D	CAT	15 1	45000	4 6	199000	218500
56	WESTPORT	HT	MY	FBG SV	IB	T500D	GM	17	55000	4 6	257500	283000
65	WESTPORT	HT	MY	FBG SV	IB	T500D	CAT	20	50T	5	527000	579000
70	WESTPORT	HT	MY	FBG SV	IB	T500D	CAT	20	53T	5	623500	685000
--- 1982 BOATS ---												
48	WESTPORT	HT	MY	FBG SV	IB	T270D	CAT	15 1	45000	4 6	190000	208500
56	WESTPORT	HT	MY	FBG SV	IB	T500D	GM	17	55000	4 6	246500	271000
65	WESTPORT	HT	MY	FBG SV	IB	T500D	CAT	20	50T	5	504500	554500
70	WESTPORT	HT	MY	FBG SV	IB	T500D	CAT	20	53T	5	595500	654000
--- 1981 BOATS ---												
48	WESTPORT	HT	MY	FBG SV	IB	T270D	CAT	15 1	45000	4 6	181500	199500
56	WESTPORT	HT	MY	FBG SV	IB	T500D	GM	17	55000	4 6	236000	259500

WESTSAIL CORPORATION
COSTA MESA CA 92626   COAST GUARD MFG ID- WSS See inside cover to adjust price for area

LOA FT IN	NAME AND/ OR MODEL	TOP/ RIG	BOAT TYPE	-HULL- MTL TP	ENGINE TP	#	HP MFG	BEAM FT IN	WGT LBS	DRAFT FT IN	RETAIL LOW	RETAIL HIGH
--- 1981 BOATS ---												
28 3	WESTSAIL 28	CUT	SA/CR	FBG KL	IB	D		9 7	13500	4 4	34900	38800
32	WESTSAIL 32	CUT	SA/CR	FBG KL	IB	D		11	19500	5	49300	54100
38 9	WESTSAIL 11.8M	CUT	SA/CR	FBG KL	IB	D	11	10	21262	5 10	59800	65700
42 11	WESTSAIL 42	CUT	SA/CR	FBG KL	IB	D		13	31500	5 8	88700	97400
42 11	WESTSAIL 42	KTH	SA/CR	FBG KL	IB	D		13	31500	5 8	89100	97900
--- 1980 BOATS ---												
28 3	WESTSAIL 28	CUT	SA/CR	FBG KL	IB	D		9 7	13500	4 4	33600	37300
32	WESTSAIL 32	CUT	SA/CR	FBG KL	IB	D		11	19500	5	47700	52400
38 8	WESTSAIL 11.8M	CUT	SA/CR	FBG KL	IB	D	11	10	21000	5 10	56800	62400
42 11	WESTSAIL 42	CUT	SA/CR	FBG KL	IB	D		13	31500	5 8	83500	93700
42 11	WESTSAIL 42	KTH	SA/CR	FBG KL	IB	D		13	31500	5 8	85600	94000
42 11	WESTSAIL 43	CUT	SA/CR	FBG KL	IB	D		13	31500	5 8	85300	93700
42 11	WESTSAIL 43	KTH	SA/CR	FBG KL	IB	D		13	31500	5 8	85600	94000
--- 1979 BOATS ---												
28 3	WESTSAIL 28	CUT	SA/CR	FBG KL	IB	D		9 7	13500	4 4	32500	36200
32	WESTSAIL 32	CUT	SA/CR	FBG KL	IB	D		11	19500	5	46200	50700
42 11	WESTSAIL 42	CUT	SA/CR	FBG KL	IB	D		13	31500	5 8	82800	90800
42 11	WESTSAIL 42	KTH	SA/CR	FBG KL	IB	D		13	31500	5 8	82800	91000
42 11	WESTSAIL 43	CUT	SA/CR	FBG KL	IB	D		13	31500	5 8	82600	90800
42 11	WESTSAIL 43	KTH	SA/CR	FBG KL	IB	D		13	31500	5 8	82800	91000
--- 1978 BOATS ---												
28 3	VOYAGER 28	CUT	SA/CR	FBG KL	IB	13D	VLVO	9 7	13500	4 4	31500	35000
32	VOYAGER 32	CUT	SA/CR	FBG KL	IB	25D	VLVO	11	19500	5	44400	49300
42 11	VOYAGER 43	CUT	SA/CR	FBG KL	VD	36D	NISS	13	31500	5 8	79700	87600
42 11	VOYAGER 43	KTH	SA/CR	FBG KL	VD	36D	NISS	13	31500	5 8	79900	87800
--- 1977 BOATS ---												
28 3	CIRCUMNAVIGATOR 28	CUT	SA/CR	FBG KL	IB	10D	VLVO	9 7	13500	4 4	37000	41100
28 3	PASSAGEMAKER 28	CUT	SA/CR	FBG KL	IB	10D	VLVO	9 7	13500	4 4	29600	32900
28 3	VOYAGER 28	CUT	SA/CR	FBG KL	IB	10D	VLVO	9 7	13500	4 4	25400	28200
32	CIRCUMNAVIGATOR 32	CUT	SA/CR	FBG KL	IB	35D	VLVO	11	19500	5	43200	48000
32	PASSAGEMAKER 32	CUT	SA/CR	FBG KL	IB	25D	VLVO	11	19500	5	40500	44700
32	VOYAGER 32	CUT	SA/CR	FBG KL	IB	25D	VLVO	11	19500	5	40200	44700
42 11	CIRCUMNAVIGATOR 42	CUT	SA/CR	FBG KL	IB	85D	PERK	13	31500	5 8	77900	85600
42 11	CIRCUMNAVIGATOR 42	KTH	SA/CR	FBG KL	IB	85D	PERK	13	31500	5 8	78100	85800
42 11	CIRCUMNAVIGATOR 43	CUT	SA/CR	FBG KL	VD	75D	NISS	13	31500	5 8	85900	94400
42 11	CIRCUMNAVIGATOR 43	KTH	SA/CR	FBG KL	VD	75D	NISS	13	31500	5 8	86100	94600
42 11	PASSAGEMAKER 42	CUT	SA/CR	FBG KL	IB	36D	PERK	13	31500	5 8	81300	89400
42 11	PASSAGEMAKER 42	KTH	SA/CR	FBG KL	IB	36D	PERK	13	31500	5 8	81400	89500
42 11	PASSAGEMAKER 43	CUT	SA/CR	FBG KL	VD	75D	NISS	13	31500	5 8	78200	85900
42 11	PASSAGEMAKER 43	KTH	SA/CR	FBG KL	VD	75D	NISS	13	31500	5 8	78300	86100
42 11	VOYAGER 42	CUT	SA/CR	FBG KL	IB	36D	PERK	13	31500	5 8	73400	80700
42 11	VOYAGER 42	KTH	SA/CR	FBG KL	IB	36D	PERK	13	31500	5 8	73500	80800
42 11	VOYAGER 43	CUT	SA/CR	FBG KL	VD	75D	NISS	13	31500	5 8	70400	77400
42 11	VOYAGER 43	KTH	SA/CR	FBG KL	VD	75D	NISS	13	31500	5 8	70600	77500
--- 1976 BOATS ---												
28 3	WESTSAIL 28	CUT	SAIL	FBG KL	IB	10D -	12D	9 7	9500	4	20300	22600
32	WESTSAIL 32	CUT	SAIL	FBG KL	IB	25D -	50D	11	19500	5	42100	46800
42 11	WESTSAIL 42	CUT	SAIL	FBG KL	IB	50D	PERK	13	31500	5 8	73400	80600
42 11	WESTSAIL 43	CUT	SAIL	FBG KL	IB	50D	PERK	13	31500	5 8	73600	80900
42 11	WESTSAIL 43	CUT	SAIL	FBG KL	IB	85D		13	31500	5 8	77900	85600
42 11	WESTSAIL 43	KTH	SAIL	FBG KL	IB	50D	PERK	13	31500	5 8	73800	81100
42 11	WESTSAIL 43	CUT	SAIL	FBG KL	IB	85D	PERK	13	31500	5 8	77900	85600
42 11	WESTSAIL 43	KTH	SAIL	FBG KL	IB	85D	PERK	13	31500	5 8	76100	83700
--- 1975 BOATS ---												
32	WESTSAIL 32	CUT	SAIL	FBG KL	IB	25D -	50D	11	19500	5	41200	45800
42 11	WESTSAIL 42	CUT	SAIL	FBG KL	IB	50D	PERK	13	32000	6	74600	82000
42 11	WESTSAIL 42	CUT	SAIL	FBG KL	IB	72D	PERK	13	32000	6	74900	82300
42 11	WESTSAIL 42	KTH	SAIL	FBG KL	IB	50D	PERK	13	32000	6	74700	82100
42 11	WESTSAIL 42	KTH	SAIL	FBG KL	IB	72D	PERK	13		6	74300	81600
--- 1974 BOATS ---												
31	WESTSAIL 32	CUT	SAIL	FBG KL	IB	25D	VLVO	11	19500	5	41300	45900
32	WESTSAIL 32	CUT	SAIL	FBG KL	IB	50D	PERK	11	19500	5	40400	44800
42 10	WESTSAIL 42	CUT	SAIL	FBG KL	IB	36D	PERK	13	32000	5 8	72700	79900
--- 1973 BOATS ---												
32	WESTSAIL 32	CUT	SAIL	FBG KL	IB	25D -	50D	11	19500	5	39600	44000
--- 1972 BOATS ---												
32	WESTSAIL 32	CUT	SAIL	FBG KL	IB	D	11		5		38800	43100
32	WESTSAIL 32	KTH	SAIL	FBG KL	IB	D	11		5		38800	43100

WESTWIND YACHTS
DIV OF NAVAL DESIGN SERVICES

Call 1-800-327-6929 for BUC Personalized Evaluation Service
Or, for 1967 to 1976 boats, sign onto www.BUCValuPro.com

WHEELER FIBRE GLASS BOAT CORP

Call 1-800-327-6929 for BUC Personalized Evaluation Service
Or, for 1961 boats, sign onto www.BUCValuPro.com

WHEELER YACHT CORP

TOMS RIVER NJ   See inside cover to adjust price for area

LOA FT IN	NAME AND/ OR MODEL	TOP/ RIG	BOAT TYPE	-HULL- MTL TP	----ENGINE--- TP # HP MFG	BEAM FT IN	WGT LBS	DRAFT FT IN	RETAIL LOW	RETAIL HIGH
------------------- 1966 BOATS --
38			SDN	WD	IB T210	13 4		2 10	37300	41500
38		FB	SDN	WD	IB T210	13 4		2 10	37400	41600
	IB T238	37500	41700, IB T277		37700 41900, IB T280				37700	41900
	IB T290	37800	42000, IB T185D		43400 48300					
------------------- 1962 BOATS --
34	9 PLAYMATE		SDN	WD	IB T125-T215				20400	23600
34	9 SPORTSMAN FAM CR	CR	WD		IB T125-T215				18200	21100
37	8	SDN	WD		IB T195				32900	36500
37	8 SPORTSMAN FAM CR	CR	WD		IB T195				25000	27800
	IB T215	25100	27900, IB T225		25100 27900, IB T238				25100	27900
	IB T120D	32800	36500							
39	10	SF	WD		IB T181D				43800	48700
39	10 PLAYMATE	SDN	WD		IB T195				37300	41500
	IB T215	37400	41500, IB T225		37400 41600, IB T238				37400	41600
	IB T120D	44300	49200, IB T181D		45700 50200					
39	10 PLAYMATE	SF	WD		IB T195				36700	40800
	IB T215	36700	40800, IB T225		36700 40800, IB T238				36800	40900
	IB T275	36900	41000, IB T120D		42900 47700					
39	10 SPORTSMAN FAM CR	CR	WD		IB T195				29100	32300
	IB T215	29100	32400, IB T225		29200 32400, IB T238				29200	32400
	IB T120D	40800	45300, IB T181D		41700 46300					
43	GULFSTREAM	FB	SDN	WD	IB T225				32100	35700
43	GULFSTREAM	FB	SDN	WD	IB T275				33600	37300
43	GULFSTREAM	FB	SDN	WD	IB T181D				36300	40300
43	GULFSTREAM	FB	SF	WD	IB T225				41700	46300
43	GULFSTREAM	FB	SF	WD	IB T275				44300	49200
43	GULFSTREAM	FB	SF	WD	IB T181D				45800	50300
43	PROMENADE DECK		MY	WD	IB T195				40800	45300
	IB T215	41600	46300, IB T225		42000 46700, IB T238				42500	47300
	IB T181D	47500	52200							
50	PROMENADE DECK		MY	WD	IB T275				49500	54400
50	PROMENADE DECK		MY	WD	IB T230D				52500	57700
55	PROMENADE DECK		MY	WD	IB T235D				69000	75800
55	PROMENADE DECK		MY	WD	IB T308D				69300	76100
60	PROMENADE DECK		MY	WD	IB T235D				80100	88000
60	PROMENADE DECK		MY	WD	IB T308D				86200	94700
64	10 PROMENADE DECK		MY	WD	IB T235D				118500	130000
64	10 PROMENADE DECK		MY	WD	IB T308D				126500	139000
------------------- 1961 BOATS --
25	BIMINI			WD	IB 200 CHRY				4450	5100
34		CR	WD		IB T195	11 6		2 6	15700	17900
34		SDN	WD		IB T195	11 6		2 6	17600	20000
37		CR	WD		IB T195	12		2 9	27800	30900
37		SDN	WD		IB T195	12		2 9	26300	29200
40		CR	WD		IB T195	12 6		2 10	32600	36200
40	FISHERMAN	SF	WD		IB	12 6		2 10	**	**
40	SEDAN CR	SDN	WD		IB	12 6		2 10	**	**
43	FISHERMAN	SF	WD		IB	13 3		3	**	**
43	PROMENADE DECK	MY	WD		IB T225	14 4		3 6	44300	49200
43	SEDAN "A"	SDN	WD		IB	13 3		3	**	**
43	SEDAN "B"	SDN	WD		IB	13 3		3	**	**
48	PROMENADE DECK	MY	WD		IB	14 6		3 6	**	**
50	PROMENADE DECK	MY	WD		IB	14 6		3 10	**	**
55	PROMENADE DECK	MY	WD		IB T235D	15 3		4	67400	74000
60	PROMENADE DECK	MY	WD		IB	16		4 6	**	**
65	PROMENADE DECK	MY	WD		IB	16 6		5	**	**
------------------- 1960 BOATS --
25	SEMI	SDN	FBG		IB 177	8 6		1 9	5250	6050
28	FAMILY CRUISER	CR	FBG		IB 225	9 6		2	7400	8500
34		CR	WD		IB T177	11 6		2 6	15300	17400
34	SPORTSMAN FAMILY CR	CR	WD		IB T177	11 6		2 6	**	**
34	SPORTSMAN FAMILY CR	CR	FBG		IB T177	11 6		2 6	15300	17400
37		SF	WD		IB T177	12		2 9	26100	29000
37	SPORTSMAN FAM CR	CR	WD		IB T177	12		2 9	27200	30200
39	10 FAMILY CRUISER	CR	WD		IB T177	16 6		2 10	25200	28000
39	10 PROMENADE DECK	MY	WD		IB T177	13 2		3	34100	37900
39	10 SPORT FISH	SF	WD		IB	12 8		2 10	**	**
39	10 TRI-CAB CRUISING SDN	TCMY	WD		IB	12 8		2 10	**	**
40		DC	WD		IB T200				43800	48600
43		SDN	WD		IB T177				29500	32800
43	GULFSTREAM	SF	WD		IB T177				37400	41500
45	PROMENADE DECK	MY	WD		IB T177	13 6		3 3	37900	42100
------------------- 1959 BOATS --
31	PLAYMATE		CR	WD	IB T125-T177	11			10400	12300
31	PLAYMATE	FB	CR	WD	IB T125-T177	11			10400	12300
34	PLAYMATE		CR	WD	IB T125-T177	11 6			14500	17100
34	PLAYMATE	FB	CR	WD	IB T125-T177	11 6			14600	17100
34	PLAYMATE		SDN	WD	IB T125-T177	11 6			16200	19000
37	PLAYMATE		CR	WD	IB T125	12			26300	29200
	IB T177	26600	29600, IB T225		26800 29800, IB T130D				31500	35000
37	PLAYMATE	FB	CR	WD	IB T125	12			26300	29300
	IB T177	26700	29600, IB T225		26900 29800, IB T130D				31500	35000
37	PLAYMATE		SDN	WD	IB T125	12			24800	27500
	IB T177	25200	28000, IB T225		25400 28200, IB T130D				30400	33800
40	PLAYMATE		CR	WD	IB T125	12 6			30900	34400
	IB T177	31300	34800, IB T225		31400 34900, IB T130D				38300	42500
40	PLAYMATE	FB	CR	WD	IB T125	12 6			31000	34400
	IB T177	31400	34800, IB T225		31500 35000, IB T130D				38300	42500
40	PLAYMATE		SDN	WD	IB T125	12 6			34900	38800
	IB T177	35300	39200, IB T225		35400 39300, IB T130D				45700	50200
43	DELUXE		SDN	WD	IB T225	13 3			29400	32700
43	DELUXE EXP		SDN	WD	IB T225	13 3			31100	34500
46	PROMENADE DECK DLX		MY	WD	IB T225	14 4			39800	44200
48	PROMENADE DECK DLX		MY	WD	IB T225	14 6			43300	48100
53	PROMENADE DECK DLX		MY	WD	IB T 71D	14 10			55800	61400
58	PROMENADE DECK DLX		MY	WD	IB T 71D	15 6			56300	61900
61	PROMENADE DECK DLX		MY	WD	IB T 71D	16			60900	66900
65	PROMENADE DECK DLX		MY	WD	IB T 71D	16 6			89700	98600
72	PROMENADE DECK DLX		MY	WD	IB T 71D	17 6			**	**
------------------- 1958 BOATS --
38			SDN	WD	IB T135				30600	34100
38			SDN	WD	IB T225				31100	34500
38			SDN	WD	IB T151D				35700	39600
43			SDN	WD	IB T225				31300	34800
43			EXP	WD	IB T225				32600	36200
43			EXP	WD	IB T275				31400	34900
43		HT	EXP	WD	IB T225				32700	36300
43		HT	EXP	WD	IB T275				30200	33600
43			SDN	WD	IB T225				29500	32800
43			SDN	WD	IB T275				34300	34300
43			SDN	WD	IB T151D				32900	36500
43			SF	WD	IB T225				38500	42800
43			SF	WD	IB T275				40900	45500
43	CONT		SDN	WD	IB T225				29900	33200
43	CONT		SDN	WD	IB T275				31300	34700
43	CONT		SDN	WD	IB T151D				35700	35700
43	PROMENADE DECK		MY	WD	IB T225				38900	43200
43	PROMENADE DECK		MY	WD	IB T275				40700	45200
43	PROMENADE DECK		MY	WD	IB T151D				44300	46600
43	PROMENADE DECK	HT	MY	WD	IB T225				39000	43400
43	PROMENADE DECK	HT	MY	WD	IB T275				40800	45400
43	PROMENADE DECK	HT	MY	WD	IB T151D				42100	46800
43	2		EXP	WD	IB T151D				37600	41700
43	2	HT	EXP	WD	IB T151D				37700	41800
46	PROMENADE DECK	HT	MY	WD	IB T275				37700	41900
46	PROMENADE DECK	HT	MY	WD	IB T151D				53000	58300
46	PROMENADE DECK		SF	WD	IB T275				41700	46300
46	PROMENADE DECK		SF	WD	IB T151D				40100	44600
48		FB	SDN	WD	IB T275				33800	37600
48		FB	SDN	WD	IB T235D				43500	48300
48	PROMENADE DECK		MY	WD	IB T275				42800	47500
48	PROMENADE DECK		MY	WD	IB T151D				55600	61100
48	PROMENADE DECK		MY	WD	IB T235D				47700	52500

96th ed. - Vol. III   CONTINUED ON NEXT PAGE   675

LOA FT IN	NAME AND/ OR MODEL	TOP/ RIG	BOAT TYPE	-HULL- MTL TP	----ENGINE--- TP # HP MFG	BEAM FT IN	WGT LBS	DRAFT FT IN	RETAIL LOW	RETAIL HIGH
					1958 BOATS					
53	PROMENADE DECK	MY	WD	IB	T235D				60900	66900
58	PROMENADE DECK	MY	WD	IB	T235D				68400	75200
61	PROMENADE DECK	MY	WD	IB	T235D				71700	78800
65	PROMENADE DECK	MY	WD	IB	T235D				110500	121500
65	PROMENADE DECK	MY	WD	IB	T289D				116000	127500
					1957 BOATS					
34		CR	WD	IB	T225				15000	17000
43	PROMENADE DECK	MY	WD	IB	T225				38300	42500
55	PROMENADE DECK	MY	WD	IB	T271D				61700	67800
					1956 BOATS					
42		SF	WD	IB	T225				20800	23100
42	DELUXE	SDN	WD	IB	T200				40300	44800
42	PROMENADE DECK	MY	WD	IB	T200				34300	38100
52	PROMENADE DECK	MY	WD	IB	T271D				47800	52500
61	PROMENADE DECK	MY	WD	IB	T275D				73100	80300
61	PROMENADE DECK	MY	WD	IB	T300D				75200	82700
					1955 BOATS					
42	PROMENADE DECK	MY	WD	IB	T225				34500	38300
50	PROMENADE DECK	HT MY	WD	IB	T D GM				**	**
57	PROMENADE DECK	MY	WD	IB	T200D				62700	68900
65	PROMENADE DECK	MY	WD	IB	T300				128500	141000
					1954 BOATS					
38		FB	SDN	WD	IB	T225				29400	32600
40		FB	SF	WD	IB	T280D GM				40200	44700
40		FB	SF	WD	RB IB	T200 CHRY				32200	35800
42		SF	WD	IB	T225				20200	22500
50		FB	FD	WD	RB IB	T216D GM				**	**
61	PROMENADE DECK	MY	WD	IB	T200D				64800	71200
					1953 BOATS					
30		SF	WD	IB	T235				8700	10000
42	PROMENADE DECK	MY	WD	IB	T165				32100	35600
48	PROMENADE DECK	MY	WD	IB	T271D				44600	49600
65	PROMENADE DECK	MY	WD	IB	T271D				107000	117500
					1952 BOATS					
42		SF	WD	IB	T225				20200	22400
48		SDN	WD	IB	T275				31200	34600
50	PROMENADE DECK	MY	WD	IB	T235				41300	45900
52	PROMENADE DECK	MY	WD	IB	T271D				45900	50400
55	PROMENADE DECK	MY	WD	IB	T271D				58000	63800
					1951 BOATS					
33		FB	SDN	WD	IB	T115				12200	13900
35		EXP	WD	IB	T125				16200	18400
44	PROMENADE DECK	MY	WD	IB	T225				27300	30300
					1950 BOATS					
36		HT	DC	WD	IB					**	**
36		HT	EXP	WD	IB					**	**
36		HT	SDN	WD	IB					**	**
40		HT	SDN	MHG	IB					**	**
43	PROMENADE DECK	MY	WD	IB	T275				37200	41300
48	PROMENADE DECK	MY	WD	IB	T200D				42300	47000
50	PROMENADE DECK	MY	WD	IB	T275				40500	45000
					1949 BOATS					
32		HT	SDN	WD	IB	CHRY				**	**
36		HT	SDN	WD	IB T	CHRY				**	**
36		HT	SF	WD	IB T	CHRY				**	**
40		HT	SDN	WD	IB T	CHRY				**	**
46		HT	SDN	WD	IB T					**	**
53		FB	MY	WD	IB T					**	**
60		HT	MY	WD	IB T					**	**
					1948 BOATS					
48	PROMENADE DECK	MY	WD	IB	T275				38200	42500
					1946 BOATS					
28	PLAYMATE	HT	SDN	WD	IB					**	**
32	SUNLOUNGER		WD	IB	T150				9150	10400
36	SUNLOUNGER	HT	SDN	WD	IB					**	**
40		HT	DC	WD	IB					**	**
40	SUNLOUNGER		WD	IB	T160				26800	29800
46		HT	DC	WD	IB					**	**
50		FB	MY	WD	IB					**	**
55		FB	MY	WD	IB					**	**
60		FB	TCMY	WD	IB					**	**
					1940 BOATS					
36			SDNSF	WD	IB	T145				21100	23500
38			SDN	WD	IB	T 95				27800	30800
					1939 BOATS					
30			SDN	WD	IB	135				7150	8200
33		HT	SDN	WD	IB					**	**
36		HT	DC	WD	IB					**	**
40		HT	SDN	WD	IB					**	**
43		HT	DC	WD	IB					**	**
45	PROMENADE DECK	MY	WD	IB	T200D				34800	38600
					1938 BOATS					
30		CR	WD	IB	85				6800	7850
35		SDN	WD	IB	140				15500	17600
42		WD	IB	T350D LEHM	23443				**	**
					1937 BOATS					
22	SEA SKIFF	WD	IB						**	**
26		SF	WD	IB						**	**
26	PLAYMATE	FB	CR	WD	IB	72 LYCO				5350	6200
28	PLAYMATE	HT	SDN	WD	IB					**	**
30	PLAYMATE	HT	CR	WD	IB					**	**
32	PLAYMATE	HT	SDN	WD	IB					**	**
35	MONTAUK	FB	SF	WD	IB					**	**
35	PLAYMATE	HT	CR	WD	IB					**	**
39	PLAYMATE	HT	DC	WD	IB T					**	**
40		CR	WD	IB	T125				25200	28000
42	PLAYMATE	HT	SDN	WD	IB T D				**	**
46	GULFSTREAM	FSH	WD	IB	T325 LYCO				38700	43000
46	PLAYMATE	HT	SDN	WD	IB					**	**
50		SF	WD	IB						**	**
54		FB	MY	WD	IB	T150D				56300	61900
65		HT	MY	WD	IB					**	**
					1936 BOATS					
35		CR	WD	IB	151				13800	15700
					1935 BOATS					
39 3		WD	IB	T325 MRCR					**	**
					1933 BOATS					
22	SEA SKIFF	OP	FSH	WD	IB					**	**
26	SEA SKIFF	FSH	WD	IB	CHRY				**	**
27	PLAYMATE	CR	WD	IB						**	**
31	PLAYMATE	CR	WD	IB						**	**
35		HT	SDN	WD	IB					**	**
38	PLAYMATE	CR	WD	IB						**	**
					1932 BOATS					
23	PLAYMATE	HT	CR	WD	IB					**	**
26	PLAYMATE	HT	CR	WD	IB					**	**
28		SF	WD	IB	110 PALM				7400	8500
28	PLAYMATE	HT	CR	WD	IB	CHRY				**	**
30	PLAYMATE	HT	SDN	WD	IB	180 STER				8450	9700
34	PLAYMATE	HT	CBNCR	WD	IB					**	**
34	PLAYMATE	HT	DC	WD	IB					**	**
38	PLAYMATE	HT	SDN	WD	IB	150 STER				30600	34000
41	PLAYMATE	HT	DC	WD	IB	150 STER				37500	41600
50	PLAYMATE	HT	MY	WD	IB	100D				56700	62300
					1931 BOATS					
22	PLAYMATE	SDN	WD	IB	CHRY				**	**
27	PLAYMATE	HT	CR	WD	IB	CHRY				**	**
30	PLAYMATE	HT	CR	WD	IB	CHRY				**	**
34	PLAYMATE	HT	DC	WD	IB	CHRY				**	**
37	PLAYMATE	HT	SDN	WD	IB	150 STER				24900	27600
62	PLAYMATE	MY	WD	IB						**	**
66		WD	IB	D GM					**	**

WHITBY BOAT WORKS LTD

WHITBY ONTARIO CANADA   COAST GUARD MFG ID- WBW See inside cover to adjust price for area

For more recent years, see the BUC Used Boat Price Guide, Volume 1 or Volume 2

LOA FT IN	NAME AND/ OR MODEL	TOP/ RIG	BOAT TYPE	-HULL- MTL TP	----ENGINE--- TP # HP MFG	BEAM FT IN	WGT LBS	DRAFT FT IN	RETAIL LOW	RETAIL HIGH
					1983 BOATS					
30 3	ALBERG 30	SLP	SA/RC	FBG KL SD	13D VLVO	8 9	9000	4 3	22600	25100
37	ALBERG 37	SLP	SA/RC	FBG KL SD	23D VLVO	10	16800	5 6	50700	55700
37 2	ALBERG 37	YWL	SA/RC	FBG KL SD	23D VLVO	10 2	16800	5 6	50700	55700
42	WHITBY 42	CUT	SA/CR	FBG KL IB	67D LEHM	13	23500	5	85700	94200
42	WHITBY 42	KTH	SA/CR	FBG KL IB	67D LEHM	13	23500	5	84000	92300
42	WHITBY 42 CUTTER RIG	KTH	SA/CR	FBG KL IB	67D LEHM	13	23500	5	87500	96100
45	WHITBY 45 MARK II	SLP	SA/RC	FBG KL IB	50D PERK	12	22100	8	102000	112500
45	WHITBY 45 MARK II	SLP	SA/RC	FBG KL IB	50D PERK	12	22100	8	99400	109000
					1982 BOATS					
30 3	ALBERG 30	SLP	SA/RC	FBG KL SD	13D VLVO	8 9	9000	4 3	21400	23800
37	ALBERG 37	SLP	SA/RC	FBG KL SD	19D VLVO	10	16800	5 6	48000	52700
37 2	ALBERG 37	YWL	SA/RC	FBG KL SD	19D VLVO	10 2	16800	5 6	48000	52700
42	WHITBY 42	CUT	SA/CR	FBG KL IB	67D LEHM	13	23500	5	81300	89300

LOA FT IN	NAME AND/ OR MODEL	TOP/ RIG	BOAT TYPE	-HULL- MTL TP	----ENGINE--- TP # HP MFG	BEAM FT IN	WGT LBS	DRAFT FT IN	RETAIL LOW	RETAIL HIGH
---	--- 1982 BOATS ---									
42	WHITBY 42	KTH	SA/CR	FBG KL IB	67D LEHM 13		23500	5	79500	87400
42	WHITBY 42 CUTTER RIG	KTH	SA/CR	FBG KL IB	67D LEHM 13		23500	5	83000	91200
45	WHITBY 45	SLP	SA/CR	FBG KL IB	51D PERK 12		23500	6	96900	106500
45	WHITBY 45	SLP	SA/RC	FBG KL IB	51D PERK 12		22100	8	94200	103500
---	--- 1981 BOATS ---									
30	3 ALBERG 30	SLP	SA/RC	FBG KL IB	13D 8 9		9000	4 3	20300	22600
37	2 ALBERG 37	SLP	SA/RC	FBG KL IB	10 2		16800	4 6	45900	50500
37	2 ALBERG 37	SLP	SA/RC	FBG KL IB	19D VLVO 10		16800	4 6	45700	50200
37	2 ALBERG 37	YWL	SA/RC	FBG KL IB	D 10		16800	4 6	45900	50500
37	2 ALBERG 37	YWL	SA/RC	FBG KL IB	19D VLVO 10		16800	5 6	45700	50200
42	WHITBY 42	CUT	SA/CR	FBG KL IB	67D LEHM 13		23500	5	77000	84600
42	WHITBY 42	KTH	SA/CR	FBG KL IB	D 13		23500	5	76800	84400
42	WHITBY 42	KTH	SA/CR	FBG KL IB	67D LEHM 13		23500	5	77000	84600
42	WHITBY 42 CUTTER RIG	KTH	SA/CR	FBG KL IB	67D LEHM 13		23500	5	77000	84600
---	--- 1980 BOATS ---									
30	3 ALBERG 30	SLP	SA/RC	FBG KL IB	13D VLVO 8 9		9000	4 3	19500	21700
37	2 ALBERG 37	SLP	SA/RC	FBG KL IB	19D VLVO 10		16800	5 6	43500	48400
37	2 ALBERG 37	YWL	SA/RC	FBG KL IB	19D VLVO 10		16800	5 6	43500	48400
42	WHITBY 42	KTH	SA/CR	FBG KL IB	67D LEHM 13		23500	5	74100	81400
---	--- 1979 BOATS ---									
30	3 ALBERG 30	SLP	SA/CR	FBG KL IB	13D VLVO 8 9		9000	4 3	19100	21200
37	2 ALBERG 37	SLP	SA/CR	FBG KL IB	19D VLVO 10		16800	5 6	42200	46800
37	2 ALBERG 37	YWL	SA/CR	FBG KL IB	19D VLVO 10		16800	5 6	42200	46800
42	WHITBY 42	KTH	SA/CR	FBG KL IB	67D LEHM 13		23500	5	71800	78900
---	--- 1978 BOATS ---									
27	7 WHITBY 27	SLP	SA/CR	FBG KL IB	D ACK 8 6		3740	5 3	7250	8300
30	3 ALBERG 30	SLP	SA/CR	FBG KL IB	13D VLVO 8 9		9000	4 4	18600	20600
37	2 ALBERG 37	SLP	SA/CR	FBG KL IB	19D VLVO 10 2		16800	5 6	40900	45500
37	2 ALBERG 37	YWL	SA/CR	FBG KL IB	19D VLVO 10 2		16800	5 6	40900	45500
42	WHITBY 42	KTH	SA/CR	FBG KL IB	67D LEHM 13		24000	5	70600	77600
---	--- 1977 BOATS ---									
27	7 WHITBY 27	SLP	SAIL	FBG KL IB	D 8 6		3740	5 3	7050	8100
30	3 ALBERG 30	SLP	SAIL	FBG KL IB	30 UNIV 8 9		9000	4 4	18000	20000
37	2 ALBERG 37	SLP	SAIL	FBG KL IB	25D VLVO 10 2		16800	4 6	39900	44400
37	2 ALBERG 37	YWL	SAIL	FBG KL IB	25D VLVO 10 2		16800	4 6	39900	44400
42	WHITBY 42	KTH	SAIL	FBG KL IB	80D LEHM 13		23500	5	68000	74800
---	--- 1976 BOATS ---									
30	3 ALBERG 30	SLP	SAIL	FBG KL IB	30 UNIV 8 9		9000	4 4	17200	19500
37	2 ALBERG 37	SLP	SAIL	FBG KL IB	25D VLVO 10 2		16800	5 6	39000	43300
37	2 ALBERG 37	YWL	SAIL	FBG KL IB	25D VLVO 10 2		16800	5 6	39000	43300
42	WHITBY 42	KTH	SAIL	FBG KL IB	67D LEHM 13		23500	5	66200	72800
---	--- 1975 BOATS ---									
30	3 ALBERG 30	SLP	SAIL	FBG KL IB	30 UNIV 8 9		9000	4 3	16800	19100
37	2 ALBERG 37 MKII	SLP	SAIL	FBG KL IB	D 10 2		16800	5 6	38200	42400
37	2 ALBERG 37 MKII	YWL	SAIL	FBG KL IB	D 10 2		16800	5 6	38200	42400
42	WHITBY 42	KTH	SAIL	FBG KL IB	63D PERK 13		23500	5	64300	70700
---	--- 1974 BOATS ---									
30	3 ALBERG 30	SLP	SAIL	FBG KL IB	30 UNIV 8 9		8500	4 3	15500	17600
37	2 ALBERG 37	SLP	SAIL	FBG KL IB	36D WEST 10 2		16800	5 6	37500	41700
37	2 ALBERG 37	YWL	SAIL	FBG KL IB	36D WEST 10 2		16800	5 6	37500	41700
42	WHITBY 42	KTH	SAIL	FBG KL IB	63D PERK 13		23500	5	63000	69300
---	--- 1973 BOATS ---									
30	3 ALBERG 30	SLP	SAIL	FBG KL IB	30 UNIV 8 9		8500	4 3	15200	17300
37	2 ALBERG 37	SLP	SAIL	FBG KL IB	36D WEST 10 2		16800	5 6	36800	40900
37	2 ALBERG 37	YWL	SAIL	FBG KL IB	36D WEST 10 2		16800	5 6	36800	40900
42	WHITBY 42	KTH	SAIL	FBG KL IB	63D PERK 13		23500	5	61900	68000
---	--- 1972 BOATS ---									
30	3 ALBERG 30	SLP	SAIL	FBG		30 UNIV 8 9		8500	4 3	14900	16900
37	2 ALBERG 37	SLP	SAIL	FBG	36D WEST 10 2		16800	5 6	36000	40000
37	2 ALBERG 37	YWL	SAIL	FBG	36D WEST 10 2		16800	5 6	36000	40000
42	WHITBY	KTH	SA/CR	FBG KL IB	D 13		23500	5	60800	66800
---	--- 1971 BOATS ---									
30	3 ALBERG 30	SLP	SAIL	FBG		30 UNIV 8 9		8500	4 3	14500	16500
37	2 ALBERG 37	SLP	SAIL	FBG	IB	30 UNIV 10 2		16800	5 6	35100	39000
45	WHITBY 45		SAIL	FBG	IB	45D WEST 12		24830	6 10	73000	80200
---	--- 1970 BOATS ---									
30	3 ALBERG 30	SLP	SAIL	FBG KL IB	30 UNIV 8 9		8500	4 3	14200	16100
37	2 ALBERG 37	SLP	SAIL	FBG KL IB	30 UNIV 10 2		16800	5 6	33700	37500
45	WHITBY 45	SLP	SAIL	FBG KL IB	36D WEST 12		24830	6 10	71100	78100
---	--- 1969 BOATS ---									
30	3 ALBERG 30	SLP	SAIL	FBG KL IB	30 8 9		9000	4 3	14700	16700
37	2 ALBERG 37	SLP	SAIL	FBG KL IB	30 10 2		16800	5 6	33000	36600
45	WHITBY 45	SLP	SAIL	FBG KL IB	36D PERK 12		24830	6 10	69100	75900
---	--- 1968 BOATS ---									
30	3 ALBERG 30	SLP	SAIL	FBG KL IB	30 8 9		9000	4 3	14400	16400
37	2 ALBERG 37	SLP	SAIL	FBG KL IB	30 10 2		16800	5 6	32300	35900
45	WHITBY	SLP	SAIL	FBG IB	36		24830		67200	73900
---	--- 1967 BOATS ---									
30	3 ALBERG 30	SLP	SAIL	FBG KL IB	30 8 9		9000	4 3	14100	16100
37	2 ALBERG 37	SLP	SAIL	FBG KL IB	30 10 2		16800	2 6	31700	35200
---	--- 1966 BOATS ---									
30	3 ALBERG 30	SLP	SAIL	FBG KL IB	30 8 9			4 4	9300	10600
---	--- 1965 BOATS ---									
30	3 ALBERG 30	SLP	SAIL	FBG IB	25				9150	10400

WHITCRAFT

LOA FT IN	NAME AND/ OR MODEL	TOP/ RIG	BOAT TYPE	-HULL- MTL TP	----ENGINE--- TP # HP MFG	BEAM FT IN	WGT LBS	DRAFT FT IN	RETAIL LOW	RETAIL HIGH
---	--- 1973 BOATS ---									
45	WHIT-CRAFT	HT	HB	FBG SV	VD T225 12		21100	3 2	32600	36200
45	WHIT-CRAFT	HT	HB	FBG SV	VD T160D 12		21100	3 2	38300	42500
50	WHIT-CRAFT	HT	HB	FBG SV	VD T280 12		24200	3 2	37100	41200
50	WHIT-CRAFT	HT	HB	FBG SV	VD T160D 12		24200	3 2	42000	46700
---	--- 1972 BOATS ---									
45	WHIT-CRAFT	HT	HB	FBG	VD T225 CHRY 12		21100	3 2	33700	37500
45	WHIT-CRAFT	HT	HB	FBG	VD T280 CHRY 12		21100	3 2	34100	37800
45	WHIT-CRAFT	HT	HB	FBG	VD T160D PERK 12		21100	3 2	41300	45900
45	WHIT-CRAFT	FB	HB	FBG	VD T225 CHRY 12			3 2	33800	37500
45	WHIT-CRAFT	FB	HB	FBG	VD T280 CHRY 12			3 2	34100	37900
45	WHIT-CRAFT	FB	HB	FBG	VD T160D PERK 12			3 2	41700	46400
50	WHIT-CRAFT	HT	HB	FBG	VD T280 CHRY 12		24200	3 2	38200	42400
	VD T330 CHRY 39100	43500, VD T160D PERK 46400 51000, VD T180D PERK 47100 51800
50	WHIT-CRAFT	HT	HB	FBG	VD T280 CHRY 12			3 2	38300	42500
	VD T330 CHRY 38900	43300, VD T160D PERK 46400 50900, VD T180D PERK 46900 51500
	VD T216D GM 46600	51200, VD T225D CAT 48400 53200
---	--- 1971 BOATS ---									
36	WHIT-CRAFT	HT	HB	FBG	IB T155 CHRY 12		11000	2 6	26400	29300
36	WHIT-CRAFT	HT	HB	FBG	IB T225 CHRY 12		11500	2 6	27500	30600
45	WHIT-CRAFT	HT	HB	FBG	IB T225 CHRY 12		21100	3 2	33400	37100
45	WHIT-CRAFT	HT	HB	FBG	IB T280 CHRY 12		21500	3 2	34000	37800
45	WHIT-CRAFT	HT	HB	FBG	IB T160D PERK 12		22500	3 2	41900	46600
---	--- 1970 BOATS ---									
31	4 WHIT-CRAFT			FBG	IB T225 12 5			2 4	8000	9200
36	WHIT-CRAFT	HT	HB	FBG SV	IO 225 12		10960	2 4	22800	25300
36	WHIT-CRAFT	HT	HB	FBG SV	IO T155 12		10960	2 4	24400	27100
36	WHIT-CRAFT	HT	HB	FBG SV	IO 225 12		10960	2 6	22800	25300
36	WHIT-CRAFT	FB	HB	FBG SV	IO T155 12		10960	2 6	24400	27100
36	WHIT-CRAFT	FB	HB	FBG SV	IO 225 12		10960	2 6	25000	27800
36	1 WHIT-CRAFT	CNV		FBG	IB 220D 12 9			3	18300	20300
38	WHIT-CRAFT	CR		FBG	IB T370D 12 7			3	25000	27800
38	4	DC		FBG	IB T283D 13 7			3 4	23900	26600
39	WHIT-CRAFT	HT	HB	FBG SV	IB T225 12		13000	2 4	26600	29600
39	WHIT-CRAFT	FB	HB	FBG SV	IB T225 12		13000	2 4	26600	29600
40	9	CNV		FBG	IB T370D 14			2 11	33700	37400
40	11	CR		FBG	IB T283D 14			3	23400	26000
44	8	CR		FBG	IB T283D 14 7			3 6	24200	26800
45	2	CNV		FBG	IB T350D 14 7			4	47600	52300
53	1	MY		FBG	IB T350D 15 10			4	45700	50200
53	7	CNV		FBG	IB T350D 16			4	49600	54600
---	--- 1969 BOATS ---									
36	WHIT-CRAFT	HT	HB	FBG	IO 225 CHRY 11 11		10500	2 4	23600	26200
36	WHIT-CRAFT	HT	HB	STL	IO 225 CHRY 11 11		10500	2 4	20300	22600
36	WHIT-CRAFT	HT	HB	FBG	IO 225 CHRY 11 11		10500	2 4	23800	26500
36	WHIT-CRAFT	HT	HB	STL	IO 225 CHRY 11 11		10500	2 4	20500	22800
36	WHIT-CRAFT	HT	HB	FBG	IO T155 CHRY 11 11		10500	2 4	25200	28100
36	WHIT-CRAFT	HT	HB	STL	IO T155 CHRY 11 11		10500	2 4	21800	24200
37	WHIT-CRAFT	HT	HB	FBG	IO T155 CHRY 11 11		10800	2 4	25300	28100
37	WHIT-CRAFT	HT	HB	STL	IO T155 CHRY 11 11		10800	2 4	20700	23000
37	WHIT-CRAFT	HT	HB	STL	IO T155 CHRY 11 11		10800	2 4	21800	24200
39	WHIT-CRAFT	HT	HB	STL	IO T155 CHRY 11 11		14900	2 4	24800	24800
39	WHIT-CRAFT	HT	HB	FBG	IO T155 CHRY 11 11		14900	2 4	29900	33200
39	WHIT-CRAFT	HT	HB	STL	IO T155 CHRY 11 11		14900	2 4	24800	27600
39	WHIT-CRAFT	HT	HB	STL	IO T225 CHRY 11 11		14900	2 4	26100	29000
39	WHIT-CRAFT	HT	HB	FBG	IO T225 CHRY 11 11		14900	2 4	30300	33700

LOA FT IN	NAME AND/ OR MODEL	TOP/ RIG	BOAT TYPE	HULL MTL TP	TP	ENGINE # HP	MFG	BEAM FT IN	WGT LBS	DRAFT FT IN	RETAIL LOW	RETAIL HIGH
						1968 BOATS						
35	WHIT-CRAFT	HT	HB	STL SV	IO	150		10 6	9800	2 3	18300	20400
37	WHIT-CRAFT	HT	HB	STL SV	IO	210		11 11	10800	2 6	19100	21300
37	WHIT-CRAFT	HT	HB	STL SV	IO	T210		11 11	10800	2 6	20900	23200
38	WHIT-CRAFT	HT	HB	STL SV	IO	210		11 11	14000	2 3	22100	24500
40	WHIT-CRAFT	HT	HB	STL SV	IO	260		11 11	13400	2 3	21500	23900
40	WHIT-CRAFT	HT	HB	STL SV	IO	T210		11 11	13400	2 6	22500	24900
40	WHIT-CRAFT	HT	HB	STL SV	IO	T260		11 11	13400	2 3	23200	25800
41	WHIT-CRAFT	HT	HB	STL SV	IO	T210		11 11	15000	2 6	23800	26500
43	WHIT-CRAFT	HT	HB	STL SV	IO	T175		11 11	16000	2 10	24700	27400
	IO T210	24900	27700, IO T250	MRCR	25500	28300, IO T260					25700	28600
						1967 BOATS						
35	WHIT-CRAFT	HT	HB	STL	IO	150				2 3	21000	23400
35	WHIT-CRAFT	HT	HB	STL	IO	210	CHRY			2 3	23000	25600
38	WHIT-CRAFT	HT	HB	STL	IO	210	CHRY			2 3	23600	26300
41	WHIT-CRAFT	HT	HB	STL	IO	T210	CHRY			2 7	25500	28300
						1966 BOATS						
34	WHIT-CRAFT	HT	HB	STL	IO	45		10	425	2	**	**
41	WHIT-CRAFT	HT	HB	STL	IO	210		12		2 6	23500	26200
						1965 BOATS						
32	WHIT-CRAFT	HT	HB	STL TR	OB			13		5	6500	7500
32	WHIT-CRAFT	HT	HB	STL TR	OB	165	INT	13		8	19900	22100
34	WHIT-CRAFT	HT	HB	STL TR	OB			14		7	10200	11600
34	WHIT-CRAFT	HT	HB	STL TR	IO	210	CHRY	14		8	20500	22800
38	WHIT-CRAFT	HT	HB	STL TR	OB			14		5	14400	16300
38	WHIT-CRAFT	HT	HB	STL TR	IO	210		14		8	23400	26000
						1964 BOATS						
32	WHIT-CRAFT	HT	HB	STL CT	OB			10		5	6350	7300
32	WHIT-CRAFT	HT	HB	STL CT	IO	120-210		10		8	19400	21700
32	WHIT-CRAFT	HT	HB	STL TR	OB			10		5	6500	7450
32	WHIT-CRAFT	HT	HB	STL TR	IB	120-160		10		8	19800	22400
32	WHIT-CRAFT	HT	HB	STL TR	IO	165-210		10		8	19800	22400
36	WHIT-CRAFT	HT	HB	STL CT	OB			11 6		5	15000	17000
	IB 120	20200	22500, IB	140		20400	22700, IB	160			20600	22900
36	WHIT-CRAFT	HT	HB	STL TR	OB			11 6		5	15200	17300
	IB 120	20600	22900, IB	140		20800	23200, IB	160			21000	23300

WHITE CANOE COMPANY
OLD TOWN ME   COAST GUARD MFG ID- WCC See inside cover to adjust price for area

LOA FT IN	NAME AND/ OR MODEL	TOP/ RIG	BOAT TYPE	HULL MTL TP	TP	ENGINE # HP	MFG	BEAM FT IN	WGT LBS	DRAFT FT IN	RETAIL LOW	RETAIL HIGH
						1964 BOATS						
16 8	1680			FBG	IO	80-110					3550	4150
16 8	1760			FBG	IO	80-110					3300	3850
18	YORK-HARBOR 1810			WD	IO	80-110					3750	4400
18	YORK-HARBOR 1820			WD	IO	80-110					3950	4600
20	HARPSWELL 2010			WD	IO	105-120					5300	6150
20	HARPSWELL 2020			WD	IO	105-120					5550	6400
20	HARPSWELL 2040			WD	IO	105-120					6250	7200
20	HARPSWELL 2050			WD	IO	105-120					6350	7300
23	YARMOUTH 2310			WD	OB						1700	2050
23	YARMOUTH 2310			WD	IO	110-190					7750	9150
23	YARMOUTH 2320			WD	OB						1750	2050
23	YARMOUTH 2320			WD	IO	110-190					7800	9200
23	YARMOUTH 2340			WD	OB						2600	3050
23	YARMOUTH 2340			WD	IO	110-190					9400	10700
23	YARMOUTH 2350			WD	OB						2500	2900
23	YARMOUTH 2350			WD	IO	110-190					9500	10800
						1961 BOATS						
21 6			CR	L/P	OB			8 2			2500	2900
21 6			RNBT	L/P	OB			8 2			3450	4050
						1960 BOATS						
18 10	RUNABOUT		RNBT	L/P RB	OB			7 6			1700	2000
21 6	CRUISER		CR	L/P RB	OB			8 2			2550	2950
21 6	RUNABOUT		RNBT	L/P RB	OB			8 2			3550	4150

WHITE WATER MARINE
COAST GUARD MFG ID- WWM

Call 1-800-327-6929 for BUC Personalized Evaluation Service
Or, for 1979 to 1988 boats, sign onto www.BUCValuPro.com

WHITEMAN YACHT CO
COAST GUARD MFG ID- WYC

Call 1-800-327-6929 for BUC Personalized Evaluation Service
Or, for 1973 boats, sign onto www.BUCValuPro.com

WHITICAR BOAT WORKS INC
STUART FL 34997   See inside cover to adjust price for area

LOA FT IN	NAME AND/ OR MODEL	TOP/ RIG	BOAT TYPE	HULL MTL TP	TP	ENGINE # HP	MFG	BEAM FT IN	WGT LBS	DRAFT FT IN	RETAIL LOW	RETAIL HIGH
						1961 BOATS						
21	SHEARWATER	SF	P/M	IB	40		7			2	3650	4250
31	SHEARWATER	SF	P/M	IB	125		11			2 8	17300	19700
36	SHEARWATER	SF	P/M	IB	T225		12			3	41900	46600
38	SHEARWATER	SF	P/M	IB	T225		12			3	59100	65000
40	SHEARWATER	SF	P/M	IB	T225		12 8			3	65600	72100
42	SHEARWATER	SF	P/M	IB	T225		13 4			3 2	45500	50000
46	SHEARWATER	SF	P/M	IB	T225		13 8			3 4	95500	105000

WHITNEY OPERATIONS INC
FARMINGDALE NY   See inside cover to adjust price for area

LOA FT IN	NAME AND/ OR MODEL	TOP/ RIG	BOAT TYPE	HULL MTL TP	TP	ENGINE # HP	MFG	BEAM FT IN	WGT LBS	DRAFT FT IN	RETAIL LOW	RETAIL HIGH
						1970 BOATS						
30 1	SYSTEM	SLP	SAIL	FBG KL	IB	8	PALM	8 6		4 8	14300	16300
35	SYSTEM	SLP	SA/CR	FBG KL	IB	D			10000	6 5	24200	26900
40	SYSTEM	SLP	SA/CR	FBG KL	IB	D			13000	6 3	37500	41700
41	CARIB 41	SLP	SAIL	FBG KL	IB	D	PERK 14		14000	6 3	40900	45400
						1969 BOATS						
30 1	SYSTEM	SLP	SAIL	FBG KL	IB	8	PALM	8 6		4 8	14000	15900
						1932 BOATS						
25	WHITNEYACHT	HT	CR	WD	IB		FARR				**	**
34	WHITNEYACHT	HT	CR	WD	IB						**	**
36	WHITNEYACHT	HT	CR	WD	IB						**	**
42	WHITNEYACHT	HT	CR	WD	IB	T200					33800	37500
47	WHITNEYACHT	HT	CR	WD	IB						**	**

WIDEBEAM LIMITED
BELL WORKS
FORMERLY BELL WOODWORKING LTD

Call 1-800-327-6929 for BUC Personalized Evaluation Service
Or, for 1965 to 2001 boats, sign onto www.BUCValuPro.com

LEE S WILBUR & CO
MANSET ME 04656   COAST GUARD MFG ID- LSW See inside cover to adjust price for area

For more recent years, see the BUC Used Boat Price Guide, Volume 1 or Volume 2

LOA FT IN	NAME AND/ OR MODEL	TOP/ RIG	BOAT TYPE	HULL MTL TP	TP	ENGINE # HP	MFG	BEAM FT IN	WGT LBS	DRAFT FT IN	RETAIL LOW	RETAIL HIGH
						1983 BOATS						
34	WILBUR 34		SF	FBG DS	IB	200		12	14000	3 9	80400	88400
38	WILBUR 38		SF	FBG DS	IB	320		12 11	24000	4	149500	164000
						1982 BOATS						
34 4	WILBUR 34		FB	CBNCR	FBG	IB		11 11	15000	3 9	**	**
38			FB	SDN	FBG DS	IB	D	12 9	24000	4	**	**
38			FB	SF	FBG DS	IB	D	12 9	24000	4	**	**
38	EXTENDED CANOPY		FB	SDN	FBG DS	IB	D	12 9	24000	4	**	**
						1981 BOATS						
38			FB	SDN	FBG DS	IB	D GM	12 9	24000	4	**	**
38			FB	SF	FBG DS	IB	D GM	12 9	24000	4	**	**
38			FB	SDN	FBG DS	IB	D	12 9	24000	4	**	**
38	WILBUR 38		SF	FBG DS	IB	320		12 11			133500	146500
						1980 BOATS						
36	WILBUR 36	HT	SF	FBG SV	OB			11		3 6	**	**
38	WILBUR 38	FB	SF	FBG SV	OB			12 9		4	**	**
38 1	CRUISER		FB	CBNCR	FBG	IB		D	13 2	28000	4	**	**
38 1	CRUISER		FB	CBNCR	FBG	IB T	D	13 2	28000	4	**	**
38 1	EXTENDED CANOPY CR		FB	CBNCR	FBG	IB	D	13 2	28000	4	**	**
38 1	EXTENDED CANOPY CR		FB	CBNCR	FBG	IB T	D	13 2	28000	4	**	**

LEE S WILBUR & CO — CONTINUED

LOA FT	IN	NAME AND/OR MODEL	TOP/RIG	BOAT TYPE	HULL MTL	TP	TP	ENG #	HP	MFG	BEAM FT	IN	WGT LBS	DRAFT FT	IN	RETAIL LOW	RETAIL HIGH
		1980 BOATS															
38	1	SPORTFISHERMAN	FB	CBNCR	FBG	IB			D		13	2	26000	4		**	**
38	1	SPORTFISHERMAN	FB	CBNCR	FBG	IB		T	D		13	2	26000	4		**	**

WILDERNESS YACHT INC
SANTA CRUZ CA 95060   COAST GUARD MFG ID- WBK See inside cover to adjust price for area

LOA FT	IN	NAME AND/OR MODEL	TOP/RIG	BOAT TYPE	HULL MTL	TP	TP	ENG #	HP	MFG	BEAM FT	IN	WGT LBS	DRAFT FT	IN	RETAIL LOW	RETAIL HIGH
		1982 BOATS															
20	6	WILDERNESS 21	SLP	SA/RC	FBG	KL	OB				7	3	1870	4		3500	4100
29	9	WILDERNESS 30SX	SLP	SA/RC	F/S	KL	IB				8	10	4300	5	6	11800	13400
38	8	WILDERNESS 40	SLP	SA/RC	F/S	KL	IB		22D	YAN	12		9500	6	5	36500	40600
		1981 BOATS															
20	4	WILDERNESS 21	SLP	SA/RC	FBG	KL	OB				7	3	1800	4		3250	3750
29	9	WILDERNESS 30SX	SLP	SA/RC	F/S	KL	IB		D		8	10	4300	5	6	11300	12800
38	3	WILDERNESS 38	SLP	SA/RC	FBG	KL	IB				12		9000	6	6	31900	35500
38	8	WILDERNESS 40	SLP	SA/RC	F/S	KL	IB		22D	YAN	12		9500	6	5	34700	38600
		1980 BOATS															
20	4	WILDERNESS 21	SLP	SA/RC	FBG	KL	OB				7	3	1800	4		3100	3600
29	9	WILDERNESS 30SX	SLP	SA/RC	F/S	KL	IB		7D	BMW	8	10	4500	5	6	11000	12600
29	9	WILDERNESS 30SX	SLP	SA/RC	FBG	KL	IB		7D	BMW	8	9	4200	5	6	10400	11900
38	8	WILDERNESS 38	SLP	SA/RC	F/S	KL	IB		35D	BMW	12		9000	6	5	31500	35000
		1979 BOATS															
20	6	WILDERNESS 21	SLP	SA/RC	FBG	KL	OB				7	3	1870	4		3050	3550
38		WILDERNESS 38	SLP	SA/RC	F/S	KL	IB		16D	REN	12		9000	6	5	28300	31500

RALPH H WILEY
OXFORD MD   See inside cover to adjust price for area

LOA FT	IN	NAME AND/OR MODEL	TOP/RIG	BOAT TYPE	HULL MTL	TP	TP	ENG #	HP	MFG	BEAM FT	IN	WGT LBS	DRAFT FT	IN	RETAIL LOW	RETAIL HIGH
		1961 BOATS															
39		FOX	SLP	SA/CR	WD	KL	OB				9			5		33900	37700
42		QUICKSILVER	SLP	SA/CR	WD		OB				11			3		52200	57400
44		MOTORSAILER	SLP	MS	WD	KL					11			3	6	54200	59500
		1960 BOATS															
39		FOX	SLP	SA/CR	WD	KL	OB				9			5		34000	37800
42		QUICKSILVER	SLP	SA/CR	WD	CB	OB				11			3		52300	57500
44		MOTORSAILER	SLP	SA/CR	WD	KL					11			3	6	64400	70800
		1959															
41				SA/CR	WD	KC	OB				10	6				34900	38800
42				SA/CR	WD	KC	OB				11			2	6	52500	57700
44				MS	WD						11			3	6	54500	59900

R B WILK COMPANY

Call 1-800-327-6929 for BUC Personalized Evaluation Service
Or, for 1967 boats, sign onto www.BUCValuPro.com

WILKER BOATS LTD
COAST GUARD MFG ID- ZWB

Call 1-800-327-6929 for BUC Personalized Evaluation Service
Or, for 1979 boats, sign onto www.BUCValuPro.com

WILKINSON MARINE
COAST GUARD MFG ID- WKN

Call 1-800-327-6929 for BUC Personalized Evaluation Service
Or, for 1978 boats, sign onto www.BUCValuPro.com

WILKINSON MARINE CORP
COAST GUARD MFG ID- WKN

Call 1-800-327-6929 for BUC Personalized Evaluation Service
Or, for 1983 boats, sign onto www.BUCValuPro.com

THE WILLARD COMPANY INC
ANAHEIM CA 92806   COAST GUARD MFG ID- WLD See inside cover to adjust price for area

For more recent years, see the BUC Used Boat Price Guide, Volume 1 or Volume 2

LOA FT	IN	NAME AND/OR MODEL	TOP/RIG	BOAT TYPE	HULL MTL	TP	TP	ENG #	HP	MFG	BEAM FT	IN	WGT LBS	DRAFT FT	IN	RETAIL LOW	RETAIL HIGH
		1983 BOATS															
30		WILLARD 30	FB	TRWL	FBG	DS	IB		50D	PERK	10	6	16000	4	8	46000	50500
30		WILLARD 8 TON	CUT	SA/CR	FBG	KL	IB		50D	PERK	10	6	17000	4	8	41000	45500
39	9	WILLARD 40	KTH	MS	FBG	KL	IB		135D	PERK	13	8	33000	4	3	92600	101500
39	9	WILLARD 40	FB	TRWL	FBG	DS	IB		135D	PERK	13	8	33000	4	3	110000	121000
55		LAPWORTH 55	CUT	SA/CR	FBG	KL	IB		135D	PERK	14	6	45000	6		216500	238000
		1982 BOATS															
30		WILLARD 30	FB	TRWL	FBG	DS	IB		50D	PERK	10	6	16000	4	8	43700	48600
30		WILLARD 8 TON	CUT	SA/CR	FBG	KL	IB		50D	PERK	10	6	17000	4	8	38800	43100
39	9	WILLARD 40	KTH	MS	FBG	KL	IB		130D	PERK	13	8	33000	4	3	87700	96400
39	9	WILLARD 40	FB	TRWL	FBG	DS	IB		130D	PERK	13	8	33000	4	3	105000	115500
		1981 BOATS															
30		WILLARD 30	FB	TRWL	FBG	DS	IB		50D	PERK	10	6	16000	4	8	42000	46700
30		WILLARD 8 TON	CUT	SA/CR	FBG	KL	IB		50D	PERK	10	6	17000	4	8	36000	40900
35	2	HORIZON II	CUT	MS	FBG	KL	IB		D		10	6	17000	4	8	39600	44000
39	9	WILLARD 40	KTH	MS	FBG	KL	IB		130D	PERK	13	8	33000	4	3	83100	91300
39	9	WILLARD 40	FB	TRWL	FBG	DS	IB		130D	PERK	13	8	33000	4	3	100000	110000
		1980 BOATS															
30		WILLARD 30	FB	TRWL	FBG	DS	IB		50D	PERK	10	6	16000	4	8	40400	44900
30		WILLARD 8 TON	CUT	SA/CR	FBG	KL	IB		50D	PERK	10	6	17000	4	8	35400	39300
35	2	HORIZON II	CUT	MS	FBG	KL	IB				10	6	17000	4	8	38100	42300
39	9	WILLARD 40	KTH	MS	FBG	KL	IB		130D	PERK	13	8	33000	4	3	80000	87900
39	9	WILLARD 40	FB	TRWL	FBG	DS	IB		130D	PERK	13	8	33000	4	3	95400	105000
54		WILLARD 54	MY		FBG	DV	IB		T185		17	2				155500	171000
65		BARROWS 65	MY		FBG	DS	IB		T460		18					388500	427000
		1979 BOATS															
30		WILLARD 30		TRWL	FBG	DS	IB		60D		10	6	16000			38900	43200
30		WILLARD 8 TON	CUT	SA/CR	FBG	KL	IB		40D	PISC	10	6	17000	4	8	34300	38100
39	9	WILLARD 40	KTH	MS	FBG	KL	IB		130D	PERK	13	8	33000	4	3	77500	85100
39	9	WILLARD 40	FB	TRWL	FBG	DS	IB		130D	PERK	13	8	32000	4	3	88700	97500
54		WILLARD 54	MY		FBG	DS	IB		T185D		17	2				161500	177500
54		WILLARD 54	MY		FBG	DS	IB		T300D		17	2				165000	181000
		1978 BOATS															
30		WILLARD 30	HT	TRWL	FBG	DS	IB		50D	PERK	10	6	17000	4	8	39700	44100
30		WILLARD 30	FB	TRWL	FBG	DS	IB		50D	PERK	10	6	17000	4	8	39700	44100
30		WILLARD 8 TON	SLP	SA/CR	FBG	KL	VD		40D	PISC	10	6	17000	4	8	33300	37000
39	9	WILLARD 40	FB	TRWL	FBG	DS	VD		130D	PERK	13	8	33000	4	3	87100	95800
		1977 BOATS															
30		HORIZON II	CUT	MS	FBG	KL	IB		50D	PERK	10	6	17000	4	8	32400	36000
30		HORIZON II	KTH	MS	FBG	KL	IB		50D	PERK	10	6	17000	4	8	32400	36000
30		VEGA-NOMAD 30	FB	TRWL	FBG	KL	IB		50D	PERK	10	6	15000	3	6	33900	37700
30		VEGA-VOYAGER 30	HT	TRWL	FBG	KL	IB		50D	PERK	10	6	15000	3	6	34800	38600
30		VEGA-VOYAGER 30	FB	TRWL	FBG	KL	IB		50D	PERK	10	6	15000	3	6	34800	38600
30		WILLARD 8 TON	CUT	SAIL	FBG	KL	IB		50D	PERK	10	6	17000	4	8	32400	36000
30		WILLARD 8 TON	KTH	SAIL	FBG	KL	IB		50D	PERK	10	6	17000	4	8	32400	36000
39	9	VEGA FISHBOAT 40	HT	TRWL	FBG	KL	IB		130D	PERK	13	9	33000	4	6	65700	72200
39	9	VEGA-FREEDOM 40	HT	TRWL	FBG	KL	IB		130D	PERK	13	9	33000	4	6	99000	109000
39	9	VEGA-NOMAD 40	FB	TRWL	FBG	KL	IB		130D	PERK	13	9	33000	4	6	83200	91400
39	9	VEGA-VOYAGER 40	HT	TRWL	FBG	KL	IB		130D	PERK	13	9	33000	4	6	84900	93200
40		WILLARD 18 TON	CUT	SAIL	FBG	KL	IB		50D	PERK	13	9	36000	5	6	77600	85300
64		WILLARD V-64	MY		FBG		IB				18			3	3	**	**
75		WILLARD V-75	MY		FBG		IB				19	6		4	2	**	**
		1976 BOATS															
30		HORIZON II	CUT	MS	FBG	KL	IB		50D	PERK	10	6	15000	3	6	27700	30800
30		HORIZON II	CUT	MS	FBG	KL	IB		50D	PERK	10	6	17000	3	6	31600	35200
30		HORIZON II	KTH	MS	FBG	KL	IB		50D	PERK	10	6	17000	3	6	31600	35200
30		VEGA-NOMAD 30	FB	TRWL	FBG	KL	IB		50D	PERK	10	6	15000	3	6	31900	35400
30		VEGA-VOYAGER 30	HT	TRWL	FBG	KL	IB		50D	PERK	10	6	15000	3	6	32700	36300
30		VEGA-VOYAGER 30	FB	TRWL	FBG	KL	IB		50D	PERK	10	6	15000	3	6	33500	37200
30		WILLARD 8 TON	CUT	SAIL	FBG	KL	IB		25D- 50D		10	6	17000	4	8	31600	35200
30		WILLARD 8 TON	KTH	SAIL	FBG	KL	IB		25D- 50D		10	6	17000	4	8	31600	35200
39	9	NOMAD	HT	TRWL	FBG	KL	IB		130D	PERK	13	9	33000	4	6	79800	87700
39	9	VOYAGER	HT	TRWL	FBG	KL	IB		130D	PERK	13	9	33000	4	6	79800	87700
40		WILLARD 18 TON	CUT	MS	FBG	KL	IB		50D	PERK	13	9	36000	5	6	75700	83200
		1975 BOATS															
30		HORIZON	CUT	MS	FBG	KL	IB		55D	PERK	10	6	15000	3	6	27100	30100
30		NOMAD	FB	TRWL	FBG	KL	IB		55D	PERK	10	6	15000	3	6	31700	35200
30		SEARCHER	HT	TRWL	FBG	KL	IB		55D	PERK	10	6	15000	3	6	31700	35200
30		VOYAGER	FB	TRWL	FBG	KL	IB		55D	PERK	10	6	15000	3	6	31700	35200
40		NOMAD	HT	TRWL	FBG	KL	IB		105D	PERK	13	9	34000			79100	86900
40		VOYAGER	FB	TRWL	FBG	KL	IB		105D	PERK	13	9	34000			79100	86900
66		WILLARD	MY		FBG	DS	IB		250		17	6	78456	4	8	229500	252500
75		WILLARD	MY		FBG	DS	IB		700		19	6		4	2	**	**

LOA FT IN	NAME AND/ OR MODEL	TOP/ RIG	BOAT TYPE	HULL MTL	HULL TP	TP #	HP	MFG	BEAM FT IN	WGT LBS	DRAFT FT IN	RETAIL LOW	RETAIL HIGH
1974 BOATS													
30	HORIZON	CUT	MS	FBG	KL	IB	50D		10 6	15000	3 6	26600	29600
30	NAVIGATOR	CUT	MS	FBG	KL	IB	50D	PERK	10 6	15000	3 6	26600	29500
30	NOMAD	FB	TRWL	FBG	DS	IB	50D		10 6	15000	3 6	30800	34200
30	SEARCHER	FB	TRWL	FBG	DS	IB	50D		10 6	15000	3 6	30800	34200
30	SEEKER	FB	TRWL	FBG	DS	IB	50D	PERK	10 6	15000	3 6	30800	34200
30	VOYAGER	HT	TRWL	FBG	DS	IB	50D		10 6	15000	3 6	30800	34200
64	WILLARD		MY	FBG		IB	T600D		18	71433	3 3	231000	253500
1973 BOATS													
30	HORIZON	CUT	MS	FBG	KL	IB	50D	PERK	10 6	15000	3 6	26100	29000
30	NOMAD	FB	TRWL	FBG	DS	IB	50D	PERK	10 6	15000	3 6	30700	34100
30	SEARCHER	FB	TRWL	FBG	DS	IB	50D	PERK	10 6	15000	3 6	29400	32600
30	TROLLER		TRWL	FBG	DS	IB	50D	PERK	10 6	15000	3 6	28700	31900
30	VEGA-ENTERPRISE		TRWL	FBG	DS	IB	50D	PERK	10 6	15000	3 6	31300	34800
30	VOYAGER	HT	TRWL	FBG	DS	IB	50D	PERK	10 6	15000	3 6	30000	33300
1972 BOATS													
30	HORIZON	CUT	MS	FBG	KL	IB	50D	PERK	10 6	15000	3 6	25500	28400
30	NOMAD	FB	TRWL	FBG	DS	IB	50D	PERK	10 6	15000	3 6	30700	34100
30	SEARCHER	FB	TRWL	FBG	DS	IB	50D	PERK	10 6	15000	3 6	27800	30900
30	VEGA-ENTERPRISE		TRWL	FBG	DS	IB	50D	PERK	10 6	15000	3 6	29300	32500
30	VOYAGER	HT	TRWL	FBG	DS	IB	50D	PERK	10 6	15000	3 6	29300	32500
1971 BOATS													
30	ATLANTIC		TRWL	FBG	DS	IB	50D		10 4		3 6	27600	30700
30	HARBOR-TUG		TRWL	FBG	DS	IB	50D		10 4	15353	3 6	29800	33100
30	PACIFIC-TROLLER		TRWL	FBG	DS	IB	50D		10 4	15353	3 6	28400	31500
30	TROPIC	CR		FBG	KL	IB	50D		10 4		3 6	29300	32600
30	VEGA 30	MS		FBG	KL	IB	50D		10 4		3 6	28400	31600
36	VEGA 36	MS		FBG	KL	IB	85		11 9	26000	3 9	45500	50000
36	VEGA CRUISER	CR		FBG	DS	IB	85D	PERK	11 9		3 9	31900	35500
36	VEGA TRAWLER		TRWL	FBG	DS	IB	85D	PERK	11 9		3 9	38300	42600
58	VEGA 58		MY	FBG	DS	IB			17 6		5	**	**
58 9	PACIFIC-CRUISER		CR	FBG	DS	IB	T275D	PERK	17 6		5 6	127000	139500
59	PACIFIC-CLIPPER		SF	FBG	SV	IB	T350D	PERK	18 3		4	157000	172500
64	PACIFIC-CLIPPER		SF	FBG	SV	IB	T500D	PERK	18 3		4 3	208000	228500
65	VEGA 65		MY	FBG	SV	IB	T370D	PERK	20		5	210500	231500
75	VEGA 75		MY	FBG	SV	IB	T500D	PERK	20		6	**	**
1970 BOATS													
36	VEGA 36		CR	FBG		IB	85D	PERK	11 9	26000	3 6	44600	49500
36	VEGA 36		MS	FBG		IB	85D	PERK	11 9		3 9	31000	34500
36	VEGA 36		TRWL	FBG		IB	85D	PERK	11 9	26000	3 6	44500	49500
53	VEGA-CLIPPER 53		CR	FBG		IB	T160		17		2 8	82800	91000
59	VEGA-CLIPPER 59		CR	FBG		IB	T283		18		3 6	166000	182500
64	VEGA-CLIPPER 64		CR	FBG		IB			18 4		3 8	**	**
1969 BOATS													
36	VEGA 36	KTH	MS	FBG	KL	IB	85D	PERK	11 9	26000	3 9	43000	47800
36	VEGA-CRUISER		CR	FBG	DS	IB	85D	PERK	11 9	26000	3 6	43100	47900
36	VEGA-TRAWLER		TRWL	FBG	DS	IB	85D	PERK	11 9	26000	3 9	43100	47900
47	DOVER 47		CR	FBG	DS	IB	T130D	PERK	15	40000	3 4	81400	89400
50	VEGA 50		TRWL	FBG		IB	T160D	PERK	15 1	44000	3 6	85500	94000
59	PACIFIC-CLIPPER		SF	FBG		IB			18	60000	3 6	**	**
65	VEGA 65		TRWL	FBG		IB			19 6	90000	4 2	**	**
1968 BOATS													
36	VEGA 36		CR	FBG	DS	IB	85D	PERK	11 9	26000	3 9	41800	46500
36	VEGA 36		CR	FBG	DS	IB	130D		11 9	26000	3 9	43100	47900
36	VEGA 36	KTH	MS	FBG	KL	IB	D		11 9		3 9	29600	32900
36	VEGA 36		TRWL	FBG	DS	IB	85D	PERK	11 9	26000	3 9	41800	46400
36	VEGA 36		TRWL	FBG	DS	IB	130D		11 9	26000	3 9	43000	47800
44	DOVER 44		MY	FBG		IB	T160D		15		3 4	60900	66900
47	DOVER 47		CR	FBG	DS	IB	T160D	PERK	15	40000	3 4	80400	88300
65	DOVER 65		MY	FBG		IB			20		4 4	**	**
1967 BOATS													
36	VEGA 36		CR	FBG		IB	85D		11 9	22000	3 6	35700	39600
47	DOVER 47		CR	FBG	DS	IB	T160D	PERK	15	40000	3 4	78000	85800
1966 BOATS													
36	VEGA 36	KTH	MS	FBG	KL	IB	D		12		3 9	28600	31800
36	VEGA 36		OFF	FBG		IB	85D		12		3 9	25700	28500
52	VEGA 52		OFF	FBG		IB	250D		17		5 9	59400	65300
1965 BOATS													
36	VEGA		CR	FBG		IB	70D		11 9		3 9	26400	29300
36	VEGA	KTH	SAIL	FBG	KL	IB			11 9		4 9	18400	20500
56	VEGA		CR	FBG		IB	235D		17		5 5	85200	93600
1963 BOATS													
36		FB	TRWL			IB	200D					30400	33700
36	OFFSHORE	OFF				IB	70D					26500	29400
36	VEGA	FB	TRWL			IB	T 70D	GRAY		20349		31700	35200
1962 BOATS													
36		FB	TRWL			IB	70D	GRAY		20349		29200	32500
36		FB	TRWL			IB	T220D	GM				32300	35900

WILLIAMS & KELLY INC

Call 1-800-327-6929 for BUC Personalized Evaluation Service
Or, for 1976 boats, sign onto www.BUCValuPro.com

JOHN WILLIAMS COMPANY INC

MT DESERT ME 04660   COAST GUARD MFG ID- JMW See inside cover to adjust price for area

For more recent years, see the BUC Used Boat Price Guide, Volume 1 or Volume 2

LOA FT IN	NAME AND/ OR MODEL	TOP/ RIG	BOAT TYPE	HULL MTL	HULL TP	TP #	HP	MFG	BEAM FT IN	WGT LBS	DRAFT FT IN	RETAIL LOW	RETAIL HIGH
1983 BOATS													
35 8	STANLEY 36	HT	YTFS	FBG	SV	IB	160D		12	14000	3 6	119000	130500
44 6	STANLEY 44	HT	YTFS	FBG	SV	IB	250D		14 7	30000	5 7	161500	177500
1981 BOATS													
35 8	STANLEY 36	HT	YTFS	FBG	SV	IB	160D		12	14000	3 6	110000	120500
44 6	STANLEY 44	HT	YTFS	FBG	SV	IB	250D		14 7	30000	5 7	146500	161000

WILLIAMS MARINA CORP

Call 1-800-327-6929 for BUC Personalized Evaluation Service
Or, for 1959 to 1961 boats, sign onto www.BUCValuPro.com

M W WILLIS & SONS BOAT WKS

COAST GUARD MFG ID- MWW

Call 1-800-327-6929 for BUC Personalized Evaluation Service
Or, for 1972 to 1973 boats, sign onto www.BUCValuPro.com

WILMAR BOAT CO INC

Call 1-800-327-6929 for BUC Personalized Evaluation Service
Or, for 1959 to 1961 boats, sign onto www.BUCValuPro.com

WILMETTE BOATWORKS INC

COAST GUARD MFG ID- WUL

Call 1-800-327-6929 for BUC Personalized Evaluation Service
Or, for 1983 to 1984 boats, sign onto www.BUCValuPro.com

WINDBOATS MARINE LTD

Call 1-800-327-6929 for BUC Personalized Evaluation Service
Or, for 1978 to 1980 boats, sign onto www.BUCValuPro.com

WINDJAMMER YACHTS

Call 1-800-327-6929 for BUC Personalized Evaluation Service
Or, for 1977 boats, sign onto www.BUCValuPro.com

WINDSEEKER YACHTS INC

COAST GUARD MFG ID- WYB

Call 1-800-327-6929 for BUC Personalized Evaluation Service
Or, for 1977 to 1979 boats, sign onto www.BUCValuPro.com

WINDSHIPS INC

CLEARWATER FL 33520   COAST GUARD MFG ID- WZI See inside cover to adjust price for area

For more recent years, see the BUC Used Boat Price Guide, Volume 1 or Volume 2

LOA FT IN	NAME AND/ OR MODEL	TOP/ RIG	BOAT TYPE	HULL MTL	HULL TP	TP #	HP	MFG	BEAM FT IN	WGT LBS	DRAFT FT IN	RETAIL LOW	RETAIL HIGH
1983 BOATS													
63 5	WINDSHIP 63	KTH	SA/CR	F/S	CB	IB	210D	CAT	17	81000	5 9	464000	509500

LOA FT IN	NAME AND/ OR MODEL	TOP/ RIG	BOAT TYPE	HULL MTL	TP	TP	ENGINE #	HP	MFG	BEAM FT IN	WGT LBS	DRAFT FT IN	RETAIL LOW	RETAIL HIGH
--- 1979 BOATS ---														
44 1	ANNAPOLIS 44	SLP	SA/CR	FBG	KL	IB		D		11	22000	6	84000	92400
--- 1978 BOATS ---														
44 1	ANNAPOLIS 44	SLP	SA/CR	FBG	KL	IB		40D	WEST	11	22500	6	82000	90100

WINDSONG YACHTS INC

Call 1-800-327-6929 for BUC Personalized Evaluation Service
Or, for 1971 boats, sign onto www.BUCValuPro.com

WINDWARD MARINE INC
COAST GUARD MFG ID- WME

Call 1-800-327-6929 for BUC Personalized Evaluation Service
Or, for 1975 to 1985 boats, sign onto www.BUCValuPro.com

WINDWARD YACHTS

Call 1-800-327-6929 for BUC Personalized Evaluation Service
Or, for 1968 to 1969 boats, sign onto www.BUCValuPro.com

WINDWARD YACHTS INC
COAST GUARD MFG ID- WYG

Call 1-800-327-6929 for BUC Personalized Evaluation Service
Or, for 1970 to 1980 boats, sign onto www.BUCValuPro.com

E F WINGATE

Call 1-800-327-6929 for BUC Personalized Evaluation Service
Or, for 1959 boats, sign onto www.BUCValuPro.com

WINNER BOATS
PESHTIGO WI 54157   COAST GUARD MFG ID- WNB See inside cover to adjust price for area
FORMERLY WIZZARD BOATS

LOA FT IN	NAME AND/ OR MODEL	TOP/ RIG	BOAT TYPE	HULL MTL	TP	TP	ENGINE #	HP	MFG	BEAM FT IN	WGT LBS	DRAFT FT IN	RETAIL LOW	RETAIL HIGH
--- 1980 BOATS ---														
16	8080	OP		FBG	DV	OB				7			1700	2050
16	SEA-FEVER 8084	OP		FBG	DV	OB				7			1750	2100
19	COUGAR		RNBT	FBG	DV	IO		120		7 4			2900	3350
19	COUGAR I	OP	RNBT	FBG	DV	OB				7 4	1300		4350	5000
21	FISHMASTER		FSH	FBG	DV	IO		120		7 8			4400	5050
24		SF		FBG	DV	IO		198		8			7000	8000
28	FAMILY FLYBRIDGE	FB	SPTCR	FBG	DV	IB		T228		10 4	9600		19400	21500
--- 1979 BOATS ---														
16 9	BIMINI	OP	RNBT	FBG	TR	OB				6 10	1250		2500	2900
16 9	BIMINI	OP	RNBT	FBG	TR	IO		120-140		6 10	2000		2400	3000
17 6	WILDCAT I	OP	RNBT	FBG	DV	IO		120-170		7 2	2000		2600	3200
17 6	WILDCAT II	OP	RNBT	FBG	DV	OB				7 2	1350		2700	3150
17 6	WILDCAT II	OP	RNBT	FBG	DV	IO		120-170		7 2	2000		2600	3200
17 8	18SS		RNBT	FBG	DV	OB				7	1075		2300	2650
17 8	18SS		RNBT	FBG	DV	JT		160	FORD	7			3300	3850
17 8	18SS		RNBT	FBG	DV	IO		170-230		7			2500	3050
18 9	COUGAR I	OP	RNBT	FBG	DV	OB				7 4	1300		2750	3150
18 9	COUGAR I	OP	RNBT	FBG	DV	IO		120-200		7 4	2200		2950	3650
18 9	COUGAR I	OP	RNBT	FBG	DV	IO		225-260		7 4	2200		3200	3900
18 9	COUGAR II	OP	RNBT	FBG	DV	OB				7 4	1300		2750	3150
18 9	COUGAR II	OP	RNBT	FBG	DV	IO		120-200		7 4	2230		2950	3700
18 9	COUGAR II	OP	RNBT	FBG	DV	IO		225-260		7 4	2230		3200	3900
18 9	X-19		RNBT	FBG	DV	IO		260		7 4	2200		3200	3700
20 8	S/F-210 2216	OP	FSH	FBG	DV	IO		165-250		7 8	2680		4400	5450
20 8	S/F-210 2216	OP	FSH	FBG	DV	IO		260		7 8	2680		4700	5650
20 8	S/F-210 2216	OP	FSH	FBG	DV	IO		120-140		7 8	2680		4400	5250
20 8	VISCOUNT 2217	OP	FSH	FBG	DV	IO		120-200		7 8	2610		4300	5250
20 8	VISCOUNT 2217	OP	FSH	FBG	DV	IO		225-260		7 8	2610		4650	5600
23 7	CONVERTIBLE 2451	OP	CUD	FBG	DV	IO		120-260		8	3700		5900	7350
23 7	CONVERTIBLE 2451	OP	CUD	FBG	DV	IO		130D	VLVO	8	3700		7200	8250
23 7	CONVERTIBLE 2451	OP	CUD	FBG	DV	IO		T120-T170		8	3700		6650	8000
23 7	FAMILY EXPRESS 2456	OP	EXP	FBG	DV	IO		185-260		8	4100		6400	7800
23 7	FAMILY EXPRESS 2456	OP	EXP	FBG	DV	IO		130D	VLVO	8	4100		7650	8800
23 7	FAMILY FB 2457	FB	CUD	FBG	DV	IO		185-260		8	4100		6400	7800
23 7	FAMILY FB 2457	FB	CUD	FBG	DV	IO		130D	VLVO	8	4100		7650	8800
23 7	S/F-240 2450	OP	SF	FBG	DV	IO		120		8	3705		6550	7700
23 7	S/F-240 2450	OP	SF	FBG	DV	IO		140-260		8	3700		6550	8100
23 7	S/F-240 2450	OP	SF	FBG	SV	IO		130D	VLVO	8	3700		8900	10100
23 7	S/F-240 2450	OP	SF	FBG	DV	IO		T120-T170		8	3700		7450	8950
28 2	EXPRESS CRUISER 2856		EXP	FBG	DV	IO		260		10 4	8000		13300	15100
	IO T165-T200	13900		16300,	VD T215-T225		16500	19100,	IO T228	MRCR	14700		16700	
	VD T228 MRCR	16700		18900,	IO T230-T240		14700	16800,	VD T250-T255		17100		19400	
	IO T260	15100		17100										
28 2	FAMILY FB 2857	FB	CBNCR	FBG	DV	IO		260		10 4	8000		15800	18000
	IO T165-T200	16900		19300,	IB T215	PCM	18900	21000,	VD T215-T225		18900		21300	
	IO T228 MRCR	17100		19400,	IB T228	MRCR	18900	21000,	VD T228	MRCR	19000		21100	
	IO T230-T240	17100		19400,	VD T250	OMC	19200	21300,	IB T255	MRCR	18900		21000	
	IB T255 PCM	18900		21000,	VD T255	MRCR	19000	21100,	IO T260		17200		19600	
31 1	FAMILY FB 3100	FB	CBNCR	FBG	DV	IB		T215-T255		11 2	8000		24100	26900
--- 1978 BOATS ---														
16 4	MARAUDER	OP	RNBT	FBG	SV	OB				6 8	850		1700	2050
16 4	STRIKE	OP	FSH	FBG	SV	OB				6 8	850		1700	2050
16 9	BIMINI	ST	RNBT	FBG	TR	OB				6 10	1150		2350	2700
16 9	BIMINI	ST	RNBT	FBG	TR	IO		120-140		6 10	2000		2450	2850
16 9	BIMINI	ST	RNBT	FBG	TR	IO		170	MRCR	6 10	2300		2650	3050
17 6	WILDCAT I	OP	RNBT	FBG	DV	IO		120-170		7 2	2000		2600	3100
17 6	WILDCAT II	OP	RNBT	FBG	DV	OB				7 2	1250		2500	2950
17 6	WILDCAT II	OP	RNBT	FBG	DV	IO		120-170		7 2	2000		2600	3150
17 7	MINIKAI	ST	RNBT	FBG	TR	OB				7 2	1250		2550	2950
17 7	MINIKAI	ST	RNBT	FBG	TR	IO		120-170		7 2	2000		2650	3150
18 9	COUGAR I	ST	RNBT	FBG	DV	OB				7 4	1350		2750	3200
18 9	COUGAR I	ST	RNBT	FBG	DV	IO		120-228		7 4	2200		2900	3600
18 9	COUGAR II	ST	RNBT	FBG	DV	OB				7 4	1350		2800	3250
18 9	COUGAR II	ST	RNBT	FBG	DV	IO		120-228		7 4	2200		2950	3650
18 9	TIGRESS	ST	CUD	FBG	DV	OB				7 4	1300		2700	3150
18 9	TIGRESS	ST	CUD	FBG	DV	IO		120-228		7 4	2200		3000	3750
20 8	S/F-210 2216	ST	FSH	FBG	DV	OB				7 8	1950		4150	4800
20 8	S/F-210 2216	ST	FSH	FBG	DV	IO		120-228		7 8	2600		4250	5250
20 8	VISCOUNT 2217	ST	FSH	FBG	DV	OB				7 8	1950		5000	5750
20 8	VISCOUNT 2217	ST	FSH	FBG	DV	IO		120-228		7 8	2600		4250	5250
23 7	CONVERTIBLE 2451	ST	CUD	FBG	DV	IO		T120-T140		8	3800		6050	7050
23 7	CONVERTIBLE 2451	ST	CUD	FBG	DV	IO		120-228		8	4300		7350	8450
23 7	EXPRESS FB 2457	FB	EXP	FBG	DV	IO		198-228		8	4300	2 7	6600	7650
23 7	EXPRESS FB 2457	FB	EXP	FBG	DV	IO		T120-T140		8	4800	2 7	7950	9150
23 7	FAMILY FLYBRIDGE 240	FB	CUD	FBG	DV	IO		198-228		8	4500	2 7	6850	7900
23 7	FAMILY FLYBRIDGE 240	FB	CUD	FBG	DV	IO		T120-T140		8	4900	2 7	8200	9300
23 7	FAMILY OVNTR 2455	FB	OVNTR	FBG	DV	IO		198-228		8	4500	2 7	6350	7400
23 7	FAMILY OVNTR 2455	FB	OVNTR	FBG	DV	IO		T120-T140		8	4800	2 7	7700	8850
23 7	HARDTOP EXPRESS 2456	HT	EXP	FBG	DV	IO		198-228		8	4500	2 7	6500	7550
23 7	HARDTOP EXPRESS 2456	HT	EXP	FBG	DV	IO		T120-T140		8	4800	2 7	7600	8700
23 7	S/F-240	FB	SF	FBG	DV	IO		198-228		8	4500	2 7	8550	9950
23 7	S/F-240	FB	SF	FBG	DV	IO		T120-T140		8	4900	2 7	10100	11500
23 7	S/F-240 2450	ST	SF	FBG	DV	IO		198-228		8	3800	2 7	6700	7800
23 7	S/F-240 2450	ST	SF	FBG	DV	IO		T120-T140		8	4300	2 7	8150	9400
23 7	WEEKENDER 2481	HT	WKNDR	FBG	DV	IO		198-228		8	3800	2 7	6300	7300
23 7	WEEKENDER 2481	HT	WKNDR	FBG	DV	IO		T120-T140		8	4300	2 7	7600	8750
28 2	FAMILY FLYBRIDGE 280	FB	CBNCR	FBG	DV	IO		T165-T198		10 4	9200	3	18100	20700
28 2	FAMILY FLYBRIDGE 280	FB	CBNCR	FBG	DV	IO		T228	MRCR	10 4	9200	3	18800	20800
28 2	FAMILY FLYBRIDGE 280	FB	CBNCR	FBG	DV	IO		T228	MRCR	10 4	9200	3	19500	21600
28 2	S/F-280	FB	SF	FBG	DV	IO		T165-T198		10 4	9200	3	18600	21100
28 2	S/F-280	FB	SF	FBG	DV	IO		T228	MRCR	10 4	9200	3	19300	21500
28 2	S/F-280	FB	SF	FBG	DV	IO		T228	MRCR	10 4	9200	3	18300	20300
31 1	SPORT FISHERMAN 3100	FB	SF	FBG	DV	IB		T198-T255		11 2	12200	3	24000	27200
--- 1977 BOATS ---														
16 4	MARAUDER 736	ST	RNBT	FBG	SV	OB				6 8	850		1700	2000
16 4	STRIKE 742	OP	FSH	FBG	TR	OB				6 8	850		1700	2050
16 9	BIMINI 784	ST	RNBT	FBG	TR	OB				6 10	1150		2300	2700
16 9	BIMINI 784	ST	RNBT	FBG	TR	IO		120-140		6 10	2000		2450	2850
17 6	WILDCAT I 821	ST	RNBT	FBG	DV	OB				7 2	1250		2500	2900
17 6	WILDCAT II 822	ST	RNBT	FBG	DV	OB				7 2	1650		3050	3550
17 6	WILDCAT II 822	ST	RNBT	FBG	DV	IO		120-175		7 2	2000		2650	3100
17 7	MINIKAI 916	ST	RNBT	FBG	DV	OB				7 2	1250		2500	2900
17 7	MINIKAI 916	ST	RNBT	FBG	DV	IO		120-175		7 2	2000		2650	3100
18 8	ELIMINATOR 1012	OP	FSH	FBG	DV	OB				8 1	1187		2500	2900
18 9	COUGAR I 965	ST	RNBT	FBG	DV	OB				7 4	1300		2650	3100

LOA FT	IN	NAME AND/ OR MODEL	TOP/ RIG	BOAT TYPE	-HULL- MTL	TP	ENGINE TP	# HP	MFG	BEAM FT	IN	WGT LBS	DRAFT FT	IN	RETAIL LOW	RETAIL HIGH
		1977 BOATS														
18	9	COUGAR I 965	ST	RNBT	FBG	DV	IO	120-235		7	4	2200			2950	3600
18	9	COUGAR II 966	ST	RNBT	FBG	DV	OB			7	4	1300			2700	3100
18	9	COUGAR II 966	ST	RNBT	FBG	DV	IO	120-235		7	4	2200			2950	3600
18	9	TIGRESS 980	ST	CUD	FBG	DV	OB			7	4	1300			2650	3100
18	9	TIGRESS 980	ST	CUD	FBG	DV	IO	120-235		7	4	2200			3050	3700
20	8	S/F-210 2214	ST	SF	FBG	DV	OB			7	8	1950			4100	4750
20	8	S/F-210 2214	ST	SF	FBG	DV	IO	120-235		7	8	2600			4550	5450
20	8	VISCOUNT 2215	ST	FSH	FBG	DV	OB			7	8	1950			4100	4750
20	8	VISCOUNT 2215	ST	FSH	FBG	DV	IO	120-235		7	8	2600			4350	5200
23	7	CONVERTIBLE 2441	ST	CUD	FBG	DV	IO	188-235		8		3700	1	4	6000	7000
23	7	CONVERTIBLE 2441	ST	CUD	FBG	DV	IO	T120-T140		8		3700	1	4	6700	7700
23	7	EXPRESS FB 2447	FB	EXP	FBG	DV	IO	188-235		8		4100	1	4	6400	7450
23	7	EXPRESS FB 2447	FB	EXP	FBG	DV	IO	T120-T140		8		4100	1	4	7150	8200
23	7	FAMILY EXPRESS 2446	HT	EXP	FBG	DV	IO	188-235		8		4100	1	4	6400	7450
23	7	FAMILY EXPRESS 2446	HT	EXP	FBG	DV	IO	T120-T140		8		4100	1	4	7150	8200
23	7	FAMILY FB 2444	FB	CR	FBG	DV	IO	188-235		8		4500	1	4	7000	8150
23	7	FAMILY FB 2444	FB	CR	FBG	DV	IO	T120-T140		8		4500	1	4	7800	9000
23	7	FAMILY OVNTR 2445	HT	OVNTR	FBG	DV	IO	188-235		8		4000	1	4	6400	7450
23	7	FAMILY OVNTR 2445	HT	OVNTR	FBG	DV	IO	T120-T140		8		4000	1	4	7150	8200
23	7	S/F-240 2440	ST	SF	FBG	DV	IO	188-235		8		3700	1	4	6600	7700
23	7	S/F-240 2440	ST	SF	FBG	DV	IO	T120-T140		8		3700	1	4	7400	8550
23	7	S/F-240 2443	FB	SF	FBG	DV	IO	188-235		8		4500	1	4	8650	10100
23	7	S/F-240 2443	FB	SF	FBG	DV	IO	T120-T140		8		4500	1	4	9600	10900
23	7	WEEKENDER 2480	ST	WKNDR	FBG	DV	IO	188-235		8		3800	1	4	6300	7300
23	7	WEEKENDER 2480	ST	WKNDR	FBG	DV	IO	T120-T140		8		3800	1	4	7000	8100
28	2	FAMILY FB 2827	FB	CR	FBG	DV	IO	T165-T190		10	4	8000	3		14100	16300
		VD T225-T230 15400 17800, IO T233 MRCR 14900 17000, VD T233 MRCR													15500	17600
		IO T235 OMC 14900 17000														
28	2	S/F-280 2826	FB	SF	FBG	DV	IO	T165-T190		10	4	8000	3		17000	19600
		VD T225-T230 16000 18500, IO T233 MRCR 18200 20200, VD T233 MRCR													16100	18300
		IO T235 OMC 18200 20200														
		1976 BOATS														
16	4	MARAUDER 735	ST	RNBT	FBG	SV	OB			6	8	850			1700	2000
16	6	STRIKE II 741	OP	FSH	FBG	TR	OB			6	2	850			1700	2000
16	9	BIMINI 783	ST	RNBT	FBG	TR	OB			6	10	1150			2300	2650
16	9	BIMINI 783	ST	RNBT	FBG	TR	IO	120-140		6	10	1150			2000	2350
17	6	WILDCAT I 819	ST	RNBT	FBG	DV	OB			7	2	1150			2300	2700
17	6	WILDCAT I 819	ST	RNBT	FBG	DV	IO	120-175		7	2	1150			2250	2650
17	6	WILDCAT II B/R 820	ST	RNBT	FBG	DV	OB			7	2	1150			2300	2700
17	6	WILDCAT II B/R 820	ST	RNBT	FBG	DV	IO	120-175		7	2	1150			2250	2650
17	7	MINIKAI 915	ST	RNBT	FBG	TR	OB			7	2	1250			2500	2900
17	7	MINIKAI 915	ST	RNBT	FBG	TR	IO	120-175		7	2	1250			2300	2700
17	7	MINIKAI 915	ST	RNBT	FBG	TR	JT	245		7	2	1250			2800	3250
18	8	ELIMINATOR 1011	OP	FSH	FBG	DV	OB			8	1	1187			2450	2850
18	9	COUGAR I 963	ST	RNBT	FBG	DV	OB			7	4	1300			2650	3050
18	9	COUGAR I 963	ST	RNBT	FBG	DV	IO	120-235		7	4	1300			2600	3150
18	9	COUGAR II B/R 964	ST	RNBT	FBG	DV	OB			7	4	1300			2650	3100
18	9	COUGAR II B/R 964	ST	RNBT	FBG	DV	IO	120-235		7	4	1300			2600	3200
21		S/F-210 2212	ST	SF	FBG	DV	OB			7	8	1950			4150	4800
21		S/F-210 2212	ST	SF	FBG	DV	IO	120-235		7	8	1950			4100	5000
21		VISCOUNT 2213	ST	FSH	FBG	DV	OB			7	8	1950			4150	4800
21		VISCOUNT 2213	ST	FSH	FBG	DV	IO	120-235		7	8	1950			3950	4800
23	7	CONVERTIBLE 2431	ST	CUD	FBG	DV	IO	165-235		8		3700	1	4	6050	7100
23	7	CONVERTIBLE 2431	ST	CUD	FBG	DV	IO	T120-T140		8		3700	1	4	6800	7850
23	7	EXPRESS FB 2437	FB	EXP	FBG	DV	IO	165-235		8			1	4	6500	7650
23	7	EXPRESS FB 2437	FB	EXP	FBG	DV	IO	T120-T140		8			1	4	7300	8400
23	7	FAMILY EXPRESS 2436	HT	EXP	FBG	DV	IO	165-235		8		4100	1	4	6450	7550
23	7	FAMILY EXPRESS 2436	HT	EXP	FBG	DV	IO	T120-T140		8		4100	1	4	7250	8350
23	7	FLYBRIDGE CR 2434	FB	CR	FBG	DV	IO	165-235		8		4500	1	4	7100	8300
23	7	FLYBRIDGE CR 2434	FB	CR	FBG	DV	IO	T120-T140		8		4500	1	4	7900	9100
23	7	OVERNIGHTER 2435	HT	CUD	FBG	DV	IO	165-235		8		4000	1	4	6400	7450
23	7	OVERNIGHTER 2435	HT	CUD	FBG	DV	IO	T120-T140		8		4000	1	4	7150	8200
23	7	S/F-240 2430	ST	SF	FBG	DV	IO	188-235		8		3700			6700	7800
23	7	S/F-240 2430	ST	SF	FBG	DV	IO	T120-T140		8		3700			7500	8650
23	7	S/F-240 2433	FB	SF	FBG	DV	IO	165-235		8		3700	1	4	7550	8900
23	7	S/F-240 2433	FB	SF	FBG	DV	IO	T120-T140		8		3700	1	4	8500	9800
28	2	FAMILY FB 2823	FB	CR	FBG	DV	VD	225		10	4	8000	3		13200	15000
		IO T165-T190 14300 16600, IO T225 15000 17100, VD T225 CHRY													14800	16800
		IO T233 MRCR 15100 17200, VD T233 MRCR 14900 16900, IO T235 OMC													15100	17200
		VD T235 OMC 15000 17100														
28	2	S/F-280 2822	FB	SF	FBG	DV	VD	225		10	4	8000	3		13800	15700
		IO T165-T190 17200 19900, IO T225 18400 20400, VD T225 CHRY													15300	17400
		IO T233 MRCR 18500 20500, VD T233 MRCR 15500 17600, IO T235 OMC													18500	20500
		VD T235 OMC 15700 17800														
		1975 BOATS														
16	6	STRIKE	OP	FSH	FBG	TR	OB			6	2	900			1750	2100
16	6	STRIKE-PRO	OP	FSH	FBG	TR	OB			6	2	950			1850	2200
16	9	BIMINI	OP	RNBT	FBG	TR	OB			6	10	1150			2300	2650
16	9	BIMINI	OP	RNBT	FBG	TR	IB	120		6	10	2000			2300	2650
17	6	WILDCAT	OP	RNBT	FBG	DV	OB			7	2	1100			2250	2600
17	6	WILDCAT	OP	RNBT	FBG	DV	IB	120		7	2	2000			2450	2850
17	7	MINIKAI	OP	RNBT	FBG	TR	OB			7	2	1250			2450	2850
17	7	MINIKAI	OP	RNBT	FBG	TR	IB	120		7	2	2000			2450	2850
18	9	COUGAR	OP	RNBT	FBG	DV	OB			7	4	1300			2600	3050
18	9	COUGAR	OP	RNBT	FBG	DV	IB	120		7	4	2200			2800	3250
21		S/F-210		SF	FBG	DV	IB	120		7	8	2600			3600	4200
21		VISCOUNT		FSH	FBG	DV	OB			7	8	1950			4100	4750
21		VISCOUNT		FSH	FBG	DV	IB	120		7	8	2600			3700	4350
23	7	SPORT FISHERMAN		SF	FBG	DV	IB	175		8		3700			5500	6300
28	2	EXPRESS CRUISER		EXP	FBG	DV	IB	T165-T235		10	4	8000			13400	16000
28	2	S/F-280		SF	FBG	DV	IB	T165-T235		10	4	8000			13300	15900
		1974 BOATS														
16	8	STRIKE		FSH	FBG		OB			6	2	900			1750	2100
16	8	STRIKE		FSH	FBG		IO	120-140		6	2	1450	2		2200	2600
16	9	BIMINI		RNBT	FBG		OB			6	2	1150			2250	2650
16	9	BIMINI		RNBT	FBG		IO	120-140		6	2	2000	1	10	2500	3100
17	6	WILDCAT I		RNBT	FBG		OB			7	2	1150			2300	2650
17	6	WILDCAT I		RNBT	FBG		IO	120-170		7	2	2000	2		2800	3400
17	6	WILDCAT II		RNBT	FBG		OB			7	2	1150			2300	2700
17	6	WILDCAT II		RNBT	FBG		IO	120-165		7	2	2000	2		2800	3450
17	6	WILDCAT II		RNBT	FBG		IO	170	VLVO	7	2	2000	2		3050	3550
17	7	BARONET		CBNCR	FBG		OB			7	2	1450			2700	3150
17	7	MINIKAI		RNBT	FBG		OB			7	2	1250			2450	2850
17	7	MINIKAI		RNBT	FBG		IO	120-170		7	2	2000	2		2800	3500
17	7	MINIKAI		RNBT	FBG		JT	185	WAUK	7	2	2000	2		2900	3400
18	9	COUGAR I		RNBT	FBG		OB			7	4	1300			2550	2950
18	9	COUGAR I		RNBT	FBG		IO	120-225		7	4	2200	2	2	3100	3850
18	9	COUGAR I		RNBT	FBG		JT	270-330		7	4	2200	2	2	3250	3750
18	9	COUGAR II		RNBT	FBG		OB			7	4	1300			2700	3100
18	9	COUGAR II		RNBT	FBG		IO	120-225		7	4	2200	2	2	3200	3900
18	9	COUGAR II		RNBT	FBG		JT	270-330		7	4	2200	2	2	3300	3850
21		VISCOUNT		FSH	FBG		OB			7	8	1950			4100	4750
21		VISCOUNT		FSH	FBG		IO	120-225		7	8	2600	2	4	4800	5700
21		VISCOUNT		FSH	FBG		JT	270-330		7	8	2600	2	4	4250	4950
23	7		FB	CR	FBG		IO	188-225		8		4500	2	11	7550	8750
23	7		FB	CR	FBG		VD	250	CHRY	8		4500	2	11	6400	7400
23	7		FB	CR	FBG		IO	T120-T170		8		4500	2	11	8450	10100
23	7			EXP	FBG		IO	165-225		8		4100	2	11	6850	7950
23	7			EXP	FBG		VD	250	CHRY	8		4100	2	11	5900	6750
23	7			EXP	FBG		IO	T120-T170		8		4100	2	11	7700	9300
23	7		HT	OVNTR	FBG		IO	165-225		8		4000	2	11	6850	7950
23	7		HT	OVNTR	FBG		VD	250	CHRY	8		4000	2	11	5850	6750
23	7		HT	OVNTR	FBG		IO	T120-T170		8		4000	2	11	7700	9300
23	7	SPORTSMAN		CNV	FBG		IO	165-225		8		3700	2	4	7050	8200
23	7	SPORTSMAN		CNV	FBG		VD	250	CHRY	8		3700	2	11	5400	6200
23	7	SPORTSMAN		CNV	FBG		IO	T120-T170		8		3700	2	4	8000	9700
28	2			EXP	FBG		IB	225-255		10	4	8000	3		12100	14000
28	2			EXP	FBG		VD	T185-T225		10	4	8000	3		13200	15400
28	2	FAMILY CRUISER	FB	CR	FBG		VD	225-330		10	4	8000	3		12300	14600
28	2	FAMILY CRUISER	FB	CR	FBG		VD	T185-T225		10	4	8000	3		13300	15500
28	2	FAMILY CRUISER	FB	CR	FBG		VD	T100D	CHRY	10	4	8000	3		17500	19800
28	2	SPORTSMAN OFFSHORE		OFF	FBG		VD	225-330		10	4	8000	3		12400	14600
28	2	SPORTSMAN OFFSHORE		OFF	FBG		VD	T185-T225		10	4	8000	3		13300	15500
28	2	SPORTSMAN OFFSHORE		OFF	FBG		VD	T100D	CHRY	10	4	8000	3		17200	19600
		1973 BOATS														
16	8	STRIKE 16		FSH	FBG		OB			6	2	900			1750	2100
16	9	BIMINI SS		RNBT	FBG		OB			6	10	1150			2250	2650
16	9	BIMINI SS		RNBT	FBG		IO	120-140		6	10	2000	1	10	2750	3200
17	6	WILDCAT I		RNBT	FBG		OB			7	2	1100			2200	2600
17	6	WILDCAT I		RNBT	FBG		IO	120		7	2	2000	2		2850	3350
		JT 130 VLVO 2650 3050, IO 140-165 2850 3350, JT 170-270													2750	3250
17	6	WILDCAT II		RNBT	FBG		OB			7	2	1150	2		2300	2700
17	6	WILDCAT II		RNBT	FBG		IO	120		7	2	2000	2		2900	3400
		JT 130 VLVO 2700 3100, IO 140-165 2950 3400, JT 170-270													2800	3300

CONTINUED ON NEXT PAGE

```
LOA  NAME AND/            TOP/ BOAT -HULL- ----ENGINE--- BEAM  WGT DRAFT RETAIL RETAIL
FT IN  OR MODEL           RIG TYPE MTL TP TP # HP MFG  FT IN  LBS FT IN  LOW   HIGH
------------------- 1973 BOATS -------------------------------------------------------
17 7 BARONET             CBNCR FBG    OB          7  2 1450        2700   3150
17 7 MINIKAI             RNBT  FBG    OB          7  2 1250 2      2450   2850
17 7 MINIKAI             RNBT  FBG    IO 120      7  2 2000 2      2900   3400
     JT  130  VLVO  2650 3100, IO 140-165   2900 3400, JT 170-270   2750   3300

18 9 COUGAR I            RNBT  FBG    OB          7  4 1300 2 2    2550   2950
18 9 COUGAR I            RNBT  FBG    IO 120      7  4 2200 2 2    3250   3750
     JT  130  VLVO  2950 3400, IO 140-165   3250 3750, JT 170 VLVO 3050   3550
     IO 188-225    3230 3900, JT 270-330    3150 3650

18 9 COUGAR II           RNBT  FBG    OB          7  4 1300 2 2    2650   3100
18 9 COUGAR II           RNBT  FBG    IO 120      7  4 2200 2 2    3250   3850
     JT  130  VLVO  3000 3500, IO 140-165   3300 3850, JT 170 VLVO 3100   3600
     IO 188-225    3350 4000, JT 270-330    3150 3700

21   VISCOUNT            FSH   FBG    OB          7  8 1950 2 4    4050   4700
21   VISCOUNT            FSH   FBG    IO 120      7  8 2600 2 4    4950   5650
     JT  130  VLVO  3900 4500, IO 140-165   4950 5700, JT 170 VLVO 4000   4650
     IO 188-225    5000 5850, JT 270-330    4100 4750

23 7 240            FB   CR    FBG    IO 188-225    8    4500 2 11 7800   9100
23 7 240            FB   CR    FBG    IO T120-T165  8    4500 2 11 8800  10100
23 7 240            HT   OVNTR FBG    IO 165-225    8    4000 2 11 7050   8250
23 7 240            HT   OVNTR FBG    IO T120-T165  8    4000 2 11 7950   9200
23 7 SPORTSMAN 240       CNV   FBG    IO 165-225    8    3700 2 11 7300   8500
23 7 SPORTSMAN 240       CNV   FBG    IO T120-T165  8    3700 2 11 8250   9550
28 2 280            FB   CR    FBG    VD 225-330  10 4  8000 3     11600  13900
     VD T185  WAUK 12600 14400, IO T188-T215  15700 18300, IO T225 MRCR 16200 18400
     VD T225        13100 14800, IO T100D CHRY 18900 21100, VD T100D CHRY 17000 19300
     IO T106D VLVO 18600 20700, VD T106D VLVO 16700 19000

28 2 280                 EXP   FBG    IB 225-255  10 4  8000 3     11700  13500
28 2 280                 EXP   FBG    VD T185-T225 10 4 8000 3     12700  14900
28 2 FAMILY 280     FB   CR    FBG    VD 225-330  10 4  8000 3     12000  14200
     VD T185  WAUK 13000 14800, IO T188-T215  16200 18800, IO T225 MRCR 16700 19000
     VD T225        13400 15200, IO T106D VLVO 19100 21200, VD T106D VLVO 17100 19400
------------------- 1972 BOATS -------------------------------------------------------
16 4 MARAUDER SS         RNBT  FBG    OB          6  8  850         1900   2250
16 9 BIMINI SS           RNBT  FBG    OB          6 10 1150         2600   3000
16 9 BIMINI SS           RNBT  FBG    IO 120-140  6 10 2000 1 10    2800   3200
16 9 BIMINI STD          RNBT  FBG    OB          6 10 1150         1850   2200
16 9 ELIMINATOR          RNBT  FBG    OB          6 10 1100         2150   2500
16 9 ELIMINATOR          RNBT  FBG    IO 120-165  6 10 2000 1 10    2750   3250
17 6 WILDCAT I           RNBT  FBG    OB          7  2 1100         2200   2600
17 6 WILDCAT I           RNBT  FBG    IO 120-188  7  2 2000 2       2950   3550
17 6 WILDCAT II          RNBT  FBG    OB          7  2 1150         2300   2700
17 6 WILDCAT II          RNBT  FBG    IO 120-165  7  2 2000 2       3000   3550
17 7 BARONET             CBNCR FBG    OB          7  2 1450         2700   3150
17 7 MINIKAI             RNBT  FBG    OB          7  2 1250         2450   2850

17 7 MINIKAI             RNBT  FBG    IO 120-165  7  2 2000 2       3000   3550
18 9 COUGAR              RNBT  FBG    OB          7  4 1300         2600   3000
18 9 COUGAR              RNBT  FBG    IO 120-225  7  4 2200 2 2     3350   4000
21   VISCOUNT            FSH   FBG    OB          7  8 1950         4050   4700
21   VISCOUNT            FSH   FBG    IO 120-225  7  8 2600 2 4     5100   6000
23 9 240            HT   CNV   FBG    IO 155-225  8    3700 2 11    7150   8850
23 9 240            HT   CR    FBG    IO 155-225  8    4000 2 11    7350   8650
23 9 240            FB   SF    FBG    IO 155-225  8    4500 2 11   10100  11700
28 2 280            FB   CR    FBG    VD 225-280  10 4 8000 3      11400  13300
     IO T155-T188 16100 18800, IO T225 MRCR 17000 19300, IO T225 OMC 17000 19200
     VD T225        12700 14600

28 2 280                 EXP   FBG    VD 225-280  10 4 8000 3      11300  13200
     IO T155-T188 15900 18600, IO T225 MRCR 16800 19100, IO T225 OMC 16800 19100
     VD T225        12600 14500
------------------- 1971 BOATS -------------------------------------------------------
16 9 BIMINI              RNBT  FBG    OB          6 10 1150 1 10    2250   2600
16 9 BIMINI              RNBT  FBG    IO 120-140  6 10 2000 1 10    2850   3450
16 9 ELIMINATOR          RNBT  FBG    OB          6 10 1100 1 10    2150   2500
16 9 ELIMINATOR          RNBT  FBG    IO 120-165  6 10 2000 1 10    2800   3400
17 6 BARONET MARK IV     SDN   FBG TR OB     80 MRCR 7 2 2200      3200   3750
17 6 WILDCAT I           RNBT  FBG    OB          7  2 1100         2200   2600
17 6 WILDCAT I           RNBT  FBG    IO 120-188  7  2 2000 2       3100   3650
17 6 WILDCAT II          RNBT  FBG    OB          7  2 1150         2300   2650
17 7 BARONET             CBNCR FBG    OB          7  2 1450         2700   3150
17 7 BARONET             CBNCR FBG    IO 120-140  7  2 2300 2       3400   3950
17 7 MINIKAI             RNBT  FBG    OB          7  2 1250         2450   2850
17 7 MINIKAI             RNBT  FBG    IO 120-165  7  2 2000 2       3100   3650

18 9 COUGAR              RNBT  FBG    OB          7  4 1300         2600   3000
18 9 COUGAR              RNBT  FBG    IO 120-215  7  4 2200 2 2     3450   4100
21   VISCOUNT            FSH   FBG    OB          7  8 1950 2 4     4500   4700
21   VISCOUNT            FSH   FBG    IO 120-215  7  8 2600 2 4     5250   6150
23                  HT   CNV   FBG    IO 155-215  8    3500 2 11    7200   8450
23                  HT   CR    FBG    IO 155-215  8    4000 2 11    7300   8550
23                  FB   SF    FBG    IO 155-215  8    4500 3      9950  11500
23   FAMILY SALON        CR    FBG    IO 155-215  8    5000 3     10800  10200
23   MONTAUK 23          CR    FBG    IO 120-140  8    3200 2 11    6350   7300
28 2 WINNER 280 6 SLEEPER CR   FBG    VD 225-330 10 4  8000 3      11000  13100
28 2 WINNER 280 6 SLEEPER CR   FBG    VD T215-T225 10 4 8000 3     12200  14000
------------------- 1970 BOATS -------------------------------------------------------
16 9 BIMINI 775          RNBT  FBG TR OB          6 10 1600         2150   2500
16 9 BIMINI 775C         RNBT  FBG DV IO 120 MRCR 6 10 1800         2850   3300
16 9 BIMINI 775D         RNBT  FBG DV IO 140 OMC  6 10 1800         2800   3300
16 9 BIMINI 775P         RNBT  FBG DV IO 120 OMC  6 10 1800         2800   3250
16 9 ELIMINATOR 738      RNBT  FBG DV OB          6 10 1600         1950   2350
16 9 ELIMINATOR 738C     RNBT  FBG DV IO 120 MRCR 6 10 1700         2800   3250
16 9 ELIMINATOR 738D     RNBT  FBG DV IO 140 MRCR 6 10 1700         2850   3250
16 9 ELIMINATOR 738K     RNBT  FBG DV IO 165 MRCR 6 10 1700         2850   3300
16 9 ELIMINATOR 738P     RNBT  FBG DV IO 120 OMC  6 10 1700         2750   3200
16 9 ELIMINATOR 738Q     RNBT  FBG DV IO 155 OMC  6 10 1700         2850   3200
17 6 BARONET MK IV 928   CBNCR FBG DV OB          7  2 1350         2550   3000
17 6 BARONET MK IV 928C  CBNCR FBG DV IO 120 MRCR 7 2 2030         3250   3800

17 6 BARONET MK IV 928D  CBNCR FBG DV IO 140 MRCR 7 2 2030         3300   3800
17 6 BARONET MK IV 928J  CBNCR FBG DV IO 160 MRCR 7 2 2130         3350   3900
17 6 BARONET MK IV 928K  CBNCR FBG DV IO 165 MRCR 7 2 2130         3350   3900
17 6 BARONET MK IV 928P  CBNCR FBG DV IO 120 OMC  7 2 2030         3300   3800
17 6 BARONET MK IV 928Q  CBNCR FBG DV IO 155 OMC  7 2 2130         3300   3850
17 6 MINIKAI 907         RNBT  FBG TR OB          7  2 1800         2250   2650
17 6 MINIKAI 907 C       RNBT  FBG TR IO 120 MRCR 7 2 1800         3100   3650
17 6 MINIKAI 907 D       RNBT  FBG TR IO 140 MRCR 7 2 1800         3150   3650
17 6 MINIKAI 907 J       RNBT  FBG TR IO 160 MRCR 7 2 1900         3200   3750
17 6 MINIKAI 907 K       RNBT  FBG TR IO 165 MRCR 7 2 1900         3200   3750
17 6 MINIKAI 907 P       RNBT  FBG TR IO 120 OMC  7 2 1800         3150   3650
17 6 MINIKAI 907 Q       RNBT  FBG TR IO 155 OMC  7 2 1900         3200   3700

17 6 WILDCAT 807         RNBT  FBG DV OB          7  2 1100         2150   2550
17 6 WILDCAT 807C        RNBT  FBG DV IO 120 MRCR 7 2 1800         3400   3450
17 6 WILDCAT 807D        RNBT  FBG DV IO 140 MRCR 7 2 1800         3450   3550
17 6 WILDCAT 807J        RNBT  FBG DV IO 160 MRCR 7 2 1900         3550   3550
17 6 WILDCAT 807K        RNBT  FBG DV IO 165 MRCR 7 2 1900         3500   3500
17 6 WILDCAT 807P        RNBT  FBG DV IO 120 OMC  7 2 1800         2950   3500
17 6 WILDCAT 807Q        RNBT  FBG DV IO 155 OMC  7 2 1900         3500   3450
17 6 WILDCAT 807T        RNBT  FBG DV IO 215 MRCR 7 2 1900         3400   3500
18 9 COUGAR 953          RNBT  FBG DV OB          7  4 1230         2450   2900
18 9 COUGAR 953D         RNBT  FBG DV IO 120 OMC  7 4 1930         3400   3950
18 9 COUGAR 953D         RNBT  FBG DV IO 140 OMC  7 4 1930         3400   3950
18 9 COUGAR 953J         RNBT  FBG DV IO 160 MRCR 7 4 2030         3450   4050

18 9 COUGAR 953K         RNBT  FBG DV IO 165 MRCR 7 4 2030         3500   4050
18 9 COUGAR 953P         RNBT  FBG DV IO 120 OMC  7 4 1930         3350   3900
18 9 COUGAR 953Q         RNBT  FBG DV IO 155 OMC  7 4 1930         3450   3900
18 9 COUGAR 953T         RNBT  FBG DV IO 215 MRCR 7 4 2030         3400   4200
21   VISCOUNT MK II 2203C FSH  FBG DV IO 120 MRCR 8 2 2350         5150   5900
21   VISCOUNT MK II 2203D FSH  FBG DV IO 140 MRCR 8 2 2350         5150   5900
21   VISCOUNT MK II 2203J FSH  FBG DV IO 160 MRCR 8 2 2450         5250   6050
21   VISCOUNT MK II 2203K FSH  FBG DV IO 165 MRCR 8 2 2450         5300   6050
21   VISCOUNT MK II 2203P FSH  FBG DV IO 120 OMC  8 2 2350         5150   5850
21   VISCOUNT MK II 2203Q FSH  FBG DV IO 155 OMC  8 2 2450         5250   6000
21   VISCOUNT MK II 2203T FSH  FBG DV IO 215 MRCR 8 2 2450         5550   6350
23   2302CC         HT   EXP   FBG DV IO T120 MRCR 8    4500      9000  10300

23   2302J          HT   EXP   FBG DV IO 160 MRCR 8    3800      7050   8100
23   2302PP         HT   EXP   FBG DV IO T120 OMC 8     3900      7050   8100
23   2302Q          HT   EXP   FBG DV IO 155 OMC 8      3700      6900   7900
23   2302R          HT   EXP   FBG DV IO 215 OMC 8      3900      7250   8300
23   2302T          HT   EXP   FBG DV IO 215 MRCR 8     3900      7300   8350
23   2303CC         FB   SF    FBG DV IO T120 MRCR 8    4800     11900  13600
23   2303J          FB   SF    FBG DV IO 160 MRCR 8     4100      9600  10900
23   2303K          FB   SF    FBG DV IO 165 MRCR 8     4100      9650  10900
23   2303PP         FB   SF    FBG DV IO T120 OMC 8     4800     11900  13500
23   2303Q          FB   SF    FBG DV IO 155 OMC 8      4200      9400  10700
23   2303R          FB   SF    FBG DV IO 210 OMC 8      4200      9800  11200
```

LOA FT	LOA IN	NAME AND/ OR MODEL	TOP/ RIG	BOAT TYPE	HULL MTL	HULL TP	ENGINE TP	ENGINE # HP	ENGINE MFG	BEAM FT	BEAM IN	WGT LBS	DRAFT FT	DRAFT IN	RETAIL LOW	RETAIL HIGH
		1970 BOATS														
23		2303T	FB	SF	FBG	DV	IO	215	MRCR	8		4200			9900	11200
23		FAMILY CNV 2300		CR	FBG	DV	OB			8		3500			6850	7850
23		FAMILY CNV 2301CC		CR	FBG	DV	IO	T120	MRCR	8		4200			8850	10000
23		FAMILY CNV 2301J		CR	FBG	DV	IO	160	MRCR	8		3600			7000	8000
23		FAMILY CNV 2301K		CR	FBG	DV	IO	165	MRCR	8		3600			7000	8050
23		FAMILY CNV 2301PP		CR	FBG	DV	IO	T120	OMC	8		4200			8650	9950
23		FAMILY CNV 2301Q		CR	FBG	DV	IO	155	OMC	8		3600			6950	7950
23		FAMILY CNV 2301R		CR	FBG	DV	IO	210	OMC	8		3700			7150	8250
23		FAMILY CNV 2301T		CR	FBG	DV	IO	215	MRCR	8		3700			7200	8300
23		FAMILY SALON 2304CC		CR	FBG	DV	IO	T120	MRCR	8		4800			9700	11000
23		FAMILY SALON 2304J		CR	FBG	DV	IO	160	MRCR	8		4100			7650	8800
23		FAMILY SALON 2304K		CR	FBG	DV	IO	165	MRCR	8		4100			7700	8850
23		FAMILY SALON 2304PP		CR	FBG	DV	IO	T120	OMC	8		4800			9650	11000
23		FAMILY SALON 2304Q		CR	FBG	DV	IO	155	OMC	8		4000			7500	8600
23		FAMILY SALON 2304R		CR	FBG	DV	IO	210	OMC	8		4200			7850	9050
23		FAMILY SALON 2304T		CR	FBG	DV	IO	215	MRCR	8		4200			7900	9100
		1969 BOATS														
16	4	SHALIMAR 726 N		RNBT	FBG	SV	IO	80	MRCR	6	8	1450			2550	3000
17	6	BARONET MK IV C/TRIM		CBNCR	FBG	DV	IO	120	MRCR	7	2	2200			3500	4050
17	6	BARONET MK IV D/TRIM		CBNCR	FBG	DV	IO	140	MRCR	7	2	2300			3550	4150
17	6	BARONET MK IV J/TRIM		CBNCR	FBG	DV	IO	160	MRCR	7	2	2400			3650	4250
17	6	BARONET MK IV N		CBNCR	FBG	DV	IO	80	MRCR	7	2	2000			3350	3900
17	6	BARONET MK IV O		CBNCR	FBG	DV	IO	80	OMC	7	2	2200			3450	4050
17	6	BARONET MK IV P		CBNCR	FBG	DV	IO	120	OMC	7	2	2200			3500	4050
17	6	BARONET MK IV Q		CBNCR	FBG	DV	IO	155	OMC	7	2	2400			3650	4200
17	6	BARONET MK IV QV		CBNCR	FBG	DV	OB			7	2	1450	2		2700	3150
17	6	MINIKAI 906 C/TRIM		RNBT	FBG	TR	IO	120	MRCR	7	2	1800			3100	3650
17	6	MINIKAI 906 D/TRIM		RNBT	FBG	TR	IO	140	MRCR	7	2	2000			3250	3800
17	6	MINIKAI 906 J/TRIM		RNBT	FBG	TR	IO	160	MRCR	7	2	2000			3300	3800
17	6	MINIKAI 906 P		RNBT	FBG	TR	IO	120	OMC	7	2	1800			3150	3650
17	6	MINIKAI 906 Q		RNBT	FBG	TR	IO	155	OMC	7	2	2000			3250	3750
17	6	MINIKAI 906 TQV		RNBT	FBG	DV	OB			7	2	1100	1	10	2200	2600
17	6	WILDCAT 806 C/TRIM		RNBT	FBG	DV	IO	120	MRCR	7		1700			3000	3500
17	6	WILDCAT 806 D/TRIM		RNBT	FBG	DV	IO	140	MRCR	7		1800			3100	3600
17	6	WILDCAT 806 H		RNBT	FBG	DV	IO	235	HOLM	7		2000			3400	3950
17	6	WILDCAT 806 J/TRIM		RNBT	FBG	DV	IO	160	MRCR	7		2000			3250	3750
17	6	WILDCAT 806 P		RNBT	FBG	DV	IO	120	OMC	7		1700			3000	3500
17	6	WILDCAT 806 Q		RNBT	FBG	DV	IO	155	OMC	7		2000			3250	3750
17	6	WILDCAT 806 QV		RNBT	FBG	DV	OB			7		1000	1	8	2000	2400
17	6	WILDCAT 806 S/TRIM		RNBT	FBG	DV	IO	200	MRCR	7		2200			3450	4000
18	9	COUGAR 952 C/TRIM		RNBT	FBG	DV	IO	120	MRCR	7	4	2000			3500	4050
18	9	COUGAR 952 D/TRIM		RNBT	FBG	DV	IO	140	MRCR	7	4	2000			3500	4100
18	9	COUGAR 952 H		RNBT	FBG	DV	IO	235	HOLM	7	4	2200			3850	4500
18	9	COUGAR 952 J/TRIM		RNBT	FBG	DV	IO	160	MRCR	7	4	2200			3700	4300
18	9	COUGAR 952 P		RNBT	FBG	DV	IO	120	OMC	7	4	2000			3500	4100
18	9	COUGAR 952 Q		RNBT	FBG	DV	IO	155	OMC	7	4	2200			3650	4250
18	9	COUGAR 952 QV		RNBT	FBG	DV	OB			7	4	1230			2500	2900
18	9	COUGAR 952 S/TRIM		RNBT	FBG	DV	IO	200	MRCR	7	4	2400			3900	4550
21		VISCOUNT MARK II H		FSH	FBG	DV	IO	235	HOLM	7	8	2750			5950	6850
21		VISCOUNT MARK II P		FSH	FBG	DV	IO	120	OMC	7	8	2550			5550	6350
21		VISCOUNT MARK II Q		FSH	FBG	DV	IO	155	OMC	7	8	2750			5700	6550
21		VISCOUNT MARKII C/TR		FSH	FBG	DV	IO	120	MRCR	7	8	2550			5500	6300
21		VISCOUNT MARKII D/TR		FSH	FBG	DV	IO	140	MRCR	7	8	2650			5600	6450
21		VISCOUNT MARKII J/TR		FSH	FBG	DV	IO	160	MRCR	7	8	2750			5750	6600
21		VISCOUNT MARKII S/TR		FSH	FBG	DV	IO	200	MRCR	7	8	2950			6050	6950
		1968 BOATS														
16	4	SHALIMAR 724 C/TRIM	OP	RNBT	FBG		IO	120		6	8	1548	2		2750	3200
16	4	SHALIMAR 724 N	OP	RNBT	FBG		IO	80	MRCR	6	8	1433	2		2650	3050
16	4	SHALIMAR 724 O		RNBT	FBG		IO	80		6	8	1433			2650	3050
17	6	MINIKAI 905 C/TRIM	OP	RNBT	FBG	TR	IO	120		7	2	1525			3050	3550
17	6	MINIKAI 905 N	OP	RNBT	FBG	TR	IO	80		7	2	1455			2950	3450
17	6	MINIKAI 905 O	OP	RNBT	FBG	TR	IO	80		7	2	1455			3050	3550
17	6	MINIKAI 905 P	OP	RNBT	FBG	TR	IO	120		7	2	1525			3100	3600
17	6	MINIKAI 905 QVT	OP	RNBT	FBG	TR	OB			7	2	940			1900	2250
17	6	WILDCAT 805 C/TRIM	OP	RNBT	FBG	SV	IO	120		7	2	1635			3100	3600
17	6	WILDCAT 805 H	OP	RNBT	FBG	SV	IO	225		7	2	2060			3550	4100
17	6	WILDCAT 805 J/TRIM	OP	RNBT	FBG	SV	IO	160		7	2	1785			3200	3750
17	6	WILDCAT 805 P	OP	RNBT	FBG	SV	IO	120		7	2	1635			3150	3650
17	6	WILDCAT 805 Q	OP	RNBT	FBG	SV	IO	155		7	2	1745			3250	3800
17	6	WILDCAT 805 QV	OP	RNBT	FBG	SV	OB			7	2	850			1750	2050
17	6	WILDCAT 805 R	OP	RNBT	FBG	SV	IO	210		7	2				3350	3900
17	6	WILDCAT 805 U	OP	RNBT	FBG	SV	IO	155		7	2	1745			3200	3750
17	7	BARONET 926 C/TRIM		CBNCR	FBG	DV	IO	120		7	2	2055	2		3500	4050
17	7	BARONET 926 N		CBNCR	FBG	DV	IO	80	MRCR	7	2	1755	2		3250	3800
17	7	BARONET 926 O		CBNCR	FBG	DV	IO	80		7	2	1755	2		3350	3900
17	7	BARONET 926 QV		CBNCR	FBG	DV	OB			7	2	1240	2		2400	2800
18	7	COUGAR 951 C/TRIM	OP	RNBT	FBG	DV	IO	120	MRCR	7	6	1735	2		3450	4050
18	7	COUGAR 951 H	OP	RNBT	FBG	DV	IO	225		7	6	2160	2		3900	4550
18	7	COUGAR 951 J/TRIM	OP	RNBT	FBG	DV	IO	160		7	6	1885	2		3600	4150
18	7	COUGAR 951 P	OP	RNBT	FBG	DV	IO	120		7	6	1735	2		3500	4050
18	7	COUGAR 951 Q	OP	RNBT	FBG	DV	IO	155		7	6	1845	2		3550	4150
18	7	COUGAR 951 QV	OP	RNBT	FBG	DV	OB			7	6	950	2		2000	2350
18	7	COUGAR 951 R	OP	RNBT	FBG	DV	IO	210		7	6		2		3750	4400
18	7	COUGAR 951 U	OP	RNBT	FBG	DV	IO	155		7	6	1845	2		3550	4100
20	6	VISCOUNT II H		FSH	FBG		IO	225		7	8	2835	2		6050	6950
20	6	VISCOUNT II J/TRIM	OP	FSH	FBG		IO	160		7	8	2460	2		5450	6300
20	6	VISCOUNT II P	OP	FSH	FBG		IO	120	MRCR	7	8	2140	2		5150	5900
20	6	VISCOUNT II Q	OP	FSH	FBG		IO	155		7	8	2420	2		5450	6250
20	6	VISCOUNT II QV C/TR	OP	FSH	FBG		IO	120	MRCR	7	8	2140	2		5100	5850
20	6	VISCOUNT II R	OP	FSH	FBG		IO	210		7	8		2		5600	6450
20	6	VISCOUNT II U	OP	FSH	FBG		IO	155		7	8	2420	2		5400	6200
		1967 BOATS														
16	4	MARATHON 605 CQV		RNBT	FBG		IO	120		6	8	1550	1	10	2800	3250
16	4	MARATHON 605 HQV		RNBT	FBG		IO	225		6	8	1750	1	10	3100	3650
16	4	MARATHON 605 NQV		RNBT	FBG		IO	80		6	8	1250	1	10	2600	3000
16	4	MARATHON 605 UQV		RNBT	FBG		IO	155		6	8	1650	1	10	2900	3350
16	4	SEVILLE 604 CG	OP	RNBT	FBG		IO	120		6	8	1500	1	7	2800	3250
16	4	SEVILLE 604 NG	OP	RNBT	FBG		IO	80		6	8	1300	1	7	2600	3050
17	7	BARONET 821 QV		CBNCR	FBG	DV	OB			7	2	1240			2400	2800
18	9	COUGAR 903 CQV		RNBT	FBG		IO	120		7	6	2000	1	8	3800	4450
18	9	COUGAR 903 HQV		RNBT	FBG		IO	225		7	6	2300	1	8	4200	4900
18	9	COUGAR 903 JQV		RNBT	FBG		IO	160		7	6	2200	1	8	4000	4650
18	9	COUGAR 903 QV		RNBT	FBG		OB			7	6	1250	1	8	2550	2950
18	9	COUGAR 903 UQV		RNBT	FBG		IO	155		7	6	2100	1	8	3900	4550
20	7	VISCOUNT 2103 CQV		FSH	FBG		IO	120		8		2350	1	8	5650	6500
20	7	VISCOUNT 2103 HQV		FSH	FBG		IO	225		8		2350	1	8	5800	6700
20	7	VISCOUNT 2103 JQV		FSH	FBG		IO	160		8		2350	1	8	5650	6500
20	7	VISCOUNT 2103 LLQV		FSH	FBG		IO	T 60		8		2350	1	8	6400	7350
20	7	VISCOUNT 2103 NNQV		FSH	FBG		IO	T 80		8		2350	1	8	6400	7350
20	7	VISCOUNT 2103 UQV		FSH	FBG		IO	155		8		2350	1	8	5650	6500
		1966 BOATS														
16	4	MARATHON		RNBT	FBG		IO	110-155		6	8				3250	3800
16	4	SHALIMAR		RNBT	FBG		IO	60-120		6	8				3150	3650
17	7	BARONET		CBNCR	FBG		OB			7	2	1400			2650	3100
17	7	BARONET		CBNCR	FBG		IO	110-150		7	2				3550	4100
17	7	ISLANDER		RNBT	FBG		OB			7	2				2450	2850
17	7	ISLANDER		RNBT	FBG		IO	110-155		7	2				3500	4050
17	7	MACKINAC		RNBT	FBG		OB			7	2	1000			2000	2400
17	7	MACKINAC		RNBT	FBG		IO	110-155		7	2				3400	4050
20	6	VISCOUNT 2101		FSH	FBG		IO	110-155							5750	6650
20	6	VISCOUNT 2101		FSH	FBG		IO	T 60							6450	7400
20	6	VISCOUNT 2102		FSH	FBG		IO	110-155							5950	6850
20	6	VISCOUNT 2102		FSH	FBG		IO	T 60							6700	7700
		1965 BOATS														
16	4	MARCHESA		RNBT	FBG		IO	60							3150	3700
16	4	MARLIN		RNBT	FBG		IO	110-165							3150	3750
17	4	ISLANDER		RNBT	FBG		OB								2350	2700
17	4	ISLANDER		RNBT	FBG		IO	110-165							3400	4000
17	7	BARONET		CBNCR	FBG		OB								2750	3150
17	7	BARONET		CBNCR	FBG		IO	110-165							3650	4250
19	2	VISCOUNT		FSH	FBG		OB								2500	2900
19	2	VISCOUNT		FSH	FBG		IO	110-165							4550	5250
28		TRAVEL YACHT	HT	HB	FBG		OB								**	**
28		TRAVEL YACHT	HT	HB	FBG		IO	110-165							**	**
		1964 BOATS														
16	4	BIMINI		RNBT	WD		OB								1700	2000
16	4	BIMINI		RNBT	WD		IO	80-160							3250	3800
16	4	SEVILLE NOVA	OP	RNBT	FBG		OB								1800	2100
16	4	SEVILLE NOVA	OP	RNBT	FBG		IO	80-160							3250	3800
17	4	BARONET		CBNCR	FBG		OB								2050	2450
17	4	BARONET		CBNCR	FBG		IO	80-140							3500	4100
19	2	VISCOUNT		FSH	FBG		OB								2500	2900
19	2	VISCOUNT		FSH	FBG		IO	80-160							4650	5400
28		TRAVEL YACHT	HT	HB	FBG		OB								**	**
28		TRAVEL YACHT	HT	HB	FBG		IO	80-160							**	**
		1963 BOATS														
16	4	SEVILLE CRITERION	OP	RNBT	FBG		OB								1700	2000
16	4	SEVILLE CRITERION	OP	RNBT	FBG		IO	80-125							3350	3900
16	4	SEVILLE NOVA	OP	RNBT	FBG		OB								1700	2000

 CONTINUED ON NEXT PAGE

LOA FT IN	NAME AND/ OR MODEL	TOP/ RIG	BOAT TYPE	HULL MTL	HULL TP	ENG TP	ENG #	ENG HP	ENG MFG	BEAM FT IN	WGT LBS	DRAFT FT IN	RETAIL LOW	RETAIL HIGH
					1963 BOATS									
16 4	SEVILLE NOVA	OP	RNBT	FBG		IO		80-125					3350	3900
16 4	SHALIMAR CRITERION		RNBT	FBG		IO		80					3350	3900
16 4	SHALIMAR NOVA		RNBT	FBG		OB							1800	2150
16 4	SHALIMAR NOVA		RNBT	FBG		IO		80					3350	3900
17 4	BARONET		CBNCR	FBG		OB							1900	2250
17 4	BARONET		CBNCR	FBG		IO		100					3600	4150
17 4	RAVINA		CBNCR	FBG		OB							2250	2600
17 4	RAVINA		CBNCR	FBG		IO		100-125					3600	4200
17 6	BIMINI-CRITERION		RNBT	WD		OB							2450	2850
17 6	BIMINI-CRITERION		RNBT	WD		IO		80-125					3750	4400
17 6	BIMINI-NOVA 100		RNBT	WD		OB							2450	2850
17 6	BIMINI-NOVA 100		RNBT	WD		IO		80-125					3750	4400
17 6	BIMINI-NOVA 150		RNBT	FBG		OB							2450	2850
17 6	BIMINI-NOVA 150		RNBT	WD		IO		80-125					3750	4400
19 2	VISCOUNT CRITERION		FSH	FBG		OB							2500	2900
19 2	VISCOUNT CRITERION		FSH	FBG		IO		100-125					4850	5550
19 2	VISCOUNT NOVA		FSH	FBG		OB							2500	2900
19 2	VISCOUNT NOVA		FSH	FBG		IO		100-125					4850	5550
20 6	BARNEGAT CRIT 100		RNBT	WD		OB							4100	4800
20 6	BARNEGAT CRIT 100		RNBT	WD		IO		100-125					5800	6650
20 6	BARNEGAT CRIT 200		RNBT	WD		OB							4100	4800
20 6	MARBLEHEAD NOVA		CBNCR	WD		OB							4100	4800
28		HT	HB	FBG		OB							**	**
28		HT	HB	FBG		IO		125					**	**
					1962 BOATS									
16 4	SEVILLE CRIT 403	OP	RNBT	FBG		OB							1700	2000
16 4	SEVILLE CRIT 403	OP	RNBT	FBG		IO		80					3450	4000
16 4	SEVILLE NOVA 404	OP	RNBT	FBG		OB							1700	2000
16 4	SEVILLE NOVA 404	OP	RNBT	FBG		IO		80					3450	4250
16 4	SHALIMAR CRIT 411		RNBT	FBG		OB							1700	2000
16 4	SHALIMAR NOVA 412		RNBT	FBG		OB							1700	2000
17 4	ISLANDER CRIT 501		RNBT	FBG		OB							2350	2750
17 4	ISLANDER CRIT 503		RNBT	FBG		IO		80					3700	4550
17 4	ISLANDER NOVA 502		RNBT	FBG		OB							2350	2750
17 4	ISLANDER NOVA 504		RNBT	FBG		IO		80					3700	4550
17 4	RAVINA CRITERION 511		CBNCR	FBG		OB							2050	2450
17 4	RAVINA CRITERION 511		CBNCR	FBG		IO		80					3700	4600
17 4	RAVINA NOVA 512		CBNCR	FBG		OB							2050	2450
17 4	RAVINA NOVA 512		CBNCR	FBG		IO		80					3700	4600
17 6	BIMINI-CRITERION 535		RNBT	WD		OB							2450	2850
17 6	BIMINI-CRITERION 535		RNBT	WD		IO		80					3900	4750
17 6	BIMINI-NOVA 536		RNBT	WD		OB							2450	2850
17 6	BIMINI-NOVA 536		RNBT	WD		IO		80					3900	4750
17 6	MACKINAC CRIT 541		RNBT	WD		OB							2450	2850
17 6	MACKINAC CRIT 541		RNBT	WD		IO		80					3900	4750
17 6	MACKINAC NOVA 542		RNBT	WD		OB							2450	2850
17 6	MACKINAC NOVA 542		RNBT	WD		IO		80					3900	4750
19 2	CAMELOT 711		CBNCR	FBG		OB							2650	3100
19 2	CAMELOT 711		CBNCR	FBG		IO		80					4900	5900
19 2	VISCOUNT 701		FSH	FBG		OB							2500	2900
19 2	VISCOUNT 703		FSH	FBG		IO		80					4950	5950
20 6	BARNEGAT CRIT 735		RNBT	WD		OB							4150	4800
20 6	BARNEGAT CRIT 735		RNBT	WD		IO		80					5950	7100
20 6	BARNEGAT-NOVA 736		RNBT	WD		OB							4150	4800
20 6	BARNEGAT-NOVA 736		RNBT	WD		IO		80					5950	7100
					1961 BOATS									
17 4	BARONET		CBNCR	FBG		OB				7 2	1300		2550	2950
17 4	ISLANDER 18		RNBT	FBG		OB				7 2	950		1950	2350
19 2	CONTESSA 20		CR	FBG		OB				7 10	1500		3000	3450
19 2	VISCOUNT		FSH	FBG		OB				7 10	1400		2800	3300
					1960 BOATS									
17 4	BARONET		CBNCR	FBG	DV	OB				7	1250		2450	2850
19 2	CONTESSA		CR	FBG	DV	OB				7 10	1500		3000	3450
19 2	VISCOUNT		FSH	FBG	DV	OB				7 10	1250		2600	3050
					1959 BOATS									
19 2	CONTESSA		CR	FBG		OB				7 10	1500		3000	3500
19 2	VISCOUNT		FSH	FBG		OB				7 10	1200		2550	2950

WINNIPESAUKEE STEAMSHIP CO

Call 1-800-327-6929 for BUC Personalized Evaluation Service
Or, for 1912 boats, sign onto www.BUCValuPro.com

WINTER YACHT BASIN INC

Call 1-800-327-6929 for BUC Personalized Evaluation Service
Or, for 1961 to 1966 boats, sign onto www.BUCValuPro.com

WISNER BROTHERS BOAT BLDRS

Call 1-800-327-6929 for BUC Personalized Evaluation Service
Or, for 1981 to 1986 boats, sign onto www.BUCValuPro.com

WITNESS CATAMARANS
COAST GUARD MFG ID- GUS

Call 1-800-327-6929 for BUC Personalized Evaluation Service
Or, for 1980 to 1986 boats, sign onto www.BUCValuPro.com

WOOD MARINE COMPANY
DIV OF BOAT BARN INC   COAST GUARD MFG ID- BXA

Call 1-800-327-6929 for BUC Personalized Evaluation Service
Or, for 1966 to 1986 boats, sign onto www.BUCValuPro.com

WORLD MARINE ENT INC
COAST GUARD MFG ID- WWJ
SEE ALSO PUGET SOUND BOAT WKS LTD

Call 1-800-327-6929 for BUC Personalized Evaluation Service
Or, for 1979 boats, sign onto www.BUCValuPro.com

WORLDCRUISER YACHT CO
COAST GUARD MFG ID- WUC

Call 1-800-327-6929 for BUC Personalized Evaluation Service
Or, for 1977 to 1985 boats, sign onto www.BUCValuPro.com

WRIGHT-BUILT BOAT CO

Call 1-800-327-6929 for BUC Personalized Evaluation Service
Or, for 1959 to 1970 boats, sign onto www.BUCValuPro.com

WYLIE DESIGN GROUP
ALAMEDA CA 94501   COAST GUARD MFG ID- TLG See inside cover to adjust price for area

LOA FT IN	NAME AND/ OR MODEL	TOP/ RIG	BOAT TYPE	HULL MTL	HULL TP	ENG TP	ENG #	ENG HP	ENG MFG	BEAM FT IN	WGT LBS	DRAFT FT IN	RETAIL LOW	RETAIL HIGH
					1979 BOATS									
28	HAWKFARM	SLP	SA/OD	FBG	KL	IB		8D	PETT	9 11	5700	5 3	13300	15200
33 9	WYLIE 34	SLP	SA/RC	FBG	KL	IB		7D	REN	10 10	7802	6	19600	21700
					1978 BOATS									
25	WYLIE 24	SLP	SA/CR	FBG	KL	IB		D		7 3		4 6	9400	10700
25	WYLIE 24	SLP	SA/OD	FBG	KL	IB		D		7 3		4 6	9400	10700
28	HAWKFARM	SLP	SA/OD	FBG	KL	IB		8D	PETT	9 11	5700	5 3	12900	14600
31	GEMINI	SLP	SA/OD	WD	KL	IB		9		3	5064	8 2	12000	13600
42	WYLIE 42	SLP	SA/RC	WD	KL	IB		40D	WEST	12 10	20500	7 5	55500	60900
50 2	RACER	SLP	SA/RC	WD	KL	IB		37D		14 2	23500	8	78000	85700
					1977 BOATS									
28	1/2 TON	SLP	SA/RC	FBG	KL	IB		8D	PETT	9 11	5000	5 1	10900	12400
28	HAWKFARM	SLP	SA/OD	FBG	KL	IB		8D	PETT	9 11	5000	5 1	11400	12900
30 6	3/4 TON	SLP	SA/RC	WD	KL	IB		12D	FARY	10 5	8000	5 11	18700	20800
30 10	OFFSHORE 31	KTH	SA/OD	WD	KL	IB		8D	PETT	9 3	5064	8	11500	13100
42 1		SLP	SA/CR	WD	KL	IB		D		12 11	20500	7 5	53700	59000
50 2	OCEAN RACER	SLP	SA/RC	WD	KL	IB		35D	WEST	14 2	23500	8	75200	82600
					1976 BOATS									
28	1/2 TON	SLP	SA/RC	FBG	KL	IB		25D		9 11	5000	5 6	10700	12200

X A X CORPORATION
HALLBERG RASSY VARV AB
FT LAUDERDALE FL 33316   COAST GUARD MFG ID- HRV   See inside cover to adjust price for area

LOA FT IN	NAME AND/ OR MODEL	TOP/ RIG	BOAT TYPE	-HULL- MTL TP	TP #	ENGINE HP	MFG	BEAM FT IN	WGT LBS	DRAFT FT IN	RETAIL LOW	RETAIL HIGH
--------------- 1976 BOATS ---------------
30 9	MONSUN 31	SLP	SAIL	FBG KL	IB	25D	VLVO	9 5	9250	4 7	26600	29500
34 6	RASMUS 35	SLP	SAIL	FBG KL	IB	75D	VLVO	10 4	12000	4 3	35000	38900
34 6	RASMUS 35	KTH	SAIL	FBG KL	IB	75D	VLVO	10 4	12000	4 3	35000	38900
41	HALLBERG-RASSY	KTH	SAIL	FBG KL	IB	75D	VLVO	11 10	22000	5 9	70600	77600
--------------- 1975 BOATS ---------------
24 1	MISIL II	SLP	SAIL	FBG KL	OB			7 7	4078	3 11	8550	9850
26	MAXI 77	SLP	SAIL	FBG KL	OB			8 3	4500	4 8	10500	12000
31	MONSUN	SLP	SAIL	FBG KL	IB	25D	VLVO	9 6	9600	4 5	26800	29800
32	MAXI 95	SLP	SAIL	FBG KL	IB	25D	VLVO	10 7	9400	4 10	26300	29200
33 5	MISTRAL	SLP	SAIL	FBG KL	IB	25D	VLVO	9 11	11464	4 10	32000	35600
35	RASMUS 35	SLP	SAIL	FBG KL	IB	75D	VLVO	10 4	13500	4 4	34000	37800
--------------- 1974 BOATS ---------------
26	NIMBUS		DC	FBG	IB	75D	VLVO	9 6	4500	2 8	8250	9500
26	NIMBUS		DC	FBG	IB	106D	VLVO	9 6	4700	2 8	9400	10700
26	NIMBUS		FSH	FBG	IB	75D	VLVO	9 6	4500	2 8	8250	9500
26	NIMBUS		FSH	FBG	IB	106D	VLVO	9 6	4700	2 8	9400	10700
31	MONSUN	SLP	SAIL	FBG	IB	25D	VLVO	9 6	10000	4 3	27200	30200
33	NIMBUS	FB	DC	FBG	IB	T106D	VLVO	11			28700	31900
35	RASMUS	SLP	SAIL	FBG	IB	75D	VLVO	10 4	13500	4 4	33100	36800
35	RASMUS	KTH	SAIL	FBG	IB	75D	VLVO	10 4	13500	4 4	33100	36800
--------------- 1973 BOATS ---------------
26	NIMBUS		DC	FBG SV	IB	75D		9 6	4500	2 8	8200	9450
29 8	P28		SAIL	FBG	IB	12D	VLVO	7 7	6500	4 3	16700	19000
32	RASMUS		SAIL	FBG	IB	25D	VLVO	10		4	25000	27800
33 5	MISTRAL		SAIL	FBG	IB	25D	VLVO	10 1	12750	4 10	33700	37500
35	RASMUS		SAIL	FBG	IB	75D	VLVO	10 4	13500	4	32300	35900
--------------- 1972 BOATS ---------------
26	NIMBUS		DC	FBG	IB	75D	VLVO	9 6	4460	2 8	7750	8900

THE YACHT HOUSE
ALAMEDA CA 94501   COAST GUARD MFG ID- YAU See inside cover to adjust price for area

LOA FT IN	NAME AND/ OR MODEL	TOP/ RIG	BOAT TYPE	-HULL- MTL TP	TP #	ENGINE HP	MFG	BEAM FT IN	WGT LBS	DRAFT FT IN	RETAIL LOW	RETAIL HIGH
--------------- 1982 BOATS ---------------
36 9	RAFIKI 37	CUT	SA/CR	FBG KL	IB	D		11 8	27000	6	66500	73100
--------------- 1980 BOATS ---------------
34 6	RAFIKI 35 COASTER	SLP	SA/CR	FBG KL	IB	40D		10 10	16500	4 6	39400	43800
36 9	RAFIKI 37	CUT	SA/CR	FBG KL	IB	35D	VLVO	11 8	27000	6	59600	65500
--------------- 1979 BOATS ---------------
34 8	RAFIKI 35	SLP	SA/CR	FBG KL	IB	27D	VLVO	10 10	16500	4 6	37800	42000
36 9	RAFIKI 37	CUT	SA/CR	FBG KL	IB	36D	VLVO	11 8	26500	6	56400	62000
--------------- 1978 BOATS ---------------
34 6	RAFIKI 35 COASTER	SLP	SA/CR	FBG KL	IB	40D		10 10	16500	4 6	36600	40600
36 9	RAFIKI 37	CUT	SA/CR	FBG KL	IB	37D	VLVO	11 8	27000	6	55200	60700
--------------- 1977 BOATS ---------------
34 6	RAFIKI 35 COASTER	SLP	SA/CR	FBG KL	IB	40D		10 10	16500	4 6	35300	39300
36 9	RAFIKI 37	CUT	SA/CR	FBG KL	IB	37D	VLVO	11 8	27000	6	53400	58600

YACHT SERVICE

Call 1-800-327-6929 for BUC Personalized Evaluation Service
Or, for 1976 boats, sign onto www.BUCValuPro.com

YACHTCRAFT CORP

Call 1-800-327-6929 for BUC Personalized Evaluation Service
Or, for 1979 to 1983 boats, sign onto www.BUCValuPro.com

YACHTSTER
COAST GUARD MFG ID- AHT

Call 1-800-327-6929 for BUC Personalized Evaluation Service
Or, for 1971 to 1973 boats, sign onto www.BUCValuPro.com

YAMAHA MOTOR CORP LTD
KENNESAW GA 30144   COAST GUARD MFG ID- YAM See inside cover to adjust price for area

YAMAHA
SHIZVOKA JAPAN

For more recent years, see the BUC Used Boat Price Guide, Volume 1 or Volume 2

LOA FT IN	NAME AND/ OR MODEL	TOP/ RIG	BOAT TYPE	-HULL- MTL TP	TP #	ENGINE HP	MFG	BEAM FT IN	WGT LBS	DRAFT FT IN	RETAIL LOW	RETAIL HIGH
--------------- 1983 BOATS ---------------
26 2	YAMAHA 26	SLP	SA/RC	FBG KL	IB	8D	YAN	9 2	4344	5 1	12400	14000
29 5	YAMAHA 30	SLP	SA/RC	FBG KL	IB	15D	YAN	10 7	7264	5 9	22200	24700
33 5	YAMAHA 33	SLP	SA/RC	FBG KL	IB	15D	YAN	11	10584	6 3	32800	36400
35 11	YAMAHA 36	SLP	SA/RC	FBG KL	IB	20D	YAN	11 10	14333	6 7	45500	50000
--------------- 1982 BOATS ---------------
24 4	YAMAHA 24MS	SLP	SA/CR	FBG KL	IB	8D	YAN	8 6	3638	2 11	9400	10700
26 2	YAMAHA 26	SLP	SA/RC	FBG KL	IB	8D	YAN	9 2	4344	5 1	11600	13200
29 5	YAMAHA 30	SLP	SA/RC	FBG KL	IB	15D	YAN	10 7	7264	5 9	20900	23200
33 5	YAMAHA 33	SLP	SA/RC	FBG KL	IB	15D	YAN	11	10584	6 3	30800	34300
35 3	YAMAHA 35CS	SLP	SA/CR	FBG KL	IB	33D	YAN	11	13780	5 3	40500	45000
35 11	YAMAHA 36	SLP	SA/RC	FBG KL	IB	22D	YAN	11 10	14333	6 7	42400	47100
--------------- 1981 BOATS ---------------
24 4	Y-25 II	SLP	SA/RC	FBG KL	IB	8D	YAN	8 11	3748	5 5	9250	10500
29 5	Y-30	SLP	SA/RC	FBG KL	IB	15D	YAN	10 7	7599	5 9	20600	22900
33 5	Y-33	SLP	SA/RC	FBG KL	IB	15D	YAN	11	9700	6 2	26600	29600
35 11	Y-36	SLP	SA/RC	FBG KL	IB	22D	YAN	11 10	12566	6 7	35400	39300
--------------- 1980 BOATS ---------------
24 4	YAMAHA 24MS	SLP	SA/CR	FBG KL	IB	8D	YAN	8 6	3638	2 11	8400	9650
24 9	YAMAHA 25 MKII	SLP	SA/RC	FBG KL	IB	8D	YAN	8 11	3749	5 5	8850	10000
33 5	YAMAHA 33	SLP	SA/RC	FBG KL	IB	12D	YAN	11	9700	6 3	25400	28200
35 11	YAMAHA 36	SLP	SA/RC	FBG KL	IB	22D	YAN	11 10	12566	6 7	33800	37600
--------------- 1979 BOATS ---------------
24 4	YAMAHA 24MS	SLP	SA/CR	FBG KL	IB	8D	YAN	8 6	3638	2 11	8050	9250
24 9	YAMAHA 25 II	SLP	SA/CR	FBG KL	IB	8D	YAN	8 11	3748	5 5	8400	9650
33 5	YAMAHA 33	SLP	SA/RC	FBG KL	IB	12D	YAN	11	9700	6 3	24400	27200
35 11	YAMAHA 36	SLP	SA/RC	FBG KL	IB	22D	YAN	11 10	12566	6 7	32500	36100

YANKEE CLIPPER YACHTS
COAST GUARD MFG ID- AFV

Call 1-800-327-6929 for BUC Personalized Evaluation Service
Or, for 1979 boats, sign onto www.BUCValuPro.com

YANKEE YACHTS INC
SANTA ANA CA 92705   COAST GUARD MFG ID- YAN See inside cover to adjust price for area

LOA FT IN	NAME AND/ OR MODEL	TOP/ RIG	BOAT TYPE	-HULL- MTL TP	TP #	ENGINE HP	MFG	BEAM FT IN	WGT LBS	DRAFT FT IN	RETAIL LOW	RETAIL HIGH
--------------- 1975 BOATS ---------------
26	YANKEE 26	SLP	SA/CR	FBG KL	IB	7D		8 9	5335	4 9	10300	11800
30	YANKEE	SLP	SA/CR	FBG KL	IB	12D		12 3	10000	3 6	21000	23300
30 1	YANKEE 30 MARK III	SLP	SA/CR	FBG KL	IB	30D		9	10000	5 5	21100	23400
38 2	YANKEE 38	SLP	SA/CR	FBG KL	IB	30D		11 9	16000	6 3	37800	42000
--------------- 1974 BOATS ---------------
26	YANKEE 26	SLP	SAIL	FBG	OB			8 9	5335	4 9	9650	11000
26	YANKEE 26	SLP	SAIL	FBG	IB	7D	WEST	8 8	5355	4 9	10200	11600
27 9	YANKEE 28	SLP	SAIL	FBG	IB	30	UNIV	8 7	6500	4 8	12700	14400
30 1	YANKEE 30 MARK III	SLP	SAIL	FBG	IB	30	UNIV	9	10000	5 5	20500	22800
30 1	YANKEE 30 MARK III D	SLP	SAIL	FBG	IB	30	UNIV	9	10000	5 5	22000	22800
38 2	YANKEE 38	SLP	SAIL	FBG	IB	30	UNIV	11 9	16000	6 3	36500	40600
38 2	YANKEE 38	SLP	SAIL	FBG	IB	25D	WEST	11 9	16000	6 3	37100	41200
--------------- 1973 BOATS ---------------
23 9	YANKEE 24	SLP	SAIL	FBG KC	OB			7 11	2900	1 8	4900	5600
26	YANKEE 26	SLP	SAIL	FBG	OB			8 9	5335	4 9	9500	10800
26	YANKEE 26	SLP	SAIL	FBG	IB	7D	WEST	8 8	5335	4 9	10000	11400
27 9	YANKEE 28	SLP	SAIL	FBG	IB	30	UNIV	8 7	6500	4 8	12500	14200
30 1	YANKEE MARK III	OP	SAIL	FBG	IB	25	UNIV	9	10000	5 5	20100	22400
30 1	YANKEE MARK III	SLP	SAIL	FBG	IB	10D	WEST	9	10000	5 5	20200	22500
38 2	YANKEE 38	SLP	SAIL	FBG	IB	50	UNIV	11 9	16000	6 3	35900	39900
--------------- 1972 BOATS ---------------
23 9	YANKEE 24	SLP	SAIL	FBG	OB			7 11	2900	1 8	4800	5500
26	YANKEE 26	SLP	SAIL	FBG KL	IB	12		8 8	5400	4 9	9650	10900
27 9	YANKEE 28		SAIL	FBG	IB	30	UNIV	8 7	6500	4 8	12200	13900
30 1	YANKEE 30		SAIL	FBG	IB	30	UNIV	9	8700	5 5	16900	19200
38 2	YANKEE 38		SAIL	FBG	IB	25D	WEST	11 9	16000	6 3	35600	39600
--------------- 1971 BOATS ---------------
23 9	SEAHORSE		SAIL	FBG	OB			7 11	2800	1 8	4550	5250
24 2	DOLPHIN		SAIL	FBG	OB			7 8	4250	2 10	6600	7600
24 2	DOLPHIN		SAIL	FBG	IB	10	KERM	7 8	4250	2 10	6900	7950
27 3	YANKEE 27	SLP	SA/CR	FBG KL	IB	10		8 6	6200	4 4	11100	12700

LOA FT IN	NAME AND/ OR MODEL	TOP/ RIG	BOAT TYPE	-HULL- MTL TP	----ENGINE--- TP # HP MFG	BEAM FT IN	WGT LBS	DRAFT FT IN	RETAIL LOW	RETAIL HIGH
				--- 1971 BOATS ---						
30 1	YANKEE 30		SAIL	FBG	IB 12- 25	9	8700	5	16400	18700
30 1	YANKEE 30		SAIL	FBG	IB 11D ALBN	9	8700	5	16500	18800
				--- 1970 BOATS ---						
24 2	DOLPHIN	SLP	SAIL	FBG KC	OB	7 8	4250	2 10	6450	7450
24 2	DOLPHIN	SLP	SAIL	FBG KC	IB 6	7 8	4250	2 10	6700	7700
30	YANKEE 30	SLP	SA/CR	FBG KL	IB ALBN	9		4 10	17300	19600
				--- 1969 BOATS ---						
24 2	DOLPHIN	SLP	SAIL	FBG KC		7 8	4250	2 10	6300	7250

YAR-CRAFT LLC
WAUSAU WI 54401   COAST GUARD MFG ID- YAR See inside cover to adjust price for area

For more recent years, see the BUC Used Boat Price Guide, Volume 1 or Volume 2

LOA FT IN	NAME AND/ OR MODEL	TOP/ RIG	BOAT TYPE	-HULL- MTL TP	----ENGINE--- TP # HP MFG	BEAM FT IN	WGT LBS	DRAFT FT IN	RETAIL LOW	RETAIL HIGH
				--- 1983 BOATS ---						
16	1678 FISH/SKI	ST	FSH	FBG SV	OB	6 6	850		1800	2150
16	AMERICANA 160		RNBT	FBG SV	IO 140	6 7	1095		2200	2550
16	AMERICANA 1683	ST	RNBT	FBG SV	OB	6 7	1060		2300	2700
16 6	EAGLE 166		RNBT	FBG TR	OB	6 5	900		2050	2450
16 6	EAGLE-SPECIAL 166		RNBT	FBG TR	OB	6 5	900		1850	2200
16 6	SPIRIT 164		UTL	FBG TR	OB	6 5	900		1900	2250
17	PATRIOT 170	ST	RNBT	FBG SV	IO 188 MRCR	6 5	1950		3000	3500
17	PATRIOT 1783		RNBT	FBG SV	OB	6 5	1000		2250	2600
19 4	FREEDOM 207		CR	FBG SV	OB	7 3	1600		3350	3900
19 4	FREEDOM 207		RNBT	FBG SV	IO 170	7 3	1620		3450	4000
19 4	LIBERTY 200		RNBT	FBG SV	IO 140	7	1620		3300	3850
19 4	LIBERTY 200 SUN		RNBT	FBG SV	IO 140	7	1620		3400	4000
				--- 1982 BOATS ---						
16	1678 FISH/SKI	ST	FSH	FBG SV	OB	6 6	850		1750	2050
16	AMERICANA 160	ST	RNBT	FBG SV	OB	6 7	1060		2200	2550
16	AMERICANA 160	ST	RNBT	FBG SV	IO 120-170	6 7	2011		2800	3300
16	AMERICANA 160 BR	ST	RNBT	FBG SV	OB	6 7	1060		2300	2650
16 6	EAGLE 166	ST	RNBT	FBG TR	OB	6 5	900		2000	2400
16 6	EAGLE 166S	ST	RNBT	FBG TR	OB	6 5	900		1800	2150
16 6	SPIRIT 164	ST	CTRCN	FBG TR	OB	6 5	900		1850	2250
17	PATRIOT 170	ST	RNBT	FBG SV	OB	6 5	1000		2150	2550
17	PATRIOT 170	ST	RNBT	FBG SV	IO 120-185	6 5	1950		2900	3400
19 4	LIBERTY 200-V-M/B	ST	RNBT	FBG SV	IO 120-230	7	2300		3700	4450
19 4	LIBERTY 200-V-S/L	ST	RNBT	FBG SV	IO 120-230	7	2300		3700	4600
19 5	FREEDOM 207	ST	RNBT	FBG SV	OB	7	1600		3300	3850
19 5	FREEDOM 207	ST	CUD	FBG SV	IO 120-230	7 3	2600		4200	5100
				--- 1981 BOATS ---						
16	1678 FISH/SKI		FSH	FBG SV	OB	6 6	850		1700	2000
16	AMERICANA 160	ST	RNBT	FBG SV	OB	6 6	1060		2100	2500
16	AMERICANA 160	ST	RNBT	FBG SV	IO 120-170	6 6	2011		2750	3250
16	AMERICANA 160 BR	ST	RNBT	FBG SV	OB	6 6	1060		2200	2600
16 6	EAGLE 166	ST	RNBT	FBG TR	OB	6 5	900		1950	2300
16 6	EAGLE 166S	ST	RNBT	FBG TR	OB	6 5	900		1750	2100
16 6	SPIRIT 164	ST	CTRCN	FBG TR	OB	6 5	900		1850	2200
17	PATRIOT 170	ST	RNBT	FBG SV	OB	6 5	1000		2050	2450
17	PATRIOT 170	ST	RNBT	FBG SV	IO 120-170	6 5	1950		2850	3350
19 4	LIBERTY 200-V-M/B	ST	RNBT	FBG SV	IO 140-230	7 1	2300		3650	4400
19 4	LIBERTY 200-V-S/L	ST	RNBT	FBG SV	IO 120-230	7 1	2300		3700	4550
19 5	FREEDOM 207	ST	CUD	FBG SV	OB	7 3	1600		3200	3750
19 5	FREEDOM 207	ST	CUD	FBG SV	IO 170-230	7 3	2600		4200	5050
				--- 1980 BOATS ---						
16	AMERICANA 160	ST	RNBT	FBG SV	OB	6 7	1060		2200	2500
16	AMERICANA 160	ST	RNBT	FBG SV	IO 120-185	6 7	2011		2750	3250
16 6	EAGLE 166	ST	RNBT	FBG TR	OB	6 5	900		1900	2300
16 6	EAGLE 166S	ST	RNBT	FBG TR	OB	6 5	900		1700	2050
16 6	SPIRIT 164	ST	CTRCN	FBG TR	OB	6 5	900		1800	2150
17	PATRIOT 170	ST	RNBT	FBG SV	OB	6 5	1000		2000	2400
17	PATRIOT 170	ST	RNBT	FBG SV	IO 120-185	6 5	1950		2800	3350
19 4	LIBERTY 200-V	ST	RNBT	FBG SV	IO 235-260	7 1			4000	4800
19 4	LIBERTY 200-V-M/B	ST	RNBT	FBG SV	IO 140-230	7 1	2300		3600	4350
19 4	LIBERTY 200-V-S/L	ST	RNBT	FBG SV	IO 140-230	7 1	2300		3750	4550
19 5	FREEDOM 207	ST	CUD	FBG SV	OB	7 3	1600		3150	3650
19 5	FREEDOM 207	ST	CUD	FBG SV	IO 170-260	7 3	2600		4150	5150
				--- 1979 BOATS ---						
16	AMERICANA 160	ST	RNBT	FBG SV	OB	6 7	1060		2050	2450
16	AMERICANA 160	ST	RNBT	FBG SV	IO 120-170	6 7	2011		2750	3250
16 6	EAGLE 166 DLX	ST	RNBT	FBG TR	OB	6 5	900		1750	2100
16 6	EAGLE 166S	ST	RNBT	FBG TR	OB	6 5	900		1750	2100
16 6	SPIRIT 164	ST	CTRCN	FBG TR	OB	6 5	900		1750	2100
17	PATRIOT 170	ST	RNBT	FBG SV	OB	6 5	1000		2000	2350
17	PATRIOT 170	ST	RNBT	FBG SV	IO 120-170	6 5	1950		2800	3300
19 4	LIBERTY 200	ST	RNBT	FBG SV	IO 140-230	7	2300		3650	4400
19 5	FREEDOM 207	ST	CUD	FBG SV	IO 170-230	7 3	2600		4150	5000
				--- 1978 BOATS ---						
16 6	EAGLE 166	ST	RNBT	FBG TR	OB	6 5	900		1750	2100
16 6	SPIRIT 165	ST	CTRCN	FBG TR	OB	6 5	900		1800	2150
17	PATRIOT 170	ST	RNBT	FBG SV	OB	6 5	1000		1950	2300
17	PATRIOT 170	ST	RNBT	FBG SV	IO 140-170	6 5	1950		2850	3300
19 4	FREEDOM 207	ST	CUD	FBG SV	IO 165-228	7	2600		4100	4900
19 4	LIBERTY 200	ST	RNBT	FBG SV	IO 140-228	7	2300		3700	4450
				--- 1977 BOATS ---						
16 6	SPIRIT-OF-76 165	ST	RNBT	FBG TR	OB	6 8	900		1850	2200
17	PATRIOT	ST	RNBT	FBG DV	OB	6 8	1195		2300	2650
17	PATRIOT	ST	RNBT	FBG DV	IO 120-140	6 8	1950		2950	3450
19 5	LIBERTY	ST	RNBT	FBG DV	IO 140-188	7 6	2500		4100	4800
19 5	LIBERTY CUDDY	ST	CUD	FBG DV	IO 165-175	7 6	3000		4750	5450
				--- 1976 BOATS ---						
16 6	EAGLE	OP	B/R	FBG TR	OB	6 7	900		1700	2000
17	PATRIOT	OP	RNBT	FBG DV	OB	6 8	900		1900	2250
17	PATRIOT	OP	RNBT	FBG DV	IO 120-140	6 8	1950		3000	3500
19 3	B/R	OP	RNBT	FBG	IO 140-190	7 2			4000	4700
				--- 1975 BOATS ---						
16 6	SPIRIT 164 TR	ST	RNBT	FBG TR	OB	6 7	900		1700	2000
17	PATRIOT 170	ST	RNBT	FBG DV	OB	6 8	1000		1850	2200
17	PATRIOT 170	ST	RNBT	FBG DV	IO 120-140	6 8	1850		3050	3550
				--- 1974 BOATS ---						
17	PATRIOT DLX	OP	RNBT	FBG DV	OB	6 8	1000		1850	2200
				--- 1973 BOATS ---						
17	PATRIOT	OP	RNBT	FBG DV	OB	6 8	1000		1850	2200

YARDWAY MARINE LTD
CONTAINER PORT RD KWAI   COAST GUARD MFG ID- XIG See inside cover to adjust price for area
ALSO HALVORSEN MARINE LTD

For more recent years, see the BUC Used Boat Price Guide, Volume 1 or Volume 2

LOA FT IN	NAME AND/ OR MODEL	TOP/ RIG	BOAT TYPE	-HULL- MTL TP	----ENGINE--- TP # HP MFG	BEAM FT IN	WGT LBS	DRAFT FT IN	RETAIL LOW	RETAIL HIGH
				--- 1983 BOATS ---						
30	ISLAND-GYPSY	HT	SDN	FBG DS	IB 120D-135D	11 6	14500	3 8	50600	56200
30	ISLAND-GYPSY	HT	SDN	FBG DS	IB T 80D-T90D	11 6	14500	3 8	50700	56200
32	ISLAND-GYPSY	DC	FBG DS	IB 120D-135D	11 6	15500	3 8	56500	62100
32 1	ISLAND-GYPSY	DC		FBG DS	IB T 80D-T90D	11 6	15500	3 8	55100	60600
32 1	ISLAND-GYPSY	HT	SDN	FBG DS	IB 120D-135D	11 6	15000	3 8	55000	60600
32 1	ISLAND-GYPSY	HT	SDN	FBG DS	IB T 80D-T90D	11 6	15000	3 8	54100	59900
36	ISLAND-GYPSY	DC		FBG DS	IB 120D FORD	12	20000	3 8	70100	77100
	IB 135D FORD	69900	76800;	IB	235D VLVO	68800 75600,	IB T120D FORD			70500	77500
	IB T135D FORD	70500	77500,	IB	T235D VLVO	71400	78500				
36	ISLAND-GYPSY	HT	SDN	FBG DS	IB 120D FORD	12 6	23000	3 11	69000	75800
	IB 135D FORD	68700	75500,	IB	235D VLVO	68000 74500,	IB T120D FORD			69500	76400
	IB T135D FORD	69900	76800;	IB	T235D VLVO	72300	79500				
44 3	ISLAND-GYPSY 44	FB	SDNSF	FBG SV	IB T450D GM	14	33000	4 3	119500	131000
44 3	ISLAND-GYPSY 44	FB	TRWL	FBG DS	IB T120D FORD	14	33000	4 3	102500	112500
44 3	ISLAND-GYPSY 44	FB	TRWL	FBG DS	IB T135D FORD	14	34000	4 3	103000	113000
44 3	ISLAND-GYPSY 44	FB	TRWL	FBG DS	IB T235D VLVO	14	34000	4 3	107500	118000
51	ISLAND-GYPSY	HT	MY		F/S DS	IB T235D VLVO	18	49000	4 3	144500	158500
51	ISLAND-GYPSY	PH		F/S DS	IB T235D VLVO	18	53000	4	124500	136500
57	ISLAND-GYPSY	FB	YTFS	F/S DS	IB T235D VLVO	18	62000	4 3	220000	242000
				--- 1982 BOATS ---						
30	ISLAND-GYPSY 30	FB	TRWL	FBG DS	IB T120D LEHM	11 6	16000	3 8	53700	59000
32 1	ISLAND-GYPSY 32	FB	TRWL	FBG DS	IB T120D LEHM	11 6	17000	3 8	61600	67700
36	ISLAND-GYPSY 36	FB	TRWL	FBG DS	IB T120D LEHM	12 6	23320	3 11	68100	74800
44 3	ISLAND-GYPSY 44	FB	TRWL	FBG DS	IB T120D LEHM	15	35000	4 3	101000	111000
50 9	ISLAND-GYPSY 51	FB	TRWL	FBG DS	IB T235D VLVO	16	49000	4 6	150500	165500
57	ISLAND-GYPSY 57	FB	TRWL	F/S DS	IB T235D VLVO	18 6	62000	4 6	166500	183000
65	ISLAND-GYPSY 65	FB	TRWL	P/M DS	IB T D	18	92000	5	**	**
72	ISLAND-GYPSY 72	FB	MY	P/M DS	IB T D	18 6	58T	5 10	**	**
				--- 1981 BOATS ---						
30	ISLAND-GYPSY 30	FB	TRWL	FBG DS	IB 120D	11 6	16000	3 8	51700	56800
32 1	ISLAND-GYPSY 32	FB	TRWL	FBG DS	IB 120D	11 6	17000	3 8	56400	62000
36	ISLAND-GYPSY 36	FB	TRWL	FBG DS	IB T120D	12	23320	3 11	64900	71300
44 3	ISLAND-GYPSY 44	FB	TRWL	WD DS	IB T120D	14	35000	4 3	97100	106500
50	ISLAND-GYPSY 50 PH	FB	TRWL	FBG DS	IB T120D	16 6			163000	179000

YARDWAY MARINE LTD -CONTINUED
See inside cover to adjust price for area

LOA FT IN	NAME AND/ OR MODEL	TOP/ RIG	BOAT TYPE	HULL MTL TP TP	ENGINE # HP	MFG	BEAM FT IN	WGT LBS	DRAFT FT IN	RETAIL LOW	RETAIL HIGH
1981 BOATS											
50 9	ISLAND-GYPSY 51	FB	TRWL	WD DS IB	T210D		16 9	49000	4 6	140500	154500
57	ISLAND-GYPSY 57	FB	TRWL	WD DS IB	T210D		17 6	53800	4 10	160500	176000
65	ISLAND-GYPSY 65	FB	TRWL	WD DS IB	T375D		18	92000	5 6	376000	413500
72	ISLAND-GYPSY 72	FB	TRWL	WD DS IB	T375D		18 6	58T	5 10	**	**
1980 BOATS											
30	ISLAND-GYPSY 30	FB	TRWL	F/W DS IB	120D		11 6	16000	3 8	49700	54600
30	ISLAND-GYPSY 30	FB	TRWL	F/W DS IB	T 80D		11 6	16000	3 8	51000	56100
36	ISLAND-GYPSY 36	FB	TRWL	F/W DS IB	T120D		12 6	23320	3 11	61900	68000
36	ISLAND-GYPSY 36	FB	TRWL	F/W DS IB	T120D		12 6	23320		64000	70300
44 3	ISLAND-GYPSY 44	FB	TRWL	F/W DS IB	T192D		14 3	35000	4 3	92600	102000
44 3	ISLAND-GYPSY 44	FB	TRWL	F/W DS IB	T192D		14 3	35000		94700	104000
50	ISLAND-GYPSY 50 PH		TRWL	WD DS IB	T192D		16 6			158500	174000
50	ISLAND-GYPSY 50 PH	FB	TRWL	WD DS IB	T120D		16 6			155500	171000
57	ISLAND-GYPSY 57	FB	TRWL	WD DS IB	T210D		17 6	53800	4 10	153500	168500
57	ICLAND-GYDCY 57	TD	TRWL	WD DG IB	T320D		17 6	53000		174000	191500
65	ISLAND-GYPSY 65	FB	TRWL	WD DS IB	T210D		18	92000	5 6	324000	356000
65	ISLAND-GYPSY 65	FB	TRWL	WD DS IB	T320D		18	92000		348500	382500
1979 BOATS											
30	ISLAND-GYPSY 30	FB	TRWL	F/W DS IB	120D		11 6	20000	3 8	58900	64700
30	ISLAND-GYPSY 30	FB	TRWL	F/W DS IB	T 80D		11 6	20000	3 8	58800	64600
36	ISLAND-GYPSY 36	FB	TRWL	F/W DS IB	T120D		12 6	23750	3 11	59800	65800
36	ISLAND-GYPSY 36	FB	TRWL	F/W DS IB	T120D		12 6	23750		61800	67900
44 3	ISLAND-GYPSY 44	FB	TRWL	F/W DS IB	T192D		14 3	34000	4 3	86800	95400
44 3	ISLAND-GYPSY 44	FB	TRWL	F/W DS IB	T192D		14 3	34000	4 3	88800	97600
50	ISLAND-GYPSY 50		TRWL	WD DS IB	T192D		16 6			151500	166500
50	ISLAND-GYPSY 50	FB	TRWL	WD DS IB	T120D		16 6			148500	163500
57	ISLAND-GYPSY 57	FB	TRWL	WD DS IB	T210D		17 6	77000	5 4	228000	250500
57	ISLAND-GYPSY 57	FB	TRWL	WD DS IB	T320D		17 6	77000	5 4	250000	275000
65	ISLAND-GYPSY 65	FB	TRWL	WD DS IB	T210D		18	92000	5 6	309500	340000
65	ISLAND-GYPSY 65	FB	TRWL	WD DS IB	T320D		18	92000		332500	365500
1978 BOATS											
30	ISLAND-GYPSY 30	FB	TRWL	F/W DS IB	120D		11 6	20000	3 8	56700	62300
30	ISLAND-GYPSY 30	FB	TRWL	F/W DS IB	T 80D		11 6	20000	3 8	56600	62200
36	ISLAND-GYPSY 36	FB	TRWL	F/W DS IB	T120D		12 6	23750	3 11	57200	62900
36	ISLAND-GYPSY 36	FB	TRWL	F/W DS IB	T120D		12 6	23750		59100	65000
44 3	ISLAND-GYPSY 44	FB	TRWL	F/W DS IB	T192D		14 3	34000	4 3	83000	91200
44 3	ISLAND-GYPSY 44	FB	TRWL	F/W DS IB	T192D		14 3	34000	4 3	84900	93300
57	ISLAND-GYPSY 57	FB	TRWL	WD DS IB	T320D		17 6	77000	5 4	239500	263000
1977 BOATS											
30	ISLAND-GYPSY 30	FB	TRWL	MHG DS IB	120D	FORD	11 6	20000	3 8	54600	60000
30	ISLAND-GYPSY 30	FB	TRWL	MHG DS IB	T 58D	FORD	11 6	20000	3 8	55200	60600
36	ISLAND-GYPSY 36	FB	TRWL	MHG DS IB	T120D	FORD	12 6	23750	3 11	52800	58100
36	ISLAND-GYPSY 36 DC	FB	TRWL	MHG DS IB	T120D	FORD	12 6	23750	3 11	56800	62400
44 3	ISLAND-GYPSY 44	FB	TRWL	MHG DS IB	T120D	FORD	14	34000	4 3	79100	86900
44 3	ISLAND-GYPSY 44 DC	FB	TRWL	MHG DS IB	T120D	FORD	14	34000	4 3	79500	87300
57 4	ISLAND-GYPSY 57	FB	TRWL	MHG DS IB	T320D	CUM	17 6	77000	5 4	228000	251000

YAWL BOATS

Call 1-800-327-6929 for BUC Personalized Evaluation Service
Or, for 1976 to 1979 boats, sign onto www.BUCValuPro.com

YEHASSO INC
COAST GUARD MFG ID- EHA

Call 1-800-327-6929 for BUC Personalized Evaluation Service
Or, for 1983 to 1984 boats, sign onto www.BUCValuPro.com

YONDER YACHT SPECIALISTS
COAST GUARD MFG ID- YYS

Call 1-800-327-6929 for BUC Personalized Evaluation Service
Or, for 1983 to 1985 boats, sign onto www.BUCValuPro.com

YORKTOWN YACHTS INC
WILMINGTON CA 90744   COAST GUARD MFG ID- KTY   See inside cover to adjust price for area

LOA FT IN	NAME AND/ OR MODEL	TOP/ RIG	BOAT TYPE	HULL MTL TP TP	ENGINE # HP	MFG	BEAM FT IN	WGT LBS	DRAFT FT IN	RETAIL LOW	RETAIL HIGH
1975 BOATS											
33	YORKTOWN	SLP	SAIL	FBG KL IB	35D	PERK	11	14000	5 6	18400	20500
35	YORKTOWN AFT COCKPIT	SLP	SAIL	FBG KL IB	35D	PERK	11 6	15500	5 8	20400	22700
35	YORKTOWN CTR COCKPIT	SLP	SAIL	FBG KL IB	35D	PERK	11 6	16000	5 8	21000	23400
39 2	YORKTOWN AFT COCKPIT	SLP	SAIL	FBG KL IB	35D	PERK	11 9	18500	6	26700	29700
39 2	YORKTOWN CTR COCKPIT	SLP	SAIL	FBG KL IB	35D	PERK	11 9	19000	6	27200	30200
1974 BOATS											
33	YORKTOWN AFT COCKPIT	SLP	SAIL	FBG KL IB	35D	PERK	11 1	12000	5 6	15100	17200
35	YORKTOWN AFT COCKPIT	SLP	SAIL	FBG KL IB	35D	PERK	11	13500	5 8	17200	19600
38 6	YORKTOWN AFT COCKPIT	SLP	SAIL	FBG KL IB	35D	PERK	11 8	15000	6	21600	24000
38 8	YORKTOWN AFT COCKPIT	SLP	SAIL	FBG KL IB	35D	PERK	11 8	15000	6	21800	24200
1973 BOATS											
33	YORKTOWN AFT COCKPIT	SLP	SAIL	FBG IB	35D	PERK	11	12000	5 6	14700	16700
35	YORKTOWN AFT COCKPIT	SLP	SAIL	FBG IB	35D	PERK	11	13500	5 8	16800	19100
38 6	YORKTOWN AFT COCKPIT	SLP	SAIL	FBG IB	35D	PERK	11 8	15000	6	21000	23300
38 8	YORKTOWN AFT CABIN	SLP	SAIL	FBG IB	35D	PERK	11 8	15000	6	21100	23500

YUKON DELTA INC
ELKHART IN 46514   COAST GUARD MFG ID- YDH   See inside cover to adjust price for area

LOA FT IN	NAME AND/ OR MODEL	TOP/ RIG	BOAT TYPE	HULL MTL TP TP	ENGINE # HP	MFG	BEAM FT IN	WGT LBS	DRAFT FT IN	RETAIL LOW	RETAIL HIGH
1982 BOATS											
25 9	MARK VII CRUISER	HT	HB	FBG TR OB			8	2200		**	**
25 9	MARK VII CRUISER	HT	HB	FBG TR IO	120		8	2200		**	**
31	COMBO-CRUISER	HT	HB	FBG TR OB			8	3600		5650	6500
31	COMBO-CRUISER	HT	HB	FBG TR IO	145		8	3600		9350	10600
1981 BOATS											
25 9	MARK V CRUISER	HT	HB	FBG TR OB			8	2200		**	**
25 9	MARK V CRUISER	HT	HB	FBG TR IO	120		8			**	**
25 9	MARK VII CRUISER	HT	HB	FBG TR IO	140	VLVO	8		1 6	**	**
25 9	MARK VII CRUISER	FB	HB	FBG TR IO	140	VLVO	8		1 6	**	**
26	MOLLY-BROWN	CR	HB	FBG TR OB	120		8			2900	3350
31	COMBO-CRUISER	HT	HB	FBG TR OB			8	3600		5600	6400
31	COMBO-CRUISER	HT	HB	FBG TR IO	140		8			9200	10500
1980 BOATS											
25 9	MARK VI CRUISER	FB	HB	FBG TR IO	120-140		8		1 4	**	**
26	MOLLY-BROWN	OP	CUD	FBG TR OB	120		8		1 4	2950	3400
31	COMBO-CRUISER III	FB	HB	FBG TR OB			8		1 6	6300	7200
31	COMBO-CRUISER III	FB	HB	FBG TR IO	140-200		8		1 6	9450	10700
31	COMBO-CRUISER LTD ED	FB	HB	FBG TR IO	200	VLVO	8		1 6	12700	14500
1979 BOATS											
25 9	MARK V CRUISER	FB	HB	FBG TR OB	120-140		8		1 4	**	**
31	COMBO-CRUISER II	FB	HB	FBG TR OB			8		1 6	6200	7100
31	COMBO-CRUISER II	FB	HB	FBG TR IO	140-200		8		1 6	9350	10800
1978 BOATS											
25 9	YUKON-DELTA	HT	HB	FBG TR OB			8	1970	1 10	**	**
25 9	MARK II CRUISER	HT	HB	FBG TR OB			8	2270	1 10	**	**
25 9	MARK II CRUISER	HT	HB	FBG TR IO	130-140		8	3700	1 10	**	**
27	MOLLY-BROWN	OP	UTL	FBG OB	120-130		8			3550	4200
27	MOLLY-BROWN	OP	UTL	FBG IO	200		8			4050	4700
27	MOLLY-BROWN			FBG IO			8			4950	5650
31	OPEN-CHALLENGE	FB	HB	FBG TR OB			8	2300	2 3	6600	7600
31	OPEN-CHALLENGE	FB	HB	FBG TR IO	130-140		8	4100	2 3	9100	10400
1977 BOATS											
25 9	MARK-II CRUISER	HT	HB	FBG TR OB			8	3700	1 10	**	**
25 9	MARK-II CRUISER	HT	HB	FBG TR IO	130-140		8	3700	1 10	**	**
27	SALMON-RUN	OP	OFF	FBG TR OB			8	2000	1 4	5950	6850
27	SALMON-RUN	OP	OFF	FBG TR IO	130-140		8	2000	1 4	3350	4000
31	OPEN-CHALLENGE	FB	HB	FBG TR OB			8	4100	2 3	6950	8000
31	OPEN-CHALLENGE	FB	HB	FBG TR IO	130-140		8	4100	2 3	9300	10600
32	ISLE-ROYALE	HT	HB	FBG DV IO	140	VLVO	12	6000	3	12100	13700
32	ISLE-ROYALE	HT	HB	FBG DV IO	T130	VLVO	12	6000	3	15500	16500
32	ISLE-ROYALE	HT	HB	FBG DV IO			12	6000	3	16700	19000
1976 BOATS											
26 4	MARK-II CRUISER	HT	HB	FBG TR IO	130-225		8	3700	8	**	**
31	COMBO CRUISER	HT	HB	FBG TR IO	130-225		8	3900	9	8550	9800
32	YUKON-DELTA	HT	HB	FBG TR IO	130-225		12	6000	2	18800	20900
1975 BOATS											
31	YUKON-DELTA COMBO	FB	HB	FBG TR OB			7 4	3600	1	5200	5950
31	YUKON-DELTA COMBO	FB	HB	FBG TR IO			7 4	3600	1	7200	8250
1973 BOATS											
25	YUKON-DELTA			FBG OB			7 6	1970	5	2900	3350
1972 BOATS											
25	YUKON-DELTA			FBG OB			7 6	1970	5	2850	3350

INDEX

A WORD OF EXPLANATION

The following is a combination of a manufacturers' index and a model name cross-reference index. It has been compiled in answer to the many requests from BUC Book users for a complete, easy-to-use reference index.

A **manufacturer name** is printed in boldface type followed by the first page on which it appears.

A **boat model name** is printed in upper case type. Indented under the model name is a list of manufacturers that made a boat with that name followed by the boat length

(rounded to the nearest foot) and basic boat type (C—canoe, D—deckboat, H—houseboat, O—outboard boat, P—powerboat with IB, IO, VD, or JT engine, S—sailboat) printed within brackets in bold type. If a manufacturer uses the name for more than one length or type, then no indicator may be shown. It is also possible that one or the other of length or boat type is undeterminable. The last item on the line is the page number. Remember, if no length or boat type is printed after a company's name, you should check the listing before eliminating it as the manufacturer you are seeking.

A **parent company or trade name** is printed in boldface type without a page number. Indented under the name is a list of the manufacturers

which are divisions of the parent company followed by their page numbers.

BOAT MANUFACTURER, TRADE NAME AND MODEL NAME INDEX

BOAT MANUFACTURER, TRADE NAME AND MODEL NAME INDEX

BOAT MANUFACTURER, TRADE NAME AND MODEL NAME INDEX

BOAT MANUFACTURER, TRADE NAME AND MODEL NAME INDEX

BOAT MANUFACTURER, TRADE NAME AND MODEL NAME INDEX

BOAT MANUFACTURER, TRADE NAME AND MODEL NAME INDEX

BOAT MANUFACTURER, TRADE NAME AND MODEL NAME INDEX

BOAT MANUFACTURER, TRADE NAME AND MODEL NAME INDEX

BOAT MANUFACTURER, TRADE NAME AND MODEL NAME INDEX

BOAT MANUFACTURER, TRADE NAME AND MODEL NAME INDEX

BOAT MANUFACTURER, TRADE NAME AND MODEL NAME INDEX

BOAT MANUFACTURER, TRADE NAME AND MODEL NAME INDEX

BOAT MANUFACTURER, TRADE NAME AND MODEL NAME INDEX

BOAT MANUFACTURER, TRADE NAME AND MODEL NAME INDEX

BOAT MANUFACTURER, TRADE NAME AND MODEL NAME INDEX

BOAT MANUFACTURER, TRADE NAME AND MODEL NAME INDEX

BOAT MANUFACTURER, TRADE NAME AND MODEL NAME INDEX